Time Out

Film Guide

Penguin Books

Week by week, for the past 34 years, London's *Time Out* magazine has provided a vivid, informed record of the capital's cultural events – in music, books, clubs, dance, theatre, film and TV, in high art and on the street. Since 1968, the previews, reviews and interviews from *TO*'s pages have marked and commented on the currents and crazes in cinema, whether in Hollywood, Iran, Hong Kong or Russia. This material – critical notices written on the actual release or re-release of each film – forms the core of the annual *Time Out Film Guide* (now in its eleventh edition), together with many reviews of movies from eras not covered in the magazine, and a number of significant feature films released straight to video or DVD.

The current edition of the *Film Guide* contains more than 540 new reviews, including a number of key festival showcase reviews, and enriched coverage of French, German, Italian and Asian cinema. This year the *Film Guide* also publishes the results of a new *Time Out* Readers' Top 100 poll taken in summer 2002 in which nearly 3,000 votes were cast for more than 400 different films. As the latest indication of what the world's critics think, *Sight and Sound* magazine's 2002 Top Ten poll is also added, together with the *TO* Cinema Centenary Top 100 poll of 1995. Icons in the text identify titles featured in all three polls.

The *Film Guide*'s credit lists and its appendices of film categories and major film-producing countries, and the actors', directors' and subject indexes, have all been updated and expanded, as has the appendix for the chief prize-winners at the Academy Awards and BAFTA ceremonies, plus those from the Cannes, Berlin and Venice film festivals. Finally, 'End Credits' marks the achievements of 114 notable film people worldwide who died between July 2001 and June 2002.

John Pym, who took over the editorship of the *Film Guide* from Tom Milne in 1994, was born in north London and spent many childhood afternoons in the 1950s and '60s in the cheapest seats of the Tolmer, the Everyman and the Odeon Muswell Hill. He was educated in England and America and began reviewing films for *Time Out* in 1975, before joining the British Film Institute for a 13-year spell on the *Monthly Film Bulletin* and *Sight and Sound*.

Edited and designed by
Time Out Guides Ltd
Universal House
251 Tottenham Court Road
London W1T 7AB
Tel +44 (0)20 7813 3000
Fax +44 (0)20 7813 6001
Email guides@timeout.com
http://www.timeout.com

Editor editions 4–11 John Pym
Editor editions 1–3 Tom Milne
Consultant Editor Geoff Andrew

Editoral Director Peter Fiennes
Managing Editor Will Fulford-Jones
Guides Co-ordinator Anna Norman

Group Art Director John Oakey
Art Director Mandy Martin
Art Editor Scott Moore
Senior Designer Lucy Grant
Designers Ben de Lotz, Sarah Edwards
Scanning/Imaging Dan Conway
Picture Editor Kerri Littlefield
Deputy Picture Editor Kit Burnet
Illustrations Simon Cooper
Audrey Hepburn cover photography Hulton Getty

Chairman Tony Elliott
Managing Director Mike Hardwick
Group Financial Director Kevin Ellis
Marketing Director Christine Cort
Group General Manager Nichola Coulthard

The Editors wish to thank the following for advice and assistance: Derek Adams, Tom Charity, Wally Hammond and Nick Bradshaw of the *Time Out* film section; Trevor Johnston, Geoffrey Macnab, Nicholas Royle and Gareth Evans; Simon Chappell and Miranda Wildi; the Greek Film Centre; Paul Fairclough; John Innes and Nick James; Martha Pym; Markku Salmi and Tom Milne.

A particular debt of gratitude is owed once again to Bob Baker, Tony Rayns, Chris Bohn and Bob Mastrangelo, and also this year to Derek Owen.

The Editors acknowledge the use of data from the British Film Institute's 'Film Index International' CD Rom in compiling the credits of films listed in this guide.

Film Guide

Edited by John Pym

Eleventh Edition 2003

Revised and Expanded

PENGUIN BOOKS

Published by the Penguin Group
Penguin Books Ltd, 80 Strand, London WC2R 0RL, England
Penguin Books USA Inc., 375 Hudson Street, New York, New York 10014, USA
Penguin Books Australia Ltd, 250 Camberwell Road, Camberwell, Victoria 3124, Australia
Penguin Books Canada Ltd, 10 Alcorn Avenue, Toronto, Ontario, Canada M4V 3B2
Penguin Books (NZ) Ltd, cnr Rosedale and Airborne Roads, Albany, Auckland, New Zealand

Penguin Books Ltd, Registered Offices: 80 Strand, London WC2R 0RL, England

First published 1989
Second edition 1991
Third edition 1993
Fourth edition 1995
Fifth edition 1996
Sixth edition 1997
Seventh edition 1998
Eighth edition 1999
Ninth edition 2000
Tenth edition 2001
Eleventh edition 2002
10 9 8 7 6 5 4 3 2 1

Printed in England by Clays Ltd, St Ives plc

Contents

Credits ii
List of Contributors vi
Foreword Geoff Andrew vii
Key to Credits viii
Time Out Readers' Film Poll 2002 x
Sight and Sound Critics' Top Ten xiv
Cinema Centenary Top One Hundred xxiv
End Credits: Obituaries 2001–2002 xxvi

FILMS A–Z 1–1375

APPENDICES
Film Categories
1. Action/Adventure 1377
2. Children's films 1379
3. Comedy 1380
4. Documentaries 1386
5. Epics 1388
6. Fantasy 1388
7. Film Noir 1389
8. Gangsters 1390
9. Horror 1390
10. Musicals 1392
11. Period/Swashbucklers 1393
12. Science Fiction 1395
13. Thrillers 1396
14. War 1400
15. Westerns 1401

Major Film-Producing Countries
16. Australian Films 1403
17. Canadian Films 1404
18. French Films 1405
19. German Films 1410
20. Italian Films 1413
21. Japanese Films 1415

Actors' Index 1417

Directors' Index 1439

General Subject Index 1509

Academy and Festival Awards
Academy of Motion Picture Arts and Sciences (Oscars) 1583
British Academy of Film and Television Arts (BAFTA Awards) 1585
Cannes Film Festival 1587
Berlin Film Festival 1589
Venice Film Festival 1591

List of Contributors

This guide is a compilation of reviews published in *Time Out* magazine's Film and TV sections since 1968. The reviews have been selected and edited by the editors. Individual reviewers can be identified by their initials, listed here, and printed at the end of each entry. Where no initials are given after an entry the identity of the reviewer is no longer known.

AC	Al Clark
ACh	Anita Chaudhuri
AG	Anton Gill
AH	Amanda Hopkinson
AHa	Arwa Haider
AJ	Alkarim Jivani
AL	Alexia Loundras
AM	Angela Mason
AMac	Angus MacKinnon
AN	Andrew Nickolds
AO	Alistair Owen
AP	Andrew Pulver
AR	Allen Robertson
AS	Allan T Sutherland
ASh	Andrew Shields
AT	Archie Tait
ATu	Adrian Turner
BB	Belkis Bhegani
BBa	Bob Baker
BC	Brian Case
BD	Bruce Dessau
BG	Brian Glasser
BP	Brian Priestley
BPa	Beverly Pagram
CA	Chris Auty
CAub	Crispin Aubrey
CB	Colin Booth
CF	Claire Fogg
CG	Carl Gardner
CGi	Chris Gilders
CL	Chris Lloyd
CM	Colette Maude
CO'S	Catriona O'Shaughnessy
CO'Su	Charlotte O'Sullivan
CPa	Claire Pajaczkowska
CPe	Chris Petit
CPea	Chris Peachment
CR	Cynthia Rose
CS	Colin Shearman
CSa	Chris Salmon
CSi	Clancy Sigal
CW	Chris Wicking
DA	Derek Adams
DAt	Don Atyeo
DC	David Curtis
DCo	Don Connigale
DD	Deke Dusinberre
DJ	DH Joseph
DJe	David Jenkins
DMcG	David McGillivray
DMacp	Don Macpherson
DO	Derek Owen
DP	David Pirie
DPe	Don Peretta
DPer	David Perry
DR	Don Ranvaud
DRo	David Rose
DS	Deborah Steels
DSi	Diana Simmonds
DT	David Thompson
DW	Dominic Wells
EG	Eve Gabereau
EP	Elaine Paterson
EPe	Emma Perry
EPr	Edward W Proctor
FD	Frances Dickinson
FF	Fiona Ferguson
FL	Frances Lass
FM	Fiona Morrow
GA	Geoff Andrew
GAd	Gilbert Adair
GB	Geoff Brown
GD	Giovanni Dadomo
GE	Gareth Evans
GM	Geoffrey Macnab
GMu	Garry Mulholland
GO	Grainne O'Kelly
GS	Gerry Sandford
GSa	Geoff Samuel
HH	Helen Hawkins
HK	Helen Van Kruyssen
HM	Helen MacKintosh
HR	Helen Rose
IA	Isabelle Appio
IB	Ian Birch
IC	Ian Christie
JB	Jerome Burne
JBa	Jane Bartlett
JC	John Collis
JCh	James Christopher
JCl	Jane Clarke
JCo	John Conquest
JCoh	Joyce Cohen
JD	Jan Dawson
JdeG	Jessica de Grazia
JDuC	John Du Cane
JE	Jane Edwardes
JF	John Ford
JFu	Jan Fuscoe
JG	John Gill
JGl	Joanne Glasbey
JK	Jeff Katz
JL	John Lewis
JM	Jo Creed-Miles
JMo	John Morrish
JMu	Jan Murray
JO'C	John O'Connell
JP	John Preston
JPi	Jim Pines
JPy	John Pym
JR	Jonathan Rosenbaum
JRo	Jonathan Romney
JS	Jennifer Selway
JW	John Wyver
JWi	Judith Williamson
JWil	Julia Williams
KC	Kieron Corless
KG	Keith Griffiths
KJ	Kevin Jackson
KM	Karen McLuskey
KW	Katy Wilkinson
LC	Laura Connelly
LD	Laura Lee Davies
LF	Lizzie Francke
LH	Liz Heron
LM	Lynda Myles
LMu	Lisa Mullen
LQ	Leonard Quart
LR	Len Richmond
LRo	Leo Robson
LS	Lindsay Shapero
LU	Lisa Ubsdell
LW	Lesley Weeks
MA	Martyn Auty
MB	Mike Bygrave
MBo	Mihir Bose
MC	Mark Cordery
MD	Melanie Dakin
MG	Michael Griffiths
MH	Matthew Hoffman
MHi	Mike Higgins
MHo	Mark Hosenball
MHoy	Martin Hoyle
MK	Mark Kermode
MM	Mandy Merck
MMc	Maitland McDonagh
MO'P	Michael O'Pray
MP	Mike Phillips
MPa	Myles Palmer
MPe	Mal Peachey
MPl	Martin Plimmer
MPo	Mike Poole
MS	Mark Sanderson
MSu	Martin Sutton
MV	Micheline Victor (now Wandor)
MW	Mark Williams
NA	Nigel Algar
NAn	Nigel Andrews
NB	Nick Bradshaw
NC	Nick Coleman
NF	Nigel Floyd
NFe	Nigel Ferguson
NJ	Nicolas Joy
NK	Naseem Khan
NKe	Nigel Kendall
NKee	Nicole Keeter
NR	Nick Roddick
NRo	Nicholas Royle
NY	Neil Young
OA	Omer Ali
OM	Olivia Maxwell
PB	Peter Ball
PBu	Pat Butcher
PBur	Paul Burston
PH	Phil Hardy
PHo	Pierre Hodgson
PK	Paul Kerr
PM	Paul Moffat
PP	Peter Paphides
PT	Paul Taylor
PW	Peter Watts
RB	Ruth Baumgarten
RC	Richard Combs
RD	Raymond Durgnat
RDo	Ray Douglas
RG	Richard Greenleaf
RGi	Ryan Gilbey
RI	Robert Irwin
RK	Rachel Kirkby
RM	Rod McShane
RMy	Robert Murphy
RP	Roger Parsons
RR	Richard Rayner
RS	Rupert Smith
RW	Richard White
RY	Robert Yates
SB	Sue Bennett
SC	Sandy Craig
SCu	Simon Cunliffe
SF	Simon Field
SFe	Suzi Feay
SFr	Sophie Frank
SFra	Susannah Frankel
SG	W Stephen Gilbert
SGa	Simon Garfield
SGo	Steven Goldman
SGr	Steve Grant
SH	Simon Hartog
SHi	Susan Hill
SJ	Steve Jenkins
SJo	Sheila Johnston
SK	Sarah Kent
SM	Scott Meek
SMac	Suzie Mackenzie
SMcA	Sarah McAlister
SP	Steve Pinder
SPr	Steve Proctor
SS	Susan Sharpe
SW	Steve Woolley
SWo	Sue Woodman
TC	Tim Clark
TCh	Tom Charity
TCo	Tom Coates
TE	Tony Elliott
TH	Tom Howard
TJ	Trevor Johnston
TM	Tom Milne
TP	Tim Pulleine
TR	Tony Rayns
TRi	Tim Rivers
VG	Verina Glaessner
WFJ	Will Fulford-Jones
WH	Wally Hammond
WI	Wendy Ide
WSG	WS Grant
WW	Winslow Wong
YS	Yvette Sitten
XS	Xanthe Sylvester

Foreword

by Geoff Andrew

I'm not, I hope, given to immodesty, but having been involved in the *Time Out Film Guide* since the first edition, I can state in all honesty that I've always felt it was the best book of its kind available, which is what it was intended to be. Over the years we've made changes to the format, notably the addition of technical credits and various appendices, but our aims have remained substantially the same as they were in 1989: to provide a collection, as up-to-date as possible, of clear, informed, incisive reviews of all the films released during the last twelve months in London, in addition, of course, to the movies both old and new covered by the magazine since its inception in the late 1960s.

We've always set out to be accessible in our writing, honest in our assessments, and accurate in our representation of films; we've always taken on board budgetary and other material considerations when evaluating films, but have never accepted that major financing, authorial reputation, lofty intentions or geographical origins automatically meant that one film might be in any way more deserving of serious appraisal than another. Films, in short, are viewed fairly and squarely on their own terms.

That's why the *Film Guide* has, perhaps, become even more valuable with each new edition. Hype has long been a feature of the film business, at least in those national industries predicated on the principles of western capitalism; after all, we're talking production, sales, profits, so advertising, personality led puff-pieces and celebratory scoops are inevitable. But film is also, or can be, an art, something many people (and not just film-makers) appear to have forgotten of late. Media coverage of cinema may be more widespread now than ever before, but only in the sense that there's more of it around; ironically, it tends to focus more exclusively on a narrower range of films: those touted, long before any remotely objective eye has seen them, as surefire hits.

But by whom? By the production companies, sales companies, distribution companies, cinemas, the trade papers, showbiz correspondents and far too many critics who, unlike most of the above, don't or shouldn't have vested interests in promoting the films. Many of those responsible for reviewing movies these days appear to be in thrall to arts editors who don't want their writers to go against the (second-guessed) grain of popular taste, but who also don't want to alienate the PRs who offer or withhold the star interviews deemed crucial to any paper or programme's high profile.

Mercifully, honest, forthright, perceptive critics do still exist, and a few of them write for *Time Out*: people who care about film enough to acknowledge its shortcomings as well as its strengths, and to look at cinema in all its variety. Hence, in the magazine's critics poll of UK releases at the end of 2001, the top ten films were from Austria, Taiwan, Sweden, Mexico, France and the US (the Americans were Terry Zwigoff and the Coens, hardly Hollywood mainstreamers). Cinema is international, after all (not that you'd know it from most of the media coverage), and during the last year our writers, while praising the likes of *The Lord of the Rings*, *Harry Potter*, *In the Bedroom* and *Ali*, also had plenty of good things to say about movies from every continent on the planet. Latin America and Austria were seen as areas requiring special attention; Asia retained and rewarded our interest; France remained true to form by leading the way in Europe, despite an uncharacteristically dismal showing at Cannes 2002, where Britain, conversely, was represented by an unusually fine clutch of titles.

Not that the Brits won any prizes, however. A problem for Messrs Leigh and Loach in particular at that festival was that some felt them merely to be marking time: more of the same, went the refrain. But is that such a flaw if it's done well? Much like a painter or composer, Jean Renoir reckoned he remade the same film over and over; to some extent, that's one mark of an auteur. And a fascinating aspect of the last year or so is that so many of the finest films have been by established directors doing what they do, revelling in or subtly refining the special idiosyncrasies of their art: Altman, Mann, Cronenberg, Rohmer, Breillat, the Dardennes, Oliveira, Kaurismäki, Kiarostami, Im Kwon-Taek and others. That's not to ignore the many promising young film-makers emerging around the world, simply to emphaise that novelty isn't everything.

That said, there is something new(ish) afoot – digital technology – and it's making its mark in all kinds of areas, from blockbuster sfx (the otherwise lamentable *Star Wars Episode II*) to films that probably couldn't be made any other way (*Atanarjuat*) and work as diversely experimental as *10* and *Waking Life*. It remains to be seen how many will use the new technology in an artistically fruitful way, and how many will see it merely as a kind of cheap shortcut. But it will certainly change the way films are conceived, made, distributed, exhibited, seen and thought about. Oh yes, and written about, too. We hope, however, that honesty, an informed perspective and an open mind will still be deemed valuable; if so, the *Time Out Film Guide* should remain ahead of the game. Happy viewing, and happy reading.

Key to the Credits

The eighth edition of the *Time Out Film Guide* was expanded with the addition of six new credit fields. Together with the director and cast, these often unsung individuals collectively represent a significant part of the creative force behind most films. Many gaps have been filled in subsequent editions and the existing material, once again, has been selectively revised. The key diagram below indicates the position of the credit fields.

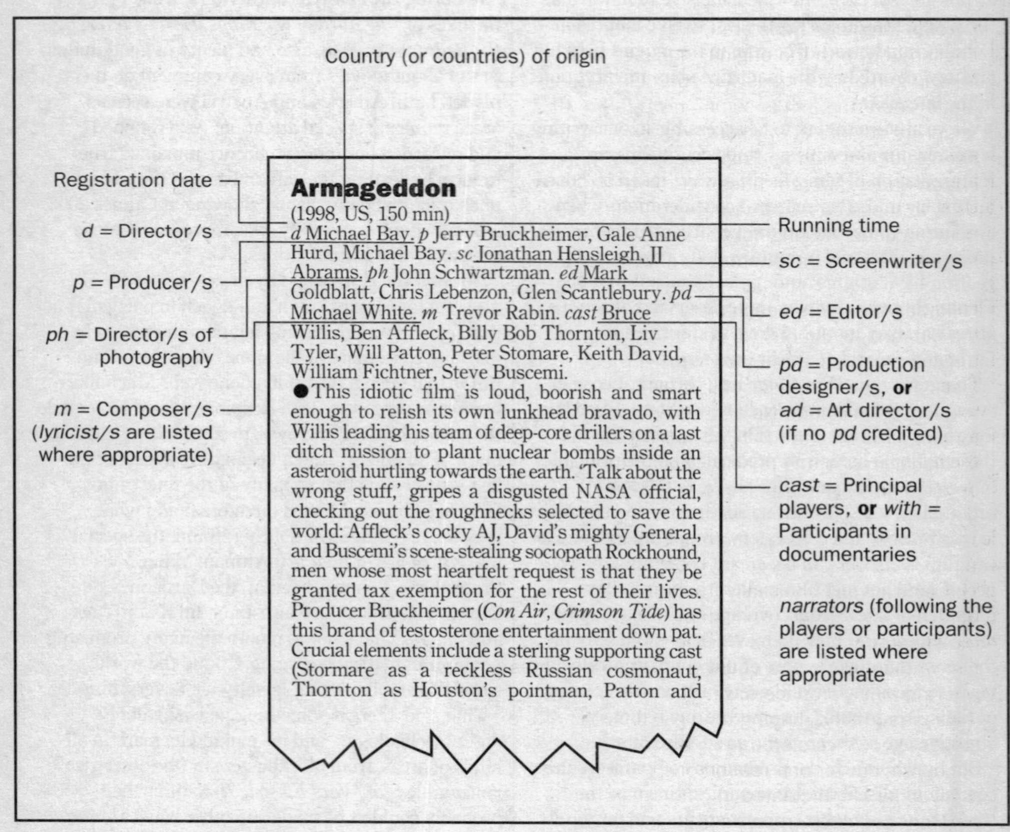

Titles are filed in directory order (ignoring word divisions). Thus: *Dancer in the Dark/Dancers/Dances with Wolves*.

American and other English-language films are listed under their original titles, followed in parentheses by their alternative American or British release titles, where different titles have been used. Thus: *Fortune Cookie, The* (aka *Meet Whiplash Willie*). Alternative titles are cross-referenced.

Foreign-language films are listed under their English title, with the original-language title following in parentheses. Exception to this rule is made where the film is commonly referred to under its original title; where a film has never been released with an English title; or where it is known under different titles in Britain and the USA. In these cases, to avoid confusion, the film is listed under its original title, with cross-references from the alternative English titles.

Following the title(s), each entry lists the date of the film and its country (or countries) of origin; the running time; the annotation 'b/w' if the film is in black-and-white, 'b/w & col' if it has one or more sequences in colour. No annotation after the running time means the film is in colour. The technical credits and principal cast then follow, as detailed on page viii. Chinese and Korean names are given with the family name first, Japanese and Thai names are given in the English order.

The date given is normally the registration date, not the release date (which may or may not be the same, depending on whether release of a film was delayed). The **country of origin** indicates where a film's producers were based, not where it was made. The running time given is that of the longest known version (many release prints are, of course, cut for one reason or another). Since many films are circulated in different versions in different countries, recorded running times are at best approximate.

In the case of silent films, which may be projected at different speeds (from 24 to 16 frames per second) for optimum effect, the length given is the footage (where known). To calculate the length of a film projected at 24 fps, divide the footage by 90; at 20 fps, by 75; at 16 fps, by 60.

The critics' initials (see page vi) follow the end of each review.

Abbreviations for producer countries

The following abbreviations, given after the registration date, are used for the countries of origin of films listed in the *Film Guide*. This refers specifically to the country or countries in which companies or organisations taking part in and providing finance for a production were officially registered at the time.

Alg	Algeria	Jap	Japan
Arg	Argentina	Leb	Lebanon
Arm	Armenia (post-1991)	Mex	Mexico
		Mor	Morocco
Aus	Austria	Moz	Mozambique
Aust	Australia	Neth	The Netherlands
Bel	Belgium	Nic	Nicaragua
Bol	Bolivia	Nor	Norway
Braz	Brazil	NZ	New Zealand
Bulg	Bulgaria	Pak	Pakistan
Can	Canada	Pan	Panama
Col	Colombia	Phil	Philippines
CR	Costa Rica	Pol	Poland
Cur	Curaçao	Port	Portugal
Cyp	Cyprus	Rus	Russia (post-1991)
Czech	Czechoslovakia		
Czech Rep	Czech Republic	SAf	South Africa
Den	Denmark	Sen	Senegal
Dom	Dominican Republic	SKor	South Korea
		Sp	Spain
EGer	East Germany	Swe	Sweden
El S	El Salvador	Switz	Switzerland
Fin	Finland	Tai	Taiwan
Fr	France	Thai	Thailand
GB	Great Britain & Northern Ireland	Trin	Trinidad
		Tun	Tunisia
		Tur	Turkey
Ger	Germany (pre-1945 & post-1990)	UAR	United Arab Republic
		Uru	Uruguay
HK	Hong Kong	US	United States of America
Hun	Hungary		
Ice	Iceland	USSR	Union of Soviet Socialist Republics
Ind	India		
Indon	Indonesia		
Ire	Ireland	Ven	Venezuela
Isr	Israel	WGer	West Germany
It	Italy	Yugo	Yugoslavia
Ivory C	Ivory Coast	Zam	Zambia
Jam	Jamaica	Zim	Zimbabwe

In addition, films produced in the most-represented countries (other than Britain and the USA) are listed separately in the following sections: Australia (Appendix 16); Canada (Appendix 17); France (Appendix 18); Germany (Appendix 19); Italy (Appendix 20); and Japan (Appendix 21). These lists cover all films involving producers based in these countries, including co-productions. Films produced elsewhere are listed under the name of the country in the General Subject Index.

Time Out Readers' Film Poll 2002

Every ten years since 1952, *Sight and Sound* magazine has polled international film critics for lists of their top ten films (augmented, over the years, by lists from film-makers), and we're delighted to reprint the 2002 *Sight and Sound* list in the new edition of the *Time Out Film Guide* (*see page xiv*). At the very least, the results constitute a fascinating barometer of changing critical fashions. Back in 1952, Chaplin, Griffith and Eisenstein were the three official geniuses of the cinema, and *Citizen Kane* was only notable for its absence from the list. By '62, *Kane* had been elected the greatest film ever, a reputation which has stuck ever since, with Renoir's *La Règle du Jeu* (*Rules of the Game*) coming second in '72, '82 and '92. Along with Eisenstein's silent *Battleship Potemkin*, *La Règle du Jeu* has been the only film to have appeared in every decade.

Still, critics are one thing, but what about the public? To complement this year's *Sight and Sound* poll, we decided to ask *Time Out* readers what they thought. The rules were simple, and in line with *Sight and Sound*'s criteria. We wanted a top ten list, though whether the nominations were for the greatest films ever made or just personal favourites was entirely up to the reader (we offered prizes both for the definitive list, which most closely resembled the final results, and for the most imaginative list). The response was very positive: we received nearly 3,000 votes for more than 400 different films.

SCORING

Some entrants placed their nominations in order of preference; many did not so we opted for the most transparent and straightforward scoring system: one point per vote. Thus, our final count is not distorted or weighted in any way, save for the subjective vagaries of time and memory. (A different and somewhat more sophisticated method of scoring was used for our Cinema Centenary poll of 1995, for which *see page xxiv*.)

It's interesting to note that while film critics tend to be suspicious of the new (in 2002, the most recent movies to make *Sight and Sound*'s top ten were the first two parts of Coppola's *Godfather* trilogy), the population at large is quick to embrace a modern classic when it sees one: check out the strong showing of *The Usual Suspects* (=8), *The Shawshank Redemption* (=15), and *The Lord of the Rings: The Fellowship of the Ring* (=17) in our poll. (Had *Time Out* followed the *Sight and Sound* scoring system, which linked the first two parts of Coppola's monumental family saga, *The Godfather* trilogy would have topped our poll with 56 votes.)

It may be that critical taste will catch up with these movies eventually. It's worth remembering that the likes of *Vertigo*, *It's A Wonderful Life*, *The Searchers* and even *2001* were not particularly well reviewed in their day. That said, the more recent movies enjoy the advantage of being fresh in the mind and widely available to the voting constituency. A fairly basic handicap system might provide a better idea of where these films might figure in the longer view: award an additional two-point bonus for every decade since a film was made, and *Shawshank* would be overtaken by the likes of *Seven Samurai*, *A Matter of Life and Death*, *Bicycle Thieves* and *Singin' in the Rain*, sliding some 12 spots down the pecking order. Such a system would also bring silent films like *Battleship Potemkin* and Buster Keaton's *The General* (which fell just outside our top 100) into the top 40. Be that as it may, we were pleasantly surprised by the relatively poor showing for recent box-office giants like *Harry Potter* and *Titanic*, both of which crept in at =90.

THE RESULTS

The highest placed subtitled film was *Les Enfants du Paradis* (*Children of Paradise*), at =17, a remarkable result for a three-hour black and white movie shot during the Occupation (and just a vote ahead of *Seven Samurai*).

In general, our poll confirms the mainstream critical consensus which has emerged since the modification (or commodification?) of auteurist criticism in the late 1960s. The directors who scored highest were Hitchcock (84 votes for 11 different films); Wilder (76 for 10); Spielberg (69 for 14) and Scorsese (62 for 9), while Akira Kurosawa (11 titles), Woody Allen and Howard Hawks (10); Michael Powell, Jean-Luc Godard, Luis Buñuel and John Huston (9 films) all had wide support. Of the next generation, the Coen Brothers, Tim Burton, David Lynch, Ridley Scott, David Fincher, Terry Gilliam and Wong Kar-Wai look set to join the pantheon.

The very notion of the canon is substantially discredited in academic circles now, and if you say that *Titanic* is your favourite movie of all time, who can say you're mistaken? Of course, it's all a matter of taste, not life and death. But polls such as these – and, for that matter, books such as the *Time Out Film Guide* – still perform an invaluable service when they remind us of the depth and diversity of film culture. After all, these are the movies we love best, and that counts for something. It's only when we think and talk and argue and dream about them that we keep these films alive. As for our surprise new Best Film of All Time: well, who ever said Nobody's perfect?

Readers' top 100 films are marked in the text with this logo: *(100)*

1. Some Like It Hot *48 votes*
(Billy Wilder, 1959, US)

2. The Godfather *38*
(Francis Ford Coppola, 1971, US)

3. Citizen Kane *34*
(Orson Welles, 1941, US)

4. Pulp Fiction *29*
(Quentin Tarantino, 1994, US)

5. Casablanca *28*
(Michael Curtiz, 1942, US)
— Vertigo *28*
(Alfred Hitchcock, 1958, US)

7. Star Wars *27*
(George Lucas, 1977, US)

8. 2001: A Space Odyssey *26*
(Stanley Kubrick, 1968, US)
— The Usual Suspects *26*
(Bryan Singer, 1995, US)

10. Blade Runner *24*
(Ridley Scott, 1982, US)

11. Jaws *23*
(Steven Spielberg, 1975, US)

12. Apocalypse Now *21*
(Francis Ford Coppola, 1979, US)
— The Third Man *21*
(Carol Reed, 1949, GB)

14. It's a Wonderful Life *20*
(Frank Capra, 1946, US)

15. The Shawshank Redemption *19*
(Frank Darabont, 1994, US)
— Taxi Driver *19*
(Martin Scorsese, 1976, US)

17. Blue Velvet *17*
(David Lynch, 1986, US)
— Chinatown *17*
(Roman Polanski, 1974, US)
— Les Enfants du Paradis *17*
(Marcel Carné, 1945, Fr)
— The Godfather Part II *17*
(Francis Ford Coppola, 1974, US)
— The Lord of the Rings: The Fellowship of the Ring *17*
(Peter Jackson, 2001, US/NZ)

22. Seven Samurai *16*
(Akira Kurosawa, 1954, Jap)

23. Psycho *15*
(Alfred Hitchcock, 1960, US)
— Withnail & I *15*
(Bruce Robinson, 1986, GB)

25. GoodFellas *14*
(Martin Scorsese, 1990, US)
— Lawrence of Arabia *14*
(David Lean, 1962, GB)
— Once Upon a Time in the West *14*
(Sergio Leone, 1968, It)
— Raging Bull *14*
(Martin Scorsese, 1980, US)

29. The Wizard of Oz *13*
(Victor Fleming, 1939, US)

30. Chungking Express *12*
(Wong Kar-Wai, 1994, HK)
— Fargo *12*
(Joel Coen, 1995, US)
— Magnolia *12*
(Paul Thomas Anderson, 1999, US)
— A Matter of Life and Death *12*
(Michael Powell/Emeric Pressburger, 1946, GB)
— Singin' in the Rain *12*
(Stanley Donen/Gene Kelly, 1952, US)

35. Bicycle Thieves *11*
(Vittorio De Sica, 1948, It)
— Don't Look Now *11*
(Nicolas Roeg, 1973, GB/It)
— Fight Club *11*
(David Fincher, 1999, US/Ger)
— The Matrix *11*
(The Wachowski Brothers, 1999, US/Aust)
— Touch of Evil *11*
(Orson Welles, 1958, US)

40. The Night of the Hunter *10*
(Charles Laughton, 1955, US)
— The Searchers *10*
(John Ford, 1956, US)
— Tokyo Story *10*
(Yasujiro Ozu, 1953, Jap)

43. A Bout de Souffle *9*
(Jean-Luc Godard, 1959, Fr)
— Delicatessen *9*
(Jean-Pierre Jeunet/Marc Caro, 1990, Fr)
— Dr Strangelove: or, How I Learned to Stop Worrying and Love the Bomb *9*
(Stanley Kubrick, 1963, GB)
— E.T. The Extra-Terrestrial *9*
(Steven Spielberg, 1982, US)
— North by Northwest *9*
(Alfred Hitchcock, 1959, US)
— Rear Window *9*
(Alfred Hitchcock, 1954, US)
— Shrek *9*
(Andrew Adamson/Vicky Jenson, 2001, US)
— Three Colours: Red *9*
(Krzysztof Kieslowski, 1994, Fr/Switz/Pol)
— Wild Strawberries *9*
(Ingmar Bergman, 1957, Swe)

52. American Beauty *8*
(Sam Mendes, 1999, US)
— Brief Encounter *8*
(David Lean, 1945, GB)
— Butch Cassidy and the Sundance Kid *8*
(George Roy Hill, 1969, US)
— Cinema Paradiso *8*
(Giuseppe Tornatore, 1988, It/Fr)
— The Deer Hunter *8*
(Michael Cimino, 1978, US)
— Double Indemnity *8*
(Billy Wilder, 1944, US)
— The Empire Strikes Back *8*
(Irvin Kershner, 1980, US)
— Gladiator *8*
(Ridley Scott, 2000, US)
— Leon *8*
(Luc Besson, 1994, Fr)
— Mirror *8*
(Andrei Tarkovsky, 1974, USSR)

— Once Upon a Time in America *8*
(Sergio Leone, 1983, US)
— Schindler's List *8*
(Steven Spielberg, 1993, US)
— Seven *8*
(David Fincher, 1995, US)
— The Terminator *8*
(James Cameron, 1984, US)
— Trainspotting *8*
(Danny Boyle, 1995, GB)

67. Aguirre, Wrath of God *7*
(Werner Herzog, 1972, WGer)
— Aliens *7*
(James Cameron, 1986, US)
— Amélie *7*
(Jean-Pierre Jeunet, 2001, Fr/Ger)
— The Apartment *7*
(Billy Wilder, 1960, US)
— L'Atalante *7*
(Jean Vigo, 1934, Fr)
— Barry Lyndon *7*
(Stanley Kubrick, 1975, GB)
— The Birds *7*
(Alfred Hitchcock, 1963, US)
— Bringing Up Baby *7*
(Howard Hawks, 1938, US)
— Cabaret *7*
(Bob Fosse, 1972, US)
— Crouching Tiger, Hidden Dragon *7*
(Ang Lee, 2000, China/Tai/US)
— Diva *7*
(Jean-Jacques Beineix, 1981, Fr)
— 8½ *7*
(Federico Fellini, 1963, It)
— In the Mood for Love *7*
(Wong Kar-Wai, 2000, HK/Fr)
— Metropolis *7*
(Fritz Lang, 1926, Ger)
— Monty Python's Life of Brian *7*
(Terry Jones, 1979, GB)
— Pierrot le Fou *7*
(Jean-Luc Godard, 1965, Fr/It)
— Les Quatre Cents Coups *7*
(François Truffaut, 1959, Fr)
— Sansho Dayu *7*
(Kenji Mizoguchi, 1954, Jap)
— The Silence of the Lambs *7*
(Jonathan Demme, 1990, US)
— The Sixth Sense *7*
(M Night Shyamalan, 1999, US)
— Stalker *7*
(Andrei Tarkovsky, 1979, USSR)
— Sunset Blvd. *7*
(Billy Wilder, 1950, US)
— West Side Story *7*
(Robert Wise/Jerome Robbins, 1961, US)

90. The Battle of Algiers *6*
(Gillo Pontecorvo, 1965, Alg/It)
— Black Narcissus *6*
(Michael Powell/Emeric Pressburger, 1946, GB)
— Buffalo '66 *6*
(Vincent Gallo, 1997, Can/US)
— Bullitt *6*
(Peter Yates, 1968, US)
— La Dolce Vita *6*
(Federico Fellini, 1960, Fr/It)
— Duck Soup *6*
(Leo McCarey, 1933, US)
— Forrest Gump *6*
(Robert Zemeckis, 1994, US)
— Four Weddings and a Funeral *6*
(Mike Newell, 1993, GB)
— Harry Potter and the Philosopher's Stone *6*
(Chris Columbus, 2001, US/GB)
— Heat *6*
(Michael Mann, 1995, US)
— Kind Hearts and Coronets *6*
(Robert Hamer, 1949, GB)
— Moulin Rouge *6*
(Baz Luhrmann, 2001, US)
— Raiders of the Lost Ark *6*
(Steven Spielberg, 1981, US)
— Requiem for a Dream *6*
(Darren Aronofsky, 2000, US)
— Reservoir Dogs *6*
(Quentin Tarantino, 1991, US)
— La Règle du Jeu *6*
(Jean Renoir, 1939, Fr)
— Three Colours: Blue *6*
(Krzysztof Kieslowski, 1993, Fr)
— Titanic *6*
(James Cameron, 1997, US)
— True Romance *6*
(Tony Scott, 1993, US)
— Wings of Desire *6*
(Wim Wenders, 1987, WGer/Fr)
— The Wicker Man *6*
(Robin Hardy, 1973, GB)
— The Wild Bunch *6*
(Sam Peckinpah, 1969, US)

SELECTED DIRECTORS

Allen, Woody *Annie Hall* (5 votes); *Bullets Over Broadway* (3); *Crimes and Misdemeanors* (2); *Husbands and Wives* (1); *Love and Death* (1); *Manhattan* (4); *The Purple Rose of Cairo* (1); *Sleeper* (3); *Stardust Memories* (2); *Sweet and Lowdown* (1).

Altman, Robert *Come Back to the 5 & Dime Jimmy Dean, Jimmy Dean* (2); *The Long Goodbye* (5); *M*A*S*H* (1); *Nashville* (4); *Popeye* (1); *Short Cuts* (1).

Bergman, Ingmar *Cries and Whispers* (2); *Fanny and Alexander* (3); *Persona* (4); *The Seventh Seal* (6); *Shame* (1); *The Silence* (1); *Through a Glass Darkly* (2); *Wild Strawberries* (9).

Buñuel, Luis *L'Age d'Or* (1); *Belle de Jour* (1); *The Discreet Charm of the Bourgeoisie* (1); *El* (1); *The Exterminating Angel* (1); *Los Olvidados* (2); *The Phantom of Liberty* (3); *Tristana* (1); *Viridiana* (1).

Burton, Tim *Batman* (1); *Edward Scissorhands* (4); *Ed Wood* (5); *Mars Attacks* (1); *The Nightmare Before Christmas* (1); *Pee-Wee's Big Adventure* (2).

Cameron, James *Aliens* (7); *The Terminator* (8); *Terminator 2: Judgment Day* (4); *Titanic* (6).

Chaplin, Charlie *City Lights* (3); *Modern Times* (3); *Monsieur Verdoux* (1).

Coen, Joel *Barton Fink* (2); *The Big Lebowski* (11); *Blood Simple* (3); *Fargo* (12); *The Hudsucker Proxy* (1); *Miller's Crossing* (1); *O Brother, Where Art Thou?* (1); *Raising Arizona* (2).

Coppola, Francis Ford *Apocalypse Now* (21); *Dracula* (1); *The Conversation* (2); *The Godfather* (38*); *The Godfather Part II* (17*); *The Godfather Part III* (1*). [* Votes for the *Godfather* trilogy were split evenly between the three films.]

Eisenstein, Sergei *Battleship Potemkin* (5); *Ivan the Terrible* (3); *October* (1).

Fellini, Federico *Amarcord* (1); *La Dolce Vita* (6); *8½* (7); *Juliet of the Spirits* (1); *Nights of Cabiria* (2); *Fellini-Satyricon* (1); *La Strada* (3).

Godard, Jean-Luc *A Bout de Souffle* (9); *Alphaville* (5); *Bande à part* (2); *Eloge de l'amour* (1); *Hail, Mary* (2); *Le Mépris* (4); *Numéro Deux* (1); *Pierrot le Fou* (7); *Weekend* (1).

Hawks, Howard *The Big Sleep* (5); *Bringing Up Baby* (7); *Gentlemen Prefer Blondes* (1); *His Girl Friday* (5); *Monkey Business* (1); *Only Angels Have Wings* (2); *Red River* (1); *Rio Bravo* (1); *Scarface* (2); *To Have and Have Not* (2).

Herzog, Werner *Aguirre, Wrath of God* (7); *The Enigma of Kaspar Hauser* (2); *Land of Silence and Darkness* (1); *Stroszek* (1).

Hitchcock, Alfred *The Birds* (7); *Dial M for Murder* (1); *North by Northwest* (9); *Notorious* (5); *Psycho* (15); *Rear Window* (9); *Rebecca* (3); *Spellbound* (1); *Strangers on a Train* (2); *The 39 Steps* (4); *Vertigo* (28).

Huston, John *The African Queen* (2); *Annie* (1); *Escape to Victory* (2); *Fat City* (2); *The Maltese Falcon* (4); *The Man Who Would Be King* (2); *The Misfits* (1); *The Treasure of the Sierra Madre* (2); *Wise Blood* (1).

Keaton, Buster *The General* (4); *Our Hospitality* (1); *The Navigator* (2).

Kieslowski, Krzysztof *Dekalog* (2); *La Double Vie de Véronique* (2); *A Short Film About Love* (1); *Three Colours: Blue* (6); *Three Colours: Red* (9).

Kubrick, Stanley *Barry Lyndon* (7); *A Clockwork Orange* (5); *Dr Strangelove: or, How I Learned to Stop Worrying and Love the Bomb* (9); *Paths of Glory* (4); *The Shining* (1); *Spartacus* (2); *2001: A Space Odyssey* (26).

Kurosawa, Akira *Akira Kurosawa's Dreams* (1); *Dersu Uzala* (1); *Dodes'ka-den* (1); *The Hidden Fortress* (2); *Ikiru* (2); *Kagemusha* (2); *Ran* (5); *Rashomon* (6); *Seven Samurai* (16); *Throne of Blood* (1); *Yojimbo* (1).

Lean, David *The Bridge on the River Kwai* (2); *Brief Encounter* (8); *Dr Zhivago* (1); *Great Expectations* (2); *Lawrence of Arabia* (14); *Oliver Twist* (1).

Leone, Sergio *A Fistful of Dollars* (1); *For a Few Dollars More* (1); *The Good, the Bad and the Ugly* (5); *Once Upon a Time in America* (8); *Once Upon a Time in the West* (14).

Lynch, David *Blue Velvet* (17); *Dune* (1); *The Elephant Man* (2); *Eraserhead* (3); *Lost Highway* (2); *Mulholland Dr.* (4); *The Straight Story* (3); *Wild at Heart* (4).

Peckinpah, Sam *The Ballad of Cable Hogue* (1); *Bring Me the Head of Alfredo Garcia* (3); *Pat Garrett and Billy the Kid* (2); *Ride the High Country* (1); *The Wild Bunch* (6).

Powell, Michael *Peeping Tom* (3); *The Thief of Bagdad* (2).

Powell, Michael and Pressburger, Emeric *A Canterbury Tale* (2); *Black Narcissus* (6); *I Know Where I'm Going!* (1); *The Life and Death of Colonel Blimp* (4); *A Matter of Life and Death* (12); *One of Our Aircraft Is Missing* (1); *The Red Shoes* (3).

Ray, Satyajit *The Apu Trilogy* [*Pather Panchali* (5); *The World of Apu* (1)].

Renoir, Jean *La Bête Humaine* (1); *Le Crime de Monsieur Lange* (2); *French Cancan* (1); *La Grande Illusion* (3); *Une Partie de Campagne* (1); *La Règle du Jeu* (6).

Scorsese, Martin *The Age of Innocence* (1); *Alice Doesn't Live Here Anymore* (1); *Casino* (2); *GoodFellas* (14); *The King of Comedy* (5); *The Last Temptation of Christ* (1); *Mean Streets* (5); *Raging Bull* (14); *Taxi Driver* (19).

Scott, Ridley *Alien* (5); *Blade Runner* (24); *Gladiator* (8); *Thelma & Louise* (4).

Spielberg, Steven *A.I. Artificial Intelligence* (1); *Close Encounters of the Third Kind* (5); *The Color Purple* (2); *Duel* (1); *Empire of the Sun* (2); *E.T. The Extra-Terrestrial* (9); *Hook* (1); *Indiana Jones and the Last Crusade* (1); *Indiana Jones and the Temple of Doom* (1); *Jaws* (23); *Jurassic Park* (4); *Raiders of the Lost Ark* (6); *Saving Private Ryan* (5); *Schindler's List* (8).

Tarkovsky, Andrei *Andrei Rublev* (4); *Ivan's Childhood* (1); *Mirror* (8); *Sacrifice* (1); *Solaris* (4); *Stalker* (7).

Truffaut, François *Les Quatre Cents Coups* (7); *Jules et Jim* (5); *Shoot the Pianist* (2).

Welles, Orson *Chimes at Midnight* (2); *Citizen Kane* (34); *It's All True* (1); *F For Fake* (1); *The Lady from Shanghai* (2); *The Magnificent Ambersons* (3); *Touch of Evil* (11); *The Trial* (1).

Wenders, Wim *Alice in the Cities* (3); *The American Friend* (1); *Kings of the Road* (1); *Paris, Texas* (3); *Wings of Desire* (6).

Wilder, Billy *Ace in the Hole* (1); *The Apartment* (7); *Avanti!* (1); *Double Indemnity* (8); *Five Graves to Cairo* (1); *The Private Life of Sherlock Holmes* (1); *Sabrina* (1); *Some Like It Hot* (48); *Stalag 17* (1); *Sunset Blvd.* (7).

Wong Kar-Wai *Chungking Express* (12); *Fallen Angels* (2); *Happy Together* (1); *In the Mood for Love* (7).

Sight and Sound Critics' Top Ten

Critics were asked by *Sight and Sound* to provide their Top Ten movies alphabetically, chronologically or in order of preference – and they are shown below as they were provided. As far as possible titles are given as they appear in the *Time Out Film Guide*, though some films – a British Airways short and a Turner Prize video work, for example – are not covered here.

1. Citizen Kane *46 votes*
(Orson Welles, 1941, US)

2. Vertigo *42*
(Alfred Hitchcock, 1958, US)

3. La Règle du Jeu *30*
(Jean Renoir, 1939, Fr)

4. The Godfather/ The Godfather Part II *23*
(Francis Ford Coppola, 1971/1974, US)

5. Tokyo Story *22*
(Yasujiro Ozu, 1953, Jap)

6. 2001: A Space Odyssey *21*
(Stanley Kubrick, 1968, US)

7. Sunrise *19*
(FW Murnau, 1927, US)
— Battleship Potemkin *19*
(Sergei Eisenstein, 1925, USSR)

9. 8½ *18*
(Federico Fellini, 1963, It)

10. Singin' in the Rain *17*
(Stanley Donen/Gene Kelly, 1952, US)

Sight and Sound Top 10 films are marked in the text with this logo: 10

Richard Allen (US, New York University): *Andrei Rublev* (Tarkovsky); *L'Atalante* (Vigo); *Citizen Kane*; *8½*; *M* (Lang); *Man With a Movie Camera* (Vertov); *The Passion of Joan of Arc* (Dreyer); *La Règle du Jeu; Ugetsu Monogatari* (Mizoguchi); *Vertigo*.

Geoff Andrew (UK, Time Out): *L'Atalante* (Vigo); *His Girl Friday* (Hawks); *The Magnificent Ambersons* (Welles); *Ma Nuit chez Maud* (Rohmer); *Ordet* (Dreyer); *Our Hospitality* (Keaton); *Les Parapluies de Cherbourg* (Demy); *Le Plaisir* (Ophuls); *Tokyo Story; The Wind Will Carry Us* (Kiarostami).

Nigel Andrews (UK, Financial Times): *Citizen Kane; Vertigo; Aguirre, Wrath of God* (Herzog); *The Night of the Hunter* (Laughton); *Spirited Away* (Miyazaki); *Hour of the Wolf* (Bergman); *Europa* (von Trier); *Happiness* (Solondz); *Careful* (Maddin); *The Godfather/The Godfather Part II*.

David Ansen (US, Newsweek): *Chimes at Midnight* (Welles); *The Conformist* (Bertolucci); *Hope and Glory* (Boorman); *Jules et Jim* (Truffaut); *McCabe & Mrs Miller* (Altman); *La Notte di San Lorenzo* (Taviani Brothers); *La Règle du Jeu; Sherlock Junior* (Keaton); *The Third Man* (Reed); *Trouble in Paradise* (Lubitsch).

Manuel Antin (Argentina, University of Cinema): *City Lights* (Chaplin); *Citizen Kane; Amarcord* (Welles); *Wild Strawberries* (Bergman); *Les Enfants du Paradis* (Carné); *Rashomon* (Kurosawa); *Viridiana* (Buñuel); *The Lady Vanishes* (Hitchcock); *Miracle in Milan* (De Sica); *Metropolis* (Lang).

Peter von Bagh (Finland, director Il Cinema Ritrovato, Bologna): *The Wedding March* (Stroheim); *Okraina* (Barnet); *Make Way for Tomorrow* (McCarey); *A Canterbury Tale* (Powell/Pressburger); *Late Spring* (Ozu); *Rio Grande* (Ford); *Edouard et Caroline* (Becker); *Bigger Than Life* (Ray); *Man of the West* (Mann); *And Life Goes On…* (Kiarostami).

Angela Baldassarre (Canada): *The Godfather/The Godfather Part II; Les Quatre Cents Coups* (Truffaut); *1900* (Bertolucci); *Citizen Kane; The Great Dictator* (Chaplin); *Gone With the Wind* (Fleming); *City Lights* (Chaplin); *La Dolce Vita* (Fellini); *Battleship Potemkin; Metropolis* (Lang).

Charles Barr (UK, University of East Anglia): *The Old Actor* (Griffith); *Ingeborg Holm* (Sjöström); *The Wind* (Sjöström); *Le Crime de Monsieur Lang* (Renoir); *The Lady Vanishes* (Hitchcock); *Random Harvest* (LeRoy); *A Canterbury Tale* (Powell/Pressburger); *My Love Has Been Burning* (Mizoguchi); *The Man Who Shot Liberty Valance* (Ford); *King Lear* (Brook).

Chris Berry (US/Australia, University of California): *A City of Sadness* (Hou Xiaoxian); *Battleship Potemkin; I Was Born, But…* (Ozu); *The Highway* (Sun Yu); *Through the Olive Trees* (Kiarostami); *A Touch of Zen* (King Hu); *In a Year with 13 Moons* (Fassbinder); *Vive l'Amour*

(Tsai Ming-Liang); *Juliet of the Spirits* (Fellini); *A One and a Two…* (Edward Yang).

Irene Bignardi (Italy, Locarno Flm Festival): *City Lights* (Chaplin); *8½; Nashville* (Altman); *Citizen Kane; Some Like It Hot* (Wilder); *Jules et Jim* (Truffaut); *Blade Runner* (Scott); *The Battle of Algiers* (Pontecorvo); *Paisà* (Rossellini); *Singin' in the Rain.*

Michaela Boland (Australia, Variety): *When Harry Met Sally…* (Reiner); *The Party* (Edwards); *Rope* (Hitchcock); *Trainspotting* (Boyle); *Citizen Kane; The Pillow Book* (Greenaway); *Grease* (Kleiser); *My Brilliant Career* (Armstrong); *To Kill a Mockingbird* (Mulligan); *Breaking the Waves* (von Trier).

Peter Bradshaw (UK, The Guardian): *The Addiction* (Ferrara); *Andrei Rublev* (Tarkovsky); *Black Narcissus* (Powell/Pressburger); *Crimes and Misdemeanors* (Allen); *In the Company of Men* (LaBute); *Kind Hearts and Coronets* (Hamer); *Paths of Glory* (Kubrick); *Raging Bull* (Scorsese); *Singin' in the Rain; Tokyo Story.*

Leon Cakoff (Brazil, São Paulo International Film Festival): *Citizen Kane; Casablanca* (Curtiz); *Rashomon* (Kurosawa); *2001: A Space Odyssey; Barren Lives* (Dos Santos); *Battleship Potemkin; And the Ship Sails On* (Fellini); *The Searchers* (Ford); *A Taste of Cherry…* (Kiarostami); *Central Station* (Salles).

Russell Campbell (New Zealand, University of Wellington): *The General* (Keaton); *L'Atalante* (Vigo); *La Règle du Jeu; Hiroshima, Mon Amour* (Resnais); *Psycho* (Hitchcock); *Jules et Jim* (Truffaut); *Vivre sa Vie* (Godard); *Au Hasard Balthazar* (Bresson); *Andrei Rublev* (Tarkovsky); *Germany, Pale Mother* (Sanders-Brahms).

Anchalee Chaiworaporn (Thailand): *A Bout de Souffle* (Godard); *Jules et Jim* (Truffaut); *Citizen Kane; Tokyo Story; La Jetée* (Marker); *And Life Goes On…* (Kiarostami); *Vertigo; Happy Together* (Wong Kar-Wai); *Rashomon* (Kurosawa); *The Celluloid Closet* (Epstein).

Paolo Cherchi-Usai (US/Italy): *Barry Lyndon* (Kubrick); *Blue* (Jarman); *Daybreak* (Sun Yu); *The Land Beyond the Sunset* (Shaw); *Land of Silence and Darkness* (Herzog); *Le Mélomane* (Méliès); *Sant Tukaram* (Fattelal/Damle); *I Am Cuba* (Kalatozov); *Surprise, Surprise* (British Airways); *Sylvester* (Pick).

Peggy Chiao (Taiwan, Arc Light Films): *Amarcord* (Fellini); *Chungking Express* (Wong Kar-Wai); *Citizen Kane; A City of Sadness* (Hou Xiaoxian); *The Godfather; La Règle du Jeu; The Searchers* (Ford); *Seven Samurai* (Kurosawa); *Tokyo Story; Vertigo.*

Michel Chion (France, University of Paris III): *Blade Runner* (Scott); *Casablanca* (Curtiz); *Fellini's Casanova* (Fellini); *City Lights* (Chaplin); *Days of Heaven* (Malick); *India Song* (Duras); *Monty Python's Life of Brian* (Jones); *Spirited Away* (Miyazaki); *Shadows of Our Forgotten Ancestors* (Paradjanov); *2001: A Space Odyssey.*

Ian Christie (UK, University of London): *Casino* (Scorsese); *Un Chien Andalou* (Buñuel); *Hitler: A Film from Germany* (Syberberg); *Ivan the Terrible* (Eisenstein); *M* (Lang); *A Matter of Life and Death* (Powell/Pressburger); *Le Mépris* (Godard); *The Story of the Late Chrysanthemums* (Mizoguchi); *Viaggio in Italia* (Rossellini); *Young Mr Lincoln* (Ford).

Michel Ciment (France, editor Positif): *Barry Lyndon* (Kubrick); *L'Atalante* (Vigo); *La Règle du Jeu; Madame de…* (Ophuls); *Sunrise; The General* (Keaton); *The Travelling Players* (Angelopoulos); *Ugetsu Monogatari* (Mizoguchi); *White Heat* (Walsh); *Salvatore Giuliano* (Rosi).

Pam Cook (UK, Southampton University): *Ballad of Little Jo* (Greenwald); *Becky Sharp* (Mamoulian); *Do the Right Thing* (Lee); *Farewell My Concubine* (Chen Kaige); *The Lodger* (Hitchcock); *Moulin Rouge* (Luhrmann); *Psycho* (Hitchcock); *The Red Shoes* (Powell/Pressburger); *Shadows* (Cassavetes); *Sunrise.*

Mark Cousins (UK, Scene by Scene, BBC): *Distant Voices Still Lives* (Davies); *The Emperor's Naked Army Marches On* (Hara); *Gold Diggers of 1933* (LeRoy); *He Who Gets Slapped* (Sjöström); *The Insect Woman* (Imamura); *Jeanne Dielman* (Akerman); *La Maman et la Putain* (Eustache); *Russian Ark* (Sokurov); *Light Sleeper* (Schrader); *Touch of Evil* (Welles).

Peter Cowie (UK, editor International Film Guide): *The Seventh Seal* (Bergman); *The Godfather Part II; Alexander Nevsky* (Eisenstein); *Jules et Jim* (Truffaut); *The Double Life of Véronique* (Kieslowski); *Les Enfants du Paradis* (Carné); *Deliverance* (Boorman); *Seven Samurai* (Kurosawa); *Vertigo; My Darling Clementine* (Ford).

Hamid Dabashi (US/Iran, Columbia University) *Close-Up* (Kiarostami); *Yol* (Gören); *Cairo Station* (Chahine); *Kadosh* (Gitai); *Moment of Innocence* (Makhmalbaf); *The Silences of the Palace* (Tlatli); *The Runner* (Naderi); *Wedding in Galilee* (Khleifi); *Bashu, The Little Stranger* (Beyzaï); *Mercedes* (Nasrallah).

Manohla Dargis (US, Los Angeles Times): *Au Hasard, Balthazar* (Bresson); *Barry Lyndon* (Kubrick); *The Godfather/The Godfather Part II; La Grande Illusion* (Renoir); *Masculin Féminin* (Godard); *The Puppetmaster* (Hou

Xiaoxian); *Scenes from Under Childhood* (Brakhage); *Some Like It Hot* (Wilder); *Tokyo Story; Touch of Evil* (Welles).

Joel David (Philippines, University of the Philippines): *Salò* (Pasolini); *Manila by Night* (Bernal); *Khalnayak* (Ghai); *The Opening of Misty Beethoven* (Metzger); *The Hour of the Furnaces* (Solanas); *La Règle du Jeu; God Told Me To* (Cohen); *La Région Centrale* (Snow); *Olympische Spiele 1936* (Riefenstahl); *The Devil in Miss Jones* (Damiano).

David Denby (US, The New Yorker): *L'Avventura* (Antonioni); *Citizen Kane; Dekalog* (Kieslowski); *The Godfather/The Godfather Part II; Seven Samurai* (Kurosawa); *Sunrise; La Règle du Jeu; The Third Man* (Reed); *Weekend* (Godard); *Vertigo.*

Malgorzata Dipont (Poland, president Polish Film Critics Club): *Battleship Potemkin; Citizen Kane; 8½; Les Enfants du Paradis* (Carné); *The Gold Rush* (Chaplin); *A Blonde in Love* (Forman); *The Devil and the Nun* (Kawalerowicz); *Rashomon* (Kurosawa); *Stalker* (Tarkovsky); *Viridiana* (Buñuel).

Phillip Dodd (UK, director Institute of Contemporary Arts): *City Lights* (Chaplin); *The Passion of Joan of Arc* (Dreyer); *Vertigo; The Battle of Algiers* (Pontecorvo); *Screen Tests* (Warhol); *Time of the Gypsies* (Kusturica); *Fires Were Started* (Jennings); *Le Mépris* (Godard); *His Girl Friday* (Hawks); *Atanarjuat: The Fast Runner* (Kunuk).

Daniil Dondurei (Russia, editor in chief Iskusstvo Kino): *Battleship Potemkin; Citizen Kane; L'Atalante* (Vigò); *Rashomon* (Kurosawa); *8½; The Passion of Joan of Arc* (Dreyer); *Wild Strawberries* (Bergman); *Dead Man* (Jarmusch); *Rocco and His Brothers* (Visconti); *One Flew Over the Cuckoo's Nest* (Forman).

Patrick Duynslaegher (Belgium, Focus Knack): *Berlin Alexanderplatz* (Fassbinder); *Citizen Kane; The Damned* (Visconti); Napoléon (Gance); *Fellini-Satyricon* (Fellini); *Seven Samurai* (Kurosawa); *Sweet Smell of Success* (Mackendrick); *Tristana* (Buñuel); *2001: A Space Odyssey; Vertigo.*

Michael Dwyer (Ireland, Irish Times): *Barry Lyndon* (Kubrick); *Bonnie and Clyde* (Penn); *Citizen Kane; Fanny and Alexander* (Bergman); *It's a Wonderful Life* (Capra); *La Nuit Américaine* (Truffaut); *Raging Bull* (Scorsese); *Three Colours Trilogy* (Kieslowski); *Vertigo; The Wild Bunch* (Peckinpah).

Richard Dyer (UK, University of Warwick): *All That Heaven Allows* (Sirk); *Il Bidone* (Fellini); *Day of the Dead* (Romero); *India Song* (Duras); *Le Goût des autres* (Jaoui); *Maciste all'Inferno* (Freda); *Pakeezah* (Amrohi); *Senso* (Visconti); *Sunrise; Loving Couples* (Zetterling).

Roger Ebert (US, Chicago Sun Times): *Aguirre, Wrath of God* (Herzog); *Apocalypse Now* (Coppola); *Citizen Kane; Dekalog* (Kieslowski); *La Dolce Vita* (Fellini); *The General* (Keaton); *Raging Bull* (Scorsese); *2001: A Space Odyssey; Tokyo Story; Vertigo.*

Klaus Eder (Germany, FIPRESCI): *Battleship Potemkin; The Gold Rush* (Chaplin); *La Règle du Jeu; Citizen Kane; Paisà* (Rossellini); *Tokyo Story; Ordet* (Dreyer); *Pather Panchali* (Ray); *Les Quatre Cents Coups* (Truffaut); *Black God, White Devil* (Rocha).

Thomas Elsaesser (Netherlands, University of Amsterdam): *Sunrise; La Règle du Jeu; Citizen Kane; The Big Sleep* (Hawks); *Letter from an Unknown Woman* (Ophuls); *Sansho Dayu* (Mizoguchi); *Vertigo; Some Like It Hot* (Wilder); *Taxi Driver* (Scorsese); *Berlin Alexanderplatz* (Fassbinder).

Jim Emerson (US): *Chinatown* (Polanski); *Citizen Kane; The Discreet Charm of the Bourgeoisie* (Buñuel); *Kings of the Road* (Wenders); *The Magnificent Ambersons* (Welles); *Nashville* (Altman); *Sherlock Junior* (Keaton); *Sunrise; 2001: A Space Odyssey; Vertigo.*

Claudio España (Argentina, University of Buenos Aires): *Breaking the Waves* (von Trier); *Citizen Kane; 8½; Memories of Underdevelopment* (Gutiérrez Alea); *Ordet* (Dreyer); *La Passion* (Godard); *Sansho Dayu* (Mizoguchi); *Sunrise; Vertigo; Viaggio in Italia* (Rossellini).

Dan Fainaru (Israel, Israeli Broadcasting Authority): *Battleship Potemkin; Dekalog* (Kieslowski); *8½; Fanny and Alexander* (Bergman); *F for Fake* (Welles); *A One and a Two…* (Edward Yang); *Shoah* (Lanzmann); *Tokyo Story; The Travelling Players* (Angelopoulos); *Vertigo.*

Edna Fainaru (Israel, Jaffa International Film Festival): *Angel* (Lubitsch); *Sullivan's Travels* (Sturges); *Floating Cloud* (Naruse); *Tokyo Story; Ikiru* (Kurosawa); *Singin' in the Rain; Providence* (Resnais); *8½; A One and a Two…* (Edward Yang); *Shoah* (Lanzmann).

Ibrahim Fawal (US/Egypt): *Bicycle Thieves* (De Sica); *Citizen Kane; 8½; Fanny and Alexander* (Bergman); *The Godfather; Lawrence of Arabia* (Lean); *Napoléon* (Gance); *On the Waterfront* (Kazan); *Rashomon* (Kurosawa); *La Règle du Jeu.*

Howard Feinstein (US): *A Clockwork Orange* (Kubrick); *Greed* (von Stroheim); *Madame de…* (Ophuls); *Nosferatu* (Murnau); *Rome, Open City* (Rossellini); *Sunset Blvd.* (Wilder); *The Passion of Joan of Arc* (Dreyer); *The Searchers* (Ford); *The Life of Oharu* (Mizoguchi); *Three Colours Trilogy* (Kieslowski).

Philip French (UK, The Observer): *The General* (Keaton); *La Grande Illusion* (Renoir); *Stagecoach* (Ford); *Citizen Kane; Singin' in the Rain; Seven Samurai* (Kurosawa); *Pather Panchali* (Ray); *Vertigo; Winter Light* (Bergman); *The Godfather.*

Jean-Michel Frodon (France, Le Monde): *A City of Sadness* (Hou Xiaoxian); *Close-Up* (Kiarostami); *M* (Lang); *The Passion of Joan of Arc* (Dreyer); *Sauve Qui Peut – la Vie* (Godard); *The Searchers* (Ford); *Shoah* (Lanzmann); *Singin' in the Rain; Van Gogh* (Pialat); *Vertigo.*

Teshome Gabriel (US, University of California at Los Angeles): *Salt of the Earth* (Biberman); *Black God, White Devil* (Rocha); *Quemada!* (Pontecorvo); *Dersu Uzala* (Kurosawa); *Ceddo* (Sembene); *Who's Singing Over There?* (Sijan); *Rue Cases Nègres* (Palcy); *El Norte* (Nava); *To Sleep with Anger* (Burnett); *Song of Exile* (Hui On-Wah).

Diego Galán (Spain): *Sunrise; The Thief of Bagdad* (Powell/ Berger/Whelan); *All About Eve* (Mankiewicz); *Touch of Evil* (Welles); *The Apartment* (Wilder); *Jules et Jim* (Truffaut); *Viridiana* (Buñuel); *The Godfather Trilogy; To Live* (Zhang Yimou); *Besieged* (Bertolucci).

June Givanni (UK): *Muna Moto* (Dikongue-Pipa); *Shadows* (Cassavetes); *Touki-Bouki* (Diop-Mambéty); *Riff-Raff* (Loach); *Paper Flowers* (Dutt); *Rue Cases Nègres* (Palcy); *Man by the Shore* (Peck); *Jungle Fever* (Lee); *To Sleep with Anger* (Burnett); *All About My Mother* (Almodóvar).

Lalitha Gopalan (US/India): *A Bout de Souffle* (Godard); *Branded to Kill* (Suzuki); *Un Chien Andalou* (Buñuel); *Dead Ringers* (Cronenberg); *Jeanne Dielman* (Akerman); *Man With a Movie Camera* (Vertov); *Night Cries – A Rural Tragedy* (Moffatt); *Sholay* (Sippy); *Solaris* (Tarkovsky); *Touch of Evil* (Welles).

Sidney Gottlieb (US, Sacred Heart University): *The Last Laugh* (Murnau); *Battleship Potemkin; La Grande Illusion* (Renoir); *Citizen Kane; Bicycle Thieves* (De Sica); *Rashomon* (Kurosawa); *The Seventh Seal* (Bergman); *Vertigo; A Bout de Souffle* (Godard); *The Godfather.*

Julian Graffy (UK, University College London): *The Life of Oharu* (Mizoguchi); *Happiness* (Medvedkin); *L'Avventura* (Antonioni); *Pierrot le Fou* (Godard); *Long Farewells* (Muratova); *Tokyo Story; Ju Dou* (Zhang Yimou); *A Life for a Life* (Bauer); *Through the Olive Trees* (Kiarostami); *Chungking Express* (Wong Kar-Wai).

Matthias Greuling (Austria, editor Celluloid): *Citizen Kane; The Apartment* (Wilder); *2001: A Space Odyssey; Battleship Potemkin; Vertigo; Les Quatre Cents Coups* (Truffaut); *Le Mépris* (Godard); *Schindler's List* (Spielberg); *La Dolce Vita* (Fellini); *L'Avventura* (Antonioni).

Alfredo Guevara (Cuba, Festival of New Latin American Cinema): *Providence* (Resnais); *Death in Venice* (Visconti); *Modern Times* (Chaplin); *Umberto D.* (De Sica); *Black God, White Devil* (Rocha); *Strawberry and Chocolate* (Gutiérrez Alea); *Los Olvidados* (Buñuel); *La Strada* (Fellini); *Battleship Potemkin; A Bout de Souffle* (Godard).

Tom Gunning (US, University of Chicago): *Day of Wrath* (Dreyer); *Vertigo; Sunrise; Ugetsu Monogatari* (Mizoguchi); *The Searchers* (Ford); *Intolerance* (Griffith); *M* (Lang); *Ivan the Terrible* (Eisenstein); *Pierrot le Fou* (Godard); *La Région Centrale* (Snow).

Peter Hames (UK): *Mirror* (Tarkovsky); *A Tale of Tales* (Norstein); *Sansho Dayu* (Mizoguchi); *Les Vacances de M. Hulot* (Tati); *The Searchers* (Ford); *Markéta Lazarová* (Vlácil); *Yeelen* (Cissé); *The Man in the White Suit* (Mackendrick); *Céline and Julie Go Boating* (Rivette); *The Trouble with Harry* (Hitchcock).

David Hanan (Australia, Monash University): *Strike* (Eisenstein); *Meshes of the Afternoon* (Deren); *A Matter of Life and Death* (Powell/Pressburger); *L'Avventura* (Antonioni); *Komal Gandhar* (Ghatak); *You Are Weighed but Found Lacking* (Brocka); *In a Year with 13 Moons* (Fassbinder); Jane Campion shorts (*Peel/ Passionless Moments/A Girl's Own Story*); *Butterfly and Flowers* (Mukdasanit); *Bitter Coffee* (Karya).

Jim Hoberman (US, Village Voice): *Flaming Creatures* (Smith); *The Girl from Chicago* (Micheaux); *Man With a Movie Camera* (Vertov); *Pather Panchali* (Ray); *La Règle du Jeu; Rose Hobart* (Cornell); *Shoah* (Lanzmann); *Deux ou Trois Choses que Je Sais d'Elle* (Godard); *Les Vampires* (Feuillade); *Vertigo.*

Yomota Inuhiko (Japan): *Kaagaz ke phool* (Dutt); *The Story of the Late Chrysanthemums* (Mizoguchi); *A Touch of Zen* (King Hu); *L'Âge d'Or* (Buñuel); *Le Vent d'Est* (Godard); *Accattone* (Pasolini); *Le Vampire* (Dreyer); *Napoléon* (Gance); *The Red Desert* (Antonioni); *Au Hasard, Balthazar* (Bresson).

Dina Iordanova (UK, University of Leicester): *The Battle of Algiers* (Pontecorvo); *Un Chien Andalou* (Buñuel); *Man With a Movie Camera* (Vertov); *Metropolis* (Lang); *Mirror* (Tarkovsky); *October* (Eisenstein); *The Round-Up* (Jancsó); *Throne of Blood* (Kurosawa); *Barren Lives* (dos Santos); *Xala* (Sembene).

Gilles Jacob (France, Cannes Film Festival): *L'Atalante* (Vigo); *Earth* (Dovzhenko); *The Empress Yang Kwei Fei*

(Mizoguchi); *Fanny and Alexander* (Bergman); *Ikiru* (Kurosawa); *The Music Room* (Ray); *My Apprenticeship* (Donskoi); *Nanook of the North* (Flaherty); *Our Daily Bread* (Vidor); *The Last Laugh* (Murnau).

Nick James (UK, editor Sight and Sound): *Andrei Rublev* (Tarkovsky); *Barry Lyndon* (Kubrick); *Black Narcissus* (Powell/Pressburger); *L'Argent* (Bresson); *Out of the Past* (Tourneur); *Singin' in the Rain; Taxi Driver* (Scorsese); *The Conformist* (Bertolucci); *A One and a Two…* (Edward Yang); *Hotel Terminus* (Ophuls).

Frederic R Jameson (US, Duke University): *The Travelling Players* (Angelopoulos); *Les Enfants du Paradis* (Carné); *High and Low* (Kurosawa); *Notorious* (Hitchcock); *Fellini-Satyricon* (Fellini); *Days of Eclipse* (Sokurov); *Lucia* (Solas); *Fantasia* (Sharpsteen); *The Thief of Bagdad* (Powell/Berger/Whelan); *La Règle du Jeu.*

Mark Jancovich (UK, University of Nottingham): *Captain Blood* (Curtiz); *El Cid* (Mann); *The Ghost and Mrs Muir* (Mankiewicz); *Jane Eyre* (Stevenson); *The Lady Eve* (Sturges); *Now, Voyager* (Rapper); *Spartacus* (Kubrick); *The Terminator* (Cameron); *The Thing from Another World* (Nyby); *To Have and Have Not* (Hawks).

Kent Jones (US, Film Comment): *Sunrise; The Story of the Late Chrysanthemums* (Mizoguchi); *Wagon Master* (Ford); *The Magnificent Ambersons* (Welles); *Viaggio in Italia* (Rossellini); *Ordet* (Dreyer); *2001: A Space Odyssey; A Woman Under the Influence* (Cassavetes); *Fanny and Alexander* (Bergman); *L'Argent* (Bresson).

Nasreen Munni Kabir (UK/India, British Film Institute): *Andaz* (Khan); *Awara* (Kapoor); *Casablanca* (Curtiz); *Citizen Kane; Pickpocket* (Bresson); *Pyaasa* (Dutt); *Seven Samurai* (Kurosawa); *Singin' in the Rain; The Maltese Falcon* (Huston); *The Third Man* (Reed).

Philip Kemp (UK): *Charulata* (Ray); *Fargo* (Coen); *Letter from an Unknown Woman* (Ophuls); *Nosferatu* (Murnau); *The Outlaw Josey Wales* (Eastwood); *La Règle du Jeu; Sansho Dayu* (Mizoguchi); *Some Like It Hot* (Wilder); *Sweet Smell of Success* (Mackendrick); *The Usual Suspects* (Singer).

Mark Kermode (UK): *The Exorcist* (Friedkin); *Brazil* (Gilliam); *Citizen Kane; The Devils* (Russell); *Don't Look Now* (Roeg); *Les Yeux sans Visage* (Franju); *It's a Wonderful Life* (Capra); *Love and Death* (Allen); *Mary Poppins* (Stevenson); *The Seventh Seal* (Bergman).

Kim Ji-Seok (South Korea): *Battleship Potemkin; Citizen Kane; Diary of a Country Priest* (Bresson); *Tokyo Story; 2001: A Space Odyssey; Still Life* (Saless); *Nostalgia* (Tarkovsky); *A Tale of the Wind* (Ivens); *A City of Sadness* (Hou Xiaoxian); *Moment of Innocence* (Makhmalbaf).

Noel King (Australia, University of Tasmania): *The General* (Keaton); *The Passion of Joan of Arc* (Dreyer); *Le Jour se lève* (Carné); *My Darling Clementine* (Ford); *Seven Samurai* (Kurosawa); *Touch of Evil* (Welles); *Vivre sa Vie* (Godard); *Performance* (Roeg/Cammell); *The Travelling Players* (Angelopoulos); *Unforgiven* (Eastwood).

Amir Labaki (Brazil): *Berlin – Die Sinfonie der Grosstadt* (Ruttmann); *Modern Times* (Chaplin); *Citizen Kane; Les Enfants du Paradis* (Carné); *Ivan the Terrible* (Eisenstein); *Sunset Blvd.* (Wilder); *Rear Window* (Hitchcock); *The Searchers* (Ford); *2001: A Space Odyssey; The Godfather.*

Gavin Lambert (US): *A Star Is Born* (Cukor); *Au Hasard, Balthazar* (Bresson); *Greed* (von Stroheim); *Madame de…* (Ophuls); *Monsieur Verdoux* (Chaplin); *Pandora's Box* (Pabst); *Notorious* (Hitchcock); *Rocco and His Brothers* (Visconti); *That Obscure Object of Desire* (Buñuel); *The Magnificent Ambersons* (Welles).

Jean-Louis Leutrat (France, University of Paris): *Ivan the Terrible* (Eisenstein); *JLG/JLG* (Godard); *Last Year in Marienbad* (Resnais); *Méditerranée* (Pollet); *Mort d'un président* (Prezydenta/Kawalerowicz); *Vaghe Stelle dell'Orsa* (Visconti); *Pickpocket* (Bresson); *The Scarlet Empress* (von Sternberg); *She Wore a Yellow Ribbon* (Ford); *Sherlock Junior* (Keaton).

Shawn Levy (US, The Oregonian): *La Belle et la Bête* (Cocteau); *Bicycle Thieves* (De Sica); *Chinatown* (Polanski); *8½; The General* (Keaton); *The Godfather/The Godfather Part II; La Grande Illusion* (Renoir); *Ran* (Kurosawa); *Vertigo; Wings of Desire* (Wenders).

Li Cheuk-To (Hong Kong, chairman Hong Kong Critics Guild): *Au Hasard, Balthazar* (Bresson); *Floating Cloud* (Naruse); *The General* (Keaton); *Mirror* (Tarkovsky); *Pather Panchali* (Ray); *The Puppetmaster* (Hou Xiaoxian); *Spring in a Small Town* (Fei Mu); *Tabu* (Murnau); *Deux ou Trois Choses que Je Sais d'Elle* (Godard); *Vertigo.*

Jacques Lourcelles (France): *While the City Sleeps* (Lang); *Forever Amber* (Preminger); *Nosferatu* (Murnau); *The 39 Steps* (Hitchcock); *Cat People* (Tourneur); *Gentleman Jim* (Walsh); *Cattle Queen of Montana* (Dwan); *Mon père avait raison* (Guitry); *Going My Way* (McCarey); *Naked Dawn* (Ulmer).

Simon Louvish (UK): *King Size Canary* (Avery); *La Dolce Vita* (Fellini); *Ikiru* (Kurosawa); *Eijanaika* (Imamura); *A Matter of Life and Death* (Powell/ Pressburger); *Greed* (von Stroheim); *Duck Soup* (McCarey); *The Godfather Part II; World of Apu* (Ray); *Sunrise.*

Tim Lucas (US, editor Video Watchdog): *Sunrise; J'Accuse* (Gance, 1937); *La Belle et la Bête* (Cocteau); *The Third Man* (Reed); *Umberto D.* (De Sica); *Le Mépris* (Godard); *2001: A Space Odyssey; Once Upon a Time in the West* (Leone); *Perceval le Gallois* (Rohmer); *Three Colours: Red* (Kieslowski).

Todd McCarthy (US, Variety): *Trouble in Paradise* (Lubitsch); *The Scarlet Empress* (von Sternberg); *Le Crime de Monsieur Lange* (Renoir); *To Have and Have Not* (Hawks); *Notorious* (Hitchcock); *Tirez sur le Pianiste* (Truffaut); *Lawrence of Arabia* (Lean); *Le Mépris* (Godard); *Chimes at Midnight* (Welles); *The Godfather Part II.*

Martin McCloone (UK, University of Ulster): *The Godfather Part II; GoodFellas* (Scorsese); *Lone Star* (Sayles); *Out of the Past* (Tourneur); *Padre Padrone* (Taviani Brothers); *The Searchers* (Ford); *The Spider's Stratagem* (Bertolucci); *The Travelling Players* (Angelopoulos); *Vertigo; Vivre sa Vie* (Godard).

Tony Macklin (US): *Citizen Kane; The Gold Rush* (Chaplin); *The General* (Keaton); *The Searchers* (Ford); *La Dolce Vita; Vertigo; 2001: A Space Odyssey; Jules et Jim* (Truffaut); *The Godfather Part II; Once Upon a Time in the West* (Leone).

Shinozaki Makoto (Japan): *Sunrise; Kawachiyama Shunso* (Yamanaka); *Day of Wrath* (Dreyer); *Ride the High Country* (Peckinpah); *Subete ga kurutteru* (Suzuki); *Minagoroshi no reika* (Kato Tai); *The Grissom Gang* (Aldrich); *Opening Night* (Cassavetes); *L'Argent* (Bresson); *Unforgiven* (Eastwood).

Derek Malcolm (UK, The Guardian): *Dekalog* (Kieslowski); *The Music Room* (Ray); *Rio Bravo* (Hawks); *The Seventh Seal* (Bergman); *The Spirit of the Beehive* (Erice); *The Story of the Late Chrysanthemums* (Mizoguchi); *The Time to Live and the Time to Die* (Hou Xiaoxian); *Tokyo Story; Touch of Evil* (Welles); *Tristana* (Buñuel).

Adrian Martin (Australia): *Love Streams* (Cassavetes); *Au Hasard, Balthazar* (Bresson); *L'Enfant secret* (Garrel); *Letter from an Unknown Woman* (Ophuls); *Once Upon a Time in America* (Leone); *Peter Ibbetson* (Hathaway); *The Awful Truth* (McCarey); *By the Bluest of Seas* (Barnet); *Badlands* (Malick); *Artists and Models* (Tashlin).

Andy Medhurst (UK, University of Sussex): *The American Soldier* (Fassbinder); *Brief Encounter* (Lean); *Chinatown* (Polanski); *Holiday* (Cukor); *Meantime* (Leigh); *Meet Me in St Louis* (Minnelli); *The Opposite of Sex* (Roos); *Red River* (Hawks); *Vertigo; Women on the Verge of a Nervous Breakdown* (Almodóvar).

David Meeker (UK): *Tih Minh* (Feuillade); *Love Me Tonight* (Mamoulian); *L'Atalante* (Vigo); *Sullivan's Travels* (Sturges); *Listen to Britain* (Jennings); *Laura* (Preminger); *Red River* (Hawks); *El* (Buñuel); *Bob le Flambeur* (Melville); *Marnie* (Hitchcock).

Joan Mellon (US): *Battleship Potemkin; Greed* (von Stroheim); *Ivan the Terrible* (Eisenstein); *The Life of Oharu* (Mizoguchi); *McCabe & Mrs Miller* (Altman); *Paisà* (Rossellini); *Pather Panchali* (Ray); *The Searchers* (Ford); *Seven Samurai* (Kurosawa); *2001: A Space Odyssey.*

Pascal Mérigeau (France, Le Nouvel Observateur): *America America* (Kazan); *Drifting Clouds* (Kaurismäki); *L'Enfance nue* (Pialat); *M* (Lang); *The Man Who Shot Liberty Valance* (Ford); *Monsieur Verdoux* (Chaplin); *The Navigator* (Keaton); *La Règle du Jeu; Sunrise; Trouble in Paradise* (Lubitsch) .

Ken Mogg (Australia, editor MacGuffin): *Barry Lyndon* (Kubrick); *Citizen Kane; Claire's Knee* (Rohmer); *The Leopard* (Visconti); *Marnie* (Hitchcock); *La Règle du Jeu; The Saga of Anatahan* (von Sternberg); *Tokyo Story; Topsy-Turvy* (Leigh); *Vertigo.*

Laura Mulvey (UK, University of London): *Viaggio in Italia* (Rossellini); *Pyaasa* (Dutt); *Through the Olive Trees* (Kiarostami); *Jeanne Dielman* (Akerman); *Liebelei* (Ophuls); *Man With a Movie Camera* (Vertov); *Xala* (Sembene); *The Man Who Shot Liberty Valance* (Ford); *Deux ou Trois Choses que Je Sais d'Elle* (Godard); *Love Me Tonight* (Mamoulian).

Kim Newman (UK): *Apocalypse Now* (Coppola); *Blue Velvet* (Lynch); *A Canterbury Tale* (Powell/ Pressburger); *Citizen Kane; Inferno* (Argento); *The King of Comedy* (Scorsese); *Let's Scare Jessica to Death* (Hancock); *Notorious* (Hitchcock); *The Shining* (Kubrick); *To Have and Have Not* (Hawks).

Katja Nicodemus (Germany, Die Zeit): *North by Northwest* (Hitchcock); *Rio Bravo* (Hawks); *All About Eve* (Mankiewicz); *2001: A Space Odyssey; Mean Streets* (Scorsese); *Pierrot le Fou* (Godard); *One, Two, Three* (Wilder); *The Wind Will Carry Us* (Kiarostami); *Ai No Corrida* (Oshima); *Céline and Julie Go Boating* (Rivette).

Jacques Noël (Belgium): *Citizen Kane; 2001: A Space Odyssey; Apocalypse Now* (Coppola); *Singin' in the Rain; Metropolis* (Lang); *Modern Times* (Chaplin); *Battleship*

Potemkin; Rio Bravo (Hawks); *A Clockwork Orange* (Kubrick); *It's a Wonderful Life* (Capra).

Barry Norman (UK): *Battleship Potemkin; Bringing Up Baby* (Hawks); *Citizen Kane; Paths of Glory* (Kubrick); *Rashomon* (Kurosawa); *La Règle du Jeu; The Searchers* (Ford); *The Seventh Seal* (Bergman); *Singin' in the Rain; Some Like It Hot* (Wilder).

Camille Paglia (US, University of the Arts in Philadelphia): *Citizen Kane; La Dolce Vita* (Fellini); *Gone With the Wind* (Fleming); *Lawrence of Arabia* (Lean); *North by Northwest* (Hitchcock); *Orphée* (Cocteau); *Persona* (Bergman); *The Ten Commandments* (DeMille); *2001: A Space Odyssey; Vertigo.*

Ellen J. Paglinauan (Philippines): *Citizen Kane; Tokyo Story; La Règle du Jeu; Battleship Potemkin; Vertigo; 2001: A Space Odyssey; 8½; Rashomon* (Kurosawa); *The Passion of Joan of Arc* (Dreyer); *The Godfather.*

David Parkinson (UK): *Intolerance* (Griffith); *Battleship Potemkin; Le Roman d'un Tricheur* (Guitry); *Citizen Kane; Rome, Open City* (Rossellini); *Rashomon* (Kurosawa); *Les Vacances de M. Hulot* (Tati); *Psycho* (Hitchcock); *2001: A Space Odyssey; Do the Right Thing* (Lee).

Milan Pavlovic (Germany, editor Steadicam): *The Wild Bunch* (Peckinpah); *Sunrise; Once Upon a Time in America* (Leone); *The Searchers* (Ford); *Some Like It Hot* (Wilder); *Taxi Driver* (Scorsese); *North by Northwest* (Hitchcock); *Touch of Evil* (Welles); *Les Amants du Pont-Neuf* (Carax); *The Purple Rose of Cairo* (Allen).

Fernando Martín Peña (Argentina): *Cries and Whispers* (Bergman); *The General* (Keaton); *The Hidden Fortress* (Kurosawa); *Un Condamné à mort s'est échappé* (Bresson); *Metropolis* (Lang); *October* (Eisenstein); *Paths of Glory* (Kubrick); *Stagecoach* (Ford); *Los Traidores* (Gleyzer); *The Trial* (Welles).

Andrey Plakhov (Russia): *A Bout de Souffle* (Godard); *Blue Velvet* (Lynch); *Breaking the Waves* (von Trier); *The Eclipse* (Antonioni); *The Lady from Shanghai* (Welles); *Mirror* (Tarkovsky); *Nosferatu* (Murnau); *8½; La Règle du Jeu; Rashomon* (Kurosawa).

Dana Polan (US, University of Southern California): *Psycho* (Hitchcock); *Sunrise; Jules et Jim* (Truffaut); *The Godfather; Rashomon* (Kurosawa); *M* (Lang); *Lawrence of Arabia* (Lean); *Intolerance* (Griffith); *Modern Times* (Chaplin); *Singin' in the Rain.*

John Powers (US, LA Weekly): *An Autumn Afternoon* (Ozu); *Bande à part* (Godard); *Belle de Jour* (Buñuel); *Les Dames du Bois de Boulogne* (Bresson); *The Godfather Part II; Meghe Dhaka Tara* (Ghatak); *The Passenger* (Antonioni); *Rio Bravo* (Hawks); *The Shop Around the Corner* (Lubitsch); *The Time to Live and the Time to Die* (Hou Xiaoxian).

MK Raghavendra (India): *L'Argent* (Bresson); *Vertigo; La Belle Noiseuse* (Rivette); *Close-Up* (Kiarostami); *L'Avventura* (Antonioni); *Solaris* (Tarkovsky); *The Phantom of Liberty* (Buñuel); *The Sweet Hereafter* (Egoyan); *An Autumn Afternoon* (Ozu); *Pulp Fiction* (Tarantino).

Tony Rayns (UK): *Zvenigora* (Dovzhenko); *Dushi Fengguang* (Muzhi); *Straits of Love and Hate* (Mizoguchi); *No. 12 (aka Heaven and Earth Magic)* (Harry Smith); *Chimes at Midnight* (Welles); *Arabian Nights* (Pasolini); *Blind Chance* (Kieslowski); *Once Upon a Time in America* (Leone); *Taipei Story* (Edward Yang); *Close-Up* (Kiarostami).

Donald Richie (US/Japan): *The Passion of Joan of Arc* (Dreyer); *Earth* (Dovzhenko); *Citizen Kane; Tokyo Story; Seven Samurai* (Kurosawa); *Pather Panchali* (Ray); *Wild Strawberries* (Bergman); *L'Avventura* (Antonioni); *Au Hasard, Balthazar* (Bresson); *Mirror* (Tarkovsky).

Pierre Rissient (France): *Night and the City* (Dassin); *The Mothering Heart* (Griffith); *Journey to the Lost City* (Lang); *Not Wanted* (Clifton); *From Saturday to Sunday* (Machaty); *Love Affair* (McCarey); *The Story of the Late Chrysanthemums* (Mizoguchi); *La Ronde* (Ophuls); *Die Wunderbare Lüge der Nina Petrowna* (Schwarz); *Pursued* (Walsh).

David Robinson (UK): *The Kid* (Chaplin); *Napoléon* (Gance); *L'Age d'Or* (Buñuel); *Stagecoach* (Ford); *La Règle du Jeu; Les Enfants du Paradis* (Carné); *Citizen Kane; Tokyo Story; Pather Panchali* (Ray); *Farewell My Concubine* (Chen Kaige).

Jonathan Romney (UK, Independent on Sunday): *The Enigma of Kaspar Hauser* (Herzog); *Hellzapoppin'* (Potter); *It's a Wonderful Life* (Capra); *Lola* (Demy); *Le Mépris* (Godard); *Sátántangó* (Tarr); *The Shining* (Kubrick); *Street of Crocodiles* (Brothers Quay); *Three Crowns of the Sailor* (Ruiz); *Touch of Evil* (Welles).

David Rooney (Australia, Variety): *Bride of Frankenstein* (Whale); *Les Quatre Cents Coups* (Truffaut); *The Last Picture Show* (Bogdanovich); *The Man Who Shot Liberty Valance* (Ford); *Out of the Past* (Tourneur); *Rear Window* (Hitchcock); *Sans Soleil* (Marker); *Tokyo Story; The Wizard of Oz* (Fleming); *Written on the Wind* (Sirk).

Jonathan Rosenbaum (US, Chicago Reader): *Les Vampires* (Feuillade); *M* (Lang); *The Story of the Late Chrysanthemums* (Mizoguchi); *Ivan the Terrible* (Eisenstein); *Gentlemen Prefer Blondes*

(Hawks); *Gertrud* (Dreyer); *Last Year in Marienbad* (Resnais); *The House Is Black* (Farokhzad); *Playtime* (Tati); *When It Rains* (Burnett).

Scott Rosenberg (Thailand): *Citizen Kane; I Am Curious, Yellow* (Sjöman); *King Kong* (Cooper/Schoedsack); *Metropolis* (Lang); *Rain Man* (Levinson); *Seven Samurai* (Kurosawa); *Singin' in the Rain; Star Wars* (Lucas); *The Graduate* (Nichols); *To Kill a Mockingbird* (Mulligan).

Jonathan Ross (UK, BBC): *8½; Blade Runner* (Scott); *Sunset Blvd.* (Wilder); *Ikiru* (Kurosawa); *The Wages of Fear* (Clouzot); *Faster, Pussycat! Kill! Kill!* (Meyer); *In the Mood for Love* (Wong Kar-Wai); *The Producers* (Brooks); *Duck Soup* (McCarey); *My Neighbour Totoro* (Miyazaki).

Bill Rothman (US, University of Miami): *A Bout de Souffle* (Godard); *Gertrud* (Dreyer); *Late Spring* (Ozu); *Letter from an Unknown Woman* (Ophuls); *The Philadelphia Story* (Cukor); *La Règle du Jeu; The Searchers* (Ford); *Sunrise; Vertigo; World of Apu* (Ray).

Jaan Ruus (Estonia, Eesti Ekspress): *L'Atalante* (Vigo); *Battleship Potemkin; A Bout de Souffle* (Godard); *Citizen Kane; 8½; Man With a Movie Camera* (Vertov); *Persona* (Bergman); *Rashomon* (Kurosawa); *La Règle du Jeu; The Wind Will Carry Us* (Kiarostami).

Sukhdev Sandhu (UK, Daily Telegraph): *The Third Man* (Reed); *Les Quatre Cents Coups* (Truffaut); *The Apple* (Makhmalbaf); *Pather Panchali* (Ray); *Breaking the Waves* (von Trier); *Good Morning, Boys!* (Varnel); *Bicycle Thieves* (De Sica); *Hue and Cry* (Crichton); *Brief Encounter* (Lean); *Exodus (1992–97)* (McQueen).

Tadao Sato (Japan, Fukuoka Film Festival): *The Story of the Late Chrysanthemums* (Mizoguchi); *Crows and Sparrows* (Zheng Junli); *Tokyo Story; Minamata* (Tsuchimoto); *Bogeyman* (Aravindan); *Where Is My Friend's House?* (Kiarostami); *My Neighbour Totoro* (Miyazaki); *Red Persimmon* (Wang T'ung); *Ferocious Saint Lord of Gobi* (Nyamgavaa); *Chunhyang* (Im Kwon-Taek).

Mark Schilling (Japan, Japan Times): *2001: A Space Odyssey; Citizen Kane; Seven Samurai* (Kurosawa); *8½; The Godfather/The Godfather Part II; Tokyo Story; Vertigo; The General* (Keaton); *GoodFellas* (Scorsese); *L'Avventura* (Antonioni).

Kim Skotte (Denmark, Politiken): *Seven Samurai* (Kurosawa); *Singin' in the Rain; On the Waterfront* (Kazan); *Stagecoach* (Ford); *The Godfather/The Godfather Part II; Fanny and Alexander* (Bergman); *Touch of Evil* (Welles); *Burnt by the Sun* (Mikhalkov); *Jules et Jim* (Truffaut); *Bicycle Thieves* (De Sica).

Anneke Smelik (Netherlands, University of Nijmegen): *Hiroshima, Mon Amour* (Resnais); *The Piano* (Campion); *Antonia's Line* (Gorris); *The Silences of the Palace* (Tlatli); *A idade maior* (Villaverde); *Daisies* (Chytilová); *Hour of the Star* (Amaral); *Orlando* (Potter); *Dust* (Hänsel); *Floating Life* (Law).

Gavin Smith (US, Film Comment): *The Passion of Joan of Arc* (Dreyer); *Sunrise; La Règle du Jeu; The Magnificent Ambersons* (Welles); *Psycho* (Hitchcock); *The Eclipse* (Antonioni); *Au Hasard, Balthazar* (Bresson); *Deux ou Trois Choses que Je Sais d'Elle* (Godard); *Taxi Driver* (Scorsese); *Days of Heaven* (Malick).

Paul Julian Smith (UK, Cambridge University): *Vertigo; Citizen Kane; Meet Me in St. Louis* (Minnelli); *A Star Is Born* (Cukor); *Imitation of Life* (Sirk); *Mildred Pierce* (Curtiz); *A Bout de Souffle* (Godard); *Chungking Express* (Wong Kar-Wai); *All About My Mother* (Almodóvar); *Amores perros* (González Iñárritu).

Jack Stevenson (Denmark/US): *Blade Runner* (Scott); *Brainstorm* (Conrad); *Europa* (von Trier); *Metropolis* (Lang); *Midnight Cowboy* (Schlesinger); *The Night of the Hunter* (Laughton); *Summer with Monika* (Bergman); *The Third Man* (Reed); *The Wizard of Oz* (Fleming); *Written on the Wind* (Sirk).

David Stratton (Australia, The Australian): *Greed* (von Stroheim); *The General* (Keaton); *La Règle du Jeu; The Grapes of Wrath* (Ford); *Citizen Kane; Letter from an Unknown Woman* (Ophuls); *Singin' in the Rain; Seven Samurai* (Kurosawa); *A Bout de Souffle* (Godard); *Nashville* (Altman).

Philip Strick (UK): *L'Avventura* (Antonioni); *Black Narcissus* (Powell/Pressburger); *Blade Runner* (Scott); *French Cancan* (Renoir); *Le Mépris* (Godard); *The Searchers* (Ford); *Solaris* (Tarkovsky); *2001: A Space Odyssey; Vertigo; Wild Strawberries* (Bergman).

Yvonne Tasker (UK, University of East Anglia): *Boys Don't Cry* (Peirce); *Chinatown* (Polanski); *The Conversation* (Coppola); *Johnny Guitar* (Ray); *M* (Lang); *Orlando* (Potter); *The Piano* (Campion); *Rebecca* (Hitchcock); *Thelma & Louise* (Scott); *Touch of Evil* (Welles).

Amy Taubin (US): *La Règle du Jeu; Au Hasard, Balthazar* (Bresson); *Man With a Movie Camera* (Vertov); *La Prise de Pouvoir de Louis XIV* (Rossellini); *Deux ou Trois Choses que Je Sais d'Elle* (Godard); *Vertigo; Shoah* (Lanzmann); *Diaries, Notes & Sketches; Walden* (Mekas); *Jeanne Dielman* (Akerman); *Spider* (Cronenberg).

Trevor Steele Taylor (South Africa): *2001: A Space Odyssey; Blow-Up* (Antonioni); *Culloden* (Watkins); *Deep Throat* (Gerard); *The Gospel According* *to St Matthew* (Pasolini); *If…* (Anderson); *The Long Day's Dying* (Collinson); *Performance* (Roeg/Cammell); *Toby Dammit* (episode in *Histoires Extraordinaires)* (Fellini); *The Wild Bunch* (Peckinpah).

Simeon Tegel (Mexico): *Day of the Beast* (Iglesia); *Herod's Law* (Estrada); *Cabeza de Vaca* (Echevarria); *Three Kings* (Russell); *Snatch* (Ritchie); *Man Bites Dog* (Belvaux/Poelvoorde); *Pulp Fiction* (Tarantino); *The Night of the Hunter* (Laughton); *Night of the Hunter* (Greene); *Fitzcarraldo* (Herzog).

Charles Tesson (France, editor Cahiers du Cinéma): *La Règle du Jeu; To Be or Not to Be* (Lubitsch); *Ordet* (Dreyer); *El* (Buñuel); *Beyond a Reasonable Doubt* (Lang); *Vertigo; Sounds from the Mountains* (Naruse); *Miss Oyu* (Mizoguchi); *The Music Room* (Ray); *Francisca* (Oliveira).

David Thomson (US, New York Times): *Blue Velvet* (Lynch); *Céline and Julie Go Boating* (Rivette); *Citizen Kane; The Conformist* (Bertolucci); *His Girl Friday* (Hawks); *Un Condamné à mort s'est échappé* (Bresson); *Pierrot le Fou* (Godard); *La Règle du Jeu; That Obscure Object of Desire* (Buñuel); *Ugetsu Monogatari* (Mizoguchi).

Sakari Toiviainen (Finland); *Battleship Potemkin; The Circus* (Chaplin); *La Grande Illusion* (Renoir); *Tokyo Story; Rear Window* (Hitchcock); *The Searchers* (Ford); *Wild Strawberries* (Bergman); *Le Mépris* (Godard); *Au Hasard, Balthazar* (Bresson); *India Song* (Duras).

Leonardo Garcia Tsao (Mexico): *Intolerance* (Griffith); *Sunrise; The Passion of Joan of Arc* (Dreyer); *King Kong* (Cooper/Schoedsack); *L'Atalante* (Vigo); *Los Olvidados* (Buñuel); *Seven Samurai* (Kurosawa); *Vertigo; La Dolce Vita* (Fellini); *Andrei Rublev* (Tarkovsky).

Kenneth Turan (US, Los Angeles Times): *Battleship Potemkin; Citizen Kane; Les Enfants du Paradis* (Carné); *The Godfather/The Godfather Part II; Madame de…* (Ophuls); *La Règle du Jeu; Seven Samurai* (Kurosawa); *Sherlock Junior* (Keaton); *Singin' in the Rain; Vertigo.*

Hulya Ucansu (Turkey, Istanbul Film Festival): *The Player* (Altman); *Three Colours Trilogy* (Kieslowski); *Pulp Fiction* (Tarantino); *Un Coeur en hiver* (Sautet); *Fargo* (Coen); *A Taste of Cherry…* (Kiarostami); *Eyes Wide Shut* (Kubrick); *Eternity and a Day* (Angelopoulos); *All About My Mother* (Almodóvar); *Clouds of May* (Ceylan).

Aruna Vasudev (India, editor Cinemaya): *The Seventh Seal* (Bergman); *Tokyo Story; Pather Panchali* (Ray); *8½; Last Year in Marienbad* (Resnais); *A Bout de Souffle* (Godard); *Antonio das Mortes* (Rocha); *Andrei Rublev* (Tarkovsky); *Singin' in the Rain; Yellow Earth* (Chen Kaige).

Walt Vian (Switzerland, editor Filmbulletin): *La Prise de Pouvoir de Louis XIV* (Rossellini); *Pierrot le Fou* (Godard); *Ugetsu Monogatari* (Mizoguchi); *La Règle du Jeu; Tokyo Story; The Round-Up* (Jancsó); *North by Northwest* (Hitchcock); *Rashomon* (Kurosawa); *Out 1: Spectre* (Rivette); *8½.*

Ginette Vincendeau (UK/France, University of Warwick): *Cléo de 5 à 7* (Varda); *Double Indemnity* (Wilder); *La Grande Illusion* (Renoir); *The Leopard* (Visconti); *The Man Who Shot Liberty Valance* (Ford); *Le Mépris* (Godard); *Pépé le Moko* (Duvivier); *Rear Window* (Hitchcock); *Le Samourai* (Melville); *Wild Strawberries* (Bergman).

Alexander Walker (UK, Evening Standard): *L'Avventura* (Antonioni); *Citizen Kane; Dr Strangelove: or, How I Learned to Stop Worrying and Love the Bomb* (Kubrick); *La Dolce Vita* (Fellini); *Les Quatre Cents Coups* (Truffaut); *The Leopard* (Visconti); *Some Like It Hot* (Wilder); *Taxi Driver* (Scorsese); *2001: A Space Odyssey; Wild Strawberries* (Bergman).

Armond White (US, New York Press): *A.I. Artificial Intelligence* (Spielberg); *L'Avventura* (Antonioni); *Intolerance* (Griffith); *Jules et Jim* (Truffaut); *Lawrence of Arabia* (Lean); *Lola* (Demy); *The Magnificent Ambersons* (Welles); *Masculin Féminin* (Godard); *Nashville* (Altman); *The Passion of Joan of Arc* (Dreyer).

Linda Williams (US, University of California, Berkeley): *L'Age d'Or* (Buñuel); *Belle de Jour* (Buñuel); *The Birth of a Nation* (Griffith); *Ai No Corrida* (Oshima); *Modern Times* (Chaplin); *Persona* (Bergman); *Sansho Dayu* (Mizoguchi); *A Star Is Born* (Cukor); *Swing Time* (Stevens); *Le Vampire* (Dreyer).

Peter Wollen (UK/US): *L'Age d'Or* (Buñuel); *The Cabinet of Dr Caligari* (Wiene); *Journeys from Berlin* (Rainer); *Modern Times* (Chaplin); *Pakeezah* (Amrohi); *La Règle du Jeu; Singin' in the Rain; Topsy-Turvy* (Leigh); *Vertigo; Vivre sa Vie* (Godard).

Michael Wood (US, Princeton University): *The Passion of Joan of Arc* (Dreyer); *Ugetsu Monogatari* (Mizoguchi); *Vertigo; Touch of Evil* (Welles); *Sunset Blvd.* (Wilder); *GoodFellas* (Scorsese); *La Jetée* (Marker); *Tristana* (Buñuel); *8½; The Cabinet of Dr Caligari* (Wiene).

Robin Wood (UK/Canada): *Rio Bravo* (Hawks); *Les Demoiselles de Rochefort* (Demy); *Heaven's Gate* (Cimino); *I Walked with a Zombie* (Tourneur); *Late Spring* (Ozu); *Marnie* (Hitchcock); *Rally 'round the Flag, Boys!* (McCarey); *The Reckless Moment* (Ophuls); *La Règle du Jeu; Ugetsu Monogatari* (Mizoguchi).

Andrew Worsdale (South Africa): *A Bout de Souffle* (Godard); *Apocalypse Now*

(Coppola); *L'Atalante* (Vigo); *Black Narcissus* (Powell/Pressburger); *Dr Strangelove: or, How I Learned to Stop Worrying and Love the Bomb* (Kubrick); *The Godfather; Once Upon a Time in America* (Leone); *Singin' in the Rain; Taxi Driver* (Scorsese); *Vertigo*.

Helena Ylänen (Finland): *8½; The Passenger* (Antonioni); *Tristana* (Buñuel); *Broken Blossoms* (Griffith); *Citizen Kane; Bonnie and Clyde* (Penn); *Red River* (Hawks); *No End* (Kieslowski); *Barry Lyndon* (Kubrick); *The Life and Death of Colonel Blimp* (Powell/Pressburger).

Slavoj Zizek (Slovenia): *Vertigo; Psycho* (Hitchcock); *Dune* (Lynch); *Ivan the Terrible* (Eisenstein); *The Fountainhead* (Vidor); *3.10 to Yuma* (Daves); *Opfergang* (Harlan); *The Sound of Music* (Wise); *Short Cuts* (Altman); *Limelight* (Chaplin).

Cinema Centenary Top One Hundred

In 1995, to mark the Centenary of Cinema, *Time Out* polled a host of directors, producers, actors, programmers and critics to find out what they felt had been the high points of that last 100 years. Each person was asked to name his or her top ten films.

Participants in the poll were each given 40 points. If they stipulated that their choices weren't in order of preference, each movie received 4 points. For those who nominated their selection in preferential order, the first choice received 7 points, the second 6, third 5, fourth 4, and fifth to tenth 3 each. Points for split/equal choices were divided appropriately. The aim of this points system was simple: to reward preferred films without pretending, say, that a number one favourite was 10 times as popular as a tenth choice, as a '10 down to 1' points system would have reflected.

Centenary Top 100 films are marked in the text with this logo: 100

1. Citizen Kane *111 points*
(Orson Welles, 1941, US)

2. The Godfather *101*
(Francis Ford Coppola, 1971/1974/1990, US)

3. La Règle du Jeu *77*
(Jean Renoir, 1939, Fr)

4. Vertigo *73*
(Alfred Hitchcock, 1958, US)

5. Seven Samurai *63*
(Akira Kurosawa, 1954, Jap)

6. Lawrence of Arabia *60*
(David Lean, 1962, GB)

7. Raging Bull *58*
(Martin Scorsese, 1980, US)

8. Touch of Evil *55*
(Orson Welles, 1958, US)

9. Tokyo Story *50*
(Yasujiro Ozu, 1953, Jap)

10. L'Atalante *49*
(Jean Vigo, 1934, Fr)

11. The Night of the Hunter *47*
(Charles Laughton, 1955, US)

12. The Conformist *46*
(Bernardo Bertolucci, 1969, It/Fr/WGer)

13. Les Enfants du Paradis *41*
(Marcel Carné, 1945, Fr)
— A Matter of Life and Death *41*
(Michael Powell/Emeric Pressburger, 1946, GB)

15. 8½ *37*
(Federico Fellini, 1963, It)
— The Magnificent Ambersons *37*
(Orson Welles, 1942, US)

17. Apocalypse Now *36*
(Francis Ford Coppola, 1979, US)
— North by Northwest *36*
(Alfred Hitchcock, 1959, US)

19. Chinatown *32*
(Roman Polanski, 1974, US)

20. La Dolce Vita *31*
(Federico Fellini, 1960, Fr/It)
— The Searchers *31*
(John Ford, 1956, US)

22. The Wild Bunch *30*
(Sam Peckinpah, 1969, US)

23. The Life and Death of Colonel Blimp *29*
(Michael Powell/Emeric Pressburger, 1943, GB)
— Some Like It Hot *29*
(Billy Wilder, 1959, US)
— Taxi Driver *29*
(Martin Scorsese, 1976, US)

26. Napoléon *28*
(Abel Gance, 1927, Fr)
— Rear Window *28*
(Alfred Hitchcock, 1954, US)

28. Battleship Potemkin *26*
(Sergei Eisenstein, 1925, USSR)
— It's a Wonderful Life *26*
(Frank Capra, 1946, US)
— Performance *26*
(Nicolas Roeg/Donald Cammell, 1970, GB)

31. The General *25*
(Buster Keaton/Clyde Bruckman, 1926, US)

32. A Bout de Souffle *24*
(Jean-Luc Godard, 1959, Fr)
— Mean Streets *24*
(Martin Scorsese, 1973, US)
— Once Upon a Time in the West *24*
(Sergio Leone, 1968, It)
— Rio Bravo *24*
(Howard Hawks, 1959, US)

36. Once Upon a Time in America *23*
(Sergio Leone, 1983, US)

37. All About Eve *22*
(Joseph L Mankiewicz, 1950, US)
— My Darling Clementine *22*
(John Ford, 1946, US)
— 2001: A Space Odyssey *22*
(Stanley Kubrick, 1968, GB)

40. The Piano *21*
(Jane Campion, 1993, Aust)

— Pierrot le Fou *21*
(Jean-Luc Godard, 1965, Fr/It)

42. L'Année Dernière à Marienbad *20*
(Alain Resnais, 1961, Fr)
— Bringing Up Baby *20*
(Howard Hawks, 1938, US)
— Gone With the Wind *20*
(Victor Fleming, 1939, US)
— The Lady Eve *20*
(Preston Sturges, 1941, US)
— Letter from an Unknown Woman *20*
(Max Ophüls, 1948, US)
— Les Quatre Cents Coups *20*
(François Truffaut, 1959, Fr)

48. The Battle of Algiers *19*
(Gillo Pontecorvo, 1965, Alg/It)

49. The Gold Rush *18*
(Charles Chaplin, 1925, US)
— La Grande Illusion *18*
(Jean Renoir, 1937, Fr)
— Une Partie de Campagne *18*
(Jean Renoir, 1936, Fr)
— The Philadelphia Story *18*
(George Cukor, 1940, US)
— Pickpocket *18*
(Robert Bresson, 1959, Fr)
— Schindler's List *18*
(Steven Spielberg, 1993, US)
— The Shining *18*
(Stanley Kubrick, 1980, GB)
— The Third Man *18*
(Carol Reed, 1949, GB)

57. Dr Strangelove: or, How I Learned to Stop Worrying and Love the Bomb *17*
(Stanley Kubrick, 1963, GB)
— The Reckless Moment *17*
(Max Ophüls, 1949, US)
— Singin' in the Rain *17*
(Stanley Donen/Gene Kelly, 1952, US)

60. Blade Runner *16*
(Ridley Scott, 1982, US)
— Blue Velvet *16*
(David Lynch, 1986, US)
— Pather Panchali *16*
(Satyajit Ray, 1955, Ind)
— Le Samourai *16*
(Jean-Pierre Melville, 1967, Fr/It)
— Sans Soleil (Sunless) *16*
(Chris Marker, 1983, Fr)
— Sweet Smell of Success *16*
(Alexander Mackendrick, 1957, US)

66. Amarcord *15*
(Federico Fellini, 1973, It/Fr)
— Greed *15*
(Erich von Stroheim, 1923, US)
— La Passion de Jeanne d'Arc *15*
(Carl Dreyer, 1928, Fr)
— Persona *15*
(Ingmar Bergman, 1966, Swe)
— Rashomon *15*
(Akira Kurosawa, 1951, Jap)
— The Treasure of the Sierra Madre *15*
(John Huston, 1948, US)

72. All That Heaven Allows *14*
(Douglas Sirk, 1955, US)
— Black Narcissus *14*
(Michael Powell/Emeric Pressburger, 1946, GB)
— Double Indemnity *14*
(Billy Wilder, 1944, US)
— Intolerance *14*
(DW Griffith, 1916, US)
— Notorious *14*
(Alfred Hitchcock, 1946, US)
— Out of the Past *14*
(Jacques Tourneur, 1947, US)
— The Red Shoes *14*
(Michael Powell/Emeric Pressburger, 1948, GB)
— Sunset Blvd. *14*
(Billy Wilder, 1950, US)

80. Casablanca *13*
(Michael Curtiz, 1942, US)
— City Lights *13*
(Charles Chaplin, 1931, US)
— Ran *13*
(Akira Kurosawa, 1985, Fr/Jap)
— The Spirit of the Beehive *13*
(Victor Erice, 1973, Sp)
— Sunrise *13*
(FW Murnau, 1927, US)

85. The Killing of a Chinese Bookie *12*
(John Cassavetes, 1976, US)
— Ordet (The Word) *12*
(Carl Theodor Dreyer, 1954, Den)
— Three Colours: Red *12*
(Krzysztof Kieslowski, 1994, Fr/Switz/Pol)

88. Aliens *11*
(James Cameron, 1986, US)
— Amadeus *11*
(Milos Forman, 1984, US)
— L'Avventura *11*
(Michelangelo Antonioni, 1960, It)
— Badlands *11*
(Terrence Malick, 1974, US)
— Barry Lyndon *11*
(Stanley Kubrick, 1975, GB)
— The Bridge on the River Kwai *11*
(David Lean, 1957, GB)
— The Colour of Pomegranates *11*
(Sergo Paradjanov, 1969, USSR)
— Don't Look Now *11*
(Nicolas Roeg, 1973, GB/It)
— Earth *11*
(Alexander Dovzhenko, 1930, USSR)
— Fanny and Alexander *11*
(Ingmar Bergman, 1982, Swe)
— La Jetée *11*
(Chris Marker, 1962, Fr)
— Kind Hearts and Coronets *11*
(Robert Hamer, 1949, GB)
— The Man Who Fell to Earth *11*
(Nicolas Roeg, 1976, US)
— Mirror *11*
(Andrei Tarkovsky, 1974, USSR)
— Pandora's Box *11*
(GW Pabst, 1928, Ger)
— The Quiet Man *11*
(John Ford, 1952, US)
— Sansho Dayu *11*
(Kenji Mizoguchi, 1954, Jap)
— The Seventh Seal *11*
(Ingmar Bergman, 1956, Swe)
— Ugetsu Monogatari *11*
(Kenji Mizoguchi, 1953, Jap)
— West Side Story *11*
(Robert Wise/Jerome Robbins, 1961, US)

End Credits
Obituaries 2001–2002

The following notes deal with some of the more significant or engaging cinema-related artists who died between July 2001 and June 2002. A complete record, of course, would be five or six times as long.

The twentieth century falls away behind us and begins slowly to turn into History, over and done with, as attitudes shift, issues change and once-familiar personalities disappear from the scene on practically a daily basis. For example, **George Harrison**, musician and, on a small scale, movie tycoon: the name alone used to be identification enough. Now the tag 'ex-Beatle' is mandatory, and it will only take another generation or two before it becomes necessary to explain who the Beatles were. So it goes.

Other relevant figures from the UK include the comic fantasist **Spike Milligan**, part of the background for the majority of the population their whole lives long. The satires and entertainments of **Roy Boulting** (mostly made in collaboration with his twin brother John, deceased 1985) reflected the national scene, directly or indirectly, for over 30 years. And the arts certainly felt the impact, intermittently at least, of **Mary Whitehouse** and her campaign, on-going since the 1960s, for more rigorous censorship, though in the end she became a figure more of fun than of influence.

Iron Curtain cinema, like all other manifestations of the Soviet empire, flourished and withered away within the span of the century. Its practitioners included the Yugoslavian **Branko Bauer**, director of orthodox, or so it's said, essays in social realism. Not at all orthodox were the grotesque animations of the Pole **Jan Lenica**, who exiled himself (to France) early on in his career. In Czechoslovakia the films of **Jaromil Jires** were typical of the output of an innovative artist working within a conservative system: often tame, but bold and imaginative (*Valerie and Her Week of Wonders*) when the chance presented itself.

In Russia itself **Grigori Chukhrai** directed the internationally successful *Ballad of a Soldier*. But international successes were hardly the hallmark of USSR cinema. The prolific **Juri Ozerov** is known in the West only for his contribution to the Olympics film, *Visions of Eight*, and you have to turn to the reference books for information on **Stanislas Rostotsky**, who specialised in World War II movies. *And the Dawns Are Quiet Here* (1972), set in a women's anti-aircraft unit, seems to have been his finest hour.

There have been the usual dispiriting confirmations that, indeed, golden lads and girls all must, as chimney sweepers, come to dust. Circa 1960 none glittered more golden than **Troy Donahue**, flaxen-haired heart-throb of *A Summer Place* and other Delmer Daves weepies; than **Dolores Michaels**, one of the last wave of Fox starlets, in *Warlock* and the nuns-in-peril shocker *5 Gates to Hell*; than the sensuous **Nobu McCarthy**, another member of the *5 Gates to Hell* cast and a Jerry Lewis foil in *The Geisha Boy*; than **Irish McCalla**, a lively exploitation heroine in the likes of *She-Demons* and, inevitably, *5 Gates to Hell*, plainly this year's chart-topper for the morbidly inclined.

Dorothy McGuire was touchingly youthful in Kazan's *A Tree Grows in Brooklyn* (1945) but so rushed, cinematically, to embrace motherhood that the strapping Troy Donahue was addressing her as Mom a mere fourteen years later in the aforementioned *A Summer Place*. Not so much glittering as smouldering in an aristocratic sort of way was **Ivan Desny**, epitome of 'the continental lover' for Lean (*Madeleine*), Antonioni (*La Signora senza camelie*), Ophüls (*Lola Montez*). Like **Barbara Valentin** ('the German Jayne Mansfield', or so she was promoted), Desny went on to become a fixture in the Fassbinder repertory company. Most disheartening of all were the deaths of the impish **Charlotte Coleman** (*Four Weddings and a Funeral*) and the pop star **Aaliyah**, just embarking on an acting career (*Queen of the Damned*), the former barely out of her twenties, the latter barely into them.

Some actors are fortunate enough to link up with a major director and become a familiar part of his or her landscape: **Sihung Lung**, elderly parent in a bunch of Ang Lee movies. Others, more fortunate still, exemplify qualities that appeal to a range of directors: **François Périer**, who could play a Cocteau angel and a Melville cop with equal facility; **Francisco Rabal**, a gruff, sometimes brutal presence in films by Antonioni, Rivette and, especially, Buñuel; and **Philippe Léotard**, a permanently bruised and groggy-looking character whose credits take in an early Pialat, several mid-period Truffauts and a late Zinnemann. Then there are those actors who only manage to register in a major way on a single occasion. Who can forget the black sailor, **Otis Young**, who accompanied Jack Nicholson on his travels in *The Last Detail* – or remember him in anything else?

Another example is **Dave Barry**, a comedian who slogged away for decades – nightclubs, radio shows, occasional bit parts in movies. But the couple of weeks he spent on *Some Like It Hot* playing Beanstalk (or Beinstock), harassed manager of the all-girl band, guaranteed his place, not perhaps in the Hall of Fame, but at least in some adjoining Cubicle of Small Renown. In a separate but related category is **Harold Russell**, non-professional, one-time only actor who lost both his hands in World War II and who most touchingly played one of the returning veterans in *The Best Years of Our Lives*.

It may be animators or designers or directors whose names begin with the letter 'K'. But in every 12-month period there seems to be one classification of film-maker which figures above all others in the obituary listings. This time around it has been the turn of producers – for example **Julia Phillips**, a major figure in 1970s Hollywood with films like *Taxi Driver* and *Close Encounters of the Third Kind*, who chronicled her own career smash-up in the acidulous memoir *You'll Never Eat Lunch in This Town Again*. In contrast to Phillips' brief passage, **Samuel Z Arkoff** – the name sounds like a parody of a Hollywood producer – was in for the long haul. In 1954 he set up (with James H Nicholson) American International Pictures, generating over the next few decades dozens – no, hundreds – of cheap, cheerful and frequently cheeky exploitation pictures with, especially if Roger Corman was involved, a touch of class. Arkoff was in the tradition of the showman-producer, as was his correlate **Herman Cohen**, whose most familiar title, *I Was a Teenage Werewolf*, was bankrolled by AIP. **Michael Todd Jr** evidently aspired to be a showman too, like his father. But his Smell-O-Vision gimmick, demonstrated in the 1960 film *Scent of Mystery*, never caught on; the logistics of the thing hardly bear thinking about. More unexpectedly Todd produced an adaptation of Sylvia Plath's *The Bell Jar* (1979), regrettably not in Smell-O-Vision.

In Britain the output of **Ivan Foxwell** was full of interesting choices. Foxwell it was who hired Harold Pinter to write a spy movie, *The Quiller Memorandum*, and *Manuela* (1957) is one of the most under-appreciated films of its decade. Numerous Americans based themselves in London in the 1960s. **John Kohn** arrived earlier than most, and his productions – such films as *The Collector* and *Figures in a Landscape* – were invariably of above average interest.

Although **Lester Persky** occasionally took a producer credit (*Hair*, *Yanks*) his name was usually at the front of the picture, as in 'Persky–Bright presents…', the company being responsible for movies by Altman, Huston and Scorsese. Similarly **Carlo Bernasconi** was head of Medusa-Film, though perhaps enjoying less autonomy than that suggests, since he was generally acknowledged to be frontman for Silvio Berlusconi in many of the tycoon's media interests. His compatriot **Tonino Cervi**, however, was the real thing, producer of Bertolucci's debut feature *La Commare Secca* and of Antonioni's *The Red Desert*, on which poor Cervi had to watch the budget soar as, notoriously, Antonioni spray-painted the countryside in various hues supposed to complement his heroine's state of mind. Thereafter Cervi restricted himself to more commercial enterprises, spaghetti Westerns and such, one of which (*Today It's Me… Tomorrow You!*) he directed himself.

Albert Band also directed from time to time but it seems he came to prefer the producer's role, on a succession of low-budget horror/sci-fi pictures (*Troll*, *TerrorVision*), some straight, some satirical; he was the father of Charles Band, who continues the dynasty with more, much more of the same. Finally **Jules Buck**: he had a peripatetic sort of career, palling around with such colourful types as John Huston and Mark Hellinger, settling in Hollywood long enough to produce Fuller's *Fixed Bayonets!*, then criss-crossing the Atlantic, as required by his business arrangements with Peter O'Toole (*Under Milk Wood*) or with the American television industry.

The traffic between television and cinema has always been brisk and two-way. **Reginald Rose** was a prolific writer for the small screen – Siegel's *Crime in the Streets* and Lumet's *12 Angry Men* were both originally Rose teleplays – but his subsequent work for theatrical movies ranged from the sublime (*Man of the West*) to the ridiculous (*Who Dares Wins*). **Roy Huggins** made a bit of a name for himself, writing an efficient Richard Quine thriller here, directing a neat Randolph Scott Western there, but it wasn't until he shifted base to television, as creator/producer of a succession of hit series (*Maverick*, *The Fugitive*, *The Rockford Files*), that he made a real impact.

A squad of illustrious television detectives, played by actors with parallel big-screen careers, finally closed their casebooks. In France **Jean Richard** was a familiar, humorous presence in features by Renoir, Clair and Carné; at the same time he was, for French tele-viewers, Inspector Maigret – in 92 episodes, according to the reference books. Across the channel, in the trail-blazingly realistic *Z Cars* of the early '60s, playing the burly Barlow, **Stratford Johns** was so imposing an authority figure that it came as quite a shock subsequently to find him cavorting campily around a brothel in *Salome's Last Dance*. As for **John Thaw**, he had a long record of crime-fighting in various guises, but it was his last big role, that of Inspector Morse, for which he was most affectionately recalled. Still, film buffs with long memories (or large video archives) might also wish to celebrate some of his earlier work: for instance, his manic Marxist in 1968's *Praise Marx and Pass the Ammunition*.

Robert B Parker's private eye Spenser had a small screen incarnation, in the person of **Robert Urich** in a bunch of tele-features; on the cinema screen, Urich starred in Alan Rudolph's eco-thriller *Endangered Species*. Ellery Queen was a more upmarket sleuth, popular in print since the 1920s. In one of several TV manifestations he was played by **George Nader** – this was in the late 1950s, providing an intermezzo in the Nader career between his routinely heroic roles in Hollywood and the same sort of thing in Europe.

So much for the cops. Turning to the robbers, we find **Lawrence Tierney**, with his great cruel slab of a face and a rap sheet extending from 1945's *Dillinger* to the heist-meister of *Reservoir Dogs* decades later. **Barry Foster** wasn't especially noted for criminal roles, but his Necktie Murderer in Hitchcock's *Frenzy* – scrambling about in the back of a potato truck to retrieve evidence from the grubby corpse of one of his victims – overwhelms the memory. In *Out of the Past*, **Jane Greer** created what for many is the definitive femme fatale, though connoisseurs of the work of Mexican actress **Maria Félix** (*Enamorada*) would probably favour her more operatic style. Their polar opposite, the female victim, might be represented by **Linden Travers**, notably in *No Orchids for Miss Blandish*, where she falls for sad-eyed sadist Jack Larue; and more ambiguously by **Hildegard Knef**, symbol of humbled post-war German womanhood, but with enough resilience and intelligence to offset the martrydom tendency.

'A faraway cinema, of which we know little...' In his obituary notices **Tolomush Okeyev** was described as 'the father of the fledgling Kyrgyz film industry.' For many, perhaps, it came as fresh news that there was a country named Kyrgyzstan somewhere on the planet, let alone that it possessed a film industry, even a fledgling one. The deaths of **Alberto Pieralisi**, prolific Brazilian director, of **John O'Shea**, New Zealand director/producer, and of **AJ Kardar**, credited with making 'Pakistan's first art house movie' (*Jago Huwa Savera*) all signposted, at least for some of us, further gaps in our awareness. In any case, for English-speaking audiences there are numerous directors who exist in a distributor-related fog, looming briefly into view then disappearing for years, perhaps forever: the Chilean-born, French-exiled **Helvio Soto** (*Il Pleut sur Santiago*), the German **Theodor Kotulla** (*Death Is My Trade*), the Italian **Carmelo Bene** (*One Hamlet Less*).

Jeanne Loriod and **Oskar Sala** weren't exactly household names either, although their work must have impinged on most people to a slight extent. They were virtuosi of, respectively, the ondes martenot and the trautonium, both contraptions dating back to a time when musical instruments that you had to plug in were something of a novelty. Loriod was mainly a concert-hall performer, but she can be heard on the soundtracks of such Maurice Jarre-scored movies as *Lawrence of Arabia* and *Mad Max Beyond Thunderdome*. Sala was as much a composer as a performer – he worked on some of Lotte Reiniger's animations, for instance. But it was his contribution to Hitchcock's *The Birds* for which he was best known. It's alleged that he devised a sound for each bird species featured in the movie, though it would take a dedicated ornithological musico-cineaste, if such exists, to verify that claim. Most widely known of instrumentalists, though, was mouth-organist **Larry Adler**, witch-hunted out of America in the early '50s, very much part of the British scene subsequently. His film work included composing/performing scores for *Genevieve* and *King & Country*.

Elsewhere on the music scene, the extravagantly creepy scores of **James Bernard** lent Hammer productions much of their distinctive flavour, while the versatility of **Mario Nascimbene** is demonstrated by two of his credits from 1958: *The Vikings*, with its rousing music-to-pillage-by, and *Room at the Top*, where the accompaniment evokes a very different, bleak and mournful mood. **Raoul Kraushaar** was a middle-of-the-road Hollywood composer whose assignments seem perfectly random, though sometimes quite distinguished. In 1953, for instance, he scored Lang's *The Blue Gardenia* and Cameron Menzies' *Invaders from Mars* – without, it must be said, adding a great deal to the merits of either. By contrast, **Bill LeSage** was a talented jazz musician under contract to the Danziger Brothers which, as anyone familiar with British movies of the 1960s will appreciate, meant that LeSage's labours were on behalf of a string of yawn-inducing, long-forgotten programme-fillers.

A number of artists associated with the Hollywood musical quit the scene. Director **George Sidney** was especially identified with the genre, via originals like *The Harvey Girls*, Broadway adaptations such as *Pal Joey* and even, with *Scaramouche*, a virtual musical, lacking any actual numbers but entirely in the mainstream as regards rhythm, design and colour. **Herbert Ross** advanced from choreographing vehicles for Cliff Richard (*Summer Holiday*) to directing vehicles for Barbra Streisand (*Funny Lady*). **Leonard Gershe** worked on the lyrics of Judy Garland's 'Born in a Trunk' number in *A Star Is Born* and scripted both *Silk Stockings* and *Funny Face*.

Singers **Dolores Gray** and **Rosemary Clooney** both enjoyed a cinematic vogue in the mid-'50s, Gray in *Kismet* and *It's Always Fair Weather*, Clooney with, notably, *White Christmas*. It was for his skills as musical arranger that **Ralph Burns** was most in demand: *Cabaret, New York New York, Annie*. But **Jay Livingston** presents a problem of categorisation: while he composed numerous movie-related popular songs (lyricist: Ray Evans) he seems never to have tackled a full-blown, straight-out musical. Doris Day sang 'Que Sera Sera' in a Hitchcock thriller, Debbie Reynolds 'Tammy' in a romantic comedy – and so, distinguishedly, on.

One of the more obscure Livingston/Evans compositions was their 'Paramount-Don't-Want-Me Blues', written for the specific plot requirements of **Billy Wilder**'s *Sunset Blvd*. Wilder's imagination seldom operated outside the twentieth century. The one exception – *The Private Life of Sherlock Holmes* – is an exception only by a year or two. Otherwise he was Twentieth Century Man through and through, finding little to admire about his time but plenty to be amused by. Wilder's range of subject matter, though not much else, was paralleled in France by **Henri Verneuil**, who busied himself with Alain Delon heist thrillers, a war film with Belmondo and even an Anthony Quinn Western. But humour (often involving Fernandel) predominated, as it did in the work of his compatriot **Yves Robert** who, Pagnol adaptations notwithstanding, was the most consistently successful French comedy director from the early '60s on. **David Swift**, another humorist, guided Hayley Mills through her first Hollywood movies and directed a couple of Jack Lemmon farces; and comedy seems to have been the forte of **Ted Demme**, a proposition which permits of no further exploration following his terribly premature exit. Casualties among the ranks of comedy players included the redoubtable **Kathleen Freeman**, talisman (talisperson?) of Jerry Lewis knockabout; **Peggy Mount**, an approximate British equivalent (*Sailor Beware*); and the erratic but highly sympathetic **Dudley Moore**.

The cartoons of **Chuck Jones** – several hundred of them – must have generated as much laughter and pleasure as any of the above-named. Taking in chase routines, conversation pieces, parodies and curious anecdotes, Jones' work occupies an unusual niche: films for grown-ups successfully passing themselves off as films for children. The droll little parables devised by **Ernest Pintoff** (*Flebus, The Critic*) were way out of the junior league on every level. He later turned to live-action features, with less fortunate results.

The taut, tough Westerns of **Budd Boetticher** had a vein of wry humour running through them that added to their distinctiveness. But the Boetticher problem persists: how come *The Rise and Fall of Legs Diamond* and his bundle of Randolph Scott Westerns are so lively and stylish, while the rest of his pictures are so routine, when not outright dreary? An enigma. A Western by **William Witney**, on the other hand, was hardly distinguishable, in terms of interest or achievement, from a Witney war film, juvenile delinquent melodrama or one of his Saturday matinee fantasy serials: which is to say that none of them is very good, though some have acquired silly cult status, especially the serials – *Captain Marvel, Dick Tracy*, etc. Also associated with the fantasy scene were **Louis M Heyward**, who functioned both as writer (*City Under the Sea*) and producer (the Dr Phibes movies); and **Chang Cheh**, director of Hong Kong martial arts movies with quaint-sounding titles like *The New One-Armed Swordsman*.

Fantasy of a different order was on offer in *Deep Throat*, in which **Linda Lovelace** did the thing she did. Also working that part of the street was **Francis Leroi**, a post-New Wave director whose early movies were sympathetically received but who in the mid-'70s veered into the production of hardcore erotica, becoming a leading French porn-smith with titles like *Mes Nuits avec Alice, Penelope, Arnold, Maud et Richard*. Britain's answer comes in the person of **Ray Selfe**, a one-man film industry functioning on various occasions as producer, director, cameraman, performer and even, with his little chain of West End cinemas, exhibitor. But this was in the '70s, when there was still a market for softcore like *Under the Bed*. By the '80s Selfe had moved on to other things.

Which no doubt we should too, scuttling away to the respectability of the West End or Broadway stage, where a number of grandes dames took their final curtain. **Irene Worth**'s entry in *Who's Who* is typical: columns of detail about her theatrical achievements, plus a couple of movie titles tacked on the end. But she was a powerful presence in Asquith's *Orders to Kill* and (admittedly a stage extension) Peter Brook's *King Lear*. Remembering the freshness of **Dorothy Tutin** in Brook's *The Beggar's Opera*, it seems a pity that quite so much of her time was spent working in the ephemeral medium of the theatre. **Kim Stanley**, a Broadway favourite, also dropped in on the movies only occasionally, notably for *The Goddess*, in which she played a Hollywood superstar, something she herself clearly had no ambitions to become. Among men of the theatre, **Nigel Hawthorne** had his greatest cinema success with another stage transposition, Alan Bennett's *The Madness of King George*. This is certainly the place to mention playwrights **Ruth Goetz** and **Anthony Shaffer**, the former the author (with husband Augustus) of *The Heiress* and adapter of *Carrie*, both for William Wyler, the latter the author of *Sleuth* and adapter on Hitchcock's *Frenzy*.

To end with, a selection of names from behind the camera – a very long way behind in some cases:

Photographed by: **Philippe Agostini**, who poeticised the spiritual values of the convent in *Les Anges du Péché*, and the violent macho ones of the Paris underworld in *Rififi*; **Subrata**

Mitra, responsible for the glittering monochrome of Satyajit Ray's early work; **Wilkie Cooper**, veteran British cinematographer with a career ranging from wartime realism (*Went the Day Well?*) to Technicolored Harryhausen fantasy (*Jason and the Argonauts*); **Dominique Chapuis**, whose resourcefulness extended to gumshoeing after aging Nazis in *Shoah*, his camera peeping out of a briefcase. More conventionally he shot movies by Claude Miller, Tonie Marshall, etc.

Art direction/production design by: **Danilo Donati**, evidently not one for rendering settings in any literal way, as demonstrated by his designs for *Amarcord* and *Pigsty*; **Richard Sylbert**, whose contributions were sometimes hard to spot (*Edge of the City*, *The Graduate*) and sometimes impossible to miss (*The Cotton Club*, *Dick Tracy*).

Costumes by: **Shirley Russell**, wife of Ken and something of a period specialist (*Reds*, *Greystoke*); **Mary Grant**, who ran up all those campy duds in *Bride of Vengeance*, not to mention the array of sharp suits in *Sweet Smell of Success*; **Tessa Prendergast**, whose designer bikini for Ursula Andress in *Dr No* succeeded in enhancing what one would have sworn was unenhanceable.

Make-up by: **John Chambers**, a somewhat macabre figure, a prosthetics genius whose experience with disfigured servicemen in World War II was reflected in the array of false noses, fake chins and bizarre appendages generally that were required by his Hollywood-related activities. The 1968 *Planet of the Apes* was, along with Mr Spock's ears, his best-known accomplishment.

Special effects by: **AD Flowers**: when the ship capsized in *The Poseidon Adventure*, when James Caan exited *The Godfather* with about a hundred bullet holes in him, Flowers it was who had made the necessary arrangements; **Glen Robinson**, whose make-believe mayhem was on an even grander scale, including the shaking apart of Los Angeles in *Earthquake* and the giant airship going up, or rather coming down, in flames in *The Hindenburg*.

Edited by: **Sophie Tatischeff**, daughter of Jacques Tati, cutter on some of his later pictures; **Evan A Lottman**, whose credits ranged from *The Muppets Take Manhattan* to a slew of Alan Pakula movies; **Ray Lovejoy**, a horror/fantasy specialist (*The Shining*, *Aliens*, the Burton Batmen); **Fredric Steinkamp**, a Frankenheimer favourite, obliged to forgo his scissors for some of the longest dissolves in movie history in *All Fall Down*; **Albert Jurgenson**, editor for Carné, Sautet, Claude Miller and, most consistently, Alain Resnais.

Distributed by: Contemporary Films, set up by **Charles Cooper** in the early 1950s, responsible for the UK circulation of work by Bergman, Satyajit Ray, Renoir and many others.

Reviewed by: the British-based **Raymond Durgnat**, who would doubtless have found something positive, if not necessarily coherent to say, in one of the numerous organs, *Time Out* included, to which he contributed; and by **Pauline Kael**, who would probably have found something negative, if not unamusing to say, from her perch at *The New Yorker*. Their paths crossed in print at least once, when Durgnat mounted a withering assault on Kael's withering assaults. But finally, the old advertisement for *Rear Window*, with its sinister message about a character who 'stared too long and saw too much' seems in both cases to be not entirely without application.

BOB BAKER

AALIYAH
16 Jan 79 – 23 Aug 01

Larry ADLER
10 Feb 14 – 6 Aug 01

Philippe AGOSTINI
11 Aug 10 – 20 Oct 01

Samuel Z ARKOFF
12 Jun 18 – 16 Sep 01

Albert BAND
7 May 24 – 14 Jun 02

Dave BARRY
26 Aug 18 – 16 Aug 01

Branko BAUER
18 Feb 21 – 11 Apr 02

Carmelo BENE
1 Sep 37 – 16 Mar 02

James BERNARD
20 Sep 25 – 12 Jul 01

Carlo BERNASCONI
15 Aug 43 – 6 Jul 01

Budd BOETTICHER
29 Jul 16 – 29 Nov 01

Roy BOULTING
21 Nov 13 – 5 Nov 01

Jules BUCK
30 Jul 17 – 18 Jul 01

Ralph BURNS
29 Jun 29 – 21 Nov 01

Tonino CERVI
14 Jun 29 – 31 Mar 02

John CHAMBERS
12 Sep 22 – 25 Aug 01

CHANG Cheh
1923 – 22 Jun 02

Dominique CHAPUIS
1948 – 4 Nov 01

Grigori CHUKHRAI
23 May 21 – 28 Oct 01

Rosemary CLOONEY
23 May 28 – 29 Jun 02

Herman COHEN
27 Aug 25 – 2 Jun 02

Charlotte COLEMAN
3 Apr 68 – 14 Nov 01

Charles COOPER
5 Jun 10 – 28 Nov 01

Wilkie COOPER
19 Oct 11 – 15 Dec 01

Ted DEMME
26 Oct 64 – 13 Jan 02

Ivan DESNY
28 Dec 22 – 13 Apr 02

Troy DONAHUE
27 Jan 36 – 2 Sep 01

Danilo DONATI
1926 – 2 Dec 01

Raymond DURGNAT
1 Sep 32 – 19 May 02

Maria FELIX
8 Apr 14 – 8 Apr 02

AD FLOWERS
1917 – 5 Jul 01

Barry FOSTER
21 Aug 31 – 11 Feb 02

Ivan FOXWELL
22 Feb 14 – 16 Jan 02

Kathleen FREEMAN
17 Feb 19 – 23 Aug 01

Leonard GERSHE
1922 – 9 Mar 02

Ruth GOETZ
12 Jan 08 – 12 Oct 01

Mary GRANT
20 Feb 17 – 2 Mar 02

Dolores GRAY
7 Jun 24 – 26 Jun 02

Jane GREER
9 Sep 24 – 24 Aug 01

George HARRISON
25 Feb 43 – 29 Nov 01

Sir Nigel HAWTHORNE
5 Apr 29 – 26 Dec 01

Louis M HEYWARD
29 Jun 20 – 26 Mar 02

Roy HUGGINS
18 Jul 14 – 3 Apr 02

Jaromil JIRES
10 Dec 35 – 24 Oct 01

Stratford JOHNS
22 Sep 25 – 29 Jan 02

Chuck JONES
21 Sep 12 – 22 Feb 02

Albert JURGENSON
1929 – 12 Jun 02

Pauline KAEL
19 Jun 19 – 3 Sep 01

AJ KARDAR
25 Nov 26 – 12 Feb 02

Hildegard KNEF (NEFF)
28 Dec 25 – 1 Feb 02

John KOHN
27 Nov 25 – 4 May 02

Theodor KOTULLA
28 Aug 28 – 20 Oct 01

Raoul KRAUSHAAR
20 Aug 08 – 13 Oct 01

Jan LENICA
4 Jan 28 – 6 Oct 01

Philippe LEOTARD
28 Aug 40 – 25 Aug 01

Francis LEROI
5 Sep 42 – 21 Mar 02

Bill LeSAGE
1927 – 31 Oct 01

Jay LIVINGSTON
28 Mar 15 – 17 Oct 01

Jeanne LORIOD
13 Jul 28 – 3 Aug 01

Evan A LOTTMAN
1931 – 25 Sep 01

Ray LOVEJOY
18 Feb 39 – 18 Oct 01

Linda LOVELACE
19 Jan 49 – 6 Apr 02

Sihung LUNG
1930 – 2 May 02

Irish McCALLA
25 Dec 29 – 1 Feb 02

Nobu McCARTHY
13 Nov 34 – 6 Apr 02

Dorothy McGUIRE
14 Jun 18 – 15 Sep 01

Dolores MICHAELS
30 Jan 33 – 25 Sep 01

Spike MILLIGAN
16 Apr 18 – 26 Feb 02

Subrata MITRA
12 Oct 30 – 8 Dec 01

Dudley MOORE
19 Apr 35 – 27 Mar 02

Peggy MOUNT
2 May 16 – 13 Nov 01

George NADER
9 Oct 21 – 4 Feb 02

Mario NASCIMBENE
28 Nov 13 – 6 Jan 02

Tolomush OKEYEV
11 Sep 31 – 18 Dec 01

John O'SHEA
1920 – 8 Jul 01

Juri OZEROV
26 Jan 21 – 16 Oct 01

François PERIER
10 Nov 19 – 28 Jun 02

Lester PERSKY
6 Jul 27 – 16 Dec 01

Julia PHILLIPS
7 Apr 44 – 1 Jan 02

Alberto PIERALISI
31 Jan 11 – 8 Oct 01

Ernest PINTOFF
15 Dec 31 – 12 Jan 02

Tessa PRENDERGAST
17 Oct 28 – Jul 01

Francisco RABAL
8 Mar 25 – 29 Aug 01

Jean RICHARD
18 Apr 21 – 12 Dec 01

Yves ROBERT
19 Jun 20 – 10 May 02

Glen ROBINSON
1914 – 27 Mar 02

Reginald ROSE
10 Dec 20 – 19 Apr 02

Herbert ROSS
13 May 27 – 9 Oct 01

Stanislas ROSTOTSKY
21 Apr 22 – 10 Aug 01

Harold RUSSELL
14 Jan 14 – 29 Jan 02

Shirley RUSSELL
11 Mar 35 – 4 Mar 02

Oskar SALA
18 Jul 10 – 26 Feb 02

Ray SELFE
18 May 32 – 3 Sep 01

Anthony SHAFFER
5 May 26 – 6 Nov 01

George SIDNEY
4 Oct 16 – 5 May 02

Helvio SOTO
21 Feb 30 – 29 Nov 01

Kim STANLEY
11 Feb 25 – 20 Aug 01

Fredric STEINKAMP
22 Aug 28 – 20 Feb 02

David SWIFT
1919 – 31 Dec 01

Richard SYLBERT
16 Apr 28 – 23 Mar 02

Sophie TATISCHEFF
22 Oct 46 – 27 Oct 01

John THAW
3 Jan 42 – 12 Feb 02

Lawrence TIERNEY
15 Mar 19 – 26 Feb 02

Michael TODD Jr
8 Oct 29 – 5 May 02

Linden TRAVERS
27 May 13 – 23 Oct 01

Dorothy TUTIN
8 Apr 30 – 6 Aug 01

Robert URICH
19 Dec 46 – 16 Apr 02

Barbara VALENTIN
15 Dec 40 – 22 Feb 02

Henri VERNEUIL
15 Oct 20 – 11 Jan 02

Mary WHITEHOUSE
13 Jun 10 – 23 Nov 01

Billy WILDER
22 Jun 06 – 28 Mar 02

William WITNEY
15 May 15 – 17 Mar 02

Irene WORTH
22 Mar 16 – 10 Mar 02

Otis YOUNG
4 Jul 32 – 12 Oct 01

a

Amélie

A

(1998, Jap, 136 min)
d Tatsuya Mori. *p* Takaharu Yasuoka. *sc/ph/ed* Tatsuya Mori, Takaharu Yasuoka. *m* Hiroshi Mutsu, Pak Poe. *with* Hiroshi Araki.

●Independent in every sense, Mori's *ciné-vérité* documentary gets inside the remnants of the Aum Shinrikyo cult after the arrest of its leaders for ordering the Tokyo subway sarin gas attack in March 1995. Mori focuses on the cult's junior spokesman Hiroshi Araki, a confused 28-year-old drop-out who has tried to sever family ties and turn his back on the materialism of 'Japan Inc'. Although it makes the most of a level of access denied to the mass media, the film doesn't attempt to analyse Aum or to account for its terrorist acts. Mori's real subject is the reason such cults exist and attract educated disciples; scrupulously impartial, he provides all the evidence necessary to ask very awkward questions about the state and the people. It rivals *The Emperor's Naked Army* as the most ornery Japanese documentary of recent times. TR

ABBA The Movie

(1977, Swe/Aust, 95 mins)
d Lasse Hallström. *p* Reg Grundy, Stig Andersson. *sc* Lasse Hallström. *ph* Paul Onorato. *ed* Lasse Hallström. *songs* Benny Anderson, Björn Ulvaeus, Clive Hicks. *cast* ABBA, Robert Hughes, Tom Oliver, Bruce Barry.

●Unashamed and supremely slick commercial for the group, maintaining a gentle air of self-parody while at the same time being a celebration of all the various apparatuses which make a merchandising phenomenon like ABBA possible. The narrative, without which the film would mostly consist of footage of the band on stage, follows ABBA through an Australian tour pursued by a Sydney deejay. If the idea's spread a bit thin, it's occasionally handled with a humour and panache worthy of Dick Lester's Beatles' movies or ABBA's own Phil Spector/Brian Wilson- inspired studio craftsmanship. RM

Abbott and Costello Meet Frankenstein (aka Abbott and Costello Meet the Ghosts)

(1948, US, 83 min, b/w)
d Charles Barton. *p* Robert Arthur. *sc* Robert Lees, Frederic I Rinaldo, John Grant. *ph* Charles van Enger. *ed* Frank Gross. *pd* Hilyard Brown. *m* Frank Skinner. *cast* Bud Abbott, Lou Costello, Bela Lugosi, Lon Chaney Jr, Glenn Strange, Lenore Aubert.

●First and possibly the best of the horror spoofs indulged by this comic duo. Not that it is particularly funny, but showing a surprising respect for Universal tradition in the matter of its monsters, it at least looks remarkably good. Graceless imitations of Laurel and Hardy (never revealing the deep-rooted affection for each other beneath the exasperations, which made Stan and Ollie so well-beloved) and of the Marx Brothers (although their verbal routines never even begin to scale the same heights of surrealist fantasy). They nevertheless made 35 movies between *One Night in the Tropics* (1940) and *Dance With Me, Henry* (1956). TM

A.B.C. Africa

(2001, Iran/Fr, 85 min)
d Abbas Kiarostami. *p* Marin Karmitz, Abbas Kiarostami. *ph* Seifollah Samadian. *ed* Abbas Kiarostami. *with* Abbas Kiarostami, Seifollah Samadian.

●Some have dismissed Kiarostami's documentary about children in Uganda orphaned by AIDS and civil war as 'conventional'; but how conventional is such a film when a few minutes only are devoted to depicting human suffering? Here, most of the kids on view – and adults, for that matter – are dancing, singing, joking and acting up for the DV camera. As such, even though the film was commissioned by the UN's International Fund for Agricultural Development in order to draw attention to a programme of teaching self-help and home economics to women who agree to adopt orphans, it's firmly in the tradition of Kiarostami's earlier work about children. It's an unsentimental, but finally very moving celebration of innocence, courage, resilience and beauty; and there's even a witty, wonderfully enthralling and subtly appropriate sequence involving an electricity blackout and a thunderstorm, a dazzlingly cinematic bit of formal play which also reflects perceptively and poetically both on the kids' lives and on cinema itself. GA

ABCD

(1999, US, 105 min)
d Krutin Patel. *p* Tejal Desai, Brian Wray, Krutin Patel. *sc* Krutin Patel, James Ambrose. *ph* Milton Kam. *ed* Ravi Subramanian. *pd* Deborah Schreier. *m* Deirdre Broderick. *cast* Madhur Jaffrey, Faran Tahir, Sheetal Sheth, Aasif Mandvi, Jennifer Dorr White, David Ari, Adriana Forlana Erdos, Rex Young.

●This saga of second generation Indians in America sorting out their cultural identity is plain fare, compared with our own Hanif Kureishi and *East Is East*. 'American-Born Confused Deshi' describes the daughter (Sheth) and son (Tahir) of a traditionalist widow (Jaffrey), concerned that neither of them has married. The son's arranged engagement has gone on too long, while his sister is torn between an old childhood friend from home and the attractions of a wealthy white suitor. All concerned have their own prejudices tested and sometimes overturned as the film ambles through the issues, but the assured performances can't compensate for a script that falls flat in the middle, while only the Asian characters really ring true. TJ

Abdication, The

(1974, GB, 103 min)
d Anthony Harvey. *p* Robert Fryer, James Cresson. *sc* Ruth Wolff. *ph* Geoffrey Unsworth. *ed* John Bloom. *pd* Terence Marsh. *m* Nino Rota. *cast* Peter Finch, Liv Ullmann, Cyril Cusack, Paul Rogers, Graham Crowden, Michael Dunn, Kathleen Byron.

●Cold Scandinavian obsession drives Queen Christina to relinquish her throne, convert to Catholicism and seek the warmer climate of Rome, where she pours out her heart to Cardinal Peter Finch ('It seems strange to call somebody father'). As an exploration of private spaces in the lives of public people (who, through circumstance or choice, are committed to celibacy), psychological insight is too often sacrificed for the sake of verbal swordplay. It ends up skirting perilously close to superior cliché ('Are we not the world's strangest couple?'). At least Garbo, playing the same role in Mamoulian's *Queen Christina*, conspired with her audience against the rest of the film. One wishes for something like that here: it all seems so remote.

Abduction

(1975, US, 97 min)
d Joseph Zito. *p* Kent E Carroll. *sc* Kent E Carroll. *ph* Joao Fernandez. *ed* James MacReading. *m* Ron Frangipane, Robbie Farrow. *cast* Judith-Marie Bergman, David Pendleton, Gregory Rozakis, Leif Erickson, Dorothy Malone, Lawrence Tierney.

●Low-budget, quasi-documentary thriller about the kidnapping of a tycoon's daughter by a revolutionary cell. Despite disclaimers in the titles and despite being based on a novel (*Black Abductors* by Harrison James) written before the event, it's obviously modelled on the Patty Hearst kidnapping. Not bad at suggesting the girl's moral and political confusion, but it founders on its own confusion of styles, methods and aims. RG

Abel

(1985, Neth, 103 min)
d Alex van Warmerdam. *p* Laurens Geels, Dick Maas, Robert Swaab. *sc* Alex van Warmerdam. *cast* Alex van Warmerdam, Henri Garcin, Olga Zuiderhoek, Loes Luca, Annet Malherbe.

●Abel is a spoilt, possibly retarded, certainly eccentric 31-year-old mummy's boy whose suffocating relationship with his mother is balanced by the constant torment which father and son inflict on each other. A final rift occurs over a TV set (father refuses to have one, mother and son smuggle a set into the loft), and Abel is booted out into the streets. Father finds solace at an establishment called 'Naked Girls', where he picks up Zus (the voluptuous Malherbe) but Abel also stumbles upon Zus, is seduced, and shares her bohemian lifestyle…Van Warmerdam, who also stars as gormless Abel, directs with brash, colourful simplicity, evidently on a minute budget. The film is self-consciously quirky, and while some of the non-stop visual jokes hit the right note of irrational oddness, others are silly and contrived. But at least it has a distinctive flavour, and some scenes display a flair for social satire. Wittily comic or tiresome, according to taste. SFe

Abendland

see Nightfall

Abenteuer des Werner Holt, Die

see Adventures of Werner Holt, The

Abgeschminkt

see Making Up

Abismos de pasión (Cumbres borrascosas/ Wuthering Heights)

(1953, Mex, 90 min, b/w)
d Luis Buñuel. *p* Oscar Dancigers. *sc* Luis Buñuel, Ardino Maiuri, Julio Alejandro de Castro. *ph* Augustin Jimenez. *ed* Carlos Savage. *ad* Edward Fitzgerald. *m* Richard Wagner. *cast* Jorge Mistral, Irasema Dilian, Lilia Prado, Ernesto Alonso.

●While it's certainly true that Emily Bronte's classic novel appealed strongly to the Surrealists, with the love between Heathcliff and Cathy an almost textbook case of *l'amour fou*, it must be said that much of Buñuel's adaptation is surprisingly lifeless, a fact perhaps attributable largely to the severe shortcomings of his lead actors. Despite impressive use of arid locations, and numerous Buñuelian 'touches' depicting man's capacity for cruelty and violence it's only in the final moments, when Alejandro/Heathcliff, consumed with passion, breaks into Catarina's funeral vault for one more kiss, that the director appears fully engaged with his material. GA

Abnormal Family: Brother's Wife (Hentai Kazoku: Aniki no Yome-san)

(1984, Jap, 62 min)
d Masayuki Suo. *p* Tasuke Asakura. *sc* Masayuki Suo. *ph* Yushi Nagata. *ad* Yohei Taneda. *m* Yoshikazu Suo. *cast* Ren Osugi, Kaoru Kaze, Miki Yamachi, Shiro Shimomoto, Kei Kubifuji.

●Suo's debut was considered so scandalous that he wasn't offered another feature for six years. His 'crime' was to shoot a sex film as a pastiche of an Ozu family melodrama. A Tokyo widower (Osugi, impersonating Ozu's regular patriarch Chishu Ryu) has three grown-up kids. Koichi marries the bouncy Yukiko but soon lurches into an SM relationship with the local bar hostess and moves out. In his absence, brother Kazuo loses his virginity to Yukiko; sister Akiko starts working in a sex sauna and eventually marries its boss. Yukiko promises to go on looking after her father-in-law. The style parodies Ozu even more sharply than the storyline (non-eyeline-match cuts, clunky music cues, establishing shots used as punctuation) and the whole thing begins by mocking the Shochiku trademark. Not very sexy, but pretty funny. TR

Abominable Dr Phibes, The

(1971, GB, 94 min)
d Robert Fuest. *p* Louis M Heyward, Ron Dunas. *sc* James Whiton, William Goldstein. *ph* Norman Warwick. *ed* Tristam Cones. *pd* Brian Eatwell. *m* Basil Kirchin, Jack Nathan. *cast* Vincent Price, Joseph Cotten, Virginia North, Hugh Griffith, Terry-Thomas, Aubrey Woods.

●Cult camp horror, with Price in fine fettle as a disfigured composer devising murders based on the ten curses of Pharaoh to avenge himself on the doctors who let his wife die on the operating table. Often amusing, occasionally sickening, always impressive for the imaginative Art Deco sets, it's pretty flatly directed, despite memorable images like the opening shot of Price hunched as manically as the Phantom of the Opera over a Hammond organ in a black plastic cowl. GA

Abominable Snowman, The

(1957, GB, 90 min, b/w)
d Val Guest. *p* Aubrey Baring. *sc* Nigel Kneale. *ph* Arthur Grant. *ed* Bill Lenny. *pd* Edward Marshall. *m* John Hollingsworth. *cast* Forrest Tucker, Peter Cushing, Maureen Connell, Richard Wattis, Robert Brown, Michael Brill, Wolfe Morris.

● Hammer's botch of Nigel Kneale's teleplay *The Creature*, about an expedition to the Himalayas. Tucker wants to exploit the Yeti, so gets killed; Cushing doesn't, so is allowed to live. The creatures, glimpsed just briefly in their gorilla suits, are hardly worth the dreary trip. TM

About a Boy

(2002, Ger/US/Fr/GB, 101 min)
d Paul Weitz, Chris Weitz. *p* Jane Rosenthal, Robert De Niro, Brad Epstein, Tim Bevan, Eric Fellner. *sc* Peter Hedges, Chris Weitz, Paul Weitz. *ph* Remi Adefarasin. *ed* Nick Moore. *pd* Jim Clay. *m* Badly Drawn Boy. *cast* Hugh Grant, Toni Collette, Rachel Weisz, Isabel Brook, Sharon Small, Victoria Smurfit, Nicholas Hoult.

● What's surprising about this film are its writer/directors, who previously made *American Pie*, and the fact that one of its five producers is De Niro, whose Tribeca optioned Nick Hornby's book. Otherwise, it's all you'd expect of a Working Title Britfilm (light, cannily international); of a Hugh Grant comedy (gently rather than raucously funny); and of a Hornby cautionary tale about a self-centred male attaining belated maturity through love's discovery. The difference here is that the catalyst for change is a child, not a woman. If Grant appears a touch uncomfortable as rich but relatively downmarket slacker and womaniser Will, he remains adept with amusing asides and flustered emotions. Indeed, the performances are mostly fine. The problem, besides occasionally clumsy editing and direction, is the story. For anyone familiar with Hornby and Grant's past fare, it's deeply predictable. Furthermore, Hornby's crises and characters can be so facile, schematic and smugly moralistic that emotional substance can get overshadowed by fluff. GA

About Adam

(2000, Ire/GB/US, 97 min)
d Gerard Stembridge. *p* Anna J Devlin, Marina Hughes. *sc* Gerard Stembridge. *ph* Bruno de Keyzer. *ed* Mary Finlay. *pd* Fiona Daly. *m* Adrian Johnston. *cast* Stuart Townsend, Frances O'Connor, Charlotte Bradley, Kate Hudson, Alan Maher, Tommy Tiernan, Rosaleen Linehan.

● Meet the Owens – a modern Irish family comprising one unconventional matriarch, daughters Lucy, Laura and Alice, and son David. Director Stembridge's comic follow-up to his intense thriller *Guiltrip* is set in a strikingly upbeat Dublin. It opens with the youngest child, the beautiful Lucy (Hudson), singing torch songs in a trendy restaurant where she also waits tables. Despite her obvious charm and no shortage of admirers, she's never had what the bookish Laura (O'Connor) would describe as 'a great passion' – then in walks Adam (Townsend), and he's perfect. 'Boring men are the curse of the world and there are just so many of them,' is how Mrs Owens (Linehan) attempts to explain Adam's unique and universal appeal. Laura believes he has a deeper, dark secret. It isn't long before Adam, the chameleon, becomes the repository for the entire family's diverse dreams and fantasies, with seduction, deception and betrayal following close behind. The implausibility is overcome by masterful use of voice-over and a clever multi-perspective structure, as well as fine performances. JFu

A Bout de Souffle 100 (100) (Breathless)

(1959, Fr, 90 min, b/w)
d Jean-Luc Godard. *p* Georges de Beauregard. *sc* Jean-Luc Godard. *ph* Raoul Coutard. *ed* Cécile Decugis. *m* Martial Solal. *cast* Jean-Paul Belmondo, Jean Seberg, Daniel Boulanger, Jean-Pierre Melville, Henri-Jacques Huet, Liliane Robin, Roger Hanin, Jean-Luc Godard.

● Godard's first feature, adapted from an existing scenario written by François Truffaut, spins a pastiche with pathos as joyrider Belmondo shoots a cop, chases friends and debts across a night-time Paris, and falls in love with a literary lady. Seberg quotes books and ideas and names; Belmondo measures his profile against Bogart's, pawns a stolen car, and talks his girlfriend into a cash loan 'just till midday'. The camera lavishes black-and-white love on Paris, strolling up the Champs-Elysées, edging across café terraces, sweeping over the rooftop skyline, Mozart mixing with cool jazz riffs in the night air. The ultimate night-time *film noir noir noir*…until Belmondo pulls his own eyelids shut when he dies. More than any other, this was the film which epitomised the iconoclasm of the early *Nouvelle Vague*, not least in its insolent use of the jump-cut. CA

About July (Qiyue Tian)

(1999, Tai, 72 min)
d Wei Desheng. *p* Liu Xiaochu. *sc* Wei Desheng. *ph* Chin Ding-Chang. *ed* Chen Bo-Wen. *pd* Shieh Lie-An. *m* Luo Jiyu. *cast* Tychicus Wang, Sima Sansan, Dong Waixiu, Zeng Mian, Zhang Long.

● When his father throws himself under a truck because of huge gambling debts, the young protagonist of this well-observed indie feature is pressed into service as a door guard at the underground gambling den to work off some of the debt. And when the place is raided by an 'untouchable' cop newly posted to the local station, he's the only one to get arrested and very brutally interrogated. Meanwhile his father's coffin sits in the family living room because there's a taboo against being buried in July. Wei worked as Edward Yang's assistant on *Mahjong* but had never made a film himself. This suitably modest debut is full of wry, darkish humour and has a touching sense of life's disappointments and humiliations. TR

About Last Night...

(1986, US, 113 min)
d Edward Zwick. *p* Stuart Oken, Jason Brett. *sc* Tim Kazurinsky, Denise DeClue. *ph* Andrew Dintenfass. *ed* Harry Keramidas. *pd* Ida Random. *m* Miles Goodman. *cast* Rob Lowe, Demi Moore, James Belushi, Elizabeth Perkins, George DiCenzo, Michael Alldredge.

● The good news? It's from a David Mamet play, *Sexual Perversity in Chicago*. The bad? Aside from the absence of any kind of plot worthy of the word, you can't tell from watching it. Lowe and Moore play a couple of desperate yuppies who hook up at a hideous Windy City singles bar and collapse first into bed and then into a more serious relationship, to the disapproval of their best friends (Perkins and a particularlyx sharp Belushi). And that's more or less it. The screenwriters work many nice little observations into their occasionally over-quippish script, but this is considerably smaller than the sum of its parts: it gets the detail, but misses the big picture. Zwick went on to create *Thirtysomething*, a series that delineated what happens when characters such as these take the time to grow up a little. WFJ

About Love, Tokyo (Ai ni tsuite, Tokyo)

(1992, Jap, 109 min)
d Mitsuo Yanagimachi. *p* Mitsuo Yanagimachi, Masaru Koibuchi. *sc* Mitsuo Yanagimachi. *ph* Shohei Ando. *ed* Nobuo Ogawa. *pd* Takeo Kimura. *m* Hajime Mizoguchi. *cast* Wu Xiao Tong, Asuka Okasaka, Hiroshi Fujioka, Qian Po.

● A scummy, indefensible picture from a once-important director. Yanagimachi's weakness has always been his uncritical fetishisation of macho bad boys, from the bike gang in *Black Emperor* to the murderous lumberjack in *Fire Festival;* his heroes this time are mainland Chinese students in Tokyo's answer to Stepney, and he sees them (with only a figleaf of detachment) as amoral, foul-mouthed misogynists slipping easily into the city's underworld of crime, gambling, violence and commercial sex. Whatever his intentions, the view of immigrant behaviour and attitudes chimes neatly with the prejudices of the Japanese Right; so it's fortunate that the visual style is as squalid as the screenplay, making the film a completely repulsive experience. TR

About Mrs Leslie

(1954, US, 104 min, b/w)
d Daniel Mann. *p* Hal B Wallis. *sc* Hal Kanter, Ketti Frings. *ph* Ernest Laszlo. *ed* Warren Low. *pd* Hal Pereira. *m* Victor Young. *cast* Shirley Booth, Robert Ryan, Alex Nicol, Marjie Millar, Eilene Janssen, Ellen Corby, Philip Ober, Harry Morgan.

● In one of her rare film roles, Shirley Booth is perfectly cast as the cheerfully competent, middle-aged owner of a Beverly Hills boarding-house, sympathetic – but not indulgent – to the various problems of her roomers. Flashbacks reveal her bitter-sweet past when, as a night-club singer, she found happiness with a mysterious, lonely tycoon (Ryan) who is able to spare only six weeks a year away from business pressures to be with her. At first resentful when she discovers that he is trapped by a marriage contracted for social and material advantage when he was young and ambitious, she learns to be grateful for what she has. It's soap, of course, especially given that Booth's story is lent a happy ending, as it were, by two roomers who turn their backs on the rat race for fame and fortune, electing instead to settle humbly for each other. But it's scripted with wit, insight and no small dash of acerbity (by Ketti Frings from a novel by Vina Delmar), while Booth and Ryan give terrific performances. Their (on the face of it) unlikely pairing lends the film a distinctly offbeat flavour. TM

About Schmidt

(2002, US, 125 min)
d Alexander Payne. *p* Harry Gittes, Michael Besman. *sc* Alexander Payne, Jim Taylor. *ph* James Glennon. *ed* Kevin Tent. *pd* Jane Ann Stewart. *m* Rolfe Kent. *cast* Jack Nicholson, Hope Davis, Dermot Mulroney, Kathy Bates, Howard Hesseman, June Squibb.

● After retirement and his wife's sudden death, insurance salesman Warren Schmidt (Nicholson) feels his life, and all the bland assumptions that have sustained it, slipping away from him. To get back on course, he travels in his Winnebago to see his beloved daughter (Davis) in the hope of preventing her marriage to a walking cliché (Mulroney) and of spending his remaining years with her. This perhaps excessively droll, even ponderous satire of Midwestern manners really takes off only when Warren reaches his prospective in-laws, allowing not only for alternative comic targets to arise but for Bates' beautifully judged turn to counterbalance Nicholson's admittedly impressive lead performance. Also enlivening are the letters to a Tanzanian child Schmidt sponsors – even though they strike a faintly false note of redemption in the final moments. GA

Above Suspicion

(1943, US, 91 min, b/w)
d Richard Thorpe. *p* Victor Saville. *sc* Keith Winter, Melville Baker, Patricia Coleman. *ph* Robert Planck. *ed* George Hively. *ad* Cedric Gibbons, Randall Duell. *m* Bronislau Kaper. *cast* Joan Crawford, Fred MacMurray, Conrad Veidt, Basil Rathbone, Reginald Owen, Andre Charlot.

● Brisk and lightly likeable spy thriller, from a novel by Helen MacInnes, with MacMurray and Crawford as newly-weds on honeymoon in Europe (hence the title), persuaded by Britain to do a bit of spying. Rathbone contributes his characteristic flair as the Nazi villain, and the whole thing gallops along in pleasant, undemanding and totally incredible fashion. GA

Above the Law (aka Nico)

(1988, US, 99 min)
d Andrew Davis. *p* Steven Seagal, Andrew Davis. *sc* Ronald Shusett, Andrew Davis, Steven Pressfield. *ph* Robert Steadman. *ed* Michael Brown. *pd* Maher Ahmad. *m* David M Frank. *cast* Steven Seagal, Pam Grier, Henry Silva, Ron Dean, Daniel Faraldo, Sharon Stone.

● Chicago cop Nico is an Italian immigrant, an aikido Black Belt, fluent in several languages, an ex-CIA operative with 'Nam experience, a fine husband and father, and possessed of the brains and brawn to back him up in his fight for what he believes is right. *Phew!* The plot concerns a Secret Service attempt to assassinate a senator about to blow the whistle on an undercover drugs trafficking/political destabilisation gimmick, and detours via scenes of a bombed church, 'Nam torture flashbacks, and numerous scraps and car chases. Through this scattergun proliferation strides Nico (Seagal in his debut) like a holy mixture of Bruce Lee, Clint Eastwood, John Wayne and Jon Miller. This he does with considerable élan. Davis' direction is *Miami*

Vice-tight, though with frequent attempts at humour: this, together with the caricature psycho-baddie (Silva), and the mixture of spectacular, bone-crunchingly realistic violence with a stab at topical socio-political commentary, makes for a *very* uncertain tone. MC

Above the Rim

(1994, US, 93 min)
d Jeff Pollack. *p* Jeff Pollack, Benny Medina. *sc* Jeff Pollack, Barry Michael Cooper. *ph* Tom Priestley. *ed* Michael Ripps, James Mitchell. *pd* Ina Mayhew. *m* Marcus Miller. *cast* Duane Martin, Leon Robinson, Tupac Shakur, David Bailey, Tonya Pinkins, Marlon Wayans, Bernie Mac.

●Forsaking teamwork to impress a university scout, high-school basketball star Kyle-Lee Watson (Martin) succeeds in alienating teammates and coach. The only person he impresses is his friend Bugaloo (Wayans), who introduces him to drug-dealer Birdie (Shakur). Seduced by the promise of fame and fortune, Kyle abandons the school squad to run instead with the Birdmen in the upcoming street basketball tournament. It's unclear if this is a realistic depiction of black youth culture, but it's certainly a moral one. A formula script, but a mobile camera, pulsing rap soundtrack and a game cast whip up the necessary fizz. AO

Above Us the Earth

(1977, GB, 85 min)
d/p/sc Karl Francis. *ph* Mike Fox. *ed* Neil Thomson. *cast* Windsor Rees, Gwen Francis, Don Osmond, Michael Foot, Neil Kinnock, Joe Gormley.

●At times inclined to substitute special pleading for analytical fact, but extremely refreshing as a study of Welsh miners and their environment, especially given the alacrity with which the British cinema has usually retreated to defensive stereotypes to characterise the working class. Documentary footage concerning the closure of Ogilvie Colliery in 1975 and the miners' attitude towards this is intercut with staged sequences of the decline and death of an old miner from lung disease. The subject is sombre and its treatment reflective, as well it might be when the director, himself a miner's son, had to mortgage his home to help complete the film. SM

Above Us the Waves

(1955, GB, 99 min, b/w)
d Ralph Thomas. *p* William MacQuitty. *sc* Robin Estridge. *ph* Ernest Steward. *ed* Gerald Thomas. *pd* George Provis. *m* Arthur Benjamin. *cast* John Mills, John Gregson, Donald Sinden, James Robertson Justice, Michael Medwin, James Kenney, Lee Patterson.

●Lamentable World War II heroics, told in muddled, would-be semi-documentary style, with the 'Tirpitz' sunk in a flood of stiff upper lips. Mills is the commander sending his midget submarines out into the studio tank. TM

Abraham Valley (Vale Abraão/aka Valley of Abraham)

(1993, Port/Fr/Switz, 187 min)
d Manoel de Oliveira. *p* Paulo Branco. *sc* Manoel de Oliveira. *ph* Mario Barroso. *ed* Manoel de Oliveira. *ad* Aria José Branco. *cast* Leonor Silveira, Cecile Sanz de Alba, Luís Miguel Cintra, Rui de Carvalho, Luís Lima Barreto, Micheline Larpin, Mário Barroso, Diogo Doria.

●This Portuguese adaptation of *Madame Bovary* – or rather a poetic meditation on the novel by Augustina Bessa-Luis – is encased in a hypnotic atmosphere, both melancholic and tranquil. Ema (Silveira), orphaned at six, house-bound till 14, grows up in a bourgeois family in the unchanging vine-terraced Duoro valley. She's slightly lame, but possesses a beauty which is 'exuberant and therefore dangerous'. Despite a taste for luxury, she marries a doctor who depends on her 'like a worm on soil'. She's twice unfaithful, but her only close bond is with a mute servant. In a world where 'the pleasures of hypocrisy exceed those of love', her spirit must die. Subtle, elegant, enigmatic, this movie by the veteran Oliveira exercises a powerful grip. Oliveira's style is hard to categorise (the director began making films in 1931): the timelessness of the modern-day setting, where the Lotuses and Maseratis seem so incongruous, is reminiscent of Resnais, but the languorous acting echoes the satiric irony of late Buñuel and the secretive minimalism of Bresson. WH

Abre los ojos

see Open Your Eyes

Abril despedaçado

see Behind the Sun

Abschied

see Farewell

Abschied vom Falschen Paradies

see Farewell to False Paradise

Abschied von Gestern

see Yesterday Girl

Absence of Malice

(1981, US, 116 min)
d/p Sydney Pollack. *sc* Kurt Luedtke. *ph* Owen Roizman. *ed* Sheldon Kahn. *pd* Terence Marsh. *m* David Grusin. *cast* Paul Newman, Sally Field, Bob Balaban, Melinda Dillon, Luther Adler, Barry Primus.

●Impeccably liberal in its orientation to 'issues' – the power and responsibilities of the press, the impact of misinformation – this avoids the excesses of Stanley Kramer-like telegraphy, only to come up looking aesthetically wet. It's not just a reliance on star casting to sugar the pill as reporter Field picks up a malicious crime squad 'leak' and smears innocent Newman. Sheer worthy dullness comes closer to describing the problem. For all the smokescreen convolutions of legalistic conspiracy and juxtapositions of ethics, 'professionalism', public interest and private morality, we're basically presented with two attractive victims on the same hook who will inevitably spar their way past one of democracy's little hiccups. PT

Absolute Beginners

(1986, GB. 108 min)
d Julien Temple. *p* Stephen Woolley, Chris Brown. *sc* Christopher Wicking, Richard Burridge, Don Macpherson. *ph* Oliver Stapleton. *ed* Gerry Hambling, Richard Bedford, Russell Lloyd. *pd* John Beard. *m* Gil Evans. *cast* Eddie O'Connell, Patsy Kensit, David Bowie, James Fox, Ray Davies, Mandy Rice-Davies, Steven Berkoff, Lionel Blair, Alan Freeman, Robbie Coltrane, Irene Handl.

●This musical taken from Colin MacInnes' book about life on the edge in the Soho and Notting Hill of 1958 is a thing of bits and shards. A pair of flyweight leads are counterbalanced by some lurid casting (including Lionel Blair as a pederast tin pan alley king, Alan Freeman's clueless trendspotter, Steven Berkoff's usual Fascist rant, and Bowie, whose face at last is taking on character). Clearly a nightmare to edit, the narrative stutters into life only occasionally. Camp is everywhere, humour thin; and the soundtrack is very contemporary for a movie which in the pre-publicity boasted of its jazz origins. The whole film is an example of the strange influence of pop promo mentality on cinema. All that noise, all that energy, so little governing thought. CPea

Absolute Giganten

see Gigantic

Absolute Power

(1996, US, 120 min)
d Clint Eastwood. *p* Clint Eastwood, Karen Spiegel. *sc* William Goldman. *ph* Jack N Green. *ed* Joel Cox. *pd* Henry Bumstead. *m* Lennie Niehaus. *cast* Clint Eastwood, Gene Hackman, Ed Harris, Laura Linney, Scott Glenn, Dennis Haysbert, Judy Davis, EG Marshall.

●When ultra-secretive master burglar Luther Whitney (Eastwood) breaks into the mansion of a politically influential millionaire (Marshall), he's surprised by the arrival of the owner's wife and the discovery (he's hiding in a closet behind a two-way mirror) that she's carrying on with the US President (Hackman). Worse, after their drunken shenanigans turn nasty, Whitney witnesses both a murder and a cover-up. He's soon being chased by the cops (Harris) and the president's aides. Surely the best defence is attack. This light, part-comic Hitchcockian thriller, scripted by William Goldman from a novel by Daniel Baldacci, doesn't rank with Eastwood's best work as actor/director, but it's nevertheless solidly enjoyable.The script may lack even a shading of political analysis or comment, but it's hard to take against a contemporary Hollywood movie which forefronts a cowardly, cynical, philandering president. GA

Absolution (aka Murder by Confession)

(1978, GB, 95 min)
d Anthony Page. *p* Elliott Kastner, Danny O'Donovan. *sc* Anthony Shaffer. *ph* John Coquillon. *ed* John Victor Smith. *pd* Natasha Kroll. *m* Stanley Myers. *cast* Richard Burton, Dominic Guard, Dai Bradley, Andrew Keir, Billy Connolly, Willoughby Gray.

●A hoary old Gothic thriller from the pen of Anthony Shaffer which should surprise nobody familiar with the plot twists wrought in *Sleuth* and *Deathtrap*. Burton as the humourless teacher-priest in a Catholic boarding school oozes fleshly torment as his prize pupil (Guard) develops a malicious rebellious streak, indulged in by a cunning manipulation of the inviolable privacy of the confessional. But, as always with Shaffer, things are not what they seem, and the last act revelations about the mystery of the missing pupil (Bradley as a grotesquely pimply cripple) tumble tediously out. RM

Abuzer Baklava (Abuzer Kadayif)

(2000, Tur, 104 min)
d Tunç Basaran. *p* Hüseyin Apaydin. *sc* Kandemir Konduk. *ph* Ali Utku. *ed* Nevzat Disiaçik. *m* Özkan Turgay. *cast* Metin Akpinar, Talat Bulut, Sibel Turnagöl, Öslem Savas, Sebnem Özinal, Ebru Destan, Melda Arat, Mazlum Kiper.

●A loopy yarn that seems, endearingly enough, to take itself fairly seriously, the film's about a college lecturer who by night transforms into – Abuzer Baklava, singing superstar! A sort of charity working Superman, he's been raising money to build a rehab centre for street kids ever since his former girlfriend was stabbed during a mugging. But his alter ego's popular success also attracts the attention of politicians and *mafiosi*; and he's getting quite comfy in his stage persona. One problem, though, he has yet to reveal his identity to his new girlfriend. It's a rather bumbling and happy-go-lucky affair, but Akpinar's performance(s) are a lot of fun. NB

Abyss, The (Afgrunden)

(1910, Den, 36 min, b/w)
d/sc Urban Gad. *ph* Alfred Lind. *cast* Asta Nielsen, Poul Reumert, Robert Dinesen, Hans Neergaard, Arne Weel, Oscar Stribolt, Emilie Sannom.

●A torturous melodrama about the inconstant passions of a young woman with a somewhat heavy-handed if emotionally sophisticated plot (piano teacher quits fiancé, a pastor's son, to follow her circus lover; it ends in bloodshed) – memorable, chiefly, for delectably risqué dance from Asta Nielsen (1881–1972). NB

Abyss, The

(1989, US, 140 min)
d James Cameron. *p* Gale Anne Hurd. *sc* James Cameron. *ph* Mikael Saloman. *ed* Joel Goodman. *pd* Leslie Dilley. *m* Alan Silvestri. *cast* Ed Harris, Mary Elizabeth Mastrantonio, Michael Biehn, Leo Burmester, Todd Graf, John Bedford Lloyd, JC Quinn.

●James Cameron's follow-up to *Aliens* abandons deep space for the spacey deep, and hits rock bottom as the submarine genre meets *Close Encounters*. A nuclear sub crashes on the floor of the Atlantic, and the motley crew of an underwater station attached to an oil rig investigate. Inevitably problems mount: a hurricane rages above, a loony marine is on the loose, and cap'n Ed Harris is forced to work with his estranged wife (Mastrantonio), who we're continually told is an utter bitch but who is actually characterised as a perfectly reasonable, efficient engineer. Moreover, there's *something out there* – though from the first glimpse of flashing lights cruising the deep, anyone who knows their Spielberg will guess the presence is benign. After a relatively gripping start, Cameron's *folie de grandeur* rapidly sinks into cliché, absurdity and hyperbole; a collapsing crane contributes one pleasingly extended chain of disasters, but the rest of this overlong concoction is scuppered by dire dialogue, histrionic performances and maudlin sentimentality. GA

Abyss: Special Edition, The

(1993, US, 171 min)
d James Cameron. *p* Van Ling. *sc* James Cameron. *ph* Mikael Saloman. *ed* Steven Quale. *pd* Leslie Dilley. *m* Alan Silvestri. *cast* Ed Harris, Mary Elizabeth Mastrantonio, Michael Biehn, Leo Burmester, Todd Graff, John Bedford Lloyd, JC Quinn.

● This is no more the 'director's cut' than the original, over which Cameron had full control; it simply incorporates footage deemed gratuitous first time round. The abyss is death, of course, and in particular the spectre of nuclear war. A sub founders on the Atlantic floor. The team of an underwater drilling rig checks out the wreck. Meanwhile, topside, a storm is blowing, and the superpowers rerun the Cuban missile crisis. Sam Goldwyn once prayed for a movie that began with a hurricane and built to a climax. This is it. The first 90 minutes are as good as anything Cameron has done: hi-tech, blue-collar film-making; tense, brittle, on-the-knuckle. The last hour-and-a-bit is increasingly OTT, sentimental and unconvincing. The new footage doesn't change much, but aggravates the problem of the climax, which now resembles *Explorers* played straight. The impression remains of a talented director drowning in the shallows of his deepest thoughts. TCh

Ação entre Amigos

see Friendly Fire

Accattone

(1961, It, 120 min, b/w)
d Pier Paolo Pasolini. *p* Alfredo Bini. *sc* Pier Paolo Pasolini. *ph* Tonino Delli Colli. *ed* Nino Baragli. *pd* Flavio Mogherini. *m* Johann Sebastian Bach. *cast* Franco Citti, Franca Pasut, Roberto Scaringella, Adele Cambria, Paola Guidi, Silvana Corsini, Adriana Asti.

● The seamy side of the sub-proletariat of Rome, a world of prostitutes, layabouts and petty thieves in which Franco Citti's Accattone, not quite making the grade as a pimp, finds himself trapped between the alternatives of working for starvation wages, or trying – with the police already on his tail – for easy pickings as a thief. Treating a social milieu Pasolini knew at first hand, his first film as a director was misunderstood by many critics when it was first released as a return to the canons of Italian neo-realism of the '40s and '50s. In fact, its editing style, use of close-ups, dialogue in the Romanesco vernacular – not to mention the Bach score – all betray an originality much more of a piece with Pasolini's later work than with neo-realism. And the character of Accattone himself, self-destructive and conscious of his situation within a class from which he cannot escape, embodies many of the contradictions in Pasolini's lifetime of coming to terms with Marxism and Catholicism. RM

Acceptable Levels

(1983, GB, 103 min)
d John Davies. *p* Angela Topping. *sc* Gordon Hann, Kate McManus, Ellin Hare, John Davies, Robert Smith, Alastair Herron. *ph* Robert Smith. *ed* Ellin Hare. *cast* Andrew Rashleigh, Kay Adshead, Sally McCafferty, Tracey Lynch, Geroge Shane, Frances Barber.

● A British TV crew assemble in Belfast to make a documentary, one of a series about children in Britain. Immured within their barricade of script, cameras and determined objectivity, they eye the disorder in which their child-subject lives for possible locations without really *seeing* anything until another child is killed by a rubber bullet. Compromises are made, images junked, ideals sacrificed to professionalism. The contrasts between crew and subject are well pointed, and the ironies, suitably loaded, trip one another domino-like. FD

Accident

(1967, GB, 105 min)
d Joseph Losey. *p* Joseph Losey, Norman Priggen. *sc* Harold Pinter. *ph* Gerry Fisher. *ed* Reginald Beck. *pd* Carmen Dillon. *m* John Dankworth. *cast* Dirk Bogarde, Stanley Baker, Jacqueline Sassard, Michael York, Vivien Merchant, Delphine Seyrig, Alexander Knox.

● A stunningly confident, oblique study of six people (three men, two wives, one girl) and the way they tear each other to pieces emotionally amid the droning calm of an Oxford summer as urbanity is ruffled by an accident that begins to send out lazy tendrils of hostility and suspicion (the performances are superb all round). With Losey's camera taking its cue for reticence from Pinter's script (adapted from the novel by Nicholas Mosley), *Accident* is an eminently civilised film, sometimes criticised for distilling a bland classicism out of the baroque provocations that made Losey's work from *The Criminal* to *The Servant* so excitingly unpredictable to watch. But what surprises is the extent to which, in discovering the real pain and the areas of darkness lurking beneath the surface of these donnish lives, Losey in fact reverts to the mood and methods of his early American masterpiece, *The Prowler*. TM

Accidental Hero (aka Hero)

(1992, US, 116 min)
d Stephen Frears. *p* Laura Ziskin. *sc* David Webb Peoples. *ph* Oliver Stapleton. *ed* Mick Audsley. *pd* Dennis Gassner. *m* George Fenton. *cast* Dustin Hoffman, Geena Davis, Andy Garcia, Joan Cusack, Kevin J O'Connor, Stephen Tobolowsky, Chevy Chase.

● When Bernie (Hoffman), a cynical petty criminal, finds himself reluctantly saving passengers from a crashed plane, little does he realise that his momentarily selfless actions will change lives, including his own. For one thing, a survivor – star TV reporter Gale Gayley (Davis) sets up a search for the anonymous 'angel of flight 204', with the result that John Bubber (Garcia) – a charismatic Vietvet down-and-out – usurps the real hero's place in the hearts of the public. For another, since Bernie's toils delayed a visit to his estranged wife (Cusack) and young son, he's in the doghouse… Intelligently written but clumsily executed, Frears' comedy-drama is frustratingly uneven. Besides a smattering of good gags, David Webb Peoples' script touches on numerous intriguing questions (notably, what constitutes heroism?) while piling irony upon irony. But while Garcia waxes credibly sincere, Hoffman hams, and Davis simply looks lost: small wonder, given Frears' leaden direction, which contrives to scupper suspense *and* comedy through sluggish pacing and misguided camera placement. GA

Accidental Legend (Fei Tian)

(1996, Tai, 120 min)
d Wang Shaudi. *cast* René Liu, Niu Chenze, Chang Shih, Miao Tien, Wei Su, Ge Hsiao-Bin.

● Splendidly anarchic first feature from a well-known TV director/screenwriter, this is a prime mix of adventure, comedy, satire and fantasy shot on spectacular locations in NW China and inspired by the long history of peasant revolts in the late-imperial era. At least three strands of storyline are intertwined, the main one centred on two boy thieves from a village of outcasts who unwittingly bring the wrath of the regional authorities down on their community. It all revolves around the authenticity (or otherwise) of gold, superstitions, good government and redeemer myths; sorting the real from the fake, Wang concludes, is not always as easy as it seems. TR

Accidental Spy, The (Tewu Mi Cheng)

(2000, HK, 108 min)
d Teddy Chen. *p* Jackie Chan, Candy Leung. *sc* Ivy Ho. *ph* Wong Wing-Hang. *ed* Kwong Chi-Leung. *pd* Kenneth Mak. *m* Peter Kam. *cast* Jackie Chan, Eric Tsang, Vivian Hsu, Kim Min-Jeong, Wu Hsing-Kuo, Alfred Cheung.

● Chan's annual HK movie is now as formalised as his annual Hollywood movie. He plays a fallible loner (no sidekick, no romance) caught up in conspiracies which take him abroad and require him to communicate in at least three languages. In this one he's Buck Yuen, a salesman suddenly tagged as the long-lost son of a dying Korean spy. He goes to Turkey in search of his inheritance and finds himself fighting off angry Turks, CIA agents and the sinister Mr Zen (Wu) for control of a bio-warfare sample of Anthrax II. Along the way he rescues a junkie floosie (Hsu), saves the life of the odd kid and drives a burning oil tanker away from built-up areas. Essentially routine, but Chan still does funnier fights and better stunts than anyone. This time they include his longest ever nude scene, fleeing from murderous thugs through a crowded indoor market in Istanbul. The coda threatens a new franchise. TR

Accidental Tourist, The

(1988, US, 121 min).
d Lawrence Kasdan. *p* Lawrence Kasdan, Charles Okun, Michael Grillo. *sc* Frank Galati, Lawrence Kasdan. *ph* John Bailey. *ed* Carol Littleton. *pd* Bo Welch. *m* John Williams. *cast* William Hurt, Kathleen Turner, Geena Davis, Amy Wright, David Ogden Stiers, Ed Begley Jr, Bill Pullman.

● In this subtly modulated romantic comedy-drama, Hurt plays a travel writer, separated from his wife (Turner) after the death of their young son, who returns to the bosom of his home-loving family when he breaks his leg. Enter wacky dog-trainer Davis, whose spontaneity disrupts Hurt's muffled life-style. That Davis has a sickly son complicates things, as does Hurt's publisher's interest in his sister Rose; and when Hurt's repentant wife tries to rekindle their marriage, he must make a choice. The screenplay by Kasdan and Frank Gelati achieves numerous shifts of tone within a compressed emotional range, while the ensemble cast responds equally well to the comic and tragic elements. Hurt excels as the writer, Davis exudes loopy charm, and Turner is brilliant as the anaesthetising wife. Even those who blew hot and cold over the slickness of *Body Heat* and *The Big Chill* should warm to Kasdan's most emotionally complex film to date. NF

Acción Mutante

(1993, Sp, 90 min)
d Alejandro de la Iglesia. *p* Esther Garcia, Pedro Almodovar, Agustin Almodovar. *sc* Alejandro de la Iglesia, Jorge Guerricaechevarria. *ph* Carles Gusi. *ed* Pablo Blanco. *m* Mariano Lozano. *cast* Antonio Resines, Enrique San Francisco, Frédérique Feder, Alex Angulo, Juan Viadas, Fernando Guillén, Karra Elejalde.

● The year is 2012 and a terrorist group, Mutant Action, is hitting back at the beauty industry and the media's focus on physical perfection. 'We don't want to smell good or lose weight!' snarls Ramón (Resines), his deformed face half covered by a leather mask. They infiltrate the society wedding of bread heiress Patricia (Feder), and just when it all looks likes a satire on terrestrial follies, take off for outer space demanding 10 million ecus in ransom for the chick. On the mining planet Axturias, peopled by sex offenders, the plot falls off, along with most of Feder's clothes. Director de la Iglesia likes tacky music, political incorrectness and TV send-ups. He is a Basque, and with some straining this could be read as a comment on his violent compatriots and their relationship with Spain. But more telling is the influence of comics, the love of the individual frame at the expense of overall coherence. SFe

Accompagnatrice, L' (The Accompanist)

(1992, Fr, 111 min)
d Claude Miller. *p* Jean-Louis Livi. *sc* Claude Miller, Luc Béraud. *ph* Yves Angelo. *ed* Albert Jurgenson. *cast* Richard Bohringer, Elena Safonova, Romane Bohringer, Bernard Verley, Samuel Labarthe, Nelly Borgeaud.

● Ever get the feeling that life is passing you by? That's how it is for 20-year-old Sophie (Bohringer) as she reaches womanhood in Occupied Paris. Brought up in tenement-block poverty by her single mother, Sophie is ecstatic when she lands a job as piano accompanist to gifted singer Irène Brice (Safonova), becoming her devoted employee and companion. Taken into the wealthy home she shares with husband Charles (Bohringer *père*), Sophie soon learns that Irène is having an affair, and the young girl enthusiastically enmeshes herself in the household's drama as a way of filling the void at the heart of her own existence. Claude Miller is a master of the lingering close-up and the subtlest nuances of character. This is essentially a film about the inner life, and the cast all deliver highly complex performances. Sophie is revealed in her fragility and passion; there's also the jealousy and bitterness she feels in her role as accompanist to the true players of life. Safonova meanwhile illuminates the absolute joy of being given a celestial voice. JBa

Accompanist, The

see Accompagnatrice, L'

Accumulator 1 (Akumulator 1)

(1994, Czech Republic, 102 min)
d Jan Sverak. *p* Petr Soukop. *sc* Jan Slovak, Jan Sverak, Zdenek Sverak, Václav Sasek. *ph* Frantisek A Brabec. *ed* Alois Fisarek. *pd* Milos Kohout. *m* Ondrej Soukoup, Jiri Svoboda. *cast* Zdenek Sverak, Petr Forman, Edita Brychta, Boleslav Polivka, Marian Labuda, Tereza Pergnerova.

●Despite its strong designs and evident ambitions, this bizarre blend of sci-fi thriller, romance and comedy is too incoherent – indeed, too obscure – to succeed as anything other than a curiosity. It has something to do with the vampiric, energy-draining powers of TV (or is that of voyeurism in general?); it's probably an allegory about complacency, enthusiasm and commitment – though it's hard to say for sure. GA

Accused, The

(1988, US, 111 min).
d Jonathan Kaplan. *p* Stanley R Jaffe, Sherry Lansing. *sc* Joan Tewkesbury, Tom Topor. *ph* Ralf D Bode. *ed* Jerry Greenberg. *pd* Richard Wilcox. *m* Brad Fiedel. *cast* Kelly McGillis, Jodie Foster, Bernie Coulson, Leo Rossi, Ann Hearn, Carmen Argenziano, Steve Antin.

●A young waitress, clothes ripped, bruised, runs screaming from a bar. Sarah Tobias (Foster, excellent) has been gang-raped, and her case is taken on by cool and efficient Deputy DA Kathryn Murphy (McGillis). When Murphy makes a deal with the accused men to reduce the charge to reckless endangerment, Sarah is enraged; and Murphy, beginning to feel the pangs of guilt, decides to prosecute the men who did not take part in the rape but encouraged the others. Surrounded by a storm of controversy – mostly generated by the inclusion of the explicit, some say exploitative, gang-rape scene –the film was written and directed by men, and produced by the Jaffe-Lansing *Fatal Attraction* stable, which hasn't helped its cause. And though it does make a clear stand on vital social and legal questions, one is left feeling distinctly uneasy at the inclusion of the scene. IA

Ace High

see Quattro dell'Ave Maria, I

Ace in the Hole (aka The Big Carnival)

(1951, US, 111 min, b/w)
d/p Billy Wilder. *sc* Billy Wilder, Lesser Samuels, Walter Newman. *ph* Charles Lang Jr. *ed* Arthur P Schmidt. *ad* Hal Pereira, Earl Hedrick. *m* Hugo Friedhofer. *cast* Kirk Douglas, Jan Sterling, Robert Arthur, Porter Hall, Frank Cady, Richard Benedict, Ray Teal.

●Wilder ran into charges of bad taste with this acid tale of reporter Chuck Tatum (Douglas), resentfully stagnating in a New Mexico backwater after being repeatedly fired from jobs in the big time, who sees a chance to manufacture a scoop when a man is trapped by a rockfall. The sheriff, calculating the publicity value to his forthcoming election campaign, agrees to spin out the rescue operation; Tatum builds his story into a nationwide sensation; and as thrill seekers, media hounds, and profiteers turn the site into a gaudy carnival, the victim quietly dies. As a diatribe against all that is worst in human nature, it has moments dipped in pure vitriol ('Kneeling bags my nylons', snaps Sterling as the victim's wife when invited to be photographed praying for her husband's safety), even though the last reel goes rather astray in comeuppance time. TM

Aces High

(1976, GB/Fr, 114 min)
d Jack Gold. *p* S Benjamin Fisz. *sc* Howard Barker. *ph* Gerry Fisher. *ed* Anne V Coates. *pd* Syd Cain. *m* Richard Hartley. *cast* Malcolm McDowell, Christopher Plummer, Simon Ward, Peter Firth, John Gielgud, Trevor Howard, Ray Milland.

●Transposition of RC Sherriff's play *Journey's End* from the trenches into the air. Off the ground the film is entertainingly cinematic (photography by Peter Allwork from Roger Corman's *The Red Baron*): the aerial battles, combining comic strip close-ups with long shots, produce a cumulative intensity that achieves the right degree of awe and horror. But on the ground the script fails to provide much more than a routine account of a young flier's brief active service. The film offers some perspective on the officer/public school product, and deals well with negatives – suppressed emotions, solitariness – but falls apart over such 'positive' clichés as the rural interlude, the brothel visit, and subsequent sexual initiation. Disappointing when you consider writer Howard Barker's stage work and Gold's TV achievements. CPe

Ace Ventura, Pet Detective

(1993, US, 86 min)
d Tom Shadyac. *p* James G Robinson. *sc* Jack B Bernstein, Tom Shadyac, Jim Carrey. *ph* Julio Macat. *ed* Don Zimmerman. *pd* William Elliott. *m* Ira Newborn. *cast* Jim Carrey, Sean Young, Courtney Cox, Tone Loc, Dan Marino, Noble Willingham, Troy Evans.

●The tale of a bumbling sleuth who specialises in finding other people's lost animals. When the emblem of the Miami Dolphins – one 'Snowflake' – is stolen on the eve of the Superbowl, our man is called in, stays one step ahead of the local police, gets the dolphin and uncovers an unfeasibly wicked plot into the bargain. In the title role is Carrey, known and loved in the States for his manic humour on the comedy show *In Living Color*. Familiarity with the character is, one assumes, why American audiences found this *Naked Gun* rip-off funny. Desperate stuff. NKe

Ace Ventura – When Nature Calls

(1995, US, 92 min)
d Steve Oedekerk. *p* James G Robinson. *sc* Steve Oedekerk. *ph* Donald Thorin. *ed* Malcolm Campbell. *pd* Stephen J Lineweaver. *m* Robert Folk. *cast* Jim Carrey, Ian McNeice, Simon Callow, Maynard Eziashi, Bob Gunton, Sophie Okonedo, Tommy Davidson.

●Topographically speaking, this sequel to Carrey's 1993 hit starts off on a high (when the pet detective fails to save a racoon, he retreats to a Tibetan mountain monastery) but from then on it's all downhill. Ventura is persuaded by a Brit diplomat (McNeice) to make tracks to an obscure African nation, where the Consul (Callow) persuades him to hunt down a stolen Great White Bat, the dowry in an inter-tribal marriage which will stop the Wachati and the Wachootoo fighting each other. Trouble is, Ventura hates bats, and even more bat guano, staple of the Wachatis' economy and cuisine. Crass. GA

Acid House, The

(1998, GB, 111 min)
d Paul McGuigan. *p* David Muir. *sc* Irvine Welch. *ph* Alasdair Walker. *ed* Andrew Hulme. *pd* Richard Bridgland, Mike Gunn. *cast* Stephen McCole, Maurice Roëves; Kevin McKidd, Michelle Gomez, Gary McCormack; Ewen Bremner, Martin Clunes, Jemma Redgrave.

●The Irvine Welsh bandwagon rolls on with this triptych of short stories. We're back in the scragend of Edinburgh where, in 'The Granton Star Cause', God (Roëves) turns up as a local drinker to reprimand laddish Boab (McCole) for wasting his life. He turns him into a fly: cue close-up of shit-eating. 'A Soft Touch' is hardly less savoury as retiring Johnny (McKidd) bides his time while his promiscuous missus (Gomez) and neighbour-from-hell (McCormack) make his life a misery. In the third tale, a rogue tab of acid sees Coco (Bremner) miraculously swap personalities with the baby just born to yuppie scum Rory and Jenny (Clunes and Redgrave), transforming the infant into a rampaging Hibs fan and Coco into even more of a dimwit than he was already. The presence in the last section of the most pitiful animatronic baby in cinema history wins the film its small niche in movie infamy. Overall, it's simply depressing to watch a capable cast devote themselves to such an irredeemably juvenile collection of banal insights and pathetic shock tactics. TJ

Acque di Primavera

see Torrents of Spring

Acordéon del Diablo, El

see Devil's Accordion, The

Across 110th Street

(1972, US, 102 min)
d Barry Shear. *p* Fouad Said, Ralph Serpe. *sc* Luther Davis. *ph* Jack Priestley. *ed* Byron 'Buzz' Brandt. *pd* Perry Watkins. *m* JJ Johnson. *cast* Anthony Quinn, Yaphet Kotto, Anthony Franciosa, Paul Benjamin, Ed Bernard, Richard Ward, Antonio Fargas.

●Unremittingly violent account of a pair of New York cops (one black, one white) assigned to track down three Harlem robbers-cum-murderers. Familiar crime movie characterisations, but as directed by Shear, who made the highly impressive *Todd Killings*, it's a gutsy affair, given a distinct lift by the Harlem locations; and between the bouts of physical aggression, there are occasional moments of insight into the fraught relationship between Quinn and Kotto. GA

Across the Pacific

(1942, US, 96 min, b/w)
d John Huston. *p* Jerry Wald, Jack Saper. *sc* Richard Macaulay. *ph* Arthur Edeson. *ed* Frank Magee. *ad* Robert M Haas, Hugh Reticker. *m* Adolph Deutsch. *cast* Humphrey Bogart, Mary Astor, Sydney Greenstreet, Victor Sen Young, Charles Halton, Roland Cot.

●Slow to begin, this accelerates into a fine, *noir*-ish thriller, set on the eve of Pearl Harbour and pitting Bogart against Jap spies plotting to destroy the Panama Canal with aerial torpedoes. Featuring the same irresistible mixture of darkness, double-cross and quirky humour as *The Maltese Falcon*, it again boasts – in addition to some superbly laconic intimations of violence – the inimitable Greenstreet, at his silkiest as a turncoat given to justifying his treachery by discoursing on the arts of judo and the *haiku*. But the real delight is the wisecracking relationship between Bogart and Astor, who pull a brilliant switch on their earlier romantic partnership – though still teased by a note of doubt – into the Nick and Nora Charles of *The Thin Man*. The absurd, flag-waving finale was added by Vincent Sherman after Huston, mobilised before completing the film, maliciously left Bogart in a tight corner from which only Superman could reasonably hope to escape. TM

Across the Sea of Time: A New York Adventure

(1997, US, 51 min)
d Steven Low. *cast* Peter Reznik, John McDonough, Donald Trump.

●A young Russian immigrant wanders the streets of the Big Apple, retracing the footsteps of his grandfather, guided by letters and photos from eight decades earlier. A terribly dull IMAX venture. Only that old 3D standby the rollercoaster ride gives much sense of vertigo, the rest is perversely static. TCh

Across the Wide Missouri

(1950, US, 77 min)
d William A Wellman. *p* Robert Sisk. *sc* Talbot Jennings. *ph* William C Mellor. *ed* John Dunning. *ad* Cedric Gibbons, James Basevi. *m* David Raksin. *cast* Clark Gable, Ricardo Montalban, John Hodiak, Adolphe Menjou, Maria Elena Marques, J Carrol Naish, Jack Holt.

●Though subjected to brutal studio cutting which largely wrecked it, an impressive Western set in Colorado in the 1820s and anticipating *Jeremiah Johnson* in its celebration of the rumbustiously idyllic life of the early fur trappers, which ended in bloodshed with the Indians aroused by the coming of greedy civilisation. Shot almost entirely on location, it's worth seeing for the landscapes alone. TM

Action for Slander

(1937, GB, 83 min, b/w)
d Tim Whelan. *p* Alexander Korda, Victor Saville. *sc* Miles Malleson. *ph* Harry Stradling. *ed* Jack Dennis. *pd* Vincent Korda. *m* Muir Mathieson. *cast* Clive Brook, Ann Todd, Margaretta Scott, Ronald Squire, Morton Selten, Felix Aylmer. Arthur Margetson.

●Upright stuff with Brook, the quintessential Englishman, being spitefully accused of cheating at cards by the husband of a woman with whom Brook is infatuated. He may be a bounder but he's not a cad, and he insists (at the cost of his good name and his army career) on proving it in court. Ann Todd (as his wife) does a passable imitation of a volcano about to blow, and Margaretta Scott has a ball as the 'other woman'. It's sincere enough but rather leaden. MA

Action in the North Atlantic

(1943, US, 127 min, b/w)
d Lloyd Bacon. *p* Jerry Wald. *sc* John Howard Lawson. *sc* Al Bezzerides, WR Burnett. *ph* Ted McCord. *ed* George Amy, Thomas Pratt. *ad* Ted Smith. *m* Adolph Deutsch. *cast* Humphrey Bogart, Raymond Massey, Alan Hale, Julie Bishop, Ruth Gordon, Sam Levene, Dane Clark.

●Tough, pacy tribute to the American Merchant Marine, with a convoy en route to Russian waters being attacked on all sides by Nazi submarines and aircraft. The rather fine special effects of explosions and fires tend to overshadow characterisation (the crew of the main ship are the usual mix of ethnic stereotypes), while the blatantly propagandist nature of the film means that the enemy are portrayed as vicious, inhuman, smiling sadists. But the performances are strong, and there is considerable curiosity value. The merchant seamen's union was Communist-controlled at the time, and fellow-travelling John Howard Lawson conceived his script in terms of Soviet cinema, with *Battleship Potemkin* as a model (and characteristic montages executed by Don Siegel). GA

Action Jackson

(1988, US, 96 min)
d Craig R Baxley. *p* Joel Silver. *sc* Robert Reneau. *ph* Matthew F Leonetti. *ed* Mark Helfrich. *pd* Virginia L Randolph. *m* Herbie Hancock, Michael Kamen. *cast* Carl Weathers, Craig T Nelson, Vanity, Sharon Stone, Thomas F Wilson, Bill Duke.

●Sometime stunt co-ordinator Baxley directs this feebly-scripted, sporadically-exciting crime pic like a showpiece for his former speciality. He fills the screen with spectacular deaths, metal-crunching car chases, and more explosions than you could shake a stick of dynamite at. In between, Weathers (in his first lead role) gets a walk-on part as Action Jackson, a disgraced cop settling old scores with ruthless businessman Dellaplane (Nelson). A few years back, Dellaplane lost Jackson his stripes, his gun, and his wife, but now Jackson has linked him to some aggressive union-busting professional hit-men. Weathers looks distinctly uncomfortable whenever the action gives way to reams of plot exposition, anti-drugs sermons, and embarrassing romantic interludes, which is often. Fans of state-of-the-art destruction would seem to be the target audience. NF

Act of Vengeance (aka Rape Squad)

(1974, US, 90 min)
d Bob Kelljan. *p* Buzz Feitshans. *sc* Betty Conklin, HR Christian. *ph* Brick Marquard. *ed* Carl Kress. *pd* Chuck Pierce. *m* Bill Marx. *cast* Jo Ann Harris, Jennifer Lee, Lisa Morre, Connie Strickland, Patricia Estrin, Lada Edmund Jr.

●Not as uninteresting as the title(s) might suggest, this deals with the negative reactions encountered by rape victims, and the tactics resorted to by a group who band themselves together as a 'rape squad', giving help and advice to other victims. Perhaps inevitably, the film becomes crippled by the demands of its exploitation format (the group seeking revenge against a particular rapist). It is further hamstrung by very obvious cuts, which may well serve to mute the male potency fantasy lurking around the edges, but also tend to make the women's revenge tactics seem singularly perfunctory. Nevertheless, the film boasts an interesting script (co-written by Betty Conklin) which puts the women's case more clearly and resonantly than you might expect, and entertains between times by building their sexual taunts somewhat in the style of a Shirelles chorus. VG

Actor's Revenge, An (Yukinojo Henge)

(1963, Jap, 113 min)
d Kon Ichikawa. *p* Masaichi Nagata. *sc* Daisuke Ito, Teinosuke Kinugasa, Natto Wada, *ph* Setsuo Kobayashi. *ed* Shigeo Nishida. *pd* Yoshinobu Nishioka. *m* Yasushi Akutagawa. *cast* Kazuo Hasegawa, Fujiko Yamamoto, Ayako Wakao, Ganjiri Nakamura, Raizo Ichikawa.

●Yukinojo, a female impersonator in a Kabuki theatre troupe, takes revenge on the three nobles who forced his parents to commit suicide. Maintaining his female role offstage, he pursues his vendetta by playing out a false courtship, and by turning his enemies against each other. A film of phenomenal all-round accomplishment, with daringly stylised visuals. Nothing is more astonishing than the twin performances of Kazuo Hasegawa as both Yukinojo and the thief who befriends him, Yomitaro – especially when you learn that Hasegawa had already played the dual role in Kinugasa's version of the story, made nearly thirty years earlier. TR

Actress (Ruan Ling-Yu)

(1991, HK/Tai, 154 min)
d Stanley Kwan Kam-Pang. *p* Leonard Ho Koon-Cheung, Jackie Chan. *sc* Yau Tai On-Ping. *ph* Poon Hang-Sang. *ed* Peter Cheung. *ad* Pok York Mok. *m* Siu Chung. *cast* Maggie Cheung, Tony Leung, Shin Hong, Carina Lau, Lawrence Ng, Cheung Chung.

●This film picks up where Kwan's *Rouge* left off, measuring people of present-day Hong Kong against their forebears of the 1930s and charting both the gains and losses of 'progress'. The forebears in question are the Shanghai film-makers who gave Chinese cinema its golden age; the film centres on the great proto-feminist actress Ruan Ling-Yu, who was hounded to suicide by gossip tabloids at the age of 25. The present-day participants are Kwan himself and his cast and crew, seen interviewing veterans from the 1930s, looking at clips from Ruan's surviving films, and discussing their own work. Nothing like an orthodox biopic, the result is tender, vivid and almost overwhelmingly moving. TR

Actress, The

(1953, US, 89 min, b/w)
d George Cukor. *p* Lawrence Weingarten. *sc* Ruth Gordon. *ph* Harold Rosson. *ed* George Boemler. *pd* Cedric Gibbons, Arthur Lonergan. *m* Bronislau Kaper. *cast* Spencer Tracy, Jean Simmons, Teresa Wright, Anthony Perkins, Ian Wolfe, Mary Wickes.

●Based on Ruth Gordon's autobiographical play *Years Ago*, chronicling her youthful experiences as a would-be actress in New England just before World War II (Gordon, with her husband Garson Kanin, wrote many screenplays for Cukor, including this one), *The Actress* is a remarkable domestic comedy. The centre of the film is not so much Jean Simmons' Broadway hopes, but rather the slow growth to understanding of her father (Tracy), who in the course of the film re-lives his own youthful hopes, and for the first time realises the compromises he made for a settled, comfortable life. Beautiful performances. PH

Actresses (Actrius)

(1996, Sp, 88 min)
d/p Ventura Pons. *sc* Ventura Pons, JM Benet i Jornet. *ph* Tomás Pladevall. *ed* Pere Abadal. *pd* Rosa Ros. *m* Carles Cases. *cast* Núria Espert, Rosa Maria Sardà, Anna Lizaran, Mercè Pons.

●Three middle-aged actresses, former disciples of a legendary diva, reunite to mull over their loves, lives, differences and similarities. This Catalan feature, from a play by JM Benet i Jornet, is unimaginately directed and betrays its stage origins at every turn. It also looks as if made for TV. Solid but less than remarkable performances. GA

Acts of Love

see Carried Away

Act Without Words – II

(2000, Ire/GB, 10 min)
d Enda Hughes. *p* Michael Colgan, Alan Moloney. *sc* Samuel Beckett. *ph* Harry Purdue. *ed* Juniper Calder. *pd* Ray Ball. *cast* Pat Kinevane, Marcello Magni.

●Enda Hughes was the youngest and least experienced director to participate in the 'Beckett on Film' project. Yet it turned out his playfully witty use of pixellated, stop-motion techniques turned out to be the most intelligent, inspired attempt to rework Beckett for a new medium. Catch an early look at a real talent in the making. KC

Adalen '31

(1969, Swe, 115 min)
d/sc Bo Widerberg. *ph* Jörgen Persson. *ed* Bo Widerberg. *cast* Peter Schildt, Kerstin Tidelius, Roland Hedlund, Stefan Feierbach, Martin Widerberg, Marie-Louise de Geer Bergenstråhle.

●Attempting to blend the sombre themes of *Raven's End* with the (superficial) lyricism of *Elvira Madigan*, Widerberg fails, in his depiction of a protracted strike at a paper mill in Sweden in 1931, to convey either the political context behind the strike or the developing political consciousness of the strikers. A beautiful, empty film. PH

Adam's Rib

(1949, US, 101 min, b/w)
d George Cukor. *p* Lawrence Weingarten. *sc* Ruth Gordon, Garson Kanin. *ph* George Folsey. *ed* George Boemler. *ad* CedricGibbons, William Ferrari. *m* Miklós Rozsa. *cast* Katharine Hepburn, Spencer Tracy, Judy Holliday, Tom Ewell, David Wayne, Jean Hagen.

●Delightful Cukor comedy in which Hepburn and Tracy are husband-and-wife lawyers engaged in a battle of the sexes as they respectively defend and prosecute a dumb blonde (the inimitable Holliday) accused of shooting her two-timing husband with intent to kill. If Hepburn's feminist arguments are a little on the wild side and too easily bounced off Tracy's paternalistic chauvinism, the script by the Kanins so bristles with wit that it scarecely matters. And in a film in which everybody is acting – a point neatly stressed by the stylised staginess of Cukor's direction – the performances (not least from Wayne and Hagen) are matchless. TM

Addams Family, The

(1991, US, 99 min)
d Barry Sonnenfeld. *p* Scott Rudin. *sc* Caroline Thompson, Larry Wilson. *ph* Owen Roizman. *ed* Dede Allen, Jim Miller. *pd* Richard MacDonald. *m* Marc Shaiman. *cast* Anjelica Huston, Raúl Julia, Christopher Lloyd, Dan Hedaya, Elizabeth Wilson, Christina Ricci, Jimmy Workman.

●'Unhappy, darling?' Gomez asks his wife. 'Totally' replies Morticia with a blissful smile. This behavioural inversion is the key, indeed the only, gag of the film. But for a one-joke movie, this adaptation of the TV series based on the *New Yorker* cartoons still summons up enough laughs. The chief pleasure is in the casting: Huston was born to play cadaverously glamorous Morticia; Julia buckles a goodly swash as her duelling, devoted husband; and Lloyd is so good as Fester that you feel the film was written as a star vehicle for him. But then Fester alone is allowed any development – is he really an impostor after the family fortune? – and it's hard to care what happens to the rest. Even the film's glorious look is second-hand (you can tell that visual effects supervisor Alan Munro worked on *Beetlejuice*), with the Coen brothers' cinematographer Barry Sonnenfeld setting a cracking pace in his directorial debut, but suggesting that Tim Burton might have given the film the edge it lacks. Ooky the Addamses may be, subversive they ain't; it plays like a paean to the nuclear family. DW

Addams Family Values

(1993, US, 94 min)
d Barry Sonnenfeld. *p* Scott Rudin. *sc* Paul Rudnick. *ph* Don Peterman. *ed* Arthur Schmidt. *pd* Ken Adam. *m* Marc Shaiman. *cast* Anjelica Huston, Raul Julia, Christopher Lloyd, Joan Cusack, Carol Kane, Christina Ricci, Jimmy Workman.

●Gomez and Morticia (Julia and Huston) have a baby, Pubert. As sequels go, this is passable: no more coherent than the episodic first instalment, but with enough sick humour to satisfy the mildly depraved. Wednesday (Ricci) and Pugsley (Workman) use a guillotine in a playful attempt to lop off the new branch of the family tree. Pubert survives. But Uncle Fester (Lloyd) looks like falling into the clutches of the new nanny, Debbie Jellinsky (Cusack), an ample-bosomed black widow with an eye on the family fortune. NF

Addicted to Love

(1997, US, 100 min)
d Griffin Dunne. *p* Jeffrey Silver, Robert Newmyer. *sc* Robert Gordon. *ph* Andrew

Dunn. *ed* Elizabeth Kling. *pd* Robin Standefer. *m* Rachel Portman. *cast* Matthew Broderick, Meg Ryan, Kelly Preston, Tcheky Karyo, Maureen Stapleton, Nesbitt Blaisdell.

● A romantic comedy without the romance. Small-town astrologer Broderick is dumped by girlfriend Preston. He follows her to New York, takes the apartment opposite (she's already moved in with French chef Karyo), and fixes up a sophisticated camera obscura so he can watch them on his sitting room wall. Enter punky black-leather biker Ryan as the chef's spurned squeeze. She's got it worse than Matthew. Together, they mike up the lovers for the full audio-visual experience, then plot revenge. These obsessives would seem to offer scope for dark, edgy humour – until, that is, you cast such overweeningly cute stars as Ryan and Broderick. Meg should give up the hardboiled masquerade and go back to being the lovable ditz she really is. The set-up's way too slow, but first-time director Dunne contrives a couple of maliciously farcical revenge sequences. TCh

Addiction, The

(1994, US, 82 min, b/w)
d Abel Ferrara. *p* Dennis Hann, Fernando Sulichin. *sc* Nicholas St John. *ph* Ken Kelsch. *ed* Mayin Lo. *pd* Charles M Lagola. *m* Joe Delia. *cast* Lili Taylor, Christopher Walken, Annabella Sciorra, Edie Falco, Paul Calderon, Fredro Starr, Robert Castle.

● Chronologically, this precedes *The Funeral* by about a year. Both were scripted by Nicolas St John after the death of his son. Both were shot quickly, on limited budgets, by much the same crew, and feature Walken and Sciorra, and a Catholic priest, Father Robert Castle. Finally, both are philosophical/religious ruminations, in genre form, on the nature of sin and redemption. *The Funeral*, though, is the far more accessible, even conventional drama. By contrast, this is one wild, weird, wired movie, the kind that really shouldn't be seen before midnight. Taylor is commanding as New York philosophy student Kathleen Conklin. Dragged into a back alley, she's vamped by Sciorra's voluptuous Casanova. Soon she starts obsessing on images of My Lai and the Holocaust, name-dropping Nietzsche, Sartre and Heidegger, and taking a syringe to a vagrant's artery for a late-night snack. Shot in b/w, with an effectively murky jungle/funk/rap score, this is the vampire movie we've been waiting for: a reactionary urban-horror flick that truly has the ailing pulse of the time. AIDS and drug addiction are points of reference, but they're symptoms, not the cause. Ferrara's chiaroscuro imagery is as striking as anything in Coppola's *Dracula*, while the voice-over narration often recalls *Apocalypse Now*. Scary, funny, magnificently risible, this could be the most pretentious B-movie ever – and I mean that as a compliment. TCh

Addition, L' (The Patsy/ The Caged Heart)

(1984, Fr, 87 min)
d Denis Amar. *p* Norbert Saada. *sc* Denis Amar, Jean-Pierre Bastid, Jean Curtelin. *ph* Robert Fraisse. *ed* Jacques Witta. *pd* Serge Douy. *m* Jean-Claude Petit. *cast* Richard Berry, Richard Bohringer, Victoria Abril, Farid Chopel, Fabrice Eberhard, Daniel Sarky.

● Berry is an actor whose short stay in jail goes wrong when he is innocently involved in a breakout. One of the guards (Bohringer) gets his knee shot off, and vengefully hounds Berry through a further prison sentence, playing sadomasochistic cat-and-mouse games spiced with a little homophobia. The psychological thriller in which the victim needs the torturer as much as vice versa is familiar territory, but any game which can only reach a sudden death resolution is always good value. Unfortunately, what the film would propose as a happy ending for the hero is in fact the point when his troubles are just beginning. CPea

Address Unknown

(1944, US, 72 min, b/w)
d/p William Cameron Menzies. *sc* Herbert Dalmas. *ph* Rudolph Maté. *ed* Al Clark. *ad* Lionel Banks, Walter Holscher. *m* Ernst Toch. *cast* Paul Lukas, Morris Carnovsky, KT Stevens, Peter Van Eyck, Carl Esmond, Mady Christians.

● Based on a novella by Kressman Taylor which sensationally exposed the Nazi threat back in 1938, this gets somewhat tangled in a Jacobean revenge plot about two old friends in San Francisco whose children plan to marry. One (Lukas) returns to Germany with the other's daughter, and, falling under the spell of Nazism, fails to intervene when she is persecuted as a Jew. Lukas' portrayal of a man haunted by guilt, and cracking when a series of anonymous letters bring him under suspicion himself, almost edges the film into *noir* territory. It's often heavy-handed, but fascinating for the way Menzies (abetted by Rudolph Maté's lighting and expressionist touches) designs the film as though he had *Things to Come* in mind. Hollywood almost invariably dwarfed its soulless Nazis within vast chambers dominated by monstrous portraits of *Der Führer*, but the syndrome never ran riot quite so headily as here. TM

Adele Hasn't Had Her Supper Yet

see Nick Carter in Prague

Adhemar ou Le Jouet de la Fatalité (Adhemar or Destiny's Plaything)

(1951, Fr, 95 min, b/w)
d Fernandel. *sc* Sacha Guitry. *ph* Noël Ramettre. *ed* Raymond Lamy. *ad* Eugène Pierac. *m* Louiguy. *cast* Fernandel, Jacqueline Bouvier, Meg Lemonnier, Andrex, Marguerite Pierry, Marcel Levesque.

● A fitfully amusing, lightly cruel series of elaborations by Guitry on the theme of the tyranny of appearance. A philanthropist with a great misshapen nose sets up a committee to help other victims of 'phenomenal physiognomy'. Along comes Fernandel, comparatively normal looking but whose misfortune, he explains, is that his face makes people laugh. All his jobs – undertaker, theatre prompt, casino detective, nurse – end by illustrating how fine feelings are at the mercy of a funny face. It's wrapped up with a grotesque final sketch and a sentimental song. Fernandel is quite subdued, both as director and star, as if aware that the subject goes too deep for mere farce. Now if Guitry himself had directed it… BBa

Adieu Bonaparte (Al-wida'a ya Bonaparte)

(1985, Egypt/Fr, 120 min)
d Youssef Chahine. *p* Marianne Khoury, Humbert Balsan, Jean-Pierre Mahot. *sc* Youssef Chahine, *ph* Mohsen Nasr. *ed* Luc Barnier. *pd* Onsi Abou Seif. *m* Gabriel Yared. *cast* Michel Piccoli, Mohsen Mohieddin, Mohsena Tewfik, Patrice Chéreau, Hoda Soltan, Gamil Ratib.

● Chahine's account of Napoleon's Egyptian campaign of 1798 is idiosyncratic, sprawling, wicked. It offers an oblique comment on Egypt's place in the world today, but typically chooses to focus on affairs of the heart, seeing international relations in terms of emotional exploitation and sexual attraction. Louis Caffarelli (Piccoli), a one-legged homosexual, arrives with Bonaparte's scientific expedition and falls in love with two Arab brothers, one for his body, the other for his mind. The film's strong gay interest is clinched by Chéreau's brilliant performance as Napoleon. Chahine is too wise to blame anyone for what happened in Egypt: he reaches for new notions of cooperation. TR

Adieu Philippine

(1962, Fr/It, 110 min, b/w)
d Jacques Rozier. *p* Georges de Beauregard. *sc* Michèle O'Glor, Jacques Rozier. *ph* René Mathelin. *ed* Monique Bonnot, Claude Durand. *m* Jacques Denjean, Paul Mattei, Maxime Saury. *cast* Jean-Claude Aimini, Yveline Céry, Stefania Sabatini, Vittorio Caprioli, André Tarroux.

● Aimini plays that familiar figure of '60s cinema, the young man awaiting his call-up papers. He works in a TV studio (very droll, these scenes) where he meets two girls, best friends, whom he joins for a holiday in Corsica. Relationships flare and fizzle, ending with the girls on the quayside and the lad on board ship, the war in Algeria beckoning. Adieu Philippine. Rozier's methods were improvisational, and evidently he cast on appearance and manner rather than on acting talent. The result is a bit long-winded but *très nouvelle vague*, with a hidden camera tailing the characters through summery Paris streets, a bunch of Franco pop oddities on the soundtrack, and a quick glimpse of Jean-Claude Brialy. BBa

Adieu, Plancher des Vaches!

see Farewell, Home Sweet Home

Adjuster, The

(1991, Can, 102 min)
d/p/sc Atom Egoyan. *ph* Paul Sarossy. *ed* Susan Shipton. *m* Mychael Danna. *cast* Elias Koteas, Arsinée Khanjian, Maury Chaykin, Gabrielle Rose, Jennifer Dale, David Hemblen, Rose Sarkisyan.

● An insurance adjuster (Koteas) arrives at the scene of a fire and takes the burned-out owner-occupier in hand. 'You may not feel it,' he tells her, 'but you're in a state of shock'. Egoyan's characters are always at a remove from the world, emotionally numb, psychically dislocated. He's fascinated by parallax and discrepancy, the gap between image and reality. Noah – the adjuster – tries to help his clients reproduce their material effects so that the clients can be exactly as they were before. Scrupulously poring over photographs for clues, he places a value on everything; and part of the special relationship he establishes with his clients is having sex with them… *The Adjuster* might almost be the third instalment in a trilogy which began with *Family Viewing* and *Speaking Parts*. It's his richest, most expansive film to date, an engrossing, deadpan tragicomedy, evocatively shot in CinemaScope, with surprisingly affecting performances from Koteas and Chaykin in particular. TCh

Admirable Crichton, The (aka Paradise Lagoon)

(1957, GB, 93 min)
d Lewis Gilbert. *p* Ian Dalrymple. *sc* Vernon Harris. *ph* Wilkie Cooper. *ed* Peter Hunt. *pd* William Kellner. *m* Douglas Gamley. *cast* Kenneth More, Diane Cilento, Cecil Parker, Sally Ann Howes, Martita Hunt, Jack Watling, Peter Graves.

● JM Barrie's comic war-horse trotted out again for More's resourceful butler to teach his shipwrecked betters the ropes of surviving with grace. It actually worked better as a musical in the 1934 Hollywood version, *We're Not Dressing*, with Bing Crosby, Carole Lombard, and Burns and Allen. PT

Adolf Hitler – My Part in His Downfall

(1972, GB, 102 mins)
d Norman Cohen. *p* Gregory Smith, Norman Cohen. *sc* Johnny Byrne. *ph* Terry Maher. *ed* Tony Lenny. *pd* Robert Jones. *m* Wilfred Burns. *cast* Jim Dale, Arthur Lowe, Bill Maynard, Tony Selby, Geoffrey Hughes, Windsor Davies, Spike Milligan.

● A clever scripting job by Johnny Byrne, some enjoyable acting, and a very real evocation of what it must have been like for an ordinary bunch of young men suddenly to be required to turn into soldiers, make this adaptation of Spike Milligan's novel a much better prospect than it might seem. The story is based on embroidered fact and takes Spike from the time he received his World War II call-up papers to the moment of embarking to tackle the Hun. In many ways the film looks like a classy *Carry On*, a feeling strengthened by the casting of Dale as Milligan (with Milligan playing his own father), though overlaid by the zaniness and compassion of Milligan's humour. The comedy is occasionally given bite by credible moments of sudden tragedy. JC

Adoption (Örökbefogadás)

(1975, Hun, 89 min, b/w)
d Márta Mészáros. *sc* Márta Mészáros, Gyula Hernadi, Ferenc Grünwalsky. *ph* Lajos Koltai. *ed* Eva Karmentö. *pd* Tamás Banovich. *m* György Kovacs. *cast* Kati Berek, László Szabo, Gyöngyvér Vigh, Arpad Perkaky, Péter Fried, István Szöke.

● Unmomentous portrait of a woman in middle-age, whose unsatisfactory romance with a married man and involvement with a delinquent girl from a nearby remand home lead her to consider adopting a child. It's a welcome change to find such a character as the subject of a movie, especially when she's as well played as she is by Kati Berek. But the direction stays locked in the hoariest 'social realist' tradition and constantly verges on cliché. TR

A Double Tour (aka Leda/Web of Passion)

(1959, Fr/It, 98 min)
d Claude Chabrol. *p* Robert Hakim, Raymond Hakim. *sc* Paul Gégauff, Claude Chabrol. *ph* Henri Decae. *ed* Jacques Gaillard. *pd* Jacques Saulnier, Bernard Evein. *m* Paul Misraki, Hector Berlioz, Wolfgang Amadeus Mozart. *cast* Madeleine Robinson, Jacques Dacqmine, Jean-Paul Belmondo, Bernadette Lafont, Antonella Lualdi, André Jocelyn, Jeanne Valérie, Mario David.

●Chabrol's third film, greeted at the time as a Hitchcock pastiche, now looks like pure Chabrol: his first demolition job on the bourgeois family as internal tensions – father (Dacqmine) is indulging a clandestine affair, mother (Robinson) worries what the neighbours will think, daughter (Valérie) struggles with her inhibitions, and son (Jocelyn) quietly strangles on his mother's apron-strings – finally succumb to spontaneous combustion. Belmondo is fun as the uncouth, outrageously *déclassé* interloper who serves as a catalyst, goading both father and daughter into an open acknowledgment of their sexual needs, but he seems to have come from another, more overt movie, at odds with the subtly detailed (and beautifully acted) portrait of social repressions and malaises. Seen in the light of Chabrol's later work, the film has gained considerably in stature. Best of several stunning scenes is the climactic murder of the mistress (Lualdi), a fragile china doll who comes gift-wrapped in a Japanese-style house. Glacial, almost serene in its inevitability, this chilling sequence reveals the first glimpses of the Fritz Lang influence later to flower in Chabrol's work. TM

Adrenaline Drive

(1999, Jap, 112 min)
d Shinobu Yaguchi. *p* Kiyoshi Mizokami. *sc* Shinobu Yaguchi. *ph* Takeshi Hamada. *ed* Shinobu Yaguchi. *pd* Yoshio Yamada. *m* Seiichi Yamamoto, Rashinban. *cast* Hikari Ishida, Masanobu Ando, Jovi Jova, Kinna Mano, Yutaka Matsushige.

●Funnier than Yaguchi's earlier comedies, this plays like a sardonic hetero variation on Kitano's *Boiling Point*,while borrowing Kitano's discovery Ando from *Kids Return*. A nerdy kid upsets a yakuza and escapes with his life, a large sack of banknotes (washed and tumble-dried to remove the bloodstains) and a shy nurse who blossoms when she loses her glasses and gets her hair done. These two go on the run, *Pierrot le Fou*-style, never quite getting it together sexually as they fend off assorted cops, bag-snatchers and vengeful yakuza. Not as fast paced as the title implies, but it strikes the right balance between motion and emotion, never confusing the two. TR

Adrenalin – Fear the Rush

(1995, US, 76 min)
d Albert Pyun. *p* Tom Karnowski, Gary Schmoeller. *sc* Albert Pyun. *ph* George Mooradian. *ed* Ken Morrisey. *pd* Nenad Pecur. *m* Antony Riparetti. *cast* Natasha Henstridge, Christophe Lambert, Norbert Weisser, Elizabeth Barondes, Craig Davis, Xavier de Clie.

●This effluent from the bowels of Hollywood is right down there with Lambert's worst. It's set in a post-apocalyptic urban Wild West landscape, a quarantine camp for immigrants to the US where Henstridge's police officer joins a SWAT-team operation to clear a killer from the estate. Shown only in extra close-up, the killer has bloodshot eyes, bloody fangs, braces, jeans and bovver boots. He also has a large knife, some virulent disease, a taste for cops' flesh and a facility for taking out whole teams of armed police. Cheap *Alien* out-takes with a dumb underground Hannibal Lecter. NB

Adrift (Hrst Plná Vody)

(1969, Czech/US, 108 min)
d Ján Kadár. *p* Julius Potocsny. *sc* Imre Gyöngyössy. *ph* Vladimir Novotny. *ed* Josef Valusiak. *pd* Karel Skvor. *m* Zdenek Liska. *cast* Rade Markovic, Milena Dravic, Paula Pritchett, Josef Kroner, Vlado Müller, Gustav Valach, Iván Darvas.

●About a fisherman's obsession for a girl he has rescued from the river. The story is not developed analytically enough to justify the extremely arty pretensions of the film's form, and the music often seems to be trying to turn it into a comedy. VG

Adult Fun

(1972, GB, 102 min)
d James Scott. *p* Tim Van Rellim. *sc* James Scott. *ph, ed* Adam Barker-Mill. *pd* Wilfred Scott. *m* Simon Standage. *cast* Peter Marinker, Deborah Norton, Judy Liebert, Roger Booth, Ann Foster, Roger Hammond.

●The influenza of Italian and French assaults on narrative film-making (during the '50s and '60s) eventually spread to Britain (in the '70s); and one of the more interesting cases is this rather opaque film. It looks very Godard-like in its combination and parody of genres (potboiler fiction, documentary, pseudo-documentary) and in its action-packed plot which pivots on underworld crime as a young stockbroker suffering from feelings of alienation becomes nightmarishly involved, Graham Greene style, in industrial espionage. Scott got one step ahead of Godard, however, in the complex mixing of the soundtrack so that words do not merely accompany the image, but must be problematically deciphered against it. DD

Advance to the Rear (aka Company of Cowards)

(1963, US, 86 min, b/w)
d George Marshall. *p* Ted Richmond. *sc* Samuel A Peeples, William Bowers. *ph* Milton Krasner. *ed* Archie Marshek. *pd* George W Davis. *m* Randy Sparks. *cast* Glenn Ford, Stella Stevens, Melvyn Douglas, Jim Backus, Joan Blondell, Andrew Prine.

●Yes, it does sound like some sub-*Carry On* lark, but the title actually masks a rather jolly comedy Western. Col Douglas and Capt Ford are members of a Union cavalry troop so inept that Gen Backus has sent them West by riverboat rather than risk losing the Civil War. Their new mission sees them more interested in professional lady Stevens, but the accident-prone twosome still manage to cover themselves in glory in this romp with a decided anti-military tone. It's not exactly *M*A*S*H* out West, but fun none the less. TJ

Adventure for Two

see Demi-Paradise, The

Adventure in Baltimore (aka Bachelor Bait)

(1949, US, 90 min, b/w)
d Richard Wallace. *p* Richard H Berger. *sc* Lionel Houser. *ph* Robert de Grasse. *ed* Robert Swink. *pd* Albert S d'Agostino, Jack Okey. *m* Frederick Hollander. *cast* Shirley Temple, John Agar, Robert Young, Albert Sharpe, Josephine Hutchinson, Charles Kemper.

●Despite hopefully provocative re-titling for British release, a very tepid comedy set in 1905. Temple plays a young woman upsetting family and social conventions when she turns to painting 'scandalous' portraits and becomes a suffragette (finally settling, of course, for domestic bliss). GA

Adventure of Sherlock Holmes' Smarter Brother, The (aka Sherlock Holmes' Smarter Brother)

(1975, US, 91 min)
d Gene Wilder. *p* Richart A Roth. *sc* Gene Wilder. *ph* Gerry Fisher. *ed* Jim Clark. *pd* Terence Marsh. *m* John Morris. *cast* Gene Wilder, Madeline Kahn, Marty Feldman, Dom DeLuise, Leo McKern, Roy Kinnear, John Le Mesurier.

●'Sheer luck,' Sigerson Holmes derisively tags his more famous older brother. Sherlock nevertheless delegates a blackmail case involving a soubrette (Kahn) to young Sigi (Wilder),while he himself concentrates on the more pressing investigation of the theft of state documents from the Foreign Secretary. The cases become entangled, however, when it transpires that the soubrette's father is the Foreign Secretary (Le Mesurier) and that her fiancé, the opera singer Gambetti (DeLuise), wants to obtain papers in papa's safe. Writer/director Wilder spins a very tangled tale, and production designer Terry Marsh has gone to town on the excessively cluttered 1890s sets, but there's a magnificent on-stage climax, when, during a production of *The Masked Ball*, documents are due to change hands and the drugged chorus progressively collapses. Hit and miss, with plums picked from all chapters of the comic handbook, and plenty of innocent lavatory humour. Kahn and DeLuise shine among the strong ensemble. JPy

Adventurers, The

(1970, US, 171 min)
d/p Lewis Gilbert. *sc* Michael Hastings, Lewis Gilbert. *ph* Claude Renoir. *ed* Anne V Coates. *pd* Tony Masters. *m* Antonio Carlos Jobim. *cast* Bekim Fehmiu, Alan Badel, Candice Bergen, Ernest Borgnine, Leigh Taylor-Young, Fernando Rey, Charles Aznavour, Olivia de Havilland.

●Revolutionary politics in a fictitious South American state seen through the eyes of Harold Robbins. Or in other words, the usual mixture of sex, fast cars and drugs with a few 'Eh gringos' and 'Viva la Revoluciones' thrown in for good measure. A really bad movie made even worse by the appearance of 'actor extraordinaire' Rossano Brazzi in a cameo role. PH

Adventures in Babysitting (aka A Night on the Town)

(1987, US, 102 min)
d Chris Columbus. *p* Debra Hill, Lynda Obst. *sc* David Simkins. *ph* Ric Waite. *ed* Frederic Steinkamp. *pd* Todd Hallowell. *m* Michael Kamen. *cast* Elisabeth Shue, Maia Brewton, Keith Coogan, Anthony Rapp, Calvin Levels, Vincent D'Onofrio, Penelope Ann Miller.

●While babysitting the neighbours' brats, 17-year-old Chris (Shue) gets an SOS call from her chubby chum Brenda (Miller), who has run away from home and is stranded at a downtown bus depot. Bundling her charges into the family Chevy, Chris sets off on a rescue mission, and ends up running the gauntlet of big city perils in a belaboured spinning-out of a weak storyline. The central issue is how the babysitters will explain away to doting parents the death, disfigurement or molestation of randy adolescents Brad and Daryl and nine-year-old Sara (a goofball of cute), should the batty lorry driver, gangsters or prostitutes they encounter have their evil way. If this family fodder is functional, it's due largely to its production design and cinematography, which endow the city of Chicago with an effectively menacing aspect. EP

Adventures of a Brown Man in Search of Civilisation (aka Nirad Chaudhuri, Adventures of a Brown Man in Search of Civilisation)

(1971, GB, 54 min)
d James Ivory. *p* Ismail Merchant. *ph* Walter Lassally. *ed* Kent McKinney. *with* Nirad Chaudhuri.

●Born in a village in East Bengal in 1897, the scholar Nirad Chaudhuri has been a lifelong enemy of received wisdom, especially Indian received wisdom. In the early '70s, he was in England researching a book on the German-born British Sanskrit scholar Max Müller. James Ivory took time out, shortly after finishing his fourth Indian feature film, *Bombay Talkie*, to observe Chaudhuri in Oxford and London dressing up in a velvet party coat with lace cuffs, commanding a dinner party, dominating a seminar, and laying down the law on every subject under the sun. The servants of the British Raj, to whose memory this diminutive gadfly dedicated his best-known book, *Autobiography of an Unknown Indian*, once behaved with a similar sort of unabashed self-assurance. JPy

Adventures of a Gnome Named Gnorm

see Gnome Named Gnorm, A

Adventures of a Private Eye

(1977, GB, 96 min)
d Stanley Long. *p* Stanley Long, Peter Long. *sc* Michael Armstrong. *ph* Peter Sinclair. *ed* Jo Gannon. *pd* Carlotta Barrow. *m* De Wolfe.

cast Christopher Neil, Suzy Kendall, Harry H Corbett, Fred Emney, Liz Fraser, Irene Handl, Jon Pertwee, William Rushton, Diana Dors.
●Surprising, really, that this rock-bottom British 'sex' comedy wasn't called *Adventures of a Private Dick* – that's about the level of the humour. A plot that isn't even worth mentioning, much playing to camera, plodding scenes and dreary gags make the whole thing instantly forgettable. Stanley Long's mercifully brief series, following in the naughty farce wake of the *Carry On* films, began and ended equally limply with *Adventures of a Taxi Driver* (1975) and *Adventures of a Plumber's Mate* (1978). CPe

Adventures of Baron Munchausen, The

(1988, GB/WGer/It, 126 min)
d Terry Gilliam. *p* Thomas Schühy. *sc* Charles McKeown, Terry Gilliam. *ph* Giuseppe Rotunno. *ed* Peter Hollywood. *pd* Dante Ferretti. *m* Michael Kamen. *cast* John Neville, Sarah Polley, Eric Idle, Charles McKeown, Winston Dennis, Jack Purvis, Valentina Cortese, Oliver Reed, Jonathan Pryce, Bill Paterson, Robin Williams, Sting.
●The tall tales of the legendary 18th-century Baron Munchausen would seem perfect subject matter for Gilliam's fertile imagination; indeed, despite production problems, the film is an engaging and dottily fantastic spectacular. The Baron (Neville) and his superhuman colleagues are rather colourless creations, but the characters they encounter during their odyssey – mafioso-like King of the Moon (Williams), love-lorn Vulcan (Reed) – are vivid and funny. Still more bizarre is the look of the film: an island transformed into a monstrous fish, a balloon sewn from underwear sailing over a war-torn city, a ship rippling through a desert strewn with statuary. But this third part of Gilliam's trilogy, about 'the triumph of imagination over rationality' and lighter in tone than *Brazil*, hardly warrants serious analysis. More of its budget should have been spent on the script – there are jarring leaps in the narrative – but it's good, intelligent fun, and occasionally truly surprising. GA

Adventures of Baron Munchhausen, The (Münchhausen)

(1943, Ger, 134 min)
d Josef von Baky. *sc* Berthold Bürger. *ph* Werner Krien, Konstantin Irmen-Tschet. *m* Georg Haentzschel. *cast* Hans Albers, Brigitte Horney, Wilhelm Bendow, Michael Bohnen, Hilde von Stolz, Leo Slezak, Eduard von Winterstein.
●A spectacular film fantasy, based on the legendary exploits of the fictional Baron Münchhausen, this escapist extravaganza (which was commissioned by Nazi propaganda minister Joseph Goebbels) is simply an excuse for a series of surreal episodes: the Baron's adventures take him from the opulent court of Catherine the Great, via a Turkish sultan's harem and Venice's Grand Canal, to the surreal landscape of the moon. NF

Adventures of Barry McKenzie, The

(1972, Aust, 114 min)
d Bruce Beresford. *p* Phillip Adams. *sc* Barry Humphries, Bruce Beresford. *ph* Donald McAlpine. *ed* John Scott. *pd* John Stoddart. *m* Peter Best, Barry Humphries, Barry Crocker. *cast* Barry Crocker, Barry Humphries, Peter Cook, Spike Milligan, Dick Bentley, Dennis Price, Joan Bakewell, William Rushton.
●Unappealing spinoff from the *Private Eye* comic strip, chronicling the adventures, with and without his Aunt Edna, of a loud-mouthed, sex-crazed innocent from Oz newly arrived in Earl's Court. The odd amusing incident, but mostly spoiled by sheer repetitiveness and the unmodulated top-of-the voice vulgarity sought at all costs. VG

Adventures of Buckaroo Banzai Across the 8th Dimension, The

(1984, US, 102 min)
d WD Richter. *p* Neil Canton, WD Richter. *sc* Earl Mac Rauch. *ph* Fred J Koenekamp. *ed* Richard Marks. *pd* J Michael Riva. *m* Michael Boddicker. *cast* Peter Weller, Ellen Barkin, John Lithgow, Jeff Goldblum, Christopher Lloyd, Lewis Smith.
●Banzai – comic-book superhero, neurosurgeon, pop star, mystic, nuclear physicist and teenage heartthrob – is testing a new jet-propelled Ford Fiesta when he crashes into one side of a mountain to exit miraculously unharmed from the other. Evil Black Lectoids from Planet 10 have been exiled within the rock, and Buck accidentally releases a few, leaving him the only one who can save the Earth from destruction. His allies include a New Jersey cowboy-brain-surgeon (Goldblum) and a six-foot extra-terrestrial rasta; their chief enemy, evil Dr Lizardo (Lithgow). Richter's comic genre hybrid comes complete with its own mythology, and team of established superheroes, and is curiously appealing. SGo.

Adventures of Bullwhip Griffin, The

(1965, US, 110 min)
d James Neilson. *p* Walt Disney. *sc* Lowell S Hawley. *ph* Edward Colman. *ed* Marsh Hendry. *ad* Carroll Clark, John B Mansbridge. *m* George Bruns. *cast* Roddy McDowall, Bryan Russell, Suzanne Pleshette, Karl Malden, Harry Guardino, Richard Haydn, Hermione Baddeley, Mike Mazurki.
●Nothing here to upset the kids, little to interest grown-ups except for Tony Hancock admirers. This was the picture for which the pride of East Cheam was summoned to Hollywood. He couldn't stay sober though, and Disney canned him, substituting Richard Haydn. The film is a pallid variation on *Ruggles of Red Gap*, with McDowall an English butler in the Wild West. The Hancock or rather Haydn role – just a turn, really – is required only to get the plot under way, but for fans even a proxy performance is worth having. For the rest, the seasoned cast and a few cartoon flourishes keep tedium at bay. BBa

Adventures of Captain Marvel, The (aka The Return of Captain Marvel)

(1941, US, 12-episode serial, 196 min, b/w)
d William Witney, John English. *p* Herbert J Yates. *sc* Ronald Davidson, Norman Shannon Hall, Arch B Heath, Joseph Franklin Poland, Sol Shor. *ph* William Nobles. *ed* Edward Todd. *m* Cy Feuer. *cast* Tom Tyler, Frank Coghlan Jr, Louise Currie, Billy Benedict, Nigel de Brulier, Reed Hadley.
●Captain Marvel was one of the greatest of comic strip characters until DC publications, creators of Superman, sued his publishers for plagarism and wiped him off the news-stands in the '50s. He was revived later by DC themselves, but when this vintage serial was put together he was at the height of his fame and glory. Young Billy Batson, who changes into superhero Captain Marvel on uttering the magic '*Shazam*', here ventures to Siam to ensure that the secrets of the Scorpion Dynasty, violated from the tomb, are not put to wicked use (naturally by a mastermind intent on world domination). Fun. DP

Adventures of Don Juan (aka The New Adventures of Don Juan)

(1948, US, 110 min)
d Vincent Sherman. *p* Jerry Wald. *sc* George Oppenheimer, Harry Kurnitz. *ph* Woody Bredell. *ed* Alan Crosland Jr. *ad* Edward Carrere. *m* Max Steiner. *cast* Errol Flynn, Viveca Lindfors, Robert Douglas, Alan Hale, Ann Rutherford, Raymond Burr, Romney Brent.
●Flynn's last swashbuckler, and – surprisingly – not half bad, even though the climactic duel with Robert Douglas had to be completed with doubles for both actors. A lavish, elegant tale of the fencing-master who trades on the queen's susceptibility to prevent Spain from raising a second Armada, it has gorgeous colour camerawork (Elwood Bredell) and a nice line in mocking wit. TM

Adventures of Elmo in Grouchland, The

(1999, US/Ger, 73 min)
d Gary Halvorson. *p* Alex Rockwell, Marjorie Kalins. *sc* Mitchell Kriegman, Joseph Mazzarino. *ph* Alan Caso. *ed* Alan Baumgraten. *pd* Alan Cassie. *m* John Debney, Martin Erskine, Michael A Regan. *cast* Mandy Patinkin, Vanessa Williams, Sonia Manzano, Roscoe Orman; voices: Kevin Clash, Fran Brill, Joseph Mazzarino, Frank Oz, Carroll Spinney, Steve Whitmire.
●Elmo, the cute little monster from TV's *Sesame Street*, gets a movie of his own, and charming it is too, for the first reel or so. We discover him snuggling up in the morning with his very favourite blanket, soft and fleecy, and quite a little groover in the first musical number. Clearly, this is one covetable 'blankie', since Elmo's soon tussling over it with pal Chloe, landing it inside the trashcan Oscar the Grouch calls home. Venturing within to retrieve it, Elmo is sucked into another dimension – Grouchland! All good messy fun, but then this Jim Henson production spoils it by introducing a fatally dull villain – Patinkin's acquisitive megalomaniac Huxley – and a fifth-rate *Wizard Of Oz* narrative. Bert and Ernie are on hand to explain the plot, but it's disappointing to see Grover and The Cookie Monster so offhandedly sidelined. TJ

Adventures of Ford Fairlane, The

(1990, US, 104 min)
d Renny Harlin. *p* Joel Silver, Steve Perry. *sc* Daniel Waters, James Cappe, David Arnott. *ph* Oliver Wood. *ed* Michael Tronick. *pd* John Vallone. *m* Yello. *cast* Andrew Dice Clay, Wayne Newton, Priscilla Presley, Morris Day, Lauren Holly, Maddie Corman.
●A poorly streamlined vehicle for America's prime exponent of the Comedy of Hate, Andrew Dice Clay, this expensively empty action comedy is as much fun as a car crash. Shortly after Heavy Metal superstar Bobby Black (Vince Neil of Motley Crue) gets fried alive on stage, 'rock-'n'roll detective' Ford Fairlane (Clay) is hired by rich bitch Colleen (Presley) to find bubble-headed groupie Zuzu Petals (Corman). When 'shock jock' Johnny Crunch (Gottfried) also gets his plug pulled, Ford starts looking for someone with lots of juice. That's it on the plot level, so the rest is padded out with Ford playing rock'n'roll (badly), driving flash cars, cracking wise, talking dirty to women, or standing around like a spare dick at a wedding while *Die Hard 2* director Harlin smashes up cars, blows up buildings, and mistimes every comic scene. Worse still is the Diceman's cynical attempt to soften his bad boy image; he still comes over as a racist, homophobic, sexist asshole who mistakes sentimentality for true feeling. NF

Adventures of Frontier Fremont, The (aka Spirit of the Wild)

(1976, US, 96 min)
d Richard Friedenberg. *p* Charles E Sellier Jr. *sc* David O'Malley. *ph* George A Stapleford. *ed* Sharron Miller. *m* Bob Summers. *cast* Dan Haggerty, Denver Pyle, Tony Miratti, Norman Goodman, Teri Hernandez, Bryan Frasier.
●Mountain-man Jacob Fremont (a wimpy Jeremiah Johnson for juniors) attempts to find harmony in nature, sporting a bushy beard, conversing endlessly ('Best thing Ah ever dun was ter lose mah gun') with the local Indians, and clearing evil crittur-killin' trappers off his mountain. Predatory adult animals he scares off merely with his shout (or is it Haggerty's acting?). This idealised, ecologically-sound, pastoral adventure seems to please young kids; but you grown-ups'd be plumb crazy to mosey along to see it. GA

Adventures of Gerard, The

(1970, GB/It/Switz, 91 min)
d Jerzy Skolimowski. *p* Henry Lester, Gene Gutowski. *sc* HAL Craig. *ph* Witold Sobocinski. *ed* Alastair McIntyre. *pd* Bill Hutchinson. *m* Riz Ortolani. *cast* Peter McEnery, Claudia Cardinale, Eli Wallach, Jack Hawkins, Mark Burns, John Neville, Norman Rossington.
●A film from Skolimowski's period of exile into the clutches of international co-production. Like his eminently Nabokovian *King, Queen, Knave*, it suffers from the semi-dubbing of an 'English version', with voices and bodies sometimes coming apart. But excused by commerce from the need to be serious, Skolimowski gives free rein to his fantasy in a careering period charade which makes amiable mockery of military

glory. McEnery is perfect as Conan Doyle's dashing French hussar, prancing through Napoleon's Peninsular campaign with one hand on hip and the other courting disasters averted only by his sublime insouciance. Not all the gags work, but enough do to make this something of a welcome – and exquisitely photographed – treat. TM

Adventures of Goopy and Bagha, The (Goopy Gyne Bagha Byne)

(1968, Ind, 132 min, b/w & col.)
d Satyajit Ray. *p* Nepal Dutta, Ashim Dutta. *sc* Satyajit Ray. *ph* Soumendu Roy. *ed* Dulal Dutta. *pd* Bansi Chandragupta. *m* Satyajit Ray. *cast* Tapen Chatterjee, Robi Ghose, Santosh Dutt, Durgadas Bannerjee, Santi Chatterjee, Prasad Mukherjee.

● Ray's 'fairytale for adults', based on a story by his own grandfather about the travels of two outcast musicians who are granted three wishes by the King of the Ghosts, has many attractions. There's much bizarre wit, some delightful songs, and (especially in the pantomime-style transformation scenes and magical manifestations) a sense of wide-eyed wonder so important to this kind of fantasy. But as its picaresque structure stretches further and further into the two-hours-plus running time (it was cut by 14 minutes for British release), even the favourably disposed may get the fidgets. GB

Adventures of Hambone and Hillie, The

see Hambone and Hillie

Adventures of Huck Finn, The

(1993, US, 108 min)
d Stephen Sommers. *p* Larry Marks. *sc* Stephen Sommers. *ph* Janusz Kaminski. *ed* Bob Ducsay. *m* Bill Conti. *cast* Elijah Wood, Courtney B Vance, Robbie Coltrane, Jason Robards, Ron Perlman, Dana Ivey.

● This Disney movie has Huck as cheeky but resourceful artful dodger – which softens the hard times and produces an efficient but unexceptional adventure side-stepping the moral dimension and pathos of Twain's original story. The film has a Gothic beginning, but that's perhaps chiefly a nod to modern horror, and is soon dropped as Huck (Wood) takes to the raft with the runaway Jim (Vance) for his unsentimental education on the Mississippi. The Grangerford/Shepherdson feud is glossed over, and it's only with the arrival of Robards' 'King' and Coltrane's 'Duke' that things begin to liven up. WH

Adventures of Huckleberry Finn, The

(1960, US, 107 min)
d Michael Curtiz. *p* Samuel Goldwyn Jr. *sc* James Lee. *ph* Ted McCord. *ed* Fredric Steinkamp. *pd* George W Davis. *m* Jerome Moross. *songs* Burton Lane. *cast* Tony Randall, Eddie Hodges, Archie Moore, Patty McCormack, Neville Brand, Buster Keaton.

● Fourth screen version of the Twain classic, made by a very tired and under-inspired Curtiz, but featuring light-heavyweight boxing champ Moore as Jim, and the great Keaton as a lion-tamer among the veteran supporting cast (which includes Andy Devine, John Carradine, Sterling Holloway, Finlay Currie, Judy Canova and Royal Dano). PT

Adventures of Huckleberry Finn, The

see Huckleberry Finn

Adventures of Ichabod and Mr Toad, The

see Ichabod and Mr Toad

Adventures of Mark Twain, The

(1943, US, 130 min, b/w)
d Irving Rapper. *p* Jesse L Lasky. *sc* Alan Le May. *ph* Sol Polito. *ed* Ralph Dawson. *ad* John Hughes. *m* Max Steiner. *cast* Fredric March, Alexis Smith, Donald Crisp, Alan Hale, C Aubrey Smith, John Carradine.

● Some soggy moments, but on the whole one of the best of the Warner biopics: solidly stylish, well acted, and with some superb camerawork from Sol Polito (especially in the riverboat sequences). It's romanticised, of course, but reasonably accurate since Twain's career (as printer, river pilot, prospector, newspaper editor, bankrupt and international lecture tourist, among other things) was colourful enough to satisfy even Hollywood. Better when it's lighthearted (the delightful jumping-frog sequence) than when it's solemn (Twain's encounter with the assembled lions of American literature). TM

Adventures of Mark Twain, The (aka Mark Twain)

(1985, US, 90 min)
d/p Will Vinton. *sc* Susan Shadburne. *ed* Kelley Baker, Michael Gall, Will Vinton. *m* Billy Scream. *cast* voices: James Whitmore, Michele Mariana, Gary King, Chris Ritchie.

● Kids will probably adore the colourful clay figures and spectacular action sequences of this technically remarkable animaed feature, but its relentless imagination will be best appreciated by adults. Born in 1835 (year of a visit by Halley's Comet), Twain prepares for death and reunion with his late wife by steering a bizarre balloon to meet the comet on its next appearance. En route, stowaways Huck Finn, Tom Sawyer and Betty Thatcher listen to the writer's fantastic fables as Vinton's sophisticated claymation puts characters and loations through strange metamorphoses to sometimes alarming, always amusing effect. Behind the laughs and lovely visuals, however, lies an astute acknowledgement of the author's embittered duality: the kindly Southern patriach is shadowed by a darker double, and for once the Twain shall meet – at the moment of death. In paying tribute to a man of originality, compassion and intelligence, Vinton has adopted those very qualities himself. GA

Adventures of Michael Strogoff, The (aka The Soldier and the Lady/Michael Strogoff)

(1937, US, 85 min, b/w)
d George Nicholls Jr. *p* Joseph Ermolieff. *sc* Mortimer Offner, Anthony Veiller, Anne Morrison Chapin. *ph* Joseph August. *ed* Frederick Knudtson. *pd* Van Nest Polglase. *cast* Anton Walbrook, Elizabeth Allan, Akim Tamiroff, Margot Grahame, Fay Bainter, Eric Blore.

● RKO's cannibalisation of the exteriors from a 1936 German adaptation of Jules Verne's historical romp, directed by Richard Eichberg (*Der Kurier des Zaren*) and simultaneously filmed in French. Appearing in all three versions, Walbrook is suitably dashing as the envoy galloping across the Steppes to prevent a Tartar uprising, getting blinded (well, not really), falling in love and fighting a duel to the death with the evil Tamiroff. Quite fun, though saddled with silly dialogue of the 'I must get to Omsk' variety. TM

Adventures of Milo and Otis, The (Koneko Monogatari)

(1986, Jap, 75 min)
d Masanori Hata. *p* Masaru Kakutani, Satoru Ogata. *sc* Mark Saltzman. *ph* Hideo Fujii, Shinji Tomita. *ed* Chizuko Osada. *m* Michael Boddicker. *cast* narrator: Dudley Moore.

● This film's international appeal (big success in the United States) was probably boosted by the fact that neither Milo nor Otis speak during the course of the picture (no subtitles or dubbing problems here). Milo, you see, is a cat, Otis a dog. After playing havoc with the other farm animals, the pesky pair go down to the river, where Milo is whisked away in a box. Stout-hearted Otis follows down the bank, but cannot keep up. All kinds of fraught encounters ensue before the pals are reunited – and I drifted off myself. A live-action feature, it scores high on the cute-ometer, what with narrator Dudley Moore working himself into a frolicsome frenzy, a singalong signature tune, and more animals than you'll find at Whipsnade. The Japanese original ran for 90 minutes. TCh

Adventures of PC 49, The (aka The Case of the Guardian Angel)

(1949, GB, 67 min. b/w)
d Godfrey Grayson. *p* Anthony Hinds. *sc* Alan Stranks, Vernon Harris. *ph* Cedric Williams. *ed* Cliff Turner. *pd* James Marchant. *m* Frank Spencer. *cast* Hugh Latimer, Patricia Cutts, John Penrose, Pat Nye, Annette Simmonds, Michael Ripper.

● Rousing little low-budget movie, a lighthearted look at the perils a London bobby faces when he witnesses a truck robbery and comes up against the dreaded Rossini gang of Manchester. Truly British stuff, based on a radio series, complete with colourful criminal slang and seamy, if hardly menacing, low-life. GA

Adventures of Pinocchio, The (aka Pinocchio)

(1996, GB/Fr/Ger/Czech Republic/US, 94 min)
d Steve Barron. *p* Raju Patel, Jeffrey M Sneller. *sc* Sherry Mills, Steve Barron, Tom Benedek, Barry Berman. *ph* Juan Ruiz-Anchia. *ed* Sean Barton. *pd* Allan Cameron. *m* Rachel Portman. *cast* Martin Landau, Jonathan Taylor Thomas, Bebe Neuwirth, Rob Schneider, Udo Kier, Geneviève Bujold, Dawn French, Griff Rhys Jones, John Sessions.

● Landau, as the lonely puppeteer Gepetto, tries his best to bring some heart to this live action version of the rich dark fantasy, and though the effects (digital technology and Jim Henson's Creature Shop) don't always seamlessly integrate Pinocchio with his surroundings, the decorative period detail still gives a strong flavour of Carlo Collodi's imagination. The film starts well with jaunty knockabout fun as the animated Pinocchio runs rings round teacher Sessions and baker's missus Dawn French, but then comes the point where it looks as though someone got cold feet. Just when you think you're about to get a solidly traditional rendering, bets are hedged by wheeling on a computer-generated cricket sounding like a sixth-rate Woody Allen, ginger-coiffed comic baddie Schneider, and a dreadfully out-of-place MOR rock ballad from Brian May. Enjoyably extravagant wickedness from Kier's rival marionette-master and tempter of naughty little boys. TJ

Adventures of Prince Achmed, The (Die Geschichte des Prinzen Achmed)

(1926, Ger, 65 min, tinted b/w)
d Lotte Reiniger. *ph* Carl Koch. *m* Wolfgang Zeller.

● Inspired by *The Arabian Nights*, Reiniger's charming silhouette animation was perhaps the first ever feature cartoon. Released in Germany in 1926 to a lukewarm reception, it proved a smash in Paris, where it was championed by Jean Renoir and the avant garde as a work of rare artistry and fluid beauty. Today, with allowances for some racial and sexual stereotyping, it impresses for its exquisite craftmanship, balletic movement, expressive romanticism and moments of potent sensuousness and poetry. In the days of super-expensive CGI technology and ever growing armies of animation technicians, it's worth noting that Reiniger and husband Carl Koch were a two-person factory. Ex-actress Reiniger designed and made all the articulated foot-high cutouts herself; Koch was in charge of the camera, and Walter Ruttmann and Berthold Bartosch helped with the special effects and backgrounds. As the original negative was lost, this DVD is based on the tinted restoration of the NFTVA answer print (1999); thankfully, the syrupy music added in the '50s has been replaced by Wolfgang Zeller's romantic original score. WH

Adventures of Priscilla Queen of the Desert, The

(1994, Aust/GB, 102 min)
d Stephan Elliott. *p* Al Clark, Michael Hamlyn. *sc* Stephan Elliot. *ph* Brian Breheny. *ed* Sue Blainey. *m* Guy Gross. *cast* Terence Stamp, Hugo Weaving, Guy Pearce, Bill Hunter, Sarah Chadwick, Mark Holmes, Alan Dargin.

● This brash, liberating and poignant road movie follows three drag queens as they travel in a silver bus – 'Priscilla' – from Sydney to a gig in

Alice Springs. 'Les Girls' are Bernadette, an ageing transsexual (Stamp), sharp-tongued Felicia (Pearce) and sensitive-flower Mitzi (Weaver), and this celebration of camp takes them where no lip-synching queens have ever been before. Unlike the bus, the film never gets bogged down, driven forward inexorably by naff disco tunes and crackling dialogue. Most impressive is the Fellini-esque panache writer/director Elliott brings to the visuals, isolating the extravagantly dressed figures in astonishing, orange-tinted landscapes and staging the production numbers like a frustrated director of musicals. Excellent, anchoring performances. Hard not to be swept along. NF

Adventures of Quentin Durward, The (aka Quentin Durward)

(1955, GB, 101 min)
d Richard Thorpe. *p* Pandro S Berman. *sc* Robert Ardrey. *ph* Christopher Challis. *ed* Ernest Walter. *pd* Alfred Junge. *m* Bronislau Kaper. *cast* Robert Taylor, Kay Kendall, Robert Morley, Alec Clunes, Marius Goring, George Cole, Ernest Thesiger, Wilfrid Hyde-White.

● If you want to be picky, Taylor is too young be playing Walter Scott's dashing young gallant, sent from Scotland to press his aged uncle's suit for the hand of the Duke of Burgundy's pretty ward, and winning her himself after her recalcitrance to an arranged marriage occasions much politicking.. Otherwise an enjoyable costume romance, colourfully done with a dash of humour, some nice Gothic touches, and the châteaux de la Loire looking really splendid as a setting. The predominantly English cast, with Clunes outstanding as the Duke of Burgundy, make the most of what is often Scott's dialogue, and the climactic duel in a blazing belltower (with the contestants doing Tarzan acts on the ropes) is terrific. TM

Adventures of Robin Hood, The

(1938, US, 111 min)
d Michael Curtiz/William Keighley. *sc* Norman Reilly Raine, Seton I Miller. *ph* Tony Gaudio. *ed* Ralph Dawson. *pd* Carl Jules Weyl. *m* Erich Wolfgang Korngold. *cast* Errol Flynn, Olivia de Havilland, Basil Rathbone, Claude Rains, Eugene Pallette, Alan Hale, Patric Knowles.

● One of the few great adventure movies that you can pretend you are treating the kids to when you are really treating yourself: the kind of Hollywood film to which *Star Wars* pays tribute, and one of the best examples of what large studio resources could produce. Glorious colour, sumptuous sets, and a brilliantly choreographed climactic sword fight between Flynn and Rathbone; the stuff of which Saturday matinee dreams were made. SM

Adventures of Robinson Crusoe

see Robinson Crusoe

Adventures of Rocky & Bullwinkle, The

(2000, US/Ger, 91 min)
d Des McAnuff. *p* Jane Rosenthal, Robert De Niro. *sc* Kenneth Lonergan. *ph* Thomas Ackerman. *ed* Dennis Virkler. *pd* Gavin Bocquet. *m* Mark Mothersbaugh. *cast* Rene Russo, Jason Alexander, Randy Quaid, Kel Mitchell, Kenan Thompson, Piper Perabo, James Rebhorn, Carl Reiner, Jonathan Winters, Robert De Niro, Janeane Garofalo, John Goodman, Billy Crystal, Whoopi Goldberg.

● Jay Ward's 1960s animated TV series is fondly remembered for its pun-filled humour.This, however, is a misguided animation/live-action crossbreed. Escaping cartoonland for the real world, Fearless Leader (De Niro) and accomplice Natasha Fatale (Russo) launch a secretly located TV station to bombard the populace with programmes of such hypnotic inanity that everyone feels compelled to vote Fearless president. Via some fantastic plot mechanism (and some average computer generated images), their arch rivals – squirrel Rocky and dim-witted moose pal Bullwinkle – are enlisted to help FBI agent Karen Sympathy (Perabo) track them down. Yes, we know the film's poking fun at Hollywood and TV, but the gags are mostly insipid, and when they do hit the mark, they're pitched too high for youngsters. DA

Adventures of Sadie, The

see Our Girl Friday

Adventures of Sherlock Holmes, The (aka Sherlock Holmes)

(1939, US, 81 min, b/w)
d Alfred Werker. *p* Darryl F Zanuck. *sc* Edwin Blum, William A Drake. *ph* Leon Shamroy. *ed* Robert Bischoff. *pd* Richard Day. *m* Cyril J Mockridge. *cast* Basil Rathbone, Nigel Bruce, Ida Lupino, George Zucco, Alan Marshal, Henry Stephenson, Terry Kilburn.

● Second in the Rathbone/Bruce series, after which it shifted from Fox to Universal, modern dress, and wartime uplift. The deer-stalkered one is here up against arch-enemy Moriarty, who has fiendish plans to commit that most heinous of all crimes: the theft of the Crown Jewels. Lightly likeable and beautifully mounted, the film succeeds thanks to some witty dialogue (Holmes to Moriarty: 'You've a magnificent brain. I'd like to present it pickled in alcohol to the London Medical Society'), and to nicely nuanced performances from Rathbone, Bruce and (as Moriarty) Zucco. GA

Adventures of Tom Sawyer, The

(1937, US, 93 min)
d Norman Taurog. *p* David O Selznick, William H Wright. *sc* John VA Weaver. *ph* James Wong Howe. *ed* Margaret Clancy. *ad* Lyle Wheeler, William Cameron Menzies. *m* Max Steiner. *cast* Tommy Kelly, Jackie Moran, Ann Gillis, May Robson, Walter Brennan, Victor Jory.

● Extraordinarily handsome to look at, with exquisite Technicolor camerawork by Wong Howe and some imaginative designs (especially the cave sequence by William Cameron Menzies). Has its longueurs, but it does capture the sense of a lazy Mississippi summer and much of the spirit of the book, with Jory making a superbly villainous Injun Joe. TM

Adventures of Werner Holt, The (Die Abenteuer des Werner Holt)

(1963, EGer, 164 min, b/w)
d Joachim Kunert. *p* Hans Mahlich, Martin Sonnabend. *sc* Claus Küchenmeister, Joachim Kunert. *ph* Rolf Sohre. *ed* Christa Stritt. *pd* Gerhard Helwig. *m* Gerhard Wohlgemuth. *cast* Klaus-Peter Thiele, Manfred Karge, Arno Wyzniewski, Günter Junghans, Peter Reusse, Dietlinde Greiff, Angelica Domröse.

● Adaptation of an autobiographical novel by Dieter Noll which sets out to tell it like it was for a young man growing up in Nazi Germany. Painstakingly worthy but excruciatingly long, and hopelessly naive in its characterisation of a hero symbolically torn since childhood between two friends, one who enjoys beating people up, the other preferring such weedy intellectual pursuits as piano-playing. Small surprise when, at long last, our hero wakes up to the truth about concentration camps while serving on the Eastern front, and becomes disaffected from Nazism. TM

Adventuress, The

see I See a Dark Stranger

Adversaire, L'

see Adversary, The

Adversary, The (L'Adversaire)

(2002, Fr/Switz/Sp, 120 min)
d Nicole Garcia. *p* Alain Sarde. *sc* Jacques Fieschi, Frédéric Bélier-Garcia, Nicole Garcia. *ph* Jean-Marc Fabre. *ed* Emmanuel Castro. *ad* Véronique Barnéoud. *m* Angelo Badalamenti. *cast* Daniel Auteuil, Géraldine Pailhas, François Cluzet, Emmanuel Devos, Bernard Fresson, François Berléand, Alice Fauvet, Jean-Marc Faure.

● January 1993: a man returns home, muddy, dazed, bloody. From this intriguing beginning, flashbacks gradually reveal that he is not the doctor he's claimed to be for the last 18 years – nor indeed has he another job – and that, finally, in shame and confusion, he has killed those nearest and dearest to him. Garcia's film suffers in comparison with *L'Emploi du Temps*, which mined the same territory but dispensed with the murder; more damagingly, it doesn't stand up on its own terms, so inert is the signposted narrative. Auteuil and Devos do their best, but the film is essentially stillborn. GA

Adversary, The (Pratidwandi)

(1971, Ind, 110 min, b/w)
d Satyajit Ray. *p* Nepal Dutta, Ashim Dutta. *sc* Satyajit Ray. *ph* Soumendu Roy. *ed* Dulal Dutta. *pd* Bansi Chandragupta. *m* Satyajit Ray. *cast* Dhritiman Chatterjee, Indiri Devi, Debraj Roy, Krishna Bose, Kalyan Chowdhuri, Joyshree Roy.

● This opens and closes with the same scene: an unemployed ex-student waiting for a job interview with some fifty others in a crowded corridor. In between, Ray takes us on a lightning excursion through the preoccupations of disenchanted urban Indian youth. Taking in concern for the underprivileged, distaste for rich hippies, hangovers of the old puritanical morality, emergent Marxism, the ground he tries to cover is almost too much; and when the hero marches into the interview room in the final scene to attack the complacent officials, it's more a dramatic device than a resolution of his conflicts. Even so, Ray's observation of human behaviour is as acute as ever, with the young man's hang-ups constantly emphasised by the gap between his actions and his dreams. CAub

Advise and Consent

(1962, US, 138 min, b/w)
d/p Otto Preminger. *sc* Wendell Mayes. *ph* Sam Leavitt. *ed* Louis Loeffler. *pd* Lyle Wheeler. *m* Jerry Fielding. *cast* Don Murray, Charles Laughton, Walter Pidgeon, Lew Ayres, Franchot Tone, Henry Fonda, Gene Tierney, Peter Lawford.

● A companion piece to *Anatomy of a Murder* and *The Cardinal*, tackling Washington politics with the best-selling mixture of sophistication and evasion characteristic of Preminger in his 'problem picture' mood. More McCarthy than Watergate, the exposé of political barter and blackmail not unnaturally looks a little quaint now, but still grips like a vice thanks to the skill with which Preminger's stunning mise en scène absorbs documentary detail. A decided bonus is the fact that the need to let every viewpoint have its say gives a starry cast opportunities gratefully grabbed all round. TM

Affair, The

(1995, GB, 105 min)
d Paul Seed. *p* John Smithson, David M Thompson. *sc* Pablo Fenjves, Bryan Goluboff. *ph* Ivan Strasburg. *ed* John Stothart. *pd* Hugo Luczyc-Wyhowski. *m* Christopher Gunning. *cast* Kerry Fox, Courtney B Vance, Leland Gantt, Ciaran Hinds, Beatie Edney, Bill Nunn, Ned Beatty.

● An efficiently performed but finally rather dull (and very televisual) study of a neglected historical subject: the reception of black GIs in Britain during WWII. The racist slurs and aggression which the soldiers endure come less from the rural, middle-class Brits, and more from their white American counterparts; indeed, Fox, whose husband is off in Europe, even goes so far as to contemplate, guiltily, an affair with the impeccably well-mannered Vance. Things turn horribly, though predictably sour. GA

Affair, The (aka Love Song)

(1973, US, 92 min)
d Gilbert Cates. *p* Aaron Spelling, Leonard Goldberg. *sc* Barbara Turner. *ph* Gerald Hirschfeld. *ed* Folmar Blangsted. *pd* Tracy Bousman. *m* George Aliceson Tipton. *cast* Natalie Wood, Robert Wagner, Bruce Davison, Kent Smith, Jamie Smith Jackson, Pat Harrington.

● For a while it seems that Cates might just pull off this modest little film, originally made for TV. Wood stars as a successful songwriter crippled by polio as a girl, with Wagner, a grey-suited straight man from her father's world of lawyers and businessmen, trying to strike up an affair with her. The predictable parallels drawn between her crippled body and emotional life are acceptable enough, because Cates handles her initial lack of interest in Wagner very sensitively, and the dialogue by Barbara Turner is exceptionally good. But about half way through, round about the time she loses her virginity (at 32), the situation runs awry. Up till then, trendy dress and soft focus visuals had been excusable because Cates handles his actors so well. Now the dialogue lapses into folksiness, then into cliché, leaving nothing but the inevitable broken glass, slashed wrists, and older but wiser body recuperating in a hospital bed. RM

Affaire du Courrier de Lyon, L'

(1937, Fr, 103 min, b/w.)
d Maurice Lehmann, Claude Autant-Lara. *p* Maurice Lehmann. *sc* Jean Aurenche, Jacques Prévert. *ph* Michel Kelber. *ed* Marguerite Beaugé. *ad* Jacques Krauss. *m* Louis Beydts. *cast* Pierre Blanchar, Dita Parlo, Charles Dullin, Jean Tissier, Dorville, Jacques Copeau, Pierre Alcover.

● This *affaire* has been troubling the French for 200 years. In 1796 the Lyons mail coach was held up and its two drivers butchered. Five suspects were quickly arrested, condemned and guillotined, though the involvement of one of them, Lesurques, was far from clear. As impossible to believe in his guilt as in his innocence, according to one commentator, though the film-makers have no doubt. Lesurques is shown as the victim of a chance resemblance (Blanchar in a double role), and the parallels between this and Hitchcock's *The Wrong Man* are striking, with Dita Parlo touching in the thankless Vera Miles role. Lehmann being a stage director, Autant-Lara was assigned to handle the cinema, in theory. At any rate, the melodramatic and the factual are kept roughly in balance, so you can't be sure, for instance, if it really did rain on the executions. Rumour has it that an uncredited Jacques Prévert wrote the dialogue. BBa

Affaire Marcorelle, L'

see Marcorelle Affair, The

Affairs of Annabel, The

(1938, US, 68 min, b/w)
d Ben Stoloff. *p* Lee Marcus, Lou Lusty. *sc* Bert Granet, Paul Yawitz. *ph* Russell Metty. *ed* Jack Hively. *m* Roy Webb. *cast* Lucille Ball, Jack Oakie, Ruth Donnelly, Bradley Page, Thurston Hall, Fritz Feld.

● Keen to cash in on the considerable comic talents of their up-and-coming Lucille Ball, RKO intended to set her up in a series. This, the first, sees her as a movie actress in need of publicity whose resourceful press agent (Oakie) contrives to have her imprisoned as a stunt. Fast, undemanding and bright, but only one more in the series followed: *Annabel Takes a Tour* (1938). GA

Affairs of Cellini, The (aka Firebrand)

(1934, US, 90 min, b/w)
d Gregory La Cava. *p* Darryl F Zanuck. *sc* Bess Meredyth. *ph* Charles Rosher. *ed* McLean. *ad* Richard Day. *m* Alfred Newman. *cast* Fredric March, Constance Bennett, Fay Wray, Frank Morgan, Jessie Ralph, Louis Calhern, Vince Barnett.

● Costume romp in 16th century Florence, with March as the roguish artist who switches his amorous attentions from his model (Wray) to a married duchess (Bennett), whose husband (Morgan) is meantime pursuing the model. Mildly diverting in a rather tiresome, bedroom farcical way, but entirely forgettable aside from Charles Rosher's attractive camerawork. TM

Affair of the Necklace, The

(2001, US, 117 min)
d Charles Shyer. *p* Charles Shyer, Redmond Morris, Andrew A Kosove, Broderick Johnson. *sc* John Sweet. *ph* Ashley Rowe. *ed* David Moritz. *pd* Alex McDowell. *m* David Newman. *cast* Hilary Swank, Jonathan Pryce, Simon Baker, Adrien Brody, Brian Cox, Joely Richardson, Christopher Walken, Paul Brooke, Peter Eyre, Simon Kunz, Diana Quick.

● Everyone seems tentative and lost in this fact-based costume drama set in the crumbling days of the ancien régime. What persuaded director Shyer he could make the massive leap from the family-movie mediocrity of *Father of the Bride Part II* to the scheming power-play of the French court? Here a disgruntled countess exposes the extravagance of Marie Antoinette and a cardinal in a sting involving an opulent piece of jewellery. Shyer tries persuade us that the Comtesse de la Motte-Valois is a righteously vengeful victim of injustice, since royal soldiers murdered her rabble-rousing aristo father. In truth, we get two hours of laborious plotting, swishy frocks and unspeakable dialogue. Swank plays a generic 'strong woman' but with little authority or focus, while her illustrious supporting cast never quite ham it up enough to add life to the prevailing stodge. TJ

Affair to Remember, An

(1957, US, 115 min)
d Leo McCarey. *p* Jerry Wald. *sc* Delmer Daves, Leo McCarey. *ph* Milton Krasner. *ed* James B Clark. *ad* Lyle Wheeler, Jack Martin Smith. *m* Hugo Friedhofer. *cast* Cary Grant, Deborah Kerr, Cathleen Nesbitt, Richard Denning, Neva Patterson, Robert Q Lewis.

● Remake of McCarey's own *Love Affair* of 1939, with Grant and Kerr taking over from Charles Boyer and Irene Dunne in this comedy drama about a shipboard romance between a wealthy playboy and an ex-chanteuse. Entertaining enough while the action's still afloat, the plot later gets bogged down in soapy clichés when the characters debark in New York, agreeing to separate and test their love before they marry. Boyer's romantic gravity is much missed in the second half. GA

Affair to Remember, An

see Love Affair

Affiche Rouge, L'

(1976, Fr, 90 min)
d Frank Cassenti. *sc* René Richon. *ph* Philippe Rousselot. *ed* Annie M Mercier. *ad* Yves Oppenheim. *m* Juan Cedron, Carlos Carlsen. *cast* Pierre Clémenti, Anicée Alvina, Maya Wodeska, Laszlo Szabo.

● Blood-red posters featuring portraits of wanted 'terrorists' decorated street walls in occupied France during World War II, and this account of how twenty-three foreigners working for the Resistance were caught and executed dramatises one of the heroic myths of the Occupation. But Cassenti adopts a radically different perspective from the humanist 'honesty' of *L'Armée des Ombres* or even *Lacombe Lucien*, and instead attempts a Marxist analysis of the myth and what it means, historically, to re-enact it. As it moves from one level of representation to another with a Brechtian approach to performance, the film occasionally obscures its aims but never fails to challenge the way we receive history in the cinema. MA

Affinità Elettive, Le

see Elective Affinities

Affliction

(1997, US, 114 min)
d Paul Schrader. *p* Linda Reisman. *sc* Paul Schrader. *ph* Paul Sarossy. *ed* Jay Rabinowitz. *pd* Anne Pritchard. *m* Michael Brook. *cast* Nick Nolte, James Coburn, Sissy Spacek, Willem Dafoe, Mary Beth Hurt, Jim True, Marian Seldes.

● Wade Whitehouse (Nolte) has a point to prove. Divorced with an eight-year-old daughter who wants as little to do with him as possible, he's the town cop, but generally considered either an irrelevance or an embarrassment. His drinking is getting worse and he's itching to square things with the old man, a bitter abusive bully (Coburn). Instead, he latches on to a fatal hunting incident to see if he can't sniff out a murderer. Like *The Sweet Hereafter*, also based on a Russell Banks novel and also shot by cameraman Paul Sarossy under a cold blanket of snow, *Affliction* puzzles over an accidental death, seeks to apportion blame, forlornly, only to skid off-track into unrelated sins of the fathers. Nolte is tremendous: poignantly floundering in his attempts to connect with his daughter and frequently flushed with anger, he's painfully aware that he's gotten a raw deal from life, while staying and blind to the consolations offered by waitress Spacek. Coburn, meanwhile, snarls savagely and chews up the scenery like a shark; no subtlety here, you can taste the violence in his blood. The heaviness is a little stifling, but not inappropriate – Schrader's American tragedy has a dull finality that is determinedly depressing. TCh

Afraid of the Dark (Double Vue)

(1991, GB/Fr, 91 min)
d Mark Peploe. *p* Simon Bosanquet. *sc* Mark Peploe, Frederick Seidel. *ph* Bruno de Keyser. *ed* Scott Thomas. *pd* Caroline Amies. *m* Jason Osborn. *cast* James Fox, Fanny Ardant, Paul McGann, Clare Holman, Robert Stephens, Susan Wooldridge, Ben Keyworth, David Thewlis.

● 11-year-old Lucas (Keyworth) is worried that his mother (Ardant) will fall victim to a psychopath who is terrorising West London with a series of razor attacks on blind women. Holding little faith in the abilities of his father (Fox) as a policeman on the case, the boy begins to suspect those around him… Screenwriter Peploe's debut as director is an ingenious psychological thriller that attempts to delve inside the dark recesses of the mind of its pre-pubescent protagonist. To some extent, it succeeds, thanks partly to genuinely touching playing from Keyworth, partly to a script that contrives to endow what is essentially a very simple plot with a wealth of Freudian symbols, cinematic references and narrative twists. It was probably more satisfying on paper than in its finished form, however: several of the performances in the first half are (perhaps deliberately) somewhat stilted, and there's a faint academicism at work which militates against real suspense. GA

Afrance, L'

see As a Man

Africa Addio (Africa, Blood and Guts)

(1966, It, 122 min)
d Gualtiero Jacopetti, Franco Prosperi. *p* Stanis Nievo. *sc* Gualtiero Jacopetti, Franco Prosperi. *ph* Antonio Climati. *ed* Franco Prosperi. *m* Riz Ortolani.

● Purporting to be a dispassionate documentary about the 'birth struggles' of an Africa freeing itself from colonialism, this was banned all over the continent except for South Africa, where it played to packed houses. Atrocity after atrocity is shown, with no real concern to analyse the context. It's all very interesting, but as one might expect from the team that produced the notorious *Mondo Cane*, the motives are undeniably exploitative.

African Elephant, The (aka King Elephant)

(1971, US, 92 min)
d Simon Trevor. *p* William N Graf, Monty Ruben. *sc* Simon Trevor, Monty Ruben. *ph* Simon Trevor. *ed* Alan L Jaggs. *m* Laurence Rosenthal. *narrator* David Wayne.

● Wild-life adventures often work like Disney cartoons – they're most successful when the animals, the heroes, are humanised to the point of being excessively charming. This documentary, which was shot in East Africa, works along these lines, especially in the way it describes the matriarchy of the elephant world and the idiosyncrasies of other socially rejected creatures. In fact the commentary written by Alan Landsburg is so full of humanly innuendos that one begins to suspect a heavy 'people' message; and it would be fair to simply dismiss the film for being into disguised (and dishonest) 'noble savagery'. Still, there's some fine photography, and some delicate observations which make this film a trillion times better than any zoo. JPi

African Queen, The

(1951, GB, 103 min)
d John Huston. *p* Sam Spiegel. *sc* James Agee, John Huston, John Collier. *ph* Jack Cardiff. *ed* Ralph Kemplen. *pd* Wilfrid Singleton. *m* Allan Gray. *cast* Katharine Hepburn, Humphrey Bogart, Robert Morley, Peter Bull, Theodore Bikel, Walter Gotell.

● Impossible to deny this film's entertainment value, even if it's hardly the great classic it's often claimed to be. Bogart, hammier than usual and thus managing to win an Oscar, is the gin-swigging, cussing river trader who helps prim missionary Hepburn to escape the Germans in East Africa during World War I. Their trying odyssey downriver, of course, gradually sees the two incompatibles falling in love, with the as always detached Bogart finally discovering commitment and attacking a German gunboat. A witty script by James Agee (from CS Forester's novel) and fine colour photography by Jack Cardiff help to counteract the basically contrived and implausible nature of the story. GA

Africa – Texas Style

(1967, GB, 109 min)
d/p Andrew Marton. *sc* Andy White. *ph* Paul Beeson. *ed* Henry Richardson. *pd* Maurice Fowler. *m* Malcolm Arnold. *cast* Hugh O'Brien, John Mills, Nigel Green, Tom Nardini, Adrienne Corri, Ronald Howard, Hayley Mills.
●Virtually a pilot movie for Ivan Tors' short-lived TV series *Cowboys in Africa*, this kiddie-market entry spiced its copious wild-life footage with a slim yarn about a Kenyan settler hiring a pair of Texans to help run his game 'ranch'. PT

After Dark, My Sweet

(1990, US, 114 min)
d James Foley. *p* Ric Kidney, Robert Redlin. *sc* James Foley, Robert Redlin. *ph* Mark Plummer. *ed* Howard Smith. *pd* David Brisbin. *m* Maurice Jarre. *cast* Jason Patric, Rachel Ward, Bruce Dern, George Dickerson, James Cotton, Corey Carrier.
●James (*At Close Range*) Foley demonstrates again his affinity for the climate of mundane evil, this time Jim Thompson's random world, where all the characters play with crooked cues. Ex-boxer and drifter Collie (Patric) seems just punchy enough to recruit as the muscle in a child kidnapping, but turns out unpredictable; and Uncle Bud (Dern) and Fay (Ward) have a testing time keeping up with his mood swings. Nobody trusts anybody, and they're right. Dern, always awkward, has matured into a showpiece of behavioural hairpin bends. Excellent. BC

Afterglow

(1997, US, 114 min)
d Alan Rudolph. *p* Robert Altman. *sc* Alan Rudolph. *ph* Tovomichi Kurita. *ed* Suzy Elmiger. *pd* François Séguin. *m* Mark Isham. *cast* Nick Nolte, Julie Christie, Lara Flynn Boyle, Jonny Lee Miller, Jay Underwood, Domini Blythe, Yves Corbeil.
●As ever, Rudolph's subject is love cross-wired. Nolte is 'Lucky Mann', a fix-it man ready, willing and able to screw away from home with the tacit consent of his wife Phyllis (Christie), a retired B-movie actress. This ageing couple can't conceal the cracks in their marriage caused by the disappearance of their only daughter some years ago. A yuppie couple represent their mirror image: Marianne (Boyle) desperately wants to have a baby, but Jeffrey (Miller) refuses to have sex. As Marianne puts Lucky to work in the spare bedroom and Jeffrey chats up Phyl, each character in turn steps through the looking glass. The film begins with a man teetering on the edge and ends in a howl of anguish – and Tom Waits' aching 'Somewhere'. In between, Rudolph's taste for monologue and metaphorical conceit may prove too arch or theatrical for some, but when he zooms in slowly on Nolte's crumpled, leonine dignity or Christie's pained, still luminous smile, he achieves a singular nakedness. If the younger couple don't achieve the same resonance, they bring a welcome off-kilter energy to the mix. This rakes over the ashes, the inflections and infractions of an unhappy, still loving, marriage with a memorable, plaintive grace. TCh

After Hours

(1985, US, 97 min)
d Martin Scorsese. *p* Amy Robinson, Griffin Dunne, Robert F Colesberry. *sc* Joseph Minion. *ph* Michael Ballhaus. *ed* Thelma Schoonmaker. *pd* Jeffrey Townsend. *m* Howard Shore. *cast* Griffin Dunne, Rosanna Arquette, Verna Bloom, Tommy Chong, Cheech Marin, Linda Fiorentino, Teri Garr, Martin Scorsese.
●A quiet New York computer programmer (Dunne) travels downtown to SoHo for a vaguely arranged date. Losing his taxi fare en route is only the first of the night's many increasingly menacing situations, with neurotic New Yorkers all apparently determined to prevent his returning home alive. Scorsese's screwball comedy is perhaps his most frightening picture to date as Dunne slowly but inexorably sinks into a whirlpool of mad and murderous emotions; but a tight and witty script and perfectly tuned performances, perilously balanced between normality and insanity, keep the laughs flowing, while the direction is as polished and energetic as ever. Only the nagging undercurrents of misogyny leave a sour taste in what is otherwise inventive film-making of the first order. GA

Afternoon Breezes (Kazetachi no Gogo)

(1980, Jap, 105 min, b/w)
d Hitoshi Yazaki. *p* Mitsuhiko Akita, Sunichi Nagasaki, Shiro Oiwake. *sc* Hitoshi Yazaki, Sunichi Nagasaki. *ph* Isamu Ishii, Atsushi Komatsubara. *m* Kazuo Shinode. *cast* Setsuko Aya, Naomi Ito, Hiroshi Sugita, Mari Atake.
●This first feature by the director of *March Comes in Like a Lion* was a seminal film for Japan's emerging independent cinema in the early 1980s. A young woman falls insanely in love with her flatmate. Unable to voice her feelings, she tries to disrupt the other woman's existing love life by seducing her boyfriend – only to find herself pregnant by him. Filmed (almost entirely in long-shots) with remarkable delicacy and restraint, it gets inside the mind of a manic obsessive with near-hallucinatory intensity. TR

After Life

(1998, Jap, 118 min)
d Hirokazu Koreeda. *p* Shiho Sato, Masayuki Akieda. *sc* Hirokazu Koreeda. *ph* Yukuru Sato, Shigeki Nakamura, Yutaka Yamazaki. *ed* Hirokazu Koreeda. *ad* Toshihiro Isomi, Hideo Gunji. *cast* Arata, Erika Oda, Taketoshi Naito, Sadao Abe, Kotaro Shiga, Yusuke Iseya.
●The second feature from the maker of the exquisite *Maborosi* returns to the theme of the relationship between life and death, but reverses the perspective. It is set in a limbo that looks like a slightly shabby school, where counsellors help new arrivals choose their most precious memory which is then recreated on a film to accompany them to eternity. The movie is about how we look back and make sense of our lives. With a strong documentary feel (many of the cast are non-professionals evidently drawing on personal experience), the film succeeds partly as an amusing and richly affecting portrait of what constitutes happiness for a wide range of modern Japanese; it is also, in passing, a little tribute to the way cinema connects with our dreams. Most poignantly, however, as it charts a revelatory encounter between a counsellor and one of his charges, it offers a subtle tribute to the healing power of love. GA

After Nightfall

see Great Jewel Robber, The

After Office Hours

(1935, US, 72 min, b/w)
d Robert Z Leonard. *p* Bernard H Hyman. *sc* Herman J Mankiewicz. *ph* Charles Rosher. *ed* Tom Held. *pd* Cedric Gibbons. *cast* Clark Gable, Constance Bennett, Stuart Erwin, Billie Burke, Harvey Stephens, Henry Travers.
●Standard Depression era plot, with Gable overdoing the brashness as a working newspaperman who resents the socialite (Bennett) he assumes to be slumming when she joins the paper's staff. Their love-hate affair, conducted in pretty flat wisecracks, comes to a head when a friend of hers is murdered and he tracks down the killer. Fine Charles Rosher camerawork, otherwise unremarkable. TM

After the Fall (Eylül Firtinasi)

(1999, Tur, 110 min)
d Atif Yilmaz. *p* Iskender Ulus, Atif Yilmaz. *sc* Gaye Boralioglü. *ph* Erdal Kahraman. *ed* Mevlüt Kocak. *pd* Cagla Ormanlar. *m* Tamer Ciray. *cast* Tarik Akan, Zara, Kutay Özcan, Hazim Körmükçü, Deniz Türkali.
●Adopting a child's viewpoint on the fallout from the anti-leftist torture and persecution campaigns following Turkey's 1980 military coup, this heartfelt, courageous, but far from strident film echoes *A World Apart* in its humanist emphasis. It focuses on individual lives and relationships rent and dislocated in that struggle. Tracing young Metim's journey from first discovering his mother in prison, to his grandfather's retreat to the countryside followed by flight and exile, this is relatively gentle, unhysterical drama. Physical abuse is represented by its results, emotional distress mostly implied, and there's plenty of time for excursions into country life and local politics, all of which rounds out the characters and fills in the emotional impact. NB

After the Fall (Nach dem Fall)

(1999, Ger, 85 min)
d Frauke Sandig, Eric Black. *p* Frauke Sandig. *sc* Frauke Sandig, Eric Black. *ph* Eric Black. *ed* Inge Schneider. *m* Janussz Stoklosa.
●In a series of outstanding interviews, this study of the death and afterlife of the Berlin Wall reveals the extent to which the 'Fall' is unfinished business, which hurriedly reunited Germany ignores at its peril. Unsettling views of the former death strip – now a huge construction site – build an appropriate atmosphere of displacement around interviews documenting the continuing presence of the vanished Wall in people's lives: the pastor who attributes to it a sinister psychic force; the homeopaths who vaunt the healing power of ground-up Wall; the psychotherapist and the Berlin pensioner who declare that knocking down the Wall has not unified Germany for them. SB

After the Fox (Caccia alla Volpe)

(1966, It/US, 102 min)
d Vittorio De Sica. *p* John Bryan. *sc* Neil Simon, Cesare Zavattini. *ph* Leonida Barboni. *ed* Russell Lloyd. *pd* Mario Garbuglia. *m* Burt Bacharach. *cast* Peter Sellers, Britt Ekland, Lidia Brazzi, Victor Mature, Paolo Stoppa, Tino Buazzelli, Mac Ronay.
●Try to imagine a comic farce co-scripted by one of the founding fathers of Italian neo-realism, Cesare Zavattini, and a wisecracking Jewish playwright, Neil Simon. Pretty funny, yes? No! Ill-fated international co-production isn't in it: we are talking turkey here as master criminal The Fox (Sellers) escapes from jail into streets full of excitable Italians, executes a gold bullion robbery, and saves his sister's honour. Marginally enlivened by Mature's witty self-mockery as a beefcake movie star fretting over his fading charms. NF

After the Thin Man

(1936, US, 111 min, b/w)
d WS Van Dyke. *p* Hunt Stromberg. *sc* Frances Goodrich, Albert Hackett. *ph* Oliver T Marsh. *ed* Robert J Kern. *pd* Cedric Gibbons. *m* Herbert Stothart. *cast* William Powell, Myrna Loy, James Stewart, Elissa Landi, Joseph Calleia. Jessie Ralph.
●Surprisingly successful sequel to the delightful, Dashiell Hammett-based comedy-mystery, *The Thin Man*, with Powell and Loy as charmingly witty as ever as the bibulous sophisticates Nick and Nora Charles, revelling in sparkling dialogue as they solve a murder. Notionally based on a story by Hammett, the plot is ingenious enough, though the then up-and-coming Stewart now seems uncomfortable cast as the culprit. After this the series grew distinctly thin, though Powell and Loy continued to give good value: Another *Thin Man* (1939), *Shadow of the Thin Man* (1941), *The Thin Man Goes Home* (1944), *Song of the Thin Man* (1947). TM

After the Truth (Nichts als die Wahrheit)

(1998, Ger/US, 128 min)
d Roland Suso Richter. *p* Werner Koenig, Edward R Pressman. *sc* Johannes W Betz, Christopher Riley, Kathleen Riley. *ph* Martin Langer. *ed* Peter R Adam. *cast* Kai Wieseinger, Götz George, Karoline Eichhorn, Doris Schade, Peter Roggisch, Bastian Trost, Stephan Schwartz, Peter Rühring, Heinz Trixner.
●This courtroom 'docu-drama' details the prosecution in Germany of Dr Josef Mengele (George), the experimenting 'Angel of Death' of Auschwitz, who, so the film has it, came home voluntarily to 'have the truth told'. The way Mengele tells it, his undenied atrocities were committed out of compassion, and his ethics were a product of the times. Taking its time to set up the credibility of Mengele's defence counsel Rohm, the film emphasises the

influence of a rightwing, possibly pro-Nazi publisher and the role of various judges, who describe the trial as a test of the German judicial system. Rohm manages to encourage his own mother to testify about her work in 'euthanasia' during the early part of the war, which weights the film's (possibly unintended) thesis about moral relativity and personal versus state responsibility. In so doing, director Richter does a disservice to the facts, not to mention the meaning and significance of Mengele's actions. WH

Against All Odds

(1984, US, 121 min)
d Taylor Hackford. *p* Taylor Hackford, William S Gilmore. *sc* Eric Hughes. *ph* Donald Thorin. *ed* Fredric Steinkamp. *pd* Richard James Lawrence. *m* Michel Colombier. *cast* Rachel Ward, Jeff Bridges, James Woods, Alex Karras, Jane Greer, Richard Widmark, Dorian Harewood.

● This places itself in much the same category as Jim McBride's *Breathless* – a glossy remake of an old and much loved classic, in this case Jacques Tourneur's 1947 *noir* thriller *Out of the Past* – and once again it is best to forget the original. Bridges is a fading football star with an iffy shoulder and friends in low places. When one of them, the owner of an iniquitous night club (Woods), sends him off to Mexico to recover an errant girlfriend, the problem of finding her, and the problem of the small murder she commits, pale beside the problem of coming back to admit they've fallen in love. There are *longueurs*; there are also compensations, however: pointed performances from Woods and Greer, passion on a Mexican beach, and as in *Breathless*, LA never looked so beautiful. CPea

Against Oblivion

see Contre l'Oubli

Against the Wind

(1947, GB, 96 min, b/w)
d Charles Crichton. *p* Michael Balcon. *sc* TEB Clarke. *ph* Lionel Banes. *ed* Alan Osbiston. *ad* J Elder Wills. *m* Leslie Bridgewater. *cast* Robert Beatty, Simone Signoret, Jack Warner, Gordon Jackson, Paul Dupuis, John Slater, Gisèle Préville.

● Above-average Ealing thriller, with a mixture of British and Belgian agents helping the resistance movement in occupied Europe during World War II. A little implausible, but backed by some semi-documentary training scenes before the group (in a plot remarkably similar to that of *13 Rue Madeleine*) set off on their mission with a traitor (Warner, cast against type) among them. Crichton, taking a break from comedy along with scriptwriter TEB Clarke, turns in some tense moments, and Signoret adds a touch of style in a pre-*L'Armée des Ombres* bout of heroism. GA

Agantuk

see Stranger, The

Agatha

(1978, US/GB, 105 min)
d Michael Apted. *p* Jarvis Astaire, Gavrik Losey. *sc* Kathleen Tynan, Arthur Hopcraft. *ph* Vittorio Storaro. *ed* Jim Clark. *pd* Shirley Russell. *m* Johnny Mandel. *cast* Dustin Hoffman, Vanessa Redgrave, Timothy Dalton, Helen Morse, Celia Gregory, Timothy West.

● The premise is superb: the (real) mystery of Agatha Christie's ten-day disappearance in 1926, during the much-reported disintegration of her marriage. The film, though, only partly fulfills its promise, despite a sensitive script and Vanessa Redgrave's excellent, introverted performance. Period re-creation – of the hotels, railway stations, dress – is almost *too* perfect, with production values tending to distract attention from the situation's intrinsic interest; and a brooding plotline is weakened by slapstick secondary characters and by Hoffman's jaunty pastiche of a performance as an arrogant American newspaperman who finds and falls in love with Agatha in the spa town of Harrogate. Though undercut by a last scene redolent of *Brief Encounter*, the brilliant, suspended twist in the central story – with its ingenious perception that one may write murder 'stories' to stave off the prospect of one's own death – remains memorable. CA

Age d'Or, L'

(1930, Fr, 63 min, b/w)
d Luis Buñuel. *p* Vicomte de Noailles. *sc* Luis Buñuel, Salvador Dali. *ph* Albert Duverger. *ed* Luis Buñuel. *ad* Pierre Schildneck. *cast* Gaston Modot, Lya Lys, Max Ernst, Pierre Prévert, Jacques Brunius, Luis Buñuel.

● 'Our sexual desire has to be seen as the product of centuries of repressive and emasculating Catholicism… it is always coloured by the sweet secret sense of sin,' mused Buñuel in his autobiography *My Last Breath*. One might describe *L'Age d'Or* as 63 minutes of *coitus interruptus*, a scabrous essay on Eros and civilisation, wherein a couple is constantly prised apart from furious love-making by the police, high society and, above all, the Church. Financed by the Vicomte de Noailles, a dream patron who loyally pronounced the film exquisite and delicious, even as right-wing extremists were pelting it with ink and stink bombs, this is a jagged memento of that Golden Age before directors forgot the art of filming erotica (the celebrated toe-sucking is sexier by far than almost anything since), the revolutionary avant-garde lost its sense of humour, and surrealism itself fell prey to advertising-agency chic. SJo

Agency (aka Mind Games)

(1981, Can, 94 min)
d George Kaczender. *p* Robert Lantos, Stephen J Roth. *sc* Noel Hynd. *ph* Miklos Lente. *ed* Kirk Jones. *pd* Bill Brodie. *m* Lewis Furey. *cast* Robert Mitchum, Lee Majors, Valerie Perrine, Saul Rubinek, Alexandra Stewart, Hayward Morse.

● An advertising agency is taken over by a political group, who inject subliminal messages into their commercials. Any potential in this idea was overlooked by Kaczender, whose dull, plodding style is a turn-off, while Lee Majors makes a blank hero. For the real dope on subliminals, see *Videodrome* or *They Live*. TCh

Age of Consent

(1969, Aust, 103 min)
d Michael Powell. *p* James Mason, Michael Powell. *sc* Peter Yeldham. *ph* Hannes Staudinger. *ed* Anthony Buckley. *pd* Dennis Gentle. *m* Peter Sculthorpe. *cast* James Mason, Helen Mirren, Jack MacGowran, Frank Thring, Neva Carr-Glynn, Andonia Katsaros.

● Not quite Powell's last film, since he followed it with *The Boy Who Turned Yellow* for the Children's Film Foundation, and his revised version of *The Edge of the World*; but it is a last return to his favourite theme of the artist taking stock of his life, which he treats with new mellowness while exploiting '60s liberality to give it a direct erotic dimension. Mason plays a commercially successful painter who retires from New York to the Great Barrier Reef; his creative drive is re-awakened when he finds there an innocent but physically mature teenager, whom he strips and paints at the first opportunity. The emotional and psychological results of the encounter are followed through with exemplary seriousness and wit, in some way anticipating the themes and visuals of Nicolas Roeg's *Walkabout*. There are some nervous insertions of redundant comic relief, but not enough to shatter the prevailing mood: brilliant sunlight illuminating all the unmomentous ins and outs of a human passion. TR

Age of Cosimo de Medici, The (L'Età de Cosimo de Medici)

(1972, It, 255 min)
d Roberto Rossellini. *sc* Roberto Rossellini, Luciano Scaffa, Marcella Mariani. *ph* Mario Montuori. *ed* Jolanda Benvenuti. *pd* Franco Velchi. *m* Manuel De Sica. *cast* Marcello Di Falco, Virginio Gazzolo, Adriano Amidei Migliano, Mario Erpichini, Tom Felleghy, Valentino Macchi.

● Rossellini's trilogy portraying the eruption of Renaissance Florence was originally made for TV (Part One: *The Exile of Cosimo de Medici*; Part Two: *The Power of Cosimo de Medici*; Part Three: *Leon Battista Alberti*). Cosimo's rise to power, his exile and return, are related in scenes of austere beauty which animate the economic, legal, military, religious and aesthetic structures of a 15th century city state. Cosimo, the artists, the merchants, the tax-collectors and the priests are all vivid Renaissance men, yet men understood not in an individual psychological frame, but in a historical materialist one. Certain sequences force a complete reappraisal of screen history: an explanation of the tax system, a discussion about architecture, an election to the ruling council, open up ways of seeing the past to which British television obstinately remains largely blind. The revealed world is both patently artificial and startlingly real. Rossellini's restless camera analyses and interrogates the continually stimulating debates about power and freewill. And the greatest achievement is the trilogy's final section, focusing on scholar and artist Leon Battista Alberti. Through him we understand the emergence of the humanist consciousness; through him we recognise the birth of our culture. JW

Age of Innocence, The

(1993, US, 138 min)
d Martin Scorsese. *p* Barbara DeFina. *sc* Jay Cocks, Martin Scorsese. *ph* Florian Ballhaus. *ed* Thelma Schoonmaker. *pd* Speed Hopkins. *m* Elmer Bernstein. *cast* Daniel Day-Lewis, Michelle Pfeiffer, Winona Ryder, Richard E Grant, Alec McCowen, Geraldine Chaplin, Mary Beth Hurt, Miriam Margolyes, Siân Phillips.

● Scorsese's magnificent film, taken from Edith Wharton's novel, is set in 1870s New York and centres on lawyer Newland Archer (Day-Lewis), whose plans to wed the impeccably connected Mary Welland (Rider) are upset by his love for her unconventional cousin, the Countess Olenska (Pfeiffer). The performances are excellent, while the director employs all the tools of his trade to bring his characters and situations vividly to life; from the start, it's clear from the speedy cutting and sumptuous mise-en-scène that Scorsese and his team are intent on drawing us into the heart of Archer's perceptions and the world around him (this is, most certainly, an expressionist film). Decor reflects and oppresses characters; posture, gesture and glance (like the witty, ironic narration) convey not only individual psychology but the ideals of an entire, etiquette-obsessed elite. Everything here serves to express an erotic fervour, imprisoned by unbending social rituals designed to preserve the status quo in favour of a self-appointed aristocracy. Scorsese's most poignantly moving film. GA

Aggression

see Agression, L'

Aggro Seizeman

(1975, Guyana, 110 min)
d/sc James Mannas, Brian Stuart-Young. *ph* Bill Green. *ed* Josephine Piñaro. *m* F Hamley Case. *cast* Gordon Case, Martha Gonsalves, Paulene McKenzie, Oscar Edwards, Cecily Robinson, Frank Pilgrim.

● Uneasy balance of late-adolescent trauma, comedy thriller and romance 'Aggro' is the hero's nickname (ie, he's rough), 'Seizeman' his occupation, meaning he repossesses goods from punters who haven't kept up their hire purchase, usually without informing his victims. His girl's parents think he's a creep, she's not so sure, and the 'seizures' are mostly meant to have us rolling in the aisles until we discover why the chip is on his shoulder. Unfortunately this is one rebel who's missing not only a cause but also a script, director, editor and any competent fellow actors. GD

Agitator (Araburu Tamashii-tachi)

(2001, Jap, 150 min)
d Takashi Miike. *p* Fujio Matsushima, Yoshihiro Masuda. *sc* Shigenori Takechi. *ph* Kiyoshi Ito. *ed* Yasushi Shimamura. *ad* Tatsuo Ozeki. *m* Koji Endo. *cast* Masaya Kato, Naoto Takenaka, Mickey Curtis, Hiroki Matsukata, Kenichi Endo, Renji Ishibashi, Takashi Miike.

● Every character and almost every incident in this sprawling yakuza gang-war saga is generic, and so Miike looks for ways to liven things up – but doesn't find many. As usual in these movies, a large crime syndicate plots to exploit the war between two smaller gangs by pretending to mediate and actually swallowing both. This was set up by Daiei Co. as a vehicle for Masaya Kato (also in Kitano's *Brother*), here playing the loose cannon who thwarts the plan with his shirt open to the navel throughout. Miike aims for 'realism' by using two cameras and shooting the whole thing in available light, but the dead weight of genre traditions proves impossible to shake off. Most striking moment: Miike's own cameo as 'depraved yakuza sadist in karaoke lounge', the man who triggers the gang-war. (The 190-minute, two-part video release also features the excellent Daisuke Ryu, not seen in this theatrical cut.) TR

Agnes Browne

(1999, Ire, 92 min)
d Anjelica Huston. *p* Jim Sheridan, Arthur Lappin, Greg Smith. *sc* John Goldsmith, Brendan O'Carroll. *ph* Anthony B Richmond. *ed* Eva Gardos. *pd* David Brockhurst. *m* Paddy Moloney. *cast* Anjelica Huston, Marion O'Dwyer, Ray Winstone, Arno Chevrier, Gerard McSorley, Niall O'Shea, Ciarán Owens, Roxanna Williams, Carl Power.

● Adapted from Irish comedian Brendan O'Carroll's autobiographical novel *The Mammy*, this would-be heartwarming melodrama offers director/star Anjelica Huston the chance to play a character so utterly noble she never convinces us for a moment. Late '60s Dublin finds the recently widowed Agnes Browne with seven young mouths to feed. She works on a fruit and veg stall, and loan shark Mr Billy (Winstone in Bill Sikes mode) is threatening to break down her door. Meanwhile, best pal Marion (O'Dwyer) gets bad news from the doctor. What's more, neither of them can afford to see the forthcoming Tom Jones concert. It sounds corny, it is corny, and although Huston's performance is indefatigable, the whole picture exists merely to offer its leading lady the chewiest of roles. It might have played better as an urban fairytale, but Huston labours under the mistaken impression that this is gritty drama. TJ

Agnes of God

(1985, US, 98 min)
d Norman Jewison. *p* Patrick Palmer, Norman Jewison. *sc* John Pielmeier. *ph* Sven Nykvist. *ed* Antony Gibbs. *pd* Ken Adam. *m* Georges Delerue. *cast* Jane Fonda, Anne Bancroft, Meg Tilly, Anne Pitoniak, Winston Rekert, Gratien Gelinas.

● When Agnes, a young novice, gives birth to a baby later found strangled, a court psychiatrist (Fonda) is despatched to the convent to discover whether the girl (who claims to remember neither conception nor pregnancy) is fit to stand trial. Fonda, a chain-smoking lapsed Catholic, is determined to find the answer within the girl's subconscious; the worldly Mother Superior (Bancroft) believes a miracle might have taken place. Thus (based on a play) the obvious and slightly spurious battle between science and faith. Splendidly shot by Sven Nykvist and with excellent performances, it's an agreeable puzzle which doesn't, thank heaven, come up with a solution to the meaning of life. JE

Agnus Dei (Nonnebørn)

(1997, Den, 90 min)
d Cæcilia Holbek Trier. *p* Nina Crone. *sc* Cæcilia Holbek Trier. *ph* Anthony Dod Mantle. *ed* Thomas Krag. *pd* Søren Kragh Sørensen. *m* Joachim Holbek. *cast* Kirsten Rolffes, Amalie Dollerup, Nastja Arcel, Bolette Engstrøm Bjerre, Stine Bjerregaard, Cecilia Eliasson, Helle Fagralid, John Hahn-Petersen, Robert Hansen, Luise Jacobsen, Bodil Jørgensen, Christina Merwald, Kurt Ravn, Kirsten Schjødt.

● First feature from the former Mrs Lars von Trier, about a young girl's pre-pubescent spell in a convent. Narratively, it's intimate but for a long time vague: young Johanne's trials and tribulations range inconsequentially across her incomprehension of her parents' reasons for abandoning her, the elder nuns' stern disapproval of her lack of religious education, and the other girls' teasing. Just when she seems better settled, the sisters start talking up her future there, striking the fear of God into her. The sequencing is distinctly choppy, and while the director aims for a sensitive touch, the prettifying sensibility (soundtrack, costumes) seems to have waylaid her. NB

Agony (Agonia/ aka Rasputin)

(1975, USSR, 148 min, b/w & col)
d Elem Klimov. *p* Semion Kutikov. *sc* Semion Lungin, Ilya Nusinov. *ph* Leonid Kalashnikov. *ed* Valery Belovoi. *pd* Yu Liublin. *m* Alfred Schnittke. *cast* Alexei Petrenko, Velta Linei, Alisa Freindlikh, Anatoly Romashin, A Romantsov, S Muchenikov.

● Headily melodramatic and overlong biopic of Rasputin, from the director of *Come and See* and *Farewell*, to which this is immeasurably inferior. The central performance by Petrenko is at best vivid and energetic, at worst mannered and over-the-top, while the whole thing, fitted out with political asides and historical footnotes, comes across as disjointed claptrap, notable only for having broken certain taboos of silence about the infamous charlatan in his native country. Obviously well-intentioned, it's nevertheless often virtually unwatchable. GA

Agony and the Ecstasy, The

(1965, US/It, 139 min)
d/p Carol Reed. *sc* Philip Dunne. *ph* Leon Shamroy. *ed* Samuel E Beetley. *pd* John F DeCuir. *m* Alex North. *cast* Charlton Heston, Rex Harrison, Diane Cilento, Harry Andrews, Alberto Lupo, Adolfo Celi, Fausto Tozzi, Tomas Milian.

● Chuck paints the Sistine Chapel while Pope Rex looks up and wonders when it will be finished. The conflict between artist and sponsor often leads to some fine and even witty interplay, though the extremely dubious love affair and the pallid battle sequences make the film lose focus. Heston is good in the role – he looks less like Michelangelo than Michelangelo's statue of Moses – and the way that Reed conveys the actual painting is impressive. The original version included a 15-minute prologue, with music by Jerry Goldsmith, which toured the world's museums so that audiences might not muddle this Michelangelo with another. ATu

Agostino d'Ippona

see Augustine of Hippo

Agression, L' (Aggression)

(1975, Fr/It, 101 min)
d Gérard Pirès. *p* Alain Poiré, Pierre Braunberger. *sc* Jean-Patrick Manchette. *ph* Silvano Ippoliti. *ed* Jacques Witta. *pd* Jacques d'Ovidio. *m* Robert Charlebois. *cast* Jean-Louis Trintignant, Catherine Deneuve, Claude Brasseur, Milena Vukotic, Jacques Rispal, Philippe Brigaud.

● A French motorcycle picture which, though based on John Buell's novel *The Shrewsdale Exit*, transcends the limitations of imitating the American genre, and offers in its place a sustained attack on French middle class values. Trintignant goes on a trail of revenge after the rape and murder of his wife and daughter; bourgeois dream disintegrates into nightmare, but the seeds of destruction are shown to be internal. Deneuve, as Trintignant's sister-in-law, provides the film's emotional core with a fine performance, her presence questioning male assumptions, even when her lines don't. CPe

Água e Sal

see Water and Salt

Aguirre, Wrath of God (100) (Aguirre, der Zorn Gottes)

(1972, WGer, 95 min)
d/p/sc Werner Herzog. *ph* Thomas Mauch. *ed* Beate Mainka-Jellinghaus. *m* Popol Vuh. *cast* Klaus Kinski, Cecilia Rivera, Ruy Guerra, Helena Rojo, Del Negro, Peter Berling.

● As in *Even Dwarfs Started Small*, the exposition of Herzog's film about the crazy, megalomaniac dream of the Spanish Conquistadors is both functional and extremely concentrated: each scene and each detail is honed down to its salient features. On this level, the film effectively preempts analysis by analysing itself as it proceeds, admitting no ambiguity. Yet at the same time, Herzog's flair for charged explosive imagery has never had freer rein, and the film is rich in oneiric moments. The extraordinary, beautiful opening scene illustrates the ambivalence. In long shot, the image of the conquistadors descending the Andes pass brims with poetic resonances: the men are situated between the peaks and the valleys, between conquered land and unexplored forests, between 'heaven' and 'earth', shrouded in mists. In close-up, the procession picking its way down the narrow path is presented and defined with specific accuracy: all the leading characters are introduced, the social hierarchy is sketched (the slave porters in chains, the women carried in chairs), and the twin poles of the expedition's ideology are signified through the loads it carries (a large Madonna figure and an even larger cannon). Neither 'reading' of the action contradicts the other: they are, rather, mutually illuminating. TR

A-Haunting We Will Go

(1942, US, 68 min, b/w)
d Alfred Werker. *sc* Lou Breslow. *ph* Glen MacWilliams. *ed* Alfred Day. *ad* Richard Day, Lewis Creber. *m* Emil Newman. *cast* Stan Laurel, Oliver Hardy, Dante the Magician, John Shelton, Sheila Ryan, Elisha Cook Jr.

● Not, frankly, one of Laurel and Hardy's better features. The pair are as likeable as ever as down-and-outs hired to deliver a coffin (containing not a corpse but a live gangster) which becomes mixed up with a magician's stage props when they act as his stooges. With pauses for Dante's stage illusions, the plot drags. TM

Ah Chung (Zhong-zai)

(1995, Tai, 98 min)
d Chang Tso-Chi. *p* Lin Tianrong, Zhang Huafu, Lin Wanyu. *sc* Chang Tso-Chi. *ph* Chang Chen. *ed* Liao Ching-Song. *ad* Chen Huai-En. *m* Hugo Pandaputra. *cast* Liu Sheng-Chung, Chiao Shio-Min, Tsai Chieh-Der, Lu Ying.

● Fresh out of school, Ah Chung is forced by his mother to join a 'Pa-Chia-Jang' troupe, performing self-flagellating rituals to please the gods at various public ceremonies. Since the troupes are run by triads and there are frequent bloody fights between rival troupes, this is tantamount to pushing Ah Chung into a life of crime. But his mother sees it as a way of warding off the family's seemingly endemic bad luck. Entirely shot on location with a non-pro cast, Chang's near plotless film offers (a) a realist picture of its characters and their milieu so intense it's almost hallucinatory; and (b) an account of fucked-up adolescence as piercing as any ever made. Too modest to be a 'masterpiece' – and all the better for that. TR

Ah Kam (A-Jin/ The Stunt Woman)

(1996, HK, 100 min)
d Ann Hui On-Wah. *p* Raymond Chow Man-Wai. *sc* Chan Man-Keung. *ph* Ardy Lam Gok-Dut. *ed* Wong Yee-Shun. *m* Otomo Yoshihide. *cast* Michelle Khan (aka Michelle Yeoh), Samo Hung Kam-Bo, James Wong Jim, Kent Cheng, Mang Hoi, Richard Ng, Ken Lo.

● Surprisingly unvarnished tribute to the unsung women and men who perform stunts in Hong Kong movies. Bond-girl-to-be Michelle Khan (who actually did break into movies doing stunts) plays Ah Kam, an immigrant from mainland China who braves her way into movie work, bungles an affair with a businessman and winds up confronting the triad gangsters who have killed her mentor (Hung). Not one of Hui's personal films, but transparently sincere. Khan did her own stunts and broke a leg during production. TR

Ah Ying (Banbianren)

(1983, HK, 116 min)
d Allen Fong Yuk-Ping. *sc* Sze Yeung-ping, Peter Wang. *ph* Chang Lok-yee. *ed* Chow Muk-leung, Ng Kam-wah. *m* Violet Lam. *cast* Hui So-Ying, Peter Wang, Hui Pui, Yao Lin-Shun, Shu Kei, Charles Ng.

● Allen Fong invents Chinese docu-drama, taking Hui So-Ying out of her job on her parents' fish market stall and following her progress in acting classes; in the background, her family acts out its real-life domestic strains and crises. Fong based the character of Ah Ying's drama teacher Cheung on his late friend Koh Wu (Peter Wang's performance is a creditable impersonation), who spent years trying but failing to raise money for a film in Hong Kong. It adds up to a wry panorama of everyday dreams and aspirations, often – but not always – doomed to be dashed. TR

A.I. Artificial Intelligence

(2001, US, 146 min)
d Steven Spielberg. *p* Kathleen Kennedy, Steven Spielberg, Bonnie Curtis. *sc* Steven Spielberg. *ph* Janusz Kaminski. *ed* Michael Kahn. *pd* Rick Carter. *m* John Williams. *cast*

Haley Joel Osment, Frances O'Connor, Sam Robards, Jake Thomas, Jude Law, William Hurt, Ken Leung, Theo Greenly, Ashley Scott, Brendan Gleeson, Michael Shamus Wiles, Clara Bellar.

●David (Osment) is a Mecha-boy, a robot prototype who thinks and feels like a real boy. Monica and Henry (O'Connor and Robards), whose natural son is in a vegetative state, afford him a wary welcome, the mother's need overcoming her trepidation. Then, when their own son makes a miraculous recovery, sibling rivalry gets out of hand, and Monica abandons the surrogate in the woods to fend for himself. A schizophrenic animal, Kubrick and Spielberg's love child begins in cerebral sci-fi mode before switching abruptly into a heart-rending fairytale redolent of *ET*, *The Wizard of Oz* and especially *Pinocchio*. Spielberg adopted the project and, whatever Kubrick's input may have been, took sole screenplay credit for the first time since *Close Encounters*. The result is surprisingly clumsy and ill-integrated. Yet *A.I.* is ambitious, personal and revealing. A film about childhood as opposed to a film for kids, it has more than its share of beauty, wonders and mysteries. The SFX are miraculous; Osment and O'Connor scarcely less so. At heart it's a terribly anguished expression of rejection, loneliness and love. If only it knew when to stop. TCh

Aïd el Kébir

(1999, Fr/Tun, 35 min)
d Karin Albou. *p* Laurent Lavolé, Isabelle Pragier. *sc* Karin Albou. *ph* Michel Sourioux. *ed* Barbara Bascou. *pd* Claude Bennys. *cast* Soria Moufakkir, Smaïl Mekki, Hichem Mesbah, Fatiha Berber, Nina Tahar.

●Set in the east of trouble-torn Algeria (though filmed in Tunisia), this intelligent, moving and highly atmospheric mini-drama examines the crisis in the heart, mind and body of a woman, Hanifa (a noble and beautifully pitched performance by Mouffakir), when her brother-in-law comes to visit her father, the dying head of an orthodox family. She's pregnant, with 'a child of sin', her neighbours say. Is the brother-in-law the father? Will she submit to family plans to marry her off quickly? This prizewinning film spends most of its time in the family home and women's bath house picking up significant glances, conversations and details, which, added up, convey what it is to be an unmarried woman in modern Islamic Algeria. A film of elegant economy, which carries its progressive attitudes lightly. WH

Aigle à Deux Têtes, L' (The Eagle Has Two Heads/ Eagle With Two Heads)

(1948, Fr, 93 min, b/w)
d Jean Cocteau. *p* Georges Dancigers. *sc* Jean Cocteau. *ph* Christian Matras. *ed* Claude Vériat. *pd* Christian Bérard. *m* Georges Auric. *cast* Edwige Feuillère, Jean Marais, Sylvia Monfort, Jean Debucourt, Jacques Varennes, Yvonne de Bray, Gilles Quéant, Ahmed Abdallah.

●One of Cocteau's more conventional films, based on his own play, with Marais as a poet/anarchist out to assassinate a 19th-century queen. But when she lays eyes on the ragged poet, it is, alas, love at first sight. He is the spitting image of her deceased husband, the King. When the emerging world of the bourgeoisie closes in (in the form of a corrupt Republican official), the couple has no other escape but death. Very Romantic, very Cocteau, and surprisingly, after 40 years, still very moving.

Aile ou la Cuisse, L' (The Wing and the Thigh)

(1976, Fr, 105 min)
d Claude Zidi. *sc* Claude Zidi, Michel Fabre. *ph* Claude Renoir. *ed* Robert Isnardon, Monique Isnardon. *ad* Michel De Broin. *m* Vladimir Cosma. *cast* Louis de Funès, Coluche, Julien Guiomar, Ann Zacharias, Raymond Bussières, Vittorio Caprioli, Marcel Dalio.

●De Funès plays the cantankerous compiler of a food guide. He steams through the movie, showing up in disguise at unsuspecting restaurants, brow beating his son, a would-be circus clown, and scrapping with a junk food manufacturer. Zidi, aka Monsieur Box Office, dispenses a string of gastronomy gags from the world of the *Dandy* and *Beano*; while trolley loads of grub are swooningly shot by the great Claude Renoir. BBa

Ailsa

(1994, Ire, 78 min)
d Paddy Breathnach. *p* Ed Guiney. *sc* Joe O'Connor. *ph* Cian De Buitléar. *ed* Emer Reynolds. *pd* Ned McLoughlin. *m* Dario Marianelli. *cast* Brendan Coyle, Andrea Irvine, Juliette Gruber, Darragh Kelly, Blanaid Irvine, Des Spillane, Gary Lydon.

●Young married Dubliner Miles (Coyle) is a genealogist – he traces family trees. When a young American (Gruber) moves into a neighbouring flat, Miles becomes obsessed with her, even stealing her mail, though he hasn't the courage to introduce himself. Structured in flashbacks by award-winning novelist Joseph O'Connor, with tracts of voice-over narration, this mood piece feels uncomfortably like an illustrated novella. First-time director Breathnach does well enough, but he might be more sparing with the blue filter next time. TCh

Aimée & Jaguar

(1998, Ger, 126 min)
d Max Färberböck. *p* Günter Rohrbach, Hanno Huth. *sc* Max Färberböck, Rona Munro. *ph* Tony Imi. *ed* Barbara Hennings, Ann Sophie Schweizer. *pd* Albrecht Konrad. *m* Jan AP Kaczmarek. *cast* Maria Schrader, Juliane Köhler, Johanna Wokalek, Heike Makatsch, Elisabeth Degen, Detlev Buck.

●Berlin, 1943: As bombs fall, the last Jews are tracked down. Felice (Schrader) helps her newspaper boss with another anti-Semitic editorial. He's unaware that she's a Jew and a lesbian. Bravado might be the best protection, but Felice and a group of Jewish girlfriends live on their nerves. This partly explains why she is drawn to Lilly (Köhler), the wife of a Nazi officer. Calling each other by pet names, Aimée and Jaguar, they strive to keep the outside world at bay. The precarious existence of Felice and her pals provides background tension, but the film leaves niggling questions unanswered. There's an imbalance in the casting, too, since the bird-like Schrader carries far more charisma than Köhler's sturdy Aryan housewife. The idea of passion defying the Nazis gives the film (based on a true story) its muted emotional charge, but, all in all, it isn't sharp enough to allow us to relive a fascinating, dangerous relationship through the lovers' eyes. TJ

Ai No Corrida (L'Empire des Sens/The Realm of the Senses/In the Realm of the Senses)

(1976, Fr/Jap, 108 min)
d Nagisa Oshima. *p* Anatole Dauman. *sc* Nagisa Oshima. *ph* Hideo Ito. *ed* Keiichi Uraoka. *pd* Jusho Toda. *m* Minoru Miki. *cast* Tatsuya Fuji, Eiko Matsuda, Aoi Nakajima, Meika Seri, Taiji Tonoyama, Hiroko Fuji.

●Oshima's erotic masterpiece, which attracted some unsavoury attention for its hardcore elements, should be seen in the context of his other films. The central couple are archetypal Oshima outsiders, turning their backs on the militarist realities of 1936 and plunging into an erotic world of their own, created and sustained by their own fantasies of hyper-virility and hyper-arousal. The film celebrates their passion, steadfastly confronting even its most alarming implications. But it's also the most involving (and hence disturbing) film about voyeurism since *Rear Window*. As ever, Oshima broaches taboos not in a spirit of adolescent daring, but in the knowledge that the most deep-rooted taboos are personal, not social. TR

Ain't Misbehavin'

(1974, GB, 85 min, b/w)
d Peter Neal, Anthony Stern. *p* David Speechley. *ed* Peter Neal.

●Intriguing collage of cinematic ephemera from the early part of this century: newsreels, blue films, fashion shorts, *What the Butler Saw* material, and glimpses of Fats Waller, George Formby, Nat King Cole, Sophie Tucker and other performers. Some of the material is fascinating, and put together in such a way that it brings home how little there is to distinguish between respectable Hollywood and its underbelly. When the film goes out for laughs, on the other hand, the results are dire in the extreme. In its way the movie porn of the '30s and '40s is as much a revelation as reading about Victorian England via the author of *My Secret Life*. It doesn't need amplification. DP

Air America

(1990, US, 118 min)
d Roger Spottiswoode. *p* Daniel Melnick. *sc* Richard Rush, John Eskow. *ph* Roger Deakins. *ed* John Bloom, Lois Freeman-Fox. *pd* Allan Cameron. *m* Charles Gross. *cast* Mel Gibson, Robert Downey Jr, Nancy Travis, Ken Jenkins, David Marshall Grant, Lane Smith, Art La Fleur, Burt Kwouk, Tim Thomerson.

●Gooood morning, Vietnam – again? Actually, the fly boys in Spottiswoode's megabudget action comedy are just over the border in Laos, but the song remains the same: innocent and not-so-innocent Americans caught up in a war they don't understand. Crazy pilot Gibson is employed by the CIA to transport humanitarian aid and heroin, the latter intended to finance the local anti-Communist warlord's private army. Despite the black comic tone, it is impossible to identify with Gibson's cynical, selfish loner whose lucrative sideline is gun-running. That leaves the uncharismatic, ineffectual Downey holding the conscience ticket – as the wide-eyed new boy whose efforts to expose such nefarious activities cause the faeces to hit the propeller – and a huge hole in the middle of the picture. Somewhere amid the *M*A*S*H*-style lunacy, magnificent flying sequences and expertly choreographed stunts, a serious political movie is struggling to make itself heard. Mostly, however, this contentious counterpoint is reduced to background noise, drowned out by maniacal laughter, deafening explosions and a slew of late-'60s pop songs. NF

Air Bud

(1997, US/Luxembourg/Can, 98 min)
d Charles Martin Smith. *p* Robert Vince, William Vince. *sc* Paul Tamasy, Aaron Mendelsohn. *ph* Mike Southon. *ed* Alison Grace. *pd* Elizabeth Wilcox. *m* Brahm Wenger. *cast* Kevin Zegers, Michael Jeter, Wendy Makkena, Eric Christmas, Bill Cobbs.

●Young Josh (Zegers) is lonely and sullen in his new home, following the death of his father, a test pilot, in a crash. He discovers an abandoned court on the way back from school, spruces it up and starts shooting hoops. Something in the undergrowth returns his ball; Josh tempts out an abandoned and bedraggled dog, Buddy, with potted blancmange, and soon discovers his prodigious ball skills. Hereafter, the plot revolves around whether Josh's mum (Makkena) will let him keep the dog. Ramshackle slapstick, upbeat life lessons and lashings of sentimentality. NB

Air de Famille, Un (Family Resemblances)

(1996, Fr, 110 min)
d Cédric Klapisch. *p* Charles Gassot. *sc* Agnès Jaoui, Jean-Pierre Bacri, Cédric Klapisch. *ph* Benoît Delhomme. *ed* Francine Sandberg. *pd* François Emmanuelli. *m* Philippe Eidel. *cast* Jean-Pierre Bacri, Jean-Pierre Darroussin, Catherine Frot, Agnès Jaoui, Claire Maurier, Wladimir Yordanoff, Sophie Simon, Cédric Klapisch.

●In a French provincial town, Henri Menard (Bacri) runs the old family restaurant where the clan convenes every Friday night. This Friday, everyone's ego is in for a bruising. A subtle, breezy comedy of manners, Klapisch's follow-up to *When the Cat's Away*... may not have quite the novelty and charm of that work, but otherwise it's a fresh and unassuming treat. Based on Bacri and Jaoui's award-winning play, the film avoids staginess, less through studied adjustment, than by naturalistic observation, delicately turned characterisation and confident performances. Pity, however, about the 'silent' dreamy flashbacks. NB

Air Force

(1943, US, 124 min, b/w)
d Howard Hawks. *p* Hal B Wallis. *sc* Dudley Nichols. *ph* James Wong Howe. *ed* George Amy. *ad* John Hughes. *m* Franz Waxman. *cast* John Garfield, John Ridgely, George Tobias, Harry Carey, Edward S Brophy, Arthur Kennedy, Gig Young, Charles Drake.

●Hawks's 'contribution to the war effort', for all its then topical anti-Japanese propaganda, now comes across as a typical Hawksian examination of the isolated, all-male group, here the crew of an American B-17 Bomber operating in the Pacific shortly after Pearl Harbor. As so often, the predominant themes are self-respect, loyalty, professionalism, and the problems of integration facing the newcomer/outsider, in this case cynical rear-gunner Garfield. Rather like a bleak version of the director's earlier *Only Angels Have Wings*, it's an unusually moving example of the 'why-we-fight' genre, with genuinely horrific scenes of widespread destruction alternating with more intimate, introspective scenes depicting the tensions between the various vividly characterised members of the crew. GA

Air Force One

(1997, US, 124 min)
d Wolfgang Petersen. *p* Wolfgang Petersen, Gail Katz, Armyan Bernstein, Jonathan Shestack. *sc* Andrew Marlowe. *ph* Michael Ballhaus. *ed* Richard Francis-Bruce. *pd* William Sandell. *m* Jerry Goldsmith. *cast* Harrison Ford, Gary Oldman, Glenn Close, Wendy Crewson, Paul Guilfoyle, William H Macy, Dean Stockwell, Jürgen Prochnow.

●Kazakhstani terrorists hijack Air Force One, the presidential 747, and the leader of the Free World puts his life on the line to rescue family and staff, then wrests control of the plane from maniac beardie Oldman. The early suspense stuff inside the plane is competently done. Ford (in Jack Ryan mode) hides in the bowels of the jet and draws on his own resources to work out the next move. Meanwhile, back at the White House, Vice-President Close runs the joint as political vultures jostle for position. Imagine *Die Hard in a Jumbo* plus action highlights from *Airport 1975*. TJ

Airheads

(1994, US, 91 min)
d Michael Lehmann. *p* Robert Simonds, Mark Burg. *sc* Richard Wilks. *ph* John Schwartzman. *ed* Stephen Semel. *m* Carter Burwell. *cast* Brendan Fraser, Steve Buscemi, Adam Sandler, Chris Farley, Joe Mantegna, Michael McKean, Michael Richards.

●Rightly despairing of ever landing a record deal, Los Angeles rockers The Lone Rangers infiltrate their favourite radio station with a demo tape and water pistols. Matters get out of control, and before they know it, Chazz (Fraser), Rex (Buscemi) and Pip (Sandler) are holding the entire station hostage, live on KPPX. The exposition is such a drag, it seems impossible that the movie won't improve once the hostage situation develops. But despite the presence of such worthies as Mantegna as a disillusioned DJ and McKean as the unctuous station manager, it never does. About airheads, and for them too. TCh

Airplane!

(1980, US, 87 min)
d Jim Abrahams, David Zucker, Jerry Zucker. *p* Jon Davison. *sc* Jim Abrahams, David Zucker, Jerry Zucker. *ph* Joseph Biroc. *ed* Patrick Kennedy. *pd* Ward Preston. *m* Elmer Bernstein. *cast* Robert Hays, Julie Hagerty, Peter Graves, Robert Stack, Lloyd Bridges, Leslie Nielsen, Kareem Abdul-Jabaar.

●Zapping every disaster movie cliché with the cartoon subtlety of *Mad* magazine may only be cannibal glee, but it prompts enough convulsions of laughter in this wacky spoof from the *Kentucky Fried Movie* team for you not to notice their dead hand at work. Imagine the same old '50s airplane yarn: pilots poisoned, passengers panic, while a traumatised war-hero lands the jalopy. It should be disastrous. But psycho ground controllers (Stack and Bridges), laff-a-second pace, and bludgeoning innuendo make this the acceptable face of the locker-room satire. DMacp

Airplane II The Sequel

(1982, US, 84 min)
d Ken Finkleman. *p* Howard W Koch. *sc* Ken Finkleman. *ph* Joseph Biroc. *ed* Dennis Virkler. *pd* William Sandell. *m* Elmer Bernstein. *cast* Robert Hays, Julie Hagerty, Lloyd Bridges, Peter Graves, Raymond Burr, Chuck Connors, Rip Torn, William Shatner, Sonny Bono, Art Fleming.

●Granted the producers wanted to repeat their success, but taking the same stars and copying the same jokes merely makes for a thin rehash. The doomed aircraft is now a moon-bound space shuttle departing on its maiden voyage from a commercial terminal with the usual bunch of loonies and loopies on board. Although Graves' paedophiliac pilot hasn't been sacrificed, nearly all the other dodgy bits have been replaced – to little avail – by a sprinkling of self-parodic guest stars such as Burr, Connors and Shatner. FL

Airport

(1969, US, 136 min)
d George Seaton. *p* Ross Hunter. *sc* George Seaton. *ph* Ernest Laszlo. *ed* Stuart Gilmore. *ad* Alexander Golitzen, Preston Ames. *m* Alfred Newman. *cast* Burt Lancaster, Dean Martin, Jean Seberg, Jacqueline Bisset, George Kennedy, Helen Hayes, Van Heflin, Maureen Stapleton, Dana Wynter.

●The first in the ghastly series spawned by Arthur Hailey's bestseller, this is the one about the mad bomber on the Rome flight, plus the statutory collection of cardboard characters with pop-up problems. Lancaster is the harassed airport manager trying to cope, in addition to the aforesaid auto-destruct passenger, with snowbound flying conditions, a wife talking divorce, an affair with another employee (Seberg), and a brother-in-law (Martin) who is not only piloting the threatened aircraft but has contrived to impregnate the stewardess (Bisset). With clichés fairly running riot, the efficient cast, at least, is a mercy. TM

Airport 1975

(1974, US, 107 min)
d Jack Smight. *p* William Frye. *sc* Don Ingalls. *ph* Philip H Lathrop. *ed* J Terry Williams. *pd* George Webb. *m* John Cacavas. *cast* Charlton Heston, Karen Black, George Kennedy, Efrem Zimbalist Jr, Susan Clark, Gloria Swanson, Linda Blair, Dana Andrews, Sid Caesar, Myrna Loy, Nancy Olson, Martha Scott, Ed Nelson.

●A ridiculous sequel, bad enough to be enjoyable, what with its jumbo jet crammed full of Hollywood celebs – Gloria Swanson, Myrna Loy, Sid Caesar, even Linda Blair (as a teenager being rushed to a kidney transplant) who looks like she is going to vomit over two nuns. Suddenly there is a mid-air collision, and the jumbo has grown a private two-seater aircraft like a facial wart. With the pilot blinded and the co-pilot killed, only stewardess Karen Black is left in the cockpit, until her lover Chuck Heston plays Tarzan by being lowered from a helicopter to save the day. Just routine procedure for any old airline nowadays. ATu

Airport '77

(1977, US, 114 min)
d Jerry Jameson. *p* William Frye. *sc* Michael Scheff, David Spector. *ph* Philip H Lathrop. *ed* J Terry Williams. *pd* George Webb. *m* John Cacavas. *cast* Jack Lemmon, Lee Grant, Brenda Vaccaro, Joseph Cotten, James Stewart, Olivia de Havilland, Darren McGavin, Christopher Lee.

●Disaster movie in which a converted luxury airliner laden with guests and art treasures is hijacked by terrorists and crashes into the sea near an oil-rig. The survivors then spend their time trying to overact their way out of the claustrophobic script, which threatens a death even more slow and painful than suffocation or drowning. NF

Airport '80 The Concorde (aka The Concorde – Airport '79)

(1979, US, 113 min)
d David Lowell Rich. *p* Jennings Lang. *sc* Eric Roth. *ph* Philip H Lathrop. *ed* Dorothy Spencer. *pd* Henry Bumstead. *m* Lalo Schifrin. *cast* Alain Delon, Susan Blakely, Robert Wagner, Sylvia Kristel, George Kennedy, Eddie Albert, Bibi Andersson, Martha Raye, Cicely Tyson.

●A deafening sonic yawn signs off this desperate finale to Universal's Arthur Hailey-inspired quartet of in-flight entertainments. A goodwill Washington-to-Moscow Concorde flight to celebrate the 1980 Olympics takes on its own heavy layer of irony, while the hazards of evasive action and depressurisation parallel the general drop in hysteria value, with even the passengers less problem-stricken than usual. An arms dealer taking disproportionate steps to cover his tracks is the cause of all cartoonish fuss. PT

Air Up There, The

(1994, US, 108 min)
d Paul M Glaser. *p* Robert W Cort, Rosalie Swedlin, Ted Field. *sc* Max Apple. *ph* Dick Pope. *ed* Michael Polakow. *m* David Newman. *cast* Kevin Bacon, Charles Maina, Yolanda Vazquez, Winston Ntshona, Mabutho 'Kid' Sithole, Sean McCann, Dennis Patrick.

●An American basketball coach talent-scouting among Kenyan tribesmen – you'd expect standard fish-out-of-water culture-clash stuff, in which the natives teach the coach as much as he teaches them, leading to a rousing we-play-as-brothers climax. Sure enough, that's exactly what you get. Give or take the odd spot of predictable arrogance, however, it's a good-humoured, good-hearted film. Bacon is the quintessential smirking and swaggering thirty-something at whom the elders initially poke fun, but to whom they eventually owe a debt of gratitude. Only in Hollywood could a single game of basketball solve a violent territorial dispute. AO

A.K.

(1985, Fr/Jap, 75 min)
d Chris Marker. *p* Serge Silberman. *sc* Chris Marker. *ph* Frans-Yves Marescot. *ed* Chris Marker. *m* Toru Takemitsu.

●A documentary shot on the black volcanic ash at the foot of Mount Fuji, where Akira Kurosawa was filming *Ran*. While Marker makes it clear why Kurosawa has earned the title 'Sensei' (master), this is not a vapid piece of hero worship. He explores some of Kurosawa's obsessions, but it is the minutiae that really attract Marker's eye: a squad of extras adjusting the fastenings of their samurai armour can expand into large speculations on the nature of film-making. Indeed it is this ability to move from the small to the very large without slick metaphor that makes this more than an expert companion to a great film, and a work of art in its own right. CPea

Akenfield

(1974, GB, 98 min)
d Peter Hall. *p* Peter Hall, Rex Pyke. *ph* Ivan Strasburg. *ed* Rex Pyke. *pd* Ian Whittaker. *m* Neville Marriner. *cast* Garrow Shand, Peggy Cole, Barbara Tilney, Lyn Brooks, Ida Page, Stanley Baxter.

●A fitfully engaging oddity, adapted by Ronald Blythe from his own study of everyday life, past and present, in a Suffolk farming village. The use of non-professional actors is for the most part effective in a sub-Loachian kind of way, but the intercutting between the largely prosaic lives of Akenfield's contemporary inhabitants, and the harsher but seemingly more lyrical existence of their Edwardian forebears, makes for some fairly simplistic contrasts. That said, Ivan Strasberg's lush, soft-focus landscape photography – especially when accompanied by the lilting pastoral strains of Tippett's 'Fantasia Concertante on a Theme of Corelli' – imbues the past with a not unappealing romantic aura. GA

Akira

(1988, Jap, 124 min)
d Katsuhiro Otomo. *p* Ryohei Suzuki., Shunzo Kato. *sc* Katsuhiro Otomo, Izo Hashimoto, Katsuji Misawa. *cast* voices: Mitsuo Iwata, Nozomu Sasaki, Mami Koyama, Taro Ishida, Tetsusho Genda.

●In 2019, some 31 years after the destruction of Tokyo in WWIII, the rebuilt city is in chaos. Pill-popping biker gangs wage deadly warfare; terrorism and riots by the unemployed are common; martial law holds sway; and the masses, duped by the leaders of fanatical religious cults, await a second coming by the legendary Akira. But would this eponymous hero be sufficiently powerful to overcome Tetsuo, a young biker with telekinetic powers who threatens to lead the world towards apocalypse? Reworked from his own hugely successful comic strip, Otomo's first excursion into movies features some of the most mind-blowing animation ever seen. Even if the human characters are flatly two-dimensional, the metropolis itself is a wondrous jumble of highways, slums, skyscrapers and labyrinthine passages, while the drawings imitate (exaggerate?) the pyrotechnical zooms, dollies and close-ups of live action camerawork to exhilarating effect. Artwork apart, the admirably complex plot is imaginative *and* serious. An impressive achievement, often suggesting a weird expressionist blend of *2001*, *The Warriors*, *Blade Runner* and *Forbidden Planet*. GA

Akira Kurosawa's Dreams (aka Dreams)

(1990, US, 119 min)
d Akira Kurosawa. *p* Hisao Kurosawa, Mike Y Inoue. *sc* Akira Kurosawa. *ph* Takao Saito, Masaharu Ueda. *m* Shinichiro Ikebe. *cast*

Chishu Ryu, Mieko Harada, Mitsuko Baisho, Chosuke Ikariya, Akira Terao, Martin Scorsese, Mitsunori Isaki, Toshihiko Nakano.
●Depicting, rather indulgently, a number of dreams vaguely intended to reflect Kurosawa's life and abiding obsessions, this is – to be frank – regrettably embarrassing. Its eight episodes, moving from childhood through war to a terror of nuclear pollution, are wholly devoid of narrative drive. Kurosawa's penchant for metaphor leads to risibly misguided and inadequate clichés: life's vicissitudes seen as a long mountain trek through a blizzard, the guilty aftermath of war as dark at the end of a tunnel, scientific fervour as a lemmings' leap into the abyss. Not a little reactionary, the film's main achievement is to show a once impressive director quite out of touch both with the world and with developments in cinema. Much of it is like a moron's guide to the Green manifesto, transforming serious issues into banal trivia, while George Lucas' Industrial Light and Magic supply surprisingly shoddy visual effects. Only during a final procession does the old Kurosawa magic get a brief look-in, but by then the hackneyed moralising and dramatic languor have ensured that, despite the well-meaning message, it's hard to care. GA

Akseli and Elina

see Täällä Pohjantähden alla

Akumulator 1

see Accumulator 1

Aladdin

(1992, US, 90 min)
d John Musker, Ron Clements. *p* Donald W Ernst. *sc* John Musker, Ron Clements, Ted Elliott, Terry Rossio. *pd* Bill Perkins. *m* Alan Menken. *cast* voices: Scott Weinger, Robin Williams, Linda Larkin, Jonathan Freeman, Frank Welker, Gilbert Gottfried.
●The most successful animated feature ever, and it's easy to see why. Visually, it's a treat, a perfect marriage of hi-tech graphics and the traditional Disney virtue of strong characterisation and colour. The script crackles with wit and life. Williams' Genie is matched by Freeman's malevolent Jafar, and by Gottfried as Jafar's wise-cracking parrot Iago. The only disappointments are the wet Aladdin and his sweetheart Jasmine and five rather ordinary original songs. NKe

Alambrista! (aka Wire Jumper/The Illegal)

(1978, US, 110 min)
d Robert M Young. *p* Michael Hausman, Irwin Young. *sc/ph* Robert M Young. *ed* Edward Beyer. *pd* Lilly Kilvert. *m* Michael Martin. *cast* Domingo Ambriz, Trinidad Silva, Linda Gillin, Ned Beatty, Paul Berrones, George Smith.
●Young's first feature. Functioning here as writer, director and cameraman, he spent over a year living among Mexican wet-backs in the US Southwest to discover what it actually feels like working illegally, and in voluntary exile, for a society barely conscious of your existence, far less your rights. His discoveries, though nothing new, remain disturbing: workers housed and transported in sub-animal conditions, slowly bled of their dignity and culture. Yet for all his righteous indignation, *Alambrista!* fails to ignite. The fictional characters through whom he dramatises his observations appear too stereotyped, caught in as many clichés as the film is trying to fight. JD.

Alamo, The

(1960, US, 192 min)
d/p John Wayne. *sc* James Edward Grant. *ph* William H Clothier. *ed* Stuart Gilmore. *pd* Alfred Ybarra. *m* Dimitri Tiomkin. *cast* John Wayne, Richard Widmark, Laurence Harvey, Richard Boone, Frankie Avalon, Linda Cristal, Patrick Wayne.
●An elephantine, historically inaccurate, stridently patriotic tribute to the handful of Texans who faced assault by 7,000 Mexican baddies. Not helped any by Avalon's vocal efforts, but occasional good patches are probably accountable to uncredited help from John Ford, while 2nd unit director Cliff Lyons certainly contributed the excellent climactic battle (which is a long, long time a-coming). TM

Alamo Bay (aka Port Alamo)

(1985, US, 99 min)
d Louis Malle. *p* Louis Malle, Vincent Malle. *sc* Alice Arlen. *ph* Curtis Clark. *ed* James Bruce. *pd* Trevor Williams. *m* Ry Cooder. *cast* Amy Madigan, Ed Harris, Ho Nguyen, Donald Moffat, Truyer V Tran, Rudy Young, Cynthia Carle.
●Malle is not normally noted for his toughness, but tackling racial prejudice head on results in one of his most compelling films. Dinh, a cheerful young Vietnamese, arrives in the Texan port to become an all-American fisherman. His reception varies from one sympathetic veteran ('good-looking women, dynamite drugs!') to the violent Shang (Harris), an embittered local with an ever-increasing family, a failing business, and a long-standing love affair with Glory (Madigan). While the conflict leads inexorably into the revival of the Ku Klux Klan, Glory's untameable obsession for Shang is cruelly tested by the surrounding tensions. Malle makes this splintering of interests a virtue by his casting of the wonderful Madigan, who adapts her forthright style (remember *Streets of Fire?*) to create one of the richest female characters in contemporary American cinema. She's teamed here with real-life husband Harris, and their scenes together really *seethe.* DT

A la Place du Coeur

(1998, Fr, 112 min)
d Robert Guédiguian. *p* Gilles Sandoz, Michel Saint-Jean, Robert Guédiguian. *sc* Jean-Louis Milesi, Robert Guédiguian. *ph* Bernard Cavalié. *ed* Bernard Sasia. *ad* Michel Vandestien. *cast* Ariane Ascaride, Christine Brücher, Jean-Pierre Darroussin, Gérard Meylan, Alexandre Ogou, Laure Raoust, Laure Raoust, Véronique Balme.
●Ever since childhood, Clim (Raoust) and Bébé (Ogou) have been in love. Indeed, such is their suitability that her parents (Ascaride and Darroussin) and his dad (Meylan) soon put aside any doubts about the couple's decision to marry so young. The only objection comes from the boy's strictly religious mother and sister, whose antipathy to the relationship intensifies when he's arrested and imprisoned for raping a woman. The others suspect he was framed by a racist cop – Bébé and his sister, who were adopted as kids, are black – and Clim determines to prove his innocence before she gives birth to their baby. But legal representation is expensive and money short. Guédiguian's gem of tender drama transposes a James Baldwin novel from New York to modern Marseilles. Specifically, the multicultural working class area of Estaque; where the director typically explores how friendship, familial support and a sense of communal purpose can alleviate and even overcome everyday social injustice. Once again, he draws warm, naturalistic performances from a cast largely made up of his wife and friends. GA

Alaska

(1996, US, 109 min)
d Fraser C Heston. *p* Carol Fuchs, Andrew Burg. *sc* Andrew Burg, Scott Myers. *ph* Tony Westman, (Baffin Island polar bears) Wolfgang Bayer. *ed* Rob Kobrin. *pd* Douglas Higgins. *m* Reg Powell. *cast* Thora Birch, Vincent Kartheiser, Dirk Benedict, Charlton Heston, Duncan Fraser, Gordon Tootoosis, Ben Cardinal, Ryan Kent, Don S Davis.
●Home comes no more remote than the Alaskan village of Quincy. Small wonder, then, that teenage Sean (Kartheiser) is disillusioned by the decision of his widower father (Benedict) to leave the city and a lucrative airline job in order to fly provisions to inaccessible outposts in a rickety light aircraft. However, Sean's younger sister Jessie (Birch) enjoys communing with nature, an attribute that stands the siblings in good stead when, following an argument, father flies off into the wilderness – and into a cliff. So begins an odyssey of survival as the pair traverse Alaska's most challenging terrain and, in the process, befriend a polar bear cub. Director Heston is clearly aware of what pleases the eye, and as a result throws in plenty of wide-angle shots of the breathtaking environment; the young leads, too, don't obtrude on the slimline plot. A taut little action pic. DA

A l'attaque!

(2000, Fr, 94 min)
d Robert Guédiguian. *p* Gilles Sandoz, Michel Saint-Jean, Robert Guédiguian. *sc* Jean-Louis Milesi, Robert Guédiguian. *ph* Bernard Cavalié. *ed* Bernard Sasia. *ad* Michel Vandestien. *m* Jacques Menichetti. *cast* Ariane Ascaride, Pierre Banderet, Frédérique Bonnal, Patrick Bonnel, Jacques Boudet, Jean-Pierre Darroussin, Alain Langlet.
●This sunny and anarchic protest comedy combines anything-goes whimsy with a steely political irreverence. It's about how ordinary working people can maintain their autonomy, dignity and spirit in the face of the modern world's arbitrary, overwhelming acts of Mammon – both in life and in cinema. Thus the film not only spins a yarn about an extended family of garage mechanics caught between an overdue bank loan and a runaway contractor's bad debt, it also regularly pulls back a creative level to poke fun at the story's altercating screenwriters (actors stand in for Guédiguian and his regular co-writer Milesi) – one intent on writing an uplifting realist fable true to the lives it represents, the other a sucker for the narrative temptations of blow-jobs and firearms. If the main drama fingers capitalist globalisation as a process of divide, deprive and rule, the film's explicit interrogation of art and entertainment values manifests the invigorating idiosyncrasy of homegrown folk and fare. NB

A la Verticale de l'été

see At the Height of Summer, The

Albero degli Zoccoli, L'

see Tree of Wooden Clogs, The

Albert, RN (aka Break to Freedom)

(1953, GB, 88 min, b/w)
d Lewis Gilbert. *p* Daniel M Angel. *sc* Vernon Harris, Guy Morgan. *ph* Jack Asher. *ed* Charles Hasse. *pd* Bernard Robinson. *m* Phillip Martell. *cast* Anthony Steel, Jack Warner, Robert Beatty, William Sylvester, Guy Middleton, Michael Balfour, Anton Diffring.
●Stolidly unimaginative World War II prison escape movie, with a dummy used as cover for head counts. The characters are dreadfully stereotypical, with the plot revolving unconvincingly around the fact that Steel, originator of the plan, is reluctant to make the break himself because he's fallen in love with a pen pal and is worried about actually meeting her. But at least the action sticks to the camp and avoids resorting to flashbacks. TM

Albino Alligator

(1996, US/Fr, 97 min)
d Kevin Spacey. *p* Brad Krevoy, Steve Stabler, Brad Jenkel. *sc* Christian Forte. *ph* Mark Plummer. *ed* Jay Cassidy. *pd* Nelson Coates. *m* Michael Brook. *cast* Matt Dillon, Faye Dunaway, Gary Sinise, William Fichtner, Viggo Mortensen, John Spencer, Skeet Ulrich.
●Three fugitive New Orleans crims make a former speakeasy their bolthole, slowly realising there's no back exit. Dillon takes charge, since a collision en route has injured brother Sinise – and the trigger finger of tight-coiled Fichtner could leap at any moment. Hostess Dunaway tries to calm nerves, enigmatic quaffer Mortensen may know more than he's letting on, and teenager Ulrich looks doomed as the boys get rolling on their negotiating tactics. A regulation stand-off, but Spacey (in his directorial debut) makes intelligent use of the single location, and the performers take care of the rest. Dillon exudes befuddled authority as he gets in deeper than he'd really like, while mama-fixated Fichtner adds the pepper, and Dunaway skilfully plays up the kidnapper/victim relationship. Regrettably, everything's a bit vacuum-packed. TJ

Al Capone

(1959, US, 103 min, b/w)
d Richard Wilson. *p* John H Burrows, Leonard J Ackerman. *sc* Malvin Wald, Henry Greenberg. *ph* Lucien Ballard. *ed* Walter Hannemann. *pd* Hilyard Brown. *m* David Raksin. *cast* Rod Steiger, Fay Spain, Murvyn Vye, James Gregory, Nehemiah Persoff, Martin Balsam, Robert Gist.
●One of the better gangster biopics, with a sure, painstaking sense of period and a general reluctance to whitewash its brutal hero, the film nevertheless stands or falls according to how you feel about Steiger. In what is undeniably his film, he gives a magnetic performance so full of detail

and mannerisms that one could accuse it of arrogance, were it not so entirely appropriate for the character of Capone. Also to be recommended are Lucien Ballard's superb monochrome camerawork and Wilson's unhurried, unsentimental direction.

Alchemist, The

(1981, US, 84 min)
d Charles Band. *p* Lawrence Appelbaum. *sc* Alan J Adler. *ph* Andrew W Friend. *ed* Ted Nicolaou. *pd* Dale A Pelton. *m* Richard Band. *cast* Robert Ginty, Lucinda Dooling, John Sanderford, Viola Kate Stimpson, Robert Glaudini.

● One of a host of movies sold on the back of the ultra-gross(ing) *The Exterminator.* The connection here is Ginty, a potato-head mumbler with a passing resemblance to Lon Chaney Jr. So too, its familiar plot owes much to the werewolf genre. Ginty is the victim of a century-old curse that keeps him young but means he goes on the blood-trail nightly (sans make-up: costly stuff, hair). Its other debt (Chaney again) is to Mummy movies, with a reincarnated lover drawn into the plot in a battered but still handsome red-and-white Plymouth that's a ringer for Stephen King's Christine. The auto and some amusingly inept demons – whack 'em with a re iron, they're out for the count – must be considered the highspots in this spectacularly low-energy multi-pastiche. GD

Alchemy

(1995, US, 96 min)
d Suzanne Myers. *p* Sarah Vogel, Kelley Forsyth. *sc* Suzanne Myers. *ph* Tami Reiker. *ed* Cecily Rhett. *pd* Teresa Mastropierro. *m* Georgia Hubley. *cast* Rya Kihlstedt, Jeff Webster, DV de Vincentis, Marian Quinn, Maggie Estep, Erica Chahoy, Jessica Stone.

● A distinguished and original indie debut that describes scenes from the life of an artist (Kihlstedt, excellent) who makes small boxes filled with meticulously arranged found objects, and also transcribes Russian fairy tales. Organised in three loose sections – titled charity, faith and hope – it's a delicate, meditative, 'mood' piece, which takes its heroine on a painful journey from loss to restoration of 'her pure heart'. Consciously feminist in tone, the film is filled with scenes of highly composed, occasionally magical, always sensitive, and often humorous appeal. Shot with Terence Davies-like attention to detail in brown or blue duotones by Tami Reiker. WH

Alcohol Years, The

(2000, GB, 50 min)
d Carol Morley. *p* Cairo Cannon. *ph* Peter Barthurst. *ed* Maggie Choyce. *ad* Annie Daniels. *m* Russell Churney. *with* Alan Wise, Howard Jones, Tony Wilson, Pete Shelley, Dave Haslam.

● Imagine if Proust had sat down, pen in hand, and found he really had lost the past, blotted out in a haze of booze, drugs and embarrassment. If he'd had Carol Morley's chutzpah, he'd have advertised in the local press for anyone with a clearer remembrance and interviewed them on camera. In Carol's case, this is a really brave move, as her interviewees remind her that between 1982 and 1987 she was the most promiscuous party animal Manchester has ever known, a universal groupie who slept with anything that moved. It may be adulterated narcissism, but Morley stays offscreen, and most of her interviewees are less than complimentary. Cleverly melding home movie footage from the '80s with new material, the result is funny, revealing, and (something Morley has never been accused of before) a bit of a tease. TCh

Al Corazón

see To the Heart

Al di là delle nuvole

see Beyond the Clouds

Aleksandr Nevski

see Alexander Nevsky

Alexander Nevsky

(1938, USSR, 112 min, b/w)
d Sergei M Eisenstein. *sc* Sergei M Eisenstein, Piotr A Pavlenko. *ph* Eduard Tissé. *ed* Sergei M Eisenstein. *m* Sergei Prokofiev. *cast* Nikolai Cherkasov, Nikolai Okhlopkov, Alexandr Abrikosov, Dmitri Orlov, Vera Ivacheva, Anna Danilova.

● Eisenstein's first project to reach completion in nearly ten years, *Alexander Nevsky* is widely regarded as an artistic and political disaster, despite its wide international popularity. Conceived as a kind of nationalist epic (and approved as such by Stalin), it resurrects the 13th-century hero Nevsky as an almost mythic guardian of the Russian heritage, and celebrates his victories against the Teutonic invaders; it was read as an anti-Nazi film during the war. It's easy to see why the mixture of religiosity, caricature and bold aestheticism has pleased many of the people some of the time. It's main interest now is that it cleared the way for the infinitely richer and more complex achievement of *Ivan the Terrible.* TR

Alexander the Great

(1955, US, 141 min)
d/p/sc Robert Rossen. *ph* Robert Krasker. *ed* Ralph Kemplen. *pd* Andre Andrejew. *m* Mario Nascimbene. *cast* Richard Burton, Fredric March, Claire Bloom, Danielle Darrieux, Barry Jones, Stanley Baker, Harry Andrews, Peter Cushing.

● A sprawling, misbegotten epic that undercuts its serious intent by constantly declaiming it, and fails to strike a balance between spectacle and speechifying. Burton's Alexander, with his hatred and fear of father figures, comes in for some heavy-handed cod-Freud analysis as he sweeps across Europe and Asia in search of glory. PT

Alexander the Great (O Megalexandros)

(1980, Greece/It, 230 min)
d/sc Theo Angelopoulos. *ph* Ghiorgos Arvanitis. *ad* Mikis Karapiperis. *m* Christodoulos Halaris. *cast* Omero Antonutti, Eva Kotamanidou, Grigoris Evangelatos, Michalis Yannatos, Laura de Marchi.

● A tale of socialism first deformed and then destroyed by an authoritarian leader, set in Greece a few years after the Paris Commune. Its Alexander is a bandit who became a popular folk hero. Following his escape from prison, he kidnaps some English aristocrats and demands as ransom that the rich local landowners hand over their property to the peasants. When a commune is set up, socialist ideals are betrayed by internal struggles as Italian anarchists, agrarian communists and radical extremists jostle for supremacy. A relentless demonstration of stylistic brilliance, it leaves one wondering why the parable is not more challenging and its point less predictable. SH

Alexandre (Alexandre le Bienheureux)

(1967, Fr, 96 min)
d Yves Robert. *p* Danièle Delorme, Yves Robert. *sc* Yves Robert, Pierre Lévy-Corti. *ph* René Mathelin. *ed* Andrée Werlin. Jacques d'Ovidio. *m* Vladimir Cosma. *cast* Philippe Noiret, Françoise Brion, Marlène Jobert, Paul le Person, Jean Carmet, Tsilla Chelton.

● Very strange movie about a farmer who goes to bed for a couple of months after his nagging wife's death; and how the villagers, who feel that he isn't living up to his status as a landowner, try to wake him up and end up falling asleep themselves; and how he almost meets his match, someone equally slothful. In fact the film makes an interesting companion piece to Nelly Kaplan's *La Fiancée du Pirate*, except that her heroine here becomes the deceitful chief baddy: the male dropout's only way of survival is to avoid alluring ladies who entice him into conformity. Pretty strongly anti-women. Has some antics with a trained dog.

Alexandria Encore (Iskandereya kaman we kaman)

(1990, Egypt/Fr, 108 min)
d Youssef Chahine. *p* Hubert Balsan. *sc* Youssef Chahine. *ph* Ramses Marzouk. *ed* Rashida Abdel-Salam. *ad* Onsy Abu Seif. *m* Mohamed Nour. *cast* Yousra, Youssef Chahine, Hussein Fahmy, Amr Abdel-Guelil, Hisham Selim, Tahia Carioca, Hoda Sultan, Ragaa Hussein.

● The third in a loose trilogy by Egypt's most widely respected director that began with *Alexandria Why?* in 1979. This takes as its starting point an argument between a film-maker (played by Chahine himself) and his favourite actor, an argument that precipitates an *8½*-style creative crisis and inspires the director to re-evaluate his work and his world. It's an exhilaratingly imaginative and sophisticated movie, embracing a number of themes and styles (including some marvellous musical sequences), beautifully shot and performed. TCh

Alex & the Gypsy

(1976, US, 99 min)
d John Korty. *p* Richard Shepherd. *sc* Lawrence B Marcus. *ph* Bill Butler. *ed* Donn Cambern. *pd* Bill Malley. *m* Henry Mancini. *cast* Jack Lemmon, Genevieve Bujold, James Woods, Gino Ardito, Robert Emhardt, Titos Vandis.

● Lemmon blusters for all he's worth, but to no effect, in this tale of a disenchanted California bail-bondsman called upon to post an immense surety for his former mistress, a sultry wind-blown gypsy (Bujold), who finds herself in the slammer awaiting sentence for the attempted murder of her oafish husband. Although patently striving for something tougher, Korty's direction achieves little more than a succession of bravura romantic flourishes. Whatever statement was intended about a couple of losers given a last chance to opt out of the system (for some sort of hazy nomadic existence) is lost in the half-hearted jokiness. JPy

Alex in Wonderland

(1970, US, 110 min)
d Paul Mazursky. *p* Larry Tucker. *sc* Paul Mazurksy. *ph* Laszlo Kovacs. *ed* Stuart H Pappe. *ad* Pato Guzman. *m* Tom O'Hagan. *cast* Donald Sutherland, Ellen Burstyn, Meg Mazursky, Glenna Sergent, Viola Spolin, Federico Fellini, Jeanne Moreau, Paul Mazursky.

● Dr Mazursky's *1.5.* Having made a box-office killing with his directing debut *Bob & Carol & Ted & Alice*, Mazursky found he was Hollywood flavour of the month and, given virtual carte blanche, didn't know how to follow his success. His financially disastrous solution to the problem was to make a movie about his own predicament: Sutherland plays a self-obsessed director whose dreams of transcending the kind of Tinseltown escapism that made his first film a hit throw him into self-indulgent doubt. Should he make a movie about racism, revolution or pollution, or buy a better house? Mazursky's most deliberately 'arty' film lacks the ironic wit of his finest work, his awe of the freedom allowed the top European directors giving rise to a cameo for Fellini himself, who turns up to console Alex in his somewhat privileged quandary. But the performances are strong, Laszlo Kovacs's camerawork is impressively dreamlike, and it's an intriguing, if deeply flawed, study of the ambitions of a Hollywood hack who fancies himself an artist. GA

Alfie

(1966, GB, 114 min)
d/p Lewis Gilbert. *sc* Bill Naughton. *ph* Otto Heller. *ed* Thelma Connell. *pd* Peter Mullins. *m* Sonny Rollins. *cast* Michael Caine, Shelley Winters, Millicent Martin, Julia Foster, Jane Asher, Shirley Anne Field, Vivien Merchant.

● Given the full swinging London mod movie treatment of the day, Bill Naughton's funny and rather moving play emerges as a terribly dated (and one might add, terribly misogynist) account of a Cockney lecher's selfish seduction and abuse of a series of compliant females. Of course he gets his comeuppance, in an ending that has all the moral weight and sincerity of a DeMille sex'n'-sawdust spectacular. Good performances, though. GA

Alfie Darling

(1975, GB, 102 min)
d Ken Hughes. *p* Dugald Rankin. *sc* Ken Hughes. *ph* Ousama Rawi. *ed* John Trumper. *pd* Harry Pottle. *m* Alan Price. *cast* Alan Price, Jill Townsend, Paul Copley, Joan Collins, Sheila White, Annie Ross, Hannah Gordon, Rula Lenska.

● In what looks like developing into an EEC movie, Price shows those M'zelles what a British leg-over is all about. But back home, this belated sequel to *Alfie* switches to the Americanisation of the Cockney skirt-chaser (Pontiac, Marlboros, etc) in a desperate bid to prove that the Affluent Society is still available, even to the working class. As for the 'birds', it's a matter of showing what those middle class dollies really want. In its efforts to sell a lifestyle, the film comes really unstuck when Alfie falls in love with hard-to-get Townsend. No one, it seems, can deal with the emotions involved: the film looks increasingly like an advert with no product to sell. CPe

Alfredo Alfredo

(1971, It/Fr, 110 min)
d/p Pietro Germi. *sc* Leo Benvenuti, Piero De Bernardi, Tullio Pinelli, Pietro Germi. *ph* Aiace Parolin. *ed* Sergio Montanari. *pd* Carlo Egidi. *m* Carlo Rustichelli. *cast* Dustin Hoffman, Stefania Sandrelli, Carla Gravina, Clara Colosimo, Daniele Patella, Danika La Loggia.
●Snails are both faster and funnier than this limp little man vs big women sex comedy, which manages to waste not only Hoffman but also Sandrelli, a fine caricaturist of the Italian female (see *The Conformist*): their subtleties of characterisation are all but steamrollered by vile mid-Atlantic dubbing. The end result is exactly the kind of mediocrity Woody Allen parodied so beautifully in *Everything You Always Wanted to Know About Sex*. GD

Algiers

(1938, US, 96 min, b/w)
d John Cromwell. *sc* John Howard Lawson. *ph* James Wong Howe. *ed* Otho Lovering. *pd* Alexander Toluboff. *m* Vincent Scotto. *cast* Charles Boyer, Sigrid Gurie, Hedy Lamarr, Joseph Calleia, Gene Lockhart, Alan Hale.
●The Hollywood remake of the Jean Gabin classic, *Pépé le Moko*, and usually compared unfavourably. Certainly there is little tension or grit in this version of the story of the supercrook who pines for Paris and is lured from the safety of the Casbah for love of a beautiful woman. Instead, there is a fantastic opulence in the black-and-white photography (by James Wong Howe), and a totally aestheticised style of acting from Boyer and Lamarr in particular. Lamarr is extraordinarily sultry (especially with her indefinable accent), and the overall effect is as if producer Walter Wanger was trying to imitate Von Sternberg's work at Paramount with Dietrich. DT

Algiers/Beirut: A Souvenir

see Algiers/Beyrouth: pour mémoire

Algiers/Beyrouth: pour mémoire (Algiers/Beirut: A Souvenir)

(1997, Fr/Leb, 95 min, b/w)
d Merzak Allouache. *p* Fabienne Servan-Schreiber. *sc* Merzak Allouache. *ph* Laurent Machuel. *ed* Claude Fréchède-Taulade. *pd* Hamza Nasrallah. *m* René-Marc Bini. *cast* Fabienne Babe, Georges Corraface, Paul Matar, Hocine Choutri, Zeina Saab Demelero, Mona Tayeh, Shadi el Zein.
●Laurence (Babe), a French-Lebanese journalist revisiting Beirut to research her late father's history, finds a once ruined city in the slow throes of revival. She also encounters an old colleague, Rachid (Corraface), a fugitive from the continuing violence in Algiers, troubled by drink and bad memories. The drama, however, remains in the past, or otherwise offscreen. Briefly sketched, the terror racking the director's home country looms like a shadow over the characters, and the film, yet remains essentially an abstraction. Despite its evocative b/w photography and warm performances, dramatically the film seems a non-starter. NB

Ali

(2001, US, 159 min)
d Michael Mann. *p* Jon Peters, Paul Ardaji, A Kitman Ho, Michael Mann. *sc* Stephen J Rivele, Christopher Wilkinson, Eric Roth, Michael Mann. *ph* Emmanuel Lubezki. *ed* William Goldenberg, Stephen Rivkin, Lynzee Klingman. *pd* John Myhre. *m* Lisa Gerrard, Pieter Bourke. *cast* Will Smith, Jamie Foxx, Jon Voight, Mario Van Peebles, Ron Silver, Jeffrey Wright, Mykelti Williamson, Jada Pinkett Smith, Nona Gaye, Joe Morton, LeVar Burton, Albert Hall.
●Mann's typically ambitious film about the former heavyweight champ is both visceral and immensely intelligent. From the virtuoso opening to the climactic re-creation of Ali's 1974 Zaire bout with George Foreman, Mann achieves a thrilling mix of action and analysis, exploiting and transcending both boxing movie and biopic conventions with a master's ease. Crucially, the film is less a psychological study than a case history of America, from the passing of the Civil Rights Act to the end of the Vietnam War. While Smith's Ali is wholly credible as an individual determined to define and remain true to himself, despite a widespread expectation that African-Americans and sportsmen should quietly accept their lot, the character also becomes an index of racial, religious, political and social changes. Most memorably, of course, he alters his name, joins the Nation of Islam, and refuses to fight in Vietnam, risking confusion, contempt and professional catastrophe. Meticulous as ever, Mann gets all this right. Smith, buoyed by a brilliant cast, is funny, sexy, conceited, deceitful, proud, loud and troubled, and he rises superbly to the occasion in the expressive fight scenes. GA

Alias Bulldog Drummond

see Bulldog Jack

Alias Nick Beal (aka The Contact Man)

(1949, US, 93 min, b/w)
d John Farrow. *p* Endre Bohem. *sc* Jonathan Latimer. *ph* Lionel Lindon. *ed* Eda Warren. *ad* Hans Dreier, Franz Bachelin. *m* Franz Waxman. *cast* Ray Milland, Thomas Mitchell, Audrey Totter, George Macready, Fred Clark.
●An undeservedly neglected film which should rank high on the list of Farrow's best. Starting out as a political thriller, almost imperceptibly it turns into fantasy, a variation on the Faust legend with honest, conscientious politician Mitchell falling under the spell of old Nick Beal (Milland) and turning into a ruthless, power-hungry monster. Working with his regular writer Jonathan Latimer, Farrow has a model screenplay of precision and construction, and adds to it careful detail, allusion and suggestion. Best of all is his visual coup of never having Milland walk into a scene: the camera continually discovers him as it or a character moves, and suddenly *there* he is when seconds ago he was nowhere. Sadly, there's a sellout religioso ending, which lessens the overall power of the suggestion of some all-pervasive, satanic evil. CW

Alice (Neco Z Alenky)

(1988, Switz, 85 min)
d Jan Svankmajer. *p* Peter-Christian Fueter. *sc* Jan Svankmajer. *ph* Svatopluk Maly. *ed* Marie Zemanova. *pd* Jan Svankmajer. *cast* Kristina Kohoutova.
●Nobody who has seen even one of Svankmajer's shorts is likely to doubt that the Czech surrealist would make the definitive version of Lewis Carroll's *Alice's Adventures in Wonderland*. For no other film-maker – and that includes David Lynch – is so consistently inventive in his ability to marry pure, startling nonsense with rigorous logic, black wit with piercing psychological insights. Here, as always, Svankmajer's methods are hugely enjoyable in their perversity: Alice (the only human in a feature debut populated by a fantastic array of superbly animated puppets) not only changes size, but actually becomes her own doll; when the White Rabbit loses his stuffing, he simply secures his gaping chest with a safety-pin and eats the sawdust. Eggs crack to reveal skulls. Rolls sprout nails. Steaks crawl. A wonderland, indeed, imbued with a grotesque, cruel, and menacing dream-logic at once distinctively Svankmajer's and true to the spirit of Carroll. GA

Alice

(1990, US, 106 min)
d Woody Allen. *p* Robert Greenhut. *sc* Woody Allen. *ph* Carlo Di Palma. *ed* Susan E Morse. *pd* Santo Loquasto. *cast* Mia Farrow, William Hurt, Joe Mantegna, Alec Baldwin, Judy Davis, Blythe Danner, Cybill Shepherd.
●Allen's eponymous heroine (Farrow) – a devoted housewife burdened with existential angst and neuroses – is suddenly plunged into mid-life crisis when she falls for nice guy saxophonist Joe (Mantegna). Is he really a worthy rival to her successful but workaholic husband (Hurt)? How do her repressed rebellious impulses square with her Catholic roots and her family? And what of her Chinese acupuncturist -hypnotist's warning that it's her heart, not her back, that ails her, and his herbal prescription that renders her invisible so that she can spy on her lover, husband and friends? Allen's renewed semi-comic exploration of the upper-crust New York psyche displays many of his worst traits, and then some. It's hard to care much about the pallid Alice's anxieties, and the silly whimsy of the fantasy interludes sits uneasily within what remains, essentially, a naturalistic comic style. A scattering of fine one-liners , but one can't help wishing that Allen would investigate pastures new. GA

Alice Adams

(1935, US, 100 min, b/w)
d George Stevens. *p* Pandro S Berman. *sc* Dorothy Yost, Mortimer Offner. *ph* Robert De Grasse. *ed* Jane Loring. *ad* Van Nest Polglase. *m* Max Steiner. *cast* Katharine Hepburn, Fred MacMurray, Fred Stone, Evelyn Venable, Frank Albertson, Ann Shoemaker, Hedda Hopper.
●Hepburn is magnificent as the small-town social climber, although the script so softens Booth Tarkington's novel that she emerges throughout as a Persil-white heroine tarnished only by a little adolescent foolishness. With Tarkington's acidly observed social satire on Midwestern attitudes carefully ironed out by the Hollywood machine, little remains beyond a glowingly nostalgic slice of Americana. But Stevens fills the gap with some brilliant set pieces, including the exemplary scene-setting of the opening sequence, the society ball at which Hepburn is reduced to endless subterfuge to mask her gauche unease, and the ghastly dinner party at which all her social pretensions finally collapse under pressure from a heatwave. TM

Alice Doesn't Live Here Anymore

(1974, US, 112 min)
d Martin Scorsese. *p* David Susskind, Audrey Maas. *sc* Robert Getchell. *pd* Toby Carr Rafelson. *ph* Kent Wakeford. *ed* Maria Lucas. *cast* Ellen Burstyn, Kris Kristofferson, Billy 'Green' Bush, Diane Ladd, Alfred Lutter, Jodie Foster, Martin Scorsese, Harvey Keitel.
●Although the ending is a bit of a cop out from a feminist point of view, Scorsese's warm and witty blending of the road movie with the conventions of the women's weepie is a delight. Burstyn is excellent as the eponymous heroine who, following the death of a husband she barely loved, sets off for the Monterey of her childhood with hopes of reviving her abandoned singing career. Her encounters, and those of her precociously witty 12-year old son, are observed with great generosity and a raw realism, while Scorsese typically makes wonderful use of music to underline character and situation. Bitter-sweet and very charming. GA

Alice et Martin

(1998, Fr/Sp/US, 124 min)
d André Téchiné. *p* Alain Sarde. *sc* André Téchiné, Gilles Taurand, Olivier Assayas. *ph* Caroline Champetier. *ed* Martine Giordano. *pd* Ze Branco. *m* Philippe Sarde. *cast* Juliette Binoche, Alexis Loret, Mathieu Amalric, Carmen Maura, Jean-Pierre Lorit, Marthe Villalonga, Pierre Maguelon, Jeremy Kreikenmayer.
●With this unorthodox love story of Alice (Binoche) and Martin (Loret), André Téchiné has produced his most mature film to date. The story traces Martin's history backwards and forwards in time. His mother (Maura) had an affair with stern industrialist Victor (Maguelon), and at ten, their son (the impressive Kreikenmayer) joins his Cahors household with devastating results. Missing since his father's death, the son arrives years later at the Paris flat shared by his sympathetic homosexual stepbrother Benjamin, a struggling actor, and sensitive violinist Alice. He stays, taking work as a model, and Alice's distanced attitude changes subtly from intrigue to love. Téchiné's trademark interests – contrasting examinations of restrictive provincial life and young urban lives – are much to the fore. For all the increasing sophistication of Téchiné's

technique, the emotions he deals with are basic, and all the more powerful for it. Loret plays Martin with an almost feral quality: he stalks Alice, his immobile arms making him look like a Bresson anti-hero. Binoche trusts her director and it shows; and Marthe Villalonga, as the step-mother, is superb. WH

Alice in the Cities (Alice in den Städten)

(1974, WGer, 110 min, b/w)
d Wim Wenders. *p* Joachim von Mengershausen. *sc* Wim Wenders, Veit von Fürstenberg. *ph* Robby Müller, Martin Schäfer. *ed* Peter Przygodda. *m* Can. *cast* Rüdiger Vogeler, Yella Rottländer, Lisa Kreuzer, Edda Köchl, Didi Petrikat, Ernest Böhm.

● A photo-journalist travels across the United States on an abortive assignment, and finds himself returning to Germany (via Amsterdam) encumbered by an independent-minded nine-year-old girl. Wenders approaches his subject with telling obliqueness, taking it – and us – continually by surprise, allowing his themes to surface gracefully from the tale, documenting and questioning the seductive overlay of American culture. VG

Alice in Wonderland

(1933, US, 79 min, b/w)
d Norman Z McLeod. *sc* Joseph L Mankiewicz, William Cameron Menzies. *ph* Henry Sharp, Bert Glennon. *ed* Ellsworth Hoagland. *ad* Robert Odell. *m* Dimitri Tiomkin. *cast* Charlotte Henry, Gary Cooper, WC Fields, Cary Grant, Edward Everett Horton, Edna May Oliver, Charles Ruggles.

● Curiouser and curiouser and that's not the half of it. With Cary Grant as the Mock Turtle, Gary Cooper as the White Knight and WC Fields as Humpty Dumpty, great things might be expected, but something went disastrously wrong in the pot. Most of the blame must rest with McLeod, whose incredibly cackhanded direction piles on the whimsy by the bucket-load and can't come to grips with the absurdity at all. Carroll may not have envisaged Alice as being totally unsullied by the ways of the world, but as played by Charlotte Henry she's as pert a piece of jailbait as ever fell down a rabbit-hole. Even the backdrops look as if they'd been lifted from Donald McGill postcards. JP

Alice in Wonderland

(1951, US/Fr/GB, 83 min)
d Dallas Bower, Lou Bunin. *p* Lou Bunin. *sc* Henry Myers, Albert E Lewin, Edward Eliscu. *ph* Gerald Gibbs. *ed* Marity Cléris. *pd* Bernyce Polifka. *m* Sol Kaplan. *cast* Carol Marsh, Stephen Murray, Pamela Brown, Felix Aylmer, Ernest Milton, David Read.

● Bunin, puppetoonist extraordinaire, encountered many frustrations during his lengthy battle to bring his Carroll to the screen (the quaint live action prologue is directed by Bower). First he came up against Technicolor, who refused to handle the processing, thus forcing him to use inferior Ansco Color. Then he was drummed off the screen for daring to release his film in the same year as Disney's all-American version. And finally, Bunin discovered that he sailed too close to the satirical winds by identifying an imperious Queen Victoria (Brown) with the off-with-his-head Queen of Hearts, thus keeping the film out of Britain. Bunin employs a diverting combination of actors and puppets against a simple Klee-like background: purists will enjoy moaning at the songs while acknowledging that elsewhere he maintains the sharpness of the original. JE

Alice's Adventures in Wonderland

(1972, GB, 101 min)
d William Sterling. *p* Derek Horne. *sc* William Sterling. *ph* Geoffrey Unsworth. *ed* Peter Weatherley. *pd* Michael Stringer. *m* John Barry. *cast* Fiona Fullerton, Michael Crawford, Robert Helpmann, Michael Hordern, Spike Milligan, Flora Robson, Ralph Richardson, Peter Sellers, Dudley Moore, Flora Robson, Dennis Waterman.

● A confectionery version of Carroll, lumbered with an unmemorable 'Curiouser and Curiouser' and other ditties by John Barry. The bevy of stars doesn't help.

Alice's Restaurant

(1969, US, 111 min)
d Arthur Penn. *p* Hillard Elkins, Joseph Manduke. *sc* Venable Herndon, Arthur Penn. *ph* Michael Nebbia. *ed* Dede Allen. *pd* Warren Clymer. *m* Arlo Guthrie. *cast* Arlo Guthrie, Pat Quinn, James Broderick, Michael McClanathan, Geoff Outlaw, William Obanhein.

● Brilliantly visualised, Arlo Guthrie's very funny 20-minute talking blues – about how, fined $50 for being a litterbug, he was subsequently rejected for service in Vietnam as an unrehabilitated criminal – is retained as the centrepiece of a film which expands into a sort of chronicle of Arlo's hippy wanderings through rural America. The context is different, but the reference point powerfully echoed throughout is his father Woody Guthrie's experience as the troubadour of the dying Dustbowl during the American Depression of the '30s, with the ballad this time asking what went wrong with the dropout dream of the '60s. Criticised at the time for a certain opportunism, Penn's lyrical vision of the end of an era looks increasingly apt in the perspective of passing time. TM

Alien

(1979, GB/US, 117 min)
d Ridley Scott. *p* Gordon Carroll, David Giler, Walter Hill. *sc* Dan O'Bannon. *ph* Derek Vanlint. *ed* Terry Rawlings. *pd* Michael Seymour. *m* Jerry Goldsmith. *cast* Tom Skerritt, Sigourney Weaver, Veronica Cartwright, Harry Dean Stanton, John Hurt, Yaphet Kotto, Ian Holm.

● In the wake of the huge commercial success of *Alien*, almost all attention has perversely focused on the provenance of the script (was it a rip-off of *It, the Terror from Beyond Space*? Of Van Vogt's fiction? Was former John Carpenter collaborator Dan O'Bannon sold out by producers Walter Hill and David Giler's rewrites?). But the limited strengths of its staple sci-fi horrors – crew of commercial spacecraft menaced by stowaway monster – always derived from either the offhand organic/Freudian resonances of its design or the purely (brilliantly) manipulative editing and pacing of its above-average shock quota. Intimations of a big-budget *Dark Star* fade early, and notions of Weaver as a Hawksian woman rarely develop beyond her resourceful reaction to jeopardy. At least Scott has no time to dawdle over redundant futuristic effects in the fashion that scuttles his later *Blade Runner*. PT

Aliens 100 (100)

(1986, US, 137 min)
d James Cameron. *p* Gale Anne Hurd. *sc* James Cameron. *ph* Adrian Biddle. *ed* Ray Lovejoy. *pd* Peter Lamont. *m* James Horner. *cast* Sigourney Weaver, Carrie Henn, Michael Biehn, Paul Reiser, Lance Henriksen, Bill Paxton.

● Fifty-seven years on, Ripley is discovered – Sleeping Beauty in space. Plagued by nightmares and surrounded by sceptics, she's forced to return to the orginal alien's home planet with a bunch of seen-it-all-before Marines. Confidently directed by James Cameron (heretofore known only for *The Terminator* and *Piranha II*), this sequel dares to build slowly, allowing Weaver to develop a multi-dimensional character even as it ups the ante by fetishising the Marines' hi-tech hardware and spawning legions of aliens (the suspense involves guessing which group will be cannon fodder). There is always an interesting tension in Cameron's work between masculine and feminine qualities. When it finally hits the fan here, we're in for the mother of all battles. TCh

Alien^3

(1992, US, 115 min)
d David Fincher. *p* David Giler, Walter Hill, Gordon Carroll. *sc* William Gibson, John Fasano, David Giler, Walter Hill, Larry Ferguson. *ph* Alex Thomson. *ed* Terry Rawlings. *m* Jonathan Sheffer. *cast* Sigourney Weaver, Charles S Dutton, Charles Dance, Paul McGann, Brian Glover, Ralph Brown, Danny Webb.

● *Aliens*, a great action movie, cheapened the original by replacing one hyper-intelligent, indestructible monster with an army of gormless critters. This third entry has only one creature, but unfortunately it's just as gormless. When Ripley (Weaver) crash-lands on a prison planet full of hard-nut slap-heads, they haven't seen a woman in years. Discovering that there's an alien loose, Ripley asks the warden to break out the guns, and can't believe it when she is told there aren't any. Nor can we. Good acting has salvaged many a poor script in the past, but not here. Dance is slaughtered in the first act, as is the regulation bastard warden (Glover), leaving only Sigourney, impressive as ever, and a motley cast of extras. Though wasteful of the expensive sets, Fincher's tight close-ups do add to the sense of claustrophobic panic. DW

Alien Nation

(1988, US, 90 min)
d Graham Baker. *p* Gale Anne Hurd. Richard Kobritz. *sc* Rockne S O'Bannon. *ph* Adam Greenberg. *ed* Kent Beyda. *pd* Jack T Collis. *m* Curt Sobel. *cast* James Caan, Mandy Patinkin, Terence Stamp, Kevin Major Howard, Leslie Bevis, Peter Jason.

● Patinkin plays a member of an alien community which, having crash-landed in the Mojave Desert some years earlier, has now established itself in California. The aliens are called 'newcomers' by those who like them, 'slags' by those who don't. Hard-nosed cop Caan is one who does not, since his partner got blown away by a newcomer robbery gang; he nevertheless volunteers to take on the inexperienced Patinkin as his partner, figuring to use the alien's inside knowledge to find the killer. Their investigations lead to ruthless businessman Stamp, another newcomer who seems to be the brains behind a drugs operation. Played hard and fast, the film might just have worked, but the decision to soft-pedal the violence merely emphasises the obviousness of the liberal point-scoring (parallels with Vietnamese or Nicaraguan refugees are so facile as to be crass). Worthy, predictable, and dull. NF

Alien Resurrection

(1997, US, 108 min)
d Jean-Pierre Jeunet. *p* Bill Badalato, Gordon Carroll, David Giler, Walter Hill. *sc* Joss Whedon. *ph* Darius Khondji. *ed* Hervé Schneid. *pd* Nigel Phelps. *m* John Frizzell. *cast* Sigourney Weaver, Winona Ryder, Dominique Pinon, Ron Perlman, Michael Wincott, Kim Flowers, Dan Hedaya, Gary Dourdan.

● Two hundred years after her suicide, Ellen Ripley's cloned by scientists intent on nurturing the alien foetus inside her. The new Ripley couldn't care less – she's dead already – but goes along for the ride when Call (Ryder) and a band of marooned space pirates fight the inevitable rear-guard action. In outline, the resilient *Alien* movies may be little more than slasher movies in space, yet equipped with strong, imaginative directors, each has proved distinctive and surprisingly resonant. Jeunet, the series' supreme fantasist, plunges deep into the nightmarish genetic whirlpool concocted by screenwriter Joss Whedon. After an ominous, memorably ghoulish opening, however, the Frenchman can't disguise a lack of engagement with the action sequences. The laziest stuff is all linear, mechanical business, much of it concerning Ryder, inadequate in a role designed simply to guarantee the teenage male fan-base. With her deep-freeze intensity and sinewy self-sufficiency, Weaver needs no such back-up. Choking as she comes face to face with earlier, aborted clones, grappling with residual maternal feelings towards the monsters she spawned and contempt for the humans she's long since left behind, Ripley Mk II is a terrifyingly ambivalent millennial saviour, more frightening than a score of aliens. TCh

Alien Thunder (aka Tonnerre Rouge)

(1973, Can, 90 min)
d/ph Claude Fournier. *sc* George Malko. *ed* Jacques Gagné. *ad* Anne Pritchard. *m* Georges Delerue. *cast* Donald Sutherland, Chief Dan George, Kevin McCarthy, Jean Duceppe, Jack Creely, Gordon Tootoosis.

● Traditionally obsessive pursuit movie, with Sutherland living up to the Mounties' motto as he tracks an Indian murder suspect across both the impressive landscape and the cultural divide. Québecois director Fournier was formerly a *vérité* documentarist with the National Film Board and the New York-based Leacock/Pennebaker axis. PT

Ali G Indahouse

(2002, Ger/US/Fr/GB, 88 min)
d Mark Mylod. *p* Tim Bevan, Eric Fellner, Dan Mazer, (LA Crew) William Green. *sc* Sacha Baron Cohen, Dan Mazer. *ph* Ashley Rowe. *ed* Paul Knight. *pd* Grenville Horner, (LA Crew) Jon Billington. *m* Adam F. *cast* Sacha Baron Cohen, Michael Gambon, Charles Dance, Kellie Bright, Martin Freeman, Rhona Mitra, Barbara New, Emilio Rivera.

●Rollin' through TV shows, celebrity cameos and a hit single with Shaggy, Sacha Baron Cohen's feckless fictional homeboy was always bound for celluloid. But beneath its glossy blaxploitation veneer, and despite an odd jumble of stars and Cohen's mock-directorial interventions, this is a parochial feature-length sitcom. Indulging his gangsta fantasies in his west Staines 'hood, Ali is horrified to learn that the community centre where he coaches a 'Keep It Real' class faces closure. Persuaded into local politics by a corrupt Chancellor (Dance), he unwittingly becomes involved in a ruse to topple the Prime Minister (Gambon). But Ali has a herbal prescription for global peace. Unpredictability and blunt irreverence ensured Ali G's classic, even subversive comic status. Though he's too ubiquitous now to dupe real authoritarians, his film nevertheless proffers plenty of cheek – even if most of its gross-out gags come signposted. AHa

Alive

(1993, US, 127 min)
d Frank Marshall. *p* Robert Watts, Kathleen Kennedy. *sc* Monte Merrick, Paul Attanasio, John Patrick Shanley. *ph* Peter James. *ed* Michael Kahn. *m* James Newton Howard. *cast* Ethan Hawke, Vincent Spano, Josh Hamilton, Illeana Douglas, Sam Behrens, Ele Keats, John Malkovich.

●1972: a plane crashes in the Andes. Despite sub-zero temperatures and scarce supplies, the survivors hold out for a rescue party. On the eighth day, they hear a radio report: they've been given up for dead. Little by little, the unthinkable becomes unavoidable. If they are to survive, they must cannibalise the corpses frozen in ice. In adapting Piers Paul Read's account of the Andes air disaster, Marshall and screenwriter John Patrick Shanley address any moral squeamishness head-on: in this do-or-die situation, they insist, the greater sin would be to die. It's not quite fair to say that this is the first tasteful cannibalism picture (the crash itself is a *tour de force*, and the camera never shies away from the meat of the matter), but this spiritual disaster movie does sometimes feel like a papal injunction. Within 30 seconds we're in the presence of God – or at least bearded John Malkovich is musing to that effect. Rosaries, prayers and carols are never far away after that, and over the end credits Aaron Neville lets fly with *Ave Maria.* Skilfully crafted and doggedly performed, the film pushes too hard and too far; it strives for the inspirational but falls well short of inspired. TCh

Alive and Kicking (aka Indian Summer)

(1996, GB, 99 min)
d Nancy Meckler. *p* Martin Pope. *sc* Martin Sherman. *ph* Chris Seager. *ed* Rodney Holland. *pd* Cecelia Brereton. *m* Peter Salem. *cast* Jason Flemyng, Antony Sher, Dorothy Tutin, Anthony Higgins, Bill Nighy, Philip Voss, Diane Parish.

●Tonio (Flemyng) is the leading light of the Ballet Luna, and probably the last: with its ranks decimated by AIDS, and Luna (Tutin) going down with Alzheimer's, the company is in an advanced stage of disrepair. Offered the lead in a valedictory production of an old success, 'Indian Summer', Tonio throws himself into the part. It could be the chance of a lifetime, because he too has AIDS; then again, perhaps the hard work is also an evasion – isolated, confused and emotionally disoriented, he's already accepted the virus as a death sentence on his love life. Then he meets Jack (Sher), HIV-negative, but interested, despite Tonio's rebuffs. How better to extend one's horizons than a relationship with a dumpy, balding older man who can't dance? This remains solidly in the tradition of gritty British realism, resolutely unglamorous and looking always rather TV-bound. However, Martin Sherman's script, adapted from his stage play, is cogent and witty, and steers clear of the downbeat worthiness of the AIDS-drama ghetto towards the more invigorating realms of contemporary gay courtship. NB

Ali Zaoua: Prince de la Rue (Ali Zaoua: Prince of the Street)

(2000, Mor/Tun/Fr, 90 min)
d Nabil Ayouch. *sc* Nabil Ayouch, Nathalie Saugeon. *ph* Vincent Mathias. *ed* Jean-Robert Thomann. *ad* Saïd Rais. *m* Krishna Levy. *cast* Mounïm Kbab, Mustapha Hansali, Hicham Moussoune, Abdelhak Zhayra, Saïd Taghmaoui.

●Street kid Ali Zaoua lives down by the harbour, begging, stealing and hustling. He dreams of leaving behind the poverty, glue-sniffing and constant danger; of becoming a sailor and journeying far from Morocco to an island with two suns. But then a run-in with rivals results in his death, and his pals Kwita, Omar and Boubker have to find a way to bury him. But they have no cash, they ought to tell Ali's estranged mother the bad news – and then there's Dib, self-appointed leader of the local urchins whose despotic insistence on total allegiance ensured the errant Ali's demise. This has a lot going for it: its sentiments are liberal, it has ambition and intelligence, it's well shot and engagingly acted, mostly by street kids, whose lot director/co-writer Ayouch hoped to improve through their association with the film. But, regrettably, the film never quite takes off. The plotting is predictable, and the characterisation of the Fagin-like Dib is symptomatic of an overall tendency towards facile sentimentality. GA

All About Eve 100

(1950, US, 138 min)
d Joseph L Mankiewicz. *p* Darryl F Zanuck. *sc* Joseph L Mankiewicz. *ph* Milton Krasner. *ed* Barbara McLean. *ad* Lyle Wheeler, George W Davis. *m* Alfred Newman. *cast* Bette Davis, Anne Baxter, George Sanders, Celeste Holm, Thelma Ritter, Marilyn Monroe, Gary Merrill.

●Davis plays the successful actress, ageing and fundamentally insecure, who employs Baxter in exchange for her flattery. From there the scheming Baxter connives her way to the top at the expense of her employer, who realises what is happening but is powerless to do anything. Mankiewicz's bitchy screenplay makes the most of the situation, being both witty and intelligent. The young Monroe gets to have a stairway entrance (introduced by cynical critic Sanders as a 'graduate of the Copacabana school of acting').

All About My Mother (Todo Sobre Mi Madre)

(1999, Sp/Fr, 106 min)
d Pedro Almodóvar. *p* Augustín Almodóvar. *sc* Pedro Almodóvar. *ph* Affonso Beato. *ed* José Salcedo. *ad* Antxón Gómez. *m* Alberto Iglesias. *cast* Cecilia Roth, Marisa Paredes, Penélope Cruz, Antonia San Juan, Candela Peña, Rosa Maria Sardá.

●After the death of her beloved teenage son in an accident, Roth leaves Madrid for Barcelona to cope with her grief, hook up with old friends, and – just maybe – contact the long-estranged father the boy never knew. As she gradually regains the will to live through her involvement with the lives of others (including her son's favourite stage diva Paredes), Almodóvar piles on the coincidences, contrivances and twists so that the film succeeds best as a beautifully crafted, semi-ironic melodrama (it cleverly alludes to – and integrates – *All About Eve*, *Streetcar*..., Capote, etc). Though the film has a fair share of camp humour, it's the formal and emotional sophistication that really impresses; like *Live Flesh*, it displays a depth and maturity lacking in Almodóvar's earlier work. GA

Alla Rivoluzione sulla Due Cavalli

see Off to the Revolution by 2CV

All At Sea

See Barnacle Bill

All Creatures Great and Small

(1974, GB, 92 min)
d Claude Whatham. *p* David Susskind, Duane Bogie. *sc* Hugh Whitemore. *ph* Peter Suschitzky. *ed* Ralph Sheldon. *pd* Geoffrey Drake. *m* Wilfred Josephs. *cast* Simon Ward, Anthony Hopkins, Lisa Harrow, Brian Stirner, Freddie Jones, TP McKenna, Brenda Bruce.

●Complacently 'charming' compendium of incidentals from the early years of vet James Herriot's Yorkshire tenure. Herriot's books later found a natural home in a TV series. PT

All Dogs Go to Heaven

(1989, Eire, 85 min)
d Don Bluth. *p* Don Bluth, Gary Goldman, John Pomeroy. *sc* David Weiss. *m* Charles Strouse, TJ Kuenster. *cast* voices: Burt Reynolds, Vic Tayback, Judith Barsi, Dom De Luise, Loni Anderson, Melba Moore.

●This animated feature from Bluth, who left Disney in 1979 to develop his own inimitably kinetic brand of animation, is a seriously flawed piece shot through with teasing glimpses of excellence. After escaping from a New Orleans dog pound, German Shepherd Charlie B Barkin (voice by Burt Reynolds) and psychotic side kick Itchy (De Luise) high-tail it to ex-partner Carface (Tayback), a casino-owning pit bull. Double-crossed by Carface, finding himself at the pearly gates without a good deed to his name, Charlie tricks his way back to earth, and liberates a young girl from Carface, who uses her ability to talk to animals to predict race-winners. The usual rompery ensues, as Charlie and Itchy exploit, then grow to love, the multi-lingual cutie. The most obvious disappointment is the songs (courtesy of Charles Strouse and TJ Kuenster), which are strikingly unmemorable, a situation worsened by Reynolds' vocal inadequacies. More worryingly, something seems to have gone seriously wrong in the editing, so that the establishment of character and scene is frequently confused. The animation is fine, but flashy visuals hardly paste over the gaping inconsistencies. MK

Allegro Non Troppo

(1976, It, 85 min, colour & b/w)
d Bruno Bozzetto. *sc* Bruno Bozzetto, Guido Manuli, Maurizio Nichetti. *ph* Mario Masini, Giuliana De Carli. *ed* Giancarlo Rossi. *m* Debussy, Dvorak, Ravel, Sibelius, Vivaldi, Stravinsky. *cast* (live-action sequences) Marialuisa Giovannini, Nestor Garay, Maurizio Michele, Maurizo Nichetti, Mirella Falco, Osvaldo Salvi.

●An animated feature parodying *Fantasia* which is sufficiently inventive to hold its own. By sticking to short popular classics and allowing different animators to interpret each one, what it loses in thematic unity and sustained trajectory it makes up for in wit, variety and even, once or twice, a fine controlling intelligence. Occasionally *kitsch* intrudes, and the interpretations remain too single-mindedly literal to allow impressionistic flights that the music might deserve, but overall very amiable, quirky fun. *Allegro*, in fact, but *non troppo*. CPea

All Fall Down

(1961, US, 110 min, b/w)
d John Frankenheimer. *p* John Houseman. *sc* William Inge. *ph* Lionel Lindon. *ed* Fredric Steinkamp. *ad* George W Davis. *m* Alex North. *cast* Warren Beatty, Eva Marie Saint, Karl Malden, Angela Lansbury, Brandon de Wilde, Barbara Baxley.

●Drawling his way round William Inge's dialogue with methodical surliness while lumbered with a Christian name – Berry-Berry – which sounds more like a disease, Beatty is the epitome of itchy, preening 'rebellion' in this marvellously silly hothouse melodrama of familial angst. In the '50s there would have been a toss-up over James Leo Herlihy's source novel becoming either a Kazan movie or a Golden Age tele-drama, but MGM accommodated that decade's slow fade by letting TV graduate Frankenheimer direct it as if remaking *East of Eden.* Lansbury and Malden head the gallery of grotesques, while de Wilde's young eyes gradually narrow in disillusion over older brother Beatty's posturing antics. PT

All I Desire

(1953, US, 79 min, b/w)
d Douglas Sirk. *p* Ross Hunter. *sc* James Gunn, Robert Blees. *ph* Carl Guthrie. *ed* Milton Carruth. *ad* Bernard Herzbrun, Alexander Golitzen. *m* Joseph Gershenson. *cast* Barbara Stanwyck, Richard Carlson, Lyle Bettger, Maureen O'Sullivan, Lori Nelson, Marcia Henderson.

●There are things wrong with *All I Desire*, but Sirk isn't responsible for them. It didn't need the forced 'happy ending' for a start, and it should clearly have been made in colour. But Hollywood producers were even more stupid in 1953 than they are now, and directors didn't often get their way. Sirk was less compromised than most, because his strategy was a kind of 'hidden' subversion of genres like musicals and weepies: appearing to deliver the producer's goods, and simultaneously undercutting them. Here, the excellent Stanwyck plays an actress who hasn't made the grade, returning to the small-town family she walked out on after a scandalous affair with a local stud. She moves from one 'imitation of life' to another: from life-on-the-run in showbiz to life-under-wraps in Hicksville, Wisconsin. Sirk's delineation of the manners and 'morality' of bourgeois middle America is devastating; and the precision with which he dissects the repressions, jealousies and joys that permeate a family has never been rivalled. TR

Alligator

(1980, US, 94 min)
d Lewis Teague. *p* Brandon Chase. *sc* John Sayles. *ph* Joe Mangine. *ed* Larry Bock. *ad* Michael Erler. *m* Craig Hundley. *cast* Robert Forster, Robin Riker, Michael Gazzo, Dean Jagger, Perry Lang, Jack Carter, Sydney Lassick.

●Ramon, the eponymous star, is flushed down the pan as a baby, grows to an inordinate size by feeding on the corpses of pets used in hormone experiments (plus the odd sewer worker), and finally hits the streets looking for food and action. The basic angle to John Sayles' script (dubious scientific research leading to a dangerous freak of nature) is a reworking of his 1978 *Piranha*, but the sense of humour, narrative economy and attention to character are as sharp and fresh as you could wish. No prizes for guessing that Ramon finally devours the shady hand that unwittingly fed him, or that the cop on his tail literally blows the lid off his own guilt problems, but Sayles and Teague never stint on incidental pleasures. The result is an effective and unpretentious treat. SJ

Alligator Eyes

(1990, US, 100 min)
d John Feldman. *p* John Feldman, Ken Schwenker. *sc* John Feldman. *ph* Todd Crockett. *ed* Cynthia Rogers. *m* Sheila Silver. *cast* Annabelle Larsen, Roger Kabler, Allen McCullough, Mary McLain, John MacKay.

●Three old college friends, Lance, Robbie and Marjorie, go on a driving holiday together. Everything goes smoothly – Lance and Marjorie reviving their youthful affair, Robbie rediscovering the bottle – until they pick up a beautiful blind hitchhiker, Pauline. Using her blindness and her body, Pauline drives a wedge between the three buddies, and then draws them into her obsessive quest to find the man who murdered her parents. An impressive psycho-thriller, and although the pace flags at times, the central enigma of Pauline's motivation is sufficient to keep you guessing. NKe

All I Want for Christmas

(1991, US, 90 min)
d Robert Lieberman. *p* Marykay Powell. *sc* Thom Eberhardt, Richard Kramer. *ph* Wade Childress. *ed* Peter E Berger. *cast* Lauren Bacall, Harley Jane Kozak, Jamey Sheridan, Ethan Randall, Kevin Nealon, Thora Birch, Amy Oberer.

●Take one street-wise adolescent (Randall), an infuriatingly precocious younger sister (Birch), a wish for Santa to bring their divorced parents back together, and stir. Throw in a couple of big names, like Lauren Bacall as Granny and Leslie Nielsen as Santa; add juvenile love interest, and *voilà!*, the perfect Christmas turkey. This is family fare for the '90s at its most shameless and formulaic. What makes the film so nauseating is not that it's badly acted or made, but that its motives are presented with such sledgehammer subtlety that even the youngest children would feel insulted by it. NKe

All Men Are Mortal

(1995, GB/Neth/Fr, 94 min)
d Ate de Jong. *p* Rudolf Wichmann, Matthijs van Heijningen. *sc* Steven Gaydos, Olwen Wymark, Ate De Jong. *ph* Bruno de Keyser. *ed* Edgar Burcksen. *m* Klaus Doldinger. *cast* Irène Jacob, Stephen Rea, Colin Salmon, Marianne Sägebrecht, Maggie O'Neill, John Nettles, Chiara Mastroianni.

●WWII is over and Regina (Jacob) is the uncrowned queen of the Parisian stage, her avant-garde Hamlet the toast of the town. It's not enough: she lusts after immortality. Thus she falls under the spell of Fosca (Rea), an anti-social derelict who claims to be 700 years old. Could she live forever in his memory? Whatever its own merits, Simone de Beauvoir's 1946 novel emerges as a pretentious farrago in this clumsily literal Dutch English-language production. As a romance, it never gets close to the heart. Quite what the narcissistic Regina sees in the near-comatose Fosca is impossible to divine – and his own motives are no clearer. In any case, we don't care about either of them. Nor are Fosca's low-budget flashbacks to centuries past particularly impressive; any con-man worth his salt could contrive his supposedly death-defying stunts. Rea is terrible, morosely confining his acting to the eyebrows and up, but at least he's supposed to be mired in ennui – Fosca has seen it all – whereas Jacob is stuck with the thankless role of Europe's greatest actress, and in English. Perhaps Kieslowski might have made us believe it, but de Jong (*Drop Dead Fred*) is not quite in that league. TCh

All My Good Countrymen (Vsichni Dobri Rodaci/ aka All Good Citizens)

(1968, Czech, 180 min)
d/sc Vojtech Jasny. *ph* Jaroslav Kucera. *ed* Miroslav Hajek. *ad* Karel Lier. *m* Svatopluk Havelka. *cast* Radoslav Brzobohaty, Vlastimil Brodsky, Vladimir Mensik, Drahoslava Hofman, Waldemar Matuska, Vaclav Lohnicky.

●Jasny, a leading light in the new wave of Czech film-makers since the late '50s, won best director at Cannes in 1969 for this kaleidoscopic portrait of a Moldavian village over the twenty-odd years since the end of WWII. The significant deaths of sundry community members throughout that time punctuate a bitter-sweet, affectionate and pointed picture of a life many Czechs would have recognised. A key film from the 'Prague Spring', it was banned in Czechoslovakia soon after the news broke of its Cannes award. TJ

Allnighter, The

(1987, US, 108 min)
d/p Tamar Simon Hoffs. sc ML Kessler, Tamar Simon Hoffs. *ph* Joseph Urbanczyk. *ed* Dan M Rich. *ad* Cynthia Sowder. *m* Charles Bernstein. *cast* Susanna Hoffs, Dedee Pfeiffer, Joan Cusack, Michael Ontkean, John Terlesky, Pam Grier.

●Dreary, misconceived sorority drama, charting the romantic adventures of its three female leads as student days come to an end. Hoffs the director is mother of Hoffs the star, but this particular project could have done with a lot more family planning. GM

All Night Long

(1981, US, 88 min)
d Jean-Claude Tramont. *p* Leonard Goldberg, Jerry Weintraub. *sc* WD Richter. *ph* Philip H Lathrop. *ed* Marion Rothman. *pd* Peter Jamison. *m* Ira Newborn. *cast* Gene Hackman, Barbra Streisand, Diane Ladd, Dennis Quaid, William Daniels, Kevin Dobson.

●Intermittently engaging comedy, with Gene Hackman as a frustrated executive who chucks up his job and family after meeting a kooky suburban sexpot (Streisand, natch), hopefully setting up his own workshop in a converted warehouse. Its dropout theme is rather too tritely familiar to generate much enthusiasm. TM

All Night Long

see Toute une Nuit

All of Me

(1984, US, 93 min)
d Carl Reiner. *p* Stephen J Friedman. *sc* Phil Alden Robinson. *ph* Richard H Kline. *ed* Bud Molin. *pd* Edward C Carfagno. *m* Patrick Williams. *cast* Steve Martin, Lily Tomlin, Victoria Tennant, Madolyn Smith, Dana Elcar, Jason Bernard, Richard Libertini.

●When wealthy heiress Tomlin dies, something goes awry with her guru's transcendental arrangements and her soul passes into Martin, or at least into one half of his body. The gag of gender-switching is not new, but here for the first time is an internal sex war on numerous levels, not the least being a woman discovering the extreme peculiarities that constitute male behaviour. Martin is his usual combination of flat cynicism and crazed childishness, indulging in some inspired Jerry Lewis-like clowning with his arms and legs hopelessly out of synch. And there are gems from a blind black sax player (Bernard). CPea

Allonsanfan

(1974, It, 111 min)
d Paolo Taviani, Vittorio Taviani. *p* Giuliani G De Negri. *sc* Paolo Taviani, Vittorio Taviani. *ph* Giuseppe Ruzzolini. *ed* Roberto Perpignani. *ad* Giovanni Sbarra. *m* Ennio Morricone. *cast* Marcello Mastroianni, Lea Massari, Mimsy Farmer, Laura Betti, Bruno Cirino.

●A film with an even greater thrust of excitement than the Tavianis' subsequent *Padre Padrone*. Mastroianni, at his most convincingly dissolute, plays a spineless aristocrat who wanders through Italy in 1816 trying to rub out his past association with a radical group, without daring to tell them he's lost their faith in Napoleonic revolution. The tangled and sumptuously melodramatic plot allows the Tavianis to lay into left-wing idealism and gullibility without departing from their own commitment for a second. Ennio Morricone's score tops a rousing and passionate entertainment. TR

All or Nothing

(2002, GB/Fr, 128 min)
d Mike Leigh. *p* Simon Channing Williams, Alain Sarde. *sc* Mike Leigh. *ph* Dick Pope. *ed* Lesley Walker. *pd* Eve Stewart. *m* Andrew Dickson. *cast* Timothy Spall, Lesley Manville, Ruth Sheen, Marion Bailey, Timothy Bateson, Alison Garland, Edna Doré.

●While Leigh has done this kind of 'working-class family in crisis' comedy-drama before, it should be emphasised that he's never done it quite so well. From the appropriately Ozu-like opening shot to the dark, almost Bergman-esque intensity of the climactic confrontation between a supermarket cashier (Manville) and the distraught minicab-driver husband she feels she no longer loves (Spall), the director and his cast provide a persuasive, dramatically powerful account of London housing-estate lives blighted by economic hardship, emotional inarticulacy, glaring resentment and impoverished hopes. A couple of the secondary characters – neighbours going through their own upheavals (mostly, as with the protagonists and their teenage kids, to do with generational tension) – are a little less subtly drawn and played, but overall the film is perceptive, often hilarious, and sometimes quite harrowing in its stark, brutal honesty. GA

All Over Me

(1996, US, 90 min)
d Alex Sichel. *p* Dolly Hall. *sc* Sylvia Sichel. *ph* Joe DeSalvo. *ed* Sabine Hoffman. *pd* Amy Beth Silver. *m* Miki Navazio. *cast* Alison Folland, Tara Subkoff, Cole Hauser, Wilson Cruz, Pat Briggs, Leisha Hailey, Ann Dowd.

●A sincere rites-of-passage movie from two first-timers (Alex Sichel directing, and sister Sylvia writing). Fifteen-year-old Claude (Folland) is loyal to her better-looking best friend Ellen (Subkoff, affecting), despite the latter's self-destructive, sex 'n' drug liaison with aggressive homophobic arsehole Mark (Hauser), who may have been involved in the sadistic murder of a gay Hell's Kitchen neighbour. It's the last day of school and as adult life beckons unenticingly, the girls' intimacy crosses over to the sexual. Music scene debutantes (Briggs from Psychotica, Hailey from the Murmurs as Claude's lesbian friend) perform impressively, but Folland is the stand-out. She doesn't overplay her teenage confusion, carries scenes with expressive looks when the script – the film's big let-down – lapses, and gears up credibly when her character's courage and assertiveness come into play. Joe DeSalvo shoots the interiors and NY streets in harmony with the movie's desultory mood, and there's a sensitive score by Miki Navazio. WH

All Quiet on the Western Front

(1930, US, 138 min, b/w)
d Lewis Milestone. *sc* George Abbott, Del Andrews, Maxwell Anderson. *ph* Arthur Edeson. *ed* Edgar Adams. *ad* Charles D Hall. *m* David Broekman. *cast* Lew Ayres, Louis Wolheim, John Wray, Slim Summerville, Russell Gleason, Raymond Griffith, William Bakewell, Owen Davis Jr.

● Based on Erich Maria Remarque's pacifist novel and renowned as *the* classic anti-war movie – it details the slow but steady extermination of a group of idealistic young German soldiers in World War I – the film's strength now derives less from its admittedly powerful but highly simplistic utterances about war as waste, than from a generally excellent set of performances (Ayres especially) and an almost total reluctance to follow normal plot structure. It is in fact the often relentless depiction of unflagging warfare and suffering that eventually pummels one into *feeling*, rather than understanding, the film's message. GA

All Quiet on the Western Front

(1980, US/GB, 158 min)
d Delbert Mann. *p* Norman Rosemont. *sc* Paul Monash. *ph* John Coquillon. *ed* Alan Pattillo. *pd* John Stoll. *m* Allyn Ferguson. *cast* Richard Thomas, Ernest Borgnine, Donald Pleasence, Ian Holm, Patricia Neal, Mark Elliott.

● A horrible instance of international packaging (past-master Lew Grade naturally got a finger in the pie) that has all the excitement of a financial balance sheet. Remarque's classic novel resists the attempts, signposted by the American presence of Thomas and Borgnine in the World War I German trenches, to make it 'relevant' to post-Vietnam. The desperate substitution of a twittering bird for the famous butterfly at the climax marks the extent to which the 1930 version remains a Milestone around director Delbert Mann's neck. Originally shown on American TV in three segments – though made as a feature film – it was cut by almost half-an-hour for release in Britain. PT

All-Round Reduced Personality – Redupers, The (Die allseitig reduzierte Persönlichkeit – Redupers)

(1977, WGer, 98 min, b/w)
d Helke Sander. *p* Clara Burckner. *sc* Helke Sander. *ph* Katia Forbert. *ed* Ursula Höf. *cast* Helke Sander, Joachim Baumann, Andrea Malkowsky, Ronny Tanner, Gesine Strempel, Gisland Nabakowski.

● Directing her first feature from her own script, Sander – a founder of the German Women's movement – also stars as an unmarried mother and freelance photographer in West Berlin, obsessed with interpreting both The Wall which separates her from the well-rounded socialists back East, and the equally divisive social structures which prevent her from uniting her different abilities in a single coherent life. A brilliant achievement: personal, political, witty, sad and rigorously dialectical. JD

All's Fair

(1989, US, 89 min)
d Rocky Lane. *p* Jon Gordon. *sc* Randee Russel, John Finegan, Tom Rondinella, William Pace. *ph* Peter Lyons Collister. *pd* Cynthia Charette. *m* Bill Meyers. *cast* George Segal, Sally Kellerman, Robert Carradine, Jennifer Edwards, Lou Ferrigno, Jane Kaczmarek.

● A dreary unfunny mess that follows a group of businessmen's wives who organise mock war games at the weekend to show their high-powered husbands they know a thing about the competitive spirit too. It didn't make it to UK cinemas, fortunately, but there is a surprise happy ending (see *Flirting with Disaster*). TJ

All Stars

(1997, Neth, 112 min)
d Jean van de Velde. *cast* Anthonie Kamerling, Danny de Munck, Paul Muller, Isa Hoes.

● Every week, come rain or shine, seven childhood friends, now in their late 20s, play football. Their Sunday get-togethers are threatened by the pressures of work and relationships, but they're determined to finish their 500th match before disbanding. This amiable rites-of-passage yarn, a hit in Holland, captures both the immaturity and idealism of its soccer-crazy characters. Although they don't want to grow up, adult responsibilities are crowding in. There's a wry, self-deprecating humour to the storytelling. The screenplay touches all the usual bases – one player is gay, one has a pregnant girlfriend, another has a disabled father – but sensitive direction combined with engaging performances from a cast of well-known Dutch TV actors ensures a freshness and delicacy which most sports movies miss by a mile. GM

All That...For This?!

see Tout ça...pour ça!!!

All That Heaven Allows 100

(1955, US, 89 min)
d Douglas Sirk. *p* Ross Hunter. *sc* Peg Fenwick. *ph* Russell Metty. *ed* Frank Gross. *ad* Alexander Golitzen, Eric Orbom. *m* Frank Skinner. *cast* Jane Wyman, Rock Hudson, Agnes Moorehead, Conrad Nagel, Virginia Grey, Charles Drake, Gloria Talbott.

● On the surface a glossy tearjerker about the problems besetting a love affair between an attractive middle class widow and her younger, 'bohemian' gardener, Sirk's film is in fact a scathing attack on all those facets of the American Dream widely held dear. Wealth produces snobbery and intolerance; family togetherness creates xenophobia and the cult of the dead; cosy kindness can be stultifyingly patronising; and materialism results in alienation from natural feelings. Beneath the stunningly lovely visuals – all expressionist colours, reflections, and frames-within-frames, used to produce a precise symbolism – lies a kernel of terrifying despair created by lives dedicated to respectability and security, given its most harrowing expression when Wyman, having given up her affair with Hudson in order to protect her children from gossip, is presented with a television set as a replacement companion. Hardly surprising that Fassbinder chose to remake the film as *Fear Eats the Soul*. GA

All That Jazz

(1979, US, 123 min)
d Bob Fosse. *p* Robert Alan Aurthur. *sc* Robert Alan Aurthur, Bob Fosse. *ph* Giuseppe Rotunno. *ed* Alan Heim. *pd* Philip Rosenberg. *m* Ralph Burns. *cast* Roy Scheider, Jessica Lange, Ann Reinking, Leland Palmer, Cliff Gorman, Ben Vereen.

● Apparently Bob Fosse thought it 'foolish' to call *All That Jazz* self-indulgent. But he did direct, choreograph and co-write this musical comedy; it's about his life; it's very pleased with itself. As translated onto screen, his story is wretched: the jokes are relentlessly crass and objectionable; the song'n'dance routines have been created in the cutting-room and have lost any sense of fun; Fellini-esque moments add little but pretension; and scenes of a real open-heart operation, alternating with footage of a symbolic Angel of Death in veil and white gloves, fail even in terms of the surreal. HM

All That Money Can Buy (aka The Devil and Daniel Webster/ Daniel and the Devil)

(1941, US, 112 min, b/w)
d/p William Dieterle. *sc* Dan Totheroh, Stephen Vincent Benet. *ph* Joseph August. *ed* Robert Wise. *ad* Van Nest Polglase. *m* Bernard Herrmann. *cast* Walter Huston, Edward Arnold, James Craig, Jane Darwell, Gene Lockhart, Simone Simon, Anne Shirley.

● A fascinating version of the Faust legend adapted from Stephen Vincent Benet's short story. Craig is the poor New Hampshire farmer in the 1840s driven to such straits that he swears he'd sell his soul for two cents, and up pops Mr Scratch (Huston in a wonderful personification of the devil of New England folklore). A rapid rise to fame and fortune follows, with Mr Scratch's handmaiden (the delightful Simon) temptingly on hand. Things get a little portentously patriotic when the seven years are up, Craig elects to have the famous orator/politican Daniel Webster (Arnold) defend him against Mr Scratch's claim for his soul, and Mr Scratch counters by summoning famous villains from history as judge and jury. But it all looks terrific, directed by Dieterle in his best expressionist mood, with superb sets (Van Nest Polglase), score (Bernard Herrmann), camerawork (the great Joe August), and a township that looks as if it came straight out of a Grant Wood painting. *Daniel and the Devil* is a cut version running 85 mins. TM

All the King's Men

(1949, US, 109 min, b/w)
d/p/sc Robert Rossen. *ph* Burnett Guffey. *ed* Al Clark. *ad* Sturges Carne. *m* Louis Gruenberg. *cast* Broderick Crawford, Joanne Dru, John Ireland, Mercedes McCambridge, John Derek, Shepperd Strudwick, Anne Seymour.

● A fine adaptation of Robert Penn Warren's Pulitzer novel, chronicling the rise and fall of Southern demagogue Willie Stark (Crawford), a thinly disguised portrait of Huey Long, the Louisiana state governor and US senator whose career – a fine record of civic improvment turned to ashes by an uncontrollable greed for power – was ended by assassination in 1935. The thesis is basically that power corrupts, with Stark presented as a man who starts out with a burning sense of purpose and a defiant honesty. Rossen, however, injects a note of ambiguity early on (a scene where Willie impatiently shrugs off his wife's dream of the great and good things he is destined to accomplish); and the doubt as to what he is *really* after is beautifully orchestrated by being filtered through the eyes of the press agent (Ireland) who serves as the film's narrator, and whose admiration for Stark gradually becomes tempered by understanding. Given that Stark's relationship with his son builds latterly to some overheated melodrama, the first half of the film is by far the best, but Rossen retains his grip throughout; and the performances (Crawford, Ireland and McCambridge especially) are superb. TM

All the Little Animals

(1998, GB, 112 min)
d/p Jeremy Thomas. *sc* Eski Thomas. *ph* Mike Molloy. *ed* John Victor Smith. *pd* Andrew Sanders. *m* Richard Hartley. *cast* John Hurt, Christian Bale, Daniel Benzali, James Faulkner, John O'Toole, Amanda Royle, Amy Robbins.

● Producer Thomas's first feature as director is an ambitious, intriguing but finally botched modern fairy tale (from a book by Walker Hamilton) in which an innocent, brain-damaged boy (Bale), threatened with incarceration by his ogre-like stepfather (Benzali) after the death of his wealthy mother, flees London for the Cornish countryside, where he meets up with an eccentric recluse (Hurt) who goes round burying animals killed in collisions with cars. It's an odd little eco-parable, clearly influenced by *Night of the Hunter* (the comparison does it no favours), with stilted dialogue, fine 'Scope camerawork, a detached performance by Benzali, and proficient work from Bale and Hurt. A brave effort, certainly different, but all too emphatically an allegory. GA

All the Marbles (aka The California Dolls)

(1981, US, 113 min)
d Robert Aldrich. *p* William Aldrich. *sc* Mel Frohman. *ph* Joseph Biroc. *ed* Irving Rosenblum, Richard Lane. *pd* Carl Anderson. *m* Frank De Vol. *cast* Peter Falk, Vicki Frederick, Laurene Landon, Burt Young, Tracy Reed, Claudette Nevins, Ursaline Bryant-King.

● Aldrich's last film, a sad summation of his attempts to gauge his contemporary audience, turns out an intermittently hilarious but generally compromised mix of '50s introspection and '70s grand-standing (last pulled off coherently in *The Mean Machine*). With Falk as manager of a female tag wrestling duo, graduating via broad road movie conventions from the steel town small halls to the MGM Grand Hotel in Reno for a championship bout, it slips in and out of styles and stylisations as if trying on each for size or for laughs, maintaining a tenuous integrity only through its director's self-deprecating self-consciousness. PT

All the President's Men

(1976, US, 138 min)
d Alan J Pakula. *p* Walter Coblenz. *sc* William Goldman. *ph* Gordon Willis. *ed* Robert L

Wolfe. *pd* George Jenkins. *m* David Shire. *cast* Dustin Hoffman, Robert Redford, Jack Warden, Martin Balsam, Hal Holbrook, Jason Robards, Jane Alexander.
● Inevitably softened by hints of self-congratulation concerning the success of Woodward and Bernstein's uncovering of the Watergate affair, Pakula's film is nevertheless remarkably intelligent, working both as an effective thriller (even though we know the outcome of their investigations) and as a virtually abstract charting of the dark corridors of corruption and power. Pakula's visual set-ups are often extraordinary, contrasting the light of the *Washington Post* newsroom with the shadows in which hides star informant Deep Throat, and dramatically engulfing Hoffman and Redford in monumental buildings to stress the enormity of their task. GA

All the Pretty Horses

(2000, US, 117 min)
d Billy Bob Thornton. *p* Billy Bob Thornton, Robert Salerno. *sc* Ted Tally. *ph* Barry Markowitz. *ed* Sally Menke. *pd* Clark Hunter. *m* Marty Stuart. *cast* Matt Damon, Henry Thomas, Lucas Black, Penélope Cruz, Rubén Blades, Robert Patrick, Julio Oscar Mechoso, Miriam Colon, Bruce Dern, Sam Shepard, Angelina Torres, JD Young.
● Thornton's film of Cormac McCarthy's novel begins with two West Texas teenagers lying under the stars, pondering mortality and itching to cross the border for high adventure. And that's just what they do, cutting out on horseback, but making the fatal acquaintance of a saddle-proud urchin name of Blevins along the way. Over the Rio Grande lies danger, love, prison, death. McCarthy's book may be knee-deep in purple sage, but his literary machismo fits square in the American canon and exerts a grievous romantic pull. Thornton's treatment is reverential – as far as can be determined from what is evidently the bare bones of the director's preferred three-hour cut. Ted Tally's adaptation doesn't omit any significant scenes, while retaining a good deal of the already spare dialogue. The movie is near perfectly cast. If Damon is a mite mature for John Grady Cole, Thomas is a shrewd choice for his sidekick Rawlins, while Black (Blevins), Cruz, Dern, Shepard and Blades all look and sound just so. Mostly simple and unaffected, the direction makes no attempt to translate McCarthy's dense poetic prose except in the loveliness of the light. Yet the film feels all wrong. The relentless, brisk linearity of the cutting doesn't allow for any breathing space; there's no punctuation, no modulation or breadth. Even the crucial sequence where Grady and Rawlins break 16 mustangs in four days feels squeezed. And the romance with Cruz is faithful to the weakest passages in the book. The result is both bathetic and broken-backed, and for once that extra hour might have helped. TCh

All the Rage (aka It's the Rage)

(1999, US, 97 min)
d James D Stern. *p* Peter Gilbert, Anne McCarthy, Ash R Shah, James D Stern, Mary Vernieu. *sc* Keith Reddin. *ph* Alex Nepomniaschy. *ed* Tony Lombardo. *pd* Judy Fleming. *m* Mark Mothersbaugh. *cast* Joan Allen, Gary Sinise, Jeff Daniels, Andre Braugher, Robert Forster, David Schwimmer, Anna Paquin, Giovani Ribisi, Josh Brolin, Bokeem Woodbine.
● A straight to small screen release, this US indie is an ensemble black comedy (allegedly) predicated on the maxim: have gun, will shoot. It begins interestingly with Daniels plugging an intruder in the middle of the night, but not fooling his wife Allen for a minute. Why is he wearing his watch, she asks. And doesn't that corpse on the carpet bear a striking resemblance to your business partner. Unfortunately, the screenplay is more interested in types than characters, the handgun motif quickly wears thin, and director Stern misses whatever comic potential presumably attracted this impressive cast. TCh

All the Right Moves

(1983, US, 91 min)
d Michael Chapman. *p* Stephen Deutsch. *sc* Michael Kane. *ph* Jan De Bont. *ed* David Garfield. *ad* Mary Ann Biddle. *m* David Campbell. *cast* Tom Cruise, Craig T Nelson, Lea Thompson, Charles Cioffi, Christopher Penn, Paul Carafotes, Gary Graham.
● Passable teen/sports movie, with a youthful Tom Cruise gunning for a football scholarship to get out of the grey Pennsylvania milltown where he lives. Chapman – who is better known as a cinematographer – aims for naturalism and sometimes gets it from his young cast (Lea Thompson makes a strong impression for once), but the script draws too heavily on the crowd-pleasing tactics of *An Officer and a Gentleman* and its ilk to stand apart. TCh

All the Way (Zou Dao Di)

(2001, China, 87 min)
d Shi Runjiu. *p* Peter Loehr. *sc* Diao Yinan. *ph* Wang Yu. *ed* Yang Hongyu. *ad* An Bin. *m* Chang Cheng-Yu, Chia Minshu, Benny Shao. *cast* Jiang Wu, Karen Mok, Chang Cheng-Yu, Guan Yue, Qi Zhi, Zhuo Kui.
● Loehr's Imar Films continues its project to reinvent Chinese mainstream entertainment cinema with a road movie/thriller set in country towns and villages in East China. An innocent businessman (Jiang) offers a ride to a hitchhiker (Mok) and finds himself taken hostage by her criminal boyfriend (Taiwanese musician Chang, who also provides some of the score). Afraid that the ensuing chase won't sustain interest on its own, the script crams in subplots and secondary characters: two comic con-men, a retired cop, a gang of swindlers, a cache of fake antique coins. Cut for pace and shot largely handheld, this is likeable, lightweight stuff. But it was the miscasting coup of the year to have sophisticated HK actress Karen Mok play a small town beautician with dodgy taste in boyfriends. TR

All the Youthful Days

see Boys from Fengkuei, The

All This, and Heaven Too

(1940, US, 140 min, b/w)
d Anatole Litvak. *sc* Casey Robinson. *ph* Ernest Haller. *ed* Warren Low. *ad* Carl Jules Weyl. *m* Max Steiner. *cast* Charles Boyer, Bette Davis, Barbara O'Neil, Virginia Weidler, Jeffrey Lynn, Walter Hampden, Harry Davenport.
● Davis in relatively subdued form as a governess accused of having an affair with a married nobleman (Boyer) in 19th century France, and of aiding and abetting in the murder of his neurotically jealous wife (O'Neil). Telling her innocent story in flashback to a class of American schoolchildren who have recognised her as a notorious woman, she is eventually rewarded by their sympathy and understanding. Adapted from a bestseller by Rachel Field, it's a pretty long, gloomy haul, though lavishly mounted (with photography by Ernest Haller) and sensitively acted. GA

All This and Money Too

see Love Is a Ball

All This and World War II

(1976, US, 88 min, b/w & col)
d Susan Winslow. *p* Sandy Lieberson, Martin J Machat. *ed* Colin J Berwick. *m* John Lennon, Paul McCartney.
● Unbelievably stupid idea of setting archive footage of the years before and during World War II to the music of the Beatles, performed by an insane assortment of singers accompanied by the London Symphony Orchestra and the Royal Philharmonic. The connections made ('The Fool on the Hill' accompanying shots of Hitler at his mountain retreat in Berchtesgaden) are crushingly crass. GA

All Through the Night

(1942, US, 107 min, b/w)
d Vincent Sherman. *p* Jerry Wald. *sc* Leonard Spigelgass. Edwin Gilbert. *ph* Sid Hickox. *ed* Rudi Fehr. *ad* Max Parker. *m* Adolph Deutsch. *cast* Humphrey Bogart, Conrad Veidt, Peter Lorre, Judith Anderson, Karen Verne, Jane Darwell, Frank McHugh.
● Lively if unremarkable Warners comedy thriller with Bogart as a wisecracking New York gambler taking on Veidt's Nazi fifth columnists, who are planning to sabotage a battleship anchored in the harbour. Shades of Runyon in the brisk banter as Bogart rallies his underworld troops, and strong acting from a superb cast (that goes on to include Jane Darwell, Jackie Gleason, Phil Silvers, Frank McHugh, Barton MacLane and Martin Kosleck) make it more than watchable, though both propaganda and direction are less than inspired. GA

All Visitors Must Be Announced

(1996, Neth, 78 min.)
d Dree Andrea.
● This profile of three New York City doormen admits us to a shadowy, purgatorial world. The doormen are gatekeepers for the rich folk of the apartment blocks they look after. They check the mail, receive parcels, allow pizza deliveries, and sometimes even help their married clients with illicit affairs. Unfortunately, the qualities which suit the doormen to their job – they're stoical, phlegmatic types – don't make them exciting subjects for a film. Despite the observational detail, the documentary is short on the adrenalin you might expect from a film set in the heart of the city. GM

Alma Gitana

see Gypsy Soul

Almonds and Raisins

(1983, GB, 90 min, b/w)
d Russ Karel. *p* Russ Karel, David Elstein. *sc* Wolf Mankowitz. *ph* Jacek Laskus. *ed* Chris Barnes, Anthony Sloman, Bridget Reiss, Kevin Hewitt. *m* John Altman. *with* Herschel Bernardi, Joseph Green, Zvee Scooler, Seymour Rechtzeit, Leo Fuchs, Miriam Kressyn, David Opatashu. *narrator* Orson Welles.
● Pictures from a galaxy far away and long ago: the 300-odd no-budget Yiddish talkies assembly-line manufactured in New York and Poland during the '30s. Very audience-specific films, too. The theme of many of them, whether melodrama or comedy (or Western!), is that of the immigrant finding a home in a new culture without sacrificing old values. For cinephiles, the extracts from the Edgar G Ulmer films are the prime attraction, but the Yiddish analogues of Abbott & Costello, Maisie and Ma Kettle exert a certain fascination in their own right. The memories of surviving participants and Wolf Mankowitz's commentary leave many points uncovered: look as well to Sylvia Paskin's excellent history *When Joseph Met Molly*. DO

Almost an Angel

(1990, US, 95 min)
d/p John Cornell. *sc* Paul Hogan. *ph* Russell Boyd. *ed* David Stiven. *ad* Mark Turnbull. *m* Maurice Jarre. *cast* Paul Hogan, Elias Koteas, Linda Kozlowski, Charlton Heston, Doreen Lang, Joe Dallesandro, Douglas Seale.
● Saving a youngster from a road accident, rough-diamond ex-con Terry Dean (Hogan) is knocked into oblivion. He hallucinates an audience with God (Heston), who refuses him entry to paradise on the grounds that he's a scumbag, sending him back to earth as a probationary angel. So far so good, as Hogan runs through his innocent abroad routine, calling God 'your honour', holding up foodstores for the poor, and attempting to fathom the extent of his imagined angelic powers ('I'm bullet-proof', he tells a bemused clergyman, 'but I can't fly yet'). Things take a nosedive, however, when he teams up with irritating do-gooder Rose (Kozlowski) and her invalid brother (Koteas), and Hogan's script ploughs into the realms of pseudo-serious philosophising. Aided and abetted by Cornell's limp direction, a hideously self-congratulatory catalogue of 'tender' set pieces ensues, revealing that Hogan is (surprise, surprise) the most wonderful, loving, caring person alive – or indeed dead. Almost a turkey. MK

Almost Famous

(2000, US, 123 min)
d Cameron Crowe. *p* Cameron Crowe, Ian Bryce. *sc* Cameron Crowe. *ph* John Toll. *ed* Joe Hutshing, Saar Klein. *ad* Clay A Griffith, Clayton R Hartley, Virginia Randolph-Weaver. *m* Nancy Wilson. *cast* Billy Crudup, Frances McDormand, Kate Hudson, Jason Lee, Patrick Fugit, Anna Paquin, Fairuza Balk, Philip Seymour Hoffman.

●You are invited aboard the Cameron Crowe Tour '73: please join us down memory lane to revisit the film-maker's own original glory days as an underage journalist with a commission to rock. Crowe's quasi-autobiographical yarn follows 15-year-old William Miller (newcomer Fugit, cute but effective) on an assignment for *Rolling Stone* to profile the fictional band Stillwater, an upcoming outfit replete with second-rate riffs, first-rate groupies, and a simmering tension between its attitudinal front man Lee and more talented guitarist Crudup. The kid sees plenty, but will he ever get his interview? And how much will he tell? Crowe points up questions of journalistic and cultural compromise, as proferred by the boy's pugnacious critical mentor, the notorious gonzo rock journalist Lester Bangs (Hoffman, enjoying himself), but he's never a film-maker to force a moral conundrum when he can let it diffuse into the general harmony of things. It's a sweet-minded, picaresque story, woolly with some of its dramatic details, but stacked with attractions: I've not even mentioned McDormand, Hudson, Taylor, Paquin. Peaches and cream. NB

Almost Perfect Affair, An

(1979, US, 93 min)
d Michael Ritchie. *p* Terry Carr. *sc* Walter Bernstein, Don Petersen. *ph* Henri Decae. *ed* Richard A Harris. *ad* Willy Holt. *m* Georges Delerue. *cast* Keith Carradine, Monica Vitti, Raf Vallone, Christian De Sica, Dick Anthony Williams, Sergio Leone, Farah Fawcett, George Peppard, Margaux Hemingway

●Ritchie's last 'personal' (and, for that matter, interesting) movie before he went blandly commercial is, like his early work, a study in the ethics of competitive rivalry. Carradine (as fine as ever) plays a self-centred independent American film-maker who meets with cute Vitti during the Cannes Film Festival. How honest are his proclamations of love? Hard to tell, given that she is the wealthy ex-actress wife of Italian producer Vallone. A strangely disenchanted romantic comedy, the film impresses with its strong performances and its ambivalent attitude towards the emotional deceptions of its lovers, while there's a bonus for buffs in the in-jokes and documentary cameo-shots of various directors caught on location along the Croisette. GA

Almost Summer

(1977, US, 89 min)
d Martin Davidson. *p* Rob Cohen. *sc* Judith Berg, Sandra Berg, Martin Davidson, Marc Reid Rubel. *ph* Stevan Larner. *ed* Lynzee Klingman. *ad* William M Hiney. *m* Charles Lloyd. *cast* Bruno Kirby, Lee Purcell, John Friedrich, Didi Conn, Thomas Carter, Tim Matheson.

●Funny but airtight tale of student electioneering and crushes in Beach Boy/Beach Baby land, contemporary in setting but as backward-looking as *The Lords of Flatbush* (which Davidson co-directed). It's the same old 'Is There Life After High School?', lubricated by mesmerising visions of material privilege - sunshine, wheels, and no parents in sight. The performances are assured, the cutting slick, the whole story runs along with compulsive familiarity: Italian-style hustler runs an unknown candidate against super-popular ball-busting cheerleader. We gawp at harsh political realities (side order of irony here), naked ambition is eventually outclassed by immense personal integrity, and everyone gets partners at the prom. RP

Almost You

(1984, US, 97 min)
d Adam Brooks. *p* Mark Lipson. *sc* Mark Horowitz. *ph* Alexander Gruszynski. *ed* Mark Burns. *ad* Nora Chavoosian. *m* Jonathan Elias. *cast* Brooke Adams, Griffin Dunne, Karen Young, Marty Watt, Christine Estabrook, Josh Mostel.

●Erica (Adams) and Alex (Dunne) have reached a marital crisis, and when Erica breaks her hip, fickle, confused Alex finds himself attracted to her young nurse, Lisa. The tension is further aggravated by Lisa's actor-lover, whose fears impel him to introduce himself, incognito, to Alex with unexpected results. Brooks' first feature distinguishes itself from superficially similar romantic comedies by its tough, unsentimental tone. Though generous towards his characters' various anxieties and foibles, Brooks never shies away from their blinkered selfishness, or from the very real unhappiness caused by Alex's philandering ways. At the same time, the sense of pain is offset by often gorgeously observed comic moments. Assured and deliciously performed. GA

Aloha, Bobby and Rose

(1975, US, 89 min)
d Floyd Mutrux. *p* Fouad Said. *sc* Floyd Mutrux. *ph* William A Fraker. *ed* Danford B Greene. *cast* Paul LeMat, Dianne Hull, Tim McIntire, Leigh French, Martine Bartlett, Robert Carradine, Noble Willingham.

●The same compulsive electric landscape of California as *American Graffiti*, but now it's a decade later and the snakes have got into the garden: LeMat (from *Graffiti*) and Hull play two disappointed fugitives from the '60s on the run after an accidental shooting. Mutrux achieves the same kind of dizzying skating-rink effect that Lucas managed in the earlier film, and gives it a vicious added edge by some unexpected juxtapositions: 'Locomotion' by Little Eva punctuates a terrifying slow-motion car accident. As the movie develops, the couple resemble human pinballs sliding back and forth among the cruelly compulsive lights and sounds. With little characterisation or depth, the plot doesn't finally add up to much more than a coda to *Graffiti*, but a sharply effective one. DP

Aloha Summer

(1988, US, 97 min)
d Tommy Lee Wallace. *p* Mike Greco, Bob Benedetto. *ph* Steven Poster. *ed* James Coblentz, Jack Mofstra, Jay Cassidy. *ad* Donald Harris. *m* Jesse Frederick, Bennett Salvay. *cast* Chris Makepeace, Yuji Okumoto, Don Michael Paul, Tia Carrere, Sho Kosugi, Lorie Griffin.

●This predictable rites-of-passage picture, directed by a John Carpenter associate and set in the summer of '59 (the year Hawaii joined the US), follows Makepeace and the gang as they square up to the glorious local surf, confront racial prejudice, and overcome their timidity in the face of bikini-clad womenfolk (including future *Wayne's World* siren Tia Carrere). *Big Wednesday* it ain't. TJ

Aloma of the South Seas

(1941, US, 76 min)
d Alfred Santell. *p* Monta Bell. *sc* Frank Butler, Seena Owen, Lillie Hayward. *ph* Karl Struss. *ed* Arthur Schmidt. *ad* Hans Dreier, William Pereira. *m* Victor Young. *cast* Dorothy Lamour, Jon Hall, Lynne Overman, Philip Reed, Katherine DeMille.

●Grin-and-bear-it melodrama of the Tropical Paradise variety, dismissed as routine nonsense even at the time. Lamour and Hall, reunited from Ford's *The Hurricane* four years earlier, mouth some unbelievable dialogue in aid of a story which manages to include the obligatory cataclysm (a volcano erupting) as part of the action. DMcG

Alone

(2001, GB, 110 min)
d Phil Claydon. *p* David Ball, John P Davies. *sc* Paul Hart-Wilden. *ph* Peter Thornton. *ed* Nick Lofting, Jonathan Rudd. *pd* Keith Maxwell. *cast* John Shrapnel, Miriam Margolyes, Laurel Holloman, Isabel Brook, Caroline Carver, Claire Goose, Susan Vidler, Claudia Harrison, Rick Wakeman.

●Derivative of its familiar American counterparts, this serial killer movie has something of a '70s atmosphere in its take on the genre and a formal quality in its PoV camerawork. The seriously disturbed Alex, moulded by childhood trauma, is searching for a special woman to take away the pain. But they all fail, and so become part of the problem. Whether it thrills or not will depend on familiarity with the models, but, given Claydon's tender age of 24, it's a confident debut. GE

Alone in the Dark

(1982, US, 93 min)
d Jack Sholder. *p* Robert Shaye. *sc* Jack Sholder *ph* Joe Mangine. *ed* Arline Garson. *ad* Peter Monroe. *m* Renato Serio. *cast* Jack Palance, Donald Pleasence, Martin Landau, Dwight Schultz, Erland Van Lidth, Deborah Hedwall.

●'I guess I just prefer psychopaths...' smiles bug-eyed Donald Pleasence, director of the fashionably liberal 'Haven' mental institute. We've already seen what the psychopaths think of *him* in a pre-credit nightmare: he hangs his victims by the ankles and splits their personalities with a meat-cleaver through the crotch. There's a sharp sense of humour at work in this school-of-Carpenter siege movie, even if, for all its ironic observations on madness in American society, it never cuts free of genre routine. A citywide blackout lets out the 370lb child molester, crazed preacher, military hardnut and faceless 'nose-bleed killer,' to put the wimpish assistant director and his family through the suspense grinder; but with the strength of the cast (Landau, Palance) on the *outside*, the siege machine seems to have slipped a gear. RP

Alone on the Pacific (Taiheiyo Hitoribotchi)

(1963, Jap, 104 min)
d Kon Ichikawa. *p* Akira Nakai. *sc* Natto Wada. *ph* Yoshihiro Yamazaki. *ed* Masanori Tsuji. *ad* Takashi Matsuyama. *m* Yasushi Akutagawa. *cast* Yujiro Ishihara, Kinuyo Tanaka, Masayuki Mori, Ruriko Asaóko, Ruriko Asaoka, Hajime Hana.

●Shot with Ichikawa's characteristically picturesque feel for the wide expanses of the 'Scope screen, this account of a yachtsman's solo trans-Pacific expedition – based on the real-life 94-day trip from Osaka to San Francisco undertaken by Kenichi Horie in 1962 – alleviates the potential tedium of its story by means of flashback inserts recalling the sailor's conflicts with a stern and dissaproving family. Storms, sharks and solitude imperil his voyage, but the real drama is psychological and spiritual: the film is ultimately a celebration of Horie's determination to free himself from a society devoted to conformism and the negation of the needs of the individual. GA

Along Came a Spider

(2001, US/Ger, 103 min)
d Lee Tamahori. *p* David Brown, Joe Wizan. *sc* Marc Moss. *ph* Matthew F Leonetti. *ed* Neil Travis. *pd* Ida Random. *m* Jerry Goldsmith. *cast* Morgan Freeman, Monica Potter, Michael Wincott, Penelope Ann Miller, Michael Moriarty, Dylan Baker, Mika Boorem, Anton Yelchin.

●In this standard prequel to the action-thriller *Kiss the Girls*, Freeman reprise his role as Washington DC's Zen detective Alex Cross, a happily married criminal profiler, writer and catch-penny philosopher who makes galleons as a hobby. But at present his confidence has been eroded by guilt over the death of his partner after a car crash at a dam. When Cross receives a tip off about an abduction direct from the perpetrator, he finds himself up against a publicity seeking psychopath intent on upstaging the Lindbergh baby kidnapping. Regrettably, every transition in this adaptation of James Patterson's novel is rammed home by the emphatic score and by the derivative enthusiasm of the brash direction. As Cross's temporary new partner, blonde, neat, pretty (and unlikely) Secret Service agent Potter is a moist-eyed, quiver-lipped and inept protector of a Senator's 12-year-old daughter Megan (Boorem, stoic). If Freeman's gravitas, feeling and expression lift the film out of the ordinary, Tamahori's over reliance on his star's 'natural dignity' leaves it tainted by self-conscious positive attitudinising. WH

Along Came Jones

(1945, US, 90 min, b/w)
d Stuart Heisler. *p* Gary Cooper. *sc* Nunnally Johnson. *ph* Milton Krasner. *ed* Thomas Neff. *pd* Wiard Ihnen. *m* Arthur Lange. *cast* Gary Cooper, Loretta Young, Dan Duryea, William Demarest, Frank Sully, Russell Simpson, Willard Robertson.

●Produced by Cooper himself, this comedy Western typecasts him as a mild-mannered wandering cowboy, given to bursts of song and hopelessly butter-fingered with a gun, who is mistaken for a dangerous outlaw (Duryea). Tickled by the respect that now attends him, Cooper soon finds himself in trouble, being manipulated by Duryea's childhood sweetheart (Young) until she has a change of heart, while assorted people try to kill him, bring him to justice, or beat him up in the hope of hijacking his loot. Scripted by Nunnally Johnson from a novel by Alan LeMay, the film demonstrates Johnson's belief that the writer is the *auteur* in cinema (the title even announces 'Nunnally Johnson's *Along Came Jones*'). Alas for illusions, but Stuart Heisler is clearly hamstrung by having to adhere to a muddled script which cries out for pruning, with more visualisation and less verbiage. The three stars do their thing adequately, but their supposed emotional cross-purposes come to grief on the strictly two-dimensional characterisations. Frequent resort to back-projected landscapes doesn't help, either. TM

Along the Sungari River (Songhua-jiang Shang)

(1947, China, 112 min, b/w)
d Jin Shan. *p* Sheng Jialun, Guan Zhibin. *sc* Jin Shan ph Yang Jiming, Chen Minhun. *ed* Jin Shan. *pd* Gao Min. *m* Li Weicai. *cast* Wang Renlu, Zhang Ruifang, Zhou Diao, Pu Ke, Yi Ping, Zhu Wenshun, Chen Zhenzhong.

●Made in very tough conditions in a Changchun studio just liberated from the Japanese, this was the pioneering attempt to dramatise Japan's invasion and annexation of Manchuria in the 1930s. Zhang Ruifang (later an iconic battleaxe in communist propaganda movies) plays a young village girl who takes to the road with her fiancé (Wang) after the Japanese have killed both her parents. The boy takes a job in a Japanese-run mine and leads the protests when it collapses in a flood. Both of them end up fighting as guerillas with the resistance. No dramatic or political surprises, but the performances are down to earth and the visuals are remarkable – much of it has the startling, pantheistic poetry once unique to Dovzhenko. A knockout debut for actor Jin Shan, who ran foul of the post-1949 government and was allowed to direct only three more features in the 1950s. TR

Alors voilà,

see So There,

Alphabet Murders, The (ABC Murders)

(1965, GB, 90 min, b/w)
d Frank Tashlin. *p* Lawrence P Bachmann. *sc* David Pursall, Jack Seddon. *ph* Desmond Dickinson. *ed* John Victor Smith. *ad* Bill Andrews. *m* Ron Goodwin. *cast* Tony Randall, Anita Ekberg, Robert Morley, Maurice Denham, Sheila Allen, Guy Rolfe.

●Adapted from *The ABC Murders*, this won't please Agatha Christie purists, with Tashlin's cool eye for the grotesque appropriately spoofing a Hercule Poirot adventure in which the famous detective has to track down a lunatic who murders his victims alphabetically. Randall plays Poirot for laughs, but did he have any choice with both Morley and Ekberg around? DMacp

Alpha Caper, The (aka Inside Job)

(1973, US, 85 min)
d Robert Michael Lewis. *p* Aubrey Schenck. *sc* Elroy Schwartz. *ph* Enzo A Martinelli. *ed* Les Green. *ad* John J Lloyd. *m* Oliver Nelson. *cast* Henry Fonda, Leonard Nimoy, James McEachin, Larry Hagman, Elena Verdugo, John Marley, Noah Beery.

●Senior citizen Fonda, forced to retire early from his job as parole officer, takes his revenge on the city officials by using his inside knowlege to rip off a mammoth gold shipment while it is being moved to a new depository. The film's success relies on the audience's complicity and the neatness of the robbery, plus a couple of good sequences thrown in as a bonus: a funeral next to a noisy freeway, an excruciating retirement party. Fonda's accomplices are rather Three Stoogish (though Larry Hagman's special cinematic special effects man is a nice idea), and the film too often betrays the limitations of its made-for-TV budget. Apart from an absurd epilogue, an undemandingly enjoyable support. CPe

Alphaville (Alphaville, Une Etrange Aventure de Lemmy Caution)

(1965, Fr/It, 98 min, b/w)
d Jean-Luc Godard. *p* André Michelin. *sc* Jean-Luc Godard. *ph* Raoul Coutard. *ed* Agnès Guillemot. *m* Paul Misraki. *cast* Eddie Constantine, Anna Karina, Howard Vernon, Akim Tamiroff, Laszlo Szabo, Michel Delahaye.

●One of Godard's most sheerly enjoyable movies, a dazzling amalgam of *film noir* and science fiction in which tough gumshoe Lemmy Caution turns inter-galactic agent to re-enact the legend of Orpheus and Eurydice in conquering Alpha 60, the strange automated city from which such concepts as love and tenderness have been banished. As in Antonioni's *The Red Desert* (made the previous year), Godard's theme is alienation in a technological society, but his shotgun marriage between the poetry of legend and the irreverence of strip cartoons takes the film into entirely idiosyncratic areas. Not the least astonishing thing is the way Raoul Coutard's camera turns contemporary Paris into an icily dehumanised city of the future. TM

Alpine Fire (Höhenfeuer)

(1985, Switz, 117 min)
d Fredi M Murer. *p* Bernard Lang. *sc* Fredi M Murer. *ph* Pio Corradi. *ed* Helena Gerber. *m* Mario Beretta. *cast* Thomas Nock, Johanna Lier, Dorothea Moritz, Rolf Illig, Tilli Breidenbach, Jorg Odermatt.

●The impact of Murer's film springs directly from its method: scrupulously detailed and naturalistic observation of a quite extraordinary reality. A family of four lives and farms in isolation near the top of a Swiss Alp. Their chief problem is a slightly retarded deaf-mute who is fast coming into puberty. In the time-honoured cure for frustrations, the father sets his son to building stone walls, as he himself did in his youth. But the boy's case is more extreme: he takes off up the mountain and builds his own small empire of fortresses, towers and phallic monuments. And when his teenage sister comes to bring him food, she stays the night with him… Murer's triumph is that he provides all the information without spelling anything out: he lets us discover these people and their relationships gradually. The tension between vision and voyeurism echoes the space between the tightness of the family and huge expanses of landscape they inhabit, pushing the film into the Surrealist key in which it finds its sublime, elegiac climax. TR

Al-Risalah (The Message/ Mohammad, Messenger of God)

(1976, Leb, 182 min)
d/p Moustapha Akkad. *sc* HAL Craig. *ph* Jack Hildyard. *ed* John Bloom. *ad* Tambi Larsen. *m* Maurice Jarre. *cast* Anthony Quinn, Irene Papas, Michael Ansara, Johnny Sekka, Michael Forest, Damien Thomas.

●An epic which trades on the conventions of the Hollywood Christpic without quite living up to DeMille vulgarity. The historical parallels of the ascendancy of Islam with early Christianity are heavily stressed throughout: a persecuted minority gradually emerging victorious with large-scale conversions; ideals of religious toleration; slave, female, and even camel liberation. Mohammad doesn't appear, and as a subjective presence (when he's there, the characters address the camera) he's mostly effective, sometimes clumsy as a narrative device. There's some fine widescreen desert location shooting, and a couple of fairish battles. All in all, a fair piece of Arab PR. RM

Alsino and the Condor (Alsino y el Condor)

(1982, Nic/Cuba/Mex/CR, 135 min)
d Miguel Littin. *sc* Miguel Littin, Isidora Aguirre, Tomás Perez Turrent. *ph* Jorge Herrera. *ed* Miriam Talavera. *m* Leo Brower. *cast* Alan Esquivel, Dean Stockwell, Carmen Bunster, Alejandro Parodi, Delia Casanova, Marta Lorena Perez.

●Set against the almost unbelievable brutality of an internecine guerilla war (Nicaragua, 1979), a young boy's dream to fly like the birds seems almost commonplace. In his dreams Alsino can fly, but when he wakes up everything is somehow different. The delightful Esquivel brings to the title role a fragile passion around which the Chilean film-maker Littin conjures an archetypal South American world of enchantment (the grandmother and her chest of secrets, the prostitute and the bird man, familiar from the writings of García Márquez and others) which can absorb intrusive realities as easily as the ever-present verdant jungle. FD

Altered States

(1980, US, 102 min)
d Ken Russell. *p* Howard Gottfried. *sc* Sidney Aaron [Paddy Chayefsky]. *ph* Jordan Cronenweth. *ed* Eric Jenkins. *pd* Richard Macdonald. *m* John Corigliano. *cast* William Hurt, Blair Brown, Bob Balaban, Charles Haid, Thaao Penghlis, Miguel Godreau.

●Based on a novel and a disowned script by the late Paddy Chayefsky, Russell's noisily grandiose swipe at psychedelia embellishes what is no more than the cosily familiar story of the obsessive Scientist Who Goes Too Far and Unwittingly Unleashes, etc. Harvard clever-dick (played with almost unconvincing solemnity by Hurt) blows his sensory deprivation experiments (with a little help from his friends and hallucinogenic drugs), and starts to regress – spectacularly – until he looks in serious danger of being sucked in down the cosmic lavatory pan into the big zilch. JS

Alternative Miss World, The

(1980, GB, 90 min)
d/p/sc Richard Gayor. *ph* Mike Davis. *ed* Rob Small. *with* Andrew Logan, Divine, Luciana Martinez, Joan Bakewell, Michael Fish, Molly Parkin.

●Documentary about the 1978 final of this drag contest, a monumental folly inaugurated in 1972 by Andrew Logan. Director Gayor charts each step in the proceedings with sycophantic relish, from the marquee being erected on Clapham Common to the walk-around itself. But if you enjoy gossip column vitriol, showbiz decadence, and a particularly vacuous brand of performance art, this is your experience. IB

Alvin Purple

(1973, Aust, 97 min)
d/p Tim Burstall. *sc* Alan Hopgood. *ph* Robin Copping. *ed* Edward McQueen-Mason. *pd* Leslie Binns. *m* Brian Cadd. *cast* Graeme Blundell, Abigail, Lynette Curran, Christine Amor, Dina Mann, Dennis Miller.

●Comedy about the sexual adventures of a clumsy, ordinary youth who nevertheless has a way with girls. It's pretty much what you'd expect from an Australian cinema enjoying its first phase of liberal censorship: an adolescent insistence on outraging 'decency' with a display of sundry organs, tits and bums; a story that could well have been written as they were going along; and jokes comprising a barrage of appalling *double entendres*. Ponderous at every level. CPe

Always

(1985, US, 105 min)
d/p/sc Henry Jaglom. *ph* Hanania Baer. *ed* Michael Kahn. *pd* James Bissell. *m* John Williams. *cast* Patrice Townsend, Henry Jaglom, Joanna Frank, Alan Rachins, Bob Rafelson, Melissa Leo, Jonathan Kaufer.

●This is not only the story of the break-up of director Jaglom's marriage, it's also an undisguised attempt to put it back together again. Using the camera as a kind of confessional, he begins by telling how his ex-wife Townsend left him. Two years later, they meet on the eve of their divorce, and chew over what went wrong as friends arrive for a Fourth of July party. He plays himself, Townsend plays herself, and most of the cast are their real-life friends. Slow to start, and intermittently tedious until the house guests begin to arrive, the film is an honest look at a particular kind of contemporary Californian relationship. Audiences will have no problem relating to the universal desire for love and affection, nor in identifying with Jaglom's predicament. What they might find difficult is actually liking any of the characters involved. CB

Always

(1990, US, 123 min)
d Steven Spielberg. *p* Steven Spielberg, Frank Marshall, Kathleen Kennedy. *sc* Ronald Bass, Steven Spielberg, Jerry Belson, Diane Thomas. *ph* Mikael Saloman. *ed* Michael Kahn. *pd* James Bissell. *m* John Williams. *cast* Richard Dreyfuss, Holly Hunter, John Goodman, Brad Johnson, Audrey Hepburn, Roberts Blossom, Keith Davis.

●Spielberg here updates the plot of the WWII movie *A Guy Named Joe*, replacing fighter pilots with firefighters. Pilot Pete (Dreyfuss) and dispatcher Dorinda (Hunter) are a loving couple who share a dangerous profession. Dorinda's worst fears are confirmed when Pete dies a fiery death, but unseen to the human eye he reemerges on earth as a guiding spirit to a novice pilot (Johnson). Divested of wartime significance, this process is rationalised as for reasons of spiritual growth (the afterlife appears distinctly New Age as a green glade inhabited by a tranquil Audrey Hepburn). After an unpromising beginning, which conveys the couple's tediously arrogant exchanges, the film gathers force in its examination of grief and longing. Pete must oversee Dorinda's burgeoning affair with his trainee; she must overcome deep-seated despair at her lover's death. The bizarre nature of the conflict never lapses into absurdity, thanks largely to sound casting and a strong supporting performance from the ever-dependable John Goodman. Spielberg's confident direction is particularly effective in the aerial sequences, but he gets carried away in an overblown conclusion. CM

Always for Pleasure

(1978, US, 58 min)
d Les Blank. *with* 'Blue Lu' Barker, Longhair Kid Thomas Valentine, Irma Thomas, Allen Toussaint, Wild Tchoupitoulas, Neville Brothers.

●Les Blank continues to map the USA's rich heritage of regional cultures, bringing to New Orleans street parades, jazz funerals, and the Mardi Gras itself, the same kind of effusively enthusiastic documentary sensibility that has turned portraits of the lifestyles surrounding blues, Cajun, and Tex-Mex music into full-blooded celebrations. Good-time film-making, ethnography with rhythm: the title says all you need to know about Blank's unique movie on the tributaries of rock'n'roll. PT

Alzire, or the New Continent (Alzire, oder der neue Kontinent)

(1978, Switz, 97 min)
d Thomas Koerfer. *p* Rolf Schmid. *sc* Dieter Feldhausen. *ph* Renato Berta. *ed* Georg Janett. *m* Jon Adams. *cast* Rüdiger Vogeler, Verena Buss, François Simon, Roger Jendly.

●Koerfer made an extremely impressive debut with *Death of the Flea Circus Director,* a genuinely Brechtian entertainment, and then promptly fell into the trap of making prettified political historiography in his second feature *The Assistant.* He hauls himself back into the real world impressively with this film, which has odd twinges of Tanner-esque liberal conscience-stroking, but mainly reconciles its politics and its fiction interestingly. It deals with a ramshackle group of actors who struggle to resurrect a Voltaire play about the conquistadors. Their internal problems and their campaign for subsidy from the Swiss authorities are counterpointed with glimpses of Voltaire and Rousseau, still hammer-and-tonging each other after all these years. TR

Ama

(1991, GB, 100 min)
d/p Kwesi Owusu, Kwate Nee-Owoo. *sc* Kwesi Owusu. *ph* Jonathan Collinson. *ed* Justin Krish. *m* Kwesi Owusu, Vico Mensah. *cast* Thomas Baptiste, Anima Misa, Roger Griffiths, Nii Oma Hunter, Joy Elias-Rilwan, Georgina Ackerman.

●This sets out to explore the themes and aesthetics of African cinema and traditional Akan story-telling in the context of contemporary Britain. Babs Ababio (Baptiste) is a middle-aged Ghanaian living in a London suburb with his wife, boxer son Joe, and 12-year-old daughter Ama (Ackerman). On a visit to the countryside, Ama has a spiritual experience, from which she brings away a golden floppy disc. She learns its contents at the office cleaned by her mother. It's a double warning from her ancestors: Babs will die unless he returns to his homeland, Joe will be paralysed if he boxes again. The women are shocked, the men too stubborn to listen… *Ama* is nothing less than an Afrocentric art film. Unfortunately, for all its ambition and the warmth of its playing, it works intermittently at best. Ploddingly shot and eccentrically scripted, it hits on a magical realism that is neither magical nor realistic. TCh

Amadeus 100

(1984, US, 160 min)
d Milos Forman. *p* Saul Zaentz. *sc* Peter Shaffer. *ph* Miroslav Ondricek. *ed* Nena Danevic. *pd* Patrizia von Brandenstein. *m* Wolfgang Amadeus Mozart. *cast* F Murray Abraham, Tom Hulce, Elizabeth Berridge, Simon Callow, Roy Dotrice, Christine Ebersole, Jeffrey Jones.

●Antonio Salieri, one of the most competent composers of his age, finds himself in competition with Mozart. This turns him into a hate-filled monster whose only aim in life is to ruin his more talented colleague. None the less Salieri emerges as the more tragic and sympathetic character, partly because he alone, of all his contemporaries, can appreciate this almost perfect music, and – more importantly, perhaps – because he speaks up for all of us whose talents fall short of our desires. The entire cast speaks in horribly intrusive American accents, but Forman makes some perceptive connections between Mozart's life and work. CS

Amant, L'

see Lover, The

Amante Perduto, L'

see Lost Lover, The

Amantes

see Lovers

Amantes del Círculo Polar, Los

see Lovers of the Arctic Circle, The

Amants, Les (The Lovers)

(1958, Fr, 88 min, b/w)
d/sc Louis Malle. *ph* Henri Decae. *ed* Léonide Azar. *ad* Bernard Evein. *m* Johannes Brahms. *cast* Jeanne Moreau, Alain Cuny, José Villalonga, Jean-Marc Bory, Judith Magre, Gaston Modot, Michèle Girardon.

●In Malle's second feature, he continued his association with new star Moreau in an (at the time) controversial study of bourgeois emptiness and sexual yearnings. She plays a chic, high society wife with money, a daughter, smart friends and a casual lover. Then one night, she makes passionate love with a young student of a few hours acquaintance, and leaves it all for a new life. If it now looks too much like an angry young sensualist's movie, the combination of highly pleasurable body language, Brahms on the soundtrack, and the ravishing, velvety monochrome photography of Henri Decaë proves hard to resist. The film established Moreau's screen persona – commanding, wilful, sultry – but it marked the stylistically-conscious Malle apart from his more tearaway *nouvelle vague* colleagues. DT

Amants Criminels, Les

see Criminal Lovers

Amants de Vérone, Les (The Lovers of Verona)

(1949, Fr, 110 min, b/w)
d André Cayatte. *p* Raymond Borderie. *sc* André Cayatte, Jacques Prévert. *ph* Henri Alekan. *ed* Christian Gaudin. *ad* René Moulaert. *m* Joseph Kosma. *cast* Pierre Brasseur, Serge Reggiani, Anouk Aimée, Martine Carol, Louis Salou, Marcel Dalio, Marianne Oswald.

●Scripted, like *Les Enfants du Paradis*, by Jacques Prévert, this is another homage to the acting profession. However, lacking the historical perspective of the earlier film, Cayatte's handling of the story of two stand-ins for the stars of a film version of 'Romeo and Juliet', who slowly become the roles they play, quickly degenerates into a simple tale of young love, despite beautiful sets and atmospheric camerawork. Though set in Italy, with the Fascist past contributing to the troubles of the star-crossed lovers, it is interesting in retrospect as an indication of the mood of the post-war, pre-New Wave French cinema. PH

Amants du Cercle Polaire, Les

see Lovers of the Arctic Circle, The

Amants du Pont-Neuf, Les

(1991, Fr, 124 min)
d Léos Carax. *p* Christian Fechner. *sc* Léos Carax, *ph* Jean-Yves Escoffier. *ed* Nelly Quettier. *pd* Michael Vendestien. *cast* Juliette Binoche, Denis Lavant, Klaus-Michael Gruber, Daniel Buain, Crichan Larson, Paulette Berthonnier, Roger Berthonnier.

●Following a spell in a hostel for the homeless after he is injured by a hit-and-run driver, fire-eater Alex (Lavant) returns to his open-air home on Paris's oldest bridge. There, besides his drugs supplier Hans (Gruber), he finds a new tenant: Michèle (Binoche), a middle-class art student who has taken to the streets for as long as her failing sight holds. Tentatively, Alex and Michèle embark on a drunken, anarchic, mutually healing affair – but she is haunted both by the prospect of blindness and by a previous, painful romance, while he is increasingly consumed by jealousy. Set against the extravagant backdrop of France's bicentennial shenanigans, Carax's tale of *amour fou* is even bolder than *Boy Meets Girl* and *Mauvais Sang*. It's filled with ecstatic imagery which manages not to jar after the gritty realism of the early scenes, and constitutes a heady anthem to abstracted, mad passion: at once a modern fairy tale and a cinephile's *folie de grandeur*, frequently exhilarating but never wholly free of pretentiousness. GA

Amarcord 100

(1973, It/Fr, 123 min)
d Federico Fellini. *p* Franco Cristaldi. *sc* Federico Fellini, Tonino Guerra. *ph* Giuseppe Rotunno. *ed* Ruggero Mastroianni. *ad* Danilo Donati. *m* Nino Rota. *cast* Puppela Maggio, Magali Noël, Armando Brancia, Ciccio Ingrassia, Nandino Orfei, Luigi Rossi.

●Fellini at his ripest and loudest recreates a fantasy-vision of his home town during the fascist period. With generous helpings of soap opera and burlesque, he generally gets his better effects by orchestrating his colourful cast of characters around the town square, on a boat outing, or at a festive wedding. When he narrows his focus down to individual groups, he usually limits himself to corny bathroom and bedroom jokes, which produce the desired titters but little else. But despite the ups and downs, it's still Fellini, which has become an identifiable substance like salami or pepperoni that can be sliced into at any point, yielding pretty much the same general consistency and flavour. JR

A ma soeur! (A mia sorella!)

(2001, Fr/It/Sp, 86 min)
d Catherine Breillat. *p* Jean-François Lepetit. *sc* Catherine Breillat. *ph* Yorgos Arvanitis. *ed* Pascale Chavance. *ad* François Renaud Labarthe. *cast* Anaïs Reboux, Roxane Mesquida, Libero De Rienzo, Arsinée Khanjian, Romain Goupil, Laura Betti, Albert Goldberg.

●Elena (Mesquida) is 15, old enough to understand the effect of her beauty on males, young enough to feel insecure and confused over how to lose her virginity to the right person. Her 12-year-old sister Anaïs (Reboux), on the other hand, is fat, envious and insists that, when the time comes, she'd rather give herself to a stranger. Holidaying with their parents, the girls reach a new phase in their bickering when Elena starts seeing Italian law student Fernando (De Rienzo), whose determination to have sex involves smooth talk that may persuade Elena of his romantic intentions, but doesn't fool little sister, reluctant witness to his siegecraft from her bed across the room. What if mum or dad were to find out? Breillat's typically tough but sensitive study of sisterly rivalry may be less philosophical in tone – not to mention less visually explicit – than its predecessor *Romance*, but it remains notable for its refusal to provide a facile, politically correct account of adolescent experience. As psychological portrait and social critique, the film offers cruelly honest insights. Dark, disturbing and hugely impressive, it's made all the more lucid by superb performances from the two young actresses. GA

Amateur

(1994, Fr/GB/US, 105 min)
d Hal Hartley. *p* Hal Hartley, Ted Hope. *sc* Hal Hartley. *ph* Michael Spiller. *ed* Steve Hamilton. *pd* Steve Rosenzweig. *m* Hal Hartley, Jeffrey

Taylor. *cast* Isabelle Huppert, Martin Donovan, Elina Löwensohn, Damian Young, Chuck Montgomery, David Simonds.
●Hal Hartley's movie – his most accessible and entertaining to date – starts with a man (Donovan) waking in a New York gutter, head bloodied, memory gone. Who is he? How did he get there? Was he a kindly soul, or a violent man linked to the Mob? Certainly for Isabelle (Huppert), an ex-nun and would-be pornographer, who lets him recuperate in her apartment, the latter seems to be true, particularly when a porn star (Löwensohn), a crazed accountant and two hitmen begin to intrude on their lives. A delightfully stylish and skewed picture of sex, violence and love in contemporary America, the film wears its more serious concerns (guilt, responsibility, exploitation, redemption) admirably lightly. Huppert is especially good, conjuring up a canny blend of hilarious melancholy and unexpected eroticism which, incidentally, provides the film-maker with his most poignant portrait yet of an ill-starred love affair. As ever, Hartley regulars do sterling service, while fine camerawork and plangent music add to the movie's more sensual pleasures. Enjoy. GA

Amateur, The

(1981, US, 112 min)
d Charles Jarrott. *p* Joe B Michaels, Garth H Drabinsky. *sc* Robert Littell, Diana Maddox. *ph* John Coquillon. *ed* Stephan Fanfara. *pd* Trevor Williams. *m* Ken Wannberg. *cast* John Savage, Christopher Plummer, Marthe Keller, Arthur Hill, Nicholas Campbell, John Marley, George Coe.
●From a compelling opening with all the sensational detachment of photojournalism – the random execution of a woman hostage by international terrorists – this turns into a lumbering vehicle for woolly idealism, trite moralising, and gung-ho action as the dead woman's boyfriend (a computer technologist) blackmails his CIA employers into helping avenge the murder. Stock characterisation and dreadful dialogue scarcely aid credibility. FD

Amazing Captain Nemo, The (aka The Return of Captain Nemo)

(1978, US, 103 min)
d Alex March. *sc* Norman Katkov, Preston Wood, Robert Dennis, William Keys, Mann Rubin, Robert Bloch, Larry Alexander. *ph* Lamar Boren. *ed* Bill Brame. *ad* Eugene Lourié. *m* Richard La Salle. *cast* José Ferrer, Burgess Meredith, Tom Hallick, Burr De Benning, Lynda Day George, Mel Ferrer, Horst Buchholz.
●There's no peace for some fictional characters. Just as Sherlock Holmes was given an extra lease of life in the '40s to fight off the Nazi threat, so Jules Verne's ascetic sea captain reappears (in a feature cobbled from the TV series) in the form of a white-bearded Ferrer and saves the free world (ie America) from Meredith's mad Professor Cunningham. You can gauge the level of this appallingly witless nonsense by the names given to the weapons Cunningham unleashes in between sucking his spectacles and patting his robot minions. They include 'delta beams', 'Z-rays' and the horrendous 'Doomsday machine' – this with seven writers credited, including Robert Bloch. GB

Amazing Colossal Man, The

(1957, US, 80 min, b/w)
d/p Bert I Gordon. *sc* Mark Hanna, Bert I Gordon. *ph* Joseph Biroc. *ed* Ronald Sinclair. *m* Albert Glasser. *cast* Glenn Langan, Cathy Downs, James Seay, Larry Thor, William Hudson.
●*King Kong* for the atomic age: US Army Colonel Manning (MAN-ing) is exposed to radiation during a nuclear bomb test, mutates into a giant, and is finally hunted down by his own army in this ferocious cold-war fable, which spins Korea, the army's obsessive secrecy, and America's post-war growth into one fantastic whole. Above-average special effects are mixed with quasi-documentary footage: armies on the move, test houses under nuclear attack, the colonel's skin shredding before our eyes under the blast. A film of uncertain politics and scathing cynicism, in which a Bible is shown shrinking to unreadable size in the giant's hand, and whose climax features an attack on Las Vegas, dream-city of the New America. CA

Amazing Doctor Clitterhouse, The

(1938, US, 87 min, b/w)
d Anatole Litvak. *sc* John Wexley, John Huston. *ph* Tony Gaudio. *ed* Warren Low. *ad* Carl Jules Weyl. *m* Max Steiner. *cast* Edward G Robinson, Claire Trevor, Humphrey Bogart, Allen Jenkins, Donald Crisp, Gale Page, Maxie Rosenbloom.
●John Huston, at the outset of his screenwriting career, helped to transfer Barre Lyndon's British play from St John's Wood to Park Avenue. It's an amusing anecdote about a psychiatrist whose research for a book on the criminal psyche leads him to burglary and murder (very *House of Games*). The characterisations are all a bit heavy-handed, but the denouement is a doozy, with the doc in the dock desperately pleading the validity of his work, even though that would make him responsible for his actions in the eyes of the law. TCh

Amazing Grace and Chuck (aka Silent Voice)

(1987, US, 115 min)
d Mike Newell. *p/sc* Davied Field. *ph* Robert Elswit. *ed* Peter Hollywood. *pd* Dena Roth. *m* Elmer Bernstein. *cast* Alex English, Joshua Zuehlke, Gregory Peck, Jamie Lee Curtis, William L Petersen, Frances Conroy.
●The concept that a 12-year-old Little League pitcher from small-town Montana could force the US and Soviet leaders to their knees, abjuring nuclear weapons, would seem to indicate that writer/producer David Field had been dropped on his head. He must have remained persuasive, however, since he got Newell to direct, and Peck and Jamie Lee Curtis to star. Chuck (Zuehlke) despairs after going on a school trip to a Minuteman missile silo, and gives up baseball in protest. Six-foot-seven basketball ace Amazing Grace Smith (English) reads the item in the press and comes out in sympathy, followed by most of the world's sportsmen, who move into Amazing's barn to coordinate the campaign. President Peck is seldom off Chuck's lawn, confessing that 'this job of mine can get a bit lonely', and offering limited reductions; but the button won't budge. Puerile. BC

Amazing Mr Beecham, The

see Chiltern Hundreds, The.

Amazing Mr Blunden, The

(1972, GB, 99 min)
d Lionel Jeffries. *p* Barry Levinson. *sc* Lionel Jeffries. *ph* Gerry Fisher. *ed* Teddy Darvas. *pd* Wilfrid Shingleton. *m* Elmer Bernstein. *cast* Laurence Naismith, Lynne Frederick, Garry Miller, Rosalyn Landor, Marc Granger, Diana Dors, James Villiers.
●A fine adaptation of Antonia Barber's novel *The Ghosts,* which begins with a quiet nostalgia reminiscent of Jeffries' earlier *The Railway Children*: a cosy suburban house, a death, and then the miraculous translation of a widowed mother and her children to a cottage in the country. The translator is a friendly ghost (Naismith), and in the crumbling old mansion where their mother is now caretaker, James and Lucy are drawn into a strange adventure where they find themselves going back 100 years to save another brother and sister from being hounded to death for their money. Handled with that sense of enchanted stillness which is one of Jeffries' great gifts as a director, the apparitions, the apprehensions, and the atmosphere of brooding menace about the house are exquisitely done. TM

Amazing Stories

(1987, US, 110 min)
d Steven Spielberg, William Dear, Robert Zemeckis. *p* David E Vogel. *sc* Menno Meyjes, Earl Pomerantz, Mick Garris, Tom McLoughlin, Bob Gale. *ph* John McPherson. *ad* Richard B Lewis. *cast* Kevin Costner, Casey Siemaszko, Kiefer Sutherland, Jeffrey Jay Cohen, Gary Mauro, John Philbin.
●Three short stories based in '50s comic book lore. Spielberg's World War II yarn of a doomed cartoonist saved through the power of imagination is the worst by far: it begins as pulp and sinks into pure slush. The second segment, in which a horror actor dressed as a mummy is mistaken by rednecks for the real thing, is almost worth the price of admission alone: directed by Dear with the speed, flash and wit of *Raiders*-era Spielberg. The Zemeckis contribution is a heavy-handed but enjoyable spoof, with two pupils terrorised by a headless English teacher spouting Shakespeare. There's salt enough to the popcorn, but as with Romero's *Creepshow*, the whole is never more than the sum of its parts. DW

Amazonia: Voices from the Rainforest (Amazonia: Vozes da Floresto)

(1991, Braz/US/Col, 70 min)
d/p/sc Glenn Switkes, Rosaines Monti Aguirre. *ph* Eduardo Poiano. *ed* Michael Rudnik. *m* Egberto Gismonti.
●This independent documentary offers a quick run-through of the history of the Amazon over the last 500 years or so, and reiterates the urgent ecological message that our complicity in the deforestation of this area is tantamount to suicide, but its real focus is the testimony of the local inhabitants. Of an estimated 800 tribes indigenous to Brazil, only 80 remain today. Increasingly, the Indians are presenting their case to the world media, and for the first time, those old adversaries the rubber trappers and the farmers are uniting against the government. *Amazonia* is a bit scrappy, but a salutary film all the same. TCh

Amazons, The (Le Guerriere dal Seno Nuda)

(1973, It/Fr/Sp, 91 min)
d Terence Young. *p* Nino E Krisman. *sc* Dino Maiuri, Massimo de Rita, Serge de la Roche. *ph* Aldo Tonti. *ed* Roger Dwyre. *pd* Mario Garbuglia. *m* Riz Ortolani. *cast* Alena Johnston, Sabine Sun, Rosanna Yanni, Helga Liné, Godela H Meyer, Rebecca Potok.
●A silly male chauvinist rewrite of the Amazon myth, specialising in bare-breasted wrestling matches and blood-and-guts action fodder, with occasional anachronisms that are meant to be funny. The sets are half-decent, and Alena Johnston has an exceptionally luscious body: too bad the dubbers gave her such a grating voice to go with it. JR

Amazon Women on the Moon

(1987, US, 84 min, b/w & col)
d John Landis, Joe Dante, Robert K Weiss, Carl Gottlieb, Peter Horton. *p* Robert K Weiss. *sc* Michael Barrie, Jim Mulholland. *ph* Daniel Pearl. *ed* Bert Lovitt, Marshall Harvey, Malcolm Campbell. *ad* Alex Hajdu. *cast* Rosanna Arquette, Ralph Bellamy, Carrie Fisher, Griffin Dunne, Steve Guttenberg, Monique Gabrielle.
●A formless compendium of sketches very loosely parodying late-night American television. The tone veers from slapstick (the predictable but delightfully over-the-top opening sketch about the perils of condo-life) through stodgy satire (the excesses of computer dating) to smutty silliness (*Video Date*). The overall result, unsurprisingly, is patchy in the extreme. Weiss' title piece – fragments guying the portentous scripts, wooden acting and non-existent budgets of Z-grade '50s sci-fi movies – is obvious but occasionally spot-on with its appalling sets and repetitive use of the same bit of landscape; Dante's *Critics Corner*, in which a pair of TV reviewers turn from movies like *Winter of My Despondency* to real lives, is pleasantly dark; and Landis' own *Blacks Without Soul*, featuring singing dork Don Simmons, who 'turned a personal affliction into a career', is a gem of brevity and precision. Slim pickings. GA

Ambassador, The

(1984, US, 95 min)
d J Lee Thompson. *p* Menahem Golan, Yoram Globus. *sc* Max Jack. *ph* Adam Greenberg. *ed* Mark Goldblatt. *ad* Yoram Barzilai. *m* Dov Seltzer. *cast* Robert Mitchum, Ellen Burstyn, Rock Hudson, Fabio Testi, Donald Pleasence, Heli Goldenberg, Michal Bat-Adam.
●The American ambassador to Israel (Mitchum) is placed in a compromising position when his wife (Burstyn) is filmed *in flagrante delicto* with a PLO leader (Testi). Resisting attempts at blackmail, Mitchum instead uses his wife's lover's influence to set up a meeting between Palestinian and Israeli students. But the success of Mitchum's personal peace initiative is threatened by the

fanatical terrorist faction SEIKA, who are determined to frustrate all attempts to negotiate a peaceful settlement. Thompson handles the cumbersome mechanics of this Cannon-financed political pot-boiler ('suggested' by Elmore Leonard's novel *52 Pick-Up*) with a singular lack of style, displacing the violence on to the mad terrorists and fudging all the major political issues. Rock Hudson plays Mitchum's sidekick in what was to be his last feature film. NF

Ambulance, The

(1990, US, 95 min)
d Larry Cohen. *p* Moctesuma Esparza, Robert Katz. *ph* Jacques Haitkin. *sc* Larry Cohen. *pd* Lester Cohen. *m* Jay Chattaway. *cast* Eric Roberts, James Earl Jones, Megan Gallagher, Richard Bright, Janine Turner, Eric Braeden, Red Buttons.

●New York comic book artist Josh Baker (Roberts) sees a young woman collapse in the street and rushes to help her. As an ambulance arrives and whisks her away, Josh catches something about Cheryl (Gallagher), diabetes, and St Francis hospital. But when he enquires there, they have no record of her having been admitted… Once again Larry Cohen transforms a familiar and benign object into something mysterious and frightening. He keeps things light and pacy, eschewing *Coma*-style medical horror in favour of a sharp comic mystery. Great supporting performances, too, from James Earl Jones as a gum-chewing cop, and Red Buttons as an ex-press photographer with a smart line in cheap patter. NF

Ambushers, The

(1967, US, 102 min)
d Henry Levin, *p* Irving Allen, *sc* Herbert Baker. *ph* Burnett Guffey. *ed* Harold F Kress. *ad* Joseph C Wright. *m* Hugo Montenegro. *cast* Dean Martin, Senta Berger, Janice Rule, James Gregory, Albert Salmi, Kurt Kasznar, Beverly Adams.

●Dire Dino vehicle, his third appearance as super-agent Matt Helm (after *The Silencers* and *Murderers' Row*), this time attempting to save the first US flying saucer from sabotage. The tongues of all concerned are firmly in cheek, as well they might be, given the awful script – but the humour is never less than indulgent.

Amélie (Le Fabuleux Destin d'Amélie Poulain/Die fabelhafte Welt der Amélie) (100)

(2001, Fr/Ger, 123 min)
d Jean-Pierre Jeunet. *p* Claudie Ossard. *sc* Guillaume Laurant, Jean-Pierre Jeunet. *ph* Bruno Delbonnel. *ed* Hervé Schneid. *ad* Aline Bonetto. *m* Yann Tiersen. *cast* Audrey Tautou, Mathieu Kassovitz, Rufus, Yolande Moreau, Flora Guiet.

●Closeted Amélie Poulain (Guiet), eight, enjoys the little things, like picking cored strawberries off the tips of her fingers. In the hectic comic overture of this sweet-hearted nostalgia fest, director Jeunet offers a colour-saturated compendium of her likes and dislikes that leaves you breathless, amazed and laughing. Cut to summer 1997: grown-up Amélie has moved to Montmartre, where she works in a café and has a revelation that her life's work should be to bring good to others. But what of herself? Love's destiny presents a puzzle: could scraps of photo-booth snaps dropped by handsome stranger Nino (Kassovitz) provide a clue? Swinging away from the grotesquerie of *Delicatessen* and *City of Lost Children* to celebratory fable, Jeunet brings the same mastery of detailed, allusive *mise-en-scène*, set design and colour composition to this love poem to *la vie Parisienne*. Central to Jeunet's vision is the anchoring performance of Tautou (as the adult Amélie), through whose innocent eyes this carnival of earthly pleasures, places and people is seen. If it errs towards the sentimentality of '30s populist comedies, it nevertheless mines a mighty vein of cinematic encouragement. WH

America, America (aka The Anatolian Smile)

(1963, US, 177 min, b/w)
d/p/sc Elia Kazan. *ph* Haskell Wexler. *ed* Dede Allen. *ad* Gene Callahan. *m* Manos Hadjidakis. *cast* Stathis Giallelis, Frank Wolff, Harry Davis, Elena Karam, Estelle Hemsley, Lou Antonio, Gregory Rozakis.

●Shot by Haskell Wexler in a stark black-and-white deliberately designed to lend the film the feel of documentary, Kazan's epic was based on his own novel, and inspired by the journey his uncle made from a Turkish peasant village, via Istanbul, to New York. For once in his career, the director employed little-known actors, with a welcome loss of theatricality; indeed, the entire movie benefits from its authenticity, geographical, historical and emotional, and may be seen as one of the peaks of Kazan's career. Certainly, it is one of the finest movies to deal with the plight of those thousands of immigrants who travelled in steerage to Ellis Island at the turn of the century. GA

America – From Hitler to M-X

(1982, US, 95 min, b/w & col)
d Joan Harvey. *p* Albee Gordon, Ralph Klein, Saul Newton. *ph* John Hazard. *ed* Joan Harvey. *with* Dick Days, Modjeska Simkins, Steve Thornton, Mike Olzsanski, Peter E Fisher, Joan Harvey.

●Despite Joan Harvey's provocative thesis – that US finance capital was deeply implicated in the Nazi armaments industry, and is involved again in today's nuclear escalation – her documentary has little of the polemical agit-prop of its companion in the nuclear controversy stakes, *The Atomic Café*. Instead, it's a painstakingly detailed compilation of archive material, investigative reportage, and masses of interviews – with ex-uranium miners, Navajos, many now critically ill; with scientists; with top military and intelligence brass – used to quietly convincing effect. SJo

Americana

(1981, US, 91 min)
d David Carradine. *p* David Carradine, Skip Sherwood. *ph* Michael Stringer. *ed* David Kern. *m* Craig Hundley, David Carradine. *cast* David Carradine, Barbara Hershey, Michael Greene, Arnold Herzstein, Sandy Ignon.

●In his independent movie, shot in 1973 with post-production work undertaken sporadically over the next seven years, Carradine plays a Vietnam veteran (no traumatised psycho, thankfully), who drifts into a small Kansas township and decides to stay on to repair a disused, dilapidated merry-go-round in the face of uncomprehending hostility from the locals. Clearly intended as an allegory both on middle American morality and on man's need for faith, it works largely due to the unsentimental depiction of the rural community, and to the fact that the potentially portentous plot never overwhelms the film's quiet atmosphere and observation. The only drawbacks, in fact, are some silly '60s style camera flourishes and the needless inclusion of Carradine's beloved Hershey, who keeps turning up wordlessly as some sort of elfin nature girl. GA

American Beauty (100)

(1999, US, 122 min)
d Sam Mendes. *p* Bruce Cohen, Dan Jinks. *sc* Alan Ball. *ph* Conrad L Hall. *ed* Tariq Anwar, Christopher Greenbury. *pd* Naomi Shohan. *m* Thomas Newman. *cast* Kevin Spacey, Annette Bening, Thora Birch, Wes Bentley, Mena Suvari, Peter Gallagher, Allison Janney, Scott Bakula, Sam Robards, Chris Cooper.

●After 14 years working in the same office, Lester Burnham (Spacey) is about to get canned. After two decades married to the same woman, he can't stand her anymore. Carolyn (Bening) is no more fond of him. And as for their daughter, Jane (Birch), she's just dying from the embarrassment of it all. And so the worm turns. Quitting his job, he takes stock of what he's lost, and he begins to bench press, smoke pot and have fun flirting with Jane's best friend, Angela. It might be madness, but at least he can look himself in the mirror without cringing. The best reviewed movie of 1999 (and winner of five Oscars) is a polished and acerbic social satire with 'countercultural' tendencies. What does Lester do but 'turn on, tune in, and drop out'? Admittedly, he's not necessarily heroic; in fact, the real hero of the piece is his neighbour's teenager, Ricky (Bentley), and the real villain is Ricky's father (Cooper). Having established a recognisably droll, sardonic voice in Spacey's narration, Alan Ball's screenplay tempers biting wit with unexpected compassion for even the most obnoxious characters. Director Mendes guides an artful path between desire and self-disgust, playing youth against experience, male against female. It's a shade too pat to be truly revelatory (and as a suspense film it's frankly unconvincing), but it repeatedly transcends its apparent limitations to insist, after Arthur Miller, 'attention must be paid'. TCh

American Blue Note (aka Fakebook)

(1989, US, 97 min)
d/p Ralph Toporoff. *sc* Gilbert Girion. *ph* Joey Forsyte. *ed* Jack Haigis. *pd* Charles M Lagola. *m* Larry Schanker. *cast* Peter MacNicol, Carl Capotorto, Tim Guinee, Bill Christopher-Myers, Jonathan Walker, Charlotte D'Amboise, Trini Alvarado.

●Low-key but sincere jazz movie follows the crisis of confidence of '60s saxman MacNicol as he realises that strolling through the standards with his quintet for weddings and local gigs isn't getting him any closer to his dreams of the big time. The movie lacks the big-name involvement of *'Round Midnight* or *Bird*, but has an acute eye for the everyday dilemmas of the working musician. TJ

American Boy

(1977, US, 55 min)
d Martin Scorsese. *p* Bert Lovitt. *ph* Michael Chapman. *ed* Amy Holden-Jones. *with* Steven Prince, Martin Scorsese, George Memmoli, Mardik Martin, Julia Cameron.

●A documentary about Steven Prince, the fever-eyed gun salesman in *Taxi Driver* (Scorsese's friend and associate since 1968), who emerges as a hip bore in a floral shirt, and dangerous to boot. A manic raconteur, his stories about working as a roadie for the old whiner Neil Young yield some intriguing anecdotage, but when he gets worked up about killing people with his Magnum, doubts about Scorsese's stance creep in: it looks suspiciously like another demonstration of his awe of violence that makes some of *Taxi Driver* look immature. CPea

American Buffalo

(1996, US/UK, 87 min)
d Michael Corrente. *p* Gregory Mosher. *sc* David Mamet. *ph* Richard Crudo. *ed* Kate Sanford. *pd* Daniel Talpers. *m* Thomas Newman. *cast* Dustin Hoffman, Sean Nelson, Dennis Franz.

●'Action talks and bullshit walks,' Don (Franz) tells his errand boy Bobby (Nelson) at the start of David Mamet's adaptation of his own play. Unfortunately, action isn't on the agenda. Talking, on the other hand, we get a-plenty. Talking about business, money, character, ethics. And this being Mamet, we get a lot of it twice. Don's working a scam with Bobby – they plan to steal a rare coin collection – but he reckons without the help of his poker buddy Teach (Hoffman), a seedy, paranoid waster, who inveigles himself into the scheme at Bobby's expense. In the theatre, this is doubtless riveting, but it's no surprise that it took two decades to make the transfer to the screen. The action's confined to Don's junk shop, and such plot as there is sneaks in by the back door about an hour into the proceedings. No complaints about the cast. Hoffman plays Teach like Ratso Rizzo twenty years on. He's good value, but Franz really nails the emotional core, painfully reconciling himself to his own flaws under the brutal tutelage of his 'friend'. Solid but stifled. TCh

American Dream, An (aka See You in Hell, Darling)

(1966, US, 103 min)
d Robert Gist. *sc* Mann Rubin. *ph* Sam Leavitt. *ed* George Rohrs. *ad* LeRoy Deane. *m* Johnny Mandel. *cast* Stuart Whitman, Janet Leigh, Eleanor Parker, Barry Sullivan, Lloyd Nolan, Murray Hamilton.

●Somewhat messy adaptation of Norman Mailer's novel, with Whitman as the ruthless TV commentator who implies that the cops are in the pay of the Mob, only to find himself winding up on a murder charge. Would-be nightmarish, it's merely tediously violent. Parker as Whitman's embittered and alcoholic ex-wife, brings the thing to life in her scenes, but otherwise it's a long haul. GA

American Dreamer

(1984, US, 105 min)
d Rick Rosenthal. *p* Doug Chapin. *sc* Jim Kouf, David Greenwalt. *ph* Giuseppe Rotunno, Jan de

Bont. *ed* Anne Goursand. *pd* Brian Eatwell. *m* Lewis Furey. *cast* JoBeth Williams, Tom Conti, Giancarlo Giannini, Coral Browne, James Staley, CB Barnes.

●Housewife Williams enters a writing competition, wins a week in Paris, and escapes from miserable husband and boring existence. After a knock on the head, she wakes up convinced she is the debonair heroine of her fantasies, and – hey, presto! – gets stuck into real-life intrigues, falls in love, etc. If you can suspend disbelief, this basically dippy story is actually quite appealing. It's not helped, though, by curiously varied performances: Conti's Englishman in Paris seems faintly embarrassed, while Giannini's villain just looks bored. But it has some amusing moments, despite slushy dialogue and a yukky happy ending. GO

American Dreamers

see Arizona Dream

American Flyers

(1985, US, 114 min)
d John Badham. p Gareth Wigan, Paula Weinstein. *sc* Steve Tesich. *ph* Don Peterman. *ed* Frank Moriss. *ad* Lawrence G Paul. *m* Lee Ritenour, Greg Mathieson. *cast* Kevin Costner, David Grant, Rae Dawn Chong, Alexandra Paul, Janice Rule.

●A pleasant, straight-down-the-road, cliché-ridden ride with two brothers (Costner and Grant) battling against a hysterical mother, a potentially fatal inheritance (cerebral aneurism), fraternal rivalry and fear of flying, and finally teaming up one last time for the gruelling 'Hell of the West' bicycle race in Golden Colorado. Badham and scriptwriter Steve Tesich keep the syrup and scenery flowing along nicely, and there's always Chong and Paul to lead the cheers. WH

American Friend, The (Der Amerikanische Freund)

(1977, WGer/Fr, 125 min)
d/sc Wim Wenders. *ph* Robby Müller. *ed* Peter Przygodda. *ad* Heidi Lüdi. *m* Jürgen Knieper. *cast* Dennis Hopper, Bruno Ganz, Gérard Blain, Lisa Kreuzer, Nicholas Ray, Samuel Fuller, Peter Lilienthal.

●Superb adaptation of Patricia Highsmith's novel *Ripley's Game*, with Hopper as her amiably cynical hero, asked to find a non-professional for a killing or two, and – in echo of *Strangers on a Train* – drawing an innocent family man (Ganz) into the game by persuading him that the blood disease he is suffering from is not merely incurable but terminal. Good Highsmith, it's even better Wenders, with Ripley, an American expatriate in Germany, first seen keeping a rendezvous with a dead man, then confiding his disorientation to a tape recorder ('There is nothing to fear but fear itself… I know less and less about who I am or who anybody else is'). Ripley, in other words, becomes the quintessential Wenders hero, the loner travelling through alien lands in quest of himself, of friendship, of some meaning to life. Emerging enviously from his solitude to wonder at the radiating warmth of Ganz' family circle, he is irresistibly attracted; but he is also condemned by his own self-disgust to approach only someone on whom he can already smell the scent of death, and by destroying whom he can complete his drive to self-destruction. TM

American Friends

(1991, GB, 95 min)
d Tristram Powell. *p* Steve Abbott, Patrick Casavetti. *sc* Michael Palin, Tristram Powell. *ph* Philip Bonham-Carter. *ed* George Akers. *ad* Andrew McAlpine. *m* Georges Delerue. *cast* Michael Palin, Trini Alvarado, Connie Booth, Bryan Pringle, Alfred Molina, David Calder, Simon Jones.

●It's 1861, and Caroline Hartley (Booth) is holidaying in Switzerland with her 18-year-old ward Elinor (Alvarado). While out walking, the impressionable teen spies bookish Oxford don Francis Ashby (Palin) through her telescope (both a literal and figurative device: as she attempts to draw Ashby out, the film focuses on what Palin has described as 'fragments of life'). From that moment on, their destinies are linked, but the gulf in their ages (he's 46) and backgrounds provides endless hurdles. This was a personal project for co-writer and star Palin, inspired by his great-grandfather's diaries. The restrained interplay and gentle gibes at English mores are precisely balanced against the forces of intellectual and emotional change, and the mood is subtle, conveying both regret and expectation in equal measure. A film of small pleasures. CM

American Gigolo

(1980, US, 117 min)
d Paul Schrader. *p* Jerry Bruckheimer. *sc* Paul Schrader. *ph* John Bailey. *ed* Richard Halsey. *ad* Ed Richardson. *m* Giorgio Moroder. *cast* Richard Gere, Lauren Hutton, Hector Elizondo, Nina Van Pallandt, Bill Duke, Brian Davies.

●Fascinating but botched attempt to update and translate Bresson's *Pickpocket* to contemporary California. Gere is the highly paid gigolo who finds himself suspected of murdering one of the women he has serviced; Hutton the rich, married woman who falls for him. Part thriller, part portrait of American malaise, it finally comes to focus on Gere's inability to get in touch with his own feelings, and therein lies the Bressonian theme of redemption. Unfortunately, the film is so determinedly stylish (Gere's costumes, Giorgio Moroder's soundtrack, John Bailey's *noir*-inflected camerawork), and the performances generally so vacuous (only Elizondo's detective really breathes), that it all becomes something of an academic, if entertaining, exercise that fails to stir the emotions. GA

American Graffiti

(1973, US, 110 min)
d George Lucas. *p* Francis Ford Coppola. *sc* George Lucas, Gloria Katz, Willard Huyck. *ph* Ron Eveslage. *ed* Verna Fields. *ad* Dennis Clark. *cast* Richard Dreyfuss, Candy Clark, Ron Howard, Paul LeMat, Cindy Williams, Charles Martin Smith, Harrison Ford.

●The film that launched a thousand careers. 'Star Wars' inventor Lucas got together a bunch of young actors who later went on to make it big in one way or another, and used them to populate his celluloid memoirs of what it was like cruising the strip back in small-town California '62. Too full of incident to reflect a typical night in reality, it's nevertheless funny, perceptive, pepped up by a great soundtrack, and also something of a text-book lesson in parallel editing as it follows a multitude of adolescents through their various adventures with sex, booze, music and cars. Its enormous success guaranteed a surfeit of imitations, only a few of which (*Big Wednesday*, *Diner*) match its glowing, controlled nostalgia. GA

American Guerilla in the Philippines (aka I Shall Return)

(1950, US, 104 min)
d Fritz Lang. *p/sc* Lamar Trotti. *ph* Harry Jackson. *ed* Robert Simpson. *ad* Lyle Wheeler, J Russell Spencer. *m* Cyril J Mockridge. *cast* Tyrone Power, Micheline Presle, Tom Ewell, Bob Patten, Jack Elam, Tommy Cook.

●Lang seems only moderately involved in this WWII flagwaver-after-the-fact, though he rouses himself for the challenge of shooting on the actual locations involved. Power and Ewell are US sailors who get caught up in the Japanese invasion and throw in their lot with the local resistance. It's not a terrible movie, but eliminating the romance with planter's wife Presle and sprucing up the script (from a book by Ira Wolfert) might have made more of it. TJ

American Heart

(1992, US, 113 min)
d Martin Bell. *p* Jeff Bridges, Rosilyn Heller. *sc* Peter Silverman. *ph* James Bagdonas. *ed* Nancy Baker. *m* James Newton Howard. *cast* Jeff Bridges, Edward Furlong, Lucinda Jenney, Don Harvey, Tracey Tyla Kapisky.

●For his first feature Martin Bell returns to the terrain of his acclaimed 1984 BBC documentary *Streetwise* – a mournful portrait of runaway kids living hand-to-mouth in downtown Seattle. Ironically, this looks grimy and drab compared to its predecessor's vivid urgency; at the same time, the feature gives more coherent expression to the downbeat romanticism which sometimes felt unduly manipulative in the non-fiction film. Bridges is Jack Kelson, a middleweight ex-con trying to go straight; he hopes to save enough money to go to Alaska, but life isn't made any easier by his teenage son Nick's decision to stick by him no matter what. With dirty ponytail and battle-scar tattoos, Jack makes no bones about being out for himself: he kicks his son out of bed and then out of the apartment when he brings a woman to their bare room late at night. It's a credible, minimalist performance, and the sad-faced Furlong responds well as his son. Compassionate; moving; heavy-going. TCh

American History X

(1999, GB, 119 min, col & b/w)
d Tony Kaye. *p* John Morrissey. *sc* David McKenna. *ph* Tony Kaye. *ed* Jerry Greenberg, Alan Heim. *pd* Jon Gary Steele. *m* Anne Dudley. *cast* Edward Norton, Edward Furlong, Fairuza Balk, Elliott Gould, Stacy Keach, Avery Brooks.

●The shock opening sums up the strength and weakness of this would-be liberal drama on American neo-Nazism: after Danny (Furlong) warns elder brother Derek (Norton) of intruders, the latter rushes out and kills two black car thieves. An energetic, taut flashback sequence, shot in b/w, sets up the working class milieu, the sibling relationship, and Derek's frightening but seductive mastery, masculinity and charisma – with the high sheen visuals fetishising Norton's hard, hairless, swastika-tattooed torso along the way. Disowned by its director and reportedly re-edited by its star, the film lurches from dramatic and visual overkill to comparative inertia as it traces (in colour) Danny's development into a favoured follower of neo-Nazi leader Cameron (Keach), his run-ins with a painstakingly reformist headmaster (Brooks), and, following Derek's release from prison, his tragic rejection of his brother's rehabilitation. Two things hold the interest: Norton's astounding performance, and a feeling for the male reality of reactionary working class environments. WH

American Hot Wax

(1977, US, 91 min)
d Floyd Mutrux. *p* Art Linson. *sc* John Kaye. *ph* William A Fraker. *ed* Melvin Shapiro. *ad* Elayne Ceder. *cast* Tim McIntire, Fran Drescher, Jay Leno, Laraine Newman, Chuck Berry, Jerry Lee Lewis.

●The early history of rock'n'roll seen through the eyes of its mentor, the New York disc jockey Alan Freed (played by McIntire), who was eventually run out of town as a payola scapegoat. With this subject, plus Chuck Berry and Jerry Lee Lewis (among others) in the cast, it seems hard to imagine any film going wrong. But *American Hot Wax* badly lacks a hard narrative core, and it makes no attempt to discipline its performers into an even approximate re-creation of their '50s acts. The result is an only occasionally moving ragbag, with a really disappointing final concert which conveys little of the raw energy of the period. DP

American in Paris, An

(1951, US, 114 min)
d Vincente Minnelli. *p* Arthur Freed. *sc* Alan Jay Lerner. *ph* Alfred Gilks, John Alton. *ed* Adrienne Fazan. *ad* Cedric Gibbons, Preston Ames. *m* George Gershwin. *cast* Gene Kelly, Leslie Caron, Oscar Levant, Nina Foch, Georges Guetary.

●A musical both ludicrously overpraised (especially in Hollywood) and underrated. The script is admittedly lax, while the Gershwin numbers defer to too many contradictory performing styles (Levant and Guetary) and can be patronisingly twee (Kelly with the children in 'I Got Rhythm'). But there are ecstatic moments, like Kelly's jazz eruption into the ballet as Toulouse-Lautrec's Chocolat, his pas-de-deux with Caron on the river-bank, his solo to 'S Wonderful'. And finally of course there is the climactic *American in Paris* ballet, which places dancers against backdrops pastiched from the paintings of Dufy, Renoir, Utrillo, Rousseau, Van Gogh, Manet and Toulouse-Lautrec. There are those who describe this as vulgar or pretentious, forgetting that the story is about Kelly as a frustrated artist. The sequence, besides being colourful, invigorating, ambitious, is also entirely appropriate to Minnelli's interest in his characters' emotions. To criticise this merging of form with content, of style with meaning – especially in a film-maker whose principal desire seems to have been to excite the senses – seems unwarranted. GA

Americanization of Emily, The

(1964, US, 115 min, b/w)
d Arthur Hiller. *p* Martin Ransohoff. *sc* Paddy Chayefsky. *ph* Philip H Lathrop. *ed* Tom

McAdoo. *ad* George W Davis. *m* Johnny Mandel. *cast* James Garner, Julie Andrews, Melvyn Douglas, James Coburn, Joyce Grenfell, Keenan Wynn, Edward Binns.
● A decidedly black comedy. Andrews is the British war widow who falls for Garner's cowardly marine, who is scheduled (For the Good of the Service) to be the first man to die in the course of the Normandy landings. In one fell swoop, writer Paddy Chayevsky celebrates American hedonism (as the prim Ms Andrews learns to have fun) and attacks the puritan conscience that turns fun into cynicism. The result is *Hospital* without the gore: witty despite Hiller's direction. PH

American Madness

(1932, US, 76 min, b/w)
d Frank Capra. *sc* Robert Riskin. *ph* Joseph Walker. *ed* Maurice Wright. *ad* Stephen Goosson. *cast* Walter Huston, Pat O'Brien, Kay Johnson, Constance Cummings, Gavin Gordon, Arthur Hoyt, Robert E O'Conner.
● Huston, the joshing, principled New York bank manager, Tom Dickson, animates this sermon (scripted by Robert Riskin) by sheer force of personality: a Depression-era bank-run is halted by the little people who rally to Dickson's defence and shame the selfish plutocrats on the bank's board. Huston's rough-hewn character is matched by a wonderfully sophisticated and seductive performance by Johnson, as the manager's somewhat neglected wife. She unwittingly abets her husband's discomfort by allowing herself to be wooed by the chief cashier (Gordon), who's been forced into dishonesty by his gambling debts. Beautifully shot by Joseph Walker, with several striking expressionistic touches, this breathtaking film from Capra's golden period with Harry Cohn's Columbia is notable among much else for its vivid depiction of how a bank operates and for a tremendous climax in which a sea of desperate depositors clamour for their cash. JPy

American Magus

(US, 2001, 93 min)
d/p/sc Paola Igliori. *ph* Paola Igliori, Bryan Sarkinen. *ed* Taryn Fitzgerald, Dan Crystal. *with* Harry Smith, Jonas Mekas, Allen Ginsberg, Robert Frank, Harvey Bialy. narrator Paola Igliori.
● Harry Smith was neglected during his life but, as more details about his work emerged since his death in 1991, he is now recognised as one of the great visionary outsiders of American art. A painter, experimental film-maker, occultist, musicologist and self-proclaimed urban anthropologist, Smith has been championed by everyone from Bob Dylan ('without Harry Smith I wouldn't have existed') to Beck and the Grateful Dead. For it was Smith who had compiled their most vital resource, the Anthology of American Folk Music LP set (released in 1952, reissued on CD in 1997), that attested to the richness of US roots music before its regional differences were erased by national radio. Igliori, who befriended Smith when he was living in the Chelsea Hotel, NY, shortly before his death, attracted contributions from such enthusiasts and acolytes as Mekas, Ginsberg and Robert Frank. She chronicles his most esoteric enthusiasms (he collected Ukranian Easter eggs and paper airplanes and liked to boast that he was the world authority on string figures), as well as cutting in clips from the films. Whatever his eccentricities, Smith's learning and ingenuity were prodigious. With its stumbling narration (from Igliori herself) and crude mix of film footage, interviews and music, this is not a polished documentary, but Smith is such a wondrously exotic subject it's easy to overlook the formal inadequacies. GM

American Movie: The Making of Northwestern

(1999, US, 104 min)
d Chris Smith. *p* Sarah Price, Chris Smith. *ph* Chris Smith. *ed* Barry Polterman, Jun Diaz. *with* Mark Borchardt, Tim Schimmels, Monica Borchardt, Alex Borchardt, Chris Borchardt, Ken Keen, Mike Schank, Matt Weisman, Bill Borchardt.
● Mark Borchardt isn't the average Hollywood wannabe director. The closest we get to the bright lights are this garrulous thirty-something's citations of *Dawn of the Dead* and *The Texas Chain Saw Massacre*, two of the inspirations behind *Coven*, the 35-minute supernatural thriller whose protracted production arc provides the narrative backbone of this delightful documentary dispatch from the no-budget neck of the woods: a tale of toil, tribulation and kooky camaraderie. We find Borchardt in his hometown of Menomonee Falls, Wisconsin, in 1995, gathering cast and crew for a more ambitious feature project, 'Northwestern', to be his own 'great American movie'. Over the next two years, we see him slack off, then pick up the reins on 'Coven', roping in his mother as assistant camera operator, his druggy pal Mike on sound, grouchy uncle Bill (and savings) as exec producer, and seemingly half the locals. It's like film-making in the folk spirit, with this eccentric backwoods auteur as a traditional rugged American individualist. Borchardt may not be quite the Henry David Thoreau of cinema – though his talent isn't the issue; his fulfilment's in the process rather than the end product – but he and his companions are bigger, bolder, more absurd and affecting characters than you'd usually find in fiction. NB

American Nightmare, The

(2000, GB, 73 min)
d Adam Simon. *p* Paula Jalfon, Colin MacCabe, Jonathan Seehring. *ph* Immo Horn. *ed* Paul Carlin. *with* George Romero, Tobe Hooper, Wes Craven, William Friedkin, John Landis, John Carpenter, Tom Savini, Carol Clover, Tom Gunning, Adam Lowenstein.
● A thorough, intelligent and stylish study of the superior brand of horror movies that emerged from America in the late '60s and '70s. The basic thesis, connecting classics like *Night of the Living Dead* and *Texas Chain Saw Massacre* to social and historical phenomena (notably the Vietnam war and its aftermath), is very familiar, but the judicious and generous use of archive footage and clips, coupled with interviews with the likes of Romero, Hooper, Craven and Carpenter, and a number of critics and cultural commentators, makes the argument all the more persuasive. Good solid stuff, though given some of the academic work done on how the films relate to concepts of family, ritual, sexual politics and so on, you sometimes feel the makers might have probed a little deeper. GA

American Ninja (aka American Warrior)

(1985, US, 95 min)
d Sam Firstenberg. *p* Menahem Golan, Yoram Globus. *sc* Paul de Mielche. *ph* Hanania Baer. *ed* Michael J Duthie. *pd* Adrian Gorton. *m* Michael Linn. *cast* Michael Dudikoff, Steve James, Judie Aronson, Guich Koock, John Fujioka.
● Joe, new to a US Army base in the Philippines, squints a lot and goes round the island zapping foreign types who steal Army weaponry for their own devious political purposes. He's a top-grade Ninja, which allows him to catch arrows in mid-flight, look serious, spout cod-Zen aphorisms, and don a natty black designer boilersuit and mask before kicking the shit out of thousands of Oriental Ninjas. This flaccid fiasco fails not merely due to the endless series of clichés and questionable political attitudes on view, but also because the script, direction and performances are so risibly inept. GA

Americano, The

(1954, US, 84 mins)
d William Castle. *p* Robert Stillman. *sc* Guy Trosper. *ph* William Snyder. *ed* Harry Marker. *ad* Jack Okey. *m* Roy Webb. *cast* Glenn Ford, Frank Lovejoy, Cesar Romero, Ursula Thiess, Abbe Lane, Rodolfo Hoyos Jr.
● Ponderously dreary Western made before Castle decided to ape Hitchcock. Ford delivers three prize bulls in Brazil, finding the buyer mysteriously murdered and tangling with bandits amid exotic scenery. The movie was a Budd Boetticher project; he directed the Brazilian location footage, but was replaced by Castle for the Hollywood studio scenes. TM

American Outlaws

(2001, US, 94 min)
d Les Mayfield. *p* Bill Gerber, James G Robinson. *sc* Roderick Taylor, John Rogers. *ph* Russell Boyd. *ed* Michael Tronick, Greg Parsons. *pd* Cary White, John Frick. *m* Trevor Rabin. *cast* Colin Farrell, Scott Caan, Ali Larter, Gabriel Macht, Gregory Smith, Harris Yulin, Will McCormack, Kathy Bates, Timothy Dalton, Ronny Cox.
● Yet another pop Western all 'bout dem dang Jesse James gang varmints. But this one's different: it says nothing about them. Think *Young Guns* without the jokes. Farrell plays Jesse as a rumblin', tumblin' wild card with a heart for one special gal, Zee Mimms (Larter), whom he has to leave back home when railroading Yankee capitalists come swooping for war-weary Missouri farmers' land deeds. JJ's rebel running mates include his non-charismatic brother Frank (Macht), their pal Cole Younger (Caan) and various secondary saddletramps who make up numbers. Pilfering railroad cash from banks across the state, they're singularly unhampered by the attentions of Dalton's egregiously drab detective-mercenary Pinkerton. Flatfooted and flat-focused, rarely has a film been so impatient to get itself over with. Not a patch on Ang Lee's underrated *Ride with the Devil.* NB

American Perfekt

(1997, US, 100 min)
d Paul Chart. *p* Irving Kershner. *sc* Paul Chart. *ph* William Wages. *ed* Michael Ruscio. *pd* Katherine Vallin. *m* Simon Boswell. *cast* Fairuza Balk, Robert Forster, Amanda Plummer, Paul Sorvino, Robert Thewlis, Geoffrey Lewis, Chris Sarandon, Joanna Gleason, Jay Patterson.
● Stealing a trick from Luke Rhinehart's cult novel *The Dice Man*, this has Forster bestowing his fate on the flip of a silver dollar. He's a doctor zigzagging across the Midwest – heads left, tails right. Bumping into Plummer's neurotic Sandra in the middle of the desert, and, taking her under his supposedly protective wing, the good doc probably isn't the answer she's looking for. Things get more intense when they run up against Thewlis's roadhog, Ernest Santini, an English magician and smalltime con operator. Then it falls apart… There's probably a great movie to be made according to the rules of chance, but this ain't it. After an intriguing first act, writer/director Chart gets confused by his own sleight of hand and winds up in banal serial-killer thriller territory. but at least he has an eye for casting. Forster's weary grace is every bit as appealing here as in *Jackie Brown*, and his subtle style is an effective counterpoint to Thewlis's manic energy and the neurotic tics of Plummer and Balk (eminently credible as Sandra's sister, Alice). TCh

American Pictures: A Personal Journey Through Black America (Amerikanske Billeder)

(1981, Den, 280 min, b/w)
d/narrator Jacob Holdt.
● For five years Jacob Holdt, a former Danish palace guard, hitchhiked around the United States, selling his blood twice a week to buy film for his camera. The result is this vast collection of stills, linked by Holdt's narrative and occasional interviews as he trudges through a land raddled by racial persecution, bigotry, chronic poverty and the enduring legacy of slavery. Here is America with its pants down: utter hopelessness in the land of plenty. By turns indignant, self-righteous, sympathetic and, occasionally, leadenly aphoristic – 'You can learn more about society from a black prostitute in a night than you can from ten universities' – this nevertheless adds up to a rare and moving indictment of the conditions that cause and foster racialism. JP

American Pie

(1999, US, 96 min)
d Paul Weitz. *p* Warren Zide, Craig Perry, Chris Moore, Chris Weitz. *sc* Adam Herz. *ph* Richard Crudo. *ed* Priscilla Nedd-Friendly. *pd* Paul Peters. *m* David Lawrence. *cast* Jason Biggs, Chris Klein, Natasha Lyonne, Thomas Ian Nicholas, Tara Reid, Mena Suvari, Eugene Levy, Jennifer Coolidge, Shannon Elizabeth, Alyson Hannigan, Clyde Kusatsu, Seann W Scott.
● Notorious for the ludicrous masturbation scene which gives the film its title, this Farrelly-like jock comedy begins as it means to go on, with Jim (Biggs) discovered by his parents unscrambling cable porn and sporting a sock on his 'third foot'.

Though Jim and his buddies make a pact to lose their virginity before the climax of the graduation ball, the wanking continues apace. The adolescent male is an ugly thing to behold, but ripe for comic humiliation. Weitz's film is enough to put you off having kids. The strange thing is, while it's told very much from the boys' point of view, the humour is almost entirely at their expense, and actually quite sensitive to a woman's needs. If this isn't feminist, exactly, at least it's laddism reconstructed. Nevertheless, it's still a crude piece of work, spottily acted and directed, albeit lifted by two or three outrageous set-pieces. TCh

American Pie 2

(2001, US, 105 min)
d JB Rogers. *p* Warren Zide, Craig Perry, Chris Moore. *sc* Adam Herz. *ph* Mark Irwin. *ed* Larry Madaras, Stuart Pappé. *pd* Richard Toyon. *m* David Lawrence. *cast* Jason Biggs, Shannon Elizabeth, Alyson Hannigan, Chris Klein, Natasha Lyonne, Thomas Ian Nicholas, Tara Reid, Seann William Scott, Mena Suvari, Eddie Kaye Thomas, Eugene Levy.

● This catches up with the original foursome on vacation after freshman year at college. Again the girls are the mature, balanced ones. Clean-cut Kevin (Nicholas) meets his ex, Vicky (Reid), and wants rather more from their friendship than she does; nice-guy jock Oz (Klein) has to deal with a summer apart from his beloved Heather (Suvari); aspiring intellectual Finch (Thomas) pines after his own Mrs Robinson; and Jim (Biggs) – the apple-pie lover – prepares for a visit from Czech sex bomb Nadia (Elizabeth) by taking lessons in love from nerdy regular Michelle (Hannigan). Base subject matter notwithstanding, the jokes are clever, original and delivered with some class. The film is surprisingly eloquent in emotional terms, as the boys begin to realise that losing their virginity didn't change their lives quite as much as they'd expected. CSa

American President, The

(1995, US, 113 min)
d/p Rob Reiner. *sc* Aaron Sorkin. *ph* John Seale. *ed* Robert Leighton. *pd* Lilly Kilvert. *m* Marc Shaiman. *cast* Michael Douglas, Annette Bening, Michael J Fox, Martin Sheen, Richard Dreyfuss, David Paymer, Anna Deavere Smith.

● Part romantic comedy, part Capra-corny political drama, this movie exudes so much sympathy, it sweats. Douglas's eminently decent, recently widowed Democratic President, 'Andy' Shepherd, is so squeaky-clean, his faults seem like the blemishes that make the perfect face. Why, the film asks, shouldn't the leader of the free world be free to form relationships like any Joe Doe? Because it's an election year, say his aides (reliable Chief of Staff Sheen, policy adviser and conscience-figure Fox, realist in-house pollster Paymer), and what's more, right-wing Presidential hopeful Dreyfuss will use any alliance to kebab his *cojones.* Aaron Sorkin's script goes light on the duplicity and corruption of office. This President's worst dilemma is being caught between mutually exclusive noble options (gun restriction law or green legislation) and the pressure of time. Bening's Sydney Wade, the environmental lobbyist Shepherd sets out to woo, is straight out of the Jean Arthur school of klutzy charm, without a diploma. An animated *Hello!* magazine spread: mildly diverting. WH

American Psycho

(2000, US/Can, 101 min)
d Mary Harron. *p* Edward R Pressman, Chris Hanley, Christian Halsey Solomon. *sc* Mary Harron, Guinevere Turner. *ph* Andrzej Sekula. *ed* Andrew Marcus. *pd* Gideon Ponte. *m* John Cale. *cast* Christian Bale, Willem Dafoe, Jared Leto, Josh Lucas, Samantha Mathis, Matt Ross, Bill Sage, Chloë Sevigny, Guinevere Turner.

● It's not easy being Patrick Bateman. Strive as he might to do the right thing, it's not clear anyone's taking any notice. And when they do he feels sullied, because they're all filthy oiks anyway. 'I like to dissect girls. Did you know I'm utterly insane?' he offers a bartender, but she doesn't even blink. And there are already enough unblinking Manhattanites filling his brushed steel fridge. Writer/director Harron (*I Shot Andy Warhol*) has sensibly excised the gratuitous gore at the sick heart of Brett Easton Ellis's yuppie slasher novel, leaving a provocative socio-psychological satire balanced tantalisingly on the cusp of chilly horror and outrageous comedy. Bateman may be the (barely) human face of a particularly '80s brand of narcissism and materialist vacuity, but he's also a spoilt dork without cause or taste. And while the production relies on '80s period trappings for much of its humour, Bateman's hollow obsession with body and status are hardly bygone phenomena. The film makes wonderfully unsettling entertainment; crucially – and gloriously – Bale nails Bateman with a sublimely dead-eyed and deadpan performance. NB

American Romance, An

(1944, US, 151 min)
d/p King Vidor. *sc* Herbert Dalmas, William Ludwig. *ph* Harold Rosson. *ed* Conrad A Nervig. *ad* Cedric Gibbons, Urie McCleary. *m* Louis Gruenberg. *cast* Brian Donlevy, Ann Richards, Walter Abel, John Qualen, Horace McNally, Ray Teal.

● Vidor's major contribution to the war effort, a huge dynastic saga (reduced by MGM to 122 minutes) that charts the progress of a Czech immigrant (Donlevy) from his arrival on Ellis Island in 1898 to the wartime conversion of his car factory to aircraft production. The fifty-year span takes in everything from '30s union-bashing to the career of the son who becomes a great musician, and adds up to the acceptable face of right wing social history. No other American director ever matched Vidor's sense of personal struggle, or the muscular poetry he found to express it. TR

American Roulette

(1988, GB, 102 min)
d Maurice Hatton. *p* Graham Easton. *sc* Maurice Hatton. *ph* Tony Imi. *ed* Barry Peters. *pd* Austen Spriggs. *m* Michael Gibbs. *cast* Andy Garcia, Kitty Aldridge, Robert Stephens, Al Matthews, Susannah York, Guy Bertrand.

● A depressingly botched political thriller from Hatton and producer Verity Lambert. Andy Garcia – who'd committed to the script just before his *Untouchables* breakthrough – is Carlos, an implausible South American poet in London. He is also a president in exile, and a target for assassination, though how and why this came to be remains a mystery for a good while. Hatton seems to be angling for an old-fashioned romantic intrigue, with chummy British secret agents, the odd suspense set-piece, and bumbling Soviet spies for comic relief. What he gets is a wayward, muddled mess. TCh

American Soldier, The (Der Amerikanische Soldat)

(1970, WGer, 80 min, b/w)
d/p/sc Rainer Werner Fassbinder. *ph* Dietrich Lohmann. *ed* Thea Eymesz. *ad* Kurt Raab, Rainer Werner Fassbinder. *m* Peer Raben. *cast* Karl Scheydt, Elga Sorbas, Jan George, Margarethe von Trotta, Hark Bohm, Ingred Caven, Kurt Raab.

● Far from Vietnam, indeed. Fassbinder's American soldier is actually a German, who comes home to roost as a hired killer in the Munich underworld. The miasma into which he sinks involves an ageing rent-boy whose time is up, a roving porn-shark-cum-supergrass called Magdalena Fuller, a mother with a pinball machine in her living-room, and a two-timing moll called Rosa von Praunheim. There is no attempt at plausibility, just a relentless insistence on mood (manic depressive) and behaviour patterns (ex-*film noir*). The gangsters in Fassbinder's earlier movies were sad, pale shadows of their American prototypes; by this time, they've become full-fledged Neuroses. In other words, this film marks a decisive step towards 'real' Fassbinder: the absurdity of its world of second-hand experience invests every cliché with a meaning it never had before. TR

American Stories (Histoires d'Amérique/aka Food, Family and Philosophy)

(1989, Fr/Be, 95 min)
d Chantal Akerman. *p* Marilyn Watelet. *sc* Chantal Akerman. *ph* Luc Ben Hamou. *ed* Patrick Mimouni. *ad* Marilyn Watelet. *m* Sonia Wieder-Atherton. *cast* Eszter Balint, Stefan Balint, Sharon Diskin, Victor Talmadge, Mark Amitin, Kirk Baltz, George Bartenieff.

● Chantal Akerman used to make great 'minimalist' movies in which very little yielded a lot. Here, sadly, she takes a lot and reduces it to a small pile of mush. The film opens with a fatuous (because completely ahistorical) evocation of the Manhattan skyline as a 'mythic' palace of dreams, and then launches into an interminable anthology of monologues and sketches about the Jewish immigrant experience, most of them played out in an open-air restaurant under the Williamsburg Bridge. The most ancient Jewish jokes are retold with agonising pedantry, and interspersed with ghetto sob stories, refugee memories, tales of persecution and pub-theatre-type recitations. Most of the material apparently comes from Isaac Bashevis Singer, but that's no excuse. Jewish culture was never this dull or maudlin. TR

American Success Company, The (aka Success)

(1979, US, 88 min)
d William Richert. *p* Daniel H Blatt, Edgar J Scherick. *sc* William Richert, Larry Cohen. *ph* Anthony B Richmond. *ed* Ralph E Winters. *pd* Rolf Zehetbauer. *m* Maurice Jarre. *cast* Jeff Bridges, Belinda Bauer, Ned Beatty, Steven Keats, Bianca Jagger, John Glover.

● Scripted by Richert (of *Winter Kills* fame) from a story by Larry Cohen, this black comedy is a delightfully offbeat satire both on capitalism and on macho posing. Bridges is excellent as the wimpy rich boy, disillusioned with wife and family business, who determines to change his life by taking on a completely new second identity as a cold, callous, misogynistic, semi-criminal type. Loosely structured and often verging on the farcical, it misses as often as it hits, but the performances are superb, and Richert manages to keep the excesses of the script nicely under control. Disarmingly unAmerican in tone and message, it was perhaps not surprisingly shot abroad in Germany. GA

American Tail, An

(1986, US, 80 min)
d Don Bluth. *p* Don Bluth, John Pomeroy, Gary Goldman. *sc* Judy Freudberg, Tony Geiss. *ed* Dan Molina. *pd* Don Bluth. *m* James Horner. *cast* voices: Phillip Glasser, Hal Smith, Christopher Plummer, Dom De Luise. Madeline Kahn.

● An animated feature set towards the end of the last century, this is a tale of persecuted Russian mice – the Mouskowitzes – travelling to America in search of a cat-free life. Inevitably, young Feivel is separated from his family and left to wander the mean streets of the Big Apple, encountering corrupt Irish-American politicians from Tammany Hall, streetwise Italian-American guttersnipes, and friendly French pigeons. For all its state-of-the-art animation techniques, Spielberg's production remains resolutely conservative: visually it's virtually indistinguishable from Walt at his wimpiest. GA

American Tail: Fievel Goes West, An

(1991, US, 75 min)
d Phil Nibbelink, Simon Wells. *p* Steven Spielberg, Robert Watts. *sc* Flint Dille. *m* James Horner. *cast* voices: Phillip Glasser, James Stewart, Nehemiah Persoff, Amy Irving, John Cleese, Dom DeLuise.

● When you're a cat-harassed, down-and-out mouse, holed up in the streets of New York, there's only one thing to do: head West, where prosperity beckons and cats and mice live in loving harmony. Or so the Mousekewitz family is led to believe by feline fiend Cat R Waul. Miles better than the overrated *American Tail*, this laugh-packed sequel boasts all the classic elements so often missing from modern cartoon features: a straightforward zip-zang-boom storyline, clearly etched characters with instantly identifiable flaws, tip-top voice-overs by well-chosen celebrities, and oodles of elasticated slapstick. There are moments of the goo which marred Don Bluth's original, but in general the sentimentality is kept to a minimum as Fievel and his fat-cat friend Tiger prepare to kick ass. MK

American Tickler or The Winner of 10 Academy Awards (aka Draws)

(1976, US, 77 min)
d Chuck Vincent. *p* Robbin Cullinen. *sc* Christopher Covino, Robbin Cullinen, Bert

Goodman, Richard Helfer, Chuck Vincent, Straw Weisman. *ph* James McCalmont. *ed* Mark Ubell. *pd* Falco Maltese. *m* Peter McKenzie. *cast* Joan Sumner, WP Dremak, Marlow Ferguson, Jeff Alin.
●Little more than a series of sketches taking satirical swipes at well-hammered American institutions, thi hodge-podge leaves almost everything to be desired. A runaway giant penis (offscreen) is lured into New York's Lincoln Tunnel; 'Jews!' yells a distraught father, his child seemingly menaced, as a bearded man in a black coat emerges from the sea. Chuck Vincent, his taste for nudity and sexual high jinks apparently dulled by having directed a string of porn movies, appears not to have lost an unamusing propensity for fevered tastelessness. JPy

American Tragedy, An

(1931, US, 96 min, b/w)
d Josef von Sternberg. *sc* Samuel Hoffenstein. *ph* Lee Garmes. *ad* Hans Dreier. *cast* Phillips Holmes, Sylvia Sidney, Frances Dee, Irving Pichel, Frederick Burton, Claire McDowell.
●Faced with Sternberg's distillation of his undeniably great but unreadably turgid novel – about a social climber who murders a factory girl when her pregnancy threatens his romance with a wealthy socialite – Dreiser sued Paramount. Not surprisingly he lost, since Sternberg uses dialogue and situations drawn directly from the book (following it much more closely than the later *A Place in the Sun*: a travesty where the socialite sticks to the social climber even unto the death cell). Where Sternberg does 'betray' Dreiser is in suggesting (with water omnipresent as a subtle Freudian motif) that sexual desire is perhaps more responsible than social circumstance for what happens. As a result, the second half of the film devoted to the trial – crucial to Dreiser but of no interest to Sternberg – is drearily expendable. But the first half, deftly sketching the hero's dreams and lonely frustrations as he struggles to shake off his bleak mission background and the dreary monotony of factory life, deserves to rank with Sternberg's best work. TM

American Warrior

see American Ninja

American Way, The (aka Riders of the Storm)

(1986, GB, 105 min)
d Maurice Phillips. *p* Laurie Keller, Paul Cowan. *sc* Scott Roberts. *ph* John Metcalfe. *ed* Tony Lawson. *pd* Evan Hercules. *m* Brian Bennett. *cast* Dennis Hopper, Michael J Pollard, Eugene Lipinski, James Aubrey, Nigel Pegram.
●Above America in a re-equipped bomber that serves as an anarchic pirate TV station, a motley crew of renegade Viet vets await amnesty from the authorities; but their captain (Hopper) cherishes his outlaw status, and jumps at the chance to wage a sabotage-and-smear campaign against a right-wing, female, war-mongering Presidential candidate. The lame suspense centres around whether S&M TV can expose her before the Pentagon blasts their hi-tech home out of the skies. There are a few endearingly naive swipes at Establishment hypocrisy, but the caricatures are too broad to constitute biting satire, political or otherwise. The celebration of rebellious rock mores is dated and embarrassing; the haywire narrative reflects Maurice Phillips' pop-promo background. Only the dependable Hopper, giving with the crazed visionary hippy once again, offers real wit or conviction, and even he is indulged. Little more than a well-intentioned oddity. GA

American Werewolf in London, An

(1981, GB, 97 min)
d John Landis. *p* George Folsey Jr. *sc* John Landis. *ph* Robert Paynter. *ed* Malcolm Campbell. *ad* Leslie Dilley. *m* Elmer Bernstein. *cast* David Naughton, Jenny Agutter, Griffin Dunne, John Woodvine, Brian Glover, Lila Kaye, Frank Oz, Don McKillop, Rik Mayall.
●Two young American hitch-hikers sample British hospitality on the Yorkshire moors (temporary shelter is proffered at The Slaughtered Lamb pub), only to be savagely attacked. Naughton recuperates in London, marvelling at the best the NHS can provide in the form of nurse Agutter, but his deceased and decomposing pal Dunne keeps popping back to clue him up on what's in store come the full moon. The mix of horror and humour felt very fresh back in 1981, and many people retain affection for this sly, witty movie – most memorable for the trashing of Piccadilly Circus. In the cold light of day, it must be admitted that Landis leans too heavily on the shock effects provided by Rick Baker's lycanthropic transformation make-up. TCh

American Werewolf in Paris, An

(1997, US/Luxembourg/Fr/GB, 103 min)
d Anthony Waller. *p* Richard Claus. *sc* Tim Burns, Tom Stern, Anthony Waller. *ph* Egon Werdin. *ed* Peter R Adam. *pd* Matthias Kammermeier. *m* Wilbert Hirsch. *cast* Tom Everett Scott, Julie Delpy, Vince Vieluf, Phil Buckman, Julie Bowen, Pierre Cosso, Tom Novembre.
●Forget Landis's fondly remembered jape, *An American Werewolf in London* (1981), this is a cash-in title. Scott (Hanks' alter ego in *That Thing You Do*) is about to make a midnight bungee-jump from the Eiffel Tower when a wan, tearful Delpy throws herself off. Seconds later, he's fallen for her and she's at the end of his tether. Too bad she has so many skeletons in her closet (including both parents). Waller's *Mute Witness* indicated he had the necessary credentials, but the most frightening thing about this effort is how unfunny it is. TCh

America's Sweethearts

(2001, US, 103 min)
d Joe Roth. *p* Billy Crystal, Susan Arnold, Donna Arkoff Roth. *sc* Billy Crystal, Peter Tolan. *ph* Phedon Papamichael. *ed* Stephen A Rotter. *pd* Garreth Stover. *m* James Newton Howard. *cast* Julia Roberts, Billy Crystal, Catherine Zeta-Jones, John Cusack, Hank Azaria, Stanley Tucci, Christopher Walken, Alan Arkin, Seth Green.
●Cusack and Zeta-Jones, a headline Hollywood ex-couple, feign renewed romance for the benefit of the watching media, and thus their new movie; Roberts is Zeta-Jones' sensible sister and long-suffering assistant, and Crystal the valiant studio publicist minding the scam. Crystal co-wrote and co-produced, and it's directed by Roth, who spent the '90s running first Fox and then Disney. But the film dishes little dirt. With Crystal's hallmark blend of lightly barbed sitcom and soft-centred storytelling, the film would rather please, yet it's an ugly piece of cinema. Roth uses the 'Scope frame like a plank of wood, battering the audience with clunky two-shots, unsubtle flashbacks and fantasy sequences, while James Newton Howard's score is so much soap. Roberts makes a convincing ugly duckling, Crystal is Crystal, and Cusack is on auto-pilot, but Zeta-Jones' prima donna comes with an unavoidable air of self-congratulation, and Christopher Walken's intervention as the unhinged, unaccountable auteur is preposterous. NB

Amerikanische Soldat, Der

see American Soldier, The

Amerikanske Billeder

see American Pictures: A Personal Journey Through Black America

Amérique des autres, L'

see Someone Else's America

Ames Fortes, Les (Savage Souls)

(2001, Fr/Bel, 119 min)
d Raul Ruiz. *p* Alain Majani d'Inguimbert, Dimitri de Clercq, Marc de Lassus Saint-Geniès. *sc* Alexandre Astruc, Mitchell Hooper, Alain Majani d'Inguimbert, Eric Neuhoff. *ph* Eric Gautier. *ed* Valeria Sarmiento. *pd* Bruno Beaugé. *m* Jorge Arriagada. *cast* Laetitia Casta, Frédéric Diefenthal, Arielle Dombasle, John Malkovich, Charles Berling, Johan Leysen, Christian Vadim, Carlos Lopez.
●Ruiz's version of Jean Giono's novel – about a young Provençal peasant (Casta), given lodgings, clothes and friendship by two rich philanthropists (the ineffably elegant Dombasle and a ludicrously coy Malkovich), who finally wreaks revenge on her toff-hating husband (Diefenthal) after his dire financial speculations have ruined them – is at once surprisingly conventional costume drama (save for his now familiar trompe l'oeil effects), and, by the second half, barely comprehensible in terms of narrative detail. It's as if Ruiz had torn pages willy-nilly from the script (written not by himself but by four others), such is the discontinuity and ambiguity – though the latter is purportedly a feature of the book, too. Whatever, Eric Gautier's fine 'Scope compositions of the brooding Provençal landscape notwithstanding, there's little of substance to savour. GA

A mia sorella!

see A ma soeur!

Amiche, Le (The Girlfriends)

(1955, It, 104 min, b/w)
d Michelangelo Antonioni. *p* Giovanni Addessi. *sc* Suso Cecchi D'Amico, Michelangelo Antonioni, Alba De Cespedes. *ph* Gianni Di Venanzo. *ed* Eraldo Da Roma. *ad* Gianni Polidori. *m* Giovanni Fusco. *cast* Eleonora Rossi Drago, Valentina Cortese, Gabriele Ferzetti, Yvonne Furneaux, Franco Fabrizi, Madeleine Fischer.
●Though seldom seen now, Antonioni's fourth feature is one of his greatest films, in which diverse plot strands, character psychology, and a masterful control of the camera are perfectly fused. Drawn from Pavese, the story begins when local-girl-made-good Clelia returns to Turin to open a fashion salon, and finds the girl in the hotel room next to her has attempted suicide. This introduces Clelia to a new set of friends, whose various amorous problems become the focus of interest. With two bravura set pieces – a picnic by the sea that foreshadows *L'Avventura*, and a troubled tea party – Antonioni's intensity and grip, and his vivid portrayal of feminine anxiety in particular, make for a film that has barely dated at all. DT

Ami de Mon Amie, L'

see My Girlfriend's Boyfriend

Amiga, La

see Girlfriend, The

Amigomio

(1993, Arg/Germ, 115 min)
d Jeanine Meerapfel, Alcides Chiesa. *p* Martin Buchhorn, Mirta Reyes. *sc* Jeanine Meerapfel, Alcides Chiesa. *ph* Victor Gonzalez. *ed* Andrea Wenzler. *m* Osvaldo Montes. *cast* Daniel Kuzniecka, Diego Mesaglio, Mario Adorf, Atillo Veronelli, Manuel Tricallotis.
●An intelligent, if meandering tale, set during the military dictatorship, of a man who leaves Argentina for Ecuador with his young son when his estranged wife, who is involved in the leftist underground, 'disappears'; en route through Bolivia, they encounter corruption, superstition, con artists and further political turmoil. Vague parallels with the flight of the man's parents from Nazi Germany do not help, but the performances and assured direction hold the film together. GA

Amin, the Rise and Fall (aka Rise and Fall of Idi Amin)

(1980, GB/Kenya, 101 min)
d/p Sharad Patel. *sc* Wade Huie. *ph* Harvey Harrison. *ed* Keith Palmer. *ad* David Minty. *m* Christopher Gunning. *cast* Joseph Olita, Geoffrey Keen, Denis Hills, Leonard Trolley, Andre Maranne, Diane Mercer.
●The music, the stilted acting, the plethora of hardware, all suggest that this reconstruction of Idi Amin's path to dictatorship might have been inspired by the puppet antics of TV's *Thunderbirds* series. True, the sickening truth of Amin's regime in Uganda should not be forgotten; but this testimony, like its subject, will probably just take its quiet leave. FD

Amir

(1986, GB, 52 min)
d John Baily. *ph* Wayne Derrick. *with* Amir Mohammed.
●The makers of the Mercedes Sosa documentary, *Será Posible el Sur*, should take a peek at this portrait of Amir Mohammed, an Afghan refugee now living in poverty in Pakistan, who

subsists on the income derived from the music he plays at Muslim weddings and functions. The music itself is a joy; but the film is also admirably lucid and informative, placing Amir's music in a clearly defined socio-political context, and letting Amir and his colleagues speak for themselves. No sycophantic pap here: the objectionable aspects of the culture on view (not one woman appears on screen, for example) are never glossed over, though the eponymous subject emerges with dignity indeed. GA

Ami retrouvé, L'

see Reunion

Amistad

(1997, US, 155 min)
d Steven Spielberg. *p* Steven Spielberg, Debbie Allen, Colin Wilson. *sc* David Franzoni, Steven Zaillian. *ph* Janusz Kaminski. *ed* Michael Kahn. *pd* Rick Carter. *m* John Williams. *cast* Morgan Freeman, Nigel Hawthorne, Anthony Hopkins, Djimon Hounsou, Matthew McConaughey, David Paymer, Pete Postlethwaite.

●For all its good intentions, Spielberg's fact-based film about African slaves fighting for their lives and freedom in 1830s America falls short of *Schindler's List*. Except for the overkill of the seizure of the Spanish ship (*La Amistad*) transporting the slaves to the New World, and a flashback of Africans being sent to a watery grave, it registers chiefly as upmarket, visually bland TV drama. As the fate of the 53 slaves charged with murder is determined in the courts, the politically and philosophically diverse factions are laboriously established: the Abolitionists (Freeman and Skarsgård); their initially dispassionate young lawyer (McConaughey); the pro-slavery attorney (Postlethwaite); President Van Buren (Hawthorne), keen to appease the South, Spain's teenage Queen Isabella, and an electorate about to vote; and former President John Quincy Adams (Hopkins), a curmudgeonly eccentric who eventually emerges from retirement to argue for brave, unbending Cinque (Hounsou) and the other defendants. In short, a wordy courtroom drama which seldom progresses beyond ciphers, stereotypes and salutary slogans. GA

Amityville Horror, The

(1979, US, 118 min)
d Stuart Rosenberg. *p* Ronald Saland, Elliot Geisinger. *sc* Sandor Stern. *ph* Fred J Koenekamp. *ed* Robert Brown. *ad* Kim Swados. *m* Lalo Schifrin. *cast* James Brolin, Margot Kidder, Rod Steiger, Don Stroud, Murray Hamilton, John Larch.

●First of three tall tales spun out of Jay Anson's supposedly factually-based bestseller. Family moves into reputedly haunted Long Island house: cue for bad smells, slamming doors, and a horrible sense of *déjà vu* as the movie churns out numerous post-*Exorcist* clichés. Tautly directed, but the thin material, and a dreadfully hammy priest from Steiger, effectively wreck what little suspense remains. GA

Amityville II: The Possession

(1982, US, 105 min)
d Damiano Damiani. *p* Ira N Smith, Stephen R Greenwald. *sc* Tommy Lee Wallace. *ph* Franco De Giacomo. *ed* Sam O'Steen. *pd* Pierluigi Basile. *m* Lalo Schifrin. *cast* James Olson, Burt Young, Rutanya Alda, Jack Magner, Andrew Prine, Diane Franklin.

●Prequel to *The Amityville Horror* which begins in much the same way, except that the tenants arriving here are presented as jerks: noisy, working class Italian Catholics who don't deserve to live in a Long Island WASP mansion, even one where blood comes out of the kitchen taps from time to time. And clearly we are not meant to care when the eldest boy (Magner), who has been contacted by a demon on his Walkman and is gradually acquiring the rotten teeth and gooseberry eyes of the possessed, wastes the entire family. Awful. JS

Amityville 3-D (aka Amityville: The Demon)

(1983, US, 93 min)
d Richard Fleischer. *p* Stephen F Kesten. *sc* William Wales. *ph* Fred Schuler. *ed* Frank J Urioste. *ad* Giorgio Postiglione. *m* Howard Blake. *cast* Tony Roberts, Tess Harper, Robert Joy, Candy Clark, John Beal, Leora Dana, Meg Ryan.

●After buying the least attractive property since the Bates Motel was left tenantless, professional sceptic Roberts spends the next hour dismissing various B-movie spooky events as freak accidents until forced to admit there's a gateway to hell under the cellar. A guy in a Creature from the Black Lagoon suit lurches through the gate waving his fins about, and the house collapses. A plummeting lift, seances, a spontaneous combustion set-piece and prophetic-of-doom photos are timed to keep us engaged, but never coalesce into a joined-up plot. To pad things out characters argue over story-lines from previous Amityville movies, while for 3-D purposes, wasps, furniture and minor players are hurled in our direction throughout. There's a nice irreverent bit by a teenage Meg Ryan. DO

Amleto di Meno, Un

see One Hamlet Less

Amnesia

(1994, Chile, 90 min)
d Gonzalo Justiniano. *p* Luis Justiniano. *sc* Gonzalo Justiniano, Gustavo Frias. *ph* Hans Burmann. *ed* Danielle Fillios. *cast* Julio Jung, Nelson Villagra, Pedro Vicuna, Marcelo Osorio, Jose Secall, Miriam Palacios.

●Stylised farcical tragedy about the cost of forgetting the pre-'democracy' dictatorship. A one-time soldier of the 'Devil's Route Battalion' comes across his sadistic former sergeant in the streets of Valparaiso and contemplates revenge. This quiet, melancholic film uses a nightmare-like flashback structure, expressionistic sound effects, surreal colour photography, wide lenses, lonely night-time locations and heightened naturalistic performances to weave a compassionate examination of the fallacy (as the sergeant puts it) that 'time erases everything'. WH

Among Giants

(1998, UK, 94 min)
d Sam Miller. *p* Stephen Garrett. *sc* Simon Beaufoy. *ph* Witold Stok. *ed* Elen Pierce Lewis, Paul Green. *pd* Luana Hanson. *m* Tim Atack. *cast* Pete Postlethwaite, Rachel Griffiths, James Thornton, Lennie James, Andy Serkis, Rob Jarvis, Alan Williams.

●It's now clear that Simon Beaufoy (writer of *The Full Monty*) belongs to a tradition that includes the kitchen sink dramas of the '60s and the working class cinema of Ken Loach – but with a comic kick. If there's a Hollywood influence here, it's the Western. Postlethwaite and his gang don't have to get to Missouri, but they do have to paint 15 miles of electricity pylons stretching out across the Yorkshire moors in three short months. This affords director Miller ample excuse for swooping, vertiginous crane and helicopter shots. Such visual heightening risks excess – a romantic clinch between Postlethwaite and Aussie hiker Griffiths on top of a water tower is oversold by a giddy camera swirl – but maybe compensates for a narrative that shies away from tension or surprise. The pleasure of the movie is in the character playing and Beaufoy's ear for Yorkshire phlegm. There's a surprising delicacy in the May/December romance, a feel for those wide horizons people hold so close – and a terrific campfire scene. TCh

Amongst Friends

(1993, US, 90 min)
d Rob Weiss. *p* Matthew Blumberg. *sc* Rob Weiss. *ph* Michael Bonvillain. *ed* Leo Trombetta. *pd* Terence Foster. *m* Mick Jones. *cast* Steve Parlavecchio, Joseph Lindsey, Patrick McGaw, Mira Sorvino, Chris Santos, Michael Artura.

●In the well-off Long Island suburbs of Five Towns, three teens act the musketeers of petty crime. But when a drugs bust puts one of them in jail for two years, the seeds of betrayal are sown. Writer/director Weiss's first feature attempts to relocate the themes and characters of *Mean Streets* to a relatively unfamiliar milieu. The bond of friendship, however, is insufficiently established to make us greatly care when it disintegrates. GA

Among the Living

(1941, US, 70 min, b/w)
d Stuart Heisler. *p* Sol C Siegel. *sc* Lester Cole, Garrett Fort. *ph* Theodor Sparkuhl. *ed* Everett Douglas. *ad* Hans Dreier, Haldane Douglas. *m* Gerard Carbonara. *cast* Albert Dekker, Susan Hayward, Frances Farmer, Harry Carey, Gordon Jones.

●A gripping piece of Southern gothic, with Albert Dekker (excellent) as identical twins. John, sent away to school as a boy, returns home after 25 years for his father's funeral, and is horrified to learn that his brother Paul is not dead as everybody thought, but shut away in the family mansion, driven insane by his father's cruelty to his mother when he was still a boy. In a nicely grisly touch, echoed in a later murder, the body of Paul's keeper is found with his hands placed over his ears (shutting out the mother's screams that Paul still hears); and in a wonderfully touching sequence, Paul goes walkabout in town, tasting freedom with the same joyous innocence as Frankenstein's monster when he first comes alive. But the violence underlying everyday life sparks a new crisis in him; the two people who know his story try to duck responsibility to preserve their own reputations; and soon the town is in the grip of lynch-fever. Script (Lester Cole/Garrett Fort), camera (Theodor Sparkuhl) and direction all conspire beautifully to keep the screws turned tight. TM

Amor Brujo, El

see Love Bewitched, A

Amore, L'

(1948, It, 79 min, b/w)
d/p Roberto Rossellini. *sc* Roberto Rossellini, Tullio Pinelli. *ph* Robert Juillard, Aldo Tonti. *ed* Eraldo Da Roma. *ad* Christian Bérard. *m* Renzo Rossellini. *cast* Anna Magnani, Federico Fellini.

●Rossellini's two-part showcase for Magnani's operatic excess. In *The Miracle*, she plays a retarded goatherd who confuses her seducer with St Joseph and her illegitimate child with a new Messiah; in *The Human Voice* (based on Cocteau's play), a middle-aged bourgeoise abandoned by her lover and clinging to the telephone as if to a lifebuoy. Basically, the first is claptrap, the second reeks of greasepaint, but the demented virtuosity of their interpreter carries all before it. GAd

Amore imperfetto, L'

see Imperfect Love

Amore Molesto, L'

(1995, It, 104 min)
d Mario Martone. *p* Angelo Curti, Andrea Occhipinti, Kermit Smith. *sc* Mario Martone. *ph* Luca Bigazzi. *ed* Jacopo Quadri. *ad* Giancarlo Muselli. *m* Steve Lacy. *cast* Anna Bonaiuto, Angela Luce, Gianni Cajafa, Peppe Lanzetta, Licia Maglietta, Anna Calato.

●Neapolitan thriller in which Anna Bonaiuto returns home to investigate the suspicious death of her 70-year-old mother (her near-naked body was found washed up on a beach). She delves into her own memory for clues about her relationship with her parent and the various men in her life. Writer/director Martone uses a *noir* mystery as an intriguing framework for the exploration of feminist, Freudian and social concerns, and thanks to his firm control of mood, it mostly works. Adventurous and unexpectedly engrossing. GA

Amore, Piomto e Furore

see China 9, Liberty 37

Amores perros (Love's a Bitch)

(2000, Mex, 154 min)
d/p Alejandro González Iñárritu. *sc* Guillermo Arriaga Jordán. *ph* Rodrigo Prieto. *ed* Alejandro González Iñárritu, Luis Carballar, Fernando Pérez Unda. *pd* Brigitte Broch. *m* Gustavo Santaolalla. *cast* Emilio Echevarría, Gael García, Goya Toledo, Alvaro Guerrero, Vanessa Bauche, Jorge Salinas, Marco Pérez, Rodrigo Murray.

●The most populous sprawl on earth proves a vivid barometer for the state of 21st-century civilisation in this feverish Mexico City triptych. González Iñárritu's Rottweiler of a movie slams street-level toughs up against glamorous, high society celebrity, then picks over the carnage. In the first story, lovelorn Octavio (García) turns to dogfighting to scrape enough money together to steal away his brother's wife. In the second, a magazine editor leaves his family for beautiful model Valeria (Toledo), just as an accident lands her in a wheelchair. The aftermath – involving an urban legend about a dog trapped under the floorboards – turns their lives inside out. The final story centres on an ex-Communist revolutionary (Echevarría) who prefers the companionship of mutts to people. Steeped in disgust, he accepts a contract to murder a businessman, but even as he confronts the worst, he somehow summons a shred of dignity and hope. Recalling *Reservoir Dogs* and *Pulp Fiction* – but edgier than both – this is a hell of a first film. For all its bonecrunching savagery, it's also a fundamentally moral work. The love of animals is one redeeming grace note, even as González Iñárritu makes it clear that the love of mankind is a far greater challenge. TCh

Amor nello specchio

see Love in the Mirror

Amorosa

(1986, Swe, 117 min)
d/sc Mai Zetterling. *ph* Rune Ericson. *ed* Mai Zetterling. *ad* Jan Oqvist. *m* Roger Wallis. *cast* Stina Ekblad, Erland Josephson, Philip Zandén, Cathérine de Seynes, Olof Thunberg, Rico Rönnbäck.

●In this Swedish art movie set in Venice, Agnes von Krusenstjerna is first seen being transported to the local asylum in a straitjacket, her career as Sweden's reviled writer of eroticism over, the history of her neurosis about to unfold. Born into the aristocracy, von K rebelled against the etiquette that was her family's foil for homosexuality, incest and insanity, jilting her noble fiancé for David Sprengel, an older man with a reputation as a lecher. Sprengel took over Agnes' life, managing her money, revising her books, and administering morphine to curb increasing fits of anxiety. There are echoes of Bergman in the themes and look of the film – beautifully shot colour-coded landscapes representing youthful summers contrast with weighty interiors for adult anguish – but Zetterling lacks the master's restraint. There's little sense of context, and we don't learn much about the author's work. Too full of its own importance, the film is completely over the top. EP

Amour à Mort, L'

(1984, Fr, 93 min)
d Alain Resnais. *p* Philippe Dussart. *sc* Jean Gruault. *ph* Sacha Vierny. *ed* Albert Jurgenson. *m* Hans Werner Henze. *cast* Sabine Azéma, Fanny Ardant, Pierre Arditi, André Dussollier, Jean Dasté, Geneviève Mnich.

●Azéma and Arditi are star-crossed lovers. When Arditi is 'resurrected' from a mysterious, fatal collapse, their love is intensified but confounded by his medical and spiritual status: is he a dead man? Has he been resurrected from an afterlife he doesn't believe in? Did he dream it? Cleric friends (Ardant and Dussollier) are enlisted to solve the conundrum, only to find their own beliefs compromised. It's shot in short, oddly stylised scenes, punctuated by mysterious footage of drifting plankton (make of that what you will). Both a discourse on love, life and belief, and a tale of extreme romantic love, it looks to be Resnais' most straightforward film to date. But there's a suspect, often humorous archness about it, to suggest he may be playing one of his biggest intellectual tricks yet. JG

Amour d'enfance (Boyhood Loves)

(2001, Fr, 102 min)
d Yves Caumon. *p* Bertrand Gore. *sc* Yves Caumon. *ph* Julien Hirsch. *ed* Sylvie Fauthoux. *ad* Stéphanie Cohen-Olivar. *m* Thierry Machuel. *cast* Mathieu Amalric, Lauryl Brossier, Fabrice Cals, Michèle Gary, Roger Souza, Bernard Blancan.

●Caumon's modest but in many respects impressive first feature centres on a typically fine performance from the dependable Mathieu Amalric. Here he's a student who makes a rare return visit to the family farm because his ailing father has little time left to live. Caumon's script deftly explores this prodigal son's sense of discomfort and guilt through the dynamics of his relationships with his parents, an old school pal and the flirtatious teenage sister of his now married and departed ex-lover. But where the film really scores is in the authenticity of its observations of rural life: how people talk and walk, the spaces between them, the rhythms of work, the changes in light and landscape. The camerawork is subtle in its precision, the attention to detail unshowy. GA

Amour de Swann, Un

see Swann in Love

Amour en Fuite, L'

see Love on the Run

Amour Existe, L'

(1960, Fr, 20 min, b/w)
d Maurice Pialat. *p* Pierre Braunberger. *sc* Maurice Pialat. *ph* Gilbert Sarthe. *ed* Kenout Peltier. *m* Georges Delerue. *narrator* Jean-Loup Reynold.

●Love may exist, but there's not much sign of it in the cold-eyed loathing with which Pialat depicts life in the Parisian suburbs. A brief evocation of his own pre-war childhood in the *banlieue*, precedes his portrait the contemporary reality: the concrete slabs ('barracks'), noise and squalor, violent teenagers with little to look forward to, bored pensioners ('people who are paid to be old') with even less, dozens of tumbledown shacks 'three kilometres from the Champs-Elysees' full of impoverished Algerians. Let's face it, Pialat is a miserable old sod at the best of times, but this hard little jewel of a documentary, perceptively shot and scored, is entirely persuasive. BBa

Amour Fou, L' (Mad Love)

(1968, Fr, 255 min, b/w)
d Jacques Rivette. *p* Georges de Beauregard. *sc* Jacques Rivette, Marilu Parolini. *ph* Alain Levent, Etienne Becker. *ed* Nicole Lubtchansky. *m* Jean-Claude Eloy. *cast* Bulle Ogier, Jean-Pierre Kalfon, Josée Destoop, Michéle Moretti, André S Labarthe, Dennis Berry.

●Rivette's claim to the status of a key innovator in contemporary cinema began with this film; it marks the beginning of his distrust of the mechanisms of fiction. A theatre director (Kalfon) mounts a production of Racine's *Andromache* starring his wife (Ogier), under the mechanical eyes of a TV documentary unit. Wife cracks under the strain and withdraws; director's former mistress takes the part. The field is thus cleared for confrontations betwen husband and wife, between theatre and TV, between ordered passion and mad love. All confrontations duly occur (plus a clash between 16mm filmstock for the theatre scenes and 35mm for the rest), at a length that exceeds all obvious expectation – and thus begins to reach areas that conventional movies don't touch. Finally, even the pretentious title is justified by the shattering, improvised ending, which sees Kalfon and Ogier demolish each other and their apartment. TR

Amour, l'Après-midi, L'

see Love in the Afternoon

Amour, l'Argent, l'Amour, L'

(2000, Ger, 134 min)
d Philip Gröning. *p* Philip Gröning, Res Balzli, Dieter Fahrer, Françoise Gazio. *sc* Philip Gröning, Michael Busch. *ph* Sophie Maintigneux, Max Jonathan Siberstein. *ed* Max Jonathan Siberstein, Valdis Oskarsdottir. *pd* Peter Menne. *cast* Sabine Timoteo, Florian Stetter, Dierk Prawdzik, Gerhard Fries, Thomas Gimbel, Michael Schech, Marquard Bohm.

●Classified as 'experimenta' by the London Film Festival, this follows two feckless young fugitives from the underclass on the road to nowhere obvious. He's an out-of-work labourer with his arm in a cast, she's a happy-go-lucky prostitute, and together they drift through the German lowlands, sometimes roughing it, sometimes selling their services, eventually reaching France and the sea. It's moody and watchable in a languorous sort of way (with doe-eyed soundtrack music from Velvet Underground and Yo La Tengo), but vague and unformulated if you're looking for drama or any sense of import. NB

Amour par terre, L' (Love on the Ground)

(1984, Fr, 127 min)
d Jacques Rivette. *p* Martine Marignac. *sc* Pascal Bonitzer, Marilù Parolini, Jacques Rivette, Suzanne Schiffman. *ph* William Lubtchansky. *ad* Roberto Plate. *cast* Geraldine Chaplin, Jane Birkin, André Dussollier, Jean-Pierre Kalfon, Laszlo Szabo, Facundo Bo, Sandra Montaigu.

●Chaplin and Birkin are actresses taken up by an enigmatic playwright (Kalfon) and installed in his fabulous suburban mansion in order to perform a play (whose last act is still unknown) for one of his house parties. With the agency of a magician and clairvoyant, melodrama gradually seeps into both life and the rehearsals of fiction; the *affaires* promoted between playwright, magician and actresses lead to premonitions, hallucination, jealousy and dark secrets, all of them threaded into a weird finale of reconciliation. As with *Céline and Julie*, the concern here is less with the contrast between fiction and reality, more with the invention of a magical realm from which reality is rigorously excluded: enchantment is discovered not from fairytale, but within life itself. Rivette creates a unique world and language, answerable finally only to himself. CPea

Amsterdam Kill, The

(1977, HK, 93 min)
d Robert Clouse. *p* André Morgan. *sc* Robert Clouse, Gregory Teifer. *ph* Alan Hume. *ed* Allan Holzman. *ad* John Blezard. *m* Hal Schaffer. *cast* Robert Mitchum, Bradford Dillman, Richard Egan, Leslie Nielsen, Keye Luke.

●Dim attempt to re-establish Hong Kong's international reputation. Mitchum plays a discredited agent who acts as liaison between ageing Triad boss who wants out and the US Drug Enforcement Agency. Results are predictably bloody, but with no one thinking beyond set pieces and international locations, the film quickly stagnates in its own violence. CPe

Amsterdamned

(1988, Neth, 113 min)
d Dick Maas. *p* Laurens Geels, Dick Maas. *sc* Dick Maas. *ph* Marc Felperlaan. *ed* Hans van Dongen. *pd* Dick Schillemans. *m* Dick Maas. *cast* Huub Stapel, Monique van de Ven, Serge-Henri Valcke, Tanneke Hartsuiker, Wim Zomer, Hidde Maas, Lou Landré, Tatum Dagelet.

●Having unleashed a killer elevator on us in *The Lift*, Dick Maas here comes up with the authentically crazy notion of a psycho-diver. By prowling (paddling?) the hundreds of canals which traverse the Dutch capital, our wetsuit wacko easily escapes detection, and can engage concurrently in his two favourite sports: diving and murder. Much of the pleasure derives from the outrageous set pieces the film wrings from a familiar formula. Aside from the eccentric psychopath, we have the divorced cop and his obnoxious kid, the bungling sidekick, the blatantly obvious suspect, and the woman relegated to an 'ooh, aargh' role. Yet Maas has talent to burn: snappy dialogue (he wrote the screenplay); brooding *Jaws*-type atmospherics (and music); and stylish execution(s). Like Dario Argento's early slasher thrillers, as a murder mystery it is frankly naff (there is at least one red herring too many); but as a spectacle it is fascinatingly gruesome. Maas murder may not be to everyone's taste, but those who take to tomato ketchup with relish – this one's for you. TCh

Amy Foster (aka Swept from the Sea – The Story of Amy Foster)

(1997, GB/US/Fr, 112 min)
d Beeban Kidron. *p* Polly Tapson, Charles Steel, Beeban Kidron. *sc* Tim Willocks. *ph* Dick Pope. *ed* Alex MacKie. *pd* Simon Holland. *m* John Barry. *cast* Vincent Perez, Rachel Weisz, Ian McKellen, Joss Ackland, Kathy Bates, Tom Bell, Zoë Wanamaker, Tony Haygarth.

●Amy (Weisz) is a Cornish servant girl, shunned by her parents, and animated only by the sight of the sea and the treasures it sweeps into her arms. A Ukrainian ship is wrecked and Amy assumes possession of Yanko (Perez), the sole survivor. He's happy with the arrangement, but Amy's community is against the match. She is a woman both behind the times and ahead of them: an unwitting revolutionary who manages to undo the punitive logic of 'civilised' society. Kidron's direction is alternately flat and glossily overwrought; the sets jar; and Tim Willocks' screenplay has drained Joseph Conrad's story of its tortuous peculiarity. This could be any TV friendly costume drama, complete with hair-centric stars and dodgy accents. CO'Su

Anaconda

(1997, US/Braz, 89 min)
d Luis Llosa. *p* Verna Harrah, Leonard Rabinowitz, Carole Little. *sc* Hans Bauer, Jim Cash, Jack Epps. *ph* Bill Butler. *ed* Michael R Miller. *ad* Barry Chusid. *m* Randy Edelman. *cast* Jennifer Lopez, Ice Cube, Jon Voight, Eric Stoltz, Jonathan Hyde, Owen Wilson, Kari Wuhrer.

●A seven-strong documentary film crew, sailing the mighty Amazon in search of a lost tribe, pick up stranded cruiser Voight. Before long he's telling them of his encounter with the elusive Shirishama tribe, and guiding them down unfamiliar tributaries. He's also beginning to act strangely, and worse, the direction in which they're heading is home to a 40ft man-eating snake. And then there were six, five, four... Voight, permanently OTT, wears a fixed scowl and tries a funny accent. The plot, meanwhile, meanders more than the river, through a series of time-filling false alarms before we get down to the big signposted main course. One never questions the realism of the remarkable animatronic and computer-generated effects, but it's hard to credit a snake that screams. DA

Analyze This

(1999, US, 103 min)
d Harold Ramis. *p* Paula Weinstein, Jane Rosenthal. *sc* Peter Tolan, Harold Ramis, Kenneth Lonergan. *ph* Stuart Dryburgh. *ed* Christopher Tellefsen, Craig P Herring. *pd* Wynn Thomas. *m* Howard Shore. *cast* Robert De Niro, Billy Crystal, Lisa Kudrow, Joe Viterelli, Chazz Palminteri, Joe Rigano, Molly Shannon.

●After the joys of Ramis' concept comedies *Groundhog Day* and *Multiplicity*, this weary Mob comedy casts De Niro as the bigtime Mafia man with an anxiety attack, and Crystal as the small-time Jewish shrink pressed into reluctant service, and follows through with resolute predictability. One or two jokes score easy points, usually at the expense of a gangster's arrested emotional development, but generally the comedy is heavy and the use of the stars lazy and clichéd, with the film smuggly dropping intermittent mugging references to *The Godfather*. A glance at *Grosse Pointe Blank* and *What About Bob?* and their comic spin on anxiety and persecution shows how good this material ought to be. NB

Anastasia

(1956, GB, 105 min)
d Anatole Litvak. *p* Buddy Adler. *sc* Arthur Laurents. *ph* Jack Hildyard. *ed* Bert Bates. *ad* Andre Andrejew. *m* Alfred Newman. *cast* Ingrid Bergman, Yul Brynner, Helen Hayes, Akim Tamiroff, Martita Hunt, Felix Aylmer, Serge Pitoeff.

●Paris, 1928: When White Russian general Brynner picks out amnesiac peasant Bergman to claim she's the daughter of the murdered Tsar, little does he know how well she'll stand up to a grilling at the hands of Hayes' formidable Empress Dowager. Glossy 'Scope historical puzzler (from the play by Marcelle Maurette and Guy Bolton) with Oscar-winning Bergman on regal form in her first Hollywood picture after her European adventure with Rossellini. TJ

Anastasia

(1997, US, 94 min)
d/p Don Bluth, Gary Goldman. *sc* Susan Gauthier, Bruce Graham, Bob Tzudiker, Noni White. *m* David Newman. *songs* Stephen Flaherty, Lynn Ahrens. *cast* voices: Meg Ryan, John Cusack, Kelsey Grammer, Christopher Lloyd, Bernadette Peters, Angela Lansbury, Hank Azaria.

●This engaging love story is free of candy flavoured characters (though not some execrable songs), and the animation's a ten-fold improvement on Bluth's recent offerings (*The Pebble and the Penguin*, etc). This being a children's film, the story of the legendary disappearance of the Romanov princess has been altered to accommodate mad magician Rasputin (voiced by Lloyd), who instigates public revolt by casting a spell on the entire royal family. As destructive forces rage in the streets of 1917 St Petersburg, panic sweeps the Imperial Palace and the royal family flees. Ten years later, confused orphan Anya (Ryan) wanders the same streets, unsure of her identity and dogged by memories of a privileged childhood. Enter con-man Dimitri (Cusack), who starts by exploiting 'Anastasia', and ends by falling in love with her. Bluth has rediscovered the ingredients of quality mainstream animation: depth and movement are more in evidence, and the action sequences are expertly staged, notably a harrowing train crash. DA

Anatahan

see Saga of Anatahan, The

Anatolian Smile, The

see America, America

Anatomy of a Murder

(1959, US, 160 min, b/w)
d/p Otto Preminger. *sc* Wendell Mayes. *ph* Sam Leavitt. *ed* Louis Loeffler. *pd* Boris Leven. *m* Duke Ellington. *cast* James Stewart, Ben Gazzara, Lee Remick, Eve Arden, Arthur O'Connell, George C Scott, Kathryn Grant.

●One of Preminger's most compelling and perfectly realised films (with a terrific Ellington score). A long, detailed account of the efforts of a smalltown lawyer (Stewart) to defend an army sergeant (Gazzara) accused of murdering the bartender who, it is claimed, raped his wife (Remick), it's remarkable for the cool, crystal clear direction, concentrating on the mechanical processes and professional performances guiding the trial, and for the superb acting. Chilling, ironic and sceptical, it is far less confident in the law than most courtroom dramas, which makes one suspect that it was this probing cynicism rather than the 'daring' use of words that caused controversy at the time of release. GA

Anchoress (aka La Recluse)

(1993, GB/Bel, 107 min, b/w)
d Christopher Newby. *p* Paul Breuls, Ben Gibson. *sc* Judith Stanley-Smith, Christine Watkins. *ph* Michel Baudour. *ed* Brand Thumim. *pd* Niek Kortekaas. *cast* Natalie Morse, Julie T Wallace, Eugene Bervoets, Peter Postlethwaite, Toyah Wilcox, Christopher Eccleston.

●This directorial debut convinces in its exploration of spiritual ferment, but fumbles the task of assembling a coherent narrative. In a medieval community, a peasant (Morse) becomes obsessed with the local chapel's statue of the Virgin, and, pronounced a holy anchoress, is walled up in the building with the object of her passion. With only a small window to the world, the girl creates a rich interior domain for herself, but in the process becomes something of a tourist attraction and longs for freedom. The film is most powerful during the cell-bound mid-section, contrasting the heroine's innocence with the machinations of Church and State. Aided by lustrous b/w cinematography, Newby delineates the textures of her pastoral surroundings to hallucinatory effect. TJ

Anchors Aweigh

(1945, US, 139 min)
d George Sidney. *p* Joe Pasternak. *sc* Isobel Lennart. *ph* Robert Planck, Charles Boyle. *ed* Adrienne Fazan. *ad* Cedric Gibbons, Randall Duell. *m* Georgie Stoll. *songs* Ralph Freed, Sammy Fain, Julie Styne. *cast* Gene Kelly, Frank Sinatra, Kathryn Grayson, José Iturbi, Leon Ames, Henry Armetta, Dean Stockwell.

●Something of a precursor to *On the Town*, with Kelly and Sinatra as sailors rushing round town (in this case Hollywood) and anxious to score with women. Thunderously patriotic (the navy is wonderful) and sentimental (kids are wonderful), it's heavily dependent on Kelly's charm and Sinatra's supposed little-boy appeal, the combination of which fuels the running gags and almost saves the scenes with Grayson. The best item is Kelly's dance with Jerry, of 'Tom and Jerry'; otherwise, in a so-so score, Kelly has his first number with a child, and Sinatra sings 'I Fall in Love Too Easily' like he means it. SG

Andalusian Dog, An

see Chien Andalou, Un

Anderson Tapes, The

(1971, US, 99 min)
d Sidney Lumet. *p* Robert M Weitman. *sc* Frank R Pierson. *ph* Arthur J Ornitz. *ed* Joanne Burke. *pd* Benjamin J Kasazkow. *m* Quincy Jones. *cast* Sean Connery, Dyan Cannon, Martin Balsam, Ralph Meeker, Alan King, Christopher Walken.

●Watchable but curiously muffled thriller in which Connery masterminds a plan to rob an entire apartment block, unaware that everybody involved is under surveillance by somebody or other. The ironies never really focus, and Lumet's hesitant direction undermines the tension. TM

And God Created Woman

see Et Dieu Créa la Femme

And God Created Woman

(1987, US, 98 min)
d Roger Vadim. *p* George Braunstein, Ron Hamady. *sc* RJ Stewart. *ph* Stephen M Katz. *ed* Suzanne Pettit. *pd* Victor Kempster. *m* Thomas Chase. *cast* Rebecca De Mornay, Vincent Spano, Frank Langella, Donovan Leitch, Judith Chapman, Jaime McEnnan.

●Vadim's update of his sensational 1956 debut offers a completely new scenario, but even so a sense of *déjà vu* prevails. Following a failed escape attempt, prisoner De Mornay is advised by slimy would-be governor Langella to slip out the back door, by marrying a solid member of the community; she therefore makes a deal with hunky carpenter Spano, with whom she has already enjoyed an encounter in the prison gym. She gets her freedom, Langella gets some useful publicity, and Spano gets $5,000 plus someone to look after him, his teenage brother, and his five-year-old son while De Mornay lives out her 12-month parole. But De Mornay's no-nookie rule provokes emotional friction, while she prefers practising with her newly formed rock band to playing domestic slave. Nevertheless, the couple survive their spats, as well as Langella's shifty manoeuvring, to resolve their differences in a corny fairytale ending. Were it not for the fleshy couplings punctuating the slim storyline, Vadim's flimsy moral tale would simply blow away. NF

...and justice for all

(1979, US, 119 min)
d Norman Jewison. *p* Norman Jewison, Patrick Palmer. *sc* Valerie Curtin, Barry Levinson. *ph* Victor J Kemper. *ed* John F Burnett. *pd* Richard Macdonald. *m* David Grusin. *cast* Al Pacino, Jack Warden, John Forsythe, Lee Strasberg, Christine Lahti, Sam Levene, Jeffrey Tambor.

●*...and justice for all* aims to do for the American judicial system what *All the President's Men* did for the presidency, and if Jewison had only maintained the tone of the superb original screenplay, he might have succeeded. The script's view of the behind-the-scenes wheeling and dealing in the criminal courts is both fascinating and horrifying: it employs a series of sharply observed episodes to expose a mountain of lies, chicanery, corruption and legalised sadism as Pacino's attorney battles to save various clients from the terrifying whims of the system. But, almost as if he were scared of becoming too serious, Jewison alternates some incredibly powerful moments with breezy farce, and also proceeds to drown the whole thing under a sub-disco score. The result is a bit like finding lumps of condensed milk in your gravy. DP

And Life Goes On... (Zendegi Va Digar Hich...)

(1992, Iran, 108 min)
d Abbas Kiarostami. *p* Ali Reza Zarrin. *sc* Abbas Kiarostami. *ph* Homayoon Payvar. *cast* Farhad Kherdamend, Buba Bayour, Hocine Rifahi, Ferhendeh Feydi, Mahrem Feydi, Bahrovz Aydini.

●Despite its narrative simplicity, this is more complex than Abbas Kiarostami's earlier film, *Where Is My Friend's House?* (1987). Learning that the region in which he shot *Where Is...* has been devastated by an earthquake, the director (played by an actor) leaves Tehran, along with his son, to see whether his actors, especially the boy who played Ahmed, have survived. Quitting the clogged main road for perilous mountain routes, he's happy to discuss with various locals the details of the disaster, and its meaning (has God abandoned them?) – but will he reach his destination? Straddling the divide between fiction and documentary with graceful ease, this is both a subtle study in the ethics of film-making, and a compassionate (but never mawkish or depressing) portrait of courage and determination in the face of overwhelming grief and hardship. GA

And Now for Something Completely Different

(1971, GB, 88 min)
d Ian Macnaughton. *p* Patricia Casey. *sc* Graham Chapman, John Cleese, Terry Gilliam, Eric Idle, Terry Jones. Michael Palin. *ph* David Muir. *ed* Thom Noble. *ad* Colin Grimes. *cast* Graham Chapman, John Cleese, Terry Gilliam, Eric Idle, Terry Jones, Michael Palin.
●Hardly very different, since this first outing for *Monty Python* on the big screen consists of a rehash of TV sketches hopefully aimed at the American market. All good stuff, though, and notably featuring 'The Upper Class Twit of the Year Race', 'Hell's Grannies' and 'The Townswomen's Guild Reconstruction of Pearl Harbor'. TM

And Now My Love (Toute une Vie)

(1974, Fr/It, 150 min)
d Claude Lelouch. *p* Pierre Pardon. *sc* Claude Lelouch, Pierre Uytterhoeven. *ph* Jean Collomb. *ed* Georges Klotz. *ad* François de Lamothe. *m* Francis Lai. *cast* Marthe Keller, André Dussollier, Charles Denner, Carla Gravina, Charles Gérard, Gilbert Bécaud.
●A film so sentimental and implausible that its emotional indulgence almost seems avant-garde as it presents the interplay of various cultural/historical/emotional threads that cause a millionairess and a film-maker to fall in love at first sight. It is stylistically dazzling, but the feelings and the characters are so shallow they could almost be part of some satire on the bourgeoisie. The fact that it's clearly autobiographical makes it even more remarkable. Cut by nearly 30 minutes for English and American release: the mind boggles. DP

...And Now the Screaming Starts! (aka Fengriffen)

(1973, GB, 91 min)
d Roy Ward Baker. *p* Max J Rosenberg, Milton Subotsky. *sc* Roger Marshall. *ph* Denys Coop. *ed* Peter Tanner. *ad* Tony Curtis. *m* Douglas Gamley. *cast* Peter Cushing, Herbert Lom, Patrick Magee, Stephanie Beacham, Ian Ogilvy, Geoffrey Whitehead.
●Disastrous feature from omnibus specialists Amicus. It's sins-of-the-fathers time again, with a disembodied hand avenging the rape of a servant's bride by an ancestral member of the Fengriffen household. The sufferers of the curse are Ogilvy and his pregnant bride Beacham, but fortunately Dr Pope (Cushing) is on hand to explain all. The film might more accurately have been called *The Screaming Never Stops*, because Beacham screeches incessantly throughout, an effect more wearing than suspenseful. NF

And Now Tomorrow

(1944, US, 85 min, b/w)
d Irving Pichel. *p* Fred Kohlmar. *sc* Frank Partos, Raymond Chandler. *ph* Daniel L Fapp. *ed* Duncan Mansfield. *ad* Hans Dreier, Hal Pereira. *m* Victor Young. *cast* Alan Ladd, Loretta Young, Susan Hayward, Barry Sullivan, Beulah Bondi, Cecil Kellaway.
●Young, left deaf by meningitis, is cured by Dr Ladd with an untried serum. She's a socialite, he's from the wrong side of the tracks, but they settle their differences by falling in love. Romantic twaddle, co-scripted by Raymond Chandler, though his touch is evident only in the briefly laconic scene of Ladd's first encounter with Young in a diner. TM

Andre

(1994, US, 95 min)
d George Miller. *p* Annette Handley, Adam Shapiro. *sc* Dana Baratta. *ph* Thomas Burstyn. *ed* Harry Hitner. *pd* William Elliott. *m* Bruce Rowland. *cast* Keith Carradine, Tina Majorino, Chelsea Field, Keith Szarabajka, Shane Meier, Aidan Pendleton, Shirley Broderick, Andrea Libman.
●Andre is an abandoned new-born seal discovered by Maine harbour master Harry Whitney (Carradine) and his seven-year-old daughter Toni (Majorino). With the help of Mum (Field), they nurse the creature to healthy adulthood. When Andre masters the art of balancing balls and dressing in Hawaiian shirts, Dad seizes the chance to attract the attention of the national press. But he's not counted on Billy Baker (Szarabajka), an ignorant seal-hating fisherman. Andre is not naturally winning, and the human characters don't seem to be giving body and soul to the enterprise. Undemanding. WH

Andrei Rublev (aka St Andrei Passion)

(1966, USSR, 182 min, b/w & col)
d Andrei Tarkovsky. *sc* Andrei Konchalovsky, Andrei Tarkovsky. *ph* Vadim Iusov. *ad* Yevgeni Tcherniaiev. *m* Vyacheslav Ovchinnikov. *cast* Anatoly Solonitsyn, Ivan Lapikov, Nikolai Grinko, Nikolai Sergeyev, Irma Rausch, Nikolai Burlyayev.
●The complete version (39 minutes longer than the print originally released) 'explains' no more than the cut version, but at least Tarkovsky's mysteries and enigmas are now intact. Rublev was a minor icon-painter of the early 1400s. Tarkovsky re-imagines him as a Christ-like cypher for the sufferings of a divided Russia under the Tartar invaders: a troubled visionary reduced to years of silence by the horrors that he witnesses, who finally rediscovers the will to speak – and to paint. The film offers eight imaginary episodes from Rublev's life: the most brilliant coup is the story of a beardless boy saving his own life by pretending that he knows how to cast a giant bell – and finding that he can do it. This boy's blind faith rekindles Rublev's confidence in himself and his people, leading the film into its blazing climax: a montage of details from Rublev's surviving icons. TR

Androcles and the Lion

(1952, US, 98 min, b/w)
d Chester Erskine. *p* Gabriel Pascal. *sc* Chester Erskine. *ph* Harry Stradling. *ed* Roland Gross. *pd* Harry Horner. *m* Frederick Hollander. *cast* Jean Simmons, Victor Mature, Alan Young, Maurice Evans, Elsa Lanchester, Robert Newton.
●Producer-elect to Bernard Shaw for *Pygmalion*, *Major Barbara* and *Caesar and Cleopatra*, Gabriel Pascal foundered in Hollywood with this pompously stagebound and unhappily cast spectacular which simply ambles through the play. The original casting of Harpo Marx as Androcles (he was fired by Howard Hughes after five weeks' shooting) might have been really something. TM

Android

(1982, US, 80 min)
d Aaron Lipstadt. *p* Mary Ann Fisher. *sc* James Reigle, Don Opper. *ph* Tim Suhrstedt. *ed* Andy Horvitch. *ad* KC Scheibel. *m* Don Preston. *cast* Klaus Kinski, Don Opper, Brie Howard, Norbert Weisser, Crofton Hardester, Kendra Kirchner.
●Built to succeed in Roger Corman's exploitation labs, this is a remarkably skilful first feature; its space-locked power struggles are in the same perilous future as *Blade Runner*, but a witty script and concise action supplant the flash and portent of megabucks sets. Kinski is Dr Daniel, illegally engaged in advanced android research, while his less advanced android assistant Max (Opper) zaps space invaders and teaches himself the history of an Earth he's never seen with rock-'n'roll and sex instruction tapes. The abrupt arrival of three fugitive convicts brings the woman Daniel needs to activate his Cassandra project, and begins a dangerous sentimental education for Max, since – unlike the characters in his pet video of Capra's *It's a Wonderful Life* – these men and women seem doomed to conflict. The result is an enjoyable genre film which never loses its sense of humour, and manages an upbeat ending instead of smoke, symbols and angst. RP

Andromeda Strain, The

(1971, US, 131 min)
d/p Robert Wise. *sc* Nelson Gidding. *ph* Richard H Kline. *ed* Stuart Gilmore. *pd* Boris Leven. *m* Gil Mellé. *cast* Arthur Hill, David Wayne, James Olson, Kate Reid, Paula Kelly.
●Soon after this fair-to-middling adaptation of his sci-fi novel, Michael Crichton took to directing his own scripts. No connection necessarily, but Wise does rather plod through the plot, so that when his scientists finally make the connection between the micro-thing from outer space and a secret bacteriologial warfare project, it seems high time indeed. After a spendidly traditional opening sequence, the message about the dangers of scientific research begins to loom ponderously large, with banks of supercomputers dedicated to science fact but the dialogue ('Good God, it's *growing*!') still mired in fiction. TM

And Soon the Darkness

(1970, GB, 99 min)
d Robert Fuest. *p* Albert Fennell, Brian Clemens. *sc* Brian Clemens, Terry Nation. *ph* Ian Wilson. *ed* Ann Chegwidden. *ad* Philip Harrison. *m* Laurie Johnson. *cast* Pamela Franklin, Michele Dotrice, Sandor Eles, John Nettleton, Clare Kell, John Franklyn.
●Unappealing women-in-peril thriller, scripted by Brian Clemens and centred on a young nurse (Franklin) whose holiday companion (Dotrice) is savagely murdered by a sex maniac on a lonely country road as they cycle through France. Predictable, implausible, and not a little nasty.

And the Band Played On

(1993, US, 141 min)
d Roger Spottiswoode. *p* Midge Sanford, Sarah Pillsbury. *sc* Arnold Schulman. *ph* Paul Elliott, Paul Ryan. *ed* Lois Freeman-Fox. *m* Carter Burwell. *cast* Matthew Modine, Alan Alda, Lily Tomlin, Ian McKellen, Richard Gere, Anjelica Huston, Steve Martin, Phil Collins.
●So keen were the makers of this adaptation of Randy Shilts' best-seller to bombard us with the facts and figures of the history of AIDS that they forgot to offer a properly dramatic human framework to make us care fully about the characters. The all-star film (from HBO Pictures) covers the early years of research: by 1980, a handful of medics had begun investigating the AIDS virus, but, despite the escalation of the numbers of those infected or dead, politicians denied them adequate funding. Meanwhile, bigots spoke of a gay plague, scientists fought for the kudos of being first to identify the virus, and disagreements beset San Francisco's gays over the closure of the bathhouses. The film, quite rightly, deals with these issues; trouble is they make for a disjointed, clichéd narrative, with Modine's honest, visionary boffin striving to make public the Truth against all odds. GA

...And the Moon Dances (Bulan Tertusuk Ilalang)

(1995, Indonesia, 125 min)
d Garin Nugroho. *p* Turino Junaidy. *sc* Garin Nugroho. *ph* Nur Hidayat. *ed* Arturo G Pradjawisastra. *cast* Ki Sutarman, Patna Paquita, Norman Wibowo, Wiwiek Handawiyah, Pramana Padmodarmaya.
●A young man and woman, both from troubled backgrounds, come to Surakarta to study under Waluyo, a master of traditional Javanese arts. The boy, Ilalang, wants to write music but seems trapped in memories of childhood traumas; the girl, Bulan (= Moon), is simply trying to find herself. The suppressed violence which haunts their lives – which, the film implies, may be endemic in Indonesian society – surfaces when their master dies in an accidental fire. Nugroho's exquisite film doesn't tell a story so much as it explores ambiguities of mood, texture, light and meaning. There's nothing folksy or 'Third World' about this daringly modernist film which uses a rich sound design to point up submerged emotional truths. TR

And Then There Were None (aka Ten Little Niggers)

(1945, US, 97 min, b/w)
d/p René Clair. *sc* Dudley Nichols. *ph* Lucien Andriot. *ed* Harvy Manger. *ad* Ernst Fegté. *m* Mario Castelnuovo-Tedesco. *cast* Walter Huston, Roland Young, Louis Hayward, June Duprez, Barry Fitzgerald, C Aubrey Smith, Judith Anderson, Mischa Auer.
●Often overrated version of Agatha Christie's play in which a group of people with no discernible connections are invited to a remote island mansion by an unknown host, only to

be murdered one by one. The macabre humour is the best thing about the movie, with the suspense rarely tightening the screws and some of the performances (Fitzgerald in particular) tending towards cartoonish caricature. Enjoyable, though, which is more than can be said for the 1965 (as *Ten Little Indians*) and 1974 remakes. GA

And Then There Were None (aka Ten Little Indians)

(1974, GB, 98 min)
d Peter Collinson. *p/sc* Harry Alan Towers. *ph* Fernando Arribas. *ed* John Trumper. *m* Bruno Nicolai. *cast* Oliver Reed, Richard Attenborough, Elke Sommer, Gert Fröbe, Adolfo Celi, Stéphane Audran, Charles Aznavour, Herbert Lom, Orson Welles.
● Glossily bland tax-shelter travesty of Agatha Christie's play, shot partly as an advert for upmarket tourism in the Shah's Iran, and featuring the disembodied voice of Orson Welles as the most palatable of its international cameos. Aznavour inevitably manages a song before he becomes the first of ten assembled strangers to receive retribution for a past murder. PT

...and the pursuit of happiness

(1986, US, 90 min)
d Louis Malle. *ed* Nancy Baker. *narrator* Louis Malle.
● A companion piece to *God's Country*, in which Malle continues his exploration of America. The theme is immigrants, starting with a lone Rumanian touring Texas on foot in homage to his adoptive home. Success stories follow, among them a whole string of bright kids winning acceptance at Ivy League universities, at MIT, as America's first immigrant astronaut. Then there is the other side of the coin: black residents driven to violent resentment on a housing development in Houston when Vietnamese start displacing them (they have more money, say the blacks; because the blacks are lazy, say the Vietnamese). The pervasive fear – of homes and jobs put at risk by immigrants – surfaces most openly in a vivid survey of the wetback problem, with so many now arriving in quest of illegal employment that all they find is illegal unemployment. A characteristically generous film, marginally less involving than *God's Country* only because the emotional ambivalence of the earlier film (where Malle fell haplessly in love with a community that invites political contempt) is lacking here. TM

And There Was Jazz (Byl Jazz)

(1981, Pol, 107 min)
d Feliks Falk. *ph* Witold Sobocinski. *cast* Jerzy Gudejko, Andrzej Chickowski, Jacek Strzemzalski, Kazimierz Wysota.
● A product of the 'X' film unit under Andrzej Wajda: one of the 'missing ten' films, banned at the time for their unsympathetic view of life in Poland. It follows the efforts to keep together, and to find venues for gigs, of a group of young, mainly 'middle class' (traditional) jazz buffs and musicians. The period is the years leading up to, and immediately following, Stalin's death in 1953: jazz is seen by the authorities as 'Western bourgeois immoralism', and the only music officially sanctioned is either martial music or dire folk songs. This group prefer listening to Charlie Parker on the Voice of America, setting up crazy jam sessions in attics etc, but their energy is finally sapped by the revelations that follow the deaths, first of 'Uncle Joe' and then, tragically, one of their company. Falk offers no searing cultural or political analysis here, but an informative and likeable depiction of growing up under Stalin's dark shadow. WH

And the Ship Sails On (E la Nave Va)

(1983, It/Fr, 132 min)
d Federico Fellini. *p* Franco Cristaldi. *sc* Federico Fellini, Tonino Guerra. *ph* Giuseppe Rotunno. *ed* Ruggero Mastroianni. *ad* Dante Ferretti. *m* Gianfranco Plenizio. *cast* Freddie Jones, Barbara Jefford, Victor Poletti, Peter Cellier, Elisa Mainardi, Norma West.
● Here we go again: the Italian *buffo* happily constructing his own world of elaborate grotesquerie in a studio far away from the problems of the real world. This time it is a marvellous ship, full of opera stars who set sail on the eve of WWI to bury one of their number. And as usual there are the anecdotes of droll inconsequence and pleasure – a symphony played on wine glasses, the divas serenading the stokers. When the boat picks up some refugees from the first flickerings of the war, a re-found social conscience seems about to edge in, only to be handled with the man's monumental off-handedness. But while Fellini may simply observe the chattering of his clowns and have absolutely nothing to say himself, it still (as usual) adds up to marginal doodlings which are unique, curious, ingratiatingly charming, and quietly nostalgic for the last great and peaceful age in Europe. CPea

And Woman...Was Created

see Et Dieu Créa la Femme

And Women Shall Weep

(1960, GB, 65 min, b/w)
d John Lemont. *sc* Leigh Vance, John Lemont. *ph* Brendan J Stafford. *ed* Bernard Gribble. *ad* Anthony Inglis. *m* Philip Green. *cast* Ruth Dunning, Max Butterfield, Gillian Vaughan, Richard O'Sullivan, Claire Gordon.
● Truly terrible cautionary tale about juvenile delinquency, with a frantically overpitched performance from Ruth Dunning as the widowed mum who hands her elder son (Butterfield) over to the police to prevent the younger one (O'Sullivan) from going the same way. TM

And Your Mother Too (Y tu mamá también)

(2001, Mex, 106 min)
d Alfonso Cuarón. *p* Jorge Vergara, Alfonso Cuarón. *sc* Carlos Cuarón, Alfonso Cuarón. *ph* Emmanuel Lubezki. *ed* Alfonso Cuarón, Alex Rodríguez. *pd* Miguel Angel Alvarez. *m* Liza Richardson, Annette Fradera. *cast* Maribel Verdú, Gael García Bérnal, Diego Luna, Marta Aura, Diana Bracho, Emilio Echevarría, Verónica Langer, Arturo Rios, Ana López Mercado.
● Julio and Tenoch (García Bernal and Luna) are old mates – well, as old as their 17 years allow. Hanging out at a ritzy society wedding they try out some moves on the gorgeous, 28-year-old, unhappily married Luisa (Verdú). To their surprise, within days they're escorting their catch out of Mexico City in search of the legendary perfect beach, Boca del Cielo ('Heaven's Mouth'). For most of the movie Luisa is in the metaphorical driving seat. When things get sticky she's quick to lay down the law. Meanwhile the guys' machismo is the butt of most of the jokes; in particular, their competitive and possessive instincts, which Luisa does her best to cure. The film's frank, uninhibited sex is refreshing, funny and true – but there's more. Divesting themselves of all the artifice and affectation, the green-tinted spectacle of their two Hollywood productions, *Great Expectations* and *A Little Princess*, Cuarón and cameraman Lubezki get their hands dirty here, for a more crisp, direct, objective approach. One side-effect is the trenchant, rueful portrait of Mexico which emerges on the margins: the vast disparities between rural and urban standards of living, old and new world cultures. TCh

Andy Warhol's Bad

(1976, US, 109 min)
d Jed Johnson. *p* Jeff Tornberg. *sc* Pat Hackett, George Abagnalo. *ph* Alan Metzger. *ed* David McKenna. *ad* Gene Rudolf. *m* Mike Bloomfield. *cast* Carroll Baker, Perry King, Susan Tyrrell, Stefania Cassini, Gordan Oas-Heim, Cyrinda Foxe.
● If ever a movie set out to live up to its title... Baker runs a home electrolysis parlour as a front for a dial-a-murder organisation: she puts her clients in touch with lethal girls who will assassinate unwanted offspring, relatives and other enemies. The New York streets are already so full of violence that the crimes pass virtually unnoticed, but the movie makes a point of lingering over its sadistic details; everything is as grotesque as possible. At the same time, it's played as much as possible like American TV soap opera, complete with its repetitions and stretches of tedium. The main plot centres on Perry King and whether he'll be cold enough to kill an autistic child. In terms of its own frames of reference, the movie is competent enough to almost transcend criticism, but its humour proved way too sick for most English critics. TR

Andy Warhol's Dracula

see Blood for Dracula

Angel

(1937, US, 91 min, b/w)
d/p Ernst Lubitsch. *sc* Samson Raphaelson. *ph* Charles Lang Jr. *ed* William Shea. *ad* Hans Dreier, Robert Usher. *m* Frederick Hollander. *cast* Marlene Dietrich, Herbert Marshall, Melvyn Douglas, Edward Everett Horton, Ernest Cossart, Laura Hope Crews.
● While the servants gossip below stairs, Dietrich flirts enigmatically between her suave English diplomat husband (Marshall) and a beguiling American old flame (Douglas). Characteristically dry Lubitsch sophistication, not much liked at the time but since hailed by enthusiasts as one of his masterpieces. To the less committed, Dietrich – caressingly photographed by Charles Lang in a manner that doesn't quite make the Sternberg grade – bats her eyelashes once too often and twice too coyly. TM

Angel

(1982, Eire, 92 min)
d/sc Neil Jordan. *ph* Chris Menges. *ed* J Patrick Duffner. *pd* John Lucas. *cast* Veronica Quilligan, Stephen Rea, Alan Devlin, Peter Caffrey, Honor Heffernan, Lise-Ann McLaughlin.
● An apocalyptic voyage into violence triggered by a chilling sectarian double murder of which Danny, a sax player in a rock showband, becomes first witness and subsequently avenger. The movie bristles with visual ironies, downbeat humour, upbeat action, and is powered by a sequence of chance encounters as Stephen Rea's Danny, like Lee Marvin in *Point Blank*, picks up the trail of the killers and, swapping his sax for a gun, pursues them through the towns and countryside of Armagh. Ostensibly a naturalistic thriller, but reaching beyond to hyper-realism and surrealism, *Angel* carries subtle echoes of Buñuel and the early Scorsese films (*Who's That Knocking at My Door?*, *Mean Streets*), but remains uniquely true to its time and place – contemporary Ireland. A stunning debut from an esteemed novelist. MA

Angel

(1983, US, 93 min)
d Robert Vincent O'Neil. *p* Roy Watts, Donald P Borchers. *sc* Robert Vincent O'Neil, Joseph M Cala. *ph* Andrew Davis. *ed* Charles Bornstein. *ad* Stephen Marsh. *m* Craig Safan. *cast* Cliff Gorman, Donna Wilkes, Susan Tyrrell, Dick Shawn, Rory Calhoun, John Diehl.
● Producer Sandy Howard appears to have stumbled on an insatiable American appetite for stories of sweet young girls who trade their sneakers for stiletto heels at sundown and cruise the street for clients. This is his second movie on the subject in a year, and has made even more money than its predecessor *Vice Squad*. But in the true tradition of such exploitation, the posters are a thousand times more suggestive than anything in the films. Much of it is played for comedy of an innocuous if tedious kind, and it's left to the psycho dredged up from *Taxi Driver* to provide the more repulsive moments. DP

Angela

(1994, US, 105 min)
d Rebecca Miller. *p* Ron Kastner. *sc* Rebecca Miller. *ph* Ellen Kuras. *ed* Melody London. *pd* Daniel Talpers. *m* Michael Rohatyn. *cast* Miranda Stuart-Rhyne, Charlotte Blythe, Anna Thomson, Johnny Ventimiglia, Hynden Walch, Ruth Maleczech.
● Ambitious but uneven indie US debut about two girls and their reaction to their mother's volatility and their father's increasing resort to the church as a provider of stability; the elder girl entertains visions of a punitive devil, and decides to purify the family of sin. An imaginative attempt to get into a young girl's mind, not unlike Ann Turner's *Celia*, but one which suffers from languid pacing and some rather overt poeticism. GA

Angela's Ashes

(1999, US/GB, 146 min)
d Alan Parker. *p* Scott Rudin, David Brown, Alan Parker. *sc* Laura Jones, Alan Parker. *ph* Michael Seresin. *ed* Gerry Hambling. *pd* Geoffrey Kirkland. *m* John Williams. *cast* Emily Watson, Robert Carlyle, Joe Breen, Ciarán Owens, Michael Legge, Ronnie Masterson, Pauline McLynn, Liam Carney, Eanna MacLiam.

●Parker's film of Frank McCourt's bestseller charts a Limerick childhood tainted by poverty, unemployment, alcoholism, bigotry and death. Young Frank's family, returning home from Brooklyn after a cot death in 1935, finds that a fresh start only makes things worse. The squalor, hunger and incessant rain finish off further children, while Dad (Carlyle) takes refuge in drink, and mum Angela (Watson) battles against her husband's feckless pride and the condescending authorities as she makes endless sacrifices for the kids. Can Frank even survive, let alone find happiness? After a shaky first half hour, which disposes of Frank's siblings so speedily that the litany of woes verges on self-parody, the film settles into a measured pace that allows for a more balanced blend of bleak drama and darkly ironic, pleasurably profane humour. Carlyle and Watson are effective, the growing boy himself is beautifully played by Breen, Owens and Legge, and the supporting roles are all vividly etched. Never quite outstaying its welcome, the stylised cinematography holds together the story's shifting moods. While most impressive of all is the sensitivity and restraint with which Parker treats the 'big' moments. GA

Angel at My Table, An

(1990, NZ, 158 min)
d Jane Campion. *p* Bridget Ikin, Jane Campion. *sc* Laura Jones. *ph* Stuart Dryburgh. *ed* Veronika Haussler. *m* Don McGlashan. *cast* Kerry Fox, Karen Fergusson, Alexia Keogh, KJ Wilson, Iris Churn, Melina Bernecker, Andrew Binns.

●Though adapted for television from three volumes of autobiography by New Zealand writer Janet Frame, Campion's film is both wholly cinematic and true to her own preoccupations. Her subject is the privations and anxieties of childhood and adolescence, the weird absurdity of ordinary life, and the disconcertingly thin line between normality and madness, all depicted with an unsentimental honesty that veers abruptly (but never jarringly) between naturalism and surrealism, comedy and tragedy. As the introverted Frame – a plain, bubble-haired redhead born into a poor, close-knit family in 1924 – progresses through school, college and erroneously diagnosed schizophrenia towards final liberation as a respected writer, Campion deploys a wealth of economically observed details to explore her heroine's passionate, deceptively placid perceptions of the world. There are none of the usual artist-biopic clichés here. Frame, as embodied by three uncannily-matched actresses, is bright but intensely, awkwardly passive, and inhabits a chaotic, arbitrary universe. Watching her hard, slow struggle for self-respect, happiness and peace becomes a profoundly moving, strangely affirmative experience. GA

Angel Baby

(1960, US, 97 min, b/w)
d Paul Wendkos. *p* Thomas F Woods. *sc* Orin Borsten, Sam Roeca, Paul Mason. *ph* Haskell Wexler. *ed* Betty J Lane. *ad* Val Tamelin. *m* Wayne Shanklin. *cast* George Hamilton, Mercedes McCambridge, Salomé Jens, Joan Blondell, Henry Jones, Burt Reynolds.

●Travelling evangelist shows get the once-over in this modestly intriguing exposé, with newcomer Salomé Jens as the mute girl Jenny Brooks who throws herself at itinerant preacher Paul Strand (Hamilton), whom she believes responsible for restoring her voice. Her exploitation (as the testifying 'Angel Baby') soon gives cause for doubt that he's for real. Reynolds (minus moustache) made his film bow as the girl's best pal. The script skilfully adapted from the novel *Jenny Angel* by Elsie Oaks Barbour is set against the telling background of the the poverty-stricken farms of the American South. Evocative low-key camerawork from Haskell Wexler, and a first-rate performance from Mercedes McCambridge as the preacher's obsessive wife. TJ

Angel Baby

(1995, Aust/US, 104 min)
d Michael Rymer. *p* Timothy White, Jonathan Shteinman. *sc* Michael Rymer. *ph* Ellery Ryan. *ed* Dany Cooper. *pd* Chris S Kennedy. *m* John Clifford White. *cast* John Lynch, Jacqueline McKenzie, Colin Friels, Deborra-Lee Furness, Daniel Daperis.

●A problematic but intense romance develops between Harry (Lynch) and Kate (McKenzie), who meet at a day-clinic for the psychologically disturbed. Family, friends and shrinks are happy about the relationship at first, but when Kate announces she's pregnant, concern grows over whether the couple can cope. True to tradition, Rymer strives to ensure that our sympathies lie with his optimistic outsiders rather than with the more conventionally settled. Happily, however, tendencies towards fairytale whimsy are mostly held in check by crisp visuals, an imaginative use of music, and down-to-earth performances. It's a sensitive, witty film, with an oddly benign take on the effects of watching TV quiz shows, and admirably ambivalent about the causes of the lovers' troubles. GA

Angel City

(1977, US, 70 min)
d/p/sc Jon Jost. *ph* Jon Jost, Robert J Schoenhut. *ed* Jon Jost. *cast* Robert Glaudini, Winifred Golden, Pierce Del Rue, Kathleen Kramer.

American independent Jon Jost must be tired of being compared with Godard, but there's no denying that his *Angel City* does for Los Angeles some of what *Alphaville* did for Paris. Both movies use private eye characters to investigate more than mere murder: Jost's Frank Goya ('like the painter') is hired to check out the death of a Hollywood starlet, and winds up identifying the villains as illusionism and monopoly capitalism. The movie is structured as a kind of countdown in twelve numbered sections, ranging in theme and tone from satire of Hollywood to American 'visionary' poetry. Interesting stuff. TR

Angel Dust

(1994, Jap, 117 min)
d Sogo Ishii. *p* Taro Maki, Kenzo Horikoshi, Eiji Izumi. *sc* Yoruzu Ikuta, Sogo Ishii. *ph* Norimichi Kasamatu. *ed* Hiroshi Matsuo. *m* Hiroyuki Nagashima. *cast* Kaho Minami, Takeshi Wakamatsu, Etsushi Toyokawa, Ryoko Takizawa, Masayuki Shionoya, Yukio Yamato.

●This psycho-thriller about urban paranoia (from the director of *Crazy Family*) suggests terrifyingly that the millennium is already with us. At 6 pm each Monday a killer strikes on the Tokyo metro, silently injecting his female victim. In shades of *Manhunter*, an expert in abnormal criminal cases (Minami) is brought in to try to enter his mind; she intuits that the perpetrator can sense the feeling of isolation and self-destructiveness in people. The trail leads to the HQ of the Ultimate Truth Church, in the shadow of Mt Fuji, a centre for rumoured reverse brainwashing. Beautifully acted, superbly shot, this erotic, enigmatic film has the compulsiveness of Gilliam's *Brazil* mixed with the darkness of Lang's *M.* Quite how many levels it works on is up to your own sympathies – or should that be empathies? The film is an uncanny pre-echo of 1995's Aum Shinrikyo's metro gas attack. WH

Angel Dust (Poussière d'Ange)

(1987, Fr, 95 min)
d Edouard Niermans. *p* Jacques-Eric Strauss. *sc* Jacques Audiard, Alain Le Henry, Edouard Niermans, Didier Haudepin. *ph* Bernard Lutic. *ed* Yves Deschamps. *pd* Dominique Maleret. *m* Léon Senza. *cast* Bernard Giraudeau, Fanny Bastien, Fanny Cottençon, Michel Aumont, Jean-Pierre Sentier, Gérard Blain, Luc Lavandier.

●For Inspector Blount (Giraudeau), life is confusing. His wife has left him. Murder investigations reveal that the victims have been sent dead rats. Then he becomes obsessed with an angelic waif (Bastien) with a callous disregard for the truth. With Blount immersed in a whirlpool of hidden pasts and shifting identities, the film resembles the layer-peeling methods of the admittedly superior *One Deadly Summer.* The elliptical *noir* plot allows plenty of space for offbeat comedy and generous characterisation, and Blount himself emerges as a sympathetic, if flawed, hero. If the denouement is less than startling, there are more than enough digressions, twists and hints of Catholic symbolism to hold the interest. GA

Angel Eyes

(2001, US, 103 min)
d Luis Mandoki. *p* Mark Canton, Elie Samaha. *sc* Gerald DiPego. *ph* Piotr Sobocinski. *ed* Jerry Greenberg. *pd* Dean Tavoularis. *m* Marco Beltrami. *cast* Jennifer Lopez, James Caviezel, Sonia Braga, Terrence Howard, Jeremy Sisto, Victor Argo, Monet Mazur, Shirley Knight.

●A multiple auto pile-up: thanks to the quick thinking of Chicago cop Sharon Pogue ('We need more ambulances here!') and much earnest hand-holding ('Look at me! Don't stop looking at me!'), a life is saved. Skip forward a year, and the fine-looking but haunted Catch (Caviezel) wanders the streets, unshaven and misunderstood, until he glimpses Pogue (Lopez). He's drawn to her and, in time, returns the favour by saving her from a crazed gangster. Their romance is excruciatingly drawn out over the second half of the film. Though both Sharon and Catch have 'issues', there's nothing that can't be resolved, it seems, by a meaningful look or a passionate embrace. Lovely Lopez is reasonably convincing as a tough cookie by day and a lonesome soft-centre by night, but despite their best efforts, neither she nor Caviezel can fight free of the turgid script. JFu

Angel Face

(1952, US, 91 min, b/w)
d/p Otto Preminger. *sc* Frank S Nugent, Oscar Millard. *ph* Harry Stradling. *ed* Frederick Knudtson. *ad* Albert S D'Agostino, Carroll Clark. *m* Dimitri Tiomkin. *cast* Robert Mitchum, Jean Simmons, Herbert Marshall, Mona Freeman, Leon Ames, Barbara O'Neil.

●Superb Freudian crime thriller, *noir*-inflected in theme but shot by and large in crisp, bright drawing-rooms. Mitchum is the archetypal *noir*-hero confronted with a devious femme fatale; as an ambulance driver who becomes so infatuated with the outwardly angelic Simmons that he moves in as her family's chauffeur and can't bring himself to admit that she is trying to murder her mother, he gives one of his most restrained and lyrical performances, perfectly offset by Simmons' demonic ingenue. Preminger, as it were, flattens the melodramatics of the story with typically cool clarity, emphasising its psychological complexities and allowing the occasional incursions of violence to emerge with shocking matter-of-factness. GA

Angel Heart

(1987, US, 113 min)
d Alan Parker. *p* Alan Marshall, Elliott Kastner. *sc* Alan Parker. *ph* Michael Seresin. *ed* Gerry Hambling. *pd* Brian Morris. *m* Trevor Jones. *cast* Mickey Rourke, Robert De Niro, Lisa Bonet, Charlotte Rampling, Stocker Fontelieu, Brownie McGhee.

●A first-person Faustian detective novel presents quite a problem to the screenwriter, and Parker's alterations to William Hjortsberg's *Falling Angel* slacken the cunning weave of strands. Private eye Harry Angel (Rourke) is hired by the mysterious and malevolent Louis Cyphre (De Niro) to find a missing crooner who dabbled in the occult; but Angel's leads all wind up dead in a series of ritual murders. The supernatural is rendered in standard props (steam from a New York grating, silent nuns, the ominous motif of the clanking ceiling fan), and the information encoded in Angel's dreams emerges in the standard approved fashion. There isn't much imagination at work, but – damagingly – there is the disastrous quirkiness of a Coney island beach scene for winter sunbathers, while a copulation scene featuring writhing bodies and a ceiling pouring blood overwhelms the final horror of the detective's situation. BC

Angelic Conversation, The

(1985, GB, 81 min)
d Derek Jarman. *sonnets* William Shakespeare. *ph* James Mackay, Derek Jarman. *ed* Cerith Wyn-Evans. *m* Coil. *cast* Judi Dench, Paul Reynolds, Phillip Williamson.

●Jarman's setting for twelve Shakespeare sonnets has no narrative as such, and the only dialogue is Judi Dench's reading of the poems. Yet even though it dispenses with such conventions, it remains a hypnotically beautiful film. Its textured, stop-frame tableaux of caves, rocks, water, and figures in strange and terrible landscapes throw up myriad painterly similarities: the lesser religious nightmares of a Bosch or Brueghel, Victorian landscape of the 'Gordale Scar school'. Very romantic. JG

Angel in Exile

(1948, US, 90 min, b/w)
d Allan Dwan, Philip Ford. *sc* Charles Larson. *ph* Reggie Lanning. *ed* Arthur Roberts. *ad* Frank Arrigo. *m* Nathan Scott. *cast* John Carroll, Adele Mara, Thomas Gomez, Barton MacLane, Alfonso Bedoya, Grant Withers, Howland Chamberlin.

● Low-budget drama about an ex-con who travels to Mexico to regain his hidden loot of gold, only to undergo a character transformation under the influence of a good woman and the local peasants who acclaim him as a saint. Carroll makes a wooden lead, but the supporting cast and Dwan's fluency with narrative (Ford took over direction for a week while he was ill) make it watchable. GA

Angel Levine, The

(1970, US, 105 min)
d Ján Kadár. *p* Chiz Schultz. *sc* Bill Gunn, Ronald Ribman. *ph* Dick Kratina. *ed* Carl Lerner. *pd* George Jenkins. *m* Zdenek Liska. *cast* Zero Mostel, Harry Belafonte, Ida Kaminska, Milo O'Shea, Eli Wallach, Anne Jackson.

● Unappealing whimsy, based on a Bernard Malamud short story, about an elderly Jewish tailor (Mostel) plagued by a bad back, a sick wife, and a business destroyed by fire, who suddenly finds an angel in his kitchen offering to help. The angel (Belafonte) is not only black but Jewish, allowing for some treacly platitudes about racial togetherness. Directed with discretion, some humour, and a soggy performance from Mostel. TM

Angel of Vengeance

see Ms .45

Angelo My Love

(1982, US, 116 min)
d/p/sc Robert Duvall. *ph* Joseph Friedman. *ed* Stephen Mack. *m* Michael Kamen. *cast* Angelo Evans, Michael Evans, Ruthie Evans, Debbie Evans, Steve 'Patalay' Tsigonoff, Timothy Phillips, Jennifer Youngs.

● The genesis of this film occurred when Duvall overheard an eight-year-old boy on a New York street having a lover's tiff with an adult woman and saying, 'If you don't love me no more, Patricia, I swear I'm gonna go back to Philadelphia'. The boy turned out to be a member of NY's little-known gypsy community, and Duvall personally financed this dramatised film about their lives, using one of his favourite films, Ken Loach's *Kes*, as a model. The thrust of the story depends upon the rites of passage of this boy into an early adulthood, the possession of an important gypsy ring stolen by some less scrupulous members of the clan, and the eventual necessity for Angelo to choose which world, the gypsy or the wider one, he wishes to inhabit. But the film's chief joy is its patient, unobtrusive observation of a culture out of synch with surrounding modern America. CPea

Angel on My Shoulder

(1997, US, 85 min)
d/p Donna Deitch. *sc* Donna Deitch, Terri Jentz. *ed/ph* Donna Deitch. *m* Bob Dylan, Harry Nilsson.*with* Gwen Welles.

● Donna Deitch (*Desert Hearts*) follows the illness of her close friend the actress Gwen Welles (*Nashville*) who died in 1993. At one point Deitch describes Welles as 'the monkey on my back, moth in my hand', and, indeed, her friend is a frustrating mix of vanity, stubbornness and vulnerability who initially sees her cancer as the fulfilment of long-held suicidal fantasies. Just as it becomes too late to escape the inevitable, she recognises her will to live. Deitch does not over-sentimentalise, nor exclude ambivalence in what is a sometimes funny, often harrowing document. FM

Angelos

(1982, Greece, 126 min)
d/p/sc Yorgos Katakouzinos. *ph* Tasos Alexakis. *ed* Aristide Karydis-Fuchs. *ad* Marilena Aravandinou. *m* Stamatis Spanoudakis. *cast* Michalis Maniatis, Dionisis Xanthos, Katerina Chelmi, Maria Alkaiou, Vasilis Tsanglos, Yorgos Bartis.

● Angelos is shy, tender, and gay, the product of a wretched family life (drunkard dad, ex-whore mom, crippled sister). When he meets a brashly confident macho marine, he therefore makes his bid for freedom and sets up a cosily domesticated flat with his lover, only to be sent out on the streets as a transvestite prostitute, with shame, humiliation, violence and death as the inevitable result. The sad-to-be-gay stance, so reminiscent of *Nighthawks*, is reinforced by the humourless central performance, while Katakouzinos' direction is frankly dull. GA

Angels

see Angels in the Outfield

Angels and Insects

(1995, US, 117 min)
d Philip Haas. *p* Belinda Haas, Joyce Herlihy. *sc* Philip Haas, Belinda Haas. *ph* Bernard Zitzermann. *ed* Belinda Haas. *pd* Jennifer Kernke. *m* Alexander Balanescu. *cast* Mark Rylance, Patsy Kensit, Saskia Wickham, Kristin Scott Thomas, Annette Badland, Jeremy Kemp, Anna Massey.

● A Victorian explorer-cum-naturalist, William Adamson (Rylance), returned from the Amazon in financial straits, arrives at the country estate of his patron, amateur entomologist Harald Alabaster (Kemp), who not only lends a surprisingly sympathetic ear to Adamson's interest in Darwin's theories on natural selection, but even looks kindly on the scientist's courtship of his daughter Eugenia (Kensit). Soon after their marriage, the newcomer has reason to feel unease: Alabaster's boorish son Edgar (Henshall) openly considers him too low-born for his sister, while Eugenia veers confusingly between brazen sexual passion and lengthy periods of locking him out of her boudoir. Happily, however, Adamson has an ally in Matty Crompton (Scott Thomas), a likewise impoverished dependant of the Alabasters, who shares his interest in insects and the discoveries of the age. Haas's intriguing adaptation of a novella by AS Byatt is not your average period drama. For one thing, the costumes, designs, music and camerawork steer clear of naturalism, highlighting both the modernity of the approach and the notion of humans as creatures to be observed dispassionately. Despite some uneven pacing and variability in performance, this is a work of clarity, ambition and intelligence. GA

Angels From Hell

(1968, US, 86 min)
d Bruce Kessler. *sc* Jerome Wish. *ph* Herman Lee Knox. *ed* William Martin. *ad* Wally Moon. *m* Stu Phillips. *cast* Tom Stern, Arlene Martel, Ted Markland, Stephen Oliver, Paul Bertoya, James Murphy.

● Routine motorcycle gang movie, violent and gory, with spurious references to Vietnam thrown in by way of an excuse.

Angel Sharks (Marie Baie des Anges)

(1997, Fr, 93 min)
d Manuel Pradal. *p* Philippe Rousselet. *sc* Manuel Pradal. *ph* Christophe Pollock. *ed* Valerie Deseine. *pd* Javier Po, Véronique Mellery. *m* Carlo Crivelli. *cast* Vahina Giocante, Frédéric Malgras, Nicolas Welbers, Swan Carpio, Jamie Harris, Andrew Clover.

● Compelling, fierce and darkly romantic, this expressionist first feature is a stylised fairy tale about young marginals stylishly shot in the stunning landscape of the Côte d'Azur. Part idealised love story, part hard-edged portrait of wild youth, it swims determinedly against the 'realist' tide of recent, cutting-edge French film-making. Related in flashback from a palatial Monte Carlo villa where 14-year-old offender Orso (Malgras) has holed up, it builds up a jaggedly poetic portrait of Orso's doomed attraction to fellow tarnished angel Marie (Giocante). Pradal takes his performances from amateurs/non-professionals as much for their rawness, power and beauty as for the sake of authenticity. Employing fluid, sensuous, saturated colour 'Scope cinematography and heightened use of sound, he presents a rhapsodic tragedy out of an almost Blake-like vision. The result is a strange, oneiric mood piece, less concerned with conventional narrative than with an individualistic, pagan exploration of the mechanics of fate and destiny, the casual savagery of life, and the lost grace of innocents. WH

Angels in the Outfield (aka Angels)

(1995, US, 102 min)
d William Dear. *p* Irby Smith, Joe Roth, Roger Birnbaum. *sc* Holly Goldberg Sloan, Dorothy Kingsley, George Wells. *ph* Matthew F Leonetti. *ed* Bruce Green. *m* Randy Edelman. *cast* Danny Glover, Brenda Fricker, Ben Johnson, Joseph Gordon-Levitt, Christopher Lloyd, Tony Danza, Milton Davis.

● Amiable remake of the 1951 MGM fantasy of the same title about divine intervention rescuing a down-at-heel baseball team. Much bat-and-ball activity, as young Gordon-Levitt's hope for a family reunion to extricate him from the care of foster mum Fricker comes to depend on an equally unlikely upturn in fortunes for local also-rans the California Angels. Soon, Lloyd's angelic helpers are improving matters on the diamond, gruff manager Glover gets convinced the kid's some kind of mascot, and even long-suffering owner Johnson starts believing that this year his boys might go all the way. The scene is set for much digital image manipulation, think-positive platitudes and a narrative line of blinding predictability; disappointing in the circumstances, given a hard-working cast, major production values and well-staged on-field action. Fans should enjoy it; parents won't suffer too much. TJ

Angels One Five

(1952, GB, 98 min, b/w)
d George More O'Ferrall. *p* John Gossage, Derek Twist. *sc* Derek Twist. *ph* Christopher Challis. *ed* Daniel Birt. *ad* Fred Pusey. *m* John Wooldridge. cast Jack Hawkins, John Gregson, Michael Denison, Andrew Osborn, Dulcie Gray, Humphrey Lestocq, Cyril Raymond, Ronald Adam.

● An unromantic view of Britain's air war, with a heavy emphasis on the mysteries of the control room. TV pioneer O'Ferrall (*Murder in the Cathedral* in 1936) brings to bear his WWII experience at Fighter Command HQ to depict a nervy, uncertain Battle of Britain. His slice-of-life realism reveals a world where heroism, pragmatism and fear are inextricably entwined, and easily ridiculed stiff-upper-lip restraint is a necessary defence against panic and despair. RMy

Angels Over Broadway

(1940, US, 80 min, b/w)
d Ben Hecht, Lee Garmes. *p/sc* Ben Hecht. *ph* Lee Garmes. *ed* Gene Havlick. *ad* Lionel Banks. *m* George Antheil. *cast* Douglas Fairbanks Jr, Rita Hayworth, Thomas Mitchell, John Qualen, George Watts.

● A characteristically slick (if moralising) script by Hecht and fine camerawork from Garmes can't quite prevent tedium setting in as the excellent cast play a group of moral down-and-outs (embezzler, con-man, dancer, disillusioned playwright) who see the light and discover that life is worth living during a night's gambling in a New York café. The problem lies less in the pacing – as one would expect with Hecht, it moves along quickly enough – than in the incursions of uplifting sentiment into the generally downbeat proceedings. GA

Angels Wash Their Faces, The

(1939, US, 85 min, b/w)
d Ray Enright. *sc* Michael Fessier, Niven Busch, Robert Buckner. *ph* Arthur L Todd. *ed* James Gibbons. *ad* Ted Smith. *cast* Ann Sheridan, Ronald Reagan, Frankie Thomas, Dead End Kids, Bonita Granville, Margaret Hamilton, Marjorie Main, Eduardo Ciannelli, Henry O'Neill.

● Quickie sequel to the classic Warners melodrama *Angels with Dirty Faces*. Minus gangster Cagney and priest Pat O'Brien, it has to content itself with Sheridan's hand-wringing over young brother Thomas and his involvement with the Dead End Kids (stars of the first film and later to land a movie series of their own). A young Ronald Reagan crops up as a kindly lawyer's son and resident romance angle. TJ

Angels With Dirty Faces

(1938, US, 97 min, b/w)
d Michael Curtiz. *sc* John Wexley, Warren Duff. *ph* Sol Polito. *ed* Owen Marks. *ad* Robert M Haas. *m* Max Steiner. *cast* James Cagney, Pat O'Brien, Humphrey Bogart, Ann Sheridan, George Bancroft, The Dead End Kids.

● A gutsy, rousing blend of gangster thriller and social comment, Curtiz's brisk film follows the lives of two slum kids who take different paths into adulthood: Cagney becomes a violent hood, O'Brien a priest. Problems arise when the local street gang – played by the Dead End Kids – come to admire Cagney for his toughness, and O'Brien has to try (the ending is hauntingly ambiguous) to persuade his former pal to pretend to be terrified as he's led to the electric chair. Great performances all round, and enough pace, shadowy camerawork and snappy dialogue to make this one of Warners' most memorable '30s dramas, despite the moralising air. GA

Angel Who Pawned Her Harp, The

(1953, GB, 76 min, b/w)
d Alan Bromly. *p* Sidney Cole. *sc* Charles Terrot, Sidney Cole. *ph* Arthur Grant. *ed* John Merritt. *ad* Ray Simm. *m* Antony Hopkins. *cast* Diane Cilento, Felix Aylmer, Jerry Desmonde, Joe Linnane, Sheila Sweet, Alfie Bass.

● A whimsical fantasy from Group 3, the low-budget production offshoot of the British Film Production Fund which operated under John Grierson and John Baxter to provide 'quality' second feature material and act as a training ground for emergent film-makers. Cilento is the heavenly visitor to Islington, dispensing good deeds from a pawnshop base, amidst an already nostalgic evocation of Cockney community life. PT

Anger Magick Lantern Cycle, The

(1947-1980, US, 151 min)
d Kenneth Anger.

● The anthology of Anger's nine released films is the most coherent (and remarkable) body of work produced by any American 'underground' film-maker. All the films are ritualistic in form and content; the later ones refer directly to the 'magick' of Anger's professed idol, Aleister Crowley. Anger's most obvious aesthetic forefathers are Eisenstein and Cocteau. *Fireworks* (1947, 14 min) and its inverse twin *Eaux d'artifice* (i.e. *Waterworks*, 1953, 13 min) show wish-fulfilment quests, the first successful (a lonely, masochistic boy survives a heart-stopping beating to earn himself a male lover), the second not (a crinolined dwarf cruises the dark gods of a water garden but isn't picked up). *Puce Moment* (1949, 6 min) salutes 1920s Hollywood, when stars were magic. In *Rabbits' Moon* (1950/79, 7 min), Harlequin snares Pierrot with a magic lantern image of Columbine, an illusion which kills him. *Inauguration of the Pleasure Dome* (1954/66, 38 min) shows a fancy dress party at which a beautiful boy is violated by intoxicated guests; the host grows stronger by subsuming everything that happens. *Scorpio Rising* (1964, 29 min) is an exhaustive tour of the death-wish in Western culture with a legendary rock'n'roll soundtrack; the word is made flesh in the person of Thanatos. In *Kustom Kar Kommandos* (1964, 3 min) a Kalifornian beach bum caresses his hot rod. *Invocation of My Demon Brother* (1969, 11 min) shows Crowleyan and other rituals; a god of light is born from the union of opposites. And *Lucifer Rising* (1980, 30 min), which features Marianne Faithfull and Donald Cammell among others, invokes Egyptian and Celtic myth (and flying saucers) to conjure the rise of Anger's own dream lover. TR

Anges du Péché, Les

(1943, Fr, 96 min, b/w)
d Robert Bresson. *p* Roger Richebé. *sc* Léopold Bruckberger, Robert Bresson, Jean Giraudoux. *ph* Philippe Agostini. *ed* Yvonne Martin. *ad* René Renoux. *m* Jean-Jacques Grünenwald. *cast* Renée Faure, Jany Holt, Sylvie, Mila Parély, Marie-Hélène Dasté, Louis Seigner.

● One of the most astonishing film debuts ever, made while France was still under Nazi occupation. Bresson chose an apparently timeless subject: the way that people affect each other's destinies. Based on the real convent of the Sisters of Béthany, a secluded order of nuns are minutely observed in their rehabilitation of women from prison. If the salvation is tangibly close to a Resistance adventure, it is the simple human confrontations that fascinate Bresson – the consuming desire of secure, bourgeois-born Anne-Marie to save the unrepentant Thérèse, wrongly imprisoned for the sake of her criminal lover. Concentrated dialogue (with a little help from Jean Giraudoux) and moulded monochrome photography by Philippe Agostini contribute to an outstanding film. Rarely have the seemingly opposite worlds of the spiritual and the erotic received such sublime, ennobling treatment. DT

Angie

(1994, US, 107 min)
d Martha Coolidge. *p* Larry Brezner, Patrick McCormick. *sc* Todd Graff. *ph* Johnny Jensen. *ed* Steven Cohen. *pd* Mel Bourne. *m* Jerry Goldsmith. *cast* Geena Davis, Stephen Rea, James Gandolfini, Aida Turturro, Philip Bosco, Jenny O'Hara, Michael Rispoli.

● Angie (Davis) is a working-class Italian from Bensonhurst, New York, who idolises her 'free-spirited' mother whom she hasn't seen since she was three, loves her devoted father (Bosco), and loathes her fussy stepmother (O'Hara). At first the only sign that she feels constricted by plumber boyfriend Vinnie (Gandolfini) is her sudden interest in art; then she discovers she's pregnant, goes to a gallery, and picks up Irish chancer Noel (Rea). Even her best friend Tina (Turturro) thinks she's crazy when she drops Vinnie, but her affair with Noel is a fairy-tale romance – until unforeseen crises force her to reassess her life. For the first hour, this adaptation of Avra Wing's novel delivers: you're carried along by the quirky romance, sharp dialogue, and the jokes about gynaecology and vibrators. But then, in the last half hour, there's a change of direction and events take an unpersuasive turn towards tragedy – a great pity, since, as a spirited comedy, the film had a lot going for it. CO'S

Angi Vera

(1978, Hun, 96 min)
d/sc Pál Gabor. *ph* Lajos Koltai. *ed* Éva Karmentó. *pd* András Gyürky. *m* György Selmeczi. *cast* Veronika Pap, Erzsi Pasztor, Eva Szabo, Tamás Dunai.

● Set in 1948 in Stalinist Hungary, *Angi Vera* tells the story of a bold, innocent girl sent on a course to improve her standing in the Party. As Gabor's camera circles, a silent witness to the emotional and moral dilemmas that surface in the group and particularly Vera herself, we gradually discover the susceptibility which turns her from apparently brave idealist to seemingly wilful liar, trading her integrity (and betraying her love) for a place in the only system which has taken an interest in her. It's a very humanist film which successfully blends melodrama, morals and political comment. It also looks tremendous. HM

Anglaise et le duc, L'

see Lady & the Duke, The

Angry Silence, The

(1959, GB, 95 min, b/w)
d Guy Green. *p* Richard Attenborough, Bryan Forbes. *sc* Bryan Forbes. *ph* Arthur Ibbetson. *ed* Anthony Harvey. *ad* Ray Simm. *m* Malcolm Arnold. *cast* Richard Attenborough, Pier Angeli, Michael Craig, Bernard Lee, Geoffrey Keen, Alfred Burke, Oliver Reed, Alan Whicker, Bryan Forbes.

● A strange mixture of melodramatic union-bashing and sharp, penetrating observations on working-class life. The villains are phantoms of an ill-informed imagination, but Attenborough's lone-wolf worker, holding out against an unofficial strike, is vivid and well thought out. The realism of his life with fading Italian bride (Angeli) and womanising lodger (Craig) is superbly realised, and hardly seems to belong to the same film as the leering Teddy boys who act as union heavies and the steely-eyed agitator (Burke) whose machinations control the fate of the sheep-like workers. As Attenborough's jaunty individualism is transmuted into paranoid hysteria, the intrusion of tragic melodrama into what looked like a realist social problem film becomes more satisfying. With the villains scattered and the hero blinded for daring to take on the world single-handed, one emerges, like the workers, suitably chastened. RMy

Angst

(1993, Aust, 56 min)
d Judy Menczel. *cast* Deb Filler, 'Austen Tayshus', Moshe Waldoks.

● This documentary looks at three Jewish comedians, whose fathers were in concentration camps. It doesn't sound like a barrel of laughs, yet the mixture of tragedy and comedy makes for a stimulating film. Character comic Deb Filler recalls how her school friends used to think her dad's tattoo was his telephone number; 'Austen Tayshus' muses on the conflict between assimilating and retaining his history; and Moshe Waldoks poses the profound question – if Jewish parents want all their children to be doctors, how did so many turn out to be comics? BD

Angst

see Schizophrenia

Angst essen Seele auf

see Fear Eats the Soul

Anguish (Angustia)

(1987, Sp, 89 min)
d Bigas Luna. *p* Pepon Caromina. *sc* Bigas Luna. *ph* Jose Maria Civit. *ed* Tom Sabin. *m* JM Pagan. *cast* Zelda Rubenstein, Michael Lerner, Talia Paul, Angel Jose.

● A strikingly original, intricately constructed, and extremely gruesome horror film about a mother-fixated opthalmologist's assistant with an unhealthy interest in eyeballs. 'Soon' says his diminutive mother (Rubenstein), 'all the eyes in the city will be ours' – and she means it. Using creepily effective ultra close-ups and a clever Chinese box structure, Luna introduces another level of voyeuristic disturbance by allowing the events in this film-within-the-film to spill out into the auditorium (it's a case of who's watching who when?), where a teenage girl in the audience is becoming increasingly disturbed by the twitchy antics of a popcorn-eating man. The execution doesn't always match the boldness of the conception, but this post-modern shocker intelligently exploits the notion that horror is in the eye of the beholder. NF

Angus

(1995, US, 90 min)
d Patrick Read Johnson. *p* Dawn Steel. *sc* Jill Gordon. *ph* Alexander Grusynski. *ed* Janice Hampton. *m* David Russo. *cast* Charlie Talbert, George C Scott, Kathy Bates, Christopher Owen, James Van Der Beek, Rita Moreno, Ariana Richards.

● Angus is a fat kid. As we know, fat kids have it rough: there's always some school-favourite out there, looking to further his own vainglory at your expense; some golden Rick Sanford (Van Der Beek), goading you, spreading scurrilities, running your over-sized underwear up the flagpole. Angus (Talbert) has it so bad he's applying to move school, but there's a more pressing problem when Rick rigs the election for the Winter Ball King and Queen, sending the unballetic Angus out to an embarrassingly public dance with the one and only Melissa Lefevre (Richards). Basic, yes, but for a teen message movie, this is surprisingly fun, and so sweetly good-natured it feels churlish to sneer. Partly that's because the film adopts such an unassuming profile: there's little preachiness or sentimentalism. If you're a tubby adolescent with girl trouble or a self-esteem problem, and in need of some sensible and reassuring escapism, this may be the one for you. NB

Animal, The

(2001, US, 83 min)
d Luke Greenfield. *p* Barry Bernardi, Carr D'Angelo, Todd Garner. *sc* Tom Brady, Rob Schneider. *ph* Peter Lyons Collister. *ed* Jeff Gourson, Peck Prior. *pd* Alan Au. *m* Teddy Castellucci. *cast* Rob Schneider, Colleen Haskell, John C McGinley, Michael Caton, Guy Torry, Louis Lombardi, Edward Asner, Bob Rubin, Pilar Schneider, Scott Wilson.

● Imagine *Police Academy*-style japes, updated with jovial bestiality and performed under the watchful eye of scatological mastermind and exec producer Adam Sandler. Desperate to get on the police force, wimpy cadet Marvin Mange (Schneider) slugs badger milk for enhanced nourishment. After a car crash, he develops superhuman powers, to the chagrin of bullying Sgt Sisk

(McGinley). It turns out Marvin was rebuilt by a mad scientist using 'pioneering animal transmutation'. Now he struggles to suppress his four-legged side. Schneider's sizeable talent for animal mimicry is revealed in a slew of visual pranks. Curiously, Marvin's magnetism somehow works on tree rescuer and insipid love interest Rianna (Haskell). His pals, however, just think that confessing to uncontrollable animal instincts means he's addicted to porn. Superbly crass. CF

Animal Attraction

see Someone Like You...

Animal Crackers

(1930, US, 98 min, b/w)
d Victor Heerman. *sc* Morrie Ryskind. *ph* George Folsey. *songs* Bert Kalmar, Harry Ruby. *cast* The Marx Brothers, Margaret Dumont, Lillian Roth, Louis Sorin, Hal Thompson, Margaret Irving.

● The Marx Brothers' second film and one of their best, satirising the rich at play as they infiltrate a society party and beome involved with a stolen painting. Groucho is Captain Spaulding the explorer, the art expert is Abey the Fishmonger, Chico and Harpo have trouble with a flash, and Groucho insults the beautiful Ms Dumont. GA

Animal Factory

(2000, US, 90 min)
d Steve Buscemi. *p* Julie Yorn, Elie Samaha, Andrew Stevens. *sc* Edward Bunker. *ph* Phil Parmet. *ed* Kate Williams. *pd* Steven Rosenzweig. *m* John Lurie. *cast* Edward Furlong, Willem Dafoe, Danny Trejo, Seymour Cassel, Steve Buscemi, John Heard, Tom Arnold, Mickey Rourke.

● *Trees Lounge* displayed confident, unshowy direction, superb low key performances, gentle wit and total credibility. Steve Buscemi's second directorial outing – adapted by Edward Bunker from his own novel – places those same virtues at the service of a rather darker story. A 21-year-old from a comfortable background, Ron Decker (Furlong) is given a harsh sentence for dealing marijuana; inside, his good looks inevitably attract attention. Fortunately, prison fixer and gangleader Earl Copen (Dafoe) commands enough respect to offer protection – though some, including the officials, reckon he just wants his own punk. A fascinating, ambiguous (hence suspenseful) portrait of the central relationship between the novice and his all-too-experienced mentor, the film also succeeds as a study of friendship, honour and the lasting effects of rough justice doled out by cons and authorities alike. John Lurie's score is terrific, the cast topnotch (watch out for Ron's tranny cellmate), and the whole thing blends tough observation with moments of surprising tenderness. GA

Animal Farm

(1954, GB, 73 min)
d/p John Halas, Joy Batchelor. *sc* John Halas, Joy Batchelor, Philip Stapp, Lothar Wolf. *m* Matyas Seiber. *cast* voices: Gordon Heath, Maurice Denham.

● Produced and directed by Halas and Batchelor, Britain's first feature length animation sticks to the letter of Orwell's 'memorable fable' on the hopes and failures of the Soviet revolution, using an avuncular narrator (Gordon Heath) and ceding all the (infrequent and largely inarticulate) character voices to Maurice Denham, rather than attempting to get under the skin of the piece. Consequently, the film feels more like an illustrated audio book (or study aid) than a fully fledged movie: an intellectual experience, not an emotional one. TCh

Animal Love

see Tierische Liebe

Animals Film, The

(1981, GB/US, 136 min)
d/p Victor Schonfeld, Myriam Alaux. *sc* Victor Schonfeld. *ph* Kevin Keating. *ed* Victor Schonfeld. *m* Robert Wyatt. *narrator* Julie Christie.

● Who cares about cruelty to animals? You should, suggests this documentary narrated by Julie Christie, not just cranks and misty-eyed pet-lovers with more sentiment than sense, because it's a basic political issue as much as a moral/emotional one. Animal abuse means mega-profits for factory farming and pharmaceutics, but the final appeal is to naked self-interest rather than compassion: when life is held cheap, it's a small step from mutilating pigs in H-bomb tests today to annihilating people tomorrow. The film uses expressive montage to drive its points home with a raw and blistering anger that can't fail to move, even if you don't always entirely agree (or care to watch the screen). SJo

Animalympics

(1979, US, 80 min)
d Steven Lisberger. *p* Steven Lisberger, Donald Kushner. *sc* Steven Lisberger, Michael Fremer. *ed* Matt Cope. *ad* Roger Allers. *pd* Richard Fernalld. *m* Graham Gouldman. *cast* voices: Gilda Radner, Billy Crystal, Harry Shearer, Michael Fremer.

● Conceived in 1976 as a 7-minute parody of the media coverage aroused by the Olympic Games, this animated film eventually turned up 73 merciless minutes longer. Using an assortment of animals and an armoury of terrible puns to run national stereotypes into the ground, it might have been tedious-but-funny. Actually it's just tedious, with a shampoo-commercial soundtrack from songsmith Graham Gouldman. CR

Anita

(1973, Swe/Fr, 95 min)
d/p/sc Torgny Wickman. *ph* Hans Dittmer. *ed* Lasse Lundberg. *m* Lennart Fors. *cast* Christina Lindberg, Stellan Skarsgård, Michel David, Danièle Vlaminck, Per Mattson.

● Swedish sex film, ludicrous and melancholy, in which Skarsgård plays a psychiatrist, an advocate of 'rational-emotive' therapy, whatever that may be, who eventually goes to bed with, and satisfies, his 17-year-old 'nymphomaniac' patient Anita (Lindberg). At the close, Anita's parents, having finally lost patience with their promiscuous daughter, change the front-door locks and have an orgy of their own. Watching this, Anita realises she is at last free. A muddled left-over from the Swinging '60s. JPy

Anita: Dances of Vice (Anita: Tänze des Lasters)

(1987, WGer, 87 min, b/w & col)
d Rosa von Praunheim. *sc* Rosa von Praunheim, Hannelene Limpach, Marianne Enzensberger, Lotti Huber. *ph* Elfi Mikesh. *ed* Rosa von Praunheim, Michael Schäfer. *ad* Inge Stiborski, Michael Fechner, Christa Kleemann, Volker März, Wolfgang Peetz. *m* Konrad Elfers. *cast* Lotti Huber, Ina Blum, Mikael Honesseau, Tillmann Lehnert, Bernd Henckels.

● On a dirty grey street in Berlin, a crowd gathers round an eccentric old woman who is performing a strip-tease. Dragged off to a psychiatric hospital, she demands cocaine instead of thorazine, tries to seduce everyone in sight, and insists that she is the legendary dancer Anita Berber, darling of the decadent '20s. Suddenly, in true *Wizard of Oz* style, the film departs from monochrome reality into the colour-drenched world of the woman's fantasies, a wildly exaggerated evocation of Weimar Berlin filmed in full-blown expressionist style. The young Anita (Blum) and her partner Droste (Honesseau) set out to be the most perverse people in the world, develop a reputation for pornographic stage performances, and have sex with anything that moves. Inevitably, both come to bad ends: Droste arrested for fraud, Anita dying of TB. The identity of the old woman (Huber) is never certain. Her belief in her own fantasy is unshakeable; and von Praunheim's film, visually astounding and performed with hilarious conviction, is an exhilarating testament to the power of the imagination. RS

Anita no perd el tren

see Anita Takes a Chance

Anita Takes a Chance (Anita no perd el tren)

(2000, Sp, 90 min)
d/p Ventura Pons. *sc* Ventura Pons, Lluís-Anton Baulenas. *ph* Mario Montero. *ed* Pere Abadal. *pd* Bel.lo Torras. *m* Carles Cases. *cast* Rosa Maria Sardà, María Barranco, José Coronado, Jordi Dauder, Roger Coma, Albert Forner.

● After running the box office of an independent cinema in Barcelona for 34 years, Anita (Sardà) is urged by her boss to take a two-week holiday. On her return she finds the cinema gone and no job for her in the multiplex rising in its place. Haunting the building site, Anita falls for the driver of an earth-mover. The ground duly moves, but Anita's beau is a married man. A likeable film with a light touch and a delight in Hollywood references. *Cinema Paradiso*, however, it is not. NRo

Ankur (The Seedling)

(1974, Ind, 131 min)
d Shyam Benegal. *p* Mohan J Bijlani, Freni Variava. *sc* Shyam Benegal. *ph* Govind Nihalani. *ed* Bhanudas. *m* Vanraj Bhatia. *cast* Anant Nag, Mirza Qadir Ali Baig, Shabana Azmi, Priya Tendulka, Dadhu Meher.

● Benegal's first narrative feature mostly recalls the modest realism of Satyajit Ray. The story is of a reluctant young rural landlord attracted to a servant whom he eventually seduces and takes as his mistress. It clearly intends some measure of social protest against an impossibly rigid caste system, the subjection of women, and traditional ruling class privilege; and if the seduction is coyly shown, the sexual nature of the relationship is at least spoken about surprisingly candidly for an Indian film. RM

Anna

(1987, US, 100 min)
d Yurek Bogayevicz. *p* Zanne Devine, Yurek Bogayevicz. *sc* Agnieszka Holland. *ph* Bobby Bukowski. *ed* Julie Sloane. *pd* Lester Cohen. *m* Greg Hawkes. *cast* Sally Kirkland, Robert Fields, Paulina Porizkova, Larry Pine, Steven Gilborn, Gibby Brand, John Robert Tillotson.

● Much-loved '60s Czech movie star Anna (Kirkland), imprisoned for criticising the authorities, is banished to the US. There her refugee spouse spurns her to make TV commercials. Now she's just a 'resting' actress. After an audition, she befriends fellow-immigrant Krystyna (the beautiful Porizkova), who has a photo of Anna clutched in her hand. Anna takes Krystyna home, and so begins the age-old tale of master and pupil. As soon as Krystyna has her teeth done, she lands a director in the Hamptons. Bigger and better roles follow, while Anna is attacked by the green-eyed monster. What price Hollywood? A must for those who *adore* all things theatrical, and a maybe for those who don't. Bogayevicz's superbly acted film is for the most part an amiable study of ageing and exile. Its low-key kookiness is reminiscent of Jarmusch; its final descent into mawkish melodrama is not. MS

Anna and the King

(1999, US, 148 min)
d Andy Tennant. *p* Lawrence Bender, Ed Elbert. *sc* Steve Meerson, Peter Krikes. *ph* Caleb Deschanel. *ed* Roger Bondelli. *pd* Luciana Arrighi. *m* George Fenton. *cast* Jodie Foster, Chow Yun-Fat, Bai Ling, Tom Felton, Syed Alwi, Randall Duk Kim, Lim Kay Siu, Melissa Campbell, Geoffrey Palmer, Ann Firbank.

● Fox threw money at this third version of the story of the widowed English governess who in 1862 forms an attachment to the strong willed but reformist king of Siam. It is, however, neither as witty as the 1946 Dunne-Harrison film, nor as lively as the 1956 Rodgers and Hammerstein musical. The logistics of the large Malay production appear to have cramped the light touch director Tennant applied to *Ever After*. Foster – playing Anna with a passable educated English accent – is a heavy proposition. But coming over like a pastiche of the passionate integrity exhibited by Holly Hunter's Ada in *The Piano*, Anna's 'feminism' feels anachronistic. She smiles a lot while tutoring the 58 royal darlings, and glows while dancing with the king at a banquet, but it's a limited performance. As King Mongkut, Chow Yun-Fat has the better, lighter measure. But it's dull and over-extended, and scenes of hanging men preclude family viewing. WH

Anna and the King of Siam

(1946, US, 128 min, b/w)
d John Cromwell. *p* Louis D Lighton. *sc* Talbot Jennings, Sally Benson. *ph* Arthur Miller. *ed* Harmon Jones. *ad* Lyle Wheeler, William Darling. *m* Bernard Herrmann. *cast* Irene Dunne, Rex Harrison, Linda Darnell, Gale Sondergaard, Lee J Cobb, Mikhail Rasumny.

● A lavish entertainment based on the real-life experiences of English governess Margaret Langdon, who arrived in Siam in 1862 to teach the King's 67 children. Sumptuous sets, exceptional photography (Arthur Miller), and some crisp verbal exchanges between the strong-willed King of Thailand and his new employee give Cromwell's light comedy the edge over the later musical version of the same story, *The King and I*, starring Yul Brynner and Deborah Kerr. NF

Annabelle partagée

(1990, Fr, 86 min)
d Francesca Comencini. *p* Sophie Deloche, Anne Fieschl. *sc* Francesca Comencini. *ph* Michel Abramowicz. *ed* Yves Deschamps. *ad* Valérie Grall. *m* Etienne Daho, Les Valentins. *cast* Delphine Zingg, François Marthouret, Jean-Claude Adelin, Florence Thomassin, Dominique Régnier, Jeanne Biras.

● It's over almost before it has begun, but you can't help noticing the close-up of an erect penis in the first few seconds; nor, despite a timely pull of focus, its subsequent discharge. This is the first and last coup in what proves to be a tedious example of the French Art Film. Annabelle (Zingg) is a 25-year-old dance student living in Paris. The obtuse angle in an Eternal Triangle, she vacillates between two lovers, the youthful Luca (Adelin), and Richard (Marthouret), an architect her father's age. The writer-director approaches this tiresome situation from an oblique, feminine perspective, but there's no insight; the film is studiously humourless, explicitly unerotic, and alienatingly disengaged. When Annabelle complains that she feels colourless, one can only agree – Mlle Zingg doesn't live up to her billing. Surely it's only in (bad) art movies that people lounge around naked staring at empty spaces, assuring a lover *ad nauseam* that 'I want you to death'. Numbing intellectual masturbation. TCh

Anna Christie

(1930, US, 90 min, b/w)
d Clarence Brown. *p* Irving Thalberg. *sc* Frances Marion. *ph* William H Daniels. *ed* Hugh Wynn. *ad* Cedric Gibbons. *cast* Greta Garbo, Charles Bickford, George F Marion, Marie Dressler, James T Mack, Lee Phelps.

● Garbo Talks. So, unfortunately, does everyone else (following an evocation of the foggy wharfside, marvellously lit by William Daniels), carefully enunciating Eugene O'Neill's quaint attempts at ethnic speech patterns for a good twenty minutes before Garbo makes her appearance as the prostitute wearily seeking haven on her father's barge (and there finding love with a young seaman). As soon as she makes her entry, hovering in the saloon doorway trailing an almost visibly murky past, one knows one is in safe hands. Even then it is several minutes before she is allowed to risk her memorable first line: 'Gimme a whisky with a ginger ale on the side. And don't be stingy, baby'. She's terrific, but she gets little support from O'Neill's play (a conventional romance tarted up with pseudo poetics) or the rest of the cast (with the exception of Dressler's gin-soaked harridan). TM

Anna Karenina

(1935, US, 95 min, b/w)
d Clarence Brown. *p* David O Selznick. *sc* Clemence Dane, Salka Viertel. *ph* William H Daniels. *ed* Robert J Kern. *ad* Cedric Gibbons. *m* Herbert Stothart. *cast* Greta Garbo, Fredric March, Basil Rathbone, Maureen O'Sullivan, Freddie Bartholomew, May Robson, Reginald Owen.

● Surprisingly, this mixture of MGM gloss, the aloof Garbo, and the labyrinthine Tolstoy works like a charm: visually and emotionally the most rarefied of Garbo's '30s films, with William Daniels' radiant photography preventing decorative blossoms, vines, banquet tables and riding-habits from congealing into the usual dull display of studio extravagance, and the dappled sunlight providing an ingenious background for Garbo's finely tortured passions. Rathbone, as usual, is enjoyably villainous as the husband; a drastically barbered March is less at ease as the lover; but the only real blot is provided by Freddie Bartholomew as the heroine's darling child, looking and sounding the way sickly chocolate tastes. GB

Anna Karenina

(1947, GB, 123 min)
d Julien Duvivier. *p* Alexander Korda. *sc* Julien Duvivier, Guy Morgan, Jean Anouilh. *ph* Henri Alekan. *ed* Russell Lloyd. *ad* Andre Andrejew. *m* Constant Lambert. *cast* Vivien Leigh, Ralph Richardson, Kieron Moore, Sally Ann Howes, Martita Hunt, Niall MacGinnis, Hugh Dempster.

● Visually opulent but lifeless Korda production which reduces Tolstoy's novel to a routine triangle situation. Leigh and Moore make a vacant duo, with Richardson's Karenin a bundle of theatrical mannerisms. TM

Anna Karenina (aka Leo Tolstoy's Anna Karenina)

(1997, US, 110 min)
d Bernard Rose. *p* Bruce Davey. *sc* Bernard Rose. *ph* Daryn Okada. *ed* Victor Du Bois. *pd* John Myhre. *cast* Sophie Marceau, Sean Bean, Alfred Molina, Mia Kirshner, James Fox, Fiona Shaw, Danny Huston, Phyllida Law.

● With the authentic backdrop of imperial Russia at his disposal, writer/director Rose luxuriates in Viscontian sumptuousness, but marble and gold leaf do not by themselves a movie make. Both Marceau's Anna and Bean's Vronsky seem tentative in the extreme, especially towards each other. We don't believe their grand passion for a moment, and without much emotional involvement to usher us along, the philosophical progress of Molina's narrator is abandoned in favour of the sixth form inanities packing Rose's turgid script. Tchaikovsky's 'Pathétique' swells every time anyone so much as coughs. TJ

Anna Pavlova

see Pavlova – A Woman for All Time

Annapolis Story, An (aka The Blue and the Gold)

(1955, US, 85 min)
d Don Siegel. *p* Walter Mirisch. *sc* Dan Ullman, Geoffrey Homes. *ph* Sam Leavitt. *ed* William Austin. *ad* David Milton. *m* Marlin Skiles. *cast* John Derek, Diana Lynn, Kevin McCarthy, LQ Jones, Pat Conway, Alvy Moore, Robert Osterloh.

● Brothers Derek and McCarthy are cadets at the Annapolis Naval Academy. During pilot training they quarrel over the affections of the vapid Lynn (50 min) then patch things up during action in the skies over Korea (35 min). Filmed on threadbare sets, with ill-matched actuality footage stitched in, this was doubtless as tiresome to shoot as it is to watch. Several of its perpetrators went on to greater things, though. Besides the director, there's Sam Peckinpah, credited as 'dialogue supervisor' and showing up as a helicopter pilot, fishing McCarthy out of the drink during what might laughingly be called the film's climax. BBa

Anne and Muriel

see Deux Anglaises et le Continent, Les

Anne Devlin

(1984, Eire, 121 min)
d Pat Murphy. *p* Pat Murphy, Tom Hayes. *sc* Pat Murphy. *ph* Thaddeus O'Sullivan. *ed* Arthur Keating. *pd* John Lucas. *m* Robert Boyle. *cast* Brid Brennan, Bosco Hogan, Des McAleer, Gillian Hackett, David Kelly, Ian McElhinney.

● Loosely based on the journals of Anne Devlin, Murphy's second feature (following *Maeve*) shows how, at the start of the 19th century, the daughter of an Irish peasant farmer becomes a collaborator with the rebel leader Robert Emmet, and proves to be stronger than any man. The fight for Irish independence is equated with the struggle for female emancipation, with the military conflict occurring off-camera, concentrating attention on the battle Anne wages at home. This restraint is maintained throughout: Murphy demonstrates rather than remonstrates. With the beauty of the Vermeer-like interiors and the towering performance of Brid Brennan compensating for the somewhat slow pace, *Anne Devlin* is a powerful, compassionate, and ultimately persuasive film. MS

Année Dernière à Marienbad, L' (Last Year in Marienbad) 100

(1961, Fr/It, 94 min, b/w)
d Alain Resnais. *p* Pierre Courau, Raymond Froment. *sc* Alain Robbe-Grillet. *ph* Sacha Vierny. *ed* Henri Colpi, Jasmine Chasney. *ad* Jacques Saulnier. *m* Francis Seyrig. *cast* Delphine Seyrig, Giorgio Albertazzi, Sacha Pitoeff, Françoise Bertin, Pierre Barbaud, Luce Garcia-Ville.

● Something of a key film in the development of concepts of cinematic modernism, simply because – with a script by *nouveau roman* iconoclast Alain Robbe-Grillet – it sets up a puzzle that is never resolved: a man meets a woman in a rambling hotel and believes he may have had an affair with her the previous year at Marienbad – or did he? Or was it somewhere else? Deliberately scrambling chronology to the point where past, present and future become meaningless, Resnais creates a vaguely unsettling mood by means of stylish composition, long, smooth tracking shots along the hotel's deserted corridors, and strangely detached performances. Obscure, oneiric, it's either some sort of masterpiece or meaningless twaddle. GA

Année Juliette, L' (The Year of Juliette)

(1995, Fr, 84 min)
d Philippe Le Guay. *p* Alain Rocca. *sc* Philippe Le Guay, Jean-Louis Richard, Brigitte Rouan, Jérôme Tonnerre. *ph* Pierre Novion. *ed* Denise de Casabianca. *ad* Jimmy Vansteenkiste. *m* Carolin Petit, Georges Arriagada. *cast* Fabrice Luchini, Valérie Stroh, Philippine Leroy Beaulieu, Marine Delterme, Didier Flamand.

● A chap takes the wrong suitcase from an airport carousel. From this creaky device evolves a haunting, salutary anecdote about Camille, an anaesthetist, who takes advantage of the suitcase confusion to end a too-pressing relationship by pretending it belongs to a fictional girlfriend, Juliette. The ideal illusory Juliette soon becomes more engrossing to Camille than disappointing, awkward reality; but the scriptwriters spring a nasty surprise on him just as the film ends. Luchini's delicate rendering of amiability turning to obsession and bewilderment, together with the movie's fitful comic streak deflect a full appreciation of just how black a tale this is. BBa

Anne of Green Gables

(1934, US, 77 min, b/w)
d George Nicholls Jr. *p* Kenneth Macgowan. *sc* Sam Mintz. *ph* Lucien Andriot. *ed* Arthur Schmidt. *ad* Van Nest Polglase, Al Herman. *m* Max Steiner. *cast* Anne Shirley, Tom Brown, OP Heggie, Helen Westley, Charley Grapewin, Sara Haden.

● A passable adaptation of LM Montgomery's children's classic, beginning well with the placidly fraught arrival in a backwoods town of the orphan girl whose horrified adoptive parents instantly protest that they actually ordered a boy (the atmosphere helped no end by Heggie's lovely performance as the henpecked husband who slyly – and mutely – rebels in her favour). After that the plot begins to develop galloping consumption in order to get everything in, while simultaneously sliding into sentimentality. A further hazard is the lead performance by former child star Dawn O'Day (who adopted the professional name of Anne Shirley after the character she enacts here): much too knowingly sophisticated in playing the wilfully imaginative child, she makes one feel that what the dear thing really rates is a sound thrashing. TM

Anne of the Indies

(1951, US, 87 min)
d Jacques Tourneur. *p* George Jessel. *sc* Philip Dunne, Arthur Caesar. *ph* Harry Jackson. *ed* Robert Fritch. *ad* Lyle Wheeler, Albert Hogsett. *m* Franz Waxman. cast Jean Peters, Louis Jourdan, Debra Paget, Herbert Marshall, Thomas Gomez, James Robertson Justice.

● Pretty much of a swashbuckling potboiler aside from the switch of having Peters, spirited but not entirely convincing, as the bloodthirsty (but she has her reasons) pirate chief. Not one of Tourneur's better films, although he does give it some of the same colourful bounce as *The Flame and the Arrow*. TM

Anne of the Thousand Days

(1969, GB, 146 min)
d Charles Jarrott. *p* Hal B Wallis. *sc* John Hale, Bridget Boland. *ph* Arthur Ibbetson. *ed* Richard Marden. *pd* Maurice Carter. *m* Georges Delerue. *cast* Richard Burton, Genevieve Bujold, Irene Papas, Anthony Quayle, John Colicos, Michael Hordern.
● Interminable plod through the story of Henry the Eighth and Anne Boleyn, sticking mainly to domestic trivia with dialogue to match. The few attempts at pageantry founder in an uneasy mixture of real locations and stagy sets, with the odd appalling painted backdrop thrown in. Burton plays throughout on a monotonous note of bluff ferocity, while Bujold remains sweetly vacuous. TM

Anne Trister

(1986, Can/Switz, 115 min)
d Léa Pool. *p* Roger Frappier, Claude Bonin. *sc* Marcel Beaulieu, Léa Pool. *ph* Pierre Mignot. *ed* Michel Arcand. *ad* Vianney Gauthier. *m* René Dupéré. *cast* Albane Guilhe, Louise Marleau, Lucie Laurier, Hugues Quester, Guy Thauvette, Nuvit Ozdogru.
● Melancholy, well-observed chronicle of a painter's self-discovery. After the death of her father, Guilhe gives up art studies in her native Switzerland and moves to Quebec, sharing an apartment with child psychologist friend Marleau, but spending much time in a nearby studio confronting her emotional upheavals through work on a huge mural. Pool's understated style captures the artistic process on the wing and isn't too heavy-handed in detailing Guilhe's growing feelings for her expat host. An impressive achievement on a minor scale. TJ

Annie

(1981, US, 128 min)
d John Huston. *p* Ray Stark. *sc* Carol Sobieski. *ph* Richard Moore. *ed* Michael A Stevenson. *pd* Dale Hennesy. *m* Charles Strouse. *cast* Albert Finney, Aileen Quinn, Carol Burnett, Ann Reinking, Bernadette Peters, Tim Curry.
● The mystery about Huston's $60m screen adaptation of the hit stage musical – an entirely ordinary and comparatively unspectacular musical fable in which perky orphan Annie (Quinn) wins the heart of mean millionaire Daddy Warbucks (Finney) – is how it could possibly have cost so much. The songs never take off into anything very much, the whole atmosphere (apart from the climax) is distinctly stagebound, and Huston merely reveals why he had never before in his long career been hired to make a musical. DP

Annie Get Your Gun

(1950, US, 107 min)
d George Sidney. *p* Arthur Freed. *sc* Sidney Sheldon. *ph* Charles Rosher. *ed* James E Newcom. *ad* Cedric Gibbons, Paul Groesse. *m* Irving Berlin. *cast* Betty Hutton, Howard Keel, Louis Calhern, Edward Arnold, Keenan Wynn, J Carrol Naish.
● It was to have been Judy Garland directed by the tasteful Charles Walters, but the lady was in one of her problem patches, and this version of Irving Berlin's barn-storming musical (a bit old-fashioned even when it appeared in 1946) finally emerged with vastly different personnel. In some ways Hutton and Sidney make a better team: they share a streak of vulgarity five miles wide, and the character of the gun-toting Annie Oakley offers Hutton ample opportunity to do 'what comes naturally', as the song has it. She screams, capers around, fires lots of bullets, and generally lets off sufficient energy to see one through the coldest winter. If you sit towards the back of the cinema, and don't mind leaving your aesthetic scruples with the usherette, you can be guaranteed an enjoyably rowdy, gaudy time. GB

Annie Hall

(1977, US, 93 min)
d Woody Allen. *p* Charles H Joffe. *sc* Woody Allen, Marshall Brickman. *ph* Gordon Willis. *ed* Ralph Rosenblum. *ad* Mel Bourne. *cast* Woody Allen, Diane Keaton, Tony Roberts, Carol Kane, Paul Simon, Shelley Duvall, Janet Margolin, Signourey Weaver.
● These were the days when Allen was still a comedian who happened to make films, rather than the comic film-maker he became. (Don't believe it? Then read film editor Ralph Rosenblum's account of the film's chaotic creation in the cutting-room, in his book *When the Shooting Stops*). The movie is therefore little more than a series of shrewd but disjointed anecdotes dealing with Allen's usual self-obsessive hang-ups and fashionable metropolitan pastimes: existential dread, masturbation, coke-sniffing, movie-going, psychoanalysis, etc. The one-liners are razor-sharp, the observations of Manhattanite manners as keen as mustard, and some of the romantic stuff even quite touching. If you can forgive the fact that it's a ragbag of half-digested intellectual ideas dressed up with trendy intellectual references, you should have a good laugh. NF

Annie Oakley

(1935, US, 83 min, b/w)
d George Stevens. *sc* Joel Sayre, John Twist. *ph* J Roy Hunt. *ed* Jack Hively. *ad* Albert S D'Agostino, Perry Ferguson. *m* Alberto Colombo. *cast* Barbara Stanwyck, Preston Foster, Melvyn Douglas, Moroni Olsen, Pert Kelton.
● Stanwyck's first Western (of sorts), aptly described as *Annie Get Your Gun* without the songs. Not strong on fact, and inclined to string out the tiresome twists that attend the crackshot lady's rivalry/romance with the resident sharpshooter (Foster) when she joins Buffalo Bill's Wild West Show. But Stevens turns it into a nice piece of nostalgic Americana, and Stanwyck is great. TM

Annie's Coming Out

(1984, Aust, 93 min)
d Gil Brealey. *p* Donald Murray. *sc* John Patterson, Chris Borthwick. *ph* Mick Van Borneman. *ed* Lindsay Frazer. *pd* Robbie Perkins. *m* Simon Walker. *cast* Angela Punch McGregor, Drew Forsythe, Tina Arhondis, Liddy Clark, Mark Butler, Monica Maughan, Philippa Baker.
● Jessie, assistant at a state institution for retarded children, comes to believe that 14-year-old Annie, despite cerebral palsy, has intelligence she is powerless to convey. Her belief leads to conflict with medical staff and eventually a court hearing, during which Annie is finally able to demonstrate her intellect and self-awareness. That is also the substance of the book by Anne MacDonald: her 'Jessie', Rosemary Crossley, discovered Annie's locked-away self in 1977, twelve years after Annie's consignment to care. But the film labours under a weight of presumably lawyer-vetted two-dimensional characters like Complacent Doctor, Kindly Judge and Nurse Dragon. Such conformism, and the related straining towards a neat story structure, mean that very little would have to change to rework this as a Sally Field or Julia Roberts vehicle for a mass market. DO

Annie Sprinkle's Herstory of Porn

(1999, US, 70 min)
d Annie Sprinkle, Scarlet Harlot. *with* Annie Sprinkle.
● After inviting audiences to examine her cervix through a speculum while on stage in the mid-'90s, what next for 'Post-Porn Modernist' and all-round spiritual sex guru Annie Sprinkle? In this docu-porn, the veteran actress turned director trawls through a selection of her own hardcore clips to chart her 25-year evolution from humble popcorn girl to present-day darling of the New York avant garde. A distinctive gem, thanks to the mediating influence of her delightfully wry and insightful commentary – as much about society's attitudes to sex as about the merits (or lack thereof) of the various excerpts on offer. SS

Anniversary, The

(1967, GB, 95 min)
d Roy Ward Baker. *p/sc* Jimmy Sangster. *ph* Harry Waxman. *ed* James Needs. *ad* Reece Pemberton. *m* Phillip Martell. *cast* Bette Davis, Sheila Hancock, Jack Hedley, James Cossins, Christian Roberts, Elaine Taylor.
● High camp black comedy from Hammer, with one-eyed momma Davis glorying in her shrill domestic tyranny over three helpless sons. Stagy evidence that Davis never really got over *What Ever Happened to Baby Jane?*, but she still had enough industrial clout to get the original director, Alvin Rakoff, fired after a week's shooting. PT

Annyong Kimchi

(1999, Jap, 52 min)
d Tetsuaki Matsue. *p* Tetsuo Yamatani, Hiraku Yoshida. *sc* Tetsuaki Matsue, Dai Nakai. *ph* Kazuki Mogi, Tetsuaki Matsue. *ed* Hiraku Yoshida, Masanori Seki. *m* Samu Okano. *with* Tetsuaki Matsue.
● Denounced as a fool by his dying grandfather, Matsue belatedly started giving thought to his Korean ancestry. Crazy about movies since childhood, he'd always thought of himself as an all-Japanese movie freak. But when he entered Imamura's film school he began 'coming out' as Korean to friends and classmates. Narrated by his younger sister Masako, *Annyong Kimchi* (literally, 'Hello, Kimchi') is a charmingly geeky essay on Korean-Japanese identity. It chronicles the history of Matsue's family (originally 'Yu', not Matsue), sketches the political and social issues and documents his first ever visit to South Korea: the self-portrait of a young man as a kimchi-hater. TR

An 01, L' (Year One)

(1972, Fr, 87 min, b/w)
d Jacques Doillon; (New York) Alain Resnais, (Niger) Jean Rouch. *sc* Gébé. *ph* Renan Pollès; Gérard de Battista, Mike Hausman, William Lubtchansky. *ed* Noëlle Boisson. *cast* Gérard Depardieu, Lee Falk, Nelly Kaplan, Patrice Leconte, Thierry Lhermitte, Lam, Damouré, Miou-Miou.
● The '60s can be heard squeaking to a close in this grab bag of sketches by the cartoonist Gébé. The premise is that the French resolve to shut the country down, talk things over and start again from scratch. Much guitar strumming follows, bras are discarded and such impositions as vacuuming and going to work are deplored and revoked. Resnais' vignette has dummies, representing distraught financiers, raining down from Wall Street skyscrapers. Rouch's contribution is even slighter: a couple of his garrulous pals in Niger discuss the situation. It's all quite genial and throwaway, and the cast is non-professional with a sprinkling of familiar names, none of whom is on screen for more than about 30 seconds. BBa

Anno Uno

see Italy: Year One

Año Perdido, Un

see One Lost Year

A Nos Amours

see To Our Loves

Another Battle (Shin Jingi Naki Tatakai)

(2000, Jap, 109 min)
d Junji Sakamoto. *p* Mitsuru Kurosawa, Hitoshi Matsuda. *sc* Koji Takada. *ph* Norimichi Kasamatsu. *ed* Takeo Araki. *ad* Yasumi Akiyoshi. *m* Tomoyasu Hotei. *cast* Etsushi Toyokawa, Tomoyasu Hotei, Sho Aikawa, Ittoku Kishibe, Koichi Sato.
● The Japanese title suggests a remake of the yakuza classic *Battles Without Honour and Humanity*, but it's actually an original and highly complex account of the battle for succession in a powerful Osaka yakuza 'family'. So complex, in fact, that the string of set-piece assassinations, provocations, negotiations and fights approaches pure abstraction; hard to say who does what to whom and why. But Sakamoto smartly anchors the whole thing in a generic male friendship between Kadoya (Toyokawa) and the Korean-Japanese Chan-Ryon (musician Hotei). Years ago Chan-Ryon killed a yakuza to save Kadoya's life. Now Kadoya decides it's time to return the favour, seeing his old friend under heavy pressure to sell his Korean business empire to the 'family'. Charismatically acted, stylishly directed, largely baffling. TR

Another Country

(1984, GB, 90 min)
d Marek Kanievska. *p* Alan Marshall. *sc* Julian Mitchell. *ph* Peter Biziou. *ed* Gerry Hambling. *pd* Brian Morris. *m* Michael Storey. *cast* Rupert Everett, Colin Firth, Michael Jenn, Robert Addie, Anna Massey, Betsy Brantley.

●In Julian Mitchell's adaptation of his own award-winning play (a naive and romanticised exploration of how ruling-class attitudes in the '30s were shaped), we are asked to believe that a brilliant young homosexual (modelled on Guy Burgess) turns eastwards to communism and the USSR when he is passed over for election to an exclusive prefects' society at his public school. Where the original play was long and more meditative, making suspension of disbelief at least possible, here it just seems like nonsense. There are compensations: Kanievska successfully overcomes the theatrical origins, and Everett turns in an electric performance. As for the rest, the film persuades you that the past is indeed another country, while offering an unreliable guide to its landscape. RR

Another Dawn

(1937, US, 75 min, b/w)
d William Dieterle. *p* Harry Joe Brown. *sc* Laird Doyle. *ph* Tony Gaudio. *ed* Ralph Dawson. *ad* Robert Haas. *m* Erich Wolfgang Korngold. *cast* Errol Flynn, Kay Francis, Ian Hunter, Frieda Inescort, Mary Forbes, Herbert Mundin.
●Flynn and Dieterle picked the short straw when the assignments were being handed out at the studio that week, for this African colonial melodrama wherein spouse Francis finds herself torn between husband Hunter and British army officer Flynn is flimsy fare indeed. Footnote: whenever a Warners movie of the '30s featured a cinema marquee in the background, the stock title *Another Dawn* was invariably featured. TJ

Another Day in Paradise

(1998, US, 101 min)
d Larry Clark. *p* Stephen Chin, Larry Clark, James Woods. *sc* Christopher Landon, Stephen Chin. *ph* Eric Edwards. *ed* Luis Colina. *pd* Aaron Osborne. *cast* James Woods, Melanie Griffith, Vincent Kartheiser, Natasha Gregson Wagner, James Otis, Branden Williams.
●After a scuffle with a guard during a bungled robbery, Bobbie (Kartheiser) is nursed back to health by Mel (Woods), who lectures him on the error of his unambitious ways. An outgoing, even generous scoundrel, Mel decides that the teenager and his girl Rosie (Wagner) should take to the road with himself and his lover Sid (Griffith) to learn the ropes. So starts an odyssey around the Oklahoma back roads for a surrogate family united in its devotion to drugs, booze and outlawdom; trouble is, the junk, Mel's crazed authoritarianism and the lowlifes they're forced to deal with take their toll. While Clark's follow-up to *Kids* shares both that film's amorality and its raw, hand held 'realism', it mostly and mercifully eschews its duplicitous sociological posturing and, despite a few truly nasty violent scenes, its all too evident desire to shock. It's considerably more appealing than its predecessor, then, and surprisingly compelling. Woods is on charismatic, virtuoso form, while Griffith is simply superb. GA

Another 48 HRS

(1990, US, 96 min)
d Walter Hill. *p* Lawrence Gordon, Robert D Wachs. *sc* John Fasano, Jeb Stuart, Larry Gross. *ph* Matthew F Leonetti. *ed* Freeman Davies. *pd* Joseph C Nemec III. *m* James Horner. *cast* Eddie Murphy, Nick Nolte, Brion James, Kevin Tighe, Ed O'Ross, David Anthony Marshall, Andrew Divoff, Bernie Casey.
●The key words here are lazy and contrived. In this pointless sequel to *48 HRS*, we get a tired replay of the classic redneck bar scene, and a desperate attempt to revive the antagonism (minus its crucial racial element) between San Francisco cop Nolte and fast-talking ex-con Murphy. The plot contortions necessary to achieve this are absurd: Nolte faces a manslaughter charge, while the resentful Murphy is about to be released after seven years in the slammer. Only when a pair of vicious bikers blow up his car does Murphy agree to team up with the gruff cop again. The sole innovation is Nolte's obsession with the mysterious Iceman, a criminal kingpin he alone believes exists. Hill's action scenes are par for the course, with plenty of shotgun slayings, vehicle chases and bodies crashing through windows. There is a certain residual pleasure, too, in Hill's atavistic efforts to introduce Western elements into an urban crime thriller, with one of the gun-toting bikers, Willie Hickok (geddit?), saying 'We're the only real outlaws left'. NF

Another Girl, Another Planet

(1992, US, 56 min, b/w)
d Michael Almereyda. *p* Michael Almereyda, Robin O'Hara, Bob Gosse. *sc* Michael Almereyda. *ph* Jim Denault. *ed* David Leonard. *cast* Nic Ratner, Elina Löwensohn, Barry Sherman, Mary Ward, Lisa Perisot, Isabel Gillies.
●Writer/director Almereyda shot his near-feature on a Fisher-Price PXL 2000 camera, a discontinued 'toy' that's been taken up by several American indie film-makers and artists for its unique visual qualities and marginal costs. The ghostly monochrome works best on an intimate scale, giving this East Village, New York, chamber drama a dreamy intensity, as its boho participants float through a late-night haze of romantic pessimism. Nic (Ratner) is married, Bill (Sherman) determinedly single; they live on different floors in the same block, pursuing the mysteries of love, sex and the sway of feminine caprice. Evocative score. Leaves an impression. TJ

Another Life

(2000, GB, 101 min)
d Philip Goodhew. *p* Angela Hart. *sc* Philip Goodhew. *ph* Simon Archer. *ed* Jamie Trevill. *pd* James Merifield. *m* James McConnel. *cast* Natasha Little, Nick Moran, Ioan Gruffudd, Imelda Staunton, Rachael Stirling, Tom Wilkinson, Diana Coupland.
●Ilford, October 1922: Percy Thompson is fatally stabbed by Freddy Bywaters, his wife Edith's lover and the couple's former lodger. The subsequent murder trial of both Edith and Bywaters was a media sensation and the judgment (she was hanged) so controversial that the Home Office closed the case files for 100 years. The focus here is on an independent-minded woman who didn't fit with the bourgeois mores of her time: a would-be free spirit who, as a milliner's book-keeper, earned more than her husband, and fantasised about killing him when she took a lover. Natasha Little's sterling performance combines the cowed suburbanite and the lusty daydreamer, making Edie as captivating as she needs to be for the film's emotional pay-off. There are, however, a few sticky moments. The visualisation of Edith's homicidal musings lacks the necessary subtle delineation of fantasy/reality, and writer/director Goodhew's deft way with dialogue sometimes deserts him when there's a point to prod home. Still, accomplished support from Moran's dull-stick husband and Wilkinson's mercurial milliner earn goodwill, and the rich material spurs an overriding sense of injustice. TJ

Another Lonely Hitman (Shin Kanashiki Hitman)

(1995, Jap, 105 min)
d Rokuro Mochizuki. *p* Yoshi Chiba. *sc* Toshiyuki Morioka. *ph* Nao'aki Imaizumi. *ed* Tekeshi Shimamura. *pd* Kunio Okamura. *m* Kazutoki Umezu. *cast* Ryo Ishibashi, Asami Sawaki, Tatsuzo Yamada, Kazuhiko Kanayama, Yukio Yamanouchi.
●This moody Osaka blues gives a new tonality and impact to the generic tale of a hitman coming out of jail and finding everything changed. Ex-rocker Ishibashi plays Tachibana, who carries out a shattering, heroin-charged hit in the opening moments and serves a 10-year term for it. Discharged, he's disgusted to find the yakuza world he knows overrun by junk and so begins a doomed mission to clean it (and a new girlfriend) up. Mochizuki shoots the film as slow-burn drama interspersed with moments of intense violence; the images are as cool as the performances. The screenplay's from a novel by Yukio Yamanouchi, former lawyer to Japan's biggest yakuza gang, who does a cameo as a slimy bank manager welshing on a golf course deal. TR

Another Man, Another Chance

see Autre Homme une Autre Chance, Un

Another Mother (De Nieuwe Moeder)

(1996, Neth, 95 min)
d Paula van der Oest. *p* René Scholten. *sc* Paula van der Oest, Stan Lapinski. *ph* Birgit Hillenius. *ed* Menno Boerema. *pd* Erly Brugmans. *m* Fons Merkies. *cast* Arijs Adamsons, Janis Reinis, Peteris Liepins, Anneke Blok, Geert de Jong, Theu Boermans, Hannah van Lunteren.
●Van der Oest's refugee road movie follows a Latvian father and son as they uproot from their homeland in search of a new family life in the Netherlands. Moon-faced 10-year-old Elvis has given up on talk since his mother died. Yuris, the boy's father, snatches him from hospital and the pair wing and pray their way across the Dutch countryside in search of Yuris' one-time pen-friend, and long-lost first love, Marie. There's a surprising amount packed into this superficially unassuming film: a generous-spirited overview that crosses borders, generations and life styles, ending on a note of hard-won, bitter-sweet optimism. A subtle and quietly touching contribution to Europe's burgeoning cinema of post-Cold War upheaval. NB

Another Shore

(1948, GB, 91 min, b/w)
d Charles Crichton. *p* Michael Balcon. *sc* Walter Meade. *ph* Douglas Slocombe. *ed* Bernard Gribble. *ad* Malcolm Baker-Smith. *m* Georges Auric. *cast* Robert Beatty, Moira Lister, Stanley Holloway, Michael Medwin, Sheila Manahan, Fred O'Donovan, Wilfred Brambell.
●Patchy and characteristically whimsical Ealing comedy, set in an unconvincingly observed Dublin, about an Irish customs clerk with dreams of moving to a South Sea paradise. An encounter with a wealthy alchoholic (Holloway) offers him his chance, but he gives it up for the sake of love. Beatty is miscast as the feckless dreamer, and the whole thing is too slim to sustain interest. GA

Another Stakeout

(1993, US, 108 min)
d John Badham. *p* Jim Kouf, Lynn Bigelow, Cathleen Summers. *sc* Jim Kouf. *ph* Roy H Wagner. *ed* Frank Morriss. *m* Arthur B Rubinstein. *cast* Richard Dreyfuss, Emilio Estevez, Rosie O'Donnell, Dennis Farina, Marcia Strassman, Madeleine Stowe, Cathy Moriarty.
●Amiable bantering Seattle PD duo Dreyfuss and Estevez keep tabs on a wealthy crime couple (Farina and Strassman) suspected of sheltering a fugitive state's witness, linchpin in a major mob investigation. This time, the catch is that brassy, inexperienced DA O'Donnell has come along for the ride, determined that the three officers should pose as a vacationing family to maintain cover. There are explosions, car chases, a climactic shoot-out, and a comic dog. Comedy and suspense sensibly packaged; but very old hat. TJ

Another Time, Another Place

(1958, GB, 95 min, b/w)
d Lewis Allen. *p* Lewis Allen, EM Smedley Aston. *sc* Stanley Mann. *ph* Jack Hildyard. *ed* Geoffrey Foot. *ad* Tom Morahan. *m* Douglas Gamley. *cast* Lana Turner, Sean Connery, Barry Sullivan, Glynis Johns, Sidney James.
●Dreary tosh with Turner as an American journalist falling in love with a married British war correspondent (Connery) during WWII. He's killed in action, and she sets off to Cornwall to comfort his family, in order to stave off her own breakdown. Yucky Muck. GA

Another Time, Another Place

(1983, GB, 102 min)
d Michael Radford. *p* Simon Perry. *sc* Michael Radford. *ph* Roger Deakins. *ed* Tom Priestley. *ad* Hayden Pearce. *m* John McLeod. *cast* Phyllis Logan, Giovanni Mauriello, Denise Coffey, Tom Watson, Gianluca Favilla, Gregor Fisher.
●Set in rural Scotland during the final year of WWII, the boldly-explored concerns of Radford's debut feature are with desire and desperation, passion and imprisonment. With a classically simple metaphor of liberation and constraint at its heart – the relationship between a trio of Italian POWs and a girl stifling in a barren environment of loveless labour – the film widens its focus on crossed cultures and connections into a productive interrogation of both the narrative and formal seductions of foreignness. Cast, shot and cut with startling effectiveness, and confidently carving its own sometimes quirky path between those territories already staked out by Bill Douglas and Bill Forsyth, the film emerges as a generous delight, almost exotically moving. PT

Another Way (Egymásra nézve)

(1982, Hun, 109 min)
d Károly Makk. *sc* Erzsébet Galgoczi, Károly Makk. *ph* Tamás Andor. *ed* György Sivo. *ad* Tamás Vayer. *m* László Dés. *cast* Jadwiga Jankowksa-Cieslak, Grazyna Szapolowska, Jozef Kroner, Gabor Reviczky.
● Opening and closing – in a circular flashback movement – on *the* classic cold war cliché of the corpse by the mist-enshrouded watchtower, this film cunningly undercuts expectations aroused by its 1958 Hungarian setting. For the body belongs to a female reporter punished for loving Truth, Freedom and Beauty – in the form of other women. Probing the interface of professional and sexual integrity, Makk troublingly links 'deviant' lesbianism with a commitment to impeccably democratic ideals. Not just a film of Big Themes, though: the love scenes sail close to the wind, steering an unsteady course between voyeurism and candour. SJo

Another Woman

(1988, US, 81 min)
d Woody Allen. *p* Robert Greenhut. *sc* Woody Allen. *ph* Sven Nykvist. *ed* Susan E Morse. *pd* Santo Loquasto. *cast* Gena Rowlands, Mia Farrow, Ian Holm, Blythe Danner, Gene Hackman, Betty Buckley, Martha Plimpton, John Houseman, Sandy Dennis, David Ogden Stiers, Philip Bosco.
● A reflective drama about a college professor in her fifties. On sabbatical to write a book on German philosophy, Marion (Rowlands) rents an apartment for the necessary solitude. There she starts overhearing sessions in the psychologist's office next door, in particular the disclosures of Hope (Farrow), who has cause to question her marriage, the meaning of life and death, etc. Marion gets to thinking, and is appalled to realise that so many assumptions about her own life and marriage are largely unfounded: in her desire for a controlled existence, she has evaded the emotional truth about relationships with her best friend (Dennis), brother (Yulin) and husband (Holm). The film shows a refinement and development of recurrent Allen themes, particularly in the characterisation of what is arguably his most complex female character to date. But in choosing a stylised approach, Allen too often obscures points in overstatement and intellectual posturing. Where the film gains considerable momentum and richness is in the marvellous performances: Rowlands' perfectly pitched approach to a demanding role is particularly stunning. CM

Another You

(1991, US, 98 min)
d Maurice Phillips. *p/sc* Ziggy Steinberg. *ph* Victor J Kemper. *ed* Dennis M Hill. *ad* Dennis Washington. *m* Charles Gross. *cast* Gene Wilder, Richard Pryor, Mercedes Ruehl, Stephen Lang, Vanessa Williams.
● The comic duo have both seen better days. In this fairly desperate romp con-man Pryor takes pathological liar Wilder under his wing after he's released from a sanatorium into the LA equivalent of 'care in the community'. Ruehl and Lang supply what plot there is (it involves a missing brewery magnate), but Pryor's health problems (the onset of multiple sclerosis some 5 years previously) have sapped his energy and much of his old gumption. (Peter Bogdanovich was replaced as director.) TJ

Antonia's Line (Antonia)

(1995, Neth/Bel/GB, 102 min)
d Marleen Gorris. *p* Hans de Weers, Gerard Cornelisse, Hans de Wolf. *sc* Marleen Gorris. *ph* Willy Stassen. *ed* Michiel Reichwein. *ad* Harry Ammerlaan. *m* Ilona Sekacz. *cast* Willeke van Ammelrooy, Els Dottermans, Dora van der Groen, Veerle van Overloop.
● A vibrant saga, from the firebrand writer/director of *A Question of Silence*, combining feminist rigour with an involving dynastic narrative. At 85, Antonia's reached her last day on earth, a moment to reflect on the last five decades since returning to her native village in Holland after WWII – years which have seen her raise daughter Danielle, make a life on the farm for herself and a small community of society's flotsam and jetsam, and part from the world a richly experienced grandmother. Judicious character development whisks us through the generations, but with ample compassion for the women's struggle against the farming patriarchy, and a voice for the innocent victims of male sexual abuse, no one in the sizeable ensemble cast ever seems left out. Solid performances and a leavening of absurd humour, but a touch airless. TJ

Anou Banou or the Daughters of Utopia (Anou Banou oder die Töchter der Utopie)

(1983, WGer, 85 min)
d/sc Edna Politi. *ph* Nurith Aviv. *ed* Elisabeth Waelchli.
● In this documentary, six Israeli women, now in their seventies, recall their roles in the founding of a nation that was to be a refuge for a battered people and a light to the world. Socialism, feminism, agricultural self-reliance were to be combined in the desert of Palestine; shibboleths were abandoned by a new generation of Jews that would think everything out anew. Now the young women of those days sit bemused in homes and gardens, more splendid than any they had ever imagined for themselves, and try to trace how their ideals seeped away. Intelligent use is made of archive footage, conversation and interviews to produce a witty, and affecting, memorial to yet another promised land. MH

A Nous la Liberté (Freedom for Us)

(1931, Fr, 104 min, b/w)
d René Clair. *sc* René Clair. *ph* Georges Périnal. *ed* René Le Hénaff. *pd* Lazare Meerson. *ad* Alexandre Trauner. *m* Georges Auric. *cast* Raymond Cordy, Henri Marchand, Rolla France, Germaine Aussey, Paul Olivier.
● With its barrel-organ score and mechanistic choreography (rather than direction) of actors, this jolly satire on automation may be dated, but no more so now than in its own time. Though it pales in comparison with the anarchic, even scatological, vulgarity of Chaplin's *Modern Times*, which it influenced, it's well worth a look today as simultaneously vindicating Clair's former high reputation and his subsequent expulsion from most critical pantheons. GAd

A Nous les Petites Anglaises!

(1976, Fr, 112 min)
d Michel Lang. *p* Irène Silberman. *sc* Michel Lang. *ph* Daniel Guadry. *ed* Thierry Derocles. *m* Mort Shuman. *cast* Rémi Laurent, Stéphane Hillel, Véronique Delbourg, Sophie Barjac.
● A larky, strung-out tale of two Parisian youths in Ramsgate struggling to lose their virginity rather than improve their English. The fun, a good deal of it at the expense of the boys' boorish, blancmange-eating hosts, is all very well for those with an appetite for sexy adolescent cuteness; but writer/director Lang might have taken more trouble to avoid getting the period (1959) so ineptly wrong. No latter-day *400 Blows*, it might well be a hazy chapter in someone's autobiography: arriving in Ramsgate after dark, one of the boys (the future cinéaste Lang?) remarks of a churchyard that it reminds him of the opening of *Moonfleet*. JPy

Ansiktet (The Face/ The Magician)

(1958, Swe, 102 min, b/w)
d/sc Ingmar Bergman. *ph* Gunnar Fischer. *ed* Oscar Rosander. *ad* PA Lundgren. *m* Erik Nordgren. *cast* Max von Sydow, Ingrid Thulin, Gunnar Björnstrand, Ake Fridell, Naima Wifstrand, Bibi Andersson, Bengt Ekerot, Erland Josephson.
● Widely underrated, probably because of its strong comic elements and a *tour-de-force* scene derived from horror movie conventions, Bergman's chilling exploration of charlatanism is in fact one of his most genuinely enjoyable films. Von Sydow is the 19th century magician/mesmerist Volger, on the run with his troupe from debts and charges of blasphemy, whose diabolical talents are put to the test by the cynical rationalist Dr Vergerus (Björnstrand); their clash results in humiliation, doubt, and death. Much of the film is devoted to wittily ironic sideswipes at bourgeois hypocrisy; more forceful, however, is the way Bergman transforms Volger's ultimately futile act of revenge into a sequence of nightmarish suspense. GA

Antagonists, The

see Masada

Anthony Adverse

(1936, US, 136 min, b/w)
d Mervyn LeRoy. *p* Henry Blanke. *sc* Sheridan Gibney. *ph* Tony Gaudio. *ed* Ralph Dawson. *ad* Anton F Grot. *m* Erich Wolfgang Korngold. *cast* Fredric March, Olivia de Havilland, Gale Sondergaard, Edmund Gwenn, Claude Rains, Anita Louise, Donald Woods, Louis Hayward, Akim Tamiroff.
● An early stab at the swashbuckler from Warner Brothers, which proved popular at the time but hasn't improved with age. A deluxe period production, adapted from Hervey Allen's doorstop novel about 'the adventures of a soul in quest of ultimate truth', it meanders along with its gallant hero through France, Africa, the Americas and countless contrivances, with little sense of discrimination or structure. Although there are plenty of welcome faces in the cast, March isn't one of them: he hasn't the dash or the zest of an adventurer, and the film quickly becomes arduous to sit through. TCh

Antichrist, The

see Anticristo, L'

Anticristo, L' (The Antichrist/The Tempter)

(1974, It, 112 min)
d Alberto De Martino. *p* Edmondo Amati. *sc* Gianfranco Clerici, Vincenzo Mannino, Alberto De Martino. *ph* Aristide Massaccesi. *ed* Vincenzo Tomassi. *ad* Umberto Bertacca. *m* Ennio Morricone. *cast* Carla Gravina, Mel Ferrer, Arthur Kennedy, George Coulouris, Alida Valli.
● An *Exorcist* rip-off to go with *The Devil Within Her*. This has got the lot, though the vomit is of a darker green than in *Devil Within Her*, less lumpy than in *The Exorcist*. Plus a few plot variations: girl becomes cripple, cripple becomes reincarnated burned witch, devil impregnates witch, witch does blow-job on goat. The cosmopolitan cast must have been selected from *Spotlight* with a pin, and the dubbing is evil. AN

Antitrust

(2000, US, 109 min)
d Peter Howitt. *p* Nick Wechsler, Keith Addis, David Nicksay. *sc* Howard Franklin. *ph* John Bailey. *ed* Zach Staenberg. *pd* Catherine Hardwicke. *m* Don Davis. *cast* Ryan Phillippe, Rachael Leigh Cook, Claire Forlani, Tim Robbins, Douglas McFerran, Richard Roundtree, Tygh Runyan, Yee Jee Tso.
● Inspired by the free 'open source' philosophy of the Linux programming software, this soon becomes a tired David and Goliath tale dressed up in shiny hi-tech clothes, as it pitches slacker intuition against the fixed mindset of the suits. When garage-based programming genius Milo (Phillippe, coasting on youthful nerves) abandons his idealistic friend and partner Teddy for a pivotal job with the NURV corporation headed by his hero, evangelical Garry Winston (Robbins, delivering the film's one complex performance), he's soon at the heart of the company's plans for the digital convergence of a satellite-based global communications system. But when several suspicious programmer deaths conveniently coincide with sudden solutions to the project's difficulties, Milo realises the cost of meeting a global deadline is much higher than he thought. GE

Antonio das Mortes (O Dragão da Maldade contra o Santo Guerreiro)

(1969, Braz, 95 min)
d Glauber Rocha. *p* Claude-Antoine Mapa, Glauber Rocha. *sc* Glauber Rocha. *ph* Affonso Beato. *ed* Eduardo Escorel. *ad* Glauber Rocha. *m* Marlos Nobre. *cast* Mauricio do Valle, Odete Lara, Hugo Carvana, Othon Bastos, Jofre Soares.
● Rocha's sequel to his own *Black God, White Devil* returns to the Brazilian Sertao in the period after 1940, the key year in which the last of the *cangaceiro* bandits was killed. The legendary 'warrior saint' Antonio is now the central character, and the movie celebrates his turn against the military regime that hires him, offering his

righteous fight as a model for all revolutionary resistance. This time, though, Rocha completely rejects the elements of realism that made his earlier films particularly obscure: the movie is styled and paced like a Leone Western, and is as flamboyantly operatic as a Jancsó parable. Interestingly, the lack of direct historical references makes the result all the more venomously agitational. TR

Antony and Cleopatra

(1972, Switz/Sp/GB, 160 min)
d Charlton Heston. *p* Peter Snell. *ph* Rafael Pacheco. *ed* Eric Boyd-Perkins. *pd* Maurice Pelling. *m* John Scott. *cast* Charlton Heston, Hildegard Neil, Eric Porter, John Castle, Fernando Rey, Freddie Jones, Juan Luis Galiardo, Carmen Sevilla.

●Shakespeare's play directed with hopeless stodginess, contriving to damp down all the fires (romantic, poetic, histrionic) to a sort of shabby naturalism, and very nearly irretrievably sunk by Hildegard Neil's petulant Cleopatra, a suburban schoolmarm having a fling on the Nile. On the credit side, the verse is very capably and clearly spoken; Heston gives an intelligently *sotto voce* reading of Antony as an old lion moth-eaten at the edges but still with a few roars in him; and there are excellent performances from Porter (Enobarbus) and Castle (Octavius). TM

Antz

(1998, US, 83 min)
d Eric Darnell, Tim Johnson. *p* Brad Lewis, Aron Warner, Patty Wooton. *sc* Todd Alcott, Chris Weitz, Paul Weitz. *ed* Stan Webb. *pd* John Bell. *m* Harry Gregson-Williams, John Powell. *cast* voices: Woody Allen, Dan Aykroyd, Anne Bancroft, Jane Curtin, Gene Hackman, Jennifer Lopez, Sylvester Stallone, Sharon Stone,Christopher Walken.

●DreamWorks' blockbuster is a revolutionary political fable set in an ant colony. Low concept, or what? CGI allows Woody Allen to 'play' Z-4195, a neurotic worker ant unhappy with his lot. A chance encounter with a slumming Princess Bala (voiced by Stone) leads Z into an impetuous uniform switch with his soldier friend Weaver (Stallone) just as scheming General Mandible (Hackman) engineers a kamikaze war against the termites. Visually striking and dynamically shot, this has strong characters and no shortage of incident. Even so, parents may enjoy it more than their children. Most of the humour springs from the whiny, cowardly Z and will probably go over younger heads. Dramatic empathy similarly derives largely from adult concerns: romantic attraction, career disenchantment, the dawning of political consciousness. Call it 'angst'. The politics are the single most intriguing aspect: the colony functions as a quasi-fascist totalitarian state. Z's rebellion is at first a blow for individual liberty, but later assumes a social dimension. Unsurprisingly, the movie ultimately advocates a benign, enlightened oligarchy. At times, the film really is as lumpen as this makes it sound. But the trip to Insectopia sticks in the mind as the one sequence that matches *Toy Story*'s inspiration and existential wit. TCh

Any Given Sunday

(1999, US, 162 min)
d Oliver Stone. *p* Lauren Shuler Donner, Dan Halsted, Clayton Townsend. *sc* John Logan, Oliver Stone. *ph* Salvatore Totino. *ed* Tom Norberg, Keith Salmon, Stuart Waks, Stuart Levy. *pd* Victor Kempster. *m* Robbie Robertson, Paul Kelly, Richard Horowitz. *cast* Al Pacino, Cameron Diaz, Dennis Quaid, James Woods, Jamie Foxx, LL Cool J, Matthew Modine, Charlton Heston, Ann-Margret, Aaron Eckhart, Jim Brown, Lauren Holly.

●There's an obvious point of comparison here with imperial Rome's taste for recreational carnage and brutality, which is why Stone includes a lengthy clip from *Ben-Hur* in this gargantuan, gung-ho American footballfest. Also included: colour filters and transitions, split-screens, freeze frames, pictures-in-pictures, assorted film and video stocks, helicopter shots, cornball weather imagery, histrionic sound effects, HipHop, heavy metal, drugs, sex, gyrating cheerleaders, colliding jocks, onfield set-pieces, off field set-tos, an encyclopaedic deployment of genre stereotypes, and stars stars stars. You may, of course, take this as a recommendation. Supercilious Europeans who insist that Americans possess no sense of irony have spent too much time in the company of Oliver Stone films. Agreed, the director has other qualities: few film-makers could hope to martial this much information into two and a half hours (fewer would try), and his flair for representational overload in itself must make Stone one of the outstanding chroniclers of American cultural decadence. Whether simply parroting the world around him makes the resulting work any good, or enjoyable, is another matter. This one's a meathead burlesque. NB

Any Wednesday (aka Bachelor Girl Apartment)

(1966, US, 109 min)
d Robert Ellis Miller. *p/sc* Julis J Epstein. *ph* Harold Lipstein. *ed* Stefan Arnsten. *ad* Alfred Sweeney. *m* George Duning. *cast* Jane Fonda, Jason Robards, Dean Jones, Rosemary Murphy, Ann Prentiss.

●Limp adaptation of a stage farce in which Robards is the wealthy businessman with a roving eye, Fonda the girl at whose flat he may be found any Wednesday, and Jones the clean-living boy who means marriage. Complications and misunderstandings are permutated to the point of screaming boredom. TM

Anywhere but Here

(1999, US, 114 min)
d Wayne Wang. *p* Laurence Mark. *sc* Alvin Sargent. *ph* Roger Deakins. *ed* Nicholas C Smith. *pd* Donald Graham Burt. *m* Danny Elfman. *cast* Susan Sarandon, Natalie Portman, Bonnie Bedelia, Shawn Hatosy, Hart Bochner, Caroline Aaron, Corbin Allred, John Diehl, Paul Guilfoyle, Michael Milhoan.

●Wang is back on the 'women's movie' track of *The Joy Luck Club*, directing Alvin Sargent's adaptation of Mona Simpson's rites of passage tale. Portman is excellent, balancing wisdom and petulance, loyalty and imposition, as Ann, a 14-year-old dragged away from Bay City, Wisconsin, in the Mercedes of her eccentric mother, speech therapist Adele (Sarandon), who's hellbent on making it in Beverly Hills. That they only get to the foothills can't be counted a real setback. Nor could the compromise apartment, nor the effects of Adele's misjudged romantic liaison, nor the pressure of Ann's increasingly pertinent contribution to family argument. Why, then, does Adele's hard earned veneer of optimism look set to crack? Wang knows his way around material like this: the trick of balancing the tears and laughs without resort to easy targets, special pleading or the diminishment of 'patsy' characters. Adele should have been a tailor made role for Sarandon. The occasional strain in her otherwise fine performance may betoken her easing back on the pedal. Wang's most telling in the quasi-comic riffs and teasing out the reversal of the pair's roles and responsibilities. Wrapping it up, there's nice 'Scope work, fine supporting performances, and a lovely cameo by Milhoan as a sympathetic LAPD officer. WH

Any Which Way You Can

(1980, US, 115 min)
d Buddy Van Horn. *p* Fritz Manes. *sc* Stanford Sherman. *ph* David Worth. *ed* Ferris Webster. *pd* William J Creber. *m* Steve Dorff. *cast* Clint Eastwood, Sondra Locke, Ruth Gordon, Geoffrey Lewis, William Smith, Harry Guardino.

●Eastwood at his least appealing in a poor sequel to the already disappointing redneck comedy of *Every Which Way But Loose*. The story is similarly thin – trucker Eastwood, accompanied by his orang-utan buddy Clyde, gets involved in repetitive brawls with sundry unsavoury brutes – while the humour is far too broad and the direction plodding. GA

Anzio

see Sbarco di Anzio, Lo

Apache

(1954, US, 87 min)
d Robert Aldrich. *p* Harold Hecht. *sc* James R Webb. *ph* Ernest Laszlo. *ed* Alan Crosland Jr. *pd* Nicolai Remisoff. *m* David Raksin. *cast* Burt Lancaster, Jean Peters, John McIntire, John Dehner, Charles Bronson.

●Aldrich's first Western is a fine, muscular piece anticipating *Ulzana's Raid* in its acceptance of the alien nature of the Apache. Set in 1886, it opens with a superbly staged skirmish in which, with Geronimo having already surrendered, one of his braves (Lancaster) launches a fresh attack and is captured, but denied the death he sought: 'You're not a warrior now, you're just a whipped Indian'. What follows, as Lancaster is forced to adapt, is very much of the '50s in its view of the alienated Indian; but the Apache's odyssey is delineated with considerable complexity, alternately confirming and challenging his distrust of the white man's ways. Sadly, the logic of the film, with the Apache eventually stranded between two worlds, was compromised by interference which imposed an upbeat ending instead of accepting the inevitability of the Apache's death. Originally, after conducting his one-man war and then abandoning it, Lancaster was to have been shot needlessly in the back by Federal troops. TM

Apache Drums

(1950, US, 72 min)
d Hugo Fregonese. *p* Val Lewton. *sc* David Chandler. *ph* Charles P Boyle. *ed* Milton Carruth. *ad* Bernard Herzbrun. *m* Hans J Salter. *cast* Stephen McNally, Coleen Gray, Arthur Shields, Willard Parker, James Griffith, Armando Silvestre.

●A modest but unusually effective B Western about a small township overrun by *Mescalero* Apaches when a warning from the gambler expelled earlier by the mayor goes unheeded. Beautifully staged by Fregonese, especially the climactic attack on the church where the survivors make their stand, with painted Apaches erupting through the high windows like demons from hell. Val Lewton's last production, it is full of touches instantly recognisable from his RKO series: the subtle ambivalence undermining attitudes and ethical principles, the generous stance against racism, the concern for childhood (the gambler distracts the frightened kids with an exhibition of sleight-of-hand), the love of traditional songs (the kids led into a chorus of 'Oranges and Lemons'; the minister countering the Apache chanting by launching into 'The Men of Harlech'). TM

Apartment, The (100)

(1960, US, 125 min, b/w)
d/p Billy Wilder. *sc* Billy Wilder, IAL Diamond. *ph* Joseph La Shelle. *ed* Daniel Mandell. *ad* Alexandre Trauner. *m* Adolph Deutsch. *cast* Jack Lemmon, Shirley MacLaine, Fred MacMurray, Ray Walston, Jack Kruschen, Edie Adams.

●Diamond-sharp satire with a brilliant performance from Lemmon as the insurance clerk who forges ahead in the rat race by lending his apartment out to philandering senior executives, only to outsmart himself when the girl of his dreams is brought there by his boss. Full of sly bits of business (MacLaine admitting to three affairs but betrayed by fingers unconsciously announcing four), and with its jaundiced vision leavened by a tender sympathy for the frailty of human motives. Even the cop-out ending (boy forgives girl and all's well) is rather moving, given the delicate skill with which Lemmon and MacLaine commute between comedy and pathos. TM

Apartment Zero

(1988, GB, 125 min)
d Martin Donovan. *p/sc* Martin Donovan, David Koepp. *ph* Miguel Rodriguez. *ed* Conrad Gonzalez. *m* Elia Cmiral. *cast* Colin Firth, Hart Bochner, Dora Bryan, Liz Smith, Fabrizio Bentivoglio, James Telfer, Mirella D'Angelo, Juan Vitali.

●No film that begins with the end of *Touch of Evil* can be all bad, but it won't win any prizes for humility either. Adrian (Firth) runs a struggling rep cinema in Buenos Aires. Empty houses oblige him to take a lodger, Jack Carney (Bochner). Carney is as laid-back and friendly as Adrian is repressed and paranoid, and soon insinuates himself into the life of the apartment block, his killer charm seducing young and old, male and female alike. He's Adrian's fantasy and his nemesis, for neither man is what he seems. Up to this point the movie comes on like Polanski's *The Tenant* buggered by Losey's *The Servant*: a heady A to Z of male melodrama with existential pretensions and film-buff iconography. Then a dose of political realism lurches us into violent thriller territory. The result is largely unconvincing; the dialogue sounds like translation, and the direction also has an affected air, An extraordinary over-emphasis on extreme close-up abandons

Bochner in particular to no man's land. Donovan clearly believes he has another James Dean on his hands, but the curling lip and arched brow more often suggest Presley's *Blue Hawaii* period. TCh

Apocalypse Now 

(1979, US, 153 min)
d/p Francis Ford Coppola. *sc* John Milius, Francis Ford Coppola. *ph* Vittorio Storaro. *ed* Walter Murch. *pd* Dean Tavoularis. *m* Carmine Coppola, Francis Ford Coppola. *cast* Martin Sheen, Robert Duvall, Marlon Brando, Frederic Forrest, Dennis Hopper, Larry Fishburne, Sam Bottoms, Harrison Ford.

●Film-as-opera, as spectacular as its plot is simple: Vietnam in mid-war, and a dazed American captain (Sheen) is sent up a long river to assassinate a renegade colonel (Brando) who is waging a brutal, unsanctioned war in Cambodia. Burdened by excessive respect for its source novel (Conrad's *Heart of Darkness)*, this is a film of great effects (a flaming bridge, Wagnerian air strikes) and considerable pretension (quotes from TS Eliot). The casting of Brando is perhaps the acid-test: brilliant as movie-making, but it turns Vietnam into a vast trip, into a War of the Imagination. CA

Apocalypse Now Redux

(2000, US, 202 min)
d Francis Ford Coppola. *p* Francis Coppola, (*Apocalypse Now Redux*) Francis Ford Coppola, Kim Aubry. *sc* John Milius, Francis Ford Coppola. *ph* Vittorio Storaro. *ed* Richard Marks (supervising); Walter Murch, Gerald B Greenberg, Lisa Fruchtman, (additional) Blackie Malkin, Evan Lottman, (associate) George Berndt, (*Apocalypse Now Redux*) Walter Murch. *pd* Dean Tavoularis. *m* Carmine Coppola, Francis Ford Coppola, Rhythm Devils. *cast* Marlon Brando, Robert Duval, Martin Sheen, Frederic Forrest, Albert Hall, Sam Bottoms, Larry Fishburne, Dennis Hopper, GD Spradlin, Harrison Ford, Christian Marquand, Aurore Clément.

●Coppola's rethink of his Vietnam War epic is intriguing, but no significant improvement. Some of the added footage is fine, some redundant. If the extra Kilgore material adds nothing, meeting the Playboy bunnies again further upriver is a touch tedious. And the lengthiest newly inserted sequence is pretty catastrophic: a visit to a French colonial plantation is dramatically ruined by incomprehensible accents, Carmine Coppola's syrupy music and a soppy sexual interlude for Sheen with simpering Aurore Clément. More Brando is fairly effective, but all the best stuff you'll have seen before.Whatever, it's wonderful to see this hallucinatory folly-cum-near masterpiece again on the big screen. GA

Apollo 13

(1995, US, 140 min)
d Ron Howard. *p* Brian Grazer. *sc* Bill Broyles, Al Reinert. *ph* Dean Cundey. *ed* Michael Hill. *pd* Michael Corenblith. *m* James Horner. *cast* Tom Hanks, Kevin Bacon, Bill Paxton, Ed Harris, Gary Sinise, Kathleen Quinlan.

●Two hundred thousand miles from home, the Apollo 13 astronauts, Jim Lovell (Hanks, highly effective), Fred Haise (Paxton) and Jack Swigert (Bacon, great fun), find that a leaking fuel tank has made a moon landing impossible. Worse, the power drops so low, and the toxic gas levels rise so high, that the mission controllers in Houston fear they may lose their first astronauts in space. Not with Harris's Gene Krantz in charge, they won't! That the rest of the story is a matter of record (they lived) is part of the problem and the interest of the film. Ron Howard's spectacular (arguably reactionary) mega-hit about the 1970 moon-shot sticks so faithfully to the version of events related in Lovell's book *Lost Moon*, that this may qualify as the most expensive drama-doc ever made. Certainly, the suspense is missing. As a result, Howard has to rig it: the tension comes from communication breakdown, the falling-out among the crew, and the battle on the ground between the boffins and the armed services. Sure, there are thrills and spills: the adrenaline rush of the well-mounted Saturn launch; the too-strange-not-to-be-true trajectory realignment as Bacon goes to manual; the race to fabricate a new filter from spare parts. Nevertheless, the film's low on dramatic scenes; furthermore, for a 'space movie', both the special effects and photography are surprisingly pedestrian. Where it scores is in subtly restating traditional notions of male heroism. WH

Apostle, The

(1997, US, 134 min)
d Robert Duvall. *p* Rob Carliner. *sc* Robert Duvall. *ph* Barry Markowitz. *ed* Stephen Mack. *pd* Linda Burton. *m* David Mansfield. *cast* Robert Duvall, Farrah Fawcett, Todd Allen, Miranda Richardson, June Carter Cash, Billy Bob Thornton, John Beasley.

●Duvall's second feature as writer/director charts the backroad to redemption travelled by Pentecostal preacher Sonny Dewey, after he takes a drunken swipe with a baseball bat at his wife Jesse's lover. Fearing imprisonment, he leaves Texas, ditches his car and his identity, and ends up in a small, poor, largely black Louisiana town, where – as 'the Apostle EF' – he sets about building himself a new church and a new life. This is far more than a beautifully observed character study and an authentic, respectful portrait of the South; it's also a thrilling, insightful, uncommonly honest study of religious experience. For while Sonny (Duvall, seldom off screen) is prone to womanising, violent anger and the odd argument with the Lord, and while his preaching style is not without its showbiz tropes, he genuinely believes. Accordingly, the film never patronises or caricatures him, his flock or their faith. The secret of the movie's emotional power lies in Duvall's unforced, witty, profoundly humane brand of realism, and in the intoxicating energy of the church gatherings. GA

Appaloosa, The (aka Southwest to Sonora)

(1966, US, 98 min)
d Sidney J Furie. *p* Alan Miller. *sc* James Bridges, Roland Kibbee. *ph* Russell Metty. *ed* Ted J Kent. *ad* Alexander Golitzen. *m* Frank Skinner. *cast* Marlon Brando, Anjanette Comer, John Saxon, Rafael Campos, Miriam Colon, Emilio Fernandez, Alex Montoya, Frank Silvera.

●Brando, virtually repeating his morose, vengeance-driven characterisation from *One-Eyed Jacks*, plays a lone wanderer who rides back to his home town with some hard-earned cash and a valuable Appaloosa stallion, planning to fulfil his dream of settling down. But a crazy Mexican bandit (Saxon) first humiliates him, then steals the horse, sparking a protracted running duel which allows Brando his regulation bout of suffering (after losing an arm-wrestling match, and paying the penalty of being stung by a scorpion). Being the good guy – you know this because he is kind to Mexican peasants – Brando comes out on top in the end. The film has its moments, but is rendered virtually unwatchable by Furie's mania for weirdly mannered camera angles (you spend half the time peering round, over or under obstacles behind which the action is strategically placed) and enormous, pointless close-ups. TM

Appartement, L'

(1996, Fr/Sp/It, 116 min)
d Gilles Mimouni. *p* Georges Benayoun. *sc* Gilles Mimouni. *ph* Thierry Arbogast. *ed* Caroline Biggerstaff. *ad* Philippe Chiffre. *m* Peter Chase. *cast* Vincent Cassel, Monica Bellucci, Jean-Philippe Ecoffey, Romane Bohringer, Sandrine Kiberlain, Olivier Granier.

●A chance encounter in a Paris café puts young exec Max (Cassel) on the trail of the girl he loved and lost. He bids goodbye to his fiancée, pretends to go on a business trip, and sets off in search of the elusive Lisa (Bellucci). Flashbacks and reminiscences with his best pal (Ecoffey) reveal the story of a passionate near-thing, while the present is complicated by the enigmatic Alice (Bohringer, simmering). The double narrative melding past and present is managed with nonchalant grace, and a leavening sense of its own ridiculousness. Hitchcock echoes through this realm of obsession, voyeurism and desire. Moreover, writer/director Mimouni toys pleasurably with the tricks of celluloid illusion: masks, mirrors and colour-coding deliver a self-consciously heightened experience almost woozy with its own playfulness. A smart, sexy, and effortlessly cool first feature. TJ

Appât, L' (The Bait)

(1995, Fr, 117 min)
d Bertrand Tavernier. *p* René Cleitman, Frédéric Bourboulon. *sc* Colo Tavernier, Bertrand Tavernier. *ph* Alain Choquart. *ed* Luce Grunenwaldt. *cast* Marie Gillain, Olivier Sitruk, Bruno Putzulu, Richard Berry, Philippe Duclos, Marie Ravel, Clotilde Courau.

●In most respects, Nathalie (Gillain) is like any other 18-year-old Parisian shopgirl: just attractive enough to do a little modelling, devoted to her boyfriend Eric (Sitruk), and bright enough to keep both of them afloat. But her means of making extra cash (chatting up rich businessmen in bars) isn't enough to fulfil their dream of going to America. So when Eric suggests they do a robbery or two, using Nathalie's promises of sex to get to her various 'acquaintances', she reluctantly agrees. But the best laid plans… Tavernier has always seemed most comfortable when dealing with ordinary people in extraordinary situations, and this proves an intriguing antidote to the slick, quick-paced thrillers favoured by Hollywood. It's not that easy a movie to watch – some of it is slow, the three main characters are not very sympathetic, and the violence (while not graphic by American standards) derives from a callousness that is quite sickening – but its quiet assurance and unsentimental intelligence makes for engrossing viewing. GA

Appel du Silence, L'

(1936, Fr, 102 min, b/w)
d Léon Poirier. *ph* Georges Million. *m* Claude Delvincourt, JE Szyfer. *cast* Jean Yonnel, Pierre de Guingand, Jacqueline Francell, Suzanne Bianchetti.

●Through a scheme sponsored by the Catholic Church, 100,000 of the faithful each stumped up a few francs to finance this movie, said sum eventually to be deductible at the box office. (The idea was instantly copied by the workers' CGT to make Renoir's *La Marseillaise*.) The result was a hero-worshipping account of the life of Charles de Foucauld, soldier, explorer, missionary ('the hermit of the Sahara'), killed by Arab rebels in 1916. The plodding Poirier's tableaux are notable only for their wholesale issue-dodging and the suppression of everything even slightly contentious to do with colonialism, race, religion and sex. BBa

Applause

(1929, US, 85 min, b/w)
d Rouben Mamoulian. *p* Jesse L Lasky, Walter Wanger. *sc* Garrett Fort. *ph* George Folsey. *ed* John Bassler. *songs* EY Harburg, Jay Gorney, Billy Rose, Fats Waller. *cast* Helen Morgan, Joan Peers, Fuller Mellish Jr, Henry Wadsworth, Jack Cameron, Dorothy Cumming.

●Despite being both Mamoulian's debut for the cinema and a very early talkie, this deeply affecting tale of *Stella Dallas*-style maternal self-sacrifice transcends its sentimental shortcomings through the fluency of direction that was to become Mamoulian's trademark. As Helen Morgan's ageing burlesque queen steadily progresses towards giving up everything – even her life – for her convent-educated daughter (Peers), Mamoulian pulls out all the stops, employing unusually mobile expressionist camerawork to convey a wealth of detail in his portrait of the seedy backstage realities of the vaudeville world. Pacy, concise and innovative, the film also benefits from a truly magnificent performance from torch-singer Morgan. GA

Apple, The (Sib/La Pomme)

(1998, Iran, 85 min)
d Samira Makhmalbaf. *sc* Mohsen Makhmalbaf. *ph* Ebrahim Ghafouri. *ed* Mohsen Makhmalbaf. *cast* Massoumeh Naderi, Zahra Naderi, Ghorbanali Naderi, Azizeh Mohamadi.

●Directed by the 18-year-old daughter of Mohsen Makhmalbaf (who wrote and edited this film), this tells the story of two gauche, innocent girls suddenly let loose on the streets of Tehran (by a pleasingly determined social worker) after being kept locked indoors for twelve years by their impoverished, elderly father and their blind, deeply insecure mother. Like so many Iranian films about children, it's simplicity itself in terms of its narrative, but cute charm is effectively offset by the harsh, unsentimental portrait of family life based on inflexibly strict, finally self-serving traditions. It's a witty, gentle but often surprisingly acerbic little movie, slowly working its way towards a quite devastating final shot which underlines the need for an open heart and mind. GA

Apple Dumpling Gang, The

(1974, US, 100 min)
d Norman Tokar. *p* Bill Anderson. *sc* Don Tait. *ph* Frank Phillips. *ed* Ray De Leuw. *ad* John B Mansbridge. *m* Buddy Baker. *cast* Bill Bixby, Susan Clark, Don Knotts, David Wayne, Slim Pickens, Tim Conway.
● A comparatively attractive Disney comedy, set in Californ-i-ay in the 1870s, about a professional gambler lumbered with three orphaned children. The traditional ingredients of homely moralising, sentimentality and raucous slapstick are used sparingly, the dialogue is fairly bright, some visual gags are neatly executed, even Knotts is bearable, and Susan Clark makes an auspicious Disney debut as the Calamity Jane-type heroine. GB

Appointment in Honduras

(1953, US, 79 min)
d Jacques Tourneur. *p* Benedict Bogeaus. *sc* Karen De Wolf. *ph* Joseph Biroc. *ed* James Leicester. *ad* Charles D Hall. *m* Louis Forbes. *cast* Glenn Ford, Ann Sheridan, Zachary Scott, Rodolfo Acosta, Jack Elam, Ric Roman, Rico Aloniz.
● A lurid jungle adventure, complete with crocodiles, piranhas, vampire bats, ants and a puma. Ford is an American planter with an urgent rendezvous in Honduras to deliver money to the former President, ousted in a coup. When the ship's captain refuses to dock because revolution is brewing, Ford frees five Nicaraguan criminals being shipped home to jail, hijacks a lifeboat with their help, and takes along a married couple (Scott, Sheridan) as hostages. Mainly because he alone knows the jungle, Ford has an edge on everyone else, and predictably wins Sheridan over from the cowardly Scott. With fine camerawork (Joseph Biroc), good performances, and a script that weaves a shallow but surprisingly complex tangle of lies and loyalties, Tourneur keeps things moving along briskly and enjoyably. His choreography of the showdown, a running fight through jungle and village, is particularly skilful. TM

Appointment With Death

(1988, US, 102 min)
d/p Michael Winner. *sc* Anthony Shaffer, Peter Buckman, Michael Winner. *ph* David Gurfinkel. *ed* Michael Winner. *pd* John Blezard. *m* Pino Donaggio. *cast* Peter Ustinov, Lauren Bacall, Carrie Fisher, John Gielgud, Piper Laurie, Hayley Mills, Jenny Seagrove, David Soul.
● Winner's tongue-in-cheek direction overplays the clichés: even Hercule Poirot (Ustinov) seems to have lost respect for his profession. Agatha Christie's story concerns a stepmother (Laurie) who cheats her adopted family out of the proceeds of their father's will; to distract their attention, she arranges a family cruise to Palestine, where the old bag is bumped off and various well-met stiff upper Britishers lengthen the list of suspects. Much is made of period (the '30s), picture-postcard settings, and a host of stars, some of them already veterans of Christie adaptations, others probably doomed to a similar tale in the future. For all the glitter and gloss that Golan and Globus can buy, the film suffers from a mind-numbing inertia, its acting anal retentive, its scene-shifts stagy. EP

Appointment with Venus (aka Island Rescue)

(1951, GB, 89 min, b/w)
d Ralph Thomas. *p* Betty E Box. *sc* Nicholas Phipps. *ph* Ernest Steward. *ed* Gerald Thomas. *ad* George Provis. *m* Benjamin Frankel. *cast* David Niven, Glynis Johns, George Coulouris, Kenneth More, Patric Doonan, Noel Purcell, Bernard Lee, Barry Jones.
● Leaden, would-be whimsical Rank comedy about a World War II British commando raid to rescue the pregnant prize-winning cow of the title from a Nazi-occupied minor Channel isle and secure its valuable breeding strain. A mere moment's meditation on the ramifications of a narrative about generic superiority (albeit bovine) should convince you that you'd be deeply offended if you were daft enough to see it. PT

Apprenticeship of Duddy Kravitz, The

(1974, Can, 121 min)
d Ted Kotcheff. *p* John Kemeny. *sc* Mordecai Richler. *ph* Brian West. *ed* Thom Noble. *pd* Anne Pritchard. *m* Stanley Myers. *cast* Richard Dreyfuss, Micheline Lanctôt, Jack Warden, Randy Quaid, Joseph Wiseman, Denholm Elliott.
● Adaptation of Mordecai Richler's serio-comic novel about a whizz-kid's no-pause-for-thought dash for the top, with Dreyfuss, playing Duddy like the kid we were all at school with who was already working on his first ulcer, confirming his earlier promise in *Dillinger* and *American Graffiti*. Set in the Jewish community of 1948 Montreal, the film has everybody parading their obsessions up front in a manner that too often makes for easy pigeon-holing (voice-of-conscience grandfather, torn Christian girlfriend, etc). Such characterisation serves the film's comic intentions better than its message, most notably in the performances of Denholm Elliott as the drunken English film director requisitioned by Duddy to film *Bar Mitzvahs*, and Randy Quaid as an innocent simpleton. CPe

Apprentis, Les

(1995, Fr, 98 min)
d Pierre Salvadori. *p* Philippe Martin. *sc* Pierre Salvadori, Philippe Harel. *ph* Gilles Henry. *ed* Hélène Viard. *ad* François Emmanuelli. *m* Philippe Eidel. *cast* François Cluzet, Guillaume Depardieu, Judith Henry, Claire Laroche, Philippe Girard, Marie Trintignant.
● Salvadori's follow-up to his eccentric debut *Wild Target* is another droll comedy of manners that milks humour from a story of outsiders. Here – more properly insiders, given the time they spend in the flat – they are two no-hopers, Antoine (Cluzet in po-faced, mildly hysteric form) and Fred (gangling Depardieu), thrown together when they find themselves permanently taking temporary residence in the vacated Paris apartment of a mutual friend. The older Antoine, an aspirant writer without a whole idea, is neurotic, ditzy and incredulous; Fred, a likeable, half-dressed slouch, is more phlegmatic. Theirs is not a marriage of true minds, more a coupling of convenience – strictly heterosexual, of course – until the going gets tough, and Antoine comes close to losing his mind. Salvadori has the confidence to gear down from the frenetic farce of the earlier movie to a laid-back observational style more suited to his odd couple's languorous misadventures. Cluzet makes a fine curmudgeon, a facial register of woe; and Depardieu (who won a César for his performance) is a seductive naïf. Marie Vermillard's script pushes too hard for significance and pathos at the end, and the film misses the gravity lent by Jean Rochefort to *Wild Target*, but it's a genuinely winning light comedy. WH

Après l'Amour

(1992, Fr, 104 min)
d Diane Kurys. *p* Alexandre Arcady, Jean-Bernard Fétoux. *sc* Diane Kurys, Antoine Lacomblez. *ph* Fabio Conversi. *ed* Hervé Schneid. *ad* Tony Egry. *m* Yves Simon. *cast* Isabelle Huppert, Bernard Giraudeau, Hippolyte Girardot, Lio, Judith Reval, Yvan Attal.
● Thirty-year-old novelist Lola (Huppert) is involved with two men: David (Giraudeau), an architect, and Tom (Girardot), a guitarist. Both are unhappily married with kids. Lola tries to maintain her independence, to conduct her affairs on her own terms, but age is catching up with her, and her freedom is an illusion of sorts, perhaps just a subtler form of entrapment. And after love, there is punishment. You may not agree with Kurys' thesis, but it's sincere. Her mise-en-scène gains in immediacy and spontaneity, and the acting is surprisingly forceful, given that the characters are mostly ineffectual. Finally, however, the narrow perspective doesn't square with the movie's pretensions to art: one longs for more dangerous liaisons, and when Kurys tries to reach out towards other people, other lives, the film loses its definition. TCh

Apri gli occhi

see Open Your Eyes

April Captains

see Captains of April

Aprile

(1998, It, 78 min)
d Nanni Moretti. *p* Nanni Moretti, Angelo Barbagallo. *sc* Nanni Moretti. *ph* Giuseppe Lanci. *ed* Angelo Nicolini. *pd* Marta Maffucci. *cast* Nanni Moretti, Silvia Nono, Pietro Moretti, Silvio Orlando, Daniele Luchetti.
● More explicitly political than *Dear Diary*, this again occupies that intriguing territory between reality and fiction as it celebrates both the birth of Moretti's son and (with some reservations) the long awaited triumph of the Left in Italy. Once again, too, it's heartfelt, eccentric and often very funny, as Moretti shares his anxieties and joys, likes and dislikes, incidentally including his own manifest shortcomings (paranoia, hysteria, self-centredness, indecision). Simultaneously sharp and gentle, rambling and to the point, it stealthily leads us into an ever stranger personal world, so that by the finale, extraordinary images of the film crew (with Moretti in cape, motorbike helmet and shades) swaying to the rhythms of a musical sequence about a Trotskyist pastry chef (!) seem perfectly normal. GA

April Fools, The

(1969, US, 95 min)
d Stuart Rosenberg. *p* Gordon Carroll. *sc* Hal Dresner. *ph* Michel Hugo. *ed* Robert Wyman. *pd* Richard Sylbert. *m* Marvin Hamlisch. *cast* Jack Lemmon, Catherine Deneuve, Peter Lawford, Jack Weston, Myrna Loy, Charles Boyer, Sally Kellerman, Melinda Dillon.
● Despite the cast, a dire romantic comedy, with Lemmon as a New York stockbroker grasping at extra-marital bliss in the shape of a married Frenchwoman. It looks as though Rosenberg had taken a crash course in Lelouch chic before making it. TM

April Story (Shigatsu Monogatari)

(1998, Jap, 67 min)
d/p/sc Shunji Iwai. *ph* Noboru Shinoda. *ed* Shunji Iwai. *pd* Yuji Tsuzuki. *m* Classic. *cast* Takako Matsu, Seiichi Tanabe, Kahori Fujii, Rumi.
● This self-consciously light miniaturist study of an 18-year-old's early days at college is in two movements. The first is a dulcet, scherzo-like rendition of the sights, sounds and sensations of starting afresh, as Uzuki (Matsu) moves into her new flat and meets her neighbour and classmates; this segues into a more rhapsodic paean to youthful rapture as the film focuses on Uzuki's motives for leaving her hometown on the northern island of Hokkaido for university in Tokyo. The delicately captured sensual minutiae, the soundtrack's childlike piano refrain, and not least the lead performance work in harmony so that the film slowly catches you up in its idyllic rhythms. NB

Apt Pupil (Un Elève doué)

(1997, US/Fr, 111 min)
d Bryan Singer. *p* Jane Hamsher, Don Murphy, Bryan Singer. *sc* Brandon Boyce. *ph* Newton Thomas Sigel. *ed* John Ottman. *pd* Richard Hoover. *m* John Ottman. *cast* Ian McKellen, Brad Renfro, Bruce Davison, Elias Koteas, Joe Morton, Jan Triska, Michael Byrne, Heather McComb, Ann Dowd, David Schwimmer.
● It begins with a high school essay question: 'Why Nazism?' Sixteen-year-old Todd (Renfro) furrows his brow and immerses himself in the library, until, taking the bus one day, he recognises a passenger (McKellen) from a 40-year-old photo of a Gestapo officer. He tracks the old Nazi down and makes him an offer he can't refuse: if Herr Dussander refuses to spill 'what they're afraid to tell us in school', Todd will expose him to the media. Unhealthily obsessed with Dussander's revelations, Todd procures him an SS uniform to spur his memory; inevitably the balance of power shifts. This intense, rather laboured adaptation of a Stephen King novella is brave or foolish enough to play with fire – making a link between fascism and suppressed homosexuality, for example – yet it leaves a nasty taste in the mouth, as if the guilty collusion between Todd and Dussander is mirrored in the relationship between viewer and film. Though director Singer works through the psychological ramifications with painstaking (and protracted) concentration, McKellen can't entirely fend off camp. You won't forget his goose step in a hurry. TCh

Apu Trilogy, The
see Pather Panchali

Arabesque
(1966, GB/US, 118 min)
d/p Stanley Donen. *sc* Julian Mitchell, Stanley Price, Peter Stone. *ph* Christopher Challis. *ed* Frederick Wilson. *ad* Reece Pemberton. *m* Henry Mancini. *cast* Gregory Peck, Sophia Loren, Alan Badel, Kieron Moore, Carl Duering, George Coulouris.
● Espionage thriller in which Peck is an American professor adrift in a tourist-eye England, coping with mysterious hieroglyphs, sinister Arabs, and an ambiguous Loren. Much flashier than Donen's earlier *Charade* (also scripted by Peter Stone, alias Pierre Marton) and very sub-Hitchcock. TM

Arabian Adventure
(1979, GB, 98 min)
d Kevin Connor. *p* John Dark. *sc* Brian Hayles. *ph* Alan Hume. *ed* Barry Peters. *pd* Elliot Scott. *m* Ken Thorne. *cast* Christopher Lee, Oliver Tobias, Emma Samms, Milo O'Shea, Mickey Rooney, Puneet Sira, John Ratzenberger, Peter Cushing.
● Lavishly mounted Arabian Nights fantasy including the usual magic carpets, evil caliphs, cheeky beggar boys and comely princesses, but lacking the requisite invention and fizz. Tobias is the heroic prince whose task it is to retrieve the legendary Rose of Elil, defeat dictator Lee and win the hand of fair Emma Samms. Crisply photographed by Alan Hume, and in terms of effects and model work an improvement on director Connor's earlier lost-world pictures. TJ

Arabian Nights (Il Fiore delle Mille e una Notte)
(1974, It/Fr, 130 min)
d Pier Paolo Pasolini. *p* Alberto Grimaldi. *sc* Pier Paolo Pasolini. *ph* Giuseppe Ruzzolini. *ed* Nino Baragli. *ad* Dante Ferretti. *m* Ennio Morricone. *cast* Ninetto Davoli, Ines Pellegrina, Franco Citti.
● If *The Decameron* represented an intense vision behind its humourous facade, and *The Canterbury Tales* – the trilogy's weak point – a loss of ground amid a welter of sexual exhibitionism, the *Arabian Nights* emerges as a wonderfully relaxed and open puzzle of interlinked tales dedicated to the multiplicity of truth. It yields an engrossing array of mysterious, profound and liberating moments. The tales revolve around slaves and kings, demons, love, betrayal, loss and atonement. Zumurrud (Pellegrina), a slave turned monarch, after her 'drag' wedding, amid delightfully conspiratorial laughter, reveals her true sexual identity to her diminutive (and equally delighted) bride. Shot on location in North Africa, the film has rarely been seen in Britain after its release in 1975 by United Artists – in an insanely dubbed version, ludicrously cut by the censor. VG

Arachnophobia
(1990, US, 109 min)
d Frank Marshall. *p* Kathleen Kennedy, Richard Vane. *sc* Don Jakoby, Wesley Strick. *ph* Mikael Saloman. *ed* Michael Kahn. *pd* James Bissell. *m* Trevor Jones. *cast* Jeff Daniels, Harley Jane Kozak, John Goodman, Julian Sands, Stuart Pankin, Brian McNamara, Mark L. Taylor.
● Dr Ross Jennings (Daniels), his wife (Kozak) and their two children uproot from the urban sprawl to a picturesque Californian small town. But the locals are distrustful of the city slickers – feelings compounded when the new doctor's patients start dropping dead. A poisonous spider, accidentally imported from the Venezuelan rain forests, has also taken up residence, and its deadly offspring are making house calls outside surgery hours. For his directorial debut, long-time Spielberg producer Frank Marshall has crammed the screen with plenty of knee-jerk thrills interlaced with black humour. Subtlety of characterisation is secondary to the antics of the 'little vampires', with victims conveniently earmarked (gluttons, a jock and an unshaven whinger receive painful lessons in social rejection), and John Goodman easily upstaging his co-stars in a glorious appearance as a bull-headed pest controller. Designed to reduce the audience to a squirming mass, the film yields plenty of grisly pleasures. CM

Araignée de Satin, L' (Satin Spider)
(1984, Fr, 83 min)
d Jacques Baratier. *p* Louis Duchesne. *sc* Jacques Baratier, Catherine Breillat, Christian Watton. *ph* Roger Fellous. *ed* Marie-Ange Baratier, Danielle Fillios. *ad* Guenolée Azerthiope. *m* Bruno Gillett. *cast* Ingrid Caven, Catherine Jourdan, Daniel Mesguich, Alexandra Scyluna, Roland Topor, Fanny Bastien, Jacques Baratier.
● In synopsis, this sounds like mainstream porn. The setting is Les Fauvettes School for Girls just after WWI, where sternly Teutonic headmistress Caven vies with Jourdan, a morphine addicted, fabric fetishist gym teacher, for the sexual favours of liquid eyed nymphet Scyluna. Meanwhile the chaplain conducts a nude exorcism and for a midnight treat the school repairs en masse to an island in the lake for sandwiches, a sing song and a lesbian orgy. But the credits – Catherine Breillat co-adapting an obscure 1921 play (*Les Détraquées* by Palau and Thiery) – suggests a more substantial project. And indeed, what is intermittently evoked is a dismal world of cemeteries, snapshots of the dead, unassuagable grief – though why the the goings-on at Les Fauvettes should be the vehicle for this evocation is far from clear, except in the light of Jacques Baratier's determination to be as peculiar as possible. BBa

Ararat
(2002, Can, 115 min)
d Atom Egoyan. *p* Robert Lantos, Atom Egoyan. *sc* Atom Egoyan. *ph* Paul Sarossy. *ed* Susan Shipton. *pd* Phillip Barker. *m* Mychael Danna. *cast* Charles Aznavour, Eric Bogosian, Brent Carver, Marie-Josée Croze, Bruce Greenwood, Arsinée Khanjian, Elias Koteas, Christopher Plummer, David Alpay.
● A director (Aznavour) shoots a historical drama (inspired by Arshile Gorky's portrait of himself with his mother) about Turkey's massacre of the Armenians; meanwhile, Armenians in Canadian exile, some involved with the shoot, some merely with one another, try to sort out their own attitudes to their cultural and personal histories. Egoyan's film, clearly close to his heart, is a summation of the themes that have preoccupied him from the start of his career. Regrettably, while one may applaud his desire to set the record straight and recognise his narrative ingenuity, the atypically heavy-handed execution suggests he may have been rather too close to the material. The dramatic contrivance extends to customs officer Plummer acting as a kind of father confessor. GA

Arbre, le Maire et la Médiathèque ou Les Sept Hasards, L' (The Tree, the Mayor and the Leisure Centre or The Seven Fortuities)
(1993, Fr, 110 min)
d/sc Eric Rohmer. *ph* Diane Baratier. *ed* Mary Stephen. *m* Sébastien Erms. *cast* Pascal Greggory, Arielle Dombasle, Fabrice Luchini, Clémentine Amouroux, Françoise-Marie Banier, Michel Jaouen.
● The mayor presides over a village in the Vendée, the *médiathèque* is the sports and culture complex he's trying to build and the tree is a schoolmaster's cherished willow which stands in the middle of the proposed development. The film hinges together are long conversations about town versus country, about ecology (progressive or reactionary?), about local and national politics. Usually with Rohmer, characters reveal themselves via their shifting affections for one another; here character emerges in discussion of the issues.The finale is also somewhat of a departure, with the actors bursting into Demy-esque song. Telling the story in seven chapters, all beginning, 'If it hadn't been for…', is a characteristic framework for a less than characteristic movie. BBa

Archangel
(1990, Can, 90 min, b/w)
d Guy Maddin. *p* Greg Klymkiw. *sc* Guy Maddin, George Toles. *cast* Kyle McCulloch, Kathy Marykuca, Sarah Neville, Ari Cohen, Michael Gottli, David Falkenberg.
● WWI. Deep in Russian snows, peg-leg Canadian soldier Boles, pining for his lost Iris, is billeted in Archangel with the family of the lovely Danchuk; but the addled Boles ignores Danchuk's feelings for him in favour of mysterious Veronkha, whom he mistakes for Iris, although she is really the spurned wife of a faithless Belgian aviator… Confused? No matter; so are the characters in this absurdist melodrama. Maddin's second feature is pitched straighter than *Tales from the Gimli Hospital*, but is every bit as inspired and patchy. Pastiche remains to the fore, with Maddin's acute sense of camp more historically motivated than before. Complete with hieratic '20s-style acting, the film is an extravagant mélange of *All Quiet on the Western Front*, Eisenstein and DeMille, all the more impressive for its cut-price *mise en scène*. The war scenes are extraordinary, although thrown in far too liberally; even better are the daft tableaux vivants which seem to comprise Archangel's only entertainment. JRo

Arche du désert, L'
(1997, Alg/Fr/Ger/Switz, 90 min)
d Mohamed Chouikh. *p* Nadjet Taibouni, Sandrine Vernet. *sc* Mohamed Chouikh. *ph* Mustapha Belmihoub. *ed* Yamina Chouikh. *m* Philippe Arthuys. *cast* Myriam Aouffen, Hacen Abdou, Messaouda Adami, Shyraz Aliane, Amin Chouikh, Abdelkader Belmokadem, Fatyha Nesserine.
● Algerian writer/director Chouikh's film – his first to be distributed in the UK – has the same mood of troubled humanity, and the same striking images and powerful performances as *The Citadel* (1988), though, if anything, the socio-political critique here is sharper. Myriam (Aouffen) embraces Amin (Abdou), a villager from a different ethnic grouping. This innocent affair has catastrophic consequences as the two families wage a war of words, and the conflict escalates to a point where only the 'wild women' of the nearby crumbling citadel, sheltering a loose community of outcasts, offer refuge or hope. As in *The Citadel*, the director makes scant allowance for Western audiences The nature of the co-existent ethnic groupings, for example, is less than clear. But one assumes he shares the consternation and dejection of one of the elders, who recognises the futility of an internal strife that threatens everyone in the symbolic despoliation of the water supply. More explicit is the role of the young and the women, whose openness and vulnerability is movingly contrasted with the folly of their elders and betters. Dark, passionate and fascinating. WH

Arch of Triumph
(1948, US, 137 min, b/w)
d Lewis Milestone. *p* David Lewis. *sc* Lewis Milestone, Harry Brown. *ph* Russell Metty. *ed* Duncan Mansfield. *pd* William Cameron Menzies. *m* Louis Gruenberg. *cast* Charles Boyer, Ingrid Bergman, Charles Laughton, Louis Calhern, Roman Bohen.
● Paris 1938, city of last resort for the stateless, including a surgeon (Boyer) whose obsession with a Nazi sadist (Laughton) leaves him vulnerable to deportation and ill-prepared for romance with Ingrid Bergman. The original Remarque novel is too hefty to fit into two hours screentime, and if Milestone chooses to focus on the tale of the doctor's revenge and his doomed romance, he also breathes life into an assembly of supporting roles: concierge, café proprietor, a general reduced to night-club doorman, none of whom is played for comic relief. Bergman seems out of place as an Italian/Romanian good-time girl, but Russell Metty gives harsh light and inky shadow to seedy hotel rooms we'll see again in *Touch of Evil* ten years on. DO

Ardilla Roja, La
see Red Squirrel, The

Arena
(1953, US, 83 min)
d Richard Fleischer. *p* Arthur M Loew. *sc* Harold Jack Bloom, Arthur M Loew. *ph* Paul C Vogel. *ed* Cotton Warburton. *ad* Cedric Gibbons, Merrill Pye. *m* Rudolf Kopp. *cast* Gig Young, Polly Bergen, Henry Morgan, Barbara Lawrence, Jean Hagen, Robert Horton, Lee Van Cleef.

●For a few months in the summer of '53, it seemed that the three-dimensional process might prevail. But those specs – the logistics of supplying them, the discomfort of wearing them – proved the death of 3-D, beaching such flattened-out relics as this, recognisable by the arrangement of planes within a shot, the slight muzziness, and by sudden movements towards the camera (e.g. a brawler's boot). It's a rodeo movie, documentary-like, approximating real time, with the usual baffled critters bearing those three rodeo stereotypes, the has-been (Morgan), the cocky upstart (Horton) and the weary veteran (Young). BBa

Arena, The

(1973, US/It, 83 min.)
d Steve Carver, Aristide Massaccesi. *p* Mark Damon. *sc* John William Corrington, Joyce H Corrington. *ph* Aristide Massaccesi. *ed* Joe Dante. *ad* Mimmo Scavia. *m* Francesco De Masi. *cast* Pam Grier, Margaret Markov, Lucretia Love, Paul Muller, Daniel Vargas.

●High camp from Roger Corman's New World Pictures, with the ancient Romans setting their women slaves to fight in the arena. Fetishistic costumes and nudity are carefully harnessed to the portrait of a decadent society keeping the mob suppressed by letting them vent their feelings on blood sports. Enjoyable to watch the actresses getting their tongues round lines like 'O Guards! Do you mean to say we have to satisfy their animal lust?'

Are You Being Served?

(1977, GB, 95 min)
d Bob Kellett. *p* Andrew Mitchell. *sc* Jeremy Lloyd, David Croft. *ph* Jack Atcheler. *ed* Al Gell. *ad* Bob Jones. *cast* John Inman, Mollie Sugden, Frank Thornton, Trevor Bannister, Wendy Richard, Arthur Brough, Andrew Sachs.

●Woefully unfunny and extremely objectionable big-screen spin-off from the woefully unfunny and extremely objectionable TV sitcom series set in a none too realistic department store. Crap of the lowest order as the staff of Grace Brothers' clothing department go on holiday to the Costa Plonka. GA

Are You Dying, Young Man?

see Beast in the Cellar, The

Argent, L'

see Dôlé

Argent, L'

(1928, Fr, 195 min, b/w)
d Marcel L'Herbier. *p* Simon Schiffrin. *sc* Marcel L'Herbier. *ph* Jules Kruger. *pd* Lazare Meerson, André Barsacq. *cast* Pierre Alcover, Alfred Abel, Brigitte Helm, Mary Glory, Raymond Rouleau, Antonin Artaud, Jules Berry, Yvette Guilbert.

●One of the great silent movies: a superlative adaptation of Zola's novel about warfare in the world of international finance when one tycoon sets out to ruin another. Full of delicate metaphorical touches, the film has an intricate narrative fluidity that never betrays its origins in a densely plotted novel. What chiefly amazes, though, is the extreme sophistication of L'Herbier's visual approach: vast architectural sets dwarf the humans scurrying in frenzied quest of fame and fortune; scenes in echoing corridors leading to the bank anticipate Antonioni as people come and go between massive pillars, aware of each other and of conflicting interests, but never quite connecting; strange, gliding movements of the camera, constantly zeroing in to isolate the private motivations of a character, or withdrawing to reorientate the context, to make new connections, to suggest wider implications. Deliberate mystification is one of L'Herbier's tools. One scene, an unmistakable premonition of *Last Year in Marienbad*, has the camera travelling sinuously through halls and corridors before discovering a benign old gentleman – the *eminence grise*, we realise, behind a Stock Exchange collapse – feeding his lapdog. Not for nothing did Resnais acknowledge his debt to L'Herbier. TM

Argent, L' (Money)

(1983, Switz/Fr, 84 min)
d Robert Bresson. *p* Jean-Marc Henchoz. *sc* Robert Bresson. *ph* Pasqualino De Santis. *ed* Jean-François Naudon. *ad* Pierre Guffroy. *cast* Christian Patey, Sylvie van den Elsen, Michel Briguet, Caroline Lang, Vincent Risterucci, Beatrice Tabourin.

●A single 500 franc forged note changes hands as a schoolboy prank; and with remorseless logic, an innocent is led down the path to becoming an axe-murderer. Taken from a Tolstoy short story, this is a return to the extremes of crime and punishment that Bresson last used in *Pickpocket;* and as in that film, crime is a model of redemption and prison a metaphor for the soul. True to a taste for Catholic paradox, the murderer may or may not 'find' himself through his acts; the family is axed in the name of spiritual release; and most powerful of all, Evil is not demeaned by any vacuous sociological explanation. Filming with his usual tranquil, austere feeling for the miraculous, Bresson still manages to make most other film-makers appear hysterical over-reachers; at nearly 80, his power to renew our faith in cinema is as firm as one could wish for. Gold, pure. CPea

Argent de Poche, L' (Small Change)

(1976, Fr, 105 min)
d François Truffaut. *p* Marcel Berbert, Rolan Thénot. *sc* François Truffaut, Suzanne Schiffman. *ph* Pierre-William Glenn. *ed* Yann Dedet. *ad* Jean-Pierre Kohut-Svelko. *m* Maurice Jaubert. *cast* Geory Desmouceaux, Philippe Goldmann, Jean-François Stévenin, Virginie Thévenet, Marcel Berbert.

●That critics hailed Truffaut's film about children as 'delightful' and 'enchanting' is a fair indication of its gross sentimentality. An initial sequence showing pupils arriving for school in a small French provincial town serves as the linking device for a series of unrelated episodes involving individual children and their families, ranging from the inconsequential to the downright mawkish. There's not a snotty nose in sight, just endless well-scrubbed faces into whose mouths Truffaut frequently puts lines of quite nauseating cuteness: 'Gregory went BOOM!' burbles the toddler who has fallen – unscathed, alas – from a ninth floor window. And most winsome of all is Julien (Goldmann), the doe-eyed welfare case whom a school medical reveals to have been beaten up by his parents: presumably this film's intended audience would have difficulty feeling sorry for an *unattractive* child. AS

Argent des Autres, L' (Other People's Money)

(1978, Fr, 105 min)
d Christian de Chalonge. *sc* Pierre Dumayet, Christian de Chalonge. *ph* Jean-Louis Picavet. *ed* Jean Ravel. *ad* Eric Simon. *m* Patrice Mestral. *cast* Jean-Louis Trintignant, Claude Brasseur, Catherine Deneuve, Michel Serrault, Juliet Berto, Umberto Orsini, Gérard Séty.

●This Prix Delluc winner is a surprisingly compulsive microcosmic political thriller, delving into the labyrinthine world of banking and high-financial manipulation. The astute casting of that perennial victim Trintignant – made the scapegoat for a scandal the bank is hushing up, he explores the system in his determination to fight back – points the cinematic connection with the more overtly violent, equally ghastly worlds of Costa-Gravas and Yves Boisset. PT

Argie

(1985, GB, 85 min)
d/p Jorge Blanco. *sc* Jorge Blanco, Sylvie Rousseau. *ph* Michel Amathieu. *ed* Jorge Blanco. *cast* Jorge Blanco, Christine Plisson, Christine von Schreitter, Ella Blanco, David Janes.

●A film whose main attraction is its wild premise: a drunken Argentinian no-hoper, settled in Britain at the time of the Falklands, decides he should declare war on the UK and opts for the rape of a barmaid as his martial overture. Unfortunately she turns out to be only too willing, and they team up together to vent their dissatisfaction on the rest of the world. It has a certain crude charm, rather like finger-painting. CPea

Aria

(1987, GB, 89 min)
d Nicolas Roeg, Charles Sturridge, Jean-Luc Godard, Julien Temple, Bruce Beresford, Robert Altman, Franc Roddam, Ken Russell, Derek Jarman, Bill Bryden. *p* Don Boyd. *sc* Nicolas Roeg, Charles Sturridge, Julien Temple, Bruce Beresford, Robert Altman, Franc Roddam, Ken Russell, Derek Jarman, Bill Bryden, Don Boyd. *ph* Harvey Harrision, Gale Tattersall, Caroline Champetier, Oliver Stapleton, Dante Spinotti, Pierre Mignot, Frederick Elmes, Gabriel Beristain, Mike Southon, Christopher Hughes. *ed* Tony Lawson, Matthew Longfellow, Neil Abrahamson, Marie-Thérèse Boiche, Jennifer Auge, Rick Elgood, Michael Bradsell, Peter Cartwright, Angus Cook. *pd* Diana Johnstone, Andrew McAlpine, Piers Plowden, Scott Bushnell, John Hay, Matthew Jacobs, Paul Dufficey, Christopher Hobbs. *m* Giuseppe Verdi, Jean-Baptiste Lully, Erich Wolfgang Korngold, Jean-Philippe Rameau, Richard Wagner, Giacomo Puccini, Gustave Charpentier, Ruggiero Leoncavallo. *cast* John Hurt, Theresa Russell, Julie Hagerty, Linzi Drew, Tilda Swinton, Marion Peterson, Valerie Allain, Nicola Swain, Peter Birch, Bridget Fonda, Sophie Ward.

●Ten directors, ten arias. Don Boyd's opera omnibus was bound to be hit-and-miss. Bryden's linking passages, and the Sturridge and Beresford sections, miss; Jarman's and Temple's are largely about Super 8 and Steadicam respectively. Roddam's *Tristan and Isolde*, like Temple's *Rigoletto*, is the work of a Brit thrilled by the neon tackiness of America, and determinedly candid in its sex and violence. Russell's *Turandot* comes on like a decorative episode of the *The Twilight Zone*. The Godard undoubtedly makes the most waves, being far out and featuring bodybuilders and nubile cleaning ladies: infuriatingly preposterous or light years ahead, its use of sound is astonishingly effective. Roeg's marvellous opener will stir memories of *The Eagle Has Two Heads, The Third Man*, and most things Ruritanian down Zenda way. Altman's typically bold decision to film the response, to a performed aria, of an audience of Hogarthian bedlamites, provides a mesmerising parallel activity which fans of Free Jazz drumming will find no difficulty in following. BC

Ariel

(1988, Fin, 72 min)
d/p/sc Aki Kaurismäki. *ph* Timo Salminen. *ed* Raija Talvio. *pd* Risto Karhula. *m* Olavi Virta, Peter Tchaikovsky, Dmitri Shostakovich. *cast* Turo Pajala, Susanna Haavisto, Matti Pellonpää, Eetu Hilkamo, Erkki Pajala, Matti Jaaranen, Hannu Viholainen.

●It begins like a road movie. When the local mine is closed, Taisto (Turo Pajala) takes his redundancy pay and his father's parting gift – a snow-white Cadillac convertible – and sets off across Finland headed nowhere in particular. Soon relieved of his money, he drifts into a few days work on the docks, and then into a relationship with Irmeli (Haavisto) and her young son. In a similarly abstracted manner the film goes through the motions of social realism, and subsequently the conventions of the prison drama, but retains the stripped-down style and cool existentialism of the road movie long after the Cadillac is sold and the journey is waylaid. With restraint worthy of Bresson, Kaurismäki defuses the dramatics, but explodes our preconceptions. Fades to black punctuate scenes of immaculate simplicity, photographed impeccably by Timo Salminen. There is an obvious affinity, too, with Jim Jarmusch's work; the prevailing gloom is undercut by the music, kitsch pop and Finnish tango, and a sense of humour dry as a Buñuelian martini. TCh

Arise, My Love

(1940, US, 113 min, b/w)
d Mitchell Leisen. *p* Arthur Hornblow Jr. *sc* Charles Brackett, Billy Wilder. *ph* Charles Lang Jr. *ed* Doane Harrison. *ad* Hans Dreier, Robert Usher. *m* Victor Young. *cast* Claudette Colbert, Ray Milland, Walter Abel, George Zucco, Dennis O'Keefe, Frank Puglia.

●Like *To Be or Not To Be*, a film that defies bad taste with a starkly low-key opening in a Spanish jail where Milland awaits the firing-squad for his part in the Civil War, but walks bemusedly out into the arms of Colbert, a stranger (and aspiring reporter) claiming him as her husband and successful in an appeal for clemency. What follows, set in Hollywood's dreamy notion of springtime in Paris as the Nazi boot relentlessly crushes

Europe, is romantic comedy at its most briliant, scripted by Brackett and Wilder with a nice line in sexual innuendo and cynical irreverence. Inspiration flags latterly, though, as the groundwork is laid for a message to democracy. Even Brackett and Wilder can't quite get away with the notion of adapting the lines quoted earlier from 'The Song of Solomon' ('Arise, my love, my fair one, come away') as a rousing appeal to America ('Arise, my love, arise, be strong'). TM

AristoCats, The

(1970, US, 78 min)
d Wolfgang Reitherman. *p* Wolfgang Reitherman, Winston Hibler. *sc* Larry Clemmons, Vance Gerry, Frank Thomas, Julius Svendsen, Ken Anderson, Eric Cleworth, Ralph Wright. *ed* Tom Acosta. *pd* Ken Anderson. *m* George Bruns. *cast* voices: Hermione Baddeley, Roddy Maude-Roxby, Eva Gabor, Phil Harris, Sterling Holloway.

● The last of the Disney animated features conceived under the great Walt's perfectionist reign of terror, this 1970 Technicolor classic marks the move towards the less labour-intensive ink-and-wash cell design which followed. The ersatz Parisian atmosphere, circa 1910, is a wonder. Maurice Chevalier may have made the theme song familiar, but the voice cast boasts a fine array of ex-pats: spinster cat-lover Mme Bonfamille is Hermione Baddeley; the conniving butler – the cad who casts her cats into the countryside to inherit her wealth – is Roddy Maude-Roxby; her beloved cat Duchess the seductive Eva Gabor. As Scatman Crothers has it: 'Everybody's picking up the feline beat, 'cos everything else is ob-so-lete!' Purr-fect. WH

Aristotle's Plot (Le Complot d'Aristote)

(1996, Fr/GB/Zim, 68 min)
d Jean-Pierre Bekolo. *p* Jacques Bidou. *sc* Jean-Pierre Bekolo. *ph* Régis Blondeau. *ed* Aurélie Ricard. *pd* Carine Tredgold. *m* Jean-Claude Petit. *cast* Ken Gampu, Albee Lesotho, Septula Sebogodi, Anthony Levendale, Dylan Wilson-Max, Rudo Hamudikuwanda.

● An ambitious, self-reflexive snapshot of the achievements of African cinema, this account of a figure called 'Cinema' and his battles to stay faithful to his art (and Aristotle's Poetics, oddly) founders on its rigidly allegorical premise. All sorts of symbolic obstacles put themselves between Cinema and his goal, most memorably a mob of blockbuster-watching gangsters. Playful and enquiring it may be, but writer/director Bekolo's dogmatism tries the patience. MHi

Arizona Bill

see Strada per Forte Alamo, La

Arizona Dream (aka American Dreamers)

(1993, Fr, 141 min)
d Emir Kusturica. *p* Claudie Ossard, Yves Marmion. *sc* David Atkins. *ph* Vilko Filac. *ed* Andrija Zafranovic. *pd* Miljen Kljakovic. *m* Goran Bregovich. *cast* Johnny Depp, Jerry Lewis, Faye Dunaway, Lili Taylor, Paulina Porizkova, Vincent Gallo.

● The first 'American' film by the director of *Time of the Gypsies* is every bit as bizarre and imaginative as his earlier work, although it's also maddeningly indulgent and erratic. Depp is persuaded to leave his job counting fish (!) to attend uncle Jerry Lewis's wedding in the Midwest; there he becomes embroiled in the lives of Taylor and her crazy mother, Dunaway, and invents a flying machine. A curate's egg with more than its share of longueurs, but its comically surreal viewpoint is infectious (an aspiring actor's *pièce de résistance* turns out to be the crop-dusting scene from *North by Northwest*). TCh

Arlington Road

(1998, US/GB, 118 min)
d Mark Pellington. *p* Peter Samuelson, Tom Gorai, Marc Samuelson. *sc* Ehren Kruger. *ph* Bobby Bukowski. *ed* Conrad Buff. *pd* Thérèse DePrez. *m* Angelo Badalamenti. *cast* Jeff Bridges, Tim Robbins, Joan Cusack, Mason Gamble, Spencer Treat Clark, Hope Davis.

● Recovering from the death of his FBI agent wife, killed in a bungled raid on a backwoods armoury, Michael Farraday (Bridges) grows suspicious of the new family across the way, since he discovered their son stumbling bloodied down the road. Though the parents – engineer Oliver (Robbins) and his wife Cheryl (Cusack) – react gratefully and graciously, and though their boy Brady (Gamble) becomes friends with his own son Grant (Clark), Michael senses that there's something hidden behind Oliver's small lies and evasions. The film sets itself up as an exploration of an America newly at war with itself, its riff on the Oklahoma bombing substantiated by Michael's lectures on anti-government extremism (a ponderous device) and one dinner table discussion. As ever with Hollywood, though, the political is personal; once sides are settled, the film concentrates on ratcheting up the cat-and-mouse tension quite effectively. NB

Armageddon

(1998, US, 150 min)
d Michael Bay. *p* Jerry Bruckheimer, Gale Anne Hurd, Michael Bay. *sc* Jonathan Hensleigh, JJ Abrams. *ph* John Schwartzman. *ed* Mark Goldblatt, Chris Lebenzon, Glen Scantlebury. *pd* Michael White. *m* Trevor Rabin. *cast* Bruce Willis, Ben Affleck, Billy Bob Thornton, Liv Tyler, Will Patton, Peter Stomare, Keith David, William Fichtner, Steve Buscemi.

● This idiotic film is loud, boorish and smart enough to relish its own lunkhead bravado, with Willis leading his team of deep-core drillers on a last ditch mission to plant nuclear bombs inside an asteroid hurtling towards the earth. 'Talk about the wrong stuff,' gripes a disgusted NASA official, checking out the roughnecks selected to save the world: Affleck's cocky AJ, David's mighty General, and Buscemi's scene-stealing sociopath Rockhound, men whose most heartfelt request is that they be granted tax exemption for the rest of their lives. Producer Bruckheimer (*Con Air*, *Crimson Tide*) has this brand of testosterone entertainment down pat. Crucial elements include a sterling supporting cast (Stormare as a reckless Russian cosmonaut, Thornton as Houston's pointman, Patton and Fichtner riding shotgun), biting down on lines beefed up by the likes of Scott Rosenberg and Robert Towne. It's just as well it's all so tongue-in-cheek, because the one thing Bay can't sell is sincerity: lovey-dovey scenes involving Tyler and the supine populations of the world are excruciatingly hokey. TCh

Armed and Dangerous

(1986, US, 88 min)
d Mark L Lester. *p* Brian Grazer, James Keach. *sc* Harold Ramis, Peter Torokvei. *ph* Fred Schuler. *ed* Michael Hill, Daniel Hanley, George Pedugo. *ad* David L Snyder. *m* Bill Meyers. *cast* John Candy, Eugene Levy, Robert Loggia, Kenneth McMillan, Meg Ryan, Brion James, Don Stroud, Steve Railsback, Jonathan Banks.

● Given the potential of the very reasonable cast, one might expect rather more than is delivered by this dim comedy-thriller about a couple of idiots (Candy and Levy) who take jobs with a security firm and end up involved with the Mob (led by Loggia). Pap of the lowest order. BC

Armeé des Ombres, L' (The Army in the Shadows)

(1969, Fr/It, 143 min)
d Jean-Pierre Melville. *p* Robert Dorfmann. *sc* Jean-Pierre Melville. *ph* Pierre Lhomme. *ed* Françoise Bonnot. *ad* Théo Meurisse. *m* Eric de Marsan. *cast* Lino Ventura, Paul Meurisse, Simone Signoret, Jean-Pierre Cassel, Claude Mann, Christian Barbier, Serge Reggiani.

● Melville's tribute to the French Resistance in World War II was a project he nurtured for 25 years, and is the summit of both his own work and his collaboration with the actor Ventura. The film was wrongly criticised for introducing the codes of the French gangster film to the sentimental heroics of the Resistance, because it was the former that borrowed and sustained the myths and rituals of the latter in the first place. Melville's style here has a quite outstanding hallucinatory quality entirely appropriate to its subject of lives and memories that are forced underground for too long. It is, in a way, the stoic alternative to Cocteau's *Orphée*, a film whose suspense derives from a state where any moment may be the moment of death. CPe

Armored Attack

see North Star, The

Armored Car Robbery

(1950, US, 67 min, b/w)
d Richard Fleischer. *p* Herman Schlom. *sc* Earl Felton, Gerald Drayson Adams. *ph* Guy Roe. *ed* Desmond Marquette. *ad* Albert S D'Agostino. *m* C Bakaleinikoff. *cast* Charles McGraw, Adele Jergens, William Talman, Steve Brodie, Douglas Fowley.

● The caper movie has since succumbed to over-familiarity and over-elaboration, but this one – pointing the way to *The Asphalt Jungle* and *The Killing* – is a model of its kind. Almost documentary in its account of the heist that goes wrong and the police procedures that are set in motion, making excellent use of LA locations, it relies on superb high contrast lighting to meld reality into the characteristic *noir* look. Vivid characterisations, too, from Talman as the vicious mastermind, Jergens as a sleazy stripper playing games, and McGraw as the steely cop out to avenge the death of his partner. TM

Armour of God, The (Long Xiong Hu Di)

(1986, HK, 88 min)
d Jackie Chan. *p* Leonard Ho Koon-Cheung, Chua Lam. *sc* Edward Tang King-Sang, Szeto Chuek-Hun, Ken Lowe, John Sheppard. *ph* Robert Thompson. *ed* Peter Cheung Yiu-Chung. *ad* William Cheung. *m* Michael Laj. cast Jackie Chan, Alan Tam, Rosamund Kwan Chi-Lam, Lola Forner.

● Since jumping into Bruce Lee's shoes, Chan has produced a furious fistful of Hong Kong-set action pictures, low on plot but high on jinks and Chan's own particular brand of self-deprecating humour. Here he strays far from home, and much of the magic evaporates with bigger budgets and the European locations which adventurer 'Asian Hawk' (Chan) and his pop star foil (Tam) pass through in their crazy quest for some relics of Crusader's armour, ending up outside Zagreb to take on a motley fraternity of malevolent troglodyte monks led by a Grand Wizard sporting Bela Lugosi's cloak. What pleasures the action sequences offer are negated by the ludicrous dubbing and half-hour tracts of tedium. WH

Army in the Shadows, The

see Armée des Ombres, L'

Army of Darkness (aka Evil Dead III)

(1992, US, 109 min)
d Sam Raimi. *p* Robert Tapert. *sc* Sam Raimi, Ivan Raimi. *ph* Bill Pope. ed Bob Murawski, ROC Sandstorm. pd Tony Tremblay. *m* Joseph Lo Duca, Danny Elfman. *cast* Bruce Campbell, Embeth Davidtz, Marcus Gilbert, Ian Abercrombie, Bridget Fonda.

● A calculated tilt at the cross-over mainstream audience, this second sequel eschews the hard-core horror of *The Evil Dead* and the splatter comedy of *Evil Dead II*, in favour of a swashbuckling comedy. Catapulted back in time, chainsaw-wielding hero Ash (Campbell) joins forces with the inhabitants of a besieged castle – and damsel in distress Sheila (Davidtz) – in their battle against an army of skeleton Deadites. With its stop-motion effects and knockabout humour, this plays more like a Ray Harryhausen version of *El Cid* than a horror movie, with plenty of slapstick but very little gore. NF

Army of Lovers or Revolt of the Perverts (Armee der Liebenden oder Revolte der Perversen)

(1979, WGer, 98 min)
d/p/sc Rosa von Praunheim. *ph* Rosa von Praunheim, Lloyd Williams, Juliana Wang, Michael Oblovitz, Ben van Meter, Nickolai Ursin, John Rome, Bob Schub, Werner Schröter. *ed* Rosa von Praunheim. *m* Tom Robinson.

● A vacuous gay liberation documentary which rapidly breaks down into a stream of talking heads – from a celebration of the anniversary of gay revolt in San Francisco to interviews with gay Nazis, gay porn movie stars and others.

Politically it seems suspect; and the crew clearly enjoyed making it a lot more than an audience will enjoy watching it. CA

Arnelo Affair, The

(1947, US, 87 min, b/w)
d/sc Arch Oboler. p Jerry Bresler. *ph* Charles Salerno. *ed* Harry Komer. *ad* Cedric Gibbons, Wade Rubottom. *m* George Bassman. *cast* John Hodiak, George Murphy, Frances Gifford, Dean Stockwell, Eve Arden.

● Arch Oboler earned himself a footnote in cinema history when he directed the first-ever 3-D feature, *Bwana Devil*, in 1952. Unfortunately, this earlier effort is two or three dimensions short of a decent thriller. Bored young wife is strangely drawn to her attorney husband's charismatic, nightclub-owning client, but soon discovers he's a murderer, and she's somehow implicated in his crime. GM

Arnold

(1973, US, 95 min)
d Georg Fenady. *p* Andrew J Fenady. *sc* Jameson Brewer, John Fenton Murray. *ph* William Jurgenson. *ed* Melvin Shapiro. *ad* Monty Elliott. *m* George Duning. *cast* Stella Stevens, Roddy McDowall, Elsa Lanchester, Shani Wallis, Farley Granger, Victor Buono.

● A thoroughly inept black comedy/horror send-up about a wealthy man who arranges for his mistress to go through a wedding ceremony with his corpse after his death. Arnold's will also entangles a number of other members of the family, who make supposedly gruesome exits via acid-laced cleansing cream, a shrinking suit, etc. The plot itself isn't so bad; it's the relentlessly chirpy American humour trowelled over everything, the impossible ballad, and the way the performers pause in delivery as if waiting for laughter, that really makes *Arnold* unbearable. VG

Arohan

see Ascending Scale

Around the Pink House (Al bayt al zahr/Autour de la maison rose)

(2000, Can/Fr/Leb, 92 min)
d Joana Hadjithomas, Khalil Joreige. *p* Anne-Cécile Berthomeau, Edouard Berthomeau, Jean Dansereau. *sc* Joana Hadjithomas, Khalil Joreige. *ph* Pierre David. *ed* Tina Baz-Le Gal. *pd* Frédéric Bénard. *m* Robert M Lepage. *cast* Hanane Abboud, Fadi Abi Samra, Asma Andraos, Nabil Assaf, Isam Bou Khaled, Joseph Bou Nasser, Zeina Saab De Melero, Georges Kehdy.

● Post-war Beirut: (re)construction everywhere. A rambling mansion is home to two refugee families. When an entrepreneur buys the place for a commercial centre, both the refugees (who have are given 10 days to get out) and the locals fall prey to confusion, fear and long-buried resentment. The script is a little too schematic and contrived, and the direction sometimes clumsy, but the shifts in loyalty are credibly handled, the pace sustained, and the whole leavened by a welcome sense of comic absurdity. How allegorical it's meant to be is unclear, but it's an intriguing account of the conflict between past and future, culture and capitalism, idealism and compromise. GA

Around the World in Eighty Days

(1956, US, 175 min)
d Michael Anderson. *p* Michael Todd. *sc* SJ Perelman, James Poe, John Farrow. *ph* Lionel Lindon. *ed* Gene Ruggiero. *ad* James W Sullivan. *m* Victor Young. *cast* David Niven, Cantinflas, Shirley MacLaine, Robert Newton, Charles Boyer, Noel Coward, Ronald Colman, Marlene Dietrich, John Gielgud, Hermione Gingold, Trevor Howard, Buster Keaton, Robert Morley, Frank Sinatra, Ava Gardner, Beatrice Lillie.

● Mike Todd's inflation of Jules Verne, with Niven as Phileas Fogg and the Mexican comedian Cantinflas as Passepartout, becomes an interminable travelogue interspersed with sketches in which star-spotting affords some relief (there are cameos from hordes of luminaries ranging from Dietrich and Beatrice Lillie to Keaton and Sinatra). Some nice period touches, but the best bit comes courtesy of Méliès, whose 'Trip to the Moon' is used at the beginning. TM

Arousers, The

see Sweet Kill

Arp Statue, The

(1971, GB, 70 min, b/w)
d/p/sc Alan Sekers. *ed* Greg Harris. *m* James L Fox. *cast* Mel Lamb, François Hugo, Monique Hugo, James L Fox, Bronson Shaw.

● A rather silly tale about a model who has her arm eaten by a lion and suffers subsequent crisis, with lots of ponderous-pretentious references to Arp's statues. The use of stills to tell the story is handled well enough.

Arrangement, The

(1969, US, 125 min)
d/p/sc Elia Kazan. *ph* Robert Surtees. *ed* Stefan Arnsten. *pd* Gene Callahan. *m* David Amram. *cast* Kirk Douglas, Faye Dunaway, Deborah Kerr, Richard Boone, Hume Cronyn.

● Having been absent from the screen since *America, America* (1963), Kazan returned with this glossy account of middle-age crack-up based on his own glossy, Harold Robbins-ish novel. Douglas plays an advertising executive who suddenly clues into the emptiness of his existence and drives serenely under a truck – there after driving his family up the wall as he follows his failed suicide attempt with the kind of high jinks that had earlier served Britain's Angry Young Men in cocking a snook at society. It all seems very forced in Kazan's case, where it isn't simply glib and indulgent (as in Douglas' sybaritic fling with Dunaway's liberated lady ad exec). GA

Arrival, The

(1996, US, 115 min)
d David Twohy. *p* Thomas G Smith, Jim Steele. *sc* David Twohy. *ph* Hiro Narita. *ed* Martin Hunter. *pd* Michael Novotny. *m* Arthur Kempel. *cast* Charlie Sheen, Ron Silver, Teri Polo, Lindsay Crouse, Richard Schiff, Leon Rippy.

● An alien-landing thriller dedicated to the proposition that even if extra-terrestrials are the scurvy planet-swiping scumbags we suspect – well, it's not as if we're keeping the place in such good nick ourselves. Sheen's a NASA boffin convinced an audio signal he's picked up is an alien transmission. Unfortunately, when he informs his boss, he finds himself on the wrong side of a mandatory personnel cutback – with apologies, of course, but we know no one as smooth as Silver can be trusted. Sure enough, after rigging up his neighbours' satellite dishes to his computer, meeting a scientist in Mexico investigating global-warming, and breaking into a secret energy installation in the jungle, Charlie finds things go deeper than anyone could've imagined. This risible hokum cashes in on TV's *The X Files* and invasion mania, but what it lacks in sophistication (everything), it partly makes up for in sheer gall. NB

Arrivederci Millwall

(1989, GB, 50 min)
d Charles McDougall. *sc* Nick Perry. *cast* Kevin O'Donohue, Sidney Cole, Peter McNamara, Tim Keen.

● Originally shown on TV in a cut form. Scripted by Nick Perry, it's not a 'football film', but rather an examination of the lives of a group of 'hardcore' Millwall supporters as they prepare for England's World Cup match in Bilbao in 1982. With the build-up and subsequent 'victory' in the Falklands as a backdrop, the gang's bigoted, nationalistic views and love of violence are exacerbated after the death, in the conflict, of their leader's brother. *Sun* readers to a man, they take an overdose of jingoism on board the ferry for Spain, where they indulge in loutish behaviour and are subsequently imprisoned. But on release, Billy's desire to avenge his brother's death ('All dagoes are the same') backfires when he steals a pistol and accidentally kills a friend. The violence is neither condoned nor glamorised, serving merely to reinforce the futility of war and aggression in all its guises. A depressing film, none the less. GBa

Ars Amandi (L'Art d'Aimer/The Art of Love)

(1983, It/Fr, 97 min)
d Walerian Borowczyk. *p* Ugo Tucci. *sc/ph/ed/ad* Walerian Borowczyk. *m* Luis Bacalov. *cast* Marina Pierro, Michele Placido, Massimo Girotti, Laura Betti, Milena Vukotic, Philippe Lemaire.

● Offbeat erotica is all we can now expect from the once highly regarded Borowczyk. The setting is Rome, AD 8, where the heroine, her mother, neighbours and servant are all engaged on a brisk round of copulation, when they're not down at the amphitheatre listening to old Ovid dispense a mixture of common sense and bathos. Sets and props are minimal, the choppy editing is made choppier by the BBFC, characters hardly exist as individuals. And any sense of the past is overwhelmed by the dubbing and lines like 'Swear it on the privates of your favourite god!' Yet Borowczyk's remote, faintly amused view of sexual arrangements is distinctive. No one else would direct a scene the way he does, at least not deliberately. BBa

Arsenal Stadium Mystery, The

(1939, GB, 84 min, b/w)
d Thorold Dickinson. *p* Josef Somlo. *sc* Patrick Kirwan, Donald Bull. *ph* Desmond Dickinson. *ed* Sidney Stone. *ad* Ralph Brinton. *cast* Leslie Banks, Greta Gynt, Esmond Knight, Ian MacLean, Brian Worth, Liane Linden, Anthony Bushell.

● More entertainment than you'd get from a Saturday afternoon at Highbury these days, this vintage thriller works Arsenal's 1938 Championship side into a murder mystery that has Slade of the Yard (Banks) pacing the marble halls in search of the killer of an opposition player, nobbled during a friendly. PT

Arsene Lupin

(1932, US, 84 min, b/w)
d Jack Conway. *sc* Carey Wilson, Bayard Veiller, Lenore Coffee. *ph* Oliver T Marsh. *ed* Hugh Wynn. *ad* Cedric Gibbons. *cast* John Barrymore, Lionel Barrymore, Karen Morley, Tully Marshall, John Miljan, Henry Armetta.

● The first time the Barrymore brothers had appeared together, John as the titled French cracksman manoeuvring Lionel's prefect of police into becoming chief suspect for his exploits (which include stealing the Mona Lisa). Very dated and sluggishly directed, but John Barrymore is fun. TM

Arsenic and Old Lace

(1944, US, 118 min, b/w)
d Frank Capra. *sc* Julius J Epstein, Philip G Epstein. *ph* Sol Polito. *ed* Daniel Mandell. *ad* Max Parker. *m* Max Steiner. *cast* Cary Grant, Priscilla Lane, Raymond Massey, Peter Lorre, Josephine Hull, Jean Adair, Jack Carson, Edward Everett Horton.

● Joseph Kesselring's black comedy about two quaint spinsters with the murderous capabilities of Venus Flycatchers comes across as dusty but gentle entertainment. As transferred to the screen by Capra, it's dusty but ferocious, with rampant overacting and little sense of comic timing. Cary Grant, doing enough double-takes to dislocate his eyeballs for life, gives a particularly horrible performance. Best value is given by Massey and Lorre (playing two wandering criminals), who don't struggle to get laughs and just act macabre. It's all weird, but not wonderful. GB

Arsonist, The (Kaki Bakar)

(1995, Malaysia, 68 min)
d/sc U-Wei Bin Haji Saari. *ph* Ali Kong Hussein. *ed* Ramli Roslan. *cast* Khalid Salleh, Ngasrizal Ngasri, Jamaludin Kadir, Azizah Mahzan.

● A very impressive transposition of William Faulkner's story *Barn Burning* to rural Malaysia, this centres on an embittered worker-for-hire who uses arson as his weapon to attack those who exploit or cheat him, but doesn't hesitate to bully his own family into submission. As the spare drama unfolds, attention focuses on the man's youngest son (Ngasri), whose instinct is to rebel against his tyrannical father but who has been more influenced by him than he realises. Everything here from the dialogue and performances to the lighting represents a break with the traditions of Malay movie melodrama. TR

Art d'Aimer, L'

see Ars Amandi

Artemisia

(1997, Fr/Ger/It, 96 min)
d Agnès Merlet. *p* Patrice Haddad. *sc* Agnès Merlet, Christine Miller, Patrick Amos. *ph*

Benoît Delhomme. *ed* Guy Lecorne. *pd* Antonello Geleng. *m* Krishna Lévy. *cast* Michel Serrault, Valentina Cervi, Miki Manojlovic, Luca Zingaretti, Brigitte Catillon, Frédéric Pierrot, Maurice Garrel.
● Artemisia Gentileschi is an icon for feminist art historians: the early 17th century Roman is the first (known) great woman artist, and her surviving paintings offer evidence of an individual who broke through the patriarchal expectations of the day. Her story is ripe for filming, but writer/director Merlet seems caught between two approaches: to deliver an arts documentary-style portrait of a woman making her way in a man's world, or to spice up the proceedings with bodice-ripping rites of passage. In the end, we get a bit of both, from the moment Artemisia (Cervi) is discovered in a nunnery, sketching her own naked body by candlelight. On seeing the drawings, her father, the successful painter Orazio Gentileschi (Serrault), allows her to study in his studio. When she becomes fascinated by experiments in perspective being shaped by the Florentine maverick, Agostino Tassi, Orazio allows her to take lessons with him. But what she learns goes far beyond the canvas – eventually her father gets Tassi (Manojlovic) arrested for rape. Beautiful costumes, elegant cinematography and assured performances, but the drama lacks the imaginative resources to get right inside its remarkable protagonist. Racy costume drama, none the less. TJ

Art for Teachers of Children

(1995, US, 80 min. b/w)
d/p/ph/ed Jennifer Montgomery. *cast* Duncan Hannah, Caitlin Grace McDonnell, Coles Burroughs, Bryan Keane, Jennifer Williams.
● Clinical-sounding title notwithstanding, Montgomery's autobiographical recollection of an illicit adolescent relationship is a courageous, incendiary and contentious exploration of attitudes to under-age sexuality. Now professor of film at a New York art school, Montgomery, who wrote, directed, shot and edited the film, was spurred to distil her experiences when pressured by the FBI in 1989 to testify against an alleged child pornographer. Montgomery was one of his photographic subjects, and her film is pitched as a fictionalised 'boarding school melodrama', charting the brief liaison that develops after 14-year-old Jennifer (poet Caitlin Grace McDonnell) poses for dorm counsellor, art teacher and aspiring photographer John (NY painter Hannah). Filmed in grainy b/w with an amateur cast, the piece has all the formal impetus of an industrial training documentary. A problem, however, is that while Montgomery has earned the right to explore her own experiences, as soon as this material appears in public its specificity evaporates, prompting the risk that it might be read as a tacit endorsement of under-age sex. TJ

Arthur

(1981, US, 97 min)
d Steve Gordon. *p* Robert Greenhut. *sc* Steve Gordon. *ph* Fred Schuler. *ed* Susan E Morse. *pd* Stephen Hendrickson. *m* Burt Bacharach. *cast* Dudley Moore, Liza Minnelli, John Gielgud, Geraldine Fitzgerald, Jill Eikenberry.
● Overrated one-joke comedy which indulges Moore's perpetual drunk act as his wastrel playboy attempts to mend his ways in order to get his hands on an inheritance and a blushing bride. Some of the lines are funny, but how can one applaud a movie which relies so heavily on the novelty value of Gielgud as a bitter butler pronouncing profanities in a posh accent? GA

Arthur 2: On the Rocks

(1988, US, 113 min)
d Bud Yorkin. *p* Robert Shapiro. *sc* Andy Breckman. *ph* Stephen H Burum. *ed* Michael Kahn. *pd* Gene Callahan. *m* Burt Bacharach. *cast* Dudley Moore, Liza Minnelli, John Gielgud, Geraldine Fitzgerald, Stephen Elliot, Paul Benedict, Cynthia Sikes.
● Multi-millionaire sot Arthur (Moore) and an ex-shopgirl Linda (Minnelli), now married five years, are sans child but happy. He's still rolling around town regaling the pofaced populace with a stale repertoire of pranks, drinking champers in the bath, laughing at his own jokes. Linda is still putting up with the shit. So far, so formula. Arthur's vindictive would-be father-in-law (Elliot) engineers a takeover coup, leaving Arthur penniless. Linda waitresses, but Arthur can't tie his own shoelaces, so he's soon hitting rock bottom. That blows the adoption plans and sets up the emotional crisis. Worst of all, Gielgud's vitriolic British butler Hobson is dead; his replacement (Benedict) is no match, so Hobson has to be resurrected, via Arthur's hallucinations, to provide homilies and set Arthur back on the path to a happy ending. As funny as a cerebral haemorrhage. WH

Artistes at the Top of the Big Top: Disorientated (Die Artisten in der Zirkuskuppel: ratlos)

(1968, WGer, 103 min, b/w & col)
d/sc Alexander Kluge. *ph* Günther Hörmann. *ed* Beate Mainka-Jellinghaus. *cast* Hannelore Hoger, Siegfried Graue, Alfred Edel, Bern Holtz, Eva Pertel, Curd Jürgens.
● Kluge's second feature is a brilliant marriage of abstract ideas and concrete images. The daughter of a trapeze artist dreams of revolutionising the circus, but comes up against reality in all its forms: the Moscow cultural chief, the capitalists who have the power but not the will to change, and her elephants – who after all remain circus elephants. Part political essay on utopia and how to achieve it, part fiction, part a 'mondo bizarro' of circus life, it's a real rarity. And, of course, it's part of the film's task to deal with such disorientating impossibilities. The circus performers – a man wrestling with a crocodile, the lion tamer, the elephants standing on their hands – would surely agree. DMacp

Artists and Models

(1955, US, 109 min)
d Frank Tashlin. *p* Hal B Wallis. *sc* Frank Tashlin, Hal Kanter, Herbert Baker. *ph* Daniel L Fapp. *ed* Warren Low. *ad* Hal Pereira, Tambi Larsen. *m* Walter Scharf. *cast* Dean Martin, Jerry Lewis, Shirley MacLaine, Dorothy Malone, Eddie Mayehoff, Eva Gabor, Anita Ekberg, Jack Elam.
● Martin and Lewis play New York bohemians, sidetracked from their artistic aspirations by Lewis' obsession with comic strips, which leads into some mild satire on their dangerously violent content as well as a daft plot involving state secrets. Tashlin's splashy use of colour, and strong contributions from the female leads (including Anita Ekberg in a cameo), help to give the film its wacky, over-heated edge. There's even the suggestion that Lewis' backward manners are the result of a childhood spent reading comics – so now we know. DT

Art of Love, The

(1965, US, 99 min)
d Norman Jewison. *p* Ross Hunter. *sc* Carl Reiner. *ph* Russell Metty. *ed* Milton Carruth. *ad* Alexander Golitzen, George Webb. *m* Cy Coleman. *cast* James Garner, Dick Van Dyke, Elke Sommer, Angie Dickinson, Ethel Merman.
● A weird comedy, set in Paris and mounted with the gloss characteristic of Ross Hunter productions, in which a struggling writer (Garner) incites his equally struggling artist friend (Van Dyke) to increase the value of his work by faking suicide. The script's few good ideas are soon flogged to death, although it all becomes interestingly tasteless towards the end when Van Dyke, nursing amorous and other grudges while in hiding, has Garner arrested for his 'murder' and saved only when his head is on the guillotine. Sommer and Dickinson give performances much too charming to be wasted on this loutish pair. DMcG

Art of Love, The

see Ars Amandi

Art of War, The

(2000, Can/US, 117 min)
d Christian Duguay. *p* Nicolas Clermont. *sc* Wayne Beach, Simon Davis Barry. *ph* Pierre Gill. *ed* Michel Arcand. *pd* Anne Pritchard. *m* Norman Corbeil. *cast* Wesley Snipes, Anne Archer, Maury Chaykin, Marie Matiko, Cary-Hiroyuki Tagawa, Michael Biehn, Donald Sutherland, Liliana Komorowska.
● This over-dressed conspiracy thriller takes its title from Sun Tsu's ancient book of military strategy, which advocated destroying one's enemies from within, thus avoiding the messy business of battle. The assassination of the Chinese ambassador jeopardises a groundbreaking UN-sanctioned trade agreement. Luckily, UN translator Matiko flees with a videotape of the incident which throws suspicion on powerful Chinese businessman Tagawa. Armed with the tape, special agent Snipes tries to untangle a web of corporate chicanery and diplomatic deceit. The hyperkinetic direction rapidly degenerates into incoherence, leaving the capable cast floundering in a sea of unspeakable dialogue. Only Archer, as a hard-nosed diplomat, and Chaykin, as a funny, phlegmatic detective, survive the death of a thousand cuts. Snipes' charisma, agility and fighting skills come into their own during the extended chase sequences and hand-to-hand combat, in which he's matched blow for blow by his character's longtime partner Biehn. NF

Art Pepper: Notes From a Jazz Survivor

(1982, US, 49 min)
d/p Don McGlynn. *ph* Mark Salvaterra. *ed* Lou Angelo. *with* Art Pepper, Laurie Pepper, Milcho Leviev, Bob Magnusson, Carl Burnett.
● In this moving documentary souvenir of the man and his music, Art Pepper speaks frankly and unsentimentally about his tortured history – his fight against heroin addiction, prison stretches, chaotic emotional affairs, bouts of depression – and still proclaims his love of life. And this rings true whenever he lifts his sax to his lips. Whether in a tight, funky blues, a plaintive Parker-ish ballad that fragments into Dolphy-like wailings, or a fast bebop shuffle, Pepper blows with an intense joy, power and passion. Avoiding adulation, this is an intelligent epitaph to a brave, restless and remarkable man. GA

Asako in Ruby Shoes (Sun Ae Bo)

(2001, SKor/Jap, 113 min)
d E J-Yong. *p* Koo Bon-Han, Masaki Tsuchida, Hitoshi Iwata. *sc* E J-Yong. *ph* Hong Kyeong-Pyo. *ed* E J-Yong, Jung Yoon-Woo. *pd* Jung Gu-Ho, Kim Jin-Cheol, Yutaka Yokoyama. *m* Cho Sung-Woo. *cast* Lee Jeong-Jae, Misato Tchibana, Ren Osugi, Kim Min-Heui, Urara Awata.
● This international co-production is another example of the increasing energy of new Korean cinema.The global village of endemic urban isolation, coupled with the new and attendant hopes of remote digital community, is explored with calm and understated poignancy. When a lonely Seoul civil servant meets an alienated Tokyo student via the latter's appearance on a webcam site, the fragile but blossoming relationship teleports the action from virtual spaces to the real landscapes of Alaska. GE

As a Man (L'Afrance)

(2001, Fr, 90 min)
d Alain Gomis. *p* Edouard Mauriat, Anne-Cécile Berthomeau. *sc* Alain Gomis. *ph* Pierre Stoeber. *ed* Fabrice Rouaud. *m* Patrice Gomis. *cast* Djolof Mbengue, Delphine Zingg, Samir Guesmi, Théophile Moussa Sowié, Thierno Ndiaye Doss, Bass Dhem.
● 'I'm fed up being a black! I want to be a Senegalese,' says El Hadj (Mbengue), a student in Paris struggling with his dissertation, his visa situation and an existential dilemma concerning his possible future. He's like a 'pink flamingo, one leg in the water, one in the air,' and it's driving him insane, not to say spoiling his relationship with understanding glass restorer Myriam. First-time director Gomis mounts a sober, politically literate and quietly effective movie that's prone, occasionally, to explode, in perfectly judged and pertinent scenes, into anger and frustration, or melancholy and pathos. Mbengue, whether doing a 'rap' of disappointment in the bathroom, showing bemusement at his colleagues' advice or caressing his lover, gives a fine and moving performance. WH

Ascendancy

(1982, GB, 85 min)
d Edward Bennett. *p* Penny Clark, Ian Elsey. *sc* Edward Bennett, Nigel Gearing. *ph* Clive Tickner. *ed* Charles Rees, George Akers. *ad* Jamie Leonard. *cast* Julie Covington, Ian Charleson, John Phillips, Susan Engel, Philip Locke.

●This continues the BFI Production Department's concern with Northern Ireland (*Cross and Passion, Maeve*) while clearly also intended to reach the art house audience hooked by *The Draughtsman's Contract*. A history lesson, around the exploitation of Irish sectarian differences in the interests of the British ruling class of 1920, is therefore rendered as costume drama. The spectator's stand-in here is Julie Covington, whose emotional/physical paralysis, occasioned by the death of her brother in World War I, gives way to an awareness of the Trouble outside. Unfortunately, and symptomatically, she functions as an obvious symbol but carries little dramatic weight (despite an excellent performance). The result seems unlikely to provoke or enlighten audiences. SJ

Ascending Scale (Arohan)

(1982, Ind, 147 min)
d Shyam Benegal. *sc* Shama Zaidi. *ph* Govind Nihalani. *ed* Bhanudas Durkar. *m* Purna Das Baul. *cast* Om Puri, Victor Banerjee, Noni Ganguly, Rajen Tarafdar, Gita Sen.

●As an agit-prop tract, designed to instruct the Indian peasant sharecropper in legal rights that are still under abuse from landowners despite government legislation, this rings loud and clear. For the Western viewer, running in at 147 minutes, it may seem to thump its tub a little too simplistically, despite stunning cinematography and some fine sequences. TM

Ascenseur pour l'Echafaud (Frantic/Lift to the Scaffold)

(1957, Fr, 89 min, b/w)
d Louis Malle. *p* Jean Thuillier. *sc* Roger Nimier, Louis Malle, *ph* Henri Decae. *ed* Léonide Azar. *ad* Rino Mondellini. *m* Miles Davis. *cast* Maurice Ronet, Jeanne Moreau, Georges Poujouly, Lino Ventura, Yori Bertin, Ivan Petrovich, Elga Andersen.

●Malle's first feature, a straightforward but classy thriller about an ex-paratrooper's attempt to dispose of his mistress' tycoon husband in a perfect murder. It became associated with the early excitements of the *nouvelle vague* mainly through the performances of Ronet (playing a prototype of the disgruntled Vietnam veteran) and Moreau (who does some moody solo wandering in the streets searching for her missing lover). The ingenious plot, using a malfunctioning lift as its deus-ex-machina, has one carefully plotted murder conjure another as its shadow image. But the cement holding the film together is really the splendid jazz score improvised by Miles Davis. TM

Ascent, The (Voskhozhdenie)

(1976, USSR, 105 min, b/w)
d Larissa Shepitko. *sc* Yuri Klepikov, Larissa Shepitko. *ph* Vladimir Chukhnov. *m* Alfred Schnittke. *cast* Boris Plotnikov, Vladimir Gostjuchin, Sergei Yakovlev, Ludmila Poliakova, Anatoli Solinitzin.

●An extraordinary, gruelling account of the partisans' fight against the Nazis in German-occupied Belorussia, *The Ascent* reflects the Russian obsession with the horrors of the Great Patriotic War, but unusually is both steeped in religious symbolism and ready to acknowledge the existence of the less than great Russian collaborator. The true battle is not with the Nazis, who hover in the background as mere extras, but between the Russian Nazi investigator and Sotnikov, the captured partisan who finds the spiritual strength to go to his death unbeaten. With its many references to the Crucifixion, the story takes on heroic proportions glorifying the sufferings of the martyr and his influence on future generations. A remarkable piece of work, not least for being filmed in black-and-white against a vast, bleak expanse of snow. SJo

As Good As It Gets

(1997, US, 138 min)
d James L Brooks. *p* James L Brooks, Bridget Johnson, Kristi Zea. *sc* Mark Andrus, James L Brooks. *ph* John Bailey. *ed* Richard Marks. *pd* Bill Brzeski. *m* Hans Zimmer. *cast* Jack Nicholson, Helen Hunt, Greg Kinnear, Cuba Gooding Jr, Skeet Ulrich, Shirley Knight.

●New York romantic novelist Melvin Udall (Nicholson) doesn't live up to his writing: an obsessive-compulsive, he's given to insulting whoever he meets. Melvin lowers his defences, however, after he's lumbered with the dog belonging to his neighbour Simon (Kinnear), a gay artist recuperating from a mugging, and after he decides to lure Carol (Hunt), a waitress at his local diner, back to work by offering to pay for her young son's treatment for asthma. So begins Melvin's unwitting progress towards something resembling normal behaviour. The film may be more ambitious and sophisticated than most Hollywood comedy-dramas, but for all the delight it takes in Melvin's outrageous sarcasm, it never quite eschews cornball cliché. Nicholson gives a committed, credible, typically charismatic performance, and the rest of the cast lends able support. The trouble lies in the rambling narrative, Brooks' cautious direction and the cosy tone which renders the whole thing reminiscent of an extended sitcom. GA

Ashanti

(1979, Switz, 117 min)
d Richard Fleischer. *p* Georges-Alain Vuille. *sc* Stephen Geller. *ph* Aldo Tonti. *ed* Ernest Walter. *pd* Mario Chiari. *m* Michael Melvoin. *cast* Michael Caine, Omar Sharif, Peter Ustinov, Rex Harrison, Beverly Johnson, William Holden.

●Faced with a dire script about the kidnapping of an Afro-American doctor into a trans-Sahara slave caravan, Fleischer opts for functional anonymity. Would that his cast had done likewise: all seem determined on self-parody in an otherwise humourless context, with Ustinov essaying a disastrous funny-voice act as the Arab slaver, and Caine, as the doctor's pursuing husband, looking totally uninterested. His recalcitrant camel remains the perfect image of and for a clapped-out primitive 'star vehicle'. PT

Ashes and Diamonds (Popiól i Diament)

(1958, Pol, 104 min, b/w)
d Andrzej Wajda. *sc* Andrzej Wajda, Jerzy Andrzejewski. *ph* Jerzy Wojcik. *ed* Halina Nawrocka. *ad* Roman Mann. *cast* Zbigniew Cybulski, Ewa Krzyzanowska, Adam Pawlikowski, Bogumil Kobiela.

●The last of Wajda's unplanned trilogy about the legacy of World War II on his generation, following *A Generation* (1954) and *Kanal* (1956), *Ashes and Diamonds* is also the most flamboyant, and features the iconic figure of Cybulski, frequently cited as the 'Polish James Dean', who died in an accident in 1967. The time is the first days of peace, though from Cybulski's dark glasses the mood could be a decade on. He plays a young fighter waiting to assassinate a recently appointed communist official in a small Polish town. But a burgeoning love affair with a hotel barmaid leads him to question the value of this continual struggle. Wajda's way is the sweet smell of excess, but some scenes remain powerfully memorable – the lighting of drinks on the bar, the upturned Christ in a bombed church, and Cybulski's prolonged death agonies at the close. DT

Ashes of Time (Dong Xie Xi Du)

(1994, HK, 95 min)
d Wong Kar-Wai. *p* Tsai Sung-Lin. *sc* Wong Kar-Wai. *ph* Christopher Doyle. *ed* Patrick Tam. *ad* William Chang Suk Ping. *m* Franky Chan, Roel A Garcia. *cast* Leslie Cheung Kwok-Wing, Brigitte Lin Ching-Hsia, Tony Leung Ka-Fai, Tony Leung Chiu-Wai, Maggie Cheung, Carina Lau, Jacky Cheung, Charlie Young.

●An all-star cast, Chris Doyle's extraordinary cinematography and innovative action sequences choreographed by Samo Hung were not enough to turn Wong Kar-Wai's most ambitious movie from an art house triumph into a commercial success. Wong takes characters from a famous martial arts novel (Jin Yong's *The Eagle-Shooting Heroes*) and deposits them in the middle of a vast desert to work through their various obsessions and manias: set in the eye of an off-screen storm, it's a tender group portrait of fallible people crawling from the wreckage of their lives. At its emotional core is Brigitte Lin playing a self dangerously divided between Yin and Yang. TR

Ashik Kerib (Ashug Qaribi/ Kerib the Minstrel)

(1988, USSR, 78 min)
d Dodo Abashidze, Sergo Paradzhanov. *sc* Giya Badridze. *ph* Albert Yavuryan. *pd* Shota Gogolashvili. *m* Djavashir Kuliev. *cast* Yuri Mgoyan, Veronika Metonidze, Levan Natroshvili, Sofiko Chiaureli.

●In a period of the undefined past, Ashik Kerib is a wandering minstrel, a lute player and singer, who falls for a rich merchant's daughter, is spurned by the father (minstrels are poor functionaries), and is despatched, to wander for 1001 nights, but not before he's made the girl promise not to marry till his return. True to Paradjanov's unique method, the ensuing episodic tale of his meetings, experiences, difficulties and growth are told in a blaze of visually splendid 'tableaux vivants' and miraculous images and symbols (doves, swans, pomegranates), intercut with religious iconic works and artefacts, and overlaid with song and poetry. The source is a story by poet Mikhail Lermontov, but the interpretation, though grounded in the world of ethnic cultural references of the Turkish (Muslim) Azerbaijani peoples, is free, open, sensual and personal. There are coded messages of the tribulations of the artist here, and also a playful, mischievous comedic tone that allays any feeling of self-absorbtion on the director's part. Astonishing. WH

Ashug Qaribi

see Ashik Kerib

Ash Wednesday

(1973, US, 99 min)
d Larry Peerce. *p* Dominick Dunne. *sc* Jean-Claude Tramont. *ph* Ennio Guarnieri. *ed* Marion Rothman. *ad* Philip Abramson. *m* Maurice Jarre. *cast* Elizabeth Taylor, Henry Fonda, Helmut Berger, Keith Baxter, Maurice Teynac, Maggie Blye.

●Liz, aged 55, sagging and wrinkled in a carefully cosmetic sort of way, secretly undergoes a face and body lift in an attempt to rejuvenate herself and her marriage. In what is little more than a homage to Taylor's face, the film spends a good deal of time looking at her reflection in the mirror and endorsing her Martini ad lifestyle up to the hilt.

Asi es la Vida

see Such Is Life

As in Heaven (Svo a Jördu sem á Himni)

(1992, Ice, 122 min)
d Kristín Jóhannesdóttir. *p* Sigurdur Palsson. *sc* Kristín Jóhannesdóttir. *ph* Snorri Thorisson. *ed* Sigurdur Jonsson. *ad* Gudrun S Haraldsdottir. *m* Hilmar Orn Hilmarsson. *cast* Alfrun Ornolfsdóttir, Pierre Vaneck, Tinna Gunnlaugsdóttir.

●The imagination of a young girl, living in a remote Icelandic fishing community in the late '30s, is so imbued with traditional superstition that she dreams herself back into the fourteenth century in order to fend off a family curse. Rather like a Nordic amalgam of *Spirit of the Beehive* and *Venus Peter*, this is a good-looking film that makes fine use of a harsh, dramatic landscape; but the adult performances, at least, tend towards the histrionic, and the whole is rather too self-consciously mysterious and slowly paced for its own good. GA

Ask Any Girl

(1959, US, 101 min)
d Charles Walters. *p* Joe Pasternak. *sc* George Wells. *ph* Robert Bronner. *ed* John McSweeney Jr. *ad* William A Horning. *m* Jeff Alexander. *cast* David Niven, Shirley MacLaine, Gig Young, Rod Taylor, Jim Backus, Elisabeth Fraser, Claire Kelly.

●MGM laid on the Fifth Avenue gloss for this obvious but not unpleasing comic romance in which Pennsylvanian hick Shirley MacLaine (very appealing in one of her first major roles) comes to New York City, beats off a queue of menfolk, and then enlists the help of suave David Niven in winning the affections of his Lothario brother Gig Young. It doesn't take X-ray vision to figure out who she's gonna end up with, but these folks know how to make the time pass amiably enough. Adapted by George Wells from the novel by Winifred Wolfe, and shot in 'Scope. TJ

Asking for Trouble

(1942, GB, 81 min, b/w)
d Oswald Mitchell. *p* Wallace Orton. *sc* Oswald Mitchell, Con West. *ph* James Wilson. *cast* Max Miller, Carol Lynne, Mark Lester, Wilfrid Hyde-White, Aubrey Mallalieu.

●The Cheeky Chappie is his usual brash self as a fishmonger (bookie on the side) who finds himself helping a damsel in distress by masquerading obnoxiously as Captain Fortescue from Africa, whom her father wants her to marry. Fast-talking but not very funny. TM

As Long as You're Healthy

see Tant qu'on a la Santé

Asoka

(2001, Ind, 158 min)
d Santosh Sivan. *p* Saket Chaudhary, Santosh Sivan. *dialogue* Abbas Tyrewala. *ph* Santosh Sivan. *ed* Sreekar Prasad. *ad* Sabu Cyril. *m* Anu Malik, (background score) Sandeep Chowta. *cast* Shah Rukh Khan, Kareena Kapoor, Danny Denzongpa, Ajit, Rahul Dev, Hrishita Bhatt, Umesh Mehra, Gerson Da Cunha.
●An Indian prince, Asoka (Khan), wages war in the third century BC, kills his brothers and ascends the throne of Magadha – only to be overcome by remorse and to denounce war in the name of Buddhism. It's the preamble to his conversion that we see most of, and especially his love affair with the independent Kaurwaki (Kapoor, convincing despite the shampoo-ad visuals). Khan embodies brutality and passion, but has to contend with an awkward mix of tragedy and comedy, which frequently jars and undercuts the action. Where director Sivan's 1998 feature, *The Terrorist*, was an intimate, slow-moving drama shot mainly in close-up, this is all whip pans, moving cameras and 'Scope action. Wonderful to look at, when you get the chance. (The director's cut runs at 158 min, while the Hindi version and the Tamil dubbed version both run at 176 min.) KW

Aspern

(1981, Port, 96 min)
d Eduardo de Gregorio. *p* Paulo Branco. *sc* Michael Graham. *ph* Acácio de Almeida. *ed* Manuela Viegas. *ad* Rita Azevedo Gomes. *m* Wolfgang Amadeus Mozart. *cast* Jean Sorel, Bulle Ogier, Alida Valli, Ana Marta, Teresa Madruga.
●A film of limpid clarity adapted from Henry James' *The Aspern Papers*, with present-day Lisbon smoothly substituting for 19th century Venice, and terrific performances from Valli and Ogier as the old lady and the spinster niece under siege from a writer determined to lay his hands on a fabulous manuscript entrusted to their keeping. Although the finer Jamesian ironies are compromised by an added subplot designed to allow the writer to explain his motivations, the central theme is subtly orchestrated as the two women fight to preserve their private feelings and memories from being made public. De Gregorio's obsession with time, memory and the sinister emanations from old dark houses (cf. his own *Sérail*, his scripts for *Celine and Julie Go Boating* and *The Spider's Strategy*) is made all the more effective here by his use of an abrupt editing style in disruptive counterpoint to the brooding atmosphere. TM

Asphaltflimmern

see Flickering Roads

Asphalt Jungle, The

(1950, US, 112 min, b/w)
d John Huston. *p* Arthur Hornblow Jr. *sc* Ben Maddow, John Huston. *ph* Harold Rosson. *ed* George Boemler. *ad* Cedric Gibbons, Randall Duell. *m* Miklós Rozsa. *cast* Sterling Hayden, Louis Calhern, Jean Hagen, Sam Jaffe, James Whitmore, John McIntire, Marilyn Monroe.
●A classic heist movie, and one of Huston's finest, this adaptation of WR Burnett's novel in which a gang of thieves falls apart after attempting a daring robbery is a taut, unsentimental study in character and relative morality. Beautifully shot by Harold Rosson, played to perfection by a less than starry cast, and directed in admirably forthright fashion by Huston, it has spawned countless imitations, few of which even remotely approach the intelligence and detail of the original. Re-made as *The Badlanders* (1958), *Cairo* (1963) and *Cool Breeze* (1972). GA

Asphalt Night (Asphaltnacht)

(1980, WGer, 90 min)
d Peter Fratzscher. *p* Michael Wiedemann. *sc/ed* Peter Fratzsche. *ph* Bernd Heiel. *ad* Holger Scholz. *m* Lothar Meid. *cast* Gerd Udo Heinemann, Thomas Davis, Ralf Herrman, Monika Rack, Gaby Helene Ruthmann.
●Two musicians, a punk and a '60s leftover, find uneasy romance during a night in Berlin. The encounter inspires the older one to complete his masterpiece, a hideous piece of bombast about 'the kids of 1984' (sic). Strictly for people who missed out on punk's heyday but needed to be reassured, after the event, that it wouldn't hurt them. A film whose seductive visual surface can't hide its reactionary musical soul. SJ

Asphyx, The (aka Horror of Death)

(1972, GB, 99 min)
d Peter Newbrook. *p* John Brittany. *sc* Brian Comport. *ph* Freddie Young. *ed* Maxine Julius. *ad* John Stoll. *m* Bill McGuffie. *cast* Robert Stephens, Robert Powell, Jane Lapotaire, Alex Scott, Ralph Arliss, Fiona Walker.
●A person's 'asphyx' is his spirit of death, which can be attracted at the moment of dying and trapped, conferring immortality on the subject. This promising notion, combined with intriguing glimpses into Victorian psychical research and a strong cast, get the film off to a good start. Sadly, it soon degenerates into formula and farce, with Stephens' theatrical delivery adding the mortal blow. DP

Assam Garden, The

(1985, GB, 90 min)
d Mary McMurray. *p* Nigel Stafford-Clark. *sc* Elisabeth Bond. *ph* Bryan Loftus. *ed* Rodney Holland. *ad* Jane Martin. *m* Richard Harvey. *cast* Deborah Kerr, Madhur Jaffrey, Alec McCowen, Zia Mohyeddin, Ian Cuthbertson.
●Though very much a two-hander and marred by the restraint that the film itself castigates, this is an often affecting study of two women – the widow of a colonial bigwig, cherishing memories of her privileged years in India, and the elderly Indian immigrant who to some extent penetrates the English woman's loneliness by forcefully offering friendship. It's a discreet and subtle movie, gradually scratching away at Kerr's veneer of happiness to reveal a core of frustration and resentment. Both the camera, prowling around the gorgeous garden that the women tend together, and Kerr's carefully controlled performance, suggest further depths of dissatisfaction. Far from original, but engaging. GA

Assassin

(1973, GB, 83 min)
d Peter Crane. *p* Peter Crane, Michael Sloan. *sc* Michael Sloan. *ph* Brian Jonson. *ed* Roy Watts. *pd* Bruce Atkins. *m* Zack Laurence. *cast* Ian Hendry, Edward Judd, Frank Windsor, Ray Brooks, Verna Harvey, John Hart Dyke.
●Charting the familiar area of spyland double-cross and disillusion, directed with much heavy 'style', this is lifted out of the run-of-the-mill by Hendry's haunting, evocative performance as the isolated, disillusioned hired killer.

Assassin, The

see Point of No Return

Assassination

(1986, US, 88 min)
d Peter Hunt. *p* Pancho Kohner. *sc* Richard Sale. *ph* Hanania Baer. *ed* James Heckert. *pd* William Cruise. *m* Robert O Ragland. *cast* Charles Bronson, Jill Ireland, Stephen Elliott, Jan Gan Boyd, Randy Brooks, Eric Stern.
●Dispirited action movie with baggy-faced Bronson, as a federal agent assigned to protect the newly instated first lady (code name One Mama), grappling listlessly with a script that gives him lines like 'The yacht was definitely blown up premeditatively'. One Mama (Ireland) doesn't hold much truck with security ('I am not going to be coerced by your chauvinistic rules'), but is forced to eat her words when it becomes clear that someone is trying to kill her. The plot, with the two going into hiding together and the sexual tension between them brewing, shambles along as predictably as a dot-to-dot quiz. EP

Assassination Bureau, The (aka The Assassination Bureau Limited)

(1968, GB, 110 min)
d Basil Dearden. *p/sc* Michael Relph. *ph* Geoffrey Unsworth. *ed* Teddy Darvas. *pd* Michael Relph. *m* Ron Grainer. *cast* Oliver Reed, Diana Rigg, Telly Savalas, Curd Jürgens, Philippe Noiret, Warren Mitchell, Beryl Reid, Clive Revill.
●None too witty black comedy, loosely based on Stevenson's unfinished novel and set in the first decade of this century. Rigg is the journalist who uncovers a secret organisation of professional killers, and manages to fight it with the help of its leader (Reed), who falls in love with her. Amid all the heavy caricaturing and the funereal pace, only Geoffrey Unsworth's photography of the Venetian scenes is of note. GA

Assassination of Trotsky, The

(1972, Fr/It/GB, 103 min)
d Joseph Losey. *p* Norman Priggen, Joseph Losey. *sc* Nicholas Mosley, Masolino D'Amico. *ph* Pasqualino De Santis. *ed* Reginald Beck. *pd* Richard MacDonald. *m* Egisto Macchi. *cast* Richard Burton, Alain Delon, Romy Schneider, Valentina Cortese, Giorgio Albertazzi, Duilio Del Prete, Jean Desailly.
●Unhistorical evocation of Trotsky's last couple of months in exile in Mexico before the Stalinist agents got to him. Burton as Trotsky is set up very deliberately as a dry, pedantic figure, and his ideas accordingly shrink in importance. Delon, too, as the enigmatic assassin, seems like an unfinished character until the brilliantly shot scene where he watches a bullfight. From there Losey's on his own, fascinatedly turning this key historical event into a Secret Ceremony. We're so starved of hard information that one can only wish for more. VG

Assassin Habite... au 21, L' (The Murderer Lives at Number 21)

(1942, Fr, 83 min, b/w)
d/p Henri-Georges Clouzot. *sc* Henri-Georges Clouzot, Stanislas-André Steeman. *ph* Armand Thirard. *ed* Christian Gandin. *ad* André Andréjew. *m* Maurice Yvain. *cast* Pierre Fresnay, Suzy Delair, Jean Tissier, Pierre Larquey, Noël Roquevert.
●Clouzot's first feature, an engaging serio-comic thriller, with Fresnay as a whimsical police inspector who poses as a pastor to infiltrate the boarding-house where a Jack the Ripper killer is hiding out. The moderately ingenious mystery is boosted by the fantastical characterisations, and there are nice touches of black humour (like the toy working models of the killer made by one of the suspects). TM

Assassino del Poliziotti, L'

see Order of Death

Assassin of the Tsar, The (Tsareubiitsa)

(1991, GB/Rus, 104 min)
d Karen Shakhnazarov. *p* Christopher Gawor, Erik Vaisberg, Anthony Sloman. *sc* Aleksandr Borodianski, Karen Shakhnazarov. *ph* Nikolai Nemolyaev. *ed* Anthony Sloman, Lidiia Miliotti. *ad* Liudmila Kusakova. *m* John Altman. *cast* Malcolm McDowell, Oleg Yankovsky, Armen Dzhigarkhanyan, Yuri Sherstnyov, Angela Ptashuk.
●Mental patient Timofeyev (McDowell, twitchy and grizzled) is convinced that he assassinated Tsar Alexander II in 1881, and that he also led the firing squad that executed Nicholas II and his family in 1918. Dr Smirnov (Yankovsky) concludes that the only way to treat Timofeyev is to enter his fantasies, and so he starts playing Tsar to his patient's executioner. Before long, present and past are blurring together and we're on a full-dress reconstruction of the last weeks of the Romanov dynasty. About halfway through this lugubrious Anglo-Russian co-production, it dawns that the film is bending over backwards to avoid being seen as just another costume-drama plod through the Kremlin's secret files. Big mistake. The historical scenes are actually credible, dignified and rather watchable, whereas the implied parallel with the collapse of the USSR doesn't begin to cohere. And the whole mental-hospital framework is a hugely tautologous way of saying that these are unhealed wounds from the past. Hard to recommend except as an oddity. TR

Assassin(s)

(1997, Fr, 134 min)
d Mathieu Kassovitz. *p* Christophe Rossignon. *sc* Mathieu Kassovitz, Nicolas Boukhrief. *ph*

Pierre Aim. *ed* Mathieu Kassovitz. *m* Carter Burwell. *cast* Michel Serrault, Mathieu Kassovitz, Mehdi Benoufa, Robert Gendreu, Danièle Lebrun.
●Kassovitz's follow-up to *La Haine* is a disappointing misfire. Jobless petty criminal Kassovitz is taken up by ageing hitman Serrault, who'd like to see his perverse code of ethics carried on into an increasingly amoral world. So far, so implausible, but once teenager Benoufa takes to their murderous world like a duck to water, and Kassovitz the writer/director starts blaming the increase in violence on watching too much TV, it's hard not to object to the facile, conservative moralising and sledge-hammer dramaturgy. The actors are indulged, the ethical stance is duplicitous (given the relish the film displays in mounting scenes of horrific violence), and the overall result is extremely tedious. GA

Assassins

(1995, US, 133 min)
d Richard Donner. *p* Richard Donner, Joel Silver, Bruce Evans, Raynold Gideon, Andrew Lazar, Jim Van Wyck. *sc* Larry Wachowski, Andy Wachowski, Brian Helgeland. *ph* Vilmos Zsigmond. *ed* Richard Marks. *m* Mark Mancina. *cast* Sylvester Stallone, Antonio Banderas, Julianne Moore, Anatoly Davydov, Muse Watson, Stephen Kahan, Kelly Rowan.
●An unusually serious, almost sombre thriller from the versatile action producer Joel Silver in which Stallone's a jaded assassin haunted by the past but unable to face the future. As Robert Rath, he gives his best performance for some time, abandoning the self-mockery of *Demolition Man* and the risible muscle-flexing of *The Specialist* in favour of a more contained stillness. If only director Donner had inspired Banderas with the same confidence in this essentially generic, but involving scenario; as Miguel Bain, however, an upstart obsessed with inheriting Rath's position as the world's number-one assassin, he's horribly embarrassing, acting throughout like a St Vitus Dance sufferer on amphetamines. Plotwise, things are straightforward. Julianne Moore has unwittingly acquired a computer disk containing dangerously incriminating information, Stallone's hired to kill her, but is having a mid-life career crisis, the bad guys and Interpol are slaughtering everything that moves, and Banderas is the joker in the pack. Between the hits, car chases and gunfire, there are numerous quiet scenes in darkened rooms in which Sly and Moore discover an affinity in their loneliness. NF

Assault, The (De Aanslag)

(1986, Neth, 148 min)
d/p Fons Rademakers. *sc* Gerard Soeteman. *ph* Theo van de Sande. *ed* Kees Linthorst. *ad* Dorus van der Linden. *m* Juriaan Andriessen. *cast* Derek De Lint, Marc Van Uchelen, Monique Van De Ven, John Kraaykamp, Huub Van Der Lubbe.
●One fateful night in a quiet Dutch street during the German occupation, a collaborator is shot by the Resistance. Fearing reprisals if the body is found outside their house, a couple of burghers park the corpse outside the neighbours', with the result that the family is executed. The only survivor is 12-year-old Anton, and these traumatic events determine the course of his life over the next 30 years, leaving him numb to the march of history and troubled by flashbacks. Anton's exorcism is a long haul, awash with madeleine cakes and intimations of the randomness of things. Rademakers never quite reconciles the needs of the psychological detective story with those of biography, settling finally for a divinity which shapes our ends, but raises interesting moral questions along the way. BC

Assault on a Queen

(1966, US, 106 min)
d Jack Donohue. *p* William Goetz. *sc* Rod Serling. *ph* William H Daniels. *ed* Archie Marshek, Jack Wheeler. *ad* Hal Pereira, Paul Groesse. *m* Duke Ellington. *cast* Frank Sinatra, Virna Lisi, Anthony Franciosa, Alf Kjellin, Errol John, Richard Conte.
●Silly nonsense about a group of adventurers who salvage a sunken U-Boat and use it to hijack the Queen Mary. A sad travesty which muddies the clean lines of Jack Finney's novel. TM

Assault on Precinct 13

(1976, US, 91 min)
d John Carpenter. *p* JS Kaplan. *sc* John Carpenter. *ph* Douglas Knapp. *ed* John Carpenter. *ad* Tommy Lee Wallace. *m* John Carpenter. *cast* Austin Stoker, Darwin Joston, Laurie Zimmer, Martin West, Tony Burton, Charles Cyphers, Nancy Loomis.
●Just as *Dark Star* undercut the solemnity of space movies like *2001* with hilarious astronaut situation comedy, Carpenter's second feature borrows the conventions of protagonists in jeopardy from *Night of the Living Dead* to produce one of the most effective exploitation movies of the decade. The gimmick is cops and cons besieged in an abandoned LA police station by a group of kamikaze urban guerillas. Carpenter scrupulously avoids any overt socio-political pretensions, playing it instead for laughs and suspense in perfectly balanced proportions. The result is a thriller inspired by a buff's admiration for Ford and Hawks (particularly *Rio Bravo*), with action sequences comparable to anything in Siegel or Fuller. It's sheer delight from beginning to end. RM

Assedio, L'

see Besieged

Associate, The

(1996, US, 113 min)
d Donald Petrie. *p* Frederic Golchan, Patrick Markey, Adam Leipzig. *sc* Nick Thiel. *ph* Alex Nepomniaschy. *ed* Bonnie Koehler. *pd* Andrew Jackness. *m* Christopher Tyng. *cast* Whoopi Goldberg, Tim Daly, Diane Wiest, Eli Wallach, Bebe Neuwirth, Austin Pendleton.
●Passed over for promotion, financial consultant Laurel Ayers (Goldberg) strikes out on her own. Prospective clients turn her down; they're impressed to a man, they say, but their partners will never support them. Thus Laurel forges Mr Robert S Cutty, a white man whose acumen, elusiveness and impressively masculine personal effects enchant Wall Street and kick start Ayers Cutty's business ventures. Then Bob Cutty gets out of hand. He takes all the praise, attracts media attention and even turns out to be an absent father. A righteous populist comedy, with some dark tinges to the element of fairy story; but also a standard Whoopi-cushion – a plot for kids, puerile characterisation, and sentimentality hammered home by the score. The present film is a remake of *L'Associé*, directed by René Gainville in 1979, which in turn was a remake of a British film, *The Mysterious Mr Davis*, directed by Claude Autant-Lara in 1936, all of them deriving from a source novel, *El Socio*, by the Chilean author Jenaro Prieto. NB

As Tears Go By (Wangjiao Jiamen)

(1988, HK, 100 min)
d Wong Kar-Wai. *p* Rover Tang. *sc* Wong Kar-Wai. *ph* Wai Keung Lau. *ed* Pi Tak Cheong. *pd* William Chang. *m* Ting Yat Chung. *cast* Andy Lau, Jacky Cheung, Maggie Cheung, Alex Man.
●A Hong Kong remake of *Mean Streets* (with emphasis on the violence and the love story, but nothing on Catholicism), this was the first feature from Wong Kar-Wai, recently [1995] established as the great romantic of the Asian avant-garde. It's more generic than either the gorgeous *Days of Being Wild* or *Chungking Express*, and less interesting, but it's clearly the work of a gifted film-maker, highly atmospheric with a number of exciting set-pieces (there's a deliriously kitschy romantic montage set to the Mandarin cover of Berlin's 'Take My Breath Away'). If it fails, ultimately, it's because the relationship between the rational gangster Lau and the impetuous Jacky Cheung never really rings true. A cut above the usual HK action melodrama all the same. TCh

Asterix & Obelix Take on Caesar (Astérix & Obélix contre César)

(1999, Fr/Ger/It, 110 min)
d Claude Zidi. *sc* Claude Zidi, Gérard Lauzier, (English adaptation) Terry Jones. *ph* Tony Pierce-Roberts. *ed* Nicole Saunier, Hervé de Luze. *pd* Jean Rabasse. *m* Jean-Jacques Goldman, Roland Romanelli. *cast* Gerard Dépardieu, Christian Clavier, Roberto Benigni, Michel Galabru, Claude Piéplu, Daniel Prévost, Pierre Palmade, Laetitia Casta, Arielle Dombasle, Sim, Marianne Sägebrecht, Hardy Kruger Jr.
●This lavish and robust live-action chapter of the famous cartoon (dubbed for export) did exceptional business at the French box office. Thanks to a dash of romance and a new improved magic potion, the 'battle with the foregone conclusion' routine still manages to surprise. There are satisfyingly bloodthirsty fights and one or two genuinely decent thrills – the best featuring a dog and a tub of tarantulas. Gauls downing drugs prompt regular helpings of glittering visual tricks which – alongside Terry Jones' inventive English adaptation full of anachronisms, insults and knowing corn – more than amply distracts from the fact that in the English version nobody's mouth seems to be working properly. SS

Asterix and the Big Fight (Le Coup de Menhir)

(1989, Fr/WGer, 81 min)
d Philippe Grimond. *p* Nicolas Pesques. *sc* George Roubicek. *ph* Craig Simpson. *ed* Jean Goudier. *pd* Nicolas Pesques. *m* Michel Colombier. *cast* voices: Bill Oddie, Bernard Bresslaw, Ron Moody, Sheila Hancock, Peter Hawkins, Brian Blessed, Michael Elphick, Andrew Sachs, Tim Brooke-Taylor.
●The sixth animated Asterix feature. Yet again the gall of the indomitable Gauls rises against the superior forces of the Roman Empire. In the only village left to be captured, Asterix and Obelix, plus faithful canine accomplice Dogmatix, are the fighters maintaining freedom against the legionnaires and their collaborators, including a surly trickster who passes himself off as a soothsayer. Unfortunately, due to an over-enthusiastic Obelix, the village druid Getafix is out of action and unable to provide the magic brew which will give the superhuman strength Asterix relies on. Magic animation and a familiarly reassuring cast of English voices contribute to an engaging film. JGl

Astérix chez les Brétons

see Asterix in Britain

Asterix Conquers America (Asterix in Amerika)

(1994, Ger, 90 min)
d Gerhard Hahn, Keith Ingham. *p* Jürgen Wohlrabe. *sc* Thomas Platt, Rhett Rooster. ed Ulrich Steinvorth. *m* Harold Faltermeyer. *cast* voices: John Rye, Craig Charles, Howard Lew Lewis, Geoffrey Bayldon.
●For those late for the news from the Gallic Wars, the French village of Asterix and Obelix is still holding out, but Caesar's disguised henchman, unable to steal village 'supplier' Getafix's recipe for their magic potion, catapults him over the edge of the flat Earth, straight into the pipe-smoking clutches of the Native Americans. The formula (for this seventh installment) is still basically the same: a good-natured punch-up heavy rescue-adventure, with Roman puns for the adults. The racism is still universally applied: massive rubber-lipped blacks on the palm island; Roman legionnaires with 'Mama Mia' accents from Italian ice-cream ads; and, interestingly, upper-crust Brits as galley-slaves rowing in competition like Edwardian varsity blues. The animation, however, is good; and while it's low on the musical count, it all rushes by too fast to notice. WH

Asterix in Amerika

see Asterix Conquers America

Asterix in Britain (Astérix chez les Brétons)

(1986, Fr, 89 min)
d Pino Van Lamsweerde. *p* Yannick Piel. *sc* Pierre Tchernia. *ph* Philippe Laine. *ed* Robert Isnardon, Monique Isnardon. *ad* Michel Guérin. *m* Vladimir Cosma. *cast* voices: Peter Hudson, Jack Beaber, Bill Kearns, Graham Bushnell, Gordon Heath, Herbert Baskind, Jimmy Shuman.
●Asterix and Obelix are once more called upon to lay waste the Romans in this third animated feature to be lifted from the marvellous text and drawings of Goscinny and Uderzo's books. It's 50 BC, and the Romans have just invaded British

shores. The Brits, however, seem more interested in their daily cuppa than fisticuffs. But one little village, still holding fort against the invaders, do call on the plucky Gauls, who come to their aid replete with a barrel of their strength-giving and intoxicating magic potion. Apart from some questionable editing and the use of slightly watered-down colours, the film stays true to the original characters. Youngsters will no doubt enjoy it, but true fans may prefer to stick with the pun-ridden books. DA

As the Beast Sleeps

(2001, GB, 75 min)
d Harry Bradbeer. *p* Tony Rowe, Robert Cooper. *sc* Gary Mitchell. *ph* Mark Garrett. *ed* Paul Endacott. *pd* Gillian Devenny. *cast* Stuart Graham, Patrick O'Kane, Colum Convey, Laine Megaw, David Hayman.

●The TV version of Belfast writer Gary Mitchell's play gauges the temperature in the Loyalist community as the IRA ceasefire brings a response in kind from the Protestant paramilitaries. The disgruntled footsoldiers of the UFF have, however, become used to free drinks and heroic status in local boozing dens. The unfolding powerplay peers through the chinks in their ideological zeal to reveal bigotry and greed, shading in the distance between them and their political masters' search for mainstream legitimacy. Dialogue with barely a false note, authentic performances and probing direction recall the glory days of BBC TV's 'Play for Today' drama strand. TJ

Asthenic Syndrome, The (Asteniceskij Sindrom)

(1990, USSR, 153 min, b/w & col)
d Kira Muratova. *sc* Kira Muratova, Sergei Popov, Alexander Tschernych. *ph* Vladimir Pankov. *ed* Valentina Olejnik. *pd* Eugeny Golubenko. *cast* Sergei Popov, Olga Antonova, Natalja Busko.

●Muratova's literally ungodly film is the most recommendable hard-to-sit-through movie of the year. It starts out in monochrome, telling the story of a woman who goes to pieces after her husband's funeral, but that turns out to be a film-within-the-film (one which empties the theatre at a preview, moreover) which prefaces an extended collage of 'fear and loathing' scenes from Russian life. Asthenia is blind aggression masking underlying weakness, and Muratova sees it as pervading her society; not only in hooliganism, vandalism and crime, but also in male-female and teacher-pupil relations, and virtually everyone's attitude to life. Not an incisive, organised movie like her long-banned *Short Meetings*, but equally distinctive and memorable. TR

Astonished Heart, The

(1950, GB, 89 min, b/w)
d Terence Fisher, Antony Darnborough. *p* Antony Darnborough. *sc* Noel Coward. *ph* Jack Asher. *ed* V Sagovsky. *pd* Maurice Carter. *m* Noël Coward. *cast* Noël Coward, Celia Johnson, Margaret Leighton, Joyce Carey, Graham Payn.

●Intriguingly schematic account (based on Coward's own playlet) of a psychiatrist's sexual obsession with a good-time girl (Leighton), and the effect it has on his devoted, self-denying, sexless wife (Johnson) as it ultimately drives him to self-destruct by throwing himself off a high building. In its way it crystallises and criticises the conventional attitudes towards sex prevalent throughout British cinema in the immediate post-war period, and which Fisher was to turn upside-down in his vampire movies, where the neurotic female altruism represented here by Celia Johnson is transformed by the cathartic presence of Dracula into ravening sexuality. DP

Astragale, L' (The Ankle Bone)

(1968, Fr/WGer, 102 min)
d Guy Casaril. *p* Pierre Braunberger. *sc* Guy Casaril. *ph* Edmond Richard. *ed* Nicole Gauduchon. *ad* Eric Simon. *m* Joss Baselli. *cast* Marlène Jobert, Horst Buchholz, Magali Noel, Claude Génia, Georges Géret, Jean-Pierre Moulin.

●Jobert plays (rather well) a juvenile delinquent who decides she can't take it when her lesbian cellmate is released from jail. So she escapes, breaking her astragalus (an ankle-bone) in the process: a metaphor for her crippled life as she hobbles around on crutches, goes on the streets to support herself, suffers agonies of jealousy when her boyfriend (Buchholz, supplanting the lesbian) starts disappearing for long periods, and lives in constant terror of being trapped by the police. It is presumably meant to be all about solitude and the prisons of the mind, but Guy Casaril's flabbily uninspired direction succeeds only in making one wish Bresson had taken over. TM

Astronaut's Wife, The

(1999, US, 109 min)
d Rand Ravich. *p* Andrew Lazar. *sc* Rand Ravich. *ph* Allen Daviau. *ed* Steve Mirkovich, Tim Alverson. *pd* Jan Roelfs. *m* George S Clinton. *cast* Johnny Depp, Charlize Theron, Joe Morton, Clea Duvall, Samatha Eggar, Donna Murphy, Nick Cassavetes, Gary Grubbs, Blair Brown.

● Astronaut Depp returns to Earth after a routine satellite repair mission, during which he and his partner Cassavetes lost radio contact with NASA for two mysterious minutes. Perplexed and hurt by her husband's refusal to talk about what happened, Depp's wife, Florida school-teacher Theron, is further unsettled by the death, from a stroke, of his partner. Then, shortly before the dead man's wife commits suicide, she tells Theron cryptically: 'He's hiding inside me.' Abandoning the space program, flyboy Depp takes a lucrative job with a NY aerospace firm with military interests. Finding herself pregnant with twins, Theron feels isolated and afraid. Is she carrying extra-terrestrial parasites? Long on atmosphere but short on momentum, the meandering plot is fleshed out by Theron's instinctive yet delicately nuanced performance – she is, by turns, vulnerable, sympathetically unhinged and fiercely strongwilled. Ravich's slick direction fills the antiseptic interiors of the couple's Manhattan designer apartment with an edgy, brooding menace, but regrettably the slow burn suspense is extinguished when too much is revealed at just the wrong moment. NF

Asya's Happiness (Istoriya Asi Klyachinoi, Kotoraya Lyubila, da nie vshla zamuzh)

(1966, USSR, 98 min, b/w)
d Andrei Mikhalkov-Konchalovsky. *p* M Zaržhitskaya. *sc* Yuri Klepikov. *ph* Georgi Rerberg. *ed* L Pokrovskoi. *ad* Mikhail Romadin. *cast* Iya Savvina, Lyubov Sokolova, Alexandre Surin, Gennady Yegorychev, Ivan Petrov.

●Shot in 1966 and subsequently banned for some twenty years, this is far superior to Konchalovsky's later work in America. Basically about a group of villagers working a collective farm, and partly focused on the options open to the lame, pregnant but proud Asya, it is an oblique, touching portrait of a remote community that is both poor and apparently forgotten by the Soviet authorities. Most of the time, the outside world barely intrudes (there is talk of Vietnam, distant tanks rumble); the farm-folk spend their non-working hours gossiping, drinking, reminiscing and, in the case of a selfish layabout and a visiting gypsy, jealously quarrelling over Asya. But plot is of less importance than atmosphere – it was probably the unglamourous vision of village life that incurred official wrath – and the fluid, even virtuoso direction. The black-and-white camerawork is very lyrical, the acting (by a cast largely made up of local non-professionals) lends the film a quiet emotional integrity, and the shifts in tone – from long contemplative shots of landscape and faces to rapidly cut, *vérité*-style sequences of joyous communal dancing and singing – are effortlessly smooth. Rarely has such a vivid, plausible sense of daily life been conveyed by a Soviet director. GA

Asylum

(1972, GB, 88 min)
d Roy Ward Baker. *p* Max J Rosenberg, Milton Subotsky. *sc* Robert Bloch. *ph* Denys Coop. *ed* Peter Tanner. *ad* Tony Curtis. *m* Douglas Gamley. *cast* Patrick Magee, Robert Powell, Geoffrey Bayldon, Barbara Parkins, Peter Cushing, Barry Morse, Britt Ekland, Charlotte Rampling, Herbert Lom, Sylvia Syms.

●The fourth Amicus horror omnibus, comprising four Robert Bloch stories, set in an asylum and boasting a fairly ingenious framing device whereby the glowering director (Magee) sets a young psychiatrist applying for a job (Powell) the task of discovering which of the patients is a former colleague gone mad. Cheerfully gruesome (especially the last tale involving Lom and a murderous manikin), but done without much wit or style. TM

Asylum

(2000, GB, 60 min)
d Chris Petit, Iain Sinclair. *p* Keith Griffiths. *ph* Chris Petit, Iain Sinclair. *ed* Emma Matthews. *with* Michael Moorcock, Ed Dorn, James Sallis, Marina Warner, David Seabrook, Françoise Lacroix, Michelle Lacroix.

●Petit and Sinclair continue their adventures in digital video in this ravishing feast for the eyes and ears (and work for the brain). Digital artist Dave McKean and sound designer Bruce Gilbert fill the same roles they filled on *The Falconer*, an earlier Petit/Sinclair project. Both films feature real people and places in a fictional context. In this case, a virus having wiped out cultural memory, an operative, Kaporal, is brought out of retirement to re-evaluate recovered, devastated files. Kaporal engages a sound recordist, Agent Matthews (editor Emma Matthews), to refill the depleted memory banks. Among her duties she must record interviews with writers believed to be Illuminati – Michael Moorcock, Ed Dorn, James Sallis. American poet Dorn, tracked down on a visit to Margate ('where the kernel of twentieth-century consciousness split open'), gives Nato a hard time for its action against Serbia and later lays into Clinton over Iraq. Sallis strums guitar in his garden in Phoenix, Arizona, while waiting for the oranges to fall from his tree. Moorcock, said to embody a thousand years of London's literary history, is located in an unseasonably rainy Bastrop, Texas. Kaporal's condition, it seems, is his realisation that what he filmed in the past he cannot now see afresh, hence this film being his final commission. 'You don't disappear. You reappear, dead,' wrote Dorn, who died in 1999. The film is dedicated to his memory. NRo

As You Desire Me

(1932, US, 69 min, b/w)
d George Fitzmaurice. *sc* Gene Markey. *ph* William H Daniels. *ed* George Hively. *ad* Cedric Gibbons. *cast* Greta Garbo, Melvyn Douglas, Erich Von Stroheim, Owen Moore, Hedda Hopper.

●Garbo in one of her archetypally enigmatic roles as a Budapest cabaret entertainer, an amnesia victim who may or may not be the wife Douglas has long believed dead, but in any case falls for him while her 'protector' Stroheim fumes malevolently. Don't expect to find too much of Pirandello's play, but Garbo (sporting a peroxide wig some of the time) brings a real erotic undertow to the love scenes, while Stroheim is terrific as the demonically sadistic writer trying to model her as one of his own creations. TM

As You Like It

(1936, GB, 96 min, b/w)
d/p Paul Czinner. *sc* Robert J Cullen, JM Barrie. *ph* Hal Rosson. *ed* David Lean. *ad* Lazare Meerson. *m* William Walton. *cast* Elisabeth Bergner, Laurence Olivier, Sophie Stewart, Leon Quartermaine, Felix Aylmer.

●Those imposing credits languish in the shadow of the one that really matters, that of the leaden, lacklustre Czinner. But even he can't entirely compromise the sweep of Walton's score or the energy of the young Olivier, in full Burt Lancaster mode as he bustles around the brambly maze of Meerson's Arden. However, showcasing the kittenish Bergner is top of the agenda here; and if her Ganymede is actually more feminine than her Rosalind, this is less likely to be about gender politics than about a director absolutely smitten with his leading lady. BBa

As You Like It

(1992, GB, 117 min)
d Christine Edzard. *p* Richard Goodwin. *ph* Robin Vidgeon. *ed* Christine Edzard. *m* Michel Sanvoisin. *cast* Cyril Cusack, James Fox, Don Henderson, Miriam Margolyes, Emma Croft, Griff Rhys Jones, Celia Bannerman.

●In Christine Edzard's modern-dress version of Shakespeare's comedy, the forest is an urban wasteland, the exiled Duke lords it over a group of down-and-outs, and Orlando versifies with an aerosol can. After the scrupulous period detail of her earlier work, this is a surprise, and the conceit weighs heavily on the entire production, putting text against context. The Duke's court appears to be a defunct town hall (with the acoustics of a swimming-pool). Andrew Tiernan plays both Orlando and his brother Oliver – but never in the same frame. Emma Croft is Rosalind, caparisoned like a man (and countless modern women) in jeans and sweater: if there be truth in sight, her Ganymede can make no sense. Both are swamped by their lines, and even Griff Rhys Jones' Touchstone makes heavy weather of the Bard's tortuous wit. It is easy to believe Edzard's claim that 'the film made itself…we just let the play do its own thing'. The wonder is that they bothered to put film in the camera, for sadly this is Shakespeare *sans* teeth, eyes, taste, *sans* everything. TCh

Atalante, L' 100 (100)

(1934, Fr, 89 min, b/w)
d Jean Vigo. *p* JL Nounez. *sc* Jean Vigo, Albert Riera. *ph* Boris Kaufman. *ed* Louis Chavance. *ad* Francis Jourdain. *m* Maurice Jaubert. *cast* Michel Simon, Jean Dasté, Dita Parlo, Louis Lefebvre, Gilles Margaritis.

● Mesmeric movie mutilated by Gaumont distributors on its first release, but subsequently restored to the form its devoted maker (the avant garde-ish son of an anarchist) intended. Not a lot happens: a sailor and his young bride share a barge home with an old eccentric, fall out, and fall in love again. But the aesthetic appeal lies in the tension between surface realism (the hardships of working class life on the canals) and the delicate surrealism of the landscapes (desolate Parisian suburbs bestraddled by pylons) and of the justly celebrated sequence where the sailor searches for his lost love. MA

Atame!

see Tie Me Up! Tie Me Down!

Atanarjuat: The Fast Runner

(2000, Can, 168 min)
d Zacharias Kunuk. *p* Paul Apak Angilirq, Norman Cohn, Zacharias Kunuk, (National Film Board) Germaine Ying Gee Wong. *sc* Paul Apak Angilirq. *ph* Norman Cohn. *ed* Zacharias Kunuk, Norman Cohn, Marie-Christine Sarda. *pd* James Ungalaaq. *m* Chris Crilly. *cast* Natar Ungalaaq, Sylvia Ivalu, Peter Henry Arnatsiaq, Lucy Tulugarjuk, Madeline Ivalu, Pauloosie Qulitalik, Eugene Ipkarnak.

● This first feature deposits us on the Arctic tundra some time in the past, before the Southerners arrived. We're in the thick of hunting by dogsled, living in igloos and the unsettling reality of shamanism. Having initiated the notion of evil abroad in the community, the central narrative about family rivalry starts to kick in. Fleetfooted Atanarjuat has his eyes on Atuat, long promised to the boorish Oki. The situation is resolved by a bout of ritual head-punching, but lust and jealousy propel events into escalating violence. Courage, endurance and the guidance of the spirits make their contribution, all engrossingly played out in the blue-white light of endless snowscapes. Shot on digital video, the film skilfully balances the intimacy of strong emotions and the scale of the daunting surroundings. Spellbinding as storytelling, it also prompts admiration for the Inuit people's patience, resilience and their overriding concern for harmony with the world around them. TJ

At Close Range

(1985, US, 115 min)
d James Foley. *p* Elliot Lewitt, Don Guest. *sc* Nicholas Kazan. *ph* Juan Ruiz-Anchia. *ed* Howard Smith. *pd* Peter Jamison. *m* Patrick Leonard. *cast* Sean Penn, Christopher Walken, Mary Stuart Masterson, Christopher Penn, Millie Perkins, Eileen Ryan.

● After young Penn is thrown out by his stepfather, he encounters his real father (Walken), who impresses the lad with his life as a successful outlaw in the Pennsylvania backwoods. He trains up the boy in stealing anything that moves, and life seems very jolly and fulfilled in a hillbilly sort of way. Then Walken is slowly revealed to the boy's eyes as a murderer and rapist; and when the boy and his friends decide to blow the whistle, the guns are turned inwards on the family. Foley has opted for a mixture of documentary 'realism' and set pieces which have clearly escaped from overlit pop promos. Mingle this with Penn and Walken going heavily over the top in usual Method fashion, and the brew is less than intoxicating. CPea

At Dawn (Po Xiao Shi Fen)

(1968, Tai, 106 min)
d Song Cunshou. *p* Li Hanxiang. *sc* Yao Fengpan. *ph* Chen Xile. *ed* Zhang Zhongmin. *ad* Tang Guoshi. *m* Wang Juren. *cast* Yang Qun, Wu Xiufang.

● The best of the 21 films produced by Li Hanxiang's company Guolian, Song's second feature is a bitter denunciation of China's feudal heritage, very much in the vein of Shi Hui's *The Whole Life of Mine*. Lu Laosan (Yang) is forced by his father into a job as a court attendant and quickly realises that the legal system is shockingly corrupt. His attempts to help a young widow (Wu) falsely accused of stealing from and murdering her husband merely draw him into the corruption; he is made to testify against her. Composed for the 'Scope frame with a formality that soon picks up an edge of irony, this resonant protest remains a high point in Taiwanese film history. TR

At First Sight

see Coup de Foudre

At First Sight

(1998, US, 129 min)
d Irwin Winkler. *p* Irwin Winkler, Rob Cowan. *sc* Steve Levitt. *ph* John Seale. *ed* Julie Monroe. *pd* Jane Musky. *m* Mark Isham. *cast* Val Kilmer, Mira Sorvino, Kelly McGillis, Steven Weber, Bruce Davison, Ken Howard, Nathan Lane, Oliver Sacks.

● A case history by Dr Oliver Sacks inspired this story about a blind masseur, Kilmer, who finds love and regains his sight. One suspects, however, that it owes as much to *Awakenings*, another celluloid Sacks adaptation, where medical science opened the doors to freedom, only for regression to set in. Winkler's film follows pretty much the same pattern, and it's far more persuasive in detailing the physical realities of its protagonist's plight than in working up a sudsy melodrama around Kilmer and Sorvino, the New York architect who changes his life. Though Winkler and cameraman John Seale convey the threatening strangeness of a world newly discovered, they ultimately opt for the Hollywood dysfunction-of-the-week routine, when the ingredients were there for something tougher. TJ

At Gunpoint (aka Gunpoint)

(1955, US, 80 min)
d Alfred Werker. *p* Vincent M Fennelly. *sc* Daniel B Ullman. *ph* Ellsworth J Fredricks. *ed* Eda Warren. *ad* David Milton. *m* Carmen Dragon. *cast* Fred MacMurray, Dorothy Malone, Walter Brennan, Skip Homeier, Whit Bissell, Jack Lambert, John Qualen, Tommy Rettig.

● MacMurray plays a storekeeper who, more by accident than marksmanship, shoots the leader of a gang robbing the town bank. From there on, this Western turns into a cross between *High Noon* and *The Man Who Shot Liberty Valance*, with the townsfolk proudly boosting MacMurray as a hero, then – as the rest of the gang come for revenge – leaving him to stand alone. The first half is quite gripping, with excellent performances from MacMurray and the ever-dependable Walter Brennan (with teeth), as the hard-drinking, cynical doctor who remains the hero's sole but overage ally. Latterly, though, Daniel B Ullman's script develops a case of creeping sententiousness, tending to speechify about civic conscience and the American Way, and throwing in an absurdly contrived upbeat ending. TM

Atlantic Adventure

(1935, US, 68 min, b/w)
d Albert Rogell. *sc* John T Neville, Nat Dorfman. *ph* John Stumar. *ed* Ted Kent. *cast* Nancy Carroll, Lloyd Nolan, Harry Langdon, Arthur Hohl, Robert Middlemass, EE Clive.

● Bracing little second-feature in which dashing reporter Lloyd Nolan is fired from the paper when he keeps a date with his fiancée rather than cover the murder of the DA. He's tipped off that the killer is fleeing to Europe on an ocean liner, so he joins him for the voyage, hoping to put his career back on track. It's a little sad to see Harry Langdon, one of the top comics of the 1920s, providing the light relief as Nolan's photographer, but the old-timer still knows how to get a laugh. GM

Atlantic City (aka Atlantic City USA)

(1980, Can/Fr, 105 min)
d Louis Malle. *p* Denis Héroux. *sc* John Guare. *ph* Richard Ciupka. *ed* Suzanne Baron. *pd* Anne Pritchard. *m* Michel Legrand. *cast* Burt Lancaster, Susan Sarandon, Kate Reid, Michel Piccoli. Hollis McLaren, Robert Joy.

● Eclectic, pacy and hard to categorise, it's part crime thriller, part love story, part fairytale, and part a gentle, generous examination of certain dying aspects of American culture. Lancaster turns in the performance of his career as the ageing petty crook, running a numbers racket, indulging in nostalgic delusions about his past experiences in the Big Time with Capone et al., and finally getting a chance to discover true self-respect when he gets involved with a young hippy who's stolen a stash of coke from the mob. Between the gripping and beautifully staged action sequences, Malle contrasts the rather sad and slightly seedy lives of various loners with their romantic dreams of success, wealth and fame, while never treating his characters with condescension or contempt. Witty, warm, but never sentimental, it also benefits from being set in the fading glories of the resort town of the title: grand seaside facades behind which lie more mundane realities, surrounded by decay and demolition. GA

Atlantis

(1992, Fr/It, 75 min)
d Luc Besson. *p* Claude Besson. *ph* Christian Petron, Luc Besson. *ed* Luc Besson. *m* Eric Serra.

● Besson's fascination with the sea continues in this wordless presentation of underwater phenomena. The point is clear: forget the Atlantis myth, there's a thriving society down there right now. Crowds of fish bustle along during some sub-marine rush hour, a pack of dolphins gossip excitedly, a couple of giant turtles gingerly make love, a diversity of glamorous and/or grotesque creatures weaves sinuously through oceanic canyons and forests. Until the very last shot, Besson's cameras stay beneath the surface, disclosing a world of topsy-turvy reflections, angry water seen from below, images that are often as abstract as a McLaren animation. Eric Serra's score, a mix of symphonic and synthetic, is discreetly complementary. There's no ecology, no biology, nothing didactic at all – simply a film-maker with a subject that enchants him. It certainly won't hurt the sale of aqualungs. BBa

Atlantis – The Lost Empire

(2001, US, 96 min)
d Gary Trousdale, Kirk Wise. *p* Don Hahn. *sc* Tab Murphy. *ed* Ellen Keneshea. *pd* Mike Mignola, Matt Codd, Ricardo Delgado, Jim E Martin. *m* James Newton Howard. *cast* voices: Michael J Fox, James Garner, Cree Summer, Don Novello, Phil Morris, Claudia Christian, David Ogden Stiers, Leonard Nimoy.

● This Disney animated spectacular is cast as an adventure story in the Jules Verne mould and played commendably straight. It ditches musical numbers and flip contemporary references in favour of a strong storyline, genuine moral dilemmas and luxuriant 'Scope. Set in 1914, it's packed with delightfully old-fangled hardware as cartographer and linguistics expert Milo Thatch finds himself on the subaquatic expedition of a lifetime to trace the legendary civilisation of Atlantis. His expertise leads Commander Rourke and his battle-hardened team to their destination, where they find treasure beyond imagination, but also a living community needing the newcomers' help. Will the Americans embrace this alien culture, or trample over it for their own ends? As such, it's probably the most grown-up animated feature Disney has produced, and with its attuned vocal performances, elegant design and pulse-quickening finale, it sets a standard of sustained craftsmanship most live-action film-makers must envy. TJ

At Long Last Love

(1975, US, 114 min)
d/p/sc Peter Bogdanovich. *ph* Laszlo Kovacs. *ed* Douglas Robertson. *pd* Gene Allen. *songs* Cole Porter. *cast* Burt Reynolds, Cybill Shepherd, Madeline Kahn, Duilio Del Prete, Eileen Brennan, John Hillerman, Mildred Natwick.

●Everybody hated Bogdanovich's homage, a trivial story slotted round some Cole Porter songs. It's an indulgent movie – Peter and Cybill having a lark with their friends – but it's also a neat parody of '30s musicals, with sets nodding to Van Nest Polglase, Hillerman taking the Eric Blore part with unerring restraint, Reynolds hamming away as if he's Cary Grant crossed with Muhammad Ali, the much-maligned Cybill Shepherd an icy honey-blonde in the Tracy Lord tradition (the Grace Kelly, not the Katharine Hepburn version). Better still, the brittle, clipped world of Porter's songs is perfectly evoked. It may be a movie we'll come back to later and find we all like it. SG

Atomic Café, The

(1982, US, 89 min, col & b/w)
d/p Kevin Rafferty, Jayne Loader, Pierce Rafferty. *ed* Jayne Loader, Kevin Rafferty.
A compilation of film clips from the late '40s and '50s, chronicling America's attempts to make the nuclear bomb an acceptable part of its cultural life. The material evidently took years to unearth, and most of it is fascinating by any standards. But like so many compilations, this emerges as much less than the sum of its parts. For one thing, the sheer bizarreness of the cultural phenomenon it displays utterly swamps some weak attempts at humour in the editing. For another, the film fails to offer even the barest social context for its material, as if atomic madness was an isolated phenomenon unrelated to the whole constellation of '50s paranoia from McCarthyism to UFOs. DP

Atomic Man, The

see Timeslip

A Toute Vitesse (Full Speed)

(1996, Fr, 85 min)
d Gaël Morel. *p* Laurent Bénégui. *sc* Gaël Morel. *ph* Jeanne Lapoirie. *ed* Catherine Schwartz. *ad* Frédérique Hurpeau. *cast* Elodie Bouchez, Stéphane Rideau, Pascal Cervo, Meziane Bardadi, Romain Auger, Salim Kechiouche.
●Morel came to film-goers' attention with his performance in *Les Roseaux sauvages* (as, indeed, did the very able Bouchez), and his directorial debut is clearly influenced by Téchiné's film. A rather unfocused, often overly elliptical study of a group of young French provincials – some from North Africa – falling in and out with each other, the film's hardly the most original account of teenage loyalties, ambitions and hedonism, but like other French films of recent years, it does attempt to treat both racism and homosexuality with some frankness. The performances, too, are strong; a pity, though, that the film finally plunges into melodramatic contrivance. GA

At Play in the Fields of the Lord

(1991, US, 187 min)
d Hector Babenco. *p* Saul Zaentz. *sc* Jean-Claude Carrière, Hector Babenco. *ph* Lauro Escorel. *ed* William Anderson. *pd* Clovis Bueno. *m* Zbigniew Preisner. *cast* Tom Berenger, John Lithgow, Daryl Hannah, Aidan Quinn, Tom Waits, Kathy Bates, Nelson Xavier.
●Babenco's ambitious eco-movie, co-scripted with Jean-Claude Carrière, condenses Peter Matthiessen's lengthy novel embracing greed, disloyalty and religious conflict in the Amazon rainforest. Martin Quarrier (Quinn) strives to understand the very culture he seeks to change: when he arrives to convert Niaruna tribesmen, clashes with his repressive wife (Bates) and dogmatic fellow-missionary Huben (Lithgow) foreshadow terrible violence. His despair is more discreetly matched by that of Huben's wife (Hannah, weak in a sketchy role), but overshadowed by that of Lewis Moon (Berenger), a part-Cheyenne mercenary who throws in his lot with the Niaruna. The film boasts a sense of conviction and wonderful natural spectacle, but lacks drive. There are also awkward lunges in tone, most evident in Bates' swift decent into madness, and the casting is problematic. Lithgow, Bates and Waits (as Moon's low-life partner) are all excellent, but Quinn's heart-throb status jars with the requirements of his role. CM

At Sundance

(1995, US, 71 min)
d Michael Almereyda, Amy Hobby. *cast* Robert Redford, Danny Boyle, Richard Linklater, Atom Egoyan, James Mangold, Whit Stillman, James Gray, Nick Gomez, Abel Ferrara, Larry Gross, Todd Haynes.
●'What are your feelings about the broad future of the movies?' That's the poser for a couple of dozen film-makers, caught in Almereyda's pixel camera lens at the 1995 Sundance film festival. Fans of American independent cinema will enjoy this glimpse of such unlikely heroes as James Mangold, Whit Stillman and James Gray, but the endless parade of talking heads speculating rather haphazardly is of marginal interest. There's a scary double act by Nick Gomez and Abel Ferrara. Scriptwriter Larry Gross quotes Gramsci ('the pessimism of the intelligence and the optimism of the will'), but it's Todd Haynes who hits the bull's eye when he claims to be 'guardedly pessimistic'. TCh

Attack

(1956, US, 103 min, b/w)
d/p Robert Aldrich. *sc* James Poe. *ph* Joseph Biroc. *ed* Michael Luciano. *ad* William Glasgow. *m* Frank DeVol. *cast* Jack Palance, Eddie Albert, Lee Marvin, Robert Strauss, Richard Jaeckel, Buddy Ebsen, Peter Van Eyck.
●Often described as hysterical, this is in fact a brilliant predecessor to Kubrick's *Paths of Glory* using a fictional slant on World War II's Battle of the Bulge – the cowardice of a CO (Albert), resulting in heavy casualties, is studiously ignored by superiors with an eye to his father's political pull – to express a virulent disgust not so much with war itself as with the systems of privilege and self-interest which perpetuate its disasters. Where Kubrick analyses, Aldrich *attacks*; and his images have precisely the same hallucinatingly twisted quality as the war-torn landscapes in which they take shape. TM

Attack of the 50 Foot Woman

(1958, US, 66 min, b/w)
d Nathan Juran. *p* Bernard Woolner. *ph* Jacques R Marquette. *ed* Edward Mann. *pd* Joseph T Garrity. *m* Ronald Stein. *cast* Allison Hayes, William Hudson, Yvette Vickers, Roy Gordon, George Douglas, Ken Terrell.
●Delirious pre-feminist horror movie about a rejected woman who suffers a dose of extra-terrestrial gigantism and finally rampages into town to twist her husband round one little finger (literally!). The special effects are dire, but the film's psycho-pathology is fascinating, and the lines have to be heard to be believed ('Put him down, Mrs Archer…'). Perfect late night indulgence. DP

Attack of the 50ft Woman

(1994, US, 89 min)
d Christopher Guest. *p* Debra Hill. *sc* Mark Hanna, Joseph Dougherty. *ph* Russell Carpenter. *ed* Harry Keramidas. *m* Nicholas Pike. *cast* Daryl Hannah, Daniel Baldwin, William Windom, Frances Fisher, Christi Conaway, Paul Benedict, O'Neal Compton.
●Searching for her errant husband one evening, Nancy Archer (Hannah) is zapped by a UFO. Although neither her husband Harry (Baldwin) nor her tycoon father (Windom) believe her story, it soon becomes transparently obvious that something extraordinary has happened: she experiences such rapid personal growth that she has to move out to the barn. This HBO remake of a notable example of '50s schlock substitutes knowing camp tackiness and post-feminist truisms for the authentic proto-feminist vulgarity of the original; but both versions are essentially about a whacking 50ft metaphor. The special effects are superior, but not a lot; and characterisation and development are still disappointingly sketchy. Of course the sexists get all the best lines. Appalled when big Nancy comes on to him, Harry pipes up: 'What do you expect me to do – buy a wetsuit and flashlight?' TCh

Attack of the Killer Tomatoes

(1979, US, 87 min)
d John DeBello. *p* Steve Peace, John De Bello. *sc* Costa Dillon, Steve Peace, John De Bello. *ph* John K Culley. *ed* John De Bello. *m* Gordon Goodwin, Paul Sundfor. *cast* Sharon Taylor, David Miller, George Wilson, Jack Riley.
●One-joke spoof on that B movie staple of the '50s, monstrously enlarged scientific mutations. The big red ones have their way with corrupt politicians and (via bloody Bloody Marys) housewife tipplers, while the pastiche '50s soundtrack croons 'I know I'm gonna miss her, a tomato ate my sister'. CR

Attack of the Puppet People (aka Six Inches Tall)

(1958, US, 79 min, b/w)
d Bert I Gordon. *sc* George Worthing Yates. *ph* Ernest Laszlo. *ed* Ronald Sinclair. *m* Albert Glasser. *cast* John Agar, June Kenny, John Hoyt, Michael Mark, Marlene Willis.
●Having already cashed in on the success of *The Incredible Shrinking Man* by rushing out (on the principle of opposites) *The Amazing Colossal Man*, producer/director Gordon went the whole hog with this tale of a lonely doll-maker (Hoyt) given to miniaturising human beings. Unsurprisingly, it's a poor second cousin to the Richard Matheson/Jack Arnold mini-classic, with poor characterisation beaten only by penny-pinching special effects, reaching a nadir with some truly laughable back projection when a couple of the unwilling little people take to the pre-dawn LA streets. Nevertheless, this is still plenty of fun, from its pseudo-science ('You know how a projector works, enlarging an image…' begins Zer Nutsy Puppeteer) to one of the shrunken gals launching reluctantly into the pop pastiche 'I'm Your Living Doll'. GD

Attack on a Bakery (Panya Shugeki)

(1982, Jap, 17 min)
d Naoto Yamakawa. *p* Masamichi Shimojo, Shigeaki Mori. *sc* Naoto Yamakawa. *ph* Yoshiharu Tezuka. *cast* Cho Ban-Ho, Taro Suwa, Shigeru Muroi, Koen Okumura.
●Novelist Haruki Murakami has always refused to sell film rights to his books, but he did allow indie pioneer Yamakawa to adapt two of his stories as short films in the early '80s. This was the first, the one about two existentially hungry labourers who 'get in character' to rob a baker's shop. But the communist baker outwits them: if they'll agree to listen to a Wagner opera, he'll give them all they can eat. They dubiously buy this deal, but later find their real 'hunger' still gnawing at them. All of the story's political and moral ambiguities are present and correct. It's brilliantly witty in both performance and film language; the sequence with future star Muroi as a customer hesitating between a croissant and a bun is not far off sublime. TR

Attack the Gas Station! (Chuyuso Supgyuk Sa Keun)

(1999, SKor, 113 min)
d Kim Sang-Jin. *p* Lee Kwan-Soo, Kim Mi-Hee. *sc* Park Jung-Woo. *ph* Choi Jung-Woo. *ed* Go Im-Pyo. *ad* Oh Sang-Man. *m* Son Mu-Hyun. *cast* Lee Seong-Jae, Yu O-Sung, Kang Sung-Jin, Yu Gee-Tae.
●In its way, Kim's anarchic comedy is as strong a blow against Korea's Confucian orthodoxy as Jang Sun-Woo's *Lies*. Four disaffected young men (flashbacks clarify their grievances against society) who have already smashed up a gas station for kicks decide in a bored moment to go back for Round Two. This time they take the place over, locking up the manager, staff and any customers who have the nerve to complain about the service. By the end of the evening, with dozens of hostages held inside and delivery boys, gangsters and cops converging on the forecourt, the four wild ones have not only shaken up people from every stratum of Korean society but also exploded the very principle of stratification. Full of surprising twists, scripted and acted with malevolent glee, this is one of the funniest and most subversive social comedies ever made. TR

Attentat, L' (Plot)

(1972, Fr/It/WGer, 124 min)
d Yves Boisset. *p* Jean-Paul Spiri-Mercanton. *sc* Ben Barzman, Basilio Franchina. *ph* Ricardo Aronovich. *ed* Albert Jurgenson. *ad* Marc Desages. *m* Ennio Morricone. *cast* Jean-Louis Trintignant, Michel Piccoli, Gian Maria Volonté, Jean Seberg, François Périer, Philippe Noiret, Michel Bouquet.
●Glossy style conflicts with content (political intrigue expanding on the known facts of the Ben Barka affair) as Boisset indicts the CIA, the media, the law, and the French political system in a tale of an all-out conspiracy to rid France of an exiled socialist who is planning to return to his own country to set up a revolutionary government, and who becomes an embarrassment to the establishment. Strong performances from an excellent cast, Morricone's music, and a script by

Jorge Semprun – who wrote Costa-Gavras' *Z* – make it a polished entertainment rather than a truly political film. GA

At the Circus

(1939, US, 87 min, b/w)
d Edward Buzzell. p Mervyn LeRoy. *sc* Irving Brecher. *ph* Leonard Smith. *ed* William Terhune. *ad* Cedric Gibbons, Stan Rogers. *m* Franz Waxman. *cast* The Marx Brothers, Margaret Dumont, Eve Arden, Nat Pendleton, Kenny Baker, Florence Rice.

● Definitely sub-standard Marxism as the brothers set about saving a circus from bankruptcy. Nice moments (much ado with badges, Groucho singing 'Lydia the Tattooed Lady', and the endless insulting repartee with Dumont), but the whole thing is rather tired and over-familiar.

At the Earth's Core

(1976, GB, 90 min)
d Kevin Connor. *p* John Dark. *sc* Milton Subotsky. *ph* Alan Hume. *ed* John Ireland. *pd* Maurice Carter. *m* Mike Vickers. *cast* Doug McClure, Peter Cushing, Caroline Munro, Cy Grant, Godfrey James, Keith Barron.

● While 1974's *The Land That Time Forgot* discovered prehistory alive at the North Pole, here Messrs Cushing and McClure run astray while testing their mechanical mole and discover the lost world of Pellucidar at the end of the journey to the centre of the earth outlined in Edgar Rice Burroughs' source novel. Scantily clad Ms Munro, vengeful telepathic pterodactyls and cut-price explosions comprise a familiar mix, but it's daft enough to enjoy if you're in a schoolboy mood. The winged dinosaurs seem specially conceived so they can be played by blokes in suits, inspiring the sort of glee now lost forever to these days of tediously flash CGI effects. TJ

At the Height of Summer (A la Verticale de l'été/aka The Vertical Ray of the Sun)

(2000, Fr/Vietnam, 112 min)
d Tran Anh-Hung. *p* Christophe Rossignon. *sc* Tran Anh-Hung. *ph* Mark Lee [Li Pingbin]. *ed* Mario Battistel. *pd* Benoît Barouh. *m* Ton That-Tiet, Velvet Underground, Arab Strap. *cast* Tran-Nu Yen-Khe, Nguyen Nhu-Quynh, Le Khanh, Ngo Quang-Hai, Chu Hung.

● Tran's third feature, the polar opposite of *Cyclo*, has a very Asian concern with 'face' – with the importance of maintaining a facade to command respect, regardless of the realities behind it. In Hanoi, three sisters prepare the family ceremony to mark the anniversary of their mother's death. Two are married, apparently happily; the youngest lives in a near-incestuous relationship with their 'little brother', an aspiring actor. By the time the family reconvenes to mark the father's death, a month later, the film has explored the emotional secrets and scandals they keep from each other and the outside world. At the same time, the sisters have hushed up a discovery that their late mother had a secret lover. The film has the structure and rhythm of a recurring dream: languid, sensual, poised between motion and stasis. Prodigious images by Taiwanese DP Mark Lee burnish a flawless illusion of harmony. TR

Attic, The

see Blackout

Attica

(1973, US, 79 min, b/w & col)
d/p/sc Cinda Firestone. *ph* Roland Barnes, Jay Lamarch, Mary Lampson, Jesse Goodman, Carol Stein, Kevin Keating. *ed* Cinda Firestone.

● A documentary revealing, among other things, that the American prison is run as an industry along capitalist lines: it has to maintain the same number of inmates in order to function properly. The film centres on the conditions and events that led up to the prisoners' rebellion in Attica State Penitentiary in 1971 which ended with the death of 43 people, some of whom, as this film shows, were actually murdered after the 'restoration of order'. A sobering and trenchant film.

Attila '74

(1975, Greece, 103 min)
d/p/sc Michael Cacoyannis. *ph* Sakis Maniatis. *ed* Michael Cacoyannis. *m* Michalis Christodoulides. *narrator* Michael Cacoyannis.

● Cacoyannis' documentary 'testimony' is a passionate massing of evidence and accusation concerning the Turkish invasion of Cyprus in 1974 that finally raises more questions than it answers, particularly about the mechanics and motivations of international power politics. The film's presiding spirit is Archbishop Makarios, shown wandering impishly at one point among the ruins of his palace while a voice on post-coup radio declares him dead, and much of the film is made up of an extended interview with him. An *Eoka B* man quotes Alexander the Great on the Gordian Knot. Puppet President Nicos Sampson, in many ways the affair's most intriguing stooge, speaks volubly but unintelligibly. And there's a vast chorus of dispossessed Greeks, mostly women, voicing personal distress, confusion and hysteria – especially the latter, for Cacoyannis is at all points longer on emotion than political analysis, which does his issue a disservice. VG

Attracta

(1983, Ire, 55 min)
d Kieran Hickey. *sc* William Trevor. *ph* Sean Corcoran. *ed* J Patrick Duffner. *cast* Wendy Hiller, Kate Thompson, Joe McPartland, John Kavanagh, Kate Flynn, Deirdre Donnelly.

● Redemption and the pain of a wasted life are the disturbing themes of this adaptation of William Trevor's short story. An ageing spinster teacher, Attracta, fastidiously played by Wendy Hiller, cracks under the strain when she realises too late her failure to teach generations of Irish pupils that good can come out of the most horrific sectarian violence. Very moving, with a manic performance from McPartland as a warped Protestant.

Auberge Rouge, L' (The Red Inn)

(1951, Fr, 94 min, b/w)
d Claude Autant-Lara. *sc* Jean Aurenche, Pierre Bost. *ph* André Bac. *ed* Madeleine Gug. *ad* Max Douy. *m* René Cloerec. *cast* Fernandel, Julien Carette, Françoise Rosay, Marie-Claire Olivia, Didier d'Yd, Jean-Roger Caussimon, Nane Germon.

● A successfully weird little tale about a 19th century inn located in the Ardèche with a history of disappearing guests, Autant-Lara's studio snow-bound black comedy is chiefly remembered now as one of the better vehicles for moose-faced Fernandel. As a gluttonous monk privy to the special service offered by the innkeeper's wife (Rosay), he is the key to saving the latest visitors from oblivion at the risk of breaking the secrecy of the confessional. The script by Aurenche and Bost has their famed polish and irony, as well as a stream of anti-clerical jibes, and is played to the hilt by an expert cast. DT

Au Coeur du mensonge

see Colour of Lies, The

Audience, The (L'Udienza)

(1972, It, 111 min)
d Marco Ferreri. *p* Franco Cristaldi. *sc* Marco Ferreri, Dante Matelli, Rafael Azcona. *ph* Mario Vulpani. *ed* Giuliana Trippa. *ad* Luciana Lev. *m* Teo Usuelli. *cast* Alain Cuny, Enzo Jannacci, Claudia Cardinale, Vittorio Gassman, Ugo Tognazzi, Michel Piccoli.

● A laboured satire of Vatican bureaucracy, this tells a would-be Kafkaesque story of a supplicant's vain attempts to get to the Pope. Only the devoutest Catholics will be able to stay awake to be outraged. As usual, Ferreri avoids the clichés of 'realism', but his mixture of high gloss, caricature, and studied seriousness is even less adequate here than in *The Last Woman.* TR

Audition

(1999, Jap, 115 min)
d Takashi Miike. *p* Akemi Suyama, Satoshi Fukushima. *sc* Daisuke Tengan. *ph* Hideo Yamamoto. *ed* Yasushi Shimamura. *pd* Tatsuo Ozeki. *m* Koji Endo. *cast* Ryo Ishibashi, Eihi Shiina, Miyuki Matsuda, Renji Ishibashi, Tetsu Kuremura, Jun Kunimura.

● Seven years after losing his wife to cancer, video producer Aoyama (Ryo *Another Lonely Hitman* Ishibashi) finds the new bride of his dreams at a casting call for a non-existent movie. Asami (Shiina) is modest, polite, sexy, a trained dancer – and, apparently, available. As Aoyama nervously begins dating her, the film slips into nightmare. Is his paranoia and guilt causing him to imagine the worst, or is Asami really a woman physically and mentally damaged by men since her childhood and out for revenge? Creatively reworked from a script by the son of director Shohei Imamura, this was a breakthrough film for Miike: his first to win festival prizes and overseas sales. It takes sex war tensions to an hallucinatory extreme and has a Grand Guignol climax that leaves many males crawling to the exits. TR

Audrey Rose

(1977, US, 113 min)
d Robert Wise. *p* Joe Wizan, Frank De Felitta. *sc* Frank De Felitta. *ph* Victor J Kemper. *ed* Carl Kress. *pd* Harry Horner. *m* Michael Small. *cast* Anthony Hopkins, Marsha Mason, John Beck, Susan Swift, Norman Lloyd, John Hillerman.

● About reincarnation, with Hopkins persuading Mason and Beck that their daughter may be his dead child returned to life, but not one in the long line of demonic kiddie pics. Wise's film is overlong, sometimes over-emphatic, and it has a staggeringly misjudged ending. But it's also notable for centering on the emotional plight of the paranormal malarkey. It is ultimately, in fact, a strikingly sober portrait of the incompatibilities of marriage, filmed with an attention to 'style' and design that is positively old-fashioned. TR

August

(1995, GB, 93 min)
d Anthony Hopkins. *p* June Wyndham-Davies, Pippa Cross. *sc* Julian Mitchell. *ph* Robin Vidgeon. *ed* Edward Mansell. *pd* Eileen Diss. *m* Anthony Hopkins. *cast* Anthony Hopkins, Leslie Phillips, Kate Burton, Gawn Grainger, Rhian Morgan, Menna Trussler, Rhoda Lewis.

● Louis Malle took Uncle Vanya to New York's 42nd Street, Michael Blakemore transplanted him to Australia in *Country Life*, and now Hopkins has brought him, via Julian Mitchell's capable adaptation, to late Victorian Wales. This directorial debut, however, leaves much to be desired. As Vanya, Hopkins indulges himself something rotten. Gentleman farmer Ieuan Davies scampers, larks, and generally behaves like a spoilt ham, but at least he's having fun. The other players barely get the measure of a film which veers from sentimental, philosophical interludes, à la Merchant Ivory, to rambunctious (unfunny) farce. Hopkins appears clueless when it comes to the camera. From time to time, he dispatches it on intrepid, ill-advised excursions around the cast with what can only be called missionary zeal. Elsewhere, he toys with depth of field and overlapping sound, but with equally unbecoming results. TCh

Augustine of Hippo (Agostino d'Ippona)

(1972, It, 120 min)
d Roberto Rossellini. *sc* Roberto Rossellini, Marcella Mariani, Luciano Scaffa, Carlo Cremono. *ph* Mario Fioretti. *ed* Jolanda Benvenuti. *ad* Franco Velchi. *m* Mario Nascimbene. *cast* Dary Berkani, Virgilio Gazzolo, Cesare Barbetti, Bruno Cattaneo, Leonardo Fioravanti.

● By concentrating on supremely important questions in a cool, apparently artless way, Rossellini's film (made for TV) forces a very dramatic tension. The life of Saint Augustine during the decadence of the Roman Empire becomes the axis for debates on politics and power, morality and conscience: how can a state survive with Christian morals? From this seemingly impossible (and un-filmable) brief, Rossellini achieves moments of devastating clarity. DMacp

August in the Water (Mizu no Naka no Hachigatsu)

(1995, Jap, 117 min)
d Sogo Ishii. *p* Binbun Furusawa. *sc* Sogo Ishii. *ph* Norimichi Kasamatsu. *ed* Hiroshi Matsuo. *pd* Yuji Hayashida. *m* Hiroyuki Onogawa. *cast* Rena Komine, Shinsuke Aoki, Masaaki Takarai, Naho Toda, Reiko Matsuo.

● After the appearance of a new black hole and the fall to earth of two meteorites, a city in Fukuoka suffers both a major drought and an epidemic of a strange disease which causes human inner organs to petrify. A boy working on the languages of fish starts dating a girl with the makings of a diving champion. But she nearly dies in a mysterious diving accident and emerges from hospital somehow changed, knowing that she has to find one of the meteors. The extraordinary climax brings it all together: the drought, the water, the flesh, the stone. Touches the parts ordinary acid doesn't reach. TR

August 32nd on Earth (Un 32 août sur terre)

(1997, Can, 98 min)
d Denis Villeneuve. *p* Roger Frappier. *sc* Denis Villeneuve, *ph* André Turpin. *ed* Sophie Leblond. *pd* Jean Babin. *m* Pierre Desrochers, Nathalie Boileau. *cast* Pascale Bussières, Alexis Martin, Richard S Hamilton, Serge Thériault, Emmanuel Bilodeau, Paule Baillargeon.
●An intriguing but only partly successful oddity about a woman who decides after a car accident that she wants an old friend (married but clearly harbouring a long term crush on her) to father her child; he agrees on condition that conception occurs in the desert – easier said than done. There are striking images here (especially in the scenes outside Salt Lake City), Martin gives a very likeable performance, and individual scenes display intelligence and wit. But it doesn't hang together very well, jump-cutting between slightly portentous artiness and light comedy, and never really adding up to very much at all. GA

Au Hasard, Balthazar (Balthazar)

(1966, Fr/Swe, 95 min. b/w)
d Robert Bresson. *p* Mag Bodard. *sc* Robert Bresson. *ph* Ghislain Cloquet. *ed* Raymond Lamy. *ad* Pierre Charbonnier. *m* Franz Schubert, Jean Wiener. *cast* Anne Wiazemsky, François Lafarge, Philippe Asselin, Nathalie Joyaut, Walter Green.
●Animal as saint: Bresson's stark, enigmatic parable, a donkey (named after one of the Three Wise Men) is both a witness to and the victim of mankind's cruelty, stupidity – and love. Taking his lack of faith in theatrical acting to its logical limit, Bresson perversely places the mute beast centre-screen as he passes from owner to owner, giving rides, heaving agricultural machinery, and receiving beatings and caresses in a coolly observed landscape of poverty and folly. The effect could not be more different from that of other films (Disney's say, or *Jaws*) that centre around animals; Balthazar's death during a smuggling expedition, amidst a field of sheep, is both lyrical and entirely devoid of maudlin sentiment. Imbued with a dry, ironic sense of humour, the film is perhaps the director's most perfectly realised, and certainly his most moving. GA

Au loin s'en vont les nuages

see Drifting Clouds

Au Nom de la Loi

(1931, Fr, 77 min, b/w)
d/sc Maurice Tourneur. *ph* Georges Benoit, Marc Bujard. *ed* Jacques Tourneur. *ad* Jacques Colombier. *cast* Charles Vanel, Marcelle Chantal, Gabriel Gabrio, Jean Marchant, Régine Dancourt.
●Men in big hats gather round The Chief to hear the word. Whether they're cops or robbers is irrelevant; it's equally unimportant why the same guys are now creeping up a stairway in single file, just before tommy gun bullets stud the wall in a chiaroscuro firefight (plenty of oscuro, not a lot of chiaro). Here is a genre in the process of fine-tuning its own imagery via the tale of a tough young *flic* lured to cocaine-soaked destruction by a soulless femme fatale. Catalogue, in other words under *noir*, antecedents of. But it's not the real thing, not quite yet, because the rhythms are all wrong, especially the cutting. This goes like a train, so Warner-esque you'd hardly be surprised if Cagney and Pat O'Brien appeared in gendarme outfits. BBa

Auntie Mame

(1958, US, 143 min)
d Morton Da Costa. *sc* Betty Comden, Adolph Green. *ph* Harry Stradling. *ed* William Ziegler. *ad* Malcolm Bert. *m* Bronislau Kaper. *cast* Rosalind Russell, Forrest Tucker, Coral Browne, Fred Clark, Roger Smith, Patric Knowles, Peggy Cass.
●Later adapted into a Broadway musical (and one of the all-time dire movies with Lucille Ball), this is the first screen version of Patrick Dennis's novel, set during the inter-war years when the larger-than-life Mame adopts a young orphan and shows the littl'un exactly how to have a high old time of it. Sadly, the movie's loud, lumpen and hellishly over-extended, notwithstanding Russell's force-of-nature star turn. TJ

Aunt Julia and the Scriptwriter

see Tune in Tomorrow

Au Pair Girls

(1972, GB, 86 min)
d Val Guest. *p* Guido Coen. *sc* Val Guest, David Adnopoz. *ph* John Wilcox. *ed* John Colville. *ad* Roy Smith. *m* Roger Webb. *cast* Gabrielle Drake, Astrid Frank, Nancie Wait, Me Me Lai, Richard O'Sullivan, John Le Mesurier.
●Feeble attempt to do what the Germans do. And if German sex films are bad, at least they're better than efforts like this, involving four au pairs on the loose in England.

Au Revoir (Tot Ziens)

(1995, Neth, 114 min)
d Heddy Honigmann. *p* Suzanne van Voorst. *sc* Heddy Honigmann, Helena van der Meulen. *ph* Stef Tijdink. *ed* Sander Vos. *pd* Frans von Gestel. *m* Wouter van Bemmel. *cast* Johanna Ter Steege, Guy Van Sande, Els Dottermans.
●A woman (Ter Steege) catches the eye of a young man (Van Sande) on the skating rink. Later, by chance, they end up cycling alongside each other. The man follows her home, and within ten minutes they're fucking on the carpet. 'Just like the 1,000-metre sprint,' the man gasps afterwards. 'You're Belgian!' she exclaims, breaking into an uncontrollable fit of giggles. Worse, he's married. Honigmann's intense relationship-drama is a mite televisual, but it doesn't pull any punches, and the performances are the real McCoy. TCh

Au Revoir les Enfants

(1987, Fr/WGer, 104 min)
d/p/sc Louis Malle. *ph* Renato Berta. *ed* Emmanuelle Castro. *ad* Willy Holt. *cast* Gaspard Manesse, Raphael Fejtö, Francine Racette, Stanislas Carré de Malberg, Philippe Morier-Genoud.
●Plotwise Malle's autobiographical film, set in a Carmelite convent school in 1944, is simplicity itself: 12-year-old Julien doesn't understand why new boy Jean Bonnet – real name, he later learns is Kippelstein – is bullied by the other pupils and protected by the teachers. Only with the arrival of the Gestapo does he see the full implications of Jean's 'difference'. If the outcome of this sombre, lovingly detailed film is unsurprising, its emotional power remains undeniable, precisely because Malle never sentimentalises his material (neither boy is particularly loveable, nor is their friendship free of petty rivalries and cruelty). Instead, he creates an authentic mood of unspoken suspicions and everyday secrecy, drawing upon performances, decor, even nature itself to paint a wintry portrait of childhood on the brink of horrific discovery. The film's quiet integrity finally depends on his avoidance of heroic cliché and stylistic bombast, and on the unindulgent generosity extended towards his characters. GA

Au revoir, mon amour (He Rijun Zai Lai)

(1991, HK, 126 min)
d Tony Au. *p* Leonard Ho. *sc* Jerry Liu, Gordon Chan. *ph* Bill Wong, David Chung, Peter Bao, Peter Ngo. *ed* Cheung Yiu Chung, Chiang Chuen Tak. *pd* Eddie Ma. *m* Anthony Kun, Terry Chan. *cast* Anita Mui, Tony Leung, Hidekazu Akai.
●Tony Au's over-designed melodrama is a vehicle for *Rouge* star Anita Mui, set (like the much less interesting *Kawashima Yoshiko*) amid the Sino-Japanese conflicts of the 1930s. Here she plays a night-club singer torn between the Chinese guerrilla who once abandoned her and a humane Japanese officer. It's one of those movies in which the script's determination to provide a murder or explosion every few minutes allows no space for character development or emotional depth. The ending in post-war Japan is the only scene in the whole two hours that isn't numbingly obvious. TR

Aurora Encounter, The

(1986, US, 90 min)
d Jim McCullough Sr. *sc* Jim McCullough Jr. *ph* Joseph Wilcots. *ed* Sheri Galloway. *pd* Drew Hunter. *m* Ron F Dilulio. *cast* Jack Elam, Peter Brown, Carol Bagdasarian, Mickey Hays, Dottie West, George 'Spanky' McFarland.
●Ever desperate to find that new miracle formula, the producers of this concoction have come up with *ET* drops in on *The Little House on the Prairie.* In a spaceship that resembles an antiquated vacuum cleaner, a particularly ugsome midget scarifies the denizens of Aurora before discovering a predilection for beer, checkers and cigars. Soon after rescuing some silly children from the local caves, the alien prangs his vessel and dies. Or does he? For small children this variation of a threadbare theme will have a certain charm, but adults are advised to watch it on video with a finger on the fast-forward button. MS

Aus einem deutschen Leben

see Death Is My Trade

Auslandstournee

see Tour Abroad

Austerlitz (aka The Battle of Austerlitz)

(1960, Fr/It/Liechtenstein/Yug, 123 min)
d Abel Gance. *p* Alexander Salkind, Michael Salkind. *sc* Abel Gance. *ph* Henri Alekan. *ed* Yvonne Martin. *ad* Jean Douarinou. *m* Jean Ledrut. *cast* Claudia Cardinale, Martine Carol, Leslie Caron, Vittorio De Sica, Jean Marais, Pierre Mondy, Jean Mercure, Jack Palance, Orson Welles, Georges Marchal, Jean-Marc Bory, Leslie Caron, Rossano Brazzi.
●Silent-cinema genius he may well have been, but by this time in his career Abel Gance was creatively a shadow of his former self. It was a bold idea of the Salkinds to hire him for this chronicle of Bonaparte's famous victory over the Austro-Prussian army, but the result, for all its lavish scale and roster of stars, is a turgid bore. The original cut ran 166 minutes. TJ

Austin Powers: International Man of Mystery

(1997, US, 95 min)
d Jay Roach. *p* Suzanne Todd, Demi Moore, Jennifer Todd, Mike Myers. *sc* Mike Myers. *ph* Peter Deming. *ed* Debra Neil-Fisher. *pd* Cynthia Charette. *m* George S Clinton. *cast* Mike Myers, Elizabeth Hurley, Robert Wagner, Michael York, Mimi Rogers, Set Green, Burt Bacharach, Carrie Fisher, Christian Slater, Rob Lowe.
●The psychedelic era's silliest secret agent is resurrected in a world that's moved on three decades. Myers (star and writer) gets so much of the detail right, it's easy to take his resourcefulness for granted. Everything, from Austin's velvet frock coats and frilly shirts, to the casting (Hurley's slinky sidekick Vanessa Kensington, scheming henchman Wagner, and York's Basil Exposition, the Ministry Man who explains the plot), and cred soundtrack (Burt Bacharach turns up in person), demonstrates how much the creator of *Wayne's World* enjoyed doing his homework. Someone, however, should have weeded out the dud gags and dissuaded Myers from playing the villain as well. Overall, though, it would take a stone face not to crumple at Austin's dodgy catchphrases and irrepressible sexual desperation. 'Shall we shag now, or shag later?' Soon, baby, soon. TJ

Austin Powers: The Spy Who Shagged Me

(1999, US, 95 min)
d Jay Roach. *p* John Lyons, Mike Myers, Suzanne Todd, Jennifer Todd, Demi Moore, Eric McLeod. *sc* Mike Myers, Michael McCullers. *ph* Ueli Steiger. *ed* John Poll, Debra Neil-Fisher. *pd* Rusty Smith. *m* George S Clinton. *cast* Mike Myers, Heather Graham, Robert Wagner, Seth Green, Mindy Sterling, Rob Lowe, Verne Troyer, Elizabeth Hurley, Tim Robbins.
●The first Austin Powers spy spoof was an affectionate ragbag of Swingin' London gags marred chiefly by Myers' decision to play the eponymous secret agent and, less amusingly, his arch enemy Dr Evil. In this wearisome sequel, he compounds those faults by playing a third character – an

obscene and grotesquely obese Scottish security guard 'Fat Bastard' – and by pitching most of the comedy at the same dismal level. Some have excused the film's many flaws by arguing that it actively revels in being a cheesy, derivative, amateurish mess full of infantile gags. Maybe, but it is, still, just that. The 'story' has Powers follow Evil back in time to 1969, when Evil purloined Powers' 'mojo' and robbed him of his libido. Cue help from dolly bird Felicity Shagwell (Graham), further dastardly opposition from Evil's dwarf clone Mini-Me, and much cameoing from Michael York, Jerry Springer, Burt Bacharach, Elvis Costello and Woody Harrelson. GA

Australia

(1989, Fr/Bel/Switz, 118 min)
d Jean-Jacques Andrien. *p* Marie Pascale Osterrieth. *sc* Jean Gruault, Jacques Audiard, Jean-Jacques Andrien. *ph* Yorgos Arvanitis. *ed* Ludo Troch. *pd* Herbert Westbrook. *m* Nicola Piovani. *cast* Jeremy Irons, Fanny Ardant, Tchéky Karyo, Agnès Sorel, Hélène Surgere.

●A period romance that attempts, unsuccessfully, to explore the blocked sensibilities of the Belgian bourgeoisie in a particular time and place (1955, Verviers, once preeminently a wool city), this quickly becomes suffocated by dramatic inertia, irrelevance and wool. Edouard Pierson (Irons, sporting two execrable accents: phony English and awesomely deliberate French) is a Belgian living, in self-imposed exile, in Southern Australia with his 12-year-old daughter, buying and selling wool for export; his Indonesian wife, met when he was a war pilot, is dead, and the daughter is a secret from his family, presumably because they might disapprove. When the wool-processing business run by brother Julien (Karyo) runs into trouble, he returns home alone, and initiates a difficult affair with a well-married country girl (Ardant, always a class act) in London and misty Verviers. Things change, and the past must be put behind. The film often looks great, but Andrien (who lives in Verviers) has clearly let his documentary instincts run riot. Wool pops up all the time, in bales, out of bales, on factory floors, felt, bought, sold and discussed. The result is inoffensive, but woolly. WH

Author! Author!

(1982, US, 109 min)
d Arthur Hiller. *p* Irwin Winkler. *sc* Israel Horovitz. *ph* Victor J Kemper. *ed* William H Reynolds. *pd* Gene Rudolf. *m* David Grusin. *cast* Al Pacino, Dyan Cannon, Tuesday Weld, Bob Dishy, Bob Elliott.

●It improves, so sit out the opening credits and the frightful theme song advising that home is where there's 'always milk and cookies and a friend'. An I-Love-New-York movie that takes its pick from *Kramer vs Kramer*, it stars Pacino as a Broadway writer left by his wife to care for the shared children of several marriages while completing his latest play. Pacino can do you a volatile, middle class intellectual with one hand behind his back, and along with his streetwise brood has all the best and funniest lines. But the women lose out. Weld's role is simply the necessary evil to prove the point that men are people too. And Cannon is, in her hairy, furry, woolly way, radiantly two-dimensional. JS

Autobiography of a Princess

(1975,GB, 59 min)
d James Ivory. *p* Ismail Merchant. *sc* Ruth Prawer Jhabvala. *ph* Walter Lassally. *ed* Humphrey Dixon. *ad* Jacquemine Charrot-Lodwidge. *m* Vic Flick. *cast* James Mason, Madhur Jaffrey, Keith Varnier, Diane Fletcher, Timothy Bateson, Johnny Stuart.

●Imperial India seen through old home movies of court life as they are watched by the besotted, blinkered daughter-in-exile of a Maharajah and the latter's former English tutor, who still meet once a year in London for tea. The film explores the gradually revealed tensions and similarities between the two as they both gravitate towards the memory of her father, the magnetic and domineering Maharajah. Her unswerving loyalty to the past empire is answered by his mounting indignation at its monstrosities and his own weaknesses. Yet nothing really happens because the two draw a veil over their true emotions, and over the true nature of the dark scandals merely hinted at (apart from one clumsy flashback). A refined, ironic exercise whose brittleness is effectively countered by Mason's playing. CPe

Autobiography of Miss Jane Pittman, The

(1973, US, 110 min)
d John Korty. *p* Robert W Christiansen, Rick Rosenberg. *sc* Tracy Keenan Wynn. *ph* James Crabe. *ed* Sid Levin. *pd* Michael Haller. *m* Fred Karlin. *cast* Cicely Tyson, Michael Murphy, Richard A Dysart, Katherine Helmond.

●Originally made for TV, this fictional recounting of the 110 years lived by one one black woman in Louisiana has a deceptively natural ring to it: what better way to reflect the range of American black experience? What greater challenge than limiting that experience to the life of one woman (ranging from Civil War to Civil Rights Movement), which has to serve as history, myth, personal story, commentary and newsreel all at once? Aiming for the stars, the film hits a magazine spread by Norman Rockwell, and obstinately stays there: a respectable enough achievement in its way, but one that ultimately dims the mind as it stirs up the emotions. JR

Autobus

see Aux Yeux du monde

Autour de la maison rose

see Around the Pink House

Autour de Minuit

see 'Round Midnight

Autre, L' (The Other)

(1999, Egypt/Fr, 106 min)
d Youssef Chahine. *sc* Youssef Chahine, Khaled Youssef. *ph* Mohsen Nasr. *ed* Rachida Abdel Salam. *pd* Hamed Hemdane. *m* Yéhia El Mouguy. *cast* Nabila Ebeid, Mahmoud Héméida, Hani Salama, Hanane Tork, Lébléba, Hassan Abdel Hamid, Ezzat Abou Aouf.

●Minor Chanine, perhaps, but still an intelligent, idiosyncratic and enjoyable movie. It's a Romeo and Juliet-style fable about the ill-starred love between the son of a a rich couple happy to deal both with dubious Western business interests and fanatical extremists, and a journalist from a poor family keen to uncover corruption in high places. As it proceeds towards its unexpectedly bleak outcome, Chahine pulls out the stops with his unique blend of melodrama, dance musical, political comment (it begins with two characters going off to an appointment with Edward Said, who cameos with a few brief words on political, national and cultural identity) and forthright sensuality. A pot-pourri held together by the director's bravura style and abiding commitment to the ideal of tolerance, and by Ebeid's extraordinary performance as the hero's scheming, insanely jealous mother, at times eerily reminiscent of Callas in Pasolini's *Medea*. GA

Autre Homme une Autre Chance, Un (Another Man, Another Chance)

(1977, Fr, 128 min)
d Claude Lelouch. *p* Alexandre Mnouchkine, Georges Dancigers. *sc* Claude Lelouch. *ph* Jacques Lefrançois, Stanley Cortez. *ed* Georges Klotz, Fabien Tordjman. *ad* Eric Moulard, Robert Clatworthy. *m* Francis Lai. *cast* James Caan, Genevieve Bujold, Francis Huster, Jennifer Warren, Susan Tyrrell.

●Lelouch's soap opera Western proves yet again that a man (Caan as a horse doctor) and a woman (Bujold as a French immigrant) will eventually find love and happiness, no matter what contrivances, colour filters or saccharine music the master puts in their way. What other Western accompanies shots of the hero on horseback with the opening chords of Beethoven's Fifth? Who but Lelouch would compound a bilingual script of disarming coyness, peppered with current phrases ('Have a nice day') and historical pinpointers ('It's too bad there's still no way to print pictures in a newspaper'). Not much dramatic interest, but the curiosity value is colossal. GB

Autumn Afternoon, An (Samma no aji)

(1962, Jap, 113 min)
d Yasujiro Ozu. *p* Shizuo Yamanouchi. *sc* Kogo Noda, Yasujiro Ozu. *ph* Yuhara Atsuta. *ed* Yoshiyasu Hamamura. *ad* Tatsuo Hamada. *m* Takanobu Saito. *cast* Chishu Ryu, Shima Iwashita, Shinichiro Mikami, Keiji Sada, Mariko Okada, Teruo Yoshida.

●A widower (Ryu) arranges for his loyal daughter (Iwashita) to be wed, and tries to drown his sorrows in sake and drunken comradeship. Given the homogeneity of Ozu's work, perhaps it is meretricious to dwell on the fact that this was his final film. Still, its sweet, mellow air is all the more moving seen in that light, and it is clearly the testament of an old man. It's also worth noting that the film-maker's mother died in the course of the shooting: Ozu had lived with her all his life. Only this film and *Good Morning* were made in colour, but Ozu applies it here with great care and precision, another mark of his sublime philosophical and cinematic continuity (incidentally, note how red and silver motifs recur throughout the picture). TCh

Autumn Crocus

(1934, GB, 86 min, b/w)
d/p/sc Basil Dean. *ph* Robert G Martin. *ed* Walter Stern. *ad* Edward Carrick. *m* Ernest Irving. *cast* Fay Compton, Ivor Novello, Esme Church, Jack Hawkins, George Zucco, Muriel Aked, Diana Beaumont.

●Despite the skimpy story and makeshift construction – the Alpine location stuff was shot by Carol Reed without the cast – this adaptation of Dodie Smith's first play emerges as a rich evocation of the hopes and dreams of the '30s. Meandering between farce, fairytale and doomed romance, the film gently explores the Cinderella story of an ageing schoolmistress who discovers her Prince is a happily married man. Compton, emanating an intensely wistful beauty, progresses convincingly from virginal exuberance to a sad knowlege that fantasy is best left as fantasy. The presence of slyly camp Novello, looking like an overgrown boy scout in his Tyrolean *lederhosen,* and an array of grubbily eccentric character actors (Hawkins unrecognisable as a sex-obsessed psychiatrist) obviates the danger of maudlin sentimentality. RMy

Autumn in New York

(2000, US, 106 min)
d Joan Chen. *p* Amy Robinson, Gary Lucchesi, Tom Rosenberg. *sc* Allison Burnett. *ph* Changwei Gu. *ed* Ruby Yang. *pd* Mark Friedberg. *m* Gabriel Yared. *cast* Richard Gere, Winona Ryder, Anthony LaPaglia, Elaine Stritch, Vera Farmiga, Sherry Stringfield, Jill Hennessy, JK Simmons, Sam Trammell, Mary Beth Hurt.

●Will Keane (Gere) is a forty-something restaurateur with an insatiable sexual appetite. One day, he spots doe-eyed hat designer Charlotte (Ryder) in his eatery, celebrating her birthday with friends. Within seconds, woof! – the old fox is after her, never mind the age difference or that in his youth he once dated her late mother. Frantic to get his leg over, he orders one of her hats, apparently fashioned from coathangers and toilet paper. When she delivers it to his loft, guess what? He'd bought it for her. To wear to a 'charity gala'! The ruse works. But as Will makes his customary morning after kiss-off speech, Charlotte drops a bombshell: she has a rare heart condition, and may have only months to live. This entirely unaffecting May–December romance is *Love Story* transposed to a Manhattan-of-the-mind. JO'C

Autumn Leaves

(1956, US, 108 min, b/w)
d Robert Aldrich. *p* William Goetz. *sc* Jean Rouverol (actual scriptwriter); Jack Jevne, Lewis Meltzer, Robert Blees (credited scriptwriters). *ph* Charles Lang Jr. *ed* Michael Luciano. *ad* William Glasgow. *m* Hans J Salter. *cast* Joan Crawford, Cliff Robertson, Vera Miles, Lorne Greene, Ruth Donnelly, Shepperd Strudwick.

●A seemingly eccentric, but in fact characteristic, Aldrich film: cutting a radical cinematic swathe through weepie material. It rattles both psychological skeletons and the skeleton of psychology as Crawford's middle-aged spinster and Robertson's seductive young liar rush first into marriage and then at each other's throats. An 'extraordinary combination of domestic Guignol and elephantised soap opera', as Richard Combs has described it. PT

Autumn Moon (Qiuyue)

(1992, HK/Jap, 108 min)
d Clara Law. *p* Clara Law, Eddie Fong, Yoko Miyake. *sc* Eddie Fong. *ph* Tony Leung Siu-Hung. *ed* Timmy Yip. *m* Lau Yee-tat. *cast* Masatoshi Nagase, Li Pui Wai, Choi Siu Wan, Maki Kiuchi.
●Clara Law's limpid, understated movie justifies its own poetic title by minimising plot and avoiding melodramatics; it's the flip-side of the slam-bang heroics that dominate Hong Kong cinema. An aimless Japanese private eye (Nagase, the Elvis fan from *Mystery Train)* catches the current autumnal mood of Hong Kong when he runs into a schoolgirl in the grip of her first crush and her dying grandmother; he has a brief sexual fling with an old flame from Japan, but nothing much else happens. The movie sees Hong Kong as a technopolis on a par with Tokyo, but regrets the waning of Chinese social and cultural traditions, and ponders the city's future in the run-up to 1997. The Brits, chasteningly, have no part to play in the film's equation. TR

Autumn Sonata (Herbstsonate)

(1978, WGer, 92 min)
d/sc Ingmar Bergman. *ph* Sven Nykvist. *ed* Sylvia Ingmarsdotter. *cast* Ingrid Bergman, Liv Ullmann, Lena Nyman, Halver Björk, Gunnar Björnstrand.
●Now about these women... Mother (concert pianist Bergman) and daughter (parson's wife Ullmann) come face to face after seven years to touch, cry and whisper – and to confront and confess – in an atmosphere pregnant with death and disease, shame and silence. Routine obsessions, routine hysteria; maybe even a routine masterpiece. Of course Bergman's actresses suffer superbly in microscopic close-up, but the nagging doubt persists as to whether this is incisive psychodrama or just those old nordic blues again. PT

Autumn Tale, An

see Conte d'automne

Aux Yeux du Monde (Autobus)

(1991, Fr, 95 min)
d Eric Rochant. *p* Alain Rocca. *sc* Eric Rochant. *ph* Pierre Novion. *ed* Catherine Quesemand. *ad* Pascale Fenouillet. *m* Gérard Torikian. *cast* Yvan Attal, Charlotte Gainsbourg, Kristin Scott-Thomas, Marc Berman, Francine Olivier, Michele Foucher.
●Desperate to impress his long-distance girlfriend (Gainsbourg), Bruno (Attal) hijacks a school bus and, at gunpoint, forces the driver, kids and teacher (Scott-Thomas) to accompany him on his long, wayward odyssey to the girl's home. Panic ensues, but the infants strike up a relationship of sorts with their often befuddled captor, while the teacher remains firm but understanding. The cops, how ever, are less forgiving... Like Hippo in Rochant's earlier *World Without Pity*, Bruno is less an angry young man than sorely in need of attention. Rochant and Attal (astonishingly good in his first lead role) certainly make him sympathetic, but never gloss over his ludicrous braggadocio or his fundamental wrong-headedness about his beloved's feelings. What makes the film so engrossing is its complexity, with a simple road thriller plot enormously enhanced by subtle performances, a telling use of landscape and psychological details, and an assured control of mood, which shifts effortlessly between manic comedy, taut suspense and more contemplative moments. GA

Avalanche

(1978, US, 91 min)
d Corey Allen. *p* Roger Corman. *sc* Claude Pola, Corey Allen. *ph* Pierre-William Glenn. *ed* Stuart Schoolnik. *pd* Sharon Compton. *m* William Kraft. *cast* Rock Hudson, Mia Farrow, Robert Forster, Jeanette Nolan, Rick Moses, Barry Primus.
●In which Hudson, as icy and mountainous as the landscape, leads a cast of generally unpleasant leisure-seekers to the belated realisation that the wages of sin is getting dumped-on by white polystyrene. The inhabitants of the wonderful world of winter sports, predictably too engrossed in sexual and commercial intrigue to heed weather warnings, undergo a semi-slapstick series of snowy effects before performing pathetic rescue dramas. Pretty lacklustre for a Roger Corman production, but as (unconscious?) disaster movie parody it's entertaining enough. GA

Avalanche Express

(1979, Eire, 88 min)
d/p Mark Robson. *sc* Abraham Polonsky. *ph* Jack Cardiff. *ed* Garth Craven. *pd* Fred Tuch *m* Allyn Ferguson. *cast* Lee Marvin, Robert Shaw, Linda Evans, Maximilian Schell, Mike Connors, Horst Buchholz, Joe Namath.
●Formulary East-West spy saga involving a KGB defector, a biological warfare programme, and running battles on the transcontinental express. Hammily acted and obviously subject to cobbling after both Robson and Shaw died before the film was completed, it's awful but given a certain fascination by the disjunctive editing style which reduces Abraham Polonsky's script to an abstraction, and which it is tempting to ascribe to Monte Hellman (called upon for 'post-production services' after Robson's death). TM

Avalon

(1990, US, 128 min)
d Barry Levinson. *p* Mark Johnson, Barry Levinson. *sc* Barry Levinson. *ph* Allen Daviau. *ed* Stu Linder. *pd* Norman Reynolds. *m* Randy Newman. *cast* Armin Müller-Stahl, Elizabeth Perkins, Joan Plowright, Kevin Pollak, Aidan Quinn, Leo Fuchs, Eve Gordon, Elijah Wood, Ronald Guttman, Israel Rubinek.
●Levinson returns to Baltimore, home of *Diner* and *Tin Men*, for this semi-autobiographical voyage into family history. Sam Krichinsky (Müller-Stahl), arriving in America from the Old Country on July 4, 1914, wanders awestruck against a night sky alive with firecrackers. He is joined by his brothers, who acquire jobs, produce children, and reside in a row-house neighbourhood. The sprawling story eventually traces four generations; changing circumstances and wider social influences are reflected in the way family circle meetings give way to internal divisions and personal ambitions. It's a shamelessly sentimental interpretation of history, with television ushering in a generation which has lost the art of communication and the ability to care. Against this blinkered vision, even Levinson's confident direction and ability to capture the absurdities and rhythms of everyday speech fail to provide sufficient compensation. CM

Avalon

(2000, Jap, 106 min, col & b/w)
d Mamoru Oshii. *p* Atsushi Kubo. *sc* Kazunori Ito. *ph* Grzegorz Kedzierski. *ad* Barbara Nowak, (digital) Hiroyuki Hayashi. *m* Kenji Kawai. *cast* Malgorzata Foremniak, Wladyslaw Kowalski, Jerzy Gudejko, Dariusz Biskupski, Bartek Swiderski, Katarzyna Bargielowska, Alicja Sapryk, Michael Breitenwald, Zuzanna Kask.
●Animation giant Oshii has made a couple of live-action films before, with undistiguished results, but this is some kind of masterpiece. Shot in Poland (in Polish!), it envisages a society in which a virtual-reality war game called Avalon is an illegal, underworld cult. Woman player Ash feels ready to leave team-play behind and go solo in Class A; the one blemish in her record is a game she is rumoured to have aborted by calling 'Reset' – a game which prompted team leader Murphy to go solo and end up apparently brain dead in hospital. Oshii presents her quest to triumph in Class A (and the two astonishing levels that lie beyond it) as a dissection of will and identity considerably more challenging than anything Cronenberg managed in *eXistenZ.* Using tinted monochrome images (only close-ups of food and the deceptive environment of Class Real are in full colour), elements of Arthurian myth, memories of Eastern Bloc war movies and CG effects of staggering sophistication, this plays like *The Matrix* re-imagined by Jan Svankmajer. TR

Avanti!

(1972, US, 144 min)
d/p Billy Wilder. *sc* Billy Wilder, IAL Diamond. *ph* Luigi Kuveiller. *ed* Ralph E Winters. *ad* Ferdinando Scarfiotti. *m* Carlo Rustichelli. *cast* Jack Lemmon, Juliet Mills, Clive Revill, Edward Andrews, Gianfranco Barra, Franco Angrisano, Gisel.
●A sunny black comedy about a stuffy American who meets an overweight Englishwoman on the tourist paradise of Ischia. Each has come to claim the body of a deceased parent – his father, her mother – only to discover that the dead pair were lovers and to find history inexorably repeating itself. The humour (derived largely from unstereotypical national stereotypes, plus the inexhaustible confusion over luggage, hotel accommodations and bureaucratic red tape) is sometimes a little leisurely, while the camera has a tendency to linger over the travelogue scenery. But any longueurs are more than made up for by the same strangely moving undercurrent of tenderness that Wilder brought to *The Private Life of Sherlock Holmes*. Marvellous performances from Lemmon and Mills. TM

Avenger, The

see Texas, Addio

Avengers, The

(1998, US, 89 min)
d Jeremiah Chechik. *p* Jerry Weintraub. *sc* Don Macpherson. *ph* Roger Pratt. *ed* Mick Audsley. *pd* Stuart Craig. *m* Joel McNeely. *cast* Ralph Fiennes, Uma Thurman, Sean Connery, Jim Broadbent, Fiona Shaw, Eddie Izzard.
●Lousy as it is, Warner Bros' big budget version of the cult '60s TV series isn't any worse than, say, the last two *Batman* flicks. Charm is a difficult quality to duplicate, and while Fiennes makes a passable stab at debonair, Uma Thurman's notion of insouciance translates as smug and spacey; she's far more convincing as Mrs Peel's deadly mute double, a robot, presumably (like so much of the plot, that remains a matter of conjecture). In some ways, the movie's inadequacies are inextricable from its virtues: heavy cuts have made a mockery of any sense of continuity, but then *The Avengers* always peddled surreal and absurdist conceits, so artificiality is the name of the game (there are a few neat ideas here: a conference in teddy bear suits, a stairway out of Escher, and an invisible cameo by Patrick Macnee). Its ersatz Englishness makes a certain sense. The trouble is, the film's decadence isn't a put-on, it is, simply, depressingly, degeneratively, decadent. TCh

Avenir d'Emilie, L'

see Future of Emily, The

Aventure Malgache

(1944, GB, 31 min, b/w)
d Alfred Hitchcock. *ph* Günther Krampf. *ad* Charles Gilbert. *cast* The Molière Players.
●The lesser of two French-language propaganda shorts made by Hitchcock in 1944 for the British Ministry of Information (see *Bon Voyage*), *Aventure Malgache* is a laboured attempt to dramatise the internal conflicts between the Gaullists, Pétanists and Vichyites in the French colonies. Welwyn Garden City stands in for Madagascar. In the event, these tensions proved so sensitive that the film was never exhibited. The plot concerns the rivalry between a corrupt Vichyite police chief and a lawyer who masterminds the local Resistance. Imaginative touches and a characteristically droll denouement. TCh

Aventures de Rabbi Jacob, Les

see Mad Adventures of 'Rabbi' Jacob, The

Aveu, L' (The Confession)

(1969, Fr/It, 160 min)
d Costa-Gavras. *p* Robert Dorfmann, Bertrand Javal. *sc* Jorge Semprun. *ph* Raoul Coutard. *ed* Françoise Bonnot. *ad* Bernard Evein. *cast* Yves Montand, Simone Signoret, Gabriele Ferzetti, Michel Vitold, Jean Bouise, Laszlo Szabo.
●The problem with Costa-Gavras movies is that they seem to feed off rather than inform the left-liberal sentiments they espouse. Thus in *L'Aveu*, an actual case history, we get no context beyond 'here is an example of the evils of Stalinism'. Instead we are offered the simple perspective of the suffering of Arthur London (Montand), a Czech party official (and his wife, Signoret), who is faced in 1951 with the problem of whether to confess to things he didn't do for the sake of the party. The result is a film which blurs as many issues as it raises. Cut by over 20 minutes for distribution in both Britain and America. PH

Aviator's Wife, The (La Femme de l'Aviateur)

(1980, Fr, 106 min)
d Eric Rohmer. *p* Margaret Ménégoz, *sc* Eric Rohmer. *ph* Bernard Lutic. *ed* Cécile Decugis. *m* Jean-Louis Valero. *cast* Philippe Marlaud, Marie Rivière, Anne-Laure Meury, Mathieu Carrière, Fabrice Luchini.

●The first in Rohmer's series *Comédies et Proverbes*, this gentle comedy laced with pain is a delight from start to finish. Erroneously assuming that his more experienced girlfriend is being unfaithful, a young student decides to investigate the identity of the man he sees leaving her room early one morning. Following the man through Paris, he meets up with a pert schoolgirl, obviously attracted but bemused by his actions, who offers to help in his ludicrous detection. The whole thing would remain at the level of whimsical farce, were it not for Rohmer's emphasis on the very real pain, confusion and wasted attempts at happiness underlying the complicated intrigues of the characters. As always, Rohmer makes clear the enormous gulf between feelings and words, intention and effect. The result is a hilarious, wonderfully bitter-sweet acknowlegment of the chasms between people trying desperately to understand and be understood. GA

A Vida em Cana

see In Cane for Life

Avventura, L' 100 (The Adventure)

(1960, It/Fr, 145 min, b/w)
d Michelangelo Antonioni. *p* Amato Pennasilico. *sc* Michelangelo Antonioni, Elio Bartolini, Tonino Guerra. *ph* Aldo Scavarda. *ed* Eraldo Da Roma. *ad* Piero Poletto. *m* Giovanni Fusco. *cast* Monica Vitti, Gabriele Ferzetti, Lea Massari, Dominique Blanchar, Renzo Ricci, James Addams.

●Though once compared to *Psycho*, made the same year and also about a couple searching for a woman who mysteriously disappears after featuring heavily in the opening reel, Antonioni's film could not be more dissimilar in tone and effect. Slow, taciturn and coldly elegant in its visual evocation of alienated, isolated figures in a barren Sicilian landscape, the film concerns itself less with how and why the girl vanished from a group of bored and wealthy socialites on holiday, than with the desultory nature of the romance embarked upon by her lover and her best friend while they half-heartedly look for her. If it once seemed the ultimate in arty, intellectually chic movie-making, the film now looks all too studied and remote a portrait of emotional sterility. GA

Awakening, The

(1980, GB, 105 min)
d Mike Newell. *p* Robert H Solo. *sc* Allan Scott, Chris Bryant, Clive Exton. *ph* Jack Cardiff. *ed* Terry Rawlings. *pd* Michael Stringer. *m* Claude Bolling. *cast* Charlton Heston, Susannah York, Jill Townsend, Stephanie Zimbalist, Patrick Drury.

●The opening section of this glossy, boringly shot mummy drama, loosely based on Bram Stoker's novel *The Jewel of Seven Stars*, is packed with cheapo Freudian parallels between an archaeologist's obsession with the tomb of an Egyptian princess, and his jealous wife's pregnancy (much intercutting between the ancient doors being thrust open and the graphic hospital birth). Though crude, this tack might have proved interesting, but the rest is part ineffective horror, part coyly underplayed element of incest as the archaeologist's daughter (aged 18) becomes the reincarnated princess and evil forces are unleashed on the world. JWi

Awakenings

(1990, US, 121 min)
d Penny Marshall. *p* Walter F Parkes, Lawrence Lasker. *sc* Steven Zaillian. *ph* Miroslav Ondricek. *ed* Jerry Greenberg, Battle Davis. *pd* Anton Furst. *m* Randy Newman. *cast* Robert De Niro, Robin Williams, Julie Kavner, Ruth Nelson, John Heard, Penelope Ann Miller, Alice Drummond, Judith Malina, Dexter Gordon.

●With Robin Williams as neurologist Oliver Sacks – here Dr Sayer – and De Niro as Leonard Lowe, the most afflicted Parkinson's case on the ward, we are deep in *Rain Man* territory (a terrain notable for its squashiness) in another homage to catatonia. The patients, frozen in what Pinter called 'A Kind of Alaska' in his play about the case, have been sealed off for decades. The good doctor treats them with L-Dopa, despite official hostility (Heard), with miraculous results. We don't get the euphoric explosions of libido detailed in Ry Cooder's 'What Makes Granny Run', nor do we get the depressions you might expect from all those wasted years. We do get Dr Sayer and Leonard relating, and – briefly – Leonard's diffident romance with a visitor (Miller) before he reverts. Dexter Gordon, one of the patients, was actually dying and looks it, which is something of a visual bring-down for the phony charades. Penny Marshall presses all the easy buttons, Williams bumbles loveably, and De Niro shakes his chassis to bits. Dramatically, it's a twin-tub, with a big slot on top to pour in the caring. BC

Away All Boats

(1956, US, 113 min)
d Joseph Pevney. *p* Howard Christie. *sc* Ted Sherdeman. *ph* William H Daniels. *ed* Ted J Kent. *ad* Alexander Golitzen, Richard H Riedel. *m* Frank Skinner. *cast* Jeff Chandler, George Nader, Julie Adams, Lex Barker, Keith Andes, Richard Boone, David Janssen, Frank Faylen, Clint Eastwood.

●Standard-issue WWII action picture (from a novel by Kenneth M Dodson) follows a US Navy transport boat as Capt Chandler and his inexperienced crew see a good deal of wide-screen combat in the Pacific. Competently staged, though the (post-war) flagwaving is as trite as the characterisation. A young Clint Eastwood appears some way down the cast list. TJ

Away from Home (Herkes Kendi Evinde)

(2001, Tur, 110 min)
d Semih Kaplanoglu. *p* Ali T Bilgen, Levent Onan, Leyla Özalp. *sc* Özden Cankaya, Semih Kaplanoglu, Serpil Kirel. *ph* Hayk Kirakosyan. *ed* Hakan Akol, Onur Tan. *pd* Çagla Ormanlar. *m* Selim Atakan. *cast* Tolga Çevik, Erol Keskin, Anna Bielska, Yalçin Akçay, Sükran Güngor, Devrim Parscan, Cüneyt Türel.

●Snapshot of three transient souls – narrator Selim, a young professional with his eye on a transfer to Manhattan; his somewhat more sympathetic uncle Nasuhi, who arrives out of the blue from half a lifetime's exile in Russia, seeking what remain of his roots; and Olga, a Russian girl after her wandering father. Both the men are self-absorbed, but Nasuhi's the one with a character and a past, and it's shame the film doesn't spend more time with him. The plot, such as it is,turns on the trio travelling from Istanbul to the old Aegean farmhouse Selim wants to sell, although there's much to admire about the film's contemplative space and pace. NB

Awfully Big Adventure, An

(1994, GB, 112 min)
d Mike Newell. *p* Hilary Heath, Philip Hinchcliffe. *sc* Charles Wood. *ph* Dick Pope. *ed* Jon Gregory. *pd* Mark Geraghty. *m* Richard Hartley. *cast* Alan Rickman, Hugh Grant, Georgina Cates, Alun Armstrong, Peter Firth, Prunella Scales, Rita Tushingham, Edward Petherbridge, Nicola Pagett, Carol Drinkwater.

●Newell's follow-up to *Four Weddings and a Funeral* offers many subtle if somewhat sombre pleasures. Charles Wood's adaptation of Beryl Bainbridge's novel about backstage theatrical life in postwar Liverpool evokes the period's dusty oppressiveness and moral hypocrisies. Cates gives a luminous performance as the starstruck trainee stagehand Stella; and Grant is cast effectively against type as Meredith Potter, the company's cruel, manipulative director who vies for Stella's innocent soul with Rickman's suave, haunted leading man PL O'Hara. When O'Hara is called back to reprise his acclaimed Captain Hook, a complex web of past and present entanglements begins to unravel. Newell's handling of the exterior scenes has a slightly cursory air, but his sharp dramatic focus draws the best from an exceptional ensemble cast. With its flawed characters and disturbingly dark centre, this fragile gem of a movie sparkles with intelligence and glows with feeling. NF

Awful Truth, The

(1937, US, 91 min, b/w)
d/p Leo McCarey. *sc* Viña Delmar. *ph* Joseph Walker. *ed* Al Clark. *ad* Stephen Goosson, Lionel Banks. *m* Ben Oakland. *cast* Cary Grant, Irene Dunne, Ralph Bellamy, Alexander D'Arcy, Cecil Cunningham.

●Zappy, sophisticated screwball comedy with Grant and Dunne displaying perfect timing as the husband and wife who get divorced and then, after enjoying quick flings with a cabaret artiste and an oil tycoon respectively, decide to get together again. A routine story perhaps, but McCarey transforms it , through his customary affection for his characters and taut pacing, into delightfully effective entertainment. The erotically teasing ending, with a black cat obstinately barring the communicating bedroom door which the *almost* un-estranged couple are praying will open, has a delicacy of touch that Lubitsch rarely managed. GA

A.W.O.L.

(1990, US, 108 min)
d Sheldon Lettich. *p* Ash R Shah, Eric Karson. *sc* Sheldon Lettich, Jean-Claude Van Damme. *ph* Robert C New. *ed* Mark Conte. *pd* Gregory Pickrell. *m* John Scott. *cast* Jean-Claude Van Damme, Harrison Page, Deborah Rennard, Lisa Pelikan, Ashley Johnson, George McDaniel, Eric Karson.

●This fight movie, despite its faults, is a considerable improvement on the cynical *Kickboxer*, *Cyborg*, etc. With Van Damme deserting from the Foreign Legion when his brother is fatally injured in an LA drug feud, the exposition suggests a revenge story, but in fact events follow an altogether livelier course: the AWOL legionnaire resolves to help his destitute sister-in-law and niece by making fast money the best way he can, as a bare-knuckle fighter. Making something of the character's immigrant status, the film-makers establish a commendably downtown perspective; the *really* seedy characters are the wealthy gamblers who get off on the bloody gladiatorial matches. This is a B-movie, crude in execution, with gimmicky set pieces, risibly caricatured villains, and overblown sentimentality. But Van Damme is beginning to come good on his promise; in particular, his friendship with the wonderful Harrison Page, as his hustling guide and mentor, bears the fruit of a more human action-movie, one that's almost worth getting excited about. TCh

Ay! Carmela

(1990, Sp/It, 103 min)
d Carlos Saura. *p* Andrés Vincente Gomez. *sc* Carlos Saura, Rafael Azcona. *ph* José Luis Alcaine. *ed* Pablo G del Amo. *ad* Rafael Palmero. *m* Alejandro Masso. *cast* Carmen Maura, Andres Pajares, Gabino Diego, Maurizio De Razza, Miguel A Rellan, Edward Zentara.

●Saura's work has so often made tacit reference to the Spanish Civil War that one might reasonably expect this, his most direct look at the conflict to date, to be one of his more heartfelt efforts. It concerns a raggedy but enthusiastic cabaret trio – lusty Carmela (Maura), husband Paulino (Pajares), and their hapless, mute dogsbody (Diego) – who, in 1938, decide to take a break from entertaining Republicans on the Aragon front and retreat to a less beleaguered Valencia. But (surprise, surprise), lost after a foggy overnight drive, they find themselves behind enemy lines, where their only hope of escaping imprisonment or execution is to fake fidelity to Franco, and stage a show for his troops with lyrics and gags doctored accordingly. As political cinema, this exceedingly broad 'tragi-comedy' falls flat on its face, never moving beyond simplistic polarities and a concept of history as sentimental as it is falsely heroic. As drama, too, it fails to transcend maudlin stereotypes (both national and sexual), while its origins as a stage play are all too obvious, and the performances given to grotesque overstatement. GA

Brazil

Babar: The Movie

(1989, Can/Fr, 76 min)
d Alan Bunce. *p* Patrick Loubert, Michael Hirsh, Clive Smith. *sc* Peter Sauder, JD Smith, John De Klein, Raymond Jaffelice, Alan Bunce. *ed* Evan Landia. *pd* Ted Bastien. *cast* voices: Gordon Pinsent, Elizabeth Hanna, Sarah Polley, Gavin Magrath, Chris Wiggins, Stephen Ouimette.
●Initial delight that Laurent de Brunhoff's elegant, courtly and very European cartoons have been rescued from the elephants' graveyard soon turns to horror: this Americanises both characters and setting beyond recognition. The premise is a staple of successful kids' movies from *Bambi* to *ET*: separation from Mommy. Babar, boy king of the elephants, must help Celeste rescue mother from the evil rhinoceros Rataxas, picking up help on the way: Zephir the monkey and a vegetarian crocodile. Somehow the precocious pachyderm overcomes all odds, indulges in some Indiana Jones-style swashbuckling, and single-handedly defeats the rhino army before his decadent and bureaucratic generals can muster so much as one soldier. Hooray! The odd good wisecrack and a cracking pace help gloss over flat and unimaginative animation, and teeny tots will adore it. DW

Baba Yaga – The Devil Witch (Baba Yaga)

(1973, It/Fr, 81 min)
d Corrado Farina. *p* Pino De Martino. *sc* Corrado Farina. *ph* Aiace Parolin. *ed* Giulio Berruti. *ad* Giulia Mafai. *m* Piero Umiliani. *cast* Carroll Baker, George Eastman, Isabelle de Funès, Ely Galleani.
●Mixture of sex and horror based on the comic strips of Guido Crepax, whose main character Valentina (played by Louis de Funès' niece Isabelle), famous fashion photographer and clothes-fetishist, gets involved in those weird adventures which all hot-blooded males are supposed to dream about. Here she meets up with lesbian witch Baba Yaga (Baker), who lures her into a murky old house with snakes, rusty sewing machines, and a bottomless pit concealed under the carpet. Followers of Crepax will find only a few moments which recall the master's style. The rest (though Farina claimed that scenes of political relevance were removed by the producers) can be safely left to connoisseurs of handsomely photographed, high class trash. GB

Babe

(1995, Aust, 94 min)
d Chris Noonan. *p* George Miller, Doug Mitchell, Bill Miller. *sc* George Miller, Chris Noonan. *ph* Andrew Lesnie. *ed* Marcus D'Arcy. *pd* Roger Ford. *m* Nigel Westlake. *cast* James Cromwell, Magda Szubanski, Zoe Burton, Paul Goddard; voices: Christine Cavanaugh, Miriam Margoyles, Danny Mann, Hugo Weaving, Miriam Flynn.
●Degree of difficulty apart – and difficulty involved making an entire farmyard of real animals talk – the merits of *Babe* are those of Dick King-Smith's classic, *The Sheep-Pig*. Piglet Babe beats the slaughterhouse and is adopted by a sheepdog who coaches him in the art of rounding up sheep. Taciturn farmer Hoggett (Cromwell) wonderingly goes along with this apprenticeship, and is gratified when Babe wins the rosette at the trials. Babe's secret is politeness which gets better results than barking, and raises lots of laughs. Charming, eccentric and very amusing. BC

Babe, The

(1992, US, 113 min)
d Arthur Hiller. *p/sc* John Fusco. *ph* Haskell Wexler. *ed* Robert C Jones. *pd* James D Vance. *m* Elmer Bernstein. *cast* John Goodman, Kelly McGillis, Trini Alvarado, Bruce Boxleitner, Peter Donat, James Cromwell, Joseph Ragno.
●A biopic of Babe Ruth, the sultan of swat and baseball's Don Bradman. Goodman gives a splendid performance as the fat-boy genius who loved life and single-handedly rescued the USA's summer sporting obsession between the wars after the Chicago White Sox scandal of 1919. Alvarado and McGillis provide strong support in a film which shows Ruth in warts-and-all mode: a boy abandoned to the priests aged seven as uncontrollable and incorrigible; a man who ate and drank like a pig, fought with fans and officials, cheated on his wife, but had a touching generosity, kindness and insecurity that stemmed from his hideous childhood. Surprisingly interesting, even if you don't know a home run from a stolen base. SGr

Bab El-Oued City

(1994, Alg/Fr, 93 min)
d Merzak Allouache. *sc* Merzak Allouache. *ph* Jean-Jacques Mrejen. *ed* Marie Collona. *m* Rachid Bahri. *cast* Nadia Kaci, Hassan Abdou, Nadia Samir, Mohamed Ourdache, Michel Such, Farida Rahaoudj.
●Frustrated by the confines of Muslim society, and angered by the religious propaganda blaring across the casbah, Boualem (Abdou) rashly steals a loudspeaker rigged up by the militants. Once they discover the culprits, the fundamentalists are determined to make an example of him. A fascinating portrait of life in contemporary Algeria – the smuggling, hypocrisy and widespread intimidation – but one that doesn't really deliver in the story department; it's cryptic to the point of impenetrability, but, paradoxically, dully predictable. TCh

Babe – Pig in the City

(1998, US/Aust, 96 min)
d George Miller. *p* George Miller, Doug Mitchell, Bill Miller. *sc* George Miller, Judy Morris, Mark Lamprell. *ph* Andrew Lesnie. *ed* Jay Friedkin, Margaret Sixel. *pd* Roger Ford. *m* Nigel Westlake. *cast* Magda Szubanski, James Cromwell, Mickey Rooney, voices: EG Daily, Steven Wright, Glenne Headley.
●Shorn of its rusticity, simplicity, the involvement of the original story's author, and, for much of the film, Cromwell's anchoring Farmer Hoggett, *Babe 2* has lost its innocence and much of its appeal. Instead of sheepdog trials, there is massive set design; a zoo-full of CGI and animatronically enhanced vignettes; a familiar, if expensively mounted, series of chases; mayhem; imperilment; and a needless clown act by Rooney. Disappointment sets in early, when Farmer Hoggett is disabled fixing the well. To save the farm, Mrs Hoggett and the pig accept a paid appearance at a distant 'Fayre', only to be drug-busted at Metropolis airport and forced to take refuge in the animal-filled Flealands hotel. Younger audiences will no doubt enjoy many of the varied, often cutesy, animal turns. But what about the pathetic orangutan, Thelonius, dressed like Max in *Sunset Blvd.*? The threatening atmosphere, furthermore, recalls the circus sequence in *Pinocchio*. There's too much emphasis on sickness and cruelty, while the underlined anthropomorphism borders on freakshow excess. WH

Babes in Arms

(1939, US, 96 min, b/w)
d Busby Berkeley. *p* Arthur Freed. *sc* Jack McGowan, Kay Van Riper. *ph* Ray June. *ed* Frank Sullivan. *ad* Cedric Gibbons. *songs* R Rodgers, L Hart, A Freed, NH Brown, H Arlen, EY Harburg. *cast* Mickey Rooney, Judy Garland, Charles Winninger, Guy Kibbee, June Preisser.
●First of the Garland-Rooney musicals, clothing a tired plot (old vaudevillians can't cope with competition from the movies, but their putting-on-a-show youngsters emphatically can) with much charm, energy and, mercifully, no Busby Berkeley chorine patterns. Sadly, one of Rodgers and Hart's best scores was mostly shed on the way to the screen, possibly considered too sophisticated for high school junketings. But the replacement numbers, including some old minstrel show favourites, have an appropriately nostalgic quality. *Babes in Arms* was followed by *Strike Up the Band* (1940), Babes on Broadway (1941) and *Girl Crazy* (1943). TM

Babes on Broadway

(1941, US, 118 min, b/w)
d Busby Berkeley. *p* Arthur Freed. *sc* Fred Finklehoffe, Elaine Ryan. *ph* Lester White. *ed* Fredrick Y Smith. *ad* Cedric Gibbons. *songs* Ralph Freed, Burton Lane, Roger Edens, EY Harburg, others. *cast* Mickey Rooney, Judy Garland, Virginia Weidler, Ray McDonald, Richard Quine, Fay Bainter.
●Perhaps the best of the Garland-Rooney musicals, only momentarily marred by some sentimentality about British war orphans. Following the usual putting-on-a-show formula, it features an unusually rich and varied collection of numbers, and gives Rooney a rare opportunity to show off his talent for impersonation. Minnelli got his first taste of direction on Garland's solos, in particular the 'Ghost Theatre' sequence. TM

Babette's Feast (Babettes Gaestebud)

(1987, Den, 103 min)
d Gabriel Axel. *p* Just Betzer, Bo Christensen. *sc* Gabriel Axel. *ph* Henning Kristiansen. *ed* Finn Henriksen. *pd* Sven Wichmann. *m* Per Norgård. *cast* Stéphane Audran, Jean-Philipe Lafont, Gudmar Wivesson, Jarl Kulle, Bibi Andersson, Bodil Kjer, Birgitte Federspiel.
●Why, in the 1870s, would a Parisienne (Audran), an acclaimed chef, be working for a pittance for two elderly sisters supervising a remote religious community on Denmark's windswept Jutland coast? The unlikely answer to that question may be found in Axel's superb adaptation of Isak Dinesen's very funny short story, a bizarre, magical concoction, seasoned to literally mouth-watering effect. The ingredients are marvellous locations, crisp photography, and an excellent cast. Axel never overstates the opposition between the villagers' God-fearing asceticism and Babette's feats of gastronomic wizardry, preferring instead a gently comic portrait of lives defined by pious austerity. It's a tale of self-sacrifice, thwarted ambitions, and lost love, but sheer sensuous joy suffuses the screen when Babette performs her own special miracle for one last supper. Axel, too, is surely an alchemist; compared to most literary adaptations, this is the word made flesh. GA

Baby

see Baby – Secret of the Lost Legend

Baby, The

(1973, US, 102 min)
d Ted Post. *p* Milton Polsky, Abraham Polsky. *sc* Abraham Polsky. *ph* Michael D Margulies. *ed* Dick Wormell. *ad* Michael Devine. *m* Gerald Fried. *cast* Anjanette Comer, Ruth Roman, Marianne Hill, Suzanne Zenor.
●What starts out as a seemingly realist study of the relationship between social worker Comer and the dysfunctional family presided over by Roman develops into a full-blown horror movie. Comer has a consuming interest in 'Baby', a man with the mind of a child, and, convinced that Roman and her sisters are bent on murder, abducts Baby. An unusual chiller, well directed by co-scripter Ted (*Magnum Force*) Post. NF

Baby Blue Marine

(1976, US, 90 min)
d John Hancock. *p* Aaron Spelling, Leonard Goldberg. *sc* Stanford Whitmore. *ph* Laszlo Kovacs. *ed* Marion Rothman. *pd* Walter Scott Herndon. *m* Fred Karlin. *cast* Jan-Michael Vincent, Glynnis O'Connor, Katherine Helmond, Dana Elcar, Bert Remsen, Richard Gere, Art Lund, Michael Conrad.
●Stodgily directed effort that rates high on curiosity value. Ostensibly dealing with WWII traumas, the film in fact attempts a weirdly fascinating washing away of post-Vietnam guilt. Vincent, then cornering the market in all-American clean-cut heroes, is the dubious choice for the part of the reject marine who finds himself playing war hero to an eager small-town audience. VG

Baby Boom

(1987, US, 111 min)
d Charles Shyer. *p* Nancy Meyers. *sc* Nancy Meyers, Charles Shyer. *ph* William A Fraker. *ed* Lynzee Klingman. *pd* Jeffrey Howard. *m* Bill Conti. *cast* Diane Keaton, Harold Ramis, Sam Wanamaker, James Spader, Pat Hingle, Britt Leach, Sam Shepard.
●A working woman's fantasy, mixing cute in both the business acumen and coochy-coo varieties. Keaton (uneasily neurotic and capable), a thrusting NY advertising exec, inherits a relative's toddler, and is forced suddenly into a crash course in adoption, diapers, child-care, and a re-examination of her own feelings. Puritan would-be adopters present a fearsome option; her lover (Ramis) finds the disruption unacceptable and leaves; her boss (Wanamaker) forgets a partnership offer. What's a wealthy single parent to do?

Take the tiny tot to leafy upstate Smallsville, and make with the chequered aprons and homemade victuals. It's played like a '40s comedy; heart-warming, sentimental, simplistic. Sickeningly calculated. WH

Baby Boy

(2001, US, 130 min)
d/p/sc John Singleton. *ph* Charles E Mills. *ed* Bruce Cannon. *pd* Keith Brian Burns. *m* David Arnold. *cast* Tyrese Gibson, Omar Gooding, AJ Johnson, Taraji P Henson, Snoop Dogg, Tamara LaSeon Bass, Ving Rhames, Candy Brown Houston.

●At 20, flirtatious Jody (Gibson) has two cute offspring, one with tempestuous longterm girlfriend Yvette (Henson), and one with jailbait Peanut (Bass). But Jody's little more than a kid himself: obsessed with his appetites, scared of responsibility, still living with his savvy momma. Days are spent scheming outside the liquor store with desperate buddy Sweetpea (Gooding), before mom's musclebound new man and Yvette's thuggish ex throw his arrested development into flux. The film's coming-of-age drama returns writer/director Singleton to South Central LA, where he's back on form (after *Shaft*). Visceral, bristling with sex and conflict, the action is bolstered by sharp, effusive dialogue and a g-funk soundtrack. Gibson is the striking lynchpin of a charismatic cast. Overall, it may not match the raw impact of Singleton's 1991 debut *Boyz N the Hood*, but his earlier preachiness has matured into a succinct sense of humour, making *Baby Boy* his most rounded delivery to date. AHa

Baby Doll

(1956, US, 115 min, b/w)
d/p Elia Kazan. *sc* Tennessee Williams. *ph* Boris Kaufman. *ed* Gene Milford. *ad* Richard Sylbert. *m* Kenyon Hopkins. *cast* Carroll Baker, Karl Malden, Eli Wallach, Mildred Dunnock, Lonny Chapman, Rip Torn.

●Based by Tennessee Williams on two of his one-act plays, this is arguably one of Kazan's least ambitious and most successfully realised movies. Essentially a black comedy about a bizarre and cruel romantic triangle, it concerns the intrusion of Wallach's cunning Sicilian businessman into the ramshackle Deep South lives of boor Malden and his immature nymphet wife Baker. Inevitably, flirtation, seduction and jealousy are the result. Condemned by the Legion of Decency upon release, its erotic content now seems tame indeed; but the grotesquely caricatured performances and the evocation of the baking, dusty, indolent homestead make for witty and compelling viewing. GA

Baby Face

(1933, US, 68 min, b/w)
d Alfred E Green. *sc* Gene Markey, Kathryn Scola. *ph* James van Trees. *ed* Howard Bretherton. *ad* Anton F Grot. *cast* Barbara Stanwyck, George Brent, Donald Cook, Henry Kolker, Douglas Dumbrille, Margaret Lindsay, John Wayne.

●Directed with more pace than style, but what matter with Stanwyck in peak form? Starting out as a barmaid in dad's speakeasy in the Pittsburgh slums, she moves to New York when he dies, and calculatingly climbs man by man from basement to penthouse. For all the moralising which has her pre-Hayes Code golddigging lead through fraught paths to true love, the character probably grew into the Phyllis Dietrichson of *Double Indemnity*. TM

Baby Face Morgan

(1942, US, 60 min, b/w)
d Arthur Dreifuss. *p* Jack Schwartz. *sc* Edward Dein, Jack Rubin, Oscar Brodney. *ph* Art Reed. *ed* Dan Milner. *ad* Frank Dexter. *m* Leon Erdody. *cast* Richard Cromwell, Mary Carlisle, Robert Armstrong, Chick Chandler, Warren Hymer, Vince Barnett.

●Very minor crime caper from the PRC stable, where they turned 'em out even cheaper and quicker than sister company Monogram Pictures, leading light on Hollywood's so-called Poverty Row. This one's about a mobster's son who's made the director of a dodgy insurance company by his dad's old partners in crime. In the midst of the ensuing tedium you may develop the suspicion that it was conceived as a comedy. Grim all the same. TJ

Baby Face Nelson

(1957, US, 83 mins, b/w)
d Don Siegel. *p* Al Zimbalist. *sc* Irving Shulman, Daniel Mainwaring. *ph* Hal Mohr. *ed* Leon Barsha. *ad* David Milton. *m* Van Alexander. *cast* Mickey Rooney, Carolyn Jones, Cedric Hardwicke, Ted De Corsia, Emile Meyer, Leo Gordon, Jack Elam.

●One of Siegel's most vigorous crime-thrillers, and a key study of the gangster as psychotic. Rooney is surprisingly and superbly cast as the Depression desperado increasingly unable to control his outbursts of irrational violence, while the supporting cast – including Gordon as John Dillinger – is expertly deployed. But it is the sheer pace and economy of Siegel's direction that lend the film its anarchic energy; recreation of period is almost ignored in favour of an emphasis on actions exemplifying the anti-hero's sexually-insecure neuroses. A superior example of the way B-movie conventions may be transcended by wit and a fertile imagination. GA

Baby It's You

(1982, US, 104 min)
d John Sayles. *p* Griffin Dunne, Amy Robinson. *sc* John Sayles. *ph* Michael Ballhaus. *ed* Sonya Polonsky. *pd* Jeffrey Townsend. *cast* Rosanna Arquette, Vincent Spano, Joanna Merlin, Jack Davidson, Nick Ferrari, Dolores Messina.

●High school in New Jersey, 1966: she's en route for college and WASPdom, he's more concerned with miming to Sinatra and curling his lip the right amount at the teachers. As usual Sayles invests his subject with great care, and breaks with tradition by pursuing the pair into post-school life: the effects of hippy culture on her, of real life (washing up in Miami) on him. There is no easy moralising, nor any patronising of the characters; their reunion is as moving and hopeless as was their first love. Arquette and Spano hit exactly the right note; and having had *Return of the Secaucus Seven* recycled by *The Big Chill*, Sayles now outdoes the Chill with his own soundtrack (uniting Sinatra, Springsteen, Shirelles). CPea

Babylon

(1980, GB, 95 min)
d Franco Rosso. *p* Gavrik Losey. *sc* Martin Stellman, Franco Rosso. *ph* Chris Menges. *ed* Thomas Schwalm. *ad* Brian Savegar. *m* Dennis Bovell. *cast* Brinsley Forde, Karl Howman, Trevor Laird, Brian Bovell, Victor Romero Evans.

●Although *Babylon* shows what it's like to be young, black and working class in Britain, the final product turns dramatised documentary into a breathless helter-skelter. Rather than force the social and political issues, Rosso lets them emerge and gather momentum through the everyday experience of his central character Blue (sensitively played by Forde). A series of increasingly provocative incidents finally polarise Blue and lead to uncompromising confrontation. Although the script runs out of steam by the end, the sharp use of location, the meticulous detailing of black culture, the uniformly excellent performances and stimulating soundtrack command attention. IB

Babylon: la paura e la migliore amica dell'uomo

see Lies to Live By (Babylon)

Babymother

(1998, GB, 82 min)
d Julian Henriques *p* Parminder Vir. *sc* Julian Henriques, Vivienne Howard. *ph* Ron Fortunato. *ed* Jason Canovas. *pd* Choi Ho Man *m* John Lunn. *cast* Anjela Lauren Smith, Caroline Chikezie, Jocelyn Esien, Wil Johnson, Suzette Llewellyn.

●Single mum Anita (Smith) is a peacock – bright and loud. She needs a nice, dun-coloured mate, but instead has Don Byron (Johnson), a reggae star who loves the limelight and panics when singing hopeful 'Nita has a chance to steal it. There's also her preachy sister Rose (Llewellyn), a serious lack of money and a sexist music industry to contend with. In crafting this kitchen sink reggae musical, writer/director Henriques has hardly made life easy for himself. While brimming with life, 'Nita is also self-obsessed, aggressive, posturing and immature. And though she looks after her children, you never feel they have an emotional connection. Clearly you need time to care for such a creature, but the numerous, often tedious musical numbers keep getting in the way. As a vocalist, however, Smith proves convincing and, in two excellent closing numbers, the 'message' that has been clumsily milling around finally assembles itself and hits home. CO'Su

Baby of Mâcon, The

(1993, GB/Neth/Fr/Ger, 122 min)
d Peter Greenaway. *p* Kees Kasander. *sc* Peter Greenaway. *ph* Sacha Vierny. *ed* Chris Wyatt. *pd* Jan Roelfs. *cast* Julia Ormond, Ralph Fiennes, Philip Stone, Jonathan Lacey, Don Henderson, Celia Gregory.

●Set halfway through the 17th century, Greenaway's film follows a church play performed for the benefit of the young aristocrat Cosimo (Lacey). In the play, a grotesque old woman gives birth to a beautiful baby boy. The child's older sister (Ormond) is quick to exploit the situation, selling blessings from the baby, and even claiming she's the true mother by virgin birth. However, when she attempts to seduce the bishop's son (Fiennes), the Church exacts a terrible revenge. An agnostic's vision of the Nativity, *The Baby of Mâcon* is an elaborate descration of Catholic iconography, and a merciless assault on superstition and religion. Greenaway breaks down the barriers between the play and the outside world, the actors and their audience, so that the performance itself becomes just another corrupt religious ritual. The film is repetitive, cold and misanthropic; everyone here is a fraud, a cynic or a simpleton; even the baby proves malign. TCh

Baby's Day Out

(1994, US, 98 min)
d Patrick Read Johnson. *p* John Hughes, Richard Vane. *sc* John Hughes. *ph* Thomas Ackerman. *ed* David Rawlins. *ad* Doug Kramer. *m* Bruce Broughton. *cast* Joe Mantegna, Lara Flynn Boyle, Joe Pantoliano, Brian Haley, John Neville, Eddie Bracken.

●Say what you like about *Home Alone* creator John Hughes, he knows how to pen a formula picture. Though heir to a fortune, Baby Bink has never had his picture in the paper, a situation his mother (Boyle) intends to rectify. But the photographers are three bungling kidnappers (led by Mantegna), who make off with the sprog and demand a tidy ransom. The baby soon escapes, proceeding to duplicate the trip round the big city described in his favourite book, as he takes in a department store, a zoo, and finally a building site. The abductors, meanwhile, suffer humiliation as they attempt to recapture him. Cartoon crude, but quite lively. NF

Baby – Secret of the Lost Legend

(1985, US, 95 min)
d Bill L Norton. *p* Jonathan Taplin. *sc* Clifford Green, Ellen Green. *ph* John Alcott. *ed* Howard Smith. *pd* Ray Storey. *m* Jerry Goldsmith. *cast* William Katt, Sean Young, Patrick McGoohan, Julian Fellowes.

●McGoohan is a nasty, glory-seeking cryptozoologist following up rumours of a brontosaurus family living deep in the Congo. His persistent assistant (Young) decides to venture into the bush herself when he dismisses her discovery of a set of bones. Then follow standard chases up and down the jungle, plus brushes with natives and soldiers, as the adversaries and their allies try to steal the creatures off each other. The bronts are brilliant, while snappy dialogue keeps the film from sinking into the absurd. Undemanding Disney family entertainment. DPe

Babysitter, The

(1995, US, 85 min)
d Guy Ferland. *p* Kevin Messick, Steve Perry. *sc* Guy Ferland. *ph* Rick Bota. *ed* Jim Prior. *pd* Phil Leonard. *cast* Alicia Silverstone, JT Walsh, Lois Chiles, George Segal, Jeremy London.

●Although sent straight to video on both sides of the Atlantic and packaged like a thousand other titillating thrillers ('Obsession is a Dangerous State of Mind,' indeed), *The Babysitter* turns out to be something a little different. Written and directed by one Guy Ferland, it's based on a story by Robert Coover, and remains true to Coover's teasing comedy of rampant sexual fantasy, that peculiar brand of esoteric erotica which deconstructionists call their own. Silverstone is the innocent babysitter who unwittingly works all the men in her life (the puberulent brat in her charge, his dad, a boyfriend, and his scheming mate) into paroxysms of polymorphous lust. The fantasy sequences grow a mite tedious – most of them centre on Alicia taking a bath – and the movie shies away from anything *too* dirty, but Walsh and Chiles have fun as the boozy parents whose marriage is on the rocks, while the true/false plotting keeps you guessing. TCh

Baby the Rain Must Fall

(1964, US, 93 min, b/w)
d Robert Mulligan. *p* Alan J Pakula. *sc* Horton Foote. *ph* Ernest Laszlo. *ed* Aaron Stell. *ad* Roland Anderson. *m* Elmer Bernstein. *cast* Steve McQueen, Lee Remick, Don Murray, Paul Fix, Josephine Hutchinson, Ruth White, Charles Watts, Kimberly Block.

●Horton Foote adapted his play *The Traveling Lady* for this vaguely literary tale of small town Texas folk, one of the string of well-meaning but amorphous pictures (*To Kill A Mockingbird* was the best) turned out by Mulligan and producing partner Alan Pakula throughout the '60s. McQueen is slightly ill-at-ease as a rebellious rockabilly singer trying to stay on the right side of the law after his release on parole, lip-synching unconvincingly on the bandstand, and unable to invest his characteristically spare acting style with the psychological insights that would enable the audience to 'read' his self-destructive character. Remick is typically radiant in a typically thankless role as the doormat wife. The impressive high-contrast b/w camerawork is by Ernest Laszlo. TJ

Baby Tramp

see Butterfly

Bachelor, The

(1999, US, 102 min)
d Gary Sinyor. *p* Lloyd Segan, Bing Howenstein. *sc* Steve Cohen. *ph* Simon Archer. *ed* Robert Reitano. *pd* Craig Stearns. *m* David A Hughes, John Murphy. *cast* Chris O'Donnell, Renée Zellweger, Hal Holbrook, James Cromwell, Artie Lange, Edward Asner, Marley Shelton, Peter Ustinov, Maria Carey, Brooke Shields.

●Who do you cast if you're remaking Keaton's 1925 classic *Seven Chances*? It's obvious, really. The Buster Keaton of the '90s, Mr Chris O'Donnell. From here on, one senses, Brit director Sinyor's Hollywood comedy was doomed. The plot's still sturdy enough: an eccentric grandfather's $100m bequest depends on the protagonist's immediate marriage (or else he loses the family business), sticking at it for a decade, and fathering at least one child. To date O'Donnell's unwillingness to commit has put off Zellweger, his girlfriend of three years, and with her out of town and out of the picture, desperation looms. Delivering his usual 'jock in a china shop' performance, O'Donnell lacks the timing to make the material play, and Sinyor's slack direction offers little assistance. Only in the final reel does the film manage a flicker of real visual wit when a misguided newspaper ad unleashes a horde of would-be brides on to the streets of San Francisco. TJ

Bachelor Bait

see Adventure in Baltimore

Bachelor Girl Apartment

see Any Wednesday

Bachelor Mother

(1939, US, 62 min, b/w)
d Garson Kanin. *p* Pandro S Berman. *sc* Norman Krasna. *ph* Robert De Grasse. *ed* Henry Berman, Robert Wise. *ad* Van Nest Polglase, Darrell Silvera. *m* Roy Webb. *cast* Ginger Rogers, David Niven, Charles Coburn, Frank Albertson, Ernest Truex.

●Rogers is superb as the brassy lady from the Bronx in this comedy of mistaken identity and parenthood, in which a young shopgirl is forced by her employers (Coburn as the department store owner, Niven as his urbanely flustered, eligible son) into becoming foster-mother to an abandoned child. It's a hilarious, snappy, loose-jointed comedy in the best Hollywood tradition, but the script and direction by Kanin have an intelligence and sense of irony which raise provocative question after provocative question – about the role of women as workers, mothers, and mistresses; about male hypocrisy. A salutary reminder that Sirk wasn't the only 'subversive' to burrow his way into the woodwork of tinsel city. CA

Bachelor Party

(1984, US, 105 min)
d Neal Israel. *p* Ron Moler, Bob Israel. *sc* Neal Israel, Pat Proft. *ph* Hal Trussell. *ed* Tom Walls. *ad* Kevin Conlin. *m* Robert Folk. *cast* Tom Hanks, Tawny Kitaen, Adrian Zmed, George Grizzard, Barbara Stuart, Robert Prescott, William Tepper, Wendie Jo Sperber, Barry Diamond.

●School bus driver Rick (Hanks) has had the same bunch of friends since grade school; mentally they're still stuck there, so it may not be the smartest move to allow them to organise his stag night. Alerted to the likely presence of drugs 'n' sluts, his fiancée and future mother-in-law crash the party dressed as hookers. And so on. Despite the donkey that arrives and ODs on the pharmaceutical buffet, the 'wild' party resembles a dance routine from an Annette Funicello beach movie. To his credit Hanks behaves throughout as though he's actually in a worthwhile movie. DO

Bachelor Party, The

(1957, US, 93 min, b/w)
d Delbert Mann. *p* Harold Hecht. *sc* Paddy Chayefsky. *ph* Joseph La Shelle. *ed* William B Murphy. *ad* Ted Haworth. *m* Paul Madeira, (uncred) Alex North. *cast* Don Murray, EG Marshall, Jack Warden, Patricia Smith, Carolyn Jones, Philip Abbott.

●Based on Paddy Chayefsky's highly successful TV play (itself a follow-up to *Marty*), this is a story about a debauch among office workers that sours as the night wears on. Praised in its day for its ensemble acting and acute analysis of middle-class anxieties, it now looks rather drab and dated. MA

Back Against the Wall

(2000, US, 94 min, b/w)
d/p/sc James Fotopoulos. *ph* John Wagner, Dennis Best. *ed/pd* James Fotopoulos. *m* Tom Nicholl, Bob Davies, Alex Horn. *cast* Debbie Mulcahy, Martin Shannon, Ernie E Frantz, Michael Wexler.

●Director Fotopoulos comes with quite a rep in the North American indie scene. Certainly this cool and highly controlled b/w study of paranoia and powerplay in the world of lingerie modelling (don't come, however, expecting lacy seductions) is formally inventive and resolutely modern. It'strong on interiors and text, and distinctively scored – early Cronenberg, without the genre trappings, comes to mind as an atmospheric cousin, but it's got its own unsettling, sometimes alienating tone. GE

Back Alley Princes (Malu Xiao Yingxiong)

(1972, HK, 100 min)
d Lo Wei. *p* Raymond Chow. *sc* Lo Wei. *ph* Chen Ching Chueh. *ed* Chang Yao Chung. *pd* Lo Wei. *m* Joseph Koo. *cast* Shangkuan Ling Feng, Samuel Hui, Angela Mao, Tien Feng.

●A socially conscious comedy which may not handle its gags with much subtlety, but does manage to portray, with deliberate casualness, life lived on the edge of desperation in Hong Kong as it charts the supposedly carefree lives of two jaunty street kids (one of whom is a girl dressed as a boy) who stage minor con-jobs for a living. The fringes of the action are littered with the activities of small-time gamblers, pimps and hustlers, while the world of bar hostesses and sexual profiteering is shown without recourse to histrionics. VG

Backbeat

(1993, GB, 100 min)
d Iain Softley. *p* Finola Dwyer, Stephen Woolley. *sc* Iain Softley, Michael Thomas, Stephen Ward. *ph* Ian Wilson. *ed* Martin Walsh. *pd* Joseph Bennett. *m* Don Was. *cast* Sheryl Lee, Stephen Dorff, Ian Hart, Gary Bakewell, Chris O'Neill, Scot Williams.

●Lively, light-hearted and long on period detail, this portrait of the pre-stardom Beatles focuses on the relationship of Lennon, his pal and 'fifth Beatle' Stuart Sutcliffe, and Astrid Kirchherr, the Hamburg photographer partly responsible for creating the band's mop-top image, with whom Sutcliffe fell in love. There's not much story – the lads' experience in Hamburg at the start of the '60s, their disagreements, their acquisition of a loyal club following, and Sutcliffe's appointment with death – so that the film depends for effect on atmosphere, performance and panache. Happily, it largely succeeds in each respect. Much of the credit must go to Hart, whose Lennon is convincingly acerbic, rebellious and petty. Dorff is adequately cool, good looking and Scousey as Sutcliffe; the other Beatles are played by fair look-alikes; and only Lee's vapid Astrid disappoints. The music is loud and raw, but nevertheless evokes the excitement it generated. GA

Back Door to Hell

(1964, US/Phil, 68 min, b/w)
d Monte Hellman. *p* Fred Roos. *sc* Richard A Guttman, John Hackett. *ph* Mars Rasca. *ed* Fely Crisotomo. *m* Mike Velarde. *cast* Jimmie Rodgers, Jack Nicholson, John Hackett, Annabelle Huggins, Conrad Maga.

●A war movie shot for around three bucks in the Philippines and seemingly pitched at the subdrive-in market. However, followers of Hellman should be able to discern traces of the futility that dominated subsequent films like *The Shooting* and *Two Lane Blacktop*. The script throws in much talk to disguise the fact that the budget couldn't accommodate more battle scenes, and amuses itself by giving a younger and greener Nicholson lines like 'You're the kinda guy who'd call Mahatma Gandhi a rabble-rouser'. CPe

Backdraft

(1991, US, 135 min)
d Ron Howard. *p* Richard B Lewis, Pen Densham, John Watson. *sc* Greg Widen. *ph* Mikael Saloman. *ed* Daniel Hanley. *ad* Albert Brenner. *m* Hans Zimmer. *cast* Kurt Russell, William Baldwin, Robert De Niro, Donald Sutherland, Jennifer Jason Leigh, Scott Glenn, Rebecca De Mornay, Jason Gedrick, JT Walsh.

●Being a fireman is just like belonging to a football team, or so screenwriter Gregory Widen would have us believe. 'You dropped the ball, you split the team up,' says scornful firefighter Stephen McCaffrey (Russell) to his rookie brother (Baldwin). As though sibling rivalry was not enough, Widen (an ex-firefighter) lumbers the plot with unnecessary complications and obvious confrontations: an investigator (De Niro) is on the trail of a skilful arsonist, the squabbling brothers have troubled romances. Ron Howard creates some promo-style sequences that would look more at home in a Gillette advert, but he does a superb job with the ultra-realistic effects. The fire sequences are stunning, and the build-up to them, complete with blaring sirens and bellowed conversations, has an aggressive immediacy. CM

Backfire

(1987, US, 91 min)
d Gilbert Cates. *p* Danton Rissner. *sc* Larry Brand, Rebecca Reynolds. *ph* Tak Fujimoto. *ed* Melvin Shapiro. *pd* Dan Lomino. *m* David Shire. *cast* Karen Allen, Keith Carradine, Jeff Fahey, Bernie Casey, Dean Paul Martin, Virginia Capers, Dinah Manoff.

●Vietnam rears its head again in this who's-haunting-who thriller about a wealthy shell-shocked veteran, Donny (Fahey), whom his wife Mara (Allen) hopes, with the help of her rekindled old flame (Martin) and some gruesome special effects, to drive to suicide. The plot backfires, and she's left with a catatonic husband whose fortune she forfeits to his devoted sister (Manoff) if she puts him in an institution. Suddenly it's Mara's turn to worry about things going bump in the night. Is she cracking up, is Donny faking his catatonia, is the sister trying to get her hands on the dough, or are the weird happenings linked to the arrival of an enigmatic stranger (Carradine)? Lacking the narrative assurance to exploit its switchback plottings, this would-be Hitchcockian mystery ends up floundering in the shallows. Only Carradine's nicely judged performance escapes the formulaic straitjacket. NF

Back from Eternity

(1956, US, 97 min, b/w)
d/p John Farrow. *sc* Jonathan Latimer. *ph* William C Mellor. *ed* Eda Warren. *ad* Albert S D'Agostino. *m* Franz Waxman. *cast* Robert Ryan, Anita Ekberg, Rod Steiger, Gene Barry, Phyllis Kirk, Keith Andes, Beulah Bondi, Cameron Prud'homme.

●Despite a typically fine, tormented performance from Ryan as the drunken pilot, Farrow's remake of his own *Five Came Back* loses out to its predecessor, partly because (without adding anything of note) it takes significantly longer to tell its tale of crashed air passengers fending off headhunters in the Amazon jungle, partly because the stereotype characters and situations had by now lost their freshness. Steiger, over-acting, is no match for the original's Joseph Calleia; Ekberg is purely ornamental; and the voluntary self-sacrifice of elderly professor Prud'homme and his scared but loving wife (Bondi) carries less weight than in the earlier film. Tense in parts, but largely formulaic. GA

Background to Danger

(1943, US, 80 min, b/w)
d Raoul Walsh. *p* Jerry Wald. *sc* WR Burnett. *ph* Tony Gaudio. *ed* Jack Killifer. *ad* Hugh Reticker. *m* Frederick Hollander. *cast* George Raft, Brenda Marshall, Sydney Greenstreet, Peter Lorre, Osa Massen, Kurt Katch.

●Maybe not up there with the best of Walsh's action pics, but still an efficient and entertaining WWII spy thriller. Raft is the American agent travelling to Turkey to prevent the country from allying itself with the Nazis, and encountering that colourful pair, Greenstreet (a Nazi) and Lorre (his Turkish opponent) en route. A bit too light to be a really good espionage drama – the genre works best when presenting a bleak world of betrayal and doubt – but Walsh keeps it moving along at a cracking pace, while the script (adapted by WR Burnett from Eric Ambler's novel) is vivid and sharp. GA

Back in the USSR

(1992, US, 89 min)
d Deran Sarafian. *p/sc* Lindsay Smith, Ilmar Taska. *ph* Yuri Neyman. *ed* Ian Crafford. *pd* Vladimir Philippov. *m* Les Hooper. *cast* Frank Whaley, Natalya Negoda, Roman Polanski, Andrew Divof, Dey Young, Brian Blessed.

●Yarn about a much-stolen Russian icon, made by Corman protégé Deran Sarafian, in which Polanski features as a black marketeer with a violent sense of humour: too farcical to be a thriller; too brutal to be a comedy; and insufficiently surefooted to be a comedy-thriller. AO

Backlash

(1986, Aust, 90 min)
d/p/sc Bill Bennett. *ph* Tony Wilson. *ed* Denise Hunter. *m* Michael Atkinson. *cast* David Argue, Gia Carides, Lydia Miller, Brian Syron, Anne Smith, Don Smith.

●Two cops drive an Aboriginal barmaid (Miller), accused of castrating her over-attentive boss with garden shears, across country to face trial. Argue is a cynical, aggressive, seen-it-all type, Caridis a rookie policewoman with starry-eyed notions about law enforcement and an increasing sympathy for their prisoner. The tensions within the group create a shifting pattern of alliances, especially when an ill-advised short cut leaves them stranded miles from anywhere. Here, the freewheeling narrative gives way to more static psychodrama. And who is the mysterious man who tracks them by day and disturbs their sleep with anguished cries by night? Former documentarist Bennett makes good use of the sun-parched landscape and improvised dialogue, while his unobtrusive camera style allows the actors ample scope to explore the drama and humour of a scenario laced with social comment. If this loosely coiled road movie doesn't always generate the kind of excitement suggested by the title, it does have a sting in its tail. NF

Back of Beyond

(1995, Aust, 85 min)
d Michael Robertson. *p* John Sexton. *sc* Paul Leadon, Anne Brooksbank. *ph* Stephen Dobson. *ed* Tim Wellburn. *pd* Ross Major. *m* Mark Moffatt. *cast* Paul Mercurio, Dee Smart, Rebekah Elmaloglou, Colin Friels, John Polson, Bob Maza.

●Blaming himself for the death of his sister, a traumatised mechanic (Mercurio) has all but given up on the lonely outback petrol station where he lives, but when a trio of jewel thieves break down in the vicinity, he's enlisted in emergency repair work at gunpoint. Gangsters holed up in a desert outpost in the company of an honest man: the set-up's at least as old as *The Petrified Forest* (1936), and though director Robertson has a few tricks up his sleeve, these are so blatantly signposted you could see them coming with your eyes shut. Friels plays the key thug, his Aryan dye job and hairnet insufficient to prevent his girl (newcomer Smart) from drifting to Mercurio's side. It's easy to understand Friels' consternation – what does she see in this sullen, monosyllabic pretty boy? He looks cute in his overalls, perhaps, but corpses have more personality. The B-movie dialogue doesn't extend to irony ('You've gotta find your purpose,' we're earnestly informed), while the director's pseudo-mystic mumbo-jumbo is strictly skin deep. TCh

Back of the World, The (La Espalda del Mundo)

(2000, Sp, 89 min)
d Javier Corcuera. *p* Elias Querejeta. *sc* Elias Querejeta, Fernando Léon de Aranoa, Javier Corcuera. *ph* Jordi Abusada. *ed* Iván Fernández, Nacho Ruiz-Capillas. *cast* Guinder Rodríguez, Mehdi Zana, Thomas Miller-El, Tomás Rangel.

●Intriguing, slightly slick, but finally affecting triptych documenting suffering and injustice around the globe. 'The Child' concerns a young Peruvian kid who toils daily in a stone quarry to help his impoverished Indian family; 'The Word' is about a Kurd exiled in Stockholm, far from his wife, for the last quarter of a century; and 'Life' deals with prisoners on Death Row in Texas, and ends with Bush on TV. For all its visual polish, the film has an air of truth, even if it doesn't really tell us much we didn't already know. GA

Back-Packers, The

see Randonneurs, Les

Back Roads

(1981, US, 95 min)
d Martin Ritt. *p* Ronald Shedlo. *sc* Gary DeVore. *ph* John A Alonzo. *ed* Sidney Levin. *pd* Walter Scott Henderson. *m* Henry Mancini. *cast* Sally Field, Tommy Lee Jones, David Keith, Miriam Colon, Michael Gazzo, M Emmet Walsh.

●Pleasantly old-fashioned romantic comedy in which two losers meet cute – he's a broken-down boxer, she a hooker angrily throwing him out after belatedly realising he's broke – then set off on a road movie odyssey through picturesque redneck locations in search of a new life. Very good on local colour but a bit sugary in its attitude to the central relationship, it would have been better taking a bleaker cue from Tommy Lee Jones' admirably dry performance. TM

Backroads

(1977, Aust, 59 min)
d/p Phillip Noyce. *sc* John Emery. *ph* Russell Boyd. *ed* David Huggett. *cast* Gary Foley, Bill Hunter, Zac Martin, Terry Camilleri, Julie McGregor.

●An Aussie male duo, one redneck dropout white, the other a young black, steal a car and joyride their way across the outback of New South Wales before coming to the inevitable end of all good movie outlaws. Very much the result of a collaborative tension between director Noyce and his black lead actor (Foley), *Backroads* is an outstanding road movie to stand beside the very best American examples of the genre. Often brilliantly funny, it manages to be both completely commercial and a scathing depiction of one of the world's most racist societies. RM

Back-Room Boy

(1942, GB, 82 min, b/w)
d Herbert Mason. p Edward Black. *sc* Val Guest, Marriott Edgar, JOC Orton. *ph* Jack Cox. *ed* Charles Saunders. *ad* Wally Murton. *m* Hans May. *cast* Arthur Askey, Moore Marriott, Graham Moffatt, Googie Withers, Vera Francis, Joyce Howard.

●Askey's an incompetent young meteorologist sent to a remote Orkney lighthouse, where he somehow rumbles a Nazi spy ring. This is typical Will Hay and the Crazy Gang territory: chaotic, childish, and much improved by the mugging of Hay's old sidekicks, Marriott and Moffatt. Co-writer Val Guest recycles many of the situations and jokes he patented in *Oh, Mr Porter!* and *The Frozen Limits*. Derivative but fun. GM

Back Street

(1932, US, 92 min, b/w)
d John M Stahl. *p* Carl Laemmle Jr. *sc* Gladys Lehman, Lynn Starling. *ph* Karl Freund. *ed* Milton Carruth. *ad* Charles D Hall. *cast* Irene Dunne, John Boles, George Meeker, ZaSu Pitts, Arlette Duncan, June Clyde.

●Fine adaptation of Fannie Hurst's tearjerking novel about a girl (Dunne) who falls in love with a man engaged to be married. An accident prevents her from pursuing the romance; he marries; and when they meet again after some years, she becomes his mistress. Soon realising the demi-paradise that awaits her alone in 'the back street' of his life, she tries to break away, only to find that the desperate need created by their love for each other makes this impossible; and remaining loyal for the rest of her life, she calmly accepts all the heartbreak and humiliation that follows. Stahl counters the danger of sentimentality by maintaining an even, beautifully controlled monotone (very moving in its quietude) that establishes a discreet distance between his camera and the excesses of the plot. One thinks, oddly, of Ozu and Dreyer as the characters find themselves quietly swept away by currents over which they have no control. TM

Back Street

(1941, US, 89 min, b/w)
d Robert Stevenson. *p* Bruce Manning. *sc* Bruce Manning, Felix Jackson. *ph* William Daniels. *ed* Ted Kent. *ad* Jack Otterson. *m* Frank Skinner. *cast* Charles Boyer, Margaret Sullavan, Richard Carlson, Frank McHugh, Tim Holt.

●While John M Stahl's 1932 version of Fannie Hurst's tearjerking romantic novel achieved the emotional charge later associated with the best of Douglas Sirk's work, this careful, well acted remake seldom ignites the explosive emotions. Sullavan is the self-annihilating mistress who lives for twenty years in shabby rooms, while her lover (Boyer) goes on with his comfortable married life. Remade, to lushly unhappy effect, in a Ross Hunter production directed by David Miller in 1961, with Susan Hayward and John Gavin. NF

Back to Back, Face to Face (Bei kao Bei, Lian dui Lian)

(1994, HK/China, 138 min)
d Huang Jianxin. *sc* Huang Jianxin, Shun Yian, Huang Xin, Liu Xinglong. *ph* Zhang Xiaoguang, Zhu Shen. *ed* Lei Quin. *pd* Li Xingri. *m* Zhang Da Long. cast Niu Zhenghua, Lei Gesheng, Li Qiang, Ju Hao, Liu Guoxiang, Xu Xuezheng.

●Huang Jianxin has been getting away with the sharpest political satire in China ever since he made *The Black Cannon Incident*, largely because he leaves viewers free to draw their own conclusions about the absurd situations he explores in his movies. This time, he dissects a power struggle for control of a cultural centre: Wang (comedian Niu Zhenhua), its vice-president, assumes his political skills and connections make him a shoo-in for the top job, but the local cultural bureau chief has other ideas. This is a combination of darkish comedy with the appeal of an ongoing soap opera. Its core is acid: here is a perfect microcosm of the way the political process works in China, with barely a whisper of exaggeration. TR

Back to Bataan

(1945, US, 97 min, b/w)
d Edward Dmytryk. *sc* Ben Barzman, Richard Landau. *ph* Nicholas Musuraca. *ed* Marston Fay. *ad* Albert S D'Agostino, Ralph Berger. *m* Roy Webb. *cast* John Wayne, Anthony Quinn, Beulah Bondi, Lawrence Tierney, Paul Fix, Fely Franquelli.

●Big John is the cowboy in colonel's clothing organising guerrilla attacks against the Japanese in the Philippines while waiting for the main forces to arrive. Designed as a tribute to the

Filipino resistance, it's fast, vigorous and quite exciting, but marred by incessant flag-waving, the usual racist depiction of the enemy, and some atrocious sentimentality (featuring not only a heroic small boy, but Quinn's Filipino sweetheart, who becomes a sort of Tokyo Rose for the Japs while passing information on the side). GA

Back to School

(1986, US, 97 min)
d Alan Metter. *p* Chuck Russell. *sc* Steven Kampmann, Will Porter, Peter Torokvei, Harold Ramis. *ph* Thomas E Ackerman. *ed* David Rawlins. *pd* David L Snyder. *m* Danny Elfman. *cast* Rodney Dangerfield, Sally Kellerman, Burt Young, Keith Gordon, Robert Downey Jr, Paxton Whitehead, Terry Farrell, M Emmett Walsh, Adrienne Barbeau, Ned Beatty, Kurt Vonnegut Jr.

● Dangerfield trundles unstoppably through the movie like a benevolent steamroller. He's Thornton Melon, motormouth millionaire, who enrolls in college to watch over his downtrodden son. He has the money, he has the confidence but mostly he has the lines: no one else gets much of a look-in here. Unusual to find a campus comedy serving as an oh-if-only fantasy for the over-50s. Otherwise it's business as usual in this acceptable time-passer. BBa

Back to the Future

(1985, US, 116 min)
d Robert Zemeckis. *p* Bob Gale, Neil Canton. *sc* Robert Zemeckis, Bob Gale. *ph* Dean Cundey. *ed* Arthur Schmidt. *pd* Lawrence G Paull. *m* Alan Silvestri. *cast* Michael J Fox, Christopher Lloyd, Lea Thompson, Crispin Glover, Thomas F Wilson, Claudia Wells.

● Teenager Marty McFly's dad is a hideous wimp, his mother a dipso, so he befriends mad scientist Dr. Brown (Lloyd). In a DeLorean time machine they travel back to 1955, the year his parents met in high school. But at that age, mom rather fancies her offspring more than his prospective father. Zemeckis takes obvious pleasure in solving not just the technical but also the emotional problems of time travel: how to avoid incest, how to unite your parents in order that you will be born, how to return to the future when both the car and the professor have blown a fuse, and above all how to avoid tampering with history. If this all sounds schematic, it shouldn't: the movie has all the benign good nature of a Frank Capra. CPea

Back to the Future Part II

(1989, US, 108 min)
d Robert Zemeckis. *p* Bob Gale, Neil Canton. *sc* Bob Gale. *ph* Dean Cundey. *ed* Arthur Schmidt. *pd* Rick Carter. *m* Alan Silvestri. *cast* Michael J Fox, Christopher Lloyd, Lea Thompson, Thomas F Wilson, Harry Waters Jr, Charles Fleischer, Joe Flaherty, Elizabeth Shue.

● No sooner has Marty McFly (Fox) returned to 1985, than Doc Brown (Lloyd) turns up to whisk him and perfunctory romantic interest Jennifer (Shue) off to 2015, in order to prevent grown-up Marty's kids going to jail. Meanwhile, mean old man Biff Tannen (Wilson) picks up an almanac of sports results, borrows the DeLorean, and heads back to the '50s to make himself rich and turn Hill valley into hell on earth. With Bob Gale, Zemeckis has fashioned a script whose complex twists, ironies and paradoxes amply compensate for the somewhat juvenile nature of the action itself. Kids will love the wham-bang-wallop, but adults will probably be more concerned with trying to fathom exactly what is going on, how and why. It's impressive entertainment, and best of all, it never degenerates into Spielbergian sentimentality: you can laugh, be thrilled and think without feeling embarrassed. GA

Back to the Future Part III

(1989, US, 119 min)
d Robert Zemeckis. *p* Bob Gale, Neil Canton. *sc* Bob Gale. *ph* Dean Cundey. *ed* Arthur Schmidt. *ad* Rick Carter. *m* Alan Silvestri. *cast* Michael J Fox, Christopher Lloyd, Mary Steenburgen, Thomas F Wilson, Lea Thompson, Elisabeth Shue, Matt Clark, Richard Dysart.

● In this exuberant final instalment of the time-travelling trilogy, with Doc (Lloyd) happily settled in 1885, Marty (Fox) realises he must go back when he learns that Doc faces death at the hands of villainous Mad Dog Tannen (Wilson) in Hill Valley, a bustling gold rush town. Marty's arrival, coinciding with an Indian charge, involves an explosive fusion of history and modern technology, with damage to the DeLorean. As Doc and Marty hastily try to assemble transport home, there comes an even more complicated development: Doc falls for a schoolmarm (Steenburgen). The resulting movie is affectionate, innovative, and vaguely lunatic. With Marty's experience of the past filtered through a lifetime of watching Westerns on TV, he struts around as though he'd wandered onto the set of a Sergio Leone movie. Western conventions are gleefully challenged, and with the camera gliding and swooping over the action (though visual pyrotechnics never obscure the emotional core), Zemeckis and writer Bob Gale – insisting that this is the final outing – bring off an audacious marriage of genres to grand and enjoyable effect. CM

Bad and the Beautiful, The

(1952, US, 116 min, b/w)
d Vincente Minnelli. *p* John Houseman. *sc* Charles Schnee. *ph* Robert Surtees. *ed* Conrad A Nervig. *ad* Cedric Gibbons, Edward Carfagno. *m* David Raksin. *cast* Kirk Douglas, Lana Turner, Barry Sullivan, Dick Powell, Gloria Grahame, Walter Pidgeon, Gilbert Roland.

● Hollywood on Hollywood: the ambitions, the dreams, the successes, the heartbreaks, all much as you'd expect. But Minnelli brings a tougher eye to his story of a young producer's meteoric rise and fall than most directors would have done, and the copious references to actual people/ movies/events anchor the melodrama in a spirit not unlike that of *Sunset Boulevard*. It's constructed as a series of three long flashbacks: the careers of a writer, a star and a director, all 'made' by producer Kirk Douglas and all disowning him now that they've reached their pinnacles of success. Fascinating as a companion piece to *Two Weeks in Another Town*, which resumes the themes and some of the characters a decade later. TR

Bad Behaviour

(1993, GB, 100 min)
d Les Blair. *p* Sarah Curtis. *ph* Witold Stok. *ed* Martin Walsh. *ad* Jim Grant. *m* John Altman. *cast* Stephen Rea, Sinead Cusack, Philip Jackson, Claire Higgins, Phil Daniels, Saira Todd, Mary Jo Randle.

● Les Blair's improvised feature is the sort of film Mike Leigh might have made if he liked people. It shares the same pleasing regard for the textures of the everyday, but gone is the malign tendency towards futile caricature; instead, this Kentish Town slice-of-life chimes with affection for its characters as they shamble their way through middle-class mid-life crisis. Gerry (Rea) is a North London council planning officer wrestling with a local permanent site for travellers. His wife Ellie (Cusack) looks after the kids and does a part-time stint in a bookshop. He's from Belfast, she's from Dublin, and even at home their heads seem to be in different places, but a chance entanglement with a building-trade scam-merchant (Leigh regular Philip Jackson), the contrasting fortunes of Claire Higgins' insecure single mum, and an office romance-that-never-was has the effect of making them realise how close and interdependent they really are. TJ

Bad Blood

(1989, US, 103 min)
d/p Chuck Vincent. *sc* Craig Horrall. *ph* Larry Revene. *ed* James Davalos. *m* Joey Mennone. *cast* Gregory Patrick, Georgina Spelvin, Linda Blair, Troy Donahue, Carolyn Van Bellinghen, Christina Veronica.

● Study the following plot synopsis: strapping young thing Ted finds that his mummy isn't his real mother, that in fact he was stolen from his real mother by his real father, who then had his brains blown out by his real mother's real father. Got that? Good. Now when Ted goes to visit his real mom with his real wife, things start to get complicated, because mommy thinks her son is actually her deceased husband, thus making her her own son's wife. Problems arise from the fact that Ted already has a real wife (in the form of the magnificent Linda Blair), so mom has to stiff her daughter-in-law in order to become her own daughter-in-law, so that she can have sex with her dead husband. Now answer the following questions: 1) How much of a bad time did the movie's writer probably have during potty training? 2) How long will it be before the above plot is reproduced in either *Neighbours* or *Dallas?* 3) How can you explain sitting through this to your friends? MK

Bad Boy Bubby

(1993, Aust/It, 112 min)
d Rolf de Heer. *p* Rolf de Heer, Domenico Procacci, Giorgio Draskovic. *sc* Rolf de Heer. *ph* Ian Jones. *ed* Suresh Ayyar. *pd* Mark Abbott. *m* Graham Tardif. *cast* Nicholas Hope, Claire Benito, Ralph Cotterill, Carmel Johnson, Sid Brisbane, Natalie Carr, Norman Kaye.

● Rolf de Heer's film is pretty much a weirdo. It begins in the sordid flat which 35-year-old Bubby (Hope) shares with his corpulent, incestuously demanding mum; since she insists the outside world is poisoned by gas, the only creatures he knows are the cat he torments and the cockroaches he eats. Then his long-lost dad turns up: jealous that he's been usurped in his mother's affections, Bubby deals with the situation the only way he knows how and, with a mixture of fear and curiosity, leaves the slum. The following adventures are somewhat predictable; but at the same time the world into which the innocent hero is cast has a singular loneliness and desolation. The film's attitude to misfits is admirable, but it's hard not to feel slightly uneasy about the use of real handicapped people in the later scenes. That said, this proficient film is never less than intriguing. It may be muddled, but one can't deny its ambitions, or the integrity of Hope's performance. GA

Bad Boys

(1983, US, 123 min)
d Rick Rosenthal. *p* Robert H Solo. *sc* Richard Di Lello. *ph* Bruce Surtees, Donald Thorin. *ed* Antony Gibbs. *pd* J Michael Riva. *m* Bill Conti. *cast* Sean Penn, Reni Santoni, Jim Moody, Eric Gurry, Esai Morales, Ally Sheedy, Clancy Brown, Robert Lee Rush.

● For O'Brien (Penn) street life is preferable to listening to his mother entertaining men beyond the paper walls. During a bungled robbery O'Brien's speeding car kills the brother of another petty criminal who opens a private war by beating and raping O'Brien's girlfriend. Unemphatic about plot development, director Rosenthal prefers to develop our understanding of his characters and their living spaces, linking without undue insistence the cramped apartments and juvenile detention cells. In the one scene where O'Brien is seen in a bright light, in his girl's bedroom, he seems as pale and bewildered as a baby. Even the borstal staff are presented as compassionate but hopelessly weary. An oxygenated, thoughtful alternative to the usual run of gangs-in-the-slammer movies. DO

Bad Boys

(1995, US, 118 min)
d Michael Bay. *p* Don Simpson, Jerry Bruckheimer. *sc* Michael Barrie, Jim Mulholland, Doug Richardson, Thomas Pope. *ph* Howard Atherton. *ed* Christian Wagner. *pd* John Vallone. *m* Mark Mancina. *cast* Martin Lawrence, Will Smith, Téa Leoni, Tchéky Karyo, Theresa Randle.

● Marcus is married and steady, Mike a lone wolf. Then, for reasons too unreasonable to explain, Marcus has to pass himself off as fellow drug-buster Mike in order to babysit a sassy murder witness (Leoni) in the latter's bachelor pad, while Mike makes himself at home with his partner's partner. As long as it's taking pot shots at macho attitudes, there's plenty of comic play in this set-up, happily exploited by the snappy, charismatic pairing of Smith and Lawrence. Unfortunately, the movie is a couple of rewrites short of 'developed', and the thriller configurations are stale. TCh

Bad Company

(1972, US, 92 min)
d Robert Benton. *p* Stanley R Jaffe. *sc* David Newman, Robert Benton. *ph* Gordon Willis. *ed* Ralph Rosenblum. *pd* Paul Sylbert. *m* Harvey Schmidt. *cast* Jeff Bridges, Barry Brown, Jim Davis, David Huddleston, John Savage, Ed Lauter.

● Benton's first film, a Western good enough to make everything he has done since seem disappointing by comparison. Set in 1863, with Union troops scouring the countryside for reluctant recruits who scurry about dressed as girls, it offers Vietnam parallels for the asking, but is really more concerned with the old mythologies as the innocent young hero sets off in best Horatio Alger fashion to seek safety, fame and fortune out West. Wandering through a land of russet melancholy (superb camerawork by Gordon Willis), he and the ragtail gang of youths he falls in with find themselves light years away from the myth of the heroic West. A few inhabitants scratch a miserable existence on chicken farms. The gunfighters are sordid, petty crooks who hit and run. Everybody else seems to be coming or going, cursing the ill luck which brought them to this wilderness. And virtue, as the young man discovers to his cost, is the first thing to go west. Elegantly and engagingly funny, it is filmed with a loving care for period detail which gives the images the feel of animated tintypes. TM

Bad Company (Mabudachi)

(2001, Jap, 98 min)
d Tomoyuki Furumaya. *p* Takenori Sento. *sc* Tomoyuki Furumaya. *ph* Masami Inomoto. *ad* Fumiaki Suzaka. *m* Masamichi Shigeno. *cast* Yamato Okitsu, Ryosuke Takahashi, Yuta Nakajima, Ken Mitsuishi, Asako Yashiro, Mikio Shimizu.

●Eight years after *This Window Is Yours*, Furumaya returns with an extremely different follow-up: loosely structured and semi-improvised rather than hyper-controlled. His protagonists are teenage boys in a small town secondary school in 1980, under the thumb of a tyrannical teacher who divides humanity into a hierarchy (scum, delinquents and people) and consigns most of his class to the lowest category. Sadatomo and his friends are hauled up for shoplifting and told to write self-criticisms. Reflection sparks their rebellion and marks the point at which they begin to think and make real moral choices for themselves. Completely believable, the film's understated subtlety makes its political attack all the more powerful. TR

Bad Day at Black Rock

(1954, US, 81 min)
d John Sturges. *p* Dore Schary. *sc* Millard Kaufman. *ph* William C Mellor. *ed* Newell P Kimlin. *ad* Cedric Gibbons, Malcolm Brown. *m* André Previn. *cast* Spencer Tracy, Robert Ryan, Anne Francis, Dean Jagger, Walter Brennan, Ernest Borgnine, Lee Marvin.

●Occasionally flabby but generally impressive thriller in which one-armed war-veteran Tracy gets off a train to encounter a desert town full of aggressive types clearly hiding a secret (involving land-grabbing and murder: Hollywood's first acknowledgement of America's less than honourable treatment of its Japanese citizens during World War II). Nicely put together by Sturges, its suspense derives largely from the excellent performances and imaginative use of the 'Scope frame by cameraman William C Mellor. GA

Badge 373

(1973, US, 116 min)
d/p Howard W Koch. *sc* Pete Hamill. *ph* Arthur J Ornitz. *ed* John Woodcock. *ad* Philip Rosenberg. *m* JJ Jackson. *cast* Robert Duvall, Verna Bloom, Henry Darrow, Eddie Egan, Felipe Luciano, Tina Cristiana.

●An attempt to out-Dirty Harry that has none of the flair of Siegel's film. Ryan (Duvall), a mean Irish cop who spends his life battling against spics and spades, finds himself suspended for having pushed a guy off a roof when in fact he fell. He hands in his badge but fights on alone, finding a cesspool (the film's definition) of gun-running to Puerto Rico and demos plastered with 'Free Puerto Rico' banners. Koch both produced and directed this ham-fistedly unpleasant film.

Bad Girls

(1994, US, 99 min)
d Jonathan Kaplan. *p* Albert S Ruddy, André Morgan, Charles Finch. *sc* Becky Johnston, Yolande Turner, Ken Friedman. *ph* Ralf D Bode. *ed* Jane Kurson. *m* Jerry Goldsmith. *cast* Madeleine Stowe, Mary Stuart Masterson, Andie MacDowell, Drew Barrymore, James LeGros, Robert Loggia, Dermot Mulroney.

●This cowgirl opus may aspire to frontier feminism, but its stale stereotypes, hackneyed plotting and fashion-conscious sensibility is more in the tradition of Howard Hughes' campfire kitsch. Discriminated against by the law, four prostitutes flee for their lives. Cody (Stowe) is the leader, a tough, sharp-shooting 'honky-tonk harlot'; Eileen (MacDowell) a Southern gentle-woman by predilection, an outlaw by destiny; Anita (Masterson) an impoverished widow; and Lilly (Barrymore, the best of them) a hard-riding, hard-drinking tomboy. There's no depth here, and precious little surface. Things move at a fair gallop, but the last 45 minutes simply rehash kidnap scenarios with one character after another. TCh

Bad Guy (Nappun Namja)

(2001, SKor, 100 min)
d Kim Ki-Duk. *p* Lee Seung-Jae, Ahn Sang-Hoon. *sc* Kim Ki-Duk. *ph* Hwang Chol-Hyun. *ed* Ham Sung-Won. *ad* Kim Sun-Ju. *m* Park Ho-Jun. *cast* Cho Jae-Hyun, Seo Won, Kim Yoon-Tae, Choi Duk-Moon, Choi Yoon-Young.

●More sexual terrorism from the self-styled badboy outsider of Korean cinema – or is that Korean society? Mute thug Han-Ki (Kim's fave actor Cho) violently kisses middle-class college girl Sun-Wha (Seo) in a park – because she's trying to ignore him. Her punishment continues when he contrives to have her press-ganged into working as a hooker in the sleaziest red-light district the director can imagine. He watches her degradation through a two-way mirror, sometimes intervening to rescue her from abusive clients, until (surprise!) she falls in love with him. This neanderthal *amour fou* comes garnished with Freudian symbolism (some of it intentional), plenty of absurdly hyperbolic violence and the rough visual poetry that is Kim Ki-Duk's one intangible asset. TR

Bad Influence

(1990, US, 99 min)
d Curtis Hanson. *p* Steve Tisch. *sc* David Koepp. *ph* Robert Elswit. *ed* Bonnie Koehler. *ad* Ron Foreman. *cast* Rob Lowe, James Spader, Lisa Zane, Tony Maggio, Marcia Cross, Kathleen Wilhoite, Christian Clemenson.

●Michael Boll (Spader) is up against a rival at work, his fiancée is boring, and he suffers mysterious stomach ailments. So when he meets smoothie Alex (Lowe), a man-about-town of independent means, he's nipping out of his hi-tech flat and into hi-tech discos before you can say 'Faust'. Work improves, sex gets kinkier. Exhausted but satisfied, Michael accepts the fact that his new friend filmed him bonking, but knows things are going too far when he falls over a dead body in his apartment…This vacuous exploration of the perils of greed lacks the intelligence and perspective to work on a subversive level. Hanson indulges in extremely obvious symbolism, and despite attempts to convey Michael's inner conflict, the dangers remain resolutely external. 'I didn't make you do anything that wasn't in you already' says Alex to his protégé. Yawn. CM

Badlanders, The

(1958, US, 83 min)
d Delmer Daves. *p* Aaron Rosenberg. *sc* Richard Collins. *ph* John F Seitz. *ed* William H Webb. *ad* William A Horning, Daniel B Cathcart. *cast* Alan Ladd, Ernest Borgnine, Katy Jurado, Anthony Caruso, Claire Kelly, Nehemiah Persoff.

●Turn-of-the-century Nevada and ex-cons Ladd and Borgnine plan a major heist on a goldmine, but aren't sure whether they can trust each other enough to stick with the complex plan they've devised to reclaim the property that's rightfully theirs. A virtual remake of *The Asphalt Jungle*, it has CinemaScope and an amiable rough-house humour, but you'd certainly never prefer it to the Huston film. TJ

Badlands 100

(1974, US, 94 min)
d/p/sc Terrence Malick. *ph* Tak Fujimoto. *ed* Robert Estrin. *ad* Jack Fisk. *m* Carl Orff, George Aliceson Tipton. *cast* Martin Sheen, Sissy Spacek, Warren Oates, Ramon Bieri, Alan Vint, Gary Littlejohn.

●One of the most impressive directorial debuts ever. On the surface, it's merely another rural-gangster movie in the tradition of *Bonnie and Clyde*, with its young 'innocents' – a James Dean-lookalike garbage collector and his magazine-addict girlfriend – first killing her father when he objects to their relationship, then going on a seemingly gratuitous homicidal spree across the Dakota Badlands. But what distinguishes the film, beyond the superb performances of Sheen and Spacek, the use of music, and the luminous camerawork by Tak Fujimoto, is Malick's unusual attitude towards psychological motivation: the dialogue tells us one thing, the images another, and Spacek's beautifully artless narration, couched in terms borrowed from the mindless media mags she's forever reading, yet another. This complex perspective on an otherwise simple plot, developed even further in Malick's subsequent *Days of Heaven*, manages to reveal so much while making nothing explicit, and at the same time seems perfectly to evoke the world of '50s suburbia in which it is set. GA

Bad Lieutenant

(1992, US, 96 min)
d Abel Ferrara. *p* Edward R Pressman, Mary Kane. *sc* Zoe Lund, Abel Ferrara. *ph* Ken Kelsch. *ed* Anthony Redman. *pd* Charles Logola. *m* Joe Delia. *cast* Harvey Keitel, Victor Argo, Anthony Ruggiero, Robin Burrows, Frankie Thorn, Victoria Bastel, Zoe Lund.

●Keitel is the depraved and corrupt New York cop of the title. Hooked on crack, heroin and alcohol, he's up to his eyeballs in debt and staking his life on the Dodgers – and they're starting to lose. Perversely, the appalling rape of a nun proffers salvation: a $50,000 reward to find the perpetrator. The film isn't so much a thriller as a slice of (low-)life. The script is cut to the bone, the set-ups have a *vérité* feel, while the editing mimics real time in long, nearly unwatchable sequences in which Keitel shoots up, or masturbates before two teenage girls. Ferrara allows his star to dictate the pace, and is rewarded with a performance of extraordinary, terrifying honesty. This is an actor laying himself bare before the camera/confessor. Astonishingly, Ferrara ups the ante. Out of degradation, he pulls redemption. It is a jarring stroke, and will divide audiences who have stayed with the film this far. It seems to me that Ferrara is an artist of the profane; his Catholicism looks suspiciously like a Scorsese hand-me-down. In this exploitation/art movie, it may just be that the truth is in the sleaze. TCh

Bad Lord Byron, The

(1949, GB, 85 min, b/w)
d David Macdonald. *p* Aubrey Baring. *sc* Terence Young, Anthony Thorne. *ph* Stephen Dade ed James Needs. ad Maurice Carter. *m* Cedric Thorpe-Davie. *cast* Dennis Price, Mai Zetterling, Joan Greenwood, Linden Travers, Sonia Holm, Raymond Lovell.

●Not as bad as its reputation would suggest, since it is well acted and stylishly shot, but the script is undeniably silly. Starting with Byron (Price) dying in Greece, it cuts to a celestial trial at which the women in his life appear to give evidence, their stories being seen in flashback. The fatuous point is to determine whether Byron is a great poet and fighter for liberty or a bad, evil rake. Very basic stuff, historically inaccurate and not made any more convincing by the eventual revelation that the judge is Byron himself (though his lines have hitherto been delivered by someone else). TM

Bad Man's River (El Hombre del Rio Malo)

(1971, Sp/It/Fr, 90 min)
d Eugenio Martin. *p* Bernard Gordon. *sc* Philip Yordan, Eugenio Martin. *ph* Alejandro Ulloa. *ed* Irving Lerner. *ad* Julio Molina. *m* Waldo de Los Rios. *cast* Lee Van Cleef, James Mason, Gina Lollobrigida, Simon Andreu, Diana Lorys.

●It took Van Cleef so long to become a star that latterly it seemed he'd accept any project which would have his name at the top. This jokey, old-fashioned Western – where his outlaw is variously bamboozled by a widow on the make (Lollobrigida) and by a revolutionary (Mason) into agreeing to blow up the Mexican army arsenal – is so out of touch that you expect Stubby Kaye to appear and sing a song. it attempts to appear modish by freezing frames with annoying irrelevance. For undemanding six-year-olds.

Bad News Bears, The

(1976, US, 103 min)
d Michael Ritchie. *p* Stanley R Jaffe. *sc* Bill Lancaster. *ph* John A Alonzo. *ed* Richard A Harris. *pd* Polly Platt. *m* Jerry Fielding. *cast* Walter Matthau, Tatum O'Neal, Vic Morrow, Jackie Earle Haley, Alfred Lutter, Joyce Van Patten.
● Amiably engrossing satire on the 'win ethic' that offers a take-it-or-leave-it approach to its serious points about enforcing precociousness on kids, but consistently delights with its panoramic comic invention. Drunken slob Matthau (perfect) coaches an abysmally inept Little League baseball team that sniffs unaccustomed success when joined by street-smart girl pitcher O'Neal, and a windmill tilt at the championship ensues. Two sequels never came close to repeating its pleasures. PT

Bad News Bears in Breaking Training, The

(1977, US, 100 min)
d Michael Pressman. *p* Leonard Goldberg. *sc* Paul Brickman. *ph* Fred J Koenekamp. *ed* John W Wheeler. *ad* Steve Berger. *m* Craig Safan. *cast* William Devane, Clifton James, Jackie Earle Haley, Jimmy Baio, Chris Barnes, Alfred Lutter.
● Bad news indeed. A quite ghastly sequel to *The Bad News Bears* in which the subject's incipient sentimentality has been left to run riot, with all charm, humour and believability lost in the process. GB

Bad News Bears Go to Japan, The

(1978, US, 91 min)
d John Berry. *p* Michael Ritchie. *sc* Bill Lancaster. *ph* Gene Polito. *ed* Richard A Harris. *pd* Walter Scott Herndon. *m* Paul Chihara. *cast* Tony Curtis, Jackie Earle Hayley, Tomisaburo Wayakama, George Wyner, Lonny Chapman, Hatsune Ishihara.
● Third and last in the *Bad News* series, with Curtis as a Hollywood hustler trying to make a buck exploiting the sad sack little league baseballers, but suffering the obligatory change of heart. Dire. TM

Bad Seed, The

(1956, US, 128 min, b/w)
d/p Mervyn LeRoy. *sc* John Lee Mahin. *ph* Harold Rosson. *ed* Warren Low. *pd* John Beckman. *m* Alex North. *cast* Patty McCormack, Nancy Kelly, Henry Jones, Eileen Heckart, Evelyn Varden, William Hopper.
● 1956 was way too soon for an unfettered treatment of the central premise: an 8-year-old serial killer. On the other hand it was too late in Mervyn LeRoy's career for him still to command enough speed and style to overcome the staginess of it all (source: a creaky Broadway play by Maxwell Anderson).The ending, with McCormack and Kelly (monster and Mom respectively) coming on in propria personae to assure us they was only funnin', must be one of the most ignominious in movie history. BBa

Bad Sleep Well, The (Warui Yatsu Hodo Yoko Nemuru)

(1960, Jap, 151 min, b/w)
d Akira Kurosawa. *p* Tomoyuki Tanaka, Akira Kurosawa. *sc* Hideo Oguni, Akira Kurosawa, Shinobu Hashimoto, Ryuzo Kikushima, Eijiro Hisaito. *ph* Yuzuru Aizawa. *cast* Toshiro Mifune, Takeshi Kato, Masayuki Mori, Takashi Shimura, Kyoko Kagawa, Ko Nishimura.
● Kurosawa's first venture for his own short-lived production company, a revenge tragedy (employee of big housing corporation marries the boss' daughter while simultaneously seeking the truth of his father's 'suicide') which attempts to indict the corruptions that go hand-in-hand with big business, ultimately hinting that even the government cannot be said to have clean hands. Freed from immediate box-office pressures, Kurosawa rather loaded the film on the side of social significance, while neglecting to capitalise on the *noir* aspects that underlie it. Even so, his use of the 'scope screen is masterly, suggesting right from the opening sequence – a wedding at which the cake is a replica of the company offices, and the crippled bride has obviously had a groom bought from among daddy's employees – a boardroom table across which manipulations gradually unfold. Exported in a 135-minute version. TM

Bad Taste

(1987, NZ, 92 min)
d/p/sc/ph/ed Peter Jackson. *ad* Caroline Girdlestone. *m* Michelle Scullion. *cast* Terry Potter, Pete O'Herne, Craig Smith, Mike Minett, Peter Jackson, Doug Wren.
● When a small New Zealand town is overrun by man-eating space aliens, it's left to gawky Derek (Jackson) and the Alien Investigation Defence Service (spot the horrible pun) to deal with them. Within the opening five minutes, one such extraterrestrial has half his head blown off. Derek himself suffers the indignity of having a cat-flap incorporated into the back of his skull, whence fall large amounts of brain matter, some of it to be replaced with assorted bowel matter. Made over four years on an incredibly low budget, the film has its moments, though ironically most of the best jokes have nothing to do with the gore: some terrifically banal conversations pass between the members of the AIDS team, and there are a few fine sequences of Three Stooges-type slapstick. Things hot up in the last 20 minutes, when Peter Jackson stops chucking intestines around and gets some serious hardware under way – we're talking rocket launchers and big chainsaws, equipment essential to the success of any movie. Indeed, a climatic rebirth-by-chainsaw scene almost makes it all worthwhile, though you may have had to visit the bathroom once or twice in the wait. MK

Bad Timing

(1980, GB, 123 min)
d Nicolas Roeg. *p* Jeremy Thomas. *sc* Yale Udoff. *ph* Anthony B Richmond. *ed* Tony Lawson. *ad* David Brockhurst. *m* Richard Hartley. *cast* Art Garfunkel, Theresa Russell, Harvey Keitel, Denholm Elliott, Daniel Massey, Dana Gillespie.
● One of Roeg's most complex and elusive movies, building a thousand-piece jigsaw from its apparently simple story of a consuming passion between two Americans in Vienna. Seen in flashback through the prism of the girl's attempted suicide, their affair expands into a labyrinthine enquiry on memory and guilt as Theresa Russell's cold psychoanalyst lover (Garfunkel) himself falls victim to the cooler and crueller investigations of the detective assigned to her case (Keitel in visionary form as the policeman turned father-confessor). But where *Don't Look Now* sustained its Gothic intensity with human intimacy, this film seems a case-example of how more could have been achieved with less editing, less ingenuity, less even of the bravura intelligence with which Roeg at one point matches Freud with Stalin as guilt-ridden spymasters. CA/DMacp

Bagdad Café (aka Out of Rosenheim)

(1987, WGer, 91 min)
d/p Percy Adlon. *sc* Eleonore Adlon, Percy Adlon. *ph* Bernd Heinl. *ed* Norbert Herzner. *ad* Bernt Capra. *m* Bob Telson. *cast* Marianne Sägebrecht, CCH Pounder, Jack Palance, Christine Kauffman, Monica Calhoun, Darron Flagg, George Aquilar.
● A radiant, oddball comedy-drama about the relationship that develops between a fat Bavarian tourist (Sägebrecht), an irritable black truckstop owner (Pounder), and a weirdo artist (Palance, smiling and delightful, in bandana and snakeskin boots), set in the dusty Arizona desert land of lonesome motels beloved of Sam Shepard. Sägebrecht, her husband ditched along the way, arrives sweatily out of the yellow haze, absurdly decked out in buttoned-up suit, green felt hat and feather, high heels and suitcase; gradually she transforms, and is transformed by, the lives of a motley band of misfits who inhabit a dilapidated diner exotically named 'The Bagdad Café'. A wish-fulfilling fable about culture-clash and the melting-pot, it's also firmly grounded in telling and cinematically original observations. Adlon's method is at once intimate, quirky and affirmative: precise evocation of place, expressive colours, and a slow build-up of characters, allow him to raise the film effortlessly into realms of fantasy, shafted with magic and moments of epiphany. WH

Bag of Marbles, A

see Sac de Billes, Un

Baie des Anges, La (Bay of Angels)

(1962, Fr, 85 min, b/w)
d Jacques Demy. *p* Paul-Edmond Decharme. *sc* Jacques Demy. *ph* Jean Rabier. *ed* Anne-Marie Cotret. *ad* Bernard Evein. *m* Michel Legrand. *cast* Jeanne Moreau, Claude Mann, Paul Guers, Henri Nassiet.
● Demy's second feature has a ravishing Jeanne Moreau, ash-blonde for the occasion and dressed all in white, as a compulsive gambler who doesn't care what happens to her so long as she has a chip to start her on the roulette tables. Ostensibly the subject is gambling, but the real theme is seduction – with Moreau casting a spell on Mann that turns him every which way – and this is above all a visually seductive film. Shot mainly inside the casinos and on the sunstruck promenades of Nice and Monte Carlo, it is conceived as a dazzling symphony in black and white. Moreau's performance is magnificent, but it's really Jean Rabier's camera which turns the whole film into an expression of sheer joy – not only in life and love, but things. Iron bedsteads make arabesques against white walls; a little jeweller's shop becomes a paradise of strange ornamental clocks; a series of angled mirrors echo the heroine as she runs down a corridor into her lover's arms; roulette wheels spin to a triumphant musical accompaniment; and over it all hangs an aura of brilliant sunshine. TM

Baise-moi

(2000, Fr, 77 min)
d Virginie Despentes, Coralie Trinh Thi. *p* Philippe Godeau. *sc* Virginie Despentes, Coralie Trinh Thi. *ph* Benoît Chamaillard, Julien Pamart. *ed* Aïlo Auguste, Francine Lemaitre, Véronique Rosa. *ad* Irène Galitzine, Paul Fayard, Christophe Mureau, Claude Veyset. *m* Varou Jan. *cast* Karen Bach, Raffaëla Anderson, Delphine McCarty, Gabor Rassov.
● Even the opening credits are terrifying: a collar of metal spikes and the face of a woman, mid-fuck, leering and grinning at the camera. Come on if you think you're hard enough. Cut to confusion and the shit lives of two seemingly unconnected women. Each flips, one murdering her brother, the other her flatmate. Then, finally, a narrative takes hold. Leaving town, Nadine (Bach) and Manu (Anderson) meet for the first time and set off on a sex and killing spree. Despentes and Trinh Thi's blistering digital film, adapted from the former's novel, is less a rape/revenge movie than an expression of freefalling anger against everything in the world as it's currently configured. It's also as unpredictable as true anger, raging against cinema, too. Set to an aggressive score, sex is not only unsimulated, but dispenses with the artifice of moaning and groaning, which it later viciously satirised. And 'Where are the witty lines?' the protagonists taunt, indifferently. Visceral, fearless, rough around the edges and luridly beautiful, this fabulous two-fingers of a film bypasses the brain and kicks in the gut. SS

Baiser mortel du dragon, Le

see Kiss of the Dragon

Baisers Volés (Stolen Kisses)

(1968, Fr, 91 min)
d François Truffaut. *p* Marcel Berbert. *sc* François Truffaut, Claude de Givray, Bernard Revon. *ph* Denys Clerval. *ed* Agnès Guillemot. *ad* Claude Pignot. *m* Antoine Duhamel. *cast* Jean-Pierre Léaud, Delphine Seyrig, Claude Jade, Michel Lonsdale, Harry Max, André Falcon, Claire Duhamel.
● A persuasively charming comedy (the third instalment of the Antoine Doinel saga), in which Léaud wanders into a job as a private detective and falls hopelessly and idealistically in love with a client's wife. The film is comprised of several flawlessly observed episodes, and Paris has never looked so nice or its inhabitants so whimsically attractive. Dedicated to Henri Langlois, the head of the Paris Cinémathèque who was nearly sacked by De Gaulle, it was made at the

time of the political upheavals of 1968 in which Truffaut was directly involved. But the film itself betrays an amazing serenity in such troubled times, transforming the anxiety and pain into a sad lyricism. DP

Bait, The

see Appât, L'

Baker's Bread (Das Brot des Bäckers)

(1976, WGer, 122 min)
d Erwin Keusch. *p* Dieter Schönemann. *sc* Erwin Keusch, Karl Saurer. *ph* Dietrich Lohmann. *ed* Lilo Krüger. *ad* Peter Herrmann. *m* Condor. *cast* Günter Lamprecht, Bernd Tauber, Maria Lucca, Silvia Reize, Anita Lochner.

●A minor key, low-budget delight with an appropriate 'small is beautiful' theme: an elaborately naturalistic account of a young baker's progress through apprenticeship and adolescence. Laced with an almost documentary insistence on the precise art of 'real' bread-making, and with a Brechtian presentation of competitive capitalism, it makes surprisingly compelling cinema from such an unlikely subject. PT

Baker's Wife, The

see Femme du Boulanger, La

Bal, Le

(1982, Fr/It/Alg, 112 min)
d Ettore Scola. *p* Giorgio Silvagni. *sc* Jean-Claude Penchenat, Ruggero Maccari, Scarpelli, Ettore Scola. *ph* Ricardo Aronovich. *ed* Raimondo Crociani. *m* Vladimir Cosma. *cast* Le Troupe du Théâtre du Campagnol.

●Scola's wordless musical-dance extravaganza traces the life of a ballroom from 1936 to the present. While couples meet, steal kisses, and separate, events in the world outside are echoed in their mimetic rituals and groupings; for the film is clearly intended as a historical and political allegory. Instead of offering any insights into France's shifting character, it relies largely on the audience's smug recognition of supposedly 'significant' cultural symbols. Fatuous stuff, really, especially when several references are anachronistic. A strong cast struggles valiantly against Felliniesque stereotypes to convey the gaucheries of human coupling. But in a movie aiming for something more ambitious, that's simply not enough. GA

Balalaika

(1939, US, 102 min, b/w)
d Reinhold Schunzel. *p* Lawrence Weingarten. *sc* Jacques Deval, Leon Gordon, Charles Bennett. *ph* Joseph Ruttenberg, Karl Freund, *ed* George Boemler. *ad* Cedric Gibbons, Eddie Imazu. *songs* George Posford, Berbard Grun. *libretto* Eric Maschwitz. *m* Herbert Stothart. *cast* Nelson Eddy, Ilona Massey, Charles Ruggles, Frank Morgan, Lionel Atwill, C Aubrey Smith.

●Draggy MGM operetta, raising some involuntary horse laughs with its notion of the Russian revolution as Bolshevik wench falls for stout Cossack. Just as you're dozing off to sleep, the bovine Eddy launches into 'The Volga Boatman's Song'. TM

Balance, La

(1982, Fr, 102 min)
d Bob Swaim. *p* Georges Dancigers, Alexandre Mnouchkine. *sc* Bob Swaim. *ph* Bernard Zitzermann. *ed* Françoise Javet. *ad* Eric Moulard. *m* Roland Bocquet, Boris Bergman. *cast* Nathalie Baye, Philippe Léotard, Richard Berry, Christophe Malavoy, Jean-Paul Connart, Bernard Freyd, Maurice Ronet.

●The mean, cobbled streets of the Belleville quartier in Paris yield up another story of love, money and death, and all the requisite shootouts, car chases and lowlife infighting are delivered with great verve and pace: but what really distinguishes this excellent thriller is Swaim's strength on the emotional front. The flics set up a pimp (Léotard) to be a new informer ('balance') by leaning on the whore he very much loves (Baye); the loyalties become more and more crossed until betrayal is the only means to salvation. Léotard is superb as the crook with a heart of glass; Baye at last breaks out of her nun's habits and gives us a tart with the strength of ten; Berry is the sympatico cop. They order these things better in France. CPea

Balkanisateur (Balkanisater)

(1997, Greece/Bulg/Switz, 98 min)
d Sotiris Goritsas. *p* Dionyssis Samiotis. *sc* Sotiris Goritsas. *ph* Stamatis Giannoulis. *ed* Takis Koumoundouros. *m* Nikos Portokaloglou. *cast* Stelios Mainas, Giota Festa, Gerassimos Skiadaressis, Sabine Berg, Bernhard Bettermann, Snejana Petrova.

●Average road movie/adventure, with two strapped-for-cash Salonikans driving through Yugoslavia, Bulgaria and Switzerland on a currency scam, enriched by telling observation and uningratiating but engaging performances. Fotis is the footloose and fancy free womaniser, Stavros the married, more educated, sensible one. Notable scenes include a pick-up at a kitschy Sofia dance hall as, afterwards at the woman's flat, Stavros refuses to make love, perturbed by the grandmother's knitting and the peering kids outside; and a meal in Belgrade, where the two men are moved by the humanising hospitality of a group of diasporan Greeks. The film may have a conventional heart, but it tries hard to avoid easy targets. WH

Ball, The (Der Ball/De Bal)

(1999, Bel/Switz/Ger/Neth, 90 min)
d Dany Deprez. *p* Jean-Claude Van Rijckeghem, Benoît Dufrasne, Rudi Teichmann. *sc* Jean-Claude Van Rijckeghem. *ph* Piotr Kukla. *ed* Ludo Troch. *ad* Michel de Graaf. *m* Vincent D'Hont*cast* Ernest Löw, Michael Pas, Martje Ceulemans, Rijk De Gooyer, Jonas De Ro, Julian Schoenaerts, Hilde van Mieghem.

●A pleasant lighthearted children's film about a group of school kids and their fight to save their playground from demolition by the town mayor. A chance meeting with the obligatory old man in the woods proves advantageous to Sophia (and the rest of the neighbourhood) when he lets her borrow his 'magic' football for a few days. For a low key (and presumably low budget) film, the effects are surprisingly well mounted. DA

Ballad in Blue (aka Blues for Lovers)

(1964, GB, 88 min, b/w)
d Paul Henreid. *p* Herman Blaser. *sc* Burton Wohl. *ph* Ronnie Taylor. *ed* Raymond Poulton. *ad* Lionel Couch. *m* Stanley Black. *cast* Ray Charles, Mary Peach, Tom Bell, Dawn Addams, Piers Bishop, Betty McDowall.

●'You're always trying to get me discovered – as if I were some new Italian restaurant': Tom Bell's composer/nightclub pianist gets the one good line in this combination of concert movie and sentimental B picture. Charles doesn't play himself off-stage too convincingly, and a cloying story of how he helps a little blind boy into the arms of a Paris specialist ('Is there a chance, doctor?' etc) doesn't help. Admirers of the man's music – about thirty percent of the movie is concert footage – will find the in-between tedium tolerable, although director Henreid could hardly get a gig with *Top of the Pops* on the evidence here. GD

Ballad of a Soldier (Ballada o Soldate)

(1959, USSR, 89 min, b/w)
d Grigori Chukhrai. *sc* Valentin Yoshov, Grigori Chukhrai. *ph* Vladimir Nikolayev. *ed* M Timofeieva. *ad* B Nemechek. *m* Mikhail Ziv. *cast* Vladimir Ivashov, Zhanna Prokhorenko, Antonina Maximova, Nikolai Kryuchkov, Ievgeni Urbansky.

●This picaresque tale was a great classic of post-war Soviet Realism – but don't let that put you off. Ivashov makes a touching figure as the teenage WWII combatant who wins four days' leave as a reward for an act of courage against the Nazis, heads off home to repair his old mother's leaking roof, yet finds himself constantly waylaid on his journey by people who need his help. Chukhrai's film may come from the stylistically more conservative wing of the Russian cinema, but its careful detail and underlying emotional clout are never in doubt. TJ

Ballad of Cable Hogue, The

(1970, US, 121 min)
d/p Sam Peckinpah. *sc* John Crawford, Edmund Penney. *ph* Lucien Ballard. *ed* Frank Santillo. *ad* Leroy Coleman. *m* Jerry Goldsmith. *cast* Jason Robards, Stella Stevens, David Warner, Strother Martin, Slim Pickens, LQ Jones, Peter Whitney.

●A strange and fascinating Western from the man renowned for the blood baths of *The Wild Bunch* and *Straw Dogs*. In gentler vein than usual, he portrays the efforts of a prospector, robbed and left to die in the desert, to turn a waterhole into a personal oasis, and to take revenge on the men who betrayed him. Hogue is probably Peckinpah's most likeable hero, and the film benefits from Robards' wry performance, as well as from the unusual mixture of comedy, action, romance, nostalgic elegy, and even song. The tone is uneven, but it's a touching and original portrait of a man trying to go it alone in the world, with tragically ironic results. GA

Ballad of Gregorio Cortez, The (aka Gregorio Cortez)

(1982, US, 105 min)
d Robert M Young. *p* Moctesuma Esparza., Michael Hausman. *sc* Robert M Young, Victor Villasenor. *ph* Ray Villalobos. *ed* Arthur Coburn, John Bertucci. *m* Michael Lewis. *cast* Edward James Olmos, James Gammon, Tom Bower, Bruce McGill, Brion James, Alan Vint.

●Set at the turn of the century, this is based on a Mexican ballad about one of the most famous manhunts in Texas history. A young Mexican farmhand kills a sheriff in self-defence, and lights out for the border with the Texas Rangers in hot pursuit. From such tawdry incidents do heroic legends grow as news of the slaying speeds down the telegraph. The longer he evades capture, the more inflated becomes the myth, and the more ironic the backlash that finally descends on the hapless, determinedly non-heroic Cortez. Beautifully shot and directed with great understatement, the result is a film of considerable poignancy and compassion. JP

Ballad of Joe Hill, The

see Joe Hill

Ballad of Josie, The

(1967, US, 102 min)
d Andrew V McLaglen. *p* Norman Macdonnell. *sc* Harold Swanton. *ph* Milton Krasner. *ed* Otho Lovering, Fred A Chulack. *ad* Alexander Golitzen, Addison Hehr. *m* Frank De Vol. *cast* Doris Day, Peter Graves, George Kennedy, Andy Devine, William Talman, Audrey Christie.

●Doris Day leads the fight for women's rights on the prairie, doing a kind of Lysistrata act to end a range war in turn-of-the-century Wyoming. A comedy Western with ideas, but lumberingly scripted and even more laboriously directed. TM

Ballad of Little Jo, The

(1993, US, 121 min)
d Maggie Greenwald. *p* Fred Berner, Brenda Goodman. *sc* Maggie Greenwald. *ph* Declan Quinn. *ed* Keith L Reamer. *pd* Mark Friedberg. *m* David Mansfield. *cast* Suzy Amis, Bo Hopkins, Ian McKellen, David Chung, Carrie Snodgress, Sam Robards, Beau Bridges.

●Maggie Greenwald's third film is inspired by the true story of a woman who in 1866 passed herself off as a man to survive the masculine brutishness of the American frontier. Expelled from her well-to-do New York home, for a pre-marital affair, Josephine Monaghan (Amis) heads West, and, taking refuge in trousers, cutting her hair and scarring her face, becomes 'Little Jo'. This is relatively unexplored terrain, and the film gets much mileage and fun out of the sex-role reversal, especially upon the arrival of Jo's lover and servant, the long-haired Tinman Wong (Chung), who sews and bakes apple pie. The mud and desperation of the frontier is vividly rendered, but the film is marred by a lack of emotional drama. JBa

Ballad of Narayama, The (Narayama Bushi-ko)

(1983, Jap, 130 min)
d Shohei Imamura. *p* Jiro Tomoda, Goro Kusakabe. *sc* Shohei Imamura. *ph* Masao Tochizawa. *ed* Hajime Okayasu. *ad* Toshio Inagaki. *m* Shinichiro Ikebe. *cast* Ken Ogata, Sumiko Sakamoto, Tonpei Hidari, Takejo Aki, Shoichi Ozawa.

●A remote village in the foothills of a great mountain, sometime in the past. A widow is approaching her 70th birthday – the age at which village law says she must go up to the mountain to die. She faces this prospect with surprising equanimity, but there are some things she wants to take care of first: to find a good new wife for her widowed eldest son, to help her runtish second son get laid for the first and only time in his life, to take her brattish eldest grandson down several pegs. The process whereby she sets about these tasks, while preparing herself serenely for her own death, amounts to a story of her personal fulfilment the like of which the cinema has rarely seen. Her society is one that is in most ways the antithesis of our own. Imamura realises this vision with shocking humour and immediacy, and then challenges us to say whether this fictitious community is more or less humane than ours. Awe-inspiring. TR

Ballad of Ramblin' Jack, The

(2000, US, 112 min)
d Aiyana Elliott. *p* Aiyana Elliott, Paul S Mezey, Dan Partland. *sc* Rick Dahl, Aiyana Elliott. *ph* Aiyana Elliott. *ed* David Baum, Susan Littenberg. *with* Jack Elliott, Arlo Guthrie, Kris Kristofferson, Alan Lomax, Odetta, DA Pennebaker, Pete Seeger, June Shelley, Dave Van Ronk.
●His obituaries will explain that Jack Elliott was the missing link between his mentor Woody Guthrie and Bob Dylan, but this poignant film by his daughter reveals a much more complex man. A Jewish doctor's boy from Brooklyn, Elliott was a cowboy in his head, and ran off to join the rodeo at fifteen. His parents circulated Missing posters advising 'Probable destination: ranch,' while the cowboys told him 'It ain't where you're from, but where you're going which counts'. He took up the guitar and started flat-picking, but it wasn't until he came across Guthrie that he really found himself. This rootless roots musician could have been one of the greats, but as pretty much every witness (Arlo Guthrie, Kristofferson, Pete Seeger) and his four wives can testify, Ramblin' Jack was always too irresponsible to build a career. He approached gigs sideways, tuning and talking as much as singing – they don't call him 'ramblin' for his travellin''. Much as he talks though, it seems he never had a heart to heart with Aiyana, a hole which fills a mite too much of this sad but loving portrait of a self-made authentic. TCh

Ballad of the Sad Café, The

(1991, US, 101 min)
d Simon Callow. *p* Ismail Merchant. *sc* Michael Hirst. *ph* Walter Lassally. *ed* Andrew Marcus. *ad* Bruno Santini. *m* Richard Robbins. *cast* Vanessa Redgrave, Keith Carradine, Cork Hubbert, Rod Steiger, Austin Pendleton, Beth Dixon.
●Callow makes his debut as a director with enormously difficult material: a strange and fantastical novella, written by the young Carson McCullers, about a barren, hayseed Georgia community. The tone is always a grainy Southern realism teetering on the edge of lunacy; and, given that the central characters are a giantess, a dwarf, and a redneck recidivist who makes the town's meat go bad, one can see the problem. Like Sartre's *Huis Clos*, this is a story of triple-unrequited passion in which fairytale and myth come to the fore, partly because (even as played by the superb Redgrave and Carradine) the main combatants are hardly made of the usual sympathetic stuff that passionate sagas need. Instead, Callow has cleverly created a company style that can encompass everyone from stand-up comedian Hubbert as the perky dwarf, Steiger as the local preacher, and Carradine, the ultimate rangy screen professional, as badman Marvin Macy. But despite traces of the English accent, it's Ms Redgrave who steals the show; the finale in which she and Carradine engage in a bloody fist-fight makes Liam Neeson's bit of bother in *The Big Man* look like handbags at dawn. SGr

Ballet Black

(1986, GB, 83 min)
d/p/sc/ph/ed Stephen Dwoskin. *ad* Bernard Trude. *m* Schaun Tozer, Leonard Salzedo. *with* Ben Johnson, Astley Harvey, Pamela Johnson, Johny Lagey, Pearl Johnson, Richie Riley, Leonard Salzedo.
●Though now nothing but historic footnote, Ballets Nègres was Europe's first all-black dance ensemble, which had its debut in London in April 1946, and its final performances in 1952. During those six years, Ballets Nègres opened doors and broke down barriers with its vibrant celebrations of Caribbean cultures. This film attempts to assemble all the scanty available documentation on the company. Lengthy sequences are jigged together from still photographs, or feature contemporary dancers trying to reconstruct one of the company's major creations. As director/writer/photographer/editor, Dwoskin should have made more choices. Had he selectively edited down his footage, the result would have been twice as compelling. As it stands, *Ballet Black* moves at a creeping, magisterial pace. Reverent, much too reverent. AR

Ball of Fire

(1941, US, 112 min, b/w)
d Howard Hawks. *p* Samuel Goldwyn. *sc* Charles Brackett, Billy Wilder. *ph* Gregg Toland. *ed* Daniel Mandell. *ad* Perry Ferguson. *m* Alfred Newman. *cast* Gary Cooper, Barbara Stanwyck, Oscar Homolka, Henry Travers, Tully Marshall, Richard Haydn, SZ Sakall.
●Marvellous performance from Stanwyck, all snap, crackle and pop as the brassy nightclub entertainer Sugarpuss O'Shea who seeks refuge with seven crusty old professors (plus Cooper) to escape unwelcome attentions from a gangster, and whose vocabulary (not to mention charms) excite delighted wonderment in the professors since they have just reached 'Slang' in the encyclopaedia they are compiling. Rather surprisingly, Hawks slightly muffs the sequence in which the gangster and his aides get their comeuppance; otherwise his handling of the sparkling Brackett-Wilder script and its subversions of *Snow White and the Seven Dwarfs* is pure joy. TM

Ballon d'Or, Le (The Golden Ball)

(1993, Guinea/Fr, 100 min)
d Cheik Doukouré. *p* Monique Annaud. *sc* Cheik Doukouré, David Carayon. *ph* Alain Choquart. *ed* Michèle Robert-Lauhac. *ad* Yan Arlaud. *m* Loy Erlich. *cast* Aboubacar Sidiki Soumah, Agnès Soral, Habib Hammoud, Salif Keita, Amara Camara.
●This deceptively light comedy-drama follows the unsentimental education of village boy Bandian (fresh-faced Sumah), a diminutive teenager mad-keen on football and hopeful of great things in the euphoric atmosphere of Cameroon's unprecedented challenge in the 1990 World Cup. Doukouré traces the condition of the boy's life in scenes that lose no power through their low-key integration into the narrative. Bandian's mother languishes ill for lack of care, and he is forced to rely on the Médecins sans Frontières centre run by doctor Isabelle (Soral); nor are the boy's skills helped by having to play with what look like coconut shells. As Bandian moves to the big city and comes under the sway of both businessman Béchir, and football manager Karim (Malian soccer star Keita), who wants to nurture Bandian's talents for the good of African football, the metaphorical resonances threaten to drown out the drama, but the gusto and vitality of the playing, the vibrancy of the photography and the sympathy of the direction pull it through. WH

Balthazar

see Au Hasard, Balthazar

Baltimore Bullet, The

(1980, US, 103 min)
d Robert Ellis Miller. *p* John Brascia. *sc* John Brascia, Robert Vincent O'Neil. *ph* James Crabe. *ed* Jerry Brady. *pd* Herman A Blumenthal. *m* Johnny Mandel. *cast* James Coburn, Omar Sharif, Ronee Blakley, Bruce Boxleitner, Jack O'Halloran, Calvin Lockhart, Michael Lerner.
●Pool-hustling saga which borrows its basic situation from *The Hustler*, much of its detail (including a New Orleans jazz funeral) from The *Cincinnati Kid*, and never comes within striking distance of either film. It's passable enough thanks to Coburn and Sharif (both grinning as toothily as Burt Lancaster), but meanders aimlessly through some lamentable direction and a silly gangster subplot. TM

Balto

(1995, US/GB, 77 min)
d Simon Wells. *p* Steven Hickner. *sc* David Steven Cohen, Roger SH Schulman. *ph* Jan Richter Friis. *ed* Nick Fletcher. *pd* Hans Bacher. *m* James Horner. *cast* Miriam Margolyes, Lola Bates-Campbell; voices: Kevin Bacon, Bob Hoskins, Bridget Fonda, Phil Collins, Jim Cummings, Donald Sinden.
●The true story of a 1925 sled team's 'serum run' across Alaska, and its husky hero Balto. Whereas Disney would have pillaged the facts for its own exacting purposes, the makers of this half-hearted animated feature let the story ramble on with a minimum of second-hand plotting and characterisation. Balto being the archetypal dog-from-the-wrong-side-of-the-tracks, when diphtheria strikes Nome, his services aren't required for the team that must fetch the life-saving anti-toxin. Injustice is compounded by the team being led by the pure-breed Steele, vain, scheming, town favourite and Balto's rival for the beautiful Jenna. The one notable spin on the story is that Balto's half-wolf. As you'd expect, we start with the old boy having internalised prejudices about his lack of pedigree; only when he's stuck down a canyon does he realise the advantages of his make-up. Mismatched TV-standard animation styles (plus some one-dimensional live action inserts); a Hoskins-voiced Russian émigré goose (fun); and a pair of comic-relief polar bears (Collins-voiced, and not fun). Probably insufficient for any but the least demanding kids. NB

Balzac and the Little Chinese Seamstress (Balzac et la petite tailleuse chinoise)

(2002, Fr/China, 116 min)
d Dai Sijie. *sc* Dai Sijie, Nadine Perront. *ph* Jean Marie Dreujou. *ed* Julia Gregory, Luc Barnier. *ad* Cao Jumping. *m* Wang Pujian. *cast* Ziiou Xun, Chen Kun, Liu Ye, Wang Shuangbao, Chung Zhijun, Wang Hongwei, Xiao Xiong.
●A touching, sensitive, lyrical tale of 'reactionary' teenage students banished to a remote but exotically beautiful village during the Cultural Revolution, Dai's film of his own semi-autobiographical bestselling novel plods from cliché to worthy cliché as if films like *King of the Children* had never been made. It's a tale (naturally) of undying friendship, of love (the lads fall for the local tailor's granddaughter, uneducated but sure to blossom thanks to their attention), of art (Western music and literature, especially) overcoming poverty, politics and prejudice, and of bittersweet memories of hard, character-forming times. Not unwatchable, but bereft of anything fresh to say, the film displays the influence of its French funding at every turn. GA

Balzac et la petite tailleuse chinoise

see Balzac and the Little Chinese Seamstress

Bamba, La

(1986, US, 108 min)
d Luis Valdez. *p* Taylor Hackford, Bill Borden. *sc* Luis Valdez. *ph* Adam Greenberg. *ed* Sheldon Kahn, Don Brochu. *pd* Vince Cresciman. *m* Carlos Santana, Miles Goodman. *cast* Lou Diamond Phillips, Esai Morales, Rosana De Soto, Danielle von Zerneck, Elizabeth Peña, Joe Pantoliano.
●An enjoyable if slightly innocuous biopic based on the brief life and short-lived fame of teen rock'n'roll idol Richie Valens ('La Bamba'). You know the kind of thing: poor but talented kid, spotted playing in local band by LA record producer, enjoys all too brief a spell of fame before dying tragically young. Plus the usual background stuff: hard-pressed but cheerful mother struggling to make ends meet, no-good brother always in trouble, girlfriend's father objecting to her dating a kid who sings 'jungle music'. The musical side of things is handled surprisingly well. Fresh-faced Phillips mimes convincingly to Los Lobos' admirably faithful cover versions of the songs, and there's a show-stealing rendition of Jackie Wilson's 'Lonely Teardrops' by Howard Huntsberry. NF

Bambi

(1942, US, 70 min)
d David Hand. *p* Walt Disney. *sc* Larry Morey. *ph* Chuck Wheeler. *ad* Robert Cormack. *m* Edward Plumb, Frank Churchill.

cast voices: Donnie Dunagan, Peter Behn, Bobby Stewart, Hardy Albright, John Sutherland, Paula Winslowe.
●From Disney's richest period, interleaving splendid animation with vulgar Americana. Babycham images occupy only a fraction of the running time in this tale of the adventures of a fawn; the rest is a strikingly impressionistic version of life in the forest and the meadow. Silhouette, panorama, and the cod use of classical music recall the best moments of *Fantasia*, while the animals are all given irresistible human traits: Bambi, Flower the skunk, and Thumper the rabbit ('Watchya doin' hibernatin'?') are like members of one of Mickey Rooney's gangs. AN

Bamboo Gods and Iron Men

(1973, Phil/US, 96 min)
d Cesar Gallardo. *p* Cirio H Santiago. *sc* Ken Metcalfe, Joseph Zucchero. *ph* Felipe Sacdalan. *ed* Gervacio Santos. *ad* Ben Otico. *m* Tito Sotto. *cast* James Iglehart, Shirley Washington, Chiquito, Marissa Delgado, Ken Metcalfe, Eddie Garcia.
●Uninspiring if innocuous offshoot of the kung-fu genre, made in the Philippines. The story revolves around some hokum about a false-bottomed Buddha in which is concealed the secret of the centuries – how to dominate the world. Supposedly novel twists are wrung on the situation by making the tourist couple who are drawn into the bizarre situation rich, young and black (genial performances, incidentally, from Iglehart and Washington). The humour is misjudged, and if the Philippine locations bring a little freshness to the film, it remains one of those efforts an audience watches in disbelief. VG

Bamboozled

(2000, US, 136 min)
d Spike Lee. *p* Jon Kilik, Spike Lee. *sc* Spike Lee. *ph* Ellen Kuras. *ed* Sam Pollard. *pd* Victor Kempster. *m* Terence Blanchard. *cast* Damon Wayans, Savion Glover, Jada Pinkett-Smith, Tommy Davidson, Michael Rapaport, Thomas Jefferson Byrd.
●Lee's satire on American TV is an intriguing failure. Its story, about the mounting of a TV revival of a blackface minstrel show, certainly has comic potential, and Lee has created a considerable figure of fun in the isolated, central figure of Pierre Delacroix (Wayans), the one black executive writer of the CNS network. Set against the venality and shallowness of his ratings hungry boss Dunwitty (Rapaport), Delacroix gains our sympathy. But, Lee also marks him as a sad dupe in sharply funny scenes where homeless tap dancer Mantan (Glover) and his buddy Womack (Davidson) are bamboozled by Delacroix and Dunwitty into playing frontmen to stereotypical 'hill-niggers' and 'Alabama porch monkeys' for the pilot. It's hard to know how to take him. The pilot of course is a hit, but success breeds failure: conflict for Mantan and Womack, deep confusion for Delacroix, the threatening attention of activists – and a loss of focus by the director. WH

Banana Ridge

(1941, GB, 88 min, b/w)
d/p Walter C Mycroft. *sc* Lesley Storm, Walter C Mycroft, Ben Travers. *ph* Claude Friese-Greene. *ed* Flora Newton. *ad* Charles Gilbert. *cast* Robertson Hare, Alfred Drayton, Isabel Jeans, Gordon McLeod, Patrick Kinsella, Nova Pilbeam.
●Veteran farceur Ben Travers had a hand in adapting his own play, set on a Malaysian rubber plantation, in which returning adventuress Isabel Jeans claims that either haughty Hare or self-regarding Drayton is actually the father of her twenty-something son. Ructions ensue, but decidedly creaky ructions. TJ

Bananas

(1971, US, 81 min)
d Woody Allen. *p* Jack Grossberg. *sc* Woody Allen, Mickey Ross. *ph* Andrew M Costikyan. *ed* Ron Kalish. *pd* Ed Wittstein. *m* Marvin Hamlisch. *cast* Woody Allen, Louise Lasser, Carlos Montalban, Jacobo Morales, Rene Enriquez, Natividad Abascal, Sylvester Stallone.
●Allen's second feature, a tribute to the Marx Brothers' *Duck Soup*, is a wonderfully incoherent series of one-liners centred around a puny New York Jew's unwitting and unwilling involvement in a South American revolution. The revolutionary party's new policies are an absurd comment on the corruption of power, especially when everyone is informed that the official, non-decadent language of the country will be Swedish. GA

Banco en el parque, Un

see Bench in the Park, A

Bande à part (The Outsiders/ Band of Outsiders)

(1964, Fr, 95 min, b/w)
d Jean-Luc Godard. *p* Philippe Dussart. *sc* Jean-Luc Godard. *ph* Raoul Coutard. *ed* Agnès Guillemot. *m* Michel Legrand. *cast* Anna Karina, Claude Brasseur, Sami Frey, Louisa Colpeyn, Chantal Darget, Ernest Menzer.
●Godard at his most off-the-cuff takes a '*Série Noire*' thriller (*Fool's Gold* by Dolores Hitchens) and spins a fast and loose tale that continues his love affairs with Hollywood and with actress Anna Karina. Karina at her most naive is taken up by two self-conscious toughs ('The little suburban couins of Belmondo in *A Bout de Souffle*', is how Godard described them), and they try to learn English, do extravagant mimes of the death of Billy the Kid, execute some neat dance steps, run around the Louvre at high speed, and rob Karina's aunt with disastrous consequences. One of Godard's most open and enjoyable films. CPe

Bande du Drugstore, La

see Dandy

Bandido!

(1956, US, 92 min)
d Richard Fleischer. *p* Robert L Jacks. *sc* Earl Felton. *ph* Ernest Laszlo. *ed* Robert Golden. *ad* John Martin Smith. *m* Max Steiner. *cast* Robert Mitchum, Gilbert Roland, Zachary Scott, Ursula Thiess, Rodolfo Acosta, Henry Brandon, Rodolfo Acosta.
●Routine plot about the Yankee soldier of fortune playing both sides as he does a spot of gun-running in revolutionary Mexico, but ending up with his heart in the right place. But the direction and performances (Mitchum and Roland especially) are excellent. TM

Bandit, The (Eskiya)

(1996, Tur, 121 min)
d Yavuz Turgul. *p* Mine Vargi. *sc* Yavuz Turgul. *ph* Ugar Ichak. *ed* Hakan Akol. *cast* Sener Sen, Sermin Sen, Ugur Yücel, Yesim Salkim, Kamuran Usluer.
●This leisurely action film spreads its tale of honour, corruption, solidarity and betrayal over a broad canvas. Sener Sen's ancient bandit, sole survivor of his gang after 35 years in jail, returns to a land that no longer remembers his legendary exploits. Back in the hill country, he finds his hunting grounds under a reservoir and his community vanished. He returns to Istanbul to seek out past accomplices – specifically best pal Mahmud, who, he learns, betrayed him all those years ago to win Keje (Sermin Sen), love of both their lives. The director mirrors the bandit's temporal and emotional displacement in his ironic uprooting of old genre codes, playfully transposing elements of mythic and American cinema into Turkey's contemporary urban reality. He films modern Istanbul like the location for a Western, and takes time out for wry and discursive asides. Warm, accessible and socially engaged. NB

Bandit of Sherwood Forest, The

(1946, US, 87 min)
d George Sherman, Henry Levin. *p* Leonard S Picker, Clifford Sanforth. *sc* Wilfred H Pettitt, Melvin Levy. *ph* Tony Gaudio, William Snyder. *ed* Richard Fanti. *pd* Stephen Goosson, Rudolph Sternard. *m* Hugo Friedhofer. *cast* Cornel Wilde, Anita Louise, Jill Esmond, Edgar Buchanan, Henry Daniell, George Macready.
●Very creditable swashbucklery with Wilde, a fencer of Olympic standard, looking much more at home as Robin Hood Junior than as Frederic ('You must stop this polonaise jangle') Chopin in *A Song to Remember*. If the dialogue is imbecilic, the villainy is splendid and Tony Gaudio's Technicolor camerawork very lush. TM

Bandit Queen

(1994, Ind/GB, 121 min)
d Shekhar Kapur. *p* Sundeep Singh Bedi. *sc* Mala Sen. *ph* Ashok Mehta. *ed* Renu Saluja. *pd* Eve Mavrakis. *m* Nusrat Fateh Ali Khan. *cast* Seema Biswas, Nirmal Pandey, Manjoj Bajpai, Rajesh Vivek, Raghuvir Yadav, Govind Namdeo, Saurabh Yadav.
●A low-caste woman who fought back, Phoolan Devi became a social outcast from her village in Uttar Pradesh when she refused to submit quietly to rape, and a folk hero when she led a group of bandits in a series of bloody raids against the higher-caste Thakurs, climaxing in the notorious Behmai massacre. This as recently as 1983 – when she finally surrendered to the authorities on her own terms. Harrowingly graphic in its treatment of violence, the film fell foul of the Indian censors and of Devi herself, but Western audiences are likely to be impressed by how director Shekhar Kapur neither sensationalises nor sermonises. The focus is squarely on Phoolan – played with blistering intensity by Seema Biswas – but Kapur doesn't glorify her, or her increasingly traumatic acts of vengeance. Instead, there's a searing anger running through the film, at the oppression of women and at the caste-system which keeps everyone in place. TCh

Bandits

(2001, US, 123 min)
d Barry Levinson. *p* Michael Birnbaum, Michele Berk, Barry Levinson, Paula Weinstein, Ashok Amritraj, David Hoberman, Arnold Rifkin. *sc* Harley Peyton. *ph* Dante Spinotti. *ed* Stu Linder. *pd* Victor Kempster. *m* Christopher Young. *cast* Bruce Willis, Billy Bob Thornton, Cate Blanchett, Troy Garity, Brian F O'Byrne, Stacey Travis, Bobby Slayton, January Jones.
●Despite a plot as old as the hills and a title that pitches for outlaw nostalgia, this is a reasonable hybrid, a character-led comic ramble along the highways and byways of genre – buddy pic, heist film, romance and road movie. Add light media satire and, with Levinson's emphasis on performance and dialogue, you have a higher-end studio project, albeit overlong and uneven, with a residue of indie spirit. It opens kinetically enough as Joe Blake (Willis), a hardman with a penchant for perusing Zen texts, breaks out of jail on a cement lorry with neurotic fellow con Terry Collins (Thornton). The two soon earn the moniker of 'the sleepover bandits' for their relaxed kidnappings of bank managers the night before a job. Along the road they pick up Kate Wheeler (Blanchett) and there ensues the inevitable falling in and out of love and trouble. This kind of picture would be dead in the saddle, if it weren't for enjoyable playing and some sprightly lines here. GE

Band of the Hand

(1986, US, 110 min)
d Paul Michael Glaser. *p* Michael Rauch. *sc* Leo Garen, Jack Baran. *ph* Raynaldo Villalobos. *ed* Jack Hofstra. *pd* Gregory Bolton. *m* Michael Rubini. *cast* Stephen Lang, Michael Carmine, Lauren Holly, John Cameron Mitchell, Daniel Quinn, Leon Robinson, Al Shannon.
●The story of a group of Miami Vice Guys turned Miami Nice Guys (sort of). Five uncontrollable teenage delinquents are dumped in the heart of the Florida Everglades where they meet Joe Tiger, a 'Nam vet turned social worker who's traded in his greens for the black Japanese designer equivalent. Joe doesn't say much, but from his allegorical one-liners we understand that he has wisdom of a profound nature to impart. The boys' education starts in the jungle, where they learn to survive or die, and ends in the urban jungle where they apply new-found self-esteem and Joe's terrorist techniques to a vigilante crusade against the entire Miami gangland. Crudely directed by Glaser, crassly acted and irresponsibly anarchistic. EP

Bandolero!

(1968, US, 106 min)
d Andrew V McLaglen. *p* Robert L Jacks. *sc* James Lee Barrett. *ph* William H Clothier. *ed* Folmer Blangsted. *ad* Jack Martin Smith, Alfred Sweeney. *m* Jerry Goldsmith. *cast* James Stewart, Dean Martin, Raquel Welch, George Kennedy, Andrew Prine, Will Geer, Clint Ritchie, Denver Pyle.

●An affably unpretentious Western, particularly attractive in its lazily offbeat opening as Stewart arrives in town to find the flophouse full because of an impending hanging, meets the hangman while luxuriating in the open-air bathhouse, waylays him for a lugubrious lecture on the secrets of the trade, and returns in the hangman's top hat and frock coat to compliment the sheriff (Kennedy) on the magnificence of his five-man gallows. Calmly staging a last-minute rescue of the condemned gang headed by his brother (Martin), he equally calmly robs the bank they failed to breach before, with the sheriff now safely in pursuit of his vanishing prisoners. A spirited chase of course ensues, with Raquel Welch as hostage, a troublesome faction in the gang, and hordes of bloodthirsty bandoleros in wait across the Mexican border. Script and direction both flag latterly, but the admirable cast keeps things going. TM

Band Waggon

(1939, GB, 80 min, b/w)
d Marcel Varnel. *p* Edward Black. *sc* John Watt, Harry Pepper, Gordon Crier, Vernon Harris, JOC Orton, Val Guest, Marriott Edgar, Bob Edmunds. *ph* Arthur Crabtree. *ed* RE Dearing, Alfred Roome. *ad* Vetchinsky. *songs* Noel Gay, Harry Parr-Davis, Kenneth Blane. *cast* Arthur Askey, Richard Murdoch, Pat Kirkwood, Moore Marriott, Peter Gawthorne, Jack Hylton, Donald Calthrop, Michael Hordern.
●'Big-Hearted' Arthur Askey, Richard 'Stinker' Murdoch and Lewis the goat live happily on the roof of the BBC: this was the premise of the 'Band Waggon' radio show, though the format was expanded for the cinema to take in a haunted castle, spies, etc. This mouldy bit of (just) pre-war England, with its jokes about long-forgotten gardening correspondents, at least mirrors the European situation by its confusion over whether the heavies are Russian or German. Askey's stridency and the way he keeps sticking out his bum by way of a funny walk will irritate all who don't keep bound copies of the *Dandy*, *Beano* and *Radio Fun*. BBa

Band Wagon, The

(1953, US, 111 min)
d Vincente Minnelli. *p* Arthur Freed. *sc* Betty Comden, Adolph Green. *ph* Harry Jackson. *ed* Albert Akst. *ad* Cedric Gibbons, Preston Ames. *songs* Howard Dietz, Arthur Schwartz. *cast* Fred Astaire, Jack Buchanan, Cyd Charisse, Oscar Levant, Nanette Fabray.
●One of Minnelli's best musicals, with an ingenious book which has Buchanan as a highbrow producer trying to turn Astaire's comeback show into an art house 'Faust', while Astaire and Charisse are meantime resolving the problem of whether their dancing styles can meld into a partnership. More importantly, it parades a stream of brilliant Howard Dietz-Arthur Schwartz numbers. Astaire is superlative in several items, notably 'By Myself' (a solitary introspection which opens the show with a purr), 'A Shine on Your Shoes', and (with Charisse) the gorgeous 'Dancing in the Dark'. So he can be forgiven for trying to do a Gene Kelly in the 'Girl Hunt' ballet (a parody of Mickey Spillane sleaze more notable for Michael Kidd's choreography and Charisse's startlingly sinuous femme fatale). All this and witty dialogue too. A treat. TM

Bang

see Big Bang Theory, The

Bangkok: Dangerous (Krung Thep Antharai)

(1999, Thai, 108 min)
d Danny Pang, Oxide Pang. *p* Pracha Maleenont, Brian L Marcar, Adirek Wattaleela, Nonzee Nimibutr. *sc* Pang Brothers. *ph* Decha Srimantra. *ed* Pang Brothers. *pd* Wut Chaosilp. *m* Orange Music. *cast* Pawalit Mongkolpisit, Premsinee Ratanasopha, Patharawarin Timkul, Pisek Intrakanchit.
●Deaf since childhood (a home movie-style flashback shows how he lost his hearing in a fight), Kong still suffers acute migraines, only partly alleviated by his job as a hitman in Bangkok. Between hits he shyly dates the girl from the drugstore who sells him painkillers – taking her, of course, to see a silent movie. By the time she discovers what he does, he's begun to realise that not all his victims are bad guys. A largely generic script gets a phenomenal treatment. There's an amazing level of visual invention, garnished with creative CGI effects, and entire reels go by without dialogue. The twin brother directors (HK Chinese, but Oxide works in Bangkok) have come up with at least two potential genre classic sequences: a hit on a HK subway train, and another in a Japanese restaurant in Bangkok, where Kong is accompanied by the ghost of his late colleague. Seriously impressive. TR

Bang Rajan – Legend of the Village Warriors (Bang Rajan)

(2000, Thai, 119 min)
d Thanit Jitnukul. *p* Adirek 'Uncle' Watleela, Nonzee Nimibutr. *sc* Kongkiat Khomsiri, Bunthin Thuaykaew, Patikarn Phejmunee, Thanit Jitnukul. *ph* Wichian Ruangwijchayakul. *ed* Sunit Asvinikul, Thanin Thiankaew. *m* Chartchai Pongprapapan. *cast* Winai Kraibutr, Bin Bunluerit, Jaran Ngamdee, Chumphorn Theppithak, Attakorn Suwannaraj.
●The all-time highest grossing film in Thailand, this uses a historical defence of the country as a metaphor for resilience in times of hardship – such as the moment the film was made, in the middle of a long recession. Bang Rajan was a village north of Ayutthaya that succeeded in blocking the advance of an invading Burmese army *eight times* in 1765–66. The script's characters and incidents are invented, but Thanit went to some lengths to ground the film in historical accuracy: he had his cast living as 18th century villagers in *jongkaben* loincloths for a month before the first frame was shot. The characters themselves are stock heroic types, but the best of them are written and played with real flair: the mercenary Tong-Menn, who can only fight when drunk, the tomboy Taeng-Onn, the reckless adventurer Inn (played by Winai, the husband in *Nang Nak*) who leads a disastrous sortie behind Burmese lines. Thanit does a fine job visually, the score is first-rate – and it's even quite sexy. TR

Bang! You're Dead (aka Game of Danger)

(1954, GB, 88 min, b/w)
d/p Lance Comfort. *sc* Guy Elmes, Ernest Borneman. *ph* Brendan J Stafford. *ed* Francis Bieber. *ad* Norman Arnold. *m* Eric Spear. *cast* Jack Warner, Derek Farr, Veronica Hurst, Michael Medwin, Gordon Harker, Anthony Richmond.
●Strange little movie about a young boy who kills a man by mistake with a gun he thought was a toy. As the police hunt goes up, with an innocent man coming under suspicion, the film can't make up its mind whether it's a thriller or a piece of social conscience, but the performance of the boy (Richmond) lends it charm. GA

Banjo on My Knee

(1936, US, 95 min, b/w)
d John Cromwell. *p/sc* Nunnally Johnson. *ph* Ernest Palmer. *ed* Robert Fritch. *ad* Hans Peters. *m* Jimmy McHugh, Harold Adamson. *cast* Barbara Stanwyck, Joel McCrea, Walter Brennan, Buddy Ebsen, Walter Catlett, Anthony Martin.
●Stanwyck carries this episodic Southern saga virtually single-handed, striking out for New Orleans on her own when Mississippi riverman McCrea does a runner after their nuptials, mistakenly believing he's accidentally killed a man during the reception. It all ends happily, but by a roundabout route. Undemanding. TJ

Bank, The

(2001, Aust, 104 min)
d Robert Connolly. *p* John Maynard. *sc* Robert Connolly. *ph* Tristan Milani. *ed* Nick Meyers. *pd* Luigi Pittorino. *m* Alan John. *cast* Anthony LaPaglia, David Wenham, Sibylla Budd, Steve Rodgers, Mandy McElhinney, Greg Stone.
●A slick Robin Hood fairytale for our age of techno-corporate feudalism and financial-market astrology, this debut from the producer of *The Boys* kicks back with a mix of protest populism and entertaining anarchism. LaPaglia is the Olympian CEO ever on the prowl for new schemes to ramp his bank's profits. A world away, a young couple's ill-advised foreign currency has brought home tragedy. Somewhere in the middle is Wenham's maths wiz, who has designed a chaos-based technique to predict stock-market crashes – think of the social benefits! – but he needs corporate resources to realise the idea. The hard, efficient design isn't absolutely matched by the occasionally hackneyed and improbable storytelling, but as a savvy, unusually conscientious audience-pleaser, it's bang on the money. NB

Bank Dick, The

(1940, US, 72 min, b/w)
d Eddie Cline. *sc* WC Fields. *ph* Milton Krasner. *ed* Arthur Hilton. *pd* Jack Otterson. *m* Charles Previn. *cast* WC Fields, Cora Witherspoon, Una Merkel, Evelyn Del Rio, Jessie Ralph, Grady Sutton, Franklin Pangborn, Bill Alston.
●By far the best of Fields' last comedies, with the great man trundling through an impeccably loony scenario of his own devising. As Egbert Souse, he does a spot of film direction, foils bank bandits, drinks in the Black Pussy Café, and marries his daughter to the gormless Og Oggilby (Grady Sutton in his greatest role). Totally ramshackle and marvellous. GB

Bank Holiday

(1938, GB, 86 min, b/w)
d Carol Reed. *p* Edward Black. *sc* Rodney Ackland, Roger Burford. ph Arthur Crabtree. *ed* RE Dearing. *ad* Alex Vetchinsky. *m* Louis Levy. *cast* Margaret Lockwood, Hugh Williams, John Lodge, Kathleen Harrison, Wally Patch, Wilfrid Lawson, Felix Aylmer.
●Comedy-drama about an August bank holiday at the seaside. Though it lacks the guts and vitality of *Millions Like Us* and *Holiday Camp* as similarly populist epics, Reed's film, in its gentle mockery of the hopes and dreams of its 'ordinary' protagonists, is unique. Lockwood, not yet a wicked lady, needs an alibi of conscientious do-gooding to mask her desire, but at least it enables her to refuse to fulfil the fantasies of her office-boy fiancé. The film's real delights, though, come from the superb working-class character acting, particularly Kathleen Harrison, resplendent in beach pyjamas, defying her Cockney caricature of a husband by dancing with a college boy, and Wilfrid Lawson, lighting up the whole film with his suggestion of undreamed of worlds of eccentricity within a sleepy Sussex station sergeant. RMy

Bank Shot

(1974, US, 83 min)
d Gower Champion. *p* Hal Landers, Bobby Roberts. *sc* Wendell Mayes. *ph* Harry Stradling Jr. *ed* David Bretherton. *ad* Albert Brenner. *m* John Morris. *cast* George C Scott, Joanna Cassidy, Sorrell Booke, Clifton James, G Wood, Bob Balaban.
●It would be nice to say that ex-MGM choreographer Champion came up with a goodie in this adaptation of Donald Westlake's novel about an escaped con (Scott) who steals an entire (mobile) bank. But despite sundry excellent ideas and the odd touch of magic (a scene shot in silhouette; Scott swimming out to sea at the end), *Bank Shot* is one of those caper films that start all stops out and have nowhere to go. Potentially good gags get lost in the rush: the jailbreak accomplished in a bulldozer; the arrival of the stolen bank in a senior citizens' mobile home park – nothing is as funny as it should be. VG

Bantsuma: The Life and Times of Tsumasaburo Bando (Bantsuma: Bando Tsumasaburo no Shogai)

(1980, Jap, 91 min)
d/p Shunsui Matsuda. *sc* Tadao Sato. *ph* Hiroshi Takasaka. *with* Tsumasaburo Bando, Takahiro Tamura, Shizuko Mori, Daisuke Ito. *narrator* Shunsui Matsuda.
●A splendid cine-history documentary about the career of the great movie actor Bando Tsumasaburo (the contraction 'Bantsuma' was his popular nickname). He started out in the 1920s as a faintly radical samurai star, turned into a gung-ho action hero in the '30s, and brought his time to an end in the '50s with mellower roles. The interest of this compilation is that the clips from the silent movies are shown complete with music and *benshi* commentary, as they were seen at the time. The narration is written by Japan's foremost critic, Tadao Sato, who also conducted the interviews with Bantsuma's colleagues and relatives. TR

BAPS

(1997, US, 93 min)
d Robert Townsend. *p* Mark Burg, Loretha Jones. *sc* Troy Beyer. *ph* Bill Dill. *ed* Patrick Kennedy. *pd* Keith Brian Burns. *m* Stanley Clarke. *cast* Halle Berry, Natalie Desselle, Martin Landau, Ian Richardson, Troy Beyer, Luigi Amodeo.

● A fish-out-of-water comedy in which 'Black American Princesses' Berry and Desselle play daft but lovable Georgia belles with dreams of Hollywood glory. Following a ridiculous pop video audition, they're brought to Landau's Beverly Hills mansion by his scheming nephew, who hopes thereby to grab the old-timer's fortune. You can see how the black, modern-day Pygmalion-type story could work, just, but not with this heap of cabbage leaves for a script, and not with such desperately goofy acting from Berry and Desselle. On first encountering a bidet, the girls can't turn off the tap, so they get very wet – that's the level of humour. Landau provides a wide and knowing smile. Richardson is easier as the stuffy butler, over-acting in more taciturn style than the other loudmouths. NB

Barabbas (Barabba)

(1961, It, 144 min)
d Richard Fleischer. *p* Dino De Laurentiis. *sc* Christopher Fry, Diego Fabbri, Ivo Perilli, Nigel Balchin. *ph* Aldo Tonti. *ed* Alberto Gallitti. *ad* Mario Chiari. *m* Mario Nascimbene. *cast* Anthony Quinn, Vittorio Gassman, Silvana Mangano, Jack Palance, Arthur Kennedy, Norman Wooland, Valentina Cortese, Harry Andrews.

● One of the most stylish and successful epics to emerge from the Hollywood-on-the-Tiber phase of film history. Quinn plays the legendary thief whose spiritual/physical journey begins at the Crucifixion and ends in the Roman arena, with a period in the sulphur mines in between. The unexpected quality owes everything to Christopher Fry's highly literate dialogue and Fleischer's very considerable abilities as a director of action. DP

Baraka (Blessing)

(1992, US, 96 min)
d Ron Fricke. *p* Mark Magidson. *ph/ed* Ron Fricke. *m* Michael Stearns.

● Technically, a wow. *Koyaanisqatsi* cinematographer Fricke offers more wordless eco-spectacle. With startling depth and luminosity, a tumble of images whirls the viewer on a world tour: ancient temples and ethnic rites, unfolding landscapes and teeming cities. Japanese snow monkeys; Angkor Wat; Grand Central Station; Auschwitz; a chicken processing plant; Mecca; the changing skies over Utah: Fricke has been there. That's the problem. Any one sequence might work powerfully in its own right, but string them together with a musical overlay and the banality of the connections becomes apparent. TJ

Barbarella

(1967, Fr/It, 98 min)
d Roger Vadim. *p* Dino De Laurentiis. *sc* Terry Southern, Roger Vadim. *ph* Claude Renoir. *ed* Victoria Mercanton. *pd* Mario Garbuglia. *m* Bob Crewe, Charles Fox. *cast* Jane Fonda, John Phillip Law, Anita Pallenberg, Milo O'Shea, David Hemmings, Claude Dauphin, Marcel Marceau, Ugo Tognazzi.

● Vadim kicks off his adaptation of Jean-Claude Forest's 'adult' comic strip by stripping Fonda starkers. From there on it's typically vacuous titillation as Barbarella takes off for the mysterious planet Sorgo in 40,000 AD, there to survive attack by perambulating dolls with vampire fangs, receive her sexual initiation from a hairy primitive, fall in love with a blind angel, be whisked off to an alarming Lesbian encounter with the tyrannical Black Queen, etc. But Terry Southern's dialogue occasionally sparkles, and the imaginative designs, as shot by Claude Renoir, look really splendid. TM

Barbarosa

(1982, US, 90 min)
d Fred Schepisi. *p* Paul N Lazarus III. *sc* William Wittliff. *ph* Ian Baker. *ed* Don Zimmerman. *ad* Michel Levesque. *m* Bruce Smeaton. *cast* Willie Nelson, Gary Busey, Gilbert Roland, Isela Vega, Danny De La Paz, George Voskovec, Alma Martinez.

● Testifying to the timelessness of the Western genre through both its ballad form and its circular narrative about the functions of legend, this is also blessed with perfect casting: Nelson and Busey as the grizzled border-country gringo and the raw German-American farmboy, both outcasts in a vast, spartan, Texan terrain – the one a resigned wanderer whose invincibility sustains a 30-year old blood feud with the family that fears his name, the other accidentally apprenticed to this mythical menace. Transplanted Australian director Schepisi confidently threads his own route through Peckinpah territory (a Mexican patriarch demanding honour; a graveyard resurrection), less concerned with Peckinpah's gothic haunting than with teasing dark, absurd ironies from the symbiosis of sworn enemies. PT

Barbary Coast

(1935, US, 97 min, b/w)
d Howard Hawks. *p* Samuel Goldwyn. *sc* Ben Hecht, Charles MacArthur. *ph* Ray June. *ed* Edward Curtiss. *ad* Richard Day. *m* Alfred Newman. *cast* Miriam Hopkins, Edward G Robinson, Joel McCrea, Walter Brennan, Frank Craven, Brian Donlevy, David Niven.

● Perhaps not one of Hawks' greatest films, but none the less interesting. Set in the isolating fog and mist that immediately removes turn-of-the-century San Francisco from time and space, it deals with the competition between nightclub owner Robinson and prospector McCrea for Miriam Hopkins' dancer. Though the Hecht-MacArthur script is surprisingly poetic and derring-do, Hawks' direction is typically matter-of-fact. PH

Barber of Siberia, The (Sibirskii Tsiriulnik)

(1999, Rus/Fr/It/Czech Republic, 177 min)
d Nikita Mikhalkov. *p* Michel Seydoux. *sc* Rustam Ibragimbekov, Nikita Mikhalkov, Rospo Pallenberg. *ph* Pavel Lebeshev. *ed* Enzo Meniconi. *pd* Vladimir Aronin. *m* Edward Nicolay Artemyev. *cast* Julia Ormond, Richard Harris, Oleg Menshikov, Alexey Petrenko, Marina Neelova, Vladimir Ilyin, Daniel Olbrychski, Robert Hardy, Elizabethg Spriggs, Nikita Mikhalkov.

● Jane Callahan (Ormond), a go-getting, worldly wise American woman, falls in love with a proud but naive young Russian cadet (Menshikov) she meets in Moscow in the 1880s. The affair ends badly. What Chekhov would have dealt with in a few pages, writer/director Mikhalkov takes three hours to tell. (His original cut was reportedly twice as long.) The casting is perverse. Mikhalkov has hired an English actress to play an American and a 40-year-old as the juvenile lead. The director himself has a small cameo as the Tsar. The 'Barber' of the title is a giant woodcutting contraption invented by the eccentric McCracken (Harris) to raze the Siberian forests. He needs the Grand Duke's backing to get the machine up and running, and is using Ormond as bait. To emphasise how vast, contradictory and magnificent Mother Russia really is, Mikhalkov throws in scenes of drunken Generals, dancing bears, cadets fighting Pushkin-like duels, postcard imagery of the grandest Moscow buildings, and shots of the untamed Siberian landscape. Like McCracken's hissing, spluttering machine, the film is lumbering and unwieldy. GM

Barb Wire

(1995, US, 99 min)
d David Hogan. *p* Brad Wyman, Mike Richardson, Todd Moyer. *sc* Chuck Pfarrer, Ilene Chaiken. *ph* Rick Bota. *ed* Peter Schink. *pd* Jean-Philippe Carp. *m* Michel Colombier. *cast* Pamela Anderson Lee, Temuera Morrison, Jack Noseworthy, Victoria Rowell, Xander Berkeley, Steve Railsback, Udo Kier.

● Hogan's credits include second unit direction of the diabolical *Batman Forever*, plus numerous pop videos. No coincidence, then, that this awful action-adventure should employ similar production principles: waste land sets, rusty warehouses, plenty of fireworks, and orange filters to depict the dying skyline of a futuristic America ravaged by its second civil war. The year's 2017, the place Steel Harbor, home to a raggle-taggle society of misfits and the legendary Hammerhead Bar and Grille, owned by the eponymous heroine, a stiletto-toed, heavy-leather blonde with a penchant for roughing it. Before long, former freedom-fighter Barb (Anderson Lee) is roped into helping some old resistance colleagues find a pair of contact lenses which will enable a government employee, who alone knows about her bosses' plans for biological warfare, to flee the country. Mean, nasty and looking not unlike Nazi extras from *Kelly's Heroes*, the Congressional Directorate always seem to be one step ahead…until Barb gets serious and tools up for a showdown. To be fair, Anderson Lee cuts a fair dash as a cartoon-style heroine (acting aside). But the film's haphazardly edited, lacks narrative clout, and rambles on to a ludicrously extended conclusion. DA

Barcelona

(1994, US, 101 min)
d/p/sc Whit Stillman. *ph* John Thomas. *ed* Chris Tellefsen. *pd* José Mareia Botines. *m* Mark Suozzo. *cast* Taylor Nichols, Chris Eigeman, Tushka Bergen, Mira Sorvino, Pep Munné, Hellena Schmied, Nuria Badia.

● Writer/director Stillman again casts an affectionate eye on the foibles of preppy young Americans, this time two cousins all at sea in the sexual, moral and political whirl of a changing Old World. It's the 'last decade of the Cold War'. Ted (Nichols) is a young, serious-minded car-company executive getting over a failed affair, his recovery hardly helped when Fred (Eigeman) – a brash naval officer – turns up uninvited to stay in his Barcelona flat. When Fred starts 'borrowing' money from his host and meddling in his encounters with various girls, tensions between the pair come to a boil. An incisive comedy of misplaced American manners, this is for the most part a very funny portrait of immaturity deceived by its own ignorance and blinkered obstinacy. Agreed, it's harder to like or care about Ted and Fred as much as their younger (and therefore more forgivably deluded) counterparts in Stillman's earlier *Metropolitan*, and the story's sudden shift into life-and-death melodrama in the final reel is a little clumsy. But the film looks good, the performances are sharp and droll, and there's more than enough originality here to confirm Stillman as a distinctive, beguiling talent. GA

Barefoot Contessa, The

(1954, US, 128 min)
d/sc Joseph L Mankiewicz. *ph* Jack Cardiff. ed William Hornbeck. *ad* Arrigo Equini. *m* Mario Nascimbene. *cast* Ava Gardner, Humphrey Bogart, Edmond O'Brien, Marius Goring, Rossano Brazzi, Elizabeth Sellars, Valentina Cortese.

● Like *The Bad and the Beautiful*, this starts with a funeral, then moves into flashback with three different guides to the scandalous life of a movie queen who started in the Spanish slums and liked to keep her feet in the dirt. Not as incisive as Minnelli's film, but still a heady Mankiewicz brew of Hollywood trash and wit. Also something of a *film à clef*, in which the millionaire producer is Howard Hughes, there are disguised caricatures (Farouk, the Duke of Windsor), and the Contessa herself is a tactful mixture (mostly Rita Hayworth). TM

Barefoot in the Park

(1967, US, 105 min)
d Gene Saks. *p* Hal B Wallis. *sc* Neil Simon. *ph* Joseph La Shelle. *ed* William A Lyon. *ad* Hal Pereira. *m* Neal Hefti. *cast* Robert Redford, Jane Fonda, Mildred Natwick, Charles Boyer, Ted Hartley.

● Disposable Neil Simon comedy about newlyweds coping with their unheated walkup apartment, a flighty mother-in-law, and a romantically disreputable neighbour. Sprightly dialogue, nice performances. TM

Barfly

(1987, US, 100 min)
d Barbet Schroeder. *p* Barbet Schroeder, Fred Roos, Tom Luddy. *sc* Charles Bukowski. *ph* Robby Müller. *ed* Eva Gardos. *pd* Bob Ziembicki. *m* Jack Baran. *cast* MickeyRourke, Faye Dunaway, Alice Krige, JC Quinn, Frank Stallone, Jack Nance, Sandy Martin.

● Rourke plays one Henry Chimaski, habitué of the Golden Horn, a '40s down-town LA dive where no iceman cometh, but one day battered princess Wanda (Dunaway) does. A few hard days' nights in Wanda's flat has the two barflies abandoning their tentative move towards a mutual expression of need in favour of rejoining the death-wish trail. Chimaski is as articulate as a lorry, so the arrival of 'beautiful' literary agent Tully (Krige) in pursuit of his genius and punchy charm comes as a surprise; his refusal of her largesse is merely a chance to show Integrity. Schroeder's direction of Charles Bukowski's script is consistent with the film's throwaway mood, stresses the upbeat, and mercifully eschews seriousness, cleverly relying on Robby Müller's efficient colour photography to create atmosphere. WH

Bargee, The

(1964, GB, 106 min)
d Duncan Wood. *p* WA Whittaker. *sc* Ray Galton, Alan Simpson. *ph* Harry Waxman. *ed* Richard Best. *ad* Robert Jones. *m* Frank Cordell. *cast* Harry H Corbett, Hugh Griffith, Eric Sykes, Ronnie Barker, Julia Foster, Miriam Karlin, Derek Nimmo, Richard Briers.
●Leaden comedy about a Casanova of the canals, scripted by Ray Galton and Alan Simpson but failing to match the flavour of their TV hit, *Steptoe and Son*. TM

Bari-Zogon

(1996, Jap, 114 min)
d Fumiki Watanabe. *cast* Fumiki Watanabe, Ryu Sasaki, Gaetano Tanaka, Makoto Akiyama.
●The title means 'Abusive Language' – a recurrent element in Watanabe's guerilla approach to indie production, which is generally rooted in his real-life investigations of personal problems and miscarriages of justice and distinguished by his un-Japanese refusal to go along with group-think. Here he reopens a case classed as 'accidental death' – a 26-year-old guy who froze to death in a cesspit – and dramatises what he believes really happened: the boy was silenced for voicing fears about the safety of nuclear power plants and refusing to go along with a related cover-up in the local mayor's election campaign. Watanabe predictably fails to get straight answers from the people involved in the case, but he puts up a persuasive argument. TR

Barking Dogs Never Bite (Puhran Dah Suh ui Geh/ aka A Higher Animal)

(2000, SKor, 106 min)
d Bong Joon-Ho. *p* Cho Min-Whan. *sc* Bong Joon-Ho, Tae-Woong Derek Son, Song Ji-Ho. *ph* Cho Yong-Gyu. *ed* Lee Eun-Soo. *pd* Lee Hang. *m* Cho Sung-Woo. *cast* Lee Sung-Jae, Bae Doo-Na, Kim Ho-Jung.
●This eloquent social comedy has a self-pitying professor hunting out the mutt who's been disturbing his sleep. He locks the creature in a closet in the basement of his apartment block and later stumbles across a janitor with a taste for dog soup (dog lovers might want to give this one a miss). The trouble is, he realises he put away the wrong hound. Ironies multiply. His pregnant wife drives him crazy. He throws the right dog from the roof of the building. His main rival for a top job is beheaded in a drunken subway accident. His wife buys a poodle. And so on. Beautifully directed, unsentimental and darkly funny. TCh

Barkleys of Broadway, The

(1949, US, 109 min)
d Charles Walters. *p* Arthur Freed. *sc* Betty Comden, Adolph Green. *ph* Harry Stradling. *ed* Albert Akst. *ad* Cedric Gibbons, Edward Carfagno. *songs* Harry Warren, Ira Gershwin. *cast* Fred Astaire, Ginger Rogers, Oscar Levant, Billie Burke, Gale Robbins.
●Originally planned by MGM as an Astaire-Garland follow-up to *Easter Parade*, but Judy dropped out, thus opening the door for one last Fred'n'Ginger movie, ten years after their previous work together. It's a pretty flat affair, with a thin story about a married dancing couple splitting up when the woman decides to take up a straight acting career. But it does, of course, have its moments: Fred cavorting with 'Shoes with Wings On', and a happy ending accompanied by 'They Can't Take That Away from Me'. GA

Barnabo of the Mountains (Barnabo delle Montagne)

(1994, Fr/It/Switz, 124 min)
d Mario Brenta. *p* Tommaso Dazzi. *sc* Angelo Pasquini, Mario Brenta, Francesco Alberti, Enrico Soci. *ph* Vincenzo Marano. *ed* Roberto Missiroli. *pd* Giorgio Bertolini. *m* Stefano Caprioli. *cast* Marco Pauletti, Duilio Fontana, Carlo Caserotti, Antonio Vecellio, Angelo Chiesura, Alessandra Milan.
●In the years after the Great War, high in the Dolomites, conflict rages between forest-rangers and gun-toting poachers. Enter soft-spoken Barnabo (Pauletti), a new ranger, whose nerve gives way during an operation to track down the gang that killed the station commander. Dismissed, the young man repairs to the solace of a peasant household, but when he receives a letter from his former superior, the call of the peaks and the chance to right old wrongs is too strong to resist. With its spare dialogue, meditative pacing and expressive use of Schubert's chamber music, this slow, rather beautiful piece is very much a European Art Movie writ large. You'll look elsewhere for snappy one-liners, but in its own way this mesmeric work has rare restorative powers. A gentle giant. TJ

Barnacle Bill (aka All At Sea)

(1957, GB, 87 min, b/w)
d Charles Frend. *p* Michael Balcon. *sc* TEB Clarke. *ph* Douglas Slocombe. *ed* Jack Harris. *ad* Alan Withy. *m* John Addison. *cast* Alec Guinness, Irene Browne, Percy Herbert, Maurice Denham, Victor Maddern, Lionel Jeffries.
●Belated addition to the Ealing comedy cycle, with Guinness as the scion of a long line of seadogs who switches to commanding a pier because he gets seasick. Much too stereotypical, with laboured jokes about bureaucracy as efforts are made to turn the pier into an entertainments centre. In a nod to *Kind Hearts and Coronets*, Guinness also plays his ancestors. TM

Barney's Great Adventure

(1998, US, 77 min)
d Steve Gomer. *p* Sheryl Leach, Dennis DeShazer. *sc* Stephen White. *ph* Sandi Sissel. *ed* Richard Halsey. *pd* Vincent Jefferds. *cast* George Hearn, Shirley Douglas, Trevor Morgan, Diana Rice, Kyla Pratt.
●This spin-off from the TV series featuring the large purple felt dinosaur of awesome good nature is emetically wholesome. The screenplay doesn't stray much from the series' 'listen, sing, and rush off to the next thing' formula. The kids (disbeliever Cody, sister Abby, friend Marcella) and their bouncy uncle figure do it at Cody and Abby's grandparents' farmhouse, a *Picture Post* rural idyll rethought by Liberace. Barney can't be seen by the oldies, who respond with serene condescension to tales of his exploits. Numbers from the 'Old McDonald' song book feature a dog playing guitar riffs on his tail. WH

Baron Fantôme, Le (The Phantom Baron)

(1943, Fr, 100 min, b/w)
d Serge de Poligny. *p* Robert Florat. *sc* Serge de Poligny, Louis Chavance, Jean Cocteau. *ph* Roger Hubert. *ed* Jean Feyte. *ad* Jacques Krauss. *m* Louis Beydts. *cast* Jany Holt, Odette Joyeux, Alain Cuny, Gabrielle Dorziat, Claude Sainval, Jean Cocteau, André Lefaur.
●A film to delight those with a taste for the slightly rarefied pleasures of a French Gothic-pastoral plot featuring a vanishing nobleman (played by Cocteau, who also served as dialogue-writer), a tumbledown castle, hidden treasure, two pairs of sparkling lovers, a gamekeeper posing as the Dauphin…and much, much more. Making light of the distinction between fantasy and reality, the kaleidoscopic tale weaves through the gradations of French society in the 1830s. Distinguished by several impeccable classical performances, Dior costumes, ravishing filtered photography and a tone of benign whimsicality, this represents the cinema of fantasy as its best and most compelling. JPy

Baron Munchhausen (Baron Prasil)

(1961, Czech, 81 min, col & b/w)
d Karel Zeman. *sc* Karel Zeman, (dialogue) Josef Kainar, (commentary) Jiri Brdecka. *ph* Jiri Tarantik. *ad* Karel Zeman. *m* Zdenek Liska. *cast* Milos Kopecky, Jana Brejchova, Rudolf Jelinek, Jan Werich, Rudolf Hrusinsky, Eduard Kohout, Karel Höger, Bohuslav Zahorsky, Nadezda Blazickova.
●Before Terry Gilliam had a go at the epic travels of fabled liar Munchhausen, Zeman had a stab in this live-action version shot in tinted b/w with occasional colour inserts. It uses collage and animation techniques that wouldn't look out of place in the work of Méliès (or Gilliam's own Python days, for that matter). Watch the Baron, moon-man and chums gruesomely outnumbered by the Turkish fleet, save the day by creating a smokescreen of the Turks' own pipe tobacco. Curious and fun. WH

Barquero

(1970, US, 114 min)
d Gordon Douglas. *p* Hal Klein. *sc* George Schenck, William Marks. *ph* Gerald Perry Finnerman. *ed* Charles Nelson. *ad* Allen Smith. *m* Dominic Frontiere. *cast* Lee Van Cleef, Warren Oates, Forrest Tucker, Kerwin Mathews, Mariette Hartley, Maria Gomez, Brad Weston.
●Uneasy derivative of the spaghetti Western's blood and guts, but with a certain fascination to its cat-and-mouse conflict between Van Cleef, as a ferryman who despises the townsfolk he serves, and Oates as the leader of an outlaw band trying to escape across the river. Terrific performance from Oates as the drug-fuddled psychopath plagued by bouts of Hamlet-like indecision, good ones from Van Cleef and Tucker. TM

Barravento (The Brute)

(1962, Braz, 70 min, b/w)
d Glauber Rocha. *p* Braga Neto, Rex Schindler. *sc* Glauber Rocha, José Telles de Magalhaes. *ph* Tony Rabatony. *ed* Nelson Pereira Dos Santos. *cast* Antonio Sampaio, Luiza Maranhão, Aldo Teixeira, Lucy Carvalho, Lidio Silva.
●Rocha's first film, a denunciation of exploitation and the superstition that helps maintain it; an exploration of 'macumba', the mixture of Christianity and African tribal religion whose superstition aids the successful subjugation and exploitation of the fishermen in the Bahia province.

Barren Illusion (Oinaru Genei)

(1999, Jap, 92 min)
d Kiyoshi Kurosawa. *p* Kenzo Horikoshi, Hiroko Matsuda. *sc* Kiyoshi Kurosawa. *ph* Takahide Shibanushi. *ed* Masahiro Onaga. *pd* Chie Matsumoto. *m treatment* Dai Soma. *cast* Shinji Takeda, Miako Tadano, Yutaka Yasui, Masamichi Matsumoto.
●Kurosawa's third film in a year, made with students at the Film School of Tokyo, is a dystopian sci-fi romance. In a near future in which allergies are epidemic, music producer Haru (Takeda) half-heartedly dates post office clerk amd mail thief Michi (Tadano). He searches for violent ways to reactivate his life, she dreams of escaping abroad; both volunteer to test a new drug which may cause impotence. But the storyline is fragmentary and oblique, the plotting is gnomic and the pace is languid; it adds up to less than the sum of its parts. TR

Barren Lives (Vidas Secas)

(1963, Braz, 135 min, b/w)
d Nelson Pereira Dos Santos. *p* Herbert Richers, Luis Carlos Barreto, Nelson Pereira Dos Santos. *sc* Nelson Pereira Dos Santos. *ph* Luis Carlos Barreto. *cast* Atila Iório, Maria Ribeiro, Orlando Macedo, Jofre Soares, I Joffre.
●Dealing with the plight of the very poor in Northeastern Brazil, this centres on a family that has been forced by drought to wander through the desert seeking some kind of work to keep them from starving. A brief respite when the man finds a job as a cattle-herder is shattered by a further drought, a disastrous gambling session, and a beating-up by the police for having insulted an officer. The film moves slowly, with a type of minimalism that emphasises the oppressive fatefulness of the family's existence: a strong comment against the landowners, priests and police, whose individualism perpetuates a needless suffering. JDuC

Barretts of Wimpole Street, The

(1934, US, 110 min, b/w)
d Sidney Franklin. *p* Irving Thalberg. *sc* Ernst Vajda, Claudine West, Donald Ogden Stewart. *ph* William Daniels. *ed* Margaret Booth. *pd* Cedric Gibbons, Harry McAffe. *m* Herbert Stothart. *cast* Norma Shearer, Fredric March, Charles Laughton, Maureen O'Sullivan, Ralph Forbes, Una O'Connor.

●Slow, deliberate, dull, and Irving Thalberg's favourite director, Franklin fittingly turned to production after Thalberg's death in 1936. This MGM prestige version of the love of Elizabeth Barrett (Shearer) and Robert Browning (March) is, as one would expect, high on production values and low on atmosphere and excitement. Even Laughton as Elizabeth's demented father does little to raise the spirits. All of which is rather surprising considering Franklin's obvious attachment to the project. In 1957, he returned briefly to directing, after a twenty year absence, with another version, once again with the producer's wife (Jennifer Jones/Selznick this time) as Elizabeth. PH

Barrier (Bariera)

(1966, Pol, 83 min, b/w)
d/sc Jerzy Skolimowski. *ph* Jan Laskowski. *ed* Halina Prugar. *ad* Roman Wolyniec. *m* Krzysztof Komeda. *cast* Jan Nowicki, Joanna Szczerbic, Tadeusz Lomnicki, Zdzislaw Maklakiewicz, Ryszard Pietruski, Maria Malicka.

●Skolimowski's third film and one of his best, an extraordinary fusion of fantasy and documentary that adds up to a bleakly disenchanted look at the Polish here-and-now. It begins with images of strange, indefinable menace that resolve themselves into one of those ritualistic Polish games (like the one in *Knife in the Water*) being played by medical students. The winner, grabbing the piggy-bank containing the spoils (no communal ownership for him) and brandishing a sabre (sole legacy of his father), sets out into streets illuminated by the ubiquitous candles of Easter, seeking the good life in a society that proves to be haunted by the oppressive weight of past glories, peopled by old age, death, disillusionment and hordes of commuters scurrying past the huge, blank new buildings. He ends clinging precariously to the front of a rattletrap tram ('There are romantic impulses left in our cynical generation') driven by the quizzical blonde he meets, loses and finally finds again as his only spark of hope. With its startling imagery and bizarre landscapes, *Barrier* is that rare bird, a genuinely surrealist film. TM

Barry Lyndon 100 (100)

(1975, GB, 187 min)
d/p/sc Stanley Kubrick. *ph* John Alcott. *ed* Tony Lawson. *pd* Ken Adam. *m* Leonard Rosenman. *cast* Ryan O'Neal, Marisa Berenson, Patrick Magee, Hardy Krüger, Steven Berkoff, Gay Hamilton, Marie Kean.

●A triumph of technique over any human content that takes Thackeray's hero and traces his rise and fall through the armies and high societies of 18th century Europe. Given the singular lack of drama, perspective or insight, the way the film looks becomes its only defence. But the constant array of waxworks figures against lavish backdrops finally vulgarises the visual sumptuousness. CPe

Bartleby

(1970, GB, 79 min)
d Anthony Friedmann. *p/sc* Rodney Carr-Smith, Anthony Friedmann. *ph* Ian Wilson. *ed* John S Smith. *ad* Simon Holland. *m* Roger Webb. *cast* Paul Scofield, John McEnery, Thorley Walters, Colin Jeavons, Raymond Mason, Charles Kinross.

●Made largely thanks to Paul Scofield's support, this was much vaunted in its day as an example of what could be done by a British independent cinema. What it actually does is betray Herman Melville's enigmatic story (about a clerk's passive withdrawal from his office responsibilities) by updating it to present-day London and anchoring its mysterious ambiguities in all-too-prosaic realities. And it vividly illustrates the pitfalls of film-making divorced from any real social, political or aesthetic context. TR

Barton Fink

(1991, US, 116 min)
d Joel Coen. *p* Ethan Coen. *sc* Ethan Coen, Joel Coen. *ph* Roger Deakins. *ed* Roderick Jaynes. *pd* Dennis Gassner. *m* Carter Burwell. *cast* John Turturro, John Goodman, Judy Davis, Michael Lerner, John Mahoney, Tony Shalhoub, Jon Polito.

●In 1941, the well-meaning, vaguely leftist Broadway playwright of the title (Turturro) tries to settle into a rancid Hollywood hotel room to write his first script for eccentric mogul Jack Lipnick (Lerner). Trouble is, it's a Wallace Beery wrestling pic, and he develops a severe case of writer's block. His only hope, it seems, is to take inspiration from a fellow writer's 'secretary' (Davis) and from his insurance salesman neighbour (Goodman), welcomed by Fink as a living paradigm of the 'Common Man'. The tortuous narrative twists that have always marked the Coens' work here inform the entire structure of the movie. As it suddenly shifts gear from its bizarre blend of brooding psychodrama and screwball satire, the film accelerates into a Gothic fantasy as outrageous as it is terrifying. Somehow everything coheres, thanks to the Coens' superb writing and assured direction, and a roster of marvellous performances. The result works on numerous levels, thrilling the mind, ears and eyes, and racking the nerves. GA

Bas-Fonds, Les (The Lower Depths)

(1936, Fr, 89 min, b/w)
d Jean Renoir. *p* Alexandre Kamenka. *sc* Eugène Zamiatine, Jacques Companéez, Charles Spaak, Jean Renoir. *ph* Fedote Bourgassoff, Jean Bachelet. *ed* Marguerite Renoir. *ad* Eugène Lourié. *m* Jean Wiener. *cast* Louis Jouvet, Jean Gabin, Suzy Prim, Vladimir Sokoloff, Junie Astor, Robert Le Vigan, André Gabriello.

●The location of Renoir's adaptation of Maxim Gorki's play is not identified, but from the distinctive acting styles the feel is very French, with the enclosed world of a studio-built courtyard suggesting the dark side to his earlier success, *Le Crime de Monsieur Lange*. But rather than building on a feeling of community, the characters assembled – among them an actor, a drunk, a fallen baron – exist more as individuals looking for a way to escape. Gabin and Jouvet are their usual glorious selves, though the tendency towards pessimism makes this one of Renoir's less rewarding films. DT

Basic Instinct

(1992, US, 127 min)
d Paul Verhoeven. *p* Alan Marshall. *sc* Joe Eszterhas. *ph* Jan De Bont. *ed* Frank J Urioste. *pd* Terence Marsh. *m* Jerry Goldsmith. *cast* Michael Douglas, Sharon Stone, George Dzundza, Jeanne Tripplehorn, Denis Arndt, Dorothy Malone, Wayne Knight.

●Nick Curran (Douglas) is a cop on the edge. Investigated for an over-zealous approach to his work, saddled with a drink and relationships problem, he becomes slowly embroiled with the case, then with the suspect, when a former rock star is found murdered at the climax of some bondage-style sex. Catherine Tramell (Stone), an ultra-clever, ultra-rich author and bisexual free spirit, is at the core of all the basic instinct paraded in the film. One scene in which she teases and bosses a roomful of hard law enforcement men is probably the best illustration of post-feminism in action that Hollywood has offered. Yet the film's depiction of not one but several bisexual women with murky, murderous pasts has angered activists, and does illustrate that sensitivity is not always the strong suit of Verhoeven or scriptwriter Joe Eszterhas. But if you like things unrestrained, hard, adult and off-the-rails, then Douglas and Stone are superb, and George Dzundza (as sidekick Gus) delivers another classic hard-boiled cameo. SGr

Basic Training

(1971, US, 80 min, b/w)
d/p/sc Frederick Wiseman. *ph* William Brayne. *ed* Frederick Wiseman.

●A companion piece to Wiseman's earlier *High School*, this is another bleak *cinéma vérité* study of institutional indoctrination: in this case, the US Army. Filmed at the Fort Knox training centre, Kentucky, it follows a group of new recruits from induction and orientation through to the regimented discipline of the graduation ceremony (prior to shipping out to Vietnam). Beneath the austere 'objectivity' of Wiseman's camera, the editing implicitly emphasises the perpetual process of dehumanisation intrinsic to the system, and finds a focal point of sorts in the maladjusted Private Hickman, whose inability to fit in leads to a suicide attempt. Hickman is a skinny precursor to Stanley Kubrick's Gomer Pyle, and the first half of *Full Metal Jacket* borrows significantly from *Basic Training*. TCh

Basilischi, I

see Lizards, The

Basil the Great Mouse Detective

see Great Mouse Detective, The

Basketball Diaries, The

(1995, US, 102 min)
d Scott Kalvert. *p* Liz Heller, John Bard Manulis. *sc* Bryan Goluboff. *ph* David Phillips. *ed* Diana Congdon. *pd* Christopher Nowak. *m* Graeme Revell. *cast* Leonardo DiCaprio, Ernie Hudson, Mark Wahlberg, James Madio, Lorraine Bracco, Bruno Kirby, Michael Imperioli.

●Jim Carroll (DiCaprio) plays basketball for his NY Catholic boys school, sniffs cleaning fluid with pals Mickey (Wahlberg) and Pedro (Madio), and writes about his life in an exercise book he carries in his back pocket. When he gets into heroin, he still keeps up the diary, transcribing the dirt in his life to eloquent hipster prose. Half-heartedly updated from the late '60s, Kalvert's adaptation faithfully tracks Carroll's descent into the realms of addiction, but fails to shed much light on the impulses which take him there. Like most drug movies, it fails to translate the highs to the screen, but dwells long and hard on the lows. Carroll's book was distinguished by the language, closer to Hubert Selby than Adrian Mole. We get snatches of this in voice-over, but not enough to make it integral to the film, which twists the material into just another cautionary tale with homophobic underpinnings. The angel-faced DiCaprio is a gifted actor, but he lacks the authority and physical presence to keep us with him. TCh

Basket Case

(1981, US, 90 min)
d Frank Henenlotter. *p* Edgar Ievins. *sc* Frank Henenlotter. *ph* Bruce Torbet. *ed* Frank Henenlotter. *ad* Frederick Loren. *m* Gus Russo. *cast* Kevin Van Hentenryck, Terri Susan Smith, Beverly Bonner, Robert Vogel, Diana Browne.

●A freak-show revenge plot that puts small ugly creatures like ET and Ewoks back where they belong: in baskets. Much of the suspense lies in the question: what is in the basket? It eats junk food in quantity, flaps its little lid, belches, and goes walkabout with deadly effect. Its custodian is a painfully fresh-faced nerd strangely adrift among the big-city low-life; and the secret of the wicker world is soon revealed to be the victim of extremely prejudicial surgery by a nympho doctor and desperate veterinarian. In a flashback, the nerd rescued his brother from a black plastic bag; now is the hour of their revenge… Same old gore and poignancy, but some garish characters and the nightmare quality of the New York hotel give it more low budget charm than it deserves. RP

Basket Case 2

(1990, US, 90 mins)
d Frank Henenlotter. *p* Edgar Ievins. *sc* Frank Henenlotter. *ph* Robert M Baldwin. *ed* Kevin Tent. *ad* Michael Moran. *m* Joe Renzetti. *cast* Kevin Van Hentenryck, Annie Ross, Jason Evers, Ted Sorel, Heather Rattray, Matt Mitler.

●With its prominent coupling motif, this sleazy romp would have perhaps been better entitled 'Bride of Basket Case'. After surviving a near-fatal fall from a New York tenement building, Duane Bradley (Van Hentenryck) and his twisted brother Belial find sanctuary from prying public eyes in the home of philanthropic granny Ruth (Ross), who presides over a menagerie of mutant misfits. While the brothers discover love is a many-splendoured thing, scheming journalist Marcie Elliot traces them to their new home, causing the normally amiable aberrations to turn nasty. Henenlotter's sequel to his shoestring-budget horror classic is an inconsistent affair which mixes comedy, shock and boredom in roughly equal proportions. Lacking the gritty, grainy quality of its predecessor, *Basket Case 2* finds itself overstretched in its ambitious attempts to parody (or perhaps honour) Tod Browning's seminal *Freaks*, despite the impressive efforts of make-up artist Gabe Bartalos. However, the gratuitous unpleasantry is present, correct, and (unsurprisingly) sexual, and the occasional snappy one-liner is welcome. MK

Basquiat

(1996, US, 106 min)
d Julian Schnabel. *p* Jon Kilik, Sigurjon Sighvatsson, Randy Ostrow. *sc* Julian Schnabel. *ph* Ron Fortunato. *ed* Michael Berenbaum. *pd* Dan Leigh. *m* John Cale. *cast* Jeffrey Wright, Christopher Walken, Dennis Hopper, David Bowie, Gary Oldman, Courtney Love, Tatum O'Neal, Willem Dafoe, Claire Forlani.

● He was a 19-year-old black graffiti artist who became the darling of the '80s New York art scene, then self-destructed at the age of 27. The film, directed by the Basquiat's old friend and rival Julian Schnabel announces itself as an insiders' view with a soundtrack reportedly cobbled together from Basquiat's record collection (Tom Waits, Iggy Pop, Charlie Parker) and a cult clique of a cast (Bowie as Warhol, Hopper as the Swiss dealer Bruno Bischofberger), but it actually tells us little about the artist, the impulses behind his art, or what drove him to his death. Wright is supremely self-possessed in the title role, but Schnabel allows him to sail through life oblivious to anything save his talent. One scene with Christopher Walken, however, hits home. He's an intrusive journalist who asks Basquiat all the right questions, about colour, celebrity, and the true value of art. They don't speak the same language, but even if we only get half-answers, it's fascinating to see Basquiat's unease when he's really being pressed. Otherwise, this is just another tale of the perils of stardom overlaid with kitsch symbolism. TCh

Bassin de J.W., Le

See Hips of John Wayne, The

Bataan

(1943, US, 114 min, b/w)
d Tay Garnett. *p* Irving Starr. *sc* Robert D Andrews. *ph* Sidney Wagner. *ed* George White. *ad* Cedric Gibbons, Lyle Wheeler. *m* Bronislau Kaper. *cast* Robert Taylor, George Murphy, Thomas Mitchell, Lloyd Nolan, Robert Walker, Lee Bowman, Desi Arnaz.

● Not exactly a gung ho WWII movie, since even Hollywood had to acknowledge American setbacks in the Pacific campaign at this stage of the war, but still contriving to have its scratch patrol of thirteen men (entrusted with a suicidal rearguard action) wipe out half the Japanese army while being decimated to tunes of glory. The ending, with the last survivor (Taylor, naturally) still firing defiantly on the advancing yellow hordes, hardly needed the closing title commending the heroism ('Their spirit will lead us back to Bataan'). So much for the realism much vaunted at the time, but – clearly modelled on *The Lost Patrol* – the film is beautifully paced by Garnett and boasts a sterling cast. TM

Bataille de San Sebastian, La

see Guns for San Sebastian

Bataille des Dix Millions, La

see Battle of the Ten Million, The

Bataille du Rail, La (Battle of the Rails)

(1946, Fr, 87 min, b/w)
d René Clément. sc René Clément, Colette Audry. *ph* Henri Alekan. *ed* Jacques Desagneaux. *m* Yves Baudrier. *cast* Antoine Laurent, Lucien Desagneux, Robert Leray, Redon, Léon Pauléon.

● The French neo-realist 'movement' began and ended with this film, whose innovations were developed neither in Clément's nor the national cinema. A semi-documentary study of World War II resistance among Breton railwaymen, using non-professional actors and natural locations, it's compromised by the director's periodic recourse to affirmative, audience-rousing set pieces, but achieves overall a sobriety that is oddly modern, even 'Bressonian' in tone. GAd

Batalett, El

see Women from the Medina

Bath House

see Oksutan

Batman

(1966, US, 105 min)
d Leslie Martinson. *p* William Dozier. *sc* Lorenzo Semple Jr. *ph* Howard Schwartz. *ed* Harry Gerstad. *ad* Jack Martin Smith, Serge Krizman. *m* Nelson Riddle. *cast* Adam West, Burt Ward, Lee Meriwether, Burgess Meredith, Cesar Romero, Frank Gorshin, Alan Napier, Neil Hamilton.

● This spin-off from the camp '60s TV series is bolstered with all the major baddies: The Penguin (Meredith), Joker (Romero), Riddler (Gorshin) and Catwoman (Meriwether). With a flip script by Lorenzo Semple Jr, it has a few inspired slapstick sequences (West trying desperately to dispose of a bomb without blowing up nuns, children or animals), but the emphatic senselessness gradually becomes tiresome. More surprisingly, the production work is by and large excellent. Nelson Riddle's musical cues are fun, and the design still looks sleek today – I'd choose Adam West's Batmobile over Michael Keaton's any day. TCh

Batman

(1989, US, 126 min)
d Tim Burton. *p* Jon Peters, Peter Guber. *sc* Sam Hamm, Warren Skaaren. *ph* Roger Pratt. *ed* Ray Lovejoy. *pd* Anton Furst. *m* Danny Elfman. *cast* Michael Keaton, Jack Nicholson, Kim Basinger, Robert Wuhl, Pat Hingle, Billy Dee Williams, Michael Gough, Jack Palance, Jerry Hall.

● In everything but its commercial success, *Batman* most resembles Lynch's *Dune*: plotless, unfocused, barely held together by mind-blowing sets, gadgets and costumes, and by director Burton's visual flair. It begins with promising angles – is Batman crazed vigilante or hero? Will journos Vicki Vale (Basinger) and Alex Knox (Wuhl) win the Pulitzer for discovering him? Why does Bruce Wayne spend millions dressing up as a bat? – but all are abandoned half-way through for a straight slugging match between Good and Evil. Cackling, dancing, killing for sheer humour value and hogging the best one-liners, Nicholson's Joker makes *The Witches of Eastwick* seem restrained and pulls off the greatest criminal coup of the decade: stealing a whole movie. Though Keaton is a perfect Bruce Wayne, at the heart of the film, where a *noir*-ish, psychologically disturbed Batman should be, there are only a small actor and a couple of stunt doubles in an inflexible rubber suit. Basinger's role, on the other hand, is over-inflated, presumably in order to prove by her prescence, as with Aunt Harriet in the '60s series, that there's nothing kinky about a hero who likes to dress up in cape and leathers. In the end, one's reaction to Burton's blockbuster is little more than that of the Joker to Batman: 'Where did he get those wonderful toys?'. DW

Batman Returns

(1992, US, 127 min)
d Tim Burton. *p* Denise DiNovi, Tim Burton. *sc* Daniel Waters, Wesley Strick. *ph* Stefan Czapsky. *ed* Chris Lebenzon. *pd* Bo Welch. *m* Danny Elfman. *cast* Michael Keaton, Danny DeVito, Michelle Pfeiffer, Christopher Walken, Michael Gough, Michael Murphy, Cristi Conaway, Andrew Bryniarski, Pat Hingle, Vincent Schiavelli.

● Bigger, louder, more relentlessly action-packed than its predecessor, *Batman Returns* batters its audience into submission. The main problems are both the lack of story and the wealth of superfluous detail in the dialogue that is sometimes barely intelligible. Precisely what the villains – Catwoman (Pfeiffer), the Penguin (DeVito) and property developer Max Shreck (Walken) – are up to, and why, is often unclear, save that they are all on some sort of power trip. Catwoman's schizophrenia, never properly explored, seems a scriptwriter's cop-out; the Penguin is merely vengeful for being consigned to the sewers at birth; and Shreck is simply a corrupt, murderous tycoon posing as Gotham's leading philanthropist. Even the epically conceived and impressively executed set pieces become wearisome after a while. If you're satisfied with stars in funny costumes playing shallow characters involved in an obscure battle to the death, fine; but if huge sets, special effects and a blaring score are not enough, it's a long haul. GA

Batman Forever

(1995, US, 121 min)
d Joel Schumacher. *p* Tim Burton, Peter Macgregor-Scott. *sc* Janet Scott Batchler, Lee Batchler, Akiva Goldsman. *ph* Stephen Goldblatt. *ed* Dennis Virkler. *pd* Barbara Ling. *m* Elliot Goldenthal. *cast* Val Kilmer, Jim Carrey, Tommy Lee Jones, Nicole Kidman, Chris O'Donnell, Michael Gough, Drew Barrymore.

● The second sequel to Tim Burton's 1989 blockbuster makes its predecessors appear models of subtlety and coherence. In theory the film marks a new lease of life for the caped crusader (new star, new faces, new director); in practice everything about *Forever* feels stale and self-conscious. Kilmer is a more sensual Bruce Wayne than Michael Keaton, but if anything his remodelled body-tight Batsuit proves even more of a straitjacket. As in *Returns*, our hero has to fight for screen time with not one, but two scene-stealing villains, Jones's (wasted) Harvey Two-Face and Carrey's Riddler, plus the love interest, Kidman's ludicrously perverse shrink Dr Meridian. As if that's not enough, he's been stuck with a partner-in-crimebusting, O'Donnell's butch young Robin, obviously designed to broaden the demographics (the queer styling even runs to a fetishistic close-up of the Bat-butt).The perfunctory plot concerns the Riddler's mass-marketing of a televisual brain drain. TCh

Batman & Robin

(1997, US, 125 min)
d Joel Schumacher. *p* Peter Macgregor-Scott. *sc* Akiva Goldsman. *ph* Stephen Goldblatt. *ed* Dennis Virkler. *pd* Barbara Ling. *m* Elliot Goldenthal. *cast* George Clooney, Arnold Schwarzenegger, Uma Thurman, Chris O'Donnell, Alicia Silverstone, Pat Hingle, Michael Gough.

● The fourth Bat-flick finds this juvenile franchise running on empty. Oozing insincerity and perplexed paternalism, Clooney plays Batman as an irrelevant bystander. Screenwriter Akiva Goldman sets up a 'revenge of nature' theme, with Schwarzenegger's lumpen Mr Freeze croaking interminable 'cool' puns ('chill'), and Thurman vamping as eco-terrorist Poison Ivy, but soon falls back on recycling random Bat-pieces with scant rhyme or reason. Robin, the blandly obnoxious O'Donnell, meets his match in Silverstone's unintentionally hilarious Oxbridge biker chick, but Batgirl is just another doll looking for a merchandising tie-in. TCh

Bats

(1999, US, 91 min)
d Louis Morneau. *p* Brad Jenkel, Louise Rosner. *sc* John Logan. *ph* George Mooradian. *ed* Glenn Garland. *pd* Philip JC Duffin. *m* Graeme Revell. *cast* Lou Diamond Phillips, Dina Meyer, Leon, Carlos Jacott, Bob Gunton, David Shawn McConnell, Marcia Dangerfield, Oscar Rowland.

● Mutant flesh-eating bats terrorise a Texas town and, it seems, the government has something to do with it (cue an anti-genetic modification message?). Diamond Phillips' sheriff joins batty zoologist Meyer and her dim assistant Leon in an effort to eradicate the creatures, alas, to no avail. Time to call in the troops. The bat attacks are a series of violent camera pans rendering everything a blur; the continuity and computer-generated imagery is dire; and the dialogue stinks, as do the performances. DA

Battaglia di Maratona, La

see Giant of Marathon, The

Batteries Not Included

(1987, US, 106 min)
d Matthew Robbins. *p* Ronald L Schwary. *sc* Brad Bird, Matthew Robbins, Brent Maddock, Steven S Wilson. *ph* John McPherson. *ed* Cynthia Scheider. *pd* Ted Haworth. *m* James Horner. cast Hume Cronyn, Jessica Tandy, Frank McRae, Elizabeth Peña, Michael Carmine, Dennis Boutsikaris.

● At the heart of this Spielberg production is a clever idea: pocket-sized flying saucers with heavy-lidded flashlights. Unfortunately, the schmaltzy tale that accompanies them would make you puke. Elderly couple Faye and Frank

(Tandy and Cronyn) are respectively loco and feisty. Their New York brownstone is threatened with demolition, so Frank prays for a miracle, which arrives in the form of little creatures from another planet. They take up residence in the tenement, where they show an amazing propensity for mending things that are damaged – bye-bye suspense. Robbins' handling of the human element is as sickly and soggy as a dunked doughnut, and the script makes gonks out of its characters. But the flirting frisbee scenes are pretty neat. EP

Battle Beneath the Earth

(1967, GB, 91 min)
d Montgomery Tully. *p* Charles Reynolds. *sc* LZ Hargreaves. *ph* Ken Talbot. *ed* Sidney Stone. *ad* Jim Morahan. *m* Ken Jones. *cast* Kerwin Mathews, Viviane Ventura, Robert Ayres, Martin Benson, Peter Arne.

●A hilarious example of Reds-under-the-bed literalism, *Battle Beneath the Earth* takes for its starting point the notion that Chinese troops are burrowing their way under America as part of a devilish plan to conquer the bastion of Western Democracy. Sadly, the film itself is neither as naive nor as adventurous as its premise. PH

Battle Beyond the Stars

(1980, US, 103 min)
d Jimmy T Murakami. *p* Ed Carlin. *sc* John Sayles. *ph* Daniel Lacambre. *ed* Allan Holzman. *ad* James Cameron. *m* James Horner. *cast* Richard Thomas, Robert Vaughn, John Saxon, George Peppard, Darlanne Fluegel, Sybil Danning, Sam Jaffe.

●Scripted by John Sayles, *Battle Beyond the Stars* rips off all sorts of nice genre items (including a feisty-talking computer and a Russ Meyerish Valkyrie) with shameless abandon, the best being the plot of *The Magnificent Seven*. Like its model, the fun comes in the gathering of the samurai: there's even the black-clad Robert Vaughn, who reprises his twitchy mercenary, exuding the awful solitude of deep space and just looking for a way to go out in style. The last quarter will please only space invader freaks, but any movie which has the line 'Have you never seen a Valkyrie go down?' surely cannot be wholly devoid of cultural merit. CPea

Battle Cries

see Haut les Coeurs

Battlefield Earth

(2000, US, 121 min)
d Roger Christian. *p* Elie Samaha, Jonathan D Krane, John Travolta. *sc* Corey Mandell, JD Shapiro. *ph* Giles Nuttgens. *ed* Robin Russell. *pd* Patrick Tatopoulos. *m* Elia Cmiral. *cast* John Travolta, Barry Pepper, Forest Whitaker, Kelly Preston, Kim Coates, Richard Tyson, Sabine Karsenti, Michael Byrne.

●This adaptation of a baggy, unfinished sci-fi novel by Scientology's L Ron Hubbard – starring famous acolyte Travolta – has a message that is loud but not at all clear. In fact, it plays more like a summer popcorn movie than a propaganda piece, with the emphasis on violent action, deafening explosions and CGI effects rather than meaningful statements. Travolta, it seems, had wanted to star in a film of *Battlefield Earth* since first reading the novel in 1982. Only the all-seeing L Ron knows why. The plodding storyline could not be simpler, or more boring. In the year 3000, the Earth is a post-war wasteland that has been colonised, *Planet of the Apes*-style, by hulking alien invaders, the Psychlos. Humans are used as slave labour, but unite to throw off the yoke of tyranny when fresh-faced hero Jonnie (Pepper), inspired by a glimpse of the Declaration of Independence in the derelict Denver library, hatches a plan to destroy the aliens' atmospherically controlled dome and overthrow the oppressors. Travolta originally coveted the 'good guy' role, but enjoys himself here as Terl, the Psychlos' sneering chief of security – although both he and his assistant Ker (Whitaker) wildly overplay the aliens' bombastic arrogance and mocking laughter. Director Roger (*Nostradamus*) Christian simply flings the action up on the screen, using visual wipes to disguise the lack of logic and continuity. NF

Battle for Anzio, The

see Sbarco di Anzio, Lo

Battle for the Planet of the Apes

(1973, US, 86 min)
d J Lee Thompson. *p* Arthur P Jacobs. *sc* John William Corrington, Joyce H Corrington. *ph* Richard H Kline. *ed* Alan L Jaggs. *ad* Dale Hennesy. *m* Leonard Rosenman. *cast* Natalie Trundy, Roddy McDowall, Claude Akins, Severn Darden, Lew Ayres, Paul Williams.

●The fifth offshoot from Pierre Boulle's novel, last and worst of the 'Ape' series. It's hampered by a banal script which, bringing the story full circle by way of an uninteresting struggle between warlike gorillas, peaceful chimps and underground mutants, seems reluctant to use the potentials for astute comic strip philosophy that all the other films revelled in to a greater or lesser extent.

Battleground

(1949, US, 118 min, b/w)
d William Wellman. *p* Dore Schary. *sc* Robert Pirosh. *ph* Paul C Vogel. *ed* John Dunning. *ad* Cedric Gibbons, Hans Peters. *m* Lennie Hayton. *cast* Van Johnson, John Hodiak, Ricardo Montalban, George Murphy, Marshall Thompson, Jerome Courtland, Denise Darcel, James Whitmore.

●A serious and frequently powerful re-enactment of WWII's Battle of the Bulge that centres on a platoon virtually lost in a blanket of fog in the harsh Ardennes winter, convincingly recreated on the back lot. It may well have been an influence on several Vietnam movies – notably *Platoon* and *Hamburger Hill* – in its unglamorous portrait of men in war. A major battle was also fought behind the scenes. It was the pet project of Dore Schary, MGM's newly arrived left wing production chief, who had the backing of MGM's president Nick Schenck in New York, but not Louis B Mayer, who hated the script and thought the film would be a disaster. Schary won the day (the film was a huge commercial success and was nominated for all the major Oscars), and Mayer's days were numbered. He was toppled in a coup led by Schary a year later. ATu

Battle Hell

see Yangtse Incident

Battle Hymn

(1957, US, 108 min)
d Douglas Sirk. *p* Ross Hunter. *sc* Charles Grayson, Vincent B Evans. *ph* Russell Metty. *ed* Russell Schoengarth. *ad* Alexander Golitzen, Emrich Nicholson. *m* Frank Skinner. *cast* Rock Hudson, Martha Hyer, Anna Kashfi, Dan Duryea, Don DeFore, Jock Mahoney, Alan Hale.

●Hudson plays a preacher who trains fighter pilots in Korea. Problem is, he is plagued with guilt for bombing a German orphanage during WWII, and sure enough a bunch of orphaned Orientals show up wanting shelter from Commie attacks. Pure sentimental slop, with accompanying choral music. Apparently based on a true story; the biggest joke is that Hudson's character is a certain Colonel Hess. ATu

Battle of Algiers, The (La Battaglia di Algeri) 100 (100)

(1965, Alg/It, 135 min, b/w)
d Gillo Pontecorvo. *p* Antonio Musu, Yacef Saadi. *sc* Franco Solinas. *ph* Marcello Gatti. *ed* Mario Serandrei. *ad* Sergio Canevari. *m* Ennio Morricone. *cast* Jean Martin, Yacef Saadi, Brahim Haggiag, Samia Kerbash, Fusia El Kader.

●The prototype for all the mainstream political cinema of the '70s, from Rosi to Costa-Gavras. It relegates the actual liberation of Algeria to an epilogue, and focuses instead on a specific phase of the Algerian guerilla struggle against the French, the years between 1954 (when the FLN regrouped, recruited new members, and tackled the problem of organised crime in the Casbah) and 1957 (when French paratroopers under Colonel Mathieu launched a systematic – and largely successful – attack on the FLN from the roots up). Some fifteen minutes were cut from prints shown in both Britain and America, removing the more graphic sequences of French torture methods, but it seems clear that even these would not have altered the film's scrupulous balance. Pontecorvo refuses to caricature the French or glamorise the Algerians: instead he sketches the way a guerilla movement is organised and the way a colonial force sets about decimating it. There's a minimum of verbal rhetoric: the urgent images and Ennio Morricone's thunderous score spell out the underlying political sympathies. TR

Battle of Austerlitz, The

see Austerlitz

Battle of Britain

(1969, GB, 131 min)
d Guy Hamilton. *p* Harry Saltzman, S Benjamin Fisz. *sc* James Kennaway, Wilfred Greatorex. *ph* Freddie Young. *ed* Bert Bates. *ad* Bert Davey. *m* Ron Goodwin, William Walton. *cast* Laurence Olivier, Michael Caine, Robert Shaw, Christopher Plummer, Susannah York, Ian McShane, Kenneth More, Trevor Howard, Ralph Richardson, Michael Redgrave.

●Dull, all-star treatment of a potentially stirring historical event, notable mainly for its lengthy, boring and far too numerous dogfight sequences, the tediousness of which is matched by the dialogue which the unfortunate actors are forced to deliver whenever they are grounded. NF

Battle of Chile, The (Batalla de Chile)

(1975, 1976, 1978, Chile, 106/99/90 min, b/w)
d/sc Patricio Guzman. *ph* Jorge Müller. *ed* Pedro Chaskel.

●Part 1: 'The Insurrection of the Bourgeoisie'; Part 2: 'The Coup d'Etat'; Part 3: 'The Power of the People'. Not only the best films about Allende and the coup d'etat, but among the best documentary films ever made, changing our concepts of political documentary within a framework accessible to the widest audience. The films (which form a unity) are committed, analytical and chronological, allowing the participants in history to explain it. The result is of an extraordinary passion. SM

Battle of Midway, The

see Midway

Battle of the Bulge

(1965, US, 167 min)
d Ken Annakin. *p* Milton Sperling, Philip Yordan. *sc* Philip Yordan, Milton Sperling. John Melson. *ph* Jack Hildyard. *ed* Derek Parsons. *ad* Eugene Lourié. *m* Benjamin Frankel. *cast* Henry Fonda, Robert Shaw, Robert Ryan, Dana Andrews, George Montgomery, Ty Hardin, Pier Angeli, Charles Bronson, Telly Savalas.

●Though writer/producer Milton Sperling dubbed his company United States Pictures after he'd seen World War II service in the Marines, the war movies he subsequently backed were notable for their avoidance of either gung-ho excess or 'war-is-hell' blandness. Both Joseph H Lewis' *Retreat, Hell!* and Fuller's *Merrill's Marauders* are riven with contradictory impulses about heroism, duty, futility and necessity; and, if finally the epic logistics of this sprawling Cinerama spectacular submerge the sparkier points of the Philip Yordan/Sperling script, *Battle of the Bulge* is no simplistic flag-waver or exorcism either. Shaw's panzer commander takes on various Allied stars in games of strategic cat-and-mouse, both lucidly and dispassionately observed, during the German counter-offensive in the Ardennes in late 1944. PT

Battle of the River Plate, The (aka Pursuit of the Graf Spee)

(1956, GB, 117 min)
d/p/sc Michael Powell, Emeric Pressburger. *ph* Christopher Challis. *ed* Reginald Mills. *pd* Arthur Lawson. *m* Brian Easdale. *cast* Peter Finch, John Gregson, Anthony Quayle, Ian Hunter, Jack Gwillim, Bernard Lee, Patrick MacNee, Christopher Lee, John Schlesinger.

●Powell and Pressburger's final collaboration as The Archers was also, perhaps, their dullest. Certainly it's a pretty routine account of the British attempt to capture of the German battleship Graf Spee in Montevideo harbour in '39, even if it is sharply shot by Chris Challis and reasonably acted by a superior cast. Admittedly, the stiff-upper-lip factor is relatively low, and the Germans are not the ususal sadistic two-dimensional villains, but those in search of the baroque romanticism usually prevalent in the team's work will be sorely disappointed. GA

Battle of the Sexes, The

(1959, GB, 84 min, b/w)
d Charles Crichton. *p/sc* Monja Danischewsky. *ph* Freddie Francis. *ed* Seth Holt. *ad* Edward Carrick. *m* Stanley Black. *cast* Peter Sellers, Constance Cummings, Robert Morley, Donald Pleasence, Ernest Thesiger, Jameson Clark, Moultrie Kelsall.

●The tone shifts uncertainly between facile farce and sharp satire in this sub-Ealing comedy (based on James Thurber's *The Catbird Seat*) about an accountant (Sellers) who plots the murder of the female efficiency expert (Cummings) who has disrupted the comfortable regime of a traditionally-run Edinburgh tweed cloth factory. Its view of women's place in the business world is unlikely to find favour with feminists and enlightened fellow travellers. NF

Battle of the Somme, The

(1916, GB, 80 min approx, b/w)
ph Geoffrey Malins, JB McDowell.

●Troops marching, artillery firing. Ominous place names: Mametz, Fricourt, La Boiselle. Those familiar but certainly faked 'going over the top' shots. Laconic titles: 'Friend and foe help each other' as British and German wounded come in arm in arm. 'Battle police' moving over heavily shelled ground, 'mopping up'. Corpse shots. Compositions tend to the painterly – foreground, centre, background, all teeming with activity. In many ways this 'official record' is a 19th century work, just as the Somme was a 19th century battle, and naturally there's no sense that 1 July 1916 was the bloodiest fiasco in British military history. Fascinating, affecting, eloquent on many levels, some of them even intended. The video released by the Imperial War Museum unfolds in dead silence. BBa

Battle of the Ten Million, The (La Bataille des Dix Millions)

(1970, Fr/Bel/Cuba, 58 min, b/w)
d Chris Marker.

●Clear, informative, well-argued account of the revolution in Cuba, looked at through the documentation of a single facet: Castro's attempt to raise the 1970 sugar harvest from 4.2 million tons to an all-time high of ten million. Beneath the level of narrative it presents an unclichéd view of the implications of revolution.

Battle of the Villa Fiorita, The

(1965, GB, 111 min)
d/p/sc Delmer Daves. *ph* Oswald Morris. *ed* Bert Bates. *ad* Carmen Dillon. *m* Mischa Spoliansky. *cast* Maureen O'Hara, Rossano Brazzi, Richard Todd, Phyllis Calvert, Martin Stephens, Olivia Hussey.

●Lushly silly soap opera about a diplomat's wife who runs off to romantic Italy with a widowed concert pianist. Even Daves and his swooping crane can do nothing to stem the tiresomeness when the children of both parties turn up to do battle for respectability. TM

Battle Royale

(2000, Jap, 113 min)
d Kinji Fukasaku. *p* Masao Sato, Masumi Okada, Teruo Kamaya, Tetsu Kayama. *sc* Kenta Fukasaku. *ph* Katsumi Yanagijima. *ed* Hirohide Abe. *pd* Kyoko Heya. *m* Masamichi Amano. *cast* 'Beat' Takeshi, Tatsuya Fujiwara, Aki Maeda, Taro Yamamoto, Masanobu Ando, Ko Shibasaki, Chiaki Kuriyama.

●A minor sensation in Japan where questions were asked in parliament, this noisy and bombastic adaptation of a recent pulp novel doesn't shape up as satire or death-sport fantasy. In the near future, the authorities respond to an epidemic of juvenile delinquency by hijacking one problem class each year to an island and ordering the kids to kill each other, leaving only one survivor. This year's choice is Class B from Zentsuji Middle School, apparently because one pupil knifed teacher Kitano (Takeshi, the sole redeeming feature). The opening shows that the massacres are big media events, but the kids here have never heard of the game before. Maybe that's why their kills are so bloodless and lacking in hardcore nastiness. Or maybe the problem is simply that veteran Fukasaku is past it. His view of teenage life (flashbacks to happier days strumming guitar in the school dorm) is positively geriatric. TR

Battleship Potemkin (Bronenosets Potyomkin) 100 10

(1925, USSR, 5,709 ft, b/w)
d/sc Sergei Eisenstein. *ph* Edward Tissé. *ed* Sergei Eisenstein. *ad* Vasili Rakhals. *cast* Alexander Antonov, Vladimir Barsky, Grigori Alexandrov, Mikhail Gomorov, Beatrice Vitoldi, Aleksandr I Levchin.

●What more can be said about *Potemkin* – the celebrated re-creation, in documentary style, of the key events of the failed 1905 Kronstadt revolution against Tsarist oppression – re-issued (in 1998) in a new print, with music by Shostakovich replacing Meisel's original score. It exemplifies, we know, Eisenstein's facination with 'montage' (the use of dialectical forms of editing to create meaning) and 'typage' (non-actors cast for physical characteristics). This, however, is propaganda, just as much as art, and looking back after more than 70 years there's something cold, academic, even manipulative about the meticulous compositions, schematic characterisations and complex choreography of massed movement. It lacks the genuinely fiery passion of Eisenstein's earlier *Strike*, not to mention the lyricism of Dovzhenko or the perky wit of Vertov. Edward Tissé's camerawork remains impressive, and there's no doubt that the whole is a technical tour de force, but the obsession with forces of power, as opposed to individual experience, is ultimately oppressive. GA

Battlestar Galactica

(1978, US, 122 min.)
d Richard A Colla. *p* John Dykstra. *sc* Glen A Larson. *ph* Ben Colman. *ed* Robert L Kimble. *ad* John E Chilberg II. *m* Stu Phillips. *cast* Lorne Greene, Richard L Hatch, Dirk Benedict, Maren Jensen, Ray Milland, Jane Seymour, Lew Ayres.

●Feature cobbled from the American TV series, complete with shots and effects repeated ad nauseam. Similar in plot and costume to *Star Wars*, but at heart a traditional space Western with less emphasis on droids and more on shootouts. Some good special effects, but with strictly tele-standard acting, straightforward space opera plot, grandiose sentiment and slushy love interest, it's really only meat for genre fans. DP

Battling Butler

(1926, US, 7 reels, b/w)
d Buster Keaton. *p* Joseph M Schenck. *sc* Paul Gerard Smith, Al Boasberg, Charles Smith, Lex Neal. *ph* Dev Jennings. *ad* Fred Gabourie. *cast* Buster Keaton, Sally O'Neil, Snitz Edwards, Walter James, Bud Fine.

●Charming comedy in which Buster, a scion of the idle rich, has to make good his supposed prowess as a prizefighter (a mistake occasioned by an unfortunate coincidence of names) in order to win the hand of a mountain girl. The first half is delightfully inventive as Keaton takes to the mountains in his Rolls for a hilariously feckless hunting trip. A slight drop in temperature latterly, despite some very funny business during the training scenes and the pseudo-championship bout, but the final grudge fight (when Buster realises how the real boxer has tricked him) is a little too nasty for comfort. TM

Bat 21

(1988, US, 105 min)
d Peter Markle. *p* David Fisher, Gary A Neill, Michael Balson. *sc* William C Anderson, George Gordon. *ph* Mark Irwin. *ed* Stephen Rivkin. *ad* Terry Weldon. *m* Christopher Young. *cast* Gene Hackman, Danny Glover, Jerry Reed, David Marshall Grant, Clayton Rohner, Erich Anderson.

●An unsatisfactory mix of low-key heroics, buddy-buddy humour, and anti-war sentiment, this downbeat Vietnam pic has reconnaissance expert Hackman (codename Bat 21) – a career colonel with no frontline experience – struggling to survive in a jungle crawling with North Vietnamese troops after ejecting from his plane. Making radio contact with spotter pilot Glover (codename Birddog), he maps out a coded route to a rendezvous. Cue for a cross-country hike punctuated by brushes with NVA patrols, a machete-wielding peasant, and an ambiguously angelic Vietnamese child. Certain scenes achieve a genuine tension, as when Hackman has to watch a captured chopper pilot sent into a waterlogged minefield by NVA soldiers; but this is immediately undercut by a retaliatory bombing raid that destroys a camouflaged NVA hideout, regardless of civilian casualties. Like the film as a whole, such scenes elicit sympathy more for the tacitly guilty Hackman than for the innocent victims. NF

Bat Whispers, The

(1930, US, 85 min, b/w)
d /sc Roland West. *ph* Ray June, Robert Plank. *ed* James Smith. *pd* Paul Roe Crawley. *m* Hugo Riesenfeld. *cast* Chester Morris, Una Merkel, Maud Eburne, William Bakewell, Gustav von Seyffertitz, Grayce Hampton.

●A talkie remake of West's silent *The Bat*, adapted from a hugely popular Broadway whodunit (by Mary Robert Rinehart and Avery Hopwood). The creaky plot, about a super-thief hiding out in an old dark house and terrifying its inhabitants, is virtually incomprehensible, a non-stop succession of spooky clichés strung together with scant regard for logic or motivation; while attempts to inject humour – centred largely around an hysterical housemaid – are often embarrassingly unfunny. Fascinating, however, is West's unusual visual sense: all enormous shadows, overhead shots, and (for the time) a surprisingly mobile camera. Remade, ineffectually, in 1958 as *The Bat*. GA

Bawdy Adventures of Tom Jones, The

(1975, GB, 93 min)
d Cliff Owen. *p* Robert Sadoff. *sc* Jeremy Lloyd. *ph* Douglas Slocombe. *ed* Bill Blunden. *ad* Jack Shampan. *m* Ron Grainer. *cast* Nicky Henson, Trevor Howard, Terry-Thomas, Arthur Lowe, Georgia Brown, Joan Collins, William Mervyn.

●Many distinguished names who should have known better lend themselves to this smutty musical version of Henry Fielding's tale. CPe

Baxter!

(1972, GB, 105 min)
d Lionel Jeffries. *p* Arthur Lewis. *sc* Reginald Rose. *ph* Geoffrey Unsworth. *ed* Teddy Darvas. *ad* Anthony Pratt. *m* Michael J Lewis. *cast* Patricia Neal, Jean-Pierre Cassel, Britt Ekland, Lynn Carlin, Scott Jacoby, Sally Thomsett, Paul Eddington.

●Jeffries' second film treats that most treacherous of subjects: the emotional deprivations of childhood. Reginald Rose's cliché-oriented script notwithstanding, Jeffries emerges successful from the project, neither wallowing in melodrama nor seeking social significance where none is to be found. Scott Jacoby is masterful as the emotionally disturbed 12-year-old caught between two worlds, California and London, and helped by an odd collection of friends. PH

Bayan Ko: My Own Country (Bayan Ko – Kapit Sa Patalim)

(1984, Phil/Fr, 108 min)
d Lino Brocka. *p* Vera Belmont. *sc* José F Lacaba. *ph* Conrado Baltazar. *ed* George Jarlego. *ad* Joey Luna. *m* Jess Santiago. *cast* Phillip Salvador, Gina Alajar, Claudia Zobel, Carmi Martin, Raoul Aragonn. Rez Cortez.

●Made under the noses of the Marcos censors in the thick of Manila's social and political turmoil, this is based on two news stories from 1980. It centres on a brawny, sympathetic Manila printshop worker, whose political naivety lands him on the wrong side during a strike, and whose anger and frustration finally drive him into crime. Shot with the urgency of newsreel, the film is a brilliantly topical thriller, and an admirable act of civil disobedience. If ever a film caught the spirit of its time, this is it. TR

Bay Boy, The (Le Printemps sous la Neige)

(1984, Can/Fr, 107 min)
d Daniel Petrie. *p* John Kemeny, Denis Héroux. *sc* Daniel Petrie. *ph* Claude Agostini. *ed* Susan Shanks. *pd* Wolf Kroeger. *m* Claude Bolling. *cast* Liv Ullmann, Kiefer Sutherland, Peter Donat, Allan Scarfe, Mathieu Carrière, Stéphane Audran.

●The trouble with this attractively photographed story of the pangs of adolescence, set against the background of a dismal mining town on the coast of Nova Scotia in 1937, is that it is too busy. So much happens to the young hero that he barely has time to react to one event before he has to be ready for the next: murder, homo- and heterosexual advances, first love, torn loyalties, loss of virginity. Thus experience changes no one, and the spectator gets little out of it. Redeeming features are some excellent performances, and two brilliantly directed seduction scenes. AG

Bay of Angels

see Baie des Anges, La

Beach, The

(2000, US/GB, 119 min)
d Danny Boyle. *p* Andrew Macdonald. *sc* John Hodge. *ph* Darius Khondji. *ed* Masahiro Hirakubo. *pd* Andrew McAlpine. *m* Angelo Badalamenti. *cast* Leonardo DiCaprio, Tilda Swinton, Virginie Ledoyen, Guillaume Canet, Robert Carlyle, Paterson Joseph, Lars Arentz Hansen, Daniel York.
●Richard (DiCaprio) finds a treasure map in which 'X' marks the location of the backpacker's Holy Grail: a virgin beach deep in the Gulf of Thailand. In persuading the stunning Françoise (Ledoyen) and her beau Etienne (Canet) to accompany him on the dangerous journey, Richard also commits the cardinal sin of passing on the map to a couple of jocks. What they find on the island is a commune living at one with nature, albeit under the disturbingly stern stewardship of Sal (Swinton). This *Heart of Darkness*-lite has a techno pulse, lustrous cinematography and stars you could eat. It's only on arrival that problems emerge: there's no flesh on the bones of this island community. Worse, Richard's descent into madness feels distinctly half-baked. Yet the movie works, just about: screenwriter John Hodge has spiked up the romance of Alex Garland's novel and put a sober spin on the finale. TCh

Beach Blanket Bingo

(1965, US, 98 min)
d William Asher. *p* James H Nicholson, Samuel Z Arkoff. *sc* William Asher, Leo Townsend. *ph* Floyd Crosby. *ed* Fred Feitshans. *ad* Howard Campbell. *m* Les Baxter. *cast* Frankie Avalon, Annette Funicello, Linda Evans, Harvey Lembeck, Don Rickles, Elsa Lanchester, Buster Keaton.
●More seafront fluff from the AIP stable, with Annette mad at Frankie for fancying starlet Evans (decades before her *Dynasty* fame) and mounting a rescue mission when she's kidnapped by a biker gang. Madhouse plot elements thrown into the mix include a passing mermaid, abrasive comic Don Rickles as the owner of a sky-diving club, and Buster Keaton as a leching old beachcomber, gamely taking falls as he chases after bikini-ed youth. Pretty dumb really, but at least it knows it, and for the record, they never actually play bingo, with beach blankets or anything else. TJ

Beach Café (Le Café de la plage)

(2001, Fr, 85 min)
d Benoît Graffin. *p* Cyriac Auriol, Pauline Duhault. *sc* Benoît Graffin, André Téchiné. *ph* Yorick LeSaux. *ed* Camille Cotte. *m* Philippe Miller. *cast* Jacques Nolot, Ouassini Embarek.
●Driss (Embarek), a young Moroccan, happens across a makeshift wooden shack on a beautiful but remote beach. The owner, Fouad (Nolot), sells tea to the occasional visitor. Driss befriends the older man, although his affection is far from reciprocated. Indeed Fouad repays his gifts with malice and deceit. André Téchiné co-wrote this simple, resonant character piece with director Graffin from Paul Bowles' transcription of a Moroccan short story. If it's not quite in the Claire Denis league, it is one of those atmospheric and sensual vignettes that lodges in the memory. TCh

Beachcomber, The

see Vessel of Wrath

Beachcomber, The

(1954, GB, 90 min)
d Muriel Box. *p* William MacQuitty. *sc* Sydney Box. *ph* Reginald Wyer. *ed* Jean Barker. *ad* George Provis. *m* Francis Chagrin. *cast* Robert Newton, Glynis Johns, Donald Sinden, Paul Rogers, Donald Pleasence, Michael Hordern.
●Lamentable version of the Somerset Maugham story about a drunken beach bum and a prissy missionary lady, previously filmed as *Vessel of Wrath* with Charles Laughton and Elsa Lanchester. Just to add to the hammy indignities, a silly *Androcles and the Lion* role has been dreamed up for an elephant. TM

Beaches

(1988, US, 123 min)
d Garry Marshall. *p* Bonnie Bruckheimer, Bette Midler, Margaret South. *sc* Mary Agnes Donoghue. *ph* Dante Spinotti. *ed* Richard Halsey. *pd* Albert Brenner. *m* Georges Delerue. *cast* Bette Midler, Barbara Hershey, John Heard, Spalding Gray, Lainie Kazan, James Read.
●CC and Hillary first meet under the boardwalk in Atlantic City. CC is a vulgar, would-be singer, Hillary a beautiful, poor little rich girl. As they grow up into Midler and Hershey, they keep their relationship alive by writing letters. Then one day Hillary turns up in New York and becomes CC's flatmate. Hillary sleeps with theatre director Heard; CC marries him. Marshall's slick and stylish flick follows the ups and downs of their marriages and careers, but because CC becomes a star, the pace is sabotaged by several Midler numbers. Even so, Midler carries the movie: nearly all the giggles are due to her cosmic skills. Two-thirds of the way through, a funny film turns tragic with the utterance of a single word, *virus*, which means that Hershey has to start gasping and preparing for death. But even though tear-jerking has never been so blatant, your tears of laughter are replaced, God damn it, by tears of grief. MS

Beach of the War Gods (Zhan Shen Tan)

(1973, HK, 100 min)
d Jimmy Wang Yu. *p* Raymond Chow Man-Wai. *sc* Jimmy Wang Yu. *ph* Chiu Yao Hu. *ed* Chang Yao-Chung. *m* Huang Mou-Shan. *cast* Jimmy Wang Yu, Lung Fei, Tien Yeh, Hsueh Han, Tsao Chien.
●Simplistic dialogue with all the subtlety of a WWII comic book mars this visually exciting effort which replays *The Magnificent Seven* on an epic scale against the background of invasion-raddled China at the end of the Ming dynasty. Wang Yu – the original one-armed swordsman – who wrote, directed and stars in the film, shows skill in shaping individual shots and keeping the project (which took three years to complete) afloat with some superb torchlit battles.

Beach Red

(1967, US, 105 min)
d/p Cornel Wilde. *sc* Clint Johnston, Donald A Peters, Jefferson Pascal. *ph* Cecil Cooney. *ed* Frank P Keller. *ad* Francisco Balangue. *m* Antonio Buenaventura. *cast* Cornel Wilde, Burr De Benning, Patrick Wolfe, Rip Torn, Jaime Sanchez, Jean Wallace, Genki Koyama.
●Wilde's neglected WWII movie is an allegory about the futility and the carnage of Vietnam. Set in the Pacific, it details a probably suicidal mission to take a Japanese-held island. The movie is massively and harrowingly brutal, almost like a horror movie, with severed limbs washing up on the beach. Although Wilde deals exclusively in pacifist clichés, the film has a genuine primitive power; in fact, it's the equal of anything made by Fuller. ATu

Beads of One Rosary, The (Paciorki Jednego Rózanca)

(1979, Pol, 111 min)
d/sc Kazimierz Kutz. *ph* Wieslaw Zdort. *ed* Józef Bartczak. *ad* Andrzej Plocki. *m* Wojciech Kilar. *cast* Augustyn Halotta, Marta Straszna, Jan Bogdol, Ewa Wisniewska, Franciszek Pieczka.
●The hero is a retired miner who stubbornly refuses to vacate his home for a new high-rise block. Everyone else has gone, but the old man remains, a last outpost defending tradition, family and freedom. And just to complicate matters, he is stoutly backed by his son, a bead from the same rosary. The relevance to the Gdansk strikes of 1980 is obvious; and an ironic ending, demonstrating the crafty compromises which can undermine rebellion, is a bitter footnote to the Polish situation. An impressive film, therefore, full of dogged humanist spirit, but also lumbering along in flat, documentary style, emerging a little like a cross between Ealing comedy and Italian neo-realism. TM

Bean

(1997, GB, 90 min)
d Mel Smith. *p* Peter Bennett-Jones, Eric Fellner, Tim Bevan. *sc* Richard Curtis, Robin Driscoll. *ph* Francis Kenny. *ed* Chris Blunden. *pd* Peter Larkin. *m* Howard Goodall. *cast* Rowan Atkinson, Peter MacNicol, Pamela Reed, Harris Yulin, Burt Reynolds, Larry Drake, John Mills.
●Rowan Atkinson's TV series *Mr Bean* enjoyed worldwide syndication, and this feature revamps the familiar material: the coffee joke, the tongue-shaving sequence, the falling-asleep-on-head joke, and the exploding air-sick-bag (very graphic). Mr Bean, a security guard at the National Gallery in London, is selected to travel to California as the gallery's representative at the unveiling of 'Whistler's Mother'. His host (MacNicol) is expecting London's finest art scholar. The jokes have a variable strike rate, and there are times when you feel that everyone's just treading water before the next big set-piece. Still, Atkinson's on peak form, witness the hilarious but risky public loo gag. The theme – a strange man in a strange land – is quite amusing too. It's just that, well, it's all a bit of a yawn. DA

Bear, The (L'Ours)

(1988, Fr, 98 min)
d Jean-Jacques Annaud. *p* Claude Berri. *sc* Gérard Brach. *ph* Philippe Rousselot. *ed* Noëlle Boisson. *pd* Toni Lüdi. *m* Philippe Sarde. *cast* Tchéky Karyo, Jack Wallace, André Lacombe.
●In *Quest for Fire*, Annaud tried to explore our primal emotions by delving into pre-history; here he attempts much the same thing, although this time it's not our ancestors but the beasts with whom we share the planet that are intended to shed light on our deepest instincts. At the turn of the century in British Columbia, a young kodiak bear, suddenly orphaned, takes up with a massive wounded grizzly. Inevitably, the cub undergoes the usual rites of passage, his awareness of death enhanced by a couple of hunters determinedly tracking his adoptive dad. Despite the enormous and very evident technical expertise involved in making the film, Annaud never manages to dispel memories of those Disney features in which animal behaviour was presented in human terms. This being the '80s, there's sex'n'violence (baby bear sees daddy bear getting it on with a local floozie bear; a clash with trappers ends in vivid realistic gore), not to mention an uplifting ecological finale. Otherwise, it's simply a ripping yarn, too prone to anthropomorphism to work successfully as a proper study either of ursine behaviour or of our own relationship to their world. GA

Bear Island

(1979, Can/GB, 118 min)
d Don Sharp. *p* Peter Snell. *sc* David Butler, Don Sharp. *ph* Alan Hume. *ed* Tony Lower. *pd* Harry Pottle. *m* Robert Farnon. *cast* Donald Sutherland, Vanessa Redgrave, Richard Widmark, Christopher Lee, Barbara Parkins, Lloyd Bridges.
●Despite a better cast than most Alistair MacLean adaptations and an interesting Arctic story about Cold War struggles to dominate the globe by weather control, this fast becomes a dodo with such elements as a former U-Boat base, most of the cast's suspiciously Nazi pasts, and an array of Teutonic accents clearly destined to play a large part in the story. Faced with such silliness, the writers panic and abandon exposition for slug-out set pieces, loud bangs and noisy chases. Left stranded, the cast must have drawn straws for lines like 'This is no place for scientists who can't control themselves'. CPe.

Bearskin – An Urban Fairytale (aka Bearskin)

(1989, GB/Port, 95 min)
d Ann Guedes, Eduardo Guedes. *p* Leontine Ruette, Eduardo Guedes. *sc* Ann Guedes, Eduardo Guedes. *ph* Michael Coulter. *ed* Edward Marnier. *ad* Jock Scott, Luis Monteiro. *m* Michael McEvoy. *cast* Tom Waits, Damon Lowry, Julia Britton, Isabel Ruth, Charlotte Coleman, Bill Paterson, Ian Dury, Alex Norton.

●If you can accept the idea of a Portuguese city standing in for London, you may just have no problem with the other weirdness dished up in this arty 'urban fairytale'. On the run from hoodlums, Lowry dons a bear-suit and prowls around Waits's Punch and Judy show; Bill Paterson as a guardian angel is a mite easier to accept than some of the film's other self-indulgent peculiarities. NF

Beast, The

see Bête, La

Beast, The (aka The Beast of War)

(1988, US/Isr, 109 min)
d Kevin Reynolds. *p* John Fiedler. *sc* William Mastrosimone. *ph* Douglas Milsome. *ed* Peter Boyle. *ad* Kuli Sander. *m* Mark Isham. *cast* George Dzundza, Jason Patric, Steven Bauer, Stephen Baldwin, Don Harvey, Frick Avari, Kabir Bedi.

●Filmed on extraordinary desert locations in Israel, this superior war movie effortlessly fuses the moral complexity of scriptwriter William Mastrosimone's original stage play with the visual spectacle and narrative drive of a full-blown cinema feature. During the second year of the Soviet invasion of Afghanistan, a Soviet tank razes an Afghan village to the ground, before becoming lost in the aptly named Valley of the Jackal. Vengeful Afghan rebels track and circle the wounded beast, taking bites out of its tough metal hide in an effort to expose the soft flesh inside. The action is tough and gripping, while the quieter scenes explore the adversaries' contrasting, sometimes self-contradictory, attitudes towards the conflict. Mark Isham's spare electronic score is an added bonus. NF

Beast from Haunted Cave

(1959, US, 75 min, b/w)
d Monte Hellman. *p* Gene Corman. *sc* Charles B Griffith. *ph* Andrew M Costikyan. *ed* Anthony Carras. *m* Alexander Laszlo. *cast* Michael Forest, Sheila Carol, Frank Wolff, Wally Campo, Richard Sinatra.

●Routine programmer made for Roger Corman in which gangsters holed up in a ski lodge tangle with the thing in the cave. Hellman's first film, but there's nothing to distinguish it from any other grade Z horror pic of the '50s. DP

Beast from 20,000 Fathoms, The

(1953, US, 80 min, b/w)
d Eugène Lourié. *p* Hal E Chester, Jack Dietz. *sc* Fred Freiberger, Lou Morheim. *ph* Jack Russell. *ed* Bernard W Burton. *ad* Edward Boyle. *m* David Buttolph. *cast* Paul Christian, Paula Raymond, Cecil Kellaway, Kenneth Tobey, Donald Woods, Lee Van Cleef, Jack Pennick.

●Freed from the Arctic ice by atomic blasts, one of Ray Harryhausen's most loveable prehistoric beasts trundles down the US coast to stomp New York, before going out in a blaze of glory at Coney Island funfair (thereby starting a stampede of similar monsters, including Godzilla). Quite what Jean Renoir made of his regular art director's switch to monster-movie auteur (*The Colossus of New York, The Giant Behemoth* and *Gorgo* followed) isn't recorded, but Lourié was merely one of a long line of designers to turn sci-fi director, alongside the likes of Harry Horner (*Red Planet Mars*), Nathan Juran (*Attack of the 50 Foot Woman*), and William Cameron Menzies (*Invaders from Mars*). From a story by Ray Bradbury. PT

Beast in the Cellar, The (aka Are You Dying, Young Man?)

(1970, GB, 87 min)
d James Kelly. *p* Graham Harris. *sc* James Kelly. *ph* Harry Waxman. *ed* Nicholas Napier-Bell. *m* Tony Macaulay. *cast* Beryl Reid, Flora Robson, Tessa Wyatt, John Hamill, TP McKenna, David Dodimead.

●Weird sisters in rural England with something in the cellar and lots of friendly army officers popping by to see that they're OK as murder spreads. Familiar stuff with the addition of a bit of nastiness and gore; very average.

Beastmaster, The

(1982, US, 118 min)
d Don Coscarelli. *p* Paul Pepperman, Sylvio Tabet. *sc* Don Coscarelli, Paul Pepperman. *ph* John Alcott. *ed* Roy Watts. *pd* Conrad E Angone. *m* Lee Holdridge. *cast* Marc Singer, Tanya Roberts, Rip Torn, John Amos, Josh Milrad.

●Rehash of *Conan the Barbarian*, with another hunk-of-the-month in a leather thong, a crisp smile, and a Buck's Fizz haircut. He also has a posse of animal friends to highlight his existential aloneness: a panther is his strength, an eagle his eyes, and two possums to handle the rest. Sorcery, ham, various hordes and polystyrene sets stalk the land (looks like Apache country), with the routine of swordfights, narrow escapes and ancient prophecies occasionally enlivened by flashes of sicko – a living eyeball ring, fluorescent blood – from the director who brought you the disgusting horror *Phantasm*. RP

Beast Must Die, The

(1974, GB, 92 min)
d Paul Annett. *p* Max J Rosenberg, Milton Subotsky. *sc* Michael Winder. *ph* Jack Hildyard. *ed* Peter Tanner. *ad* John Stoll. *m* Douglas Gamley. *cast* Calvin Lockhart, Peter Cushing, Charles Gray, Anton Diffring, Marlene Clark.

●The Amicus studio is better known for omnibus horror films like *Torture Garden* and *Tales from the Crypt*, and this flaccid feature suggests they would have done better to stick to that winning formula. Rich eccentric Lockhart invites a group of guests to his country mansion to discover which of them is a werewolf: a standard country house mystery, in fact, with werewolf substituted for murderer. Worse still, the film employs an awkward device whereby the audience is also invited to wade through the shoals of red herrings to guess the werewolf's identity for themselves. NF

Beast of War, The

see Beast, The

Beast With Five Fingers, The

(1947, US, 88 min, b/w)
d Robert Florey. *p* William Jacobs. *sc* Curt Siodmak. *ph* Wesley Anderson. *ed* Frank Magee. *ad* Stanley Fleischer *m* Max Steiner. *cast* Peter Lorre, Victor Francen, Robert Alda, Andrea King, J Carrol Naish, Charles Dingle.

●Effective supernatural thriller in which a famous pianist (Francen) who has suffered a stroke ekes out his last days in an Italian Gothic mansion, surrounded by grasping relatives. When he finally dies, leaving his fortune to a young niece, the other relatives are well pissed off; so too is secretary Lorre, who wanted not only the old man's loot but also access to his library of books on the occult. Then the dead man's severed hand starts tinkling the ivories, dislodging books, and crawling around the terrified Lorre. The fudged ending imposed by the studio deflates much of the mystery, but the animated hand, creepy piano music, and Lorre's eye-popping performance are all memorable. Fans of Sam Raimi's *Evil Dead II* will note the derivation of that film's hilarious disembodied hand sequence. NF

Beast Within, The (Menneskedyret)

(1995, Den, 79 min)
d/sc Carsten Rudolf. *ph* Anthony Dod Mantle. *ed* Morten Giese. *m* Anders Koppel. *cast* Cyron Bjørn Melville, Jens Okking, Michelle Bjørn-Andersen, Søren Pilmark, Morten Suurballe, Benedikte Hansen, Freja Johansen, Joan Maquardsen.

●A 'troubled kid' drama intermittently flagging itself as a supernatural thriller, this actually belongs in the less vaunted generic territory known as the 'bloody mess'. Young Frederik (Melville), alarmed by what he sees when he peeps in on mum's massage therapy, is taken with the idea that he's become 'the human beast' after supping from his girlfriend Henriette's witch's broth. When a dead cow lands on his beloved dad at his abattoir workplace, Frederik flips. The setting is a small backwoods town where all the grown-ups – two women and three men, including the vicar – seem to have known each other, in a murkily biblical but not very interesting way. The storyline flails like a cat drowning in a cauldron. NB

Beat Girl (aka Wild for Kicks)

(1959, GB, 85 min, b/w)
d Edmond T Gréville. *p* George Willoughby. *sc* Dail Ambler. *ph* Walter Lassally. *ed* Gordon Pilkington. *ad* Elven Webb. *m* John Barry. *cast* Gillian Hills, David Farrar, Noelle Adam, Christopher Lee, Adam Faith, Shirley Anne Field.

●Hills is the resentful teenager, daughter of a middle class father remarried to a gorgeous 'woman with a past', who decides to rebel by playing juke-box records and mixing with Beatniks. Fascinating partly for the sheer prurience of its content and for Adam Faith's first film appearance.

Beat Street

(1984, US, 106 min)
d Stan Lathan. *p* David V Picker, Harry Belafonte. *sc* Andrew Davis, David Gilbert, Paul Golding. *ph* Tom Priestley Jr. *ed* Dov Hoening. *pd* Patrizia von Brandenstein. *cast* Rae Dawn Chong, Guy Davis, Jon Chardiet, Leon W Grant, Saundra Santiago, Robert Taylor, Dean Elliott.

●While Charlie Ahearn's 1982 independent feature *Wild Style* worked frontline reportage of New York's nascent rap and breakdance scene into an otherwise anodyne teenage romance, this rather glossier affair sprinkles the latest happening sounds over a selection of familiar narrative moves. So we get troubled cross-ethnic relationships, the drama of a young dj's first night on the decks at a big club, the dangers of spraying graffiti on subway trains – all of it unfolding against the streetwise setting of the Bronx, but with a strictly PG-rated filter on sex and bad language. Pretty bland, but you have to admit co-producer Belafonte had an eye for talent, spotlighting HipHop legends-in-the-making Afrika Bambaata and the Soul Sonic Force, the Rock Steady Crew, and Grand Master Melle Mel and The Furious Five. TJ

Beat the Devil

(1953, US, 100 min, b/w)
d John Huston. *p* Jack Clayton. *sc* Truman Capote, John Huston. *ph* Oswald Morris. *ed* Ralph Kemplen. *ad* Wilfrid Shingleton. *m* Franco Mannino. *cast* Humphrey Bogart, Jennifer Jones, Gina Lollobrigida, Robert Morley, Peter Lorre, Ivor Barnard, Edward Underdown.

●In this offbeat spoof of *Maltese Falcon*-type thrillers, an ill-assorted group of travellers are en route to the African coast, where they each plan to stake a claim to a plot of uranium-rich land. Truman Capote's absurdly talky script is stuffed with in-jokes and bizarre characters, but is seldom as clever as it thinks it is. Despite slack plotting and a complete lack of suspense, the film has achieved an undeserved cult status. NF

Beau Geste

(1939, US, 120 min, b/w)
d/p William A Wellman. *sc* Robert Carson. *ph* Theodor Sparkuhl, Archie Stout. *ed* Thomas Scott. *ad* Hans Dreier, Robert Odell. *m* Alfred Newman. *cast* Gary Cooper, Ray Milland, Robert Preston, Brian Donlevy, J Carrol Naish, Susan Hayward, Albert Dekker, Broderick Crawford.

●The finest of three screen versions of PC Wren's tale of heroism in the French Foreign Legion (the others were made in 1926 and 1966, the latter a travesty). Pictorially ravishing, it features a memorable opening with a fort garrisoned by corpses, and the high adventure tone carries on from there. Cooper is suitably strong in his usual taciturn and gentle way as 'Beau', eldest of the three brothers who join the Legion to cover the mysterious 'theft' of a valuable jewel, but it is really Donlevy who leaves the most lasting impression as the sadistic Legion sergeant. Boys' Own stuff, maybe, but fun. GA.

Beau James

(1956, US, 106 min)
d Melville Shavelson. *p* Jack Rose. *sc* Jack Rose, Melville Shavelson. *ph* John F Warren. *ed* Floyd Knudtson. *ad* Hal Periera, John Goodman. *m* Joseph J Lilley. *cast* Bob Hope, Vera Miles, Paul Douglas, Alexis Smith, Darren McGavin, Jimmy Durante, Jack Benny. *narrator* Walter Winchell.

●Lightly likeable but awkward attempt by Hope to sustain a more dramatic role than usual in a romanticised biopic of Jimmy Walker, the not altogether honest mayor of New York during the roaring '20s. Good period atmosphere and a few charming guest appearances from Jimmy Durante, Jack Benny and others, but it's all very slight. GA

Beaumarchais (Beaumarchais l'insolent)

(1996, Fr, 100 min)
d Edouard Molinaro. *p* Charles Gassot. *sc* Edouard Molinaro, Jean-Claude Brisville. *ph* Michael Epp. *ed* Véronique Parnet. *ad* Jean-Marc Kerdelhue. *m* Jean-Claude Petit. *cast* Fabrice Luchini, Manuel Blanc, Sandrine Kiberlain, Michel Serrault, Jacques Weber, Michel Piccoli, Dominique Besnehard.
●None too subtle in borrowing the boisterous but lyrical mood and certain dramatic elements from both *Les Enfants du Paradis* and *Cyrano de Bergerac*, this costume romp soons runs out of steam. It starts, in 1770s Paris, with the playwright Beaumarchais taking on a young friend of Voltaire as his secretary and, it transpires, his conscience. The bustling crowds, the lively word play, the solid camerawork and designs, and the overall theatricality bode well. As the episodic narrative proceeds, however, outlining the insolent hero's multifarious talents (scourge of the nobility and champion of the people; unrepentant womaniser; arms dealer, spy, supporter of American independence; dramaturgical iconoclast), the film meanders and rapidly becomes a series of decorous, undifferentiated historical tableaux inhabited by venerables of the French acting world. That said, Luchini gives Beaumarchais an exquisite, mellifluous air of arrogance and irony, notably offset by Sandrine Kiberlain as his devout wife. GA

Beau Mariage, Le (A Good Marriage)

(1981, Fr, 97 min)
d Eric Rohmer. *p* Margaret Ménégoz. *sc* Eric Rohmer. *ph* Bernard Lutic. *ed* Cécile Decugis, Maria-Luisa Garcia. *m* Ronan Girre. *cast* Béatrice Romand, André Dussollier, Arielle Dombasle, Huguette Faget, Thamila Mezbah, Féodor Atkine.
●The second in Rohmer's series of 'Comedies and Proverbs' tells the cautionary tale of a girl who impulsively decides to marry, picks out a suitable mate in the conviction that he finds her equally eligible, and then suffers agonies of humiliation when she discovers that he does not. Funny, touching and beautifully acted, it is acutely exact both psychologically and socially, not least in the way the troubled heroine shuttles between the busy highways of Paris and the ancient cobbled streets of Le Mans, with the different settings ironically reflecting the paradox that this paragon of women's lib chooses to see liberation as allowing her to live like a Victorian lady of leisure. TM.

Beau-père

see Stepfather

Beau Serge, Le

(1959, Fr, 97 min, b/w)
d Claude Chabrol. *p* Jean Cotet. *sc* Claude Chabrol. *ph* Henri Decae. *ed* Jacques Gaillard. *m* Emile Delpierre. *cast* Gérard Blain, Jean-Claude Brialy, Michèle Meritz, Bernadette Lafont, Jeanne Perez, Claude Cerval, Edmond Beauchamp.
●Chabrol's first film – one of the first manifestations of the *Nouvelle Vague* – is about a young student (Brialy) who returns to his native village to convalesce from an illness, finds that his childhood friend and hero (Blain) has become a hopeless drunk, and attempts to reclaim him at the cost of his own health. As mirror images of each other, the two men reflect the interest in Hitchcockian themes of transference later elaborated in Chabrol's work, but here expressed rather too overtly in terms of Christian allegory (a transference not so much of guilt as of redemption). Shot entirely on location in the village of Sardent (where Chabrol spent much of his childhood), it presents a bleak, beautifully observed picture of provincial life, later revisited to even more stunning effect in *Le Boucher*. TM

Beauté du Diable, La (Beauty and the Devil)

(1949, Fr/It, 100 min, b/w)
d René Clair. *p* Salvo D'Angelo. *sc* René Clair, Armand Salacrou. *ph* Michel Kelber. *ed* James Cuenet. *ad* Léon Barsacq. *m* Roman Vlad. *cast* Michel Simon, Gérard Philipe, Nicole Besnard, Simone Valère, Carlo Ninchi, Paolo Stoppa, Raymond Cordy.
●In spite/because of what must have seemed impeccable credentials – Clair, the two leads, a screenplay by dramatist Armand Salacrou, and nostalgic, Méliès-inspired sets by Barsacq – this version of the Faust legend is a turgidly literary cocktail of escapist fantasy and Sartrean *engagement,* which could not even plead the excuse of Carné's comparable *Les Visiteurs du Soir* of having been filmed during the Occupation. (A colour and detail-enhanced IMAX version restores a previously omitted 11-minute song-and-dance number. GAd

Beauté Volée

see Stealing Beauty

Beauties of the Night

see Belles de nuit, Les

Beautiful Blonde from Bashful Bend, The

(1949, US, 77 min)
d/p/sc Preston Sturges. *ph* Harry Jackson. *ed* Robert Fritch. *ad* Lyle Wheeler, George W Davis. *m* Cyril J Mockridge. *cast* Betty Grable, Rudy Vallee, Cesar Romero, Olga San Juan, Sterling Holloway, Hugh Herbert, Danny Jackson.
●Fast-moving and witty spoof of Western conventions from one of Hollywood's finest writer/directors of comedy. Grable is the crack-shot chanteuse hiding from the law as a schoolmarm (after accidentally shooting a judge in the rear when two-timed by her lover Romero) and getting involved in the numerous shootouts between the local townsmen. It relies a little too much on zany slapstick, but the dialogue is sharp and the Technicolor photography by Harry Jackson adds a pleasant gloss. GA

Beautiful Creatures

(2000, GB, 88 min)
d Bill Eagles. *p* Alan J Wands, Simon Donald. *sc* Simon Donald. *ph* James Welland. *ed* Jon Gregory. *pd* Andy Harris. *m* Murray Gold. *cast* Rachel Weisz, Susan Lynch, Iain Glen, Maurice Roëves, Alex Norton, Jake D'Arcy, Tom Mannion.
●You can certainly see the fun in the ideas behind this blackly comic female buddy picture. Regrettably, the execution proves patchy. The uneasy combination of high farce and crunching violence is established early on. When Petula (Weisz) is in the midst of rough-house treatment from her boyfriend (Mannion), passer-by Dorothy (Lynch) interrupts the altercation, and a hefty whack from an iron bar soon quietens him down. Accidentally, of course, but permanently. Once the two gals collect themselves, they cook up a kidnapping scam, hoping to collect a million quid while the corpse gathers dust. The strength of the movie is the way the female leads play off one another; together they manage to create an effective partnership, shaping an amusing learning curve in the face of the escalating mayhem. There's a vague female empowerment vibe and some ill-defined notion about male objectification of women, but it's hard to credit much of it when the movie inflicts harm on humans and dog alike with would-be shocking relish. TJ

Beautiful Dreamers

(1988, Can, 108 min)
d John Harrison. *p* Martin Walters, Michael Maclear. *sc* John Harrison. *ph* François Protat. *ed* Ron Wisman. *pd* Seamus Flannery. *m* Lawrence Shragge. *cast* Colm Feore, Rip Torn, Wendel Meldrum, Sheila McCarthy, Colin Fox, David Gardner, Marsha Moreau.
●In 1880, progressive doctor Maurice Bucke invited American poet Walt Whitman to London, Ontario, where he was superintendent of the mental asylum. Whitman, whose brother was mentally ill, was a source of spiritual enlightenment for the doctor: they formed a lifelong friendship, and Bucke eventually went on to write the poet's biography. Writer-director Harrison uses these facts to develop a tale primarily of emotional rediscovery and sexual awakening. Bucke (Feore) finds his strait-laced wife (Meldrum) antagonistic to Whitman, until she too throws convention aside and goes skinny-dipping with the guys. Where the film drags is in its earnest attempt to convey the doctor's euphoric response to Whitman's message: applying the tone of Bucke's writings to the screen doesn't always make for credible exchanges. More involving are the scenes within the asylum which indicate the value of compassionate treatment, and Torn's glorious performance as Whitman. CM

Beautiful Girls

(1996, US, 113 min)
d Ted Demme. *p* Cary Woods. *sc* Scott Rosenberg. *ph* Adam Kimmel. *ed* Jeffrey Wolf. *pd* Dan Davis. *cast* Timothy Hutton, Michael Rapaport, Matt Dillon, Noah Emmerich, Annabeth Gish, Lauren Holly, Martha Plimpton, Rosie O'Donnell, Max Perlich, Natalie Portman.
●A bunch of guys share beer and bewilderment over the course of a wintry reunion weekend. They talk sports and missed chances, but it's women they obsess about: the ones that got away, and the ones that won't let them get away with a thing. Willie (Hutton) is back home alone, contemplating marriage like it's a slow death sentence. His buddies Birdman (Dillon), Paul (Rapaport) and Kev (Perlich) aren't much help: they're hopelessly stuck on the beauty myth. And then he meets this amazing woman (Portman) – too bad she's just 13. With this cast, the title's no misnomer, but the point of view basically belongs to the unreconstructed male. Women may be unimpressed, but men will squirm with recognition. The sensibility's very *Diner*, and rather smart-alecky, but this is a picture worth listening to. You don't have to check your brain at the box-office, just your PC sensibilities. TCh

Beautiful Mind, A

(2001, US, 135 min)
d Ron Howard. *p* Brian Grazer, Ron Howard. *sc* Akiva Goldsman. *ph* Roger Deakins. *ed* Mike Hill, Dan Hanley. *pd* Wynn Thomas. *m* James Horner. *cast* Russell Crowe, Ed Harris, Jennifer Connelly, Paul Bettany, Adam Goldberg, Judd Hirsch, Josh Lucas, Anthony Rapp, Christopher Plummer, Vivien Cardone, Austin Pendleton.
●As a math student at Princeton in 1947, John Forbes Nash (Crowe) was eccentric, uncouth and arrogant, but his PhD thesis on 'Non-Cooperative Games' justified his self-esteem, and he was promptly ushered into top level government think tanks. At the age of 30, however, Nash was diagnosed with schizophrenia after claiming he was communicating with 'abstract powers from outer space – or perhaps foreign governments' via the *New York Times*. Screenwriter Akiva Goldsman takes this last detail from Sylvia Nasar's biography and makes a meal of it, inventing characters, erasing Nash's bisexuality and omitting his divorce from (and subsequent remarriage to) Alicia (Connelly). You couldn't ask for a more dramatic contrast to, say, the softly, softly approach Richard Eyre takes in *Iris*, a contemporaneous biopic about the intellect and the heart. Surprisingly, given Goldsman's lamentable track record (*A Time to Kill*, *Batman and Robin*), his artistic trespass pays dividends, sucking us into the mind of a genius in a way Eyre never quite managed, thanks largely to Roger Deakins' imaginative cinematography. At its most effective when it seems to lose the plot in a scrambled second act that posits the Cold War as a collective paranoid delusion, the film reverts to type (and to fact) for a sentimental anti-climax. TCh

Beautiful Mystery – Legend of Big Horn (Utsukushiki Nazo: Kyokon Densetsu)

(1983, Jap, 61 min)
d Genji Nakamura. *sc* Rokuro Mochizuki. *ph* Hideo Ito. *ed* Makoto Sawada. *cast* Nagamoto Tatuya, Shiyuto Kei, Yamashina Kaoru, Osugi Ren.
●Scripted by Rokuro Mochizuki, Nakamura's film dramatises the gay bar legends about Yukio Mishima and his private army. Aspiring muscle queen Shinohara is recruited into the 'militia' run by famous writer/demagogue Mitani and whisked off to boot camp, where his roommate buggers him at the first opportunity. He soon overcomes his prim objections and relaxes into the gruelling regimen of gay orgies – only to oversleep and miss his leader's attempted coup d'état. This ribald, highly entertaining film was Japan's first gay exploitation feature. Amazing that it was made at a time when discussion of Mishima's sexuality was a virtual taboo in Japan. TR

Beautiful People

(1974, SAf, 93 min)
d/p/sc/ph/ed Jamie Uys. *narrator* Paddy O'Byrne.

● Abysmally anthropomorphic wild-life documentary which persists in lumbering its poor subjects with the attributes of people ('The jackal is a slob', etc).

Beautiful People

(1999, GB, 107 min)
d Jasmin Dizdar. *p* Ben Woolford. *sc* Jasmin Dizdar. *ph* Barry Ackroyd. *ed* Justin Krish. *pd* Jon Henson. *m* Garry Bell. *cast* Edin Dzandzanovic, Charlotte Coleman, Nicholas Farrell, Danny Nussbaum, Gilbert Martin, Siobhan Redmond.

● Written and directed by a Bosnian, this boisterous black comedy, about the encounters of assorted Londoners with various Bosnian exiles, is quite unlike any other British film. It's a *Short Cuts*-style jigsaw of interlocking characters, and in the early scenes it's easy to become a little irritated by some of the broad stereotypes and the rather insistent narrative ingenuity. Then, after a paralytically hungover British football hooligan finds himself dropped into wartorn Bosnia on an aid pallet, each narrative strand suddenly takes an exhilarating turn, and the overall absurdity pays dividends. With its echoes of early Forman and Kusturica, this suggests Dizdar is a talent to watch. GA

Beautiful Thing

(1996, GB, 89 min)
d Hettie MacDonald. *p* Tony Garnett, Bill Shapter. *sc* Jonathan Harvey. *ph* Chris Seager. *ed* Donald Fairservice. *pd* Mark Stevenson. *m* John Altman. *cast* Glen Berry, Linda Henry, Scott Neal, Tameka Empson, Ben Daniels, Meera Syal.

● A real winner this, from producer Tony Garnett and Channel 4: an 'urban fairytale' set in darkest Thamesmead, South London. Jamie (Berry) is in love with next-door neighbour Ste (Neal), but he's terrified his mum will find out, and Ste has plenty of troubles of his own. It may sound like a feelgood movie, but throw in the timeless tunes of Mama Cass, a funny romantic screenplay by Jonathan Harvey (skillfully adapting his own play), and a formidable performance from Linda Henry as Jamie's independent-minded mother, and you have the likeliest gay crossover hit since *My Beautiful Laundrette*. TCh

Beautiful Troublemaker

see Belle Noiseuse, La

Beau Travail

(1998, Fr, 90 min)
d Claire Denis. *p* Jérôme Minet. *sc* Claire Denis, Jean-Pol Fargeau. *ph* Agnès Godard. *ed* Nelly Quettier. *pd* Arnaud de Moleron. *m* Eran Tzur. *cast* Denis Lavant, Michel Subor, Grégoire Colin, Marta Tafesse Kassa, Richard Courcet.

● Inspired by *Billy Budd*, this extraordinary film concerns the experiences of a sergeant in the Foreign Legion in Djibouti. It's an ellipitical but entirely accessible tale of repressed homo-erotic desire leading to deadly jealousy, though little is spelt out explicitly (Lavant's protagonist himself hardly speaks). The intensity of mood and thematic resonance derive almost wholly from the poetic juxtaposition of images of sustained beauty and strangeness. GA

Beauty and the Beast

see Belle et la Bête, La

Beauty and the Beast

(1976, US, 91 min)
d Fielder Cook. *p* Hank Moonjean. *sc* Sherman Yellen. *ph* Jack Hildyard, Paul Beeson. *ed* Frederick Wilson. *ad* Elliot Scott. *m* Ron Goodwin. *cast* George C Scott, Trish Van Devere, Virginia McKenna, Bernard Lee, Michael Harbour, William Relton, Patricia Quinn.

● Made for TV but theatrically released, this retelling of the Perrault fairytale falls flat on its face by comparison with Cocteau's marvellous *La Belle et la Bête*. Cook introduces us to the Beast's castle by way of a distorting lens that promptly robs it of any magic whatsoever; its interiors remind one of nothing so much as a slightly seedy stately home in which things have a tiresome habit of appearing or disappearing. Even more dispiritingly, Scott's Beast, turned into a snouty pig with tusks and a waistline to match, has been robbed of the heady eroticism Jean Marais brought to the part. Small wonder that Belle (Van Devere), behaving like a callow coed with a beady eye for the material benefits provided by magic, keeps inventing little games of hide-and-seek and suchlike to keep her suitor occupied. TM

Beauty and the Beast

(1991, US, 84 min)
d Gary Trousdale, Kirk Wise. *p* Don Hahn. *sc* Linda Woolverton. *ph* Joe Jiuliano. *ed* John Camochan. *ad* Brian McEntee. *m* Alan Menken, Howard Ashman. *cast* voices: Paige O'Hara, Robby Benson, Richard White, Jerry Orbach, David Ogden Stiers, Angela Lansbury.

● Disney animation enters the '90s, embraces the stunning technical advances of computer-generated imagery, and updates the traditional dependent heroine. Belle, besides representing a move away from the usual Barbie Doll looks, is resourceful, bookish, and vigorous in resisting the chauvinist advances of Gaston, the character who turns out to bear the true mark of the beast. Gaston was based on LA's Medallion Man narcissists, and is well and truly lampooned in the barroom waltz. Beast, based on a menagerie of brooding buffalo, bear, boar and gorilla, learns to master his temper, and his growing relationship with Belle is infinitely touching. His bewitched castle is enlivened by an antic household including a candelabra with the panache of a French maître d', a neurotic clock, and a mother-and-son teapot and cup. The six musical numbers either reveal character or push the action, with 'Be Our Guest' an outstanding example of cartoon choreography. Dazzlingly good. BC

Beauty and the Devil

see Beauté du Diable, La

Beauty Jungle, The

(1964, GB, 114 min)
d/p Val Guest. *sc* Robert Muller, Val Guest. *ph* Arthur Grant. *ed* Bill Lenny. *ad* Maurice Carter. *m* Laurie Johnson. *cast* Ian Hendry, Janette Scott, Ronald Fraser, Edmund Purdom, Jean Claudio, Kay Walsh, Norman Bird, Tommy Trinder, Sid James, Lionel Blair.

● Typist Janette Scott signs up for a beauty contest and before long she's wearing the 'Miss Globe' crown and sash in this vapid would-be exposé. The path to the gutter is, however, as swift as it is predictable. Shot in 'Scope with guest appearances by, among others, Sid James, Sterling Moss and the Duchess of Bedford. TJ

Beavis and Butt-head Do America

(1996, US, 80 min)
d Mike Judge. *p* Abby Terkuhle. *sc* Mike Judge, Joe Stillman. *ed* Terry Kelley. *ad* Jeff Buckland. *m* John Frizzell. *cast* voices: Mike Judge, Robert Stack, Cloris Leachman, Eric Bogosian, Jacqueline Barba, Bruce Willis, Demi Moore.

● Beavis and Butt-head are the no-brain buddies who laugh like worried sheep and move as gracefully as ironing boards. From their rightful place – in front of the TV and on it – the sedentary duo have been forced on to the celluloid highway. The point is, barring the loss of the naff music videos, nothing much about Mike Judge's creation has changed. Under the happy delusion that someone will pay them to have sex with a beautiful chick, the pair get caught up in an international spy ring, with all roads leading to the White House and much classic American scenery studiously ignored in favour of obsessive word play. This can pall after a while, yet what holds the interest is the attention to character, with B&B the latest incarnation of the Odd Couple. Beavis can't handle caffeine and hates the idea of flying. He's a '90s icon, but a jibbering fit on a plane highlights his acute discomfort with modernity. The pair are also all at sea in pioneer country. In the film's finest moment, when the boys meet up with their roadie fathers in the desert, the cry from the heart is: 'We need a 7-Eleven!' Without a TV, they have no rightful place and only mind-altering substances can restore equilibrium. With most mainstream US movies rabidly anti-drugs, this is a strikingly contrary message, rammed home by a splendid Butthole Surfers' song, which even the sober happy-clappy ending can't erase. CO'Su

Because of That War (Biglal Hamilkhama Hahi)

(1988, Isr, 93 min)
d Orna Ben-Dor Niv. *p* David Schutz, Samuel Altman. *sc* Orna Ben-Dor. *ph* Oren Schmukler. *ed* Rachel Yagil. *m* Yehuda Poliker. *with* Yehuda Poliker, Jacko Poliker, Ya'acov Gilad, Halina Birnbaum.

● An affecting 'talking heads' documentary which traces the stories of four Israelis: Yehuda Poliker and Ya'acov Gilad, two rock musicians bound together not only by their music, but also by their common experience as the offspring of survivors of the Nazi extermination camps; and those survivors themselves – Yehuda's father Jacko (from Salonika, taken to Treblinka), and Yaakov's mother Halina (from Warsaw, taken to Auschwitz as a teenager). The film is punctuated by renderings of songs, both live and studio performances, which reflect the traumas of dealing with the aftermath of the Holocaust, and some of which use the work of Halina, a writer and poet. It is a thoughtful and thought-provoking film which, despite the harrowing sequences (Jacko breaking down recalling the death of one of his brothers – his whole family was wiped out; Halina describing, in a lengthy sentence with a group of students, her experience of the camps and the 'death march') maintains a considerable control, which allows space for difficulties and ambivalences to be expressed without losing sympathy for its witnesses. As much is said here on what it means to live so continuously and intimately with death, loss and guilt, as is understood, unspoken, about the need for love. WH

Beck (aka The Locked Room)

(1992, Neth/Bel, 100 min)
d Jacob Bijl. *p* Antonino Lombardo, Rolf Orthel. *sc* Jacob Bijl. *ph* Tom Erisman. *ed* Wim Louwrier. *ad* Philippe Graff. *m* Lodewijk de Boer. *cast* Jan Decleir, Els Dottermans, Warre Borgmans, Jakob Beks.

● When chief inspector Beck returns to work upon recovery from a shooting incident, he is asked to look into the case of an apparent suicide; colleagues, meanwhile, are investigating a series of robberies. But both cases merge when single mother Monita is asked to act as a courier for an unscrupulous photographer... This modest, competent thriller works effectively as a police procedural; but more interestingly, with studious detachment, it explores how far chance determines one's destiny. From the novel by Maj Sjöwall and Per Wahlöö. CM

Beckoning Light, The

see Maborosi

Becky Sharp

(1935, US, 84 min)
d Rouben Mamoulian. *p* Kenneth MacGowan. *sc* Francis Edward Faragoh. *ph* Ray Rennahan. *ed* Archie Marshek. *pd* Robert Edmond Jones, Wiard Ihnen. *m* Roy Webb. *cast* Miriam Hopkins, Cedric Hardwicke, Nigel Bruce, Frances Dee, Billie Burke, Alison Skipworth.

● So much has been made of the fact that this was the first feature to be shot in three-strip Technicolor that it's often forgotten just how marvellous a film it actually is. A sophisticated, witty, and beautifully economical adaptation of Thackeray's *Vanity Fair* as it charts its cunning heroine's meteoric rise in society, it rightly and explicitly treats her entirely amoral manipulation of sympathetic women and besotted men as an on-going performance of immense versatility. But the colour is supremely important, in that Mamoulian uses costume, decor and lighting to precise symbolic effect, most memorably, perhaps, in the famous ballroom sequence on the eve of Waterloo when, as battle is announced, the pastel gowns are suddenly replaced by the crimson cloaks of soldiers rushing to war. Its enormously funny script might nevertheless seem precious, even stilted, were it not for the excellence of the performances, of which Miriam Hopkins' Becky is merely the most dazzling. GA

Bed and Board

see Domicile Conjugal.

Bedazzled

(1967, GB, 103 min)
d/p Stanley Donen. *sc* Peter Cook. *ph* Austin Dempster. *ed* Richard Marden. *ad* Terence Knight. *m* Dudley Moore. *cast* Peter Cook, Dudley Moore, Eleanor Bron, Michael Bates, Raquel Welch, Barry Humphries.

●Pete and Dud's update of the Faust legend is a hit-and-myth affair in which diminutive cook Dud, finding his love for waitress Eleanor Bron unrequited, attempts suicide and is offered seven wishes in return for his soul by the devilish Pete. Good fun sometimes but a little too sketchy, with a plot that is almost as threadbare as the outfit worn by the voluptuous Raquel Welch in her cameo role as one of the Seven Deadly Sins – need one add which?

Bedazzled

(2000, US/Ger, 93 min)
d Harold Ramis. *p* Trevor Albert, Harold Ramis. *sc* Larry Gelbart, Harold Ramis, Peter Tolan. *ph* Bill Pope. *ed* Craig P Herring. *pd* Rick Heinrichs. *m* David Newman. *cast* Brendan Fraser, Elizabeth Hurley, Frances O'Connor, Miriam Shor, Orlando Jones, Paul Adelstein, Toby Huss, Gabriel Casseus.

●Harold Ramis might have had fun with seven magic wishes and a Faustian pact, but this update of a 1967 update of a well-worn legend fails to ignite. The hero, Elliot Richards (Fraser), tempted by the Devil for the sake of a Big Mac and Coke, wastes his wishes, while his so-called adversary, the Princess of Darkness in a red dress, catsuit, traffic-cop and nurse outfits (Hurley, barkingly mediocre), exploits and indulges him in an ad hoc way, thus undermining the rules of their game. Essentially, a computer geek learns a wholesome lesson about not dreaming his life away and being rewarded with, er, the girl of his dreams, albeit a transmogrified version. That said, the visual gags generally come off and the leads have some canny lines. SS

Bedevil

(1993, Aust, 90 min)
d Tracey Moffatt. *p* Anthony Buckley, Carol Hughes. *sc* Tracey Moffatt. *ph* Geoff Burton. *ed* Wayne Le Clos. *pd* Stephen Curtis. *m* Carl Vine. *cast* Lex Marinos, Tracey Moffatt, Diana Davidson, Jack Charles, Dina Panozzo.

●The brash '60s-style credits are promising, but what follows doesn't live up to the expectations raised by Moffatt's shorts. This trilogy of vaguely supernatural tales may look striking – it was shot, very noticeably, in the studio, for control of colour and camera movement – but the 'elliptical' stories remain bafflingly obscure. To put it kindly: pretentious as hell. GA

Bedford Incident, The

(1965, GB, 102 min, b/w)
d/p James B Harris. *sc* James Poe. *ph* Gilbert Taylor. *ed* John Jympson. *ad* Arthur Lawson. *m* Gerard Schurmann. *cast* Richard Widmark, Sidney Poitier, James MacArthur, Eric Portman, Martin Balsam, Wally Cox, Donald Sutherland.

●Harris, Stanley Kubrick's former producer, here came up with his own *Dr Strangelove* variant, muting the black humour but just as incisively diagnosing nuclear insanity, as Widmark's super-patriot warship captain hunts a Soviet sub in Arctic waters, justifying his brinkmanship to Poitier's junketing journalist (along to do a story) and a sorely tried crew. PT

Bedknobs and Broomsticks

(1970, US, 117 min)
d Robert Stevenson. *p* Bill Walsh. *sc* Bill Walsh, Don Da Gradi. *ph* Frank Phillips. *ed* Cotton Warburton. *ad* John B Mansbridge. *m* Richard M Sherman, Robert B Sherman. *cast* Angela Lansbury, David Tomlinson, Roddy McDowall, Sam Jaffe, John Ericson, Bruce Forsyth, Cindy O'Callaghan.

●Disney comedy about an apprentice witch in good old cutesy-pie England, helped by three kids in making a contribution to the war effort. Never boring, and has a well-animated soccer match with animals. Must all films for kids be so shoddy, though? The music is appalling.

Bedlam

(1946, US, 79 min, b/w)
d Mark Robson. *p* Val Lewton. *sc* Val Lewton, Mark Robson. *ph* Nick Musuraca. *ed* Lyle Boyer. *ad* Albert S D'Agostino, Walter E Keller. *m* Roy Webb. *cast* Boris Karloff, Anna Lee, Billy House, Richard Fraser, Glenn Vernon, Ian Wolfe, Jason Robards Sr.

●Even Val Lewton's staunchest fans don't claim *Bedlam* as one of his most successful productions, but its tale of the celebrated 18th century madhouse is both intelligently written and admirably acted. Its major pretension is also its greatest weakness: the design is scrupulously modelled on Hogarth prints, and the aestheticism finally swamps most of the gusto in the plot. Robson's notably unpoetic direction doesn't help, either; yet few Hollywood films ever had such ambition. TR

Bed of Roses

(1996, US, 87 min.)
d Michael Goldenberg. *p* Alan Mindel, Denise Shaw. *sc* Michael Goldenberg. *ph* Adam Kimmel. *ed* Jane Kurson. *pd* Stephen McCabe. *m* Michael Convertino. *cast* Christian Slater, Mary Stuart Masterson, Pamela Segall, Josh Brolin, Ally Walker, Debra Monk.

●Lisa (Masterson), an industrious New York investment banker, learns in quick succession of the deaths of her father Stanley and goldfish Melville. Next day she receives a lavish bouquet via deliveryman Lewis (Slater). Despite her best efforts, the sender's identity remains a mystery, until she wakes up one night to see Lewis staring longingly at her apartment window. It's a modestly engaging set-up, but once love has blossomed, what's to keep our attention? There's a well-signposted consideration of the discrepancies betwixt fantasy and reality, more talked about than enacted. As for the basic story-line, the characters are too anodyne to keep us involved in their repetitive cycle of break-ups and reconciliations; Slater especially, in the more passive role, is almost terminally nice. Humdrum. NB

Bedrooms and Hallways (Des Chambres et des Couloirs)

(1998, GB/Fr/Ger, 96 min)
d Rose Troche. *p* Ceci Dempsey, Dorothy Berwin. *sc* Robert Farrar. *ph* Ashley Rowe. *ed* Christopher Blunden. *pd* Richard Bridgland. *m* Alfredo D Troche, Ian MacPherson. *cast* Kevin McKidd, Hugo Weaving, Jennifer Ehle, Tom Hollander, Simon Callow, Harriet Walter, James Purefoy.

●A weekly all-male encounter session allows straight men to unburden their emotions, until McKidd comes along, gets handed the 'honesty stone', and admits to a stirring desire for fellow member Purefoy. The latter in turn is having woman troubles of his own, and might just be tempted to take up on the offer. This contemporary London comedy from Rose Troche admits (like her earlier *Go Fish*) that sexuality is often not as cut and dried as we might think, and is much more diverting for it. McKidd makes a believably befuddled leading man, and there's agreeable support from Callow (wonderfully pretentious guru of 'Iron John' psycho-babble) and Hollander (ultra-camp bitchy flatmate). Slightly one-paced, occasionally contrived, but an amiable diversion for the open-minded. TJ

Bedroom Window, The

(1987, US, 113 min)
d Curtis Hanson. *p* Martha De Laurentiis. *sc* Curtis Hanson. *ph* Gilbert Taylor. *ed* Scott Conrad. *pd* Ron Foreman. *m* Michael Shrieve. *cast* Elizabeth McGovern, Steve Guttenberg, Isabelle Huppert, Paul Shenar, Carl Lumbly, Wallace Shawn, Brad Greenquist.

●Terry Lambert (Guttenberg) is not a bright man. Having just bonked his boss's wife Sylvia (Huppert), he gets up to take a leak. While he is in the bathroom, the rich bitch witnesses an assault on a young woman (McGovern) from the bedroom window, and scares the attacker off. The next day, the corpse of a woman is found in a dumpster a few blocks away. Because Terry wants to do the right thing, and his affair with Sylvia must remain secret, he tells the cops that he saw the attack. So when the accused is released due to lack of evidence, the boys in blue start leaning on Terry. Writer/director Hanson has created a plausible thriller with several neat twists; but the last half-hour, while never quite losing its grip, degenerates into pure flapdoodle, with McGovern coming to the rescue by using herself as bait to trap the real sicko. MS

Bed Scenes

see Scènes de lit

Bed Sitting Room, The

(1969, GB, 91 min)
d/p Richard Lester. *sc* John Antrobus. *ph* David Watkin. *ed* John Victor Smith. *pd* Assheton Gorton. *m* Ken Thorne. *cast* Ralph Richardson, Rita Tushingham, Michael Hordern, Arthur Lowe, Mona Washbourne, Peter Cook, Dudley Moore, Spike Milligan, Roy Kinnear, Marty Feldman, Dandy Nichols, Harry Secombe.

●Surreal after-the-bomb comedy (adapted from the play by Spike Milligan and John Antrobus) that suffers from being too hit-and-miss, despite flashes of brilliance and some dazzling photography. However, if time as we know it will cease after the bomb, then the film offers an adequate representation of temporal dislocation: its non-plot frequently makes the 91 minutes seem interminable. CPe

Bee Keeper, The (O Melissokomos)

(1986, Greece/Fr, 122 min)
d/p Theo Angelopoulos. *sc* Theo Angelopoulos, Dimitris Nollas, Tonino Guerra. *ph* Yorgos Arvanitis. *ed* Takis Yannopoulos. *ad* Mikes Karapiperis. *m* Eleni Karaindrou. *cast* Marcello Mastroianni, Nadia Mourouzi, Serge Reggiani, Jenny Roussea, Dinos Iliopoulos.

●Angelopoulos' odyssey of a middle-aged man in the grip of terminal emptiness has a stately pace and a shortage of event or information that are a lot to take. It's always raining, usually evening, and the settings are mainly petrol stations and sad rooming houses in Greek tank towns. Spyros (Mastroianni) resigns his job as a schoolmaster, leaves his wife, and drives off with his beehives to follow the pollen route. A teenage hitchhiker (Mourouzi) attaches herself, bumming fags and food, and even using his room to score with a passing soldier. Spyros remains uncomplaining, wordless and lifeless throughout. They finally get it on in a neglected cinema, which not only fails to buck up his ideas, but appears to confirm his disenchantment, because the next day he surrenders to death by bee-sting. A muffled, deeply interior film. BC

Beethoven

(1992, US, 88 min)
d Brian Levant. *p* Michael C Gross, Joe Medjuck. *sc* Edmond Dantes, Amy Holden-Jones. *ph* Victor J Kemper. *ed* Sheldon Kahn. *pd* Alex Tavoularis. *m* Randy Edelman. *cast* Charles Grodin, Bonnie Hunt, Dean Jones, Nicholle Tom, Christopher Castille, Sarah Rose Carr, David Duchovny.

●Sounds horrible: a comedy about a big shaggy dog which wins the love of a suburban family by destroying their home. Things start out badly when baby Beethoven (a St Bernard so named for his musicality) piddles on a pet shop patron before the credits are finished. Mercifully, the excrement gags are soon exhausted and things take a turn for the better, thanks largely to the sublimely sour-faced antics of Charles Grodin as dad, a neurotic dog-hater who markets air-fresheners for a living. Elevated from the doldrums of *Digby*-esque sentimentality by a surprisingly bouncy script, the film is also redeemed by regular interludes of acerbic dialogue and a brace of fine supporting performances (notably David Duchovny as a slimy yuppie git who says 'Ciao, bello!' and criticises the cappuccino). MK

Beethoven's 2nd

(1993, US, 88 min)
d Rod Daniel. *p* Joe Medjuck, Michael C Gross. *sc* Len Blum. *ph* Bill Butler. *ed* Sheldon Kahn, William Gordean. *pd* Lawrence Miller. *m* Randy Edelman. *cast* Charles Grodin, Bonnie Hunt, Debi Mazar, Nicholle Tom, Christopher Castile, Sarah Rose Karr, Chris Penn.

●Daniel's hit Beethoven sequel builds on the high slobber and house-destruct factor of the earlier film by adding aahhh! appeal in the shape of four puppies. The soulful St Bernard – now secure in the household of persuadable grump Grodin and supermum Hunt – finds a pedigree chum in Sissy, owned by evil stack-heeled

Mazar. The plot follows the dogs' romance, passes discreetly over the sex, and has Grodin's three brats engaging in benign subterfuge, hiding the fruits of the union from daddy in the basement cupboard. Then the evil stack-heeled one wants Sissy back in some palaver over an emotional tug-of-love divorce settlement. *Then* she wants to sell the offspring for *profit*! Then... It's a shaggy-dog story, targeted at children and the softer cinemagoer, but amiable enough not to offend the hard-boiled. WH

Beetlejuice

(1988, US, 92 min)
d Tim Burton. *p* Michael Bender, Larry Wilson, Richard Hashimoto. *sc* Michael McDowell, Warren Skaaren. *ph* Thomas Ackerman. *ed* Jane Kurson. *pd* Bo Welch. *m* Danny Elfman. *cast* Michael Keaton, Alec Baldwin, Geena Davis, Jeffrey Jones, Winona Ryder, Catherine O'Hara, Glenn Shadix, Sylvia Sidney, Annie McEnroe.
●This ghost story from the haunters' perspective (co-scripted by Michael McDowell) provides some of the most surprisingly enjoyable viewing in years. The drearily happy Maitlands (Baldwin and Davis) drive into the river, come up dead, and return to their beloved, quaint house as spooks intent on despatching the hideous New York yuppie family which had usurped their property. The humour unfolds as the horrible Deetzes (Jones and O'Hara) fill the house with revolting avant-garde art, bulldozers, and camp interior designers spitting venom; while only their mournful teenage daughter (Ryder) seems either aware of or in tune with the ghostly couple, whose failure to shine in the scare stakes finally drags them into the arms of the gunslinger-exorcist Betelgeuse (Keaton), a kind of OTT demonic Clint Eastwood of the underworld (who rids houses of unwanted humans). Off-the wall humour and some sensational sight gags make the movie, maddeningly disjointed though it sometimes is, a truly astonishing piece of work. SGr

Before and After

(1996, US, 108 min)
d Barbet Schroeder. *p* Barbet Schroeder, Susan Hoffman. *sc* Ted Tally. *ph* Luciano Tovoli. *ed* Lee Percy. *pd* Stuart Wurtzel. *m* Howard Shore. *cast* Meryl Streep, Liam Neeson, Edward Furlong, Julia Weldon, Alfred Molina, Daniel von Bargen, John Heard.
●A director who still thinks like a producer, Barbet Schroeder has a way of making decent, intelligent, rather boring films (*Reversal of Fortune*, *Kiss of Death*), but this is simply more mediocre than most: a fraught family drama which never really hits home. When a local teenager turns up dead, Ben and Carolyn Ryan (Neeson and Streep) have no inkling that their lives will be affected. Even when son Jacob (Furlong) runs off, Carolyn can't believe he's done anything wrong; but a police inquiry soon persuades Ben otherwise, and he angrily destroys incriminating evidence, a course of adamant non-cooperation which horrifies his wife and daughter. Plenty of dramatic meat here, but the talky screenplay by Ted (*Silence of the Lambs*) Tally, from the book by Rosellen Brown, soon forgoes any semblance of suspense in favour of supposedly subtle character study and a thorny ethical conundrum: what price truth when your own flesh and blood faces life behind bars? While the script pays brief lip service to class questions, the movie runs away from guilt as surely as young Jacob. Streep has virtually nothing to play with, while Neeson's bullish chauvinism is indulged right up to a phoney prison-scene showdown. It's not a stupid film, exactly, but badly made, stagnant, humourless, and sorely lacking in authentic human behaviour. TCh

Before and After Sex (Prima e Dopo l'Amore ... Un Grido d'Allarme)

(1972, It, 91 min)
d Giovanni Crisci. *p* Renzo Renzi. *sc* Aldo Calamara, Giovanni Crisci, Fabrizio Diotallevi, Guido Quattrone, Renzo Renzi. *ph* Giovanni Crisci. *ed* Fedora Zincone. *ad* Annamaria Lentini. *m* Pat Bodie. *cast* Farid Bendali, Franco Jamonte, Leonora Vivaldi, Richard Melville, Valeria Loredana Mongardini.
●Unappetising and repressive film that presumably attempts to act as a Trojan horse by infiltrating a dire warning about syphilis through the medium of a sexploitation piece. It fails primarily through doing nothing to explain the disease in rational, helpful terms, and everything to play on panic and mystification. VG

Before Dawn

(1933, US, 60 min, b/w)
d Irving Pichel. *sc* Garrett Fort. *ph* Lucien Andriot. *ed* William Hamilton. *ad* Van Nest Polglase. *m* Max Steiner. *cast* Stuart Erwin, Warner Oland, Dorothy Wilson, Dudley Digges, Jane Darwell, Gertrude W Hoffman.
●RKO cheapie based on Edgar Wallace's *Death Watch*, with Wilson as the pretty spiritualist involved in the unmasking of a murderer. Set in an old dark house where loot lies hidden, it's watchable (with a nicely sinister performance from Oland), but pretty routine when one recalls that Pichel made *The Most Dangerous Game* a year earlier. TM

Before Dawn (Di Ba Zhan)

(1983, HK, 88 min)
d Clarence Ford [Fok Yiu-Leung]. *cast* Deannie Ip, Lau Dan, Loletta Lee, Ku Feng, Wong Sue-Kei, Leung Saan.
●Ah Po, aged 17, has been spoiled all his life by his mother, a nightclub dancer dumped by his father and a succession of other men. He considers himself straight but one night's service as a rent boy leaves him implicated in a series of murders of gay men – which are actually being carried out by the bent cop who is charged with investigating them. Fok's hysterical, barely coherent melodrama throws in everything from kitchen sink realism to forced-sodomy fantasies with fluttering doves but centres on the chasm between adults and kids. It had the distinction of being the first Hong Kong feature to imagine a gay sub-culture and broach the possibility of its protagonist's sexual ambivalence. No 'positive images', but it was a cult favourite in underground gay circles in the unliberated '80s. TR

Before Hindsight

(1977, GB, 78 min, b/w & col)
d Jonathan Lewis. *p* Elizabeth Taylor-Mead. *sc* Jonathan Lewis, Elizabeth Taylor-Mead. *ph* Roger Deakins. *ed* Jonathan Lewis. *with* James Cameron, Edgar Anstey, George Elvin, Leslie Mitchell, Ivor Montagu, Jonathan Dimbleby.
●Newsreels from the '30s constitute the bulk of this fascinating documentary, clearly illustrating that the public was fed an extremely biased view of events: straight propaganda, the stricture to provide entertainment, and the attempt to be objective all contributing to this. Lewis and producer Elizabeth Taylor-Mead have constructed their argument well, but it is Jonathan Dimbleby's brief comments towards the end that contain the crucial lesson: forty years on, the same forces work to distort our view of Northern Ireland. The film only indicates this to be the case, but it is precise and coherent enough to make the point with considerable force. JW

Before I Hang

(1940, US, 71 min, b/w)
d Nick Grindé. *sc* Robert Hardy Andrews. *ph* Benjamin Kline. *ed* Charles Nelson. *ad* Lionel Banks. *m* Morris W Stoloff. *cast* Boris Karloff, Evelyn Keyes, Bruce Bennett, Edward Van Sloan, Pedro de Cordoba.
●Karloff brings his usual injection of class to this middling B-pic about a scientist working in the field of rejuvenation through blood plasma treatment, which comes in handy when he's sentenced to death for a mercy killing and is able to rejuvenate himself behind bars to escape the sentence. The catch is, of course, that he's had to use the blood of a convicted murderer – definitely not a good idea, as any genre buff knows. TJ

Before Night Falls

(2000, US, 133 min)
d Julian Schnabel. *p* Jon Kilik. *sc* Cunningham O'Keefe, Lázaro Gómez Carriles, Julian Schnabel. *ph* Javier Pérez Grobet, Guillermo Rosas. *ed* Michael Berenbaum. *pd* Salvador Parra. *m* Carter Burwell. *cast* Javier Bardem, Johnny Depp, Sean Penn, John Ortiz, Santiago Magill, Michael Wincott, Najwa Nimri, Alfredo Villa, Hector Babenco, Jerzy Skolimowski.
●Schnabel's biopic of Cuban writer Reinaldo Arenas – betrayed by the revolution because of his homosexuality – is evidently a labour of love, and at the same time surprisingly conventional. It has a richly imagined look (much more assured than *Basquiat*) and a real feel for the words (Bardem's Oscar-nominated performance combines overt sensuality with intellectual curiosity and pride), but you may have qualms about the stunt casting of Penn and Depp. TCh

Before Stonewall

(1984, US, 87 min, b/w & col)
d Greta Schiller, Robert Rosenberg. *p* Robert Rosenberg, John Scagliotti, Greta Schiller. *ph* Jan Kraepelin, Sandi Sissel, Cathy Zheutlin. *ed* Bill Daughton. *narrator* Rita Mae Brown.
●Films like *Word Is Out* and *The Times of Harvey Milk* have done valuable lesbian and gay archaeology, but none so well as this documentary. Mixing up-to-the-minute footage with older material mined from Hollywood newsreel and home movie, it achieves a near-perfect balance between historical and political perspectives, and sometimes unconsciously hilarious archive footage. Its politics are sensible, the life stories touching, warm and funny, and the archive stuff camper than Butlin's empire. JG

Before Sunrise

(1995, US, 101 min)
d Richard Linklater. *p* Anne Walker. *sc* Richard Linklater, Kim Krizan. *ph* Lee Daniel. *ed* Sandra Adair. *pd* Florian Reichmann. *cast* Ethan Hawke, Julie Delpy, Andrea Eckert, Hanno Pöschl, Erni Mangold.
●Céline (Delpy), an easy-going Parisian, is on her way back from Budapest to study at the Sorbonne; Jesse (Hawke), a young American, is at the end of a Eurorail tour. They meet on a train just outside Vienna; by the time they reach the station, they've hit it off well enough for Jesse to propose that Céline spend the next 14 hours wandering the city with him, until his flight leaves for the States. Intrigued, she accepts. So begins an unexpected adventure of the heart. What's magical about Linklater's entrancing movie is the way he and his actors manage to convey the emotional truths that underlie all the talk as the potential lovers test each other's opinions and commitment. Funny, poignant and perceptive, this is a brilliant gem. GA

Before the Nickelodeon: The Early Cinema of Edwin S Porter

(1982, US, 60 min, b/w & col)
d/p Charles Musser. *sc* Warren D Leight, Charles Musser. *ed* Charles Musser. *voices* Jay Leyda, Bob Rosen, Mitchell Kriegman, Peter Davis, Milos Forman, Louis Malle, Robert Altman. *narrator* Blanche Sweet.
●Edwin S Porter's contribution to the history of the movies is enormous. At a time when most film-makers were content with crude one-take shorts of straightforward dramatic design, Porter was already experimenting with editing his stories to include different points of view and various trick special effects which he may have learned from Méliès. His *Western The Great Train Robbery* (1902) set the stamp on what was to become Hollywood's greatest genre, and was the most popular film until *The Birth of a Nation* (1915), directed by DW Griffith, an actor who was given his first movie break by Porter. Musser's enchanting piece of movie archaeology traces the life of this key figure, with plenty of clips from his greatest hits, a commentary from Blanche Sweet (the Griffith star), and just the right note of amused genuflection to a master. Also included, complete, are four of Porter's short films. CPea

Before the Rain (Pred Dozdot)

(1994, Macedonia/GB/Fr, 115 min)
d Milcho Manchevski. *p* Judy Counihan, Sam Taylor, Cat Villiers, Cedomir Kolar, Gorjan Tozija. *sc* Milcho Manchevski. *ph* Manuel Teran. *ed* Nick Gaster. *pd* Sharon Lamofsky. *m* Anastasia. *cast* Rade Serbedzija, Katrin Cartlidge, Grégoire Colin, Labina Mitevska, Jay Villiers, Phyllida Law.
●A solemn triptych that transports us from the ethnic tensions of Macedonia to the urban strife of London, and back again. In 'Words', we see a

monk break his vow of silence to shelter an Albanian girl from a lynch mob; in 'Faces', Anne (Cartlidge), an English picture-editor, refuses to accompany her photographer lover Aleksandar (Serbedzija) to the village where he grew up, and tells her estranged husband that she's pregnant; while in part three, 'Pictures', Aleksandar returns home for the first time in 20 years, and struggles to make sense of the madness infesting his country. As a director, Manchevski is still finding his feet. The tragic portents of the first story are heavily signalled, and the attempt to convey the rhythm of London life in nervy edits is unconvincing, but the boldness of the conception sees him through. Flawed, certainly, and a little infatuated with its own tragic aura, but a brave, compelling work which repays serious attention. TCh

Before the Revolution (Prima della Rivoluzione)

(1964, It, 112 min, b/w)
d/sc Bernardo Bertolucci. *ph* Aldo Scavarda. *ed* Roberto Perpignani. *ad* Romano Pampaloni. *m* Gino Paoli, Ennio Morricone. *cast* Francesco Barilli, Adriana Asti, Allen Midgette, Morando Morandini, Domenico Alpi, Giuseppe Maghenzani.

●In all of Bertolucci's movies, there's a central conflict between the 'radical' impulses and a pessimistic (and/or willing) capitulation to the mainstream of bourgeois society and culture. It's a contradiction that takes on juggernaut proportions in '1900', but it stands as a major source of tension and interest in many of the earlier films. Both *Before the Revolution* (Bertolucci's second feature) and *Partner* try to examine it head-on. *Revolution* is about a middle-class 20-year-old who 'discovers' Marxism and tries – for a while – to change his life; *Partner* is an exuberant response to the student riots of '68, with Pierre Clémenti as a timid drama student confronting his own anarchic revolutionary alter ego. The first is mostly 'classical' in style, while the second is aggressively 'new wave', but both are full of interruptions and digressions: they throw out ideas and allusions (usually to other movies) with reckless enthusiasm, and they remain invaluable aids to an understanding of the '60s. TR

Before Winter Comes

(1968, GB, 103 min)
d J Lee Thompson. *p* Robert Emmett Ginna. *sc* Andrew Sinclair. *ph* Gilbert Taylor. *ed* Willy Kemplen. *ad* John Blezard. *m* Ron Grainer. *cast* David Niven, Topol, Anna Karina, John Hurt, Ori Levy, Anthony Quayle, John Collin.

●Towards the end of WWII, Major Niven has the difficult task of deciding the fate of displaced persons: send them to the Free World, or to Russia? His job is made rather easier when co-star Topol arrives, a valued linguist who claims to be a Yugoslav refugee but is in fact a Russian deserter. Scripted by Andrew Sinclair from a short story by Frederick L Keefe, it's impeccably humanistic, unusually contrived and incredibly dull. It should have been a comedy or a musical. ATu

Beggars of Life

(1928, US, 7,560 ft, b/w)
d William A Wellman. *sc* Benjamin Glazer. *ph* Henry Gerrard. *ed* Allyson Shaffer. *cast* Louise Brooks, Richard Arlen, Wallace Beery, Edgar Washington, HA Morgan, Andy Clark.

●If it weren't for two of its lead performances, this would be a simple period curiosity, one of Hollywood's first sympathetic portraits of life on the run from the police. A vagrant falls in with a young woman wanted for murder; the two of them seek refuge with a group of hoboes, but find their own kind as hostile as the rest of society. Wellman sketches the hobo mentality with a fine economy, but cannot deliver the pace and suspense that the plot demands. Hence the importance of the players. Beery, entering with a pilfered beer-barrel on his shoulder, offers an extravagantly randy, bullying and sentimental performance as Oklahoma Red, leader of the hoboes. Despite his excellence, though, all eyes are on the 22-year-old Louise Brooks, who was about to leave for Germany to star in *Pandora's Box*. As the movie opens, she has just shot her adoptive father, who tried to rape her. She flees in boy's clothes, tough and vulnerable in equal proportions. The camera loves her, and she rewards it with a performance that radiates inner life. TR

Beggar's Opera, The

(1952, GB, 94 min)
d Peter Brook. *p* Laurence Olivier, Herbert Wilcox. *sc* Denis Cannan, Christopher Fry. *ph* Guy Green. *ed* Reginald Beck. *ad* William C Andrews, Georges Wakévitch. *m* Arthur Bliss. *cast* Hugh Griffith, Laurence Olivier, Dorothy Tutin, Stanley Holloway, Daphne Anderson, Sandra Dorne, Yvonne Furneaux, George Devine, Laurence Naismith, Athene Seyler, George Rose, Kenneth Williams.

●A commercial disaster, Peter Brook's first movie has gradually grown in stature as more people have discovered its delights. John Gay's original concoction satirised the conventions of Italian opera and dumped them into Merrie England's morass of highwaymen, whores and hangmen. The movie, with the music adapted by Arthur Bliss, and the script adapted by Dennis Cannan and Christopher Fry, sets out to send up what was already partly a send-up; and Brook, of course, was the ideal director, committed to radical theatre and disrespectful (or innocent) of cinematic forms. He has trouble when dialogue gives way to song (though even here one might call this a Brechtian device, as in *The Threepenny Opera*), but gets performances from Olivier (as the swashbuckling MacHeath) and Tutin (as Polly Peachum) of such mellifluous exuberance that the cracks are neatly sealed. ATu

Begging the Ring

(1978, GB, 55 min)
d/p Colin Gregg. *sc* Colin Gregg, Hugh Stoddart. *ph* John Metcalfe. *ed* Colin Gregg. *cast* Danny Simpson, Jon Croft, Janette Legge, Kenneth Midwood, Terence Conoley, Alan Penn.

●Typical attempt at social realism by the independent team of Gregg and writer Hugh Stoddart. An investigation of a family's dilemma when the 18-year-old son, trained by his ambitious father for the local wrestling championships, receives his call-up papers for WWI, its failure derives not only from the limitations of the realist, semi-documentary style (Gregg fails to tease out the knotty problems of enforced conscription clearly); but also from the difficulty of following some of the Cornish dialect; and, most noticeably, from the awkward insertion of an intellectual-outsider, commenting chorus-fashion with lines like 'We're all wrestling with the angel of darkness, lad'. GA

Beginner's Luck

(2001, GB, 90 min)
d Nick Cohen, James Callis. *p* Harriet Evans-Lombe. *sc* Nick Cohen, James Callis. *ph* Chris Preston. *ed* Alistair Waterson. *pd* Tracy Ann Baines. *m* Shriek Music. *cast* Julie Delpy, Steven Berkoff, Christopher Cazenove, Fenella Fielding, Jean Yves Bertolot, James Callis, Tom Redhill, Rosanna Lowe, Sarah Belcher, Amelia Lowdell.

●The world of luvvies, as depicted by these first time film-makers, in a touring theatre production, may be offputting, but there are laughs to be had in the wildly careering road show. Parallels with the play-within-the-film, *The Tempest*, are portentous, but you have to admire the makers' chutzpah in landing Berkoff – madly OTT as a Soho porn baron – and Delpy, playing a mysterious actress who catalyses relationships within the troupe. OA

Beginning, The (Nachalo)

(1970, USSR, 90 min, b/w)
d Gleb Panfilov. *sc* Evgeny Gabrilovich, Gleb Panfilov. *ph* Dmitri Dolynin. *ad* Marksen Gaukhman-Sverdlov. *m* Vadim Bibergan. *cast* Inna Churikova, Leonid Kuravlev, Valentina Telichkina, Yuri Klepikov, Mikhail Kononov.

●About a girl who works in a factory, spends her spare time acting in a local drama group, and is discovered by a film director looking for an unknown to play Joan of Arc in his next movie, *The Beginning* avoids all the clichés you'd expect from a plot like this, souping the whole thing up by interweaving segments from the 'Joan' film with sequences around the girl's life. This is Panfilov's second film, and he has obviously absorbed his fair share of Bergman, Bresson, Forman and Godard, but generally without allowing their influence to get in the way. The film also says something about the manufacturing of stereotypes. At the end the girl is unemployed, doing the agency rounds before going back to where she came from, while the camera lingers on an impossibly glamorous poster of her outside a cinema.

Beguiled, The

(1970, US, 105 min)
d/p Don Siegel. *sc* John B Sherry, Grimes Grice. *ph* Bruce Surtees. *ed* Carl Pingitore. *pd* Ted Haworth. *m* Lalo Schifrin. *cast* Clint Eastwood, Geraldine Page, Elizabeth Hartman, Jo Ann Harris, Darleen Carr, Mae Mercer.

●Combining the conventions of both Western and Grand Guignol chiller, and often directed as if it were an art movie, this is one of Siegel and Eastwood's strangest – and most beguiling – collaborations. Eastwood is the Yankee soldier, who after being wounded during the Civil War, takes refuge in an isolated Southern seminary for young women. Shut away from the world, the women project their romantic fantasies onto him, and he responds with callous, male manipulation. But jealousy and resentment raise their heads, and he finds himself in a world of brutal revenge. Beautifully shot by Bruce Surtees, carefully paced, it's a haunting, elegant work that seems to have influenced the troubled sexuality of Eastwood's own *Play Misty for Me* and *Tightrope*. GA

Béguines, The

see Rempart des Béguines, Le

Behind Closed Eyes (Achter gesloten ogen)

(2000, Neth, 100 min)
d Duco Tellegen.

●Profiles of kids damaged in recent wars, trying to rebuild themselves a normality. Spencer (18), one of Liberia's ex-child soldiers (and murderers), is treated gingerly; Eranda (7), a Kosovan refugee, reluctantly communicates his feelings about war; one-legged landmine orphan Nhom (13) gets on with school and a new prosthesis, but never smiles; Jacqueline (18), a raped and now ostracised new mother, struggles for the courage to enter her village, and adulthood. Quietly affecting. NB

Behind Convent Walls (L'Interno di un Convento)

(1977, It, 96 min)
d Walerian Borowczyk. *p* Giuseppe Vezzani. *sc* Walerian Borowczyk. *ph* Luciano Tovoli. *ed* Walerian Borowczyk. *ad* Luciano Spadoni. *m* Sergio Montori. *cast* Ligia Branice, Marina Pierro, Gabriella Giaccobe, Loredana Martine, Mario Maranzana.

●Borowczyk has fetishised prostitution (*The Streetwalker*) and bestiality (*The Beast*), so turning out this pastiche of sex-movie staple (the convent as a sexual greenhouse) can't have been too challenging. The film's pace is too slow, and interest in detail overwhelms the narrative. But this waywardness allows some unusual inflexions: masturbation as a real centre of interest, Christ as a laughable sex-martyr. Ultimately the convent-as-haven is exploded: patriarchy intrudes to deliver punishment, and the tale ends (?) with the murder of the abbess and multiple suicide by the nuns. CA

Behind Enemy Lines

(2001, US, 106 min)
d John Moore. *p* John Davis. *sc* David Veloz, Zak Penn. *ph* Brendan Galvin. *ed* Paul Martin Smith. *pd* Nathan Crowley. *m* Don Davis. *cast* Owen Wilson, Gene Hackman, Gabriel Macht, Joaquim de Almeida, David Keith, Olek Krupa, Vladimir Mashkov, Charles Malik Whitfield.

●Hackman is too old for the derring-do – this time he's the gruff admiral trying to get reckless crashed fly-boy Wilson home before Serbs lay their murderous hands on him – but otherwise it's the same old same old. The cavalier script doesn't exactly tread cautiously through the political minefield that is the Balkans; it's more like a hell-for-leather sprint, head down, hoping for the best. Of course, the film isn't trying to catch your conscience, only to stir the blood. If the Serbs weren't such cartoonish villains or Wilson so invulnerable to bullets, it might have been more effective. Brit director Moore comes from advertising. His hyper Gameboy visuals render war as an especially obscene pop promo.

It's also worth noting how this Fox production shoehorns in several blatant plugs for Murdoch's Sky News. TCh

Behindert

see Hindered

Behind the Iron Curtain

see Iron Curtain, The

Behind the Rent Strike

(1974, GB, 50 min)
d/p/sc/ph/ed Nicholas Broomfield.

●Brilliant documentary attempt to understand the 14 months' rent strike by the people of Kirkby New Town, near Liverpool, which started just before Christmas in 1973. An analysis of the social conditions is preceded by an interview between the film-maker and an extremely shrewd working-class housewife who debunks this and all other investigations by the media as just another form of bourgeois masturbation. This in itself makes a complacent viewing, which might normally act as an appeaser to liberal conscience, impossible. RM

Behind the Sun (Abril despedaçado)

(2001, Braz/Switz/Fr, 92 min)
d Walter Salles. *p* Arthur Cohn. *sc* Walter Salles, Sérgio Machado, Karim Aïnouz. *ph* Walter Carvalho. *ed* Isabelle Rathéry. *pd* Cássio Amarante. *m* Antônio Pinto. *cast* José Dumont, Rodrigo Santoro, Rita Assemany, Luiz Carlos Vasconcelos, Flavia Marco Antonio, Ravi Ramos Lacerda, Caio Junqueira.

●The arid badlands of Bahia, northern Brazil, in 1910. Among those subsisting off the sugarcane are the Breves: rigid authoritarian patriarch (Dumont), long-suffering but loyal wife (Assemany), young Pacu (Lacerda) and 20-year-old Tonho (Santoro) – unlikely to see 21, given the age-old feud between his family and the Ferreiras, who just slew his elder brother. Age-old notions of honour dictate the eldest son take revenge, thus ensuring the deadly cycle endures. So assured, bold, harmonious and fertile a mix of form and content is Salles' follow-up to *Central Station*, you'd never guess it was taken from an Albanian novel about Balkan animosities. Transposing the tale to his own country's harshest region at a time when farmers' feuds were rife, Salles uses the milieu not only to assemble some astonishingly luscious images, but to reflect on the relationship of economics and tradition to individual freedom. At the same time, by highlighting ritual and metaphor, he inflects the narrative (in its essential dynamics not unlike a Western) with a poetic clarity and richness reminiscent of Greek tragedy and myth. GA

Beijing Bastards (Beijing Zazhong)

(1993, HK/China, 95 min)
d Zhang Yuan. *p* Cui Jian, Zhang Yuan, Shu Kei, Christopher Doyle. *sc* Zhang Yuan, Tang Dalian, Cui Jian. *ph* Zhang Jian. *ed* Feng Shungyuan. *ad* Liu Xiaodong. *m* Cui Jian, Dou Wei, Ha Yong. *cast* Cui Jian, Li Wei, Wu Lala, Tang Dalian.

●This is a film without precedent in Chinese cinema: a seemingly free-form portrait of rock-generation kids in the city, its own quest for a structure mirroring their search 'for something to help them live'. One broken relationship provides the overall frame (a young guy named Karzi searches for the pregnant girlfriend who has left him), but half a dozen other characters also clamour for the film's attention, chief among them Cui Jian, China's rock pioneer, who plays himself and contributes several songs. Zhang Yuan has an acute feel for street-level realities, and gets very close to these kids blowing their lives on drink, dope and petty squabbles. Not exactly a blank generation, but they sure do look lost. TR

Beijing Bicycle (Shiqi Sui de Danche)

(2000, Tai/China/Fr, 113 min)
d Wang Xiaoshuai. *p* Peggy Chiao, Hsu Hsiao-Ming, Han Sanping. *sc* Wang Xiaoshuai, Tang Danian, Peggy Chiao, Hsu Hsiao-Ming. *ph* Liu Jie. *ed* Liao Qingsong. *ad* Tsai Chao-Yi, Cao Anjun. *m* Wang Feng. *cast* Cui Lin, Li Bin, Zhou Xun, Gao Yuanyuan, Li Shuang, Zhao Yiwei, Pang Yan.

●Enjoyable but less resonant than his earlier work, Wang's third 'above-ground' film centres on two contrasted 17-year-olds in present-day Beijing. Country kid Guei (Cui), slow-witted and awesomely stubborn, is a newly arrived economic migrant who gets a job as a bike courier and works hard to cover the cost of the bike. But his treasure is stolen and later bought from a street market by schoolkid Jian (Li Bin). Guei finds it and tries to steal it back. After much wrangling, the two agree to a timeshare arrangement. Then Jian's clumsy handling of his first crush brings trouble down on both their heads. There's plenty of good sociological observation in the background (Jian's fraught dealings with his remarried father yield two great scenes), but the best thing here is the stand-off between the two boys, on the cusp of a friendship. TR

Beim jodeln juckt die Lederhose

see There's No Sex Like Snow Sex

Being at Home with Claude (Seul, avec Claude)

(1992, Can, 85 min, b/w & col)
d Jean Beaudin. *p* Louise Gendron. *sc* Jean Beaudin, René-Daniel Dubois. *ph* Támas Vamos. *ed* André Corriveau. *m* Richard Grégoire. *cast* Roy Dupuis, Jacques Godin, Jean-François Pichette, Gaston Lepage, Hugo Dubé.

●Adapted from René-Daniel Dubois' controversial stage hit, this is everything Gregg Araki's *The Living End* was hyped up to be, but fell sorely short of. Queer criminality meets aching romanticism in a daring, moving illustration of Wilde's maxim 'each man kills the thing he loves'. Opening with an explosive sequence in which a man is literally fucked to death, the mystery of the film is not whodunit, but why. A hustler (Dupuis) confesses to the murder, but the law, in the shape of a nameless police inspector (Godin) requires a motive. What follows is an extended dialogue between a gay outlaw and the voice of a shocked society. The prospect of 85 minutes in the company of two characters enclosed in a single set might not sound like such a thrilling ride, but there's more drama to be found contained in these four walls than on the run through all Araki's wide-angle landscapes. The lead performances are superb, Beaudin's direction is tighter than a rent boy's vest, and if the opening scene doesn't leaving you gasping, you're probably already dead. PBur

Being Human

(1994, US, 125 min)
d Bill Forsyth. *p* David Puttnam, Robert F Colesberry. *sc* Bill Forsyth. *ph* Michael Coulter. *ed* Michael Ellis. *ad* Norman Garwood. *m* Michael Gibbs. *cast* Robin Williams, John Turturro, Anna Galiena, Vincent D'Onofrio, Hector Elizondo, Robert Carlyle; voice: Theresa Russell.

●Forsyth's most ambitious film disappeared after its disastrous US opening. Warners sat on it for a year, trying to figure out a recut which would make sense. They eventually gave the film back to the director who added Russell's voice-over narration as a sign of good faith. It's a difficult picture to get a handle on (five stories spanning 6,000 years): in each tale, Williams plays a human being (sic), Hector – a caveman, Roman slave, medieval traveller, 17th century aristocrat, and finally a contemporary New Yorker. The stories are low-key and deliberately anti-climactic, but they coalesce into a tender, contemplative whole that's profound and moving. While Hector may not be reincarnated, exactly, each story feeds on what has gone before, so that after losing his family in the Bronze Age, he's separated from them in every other tale. Other motifs recur: fear and anxiety, superstition and sacrifice; the nature of partnership, how men treat women (and other men) as chattels; the significance of water-crossings; the need and difficulty of filling other men's shoes; the abused integrity of a name. The studio was probably right: there is no general audience for this mid-life crisis of a movie, but it's singular and fascinating all the same. TCh

Being John Malkovich

(1999, US, 113 min)
d Spike Jonze. *p* Michael Stipe, Sandy Stern, Steve Golin, Vincent Landay. *sc* Charlie Kaufman. *ph* Lance Acord. *ed* Eric Zumbrunnen. *pd* KK Barrett. *m* Carter Burwell. *cast* John Cusack, Cameron Diaz, Catherine Keener, Orson Bean, Mary Kay Place, Charlie Sheen, John Malkovich.

●A true original, this one, from the demented minds of director Jonze (famous for his lo-fi pop promos for Fatboy Slim and Björk) and screenwriter Kaufman (not famous for anything yet). Taking a job as a filing clerk on the seventh-and-a-half floor (don't ask), Cusack happens across a portal into the head of John Malkovich, the actor. Chivvied along by maneater Keener, he starts selling tickets to interested parties, but not before his wife (an unrecognisably frumpy Diaz) has decided she likes being a man so much she needs a sex change operation. Yes, it loses its way a little in the sex war department, but this must be seen to be believed, a hundred carat cult item – and all credit to Malkovich for playing along. TCh

Being There

(1979, US, 130 min)
d Hal Ashby. *p* Andrew Braunsberg. *sc* Jerzy Kosinki. *ph* Caleb Deschanel. *ed* Don Zimmerman. *pd* Michael Haller. *m* Johnny Mandel. *cast* Peter Sellers, Shirley MacLaine, Melvyn Douglas, Jack Warden, Richard Dysart, Richard Basehart.

●Sellers' performance – as the innocent neuter figure who rises accidentally to political power on the strength of vacant homilies – is remarkable. But Ashby's direction is marred by the same softness that made *The Last Detail* and *Coming Home* so morally bland. What emerges in the end is a strange ambiguity of attitude to the American political system and a hollow humour about cultural values. The cinema of cynicism, really. CA

Bel Ami

(1939, Ger, 102 min, b/w)
d/p Willi Forst. *sc* Willi Forst, Axel Eggebrecht. *ph* Ted Pahle. *ed* Hans Wolff. *ad* Werner Schlichting, Robert Herlth. *m* Theo Mackben. *cast* Willi Forst, Johannes Riemann, Olga Tschechowa, Lizzi Waldmüller, Hilde Hildebrandt, Ilsa Werner.

●'Bubblier than champagne and lighter than the air of Paris' has been the verdict of French critics on the co-scenarist, director and star of *Bel Ami*. In the congenial role of Maupassant's irresistible womaniser, who uses his charm to get to the top, the Viennese Forst managed to resurrect the frivolous light-heartedness of a waltzing never-never land in the shape of turn-of-the-century Paris. A delightful parade of Germany's most forceful female stars as Bel Ami's victims (?), and satirical comments on bourgeois parliamentarianism and the free press make it doubly interesting to watch, considering its market was Nazi Germany in 1939. RB

Believe in Me

(1971, US, 88 min)
d Stuart Hagmann. *p* Irwin Winkler, Robert Chartoff. *sc* Israel Horovitz. *ph* Dick Kratina, Richard C Brooks. *ed* John C Howard. *ad* Robert Gundlach. *m* Fred Karlin. *cast* Michael Sarrazin, Jacqueline Bisset, Jon Cypher, Allen Garfield, Kurt Dodenhoff.

●Hagmann, of *The Strawberry Statement*, shows the same concern here to isolate his audience from his subject by glossy technique. The story tracks a sensitive young doctor driven to speed by the strain of watching kids die daily in his ward. He meets Bisset, turns her on, brings her down, etc. A pernicious film that trades on deliberate confusion of values, and glamorises mainlining as effectively as a Tube ad.

Believer, The

(2001, US, 98 min)
d Henry Bean. *p* Susan Hoffman, Christopher Roberts. *sc* Henry Bean. *ph* Jim Denault. *ed* Mayin Lo, Lee Percy. *pd* Susan Block. *m* Joel Diamond. *cast* Ryan Gosling, Summer Phoenix, Glenn Fitzgerald, Garret Dillahunt, Kris Eivers, Joel Garland, Joshua Harto, Tommy Nohilly, Theresa Russell, Billy Zane.

●Danny Balint (Gosling) is a skinhead. He'll cross the street to shout abuse in the face of a Jew, hit him and kick him when he's down. But he's articulate, too, more than capable of holding his own in theological debate – so much so that he comes to the attention of American fascist organisers Curtis Zampf (Zane) and Lina Moebius

(Russell). They want to groom him for a political role, but Danny impatiently advocates direct action: terror and assassination. Hard to believe Danny is a Jew born and bred. Screenwriter Bean's first film as writer/director is defiantly personal and provocative. Inspired by a news story about a Jewish anti-Semite, it takes this hard kernel of unpalatable truth as licence to pick over the elusive threads separating devotion from zealotry, love from hate, the sacred from the profane. Visually undistinguished, and marred by over-literal flashback and fantasy sequences, the film is driven by Gosling's revelatory performance. No polemic, the movie puts our own religious sensibilities and prejudices to the test. The result is arresting, prickly, vaguely funny, even – 'difficult' in the best sense. TCh

Believers, The

(1987, US, 114 min)
d John Schlesinger. *p* John Schlesinger, Michael Childers, Beverly J Camhe. *sc* Mark Frost. *ph* Robby Müller. *ed* Peter Honess. *pd* Simon Holland. *m* J Peter Robinson. *cast* Martin Sheen, Helen Shaver, Harley Cross, Robert Loggia, Elizabeth Wilson, Harris Yulin, Lee Richardson.

●There's a shocking start: due to a dodgy coffee machine, Cal Jamison's wife ends up frying over spilt milk. To get over their loss, Cal (Sheen), a trick cyclist for cops, and his 7-year-old son move to New York, where they become involved with the age-old religion Santeria, which worships African spirits in the shape of Christian saints. As one little boy after another dies a grisly death – sacrificed, it turns out, in return for perpetual parental gratification – the ever more ridiculous plot encompasses auto-suggestion, voodoo, and not-so-special effects. It's not at all scary, but there's one good bit where this bubo on a woman's cheek bursts open and all these itsy-bitsy spiders scurry out. The real mystery is what Schlesinger and Sheen are doing making this schlock. MS

Bella Vita, La

see Living It Up

Bellboy, The

(1960, US, 72 min, b/w)
d/p/sc Jerry Lewis. *ph* Haskell Boggs. *ed* Stanley Johnson. *ad* Hal Pereira. *m* Walter Scharf. *cast* Jerry Lewis, Alex Gerry, Bob Clayton, Sonny Sand, Herkie Styles, Milton Berle, Walter Winchell.

●For his first venture into direction, Lewis forsook the saccharine plotlines of his previous work for a film of sketches based on the character of a bumbling bellboy at the Fontainebleau Hotel in Miami. The result, each scene working like a fully achieved comic short, boasts more hits than misses, including such superbly timed gags as the speedy assembling of chairs in a hall and the relapse of a hopeless diet-watcher, as well as guest appearances by Walter Winchell, Milton Berle and 'Jerry Lewis' (revealingly irascible). Lewis even throws in a tribute to his great mentor, Stan Laurel. Perhaps to the relief of many, Lewis (in his bellboy character) remains entirely mute for most of the movie. DT

Belle

(1973, Bel/Fr, 93 min)
d/sc André Delvaux. *ph* Ghislain Cloquet. *ed* Emmanuelle Dupusi. Pierre Joassin. *ad* Claude Pignot. *m* Frédéric Devreese. *cast* Jean-Luc Bideau, Danièle Delorme, Adriana Bogdan, Roger Coggio, René Hainaux.

●Delvaux again reveals his preoccupation with illusion and reality. Mathieu (Bideau) is a successful academic and family man until, profoundly threatened by his daughter's imminent marriage, he retreats into a barren landscape inhabited by a beautiful, silent stranger (Delorme). What develops is a love story turned surreal thriller, an investigation of the male ego and sexual paranoia. However, overlong and with some very obvious symbolism (a dull wasteland for isolation; windblown grass for sexual fulfilment; guns, trains and furs for good measure), the film is visually disappointing and fails to sustain its interesting ideas. HM

Belle Captive, La

(1982, Fr, 85 min)
d Alain Robbe-Grillet. *p* Anatole Dauman. *sc* Alain Robbe-Grillet. *ph* Henri Alekan. *ed* Bob Wade. *cast* Daniel Mesguich, Cyrielle Claire, Daniel Emilfork, François Chaumette, Gabrielle Lazure, Arielle Dombasle.

●On his way to deliver an important letter to the Comte de Corinthe for his glamorous, motorcycling boss Sara (Claire), Walter (Mesguich) comes across an injured woman, Marie-Ange (Lazure), lying in the road. In search of help, he takes her to an isolated villa where a mysterious convocation of sinister-looking gentlemen is in progress. A man calling himself a doctor (Chaumette) locks them in a bedroom where they make love. In the morning, Marie-Ange is gone and the villa deserted. A painting over the bed – Magritte's *La Belle Captive* – stirs echoes in Walter's mind. He has been experiencing visions of a theatre curtain framing part of a windswept beach, where the waves roll in remorselessly. The narrative, littered with false starts and dead ends, dreams within dreams, is pure Robbe-Grillet, recalling some of his startling early novels (*Dans le Labyrinthe*, *La Maison de rendez-vous*). Robbe-Grillet habitué Wade helps the viewer make sense of it all and assists his director in augmenting the tension as the sense of nightmarish claustrophobia builds towards the climax. NRo

Belle de Jour

(1967, Fr/It, 100 min)
d Luis Buñuel. *p* Robert Hakim, Raymond Hakim. *sc* Luis Buñuel, Jean-Claude Carrière. *ph* Sacha Vierny. *ed* Walter Spohr. *ad* Robert Clavel. *cast* Catherine Deneuve, Jean Sorel, Michel Piccoli, Genevieve Page, Francisco Rabal, Pierre Clémenti, Georges Marchal.

●Buñuel's cool, elegant version of Joseph Kessel's novel is an amoral comedy of manners. Beautiful, bored and bourgeoise Séverine, married to a surgeon, decides to while away her afternoons by working in a high-class whorehouse, where she encounters a variety of characters – a Chinaman with a strangely erotic box, a depraved Duke, and a gangster with gold teeth, with whom she falls in love. Or does she? Allowing us no indication of what is real, what is not, Buñuel constructs both a clear portrait of the bourgeoisie as degenerate, dishonest and directionless, and an unhysterical depiction of Deneuve's inner fantasy life, where she entertains dreams of humiliation galore. For a film about such a potentially sensationalist subject, it's remarkably discreet and chaste. GA

Belle Epoque

(1992, Sp, 110 min)
d/p Fernando Trueba. *sc* Rafael Azcona, Fernando Trueba, José Luis Garcia Sanchez. *ph* José Luis Alcaine. *ed* Carmen Frias. *ad* Juan Botella. *m* Antoine Duhamel. *cast* Fernando Fernán Gómez, Jorge Sanz, Maribel Verdú, Ariadna Gil, Miriam Diaz-Aroca, Mary Carmen Ramírez, Penelope Cruz.

●Provincial Spain, 1931. Elderly artist Manolo (Gómez) shelters a young deserter from the royalist army. Fernando (Sanz) is happy to accept, especially when he sets eyes on Manolo's four daughters. To his surprise, the bugle boy is seduced by each in turn, but even in this rural backwater the etiquette of love is more sophisticated than he appreciates. Trueba's rich, sunny film harks back to the sort of pastoral idyll that only exists in romances. Despite the conventional farce structure, it's never quite the straight male fantasy you might imagine. There's a marvellous cameo by Mary Carmen Ramírez as Manolo's operatically inclined wife; but all the women are marvellous. Somehow the film's wistful and ironic leanings are embodied in Gómez's bemused patriarch: a self-confessed libertine who can only make love to his wife. Ultimately the movie's too flirtatious to be for real – but you might indulge yourself this once. TCh

Belle Equipe, La

(1936, Fr, 94 min, b/w)
d Julien Duvivier. *sc* Julien Duvivier, Charles Spaak. *ph* Jules Kruger. *ed* Marthe Poncin. *ad* Jacques Krauss. *m* Maurice Yvain. *cast* Jean Gabin, Viviane Romance, Charles Vanel, Aimos, Charles Dorat, Micheline Cheirel.

●An amiable group of misfits living together in destitution win a sweepstake, and with their pooled resources decide to turn a derelict old building on the Marne embankment into a café-concert. With its pervasive odour of fried sausages and bicycle tyres, the gruff voices of Gabin, Vanel et al, and an authentic whiff of the Popular Front (dispersed all too soon by a mixture of wanderlust and woman-lust among the five), this minor 'classic' – once intended for Renoir – is a Cartier-Bresson photograph teased into life. GAd

Belle et la Bête, La (Beauty and the Beast)

(1946, Fr, 100 min cut to 92, b/w)
d Jean Cocteau. *p* André Paulvé. *sc* Jean Cocteau. *ph* Henri Alekan. *ed* Claude Héria. *ad* René Moulaert, Christian Bérard, Lucien Carré. *m* Georges Auric. *cast* Jean Marais, Josette Day, Marcel André, Mila Parély, Michel Auclair, Nane Germon.

●Cocteau's fairytale set standards in fantasy which few other film-makers have reached. Despite the Vermeer-like compositions, he has some trouble capturing the right tone for the 'realistic' scenes, but the sequences in the enchanted castle – wonderfully designed by Christian Bérard complete with fantastic living statuary, and dignified by a Beast at once ferocious, erotic and genuinely tragic – are pure magic. René Clément is credited as co-director, but had very little to do with the *mise en scène*. TM

Belle Fille comme moi, Une (A Gorgeous Bird Like Me/Such a Gorgeous Kid Like Me)

(1972, Fr, 98 min)
d François Truffaut. *p* Marcel Berbert, Claude Ganz. *sc* Jean-Loup Dabadie, François Truffaut. *ph* Pierre-William Glenn. *ed* Yan Dedet. *ad* Jean-Pierre Kohut-Svelko. *m* Georges Delerue. *cast* Bernadette Lafont, Claude Brasseur, Charles Denner, Guy Marchand, André Dussollier, Philippe Léotard, Anne Kreis.

●Truffaut's weakest movie, a black comedy which totally misfires. Lafont languishes in prison and relates to a sociologist (Dussollier) her life of crime, which begins with patricide (at the age of nine) and goes down from there. While there is nothing objectionable about the story – she is a real slut and the men are an awful lot who get their just deserts, thus sidestepping charges of misogyny – Truffaut miscalculates the tone. He was normally the most civilised of directors, but this is a loud and crude film. ATu

Belle Noiseuse, La (The Beautiful Troublemaker)

(1991, Fr, 239 min)
d Jacques Rivette. *p* Martine Marignac. *sc* Pascal Bonitzer, Christine Laurent, Jacques Rivette. *ph* William Lubtchansky. *ed* Nicole Lubtchansky. *ad* Emmanuel de Chauvigny. *m* Igor Stravinsky. *cast* Michel Piccoli, Jane Birkin, Emmanuelle Béart, David Bursztein, Marianne Denicourt, Gilles Arbona, Marie Belluc.

●Confronting the issue of creativity with honesty and insight, Rivette's loose adaptation of Balzac's short story 'The Unknown Masterpiece' is for the most part hypnotically fascinating. Hidden away with wife Liz (Birkin) in their rambling Languedoc mansion, Edouard Frenhofer (Piccoli) has painted next to nothing for years; but when a friend introduces painter Nicolas (Bursztein) and his lover Marianne (Béart), Frenhofer is so taken with the girl that he asks her to pose for a masterpiece he abandoned a decade earlier. So begins a battle of wills waged between the artist, his recalcitrant model, her increasingly jealous lover, a wife wary of his motives, and his own self-doubt. Firmly anchored by a strong cast, the relationships are explored in exhaustive detail, so that the tensions arising, as the painter's cauterising work proceeds, are convincing throughout. (Rather less plausible is the suggestion that Frenhofer is a genius, since the canvases we see – painted by the off-screen hand of Bernard Dufour – are hardly wonderful). As impeccably shot as its subject deserves, the film is more accessible than most of Rivette's work, with characteristically playful passing nods to the relationship between life and performance. GA

Belle Noiseuse – Divertimento, La

(1991, Fr, 126 min)
d Jacques Rivette. *p* Martine Marignac. *sc* Pascal Bonitzer, Christine Laurent, Jacques

Rivette. *ph* William Lubtchansky. *ed* Nicole Lubtchansky. *ad* Emmanuel de Chauvigny. *m* Igor Stravinsky. *cast* Michel Piccoli, Jane Birkin, Emmanuelle Béart, David Bursztein, Marianne Denicourt, Gilles Arbona, Marie Belluc.

● Rivette here remodels *La Belle Noiseuse* into another film entirely, using alternative takes, recutting to a much brisker rhythm, and bookending it with a discreetly but crucially different beginning and ending. The lengthy close-ups of painter Bernard Dufour's hand in action have gone; so have most of the agonising sittings in which Piccoli tries to wring out of Béart the realisation of his ideal masterpiece. This makes for a less tangible sense of painting's material nature, and makes more of a mystery out of the artist-model relationship; the emphasis shifts radically on to Piccoli's wife (Birkin), who now sees the sittings from outside, much as we do. It's a lighter film, but by no means slighter, more like the difference between a Henry James short story and an extended performance piece. JRo

Belle of New York, The

(1951, US, 81 min)
d Charles Walters. *p* Arthur Freed. *sc* Robert O'Brien, Irving Elinson, Chester Erskine. *ph* Robert Planck. *ed* Albert Akst, Jack Martin Smith. *ad* Cedric Gibbons. *songs* Harry Warren, Johnny Mercer. *cast* Fred Astaire, Vera-Ellen, Marjorie Main, Keenan Wynn, Alice Pearce, Clinton Sundberg.

● Classically simple Arthur Freed musical with Vera-Ellen in the unlikely guise of a high-kicking 'Daughter of the Right' who proves capable of moving from primness to flamboyant sauciness with remarkable efficacy, while her doll-like dancing is overshadowed but never overawed by Astaire's light-footed zaniness. The plot – dissolute playboy seeks redemption in the arms of purer-than-the-driven-snow maiden – is merely the minimal requirement for an escape into fantasy. If it isn't quite on the level of Minnelli's jagged surrealism, the film's central conceit – that those truly in love can walk on air – allows for some spectacular special effects as the lovers levitate up and away over the star-spangled roofs of New York. RMy

Belles de nuit, Les (Beauties of the Night)

(1952, Fr/It, 90 min, b/w)
d René Clair. p Henry Deutschmeister. René Clair. *ph* Armand Thirard. *ed* Louisette Hautecoeur. *ad* Léon Barsacq. *m* Georges Van Parys. *cast* Gérard Philipe, Martine Carol, Gina Lollobrigida, Magali Vendeuil, Raymond Bussières, Raymond Cordy, Paolo Stoppa.

● Clair's engaging fantasy stars Philipe as a frustrated young composer who escapes from poverty, noise and failure into dreams of *la belle époque*, where his music is the talk of the Paris Opéra, and a lovely married woman (Carol, in reality mother of one of his pupils) melts in his arms. But old men lamenting, first that the real belle époque was 1830, then 1789, drive his dreams back in time to military conquest and an exotic princess (Lollobrigida, in reality the cashier in the local café), then to revolutionary fervour and the love of a pretty aristocrat (Vendeuil, in reality the girl next door). At the risk of seeming scrappy (a risk not always avoided), his fantasies obey dream logic by arbitrarily chopping, changing and melting into each other; but they are often witty (nightmarishly, his opera turns into a symphony for motor horns, pneumatic drills and vacuum cleaners), and they borrow an overall structure from Griffith and *Intolerance* (building to simultaneous perils from a jealous husband's duelling pistol, from harem scimitars, and from the guillotine). The trouble with the film is that its reality, pretty much duplicating the cosily antiquated world of *Le Million*, is in itself a dream: all too predictably, love and success await the dreamer. TM

Belles of St Trinian's, The

(1954, GB, 91 min, b/w)
d Frank Launder. *p* Sidney Gilliat, Frank Launder. *sc* Frank Launder, Sidney Gilliat, Val Valentine. *ph* Stan Pavey. *ed* Thelma Connell. *ad* Joseph Bato. *m* Malcolm Arnold. *cast* Alastair Sim, Joyce Grenfell, Hermione Baddeley, George Cole, Joan Sims, Beryl Reid, Betty Ann Davies, Irene Handl.

● First in the highly enjoyable if hardly sophisticated series of Launder and Gilliat comedies based on Ronald Searle's cartoons about unruly brats and incompetent staff at a seedy girls' school. Predictable, perhaps, but it's hard to resist the performances of Cole as a conniving spiv and Sim (in drag) as the bumbling headmistress. GA

Belle Verte, La (The Good Green World)

(1996, Fr, 95 min)
d Coline Serreau. *p* Alain Sarde. *sc* Coline Serreau. *ph* Robert Alazraki. *ed* Catherine Renault. *ad* Guy-Claude François. *m* Coline Serreau. *cast* Coline Serreau, Vincent Lindon, Marion Cotillard, Patrick Timsit, Paul Crauchet, Didier Flamand, Francis Perrier.

● Mila (Serreau) lives in a leafy utopia in another neck of the galaxy but, with her part Earth ancestry, has a hankering to look the old place over. She's dismayed to find inedible food, unbreathable air, noise and a bad idea called money. With her superior mental powers, though, she easily copes with bad tempered motorists, heartless social workers and the like, brainwashing them until they can appreciate the beauty in a lettuce leaf. The film offers acrobats, kittens, an orphan Serbian baby and an unwittingly offputting account of the Green Party line. BBa

Bell from Hell, The

see Campana del Infierno, La

Bellissima

(1951, It, 108 min, b/w)
d Luchino Visconti. *p* Salvo D'Angelo. *sc* Suso Cecchi D'Amico, Francesco Rosi, Luchino Visconti. *ph* Piero Portalupi. *ed* Mario Serandrei. *ad* Gianni Polidori. *m* Franco Mannino. *cast* Anna Magnani, Walter Chiari, Tina Apicella, Gastone Renzelli, Alessandro Blasetti, Tecla Scarano.

● A curiously sentimental satire on Cinecittà Film Studios, in which half of Rome's adoring mothers stridently cajole their untalented offspring into a studio child-star competition. It rivals most Hollywood-on-Hollywood movies in ironic entertainment value, but the abiding memory is of Magnani at full throttle contributing to quite the noisiest film ever made. PT

Bellman and True

(1987, GB, 122 min)
d Richard Loncraine. *p* Michael Wearing, Christopher Neame. *sc* Desmond Lowden, Richard Loncraine, Michael Wearing. *ph* Ken Westbury. *ed* Paul Green. *pd* Jon Bunker. *m* Colin Towns. *cast* Bernard Hill, Derek Newark, Richard Hope, Ken Bones, Frances Tomelty, Kieran O'Brien.

● There are kiss-off points in Loncraine's caper thriller – notably a silky Mister Big who calls his victim 'Dear Heart' while the muscle brandishes a Stanley knife – but the complexity of the characters more than compensates. More crucially, the balance of the film is off in the telling, and after a gabbled scene-setter, we spend too long bogged down in an empty mansion with alcoholic computer expert Hiller (Hill), his small stepson (O'Brien), and Mr Big (Hope), as pressure is put on Hiller to hack into a bank's security system and take out the alarms. The villainy braces up with the appearance of Guv'nor (Newark), whose threats are convincing enough to cause Hiller an involuntary evacuation, and the actual robbery powers along on a nice mixture of humour and tension, topped by a getaway containing a memorably tight squeeze. Hill is grimly anxious as the reluctant pawn, and his bedtime story sessions with the boy are suitably transparent. Nice try. BC

Bells Are Ringing

(1960, US, 125 min)
d Vincente Minnelli. *p* Arthur Freed. *sc* Betty Comden, Adolph Green. *ph* Milton Krasner. *ed* Adrienne Fazan. *ad* George W Davis, Preston Ames. *songs* Jule Styne, Betty Comden, Adolph Green. *cast* Judy Holliday, Dean Martin, Fred Clark, Eddie Foy Jr, Frank Gorshin, Jean Stapleton, Ruth Storey.

● Minnelli's last musical before *On a Clear Day You Can See Forever*, and like it a curate's egg. The two stars are a pleasure to behold, particularly the genially dizzy Holliday, a telephone answering-service operator who can't help involving herself in the lives and hopes of her clients. And old Mr Nonchalance Martin sidles through his part as a doubting, drunken playwright with his customary charm. But their material just isn't up to the mark: Betty Comden and Adolph Green's script involves much jaded satire of jaded topics like Method acting, pop music and smart parties, while Jule Styne's infrequent songs don't really get the bells ringing. Something is also wrong with Minnelli's presentation, for the action tends to hang inside the 'Scope frame looking theatrical and inert; even the location stuff seems phony. GB

Bells Go Down, The

(1943, GB, 90 min, b/w)
d Basil Dearden. *p* Michael Balcon. *sc* Roger MacDougall. *ph* Ernest Palmer. *ed* Mary Habberfield. *ad* Michael Relph. *m* Roy Douglas. *cast* Tommy Trinder, James Mason, Beatrice Varley, Philip Friend, Mervyn Johns, William Hartnell, Finlay Currie.

● Uncomfortable war effort from Ealing, semi-documentary in intent but getting bogged down in silly histrionics as one auxiliary fireman has to work on a blazing warehouse while his own home burns, and another perishes in an attempt to save his hated chief while his wife has a baby in the blitz. Horribly patronising in its view of the humble doing their bit for Britain (even the crook turns up trumps), and knocked sideways as a tribute to the Auxiliary Fire Service by Humphrey Jennings' *Fires Were Started*, coincidentally released the same month. TM

Bells of St Mary's, The

(1945, US, 126 min, b/w)
d/p Leo McCarey. *sc* Dudley Nichols. *ph* George Barnes. *ed* Harry Marker. *ad* William Flannery. *m* Robert Emmett Dolan. *cast* Bing Crosby, Ingrid Bergman, Henry Travers, William Gargan, Ruth Donnelly, Rhys Williams.

● Rambling, embarrassingly winsome sequel to *Going My Way*, with Crosby's crooning priest transferred to a rundown parish where Barry Fitzgerald's roguish twinkle is replaced by Bergman's wholesome (but roguish) nun. TM

Belly

(1998, US, 96 min)
d Hype Williams. *p* Ron Rotholz, Hype Williams, Robert Salerno, Larry Meistrich. *sc* Hype Williams. *ph* Maleek Sayeed. *ed* David Leonard. *pd* Regan Jackson. *m* Stephen Cullo. *cast* Nas [Nasir Jones], DMX [Earl Simmons], Taral Hicks, Tionne 'T-Boz' Watkins, Method Man [Clifford Smith].

● The unremarkable presence of a gaggle of rap stars is just part of the problem with this ill advised first feature. Working with Spike Lee's cinematographer Maleek Sayeed, HipHop promo director Williams indulges in a stream of stylised compositions: characterisation is absent and the narrative feels like a cosmetic overlay. Insofar as there's any story, it's about a posse of drug dealers falling out over their vision of the future. (Nasty, brutish and short? Or to retire and start a family?) An unrelenting spectacle of guns, girls, drugs, cash, cars, clubs and cool apartments, scored to endless use of the term 'nigga', it looks suspiciously like a deliberate exercise in audience alienation. NB

Belly of an Architect, The

(1987, GB/It, 118 min)
d Peter Greenaway. *p* Colin Callender, Walter Donohue. *sc* Peter Greenaway. *ph* Sacha Vierny. *ed* John Wilson. *ad* Luciana Vedovelli. *m* Wim Mertens. *cast* Brian Dennehy, Chloe Webb, Lambert Wilson, Sergio Fantoni, Stefania Casini, Vanni Corbellini.

● When middle-aged American architect Stourley Kracklite (Dennehy) visits Rome to oversee an exhibition in tribute to an 18th century predecessor, Boullée, his grand ambitions founder in a morass of disease, doubt and intrigue. Is his pregnant wife (Webb) having an affair with the insidiously reptilian Caspasian (Wilson), himself possibly plotting to steal the kudos for the exhibition? Is she even poisoning him, thus causing debilitating cramps in Kracklite's up-ended dome of a stomach? The story is decorated in the usual Greenaway style;

visual and symbolic rhymes galore produce a quizzical and quirky meditation on a multitude of themes. But where the film perhaps wins out over Greenaway's earlier movies is in its admission of feeling. The exquisitely framed images, the allusive script, the droll witticisms are counterbalanced by Dennehy's literally enormous performance, which threatens to tear the film's formal symmetries to vividly memorable shreds. GA

Beloved

(1998, US, 172 min)
d Jonathan Demme. *p* Edward Saxon, Jonathan Demme, Gary Goetzman, Oprah Winfrey, Kate Forte. *sc* Akosua Busia, Richard LaGravenese, Adam Brooks. *ph* Tak Fujimoto. *ed* Carol Littleton, Andy Keir. *pd* Kristi Zea. *m* Rachel Portman. *cast* Oprah Winfrey, Danny Glover, Thandie Newton, Kimberly Elise, Beah Richards, Lisa Gay Hamilton, Albert Hall.

●From the breathtaking opening scene, it's clear that Demme won't be content to sit back and preach. Inspired by the true story of a runaway slave driven to commit unspeakable murder rather than re-submit to her chains, Toni Morrison's ghost story takes the lid off the blistering, restless tumult, the 'screaming baboon' that is the legacy of American racism. When Paul D (Glover) arrives at the home of his old friend Sethe (Winfrey), he's confronted with a spectre of violence more powerful than he can comprehend, and peremptorily ousted by Newton's malign innocent, Beloved. On one level, this is pure horror, an extraordinary yarn of the supernatural, torture and abuse, physical endurance, hope crushed, love corrupted. The script has compressed the novel, but in struggling to honour its depth has saddled itself with a difficult and anti-climactic structure which draws you in, but keeps you waiting. That said, the film makes a good fist of approximating Morrison's densely textured, incantatory style, steers clear of sentimentality, and snatches heart-rending performances from Winfrey, Newton and Elise, as Sethe's daughter Denver. TCh

Beloved Enemy

(1936, US, 89 min, b/w)
d HC Potter. *p* Samuel Goldwyn. *sc* John L Balderston, Rose Franken, William Brown Meloney. *ph* Gregg Toland. *ed* Sherman Todd. *ad* Richard Day. *m* Alfred Newman. *cast* Merle Oberon, Brian Aherne, Karen Morley, Henry Stephenson, Jerome Cowan, David Niven, Donald Crisp.

●Sam Goldwyn turned the Irish Troubles of 1921 into the backdrop for a tale of doomed love. Oberon's the daughter of a stuffy English civil servant sent to Dublin, Aherne a fiery rebel leader, but the drawstrings of romance bind them together in this hokey tale of passion, duty, betrayal, etc. First-time director Henry Codman Potter was later to find fame with *Hellzapoppin'*, which gives some idea where his talents lay. Not here, in other words. TJ

Beloved Infidel

(1959, US, 123 min)
d Henry King. *p* Jerry Wald. *sc* Sy Barlett. *ph* Leon Shamroy. *ed* William H Reynolds. *ad* Lyle Wheeler, Maurice Ransford. *m* Franz Waxman. *cast* Gregory Peck, Deborah Kerr, Eddie Albert, Philip Ober, Herbert Rudley, Ken Scott, Karin Booth.

●An adaptation of the book by journalist Sheilah Graham about her affair with the permanently sozzled F Scott Fitzgerald during his ill-fated last days as a '30s Hollywood screenwriter. This is a great artist's life as grimly self-conscious soap opera. Peck and Kerr are awkwardly stiff, burdened by literary history. Vaguely caustic attitude towards Tinseltown mores; and notable 'Scope photography from Leon Shamroy. TJ

Below the Belt

(1980, US, 98 min)
d/p Robert Fowler. *sc* Robert Fowler, Sherry Sonnett. *ph* Alan Metzger, Misha Suslov. *ed* Steven Zaillian. *ad* Eugene Gurlitz. *m* Jerry Fielding. *cast* Regina Baff, John C Becher, Jane O'Brien, Mildred Burke, James Gammon, Annie McGreevey, Billie Mahoney.

●A cheapo independent precursor of Aldrich's *California Dolls*, adapting road movie clichés to the women's wrestling circuit, which lacks – if you'll excuse the expression – the balls of classic exploitation. Baff (cast as virtually the same waif she patented as truckers' moll Janice for Joseph Strick) quits the urban dead-end for an apprenticeship of grappling gigs in the Southern States, learning the ropes before inevitably bringing an old pro favourite to her knees and the crowd to its feet. PT

Belstone Fox, The

(1973, GB, 103 min)
d James Hill. *p* Sally Shuter. *sc* James Hill. *ph* John Wilcox. *ed* Peter Tanner. *ad* Hazel Peiser. *m* Laurie Johnson. *cast* Eric Porter, Rachel Roberts, Jeremy Kemp, Bill Travers, Dennis Waterman, Heather Wright.

●A dismayingly literal and unimaginative version of David Rook's novel *Ballad of the Belstone Fox*, a simple country tale of fox-hunting and the havoc wrought upon an ageing huntsman through his moment of kindness in nurturing a young fox cub.

Bemani (Stay Alive)

(2002, Iran, 97 min)
d Dariush Mehrjui. *p* Mohammad Nikbin, Tahmineh Milani, Dariush Mehrjui. *sc* Dariush Mehrjui, Vahideh Mohammadifar. *ph* Bahram Badakshani. *ed* Dariush Mehrjui, Mastaneh Mohajer. *cast* Masoumeh Bakhshi, Shadi Heydari, Neda Aghaei.

●Set in a region of Iran close to the Iraqi border, Mehrjui's film concerns the apparently all-too-common phenomenon of young women setting themselves alight in protest against the prison-like conditions of their lives in a society founded on repressive patriarchal tradition. The film focuses on three different women, reacting variously to their predicaments, and is undoubtedly both heartfelt and affecting; but while its narrative style – elliptical, fragmented, even eccentric at times – is ambitious and imaginative, it sometimes makes for a loss of clarity and momentum. GA

Be My Star (Mein Stern)

(2001, Aus/Ger, 65 min)
d/p/sc Valeska Grisebach. *ph* Bernhard Keller. *ed* Anja Salomonowitz. *pd* Beatrice Schultz. *cast* Nicole Gläser, Christopher Schöps, Monique Gläser, Jeanine Gläser, Sebastian Rinke, Christina Sandke.

●Like *Lovely Rita*, this is another fine slice of realism from Austria, albeit one shot in Berlin. It charts the ups and downs in the relationship between 14-year-old Nicole and Christopher, who is hardly any older for all his faintly ludicrous pretensions to coolness, experience and maturity. Beautifully acted and observed, the film picks up on how tiny things can seem a matter of life or death in teenage relationships; the spotty, awkward daters may look risible to those of us with the advantage of hindsight, but that doesn't lessen their pain and pleasure. Their dignity and humanity are wisely respected by writer/director Grisebach in her lovely debut, which features one of the finest dance scenes in recent cinema. GA

Ben

(1972, US, 94 min)
d Phil Karlson. *p* Mort Briskin. *sc* Gilbert A Ralston. *ph* Russell Metty. *ed* Harry Gerstad. *ad* Rolland M Brooks. *m* Walter Scharf. *cast* Lee Harcourt Montgomery, Joseph Campanella, Arthur O'Connell, Rosemary Murphy, Meredith Baxter.

●Small boy with heart condition finds (to music) that 'he has a friend in Ben', which is more than the audience is likely to have. Carried on from *Willard* and its wonder rat. The rats next door make their presence known, and Ben leads them to a safer life in the drain, helped by this same small boy (with heart condition). The whole nature-rising-against-man fable becomes a kind of sub-Disney lark. Ben himself is a sleek well-trained creature. Can't say the same for those who dreamed up the project.

Bench in the Park, A (Un banco en el parque)

(1999, Sp, 82 min)
d Agusti Vila. *p* Fernando Colomo. *sc* Agusti Vila. *ph* David Omedes. *ed* Miguel Angel. Santamaria. *ad* Sofía Pape. *m* Ian Briton. *cast* Alex Brendemül, Ingrid Rubio, Rosana Pastor, Vicenta N'Dongo, Victoria Freire, Mónica López, Aitor Merino, Gary Piquer.

●Juan is a bit of a prat when it comes to relationships. When his girlfriend goes to study in London, his pride demands he finish with her, even though he immediately feels lost and lonely. He's too proud, too, to be paired off by pals, so he decides to spend a little time in the park every day, on the very same bench, in the hope of meeting someone. Indeed, he reckons, doing the same in a bar will double his chance of success. Absurd – but quite right, as it turns out, and then the problems really start. If this sounds a little reminiscent of Rohmer, it is (there's even a verbal allusion to *The Green Ray*), and all the better for it. A beautifully unsentimental low key comedy of manners, full of delicious ironies, engagingly acted, and written and directed with real intelligence and insight. GA

Bend It Like Beckham

(2002, Ger/GB, 112 min)
d Gurinder Chadha. *d* Deepak Nayar, Gurinder Chadha. *sc* Gurinder Chadha, Guljit Bindra, Paul Mayeda Berges. *ph* Lin Jong. *ed* Justin Krish. *pd* Nick Ellis. *m* Craig Pruess. *cast* Parminder Nagra, Keira Knightley, Jonathan Rhys Meyers, Anupam Kher, Archie Panjabi, Shaznay Lewis, Frank Harper, Juliet Stevenson, Shaheen Khan, Zohra Segal, Nina Wadia.

●Football's uncommon ability to bring a nation together is celebrated in this sweet, positive youth movie. Jess (Nagra) loves nothing better than kicking a ball about – unless it's her idol, Becks. Unfortunately her family cling to traditional Asian values. While they're willing to tolerate her fanaticism, the very idea of their daughter joining a local girls' team makes them see red. But, encouraged by her new best pal Jules (Knightley) and dishy Irish coach Joe (Rhys Meyers), she defiantly signs on with the team, even though she has to go to extreme lengths to keep it secret. It's heartening to find Chadha exercising feminist, multicultural themes organically in an unpretentious mainstream entertainment. Nagra and Knightley have winning personalities, but credit should also go to writer/director Chadha for getting the balance right between humour and pathos, and sporting and romantic action, not to mention negotiating the tricky business of filming football action with originality and finesse. Poppy and fun, this game underdog deserves to get a result. TCh

Bend of the River (aka Where the River Bends)

(1952, US, 91 min)
d Anthony Mann. *p* Aaron Rosenberg. *sc* Borden Chase. *ph* Irving Glassberg. *ed* Russell Schoengarth. *ad* Bernard Herzbrun, Nathan Juran. *m* Hans J Salter. *cast* James Stewart, Julia Adams, Arthur Kennedy, Rock Hudson, Lori Nelson, Jay C Flippen, Harry Morgan.

●Mann's finest Western casts Stewart as a wagon train leader, guiding a group of settlers through Indian country to the Oregon Territory. Stewart is a man haunted by a secret, his violent past as a Missouri border raider – a past which catches up with him when another former raider (Kennedy) joins the wagon train. The two men are paralleled throughout, Kennedy representing the old violence which may yet erupt in the reformed Stewart, and the whole film is concerned with the testing of Stewart's capacity for change. Continually provoked by his spiky relationship with Kennedy, Stewart is a man who must clarify and reaffirm his new relationship with a peaceful society. Lighthearted comedy, majestic scenery, and superbly handled action are fused into a unifying moral vision which, though it deals with abstractions, always expresses itself through visible actions and tangible symbols. NF

Beneath the Planet of the Apes

(1970, US, 94 min)
d Ted Post. *p* Arthur P Jacobs. *sc* Paul Dehn, Mort Abrahams. *ph* Milton Krasner. *ed* Marion Rothman. *ad* Jack Martin Smith. *m* Leonard Rosenman. *cast* James Franciscus, Charlton Heston, Kim Hunter, Maurice Evans, Victor Buono, Linda Harrison.

●Beneath the planet of the apes is discovered an older civilisation: a tribe of mutant humans living in the ruins of New York and now maniacally worshipping an atom bomb. This first sequel to *Planet of the Apes* isn't bad, but already shows the way the original conception was to degenerate into routine comic strip adventure. TM

Beneath the 12-Mile Reef

(1953, US, 102 min)
d Robert D. Webb. *p* Robert Bassler. *sc* AI Bezzerides. *ph* Edward Cronjager. *ed* William H Reynolds. *ad* Lyle Wheeler, George Patrick. *m* Bernard Herrmann. *cast* Robert Wagner, Terry Moore, Gilbert Roland, J Carrol Naish, Richard Boone, Peter Graves, Angela Clark.
●Wagner and Moore replay *Romeo and Juliet* in Tarpon Springs, Florida, with rival sponge fishermen standing in for the Montagues and Capulets. One of the earliest CinemaScope pictures, it looks better than it ought to, and Bernard Herrmann provides an eerie score. But it's best remembered for the incredibly young Robert Wagner scrapping with an octopus (you won't get that in staged Shakespeare). TCh

Beneath the Valley of the Ultra Vixens

(1979, US, 93 min)
d/p Russ Meyer. *sc* Roger Ebert, Russ Meyer. *ph/ed* Russ Meyer. *ad* Michele Levesque. *m* William Tasker. *cast* Francesca 'Kitten' Natividad, Anne Marie, Ken Kerr, June Mack, Russ Meyer.
●Delirious proof that Meyer deserves to be considered as one of America's foremost satirists. His use of ludicrously pneumatic female 'stars' has come to seem less like simple soft-core titillation and more a turning of their over-endowed bodies into a grand metaphor for Female sexual appetite, the central nightmare of the all-American Male psyche. Less subversive than his earlier work; still hilarious, though.

Benefit of the Doubt

(1993, US/Ger, 90 min)
d Jonathan Heap. *p* Michael Spielberg, Brad Gilbert. *sc* Jeffrey Polman, Christopher Keyser, Michael Lieber. *ph* Johnny Jensen. *ed* Sharyn L Ross. *pd* Marina Kiesner. *m* Hummie Mann. *cast* Donald Sutherland, Amy Irving, Rider Strong, Christopher McDonald, Graham Greene, Theodore Bikel.
●Paroled wife-murderer (Sutherland) returns to eye-pleasing Cottonwood, Arizona, to haunt his daughter Karen (Irving), 22 years after her testimony put him in jail. He insinuates his way into her life by doting on her 11-year-old son (Strong). While father Frank remains ambiguous, this is mildly unsettling; once he goes loco and killing or terrorising everyone in sight, it loses all credibility. Most contrived. NF

Bengazi

(1955, US, 78 min. b/w)
d John Brahm. *p* Sam Wiesenthal, Eugene Tevlin. *sc* Endre Bohem, Louis Vittes. *ph* Joseph Biroc. *ed* Robert Golden. *ad* Jack Okey. *m* Roy Webb. *cast* Richard Conte, Victor McLaglen, Richard Carlson, Mala Powers, Richard Erdman, Hillary Brooke.
●A risibly dud script never gives Brahm's stylish direction or Joseph Biroc's fine camerawork a chance to make anything of this adventure set in postwar Bengazi. Conte and McLaglen, unscrupulous co-owners of a seedy café (shades of *Casablanca*), set out for a desert oasis to hijack a cache of gold, only to find themselves surrounded by hostile Bedouins (shades of *The Lost Patrol*). Also trapped are a pursuing police chief (Carlson) and McLaglen's anxious daughter (Powers), a colleen fresh from the Dublin convent: cue for both bad boys to outdo each other in heroic self-sacrifice. Conte is excellent, but McLaglen as usual overdoes his loveable Irish rogue bit, while Carlson ('I'm thinkin' of the wee village in Scotland where I was born') offers one of the screen's most excruciating accents. TM

Ben-Hur A Tale of the Christ

(1925, US, 145 min, b/w & col)
d Fred Niblo. *p* Louis B Mayer, Samuel Goldwyn, Irving Thalberg. *sc* Carey Wilson, June Mathis. *ph* René Guissart, Percy Hilburn, Karl Struss, Clyde De Vinna. *ed* Lloyd Nosler. *pd* Cedric Gibbons, Horace Jackson. *cast* Ramon Novarro, May McAvoy, Francis X Bushman, Betty Bronson, Claire McDowell, Kathleen Key.
●Despite the numerous disasters encountered during its production in Italy and Hollywood, MGM's spectacular about a Jew's conflicts with the authority of the Roman Empire remains one of the most impressive silent epics, largely thanks to the sheer scale of its conception and to the execution of its several set pieces (most notably the famed chariot race). The print under review, refurbished by Kevin Brownlow and David Gill for the 'Thames Silents' series with a new score by Carl Davis, has the added delight of a careful restoration of the several Technicolor sequences. GA

Ben-Hur

(1959, US, 217 min)
d William Wyler, Andrew Marton. *p* Sam Zimbalist. *sc* Karl Tunberg. *ph* Robert Surtees. *ed* Ralph E Winters, John D Dunning. *ad* William A Horning, Edward Carfagno. *m* Miklós Rozsa. *cast* Charlton Heston, Jack Hawkins, Haya Harareet, Stephen Boyd, Hugh Griffith, Martha Scott, Cathy O'Donnell.
●Although a bit like a four-hour Sunday school lesson, 'Ben-Hur' is not without its compensations, above all, of course, the chariot race (which was directed not by Wyler but by Andrew Marton, and it shows). The rest is made interesting by the most sexually ambivalent characters sporting togas this side of *Satyricon.* When not fondling phallic substitutes, Heston and Boyd gaze admiringly into each other's eyes, but when they fall out - well, hell hath no fury like a closet queen scorned. Heston ends up naked in the galleys where he's rowing and Jack Hawkins is commanding; one look at Chuck's rippling muscles, and Hawkins adopts him. Heston goes back for revenge on Boyd, who's lying around in the baths with his men looking like they're auditioning for *Sebastiane.* Along the way, an unbilled Jesus performs miracles for Ben's kinsfolk, which are convincing enough to convert him. The movie could be trying to say that for some people religion is an escape from their sexuality, but it seems unlikely. SM

Benjamin Smoke

(2000, US, 76 min)
d/p/ph Jem Cohen, Peter Sillen. *ed* Nancy Roach. *m* Smoke.
●Cohen's is a cinema of transience and dissipation, of patient archiving and spontaneous revelation. Drawn to the derelict and dilapidated, he records his subjects – musicians, townscapes – piecemeal over time, sometimes on scraps of different film stock. Cohen and collaborator Peter Stillen outline the bare bones of dissolute drag queen and singer-songwriter Benjamin's biography, mostly as expounded by the man himself: early flirtations with his mother's wardrobe; musical and other adventures fronting the Opal Foxx Quartet and Smoke; his affliction with 'the HIV thing'; his death in 1999, aged 39. Cohen first arrived on the scene in '89, whence the film's scratchy, present tense scrapbook proceeds in fits and starts, with an eye for the changes fermenting in his locale of Cabbagetown, Alabama. Benjamin's music, meanwhile, heard in snatches of rehearsals and shows, occupies that dark hollow between American folk and punk, Harry Smith and Patti Smith. NB

Benji

(1974, US, 86 min)
d/p/sc Joe Camp. *ph* Don Reddy. *ed* Leon Seith. *ad* Harland Wright. *m* Euel Box. *cast* Peter Breck, Edgar Buchanan, Terry Carter, Christopher Connelly, Patsy Garrett.
●Big-grossing film in the States, about the life'n'love of a stray mongrel, told from the dog's point of view. Against the novelty of the canine stunts one has to balance some terribly variable acting, poor lighting, and spotty photography. Attendant adults will probably find it a long haul. A sequel ensued, *For the Love of Benji* (1977).

Benny and Joon

(1993, US, 99 min)
d Jeremiah Chechik. *p* Susan Arnold, Donna Roth. *sc* Barry Berman. *ph* John Schwartzman. *ed* Carol Littleton. *ad* Neil Spisak. *m* Rachel Portman. *cast* Johnny Depp, Mary Stuart Masterson, Aidan Quinn, Julianne Moore, Oliver Platt, CCH Pounder.
●Another one flies over the cuckoo's nest in this soft-hearted romantic three-hander. Joon (Masterson) plays cooky – sorry, severely emotionally unstable. She's a vegetarian painter in airy print dresses and bobby sox. Sam (Depp) is a kind of gentle man-child fantasy creation, who expresses himself through Chaplin and Keaton mime routines. Piggy-in-the-middle is Quinn's blue-collar straight man, Joon's together brother Benny, who looks after her at home, just managing to keep her from being institutionalised. He refuses to bless Sam and Joon's marriage of true minds…It's acted out in the secondary emotional register of the glass menagerie: whimsical, delicate, idiosyncratic, barmy. WH

Benny's Video

(1992, Aus/Switz, 105 min)
d Michael Haneke. *p* Veit Heiduschka, Bernard Lang. *sc* Michael Haneke. *ph* Christian Berger. *ed* Marie Homolkova. *ad* Christoph Kanter. *cast* Arno Frisch, Angela Winkler, Ulrich Mühe, Ingrid Strassner, Stephanie Brehme.
●An unsettling if not entirely successful social-cum-psychological drama. Benny – a well-off 14-year-old whose none too warmly affectionate parents have bought him an amazing array of video equipment – has become so desensitised to reality by watching endless violent images on the small screen that he ends up killing an almost total stranger. So far, so unremarkable; but his remorseless, Psycho-style reaction to the deed, his mute 'confession' to his parents via video, and their reaction in turn, are quietly chilling. As a study in the complex relationship between violence and cinema, it's an unsensational alternative to *Henry: Portrait of a Serial Killer* and *Man Bites Dog*. GA

Bent

(1996, GB/US/Japan, 116 min)
d Sean Mathias. *p* Michael Solinger, Dixie Linder. *sc* Martin Sherman. *ph* Yorgos Arvanitis. *ed* Isabelle Lorente. *pd* Stephen Brimson Lewis. *m* Philip Glass. *cast* Lothaire Bluteau, Clive Owen, Brian Webber, Ian McKellen, Mick Jagger, Jude Law, Suzanne Bertish, Rupert Graves, Charlie Watts.
●Fassbinder and Costa-Gavras both wanted to film Martin Sherman's 1979 play about gay persecution under the Nazis, but it was theatre director Mathias who finally got it on screen. In this visually daring adaptation a ruined power station on the Clyde stands in for '30s Berlin, and Dachau is represented by a disused cement factory outside Tring. Owen and Bluteau are the gay men, Max and Horst, who trace a line between these points. Leaving the decadent nightlife over which Jagger's club owner, Greta, holds court, the two eventually meet in line at the concentration camp. Horst wears the homosexual's pink triangle and Max has been trying to pass as a Jew. That way, he reckons, he's not quite the lowest of the low. Although Sherman's ranking of the gays as even more oppressed than the Jewish prisoners seems unnecessary, the anger behind his screenplay is never in doubt. Life on the run keeps the first half moving, but it's hard to connect with the performers when Owen and Bluteau are dwarfed by the post-industrial surroundings. TJ

Benvenuta

(1983, Bel/Fr/It, 106 min)
d André Delvaux. *p* Jean-Claude Batz. *sc* André Delvaux. *ph* Charlie van Damme. *ed* Jean Goudier, Albert Jurgensa. *ad* Claude Pignot. *m* Fréderic Devreese. *cast* Fanny Ardant, Vittorio Gassman, Françoise Fabian, Mathieu Carrière, Claire Wauthion.
●A film about fictions, their fascination, and the processes by which they are created. A young screenwriter visits a famous novelist, seeking background for a script based on the scandalous love story she published twenty years before. As they talk, two romances are rhymed: one, from the novel as remembered by her and imagined by him, is strange, exalted, melodramatic (played by Gassman and Ardant); the other is shy, tender, hesitant as the two writers (Fabian, Carrière) warm to their collaboration. Meanwhile, conjured out of the network of memories, cross references, musical and visual analogies, an entirely different story

gradually emerges. Working through subtle Jamesian nuance, it's not an easy film but an immensely rewarding one. TM

Bequest to the Nation (aka The Nelson Affair)

(1973, GB, 116 min)
d James Cellan Jones. *p* Hal B Wallis. *sc* Terence Rattigan. *ph* Gerry Fisher. *ed* Anne V Coates. *pd* Carmen Dillon. *m* Michel Legrand. *cast* Glenda Jackson, Peter Finch, Michael Jayston, Anthony Quayle, Margaret Leighton, Dominic Guard.

● Terence Rattigan's adaptation of his own play in which Finch (Nelson) and Jackson (Lady Hamilton) attempt to take the lid off a relationship which 'changed the course of British history'. Histrionics apart, you come out wondering whether it really matters.

Berdel

(1991, Tur, 86 min)
d Atif Yilmaz. *sc* Atif Yilmaz, Yildirim Turker. *ph* Erdal Kahraman. *ed* Mevlüt Koçak. *pd* Mustafa Ziya Ulkenciler. *m* Selim Atakan. *cast* Türkan Soray, Tarik Akan, Mine Çayiroglu, Füsun Demirel, Erdinc Özkan.

● Yilmaz' powerful film starts with Hikmet the Supermarket, a travelling purveyor of essential goods to this rural clime of Turkey, shouting 'Quinine for men! Condoms for women!' Meanwhile, Hanim (Soray), wife to Ömer (Akan), is giving birth to her fifth girl – a disaster in this patriarchal community – and Ömer is wandering the coffee-houses in a terminal state of anxiety. He must have a boy. Nobody's happy, least of all Hanim's daughter Beyaz (Çayiroglu). It is she who will be forced to become the second wife of an older man so that her father may himself take a second wife and avoid the dowry – the custom of 'Berdel'. This moving and finely acted drama describes the tragic implications of these events with compassion, restraint and a close attention to detail; and in so doing, paints a forceful portrait of a society painfully entering the modern world. WH

Berlin Affair, The (Interno Berlinele)

(1985, It/WGer, 121 min)
d Liliana Cavani. *p* Menahem Golan, Yoram Globus. *sc* Liliana Cavani, Roberta Mazzoni. *ph* Dante Spinotti. *ed* Ruggero Mastroianni. *ad* Luciano Ricceri. *m* Pino Donaggio. *cast* Gudrun Landgrebe, Kevin McNally, Mio Takaki, Hanns Zischler, Massimo Girotti, Philippe Leroy, William Berger.

● Cavani's monumentally dull opus has little to offer even the raincoat trade. Darling Lili is back among the kinky Nazis (remember Charlotte and Dirk smearing each other with jam in *The Night Porter*?). This time it's Berlin, 1938, where bored diplomat's wife Louise joins an art class and encounters the sensuous Mitsuko, daughter of the Japanese ambassador. Soon they're fumbling away inside each other's kimonos, until Louise's ambitious hubby discovers the awful truth. Filmed with a curious kind of glazed indifference, never has sex every which way seemed so boring, interminable and *unnecessary*. DT

Berlin Alexanderplatz

(1979/80, WGer, 15 hr. 30 min)
d Rainer Werner Fassbinder. *p* Peter Marthesheimer. *sc* Rainer Werner Fassbinder. *ph* Xavier Schwarzenberger. *ed* Jiliane Lorenz. *ad* Harry Baer. *m* Peer Raben. *cast* Günter Lamprecht, Hanna Schygulla, Barbara Sukowa, Karin Baal, helmut Griem, Ivan Desny, Udo Kier.

● This shattering adaptation of Alfred Döblin's masterpiece – made for TV in 13 episodes with a two-hour epilogue – offers a level-headed account of protagonist Biberkopf's key weakness: his quasi-sexual infatuation with the psychotic pimp Reinhold. Aided by great design, cinematography, and, not least, performances, Fassbinder tells the story surprisingly naturalistically. Then in the epilogue, he offers a disturbing meditation on his own fantasies about Biberkopf. This phantasmagoria is Fassbinder's most daring act of self-exposure: a movie time-bomb that forces you to rethink the series as a whole. The work of a genuine master with nothing left to lose or hide. TR

Berlin – Die Sinfonie der Grosstadt (Berlin – Symphony of a Great City)

(1927, Ger, 70 min approx, b/w)
d Walter Ruttmann. *ph* Karl Freund, Reimar Kuntze, Robert Baberski, Laszlo Schaeffer. *ed* Walter Ruttmann.

● A textbook classic to which the years have not been kind. The portrait of a city dawn-to-dusk may not have been a hackneyed project in 1927, but it would soon become so. The unsophisticated structure, the mundane content of the images, the exclusion of overt human or social significance were all presumably deliberate, the better to centre attention on the montage, which is indeed dynamic and possibly 'symphonic', for those able to concentrate on editing rhythms for any length of time. Today it's the hidden camera banalities that hold the real interest, while the turbulent cutting ironically becomes a hindrance to actually engaging with these fragments of long ago and far away. Reissued in the '30s with an added score by Edmund Meisel. BBa

Berlin Express

(1948, US, 87 min, b/w)
d Jacques Tourneur. *p* Bert Granet. *sc* Harold Medford. *ph* Lucien Ballard. *ed* Sherman Todd. *ad* Albert S D'Agostino, Al Herman. *m* Frederick Hollander. *cast* Merle Oberon, Robert Ryan, Paul Lukas, Charles Korvin, Robert Coote.

● Four representatives of the Occupying Powers join forces to aid a 'good' German with an unspecified plan to unify his country in the immediate aftermath of WWII. Minor stuff, if diverting enough in its absurdity (Oberon picking her way through the rubble of Berlin in a series of Orry-Kelly gowns). But the train itself whisks the narrative along, and Tourneur's unflinching stare at postwar devastation owes less to any documentary pretensions that to an almost Langian beadiness of eye. GAd

Berlin Is in Germany

(2001, Ger, 93 min)
d Hannes Stöhr. *p* Gudrun Ruzicková-Steiner. *sc* Hannes Stöhr. *ph* Florian Hoffmeister. *ed* Anne Fabini. *ad* Anke Bistein, Natalja Meier. *m* Florian Appl. *cast* Jörg Schüttauf, Edita Malovcic, Tom Jahn, Robert Loehr, Valentin Platareanu, Oscar Martinez, Carmen-Maja Antoni, Robin Becker, Dirk Borchardt, Udo Kroschwald, Julia Jäger.

● This liberal, semi-metaphorical tale of the difficulties of adjustment and change for East Germans in the new united Germany sees ex-soldier Martin (Schüttauf) leaving Brandenburg gaol ten years after the fall of the Wall having been incarcerated for murdering the apartment official who had discovered his plans for escape to the West. It crosses familiar territory as it follows Martin's efforts to reaquaint himself with his 11-year-old son, ex-wife and old prison chums, cope with innovations (train ticket machines, Gameboys) and a panoply of worklessness, homelessness and complex social security provisions. Notable, however, is writer/director Stöhr's light touch, patience and restraint and the the strength of the main performances, especially that of Schüttauf as the sympathetic Pushkin-reading ex-con. WH

Berlin Jerusalem

(1989, Fr, 89 min)
d/p Amos Gitai. *sc* Amos Gitai, Gudie Lawaetz. *ph* Henri Alekan. *ed* Luke Barnea. *ad* Emannel Amrani. *m* Markus Stockhausen. *cast* Lisa Kreuzer, Rivka Neuman, Markus Stockhausen, Benjamin Lévy, Danny Roth, Bernard Eisenschitz.

● By telling the story of two historical pioneers reclaimed from the amber of Israeli mythology, Gitai explores nothing less than the journey to the Promised Land, the Zionist dream made reality. Else Lasker-Schüler (Kreuzer) is a German expressionist poet, Tania Shocat (Neuman) a Russian socialist activist. In a boldly conceptualised Berlin, Tania takes leave of Else and sets off for the Holy Land, where she participates in one of the original agricultural collectives. Meanwhile, as Hitler rises to power, Else finds herself a stranger in her own land; she too must take the road from Berlin to Jerusalem. In a sense, both women are revolutionaries – Else in art, Tania in politics – and Gitai juxtaposes their different perspectives on life, adopting a relevant style for each. In Berlin (actually Paris), master cinematographer Henri Alekan visualises a blue-black city with explicit references to expressionism; in Tania's story, the arid landscape and low-key drama are photographed realistically by Nurith Aviv. If this subtle and restrained film struggles to accommodate Else's flamboyant personality, it nevertheless climaxes with her, amid a shattering sonic barrage of death and destruction that brings it bang up to date. 'There is lamentation in the world/As if God had died/And we are in his cemetery'. TCh

Berlin Report

(1991, SKor, 100 min)
d Park Kwang-Su. *p* Byung-Gi Suh. *sc* Park Kwang-Su. *ph* Kwang-Suk Chung. *ed* Kim Hyun. *cast* Ahn Song-Gi, Kang Soo-Yeon, Moon Sung-Kuen, Marianne Loyen, Jacques Seiler, Jean-Marie Bonne Fon.

● Shot entirely in Europe, much of it on trans-continental autoroutes, Park's weird political allegory doesn't manage to say much about the prospects or perils of Korean reunification but it sort of delivers as a mystery thriller. Raised in France by foster parents, a Korean brother and sister have gone separate ways. The boy, an artist and socialist, has vanished into East Germany; the girl has sunk into a reclusive silence since the unexplained death of her adoptive father. Ahn plays a Paris-based journalist who sets out to break the girl's silence by locating her brother – just after the Berlin Wall has come down. Stylishly shot, decently acted, intriguing. TR

Berlin – Symphony of a Great City

see Berlin – Die Sinfonie der Grosstadt

Bermuda Triangle, The

(1978, US, 94 min)
d Richard Friedenberg. *p* Charles E Sellier Jr, James L Conway. *sc* Stephen Lord. *ph* Henning Schellerup. *ed* John F Link. *ad* Charles Bennett. *m* John Cameron. *cast* Donald Albee, Lin Berlit, Vickery Turner, Howard W Bishop Jr. *narrator* Brad Crandall.

● This speculative grab-bag spends most of its running time in dull, badly acted reconstructions of boats, planes and people disappearing in a welter of tacky special effects, and then wheels in the loony fringe psychics, conspiracy theorists and UFO freaks for a decidedly 'unbalanced' appraisal of the Triangle's enigma. PT

Bermude: La Fossa Maledetta

see Sharks' Cave, The

Bernadette

(1988, Fr, 119 min)
d Jean Delannoy. *p* Giancarlo Parretti. *sc* Robert Arnaut, Jean Delannoy. *ph* Jean-Bernard Penzer. *ed* Annie Charvein. *ad* Alain Paroutaud. *m* Francis Lai. *cast* Sydney Penny, Jean-Marc Bory, Philippe Rondest, Arlette Didier, Roland Lesaffre, Michel Duchaussoy.

● Veteran director Delannoy keeps things simple in his account of the peasant girl who claimed to have seen a vision at Lourdes. Bernadette lives with her family in appalling poverty, suffers from asthma, and is a slow learner, unable to grasp the intricacies of the catechism. One day a lady in white bathed in a heavenly glow appears in a grotto (the first of 17 such sightings). The peasant community believes her unhesitatingly, but official bodies sceptically search for scientific explanations or even political conspiracies. There's no doubting Delannoy's allegiance: he takes time to establish Bernadette's goodness and humility, painting as insipid a character as is usual for cinematic saints, while Sydney Penny brings to the part a naive allure. Long takes and Francis Lai's haunting music set a solemn tone that hints at big implications, but spirituality finally swamps the facts, and at two hours, this small story seems overstretched. EP

Bernie

(1996, Fr, 87 min)
d Albert Dupontel. *p* Alain Belmondo, Gérard Crosnier, Jean-Michel Rey, Philippe Liegeoise. *sc* Albert Dupontel, Gilles Laurent. *ph*

Guillaume Schiffman. *ed* Juliette Welfling. *ad* Laurent Allaire. *m* Ramon Pipin. *cast* Albert Dupontel, Claude Perron, Roland Blanche, Hélène Vincent, Roland Bertin.

●Released from an institution 30 years after his parents dumped him down a garbage chute, Bernie Noel (Dupontel) finds a Paris apartment, buys a video camera, and sets about tracking down his folks. His tenuous grip on reality isn't improved by contact with the world at large; he leaves a trail of corpses and headless budgies in his wake. To complain that a black comedy is tasteless and offensive is probably to miss the point, but there it is. The violence against women of all ages is particularly grating. A hit in France. TCh

Bert Rigby, You're a Fool

(1989, US, 94 min)
d Carl Reiner. *p* George Shapiro. *sc* Carl Reiner. *ph* Jan de Bont. *ed* Bud Molin. *pd* Terence Marsh. *m* Ralph Burns. *cast* Robert Lindsay, Anne Bancroft, Corbin Bernsen, Robbie Coltrane, Cathryn Bradshaw, Jackie Gayle, Bruno Kirby, Liz Smith.

●Reiner scripted this musical after seeing Robert Lindsay's acclaimed stage performance in *Me and My Girl*. Such is the apparent admiration, all perspective has been lost. Details from Lindsay's own life are loosely incorporated into the plot, which becomes progressively inflated and thus – paradoxically – a thoroughly inadequate showcase for the star's more intimate style. Striking miner Bert Rigby (Lindsay) enlivens his humdrum life with impersonations of Kelly and Astaire. When an amateur talent show comes to town, Bert's bungled rendition of 'Isn't It Romantic' proves a huge hit, and sets the chirpy singer-dancer on the road to Hollywood. Stock characters litter his progress: manipulative agent (Coltrane), producer's frustrated wife (Bancroft), pretentious TV commercials director (Kirby), egocentric movie star (Bernsen). Certainly the performances aren't at fault, but it's difficult to imagine what sort of audience has been targeted for this bizarre hybrid of cinematic styles. One thing's for sure: a musical it ain't. Even the numbers reviving Cole Porter, Noël Coward and Irving Berlin fail to light up the screen; along with the star, they're hopelessly misused. CM

Besieged (L'Assedio)

(1998, It, 94 min)
d Bernardo Bertolucci. *p* Massimo Cortesi. *sc* Clare Peloe, Bernardo Bertolucci. *ph* Fabio Cianchetti. *ed* Jacopo Quadri. *pd* Gianni Silvestri. *m* Alessio Vlad. *cast* Thandie Newton, David Thewlis, Claudio Santamaria, John C Ojwang, Massimo de Rossi, Cyril Nri.

●Shandurai (Newton), an African refugee in Rome, pays her way through medical school as a live-in cleaner for English pianist and composer Kinsky (Thewlis). Shy and timid, he woos her with gifts and music, but she rejects his overtures; her husband's a political prisoner in her homeland, she says. Kinsky responds with an act of love simple, profound and pivotal. Like Welles' *The Immortal Story*, this is a beautiful cameo from a mature artist. The scale doesn't signify a retreat – unless love is counted a minor theme – but it does seem to have had a liberating effect on the director, who embellishes a piquant short story by James Lasdun with dazzling mise en scène: delirious travelling shots, jumpcuts and an innovative soundtrack, all edited with seamless flair. This is cinema with music's fluid purity of form – indeed, it runs for 15 minutes before Bertolucci has recourse to anything so base as the spoken word. Kinsky plays Bach and Mozart; Shandurai, Salif Keita and Youssou N'dour. Some may find it pretentious, but Thewlis (clumsy, remote, rarefied) and Newton (contained, honestly bewildered) provide innumerable points of entry. It's a film about the limits of art, about civilization at this moment of flux, and about a gentle connection between a man and a woman. TCh

Best

(1999, GB/Ire, 106 min)
d Mary McGuckian. *p* Mary McGuckian, Chris Roff, Elvira Bolz. *sc* John Lynch, Mary McGuckian. *ph* Witold Stok. *ed* Kant Pan. *pd* Max Gottlieb. *m* Mark Stevens. *cast* John Lynch, Ian Bannen, Jerome Flynn, Ian Hart, Patsy Kensit, Cal MacAninch, Linus Roache, Adrian Lester, David Hayman, James Ellis, Roger Daltrey, Stephen Fry, Clive Anderson.

●From the opening – a studio mock-up ringing to awkward laughter, where an embarrassed George Best (Lynch, subdued), minded by fellow footballer Rodney Marsh (Daltrey), defends his reputation to interviewer Clive Anderson – the uneasy tone of this part tribute (Best served as script consultant), part history of the great Manchester United player is established. It's a familiar tale: of a boy uprooted (he was taken from Belfast as a 15-year-old), his long wait, his glory years on the field, his 'pop' celebrity, his women (represented by Kensit's Anna), and then the long, slow descent as gambling and booze take over. The film is scrappily put together, the re-creations of the great footballing moments don't work, the 30-year 'father-son' relationship of Best and Matt Busby (Bannen) is overly drawn out, and the whole is slightly seedy and unenlightening. Lynch's professional gives the impression of a completely unremarkable man as much damned as blessed by an extraordinary talent. WH

Best Age, The (Nejkrasnejsi Vek)

(1968, Czech, 80 min, b/w)
d Jaroslav Papousek. *p* Jaroslav Solnicka. *sc* Jaroslav Papousek. *ph* Joseph Ort-Snep. *ed* Jirina Lukesová. *ad* Karel Cerny. *m* Karel Mares. *cast* Hana Brejchová, Vera Kresadlová, Ladislava Jakim, Jan Stöckl, Anna Pisarikova.

●One of those pleasingly elliptical Czech comedies which flourished briefly during the '60s, never quite confronting their subjects head on, and in not doing so managing to speak volumes about the foibles of humanity. Querulous old men queue up for the privilege of adding a few pence to their pensions by acting as models at an art school; callow young students ponder the mysteries of death behind the tired old skulls they are set to sculpt; and a strange, yearning discontent permeates the air, with each age group firmly convinced that the other has the best of things. It's very slight, but although Papousek hasn't quite the same infallible command of timing as a film like Milos Forman's *A Blonde in Love*, he does extract very much the same flavour of dry, deadpan humour from his sidelong view of the human comedy. TM

Best Boy

(1979, US, 111 min)
d/p/sc Ira Wohl. *ph* Tom McDonough. *ed* Ira Wohl. *pd* Tom McDonough. *with* Philip Wohl, Max Wohl, Pearl Wohl, Ira Wohl, Frances Wohl, Christine O'Connor.

●About the director's cousin, Philly, who's 52, says he's 16, and actually has the mental age of a five-year-old. When Wohl started filming, it was because he'd convinced Philly's protective, elderly parents that they had to help their son towards greater independence. The result is in part a sensitive record of that three year process, in a film which never preaches but almost incidentally points out what help is available, where it works and where it falls short. It's also a tale of the love, guilt and stoicism of Philly's parents, and despite moments of real sorrow, the final impression left by the film is one of optimism – in the way it discovers dignity in ordinary people, an infectious sense of humour in adversity, and the songs in the heart of a mentally disabled man. HM

Best Defence

(1984, US, 94 min)
d Willard Huyck. *p* Gloria Katz. *sc* Gloria Katz, Willard Huyck. *ph* Don Peterman. *ed* Sidney Wolinsky. *pd* Peter Jamison. *m* Patrick Williams. *cast* Dudley Moore, Eddie Murphy, Kate Capshaw, George Dzundza, Helen Shaver, Peter Michael Goetz, Tom Noonan.

●Sometime George Lucas associates Huyck and Katz had disastrous previews with their 'comedy' about engineer Dud's bumbling attempts to perfect the crucial on-board gyroscope for the new XM-10 Annihilator tank. So it was off for reshoots, drafting in 'strategic guest star' Murphy (it says so on the opening titles) as a US army tank commander putting said vehicle through its slapstick paces on test manoeuvres. Cutting back and forth between the two points, the film's a dismally unfunny shambles in which the leads never meet, enlivened only by a baleful cameo from hardware designer Tom Noonan, and the jaw-dropping plot development that has Iraq invading Kuwait, six years before Saddam did it for real. Never thought you'd get to hear Eddie Murphy say 'I love Iraq!'? Well, he does here, feigning cowardice to bamboozle enemy firepower. TJ

Best Foot Forward

(1943, US, 95 min)
d Edward Buzzell. *p* Arthur Freed. *sc* Irving Brecher, Fred Finklehoffe. *ph* Leonard Smith. ed Blanche Sewell. ad Cedric Gibons, Edward Carfagno. *m* Hugh Martin, Ralph Blane. *cast* Lucille Ball, William Gaxton, Tommy Dix, Virginia Weidler, Nancy Walker, June Allyson, Gloria De Haven, Kenny Bowers.

●A breezy but bland adaptation of the Broadway musical, with Lucille Ball as a movie star called Lucille Ball who, as a publicity stunt designed to revive a flagging career, accepts an invitation from a star-struck cadet (Dix) to attend a prom at his military academy. Much farcical ado ensues since the star's presence has to be kept secret from the authorities and the cadet's regular girlfriend (Weidler), while Ball herself is not pleased at having to garner publicity while remaining incognito. Buzzell's direction is laboured, and the merely passable musical numbers are staged by Charles Walters with surprisingly little flair. Harry James, providing the brash big band swing for the prom, manages to squeeze in his flashy rendition of 'Flight of the Bumble Bee' (not much cop there for the dancers on the floor). TM

Best Friends

(1982, US, 109 min)
d Norman Jewison. *p* Norman Jewison, Patrick Palmer. *sc* Valerie Curtin, Barry Levinson. *ph* Jordan Cronenweth. *ed* Don Zimmerman. *ad* Josan F Russo. *m* Michel Legrand. *cast* Burt Reynolds, Goldie Hawn, Jessica Tandy, Barnard Hughes, Audra Lindley, Keenan Wynn.

●Screenwriters Barry Levinson and Valerie Curtin present a semi-autobiographical study of two people who have lived together successfully for years, but find that the act of marriage virtually destroys their relationship. Hawn and Reynolds play two screenwriters who keep the ceremony secret from everyone except their parents, but still find the pressures almost too much to bear. The script is sharply written, while Jewison is a lot more sensitive to the material than he was on that earlier Levinson-Curtin effort, *And Justice For All*. But though engaging and agreeable, the film is never wildly funny. DP

Best Hotel on Skid Row

(1990, US, 47 min)
d Christine Choy, Renee Tajima. *p* Peter Davis, Christine Choy, Renee Tajima. *sc* Renee Tajima. *ph* Christine Choy. *ad* Geoffrey Bartz. *narrator* Charles Bukowski.

●In the City of Angels, Skid Row covers 50 square blocks. This rather scattershot documentary introduces us to the residents of the Madison Hotel ($8.20 a night): drunks, drug addicts, the walking wounded. Charles Bukowski's w(h)iney voice-over and music by Tom Waits, Coltrane, et al, threaten to romanticise the film, and at times it does feel like an old Disney travelogue gone badly off course, but gradually the lives of these people take over. Billy hasn't left the fifth floor in two months. He pays Adam to run his errands. Adam, he explains, can't talk – lung cancer – can't read or write, he's 'in a world of trouble'. They all are. TCh

Best in Show

(2000, US, 90 min)
d Christopher Guest. *p* Karen Murphy. *sc* Christopher Guest, Eugene Levy. *ph* Roberto Schaefer. *ed* Robert Leighton. *pd* Joseph T Garrity. *m* Jeffery CJ Vanston. *cast* Parker Posey, Michael Hitchcock, Catherine O'Hara, Eugene Levy, Bob Balaban, Christopher Guest, Michael McKean, John Michael Higgins, Jennifer Coolidge, Jane Lynch, Fred Willard, Jim Piddock.

●It's a commonplace that pets resemble their owners (or vice versa), but the phenomenon has rarely been explored with such dogged glee. A 'mockumentary' tracking half-a-dozen contestants as they prepare for the annual Mayflower Dog Show in Philadelphia, Christopher Guest's film combines flea-on-the-wall observation with direct-to-camera interviews. The similarities with

This Is Spinal Tap are plain, although most of the gags here are more of a smile than laugh-out-loud. Co-written by Guest and Eugene Levy, but apparently largely improvised, this caricatures a broad cross-section of social archetypes, from the gay couple (McKean and Higgins) with their shih-tzu, to the neurotic yuppies (Posey and Hitchcock) with their Weimaraner, and Guest's backwoods cajun, with his bloodhound Hubert. The performances are perfect, and the actors aren't bad either, but while it rightly celebrates the underdogs, the film doesn't humanise its stereotypes the way *Spinal Tap* did. The dog show itself is enlivened by an outrageous comic turn from Fred Willard as an addled TV commentator suffering from a bad case of foot-in-mouth disease. Levy is fun, too, as a cuckolded salesman with two left feet (literally). TCh

Best Intentions, The (Den Goda Viljan)

(1992, Swe, 181 min)
d Bille August. *p* Lars Bjälkeskog. *sc* Ingmar Bergman. *ph* Jörgen Persson. *ed* Janus Billeskov Jansen. *pd* Anna Asp. *m* Stefan Nilsson. *cast* Samuel Fröler, Pernilla August, Max von Sydow, Ghita Norby, Lennart Hjulström, Mona Malm.

● Ingmar Bergman's *Fanny and Alexander* mined his childhood for inspiration; next came the autobiography, *The Magic Lantern*; and now, his screenplay recounting his parents' courtship and early days of marriage preceding his birth. But the joy which finally infused the earlier film is lacking in this much bleaker affair. Henrik Bergman (Fröler) is an impoverished theology student when he meets spoiled, rich Anna (Pernilla August). Instantly attracted, the couple spend the next two years battling parental obstruction; once together, their problems really begin… Bille August has space to develop relationships and explore the emotional nuances which lead to numerous confrontations; with cinematographer Jörgen Persson, he conveys a firm sense of oppressive natural forces; and the film boasts impeccable performances (von Sydow is splendid as Anna's father). But with a running time of three hours, this weighty drama tests the most patient soul. CM

Best Laid Plans

(1999, US, 93 min)
d Mike Barker. *p* Alan Greenspan, Betsy Beers, Chris Moore, Sean Bailey. *sc* Ted Griffin. *ph* Ben Seresin. *ed* Sloane Klevin. *pd* Sophie Becher. *m* Craig Armstrong. *cast* Alessandro Nivola, Reese Witherspoon, Josh Brolin, Rocky Carroll, Michael G Hagerty, Terrence Howard, Jamie Marsh.

● Tropico is small town anywhere, USA, and Nick (Nivola) has a scummy job in a recycling plant. Meeting Lissa (Witherspoon) is just about the only highlight in his life just now, and he'd hoped that an inheritance from his late father would be their ticket to somewhere else. No chance. The taxman has swallowed the lot, leaving Nick all too susceptible when pals at work tell him of a robbery they're setting up. What sounds like no-risk turns into a nightmare with Nick left owing serious money to the heaviest dude in town. There are surprises for even the veteran twist-spotter, but the film is far from an exercise in empty narrative mechanics: friendship, loyalty, moral choices move events this way and that. Nivola gives a canny performance, while Witherspoon's sympathetic support and Brolin's seeming fall guy provide a persuasive foundation for all the slipperiness that follows. British director Barker keeps the cast believable but fabricates a *noir*-ish Edward Hopper backdrop around them, delivering a tantilising hyper-reality. TJ

Best Little Whorehouse in Texas, The

(1982, US, 114 min)
d Colin Higgins. *p* Thomas L Miller, Edward K Milkis, Robert L Boyett. *sc* Larry L King, Peter Masterson, Colin Higgins. *ph* William A Fraker. *ed* Pembroke J Herring. *pd* Robert Boyle. *m* Patrick Williams. *songs* Carol Hall. *cast* Burt Reynolds, Dolly Parton, Dom DeLuise, Charles Durning, Robert Mandan, Lois Nettleton.

● The brothel as soul of the community, charitable institution, or social therapy on a par with raffia work? This musical avoids sensitive issues like the clap, settling for stock tarts-with-hearts, loyal regulars, virginal jocks, and an outraged clean-up-the-state prude (DeLuise) of monstrously miscamped proportions. Clumsy chorus-lining, a penchant for ostrich plumes, and a tinny musical sameness betray the film's stage origins. One good number: Durning's Governor tripping a neat political 'Sidestep'. But the dialogue is Texas crude, the sentiment Bible Belt coy, and the songs conveyor-belt Broadway: stale air on a G-string. AM

Best Man

(1997, US, 89 min)
d/p/ed Ira Wohl. *ph/pd* Tom McDonough.

● We revisit Philip Wohl (see *Best Boy*), now 70 years old and, so far as we can decode his words and looks, deriving interest and pleasure from his simply structured life. Clearly, the process of achieving semi-independence, so movingly recorded in the earlier film, was decisive. Subtitled '*Best Boy* and all of us 20 years later,' this is nothing more urgent than an update – worth having, despite the sense of events being arranged as much for our benefit as Philly's: a visit to his parents' grave, a trip to California, his belated bar mitzvah. Most touching is the mutually sustaining relationship between Philly and his now-widowed sister Fran. And inevitably there is the action of the years, so manifest in an extended project like this: the deaths, the losing touch, the sadness alongside the affection and humour. BBa

Best Man, The

(1964, US, 104 min, b/w)
d Franklin Schaffner. *p* Stuart Millar, Lawrence Turman. *sc* Gore Vidal. *ph* Haskell Wexler. *ed* Robert E Swink. *ad* Lyle Wheeler. *m* Mort Lindsey. *cast* Henry Fonda, Cliff Robertson, Edie Adams, Margaret Leighton, Ann Sothern, Lee Tracy, Shelley Berman.

● Presidential politics may loom larger and darker since Watergate, but this disenchanted peek behind the scenes of an American election still bites, thanks to a Gore Vidal script (based on his own play) which dissects with gleeful cynicism the machinery of tub-thumping, image-building and chicanery that goes into motion as rival presidential candidates (Fonda the nice liberal, Robertson the nasty extremist) fight to cut each other's throats. Memorable lines galore, like the Southern senator's all-purpose reply to awkward questions about how many integrated schools there are in his state ('None, thank God, but we're making remarkable progress'), and a whole string of brilliant performances. TM

Best Man, The

(1999, US, 120 min)
d Malcolm D Lee. *p* Spike Lee, Sam Kitt, Bill Carraro. *sc* Malcolm D Lee. *ph* Frank Prinzi. *ed* Cara Silverman. *pd* Kalina Ivanov. *m* Stanley Clarke. *cast* Taye Diggs, Nia Long, Morris Chestnut, Harold Perrineau Jr, Terrence Howard, Sanaa Lathan, Monica Calhoun, Melissa De Sousa.

● As Harper Stewart (Diggs) prepares to act as best man at a friend's wedding, it emerges that his about-to-be-published first novel, 'Unfinished Business', is a thinly disguised roman-à-clef. The wedding guests gather – among them Jordan (Long), one of the affianced author's old flames – former times recalled, and the talk gets round to putting real names to Harper's literary faces. So much for the under-powered plot, from tyro writer/director Malcolm D Lee, to which the tiresome unearthing of nice guy Harper's previous dalliances contributes little. The strong cast riff on fidelity, loyalty and commitment, and unsurprisingly the nuptial schmaltz is ladled on in the final reel. MHi

Best Men

(1997, US, 89 min)
d Tamra Davis. *p* Brad Krevoy, Steve Stabler, Brad Jenkel, Deborah Ridpath. *sc* Art Edler Brown, Tracy Fraim. *ph* James Glennon. *ed* Paul Trejo. *pd* Tony Corbett, Mark Mothersbaugh. *cast* Luke Wilson, Drew Barrymore, Dean Cain, Andy Dick, Mitchell Whitfield, Sean Patrick Flanery, Fred Ward, Brad Dourif, Tracy Fraim.

● Independence, California, July 4th. The day Jesse (Wilson) gets out of jail, he heads for church to marry his sweetheart (Barrymore). Unfortunately, one of his four best men, Billy (Flanery), needs to stop at the bank en route. Billy is the town sheriff's son, but unknown to his pals, he's also the notorious bank robber Hamlet, so-called for his propensity to spout Shakespeare during heists. A dog day situation soon develops, with the nuptials transferred to the bank and the FBI roped in as witnesses. Yet another quirky crime comedy, but on its own terms entertaining enough, with a distinctively sharp take on masculine behaviour and a surprising amount of the Bard. TCh

Best of the Best

(1989, US, 95 min)
d Bob Radler. *p* Phillip Rhee, Peter Strauss. *sc* Paul Levine. *ph* Douglas Ryan. *ed* William Hoy. *pd* Maxine Shepard. *m* Paul Gilman. *cast* Eric Roberts, James Earl Jones, Louise Fletcher, Sally Kirkland, Christopher Penn, Phillip Rhee, John P Ryan.

● 'No women, no alcohol, no drugs. You will eat, drink and shit competition' warns coach James Earl Jones, pretty much summing up the attraction of this particular 'entertainment'. The perfunctory plot concerns the selection and training of a five-man US karate team to take on the formidable Koreans. This might have made an interesting documentary, but the film-makers opt instead for hokey drama. The squad includes Penn's two-dimensional red-neck Travis Bickley (!), Roberts as a comparatively enlightened old hand, and Phillip Rhee as the young hopeful with the obligatory revenge motif. This surprisingly heavyweight cast – Louise Fletcher and Sally Kirkland lend spiritual support – manages to lower itself to the exploitation level material without apparent strain; indeed the performances are all truly atrocious. After much fist-clenching, the movie closes to a draw – a small mercy to be grateful for, though kamikaze kids inclined to stay the course will probably be disappointed by the shallow sentimentality. TCh

Best of the Best 2

(1992, US, 100 min)
d Robert Radler. *p* Phillip Rhee, Peter Strauss. *sc* Max Strom, John Allen Nelson. *ph* Fred Tammes. *ed* Bert Lovitt. *pd* Gary Frutkoff. *m* David Michael Frank. *cast* Eric Roberts, Phillip Rhee, Christopher Penn, Wayne Newton, Ralph Moeller, Meg Foster, Edan Gross.

● Three years ago, Roberts, Rhee and a surprisingly mercenary supporting cast enacted the Olympian efforts of the US karate team against the mighty Koreans; but this effort, less sequel than cast reunion, jettisons the comparatively ascetic demands of the sports movie formula for the more demonstratively decadent pleasures of action-melodrama. Newton invites a select group of high-rollers to the Las Vegas Colosseum's nightly no-rules blood bout, where our horizontally-challenged pair vow to avenge the death of their team-mate (Penn). Radler's contemporary gladiator movie is little more than a crude pastiche: no matter that its prime role models come from sci-fi (*Rollerball, The Running Man*), at least it musters the courage of its shameless contrivance. TCh

Best of Times, The

(1986, US, 104 min)
d Roger Spottiswoode. *p* Gordon Carroll. *sc* Ron Shelton. *ph* Charles F Wheeler. *ed* Garth Craven. *ad* Anthony Brockliss. *m* Arthur B Rubinstein. *cast* Robin Williams, Kurt Russell, Pamela Reed, Holly Palance, Donald Moffat, Margaret Whitton.

● At 9.22 pm on November 15, 1972, Jack Dundee (Williams) dropped a catch in a game of American football and caused his team, the Taft Rockets, to lose to the rival town of Bakersfield. Thirteen years later he is still haunted by his error, which is hardly surprising considering that no one will let him forget it. Prompted by the friendly neighbourhood whore, Dundee decides to stage a rematch, and persuades his buddy, quarterback Russell, to help him. When their wives find out, they chuck them out, so both men have more than just their reputations to regain. Though it does have its moments, the result is never as funny as it should be. Williams and Russell, although fine individually, don't spark off each other as a comic duo should, and the ending is so predictable it's almost unexpected. MS

Best of Walt Disney's True Life Adventures, The

(1975, US, 89 min)
d James Algar. *p* Ben Sharpsteen, James Algar. *sc* James Algar. *ph* Alfred G Milotte, Elma Milotte, N Paul Kenworthy Jr, Robert H Crandall, Hugh A Wilmar, James R Simon, Herb Crisler, Lois Crisler, Tom McHugh, Jack Couffer. *ed* Norman Palmer. *m* Paul Smith, Oliver Wallace.
● True life? The 'adventures' in this compilation are about as true to life as those ads with cats wearing bow-ties and sheep sauntering by washing-machines. Disney's field photographers procured fine and rare footage, only to have it dolled up with jokey editing, cute music, and a patronising commentary: scorpions doing a barn dance, polar bears rolling down ice-caps by mistake, ducks slipping on a frozen pond, and Skinny the bravado squirrel demonstrating his bravado. The final image consists of a skyful of birds: you expect them to form the words 'The End', but they never do. GB

Best Revenge

(1983, Can, 96 min)
d John Trent. *p* Michael Lebowitz. *sc* David Rothberg, Rick Rosenthal, John Hunter. *ph* John Coquillon. *ed* Alban Streeter. *pd* William Beeton. *m* Keith Emerson. *cast* John Heard, Levon Helm, Alberta Watson, Stephen McHattie, Moses Znaimer, John Rhys-Davies.
● A rather obvious Canadian spin on *Midnight Express* (right down to the domineering Keith Emerson electronic score) has Heard as the small-time drugs runner inveigled into making a marijuana pick-up in Morocco, since his best mate McHattie is being held captive by gangland boss Znaimer. Linking up with bohemian cohort Helm (previously the singing drummer in The Band), their plan starts going awry when Moroccan contact Rhys-Davies takes them to sample the goods. Subsequent developments marry wearying predictability with an undercurrent of xenophobia, suspense being predicated on the notion that Moroccan policemen in dark glasses are invariably up to no good. TJ

Best Seller

(1987, US, 95 min)
d John Flynn. *p* Carter de Haven. *sc* Larry Cohen. *ph* Fred Murphy. *ed* David Rosenbloom. *pd* Gene Rudolf. *m* Jay Ferguson. *cast* James Woods, Brian Dennehy, Victoria Tennant, Allison Balson, Paul Shenar, George Coe.
● This Larry Cohen-scripted thriller reworks the old idea of the symbiotic relationship between cop and killer, adding a new twist. LA Detective Meechum (Dennehy) is a burnt-out wreck whose sideline as a crime novelist has dried up since his wife's death. Sleazy, amoral hit-man Cleve (Woods) steps out of Meechum's past and offers him the dirt on his ex-boss, major league criminal turned legitimate corporation boss Madlock. The deal is that Meechum gets to write again and Cleve gets to be the hero of a hard-hitting exposé of Madlock's bloodstained past. Tough action, hardboiled dialogue and a tightly constructed script keep the action brisk and bloody, while the jaundiced sideswipes at American capitalism are laced with cynicism. Sadly, the potentially explosive confrontation between Dennehy and Woods never quite lives up to expectations; but Flynn's lean direction achieves a gritty B movie edge as the sparks fly and Dennehy moves towards a grudging respect for his manic alter ego. NF

Best Shot

see Hoosiers

Best Things in Life Are Free, The

(1956, US, 104 min)
d Michael Curtiz. *p* Henry Ephron. *sc* William Bowers, Phoebe Ephron. *ph* Leon Shamroy. *ed* Dorothy Spencer. *ad* Lyle Wheeler, Maurice Ransford. *cast* Gordon MacRae, Dan Dailey, Ernest Borgnine, Sheree North, Murvyn Vye, Tommy Noonan, Tony Galento.
● One of the very best of the musical biopics (of the DeSylva/Henderson/Brown songwriting team): a strangely neglected film, perhaps because the superb string of numbers are mostly 'thrown away' on delightfully modest, off-the-cuff renditions, either by Sheree North or by the songwriters themselves (with Borgnine keeping his end up admirably). The two big production numbers are gems: 'Black Bottom' done as a spirited gangster movie parody, and 'Birth of the Blues' as a brilliantly evocative, mostly all-black mood piece. Even the plot is livelier than usual, centering on DeSylva's defection from the team to try his hand as a Hollywood producer. A lot can be forgiven, in any case, for its maliciously illustrated anecdote about how the trio, regally ordered to write a song for Al Jolson (who wasn't above neglecting to pay), concocted one so trashily treacly that nobody could sing it. Jolson was thrilled. The song: 'Sonny Boy'. TM

Best Way to Walk, The (La Meilleure Façon de Marcher/ aka The Best Way)

(1976, Fr, 86 min)
d Claude Miller. *sc* Claude Miller, Luc Béraud. *ph* Bruno Nuytten. *ed* Jean-Bernard Bonis. *ad* Hilton Mac Connico. *m* Alain Jomy. *cast* Patrick Dewaere, Patrick Bauchitey, Christine Pascal, Claude Piéplu, Michel Blanc.
● A film about getting off on the 'right' foot. Dealing with the confusions of adolescent sexuality, it's less about groping one's way towards adulthood than about the search for sexual identity. Set in 1960 in a boys' summer camp, it traces the ambiguous relationship between two camp monitors. Claude Miller, Truffaut's former assistant, handles the contrasts of his script with assurance, especially those between group conformity and private individual feelings. Only at the end does his touch falter, because until then his perception of emotional nuances effectively masks the stereotypical equations he makes between sex, class and, to a lesser extent, politics. But overall it's a highly assured first feature. CPe

Best Years of Our Lives, The

(1946, US, 172 min, b/w)
d William Wyler. *p* Samuel Goldwyn. *sc* Robert E Sherwood. *ph* Gregg Toland. *ed* Daniel Mandell. *ad* Perry Ferguson, George Jenkins. *m* Hugo Friedhofer. *cast* Fredric March, Myrna Loy, Dana Andrews, Teresa Wright, Virginia Mayo, Harold Russell, Hoagy Carmichael.
● Overlong, perhaps, but this tender and occasionally tough look at the plight of returning war veterans is one of Wyler's best films. Robert Sherwood's script is thorough without falling into undue sentimentality or bombast, the performances throughout are splendid (including that of Russell, an amateur actor who was himself an amputee), and Gregg Toland's masterly camerawork serves as a textbook on the proper use of deep focus. Maybe not the masterpiece it would like to be, but a model of fine Hollywoood craftsmanship all the same. GA

Bête, La (The Beast)

(1975, Fr, 102 min)
d Walerian Borowczyk. *p* Anatole Dauman. *sc* Walerian Borowczyk. *ph* Bernard Daillencourt, Marcel Grignon. *ed* Walerian Borowczyk. *ad* Jacques d'Ovidio. *m* Domenico Scarlatti. *cast* Sirpa Lane, Lisbeth Hummel, Elisabeth Kahson, Pierre Benedetti, Marcel Dalio, Guy Tréjean.
● Once upon a time, in the 18th century, a beast lived in the woods of an aristocratic estate. And this beast, possessed of a giant phallus and an insatiable lust, set upon the beautiful young lady of the house. But the lady was of an even greater sexual appetite, and laid the beast to eternal rest. Two centuries later, the tale of the beast would return in the dreams of an American heiress contracted to carry the male descendant of the same crumbling aristocratic family… Borowczyk's all-out assault on social conventions and repressed desires, an outrageously ironic blend of French farce and surrealist poetry, can be seen as signposting both the peak of his sexual fables (Blanche, Immoral Tales) and his subsequent decline into ephemeral soft porn. Its shameless shuffling of equine couplings, pederastic priests and priapic black manservants earns it nul points for political correctness. But seen from its own amoral perspective, aided by Borowczyk's remarkable sense of framing and rhythm, *La Bête* is that rare achievement, a truly erotic film. DT

Bête Humaine, La (The Human Beast/Judas Was a Woman)

(1938, Fr, 104 min, b/w)
d Jean Renoir. *p* Robert Hakim. *sc* Jean Renoir. *ph* Curt Courant. *ed* Marguerite Renoir. *pd* Eugène Lourié. *m* Joseph Kosma. *cast* Jean Gabin, Simone Simon, Fernand Ledoux, Julien Carette, Blanchette Brunoy, Jean Renoir.
● Stunning images of trains and railway lines as a metaphor for the blind, immutable forces that drive human passions to destruction. Superb performances from Gabin, Simon and Ledoux as the classic tragic love triangle. The deterministic principles of Zola's novel, replaced by destiny in Lang's remake *Human Desire*, are slightly muffled here. But given the overwhelming tenderness and brutality of Renoir's vision, it hardly matters that the hero's compulsion to kill, the result of hereditary alcoholism, is left half-explained. TM

Betelnut Beauty (Ai Ni Ai Wo)

(2000, Tai/Fr, 106 min)
d Lin Cheng-Sheng. *p* Peggy Chiao, Hsu Hsiao-Ming, Fabienne Vonier. *sc* Lin Cheng-Sheng. *ph* Han Yun-Chung. *ed* Liao Qingsong, Hsiao Ju-Kuan. *ad* Hsia Shao-Yu. *m* A-Chi and the Chairman. *cast* Chang Chen, Sinje, Tsai Chen-Nan, Gao Mingjun.
● Far less measured and 'artful' than Lin's previous films, this low-life romance fizzily blends humour and violence, tragedy and sex. Betelnuts offer a mild (legal) high, sold in Taiwan – mostly to passing truckers and taxi drivers – from roadside stands staffed by under-dressed young women with links to organised crime. Fei-Fei (Sinje) runs away from her prying mother to run a betelnut stand. Feng (Chang), a young assistant baker just out of military service, falls hard for her and gets drawn into the world of her 'protector' Tiger and his rival Guang (Gao, in dreadlocks, shaping up as one of Taiwan's best actors). Things end badly, but there's none of the forced melancholy found elsewhere in Taiwanese cinema. TR

Betrayal

(1982, GB, 95 min)
d David Jones. *p* Sam Spiegel. *sc* Harold Pinter. *ph* Mike Fash. *ed* John Bloom. *pd* Eileen Diss. *m* Dominic Muldowney. *cast* Jeremy Irons, Ben Kingsley, Patricia Hodge, Avril Elgar, Ray Marioni, Caspar Norman.
● Stagy adaptation by Pinter of his own theatrical success about a determinedly upper-middle class romantic triangle between Kingsley's publisher, wife Hodge, and glacial lover Irons. Hodge is fine, Kingsley tries his best, and Irons is as tight-assed as ever. But it's all so uncinematic as to make one wonder why it was ever made in the first place. GA

Betrayed

see When Strangers Marry

Betrayed

(1988, US, 127 min)
d Costa-Gavras. *p* Irwin Winkler. *sc* Joe Eszterhas. *ph* Patrick Blossier. *ed* Joele van Effenterre. *pd* Patrizia von Brandenstein. *m* Bill Conti. *cast* Debra Winger, Tom Berenger, John Heard, Betsy Blair, John Mahoney, Ted Levine, Jeffrey DeMunn.
● After the Chicago killing of a controversial radio talk-show host by right wing extremists, FBI agent Winger goes undercover to investigate prime suspect Berenger. A widowed family man farmer, he's as clean-living and charming as they come; inevitably she falls for him, uncertain of his guilt until he takes her hunting by night…for human prey. Winger wants out, but when her boss and ex-lover (Heard) refuses the request, she finds herself involved in a white supremacist conspiracy against blacks, Jews and gays, and living with a man she detests and fears. If the forte of Costa-Gavras' political thriller is its acting, that only underlines the flaws in Joe *Jagged Edge* Eszterhas' murky, often contrived script. The racist sentiments and deeds on view are plausible; it's the plot details that suspend disbelief (why for instance, doesn't Berenger notice Winger's deceptions earlier?). The film has its fair share of chilling moments, and its determination to expose the moral sickness infesting the Midwest's conservative heartlands is admirable. But Winger's emotional dilemma is clumsily sketched, leaving the film relying for suspense on a handful of set pieces; and that isn't quite enough. GA

Betsy, The

(1978, US, 125 min)
d Daniel Petrie. *p* Robert R Weston. *sc* Walter Bernstein, William Bast. *ph* Mario Tosi. *ed* Rita Roland. *pd* Herman A Blumenthal. *m* John Barry. *cast* Laurence Olivier, Robert Duvall, Katharine Ross, Tommy Lee Jones, Jane Alexander, Lesley-Anne Down.

●Power struggles in the motor industry are personified by young Tommy Lee Jones, who should be dynamic but lacks the energy of a suburban second-hand car salesman, and old Laurence Olivier. But not even decades as a 'great actor' allow Olivier to invest dialogue like 'Never shit a shitter' with feeling, so he plays with his American accent instead. All the sex is so discreet that the movie never allows itself to get as trashy as a Harold Robbins bestseller should be. SM

Betsy's Wedding

(1990, US, 94 min)
d Alan Alda. *p* Martin Bregman, Louis A Stroller. *sc* Alan Alda. *ph* Kelvin Pike. *ed* Michael Polakow. *pd* John Jay Moore. *m* Bruce Broughton. *cast* Alan Alda, Molly Ringwald, Madeline Kahn, Joe Pesci, Ally Sheedy, Anthony LaPaglia.

●When fashion student Betsy (Ringwald) visits her parents in the West Hamptons, she announces to dad and mom – motormouth Italian-American architect Eddie (Alda) and talkative Jewish-American Lola (Kahn) – that she's gonna marry straight WASP Jake: it's Betsy's last word on the matter. Mom wants the wedding Jewish; financially-overstretched Dad, despite killing looks from his wife, wins a verbal poker game with the wealthy in-laws and gets to foot the bill. Plans are laid for a reception tent larger than Yankee Stadium, and the invitation list takes on telephone book proportions. Betsy and Jake are tempted to call the whole thing off. Alda's foray into the wedding movie may lack the acerbity of Minnelli or the cinematic competence of Altman, but it's a warm, wordy, middlebrow crowd-pleaser. Alda's skill is with witty, fast-talking patter and in coaxing fine performances from his actors (playing an extended family of gently caricatured New York types). The values are bollocks, but the film is fun. WH

Better Late Than Never

(1983, GB, 95 min)
d Bryan Forbes. *p* Jack Haley Jr, David Niven Jr. *sc* Bryan Forbes. *ph* Claude Lecomte. *ed* Philip Shaw. *ad* Peter Mullins. *m* Henry Mancini. *cast* David Niven, Art Carney, Maggie Smith, Lionel Jeffries, Kimberly Partridge, Catherine Hicks.

●Forbes seemed to have hit rock bottom with the ghastly *International Velvet*. But he found even more abject depths with this comedy about a moppet and two elderly parties scrabbling to claim (illegitimate) grandpaternity, initially because there's a fortune involved, but then love… TM

Better Than Sex

(2000, Aust, 90 min)
d Jonathan Teplitzky. *p* Bruna Papandrea, Frank Cox. *sc* Jonathan Teplitzky. *ph* Garry Phillips. *ed* Shawn Seet. *pd* Tara Kamath.*m* David Hirschfelder. *cast* David Wenham, Susie Porter, Catherine McClements, Kris McQuade, Simon Bossell, Imelda Corcoran.

●Despite decent lead performances, this tedious account of a one-night stand between two self-consciously non-committal types resulting in – to their surprise, if no one else's – lasting romance makes woefully limp entertainment. The film strains to be hip, sexy and modern, but in wanting to have its cake and eat it, the blend of fashionable cynicism and hoary sentimentality ensures that a depressing sense of déjà vu rapidly sets in. As for the excessive use of voice-over, facile 'insights' and tricksy camera angles trying to conceal the stagey mise-en-scène, the less said the better. GA

Better Tomorrow, A (Yingxiong Bense)

(1986, HK, 95 min)
d John Woo. *p* Tsui Hark. *sc* Chan Hing Kai, Leung Suk Wah. *ph* Wong Wing Hang. *ed* Kam Ma. *ad* Bennie Lui. *m* Joseph Koo. *cast* Chow Yun-Fat, Leslie Cheung, Ti Lung, Emily Chu, Waise Lee, Tian Feng.

●Woo's career was at its nadir when Tsui Hark brought him into Film Workshop and proposed this 'remake' of Patrick Lung's 1967 movie *Story of a Discharged Prisoner* (also called *Yingxiong Bense* – 'The Nature of Heroes' – in Chinese). It's known that Tsui 'helped out' with the direction and editing, but the focus on codes of honour between men and wildly hyperbolic gunplay is 100 per cent Woo. Sung (Ti Lung) and Lee (Chow), traffickers in forged banknotes, are set up for a bust. Sung serves time in Taiwan while the wounded Lee hits the skids in Hong Kong. Three years later they team up to revenge themselves on their betrayer. Matters are complicated by Sung's brother Kit (Cheung, hilariously miscast in a macho role), a cop who blames Sung for the death of their father. Floridly romantic and serenely excessive (men shot a dozen times don't die, guns never need reloading), it has the bravado of a minor classic. TR

Better Tomorrow II, A (Yingxiong Bense II)

(1987, HK, 104 min)
d John Woo. *p* Tsui Hark. *sc* John Woo. *ph* Wong Hing Hung. *pd* Andy Lee. *m* Joseph Koo. *cast* Chow Yun-Fat, Leslie Cheung, Ti Lung, Dean Shek, Emily Chu.

●Chuffed by the success of *A Better Tomorrow*, Woo wanted to go straight on to *The Killer* and *Bullet in the Head*. But Tsui Hark insisted on a sequel, and came up with a storyline to press his point. The result is not 'the worst film ever made' (as Woo has been heard to describe it), but it's clear that his heart wasn't in it. The plot is a virtual rerun of the first one: ex-hoods and cops team up to beat ruthless counterfeiting racketeers by any means necessary. Since the Mark Lee character was killed off last time, it was necessary to invent Ken Lee, a twin brother in New York, to bring back Chow Yun-Fat – who (not surprisingly in the circumstances) treats the whole thing as a joke. There are odd flashes of Woo's talent, but the endless cross-cutting between characters generates no tension and the vast expenditure of (mostly ineffective) bullets and grenades looks more like *Death Wish* than a sign of visionary excess. TR

Betty Blue (37°2 le Matin)

(1986, Fr, 121 min)
d/sc Jean-Jacques Beineix. *ph* Jean-François Robin. *ed* Monique Prim. *ad* Carlos Conti. *m* Gabriel Yared. *cast* Béatrice Dalle, Jean-Hugues Anglade, Consuelo De Haviland, Gérard Darmon, Clementine Celarié.

●Betty (Dalle) is in her boyfriend Zorg's (Anglade) beach house, bonking his brains out first thing in the morning. They do a lot of that. Then she discovers his notebooks in which he has been scribbling his novel (he does a lot of that), promptly burns down the house and forces him to go to Paris in search of fame with her. Here they team up with another wiggy couple who run a pizza joint, and they do a lot of funny things. This mid-section provides the film's humorous and good-natured antics. From there, the couple move to the south, and finally dissolve to a sad attack of *amour fou*. Full of comic asides, the whole thing is all rather wonderful in the traditional Gallic way. The fullness of life, while not exactly celebrated, is certainly lived through; mostly without clothes on. CPea

Betty Blue (37°2 le Matin)

(1986, Fr, 183 min)
d/sc Jean-Jacques Beineix. *ph* Jean-François Robin. *ed* Monique Prim. *ad* Carlos Conti. *m* Gabriel Yared. *cast* Béatrice Dalle, Jean-Hugues Anglade, Consuelo De Haviland, Gérard Darmon, Clementine Celarié.

●Beineix's basic story – the obsessive passion of Betty and Zorg and her descent into madness – remains the same in this 'director's cut', it just takes longer. Most of the restored sections simply add to Beineix's musings on the nature of obsession: there's a mattress-hating binman, a drunken olive salesman, and a detective who, like Zorg, is a frustrated writer, and who, like Betty, wants to kill all publishers. The problem with all this light relief is that it unbalances the rest of the film. Whereas in the shorter cut Eddy and Lisa played a crucial role, by the time this version finishes you've forgotten they ever existed. Granted, the reintroduction of a long child-kidnapping scene and a security guard robbery slows down the advance of Betty's illness, which in the original turned her from wild lover to crazed demon overnight. Otherwise, though, Beineix's determination to tell the full story results in a bum-numbing and often downright dull three hours. NKe

Betty Boop Follies, The

(1972, US, 93 min)
d Dave Fleischer. *p* Max Fleischer. *cast* voice: Mae Questel.

●A random collection of fourteen cartoons featuring the cartoon vamp created by Max Fleischer, the only real rival of the Disney and Ub Iwerks team in American animation of the early '30s. The mini-skirted and gartered Betty resembles the dumb broad sex-object satirised by Wilder in *Some Like It Hot*, but it's difficult to see why the Hayes Office considered the character too risqué. Fleischer's style at times borders on surrealism, the animation feeding off the rhythms of the soundtrack popular jazz music. The cartoons, originally in black-and-white, have been brightly coloured electronically. RM

Betty's Brood

(1991, GB, 70 min)
d Mick McConnell. *p* Diane Allison, Eileen Cumming. *sc* Tom McEnroe. *ph* Gordon Gronbach. *ed* Mick McConnell, Gordon Gronbach. *pd* Anne-Marie Murray. *m* Grant Urquhart, Mario D'Agostino. *cast* Marjory McCavigan, Diane Kurys, Eileen Cumming.

●Though certainly a little rough-and-ready (particularly in the editing), this very low-budget feature, made for just £2000 by the Gorbals Unemployed Workers' Centre, gets by on an intelligent script and naturalistic performances of great conviction from an almost entirely non-professional cast. A look at life in contemporary Britain, as evidenced by the Gorbals, it tells of one family's attempts to deal with death, drug addiction, disease and the threat of dissolution. Very much in the Loach/Amber mould, but none the worse for that. GA

Between Friends

(1973, Can, 90 min)
d Donald Shebib. *sc* Claude Harz. *ph* Richard Leiterman. *ed* Tony Lower. *ad* Claude Bonnière. *m* Matthew McCauley. *cast* Michael Parks, Bonnie Bedelia, Chuck Shamata, Henry Beckman, Hugh Webster.

●After days of youthful glory in the '60s as a surfboard champion, a young Californian (Parks) drifts into petty crime. Teaming up in Toronto with an old friend (Shamata), his girl (Bedelia), and her father (Beckman), he plans the big robbery. The tensions among the group, sparked by the inevitable attraction between Parks and Bedelia, gradually emerge and take over. Laconic and low-keyed, set in a decaying winter. CPe

Between Heaven and Hell

(1956, US, 94 min, b/w)
d Richard Fleischer. *p* David Weisbart. *sc* Harry Brown. *ph* Leo Tover. *ed* James B Clark. *ad* Lyle Wheeler, Addison Hehr. . *m* Hugo Friedhofer. *cast* Robert Wagner, Terry Moore, Broderick Crawford, Buddy Ebsen, Brad Dexter, Robert Keith, Mark Damon.

●Haughty Southern gentleman Wagner is forced to buck up his ideas when he's sent to the Pacific campaign during WWII and finds himself in the 'suicide' platoon commanded by the psychotic Crawford. Needless to say, Wagner's reforming snob learns all about humanity and humility in the tough times that follow. Fleischer keeps his head down, knits the action together, and tries not to let the worthy sentiments saturate the proceedings entirely. TJ

Between Midnight and Dawn

(1950, US, 92 min, b/w)
d Gordon Douglas. *p* Hunt Stromberg. *sc* Eugene Ling. *ph* George Diskant. *ed* Gene Havlick. *ad* George Brooks. *m* George Duning. *cast* Edmond O'Brien, Mark Stevens, Gale Storm, Donald Buka, Gale Robbins.

●An expressive *noir* title, lifted from Eliot: 'Between midnight and dawn, when the past is all deceit,' is squandered on this routine police procedural/buddy movie. O'Brien and Stevens nose around the mean streets in their prowl car, rivals for the affections of the pretty dispatcher but united in pursuit of a slimy Mr Big. The late appearance of a revenge motif works up a little head of steam, and Douglas directs with his customary autopilot efficiency. BBa

Between the Lines

(1977, US, 101 min)
d Joan Micklin Silver. *p* Raphael D Silver. *sc* Fred Barron. *ph* Ken Van Sickle. *ed* John Carter. *pd* Stuart Wurtzel. *m* Southside Johnny and the Asbury Jukes. *cast* John Heard, Lindsay Crouse, Jeff Goldblum, Jill Eikenberry, Bruno Kirby, Gwen Welles, Michael J Pollard.

●An odd film. Ostensibly an examination (and celebration?) of the counter-culture from within, in the form of the story of trials and tribulations of the staff of the *Back Bay Mainline* (a Boston fringe paper) as the '60s edge into the '70s, *Between the Lines* is soon revealed to be an unabashedly Hollywoodian paean to journalism and the free drink. The various reporters ache for fame and brood about the commercialisation of their craft with cynical detachment. That said, Silver's penny plain direction is surprisingly effective. An odd film. PH

Between Wars

(1974, Aust, 100 min)
d/p Michael Thornhill. *sc* Frank Moorhouse, Michael Thornhill. *ph* Russell Boyd. *ed* Max Lemon. *pd* Bill Hutchinson. *cast* Corin Redgrave, Arthur Dignam, Judy Morris, Patricia Leehy, Gunter Meisner.

●The story of an Australian doctor between the wars. Ostensibly the subject is the young war surgeon's early exposure to the theories of Freud, through to his eventual disillusioned settlement in a comfortable Sydney psychiatric practice. But the real concern is with the texture of Australian social life (in its broadest possible terms) between the wars. Thornhill's direction of the actors is low-key enough to allow the repressive nature of Australian life to emerge from a meticulously controlled *mise en scène*. RM

Beverly Hillbillies, The

(1993, US, 93 min)
d Penelope Spheeris. *p* David Permut, Dale Launer, Penelope Spheeris. *sc* Lawrence Konnor, Mark Rosenthal. *ph* Robert Brinkmann. *ed* Ross Albert. *pd* Peter Jamison. *m* Lalo Schifrin. *cast* Lily Tomlin, Dabney Coleman, Rob Schneider, Cloris Leachman, Zsa Zsa Gabor, Buddy Ebsen, Dolly Parton.

●Savour the music and lyrics from the original TV series – it's one of the highlights of this lamentable half-hour sit-com masquerading as a movie. Rich bumpkin family takes over Hollywood mansion and evil scheming couple try to cheat them of their wealth. No unexpected twists; very few jokes; not much talent. After the glory that was *Wayne's World*, director Spheeris should be ashamed of herself. NKe

Beverly Hills Brats

(1989, US, 91 min)
d Dimitri Sotirakis. *p* Terry Moore, Jerry Rivers. *sc* Linda Silverthorn. *ph* Harry Mathias. *ed* Jerry Frizell. *pd* George Costello. *m* Barry Goldberg. *cast* Martin Sheen, Peter Billingsley, Burt Young, Terry Moore, Ramon Estevez, Whoopi Goldberg.

●Teenager Billingsley is at home alone in his folks' ritzy Hollywood pad when burglar Young breaks in and the pair hatch a plan to make the kid's parents sit up and take notice of him, while the latter pockets a bob or two for himself. Sometimes the movie goes for satire, sometimes it goes for sentiment, either way it's difficult to care. TJ

Beverly Hills Cop

(1984, US, 105 min)
d Martin Brest. *p* Don Simpson, Jerry Bruckheimer. *sc* Daniel Petrie Jr. *ph* Bruce Surtees. *ed* Billy Weber. *pd* Angelo Graham. *m* Harold Faltermeyer. *cast* Eddie Murphy, Judge Reinhold, John Ashton, Lisa Eilbacher, Ronny Cox, Steven Berkoff.

●Constructed purely to allow Murphy full rein, the movie leads with its strongest card: Murphy as a cop, black, dirty, fast, on a case of stolen Marlboros in Detroit. When he begins unofficially to investigate the death of a friend, the trail leads him to Beverly Hills. The only black comic who doesn't make white audiences feel guilty expertly steps into the gaping holes left specifically for him in the film, but the connecting stuff is just bagatelle. CPea

Beverly Hills Cop II

(1987, US, 103 min)
d Tony Scott. *p* Don Simpson, Jerry Bruckheimer. *sc* Bud Shrake, Dan Jenkins, Larry Ferguson, Warren Skaaren. *ph* Jeffrey Kimball. *ed* Billy Weber. *pd* Ken Davis. *m* Harold Faltermeyer. *cast* Eddie Murphy, Judge Reinhold, Jürgen Prochnow, Ronny Cox, John Ashton, Brigitte Nielsen, Allen Garfield.

●Whatever was fresh and funny about Murphy's Detroit street cop in the original has disappeared: all of his fast-talking con-man impersonations are uniformly yammering and repetitive. Called off a credit card case in Detroit to help his old LA buddies solve The Alphabet Crimes, Murphy is soon on the track of an illegal arms dealer (Prochnow) and his Bondish hit-lady (Nielsen). Scott's direction is a mixmaster without a compass. Depressing. BC

Beverly Hills Cop III

(1994, US, 104 min)
d John Landis. *p* Mace Neufeld, Robert Rehme. *sc* Steven E De Souza. *ph* Mac Ahlberg. *ed* Dale Beldin. *m* Nile Rodgers. *cast* Eddie Murphy, Judge Reinhold, Hector Elizondo, Theresa Randle, Timothy Carhart, John Saxon, Stephen McHattie.

●After a colleague is murdered Detroit cop Axel Foley (Murphy) tracks the killers to – you guessed it! – Beverly Hills. The best screenwriter Steven de Souza can do by way of novelty is to locate the action in an LA amusement park, Wonder World. This is an incredibly cheap looking production. You can see the joins in the matte work; and hear the joins in the dialogue, huge chunks of clumsy exposition in what should be a straightforward thriller. There are germs of interest – America's theme-park culture and obsession with weapons – but on the whole Landis aims for the obvious. TCh

Beverly Hills Nightmare

see Bone

Beware, My Lovely

(1952, US, 77 min, b/w)
d Harry Horner. *p* Collier Young. *sc* Mel Dinelli. *ph* George E Diskant. *ed* Paul Weatherwax. *ad* Albert S D'Agostino. *m* Leith Stevens. *cast* Ida Lupino, Robert Ryan, Taylor Holmes, Barbara Whiting, OZ Whitehead, James Willmas.

●Not uninteresting woman in jeopardy thriller, worth a look for Lupino and Ryan: she as a lonely war widow, he as the itinerant handyman who suddenly goes funny, locks her up, and alternates unpredictable moods of tenderness and violence. Let down by broodingly sluggish direction (production designer Horner's debut) and by a script which gets bogged down in repetitive action instead of exploring the characters. The deliberately anticlimactic ending should have been much more effective than it is. TM

Beware of a Holy Whore (Warnung vor einer heiligen Nutte)

(1970, WGer, 103 min)
d/sc Rainer Werner Fassbinder. *ph* Michael Ballhaus. *ed* Franz Walsch [Rainer Werner Fassbinder], Thea Eymèsz. *ad* Kurt Raab. *m* Peer Raben. *cast* Lou Castel, Hanna Schygulla, Eddie Constantine, Rainer Werner Fassbinder, Marquard Bohm, Marcella Michelangeli.

●A film about film-making with roots in Fassbinder's unhappy experience shooting Whity in Spain. A German unit stalled by financial and technical problems, lethargically brooding in a Spanish hotel, is finally galvanised by the arrival of the manic director (Castel) and laconic star (Constantine) into a frenzy of activity which ends – the film they are making is a denunciation of state-sanctioned violence – in a concerted attack on the director. Tediously self-indulgent yet fascinating, it works better in its exploration of sexual frustrations than in its thesis that cinema should not be allowed to remain 'a holy whore of entertainment'. TM

Beware of Pity

(1946, GB, 102 min, b/w)
d Maurice Elvey. *p* WP Lipscomb. *sc* WP Lipscomb, Elizabeth Baron, Marguerite Steen. *ph* Derick Williams. *ed* Grace Garland. *ad* Alex Vetchinsky. *m* Nicholas Brodszky. *cast* Lilli Palmer, Albert Lieven, Cedric Hardwicke, Gladys Cooper, Linden Travers, Ernest Thesiger, Anthony Dawson.

●A cavalry officer takes to visiting the permanently wheelchair-bound daughter of a local bigwig, with catastrophic results. This adaptation of Stefan Zweig's novel was a box office disaster, after which Elvey didn't work again for five years. Turning on the distinction between pity and compassion must have seemed timely in the context of so much post-war affliction. But alas, the director shows little cinematic flair, while the sets and Cecil Beaton's costumes would better suit an Ivor Novello operetta. Worth seeing though, to salute its good intentions and to enjoy Hardwicke's turn as a sympathetic doctor. BBa

Beware! the Blob (aka Son of Blob)

(1972, US, 88 min)
d Larry Hagman. *p* Anthony Harris. *sc* Jack Woods, Anthony Harris. *ph* Al Hamm. *ed* Tony De Zarraga. *m* Mort Garson. *cast* Robert Walker, Gwynne Gilford, Godfrey Cambridge, Richard Stahl, Richard Webb, Carol Lynley, Shelley Berman, Larry Hagman.

●A tongue-in-cheek sequel to *The Blob* (around the time of the spin-off hit single by The Five Blobs which went: 'It creeps, it crawls, it slithers up the walls'), this is Mary Martin's son's only directorial effort, and he plays a cameo part as a hobo. The best moment occurs when the Blob (what is it made of?) takes over a bowling alley, then an ice-skating rink. For the rest, assorted guest stars are trundled on to do unfunny turns before getting eaten. CR

Bewegte Mann, Der (The Most Desired Man/ Maybe...Maybe Not)

(1994, Ger, 94 min)
d Sönke Wortman. *p* Bernd Eichinger. *sc* Sönke Wortman. *ph* Gernot Roll. *ed* Ueli Christen. *pd* Monika Bauert. *m* Torsten Breuer. *cast* Til Schweiger, Katja Riemann, Joachim Król, Rufus Beck, Antonia Lang, Nico van der Knapp.

●Doro (Riemann) catches boyfriend Axel (Schweiger) in flagrante and kicks him out; he winds up sharing a place with gay acquaintance Norbert (Król); but, after learning she's pregnant, she begins to suspect there's something going on between her ex and his new flatmate. By way of proof, she finds Norbert naked in the wardrobe. Preening cross-dresser Walter (Beck) and sad-faced Norbert offer us a choice of gay stereotypes, but director Wortmann has nothing but sympathy for their pangs of lust for the leading man, and even suggests that his desires are a lot less straight and narrow than he'd care to admit. Unfortunately, just when you think the film's turned all liberating and subversive, it wheels on a brazenly throwaway finale and, disappointingly, ends up endorsing the heterosexual coupledom it's been trying to undercut. Billed as the most successful German comedy of all time. Moderately diverting. TJ

Beyond, The (...E Tu Vivrai nel Terrore! L'Aldila)

(1981, It, 88 min)
d Lucio Fulci. *p* Frabrizio De Angelis. *sc* Lucio Fulci, Giorgio Mariuzzo, Dardano Sacchetti. *ph* Sergio Salvati. *ed* Vincenzo Tomassi. *pd* Massimo Lentini. *m* Fabio Frizzi. *cast* Katherine McColl, David Warbeck, Cinzia Monreale, Antoine Saint Jean.

●A shamelessly artless horror movie whose senseless story – a girl inherits a spooky, seedy hotel which just happens to have one of the Seven Doors of Hell in its cellar – is merely an excuse for a poorly connected series of sadistic tableaux of torture and gore. Suspense takes second place to repulsion as faces melt into bubbling, psychedelic disfigurements, crumbling zombies appear everywhere for no apparent reason other than to crumble a little more, and characters sporting strange green contact lenses stare ominously into the camera. GA

Beyond a Reasonable Doubt

(1956, US, 80 min, b/w)
d Fritz Lang. *p* Bert Friedlob. *sc* Douglas Morrow. *ph* William Snyder. *ed* Gene Fowler Jr. *ad* Carroll Clark. *m* Herschel Burke Gilbert. *cast* Dana Andrews, Joan Fontaine, Sidney Blackmer, Barbara Nichols, Philip Bourneuf, Shepperd Strudwick, Arthur Franz.

●Lang's most austere film, reducing the characters to pawns arbitrarily shifted in demonstration of a fascinating theorem. Andrews plays a writer who plans, with the cooperation of a newspaper publisher, to discredit the concept of capital punishment: by deliberately implicating himself as a murderer, he will prove the ease with which circumstantial evidence can lead to wrongful conviction. But after he is duly convicted, the publisher (his sole confidant) is accidentally killed and evidence of the plan destroyed. Despite the ingenious/ingenuous twist that ensues, the film is not concerned with innocence or guilt but with demonstrating that justice, finally, lies in the hand of fate. Not a forthcoming film, but one which repays attention. TM

Beyond Bedlam

(1994, GB, 95 min)
d Vadim Jean. *p* Paul Brooks. *sc* Rob Walker, Vadim Jean. *ph* Gavin Finney. *ed* Liz Webber. *pd* James Helps. *m* David Hughes. *cast* Craig Fairbrass, Elizabeth Hurley, Keith Allen, Anita Dobson, Jesse Birdsall, Georgina Hale, Craig Kelly.

●Jean's second feature (after *Leon the Pig Farmer*) is pitched somewhere between a psychological thriller and an out-and-out horror movie. In his cell, thanks to Dr Hurley's mind-control drug experiments, 'Bone Man' Allen amuses himself as a dream-invading serial killer. Alerted by a string of suicides at the block of flats where Hurley lives, cynical cop Fairbrass soon realises that she's been experimenting on herself too. Sucked into a dream world where reality and illusion blur, Fairbrass must confront not only his old criminal nemesis, but the guilty memories lurking in his unconscious. The film ends with a brutal punch-up in which Fairbrass finally faces the seemingly indestructible Allen. Like the film as a whole, this scene is skilfully shot, creatively designed and well edited – but it also undermines the story's premise, that the killer's power now lies in his ability to manipulate the unconscious rather then to punish the flesh. NF

Beyond Evil (Al di là del Bene e del Male)

(1977, It/Fr/Ger, 127 min)
d Liliana Cavani. *p* Robert Gordon Edwards. *sc* Liliana Cavani, Franco Arcalli, Italo Moscati. *ph* Armando Nannuzzi. *ed* Franco Arcalli. *pd* Lorenzo Mongiardino. *m* Daniele Paris. *cast* Dominique Sanda, Robert Powell, Erland Josephson, Virna Lisi, Philippe Leroy, Umberto Orsini.

●Cavani's biopic tracing the relationship between Friedrich Nietzsche (Josephson), minor writer Paul Rée (Powell), and Lou Salomé (Sanda), successful novelist and later student of Freud. Its celebration of a 'pure' and passionate friendship committed to Nietzsche's ideas (of a life transcending ethics) is given a handsomed Cinecittà period production. But Cavani's curious dramatic conceit that the writings of the Superman himself can be injected into flesh-and-blood historical characters – as dialogue, as models for outrageous social behaviour – finally ends up as ambiguous, sensationalistic and overblown as its true precursor, Ken Russell's *Women in Love*, a film to which *Beyond Evil*, to put it politely, more than pays homage. RM

Beyond Forgivin' (Dokmai nai Tangpuen)

(1999, Thai, 112 min)
d Manop Udomdej. *p* Sorajak Kasemsuvan, Chochart Toprateep. *sc* Manop Udomdej. *ph* Sutas Intranupakorn. *ed* Manop Jenjarassakul. *pd* Pongrat Meesaiyart. *m* Tewan Sapsanyakom. *cast* Dom Hetrakul, Nuchnart Saichompoo, Juthamas Chantasorn, Chatanant Trisarnsri, Kajornsak Ratananisai.

●Manop returns to film-making from an eight-year lay-off with a stylish but garbled thriller. It starts from a characteristically witty premise: a professional hitman falls in love with a woman who sells life insurance. Before he retires from crime and opens a flower shop, though, Lop (Dom Hetrakul, *Crime Kings*) has one last job to do: a straightforward heroin delivery run. But someone steals the junk and Boss Klang blames Lop, whose pregnant fiancée is murdered in a raid on his house. Manop never quite finds the right balance between shoot 'em up scenes and more reflective musings on mortality, relationships and ethics, and the film sometimes meanders when it should be powering forwards. But the casting and cinematography help compensate. TR

Beyond Rangoon

(1995, US, 99 min)
d John Boorman. *p* John Boorman, Eric Pleskow, Barry Spikings. *sc* Naomi Foner, Bill Rubinstein, Alex Lasker, John Boorman. *ph* John Seale. *ed* Ron Davis. *pd* Anthony Pratt. *m* Hans Zimmer. *cast* Patricia Arquette, U Aung Ko, Frances McDormand, Spalding Gray, Tiara Jacquelina, Victor Slezak.

●1988: Profoundly scarred by the deaths of her husband and son, American doctor Patricia Arquette remains largely unmoved by what she sees around her in Burma, until she is suddenly thrown into the midst of the conflict between the ruling fascist regime and the dissident democracy movement, incarnated here by the wise old tour guide U Aung Ko. While it's hard, finally, to care much about Arquette's road to redemption (especially given her flat and unappealing performance), and while some of the mystical/philosophical homilies advanced by the screenplay simply sound banal, there's no denying Boorman's commitment to the cause of freedom, nor his assured handling of the scenes depicting the larger chaos of a beautiful land torn apart by violence. Illuminating fare. GA

Beyond Reasonable Doubt

(1980, NZ, 108 min)
d John Laing. *p* John Barnett. *sc* David Yallop. *ph* Alun Bollinger. *ed* Michael Horton. *ad* Kai Hawkins. *m* Dave Fraser. *cast* David Hemmings, John Hargreaves, Tony Barry, Martyn Sanderson, Grant Tilly, Diana Rowan.

●'You wouldn't want me to confess to something I didn't do, would you?...Would you?' But that's just what Inspector David Hemmings does want in this true tale of Rough Justice Down Under, based on a controversial court case involving a New Zealand farmer charged with a double killing, which occupied the country's courts from 1970 till the Prime Minister's pardon in 1979. This modest but enjoyable film wears its pessimistic *noir* trappings well: cops who believe everyone's got something to hide, everybody's guilty, and rigging evidence and jury lists accordingly; the wife who almost cracks under the strain; most of all, the lack of faith in the truism that justice will out. RM

Beyond Silence (Jenseits der Stille)

(1996, Ger, 110 min)
d Caroline Link. *p* Jakob Claussen. *sc* Caroline Link, Beth Serlin. *ph* Gernot Roll. *ed* Patricia Rommel. *pd* Susann Bieling. *m* Niki Reiser. *cast* Sylvie Testud, Tatjana Trieb, Howie Seago, Emmanuelle Laborit.

●A study of living with deafness, which approaches the disability through the eyes and ears of someone who can see and hear. Young Lara (Trieb) can hear fine, but both her parents are deaf, and thus somewhat reliant on her – provoking small frictions, with her stubborn-minded father in particular. Given a clarinet by her aunt, Lara takes it up eagerly, defiantly, and successfully. Cut (mid-performance) to Lara as a young adult (Testud). Her aunt now suggests she move to music college in Berlin. Thanks to rich characterisation (wonderfully acted by all concerned, the Laras especially) and Caroline Link's impressively controlled direction, the film's possessed of a quiet beauty. It tails off toward the close, but still there are some scenes to cherish (how about a deaf church congregation sign singing in unison). NB

Beyond the Blue Horizon

(1942, US, 76 min)
d Alfred Santell. *p* Monta Bell. *sc* Frank Butler. *ph* Charles Boyle, William Mellor. *ed* Doane Harrison. *ad* Hans Dreier, Earl Hedrick. *m* Victor Young. *cast* Dorothy Lamour, Richard Denning, Jack Haley, Patricia Morison, Walter Abel.

●Silly stuff indeed, but OK if you like the lady in the sarong's jungle epics, especially since this is slightly more tongue-in-cheek than most. Here she's an heiress to a fortune, ignorant of her wealth because she's lived on an exotic island since childhood. But then she's rescued, true love calls, and intrigue beckons. GA

Beyond the Clouds (Par-delà les Nuages/Al di là delle nuvole/Jenseits der Wolken)

(1995, Fr/It/Ger, 115 min)
d Michelangelo Antonioni. *p* Stéphane Tchalgadjieff, Arlette Danys, Philippe Carcassonne. *sc* Wim Wenders, Michelangelo Antonioni, Tonino Guerra. *ph* Alfio Contini, Robby Müller. *ed* Claudio Di Mauro, Peter Przygodda. *ad* Thierry Flamand. *m* Lucio Dalla, Laurent Petitgrand, Van Morrison, U2. *cast* John Malkovich, Vincent Perez, Sophie Marceau, Irène Jacob, Peter Weller, Fanny Ardant, Marcello Mastroianni.

●Antonioni's first film in ten years, and it's like he's never been away. This is European art cinema as it used to be known: composed, stately, meditative, in every sense formal. (Modernism looks better than ever, now it's so old fashioned.) The film tells four stories – four potential films in the mind of director Malkovich (the linking material is by Wim Wenders) – in Italian, English, French, music and silence. Four brief encounters are imbued with concerted philosophical and spiritual gravitas by the grace and patience of the camera: 'I only discovered reality when I began to photograph it,' muses Malkovich. Antonioni has always been one to exercise his metaphoric *droit de seigneur*, and women may feel uncomfortable with the intensity of the director's gaze here, but it makes for entrancing cinema. TCh

Beyond the Door

see Chi Sei?

Beyond the Door (Oltre la Porta)

(1982, It, 116 min)
d Liliana Cavani. *p* Francesco Giorgi. *sc* Liliana Cavani, Enrico Medioli. *ph* Luciano Tovoli. *ed* Ruggero Mastroianni. *ad* Dante Ferretti. *m* Pino Donaggio. *cast* Marcello Mastroianni, Eleonora Giorgi, Tom Berenger, Michel Piccoli, Paolo Bonetti.

●There is something to be said for Liliana Cavani, but it is difficult to remember what it is. The cruelty of her *Night Porter* was ruined by sentimentality, and *Beyond Good and Evil* managed to conflate Nietzsche and Robert Powell in a ménage à trois. *Beyond the Door* is the usual mix of cheapjack sentiment, cutprice Freudian familial relations, and a baffled cast running way over boiling point. Giorgi (a madonna face) keeps her stepfather Mastroianni (or *maybe* he's her father) in a Moroccan prison after faking evidence against him over her mother's death, so that she can keep her claws on his body, which she desires far more than the American oilman (Berenger, looking like a young Paul Newman) who desires her like mad but can't understand what's going on here. Un peu tortueuse, hein? There are some dinky touristique scenes in the brothels of Marrakesh, that mosaic city which caters to the devices and desires of your heart; but it should all have been made in hardcore by Gerard Damiano (*Behind the Green Door*). CPea

Beyond the Forest

(1949, US, 96 min, b/w)
d King Vidor. *p* Henry Blanke. *sc* Lenore J Coffee. *ph* Robert Burks. *ed* Rudi Fehr. *ad* Robert M Haas. *m* Max Steiner. *cast* Bette Davis, Joseph Cotten, David Brian, Ruth Roman, Dona Drake, Regis Toomey, Minor Watson.

●Rosa Moline (Davis) is a twelve o'clock girl in a nine o'clock town. Loyalton is the burg in question, and Rosa doesn't like it one bit: 'What a dump…like sitting in a coffin and waiting to be carried out!' Her personal rebellion takes the form of adultery, miscarriage and murder, in King Vidor's most demented film from his most frenzied period, immediately after *Duel in the Sun* and *The Fountainhead* and before *Ruby Gentry*. Davis, done up for all the world like Jennifer Jones, is too old for the part, but gives it her all (she used the film for her own rebellion, escaping a Warner Bros contract that still had ten years to run). She's like a caricature of herself, and the movie, too, is soap gone into lather. Laugh it off, by all means, but American melodrama at this pitch of alienation is quite fascinating. TCh

Beyond the Limit

see Honorary Consul, The

Beyond the Mat

(1999, US, 103 min)
d Barry W Blaustein. *p* Brian Grazer, Ron Howard, Michael Rosenberg, Barry Bloom, Barry W Blaustein. *sc* (narrative) Barry W Blaustein. *ph* Michael Grady. *ed* Jeff Werner. *m* Nathan Barr. *with* Vince McMahon, Darren

Drozdov, Roland Alexander, Tony Jones, Mike Modest, Terry Funk, Vicki Funk, Stacey Funk, Brandee Funk, Paul Heyman, Jake 'The Snake' Roberts, Mick Foley, Barry W Blaustein.

● Barry Blaustein was once a *Saturday Night Live* producer and scriptwriter for Eddie Murphy. For this homespun documentary about the off-mat lives of US wrestlers he took his long-standing fascination with the lucrative spectacle on the road, looking to answer the question: What sort of human being bashes another man's skull into a ringpost for a living? His first port of call was the office of Vince McMahon, scion of the World Wrestling Federation's controlling family, who has overseen the transformation of the federation (current worth $1 billion) into the movie studio it is today, with writers, composers and wardrobe designers all engaged in the production of its violent pantomimes. We tour the All-Pro Wrestling School in California and Philadelphia's fearsome Extreme Championships, but it's the studies Blaustein makes of several wrestlers that root the film. He hangs out with 53-year-old Terry Funk, still stuck on the sport despite severe arthritis; with lost legend Jake 'The Snake' Roberts, slumming on the inter-state circuit and musing on his fuck-ups with sex, drugs and family; and, most compellingly, with Mick Foley (aka 'Mankind'), a genuinely sweet family man who likes bringing his wife and young kids to watch his work. NB

Beyond the Poseidon Adventure

(1979, US, 122 min)
d/p Irwin Allen. *sc* Nelson Gidding. *ph* Joseph Biroc. *ed* Bill Brame. *pd* Preston Ames. *m* Jerry Fielding. *cast* Michael Caine, Sally Field, Telly Savalas, Peter Boyle, Jack Warden, Shirley Knight, Shirley Jones.

● After the disaster of *The Poseidon Adventure*, the Salvage Operation. It provides the thinnest of excuses for rerunning the 'dramas' of the night before, but it doesn't do anything to salvage the venerable formula. This time it's the ship that sinks. JCR

Beyond Therapy

(1986, US, 93 min)
d Robert Altman. *p* Steven Haft. *sc* Christopher Durang, Robert Altman. *ph* Pierre Mignot. *ed* Jennifer Agué. *pd* Stephen Altman. *m* Gabriel Yared. *cast* Julie Hagerty, Jeff Goldblum, Glenda Jackson, Tom Conti, Christopher Guest, Genevieve Page, Cris Campion.

● Having dealt with computer dating in the insanely neglected *A Perfect Couple*, Altman turns his attention to Lonely Hearts subscribers in a film that merges the romantic merry-go-round antics of *La Ronde* with the clamorous, overflowing narrative tactics of *Nashville*. Based on a stage play – though you wouldn't know it – the movie commences in a ritzy French restaurant where goofy Goldblum meets nutsy nice girl Hagerty; he's bisexual, she's scared stiff of virtually everything. On the fringes of their frantic, stop-go love affair jabbers a gaggle of eccentric lovers, mothers and shrinks. Besides their evidently loose grip on sanity, the members of this group share a desire for a protector. Altman's brash, broad satire retains the ability to touch the heart, evincing a very real sense of pain in certain otherwise contrived scenes. Stunningly designed and shot, it's a weird and sometimes wonderful excursion into New York neurotica that will offend, disturb and intrigue. GA

Beyond the Stars (aka Personal Choice)

(1989, US, 88 min)
d David Saperstein. *p* Joseph Perez. *sc* David Saperstein. *ph* John Bartley. *ed* Frank Irvine. *pd* John J Moore. *m* Geoff Levin, Chris Many. *cast* Christian Slater, Martin Sheen, Sharon Stone, F Murray Abraham, Robert Foxworth, Olivia d'Abo.

● An expensive cast assembles for this dreary and cliché-intensive chronicle of would-be astronaut Slater's loss of innocence when he meets up with old hand Sheen, a man who's been up there, done it, and suffered a hefty dose of radiation poisoning for his troubles. TJ

Beyond the Valley of the Dolls

(1970, US, 109 min)
d/p Russ Meyer. *sc* Roger Ebert. *ph* Fred J Koenekamp. *ed* Dann Cahn. *ad* Jack Martin Smith. *m* Stu Phillips. *cast* Dolly Read, Cynthia Myers, Marcia McBroom, John La Zar, Michael Blodgett, Pam Grier.

● With his first movie for a major studio, Meyer simply did what he'd been doing for years, only bigger and better. That's to say, he turned the homely story of an all-girl rock band's rise to fame under their transsexual manager into a delirious comedy melodrama, soused in self-parody but spiked with dope, sex and thrills. TR

Beyond the Walls (Me'Achorei Hasoragim)

(1984, Isr, 103 min)
d Uri Barbash. *p* Rudy Cohen. *sc* Benny Barbash, Ean Preis. *ph* Amnon Salomon. *ed* Toya Asher. *ad* Eitan Levi. *m* Ilan Virtzberg. *cast* Arnon Zadok, Muhamad Bakri, Hilel Ne'eman, Assi Dayan, Boaz Sharaabi, Roberto Polak.

● Prison as a metaphor for society at large: there are the rulers/jailers and the ruled/prisoners; the governors play a game of divide and rule with the governed in order to ensure their dominance. *Beyond the Walls* hammers home this cliché in an Israeli prison, where the authorities are ugly sadists and the prisoners' leaders – both Arab and Jew – tall, handsome figures of heroic moral stature. The enduring impression is not the liberal homiletics, however, but rather the unremitting beastliness of the prisoners' lives: a foul stew of humiliation, beatings and homosexual rape. Still, if you like your politics simplistic and your movies brutal – as apparently do the judges who awarded this film the International Critics Prize at the 1984 Venice Festival – you might enjoy the touching details, good character performances, and overall enthusiasm that embellish this thin allegory. MH

B.F.'s Daughter (aka Polly Fulton)

(1948, US, 108 min, b/w)
d Robert Z Leonard. *p* Edwin H Knopf. *sc* Luther Davis. *ph* Joseph Ruttenberg. *ed* George White. *ad* Cedric Gibbons, Daniel Cathcart. *m* Bronislau Kaper. *cast* Barbara Stanwyck, Charles Coburn, Van Heflin, Richard Hart, Spring Byington, Keenan Wynn, Margaret Lindsay.

● Stanwyck weds poor pinko prof Heflin, then surprises him by giving him a mansion and revealing that her dad is actually millionaire Coburn. This trite social comedy makes a real mess of a then-admired novel by JP Marquand. Nobody's finest hour. TJ

Bhaji on the Beach

(1993, GB, 101 min)
d Gurinder Chadha. *p* Nadine Marsh-Edwards. *sc* Meera Syal, Gurinder Chadha. *ph* John Kenway. *ed* Oral Ottle. *pd* Derek Brown. *m* John Altman. *cast* Kim Vithana, Jimmi Harkishin, Sarita Khajuria, Mo Sesay, Lalita Ahmed, Zohra Segal, Peter Cellier.

● A group of Asian 'sisters' go on a women's trip to Blackpool, only to be pursued and confronted by their menfolk. Plot and motivation are both contrived, but once the story gets going, first-time director Gurinder Chadha extracts maximum fun from her sedate matrons and wild teenagers let loose in a working-class holiday hell; she is, in fact, as comfortable with the bhaji as the beach. Segal is wonderfully wrong-headed as chief of the censorious aunties, and Ahmed delightful as the wistful shopkeeper Asha, who meets a camp old English actor (Cellier) and cavorts with him in Bollywood daydreams. The men - the stage villains of the piece - do the best they can. SFe

Bhowani Junction

(1956, GB, 110 min)
d George Cukor. *p* Pandro S Berman. *sc* Sonya Levien, Ivan Moffat. *ph* Freddie Young. *ed* Frank Clarke. *ad* Gene Allen, John Howell. *m* Miklós Rozsa. *cast* Ava Gardner, Stewart Granger, Francis Matthews, Bill Travers, Abraham Sofaer, Marne Maitland, Marne Maitland.

● Cukor's abiding interest in both the predicament of women in a male-dominated society and the problems of role-playing are given their most explicitly political expression in this marvellous melodrama set in India during the last gasps of British colonialism. Focusing on an Anglo-Indian girl torn apart by her feelings for three men – an English soldier, an Indian, and another Anglo-Indian – it's one of those rare films that successfully and intelligently combine personal and political issues, in that Gardner's status as a woman without a recognised racial/national idenity dramatically embodies widely conflicting cultural and political ideas. As such, it's very much an intimate epic, drawing an unsentimental portrait of a society in transition, and a vivid, moving account of its heroine's tragic dilemma. Beautiful to look at, and perfectly acted throughout. GA

Bhumika

see Role, The

Bible...In the Beginning, The (La Bibbia)

(1966, It/US, 175 min)
d John Huston. *p* Dino De Laurentiis. *sc* Christopher Fry. *ph* Giuseppe Rotunno. *ed* Ralph Kemplen. *ad* Mario Chiari. *m* Toshiro Mayuzumi. *cast* Michael Parks, Ulla Bergryd, Richard Harris, John Huston, Stephen Boyd, George C Scott, Ava Gardner, Peter O'Toole.

● Turgid account of Old Testament events from the Creation to Abraham's sacrifice of Isaac. Huston himself adds a touch of life as Noah, and the Tower of Babel scene is fairly well done, but overall it's a long haul which manages to suggest that places like Eden and Sodom weren't much fun at all. GA

Bicentennial Man

(1999, US, 131 min)
d Chris Columbus. *p* Wolfgang Petersen, Gail Katz, Neal Miller, Laurence Mark, Chris Columbus, Mark Radcliffe, Michael Barnathan. *sc* Nicholas Kazan. *ph* Phil Meheux. *ed* Neil Travis. *pd* Norman Reynolds. *m* James Horner. *cast* Robin Williams, Sam Neill, Embeth Davidtz, Oliver Platt, Wendy Crewson, Hallie Kate Eisenberg, Stephen Root, Lynne Thigpen.

● Williams dons a robot suit for this sentimental sci-fi family epic based on the writings of Isaac Asimov. It's 2005, and 'Sir' (Neill) has just taken delivery of Andrew, a chromium butler-cum-nanny, with ideas above his station. When Andrew displays simple human emotions, Sir teaches him all about the human condition, thus setting off a chain of events spanning 200 years: Andrew goes on a pilgrimage, only to return decades later to find that his former charge Little Miss (Davidtz) is now an ancient and grandmother of Portia (Davidtz again). Love, it appears, is in the air, encouraging Andrew to change from automaton to a human. Cue a fully fleshed Williams and sermonising about anthropomorphism, immortality, euthanasia, etc. DA

Biches, Les (The Does)

(1968, Fr/It, 99 min)
d Claude Chabrol. *p* André Génoves. *sc* Paul Gégauff, Claude Chabrol. *ph* Jean Rabier. *ed* Jacques Gaillard. *ad* Marc Berthier. *m* Pierre Jansen. *cast* Stéphane Audran, Jacqueline Sassard, Jean-Louis Trintignant, Nane Germon, Henri Attal, Dominique Verdi, Serge Bento, Claude Chabrol.

● The film with which Chabrol returned to 'serious' film-making after his series of delightful thriller/espionage spoofs, this was also the film in which he began transferring his allegiance from baroque Hitchcockery to the bleak geometry of Lang. A calm, exquisite study, set in an autumnal Riviera, of the permutational affairs of one man and two women which lead to obsession, madness and despair. Each sequence is like a question-mark adding new doubts and hypotheses to the circular (as opposed to triangular) relationship as a rich lady of lesbian leanings (Audran) picks up an impoverished girl (Sassard), and whisks her off to her St Tropez villa. There, much to the distress of her benefactress, the girl embarks on an affair with a handsome young architect (Trintignant), only to find in her turn that architect and lesbian lady are in the throes of a mutual passion. Impeccably performed, often bizarrely funny, the film winds, with brilliant clarity, through a maze of shadowy emotions to a splendidly Grand-Guignolesque ending. TM

Bicycle Thieves (100) (Ladri di Biciclette)

(1948, It, 96 min, b/w)
d Vittorio De Sica. *p* Umberto Scarpelli. *sc* Vittorio De Sica, Cesare Zavattini, Suso Cecchi D'Amico, Oreste Biancoli, Adolfo Franci,

Gherardo Gherardi, Garardo Guerrieri. *ph* Carlo Montuori. *ed* Eraldo Da Roma. *ad* Antonio Traverso. *m* Alessandro Cicognini. *cast* Lamberto Maggiorani, Enzo Staiola, Lianella Carell, Gino Saltamerenda, Vittorio Antonucci, Giulio Chiari.

● A working class Italian, out of work for some time, has the bicycle stolen which he needs for a new job; he and his son wander round Rome looking for it. Often hailed as an all-time classic, *Bicycle Thieves* tries to turn a simple story into a meditation on the human condition, but its greatest achievement is in bringing the lives of ordinary Italian people to the screen. However, like so many of the films grouped together under the heading of Italian neo-realism, its grainy monochrome images and simple storyline never delve beneath the surface of the characters' lives to reveal the social mechanisms at work there. It is as if, just by portraying the events unobtrusively, De Sica imagines that they will yield up their essential truth by a process of revelation – a very appropriate image for a strain of liberal humanism strongly influenced by Catholicism. Observant and sympathetic it is, politically perceptive it is not. NF

Biddy

(1983, GB, 85 min)
d Christine Edzard. *p* Richard Goodwin. *sc* Christine Edzard. *ph* Alec Mills. *m* Michel Sanvoisin. *cast* Celia Bannerman, Sam Ghazoros, Patricia Napier, John Dalby, Kate Elphick, Sally Ashby.

● A meticulously realised, perfectly nostalgic picture whose subject is a Victorian nurserymaid. Biddy's voice, decorated equally with passages from English literature and pithy homilies, runs on and on (all other voices are surreal noises-off) marshalling the forces of the nursery and the pattern of her charges' lives. She revels, Mrs Tiggy-Winkle-like, in mending, clean linen and the laying of tea, happiest when 'everything is in its proper place, everything is in order'. But even as this spare, deliberately wrought film so carefully points and extolls the virtues of Biddy and those many others like her, it is apparent that what is really being celebrated is the paraphernalia of these lives. The sewing-boxes, the button-hooks, the pieces of treen and piles of handworked lace, these are the real stars of the film. FD

Bidone, Il (The Swindlers)

(1955, It/Fr, 114 min, b/w)
d Federico Fellini. *sc* Federico Fellini, Ennio Flaiano, Tullio Pinelli. *ph* Otello Martelli. *ed* Mario Serandrei. *ad* Dario Cecchi. *m* Nino Rota. *cast* Broderick Crawford, Giulietta Masina, Richard Basehart, Franco Fabrizi, Alberto De Amicis.

● A pair of provincial con-men (Crawford and Basehart) pose as priests to swindle ignorant peasant farmers, but what begins as comedy turns sour, cruel, and finally tragic. Characteristically, Fellini stacks the pack with a final victim of great facial beauty, palsied legs and obscurantist belief, after which it is only a matter of time before bad Brod receives his comeuppance on a stony hillside. Most of Fellini's preoccupations are present, but in 1955 had not yet blown the obligation to tell a story off-course. BC

Big

(1988, US, 104 min)
d Penny Marshall. *p* James L Brooks, Robert Greenhut. *sc* Gary Ross, Anne Spielberg. *ph* Barry Sonnenfeld. *ed* Barry Malkin. *pd* Santo Soquasto. *m* Howard Shore. *cast* Tom Hanks, Elizabeth Perkins, Robert Loggia, John Heard, Jared Rushton, David Moscow, Jon Lovitz.

● It's no fun being in your early teens, especially if you're none too tall. So thinks Josh Baskin, having been denied a ride on a fairyground superloop. But neither is being a kid in a grown-up body so hot, as Josh discovers after a carnival wishing-machine grants the change overnight. What do you do when Mom doesn't recognise you, and thinks you're your own abductor? How do you get a job when you can't drive and have no social security number? And when you do find work with a toy-design company, how do you cope with board meetings, office rivalries, and swish staff parties? Marshall's movie may be a mite predictable, but it's genuinely funny, thanks partly to Hanks' engagingly gauche and gangly performance as the overgrown Josh, and partly to a script that steers admirably clear of gross innuendo. Much of the humour derives from Josh's inability to comprehend adult life; much of its charm from the way his forthright innocence steadily revitalises those around him. Admittedly, this latter theme makes for an ending oozing with saccharine sentiment; but until then Marshall, Hanks, and his co-stars seldom put a foot wrong. GA

Bigamist, The

(1953, US, 80 min, b/w)
d Ida Lupino. *p/sc* Collier Young. *ph* George E Diskant. *ed* Stanford Tischler. *ad* James W Sullivan. *m* Leith Stevens. *cast* Edmond O'Brien, Ida Lupino, Joan Fontaine, Edmund Gwenn, Jane Darwell, Kenneth Tobey.

● One of Lupino's sympathetic little problem pictures. Its weakness, perhaps, is that in trying to avoid the obvious of making a whipping-boy of the bigamous husband, it creates characters who are a shade too good to be true. But the three lead performances are terrific, movingly illuminating the impasse whereby O'Brien's travelling salesman finds himself in love with two women – Fontaine as the outgoing career-woman who can't have children, Lupino as the quiet home-lover who has borne him a child – each of whom brings him something the other can't. The complex issues are sketched in with both tact and compassion. TM

Big Animal, The (Duze zwierze)

(2000, Pol, 75 min)
d Jerzy Stuhr. *p* Slawomir Rogowski. *sc* Krzysztof Kieslowski. *ph* Pawel Edelman. *ed* Elzbieta Kurkowska. *pd* Monika Sajko-Gradowska. *m* Abel Korzeniowski. *cast* Anna Dymna, Jerzy Stuhr.

● A middle-aged couple in an isolated, picturesque Polish village find a camel in their garden left behind by a visiting circus. When they subsequently adopt the creature, their relationship with fellow villagers, and particularly those officials handling bureaucratic licences, subtly changes. Some want rid of the new pet; others see it as a source of profit. Is it of use to the community, or a nuisance? Less rewarding and ambitious than actor Stuhr's earlier *Love Stories*, this gentle satire is nevertheless neatly observed, shrewdly performed, and not without interest as a parable about freedom, habit, bigotry, materialism and – yes! – love (for the exotic beast). If it all looks a little old-fashioned, well, it was written years ago by (somewhat surprisingly) one Krzysztof Kieslowski. GA

Big Bad Mama

(1974, US, 85 min)
d Steve Carver. *p* Roger Corman. *sc* William Norton, Frances Doel. *ph* Bruce Logan. *ed* Tina Hirsch. *ad* Peter Jamison. *m* David Grisman. *cast* Angie Dickinson, William Shatner, Tom Skerritt, Susan Sennett, Robbie Lee, Noble Willingham, Dick Miller.

● Roger Corman's production, following up on his own *Bloody Mama*, is something of a delight. Although covering the familiar ground of bank robbing during the Depression, the film persistently and boisterously treads its own path. Dickinson and her two daughters, the one practised beyond her years, the other pretty dumb, move through rural and small-town America selling bootleg liquor, picking up men, robbing banks, and kidnapping rich daughters, arguing that if Ford, Rockefeller, Capone and the rest can have a slice of the cake, why can't they? The ribald script, pausing occasionally for insight, sets up various wayward characters (most of them hot for Mama and her girls) and indulges a capacity for ménages à trois.

Big Banana Feet

(1976, GB, 77 min)
d/p/sc Murray Grigor, Patrick Higson. *ph* David Peat. *ed* Patrick Higson. *m* Billy Connolly. *with* Billy Connolly.

● The paradoxical fascination with showbiz exhibited by *cinéma-vérité* film-makers continues unabated. And this record of Billy Connolly's 1975 Irish tour survives inevitable comparisons with Pennebaker, Graef and the Maysles, largely because its subject is caught at the peak of his form, and because Connolly remains resolutely immune to standard showbiz poses; offstage he effortlessly extends his wit to the grotesqueries of touring. A thoroughly entertaining film. PT

Big Bang, The (Le Big Bang)

(1987, Fr/Bel, 90 min)
d Picha. *p* Boris Szulzinger. *sc* Tony Hendra. *ed* Nicole Garnier-Klipfel. *m* Roy Budd. *cast* voices: Luis Rego, Georges Aminel, Perrette Pradier, David Lander, Carole Androsky, Marshall Efron.

● A far cry from Raymond Briggs' nuclear warning, Picha's 'adult cartoon' combines both readings of its title in what '60s counter-culture would probably have mistaken for Swiftian satire. Following the Bomb, Planet Earth has polarised into two nations, both deficient in the standard number of limbs and sexual characteristics. All the men, who have their arses blown off, are gay and live in an American-Soviet zone, while the multi-breasted women live in Vaginia. A fourth world war threatens, and only Fred, the last possible superhero, can avert it. The final conflict is fought out by a megaton tit and a megaton prick. It is all determinedly gross, with something to offend everyone. BC

Big Bang, The

(1989, US, 81 min)
d James Toback. *p* Joseph H Kanter. *ed* Stephanie Kempf. *ad* Nicole C Nicola. *with* James Toback, Don Simpson, José Torres, Eugene Fodor, Darryl Dawkins, Barbara Traub, Charles Lassiter.

● James Toback has his own theory about the universe to set against Genesis and the Big Bang: 'It all started with the orgasmic explosion of God,' he announces with revelatory fervour at the beginning of this film, which starts with his pitch to independent financier Joe Kanter: it's got no script, no actors, no story, just a bunch of people talking about their lives and beliefs. And this is what we get: a gangster who had a bit part in *GoodFellas* explains that the best day of his life was when he fell out of love; a basketball star momentarily lays aside his macho bluff to reveal how his wife committed suicide. Movie jock Don Simpson is opaque, Auschwitz survivor Barbara Traub reflective, and no, painter Charles Lassiter couldn't kill even in self-defence, he's more the victim type. Toback asks the big questions, and elicits honest, thoughtful responses from his 19 subjects. His quietly composed picture engages right from its exuberant, staccato opening to a subtle, affecting coda. Sex, love, life, death and the whole damn thing… TCh

Big Bang Theory, The (aka Bang)

(1995, US, 100 min)
d Ash. *p* Daniel M Berger, Ladd Vance. *sc* Ash. *ph* Dave Gasperik. *ed* Ash, Daniel M Berger. *pd* Daniel M Berger. *m* Orlando Aquillen. *cast* Darling Narita, Peter Greene, Everlast, Michael Arturo, James Sharpe, Luis Guizar, Art Cruz.

● A bad day in Los Angeles: get up, lose your apartment, go to a film audition (plus casting couch), get arrested by a cop who'll release you only if you give him head. So far, so demeaning. The Girl (with no name) handcuffs the officer to a tree, takes his uniform and motorbike – and checks out how all that power feels by patrolling the local environs, whereupon various subdivisions of hell break loose. Written and directed by a young LA Brit named Ash, this is defiantly independent film-making, shot guerilla-style, fast and without permits. The *vérité* ambience is less affected than usual, and a genuine sense of recalcitrant rage distinguishes the film from the fraudulent nonsense of *Falling Down*. Things improve after a shaky start, and Narita delivers a gutsy performance as the Girl. Ash, however, shows little idea of how each narrative appendix fits into his half-formed overall design. NB

Big Bankroll, The

see King of the Roaring 20's – The Story of Arnold Rothstein

Big Blockade, The

(1942, GB, 68 min, b/w)
d Charles Frend. *p* Alberto Cavalcanti. *sc* Charles Frend, Angus Macphail. *ph* Wilkie Cooper. *ed* Charles Crichton, Compton Bennett. *ad* Tom Morahan. *m* Richard Addinsell. *cast* Leslie Banks, Michael Redgrave, Will Hay, John Stuart, John Mills, Bernard Miles, Robert Morley.

●Like *Next of Kin*, this was expanded by Ealing from what had been planned as a propaganda short explaining the work of the Ministry of Economic Warfare. Much more didactic than Dickinson's film, and much less well directed, it's strictly a museum piece. TM

Big Blue, The

(1988, US, 119 min)
d Luc Besson. *p* Patrice Ledoux. *sc* Luc Besson, Robert Garland, Marilyn Goldin, Jacques Mayol, Marc Perrier. *ph* Carlo Varini. *ed* Olivier Mauffroy. *pd* Dan Weil. *m* Bill Conti. *cast* Rosanna Arquette, Jean-Marc Barr, Jean Reno, Paul Shenar, Sergio Castellitto, Jean Bouise, Griffin Dunne.
●The action centres on the rivalry between free-divers Barr and Reno – they dive deep without an aqualung – which begins when they are little boys. The first time you see someone plunging into alien blackness is exciting, but the novelty soon wears off. The first half-hour is the best part of the movie. Going through her usual kooky routine, Arquette plays a New York insurance agent who encounters Barr in Peru, and is captivated by his wide-eyed innocence (which others might describe as bovine stupidity). Her sole purpose seems to be to reassure the audience that there is nothing funny going on between best buddies Barr, who talks to dolphins, and Reno, a macho mother's boy (a performance of much comic credibility). The ending is the worst part of the movie: Barr rejects the pregnant Arquette in favour of going under one last time to become a dolphin-man. Such bathos reeks of cod-Camus. What lies in between is a series of CinemaScopic swathes of blue seas and white cliffs. Besson's film is exactly like his hero: very pretty but very silly. MS

Big Boss, The (Tangshan Daxiong/aka Fists of Fury)

(1971, HK, 100 min)
d Lo Wei. *p* Raymond Chow. *sc* Lo Wei. *ph* Chen Ching Cheh. *ed* Fan Chia Kun. *ad* Chien Hsin. *m* Wang Fu Ling. *cast* Bruce Lee, Maria Yi, James Tien, Nora Miao, Miss Malarin, Han Yingjie.
●Lee had been a child star in Hong Kong movies of the 1950s; this crudely made but highly enjoyable revenge drama marked his return to Hong Kong (after his failure to escape stereotyped bit-parts in the US) and launched a worldwide fashion for 'kung fu' movies. Cheng (Lee) arrives in Thailand to join relatives working in an ice-packing plant. When he learns that the place is a front for heroin smuggling, he reveals his martial prowess and takes on the villainous boss (Han Yingjie, also the film's martial arts choreographer) in a frighteningly intense duel to the death. The mix of authentic martial arts skills, cartoon-like violence, righteous anger and filial piety (Cheng never forgets his promises to dear old mum, back in Hong Kong) struck a chord with audiences everywhere in a way rarely seen since the heyday of the James Dean cult, making Lee a global star overnight. TR

Big Brass Ring, The

(1998, US, 104 min)
d George Hickenlooper. *p* Fuller French, Andrew Pfeffer, Donald Zuckerman. *sc* FX Feeney, George Hickenlooper, (original script) Orson Welles, Oja Kodar. *ph* Kramer Morgenthau. *ed* Jim Makiej. *pd* Jerry Fleming. *m* Thomas Morse. *cast* William Hurt, Nigel Hawthorne, Irène Jacob, Miranda Richardson, Ewan Stewart, Gregg Henry, Ron Livingston, Jefferson Mays, Jim Metzler.
●Noteworthy for being based on a flawed but fascinating script by Orson Welles, this conspiracy thriller from the documentarist who gave us *Hearts of Darkness* is a bit of a mess. Hurt's the political candidate being funded by wife Richardson, investigated by crusading journo Jacob (greatly changed from her Kieslowski days), and generally hassled by Hawthorne, a figure from his past.The story's a little predictable, anyway, but the somewhat unenthusiastic performances and the pedestrian direction don't help. A curiosity for Welles nuts, but not a patch on even the least of the Master's films. GA

Big Brawl, The

(1980, US, 95 min)
d Robert Clouse. *p* Fred Weintraub, Terry Morse Jr. *sc* Robert Clouse. *ph* Robert Jessup. *ed* George Grenville. *ad* Joe Altadonna. *m* Lalo Schifrin. *cast* Jackie Chan, José Ferrer, Kristine De Bell, Mako, Ron Max, David S Sheiner.
●No prizes for sophistication, but a much less botched job than *Enter the Dragon*. The first half, at least, is an adequate showcase for the not inconsiderable talents of Jackie Chan (trained in a Cantonese Opera school, he is less a martial artist than a highly skilled and inventive acrobat, with a sharp sense of physical comedy). The thinly motivated plot (involving mafiosi, kidnapping, and a brawl tournament in '30s Texas) is as implausible, sexist and naive as an average Hong Kong movie, but Chan gets enough of his own way to emerge radiating charm and to perform a few genuinely amazing stunts. TR

Big Bus, The

(1976, US, 89 min)
d James Frawley. *p/sc* Fred Freeman, Lawrence J Cohen. *ph* Harry Stradling Jr. *ed* Edward A Warschilka. *pd* Joel Schiller. *m* David Shire. *cast* Joseph Bologna, Stockard Channing, John Beck, Rene Auberjonois, Ned Beatty, José Ferrer, Ruth Gordon.
●Frawley's experience directing the Monkees serves him well in timing the one-liners which make up this engaging parody of the airport disaster movie. The maiden voyage of the first nucelar-powered bus – dogged by cannibalistic bus driver, saboteur from the oil companies, and ecstatically stereotyped passengers rediscovering God, sex and wills to live in moments of crisis – is very funny even if the film never gets anywhere. TM

Big Business

(1988, US, 98 min)
d Jim Abrahams. *p* Steve Tisch, Michael Peyser. *sc* Dori Pierson, Marc Reid Rubel. *ph* Dean Cundey. *ed* Harry Keramidas. *pd* William Sandell. *m* Lee Holdridge. *cast* Bette Midler, Lily Tomlin, Fred Ward, Edward Herrmann, Michele Placido, Daniel Gerroll, Barry Primus, Michael Gross.
●Two sets of identical twins, one of each having been accidentally swapped at birth by a short-sighted nurse, are finally, and confusingly, reunited years later in New York. You get the picture, they check into the same hotel, and spend the whole film rushing from room to room, being mistaken for each other by an assortment of bell-boys, conspiratorial executives, and conniving Italian businessmen. Midler gets to play her vulgar, trashy self twice over, Tomlin introduces a little comic variety as the gutsy blue collar worker and the drippy sister, and Abrahams handles the mechanical plot with skill, if not style. The frenetic fun reduces everyone to a cipher; it's difficult to care about any of them. NF

Big Carnival, The

see Ace in the Hole

Big Chill, The

(1983, US, 105 min)
d Lawrence Kasdan. *p* Michael Shamberg. *sc* Lawrence Kasdan, Barbara Benedek. *ph* John Bailey. *ed* Carol Littleton. *pd* Ida Random. *cast* Tom Berenger, Glenn Close, Jeff Goldblum, William Hurt, Kevin Kline, Mary Kay Place, Meg Tilly, JoBeth Williams.
●A funeral reunites a group of friends from the idealistic '60s who have gone their separate ways in the pragmatic '80s. Over the weekend they eat a lot, argue, go jogging, try to bed one another, and reminisce endlessly to the accompaniment of a host of '60s greats on the soundtrack. However, the script deftly avoids the twin pitfalls of solemnity or sentimentality which threaten such a scenario; instead it's perceptive, affectionate and often very funny. JB

Big Circus, The

(1959, US, 108 min)
d Joseph M Newman. *p* Irwin Allen. *sc* Irwin Allen, Charles Bennett, Irving Wallace. *ph* Winton C Hoch. *ed* Adrienne Fazan. *ad* Albert S D'Agostino. *m* Paul Sawtell, Bert Shefter. *cast* Victor Mature, Red Buttons, Rhonda Fleming, Kathryn Grant, Vincent Price, Peter Lorre.
●Hitchcock's old scriptwriter from *Blackmail*, Charles Bennett, worked on the screenplay of this pleasing big-top melodrama. Circus owner Mature is left bankrupt when his erstwhile partners walk out on him. He begs a bank loan and puts the show back on the road. But somebody is out to get him. The story is straggly but there are plenty of incidental pleasures: Peter Lorre does a turn as a clown, and matters close with a walk across Niagara Falls. GM

Big City, The

see Mahanagar

Big Clock, The

(1947, US, 95 min, b/w)
d John Farrow. *p* Richard Maibaum. *sc* Jonathan Latimer. *ph* John F Seitz. *ed* Eda Warren. *ad* Hans Dreier, Roland Anderson, Albert Nozaki. *m* Victor Young. *cast* Ray Milland, Charles Laughton, Maureen O'Sullivan, George Macready, Rita Johnson, Elsa Lanchester.
●Excellent *noir* thriller in which crime-journalist Milland, innocently involved with a girl subsequently murdered by his megalomaniac boss Laughton, is then commissioned by Laughton to find the culprit. When he himself becomes the framed suspect, the trap seems closed....With strong performances (especially Laughton as the gross, sexually insecure tycoon, confident in his ability to control the law through his wealth and status), the film also delights through Farrow's evocative direction: the newspaper conglomerate's enormous clock indicating not only the race against time but also the inhumanly inflexible world in which the action takes place; the phallic ornament with which the impotent murderer kills his mocking mistress; and John Seitz's marvellous high contrast photography, portraying a world of isolation in which nothing is as it seems. The source novel by Kenneth Fearing was remade, much altered, as *No Way Out* (1986). GA

Big Combo, The

(1955, US, 89 min, b/w)
d Joseph H Lewis. *p* Sidney Harmon. *sc* Philip Yordan. *ph* John Alton. *ed* Robert S Eisen. *pd* Rudi Feld. *m* David Raksin. *cast* Cornel Wilde, Richard Conte, Jean Wallace, Brian Donlevy, Lee Van Cleef, Earl Holliman, Robert Middleton.
●Terrific gangster movie, although – despite the syndicate shenanigans promised by the title – it's more of a *film noir* focusing on the private, obsessional duel between Wilde's cop and Conte's gangster, each variously haunted by a woman and virtually becoming the other's alter ego during the course of their deadly vendetta. A film structured by viciousness and pain (amplified by two peculiarly hideous torture scenes involving a hearing aid), it's a dark night of several souls perfectly visualised in John Alton's extraordinary camerawork. Even better than Lewis' earlier – and remarkable – *Gun Crazy*. TM

Big Country, The

(1958, US, 166 min)
d William Wyler. *p* William Wyler, Gregory Peck. *sc* James R Webb, Sy Bartlett, Robert Wilder. *ph* Franz Planer. *ed* Robert Belcher, John Faure. *ad* Frank Hotaling. *m* Jerome Moross. *cast* Gregory Peck, Burl Ives, Jean Simmons, Charlton Heston, Carroll Baker, Charles Bickford, Chuck Connors.
●One of those Big Westerns – feuding families with rival patriarchs back on the farm – which aren't so much epic as long. Finely crafted, though, with some marvellous camerawork (Franz Planer), an outstanding performance from Heston, and a vague message about violence predictably underscored by a marathon fist-fight between Peck and Heston. TM

Big Daddy

(1999, US, 93 min)
d Dennis Dugan. *p* Sid Ganis, Jack Giarraputo. *sc* Steve Franks, Tim Herlihy, Adam Sandler. *ph* Theo Van de Sande. *ed* Jeff Gourson. *pd* Perry Andelin Blake. *m* Teddy Castellucci. *cast* Adam Sandler, Kirsty Swanson, Cole Sprouse, Dylan Sprouse, Joey Lauren Adams, Jon Stewart, Allen Couvert, Josh Mostel, Leslie Mann, Joe Bologna, Steve Buscemi.
●An educated thirty-something slacker, Sonny (Sandler), has shunned a career for a life of part-time work, pizza, beer and sports. In an attempt to prove to his impatient girlfriend Vanessa (Swanson) that he's capable of handling responsibility, Sonny adopts the bed-wetting five-year-old Julian (twins Cole and Dylan Sprouse), whom he attempts to raise with unorthodox parenting skills. This lightweight, bubblegum caper synthesises robust, physical humour, self-deprecation and witty one liners. The main problem, as

with most other dumb boy pictures, is that the supporting characters are underwritten. Here, the women are dollies wallpapering Sandler's universe, an irritating but indispensable component of the lad's survival kit, providing ample opportunity for puerile humour. HK

Big Deal at Dodge City

see Big Hand for the Little Lady, A

Big Deal on Madonna Street

see Soliti Ignoti, I

Big Easy, The

(1986, US, 101 min)
d Jim McBride. *p* Stephen J Friedman. *sc* Jim McBride, Daniel Petrie Jr, Jack Baran. *ph* Affonso Beato. *ed* Mia Goldman. *pd* Jeannine C Oppewall. *m* Brad Fiedel. *cast* Dennis Quaid, Ellen Barkin, Ned Beatty, Ebbe Roe Smith, John Goodman, Lisa Jane Persky.

● Lieutenant Remy McSwain of Homicide (Quaid) comes from a long line of venal cops, and although he does little more than run red lights, eat on the cuff in restaurants, and subscribe to the mildly extortionate Widows and Orphans Fund, he is not about to blow the whistle on his 'family's' fancier deals. Crusading Assistant DA Anne Osborne (Barkin) soon locks horns with him in and out of bed, but it takes a multiple murder and heroin scam to make him face up to his own corruption. You might take issue with the ratio of romance to detection, and to the toy alligator he cuddles in bed, but there is a gusto to the movie and a rush of incidental delights. Highly enjoyable. BC

Big Fella

(1937, GB, 73 min, b/w)
d James Elder Wills. *p* Henry Passmore, J Elder Wills. *sc* Ingram D'Abbes, Fenn Sherie. *ph* George Stretton, HAR Thomson. *ed* Brereton Porter, Douglas Robertson. *ad* J Elder Wills. *m* Eric Ansell. *cast* Paul Robeson, Eldon Grant, Elizabeth Welch, Marcelle Rogez, Roy Emerton, James Hayter.

● Sentimental tosh leavened only by the easy-going acting and powerful singing of its star. Robeson plays a Marseilles layabout hired by a wealthy English couple to find their missing son; when he finally discovers the boy's whereabouts, the latter prefers to stay with Robeson rather than return to Mater and Pater. A comedy drama that fails to tug the heartstrings or tickle the funnybone. GA

Big Fix, The

(1978, US, 108 min)
d Jeremy Paul Kagan. *p* Carl Borack, Richard Dreyfuss. *sc* Roger L Simon. *ph* Frank Stanley. *ed* Patrick Kennedy. *pd* Robert Boyle. *m* Bill Conti. *cast* Richard Dreyfuss, Susan Anspach, Bonnie Bedelia, John Lithgow, Ofelia Medina, Nicholas Coster.

● Much underrated wry thriller with a nice sense of its own scale and an occasionally tough way with eccentricity, in which Dreyfuss' sort-of-private-eye ('a would-be marxist gumshoe') finds nostalgia for an activist past turning sour as an unlikely rightist backlash violently hits a Californian gubernatorial election campaign, and his counter-culture quipping has to be put on hold. A more characteristically quirky work from the oddball Kagan than *The Chosen*. PT

Bigfoot and the Hendersons

see Harry and the Hendersons

Bigger Splash, A

(1974, GB, 105 min)
d/p Jack Hazan. *sc* Jack Hazan, David Mingay. *ph* Jack Hazan. *ed* David Mingay. *m* Patrick Gowers. *cast* David Hockney, Peter Schlesinger, Celia Birtwell, Mo McDermott, Henry Geldzahler, Ossie Clark.

● Elegantly framed improvisation around the lifestyle of painter David Hockney and friends. Like its protagonists, the film's main preoccupations are composition and style, which often leaves it unquestioningly reflecting their vapid antics.

Bigger Than Life

(1956, US, 95 min)
d Nicholas Ray. *p* James Mason. *sc* Cyril Hume, Richard Maibaum. *ph* Joseph MacDonald. *ed* Louis Loeffler. *ad* Lyle Wheeler, Jack Martin Smith. *m* David Raksin. *cast* James Mason, Barbara Rush, Walter Matthau, Robert Simon, Roland Winters, Christopher Olsen.

● Mason's furrowed brow and brooding presence have rarely (never?) been used to better effect: 30 years on, his performance as the mild schoolteacher who is prescribed the wonder drug cortisone and becomes a raving megalomaniac addict remains profoundly disturbing. Suburbia is haunted by psychosis; family life torn apart by Oedipal bloodlust. Ray's direction (in 'Scope and Eastman Colour) is as moving as ever - delicate compositions and fluid camerawork contradicted by the image of weak men locked into obsessive self-destruction. At every level the banal props of '50s prosperity are turned into symbols of suffocation and trauma, from the X-ray machine used to diagnose Mason's 'disease' to the bathroom cabinet mirror shattering under a desperate blow. Trashed on first release, resurrected by Truffaut and Godard, lovingly imitated by Wim Wenders (in *American Friend*): this is *Rebel Without a Cause* for the grown-up world. CA

Biggest Heroes, The

see Greatest Heroes, The

Big Girls Don't Cry...They Get Even (aka Stepkids)

(1992, US, 104 min)
d Joan Micklin Silver. *p* Laurie Perlman, Gerald T Olson. *sc* Frank Mugavero. *ph* Theo van de Sande. *ed* Janice Hampton. *m* Patrick Williams. *cast* Griffin Dunne, Dan Futterman, Patricia Kalember, Jenny Lewis, Ben Savage, Adrienne Shelly, David Strathairn, Trenton Teigen, Margaret Whitton, Hillary Wolf.

● Precocious adolescent Laura (Wolf), who remonstrates straight to camera and consoles herself from a miniature book of quotes (Thoreau, etc), is related to half of California through multiple marriages. Fed up, she is the hub of this entirely predictable ensemble piece. There are those with whom she lives: couture-obsessed mom (Whitton) and her clone stepdaughter; pint-sized 'GI Joe' stepbrother (Teigen); neglectful stepdad (Strathairn). And those with whom she doesn't, including estranged man-child dad (Dunne, excellent as usual), temporarily shacked up with a winsome air-head hippy (Shelly), and favourite stepbrother Josh (Futterman). The extended family finally all meet up in a wood cabin by a lake for a *Big Chill*-out, awaiting Laura's return from an attempted runaway. Directed by numbers, this continues a sad decline which has taken Joan Micklin Silver from *Hester Street* through *Loverboy* to this. WH

Biggles

(1986, GB, 92 min)
d John Hough. *p* Kent Walwin, Pom Oliver. *sc* John Groves, Kent Walwin. *ph* Ernest Vincze. *ed* Richard Trevor. *pd* Terry Pritchard. *m* Stanislas. *cast* Neil Dickson, Alex Hyde-White, Fiona Hutchinson, Peter Cushing, Marcus Gilbert, William Hootkins, Alan Polonsky, Francesca Gonshaw, Michael Siberry, Daniel Flynn.

● This potty venture seeks to resurrect Capt WE Johns' RAF hero from years ago, via a sci-fi time-travel scenario. Biggles on the Western Front in 1917 and Jim Ferguson, New York entrepreneur in 1986 are 'time-twins', flitting back and forth across the decades at the scriptwriters' convenience, with a Hun secret weapon as McGuffin. Not bold enough, not comical enough, not camp enough, not anything enough; and frustratingly there's no sign of Worralls, female counterpart of Biggles in the Johns canon. BBa

Big Hand For the Little Lady, A (aka Big Deal at Dodge City)

(1966, US, 96 min)
d/p Fielder Cook. *sc* Sidney Carroll. *ph* Lee Garmes. *ed* George Rohrs. *ad* Robert Smith. *m* David Raksin. *cast* Henry Fonda, Joanne Woodward, Jason Robards, Charles Bickford, Burgess Meredith, Kevin McCarthy, Paul Ford, Robert Middleton.

● A superb cast makes up for indifferent direction in this engaging O Henryish yarn about a marathon poker game (in Laredo, despite the British release title) and the little lady who uses her feminine wiles to scoop the pot. To be fair to Cook, this started life as a 48-minute teleplay by Sidney Carroll; the rest he has to pad out with close-ups and irrelevancies. TM

Big Heat, The

(1953, US, 90 min, b/w)
d Fritz Lang. *p* Robert Arthur. *sc* Sydney Boehm. *ph* Charles Lang Jr. *ed* Charles Nelson. *ad* Robert Peterson. *m* Daniele Amfitheatrof. *cast* Glenn Ford, Gloria Grahame, Jocelyn Brando, Lee Marvin, Carolyn Jones, Alexander Scourby.

● Homicide Sgt Dave Bannion (Ford), a seemingly wholesome family man, investigates a fellow officer's suicide. Lifting the lid off the garbage can, he uncovers a world where megalomaniac crime bosses, police commissioners and city councillors share the same poker table, and all opposition is put on the payroll. Pulled off the case and suspended from duty, personal tragedy and a growing contempt for his peers lead him into a vengeful vendetta that equates his actions with those of his enemies. Lang strips down William P McGivern's novel to essentials, giving the story a narrative drive as efficient and powerful as a handgun. The dialogue is functional. Every shot is composed with economy and exactitude, no act gratuitous. The most celebrated scene, where Marvin's psychopathic gangster mutilates his moll Grahame's face with scalding coffee, is remarkable in that you never see him do it; the contract killings are also sex murders, but again unseen. Bannion's redemption comes as he (and we) are moved by the courage of others; a crippled woman gives him a lead, a band of old army chums protect his daughter, and finally Grahame, in whose retributive act lies his purgation. WH

Big Hit, The

(1998, US, 91 min)
d Che-Kirk Wong. *p* Warren Zide, Wesley Snipes. *sc* Ben Ramsey. *ph* Danny Nowak. *ed* Robin Russell, Pietro Scalia. *pd* Taavo Soodor. *m* Grame Revell. *cast* Mark Wahlberg, Lou Diamond Phillips, Christina Applegate, Avery Brooks, Bokeem Woodbine, Antonio Sabata Jr, Lainie Kazan, Elliott Gould, Sab Shimono, China Chow, Lela Rochon.

● Wahlberg exudes a dopey charm as Mel, a hitman for whom a lucrative kidnapping-on-the-side turns sour. The victim, industrialist's daughter Keiko (China Chow), is the godchild of his day-job boss. Betrayed by his back-up Cisco (Phillips), Mel finds himself on the wrong end of a lot of firepower. Meanwhile, his personal life is approaching meltdown. His fiancée, Jewish princess Pam (Applegate), has asked her disapproving parents to visit for the weekend; his money-grabbing mistress, Chantel (Rochon), is taking him for everything he's got; and an zealous video-store clerk is hassling him about an overdue tape. Substituting a frenzied pace and hyperkinetic editing for style and panache, HK film-maker Che-Kirk Wong flings together a series of ludicrously choreographed, gravity-defying set pieces. Those elements of Ben Ramsey's screenplay that survive this death of a thousand cuts provide a hint of what might have been, especially the quieter scenes between the terminally harassed Mel and his smart, disarmingly matter-of-fact kidnap victim. NF

Big Jake

(1971, US, 110 min)
d George Sherman. *p* Michael A Wayne. *sc* Harry Julian Fink, RM Fink. *ph* William Clothier. *ed* Harry Gerstad. *ad* Carl Anderson. *m* Elmer Bernstein. *cast* John Wayne, Richard Boone, Maureen O'Hara, Patrick Wayne, Chris Mitchum, Bobby Vinton, Bruce Cabot, Glenn Corbett, Harry Carey Jr, John Ethan Wayne.

● A late Wayne Western, depending heavily on recycling better (and no better) earlier pictures. Strung together in a one-suspect kidnapping yarn are the family feuds and father/son reconciliations first encountered in *Shepherd of the Hills*, with *Hondo*, *The Searchers* and *McLintock* plundered along the way. But this is 1971, the year of *Dirty Harry*, so a new brutality attaches awkwardly to the familiar goings on; and where the humour in *The Searchers* served to mark that film's epic passages of time, Big Jake's knockabout with motorbikes and mud fights merely, and tiresomely, prolongs the pursuit. DO

Big Job, The

(1965, GB, 88 min, b/w)
d Gerald Thomas. *p* Peter Rogers. *sc* Talbot Rothwell. *ph* Alan Hume. *ed* Rod Keys. *ad* Bert Davey. *m* Eric Rogers. *cast* Sidney James, Sylvia Syms, Dick Emery, Joan Sims, Lance Percival, Jim Dale, Deryck Guyler, Edina Ronay.

●Director Thomas, writer Rothwell, producer Thomas, and the familiar cast ensure that this 'unofficial' Carry On reproduces the familiar formula of its virtually institutionalised predecessors. Here Sid's hapless gang emerge from jail fifteen years after the eponymous disaster, and attempt to recover their hidden loot from the grounds of a police station that has sprung up on the site. PT

Big Knife, The

(1955, US, 111 min, b/w)
d/p Robert Aldrich. *sc* James Poe. *ph* Ernest Laszlo. *ed* Michael Luciano. *ad* William Glasgow. *m* Frank De Vol. *cast* Jack Palance, Ida Lupino, Shelley Winters, Rod Steiger, Everett Sloane, Jean Hagen, Wendell Corey, Wesley Addy.

●Hollywood on Hollywood: 'They louse you up, and then they call you a louse'. Aldrich coaxes independent, intense performances from Clifford Odets' wordy and stagebound script, which is left to wrestle with its own rather precious liberal conscience while Aldrich concentrates upon what interests him more: the problems of survival and redemption. Undoubtedly daring in its day, *The Big Knife* remains intelligent and literate, but saved from 'safety' by Palance and Steiger's obviously mutual loathing. Palance's performance as the cracking star shows that he once had a great capacity for suffering, and Steiger's hammy outrageousness (playing a mixture of studio bosses Cohn and Mayer) has never been so adroitly exploited. CPe

Big Lebowski, The

(1998, US/GB, 127 min)
d Joel Coen. *p* Ethan Coen. *sc* Joel Coen, Ethan Coen. *ph* Roger Deakins. *ed* Roderick Jaynes, Tricia Cooke. *pd* Rick Heinrichs. *m* Carter Burwell. *cast* Jeff Bridges, John Goodman, Julianne Moore, Steve Buscemi, David Huddleston, Philip Seymour Hoffman, Tara Reid, John Turturro, David Thewlis, Ben Gazzara, Sam Elliott.

●This comic update of the world crystallised by Raymond Chandler charts the disastrous involvement of laidback dopehead Jeff 'the Dude' Lebowski (Bridges) in a kidnapping case involving the wife of his millionaire namesake (Huddleston). The Dude is hired as bagman and of course finds himself increasingly at risk as he makes his way about an LA populated by the rich, strange and dangerous. Nor do his bowling buddies help: Donny (Buscemi) is frankly several pins short of a strike; while Walter (Goodman), a crazed, irascible Viet vet, is so determined to stand his (and the Dude's) ground that he causes more trouble than he solves. Immensely inventive and entertaining, the film may not have the enigmatic elegance or emotional resonance of *Barton Fink* or *Fargo,* but it's still a prime example of the Coens' effortless brand of stylistic and storytelling brilliance. Thanks to Roger Deakins' gleaming camerawork, T-Bone Burnett's eclectic soundtrack selection and the Coens' typically pithy dialogue, it looks and sounds wonderful. Moreover, far from being shallow pastiche, it's actually about something: what it means to be a man, to be a friend, and to be a 'hero' for a particular time and place. GA

Big Lift, The

(1950, US, 120 min, b/w)
d George Seaton. *p* William Perlberg. *sc* George Seaton. *ph* Charles G Clarke. *ed* Robert Simpson, William Reynolds. *ad* Lyle Wheeler, Russell Spencer. *m* Alfred Newman. *cast* Montgomery Clift, Paul Douglas, Cornell Borchers, Bruni Löbel, OE Hasse, Danny Davenport.

●Filming in Germany against the backdrop of the Berlin Airlift adds an extra element of historical interest to this social-conscience picture exploring differing American attitudes to the former enemy five years after the war. Clift is good value as the young idealist airman who discovers that girlfriend Borchers has been lying to him about her past, while radio operator Douglas, soured by his experiences during combat, can barely disguise his xenophobia, even though he's going out with attractive fraulein Löbel. TJ

Big Man, The

(1990, GB, 116 min)
d David Leland. *p* Stephen Woolley. *sc* Don Macpherson. *ph* Ian Wilson. *ed* George Akers. *pd* Carol Amies. *m* Ennio Morricone. *cast* Liam Neeson, Joanne Whalley-Kilmer, Billy Connolly, Ian Bannen, Maurice Roëves, Kenny Ireland, John Beattie, Hugh Grant.

●By adhering to the classic fight-movie formula of beleaguered pugilist vs manipulative crime boss in this adaptation of William McIlvanney's novel, Leland and scriptwriter Don Macpherson have made one of Britain's finest existential thrillers in ages. When unemployed Scottish miner Danny Scoular (Neeson) agrees to fight a one-off bare-knuckle bout, he not only risks losing his wife (Whalley-Kilmer) and kids, but enters a hellish domain lorded over by ruthless Glasgow gang boss Matt Mason (Bannen). The tortuous, taciturn script centres on questions of integrity, courage, commitment and betrayal; and the mood of corruption, paranoia and violence is palpable throughout, thanks in no small measure to excellent performances from Neeson and Bannen. There are minor flaws, but as a portrait of one man's desperate struggle to survive against all odds, the film is tough, taut and intelligently critical of the man's world it depicts. GA

Big Meat Eater

(1982, Can, 82 min)
d Chris Windsor. *p* Laurence Keane. *sc* Phil Savath, Laurence Keane, Chris Windsor. *ph* Doug McKay. *ed* Chris Windsor, Laurence Keane, Lilla Pedersen. *m* J Douglas Dodd. *cast* George Dawson, Big Miller, Andrew Gillies, Stephen Dimopoulous, Georgina Hegedos, Ida Carnevali.

●In response to the slander that all Canadian movies look as though they're made by social workers: a sci-fi cannibal zombie musical. Bob the butcher's right-hand man has real right hands in the freezer, one of which is attached to the mayor, who returns as a walking dead ambassador for robotic aliens desperate for a rare fuel only to be found, as it happens, under the butcher shop. If you don't care for that plotline, there are three or four others defrosting simultaneously. Abdullah, indiscriminate master of the chill cabinet, is played by frame-filling blues veteran Big Miller, who also provides the musical choice cuts. The nearest Hollywood equivalent (not that one springs to mind) would have spent more on catering than the small change that this carnivore evidently consumed. DO

Big Momma's House

(2000, US/Ger, 98 min)
d Raja Gosnell. *p* David T Friendly, Michael Green. *sc* Darryl Quarles, Don Rhymer. *ph* Michael D O'Shea. *ed* Bruce Green, Kent Beyda. *pd* Craig Stearns. *m* Richard Gibbs. *cast* Martin Lawrence, Nia Long, Paul Giamatti, Jascha Washington, Terrence Howard, Anthony Anderson, Ella Mitchell, Carl Wright, Phyllis Applegate.

●To corner an escaped bank robber, crack FBI agent and master-of-disguise Malcolm Turner (Lawrence) goes undercover as the obese, grits-cookin', Bible-thumpin' grandmother of the fugitive's former girlfriend Sherry (Long). This contrived set-up precariously in place, Turner predictably falls for comely Sherry. Thereafter, matters alternate between scatological farce and ersatz romantic comedy. The likeable star's characteristic energy is not much in evidence. MHi

Big Mouth, The

(1967, US, 107 min)
d/p Jerry Lewis. *sc* Jerry Lewis, Bill Richmond. *ph* W Wallace Kelley, Ernest Laszlo. *ed* Russel Wiles. *pd* Lyle Wheeler. *m* Harry Betts. *cast* Jerry Lewis, Harold J Stone, Susan Bay, Buddy Lester, Del Moore, Paul Lambert.

●A prime example of a comic genius on the border line between comedy and tragedy, Lewis is the double of a wanted diamond smuggler in this intricate, machine-like movie. Frustrating and embarrassing, it's one of the few children's films to treat paranoia seriously and humorously at the same time. DMacp

Big Night

(1995, US, 108 min)
d Campbell Scott, Stanley Tucci. *p* Jonathan Filley. *sc* Stanley Tucci, Joseph Tropiano. *ph* Ken Kelsch. *ed* Suzy Elmiger. *pd* Andrew Jackness. *m* Margot Core. *cast* Stanley Tucci, Tony Shalhoub, Isabella Rossellini, Ian Holm, Minnie Driver, Allison Janney, Marc Anthony, Campbell Scott.

●New Jersey, the late '50s: Italian immigrants Primo and Secondo Pilaggi (Shalhoub and Tucci) are struggling to make a go of their restaurant, The Paradise. While Primo is a master chef with a near-mystical faith in the traditional food of the old country – too subtle for the locals, who'd rather dine down the street at the glitzy Americanised eatery owned by the flamboyant Pascal (Holm) – Secondo tactfully suggests his older brother offer a few compromises on the menu before the bank forecloses. Ironically, potential salvation comes from Pascal, who promises that, as a publicity stunt, he'll get his friend, the crooner Louis Prima, to visit The Paradise. It's their last chance, and the brothers prepare a banquet no one will ever forget. Directed by actors Tucci and Scott, and written by Tucci with his cousin Joseph Tropiano, this beautifully acted film is a modest but big-hearted delight. Focusing firmly on mood, character and situation, it finds time not only for a generous, balanced appraisal of the brothers' relationship, but for a wealth of other deftly drawn personalities. Much is made of the big night and its preparation, with mouth-watering results, but it's the long, final shot of an omelette being cooked and eaten that best characterises the film's prime virtues: simple, unpretentious, to the point, and warmly human. GA

Big Night, The

(1951, US, 75 min, b/w)
d Joseph Losey. *p* Philip A Waxman. *sc* Stanley Ellin, Joseph Losey. *ph* Hal Mohr. *ed* Edward Mann. *ad* Nicolai Remisoff. *m* Lyn Murray. *cast* John Barrymore Jr, Preston Foster, Howland Chamberlin, Howard St John, Dorothy Comingore, Joan Lorring, Philip Bourneuf.

●Losey's last American film before his European exile opens on a note strikingly reminiscent of *The Killers*: a sensitive 17-year-old boy (Barrymore) watches in shattered disbelief as the father he hero-worships (Foster) tamely submits to a brutal thrashing at the hands of a crippled sports reporter (St John). Then, wandering with vengeful gun through a seedy nighttown inferno of bars, boxing-rings and nightclubs, he gradually discovers why in a process of growing up. Intense, sharply characterised, brilliantly shot by Hal Mohr, it works extremely well even though Losey subsequently objected to the chronological narrative imposed by producer Philip Waxman: 'It had been planned in a frame of flashback.' TM

Big Parade, The

(1925, US, 12,550 ft, b/w & col)
d King Vidor. *sc* Harry Behn, Laurence Stallings. *ph* John Arnold. *ed* Hugh Wynn. *ad* Cedric Gibbons, James Basevi. *m* William Axt. *cast* John Gilbert, Renée Adorée, Hobart Bosworth, Claire McDowell, Claire Adams, Robert Ober, Tom O'Brien, Karl Dane.

●Time has not dealt altogether kindly with Vidor's silent blockbuster which, like *All Quiet on the Western Front* five years later, made both art and box-office out of the disillusionments of WWI. Too much of it is plain embarrassing: the buddy humour which scriptwriter Laurence Stallings carries over from *What Price Glory?*; the snatches of all-American whimsy (French girl introduced to the mysteries of chewing gum; the sentimentality of the hero's return minus a leg but plus superimpositions showing his mother remembering him as a child falling and grazing his knee. Yet even if it romanticises the true horrors beyond all recognition, there is undeniable power in Vidor's vision of a doughboy's episodic odyssey through the vast landscape of war. One is never left in any doubt that he was, even then, a major talent. TM

Big Parade, The (Da Yuebing)

(1986, China, 103 min)
d Chen Kaige. *p* Chen Liguo. *sc* Gao Lili. *ph* Zhang Yimou. *ed* Zhou Xinxia. *ad* He Qun. *m* Qu Xiaosong, Zhao Jiping. *cast* Wang Xueqi, Sun Chun, Lu Lei, Wu Ruofu, Guan Qiang.

●Chen sees his follow-up to *Yellow Earth* as a metaphor for life in China today: the need to overcome personal frustrations and failings for the common good. It also works extremely well simply as a film about men under stress. Four hundred-odd volunteers, many of the fresh recruits still in their teens, come to a training camp for eight months of intensive drilling. Some of them will win places in China's National Day parade. The film focuses on four of the young squaddies and two of the officers, looking at the ways they bond and split apart, but also at their most intimate feelings; their sense of physical inadequacy, for instance, or their hypocrisy in presenting an exterior they know to be false. It's surprisingly humane and moving. As in *Yellow Earth*, Zhang Yimou's photography lifts the drama into another dimension; there are images here whose power and grace burn themselves into the mind. TR

Big Picture, The

(1988, US, 101 min)
d Christopher Guest. *p* Michael Varhol, Richard Gilbert Abramson. *sc* Michael Varhol, Christopher Guest, Michael McKean. *ph* Jeff Jur. *ed* Martin Nicholson. *pd* Joseph T Garrity. *m* David Nichtern. *cast* Kevin Bacon, Emily Longstreth, JT Walsh, Jennifer Jason Leigh, Martin Short, Michael McKean, Kim Miyori, Teri Hatcher, Tracy Brooks Swope, Elliott Gould, Roddy McDowall, John Cleese, Eddie Albert.
●Actor-turned-director Guest presents a comic cautionary tale about a young film school graduate (Bacon) seduced into the compromises necessary to make his first big picture – a snowbound country-house drama that almost ends up as a teen comedy called 'Beach Nuts'. Bacon is engagingly naive as the starstruck director whose artistic pretensions are whittled away by a slimy studio exec (Walsh). He also becomes increasingly estranged from homely girlfriend (Longstreth) and best pal cinematographer (McKean), and carnal temptation comes in the heavenly form of a TV starlet (Hatcher) who sees him as a ticket to big screen fame. The movie references may strike some as in-jokey, but Guest's likeable film has enough jaundiced sideswipes and lighter chuckles to see it through its slacker spells. Even so, an increasing sense of bittiness creeps in, emphasised by a series of cameos: loopy Jennifer Jason Leigh, an Irish John Cleese, judge Roddy McDowall, and spaced-out agent Martin Short (whose contribution alone is worth the price of admission). NF

Big Red One, The

(1980, US, 113 min)
d Samuel Fuller. *p* Gene Corman. *sc* Samuel Fuller. *ph* Adam Greenberg. *ed* Morton Tubor. *ad* Peter Jamison. *m* Dana Kaproff. *cast* Lee Marvin, Mark Hamill, Robert Carradine, Bobby DiCicco, Kelly Ward, Stéphane Audran.
●In outline, a chronicle of the movements of a squad from the 1st US Infantry Division through WWII, from a beach-head assault in North Africa to the liberation of a concentration camp in Czechoslovakia. The sergeant is played by Marvin, and four young riflemen are the only members of his squad who survive the war with him; one of them (Carradine) is Fuller's surrogate – because this is Fuller telling his own story, synthesising every thought he ever had about the experience of warfare. No heroics, no anti-heroics, no 'drama' to speak of; instead a racy description of incidents from a great war correspondent, married with a Bressonian concentration on feelings of isolation and dislocation. Visually and philosophically, it's Fuller's equivalent of Kurosawa's *Kagemusha*, although Fuller's film is more complex, more absurd and more haunted. TR

Big Shot, The

(1942, US, 82 min, b/w)
d Lewis Seiler. *p* Walter MacEwen. *sc* Bertram Millhauser, Abem Finkel, Daniel Fuchs. *ph* Sid Hickox. *ed* Jack Killifer. *ad* John Hughes. *m* Adolph Deutsch. *cast* Humphrey Bogart, Irene Manning, Richard Travis, Susan Peters, Stanley Ridges, Minor Watson, Chick Chandler, Howard Da Silva.
●Tired gangster movie covering much the same ground as the infinitely superior *High Sierra* from the previous year. Bogart is fine as the three-time loser trying to go straight, framed back into jail, and breaking out again to meet his doom, but the film goes downhill around him. TM

Big Silence, The (Il Grande Silenzio)

(1968, Fr/It, 115 min)
d Sergio Corbucci. *p* GA Giurgola. *sc* Sergio Corbucci, Vittoriano Perili, Mario Amendola, Bruno Corbucci. *ph* Silvano Ippoliti. *ad* Riccardo Domenici. *m* Ennio Morricone. *cast* Jean-Louis Trintignant, Klaus Kinski, Vonetta McGee, Gastone Moschin, Frank Wolff.
●While *Django* remains the erratic Corbucci's best picture, this slightly later spaghetti Western does well by an inventive set-up, which has unusually heavy snowfalls on the US-Mexican border bringing various outlawis down from the mountains, where Kinski's ruthless bounty hunter is waiting for them. Trintignant is 'Silenzio', the mute gunfighter determined to stop the carnage, and between the bullets there's engaging stuff from the two stars and an unmistakable chill in the air. TJ

Big Sky, The

(1952, US, 122 min, b/w)
d/p Howard Hawks. *sc* Dudley Nichols. *ph* Russell Harlan. *ed* Christian I Nyby. *ad* Albert S D'Agostino, Perry Ferguson. *m* Dimitri Tiomkin. *cast* Kirk Douglas, Dewey Martin, Steve Geray, Elizabeth Threatt, Arthur Hunnicutt, Buddy Baer, Michael Douglas.
●While not up to the standard of Hawks' best Westerns (*Red River, Rio Bravo*), still an evergreen delight. Douglas and Martin are the two Kentuckians who join a pioneering trading expedition up the Missouri River to buy furs from the Blackfoot Indians. Problems are many, what with the dangers of the landscape and the hostility of certain Indians. But Hawks is less concerned with the adventurous aspect of the odyssey than with the relationship between the two men, who slowly discover a deep mutual respect, only to have it threatened by their both loving the same woman (an Indian they capture as a hostage against trouble). Episodic, rambling and very amiable, with a nice line in black humour (most evident in the marvellous sequence where Douglas has his finger amputated, only to lose it in the undergrowth). First shown in a 140-minute version. GA

Big Sleep, The

(1946, US, 114 min, b/w)
d/p Howard Hawks. *sc* William Faulkner, Leigh Brackett, Jules Furthman. *ph* Sid Hickox. *ed* Christian I Nyby. *ad* Carl Jules Weyl. *m* Max Steiner. *cast* Humphrey Bogart, Lauren Bacall, John Ridgely, Martha Vickers, Dorothy Malone, Regis Toomey, Elisha Cook Jr, Peggy Knudsen.
●One of the finest mainstream *noir*-thrillers ever made. As Bogart's Marlowe gets involved with the Sternwood family's many problems (drugs, blackmail, nymphomania and murder), Hawks never allows the plot to get in the way of his real interest: the growing love, based on remarkably explicit sexual attraction, between Bogie and Bacall, and the way that emotion causes both of them to modify their initial positions regarding the criminal goings-on. In fact, the story is virtually incomprehensible at points, but who cares when the sultry mood, the incredibly witty and memorable script, and the performances are so impeccable? GA

Big Sleep, The

(1978, GB, 99 min)
d Michael Winner. *p* Elliot Kastner, Michael Winner. *sc* Michael Winner. *ph* Bob Paynter. *ed* Frederick Wilson. *pd* Harry Pottle. *m* Jerry Fielding. *cast* Robert Mitchum, Sarah Miles, Richard Boone, Candy Clark, Joan Collins, Edward Fox, John Mills, James Stewart, Oliver Reed.
●The residue of Chandler in Winner's remake of *The Big Sleep* might just con audiences unfamiliar with the novels and who haven't seen the 1946 Hawks/Bogart version. Otherwise, it's on very shaky ground indeed. Spuriously relocated in London (Winner's facility with luxurious location set pieces is anything but masterful), and with Marlowe dressed by Savile Row (Mitchum seems to sleepwalk through the part), the film sorely lacks any of the seediness and menace which made the 1973 remake of *Farewell My Lovely* at least watchable. Winner's insistence as a director on making everything as explicit as possible is often stultifying beyond belief. RM

Big Steal, The

(1949, US, 71 min. b/w)
d Don Siegel. *p* Jack J Gross. *sc* Daniel Mainwaring, Gerald Drayson Adams. *ph* Harry J Wild. *ed* Samuel E Beetley. *ad* Albert S D'Agostino, Ralph Berger. *m* Leigh Harline. *cast* Robert Mitchum, Jane Greer, William Bendix, Ramon Novarro, Patric Knowles, John Qualen.
●Reuniting the team of Mitchum, Greer and ace-scriptwriter Daniel Mainwaring after the classic *noir*-romance *Out of the Past*, this takes a typical thriller situation (for that matter, a common Siegel motif: society's outsider up against authority) and turns it into a fast-moving, witty parody. Mitchum is the GI framed for a payroll robbery, on the run from dumb officer Bendix, falling in love with the delectable Greer, and in pursuit of the real culprit. Dialogue sparkles, the Mexican locations are atmospherically shot by Harry Wild, and Siegel handles the action with characteristic pace and vigour. The numerous plot twists are in themselves an exhilaratingly tongue-in-cheek exaggeration of noir conventions, while remaining central to the excitement of the film. Vigorous, playful stuff. GA

Big Steal, The

(1990, Aust, 100 min)
d Nadia Tass. *p* Nadia Tass, David Parker. *sc* David Parker, Maxwell Dunn. *ph* David Parker. *ed* Peter Carrodus. *pd* Paddy Reardon. *m* Philip Judd. *cast* Ben Mendelsohn, Claudia Karvan, Steve Bisley, Marshall Napier, Damon Herriman, Angelo D'Angelo.
●Australian teen Danny (Mendelsohn) craves only two things from life: a Jaguar and fellow-student Joanna (Karvan). He's working class, she's not, so Danny convinces himself that she will only go out with him if he possesses the dream car. Cue large debts and a spiralling nightmare with shady car-dealer Gordon Farkas (Bisley), setting the scene for a ruined date and desperate revenge. In this unevenly paced film, the directing-writing team of Tass and David Parker have retained some of the absurdity of their earlier *Malcolm*. The film eventually veers off into slapstick: a shame, because the prolonged chase scenes detract from the offbeat view of suburbia and peer pressure which lifts this above more mundane offerings in the genre. Mendelsohn's combination of vulnerability and bravado is a consistent delight. CM

Big Store, The

(1941, US, 83 min, b/w)
d Charles Riesner. *p* Louis K Sidney. *sc* Sid Kuller, Hal Fimberg, Ray Golden. *ph* Charles Lawton. *ed* Conrad A Nervig. *ad* Cedric Gibbons, Stan Rogers. *songs* Sid Kuller, Ray Golden Hal Borne, Milton Drake, Artie Shaw. *cast* The Marx Brothers, Tony Martin, Virginia Grey, Margaret Dumont, Douglas Dumbrille, Virginia O'Brien, Henry Armetta.
●Kitsch wins over comedy in the Marx Brothers' last MGM film, which remains in the mind mainly because of the amazingly awful 'Tenement Symphony', in which Tony Martin and a screen full of sparkling urchins warble a lyric of the finest drivel: 'The songs of the ghetto inspired the allegretto'. Nothing the Marx Brothers do is funnier than this, though Harpo and Chico's musical bits are livelier than usual. Dumont is prominently featured and totally mishandled, Groucho seems half asleep, and the plot (centred on a department store) doesn't bear thinking about. GB

Big Street, The

(1942, US, 88 min, b/w)
d Irving Reis. *p* Damon Runyon. *sc* Leonard Spigelgass. *ph* Russell Metty. *ed* William Hamilton. *ad* Albert S D'Agostino, Al Herman. *m* Roy Webb. *cast* Henry Fonda, Lucille Ball, Ray Collins, Sam Levene, Eugene Pallette, Agnes Moorehead, Barton MacLane.
●Adapted from a story by Damon Runyon ('Little Pinks'), this captures much of his low-life spirit and colourful vernacular, but occasionally spoils it all by wallowing in unnecessary sentimentality. Busboy Fonda idolises nightclub chanteuse Ball so much that when she's crippled by her gangster friend, he devotes himself to her well-being, even to the extent of pushing her wheelchair to Florida. Most appealing are the performances by the likes of Pallette, Collins and

Levene, although Ball, in a rare straight role, is stunning as the hard-as-nails, embittered exploiter of Fonda's affections. GA

Big Swap, The

(1997, GB, 122 min)
d/p/sc Niall Johnson. *ph* Gordon Hickie. *ed* David Thrasher. *pd* Craig Johnson. *m* Jason Flinter, Craig Johnson. *cast* Antony Edridge, Sorcha Brooks, Richard Cherry, Julie-Ann Gillitt, Kevin Howarth, Alison Egan, Mark Caven, Clarke Hayes, Jackie Sawiris.
● An adult British movie about sex and its role in modern relationships. Five comfortably off, thirty-something couples decide one weekend to try, just for fun, partner swapping. The group embraces diverse characteristics – shy, candid, cautious, adventurous, sensitive, misogynist, closet lesbian, man dependent – without ever offering one rounded human being. Not withstanding a few lame attempts at humour, the film is dreadfully earnest in its remorseless attempts to touch on every imaginable insecurity, jealousy, anxiety, need and sexual proclivity. GA

Big Tease, The

(1999, US/GB, 86 min)
d Kevin Allen. *p* Philip Rose. *sc* Sacha Gervasi, Craig Ferguson. *ph* Seamus McGarvey. *ed* Chris Peppe. *pd* Joseph Hodges. *m* Mark Thomas. *cast* Craig Ferguson, Frances Fisher, Mary McCormack, Donal Logue, Larry Miller, Charles Napier, Michael Paul Chan, Sara Gilbert, Chris Langham.
● Crawford Mackenzie (character comedian Ferguson) is a Scottish stylist, 'the Red Adair of Hair', intent on winning the World Freestyle Hairdressing Championships in Hollywood. Cue excitement and the attentions of a BBC director. But when Crawford arrives in LA, plus camera crew, he discovers he's been invited to watch, not compete. It doesn't take a genius to spot the template for this Celtic-American 'mock-umentary'. But in the words of Nigel Tufnell, 'it's a thin line between clever and – stupid', and that's the difference between *Spinal Tap* and this. Rob Reiner's film looked, felt and smelt like a fly on the wall documentary, Kevin Allen's can't be bothered to maintain the pretence. Ferguson inclines to play it for pathos over laughs, with Mackenzie emerging as the resilient underdog, intrepidly bidding to qualify for a union card, enlisting help from Sean Connery and his high powered agent along the way. The mind boggling finale sashays into kitsch *Strictly Ballroom* territory and falls flat on its nationalist coiffure. TCh

Big Time

(1988, US, 87 min)
d Chris Blum. *p* Luc Roeg. *sc* Keith Reddin. *ph* Daniel Hainey. *ed* Glenn Scantlebury. *ad* Sterling Storm. *m* Tom Waits. *cast* Tom Waits, Michael Blair, Ralph Carney, Greg Cohen, Marc Ribot, Willy Schwarz.
● This magnificent movie, filmed on a set consisting of a red-and-black checked floor and neon light boxes, cross-cut with scenes shot around the theatre, sees Waits adopt a variety of guises; the pencil-moustached ticket-seller who 'dreams the film', a sit-down comedian in stained white tuxedo and glitter-flecked face – sort of Victor Borge from Hell – and more or less straight troubadour. The music is from *Frank's Wild Years, Rain Dogs* and *Swordfishtrombones*. Musical, visual and verbal puns abound; elements of vaudeville, burlesque and soulful balladry are orchestrated by what is evidently, for all the downbeat, offbeat imagery, a fantastically energetic imagination. A concert film unlike any other, owing something to the work of '40s fashion photographer/jazz film-maker Djon (*Jammin the Blues*) Mili, and with no shots of an audience at all. MC

Big Top Pee-Wee

(1986, US, 90 min)
d Randal Kleiser. *p* Paul Reubens [Paul Reubenfeld], Debra Hill. *sc* Paul Reubens, George McGrath. *ph* Steven Poster. *ed* Jeff Gourson. *ad* Stephen Marsh. *m* Danny Elfman. *cast* Paul Reubens, Penelope Ann Miller, Kris Kristofferson, Valeria Golino, Susan Tyrrell, Albert Henderson, Kevin Peter Hall, Kenneth Tobey.
● This second feature from minor-comedian-cum-notorious-cult-figure Paul Reubens (alias Pee-Wee Herman) isn't in the same class as *Pee-Wee's Big Adventure*, but still provides plenty of prize pickings for kids, kooks and academics. Pee-Wee is down on the farm with his talking pig Vincent when a circus pitches tent in the adjacent field. Soon our hero is convinced there's sawdust in his veins. So are we, because comedians don't come much stranger than Pee-Wee. You'd think twice about taking candy from this baby, but his deadpan perversity is both funny peculiar and funny ha-ha. TCh

Big Town, The

(1987, US, 110 min)
d Ben Bolt. *p* Martin Ransohoff, Don Carmody. *sc* Robert Roy Pool. *ph* Ralf D Bode. *ed* Stuart H Pappé. *pd* Bill Kenney. *m* Michael Melvoin. *cast* Matt Dillon, Diane Lane, Tommy Lee Jones, Bruce Dern, Lee Grant, Tom Skerritt.
● Gambler JC Cullen (Dillon) meets Hooker, a retired diceman in his Indiana hometown, who urges him to chance his arm in Chicago, and gives him his lucky dollar and an introduction to a husband and wife team (Dern and Grant) who have the action sewn up. He shoots dice for them for percentages, but itches to crack the big game in the back room of the strip club run by badman Cole (Jones). Yorn between good girl Aggie and Cole's coonniving stripper wife (Lane), JC has to discover the things that are meanfingful and enduring the hard way. Just about the only pleasure in this formula effort is matching up memories of Rip Torn in *The Cincinnati Kid* with Bruce Dern. Edward G and McQ still have the only game in town. BC

Big Trail, The

(1930, US, 157 min, b/w)
d Raoul Walsh. *sc* Jack Peabody, Marie Boyle, Florence Postal. *ph* Lucien Andriot, Arthur Edeson. *ed* Jack Dennis. *ad* Harold Miles, Frank Serson. *m* Arthur Kay. *cast* John Wayne, Marguerite Churchill, El Brendel, Tully Marshall, Ward Bond, Tyrone Power Sr, David Rollins.
● Walsh's epic Western has gone down in cinema history as the film that made bit-part actor Marion Morrison into leading man John Wayne (though it needed Ford's *Stagecoach* to revive his career a decade later). Originally made simultaneously in normal 35mm and a short-lived 70mm process called 'Grandeur', it has recently been restored to its spectacular wide-screen glory. The saga of a wagon trail, the film is more striking now for its wide shots - vast landscapes, wagons being hauled up impossibly steep cliffs - than for the knockabout humour of the character scenes. DT

Big Trouble

(1986, US, 93 min)
d John Cassavetes. *p* Mike Lobell, Andrew Bergman. *sc* Warren Bogle, Andrew Bergman. *ph* Bill Butler. *ed* Don Cambern. *pd* Gene Callahan. *m* Bill Conti. *cast* Peter Falk, Alan Arkin, Beverly D'Angelo, Charles Durning, Paul Dooley, Robert Stack, Valerie Curtin.
● Presumably directed as a favour to old buddy Falk, Cassavetes' last film is a far cry from the glories of *Gloria, Husbands, Shadows* and the rest. Indeed, it's absolutely unrecognisable as his work, being a conventionally glossy spoof thriller in which insurance salesman Arkin, desperate for finance to send his musical triplets through Yale, agrees to forge a double indemnity policy on Falk's life for his third wife D'Angelo. Sounds familiar? For the first third, this is a comic reshuffle of moments from Wilder and Chandler's classic *Double Indemnity*, but then out come the wacky surprises in a chaotically inventive mish-mash of black neurotic humour. Never hysterically funny but scattered with pleasingly OTT moments and throwaway lines, it looks as if Cassavetes merely wanted a).to prove he could make a blandly stylish commercial piece, and b) the cash. GA

Big Trouble in Little China

(1986, US, 100 min)
d John Carpenter. *p* Larry Franco. *sc* Gary Goldman, David Z Weinstein. *ph* Dean Cundey. *ed* Mark Warner. *pd* John J Lloyd. *m* John Carpenter, Alan Howarth. *cast* Kurt Russell, Kim Cattrall, Dennis Dun, James Hong, Victor Wong, Kate Burton.
● 'Ready, Jack?' asks Kurt Russell's Chinese buddy before another fraught round of mayhem beneath the streets of San Francisco's Chinatown. 'I was born ready', comes back the growled response; and it is this level of conscious self-mockery which saves the John Wayne posturing and genre high kicks from being just another climber on the *Raiders of the Lost Ark* band wagon. Russell is the T-shirted bozo trucker, who only has to fire his gun into the ceiling for the plaster to fall on his head. Down the mean catacombs and underground streams of Chinatown he goes, in search of something or other and encountering every Chinese cliché known to man: devil women, 900-year-old sages, water tortures, black magic monsters. The icing on all this cake is a load of kung-fuey, which in spite of three nifty warlords who come equipped with their own static electricity and interesting hats, isn't really up to the mark established in the meanest of Hong Kong martial arts movies. Carpenter has always been a skilful genre mechanic, breathing life into old forms; if he stubs his toes up against the bamboo curtain this time, there is still more enjoyable sly humour than in most slug-fests. CPea

Big Wednesday

(1978, US, 119 min)
d John Milius. *p* Fuzz Feitshans. *sc* John Milius, Dennis Aaberg. *ph* Bruce Surtees, Greg MacGillivray. *ed* Robert L Wolfe. *pd* Charles Rosen. *m* Basil Poledouris. *cast* Jan-Michael Vincent, William Katt, Gary Busey, Patti D'Arbanville, Lee Purcell, Sam Melville.
● A personal epic (and a celebration of traditional values) that follows three male friends over a decade of surfing – the '60s – under the gradual encroachment of external considerations: age, the war, responsibility. Misguided occasionally, suspect even, it represents the painful growing-up of the beach/youth movie; possibly one of the best American films of the '70s. CPe

Big Wheels and Sailor

(1979, GB, 55 min)
d Doug Aitken. *cast* Nigel Humphries, Julian Curry, Sheila Reid, Dominic Letts, Glen Cunningham.
● Lively, innocent and highly characteristic Children's Film Foundation offering in which the 'Big Wheels' of a decidedly well-spoken truck-driver (plus two kids) is hijacked by 'Mother', the cigar-smoking owner of a cab company (Reid), slit-eyed and hissingly dismissive of her incompetent 'children'. Plenty of wheezing hydraulic brakes, junior motorbike rough-riding, and chasing over teetering industrial structures. No less implausible than *Teenage Mutant Ninja Turtles*, but from a different age. JPy

Big Zapper

(1973, GB, 94 min)
d/p Lindsay Shonteff. *sc* Hugh Brody. *ph* John C Taylor. *ed* Spencer Reeve. *m* Colin Pearson. *cast* Linda Malowe, Richard Monette, Gary Hope, Sean Hewitt, Jack May, Michael O'Malley.
● Imagine TV's *The Avengers* yoked to a British sex movie, add some conscious efforts to imitate Hong Kong kung-fu movies, and you have some idea of this lamentable enterprise. Totally raddled effort devoid of any finer judgment or humour.

Bike Boy

(1967, US, 96 min)
d/p/sc Andy Warhol, Paul Morrissey. *ph* Paul Morrissey. *cast* Joe Spencer, Viva, Bridgit Polk, Ingrid Superstar, Ed Hood, Valerie Solanas.
● The idea in this one was to take a typical American stud (Spencer, never seen before or since) and place him in 'situations' with experienced Warhol actresses. How did he acquit himself? Impassively. The funniest things are the finale, which has Viva racing to get the guy to drop his pants before the film runs out, and the added prologue, with Spencer showing off his scrumptious physique in the shower, included in order to step up the film's nudity quotient. TR

Bilitis

(1976, Fr, 95 min)
d David Hamilton. *sc* Catherine Breillat. *ph* Bernard Daillencourt. *ed* Henri Colpi. *ad* Eric Simon. *m* Francis Lai. *cast* Patti D'Arbanville, Mona Kristensen, Bernard Giraudeau, Mathieu Carrière, Gilles Kohler.

●The source for this debilitatingly tasteful tosh is the *Chansons de Bilitis* by Pierre Louys. Surprisingly, a strong hint of Louys' erotic spirit survives, transmitted mainly through the effective playing and poise of the two leading characters. But it needs much more than a strong hint to counteract Hamilton's fey and phony style. GB

Bill & Ted's Excellent Adventure

(1988, US, 89 min)
d Stephen Herek. *p* Scott Kroopf, Michael S Murphey, Joel Soisson. *sc* Chris Matheson, Ed Solomon. *ph* Timothy Suhrstedt. *ed* Larry Bock, Patrick Rand. *pd* Roy Forge Smith, Lynda Paradise. *m* David Newman. *cast* Keanu Reeves, Alex Winter, George Carlin, Terry Camilleri, Bernie Casey, Dan Shor, Robert V Barron.
●Bill (Winter) and Ted (Reeves) are cool dudes, but to their teacher, they're high school no-hopers. They fantasise about forming a rock band called 'Wyld Stallyns'; one day they'll pull themselves together and learn how to play guitar. Unless he achieves the seemingly impossible and passes a history presentation, Ted will be shipped off to military school; end of friendship! A figure from the future (Carlin) appears in the nick of time, providing a time-travelling phone booth. The two jump in and out of different epochs, collecting historical figures (from Socrates to Billy the Kid) and confronting them with West Coast culture. This is extremely silly, good natured, superficial stuff; a lot depends on whether you take to Bill and Ted's unique lingo (which contorts surfers' expressions) and their gormless behaviour. The funniest scenes involve Napoleon (Camilleri) adrift in Southern California: pompous and power-hungry, he devours the menu in an ice-cream parlour and hogs the rides in a waterslide park. CM

Bill & Ted's Bogus Journey

(1991, US, 98 min)
d Peter Hewitt. *p* Scott Kroopf. *sc* Chris Matheson, Ed Solomon. *ph* Oliver Wood. *ed* David Finfer. *m* David Newman. *cast* Alex Winter, Keanu Reeves, George Carlin, Joss Ackland, William Sadler, Pam Grier, Sarah Trigger, Amy Stock-Poynton, Jeff Miller, David Carrera.
●The Utopia created in *Bill & Ted's Excellent Adventure* is threatened by two robot doppelgängers of the meat-headed, mop-topped duo. These two Terminators travel back in time to present-day San Dimas, California, and swiftly despatch the real Bill & Ted. But death is only the beginning... The first Bill & Ted movie remained a minor cult in Britain, but this far more cinematic sequel deserves a wider audience. Winter (Bill) and Reeves (Ted) make a comic pairing to rival Laurel and Hardy, blundering through life – and the afterlife – with an endearing naivety (when the Grim Reaper promises them their lives if they beat him at chess, they suggest a game of Battleships). The eventual triumph of US junk culture is somewhat offensive, even if prophetic, and there are a few naff ideas; but for those who appreciate dude-speak and bozo humour, this is a very funny film. DW

Billion Dollar Brain

(1967, GB, 111 min)
d Ken Russell. *p* Harry Saltzman. *sc* John McGrath. *ph* Billy Williams. *ed* Alan Osbiston. *pd* Syd Cain. *m* Richard Rodney Bennett. *cast* Michael Caine, Karl Malden, Françoise Dorléac, Oscar Homolka, Ed Begley, Guy Doleman, Milo Sperber.
●One of Russell's most enjoyable movies, completely free of the pretentious bombast that has become his trademark, so that its meaning is embodied in the narrative rather than imposed on it with a directorial sledgehammer. This was the third and last of Caine's appearances as Len Deighton's Harry Palmer, dominated by Russell's skill and visual flair. The plot is a particularly good one about a fascist Texan general called Midwinter (Begley) who plans the invasion of Russia with the aid of a computer and his own private army (the computer has a screen personality almost as distinctive and pleasing as Hal's in *2001*). In an excellent supporting cast, Homolka is outstanding as the Russian general who collaborates with Palmer to prevent the war, and Russell ingeniously constructs the invasion as a parody of the famous ice-breaking sequence in Eisenstein's *Alexander Nevsky*. DP

Bill of Divorcement, A

(1932, US, 75 min. b/w)
d George Cukor. *p* David O Selznick. *sc* Howard Estabrook, Harry Wagstaff Gribble. *ph* Sid Hickox. *ed* Arthur Roberts. *ad* Carroll Clark. *m* Max Steiner. *cast* John Barrymore, Katharine Hepburn, Billie Burke, David Manners, Henry Stephenson, Elizabeth Patterson.
●Skilfully canned version of Clemence Dane's terribly dated problem play about a shellshocked WWI veteran (possibly suffering from hereditary insanity) who returns from the asylum after 15 years to find his wife planning divorce and his daughter a stranger. Full of strangled sentiments and easy options, with a rather too carefully studied performance by Barrymore. But fascinating to see Hepburn's raw-boned talent already at work in her first film, and Cukor already responding to it. Remade in 1940 with Adolphe Menjou and Maureen O'Hara. TM

Billy Bathgate

(1991, US, 107 min)
d Robert Benton. *p* Arlene Donovan, Robert F Colesberry. *sc* Tom Stoppard. *ph* Nestor Almendros. *ed* Alan Heim. *pd* Patrizia von Brandenstein. *m* Mark Isham. *cast* Dustin Hoffman, Nicole Kidman, Loren Dean, Bruce Willis, Steven Hill, Steve Buscemi, Billy Jaye, John Costelloe, Tim Jerome, Stanley Tucci.
●Despite a Tom Stoppard script and diligent direction, EL Doctorow's novel about a youngster's experience of the life and times of Dutch Schultz seldom takes off as a movie. An early scene, in which the gangster (Hoffman) sees 16-year-old Billy (Dean) juggling balls high above the street on a railway bridge, catches the magic realism of the novel, but little else does. Schultz, past his peak and awaiting trial, is a changeable mixture of the kindly and the murderous, but Hoffman's performance seems to be based on Arturo Ui, and his voice sounds as if it has been dredged up from the river, along with the corpse of Bo (Willis), first encountered with his feet in a bucket of cement. Dutch's mistress (Kidman), a society woman slumming, takes a shine to Billy, and their affair provides some necessary development to relationships within the gang. The best performance comes from Steven Hill as Otto, the gangster's faithful retainer, and although Dean is OK as the kid with luck, the role of talisman doesn't play on film. BC

Billy Budd

(1962, GB, 125 min. b/w)
d/p Peter Ustinov. *sc* Peter Ustinov, DeWitt Bodeen. *ph* Robert Krasker. *ed* Jack Harris. *pd* Don Ashton. *m* Antony Hopkins. *cast* Robert Ryan, Peter Ustinov, Terence Stamp, Melvyn Douglas, Paul Rogers, John Neville, Ronald Lewis, David McCallum.
●Ustinov directs this adaptation of Melville's last work in uncharacteristically serious vein. There is a decided shift in emphasis from Melville's allegory of absolute good and evil to a poignant examination of the blindness of justice and law. The angelic Billy is played by a blond Stamp in his first film role; Ustinov himself is Man-o-War Captain Vere, forced to try the naif Billy for the accidental murder of master-at-arms Claggart; and Ryan's performance as the evil Claggart, a role he had long coveted, is staggeringly authoritative, right up to the smile on his face as he dies knowing Billy will hang for his murder. There are many powerful scenes unspoilt by attempts from Ustinov to be cinematic; in fact his self-effacing direction allows the actors to give uniformly sincere performances. Only marginally spoiled by such visual conceits as the lurching ship representing the tilting scales of justice during Vere's debate on whether Billy should hang. RM

Billy Elliot

(2000, GB, 110 min)
d Stephen Daldry. *p* Greg Brenman, Jon Finn. *sc* Lee Hall. *ph* Brian Tufano. *ed* John Wilson. *pd* Maria Djurkovic. *m* Stephen Warbeck. *cast* Julie Walters, Gary Lewis, Jamie Draven, Jean Heywood, Jamie Bell, Adam Cooper, Stuart Wells, Mike Elliot, Patrick Malahide.
●During the miners' strike of 1984, a motherless boy from a pit village takes up dancing against the wishes of his collier dad and older brother. Regrettably, the unsentimental depiction of the working class Northeast in Lee Hall's semi-autobiographical script has been tinged with caricature in stage director Daldry's first feature. That said, the film's real heart – the relationship that Billy (Jamie Bell) strikes up with his dance teacher Mrs Wilkinson (Walters) – provides the conventional dramatic arc with a supple emotional springboard. Mrs Wilkinson is a dispirited soul who finds as much genuine pleasure in nurturing the talent and hope of this 11-year-old as he does in the discipline and support of her surrogacy. Walters is first rate when she checks her tendency to mannerism and harnesses her natural emotionalism. Bell is fine, too, but Daldry overuses the dance as a metaphor for escape and frustration, and choreographer Peter Darling's grandstanding ballet numbers sit a little uneasily, given the realist comedy pitch. WH

Billy Jack

(1971, US, 113 min)
d TC Frank [Tom Laughlin]. *p* Mary Rose Solti. *sc* Tom Laughlin, Delores Taylor. *ph* Fred J Koenekamp, John M Stephens. *ed* Larry Heath , Marion Rothman. *m* Mundell Lowe. cast Tom Laughlin, Delores Taylor, Clark Howat, Bert Freed, Julie Webb, Kenneth Tobey.
●One of the most significant American films of the '70s, not because it's good – it's terrible – but because of the way in which producer/writer/director/star Laughlin marketed it. After it flopped when first distributed through Warners, Laughlin sued the company for nonfulfilment of their contract – a step few independent producers have ever taken – and then independently distributed it across America, carefully balancing promotional expenditure in accordance with daily examinations of the film's local box-office returns. This marketing of the film, as though it were a rock record rather than a film, produced a bonanza for Laughlin and subsequently set the pattern for the intensive promotions of selective films to their 'natural' markets. The film itself is a down market youth pic with Laughlin as the half-breed Vietnam veteran who stands up for America's misunderstood youth and operates a sort of one-man Countryside Commission. PH

Billy Liar!

(1963, GB, 98 min, b/w)
d John Schlesinger. *p* Joseph Janni. *sc* Keith Waterhouse, Willis Hall. *ph* Denys Coop. *ed* Roger Cherrill. *ad* Ray Simm. *m* Richard Rodney Bennett. *cast* Tom Courtenay, Julie Christie, Wilfred Pickles, Mona Washbourne, Ethel Griffies, Finlay Currie, Rodney Bewes, Helen Fraser.
●Courtenay as the undertaker's clerk in a dull Northern town who escapes, Walter Mitty-like, into fantasy, scripted by Keith Waterhouse from his own novel (and the play he adapted from it with Willis Hall). Made three years later than *Saturday Night and Sunday Morning*, this is already in a different world. The back-to-backs are being torn down to make way for high-rise flats and supermarkets, gritty realism blossoms into flamboyant fantasy, and the feminine is now represented by kookie 'swinging '60s' Christie. A warm, witty, sensitive film: whatever happened later, something stirred in British cinema in the '60s. RMy

Billy Rose's Jumbo (aka Jumbo)

(1962, US, 125 min)
d Charles Walters. *p* Joe Pasternak, Martin Melcher. *sc* Sidney Sheldon. *ph* William H Daniels. *ed* Richard W Farrell. *ad* George W Davis, Preston Ames. *songs* Richard Rodgers, Lorenz Hart. *cast* Doris Day, Stephen Boyd, Jimmy Durante, Martha Raye, Dean Jagger, Joseph Waring.
●'Oh my God! There she is' screams Ignatius Reilly, the film buff who loves to fan his pet hates in John Kennedy Toole's *A Confederacy of Dunces*. She, of course, is Doris Day, here involved in the direst of circus plots ('What degenerate produced this abortion?' asks the indignant Reilly; answer, Hecht and McArthur). A former choreographer and a fine hand at musicals (*Good News, Easter Parade, Summer Stock*), Walters almost makes up for the three-ring vulgarities with some beautifully staged Rodgers and Hart numbers, although the best of them (the opening sequence) clearly reveals the hand of Busby Berkeley, credited as second unit director. TM

Billy's Hollywood Screen Kiss

(1998, US, 93 min)
d Tommy O'Haver. *p* David Moseley. *sc* Tommy O'Haver. *ph* Mark Mervis. *ed* Jeff Batancourt. *pd* Franco-Giacomo Carbone. *m* Alan Ari Lazar. *cast* Sean P Hayes, Brad Rowe, Richard Ganoung, Meredith Scott Lynn, Matthew Ashford, Christopher Bradley, Paul Bartel, Armando Valdes-Kennedy.
●First time writer/director O'Haver sets the tone by giving his presumed alter ego, aspiring photographer Billy (Hayes), a straight to camera speech. Half confessional, half mock lecture illustrated with Polaroids, it lays down Billy's sexual-political and cinematic aesthetics and the film's modest intentions and survivalist agenda. The plot is old fashioned boy loves boy. Dissatisfied with his less romantic lover Fernando (Valdes-Kennedy), Billy notices square-jawed Gabriel (Rowe) at an art gallery, seeing in him a potential model for his Hollywood Screen Kiss photo project and, perhaps, a lover. Gabriel quickly accepts the former role but dead bats the latter, and shows signs of venality by accepting an invitation to the yacht party of a mutual gay acquaintance, big shot artist Rex (Bartel). Will it be kiss or kiss-off for Billy? Despite being shot in 'Scope and saturated colour, this is closer to the 'hell, let's give it a go' spirit of '90s indie explorers like Kevin Smith. The dialogue may lack Smith's snap and wit, but the overall effect is warm and direct. WH

Billy the Kid

(1941, US, 95 min)
d David Miller. *p* Irving Asher. *sc* Gene Fowler. *ph* Leonard Smith, William V Skall. *ed* Robert J Kern. *ad* Cedric Gibbons. *m* David Snell. *cast* Robert Taylor, Brian Donlevy, Ian Hunter, Mary Howard, Gene Lockhart, Lon Chaney Jr.
●As a studio, MGM was never very happy on the range – indeed its main units rarely got out there, staying in front of process screens and depending on 2nd units. This is a typically lumbering brew, with Taylor as an unlikely Billy Bonney; but then the film has little to do with 'myth', let alone any of the 'reality' behind it. Of interest only as proof of how important it was for Ford to discover Monument Valley. CW

Billy the Kid and the Green Baize Vampire

(1985, GB, 93 min)
d Alan Clarke. *p* Simon Mallin. *sc* Trevor Preston. *ph* Clive Tickner. *ed* Stephen Singleton. *pd* Jamie Leonard. *m* George Fenton. *cast* Phil Daniels, Alun Armstrong, Bruce Payne, Louise Gold, Eve Ferret, Don Henderson.
●So utterly crazed in conception and so defiantly weird in execution that one can't help harbouring a sneaking *something* for it. A very simple story of the challenge and run-up to the final snooker showdown between the reigning champion (Armstrong) and the would-be contender (Daniels) is confined in a nondescript studio-built breeze-block nightmare interior of dark labyrinthine corridors, featureless rooms and odd pool parlours. A musical, it rattles along in its own funny way to the final grudge match filmed in great swooping takes on a louma crane. It has a kind of balls-out courage. One can certainly see why, but they don't make many films like this. CPea

Billy the Kid vs Dracula

(1965, US, 89 min)
d William Beaudine. *p* Carroll Case. *sc* Carl K Hittleman. *ph* Lothrop Worth. *ed* Roy Livingston. *ad* Paul Sylos, Harry Reif. *m* Raoul Kraushaar. *cast* Chuck Courtney, John Carradine, Melinda Plowman, Virginia Christine, Harry Carey Jr, Olive Carey, Walter Janovitz.
●Billy has made an honest Kid of himself around Betty Bentley's Bar-B Ranch until Carradine's Count Dracula enters the plot, posing as Betty's prodigal uncle. An unlikely combination of prairie chases and deftly-wielded crucifixes ensues in what *may* be intended as a campy spoof. CR

Billy Two Hats

(1973, GB, 99 min)
d Ted Kotcheff. *p* Norman Jewison, Patrick Palmer. *sc* Alan Sharp. *ph* Brian West. *ed* Thom Noble. *ad* Anthony Pratt. *m* John Scott. *cast* Gregory Peck, Desi Arnaz Jr, Jack Warden, Sian Barbara Allen, David Huddleston, John Pearce.
●Given that it was scripted by Alan Sharp, who wrote Penn's wonderful *Night Moves* and Aldrich's *Ulzana's Raid*, a disappointing attempt to merge serious statements about racial prejudice with a Western pursuit story. Peck is miscast as the ageing Scots outlaw who befriends a half-breed Indian (Arnaz), only to be hounded after a bank raid by Warden's ruthless, bigoted sheriff. Shot in Israel, it looks like Kotcheff was more interested in the scenery than in the characters. GA

Biloxi Blues

(1987, US, 107 min)
d Mike Nichols. *p* Ray Stark. *sc* Neil Simon. *ph* Bill Butler. *ed* Sam O'Steen. *pd* Paul Sylbert. *m* Georges Delerue. *cast* Matthew Broderick, Christopher Walken, Matt Mulhern, Corey Parker, Markus Flanagan, Casey Siemaszko, Michael Dolan, Penelope Ann Miller, Park Overall.
●As predictable as *Brighton Beach Memoirs*, Neil Simon's army reminiscences (adapted from his own play) interest – if at all – through the appropriateness of the playing. It's the ethnic mixture as usual at boot camp, from Jewish intellectual (Parker) to dumb, bullying Polack (Mulhern). Again our narrator is wry, sensitive would-be writer Broderick, so we hear the cues and cadences of Simon's Broadway plays. The new recruits have standard issue hilarious-style problems – route marching, press-ups, food, the local brothel – but most of all they have psychotic, cruel-to-be-kind drill sergeant Walken, who longs to be included in their banal bunkhouse fantasy quizzes, but not the sodomy in the showers, of course. Why Walken plays him so dulcet and limp is beyond comprehension. Suffice it to say it is suicidally against the grain. BC

Bim

(1974, Trinidad, 102 min)
d/p Hugh A Robertson. *sc* Raoul Pantin. *ph* Bruce Sparks. *ed* Paul L Evans. *m* Andre Tanker. *cast* Ralph J Maharaj, Anand Maharaj, Hamilton Parris, Wilbert Holder, Joseph Gilbert, Anna Seeratan.
●Set in colonial Trinidad of the '40s, and using the racial conflict between Indian sugar-cutters and black Trinidadians as the dramatic spring (centred on a *Harder They Come*-type fugitive outlaw protagonist), *Bim* continually throws up intriguing facets of the social texture. Best is the casual acceptance of violence (if not fear or pain) as a fact of life; worst is the treatment of the avuncular British godparents of independence, looking for all the world as if there were no past of colonial exploitation to answer for. RM

Bingo

(1991, US, 87 min)
d Matthew Robbins. *p* Thomas Baer. *sc* Jim Strain. *ph* John McPherson. *ed* Maryann Brandon. *m* Richard Gibbs. *cast* Cindy Williams, David Rasche, Robert J Steinmiller Jr, David French, Kurt Fuller, Joe Guzaldo, Glenn Shadix.
●Canine caper in which a mutt forsakes the circus for the company of a boy whose parents have warned him he can't have a dog. Unsuitable for grown-ups. TJ

Bingo Long Travelling All-Stars & Motor Kings, The

(1976, US, 111 min)
d John Badham. *p* Rob Cohen. *sc* Hal Barwood, Matthew Robbins. *ph* Bill Butler. *ed* David Rawlins. *pd* Lawrence G Paull. *m* William Goldstein. *cast* Billy Dee Williams, James Earl Jones, Richard Pryor, Rico Dawson, Jophery Brown, Sam 'Birmingham' Brison.
●After two disasters (*Lady Sings the Blues*, *Mahogany*), Motown's affair with the cinema produced this over-glossy but attractive period comedy (the setting is 1939, with music to match) about a group of black baseball players trying to make the big time. Excellent performances, but the best thing about it is the sharp, sceptically witty script by Hal Barwood and Matthew Robbins (of *The Sugarland Express*) which teases one or two old sores (notably the black man's recipe for success in a white world: be a clown). TM

Bird

(1988, US, 160 min)
d/p Clint Eastwood. *sc* Joel Oliansky. *ph* Jack N Green. *ed* Joel Cox. *pd* Edward C Carfagno. *cast* Forest Whitaker, Diane Venora, Michael Zelniker, Samuel E Wright, Keith David, Michael McGuire, James Handy, Diane Salinger.
●Eastwood's Bird is bravely the Bird of the jazz faithful, with few concessions. Most of the exaggerations and telescopings of place and time will offend only the discographical mentality. The treatment of narcotics, race, and racism is matter-of-fact, nor is the sense of period insisted upon as it was in The Cotton Club; above all, brave beyond the call of duty, the director trusts the music, tricky old bebop. Music properly dominates the biopic, explaining Chan's long-suffering love for Bird and Bird's whole outlook on the world. The way the narrative leaps back and forth in time parallels the neurotic speed of uptake in bebop itself. Whitaker looks as if he's really playing, indicates the protean nature of the genius, and grabs the part of a lifetime with both hands. Venora's Chan is a miracle. The progression from the Chan of the courtship days,, with her hip, sassy dancer's walk, to the set face and shoulders of the common-law wife, tells a touching story of betrayed dreams. At last American cinema has done black music proud. Unforgettable. BC

Birdcage, The

(1996, US, 119 min)
d/p Mike Nichols. *sc* Elaine May. *ph* Emmanuel Lubezki. *ed* Arthur Schmidt. *pd* Bo Welch. *m* Jonathan Tunick, Steven Goldstein. *cast* Robin Williams, Gene Hackman, Nathan Lane, Dianne Wiest, Dan Futterman, Calista Flockhart, Hank Azaria, Christine Baranski.
●Anodyne Hollywood remake of the 1978 gay farce *La Cage aux Folles*. Homely Armand (Williams) and drag queen Albert (Lane) are thrown into a flap by the imminent arrival of Armand's son Val (Futterman), his fiancée Barbara (Flockhart), and her parents, bigoted Senator Keeley (Hackman) and his well-meaning wife Louise (Wiest). While Albert sulks and minces, Armand removes the soft furnishings and objets d'art. But from the moment their lisping Hispanic houseman Agador (Azaria) trips in on high heels, the edifice of lies starts to totter. Williams' unusually restrained performance is his best for years, Hackman again reveals his underused gift for comedy, and the build-up to the hysterical finale is dotted with slick flourishes. Lane's squealing Albert, on the other hand, is a test. Director Nichols and scriptwriter Elaine May obviously see this as a satire on moralistic, right-wing Republicanism. In fact, it doesn't so much champion diversity as celebrate conformity, stressing the gay and straight characters' shared investment in the idea of 'family', however that mutable institution may now be defined. NF

Birdland (Chengshi Feixing)

(2000, Tai, 56 min)
d Huang Min-Chen [Huang Mingzheng]. *p* Chang Chih-Yuan, Kien Chen-Hui. *sc* Huang Min-Chen. *ph* Chin Ting-Chan. *ed* Lei Chen-Ching. *m* Lin Hui-Ling, Chen Shih-Hsing, Chang 43. *cast* An Yuan-Liang, Mo Tzu-Yi, Liu Yu-Yi, Chang Feng-Shu, Luo Yi-Hsuan, Chou Heng-Yin.
●Huang's follow-up to the exceptional *Too Young* is an ambitious short feature that tries to construct a bird's-eye panorama of contemporary Taiwan. An illegal immigrant from Mainland China reaches Taipei and is taken for A-Xiang, a cab driver who went missing while flying a light plane two years ago. He nervously assumes A-Xiang's identity and begins driving his taxi. His story is cross-cut with two others, one about a young motorcycle courier, the other about a betel-nut vendor who works as an extra in a crummy movie and then (without trying) picks up a surrogate family. And we eventually catch up with the real A-Xiang, who crashed his plane and began a new life with one of Taiwan's aboriginal tribes. Wittily observed and skilfully put together, but as a state-of-the-nation sketch of a troubled island it's too slight to add up. TR

Bird Man of Alcatraz

(1961, US, 148 min, b/w)
d John Frankenheimer. *p* Stuart Millar, Guy Trosper. *sc* Guy Trosper. *ph* Burnett Guffey. *ed* Edward Mann. *ad* Fernando Carrere. *m*

Elmer Bernstein. *cast* Burt Lancaster, Karl Malden, Thelma Ritter, Betty Field, Neville Brand, Edmond O'Brien, Hugh Marlowe.
●Striking performance by Lancaster in this factually based story of a double killer, sentenced to life in solitary, who gets hooked on birds after rescuing a fledgling sparrow, and gradually turns himself into a noted ornithologist. Despite some embarrassing sociological trimmings and an overwrought Ritter as mom fighting for her boy, a likeable film, particularly in its observation of the evolving relationship between the anti-social prisoner and the hostile warder (Brand, excellent) from whom he is forced to beg favours. TM

Bird Now

(1987, Bel/Fr, 90 min)
d Marc Huraux. *p* Hengameh Panaki. *sc* Marc Huraux, David Aronson. *ph* Richard Copans. *ed* Marc Huraux. *with* Chan Parker, Doris Parker, Bill Miles, Dizzy Gillespie, Walter Bishop Jr, Lester Bowie, Henry Threadgill.
●Huraux's semi-documentary purports to view the phenomenon of Charlie Parker through the cityscapes of New York, but often looks like footage in search of a peg. Wouldn't Kansas City have been more germane to the subject, since Bird was formed before he hit the Apple? The interviews with the bebop veterans are intermittently informative but largely over-familiar, though the real Chan and the rarer Doris are a find. Henry Threadgill comes over as a pretentious twit. A ragbag premise. BC

Bird on a Wire

(1990, US, 111 min)
d John Badham. *p* Rob Cohen. *sc* David Seltzer, Louis Venosta, Eric Lerner. *ph* Robert Primes. *ed* Frank Morriss, Dallas Puett. *ad* Philip Harrison. *m* Hans Zimmer. *cast* Mel Gibson, Goldie Hawn, David Carradine, Bill Duke, Stephen Tobolowsky, Joan Severance, Harry Caesar, Jeff Corey.
●Beware films which boast hybrid classifications like action-romantic comedy and credit three screenwriters (one per genre?). This formulaic offering teams Gibson and Hawn – a love match made in casting heaven – as ex-lovers, reunited after years apart, who find themselves on the run from vengeful criminals. Rick (Gibson), hiding under the Federal Witness Protection Program, changes identities and jobs like most people change socks; Marianne (Hawn) is a lawyer who, in taking up Rick's dangerous life-style, bears the permanent expression of a kid on a rollercoaster. Within the first half-hour, we've met the baddies (led by a taciturn Carradine), heard Rick and Marianne's teasing banter, and experienced the thrills of a shootout and car chase. As for what follows, this drearily repetitious film offers more of the same with variations in backdrop, all directed in perfunctory fashion by Badham. It does have a nice '60s soundtrack; shame about the rest. CM

Bird People in China, The (Chugoku no Chojin)

(1998, Jap, 118 min)
d Takashi Miike. *p* Toshiaki Nakazawa. *sc* Masa Nakamura. *ph* Hideo Yamamoto. *ed* Taiji Shimamura. *pd* Chihiro Masumoto. *m* Kojo Endo. *cast* Masahiro Motoko, Renji Ishibashi, Mako, Wang Lili.
●Very different from Miike's gangster movies but equally rooted in his obvious passion for all things Chinese, this 'adult fairytale' sends two ill-matched Japanese men on a mission to investigate a seam of jade in a remote area of Yunnan (China's deep south-west). Wada (Motoko) is a lily-livered company man; Ujiie (Ishibashi) is a bad mannered, foul mouthed and latently psychotic yakuza who muscles in on the trip because Wada's firm owes money to his gang. The perilous quest takes up the first half of the film, but the second is something else again: both men fall under the spell of the village and Wada grows fascinated by the (mysteriously blue-eyed) girl who claims to be teaching the local children to fly. Pitched somewhere between *King of the Children* and *Mad Max: Beyond Thunderdome*, the film's mix of adventure-comedy and magic realism confirms Miike as a genuinely innovative talent. TR

Birds, The (100)

(1963, US, 119 min)
d/p Alfred Hitchcock. *sc* Evan Hunter. *ph* Robert Burks. *ed* George Tomasini. *pd* Robert Boyle. *cast* Tippi Hedren, Rod Taylor, Suzanne Pleshette, Jessica Tandy, Ruth McDevitt, Veronica Cartwright, Ethel Griffies, Charles McGraw.
●'The Birds Is Coming' the advance posters twittered ungrammatically but with justifiable excitement. With death dropping blandly out of a clear sky – its menace magnified into apocalypse from the crop-dusting scene in *North by Northwest* – this is Hitchcock at his best. Full of subterranean hints as to the ways in which people cage each other, it's fierce and Freudian as well as great cinematic fun, with ample fodder for the amateur psychologist following up on Hitch's tortuous involvement with his leading ladies. TM

Birds and the Bees, The

(1956, US, 94 min)
d Norman Taurog. *p* Paul Jones. *sc* Sidney Sheldon, Preston Sturges. *ph* Daniel L Fapp. *ed* Archie Marshek. *ad* Hal Pereira. *m* Walter Scharf. *cast* George Gobel, Mitzi Gaynor, David Niven, Reginald Gardiner, Harry Bellaver, Fred Clark.
●Flat remake of *The Lady Eve* in which the humour relies more heavily on crude slapstick. Gaynor is no Barbara Stanwyck, and Gobel (in the Henry Fonda part) was here making what was to be the start of a very short-lived film career. DMcG

Bird's Singing, The (Para Recibir el Canto de los Pájaros)

(1995, Bol, 97 min)
d Jorge Sanjines. *p* Beatriz Palacios. *sc* Jorge Sanjines. *ph* Raúl Rodriguez. *ed* Pedro Chaskel, Jorge Sanjines. *m* Cergio Prudencio. *cast* Guido Arce, Marcelo Guzman, Reynaldo Yujra, Lineth Herbas, Geraldine Chaplin.
●A heavy-handed allegory by a veteran Bolivian film-maker about the racism endemic in his country and the more universal inability to learn from history. It opens with masked conquistadors (the harquebus angels) lined against the Andean *altiplano* skyline, as a mainly *mestizo* film crew track up the hill like Aguirre's invading army in Herzog's *Wrath of God*. Thus begins a series of broad parallels, culminating in a siege, whereby the crew, assailed by the Indian community (who have refused to be in their historical movie), almost resort to the use of the ancient harquebuses in their possession. The song of the title refers to the birds of the Indians' annual music festival: the crew shoot them for sport. Beautiful scenery. WH

Bird with the Crystal Plumage, The

see L'Uccello Dalle Piume de Cristallo

Birdy

(1984, US, 120 min)
d Alan Parker. *p* Alan Marshall. *sc* Sandy Kroopf, Jack Behr. *ph* Michael Seresin. *ed* Gerry Hambling. *pd* Geoffrey Kirkland. *m* Peter Gabriel. *cast* Matthew Modine, Nicolas Cage, John Harkins, Sandy Baron, Karen Young, Bruno Kirby.
●A trifle self-indulgent – well, it is directed by Alan Parker – but never boring, this tells of the strange, trusting friendship between Birdy (Modine), an introverted teenager whose ideal companion is one of his pet birds, and his protective mate Al (Cage). Their relationship is explored both through flashback, larking about at school and fighting as Vietnam conscripts, and in the present: interned in an army mental hospital, the lonely Birdy appears to believe that he has actually turned into one of his own feathered pets. A military doctor has sent for Al in the hope that he can bring his pal back to his senses. But is he mad? Or can genuine freedom exist only in someone's head? You come away convinced that all that RD Laing stuff about the integrity of mad people ought not to be consigned to the dustbin of the '60s after all. CS

Birth, The

see Piravi

Birthday Party, The

(1968, GB, 124 min)
d William Friedkin. *p* Max J Rosenberg, Milton Subotsky. *sc* Harold Pinter. *ph* Denys Coop. *ed* Antony Gibbs. *pd* Edward Marshall. *cast* Robert Shaw, Patrick Magee, Dandy Nichols, Sydney Tafler, Moultrie Kelsall, Helen Fraser.
●Film version of Pinter's first full-length play, a rather unsubtle and flashy piece of seaside gothic in which a scruffy, stay-at-home boarding-house lodger is terrorised by two sinister visitors: rather clever inversions of the stereotypic stage Jew and Irishman. Seems long and fussy, partly the fault of both play and director, but some marvellous performances (Nichols creating her Silly Moo character, Tafler superb as the anecdotal Goldberg) make it worth seeing. SG

Birth of a Butterfly (Tavalod-e-yek Parvaneh)

(1998, Iran, 110 min)
d Mojtaba Raei. *p* Seyed Said Seyedzadeh. *sc* Saeid Shapouri. *ph* Mohammad Davoudi. *ed* Hassan Hassandost. *m* Kambiz Roshan-Ravan. *cast* Rahim Jahani, Yashar Mahmoudi, Hamed Manafizadeh, Rakhshandeh Ziraz, Mahmud Nazar Alian, Mohammad M Faqih, Zahra Farhadi.
●Three stories encapsulate different aspects of traditional moral instruction. The first sees a stern father banishing his young son from the household to spare him the sight of his dying mother; the second follows the good deeds of a devout disabled boy left at home when his family visit a religious shrine; the third shows the dilemma in which a teacher finds himself when local villagers are eager to believe he possesses spiritual powers. The didactic lessons will be more obvious to Iranian audiences than to Western eyes. That said, the rugged landscapes are striking and there is a captivating reverence in the way the director films a bowl of apples, for instance, or a rippling pool. TJ

Birth of a Nation, The

(1915, US, 13,058 ft. b/w)
d DW Griffith. *p* DW Griffith, Harry E Aitken. *sc* DW Griffith, Frank E Woods. *ph* GW Bitzer. *ed* James Smith. *m* Joseph Carl Breil. *cast* Lillian Gish, Mae Marsh, Henry Walthall, Miriam Cooper, Mary Alden, Ralph Lewis, Raoul Walsh.
●Based on the Rev. Thomas Dixon Jr's deliriously racist *The Clansman*, a melodramatic novel about the American Civil War and its aftermath, Griffith's film is remarkable for its technical innovations and for the truly epic feel created by the carefully orchestrated, swirling masses of figures in the battle scenes. It's also remarkable for having had no written scenario, costumes that were made by Lillian Gish's mother, battle scenes that were shot in a day, and a cost that meant Griffith had nothing left but the shirt on his back. The biggest challenge the film provided for its audiences is perhaps to decide when 'ground-breaking, dedicated, seminal cinematic art' must be reviled as politically reprehensible. The film's explicit glorification of the Ku Klux Klan has never tempered with time. MSu

Birth of a Nation, The (Die Geburt der Nation)

(1973, WGer, 70 min, b/w & col)
d/p/sc/ph/ed/m/narrator Klaus Wyborny. *cast* Christoph Hemmerling, Peter Flak, Nick Busch, Hannes Hatje, Angelika Düsing.
●Authentically 'New' German Cinema, and, simultaneously, an archaeology of narrative film itself, Wyborny's avant-garde landmark defines cinema as a 'nation' that has perversely acquired rulers, laws and hierarchies before it has even been physically mapped out. At first appearing to spin an elementary yarn of social organisation (the predictably fraught establishment of a rudimentary commune in the Moroccan desert of 1911) in the 'authoritative' film language of DW Griffith, Wyborny proceeds to break down that language to its constituent elements and produce fragmentary hints of alternatives. Structural film-making of a rare wit and accessibility results, with flashes of appropriate absurdity (like the sudden intrusion of Randy Newman's 'Lonely at the Top') highlighting the redundancy of closed systems, whether social or cinematic. PT

Birth of the Blues

(1941, US, 86 min, b/w)
d Victor Schertzinger. *p* Buddy DeSylva. *sc* Harry Tugend, Walter DeLeon. *ph* William C Mellor. *ed* Paul Weatherwax. *ad* Hans Dreier, Ernst Fegté. *songs* Johnny Mercer, WC Handy, others. *cast* Bing Crosby, Mary Martin, Brian Donlevy, Carolyn Lee, Eddie 'Rochester' Anderson, Jack Teagarden.
● White man invents the blues! Not even that, actually: White man sings Tin Pan Alley medley, as Bing Crosby's quintet takes the New Orleans jazz scene by storm, aided by Mary Martin and red-hot trumpet man Brian Donlevy. Real jazz presence comes in the form of Jack Teagarden and his trombone, and for anyone expecting at least some black presence in the birth of the blues, Eddie 'Rochester' Anderson plays Bing's loyal factotum. DO

Bis ans Ende der Welt

see Until the End of the World

Bisexual (Les Onze Mille Vierges)

(1975, Fr/It, 98 min)
d Eric Lipmann. *p* Bernard Lapeyre, Adolphe Viezzi. *sc* Eric Lipmann, Bernard Lapeyre. *ph* Bernard Joliot. *ed* Renée Lichtig. *ad* Claude Pignot. *m* Michel Colombier. *cast* Yves-Marie Maurin, Florence Cayrol, Nathalie Zeiger, Jenny Arasse, Marion Game, Bernadette Robert.
● This better-than-average sex film is based on Guillaume Apollinaire's erotic novel of the same title. Narrative development is largely jettisoned in favour of films-within films, Freudian slips, and Surrealist elements of nightmare. The direction, though, remains sadly unimaginative. CPe

Bishop's Story, The

(1993, Ire, 82 min, b/w)
d/sc Bob Quinn. *ph* Seamus Deasy. *ed* Martin Duffy. *ad* Tom Conroy. *m* Roger Doyle. *cast* Donal McCann, Maggie Fegan, Ray McBride, Paedar Lamb, Tomás O Flaitheara, Sean O Coisdealbha.
● In this deliberate b/w homage to the silent era, a bishop (McCann) relates to a fellow priest (McBride) at a Roman Catholic retreat the story of how as a young man in a coastal village in the West of Ireland he fell in love with a girl (Fegan). The flashbacks which make up the body of the film are printed in sepia and shot in a style reminiscent of Flaherty and Sjöström. It's a nostalgic, memorable piece, from the veteran Bob Quinn, not so much for the resigned mood of the storyteller, as for the deeply moving imagery – a collie running up a hill; the white-clothed ankle of a girl; the dancing torches of a midnight search party; the expressive, weather-beaten faces of the villagers. The dialogue is in Gaelic, post-synched and quiet, as if heard from down the tunnel of memory. WH

Bishop's Wife, The

(1947, US, 108 min, b/w)
d Henry Koster. *p* Samuel Goldwyn. *sc* Robert E Sherwood, Leonardo Bercovici. *ph* Gregg Toland. *ed* Monica Collingwood. *ad* George Jenkins. *m* Hugo Friedhofer. *cast* Cary Grant, Loretta Young, David Niven, Monty Woolley, Gladys Cooper, Elsa Lanchester, James Gleason, Sam Haden.
● Pleasant enough Goldwyn-produced whimsy, cashing in on the success of '40s angelic fantasies such as *Here Comes Mr Jordan* and *It's a Wonderful Life*. Angel Grant responds to a bishop's plea for help after his devotion to his plans for a new cathedral has alienated him from family and parishioners. Cary's charm works as successfully upon audiences as it does upon the film's characters, and his relaxed wit plus Loretta Young's delicate loveliness makes for a frothily touching comedy. GA

Bitch, The

(1979, GB, 94 min)
d Gerry O'Hara. *p* John Quested. *sc* Gerry O'Hara. *ph* Denis Lewiston. *ed* Eddy Joseph. *ad* Malcolm Middleton. *m* Biddu. *cast* Joan Collins, Michael Coby, Kenneth Haigh, Ian Hendry, Carolyn Seymour, Mark Burns.
● Dreadful sequel to *The Stud* from the Collins sisters, cynically predicated on the supposed desire of the depressed masses to glimpse the Mayfair disco-culture high-life they otherwise can't afford. JS

Bite the Bullet

(1975, US, 131 min)
d/p/sc Richard Brooks. *ph* Harry Stradling Jr. *ed* George Granville. *ad* Robert Boyle. *m* Alex North. *cast* Gene Hackman, Candice Bergen, James Coburn, Ben Johnson, Ian Bannen, Jan-Michael Vincent, Paul Stewart.
● A straining think-piece on Western/American morality and values, Brooks' would-be epic charts a 700-mile horse race as a simplistic graph of courage, caring and callousness, with Hackman and Coburn emerging as *Professional*-like pillars of integrity from a meltingly macho proving ground. Any random thought ever committed to paper about the intrinsic 'messages' of the Western genre here turns up as a line of speechifying dialogue: the result is a folly stultified by its own seriousness. PT

Bit of Scarlet, A

(1996, GB, 75 min)
d Andrea Weiss. *p* Rebecca Dobs. *sc* Andrea Weiss, Stuart Marshall. *ed* Andrea Weiss. *m* John Eacott. *narrator* Ian McKellen.
● This documentary, a companion piece to *The Celluloid Closet*, examines gay and lesbian cinematic representation (or non-representation) in mainstream British cinema and TV. Basically, it's a clipfest, with Andrea Weiss and Stuart Marshall's tart narration spoken by Ian McKellen, which trawls the sound era from the Rathbone/Bruce pairing in *The Hound of the Baskervilles* (1939), through the recidivist belles of St Trinian's, the *Carry On* movies, Dirk Bogarde in *Victim* and Malcolm McDowell in *If....*, to Terence Davies and the present. Serious but light, the film presents a provocative, more or less orthodox gay reading, broken down into chapters and using mock 'rules' of behaviour to ironic effect. The participation of various archives (including Britain's NFTVA) is a plus: the shot, for instance, of Kathleen Byron's glare at fellow nun Deborah Kerr in Black Narcissus wouldn't seem half so powerful or erotic if it weren't shown in a plush Technicolor print. WH

Bits and Pieces (Il cielo è sempre più blu)

(1996, It, 110 min)
d Antonello Grimaldi. *p* Domenico Procacci, Maurizio Totti. *sc* Daniele Cesarano, Paolo Marchesini. *ph* Alessandro Pesci. *ed* Angelo Nicolini. *ad* Giada Calabria. *m* Enzo Favata, Jana Project. *cast* Enrico Lo Verso, Asia Argento, Dario Argento, Gabriele Salvatores, Monica Bellucci, Daniele Lucchetti. Luca Barbareschi, Roberto Citran.
● This kaleidoscopic portrait of Rome is peppered with small, intriguing pleasures and leaves a strangely lasting impression. Whether it adds up to an essay on the mind's ability to comprehend something so vast as a city (or the world for the matter) is a moot point. The myriad separate (if slowly relating) scenes offer much droll, mysterious and uniquely Roman amusement. It's one of those idiosyncratic movies that turn up once in a while, usually by people like Otar Iosseliani or Nanni Moretti. Among the throng, Romans and film buffs will spot any number of cameos (Dario Argento, Gabriele Salvatores). WH

Bitter Cane

(1983, US, 74 min)
d Jacques Arcelin. *m* Manno Charlemagne, Nicol Levy, Georges 'Moumousse' Wilson, Anaika, Rulx Rosefort. *narrator* Jean-Claude Martineau.
● Haiti was first colonised by the French, who turned the island into a giant coffee plantation. In 1804, it witnessed the world's first successful slave revolution. The US Marines arrived in 1915, introduced American capital investment, shifted the economy towards producing crops and products for export, and set up the first in a series of puppet dictators to protect their interests. And, aside from a brief hiccough under Papa Doc Duvalier, that's the way it's been ever since. This history is outlined eloquently and succinctly in Arcelin's documentary, shot clandestinely in Haiti in collaboration with the Mouvement Haitien de Libération. The film avoids all the pitfalls of agitprop rhetoric; its only (forgivable) weakness is that it gets emotionally carried away by some of its ghastly human testimonies. TR

Bitteren Tränen der Petra von Kant, Die

see Bitter Tears of Petra von Kant, The

Bitter Harvest

(1963, GB, 96 min)
d Peter Graham Scott. *p* Albert Fennell. sc Ted Willis. *ph* Ernest Steward. *ed* Russell Lloyd. *ad* Alex Vetchinsky. *m* Laurie Johnson. *cast* Janet Munro, John Stride, Anne Cunningham, Alan Badel, Vanda Godsell, Norman Bird, Terence Alexander, Thora Hird.
● A tepid sex drama, one of a number of tedious and supposedly 'realistic' British films that attempted to cash in on the success of *Saturday Night and Sunday Morning*, etc, in the early '60s. Janet Munro is the Welsh village girl who becomes caught up in the vice-ridden world of the big city. DP

Bitter Moon (Lunes de fiel)

(1992, Fr/GB, 139 min)
d/p Roman Polanski. *sc* Roman Polanski, Gérard Brach, John Brownjohn. *ph* Tonino Delli Colli. *ed* Hervé de Luze. *pd* Willy Holt, Gérard Viard. *m* Vangelis. *cast* Hugh Grant, Kristin Scott-Thomas, Emmanuelle Seigner, Peter Coyote, Victor Bannerjee, Sophie Patel, Stockard Channing, Patrick Albenque.
● Like Polanski's debut feature *Knife in the Water*, this is set partly on a boat, and charts the shifts in power between characters performing complex sexual/emotional manoeuvres. Nigel (Grant) and Fiona (Scott-Thomas), a wealthy English couple on a second honeymoon, meet Oscar (Coyote) and Mimi (Seigner) on a Mediterranean cruise. The wheelchair-bound Oscar is determined to regale Nigel with a lurid tale of his awful love for Mimi, and exploits her charms to ensure that Nigel hears the story to its bitter end. Characteristically, Polanski treats this slightly protracted tale of erotic obsession partly as deeply ironic black comedy. But there's also real seriousness in the way the film condenses a whole range of feelings into one crazed, cruel relationship and its effect on another couple, so that it becomes both a grotesque portrait of love's variety and a queasy commentary on the perverse pleasures we derive from the suffering of others. Rich and darkly disturbing, it's also wickedly entertaining. GA

Bitter Rice (Riso Amaro)

(1948, It,108 min, b/w)
d Giuseppe De Santis. *p* Dino De Laurentiis. *sc* Corrado Alvaro, Giuseppe De Santis, Carlo Lizzani, Carlo Musso, Ivo Perilli, Gianni Puccini. *ph* Otello Martelli. *ed* Gabriele Barriale. *ad* Carlo Egidi. *m* Goffredo Petrassi. *cast* Silvana Mangano, Vittorio Gassman, Raf Vallone, Doris Dowling, Lia Corelli, Checco Rissone.
● Intended as a hard-hitting social critique of the exploitation of rice-field workers in the Po Valley, this was much criticised at the time for compromising its neo-realism by sugaring the bleak message with some souped-up sex and violence. Actually it all seems very mild now, but De Santis' bold camera style and superb handling of crowd movement are well worth a look. TM

Bitter Sweet

(1940, US, 92 min)
d WS Van Dyke. *p* Victor Saville. *sc* Lesser Samuels. *ph* Oliver T Marsh, Allen Davey. *ed* Harold F Kress. *ad* Cedric Gibbons, John S Detlie. *m* Noël Coward. *cast* Jeanette MacDonald, Nelson Eddy, George Sanders, Felix Bressart, Lynne Carver, Ian Hunter, Fay Holden, Sig Ruman.
● Second screen version of the Noël Coward operetta (adapted by Lesser Samuels) about young love in turn-of-the-century Vienna. MacDonald pips, squeaks and chirps in her melodious fashion as the red-cheeked English rose who elopes to Austria. Eddy is her music teacher and sweetheart. Shot in best MGM Technicolor, the film looks a treat, but there's no disguising the flimsy, winsome storyline. GM

Bitter Tea of General Yen, The

(1933, US, 89 mins, b/w)
d/p Frank Capra. *sc* Edward Paramore. *ph* Joseph Walker. *ed* Edward Curtiss. *m* W

Franke Harling. *cast* Barbara Stanwyck, Nils Asther, Gavin Gordon, Toshia Mori, Richard Loo, Walter Connolly.

● Light years away from the homespun, small-town Capracorn for which the director is best known, this exotic, erotic melodrama is by far his finest achievement. Stanwyck, subtly radiant, is the American missionary in Shanghai who is abducted by a highly sophisticated Chinese warlord (Asther); like the film itself, she is both fascinated and repelled by the prospect of miscegenation. Where Capra's other films are largely stolid, prosaic and talky, this is sensuous and profoundly cinematic, perhaps most notably in a sequence in which Stanwyck dreams of her seduction by a forceful Asther. Odd, but oddly moving. GA

Bitter Tears of Petra von Kant, The (Die Bitteren Tränen der Petra von Kant)

(1972, WGer, 124 min)
d/p/sc Rainer Werner Fassbinder. *ph* Michael Ballhaus. *ed* Thea Eymèsz. *pd* Rainer Werner Fassbinder. *cast* Margit Carstensen, Hanna Schygulla, Irm Hermann, Katrin Schaake, Eva Mattes, Gisela Fackeldey.

● If *Fear Eats the Soul* used Emmi and Ali's improbable relationship as a key to deep-set patterns of social prejudice and fear, then the slightly earlier *Bitter Tears* sketches the currents of dominance and submission that lie beneath the surface of any human relationship. This time, the focus is gay rather than straight: fashion designer Petra (once widowed, once divorced) develops a fiercely possessive crush on her model Karin, and, as soon as the one-sided affair reaches its necessary end, starts wallowing in theatrical self-pity. Coldly described, the set and costume design and the hothouse atmosphere represent so much high-camp gloss; but once again this careful stylisation enables Fassbinder to balance between parody of an emotional stance and intense commitment to it. He films in long, elegant takes, completely at the service of his all-female cast, who are uniformly sensational. TR

Bitter Victory (Amère Victoire)

(1957, Fr, 100 min, b/w)
d Nicholas Ray. *p* Paul Graetz. *sc* René Hardy, Nicholas Ray, Gavin Lambert. *ph* Michel Kelber. *ed* Léonide Azar. *ad* Jean d'Eaubonne. *m* Maurice Le Roux. *cast* Richard Burton, Curd Jürgens, Ruth Roman, Raymond Pellegrin, Nigel Green, Christopher Lee, Anthony Bushell.

● The title tells all. Though Jürgens and Burton lead a successful World War II assault on Rommel's desert headquarters (for which Jürgens is undeservedly decorated), in the course of the raid both men are broken. Jürgens falls prey to indecision and cowardice brought on by his envy of the seeming ease with which Burton handles both the military situation and his personal affairs (including a past liaison with Jürgens' wife), while Burton's romantic veneer is shattered by the conflicting emotions he discovers within himself. The resulting personal anguish, summed up in Burton's blank delivery of the line 'I kill the living and save the dead', seeps into the very grain of Ray's magisterial black-and-white 'Scope set-ups. PH.

Bix: 'Ain't None of Them Play Like Him Yet'

(1981, Can, 116 min, b/w & col)
d/p/ed Brigitte Berman. *with* Mary Louise Shoemaker, Hoagy Carmichael, Bill Challis, Esten Spurrier, Artie Shaw, Louis Armstrong. *narrator* Richard Basehart.

● A documentary in which the legendary jazz cornettist Bix Beiderbecke, who blew his one chance to get on film (*The King of Jazz*) through his ultimately fatal alcoholism, is brought to life with interviews and well-chosen records though he died over fifty years ago. Overlong towards the end but beautiful to look at, the pastel tones on the new material blending with black-and-white archive still and movie footage, which instead of distancing the music even further places it vivdly in its period. BP

Bizarre, Bizarre

see Drôle de Drame

Black and Silver

(1981, GB, 75 min, b/w & col)
d/sc William Raban, Marilyn Raban. *ph* William Raban. *ed* William Raban, Marilyn Raban. *m* Ben Mason. *cast* Marilyn Raban, Jessica Bennett, Lily Dragalla, Juliette Tully, Roger Tully.

● This radical reworking of an Oscar Wilde tale (*The Birthday of the Infanta*) based on Velasquez' painting 'Las Meninas', marked the Rabans' first venture into 'experimental narrative' territory. A film of often glacial beauty and formal dexterity, it is also, in its continually looping themes of duplicity, self-deception and loss, a subtle and intuitive essay on the nature of film itself. One of the more successful films from the avant-garde, and for its imagery alone well worth seeing. MO'P

Black and White

(1999, US, 99 min)
d James Toback. *p* Michael Mailer, Daniel Bigel, Ron Rotholz. *sc* James Toback. *ph* David Ferrara. *ed* Myron Kerstein. *pd* Anne Ross. *m* American Cream Team, Oli 'Power' Grant. *cast* Robert Downey Jr, Stacy Edwards, Gaby Hoffmann, Jared Leto, Joe Pantoliano, Bijou Phillips, Power, Claudia Schiffer, William Lee Scott, Brooke Shields, Ben Stiller, James Toback.

● Autumn in Central Park: two girls and a guy are making the beast with three backs. They split: uptown, white teen Charlie (Phillips) takes her seat for supper (quail) and a spat with her patrician family; downtown, black teen Rich (Wu-Tang Clan's Power) comes up against the prejudice of a recording studio manager (Toback) who equates Rich's HipHop ambitions with the prospect of gang warfare landing on his lobby. In Rich's wake trail a host of friends, false friends, hangers-on and schemers, seeking sex, glamour and perhaps some sort of liberation, while stirring up betrayal and a murder. It looks like a mess – if one stuffed with incident, issues and intrigue. Hugely improvised, the film bounces between a host of characters, settings, and means and modes of expression; it couches its questions of cross-cultural sharing and borrowing in dialogue, rapped lyrics on the soundtrack, even on a classroom blackboard, as well as in its own magpie compositional style. The tone is intriguing: where does observation (or ogling) end and suggestion or satire begin? Should a film about the vagaries of identity and ethics be so loose itself? At least the cast get a chance to flex themselves: Stiller and Pantoliano especially are great value, and Downey is just uproarious. NB

Black and White in Color (La Victoire en Chantant)

(1976, Fr/Switz/Ivory Coast, 100 min)
d Jean-Jacques Annaud. *p* Arthur Cohn, Jacques Perrin, Giorgio Silvagni. *sc* Georges Conchon, Jean-Jacques Annaud. *ph* Claude Agostini, Eduardo Serra, Nanamoudou Magassouda. *ed* Françoise Bonnot. *ad* Max Douy. *m* Pierre Bachelet, Mat Camison. *cast* Jean Carmet, Jacques Dufilho, Catherine Rouvel, Jacques Spiesser,Dora Doll, Maurice Barrier.

● It would be difficult to imagine how this supposedly liberal satire on colonialism and racism could be more offensive. Set in the Ivory Coast French colony of 1915, it concentrates on the disruption caused to a sleepy French community by the belated news of the outbreak of World War I. Pricking the pretensions of characters stirred by patriotism as they mobilise the natives into battle against the neighbouring German community, writer/director Annaud unfortunately also manages to reinforce some of the worst racist and sexist stereotypes (funny, gullible niggers; giggly, busty women), and couch the whole thing in a broad, farcical style of comic acting familiar from the French cinema of the '30s. RM

Black Angel

(1946, US, 80 min, b/w)
d Roy William Neill. *p* Roy William Neill, Tom McKnight. *sc* Roy Chanslor. *ph* Paul Ivano. *ed* Saul A Goodkind. *ad* Jack Otterson. *m* Frank Skinner. *cast* Dan Duryea, June Vincent, Peter Lorre, Broderick Crawford, Wallace Ford, Constance Dowling.

● Not exactly a pristine Cornell Woolrich adaptation, since the brooding subjectivism (so lovingly preserved in a real poverty row quickie like *Fear in the Night*) has been partly pruned to leave a moody thriller along the lines of *Phantom Lady*, beautifully crafted with the sort of unpretentious skill Neill brought to the Rathbone-Bruce Sherlock Holmes series. The authentic tang of *noir* is lent by Duryea, superb in (for once) a sympathetic role as the tormented musician with the faithless wife who finds the solution to the mystery of her murder surfacing through the alcoholic haze of his memory. Lovely supporting cast too. TM.

Blackbeard's Ghost

(1967, US, 107 min)
d Robert Stevenson. *p* Bill Walsh. *sc* Bill Walsh, Don DaGradi. *ph* Edward Colman. *ed* Robert Stafford. *ad* Carroll Clark, John B Mansbridge. *m* Robert F Brunner. *cast* Peter Ustinov, Dean Jones, Suzanne Pleshette, Elsa Lanchester, Joby Baker, Michael Conrad.

● A typically larky Disney film, heavily over-directed and under-written, in which the ghost of a fearsome pirate is summoned from limbo (where he is condemned to wander until he manages to do one good deed). His task is to save a bevy of poor old ladies – his proud descendants, collectively known as the Daughters of Blackbeard, and running an inn dedicated to his memory – from eviction by developers who have a gambling-joint in mind. Ustinov has his moments as the ghostly pirate, but seems to have got bogged down in an imitation of Peter Cook's inimitably peculiar Cockney whine – which Peter Cook does so much better. TM

Blackbeard the Pirate

(1952, US, 99 min)
d Raoul Walsh. *p* Edmund Grainger. *sc* Alan LeMay. *ph* William Snyder. *ed* Ralph Dawson. *ad* Albert S D'Agostino. *m* Victor Young. *cast* Robert Newton, Linda Darnell, Keith Andes, William Bendix, Torin Thatcher, Richard Egan, Alan Mowbray.

● Despite the combination of Walsh, Darnell and Bendix, a mediocre swashbuckler with Sir Henry Morgan (Thatcher) swishing about on the high seas in pursuit of the deadly Blackbeard (Newton, overdoing the ham, as usual). At best, colourful; at worst, drearily predictable. GA

Black Beauty

(1994, GB/US, 88 min)
d Caroline Thompson. *p* Peter MacGregor-Scott, Robert Shapiro. *sc* Caroline Thompson. *ph* Alex Thomson. *ed* Claire Simpson. *pd* John Box. *m* Danny Elfman. *cast* Sean Bean, David Thewlis, Jim Carter, Peter Davison, Andrew Knott, Alun Armstrong, John McEnery, Eleanor Bron, Peter Cook.

● This version slow-burns with an old-fashioned sense of injustice. The story is told from Black Beauty's point of view (voice, Alan Cumming), and it's a Dickensian catalogue of conscience-pricking social and class conditions. Directing her first feature, screenwriter Caroline Thompson adopts a level-headed tone, avoiding the twin traps of sentimentality and sermonising. The film is shot with a good eye for scenery and composition, and Thompson shows total commitment to the story. But what can a horse do to engage the emotions? On the whole, it's just an undramatic working life, enlivened somewhat by David Thewlis' performance as a cabman, the most fully realised character among a gallery of quick-sketch ciphers. WH

Black Belt Jones

(1973, US, 87 min)
d Robert Clouse. *p* Fred Weintraub, Paul Heller. *sc* Oscar Williams. *ph* Kent Wakeford. *ed* Michael Kahn. *m* Luchi De Jesus. *cast* Jim Kelly, Gloria Hendry, Malik Carter, Scatman Crothers, Alan Weeks, Eric Laneuville.

● The crew from *Enter the Dragon* strike again with the irritating tendency to cram in every feasible plot variation, confusing good with more and bigger. Where the film diverges from its Chinese forebears is in making its hero not just one of the karate students whose school is threatened – here by a collusion between civic developers and Mafia money men – but a rich outsider in the employ of the US government, thus losing whatever subversive qualities the Chinese originals contain. VG.

Black Bird, The

(1975, US, 98 min)
d David Giler. *p* Michael Levee, Lou Lombardo. *sc* David Giler. *ph* Philip H Lathrop. *ed* Lou Lombardo. *pd* Harry Horner. *m* Jerry Fielding. *cast* George Segal, Stéphane Audran, Lionel Stander, Lee Patrick, Elisha Cook, Signe Hasso, John Abbott.

●Giler's first film, a parody-sequel to John Huston's *The Maltese Falcon*, has Segal as Bogie's inept son, Sam Spade Jr, bumbling about present-day San Francisco, harried by father's blowsy secretary (Lee Patrick, from the original) and pursued by Elisha Cook, three murderous Hawaiians, and a crazy dwarf. Giler's earnest screenplay scrupulously updates the Hammett novel: Audran plays the daughter of the late General Kemidov who, you may remember, was the last legitimate owner of the priceless black bird. However, despite a strong cast which pulls together several sharply written episodes, as a whole the movie fails to top the wry tone of Huston's classic or to produce a surprise denouement equal to the impact of Mary Astor's treachery. JPy

Blackboard Jungle

(1955, US, 101 min, b/w)
d Richard Brooks. *p* Pandro S Berman. *sc* Richard Brooks. *ph* Russell Harlan. *ed* Ferris Webster. *ad* Cedric Gibbons, Randall Duell. *cast* Glenn Ford, Anne Francis, Vic Morrow, Louis Calhern, Sidney Poitier, Richard Kiley, Maggie Hayes.

●This was the movie which featured 'Rock Around the Clock' over the credits and had Teds ripping up the seats on its first release in Britain. But this notoriety gives a false impression of the film. It's based on Evan Hunter's moralistic best-seller about a young New York teacher at a tough school, and is very worthy in its intentions. Highlights include Vic Morrow as a confused knife-wielding delinquent, but the studied pseudo-documentary atmosphere never quite convinces.

Blackboard Massacre

see Massacre at Central High

Blackboards (Takhté Siah)

(2000, Iran/It, 85 min)
d Samira Makhmalbaf. *p* Mohsen Makhmalbaf. *sc* Mohsen Makhmalbaf, Samira Makhmalbaf. *ph* Ebrahim Ghafori. *ed* Mohsen Makhmalbaf. *m* Mohamed Reza Darvishi. *cast* Saïd Mohamadi, Bahman Ghobadi, Behnaz Jafari, Rafat Moradi.

●Just as assured as *The Apple*, and considerably more ambitious, 20-year-old Makhmalbaf's second feature – co-written and edited by her father Mohsen – is an enigmatic, metaphorical fable set in Iranian Kurdistan, hard by the Iraqi border. Two teachers break away from their nomadic group in search of pupils; one joins up with kids smuggling contraband across the mountains, the other with a bunch of elderly exiles trying to return to their homeland. Neither group is interested in education, especially as they're too busy watching out for unseen border patrols. There are astonishing images here, and some extraordinarily tense, suggestive set-pieces, particularly in the bleak final half-hour; but the occasionally repetitive narrative, the often oblique script, and the overall austerity make it less immediately accessible than its predecessor. Memorably poetic film-making, all the same. GA

Black Book, The

see Reign of Terror

Black Bounty Killer, The

see Boss Nigger

Black Bunch, The (aka Jungle Sex)

(1972, US, 67 min)
d Henning Schellerup. *p* Daniel B Cady. *sc* Chester H Carlfi. *ph* Ward Williams. *ed* HA Marshall. *ad* Earl Marshall. *m* Jack Millman. *cast* Gladys Bunker, Betty Barton, Yvonne, Marshall Breedson, Evan Renshaw, Kurt Horst.

●Four African village women, sole survivors of a mercenary massacre, swear vengeance. They join an unsavoury party of bounty hunters on the trail of a millionaire's kidnapped son. The women seduce the bounty hunters but fail to obtain their weapons. The mercenaries harry the party; a pouch of diamonds is introduced into the script; and almost everybody ends up dead. Shoddy and reprehensible. JPy

Black Caesar (aka The Godfather of Harlem)

(1973, US, 96 min)
d/p/sc Larry Cohen. *ph* Fenton Hamilton. *ed* George Folsey Jr. *pd* Larry Lurin. *m* James Brown. *cast* Fred Williamson, D'Urville Martin, Gloria Hendry, Art Lund, Val Avery, Minnie Gentry, Julius W Harris.

●Retitled for release in Britain, although *Black Caesar* gives a more accurate indication of the film's theme of the hero as over-reacher. James Brown belts out 'Ain't It Cool to Be a Boss' as Williamson decides to take over Harlem's crime from the whites, ostensibly to give the blacks a better deal. In doing so, he ends up a white man's nigger, aping all that he has intended to destroy, and losing his girl into the bargain. Unfortunately it all remains too crude to convince one of its better intentions. What survives is a chase with the wounded Williamson riding taxi through snarled-up streets, his pursuers on foot; an extraordinary wish-fulfilment fantasy where a white middle class party (albeit of gangsters) is mown down; and an ending that caters for the inevitable sequel 'Hell Up in Harlem'. CPe

Black Cannon Incident, The (Heipao Shijian)

(1985, China/WGer, 99 min)
d Huang Jianxin. *p* Wu Tiangming, Manfred Durniok. *sc* Li Wei. *ph* Wang Xinsheng, Feng Wei. *ed* Chen Dali. *ad* Liu Yichuan. *m* Zhu Shirui. *cast* Liu Zifeng, Gerhard Olschewski, Gao Ming, Wang Yi, Yang Yazhou, Ge Hui.

●An inoffensive engineer comes under suspicion of industrial espionage. The Security Bureau finds plenty to worry over in his file: raised as a Catholic, never married, he'd had a mysterious argument with a visiting expert from Germany. And so he's packed off to the maintenance depot (where, of course, there is nothing to do) while a pea-brained investigation is launched. Take the resulting chaos as comedy or tragedy; either way, there's no doubt the Chinese ruling class comes in for an unsparing hammering. What's more, the film's political daring is matched by a torrent of bright ideas in the plotting, design and colour-control departments. TR

Black Cat, The

(1941, US, 70 min, b/w)
d Albert S Rogell. *p* Burt Kelly. *sc* Robert Lees, Frederic Rinaldo, Eric Taylor, Robert Neville. *ph* Stanley Cortez. *ed* Ted J Kent. *ad* Jack Otterson. *m* Hans J Salter. *cast* Basil Rathbone, Broderick Crawford, Bela Lugosi, Hugh Herbert, Gale Sondergaard, Anne Gwynne, Gladys Cooper.

●Undistinguished comedy-chiller involving the familiar routine of old dark house, reading of a will, assorted murders. Nothing to do with Poe's story except for some business involving cats, it's worth watching mainly for the admirable Stanley Cortez camerawork. Alan Ladd has a small role as Rathbone's son. TM

Black Cat, The (aka House of Doom)

(1934, US, 65 min, b/w)
d Edgar G Ulmer. *p* EM Asher. *sc* Peter Ruric. *ph* John J Mescall. *ed* Ray Curtiss. *ad* Charles D Hall. *m* Liszt, Schumann, Tchaikovsky. *cast* Boris Karloff, Bela Lugosi, David Manners, Lucille Lund, Julie Bishop, Egon Brecher.

●Devised and directed by Ulmer, most obscure of all the German émigrés in Hollywood, *The Black Cat* owes nothing at all to the Poe short story but everything to the splendours of the German-American expressionist fantasy tradition. Virtually plotless, it describes the sadistic, guilt-ridden clash between Karloff and Lugosi, enemies from WWI; the Karloff character was reputedly inspired by Aleister Crowley. The arena of combat is Karloff's futuristic mansion, built on the site of a concentration camp; enthralling design and camerawork conjure disquiet from the smallest detail or gesture; the classic highpoint is the game of chess for the life of the heroine. Sumptuously subversive…one of the very best horror movies Universal ever made. TR

Black Cat White Cat

(1998, Ger/Fr/Yugo/Aus/Greece, 129 min)
d Emir Kusturica. *p* Karl Baumgartner. *sc* Gordan Michic. *ph* Thierry Arbogast. *ed* Svetolik-Mica Zajc. *pd* Milenko Jeremic. *m* Dr Nele Karajlic, Vojislav Aralica, Dejan Sparavalo. *cast* Bajram Severdzan, Srdjan Todorovic, Branka Katic, Florijan Ajdini, Ljubica Adzovic, Zabit Memedov.

●This Yugoslavian saga about two gypsy patriarchs and their unruly families is staged as a kitsch comedy in the Fellini vein. The slapstick is grotesque, cruel, and at its best, riotously funny. Mack Sennett would have been proud of the intricately choreographed sight gag which ends up with the gun-toting gypsy warlord Dadan literally in the shit. There are some quieter, more lyrical moments too – young lovers disappearing into a field of sunflowers; a rheumy-eyed old gangster watching a *Casablanca* video again and again. Flaunting Kusturica's usual disregard for conventional narrative, this is storytelling on the hoof, rambling, self-indulgent, but with enough warmth and humour to overcome its own excesses. GM

Black Cauldron, The

(1985, US, 80 min)
d Ted Berman, Richard Rich. *p* Joe Hale. *sc* David Jonas, Vance Gerry, Ted Berman, Richard Rich, Al Wilson, Roy Morita, Peter Young, Art Stevens, Joe Hale. *ed* James Melton, Kim Kofrod, Armetta Jackson. *m* Elmer Bernstein. *cast* voices: Pete Renaday, Phil Nibbelink.

●The long-touted magnum opus – an animated feature – supposed to revive Disney's flagging fortunes. Ostensibly a sinister sword and sorcery epic, it comes across as a major disappointment. Of course there's the statutuory naughty, cute furry animal to keep the very small children happy, but the rest of us kiddies walk out wondering when Jiminy Cricket is going to dust off his whistle. As usual it is technically excellent, but the charm, characterisation and sheer good humour that made features like *Pinocchio* and *Jungle Book* so enjoyable are sadly absent. DPe

Black Christmas

(1974, Can, 97 min)
d/p Bob Clark. *sc* Roy Moore. *ph* Reginald Morris. *ed* Stan Cole. *ad* Karen Bromley. *m* Carl Zitter. *cast* Olivia Hussey, Keir Dullea, Margot Kidder, Andrea Martin, John Saxon, Marian Waldman.

●Just who is making all those obscene phone calls and murdering the inmates of a sorority house before the girls go off on their Christmas holidays? A vague knowledge of the cast's previous experience will provide the answer, but for all one's accurate guesswork, the film still manages a good slice of old-fashioned suspense. CPe

Black Diamond Rush

(1993, US, 100 min)
d/p Kurt Miller, Peter Speek. *sc* Warren Miller. *ph* Don Brolin. *ed* Paul Burack, Kim Schneider. *m* Middleman. *narrator* Warren Miller.

●Writer/narrator Warren Miller has been making ski films in the US for more than 40 years. In this documentary, a clutch of bold American skiers and snow-boarders (prone to pulling faces for the camera) search out slopes far removed from the manicured motorways populated by the rest of us. After a while the mountains tend to merge, and the high-speed wipe-outs begin to lose their bone-crunching impact. Breathtaking camerawork. ASh

Black Eagle

(1988, US, 104 min)
d Eric Karson. *p* Shimon Arama. *sc* AE Peters, Michael Gonzales. *ph* George Koblasa. *ed* Michael Kelly. *m* Terry Plumeri. *cast* Sho Kosugi, Jean-Claude Van Damme, Doran Clark, Bruce French, Vladimir Skomarovsky, William H Bassett.

●Codename Black Eagle (Kosugi) is summoned to Malta to thwart KGB plans to steal a sunken laser device. And, barring sundry explosions, killings, a subplot in which his two children are kidnapped, and a car chase (visibly at 33 mph) through the streets of Malta, that's about it. Directed without flair, this is a movie that defies easy classification: it's either a spy thriller without glamour, gadgets, or twists, or a martial arts movie with only two real fights; and if the script ever had a good line, it's fumbled somewhere between the Russian and Japanese accents. The only difference between this and countless other low-budget action movies is that the hero is not macho: he's thin, doesn't screw around, and even fails to defeat the KGB's balletic kung-fu king (Van Damme). In fact, he does nothing of any interest at all: refile under codename Black Turkey. DW

Black Emanuelle (Emanuelle Nera)

(1976, It, 96 min)
d Adalberto Albertini. *p* Mario Mariana. *sc* Adalberto Albertini. *ph* Carlo Carlini. *ed* Vincenzo Tomassi. *ad* Alberto Boccianti. *m* Nico Fidenco. *cast* Laura Gemser, Karin Schubert, Angelo Infanti, Isabelle Marchall, Venantino Venantini, Gabriele Tinti.

●'They're a peaceful tribe, but when they get carried away with their rites nothing can stop them,' Emanuelle is warned as she totes her Nikon through the bush in search of the origins of African civilisation. And you can bet she finds more than she bargained for. Her journey is one of inner discovery too – is she a lesbian, as beach and poolside scenes would seem to testify? Does she prefer it with white men or black? And what of the hockey team who finish the film by raping her on the night train through Nairobi? Crude symbolism, with the couplings shot as dully as the travelogue stuff. AN

Black Eye

(1973, US, 97 min)
d Jack Arnold. *p* Pat Rooney. *sc* Mark Haggard, Jim Martin. *ph* Ralph Woolsey. *ed* Gene Ruggiero. *m* Mort Garson. *cast* Fred Williamson, Rosemary Forsyth, Teresa Graves, Floy Dean, Richard Anderson, Cyril Delevanti.

●Not a bad stab at all at turning out a private eye film in the Chandler mould around a black investigator called Stone, played not brilliantly but well enough by Williamson. The Southern Californian environment is sketched in well, a superficially bland jungle populated by eccentric mystics, phony Godmongers, smooth society women, and a seemingly eclectically chosen array of corpses. Having Stone too out-of-pocket to afford an office but operating out of a neighbourhood bar is also a nice touch. And several of the women characters remain firmly in the mind. Unexpected place to find the director of *The Creature from the Black Lagoon*. VG

Black Flowers for the Bride

see Something for Everyone.

Black Fox

(1962, US, 89 min, b/w)
d/p/sc Louis Clyde Stoumen. *ed* Kenn Collins, Mark Wortreich. *m* Ezra Laderman. *narrator* Marlene Dietrich.

●A documentary produced by Jack Le Vien and narrated by Marlene Dietrich, this semi-allegorical account of Adolf Hitler's rise and fall offers no surprises but reiterates some interesting points. Selected factual details of his career are projected against the backcloth of Goethe's adaptation of the fable of *Reynard the Fox* – 'who some would say was a liar, a thief and a murderer – but often spoke of God'. Hitler is placed firmly and intelligently in his historical context, and is shown to be as much a product of his time (the world recession, Versailles, the foundering of the German democratic experiment) as of his personal genius. In other words, the German people and the world got the dictator they deserved, and the German people at least were glad to have him. FD

Black Fury

(1934, US, 92 min, b/w)
d Michael Curtiz. *p* Robert Lord. *sc* Abem Finkel, Carl Erickson. *ph* Bryon Haskin. *ed* Tom Richards. *ad* John Hughes. *m* Leo Forbstein. *cast* Paul Muni, Karen Morley, William Gargan, Barton MacLane, John Qualen, J Carrol Naish, Mae Marsh, Akim Tamiroff, Vince Barnett.

●'Torn from the front-page headlines', this strike drama is a good example of the extent to which Warner Bros was the proletarian studio: it plays with political dynamite while preaching conciliation and moderation. Fielding a Polish accent only Meryl Streep could understand, Muni is Joe Radek, an easy-going miner whose popularity among his workmates makes him the perfect dupe for a labour agitator planted by strike-breaking racketeers. Something of a buffoon, Radek finds himself leading a walk-out which wrecks the delicate relations between union and management, who are compelled to bring in scabs and industrial police. These last are the real villains of the piece – not the bosses – but at least there is no question that the heroes are the 'bohunks', immigrant workers whose harsh living and working conditions are vividly recreated in Warner's specially constructed 'Coal Town', an impressive complex of wooden shacks, drills and mineshafts. Inspired by the case of Mike Shemanski, a Pittsburgh miner murdered by three company policemen, it is hardly surprising that the film was censored in some states and banned outright in Pennsylvania itself. TCh

Black Girl (La Noire de...)

(1966, Sen, 55 min, b/w)
d Ousmane Sembene. *p* André Zwobada. *sc* Ousmane Sembene. *ph* Christian Lacoste. *ed* André Gaudier. *cast* Mbissine Therese Diop, Anne-Marie Selinek, Robert Fontaine, Momar Nar Sene, Ibrahima Roy.

●Originally intended to be feature length, Sembene's third film tells of the destruction of a young woman who leaves to work as a maid in Antibes. Sembene, who abandoned the novel for film, who trained in Moscow with Donskoi, and whose commitment to African cinema was in part provoked by the racism of Leni Riefenstahl's *Olympiad*, has here contrived a masterful if not entirely flawless rendering of the key themes in Francophone African cinema. It is an essential step in his project to 'totally Africanise the style and conception of my cinema'. SH

Black God, White Devil (Deus e o Diabo na Terra do Sol)

(1964, Braz, 110 min, b/w)
d Glauber Rocha. *p* Luiz Augusto Mendes. *sc* Glauber Rocha. *ph* Waldemar Lima. *ed* L Ririra. *ad* Glauber Rocha. *m* Heitor Villa-Lobos, Johann Sebastian Bach, Sergio Ricardo. *cast* Yona Magalhaes, Geraldo Del Rey, Othon Bastos, Mauricio do Valle, Lidio Silva, Sonia dos Humildes.

●Rocha's first major film introduced most of the methods, themes and even characters that were developed five years later in his *Antonio das Mortes*. Set in the drought-plagued Brazilian Sertao in 1940, it explores the climate of superstition, physical and spiritual terrorism and fear that gripped the country: the central characters, Manuel and Rosa, move credulously from allegiance to allegiance until they finally learn that the land belongs not to god or the devil, but to the people themselves. The film's success here doubtless reflects the 'exoticism' of its style, somewhere between folk ballad and contemporary myth, since the references to Brazilian history and culture are pervasive and fairly opaque to the uninitiated. But Rocha's project is fundamentally political, and completely unambiguous: he faces up to the contradictions of his country in an effort to understand, to crush mystiques, and to improve. TR.

Black Gunn

(1972, US, 95 min)
d Robert Hartford-Davis. *p* John Heyman. *sc* Franklin Coen. *ph* Richard H Kline. *ed* David De Wilde. *ad* Jack DeShields. *m* Tony Osbourne, Pat Somerset. *cast* Jim Brown, Martin Landau, Brenda Sykes, Luciana Paluzzi, Vida Blue, Stephen McNally, Keefe Brasselle.

●Hartford-Davis crucifies Jim Brown (figuratively speaking) by directing this tale of a black capitalist avenging his brother's death with startling lack of inspiration. The modulation of the pimp image, however, after the explicitness of *Superfly*, is a wonder to behold. Collectors only.

Black Hand

(1949, US, 93 min, b/w)
d Richard Thorpe. *p* William H Wright. *sc* Luther Davis. *ph* Paul C Vogel. *ed* Irvine Warburton. *ad* Cedric Gibbons, Gabriel Scognamillo. *m* Alberto Colombo. *cast* Gene Kelly, J Carrol Naish, Teresa Celli, Marc Lawrence, Frank Puglia, Barry Kelley.

●Kelly in a rare dramatic role is an Italian-American out for revenge on the Black Hand, the Mafia-like organisation of extortionists who murdered his lawyer father. Training in the law himself, he enlists the help of New York police inspector Naish, who makes a courageous trip to Sicily to retrieve the information they need to crack the organisation. Although the two Irish-American leads aren't ideally cast, they both give a decent account of themselves in an unusual, neatly plotted little thriller. TJ

Black Hawk Down

(2001, US, 144 min)
d Ridley Scott. *p* Jerry Bruckheimer, Ridley Scott. *sc* Ken Nolan. *ph* Slawomir Idziak. *ed* Pietro Scalia. *pd* Arthur Max. *m* Hans Zimmer. *cast* Josh Hartnett, Ewan McGregor, Tom Sizemore, Eric Bana, William Fichtner, Ewen Bremner, Sam Shepard, Gabriel Casseus, Ioan Gruffudd.

●Mogadishu, Somalia, 1993. US Rangers and Delta Force troops descend on a stronghold to snatch lieutenants in Gen Aidid's Habr Gidr clan. The mission involves some 140 men, but when a Black Hawk helicopter is shot down chaos ensues. Surrounded by angry hordes, the troops are trapped in a nightmarish 15-hour firefight in which nearly a thousand Somalis are killed. Scott's film is drawn in harrowingly accurate detail (surprising for an all-star Bruckheimer production) from Mark Bowden's authoritative minute-by-minute account of the Battle of the Black Sea. There's zero backstory, and the last two hours reconstruct the battle as experienced by everyone involved. On a technical level this is accomplished, credible, and (almost) devoid of sentimentality. If you want to know what combat feels like, this is hardcore. Scott honours the troops and doesn't shy from the confusion and cock-up of this misadventure. He also does a reasonable job sketching the complicated and contradictory political context, but attempts to bring in the odd Somali perspective are grossly inadequate. TCh

Black Hole, The

(1979, US, 98 min)
d Gary Nelson. *p* Ron Miller. *sc* Jeb Rosebrook, Gerry Day. *ph* Frank Phillips. *ed* Gregg McLaughlin. *pd* Peter Ellenshaw. *m* John Barry. *cast* Maximilian Schell, Anthony Perkins, Robert Forster, Joseph Bottoms, Yvette Mimieux, Ernest Borgnine.

●Disney's most ambitious and costly production to date – about a spaceship crew which encounters a Black Hole and a long-lost madman – and if looks were everything you could hardly fault it. The company's effects team have excelled themselves in the creation of spectacular settings and holograms, but the script reads as though they simply ordered up a melange of *Forbidden Planet* and *20,000 Leagues Under the Sea* (with a little bit of R2D2 on the side). Next time around they ought to pension off a few designers to pay for a decent screenplay. DP

Black Holes, The (I Buchi Neri)

(1995, It, 92 min)
d Pappi Corsicato. *p* Aurelio De Laurentiis. *sc* Pappi Corsicato. *ph* Petriccione Italo Daniele. *ed* Nino Baragli, Fabio Nunziata. *pd/m* Pappi Corsicato. *cast* Iaia Forte, Vincenzo Peluso, Marinella Anaclerio, Manuela Arcuri, Anna Avitabile, Maurizio Bizzi.

●Some may claim Corsicato as a Neapolitan Almodóvar, but this tale of the offbeat relationship between a roadside hooker and an enigmatic, idle, sexually ambivalent hunk visiting his hometown for his mother's funeral, is too inconsequential to hold the attention. Much of it is a none-too-witty kitsch pastiche of '60s B-movies, though heaven knows where the mystical whimsy about chickens and epiphanies fits in. The hero resembles Keanu Reeves in a bleach-blond wig. GA

Black Holiday (La Villeggiatura)

(1973, It, 112 min, b/w)
d Marco Leto. *sc* Marco Leto, Lino Del Fra, Cecilia Mangini. *ph* Wolfgang Alfi. *ed*

Giuseppe Giacobino. *ad* Giorgio Lippi. *m* Giuseppe Verdi. *cast* Adalberto Maria Merli, Adolfo Celi, Milena Vukotic, John Steiner, Roberto Herlitzk.
●Set in Fascist Italy and focused around the internment of a young professor of law on a prison island, *Black Holiday* maintains an impressive ideological urgency and relevance. Inspector Rizzuto (Celi, excellent) attempts to 'contain' and control the renegade teacher through the most telling, 'civilised' and classist of methods, by wrapping him in privileges. And the professor (Merli), class-bound but initially blind to the implications of the fact, begins to succumb. The parameters of middle class compromise are very clearly drawn. The precision is admirable, the images spare; and if the hero of the film is the inarticulate Communist who dislocates the professor's essential complacency, its heart can be perceived in the owlish anarchist who remains rousingly defiant to the end. VG

Black Jack

(1979, GB, 110 min)
d Ken Loach. *p* Tony Garnett. *sc* Ken Loach. *ph* Chris Menges. *ed* William Shapter. *ad* Martin Johnson. *m* Bob Pegg. *cast* Stephen Hirst, Louise Cooper, Jean Franval, Phil Askham, Pat Wallis, John Young.
●An amiable adaptation of the classic kids' novel by Leon Garfield, which tells the adventures of a boy on the road in brutal, colourful 1750s England. Loach shoots the film with characteristic sensitivity (and scrupulous period realism), but his unwillingness to face the challenges of social history, and his failure to capture the magical spirit of the novel, let him down. CA

Black Joy

(1977, GB, 109 min)
d Anthony Simmons. *p* Elliott Kastner, Martin Campbell. *sc* Jamal Ali, Anthony Simmons. *ph* Philip Meheux. *ed* Thom Noble. *ad* Brian Savegar. *cast* Norman Beaton, Trevor Thomas, Floella Benjamin, Oscar James, Dawn Hope, Paul Medford.
●A comedy of social manners which manages a fair penetration of Brixton realities and immigrant culture despite its predictable format: survival of the fittest in a jungle of squatters, hookers, urchins and conmen. The ending lacks music, but most of the film has a pace and energy not often seen in British movies. TR

Black Knight, The

(1954, GB, 85 min)
d Tay Garnett. *p* Irving Allen, Albert R Broccoli. *sc* Alec Coppel, Bryan Forbes. *ph* John Wilcox. *ed* Gordon Pilkington. *ad* Alex Vetchinsky. *m* John Addison. *cast* Alan Ladd, Patricia Medina, Andre Morell, Harry Andrews, Peter Cushing, Anthony Bushell, Patrick Troughton.
●Low-budget Arthurian antics featuring vengeful armourer Ladd's specially scaled-down sword and very little cinematic sorcery. Erratic veteran Garnett coasts through the second-hand motions of a hastily concocted patchwork script. PT

Black Lizard, The (Kuro Tokage)

(1968, Jap, 86 min)
d Kinji Fukasaku. *sc* Masashige Narusawa, Kinji Fukasaku. *ph* Hiroshi Dowaki. *ad* Kyohei Morita. *m* Isao Tomita. *cast* Akihiro Maruyama, Isao Kimura, Junya Usami, Kikko Matsuoka, Yukio Mishima.
●A latter-day cult favourite in the US, but Fukasaku (generally a specialist in macho genres) was far too 'straight' a director to make the most of this camp extravaganza. Black Lizard is a glamorous thief who holds a jeweller's daughter to ransom against a fabled diamond, but then falls in love with the detective who tracks her to her secret island hideaway, home to her bizarre collection of human 'statues'. Yukio Mishima adapted the original Edogawa Ranpo (the Japanese 'Edgar Allan Poe') story as a stage vehicle for his friend Maruyama, a celebrated drag queen, and he demanded a guest spot in the movie version as one of the 'statues'. (He appears naked with a silver figleaf.) Lamentably, Fukasaku tries to treat it as a hip action-adventure and thinks no further than pastiche James Bond. Hints of queer perversity glimmer through, but it's mostly leaden. TR

Blackmail

(1929, GB, 82 min, b/w)
d Alfred Hitchcock. *p* John Maxwell. *sc* Alfred Hitchcock, Garnett Weston, Charles Bennett. *ph* Jack Cox. *ed* Emile De Ruelle. *ad* Wilfred Arnold. *m* James Campbell, Reg Connelly. *cast* Anny Ondra, John Longden, Sara Allgood, Donald Calthrop, Cyril Ritchard, Charles Paton.
●*Blackmail* marked Hitchcock's first use of sound, and it remains famous for its innovations in that area. But it's now more stimulating for its experiment with narrative structure: an efficient, impersonal police investigation that elides into a messy, personal story of attempted rape, murder in self-defence, blackmail and chase to the death. TR

Blackmail

(1939, US, 81min, b/w)
d HC Potter. *p* John Considine Jr. *sc* David Hertz, William Ludwig. *ph* Clyde de Vinna. *ed* Howard O'Neill. *ad* Cedric Gibbons, Howard Campbell. *m* Edward Ward, David Snell. *cast* Edward G Robinson, Ruth Hussey, Gene Lockhart, Guinn Williams, John Wray, Arthur Hohl, Bobs Watson.
●Robinson is excellent as a fugitive from a chain gang, convicted of a crime he didn't commit, who nine years later has become a pillar of society with wife, child and enviable reputation as an oil-well troubleshooter. Lockhart is even better as the blackmailer, oozing sleazy, scalp-crawling bonhomie, who confesses that *he* committed the crime, plausibly claims to be anxious to set the record straight, and engineers a scam which puts Robinson back on the chain gang. Potter handles the sharply shifting moods very well: the authentic excitement of the oil-rig fire at the beginning; the *ordinariness* of the family background and the blackmailer's scenes; the dark, brooding brutality (mental as much as physical) of the chain gang sequences. Much of the film's edge is guaranteed by a fine script from David Hertz and William Ludwig, which cleverly paces its action to a parabola between two oil fires (the first a blaze of glory for Robinson, the second his season in hell). Pity about the totally duff upbeat ending. TM

Black Marble, The

(1980, US, 113 min)
d Harold Becker. *p* Frank Capra Jr. *sc* Joseph Wambaugh. *ph* Owen Roizman. *ed* Maury Winetrobe. *pd* Alfred Sweeney. *m* Maurice Jarre. *cast* Robert Foxworth, Paul Prentiss, Harry Dean Stanton, Barbara Babcock, John Hancock, James Woods.
●Repeat teaming for Becker and Joseph Wambaugh after *The Onion Field*, mining the latter's usual preoccupation in an adaptation of his novel about a cop driven to drink by the pressures of his job, but pulling himself together when he is teamed with policewoman Prentiss as his new partner. Sound in most departments and with an excellent cast, but not all that interesting. TM

Black Moon

(1974, Fr, 101 min)
d Louis Malle. *p* Claude Nedjar. *sc* Louis Malle, Ghislain Uhry, Joyce Bunuel. *ph* Sven Nykvist. *ed* Suzanne Baron. *ad* Ghislain Uhry. *m* Diego Masson. *cast* Cathryn Harrison, Thérèse Giehse, Alexandra Stewart, Joe Dallesandro.
●Malle's weird surrealist fantasy updates *Alice in Wonderland* into a future society where men and women are engaged in deadly combat, seemingly coexistent with an alternative comradeship of talking rats and enchanted unicorns. Malle offers no explanation for his heroine's visionary odyssey through a world in which all history runs parallel with all realities. Yet a logic is there, even if its reference point is jabberwocky. A black moon, in astrological terms, refers to the time of chaos that preludes some cataclysmic change. And like Malle's other films around this time, *Black Moon* hopefully posits a social revolution in which such outmoded concepts as innocence and sin will appear in new guises. TM

Black Moon Rising

(1985, US, 100 min)
d Harley Cokliss. *p* Joel B Michaels, Douglas Curtis. *sc* John Carpenter, Desmond Nakano, William Gray. *ph* Mikhail Suslov. *ed* Todd Ramsay. *pd* Bryan Ryman. *m* Lalo Schifrin. *cast* Tommy Lee Jones, Linda Hamilton, Robert Vaughn, Richard Jaeckel, Lee Ving, Bubba Smith.
●Pulling a quick theft of a dodgy company's computer cassette for the Government, Jones then finds himself pursued by both company and Government, and hides the merchandise in the back of a passing car. The car can do an improbable 350 mph. Unfortunately it is stolen by a gang, so his task is to penetrate the impregnable lair of Vaughn's carnapping set-up. It all gets off to a cracking start, only to dwindle very rapidly into thin and predictable variations on the formulaic ploys. And Vaughn gives his usual performance of perfect menace, which suggests that he should be about to engage in world domination, not just nicking motors. CPea

Black Narcissus 100 (100)

(1946, GB, 100 min)
d/p/sc Michael Powell, Emeric Pressburger. *ph* Jack Cardiff. *ed* Reginald Mills. *pd* Alfred Junge. *m* Brian Easdale. *cast* Deborah Kerr, Sabu, David Farrar, Flora Robson, Kathleen Byron, Jean Simmons, Jenny Laird, Esmond Knight.
●Interesting to compare with another version of a Rumer Godden story, Renoir's *The River*, in that whereas Renoir shot on location in India and created an almost documentary feel to his film, Powell refused to go to the Himalayas and shot at Pinewood, coming up with a heady melodrama that treats India as a state of mind rather than a real country. A group of nuns lead a tough, isolated existence in a mountain convent, and find themselves psychologically disturbed by all manner of physical phenomena: extremes of weather and temperature, illness, a local agent's naked thighs, a young prince's perfume purchased, ironically, at London's Army and Navy stores. As temptation draws the women away from their vocation, they fall prey to doubt, jealousy and madness. Powell's use of colour, design and music was never so perfectly in tune with the emotional complexities of Pressburger's script, their talents combining to create one of Britain's great cinematic masterpieces, a marvellous evocation of hysteria and repression, and incidentally one of the few genuinely erotic films ever to emerge from these sexually staid isles. GA

Black Night

see Lumière Noire

Black on White (Mustaa Valkoisella)

(1967, Fin, 95 min)
d Jörn Donner. *p* Arno Carlstedt. *sc* Jörn Donner. *ph* Esko Nevalainen. *ed* Jörn Donner. *m* Georg Riedel. *cast* Jörn Donner, Kristiina Halkola, Liisamaija Laaksonen, Lasse Martenson.
●A simple triangle affair, shot in stunning colour, which somehow contrives to make capital out of its own banality. Nothing much happens, but a great deal is revealed about the illusion of happiness, as a young businessman (well played by Donner himself) breaks up his 'perfect' marriage to pursue a short-lived affair with a flighty young secretary (Halkola). He manoeuvres to get her away on an imaginary business trip; he begins to get caught up in a tissue of lies both at home and at the office; and he watches helplessly as the girl gradually drifts indifferently away, leaving him forlornly dogging her footsteps. With quiet, unobtrusive compassion, always revealing more than is said, Donner records the hell on earth of man's quest for happiness. TM

Black Orchid, The

(1959, US, 96 min, b/w)
d Martin Ritt. *p* Carlo Ponti, Marcello Girosi. *sc* Joseph Stefano. *ph* Robert Burks. *ed* Howard Smith. *ad* Hal Pereira, Roland Anderson. *m* Alessandro Cicognini. *cast* Sophia Loren, Anthony Quinn, Ina Balin, Jimmie Baird, Mark Richman, Naomi Stevens, Frank Puglia.
●A seriously bad tearjerker. Loren's life is in ruins – her gangster husband has died, her son has become James Dean – until she meets up with nice widower Mr Quinn, who shows her his farm and daughter. Cue for the daughter to go round the twist at the thought of Loren as a stepmother. One in a long line of clinkers (except for the masterly *Hud*) from Ritt, and a first script by composer Joseph Stefano, who got his act together with his next picture, which was *Psycho*. ATu

Black Orpheus (Orfeu Negro)

(1959, Fr/It/Braz, 106 min)
d Marcel Camus. *p* Sacha Gordine. *sc* Vinicius de Moraes. *ph* Jean Bourgoin. *ed* Andrée Feix. *m* Antonio Carlos Jobim, Luis Bonfa. *cast* Breno Mello, Marpessa Dawn, Adhemar da Silva, Lourdes de Oliveira, Lea Garcia.
●In recreating the Orpheus legend in Rio de Janeiro with an all black cast, Camus celebrates not only the universality of the story, but the exoticism and poetry of Brazil and her culture. Orpheus, a charismatic trolley car conductor and star of one of the Carnival's Samba schools, is betrothed to the wonderfully brassy Mira but in love with Eurydice. Pursued by Death and the vengeful Mira, the doomed lovers weave their way through a carnival-mad Rio that seethes and strains towards the sweaty release of Carnival night. Although certain of the more sentimental scenes seem rather dated, the relentless – almost abstract – onslaught of colour, noise and frenetic movement stands up very well, compelling one towards the visual splendour of the inevitably poignant ending. FD

Blackout

see Contraband

Blackout (aka The Attic)

(1988, US, 91 min)
d Doug Adams. *cast* Carol Lynley, Gail O'Grady, Michael Keys Hall, Joseph Gian, Deena Freeman, Joanna Miles.
●Years after the mysterious disappearance of her father, plucky runaway Caroline Boyle (O'Grady) receives a letter from him requesting that she return for a family reunion. Intrigued, she goes home, to be met by her unwelcoming mother (Lynley) and a strange new boyfriend. Confused, she embarks on a fact-finding mission which, via many a knife-wielding flashback, eventually leads her to the attic… A cheaply made psychological thriller, scripted by Joseph Stefano, this certainly has its fair share of claret, but is strictly fodder for slasher fans. DA

Blackout, The

(1997, US/Fr, 98 min)
d Abel Ferrara. *p* Edward R Pressman, Clayton Townsend. *sc* Marla Hanson, Chris Zois, Abel Ferrara. *ph* Ken Kelsch. *ed* Anthony Redman. *pd* Richard Hoover. *m* Joe Delia, Schoolly D. *cast* Matthew Modine, Claudia Schiffer, Béatrice Dalle, Sarah Lassez, Dennis Hopper.
●So incoherent, sloppy and determinedly sleazy that it looks like self-parody, Ferrara's psycho-drama tells of a movie star (Modine) heavily into drugs and booze. Ignoring girlfriend Dalle's objections to his lifestyle, he ODs and blacks out; 18 months later, cleaned up and living quietly with Schiffer, he's nevertheless haunted by fantasies that he may have murdered Dalle. Neither the pretentious dialogue nor the sudden shifts in character (particularly that of Hopper's crazed director) makes sense; and the visuals are often pitifully voyeuristic in their emphasis on female flesh and all-round degeneracy. GA

Black Panther, The

(1977, GB, 98 min)
d/p Ian Merrick. *sc* Michael Armstrong. *ph* Joe Mangine. *ed* Teddy Darvas. *ad* Carlotta Barrow. *m* Richard Arnell. *cast* Donald Sumpter, Debbie Farrington, Marjorie Yates, Sylvia O'Donnell, Andrew Burt, Ruth Dunning, Alison Key.
●Based on the case of Donald Neilson, who killed three sub-postmasters and 17-year-old heiress Lesley Whittle, this dull but earnest movie bends over backwards not to exploit its subject. But strained realism and an obsession with facts permit little insight and even less drama. The film does little more than plod after the central character on his criminal rounds.

Black Pirate, The

(1926, US, 8,312 ft)
d Albert Parker. *p* Douglas Fairbanks. *sc* Jack Cunningham, Douglas Fairbanks. *ph* Henry Sharp. *ed* William Nolan. *ad* Carl Oscar Borg, Dwight Franklin. *cast* Douglas Fairbanks, Billie Dove, Donald Crisp, Anders Randolf, Tempe Pigott, Sam De Grasse, Charles Stevens.
●Alongside Keaton and Gene Kelly, Fairbanks was perhaps the most gracefully athletic mover in the history of the movies, and *The Black Pirate* perfectly captures his relaxed, exuberant optimism. A pacy tale of romance and revenge on the high seas, it sees Doug swashing his buckle with unsurpassed ease: the daring stunts are breathtakingly stylish (none more so than the celebrated descent down a sail on the point of a dagger), while scenes like the shoal of soldiers swimming underwater to invade the pirate ship are shot through with a poetic beauty. An added bonus is that the film was shot in two-strip Technicolor, a lovely pastel process that defies description. GA

Black Rain

(1989, US, 125 min)
d Ridley Scott. *p* Stanley R Jaffe, Sherry Lansing. *sc* Craig Bolotin, Warren Lewis. *ph* Jan de Bont. *ed* Tom Rolf. *pd* Norris Spencer. *m* Hans Zimmer. *cast* Michael Douglas, Andy Garcia, Ken Takakura, Kate Capshaw, Yusaku Matsuda, Shigeru Koyama, John Spencer.
●Dishonoured detective Nick Conklin (Douglas) and easygoing partner Charlie Vincent (Garcia) escort a desperately ruthless yakuza from New York to Osaka. When he is snatched from under their noses, they join forces with the Japanese police to recover their man. Most of the interplay is between Conklin, under investigation back home, and his Japanese colleague Matsumoto (Takakura), who upholds group loyalty over the American's individualism. 'You must have patience', Conklin is warned by his Japanese hosts. 'Fuck patience', he retorts, and goes about cutting corners. Their quarry belongs to a counterfeiting ring which schemes to infiltrate the American economy – Japanese revenge, it would seem, for losing the war (black rain refers to radioactive fallout after Hiroshima and Nagasaki). Tiresome gags abound at the expense of the uptight Japanese detective, with Conklin revelling in language misunderstandings, and prejudices are aired until some sort of reconciliation is reached – *after* Matsumoto has adopted vigilante methods. Obvious stuff. CM

Black Rain (Kuroi Ame)

(1989, Jap, 123 min, b/w)
d Shohei Imamura. *p* Hisa Iino. *sc* Shohei Imamura, Toshiro Ishido. *ph* Takashi Kawamata. *ed* Hajime Okayasu. *ad* Hiasao Inagaki. *m* Toru Takemitsu. *cast* Yoshiko Tanaka, Kazuo Kitamura, Etsuko Ichihara, Shoichi Ozawa, Norihei Miki, Kaisuka Ishide.
●On an August morning in 1945, the inhabitants of Hiroshima set out for another day at work. In minutes a sudden flash reduces the city to a nightmarish furnace strewn with rubble, crumbling corpses and charred survivors. Presently, this gut churningly graphic opening switches to what appears to be a rural idyll some five years later; in a small village, a family who escaped have settled down in an attempt to regain some sense of purpose in life. But radiation sickness takes its toll, and the bulk of Imamura's emphatically serious domestic drama charts the inexorable decay of the entire social, psychological and moral fabric of a community. Rarely does the film preach, and only the repeated rantings of a demented army veteran – so OTT as to be unintentionally comic – break the consistently understated mood. But despite the largely sensitive depiction of waste, suffering and despair, the often ponderous pacing and the script's solemnity tend to work against emotional involvement. Grimly compelling viewing, but perhaps a little too determinedly gloomy for its own good. GA

Black Rainbow

(1989, GB, 103 min)
d Mike Hodges. *p* John Quested, Geoffrey Helman. *sc* Mike Hodges. *ph* Gerry Fisher. *ed* Malcolm Cooke. *pd* Voytek. *m* John Scott. *cast* Rosanna Arquette, Jason Robards, Tom Hulce, Mark Joy, Ron Rosenthal, John Bennes, Linda Pierce, Olek Krupa.
●Spiritualist Martha Travis (Arquette) puts the recently bereaved in touch with their loved ones, reassuring them of a happy hereafter; but when she develops the gift – or rather curse – of prophecy, she becomes the disembodied witness to a brutal killing, and the hit-man's next target. As she fights to convince her drunken father (Robards) and a sceptical journalist (Hulce) that her powers are real, the rainbow colours of her visions are painted black, and she slips towards madness and despair… Writer-director Hughes has coaxed superbly understated performances from his cast, even down to the suburban black-gloved assassin who commutes to killings after kissing his wife and kids. The pacing, too, is tight and restrained, building slowly so that the climax, when it comes, packs a real wallop (though he can't resist an ambiguous coda). The result is Hodges' best film since his debut with *Get Carter*: a psychological thriller with a brain and a heart, which challenges the audience to explore their assumptions about reality, religion and the supernatural. DW

Black Republic (Keduldo Urichorum)

(1990, SKor, 100 min)
d Park Kwang-Su. *p* Lee Kwon-Suk. *sc* Park Kwang-Su, Kim Kwang-Su. *ph* Yoo Young-Kil. *ed* Kim Hyun. *ad* Dou Yong-woo. *m* Kim Soo-chui. *cast* Moon Sung-Keun, Shim Hye-jin, Park Joong-hoon.
●Park Kwang-Su is the foremost director of the New Korean Cinema, and this is the best of his three features to date. Soon after the brutal suppression of the Kwangju Uprising in 1980, a student activist on the wanted list hides out in a dying mining town near the North Korean border. Very little happens in plot terms, but his edgy relationships with others (a prostitute who's also on the run from something in her past, a mother-fixated thug who turns out to be the spoiled son of the town's last employer) give the film all the grip of a hard-boiled thriller. It adds up to a persuasive account of the terrible state of South Korean society a decade ago (and by implication, still). TR

Black Rider, The

(1954, GB, 66 min, b/w)
d Wolf Rilla. *p/sc* AR Rawlinson. *ph* Geoffrey Faithfull. *ed* John Trumper. *ad* John Stoll. *m* Wilfred Burns. *cast* Jimmy Hanley, Rona Anderson, Leslie Dwyer, Lionel Jeffries, Beatrice Varley, Kenneth Connor.
●Workaday British support feature from years gone by in which tyro reporter Hanley and the chaps from the local motorcycle club investigate the apparent haunting of a nearby castle. Could it possibly have something to do with the nefarious activities of a bunch of smugglers? Director Wolf Rilla was in more genuinely spooky territory six years later with *Village of the Damned*. TJ

Black River

(1993, Aust, 60 min)
d Kevin Lucas. *p* Aanya Whitehead, Kevin Lucas, Sue Maslin. *sc* Kevin Lucas. *ph* Kim Batterham. *ed* Dany Cooper. *pd* Tim Ferrier. *m* Andrew Schultz. *cast* Marocchy Barambah, John Pringle, James Bonnefin, Clive Birch, The Bangarra Dance Theatre.
●This is a bold transfer of a Sydney Metropolitan Opera production (words by journalist Julianne Schultz, music by brother Andrew) inspired by a human rights enquiry into the fractious state of race relations in a small outback town. The action centres on an angry Aboriginal woman Miriam (mezzo Barambah), who's come to the local jail after her son's suspicious death in custody and finds herself thrown together with a judge on a fact-finding visit (baritone Pringle), the village drunk (tenor Bonnefin) and a surprisingly easygoing cop (bass Birch) – all marooned in the cells as the waters of a flash flood rise around them. The score builds in intensity as Barambah recounts centuries of her people's oppression. Piercing the innermost conflicts of the Australian psyche, all this might mean more on home ground, but to an outsider the result plays rather like a high art music video. The blending of realist and supernatural elements is ambitious, but the relative compactness of the material hardly allows convincing characterisation to emerge. A genuine curio, if not an unqualified success. TJ

Black Robe

(1991, Can/Aust, 100 min)
d Bruce Beresford. *p* Robert Lantos, Stéphane Reichel, Sue Milliken. *sc* Brian Moore. *ph* Peter James. *ed* Tim Wellburn. *pd* Herbert Pinter. *m* Georges Delerue. *cast* Lothaire Bluteau, Aden Young, Sandrine Holt, August Schellenberg, Tantoo Cardinal, Billy Two Rivers, Lawrence Bayne.

●Brian Moore here adapts his own savage, elegiac novel about the Jesuit mission to 'reap souls' among the Iroquois in 1630s Quebec. The film details the harrowing canoe trip undertaken in intense cold by idealistic Father Laforgue (Bluteau), a young carpenter named Daniel (Young) and a band of Algonquin Indians, way up into Huron territory to reach a disease-stricken outpost. It's a Conradian journey into the heart of darkness. Laforgue's mind and body are assaulted by privation, doubt, sexual arousal and horror, which sends him into faith-destroying anguish, with worse to come. The film is essentially illustrative, and Moore's screenplay understandably softens the text somewhat, but it still contains shocking scenes of torture and murder. What distinguishes the result is the brutal, cleareyed honesty with which the Native American (and the missionary) culture is represented. Beautifully shot, too. WH

Black Room, The

(1935, US, 67 min, b/w)
d Roy William Neill. *sc* Henry Myers, Arthur Strawn. *ph* Allen Siegler. *ed* Richard Cahoon. *ad* Stephen Goosson. *m* Louis Silvers. *cast* Boris Karloff, Marian Marsh, Robert Allen, Katherine DeMille, Thurston Hall.
●Moodily stylish Gothic melodrama, with Karloff in a dual role as twins fulfilling a family curse. Solid rather than distinguished (striking sets but too many rhubarbing villagers), although Karloff's performance is outstanding, especially in a subtle pantomime sequence where the bad twin rehearses his transformation into the brother he has killed. TM

Black Sabbath (I Tre Volti della Paura)

(1963, It/Fr, 99 min)
d Mario Bava. *sc* Marcello Fondato, Alberto Bevikiqua, Maris Buva. *ph* Ubaldo Terzano. *ed* Mario Serandrei. *ad* Giorgio Giovannini. *m* Les Baxter. *cast* Jacqueline Pierreux, Harriet, Michèle Mercier, Lidia Alfonsi, Boris Karloff, Mark Damon.
●Vintage Bava in which Karloff introduces three adaptations from famous tales of the supernatural (and also stars in the last): *The Drop of Water* by Chekhov, *The Telephone* by Howard Snyder, and *The Wurdalak* by Tolstoy. Pictorially it's amazing, and even the script and dubbing are way above average. If only Amicus, who subsequently cornered the horror omnibus market, had taken heed they might have got some ideas as to what can be done with the format. DP

Blacks Britannica

(1978, US, 57 min)
d David Koff.
●Of all the films which have so far been made about the black community in Britain, this one comes closest to telling it how it is. The thesis is that the black community in Britain is the most oppressed section of an oppressed working class. The fact that young blacks reject their decreed role in the country's social and economic structure has meant that the state has been obliged to use a number of devices to reinforce its intentions, including the police, the judiciary, the media and the schools. The whole picture is linked by a number of interviews with activists in the black community, which means that the picture which emerges is an authentic black view of affairs. British TV could have, and should have, done this years ago. MP

Black Shack Alley (Rue Cases Nègres/ aka Sugar Cane Alley)

(1983, Fr, 106 min)
d/sc Euzhan Palcy. *ph* Dominique Chapuis. *ed* Marie-Josephe Yoyotte. *ad* Thanh At Hoang. *m* Roland Louis. *cast* Garry Cadenat, Darling Legitimus, Douta Seck, Joby Bernabé, Francisco Charles.
●Palcy's first feature is set in her native Martinique of the '30s: an 11-year-old boy lives in a shanty row (Rue Cases Nègres) in the middle of the back-breaking regime of the sugar cane plantations. Thanks to the selfless devotion of his grandmother, and the spiritual awakening offered by an ancient mentor, whose father was an African slave, he prospers at school, and manages to escape the grinding round of poverty by dint of education. Shot in ochre hues, with a remarkable polish, the movie never allows itself the easy route of angry misery, but actively engages its themes with optimism and its characters with love. The old people, especially, are treated with great dignity, while the boy's slow awakening to a poetic understanding of his condition is imbued with potent, primitive magic. CPea

Black Sheep

(1996, US, 87 min)
d Penelope Spheeris. *p* Lorne Michaels. *sc* Fred Wolf. *ph* Daryn Okada. *ed* Ross Albert. *pd* Peter Jamison. *m* William Ross. *cast* Chris Farley, David Spade, Tim Matheson, Christine Ebersole, Gary Busey, Grant Hershov, Timothy Carhart, Bruce McGill.
●In freefall since *Wayne's World*, Penelope Spheeris' career has descended halfway down the deep-sea Marianas Trench, whence comes this soggy comedy, guaranteed to induce the bends. It features Farley and Spade, the director's co-fugitives from *Saturday Night Live* (previously paired in *Tommy Boy*), and revolves around the gubernatorial candidacy of Al Donnelly (Matheson). Al's riding high in the polls against the unscrupulous incumbent (Ebersole), which is why his campaign can't afford the damaging presence of brother Mike (Farley), a sweet but self-destructive oaf. Mike's packed off with some guy called Steve (Spade) to an isolated cabin, where the duo perform incompetent slapstick. Mike slips and falls down a hill; a big boulder rolls on to the hut; Mike, trying to use his mobile phone, walks into a tree. NB

Black Sheep of Whitehall, The

(1941, GB, 80 min, b/w)
d Will Hay, Basil Dearden. *p* Michael Balcon. *sc* Angus MacPhail, John Dighton. *ph* Günther Krampf, Eric Cross. *ed* Ray Pitt. *ad* Tom Morahan. *m* Ernest Irving. *cast* Will Hay, John Mills, Basil Sydney, Felix Aylmer, Henry Hewitt, Thora Hird.
●The traditional Hay formula – his seedy correspondence course lecturer is mistaken for an economics expert kidnapped by spies, allowing him to indulge in much pretence and buffoonery, and to end up in a manic chase – is inserted into a predictably patriotic plot about plucky little Brits outwitting the Nazi villains. Funny in parts. GA

Blacksnake (aka Slaves)

(1973, US, 82 min)
d/p Russ Meyer. *sc* Russ Meyer, Len Neubauer. *ph* Arthur J Ornitz. *ed* Russ Meyer. *ad* Rick Heatherly. *m* Bill Loose, Almon R Teeter. *cast* Anouska Hempel, David Warbeck, Percy Herbert, Milton McCollin, Thomas Baptiste, Bernard Boston.
●A gorgeous mix of sex, violence, social comment, and film parody, set in the Caribbean in 1853, with Hempel as the whip-wielding plantation mistress taking black slaves as studs until they finally revolt. Catch the super sermon by a crucified rebel (complete with choral backing), and Meyer's final eulogy to racial harmony (i.e. miscegenation). Makes even *Mandingo* look serious.

Black Snow (Ben Ming Nian)

(1989, China, 107 min)
d Xie Fei. *sc* Liu Heng. *ph* Xiao Feng. *pd* Long Yongxin. *cast* Jiang Wen, Cheng Lin, Yue Hong, Liu Xiaoning, Cai Hongxing, Lui Bin.
●This was adapted by young writer Liu Heng from his own short story about an ex-con trying to go straight in the back alleys of Beijing, but finding himself dragged down by the crime and violence he encounters. Film-school teacher Xie Fei keeps it all very low-key, but has no obvious point of view about the characters or the material. What brings the film to life is the writing (realistic to a fault, but very sharply observed), and the superb central performance of Jiang Wen, previously seen in films like *Red Sorghum* and *Hibiscus Town*. Jiang really is in the class of Gary Oldman: a young actor capable of inhabiting a role in a way that makes his smallest gesture count. TR

Black Stallion, The

(1979, US, 117 min)
d Carroll Ballard. *p* Fred Ross, Tom Sternberg. *sc* Melissa Mathison, Jeanne Rosenberg, William D Witliff. *ph* Caleb Deschanel. *ed* Robert Dalva. *ad* Aurelio Crugnola, Earl Preston. *m* Carmine Coppola. *cast* Kelly Reno, Mickey Rooney, Teri Garr, Clarence Muse, Hoyt Axton, Michael Higgins.
●Walter Farley's classic tale has been adapted with amazing facility by Ballard and executive producer Coppola. Even though its essential features (shipwrecked child, desert island, magical stallion, '40s New York) represented appalling production problems, the film jettisons most of the cuteness implicit in its theme and handles the material with dream-like clarity. A magnificently well-crafted movie. DP.

Black Stallion Returns, The

(1983, US, 103 min)
d Robert Dalva. *p* Tom Sternberg, Fred Roos, Doug Claybourne. *sc* Richard Kletter, Jerome Kass. *ph* Carlo Di Palma. *ed* Paul Hirsch. *ad* Aurelio Crugnola. *m* Georges Delerue. *cast* Kelly Reno, Vincent Spano, Allen Garfield, Woody Strode, Ferdy Mayne, Teri Garr.
●Fun follow-up to *The Black Stallion* (which Dalva edited), with the horse stolen by enigmatic Arabs, and a determined Alec Ramsay (now the archetypal '50s teenager) stowing away on a plane bound for Casablanca, landing in the very middle of a sticky web of tribal rivalries and desert traditions. As in the original, the character of Alec distinguishes the film: he's resourceful, single-minded, but it is perhaps his very ordinariness that matters. FD

Black Sunday

see Maschera del Demonio, La

Black Sunday

(1976, US, 143 min)
d John Frankenheimer. *p* Robert Evans. *sc* Ernest Lehman, Kenneth Ross, Ivan Moffat. *ph* John A Alonzo. *ed* Tom Rolf. *ad* Walter Tyler. *m* John Williams. *cast* Robert Shaw, Bruce Dern, Marthe Keller, Fritz Weaver, Steven Keats, Bekim Fehmiu, Michael V Gazzo, William Daniels.
●Black September terrorists attempt to wipe out a US football crowd by hijacking the TV blimp. Besides some good suspense sequences, Frankenheimer tries to utilise his well-known skill with actors to open up all sides of the issue. Unfortunately, all the major characters have a whiff of Hollywood artifice, largely because (as has happened too often before in his career) Frankenheimer gets carried away by their verbosity. But perhaps any Hollywood film giving the Palestinian case an airing deserves to be welcomed. DP

Black Swan, The

(1942, US, 85 min)
d Henry King. *p* Robert Bassler. *sc* Ben Hecht, Seton I Miller. *ph* Leon Shamroy. *ed* Barbara McLean. *ad* Richard Day, James Basevi. *m* Alfred Newman. *cast* Tyrone Power, Maureen O'Hara, Laird Cregar, Thomas Mitchell, George Sanders, Anthony Quinn, George Zucco, Fortunio Bonanova.
●A splendidly overripe swashbuckler, with Power as an adventurer who lends a sword to his old comrade Henry Morgan (Cregar) when he is appointed governor of Jamaica, seconding his bid to rid the Caribbean of buccaneers, in the process wooing and winning O'Hara's feisty damsel in distress, daughter of the former governor (Zucco). Sanders is the villain of the piece, one Captain Leech, an unreformed pirate with a brazen red hairpiece and the beard to go with it. Excitingly staged, boldly photographed in Technicolor, and boasting a flamboyant cast, this is a classic of its type. TCh

Black Tent, The

(1956, GB, 93 min)
d Brian Desmond Hurst. *p* William MacQuitty. *sc* Robin Maugham, Bryan Forbes. *ph* Desmond Dickinson. *ed* Alfred Roome. *ad* George Provis. *m* William Alwyn. *cast* Anthony Steel, Donald Sinden, Anna Maria Sandri, Andre Morell, Donald Pleasence, Michael Craig, Anton Diffring, Ralph Truman.
●WWII romance mystery (scripted by Robin Maugham and Bryan Forbes) has the folk at the ancestral seat worried when son and heir Steel fails to return home from the North African campaign. Brother Sinden is packed off to discover that he's fallen for a sheikh's daughter and

thrown in his lot with the bedouin. Director Hurst and a stiff cast manage to flatten the interest out of potentially intriguing material. TJ

Black Torment, The

(1964, GB, 85 min)
d/p Robert Hartford-Davis. *sc* Donald Ford, Derek Ford. *ph* Peter Newbrook. *ed* Alastair McIntyre. *ad* Alan Harris. *m* Robert Richards. *cast* John Turner, Heather Sears, Ann Lynn, Peter Arne, Francis de Wolff, Edina Ronay, Joseph Tomelty, Raymond Huntley.

● Occasionally effective ghost chiller, detailing an 18th century aristocrat's investigations into a series of hauntings that follow his first wife's suicide. The explanation, when it comes, its both rational and unsurprising, but the general mood of the piece carries it through despite atrocious direction. GA

Black Wax

(1982, GB/US, 79 min)
d/p Robert Mugge. *ph* Lawrence McConkey. *ed* Robert Mugge. *m* Gil Scott-Heron. *with* Gil Scott-Heron and the Midnight Band.

● Admirers of the special blend of tight jazzy funk and intelligently political lyrics that is the hallmark of singer/composer/poet Gil Scott-Heron will find much to enjoy in this engaging documentary. A mixture of coolly shot concert footage and scenes of Scott-Heron taking us on an 'alternative' tour of Washington while pronouncing on politics, poetry and prejudice, the film displays both the man's exhilarating musical eclecticism and his sharply ironic, often cynical vision of an America torn apart by fear, loathing and misguided ideals. Highly watchable and listenable material. GA.

Black Widow

(1954, US, 95 min)
d/p/sc Nunnally Johnson. *ph* Charles G Clarke. *ed* Dorothy Spencer. *ad* Lyle Wheeler, Maurice Ransford. *m* Leigh Harline. *cast* Van Heflin, George Raft, Gene Tierney, Ginger Rogers, Reginald Gardiner, Peggy Ann Garner, Otto Kruger.

● An adaptation of Patrick Quentin's fine thriller which starts promisingly with Heflin's distinguished Broadway producer, meeting a sweetly aspiring young playwright (Garner), helplessly bemused when (actually vampirically ambitious) she virtually takes over his apartment on the excuse that the surroundings are conducive to inspiration. When she is subsequently found murdered there and he becomes the prime suspect, the film degenerates into a routine whodunnit. Worth seeing for the fine cast, Raft (dreary as ever as the investigating cop) and Rogers (unexpectedly overdoing it as a bitchy actress) excepted. TM

Black Widow

(1987, US, 102 min)
d Bob Rafelson. *p* Harold Schneider. *sc* Ronald Bass. *ph* Conrad Hall. *ed* John Bloom. *pd* Gene Callahan. *m* Michael Small. *cast* Debra Winger, Theresa Russell, Sami Frey, Dennis Hopper, Nicol Williamson, Diane Ladd.

● From its opening shot – Theresa Russell's split reflection in a make-up mirror – both the theme and the over-schematic symbolism of Rafelson's thriller are immediately apparent. For Russell plays a homicidal psychopath whose killings of various wealthy husbands are investigated by a Justice Department workaholic (Winger), who slowly but surely becomes a kind of mirror-image of her Protean prey. The story and treatment are familiar from '40s *noir* thrillers, but it's clear that Rafelson is attempting something more than mere homage. Disappointingly, the femme fatale – apparently in love with her husbands even as she plans their demise – is presented as somehow more female, fulfilled and complete than the career woman, who in turn eventually discovers both dress sense and the joy of sex with her opposite's next victim-to-be. There are things to enjoy – committed performances, Conrad Hall's elegant camerawork, a script that becomes pleasurably tortuous towards the end – but the film finally offers far less than meets the eye. GA

Black Windmill, The

(1974, US, 106 min)
d/p Don Siegel. *sc* Leigh Vance. *ph* Ousama Rawi. *ed* Antony Gibbs. *ad* Peter Murton. *m* Roy Budd. *cast* Michael Caine, Joseph O'Connor, Donald Pleasence, John Vernon, Janet Suzman, Delphine Seyrig, Joss Ackland, Clive Revill.

● Although received with critical disappointment, mainly because Siegel had forsaken his exploration of American mythology and violence for what seemed to be a rather old-fashioned British thriller, there is in fact a lot to enjoy in *The Black Windmill*. It's a very playful piece at the expense of the British stiff-upper lip, made with a discerning American's eye for London. The plot is a shaggy dog story (with just the right degree of nightmarishness) revolving around intelligence agent Caine's single-handed attempts to retrieve his kidnapped son. Though by no means a perfect film, it is a much more coherent work than it is given credit, held together by Siegel's exuberant eye for the incongruous. CPe

Blacula

(1972, US, 93 min)
d William Crain. *p* Joseph T Naar. *sc* Joan Torres, Raymond Koenig. *ph* John Stevens. *ed* Allan Jacobs. *ad* Walter Scott Herndon. *m* Gene Page. *cast* William Marshall, Vonetta McGee, Denise Nicholas, Thalmus Rasulala, Gordon Pinsent, Charles Macaulay, Elisha Cook Jr.

● Disappointing black horror movie which followed in the successful wake of *Shaft*. The script by Joan Torres and Raymond Koenig seems to be the real problem: apart from a garbled opening in which Blacula is vampirised while trying to liberate his people, the plot simply turns away from all the obvious political/social/sexual implications, even on the level of action. Instead, Blacula becomes a less than impressive lovesick vampire chasing his reincarnated wife through LA (one of the dullest plot mechanisms of all), and the film remains a lifeless reworking of heroes versus vampires with soul music and a couple of good gags. Not a particularly promising debut for Crain, whose TV background is all too obvious in the cramped over-emphatic style. DP.

Blade

(1998, US, 120 min)
d Stephen Norrington. *p* Peter Frankfurt, Wesley Snipes, Robert Engelman. *sc* David S Goyer. *ph* Theo van de Sande. *ed* Paul Rubell. *pd* Kirk M Petruccelli. *m* Mark Isham. *cast* Wesley Snipes, Stephen Dorff, Kris Kristofferson, N'Bushe Wright, Donal Logue, Udo Keir, Traci Lords.

● An attempt to redefine cutting edge horror, this techno-vampire pic is spoiled by the same weak storytelling and flashy, computer game visuals seen in the director's first feature *Death Machine*. Shortly before dying in childbirth, a woman is bitten by a vampire, and her son, Blade, becomes a hybrid, half-human, half-vampire. Suppressing a thirst for blood with garlic injections, Blade (Snipes) wages war against the bloodsuckers; however, he and his human sidekick Whistler (Kristofferson) meet their match in Deacon Frost (Dorff), who dreams of an apocalypse that will install vampires as rulers of Earth. Ostensibly this is about a complex, ambiguous hero, but too little time is spent exploring Blade's tortured soul. Instead, the demons get the best tunes and the best scenes. The rest is a series of messily choreographed, gloatingly sadistic fights, tricked out with embarrassing one liners and reams of exposition. NF

Blade II

(2002, US/Ger, 117 min)
d Guillermo del Toro. *p* Peter Frankfurt, Wesley Snipes, Patrick Palmer. *sc* David S Goyer. *ph* Gabriel Beristain. *ed* Peter Amundson. *pd* Carol Spier. *m* Marco Beltrami. *cast* Wesley Snipes, Kris Kristofferson, Ron Perlman, Leonor Varela, Norman Reedus, Thomas Kretschmann, Luke Goss, Matthew Schulze, Danny John Jules, Donnie Yen.

● This flashy, eye-catching sequel recaps the first film in the credit sequence, re-introducing Snipes' 'day-walker' (half-man, half-vampire), scourge of the bloodsuckers. Upping the ante on the original, Blade and Whistler (Kristofferson) are drawn into an alliance with their foe against a new, bald, cannibalistic strain that is invulnerable to garlic and silver, but unlikely to get a suntan anytime soon. The influences are eclectic as before – Marvel comics, Hong Kong martial arts and Japanese samurai movies, video games and rap music – but stripped down to such basics as story and dialogue, it's nothing to get excited about. TCh

Blade, The (Dao)

(1995, HK, 104 min)
d Tsui Hark. *p* Raymond Chow. *sc* Tsui Hark. *ph* Keung Kwok-Man. *ed* Tsui Hark. *cast* Wing Zhao, Xiong Xinxin, Su Tsui-Yu, Wai Tin-Chi. Chan Ho, Valerie Chow.

● Nominally a remake of the old Shaw Brothers/Wang Yu *One-Armed Boxer*, this is actually a (not very) original story: a young man discovers belatedly that he should be out avenging the father he never knew, loses an arm while rescuing a girl from kidnappers, and trains himself to overcome his handicap so as to confront the worst of the bad guys in the final reel. As rife with continuity errors and other signs of haste as most later-day Tsui Hark movies, this is chiefly notable for its emphasis on naked male flesh; the girl's first-person voice-over is there to deflect suspicions of homo-eroticism. TR

Blade Runner 100 (100)

(1982, US, 117 min)
d Ridley Scott. *p* Michael Deeley. *sc* Hampton Fancher, David Webb Peoples. *ph* Jordan Cronenweth. *ed* Marsha Nakashima. *pd* Lawrence G Paull. *m* Vangelis. *cast* Harrison Ford, Rutger Hauer, Sean Young, Edward James Olmos, M Emmet Walsh, Daryl Hannah.

● An ambitious and expensive adaptation of one of Philip K Dick's best novels (*Do Androids Dream of Electric Sheep?*), with Ford as the cop in 2019 Los Angeles whose job is hunting mutinous androids that have escaped from the off-world colonies. The script has some superb scenes, notably between Ford and the (android) femme fatale Young, while Scott succeeds beautifully in portraying the LA of the future as a cross between a Hong Kong street-market and a decaying 200-storey Metropolis. But something has gone badly wrong with the dramatic structure: the hero's voice-over and the ending feel as if they've strayed in from another movie, and the android villains are neither menacing nor sympathetic, when ideally they should have been both. This leaves Scott's picturesque violence looking dull and exploitative. DP

Blade Runner – The Director's Cut

(1982/1991, US, 112 min)
d Ridley Scott. *p* Michael Deeley. *sc* Hampton Fancher, David Webb Peoples. *ph* Jordan Cronenweth. *ed* Marsha Nakashima. *pd* Lawrence G Paull. *m* Vangelis. *cast* Harrison Ford, Rutger Hauer, Sean Young, Edward James Olmos, M Emmet Walsh, Daryl Hannah.

● More notable for what's been removed than for what's been added, this restored version of Scott's seminal sci-fi movie makes it clear that all its former faults were introduced by nervous studio executives, who thought the narrative too confusing, the ending too bleak. Gone is the redundant *noir*-style voice-over by Harrison Ford's blade runner (the plot makes more sense without it). Gone, too, the obviously tacked-on happy ending in which Ford and the replicant (Young) flew off into the sunset (which contradicted what we already knew about the replicant's built-in obsolescence). With one crucial exception, the effect of the restorations is less radical, although the extended romantic scenes between Ford and Young do flesh out their relationship. More cryptically, Ford's restored 'unicorn dream' is echoed later by an origami figure left by police chief Bryant's right-hand man Gaff (Olmos) – possibly hinting that Ford himself is a replicant. Perhaps this, too, like Young's treasured childhood memories, is just an implant. In its earlier incarnation, the film was a flawed masterpiece; in Scott's restored version, it is, quite simply, a masterpiece. NF

Blair Witch Project, The

(1999, US, 81 min)
d Daniel Myrick, Eduardo Sanchez. *p* Gregg Hale, Robin Cowie. *sc* Daniel Myrick, Eduardo Sanchez. *ph* Neal Fredericks. *ed* Daniel Myrick, Eduardo Sanchez. *pd* Ben Rock. *m* Tony Cora. *cast* Heather Donahue, Michael Williams, Joshua Leonard.

● Heather, Michael and Josh (Donahue, Williams and Leonard) disappeared on 21 October 1994 while shooting a documentary in the forest of the Black Hills, Maryland. A year later, their footage was found. This movie is the last trace of them. This is a horror film made against the grain, in defiance of the genre as it has evolved over the last three decades. After a handful of interviews with the natives, the trio starts to trek through the woods to check out the 'cemetery' rumoured to mark the graves of missing children. At first, they joke around. Then, as they come across strange talismans made of twigs and stones, the mood becomes apprehensive. At night, inexplicable sounds disrupt their sleep. They lose their way in the trees, and the next night, the sounds are closer, stranger, much more frightening. This is back to basics horror: we're in deep dark woods among things that go bump in the night. The actors never put a foot wrong; the video diary form allows no artifice, so that as terror mounts, the dread is infectious. Indeed, the gradual social and psychological breakdown which ensues is often painful to watch. And to listen to, the sound design being extraordinarily evocative. Worse, it stays with you: the film issues a kind of shadow horror that only comes into play later, at night, when you want to forget it. TCh

Blair Witch 2

see Book of Shadows Blair Witch 2

Blaise Pascal

(1972, Fr/It, 131 min)
d/p Roberto Rossellini. *sc* Roberto Rossellini, Marcella Mariani, Luciano Scaffa. *ph* Mario Fioretti. *ed* Jolanda Benvenuti. *ad* Franco Velchi. *m* Mario Nascimbene. *cast* Pierre Arditi, Rita Forzano, Giuseppe Addobbati, Christian De Sica, Claude Baks, Livio Galassi.

●A thrilling, intense chronicle analysing the thought and development of 'a very boring man who never made love in his life' (Rossellini). The 17th century scientist and philosopher struggles with a society which believes in witchcraft and ridicules his discovery of the vacuum. Notions of both are made concrete as the film illustrates Pascal painfully pushing Europe towards Enlightenment. Discoursing with Descartes, he explains the necessity of limits to reason for the existence of God. And the 20th century audience *understands,* recognising a world explored with extraordinary lucidity and simplicity. Faith grapples with empiricism, reason routs superstition, and with every frame, Rossellini reinvents the historical biography. JW

Blame It On Rio

(1984, US, 100 min)
d/p Stanley Donen. *sc* Charlie Peters, Larry Gelbart. *ph* Reynaldo Villalobos. *ed* George Hively, Richard Marden. *ad* Marcos Flacksman. *m* Ken Wannberg, Oscar Castro-Neves. *cast* Michael Caine, Joseph Bologna, Valerie Harper, Michelle Johnson, Demi Moore.

●Two middle-aged businessmen (Caine and Bologna) take a holiday in Rio without their wives but with their teenage daughters. When Bologna's daughter, a pyrogenic half-pint with the subtle approach of a heat-seeking missile, homes in on Caine, the result is a very predictable sort of French farcing about. Aside from a good exchange rate of one-liners, the chief feeling left by the movie (a remake of Claude Berri's *Un Moment d'Egarement*) is of a thin, cynical calculation. Sole reason to catch it would be to monitor one more step of Caine's increasing excellence as middle age overtakes him. CPea

Blame It on the Bellboy

(1992, GB, 78 min)
d Mark Herman. *p* Jennifer Howarth. *sc* Mark Herman. *ph* Andrew Dunn. *ed* Michael Ellis. *ad* Gemma Jackson. *m* Trevor Jones. *cast* Dudley Moore, Bryan Brown, Richard Griffiths, Andreas Katsulas, Patsy Kensit, Alison Steadman, Penelope Wilto, Bronson Pinchot.

●Confusion over a name by a bellboy (Pinchot) in a Venetian hotel leads to lots of Benny Hill-style sexual innuendo, torture of the wrong man by the Mafia, and a hitman unable to work out who he's to hit. Meek Melvyn (Moore) is visiting Venice to buy a property for his boss, but falls into the hands of villainous Scarpa (Katsulas). Estate agent Caroline (Kensit) is mistaken for a sure bonk by porky Maurice (Griffiths), whose wife (Steadman) turns up unexpectedly. Only Bryan Brown (the hitman) and Penelope Wilton (the girl Maurice expected to meet) manage to do anything with their roles, even though she's cast as a Mickey Spillane fan. Mark Herman wrote as well as directed this leaden farce. BC

Blame It on Voltaire

see Faute à Voltaire, La

Blanche

(1971, Fr, 92 min)
d Walerian Borowczyk. *p* Dominique Duvergé, Philippe d'Argila. *sc* Walerian Borowczyk. *ph* Guy Durban. *ed/ad* Walerian Borowczyk. *cast* Ligia Branice, Michel Simon, Lawrence Trimble, Jacques Perrin, Georges Wilson, Denise Peronne.

●In this remarkable film, Borowczyk, through his commitment to ambiguity (notably in his framing, which forever denies the foreground/background opposition) and his belief in almost entomological observation, transforms his 13th century characters – a foolish old Baron, an over-proud King, a lecherous page and a stupidly handsome lover, all of whom are in love with and/or lust after the simple Blanche, the Baron's young wife – into tragic figures caught up in a dance of death over which they have no control. In exactly the same way, the castle and its decor, photographed by Borowczyk as though it were living and its inhabitants were mere dolls for the most part, is seen as the backdrop to a happy fairytale, and at the same time as the root of all evil, as rooms and bizarre machines are opened and set in motion. PH

Blanche Fury

(1947, GB, 95 min)
d Marc Allégret. *p* Anthony Havelock-Allan. *sc* Audrey Erskine Lindop, Hugh Mills, Cecil McGivern. *ph* Guy Green, Geoffrey Unsworth. *ed* Jack Harris. *ad* Wilfrid Shingleton. *m* Clifton Parker. *cast* Valerie Hobson, Stewart Granger, Walter Fitzgerald, Michael Gough, Maurice Denham, Sybilla Binder, Suzanne Gibbs.

●A strikingly designed Victorian melodrama, produced by Cineguild, which had made David Lean's two Dickens adaptations and was now trying to get into the Gainsborough market. Hobson plays a poor-relation governess who marries a widowed cousin and falls in love with Granger, a bastard who believes he has been disinherited. What makes the film rather distinctive is its eagerness to kill off the cast, whose acting is too lightweight for the material. ATu

Blank Check (aka Blank Cheque)

(1994, US, 93 min)
d Rupert Wainwright. *p* Gary Adelson, Craig Baumgarten. *sc* Blake Snyder, Colby Carr. *ph* Bill Pope. *ed* Hubert C de la Bouillerie, Jill Savitt. *pd* Nelson Coates. *m* Nicholas Pike. *cast* Brian Bonsall, Karen Duffy, James Rebhorn, Jayne Atkinson, Michael Faustino, Miguel Ferrer, Tone Loc.

●Neglected by his parents in favour of his older brother, 11-year-old Preston (Bonsall) wants money and his own house for his birthday. His wish is granted when crook Quigley (Ferrer) drives over his bike, since damages consist of a blank cheque; but when Preston fills in the amount as $1 million, he gets more than he bargained for, bringing both Quigley and the FBI down on top of him. A Disney feature from a first-time British director: inauspicious. AO

Blast from the Past

(1998, US, 109 min)
d Hugh Wilson. *p* Renny Harlin, Hugh Wilson. *sc* Bill Kelly. *ph* José Luis Alcaine. *ed* Don Brochu. *pd* Robert Ziembicki. *m* Steve Dorff. *cast* Brendan Fraser, Christopher Walken, Sissy Spacek, Alicia Silverstone, Dave Foley.

●What if Cold War fallout had frozen humankind's development, or plunged it back into the Dark Ages? Actually, the bomb only drops for one Californian family, inventor and borderline paranoiac Calvin (Walken) and his pregnant wife Helen (Spacek), whose 'prayerful watch and wait stance' during the Cuban Missile Crisis – plus a plane falling on their house – necessitates withdrawal to their radiation shelter for a 35-year stretch. When the bunker's time locks open, '90s LA look post-apocalyptic, but armed with some valuable baseball cards, son Adam (Fraser) ventures forth in search of supplies and a mate, finding an Eve (Silverstone) rather more knowing than himself. The story is humdrum and lackadaisical, the sociology merely decorative and witlessly conservative. Director Wilson takes credit for *The First Wives Club* and *Police Academy*, but this one has its redeeming qualities. The broad obvious jokes are generally tossed away with a panache that might be mistaken for subtlety; the performances are affable (good to see Walken for once comically underplaying – okay, coasting, but nicely); and there's even the odd surprise along the way. NB

Blaue Licht, Das (The Blue Light)

(1932, Ger, 72 min, b/w)
d/p Leni Riefenstahl. *sc* Leni Riefenstahl, Bela Balazs. *ph* Hans Schneeberger. *ed* Leni Riefenstahl. *m* Giuseppe Becce. *cast* Leni Riefenstahl, Mathias Wieman, Beni Führer.

●A majestic waterfall cascading down a rugged mountainside, a horse grazing in the clearing of a sun-dappled forest: cliché prose for cliché images, as Riefenstahl indulges her taste for wildly idealised Nature. She plays Junta, the outcast of the Dolomites, shunned by the locals as a witch, her only friends a boy goatherd and a visiting artist. She communes mystically with a crystal grotto, source of the Blue Light, associated with truth and purity. At least until the villagers desecrate it, prompting her to check out. Riefenstahl's affirmation of the occult has a certain morbid interest, but it's as a performer, posing leggily atop cloudswept crags, that she most compels attention – though a certain Thatcheresque cast to her features is hard to rise above, once you've spotted it. BBa

Blaze

(1989, US, 117 min)
d Ron Shelton. *p* Gil Friesen, Dale Pollock. *sc* Ron Shelton. *ph* Haskell Wexler. *ed* Robert Leighton. *ad* Armin Ganz. *m* Bennie Wallace. *cast* Paul Newman, Lolita Davidovich, Jerry Hardin, Gailard Sartain, Jeffrey DeMunn, Garland Bunting, Richard Jenkins, Brandon Smith, Jay Chevalier.

●In the late '50s, Louisiana governor Earl K Long (brother of Huey) scandalised voters when news broke of his affair with stripper Blaze Starr. In what is essentially a vehicle for Paul Newman, Long comes over as gangling eccentric and political visionary: he keeps his boots on while love-making, and at a time of entrenched prejudice approves voting rights for blacks. While opponents plot his abduction. supporters applaud his outspokenness. The film's overall tone is light, and against this Newman cuts an imposing, vigorous figure. But Ron Shelton's script is inconsistent. Co-star Davidovich attempts a sympathetic rendering of Blaze Starr, but her role is underdeveloped; given that the central relationship prevails over the political agenda, it's an oversight which leaves dialogue one-sided and often toothless. Considering the awareness of post-Watergate audiences, it's not enough merely to portray a gutsy, glitzy couple who both, by Starr's definition, work in 'showbiz'. The film has a certain candour, but it would have been enhanced by a less superficial approach. CM

Blazing Guns (Uomo avvisato, mezzo ammazzato ...parola di Spirito Santo)

(1972, It/Sp, 91 min)
d Antony Ascott [Giuliano Carnimeo]. *sc* Tito Carpi, Federico de Urrutia. *ph* Miguel F Mila. *ed* Ornella Micheli. *ad* Cubero Galicia. *m* Bruno Nicolai. *cast* Gianni Garko, Pilar Velasquez, Chris Huerta, Polda Bendandi, Jorge Rigaud, Paolo Gozlino.

●Gory (and excremental) spaghetti Western about a goldmine won in a poker game and the trouble it causes in revolution-torn Mexico. The white-cloaked protagonist, Harold 'Holy Ghost' (Garko), owner of a dove named 'Eagle', is a pretty unconvincing avenging angel. JPy

Blazing Saddles

(1974, US, 93 min)
d Mel Brooks. *p* Michael Hertzberg. *sc* Mel Brooks, Norman Steinberg, Andrew Bergman, Richard Pryor, Alan Uger. *ph* Joseph Biroc. *ed* John C Howard, Danford B Greene. *pd* Peter Wooley. *m* John Morris. *cast* Cleavon Little, Gene Wilder, Slim Pickens, Harvey Korman, Madeline Kahn, Mel Brooks, David Huddleston.

●'Oh Lord', says the preacher in a suitably grave voice, 'do we have the strength to carry out this task in one night, or are we just jerking off?' Maybe Mel Brooks should have asked himself that question about this movie. The screenplay is credited to five writers, and it shows in the confused melange of styles. There are some lovely touches, and a score of lines like the preacher's which start pompous and end crude; or the contrast between picture – archetypal white-haired old lady – and words – 'Up yours, Nigger!' But if part is delightful, a larger part proves that there is more corn in Hollywood than Oklahoma, and a lot is just Hollywood jerking off. PB

Blazing Sun

see Plein Soleil

Bleak Moments

(1971, GB, 111 min)
d Mike Leigh. *p* Les Blair. *sc* Mike Leigh. *ph* Bahram Manocheri. *ed* Les Blair. *ad* Richard Rambaut. *songs* Mike Bradwell. *cast* Anne Raitt, Sarah Stephenson, Eric Allan, Joolia Cappleman, Mike Bradwell, Linda Beckett, Liz Smith.

●A girl left at home with her mentally retarded sister tries to work out her own communication problems. She fails with a well-meaning teacher, especially in a Chinese restaurant where the only other diner gobbles down his food in contrasting extravagance, and also with a long-haired would-be guitarist, who buries his head in his own silence. Says a lot about repressed feelings, with none of the social propaganda of Ken Loach's *Family Life*. The bleak moments are everywhere, and pretty harrowing.

Bleeder

(1999, Den, 97 min)
d Nikolas Winding Refn. *p* Nikolas Winding Refn, Henrik Danstrup, Thomas Falck. *sc* Nikolas Winding Refn. *ph* Morten Søborg. *ed* Anne Østerud. *pd* Peter de Neergaard. *m* Peter Peter. *cast* Kim Bodnia, Mads Mikkelsen, Rikke Louise Andersson, Liv Corfixen, Levino Jensen, Zlatko Buric, Claus Flüggare, Gordana Radosavljevic, Marko Zecewic, Dusan Zecewic.

●This gruelling drama finds the director of *Pusher* seeking to broaden his emotional range and break out of crime genre histrionics. But he's so good at that stuff, he can't quite keep the blood and guts off the screen. A grimly funny portrait of a group of immature friends in deadend jobs failing to connect with women (or indeed reality), this feels a little like a Danish *Nil by Mouth* with a touch of *Clerks* thrown in. Bodnia especially has some powerful scenes. Yet the more intense the movie gets, the less credible it becomes. A lovely sequence in which a woman simply browses in a bookshop shows how much more the director has to offer; at the moment he's still too close to these self-punishing men. TCh

Blended

see Métisse

Bless the Child

(2000, US/Ger, 108 min)
d Chuck Russell. *p* Mace Neufeld. *sc* Tom Rickman, Clifford Green, Ellen Green. *ph* Peter Menzies Jr. *ed* Alan Heim. *pd* Carol Spier. *m* Christopher Young. *cast* Kim Basinger, Jimmy Smits, Rufus Sewell, Ian Holm, Angela Bettis, Holliston Coleman, Christina Ricci, Lumi Cavazos.

●Oscar winner Kim Basinger's search for a strong female role to follow *LA Confidential* has taken her down a particularly gruesome blind alley with this occult thriller. She plays a successful nurse, a single woman whose maternal instincts are unexpectedly stirred when wayward younger sister Bettis lumbers her with a baby daughter. As time passes, she comes to understand that the little girl is 'special', and she's prepared to fight for custody when the reformed smackhead mum pitches up to reclaim her offspring. The latter arrives supported by Sewell, a celebrity self-help guru with a dark secret. Not only is he trying to conceal an English accent, but he and his national organisation are footsoldiers of Satan, and bent on eliminating the telekinetic moppet sent from above as our earthly salvation. The use of child jeopardy as a cheap suspense mechanism is somewhat dubious, but one's unease is slightly mollified by the fact that much of this is far too silly to take seriously. TJ

Blind Alley

(1939, US, 71 min, b/w)
d Charles Vidor. *sc* Michael Blankfort, Albert Duffy. *ph* Lucien Ballard. *ed* Otto Meyer. *ad* Lionel Banks. *m* Morris Stoloff. *cast* Chester Morris, Ralph Bellamy, Ann Dvorak, Joan Perry, Melville Cooper, Rose Stradner, Marc Lawrence.

●Interesting but somewhat ramshackle chunk of Freudiana adapted from a stage play, in which an escaped convict (Morris) and his associates hold a remote household hostage while waiting for their getaway transport. The house happens to belong to a psychiatrist (Bellamy), and the process by which he gradually asserts his dominance, realising that the convict is a compulsive killer who is afraid he's going mad, is persuasively done; the miracle analysis he achieves within hours (programming the killer so that he can no longer pull the trigger), is ludicrous, to say the least. The best sequence details the killer's recurring nightmare of cowering from a relentless shower of blood under a perforated umbrella, simply but very effectively staged in negative; and throughout, Lucien Ballard's deep focus compositions enhance the otherwise routine tensions. Remade in 1948 as *The Dark Past*. TM

Blind Alley (Mienai)

(1985, Jap, 58 min)
d Go Riju. *p* Tsuyoshi Ozawa. *sc* Go Riyuji. *ph* Go Abe. *ed* Koji Tanaki. *m* Gulliver Otsuka. *cast* Koji Sano, Asao Kobayashi, Go Riju.

●A sort of documentary by a bright young actor-director (he plays the young Mishima in Paul Schrader's *Mishima*), shot on video and transferred to 16 mm film. Riju starts out talking about his own inability to feel political commitment and his uncertainties about cinema, then stumbles on an inarticulate and reclusive young truck-driver and decides to make a film about him. The film records their encounters over a period of weeks, with Riju driven into a frenzy of frustration by the boy's passivity and lack of interest in 'important' questions, until they finally come to blows. This is funny and surprisingly engrossing – and a surprise ending rockets it into another dimension entirely. TR

Blind Chance (Przypadek)

(1982, Pol, 122 min)
d Krzysztof Kieslowski. *p* Jacek Szeligowski. *sc* Krzysztof Kieslowski. *ph* Krzysztof Pakulski. *ed* Elzbieta Kurkowska. *pd* Rafal Waltenberger. *m* Wojciech Kilar. *cast* Boguslaw Linda, Tadeusz Lomnicki, Zbigniew Zapasiewicz, Boguslawa Pawelec, Jerzy Stuhr, Marzena Trybala.

●Kieslowski's film was originally suppressed under Martial Law for its gloomy political prognosis. It offers three quite distinct possibilities for Poland's future by having a former medical student running to catch a train from Lodz to Warsaw. First, he catches the train, meets an old-style Stalinist, and joins the Party. Second, he misses the train, gets arrested, and is jailed with dissident students. Lastly, he misses the train again, gets married, and settles down to sexy and apolitical bliss. A fourth story, in which Poland throws out the Communist Party, was presumably unthinkable in 1982… ATu

Blind Corner

(1963, GB, 80 min, b/w)
d Lance Comfort. *p* Tom Blakeley. *sc* James Kelly Peter Miller. *ph* Basil Emmott. *ed* John Trumper. *ad* John Earl. *m* Brian Fahey. *cast* William Sylvester, Barbara Shelley, Elizabeth Shepherd, Alex Davion, Mark Eden, Ronnie Carroll.

●An unassuming but occasionally effective second feature thriller which is marred by some phony characterisation. Sylvester plays a blind pop music composer, with Shelley as his apparently loving wife who plans to murder him and go off with her lover. Of interest chiefly to admirers of Barbara (Cat Girl) Shelley or Elizabeth (Ligeia) Shepherd.

Blind Date (aka Chance Meeting)

(1959, GB, 95 min, b/w)
d Joseph Losey. *p* David Deutsch. *sc* Ben Barzman, Millard Lampell. *ph* Christopher Challis. *ed* Reginald Mills. *ad* Edward Carrick. *m* Richard Rodney Bennett. *cast* Hardy Krüger, Stanley Baker, Micheline Presle, Robert Flemyng, Gordon Jackson, John Van Eyssen, Jack MacGowran.

●Made four years before the Profumo affair gave such scandals a real-life significance, Losey's thriller – based on Leigh Howard's novel – deals with the murder of a diplomat's French mistress (Presle), and the pressures on a cynical cop (Baker) to pin the case on her other lover (Krüger), a Dutch artist from the lower classes. Although the script is dramatically weak, Losey's precise view of the characters in terms of class conflict and erotic obsession gives the film an edge absent in the work of most resident British directors of the period. DT

Blind Date

(1984, US, 99 min)
d/p Nico Mastorakis. *sc* Nico Mastorakis, Fred C Perry. *ph* Andreas Bellis. *ed* George Rosenburg. *pd* Anne-Marie Papadelis. *m* Stanley Myers. *cast* Joseph Bottoms, Kirstie Alley, James Daughton, Lana Clarkson, Keir Dullea, Charles Nicklin.

●Bottoms becomes traumatically blind after witnessing his object of desire with another man, and so has a computer embedded in his brain. The resulting Dayglo vision turns the world into one huge video game inside his head; but the picture quality isn't good enough to enable him to see the face of the killer who is carving up the women of Athens with a scalpel. Unfortunately not enough is made of this blurring of the interface between man and machine; and the key concept of voyeurism is kept strictly on the exploitative level. The rest of the film (shot in Greece) is largely composed of women in slashed blouses or wet bikinis undergoing humiliation. It needs the kind of nasty thoughtfulness of a De Palma behind it; but it just comes out a Babycham picture in a Moet bottle. CPea

Blind Date

(1987, US, 95 min)
d Blake Edwards. *p* Tony Adams. *sc* Dale Launer. *ph* Harry Stradling Jr. *ed* Robert Pergament. *pd* Rodger Maus. *m* Henry Mancini. *cast* Kim Basinger, Bruce Willis, John Larroquette, William Daniels, George Coe, Mark Blum.

●Walter (Willis) needs a date for that all-important business dinner, but the lady his brother fixes him up with should carry a blue-touch-paper warning. Nadia (Basinger) can't drink without going ape. She loses him his job, wrecks his car, and inadvertently sets her insanely jealous ex-boyfriend David (Larroquette) on his case. Most of the set pieces are predictable in this formula comedy, though there is a sprinkling of chuckles in the sight gags. BC

Blindfold

(1965, US, 102 min)
d Philip Dunne. *p* Marvin Schwartz. *sc* Philip Dunne, WH Menger. *ph* Joseph MacDonald. *ed* Ted J Kent. *ad* Alexander Golitzen, Henry Bumstead. *m* Lalo Schifrin. *cast* Rock Hudson, Claudia Cardinale, Guy Stockwell, Jack Warden, Brad Dexter, Anne Seymour.

●A wryly self-mocking spy thriller coating a convoluted international plot and stock genre characters (psychologist, mad scientist, security chief, et al) in the requisite '60s gloss. The final film as director of former Fox contract writer (*How Green Was My Valley*, *Forever Amber*, *The Robe*, etc) Dunne. PT

Blind Fury

(1989, US, 86 min)
d Phillip Noyce. *p* Daniel Grodnik, Tim Matheson. *sc* Charles Robert Carner. *ph* Don Burgess. *ed* David Simmons. *pd* Peter Murton. *m* J Peter Robinson. *cast* Rutger Hauer, Terrance O'Quinn, Brandon Call, Noble Willingham, Lisa Blount, Nick Cassavetes, Rick Overton, Randall 'Tex' Cobb, Meg Foster, Sho Kosugi.

●Like many a damaged hero, Nick Parker (Hauer) is a Vietvet, but his experiences left him blind, not batty. A credits sequence shows how the stricken Parker was rescued from the battlefield by gentle Vietnamese and taught some nifty (if not downright supernatural) sword skills. He also (Rambo, please note) learns tolerance, self-restraint and compassion. Pair him with a cute menaced kid whose mum has been offed by the

Mob, and whose dad (O'Quinn) is Parker's long-lost army pal, and you have a New Man with a Mission. Hauer's Parker, shambling, shrewd and powerful, is humorous and appealing, and Noyce skilfully orchestrates a hilarious army of gurning baddies. It thunders along admirably, if rather unbelievably, and to counter the sickly moments with the cute kid (Call), there's plenty of pleasurable ass-kicking. SFe

Blind Goddess, The

(1948, GB, 87 min, b/w)
d Harold French. *p* Harold French, Betty Box. *sc* Muriel Box, Sydney Box. *ph* Ray Elton. *ed* Gordon Hales. *ad* Norman Arnold. *m* Bernard Grun. *cast* Eric Portman, Michael Denison, Claire Bloom, Anne Crawford, Hugh Williams, Frank Cellier, Clive Morton, Maurice Denham, Thora Hird.

●Apapted from a play by Sir Patrick Hastings, this class-bound courtroom drama is utterly of its time, what with its nice young hero ('Darling, I've been a blithering idiot'), its masterful King's Counsel ('I object – to nothing'), its sternly impartial judge. Add Maurice Denham and Thora Hird as the servant class ('Cook would like a word, ma'am'), plus the thought that rock'n'roll was still eight years away, and you catch a glimpse of the hell that must have been 1948. Of mild interest are Portman's delivery, a cadenced gabble, with words hurtling into one another like a motorway pile-up; and the way in which, having dared to make Lord and Lady Brasted the stop-at-nothing villains, the writers still can't forbear from finding them really rather admirable and splendid. The title refers to Justice. BBa

Blind Husbands

(1918, US, 8 reels, b/w)
d Erich von Stroheim. *p* Carl Laemmle. *sc* Erich von Stroheim. *ph* Ben Reynolds. *ed* Erich von Stroheim, Frank Lawrence, Eleanor Fried. *ad* Erich von Stroheim. *cast* Erich von Stroheim, TH Gibson Gowland, Sam de Grasse, Francelia Billington, Fay Holderness.

●Stroheim's first film as director (he also wrote, starred in, and designed the sets for it). Apart from the naturalistic acting styles from all the principals, *Blind Husbands* is not particularly remarkable in itself; but it adequately signposts many of the aspects of Stroheim's later work which make him unique. Stroheim himself plays the aristocratic officer attempting to seduce the neglected wife of a young American on holiday in the Austro-Italian Alps. It's a moral tale, as simplistic as it sounds, but what makes it distinctive is the use of design and the characters' personal mannerisms as fully functional elements of the director's overall moral purpose. RM

Blindman

(1971, US/It, 105 min)
d Ferdinando Baldi. *p* Tony Anthony, Saul Swimmer. *sc* Tony Anthony, Piero Anchisi, Vincenzo Cerami. *ph* Riccardo Pallottini. *ed* Roberto Perpignani. *ad* Gastone Garsetti. *m* Stelvio Cipriani. *cast* Tony Anthony, Ringo Starr, Agneta Eckemyr, Lloyd Batista, Magda Konopka.

●Alternately amusing and embarrassing sub-Leone Western, with a blind pudgy-faced hero who can nevertheless shoot straight and enjoys a psychic understanding with his horse. Despite some striking widescreen photography, the hero and the silly plot, involving his attempts to regain fifty stolen mail order brides, relegates it to passable viewing for a local double bill, but that's about all.

Blind Spot (Die Reise nach Lyon)

(1980, WGer, 111 min)
d/sc Claudia von Alemann. *ph* Hille Sagel. *ed* Monique Dartonne. *m* Frank Wolff. *cast* Rebecca Pauly, Jean Badin, Denise Péron, Sarah Stern, Maurice Garden, Pierre-Emile Legrand.

●Flora Tristan was a 19th century utopian socialist feminist, notorious in her day, now largely forgotten. A young historian (Pauly) leaves husband and child to seek traces of Tristan in contemporary Lyons. Disillusioned with the records-and-monuments methods of historians, she roams the streets recording sounds Tristan may have heard. A film about the impossibility of knowing the past; the camera looks and looks but only yields implacably closed images. Sound's the thing, and in the final, long-held shot of the woman ecstatically playing her violin, the film's complex and compelling themes come together. JR.

Blink

(1994, US, 106 min)
d Michael Apted. *p* David Blocker. *sc* Dana Stevens. *ph* Dante Spinotti. *ed* Rick Shaine. *pd* Dan Bishop. *m* Brad Fiedel. *cast* Madeleine Stowe, Aidan Quinn, James Remar, Peter Friedman, Bruce A Young, Laurie Metcalf.

●Suddenly, after 20-odd years of living in darkness, Emma Brody has seen too much – or has she? Well, you can join the dots to complete Apted's thriller from the blurb, except for the question bit at the end. That's the hook. Retroactive vision is a rare phenomenon which accompanies the early stages of restored sight, involving flashbacks and, for the purposes of movies, lots and lots of computer-generated effects. Emma (Stowe), a folk fiddle player, suffers from the above, which makes her an unreliable murder witness. Who believes her? The murderer for one, and the coarse cop Hallstrom (Quinn) for another, and it isn't long before he becomes someone to watch over her. The handling of both plot and romance is muddled, and the film is largely fuelled by Stowe's tough, independent characterisation. She plays against the sentimentality inherent in her predicament, but isn't consistently helped by either script or sugary compositions. Fairly functional time-passer, but it would've passed anyway. BC

Bliss

(1985, Aust, 112 min)
d Ray Lawrence. *p* Anthony Buckley. *sc* Ray Lawrence, Peter Carey. *ph* Paul Murphy. *ed* Wayne Le Clos. *ad* Owen Paterson. *m* Peter Best. *cast* Barry Otto, Lynette Curran, Helen Jones, Gia Carides, Miles Buchanan, Jeff Truman.

●Lawrence's adaptation of Peter Carey's novel in no way pants after American prototypes. Part surrealist comedy and part mid-life crisis drama, its madcap energy and anarchic intelligence put it in a class of its own. Harry Joy (Otto), rich advertising executive, is loved by everyone except his wife, who is having an affair with his partner and best friend. Harry only discovers this after a four-minute clinical death from a heart attack, when he begins to see his life in perspective: his marriage is in ruins, his son swaps drugs for sex from his daughter, all around him people are dying of cancer, and his wife has him committed to an asylum. Then into his life steps the young and beautiful Honey (Jones), and the sweet-toothed Harry falls in love as she beckons him into the bush and a back-to-nature idyll. Witty and profoundly enjoyable. CB.

Bliss of Mrs Blossom, The

(1968, GB, 93 min)
d Joseph McGrath. *p* Josef Shaftel. *sc* Alec Coppel, Denis Norden. *ph* Geoffrey Unsworth. *ed* Ralph Sheldon. *pd* Assheton Gorton. *m* Riz Ortolani. *cast* Shirley MacLaine, Richard Attenborough, James Booth, Freddie Jones, William Rushton, Bob Monkhouse, Patricia Routledge.

●Coarse comedy which looks a little like Joe Orton gone disastrously wrong (actually it's based on a play by Alec Coppel) as Attenborough's downtrodden brassière manufacturer dreams of being an orchestra conductor, his wife secretly instals a lover in the attic, and an effeminate detective prowls in quest of a crime. Any sparks in the script or performances are ruthlessly extinguished by atrocious direction. TM

Blithe Spirit

(1945, GB, 96 min)
d David Lean. *p* Anthony Havelock-Allan. *sc* Noël Coward. *ph* Ronald Neame. *ed* Jack Harris. *ad* CP Norman. *m* Richard Addinsell. *cast* Rex Harrison, Constance Cummings, Kay Hammond, Margaret Rutherford, Hugh Wakefield, Joyce Carey.

●A classy adaptation of Noël Coward's successful stage play, in which the wedded bliss of cynical remarried novelist Harrison is threatened by the mischievous ghost of his first wife (Hammond), who appears at a seance presided over by Rutherford's eccentric medium and proceeds to bother his none-too-amused second wife (Cummings). Nifty special effects for the time, and plenty of Coward's inimitable wit and repartee. NF

Blob, The

(1958, US, 86 min)
d Irwin S Yeaworth Jr. *p* Jack H Harris. *sc* Theodore Simonson, Kate Phillips. *ph* Thomas E Spalding. *ed* Alfred Hillman. *ad* William Jersey, Karl Karlson. *m* Ralph Carmichael. *song* Burt Bacharach, Mack David. *cast* Steve McQueen, Anita Corseaut, Earl Rowe, Olin Howlin.

●Arriving from outer space (for which read Russia), a large ball of interstellar snot terrorises a small American town by eating everything in sight. McQueen turns in a commendable performance as the (not so) young rebel without a car, who attempts to alert his townsfolk to the threat of the amorphous alien, demonstrating in the process that tearaway teens can still be steadfast, loyal and true when the shit comes down. Despite producer Jack Harris' pooh-poohing of the 'political subtext' theory, rampant Commie-phobia pervades as the ever-redder blob sucks the life-blood out of every sacred American institution, climaxing in a truly marvellous scene in which the enemy within devours an entire diner, over easy, with a side salad and fries to go. MK

Blob, The

(1988, US, 95 min)
d Chuck Russell. *p* Jack H Harris, Elliot Kastner. *sc* Chuck Russell, Frank Darabont. *ph* Mark Irwin. *ed* Terry Stokes, Tod Feuerman. *pd* Craig Stearns. *m* Michael Hoenig. *cast* Shawnee Smith, Donovan Leitch, Kevin Dillon, Billy Beck, Candy Clark, Del Close, Jeffrey DeMunn.

●This reworking of the 1958 cheapie clearly illustrates one thing: that no increase in budget and no amount of state-of-the-art special effects can compensate for a slim B-movie plot. After a meteorite crashes to earth, the amorphous Blob slimes its way through the small town of Arborville, ingesting en route a varied diet of dogs, groping couples, cinema patrons, and other disposable teens. The gelatinous monster slides from one set piece to the next more smoothly than the stop-start plot, which (as in the original) consists largely of the efforts of cheerleader Smith and rebellious biker Dillon to alert sceptical adults to the alien threat. More successful is the film's main innovation, a government conspiracy subplot in which a biological containment team seal off the town and put the monster's potential as a weapon above the safety of the townspeople. It's the effects that carry the day, however with the sluggish, oozing blob of the original now a clear pink amoebic predator that lashes out sticky tendrils and digests its victims in full view. NF

Blockade

(1938, US, 85 min, b/w)
d William Dieterle. *p* Walter Wanger. *sc* John Howard Lawson. *ph* Rudolph Maté. *ed* Dorothy Spencer. *ad* Alexander Toluboff. *m* Werner Janssen. *cast* Henry Fonda, Madeleine Carroll, Leo Carrillo, Reginald Denny, John Halliday, Vladimir Sokoloff.

●Classic example of Hollywood easing its conscience about the Spanish Civil War (never identified by name) while carefully hedging its bets. Scripted by John Howard Lawson (later one of the Hollywood Ten), it's littered with pseudo-echoes of Soviet movies as Fonda's peasant rabbits on about his love of the soil, while Carroll does the Dietrich bit as a spy suffering romance and a change of heart. Totally spurious, though well shot (Rudolph Maté) and directed, it ends in cringing embarrassment with Fonda making an appeal to camera for the world to stop this war. TM

Block-Heads

(1938, US, 57 min, b/w)
d John G Blystone. *p* Hal Roach, Stan Laurel. *sc* James Parrott, Harry Langdon, Felix Adler, Charles Rogers, Arnold Belgard. *ph* Art Lloyd. *m* Marvin Hatley. *cast* Stan Laurel, Oliver Hardy, Billy Gilbert, Patricia Ellis, James Finlayson, Minna Gombell.

●Planned as the last Laurel & Hardy film (which fortunately turned out not to be the case), this remains one of their best features. From its opening sequence– Stan guarding the front, twenty years after the end of World War I hostilities – through the chance re-meeting of Stan and a horribly domesticated Ollie, to the climax of disaster caused by Stan's good intentions, *Blockheads* (co-scripted by Harry Langdon) is a triumphant exploration of the quality and kind of relationship between Stan and Ollie that underlies their best comedy. PH

Blockhouse, The

(1973, GB, 92 min)
d Clive Rees. *p* Anthony Rufus-Isaacs, Edgar M Bronfman Jr. *sc* John Gould, Clive Rees. *ph* Keith Goddard. *ed* Peter Gold. *ad* Leo Austin, George Lack. *m* Stanley Myers. *cast* Peter Sellers, Charles Aznavour, Per Oscarsson, Peter Vaughn, Alfred Lynch, Jeremy Kemp.

● A group of slave workers, drafted by the Nazis to help construct their coastal defences in 1944, are sealed underground during an Allied naval bombardment. They find huge stores of food, but candles to last only so long. The slow dying of their light provides the film with its meagre dramatic impetus, as one by one they are done in by boredom, illness, jealousy. Incongruous casting lends piquancy to their fate, but like them the film seems designed for terminal obscurity. RC

Block-Notes di un Regista

see Fellini A Director's Notebook

Blonde Ambition

(1980, US, 81 min)
d/p John Amero, Lem Amero. *sc* LeRue Watts. *ph* Roberta Findlay. *ed* Lem Amero. *ad* LaRue Watts. *m* Firth De Mule. *cast* Suzy Mandel, Dory Devon, Eric Edwards, George Payne, Kurt Mann, Jamie Gillis.

● A bawdy rip-off of *Gentlemen Prefer Blondes* from the porn circuit. The storytelling is paltry, most of the acting aboriginal, but there is a pyrogenic half-pint in the shape of Mandel, who has all the dumb-puckering ingenuousness of the early Monroe. At the drop of a champagne glass, she is rending her garments and preparing to break the seventh commandment with some humdinger in a stetson, only the infuriating cuts for the British market (six minutes gone) coming between her and you and the fun. There is also evidence of a certain crude humour at work: an amorous version of *Gone With the Wind* ('The Yankees are coming!') being directed by Jamie Gillis, NY porn star. And the bizarre spectacle of someone's front room transformed into a skating rink for a set piece of troilism on ice, yet. CPea

Blonde Fist

(1991, GB, 99 min, b/w & col)
d Frank Clarke. *p* Joseph D'Morais, Christopher Figg. *sc* Frank Clarke. *ph* Bruce McGowan. *ed* Brian Peachey. *pd* Colin Pocock. *m* Alan Gill. *cast* Margi Clarke, Carroll Baker, Ken Hutchinson, Sharon Power, Angela Clarke, Lewis Bester, Gary Mavers.

● A pugnacious but misbegotten celebration of working-class values, Clarke's directorial debut (he wrote *Letter to Brezhnev*) is a sad disappointment. Ronnie (Margi Clarke) is an embodiment of female working-class strengths. She also has a deadly right fist, inherited from her bare-knuckle fighter father, which lands her in gaol for assaulting her husband's girlfriend, and later – after she's escaped to America in search of her father – gives her a chance to make some desperately needed money on the female boxing circuit. The film starts intriguingly, with a black-and-white sequence set in the late '50s, in which dad (Hutchinson) fights round the back while mum gives birth. But as we move into colour and modern times, it falls apart: ploddingly paced and cliché-filled. WH

Blonde in Love, A

see Lásky Jedné Plavovlásky

Blonde Venus

(1932, US, 97 min, b/w)
d/p Josef von Sternberg. *sc* SK Lauren, Jules Furthman. *ph* Bert Glennon. *ad* Wiard B Ihnen. *cast* Marlene Dietrich, Herbert Marshall, Cary Grant, Sidney Toler, Dickie Moore, Hattie McDaniel.

● With characteristic exaggeration, Sternberg himself wrote off *Blonde Venus* as a disaster. He made it (under protest) in response to studio pressure for another Dietrich vehicle, and seems to have attempted to work a number of autobiographical elements into its sprawling extremes of glamour and squalor. The film is certainly a mess at one level, with damaging fluctuations in tone and pace, and some ropey supporting performances, but it remains enough of a visual triumph to earn its place in the series of Dietrich movies. Dietrich is here not only married but also a mother, forced into a career as a nightclub singer to pay for her husband's medical fees, and then lured into an affair with playboy Grant. Her misadventures (including a flight into seedy hotels in the Deep South) are a bizarre mixture of fairytale and social-realist drama, snapping into sharpest focus when she performs the legendary 'Hot Voodoo' number while emerging from a gorilla-skin. TR

Blondie

(1938, US, 69 min, b/w)
d Frank Strayer. *sc* Richard Flournoy. *ph* Henry Freulich. *ed* Gene Havlick. *cast* Penny Singleton, Arthur Lake, Gene Lockhart, Ann Doran, Larry Simms, Jonathan Hale.

● First in the series based on Chic Young's comic strip about the bumbling Dagwood Bumstead and his dizzy blonde wife (who wore the pants, but pretended not to). Popular at the time, brightly and breezily done, it ran to twenty-seven sequels ending in 1950, during which time Baby Dumpling (played throughout by Simms) grew up to become the adolescent Alexander. A prototype of the average TV sitcom today. TM

Blood and Concrete

(1991, US, 99 min)
d Jeffrey Reiner. *p* Richard Labrie. *sc/ed* Jeffrey Reiner, Richard Labrie. *ph* Declain Quinn. *pd* Pamela Woodbrudge. *m* Vinny Golia. *cast* Billy Zane, Jennifer Beals, Darren McGavin, James Le Gros, Nicholas Worth, William Bastiani.

● A black comic cocktail of '50s B *film noir* and post-modern irony, with a bitter twist. Small-time criminal Joey Turks (Zane) stumbles into a scam involving an addictive aphrodisiac drug, Libido, then hooks up with damaged romantic Mona (Beals). Veteran cop Hank Dick (McGavin), meanwhile, wants to settle a long-standing score with the package's real owner, criminal big-shot Spuntz, whose gay psycho hoodlum Lance (Le Gros) has become Joey's shadow. Jim Thompson might have recognised the survival ethic and scuzzy characters, but this is soft-boiled pastiche rather than hard-boiled parody. NF

Blood and Sand

(1922, US, 7,100 ft, b/w)
d Fred Niblo. *sc* June Mathis. *ph* Arthur Edeson. *ed* Dorothy Arzner. *cast* Rudolph Valentino, Nita Naldi, Lila Lee, George Field, Walter Long.

● Matador Valentino and vamp Naldi tango this rise-and-fall *corrida* melodrama towards the realm of the senses. But Niblo's prosaic direction is at odds with the Iberian exotica, and it is left to the odd inventions of June Mathis' script, and the bullfight sequences constructed by editor Dorothy Arzner, to add anything to the curiosity value of the Great Lover's work. PT

Blood and Sand

(1941, US, 123 min)
d Rouben Mamoulian. *p* Darryl F Zanuck, Robert T Kane. *sc* Jo Swerling. *ph* Ernest Palmer. *ed* Robert Bischoff. *ad* Richard Day, Joseph C Wright. *m* Alfred Newman. *cast* Tyrone Power, Linda Darnell, Rita Hayworth, Laird Cregar, Anthony Quinn, J Carrol Naish, John Carradine, Alla Nazimova.

● One of *the* great colour films (with Mamoulian taking the inspiration for his lush visuals from Spanish masters like Goya, Velasquez and El Greco), this is melodramatic romance of the first order. The story is hardly a stunner, taken from Ibañez and telling of a young man's rags-to-riches rise as a matador, only to fall under the spell of Hayworth's aristocratic temptress, who lures him away from virginal childhood sweetheart Darnell. What makes the film so enjoyable is the sheer elegance of the execution, with Mamoulian's sense of rhythm, the rich Technicolor, and Richard Day's sets conjuring up an imaginary Spain of the heart, poignant location of love in the shadows and death in the afternoon. GA

Blood and Wine

(1996, US/GB, 100 min.)
d Bob Rafelson. *p* Jeremy Thomas. *sc* Nick Villiers, Alison Cross. *ph* Tom Sigel. *ed* Steven Cohen. *pd* Richard Sylbert. *m* Michal Lorenc. *cast* Jack Nicholson, Michael Caine, Stephen Dorff, Jennifer Lopez, Judy Davis, Harold Perrineau Jr, Robyn Peterson.

● The theft of a $1m diamond necklace from a wine dealer's wealthy client is merely the generic hook for Rafelson's insidious character study, which teams Nicholson's over-reaching vintner with Caine's terminally seedy safe cracker. As in *The Postman Always Rings Twice*, the crime itself proves deceptively easy; it's the ensuing complications that expose the subtly shifting alliances, the sly deceptions and the murky motives. With his crudely dyed black hair and big talk, the has-been Caine's professional competence is as shaky as his health, and everything is complicated by Nicholson and his unwitting son Dorff's mutual lust for the inside connection, the client's sexy, manipulative nanny, Jennifer Lopez. An engrossing thriller – and one sparkling with intelligence, with the surprising twists grounded in credible human behaviour. NF

Bloodbath at the House of Death

(1983, GB, 92 min)
d/p Ray Cameron. *sc* Ray Cameron, Barry Cryer. *ph* Brian West, Dusty Miller. *ed* Brian Tagg. *ad* John Sunderland. *m* Mike Moran, Mark London. *cast* Kenny Everett, Pamela Stephenson, Vincent Price, Gareth Hunt, John Fortune, Sheila Steafel.

● Headstone Manor saw the disappearance of 18 souls in 18 grisly ways, which the locals have variously put down to some dodgy monkey business, visitors from outer space, or fast food excess. Ten years on, strong radiation readings bring the one-legged Dr Mandeville (Everett) to do some paranormal research, and the carnage begins. The spoofings of so many genre films in a barrage of visual gags quickly becomes predictable; only Sheila Steafel's *Carrie* sketch is done with any imagination. FL

Blood Beach

(1980, US, 89 min)
d Jeffrey Bloom. *p* Steven Nalevansky. *sc* Jeffrey Bloom. *ph* Steve Poster. *ed* Gary Griffen. *ad* William Sandell. *m* Gil Mellé. *cast* David Huffman, Mariana Hill, John Saxon, Otis Young, Stefan Gierasch, Burt Young.

● Bringing the fear of the thing that may lurk under the water and nibble your toes one step further inland, *Blood Beach* locates its murderous monster under the sand. Its debt to *Jaws* is implicit from the setting (seaside town loses tourists and trade) to the music (subterranean bass rumbles signal monster's approach), but the bad-taste jokes and the light-hearted approach inspire laughter, not the thrill of fear. Good, cheap B-movie fun.

Blood Beast from Outer Space

see Night Caller, The

Blood Beast Terror, The (aka The Vampire Beast Craves Blood)

(1967, GB, 88 min)
d Vernon Sewell. *p* Arnold Louis Miller. *sc* Peter Bryan. *ph* Stanley Long. *ed* Howard Lanning. *ad* Wilfred Wood. *m* Paul Ferris. *cast* Peter Cushing, Robert Flemyng, Wanda Ventham, Vanessa Howard, David Griffin, Roy Hudd.

● Tacky, indifferently acted horrors involving a weremoth (Ventham, who metamorphoses into a giant death's head) loose in rural England. Flemyng is the loony entomologist, Cushing the cop investigating a series of murders. TM

Bloodbrothers

(1978, US, 116 min)
d Robert Mulligan. *p* Stephen J Friedman. *sc* Walter Newman. *ph* Robert Surtees. *ed* Sheldon Kahn. *pd* Gene Callahan. *m* Elmer Bernstein. *cast* Paul Sorvino, Tony Lo Bianco, Richard Gere, Lelia Goldoni, Yvonne Wilder, Kenneth McMillan.

●A ludicrously overblown soap opera set in Italian Brooklyn which races from childhood anorexia to adolescent sexual trauma via wife-battering. Gere, as the pretty school-leaver who wants to be a social worker but comes up against his father's hard-hat ambitions, is fine, but his sensitive performance is simply mangled by the movie's muddled glorification of the macho ethos. Mulligan recut the film to 98 minutes for TV.

Blood Brothers, The (Cia Ma/ aka Chinese Vengeance)

(1973, HK, 117 min)
d Chang Cheh. *p* Run Run Shaw. *sc* I Kuang, Chang Cheh. *ph* Kung Mu To. *ed* Kuo Ting-Hung. *ad* Chuang Sheng. *cast* David Chiang, Ti Lung, Chen Kuan Tai, Ching Li.
●Visually rich and one of Chang Cheh's most satisfying efforts, a heady mixture of heroism, fatalism and sensuality. The slow unravelling of the relationship between the three 'blood brothers' of very different character – the noble knight (Ti Lung), the fraught avenger (David Chiang) and the loose, 'innocent' victim (Chen Kuan Tai) – fits well with the rigorous ethical structure that is glimpsed from time to time beneath the exotic surface trappings of dynastic China. There is also bold use of superimposition and collage. VG

Blood for Dracula (Dracula Vuole Vivere: Cerca Sangue di Vergine!/aka Andy Warhol's Dracula)

(1974, It/Fr, 103 min)
d Paul Morrissey. *p* Andrew Braunsberg. *sc* Paul Morrissey. *ph* Luigi Kuveiller. *ed* Jed Johnson, Franca Silvi. *pd* Enrico Job. *m* Claudio Gizzi. *cast* Joe Dallesandro, Udo Kier, Maxime McKendry, Vittorio De Sica, Milena Vukotic, Roman Polanski.
●The time-honoured myth refracted through the lens of New York lifestyle. Dracula (Kier) becomes just another junkie searching for his fix, having quit Romania on a quest for the virgin blood that he desperately needs in Catholic Italy. Little Joe, as per, hunkers around after anything in skirts, looks puzzled, and spouts neo-Marxist claptrap. The deadpan dialogue is improved no end by wayward dialectic from De Sica, incomprehensible as an Italian with four sexy daughters. Often startlingly beautiful to look at. CPea

Blood from the Mummy's Tomb

(971, GB, 94 min)
d Seth Holt, Michael Carreras. *p* Howard Brandy. *sc* Christopher Wicking. *ph* Arthur Grant. *ed* Peter Weatherley. *ad* Scott MacGregor. *m* Tristram Cary. *cast* Andrew Keir, Valerie Leon, James Villiers, Hugh Burden, George Coulouris, Rosalie Crutchley.
●An adaptation of Bram Stoker's *Jewel of the Seven Stars*, scripted by former TO contributor Chis Wicking, and directed by cult horror-merchant Holt (who sadly died during production, leaving Carreras to finish it off). A stylish addition to the mummy genre, with members of an expedition which brought a mummy back to Britain suddenly kicking the bucket years later, and the expedition leader's daughter being possessed by the ancient princess. One of the better late efforts from Hammer. GA

Bloodhounds of Broadway

(1989, US, 93 min)
d/p Howard Brookner. *sc* Howard Brookner, Colman DeKay. *ph* Elliot Davis. *ed* Camilla Toniolo. *ad* Linda Conaway-Parsloe. *m* Jonathan Sheffner, Roman Baran. *cast* Madonna, Jennifer Grey, Rutger Hauer, Matt Dillon, Randy Quaid, Julie Hagerty, Josef Sommer.
●An American Playhouse production of a '20s musical pastiche based on four Damon Runyon stories, featuring Madonna as a nightclub singer, Hauer as a gangster, Dillon as a gambler, Quaid as a hapless swain, Grey as 'Lovely Lou', and Hagerty as a society dame. Actually, the performances aren't too bad – even Madonna's, although her squeaky disco voice is manifestly unsuited to period crooning. But even the all-star cast can't impose order or interest on the ludicrous and mystifyingly convoluted plot. Madonna's confession that she wants to drop being a jazz baby and retire to a 'quarter-acre in Newark' to raise babies and chickens might just be worth your attention. But ultimately the film delivers its own epitaph: 'The Brain is dead'. I'm afraid so. SFe

Blood In Blood Out

see Bound by Honor

Blood Is Not Fresh Water

(1998, Ethiopia/It, 57 min)
d/p/sc Theo Eshetu. *ph* Eric Black, Rory Logsdail. *ed* Stephen Natanson, Flavia Medusa. *with* Julian Warde Jones, Rinaldo Rainero, Emma Stowe, Monica Piseddu, Alan Jones.
●Eshetu's essay on his ancestral homeland of Ethiopia is a melange of travelogue, history and myth. Ostensibly a portrait of the video-maker's grandfather, who held many ministerial posts during the reign of Haile Selassie, this intelligently constructed work is a lyrical exploration of the country which Eshetu terms 'a place of the imagination', yet it also tackles head-on contemporary and historical Eurocentrist assumptions. A vibrant sense of place is caught with visual flair on scant resources. FM

Bloodline (aka Sidney Sheldon's Bloodline)

(1979, US/WGer, 127 min)
d Terence Young. *p* David V Picker, Sidney Beckerman. *sc* Laird Koenig. *ph* Freddie Young. *ed* Bud Molin. *pd* Ted Haworth. *m* Ennio Morricone. *cast* Audrey Hepburn, Ben Gazzara, James Mason, Claudia Mori, Irene Papas, Michelle Phillips, Maurice Ronet, Romy Schneider, Omar Sharif.
●Boardroom fun and games and lots of soap opera antics occur when Hepburn takes over the family multi-million, multi-national company after dad gets bumped off. Like Sheldon's *The Other Side of Midnight*, it's expensive, old-fashioned and overlong.

Blood Money (aka The Stranger and the Gunfighter)

(1974, HK/It/Sp/US, 107 min)
d Antonio Margheriti. *p* Run Run Shaw, Gustave Berne. *sc* Barth Jules Sussman. *ph* Alejandro Alloa. *ed* George Serrallonga. *m* Carlo Savina. *cast* Lee Van Cleef, Lo Lieh, Karen Yeh, Julian Ugarte, Goyo Peralta, Al Tung.
●Ludicrous Chinese/Italian Western, shot in Spain on mostly American money, teaming up a bemused Lee Van Cleef with an embarrassed Lo '*King Boxer*' Lieh. The vulgar plot centres on a treasure map tattooed in segments on female buttocks; the action scenes are uniformly buggered up by the director. TR

Blood Oath

(1990, Aust, 108 min)
d Stephen Wallace. *p* Charles Waterstreet, Denis Whitburn, Brian Williams. *sc* Brian Williams, Denis Whitburn. *ph* Russell Boyd. *ed* Nicholas Beauman. *ad* Bernard Hides. *m* David McHugh. *cast* Bryan Brown, George Takei, Terry O'Quinn, John Bach, Toshi Shioya, John Clarke, Tetsu Watanabe, Deborah Unger, John Polson, Jason Donovan.
●Ambon Island, Indonesia, 1946: dejected Japanese PoWs lead members of the Australian Army Legal Corps to a hidden clearing where scores of Australian PoWs were executed by prison camp guards. What follows is run-of-the-mill courtroom drama as Captain Robert Cooper (Brown, predictably curt), the hard-line prosecutor assigned to the war crimes case, questions suspects: Vice-Admiral Baron Takahashi (Takei, impressive), his sadistic underling Captain Ikeuchi (Watanabe), and a young Japanese signals officer (Shioya). The result may be of historical interest to those unfamiliar with some of the lesser-known details of WWII, and goes some way towards highlighting cultural differences and opposing views of war. Jason Donovan makes his big screen debut: two minutes and the immortal line, 'Do you need anything?' Quite. DA

Blood of a Poet, The,

see Sang d'un Poète, Le

Blood of Doctor Jekyll, The

see Docteur Jekyll et les Femmes

Blood of Hussain, The

(1980, GB/Pak, 112 min)
d/p/sc Jamil Dehlavi. *ph* Walter Lassally, Jamil Dehlavi. *ed* Sue Collins, Jamil Dehlavi. *cast* Salmaan Peerzada, Kika Markham, Durriya Kazi, Kabuli Baba, Mirza Ghazanfar Beg, Fauzia Zareen.
●A startling premonition and damning indictment of General Zia's Pakistan, this is nonetheless the very antithesis of crude agit-prop. The eruption of a white stallion from beneath the red desert earth strikingly exemplifies writer/director Dehlavi's accessible use of mythical metaphor to underpin his fiction of contemporary rebellion and martyrdom; and such visual coups abound as he interrogates notions of power and responsibility in the family and the state. PT

Blood of Others, The (Le Sang des Autres)

(1984, Can/Fr, 130 min)
d Claude Chabrol. *p* Denis Héroux, John Kemeny. *sc* Brian Moore. *ph* Richard Ciapka. *ed* Yves Langois. *pd* François Comtet. *m* François Dompierre. *cast* Jodie Foster, Michael Ontkean, Sam Neill, Stéphane Audran, Alexandra Stewart, Jean-Pierre Aumont, Kate Reid, John Vernon, Micheline Presle, Samuel Fuller.
●Chabrol was an unlikely choice to film Simone de Beauvoir's 1945 novel about moral growth and sacrifice during the Occupation – he being more your man for moral decay, egotism and such. His response to the heroine's progress from frivolity to engagement wavers between disinterested and uninterested. And considering the Mills & Boon trimmings one sort of sympathises, what with a lovelorn Nazi (Neill), a lovelorn resistance fighter (Ontkean) and Foster – patently modern American – at the centre. An occasional scene catches fire, but mostly it's an uninspired plod through very routine material. This is the theatrical version of a three-hour TV mini-series. BBa

Blood of Revenge (Meiji Kyokyakuden Sandaime Shumei)

(1965, Jap, 90 min)
d Tai Kato. *p* Koji Shundo. *sc* Ko Murao, Norifumi Suzuki. *ph* Motoya Washio. *ed* Katsumi Kawai. *ad* Norimichi Ikawa. *m* Shunsuke Kikuchi. *cast* Koji Tsuruta, Junko Fuji, Minoru Oki, Tetsuro Tamba, Masahiko Tsugawa.
●An absolutely standard period yakuza movie from the Toei conveyorbelt, lifted above the ruck by Tsuruta's wonderful performance (he was the genre's first star) and by Kato's distinctive mise en scène of long takes and wide-angle, deep focus compositions. The Kiyatatsu Clan is trying to go straight as a legitimate construction company in Osaka, 1907, but the renegade Hoshino Clan stops at nothing to sabotage its efforts. Asajiro (Tsuruta) has to keep civic building projects on schedule, preach non-violence, tame his late *oyabun*'s son and suffer heartbreak because he can't save his beloved geisha Hatsue (Fuji). It ends, of course, in rivers of blood. TR

Blood of the Condor (Yawar Mallku)

(1969, Bol, 74 min, b/w)
d Jorge Sanjines. *p* Ricardo Rada. *sc* Jorge Sanjines, Oscar Soria. *ph* Antonio Eguino. *m* Alberto Villalpando, Alfredo Dominguez, Gregorio Yana, Ignacio Quispe. *cast* Marcelino Yanahuaya, Benedicta Mendoza Huanca, Vicente Salinas.
●About a conflict between the Peace Corps and a local tribe in Bolivia , used to dramatise the racism latent in 'Western Aid' programmes. The Peace Corps were discovered to be practising sterilisation on Indian women without their knowledge. Sanjines' film explores the implications of this policy.

Blood of the Dragon (Satsujinken 2)

(1974, Jap, 88 min)
d Shigehiro Ozawa. *p* Norimichi Matsudaira. *sc* Shigehiro Ozawa, Hajime Takaiwa. *ph* Teiji Yoshida. *ed* Kozo Horiike. *ad* Tokumichi Igawa. *m* Toshiaki Tsushima. *cast* Shinichi Chiba, Yoko Ichiji, Masafumi Suzuki, Kaoru Nakajima.

●From the same unarmed combat series as *Kung Fu Street Fighter* (qv. since the same general remarks apply). Chiba again stars as Terry Tsuguri, with a lot of flashbacks to the earlier film. But new linking material includes at least one devastating fight scene: an all-but-naked Tsuguri fighting off an ambush in a sauna. TR

Blood of the Vampire

(1958, GB, 85 min)
d Henry Cass. *p* Robert S Baker. *sc* Jimmy Sangster. *ph* Monty Berman. *ed* Douglas Myers. *ad* John Elphick. *m* Stanley Black. *cast* Donald Wolfit, Barbara Shelley, Vincent Ball, Victor Maddern, William Devlin, Andrew Faulds, John Le Mesurier.

●The barnstorming Wolfit as a mad doctor returning to life after execution, taking control of a lunatic asylum (which comes complete with torture dungeon, useful for chastising the recalcitrant Shelley and her lover), and using the patients as a blood bank for his vampirism. As produced by Baker and Berman, never a guarantee of anything very much, it's lusty but not exactly subtle, with one or two florid colour effects. TM

Blood on Satan's Claw

see Satan's Skin

Blood on the Moon

(1948, US, 88 min, b/w)
d Robert Wise. *p* Theron Warth. *sc* Lillie Hayward. *ph* Nick Musuraca. *ed* Samuel E Beetley. *ad* Albert S D'Agostino, Walter Keller. *m* Roy Webb. *cast* Robert Mitchum, Barbara Bel Geddes, Robert Preston, Walter Brennan, Tom Tyler, Harry Carey Jr.

●A bevy of late '40s RKO talent, including ace cameraman Nick Musuraca, combine to make an intriguing *noir* Western. A complex tale of duplicity and split loyalties is played out against a noir backdrop of low-ceilinged bars and rain-soaked windswept darkness. Mitchum delivers his customarily immaculate, stoned performance as a reluctant hired gun duped into heading a trumped-up homesteaders' revolt, and Bel Geddes plays the spunky cowgirl who engages him in erotic gun-play. NA

Blood on the Streets

see Borsalino & Co.,

Blood on the Sun

(1945, US, 94 min, b/w)
d Frank Lloyd. *p* William J Cagney. *sc* Lester Cole. *ph* Theodor Sparkuhl. *ed* Truman K Wood, Walter Hannemann. *pd* Wiard Ihnen. *m* Miklos Rozsa. *cast* James Cagney, Sylvia Sidney, Wallace Ford, Rosemary DeCamp, John Emery, Robert Armstrong.

●Based on fact but a typical Cagney actioner for which, playing a newspaperman in Japan during the late '20s who uncovers a dastardly plot to conquer the world, he added martial arts skills to his usual two-fisted armoury. Marred by crude Jap-baiting propaganda and a silly romantic complication (Sidney as a Chinese American spy) but fun. TM

Blood Red

(1989, US, 91 min)
d Peter Masterson. *p* Judd Bernard, Patricia Casey. *sc* Ron Cutler. *ph* Toyomichi Kurita. *ed* Randy Thornton. *ad* Bruno Rubeo. *m* Carmine Coppola. *cast* Eric Roberts, Giancarlo Giannini, Dennis Hopper, Burt Young, Carlin Glynn, Lara Harris, Elias Koteas, Marc Lawrence, Frank Campanella, Aldo Ray, Susan Anspach, Julia Roberts.

●This liberal quasi-Western is like the Jesse James story updated by the right-on, socially-minded Sundance Institute. Eric Roberts plays the no-good son of a 19th century immigrant Sicilian wine-grower whose livelihood is threatened by the railroad which a ruthless Irish carpetbagger (Hopper) plans to drive through the vineyards. After his father is killed, Roberts takes the law into his own hands, becoming an outlaw and rallying the hitherto pacifist Sicilians to the cause. What started as a sincere social drama suddenly explodes into a fully-fledged Western, with plenty of fisticuffs and gunplay. Julia Roberts stands around in the background looking pretty, with only a dozen or so lines. NF

Blood Red Roses

(1986, GB, 150 min)
d John McGrath. *p* Steve Clark-Hall. *sc* John McGrath. *ph* Mark Littlewood. *ed* Jane Wood, Jo Nott. *ad* Andy Harris. *m* Eddie McGuire. *cast* Elizabeth MacLennan, James Grant, Gregor Fisher, Dawn Archibald, Louise Beattie, Amanda Walker, Julie Graham.

●Originally a stage play and reverting to TV after its theatrical screening, John McGrath's feminist saga is what might be termed a curate's scotch egg. In parts it's moving, funny and warm, in others (notably much of the last third) it's mind-numbingly boring, self-righteous and over-prone to the use of that terrible short-cut of having its characters reacting to world events (the Falklands, the Miners' Strike, Thatcher's victories) on TV. Its story is that of one woman, Bessie Gordon, moving from Highland childhood to Glasgow, where she works in an engineering factory, marries the shop steward, becomes politicised, alienated from her sexist-but-leftist hubby, and ends up still optimistic, independent, divorced and recovering from her (deserved?) reputation as a red wrecker in '86. There are some brilliant moments, but the pace is often achingly slow, the dice overloaded in obvious directions, and nothing is helped by the abrupt switch of actresses as Bessie ages from the charming Louise Beattie to the hectoring Elizabeth MacLennan. SGr

Blood Reincarnation (Yin-yang Jieh)

(1974, HK, 99 min)
d Ding Shanxi. *p* Yu Feng-Chih. *sc* Ting Shan-Hsi *ph* Chen Ching-Chu. *ad* Yang Shih-Cheng. *m* Chou Fu-Liang. *cast* Yang Qun, Tang Baoyun, Suzy Mang, Henry Yue Young, Dean Shek, Shih Tien, Shirley Huang.

●An anthology of three ghost/horror stories, each of them something of a tour de force. The first is gutsy and visceral: a wronged woman returns to haunt the couple who killed her while the wife is in labour. The second is played for black laughs: a drowned husband gets his revenge on his wife and her lover by haunting them as a water spirit (amazing scenes when the lover can't stop drinking, and then can't stop peeing). And the third is sad and elegiac: an unjustly executed acupuncturist uses a 'blood reincarnation' spell to live on as a spirit in order to complete his medical text-book. Horror movie fans will emerge rejuvenated. TR

Blood Relatives (Liens de Sang)

(1977, Can/Fr, 95min)
d Claude Chabrol. *p* Denis Héroux, Eugène Lepicier. *sc* Claude Chabrol, Sydney Banks. *ph* Jean Rabier. *ed* Yves Langlois. *pd* Anne Pritchard. *m* Howard Blake. *cast* Donald Sutherland, Aude Landry, Lisa Langlois, Laurent Malet, Stéphane Audran, Donald Pleasence, David Hemmings.

●Uneasy and only partly successful thriller, taken from one of Ed McBain's 87th Precinct novels, with Sutherland overshadowing the rest of the cast as the detective investigating the assault and murder of a young girl in Montreal. The result is pretty much par for the Chabrol course, with the girl's family – a hive of incest that provides the chief suspects – pictured as a typically degenerate example of the bourgeoisie. But it's mainly rather wooden, and shot in a flat television style; only towards the end do suspense and the director's full talent really take hold. GA

Blood River (Dio Perdona...Io No!)

(1967, It/Sp, 115 min)
d Giuseppe Colizzi. *p* Enzo D'Ambrosio. *sc* Giuseppe Colizzi. *ph* Alfio Contini. *ed* Sergio Montanari. *ad* Luis Vazquez, Gastone Corsetti. *m* Angel Oliver Pina. *cast* Terence Hill, Bud Spencer, Frank Wolff, Gina Rovere, José Manuel Martin, Tito Garcia.

●Stock spaghetti Western, predating the much wittier 'Trinity' series featuring the same stars. A brilliant opening sequence has a train, apparently empty, pull into an isolated station decked out with a welcoming band and all; gradually it is revealed that the carriage is a sea of corpses with only one man left alive. The rest of the plot, told in flashback without much dash, involves a gambling duel with a gun loaded with blanks, a gold robbery, an insurance investigator, a fight to the death.

Blood Simple

(1983, US, 99 min)
d Joel Coen. *p* Ethan Coen. *sc* Joel Coen, Ethan Coen. *ph* Barry Sonnenfeld. *ed* Roderick Jaynes, Don Wiegmann. *pd* Jane Musky. *m* Carter Burwell. *cast* John Getz, Frances McDormand, Dan Hedaya, M Emmet Walsh, Samm-Art Williams, Deborah Neumann.

●Hugely enjoyable *film noir* in which a Texan bar-owner hires a seedy private eye, first to spy on his wife, then to kill her and her lover. Instead, the eye (a marvellous performance from Walsh), having collected his fee, executes a variation on the contract. Whereupon things take off in a maelstrom of misunderstanding that spreads guilt and fear like a plague through the characters, and escalates a nightmarish terror (premature burial, murder by battery, crucifying impalement) that owes some debt to the horror comic. A remarkably assured debut for Coen, formerly assistant editor on *The Evil Dead*. TM

Blood Sisters

see Sisters

Bloodsport

(1987, US, 92 min)
d Newt Arnold. *p* Mark DiSalle. *sc* Sheldon Lettich, Christopher Crosby, Mel Friedman. *ph* David Worth. *ed* Carl Kress. *m* Paul Hertzog. *cast* Jean-Claude Van Damme, Donald Gibb, Leah Ayres, Norman Burton, Forest Whitaker, Roy Chiao, Philip Chan, Bolo Yeung.

●Sporting the charisma of a lobotomised newt, hunky US Defense Intelligence agent Van Damme goes AWOL and turns up in Hong Kong, where he bumps into mountain man Gibb who, like Van Damme, is there to take part in a secret international martial arts competition. They become good buddies. This gives Van Damme extra reason to get riled when he eventually faces Yeung in the final, since this murderous, cheating inscrutable, yellow-bellied Korean villain has stomped all over his friend's head in the semis. Journalist Ayres tags along to provide a modicum of hero worship and heterosexuality. Forest Whitaker's cameo adds plumage to what is otherwise a well-plucked turkey, humourless and plagued by a script full of stilted mumbo-jumbo. SCu

Blood: The Last Vampire

(2000, Jap, 45 min)
d Hiroyuki Kitakubo. *p* Yukio Nagasaki. *sc* Kenji Kamiyama. *ad* Yusuke Takeda. *m* Yoshihiro Ike. *cast* voices: Youki Kudoh, Saemi Nakamura, Joe Romersa; Rebecca Forstadt, Paul Carr, David Mallow.

●Purportedly Japan's first fully digitally animated feature – although 'featurette' seems more accurate – this Team Oshii (*Ghost in the Shell*) effort is intermittently a marvel of computer generated and/or processed visuals. Much of the imagery has a spookily redolent industrial texture – witness the opening scenes of a desolate underground train line – yet much of it is flat and static. The story about a secret service hunt for shape-changing demons set on an American army base in Japan over Halloween 1966 is thick with cliché and po-faced exposition; and just when it's getting somewhere, the film ends. NB

Blood Ties (Il Cugino Americano)

(1986, It, 120 min)
d Giacomo Battiato. *p* Giovanna Genoese, Alessandro Fracassi. *sc* Corrado Augias, Giacomo Battiato. *ph* Romano Albani. *ed* Maria Morra. *ad* Paolo Biagetti. *m* Celso Valli. *cast* Brad Davis, Tony Lo Bianco, Vincent Spano, Barbara De Rossi, Arnoldo Foà, Delia Boccardo,

●Snivelling punk Spano is a coke-snorting American mafioso. Lo Bianco is a Sicilian judge putting the heat on Palermo's drug-trafficking mobsters. And good guy Davis, who 'owes' the Mafia, is a respectable New England academic 'persuaded' by Spano to fly to the old country, wheedle his way into cousin Lo Bianco's affections, and kill him, in return for the life of his kidnapped father. The film (a feature carved out of a 4-hour TV series, and cut by a further 22 minutes for release in Britain) is a collection of Coppola-derived clichés. The action consists of repeated macho standoffs and routine car chases, the women are disposable chattels, and the performances range from the wooden set-jaw squinting of Davis to the effulgent Method mannerisms of Spano at his most sweatily unappealing, with little in between. Lo Bianco alone reveals true class. GA

Blood Virgin, The

see Symptoms

Blood Wedding

see Noces Rouges, Les

Blood Wedding (Bodas de Sangre)

(1981, Sp, 71 min)
d Carlos Saura. *p* Emiliano Piedra. *ph* Teo Escamilla. *ed* Pablo G del Amo. *ad* Rafael Palmero. *m* Emilio de Diego. *cast* Antonio Gades, Cristina Hoyos, Juan Antonio Jiménez, Pilar Cárdenas, Carmen Villena.

●Choreographed by Gades from the play by Lorca, with Saura recording not the polished final production but a day-lit dress rehearsal in a bare studio with no scenery and minimal props. This visual austerity accentuates gesture, ceremony and convention, in both the ballet itself (a drama of outraged honour and revenge) and the dancers' parallel, ritual preparations for performance. Saura uses cinematic effects sparingly, at dramatic highpoints (in particular the climactic knife-fight, filmed in a vertiginous circular tracking shot) which draw the viewer from beyond the metaphorical footlights into the very heart of passion and desire. Dance-lovers will need no further encouragement, but it's seductive enough to fascinate even balletophobes. SJo

Bloody Angels (1732 Høtten)

(1998, Nor, 100 min)
d Karin Julsrud. *p* Tom Remlov. *sc* Kjetil Indegaard. *ph* Philip Øgaard. *ed* Sophie Hesselberg. *pd* Billy Johanson. *m* Kjetil Bjerkestrand, Magne Furuholmen. *cast* Reidar Sørenson, Gaute Skjegstad, Trond Høvik, Simon Norrthon, Laila Goody, Stig Henrik Hoff, Kjersti Holmen, Bjørn Floberg, Bjørn Sunquist.

●A cool, quirky, serio-comic cop thriller-cum-social satire in which an Oslo detective visits a hick town to investigate a series of murders rumoured by the locals to have been the work of 'angels'. More likely, given the unsavoury types he meets, one killing was a vigilante act perpetrated against a family of misfits as vengeance for the murder of a girl. So will they obstruct the course of justice? Essentially a fable of violence begetting violence, the film looks good, is imbued with a deadpan wit, and gets tauter, tenser and weirder as it proceeds, with only the eccentric use of music over-egging the cake. Oddball stuff, variously evocative of *Seven*, *Fargo*, *Dirty Harry* and Aki Kaurismäki (no bad mix), and an intriguing, promising debut. GA

Bloody Fists, The (Dangkou Tan)

(1972, HK, 100 min)
d Ng Sze-Yuen. *p* Jimmy L Pascual. *ed* Cuo Teng Hong. *m* Chao Fu Liang. *cast* Chen Xing, Henry Yue Young, Chen Kuan-Tai, Lindy Lam, Liu Daqian

●A lively example of the work of Chinese filmmakers outside the major studios, with a good portrait of collective villainy led by Chen Kuan Tai, evocatively kitted out in flowing mane, black mask, and black gloves which conceal equally blackened hands (due to the 'iron fist' martial arts technique). Matters are helped, too, by stylish visuals and the care taken to provide adequate motivation for the usual conflict of interests between the Chinese and the Japanese.VG

Bloody Kids

(1979, GB, 91 min)
d Stephen Frears. *p* Barry Hanson. *sc* Caroline Embling, Stephen Poliakoff. *ph* Chris Menges. *ed* Peter Coulson. *ad* Martin Johnson. *m* George Fenton. *cast* Derrick O'Connor, Gary Holton, Richard Thomas, Peter Clark, Gwynneth Strong, Caroline Embling, Jack Douglas.

●Night time on the streets of Southend, and a dazzled 11-year-old schoolboy wanders through the floodlit aftermath of an auto accident, transfixed by the chaos with which the grown-ups can hardly cope. He teams up with his 11-year-old mate and the two stage their own happening, a knife-fight that goes slightly wrong and puts one in hospital and the other on the run through the night. School hasn't a clue, the hospital is a ringing void, the cops don't know where to begin, and the only ones left in Thatcherite Britain with any energy are the kids, with nothing to do except bugger about. Frears' film (scripted by Stephen Poliakoff and originally made for TV) has dark humour, a taste for the surreal aspects of this crashed world, and a head-on energy which leaves most contemporary offerings on the state-of-the-nation looking distinctly lame. CPea

Bloody Mama

(1970, US, 90 min)
d/p Roger Corman. *sc* Robert Thom. *ph* John A Alonzo. *ed* Eve Newman. *m* Don Randi. *cast* Shelley Winters, Pat Hingle, Don Stroud, Bruce Dern, Diane Varsi, Robert De Niro, Robert Walden, Clint Kimbrough.

●'The family that slays together stays together', ran the ads. Immersed in Freudian motifs, Corman's foray into rural gangsterdom makes no bones about its anti-social anti-heroes: the Barker clan are blatantly public enemies. A prologue sees young Kate Barker raped by her brothers; 'Blood's thicker than water' says her Pa. It's advice she clings to. Cutting to the Depression years, Corman finds Ma Barker abandoning her weak husband and taking her brood off on a brutal crime spree. This family unit comprises a sadist, a homosexual, a junkie (De Niro, sniffing glue like there's no tomorrow) and a lady-killer, and it's held together by incest and murder. Despite such sleazy subject matter, the cast is outstanding, dominated by a fierce Shelley Winters, and Corman pulls no punches, delivering a searing Jacobean tragedy of a gangster movie. TCh

Bloody Morning (Xuese Qingchen)

(1992, China, 100 min)
d Li Shaohong. *p* Liao Xiaogeng, Tian Yuping. *sc* Li Shaohong, Xiao Mao. *ph* Zeng Nianping. *ad* Shi Jiandu. *m* Meng Weidong. *cast* Hu Yajie, Kong Lin, Zhao Jun, Wang Guangquan.

●Finally unbanned by China's political thaw, this is the finest movie made in China since the Beijing massacre. Fifth-generation woman director Li Shaohong has freely adapted the Garcia Márquez novel *Chronicle of a Death Foretold* to produce a truly shocking account of the consequences of poverty and backwardness in a North China village. In her version, the victim of the all-too-preventable killing is not a wealthy man but the village teacher, the only intellectual in a community of peasants. The build-up to the crime, explored in a web of flashbacks, turns out to hinge on the inner rage of a 36-year-old male virgin and on the puritanical stance of traditional village society; but what Li ultimately lays bare is the psyche of a people for whom existence means no more than survival. TR

Bloody Sunday

(2001, GB/Ire, 110 min)
d Paul Greengrass. *p* Mark Redhead. *sc* Paul Greengrass. *ph* Ivan Strasburg. *ed* Clare Douglas. *pd* John Paul Kelly. *m* Dominic Muldoon. *cast* James Nesbitt, Tim Pigott-Smith, Nicholas Farrell, Gerard McSorley, Kathy Kiera Clarke, Allan Gildea, Gerard Crossan, Mary Moulds.

●Thirteen died in Londonderry on Sunday, 30 January 1972, and this dramatic reconstruction, based on eyewitness accounts, uses a 24-hour timeframe to piece together the tragic course of events. Confrontation looms as local Protestant MP Ivan Cooper (Nesbitt) decides to press ahead with a banned march against internment without trial. He determinedly distances himself from the IRA, but the British army decides to target the occasion to take out the ringleaders. With a prowling handheld camera and relentless cutting, the film builds almost unbearable tension (comparisons with *The Battle of Algiers* are not inappropriate) before erupting into carnage. Although its assertion that the Paras fired first remains contentious, it's still a persuasive picture of fateful circumstances falling into place, carefully portraying the differences of attitude among the army personnel, some of whom realise the iniquity of their actions, with Nesbitt's stand-out performance putting an anguished human face on the day ideals died. TJ

Bloomfield (aka The Hero)

(1969, GB, 95 min)
d Richard Harris. *p* John Heyman, Wolf Mankowitz. *sc* Wolf Mankowitz. *ph* Otto Heller. *ed* Kevin Connor. *pd* Richard MacDonald. *m* Johnny Harris. *cast* Richard Harris, Romy Schneider, Kim Burfield, Maurice Kaufmann, Yossi Yadin.

●Harris, directing himself (an embarrassing debut in that department) as an ageing Israeli soccer star, has a row with his plump sculptress girlfriend (Schneider). 'Give eet up!' she begs. 'You don't understand. They need me' he says, miming exasperation. There's even a clock ticking in the background. All this plus potted music and long shots of architecture and desertscapes. *Bloomfield* never approaches even the energy level of those hilariously dated commercials which send you scurrying to the ice-cream girl as a hero-worshipping kid hovers and Harris is offered a car to throw the game. Hanging up by your nipples may be masochism, but this is suicide. MPa

Blossoms in the Dust

(1941, US, 100 min)
d Mervyn LeRoy. *p* Irving Asher. *sc* Anita Loos. *ph* Karl Freund, W Howard Greene. *ed* George Boemler. *ad* Cedric Gibbons, Urie McCleary. *m* Herbert Stothart. *cast* Greer Garson, Walter Pidgeon, Felix Bressart, Marsha Hunt, Fay Holden, Samuel S Hinds.

●Glossy biopic of Edna Gladney, a childless Texan lady who channelled her frustration into taking up the cause of illegitimate children and running foster homes. Pretty Technicolor, but the tearjerking is shameless. TM

Blossom Time

(1934, GB, 91 min, b/w)
d Paul L Stein. *p* Walter C Mycroft. *sc* Franz Schulz, John Drinkwater, Roger Burford, GJ Clutsam. *ph* Otto Kanturek, Bryan Langley. *ed* Leslie Norman. *ad* David Rawnsley, Clarence Elder. *m* Franz Schubert. *lyrics* John Drinkwater, GH Clutsam. *cast* Richard Tauber, Jane Baxter, Carl Esmond, Athene Seyler, Paul Graetz, Charles Carson.

●Where Hitchcock's near contemporary *Waltzes from Vienna* relied on poorly worked-out gimmicks and the rather irrelevant talents of Jessie Matthews, Stein's Berlin/Hollywood apprenticeship enabled him to produce a classic musical biopic. Purists may sneer at the representation of Franz Schubert as a popular singer/songwriter, but Tauber's voice is magnificent and his minimally melodramatic acting fits perfectly this Ruritanian world where a fire-eating, snuff-sniffing duchess stands in the path of true love. The story may be flimsy, but the way Stein deftly moves it forward to its wedding-ritual finale is superb. RMy

Blow

(2001, US, 123 min)
d Ted Demme. *p* Ted Demme, Joel Stillerman, Denis Leary. *sc* David McKenna, Nick Cassavetes. *ph* Ellen Kuras. *ed* Kevin Tent. *pd* Michael Hanan. *m* Graeme Revell. *cast* Johnny Depp, Penélope Cruz, Franka Potente, Rachel Griffiths, Paul Reubens, Jordi Mollá, Cliff Curtis, Max Perlich, Ray Liotta.

●Perhaps because it sticks too closely to Bruce Porter's source book, this account of George Jung's rise from small-time dope dealer to major league coke player feels both too long and yet not epic enough; the storyline sprawls over several decades before sliding into sentimental anti-climax. Flashing back from the aged Jung's 'last big deal', it chronicles an unhappy Boston childhood. Jung's post-college escape to California is liberating, as he and his buddies enjoy the beach bum life, with freeloving chicks and a lively trade in marijuana. A prison term brings Jung in contact with Colombian Diego Delgado (Mollá), who helps set him up as the US connection for Pablo Escobar's burgeoning cocaine operation. But as dope-smoking '70s hippie hedonism gives way to snow-nosed '80s greed, friendships are strained, loyalties snap and the whole thing implodes. As the likeable Jung, Depp wears a succession of ill-fitting hippie wigs, drawing attention to his unusually ordinary acting, which feels more like an impersonation than a characterisation. Cruz turns up late in the day, as Jung's second wife Mirtha, but her coke-fuelled Latino spitfire only underscores how the rest of the cast are just coasting towards the disappointing denouement. NF

Blow Dry

(2000, Ger/GB/US, 90 min)
d Paddy Breathnach. *p* Ruth Jackson, William Horberg, David Rubin. *sc* [based on the screenplay *Never Better* by] Simon Beaufoy. *ph* Cian de Buitléar. *ed* Tony Lawson. *pd* Sophie Becher. *m* Patrick Doyle. *cast* Alan Rickman, Natasha Richardson, Rachel Griffiths, Rachael Leigh Cook, Josh Hartnett, Bill Nighy, Rosemary Harris, Warren Clarke.
●Presumably, this barely amusing, would-be-whimsical Anglo-American blah from the writer of *The Full Monty* started out along familiar but workable lines, the occasion of the National Hair Championships in glamorous Keighley offering an opportunity for a divided family to put aside differences, make a stand in the face of terminal illness and relish their underdog status in the competition. The direction, however, makes this as calculating as it sounds; and, lacking any emotional pull, it has only the imagined comic value of crazy hairstyles to fall back on. The cast deliver the basics and little more. TJ

Blow for Blow

see Coup pour Coup

Blowing Wild

(1953, US, 88 min, b/w)
d Hugo Fregonese. *p* Milton Sperling. *sc* Philip Yordan. *ph* Sid Hickox. *ed* Alan Crosland Jr. *ad* Al Ybarra. *m* Dimitri Tiomkin. *cast* Gary Cooper, Barbara Stanwyck, Anthony Quinn, Ruth Roman, Ward Bond, Ian MacDonald.
●The calculated absurdities and violent romanticism of this *Johnny Guitar* precursor (also scripted by Philip Yordan) were greeted with derision on the film's first appearance. It's set somewhere South of the Border, where bandidos, chests criss-crossed with cartridge belts, open fire on trucks laden with nitro-glycerine. Things are no less volatile back at the rancho, where Stanwyck can't have Cooper ('You're no good, Marina') and consoles herself with booze and a state of permanent fury, as a symbolic oil well pumps away outside her bedroom window. It's clear from the off that most of the characters will wind up killing one another. Inventive, unrestrained film-making, and another under-appreciated entertainment from the uneven but talented Fregonese. BBa

Blown Away

(1994, US, 121 min)
d Stephen Hopkins. *p* John Watson, Pen Densham, Richard Lewis. *sc* Joe Batteer, John Rice. *ph* Peter Levy. *ed* Tim Wellburn. *pd* John Graysmark. *m* Alan Silvestri. *cast* Jeff Bridges, Tommy Lee Jones, Suzy Amis, Lloyd Bridges, Forest Whitaker, Stephi Lineburg.
●This action-thriller is a tense, effective bomb-fest; technically high-powered and unsophisticated enough in narrative and cultural terms to raise more than the odd laugh. Boston, it seems, has a bomb problem, with a disposal squad larger than the London Met. Dove (Bridges) is its maverick expert, of the breed who are mad, brave and cool, who crack jokes as the seconds tick away and vomit later in alleys, unseen. He's on the point of jacking it in for marriage and surrogate fatherhood when a spate of blasts are caused by ex-IRA loon Gaerity (Jones). The explosions dog Dove's path and he scents a 'this-time-it's-personal' scenario. Bridges walks through the bravura sequences and his père (Lloyd), as Dove's 'dad', does the funniest pixie American-Irishman. Jones, as ever, is menace incarnate. WH

Blow Out

(1981, US, 108 min)
d Brian De Palma. *p* George Litto. *sc* Brian De Palma. *ph* Vilmos Zsigmond. *ed* Paul Hirsch. *pd* Paul Sylbert. *m* Pino Donaggio. *cast* John Travolta, Nancy Allen, John Lithgow, Dennis Franz, John Aquino, Peter Boyden.
●The recipe for this is two parts Antonioni's *Blow-Up* to one part Coppola's *The Conversation*: mix well and garnish with stars Travolta and Allen. Sound man Travolta witnesses what may or may not be murder. Can he prove the US Presidential aspirant's car crash was no accident? Will happy hooker Allen stay alive long enough to help him? Where Antonioni's images made you think, De Palma's merely make you blink, and the baroque plot confuses as often as it frightens. Still, plenty of style, a modicum of thrills, and a suitably s(l)ick ending. Collectors of character performances will enjoy Lithgow's right-wing nut. MB

Blow-Out (La Grande Bouffe)

(1973, Fr/It, 133 min)
d Marco Ferreri. *p* Jean-Pierre Rassam. *sc* Marco Ferreri, Rafael Azcona, Francis Blanche. *ph* Mario Vulpiani. *ed* Claudine Merlin. *ad* Michel de Broin. *m* Philippe Sarde. *cast* Marcello Mastroianni, Ugo Tognazzi, Michel Piccoli, Philippe Noiret, Andrea Ferreol, Monique Chaumette.
●Sade's *120 Days of Sodom* reworked, with few of the resonances and none of the rigour of Pasolini's *Salò*. Four men immure themselves in a mansion for protracted orgies of eating and screwing: their excesses make for a colourful social satire, but when the tone turns sombre it looks awkwardly as if Ferreri was trying for something more. TR

Blow to the Heart (Colpire al Cuore)

(1982, It, 105 min)
d Gianni Amelio. *p* Enzo Porcelli. *sc* Gianni Amelio, Vincenzo Cerami. *ph* Tonino Nardi. *ed* Anna Napoli. *ad* Marco Dentici. *m* Franco Piersanti. *cast* Jean-Louis Trintignant, Laura Morante, Fausto Rossi, Sonia Gessner, Vanni Corbellini, Laura Nucci.
●A middle-aged professor flirts with the Red Brigade, more for the frisson it brings than through any great political commitment. His inquisitive, priggish adolescent son watches with mounting disgust and determines to bring him to justice. At first the pace is stultifyingly slow. Amelio seems determined to excise any tension he creates by constantly undercutting the narrative with long (very long) reflective scenes. Gradually, though, the rhythm begins to establish itself as Trintignant (excellent as always) realises he's being outmanoeuvred by his son, whom he continues to dote on. A curiously bewitching movie, originally made for TV. JP

Blow-Up

(1966, GB, 111 min)
d Michelangelo Antonioni. *p* Carlo Ponti. *sc* Michelangelo Antonioni, Tonino Guerra. *ph* Carlo Di Palma. *ed* Michelangelo Antonioni, Frank Clarke. *ad* Assheton Gorton. *m* Herbie Hancock. *cast* David Hemmings, Vanessa Redgrave, Peter Bowles, Sarah Miles, John Castle, Jane Birkin, Veruschka, Julian Chagrin.
●As often with Antonioni, a film riddled with moments of brilliance and scuppered by infuriating pretensions; full of longueurs, it works neither as a portrait of Swinging London, nor as a *bona fide* thriller. But as it establishes its metaphysical mystery – Hemmings' vacuously trendy photographer discovers a purpose to his life when he enlarges a picture that may or may not prove that a murder has taken place – it does become strangely gripping, questioning the maxim that the camera never lies, and settling into a virtually abstract examination of subjectivity and perception. Deep stuff, then, though the surrounding dross – sex'n'fashion'n'rock'n'roll – makes it pretty hard to watch. Still, at least Carlo Di Palma's camerawork leavens the brew. GA

Blue

(1968, US, 113 min)
d Silvio Narizzano. *p* Judd Bernard, Irwin Winkler. *sc* Meade Roberts, Ronald M Cohen. *ph* Stanley Cortez. *ed* Stewart Linder. *ad* Hal Pereira. *m* Manos Hadjidakis. *cast* Terence Stamp, Joanna Pettet, Karl Malden, Ricardo Montalban, Anthony Costello, Joe De Santis, Stathis Giallelis.
●A grotesque, pretension-ridden Western which falls flat on its face with a ponderous yarn about a white boy, raised by Mexican bandits, who returns to civilisation with a war-whoop and a chip on his shoulder the size of Brooklyn Bridge about which side he belongs to. Terence Stamp struggles unavailingly against the ludicrous dialogue, and some fine landscape photography by Stanley Cortez is wrecked by a penchant for gaudy filters and even gaudier sunsets. TM

Blue

(1993, GB, 76 min)
d Derek Jarman. *p* James Mackay, Takashi Asai. *sc* Derek Jarman. *m* Simon Fisher Turner. *voices* Nigel Terry, John Quentin, Derek Jarman, Tilda Swinton.
●The screen is a perfect blue throughout as Derek Jarman faces up to AIDS, the loss of loved ones, the breakdown of the body, blindness, his own approaching fall into the void. The film embodies the spiritual transcendence which Cyril Collard sought to convey in the last reel of his anguished melodrama *Savage Nights*, crucially in the serene contemplation of the screen itself, but also in Jarman's beautiful poetry. Extracts from the film-maker's diary supply an ironic commentary on the 'progress' of his illness so that the movie becomes a juxtaposition between the finite and the infinite, the sublime and the ridiculous. Greatly helped by Simon Fisher Turner's soundtrack. Moving beyond words. TCh

Blue and the Gold, The

see Annapolis Story, An

Blue Angel, The (Der blaue Engel)

(1930, Ger, 108 min, b/w)
d Josef von Sternberg. *p* Erich Pommer. *sc* Karl Zuckmayer, Karl Vollmuller, Robert Liebmann. *ph* Günther Rittau, Hans Schneeberger. *ed* Sam Winston. *ad* Otto Hunte, Emil Hasler. *songs* Frederick Hollander, Robert Liebmann, Richard Rillo. *cast* Emil Jannings, Marlene Dietrich, Kurt Gerron, Rosa Valetti, Hans Albers, Eduard von Winterstein.
●Lola, star at the sleaziest nightclub in screen history, meets, seduces and ultimately destroys the upright bourgeois schoolteacher, Professor Rath. A tragedy? A comedy? It's actually a surprisingly complex morality play: a celebration of Lola's sexuality (it was Dietrich's first major role) and an ironic observation of Rath's repression and masochism (Jannings never suffered more or better). The film looks and sounds its age, but remains enthralling. Sternberg shot English and German versions simultaneously. TR

Bluebeard

(1944, US, 73 min, b/w)
d Edgar G Ulmer. *p* Leon Fromkess. *sc* Pierre Gendron. *ph* Arthur Feindel. *ed* Carl Pierson. *pd* Eugen Schüfftan. *m* Leo Erdody. *cast* Jean Parker, John Carradine, Nils Asther, Ludwig Stossel, Iris Adrian, George Pembroke.
●Ulmer (Murnau's one time art director and assistant) is the most subterranean of all directors, and here turns out a triumph of mind, eye and talent over the matter handed him by a PRC budget. Carradine is the turn-of-the-century painter, part-time puppeteer and pathological killer in some spellbinding schizophrenic sleaze. CW

Bluebeard's Castle

(1964, WGer, 60 min)
d Michael Powell. *p* Norman Foster. *libretto* Bela Balazs. *ph* Hannes Staudinger. *ed* Paula Dvorak. *pd* Hein Heckroth. *m* Bela Bartok. *cast* Norman Foster, Anna Raquel Sartre.
●An intriguing rarity for Powell completists, this straightforward performance film of Bartok's opera was shot only after the score had already been recorded in Zagreb. As a result, Powell was free to indulge himself with the look of the film, so long-term collaborator Hein Heckroth went to town on the cobwebby gauzes and nets. And indeed, it does look terrific, if rather too busy, a brooding tapestry of browns, blues and greys. That said, it's inevitably of limited interest only, and finally something of a footnote from (two of) the men behind *The Red Shoes* and *The Tales of Hoffmann*. GA

Bluebeard's Eighth Wife

(1938, US, 85 min, b/w)
d/p Ernst Lubitsch. *sc* Charles Brackett, Billy Wilder. *ph* Leo Tover. *ed* William Shea. *ad* Hans Dreier, Robert Usher. *m* Frederick Hollander, Werner R Heymann. *cast* Claudette Colbert, Gary Cooper, David Niven, Edward Everett Horton, Elizabeth Patterson, Herman Bing, Franklin Pangborn.
●The film in which Brackett and Wilder supposedly perfected the Hollywood ploy of 'meeting cute' with a Riviera department store scene

where Coop wants to buy pyjama tops and Colbert the bottoms. Otherwise a sporadically funny, somewhat contrived comedy, with Lubitsch softening the script's acidity (thereby giving the wrong sort of discomfort to the closing scenes in a lunatic asylum), and Cooper miscast as a playboy millionaire who has divorced seven wives and has a comeuppance coming up from the eighth. TM

Blue Belle

(1975, GB/It, 87 min)
d Massimo Dallamano. *p* Harry Alan Towers. *sc* Massimo Dallamano, Harry Alan Towers, Marcello Coscia. *ph* Franco Delli Colli. *ed* Nicholas Wentworth. *m* Bixio, Frizzi, Tempera. *cast* Annie Belle, Charles Fawcett, Felicity Devonshire, Ciro Ippolito, Maria Rohm.

●This Harry Alan Towers film has nothing to offer except some widescreen Chinese locations (much beloved of Towers, who also produced the *Fu Manchu* series) and a variety of sexual venues: art gallery, riding stables, Tibetan monastery. Otherwise it's 'Convent-bred Emanuelle 3 Goes East' as Eponymous Annie meets up with Felicity Devonshire – looking as though she's on a modelling trip for *The Sun* – and they both strip off a lot. A Jane Birkin-type song plays endlessly in the background. Someone says 'There is a Chinese legend – when you throw in lead, you can fish out gold'. Not here. AN

Blue Bird, The

(1976, US/USSR, 99 min)
d George Cukor. *p* Paul Maslansky, Lee Savin, Paul Radnia. *sc* Hugh Whitemore, Alfred Hayes, Alexei Kapler. *ph* Freddie Young. *ed* Ernest Walter. *ad* Brian Wildsmith. *m* Irwin Kostal. *cast* Elizabeth Taylor, Jane Fonda, Ava Gardner, Cicely Tyson, Will Geer, Robert Morley, George Cole, Harry Andrews, Patsy Kensit.

●Forget the alluring cast (incorporating some Russian dancers for the ballet sequences), this is a desperately pedestrian, hideously glitzy version of Maeterlinck's delicate fantasy about two kids and their quest for the blue bird of happiness. You'd never believe in a month of Sundays that Cukor directed it. TM

Blue Black Permanent

(1992, GB, 86 min)
d Margaret Tait. *p* Barbara Grigor. *sc* Margaret Tait. *ph* Alex Scott. *ed* John MacDonnell. *pd* Andrew Semple. *m* John Gray. *cast* Celia Imrie, Jack Shepherd, Gerda Stevenson, James Fleet, Sean Scanlan, Hilary Maclean.

●A first feature from veteran avant-garde filmmaker Tait, a septuagenarian Orcadian. A work of extraordinary emotion, the film takes the form of a remembrance, with troubled Edinburgh photographer Barbara (Imrie) attempting to tell her boyfriend (Shepherd) the story – sketched in flashback – of her mother Greta (Stevenson), who died in the sea off Orkney when Barbara was nine, some 40 years earlier, leaving her guilty and confused. This is about the struggle to give shape and meaning to life, and it's rare to see a film that attempts to do this so directly. The presiding spirit (and imagery) is that of the sea: its intimations of mystery, overwhelming elemental and impersonal forces, rhythm and eventual balm. But Tait also seems miraculously to invest the ordinary (scenes are simply and unostentatiously shot) with equal mystery, cutting to a close-up of a pebble beach, not a face, at moments of revelation. Even the awkwardness of the present-day scenes with Imrie and Shepherd, as they wander in their car or through the streets, she talking, he listening, seems surreal. A film that strikes deep chords. WH

Blue Chips

(1994, US, 101 min)
d William Friedkin. *p* Michelle Rappaport. *sc* Ron Shelton. *ph* Tom Priestley. *ed* Robert K Lambert, David Rosenbloom. *pd* James D Bissell. *m* Nile Rodgers, Jeff Beck, Jed Leiber. *cast* Nick Nolte, Mary McDonnell, JT Walsh, Shaquille O'Neal, Alfre Woodard, Ed O'Neill, Bob Cousy, Anfernee 'Penny' Hardaway, Matt Nover, Larry Bird, Lou Gossett Jr.

●This hard-hitting college basketball drama (unreleased in UK cinemas) marks a notable return to form for William Friedkin. The movie has parallels with the documentary *Hoop Dreams*: both use the fate of promising young players to criticise capitalist structures. Heading an exceptionally strong cast, Nolte is magnificent as the team coach Pete Bell: a wounded, angry bear of a man. He loves the game, but under pressure from the college authorities to produce a winning team, he's tempted to bend the rules, to bribe three youngsters to sign for Western Uni. The pithy script is by Ron (*White Men Can't Jump*) Shelton, and Friedkin gets in so close to the games you feel on court yourself. Highly recommended. TCh

Blue City

(1986, US, 83 min)
d Michelle Manning. *p* William L Hayward, Walter Hill. *sc* Lukas Heller, Walter Hill. *ph* Steven Poster. *ed* Ross Albert. *ad* Richard Lawrence. *m* Ry Cooder. *cast* Judd Nelson, Ally Sheedy, David Caruso, Paul Winfield, Scott Wilson, Anita Morris.

●An addition to the sub-genre of Hollywood movies that involves fashionable youth striking aggressive postures, riding motorcycles, smashing up bars, and getting a good beating to the sound of loud rock music. Wild boy Nelson returns to his home town to find that his father, the slightly crooked ex-mayor, has been bumped off by persons unknown. Aided by his best chum (who can't walk properly) and his best chum's sister, he embarks on the unlikely programme of harassing the local heavies, with a view to obtaining a lead. The inevitable final shootout reveals all and justice is seen to be done. Fast, stylish, but the formula palled ages back and it hardly does justice to the Ross Macdonald novel on which it is based. DPe

Blue Collar

(1978, US, 114 min)
d Paul Schrader. *p* Don Guest. *sc* Paul Schrader, Leonard Schrader. *ph* Bobby Byrne. *ed* Tom Rolf. *pd* Lawrence G Paull. *m* Jack Nitzsche. *cast* Richard Pryor, Harvey Keitel, Yaphet Kotto, Ed Begley Jr, Harry Bellaver, George Memmoli, Lucy Saroyan.

●Very probably the most clear-sighted movie ever made about the ways that shopfloor workers get fucked over by 'the system'. Three guys (two black, one Polack) work on the production line in a Detroit automobile factory. One day they figure their union does them no more favours than their bosses. They pull a clumsy robbery at union HQ, and get no more than some suspicious documents that point to union links with organised crime. Suddenly they're out of their league: violence, paranoia, rivalry and recrimination erupt around them. This movie was directed and co-written by a theology graduate. TR.

Blue Dahlia, The

(1946, US, 98 min, b/w)
d George Marshall. *p* John Houseman. *sc* Raymond Chandler. *ph* Lionel Lindon. *ed* Arthur P Schmidt. *ad* Hans Dreier, Walter Tyler. *m* Victor Young. *cast* Alan Ladd, Veronica Lake, William Bendix, Howard Da Silva, Hugh Beaumont, Doris Dowling.

●Ladd's returning war veteran stalks stoically down those mean streets once more in search of the killer of his wife (Dowling), a faithless floozie undeserving of his concern. Raymond Chandler's script never quite recovers from the Navy Department's objection to having Ladd's war-wounded buddy Bendix, wandering around with a steel plate in his head and intermittent amnesia, turn out to have done the killing (out of outraged loyalty to his friend, then blanking it out in his memory). The plot rewrite involves one or two arbitrary connections and a much less satisfactory conclusion. A fine hardboiled thriller for all that, with excellent dialogue and performances, and much more apt direction from Marshall than one might expect. TM

Blue Denim (aka Blue Jeans)

(1959, US, 89 min, b/w)
d Philip Dunne. *p* Charles Brackett. *sc* Edith Sommer, Philip Dunne. *ph* Leo Tover. *ed* William H Reynolds. *ad* Lyle Wheeler, Leland Fuller. *m* Bernard Herrmann. *cast* Carol Lynley, Brandon de Wilde, Macdonald Carey, Marsha Hunt, Warren Berlinger, Roberta Shore.

●A controversial film in its time, this now looks hilariously dated. It's a prototype youth movie about kids who Go Too Far, with Lynley and de Wilde having to face the consequences of her pregnancy. The backstreet abortionist is naturally presented as the summit of all depravity, and the pair seem idiotically naive by present standards, but it does carry '50s atmosphere and the performances (Lynley especially) aren't too bad. But unlike Nicholas Ray's *Rebel Without a Cause*, there is no attempt here to come within a thousand miles of the real problems of adolescence. DP

Blue Exile, The (Mavi Sürgün)

(1993, Tur/Ger, 113 min)
d Erden Kiral. *sc* Erden Kiral, Kenan Ormanlar, Elly Schellerer-Omanlar. *ph* Kenan Ormanlar. *ed* Karin Fischer. *m* Timur Selcuk. *cast* Can Togay, Hanna Schygulla, Ozay Fecht, Ayse Romey, Tatiana Papamoskou.

●This ambitious co-production, based on Cevat Sakir's autobiographical novel *The Fishermen of Helicarnassus* (*Mavi Sürgün*), describes the author's six-month journey in 1925 from Ankara to exile in the SW fishing port that is now Bodrum, where he was to serve the second half of a sentence for writing about WWI deserters. Kiral uses the epic journey as a poetic meditation on the writer's life, and also on memory, history and the meaning of life. Replete with quotes from Dante and mysterious dark episodes (such as one on a train in which Schygulla's 'Levant Marie' reminds the exile of his first wife), it's an enigmatic confusing drama, but one which often succeeds in triggering 'the unbearable smell of the past'. WH

Blue Eyes of Yonta, The (Udju Azul di Yonta)

(1992, Guinea-Bissau/Port, 95 min)
d Flora Gomes. *p* Paulo De Sousa. *sc* Flora Gomes. *ph* Dominique Gentil. *ed* Dominique Paris. *ad* Miguel Mendes. *m* Adriano G Ferreira-Atchutchi. *cast* Maysa Marta, António Simão Mendes, Pedro Dias.

●Only the second film to emerge from Guinea-Bissau, this is an engaging domestic drama about Yonta, a young girl in love with Vicente, an older man home from the war. Vicente has other fish to fry – literally, a consignment of them to be sold – but Yonta has a secret admirer, whose florid declarations of passion are, to her embarrassment, getting read out in the local disco. Kid brother Amilcar just stands back and revels in the flying sparks. Stylistically, it's low-key, apart from the remarkable final tracking shot that comes as a genial surprise. Thanks to the diversity of the narrative, and the real presence of its leads, this state-of-Guinea domestic drama comes across as something more than *Neighbours* with Creole dialogue. JRo

Blue Fin

(1978, Aust, 90 min, b/w)
d Carl Schultz. *p* Hal McElroy. *sc* Sonia Borg. *ph* Geoff Burton. *ed* Rod Adamson. *m* Michael Carlos. *cast* Greg Rowe, Hardy Krüger, John Jarrett, Elspeth Ballantyne, Liddy Clarke.

●Boy's adventure material from the *Storm Boy* stable, with Rowe this time the son of tuna-fishing captain Kruger, eventually disproving his father's estimation of his unsuitability as a sailor by saving his boat and his life. The early fishing scenes are fascinating on a quasi-documentary level, but the yarn itself is too slight and predictable, even down to its routine tragedies and satirical digs at landlubbing poms. PT

Blue Gardenia, The

(1953, US, 90 min)
d Fritz Lang. *p* Alex Gottlieb. *sc* Charles Hoffman. *ph* Nick Musuraca. *ed* Edward Mann. *ad* Daniel Hall. *m* Raoul Kraushaar. *cast* Anne Baxter, Richard Conte, Ann Sothern, Raymond Burr, Jeff Donnell, Richard Erdman, Nat 'King' Cole.

●Relatively minor but still gripping *film noir*, in which Baxter, jilted by her soldier fiancé, goes on a blind date with Burr, gets drunk…and awakes to discover that the pushy playboy has been murdered, quite possibly by herself. The story, which continues with news-reporter Conte's attempts first to get the killer to come forward and then to clear Baxter's name, is not altogether original, but Lang, his cast, and cameraman Nic Musuraca manage to inject the proceedings with a grimly compelling atmosphere. And the title? It's the name of the nightclub where Baxter's fateful encounter with Burr occurs, and where Nat King Cole contributes a welcome musical cameo. GA

Blue Hawaii

(1961, US, 101 min)
d Norman Taurog. *p* Hal B Wallis. *sc* Hal Kanter. *ph* Charles Lang Jr. *ed* Warren Low. *ad* Hal Pereira, Walter Tyler. *songs* Hugo Peretti, Fred Wise, Ben Weisman, Sid Tepper, Roy C Bennett, others. *cast* Elvis Presley, Joan Blackman, Angela Lansbury, Roland Winters, Nancy Walters, Iris Adrian, John Archer.
● Presley escapes the *GI Blues* and takes a job with a Hawaii tourist agency in this innocuous star vehicle/holiday brochure. Lots of scenery and one tolerable song, 'Can't Help Falling in Love'. NF

Blue Heat

see Last of the Finest, The

Blue Ice

(1992, US, 105 min)
d Russell Mulcahy. *p* Martin Bregman, Michael Caine. *sc* Ron Hutchinson. *ph* Denis Crossan. *ed* Seth Faum. *pd* Grant Hicks. *m* Michael Kamen. *cast* Michael Caine, Sean Young, Ian Holm, Bobby Short, Alun Armstrong, Sam Kelly, Jack Shepherd, Phillip Davis, Patricia Hayes, Alan MacNaughtan, Bob Hoskins.
● It is a testament to Caine's screen presence that, as an ex-MI6 agent turned jazz club-owner, he almost single-handedly carries this routine thriller. Young is glamorously sexy as the US ambassador's wife whose passionate advances embroil Caine once more in the dangerous world of espionage, while director Mulcahy tempers his flashy visual style and unobtrusively propels the narrative forward. Ageing romantic Caine falls hard for Young, and agrees to help find an ex-lover who, she claims, is threatening to tell the tabloids about their torrid affair. But when Caine and a friendly copper track her old flame to a seedy hotel, the bodies start piling up and Caine finds himself on the wrong end of a murder investigation. You don't need a billion dollar brain to discern the echoes of Caine's Harry Palmer character. So despite a promising set-up, not even Caine can dispel an air of desperate atavism. NF

Blue in the Face

(1995, US, 89 min)
d Wayne Wang, Paul Auster. *p* Greg Johnson, Peter Newman. *sc* Wayne Wang. *ph* Adam Holender. *ed* Chris Tellefsen. *pd* Kalina Ivanov. *m* John Lurie. *cast* Harvey Keitel, Roseanne Barr, Michael J Fox, Lily Tomlin, Giancarlo Esposito, Mel Gorham, Jared Harris, Madonna, Mira Sorvino, Victor Argo, Lou Reed, Jim Jarmusch, RuPaul.
● Wang and Auster had so many ideas and incidents left over from *Smoke* that they knocked out this mostly improvised feature in one week after finishing the shoot of the other film. Prior commitments prevented most of the Smoke cast from sticking around, so this centres on Keitel's Auggie Wren and makes his tobacco store the centre of a freewheeling Brooklyn universe. Roseanne barges in as the semi-detached wife of the owner, Lily Tomlin hangs around as the bag lady, Fox intercepts passers-by with a questionnaire, Jim Jarmusch buys what he says will be his last packet of cigarettes and Madonna drops in to sing a telegram. It's hit and miss, of course, but its slacker charm perfectly complements the dovetailed plotting of *Smoke*. A celebration of loose ends that will have you thinking of a move to Brooklyn. TR

Blue Jean Cop

see Shakedown

Blue Jeans

see Blue Denim

Blue Juice

(1995, GB, 100 min)
d Carl Prechezer. *p* Peter Salmi, Simon Relph. *sc* Peter Salmi, Carl Prechezer. *ph* Richard Greatrex. *ed* Michael Ellis. *pd* Mark Tildesley. *cast* Sean Pertwee, Catherine Zeta Jones, Steven Mackintosh, Ewan McGregor, Peter Gunn, Heathcote Williams, Jenny Agutter.
● Fast approaching 30, JC (Pertwee) is torn – between his love for Chloe (Jones) and his obsession with surfing; between travelling the globe with his girl and staying in Cornwall with old mates down from London. In short, JC is worried about getting old. British surfing movies might not be everyone's cup of tea, but this is a droll feature debut revelling in odd juxtapositions and riding along with enough flair to distract from its shortcomings. GA

Blue Kite, The (Lan Fengzheng)

(1993, HK/China, 138 min)
d Tian Zhuangzhuang. *sc* Xiao Mao. *ph* Hou Yong. *ed* Quian Lengleng. *ad* Zhang Xiande. *m* Youshihide Otomo. *cast* Yi Tian, Zhang Wenyao, Chen Xiaoman, Lu Liping.
● About the experiences of a Beijing family – seen largely through the eyes of its youngest member, Tietou – between 1953 and 1967, Tian's epic domestic drama is a direct, honest account of how Mao's policies affected the lives of ordinary people. While the steadily darkening tale makes for a film at least partly about death and absence, it focuses not on those who are exiled or die, but on those left behind. Tian's method is understatement, with the result that the trials faced by Shujuan (Lu Liping), her brothers and sister, her three husbands and her son Tietou become all the more plausible and affecting. There's an immense amount of telling detail, and Tian manages to express both sympathy and righteous anger without once resorting to bombast or sentimentality. A masterly blend of the personal and the political. GA

Blue Knight, The

(1973, US, 96 min)
d Robert Butler. *p* Walter Coblenz. *sc* E Jack Neuman. *ph* Michael D Margulies. *ed* Marjorie Fowler, Samuel E Beetley, Jr Gene Fowler. *ad* Hilyard Brown. *m* Nelson Riddle. *cast* William Holden, Lee Remick, Joe Santos, Eileen Brennan, Emile Meyer, Sam Elliott.
● Feature cut-down of US TV's first ever mini-series (originally aired over four nights in November 1973), perhaps now less interesting as a digest of a fair LAPD drama (covering the lead-up to veteran cop Holden's retirement from the force) than for its intriguingly tentacular influence over subsequent developments in US police representation, primarily exerted via creative personnel Butler, E Jack Neuman and Joseph Wambaugh. The quality anthology series *Police Story* was the first result, supervised by writer Neuman and shadowed by cop-turned-novelist Wambaugh who, as that series began spinning off its own variants, moved his awareness of law'n'order contradictions and his own brand of special pleading to the big screen (*The Onion Field*, *The Black Marble*). Butler, after playing shy of the cop genre for some time, then reemerged to establish the particular radical texture of the opening series of *Hill Street Blues*. Seminal stuff. PT

Blue Lagoon, The

(1949, GB, 103 min)
d Frank Launder. *p* Sidney Gilliat, Frank Launder. *sc* Frank Launder, John Baines, Michael Hogan. *ph* Geoffrey Unsworth. *ed* Thelma Myers. *ad* Edward Carrick. *m* Clifton Parker. *cast* Jean Simmons, Donald Houston, Susan Stranks, Peter Jones, Maurice Denham, Noel Purcell, James Hayter, Cyril Cusack.
● Previously an unrealised Carol Reed project, and subsequently a risibly coy teen-sex tease from Randal Kleiser, H de Vere Stacpoole's novel was first filmed by Launder and Gilliat's Individual Pictures, who utilised Technicolor for the first time and split their schedule between Fiji and Pinewood. Stranks and Jones are the child castaways who mature into Simmons and Houston's supposedly unsocialised adolescent lovers on a Pacific paradise. Audiences flocked, as they have since, at the mere promise. PT

Blue Lagoon, The

(1980, US, 104 min)
d/p Randal Kleiser. *sc* Douglas Day Stewart. *ph* Nestor Almendros. *ed* Robert Gordon. *ad* Jon Dowding. *m* Basil Poledouris. *cast* Brooke Shields, Christopher Atkins, Leo McKern, William Daniels, Elva Josephson, Glenn Kohan.
● This remake of the H de Vere Stacpoole novel about two shipwrecked kids growing up on a desert island was hyped as being about 'natural love'; but apart from 'doing it in the open air', there is nothing natural about two kids (unfettered by the bonds of society from their early years) subscribing to marriage and traditional role-playing. The only thing blue about the movie is the sea, and the way you'll feel after wasting your time on this dose of 'tasteful', TV commercial-style, nudity. FF

Blue Lamp, The

(1949, GB, 84 min, b/w)
d Basil Dearden. *p* Michael Balcon. *sc* TEB Clarke. *ph* Gordon Dines. *ed* Peter Tanner. *ad* Jim Morahan. *m* Ernest Irving. *cast* Jack Warner, Jimmy Hanley, Dirk Bogarde, Peggy Evans, Patric Doonan, Robert Flemyng, Bernard Lee, Meredith Edwards, Gladys Henson.
● The film that spawned George Dixon, of 'Dock Green' fame, here presented as the perfect friendly bobby, teaching new recruit Hanley the rules of the game, until half way through he is shot and killed by Bogarde's reckless delinquent. Thereafter the film details the search for the killer, but it's less interesting as a thriller than as a cosy, rosy depiction of both the police and the society in which they function, ever ready to help the bobbies in their quest for justice. Very, very British, and not a patch on its far tougher, darker Hollywood counterparts. GA

Blue Light, The

see Blaue Licht, Das

Blue Max, The

(1966, GB, 155 min)
d John Guillermin. *p* Christian Ferry. *sc* David Pursall, Jack Seddon, Gerald Hanley. *ph* Douglas Slocombe. *ed* Max Benedict. *pd* Wilfrid Shingleton. *m* Jerry Goldsmith. *cast* George Peppard, James Mason, Ursula Andress, Jeremy Kemp, Karl Michael Vogler, Anton Diffring.
● Guillermin has made rather a career of the sort of film which is remembered for its special effects and pyrotechnical action sequences, usually in a context of unashamed banality. *The Blue Max* deserves plaudits for its WWI dogfight sequences, but the human drama (overweeningly ambitious pilot scuppers himself by playing footsy with his superior's wife) never gets off the ground, despite the novelty of its involving German airmen (on which score it was later wiped out of the skies by Roger Corman's *The Red Baron*). GA

Blue Moon (Lan Yue)

(1997, Tai, 99 min)
d Ko I-cheng. *p* Cheng Aaton. *sc* Ko I-cheng, Joe Liu. *ph* Le Jack. *ed* Lin Hokka. *pd* Michael Hsu. *m* Tseng Szu-ming. *cast* Tarcy Su, Leon Dai, David Wang, Chang Han, Teddy Lo.
● In Godard's words, this is a film with a beginning, a middle and an end – but not necessarily in that order. It's a fascinating experiment: five reels – each centred on the tangled relationship between a divorced author, a volatile film producer and a determinedly free spirited young woman, all involved at some point or another with gun toting hoods – which may be shown in any order. The arrangement I saw definitely worked, since the themes of chance, predestination, choice and indecision were well to the fore. Witty, perceptive and consistently intriguing. GA

Blue Mountains (Golubye Gory Ely Nepravdopodobnaya Istoria)

(1983, USSR, 97 min)
d Eldar Shengelaya. *sc* Rezo Cheishvili. *ph* Levan Paatashvili. *ed* Leila Ashiani. *ad* Boris Tskhakaya. *m* Gia Kancheli. *cast* Ramaz Giorgobiani, V Kakhniashvili, T Chirgadze, I Sakvarelidze, Teimuraz Chirgadze.
● Transcending its status as a somewhat over-familiar allegorical satire on the shortcomings of bureaucracy, this most enjoyable Russian comedy becomes, through richly detailed observation, a wicked, winning farce about universal human foibles. Detailing a year in the life of a chaotic, literally crumbling publishing house as viewed through the initially hopeful eyes of a young writer, it quickly establishes a vivid tapestry of eccentrics, layabouts, liggers, obsessives, and incompetents, all too preoccupied with their own ludicrously personal concerns ever to get *anything* done. The realism of the beginning gradually yields to spiralling fantasy, surreal and

revealing in the Buñuel style; the strangely formal repetitive narrative only serves to underline the hilarious absurdity of the imaginative script, while the dark, 'meaningful' currents beneath the brightly sparkling surface are clear but never laboured. GA

Blue Movie

(1968, US, 133 min)
d/p Andy Warhol. *sc* Viva, Louis Waldon. *ph/ed* Andy Warhol. *cast* Viva, Louis Waldon.
● A totally inoffensive introduction to a fairly natural and often witty couple learning to improvise a bantering fuck for the camera. The sex is no stronger than the light and pretty blue in which it's photographed. No doubt it's the very naturalness of it which some find so disturbing; there's no attempt to get in the way of our straight appreciation of the camera's appreciation of their having some offhand fun one lazy sunny day. It's worth seeing, if only as a strong reminder of the enormous dishonesty and guilt-coyness with which sex is normally dealt with in the commercial cinema. JDuC

Blue Murder at St Trinian's

(1957, GB, 86 min)
d Frank Launder. *p* Sidney Gilliat, Frank Launder. *sc* Frank Launder, Val Valentine, Sidney Gilliat. *ph* Gerald Gibbs. *ed* Geoffrey Foot. *ad* Alan Harris. *m* Malcolm Arnold. *cast* Alastair Sim, George Cole, Joyce Grenfell, Terry-Thomas, Lionel Jeffries, Judith Furse, Sabrina.
● Jewel thief Jeffries is forced to masquerade as a St Trinian's mistress while the school is making a Grand Tour of Europe. Inventive situations utilising a classic British blend of comedy and crime make it the best (if you like this sort of thing) in the series which followed *The Belles of St Trinian's*. With all the regulars, plus Terry-Thomas and the legendary Sabrina as a big schoolgirl. DMcG

Blue Note: A History of Modern Jazz

(1997, Ger, 92 min)
d Julian Benedikt. *p* Ulli Pfau. *sc* Julian Benedikt. *ph* William Rexer II. *ed* Andrew Hulme. *with* Ron Carter, André Previn, Carlos Santana, Bertrand Tavernier, Taj Mahal, Bud Powell, Dexter Gordon, Thelonious Monk, Art Blakey, Cassandra Wilson, Max Roach, Lou Donaldson.
● You couldn't make any great claims for this as an outstanding example of documentary film-making – it traces the history faithfully and talks to a lot of the right people, but its choppy, syncopated style is really just a gloss on the facts. Even so, it's most enjoyable. Alfred Lion and Frank Wolff emigrated from Germany in the '30s and created the most significant label in the history of jazz. Blue Note brought the best out of the best, including Thelonious Monk, Bud Powell, Dexter Gordon, Art Blakey and Sonny Rollins. Propelled by 'Cherokee' and a dizzy set of modern classics, augmented by revealing anecdotes from Max Roach, Lou Donaldson, Bertrand Tavernier and André Previn, as well as Wolff's stunning studio photographs, this swings like a hepcat. TCh

Blue Notes and Exiled Voices

(1991, GB, 52 min)
d Imruh Bakari. *p* Henry Martin. *ph* Chris Morphet. *ed* Stuart de Jong.
● An informative, well-made documentary from the Ceddo workshop about the experience of exile of the generations of black South African musicians who have emigrated to Britain since the mid-'50s. It's a mixture of talking head interviews, archive footage, stills and well-integrated performances – from the Mervyn Africa Quintet, the Brotherhood of Breath, and the Hugh Masakela Band (which ends the film with a deeply expressive rendition of 'Healing'). The interviewees came over in different waves: Masakela as a reaction to the 1960 Sharpeville massacre, for instance, and many others to join their already exiled friends; many stayed – like Pinise Saul – after London shows such as *King Kong* and *Ipi Tombi*. Mervyn Africa describes the stresses – SA was never out of their hearts – and how too many of his fellow musicians have died young. The film sheds additional light on the pervasive tragic effects of apartheid. WH

Blue Peter, The (aka Navy Heroes)

(1955, GB, 94 min)
d Wolf Rilla. *p* Herbert Mason. *sc* Don Sharp, John Pudney. *ph* Arthur Grant. *ed* John Trumper. *ad* Ray Simm. *m* Antony Hopkins. *cast* Kieron Moore, Greta Gynt, Sarah Lawson, Mervyn Johns, Harry Fowler, Anthony Newley, John Charlesworth.
● Basically a new recruits army drama transposed to an Outward Bound camp for sea cadets, with nervy Korean vet Moore subsuming his own problems beneath those of his young charges, including Fowler and Newley. Flatly directed by the man who sounds more like a Japanese movie monster; acted with apparent conviction by Moore, who himself subsequently directed several Catholic-backed documentaries. PT

Blues Brothers, The

(1980, US, 133 min)
d John Landis. *p* Robert K Weiss. *sc* Dan Aykroyd, John Landis. *ph* Stephen M Katz. *ed* George Folsey Jr. *pd* John J Lloyd. *m* Ira Newborn. *cast* John Belushi, Dan Aykroyd, Kathleen Freeman, James Brown, Henry Gibson, John Landis, Frank Oz, Cab Calloway, Aretha Franklin, Carrie Fisher.
● A dispiriting indulgence, Landis' $27 million whoopee cushion embodies the current well-meaning but directionless predicament of the Rolling Stone generation. Belushi and Aykroyd evolved the fraternal idea (spivvy white kids obsessed with R & B) when it tackled real prejudices with a liberating directness. Now that incisiveness is blunted and the energy funnelled into extravagant spectacle. What should have been an epic, surreal romp through the America of Howard Johnsons, turns out like a grandiose TV variety show stuffed to the gills with dislocated cameo appearances. They're either pointless (Twiggy, Carrie Fisher) or come close to being patronising (Ray Charles, James Brown, Aretha Franklin, Cab Calloway). IB

Blues Brothers 2000

(1998, US, 123 min)
d John Landis. *p* John Landis, Dan Aykroyd, Leslie Belzberg. *sc* Dan Aykroyd, John Landis. *ph* David Herrington. *ed* Dale Beldin. *pd* Bill Brodie. *m* Paul Shaffer. *cast* Dan Aykroyd, John Goodman, Joe Morton,., J Evan Bonifant, Aretha Franklin, James Brown, BB King, Steve Cropper.
● In 1980 John Landis' rhythm 'n' blues demolition derby was slated by critics (see above) and written off as a box office flop. It became a cult hit, and must now be counted a popular classic. Eighteen years since his last public engagement, Elwood Blues (Aykroyd) is broke and all but washed up. Despite the death of his brother Jake (John Belushi), he decides to put the band back together for one last throw of the dice. This isn't a sequel, it's a remake. Some ingredients have been substituted, but it's the same recipe of R & B and comic overkill. As before, the best thing is the music: Aretha Franklin, Sam Moore, James Brown. The rest is stale, cynical and hamfisted. TCh

Blues entre les Dents, Le

see Blues Under the Skin

Blues for Lovers

see Ballad in Blue

Blues Harp

(1998, Jap, 106 min)
d Takashi Miike. *p* Naoya Narita. *sc* Toshihiko Matsuo, Toshiyuki Morioka. *ph* Hideo Yamamoto. *ed* Taiji Shimamura. *ad* Akira Ishige. *m* Atsushi Okuno. *cast* Hiroyuki Ikeuchi, Seiichi Tanabe, Saori Sekino, Mickey Curtis.
● The plot has a kinship with *Performance*: a middle-ranking yakuza hides out from enemies in a small blues club and finds himself falling in love with its (straight) owner, the son of a black American GI and an Okinawan woman. It turns out to be a fatal attraction, because the gangster's deputy gets so jealous that he works up a plan to get the musician killed. Characteristically, Miike tackles the material head-on, using the setting (Yokosuka, the US military base seen in Imamura's *Pigs and Battleships*) and strong images (Yamamoto also shot *Hana-Bi*) to orchestrate a 'blues' for a doomed and predominantly one-sided love affair. With great performances from Ikeuchi (the musician) and Tanabe (the yakuza), it's as soulful as they come. TR

Blue Skies

(1946, US, 104 min)
d Stuart Heisler. *p* Sol C Siegel. *sc* Arthur Sheekman, Allan Scott. *ph* Charles Lang Jr, William Snyder. *ed* LeRoy Stone. *ad* Hans Dreier, Hal Pereira. *songs* Irving Berlin. *cast* Bing Crosby, Fred Astaire, Joan Caulfield, Billy de Wolfe, Olga San Juan, Frank Faylen.
● Unusually lavish Paramount musical with a generous quota of 21 Irving Berlin songs (only four of them new). Negligible backstage plot, but the numbers are fine (even if Crosby does groan his tiresomely soulful way through 'White Christmas' *and* 'How Deep is the Ocean'), with a particularly spirited Carmen Miranda-ish rendering of 'Heat Wave' by Olga San Juan. High spot is undoubtedly Astaire's great interpretation of 'Puttin' on the Ritz' accompanied, courtesy of trick photography, by a chorus line of Astaires each doing a solo act. TM

Blue Sky

(1991, US, 101 min)
d Tony Richardson. *p* Robert H Solo. *sc* Rama Laurie Stagner, Jerry Leichtling, Arlene Sarner. *ph* Steve Yaconelli. *ed* Robert K Lambert. pd Timian Alsaker. *m* Jack Nitzsche. *cast* Tommy Lee Jones, Jessica Lange, Powers Boothe, Carrie Snodgress, Amy Locane, Anna Klemp, Chris O'Donnell, Mitchell Ryan.
● Hank (Jones) is besotted with his sexy, manic-depressive wife Carly (Oscar-winner Lange) to the extent that their daughters (Locane and Klemp) more or less raise themselves. He's an Army scientist researching levels of radiation after '60s nuclear tests in the desert, and official pressure on him to massage his readings gets heavier after a pair of cowboys stray into the fall-out. But the real drama here is his marriage, neatly delineated by Carly sashaying about like Marilyn on Jones Beach, half-naked under a gauze scarf, and later breaking down in public as she sees their sordid quarters on camp. She's infantile, a fantasist dreaming of Hollywood, and easy prey for the horny commanding officer (Boothe). In this portrait of a complex, painful, dependent relationship, the two leads deliver their blazing best, helped by an intelligent, unsparing script. BC

Blue Spring (Aoi Haru)

(2001, Jap, 83 min)
d Toshiaki Toyoda. *p* Dai Miyazaki. *sc* Toshiaki Toyoda. *ph* Norimichi Kasamatsu. *ed* Mototaka Kusakabe. *ad* Mitsuo Harada. *m* Kenji Ueda. *cast* Ryuhei Matsuda, Hirofumi Arai, Sosuke Takaoka, Yusuke Oshiba, Yuta Yamazaki.
● High-school delinquent Kujo (Matsuda, evidently trying to erase memories of *Gohatto* by playing macho) becomes top dog in class and is idolised by his buddy Aoki. But as graduation approaches he turns away from his likely future as a yakuza, leaving Aoki bereft and increasingly unstable. Very disappointing after Toyoda's non-fiction *Unchain*, this is an object lesson in how *not* to adapt a manga. The director flails around for the right blend of realism and stylisation, and ends up staking everything on scenes of hyperbolic (and pitifully unconvincing) violence. TR

Blue Steel

(1989, US, 102 min)
d Kathryn Bigelow. *p* Edward R Pressman, Oliver Stone. *sc* Kathryn Bigelow, Eric Red. *ph* Amir Mokri. *ed* Hal Levinsohn. *pd* Tony Corbett. *m* Brad Fiedel. *cast* Jamie Lee Curtis, Ron Silver, Clancy Brown, Elizabeth Pena, Louise Fletcher, Philip Bosco, Clancy Brown.
● On her first day of active duty, rookie NY cop Megan Turner (Curtis) surprises a supermarket robber and blows him away. Suspended for shooting an unarmed suspect (his gun has mysteriously disappeared), Megan is later seduced by charming commodities-broker Eugene Hunt (Silver). Then dead bodies start turning up all over town, killed with bullets fired from her gun and etched with her name. Detective Nick Mann (Brown) takes Megan under his wing, but even

when Hunt virtually confesses to the crimes, the disturbing cat-and-mouse games have just begun. Curtis gives her most complex performance to date as the reckless Megan, whose obsessive behaviour and over-reactions have more to do with turning the tables on violent men than balancing the scales of justice. Short on plausibility but preserving the psycho-sexual ambiguities throughout, Bigelow's seductively stylish, wildy fetishistic thriller is proof that a woman can enter a traditionally male world and, like Megan, beat men at their own game. NF

Blue Streak

(1999, US, 94 min)
d Les Mayfield. *p* Toby Jaffe, Neal H Moritz. *sc* Michael Berry, John Blumenthal, Steve Carpenter. *ph* David Eggby. *ed* Michael Tronick. *pd* Bill Brzeski. *m* Edward Shearmur. *cast* Martin Lawrence, Luke Wilson, Dave Chappelle, Peter Greene, Nicole Ari Parker, Graham Beckel, Robert Miranda, Olek Krupa.

● Lawrence and his cohorts are in the midst of a diamond heist when he's nabbed by the cops on a nearby construction site. Reluctant to be collared redhanded, he hides the hot rock in a ventilation duct, resolving to return and retrieve it. After a two-year stretch, he looks up the old address and discovers it's LA's largest police station. Posing as a pizza delivery boy doesn't get him past the front desk, but when he comes up with convincing ID to pass as a newly transferred detective, he's in. None of this is within hailing distance of plausibility, but it does make a certain skewed sense that the crook's streetwise *nous* is what makes him a successful, if unconventional cop. The conceit is fun, but the movie doesn't give Lawrence anything challenging to do. TJ

Blues Under the Skin (Le Blues entre les Dents)

(1972, Fr, 88 min)
d Robert Manthoulis. *sc* Robert Manthoulis, Claude Fléouter. *ph* Fotis Mestheneos, Louis Soulanes. *ed* Dominique Colonna, Olivier Grégoire. *ad* Jean Gallaud. *cast* Amelia Cortez, Onike Lee, Roland Sanchez, BB King, Brownie McGhee, Sonny Terry, Mance Lipscomb, Furry Lewis.

● A mixture of documentary and fiction that alternates between bluesmen – from those on the chain gangs right up to BB King – singing and talking about their work, and a classic blues story set in Harlem about a girl who quits her man. The mixture is not a wholly comfortable one, the story and the acting of the young couple being too self-conscious to stand up to the naturalness of the bluesmen themselves. But the music survives on its own, and Amelia Cortez, a real old blues lady playing the mother-in-law, holds the story together with her reminiscences.

Blue Sunshine

(1977, US, 95 min)
d Jeff Lieberman. *p* George Manasse. *sc* Jeff Lieberman. *ph* Don Knight. *ed* Brian Smedley-Aston. *ad* Ray Storey. *m* Charles Gross. *cast* Zalman King, Deborah Winters, Mark Goddard, Robert Walden, Charles Siebert, Ann Cooper.

● An intriguing premise: what if a certain species of LSD, a decade later, should begin to have an unexpected effect on its users' chromosomes? All over an American city, isolated individuals inexplicably slaughter their loved ones before going on the rampage. The film has a phenomenal opening, and makes the most of its plot possibilities, but the police's continual arrival at the scene of murder just in time to implicate the investigative hero will put a strain on any audience's credulity. Exploitation of a superior kind, none the less. DP

Blue Thunder

(1982, US, 110 min)
d John Badham. *p* Gordon Carroll. *sc* Dan O'Bannon, Don Jakoby. *ph* John A Alonzo. *ed* Frank Morriss, Edward Abroms. *ad* Sydney Z Litwack. *m* Arthur B Rubinstein. *cast* Roy Scheider, Warren Oates, Candy Clark, Daniel Stern, Paul Roebling, David S Sheiner, Malcolm McDowell.

● Maverick LA cop Frank Murphy (Scheider), never happier than when he's in the pilot's seat conducting irregular surveillance of the nearest nude yoga fanatic, is assigned to test-fly Blue Thunder, the last word in hi-tech attack helicopters. When Murphy twigs that the military has sinister designs for the super-chopper, his liberal hackles rise. They rise still further when the sardonic Col Cochrane (McDowell) makes it personal: the two last met on a tour of duty in Vietnam. The opposition of good and evil is devoid of any subtle shading, so just sit back and enjoy the spectacular dogfight over downtown Los Angeles. The sight of aircraft smashing into tall buildings, however, slightly takes the edge off the fun after 9/11, but director Badham wasn't to know that two decades earlier. Warren Oates is good value as Murphy's grizzled and grumpy superior. NRo

Blue Tiger

(1994, US, 88 min)
d Norberto Barba. *p* Mike Leahy, Aki Komine. *sc* Joel Soisson. *ph* Christopher Walling. *ed* Caroline Ross. *pd* Markus Canter. *cast* Virginia Madsen, Toru Nakamura, Ryo Ishibashi, Harry Dean Stanton, Dean Hallo.

● A directorial debut which takes a formula, straight-to-video screenplay and gives it a huge shot of adrenaline in the heart. It's the familiar exploitation story of a single mother who takes up arms when her child is killed in a mob shootout, but with gleaming cinematography, tight editing and top-notch performances across the board, this is worth a detour. Barba has an eye for detail (a new tattoo bleeding through Madsen's blouse) and a special way with action sequences – could John Woo be replacing David Lynch as the American indies' spiritual mentor for the mid-'90s? TCh

Blue Velvet 100 (100)

(1986, US, 120 min)
d David Lynch. *p* Richard Roth. *sc* David Lynch. *ph* Frederick Elmes. *ed* Duwayne Dunham. *pd* Patricia Norris. *m* Angelo Badalamenti. *cast* Kyle MacLachlan, Isabella Rossellini, Dennis Hopper, Laura Dern, Hope Lange, Dean Stockwell, George Dickerson.

● Jeffrey (MacLachlan) is the contemporary knight in slightly tarnished armour, a shy and adolescent inhabitant of Lumberton, USA. After discovering a severed ear in an overgrown backlot, he embarks upon an investigation that leads him into a hellish netherworld, where he observes – and comes to participate in – a terrifying sadomasochistic relationship between damsel-in-distress Dorothy (Rossellini) and mad mobster Frank Booth (Hopper). Grafting on to this story his own idiosyncratic preoccupations, Lynch creates a visually stunning, convincingly coherent portrait of a nightmarish substratum to conventional, respectable society. The seamless blending of beauty and horror is remarkable – although many will be profoundly disturbed by Lynch's vision of male-female relationships, centred as it is on Dorothy's psychopathic hunger for violence – the terror very real, and the sheer wealth of imagination virtually unequalled in recent cinema. GA

Blue Villa, The (Un bruit qui rend fou)

(1994, Belg/Fr/Switz, 100 min)
d Alain Robbe-Grillet, Dimitri de Clercq. *p* Jacques de Clercq. *sc* Alain Robbe-Grillet. *ph* Hans Meier. *ed* France Duez. *ad* Alain Chennaux. *m* Nikos Kypourgos. *cast* Fred Ward, Arielle Dombasle, Charles Tordjman, Sandrine Le Berre, Dimitri Poulikakos, Christian Maillet.

● Perhaps the French title – *Un bruit qui rend fou* (a maddening noise) – evokes more accurately the particular qualities of Robbe-Grillet's movie. As in *Last Year in Marienbad* and *L'Immortelle*, the writer/director can't simply let a story unfold, but worries away at it with question after question, hypothesis after hypothesis. Thus, when a Mediterranean island is revisited by Frank (Ward), a sailor said to have drowned a year earlier when he fled after allegedly killing 16-year-old Santa, we're unsure not only whether he's a ghost, but whether the girl is actually dead or hidden in a bordello, the Blue Villa, run by a shady chanteuse (Dombasle). We're unsure even whether Frank's return is for real, or something imagined by Santa's father, a screenwriter (Tordjman), whom, naturally, the police chief suspects of being behind the crime, if it ever happened. Despite the longueurs, fans of Ruiz, Greenaway or Welles' *Confidential Report* may find much to enjoy. Nevertheless, just as the whiff of sexual perversity now seems both dubious and dated, so the film's arch artifice seems strangely out of touch with current film-making concerns. GA

Blue Water, White Death

(1971, US, 99 min).
d Peter Gimbel, James Lipscomb. *p/sc* Peter Gimbel. *ph* James Lipscomb. *ed* John Maddox. *with* Ron Taylor, Rodney Jonklas, Stanton Waterman, Valerie Taylor.

● A pre-*Jaws* documentary on the search by a team of cameramen/divers for the Great White Shark. Still surprisingly uncliched; a film definitely to get your teeth into.

Blume in Love

(1973, US, 116 min)
d/p/sc Paul Mazursky. *ph* Bruce Surtees. *ed* Donn Cambern. *pd* Pato Guzman. *m* Bill Conti. *cast* George Segal, Susan Anspach, Kris Kristofferson, Marsha Mason, Shelley Winters, Paul Mazursky.

● As *Willie & Phil* demonstrated conclusively, Mazursky's exposure to European art cinema (*Jules et Jim*) must have come at an impressionable age. Almost all the affectedly ampersanded characters of his rollcall filmography (Bob & Carol & Ted & the rest) are adrift in the emotional flux of infinitely permutated relationships, and there's only so much mileage to be gained from glossing the '50s Hollywood sex comedy with 'sophisticatedly' ambivalent light satire. Here the never-ending game of musical beds is played by divorce lawyer Segal, ex-wife Anspach, and assorted lovers Mason and Kristofferson, with Venice the cultural postcard backdrop. PT

Blush (Hongfen)

(1995, HK/China, 119 min)
d Li Shaohong. *p* Chen Kunming, Jimmy Tan. *sc* Li Shaohong, Ni Zhen. *ph* Zeng Nianping. *ed* Zhou Xinxia. *pd* Chen Yiyun, Lin Chaoxiang. *m* Guo Wenjing. *cast* Wang Ji, Wang Zhiwen, He Saifei, Zhang Liwei, Wang Rouli, Song Xiuling.

● Based on a story by Su Tong (original author of *Raise the Red Lantern*), this explores the contrasted but linked fates of two Suzhou prostitutes in the years after the communist victory in 1949. Neither adapts to 'New China': one marries a former client, imagining he'll bring back the good times, and the other finds herself pregnant in a Buddhist nunnery. Li's previous films blended spot-on social realism with sharp psychological insights; here she adds a knowingly decadent languor to the mix, producing a Chinese 'women's movie' like no other. TR

Blutigen Geier von Alaska, Die

see Hellhounds of Alaska, The

B. Monkey

(1998, It/GB/US, 90 min)
d Michael Radford. *p* Stephen Woolley, Colin Vaines. *sc* Michael Radford, Chloe King, Michael Thomas. *ph* Ashley Rowe. *ed* Joelle Hache. *pd* Sophie Becher. *m* Jennie Muskett. *cast* Asia Argento, Jared Harris, Rupert Everett, Jonathan Rhys Meyers, Julie T Wallace, Ian Hart, Tim Woodward, Bryan Pringle, Clare Higgins.

● Strait-laced teacher Alan (Harris) moonlights as a hospital DJ playing Django Reinhardt and confiding in his captive audience (they'd run a mile if only they could). He chats up Beatrice (Argento) after spotting her in a bar. Romance blossoms between geek and goddess, yet 'B Monkey' – as Beatrice is known on the street – is an armed robber. She wants to quit, but the underworld won't let go, and B doesn't help by shooting a racketeer creditor of her best friend Paul (Everett). In a last-ditch break with the past, Alan and B flee to Yorkshire, but London is never far away. Despite the implausible romance and a lack of gritty authenticity – both in the Dales and in the Smoke – there's much to enjoy, from Everett's morose dandy to Pringle's bisexual headteacher. Excellent cameos from Higgins as a jealous teaching colleague and Wallace as an abusive parent. Rhys Meyers shoots a lowering glare as Paul's ex-lover, while Argento's performance is an electrifiying mix of kittenish vulnerability and tattooed carnality. NRo

B. Must Die (Hay que Matar a B)

(1973, Sp/Switz, 102 min)
d José Luis Borau. *p* Luis Megino, Irving Lerner. *sc* Antonio Drove, José Luis Boran. *ph* Luis Cuadrado. *ed* Pablo G Del Amo. *ad* Federico Gonzales Mas. *cast* Burgess Meredith, Stéphane Audran, Patricia Neal,Darren McGavin.
●Somewhere in South America, there's a country on the brink of chaos, a no-hope Hungarian recruited as an unwilling hit man, a popular politician called B. A simple, no frills thriller with an international cast and a rather bland international taste. The plot ticks over efficiently enough, and could be seen as a covert fable on fascist Spain, but it's mainly surprising as a conspicuous contrast to the later, much more poetic/fantastical 'new-wave' Spanish cinema. SJo

BMX Bandits

(1983, Aust, 90 min)
d Brian Trenchard-Smith. *p* Tom Broadbridge, Paul F Davies. *sc* Patrick Edgeworth. *ph* John Seale. *ed* Alan Lake. *pd* Ross Major. *m* Colin Stead, Frank Strangio. *cast* David Argue, John Ley, Nicole Kidman, Angelo D'Angelo, James Lugton, Bryan Marshall.
●Two teenage boy BMXers gang up with a young supermarket girl after an unexpected meeting with one of her trolleys. While oyster-catching to raise readies for the bike repairs, they stumble on a stash of illegal walkie-talkies intended for use in a bank job, which leads to a slapstick bike/car chase, culminating in a mass rally of young bikers. Obviously made on a TV budget, the plot is weedy, and the film is saved only by some neat stunts and the splendour of the Australian landscape. DA

Bo's Bolero

see Bolero

Boardwalk

(1979, US, 100 min)
d Stephen Verona. *p* George Willoughby. *sc* Stephen Verona, Leigh Chapman. *ph* Billy Williams. *ed*Thom Noble. *pd* Glenda Ganis. *m* William S Fischer, Michael Kamen, Rob Mounsey, Coleridge Taylor-Perkinson. *cast* Ruth Gordon, Lee Strasberg, Janet Leigh, Joe Silver, Eddie Barth, Merwin Goldsmith, Kim Delgado.
●Disappointing after Verona's earlier *Lords of Flatbush*, this tale of elderly Strasberg and Gordon, a loving couple living on Coney Island, standing up to the marauding, mugging youth gangs that forever threaten them, is smug, sentimental, and more than a mite objectionable in some if its implications. *Death Wish* meets *On Golden Pond* – eminently avoidable. GA

Boat, The (Das Boot)

(1981, WGer, 149 min)
d Wolfgang Petersen. *p* Günter Rohrbach. *sc* Wolfgang Petersen. *ph* Jost Vacano. *ed* Hannes Nikel. *pd* Rolf Zehetbauer. *m* Klaus Doldinger. *cast* Jürgen, Prochnow, Herbert Grönemeyer, Klaus Wennemann, Hubertus Bengsch, Martin Semmelrogge, Claude-Oliver Rudolph.
●This belongs to that least enticing of genres, the submarine movie. Yet, despite a narrative almost wholly confined to the cramped interior of a U-boat patrolling the Atlantic, it isn't hard to understand why Germany's most expensive film ever became an international hit. Apart from the fact that, like *Chariots of Fire*, it exploits a contemporary soft spot for nostalgic, non-sectarian patriotism, Petersen's shooting style displays a breathtaking, if impersonal and faintly academic, virtuosity comparable to that of Lean or Coppola. As the brilliantly deployed Steadicam whizzes through the sweaty clutter of the vessel's living quarters, the film's unfailing (and paradoxical) sense of spectacle is rendered even more dynamic by appearing about to burst at the seams of its own claustrophobia. A pity, then, that its ironies on the futility of warfare prove trite beyond belief. GAd

Boat: The Director's Cut, The (Das Boot)

(1981, WGer, 209 min)
d Wolfgang Petersen. *p* Günter Rohrbach. *sc* Wolfgang Petersen. *ph* Jost Vacano. *ed* Hannes Nikel. *pd* Rolf Zehetbauer. *m* Klaus Doldinger. *cast* Jürgen, Prochnow, Herbert Grönemeyer, Klaus Wennemann, Hubertus Bengsch, Martin Semmelrogge, Claude-Oliver Rudolph.
●Restored footage from the original German TV version brings this portrait of life on a WWII U-boat close to three and a half hours. As captain Prochnow and his crew hunt British convoys in the North Atlantic, it's hard to think of any other film that makes the experience of combat so palpable. Although the bursts of action are appropriately visceral and the travails of sinking to the ocean floor unbelievably tense, what makes the film so powerful is the space it gives to characterisation. We get to know these people, and thus care desperately about their survival. Perhaps Petersen's script dissociates them to easily from the Nazi cause, but it's clear that these so-called 'Grey Wolves' (all volunteers, most of whom never returned) were the true mavericks of the German war machine. TJ

Boatman

(1993, It, 56 min, b/w)
d/p/sc/ph/ed Gianfranco Rosi.
●Excellent look at life on and around the Ganges at Benares, where the dead are cremated, buried or dumped, according to caste or wealth, and the living come to mourn, worship, bathe, gawp and ply their trades. Besides the non-judgmental tone, what impresses about this documentary is the way it balances the many contradictions in the teeming lives it reveals, and the way poetry is combined with wit. There's understanding here (though Rosi never pretends to be other than an outsider); the only pity is that it's not in colour. GA

Boatman (Ang Bangkero)

(1984, Phil, 120 min)
d Tikoy Aguiluz. *cast* Ronnie Lazaro, Sarsi Emmanuelle, Jonas Sebastian, Suzanna Love.
●A gauche young boatman from the sticks makes his way to the Big City, finds work in live sex shows, and winds up starring in soft-porn movies with two women fighting over his body off-screen. The London Festival described this spineless and exploitative mess as 'audacious', clearly forgetting that Lino Brocka covered very similar ground with very much more integrity ten years earlier, when martial law was still in force. At best this is embarrassing, at worst it's amateur night in Manila. TR

Boatman (Kayikci)

(1999, Tur/Greece/Bulg, 88 min)
d/p Biket Ilhan. *sc* Metin Belgin, Ulku Karaosmanoglu. *ph* Colin Mounier. *ed* Nikos Kanakis. *ad* Jale Basaran.*m* Thesia Panayiotou. *cast* Memet Ali Alabora, Katerina Moutsatsos, Elena Filippa, Pericles Lianos, Stelios Goutis, Levent Ozdilek.
●A confused but ineffably sweet 'love across the divide' story set aroud the fishing towns and islands of the Aegean. Deaf mute Turkish boatman Kayikci pines for Evdokia, a Greek singer from Chios, so one night he swims there. No one quite understands what he's up to – the Greeks suspect him for a Turkish spy and send him back – except Evdokia, who takes him for her own Leander. *Il Postino* territory, only more naive. NB

Boat People (Touben Nuhai)

(1982, HK, 111 min)
d Ann Hui. *p* Xia Meng. *sc* Yau-Tai On-Ping. *ph* Huang Zongji. *ed* Kin Kin. *ad* Tony Au. *m* Law Wing-Fai. *cast* George Lam, Season Ma, Cora Miao, Andy Lau, Gus Wong.
●Hui's impressive film sets out to explain why so many Vietnamese (mostly of Chinese descent) took to the South China Sea as refugees in the late 1970s. A Japanese photo-journalist covers the 'liberation' of Danang in 1975 and returns to report on 'New Vietnam' three years later. Initially a pawn of the propaganda bureau, he gradually realises the truth about forced labour camps, poverty and corruption, not to mention the generational in-fighting within the communist party. On first release it was taken as a pessimistic prophecy of Hong Kong's likely fate after the 1997 reversion to China's sovereignty – a reading it only half invites. The major weakness is the central casting: Lam is hopelessly unconvincing as both a Japanese and a professional photographer. TR

Bob & Carol & Ted & Alice

(1969, US, 105 min)
d Paul Mazursky. *p* Larry Tucker. *sc* Paul Mazursky, Larry Tucker. *ph* Charles E Lang. *ed* Stuart H Pappé. *ad* Pato Guzman. *m* Quincy Jones. *cast* Natalie Wood, Robert Culp, Elliott Gould, Dyan Cannon, Horst Ebersberg.
●Mazursky's sharp but sympathetic satire on the Encounter-group mindset and free-love ethos that swept certain areas of Californian life (Hollywood included, of course) in the late '60s. Too often dismissed as modish, it's in fact a mostly very funny, insightful, gently romantic account of well-meaning couples – documentarist Culp and wife Wood (seriously sincere and 'liberated'), and their relatively straitlaced pals Gould and Cannon – striving valiantly but vainly to balance personal needs and desires with changing social fads and theories. The closing moments are a touch trite, but until then the subtlety of writing and playing – coupled with a spontaneity and readiness to let scenes sprawl at times almost reminiscent of Cassavetes – make for pleasures aplenty. GA

Bobby Deerfield

(1977, US, 123 min)
d/p Sydney Pollack. *sc* Alvin Sargent. *ph* Henri Decaë. *ed* Fredric Steinkamp. *pd* Stephen Grimes. *m* David Grusin. *cast* Al Pacino, Marthe Keller, Anny Duperey, Walter McGinn, Romolo Valli.
●A classic example of a Hollywood director being struck down by a lethal 'art' attack as soon as he sets foot in Europe. Pacino's cripplingly introverted racing driver falls in love with dying heiress. Although Pollack at times seems to be struggling to avoid the obvious pitfalls, he ultimately wallows in all of them, making the characters and settings into something very like a prolonged Martini ad. DP

Bob le Flambeur (Bob the Gambler)

(1956, Fr, 95 min, b/w)
d/p Jean-Pierre Melville. *sc* Jean-Pierre Melville, Auguste Le Beton. *ph* Henri Decaë. *ed* Monique Bonnot. *ad* Jean-Pierre Melville, Claude Bouxin. *m* Eddie Barclay, Jo Boyer. *cast* Roger Duchesne, Isabelle Corey, Daniel Cauchy, Guy Decomble, André Garret, Claude Cerval, Simone Paris, Howard Vernon.
●The cable car leads us down from the 'heaven' of the Sacré Coeur in Montmartre to the 'hell' of Pigalle, and as the neon is extinguished for another dawn, a weary Bob the Gambler treads his way home from the tables. Melville's 'love letter to Paris' is shot, like all good city films, between the hours of dusk and dawn, and is a loving recreation of all that is wonderful about the dark American city thrillers of the '30s and '40s. What doubles the pleasure, however, is that in spite of the heist, the double-crosses and the sudden death, it is still remarkably light in tone: an underworld comedy of manners. The courtly Monsieur Bob may wear a trenchcoat and fedora, but he rescues young ladies adrift in the milieu, remains loyal to his friend *l'inspecteur*, and gives the impression of wanting to rob the casino, not to assuage his gambling fever, but simply so that he can perform a robbery in dinner jacket. A wonderful movie with all the formal beauty, finesse and treacherous allure of green baize. CPea

Bobo, The

(1967, GB, 103 min)
d Robert Parrish. *p* Elliott Kastner, Jerzy Gershwin. *sc* David R Schwartz. *ph* Gerry Turpin. *ed* John Jympson. *pd* Don Ashton. *m* Francis Lai. *cast* Peter Sellers, Britt Ekland, Rossano Brazzi, Adolfo Celi, Hattie Jacques, Ferdy Mayne, Kenneth Griffith, John Wells.
●A sourly unfunny comedy, set in Spain (local colour has the characters lisping when talking about Barthelona), with Sellers as a singing matador and Ekland as a gold-digging floozie. The ghastly plot calls for the impoverished Sellers to seduce the mercenary Ekland within three days to win a bet (his prize, the contract he yearns for as a professional crooner). He does so, at great length. Inevitably but improbably, the pair fall in love; and an even ghastlier finale has Ekland discovering the truth, Sellers performing a noble act of self-sacrifice, and bitter-sweetness reigning on

the screen. Even more embarrassing than Sellers' efforts to be funny is the realisation that he is trying to be moving too. TM

Bob Roberts

(1992, US, 104 min)
d Tim Robbins. *p* Forrest Murray. *sc* Tim Robbins. *ph* Jean Lépine. *ed* Lisa Churgin. *pd* Richard Hoover. *m* David Robbins. *cast* Tim Robbins, Giancarlo Esposito, Alan Rickman, Ray Wise, Brian Murray, Gore Vidal, Rebecca Jenkins, Susan Sarandon, David Strathairn, John Cusack, James Spader, Peter Gallagher.

●Bob Roberts (Robbins, in his first film as writer/director) is a senatorial candidate in Pennsylvania in 1990. As a successful folk-singer, he knows how to use easy sentiment and emotive words to win support for his reactionary manifesto; as a self-made millionaire who took against a '60s childhood spent in a hippy commune, he is the living embodiment of the materialistic message he preaches; and he knows how to conduct a ruthless smear campaign against his rival, incumbent Democrat Senator Paiste (Vidal). Presenting itself as a documentary, *Bob Roberts* is not merely a satirical fictional biopic, but a wry exploration of the relationship between political reality and manufactured image, showing how far contemporary politics has been reduced by the media to the level of easy-to-handle entertainment. It does have flaws, but its confidence and courage in going against the grain of an increasingly conservative America are impressive. GA

Bob's Weekend

(1996, GB, 93 min)
d/p Jevon O'Neill. *sc* Jevon O'Neill, Jayson Rothwell. *ph* Roy D Smith. *ed* Nick Thompson. *pd* Mark Ingham. *m* Don Gould, David Mindel. *cast* Bruce Jones, Charlotte Jones, Ricky Tomlinson, Brian Glover, Anna Jaskolka.

●Likeable realist-tinged fantasy adventure by debut director (and co-writer) O'Neill: the last journey of a sacked security guard (Bruce Jones) who high-tails to Blackpool to end it all after discovering his wife's infidelity. This diffident, dictionary-reading man buys a Bolivian admiral's uniform (the Bolivians' have a land-locked cardboard navy, he's told) and pile of Encyclopedia Britannicas. He's intent on jumping off the pier thus laden, until a pretty student gets interested in his case. WH

Bob the Gambler

see Bob le Flambeur

Boca a Boca

see Mouth to Mouth

Boccaccio '70

(1961, It, 210 mins)
d Federico Fellini, Mario Monicelli, Vittorio de Sica, Luchino Visconti. *p* Tonino Cervi, Carlo Ponti. *sc* Federico Fellini, Ennio Flaiano, Tullio Pinelli, Luchino Visconti, Suso Cecchi D'Amico, Cesare Zavattini, Giovanni Arpino, Italo Calvino, Mario Monicelli. *ph* Otello Martelli, Giuseppe Rotunno, Armando Nanuzzi. *ed* Leo Catozzo, Mario Serandrei, Adriana Novelli. *ad* Piero Zuffi, Mario Garbuglia, Elio Costanzi, Piero Gherardi. *m* Nino Rota, Armando Trovaioli, Piero Umiliano. *cast* Anita Ekberg, Sophia Loren, Romy Schneider, Peppino de Filippo, Tomas Milian, Romolo Valli, Paolo Stoppa.

●Probably the best remembered of that exasperating sub-genre, the portmanteau film, largely because the directors concerned (the undisputed heavyweights of their time) let rip in their most vulgar styles in an attempt to recapture the spirit of Boccaccio. The filmettes also reveal a startling fear of women in general. Fellini's episode concerns an outsize Ekberg who steps out of a billboard poster to torment an ineffectual puritan; while Visconti delivered a vicious tale of a beautiful young wife (a stunning performance by Schneider) who takes revenge on her husband by making him pay for her body. De Sica and Monicelli went for broader, more traditional comedic effect – less pretentious, but perhaps inevitably in this company, less memorable. DT

Bodas de Sangre

see Blood Wedding

Boda secreta

see Secret Wedding

Bodies, Rest & Motion

(1993, US, 94 min)
d Michael Steinberg. *p* Allan Mindel, Denise Shaw, Eric Stoltz. *sc* Roger Hedden. *ph* Bernd Heinl. *ed* Jay Cassidy. *ad* Stephen McCabe. *m* Michael Convertino. *cast* Phoebe Cates, Bridget Fonda, Tim Roth, Eric Stoltz, Alicia Witt.

●Roger Hedden's adaptation of his own play charts the reverberations of a collision between four young dead-enders in an Arizona desert town. Selfish, nihilistic TV salesman Nick (Roth) is determined to head for Bute, Montana; Beth (Fonda), his current partner, is altogether less restless, while Carol (Cates) – friend to both and Nick's former (?) lover – seems to want them around. Into this unappealing ménage stumbles Sid (Stoltz), a decorator come to paint Nick and Beth's house for the next tenant, a banal doper with the hots for Beth. A laid-back look at youthful rootlessness which never really catches fire. GA

Bodo (Baodao Dameng)

(1993, Tai, 80 min)
d Huang Ming-Chuan. *p* Tzou Bukam. *sc* Huang Ming-Chuan, Angel Chen. *ph* Huang Mingchuan. *ed* JJ Chen. *cast* Bodo, Tsai Yi, Shi Nanhua, Huang Hongbin, Huang Zhiqi, Lin Wenyi, Wang Yiyan.

●Highly imaginative – not to say seriously hallucinatory – indie feature in which Huang sets out to exorcise Taiwan's problems with militarism, past and present. The chief setting is a southern garrison, first line of defence against invaders from the sea – who never come. Boredom, inactivity and tropical torpor take their toll and, as usual, the sleep of reason begets monsters: dangerous games, dark desires and nightmarish fantasies which afflict everyone from the kids doing military service, to the deserters living rough, and the pretty, vacant locals. Bodo, incidentally, is the Taiwanese-dialect nickname for Taiwan; it means 'Treasure Island'. TR

Body (Deham)

(2001, Ind, 120 min)
d/p/sc/ph Govind Nihalani. *ed* Deepa Bhatia. *pd* Deepali Meher. *m* Roy Venkataraman. *cast* Joy Sengupta, Kitu Gidwani, Aly Khan, Surekha Sikiri-Rege, Julie Ames, Mohan Kapoor.

●Although the opening shot appears to be a homage to *Blade Runner*, don't expect Ridley Scott impact from veteran Nihilani's somewhat rudimentary sci-fi movie. A young man, Sanjoy (Sengupta), sells his body, or significant parts of it, to a major Western conglomerate that will harvest his organs as and when they're needed by a client family in the West. Sanjoy's own family, however, with whom he shares cramped living quarters, are not best pleased, despite his honorable motives. An ambitious curiosity. NRo

Body, The

(2001, US/Ger, 109 min)
d Jonas McCord. *p* Rudy Cohen. *sc* Jonas McCord. *ph* Vilmos Zsigmond. *ed* Alain Jakubowicz. *pd* Allan Starski. *m* Serge Colbert. *cast* Antonio Banderas, Olivia Williams, John Shrapnel, John Wood, Jason Flemyng, Makhram J Khoury, Ian McNeice, Vernon Dobtcheff, Derek Jacobi.

●'Who would believe this? It reads like tabloid journalism, not an archaeological report,' maunders Father Guttierez (Banderas), an ex-soldier unimpressed by his latest mission from God. Seems one Dr Golden (Williams) has unearthed a crucified corpse and dated it back to AD 32. She believes she may have the body of Christ on her hands. But isn't Resurrection the whole enchilada? Obviously, the future of the Christian faith is at stake. Guttierez hotfoots it from the Vatican to Jerusalem where the doc generously allows him to check out her credentials. Meanwhile sinister Palestinian agents and shady Israeli security forces vie to trade a cover-up for papal favours. Writer/director McCord doesn't do much to flesh out the bare bones of his airport novel material, but treats it with an earnestness which precludes the promised trashy thrills. Flemyng and Jacobi compete for the dodgy accent award – a pointless effort in any Banderas movie. TCh

Body and Soul

(1947, US, 104 min, b/w)
d Robert Rossen. *p* Bob Roberts. *sc* Abraham Polonsky. *ph* James Wong Howe. *ed* Robert Parrish. *ad* Nathan Juran. *m* Hugo Friedhofer. *cast* John Garfield, Lilli Palmer, Hazel Brooks, Anne Revere, William Conrad, Joseph Pevney, Canada Lee.

●With its mean streets and gritty performances, its ringside corruption and low-life integrity, *Body and Soul* looks like a formula '40s boxing movie: the story of a (Jewish) East Side kid who makes good in the ring, forsakes his love for a nightclub floozie, and comes up against the Mob and his own conscience when he has to take a dive. But the single word which dominates the script is 'money', and it soon emerges that this is a socialist morality on Capital and the Little Man – not surprising, given the collaboration of Rossen, Polonsky (script) and Garfield, all of whom tangled with the HUAC anti-Communist hearings (Polonsky was blacklisted as a result). A curious mixture: European intelligence in an American frame, social criticism disguised as noir anxiety (the whole film is cast as one long pre-fight flashback). But Garfield's bullish performance saves the movie from its stagy moments and episodic script. CA

Body and Soul

(1981, US, 122 min)
d George Bowers. *p* Menahem Golan, Yoram Globus. *sc* Leon Isaac Kennedy. *ph* James Forrest. *ed* Sam Pollard, Skip Schoolnik. *ad* Bob Ziembicki. *m* Webster Lewis. *cast* Leon Isaac Kennedy, Jayne Kennedy, Muhammad Ali, Michael Gazzo, Perry Lang, Kim Hamilton, Gilbert Lewis.

●With great predecessors like *The Set-Up*, *Fat City* and *Raging Bull*, it's hard to see how this travesty (rather than remake) of the Rossen/Polonsky original could be so agonisingly awful. Sketchily skipping through the predictable vacillations of its boxer-hero's career, the film's plastic performances, saccharine sentiments, inept fight scenes, and sexist fantasy all vie for the honour of pummelling the audience into mindless shock. Garbage. GA

Body Bags

(1993, US, 95 min)
d John Carpenter, Tobe Hooper, Larry Sulkis. *p* Sandy King. *sc* Billy Brown, Dan Angel. *ph* Gary B Kibbe. *ed* Edward A Warschilka. *pd* Dan Lomino. *m* John Carpenter, Jim Lang. *cast* Stacy Keach, Mark Hamill, Robert Carradine, David Warner, David Naughton, Alex Datcher, Sheena Easton, Deborah Harry, Roger Corman, Sam Raimi, Wes Craven, John Agar, John Carpenter, Tobe Hooper.

●With its trio of warmed-over stories (a killer eye, some killer hair, even a boring old serial killer), this is an attempt by a pair of one-time horror auteurs to emulate the successful *Tales from the Crypt* formula, only now it's nowhere near as happening. Not content with exposing his directorial shortcomings in two of the segments (Hooper directs the third in equally average fashion), Carpenter also inflicts a half-assed imitation of Michael Keaton's Betelgeuse on his audience as he presents all three parts from a morgue. Made for cable with many has-beens from hell. AO

Body Count

(1997, US/GB, 84 min)
d Robert Patton-Spruill. *p* Mark Burg, Doug McHenry, George Jackson. *sc* Theodore Witcher. *ph* Charles Mills. *ed* Richard Nord. *pd* Tim Eckel. *m* Curt Sobel. *cast* David Caruso, Linda Fiorentino, John Leguizamo, Ving Rhames, Donnie Wahlberg, Forest Whitaker.

●Slow-drawling Crane (Whitaker) invites steady two-time loser Pike (Rhames) to join a wild card Puerto Rican (Leguizamo), a racist psycho (Caruso), and a half-brain (Wahlberg) in a Boston art gallery heist. A guard is shot, Crane's gunned down by the law, and as the carload of villains escapes to rendezvous with the fence, the paranoia and bickering kicks straight in – and that's before they pick up dame-in-distress Fiorentino, who adds sexual rivalry to the deadly brew. The director seems unsure whether this is a violent thriller or a *Ladykillers*-style black comedy, so goes for both with disconcerting consequences. Peppered with darkly humorous set-pieces, the script is laced with elaborate non sequiturs. WH

Body Double

(1984, US, 114 min)
d/p Brian De Palma. *sc* Robert J Avrech, Brian De Palma. *ph* Stephen H Burum. *ed* Jerry Greenberg, Bill Pankow. *pd* Ira Random. *m* Pino Donaggio. *cast* Craig Wasson, Melanie Griffith, Gregg Henry, Deborah Shelton, Guy Boyd, Dennis Franz.
● De Palma actually has the gall to combine the plots from both *Vertigo* and *Rear Window* in one big voyeur-fest and pull it off with a certain sly efficiency. Struggling actor Wasson is fired from his role as a punk vampire because of claustrophobia. While flat-sitting for a friend, he spends his hours glued to the telescope watching an interesting lady opposite. But who is the scarred Indian, coming at her with a power drill? And why is he so obviously wearing a mask? Unblinking tosh of this order needs to be put on the protected list. CPea

Body Drop Asphalt

(2000, Jap, 90 min)
d Junko Wada. *p* Takashi Echigoya, Koichi Fujita. *sc* Junko Wada. *ph* Kazuhiro Shirao, Noboru Miyashita. *ed* Kazuhiro Shirao. *ad* Junko Wada. *m* Comoesta Yaegashi. *cast* Sayuri Oyamada, Makoto Ogi, Yoji Tanaka, Yuichi Kishino, Matthieu Manche, Katsu Kanai.
● The first 30 minutes of Wada's fabulous debut feature looks like one of her bouncy, erotic short films: a litany of hesitations, a flurry of fetishes, a molehill of cute self-doubt. Then the narrative kicks in, and the film turns into an epically enjoyable comedy satire with everything from literary pretensions to doomsday fantasies in its sights. Eri (Oyamada) is a lonely city singleton who knocks out a trashy romantic novel and is amazed to find herself feted by the lit-crit establishment. She succumbs to a fashionable lifestyle, but since her own romantic experiences fall somewhat short of her fiction she starts writing a sequel in which her heroine Rie suffers the tortures of the damned and commits suicide. But then Rie (Ogi) emerges from the laptop to demand a rethink. With a wonderful score, zippy primary colour images, great UFO jokes and a guest appearance by veteran avant-gardist Katsu Kanai as God, this is the most fun of its kind since Godard's *Une Femme est une femme*. TR

Bodyguard, The

see Garde du Corps, Le

Bodyguard, The

(1992, US, 129 min)
d Mick Jackson. *p* Lawrence Kasdan, Jim Wilson, Kevin Costner. *sc* Lawrence Kasdan. *ph* Andrew Dunn. *ed* Richard A Harris. *pd* Jeffrey Beecroft. *m* Alan Silvestri. *cast* Kevin Costner, Whitney Houston, Gary Kemp, Bill Cobbs, Ralph Waite, Tomas Arana, Michele Lamar Richards.
● Whitney Houston's screen debut sees her as famous singer/actress Rachel Marron. Bodyguard Frank Farmer (Costner) turns up at her mansion, ready to protect her in the wake of a series of death threats, but he encounters resentments as the Oscar-nominated megastar insists on following a demanding schedule in the run-up to the awards. Is the killer her slimy press agent (Kemp), the loon who keeps a shrine to her in his locker, or dodgy bodyguard Greg (Arana) with the strange squint and roving hands? Farmer and Marron fall in love and escape to the lakeside home of his dad (Waite); but even there danger lurks. Jackson's showy technique does little to lighten the over-earnest heroics and ponderous references to samurai, which are punctuated by assorted numbers and costume changes for Houston. Lawrence Kasdan, it seems, mulled over the first draft of his screenplay twenty years ago; it should have been left to languish in development purgatory. CM

Body Heat

(1981, US, 113 min)
d Lawrence Kasdan. *p* Fred T Gallo. *sc* Lawrence Kasdan. *ph* Richard H Kline. *ed* Carol Littleton. *pd* Bill Kenney. *m* John Barry. *cast* William Hurt, Kathleen Turner, Richard Crenna, Ted Danson, JA Preston, Mickey Rourke.
● Hot and sticky, though never less than sumptuously deodorised, this is a neon-shaded contemporary *noir* romance: all lust, greed, murder, duplicity and betrayal. As credulously myopic lawyer Ned and slinky femme fatale Matty progress from dirty talk to dirty deeds (a disposable husband, a contestable will), there's the pleasure of unravelling a confidently dense yarn for its own sake, alongside the incongruous experience of finding yellowing pulp fiction classily rebound, or hearing a '40s standard of romantic unease re-recorded with digital precision. Whether the movie-movie cleverness becomes as stifling as the atmosphere Kasdan casts over his sunstruck night people is all down to personal taste, but there's no denying the narrative confidence that brings the film to its unfashionably certain double-whammy conclusion. PT

Body in the Forest, A (Cuerpo en el Bosque)

(1996, Sp, 91 min)
d Joaquin Jordá. *p* José Antonio Pérez Giner, Josep Maria Forn. *sc* Joaquin Jorda. *ph* Carles Gusi. *ed* Ivan Aledo. *pd* Antonion Belart. *m* Sergei Jorda. *cast* Rossy de Palma, Núria Prims, Ricardo Borràs, Pep Molina, Joan Masdeu, Julieta Serrano.
● Catalonia: four men on a boar hunt discover the remains of a girl, Montse. The corpse is cut up and daubed 'whore' in blood. The Civil Guard send in an outside investigator, Lt Cifuentes (Rossy de Palma). Ignoring the local policeman, who focuses on the centuries of ill fate that have befallen the girl's family, Cifuentes interviews Montse's last few acquaintances, treating them with mounting contempt as she reconstructs events. Occasionally we hear the girl's voice, winding its way through the film's staggered flashback structure. Writer/director Jordá has an elliptical way with film grammar, and plays similar insouciant games with the audience's identification. Rather than an unreliable narrator, it's the protagonist who proves, well, ethically double-jointed. The film works as an enjoyably overheated investigative thriller, but also as a bleak indictment of a community where superstition and bigotry conceal a contemporary culture of callous opportunism. NB

Body Melt

(1993, Aust, 84 min)
d Philip Brophy. *p* Rod Bishop, Daniel Scharf, Lars Michalak. *sc* Philip Brophy, Rod Bishop. *ph* Ray Argall. *ed* Bill Murphy. *pd* Maria Kozic. *m* Philip Brophy. *cast* Gerard Kennedy, Andrew Daddo, Ian Smith, Vince Gill, Regina Gaigalas, Maurie Annese.
● A vitamin drink delivered free to residents of idyllic housing development Pebbles Court provokes a series of ghastly body mutations. Two investigating cops trace the trouble to the futuristic 'health farm' of Dr Carrera (Smith) where guests are being used for crazed experiments. Despite its emetic preoccupations – exploding stomachs, elongating tongues, etc – this mordant debut feature is in fact less a splatterfest than a consumerist satire. It's overlaid with black humour and takes swipes at health fads, body building, soap operas and the false utopia of suburban living. NF

Body of Evidence

(1992, US, 101 min)
d Uli Edel. *p* Dino De Laurentiis, Martha De Laurentiis. *sc* Brad Mirman. *ph* Douglas Milsome. *ed* Thom Noble. *pd* Victoria Paul. *m* Graeme Revell. *cast* Madonna, Willem Dafoe, Joe Mantegna, Anne Archer, Jürgen Prochnow, Julianne Moore, Frank Langella.
● Whatever aims Uli (*Last Exit to Brooklyn*) Edel set out with, this turned into a tributary to *Sex* as soon as Madonna came aboard. She plays a dominatrix, and what she gets up to with her defence attorney (Dafoe) is what will pull audiences, rather than the courtroom debate. As a child, she confides, she observed that the strawberries one had to wade through thorns to reach were the sweetest, after which she introduces Dafoe to SM. Enumerating these strawberries, we get the following. She drips hot candle-wax on to his body, registering a consensual moment before dripping it on to his dick. She rummages in his flies in a crowded lift. He muff-dives her in an underground car park. She has a wank. There's bondage, buggery, and a clothes-ripping chase up the stairs. Apart from that, there's a bit of verbal back-and-forth in court between the DA (Mantegna) and defence about whether she used her body as a lethal weapon to kill her millionaire lover and inherit; a brace of shifty witnesses (Archer and Prochnow); no tension; and Portland, Oregon in the rain. BC

Body Parts

(1991, US, 94 min)
d Eric Red. *p* Frank Mancuso Jr. *sc* Eric Red, Norman Snider. *ph* Theo van de Sande. *ed* Anthony Redman. *pd* Bill Brodie. *m* Loek Dikker. *cast* Jeff Fahey, Lindsay Duncan, Kim Delaney, Zakes Mokae, Brad Dourif, John Walsh, Paul Benvictor.
● Director Eric Red, screenwriter of *The Hitcher*, gives a grungy new spin to a familiar genre theme in this tacky but vigorous mad doctor movie. Fahey's a criminal psychologist who has a new arm grafted on by doc Duncan, but after his behaviour turns erratic, he discovers that the limb in question once belonged to an executed killer – and that there are other recipients of the deceased slayer's bits and pieces also going haywire around town. Dourif's an artist who received the killer's left arm: in the old days he used to execute tepid watercolours of Cape Cod; now he hurls paint at the canvas with the intensity of Jackson Pollock on a bad day. Loosely based on *Choice Cuts*, by the French team Narcejac and Boileau, whose novels inspired *Vertigo* and *Les Diaboliques*. TJ

Body Rock

(1984, US, 94 min)
d Marcelo Epstein. *p* Jeffrey Schechtman. *sc* Desmond Nakano. *ph* Robby Müller. *ed* Richard Halsey, Lorenzo DeStefano. *pd* Guy Comtois. *m* Sylvester Le Vay. *cast* Lorenzo Lamas, Vicki Frederick, Cameron Dye, Michelle Nicastro, Ray Sharkey, Seth Kaufman.
● A breakdancing morality tale. Chilly D (Lamas), a singer/dancer from downtown New York, becomes the darling of a trendy niterie. He snubs his pals, throws over his nice girlfriend for a high-living rich bitch, and gets his comeuppance, before honest poverty and spontaneous street culture triumph over capricious uptown exploitation at a hijacked 'Rapstravaganza' event. Drearily reminiscent of a souped-up Marcel Marceau. GA.

Body Shots

(1999, US, 106 min)
d Michael Cristofer. *p* Jennifer Keohane, Harry Colomby. *sc* David McKenna. *ph* Rodrigo García. *ed* Eric Sears. *pd* David J Bomba. *m* Mark Isham. *cast* Sean Patrick Flanery, Jerry O'Connell, Amanda Peet, Tara Reid, Ron Livingston, Emily Procter, Brad Rowe, Sybil Temchen.
● The LA singles scene has rarely looked less appealing. Eight glossy twenty-somethings meet to trawl bars and nightclubs. After rather too many vodka jellies, they pair off: the two lawyers together; the actress and the pro-football player; the cocktail waitress and the fool in golfing trousers. By morning, the camaraderie and good feeling are shaken by one girl accusing her partner of date rape. The characters are shallow, self-obsessed and charmless, and matters aren't helped by contrived, straight-to-camera interviews with each actor. WI

Body Snatcher, The

(1945, US, 78 min, b/w)
d Robert Wise. *p* Val Lewton. *sc* Philip MacDonald, Val Lewton. *ph* Robert De Grasse. *ed* Jack Whittredge. *ad* Albert S D'Agostino. *m* Roy Webb. *cast* Boris Karloff, Bela Lugosi, Henry Daniell, Edith Atwater, Russell Wade, Rita Corday, Sharyn Moffett, Donna Lee.
● Not one of the really top-notch Val Lewton productions: unlike Jacques Tourneur, Wise could never control Lewton's tendency to stuff every scene to the hilt with bookish period detail and fusty dialogue. But this adaptation of the old Burke and Hare business (based on a Robert Louis Stevenson story) is still great entertainment, with Karloff, Lugosi and Daniell (Hollywood's greatest sourpuss) leaving no dead body unturned in 19th century Edinburgh. Lewton's Edinburgh is predictably full of cobbles, clip-clopping horses, street singers and other atmospheric bric-à-brac – all very nice, but they do slow proceedings down. However, the film accelerates to great effect towards the end. GB

Body Snatchers

(1993, US, 87 min)
d Abel Ferrara. *p* Robert H Solo. *sc* Nicholas St John, Dennis Paoli, Stuart Gordon. *ph* Bojan Bazelli. *ed* Anthony Redman. *pd* Peter Jamison. *m* Joe Delia. *cast* Gabrielle Anwar, Meg Tilly, Forest Whitaker, Terry Kinnelly, Billy Wirth, Christine Elise.

● This remake of the classic '50s paranoia movie, Don Siegel's *Invasion of the Body Snatchers*, is evidence that the end of the Cold War hasn't dispelled fears of creeping authoritarianism and loss of individuality. The story is relocated to a southern military base – a more credible breeding ground for insurgency than the San Francisco of Phil Kaufman's chilling 1978 version – with disaffected teenager Anwar at the centre of the drama. At first this seems like a sop to Hollywood fashion, but in fact it's a switch which lends an intriguing perspective as the nuclear family approaches meltdown. Tilly (and her body double) are excellent as the teenager's stepmom; and there's a good tight script from Stuart Gordon, Dennis Paoli and longtime Ferrara collaborator Nicholas St John. This slick, polished film is a change of pace for Ferrara, but fans of his more abrasively challenging work are unlikely to feel short-changed – 'I always loved *Martian* movies,' Ferrara has said. 'I used to dress up as a Martian when I was a kid and go out and terrify the neighbours…' TCh

Body Stealers, The (aka Thin Air/Invasion of the Body Stealers)

(1969, GB/US, 91 min)
d Gerry Levy. *p* Tony Tenser. *sc* Mike St Clair, Peter Marcus. *ph* Johnny Coquillon. *ed* Howard Lanning. *ad* Wilfred Arnold. *m* Reg Tilsley. *cast* George Sanders, Maurice Evans, Patrick Allen, Neil Connery, Hilary Dwyer, Robert Flemyng, Lorna Wilde, Allan Cuthbertson.

● Parachutists testing new gear are taken over by aliens after descending through a strange red cloud. Gen Sanders orders US Air Force special investigator Allen to come up with some answers. A threadbare Anglo-American enterprise, with too much vapid chat and too little action, ending very feebly (in a British sort of way) with alien girl Lorna Wilde coming over to our side and Allen agreeing to find volunteers to boost her planet's diminishing population. TJ

Bodywork

(1999, GB, 93 min)
d Gareth Rhys Jones. *p* Richard McGill. *sc* Gareth Rhys Jones. *ph* Thomas Wuthrich. *ed* Susan Spivey. *pd* Jeremy Bear. *m* Srdjan Kurpjel, Black Tooth. *cast* Hans Matheson, Charlotte Coleman, Peter Ferdinando, Beth Winslet, Lynda Bellingham, Clive Russell.

● Luckless yuppie Virgil Guppy (Matheson) is framed for murder when the body of a prostitute turns up in the boot of his Jag. The evidence points to a set-up involving the crooks who sold him the car. But the 'comic coppers' on the case aren't listening, and girlfriend Fiona (Winslet), about to take off in the direction of his best friend's bed, is asking awkward questions like, why did he come home from the launderette without his trousers on. Enter incurably ill car thief-cum-tattoo artist Tiffany (Coleman), her super-smart kid and their East European(ish) sidekick, offering sanctuary. This plays like the first episode of a one-series sitcom; and if writer/director Rhys Jones had any designs on subverting peekaboo games in the changing room, he fails to deliver them. The juxtaposition of humour and violence is self-conscious, the symbolism leaden, the suspense non-existent and the killer's excuse of a *Rope*-style motive risible. SS

Boesman and Lena

(1973, SAf, 102 min)
d Ross Devenish. *p* Johan Wicht. *sc* Athol Fugard. *ph* David Muir. *ed* John Scott, Roger Harris. *ad* Ken Robinson. *m* Alan Kwela, Tommy Mosemola, Ernest Mothle, Nelson Mgwaza. *cast* Athol Fugard, Yvonne Bryceland, Sandy Tubé, Val Donald, Percy Sieff, Bert Coppin, Frank Zietsman.

● A sour film about down-and-out coloured people trying to scrabble an existence in South Africa. When the government bulldozers move in, Boesman and Lena set out on the road. There's little story, beyond the separate reactions of each of them to an old, sick Kaffir who comes to their fire. What it's about is simply the situation of dereliction, of being without homes, roots, dignity. And although there are faults in the film – it still smells heavily of the stage for which it was originally written by Athol Fugard – enough of that feeling still comes through to make it valid. NK

Boesman & Lena

(1999, Fr/SAf, 88 min)
d John Berry. *p* François Ivernel, Pierre Rissient. *sc* John Berry. *ph* Alain Choquart. *ed* Claudine Bouché, Jeanne Moutard. *pd* Max Berto. *m* Wally Badarou. *cast* Danny Glover, Angela Bassett, Willie Jonah, Graham Weir, Anton Stoltz.

● The career of John Berry, a victim of Hollywood's anti-communist blacklist, took him to France, where most of his subsequent movies were made. Berry was behind the first New York stage production of Athol Fugard's classic play in 1970, so it's somehow fitting that he should bow out (he died in Paris in 1999, aged 82) with a French-financed screen adaptation of this anguished exploration of the injustices of apartheid. The selling point here is obviously the presence of Glover and Bassett, squaring up to the meaty material as the two scavengers left sleeping out on waste ground after the white authorities demolished their shantytown home. Both actors give everything asked of them, yet however much one respects the eloquence of the writing, its declamatory style is rather more suited to the stage than Berry's realistic settings and portentous close-ups Berry affords it here. However, as a visual record of the play, it serves well enough for current and future students. TJ

Bof!

(1971, Fr, 94 min)
d/sc Claude Faraldo. *ph* Sacha Vierny. *ed* Joselyne Triquet. *ad* Pierre Guffroy. *m* Jean Guérin. *cast* Marie Dubois, Julian Negulesco, Paul Crauchet, Marie-Hélène Breillat, Marie Mergey, Mamadiou Diop.

● Social fantasy about a young French worker whose father decides to murder his melancholy wife and set up a free-wheeling commune with his son and daughter-in-law. The film has considerable humour and charm, but in illustrating this engaging interpersonal revolution, Faraldo has to skate over so many psychological and social obstacles that the film finally ends up Utopian rather than fantastic, wish fulfilment rather than satire. DP

Bofors Gun, The

(1968, GB, 105 min)
d Jack Gold. *p* Robert A Goldston, Otto Plaschkes. *sc* John McGrath. *ph* Alan Hume. *ed* Anne V Coates. *ad* Terence Knight. *m* Carl Davis. *cast* Nicol Williamson, Ian Holm, David Warner, Richard O'Callaghan, Barry Jackson, Donald Gee, John Thaw, Peter Vaughan, Barbara Jefford.

● A British army camp in Occupied Germany, 1954. John McGrath's adaptation of his own play perfectly captures the tang of the barrack room in all its brutish, scarifyingly jocular destructiveness as he sets up a classic situation. A young National Serviceman (Warner), obvious officer material, nervously prepares to exercise authority for the first time as corporal of the guard; facing him are six old hands, eager to slope off, probing for signs of weakness. Basically, the conflict is between authority and responsibility. Warner is responsible, all right, but the authority is all in the hands of the drunken, totally irresponsible Irishman (Williamson) who goads his man like a matador tormenting a bull. If the explosive climax is a shade too melodramatic to be entirely convincing, the performances are first-rate, and Gold (his debut feature) directs with precise, self-effacing control. TM

Bogey Man, The (Kummatty)

(1980, Ind, 90 min)
d/sc G Aravindan. *ph* Shaji. *cast* Ramunni, Master Ashokan, Vilasini.

● A little myth, a little magic, folklore and folk-songs combine in this story of an Indian Pied Piper's visit to a small village, and the dusty band of children he befriends there. Though sometimes slow, what makes the film so beguiling is its conviction and lack of condescension in depicting a world where fact and fantasy collide. FF

Bohème, La

(1988, Fr/It, 107 min)
d Luigi Comencini. *ph* Armando Nannuzzi. *ed* Sergio Buzi, Reine Wekstein. *ad* Paola Comencini. *m* Giacomo Puccini. *cast* Barbara Hendricks, Luca Canonici, Angela Maria Blasi, Gino Quilico, Richard Cowan, Francesco Ellera D'Artegna. *voices* José Carreras, Michel Sénéchal, Federico Davia.

● In adapting the story of Puccini's opera, Comencini has created a cogent, perceptive, and often illuminating visual narrative. In the opening scenes, Mimi (Hendricks) overhears the boisterous bohemians in the attic above, and later, knowing Rodolfo (Canonici, sung by José Carreras) has been left alone, initiates a meeting by knocking on his door, pretending her candle has gone out. It makes sense, although the aura of twinkling lights that surrounds her during his passionate outpourings in '*Che gelida manina!*' is unfortunate. But that is Comencini's only trespass into outright kitsch. Other variations on the storyline are perfectly acceptable: musicians of the Cafè Momus accompany Musetta (Blasi) in '*Quando me'n vo soletta*'; the introduction of a silent, older admirer in the third act deftly explains Marcello's outrage; while Mimi's '*Addio*' is beautifully observed. James Conlon conducts the Orchestre National de France with passion in his gut. Don't forget the tissues… OM

Bohemian Life

see Vie de Bohème, La

Boiler Room

(2000, US, 120 min)
d Ben Younger. *p* Suzanne Todd, Jennifer Todd. *sc* Ben Younger. *ph* Enrique Chediak. *ed* Chris Peppe. *pd* Anne Stuhler. *m* The Angel. *cast* Ben Affleck, Giovanni Ribisi, Vin Diesel, Nia Long, Scott Caan, Ron Rifkin, Jamie Kennedy, Bill Sage.

● This beady-eyed morality play is set in the hothouse environment of an illicit share-ramping operation, which 19-year-old numbers whizz Seth Davis (Ribisi) takes to the NY stockbroking firm JT Marlin after his father, a stern judge, shuts down his home gambling den. JT Marlin is a quicksilver enterprise founded on the get-rich-quick dreams of its customers and recruits alike. Everyone can become a millionaire here, Affleck's recruiting officer tells the new intake, 'the only question is how many times over.' Of course, other questions arise: Seth's secret affair with his boss's ex, company secretary Abbie (Long); his dad's continuing stern attentions; the customers fleeced of their life savings; and the attentions of the FBI. Not all of this works – the Oedipal angst of Seth's relationship with his dad is unnecessary and close to unbearable – but enough's credible and thought through to mark the film as a praiseworthy and auspicious achievement for first time writer/director Younger. Turns of dialogue ring compellingly true, and the well chosen cast (especially Ribisi) carry the inflections of the drama with some style. NB

Boiling Point

(1993, US, 90 min)
d James B Harris. *p* Marc Frydman, Leonardo de la Fuente. *sc* James B Harris. *ph* King Baggot. *ed* Jerry Brady. *pd* Ron Foreman. *m* Cory Lerios, John D'Andrea. *cast* Dennis Hopper, Wesley Snipes, Viggo Mortensen, Valerie Perrine, Lolita Davidovich, Tony Lo Bianco, Seymour Cassel.

● A slow-burning study of a Treasury agent and a con-artist separated by the law but united by their need for love. Fresh out of jail, doper conman Red Diamond (Hopper) teams up with psychotic sidekick Ronnie (Mortensen) to raise the $50,000 he owes a Mafia boss. But the 'buyer' Ronnie kills during a funny-money transaction is the partner of Treasury agent Jimmy Mercer (Snipes), who swears revenge. From then on, Red and Jimmy's lives run in parallel, the two men passing and repassing each other until their paths finally cross. Director Harris's strength is his ability to flesh out routine crime scenarios with credibly motivated characters, adding emotional depth and texture to familiar generic pleasures. That said, Snipes never quite finds the measure of his role; so, despite Hopper's unusually funny and warm performance, the final impression is tepid. NF

Boiling Point (3-4x Jugatsu/San tai Yon x Jugatsu)

(1990, Jap, 96 min)
d Takeshi Kitano. *p* Hisao Nabeshima, Masayuki Mori, Takio Yoshida. *sc* Takeshi Kitano. *ph* Katsumi Yanagishima. *ed* Toshio Taniguchi. *ad* Osumu Sasaki. *cast* Masahiko Ono, Yuriko Ishida, Takahito Iguchi, Minoru Iizuka, Makoto Ashikawa, Hisashi Igawa, Takeshi Kitano.
●Diffident, dreamy, dim-witted Masaki hasn't a lot going for him. Moreover, he habitually misreads a situation, so that when he hits out at a dissatisfied customer who's quite clearly a yakuza, he gets his boss into big trouble with the Mob. Fortunately, there's help in the form of his ex-yakuza pal Takashi, who takes on the hoods but who, after being beaten up, is forced to ask the hapless Masaki to go buy him a gun in Okinawa. There the boy falls in with the nastiest gangster of 'em all: the drunken, sadistic, conspicuously crazy Uehara, played by the film's writer/director Kitano. Ono's gormless protagonist and Kitano's charismatic but despicable psycho are particularly memorable comic creations. The funniest film to date from a key '90s film-maker. GA

Bolero

see Uns et les autres, Les

Bolero

(1934, US, 85 min, b/w)
d Wesley Ruggles. *sc* Carey Wilson, Kubec Glasmon, Ruth Ridenour, Horace Jackson. *ph* Leo Tover. *ed* Hugh Bennett. *cast* George Raft, Carole Lombard, Sally Rand, Gertrude Michael, Ray Milland, William Frawley.
●Ravel's mesmeric theme provides the inspiration for this largely undistinguished tale of an exhibition dancer's rise to fame and fortune. Raft at his most wooden (from the waist up), Lombard at her most decorative (all over), a dumb script, and much early '30s decolletage (before the Hayes Code was strictly enforced). RM

Bolero

(1984, US, 104 min)
d John Derek. *p* Bo Derek. *sc/ph/ed* John Derek. *pd* Alan Roderick-Jones. *m* Peter Bernstein; (love scene) Elmer Bernstein. *cast* Bo Derek, George Kennedy, Andrea Occhipinti, Ana Obregon, Greg Bensen, Olivia D'Abo, Ian Cochrane.
●The credits signal the unappetising prospect of aging hulk George Kennedy starring in a sex movie, but that turns out to be the least of the audience's worries. John Derek deploys a bunch of perfunctory props (the 1920s, wealth, a sheik, a bullfighter) as starting points for the adventures of his blankly beauteous missus. Erotic, surely, only for the very easily pleased, with Dereks J and B and Cannon Films converging to form a matrix of sustained, tawdry silliness. BBa

Bolivia

(2001, Arg, 76 min, b/w)
d Israel Adrián Caetano. *p* Matias Mosteirin. *sc* Israel Adrián Caetano. *ph* Julián Apezteguia. *ed* Lucas Scavini, Santiago Ricci. *pd* Maria Eva Duarte. *m* Los Kjarcas. *cast* Freddy Waldo Flores, Rosa Sánchez, Oscar Bertea, Enrique Liporace, Marcelo Videla.
●Café society, Argentine-style: a simmering mix of drugs, debts and racism. Freddy (Flores) is a Bolivian immigrant without a work permit. Displaced when the Yankees burned down the fields where he worked, he's taken on by a wary coffee-shop proprietor whose other cheap labour is half-Paraguayan Rosa (Sánchez), and whose customers generally confuse Freddy for Peruvian, when they're not hassling Rosa or bemoaning their own crises. Life here is cheap. Shot in grainy b/w, spanning 60 hours or so and only thrice venturing outside the café bounds, this gritty little number sketches with matter of fact realism the vagaries and desolation of the urban uprooted and marginalised, with flashes of human connection jostling with random intimidation. Wonderfully (under)played by the cast. NB

Bollywood Calling

(2000, Ind, 100 min)
d Nagesh Kukunoor. *p* B Satyanarayana, Nagesh Kukunoor, Elahé Hiptoola. *sc* Nagesh Kukunoor. *ph* Keshav Prakash. *ed* Renu Saluja. *m* Ashirvad. *cast* Om Puri, Pat Cusick, Navin Nischol, Perizad Zorabian, Vikram Inamdar, Monique Curnen, Chet Dixon.
●A dire 'satire' on the absurdities and egomanias of both the Western and Indian film industries. The unconvincing Cusick, a depressive, alcoholic and ailing B-movie actor, is seduced by producer Om Puri into taking what he fears will be his last role in a Bollywood extravaganza. Cue culture clash a-plenty, since film-making methods and culture are so different as to be incomprehensible to the American, not least the hypocritical devotion shown by all to the ageing star. Puri does his best, and some of the supporting performances are passable, but this is sentimental, predictable, moralistic tosh, as contrived and melodramatic as the films it affectionately mocks. The use of serious illness as a plot device effectively sours the enterprise. GA

Bolshe Vita (Bolse Vita)

(1995, Hun, 101 min)
d Ibolya Fekete. *p* Istvan Darday. *sc* Ibolya Fekete. *ph* Andras Szalai. *ed* Klara Majoros. *pd* Zsolt Juhász. *m* Yuri Fomichev, Ferenc Muk. *cast* Yuri Fomichev, Igor Chernievich, Alexei Serebriakov, Agnes Máhr, Helen Baxendale, Caroline Loncq.
●This first feature is a mellow high of a trip through that fleeting moment after the overthrow of the Soviet empire, 'when Eastern Europe was happy,' flush with optimism and self-determination, before darker forces again asserted their control. From the Bolshe Vita – a bohemian club in Budapest and point of convergence, like the city itself, for pilgrims and wayfarers from all directions – the film follows a diverse and divergent troupe of characters through a tender, melancholic, unsentimental and very funny celebration of this evanescent period of openness and freedom. Rough around the edges, but if it seems rambling and uneventful, that's because writer/director Fekete understands that life's memorable moments aren't about what you did so much as who you were with. NB

Bolwieser (The Stationmaster's Wife)

(1977, WGer, 111 min)
d/sc Rainer Werner Fassbinder. *ph* Michael Ballhaus. *ed* Ila von Hasperg, Rainer Werner Fassbinder, Juliane Lorenz. *ad* Kurt Raab. *m* Peer Raben. *cast* Kurt Raab, Elisabeth Trissenaar, Bernhard Helfrich, Karl-Heinz von Hassel, Udo Kier.
●Marvellous performance from Trissenaar – justifiably compared to Garbo and Dietrich – as the enigmatically errant wife of a provincial stationmaster, doting but hardly of the stallion breed. In mood, something of a cross between *Fear of Fear* and *Chinese Roulette* as Fassbinder continues his Sirkian task of exploring the cheerless grey world of petit bourgeois morality (the time is just after the First World War), highlighting a series of melodramatic sexual betrayals in order to dissect (with surprising compassion) the tissue of lies and deceptions that makes them inevitable while simultaneously keeping society going (towards the fascism that clearly lies just ahead). A feature drawn from the original 2-part, 200 minute TV film. TM

Bombay Our City (Hamara shaher)

(1985, Ind, 82 min)
d/p/sc Anand Patwardhan. *ph* Ranjan Palit, Anand Patwardhan. *ed* Anand Patwardhan.
●Double-deckers and Victorian Gothic are ironically glimpsed past Bombay's shantytowns. Unforgettable images of brutality (the police sporadically demolish the huts, beat the inhabitants, destroy their possessions and livelihood) jostle the resigned: a girl recalls her teenage brother, shot by the police. 'Nothing remains. I do my work. When I think of my brother, I keep quiet'. An untouchable gratefully describes his 'good municipal job': unblocking open gutters, carting off the filth. The Advertising Club discusses improving the police's image. A cripple hobbles through floods on a peg-leg that turns out to be his limb, withered to a stick. Shot over three years, this is documentary to make you angry; for once, not with the British. MHoy

Bombay Talkie

(1970, Ind, 105 min)
d James Ivory. *p* Ismail Merchant. *sc* Ruth Prawer Jhabvala, James Ivory. *ph* Subrata Mitra. *ed* David Gladwell. *ad* A Ranga Raj. *songs* Shankar-Jaikishan, Hasrat Jaipuri. *cast* Shashi Kapoor, Jennifer Kendal, Zia Mohyeddin, Aparna Sen, Utpal Dutt, Nadira.
●Misjudged attempt at examining the popular Indian cinema while trying to reach both its audience and a wider international one. American writer arrives in Bombay, starts affair with film star, and slights would-be-poet – with tragic consequences. With the playing not quite satire, not quite straight, the compromises leap from every frame. Gentle and pleasing in a perverse way, but entirely insubstantial. JW

Bombsight Stolen

see Cottage to Let

Bone (aka Dial Rat for Terror/Beverly Hills Nightmare)

(1972, US, 92 min)
d/p/sc Larry Cohen. *ph/ed* George Folsey Jr. *m* Gil Mellé. *cast* Andrew Duggan, Joyce Van Patten, Yaphet Kotto, Jeannie Berlin, Casey King.
●Cohen's first feature is a strange black comedy with Kotto as a reluctant rapist confronting a smart couple in their home, and finally colluding with the wife against the husband. Cohen himself says he was attempting 'something like Joe Orton's work', and although it's pretentious in places, the Orton themes are not hard to spot. Critic Robin Wood went so far as to call it 'one of the most remarkable debuts in American cinema'. DP

Bone Collector, The

(1999, US, 118 min)
d Phillip Noyce. *p* Martin Bregman, Louis A Stoller, Michael Bregman. *sc* Jeremy Iacone. *ph* Dean Semler. *ed* William Hoy. *pd* Nigel Phelps. *m* Craig Armstrong. *cast* Denzel Washington, Angelina Jolie, Queen Latifah, Michael Rooker, Mike McGlone, Luis Guzmán, Leland Orser, John Benjamin Hickey.
●Lincoln Rhyme (Washington) is a legendary forensics cop bedridden after an accident, but that doesn't stop him leading an investigation to track down a serial killer, since patrolwoman Amelia Donaghy (Jolie) is on hand to do all the legwork. It isn't too hard to figure what follows from this contrived scenario: lots of gruesome slayings to be picked over, set-pieces where Jolie has to creep around in the dark wondering if the maniac is going to leap out, and a romance angle between her and Washington. The material is dreck, no doubt, but all concerned give it top class treatment. Washington is commanding as he barks orders to the support team, director Noyce is enough of a technician to make sure the film pushes the right suspense buttons, and the art direction at the crime scenes is so hideous you suspect they had real life psychos place the dismembered limbs just so. In the end, though, a final reel of chin dropping idiocy makes all this a wasted effort, and you leave with the feeling that a nasty bit of work has merely been tarted up for our delectation. TJ

Bones

see Ossos

Bonfire of the Vanities, The

(1990, US, 125 min)
d/p Brian De Palma. *sc* Michael Cristofer. *ph* Vilmos Zsigmond. *ed* David Ray, Bill Pankow. *pd* Richard Sylbert. *m* Dave Grusin. *cast* Tom Hanks, Bruce Willis, Melanie Griffith, Kim Cattrall, Saul Rubinek, Morgan Freeman, F Murray Abraham, John Hancock, Kevin Dunn, Clifton James, André Gregory, Robert Stephens.
●De Palma's film of Tom Wolfe's dark, hilarious magnum opus bombed in the States – amid charges of racism – and it's easy to see why. It's norra lorra laffs. Wolfe's book about the inhabitants of the Big Bad Apple has a Dickensian scope and a Faustian dynamic: 'What shall it profit a man, if he gain the whole, but lose his soul?' His view of an ethnic pressure-cooker society is ironic and caustic but even-handed. In the movie,

simplification and scaling down – plus significant changes in ethnicity – lose the balance. In a twin-track movie, we watch dipso journo Peter Fallow (Willis) – who narrates – rise as adulterous Wall Street trader Sherman McCoy (Hanks) falls. Fallow is put onto a story: a poor Bronx black is a near-fatal hit-and-run casualty. The car turns out to be McCoy's Mercedes – scoop! – and the jackals descend. What De Palma delivers is merely a mediocre yuppy nightmare movie, stylistically flashy but with little pace, bite or pathos. As usual with De Palma, the woman gets shafted (here Griffith as McCoy's mistress). If anything, it's a Hanks 'little boy lost' movie, more in the Big tradition than The Big Tradition. WH

Bongo Man

(1981, WGer, 93 min)
d Stefan Paul. *p* Gerd Unger, Edgar Deplewski. *sc* Stefan Paul. *ph* Heinz Rexer, Mike Condé, Udo Hitzler. *ed* Hildegard Schröder. *with* Jimmy Cliff and the Oneness Band, Miriam Makeba, Barbara Jones, Nadine Sullivan, Bob Marley and the Wailers. *narrator* Lister Hewan-Lowe.

●Having to wait ten years before seeing Jimmy Cliff on film again after *The Harder They Come* was bad enough; having to watch him witlessly lionised is rubbing salt into the wounds. As if director Paul had got his artistic needle stuck, *Bongo Man* is little more than a repeat of his *Reggae Sunsplash* formula: sliced up concert footage and interviews over which a narrator/commentator intones lines like 'politicans divide, musicians unite'. Not that it doesn't have its moments, as Cliff is followed through a series of concerts, walkabouts and rasta raps set against the politically volatile atmosphere of 1980s Jamaican elections; most of them spring from the thirteen or so resonant reggae anthems and the odd bit of wit in the face of 'babilan'. But overall it's a sprawling muddy mess of a movie. FL

Bonheur, Le (Happiness)

(1965, Fr, 79 min)
d Agnès Varda. *p* Mag Bodard. *sc* Agnès Varda. *ph* Jean Rabier, Claude Beausoleil. *ed* Janine Verneau. *ad* Hubert Monloup. *m* Wolfgang Amadeus Mozart. *cast* Jean-Claude Drouot, Claire Drouot, Sandrine Drouot, Olivier Drouot, Marie-France Boyer.

●The sheer visual elegance and romantic splendour of Varda's film aroused the kind of critical suspicions that quite rightly surround *Un Homme et une Femme*. But although the sexual politics of its plot (about a man trying to love two women) may seem stilted, the film retains two huge advantages. In the first place, Varda is trying to explore on film the kind of romantic areas that have so often (and so wrongly) been the exclusive province of male directors. And in the second, the overwhelming beauty of the movie's surface is not so much used to glamorise its characters as to illuminate their own dream worlds. DP

Bonheur est dans le pré, Le

(1995, Fr, 106 min)
d Etienne Chatiliez. *p* Charles Gassot. *sc* Florence Quentin. *ph* Philippe Welt. *ed* Anne Lafarge. *ad* Stéphane Makedonshy. *m* Pascal Andreacchio. *cast* Michel Serrault, Eddy Mitchell, Sabine Azéma, Carmen Maura, François Morel, Jean Bosquet, Eric Cantona.

●Francis (Serrault) is undergoing a late-life crisis – the workers at his Paris factory are on strike, his imbecile wife Nicole (Azéma) and daughter are as insensitive as always, and his best friend Gérard (Mitchell) has misremembered his birthday – and the easiest solution seems to be a heart attack. Nope, try again. As he watches a plaintive TV show with his gawping family, his face suddenly appears accompanying a piece on a woman (Maura) looking for her long-lost husband. He's hesitant, but hey-ho, it's off to the South we go: a change of scene, good weather, food, wine, love, a new life. Thereafter we make a gentle approach-landing on to a firm ground of lower-middlebrow escapism. A well-adorned buddy movie, with a faint whiff of misogyny. NB

Bonjour, Monsieur Doisneau

(1992, Fr, 55 min)
d/sc Sabine Azéma. *p* Alain Taieb. *ph* E Carton Grammont. *ed* Luce Grunenwaldt. *with* Robert Doisneau, Sabine Azéma.

●That pavement super-snog 'Le Baiser de l'Hôtel de Ville' must be the most familiar of Robert Doisneau's street shots. Azéma, star of *Life and Nothing But* and *No/Smoking*, chats to the 80-year-old photographer in various locations, including a rose garden – 'This is not who I am,' he objects – and outside the Renault car works.Topics include childhood memories, how to pose (the secret's in the feet), the suburbs. This is conventional, slightly skittish reportage, with the bonus that Doisneau (irascible, tender) and Azéma (puckish, steely) are such strong individuals that their relationship becomes an auxiliary subject of the film. BBa

Bonjour Tristesse

(1958, US, 94 min, b/w & col)
d/p Otto Preminger. *sc* Arthur Laurents. *ph* Georges Périnal. *ed* Helga Cranston. *pd* Roger Furse. *m* Georges Auric. *cast* Deborah Kerr, David Niven, Jean Seberg, Mylène Demongeot, Geoffrey Horne, Juliette Greco, Martita Hunt, Jean Kent.

●The flirtation with incest at the centre of this adaptation of Françoise Sagan's novel is tame by modern standards, but the evil scheming of Seberg as the daughter set on separating her father and his mistress is still forceful. But is it 'evil' scheming? Preminger's cool, detached camera scuttles between a wintry black-and-white present and Technicolor flashbacks to summer on the Riviera to provide the necessary evidence, but leaves us, the audience, to draw the conclusions. PH

Bonne Année, La (Happy New Year)

(1973, Fr/It, 115 min)
d/p/sc/ph Claude Lelouch. *ed* Georges Klotz. *m* Francis Lai. *cast* Lino Ventura, Françoise Fabian, Charles Gérard, André Falcon, Silvano Tranquilli, Claude Mann.

●*Un Homme et une Femme* revisited seven years on (with different leads). Ventura plays an ageing thief, pulling a diamond job in Cannes and falling for Fabian's elegant antique-dealer. The robbery is slickly done, but treatment of the affair is less certain. Opening with a clip from *Un Homme et une Femme*, the film by implication yearns nostalgically for the relative simplicity and certainty of that relationship. The present couple have become less sure but more knowing. Twice divorced, she feels obliged to take lovers while he's in prison; he looks far from convinced by their final reconcilation. But any exploration of such cynicism is largely dissipated by the surfeit of Gallic charm, with Lelouch's camera fidgeting away as he bolsters up his story with a layer of chic, some pat phrase-making, and a lot of modish references. Ventura's presence nevertheless lends weight.

Bonne Nouvelle

(2001, Fr, 60 min)
d Vincent Dieutre. *p* Christian Baute. *sc* Vincent Dieutre. *ph* Benoît Chamaillard, Viken Armenian. *ed* Dominique Auvray. *voices* Eva Truffaut, Bojena Horackova, Vincent Dieutre.

●The opening 360 degree shot of a Paris street-corner should alert you to the artiness of this precious, rather pretentiously 'poetic' offering which combines fairly redundant images of streets, buildings, rooms, crowds and cars with voice-overs relating anecdotes evoking life in the city. The emphasis on sex and death notwithstanding, it's hard to see much point to it all. GA

Bonnes Femmes, Les (The Girls)

(1960, Fr/It, 102 min, b/w)
d Claude Chabrol. *p* Robert Hakim, Raymond Hakim. *sc* Paul Gégauff. *ph* Henri Decaë. *ed* Jacques Gaillard. *ad* Jacques Mély. *m* Paul Misraki, Pierre Jansen. *cast* Bernardette Lafont, Stéphane Audran, Clothilde Joano, Lucile Saint-Simon, Claude Berri, Mario David.

●Guilt, complicity, bourgeois aspirations and murder: Chabrol's fourth feature clearly illuminates his abiding interests, even as it achieves a dazzling formal complexity in its arrangement of a series of events charting the dreams of a better life entertained by four Parisian shopgirls desperate to escape the daily monotony of their existence. One longs for success in the music halls, one the staid security of marriage, another a good time and little else; and the last, seeking romance, is the most vulnerable… At once a detailed portrait of Parisian life and an ironic, witty study of human foibles, the film remains emotionally affecting thanks to Chabrol's unsentimental compassion for his subjects. GA

Bonnie and Clyde

(1967, US, 111 min)
d Arthur Penn. *p* Warren Beatty. *sc* David Newman, Robert Benton. *ph* Burnett Guffey. *ed* Dede Allen. *ad* Dean Tavoularis. *m* Charles Strouse. *cast* Warren Beatty, Faye Dunaway, Michael J Pollard, Gene Hackman, Estelle Parsons, Denver Pyle, Dub Taylor, Gene Wilder.

●Reclaiming the American gangster movie after it had been stolen by the *Nouvelle Vague*, Penn's film was so successful (and so imitated) that it inevitably met with some grudging devaluation. But it's still great: half comic fairytale, half brutal fact, it reflects the essential ambiguity of its heroes (faithfully copied from history and the real-life Barrow gang which terrorised the American South in the early '30s) by treading a no man's land suspended between reality and fantasy. With its weird landscape of dusty, derelict towns and verdant highways, stunningly shot by Burnett Guffey in muted tones of green and gold, it has the true quality of folk legend. TM

Bonnie Scotland

(1935, US, 80 min, b/w)
d James W Horne. *p* Hal Roach. *sc* Frank Butler, Jefferson Moffitt. *ph* Art Lloyd. *ed* Bert Jordan. *cast* Stan Laurel, Oliver Hardy, Anne Grey, David Torrence, James Finlayson, June Lang, William Janney.

●Little to do with life north of the border, since this parody of *Lives of a Bengal Lancer* sees the darling duo travelling from America to Scotland to collect an inheritance, and thereafter enlisting (accidentally, natch) with the army to serve in India. Not one of the pair's funniest features – which are almost all inferior to the shorts, anyway – but there are a few memorable moments, not least when they improvise one of their little dances while supposedly cleaning up the parade-ground. GA

Bon Voyage

(1944, GB, 26 min, b/w)
d Alfred Hitchcock. *sc* John Orton, Angus Macphail, Arthur Calder-Marshall. *ph* Günther Krampf. *ad* Charles Gilbert. *cast* John Blythe, The Molière Players.

●In 1944 Hitchcock made two British shorts – *Bon Voyage* and *Aventure Malgache* – for the Ministry of Information; they were shot in French and intended exclusively as propaganda for liberated French territories. *Bon Voyage*, from an idea by Arthur Calder-Marshall, unfolds through flashbacks. A Scottish RAF officer (with an Etonian burr) is debriefed in London after his escape through Occupied France. Hitch is right at home with the man-on-the-run scenario, but what's most interesting is the cleverly structured shift in perspective, from the subjective testimony of the officer to the overview afforded by his superiors. Essential viewing for completists, but not, perhaps, for others. TCh

Bonzesse, La

(1974, Fr, 103 min)
d François Jouffa. *p* Francis Leroi. *sc* François Jouffa, Jean-Pierre Gambert. *ph* Jean Gonnet. *ed* Annabelle. *m* Hadi Kalafate. *cast* Sylvie Meyer, Bernard Verley, Olga Valery, Christine Aurel, Bernard Tixier, Eva Damien.

●An astonishingly uncoordinated sex film with a false air of seriousness: the title, meaning 'The Priestess', refers to a spurious ending which sees plucky Sylvie Meyer hoof off to Katmandu to get her head together and shaved. Ostensibly a detailed account of the techniques and mechanics of prostitution – Meyer is a philosophy student who supplements her grant, gains insight, and gets laid simultaneously – it's enjoyable enough so long as it sticks to the minutiae (bidets, poor pervs in crocodile suits, business chat in the brothel kitchen). But then it lurches out into the world of admen and nightclubs, and is conventionally angled towards the sex scenes. There's also a strange subplot about a servant who keeps a poster for *The Servant* on his wall. Uncensored, it might have made more sense. AN

Boogie Man Will Get You, The

(1942, US, 66 min, b/w)
d Lew Landers. *p* Colbert Clark. *sc* Edwin Blum. *ph* Henry Freulich. *ed* Richard Fantl. *ad* Lionel Banks. *m* MW Stoloff. *cast* Boris Karloff, Peter Lorre, Jeff Donnell, Larry Parks, Maxie Rosenbloom, Frank Puglia, Don Beddoe.
● Irresistibly ramshackle horror spoof, with Karloff – abetted by a puckish Lorre, who's the town mayor, police chief, estate agent and everything else – as a mad scientist busily at work in the basement of a house let to newlyweds, trying to help the war effort by creating a superman out of raw materials obtained by bumping off the living. Often crudely farcical but still surprisingly inventive, and the cast (Lorre especially) do wonders. TM

Boogie Nights

(1997, US, 156 min)
d Paul Thomas Anderson. *p* Lloyd Levin, John Lyons, Paul Thomas Anderson, Joanne Sellar. *sc* Paul Thomas Anderson. *ph* Robert Elswit. *ed* Dylan Tichenor. *pd* Bob Ziembicki. *cast* Mark Wahlberg, Burt Reynolds, Julianne Moore, Don Cheadle, Heather Graham, Alfred Molina, Philip Baker Hall, Nicole Ari Parker, Luis Guzman, William H Macy, Phil Hoffman.
● Anderson's second feature – a dazzling, highly confident, atmospherically original and refreshingly non-prurient take on the LA porn movie community – may not be a '90s *Citizen Kane*, as some claim, but in terms of sweep, ambition and precocious cinematic competence, it heralds the arrival of a new talent. Charting the rise and fall of well-endowed teenage ingénu Dirk Diggler (Wahlberg), from dishwasher to subcultural skinflick superstar, and back to washed-out junkie, the film is less a cautionary tale than a freewheeling, talent-showcasing homage to the glitter, tack and kitsch excesses of the drug-fuelled late '70s and the hangover '80s. The sense of homage/pastiche goes further still: if the rambling ensemble construction derives from *Nashville*, the swooping long takes and whiplash pans come courtesy of Scorsese. But it's the music that calls the tune with the energetic soul and disco records of the period dictating the editing, pacing and the slightly sleazy, morally neutral tone. This is style condescending magnificently to content, but what stiffens this unashamedly exhibitionist movie's muscles are the 'family' of beautifully judged performances, from Reynolds' stand-out as porn-king auteur/father figure, to Moore's superb cokehead survivor-star and Macy's humiliated cuckold, right down to Hoffman's gut-wrenching gay crew member. WH

Book of Life, The

(1998,US/Fr, 63 min)
d Hal Hartley. *p* Simon Arnal, Caroline Benjo, Jerome Brownstein, Thierry Cagianut, Pierre Chevalier, Chelsea Fuhrer, Matthew Myers, Caroline Scotta. *sc* Hal Hartley. *ph* Jim Denault. *ed* Steve Hamilton. *ad* Andy Biscontini. *cast* Martin Donovan, Thomas Jay Ryan, Dave Simonds, PJ Harvey, Miho Nikaido, Anna Köhler, Martin Pfeffercorn, Paul Albe, Olga Alexandrovna, Michael Ornsetin, William S Burroughs, James Urbaniak.
● Hartley's typically wry, witty and inventive contribution to Haut et Court's Millennium series envisages Christ (Donovan) reluctantly sent by dad to NYC to supervise the Day of Judgment; meanwhile Satan (Ryan) hopes to put a stop to the Apocalypse, while continuing his quest for wayward souls. The plotting, the philosophical discussions and the playing are as enjoyable as ever, but what makes this Hartley film special is his invigorating use of digital video and experiments with sound and music. GA

Book of Love

(1990, US, 87 min)
d Robert Shaye. *p* Rachel Talalay. *sc* William Kotzwinkle. *ph* Peter Demin. *ed* Terry Stokes. *pd* CJ Strawn. *cast* Chris Young, Keith Coogan, Josie Bissett, Tricia Lee Fisher, Danny Nucci, John Cameron Mitchell, Michael McKean, Aeryk Egan.
● Adapted by William Kotzwinkle from his novel *Jack in the Box*, this tale of young lust in the '50s utilises all the usual period memorabilia: good-looking cars, better-looking hairstyles, psychotically uptight parents, and the obligatory Greatest Hits soundtrack. Against this formulaic backdrop, Shaye offers vignettes of hyper-hormonal teen torment, from whackin' off in class to being buggered with a candle on a Merry Ranger camp outing. 'I suppose it's time for another dick-measuring contest,' opines one poor sap when all other forms of entertainment seem exhausted. Unlike so many first-fumbling '50s movies, however, this one tempers its scrotal obsessions with a sense of naive wide-eyed delight, for which credit is largely due to the fresh-faced cast (Chris Young in particular). Hardly *American Graffiti*, but way above the inanities of *Lemon Popsicle*. MK

Book of Shadows Blair Witch 2

(2000, US, 90 min)
d Joe Berlinger. *p* Bill Carraro. *sc* Dick Beebe, Joe Berlinger. *ph* Nancy Schreiber. *ed* Sarah Flack. *pd* Vince Peranio. *m* Carter Burwell. *cast* Kim Director, Jeffrey Donovan, Erica Leerhsen, Tristen Skyler, Stephen Barker Turner, Kurt Loder, Chuck Scarborough.
● Forget curiosity. Seeing this will only taint your memory of the terrifying original. Berlinger claims this is a postmodern commentary on the entire 'Blair Witch' phenomenon, yet it fails on every level: it isn't scary or innovative, and its 'insights' are obvious and spurious. It's mostly shot on 35mm, and no amount of digital video footage, Hi-8 images and tricksy computer graphics can disguise that it's a sell-out travesty. The original leads were three average slacker types. Here, they're five horror clichés: a crazy Burkittsville local whose Blair Witch obsession has spawned a merchandising and tour group business, and four clients – a psychic goth, a practising wiccan, a sceptical academic and his more susceptible girlfriend. Camped for the night at child killer Rustin Parr's house, they're disturbed by a rival tour group. Later, they get smashed on drink and drugs, then awake to find their memories have been wiped. Taking refuge in the tour operator's woodland warehouse loft, they try to figure out, with the help of video footage, what happened during the 'lost hours'. NF

Book That Wrote Itself, The

(1999, Ire, 70 min)
d/p/sc Liam O'Mochain. *ph* Oisin Bourke. *ed* Ray Fallon. *pd* Conner Arrigan, Damien Creagh. *m* Paul Dwyer. *cast* Liam O'Mochain, Antoinette Guiney, Marco Van Belle, Kristen Marken, Carol Myers, Angel Bond, Mike Carberry. *with* Kenneth Branagh, George Clooney, Catherine Deneuve.
● Mochin's cheap but inventive comedy 'docu-drama' (in fact it'sa drama about a docu-drama) is a fledgling effort that proves surprisingly memorable. A young writer with a blag artist's charm hires a novice female assistant to help turn his book into a movie that ends up at the Venice film festival. Minor, talky, occasionally irksome, but energetic. WH

Boom

(1968, GB, 113 min)
d Joseph Losey. *p* John Heyman, Norman Priggen. *sc* Tennessee Williams. *ph* Douglas Slocombe. *ed* Reginald Beck. *pd* Richard MacDonald. *m* John Barry. *cast* Elizabeth Taylor, Richard Burton, Noël Coward, Joanna Shimkus, Michael Dunn, Romolo Valli, Veronica Wells.
● A typically heady serio-comic brew, adapted by Tennessee Williams from his own playlet *The Milk Train Doesn't Stop Here Any More*, in which an ageing beauty, awaiting death immured in her fortress home, finds fanciful comfort in the attentions of a wandering poet, known as the Angel of Death because he has a knack of being in at the kill when rich women die. Clearly written for an older woman and younger man, it gets Burton and Taylor, comfortably matched, making nonsense of theme and relationships, and giving monotonously unsubtle performances (she screeches, he glooms). The setting, not a fading Southern mansion but a bleakly beautiful Mediterranean island, also seems peculiarly alien to the atmosphere of hothouse decadence. Still, Losey and cameraman Douglas Slocombe make it look gorgeous in a pile-up of baroque detail; at times it almost seems as though it might blossom wittily into a chronicle of the declining years of Modesty Blaise. TM

Boomerang

(1947, US, 86 min, b/w)
d Elia Kazan. *p* Louis De Rochemont. *sc* Richard Murphy. *ph* Norbert Brodine. *ed* Harmon Jones. *ad* Richard Day, Chester Gore. *m* David Buttolph. *cast* Dana Andrews, Jane Wyatt, Lee J Cobb, Arthur Kennedy, Sam Levene, Ed Begley, Karl Malden.
● Kazan's third film, a semi-documentary thriller loaded with social conscience (it was produced by Louis de Rochemont, the man behind *The March of Time*). Shot on location in a small New England town, it follows State Attorney Andrews' attempts to prove that a tramp (Kennedy) accused of murdering an elderly priest may, despite the town's prejudices, be innocent. The unemphatic presentation of details, the use of locations, and strong performances from a largely non-professional supporting cast, lend the film authenticity and power. But as Kazan himself later stated: 'There is a dramatic trick in it; it turns out there is a villain, and at a certain point the author uncovers him... Actually civic corruption is much more widespread. It is much more complex, and I know that now'. GA

Boomerang (Comme un Boomerang)

(1976, Fr/It, 100 min)
d José Giovanni. *p* Raymond Danon, Alain Delon. *sc* José Giovanni, Alain Delon. *ph* Pierre-William Glenn. *ed* Françoise Javet. *ad* Willy Holt. *m* Georges Delerue. *cast* Alain Delon, Carla Gravina, Suzanne Flon, Dora Doll, Charles Vanel.
● A good *série noire* novelist, Giovanni took less happily to film-making, and does little right with this melodrama-plus-message produced by Delon as a vehicle for Delon. The latter plays a prominent businessman attempting to save his son, who killed a cop while turned on at a wild party. But the truth of his own criminal past emerges, the son decides to emulate dad by busting out, and predictable complications bolster the argument against hysterical media campaigns demanding the death penalty. The general air of cliché is sealed by the inevitable final freeze-frame as Delon and son, trying to escape on foot across the border, make it and/or are nailed by a pursuing helicopter. TM

Boomerang

(1992, US, 117 min)
d Reginald Hudlin. *p* Brian Grazer. *sc* Barry W Blaustein, David Sheffield. *ph* Woody Omens. *ed* Earl Watson. *ad* Jane Musky. *m* Marcus Miller. *cast* Eddie Murphy, Robin Givens, Halle Berry, David Alan Grier, Martin Lawrence, Grace Jones, Geoffrey Holder , Eartha Kitt, Tisha Campbell, Melvin Van Peebles.
● Patchy sex comedy about an irresistible adman who meets his match after feeling what it's like to be a sex object. It's hard not to wonder at Eddie Murphy's seemingly limitless egotism, which allows him to waltz through a movie in which he not only 'comes' on camera but is described as having 'the best ass' in the world. Not that there isn't a lot to laugh at: one scene where Murphy's shy pal is embarrassed by his horny, sassy parents is a side-splitter. The film is far too slick to be ineffective, but its attempts to play with the sex-war theme are often unbelievably crass. Mike Tyson's ex-wife Givens gives an understandably convincing performance as a ball-buster, and it's good to see a black-based film *not* concerned with guns, drugs and dem dere pigs. SGr

Boom Town

(1940, US, 116 min, b/w)
d Jack Conway. *p* Sam Zimbalist. *sc* John Lee Mahin. *ph* Harold Rosson. *ed* Blanche Sewell. *ad* Cedric Gibbons. *m* Franz Waxman. *cast* Clark Gable, Spencer Tracy, Claudette Colbert, Hedy Lamarr, Frank Morgan, Lionel Atwill, Chill Wills.
● All the clichés as two buddies tangle over romance while undergoing ups and downs in the oil business. The cast keep things going as Gable wins Colbert, Tracy is decent about it, then Lamarr hoves in view... TM

Boon, The (Kondura)

(1977, Ind, 132 min)
d/sc Shyam Benegal. *ph* Govind Nihalani. *m* Vanraj Bhatia. *cast* Vanishree, Anant Nag, Smita Patil, Satyadev Dubey, Amrish Puri.

●The boon bestowed on the self-pitying black sheep of a rural Indian family by a gnarled deity is a decidedly mixed blessing: a magic root guaranteeing power at the price of celibacy, and bringing knowledge at the price of tragedy. Benegal's delineation – hardly revelatory – of the community's hopeless subjection to the mutually reinforcing tyranny of religious superstition and the local landowner is similarly a mixed bag of fantasy and realism; its intricately established humanist dilemma is undermined by caricatured villainy. PT

Boost, The

(1988, US, 95 min)
d Harold Becker. *p* Daniel H Blatt. *sc* Darryl Ponicsan. *ph* Howard Anderson. *ed* Maury Winetrobe. *ad* Ken Hardy. *m* Stanley Myers. *cast* James Woods, Sean Young, John Kapelos, Steven Hill, Kelle Kerr, John Rothman, Amanda Blake.
●A well-crafted, hard-hitting look at an ideal marriage torn apart by personal insecurity, material greed and designer drugs. After years of frustration, Woods meets a sympathetic Californian businessman (Hill), who soon has him selling tax-shelter real estate investments as if his life depended on it. The market is wiped out overnight. Woods is left with no job and a lot of bills. He still has his beautiful wife (Young), but his fragile self-respect is shattered. Offered a little 'boost' by a pal, Woods snorts coke for the first time, instantly dispelling despair but also tapping into an already dangerously addictive personality. The addiction scenario is standard stuff: stress and temptation followed by steep decline, short-lived clean up, and final tragic lapse. The real fascination, though, is the sense that Woods is a disaster waiting to happen, a hollow man constantly on the verge of implosion. The approach here is slightly too monotone and distanced, curiously at odds with Woods' compulsively energetic performance. NF

Boot, Das

see Boat, The

Bootleggers

(1974, US, 110 min)
d/p Charles B Pierce. *sc* Earl E Smith. *ph* Tak Fujimoto. *ed* Frank Ford. *ad* Tommy Hasson, Larry Bishop. *m* Jaime Mendoza-Nava. *cast* Slim Pickens, Paul Koslo, Dennis Fimple, Jaclyn Smith, Seamon Glass, Daryle Ann Lindley.
●Any film which actually stars Slim Pickens can't be all good, and *Bootleggers* isn't remotely good. It's a thuddingly dull yarn about two Arkansas roisterers and their feud with a neighbouring family. The actors show an understandable reluctance to give their dialogue zing ('I gotta do what I gotta do' is the most notable chestnut), and director Pierce (whose name proliferates over the credits to an unseemly degree) stages events with a dramatic ineptness and visual crudity usually consigned to rock-bottom porno. GB

Bootmen

(2000, Aust/US, 95 min)
d Dein Perry. *p* Hilary Linstead. *sc* Steve Worland, Hilary Linstead, Dein Perry. *ph* Steve Mason. *ed* Jane Moran. *pd* Murray Picknett. *m* Cezary Skubiszewski. *cast* Adam Garcia, Sophie Lee, Sam Worthington, William Zappa, Richard Carter, Susie Porter, Anthony Hayes, Christopher Horsey, Drew Kaluski.
●Steelworker/tap-dancer Sean (Garcia) quits Newcastle, Australia, and heads for Sydney, despite Dad's 'no son of mine' speech (think *Billy Elliot*, transposed). He leaves behind his newfound love, hairdresser Linda (Lee), and brother Mitch (Worthington), who gave up tapdancing and took up stealing, usually cars but, in his brother's absence, Sean's girlfriend too. Sydney doesn't work out and Sean returns home determined to set up his own gig – one that better showcases his roots – cue steel toecaps tapping on girders, metal pipes and tinpan dunnies. Garcia makes a fine-looking lead and his fancy footwork throughout is reasonably entertaining, but it's not enough to save this turkey. Directed by the founder of the Australian dance troupe Tap Dogs, the script is weak, the characters clichéd and the plot bubblegum. JFu

Booty Call

(1997, US, 79 min)
d Jeff Pollack. *p* John Morrissey. *sc* Takashi Bufford, Bootsie. *ph* Ron Orieux. *ed* Chris Greenbury. *pd* Sandra Kybartas. *m* Robert Folk. *cast* Jamie Foxx, Tommy Davidson, Vivica A Fox, Tamala Jones, Scott LaRose, Ric Young, Art Malik.
●A teen friendly sitcom stretched to cinema length. Two soul brothers want to score before the night's out: bland Rushon (Davidson) with his demure girl Nikki (Jones), and big mouth Bunz (Jamie Foxx) with her classy, but wild best friend, Lysterine (Vivica A Fox). The hip-hop soundtrack may be full of new tunes, but racial stereotypes abound and the battle of the sexes strikes a wretchedly familiar note. As in: Woman with moustache, she scary. Woman in fussy lingerie, she sexy! Or: Men will do anything to get sex, but clever women use it as a bargaining chip. Very occasionally, there's a surreal sparkle. 'You go to a club and a girl looks great,' Bunz explains. 'Come high noon, there's a sea donkey climbing into your car!' But don't hold your breath. CO'Su

Bopha!

(1993, US, 120 min)
d Morgan Freeman. *p* Lawrence Taubman. *sc* Brian Bird, John Wierick. *ph* David Watkin. *ed* Neil Travis. *pd* Michael Philips. *m* James Horner. *cast* Danny Glover, Alfre Woodard, Malcolm McDowell, Marius Weyers, Maynard Eziashi, Malick Bowens.
●After *Cry Freedom*, *A Dry White Season* and *The Power of One*, it's good to see a Hollywood movie about apartheid-era South Africa that comes from a black perspective. Adapted from a play by Percy Mtwa, Freeman's directorial debut is the involving and complex study of a proud black policeman (Glover) who believes he's doing right by upholding the rule of white law. His life is about to crumble around him when his son takes part in the protest against schooling in Afrikaans, and a hardline Special Branch officer (McDowell) is brought in to snuff out the agitation. Video release only in Britain. TJ

Border, The

(1981, US, 108 min)
d Tony Richardson. *p* Edgar M Bronfman Jr. *sc* Deric Washburn, Walon Green, David Freeman. *ph* Ric Waite. *ed* Robert K Lambert. *pd* Toby Carr Rafelson. *m* Ry Cooder. *cast* Jack Nicholson, Harvey Keitel, Valerie Perrine, Warren Oates, Elpidia Carrillo, Dirk Blocker.
●A Tex-Mex stew that looks to have all the right spicy ingredients, but emerges under gringo chef Richardson as not exactly indigestible, merely flavourless. Limping home late and lost amid numerous exposés of tragedy and corruption along America's chain-link southern frontier, it simply hands us Nicholson moodily scratching his conscience as a patrolman pitying the poor immigrants (one young wetback madonna in particular), and going up against his superiors' smuggling operation. PT

Border Incident

(1949, US, 96 min, b/w)
d Anthony Mann. *p* Nicholas Nayfack. *sc* John C Higgins. *ph* John Alton. *ed* Conrad A Nervig. *ad* Cedric Gibbons, Hans Peters. *m* André Previn. *cast* Ricardo Montalban, George Murphy, Howard da Silva, James Mitchell, Arnold Moss, Alfonso Bedoya, Teresa Celli, Charles McGraw.
●Conventional script about two immigration service agents who join hands across the border to smash a murderous racket exploiting cheap Mexican labour. Lifted right out of the rut by John Alton's camerawork, which helps Mann to transform routine heroics into the stuff of *film noir*. However well-trodden its path, the film shines bright by comparison with Tony Richardson's later *The Border*, which treated a similar subject with twice the ambition and half the conviction. TM

Borderline

(1980, US, 105 min)
d Jerrold Freedman. *p* James Nelson. *sc* Steve Kline, Jerrold Freedman. *ph* Tak Fujimoto. *ed* John F Link II. *ad* Michel Levesque. *m* Gil Mellé. *cast* Charles Bronson, Bruno Kirby, Bert Remsen, Michael Lerner, Kenneth McMillan, Ed Harris.
●Entirely bland actioner, with Bronson as the laconic border patrolman on the track of the bad guys bringing illegal immigrants in. Only Tak Fujimoto's typically professional camerawork offers any interest. GA

Border Shootout

(1990, US, 110 min)
d/sc CJ McIntyre. *ph* Dennis Dalzell. *ed* Grant Johnson. *pd* Craig B Stein. *m* Coley Music Group. *cast* Cody Glenn, Jeff Kaake, Glenn Ford, Lizabeth Rohovit, Michael Horse, Russell Todd, Michael Ansara.
●Another Elmore Leonard novel bites the dust, this time in a poor latter-day Western in which greenhorn rancher Cody Glenn is appointed sheriff of a frontier town which has grown impatient with veteran lawman Glenn Ford. Unfortunately, the town council don't make it easy for themselves by deciding to hang a couple of cattle rustlers, thus pitching retribution down on everyone's head. TJ

Bordertown

(1934, US, 90 min, b/w)
d Archie Mayo. *p* Robert Lord. *sc* Laird Doyle, Wallace Smith. *ph* Tony Gaudio. *ed* Thomas Richards. *ad* Jack Okey. *m* Bernhard Kaun. *cast* Paul Muni, Bette Davis, Margaret Lindsay, Eugene Pallette, Robert Barrat, Soledad Jimenez.
●Muni, in one of his careful ethnic portraits, plays a streetwise Mexican from the LA ghetto who graduates from night school as a lawyer after five tough years, only to be disbarred when he loses his temper and first court case – against a pretty socialite (Lindsay) charged with drunken driving – because influence and legal skills are stacked against him. Disillusioned, he heads across the border to make money, convinced that nothing else matters in the Land of Opportunity; and does so by working his way up from bouncer to partner in Pallette's Tijuana night-club, in the process becoming an object of desire to Pallette's bored wife (Davis, incandescent in a sketchy part). Misreading his lack of interest, she clears the decks by murdering her husband; then, driven insane by guilt, she tries (but fails) to frame him for the murder. Muni, now affluent, meanwhile takes up with his dream girl, the socialite from his court case, who is happy to flirt while slumming in Tijuana, but laughs him off ('You belong to a different tribe, savage') when he proposes marriage. Beautifully shot by Tony Gaudio, well acted, grippingly directed, the film makes acutely acerbic points about privilege and prejudice; but typically of Warners in its social conscience mode, settles in the end for the status quo. The Mexican decides to go 'back where I belong, with my own people', and the message is clear: had he respected the principles of apartheid, he'd have earned himself a gold star. TM

Borges, Books and the Night (Borges, los libros y las noches)

(1999, Arg, 83 min)
d Tristán Bauer. *sc* Tristán Bauer, Carolina Scaglione. *ph* Javier Julia, Alejandro Fernando Moujan. *ed* Alejandro Brodersohn. *m* Frederico Bonasso. *cast* Walter Santa Ana, Lorenzo Quintero, Leonardo Sbaraglia.
●A realisation in film of the extraordinary literary universe of definitive modernist writer Jorge Luis Borges was always going to be a huge challenge. To his credit, however, Bauer makes a very effective shot at it. Using found footage, interviews, biographical reconstructions, dramatised extracts and an allusive imagery, he constructs a multi-layered portrait of the author's life and work, tracing the Möbius strip of overlaps and collusions between the two. And if he denies Borges his self-declared 'hope to be anonymous, it is the highest kind of glory,' he does admit the uncategorisable mystery at the heart of his unique literary project. GE

Born for Glory

see Forever England

Born in East L.A.

(1987, US, 87 min)
d Cheech Marin. *p* Peter Macgregor-Smith. *sc* Cheech Marin. *ph* Alex Philips. *ed* Don Brochu. *m* Lee Holdridge. *cast* Cheech Marin, Daniel Stern, Paul Rodriguez, Jan-Michael Vincent, Kamala Lopez, Alma Martinez, Tony Plana.

●Minus his old smoking partner Tommy Chong, writer/director/star Cheech Marin obviously put a lot into this story of a third generation Hispanic American who's unwittingly dumped back in Tijuana by US immigration authorities, doesn't speak a word of Spanish, and spends the rest of the movie trying to get back Stateside. The result is a well-meaning bore, which isn't sure whether to play it for laughs or to make a serious point, and ends up missing out on both fronts. Based on a routine Marin built around Bruce Springsteen's 'Born in the USA'. TJ

Born in Flames

(1983, US, 80 min)
d/p/sc Lizzie Borden. *ph* Ed Bowes, Al Santana. *ed* Lizzie Borden. *m* The Bloods, The Red Crayolas, Ibis. *cast* Honey, Adele Bertei, Jeanne Satterfield, Flo Kennedy, Pat Murphy, Kathryn Bigelow, Becky Johnston.

●'The right to violence is like the right to pee: you've gotta have the right place and the right time'. The time: the near future. The place: New York, ten years after a peaceful revolution has recreated all men equal. All men, leaving the women to mouth their discontent: like Adele (Satterfield) as a member of the militant women's army; like Honey, beautiful and black, presenter for the pirate Phoenix radio; or Isabel (Bertei), who performs nightly on Radio Ragazza. Borden charts the explosive coming together of the women as they forge their own liberation, handling her story with audacity and making even the driest argument crackle with humour, while the more poignant moments burn with a fierce white heat. FD

Born Losers, The

(1967, US, 114 min)
d TC Frank [Tom Laughlin]. *p* TC Frank, Don Henderson. *sc* James Lloyd. *ph* Gregory Sandor. *ed* John Winfield. *ad* Richard Beck-Meyer. *m* Mike Curb. *cast* Tom Laughlin, Elizabeth James, Jane Russell, Jeremy Slate, Paul Bruce, William Wellman Jr.

●Unprepossessing meet-violence-with-vengeance movie in which Hell's Angels terrorise a California town, rape teenagers, and receive their comeuppance from a taciturn halfbreed Vietnam veteran. Of interest only to cult buffs as the home movie which launched Laughlin's money-spinning 'Billy Jack' series. Laughlin subsequently cut much of the copious violence, but could do nothing to improve the rock-bottom acting and production values. JPy

Born of Fire (aka The Master Musician)

(1987, GB, 84 min)
d Jamil Dehlavi. *p* Jamil Dehlavi, Thérèse Pickard. *sc* Raficq Abdullah. *ph* Bruce McGowan. *ed* Robert Hargreaves. *ad* Michael Porter. *m* Colin Towns. *cast* Peter Firth, Suzan Crowley, Stefan Kalipha, Oh-Tee, Nabil Shaban, Jean Ainslie.

●A virtuoso English flautist (Firth) is lured to Turkey to confront a seductive djinn and a naked devil in order to learn the secret of his father's death. The story, which starts quite sensibly in the Wigmore Hall, London, becomes increasingly cocooned in impenetrable mysticism. Strikingly weird mountain locations of jagged caves and calcified rock pools, but the whole concoction's decidedly rum. JPy

Born on the Fourth of July

(1989, US, 144 min)
d Oliver Stone. *p* A Kitman Ho, Oliver Stone. *sc* Oliver Stone, Ron Kovic. *ph* Robert Richardson. *ed* David Brenner. *pd* Bruno Rubeo. *m* John Williams. *cast* Tom Cruise, Kyra Sedgwick, Raymond J Barry, Willem Dafoe, Jerry Levine, Frank Whaley, Caroline Kava.

●Broadening the sweep of *Platoon*, this is a more ambitious, accomplished film about Vietnam, but not because it treads the now familiar path from innocence to enlightenment. Rather, its strength stems from the intense depiction of a man stripped of dignity and sexuality as a result of appalling injuries. Based on the experiences of veteran Ron Kovic (who co-scripted, with Stone, this adaptation of his book), the film encompasses two decades. From an upright, Catholic background, Kovic (Cruise) emerges ready to kill Commies. After being wounded, he ends up in the veterans' hospital back home – a hellish place short on funds and sentiment. Starting the slow process of re-education, from the confines of a wheelchair he begins active participation in the anti-war movement. Cruise's performance is a powerful, credible interpretation; but Stone can't resist sermonising, particularly when he overplays Kovic's tortured attempts at catharsis after he accidentally shoots a fellow soldier. Idyllic childhood scenes signpost all too clearly the ensuing nightmare. But things progressively improve, the sheer scope of the action accomodating the more vigorous approach applied to later sequences. A compelling, elegiac film, particularly encouraging after the simplified morality of Platoon. CM

Born Romantic

(2000, GB, 96 min)
d David Kane. *p* Michele Camarda. *sc* David Kane. *ph* Robert Alazraki. *ed* Michael Parker. *pd* Sarah Greenwood. *m* Simon Boswell. *cast* Craig Ferguson, Ian Hart, Jane Horrocks, Adrian Lester, Catherine McCormack, Jimi Mistry, David Morrissey, Olivia Williams, Kenneth Cranham.

●Born with two left feet, more like. That doesn't mean just the cast, as they take to the floor of the salsa club we're asked to believe they frequent, but also director Kane's script which bears scant resemblance to life as we know it in London or, for that matter, anywhere else on the planet. Lester's cabbie, the fount of all wisdom (earthly rather than divine, but still saintly and implausible), is a common denominator in the lives of six stereotypes, all, wittingly or not, in need of love. On the distaff side, there's standoffish posh Williams, hypochondriac neurotic McCormack and promiscuous hairdresser Horrocks; the lads making predictable play for them are MOR-obsessed smoothie Ferguson, inept thief Mistry and failed Scouse muso Morrissey, who let Horrocks down ages ago. As the actors playing these less than engaging characters mug their way through the flaccid sitcom conceits that pass for a plot, the question's not 'Who will that nice minicab driver end up with?' – that's obvious pretty early on – but 'Please can we take a short cut and get this over with?' GA

Born to Be Bad

(1950, US, 94 min, b/w)
d Nicholas Ray. *p* Robert Sparks. *sc* Edith Sommer, Charles Schnee. *ph* Nick Musuraca. *ed* Frederick Knudtson. *ad* Albert S D'Agostino, Jack Okey. *m* Frederick Hollander. *cast* Joan Fontaine, Robert Ryan, Zachary Scott, Joan Leslie, Mel Ferrer, Harold Vermilyea, Virginia Farmer.

●While far from being one of Ray's finest films – he himself was decidedly unhappy with the basic material – this is still a highly watchable bitchy melodrama. Fontaine is admirably cast as the deceitful, ambitious go-getter dying to get her claws into a rich husband and playing off various suitors against one another; her customary 'nice' image is undermined throughout, exposing the wiles that may underlie traditional 'feminine innocence', and at the same time revealing that men gullible enough to believe in such sweetly simpering pleasantry deserve what they get. A pretty predictable story, in fact, but directed by Ray with great attention to emotional states and telling camera compositions (all those staircases!). GA

Born to Boogie

(1972, GB, 67 min)
d/p Richard Starkey [Ringo Starr]. *sc* Ringo Starr, Marc Bolan. *ph* Nic Knowland, Ringo Starr, Mike Dodds, Mike Davis, Jeremy Stavenhagen, Richard Stanley. *ed* Graham Gilding. *cast* Marc Bolan, T. Rex, Ringo Starr, Elton John.

●The inevitable mixture of concert footage (Empire Pool, Wembley, 1972) and would-be surrealist horseplay. Even more gruesome than you might fear, despite Elton John's energetic rendition of 'Tutti Frutti'.

Born to Dance

(1936, US, 105 min, b/w)
d Roy Del Ruth. *p* Jack Cummings. *sc* Jack McGowan, Sid Silvers, BG de Sylva. *ph* Ray June. *ed* Blanche Sewell. *ad* Cedric Gibbons. *songs* Cole Porter. *cast* Eleanor Powell, James Stewart, Virginia Bruce, Una Merkel, Sid Silvers, Frances Langford, Raymond Walburn, Buddy Ebsen, Alan Dinehart, Reginald Gardiner.

●Planned as a revue with Cole Porter numbers, this evolved into a full-fledged musical with *On the Town* plot: three sailors on shore leave (Stewart, Silvers, Ebsen) become involved with a trio of girls (Powell, Merkel, Langford). Reminders of the original conception surface in a series of specialty acts – a ballroom dance duo, comic monologues for store floor-walker and switchboard girl, a Chaplinesque mime by a cop with a yen to be an orchestra conductor – which are surprisingly good and cleverly integrated with the main action, concerning Stewart's efforts to resolve a romantic misunderstanding with Powell and to secure her big break as a dancer. The grand finale is one of Powell's rather mechanical tap numbers, complete with spectacular chorus, on the foredeck of a battleship, but she comes up with much more inventive routines to 'Rap Tap on Wood' and 'Easy to Love' (the latter in rapturous response to a crooning Stewart in moonlit Central Park). Cole Porter's excellent score also includes 'I've Got You Under My Skin', and a delightful Gilbert & Sullivan pastiche for Raymond Walburn's gallant captain and his crew. TM

Born to Kill (aka Lady of Deceit)

(1947, US, 92 min, b/w)
d Robert Wise. *p* Herbert Schlom. *sc* Eve Greene, Richard Macaulay. *ph* Robert de Grasse. *ed* Les Millbrook. *ad* Albert S D'Agostino, Walter E Keller. *m* Paul Sawtell. *cast* Claire Trevor, Lawrence Tierney, Walter Slezak, Philip Terry, Audrey Long, Elisha Cook Jr, Isabel Jewell, Esther Howard.

●A touch of the old mutilated ecstasy, this. One of the B movies that Wise directed before his career took off, it's an unthrilling *noir* thriller about a psychopathic slum kid (Tierney) marrying into wealth, and his relationship on the side with a woman (Trevor) who gets her kicks from living dangerously. Not a frame of it is convincing at the intended level, but it is consistently fascinating in its relentless emphasis on cruelty, degradation and duplicity – and the scene in which a lurid description of two corpses provokes paroxysms of lust in Tierney and Trevor is a classic of its kind. It also boasts Slezak as a rotundly philosophical (and corrupt) gumshoe, Elisha Cook as the usual fall-guy with a viciousness all his own, and a lot of surprising 'dirty' talk for the period. The pervasive misogyny is given some engagingly fresh angles too. TR

Born Yesterday

(1950, US, 103 min, b/w)
d George Cukor. *p* S Sylvan Simon. *sc* Albert Mannheimer. *ph* Joseph Walker. *ed* Charles Nelson. *pd* Harry Horner. *m* Frederick Hollander. *cast* Judy Holliday, William Holden, Broderick Crawford, Howard St John, Frank Otto, Larry Oliver.

●Despite the tendency of Garson Kanin's play to go all dewy-eyed in its celebration of American democratic ideals, Cukor's screen version is still a delight. The story – rehashed later in *The Girl Can't Help It* – concerns the apparently dumb chorus-girl mistress of a ruthless tycoon-cum-gangster; the big shot decides she should become more sophisticated and knowledgeable (purely for the sake of appearances), and employs Holden to give her a few lessons. But the plan backfires, both because she falls for the teacher and because her education turns her against her brutish lover's rather dubious moral practices. A very simple idea, but enlivened by a sharp, witty script, and by Cukor's effortless handling of the brilliant performances: especially fine are Holliday as the dumb blonde who makes good, and Crawford as the confused sugar-daddy, nowhere more so than in the marvellous scene where her mindless singing disturbs his concentration over a game of gin rummy. Magic. GA

Born Yesterday

(1993, US, 100 min)
d Luis Mandoki. *p* D Constantine Conte. *sc* Douglas McGrath. *ph* Lajos Koltai. *ed* Lesley Walker. *pd* Lawrence G Paull. *m* George Fenton. *cast* Melanie Griffith, John Goodman, Don Johnson, Edward Herrmann, Max Perlich, Michael Ensign.

●The triumphant trio of Holliday, Holden and Crawford in Cukor's 1950 version of Garson Kanin's sharp stage comedy is a hard act to follow. Ironically, however, in this once-more-without-feeling remake, sketchily updated to the '90s, Griffith's performance in the not-so-dumb broad role is closer in some ways to Kanin's conception than Holliday's. Kanin wanted to play on opposites, requiring gangster Harry's moll to be a clean slate on which the not-so-smart journo (Johnson), hired by Harry to give her class, could write. Where Holliday was always too sophisticated a butterfly right from the off, Griffith's copycat performance starts dumb – but then never takes wing. WH

Borrowed Life, A (Duo-sang)

(1994, Tai, 165 min)
d Wu Nianzhen. *p* Wang Ying-Hsiang, Chou Chun-Yu, Jan Hung-Tze. *sc* Wu Nien-Jen. *ph* Liu Cheng-Chuan. *ed* Liao Ching-Song. *cast* Tsai Chen-Nan, Tsai Chiou-Feng, Fu Jun, Peng Wan-Chun.

●Taiwan's foremost scriptwriter turned director to make this sprawling and highly resonant autobiographical film. Spanning the years from his childhood in the 1950s to the present, it centres on his often difficult relationship with his father, a coal miner turned gold miner who considered himself Japanese rather than Chinese and never fulfilled his role as head of the family. Wu not only uses his own story as a yardstick for the social, cultural and economic changes Taiwan has seen over four decades, but offers an indelible picture of the mining community in which he grew up. Regrettably, the protracted closing scenes flirt with the clichés of melodrama. TR

Borrower, The

(1989, US, 97 min)
d John McNaughton. *p* RP Sekon, Steven A Jones. *sc* Mason Nage, Richard Fire. *ph* Julio Mercat, Robert C New. *ed* Elena Maganini. *pd* Robert Henderson. *m* Robert McNaughton, Ken Hale, Steven A Jones. *cast* Rae Dawn Chong, Don Gordon, Tom Towles, Antonio Fargas, Neil Giuntoli, Larry Pennell, Tony Amendola, Pam Gordon.

●McNaughton's second movie (following *Henry: Portrait of a Serial Killer*) is a low-budget sci-fi shocker about an Earth-bound, 'genetically devolved' alien whose modus operandi is not unlike the host-seeking creature in *The Hidden*, only messier. Instead of invading a human body, the mutating monster simply rips the head off some unsuspecting Earthling, squishes it down on its shoulders, and goes about its business. Meanwhile, smart-mouthed female cop Chong is chasing an escaped psycho, the two plot threads coming together when the killer and the headhunter meet up and form a gruesome, deadly composite. *Henry* it ain't, but this black comic gore fest has its moments, the best of which are reminiscent of Stuart Gordon's *Re-Animator*. NF

Borrowers, The

(1997, GB, 87 min)
d Peter Hewitt. *p* Tim Bevan, Eric Fellner, Rachel Talalay. *sc* Gavin Scott, John Kamps. *ph* John Fenner. *ed* David Freeman. *pd* Gemma Jackson. *m* Harry Gregson-Williams. *cast* John Goodman, Jim Broadbent, Mark Williams, Celia Imrie, Hugh Laurie, Ruby Wax, Flora Newbigin.

●The nice Lender family don't realise they have Borrowers nestling under the floorboards and living off domestic scraps. Digital technology brings the tiny folk of Mary Norton's children's books to life as never before. Scampering round the kitchen, Arietty Borrower (Newbigin) is almost locked in the freezer when the lure of ice-cream proves too strong. Mum and dad (Imrie and Broadbent, a terrific team) administer a scolding, but this little fracas is as nothing compared to the upheaval that's to follow. The Lenders' great aunt, owner of the house, has died, and since lawyer Ocious Potter (Goodman) can find no will, he's announced his intention to demolish the place. Exemplary entertainment. TJ

Borsalino

(1970, Fr/It, 126 min)
d Jacques Deray. *p* Alain Delon. *sc* Jean-Claude Carriere, Claude Sautet, Jacques Deray, Jean Cau. *ph* Jean-Jacques Tarbes. *ed* Paul Cayatte. *ad* François de Lamothe. *m* Claude Bolling. *cast* Jean-Paul Belmondo, Alain Delon, Michel Bouquet, Catherine Rouvel, Corinne Marchand, Françoise Christophe, Julien Guiomar.

●Competent but stereotypical performances from the two stars as small-time hoodlums working their way up in the Marseilles underworld of the '30s. Fairly basic as a gangster pastiche, despite its nods to Hawks, Melville, et al; but not unenjoyable thanks to its loudly stressed period detail and Claude Bolling's jolly score for mechanical piano. TM

Borsalino & Co (Blood on the Streets)

(1974, Fr/It/WGer, 91 min)
d Jacques Deray. *p* Alain Delon. *sc* Pascal Jardin. *ph* Jean-Jacques Tarbes. *ed* Henri Lanoe. *ad* François de Lamothe. *m* Claude Bolling. *cast* Alain Delon, Catherine Rouvel, Riccardo Cucciolla, Reinhardt Kolldehoff, Daniel Ivernel, André Falcon.

●Produced by Delon primarily, it seems, as a showcase for himself (his wardrobe is prodigious), this takes up the story of the underworld struggle for the supremacy of Marseilles in the '30s where the immeasurably superior *Borsalino* left off. Delon's brutality is presented as somehow less reprehensible than that of Mafia capo Cucciolla (who aims to promote Fascism through heroin) because he is sustained by the love of Rouvel's golden-hearted tart (the violins are almost audible). Delon's overblown reprise of Gene Hackman's drug addiction in *French Connection II* effectively tips the movie into the realm of hackneyed but not altogether unenjoyable fantasy. JPy

Bosna!

(1994, Fr, 117 min)
d Bernard-Henri Lévy, Alain Ferrari. *sc* Bernard-Henri Lévy, Gilles Hertzog. *ph* Pierre Boffety. *ed* Frédéric Lossignol, Yann Kassile. *m* Denis Barbier, Raoul Breton.

●This two-hour essay-reportage goes behind Bosnian lines to show horrors and hear testimonies that will never reach the TV news; it makes incisive use of archive footage to back up its argument. In the future, the directors assert, no one will be able to plead ignorance as happened with the Holocaust. Bernard-Henri Lévy is a writer, philosopher and art critic, and his voice-over narration is prone to a rhetorical excess that can only be described as 'very French'. But the accuracy – and urgency – of his polemic is undeniable. The Bosnians are fighting fascism, their own localised version of the Spanish Civil War or WWII, against empire-building, book-burning neo-Hitlers named Milosevic and Karadzic. Pitched somewhere between Orwell and Robert Fisk, *Bosna!* is cultured, humane and carefully reasoned – but above all angry. TR

Boss Nigger (aka The Black Bounty Killer)

(1974, US, 92 min)
d Jack Arnold. *p* Jack Arnold, Fred Williamson. *sc* Fred Williamson. *ph* Bob Caramico. *ed* Gene Ruggiero, Eva Ruggiero. *pd* Design Consultants. *m* Leon Moore, Tom Nixon. *cast* Fred Williamson, D'Urville Martin, RG Armstrong, William Smith, Carmen Hayworth, Barbara Leigh.

●Williamson parodies his own star image from numerous violent black movies in this cod Western which he wrote for his own production company. Bounty hunter Williamson, self-appointed sheriff of terrorised San Miguel, having outsmarted the cowardly white mayor and extricated himself from romance with an orphaned black girl and a nubile Boston schoolmarm, despatches villainous William Smith with a sawn-off rifle. Cobbled together as though made for TV, this is an entertaining mix of clichéd lines delivered straightfaced and an invigorating dose of old-fashioned bloodless violence. Despite moments of glutinous sentimentality, an interesting and intermittently amusing black picture. JPy

Bossu, Le (On Guard!)

(1997, Fr/It/Ger, 129 min)
d Philippe de Broca. *p* Patrick Godeau. *sc* Philippe de Broca. Jean Cosmos, Jérôme Tonnere. *ph* Jean-François Robin. *ed* Henri Lanoë. *ad* Bernard Vézat. *m* Philippe Sarde. *cast* Daniel Auteuil, Fabrice Luchini, Vincent Perez, Marie Gillain, Yann Collette, Jean-François Stévenin, Philippe Noiret.

●France, 1699. Count Gonzague (Luchini) stands to inherit a fortune from his cousin, the Duc de Nevers (Perez), but not if the dashing duke produces an heir before Gonzague can bump him off. Lagardère (Auteuil), a promising young swordsman, is paid to do the dirty deed, but instead wins the Duke's trust when he warns him of a cowardly ambush. The pair then set off from Paris to provincial Caylus, where a one-night stand has given Nevers a child by the daughter of a local nobleman. A wedding beckons, but not before Gonzague unleashes his worst, leaving Lagardère holding the baby, and swearing vengeance on those who sought to bloody such a happy day. This is a swashbuckler in the classic mode, and rather good at that. De Broca displays a veteran's assurance in knowing that too much tongue-in-cheek irony would devalue the cut and thrust of a traditional well turned plot. Luchini makes an exquisite villain, Perez a delightful none too bright aristo, and the reliably wonderful Auteuil simply eats up costume changes, romantic longing and breathtaking swordplay alike – all played absolutely straight. TJ

Bostonians, The

(1984, GB, 122 min)
d James Ivory. *p* Ismail Merchant. *sc* Ruth Prawer Jhabvala. *ph* Walter Lassally. *ed* Katherine Wenning, Mark Potter. *pd* Leo Austin. *m* Richard Robbins. *cast* Christopher Reeve, Vanessa Redgrave, Madeleine Potter, Jessica Tandy, Nancy Marchand, Wesley Addy, Linda Hunt.

●Ruth Prawer Jhabvala's finely honed script cuts through both Henry James' cynicism and the dense jungle of his prose to reveal a story of unexpected passion, a love triangle set against the early stirrings of the suffragette movement in late 19th century Boston. The core of the film is the battle between shy, intense proto-feminist and struggling, reactionary lawyer for the love, and allegiance, of a young girl who also happens to be a formidably gifted orator. At times too decorous, too slow for its own good, it is given guts by intense, acutely observed performances from Reeve and Redgrave. RR

Boston Kickout

(1995, GB, 110 min)
d Paul Hills. *p* Paul Hills, Tedi De Toledo. *sc* Paul Hills, Diane Whitley, Roberto Troni. *ph* Roger Bonnici. *ed* Melanie Adams. *pd* Simon Elliott. *m* Robert Hartshorne. *cast* John Simm, Emer McCourt, Marc Warren, Nathan Valente, Derek Martin, Richard Hanson.

●For disillusioned teenager Phil (Simm) and his three closest pals, 'coming of age' in Stevenage in the late '70s is no picnic. New Town utopianism has given way to an alienated reality of unemployment, violence, crime, alcoholism and drug abuse. The performances are heartfelt, if a little uneven, with Valente's skinhead nutter threatening to steal the show. Shrewdly observed, full of incident and unafraid of emotion. NF

Boston Strangler, The

(1968, US, 120 min)
d Richard Fleischer. *p* Robert Fryer. *sc* Edward Anhalt. *ph* Richard H Kline. *ed* Marion Rothman. *ad* Jack Martin Smith, Richard Day. *m* Lionel Newman. *cast* Tony Curtis, Henry Fonda, George Kennedy, Mike Kellin, Hurd Hatfield, Murray Hamilton, Jeff Corey, Sally Kellerman.

●A nasty case of multiple schizophrenia. Not only are the images tiresomely fragmented by the then fashionable split-screen technique, but the character of Albert DeSalvo, self-confessed perpetrator of 11 stranglings, has been tailored into a straightforward case of split personality, so that we may weep sympathetically as we watch a happy family man being gradually forced to face the crimes committed by his other self without his conscious knowledge. Curtis gives a careful performance, but can breathe little life into this expurgated cliché. Boston in panic (split-screen images of old ladies gossiping on one side of the screen while a corpse awaits detection on the other) is not exactly compulsive. And the interrogation scenes are interminable. Nice stuff around the middle, though, when the stones turned over by the police during their investigations reveal a fine collection of pallid, squirming perverts. TM

Botany Bay

(1952, US, 94 min)
d John Farrow. *p* Joseph Sistrom. *sc* Jonathan Latimer. *ph* John F Seitz. *ed* Alma Macrorie. *ad* Hal Pereira, Joseph McMillan Johnson. *m* Franz Waxman. *cast* Alan Ladd, James Mason, Patricia Medina, Cedric Hardwicke, Jonathan Harris, Murray Matheson, Malcolm Lee Beggs.
●Floggings and keelhaulings as Ladd, a medical student condemned to transportation on the first British convict ship bound for Australia in 1787, suffers stoically while Mason's captain sneers sadistically and Medina hovers prettily. Even dumber when Australia is reached, aborigines attack, and plague breaks out. Farrow and Ladd, with Howard da Silva in the Mason role, had already tackled a similar yarn much more creditably with *Two Years Before the Mast.* TM

Both Sides of the Street (La Contre-allée)

(1991, Fr, 83 min)
d/sc Isabel Sébastian. *p* Chantal Perrin. *sc* Isabel Sébastian, Jean-Paul Lilienfeld, Alan David. *ph* Willy Kurant. *ed* Raymonde Guyot. *ad* Claude Lenoir. *m* Didier Vasseur. *cast* Caroline Cellier, Jennifer Covillault, Jacqueline Maillan, Jacques Perrin, Massim Ghini.
●Lilas and Marie are the unlikeliest of friends – one a prostitute, the other a young virgin – but their relationship prompts Lilas' discovery of maternal urges, while Marie learns to embrace her sexuality. Meanwhile, playboy Pierre is on hand to offer advice to his young friend. Writer/director Sébastian tones down sensationalism, but she also strips the film of credibility; some sequences prove titillating, and the characters remain woefully two-dimensional. Superficial and unaffecting. CM

Bottle Rocket

(1996, US, 91 min)
d Wes Anderson. *p* Polly Platt, Cynthia Hargrave. *sc* Owen C. Wilson, Wes Anderson. *ph* Robert Yeoman. *ed* David Moritz. *pd* David Wasco. *m* Mark Mothersbaugh. *cast* Owen C. Wilson, Luke Wilson, Robert Musgrave, Lumi Cavazos, James Caan.
●Less idiosyncratic than *Rushmore*, Anderson's debut is none the less offbeat enough to defy easy analysis. Three friends, already old enough to have started growing apart, team up to indulge the flakey Dignan (Owen Wilson) in his fantasy of pulling off a major heist. The other two are Anthony (Luke Wilson), just recovering from a breakdown, and the interestingly named Bob Mapplethorpe (Musgrave), a rich kid desperate to escape from domination by his macho brother. The plot throws several curveballs (such as Anthony falling charmingly in love with a Latina motel worker), but the core of the film is the strength/fragility of the central friendships, bounded by motifs of sanity and craziness, imprisonment and escape. Caan does a funny cameo as the local crimelord but the film belongs to Anderson's co-conspirator Wilson, whose wired performance leaps off the screen. TR

Boucher, Le (The Butcher)

(1970, Fr/It, 94 min)
d Claude Chabrol. *p* André Génoves. *sc* Claude Chabrol. *ph* Jean Rabier. *ed* Jacques Gaillard. *ad* Guy Littaye. *m* Pierre Jansen. *cast* Stéphane Audran, Jean Yanne, Antonio Passalia, Mario Beccaria, Pasquale Ferone, Roger Rudel.
●Classically simple but relentlessly probing thriller, set in a French village shadowed by the presence of a compulsive killer. Some lovely Hitchcockian games, like the strange ketchup that drips onto a picnic hamburger from a clifftop where the latest victim has been claimed. But also more secretive pointers to social circumstance and the 'exchange of guilt' as Audran's starchy schoolmistress finds herself irresistibly drawn to the ex-army butcher she suspects of being the killer: the fact, for instance, that alongside the killer as he keeps vigil outside the schoolhouse, a war memorial stands sentinel with its reminder of society's dead and maimed. With this film Chabrol came full circle back to his first, echoing not only the minutely detailed provincial landscape of *Le Beau Serge* but its theme of redemption. The impasse here, a strangely moving tragedy, is that there is no way for the terrified teacher, bred to civilised restraints, to understand that her primeval butcher may have been reclaimed by his love for her. TM

Boudu Sauvé des Eaux (Boudu Saved from Drowning)

(1932, Fr, 87 min b/w)
d Jean Renoir. *p* Michel Simon. *sc* Jean Renoir, Albert Valentin. *ph* [Georges] Asselin. *ed* Suzanne de Troeye. *ad* [Hugues] Laurent, [Jean Castanier]. *cast* Michel Simon, Charles Granval, Marcelle Hainia, Sévérine Lerczinska, Jean Dasté, Max Dalban, Jacques Becker.
●Boudu, a scrofulous, anarchic tramp, is saved from a watery suicide by the well-intentioned but irredeemably bourgeois bookseller Lestingois, and repays his favour by becoming the most morally, socially, sexually and philosophically disruptive house-guest of all time. Renoir's most Buñuelesque movie remains as fresh and 'scandalous' as it must have been in 1932, a delicious clash of manners between the unregenerate tramp with bizarre principles of his own and the ultra-proper middle class household where the principles are showing signs of tarnish. Michel Simon's outrageous performance as Boudu, and Renoir's 'liberated' location camerawork are still wholly seductive. TR

Boulangère de Monceau, La

(1962, Fr, 26 min)
d Eric Rohmer. *p* Barbet Schroeder. *sc* Eric Rohmer. *ph* Jean-Michel Meurice, Bruno Barbey. *ed* Eric Rohmer. *cast* Barbet Schroeder, Michèle Girardon, Claudine Soubrier, Michel Mardore.
●Before he shot any of them, Rohmer announced the titles of his 'Six Moral Tales', the series that would occupy him for the next decade and make the French critic and academic an international name as a writer/director. Shot in 16mm and never released theatrically, this fledgling effort (though Rohmer had already made his first feature *Le Signe du Lion* in 1959) is narrated by Bertrand Tavernier and follows the fortunes of a student, Barbet Schroeder, who returns each day to the spot where he fell in love with a girl he met in the street. On the way though, there's a bakery where he stops for his daily cakes, and a very alluring young lady behind the counter. TJ

Boule de Suif

(1945, Fr, 102 min, b/w)
d Christian-Jacque. *sc* Louis d'Hée, Henri Jeanson, Christian-Jacque. *ph* Christian Matras. *ed* Jacques Desagneaux. *ad* Léon Barsacq. *m* Marius-Paul Huillot. *cast* Micheline Presle, Louis Salou, Alfred Adam, Jean Brochard, Berthe Bovy, Roger Karl.
●'We've been betrayed,' snarls the bedraggled soldier, arriving with news of Sedan and the surrender of the Prussians. But for 1870, read 1940. This was hustled into production after the Liberation and while the war was still in progress, an instant response to the trauma of defeat and occupation. Two de Maupassant stories are harnessed together for an account of a coach journey across a landscape dominated by fear, compromise and humiliation. With its not very hidden agenda the film can only elicit concern for its characters as representative types rather than individuals. But the moral climax is exemplary, with plucky hooker Presle spitting on a Prussian cur – no genteel miming of the act, either, but a great messy oyster, delivered full face. You can even now sense the straining towards catharsis, and if the film's first audiences were still capable of cheering, then cheer they probably did. BBa

Boulevard Nights

(1979, US, 102 min)
d Michael Pressman. *p* Bill Benenson. *sc* Desmond Nakano. *ph* John Bailey. *ed* Richard Halsey. *pd* Jackson De Govia. *m* Lalo Schifrin. *cast* Richard Yniguez, Danny de la Paz, Marta Dubois, James Victor, Betty Carvalho, Carmen Zapata, Victor Millan.
●An unexceptional cocktail of traditional underdog ingredients: gangland rivalry, James Dean-type angst, and some simplistic social comment – poverty Mexican-American style, where the only entertainment comes from cruising custom cars and protecting territorial rights. The downtrodden side of LA is well shot, and Danny de la Paz is excellent as the non-conforming youngster. But that's not enough to save the film or provide it with an identity of its own.

Bounce

(2000, US, 106 min)
d Don Roos. *p* Steve Golin, Michael Besman. *sc* Don Roos. *ph* Robert Elswit. *ed* David Codron. *pd* David Wasco. *m* Mychael Danna. *cast* Ben Affleck, Gwyneth Paltrow, Joe Morton, Natasha Henstridge, Tony Goldwyn, Johnny Galecki, David Paymer, Alex D Linz, Jennifer Grey.
●Roos' follow-up to his sassy, sardonic *The Opposite of Sex* substitutes a heartfelt sentiment for casual sarcasm. Paltrow is a vulnerable, widowed mother and Affleck a slick, womanising ad company exec. The twist is that, following a chance pre-Christmas meeting at a snowbound airport, Affleck gives Paltrow's husband his ticket and enjoys a 'lay-over' with Henstridge; but the plane crashes, making him indirectly responsible for her loss. A year later, he emerges from alcoholic rehab with a bad case of survivor's guilt and a need to make amends. Things get complicated when he and Paltrow, who doesn't know about the ticket switch, fall for one another. The air of contrivance inherent in this set-up is initially kept at bay by the sombre tone, the sincere performances, and Roos' instinct for finding the emotional heart of individual scenes. Luminous as ever, Paltrow quivers with emotion, her panicky fear of intimacy and concern for her children contrasting starkly with Affleck's ambiguous, guarded opportunism. But while it's easy to believe Affleck as the confident guy who closes every deal, he's too lightweight and likeable to pull off the more complex, contradictory aspects of his character's transition. NF

Bound

(1996, US, 109 min)
d Andy Wachowski, Larry Wachowski. *p* Andrew Lazar, Stuart Boros. *sc* Andy Wachowski, Larry Wachowski. *ph* Bill Pope. *ed* Zach Staenberg. *pd* Eve Cauley. *m* Don Davis. *cast* Jennifer Tilly, Gina Gershon, Joe Pantoliano, John P Ryan, Christopher Meloni, Richard C Sarafian.
●Chicago: when hood's moll Violet (Tilly) and ex-con Corky (Gershon) size each other up across a corridor, things soon get plenty biblical. They're made up, they've made out, and now Violet wants to make off with Corky and $2m that hubby's laundering for his boss. Lusty lesbian leads, looting lots of lolly! One of the most blatantly calculated, artistically bankrupt Hollywood calling-cards in ages, this by-the-numbers neo-*noir* has one gimmick – dyke desire – and no ideas. Circumstantial evidence against the Wachowskis points to fraternal band-wagoning, deliberate marketing to both icon-starved lesbian audiences and the dirty-mac brigade, and cynical courting of lascivious media hype. NB

Bound and Gagged: A Love Story

(1992, US, 94 min)
d Daniel B Appleby. *p* Dennis Mahoney. *sc* Daniel B Appleby. *ph* Dean Lent. *ed* Kaye Davis. *pd* Dane Pizzuti Krogman. *m* William Murphy. *cast* Ginger Lynn Allen, Elizabeth Saltarrelli, Karen Black, Mary Ella Ross, Chris Denton, Chris Mulkey.
●A first feature less about sex than emotional baggage – the real ties that bind. Leslie (Allen) seeks refuge from brutal Steve (Mulkey) in the arms of another woman, Elizabeth (Saltarrelli). But Elizabeth also resorts to force. Helped by suicidal Cliff (Denton), she kidnaps Leslie after the latter refuses to divorce her husband. A black comic road movie and a rather paternalistic post-feminist parable, this might have worked better with a more consistent tone. Director Appleby is uncomfortable with stereotypes, and Denton's running suicide-gag is misjudged. On the other hand, the tug-of-love between the besotted, powerful Elizabeth and the weak, resistant Leslie is more confidently handled – with both actresses making the most of meaty roles. TCh

Bound by Honor (aka Blood In Blood Out)

(1993, US, 180 min)
d Taylor Hackford. *p* Taylor Hackford, Jerry Gershwin. *sc* Jimmy Santiago Baca, Jeremy Iacone, Floyd Mutrux. *ph* Gabriel Beristain. *ed* Frederic Steinkamp, Karl F Steinkamp. *pd*

Bruno Rudeo. *m* Bill Conti. *cast* Damian Chapa, Jesse Borrego, Benjamin Bratt, Enrique Castillo, Victor Rivers, Delroy Rivers.
●Few films justify three-hour running times, and, despite solid performances, this epic tale of a Chicano sub-culture isn't one of them. Certainly, there are moments of powerful physical and emotional violence as half-caste hero Miklo (Chapa) attempts to consolidate his gangland heritage. Convicted of a shooting, Miklo rises to prominence within prison walls, while his former accomplices on the outside turn variously to drug abuse and law enforcement. What bond can remain between the blood brothers when circumstances divide them so dramatically? Clearly a labour of love for director Hackford, the film oozes integrity and is heavy with the stench of an authentic milieu; but forceful set-pieces and astute cultural observations are lost amid a sea of confusing (and eventually dull) stand-offs between warring gangs. MK

Bound for Glory

(1976, US, 148 min)
d Hal Ashby. *p* Robert F Blumofe, Harold Leventhal. *sc* Robert Getchell. *ph* Haskell Wexler. *ed* Robert C Jones, Pembroke J Herring. *pd* Michael Haller. *m* Leonard Rosenman. *cast* David Carradine, Ronny Cox, Melinda Dillon, Gail Strickland, John Lehne, Randy Quaid.
●Ashby forsakes the bleak satire of *The Last Detail* and *Shampoo* for an overlong, sentimental and lifeless biopic of Woody Guthrie. The film glosses the legendary folksinger-cum-hobo into a beatific eccentric who mimics the actions of others more than forges a radical lifestyle. Within these confines, Carradine's studious underplaying is impressive, and Haskell Wexler's Oscar-winning photography evokes a lyrical sense of atmosphere and location. IB

Bounty, The

(1984, GB, 133 min)
d Roger Donaldson. *p* Bernard Williams. *sc* Robert Bolt. *ph* Arthur Ibbetson. *ed* Tony Lawson. *pd* John Graysmark. *m* Vangelis. *cast* Mel Gibson, Anthony Hopkins, Laurence Olivier, Edward Fox, Daniel Day-Lewis, Bernard Hill, Philip Davis, Liam Neeson.
●Definitely not a remake of the MGM classic, but a Robert Bolt-scripted meditation on the conflict between Bligh's puritanism and Christian's surrender to Polynesian paganism. The floggings and sadism are thus kept to a minimum, with Hopkins' Bligh emerging less as a hissable villain than as a credibly sympathetic but flawed character. It's all a brave try, though Gibson is perhaps not up to the demands of a Christian's progress from naive rating to self-loathing exile, and Donaldson's direction often verges on the stolid. GA

Bowery, The

(1933, US, 90 min, b/w)
d Raoul Walsh. *sc* Howard Estabrook, James Gleason. *ph* Barney McGill. *ed* Allen McNeil. *ad* Richard Day. *m* Alfred Newman. *cast* Wallace Beery, George Raft, Jackie Cooper, Fay Wray, Pert Kelton, Herman Bing, George Walsh, Esther Muir, Lillian Harmer.
●A cheerfully colourful portrayal of New York City low-life during the 1880s (or Gay Nineties, as a title declares), not long on historical accuracy, despite token appearances by John L Sullivan (Walsh) and Carrie Nation (Harmer), and a reconstruction of Steve Brodie's famous jump off the Brooklyn Bridge for a bet in 1888. Basically, it's a sentimentally rumbustious buddy movie in which gambler Brodie (Raft) and saloon-owner Chuck Connors (Beery) indulge in furious rivalry for the title of 'King of the Bowery', as well as for the affections of pretty Lucy Calhoun (Wray) and a pouting streetwise moppet (Cooper). It's entertaining enough in its raucous way, but marred by a complacently racist attitude to the Chinese community. TM

Bowery to Broadway

(1944, US, 94 min, b/w)
d Charles Lamont. *p* John Grant. *sc* Edmund Joseph, Bart Lytton, Arthur T Horman. *ph* Charles van Enger. *ed* Arthur Hilton. *ad* John B Goodman, Martin Obzina. *m* Edward Ward. *cast* Jack Oakie, Donald Cook, Maria Montez, Susanna Foster, Turhan Bey, Louise Albritton, Ann Blyth.
●Patchy (and worse) musical set in the naughty nineties, with Oakie and Cook as rival impresarios climbing from beergarden to Broadway. Montez is awful as an exotic European star, Foster not much better doing her operetta bit. But the period numbers are bright, and there is one delightful song-and-dance routine from Donald O'Connor and Peggy Ryan. TM

Bowfinger

(1999, US, 97 min)
d Frank Oz. *p* Brian Grazer. *sc* Steve Martin. *ph* Ueli Steiger. *ed* Richard Pearson. *pd* Jackson DeGovia. *m* David Newman. *cast* Steve Martin, Eddie Murphy, Heather Graham, Christine Baranski, Jamie Kennedy, Barry Newman, Adam Alexi-Malle, Kohl Sudduth, Terence Stamp, Robert Downey Jr.
●Martin reminds us why he was once considered the funniest white man in America with this silly, savvy satire on Hollywood's lunatic fringe. He's Bobby Bowfinger, a producer/director with no credits and no credit. Even the self-deluded BB knows it's now or never time when his accountant gifts him a screenplay, the alien invasion story 'Chubby Rain'. Bobby rounds up the best cast and crew $2,100 can buy, and convinces them he's landed action superstar Kit Ramsey (Murphy) for the lead. His conceit has an oblivious Ramsey re-acting for hidden cameras in a *vérité* action movie. '*Cinéma nouveau*', Bobby calls it. Directed by Frank Oz from Martin's own laugh out loud script, this endows showbiz stereotypes with a hardbitten narcissism that doesn't preclude a certain innocence. The supporting turns are generous by any standards, with Murphy near his best (he doubles as his own stand-in), and Graham having a ball as the world's worst actress. Preposterous and utterly self-absorbed, this has la-la land down to a tee. TCh

Bowling for Columbine

(2002, US, 120 min)
d Michael Moore. *p* Charles Bishop, Michael Donovan. *ph* Brian Danitz, Michael McDonough. *m* Jeff Gibbs.
●In which Moore, in the aftermath of both the 1999 massacre at Columbine High School, and 11 Sept 2002, asks what it is that makes the US so prone to violent killings. While laying much of the blame on the country's self-defeating gun laws and pillorying the National Rifle Association in general and its mouthpiece Charlton Heston in particular, he acknowledges that there's more to the issue than that, and asks, for example, why other at least superficially similar countries, notably Canada, don't suffer/produce Columbine-style catastrophes. The free-wheeling argument gets lost here and there, and there's no denying either the self-aggrandising or the over-simplifying aspects of Moore's muck-raking methods. But overall his argument is pretty persuasive and, of course, often hilariously delivered. GA

Boxcar Bertha

(1972, US, 88§ min)
d Martin Scorsese. *p* Roger Corman. *sc* Joyce H Corrington, John William Corrington. *ph* John M Stephens. *ed* Buzz Feitshans. *m* Gib Guilbeau, Thad Maxwell. *cast* Barbara Hershey, David Carradine, Barry Primus, Bernie Casey, John Carradine.
●Superior formula stuff, injected with a rare degree of life by enthusiastic direction that occasionally tries for virtuosity and succeeds, and by a neat performance from Hershey that avoids the yawning traps in the script (built-in sex sequences, the she-loved-her-man theme in general). She plays Bertha, the Arkansas farm girl who hits the road, with the right degree of matter-of-factness and a lot of humour. The film traces the alienation of Bertha, a trade unionist she meets, a black friend of his, and a small-time Yankee conman – slipping into crime, stealing from the railroad bosses, and sending part of the haul back to the railway union. Produced by Cormans Roger and Julie, from the memoirs of the real Bertha Thompson. VG

Boxer, The

(1977, Jap, 94 min)
d Shuji Terayama. *p* Yoshihiro Kojima. *sc* Shiro Ishimori, Masao Kishida, Shuji Terayama. *ph* Tatsuo Suzuki. *ed* Fumio Soda. *ad* Tadayuki Kuwana. *m* JA Seazer. *cast* Kentaro Shimizu, Bunta Sugawara, Masumi Harukawa, Yoko Natsuki, Keiko Niitaka, Yoko Ran.
●Terayama has here brilliantly fused the elements of his previous film and theatre work – surrealism, a sense of the essential anarchy of relationships, and a flair for startling and beautiful images – with a compulsively exciting Hollywood-style narrative about a young man's relentless ambition to be a champion boxer. The film synthesises these seemingly disparate approaches while allowing them separate existences, and through this evokes not only a poetic vision of modern industrial Tokyo and the fading dreams of the city's losers, but also a tense and realistic portrayal of the sheer brutality of the world of boxing, in its inexorable attraction and its heroic despair. SM

Boxer, The

(1997, Ire/GB/US, 114 min)
d Jim Sheridan. *p* Jim Sheridan, Arthur Lappin. *sc* Jim Sheridan, Terry George. *ph* Chris Menges. *ed* Gerry Hambling, Clive Barrett. *pd* Brian Morris. *m* Gavin Friday, Maurice Seezer. *cast* Daniel Day-Lewis, Emily Watson, Brian Cox, Ken Stott, Gerard McSorley, Eleanor Methven, Ciaran Fitzgerald.
●Danny Flynn (Day-Lewis) returns to Belfast after 14 years in prison for IRA activity. He's an outcast, castigated by a former boxing colleague Ike (Stott) for having wasted his talents; by old flame Maggie (Watson), now married to a jailed terrorist, for the ruin of their relationship; and by Republican militants for having renounced violence outside the ring. Despite the disapproval of Maggie's son and father (Cox), a peace-seeking Republican leader who views the resumption of their affair as personally and politically dangerous, Danny and Maggie find themselves drawn together again. Moreover, Danny teams with Ike to set up a gym where training and bouts ignore the sectarian divide. But even love and the most modest projects can fall foul of ingrained prejudice. This may not offer a hugely original take on the Troubles, but it does deliver dramatically. Day-Lewis, taciturn and strong-willed, is as persuasive as ever, while Stott and Cox offer strong support. While Sheridan (who co-wrote) weighs in with gutsy, gritty direction, shooting the fight scenes with panache and cutting sharply throughout for suspense and pace. Politically, too, it's sensitive and sensible. GA

Boxing Helena

(1993, US, 105 min)
d Jennifer Chambers Lynch. *p* Philippe Caland, Carl Mazzocone. *sc* Jennifer Chambers Lynch. *ph* Frank Byers. *ed* David Finfer. *m* Graeme Revell. *cast* Julian Sands, Sherilyn Fenn, Art Garfunkel, Bill Paxton, Kurtwood Smith.
●Fenn is the free-spirited Helena, unfortunate object of surgeon Sands' sexual obsession. His courtship only invites scorn – but, when Helena is hit by a car outside his family mansion, the doc sees a chance to cut her down to size. Lynch in her first stab at directing tries for the black-comic, blue velvet knife-edge between surrealism and perversity, but the results – neither graphic, nor gruesome – are simply incongruous. Grotesquely misconceived. TCh

Box of Moon Light

(1996, US, 112 min)
d Tom DiCillo. *p* Macus Viscidi, Thomas A Bliss. *sc* Tom DiCillo. *ph* Paul Ryan. *ed* Camilla Toniolo. *pd* Thérèse DePrez. *m* Jim Farmer. *cast* John Turturro, Sam Rockwell, Catherine Keener, Lisa Blount, Annie Corley, Rica Martens.
●After DiCillo's delicious *Living in Oblivion*, this comes as a disappointment. Turturro's on form as the straitlaced, clock-watching, by-the-book construction foreman who cracks up when a job is cancelled and goes looking for a happy-holiday lake from his youth. Fair enough, but when he falls in with Rockwell, a half-crazed hippy kid into self-sufficient country life and irresponsible behaviour, you know Turturro's in for a trite lesson in living. Not as funny, deep or original as it would like to be, although things pick up with yet another fine turn from Catherine Keener. GA

Boy (Shonen)

(1969, Jap, 97 min)
d Nagisa Oshima. *p* Masayuki Nakajima, Takuji Yamaguchi. *sc* Tsutomu Tamura. *ph* Tashuhiro Yoshioka, Seizo Sengen. *ed* Sueko

Shiraishi. *ad* Jusho Toda. *m* Hikaru Hayashi. *cast* Tetsue Abe, Fumio Watanabe, Akiko Koyama, Tsuyoshi Kinoshita.
●It came from a Japanese newspaper story: a down-and-out family were making their young son fake road accidents in order to blackmail motorists for 'hospital fees'. Oshima starts from character studies of the members of the family as outsiders in Japanese society: the lazy, facilely embittered father, the tackily glamorous mother longing for her stepson's love, the 10-year-old boy hopelessly confused about his role as the family breadwinner. With characteristic tender roughness, Oshima then develops this extraordinary story into an open-ended question about the truth of appearances, centering on the boy's own fantasies about his sci-fi hero. A key film in the struggle for a modern, political cinema. TR

Boy and Bicycle

(1965, GB, 28 min, b/w)
d/p/sc/ph/ed Ridley Scott. *m* John Baker, John Barry. *cast* Tony Scott.
●A schoolboy puts in a hard day's truanting, cycling around photogenic town and seafront locations in County Durham, while musing, stream of consciousness style, on everything from time (Will I remember today when I'm 80?) to the significance of the dead lion on the Tate & Lyle Syrup label. Shot in 1961, post-produced by the BFI Experimental Film Fund and presented under their auspices, it's imaginative, unpretentious, fluent and professional, and just a little thin: Scott beginning as he meant to go on. Young Tony, on this evidence, could have had a decent career as an actor. BBa

Boy and His Dog, A

(1974, US, 89 min)
d LQ Jones. *p* Alvy Moore. *sc* LQ Jones. *ph* John Arthur Morrill. *ed* Scott Conrad. *pd* Ray Boyle. *m* Tim McIntire. *cast* Don Johnson, Susanne Benton, Jason Robards, Alvy Moore, Helene Winston, Charles McGraw.
●Based on Harlan Ellison's novella, this covers familiar territory – vigorously and imaginatively – as feuding clans of scavengers prowl the desolate American landscape left by a nuclear holocaust. What lifts things right out of the rut is the cynical commentary provided by the hero's dog, communicating telepathically (in voice-off admirably spoken by Tim McIntire) and kicking the daylights out of all those boy-and-his-dog yarns (canine values win out, for example, when with barely a qualm the hero consigns his girl to serve as dogfood). The second half, venturing underground to find Middle America miraculously preserved but rapidly dying, is less good. Jones' debut as a director nevertheless has a distinctive tang, as affably unprincipled as the series of villains he played for Sam Peckinpah. TM

Boy Called Charlie Brown, A

see Boy Named Charlie Brown, A

Boy Called Hate, A

(1995, US, 95 min)
d Mitch Marcus. *p* Steve Nicolaides. *ph* Paul Holahan. *ed* Michael Ruscio. *pd* Caryn Marcus. *m* Pray For Rain. *cast* Scott Caan, Missy Crider, James Caan, Adam Beach, Elliott Gould.
●Extravagantly praised in some quarters ('there haven't been many better US studies in adolescent ennui since Jonathan Kaplan's equally uncompromising *Over the Edge*,' according to *Sight and Sound*), this direct-to-video debut isn't worth getting too worked up about. The very familiar tale has Caan Jr as a misunderstood kid who takes off through the Midwest with a tearaway gal (Crider) after putting a bullet in the man who was attacking her. It's photographed with some élan, but Marcus's own script is mired in cliché, to the point where our runaways are inducted in Native American lore by a wild Indian (Beach) who seems to have strayed from the Oliver Stone reservation. Scott Caan is a bit of a pudding, but at least Crider gives good attitude. TCh

Boy Called Third Base, A (Third)

(1978, Jap, 102 min)
d Yoichi Higashi. *p* Katsuhiro Maeda. *sc* Shuji Terayama. *ph* Koichi Kawakami. *ed* Keiko Ichihara. *ad* Ikuro Ayabe. *m* Michi Tanaka. *cast* Toshiyuki Nagashima, Tsuguaki Yoshida, Aiko Morishita, Akiko Shikata, Takeshi Wakamatsu, Yutaka Nemoto.
●This borstal-boy movie, so different from our own dear *Scum*, contains little violence and less sociology; it subsumes all the usual puberty blues stuff into an exceptionally moving account of one boy learning the hard way that it's best to 'run at your own pace' – a daring leap into individualism for Japan in the late 1970s. The key name on the credits is Terayama, who not only adapted Haku Kenju's novel but also provided much of the cast and several of the crew from his theatre company Tenjo-sajiki. A lot of the themes are pure Terayama too: confinement as the door to fantasy, an obsession with flying, the kid nicknamed 'Mr Poetry' who writes *haiku* about borstal life. In his first major role as the baseball playing anti-hero, Nagashima registers strongly: a brooding, volatile presence. TR

Boy Friend, The

(1971, GB, 125 min)
d/p/sc Ken Russell. *ph* David Watkin. *ed* Michael Bradsell. *pd* Tony Walton. *m* Sandy Wilson. *cast* Twiggy, Christopher Gable, Barbara Windsor, Moyra Fraser, Bryan Pringle, Max Adrian, Catherine Wilmer, Vladek Sheybal, Tommy Tune, Glenda Jackson .
●Sandy Wilson's delightfully lightweight musical is given the unnecessary avoirdupois that seems unavoidable with Russell. Some things work beautifully: Tommy Tune's deliriously leggy Charleston, the bathing beauty inanities of 'Sur la Plage', almost everything Twiggy does as the wide-eyed ingenue. But there are also some bloated Busby Berkeley pastiches which clash horribly with Wilson's mock-'20s score. Consistency was never Russell's strong point. TM

Boyfriend School, The

see Don't Tell Her It's Me

Boyfriends

(1996, GB, 81 min)
d/p/sc Neil Hunter, Tom Hunsinger. *ph* Richard Tisdall. *ed* John Trumper. *ad* James Dearlove. *cast* James Dreyfus, Mark Sands, Andrew Ableson, Michael Urwin, David Coffey, Darren Petrucci, Michael McGrath, Russell Higgs.
●This low-budget first feature takes a wry look at the ideals, desires and neuroses of a bunch of mostly middle-class gay men who come together for a country weekend. Tetchy video documentarist Paul (Dreyfus) and passive Ben (Sands) have decided to end their five-year relationship; after just three months, romantic Matt (Urwin) reckons he's met Mr Right in Owen (Ableson), who's wary of the suggestion that they move in together; meanwhile, social-worker Will (Coffey) brings along young, working-class Adam (Petrucci), yet to succumb to emotional or sexual commitment. Attraction, betrayal, jealousy and misunderstanding run their course. The performances are on the whole convincing, while every so often the petty, ratty tensions, coupled with lines of acerbic wit, hint at a more complex scenario of genuine pain and confusion. GA

Boy from Mercury, The

(1996, GB/Fr/Ire, 87 min)
d Martin Duffy. *p* Marina Hughes. *sc* Martin Duffy. *ph* Seamus Deasy. *ed* John Victor Smith. *pd* Tom Conroy. *m* Stephen McKeon. *cast* Rita Tushingham,Tom Courtenay, Hugh O'Conor, James Hickey, Ian McElhinney.
●Writer/director Duffy's semi-autobiographical first feature breathes life into the rites-of-passage movie, mostly by respecting the scale and nature of childhood experience. Set in Dublin sometime between the Sputnik going up and Gagarin going round, it concerns an eight-year-old, James Cronin (Hickey), who becomes convinced that he and his dog are Mercurians with special powers. His doting mother (Tushingham) is as acquiescent as his brother and schoolmates are derisive: her forbearance is based on concern – and maybe guilt – following her husband's death. As the boy's delusions persist, uncle Tony (Courtenay), a gentle, almost foolish man wedded to his scooter, is called in. An opening quote from Terence Davies' *The Long Day Closes* proves an affectionate homage not a stylistic introduction. Thereafter Duffy settles down to his own narrative style: one of gradually beguiling understatement. The early '60s era of Bakelite and pinafores is unobtrusively caught by cinematographer Seamus Deasy. Courtenay's turn errs on the side of mannerism, but otherwise Hickey's unfussy playing has fine support. A sweetheart of a movie. WH

Boyhood Loves

see Amour d'enfance

Boy Is Ten Feet Tall, A

see Sammy Going South

Boy Meets Girl

(1938, US, 86 min, b/w)
d Lloyd Bacon. *p* Sam Bischoff. *sc* Bella Spewack, Samuel Spewack. *ph* Sol Polito. *ed* William Holmes. *ad* Esdras Hartley. *m* Leo Forbstein. *cast* James Cagney, Pat O'Brien, Marie Wilson, Ralph Bellamy, Frank McHugh, Dick Foran, Ronald Reagan.
●Not as sharp a satire on Hollywood as Kaufman and Hart's *Once in a Lifetime*, but a lively jibe all the same, with Cagney and O'Brien striking sparks off each other as the slap-happy screenwriters who decide to take their revenge on producer Bellamy and an arrogant cowboy star (Foran) by cooking up an ingenious, if unlikely, script for their next movie. Fast, funny and none too demanding. GA

Boy Meets Girl

(1984, Fr, 104 min, b/w)
d Léos Carax. *p* Patricia Moraz. *sc* Léos Carax. *ph* Jean-Yves Escoffier. *ed* Nelly Meunier, Francine Sandberg. *ad* Serge Marzolff, Jean Bauer. *m* Jacques Pinault. *cast* Denis Lavant, Mireille Perrier, Carroll Brooks, Elie Poicard, Maïté Nahyr, Christian Cloarec.
●Shy young Alex wanders the dark Parisian streets gazing in confusion at the passers-by. Meanwhile Mireille is being given the brush-off by her live-in lover. Eventually, their paths cross as if by destiny; in the meantime, numerous other loners have wandered in and out of Carax's meandering, moody narrative. Easy but unfair to fault Carax's first feature when he has conjured up a persuasively poetic atmosphere for his meditation on the failings of human intercourse. Credit must go to Jean-Yves Escoffier's astonishing black-and-white camerawork, and to the largely wordless, eloquent performances. Finally, however, the film's greatest coup is its creation of a Parisian purgatory of lost souls, bathed eternally in night. Absurd humour counteracts the morbid philosophising, while the alternately surreal and expressionist imagery is reminiscent of silent cinema at its most elegant. GA

Boy Named Charlie Brown, A (aka A Boy Called Charlie Brown)

(1969, US, 86 min)
d Bill Melendez. *p* Lee Mendelson, Bill Melendez. *sc* Charles M Schulz. *ph* Nick Vasu. *ed* Robert T Gillis. *pd* Bernard Gruver. *songs* Rod McKuen, Vince Guaraldi. *cast* voices: Peter Robbins, Pamelyn Ferdin, Glenn Gilger, Andy Pforsich, Sally Dryer, Anne Altieri.
●An animated feature derived from the cartoon strip. Very flat animation, occasionally carelessly painted, with the characters often 'out of tune' with the style of the background. Schulz's script maintains much of the irony of the strips, but the injections of whimsy put its appeal uneasily between adults and children. Snoopy has some beautiful moments, though.

Boy of Two Worlds

see Paw

Boys

(1995, US, 86 min)
d Stacy Cochran. *p* Peter Frankfurt, Paul Feldsher, Eric Huggins. *sc* Stacy Cochran. *ph* Robert Elswit. *ed* Camilla Toniolo. *pd* Dan Bishop. *m* Stewart Copeland. *cast* Winona Ryder, Lukas Haas, John C Reilly, James LeGros, Skeet Ulrich, Chris Cooper, Bill Sage.
●Scholarship student at an all-male boarding school, John Baker (Haas) is under pressure from his ambitious dad, but feels gnawing restlessness at the prospect of another term. But while he can't wait for his life to begin, dissolute twenty-something Patty Vare (Ryder) probably wishes she could rewind hers a little. It's the morning after

the night before, the police are at the door talking about a stolen car, and she may already have reached the wreckage stage herself. Horse-riding provides a few hours' distraction, but a fall leaves her prone on the ground and, soon, an unwitting, forbidden guest in John's dorm. From such circumstances springs a hesitant if unlikely attraction that fulfils a need in each, but which might take some explaining to the outside world. Writer/director Cochran is stronger on capturing the texture surrounding her characters' converging experiences than making much of it when they do get together. Most striking is the background detail at the boys' school, where the unfolding girl-in-the-room crisis hits a properly complex note of panic, excitement, embarrassment and yearning. TJ

Boys, The

(1998, Aust/GB, 85 min)
d Rowan Woods. *p* Robert Connolly, John Maynard. *sc* Stephen Sewell. *ph* Tristan Milani. *ed* Nick Meyers. *pd* Luigi Pittorino. *m* The Necks. *cast* David Wenham, Toni Collette, Lynette Curran, John Polson, Jeanette Cronin, Anthony Hayes, Anna Lise.
● Woods' brilliantly controlled feature debut is a fierce study of male violence, family loyalty and domestic imprisonment. Yet despite a Ken Loach-style attention to social context and non-judgmental observation, his dissection of the twisted psycho dynamics of an imploding 'white trash' family pushes beyond naturalism into a realm of forced hyper-realism. Fresh out of prison, sentimental psychopath Brett Sprague (Wenham) struggles to contain the seething resentments and external pressures that threaten to tear his family apart. In the course of one drink'n'drug-fuelled day, the fraught relationships between Brett, his downtrodden mother (Curran), his two brothers Glenn (Polson) and Stevie (Hayes), and his sullen girlfriend Michelle (Collette) reach breaking point; caught in the crossfire are Stevie's timid, pregnant girlfriend Nola (Lise) and Glenn's socially aspiring wife Jackie (Cronin). Trapped in a destructive cycle of social deprivation and self-exclusion, the brothers lash out, particularly at the women. Intercutting spiralling domestic madness with flashes forward to its consequences, this terrifying vision of social exclusion, male insecurity and frustrated rage builds inexorably to a controlled explosion of savagery. NF

Boy's Choir (Dokuritsu Shonen Gasshodan)

(1999, Jap, 130 min)
d Akira Ogata. *p* Takenori Sento. *sc* Kenji Aoki. *ph* Masami Inomoto. *ed* Shuichi Kakesu. *ad* Hidefumi Hanatani. *m* Shinichiro Ikebe. *cast* Atsushi Ito, Sora Toma, Tarayuki Kagawa, Ryoko Takizawa, Ken Mitsuishi, Kihachi Okamoto.
● The early 1970s. Shy and stuttering, Michio (Ito) is sent to a Catholic orphanage when his father dies and there befriends Yasuo (Toma), a boy soprano who draws him into the school choir. These volatile kids are pulled into political activism by a fateful encounter with the ex-lover of their choirmaster, a woman on the run from the police. There's something endearingly barmy about a project to trace the roots of an entire generation back to the '70s crazes for the Vienna Boys' Choir and leftie nihilism, and first-time director Ogata almost makes his thesis stick. But he's helped more by strong and committed performances from the two leads than by the script, which lurches from cliché (will his voice break before the concert?) to crude shock effects (severed limbs from a suicide bomber rain down). TR

Boys Don't Cry

(1999, US, 118 min)
d Kimberly Peirce. *p* Jeffrey Sharp, John Hart, Eva Kolodner, Christine Vachon. *sc* Kimberly Peirce, Andy Bienen. *ph* Jim Denault. *ed* Lee Percy, Tracy Granger. *pd* Michael Shaw. *m* Nathan Larson. *cast* Hilary Swank, Chloë Sevigny, Peter Sarsgaard, Brendan Sexton III, Alison Folland, Alicia Goranson, Matt McGrath, Rob Campbell, Jeanetta Arnette.
● The grimly compelling true story of Teena Brandon, a 21-year-old Nebraskan who chose to carry herself off as a boy, 'Brandon'. When her hometown of Lincoln gets too hot, s/he picks up with a rough, rootless bunch from Fall City, including ex-con John (Sarsgaard), who has 'no impulse control', his buddy Tom (Sexton), who's into self-inflicted pain and arson, and the white trash glamour girl Lana (Sevigny). When Brandon falls in love with the latter, it's a safe bet things aren't going to work out. Like a number of Christine Vachon productions, this deals in sexual transgression and retribution, but director Peirce keeps a lid on her artier tendencies, with the focus squarely on the actors. Given Hilary Swank's brave, enthralling and Oscar-winning performance, and the dismaying power of the story, that makes a lot of sense. TCh

Boys from Brazil, The

(1978, US, 125 min)
d Franklin J Schaffner. *p* Martin Richards, Stanley O'Toole. *sc* Heywood Gould. *ph* Henri Decaë. *ed* Robert Swink. *pd* Gil Parrondo. *m* Jerry Goldsmith. *cast* Gregory Peck, Laurence Olivier, James Mason, Lilli Palmer, Uta Hagen, Steven Guttenberg, Denholm Elliot, Rosemary Harris, John Dehner.
● Ira Levin's novel was so obviously devised for the cinema that it reads more like a script. Its premise was ingenious: why has a Nazi hit team from South America begun a systematic slaughter of innocuous middle-aged professional men all over Europe? The answer should have made a great thriller, but the film is sunk by a series of preposterous performances. There are more phony German accents than in a prep school version of *Colditz*, and Levin's expert plotting is buried beneath an avalanche of lines like 'Vat are we goink to do?'. Easy answer. DP

Boys from Fengkuei, The (Fenggui Lai-de Ren/ aka All the Youthful Days)

(1983, Tai, 98 min)
d Hou Xiaoxian. *p* Lin Rongfeng, Zhang Huakun. *sc* Zhu Tianwen. *ph* Chen Kunhou. *ed* Liao Qingsong. *m* Bach, Vivaldi. *cast* Niu Chengze, Zhang Shi, Lin Xiuling, Zhao Pengju, Du Zonghua.
● Hou's first indie production was also a creative breakthrough, the film in which he turned away from commercial formulas and began experimenting with long takes, wide-angle shots and melodrama-free plotlines. Three young men from Fengkuei, a backwater village in the Penghu Islands, decamp to Kaohsiung, Taiwan's southern port, for what they think will be a life of laddish fun; like Fellini's *Vitelloni*, they are pushed towards maturity by encounters with crime, death, work and women. Hou soon went far beyond these rather obvious social and psychological observations, but the film retains a real freshness and charm; it launched several acting careers. The classical music track doesn't work in this context, but it's a small improvement on the Taiwanese version (three minutes longer, thanks to a now-cut theme song), which had a dreadul pop soundtrack. TR

Boys in Blue, The

(1983, GB, 91 min)
d Val Guest. *p* Greg Smith. *sc* Val Guest. *ph* Jack Atcheler. *ed* Peter Weatherley. *ad* Geoffrey Tozer. *m* Ed Welch. *cast* Bobby Ball, Tommy Cannon, Suzanne Danielle, Roy Kinnear, Eric Sykes, Jack Douglas, Edward Judd, Arthur English.
● This is matriarch humour, strayed from the bosom of clubland; only a Lancashire mother can truly appreciate the feature-length witless babble of Cannon and Ball dressed as bobbies. Cannon has the brain cell, Ball has the catchphrase ('Rock on, Tommy'); they both talk about pulling birds and going to the pictures, repeating each other's lines endlessly, thereby requiring only half a script. Which is all they get; it's about country coppers whose station is under threat until Big Crime turns up on their doorstep. To complete the picture of the typical British film comedy cashing in on TV success, just look at the cast list, halve the budget you first thought of, and add a gratuitous advert for British Leyland. RP

Boys in Brown

(1949, GB, 84 min, b/w)
d Montgomery Tully. *p* Antony Darnborough. *sc* Montgomery Tully. *ph* Gordon Lang, Cyril Bristow. *ed* James Needs. *ad* Douglas Daniels. *m* Doreen Carwithen. *cast* Jack Warner, Jimmy Hanley, Richard Attenborough, Dirk Bogarde, Barbara Murray, Thora Hird, Michael Medwin.
● Sentenced to three years in Borstal, young Attenborough gets off to a dismaying start: outfitted with regulation short pants then propositioned by a Welsh-accented Dirk Bogarde, eager to become his 'special pal'. The fairly outspoken (for 1949) script criticises a system portrayed as suffering from cash starvation (echoed by the film's own rock-bottom budget) yet required to cope with hordes of incorrigibles: a recidivism rate of 75 per cent is indicated. It's a blend of cosy stereotypes, reforming zeal and post-war disillusion amounting to a gloomy admonition not to expect very much from life. A British *noir*, in that sense. From a play by actor Reginald Beckwith. BBa

Boys in Company C, The

(1977, HK, 128 min)
d Sidney J Furie. *p* André Morgan. *sc* Rick Natkin, Sidney J Furie. *ph* Godfrey Godar. *ed* Michael Berman. *ad* Robert Laing. *m* Jaime Mendoza-Nava. *cast* Stan Shaw, Michael Lembeck, James Canning, Craig Wasson, Andrew Stevens, Noble Willingham.
● Gruelling yet humorous look at a bunch of Marines through training and posting to Vietnam in 1968, this turns every war film cliché upside down: transistor radios grind out rock music over the life-and-death patrols, and the GIs behave less like soldiers than shambling tourists. DP

Boys Next Door, The

(1985, US, 91 min)
d Penelope Spheeris. *p* Keith Rubinstein, Sandy Howard. *sc* Glenn Morgan, James Wong. *ph* Arthur Albert. *ed* Andy Horvitch. *ad* Jo-Ann Chorney. *m* George S Clinton. *cast* Maxwell Caulfield, Charlie Sheen, Patti D'Arbanville, Christopher McDonald, Hank Garrett, Paul C Dancer.
● When Bo and Roy, 18-year-olds fresh from school and seemingly normal, decide to hit LA for one last fling before settling into factory jobs, neither they nor the audience are prepared for their sudden descent into committing a series of brutal, apparently motiveless murders. Whereas Spheeris' *The Wild Side* was weakened by sentimentalising its disaffected punk heroes, her second feature presents a tougher and more balanced view of teen violence; while we're allowed a glimmer of understanding into the murderers' feelings, we never indulge them with misplaced sympathies: these boys are monsters. GA

Boy Soldier

(1986, GB, 100 min)
d Karl Francis. *p* Karl Francis, Hayden Pearce. *sc* Karl Francis. *ph* Roger Pugh Evans. *ed* Aled Evans. *ad* Hayden Pearce. *m* Graham Williams. *cast* Richard Lynch, Bernard Latham, Dafydd Hywel, James Donnelly, WJ Phillips, Timothy Lyn, Robert Pugh.
● When Wil Thomas, tired of unemployment and a nagging mother, enlists in a Welsh army regiment for a stretch in Belfast, he makes friends, falls in love, and shapes up as an efficient cog in the military machine. Suddenly, however, there's a shooting, and Wil is imprisoned for murder. The complex but lucid account of his political education is performed partly in Welsh, no nationalist gimmick but a dramatically essential device. For the boy's resort to his native tongue not only signifies his growing solidarity with the 'enemy'; it also serves as a vital strategy of self-defence in his war with the English officers. The occasionally needless fragmentation of the narrative at times weakens the film's emotional punch, while the almost universal depiction of Wil's would-be moral guardians as corrupt and hypocritical brutes might seem overemphatic. But it's a brave, sincere and intelligent movie, forcefully grasping a thorny subject all too often handled with kid gloves. GA

Boys on the Beach

see Ciel, les Oiseaux et… Ta Mère!, Le

Boys on the Side

(1995, US, 117 min)
d Herbert Ross. *p* Arnon Milchan, Steven Reuther, Herbert Ross. *sc* Don Roos. *ph* Donald Thorin. *ed* Michael R Miller. *pd* Ken Adam. *m* David Newman. *cast* Whoopi Goldberg, Mary-Louise Parker, Drew Barrymore, Matthew McConaughey, James Remar, Estelle Parsons.
● Goldberg's in her element here as Jane, a lesbian singer with attitude to spare who shares a cross-country drive first with Robin (Parker) and

then with wild-child Holly (Barrymore). On the road, this female buddy-movie plays like a camper *Thelma & Louise* (rescued from her abusive boyfriend, Holly finds herself on the run when his corpse turns up on the front pages); it changes gears abruptly at the halfway mark, when Robin goes down with an AIDS-related illness. This tender, ticklish chicks' flick pushes a good many emotional buttons, but resists at least some of the easier options. TCh

Boys Will Be Boys

(1935, GB, 75 min, b/w)
d William Beaudine. *p* Michael Balcon. *sc* Will Hay, Robert Edmunds. *ph* Charles Van Enger. *ed* Alfred Roome. *pd* Alex Vetchinsky. *m* Louis Levy. *cast* Will Hay, Gordon Harker, Claude Dampier, Jimmy Hanley, Davy Burnaby, Norma Varden.

●Typically hectic Hay farce in which, thanks to a bit of crookery, he graduates from prison teacher to headmaster of a decidedly unorthodox school. Underhand dealing and batty backchat galore, lorded over by its garrulous star and the marvellous Harker. GA

Boy Who Could Fly, The

(1986, US, 114 min)
d Nick Castle. *p* Gary Adelson. *sc* Nick Castle. *ph* Steven Poster, Adam Holender. *ed* Patrick Kennedy. *pd* James D Bissell. *m* Bruce Broughton. *cast* Lucy Deakins, Jay Underwood, Bonnie Bedelia, Fred Savage, Colleen Dewhurst, Fred Gwynne, Mindy Cohen.

●With such a promising premise, it's a shame that *The Boy Who Could Fly* so quickly descends into Disneyland. Milly (Deakins) is the new kid on the block. The boy next door is Eric (Underwood), an autistic child who spends his days perched on a bedroom windowsill with arms outstretched in dreams of flight. The two outsiders are at once drawn to one another, and a sympathetic teacher (Dewhurst) plays upon their developing relationship, hoping to reintegrate Eric into the classroom and prevent the authorities from institutionalising him. As the adults close in, the young dreamers are chased on to the school roof, with nowhere to turn but up or down. Director Castle gets lost in fantasy, spoiling a promising portrait with some heavy-handed emotional manipulation and an escapist conclusion. SGo

Boy Who Cried Bitch, The

(1990, US, 105 min)
d Juan José Campanella. *p* Louis Tancredi. *sc* Catherine May Levin. *ph* Daniel Shulman. *ed* Darren Kloomak. *pd* Nancy Deren. *m* Wendy Blackstone. *cast* Harley Cross, Karen Young, Dennis Boutsikaris, Adrien Brody, Gene Canfield, Moira Kelly, Jesse Bradford.

●An unevenly pitched, resolutely sincere adaptation by scriptwriter Catherine May Levin of her novel about a delinquent 12-year-old boy whose guilt-ridden mother is forced by an emotional war of attrition to commit her potentially violent son to a series of unsuitable psychiatric institutions. Although Cross, as the delinquent boy, and Young as his long-suffering mother, lend a powerful conviction to their demanding roles, Campanella's aimlessly roaming camera and elliptical scene transitions are curiously at odds with the predominantly naturalistic tone. NF

Boy Who Had Everything, The

(1984, Aust, 94 min)
d Stephen Wallace. *p* Richard Mason, Julia Overton. *sc* Stephen Wallace. *ph* Geoff Burton. *ed* Henry Dangar. *pd* Ross Major. *m* Ralph Schneider. *cast* Jason Connery, Diane Cilento, Laura Williams, Lewis Fitz-Gerald, Ian Gilmour, Nique Needles.

●*Chariots of Fire*, ocker-style, with its over-achieving hero caught between mother, a brassy blonde parvenue, and alma mater, a pretentious private college with sadistic humiliation rites. Wallace bodges around the early '60s context and his golden boy's Oedipal inclinations, and understandably there's an awkwardness here in the performances of real-life mother and son Cilento and Connery, who evinces little of father Sean's cruel charisma or acting ability. SJo

Boy with Green Hair, The

(1948, US, 82 min)
d Joseph Losey. *p* Stephen Ames. *sc* Ben Barzman, Alfred Lewis Levitt. *ph* George Barnes. *ed* Frank Doyle. *ad* Albert S D'Agostino, Ralph Berger. *m* Leigh Harline. *cast* Dean Stockwell, Pat O'Brien, Robert Ryan, Barbara Hale, Samuel S Hinds, Walter Catlett.

●Imagine a cosy Disney feature crossed with an allegory on war and racism, and you have some idea of the bizarre flavour of Losey's first feature. A rather simplistic symbolic tale about a war-orphan whose hair turns green in protest against his plight, only to be rejected by friends and strangers alike, it's muddled, awkward, pretentious, and often downright embarrassing. But the very fact that it is so ridiculous, with absurd moments like the garrulous old grandfather (O'Brien) singing silly songs, lends it a certain off-beat charm. GA

Boyz N the Hood

(1991, US, 107 min)
d John Singleton. *p* Steve Nicolaides. *sc* John Singleton. *ph* Chuck Mills. *ed* Bruce Cannon. *pd* Charles Mills. *m* Stanley Clarke. *cast* Larry Fishburne, Cuba Gooding Jr, Ice Cube, Morris Chestnut, Nia Long, Tyra Ferrell, Angela Bassett.

●South Central LA, 1984: anxious that her son will fall prey to the drug-related violence of the local gangs, ten-year-old Tre Styles' mother hands the boy over to her estranged husband, Furious (Fishburne). Seven years later, his father's strict lessons in the art of taking responsibility have ensured Tre's moral strength, black pride and rigorous self-discipline; but in a community ravaged by crack, poverty, police harassment and guns, it's hard to stay true to one's principles when life-long friends are shot at and revenge is called for. If the coming-of-age story is in itself hardly original, and the speeches are sometimes a mite preachy, writer/director Singleton (his debut) mounts his arguments forcefully and clearly. But what makes the film so affecting is the no-nonsense direction and Singleton's sure, specific sense of the rewards and hardships of community; in this, he is lent excellent support from a fine cast. GA

Brady Bunch Movie, The

(1995, US, 89 min)
d Betty Thomas. *p* Sherwood Schwartz, Lloyd J Schwartz, David Kirkpatrick. *sc* Bonnie Turner, Laurice Elehwany, Jerry Turner, Rick Copp. *ph* Mac Ahlberg. *ed* Peter Teschner. *ad* Steven Jordan. *m* Guy Moon. *cast* Shelley Long, Gary Cole, Christopher Daniel Barnes, Christine Taylor, Michael McKean, Jean Smart, Henriette Mantel, Paul Sutera, Jennifer Elise Cox, Jesse Lee.

●An anodyne family-values sitcom, *The Brady Bunch* ran from 1969 to 1974, and somehow reflected the Nixon presidency without mentioning drugs, Vietnam or Watergate. Two decades later, how relevant can the Brady Bunch be? The screenwriters' answer, subverting the original, is simply to plonk the family in the middle of contemporary LA. All around is greed, apathy and dog-eat-dog, but the Brady home remains a haven of cheesy smiles and moral certitude. Director Thomas (once Sgt Lucy Bates of *Hill Street Blues*) has recreated '70s sitcom-land with the kind of unerring attention to detail Merchant-Ivory lavish on a society ball, and she's drawn hilariously synthetic performances from a shrewdly cloned cast. TCh

Brain Damage

(1987, US, 86 min)
d Frank Henenlotter. *p* Edgar Ievins. *sc* Frank Henenlotter. *ph* Bruce Torbet. *ed* James Kwei, Frank Henenlotter. *ad* Ivy Rosovsky. *m* Gus Russo, Clutch Reiser. *cast* Rick Herbst, Gordon MacDonald, Jennifer Lowry, Theo Barnes, Lucille Saint-Peter, Vicki Darnell.

●Escaping from a nice old Jewish couple unwilling to cater for his unusual dietary needs, the phallic Elmer, a parasitic creature, fastens on to Brian (Herbst) as a more promising victim. By tapping into the back of Brian's neck, Elmer blue-rinses his brain with a euphoria-inducing liquid. Brian thinks he can handle it, but it's addictive, and pretty soon he's helping Elmer to obtain his preferred food, human brains. While it would win few prizes for narrative sophistication and visual imagination – the euphoric hallucinations seem to have strayed from a '60s LSD movie – *Brain Damage* does display a commendable social conscience in deploring the perils of mindbending substances. By way of aversion therapy, it presents gruesome scenes like that in which Brian pulls a bloody string of mental floss from out of his left ear. Similarly, the most disgusting scene will deter impressionable young women from performing the act of fellatio for life. There are some nice comic moments though; in fact relying as heavily on its disquieting black humour as on images of physical disgust, the whole thing works far better as comedy than horror. NF

Braindead

(1992, NZ, 104 min)
d Peter Jackson. *p* Jim Booth. *sc* Peter Jackson, Stephen Sinclair, Frances Walsh. *ph* Murray Milne. *ed* Jamie Selkirk. *pd* Kenneth Leonard-Jones. *m* Peter Dasent. *cast* Timothy Balme, Diana Peñalver, Elizabeth Moody, Ian Watkin, Brenda Kendall, Stuart Devenie.

●Peter Jackson's zombiefest follow-up to *Bad Taste*, set in suburbia in the late '50s, is 'a slapstick comedy with blood and guts instead of custard pies'. When 25-year-old virgin Lionel (Balme) falls for the lovely Paquita (Peñalver), he provokes his domineering mother's jealousy. Soon after, a toxic nip from a Sumatran rat-monkey at the local zoo transforms Lionel's mother – through several putrescent stages – into a hideous, pustulant monster with a craving for human flesh. The finale, in which Lionel reduces a horde of flesh-eaters to a mulch of blood, flesh and offal with the aid of a flymo, is probably the goriest scene ever. NF

Brain Machine, The

(1954, GB, 83 min, b/w)
d Ken Hughes. *p* Alec C Snowden. *sc* Ken Hughes. *ph* Josef Ambor. *ed* Geoffrey Muller. *ad* George Haslam. *m* Richard Taylor. *cast* Patrick Barr, Elizabeth Allan, Maxwell Reed, Russell Napier, Gibb McLaughlin, Vanda Godsell.

●When the reading on psychiatrist Allan's electro-encephalograph indicates that amnesiac hospital patient Reed is none other than a dangerous psychopath she'd previously tested, the patient in question kidnaps the doctor and threatens her life – leaving medic husband Barr racing against time to track down the villain's hide-out. Pacy little British B-pic which finds an interesting early techno angle on a pretty familiar storyline. TJ

Brainscan

(1994, US, 95 min)
d John Flynn. *p* Michael Roy. *sc* Andrew Kevin Walker. *ph* François Protat. *ed* Jay Cassidy. *pd* Paola Ridolfi. *m* George S Clinton. *cast* Edward Furlong, Frank Langella, T Ryder Smith, Amy Hargreaves, Jamie Marsh, Victor Ertmanis.

●The titular computer game, 'the ultimate experience in inter-active horror', gets a little too real for high-school misfit Michael (Furlong) in this dumb hi-tech horror movie. While playing Brainscan and seeing through the eyes of a killer, Michael breaks into a suburban house, grabs a kitchen knife, climbs the stairs and stabs to death a sleeping, middle-aged man. Next day, he learns that a middle-aged man has been murdered in his quiet suburban neighbourhood. Was it real or was it virtual reality? 'Reality, unreality, what's the difference?' asks the cadaverous Trickster (Smith), who emerges from the screen as the personification of the game's malevolent electrical impulses. Director Flynn presents the dogged investigation by smoothly insinuating detective Hayden (Langella) with some style; but he seems much less interested in the fantastic elements, the self-conscious in-jokes and lacklustre visual effects. NF

Brainstorm

(1983, US, 106 min)
d/p Douglas Trumbull. *sc* Robert Stitzel, Philip Messina. *ph* Richard Yuricich. *ed* Edward A Warschilka, Freeman Davies. *pd* John Vallone. *m* James Horner. *cast* Christopher Walken, Natalie Wood, Louise Fletcher, Cliff Robertson, Jordan Christopher, Donald Hotton.

●On paper, with its fascinating premise – a helmet-like device to enable people to experience other people's experiences – this has a lot going for it. On screen, however, it's an interesting and ambitious package that doesn't quite work. Use of the device is limited to the obvious, like sex and racing cars, or to the impossibly mystical, which fails to crack the old problem that hell is always more vivid than heaven. The drama comes from the battle between the mad scientist (Walken) who wants the device to benefit mankind, and the mysterious men in dark suits who want to keep it all under wraps for the military. As a thriller it's a bit soft, as sci-fi it's a bit simple. JB

Brainwaves

(1983, US, 80 min)
d/p/sc Ulli Lommel. *ph* Jon Kranhouse, Ulli Lommel. *ed* Richard Brummer. *ad* Stephen E Graff. *m* Robert O Ragland. *cast* Keir Dullea, Suzanna Love, Tony Curtis, Vera Miles, Ossie Davis, Corinne Alphen.
●Ulli Lommel graduated from playing twitchers and fruitcakes in Fassbinder movies by directing *Tenderness of the Wolves*, a touching account of a gay paedophile butcher. He then decamped to Hollywood to essay a career pitched somewhere between Dennis Hopper and Paul Morrissey. Mostly he made no-budget schlock, like this ludicrously straightfaced 'thriller' about brainwave transplants. A black hole for fading stars in which Dr Curtis kindly operates on the heroine (Love) who is in a coma after suffering a traumatic blow to the brain. The donor is a murder victim, unexpectedly supplying not only motor reflexes but memories, so that the poor recipient is soon being stalked herself. ATu

Bramble Bush, The

(1959, US, 105 min)
d Daniel Petrie. *p* Milton Sperling. *sc* Milton Sperling, Philip Yordan. *ph* Lucien Ballard. *ed* Folmer Blangsted. *ad* John S Poplin. *m* Leonard Rosenman. *cast* Richard Burton, Barbara Rush, Jack Carson, Angie Dickinson, James Dunn, Henry Jones, Tom Drake.
●Alcohol, adultery and euthanasia loom large in this glossy version of Charles Mergendahl's sub-*Peyton Place* novel about a New England doctor going home to Cape Cod and falling for his dying friend's wife. One of Burton's take the money and run performances. TM

Bram Stoker's Dracula

see Dracula

Branches of the Tree (Shakha Proshakha)

(1990, Ind/Fr, 120 min)
d Satyajit Ray. *p* Daniel Toscan du Plantier, Gérard Depardieu. *sc* Satyajit Ray. *ph* Sandip Ray. *ed* Dulal Dutt. *m* Satyajit Ray. *cast* Ajit Banerjee, Maradan Banerjee, Lily Charraborty, Soumitra Chatterjee, Mamata Shankar.
●A sombre family drama occasioned by the heart attack of a venerable businessman and philanthropist, who lives with his senile father and mentally disturbed son, but derives hope and a measure of satisfaction from his other three sons, successful men instilled with his principles of hard work and integrity. The family dutifully gathers at his bedside and awaits some sign of recovery; but old resentments cloud the air as first one son, then another, admit that their father's values are no longer tenable in a modern society where corruption distinguishes winners from losers. Ray stressed that the scenario for this, his second film since his serious coronary problems, was written 25 years ago and should not be taken as autobiographical. For all that, it is evidently an old man's film. With a single principal setting, and long passages of unwieldy exposition or earnest sermonising, the script might have been intended for the stage; and although it reclaims some of the ground lost in *An Enemy of the People*, Ray's functional, inelegant *mise en scène* provides little embellishment. TCh

Branded to Kill (Koroshi No Rakuin)

(1966, Jap, 91 min, b/w)
d Seijun Suzuki. *p* Kaneo Iwai. *sc* Hachiro Guryu. *ph* Kazue Nagatsuka. *ed* Mutsuo Tanji. *ad* Sukezo Kawahara. *m* Naozumi Yamamoto. *cast* Jo Shishido. Nanbara Koji, Ogawa Mariko, Annu Mari, Isao Tamagawa.
●The film that got Suzuki fired by Nikkatsu, and it's not hard to see why. It starts almost straightforwardly as a bluesy gangster thriller in pared-down Melville mould. But as 'number three killer' Shishido (a Suzuki regular) moves from some beautifully staged hits to perverse obsession with an ultra cool femme fatale and a set-to with 'number one killer', the weirder the film becomes. Just as Shishido cracks up and enters a surreal nightmare world, so Suzuki breaks the film down into a bizarre but beguiling chain of absurdist, OTT, barely related elements. It looks a little like golden-age Godard (but far more stylish). The climax, oddly reminiscent of *Point Blank* (made the same year), shows how much further Suzuki was prepared to push even than Boorman, let alone Hollywood. Occasionally mystifying, but always witty, inventive and dazzling to look at. GA

Brandy Ashore

see Green Grow the Rushes

Brannigan

(1975, GB, 111 min)
d Douglas Hickox. *p* Jules Levy, Arthur Gardner. *sc* Christopher Trumbo, Michael Butler, William P McGivern, William Norton. *ph* Gerry Fisher. *ed* Malcolm Cooke. *ad* Edward Marshall. *m* Dominic Frontiere. *cast* John Wayne, Richard Attenborough, Judy Geeson, Mel Ferrer, John Vernon, Daniel Pilon, John Stride.
●Wayne playing national monument (in the guise of a Chicago cop) is exported to London to get his man and take in the sights. What follows is flatly predictable: some grousing about wearing neckties in the Garrick Club; tedious 'language' problems; relentless use of tourist locations and some jokey fisticuffs in a pub brawl that's geared solely for the American market. CPe

Brasher Doubloon, The (aka The High Window)

(1946, US, 72 min, b/w)
d John Brahm. *p* Robert Bassler. *sc* Dorothy Hannah, Leonard Praskins. *ph* Lloyd Ahern. *ed* Harry Reynolds. *ad* James Basevi, Richard Irvine. *m* David Buttolph. *cast* George Montgomery, Nancy Guild, Florence Bates, Fritz Kortner, Conrad Janis, Roy Roberts, Marvin Miller, Houseley Stevenson.
●Usually shrugged aside as a negligible Chandler adaptation, but Brahm has other fish to fry. The tone is set by the opening shot of an old dark house as Philip Marlowe's offscreen voice complains about the wind blowing eternally off the Mojave. That wind continues throughout, stirring the mood of malaise as swaying branches set shadows flickering in dim-lit rooms where the heroine is being slowly driven mad. The opening interview, with the marvellously malevolent Florence Bates easily outgunning General Sternwood in flesh-crawling unease, challenges *The Big Sleep* on its own ground. The middle stretches, with Kortner outstanding in the Lorre role, produce as vivid a set of grotesques as *The Maltese Falcon*. But what keeps the last third afloat owes less to Chandler or Hammett than to the sense of brooding Gothic melodrama in which Brahm specialised. Forget Philip Marlowe, enjoy a fine companion piece to *The Lodger*, *Guest in the House*, *Hanover Square* and *The Locket*. TM

Brassed Off

(1996, GB/US, 107 min)
d Mark Herman. *p* Steve Abbott. *sc* Mark Herman. *ph* Andy Collins. *ed* Michael Ellis. *pd* Don Taylor. *m* Trevor Jones. *cast* Pete Postlethwaite, Ewan McGregor, Tara Fitzgerald, Stephen Tompkinson, Jim Carter, Philip Jackson, Stephen Moore.
●This is an angry, tragic film, which softens you up with a few off-the-peg stereotypes and colloquial laughs and then rams them back down your throat. Postlethwaite is Danny, the devoted leader of the Grimley Colliery Band. Music is so important to him, he barely notices that the pit's on the verge of closure, and can't begin to understand why members like Andy (McGregor), Harry (Carter) and even his own son, Phil (Tompkinson), are finding it hard to cough up their subs. Matters come to a head with the band competing in the national championships and the miners voting for voluntary redundancy. Writer/director Herman pulls off a popular, proletarian comedy which might actually appeal to the people it's about. He uses comic shorthand – not all the relationships are as developed as they might be – but captures a credible sense of the tensions within the community at large, and the devastating impact of the pit closures. He's not shy about laying the blame, either. Tompkinson, Postlethwaite and Carter are stand-outs in an impressive ensemble cast, but for many, the brass band music will come as the real revelation. TCh

Brass Monkey, The (aka Lucky Mascot)

(1948, GB, 84 min, b/w)
d Thornton Freeland. *p* NA Bronsten. *sc* Alec Coppel. *ph* Basil Emmott. *ed* David Hawkins. *ad* Walter M Scott. *m* Bernard Grun. *cast* Carroll Levis, Carole Landis, Herbert Lom, Avril Angers, Ernest Thesiger, Terry-Thomas.
●Radio personality Levis, who hosted a long-running talent-spotting show on Radio Luxembourg, made an unlikely transition to the big screen in this ramshackle support feature that sat on the shelf for three years before its eventual release in 1951. Levis more or less plays himself, implicated in Buddhist connoisseur Thesiger's search for a trio of valuable brass monkeys, with villainous Lom under suspicion of theft. A curio, but not really a collectible. TJ

Brass Target

(1978, US, 111 min)
d John Hough. *p* Arthur Lewis. *sc* Alvin Boretz. *ph* Tony Imi. *ed* David Lane. *pd* Rolf Zehetbauer. *m* Laurence Rosenthal. *cast* Sophia Loren, John Cassavetes, George Kennedy, Robert Vaughn, Patrick McGoohan, Bruce Davison, Edward Herrmann, Max von Sydow.
●Mining the profitable vein of *Day of the Jackal*, this tale of conspiracy and assassination has General Patton murdered by subordinates involved in a vast gold heist. The movie goes for several targets – historical significance, murky intrigue, Bond-style techno-glamour – but misses them all. Loren, as the woman with a past, drifts in and out of a defiantly labyrinthine plot which reaches rock bottom with the revelation that Patton's adjutant's mistress' ex-husband was (maybe) a Nazi cabinet minister. Pretty thin. CA

Bravados, The

(1958, US, 98 min)
d Henry King. *p* Herbert B Swope. *sc* Philip Yordan. *ph* Leon Shamroy. *ed* William Mace. *ad* Lyle Wheeler, Mark Lee Kirk. *m* Lionel Newman. *cast* Gregory Peck, Stephen Boyd, Albert Salmi, Henry Silva, Lee Van Cleef, Joan Collins, Joe De Rita, Andrew Duggan, George Voskovec, Gene Evans.
●Nine years after the impressive *Twelve O'Clock High*, eight after the magnificent *The Gunfighter*, King and Peck teamed up again for this revenge Western. For a while, it looks as though the magic is going to work again, as Peck rides grimly into a small town, announces that his purpose is to watch four outlaws hang, and – when they contrive to escape – outrides the posse to exterminate the outlaws one by one. Ironically, although guilty of similar crimes, the quartet (Boyd, Salmi, Van Cleef and Silva) turn out to be not guilty of the rape/murder of Peck's wife. Cue for a crisis of conscience which is worked out in perfunctory religious terms, with Joan Collins conveniently on hand as an image of salvation. With good performances and excellent 'Scope camerawork from Leon Shamroy, the action sequences are fine, but the religious motifs are as maudlin as *The Song of Bernadette*. TM

Brave, The

(1997, US, 123 min)
d Johnny Depp. *p* Charles Evans, Carroll Kemp. *sc* Paul McCudden, Danny Depp, Johnny Depp. *ph* Vilko Filac. *ed* Pascale Buba. *pd* Miljen 'Kreka' Kljakovic. *m* Iggy Pop. *cast* Johnny Depp, Marlon Brando, Elpidia Carrillo, Marshall Bell, Frederic Forrest, Max Perlich.
●Depp's directorial debut is a *folie de grandeur*. There's nothing intrinsically wrong with the story, in which Depp, a Latin or Native American – it's unclear which – living with his wife and kids in a shanty town next to a garbage dump, decides to help his family escape poverty by being paid a fortune for his own death. But after the scenes in which he makes his deal with Brando – a snuff-movie producer? (again it's unclear) – the film goes seriously off the rails as it forsakes glum realism for maudlin sentiment and whimsical, symbolic fantasy (Depp gets back in touch with his kids and builds a fairground for the other dispossessed). Besides the implausibilities, the direction has two fatal flaws: it's both tediously slow and hugely narcissistic as the camera focuses repeatedly on Depp's bandana'd head and rippling torso. GA

Brave Don't Cry, The

(1952, GB, 90 min, b/w)
d Philip Leacock. *sc* Montagu Slater. *ph* Arthur Grant. *ed* John Trumper. *ad* Michael Stringer. *cast* John Gregson, Meg Buchanan, John Rae, Fulton Mackay, Andrew Keir, Russell Waters, Jameson Clark.

●By rights a title like this should herald some high-flown best-seller garbage, but in fact this is quite a decent little film from the short-lived Group 3 venture, produced by John Grierson and John Baxter: a semi-documentary reenactment of the 1950 Knockshinnoch mine disaster in Scotland. Sober, careful, making excellent use of locations and a cast drawn largely from the Glasgow Citizens' Theatre, it is only occasionally inclined to over-emote. TM

Braveheart

(1995, US, 177 min)
d Mel Gibson. *p* Alan Ladd Jr, Bruce Davey, Mel Gibson. *sc* Randall Wallace. *ph* John Toll. *ed* Steven Rosenblum. *pd* Tom Sanders. *m* James Horner. *cast* Mel Gibson, Sophie Marceau, Patrick McGoohan, Catherine McCormack, Alun Armstrong, Ian Bannen, Brendan Gleeson, James Cosmo.

●Scotland at the end of the 13th century: William Wallace (Gibson) purposes to free his country from the tyranny of Edward Longshanks (McGoohan). From the opening shots, swirling through the mists o' time over snowy peaks and silvery lochs, to the final torture scenes in which disembowelment provokes only a brave grimace, Gibson's epic offers a stew of Hollywood clichés. Political analysis is not on the menu; this is a tale of heroes 'n' villains, pure and simplistic. The Sassenachs are rude stereotypes, while the Scots are either macho hunks or, should they be aristos, dour quislings. The battle scenes are staged effectively, but for the most part this is a vehicle for Gibson, graduating from cocky *Lethal Weapon* register to something more one-dimensional and rhetorically solemn. Pure hokum. GA

Brave Little Toaster, The

(1987, US, 90 min)
d Jerry Rees. *p* Donald Kushner, Thomas L Wilhite. *sc* Jerry Rees, Joe Ranft. *m* David Newman. *cast* voices: Jon Lovitz, Tim Stack, Timothy E Day, Thurl Ravenscroft, Deanna Oliver, Phil Hartman.

●This gem of an adventure, from a novel by Thomas M Disch, is essentially *The Incredible Journey* with five animated electrical appliances (toaster, lamp, vacuum-cleaner, electric blanket and portable radio) that are not so much live as *alive!* Abandoned by their 'master', a spotty kid who moves off with parents to the big city, the plucky quintet are left with no option but to up cables and set off into the wild blue yonder. A winning combination of inventive characters, amusing dialogue, excellent voice-overs, likeable tunes (courtesy of former Beach Boys collaborator Van Dyke Parks), and first-rate animation. Indeed, one of the most enchanting animated films since *The Snowman*. A volt from the blue. DA

Brazil

(1985, GB, 142 min)
d Terry Gilliam. *p* Arnon Milchan. *sc* Terry Gilliam, Tom Stoppard, Charles McKeown. *ph* Roger Pratt. *ed* Julian Doyle. *pd* Norman Garwood. *m* Michael Kamen. *cast* Jonathan Pryce, Robert De Niro, Katherine Helmond, Ian Holm, Bob Hoskins, Michael Palin, Ian Richardson.

●Fortunately the story of an alternative future is realised with such visual imagination and sparky humour that it's only half way through that the plot's weaknesses become apparent. Like 1984, it looks forward from the '40s to a vast urban society ruled by an oppressive bureaucracy that has developed primitive valve computers. Pryce plays a worker in the all-powerful Ministry of Information, and the best moments arise when his flat's central heating system becomes a kind of spiritual battleground between guerrilla engineer De Niro and his state opposite number Hoskins. Here Gilliam fuses terror and comedy with real brilliance; elsewhere the plot's gaping holes reduce the film to a glittering novelty. DP

Bread and Chocolate (Pane e Cioccolata)

(1973, It, 112 min)
d Franco Brusati. *p* Maurizio Lodi-Fé. *sc* Franco Brusati, Iaia Fiastri, Nino Manfredi. *ph* Luciano Tovoli. *ed* Mario Morra. *ad* Luigi Scaccianoce. *m* Daniele Patucchi. *cast* Nino Manfredi, Anna Karina, Johnny Dorelli, Paolo Turco, Ugo D'Alessio.

●Production-line Italian comedy only slightly helped by the tragi-comic skills of Nino Manfredi, as a guest-worker in oh-so-clean Switzerland desperately trying to break into the Aryan leisure culture. Brusati fatally miscalculates this comedy of failure, despising his protagonist, confusing pathos with camp. Almost as sad, the sublime Karina is thrown away in a bland Euro cameo (as a Greek exile on the run). Good acting, dreadful everything else. CA

Bread and Roses

(2000, GB/Ger/Sp/Fr/It, 110 min)
d Ken Loach. *p* Rebecca O'Brien. *sc* Paul Laverty. *ph* Barry Ackroyd. *ed* Jonathan Morris. *pd* Martin Johnson. *m* George Fenton. *cast* Pilar Padilla, Adrien Brody, Elpidia Carrillo, Jack McGee, Monica Rivas, Frank Dávila, Lillian Hurst, Mayron Payes, Maria Orellana.

●Loach's first North American film assumes a seriously unironic Latino perspective on the great economic divide. Maya (Padilla) has no sooner been ferreted across the border than the traffickers are seeking to exact their pound of flesh. She escapes and hooks up with sister Rosa (Carrillo), who reluctantly gets her a job as an office cleaner. Intelligent and forthright, Maya becomes involved first with Ruben, a colleague saving for college, then with Sam (Brody), a union activist. Loach's committed progressive agenda commands respect, and the film reminds us how unskilled workers in the States are routinely exploited – and of the extent to which they're ignored by the media in general and Hollywood in particular. Padilla makes a good fist of her first film role; Maya's idealism has an irrepressible flirty, impetuous side. It's a pity, though, that Loach and screenwriter Laverty are less interested in the character's emotional life than in her political education. For the one genuinely gripping dramatic confrontation comes between the two sisters, a searingly intimate argument which overshadows everything else in the movie. TCh

Bread and Tulips (Pane e Tulipani)

(2000, It, 110 min)
d Silvio Soldini. *p* Daniele Maggioni. *sc* Doriana Leondeff, Silvio Soldini. *ph* Luca Bigazzi. *ed* Carlotta Cristiani. *pd* Paola Bizzarri. *m* Giovanni Venosta. *cast* Licia Maglietta, Bruno Ganz, Giuseppe Battiston, Marina Massironi. Antonio Catania, Felice Andreasi, Tatiana Lepore.

●Rosalba (Maglietta), a forty-something housewife, is on holiday with her husband, a sanitary fittings manufacturer, and their family when she's left behind by the coach and stranded at a roadside diner. Deciding not to wait for their return, Rosalba embarks on her own adventure and hitchhikes to Venice. She meets and develops relationships with some very special people: an anarchic florist, a suicidal Icelandic restaurateur with an eccentric take on the world, and other quirky characters who give her life a hitherto unknown richness and colour. Funny, idiosyncratic and uplifting. JFu

Break, The

see Further Gesture, A

Breakdance

see Breakin'

Breakdown

(1997, US, 93 min)
d Jonathan Mostow. *p* Martha De Laurentiis, Dino De Laurentiis. *sc* Jonathan Mostow, Sam Montgomery. *ph* Douglas Milsome. *ed* Derek Brechin, Kevin Stitt. *pd* Victoria Paul. *m* Basil Poledouris. *cast* Kurt Russell, JT Walsh, Kathleen Quinlan, MC Gainey, Jack Noseworthy, Rex Linn.

●East Coast sophisticate Russell drives across the Southwest with wife Quinlan in a new Jeep. Breaking down in the middle of nowhere, he stays with the vehicle while Quinlan accepts a lift from trucker Walsh to the nearest phone. The thing is, Kurt gets the jeep going again, and by the time he's caught up with the truck, Kathleen has vanished and JT claims he must have the wrong fella – he's never seen him before in his life. There's not much fuel in the tank, but co-writer/director Mostow keeps this belated *Duel* retread streamlined and reasonably efficient. But it has no real credibility except for the gritty conviction of the stars, especially the late JT Walsh, oozing his singularly malevolent bonhomie. Mostow makes the most of the deserted truckstop landscapes but rehashes all the paranoid Hollywood clichés about the dangers lurking behind the gap-toothed smiles of Middle America – and caps it all with an insultingly brutal OTT ending. TCh

Breaker Morant

(1979, Aust, 107 min)
d Bruce Beresford. *p* Matthew Carroll. *sc* Jonathan Hardy, David Stevens, Bruce Beresford. *ph* Donald McAlpine. *ed* William Anderson. *pd* David Copping. *m* Phil Cuneen. *cast* Edward Woodward, Jack Thompson, John Waters, Bryan Brown, Charles Tingwell, Terence Donovan, Lewis Fitz-Gerald.

●Three lieutenants (Woodward, Brown, Fitz-Gerald), members of an Australian platoon fighting in the Boer War, are court-martialled for murdering Boer prisoners and a German missionary, and Jack Thompson steps in to try to prove their innocence. It's a *Paths of Glory* situation, complete with righteous anger at the expedient conniving authorities, distinguished by some strong courtroom scenes and an overwhelming pessimism. If it hardly breaks any new ground either formally or politically, it's nevertheless a moving and highly professional affair, in which Brown and Thompson give particularly good performances. GA

Breakfast at Tiffany's

(1961, US, 115 min)
d Blake Edwards. *p* Martin Jurow, Richard Shepherd. *sc* George Axelrod. *ph* Franz Planer. *ed* Howard Smith. *ad* Hal Pereira, Roland Anderson. *m* Henry Mancini. *cast* Audrey Hepburn, George Peppard, Patricia Neal, Buddy Ebsen, Mickey Rooney, John McGiver, Martin Balsam.

●Bowdlerised but pleasant enough adaptation, by George Axelrod, of Truman Capote's novel, with Hepburn rather too winsome as the Manhattan callgirl Holly Golightly, who has an on-off relationship with Peppard's writer, himself juggling an affair with a (Neal) wealthy patroness. The party scenes and intimations of hipness now look dated, and it's all rather too sugary for its own good (Henry Mancini's award-winning 'Moon River' being symptomatic); but taken as a shallow fairytale it has a certain charm. GA

Breakfast Club, The

(1984, US, 97 min)
d John Hughes. *p* Ned Tanen, John Hughes. *sc* John Hughes. *ph* Thomas Del Ruth. *ed* Dede Allen. *pd* John W Corso. *m* Keith Forsey. *cast* Emilio Estevez, Paul Gleason, Anthony Michael Hall, John Kapelos, Judd Nelson, Molly Ringwald, Ally Sheedy.

●An iconic movie of the '80s, with all the unappealing baggage that suggests. Five mutually antipathetic teens are called in for Saturday detention at a suburban American high school. Initial bouts of verbal jousting fade, making way for a bonding session fugged in pot smoke, the development of friendship everlasting (or until bell rings for class on Monday morning, whichever is the sooner) and That Simple Minds Song. Which would be fine, were the characters not a punchable quintet of overdrawn saps, the acting (Ringwald and Hall excepted) overplayed and unsympathetic, and the script the wrong side of the line that separates smart from smart-arse. Its continuing cult popularity is mystifying; as teen movies go, this is a long way off, say, *Fast Times at Ridgemont High* or *Pretty in Pink*. Hughes: stay behind for detention afterwards. And write me four sides on why this, uh, sucks. WFJ

Breakfast of Champions

(1999, US, 110 min)
d Alan Rudolph. *p* David Blocker, David Willis. *sc* Alan Rudolph. *ph* Elliot Davis. *ed* Suzy Elmiger. *pd* Nina Ruscio. *m* Mark Isham. *cast* Bruce Willis, Albert Finney, Nick Nolte, Barbara Hershey, Glenne Headley, Lukas Haas, Omar Epps, Vicki Lewis, Buck Henry, Will Patton.

●Everyone loves retail king Dwayne Hoover (Willis). Still, Dwayne starts every day sticking a gun in his mouth. His wife Celia (Hershey) is bed-bound and their son Bunny (Haas) hides in a subterranean bolthole while at work. Wayne's old pal Harry (Nolte) is so paranoid about his fetish for women's underwear he's oblivious to Dwayne's affair with his secretary Francine (Headley). Welcome to Midland City. But what welcome will Midland give Kilgore Trout (Finney), a man neither loved nor, like his writing, even known by the world at large? For someone has invited this raving troglodyte to the town's first Fine Arts festival. Barely recognisable from the signature romantic meditations of its director, this awesomely misconceived farce is in fact a project Rudolph has been harbouring ever since the early '70s, when Kurt Vonnegut's source novel first appeared. If the author's satire of parochial consumer society may be decidedly of its time, Rudolph dives into it with such abandon that he loses sight of any notion of a target or comprehensibility. Some spectacular moments, not least Nolte in red lingerie. NB

Breakheart Pass

(1975, US, 94 min)
d Tom Gries. *p* Jerry Gershwin. *sc* Alistair MacLean. *ph* Lucien Ballard. *ed* Byron 'Buzz' Brandt. *pd* Johannes Larsen. *m* Jerry Goldsmith. *cast* Charles Bronson, Ben Johnson, Jill Ireland, Richard Crenna, Charles Durning, Archie Moore, Ed Lauter.

●Pretty typical Alistair MacLean adventure with all the usual failings: minimal characterisation, terrible dialogue, too much plot, and too little real, inherent dynamism as opposed to weightily set up action pieces. This one manages to combine a basic *Ten Little Indians* plot with murder on a train à la Orient Express, set in the old West. VG

Breakin' (aka Breakdance)

(1984, US, 87 min)
d Joel Silberg. *p* Allen DeBevoise, David Zito. *sc* Charles Parker, Allen DeBevoise, Gerald Scaife. *ph* Hanania Baer. *ed* Mark Helfrich. *pd* Ivo Cristante. *m* Gary S Remal, Michael Boyd. *cast* Lucinda Dickey, Adolfo 'Shabba-Doo' Quinones, Michael 'Boogaloo-Shrimp' Chambers, Ben Lokey.

●A vehicle for the astonishing form of 'breaking' in which athletic types perform as if they were having a molar drilled without anesthetic while being simultaneously kneecapped…all to that disco beat. On the athletic level alone it trashes *Flashdance* into the boards, and the film's three heroes, Dickey, Shabba-Doo and Boogaloo-Shrimp (Oscars all round, just for the names) are all spellbinding; the soundtrack is also a treat, and the storyline, if lame (boy meets girl, sticks two fingers up at the dance establishment, and still wins prestigious audition) is peppered with enough modern motifs to suspend disbelief. DS

Breaking Away

(1979, US, 101 min)
d/p Peter Yates. *sc* Steve Tesich. *ph* Matthew F Leonetti. *ed* Cynthia Scheider. *ad* Patrizia von Brandenstein. *m* Patrick Williams. *cast* Dennis Christopher, Dennis Quaid, Daniel Stern, Jackie Earle Haley, Barbara Barrie, Paul Dooley, Robyn Douglass.

●Class conflict and small town chauvinism are the subject of Yates' ingenious youth movie, a film which intrigues as much by its portait of working-class America bitterly opposed to the affluent society as by its large measure of lovingly-crafted fantasy. Hero Dave (Christopher) and his mates try to win the annual 'Little Indy' team cycle race in their home town (Bloomington, Indiana), as a gesture of defiance to the richly privileged college boys. Scripted by Steve Tesich, it's Yates' best film since *The Friends of Eddie Coyle* and displays the kind of unsentimental optimism that went out of fashion with Hawks. DP

Breaking Glass

(1980, GB, 104 min)
d Brian Gibson. *p* Davina Belling, Clive Parsons. *sc* Brian Gibson. *ph* Stephen Goldblatt. *ed* Michael Bradsell. *ad* Evan Hercules. *songs* Hazel O'Connor. *cast* Phil Daniels, Hazel O'Connor, Jon Finch, Jonathan Pryce, Peter-Hugo Daly, Paul McCartney, Rod Stewart.

●Super-cynical first feature by ex-TV director Gibson. Its version of punk London in the '80s is a bizarre mix of Big Brother fantasy and shallow realism, with rock singer Kate (O'Connor) making it to rock star and losing her marbles on the way. *The Glenn Miller Story* meets *Rude Boy*.

Breaking In

(1989, US, 94 min)
d Bill Forsyth. *p* Harry Gittes. *sc* John Sayles. *ph* Michael Coulter. *ed* Michael Ellis. *ad* Adrienne Atkinson. *m* Michael Gibbs. *cast* Burt Reynolds, Casey Siemaszko, Sheila Kelley, Lorraine Toussaint, Albert Salmi, Harry Carey, Maury Chaykin, Stephen Tobolowsky.

●Forsyth's second American picture (the first actually shot in the States) is a gentle comedy about a couple of guys who happen to break into the same house at the same time. Mike (Reynolds) is an old-time pro, but Ernie (Siemaszko) is a kid, only in it for thrills. Declaring he'd sooner have a partner than a witness, Mike sets about showing Ernie the ropes. Despite the caper movie framework, John Sayles' screenplay is not as far from *That Sinking Feeling* as you might think. Forsyth has a rare talent for locating the comic in the real world. His heroes and heroines never quite fit in, and who can blame them? There's something funny going on: a guard dog more inquisitive than aggressive, a Christian hostel with thousands of dollars in its safe, a poetic prostitute who muses, 'What would I do with your balls were they mine?'. Reynolds reminds one of the easy charm he commands when he doesn't force it, and young gun Siemaszko is marvellous as a likeable schmuck who wants only to belong; together they're poignant and very funny. A subtle, masterly film, a series of life lessons which never ducks the moral ironies, no less precious for their simplicity. TCh

Breaking Point

(1976, Can, 92 min)
d Bob Clark. *p* Claude Héroux, Bob Clark. *sc* Roger E Swaybill, Stanley Mann. *ph* Marc Champion. *ed* Stan Cole. *pd* Dave Deyell. *m* David McLey. *cast* Bo Svenson, Robert Culp, Belinda J Montgomery, Stephen Young, John Colicos, Linda Sorenson.

●Canadian version of *Death Wish*. If the thrust of the film is a rising curve of violence, Clark's direction is far less certain, with the result that odd touches in the script suggest the film has aspirations which are never fulfilled. Instead stock resolutions abound. PH

Breaking Point, The

(1950, US, 97 min)
d Michael Curtiz. *p* Jerry Wald. *sc* Ranald MacDougall. *ph* Ted McCord. *ed* Alan Crosland Jr. *ad* Edward Carrere. *m* Ray Heindorf. *cast* John Garfield, Patricia Neal, Phyllis Thaxter, Juano Hernandez, Wallace Ford, Edmon Ryan.

●Hawks messed around with Hemingway and made *To Have and Have Not* (1944); six years later Curtiz played it straighter and wound up with this thoroughly competent smuggling drama, which, without Bogey and Bacall on board, has faded into the celluloid woodwork. Garfield works hard though as the Southern California boat-owner who puts himself in danger when he agrees to take on illegal cargo to pay his debts, and even if you know and love the Hawks' movie there's still much to intrigue here. (Don Siegel directed a third version, *The Gun Runners*, with Audie Murphy in 1958.) TJ

Breaking Point, The (aka The Great Armored Car Swindle)

(1960, GB, 59 min, b/w)
d Lance Comfort. *p* Peter Lambert. *sc* Peter Lambert. *ph* Basil Emmott. *ed* Peter Pitt. *ad* John Earl. *m* Albert Elms. *cast* Peter Reynolds, Dermot Walsh, Joanna Dunham, Lisa Gastoni, Brian Cobby.

●Humdrum, mercifully brief British thriller adapted by producer Peter Lambert from a not-bad novel by Laurence Meynell: matters revolve around attempts to flood a small Middle Eastern country, Lalvadore, with counterfeit notes. The story, too, has a flat, forged feel. GM

Breaking the Sound Barrier

see Sound Barrier, The

Breaking the Waves

(1996, Den/Swe/Fr/Neth/Nor, 159 min)
d Lars von Trier. *p* Vibeke Windelov, Peter Aalbaek Jensen. *sc* Lars von Trier. *ph* Robby Müller. *ed* Anders Refn. *ad* Karl Juliusson. *m* Joachim Holbek. *cast* Emily Watson, Stellan Skarsgård, Katrin Cartlidge, Jean-Marc Barr, Adrian Rawlins, Jonathan Hackett, Sandra Voe.

●The '70s, North-West Scotland: despite opposition from the Calvinist community in which she lives, Bess (Watson) is sufficiently sure God looks kindly on her love for oil-rig worker Jan (Skarsgård) that she marries him. When he returns to the rig, however, she can barely tolerate his absence, and prays for his return – which he does, paralysed and perhaps brain-damaged by an accident. Distraught that his wife's brief sexual bliss is over, Jan suggests she take lovers and describe her liaisons afterwards, so they might still enjoy sex by proxy. Bess consents reluctantly – until, that is, she comes to believe that the sacrifices she's making will restore Jan's health, or at least save his life. Meanwhile, the villagers ostracise her as a whore. This epic melodrama about love, faith, suffering and redemption is emotionally overwhelming. Its raw power is assured not only by the forthright performances and the increasingly cruel, violent events of the last hour, but by Robby Müller's edgily realist 'Scope camerawork. It's a rapt movie, and so wrapped up in its own harrowing dynamics that it finally, perhaps, goes too far in subjecting its selfless heroine to pain and indignity; is this sympathy or sadism? That said, it's a remarkable achievement for all concerned, with Katrin Cartlidge, as Bess's widowed sister-in-law, sharing the acting laurels with the radiant Emily Watson, and writer/director Lars von Trier building the emotional and dramatic intensity with consummate skill. GA

Breaking Up

(1996, US, 89 min)
d Robert Greenwald. *p* Robert Greenwald, George Moffly. *sc* Michael Cristofer. *ph* Mauro Fiore. *ed* Suzanne Hines. *pd* Terrence Foster. *m* Mark Mothersbaugh. *cast* Russell Crowe, Salma Hayek, Abraham Alvarez.

●Steve (Crowe) and Monica (Hayek) keep breaking up. Nothing can stop them. They try to make a clean break by getting married, but it doesn't work. Almost the only other thing in the lives of this pair is the camera, with which, admittedly, they have a healthy interaction, inviting it over for dinner, into the shower, or, when apart, gregariously telling it about their feelings. There's hardly any sign of work, friends, family, and no suggestion that social or professional influences inform a relationship. And there's no attempt at rounded storytelling, or any insight into this self-contradictory love affair – merely a skin-deep litany of symptoms. NB

Break of Dawn

(1988, US/Mex, 115 min)
d Isaac Artenstein. *p* Jude Pauline Eberhard. *sc* Isaac Artenstein. *ph* Stephen Lighthill. *ed* John Nutt. *m* Mark Adler. *cast* Oscar Chavez, Maria Rojo, Peter Henry Schroeder, Pepe Serna, Socorro Valdez.

●A fairly workmanlike movie, but the fascinating subject matter intrigues. Mexican actor and singer Oscar Chavez stars as Pedro J Gonzalez, the first Spanish-speaking radio star to make it in the US. His career ended prematurely in the 1930s when his outspoken comments on the forced deportation of Mexican immigrants were met by a vindictive response from a publicity-seeking DA. Unjustly convicted of the rape of an under-age girl and sentenced to 50 years in San Quentin, his plight mobilised the Mexican-American community in the fight to clear his name. TJ

Breakout

(1975, US, 96 min)
d Tom Gries. *p* Robert Chartoff, Irwin Winkler. *sc* Howard B Kreitsek, Frank Kowalski. *ph* Lucien Ballard. *ed* Bud S Isaacs. *ad* Alfred Sweeney Jr. *m* Jerry Goldsmith. *cast* Charles Bronson, Robert Duvall, Jill Ireland, Randy Quaid, Sheree North, Emilio Fernandez, Alan Vint.

●A routinely spectacular adventure, set in Mexican border country and featuring Bronson as the mastermind behind a series of attempts to spring a framed man from jail. It offers little of substance beyond some fancy stunts, a number of obvious plagiarisms (*Chinatown*, *Charley Varrick*, *Thunderbolt* and *Lightfoot*), and a strong support cast who deserved better.

Break to Freedom

see Albert RN

Breath

(2000, Ire/GB, 45 sec)
d Damien Hirst. *p* Michael Colgan, Alan Moloney. *sc* Samuel Beckett. *ph* Brendan Galvin. *ad* (sup) Clodagh Conroy. *cast* voice: Keith Allen.
● At under a minute, this is Beckett's shortest play. Damien Hirst directs and Keith Allen provides the long exhalation. The camera sweeps over an island of medical and technical debris, lingering finally over an ashtray and a bottle of pills. Rendering it as a Pharmacy hit by a bomb, Hirst gets some sardonic humour into Beckett's most uncompromising vision of life. EPe

Breathless

(1983, US, 100 min)
d Jim McBride. *p* Martin Erlichman. *sc* LM Kit Carson, Jim McBride. *ph* Richard H Kline. *ed* Robert Estrin. *pd* Richard Sylbert. *m* Jack Nitzsche. *cast* Richard Gere, Valerie Kaprisky, William Tepper, John P Ryan, Art Metrano, Robert Dunn.
● Neither straight remake nor looser homage to Godard's *A Bout de Souffle*; better by far to just enjoy it on its own terms when it turns out at least three parts better than anyone predicted. Gere is the rockabilly punk living permanently on the edge, on the run from a cop-killing, and certain of at least two things: how to steal cars and his obsession with his girl. Together they conduct a fugitive romance across LA, a common enough idea from Hollywood (Gun Crazy is a motif) but one which is burning with a rarely seen passion. The breathless shooting style lingers forever on Gere's pumping, preening narcissism, which leaves you in no doubt that the true romance is not between boy and girl, but between Gere and camera. The film's other star is LA, which is filmed as a series of dazzling pop art backdrops – cultural vacancy and hedonism, yoked together by violence: a city for the '80s. A wanton, playful film, belying the stated despair by its boiling energy. CPea

Breathless

see A Bout de Souffle

Breezy

(1973, US, 107 min)
d Clint Eastwood. *p* Robert Daley. *sc* Jo Heims. *ph* Frank Stanley. *ed* Ferris Webster. *ad* Alexander Golitzen. *m* Michel Legrand. *cast* William Holden, Kay Lenz, Roger C Carmel, Marj Dusay, Joan Hotchkis, Jamie Smith Jackson.
● Eastwood has often been noted for his sudden, surprising and adventurous switches in direction, but none of them (not even *Tightrope*) is quite as extraordinary as this. For one thing he does not appear in it himself (well, only in a Hitchcock-style shot); for another, the subject matter is hardly what one would associate with 'Dirty Harry'. A middle-aged real-estate broker meets a hippy hitchhiker less than half his age. They fall in love. A project full of pitfalls, all of which Eastwood, remarkably, manages to avoid. The film is sentimental only in that its characters, being human and in love, are sentimental; otherwise the script (by Jo Heims, who also wrote *Play Misty For Me*) and direction clearly chart the many obstacles facing the pair in terms of age, background, ideals and so on. It's performed beautifully, laced with a quietly ironic wit, and quite lovely to look at. GA

Breve Vacanza, Una

see Brief Vacation, A

Brewster McCloud

(1970, US, 105 min)
d Robert Altman. *p* Lou Adler. *sc* Doran William Cannon. *ph* Lamar Boren, Jordan Cronenweth. *ed* Louis Lombardo. *ad* Preston Ames, George W Davis. *m* Gene Page. *cast* Bud Cort, Sally Kellerman, Michael Murphy, Shelley Duvall, William Windom, Rene Auberjonois, Stacy Keach, John Schuck.
● Though it bears more than a few traces of the forced outrageousness that marked Doran William Cannon's previous screenplay, for Preminger's lamentable comedy *Skidoo*, Altman's unexpected follow-up to *M*A*S*H* is pitched fairly successfully between escapist fantasy and satirical comment on the same. Cort is the Icarus figure attempting to become airborne in the Houston Astrodome, Kellerman the sort of guardian angel who appears to have wandered in from a Dennis Potter play, and Murphy the cop mulling connections between bird shit and murder. PT

Brewster's Millions

(1945, US, 79 min, b/w)
d Allan Dwan. *sc* Siegfried Herzig, Charles Rogers, Wilkie Mahoney. *ph* Charles Lawton Jr. *ed* Grant Whytock, Richard Heermance. *ad* Joseph Sternad. *m* Hugo Friedhofer. *cast* Dennis O'Keefe, Helen Walker, Eddie 'Rochester' Anderson, June Havoc, Gail Patrick, Mischa Auer.
● The fifth adaptation of the perennial play about a young man (here an ex-GI, engagingly played by O'Keefe) who stands to inherit seven million dollars provided he can get rid of one million (in secret, no giving it away) within a couple of months. No masterpiece but really quite inventive, it was one of three breathless farces directed by Dwan during the '40s (the other two, marginally superior, were *Up in Mabel's Room* and *Getting Gertie's Garter*). TM

Brewster's Millions

(1985, US, 101 min)
d Walter Hill. *p* Lawrence Gordon, Joel Silver. *sc* Herschel Weingrod, Timothy Harris. *ph* Ric Waite. *ed* Freeman Davies, Michael Ripps. *pd* John Vallone. *m* Ry Cooder. *cast* Richard Pryor, John Candy, Lonette McKee, Stephen Collins, Jerry Orbach, Pat Hingle, Hume Cronyn.
● Hill's first attempt at straight comedy is less than happy. Pryor is the pitcher for the Hackensack Bulls baseball team, suddenly left $300 million in a will. But he first has to spend 30 million in a month without revealing the wheeze and ending up with no assets. The ideas here aren't nearly up to the scratch that writers Herschel Weingrod and Timothy Harris established in *Trading Places*. That the story has been filmed successfully seven times previously might have sounded warning bells that a more modernist treatment was called for than simply updating the amount involved to take inflation into account. CPea

Bribe, The

(1949, US, 98 min, b/w)
d Robert Z Leonard. *p* Pandro S Berman. *sc* Marguerite Roberts. *ph* Joseph Ruttenberg. *ed* Gene Ruggiero. *ad* Cedric Gibbons, Malcolm Bray. *m* Miklos Rozsa. *cast* Robert Taylor, Ava Gardner, Charles Laughton, Vincent Price, John Hodiak, John Hoyt.
● Price and Laughton make a formidable pair of heavies in this otherwise feeble thriller shot on a cheaply rigged-up corner of the MGM backlot. Taylor isn't up to moral dilemma as a US government agent sent to crack illicit aircraft engine trading in the Caribbean, yet tempted by a lucrative cash offer and the irresistible charm of café chanteuse Gardner. TJ

Bridal Path, The

(1959, GB, 95 min)
d Frank Launder. *p* Sidney Gilliat, Frank Launder. *sc* Frank Launder, Geoffrey Willans. *ph* Arthur Ibbetson. *ed* Geoffrey Foot. *ad* Wilfrid Shingleton. *m* Cedric Thorpe Davie. *cast* Bill Travers, Fiona Clyne, George Cole, Gordon Jackson, Dilys Laye, Duncan Macrae, Charlotte Mitchell, Bernadette O'Farrell.
● Travers donned a kilt and spruced up his braw bricht accent one more time for this Launder and Gilliat frolic (from a novel by Nigel Tranter), in which a cheery Hebridean islander, Ewan McEwan, is despatched to the mainland to search for a wife. Along the way, he gets himself mistaken for a notorious salmon poacher. In the end, however, he's allowed to marry his island sweetheart (Fiona Clyne), who turns out not to be his cousin after all (the island Elders had been worried about inbreeding). Everything's handled very decorously (this being 1959), but the jokes are a bit thin, and the Technicolor landscape (photographed by Arthur Ibbetson) is laid on rather thick. TJ

Bride, The

(1985, GB, 119 min)
d Franc Roddam. *p* Victor Drai. *sc* Lloyd Fonvielle. *ph* Stephen H Burum. *ed* Michael Ellis. *pd* Michael Seymour. *m* Maurice Jarre. *cast* Sting, Jennifer Beals, Anthony Higgins, Clancy Brown, David Rappaport, Geraldine Page, Alexei Sayle, Quentin Crisp, Timothy Spall.
● A monster movie with a difference: Roddam's update of the classic *The Bride of Frankenstein* is not so much a movie, more a monster. Sting looks like he's smelt something rotten (the script?) as Baron Frankenstein, he with other people's bits in his mitts, a man determined to create the perfect bride for his less than perfect monster. Uncertain in tone, uneasy in conception, preposterous as a love story and possessing all the horror of an advert for Holsten Pils, this is perhaps the silliest film of the year. RR

Bride of Chucky

(1998, US, 89 min)
d Ronny Yu. *p* David Kirschner, Grace Gilroy. *sc* Don Macini. *ph* Peter Pau. *ed* David Wu. Randolph K Bricker. *pd* Alicia Keywan. *m* Graeme Revell. *cast* Jennifer Tilly, Katherine Heigl, Nick Stabile, John Ritter, Alexis Arquette, Gordon Michael Woolvett, Lawrence Dane, Michael Johnson.
● The sensational, virtually irrational association of the *Child's Play* films with the murder of the Liverpool boy Jamie Bulger has proved one of the more enduring instances of tabloid opportunism. Assuming we can address this third sequel on its merits as opposed to its demonic properties, it's by some way the best of the killer doll series, and as stylish and witty a horror movie as you could want. Tilly has a lot of fun as bleached blonde trailer trash Tiffany, Chucky's old chick when he was still just your average flesh-and-blood psychotic. Having studied 'Voodoo for Dummies', Tiffany reckons she can bring her rubber lover back to life. Unfortunately, things don't exactly go to plan, and a revitalised but still pissed off Chucky (voiced by Brad Dourif) decides he has to cut Doll face down to size. With the unwitting aid of runaway teens Stabile and Heigl, the deadly duo embark on a cross-country murder spree. HK director Ronny Yu and screenwriter Don Mancini approach their assignments with infectious absurdist glee. Cinematic in-jokes (notably alluding to Whale's *Bride of Frankenstein*) and ingenious murders (it must be a challenge to make these pint pots threatening) give it a *Scream*-like postmodern sensibility, but with a surreal quality all its own. TCh

Bride of Frankenstein, The

(1935, US, 80 min, b/w)
d James Whale. *p* Carl Laemmle Jr. *sc* William Hurlbut. *ph* John Mescall. *ed* Ted J Kent. *ad* Charles D Hall. *m* Franz Waxman. *cast* Boris Karloff, Colin Clive, Valerie Hobson, Ernest Thesiger, Elsa Lanchester, Una O'Connor, Dwight Frye, Gavin Gordon.
● Tremendous sequel to Whale's own original, with a clever prologue between Byron and Mary Shelley setting the scene for the revival of both Frankenstein and his monster. Thereafter Thesiger's loony Dr Praetorius arrives on the scene, complete with miniaturised humans, and tries to persuade the good doctor to have another go at creating life, this time in the form of a female companion for Karloff. What distinguishes the film is less its horror content, which is admittedly low, than the macabre humour and sense of parody. Strong on atmosphere, Gothic sets and expressionist camerawork, it is – along with *The Old Dark House*, Whale's most perfectly realised movie, a delight from start to finish. GA

Bride of Vengeance

(1949, US, 91 min, b/w)
d Mitchell Leisen. *p* Richard Maibaum. *sc* Cyril Hume, Michael Hogan, Clemence Dane. *ph* Daniel Fapp. *ed* Alma Macrorie. *ad* Hans Dreier, Roland Anderson, Albert Nozaki. *m* Hugo Friedhofer. *cast* Paulette Goddard, John Lund, Macdonald Carey, Raymond Burr, John Sutton, Albert Dekker.
● In this poker-faced absurdity the Duke of Ferrara adopts the Zorro gambit, pretending to be a fop, so the Borgias won't suspect he means to fight them with the enormous cannon he's building in his cellar. This business of the cannon ('Jupiter') is the sort of dream one of Freud's more humorous patients might have made up, though it's of a piece with the extraordinary men's costumes, designed by Leisen himself; with the nude male statuary discreetly decorating the ducal estate; and with Paulette Goddard's demonstrations of passionate agitation, not least when

she first claps eyes on Jupiter. Otherwise, Lucrezia and Cesare are on form ('Remove his tongue and an arm'), suggesting the idea of incest as clearly as Paramount would then permit. Traces of Leisen's intermittently fastidious directorial personality remain, though the notion of fastidious camp may be too paradoxical to sustain. BBa

Brides of Dracula, The

(1960, GB, 85 min)
d Terence Fisher. *p* Anthony Hinds. *sc* Jimmy Sangster, Peter Bryan, Edward Percy. *ph* Jack Asher. *ed* Alfred Cox. *pd* Bernard Robinson. *m* Malcolm Williamson. *cast* Peter Cushing, David Peel, Martita Hunt, Yvonne Monlaur, Miles Malleson, Mona Washbourne, Freda Jackson.

●Patchy but striking, and directed with Fisher's usual flair. Not really a sequel to Hammer's *Dracula*, since Christopher Lee refused to repeat his role, it has Peel as a youthful and somewhat pallid relative who is kept locked up (though thoughtfully provided with suitable victims) by a fond mamma, but escapes to get within biting distance of an academy for young ladies. Hunt (the mother) and Jackson (a crazed retainer) are fun. TM

Brides of Fu Manchu, The

(1966, GB, 91 min)
d Don Sharp. *p/sc* Harry Alan Towers. *ph* Ernest Steward. *ed* Alan Morrison. *ad* Frank White. *m* Johnny Douglas. *cast* Christopher Lee, Douglas Wilmer, Marie Versini, Heinz Drache, Howard Marion Crawford, Tsai Chin.

●This was the second of the two movies that the talented Sharp made for producer Harry Alan Towers in the Fu Manchu series, based on Sax Rohmer's vintage yellow bogeyman. Although nothing like as stylish as its predecessor, *The Face of Fu Manchu*, it manages to get quite a lot of fun out of a Bondish plot in which the evil doctor (played with as much sinister menace as ever by Christopher Lee) kidnaps a dozen girls so as to force key relatives to develop a deadly new energy ray. DP

Bride Wore Black, The (La Mariée était en Noir)

(1967, Fr/It, 107 min)
d François Truffaut. *p* Marcel Berbert. *sc* François Truffaut, Jean-Louis Richard. *ph* Raoul Coutard. *ed* Claudine Bouché. *ad* Pierre Guffroy. *m* Bernard Herrmann. *cast* Jeanne Moreau, Claude Rich, Jean-Claude Brialy, Michel Bouquet, Michel Lonsdale, Charles Denner, Daniel Boulanger, Alexandra Stewart.

●Truffaut has stated that this elegant detective thriller, based (like his *Mississippi Mermaid*) on a novel by Cornell Woolrich, was an attempt to reconcile his two cinematic idols, Alfred Hitchcock and Jean Renoir. It's about Julie Kohler (Moreau), whose husband is inexplicably shot dead on the church steps after their wedding. Truffaut follows Julie's systematic and deadly revenge with a light, idyllic style as she ruthlessly hunts and kills her victims (by methods which include pushing the first over a balcony, poisoning the next, and suffocating the third). Perhaps the mixture of crime fiction and Renoir never quite jells, but it's all highly entertaining, and Hitchcock buffs will enjoy picking out the many echoes (of *Marnie* especially). DP

Bridge, The

(1990, GB, 99 min)
d Sydney MacCartney. *p* Lyn Goleby. *sc* Adrian Hodges. *ph* David Tattersall. *ed* Michael Ellis. *pd* Terry Pritchard. *m* Richard G Mitchell. *cast* Saskia Reeves, David O'Hara, Joss Ackland, Rosemary Harris, Anthony Higgins, Geraldine James.

●Another of those parasol and starched linen Vic-wardian costumers of TV drama dimensions, this time the account of an impossible romantic liaison between a beautiful and sensitive married mother (Reeves) and the youthful Impressionist painter Philip Wilson Steer (O'Hara). Based on the novel by Maggie Hemingway, the film takes its mood from a Steer painting: an enigmatic depiction of a lone woman on a remote Suffolk bridge. Despite being well acted (especially by Reeves), well scripted, finely shot by David Tattersall, and directed with discretion and sensitivity, the result is enervatingly familiar and too tastefully corseted in propriety to arouse the least passion. The working classes, of course, are the ones who don't have sunlight artistically highlighting their despairing faces. WH

Bridge at Remagen, The

(1969, US, 116 min)
d John Guillermin. *p* David L Wolper. *sc* Richard Yates, William S Roberts. *ph* Stanley Cortez. *ed* William Cartwright. *ad* Alfred Sweeney. *m* Elmer Bernstein. *cast* George Segal, Robert Vaughn, Ben Gazzara, Bradford Dillman, EG Marshall, Peter Van Eyck, Matt Clark.

●Cliché runs riot in this WWII yarn, where much ado about a bridge that nobody wants spells that old war-is-madness message trumpeted by *The Bridge on the River Kwai*. Segal, Gazzara and some fine camerawork by Stanley Cortez more or less save the day. TM

Bridge on the River Kwai, The

(1957, GB, 160 min)
d David Lean. *p* Sam Spiegel. *sc* Carl Foreman, Michael Wilson [credited to Pierre Boulle]. *ph* Jack Hildyard. *ed* Peter Taylor. *ad* Don Ashton. *m* Malcolm Arnold. *cast* William Holden, Alec Guinness, Jack Hawkins, Sessue Hayakawa, James Donald, Andre Morell.

●A classic example of a film that fudges the issues it raises: Guinness restores the morale of British PoWs by building a bridge which it transpires is of military value to the Japanese, and then attempts to thwart Hawkins and Holden's destruction of it – or does he? etc. The film's success also marked the end of Lean as a director and the beginnings of American-financed 'British' films. PH

Bridges at Toko-Ri, The

(1954, US, 103 min)
d Mark Robson. *p* William Perlberg, George Seaton. *sc* Valentine Davies. *ph* Loyal Griggs. *ed* Alma Macrorie. *ad* Hal Pereira, Henry Bumstead. *m* Lyn Murray. *cast* William Holden, Grace Kelly, Fredric March, Mickey Rooney, Robert Strauss, Charles McGraw, Earl Holliman.

●Big-budget adaptation of James Michener's Korean war novel, making some noises about the essential futility of the conflict but concluding that the bridges must be bombed to stop the spread of Communism. Competent, well acted and with some excellent aerial special effects, but flawed by mawkish sentimentality in orchestrating its nobility of self-sacrifice theme. Holden is the WWII pilot, now married and established in a civilian career, who resents being recalled to risk his life in a forgotten war; Rooney (sporting a non-regulation green silk topper) and Strauss are on hand to provide the other-ranks humour. TM

Bridges of Madison County, The

(1995, US, 135 min)
d Clint Eastwood. *p* Clint Eastwood, Kathleen Kennedy. *sc* Richard LaGravenese. *ph* Jack N Green. *ed* Joel Cox. *pd* Jeannine C Oppewall. *m* Lennie Niehaus. *cast* Clint Eastwood, Meryl Streep, Annie Corley, Victor Slezak, Jim Haynie, Phyllis Lyons.

●When the daughter and son of the late Francesca Johnson (Streep) return home to Madison County, Iowa, to oversee the funeral arrangements, they're shocked to learn that their mother wished to have her ashes scattered from the Roseman Bridge, not buried beside their father. Worse, they find Francesca's diary, relating how, in '65 while they were off with dad on a visit to Illinois, she met and fell for *National Geographic* photographer Robert Kincaid (Eastwood): an affair which was to affect her entire life. Immaculately performed, and assembled with wit and sensitivity, this is one of the most satisfying weepies in years. Indeed, it's hard to imagine anyone but Eastwood doing such a fine job of adapting Robert James Waller's bestseller for the screen. Typically, his clean, pared direction, coupled with Richard LaGravenese's mostly no-frills script, ensures that the film avoids sentimentality even as the two lovers rush to embrace it. GA

Bridget

(2002, Fr/US, 94 min)
d Amos Kollek. *p.* Frédéric Robbes. *sc* Amos Kollek. *ph* Ed Talavera. *ed* Jeffrey Marc Harkavy, Ron Len. *pd* Jon Nissenbaum. *m* Joe Delia. *cast* Anna Thomson, Julie Hagerty, David Wike.

●Kollek's wilful, meandering and hugely self-indulgent drama is pitched somewhere between a murky Cassavetes-style gangster thriller (in the vein of *Killing of a Chinese Bookie*), a Paul Morrissey exploitation pic and a lush melodrama about a mom fighting to get her kid back. The director's regular muse Anna Thomson brings a little dignity to her underwritten role as the long-suffering heroine who's left holding the baby after her husband is killed by the Mob. Bridget – a sort of latter-day Moll Flanders – is sexually exploited, becomes a drug mule in the Middle East, and marries for money, but the film is so chaotically structured and so ponderous in its pacing that it's hard to care much what happens to her. GM

Bridget Jones's Diary

(2001, US/Fr/GB, 97 min)
d Sharon Maguire. *p* Tim Bevan, Eric Fellner, Jonathan Cavendish. *sc* Helen Fielding, Andrew Davies, Richard Curtis. *ph* Stuart Dryburgh. *ed* Martin Walsh. *pd* Gemma Jackson. *m* Patrick Doyle. *cast* Renée Zellweger, Colin Firth, Hugh Grant, Jim Broadbent, Gemma Jones, Sally Phillips, Shirley Henderson, James Callis, Embeth Davidtz, Celia Imrie, Honor Blackman, James Faulkner.

●Now here's a plot to make a Marxist-Leninist weep: posh girl meets posh bloke, then realises his posh pal is nicer. The end. And yet this ultra-hyped adaptation of the ultra-successful Helen Fielding novel sends you out with a smile on your face. For a simple reason: where *Four Weddings* and *Notting Hill* ask you to feel sympathy for a privileged git who radiates self-love, Bridget Jones (Zellweger) really does seem a hopeless case. Why? Because she's overweight and stays that way – for all Bridget's New Year resolutions, there's no 'ugly duckling blossoms into swan' scenario here. She's also witty, and has a quivery way with her chunky nose and mouth that makes watching her feel refreshingly non-voyeuristic. Like a prodigious toddler, Bridget wears a permanent expression of concentration and it rubs off on us. That Grant is for once supposed to be shallow is another plus. As for Firth, how he manages to make Mr Darcy (aka Mr Right) non-ludicrous is a mystery. In a romantic comedy that runs suspiciously like clockwork, Darcy's embarrassment, like Bridget's body, feels blissfully warm to the touch. CO'Su

Bridge Too Far, A

(1977, GB, 175 min)
d Richard Attenborough. *p* Joseph E Levine, Richard P Levine. *sc* William Goldman. *ph* Geoffrey Unsworth. *ed* Antony Gibbs. *pd* Terence Marsh. *m* John Addison. *cast* Dirk Bogarde, James Caan, Michael Caine, Sean Connery, Edward Fox, Elliott Gould, Gene Hackman, Anthony Hopkins, Laurence Olivier, Robert Redford, Ryan O'Neal, Liv Ullmann.

●Attenborough's trumpeted entry into the all-time blockbuster stakes (based on the book by Cornelius Ryan) is noisy and protracted and has a name cast list as long as your arm. Bogarde, as the ranking officer-actor, presides over the execution of Montgomery's bold plan to seize six Dutch bridges. It turns out to be an overworked, very old and very tired warhorse. Glossy, ponderous, predictable. JPy

Brief Ecstasy

(1937, GB, 71 min, b/w)
d Edmond T Gréville. *p* Hugh Perceval. *sc* Basil Mason. *ph* Ronald Neame. *ad* R Holmes Paul. *m* George Walter. *cast* Paul Lukas, Linden Travers, Hugh Williams, Marie Ney, Renee Gadd, Fred Withers.

●A remarkable film, thematically not dissimilar to *Brief Encounter*, except that lust is given a fair crack of the whip. A strong erotic undertow runs through the witty opening scene: in the exchange of covert glances as Williams comes into a snack bar where Travers is having coffee; in the 'accidental' pawing of her person as he mops the coffee he has spilt; in the over-pitched fury with which she slaps him. His subsequent apology accepted, a superb montage (soft music, silhouettes, champagne, whispered exchanges) heralds a brief night of ecstasy, after which he announces his imminent departure for India. Five years later, he returns to find her the beloved wife of a distinguished, much older scientist (Lukas), and desire is reborn. The excellent script plays fair by all the characters (one scene has Lukas start skipping gaily upstairs to bed in his wife's wake, only to pause, puffing, before he makes it). And Travers' inner struggle, no becoming yes then no again as she realises what she means to her husband, is beautifully detailed in both performance and Gréville's expressionist-tinged direction, which makes it clear that her choice of love is made at the bitter cost of the other thing. TM

Brief Encounter (100)

(1945, GB, 86 min, b/w)
d David Lean. *p* Noël Coward. *sc* Noël Coward, David Lean, Anthony Havelock-Allan. *ph* Robert Krasker. *ed* Jack Harris. *ad* LP Williams. *m* Sergei Rachmaninov. *cast* Celia Johnson, Trevor Howard, Stanley Holloway, Joyce Carey, Cyril Raymond, Valentine Dyall.

●Much beloved, but still exemplary in demonstrating exactly what is wrong with so much of British cinema. OK, so after the war people weren't as quick to jump into bed with other people's spouses as they are now (or were before AIDS), nor were they as open about it. But the stiff-lipped restraint that marks and mars this piece about mild extra-marital petting pertains not merely to the depiction of physical attraction and activity but, more importantly, to the emotions. Much ado about nothing, really, with a classy veneer of sugary romanticism added in the use of Rachmaninov on the soundtrack. GA

Brief Vacation, A (Una Breve Vacanza)

(1973, It/Sp, 112 min)
d Vittorio De Sica. *p* Marina Cicogna, Arthur Cohn. *sc* Cesare Zavattini. *ph* Ennio Guarnieri. *ed* Franco Arcalli. *ad* Luigi Scaccianoce. *m* Christian De Sica. *cast* Florinda Bolkan, Renato Salvatori, Daniel Quenaud, José Maria Prada, Teresa Gimpera, Adriana Asti.

●De Sica and Zavattini administer the last rites over the corpse of neo-realism in this travesty which starts with one of those vociferous Italian domestic squabbles, but soon switches to masturbatory fantasy with a gushy celebration of romance in a mountain TB sanatorium. Bolkan, as the working-class housewife drudging to feed a thankless family who is sent to the clinic at the government's expense, deserves better. TM

Brigadista, El

see Teacher, The

Brigadoon

(1954, US, 108 min)
d Vincente Minnelli. *p* Arthur Freed. *sc* Alan Jay Lerner. *ph* Joseph Ruttenberg. *ed* Albert Akst. *ad* Cedric Gibbons, Preston Ames. *songs* Frederick Loewe, Alan Jay Lerner. *cast* Gene Kelly, Van Johnson, Cyd Charisse, Elaine Stewart, Barry Jones, Hugh Laing.

●A classic – if not *the* classic – Minnelli musical, *Brigadoon* is an explicit statement about (and partial criticism of) the notion that an artist only lives through his art, preferring its reality to the world's. The film begins with a disenchanted Kelly in flight from 'civilised' New York, lost in the Scottish Highlands and stumbling on the legendary village of Brigadoon which only appears for one day each century. There he meets the love of his life Fiona (Charisse), only to discover both the truth about Brigadoon and that some of its inhabitants want the real life he is fleeing from, even though it will destroy Brigadoon. Disillusioned when the villagers kill the would-be escapees, Kelly leaves. But in New York, amidst the chaos of modern living, he discovers he is yearning for Fiona and Brigadoon. He returns to Scotland where his faith (and Fiona's love) conjures up Brigadoon. This time he settles there, accepting that the price of happiness is to live but one day a century. As this description of the film makes clear, it (and Minnelli's musicals in general) is escapist to say the least. However, Minnelli's musicals must be seen alongside his dramas which examine the other side of the coin, the problems of confronting reality, rather than evading it or constructing one's own. PH

Brigand of Kandahar, The

(1965, GB, 81 min)
d John Gilling. *p* Anthony Nelson Keys. *sc* John Gilling. *ph* Reginald Wyer. *ed* James Needs. *pd* Bernard Robinson. *m* Don Banks. *cast* Ronald Lewis, Oliver Reed, Yvonne Romain, Duncan Lamont, Glyn Houston, Catherine Woodville.

●Minor 'Cinema of Empire' episode from the erratic Gilling, who found his happiest niche with Hammer (who produced this) but in their horror mode. India in 1850 provides the backdrop (supposedly, at least, since papier mâché rocks and rural England are much in evidence) for a routine military adventure, with a half-caste officer (Lewis) facing court-martial for cowardice as the natives indicate their restlessness in time-honoured style. PT

Brigands

(1996, Fr, 129 min)
d Otar Iosseliani. *p* Martine Marignac. *sc* Otar Iosseliani. *ph* William Lubtchansky. *ed* Otar Iosseliani. *pd* Emmanual de Chauvigny, Jean-Michel Simonet, Lena Joukova. *m* Nicolas Zourabichvili. *cast* Amiran Amiranachvili, Dato Gogibedachvili, Guio Tzintsadze, Nino Ordjonikidze, Keti Kapanadze.

●More properly, 'Brigands, Chapter VII', this mournful, over-long, virtually dialogue-free account of man's inhumanity to man cuts between the centuries, from the recent civil war in Georgia to medieval feuding and Stalinist torture chambers, using the same group of actors in each setting. The film's deadpan tone is eloquence itself, but there's no narrative momentum when everything is so clearly hopeless. TCh

Brigham Young – Frontiersman

(1940, US, 112 min, b/w)
d Henry Hathaway. *p* Kenneth Macgowan. *sc* Lamar Trotti. *ph* Arthur Miller. *ed* Robert Bischoff. *ad* William Darling, Maurice Ransford. *m* Alfred Newman. *cast* Tyrone Power, Linda Darnell, Dean Jagger, Brian Donlevy, John Carradine, Jane Darwell, Mary Astor, Vincent Price.

●1840s. Brigham Young (Jagger) joins Joseph Smith's Mormon Church just as persecution drives the faithful Utah-wards. The community they establish is riven with conflict and almost perishes in the harsh winter, until seagulls arrive to eat the locusts that are ruining the make-or-break wheat crop. Tensions are also evident between Mormon history and 1940 sensitivities, so that although Brigham's polygamy is alluded to, Mary Astor never shares the frame with another Mrs Young. Common ownership of land and crops is acknowledged, but greater emphasis is placed on the Mormons exercising their Constitutional rights and on their status as Fordian pioneers. Still, Hathaway resists mythologising a narrative already laden with Biblical symbolism: Smith and Young are portrayed as tetchy zealots. And there is richness in the detail: the practicalities of how a town uproots itself, how birth, death and schooling go on inside a moving wagon. DO

Brighter Summer Day, A (Guling Jie Shaonian Sha Ren Shijian)

(1991, Tai, 237 min)
d Edward Yang. *p* Yu Weiyen. *sc* Edward Yang, Yan Hongya, Yang Shunqing, Lai Mingtang. *ph* Zhang Huigong, Li Longyu. *ed* Chen Bowen. *pd* Yu Weiyan, Edward Yang. *m* Zhan Hongda. *cast* Zhang Zhen, Lisa Yang, Zhang Guozhu, Elaine Jin, Wang Juan, Zhang Han.

●Slow, elliptical, and for the most part understated, Yang's masterly account of growing up in Taiwan at the start of the '60s is as visually elegant as his own *Taipei Story* and *The Terroriser*, and as epic in scope as Hou Xiaoxian's *City of Sadness* (which Yang produced). On the surface, it's about one boy's involvement in gang rivalry and violence (on which level, it's often a little obscure, so numerous are the characters) and his experience of young love. On a deeper level, however, it's about a society in transition and in search of an identity, forever aware of its isolation from mainland China, and increasingly prey to Americanisation. The measured pace may be off-putting, but stay with it – the accumulated wealth of detail invests the unexpected final scenes with enormous, shocking power. GA

Bright Lights, Big City

(1988, US, 107 min)
d James Bridges. *p* Mark Rosenberg, Sydney Pollack. *sc* Jay McInerney. *ph* Gordon Willis. *ed* John Bloom. *pd* Santo Loquasto. *m* Donald Fagen. *cast* Michael J Fox, Kiefer Sutherland, Phoebe Cates, Swoosie Kurtz, Frances Sternhagen, Tracy Pollan, John Houseman, Jason Robards, Dianne Wiest.

●It's hard to care much about Jamie Conway, an aspiring novelist who is dissipating his substance in New York on cocaine and parties: Fox hasn't the range to play anguish, so the explanatory voice-over is less a survival from the best-selling novel than a necessity. Why is he doing this to himself? It's a cry for help, of course, and there's a lengthy monologue at a concerned colleague's apartment that brings any dramatic thrust to a stop. Jamie's wife (Cates) has left him, and his beloved mother (Wiest) has died of cancer, so he clings to bad influences like Tad the Lad (Sutherland). 'The Bolivian Marching Powder' finally gives him a nose-bleed, which forces him to take stock of his soul, and in a risible piece of symbolism, he trades his shades for a loaf of bread like Mother use to bake. Some telling cameos, however: Robards as a boozy bore who once hobnobbed with the greats of American Lit; Houseman as an etymological pedant; Wiest in a wonderfully moving death-bed scene. BC

Brightness

see Yeelen.

Brighton Beach Memoirs

(1986, US, 110 min)
d Gene Saks. *p* Ray Stark. *sc* Neil Simon. *ph* John Bailey. *ed* Carol Littleton. *pd* Stuart Wurtzel. *m* Michael Small. *cast* Blythe Danner, Bob Dishy, Brian Drillinger, Stacey Glick, Judith Ivey, Jonathan Silverman.

●Neil Simon's autobiographical play, a Jewish *Dear Octopus*, makes for mildly diverting comedy in overexposed terrain. 15-year-old Eugene (Silverman) is the tour guide of his Brooklyn household, staring into the camera and commentating. His adolescent fantasies of sex and baseball are continually interrupted by his mother (Danner), who keeps him running errands. Danner does what she can with the stereotype between cooking, tidying and *kvetching*, while dad (Dishy) overworks, worries about Hitler, and denies that he's a saint. All social life revolves around the liver-and-cabbage, all unsocial life around the bathroom. All grievances come to a head dramatically, but blood is the rap you can't beat. BC

Brighton Rock

(1947, GB, 92 min. b/w)
d John Boulting. *p* Roy Boulting. *sc* Graham Greene, Terence Rattigan. *ph* Harry Waxman. *ed* Peter Graham Scott. *ad* John Howell. *m* Hans May. *cast* Richard Attenborough, Carol Marsh, Hermione Baddeley, William Hartnell, Harcourt Williams, Alan Wheatley.

●Thanks to a marvellous source in Graham Greene's novel, one of the finest British thrillers ever. Attenborough puts in his most memorable performance (with the possible exception of his Christie in *10 Rillington Place*) as Pinky, the psychopathic and murderous leader of a Brighton gang working the racetrack, who courts and marries a waitress (witness to one of his crimes) in order to keep her silent. Beautifully shot by Harry Waxman, it's perhaps the nearest thing to a British *noir* thriller, and as David Thomson has written, has the authentic 'tang of fish and chips'. And the ending is less a happy cop-out than a climax of superb irony. GA

Brighton Strangler, The

(1945, US, 67 min, b/w)
d Max Nosseck. *p* Herman Schlom. *sc* Arnold Phillips, Max Nosseck. *ph* J Roy Hunt. *ed* Les Millbrook. *ad* Albert S D'Agostino, Ralph Berger. *m* Leigh Harline. *cast* John Loder, June Duprez, Michael St Angel, Miles Mander, Rose Hobart, Gilbert Emery, Ian Wolfe.

●Good old amnesia gets a none too convincing outing as Loder, star of a play called *The Brighton Strangler* in London's West End, gets hit on the head when the theatre is bombed in an airraid on closing night, and revives – presumed killed – under the impression that he is the character he played for 300 performances. Ingenious plotting gets him to Brighton in circumstances similar enough to the play to keep him on the rails; and the script is ruthless enough to have him bring off a couple of garrottings before reality catches up with him. Nosseck keeps things moving along smoothly enough, despite an irritating penchant for little 'mood' montages (generally when Loder's mind stutters between fiction and reality); but the credibility quotient, already low, is not improved by studio sets and backdrops which make what is supposedly happening in real life look very much like theatrical artifice. TM

Brilliant Lies

(1996, Aust, 94 min)
d Richard Franklin. *p* Richard Franklin, Sue Farrelly. *sc* Richard Franklin, Peter Fitzpatrick. *ph* Geoff Burton. *ed* David Pulbrook. *pd* Tracy Watt. *m* Nerida Tyson-Chew. *cast* Gia Carides, Anthony LaPaglia, Zoe Carides, Ray Barrett, Michael Veitch, Neil Melville, Catherine Wilkin.

●Franklin's adaptation of David Williamson's play about sexual harassment in the workplace is a huge improvement on his abysmal *Hotel Sorrento*, but still suffers from staginess. Centred on the accusations of flirty, money-grabbing Gia Carides against slimy, misogynist boss LaPaglia, the script delves into a range of heavily conflicting attitudes (to sexual politics, family relationships, honesty, ethics), remaining sensitive throughout to male paranoia and female resentment. Motivation and resolution, finally, are a little pat, but the sturdy performances flesh out the schematic scenario and, clumsy flashbacks aside, Franklin directs with a fair sense of irony and immediacy. GA

Brimstone and Treacle

(1982, GB, 87 min)
d Richard Loncraine. *p* Kenith Trodd. *sc* Dennis Potter. *ph* Peter Hannan. *ed* Paul Green. *pd* Millie Burns. *m* Sting, Michael Nyman. *cast* Sting, Denholm Elliott, Joan Plowright, Suzanna Hamilton, Benjamin Whitrow, Dudley Sutton.

●Into the musty atmosphere of the Bates' suburban household comes incubus/angel figure Martin Taylor (a pleasing performance from Sting in a role which conveniently requires the star to be seen to be acting). Posing as a friend of their recently brain-damaged child, the narcissistic Taylor charms the prayer-trusting, lightbrained mother (Plowright) and challenges the lustfully guilt-ridden father (Elliott), while doing dirty deeds to their daughter in the front room. The quality and ambiguities of good and evil get a thorough, if predictable going-over as Taylor manoeuvres around the parents like a clay-footed Pan. Betrayed by an over-familiar plotline (Orton's *Entertaining Mr Sloane* and Pasolini's *Theorem* for a start) it also suffers from a mild case of stagebounditis as a TV play transferred to the big screen. Otherwise very watchable, thanks to a trio of superb performances, and confident, well-paced direction which only goes overboard in the fantasy sequences. FL

Bringing Out the Dead

(1999, US, 121 min)
d Martin Scorsese. *p* Scott Rudin, Barbara De Fina. *sc* Paul Schrader. *ph* Robert Richardson. *ed* Thelma Schoonmaker. *pd* Dante Ferretti. *m* Elmer Bernstein. *cast* Nicolas Cage, Patricia Arquette, John Goodman, Ving Rhames, Tom Sizemore, Marc Anthony, Mary Beth Hurt, Cliff Curtis, Nestor Serrano, Aida Turturro.

●New York, the early '90s. Frank Pierce (Cage) drives an ambulance for the Emergency Medical Services. He's wired, confused, lonely – and haunted by the lives he's failed to save. Not that Hell's Kitchen, his territory, or his paramedic partners (Goodman, Rhames and Sizemore) over three wild nights help much. The sole source of peace for Frank would seem to be Mary (Arquette), daughter of a heart attack victim – but even she's an ex-junkie afraid that the underfunded hospital won't save her dad. Scorsese's film of Joe Connelly's novel has been likened to *Taxi Driver*. A more apposite comparison, however, might be the closing, coke fuelled coda of *GoodFellas*, since this sees Scorsese pulling out all the stylistic stops to play Frank's story in the fortissimo register. It's a pity the tone veers awkwardly between philosophical speculation, black comedy, Kazan-like drama and souped-up Expressionism. Also the performances of Cage and Sizemore are too manic, and a sense of déjà vu often creeps in. Of course, it's immaculately crafted and exhilaratingly paced, but in the end it's never as emotionally involving as it could and should be. GA

Bringing Up Baby  (100)

(1938, US, 102 min, b/w)
d Howard Hawks. *p* Howard Hawks. *sc* Dudley Nichols, Hagar Wilde. *ph* Russell Metty. *ed* George Hively. *ad* Van Nest Polglase. *m* Roy Webb. *cast* Cary Grant, Katharine Hepburn, Charles Ruggles, May Robson, Barry Fitzgerald, Walter Catlett, Fritz Feld.

●One of the finest screwball comedies ever, with Grant – a dry, nervous, conventional palaeontologist – meeting up with madcap socialite Hepburn and undergoing the destruction of his career, marriage, sanity and sexual identity. The catalyst in the process is Baby, a leopard that causes chaos wherever he goes, and finally awakens Grant to the attractions of irreponsible insanity. Fast, furious and very, very funny. GA

Bring It On

(2000, US, 99 min)
d Peyton Reed. *p* Marc Abraham, Thomas A Bliss. *sc* Jessica Bendinger. *ph* Shawn Maurer. *ed* Larry Bock. *pd* Sharon Lomofsky. *m* Christopher Beck. *cast* Kirsten Dunst, Eliza Dushku, Jesse Bradford, Gabrielle Union, Sherry Hursey, Holmes Osborne, Clare Kramer.

●Torrance (Dunst), captain of the Toro cheerleading squad at a San Diego high school, is hellbent on taking the team to victory in the national championships for the sixth consecutive year. But pressure builds when she discovers that her predecessor stole their well rehearsed routines from the Clovers, a HipHop squad out for revenge. Meanwhile, there's a cheating boyfriend and her confusing feelings for Cliff, brother of Missy (Dushku, feisty), the Toro's new key recruit. The script contains few surprises, but the dynamics of female friendships are well observed, as is the reality (or surreality) of the cheerleading world. Lightweight, but unexpectedly feelgood. KW

Bring Me the Head of Alfredo Garcia

(1974, US/Mex, 112 min)
d Sam Peckinpah. *p* Martin Baum. *sc* Gordon Dawson, Sam Peckinpah. *ph* Alex Phillips. *ed* Garth Craven. *ad* Agustín Huarte. *m* Jerry Fielding. *cast* Warren Oates, Isela Vega, Gig Young, Robert Webber, Helmut Dantine, Emilio Fernandez, Kris Kristofferson.

●After the deathwish of *Pat Garrett and Billy the Kid*, it's logical that the spirit of a dead man should dominate its successor. And for a director so preoccupied with male virility, it's hardly surprising that Peckinpah has made a film primarily about impotence: Oates, a washed-up American barroom pianist, hunts for the head of the stud Garcia and for his own machismo through a contemporary Mexico that reflects Peckinpah's continuing love affair with that country. There's no suspense; what happens is as predictable as it is inevitable. Peckinpah has structured a slow, almost meditative film out of carefully fashioned images that weave inextricable links between sex, death, music and violence. CPe

Bring Me the Head of Mavis Davis

(1997, GB, 99 min)
d John Henderson. *p* Stephen Colegrave, Joanne Reay. *sc* Craig Strachan. *ph* Clive Tickner. *ed* Paul Endacott. *pd* Michael Carlin. *m* Christopher Tyng. *cast* Rik Mayall, Jane Horrocks, Danny Aiello, Ronald Pickup, Philip Martin-Brown, Heathcote Williams.

●Marty Starr (Mayall) is a bullying record producer. In 1980, Marty discovered mousy Mavis Davis (Horrocks), and threw her back to the world as glamorous Marla Dorland. Now he's in trouble: Marla's sales aren't flourishing and she wants out of the contract. But debt-ridden, disaster-prone Marty has a plan: an early death would be the perfect end to Marla's career, and the rebirth of his. Horrocks seems unaware that this is not some ditzy ad, but the unforgiving big screen; her warbling is neither bad enough to be entertaining, nor good enough to engross. As for Mayall, he never stops being Mayall, and thus deserves every cheap line he gets. The sterling presence of Aiello as a mobster only adds to the embarrassing sense of resources being frenetically whooshed down the drain. CO'Su

Bring On the Night

(1985, US, 97 min)
d Michael Apted. *p* David Manson. *ph* Ralf D Bode. *ed* Robert K Lambert, Melvin Shapiro. *pd* Ferdinando Scarfiotti. *with* Sting, Omar Hakim, Darryl Jones, Kenny Kirkland, Branford Marsalis, Miles Copeland.

●One of the more intelligent, slick and witty shots at the bronzed, big-named rockumentary. Tracing the 'Dream of the Blue Turtles' live project from press conference through rehearsals to the first night in Paris, we get about two-thirds music and one-third chat, both elements varying greatly in quality. Sting, though central, is seldom as colourful or revealing as jazz-rooted band members Marsalis, Kirkland or Hakim. Things are also a little too clean and easy throughout, but then there's always the music – never jazz, of course, but at its best tuneful, highly politicised rock in the hands of some of the most talented musicians in the world. SGa

Brink of Hell

see Toward the Unknown

Brink's Job, The

(1978, US, 103 min)
d William Friedkin. *p* Ralph Serpe. *sc* Walon Green. *ph* Norman Leigh. *ed* Bud Smith, Robert K Lambert. *pd* Dean Tavoularis. *m* Richard Rodney Bennett. *cast* Peter Falk, Peter Boyle, Allen Garfield, Warren Oates, Gena Rowlands, Paul Sorvino.

●Despite Friedkin's strong track record – *The French Connection, The Exorcist* – this is a comedy thriller as lacking in skill, direction or wit as it's possible to imagine. Falk, as the leader of a gang of fools engaged in a multi-million dollar heist, hams his way anxiously through a plot full of childish hiccups, with only Warren Oates (as a weak, tormented accomplice) injecting even a minimum of conviction. CA

Britannia Hospital

(1982, GB, 116 min)
d Lindsay Anderson. *p* Davina Belling, Clive Parsons. *sc* David Sherwin. *ph* Mike Fash. *ed* Michael Ellis. *pd* Norris Spencer. *m* Alan Price. *cast* Leonard Rossiter, Graham Crowden, Joan Plowright, Jill Bennett, Marsha Hunt, Malcolm McDowell, Fulton Mackay.

●It's not merely the rather obvious and all-embracing metaphor of a chaotic and run-down hospital standing in for Britain that is the problem with Anderson's vitriolic attempt at a comedy on the state of the nation; what is perhaps more annoying, finally, is his general tone, that of a cynical old sourpuss with an enormous chip on his shoulder and little – if any – sympathy for anybody. As the caricatures of authoritarians, strikers, media hacks and so on go through the nightmarish events surrounding a royal visit to the hospital on its 500th anniversary, one can't help feeling that so much contempt on the director's part only hides a lack of commitment and focus; the result is less neo-Swiftian satire than a 'Carry On Down the Drain, Britain' with pretensions to deep significance. GA

British Sounds

(1969, GB, 52 min)
d Jean-Luc Godard. *p* Irving Teitelbaum, Kenith Trodd. *sc* Jean-Luc Godard. *ph* Charles Stewart. *ed* Elizabeth Kozmian-Ledward.

●The film that was made for and then banned from London Weekend TV. Essentially a documentary, it's a genuine political artefact in which Godard contrives to assault the British sensibility with a series of images and provocations (the slogans flashed on the screen are sometimes humorous and always to the point). The parts where people just talk really work; when Ford Dagenham workers discuss the company-employee situation, the effect is simple and uncluttered but devastatingly effective. Sometimes, however, the control vanishes – the sequence with Essex students making posters, for instance – and this confirms the impression that revolution in Britain will only come from the industrial army who need it, not the middle class academics who play it. TE

Broadcast News

(1987, US, 132 min)
d/p/sc James L Brooks. *ph* Michael Ballhaus. *ed* Richard Marks. *pd* Charles Rosen. *m* Bill Conti. *cast* William Hurt, Albert Brooks, Holly Hunter, Jack Nicholson, Robert Prosky, Lois Chiles, Joan Cusack, Peter Hackes.

● Writer/director Brooks is knowing about the wisecracks, back-stabbings, political shifts, and innate decencies of the media game, and underpinning what is a charming, protean love-triangle is a serious statement about the function, value, and direction of television news. Aaron Altman (Albert Brooks) is brave, decent, witty, committed, and hopelessly in love with his Mensa-plus producer Jane Craig (Hunter, magnificent), a skilful but personally unfulfilled member of their Washington bureau. Enter Hurt's Tom Grunick, irresistable to women and station executives alike. Aaron is exceptional, but Tom has the looks and presentation to please corporate media America. He just can't grasp or weigh facts. So who gets the jobs, and who gets Jane? Brooks' script has some superb set pieces, crackles with furious one-liners, and mirrors fact. Though a little soft-centred, and closing with a too open-ended postscript, it confirms all the camaraderies and care beyond and behind the pressures and pratfalls, and manages to knock rivals in Yuppie-tography like *Wall Street* and *Fatal Attraction* sideways. SGr

Broadway

(1942, US, 91 min, b/w)
d William A Seiter. *p* Bruce Manning. *sc* Felix Jackson, John Bright. *ph* George Barnes. *ed* Ted J Kent. *ad* Jack Otterson. *m* Frank Skinner. *cast* George Raft, Pat O'Brien, Janet Blair, Broderick Crawford, Marjorie Rambeau, SZ Sakall, Anne Gwynne.

● The George Abbott and Philip Dunning play (first filmed by Paul Fejos in 1929) reshaped as a vehicle for Raft who, playing himself, recalls his days as a nightclub dancer and his association with Prohibition racketeers. He gets to tango and to tangle with a tough gangster (Crawford) over his girl. But studded with songs and all a bit hackneyed, it's more a curiosity than anything else. TM

Broadway Ahead

see Sweetheart of the Campus

Broadway Bill (aka Strictly Confidential)

(1934, US, 104 min, b/w)
d Frank Capra. *p* Harry Cohn. *sc* Robert Riskin. *ph* Joseph Walker. *ed* Gene Havlick. *cast* Warner Baxter, Myrna Loy, Walter Connolly, Helen Vinson, Douglas Dumbrille, Raymond Walburn, Lynne Overman, Clarence Muse, Margaret Hamilton, Jason Robards Sr, Lucille Ball.

● Scripted by Robert Riskin from a story by Mark Hellinger, this is an early sample of Capracorn, with Connolly as a tyrannical tycoon who uses his three sons-in-law as yes men. One of the three (Baxter) rebels, tells Connolly he is a shark preying on small businesses, and goes back to his earlier life on the racetrack, hoping to make a champion of his horse Broadway Bill. His wife (Vinson) turns her back on him, but her rebellious younger sister (Loy) delightedly abets him. Complications ensue, since the horse won't run unless its rooster pal is on hand, conmanship is required to raise the Derby entrance fee, and the fix proves to be on. Gallant Broadway Bill nevertheless wins (though his heart bursts with the effort), justifying the faith of all the small-time punters who had bet on him. Baxter is consoled by his realisation that Loy loves him, and the chastened Connolly (surprise, surprise) gives his empire back to the little people. Ethically dubious and mostly tedious, it was remade by Capra as *Riding High* in 1950, re-using some of the racetrack footage. TM

Broadway Bound

(1991, US, 94 min)
d Paul Bogart. *p* Terry Nelson. *sc* Neil Simon. *ph* Isidore Mankofsky. *ed* Andy Zall. *pd* Ben Edwards. *m* David Shire. *cast* Anne Bancroft, Hume Cronyn, Corey Parker, Jonathan Silverman, Jerry Orbach, Michele Lee, Marilyn Cooper.

● Made as a TV movie, the last part of Neil Simon's autobiographical trilogy – following *Brighton Beach Memoirs* and *Biloxi Blues* – is also the nadir. All together now – let my people go! This Jewish family seems to have been with us as long as the Archers, with Momma (Bancroft) cooking, Poppa (Orbach) kvetching, Granddad (Cronyn) complaining, the boys (Parker and Silverman) spoiled and getting ahead, and typicality ruling unchallenged for the first half. A little drama is injected when the boys, trying out as radio script writers, put their own family on the air, which pisses off Poppa in a big way. Momma and Poppa and the boys go their separate ways; Momma remembers dancing as a teenager with George Raft. That's it. Bancroft does her considerable best with a squashy role, but the marvellous Cronyn is stuck with an unbudgeable garden gnome. Barely endurable. BC

Broadway Danny Rose

(1984, US, 84 min, b/w)
d Woody Allen. *p* Robert Greenhut. *sc* Woody Allen. *ph* Gordon Willis. *ed* Susan E Morse. *pd* Mel Bourne. *cast* Woody Allen, Mia Farrow, Nick Apollo Forte, Sandy Baron, Corbett Monica, Jackie Gayle, Morty Gunty, Milton Berle.

● Admittedly slighter than its immediate predecessor *Zelig*, this is still a delightful comedy that sees Allen as a no-hope theatrical agent (his clients include balloon twisters, wine-glass players and bird trainers, who *all* leave him when the Big Time beckons) who acts as beard for an adulterous, unmusical crooner on his books, and gets involved with a brassy Mafia widow (Farrow, unrecognisable). The jokes are firmly embedded in plot and characterisation, and the film, shot by Gordon Willis in harsh black-and-white, looks terrific; but what makes it work so well is the unsentimental warmth pervading every frame. GA

Broadway Melody of 1936

(1935, US, 102 min, b/w)
d Roy Del Ruth. *p* John W Considine Jr. *sc* Jack McGowan, Sid Silvers. *ph* Charles Rosher. *ed* Blanche Sewell. *ad* Cedric Gibbons. *songs* Nacio Herb Brown, Arthur Freed. *cast* Eleanor Powell, Robert Taylor, Jack Benny, Una Merkel, Sid Silvers, Buddy Ebsen, Frances Langford.

● 'She put 'em down like a man, no ricky-ticky-sissy stuff with Ellie,' Fred Astaire once observed of Eleanor Powell, a dancer he admired enormously. She blazes through this otherwise routine (if very luxurious) MGM musical. Moss Hart's contrived story (unaccountably nominated for an Oscar) casts her as a struggling actress who pretends to be a famous French star in order to land the plum role in Robert Taylor's forthcoming Broadway extravaganza. Comedian Jack Benny, in a role modelled on newsman Walter Winchell, plays a columnist with a grudge against Taylor. And yes, as always in these backstage musicals, everything comes right on the night. GM

Brokedown Palace

(1999, US, 101 min)
d Jonathan Kaplan. *p* Adam Fields, (Philippines) Lope V Juban Jr. *sc* David Arata. *ph* Newton Thomas Sigel. *ed* Curtiss Clayton. *pd* James Newport. *m* David Newman. *cast* Claire Danes, Bill Pullman, Kate Beckinsale, Lou Diamond Phillips, Jacqueline Kim, Daniel LaPaine, Tom Amandes.

● Alice (Danes) and Darlene (Beckinsale) take a high school graduation trip to Bangkok, but are nabbed with drugs planted by heroin runner Nick (Lapaine). They protest their innocence, but receive long sentences after Alice is conned into signing a confession. Hopes of a speedy release are dashed, the efforts of family and friends prove fruitless, so the young women are forced to settle down to serve their time. This far from passive experience rapidly exposes the differences in their characters and brings to a crisis their notions of trust, belonging and loyalty. Topical, in the UK at least, this revisits every Western backpacker's nightmare: their own private *Midnight Express*. Complex issues are raised and, true to form, director Kaplan reduces them to 'issue movie' proportions. But that said, and setting aside the possibly racist representations, the film exerts a fascination. The open possibility that one of the women may in fact be guilty is an intriguing intellectual catalyst. However, Alice's underwritten role is made to carry an unreasonably heavy burden, and it's a credit to the excellent Danes that she carries it off so lightly. WH

Broken Arrow

(1950, US, 93 min)
d Delmer Daves. *p* Julian Blaustein. *sc* Albert Maltz [credited to Michael Blankfort]. *ph* Ernest Palmer. *ed* J Watson Webb Jr. *ad* Lyle Wheeler, Albert Hogsett. *m* Hugo Friedhofer. *cast* James Stewart, Jeff Chandler, Debra Paget, Will Geer, Jay Silverheels, Arthur Hunnicutt.

● The Western that launched the be-nice-to-the-Indian cycle of the '50s now looks a little on the self-consciously liberal side, making something of a meal of its plea for racial tolerance and peaceful coexistence, as Stewart's army scout and Chandler's Cochise strive to bring peace to the Apache. A little awkward, too, in its bows to convention while trying to present an authentic picture of the Indian way of life (lots of Apache extras, but the leads are played by white actors; the Apache language rendered into 'poetic' English). A fine film all the same, despite the compromised ending, quite beautifully shot by Ernest Palmer. TM

Broken Arrow

(1996, US, 86 min)
d John Woo. *p* Mark Gordon, Terence Chang, Bill Badalato. *sc* Graham Yost. *ph* Peter Levy. *ed* John Wright, Steve Mirkovich, Joe Hutshing. *pd* Holger Gross. *m* Hans Zimmer. *cast* John Travolta, Christian Slater, Samantha Mathis, Delroy Lindo, Bob Gunton, Frank Whaley, Howie Long.

● There are no rough edges in Woo's second Hollywood outing. Working with more money than on his first (the unhappy *Hard Target*), a better cast and a script by Graham Yost (*Speed*), the director has fashioned a high-powered, streamlined, comfortably ludicrous entertainment in which bomber pilots Travolta and Slater go *mano-a-mano* in the Arizona desert, with two hot nuclear warheads between them. If movies were censored for implausiblility, this would be deemed unfit for public viewing. It's incredible in both senses of the word. You're never bored in a Woo movie: he's the kind of stylist who does everything to the max. Mostly what he does is action, and this script is tailor-made: a series of superb set-pieces in which a nuclear explosion is far from the climax. If the movie feels more callous than *Speed*, that's partly because Slater and spunky park ranger Mathis lack the warmth of Reeves and Bullock, but the charismatically crazy Travolta has the measure of it. This is just what Hollywood wanted of John Woo: more bang for the buck. The scary part is, where does he go from here? TCh

Broken Arrow 29

(1986, GB, 72 min)
d/p/sc Dina Hecht. *ph* Gabriel Beristain. *ed* Monica Henriquez. *pd* Kennedy Bradley. *m* Los Iberos.

● In January 1966, a US B-52 carrying four nuclear bombs crashed near the Spanish villages of Palomares and Villaricos. Dina Hecht returned to the scene of the crime and subsequent cover-up twenty years later, using a classified US Defence Department report as her guide. Though the Americans don't come up smelling like anything particularly fragrant (despite some archive footage showing the former US ambassador bathing in the now 'decontaminated' sea), Hecht does not engage in a melodramatic plutonium slinging match. Most interesting is her examination of the local politicians and their use of the incident, the small seaside villages serving as a microcosm of the national government's inability – and seeming lack of real desire – to effect change in Spain. SGo

Broken Blossoms

(1919, US, 6,013 ft, b/w)
d/p/sc DW Griffith. *ph* Billy Bitzer. *ed* James Smith, Rose Smith. *ad* Charles E Baker. *cast* Lillian Gish, Richard Barthelmess, Donald Crisp, Arthur Howard, Edward Peil, George Beranger, Norman Selby.

●There's a marvellous moment when Barthelmess, as the gentle Chinese who offers Gish shelter from her brutal father, gathers an imaginary spray of moondust to sprinkle on her hair as she huddles in bed. But for all that he is making a fervent plea for tolerance, Griffith is careful to let the hint of romance go no further: miscegenation has no place in his hoarily traditional melodrama of waifs and strays and the villains who make them so. This is in fact Griffith at his best and worst. On the debit side, some risibly highfalutin titles, some naive attempts to impose wider contexts on what is essentially a fragile short story (already stretched dangerously thin), and a monotonously simplistic view of the drunken prize-fighter father's brutality. Very much on the credit side, though, are stretches of pure Griffith poetry, marvellous use of light and shadow in cameraman Billy Bitzer's evocation of foggy Limehouse, and a truly unforgettable performance from Gish. TM

Broken Blossoms

(1936, GB, 78 min, b/w)
d John Brahm. *p* Julius Hagen. *sc* Emlyn Williams. *ph* Curt Courant. *ed* Jack Harris. *ad* James Carter. *m* Karol Rathaus. *cast* Dolly Haas, Emlyn Williams, Arthur Margetson, Gibb McLaughlin, Donald Calthrop, Ernest Sefton, Jerry Verno.

●A pale shadow of Griffith's film, with Haas struggling vainly to emulate the limpid Lillian Gish, and Williams (who also scripted) coming a ludicrous cropper compared to the marvellously expressive passivity of Richard Barthelmess' Chinaman. With no performances to speak of, the whole rickety structure collapses like a pricked balloon. Very pleasing to the eye, all the same, with Brahm giving the whole thing a moody veneer of UFA expressionism. TM

Broken Branches (Naeil ui Hyahae Hurunun Kang)

(1995, SKor, 96 min)
d Park Jae-Ho. *p* Kim Sang-Beom. *sc* Park Jae-Ho. *ph* Park Seung-Ho. *ed* Park Kok-Jee. *cast* Kim Ye-Ryung, Lee Hong-Sung, Lee Dae-Yun, Lee In-Chul, An Hae-Sook.

●The first 'gay movie' ever made in Korea, a country more homophobic than most, spans the years from 1955 to the present, rhyming the country's social and political changes with the fortunes of one extended family. Each of the three chapters marks a phase in the breakdown of the traditional Confucian-patriarchal family; the tone gradually shifts from tragedy to comedy. Most attention has been focused on the third chapter, in which the narrator comes out as gay and describes the joys and miseries of his affair with a married man. Let down by some dodgy performances in minor roles and some spasms of melodrama, but the overall scope is impressive for an indie feature – and the candour and sincerity are piercing. TR

Broken Butterfly

see Butterfly

Broken English

(1996, NZ, 92 min)
d Gregor Nicholas. *p* Robin Scholes. *sc* Gregor Nicholas, Johanna Pigott, Jim Salter. *ph* John Toon. *ed* David Coulson. *pd* Michael Kane. *m* Murray Grindlay, Murray McNabb. *cast* Rade Serbedzija, Aleksandra Vujcic, Julian Arahanga, Marton Csokas, Madeline McNamara, Zhao Jing.

●An ethnic drama set in Auckland: violent Croatian immigrant (Serbedzija) is unhappy when daughter Nina (Aleksandra Vujcic, overflowing with sensual vitality) falls for fellow restaurant worker Eddie (Arahanga). Eddie, a Maori, hot foots it home; Nina's battened in her room. The future looks grim. This first feature is prone to over-emphatic contrasts: from the Croatians' Independence Day feast, for example, the camera travels to the Maori feast over the fence like an equal opportunities arbiter. And stylistically, there's an element of schizophrenia: painting a kinetic ad-style gloss over sombre realism tends to trivialise the director's evident concern to escape the confines of conventional drama. That said, the film gets by on its energy and self-belief. Arahanga has an easy, uningratiating charm, and Serbedzija, a bit of a cartoon bastard as written, gives a discomforting power to his role. (The music includes so-called 'Croatian Barbecue Songs' and work from the Taokotaianga Cultural Group.) WH

Broken Glass

(1996, GB/US, 96 min)
d David Thacker. *p* Fiona Finlay. *sc* David Holman, David Thacker. *ph* John Daly. *ed* Kate Evans. *pd* Bruce Macadie. *m* Adrian Johnston. *cast* Mandy Patinkin, Henry Goodman, Margot Leicester, Elizabeth McGovern, Julia Swift, Ed Bishop.

●Arthur Miller's greatest work may be well behind him, but this strikes with the dramatic power of a sledgehammer. Young Vic director David Thacker and playwright David Holman (the co-adaptors) have made a gripping movie out of the play. The troubled matter of Jewish identity is the subject, and the ramifications take in everything from society to marriage. Sylvia (Leicester) reads about Nazi Party attacks on Jews in Berlin and is struck down with hysterical paralysis. Her husband Gellburg (Goodman) sends for a specialist (Patinkin) who begins to uncover the unlovely facts about their marriage, a union entered into for everyone's sake but hers. Fear has brought them to this state and, thanks to faultless playing and exemplary writing, the tragedy becomes universal. BC

Broken Harvest

(1994, Ire, 101 min)
d Maurice O'Callaghan. *p* Gerry O'Callaghan. *sc* Maurice O'Callaghan, Kate O'Callaghan. *ph* Jack Conroy. *ed* J Patrick Duffner, Arthur Keating. *ad* Alan Galett. *m* Patrick Cassidy. *cast* Colin Lane, Marian Quinn, Niall O'Brien, Darren McHugh, Joe Jeffers, Jim Queally.

●A lyrical but relatively unsentimental tale of the tensions that beset Ireland for years after the Civil War. Focused on local rivalries, particularly between two men who fell out over a woman and over political differences, the film is good on the conflicting impulses of hating and forgiving, forgetting and remembering, but less certain in its execution: visuals, editing and story are a shade obvious, the acting a little unsure. GA

Broken Hearts Club, The

(2000, US, 95 min)
d Greg Berlanti. *p* Mickey Liddell, Joseph Middleton. *sc* Greg Berlanti. *ph* Paul Elliott. *ed* Todd Busch. *pd* Charlies Daboub. *m* Christophe Beck. *cast* Zach Braff, Dean Cain, Andrew Keegan, Nia Long, John Mahoney, Mary McCormack, Matt McGrath, Timothy Olyphant.

●The club is like this big, gay support group thing: they meet and hang out, play softball, drink, gossip, bitch and joke around. The club has its own code language, its rituals, and its own elastic membership standards, encompassing half a dozen guys of mixed dispositions, augmented by the occasional 'newbie'. Berlanti's moderately diverting movie, subtitled 'a Romantic Comedy', speaks the smart, self-obsessed language of the hip twenty-something set, pores over their dating rituals, and ignores everything outside this narrow range of comfortable urban angst. The characters here are homosexual, but the film contains them – *constrains* them – as if it were television: it's like *ER* without the white coats. It's precisely this blandness that makes the film easy to watch and even enjoy. Like better American television, it's utterly inclusive and non-threatening, scripted with a patina of wit, unobtrusively crafted and cast with attractive nonentities. TCh

Broken Lance

(1954, US, 96 min)
d Edward Dmytryk. *p* Sol C Siegel. *sc* Richard Murphy. *ph* Joe MacDonald. *ed* Dorothy Spencer. *ad* Lyle Wheeler, Maurice Ransford. *m* Leigh Harline. *cast* Spencer Tracy, Robert Wagner, Jean Peters, Richard Widmark, Katy Jurado, Earl Holliman, Hugh O'Brien.

●Internecine family struggles, hijacked from Mankiewicz's excellent *House of Strangers* to provide a gripping if hardly original Western. Tracy is the Lear-like patriarch dismayed to discover that filial strife and betrayal is threatening his cattle empire. Strong performances, ably augmented by Joe MacDonald's lovely 'Scope camerawork.

Broken Mirrors (Gebroken Spiegels)

(1984, Neth, 116 min)
d Marleen Gorris. *p* Matthijs van Heijningen. *sc* Marleen Gorris. *ph* Frans Bromet. *ed* Hans van Dongen. *ad* Harry Ammerlaan. *m* Lodewijk de Boer. *cast* Lineke Rijxman, Henriette Tol, Edda Barends, Coby Stunnenberg, Carla Hardy.

●Humour, the currency of Dutch director Gorris' first feminist thriller, *A Question of Silence*, is exchanged in her second for the much darker coinage of horror. A murderer is at large: a well-dressed businessman who incarcerates his victims, chains and starves them, and documents their death amid their filth with instamatic snaps. Meanwhile, in another part of town, a woman joins a brothel. These two simple strands of plot come together within the film, and are united by a single theme: that women's suffering is basic to man's pleasure. A film directed by a duller dog than Gorris would remain just this: a bleak message wagged by a compelling tale. But Gorris' talent as a director is to mobilise ideas to grip an audience, with characters that fill us with compassion and respect and allow us to derive a guilty pleasure from this very special film about the ordinary pain of others. FD

Broken Noses

(1987, US, 77 min, b/w & col)
d Bruce Weber. *p* Emie Amemiya. *ph* Jeff Preiss. *ed* Phyllis Famiglietti. *ad* Sam Shahid. *with* Andy Minsker.

●Black-and-white pix of male models in Calvin Klein knickers – that's photographer Bruce Weber. Or is it? His first feature, an experimental documentary in mono and colour, breaks the mould. It follows boxing lightweight Andy Minsker, a ringer for Chet Baker, round Portland, Oregon: he talks to camera, engages parents and friends in tense, hearty conversation, and hangs out with his adopted gang, the tough kids he trains in his Mt Scott boxing club. Weber's eye is insistent and very subtle, and what emerges from a somewhat mawkish tale is deeply engaging. The unstable foundations of *faux* machismo gently rock his various encounters, and truth leaks out: his separated parents, for instance, unwittingly delineate a nasty family tableau from his youth when they get enthusiastic about the need for stern but fair discipline. Weber leaves joins showing and takes risks: a colour sequence of Minsker in a rose garden reluctantly reading from *Richard II* works against all odds. Throughout, the sounds of such as Gerry Mulligan, Julie London, and Chet Baker overlay these curiously tender images. TC

Broken Vessels

(1999, US, 91 min)
d Scott Ziehl. *p* Roxana Zal, Scott Ziehl. *sc* David Baer, John McMahon, Scott Ziehl. *ph* Antonio Calvache. *ed* David Moritz, Chris Figler. *pd* Rodrigo Castillo. *m* Bill Laswell, Martin Blasick, Brent David Fraser. *cast* Todd Field, Jason London, Roxana Zal, Susan Traylor, James Hong, Brent David Fraser, William Smith, David Baer.

●Saddling up in LA with veteran paramedic Jimmy (Field), young Tom (London) wants to put some miles between himself and a dark episode back East. However, Jimmy's blooding of the greenhorn snuffs out any fantasies Tom might have entertained of redemptive good works. Saving lives, he learns, is what you do when you're not whoring, boozing, thieving, shooting up or subduing uppity patients with the defib paddles. Who then, the film asks, are the real casualties: the unfortunates in the back of the rig or the strung-out pair riding upfront? Recalling elements of *Repo Man* and *Trainspotting*, this striking first feature is best enjoyed as an amoral trip to the (needle) sharp end of US healthcare. Desaturated film, overlap editing and time-lapse traffic sequences impart Jimmy and Tom's downward spiral with an impressively entropic feel; the performances too, particularly from Field, are suitably wearied. It's a pity then that this beguilingly textured surface conceals some sketchy characterisation and a standard plot. MHi

Bronco Billy

(1980, US, 119 min)
d Clint Eastwood. *p* Dennis Hackin, Neal Dobrofsky. *sc* Dennis Hackin. *ph* David Worth. *ed* Ferris Webster, Joel Cox. *ad* Eugene Lourié.

cast Clint Eastwood, Sondra Locke, Geoffrey Lewis, Scatman Crothers, Bill McKinney, Sam Bottoms, Dan Vadis, Sierra Pecheur, Woodrow Parfrey, Hank Worden.

● A disarming movie, standing somewhere between a comic, contemporary version of *The Outlaw Josey Wales* (bunch of no-hopers finding fulfilment together) and Frank Capra (good 'little people', runaway heiress, scheming Eastern bureaucrats). Basically, it's the charming tale of a New Jersey shoe-salesman who fantasises about being a cowboy, and takes a group of assorted weirdos on the road with a travelling show. Not a lot to it in terms of plot, but Eastwood manages to both undermine and celebrate his character's fantasy life, while offering a few gentle swipes at contemporary America (the Stars and Stripes tent sewn together by mental hospital inmates). Fragile, fresh, and miles away from his hard-nosed cop thrillers, it's the sort of film only he would, and could, make. GA

Bronco Bullfrog

(1970, GB, 86 min, b/w)
d Barney Platts-Mills. *p* Andrew St John. *sc* Barney Platts-Mills. *ph* Adam Barker-Mill. *ed* Jonathan Gili. *m* Howard Werth, Tony Connor, Keith Gemmell, Trevor Williams. *cast* Del Walker, Anne Gooding, Sam Shepherd, Roy Haywood, Freda Shepherd.

● This healthy antidote to the 'classless' swinging '60s was made for £17,000, a major achievement in itself. What one least expects from the subject – the drift into aimless petty crime and misdemeanours of a trio of working class youths in London's East End – is the dominant mood of shyness that gives the film much of its effect. This can be attributed mainly to a cast of non-professionals unconcerned with showing off by 'acting', and to Platts -Mills' understated storyline and direction. *Bronco Bullfrog*'s true subject is the mediocrity of British life, but at exactly the points where one begins to fear a customary excess of bathos, the film discovers its sense of humour. As such, its feelings are truer to its subject than later, more vaunted youth pictures like *Quadrophenia*. CPe

Bronx Tale, A

(1993, US, 121 min)
d Robert De Niro. *p* Robert De Niro, Jane Rosenthal, Jon Kilik. *sc* Chazz Palminteri. *ph* Reynaldo Villalobos. *ed* David Ray, Robert Q Lovett. *pd* Wynn Thomas. *m* Butch Barbella. *cast* Robert De Niro, Chazz Palminteri, Lillo Brancato, Francis Capra, Taral Hicks, Joe Pesci.

● De Niro takes a confident stab at familiar material in his first film as director. He plays an unassuming bus driver, a straight-arrow good father, appalled when son Calogero (Capra at 9, Brancato at 17) falls under the influence of local wiseguy Sonny. The first hour or so, set in 1960, is a delight. De Niro knows the flavour inside out. He gets the music right, the speech rhythms and the faces – and a largely unknown cast does wonders. Despite a charismatic performance from Chazz Palminteri (author of the play from which the film is drawn), Sonny is, however, just too good to be true: a Mafia kingpin, who comes on more like a radical priest, steering young 'C' away from racism, sexism and guns. When the scene switches to 1968, problems become more pronounced: C falls for a black girl (Hicks), and has to choose between his crazy pals and his own heart. Not an unalloyed success, but the performances and youthful vigour make up for the somewhat clumsy structure. TCh

Bronx Warriors (1990 I Guerrieri del Bronx)

(1982, It, 84 min)
d Enzo G Castellari. *p* Fabrizio De Angelis. *sc* Dardano Sacchetti, Elisa Livia Briganti, Enzo G Castellari. *ph* Sergio Salvati. *ed* Gianfranco Amicucci. *pd* Massimo Lentini. *m* Walter Rizzati. *cast* Vic Morrow, Christopher Connolly, Fred Williamson, Mark Gregory, Stefania Girolami.

● Interleaving script pages from *The Warriors* and *Escape from New York* has proved a cheap departure for Italian schlock-merchants. Here, we're offered the Bronx of 1990, surrendered to the gangs, but now invaded by freelance psychopath Morrow, hired to liberate a runaway heiress (happily slumming as a biker's moll until kidnapped by rival sickies) from across the river, but more intent on wiping out all scummy life in his former habitat. Muddy, muddled and moronic: heavily censored ultra-violence, interval-style ice-cream score, insultingly perfunctory climax and all. Next from the Cinecittà carbon factory – *Mad Mario 3*? PT

Bronzés, Les

(1978, Fr, 95 min)
d Patrice Leconte. *sc* l'equipe du 'Splendid', Patrice Leconte. *ph* Jean-François Robin. *ed* Noëlle Boisson. *ad* Jacques D'Ovidio. *m* Michel Bernholc. *cast* Josiane Balasko, Michel Blanc, Marie-Anne Chazel, Gérard Jugnot, Dominique Lavanant, Thierry Lhermitte.

● This is a little seaside memento from the early part of Leconte's career, when he was associated with the café theatre group 'Splendid'. It's an ensemble piece comprising a series of sketches and anecdotes set in a holiday camp on the Ivory Coast, a sort of African Butlins minus the rides. Basically it's Monsieur Hulot with a sex life, and though Tati would probably have disapproved of the ribaldry, the attitudes are not dissimilar. It certainly bubbles along amusingly enough, and on home ground it did well enough to prompt a sequel, *Les Bronzés font du ski*. BBa

Brood, The

(1979, Can, 91 min)
d David Cronenberg. *p* Claude Héroux. *sc* David Cronenberg. *ph* Mark Irwin. *ed* Alan Collins. *ad* Carol Spier. *m* Howard Shore. *cast* Oliver Reed, Samantha Eggar, Art Hindle, Cindy Hinds, Nuala Fitzgerald, Henry Beckman.

● Despite his protestations to the contrary, Cronenberg's films are epics of sexual anxiety boasting an almost Calvinistic focus on the human body as the centre of evil: a strain of sexual rabies in *Rabid*; slug-like parasites (curiously resembling faeces) in *Shivers*. In *The Brood* the threat seems initially more exterior (and so less threatening), with deranged patients from the sinister 'Institute of Psychoplasmics' on release, and small mutant murderers leaping out from behind doors and out of cupboards. But the source of the mayhem, it transpires, is Samantha Eggar, an improbably psychotic mother, busy unleashing hatred on her husband (and on Family Life generally). It's a strong theme, unfortunately undercut by faulty pacing and odd lapses in the tension. Still worth seeing for its latently political story and its gory special effects. CA

Brot des Bäckers, Das

see Baker's Bread

Brother (Brat)

(1997, Rus, 99 min)
d Aleksei Balabanov. *p* Sergei Selianov. *sc* Aleksei Balabanov. *ph* Sergei Astakhov. *ed* Marina Lipartiia. *m* Viacheslav Butusov. *cast* Sergei Bodrov, Viktor Sukhorukov, Svetlana Pismichenko, Maria Zhukova, Iurii Kuznetsov, Viacheslav Butusov, Irina Rakhshina.

● Balabanov's third feature is a snappily edited, contemporary gangster thriller, shot in semi-documentary style, which is a far cry from the elusive b/w art house teasers he's getting a reputation for. As an incidental portrait of Russia (or at least St Petersburg), it paints a sorry if fascinating picture. Though the social focus is relatively narrow – following a recently demobbed soldier caught up in his mobster brother's internecine world of seedy corruption, soulless materialism and frequent violence and death – the carefully depicted environment of cold markets, dossers' hang outs and cheerless workers' flats build a convincing account of a country's disaffection, lack of direction and yearning stoicism. Not that the film is depressing. Bodrov brings a broody matter-of-factness to his role as the reluctant killer Danila, obsessed with a Soviet-era underground rock group. He's in many ways an innocent and a romantic: his rationale, his racism, received not self-developed. Balabanov shows again his rare talent for deriving entirely credible performances, shooting with a no-fuss efficiency and assurance, while retaining an authorial distance that leaves the moral lessons open. WH

Brother

(2000, Jap, 117 min)
d Takeshi Kitano. *p* Masayuki Mori, Jeremy Thomas. *sc* Takeshi Kitano. *ph* Katsumi Yanagijima. *ed* Takeshi Kitano. *pd* Norihiro Isoda. *m* Joe Hisashi. *cast* 'Beat' Takeshi, Owen Epps, Claude Maki, Susumu Terajima, Ren Osugi, Ryo Ishibashi, Tetsuya Watari.

● Kitano adapts to the demands of 'international' film-making in very characteristic ways: by adopting the uncomplicated directness of Hollywood movies (no trace of the 'philosophical' dimensions of *Sonatine* or *Hana-Bi* here) and by remaining absolutely true to himself. He plays Tokyo yakuza Yamamoto, forcibly retired from his gang after a hostile takeover; fitted with a fake identity, he moves to Los Angeles to join his younger brother, who (he seems unsurprised to discover) has dropped out of college and started dealing drugs with a black gang. He brings just two items of baggage: the urge to dominate and a death wish, both of which infect his new associates like a virus. They put paid to a local Latino gang and assimiliate the Little Tokyo yakuza, but then run into the brick wall of the Mafia. Characterisation is present and resonant – the development of the relationship between Yama moto and the black con-artist (Epps) is even quite touching – but subordinated to ruthless analysis of quasi-military tactics and strategies in the gang subculture. A film of almost diagrammatic clarity, in which questions of loyalty, honour and, yes, brotherhood are mere pieces on the chessboard. TR

Brother and Sister (Ani Imoto/aka Mon and Ino)

(1976, Jap, 98 min)
d Tadashi Imai. *p* Hideyuki Shino, Masatada Kaneko. *sc* Yoko Mizuki. *ph* Kazutami Hara. *ed* Nobuo Ogawa. *ad* Kazuo Takenaka. *m* Takeshi Shibuya. *cast* Kumiko Akiyoshi, Masao Kusakari, Kimiko Ikegami, Shuji Otaki, Natsuko Kahara.

● Refreshing to be given the opportunity to see a Japanese film that is neither 'high art', nor period dramatics or grinding social realism. Imai is not always in total control of his subject – the reaction of a Japanese family to the pregnancy of one of two unmarried daughters – but the directness and charm of his unassuming approach make this a film well worth seeing. Excellent performances, too, from Kahara as the mother, Akiyoshi and Ikegame as the sisters. VG

Brother, Can You Spare a Dime?

(1975, GB, 109 min, b/w)
d Philippe Mora. *p* Sandy Lieberson, David Puttnam. *sc* Philippe Mora. *ed* Jeremy Thomas.

● A maddening mixture, with fascinating material put to often questionable uses, this compilation film tries to chronicle the history of America from the Wall Street Crash to Pearl Harbor, using only contemporary newsreels and Hollywood features (without commentary) to tell the story. Extracts from movies are strung together to make James Cagney an all-purpose hero (setting jauntily out in life with his sweetheart, surviving the train crash wrought by King Kong, joining the queue of hungry unemployed, getting rich quick as a mobster, etc); meanwhile, newsreels offer starker visions of the Depression and the political manoeuvrings behind the scenes (including the insidious, fascistic appeal of 'a strong man to put things right'). Beautifully put together to the ironic accompaniment of songs from Bessie Smith, Billie Holiday, Woody Guthrie and others, the film is highly entertaining but also highly specious. Not only because it misrepresents the material (dubbing new sound, deliberately blurring the distinction between fiction and newsreel), but because it imposes a frivolous, one-dimensional interpretation that often obscures the real implications of the period. TM

Brother from Another Planet, The

(1984, US, 108 min)
d John Sayles. *p* Peggy Rajski, Maggie Renzi. *sc* John Sayles. *ph* Ernest Dickerson. *ed* John Sayles. *pd* Nora Chavooshian. *m* Mason Daring. *cast* Joe Morton, Tom Wright, Caroline Aaron, Herbert Newsome, Dee Dee Bridgewater, Darryl Edwards, John Sayles.

● A mute, black extra-terrestrial fetches up in Harlem to be greeted first with bewildered hostility, then with a certain casual friendliness. The slim, episodic, but thoroughly enjoyable story shoots off like a firework in numerous directions: droll comedy among a group of cheery, bleary barflies; unforced intimations of a streetwise messiah as Bro's peculiar powers put paid to a drugs ring; delicate insights into Harlem's social mores, wrapped up in unpretentious fashion without a trace of stereotyping. Central to the film's deft balancing act between shaggy dog humour and something just a little more serious is Morton's expressive performance as the alien, though the rest of the cast also plays admirably. GA

Brotherhood, The

(1968, US, 98 min)
d Martin Ritt. *p* Kirk Douglas. *sc* Lewis John Carlino. *ph* Boris Kaufman. *ed* Frank Bracht. *ad* Tambi Larsen. *m* Lalo Schifrin. *cast* Kirk Douglas, Alex Cord, Irene Papas, Luther Adler, Susan Strasberg, Murray Hamilton, Eduardo Ciannelli, Joe De Santis.

● Douglas, dressed up in droopy moustache and dyed hair, plays a board member of the New York Syndicate who has nostalgic memories of how much better things were done in the old Mafia days. Not surprisingly, he falls foul of the syndicate, flees into retirement in Sicily, and confronts the man sent to kill him – none other than the younger brother (Cord) he raised with selfless devotion. Ritt can do very little with the breast-beating which attends this tale of brotherly love and self-sacrifice. It therefore wends its way, slowly and stolidly, to the bitter end, pausing to allow Luther Adler to brighten things up briefly as a plump, greasy and rather engaging stool pigeon turned respectable. TM

Brotherhood of the Wolf (Le Pacte des loups)

(2001, Fr, 134 min)
d Christophe Gans. *p* Richard Grandpierre, Samuel Hadida. *sc* Stéphane Cabel. *ph* Dan Laustsen. *ed* Sébastien Prangère, David Wu, Xavier Loutreuil. *pd* Guy-Claude François. *m* Joseph Lo Duca. *cast* Samuel Le Bihan, Vincent Cassel, Emilie Dequenne, Monica Bellucci, Jérémie Rénier, Mark Dacascos, Jean Yanne, Jean-François Stévenin, Edith Scob.

● Is it a scary monster movie about a werewolf? A sumptuous period drama with dashing hero, beautiful heroine and mysterious courtesan caught up in political and religious intrigues? A *Last of the Mohicans*-style adventure with an Iroquois brave fighting alongside his white blood brother? Or a swashbuckling romp? No, it's all four. Astonishingly, the scope, ambition and panache of Gans' alchemical fusion of cinematic elements turns potentially base metal into gold. Sent by King Louis XV to investigate a wolf-like creature that has been slaughtering the people of the Gévaudan region, historian Grégoire de Fronsac (Le Bihan) and his Iroquois friend Mani (Dacascos) gain help from a young marquis, Thomas d'Apcher (Rénier), and encouragement from the beautiful Marianne de Morangias (Dequenne). But they're hindered by Marianne's jealous brother Jean-François (Cassel), by rampant superstition, and by the vested interests of local aristos. A massive wolf-hunt produces a pile of carcasses, but the attacks continue. Set in 18th century France, but imbued with a 21st century sensibility, the film offers a pick 'n' mix selection of genres. A little rich for refined palates, perhaps, but open-minded genre fans will wolf it down. NF

Brotherly Love

see Country Dance

Brother Orchid

(1940, US, 91 min, b/w)
d Lloyd Bacon. *sc* Earl Baldwin. *ph* Tony Gaudio. *ed* William Holmes. *ad* Max Parker. *m* Heinz Roemheld. *cast* Edward G Robinson, Ann Sothern, Humphrey Bogart, Donald Crisp, Ralph Bellamy, Allen Jenkins, Charles D Brown.

● Racketeer Robinson, Little John Sarto, takes time out from a life of crime, but when he returns to the fray, he discovers Bogart's now running the old gang and his presence is no longer required. Brother Superior Crisp's monastery provides unlikely sanctuary in this enjoyable, though not unpredictable star comedy made when Bogie's career hadn't yet peaked and he was still doing second-string roles, like tough Jack Buck here. TJ

Brothers (Bratan)

(1991, Tajikistan, 100 min, b/w)
d Bakhtiar Khudojnazarov. *sc* Leonid Machkamov, Bakhtiar Khudojnazarov. *ph* Georgy Dzalaiev. *ed* Tatjana Malceva. *ad* Negmat Jouraiev. *m* Achmad Bakaev. *cast* Timur Tursunov, Firuz Sabzaliev, N. Begmurodov, N. Afirova, R Kurpanov.

● Seventeen-year-old Farukh and his lisping, mischievous kid brother Azamat (known as 'Bunny') leave their leaky home in a Tajik village and hitch a ride on a goods train to the small town where their father works as a doctor. But he and his girlfriend aren't that pleased to see them, and so Farukh decides to travel further – finally taking Azamat along too. Shown in golden yellow-tinted monochrome, Khudojnazarov's debut feature (he was 26 at the time) is a picaresque rail-movie in which the underlying trauma is Azamat's habit of eating earth, the adventures are fleeting encounters with oddball friends and strangers, and the landscape is startlingly bleak. Funny and sad in equal parts, it stays just this side of cute. The glimpse of an open-air cinema where the projector breaks down acknowledges a debt to early Wenders. TR

Brothers

(1999, GB, 98 min)
d Martin Dunkerton. *p* Martin Dunkerton, Joanna Garvin. *sc* Martin Dunkerton, Nick Valentine. *ph* Richard Terry. *ed* John Grover. *pd* Conrad Butlin. *m* Julian Stewart Lindsey. *cast* Justin Brett, Daren Jacobs, Daniel Fredenburgh, Rebecca Cardinale, Nick Valentine, Fin Wild, Leigh Tapper.

● Apparently a series of Mediterranean holidays was the inspiration for this laddish ode to hedonism. Five British blokes go on a Greek vacation with just two things on their minds: getting laid and getting drunk. They're the sort of testosterone charged fools one actively avoids on foreign holidays. But then, presumably, they're also closely related to the film's target audience; no one else would want to sit through scenes of blokes pissing on each other, downing 20 schnapps at a sitting, and then falling into bed only to wake up in a pool of vomit. Most of the performers are from TV and act with conviction; worryingly, their images remain burnt into the mind well after leaving the cinema. Fortunately, though, a few pints of lager and five tequila slammers will erase the whole experience. DA

Brothers, The

(2001, US, 102 min)
d Gary Hardwick. *p* Darin Scott, Paddy Cullen. *sc* Gary Hardwick. *ph* Alexander Gruszynski. *ed* Earl Watson. *pd* Amy Ancona. *m* Marcus Miller. *cast* Morris Chestnut, DL Hughley, Bill Bellamy, Shemar Moore, Tamala Jones, Tatyana Ali, Jenifer Lewis, Clifton Powell, Gabrielle Union.

● The sound of wedding bells threatens to split asunder four African-American buddies in this serio-comic survey of modern manhood. When exec Terry (Moore) announces his nuptials, his friends are unimpressed: teacher Derrick (Hughley) is dead against it since he got hitched too young, and eligible pediatrician Jackson (Chestnut) reckons there's still time to play the field, like lawyer Brian (Bellamy). Subsequent events conspire to alter their opinions, however, since Jackson in particular is about to face character-building woman trouble, when he meets sassy photographer Denise (Union). Writer/director Hardwick's debut is a patchy assemblage of soap opera devices, often hilarious incidental dialogue, and an occasionally trenchant look at blinkered machismo. Although aspirational upper income-bracket settings help smooth over the joins, the film's inconsistency is exasperating. TJ

Brothers and Sisters

(1980, GB, 101 min)
d Richard Woolley. *p* Keith Griffiths. *sc* Richard Woolley, Tammy Walker. *ph* Pasco MacFarlane. *ed* Mick Audsley. *ad* Miranda Melville. *m* Trevor Jones. *cast* Carolyn Pickles, Sam Dale, Robert East, Jennifer Armitage, Elizabeth Bennett, Barry McCarthy.

● Prompted by the terrible murders of 'The Yorkshire Ripper' (and made before he was caught), this examination of contemporary sexual politics and violence is too simplistic by half. After a prostitute is murdered, two brothers (one apparently right wing, one left) are suspected, and the film investigates their attitudes towards women as police proceedings continue. Despite its obvious sincerity and ambitions, the film is wrecked by its half-hearted adherence to the thriller format (neither implicating its audience in the sadistic impulses behind voyeurism and film-watching, nor denying them that excitement by avoiding thriller-style scenes), by its schematic approach towards characterisation, and by its complacent sense of male guilt, simply asserting (in too direct a way) that all men are responsible for violence towards women. GA

Brothers in Law

(1956, GB, 94 min, b/w)
d Roy Boulting. *p* John Boulting. *sc* Frank Harvey, Jeffrey Dell, Roy Boulting. *ph* Max Greene. *ed* Anthony Harvey. *ad* Albert Witherick. *m* Benjamin Frankel. *cast* Ian Carmichael, Richard Attenborough, Terry-Thomas, Jill Adams, Miles Malleson, Irene Handl, John Le Mesurier, Leslie Phillips, Kenneth Griffith, John Le Mesurier, Nicholas Parsons.

● This Boulting brothers comedy (from a novel by Henry Cecil) about the absurdities of the British legal system chugs along amiably but lacks real satirical bite. The usual gallery of eccentric British character actors are out in force (Malleson the absent-minded pupil master, Terry-Thomas the court-hardened swindler), giving their usual mannered but doughty performances. Carmichael is the innocent abroad, a newly qualified barrister exposed to the baffling rituals and bizarre antics of his peers. GM

Brothers in Trouble

(1995, GB, 102 min)
d Udayan Prasad. *p/sc* Robert Buckler. *ph* Alan Almond. *ed* Barrie Vince. *pd* Chris Townsend. *m* Stephen Warbeck. *cast* Om Puri, Angeline Ball, Pavan Malhotra, Pravesh Kumar, Ahsen Bhatti, Bhasker.

● Illegal Pakistani immigrants, packed into a London house in the 1960s, work non-stop in abysmal conditions to send paltry sums home to their families. The arrival of Mary (Ball, proving *The Commitments* was no fluke) introduces a spark of humanity into their miserable existence, but also ultimately destroys it. This over-long film, a BBC production with German and Italian backing, is at its best when concentrating on the relationship between the newest immigrant Amir (Malhotra) and the studious Sakib (Kumar), but the pace is uneven and the final scene badly misjudged. FM

Brothers Karamazov, The

(1958, US, 146 min)
d Richard Brooks. *p* Pandro S Berman. *sc* Richard Brooks. *ph* John Alton. *ed* John Dunning. *ad* William A Horning. *m* Bronislau Kaper. *cast* Yul Brynner, Claire Bloom, Richard Basehart, Lee J Cobb, Maria Schell, Albert Salmi, William Shatner.

● Painstaking attempt to reduce Dostoevsky's novel to manageable proportions, retaining most of the major episodes but contriving to miss the point – the tortuous quest for God – by giving one brother (Brynner) the star role whereas all four should contribute equally to the theme. Very uncertain in period and atmosphere, and saddled with some terrible performances. TM

Brothers Karamazov, The (Bratya Karamazovy)

(1968, USSR, 220 min)
d/sc Ivan Pyriev. *ph* Sergei Vronsky. *ed* B Kremnev. *pd* Vitali Levitsky. *m* Isaac Schwartz. *cast* Mikhail Ulianov, Lionella Pyrieva, Kiril Lavrov, Andrei Myahkov, Marc Prudkin, Leonela Skirda, Svetlana Korkoshko.

● Given essentially theatrical performances, Dostoevsky's tale – of the tensions and ties between three sons of a divisive father – comes across as akin to Grand Soap Opera, while the brown-rich Soviet colour stock, the wooden buildings and the 19th century outfits lend an aura reminiscent of '50s Gothic Westerns. Most of the characters are delightfully sozzled, brooding deeply over thoughts of murderous passion or hopes of saintly redemption, and lamenting things like, 'Beauty is terrible! A clash of good and evil fought out on the battlefield of the human heart!' This refers to the effect good-time girl Grusha has on old Karamazov and his son Dimitri. It's Dimitri's jealousy, and his resentment at getting the short straw with an inheritance, that sparks tragic events. Through the misery these events bring, Dimitri and his two brothers are finally united – in guilt. And there's a twist! Overlong, but fun. WH

Brothers McMullen, The

(1995, US, 108 min)
d/p/sc Edward Burns. *ph/ed* Dick Fisher. *m* Seamus Egan. *cast* Jack Mulcahy, Edward Burns, Mike McGlone, Connie Britton, Maxine Bahns, Elizabeth P McKay.

● Burns' engaging first feature is a witty romantic comedy about God, sex and commitment in Long Island, New York. The brothers are: Jack (Mulcahy), happily married and about to fall into a reckless affair; Barry (Burns himself), a bachelor who may just have got the woman of his dreams; and Patrick (McGlone), a devoutly Catholic graduate whose Jewish girlfriend has their whole future mapped out. Circumstances bring the three together again under one roof, where they pool their guilt, bafflement and indecision. Burns wrote and directed the film on a shoestring, but if his stamping ground is determinedly working-class Irish-American, the tone is closer to the gentle Uptown ironies of Woody Allen than to Hal Hartley or Jim Jarmusch. Macho pride is the font of most of the comedy, and it's only in the rather pat conclusion that the clan work out an uneasy rapprochement with their female partners. Burns is hardly the most innovative talent to have emerged this year, but he's found plenty of comic mileage in his own backyard. TCh

Brother Sun, Sister Moon (Fratello Sole, Sorella Luna)

(1972, It/GB, 122 min)
d Franco Zeffirelli. *p* Luciano Perugia. *sc* Suso Cecchi D'Amico, Kenneth Ross, Lina Wertmüller, Franco Zeffirelli. *ph* Ennio Guarnieri. *ed* Reginald Mills. *pd* Lorenzo Mongiardino. *m* Donovan. *cast* Graham Faulkner, Judi Bowker, Leigh Lawson, Kenneth Cranham, Lee Montague, Valentina Cortese, Alec Guinness.

● Hello flowers, hello sky: the life of St Francis of Assisi, viewed as a wimpy hippy by the unspeakably daft Zeffirelli, wandering through soft focus landscapes accompanied by the strains of Donovan. Avoid at all costs. GA

Browning Version, The

(1951, GB, 90 min, b/w)
d Anthony Asquith. *p* Teddy Baird. *sc* Terence Rattigan. *ph* Desmond Dickinson. *ed* John D Guthridge. *ad* Carmen Dillon. *cast* Michael Redgrave, Jean Kent, Nigel Patrick, Ronald Howard, Wilfrid Hyde-White, Brian Smith.

● A careful adaptation of Terence Rattigan's play – in effect a re-run of *Goodbye Mr Chips* seen through dark-tinted glasses – which draws what little venom the original had by adding an absurdly sentimental coda. Worth watching for Redgrave's powerfully detailed performance as the schoolmaster who has masked his feelings of inadequacy by turning into a petty tyrant over the years, and whose facade is disastrously breached by a small act of kindness from one of the boys. But the rest of the characters are strictly cardboard. TM

Browning Version, The

(1994, GB, 97 min)
d Mike Figgis. *p* Ridley Scott, Mimi Polk. *sc* Ronald Harwood. *ph* Jean-François Robin. *ed* Hervé Schneid. *pd* John Beard. *m* Mark Isham. *cast* Albert Finney, Greta Scacchi, Matthew Modine, Julian Sands, Bern Silverstone.

● Considered dispassionately, Figgis' lavish update of Terence Rattigan's play must be judged redundant, even meaningless, as an account of contemporary British manners. However much Ronald Harwood's screenplay tries to 'modernise' things, the story belongs inescapably to a different world with different social mores. That said, as Crocker-Harris, the buttoned-up classics teacher (Finney), faces an enforced retirement, not to mention rumours that his wife Laura (Scacchi) might be having an affair with his friend, the chemistry teacher Frank Hunter (Modine), the film contrives, despite its conspicuous faults, to work surprisingly well as a full-blown weepie. Most of the credit must go to Finney, whose quiet but overwhelmingly moving performance lends the film an emotional truth its heritage trimmings hardly deserve. GA

Brown on Resolution

see Forever England

Brown's Requiem

(1998, US, 104 min)
d Jason Freeland. *p* Tim Youd, David Rubin. *sc* Jason Freeland. *ph* Sead Mutarevic. *ed* Toby Yates. *pd* Marc Rizzo. *m* Cynthia Millar. *cast* Michael Rooker, William Sasso, Kevin Corrigan, Selma Blair, Tobin Bell, Harold Gould, Brion James, Brad Dourif, Valerie Perrine.

● Not so much *LA Confidential* as 'LA Cliché', this is based on James Ellroy's first book and feels like a dry run for themes and attitudes he went on to explore with far greater complexity and skill. The eternally hoarse Rooker is well cast as Fritz Brown, ex-cop, repo man, and occasional shamus: $500 a day, plus expenses. Hired by one 'Fatdog' to trail his sister's Jewish sugardaddy, Brown soon starts stumbling across your standard cross-section of corrupt cops, cruel corpses and cantankerous caddies. Cantankerous caddies? Well, okay, the film does have its inventive moments, but the rough edit I saw was stymied by too much voice-over and a funereal pace. TCh

Brubaker

(1980, US, 130 min)
d Stuart Rosenberg. *p* Ron Silverman. *sc* WD Richter. *ph* Bruno Nuytten. *ed* Robert Brown. *ad* J Michael Riva. *m* Lalo Schifrin. *cast* Robert Redford, Yaphet Kotto, Jane Alexander, Murray Hamilton, David Keith, Morgan Freeman.

● Redford is Brubaker, all gritty integrity and inner resolve as the new warden of a Southern prison farm, who arrives disguised as a prisoner so that he may better expose the mugging, raping and murdering cesspit he discovers. By its attribution of every evil to simple human greed, the melodrama remains hamfisted; while Rosenberg's direction (the original director, Bob Rafelson was fired for thumping the producer) signals 'realism' with crude denim-blue tints in every image. After two hours and ten minutes one is left only with a numbing awareness of Redford's charmless charm, the macho image unable (unlike Eastwood or Reynolds) to even contemplate self-irony. CA

Bruce Lee Story, The

see Dragon Dies Hard, The

Bruce Lee: The Man, The Myth (Li Xiaolong Chuanqi/aka Bruce Lee – True Story)

(1976, HK, 104 min)
d Wu Szu-Yuen. *p* Chang Ch'uan. *sc* Wu Szu-Yuan. *ph* Chang Ch'i. *ed* Sung Ming, P'an Hsiung Yao. *m* Chou Fu-Liang. *cast* Bruce Li, Liang Shao-Sung, Ch'en Chien-Po. Hsiao Ch'i Lin, Hsu Chung-Hsin.

● Numbingly unimaginative and exploitative biography. Would you trust a film that opens on a '70s street scene and captions it 'Hong Kong 1958'?

Bruit qui rend fou, Un

see Blue Villa, The

Brute, The

(1976, GB, 90 min)
d Gerry O'Hara. *p* John Quested. *sc* Gerry O'Hara. *ph* Denis Lewiston. *ed* Gerry Hambling. *ad* Terry Pritchard. *m* Kenneth Jones. *cast* Sarah Douglas, Julian Glover, Bruce Robinson, Jenny Twigge, Suzanne Stone, Peter Bull.

● Crazy collision of sensationalism and social concern makes this wife-battering study seem more like a horror movie – which is both endearing and disturbing. CW

Brute, The

see Barravento

Brute, The

see Bruto, El

Brute Force

(1947, US, 98 min, b/w)
d Jules Dassin. *p* Mark Hellinger. *sc* Richard Brooks. *ph* William Daniels. *ed* Edward Curtiss. *ad* Bernard Herzbrun, John F DeCuir. *m* Miklos Rozsa. *cast* Burt Lancaster, Hume Cronyn, Charles Bickford, Sam Levene, Whit Bissell, John Hoyt, Art Smith, Howard Duff, Yvonne De Carlo, Ann Blyth, Ella Raines.

● Despite a loss of temperature through the flashbacks which let in some female interest, this is one of Dassin's best films. Less coherent than Siegel's *Riot in Cell Block 11* in its challenge to prison conditions, it draws on WWII experience to draw a powerful analogy between the prison (where Cronyn's sadistic chief guard beats up prisoners to the strains of Wagner) and a fascist state. With brutality breeding brutality in this world which the dialogue (script by Richard Brooks) defines as an existentialist hell from which there is no escape, *Brute Force* was a notably violent film in its day. The scene in which an informer is herded by blow-torches to execution in a steam press still chills. TM

Bruto, El (The Brute)

(1952, Mex, 83 min, b/w)
d/sc Luis Buñuel. *ph* Augustin Jimenez. *sc* Luis Buñuel, Luis Alcoriza. *ed* Jorge Bustos. *ad* Gunther Gerszo. *m* Raúl Lavista. *cast* Pedro Armendariz, Katy Jurado, Rosita Arenas, Andres Soler.

● One of the fascinating melodramas Buñuel made during his early years in Mexico. The landlord of a block of tenements tries to throw his tenants out to make way for a luxurious new house for himself and his mistress. To implement this, he hires a 'strong and devoted' slaughterhouse worker, and talks him into eliminating the community's leading resisters. Unusually, the film concentrates not on the heroic resistance of the tenants but on El Bruto himself, and his growing awareness of the iniquities of the paternalistic order he is helping. Buñuel sharpens the political edge by having El Bruto discover that his boss is also his natural father. The images are powerful, not to say – in a nightime chase sequence – magnetic, and the character of the reliable worker-cum-hired 'brute', who discovers who his real enemies are, unforgettable.

Brutti, sporchi e cattivi (Ugly, Dirty and Bad/Ugly, Dirty and Mean/Down and Dirty)

(1976, It, 115 min)
d Ettore Scola. *p* Carlo Ponti. *sc* Ettore Scola, Ruggero Maccari. *ph* Dario Di Palma. *ed* Raimondo Crociani. *ad* Luciano Ricceri, Franco Velchi. *m* Armando Trovaioli. *cast* Nino Manfredi, Francesco Anniballi, Maria Bosco, Franco Merli, Ettore Garofolo, Alfredo D'Ippolito.

● Scola picked up the best director prize at Cannes for this grim comedy about a large, degenerate family living in a shanty town on the outskirts of Rome. Manfredi is the pathetic and monstrous one-eyed patriarch Giacinto, consumed with fear that his bundle of insurance money (a million lire!) will be stolen by his scheming relatives. They would too! Scola by no means romanticises the poor (drinking, thieving and copulation is about all they're interested in), but in this environment it's hard to see how it could be otherwise. Depressing and funny at the same time: cross *Bicycle Thieves* and *Steptoe and Son* and you're in the right vicinity. TCh

Brylcreem Boys, The

(1996, GB, 106 min)
d Terence Ryan. *p* Paul Madigan, Alan Latham, Bernie Stampfer, Terence Ryan. *sc* Terence Ryan, Jamie Brown. *ph* Gerry Lively. *ed* Emma Hickox. *pd* Steve Hardie. *m* Richard Hartley. *cast* Bill Campbell, William McNamara, Angus MacFadyen, John Gordon Sinclair, Gabriel Byrne, Jean Butler.

● WWII, neutral Ireland: German and Allied soldiers share the same prison camps. The potentially rewarding premise is wasted in a whimsical comedy that resorts to predictable plot twists and character development, to national stereotyping, and to the convention of having two guys on different sides fall for the same girl. Byrne does his best as the camp commander, but the dice are loaded. GA

BS I Love You

(1971, US, 98 min)
d Steven Hillard Stern. *p* Arthur M Broidy. *sc* Steven Hillard Stern. *ph* David Dans. *ad* Ernst Fegté. *m* Jimmy Dale, Mark Shekter. *cast* Peter Kastner, Joanna Cameron, Louise Sorel, Gary Burghoff, Joanna Barnes, Richard B Shull.

● 'BS' is revealed during the credits to stand for 'bullshit', which is an indication of the desperately trendy nature of the film. Kastner, star of *You're a Big Boy Now*, plays a similar character a few years on, an adman beset by women. Some good gags, but forget it.

Buccaneer, The

(1958, US, 121 min)
d Anthony Quinn. *p* Henry Wilcoxon. *sc* Jesse L Lasky Jr, Berenice Mosk. *ph* Loyal Griggs. *ed* Archie Marshek. *ad* Hal Pereira, Walter Tyler, Albert Nozaki. *m* Elmer Bernstein. *cast* Yul Brynner, Charlton Heston, Claire Bloom, Charles Boyer, Inger Stevens, EG Marshall, Henry Hull.

● Lavish spectacle produced for DeMille (who had directed his own version in 1938, and whose last production this was), misfiring lamely in its attempt to make swashbuckling entertainment out of the historical fact of pirate Jean Lafitte's patriotic gesture in fighting the Battle of New Orleans in 1815. Very stodgy. TM

Buchanan Rides Alone

(1958, US, 78 min)
d Budd Boetticher. *p* Harry Joe Brown. *sc* Charles Lang. *ph* Lucien Ballard. *ed* Al Clark. *ad* Robert Boyle. *cast* Randolph Scott, Craig Stevens, Barry Kelley, Tol Avery, Peter Whitney, Manuel Rojas, LQ Jones, Joe De Santis, Roy Jenson.

● Randolph Scott rides into a small border town, becomes innocently involved in a killing (Mexican youth of wealthy family avenges the rape of his sister), and is escorted out again at gunpoint with his life spared but his money-belt emptied. Being Scott, he naturally turns right around to recover his money, in the process stoutly righting assorted wrongs without ever really knowing what is going on as Charles Lang's script drives with admirable lucidity through a morass of enigmatic loyalties and abruptly shifting partnerships, mainly involving the frenzied efforts of the three corrupt brothers who run the town to doublecross each other for profit by alternatively hanging, ransoming or kidnapping the Mexican youth. A minor film compared to *The Tall T* or *Ride Lonesome*, maybe, but foregrounding the poker-faced sense of absurdity that lurks never far below the surface through the entire Boetticher/Scott series, it is still a marvel of economical craftsmanship. TM

Bûche, La (Season's Beatings)

(1999, Fr, 107 min)
d Danièle Thompson. *p* Alain Sarde. *sc* Danièle Thompson, Christopher Thompson. *ph* Robert Fraisse. *ed* Emmanuelle Castro. *pd* Michèle Abbé-Vannier. *m* Michel Legrand. *cast* Sabine Azéma, Emmanuelle Béart, Charlotte Gainsbourg, Claude Riche, Françoise Fabian, Christopher Thompson, Jean-Pierre Darroussin, Isabelle Carré.

● The daughters of a separated Russian Jewish family in Paris, single singer Louba (Azéma), successful married Sonia (Béart) and sharp-mouthed gamine Milla (Gainsbourg), convene before Christmas for their stepfather's funeral. As the 25th approaches, they argue about the cake (*Bûche de Noël*), and revelations tumble on the girls, their husbands/lovers and their parents. The daughters' real father is hospitalised for heart problems, and emotions burst out all over. Legrand's lush jingles accompany the deliberately kitsch 'Xmas' inserts; Dean Martin croons the Yuletide classics; and it ends with a flood of violins accompanying 'My Yiddisher Momma'. WH

Buchi Neri

see Black Holes, The

Büchse der Pandora, Die

see Pandora's Box

Buck and the Preacher

(1971, US, 103 min)
d Sidney Poitier. *p* Joel Glickman. *sc* Ernest Kinoy. *ph* Alex Phillips. *ed* Pembroke J Herring. *pd* Sydney Z Litwack. *m* Benny Carter. *cast* Sidney Poitier, Harry Belafonte, Ruby Dee, Cameron Mitchell, Denny Miller, Nita Talbot.

● Poitier's first film as director has an excellent subject which is rather reminiscent of Ford's *Wagon Master*: the long, hard trek through the wilderness, harassed by marauding white nightriders all the way, of a group of Negro slaves freed after the end of the Civil War. It is pleasant enough, but somehow – despite excellent performances by Poitier (the intrepid wagonmaster) and Belafonte (a roguish preacher) – it never quite clicks. Nice, though, to see the Indians riding to the rescue instead of the Cavalry. TM

Bucket of Blood, A

(1959, US, 66 min, b/w)
d/p Roger Corman. *sc* Charles B Griffith. *ph* Jacques R Marquette. *ed* Anthony Carras. *ad* Daniel Haller. *m* Fred Katz. *cast* Dick Miller, Barboura Morris, Anthony Carbone, Julian Burton, Ed Nelson, John Brinkley.

● Corman's first full-blooded horror comedy was put in a class of its own by Charles Griffith's unusually witty script. Walter, hapless waiter in a Greenwich Village hangout, yearns to be as famous as the poets and musicians he serves endless coffee to. After a lucky break (straight out of Poe), he begins to make it as a prolific sculptor of gruesome corpses… Not surprisingly, the parody of the 'beat scene' (including a hilarious caricature of Allen Ginsberg) is closer to the truth than those attempted in many mainstream movies.

Buck Rogers in the 25th Century

(1979, US, 89 min)
d Daniel Haller. *p* Richard Caffey. *sc* Glen A Larson, Leslie Stevens. *ph* Frank Beascoechea. *ed* John J Dumas. *ad* Paul Peters. *m* Stu Phillips. *cast* Gil Gerard, Pamela Hensley, Erin Gray, Henry Silva, Tim O'Connor, Joseph Wiseman.

● The way space jock and cosmic smartass Buck Rogers does his thing, launched into the 25th century from 1987, the audience will soon twig that he's been deep-frozen for at least 30 years longer than the script lets on: his humour is pure *Playboy* '50s. Same for the sexual rivalry between Good and Bad: the competent but prudish Captain Wilma Deering ('Commander of the Earth's Defences') and languorous but evil Princess Ardala ('With a man like you, I could defy my father'). In homage to Buck's cartoon strip origins, blonde Deering wears crisp and manly uniform, while the dark Princess sports barbarian gear right out of *Conan* by *Barbarella*. At best, the formula works like vintage Bond (explicitly so in the title sequence). But too much time is wasted with stale *Star Wars* plagiarisms, including the screen's dullest robot. Better to have made more of the best urban gang for some time: nuclear mutants roaming what's left of Chicago. CR

Bucktown

(1975, US, 94 min)
d Arthur Marks. *p* Bernard Schwartz. *sc* Bob Ellison. *ph* Robert Birchall. *ed* George Folsey Jr. *ad* George Costello, John Carter. *m* Johnny Pate. *cast* Fred Williamson, Pam Grier, Thalmus Rasulala, Tony King, Bernie Hamilton, Art Lund.

● Reactionary vengeance movie, blaxploitation style. Having effortlessly wiped out the entire corrupt white police department of Buchanan (known as Bucktown to the police grafters) to avenge his brother, Williamson's super ghetto-black Duke Johnson falls for the uncharacteristically simpering Pam Grier and opts for a life of macho domestic bliss. But not before he has disposed of all his former street buddies (who have taken over the graft) in a finale of massive retribution. JPy

Buddha Bless America (Taiping Tianguo)

(1996, Tai, 125 min)
d Wu Nianzhen. *p* Yang Teng-Kuei, Yeh Wen-Li. *sc* Wu Nianzhen. *ph* Li Ping-Bin. *ed* Chen Bo-Wen. *ad* Lee Fu-Hsung. *m* Jiang Hsiao-wen. *cast* Lin Cheng-Sheng, Jiang Shuna, Yang Congxian, Lee Hsin-Tzong. Bai Ming-Hwa.

● The second feature by Taiwan's pre-eminent scriptwriter is a wonderfully wry comedy with undertones of melancholy. In the late '60s, a remote village in southern Taiwan is chosen as the site for some US Army war games; the villagers, promised compensation for the damage to their homes and crops, are resettled in the schoolhouse while the smartest local entrepreneur builds a temporary nightclub to keeps the GIs entertained. Against the backdrop, the smartest guy in the community (played by Lin, himself a distinguished director) fights a losing battle to maintain his dignity and honour. Wise, worldly and only gently anti-American. TR

Buddha's Lock (Tian Pusa)

(1987, HK/China, 96 min)
d Yim Ho. *p* Li Weiyan, Chen Jindi. *sc* Kong Liang. *ph* Lu Yue, Wang Xiaolie. *ed* Jiang Guoquang. *pd* Kang Lin, Zhao Jiping. *cast* John X Heart, Zhang Lutong, Yan Bide, Sun Feihu, Wei Zongwan, Steve Horowitz.

● This has a fascinating subject, based on fact: the arrest and enslavement of a crashed American airman by a backward tribe of the Yi people in central Sichuan during WWII. Unfortunately, it also has a script (by a Mainland Chinese writer) that has no real idea how to set up or develop characters, and constantly lets ethnographic elements get in the way of the narrative. The result is a strange mixture of excellence and hopeless misjudgements, never quite strong enough to overcome the handicap of a weak performance from the main America actor. At its best, it plays like an early Herzog movie: an assault on the very concept of human dignity in primitive, elemental landscapes. TR

Buddies

(1985, US, 79 min)
d/p/sc Arthur Bressan Jr. *ph* Carl Teitelbaum. *ed* Arthur Bressan Jr. *m* Jeffrey Olmsted. *cast* Geoff Edholm, David Schachter, Billy Lux, David Rose, Libby Saines, Damon Hairston, Tracy Vivat.

● An angry film, but it's a quiet, calm, insistent kind of anger which is all the more effective for its undestatement. The action is based in New York, and set around a dying AIDS patient and his 'buddy', a voluntary counsellor/visitor sent by the local gay centre. Edholm acts with intensity and conviction as the dying man railing against a government and a system that rejects him; Schachter is weaker and less believable as his buddy, though he improves as the film progresses, until by the end, as he parades outside the White House, his character and commitment are fully realised. It's a clever film, a good campaigning and educational piece, moving, funny, depressing and yet ultimately uplifting in its acknowledgment that people were beginning to realise that something had to be done, and were willing to commit themselves to doing it. The US government is seen as the ultimate villain, and mankind as the victim of a problem which can only be fought by more research, action and government money. MG

Buddy Buddy

(1981, US, 96 min)
d Billy Wilder. *p* Jay Weston. *sc* Billy Wilder, IAL Diamond. *ph* Harry Stradling. *ed* Argyle Nelson. *pd* Dan Lomino. *m* Lalo Schifrin. *cast* Jack Lemmon, Walter Matthau, Paula Prentiss, Klaus Kinski, Dana Elcar, Miles Chapin.

● After failing to set the box-office on fire with such sublime achievements of the '70s as *The Private Life of Sherlock Holmes* and *Fedora*, Wilder was understandably playing safe this time around. One is therefore less inclined to condemn than to overlook this farce about a hardboiled hit man and the suicidal pest next door (previously filmed by Edouard Molinaro in 1973 as *L'Emmerdeur*). What makes it even easier to ignore is that it looks so little like a Wilder film. There is some byplay with doubles, disguises and mistaken identity, but the rest is all bland Panavision, dreary back projection, and laboured dialogue. RC

Buddy Holly Story, The

(1978, US, 114 min)
d Steve Rash. *p* Freddy Bauer. *sc* Robert Gittler. *ph* Stevan Larner. *ed* David Blewitt. *pd* Joel Schiller. *m* Joe Renzetti. *cast* Gary Busey, Don Stroud, Charles Martin Smith, Conrad Janis, William Jordan, Maria Richwine.

●Fine biopic which showcases a brilliant performance by Busey as Holly, and conveys a real, raw feeling for the music. The opening sequence, for example – a roller-rink gig to a stunned Hicksville audience – was done 'live' and it shows. Streets ahead of most rock celluloid. CA

Buddy's Song

(1990, GB, 106 min)
d Claude Whatham. *p* Roy Baird, Bill Curbishley, Roger Daltrey. *sc* Nigel Hinton. *ph* John Hooper. *m* Roger Daltrey, Alan Shacklock. *cast* Roger Daltrey, Chesney Hawkes, Sharon Duce, Michael Elphick, Douglas Hodge, Paul McKenzie, James Aubrey, Liza Walker.

●Not quite a British musical, more a *Minder*-ish comedy-drama with songs. Daltrey plays Terry, a superannuated Teddy Boy ducking and diving on the fringes of the criminal world, who gets landed with some stolen property and ends up in jail. Meanwhile his wife Carol (Duce) decides to better herself by taking an interest in computers and having it off with her boss, leaving son Buddy (Hawkes) sufficiently perturbed to pick up a guitar and sing some New Town blues. Dad, now out of jail, wants to make him a star. Sadly, he's the all-time nightmare parent: he fails to resurrect his marriage, build a new life, or steer his boy's talents in the right direction. The usual teenage rock-band incidents pile up alarmingly, but Hawkes greets triumph and disaster alike with the same sullen depressed-adolescent expression (perhaps because the loathsome 'Lite Rock' songs he's been given make him sound like a secular Cliff Richard). Daltrey's central performance, on the other hand, is fearless and compelling. JMo

Buena Vida, La

see Good Life, The

Buena Vista Social Club

(1999, Ger, 101 min)
d Wim Wenders. *p* Wim Wenders, Ulrich Felsberg, Rosa Bosch. *ph* Jörg Widmer, Robby Müller, Lisa Rinzler. *ed* Brian Johnson, Monica Anderson. *with* Ry Cooder, Compay Segundo, Eliades Ochoa, Ibrahim Ferrer, Omara Portuondo, Orlando 'Cachaito' Lopez.

●Hard to credit that Wenders can still come up with a film that people actually want to see, but this project (handed to him on a plate by Ry Cooder) is a blinder. It documents the second phase in Cooder's reactivation of a group of elderly *soneros* musicians in Cuba: a trip to Havana in early 1998 to record with the amazing Ibrahim Ferrer, which prompts a reunion of the musicians who'd worked with Cooder on the original 'Buena Vista Social Club' album and leads to SRO concerts in Amsterdam and New York. The film-making is workmanlike and never gets in the way of the pleasure of seeing these incredible oldsters getting the standing ovations they've deserved all their lives. TR

Buenos Aires Vice Versa

(1996, Arg, 122 min)
d Alejandro Agresti. *p* Emjay Rechsteiner, Karen Javoneski, Polly Tapson, Axel Harding. *sc* Alejandro Agresti. *ph* Ramiro Aisenson. *ed* Alejandro Agresti, Alejandro Brodersohn. *cast* Vera Fogwill, Fernan Miras, Mirta Busnelli, Nicolas Pauls, Carlos Roffe.

●Agresti returned home from Europe to film this colourful, deceptively casual kaleidoscopic look at life in contemporary Buenos Aires: a city, as the various fragmented stories show, where the past – particularly in the form of absent (i.e. 'disappeared') families – exerts a strong, even tragic influence on the present. If that sounds heavy and obvious, the film has the same steadily intoxicating blend of passion and wit, romance and melancholy, meditation and vitality as the Astor Piazzolla tangos argued over in one café scene. And the characters, from a young woman hired to shoot a video of city life by a reclusive old couple, to a shunned woman who bellows at her ex when he's on the TV, and a kid who lives on the streets, are as engaging and easy to watch as the relaxed but vibrant camerawork. GA

Buenos Aires Zero Degree

(1999, HK, 59 min)
d Kwan Pun-Leung, Amos Lee. *p* Wong Kar-Wai, Jacky Pang, Chan Ye-Cheng. *sc/ph/ed* Kwan Pun-Leung, Amos Lee. *with* Tony Leung, Shirley Kwan.

●Co-directors Kwan and Lee (a video-art team; Kwan also shot Stanley Kwan's recent features) did go to Argentina to retrace some of the steps Wong Kar-Wai took when making *Happy Together* and did interview some of the participants in that fraught adventure, but their film is nothing like a conventional 'Making of'. Around three-quarters of *Buenos Aires Zero Degree* is composed of unused rushes from Wong's film: abandoned narrative twists, alternative endings, and a generous sampling of Shirley Kwan's performance in a role cut from the film. There's even a 'forbidden' glimpse of Leslie Cheung in drag, shown in negative. Anyone who knows *Happy Together* itself will find here real insights into Wong's aleatory methods of storytelling and film-making. TR

Buffalo Bill and the Indians, or Sitting Bull's History Lesson

(1976, US, 123 min)
d/p Robert Altman. *sc* Alan Rudolph, Robert Altman. *ph* Paul Lohmann. *ed* Peter Appleton, Dennis M Hill. *pd* Tony Masters. *m* Richard Baskin. *cast* Paul Newman, Joel Grey, Burt Lancaster, Kevin McCarthy, Harvey Keitel, Allan Nichols, Geraldine Chaplin, Will Sampson.

●Altman's continuing fascination with the lunatic reality underlying America's popular myths finds an obvious subject in Buffalo Bill. William F Cody was a nonentity who utilised the heroic Western image of 'Buffalo Bill' to create a capitalist showbiz enterprise grossing a million a year. With typical fast-paced wit, Altman focuses on Cody's blinkered, scatter-brained retinue, contrasting their alcoholic self-deception with the mystical reality and strength of the Indians destroyed in their grand distortion of history. Some of it comes off well, and Newman is superb. But the film shows tiresome signs of its origins as a stage play (by Arthur Kopit), and the good moments aren't quite enough to make up for its overall predictability. DP

Buffalo '66 (100)

(1997, Can/US, 110 min)
d Vincent Gallo. *p* Chris Hanley. *sc* Vincent Gallo, Alison Bagnall. *ph* Lance Acord. *ed* Curtiss Clayton. *pd* Gideon Ponte. *m* Vincent Gallo. *cast* Vincent Gallo, Christina Ricci, Ben Gazzara, Mickey Rourke, Rosanna Arquette, Jan-Michael Vincent, Anjelica Huston.

●Gallo's directorial debut is one of a kind, an eccentric, provocative comedy which laces a poignant love story with both a sombre, washed-out naturalism and surreal musical vignettes. Throwing out the standard repetitions of shot/reverse shot, Gallo brings an individual film grammar to the screen, a beguiling mix of formal tropes and apparently impetuous conceits. If not autobiographical, then at least deeply personal, the film follows one Billy Brown (Gallo) out of prison and back to his hometown, Buffalo, NY. There he kidnaps a girl, Layla (Ricci) a busty, blonde in two-inch skirt and dazzling fairy tale slippers, and entreats her to play his loving wife for his parents' benefit. The homecoming goes a long way to explain Billy's aggressive insecurity: his indifferent mom (Huston) is a rabid football obsessive, while his dad (Gazzara) is taciturn and hostile, though taken with Layla. The cruel caricature of this sourly funny episode is tempered by Layla's sweetness. Billy's turmoil is redeemed in her simplicity. You may scoff at such blatant male wish-fulfilment, but when Billy finally opens himself to the threat of intimacy, it's a heart-rending moment. A brave, honest, stimulating film, this reaches parts other movies don't even know exist. TCh

Buffet Froid

(1979, Fr, 93 min)
d Bertrand Blier. *p* Alain Sarde. *sc* Bertrand Blier. *ph* Jean Penzer. *ed* Claudine Merlin. *ad* Theo Meurisse. *cast* Gérard Depardieu, Bernard Blier, Jean Carmet, Genevieve Page, Denise Gence, Carole Bouquet, Michel Serrault.

●Rigorously absurd contemporary *film noir* which presents every character, incident and situation known to the genre, but none of the customary explanations, motivations or consequences. A blackly surreal procession of amoral and/or illegal acts proceed haphazardly from Depardieu's discovery of his lost penknife embedded in a dying Métro traveller, and his subsequent alliance with his wife's murderer and a police inspector, producing a cherishably Buñuelian depiction of the far-from-discreet crimes of the bourgeoisie. PT

Buffy the Vampire Slayer

(1992, US, 94 min)
d Fran Rubel Kuzui. *p* Howard Rosenman, Kaz Kuzui. *sc* Joss Whedon. *ph* James Hayman. *ed* Camilla Toniolo, Jill Savitt. *pd* Lawrence Miller. *cast* Kristy Swanson, Donald Sutherland, Paul Reubens, Rutger Hauer, Luke Perry, Michele Abrams, Hilary Swank, Pee Wee Herman [Paul Reuben].

●Buffy (Swanson) and her vacuous valley-girl pals are, like, *rilly* irritating: they have a keen fashion sense and an imaginative line in vapid chat, but they're in desperate need of a reality check. Enter creepy old Merrick (Sutherland), who tells Buffy her weird dreams are the result of her being The Chosen One, the Slayer. So off they wander to a moonlit cemetery, where a recently fanged victim emerges from a fresh grave, and Buffy instinctively stabs him through the heart. But what will her pals say? Should she skip cheerleading practice? 'The world is under threat from the legions of the Undead, and you're worried about the Seniors' Dance', gasps exasperated hunk Pike (Perry), who's smitten but can't believe her attitude. Unfocused stuff, pitched at undemanding teenagers. Swanson can't act but moves well, while Hauer is far too louche to be a scary vampire villain. NF

Bug

(1975, US, 101 min)
d Jeannot Szwarc. *p* William Castle. *sc* William Castle, Thomas Page. *ph* Michel Hugo. *ed* Alan Jacobs. *ad* Jack Martin Smith. *m* Charles Fox. *cast* Bradford Dillman, Joanna Miles, Richard Gilliland, Jamie Smith Jackson, Alan Fudge, Jesse Vint.

●Basically a mad scientist story enlivened by eco-subtexts, in which horrible self-combusting cockroaches are thrown up from beneath the earth's crust during an earthquake, only to commence setting fire to everyone and everything they touch; meanwhile Dillman's hermit-like scientist investigates, analyses, and comes to play God. Therein lies the film's interest: biblical and religious images (heads aflame with tongues of fire, winged demons) hold sway right from the film's opening, set effectively in a remote desert church, to establish a schlock-horror allegory on the creation myth. Tacky in parts – as one might expect from producer William Castle (his last film; he also co-scripted) – and occasionally lacking in plot logic, it's nevertheless an imaginative little B thriller that manages to be genuinely suspenseful. GA

Bugis Street

(1994, Singapore, 101 min)
d Manshi Yonfan. *p* Katy Yew. *sc* Manshi Yonfan. *ph* Jacky Tang. *cast* Hiep Thi Le, Michael Lam, Benedict Goh, Ernest Seah, Gerald Chen, Maggie Lye.

●Before the ultimate nanny state tidied away all signs of 'dirt', Bugis Street was Singapore's centre for transvestite hookers. This movie, by a Hong Kong fashion photographer turned director, is a fey evocation of those days, centred on the imaginary Sin-Sin Hotel, crammed to the rafters with she-males and their drunken sailor pick-ups. There's no plot; the film explores its world through the eyes of the newly arrived maid (Le, from Oliver Stone's *Heaven & Earth*), an innocent who winds up learning all she'll ever need to know about eye-liner, falsies, penises and putting a brave face on things. Better as censor-bait than as drama, but it contains several powerful direct-to-camera monologues by real life drag queens. TR

Bugles in the Afternoon

(1952, US, 85 min)
d Roy Rowland. *p* William J Cagney. *sc* Daniel Mainwaring, Harry Brown. *ph* Wilfred M Cline. *ed* Thomas Reilly. *ad* Edward Carrere. *m* Dimitri Tiomkin. *cast* Ray Milland, Helena Carter, Hugh Marlowe, Forrest Tucker, Barton MacLane, George Reeves, James Millican, Gertrude Michael.

●Derived from an Ernest Haycox Western, this begins well, with unusually cool, composed performances from Carter (as the heroine) and

Michael (a striking cameo as a saloon girl). Milland, cashiered from the army after running a fellow officer through with his sabre (for pressing his attentions on Milland's fiancée, it eventually emerges), enlists as a private in the frontier cavalry, only to find the same officer (Marlowe) installed as his commanding officer and getting up to his old tricks again. Though Daniel Mainwaring and Harry Brown provide some good scenes and intelligent dialogue, the plot works too hard to prove Marlowe a double-dyed villain, cheerfully sacrificing lives if only Milland's can be one of them, and ending in absurdity as the pair work up to their grudge fight while the Sioux are busy massacring everybody in sight at the Little Big Horn. A pity, because Rowland directs with a fine control of mood and pace, and there are sterling performances from Milland and Tucker to add to those by the two women. TM

Bug's Life, A

(1998, US, 95 min)
d John Lasseter. *p* Darla K Anderson, Kevin Reher. *sc* Andrew Stanton, Donald McEnery, Bob Shaw. *ph* Sharon Calahan. *ed* Lee Unkrich. *pd* William Cone. *m* Randy Newman. *cast* voices: Dave Foley, Kevin Spacey, Julia Louis-Dreyfus, Phyllis Diller.

●An underworld film in the truest sense, Disney/Pixar's animated story takes elements from the gangster and adventure genres and shrinks them down to a microscopic grass-root level. Flik is like any other worker ant gathering harvest before the onset of winter; he's a bit clumsy and not terribly bright. At least he means well, though his actions get the colony into trouble with extortionist Hopper and his band of gangly grasshoppers. The gist is simple: supply double the annual food quota to Hopper and his mates, or the colony gets it. Since Flik feels responsible for this mess, he volunteers to fetch help, and returns some time later with – an inept circus act! As expected, from the makers of *Toy Story*, the computer-generated imagery in this *Magnificent Seven*-style critterfest is exceptional throughout. Most of the (four-legged) cast, too, are imaginatively rendered, their predominantly jokey dialogue keeping the motor running whenever the film threatens to stall. Add a cluster of hilarious incidentals and the funniest post-closing-credits sequence in years, and the final result is pixel perfect. DA

Bugsy

(1991, US, 136 min)
d Barry Levinson. *p* Mark Johnson, Warren Beatty, Barry Levinson. *sc* James Toback. *ph* Allen Daviau. *ed* Stu Linder. *pd* Dennis Gassner. *m* Ennio Morricone. *cast* Warren Beatty, Annette Bening, Harvey Keitel, Ben Kingsley, Elliott Gould, Joe Mantegna, Richard Sarafian, Bebe Neuwirth, Wendy Phillips, Robert Beltran, James Toback.

●Sent by Meyer Lansky and Lucky Luciano to take care of West Coast business, the womanising Benjamin 'Bugsy' Siegel (Beatty) settles down to a life of Hollywood glitz. His fraught affair with starlet Virginia Hill (Bening), which places great strain on Siegel's otherwise happy marriage, is only one of the psychopathically violent mobster's obsessions. For he dreams, too, of building a casino-hotel in Las Vegas. But Bugsy's twin passions put him at risk: his extravagance with Mob money and his high profile turn the crime barons against him… One can, of course, remain sceptical about the film's unabashedly romantic portrait of Siegel (though Beatty is truly unsettling when called on to come up with murderous rage), but its virtues are many: Bugsy's risible efforts at self-improvement through language; a farcical tour de force where he juggles a daughter's birthday meal, phone calls from Virginia and a business meeting; mad plans to kill Mussolini; brutal humiliations meted out to disloyal wiseguys. With a sparklingly witty script (James Toback), classy direction and terrific performances all round, Beatty's return to the fray is his best movie since *McCabe and Mrs Miller*. GA

Bugsy Malone

(1976, GB, 93 min)
d Alan Parker. *p* Alan Marshall. *sc* Alan Parker. *ph* Michael Seresin, Peter Biziou. *ed* Gerry Hambling. *pd* Geoffrey Kirkland. *songs* Paul Williams. *cast* Scott Baio, Jodie Foster, Florrie Dugger, John Cassisi, Martin Lev.

●Novelty gangster pic with an entire cast of children who use guns which fire ice cream, Adults may be diverted by the affectionate pastiche of old gangster movies and by Paul Williams' pleasant Nilsson-like song'n'dance numbers. CPe

Build My Gallows High

see Out of the Past

Bulldog Drummond

(1929, US, 89 min, b/w)
d F Richard Jones. *p* Samuel Goldwyn. *sc* Sidney Howard. *ph* George Barnes, Gregg Toland. *ed* Viola Lawrence, Frank Lawrence. *ad* William Cameron Menzies. *cast* Ronald Colman, Joan Bennett, Montagu Love, Lilyan Tashman, Claud Allister, Lawrence Grant.

●No less than 13 different actors have impersonated Sapper's perennially gentlemanly hero in films, ranging from Carlyle Blackwell in 1922 to Richard Johnson in 1966 and 1968. In theory, at least, Colman is perfect casting, well able to cope with both the suavity and the built-in humour, and his talkie debut (with its Chandlerian plot about a girl trying to rescue her uncle from a sanitorium where he is being coerced into signing away his fortune) was a huge success at the time. If the pre-Bond formula and the military clubman hero prove a little jaded now, there is compensation in the careful Goldwyn packaging: direction by a graduate of the Sennett school, sets by William Cameron Menzies, low-key camerawork from Gregg Toland. TM

Bulldog Drummond Comes Back

(1937, US, 64 min, b/w)
d Louis King. *sc* Edward T Lowe. *ph* William C Mellor. *ed* James Smith. *ad* Hans Dreier, Franz Bachelin. *m* Boris Morros. *cast* John Howard, John Barrymore, Louise Campbell, Reginald Denny, EE Clive, J Carrol Naish, John Sutton.

●Second – and perhaps the best – in Paramount's *Bulldog Drummond* series, with Howard taking over the lead from Ray Milland (whose star was rising). It boasts a waspishly nasty villain (Naish), and the Holmesian revenge plot, complete with clues in rhyming couplets, is considerably enhanced by Barrymore as a Scotland Yard detective with an irresistible flair for disguises. Then on the downgrade, Barrymore belies his demotion to a B movie series with a performance of witty relish, at one point musing (as he applies his make-up) 'You know, I really think I should have been an actor.' The series, featuring Howard throughout, continued with *Bulldog Drummond's Peril, Bulldog Drummond's Revenge, Bulldog Drummond in Africa* (1938), *Arrest Bulldog Drummond, Bulldog Drummond's Secret Police* and *Bulldog Drummond's Bride* (1939). TM

Bulldog Drummond Escapes

(1937, US, 67 min. b/w)
d James Hogan. *sc* Edward T Lowe. *ph* Victor Milner. *ed* William Shea. *ad* Hans Dreier, Earl Hedrick. *cast* Ray Milland, Heather Angel, Reginald Denny, Porter Hall, Guy Standing, EE Clive, Walter Kingsford.

●First in Paramount's series of B movies devoted to 'Sapper' HC McNeile's British ex-army officer with a taste for adventure. A fine if familiarly atmospheric opening as our hero, driving through the inescapable English fog, is hailed by a damsel in distress, has his car stolen from under his nose, and finds a corpse lurking in the marshes. Thereafter the scene shifts to a country mansion complete with the usual equipment ranging from shifty butler to secret passages, and everything begins to creak audibly. TM

Bulldog Jack (aka Alias Bulldog Drummond)

(1935, GB, 72 min, b/w)
d Walter Forde. *p* Michael Balcon. *sc* Gerard Fairlie, John Orton, Sidney Gilliat. *ph* Max Greene. *ed* Otto Ludwig. *pd* Alfred Junge. *cast* Jack Hulbert, Fay Wray, Ralph Richardson, Claude Hulbert, Paul Graetz, Gibb McLaughlin, Athol Fleming.

●Sleuthing send-up from Michael Balcon's Gaumont with Jack Hulbert masquerading as the famous English detective in order to track down criminal mastermind Richardson, who's been snaffling gems from the British Museum. A jolly jape, and comedy man Forde slings together a cracking climactic chase through the London underground. TJ

Bull Durham

(1988, US, 108 min)
d Ron Shelton. *p* Thom Mount, Mark Burg. *sc* Ron Shelton. *ph* Bobby Byrne. *ed* Robert Leighton, Adam Weiss. *pd* Armin Ganz. *m* Michael Convertino. *cast* Kevin Costner, Susan Sarandon, Tim Robbins, Trey Wilson, Robert Wuhl, William O'Leary, David Neidorf, Danny Gans, Tom Silardi, Max Patkin.

●Less a baseball movie than a romantic comedy based around the sacred diamond. Each season, Annie (Sarandon) – devout believer in the Church of Baseball – favours one member of the Durham Bulls minor league team with her patented instruction in the subtle arts of baseball and love-making. Selecting young acolyte Ebby (Robbins), she initiates him into the secret of 'breathing through your eyelids', encourages him to wear a suspender belt while pitching, and ties him to a bed to read him extracts from Whitman's erotic poem 'I Sing the Body Electric'. The seasoned Crash (Costner) meanwhile grooms the youngster for a shot at the major league, concentrating on his fast but undisciplined pitching, because he throws like he fucks, all over the place. Paradoxically, writer/director Shelton's intimate knowledge of baseball allows him to convey the feel of the game, its esoteric mythology and quirky superstitions, without losing sight of the real issue: when will Annie and Crash get it together? The film's delicious charge stems not from a rush towards a big game climax, but from the aching pleasure of Crash and Annie's potential consummation. Exuding easy charm, Costner confirms his status as *the* romantic leading man of the late '80s; Sarandon is sexier reading Emily Dickinson's poems fully clothed than most actresses would be writhing naked on a bed; together, they are indeed the bodies electric. Marvellous stuff. NF

Bullet Ballet

(1998, Jap, 98 min)
d/p/sc/ph/ed/pd Shinya Tsukamoto. *m* Chu Ishikawa *cast* Shinya Tsukamoto, Kirina Mano, Tatsuya Nakamura,Takahiro Murase, Kyoka Suzuki, Hisashi Igawa.

●A cult figure for his *Tetsuo* films and *Tokyo Fist*, Shinya Tsukamoto is the ultimate auteur: he writes, directs, designs, photographs, edits and stars – surprisingly, he doesn't supply his own critique. Goda is a characteristic role: a middle class worm who turns into a gun-fixated revenge junkie after his girlfriend shoots herself and he's mugged by a gang of street punks. The plot wouldn't translate to America: Goda can't get himself a gun for love or money. The industrial-primitive aesthetic has a ricochet trajectory: jittery, super-fast, elliptical shock cuts, culminating in melancholy death. It's aggro art, intense, gut-felt – but also, like all Tsukamoto's work, numbingly over-stretched. TCh

Bullet for the General, A (¿Quién sabe?)

(1966, It, 135 min)
d Damiano Damiani. *p* Bianco Manini. *sc* Salvatore Laurani. *ph* Antonio Secchi. *ed* Renato Cinquini. *ad* Sergio Canevari. *m* Luis Enriquez Bacalov. *cast* Gian Maria Volonté, Klaus Kinski, Martine Beswick, Lou Castel, Jaime Fernández, Andrea Checchi.

●A spaghetti Western on a par with Leone's. It shares Volonté and Kinski with *For a Few Dollars More*, and Luis Bacalov's haunting score was 'supervised' by Ennio Morricone, but the politics are more radical than anything Leone stood for (it ends with a ringing call to arms: 'Don't buy bread, buy dynamite!'). Lou Castel plays a tight-lipped gringo who insinuates himself into Volonté's gang of Mexican bandits on the fringes of the revolution. The film charts the peculiar friendship between these two blinkered mercenaries, and Volonté's belated arrival at a political consciousness. This intelligent, compelling reversal of the archetypal Hollywood schema (in which an American star lends his gun to the peasants' cause) was scripted by Franco Solinas, who also contributed to Rosi's *Salvatore Giuliano*, Costa-Gavras' *State of Siege*, Pontecorvo's *Battle of Algiers* and *Queimada!* TCh

Bullet in the Head (Diexue Jietou)

(1990, HK, 136 min)
d/p John Woo. *sc* John Woo, Patrick Leung, Janet Chun. *ph* Ardy Lam, Wilson Chan, Somcahi Kittikun, Wong Wing-Hang. *ed* John Woo. *ad* James Leung. *m* James Wong, Romeo Diaz. *cast* Tony Leung, Jacky Cheung, Waise Lee, Simon Yam, Fennie Yeun, Yolinda Yan.
●Highly ambitious Vietnam epic about the dehumanising effects of greed and repression. Ben (Leung) grows up in the Hong Kong slums in the late '60s with best friends Paul (Waise Lee) and Frank (Cheung). Fleeing to Saigon after a fight with a gangster, the three attempt to profit from the war, smuggling first penicillin, then gold. Their enterprise comes at a heavy price. Paul becomes obsessed with the gold, and after capture by the Vietcong, they are forced to choose between murder or death. The governing metaphor is spelled out in the title: Woo recreates the infamous news photo of a Vietnamese executed by a gun to his head, ups the ante on the Russian roulette sequence in *The Deer Hunter*, and puts his own macabre spin on Peckinpah's *Bring Me the Head of Alfredo Garcia*. The early sequences play like one of Woo's gangster films, with their heroic rhetorical imagery, slow motion, dissolves and freeze frames, but the director tightens the screw when the action shifts to Vietnam. Sometimes incoherent, over-pitched or simply painful to watch, this is Woo's most personal and political morality tale – a substantial movie all but consumed in the flames of its own madness. TCh

Bulletproof

(1987, US, 94 min)
d Steve Carver. *p* Paul Hertzberg. *sc* TL Lankford, Steve Carver. *ph* Francis Grumman. *ed* Jeff Freeman. *pd* Adrian Gorton. *m* Tom Chase, Steve Rucker. *cast* Gary Busey, Darlanne Fluegel, Henry Silva, Thalmus Rasulala, LQ Jones, René Enriquez, Mills Watson, RG Armstrong.
●In order to flush out Communist guerillas gathering near the Mexican/US border, the CIA use a prototype super-tank as bait, and lure former Special Forces agent Frank 'Bulletproof' McBain (Busey) out of retirement. One of the 'expendable' US soldiers captured at the same time is McBain's ex-lover (Fluegel). The terrorists are a motley rabble: Arab rapists, Mexican toy soldiers, and Nicaraguan sadists with a strong line in priest-slapping, nun-wasting and church-burning – atheistic Commies and racial stereotypes to a man. The Russkies, for whom the stolen tank is destined, are icy killers armed with a flimsy-looking helicopter gunship and AK47s that don't shoot straight. The excellent Busey is here wasted in a comic-strip hero role which taxes only his muscles and lopsided grin; Fluegel, meanwhile, scowls attractively while never quite pulling off her tough-girl act. Awkward slo-mo flashbacks and cheapskate production values add technical insult to artistic injury, and the whole thing is reminiscent of early Chuck Norris. NF

Bullets or Ballots

(1936, US, 82 min, b/w)
d William Keighley. *sc* Seton I Miller. *ph* Hal Mohr. *ed* Jack Killifer. *ad* Carl Jules Weyl. *m* Heinz Roemheld. *cast* Edward G Robinson, Joan Blondell, Barton MacLane, Humphrey Bogart, Frank McHugh, Joseph King, Richard Purcell, George E Stone.
●Dark Warners gangster film scripted by Seton I Miller (*G-Men*) and directed at a fair lick by studio journeyman Keighley. The war on crime won't easily be won. Robinson's on the side of the law for the first time, and relishes it. He's a New York cop who goes undercover to bust a racket. The machine guns keep rattling, Blondell reprises her sassy siren routine, and Bogart snarls away as the gangster Nick 'Bugs' Fenner. Both Bogey and Robinson go down at the close. GM

Bullets Over Broadway

(1994, US, 99 min)
d Woody Allen. *p* Robert Greenhut. *sc* Woody Allen, Douglas McGrath. *ph* Carlo Di Palma. *ed* Susan E Morse. *pd* Santo Loquasto. *cast* John Cusack, Jack Warden, Chazz Palminteri, Tony Sirico, Joe Viterelli, Dianne Wiest, Jim Broadbent, Jennifer Tilly, Mary-Louise Parker, Tracey Ullman, Rob Reiner, Harvey Fierstein.
●Set in the Runyonesque New York of the Jazz Age, when artists rubbed shoulders with gangsters at speakeasies, this is the story of idealistic young playwright David Shayne (Cusack). With backing from mob boss Nick Valenti (Viterelli), Shayne can direct his new work on Broadway, and even attract stars of the magnitude of Helen Sinclair (Wiest) and Warner Purcell (Broadbent). There's just one catch: Valenti insists that his flapper girlfriend Olive (Tilly) play a leading role. Not only is she terrible, she comes with a shadow, Nick's bodyguard Cheech (Palminteri), who oversees the rehearsals with barely concealed impatience. A merciless satire on the pretensions, hypocrisies and indulgences of theatre folk, this is Allen's fizziest piece in years. It's propped up by two fiercely competitive caricatures from Tilly and Wiest, who completely and appropriately overshadow Cusack's approximation of the inexperienced author. It must be said that this is scarcely new ground, and that the staging is sometimes clumsy, but just when you wonder how much life is left in these stereotypes, Allen pulls off a doozy of a dramatic switch which takes the farce to unexpected, dizzy heights. No! Don't speak! See it! TCh

Bullets Over Summer (Baolie Xingjing)

(1999, HK, 92 min)
d Wilson Yip. *p* Joe Ma. *sc* Matt Chow, Wilson Yip, Ben Cheung. *ph* Lam Wah-Chuen. *ed* Cheung Ka-Fai. *ad* Stanley Cheung. *m* Tommy Wai. *cast* Francis Ng, Louis Koo, Michelle Alicia Saram, Stephanie Lin, Helena Law, Lai Yiu-Cheung.
●One of the livelier teams working to reactivate the HK film industry, director Yip and producer Ma aim quite high in this comedy-thriller about a protracted stake-out. Two ill-matched cops take over a dotty old lady's apartment to watch the one opposite, believed to be a base for a gang of murderous robbers. The volatile elder cop Mike (Ng), supposedly terminally ill, grows fascinated by the pregnant, unmarried girl at the local dry cleaner's; his young partner Brian (Koo) is lazy, unfocused and more interested in dating a new girlfriend than in the job in hand. The cops-in-love motif and the off-the-wall humour doubtless owe something to *Chungking Express*, but the film is at heart glad to be generic.This stance pays off in the climactic confrontation, which comes out of the blue and manages to be funny, suspenseful *and* intense. TR

Bullet Train, The (Shinkansen Daibakuha)

(1975, Jap, 89 min)
d Junya Sato. *p* Kanji Amao, Jun Sakagami. *sc* Ryunosuke Oko, Junya Sato, Shigeko Katsuhara. *ph* Masahiko Iimura. *ed* Keiichi Kawai. *cast* Ken Takakura, Shin-ichi Chiba, Akira Oda, Kei Yamamoto, Fumio Watanabe, Takashi Shimura.
●A terrific central concept: a bomb is planted on one of Japan's 200 mph Shinkansen expresses, primed to explode as soon as the train slows to a certain speed. Savour it, because it's virtually all there is; the clumsy plotting, low-octane direction and muffled performances certainly don't add up to much of a movie. All that's required from Ken Takakura (as the chief bomber) is his presence, which he delivers adequately. Maybe the original Japanese version (running at 155 minutes) made more of the political undercurrents, but all that's left here are glimmerings of suspense in the final half-hour. TR

Bullfighter and the Lady

(1951, US, 87 min, b/w)
d Budd Boetticher. *p* (uncred) John Wayne. *sc* James Edward Grant. *ph* Jack Draper. *ed* Richard L Van Enger. *ad* Alfred Ybarra. *m* Victor Young. *cast* Robert Stack, Gilbert Roland, Joy Page, Katy Jurado, Virginia Grey, John Hubbard.
●Produced by John Wayne, and shorn down to 87 minutes by John Ford for a release print that surely must have had more dramatic bite than the complete version (a director's cut running 124 minutes has since been made available), this sees Boetticher getting far too close to the subject of his beloved bullfighting for the film's good. Stack is the arrogant American film-maker who, on a trip to Mexico, enlists Roland's champion toreador to pass on his skills. Inevitably, there must be death in the afternoon – not to mention many hard lessons in the Latin sense of honour – before Stack grows up enough to become a true man and great artist. Dire continuity and shifts in point of view, endless didactic sequences extolling the bullfighter's grace, and generally wooden performances result in a surprising fiasco of almost unbearable tedium. GA

Bullitt (100)

(1968, US, 114 min)
d Peter Yates. *p* Philip D'Antoni. *sc* Alan R Trustman, Harry Kleiner. *ph* William A Fraker. *ed* Frank P Keller. *ad* Albert Brenner. *m* Lalo Schifrin. *cast* Steve McQueen, Robert Vaughn, Jacqueline Bisset, Don Gordon, Robert Duvall, Simon Oakland, Norman Fell, Carl Reindel.
●A thriller which begins, as it means to go on, with a bang. Only minutes after the preliminaries are over, a door bursts open, a shotgun is fired, and the victim is blasted clean off the bed into the wall behind him. The plot, concerning the battle of wits between an honest cop and an ambitious politician for possession of the key witness in a Mafia exposé, is serviceable but nothing special. But the action sequences are brilliant, done without trickery in real locations (including a great car chase which spawned a thousand imitations) to lend an extraordinary sense of immediacy to the shenanigans and gunfights. TM

Bullseye!

(1990, US, 92 min)
d/p Michael Winner. *sc* Leslie Bricusse, Laurence Marks, Maurice Gran. *ph* Alan Jones. *ed* Arnold Crust [Michael Winner]. *pd* John Blezard. *cast* Michael Caine, Roger Moore, Sally Kirkland, Deborah Barrymore, Lee Patterson, Mark Burns, Derren Nesbitt, John Cleese, Patsy Kensit.
●In Winner's frantic and seriously unfunny comedy, Caine and Moore play a couple of recently reunited colourful conmen, respectively donkey-jacketed Sid and suave Gerald. What they have in common is severe cash-flow problems and remarkable resemblances to two dishonest scientists – Dr Hicklar (Caine), a Yank, and Sir John Bavistock (Moore), a nob – whom they see on the box talking guardedly about their potentially invaluable experiments in initiating cold fusion in a test-tube. Sid and Gerald bone up on their respective accents – Caine's American accent is funny – don cunning disguises, and assume the roles of Hicklar and Bavistock in order to perpetrate a heist. The whole thing then spirals off into total chaos with an all-nonsense plot about selling the plans to the highest bidder, involving gunfights on the Orient Express, double-crosses, and a visit to every stately home in Britain. No actor comes out unscathed from this stinker. Menahem Golan produced. WH

Bullshot

(1983, GB, 88 min)
d Dick Clement. *p* Ian La Frenais. *sc* Ron House, Diz White, Alan Shearman. *ph* Alex Thomson. *ed* Alan Jones. *pd* Norman Garwood. *m* John Du Prez. *cast* Alan Shearman, Diz White, Ron House, Frances Tomelty, Michael Aldridge, Mel Smith, Billy Connolly.
●A movie based on a stage spoof of Sapper McNeile's Bulldog Drummond secret agent stories, and from almost the first five minutes of exploding test-tubes and pratfalls and false wigs, it's obvious that what might have worked in the theatre is all wrong for the screen. It is not simply that banana-skin jokes look a bit ridiculous when we're used to modern stuntwork. By now films like *Superman* and *Raiders of the Lost Ark* have also shown that it's quite possible to take pulp heroes, and make the audience care for them without resorting to the banality of all-out camp. This basic disability is all the more regrettable since the film is very handsomely mounted and performed with gusto. DP

Bully

(2001, Fr/US, 112 min)
d Larry Clark. *p* Don Murphy, Fernando Sulichin, Chris Hanley. *sc* Zachary Long [David McKenna], Roger Pullis. *ph* Steve Gainer. *ed* Andrew Hafitz. *pd* Linda Burton. *cast* Brad Renfro, Bijou Phillips, Rachel Miner, Michael Pitt, Kelli Garner, Daniel Franzese, Leo Fitzpatrick, Nick Stahl, Nathalie Paulding.

●Harmony Korine calls Clark 'an artistic vampire who sucks the lifeforce out of the young and un-corrupt'. At first, this film confirms Korine's misgivings. Based on writer Jim Schutze's true story about a group of bored Florida teenagers who turn to murder, it's a relentlessy voyeuristic affair. Clark is fascinated by the bodies of his protagonists. Still, this is more than an old man's wet dream. Shot with an excellent cast on the South Florida locations where the real Bobby Kent was killed, it comes across in its better moments like a 'slacker' version of *In Cold Blood*. In its own macabre way, it is often also very funny. Even so, it's hard to fathom the director's attitude toward his own characters. He both drools over them and attempts to lay bare the emptiness of their lives in stern, moralistic fashion. GM

Bulto, El (Excess Baggage)

(1992, Mex, 114 min)
d/p Gabriel Retes. *sc* Gabriel Retes, Maria del Pozo. *ph* Chuy. *ed* Saul Aupart. *cast* Gabriel Retes, Hector Bonilla, Lourdes Elizarraras, José Luis Alonso, Delia Casanova.
●A radical photo-journalist is knocked down by a Government riot control squad ('The Hawks') in 1971, is put into a coma, and finally awakes 20 years later. The household he re-enters – which includes the son and daughter he never knew he had, his wife has remarried – has moved into the modern world, with its Nintendos, Walkmans, and shifted political and social perspectives. 'El Bulto' ('The Lump', as they have referred to him) has to learn to walk again and to live in the present. Director Retes finely calibrates his re-entry from his 'space capsule', and in so doing makes many acute points about the history of social and political change for the Mexico City middle-class intelligentsia. WH

Bulworth

(1998, US, 108 min)
d Warren Beatty. *p* Warren Beatty, Pieter Jan Brugge. *sc* Warren Beatty, Jeremy Pikser. *ph* Vittorio Storaro. *ed* Robert C Jones, Billy Weber. *pd* Dean Tavoularis. *m* Ennio Morricone. *cast* Warren Beatty, Oliver Platt, Don Cheadle, Paul Sorvino, Halle Berry, Jack Warden, Isaiah Washington, Christine Baranski, Richard Sarafian.
●This opens with an image of disillusionment: alone in his study, a Democrat Senator (Beatty), up for re-election in 1996, sits in front of his VCR, weeping at repeated shots of himself extolling 'liberal' values. At the end of his rope, he takes out a contract on his life (after lining up massive life insurance for his daughter), then goes to a rally in South Central LA where, to the horror of his aides, he tells the black assembly how little they and other impoverished groups mean to politicians of every hue. Aroused both by their response and by the sight of a young woman in the audience (Berry), Bulworth accompanies her to a club where, driven and dazed by desire, drugs and dance, he rediscovers the will both to live and to make a difference simply by telling the awful truth. This is that rare thing: a Hollywood satire/conspiracy thriller that takes its politics seriously, is prepared to provoke and even offend, and actually takes risks, dramatic and otherwise. It's a sharp, brave movie, a little ragged around the edges, but that's to its advantage. Notwithstanding the faintly predictable romantic subplot, this is not pre-packaged high-concept entertainment. Intriguing, intelligent and ambitious. GA

Bundled (Wo Jiao A-Ming-la)

(2000, Tai, 75 min)
d Singing Chen. *p* Huang Ming-Chuan. *sc* Singing Chen. *ph* Shen Ko-Shang. *ed* Singing Chen, Carol Chen. *ad* Max Huang. *m* Singing Chen. *cast* Yen Mu-Tsuen, Chen Li-Te, Zhang Yui-Wei, Lin Zhong-Ying, John Lee.
●A *Dodes'kaden* for the post-punk generation, Chen's remarkable debut presents itself as a series of interlocking dreams. It centres on dropouts and misfits in Taipei, sleeping rough in abandoned buildings and under bridges, and the core of the film is her engagement with these variously frustrated and other-worldly outsiders. Two elements give it shape and structure. First, the quest by an insensitive TV journalist to track down a prizewinning writer who has turned his back on mainstream society. Second, the juxtaposition of the worlds of Ah Ming (Yen, a real-life homeless man) and a middle-class mother and daughter. Ah Ming finds a camcorder which replays images of the little girl's birthday party, and imagines that it shows his own long-lost family. Meanwhile, the girl on the tape imagines (or intuits?) the grandpa she never knew. Highly original and often magical. TR

Bundle of Joy

(1956, US, 98 min)
d Norman Taurog. *p* Edmund Grainger. *sc* Norman Krasna, Robert Carson, Arthur Sheekman. *ph* William Snyder. *ed* Harry Marker. *ad* Albert S D'Agostino. *songs* Josef Myrow, Mack Gordon. *cast* Debbie Reynolds, Eddie Fisher, Adolphe Menjou, Tommy Noonan, Una Merkel, Melville Cooper.
●Lame remake of *Bachelor Mother* with songs. As the shopgirl who finds an abandoned baby, and by looking after it prompts a sacndal when everyone thinks it's hers, Reynolds is cute but lacks the sparky vivacity of Ginger Rogers, while Fisher is simply no match for David Niven. GA

Bunker, The

(2001, US, 95 min)
d Rob Green. *p* Daniel Figuero. *sc* Clive Dawson. *ph* John Pardue. *ed* Richard Milward. *pd* Richard Campling. *cast* Nicholas Hamnett, Charley Boorman, John Carlisle, Jack Davenport, Christopher Fairbank, Jason Flemyng, Simon Kunz, Andrew Lee-Potts, Eddie Marsan, Andrew Tiernan.
●Green's first feature is an assured, atmospheric slice of psychological horror about the remnants of a platoon of German soldiers trapped in a bunker near the Belgian border at the end of the WWII. Despair, disenchantment, delirium and fear add to the usual tensions between men of diverse character, rank and background forced by the advancing Allies into claustrophobic proximity with one another. But then rumours about a tunnel raise hopes of escape. In some regards it's a strangely old-fashioned film (far from a bad thing!), acted with assurance and building tension through suggestion, pacing and *mise-en-scène*. At times, Clive Dawson's script gets a little cluttered and loses focus, but anyone who recalls Michael Mann's *The Keep* or even Val Lewton's *Isle of the Dead* with affection is likely to be impressed. GA

Bunker Palace Hotel

(1989, Fr, 96 min)
d Enki Bilal. *p* Maurice Bernart. *sc* Enki Bilal, Pierre Christin. *ph* Philippe Welt. *ed* Thierry Derocles. *ad* Michèle Abbé-Vannier. *m* Philippe Eidel, Arnaud Devos. *cast* Jean-Louis Trintignant, Carole Bouquet, Maria Schneider, Benoît Régent, Jean-Pierre Léaud, Roger Dumas.
●Connoisseurs of dire futures and admirers of the colour grey will find most to relish in this haunting but rather heartless picture. As civil war rages, a bunch of variously weird Establishment figures takes refuge in an underground hideaway staffed by erratically functioning robots. A shaven headed Trintignant, oozing sinister emollience, dominates the scene; his encounters with Bouquet, a tightlipped revolutionary who has infiltrated the group, are gripping. Bilal is a leading strip-cartoon artist (and designer for Alain Resnais) and his imaginary ash coloured setting is certainly striking. But finally the stylishness and the deadpan comedy seem attached to little beyond a skin deep misanthropy. BBa

Bunny Caper, The

see Sex Play

Bunny Lake is Missing

(1965, GB, 107 min, b/w)
d/p Otto Preminger. *sc* John Mortimer, Penelope Mortimer. *ph* Denys Coop. *ed* Peter Thornton. *pd* Don Ashton. *m* Paul Glass. *cast* Keir Dullea, Carol Lynley, Laurence Olivier, Martita Hunt, Noël Coward, Lucie Mannheim, Adrienne Corri, Anna Massey, Finlay Currie, Clive Revill.
●A middling thriller scripted by John and Penelope Mortimer (from Evelyn Piper's novel) in which weary Inspector Olivier cruises a cameo-strewn London in search of Lynley's mislaid (and just possibly non-existent) child, and Preminger characteristically nags away at the minor-key ambiguities as if the investigation were philosophical rather than criminal. A brief appearance by The Zombies places the time of the season quite neatly, though London doesn't so much swing as creak eerily. PT

Bunny O'Hare

(1971, US, 92 min)
d Gerd Oswald. *p* Gerd Oswald, Norman T Herman. *sc* Stanley Z Cherry, Coslough Johnson. *ph* Loyal Griggs, John M Stephens. *ed* Fred R Feitshans. *m* Billy Strange. *cast* Bette Davis, Ernest Borgnine, Jack Cassidy, Joan Delaney, Jay Robinson, John Astin.
●Embarrassingly unfunny caper in which Davis and Borgnine masquerade as hippies to commit a series of 'social revenge' bank robberies. Davis, supported by Oswald, understandably sued producers AIP for post-production tampering which ineptly stressed the knockabout aspects. TM

Buona Sera, Mrs Campbell

(1968, US, 113 min)
d/p Melvin Frank. *sc* Melvin Frank, Denis Norden, Sheldon Keller. *ph* Gabor Pogany. *ed* William Butler. *ad* Arrigo Equini. *m* Riz Ortoloni. *songs* Melvin Frank, Andrew Frank. *cast* Gina Lollobrigida, Phil Silvers, Telly Savalas, Peter Lawford, Shelley Winters, Lee Grant, Janet Margolin.
●Lollobrigida as an unmarried Italian mum (the Mrs Campbell derives from a soup can) whose deception – she has been enjoying child support from three different US airmen since World War II – is threatened by a squadron reunion. Formulary but mildly amusing until it gravitates to sentimentality. TM

'burbs, The

(1988, US, 102 min)
d Joe Dante. *p* Michael Finnell, Larry Brezner. *sc* Dana Olsen. *ph* Robert Stevens. *ed* Marshall Harvey. *pd* James Spencer. *m* Jerry Goldsmith. *cast* Tom Hanks, Bruce Dern, Carrie Fisher, Rick Ducommun, Corey Feldman, Wendy Schaal, Courtney Gains, Gale Gordon, Dick Miller, Robert Picardo.
●When Ray Peterson (Hanks) opts to take his vacation at home in Hinckley Hills – the epitome of suburban conformism – he soon becomes infected by his neighbours' paranoia over the Klopeks, new arrivals to the scuzziest house in the street. Okay, they're ugly, they keep a dog called Landru, dig up the garden by night, and have a noisy basement; but are they really 'neighbours from hell'? After all, Ray's pals are pretty weird: Mark (Dern) is a rabid militarist, Art (Ducommun) is obsessed with macabre murders, and Ricky (Feldman) is a thrill-crazy Heavy Metal freak. Joe Dante's manic black satire portrays the investigations of this quartet of eternal adolescents into the Klopeks' admittedly unusual lifestyle with enormous glee, revelling in OTT behaviour and absurd dialogue, and tossing out film parodies with reckless abandon. Characteristically, Dante's nonchalant attitude towards plot structure makes for erratic pacing (the last half hour does flag), but that's part and parcel of his breathless, anarchic style. It's very silly, of course, but Hanks' fine timing is matched by a strong supporting cast, and thanks to Dante's wicked, comic-strip view of the world, the movie achieves an admirably wacky consistency as it debunks American mores and movie clichés, from Hitchcock and Leone to Michael Winner and Tobe Hooper. GA

Burden of Dreams

(1982, US, 95 min)
d/p/ph Les Blank. *ed* Maureen Gosling. *with* Werner Herzog, Klaus Kinski, Claudia Cardinale, Jason Robards, Mick Jagger. *narrator* Candace Laughlin.
●Blank's special brand of ethnographic film documentary finds a curiously appropriate subject in that weirdest of all capsule cultures: the on-location film crew. Blank chronicles Herzog's notorious and near-disastrous filming of his epic *Fitzcarraldo* in the face of a temperamental cast (including at various stages Mick Jagger, Jason Robards and Kinski), Amazon locations, the local populace, and the fates in general. Blank's footage, which at times must have looked like being the only cinematic record that would come out of the jungle, clarifies many of the rumours about the shooting, and also takes on a crazy life of its own as the Amazon tributary becomes a blackly comic shit creek of (off camera) tribal skirmishes. But ultimately it's left to us to decide where Herzog could or should have drawn the line. PT

Bureau of Missing Persons

(1933, US, 74 min, b/w)
d Roy Del Ruth. *sc* Robert Presnell. *ph* Barney McGill. *ed* James Gibbon. *ad* Robert M Haas. *cast* Pat O'Brien, Bette Davis, Lewis Stone, Glenda Farrell, Allen Jenkins, Hugh Herbert, Ruth Donnelly, Alan Dinehart.
●Not a Davis vehicle, since she only appears halfway through, playing a girl wanted for murder. Based on a book by former police captain John Ayres, it cross-breeds an attempt to document the range of work covered by the NY Missing Persons Bureau (a number of unconnected cases are developed in parallel) and a healthily cynical vein of macabre humour. With Del Ruth directing at screwball pace, things sometimes get a little too jokey; but at its best, in noting the obsessive quirks developed by officers, it has some claim to be considered an ancestor of *Hill Street Blues*. TM

Burglar

(1987, US, 102 min)
d Hugh Wilson. *p* Kevin McCormick, Michael Hirsch. *sc* Joseph Loeb III, Matthew Weisman, Hugh Wilson. *ph* William A Fraker. *m* Sylvester Levay. *cast* Whoopi Goldberg, Bob Goldthwait, GW Bailey, Lesley Ann Warren, James Handy, John Goodman.
●A fairly grim work-out for Whoopi Goldberg as a likeable cat burglar who witnesses a murder then turns amateur 'tec to nail the culprit before she's charged with the crime herself. Memorable one-liners in short supply. TJ

Burglar (Vzlomshchik)

(1987, USSR, 89 min)
d Valery Ogorodnikov. *sc* Valery Priyemkikhov. *ph* Valerii Mironov. *ed* T Demsovoi. *pd* Viktor Ivanov. *m* Viktor Kisin. *cast* Oleg Elykomov, Konstantin Kinchev, Yuri Tsapnik, Svetlana Gaitan, Polina Petrenko.
●With a brother dedicated to punk rock stardom at any cost and a drunken father who chases skirt between robotic dancing lessons from the TV, young Senka stands as much chance of nurture as the hero of Truffaut's *400 Blows*. The amazing thing about Ogorodnikov's film is that it was made in Russia. Clearly, plenty of Soviet teenies share the nihilistic feelings of their Western counterparts, and the extensive footage of safety-pin chic at concerts perhaps points to a sound export instinct on the director's part. Senka's brother Kostya is under pressure from Howmuch, a very heavy rocker, to steal a synthesiser from the Community Centre, so to protect him Senka steals it himself. The story occupies little more space than the music, but the performances are splendid enough to lodge Senka's predicament in the heart. BC

Burglars, The (Le Casse)

(1971, Fr/It, 120 min)
d/p Henri Verneuil. *sc* Vahé Katcha, Henri Verneuil. *ph* Claude Renoir. *ed* Pierre Gillette. *ad* Jacques Saulnier. *m* Ennio Morricone. *cast* Jean-Paul Belmondo, Omar Sharif, Dyan Cannon, Robert Hossein, Nicole Calfan, Renato Salvatori.
●Fine *film noir* material (David Goodis' novel *The Burglar*, previously filmed as Paul Wendkos' impressive debut in 1956), but here it suffers an overdose of sunshine and multi-national production values to emerge as just another glossy heist replete with sparring jewel thief and detective. PT

Buried Alive

(1990, US, 91 min)
d Gerard Kikoine. *p* Harry Alan Towers. *sc* Jake Clesi, Stuart Lee. *ph* Gerard Loubeau. *ed* Gerard Kikoine. *ad* Dankert Guilliaume. *cast* Robert Vaughn, Donald Pleasence, Karen Witter, John Carradine, Arnold Vosloo, Ashley Hayden.
●Bits of several Edgar Allan Poe stories make up this schlock offering, shot on the cheap in South Africa. It's set in a school for delinquent young ladies (cue shower scene), where new teacher Karen Witter is about to connect the shock disappearance of several pupils with the nefarious activities of mad doctor Vaughn. A sad checkout for John Carradine in his final role. TJ

Burke and Hare

(1971, GB, 91 min)
d Vernon Sewell. *p* Guido Coen. *sc* Ernie Bradford. *ph* Desmond Dickinson. *ed* John Colville. *ad* Scott MacGregor. *m* Roger Webb. *cast* Derren Nesbitt, Glynn Edwards, Harry Andrews, Dee Shenderey, Yootha Joyce, Françoise Pascal.
●Vacillating between melodrama and bathos, this moves uneasily from one unfulfilled promise to another, dogged from first image to last by an overwhelming mediocrity. The film attempts a historical reconstruction of the murderous activities of the infamous bodysnatchers, with a concurrent reinterpretation of the economic and sexual contexts of the Edinburgh of the 1820s within which they operated. Needless to say, the sexuality is prudish, coarse and vicarious in the 'Carry On' style, and the attempts at horror are unconvincing in the extreme. JDuC

Burmese Harp, The (Biruma no Tategoto)

(1956, Jap, 116 min, b/w)
d Kon Ichikawa. *p* Masayuki Takagi. *sc* Natto Wada. *ph* Minoru Yokoyama. *ad* Takashi Matsuyama. *m* Akira Ifukube. *cast* Shoji Yasui, Rentaro Mikuni, Tatsuya Mihashi, Tanie Kitabayashi, Yunosuke Ito.
●Lyrical and rather ostentatiously humanist, Ichikawa's film tells of a Japanese soldier in Burma, so appalled by the bloody carnage of war that he refuses to return home after his country's defeat, and stays on, garbed as a Buddhist monk, to bury the dead. If the film was clearly a sincere castigation of the militarist fervour that swept Japan during the war, it nevertheless suffers from its rather deliberate heart-warming tone and a too leisurely pace that tends to over-emphasise moments of pathos. That said, it is hard not to be swayed by the pacifist sentiments. GA

Burn!

see Queimada!

Burning, The

(1980, US, 91 min)
d Tony Maylam. *p* Harvey Weinstein. *sc* Peter Lawrence, Bon Weinstein. *ph* Harvey Harrison. *ed* Jack Sholder. *ad* Peter Politanoff. *m* Rick Wakeman. *cast* Brian Matthews, Leah Ayres, Brian Backer, Larry Joshua, Jason Alexander, Lou David, Holly Hunter.
●In the tradition of such horror pix as *Halloween* and *Friday the 13th*, this portrays the gruesome extermination of a group of charmless adolescents by a bogey man. This time it's a hulk of burnt flesh wielding garden shears and terrorising a summer camp; and true to cycle, it's the teenage girls who are the chief victims of both the murderer's savage cuts and the camera's leering gaze. Presented as provocative teasers, they're despatched while the mini-machos laugh, lust, bully, build rafts and, finally become heroes. Suspensewise, it's proficient enough, but familiarity with this sort of stuff can breed contempt. GA

Burning an Illusion

(1981, GB, 111 min)
d/sc Menelik Shabazz. *ph* Roy Cornwall. *ed* Judy Seymour. *ad* Miranda Melville. *m* Seyoum Nefta. *cast* Cassie McFarlane, Victor Romero, Beverley Martin, Angela Wynter, Malcolm Fredericks.
●A young British-born black woman is forced into encounters with sexism and racism in her attempt to negotiate some kind of future in a community where patriarchal power often erupts into street violence. As the heroine finds herself drawn into black militancy and feminism, a good chance is missed to develop the character of her more passive friend who wants no truck with 'Africa'. An important film for Britain in 1981, nevertheless, though in need of cutting to sharpen its edge. MA

Burning Hills, The

(1956, US, 93 min)
d Stuart Heisler. *p* Richard Whorf. *sc* Irving Wallace. *ph* Ted McCord. *ed* Clarence Kolster. *ad* Charles H Clarke. *m* David Buttolph. *cast* Tab Hunter, Natalie Wood, Skip Homeier, Eduard Franz, Earl Holliman, Claude Akins, Ray Teal, Frank Puglia.
●A stock revenge Western, nicely shot in 'Scope by Ted McCord. When his brother is murdered, Trace Jordan (Hunter) confronts the local cattle baron, Sutton (Teal), knowing that he has had settlers killed before in his determination to keep the whole range to himself. Both men are wounded after Sutton denies it and draws his gun; but with the aid of a feisty half-Mexican girl (Wood) whose father was one of the settlers killed, Jordan manages to get away, eventually outwitting a posse of pursuing gunmen led by Sutton's vicious son (Homeier). Heisler keeps the single-minded action admirably taut, while the script, based on a novel by Louis L'Amour, tries (without much success) to ring a few changes by detailing some uncertain loyalties among the characters. A less bland hero than Tab Hunter might have helped; Natalie Wood, though miscast, is not at all bad. TM

Burning Life

(1994, Ger, 105 min)
d Peter Welz. *p* Alexander Gehrke. *sc* Stefan Kolditz. *ph* Michael Schaufert. *ed* Helga Wardeck. *pd* Dieter Adam, Claudia Sembach. *m* Neil Quinton. *cast* Maria Schrader, Anna Thalbach, Max Tidof, Jaecki Schwarz, Andreas Hoppe.
●This strangely dated road movie (very loosely in the *Thelma & Louise* mould) sees two women go on a bank robbing spree along the backroads of post-Wall East Germany, pursued by a showman/fakir in a hippie van, and assorted fascistic cops in leathers. The 'chicks', one a frustrated history teacher maddened by her father's suicide, the other a frustrated cabaret-style chanteuse (she gets to do an embarrassing microphone caressing number) sport the complete range of guns, specs and threads from the renta-cool catalogue. Audaciously unoriginal. WH

Burning Memory (Resism)

(1988, Isr, 93 min)
d Yossi Somer. *p* Ami Amir. *sc* Ami Amir, Yossi Somer. *ph* Yovav Kosh. *ed* Ya'akov Dagan, Rifka Yogev. *ad* Robert Bassal. *m* Jan Garbarek. *cast* Danny Roth, Shmeul Edelman, Pauli Reshef, Etty Ankri, Alon Oliarchick, Renven Dayan.
●Writer/director Somer poured experience gained as a paramedic during the Israeli-Lebanese conflict into this impassioned first feature. Roth goes through it as the shell-shocked soldier treated to a course of military-style psychotherapy, the object being to get him back in the field as soon as possible. It's not exactly a polished effort, but Somer knows the milieu and we're never in doubt where his sympathies lie. TJ

Burning Paradise (Huoshao Honglian Si)

(1993, HK, 104 min)
d Ringo Lam. *cast* Willie Chi, Carmen Lee, Cheng Dong, Yang Sheng, KK Huang, Lin Quan.
●A box office disaster in Hong Kong and straight-to-video in Britain, this finds Lam working with a cast of unknowns in Mainland China, trying to freshen up an often-told story first filmed in Shanghai in 1928. (Tsui Hark, doyen of remaking/remodelling jobs, served as producer.) Fong Sai-Yuk (Chi) is one of many Shaolin monks arrested for fomenting anti-Manchu resistance and imprisoned in the Red Lotus Temple. Lam's big idea is to see the prison as a literal hell, governed by a depraved psychotic whose project is to create the Anti-Buddha; the best scenes pursue this dark vision, which extends to presenting the Shaolin hero Hong Xiguan (Yang) as an apparent traitor. Some of the acrobatic fights do seem grimly anarchic, but the endless booby traps grow tiresome and the film's 'dark side' is undercut by feeble elements of humour and romance. As a genre piece: too little, too late. TR

Burning Secret

(1988, GB/US, 107 min)
d Andrew Birkin. *p* Norma Heyman, Eberhard Junkersdorf, Carol Lynn Greene. *sc* Andrew Birkin. *ph* Ernest Day. *ed* Paul Green. *pd* Bernd Lepel. *m* Hans Zimmer. *cast* David Eberts, Faye Dunaway, Klaus Maria Brandauer, Ian Richardson, John Nettleton.
●Based on a short story by Stefan Zweig, set in post-World War I Austria. Asthmatic Edmund (Eberts) is the 12-year-old son of an American diplomat. In an attempt to cure his wheezing, his mother (Dunaway) takes him to stay in a remote mountain spa where he falls under the spell of the Baron (Brandauer), who fills his head with stories of his war exploits. What Edmund doesn't know is that the Baron is only using him to reach his mother. Of course, it all ends in tears. Snowbound Marienbad looks splendid, Brandauer oozes his usual sinister charm, and Dunaway is at her most haughtily

haunted. The well-meaning sensitivity is seriously weakened, though, by the way Edmund's asthma appears to be caused by telepathy: before his mother has had a chance to become breathless in the Baron's bed, the boy's lungs have already collapsed in sympathy, leaving the audience gasping for air. It isn't meant to be funny – this is a tale about adult cruelty and the tragic loss of childhood innocence – but the end quotation from Goethe's *Erl King* has all the crashing finality of a coffin-lid. MS

Burning Wall, The

(2001, US, 115 min)
d/p/sc Hava Kohav Beller. *ph* Christopher Lerch, Judith Kaufmann, Harald Klix. *ed* Markus Akira Peters, Lawrence Silk. *m* Joel Goodman, Elliot Sokolov.

● Midway through Beller's documentary about the secret history of East Germany, the camera shows an enormous safe door being unlocked, then another. This is the entrance to a vast hangar-like building housing the thousands of boxes and documents that constitute the Stasi's archives, 50 years' worth of transcripts and recordings made by an organisation which prided itself on its surveillance techniques and its uncanny ability to make East German citizens denounce one another. Beller interviews officers of the Stasi secret police as well as former dissidents, while chronicling the events leading up to the destruction of the Berlin Wall. There's a grim humour as well as considerable pathos in her account of how the ideals on which the state was founded were so quickly corrupted. GM

Burnt by the Sun (Utomlennye solntsem/ Soleil trompeur)

(1994, Rus/Fr, 134 min)
d Nikita Mikhalkov. *p* Nikita Mikhalkov, Michel Seydoux. *sc* Nikita Mikhalkov, Rustam Ibragimbekov. *ph* Vilen Kaliuta. *ed* Enzo Meniconi. *ad* Vladimir Aronin, Aleksandr Samulekin. *m* Edouard Artemiese. *cast* Nikita Mikhalkov, Ingeborga Dapkounaite, Nadia Mikhalkov, Oleg Menchikov, Andre Oumansky.

● A summer's day at a dacha in Stalinist Russia, 1936. A hero of the Revolution, Kotov (director Mikhalkov), basks in the affection of his wife Maroussia (Dapkounaite) and their daughter Nadia (Nadia Mikhalkov), but his cosy world is disturbed by the arrival of Dimitri (Menchikov), Maroussia's first love. In the course of a day, Dimitri charms the household with his bravado and good looks, but Kotov grows uneasy as the reason for Dimitri's presence emerges. This is a careful, telling portrait of a community blinded by its illusions. For most of its running time, the film seems to follow suit: it's a placid, languorous country-house comedy far removed from the realities of the Stalinist terror. This is a masquerade, however. Dimitri's first appearance isn't quite the idle jape it first seems, while Kotov's dacha really is some kind of madhouse. Mikhalkov is a quintessentially Russian director: awkwardly, theatrically expansive, somewhat lugubrious even in the midst of an idyll, but unafraid of ideas and complexity. His own performance is impeccable, and the scenes with his daughter Nadia achieve a rare poignancy. TCh

Burnt Offerings

(1976, US, 115 min)
d/p Dan Curtis. *sc* William F Nolan, Dan Curtis. *ph* Jacques R Marquette. *ed* Dennis Virkler. *ad* Eugène Lourié. *m* Robert Cobert. *cast* Karen Black, Oliver Reed, Burgess Meredith, Eileen Heckart, Lee Montgomery, Dub Taylor, Bette Davis.

● The current minor boom in American horror films has two notable features: the single-minded concentration on the nuclear family as a point of attack, and the consistent rejection of happy endings. This tale of a family taking a spooky old mansion for the summer would be strictly formula stuff were it not for these elements; but veteran Eugène Lourié's art direction helps. DP

Burn, Witch, Burn!

see Night of the Eagle

Burra Sahib

(1975, GB, 55 min)
d Nick Gifford.

● Taken together with its companion piece *General Sahib* (Nick Gifford, 1976), this forms an unforgettable documentary portrait of curious lives from the days of the Raj. The first deals with Gifford's three uncles, all Boer expatriates, who run a taxidermy business in India. With patient elaboration, a picture of a time-warped Imperial past emerges alongside the personal details. Sepia photographs of polo and pig-sticking compare with Uncle Joubert's contemporary sporting life – duck-shooting or fishing from the same hide coracle that he has used for forty years. Few words, the images speak for themselves. 'General Sahib' follows the daily duties of a retired Major-General (MC) from the Indian Army who runs a hospital for lepers, mental cases and children – poor creatures who have lost their bodies and minds and wander in the other world of sickness. The bristling, leonine General is also seen visiting his old military barracks at Poona, and indulging in a chukka of polo. His manner does not change, he still has a word for everyone. A slightly unnerving reminder that compassion is not necessarily excluded from the military cast of mind, although its expression may appear rather odd. Two great portraits of anachronism. CPea

Business Affair, A

(1993, GB/Fr/Ger/Sp, 98 min)
d Charlotte Brandström. *p* Xavier Larrere, Olivia Stewart, Clive Parsons, Davina Belling. *sc* William Stadiem. *ph* Willy Kurant. *m* Didier Vasseur. *cast* Christopher Walken, Jonathan Pryce, Carole Bouquet, Sheila Hancock, Tom Wilkinson, Anna Manahan.

● Carole Bouquet is a floor-walking model and would-be writer caught between two contrasting but equally self-absorbed men in this well-written romantic comedy with a gently feminist undertow. While nursing her novelist husband through a chronic bout of writer's block, she is seduced by the brash charm of her publisher. Sold short by both men, Bouquet eventually opts for a literary identity of her own. Greatly helped by Pryce's atypically unsympathetic performance and Walken's easy charm, writer William Stadiem and director Brandstrom cut to the intellectual root, if not the emotional heart, of this ill-fated triangle of ambition and desire. Ultimately, perhaps, slightly too modest to attract the thoughtful art-house audience it's aimed at. NF

Business As Usual

(1987, GB, 89 min)
d Lezli-An Barrett. *p* Sara Geater. *sc* Lezli-An Barrett. *ph* Ernest Vincze. *ed* Henry Richardson. *ad* Hildegard Betchler. *cast* Glenda Jackson, John Thaw, Cathy Tyson, Mark McGann, Eamon Boland, James Hazeldine.

● When Babs (Jackson, uncharacteristically warm), manageress of a Liverpool fashion store, confronts the area manager (Boland) about his indecent advances towards one of her staff (Tyson), she is promptly sacked. The incident exacerbates existing friction at home between her unemployed ex-shop steward husband (Thaw) and her left-wing son (McGann), who quarrel over tactics for fighting her unfair dismissal. An accomplished first feature, this is no strident feminist sermon, the main theme being Babs' awakening to an untapped inner strength and confidence. Barrett's unsensational approach, offset by the raw indignation piercingly communicated by a superb cast, puts sexual intimidation powerfully in perspective as part of what is, for many, a broader everyday campaign. EP

Business Is Business (Wat Zien Ik)

(1971, Neth, 89 min)
d Paul Verhoeven. *p* Rob Houwer. *sc* Gerard Soeteman. *ph* Jan De Bont. *ed* Jan Bosdriesz. *pd* Massimo Gotz. *m* Julius Steffaro. *cast* Ronnie Bierman, Sylvia De Leur, Piet Romer, Jules Hamel, Bernard Droog.

● Verhoeven's first feature is an incongruously jaunty tale, based on Albert Mol's novel, about two Dutch prostitutes, Greet (Bierman) and Nel (De Leur). Keen to avoid the self-consciousness of European art house cinema, the director opts for a knockabout style oddly reminiscent of Robin Askwith comedies. The encounters between the women and their clients, most of them looking like they've escaped from a George Grosz cartoon, are invariably played for laughs, but the slapstick with cream cakes and feathers is inappropriate given the humiliation the women endure. The endlessly put-upon Nel has an abusive boyfriend; Greet is more self-reliant, but can't escape her way of life. Whatever his reputation now as a master cinematographer, Jan De Bont shoots the film in a plain uninspiring fashion. Not the most auspicious of debuts. GM

Business of Strangers, The

(2001, US, 84 min)
d Patrick Stettner. *p* Susan A Stover, Robert H Nathan. *sc* Patrick Stettner. *ph* Teo Maniaci. *ed* Keiko Deguchi. *pd* Dina Goldman. *m* Alexander Lasarenko. *cast* Stockard Channing, Julia Stiles, Frederick Weller, Mary Testa, Jack Hallett, Marcus Giamatti, Buddy Fitzpatrick.

● Drink and a mutual fascination soften the initial antipathy between tough middle-aged exec Julie (Channing, excellent) and her her sour underling Paula (Stiles) as they while away a few hours enjoying the sterile comforts of an airport hotel. Tensions resurface with the arrival of headhunter Nick (Weller), one of Julie's associates, whom Paula alleges is a rapist from her past. What to think? He's shifty, she's manipulative. There's no dreary vying for sexual attention, however; first-time writer/director Stettner immediately puts the headhunter into a drug-induced coma, leaving his female companions to play out a taut generational power game after scrawling obscenities over every inch of his body. What have they both come to? Intelligently scripted and thoroughly absorbing. SS

Bus Riley's Back in Town

(1965, US, 93 min)
d Harvey Hart. *p* Elliot Kastner. *sc* Walter Gage [Willliam Inge]. *ph* Russell Metty. *ed* Folmar Blangsted. *ad* Alexander Golitzen, Frank Arrigo. *m* Richard Markowitz. *cast* Michael Parks, Ann-Margret, Jocelyn Brando, Janet Margolin, Kim Darby, Brad Dexter, Mimsy Farmer.

● Universal, attempting to cash in on the success of the French New Wave in the States, set up two films starring Michael Parks, of which this was the second, and allowed the directors comparative studio freedom. Although romantic and heavy-handed, Hart's piece is a well-intentioned study of small-town life in America, centred round Parks as a hellraiser back from the navy and determined to mend his ways. A handful of jobs later and he's serving as a stud to Ann-Margret before sinking into suitable obscurity, married and contemplating work in a garage. When Universal saw the poor returns from *Wild Seed*, the first film, they intervened, shot extra footage involving Ann-Margret, and demanded so many cuts that scriptwriter William Inge removed his name from the credits: probably no great loss, since the script was the weakest aspect of the whole thing. But it did set back the career of a promising director a good few years. DP

Bus Stop

(1956, US, 96 min)
d Joshua Logan. *p* Buddy Adler. *sc* George Axelrod. *ph* Milton Krasner. *ed* William H Reynolds. *ad* Lyle Wheeler, Mark-Lee Kirk. *m* Alfred Newman, Cyril J Mockridge. *cast* Marilyn Monroe, Don Murray, Betty Field, Arthur O'Connell, Eileen Heckart, Hope Lange, Hans Conried.

● Although it's not explicitly a musical, *Bus Stop* is certainly a product of that imagination which says the best things in life are free, and if you don't have a dream how you gonna have a dream come true. Once that's understood, it's easier to go beyond the bizarre misogyny and stilted theatricality of the plot in which a naive, loud-mouthed cowboy (Murray) tries to kidnap a saloon singer from the Ozarks played by Monroe. Apart from her engaging performance, the film's real interest lies in the unpleasant nature of its subtext: equations of poverty with personal unworthiness, and the uneasiness of an implicitly homosexual focus on Murray. CR

Buster

(1988, GB, 102 min)
d David Green. *p* Norma Heyman. *sc* Colin Shindler. *ph* Tony Imi. *ed* Lesley Walker. *pd* Simon Holland. *m* Anne Dudley. *cast* Phil Collins, Julie Walters, Larry Lamb, Stephanie Lawrence, Ellen Beaven, Michael Attwell, Sheila Hancock, Anthony Quayle.

●This is a love story, not a crime adventure. When Buster Edwards (Collins) receives his share of the 1963 Great Train Robbery, he doesn't know what to do with it except spend it. Soon he and his wife June (Walters) are stuck in Acapulco, down to £20,000. June, who can't bear to be without chips, rain, and bingo, takes their darling daughter Nicky back to the Elephant and Castle, and Buster, though he knows he'll get nicked, soon follows. We're invited to view Edwards as the archetypal cheeky Cockney, to condone his crimes, and commiserate when he gets his comeuppance: character development, moral perspective, and cinematic style are out of the question. The re-enactment of the heist, for instance, has no place for the iron bar used to 'persuade' the engine driver. There are a couple of good moments – the Edwards family emerging into the Mexican sun swathed in winter coats, the massive police presence at the inevitable arrest – while Collins and Waters make the most of seriously underwritten roles. MS

Buster and Billie

(1973, US, 100 min)
d Daniel Petrie. *p* Ron Silverman. *sc* Ron Turbeville. *ph* Mario Tosi. *ed* Michael Kahn. *ad* Carol Wenger. *m* Al DeLory. *cast* Jan-Michael Vincent, Joan Goodfellow, Pamela Sue Martin, Clifton James, Robert Englund.
●An attempt to come to grips with repressed adolescent sexuality in backwoods Georgia by way of the touching relationship that develops between the high school's clean-cut good-looker and the dumb ugly duckling who gets used for the boys' gang bangs. The handling of the aggression that inevitably disrupts the idyllic affair is adequate, but the film falls down over its attempts to give credibility to the central relationship. Meticulous period (1948) detail. CPe

Buster's World (Busters Vedren)

(1984, Den, 91 min)
d Bille August. *p* Mads Egmont Christensen, Nina Crone. *sc* Bjarne Reuter. *ph* Fritz Schrøder. *ed* Thomas Gislason. *ad* Søren Kragh Sørensen. *m* Bo Holten. *lyrics* Nanna Lüders Jensen. *cast* Mads Bugge Andersen, Katerina Stenbeck, Peter Schrøder, Katja Miehe-Renard, Signe Dahl Madsen, Kirsten Rolffes, Martin Krakaver, John Riedl, Berthe Qvistgaard.
●August's second feature proper is a genial yarn about a freckled boy – Buster Oregon Mortensen, as he likes to announce himself – ambling through the days with his head in the clouds. This means trouble with teachers and the neighbourhood bully, but a generally fanciful outlook, as Buster plies his summer trade as the village delivery boy, with his penchant for magical tricks and surprises. The film, which began as a children's TV series, keeps the right side of cute, and the comedy picks up after a lumbering start. 'Life is really something' is the moral. NB

Busting

(1973, US, 92 min)
d Peter Hyams. *p* Irwin Winkler, Robert Chartoff. *sc* Peter Hyams. *ph* Earl Rath. *ed* James Mitchell. *m* Bill Goldenberg. *cast* Elliott Gould, Robert Blake, Allen Garfield, Antonio Fargas, Michael Lerner, Ivor Francis, William Sylvester, Logan Ramsey.
●Slick and often witty cop thriller, with Gould and Blake in fine form as the vice-squad detectives going it alone in the face of apathy and corruption among their superiors in their attempts to clean up LA. Cynical and rather too determinedly hip, it nevertheless entertains – thanks to some good action sequences and firm control of atmosphere – and, as Hyams' first feature, presages the delights to come in *Capricorn One* and *Outland*. GA

Bustin' Loose

(1981, US, 94 min)
d Oz Scott. *p* Richard Pryor, Michael S Glick. *sc* Roger L Simon. *ph* Dennis Dalzell. *ed* David Holden. *ad* Charles R Davis. *m* Mark Davis, Roberta Flack. *cast* Richard Pryor, Cicely Tyson, Angel Ramirez, Jimmy Hughes, Edwin DeLeon, Robert Christian.
●A remarkable change of direction for the subsequently self-immolating Pryor, whose biting stand-up barrage had put him in the Lenny Bruce class of hard-core comic satire. A 'warm-hearted comedy' involving a bunch of orphan kids promises neither a rewarding evening nor the best use of Pryor's considerable talent. However, in spite of an impractically pat 'happy ending' and liberal spoonfuls of sugar, we are kept some way from Walt Disney territory. Some of the set pieces, notably Pryor's encounter with the Ku Klux Klan, are beautifully achieved; the sentimentality is usually effective, and protected by a hard edge of fast-rap comedy; the kids are bearable. The plotting is sloppy at times and this is undoubtedly a minor film, but its rewards are surprising. JC

Butch and Sundance: The Early Days

(1979, US, 112 min)
d Richard Lester. *p* Gabriel Katzka, Steven Bach. *sc* Allan Burns. *ph* Laszlo Kovacs. *ed* Antony Gibbs. *pd* Brian Eatwell. *m* Patrick Williams. *cast* William Katt, Tom Berenger, Jeff Corey, John Schuck, Michael C Gwynne, Peter Weller, Brian Dennehy, Jill Eikenberry.
●As a star-less 'prequel' to the Goldman/Hill, Redford/Newman moneyspinner, this was always a commercial no-hoper, but early signposted ambitions to dig beneath its predecessor's ingratiating lyricism don't really pan out either. Allan Burns' script contents itself with episodic variations on its model, while notions of a myth in-the-making hang a little too heavily on the self-conscious dialogue, and Lester merely pumps up the quirk quotient. PT

Butch Cassidy and the Sundance Kid (100)

(1969, US, 110 min)
d George Roy Hill. *p* John Foreman. *sc* William Goldman. *ph* Conrad Hall. *ed* John C Howard, Richard C Meyer. *ad* Jack Martin Smith, Philip M Jefferies. *m* Burt Bacharach. *cast* Paul Newman, Robert Redford, Katharine Ross, Strother Martin, Henry Jones, Jeff Corey, Cloris Leachman, Ted Cassidy.
●You could do worse than catch Redford and Newman in one of the funniest if slightest Westerns of recent years. Unashamedly escapist, it rips off most of its plot (from pursuit to final shootout) and much of its visual style from Peckinpah's *The Wild Bunch*, and even parodies *Jules and Jim*. It's slightly the worse for some of the borrowings, but the script is often hilarious, Newman and Redford making the best use of it when they get to parry dialogue with each other (eg, during the pursuit). It is much better and funnier than the *The Sting* precisely because it allows the two stars to play off each other. RM

Butcher, The

see Boucher, Le

Butcher Boy, The

(1997, US, 110 min)
d Neil Jordan. *p* Redmond Morris, Stephen Woolley. *sc* Neil Jordan, Patrick McCabe. *ph* Adrian Biddle. *ed* Tony Lawson. *pd* Anthony Pratt. *m* Elliot Goldenthal. *cast* Stephen Rea, Fiona Shaw, Eamonn Owens, Alan Boyle, Niall Buggy, Brendan Gleeson, Gerard McSorley, Ardal O'Hanlon, Milo O'Shea, Sinéad O'Connor, Aisling O'Sullivan.
●Set in an Irish town in the early '60s, Jordan's film of Patrick McCabe's novel centres on troubled teen Francie Brady (Owens), a lippy lad who withdraws from family strife – dad (Rea) is almost permanently drunk, mum (O'Sullivan) sliding towards insanity – into fantasies inspired by comics, sci-fi movies and TV shows, and into blood brother pacts with best pal Joe (Boyle). His renown as an ill-mannered hothead, however, is such that he's denied access to his friend. Moreover, after a spell in a church-run remand home, he returns to find his family in tatters. This consistently surprising, even shocking work moves from sly social comedy to something more darkly disturbing as Francie's sense of control begins to crumble. Though the movie sometimes looks as if the authentic Irish wit, colour and blarney has been filtered through the sensibility of a Buñuel or Polanski, Jordan never allows the surreal/expressionist aspects to dominate. GA

Butcher's Wife, The

(1991, US, 105 min)
d Terry Hughes. *p* Wallis Nicita, Lauren Lloyd. *sc* Ezra Litwik, Marjorie Schwartz. *ph* Frank Tidy. *ed* Donn Cambern. *ad* Charles Rosen. *m* Michael Gore. *cast* Demi Moore, Jeff Daniels, George Dzundza, Mary Steenburgen, Frances McDormand, Margaret Colin, Miriam Margolyes.
●Lovelorn psychic Marina (Moore) wafts about her North Carolina look-out tower, putting all her considerable mental energies into finding Mr Right. Tell-tale signs indicate a lover is on his way, and before you can say crystal ball, the tide washes up portly New York butcher Leo (Dzundza). Is this fate, or did Leo simply make a wrong turn at the last island? Within days they're married and setting up home in Greenwich Village, where Marina starts dishing out clairvoyant advice with the pork chops, a development which pleases everyone but Leo and psychiatrist Dr Alex Tremor (Daniels). Moore sports blonde hair and – less convincingly – a Southern accent, but these are the only elements which jar in this hugely engaging romantic comedy. Hughes' direction and crisp visuals turn studio artifice into something altogether magical. CM

But I'm a Cheerleader

(1999, US, 92 min)
d Jamie Babbit. *p* Andrea Sperling, Leanna Creel. *sc* Brian Wayne Peterson. *ph* Jules Labarthe. *ed* Cecily Rhett. *pd* Rachel Kamerman. *m* Pat Irwin. *cast* Natasha Lyonne, Clea DuVall, Dante Basco, RuPaul Charles, Eddie Cibrian, Bud Cort, Melanie Lynskey, Mink Stole, Cathy Moriarty, Ione Skye, Julie Delpy.
●The aptly misleading title (the theme is flawed assumptions) refers to the refusal of teenage golden girl Megan (Lyonne) to agree with her bible-bashing parents that she's gay. Denial seals her fate: heterosexual conversion therapy under the neurotic tutelage of Mary (Moriarty) and Mike (RuPaul) at True Directions reform school for homosexual youth, a Christian set-up – with single-sex dorms. How far, the film asks, do all things 'masculine' and 'feminine' serve as reliable indicators of sexuality? The more Mary and Mike force models of hetero perfection on their amiable charges, the more their efforts end in glaring extremes of camp. That this doesn't feel like the gender studies lesson it is, is mostly down to the tone of intelligent mischief, punctuated by tender moments when illicit romance beckons. First rate performances all round. SS

Butley

(1973, US/GB/Can, 130 min)
d Harold Pinter. *p* Ely Landau. *sc* Simon Gray. *ph* Gerry Fisher. *ed* Malcolm Cooke. *ad* Carmen Dillon. *cast* Alan Bates, Jessica Tandy, Richard O'Callaghan, Susan Engel, Michael Byrne, Georgina Hale.
●One of the American Film Theatre series of filmed plays, which racked up a considerable amount of transcribed contemporary drama in the early '70s before the experiment dried up in the face of audience indifference. Simon Gray's account of an academic with rather too much wit, acerbity and withering honesty than is good for him follows a predictable course, in which one is allowed to enjoy Butley's lacerations of those around him until the play shows its moral side by revealing Butley to be a hopelessly self-deceived bastard who has cut himself to pieces in the process. A tour de force, as these things are evidently stacked to be, for Alan Bates. GA

Buttane, Le

see Whores, The

Buttercup Chain, The

(1970, GB, 95 min)
d Robert Ellis Miller. *p* John Whitney, Philip Waddilove. *sc* Peter Draper. *ph* Douglas Slocombe. *ed* Thelma Connell. *pd* Wilfrid Shingleton. *m* Richard Rodney Bennett. *cast* Hywel Bennett, Leigh Taylor-Young, Jane Asher, Sven-Bertil Taube, Clive Revill, Roy Dotrice, Michael Elphick.
●Awesomely arty tosh in which Bennett and Asher play the children of identical twins. In love but inhibited from making love with each other, they console themselves with an American girl who drives on the wrong side of the road (Taylor-Young) and a Swede called Fred who swims in the nude (Taube). Resolutely globe-trotting from one tourist attraction to the next, the camera follows the quartet to Spain, Sweden and Italy as they pair off into various combinations, meanwhile suffering self-inflicted torments. Miller's fulsome direction very nearly puts even Lelouch in the shade. TM

BUtterfield 8
(1960, US, 109 min)
d Daniel Mann. *p* Pandro S Berman. *sc* Charles Schnee, John Michael Hayes. *ph* Joseph Ruttenberg, Charles Harten. *ed* Ralph E Winters. *ad* George W Davis, Urie McCleary. *m* Bronislau Kaper. *cast* Elizabeth Taylor, Laurence Harvey, Eddie Fisher, Betty Field, Dina Merrill, Mildred Dunnock.
●Once thought of as racy and adventurous in its treatment of sex, this turgid nonsense about a high-class whore with love in her heart has dated atrociously. Taylor hams away and Harvey in his debonair mood is distinctly unappealing, while the overall effect is too excruciating even to be unintentionally funny. GA

Butterflies Are Free
(1972, US, 109 min)
d Milton Katselas. *p* MJ Frankovich. *sc* Leonard Gershe. *ph* Charles Lang Jr. *ed* David Blewitt. *pd* Robert Clatworthy. *m* Bob Alcivar. *cast* Goldie Hawn, Edward Albert, Eileen Heckart, Paul Michael Glaser, Michael Warren.
●A piece of (barely) stage-adapted nonsense, scripted by Leonard Gershe from his own play, about blind-boy-meets-emotionally-immature girl and how his mum brings them together. With some funny lines from Goldie Hawn and little else.

Butterfly (aka Broken Butterfly/Baby Tramp)
(1972, Switz, 86 min)
d Joseph W Sarno. *p* Chris D Nebe. *sc* Joseph W Sarno. *ph* Paul Rohe. *m* Guenter Moll. *cast* Marie Forsa, Harry Reems, Rob Everett, Zoe.
●Intriguing title, but don't be tempted: it's the same old slop with a young and pure country girl running away from her auntie's farm ('I must find out what lies on the other side of our fields') and discovering a disgusting new life in Munich. The chief perverter is played by Harry Reems, later to appear in *Deep Throat*. Sarno's direction has a slight plodding charm, and the foreigners in the cast speak deliciously wayward English. GB

Butterfly
(1981, US, 108 min)
d/p Matt Cimber. *sc* John Goff, Matt Cimber. *ph* Eduard van der Enden. *ed* Brent A Schoenfeld, Stan Siegel. *ad* Dave De Carlo. *m* Ennio Morricone. *cast* Stacy Keach, Pia Zadora, Orson Welles, Lois Nettleton, Edward Albert, Stuart Whitman, Ed McMahon, June Lockhart, James Franciscus.
●A blatant vehicle for much-hyped sex symbol Zadora, who looks less like a backwoods baby doll than an ageing Barbie doll, and whose millionaire husband funded the film. Co-starring Keach as the long-lost Daddy who can't keep his hands off her, this is less an adaptation of James M Cain's novel than a grotesque parody of Tennessee Williams, and by the time the plot reaches its incest trial climax it is close to open farce, despite a pleasing cameo from Welles as the judge. DP

Butterfly and Flowers (Peesua lae dokmai)
(1985, Thai, 126 min)
d Euthana Mukdasanit. *p* Chareon Iamphungporn. *sc* Euthann Mukdasanit. *ph* Panya Nimchareonpong. *ed* ML Varapa Kasaemsri. *m* Butterfly. *cast* Suriya Yaovasang, Vasana Pholyiem, Suchow Phongvilai, Rome Isra.
●An exceptionally beautiful movie set among Thailand's Muslim minority in villages near the Malaysian border, and centering on a bright teenage kid forced to drop out of school and support his family by turning small-time smuggler. Impossible to convey its qualities without falling back on turn-off words like 'charm' and 'sensitivity', but the fact is that it succeeds in evoking the trials, terrors and excitements of childhood with an immediacy that's both sweet *and* tough. There's an eye-opening blend of universal and local elements: trouble with punks at a rock concert, daredevil feats on the roof of a moving train. And it offers the joy of seeing a director in full control of his medium. TR

Butterfly Ball, The
(1976, GB, 87 min)
d/p/sc Tony Klinger. *ph* Ian Wilson. *ed* Anthony Klinger. *ad* Tony Curtis. *songs* Roger Glover. *with* Glenn Hughes, Eddie Hardin, Roger Glover, Earl Jordan, Mickey Lee Soule, Twiggy.
●One of the worst of the spate of rock extravaganzas churned out around this time. The core, with linking commentary by Vincent Price, is a live performance at the Albert Hall of the music Roger Glove scored for William Plomer's book (an adaptation of a 19th century fairytale), which is embroidered with 'imaginative' sequences meant to highlight the different songs. Klinger, who wrote, produced and directed this dinosaur, shows absolutely no insight into the visual presentation of hard rock or fantasy fiction. The imaginative sequences employ the most hackneyed of rock movie clichés, mushroom clouds, some Walt Disney wild life, a masked magician, and an *Alice in Wonderland* tea party. The only hint of life emerges in a brief animation sequence, which returns to Alan Aldridge's illustrations for the book. The music is equally arthritic. Devastatingly boring. IB

Butterfly Effect, The (El Efecto Mariposa)
(1995, Sp/Fr/GB, 109 min)
d Fernando Colomo. *p* Beatriz de la Gandara. *sc* Joaquin Oristrell, Fernando Colomo. *ph* Jean-François Robin. *ed* Miguel Angel Santamaria. *ad* John Roberts. *m* Ketama. *cast* María Barranco, Coque Malla, Rosa Maria Sardá, James Fleet, Peter Sullivan, Cécile Pallas, José María Pau.
●Fernando Colomo, the Spanish producer/director best known for *Skyline*, based on his experiences in New York, transfers his gently satirical gaze to London. Straitlaced Luis (Malla) enrols in a summer course at the London School of Economics. Soon after he finds lodgings in a Camberwell council flat with untidy *Star Trek* fanatic Oswald (Fleet), their neighbour, Luis's free-spirited aunt Olivia (Barranco), has a bust-up with her philandering actor partner (Sullivan). Luis offers comfort, but, when his mum (Sardá) asked her younger sister to shake him out of his conservative ways, was an affair what she had in mind? The movie's scores on its vitality and because Colomo has an evident feel for London life, especially as experienced by foreigners. Less successful is the ambitious attempt to relate Chaos Theory (direct-to-camera explanations) to human personalities, emotions and behaviour, and the predictable half-hearted celebration of 'liberated' ethics in an otherwise conventional romance. GA

Butterfly Kiss
(1995, GB, 88 min)
d Michael Winterbottom. *p* Julie Baines. *sc* Frank Cottrell-Boyce. *ph* Seamus McGarvey. *ed* Trevor Waite. *ad* Rupert Miles. *m* John Harle. *cast* Amanda Plummer, Saskia Reeves, Kathy Jamieson, Des McAleer, Lisa Jane Riley, Paul Brown.
●When punky weirdo Eunice wanders into a service-station in search of a friend, the dowdy girl at the counter, Miriam, is so drawn to the belligerent vagrant that she takes her home. That night, to Miriam's bemusement, Eunice strips off to reveal a bruised, chained, pierced body and seduces her; the next morning, however, finding her guest gone, Miriam feels impelled to head off in pursuit, a move that will draw her into Eunice's brutal world of seedy sexual encounters and habitual murder. This bleak, provocative debut is at once emphatically English and clearly indebted to American crime and road movies. It's an odd, unsettling little movie, graced with an uneven but authentically raw performance from Plummer as the ranting sociopath and a subtler, sometimes touching turn from Reeves as her beguiled accomplice/would-be redeemer. GA

Butterfly Murders, The (Die Bian)
(1979, HK, 88 min)
d Tsui Hark. *p* Wu Sijian, Zhang Quan. *sc* Lin Fan [Lin Zhiming and Liang Nonggang]. *ph* Fan Jinyu. *ed* Huang Zhixiong. *pd* Kong Quankai, Liu Lili. *cast* Liu Zhaoming, Michelle Mee, Huang Shutang,Zhang Guozhu.
●A dazzling movie from the vanguard of the 'new wave' in Hong Kong Chinese cinema. Swarms of killer butterflies lay siege to a medieval castle while, inside, the scholar-hero unravels a tangle of secret identities, arcane plots and cruel inventions. Enough plot ideas and visual flair to sustain a dozen average 'thrillers'. Here making his debut, Tsui does what Corman would have done, had he been Chinese and had a million butterflies to play with. TR

Butterfly's Tongue (La Lengua de las Mariposas/aka The Tongue of the Butterfly
(1998, Sp, 96 min)
d José Luis Cuerda. *sc* Rafael Azcona. *ph* Javier Salmones. *ed* Nacho Ruiz Capillas. *ad* Josep Rosell. *m* Alejandro Amenábar. *cast* Fernando Fernán-Gómez, Manuel Lozano, Uxía Blanco, Gonzálo M Uriarte, Alexis de los Santos, Tamar Novas, Guillermo Toldeo, Elena Fernández.
●Galicia, 1936. Eight-year-old Moncho (Lozano) runs away from his first day in school, terrified that his teacher Don Gregorio (Fernán-Gómez) is a flogger. His concerns are misplaced and, once he's coaxed back, he finds Don Gregorio a learned tutor and ally. Over the following months, Moncho learns about spiders and butterflies, potatoes and poetry; befriends a classmate, Roque, with whom he spies on a torrid backwoods love affair; and accompanies his budding saxophonist brother (de los Santos) abroad to the Santa Maria de Lombas Fair, where they meet a beguiling mute girl bearing the scar of a wolf. In the background the nation's political ferment looms, threatening to disrupt the benign course of Moncho's life lessons. A simple colourful fable underscoring the fragility of liberal romantic values, the film combines three Manuel Rivas short stories to slightly rambling effect. Beautifully filmed and lovingly performed, it paints a rather rose-tinted vision of pastoral arcadia, so the sobering finale comes as quite an abrupt change of mood. NB

...But Then, She's Betty Carter
(1980, US, 53 min)
d/p/sc Michelle D Parkerson. *ph* S Norman, M Boyer. *ed* Jom Brown. *cast* Betty Carter, Lionel Hampton.
●A profile of Betty 'Bebop' Carter, intercutting interview material with footage from a public concert sponsored by Howard University at the Cranston Auditorium. Roughly slapped together in a manner not entirely inappropriate to the lady's brash personality and scat-singing style, the numbers tend to be truncated by conversations which reveal remarkably little. Even Lionel Hampton, in a guest spot, seems infected by the air of self-congratulation. TM

Buttoners (Knoflíkári)
(1997, Czech Republic, 108 min, b/w & col)
d Petr Zelenka. *p* Alexej Guha. *sc* Petr Zelenka *ph* Miro Gábor. *ed* David Charap. *pd* David Cerny. *m* Ales Brezina. *cast* Seisuke Tsukahara, Richard Toth, David Charap; Vladimír Dlouhy; Jirí Kodet, Borivoj Navrátil; Rudolf Hrusínsky, Eva Holubová.
●Popular winner of a Rotterdam 1998 Tiger Award, this delightfully droll feature consists of six stories: the first, set in Japan, take place just before the bomb drops on Hiroshima, and the rest, set in the Czech Republic, take place 50 years later to the day. Initially, it's hard to discern a linking theme between Japanese mystified by American swearing, lovers indulging their passion in the back of a taxi, a man with a very bizarre perversion, and another whose expertise lies in spitting at trains, but gradually, as the film becomes increasingly offbeat and hilarious, Zelenka's concern with cause and effect, chance and destiny, responsibility and forgiveness emerges with intriguing, consistently surprising results. The imaginative blend of social satire, historical speculation, sci-fi and downright surrealism is sometimes reminiscent of late Buñuel, though the lasting impression is of a highly original black comedy not quite like anything else. GA

Bwana
(1995, Sp, 87 min)
d Imanol Uribe. *sc* Imanol Uribe, Juan Potau, Paco Pino. *ph* Javier Aguirresarobe. *ed* Teresa Font. *m* José Nieto. *cast* Andrés Pajares, Maria Barranco, Emilio Buale, Alejandro Martinez, Andrea Granero, Miguel del Arco.

●This begins promisingly, as a broad comedy about a taxi driver and his family stranded on a remote beach with an enigmatic, non-Spanish-speaking black man. The authority of Pajares' bullying yet ineffectual father is repeatedly undercut by his wife, Barranco's sly mockery, his fractious children's unruly behaviour, and the dignified stillness of Buale's iconic black man. However, with the subsequent arrival of three skinhead neo-Nazis, Basque director Uribe's broken-backed film suddenly becomes a facile social allegory about everyday racism. NF

By Candlelight

(1933, US, 70 min, b/w)
d James Whale. *sc* Hans Kraly, Karen de Wolf, F Hugh Herbert, Ruth Cummings. *ph* John Mescall. *ed* Ted Kent. *ad* Charles D Hall. *m* Franke Harling. *cast* Paul Lukas, Elissa Landi, Nils Asther, Dorothy Revier, Lawrence Grant.
●A dazzling display of romantic confidence trickery which takes on Lubitsch in his own territory. Convinced that he too can be a Casanova, a butler (Lukas) seizes his chance when his aristocratic employer (Asther) goes underground to avoid an importunate mistress, but discovers that upstairs and downstairs aren't quite the same thing. Delightful in its complications and malicious social implictions, the whole film – designed as a theatrical charade in which the butler casts himself above his station – fairly glitters with wit. TM

Bye-Bye Babushka

(1997, US, 80 min, b/w & col)
d Rebecca Feig. *p* Rebecca Feig, Mitchell Rosenbaum. *ph* Mitchell Rosenbaum. *ed* Daisy Wright.
●Rebecca Feig and her co-producer/camerman, Mitchell Rosenbaum, spent two years in Russia during the shooting of this empathetic documentary about the daily lives of a handful of Russian grandmothers. 'We are not women, we are horses.' The women, some in their eighties or nineties, are still working – simply to survive. In the cities they must scrape together the money for food, in the country they break their backs on scraps of land. War, revolution and toil have taken away most of their children. They are together, alone, with a combined stoicism and spirit which is humbling. FM

Bye Bye Birdie

(1963, US, 112 min)
d George Sidney. *p* Fred Kohlmar. *sc* Irving Brecher. *ph* Joseph Biroc. *ed* Charles Nelson. *ad* Paul Groesse. *songs* Charles Strouse, Lee Adams. *cast* Ann-Margret, Janet Leigh, Dick Van Dyke, Bobby Rydell, Maureen Stapleton, Jesse Pearson, Paul Lynde, Ed Sullivan.
●One of the more unsung '60s musicals, this is a big, splashy, Broadway-derived mix of boisterous rock'n'roll satire and breezy showbiz formulas. Hip-swivelling singing idol Conrad Birdie (Pearson in a juicy send-up of Elvis-style narcissism) gets drafted into the army, but not before his managers ('oldsters' Leigh and Van Dyke) arrange for him to bestow a last, symbolic kiss on one lucky Middle American Miss (Ann-Margret). Released just months before Kennedy's assassination, this enjoyable timepiece is notable today for its peppy score, energetic dancing, and for having made a star of the extremely nubile Ann-Margret, 22 passing for 16. Her fresh, wholesome eroticism fairly bursts off the screen. DJ

Bye Bye Blues

(1989, Can, 117 min)
d/p/sc Anne Wheeler. *ph* Vic Sarin. *ed* Christopher Tate. *ad* Scott Dobbie. *m* George Blondheim. *cast* Michael Ontkean, Rebecca Jenkins, Luke Reilly, Stuart Margolin, Wayne Robson, Robyn Stevan, Leon Pownall.
●When WWII breaks out, the idyllic colonial existence of Daisy Cooper (Jenkins) and her husband Teddy (Ontkean) is destroyed: a doctor, he is transferred from India to Singapore, while she returns to Canada and the demands of prying neighbours and parochial constraints. But seizing an opportunity to make extra cash singing and playing piano for a dance band, she falls under the spell of Max (Reilly), a rakish trombone player. Will she wait dutifully for Teddy, or dump the kids with relatives and hit the road? Unimaginative direction makes too much use of hackneyed conventions: rain-spattered windows, lonely silhouettes in the night, Max playing a pensive tune beneath a flickering hotel sign. Such techniques are a little like the plot: you've seen it all before. CM

Bye Bye Brasil

(1979, Braz/Fr, 100 min)
d Carlos Diegues. *p* Luis Carlos Barreto. *sc* Carlos Diegues. *ph* Lauro Escorel. *ed* Mair Tavares. *m* Chico Buarque, Roberto Menescal, Dominguinhos. *cast* Betty Faria, José Wilker, Fabio Junior, Zaira Zambelli.
●About a group of travelling players and their adventures on the road, this is designed as a fairytale with social asides. It wears its Brazilian charm heavily on its sleeve, but its picture of social changes is so resolutely apolitical – and its tale so commercially upbeat – that finally it leaves only the impression of a series of friendly and not very perceptive postcards. SM

Bye Bye Braverman

(1968, US, 94 min)
d/p Sidney Lumet. *sc* Herbert Sargent. *ph* Boris Kaufman. *ed* Gerald Greenberg. *ad* Ben Kasazkow. *m* Peter Matz. *cast* George Segal, Jack Warden, Joseph Wiseman, Sorrell Booke, Jessica Walter, Phyllis Newman, Zohra Lampert, Godfrey Cambridge.
●One of Lumet's New York movies, based on Wallace Markfield's acidly funny novel *To an Early Grave*, about four literary mediocrities driving around in search of a friend's funeral (the eponymous Braverman, a lionised success), meanwhile giving vent to their spleen in conversations haunted by middle-age, failure and death. Unreleased in Britain, perhaps because of its 'doubtful' taste (at one point the four find themselves hilariously stalled at the wrong funeral), it's a little unfocused but bristles with Jewish wit and fine performances. TM

Bye Bye Love

(1995, US, 106 min)
d Sam Weisman. *p* Gary David Goldberg, Brad Hall, Sam Weisman. *sc* Gary David Goldberg, Brad Hall. *ph* Kenneth Zunder. *ed* Roger Bondelli. *pd* Linda DeScenna. *m* JAC Redford. *cast* Matthew Modine, Randy Quaid, Paul Reiser, Janeane Garofalo, Amy Brenneman, Eliza Dushku, Lindsay Crouse, Rob Reiner.
●This anodyne domestic caper is one of those movies where you keep waiting for the ad breaks. The star power is strictly middle-ranking: an ill-at-ease Modine is recently divorced womaniser Dave; remarkably chummy Quaid is recently divorced Vic, stuck in blind-date purgatory; and Reiser is Donny, also recently divorced but still in love with his ex-wife. All three have kids, all three have custody during one weekend of meticulously organised fun and extra-curricular romantic intrigue. It's hard to be much concerned about these plastic people and their travails. Even so, you have to admit a certain grudging admiration for the way the slick construction and the stream of mildly amusing one-liners keep you watching despite yourself. TJ

By Nightfall (Verso sera)

(1990, It, 99 min)
d Francesca Archibugi. *p* Leo Pescarlo, Guido De Laurentiis. *sc* Francesca Archibugi, Gloria Malatesta, Claudia Sbarigia. *ph* Paolo Carnera. *ed* Roberto Missiroli. *pd* Osvaldo Desideri, Paola Marchesia. *m* Roberto Gatto. *cast* Marcello Mastroianni, Sandrine Bonnaire, Lara Pranzoni, Zoe Incrocci, Giorgio Tirabassi, Victor Cavallo.
●Archibugi returns to the family strife of her previous *Mignon Has Left* for this drama about a university professor (Mastroianni) whose life is turned upside-down when his young granddaughter and her free-wheeling mother (Bonnaire) take up residence in his house. He is forced to re-examine rigid priorities, but new-found affections prove more difficult to comprehend. Some scenes strain towards didacticism, but these are tempered by touching performances and the film's gentle exploration of love's restorative qualities. CM

By the Law (Dura Lex)

(1926, USSR, 5,489 ft, b/w)
d Lev Kuleshov. *sc* Victor Chkovski. *ph* Konstantin Kuznetsov. *ad* Isaac Makhlis. *cast* Alexandra Khokhlova, Sergei Komarov, Vladimir Fogel, Pyotr Galadzhez.
●Rough justice in the remote Klondike, when a husband and wife have to cope not only with the extremes of Nature, but with the discovery of a murderer in their midst. Adapted from Jack London's story *The Unexpected*, the picture runs barely an hour, working up an impressive degree of intensity. Apparently Kuleshov saw the project as a vehicle for his theories about acting, montage and the dynamics of the relationship between the two. Nevertheless, its human values emerge as paramount. BBa

By the Light of the Silvery Moon

(1953, US, 102 min)
d David Butler. *p* William Jacobs. *sc* Robert O'Brien, Irving Elinson. *ph* Wilfred M Cline. *ed* Irene Morra. *ad* John Beckman. *songs* Gus Edwards, Edward Madden, Clifford Grey, Nat D Ayer, others. *cast* Doris Day, Gordon MacRae, Leon Ames, Rosemary DeCamp, Mary Wickes, Billy Gray.
●Harmless sequel to *On Moonlight Bay*, which left Day and MacRae on the brink of marriage at the end of World War I. Manufactured delays for the wedding provide a tiresomely thin plot, but leaves more time for comedy involving young brother, who becomes convinced that dad is romancing a French actress. The gaps are plugged by another batch of nostalgic songs like 'If You Were the Only Girl in the World' and 'Be My Little Bumble Bee'. TM

By the Sword

(1991, US, 91 min)
d Jeremy Paul Kagan. *p* Marlon Staggs, Peter E Strauss. *sc* James Donadio. *ph* Arthur Albert. *ed* David Holden. *pd* Gary Frutkoff. *m* Bill Conti. *cast* Eric Roberts, F Murray Abraham, Chris Rydell, Mia Sara, Elaine Kagan, Brett Cullen.
●Inevitably reminiscent of *Amadeus*, what with Abraham playing Max Suba, an ex-fencing star faced with a younger, more brilliant exponent of the art (compare 'You are the best composer known to me' with 'You're the best fencer I've ever known'). Just like in *Amadeus*, Abraham gets to flash that sinister smile – both sets of teeth showing – and cry 'Maestro!' Roberts is an unbelievably mannered actor, but as Villard, he's playing an unbelievably mannered man, 'a freak who thinks he's living in the fourteenth century,' as one of the students complains. Villard runs a viciously competitive Salle (fencing school), and Suba, 25 years in the slammer, turns up to try for an instructor's post. Sternly repulsed ('One must learn, before one teaches'), he accepts a job as janitor. After many shots of him practising with a duster, a paint brush and a french stick, he begins to teach, but his gentle, philosophical style clashes with the Maestro's macho technique. A deeper secret links the two men, spelled out in nightmarish flashback, and there's an inevitable showdown. Right down to the painful fencing-to-disco-music routine, this is embarrassingly fab. SFe

Byzantium (Kahpe Bizans)

(1999, Tur, 90 min)
d Gani Müjde. *p* Ferdi Egilmez, Mehmet Soyarslan. *sc* Kemal Kenan Ergen, Gani Müjde. *ph* Ugur Icbak. *ed* Onur Tan. *m* Ugur Dikmen. *cast* Sümer Tilmaç, Aysegül Aldinç, Nurseli Idiz, Mehmet Ali Erbil, Cem Davran, Demet Sener, Hande Ataizi.
●Base your medieval history test on this and you won't rise up the ranks of academia. Dumb comedy Turkish-style, it begins with a cultivated warrior tribe called the Najar decamping from Australia to the Turkish plains, only to meet with keen persecution by the effeminate but bloodthirsty Byzantine emperor Horribilis XVI. On the day the Najar's chief, a fat fellow by the name of Superwarrior, and his wife are delivered of triplets, Horribilis is given to understand he'll be topped by one of their number, so he pulls a Herod with the Najar's newborn. But the triplets in turn pull something of a Romulus and Remus, or maybe a baby Oedipus, and a generation down the line everyone's set up for mix and match court intrigue and a farcical revolt. Most of the jokes fall very flat, but full marks for irrepressibility. NB

C

Chinatown

Cabaret (100)

(1972, US, 123 min)
d Bob Fosse. *p* Cy Feuer. *sc* Jay Presson Allen. *ph* Geoffrey Unsworth. *ed* David Bretherton. *pd* Rolf Zehetbauer. *songs* John Kander, Fred Ebb. *cast* Liza Minnelli, Michael York, Helmut Griem, Joel Grey, Fritz Wepper, Marisa Berenson.
● A maddening mixture, this adaptation of John Kander's fine musical based on Christopher Isherwood's Berlin stories. Superbly choreographed by Fosse, the cabaret numbers evoke the Berlin of 1931 – city of gaiety and perversion, of champagne and Nazi propaganda – so vividly that only an idiot could fail to perceive that something is rotten in the state of Weimar. Doubling as director, Fosse unfortunately feels the need to put the boot in with some crude cross-cutting (eg from a man being beaten up by Nazis in the street to the leering faces of the cabaret performers) which lands the film in a queasy morass of overstatement. TM

Cabaret Balkan (Bure Baruta/Baril de Poudre/ aka The Powder Keg)

(1998, Fr/Greece/Macedonia/Tur/Yugo, 100 min)
d/p Goran Paskaljevic. *sc* Dejan Dukovski, Goran Paskaljevic, Filip David, Zoran Andric. *ph* Milan Spasic. *ed* Petar Putnikovic. *pd* Milenko Jeremic. *m* Zoran Simjanovic. *cast* Miki Manojlovic, Sergei Trifunovic, Mirjana Jokovic, Lazar Ristovski, Mira Banjac, Ivan Bekjarev.
● Adapted from a play by Dejan Dukovski, Paskaljevic's freewheeling black comedy charts an eventful night in the life of various inhabitants of Belgrade following the break-up of Yugoslavia. As their paths intersect and intertwine, the Serbian writer/director explores, somewhat insistently, his fellow citizens' almost absurd and very dangerous tendency to argue, fall out, fight, hate, maim and mutilate, and make up again over a sentimental laugh. Much more tightly controlled than the work of his (reputedly detested) compatriot Kusturica, but occasionally painted in similarly broad, exuberant strokes, this is a sometimes scary, sometimes hilarious, consistently compassionate portrait of a culture in crisis. GA

Cabbie, The (Yun Zhuanshou de Lian)

(2000, Tai, 94 min)
d Chen Yiwen, Chang Hwa-Kun. *p* Huang Lin-Shyang, Chiu Shun-Ching, Chang Hwa-Kun. *sc* Su Zhaobin. *ph* Tsai Cheng-Tai. *ed* Chen Bowen. *ad* Tsai Chao-Yi. *m* Luo Dayou. *cast* Rie Miyazawa, Chu Chung-Heng, Tai Bo, Cheng Hsiu-Ying, Leon Dai, Duan Chun-Hao.
● Vastly enjoyable, Chen's third feature (producer Chang is credited as co-director for legal reasons, apparently) could be cinema's answer to *Tristram Shandy*: the life/love-story of taxi driver Daquan (Chu) is interspersed with so many vignettes, digressions, direct-to-camera interruptions and flashbacks that it defies description, let alone synopsis. The first half mixes episodes from Daquan's personal history (how and why his coroner mother married his cabbie father, why he became a driver, why dad's office is located next to an accident black-spot) with reflections on the way people confide their darkest secrets to cabbies. The second half is mostly the love story: confirmed bachelor Daquan falls for policewoman Jingwen (Japanese star Miyazawa, well-dubbed into Chinese) and sets about committing every moving violation in the book as many times as it takes to catch her attention. Wise, worldly and put together with unfailing dark wit, this is an absolute joy. TR

Cabeza de Vaca

(1990, Mex/Sp, 112 min)
d Nicolas Echevarria. *p* Rafael Cruz, Jorge Sanchez, Julio Solorzano Foppa. *sc* Nicolas Echevarria, Guillermo Sheridan. *ph* Guillermo Navarro. *ed* Rafael Castenedo. *pd* José Luis Aguilar. *m* Mario Lavista. *cast* Juan Diego, Daniel Jiménez Cacho, Roberto Sosa, Carlos Castañon, Gerardo Villarreal, Roberto Cobo, Jose Flores.
● An expiatory historical epic based on the journal of the Spanish conquistador Cabeza de Vaca. Shipwrecked with his crew in what is now Florida in 1528, de Vaca went native with the local Americans. It's a spectacular, beautifully shot, anti-imperialist bloodbath of a movie, which plays like a demented mix of Herzog, Jodorowsky and Tarkovsky. WH

Cabinet of Dr Caligari, The (Das Kabinett des Dr Caligari)

(1919, Ger, 5,587 ft, b/w)
d Robert Wiene. *p* Erich Pommer. *sc* Carl Mayer, Hans Janowitz. *ph* Willy Hameister. *ad* Hermann Warm, Walter Reimann, Walter Röhrig. *cast* Werner Krauss, Conrad Veidt, Lil Dagover, Friedrich Feher, Hans Heinz von Twardowski.
● Undoubtedly one of the most exciting and inspired horror movies ever made. The story is a classic sampling of expressionist paranoia about a hypnotist who uses a somnambulist to do his murders, full of the gloom and fear that prevailed in Germany as it emerged from WWI. There are plenty of extremely boring sociological/critical accounts of the film; best to avoid them and enjoy the film's extraordinary use of painted light and Veidt's marvellous performance. Incidentally, the influence of *Caligari* on the cinema is much more problematic than some historians suppose. Thematically it has rarely been copied, and the style only really infiltrated in dream sequences and other odd devices. DP

Cabin in the Cotton, The

(1932, US, 79 min, b/w)
d Michael Curtiz. *associate d* William Keighley. *sc* Paul Green. *ph* Barney McGill. *ed* George Amy. *ad* Esdras Hartley. *m* Leo Forbstein. *cast* Richard Barthelmess, Bette Davis, Dorothy Jordan, Berton Churchill, Russell Simpson, Tully Marshall, Henry B Walthall.
● A good example of Warner's social crusading style. The script takes care to include some shifty sharecroppers, but mostly it's about wealthy planters exploiting their poverty stricken tenants, with Barthelmess as the man in the middle. At the climax our hero advocates lawbreaking to change the system, but even then the characters remain those of a formula melodrama of the day. Blonde Bette Davis is very lively as the boss's daughter, teasing guileless Barthelmess ('Cute! I'd like to kiss ya, but I just washed my hair'), making him dance the Peckerwood Wiggle and singing 'Willie the Weeper' as she slips into 'something more restful,' i.e. nothing at all. BBa

Cabin in the Sky

(1943, US, 99 min, b/w)
d Vincente Minnelli. *p* Arthur Freed. *sc* Joseph Schrank. *ph* Sidney Wagner. *ed* Harold F Kress. *ad* Cedric Gibbons. *m/songs* John Latouche, Vernon Duke, Harold Arlen, EY Harburg, Ted Fetter. *cast* Eddie 'Rochester' Anderson, Lena Horne, Ethel Waters, Louis Armstrong, Rex Ingram, Duke Ellington.
● One can easily criticise this all-black musical (Minnelli's first feature) for falling prey to the same 'Uncle Tom' stereotyping that characterised *Green Pastures*, but there's no denying both the compassion with which Minnelli treats his characters and the immense cinematic talent on view. The gorgeous dreamlike sets and consummate control of the fantastic atmosphere that imbues the story (an idle, poverty-stricken farmer dreams of being sent to Hell upon dying) are already well developed. And the cast are magnificent, delivering the lovely Harold Arlen score with style and power. GA

Cabiria

see Notti di Cabiria, Le

Cable Guy, The

(1996, US, 96 min)
d Ben Stiller. *p* Andrew Licht, Jeffrey A Mueller, Judd Apatow. *sc* Lou Holtz Jr, Judd Apatow. *ph* Robert Brinkmann. *ed* Steven Weisberg. *pd* Sharon Seymour. *m* John Ottman. *cast* Jim Carrey, Matthew Broderick, Leslie Mann, Jack Black, Diane Baker, George Segal, Ben Stiller, Eric Roberts, Janeane Garofalo.
● A twisted and often nasty black comedy. When naive suburbanite Broderick asks Carrey's over-eager Cable Guy to give him a few extra channels for free, he has no idea he's inviting the wired-up plugster into his life. Newly separated from his girlfriend, Broderick is sucked into his socially inept pal's deranged fantasy world, the result of a lonely boyhood spent watching TV. Carrey's whirlwind comic energy is too spontaneous and elusive to be contained by Lou Holtz Jr's initially unsettling script. Also, Stiller's erratic direction fails to establish a consistent tone, so that obvious, crowd pleasing set-pieces alternate with creepy, disturbing weirdness. Compare, for instance, Carrey's typically berserk karaoke rendition of Jefferson Airplane's 'Somebody to Love?' with the nightmarish sequence in a kitschy Arthurian theme restaurant, where he and Broderick quaff ale and gnaw chicken before fighting, virtually to the death, with swords, axes, maces and jousting lances. Nevertheless, because it dares to expose the dark side of Carrey's persona, and to take chances at this pivotal stage in his meteoric career, Stiller's film ranks as an honourable failure. NF

Caboblanco

(1979, US, 87 min)
d J Lee Thompson. *p* Lance Hool, Paul A Joseph. *sc* Morton Fine, Milton Gelman. *ph* Alex Phillips. *ed* Michael F Anderson. *ad* José Rodriguez Granada. *m* Jerry Goldsmith. *cast* Charles Bronson, Jason Robards, Dominique Sanda, Fernando Rey, Simon MacCorkindale, Camilla Sparv, Gilbert Roland.
● Appalling rehash of *Casablanca*, with Bronson as the expat living on the coast of Peru after the war and coming into conflict with Nazis over treasure at the bottom of the sea. Indescribably inept. GA

Cachetonneurs, Les (The Music Freelancers/ aka The Freelancers)

(1999, Fr, 91 min)
d Denis Dercourt. *p* Tom Dercourt. *sc* Denis Decourt. *ph* Jérôme Peyrebrune. *ed* Yann Coquart. *ad* Suen Mounicq. *cast* Pierre Lacan, Marc Citti, Philippe Clay, Henri Garcin, Marie-Christine Laurent, Serge Renko, Wilfred Benaïche, Clémentine Benoît, Ivry Gitlis, Sonia Mankaï, Meyong Békaté.
● Another day, another gig. As one rehearsal ends, bass player Roberto (Lacan) is networking among his regular freelancers on the fringes of the classical music scene. The job on offer means good money, meeting in a country chateau and rehearsing with veteran Austrian conductor Svarowski (Garcin) for a private New Year's Eve concert. Roberto has five takers – among them a pregnant flautist, a kleptomaniac cellist, and an abrasive viola player – who join a nervy local clarinettist to await the the maestro's arrival. Quite why this famous baton waver should have agreed to work with such a modest ensemble, it takes a while to find out, but the group certainly needs him to stamp his authority on their conflicting personalities. This first feature makes up in authenticity what it lacks in excitement; the musical sequences are convincing, as is the depiction of the daily grind of providing light classics to anyone who'll cough up. Beyond that, however, it fights shy of delving too deep into its characters' frazzled emotions. TJ

Ça commence aujourd'hui

see It All Starts Today

Cactus

(1986, Aust, 96 min, b/w)
d Paul Cox. *p* Jane Ballantyne, Paul Cox. *sc* Paul Cox, Bob Ellis, Norman Kaye. *ph* Yuri Sokol. *ed* Tim Lewis. *pd* Asher Bilu. *m* Giovanni Battista Pergolese. *cast* Isabelle Huppert, Robert Menzies, Norman Kaye, Monica Maughan, Banduk Marika, Sheila Florance.
● Separated from her husband, partially blinded in a car crash, Colo (Huppert) takes refuge in friendship with Robert (Menzies), himself completely blind since birth. Love blooms… Given the subject matter, Cox's bitter-sweet romance might have been pure soap; but thanks to superior performances and Cox's strangely detached tone, sentimentality is held at bay. This is due partly to his characteristically elevated concerns – occasionally stilted 'telling' dialogue suggests that he views blindness as a perversely privileged path towards self-awareness – and partly to his seeming determination to become the Australian *auteur sans pareil*: the flower symbolism, the use of classical music, and the flickery flashbacks are

all familiar from his earlier *Lonely Hearts, Man of Flowers* and *My First Wife*. It's an often over-schematic movie that holds the attention through its extreme elegance, the camera slowly prowling to explore a luscious Eden-like landscape that Huppert is increasingly unable to see. Best, however, are the film's apparently most inconsequential moments – a tipsy birthday party peopled by elderly eccentrics, a stormy cactus-growers' committee meeting – which exude a vitality and humour to carefully counterpoint the solemnity of the story proper. GA

Cactus Jack

see Villain, The

Cadaveri Eccellenti

see Illustrious Corpses

Caddie

(1976, Aust, 106 min)
d Donald Crombie. *p* Anthony Buckley. *sc* Joan Long. *ph* Peter James. *ed* Tim Wellburn. *ad* Owen Williams. *m* Peter Flynn. *cast* Helen Morse, Takis Emmanuel, Kirrily Nolan, Jacki Weaver, Jack Thompson, Lynette Curran, Melissa Jaffer.

●An intelligent script, based on an anonymous autobiography, and charting the struggles of an independent woman in Depression-era Australia, gets an unfortunate sentimentalising gloss from Crombie's direction, which attempts to realign essentially tough-minded material with the prevalent trend to retro prettiness. Morse is fine as the abandoned wife who becomes a barmaid to support herself and her two kids, though her retention of plucky charm under her 'deviate' circumstances rings a little too good to be true. PT

Caddyshack

(1980, US, 98 min)
d Harold Ramis. *p* Douglas Kenney. *sc* Brian Doyle-Murray, Harold Ramis, Douglas Kenney. *ph* Stevan Larner. *ed* David Bretherton, Robert Barrere. *pd* Stan Jolley. *m* Johnny Mandel. *cast* Chevy Chase, Rodney Dangerfield, Ted Knight, Michael O'Keefe, Bill Murray, Sarah Holcomb, Scott Colomby, Cindy Morgan.

●If you're still at the age when farting and nose-picking seem funny, then *Caddyshack* should knock you dead. Buried deep – very deep – beneath the rising tide of effluent is a pleasant enough story of a kind about trying to make it to the top as a caddy while yet remaining human; a movie which could have done for golf what *Breaking Away* did for cycling. Instead it allows a string of resistible TV comics (Chase excepted) to mug through an atrocious chain of lame-brained set pieces, the least vulgar of which involves a turd in a swimming pool. Going a bit far? Well, then someone eats it. And then some-one sits in a pile of vomit. And then…it just gets worse. CPea

Cadillac Man

(1990, US, 97 min)
d Roger Donaldson. *p* Charles Roven, Roger Donaldson. *sc* Ken Friedman. *ph* David Gribble. *ed* Richard Francis-Bruce. *ad* Gene Rudolf. *m* J Peter Robinson. *cast* Robin Williams, Tim Robbins, Pamela Reed, Fran Drescher, Zack Norman, Annabella Sciorra, Lori Petty, Paul Guilfoyle.

●Robin Williams' role here as ruthless, womanising auto-salesman Joey O'Brien seems at first ideally suited to his motormouth persona. When the company secretary's jealous, machine gun-toting husband Larry (Robbins) roars into the showroom, takes everyone hostage, and demands to know the identity of his wife's lover, Joey's quick-fire patter undergoes the ultimate road test: as a SWAT team, TV crews and spectators gather outside, he tries to stop Larry shooting or blowing up the hostages. To his credit, Robbins more than holds his own, his credibly unhinged husband alternating between frustrated ranting, nervy panic and childlike vulnerability. Very soon, however, the film swerves violently into overpitched farce, then plummets into irksome, *Good Morning, Vietnam*-style sentimentality. While he's lying through his teeth or improvising a sales pitch that might save his skin, Williams is funny and convincing; but once he starts getting dewy-eyed and sincere, flesh-crawling embarrassment takes over. NF

Caesar and Cleopatra

(1945, GB, 138 min)
d/p Gabriel Pascal. *sc* George Bernard Shaw. *ph* Freddie Young, Jack Hildyard, Jack Cardiff. *ed* Frederick Wilson. *ad* Oliver Messel, John Bryan. *m* Georges Auric. *cast* Claude Rains, Vivien Leigh, Cecil Parker, Stewart Granger, Flora Robson, Francis L Sullivan, Basil Sydney, Ernest Thesiger.

●Lavish but frequently dull and theatrical adaptation of Bernard Shaw's play about imperial romance up the Nile. Some of the wit survives despite being swamped by the spectacle, the Technicolor photography (by a number of cameramen) is eye-catching, and Rains turns in his usual sturdy performance. But it's all something of an overwrought folly. GA

Cafe au Lait

see Métisse

Café de la plage, Le

see Beach Café

Café Flesh

(1982, US, 76 min)
d Rinse Dream [Stephen Sayadian]. *p* FX Pope, Stephen Sayadian. *sc* Herbert W Day, Rinse Dream. *ph* FX Pope. *ed* Sidney Katz. *pd* Paul Bertell. *m* Mitchell Froom. *cast* Pia Snow, Kevin Jay, Marie Sharp, Andrew Nichols.

●Though hardly on a par with the 1898 novel which foreshadowed, in most significant details, the wreck of the *Titanic* 14 years later, this slice of sci-fi porn does show a certain eerie prescience. Produced on the very eve of the AIDS pandemic, it proposes a future in which, following some plague-like visitation, the world's population is either Sex Positive or Sex Negative. In this tale, though, 'Positive' is good, means you can do it, whereas the unhappy Negatives can only congregate at Café Flesh, just to sit and watch. This is merely the framework for the standard hard-core action that follows – thought-provoking framework all the same. BBa

Cage aux Folles, La (Birds of a Feather)

(1978, Fr/It, 91 min)
d Edouard Molinaro. *p* Marcello Danon. *sc* Francis Veber, Edouard Molinaro, Marcello Danon, Jean Poiret. *ph* Armando Nannuzzi. *ed* Robert Isnardon, Monique Isnardon. *ad* Mario Garbuglia. *m* Ennio Morricone. *cast* Michel Serrault, Ugo Tognazzi, Michel Galabru, Claire Maurier, Rémi Laurent, Benny Luke, Carmen Scarpitta.

●Barefoot black butler can't decide whether he's a Pearl Bailey or Paul Robeson. Father of the family has a teenage son by a heterosexual fling, and 'mother' is a drag star. Between them they make John Inman look like Richard Harris. But the son wants to marry the daughter of a morality campaigner, and the in-laws must meet… High camp and farce are acquired tastes, but even those who usually resist should find amusement in the last act's mounting hysteria. Although theatrical, it remains very funny, and uses the overt stereotyping with great sympathy. SM

Cage aux Folles II, La

(1980, Fr/It, 99 min)
d Edouard Molinaro. *p* Marcello Danon. *sc* Jean Poiret, Francis Veber, Marcello Danon. *ph* Armando Nannuzzi. *ed* Robert Isnardon, Monique Isnardon, Carlo Della Corte. *ad* Luigi Scaccianoce. *m* Ennio Morricone. *cast* Michel Serrault, Ugo Tognazzi, Marcel Bozzuffi, Paola Borbini, Giovanni Vettorazzo, Glauco Onorato, Michel Galabru.

●This time round, Renato (still phlegmatic and long-suffering) and Albin (still squawking like a constipated parrot) find themselves on the run from the macho world of spy rings, counter-espionage, and all manner of things that go wrong on the night. It's a finely timed and often hilarious airy-fairy farce, full of ironies with so many twists that they make Chubby Checker look like a slide rule. FL

Cage aux Folles III: The Wedding, La (La Cage aux Folles: Elles se Marient)

(1985, Fr/It, 91 min)
d Georges Lautner. *p* Marcello Danon. *sc* Michel Audiard, Jacques Audiard, Marcello Danon, Georges Lautner, Gérard Lamballe. *ph* Luciano Tovoli. *ed* Michelle David, Elisabeth Guido, Lidia Pascolini. *ad* Mario Garbuglia. *m* Ennio Morricone. *cast* Michel Serrault, Ugo Tognazzi, Marcel Bozzuffi, Michel Galabru, Antonella Interlenghi, Benny Luke, Saverio Vallone, Stéphane Audran.

●The huge success of the original rested on Mr and Mrs Popcorn's delighted discovery that, deep down, all those raving queers were very wonderful human beings just like them, while hipper viewers savoured its sly send-up of sexual stereotypes. Fat chance of either happening in this silly farrago of a second sequel, wherein Serrault's flamboyant drag artiste (his ample form, encased in a black-and-yellow striped leotard, bringing new meaning to the term Queen Bee) must sire a child to inherit a fortune. Serrault is too, too outré as the shrieking Zaza, Tognazzi approaches rigor mortis as his straightman, and Lautner (taking over from Edouard Molinaro) directs with zero comic flair. SJo

Caged

(1949, US, 96 min, b/w)
d John Cromwell. *p* Jerry Wald. *sc* Virginia Kellogg, Bernard C Schoenfeld. *ph* Carl Guthrie. *ed* Owen Marks. *ad* Charles H Clarke. *m* Max Steiner. *cast* Eleanor Parker, Agnes Moorehead, Ellen Corby, Hope Emerson, Jan Sterling, Jane Darwell.

●Writer Virginia Kellogg spent time behind bars to research this women-in-prison saga, which gained Parker an Oscar nomination as the teenager who's jailed for a crime committed by her man, has his baby while she's inside, and winds up a hard case. Agnes Moorehead's the concerned warden, Emerson the sadistic bull-dyke guard, staples of a genre which started here and has the likes of *Prisoner Cell Block H* and *Bare Behind Bars* to answer for. TJ

Caged Heart

see L'Addition

Caged Heat

(1974, US, 83 min)
d Jonathan Demme. *p* Evelyn Purcell. *sc* Jonathan Demme. *ph* Tak Fujimoto. *ed* Johanna Demetrakas, Carolyn Hicks, Michael Goldman. *ad* Eric Thierman. *m* John Cale. *cast* Juanita Brown, Roberta Collins, Erica Gavin, Ella Reid, Lynda Gold, Warren Miller, Barbara Steele, Toby Carr Rafelson.

●The US drive-in audience's taste for renegade women has thrown up some pretty bizarre movies, but few more distinctive than Demme's directorial debut. It starts out as a bare-knuckled women's prison pic and turns into a 'girl gang' rampage, by way of a lot of witty feminist gags and the incursion of what William Burroughs would call a 'technological psychiatry' theme. A percussive, Velvet-y score by John Cale and several casting surprises (including the long-absent Barbara Steele) help keep both pace and interest high. It's no more than passable as a thriller, but the density of invention and energy in other respects is enough to shame a dozen contemporary major studio movies. TR

Cage of Gold

(1950, GB, 83 min, b/w)
d Basil Dearden. *p* Michael Balcon. *sc* Jack Whittingham. *ph* Douglas Slocombe. *ed* Peter Tanner. *pd* Michael Relph. *m* Georges Auric. *cast* Jean Simmons, David Farrar, James Donald, Madeleine Lebeau, Herbert Lom, Bernard Lee, Gladys Henson.

●Middling Ealing thriller which sees Simmons marrying the caddish Farrar, only to be deserted when he discovers she has no money. Then, when she marries her childhood sweetheart, believing Farrar dead, he returns to blackmail her. It takes far too long to get going, and even during the melodramatic climax, never really convinces. Nicely shot, though, by Douglas Slocombe. GA

Cahill – US Marshal

(1973, US, 103 min)
d Andrew V McLaglen. *p* Michael A Wayne. *sc* Harry Julian Fink, Rita M Fink. *ph* Joseph Biroc. *ed* Robert L Simpson. *pd* Walter M Simonds. *m* Elmer Bernstein. *cast* John Wayne, George Kennedy, Gary Grimes, Neville Brand, Marie Windsor, Harry Carey Jr.

●Wayne, running to fat and covered in pancake, finds that even he has trouble with his kids in this rather slow Western. Seventeen-year-old Danny and little Billy Joe Cahill collude with a gang to rob a bank...all on account of Big Daddy's been out huntin' villains and neglecting them.

Caine Mutiny, The

(1954, US, 125 min)
d Edward Dmytryk. *sc* Stanley Roberts. *ph* Franz Planer. *ed* William A Lyon, Henry Batista. *pd* Rudolph Sternad. *m* Max Steiner. *cast* Humphrey Bogart, José Ferrer, Van Johnson, Robert Francis, Fred MacMurray, EG Marshall, Lee Marvin, Claude Akins.
●Having aligned himself with producer Stanley Kramer after naming names during the HUAC witch-hunt trials, Dmytryk opted for ever more turgidly serious subject matter. This, the last and perhaps the best of his films for Kramer, was an adaptation of Herman Wouk's Pulitzer Prize-winning novel about the court martial carried out against peacetime naval destroyer officers Francis and Johnson after they have mutinied against Bogart's Captain Queeg, who panics during a storm. Bogie's considerable charisma is visibly weakened by his tired appearance, and the strong cast is never really allowed full rein by Dmytryk, whose abiding concern that fair play be seen to be done, with regard to all the characters' various motivations, makes for a stodgily liberal courtroom drama. GA

Cairo Road

(1950, GB, 95 min)
d David Macdonald. *p* Aubrey Baring. *sc* Robert Westerby. *ph* Oswald Morris. *ed* Peter Taylor. *ad* Duncan Sutherland. *m* Robert Gill. *cast* Eric Portman, Laurence Harvey, Maria Mauban, Camelia, Harold Lang, Karel Stepanek, John Gregson, Peter Jones.
●Britain's Anti-Narcotics Bureau takes the fight against the dope smugglers to the Egyptian capital in this workaday thriller, whose makers actually took the trouble to go to Cairo and Port Said to shoot it. Twenty-something Harvey makes an early appearance as Inspector Portman's bumbling, keen-as-mustard assistant. TJ

Cal

(1984, GB, 102 min)
d Pat O'Connor. *p* Stuart Craig, David Puttnam. *sc* Bernard MacLaverty. *ph* Jerzy Zielinski. *ed* Michael Bradsell. *pd* Stuart Craig. *m* Mark Knopfler. *cast* Helen Mirren, John Lynch, Donal McCann, John Kavanagh, Ray McAnally, Stevan Rimkus, Catherine Gibson.
●Too sensitive for the abattoir where his father works and with no stomach for the IRA driving jobs he is pressured into, Cal tries to dodge the Protestant gangs that roam his predominantly Loyalist estates and yearns after the local librarian. That he should have driven the car carrying the gunman who killed her husband, entails a familiar pattern of love laced with guilt and doomed to founder in the great divide. Bernard MacLaverty's fine script keeps the action batting along and the focus narrow, concentrating on the human tragedy rather than plugging any partisan line. The symbolism is thrashed just a little hard at times, but on the whole it's a most impressive debut from O'Connor, strongly acted all round. JP

Calamity Jane

(1953, US, 101 min)
d David Butler. *p* William Jacobs. *sc* James O'Hanlon. *ph* Wilfred M Cline. *ed* Irene Morra. *ad* John Beckman. *songs* Sammy Fain, Paul Francis Webster. *cast* Doris Day, Howard Keel, Allyn McLerie, Philip Carey, Gale Robbins.
●Deadwood Stage, Black Hills of Dakota, (Just Blew in from the) Windy City: Fain-Webster evidently believed in the efficacy of place names, rightly as it turned out, since virtually all their songs for this modestly produced musical became standards. Biggest hit of all was 'Secret Love', the title of which, combined with the spectacle of Doris tomboyin' around in buckskins and britches (her exploits include the abduction of pouting showgirl McLerie), anecdotally made the film quite precious to lesbian audiences of the time. The energy of the music and of the supercharged Day just about prevail over the lethargy of Butler's (non-)direction. BBa

Calcutta

(1946, US, 83 min, b/w)
d John Farrow. *p/sc* Seton I Miller. *ph* John F Seitz. *ed* Archie Marshek. *ad* Hans Dreier, Franz Bachelin. *m* Victor Young. *cast* Alan Ladd, Gail Russell, William Bendix, June Duprez, Lowell Gilmore.
●Although shot entirely in the black hole of the backlot, this is a seasoned programmer with hard-living pilot Ladd, a mainstay of the Calcutta-Chungking air route, braving the bazaars of the Indian city in search of his best pal's killer. Evidence points to the Chalgani Club and Ms Russell. TJ

Calendar

(1993, Can/Arm/Ger, 75 min)
d/p/sc Atom Egoyan. *ph* Norayr Kasper. *ed* Atom Egoyan. *m* Duduk. *cast* Atom Egoyan, Arsinée Khanjian, Ashot Adamian, Michelle Bellerose, Natalia Jasen.
●After photographing a series of churches in his native Armenia for a calendar commission, a man looks back on the trip to retrace the disintegration of his relationship with his then partner. In Canada, a year later, the glossy prints look down from the walls on his loneliness, while his ex's occasional telephone calls go miserably unanswered. A certain piquancy (for those in the know) is gained from the Armenian-born Egoyan's casting of himself as the lovelorn lensman and spouse Khanjian as the woman he left behind. Egoyan filters his customary themes – the difficulties of personal communication, the relationship between emotional lives and video technology – in a film which incisively balances metaphor and awkward realism, while shuttling nimbly through time and space, between celluloid and video formats. TJ

California Dolls, The

see All the Marbles

California Man

see Encino Man

California Split

(1974, US, 109 min)
d Robert Altman. *p* Robert Altman, Joseph Walsh. *sc* Joseph Walsh. *ph* Paul Lohmann. *ed* Lou Lombardo. *pd* Leon Ericksen. *m* Phyllis Shotwell. *cast* Elliott Gould, George Segal, Ann Prentiss, Gwen Welles, Edward Walsh, Joseph Walsh, Bert Remsen, Jeff Goldblum.
●Gould and Segal on some wild casino sprees in Los Angeles and Reno, speeding through a compulsive night world of frenzied overlapping chatter. Like Hawks, Altman feels rather than thinks his way into a subject, with a special interest in how people relate to one another in moments of crisis. In the process he shows more of what's happening in America than most newsreels, coaxes jazzy and inventive performances out of his actors (Prentiss and Welles are particular treats), and asks for a comparable amount of creative improvisation from his audience while busily hopping from one distraction to the next. JR

California Suite

(1978, US, 103 min)
d Herbert Ross. *p* Ray Stark. *sc* Neil Simon. *ph* David M Walsh. *ed* Michael A Stevenson. *pd* Albert Brenner. *m* Claude Bolling. *cast* Alan Alda, Michael Caine, Bill Cosby, Jane Fonda, Walter Matthau, Elaine May, Richard Pryor, Maggie Smith.
●Quick and varied comedy, highly suited to Neil Simon's machine-gun gag-writing. The four sketches about guests in a Hollywood hotel range from out-and-out banana peel slapstick (Cosby and Pryor) to tragi-comedy of a superior kind (Fonda). Inevitably Fonda provides the film with its centre, giving another performance of unnerving sureness. Also on the credit side is a bedroom farce of epic proportions from Matthau and May. The other vignettes are a bit glum. DP

Caligula

(1979, US/It, 160 min)
d Tinto Brass. *p* Bob Guccione, Franco Rossellini. *sc* Gore Vidal. *ph* Silvano Ippoliti. *ed* Nino Bragli. *ad* Danilo Donati. *m* Paul Clemente. *cast* Malcolm McDowell, Teresa Ann Savoy, Guido Mannari, John Gielgud, Peter O'Toole, Helen Mirren.
●Nobody wanted anything to do with *Caligula*: Gore Vidal didn't want his name on it, producer Bob Guccione of *Penthouse* didn't want the Italian director to finish it (then didn't want reviewers to see it), the stars didn't want to be associated with it. The appealing idea of a raging loony who has the power to pursue his little whims has attracted and sunk better talents than these. Indeed, dotted throughout there are glimpses of what might have been: Caligula enquiring of an ebbing Gielgud what it's like to die, a death machine that operates like a combine harvester, some exotic sets in Italo-barbaric style. But all in all it's a dreary shambles, directed by Brass *toto drosso con abandimento*. CPea

Callan

(1974, GB, 106 min)
d Don Sharp. *p* Derek Horne. *sc* James Mitchell. *ph* Ernest Steward. *ed* Teddy Darvas. *ad* John Clark. *m* Wilfred Josephs. *cast* Edward Woodward, Eric Porter, Carl Mohner, Catherine Schell, Peter Egan, Russell Hunter, Kenneth Griffith, Veronica Lang.
●If any TV spin-off should work, it's *Callan*, a descendant of Michael Caine's Harry Palmer, a loner, a technician who finds conscience clogging the wheels and his actions reverberating within an ever more disillusioning environment. In fact the film is solid rather than inspired, disastrously taking a good third of its running-time to establish its authority over the big screen. Apart from one brilliant cat-and-mouse game played in cars, most of the ideas seem to remain firmly in the admittedly strong script. Callan has even been awarded a Magnum à la Dirty Harry, and a tricksily filmed 'iron fist' technique to rival Lo Lieh's. VG

Callejon de los Milagros, El

see Midaq Alley

Calle Mayor (The Love Maker/Main Street)

(1956, Sp/Fr, 95 min, b/w)
d/sc Juan Antonio Bardem. *ph* Michel Kelber. *ed* Margarita Ochoa. *ad* Enrique Alarcon. *m* Joseph Kosma. *cast* Betsy Blair, José Suárez, Yves Massard, René Blancard, Dora Doll, Lila Kedrova.
●*Calle Mayor* is adapted from a classic novel of Spanish provincial life by Carlos Arniches, which had previously been filmed in the '30s. Bardem's version of this bitter tale of a woman's oppression was made at the height of Francoism, and had to carry an unconvincing foreword claiming that the story could happen 'anywhere'. When a group of idle young men decide as a joke that one of them should seduce an unmarried woman in her mid-30s, she becomes smitten by him, and the situation turns sourly serious. Bardem's neo-realist pretensions look a trifle thin now, but the film's portrait of a town riddled with prejudice and hypocrisy still packs a weighty punch. The central performance by the un-Spanish seeming Betsy Blair is especially touching. DT

Call Harry Crown

see 99 and 44/100% Dead

Calling All Cats

see 6.5 Special

Call Me

(1987, US, 98 min)
d Sollace Mitchell. *p* John E Quill, Kenneth F Martel. *sc* Karyn Kay. *ph* Zoltan David. *ed* Paul Fried. *pd* Stephen McCabe. *m* David Frank. *cast* Patricia Charbonneau, Stephen McHattie, Boyd Gaines, Sam Freed, Steve Buscemi, Patti D'Arbanville, John Seitz, David Strathairn.
●Anna's boyfriend Alex (Freed) is a supercilious nerd who fits in his fucking around his work and the evening news. When Anna (Charbonneau) starts receiving velvet-voiced phone calls exhorting her to dress sexily and meet in a downtown New York bar, she is intrigued and complies, believing the caller to be Alex. There follows a wonderfully uncomfortable scene when she waits in a sleazy drinking hole surrounded by looming off-cue characters, but Alex doesn't show. In the loo, she earwigs a brutal killing, thus becoming a risk to an organised crime syndicate. Meanwhile the mysterious calls continue, and she

finds herself drawn to someone who, besides alerting her to the erotic potential of oranges, expresses concern for her safety... While Mitchell's directing debut is not slick, it is highly enjoyable, and should do for Jaffa what *Last Tango* did for butter. EP

Call Northside 777

(1947, US, 111 min, b/w)
d Henry Hathaway. *p* Otto Lang. *sc* Jerome Cady, Jay Dratler. *ph* Joseph MacDonald. *ed* J Watson Webb Jr. *ad* Lyle R Wheeler, Mark-Lee Kirk. *m* Alfred Newman. *cast* James Stewart, Richard Conte, Lee J Cobb, Helen Walker, Betty Garde, Kasia Orzazewski, Joanne De Bergh.

●One of the most impressive of Fox's semi-documentary *noir* thrillers shot on location (here Chicago), this sees Stewart as a hard-boiled newspaper reporter latching on to a 'human interest' story of a woman slaving away for years to save the money which may help free her son from prison, and then setting out to prove the man innocent of murder. Besides the generally strong performances and Joe MacDonald's fine monochrome camera-work, what finally impresses about the film is Stewart's gradual development from sceptical scoop-hunter to a committed crusader for justice. Add to that the suggestion that the police are less than willing to be proved wrong in their conviction of Conte (it was a cop that he allegedly killed), and you have an absorbingly intelligent thriller. GA

Call of the Wild, The

(1972, GB/WGer/Sp/It/Fr, 105 min)
d Ken Annakin. *p* Harry Alan Towers. *sc* Harry Alan Towers, Wyn Wells, Peter Yeldham. *ph* John Cabrera. *ed* Thelma Connell. *ad* Knut Solberg. *m* Carlo Rustichelli. *cast* Charlton Heston, Michèle Mercier, Raimund Harmstorf, George Eastman, Maria Rohm.

●Jack London's Yukon yarn of an Alsatian sled-dog and his master has been filmed three times. The 1935 William Wellman version compensated for a tame adaptation by the presence of Clark Gable and Loretta Young; the 1976 telemovie benefited from a tougher James (*Deliverance*) Dickey script; all this has to boast is dreaded multi-national packager Harry Alan Towers, who was still mining the same seam of fool's gold in 1979 with the tax-sheltered *Klondike Fever*. At least Canadian money ensured the right locations for that; here Norwegian snowscapes substitute. PT

Calmness (Shantham)

(2000, Ind, 95 min)
d Jayaraj. *p* PV Gangadharan. *sc* Maadambu. *ph* Ravi Varman. *ed* NP Sathish. *pd* Nemom Pushparaj. *m* Kaithapram. *cast* Seema Biswas, IM Vijayan, KPAC Lalitha, MG Sasi.

●Two old friends grow further and further apart in early adulthood due to their commitment to opposing extremist political parties; the result is hatred, murder and revenge, not to mention grief for their mothers. Well-meaning but schematic, facile, and none too lucid in terms of narrative organisation. Not bad looking, though. GA

Caluga o Menta

(1990, Chile, 100 min)
d Gonzalo Justiniano. *p* Patricia Navarrete. *sc* Gustavo Frias, Gonzalo Justiniano, Juan Andrés Peña. *ph* Gaston Roca. *ed* Claudio Martinez. *m* Jaime de Aguirre. *cast* Mauricio Vega, Aldo Parodi, Patricia Rivadeneira, Cecilia Godoy, Miriam Palacios, Luis Alarlon.

●An effectively gritty account of the nihilistic existence led by a selection of petty criminals, druggies, down-and-outs and prostitutes living on the margins of Chilean society. There's nothing particularly original or insightful about its portrait of disaffected youth, but the actors have talent and the right faces, and Justiniano directs his rambling story with a good sense of economy and detail. GA

Came a Hot Friday

(1984, NZ, 101 min)
d Ian Mune. *p* Larry Parr. *sc* Dean Parker, Ian Mune. *ph* Alun Bollinger. *ed* Ken Zemke. *pd* Ron Highfield. *m* Stephen McCurdy. *cast* Peter Bland, Phillip Gordon, Billy T James, Michael Lawrence, Marshall Napier, Don Selwyn.

●A splendidly engaging Kiwi comic Western set in 1949 and based on the novel by the highly regarded novelist Ronald Hugh Morrieson. Two con-men who make a tidy if perilous living from scamming village bookmakers descend on a one-lamb town just as the local club-owner is committing a spot of arson and murder for the insurance money. After falling out with both clubman and bookie, the merry pranksters meet up with a bizarre Maori who lives in the woods and thinks he's a Mexican bandit, endure much violence, sexual chicanery and sundry perils, and don't end up with the gold. It's sometimes too chirpy and bumptious, and has a hideous soundtrack, but it holds one and cheers the parts that even mint sauce cannot reach. SGr

Camelot

(1967, US, 181 min)
d Joshua Logan. *p* Jack L Warner. *sc* Alan Jay Lerner. *ph* Richard H Kline. *ed* Folmar Blangsted. *pd* John Truscott. *m* Frederick Loewe. *cast* Richard Harris, Vanessa Redgrave, Franco Nero, David Hemmings, Lionel Jeffries, Laurence Naismith, Estelle Winwood.

●This thuddingly dull musical (all false eyelashes and kohl) drowns the Arthurian legend in a sea of pink blancmange and leaves one desperately scanning the horizon for flotsam. All hands lost. Can the actors possibly be taking this farrago seriously? One looks in vain for their private signals to indicate the contrary. Redgrave, to her lasting embarrassment, one suspects, plays Guenevere with absolute sincerity, even when singing 'Where Are the Simple Joys of Maidenhood?' The men's vocal mannerisms make them sound as though they're on the far end of a long-distance telephone. CPe

Camels Are Coming, The

(1934, GB, 80 min, b/w)
d Tim Whelan. *p* Michael Balcon. *sc* Guy Bolton. *ph* Glen MacWilliams, Bernard Knowles. *ed* Frederick Y Smith. *ad* OF Werndorff. *m* Ray Noble, Max Kester, Noel Gay, Jack Beaver. *cast* Jack Hulbert, Anna Lee, Hartley Power, Harold Huth, Allan Jeayes, Peter Gawthorne.

●This wobbly Gainsborough vehicle, produced by Michael Balcon, sends Hulbert of the Camel Corps on an Egyptian drug trafficking investigation; he faces hostile tribesmen and an extremely disobliging 'ship of the desert'. TJ

Camera Buff (Amator)

(1979, Pol, 112 min)
d/sc Krzysztof Kieslowski. *ph* Jacek Petrycki. *ed* Halina Nawrocka. *ad* Rafal Waltenberger. *m* Krzysztof Knittel. *cast* Jerzy Stuhr, Malgorzata Zabkowska, Ewa Pokas, Stefan Czyzewski, Jerzy Nowak.

●Fairly impressive account of an amateur movie-maker who progresses from home movies, via the factory film club, to documentaries of a more political kind. But in improving his technique and his status as a film-maker, he lays himself open to criticism and censorship from the local authorities, and so begins the ideological battle – artistic expression vs political oppression – of Kieslowski's satire. It's not as funny as some critics would have it, and the basic theme is hardly original in Eastern European cinema, but the evocation of the hero's passion for movies, and Stuhr's central performance, manage to make it intelligent entertainment. GA

Camera: Je, The

(1977, US, 88 min)
d Babette Mangolte. *with* Babette Mangolte, Chantal Akerman, Lucinda Childs, Epp Kotkas, Kim Ginsberg.

●This self-portrait of the artist in 1976/77 achieved through subjective camera technique, is actually a kind of diptych. On one side, a photographic session with a series of interesting subjects, some relaxed, some tense and reluctant, whose encounters with the camera emerge as a power struggle, a remorseless battle of wills. On the other, an interminable tour through New York on a clear winter's day, snapping random images of street corners and skyscrapers. Designed to set up a number of dichotomies (people/ cityscapes, interior/exterior, stasis/movement, flatness/depth of field), it all has a sort of satisfying symmetry, but doesn't entirely escape degenerating into a sterile academic exercise. SJo

Cameraman, The

(1928, US, 6,995 ft, b/w)
d Edward Sedgwick. *p* Lawrence Weingarten. *sc* Clyde Bruckman, Lex Lipton, Richard Schayer. *ph* Elgin Lessley, Basil Wrangell. *ed* Hugh Wynn, Basil Wrangell. *cast* Buster Keaton, Marceline Day, Harry Gribbon, Harold Goodwin, Sidney Bracy.

●Keaton's first feature after moving to MGM. That this meant the eventual sacrifice of his career can be seen in the story – Keaton becomes an MGM newsreel camera-man in order to get the girl, who works in the MGM office – and the first half of the film, a series of gags (collapsing bed, reflex-testing, mixed-up bathing suits) second-hand enough to have come out of *Nickelodeon*. But the final sequences make up for this disappointment: Keaton gets involved in a Tong war and (inadvertently) with an organ-grinder's monkey. He shoots exclusive footage, but the monkey steals the film. Keaton returns with an empty camera and is kicked out. Gloomily he goes to the beach. His girl is in a boating accident. Forsaking his camera, he rescues her. The monkey keeps the camera rolling. Keaton gets the girl, and back at MGM, it's the greatest news film they've ever seen...shot by the monkey. A delightful piece of film-making within-a-film which is both an insight into Keaton's own logic, and also, alas, a sort of epitaph. AN

Camera Obscura

(2000, US, 114 min)
d Hamlet Sarkissian. *p* Tassos Kazinos. *sc* Hamlet Sarkissian. *ph* Haris Zambarloukos. *ed* Andrea Zondler. *m* Tigran Mansuryan. *cast* Adam Trese, Ariadna Gil, Cully Fredricksen, VJ Foster, Molly Bryant, Kirk Ward.

●When Jimmy gets a job as crime scene photographer for the LAPD, he enters a world of problems. Unable to cope with the horror he sees, he starts beautifying the corpses and gets involved with police drug deals, causing his domestic life to head for meltdown. From a neat concept, writer/director Sarkissian has fashioned a fast-moving and good-looking thriller that only occasionally overdoes its penchant for visual effects. But the film casts its net too wide. Unsure of its primary focus, it tries to deliver a relationship drama, (corrupt) cop precedural and styleled investigation into the nature of reality and appearances, not pursuing the latter rigorously enough really to lift the project. GE

Cameron's Closet

(1987, US, 87 min)
d Armand Mastroianni. *p* Luigi Cingolani. *sc* Gary Brandner. *ph* Russell Carpenter. *ed* Frank De Palma. *pd* Michael Bingham. *m* Harry Manfredini. *cast* Cotter Smith, Mel Harris, Scott Curtis, Chuck McCann, Leigh McCloskey, Kim Lankford, Gary Hudson, Tab Hunter.

●If nothing else, this muddled horror pic contains so many diverse elements that you can't help wondering what Mastroianni might throw in next. Here, in no particular order, are telekinetic mayhem, psychic premonitions, wigged-out scientists, disconnected dream sequences, a female shrink, a Mayan fetish doll, the now obligatory running down corridors, and an evil, cupboard-dwelling monster which can only be summoned by the innocent mind of a child. Curtis plays a young boy whose exceptional psychic powers have been allowed to run out of control by his scientist father (Hunter) and the latter's assistant (McCann). As a result, Cameron's fertile imagination has conjured up a red-eyed monster which lives in the closet (*any* closet) and tends to do nasty things to anyone he doesn't much like. With its mix of mawkish family stuff and graphic mutilations, this is one closet you'll be happy to come out of. NF

Camila

(1984, Arg/Sp, 105 min)
d Maria Luisa Bemberg. *p* Angel Baldo, Hector Gallardo, Edecio Imbert. *sc* Maria Luisa Bemberg, Beda Cocampo Feijoo, Juan Bautista Stagnaro. *ph* Fernando Arribas. *ed* Luis César d'Angiolillo. *ad* Miguel Rodriguez. *m* Luis Maria Serra. *cast* Susu Pecoraro, Imanol Arias, Hector Alterio, Elena Tasisto, Carlos Muñoz.

●Described by the director as 'a passionate woman's intellectual and sexual seduction of a man she found morally desirable', this is the true story of the doomed amours of a young socialite from the beau monde of Buenos Aires and her Jesuit priest. The historical background (the Rosas dictatorship, 1847) is left somewhat sketchy, and Bemberg, a 62-year-old feminist who made her first film at 58, evidences an over-fondness for the Laura Ashley school of costume drama, all starched petticoats and soft-focus cinematography. But, presided over by an unholy trinity of Church, State and family, Susu Pecoraro as Camila conducts her romance with proper abandon and a vibrant intelligence that burns bright and true amid the frilly period fashions. SJo

Camilla

(1993, Can/GB, 95 min)
d Deepa Mehta. *p* Christina Jennings, Simon Relph. *sc* Paul Quarrington. *ph* Guy Dufaux. *ed* Barry Farrell. *pd* Sandra Kybartas. *m* John Altman, Daniel Lanois. *cast* Jessica Tandy, Bridget Fonda, Elias Koteas, Maury Chaykin, Graham Greene, Hume Cronyn, Atom Egoyan.
●Freda Lopez (Fonda), an aspiring songwriter, is going nowhere fast with her career, and her marriage has lost its sparkle; she and her graphic-artist husband (Koteas) take a vacation on Peabo Island, in the Deep South, in the hope of re-energising their lives. Freda forms a close friendship with Camilla (Tandy), eccentric owner of their beach home, who enjoys launching into a fantasy world concerning her own past career as a classical violinist. The pair hit the road and bond, each inspiring the other to unfold her life that little bit more fully. A feel-good romantic comedy which wears its heart a little too obviously on its sleeve. JBa

Camille

(1922, US, 5,600 ft, b/w)
d Ray Smallwood. *sc* June Mathis. *ph* Rudolph Bergquist. *ad* Natacha Rambova. *cast* Alla Nazimova, Rudolph Valentino, Arthur Hoyt, Zeffie Tilbury, Rex Cherryman, Edward Connelly.
●Typically cockeyed Hollywoodian notion of how to approach Art, from self-styled exoticist Nazimova. Pointlessly updating Dumas' tale of the tubercular Mlle Gautier's doomed romance with her too socially respectable lover to 1920s Paris, the movie is all Style and no substance: art deco sets (designed by Rudy's later wife Natacha Rambova), hammy histrionics from Nazimova, and not a camera movement in sight. A pity, then, that the initially subdued Valentino's rather impressive performance is allowed to degenerate into overstatement, and then to disappear, as Alla indulges in interminable death throes. GA

Camille

(1936, US, 108 min, b/w)
d George Cukor. *sc* Zoe Akins, Frances Marion, James Hilton. *ph* William H Daniels, Karl Freund. *ed* Margaret Booth. *ad* Cedric Gibbons. *m* Herbert Stothart. *cast* Greta Garbo, Robert Taylor, Lionel Barrymore, Elizabeth Allan, Henry Daniell, Laura Hope Crews
●MGM's high camp 'funereal' decor, the judicious adaptation of Dumas' play, Cukor's gay sensibility in directing women, and William Daniels' atmospheric photography – all these made *Camille* Garbo's most popular film. Her aura of self-knowledge, inner calm and strength of purpose intermeshed finely with elements of the production to produce a tragedy of love-as-renunciation which was closer in spirit to *Hedda Gabler* than to Dumas. As Roland Barthes says of the character: 'Marguerite is aware of her alienation, that is to say she sees reality as alienation…she knows herself to be an object but cannot think of any destination for herself other than that of ornament in the museum of the masters'. The camera's reliance upon 'The Face' of Garbo was never more obvious than in the final shot of the film. It is through the face that death is signalled, in a long-held close-up of Camille's last few moments that fades into darkness on the point of her demise. MSu

Camille Claudel

(1988, Fr, 174 min)
d Bruno Nuytten. *p* Bernard Artigues. *sc* Bruno Nuytten, Marily Goldin. *ph* Pierre Lhomme. *ed* Joelle Hache, Jeanne Kef. *pd* Bernard Vézat. *m* Gabriel Yared. *cast* Isabelle Adjani, Gérard Depardieu, Alain Cuny, Laurent Gréville, Philippe Clévenot, Katrine Boorman, Danielle Lebrun, Madeleine Robinson.
●Paris 1885: by night, a sculptress fills a suitcase with clay from a workman's trench. Such is the intense dedication of Camille Claudel (Adjani), whose desire to win favourable patronage from Rodin (Depardieu) drives her into a disastrous affair with that womanising egotist, thus alienating her family (including poet Paul). As ever in movies about artistic genius, a break-up sends Camille round the bend – a surefire guarantee of prolific productivity, the inevitable neglect of which, by a blinkered bourgeois intelligentsia, pushes her into ever more manic creativity and misery. Nuytten's film would seem far less banal if it were half the length; at almost three hours, we are simply left with trite ideas about artistic inspiration, and a glossy costumer that makes all too predictable points about the ambivalent nature of insanity, the importance of status and money in the art world, and the position of women in a male-dominated society. GA

Camille without Camellias

see Signora senza camelie, La

Camisards, Les

(1971, Fr, 110 min)
d/p René Allio. *sc* René Allio, Jean Jourdheuil. *ph* Denys Clerval. *ed* Sylvie Blanc. *ad* Nicole Rachevine. *m* Philippe Arthurys. *cast* Philippe Clevenot, Jacques Debary, Gérard Desarthe, Dominque Labourier, François Marthouret, Rufus, Hubert Gignoux.
●Set in the Cévennes region of France in the 18th century, *Les Camisards* is about a band of Huguenot rebels who turn their anger at the repressive tactics of a Catholic state into active confrontation (burning churches, hanging informers, guerilla tactics against the army). When it first appeared at the London Film Festival in 1972, it was described as 'Brechtian, distanced, cool rather than emotional and romantic'. True, but it sometimes falls *between* the stools of an all-out costume drama and a political film about repression. It has fine moments though. The rebels roam about a lazy summer countryside, egged on by religious fanatic Abraham Mazel (Desarthe), occasionally meeting the incompetent state troopers in miniature pitched battles. As the red-jacketed soldiers fall to their knees to fire, the camisards respond by singing a song of solidarity: enough to make your heart beat a little faster.

Cammina Cammina

(1983, It, 155 min)
d/p/sc/ph/ed/ad Ermanno Olmi. *m* Bruno Nicolai. *cast* Alberto Fumagalli, Antonio Cucciarrè, Eligio Martellacci, Renzo Samminiatesi.
●Directed, produced, written, photographed and edited all by Ermanno Olmi, this vast film follows the ramblings of a ragged caravan across an Africa that looks suspiciously like Lower Tuscany. After a deal of time it becomes apparent that these are the Magi, following yonder star, while clad in ethnic sacking. Olmi treats the whole escapade with a delightful irreverence, which apparently has not amused the Vatican.

Campana del Infierno, La (The Bell of Hell/The Bell from Hell)

(1973, Sp/Fr, 106 min)
d/p Claudio Guerin Hill. *sc* Santiago Moncada. *ph* Manuel Rojas. *ed* Magdalena Pulido. *ad* Eduardo Torre de la Fuente. *m* Adolfo Waitzman. *cast* Renaud Verley, Viveca Lindfors, Alfredo Mayo, Maribel Martin.
●On the whole a reasonably thought out baroque tale about a young man whose aunt is trying to get him certified in order to collect his inheritance. In return, he plans elaborate revenge against her and her three beautiful daughters. The complexities of the central character are well handled, and there's enough evidence to suggest that some care went into the film's making. So even when the plot flags, it remains good to look at (a mixture of Buñuel and Roger Corman), apart from some graphic scenes in an abattoir. Lindfors is excellent as the aunt. In a tragic irony, the director jumped or fell to his death from the bell-tower after shooting was completed. CPea.

Campsite Massacre

see Final Terror

Camp Thiaroye (Camp de Thiaroye)

(1987, Sen/Tun/Alg, 152 min)
d Ousmane Sembene, Thierno Faty Sow. *p* Mamadou Mbengue, Mustapha Ben Jemia. *sc* Ousmane Sembene, Thierno Faty Sow. *ph* Ismail Lakhdar Hamina. *ed* Kahen Attia. *ad* El-Hadj Abdoulaye Diouf. *m* Ismaila Lo. *cast* Ibrahima Sane, Sigiri Bakara, Gustave Sorgho, Camara Med Donsogho, Hamed Camara, Ismaila Cissé.
●In 1939, young men in French African colonies were recruited to fight the 'World's' war in Europe. Five years later, some returned to Camp Thiaroye to await back pay and demobbing. Tension between men and officers, complaints about chow, a misadventure in a brothel: staples of the basic training and/or prison camp genre are all present and correct. But although the influence of years in France is apparent (he fought in WWII himself), Sembene's is an African sensibility; and the after-effects of the culture clash (literal and metamorphical) precipitated by Hitler is but one of the themes in a subtle and moving picture. Through a series of everyday incidents, we gradually realise the extent of the French (white) officers' racism; the hypocritical games they play seem ironic at first, but lead to a shameful and bloody end. This, in microcosm, is a story of colonialism, told from the receiving end and taken to a radical conclusion. Sembene and Sow have made what is not only a humane, passionate film, but an honest and vital memorial to those men who died, after the war, at Camp Thiaroye. TCh

Canadian Bacon

(1995, US, 90 min)
d Michael Moore. *p* Michael Moore, David Brown, Ron Rotholz, Steve Golin. *sc* Michael Moore. *ph* Haskell Wexler. *ed* Geraldine Peroni, Wendey Stanzler, Michael Berenbaum. *pd* Carol Spier. *m* Elmer Bernstein. *cast* Alan Alda, John Candy, Kevin Pollak, Rhea Perlman, Bill Nunn, Rip Torn, Kevin J O'Connor, James Belushi, Dan Aykroyd.
●Moore took a mischievous but pointed look at American mores in *Roger & Me* and in his small-screen series *TV Nation.* This satirical sideswipe at the Land of the Free is, however, a stifferoonie. The plot has one joke: hard-pressed US President Alda, a fumbling liberal in the Clinton tradition, needs a war, or something, to up his ratings and win a second term, but after the end of the Cold War there are no enemies left – so the White House staff decide to take on the evil empire to the north, *Canada!* Dismal days. TJ

Canadians, The

(1961, US, 85 min)
d Burt Kennedy. *p* Herman E Webber. *sc* Burt Kennedy. *ph* Arthur Ibbetson. *ed* Douglas Robertson. *m* Muir Mathieson. *cast* Robert Ryan, John Dehner, Torin Thatcher, John Sutton, Teresa Stratas, Burt Metcalfe.
●Kennedy's first feature, a Western about the Sioux flight to Canada following the death of Custer at Little Big Horn, running into trouble with a rancher (Dehner), but kept to the straight and narrow by Ryan's Mountie. Despite Ryan's performance, a completely inferior film, with a trite script constantly slanted by the presence of Brooklyn opera singer Teresa Stratas as a squaw. DP

Canal Zone

(1977, US, 175 min, b/w)
d/p/ed Frederick Wiseman. *ph* William Brayne.
●First of a disappointing trilogy of Wiseman documentaries on export versions of Americana (followed by the military sketches of *Sinai Field Mission* and *Manoeuvre*), in which the pettily formal rituals of life around the Panama Canal are registered as if the politically sensitive zone had no social, economic, cultural or geographic identity beyond its backdrop function as a bicentennial home from home. Unilluminating and, at nearly three hours, deadly boring. PT

Canary Yellow Bicycle, The (To Kanarini Podilato)

(1999, Greece, 91 min)
d Dimitris Stavrakas. *p* Alekos Papayorgiou. *sc* Dimitris Stavrakas, Stavros Tsiolis, Vasilis Spiliopoulos. *ph/ed* Dinos Katsouridis. *ad*

Tassos Zografos. *m* Nikos Kypourgos. *cast* Dimitris Alexandris, Giorgos Halaris, Thanos Grammenos, Manos Vakoussis, Nikos Georgakis.
● Aris (Alexandris), a new teacher at an Athens primary school, slowly realises that Lefteris (Halaris), a slow learner from a neglectful home, has suffered years of disabling ridicule from his classmates, and misunderstanding, if not downright prejudice, from the teaching staff. Aris realises from Lefteris' ability to build his own bike (the yellow one of the title) that the boy's abilities have not been sufficiently tapped. Can Aris build up the boy's confidence in the face of indifference/hostility from all around? Stavrakas nurtures fine performances from his tow principles, and his heart is in all the right places, but despite the film's undoubted worthiness and charm, occasional overemphatic direction and an under-contextualised screenplay, render it overly simplistic and ultimately unsatisfying. WH

Can-Can

(1960, US, 131 min)
d Walter Lang. *p* Jack Cummings. *sc* Dorothy Kingsley, Charles Lederer. *ph* William H Daniels. *ed* Robert Simpson. *ad* Lyle Wheeler, Jack Martin Smith. *songs* Cole Porter. *cast* Frank Sinatra, Shirley MacLaine, Maurice Chevalier, Louis Jourdan, Juliet Prowse.
● Sinatra is the lawyer who defends the aesthetic merits of the can-can in the Paris of the 1890s in this vulgar and gaudy version of the Cole Porter musical. MacLaine and Prowse provide the dancing, while Jourdan and Chevalier inject Hollywood's idea of Gallic charm. The film has a small place in cinema history for being savaged by Nikita Khrushchev in the course of his visit to America. Terrible. PH

Candidate, The

(1972, US, 110 min)
d Michael Ritchie. *p* Walter Coblenz. *sc* Jeremy Larner. *ph* John Korty, Victor Kemper. *ed* Richard A Harris, Robert Estrin. *pd* Gene Callahan. *m* John Rubinstein. *cast* Robert Redford, Peter Boyle, Don Porter, Allen Garfield, Karen Carlson, Quinn Redeker, Melvyn Douglas.
● Ritchie and Redford's follow-up to *Downhill Racer* is one of the more intelligent films to have been made about political machinations in America. Redford plays an idealistic young lawyer, concerned with grass roots issues, refusing to play the media games that are so much part of the political campaign he becomes involved in, and determined to do and say exactly what he feels. But gradually the desire for the power by which he can implement his ideas leads him into fatal compromise. A fairly obvious story, perhaps, but one that is helped enormously both by Ritchie's reluctance to move away from simulated realism into melodramatic plotting, and by his customary generosity, clear-eyed and unsentimental, towards his characters. And the trap of blaming the inexorable move towards compromise and sellout either on a lone individual (which would suggest that otherwise everything would be all right) or on the system (a vague concept which would excuse the protagonist) is carefully avoided. Rather, the symbiotic relationships into which Redford and his agents, publicists and colleagues willingly, if reluctantly, allow themselves to fall, make for a far more thorough depiction of the seductive nature of power. GA

Candido Erotico

(1978, It, 94 min)
d Claudio De Molinis. *p* Dino Di Salvo. *sc* Romano Bernardi. *ph* Emilio Loffredo. *ed* Giancarlo Venarucci. *ad* Marco Canevari. *m* Nico Fidenco. *cast* Lilli Carati, Mircha Carven, Maria Baxa, Ajita Wilson.
● Another immaculate conception from Cinecittà's booming 'Vatican' stable, a solemn rehearsal of soft-core rituals: troilism, voyeurism, snide cracks at women's liberation. The glossy young gigolo-hero fucks mother for her money and daughter for lurv, but on the Catholic fun-first-pay-later principle ends up both married *and* impotent. Oedipus + hip guilt = yuk! CA

Candleshoe

(1977, US, 101 min)
d Norman Tokar. *p* Ron Miller. *sc* David Swift, Rosemary Anne Sisson. *ph* Paul Beeson. *ed* Peter Boita. *ad* Albert Witherick. *m* Ron Goodwin. *cast* David Niven, Helen Hayes, Jodie Foster, Leo McKern, Veronica Quilligan, Ian Sharrock.
● Comedy-adventure with a hit-and-miss list of Disney ingredients: street-smart (formerly 'spunky') Jodie Foster, Uncle David Niven wearing eccentric disguises, sweet Ms Hayes, winsome orphans, a slapstick climax. Candleshoe is the stately Warwicks manor occupied by Lady Gwendolyn, her butler and her multi-racial brood. The problem of its upkeep would be solved by the discovery of the treasure buried by a pirate ancestor; Foster, the delinquent double of Hayes' long-lost granddaughter is imported by the villains to find it first. AN

Candy

(1968, US/It/Fr, 124 min)
d Christian Marquand. *p* Robert Haggiag. *sc* Buck Henry. *ph* Giuseppe Rotunno. *ed* Giancarlo Cappelli. *ad* Dean Tavoularis. *m* David Grusin. *cast* Ewa Aulin, Marlon Brando, Richard Burton, James Coburn, Walter Matthau, Charles Aznavour, John Huston, John Astin, Elsa Martinelli, Ringo Starr.
● As adapted by Buck Henry, Terry Southern's genuinely, wickedly funny novel – a *Candide*-style sex satire, about a naive American teenage girl whose innocence automatically provokes the men she meets to feverish, rapacious lust – is neither erotic nor funny. Aulin, besides being unable to act, can't manage an American accent; her various sexual encounters are ludicrously over-long; and quite what the film is meant to be satirising remains obscure throughout. Indeed, it's a typically undisciplined example of late '60s movie-making, dependent on a bland series of caricature cameos from decent actors who should have known better. Burton's Dylan Thomas parody alleviates the tedium temporarily, but Marquand simply doesn't seem to know what directing is all about; the overall effect is profoundly exhausting. GA

Candyman

(1992, US, 98 min)
d Bernard Rose. *p* Alan Poul, Steve Golin, Sigurjon Sighvatsson. *sc* Bernard Rose. *ph* Anthony B Richmond. *ed* Dan Rae. *ad* Jane Ann Stewart. *m* Philip Glass. *cast* Virginia Madsen, Tony Todd, Xander Berkeley, Kasi Lemmons, DeJuan Guy, Vanessa Williams.
● This faithful, scary and visually imaginative adaptation of Clive Barker's story 'The Forbidden' casts Madsen as a Chicago doctoral student researching an urban myth about a hook-handed killer called Candyman. A series of murders in the city's run-down projects are linked with stories about a figure who appears when you say his name five times in front of a mirror. But are the frightened residents and elaborate graffiti proof that Candyman exists, or simply evidence of their wish to believe in the bogeyman? Following up on *Paperhouse*, Rose stages the suspense and horror with skill and panache, making this one of the best sustained horror movies for some years. NF

Candyman 2: Farewell to the Flesh

(1995, US, 94 min)
d Bill Condon. *p* Sigurjon Sighvatsson, Steve Golin, Gregg Fienberg. *sc* Rand Ravich, Clive Barker, Mark Kruger. *ph* Tobias Schliessler. *ed* Virginia Katz. *pd* Barry Robison. *m* Philip Glass. *cast* Tony Todd, Kelly Rowan, Timothy Carhart, Veronica Cartwright, William O'Leary, Bill Nunn, Matt Clark.
● *Candyman* was the best Clive Barker adaptation to date. This follow-up is a travesty of both its literary source and the original film. The only logical sequel would have been 'Candywoman', centred on Virginia Madsen's transformed character. Instead, we have a tedious, fright-free prequel featuring Todd's vanquished Candyman. Director Condon and his writers have misunderstood the myth, which holds that the legendary hook-handed killer exists only in the spaces between the many stories about him; there can, therefore, be no definitive account of his origins. Most of this film, however, is spent explaining how, after the Civil War, Daniel Robataille, the artistic son of a black slave, fell in love with a landowner's daughter, made her pregnant and was punished for his sins. All of which we already knew, and little of which is relevant to a modern-day story about New Orleans schoolteacher Annie Tarrant (Rowan), whose father was slashed to death some years ago. Now Annie is intrigued by her pupil Matthew's obsessive drawings, all of which depict a tall black figure being pursued by a vengeful white mob. Atrocious. NF

Candy Mountain

(1987, Switz/Fr/Can, 92 min)
d Robert Frank, Rudy Wurlitzer. *p* Ruth Waldburger. *sc* Robert Frank, Rudy Wurlitzer. *ph* Pio Corradi. *ed* Jennifer Augé. *pd* Brad Ricker, Keith Currie. *m* Dr John, David Johnsen, Leon Redbone. *cast* Kevin J O'Connor, Harris Yulin, Tom Waits, Bulle Ogier, Roberts Blossom, Leon Redbone, Dr John, Rita MacNeil, Joe Strummer, Laurie Metcalf, Jayne Eastwood, Kazuko Oshima.
● A witty anti-road-movie with a subplot on the nature of the artist. Julius (O'Connor, who looks streetwise but plays with aching vunerability) is young, broke, and dreams of rock star fame and fortune. He lands a job with a dodgy band and an assignment to track down Elmore Silk (Yulin), a reclusive, masterly maker of acoustic guitars. Things don't go well: Julius loses his girl and car at the first gas station. From then on, his search is determined by providence and a host of (perfectly cast) off-the-wall characters – a glamorous Frenchwoman (Ogier) stuck out in the middle of the prairies, a father and son laying down the law in barely inhabited North Canada, a woman who kidnaps him for company. As Silk's plaid-clad brother, Tom Waits rasps credibility into the script, telling Julius to 'play golf instead of travelling without knowing where you're going': so begins a steady undermining of the road as a symbol of freedom. The journey ends in Nova Scotia with our James Dean-ish hero humbled by the road but not quite broken. It's left to Elmore Silk to hammer the nail in the coffin of his ideals. Not beat and not downbeat, the general message is a reaffirmation of life after Kerouac. EP

Candy Stripe Nurses

(1974, US, 77 min)
d Alan Holleb. *p* Julie Corman. *sc* Alan Holleb. *ph* Colin Campbell. *ed* Allan Holzman. *ad* Jane Rum. *m* Eron Tabor, Ron Thompson. *cast* Candice Rialson, Robin Mattson, Maria Rojo, Kimberly Hyde, Roger Cruz, Rick Gates, Rod Haase, Dick Miller.
● A terrific pulp B feature which relates the adventures of three such renegade 'stripers' (young orderlies) who variously cure the ailments, physical and spiritual, of a Chicano wrongly accused of masterminding a robbery, a self-consumed rock star in an advanced state of doped lethargy, and a basketball player hooked on rippling muscles and amphetamines. Holleb keeps the pace exuberantly frenetic, darting from genuine pathos to quality Cheech and Chong styled humour within the comic strip framework. Particularly effective are the performances which, apart from an excessive parody of the rock star, stay on the restrained side of caricature. In addition, numerous sharply observed details, a tight and spicy script, a splendidly brash punk rock score, and good use of location (including loudly coloured street graffiti and a labyrinthine car repairs yard) make this New World production fairly essential viewing for devotees of exploitation movies. IB

Cane Toads – An Unnatural History

(1987, Aust, 46 min)
d/sc Mark Lewis. *ph* Jim Frazier, Wayne Taylor. *ed* Lindsay Frazer. *m* Martin Armiger. *narrators* Stephanie Lewis, Paul Johnstone.
● Optimistically imported into Australia to curb the destructive sugar cane beetle in 1935 – 'Now we've got these cane grubs by the balls!' – the cane toad proved useless. Worse, it bred at an astonishing rate, choked the billabongs, ate everything including ping-pong balls, emitted toxins to the touch, and possessed a sex drive so strong that it would mate with mud. 'They're a bit of a rough bunch', comments one of the numerous and hilarious interviewees. But in some areas of Queensland, the cane toad is regarded with reverence and even affection – 'They're mates' – and statues have been erected to the warty oversized amphibian. Little girls put little frocks on them and put them in little beds;

junkies smoke them and hallucinate; a citizen impersonated one on the highway and was fined. The most curious nature film since *The Hellstrom Chronicle*. BC

Cannery Row

(1982, US, 120 min)
d David S Ward. *p* Michael Phillips. *sc* David S Ward. *ph* Sven Nykvist. *ed* David Bretherton. *pd* Richard MacDonald. *m* Jack Nitzsche. *cast* Nick Nolte, Debra Winger, Audra Lindley, Frank McRae, M Emmet Walsh, Tom Mahoney.

● Based on John Steinbeck's novel about a skid row community full of lovable tramps and prostitutes. Nolte is the ex-baseball star turned marine biologist whose life is changed by the love of a good woman, Winger. Sentimental comedies must walk a fine line between mawkishness and insipidity: although this one slips off the wire occasionally, a strong script, careful treatment and some spirited performances keep it aloft. John Huston serves as narrator. MH

Cannibal (Ultimo Mondo Cannibale)

(1976, It, 92 min)
d Ruggero Deodato. *p* Giorgio Carlo Rossi. *sc* Tito Carpi, Gianfranco Clerici, Renzo Genta. *ph* Marcello Masciocchi. *ed* Daniele Alabiso. *pd* Walter Patriarca. *m* Ubaldo Continiello. *cast* Massimo Foschi, Me Me Lai, Ivan Rassimov, Sheik Razak Shikur, Judy Rosly.

● An oil prospector is captured in a remote Philippine rain forest by a tribe of stone age cannibals, and imprisoned until rescued by the inevitable lustful lady cannibal. Cheapo exploitation director Deodato takes his 'true story' plot, average exploiter rituals and distinctly paunchy hero far too seriously for the film not to be laughable despite its two strong ingredients: excellent cro-magnon acting and a surprising amount of 'frank' (because anthropological?) male nudity. CA

Cannibal Holocaust

(1979, It/Col, 98 min)
d Ruggero Deodato. *p* Franco Di Nunzio, Franco Palaggi. *sc* Gianfranco Clerici. *ph* Sergio d'Offizi. *ed* Vincenzo Tomassi. *pd* Massimo Antonello Geleng. *m* Riz Ortolani. *cast* Robert Kerman, Francesca Ciardi, Perry Pirkanen, Luca Barbareschi, Salvatore Basile, Ricardo Fuentes, Gabriel Yorke, Paolo Paolini.

● A young film crew vanishes in the Colombian rainforest while shooting an anthropology documentary. Their footage, boldly retrieved by a university prof (Kerman), reveals the horrible truth behind their disappearance. Slightly foreshadowing *Blair Witch* then, but here the evils wrought by – and significantly upon – a barbaric tribe of cannibals are not left to the imagination. Despite poor dubbing, this is a more interesting and unusual film than its schlock-horror title and subject matter might suggest. The intense climax is approached with excellent cinematography and editing, as savage cruelty is eerily juxtaposed with beautiful scenery and Riz Ortolani's terrific score. Its pointed attack on exploitative film-making seems somewhat rich in the circumstances, but this is well made, uniquely unpleasant and almost deserving of its huge cult status. DCo

Cannibals, The (I Cannibali)

(1969, It, 87 min)
d Liliana Cavani. *p* Enzo Doria, Bino Cicogna. *sc* Italo Moscati, Liliana Cavani, Frabrizio Onofri. *ph* Giulio Albonico. *ed* Nino Baragli. *ad* Ezio Frigerio. *m* Ennio Morricone. *cast* Britt Ekland, Pierre Clémenti, Tomas Milian, Francesco Leonetti, Delia Boccardo, Marino Mase.

● Made directly after *Galileo*, whose strengths Cavani enlarges and develops, this also postulates a primacy of human and emotional response over the nihilism of *The Night Porter* (made four years later). In this modern day reworking of *Antigone*, Cavani's striking visual sense illuminates her subject sufficiently to overcome doubts about some of the '60s conceits. Where she manages to evoke her Fascist state as exceptionally normal, the film works exceptionally well; where she obsessively indulges in hyperbolic scenes of Fascist ritual, it all but scuttles itself. VG

Cannibal Women in the Avocado Jungle of Death (aka Piranha Women in the Avocado Jungle of Death)

(1988, US, 90 min)
d JD Athens. *p* Gary W Goldstein. *sc* JD Athens. *ph* Robert G Knouse. *ad* Kimberly Charles Rees. *m* Carl Dante. *cast* Shannon Tweed, Bill Maher, Barry Primus, Adrienne Barbeau, Karen Mistal, Brett Stimely.

● Following a military failure, ethno-historian Margaret Hunt (Tweed) is sent by the CIA into the Avocado Jungle to track down eminent radical feminist Dr Kurtz, a former chat-show personality turned man-eating Piranha Woman. Aided only by dong-headed guide Maher (not so much a walking erection as a semi-ambulant willy) and the vacuous Bunny, a student whose idea of a good time involves licorice ropes, Hunt sets off into the heart of trashiness where she encounters The Donahews, a tribe of emasculated men who shower her with gifts of handmade pot-holders, and a splinter tribe of women who hate the Piranha's penchant for eating men with guacamole dip (they opt for clam dip themselves). Amid a plethora of 'garbage genre' movies which fail to fulfil the promise of their titles, this is something of a relief, aided by a genuinely funny script, a tip-top performance from Maher, and film trivia aplenty for those who want it. MK

Cannonball (aka Carquake)

(1976, US/HK, 93 min)
d Paul Bartel. *p* Samuel W Gelfman. *sc* Paul Bartel, Donald C Simpson. *ph* Tak Fujimoto. *ed* Morton Tubor. *ad* Michel Levesque. *m* David A Axelrod. *cast* David Carradine, Bill McKinney, Veronica Hamel, Gerrit Graham, Robert Carradine, Judy Canova, Martin Scorsese, Joe Dante.

● In many ways this is the film Bartel wanted *Death Race 2000* to be. Once again starring David Carradine and constructed around another Trans-American race, it is both better and worse. The comedy cut from *Death Race* by producer Roger Corman – here guesting as the DA who tries to ban the race – is now present with a vengeance: Gerrit Graham's would-be country singer and a marvellous comic-strip pile-up of cars provide the film's highlights. That said, *Cannonball* lacks its predecessor's dramatic tension, and by the middle of the film Bartel's disregard for narrative in favour of a series of jokes leaves no dramatic resolution. The movie also features a number of in-joke guest appearances, including (in addition to Corman and Bartel himself) Martin Scorsese, Jonathan Kaplan, Joe Dante, Allan Arkush and Sylvester Stallone. PH

Cannonball Run, The

(1980, US, 95 min)
d Hal Needham. *p* Albert S Ruddy. *sc* Brock Yates. *ph* Michael Butler. *ed* Donn Cambern, William Gordean. *ad* Carol Wenger. *m* Al Capps. *cast* Burt Reynolds, Roger Moore, Farrah Fawcett, Dom DeLuise, Dean Martin, Sammy Davis Jr, Jack Elam, Adrienne Barbeau, Jackie Chan, Peter Fonda.

● Stars' home movie, with Burt Reynolds and the gang having a terrific time with the camera and each other. Looks like something knocked off on rest days from *Smokey and the Bandit II*. The last five minutes, when they show out-takes of flubbed lines, etc, are hysterical. The rest is strictly for those willing to pay for a series of TV chat show performances. MB

Cannonball Run II

(1983, US, 108 min)
d Hal Needham. *p* Albert S Ruddy. *sc* Hal Needham, Albert S Ruddy, Harvey Miller. *ph* Nick McLean. *ed* William Gordean, Carl Kress. *ad* Thomas E Azzari. *m* Al Capps. *cast* Burt Reynolds, Dom DeLuise, Dean Martin, Sammy Davis Jr, Marilu Henner, Telly Savalas, Shirley MacLaine, Ricardo Montalban, Henry Silva, Frank Sinatra, Sid Caesar, Jackie Chan.

● Cannonball Baker set the first New York to LA road record back in the '20s with a time of 60 hours for the 3,000 miles. When Congress effectively castrated the big-engined muscle cars of the '60s with smog emission laws and a blanket 55mph speed limit, Brock Yates, a motoring journalist, inaugurated the highly illegal 'Cannonball Baker Sea-to-Shining-Sea Memorial Trophy Dash' in 1971. US Grand Prix star Dan Gurney brought the time down to 35 hrs 54 mins, and Hollywood stuntman Needham once took part in a camouflaged ambulance, went on to make the first *Cannonball Run*, a lot of money, and then this sequel, in which the old Hollywood 'Rat Pack' of Sinatra, Martin, Davis and MacLaine are reunited for the first time since *Ocean's 11* (1960). There are nun jokes, mafia jokes, big breast jokes, karate jokes, *Jaws* jokes, more big breasts. It's a long ride. CPea

Can She Bake a Cherry Pie?

(1983, US, 90 min)
d/sc Michael Emil. *p* MH Simonsons. *sc* Henry Jaglom. *ph* Robert Fiore. *ed* Henry Jaglom. *m* Karen Black. *cast* Karen Black, Michael Emil, Michael Margotta, Frances Fisher, Martin Harvey Friedberg.

● This takes Jaglom one step further in cornering the US market in the lost and the lonely, with a personal style that is pure innocent delight. Emil is the sort of middle-aged baldy who combs the few remaining strands over his dome, wears socks under his sandals, and spends his time busking his way through endless free-form monologues about his tottering love-life. Crossing over his shambling rhetoric is Black, giving the performance of her career, as an unfocused kook who hasn't a clue what she wants but is fairly certain that she's being followed by her ex-husband. The film is essentially a plotless reverie of lyrical whimsy encircling the usual New York crazies in a slow waltz. There is more than a little magic abroad: Orson Welles (in footage borrowed from Jaglom's own *A Safe Place*) tries to make some very large animals disappear; Black can sing a mean blues. It ought to fall apart in its own cheerful indulgence, leaving all concerned with egg on their faces; but somehow it's all done with such a loopy benevolence that it emerges as the damn nicest film since Astaire stopped dancing. CPea

Cantata of Chile (Cantata de Chile)

(1976, Cuba, 119 min)
d Humberto Solás. *p* Orlando de la Huerta, Camilo Vives. *sc* Humberto Solas. *ph* Jorge Herrera. *ed* Nelson Rodriguez. *ad* Luis Lacosta. *m* Leo Brouwer. *cast* Nelson Villagra, Shenda Román, Eric Heresmann, Alfredo Tornquist, Leonardo Perucci, Peggy Cordero.

● A stylised fresco of constant class struggle interfacing the mythic dimensions of a reconstruction of the 1907 Iquique massacre, when 3,600 Latin American workers died following strikes in the British-owned nitrate mines. A fervent, inspirational hymn to resistance and solidarity, the film encodes its political analysis in its montage of sounds and images, which occasionally overwhelm in their emotive intensity (unfortunately so in a couple of passages of excruciating violence). In part it recalls Jancsó, and is in some way the film Bertolucci would have liked to have made of *1900*, vindicating the epic spectacle as a progressive form. PT

Can't Buy Me Love

(1987, US, 94 min)
d Steve Rash. *p* Thom Mount. *sc* Michael Swerdlick. *ph* Peter Lyons Collister. *ed* Jeff Gourson. *pd* Donald Light Harris. *m* Robert Folk. *cast* Patrick Dempsey, Amanda Peterson, Courtney Gains, Tina Caspary, Seth Green, Sharon Farrell, Dennis Dugan.

● Ronald Miller (Dempsey) is a nerd who wants to be in with the cool clique: the elite jocks and cheerleaders of your average American co-ed high school. Miller pays cheerleading princess (Peterson) to step out with him for a month; the ploy works, and pretty soon Ronald has gained a whole new wardrobe and a whole new attitude. So cool does he become that he fails to notice the real warm feelings that the lovely Cindy has developed for him; so when their time is up, he drops her as planned and begins to work his way through her friends. The director has a feel for this shopping-with-Mummy's- plastic milieu, but the theme of peer group pressure and the almost universal human need for acceptance is compromised by a script of very Californian piety. Otherwise a slight but not unenjoyable movie. MC

Canterbury Tale, A

(1944, GB, 124 min, b/w)
d/p/sc Michael Powell, Emeric Pressburger. *ph* Erwin Hillier. *ed* John Seabourne. *pd* Alfred

Junge. *m* Allan Gray. *cast* Eric Portman, Sheila Sim, John Sweet, Dennis Price, Esmond Knight, Charles Hawtrey, George Merritt, Edward Rigby.
●Michael Powell's extraordinary film proceeds from the faintly bizarre story of three characters (a land girl, a British sergeant and a US sergeant) who, arriving by the same train in a small Kent village, make friends and set out to unmask the mysterious 'glue man' who pours glue on to the hair of girls out late at night with servicemen. But the film shows a sharp awareness of the tensions underlying a country community in wartime – from rural resentment of the influx of outsiders to more long-term fears of the decay of a traditional social order. An assertion of stability to counterbalance these is provided by Powell's almost mystical sense of historical continuity, epitomised by Canterbury Cathedral and the Pilgrims' Way as captured in Erwin Hillier's lyrical photography. Though infuriatingly difficult to categorise, the film is bold, inventive, stimulating and extremely entertaining. AS

Canterbury Tales, The (I Racconti di Canterbury)

(1971, It/Fr, 109 min)
d Pier Paolo Pasolini. *p* Alberto Grimaldi. *sc* Pier Paolo Pasolini. *ph* Tonino Delli Colli. *ed* Nino Baragli. *ad* Dante Ferzetti. *cast* Pier Paolo Pasolini, Laura Betti, Franco Citti, Ninetto Davoli, Hugh Griffith, Derek Deadman, Jenny Runacre.
●Like *The Decameron*, a broad canvas on which is writ large and bawdy the life of the people. We are again plummeted into a world of lecherous ladies, ugly old husbands, willing and ready pages, ending with a superb final fling in a gaudy red Sicilian hell, accompanied by a salvo of farts. As usual Pasolini creates visual magic where other directors would never see beyond the banal, and the humour is as rich as ever; but there is a distinct feeling of strain, not to say waste, about this film. The best tales are of course the blacker ones: Franco Citti as the Devil, in the Friar's tale, blackmailing sexual offenders; or the Steward's tale, a neat variation on one of the hoariest sex gags around.

Can't Help Singing

(1944, US, 89 min)
d Frank Ryan. *p* Felix Jackson. *sc* Lewis R Foster, Frank Ryan. *ph* Woody Bredell, W Howard Greene. *ed* Ted J Kent. *ad* John B Goodman, Robert Clatworthy. *songs* Jerome Kern, EY Harburg. *cast* Deanna Durbin, Robert Paige, Akim Tamiroff, David Bruce, Ray Collins, Thomas Gomez.
●Lively Technicolor musical bearing more than a slight resemblance to *Oklahoma*, with a grown-up Durbin as the girl travelling against her father's wishes to meet her fiancé in California but falling for another man instead. A spirited score by Jerome Kern and EY Harburg, plus some fine location photography, allow a strong supporting cast to display its talents. GA

Can't Stop the Music

(1980, US, 124 min)
d Nancy Walker. *p* Allan Carr, Jacques Morali, Henri Belolo. *sc* Bronte Woodard, Allan Carr. *ph* Bill Butler. *ed* John F Burnett. *pd* Stephen Hendrickson. *m* Jacques Morali. *cast* The Village People, Valerie Perrine, Bruce Jenner, Steve Guttenberg, Tammy Grimes, June Havoc, Barbara Rush.
●The big joke in this disco-musical is having gay butch stereotypes of both sexes carry on as if they were straight. Six dopey members of the Village People, all with bursting flies, fall for Valerie Perrine (who has a just-platonic relationship with her male room-mate), while the Lesbian advertising agent swoons into the arms of a man. It follows that most of the dialogue is gay in-jokes, with the odd music biz joke for variety. A wretchedly sub-standard score from Jacques Morali and production numbers of exceptional tackiness round things off. Oh, and yes, there is fun in the showers in the 'YMCA' number. TR

Can You Keep It Up for a Week?

(1974, GB, 94 min)
d Jim Atkinson. *p* Elton Hawke. *sc* Robin Gough. *ph* Ricky Briggs. *ed* David Docker. *ad* Jacquemine Charrot-Lodwidge. *m* Dave Quincy. *cast* Jeremy Bulloch, Jill Damas, Neil Hallett, Richard O'Sullivan, Sue Longhurst, Valerie Leon.
●Embarrassing British sex comedy, featuring Jeremy Bulloch (late of the *Billy Bunter* TV series) and – God help him – Richard O'Sullivan. The solitary laugh comes in the credits at the end: 'The producers acknowledge the assistance of the management of the Holiday Inn hotels at Swiss Cottage and Heathrow in making this film'. Surprising that it took as long as 12 days to shoot…mind you, it was quite a trek out to the airport in those days before the Piccadilly Line extension was complete. AN

Cape Fear

(1961, US, 105 min, b/w)
d J Lee Thompson. *p* Sy Bartlett. *sc* James R Webb. *ph* Sam Leavitt. *ed* George Tomasini. *ad* Alexander Golitzen, Robert Boyle. *m* Bernard Herrmann. *cast* Gregory Peck, Robert Mitchum, Polly Bergen, Lori Martin, Martin Balsam, Jack Kruschen, Telly Savalas, Barrie Chase.
●An irredeemable criminal exacts his revenge on the family of a lawyer who put him away. This supremely nasty thriller – originally severely cut by the British censor – boasts great credentials: a source in John D MacDonald's novel *The Executioners*, Mitchum as the sadistic villain (a bare-chested variant on his *Night of the Hunter* role), Peck as the epitome of threatened righteousness, seedy locations in the Southern bayous, and whooping music by Bernard Herrmann. If director Thompson isn't quite skilful enough to give the film its final touch of class (many of the shocks are just too planned), the relentlessness of the story and Mitchum's tangibly sordid presence guarantee the viewer's quivering attention. DT

Cape Fear

(1991, US, 128 min)
d Martin Scorsese. *p* Barbara DeFina. *sc* Wesley Strick. *ph* Freddie Francis. *ed* Thelma Schoonmaker. *m* Bernard Herrmann, Elmer Bernstein. *cast* Robert De Niro, Nick Nolte, Jessica Lange, Juliette Lewis, Joe Don Baker, Robert Mitchum, Gregory Peck, Martin Balsam, Illeana Douglas.
●While one can't deny the technical bravura of this remake of J Lee Thompson's 1961 thriller, it's hard not to feel that Scorsese is selling himself short. Max Cady (De Niro) – the manic, bible-quoting rapist who sets out to wreak sadistic revenge on the family of defence attorney Sam Bowden (Nolte), who suppressed evidence that might have kept him out of jail – comes over less as a credible human being or as Scorsese's 'malignant spirit' of the Bowdens guilt, more as a virtually indestructible monstrosity. Likewise, the Bowdens' newly acquired 'sins' – flirtations with adultery for Sam, unforgiving neuroses for his wife (Lange), nascent interest in sex for his daughter (Lewis) – neither deserve the punishment the film inflicts on them, nor lend substance to the conceit that the family must embrace the violent nemesis Cady represents if it is to find redemption. Except for Lewis and a typically solid turn by Baker, the performances are largely unimaginative in this overblown horror-schlocker. GA

Caper of the Golden Bulls, The (aka Carnival of Thieves)

(1966, US, 105 min)
d Russell Rouse. *p* Clarence Greene. *sc* Ed Waters, David Moessinger. *ph* Harold Stine. *ed* Chester W Schaeffer, Robert Wyman. *ad* Hal Pereira. *m* Vic Mizzy. *cast* Stephen Boyd, Yvette Mimieux, Giovanna Ralli, Walter Slezak, Vito Scotti.
●Abominable caper movie in which a jewel robbery is planned to occur (cue for much gaudy local colour) during the festival of bulls at Pamplona. So manaically dreary that even the ever-reliable Walter Slezak can do nothing to save it. TM

Cape Town Affair, The

(1967, US/SAf, 103 min)
d/p Robert D Webb. *sc* Harold Medford, Samuel Fuller. *ph* David Millin. *ed* Peter Grossett. *ad* Bert Aurik. *m* Bob Adams. *cast* James Brolin, Jacqueline Bisset, Claire Trevor, John Whiteley, Bob Courtney, Siegfried Mynhardt.
●Horrendously unworthy remake of Fuller's classic *Pickup on South Street*, with the action switched to South Africa. Brolin takes over Richard Widmark's role as the pickpocket stealing a girl's handbag, only to discover in it microfilm which leads them both into espionage and murder. GA

Capitães de Abril

see Captains of April

Capitaine Conan

(1996, Fr, 132 min)
d Bertrand Tavernier. *p* Alain Sarde. *sc* Jean Cosmos, Bertrand Tavernier. *ph* Alain Choquart. *ed* Luce Grunenwaldt. *ad* Guy-Claude François. *m* Oswald D'Andrea. *cast* Philippe Torreton, Samuel Le Bihan, Bernard Le Coq, Catherine Rich, Claude Rich, Claude Brosset.
●It's 1918 and all is strangely quiet on the Bulgarian front, where a French regiment is fighting an odd sort of war with crossbows and sling-shots. After the armistice the unit is posted to Bucharest, where discipline slackens (armed robbery, desertion) and trench pals Conan and Lt Norbert fall out over questions of loyalty. To their dismay the regiment entrains eastward to crush the Bolsheviks, and further slaughter ensues. A peacetime coda shows Conan, aggressive dynamo in combat, pottering ineffectually around his provincial backwater. For all the lavish production values and thoughtful performances, this adaptation of Roger Vercel's novel is disappointing. The narrative lacks focus, and Tavernier's fastidiousness (no horrors of war here) rules out the sort of close-up detail that might have jolted the thing to life. BBa

Capitaine Fracasse, Le

(1942, Fr, 108 min, b/w)
d Abel Gance. *sc* Abel Gance, Claude Vermorel. *ph* Nicholas Hayer. *ed* Lucienne Déméocq. *ad* Henri Mahé. *m* Arthur Honegger. *cast* Fernand Gravey, Assia Noris, Jean Weber, Jean Fleur, Paul Oettly, Maurice Escande.
●Forget *Napoleon* and its vaulting ambition. Directed with bare competence, this is a limp adaptation of Théophile Gautier's historical fantasy (one of the source books of camp) about a penniless baron who joins a group of travelling players after falling for the *ingénue*. Both the theatrical and the swashbuckling larks remain dispiritingly lifeless. TM

Capitanes d'avril

see Captains of April

Capitano, Il

(1991, Swe/Fin/Ger/Den, 110 min)
d Jan Troell. *p* Jan Troell, Göran Setterberg. *sc* Per Olov Enquist. *ph/ed* Jan Troell. *pd* Stig Limer. *m* Lars Akerlund, Sebastian Öberg. *cast* Antti Reini, Maria Heiskanen, Berto Marklund. Antti Vierikko, Harri Mallenius.
●Jan Troell's plodding tale of a punkish teenage couple thieving their way across Finland suffers from memories of Malick's *Badlands*. The girl wants out after the boy kills her rabbits, but can't break the spell of the tyrannical psycho who winds up shooting a family. All we know about him is generic: he watches Sid Vicious doing 'My Way' on the motel TV, likes car crash video games, and cuts the cards to determine their destination. Inordinately slow, with endlessly similar highways and little faith in the audience's uptake. Unsensational. BC

Capone

(1975, US, 101 min)
d Steve Carver. *p* Roger Corman. *sc* Howard Browne. *ph* Vilis Lapenieks. *ed* Richard C Meyer. *ad* Ward Preston. *m* David Grisman. *cast* Ben Gazzara, Susan Blakely, Harry Guardino, John Cassavetes, Sylvester Stallone, Frank Campanella, Royal Dano, Dick Miller.
●The failure of Corman's *St Valentine's Day Massacre* apparently led to his quitting directing. So quite why he produced this lavish though palpably inferior version of the Capone story remains something of a mystery. Tracing the rise and fall of its hero from Union Street punk to syphilitic madman, *Capone* begins well enough as a resolutely profane alternative to Corman's version ('Give you five grand? I wouldn't piss up

your arse if you were on fire'), and emphasises well enough that in an amoral world of 'free enterprise' gangsters are merely less hypocritical than anyone else. But as the complex internecine warfare unfolds (with good emphasis on the nationalities involved), the script becomes increasingly schematic, finally degenerating into one endless shoot-out. CPe

Caporal Epinglé, Le (The Elusive Corporal/ The Vanishing Corporal)

(1962, Fr, 106 min, b/w)
d Jean Renoir. *p* JW Beyer. *sc* Jean Renoir, Guy Lefranc. *ph* Georges Leclerc. *ed* Renée Lichtig. *ad* Wolf Witzmann. *m* Joseph Kosma. *cast* Jean-Pierre Cassel, Claude Brasseur, Claude Rich, OE Hasse, Jean Carmet, Mario David, Jacques Jouanneau.

● A deceptively slight tale of the attempts by three Frenchmen to escape from a Nazi prison camp during World War II, this late addition to Renoir's impressively wide-ranging oeuvre is nevertheless suffused with the same warm and generous humanism as the great *Règle du Jeu* or *Grande Illusion*. Though the whole thing is played as a comedy, the scenes in the prison camp display Renoir's characteristically sharp eye for regional and class differences, even under the yoke of common suffering. The final parting on the bridge in Paris is a scene which will ring loud and true for anyone with the slightest sense of the value of freedom and friendship. NF

Caprice

(1967, US, 98 min)
d Frank Tashlin. *p* Aaron Rosenberg, Martin Melcher. *sc* Jay Joyson, Frank Tashlin. *ph* Leon Shamroy. *ed* Robert Simpson. *ad* Jack Martin Smith, William J Creber. *m* Frank De Vol. *cast* Doris Day, Richard Harris, Ray Walston, Jack Kruschen, Lilia Skala, Edward Mulhare.

● Characteristically dotty Tashlin comedy about industrial espionage. Incoherently scripted, heavily miscast (Day and Harris hardly add up to a Jerry Lewis), with its few bright moments bogged down in a wearisome spoof of the then fashionable spy cycle. TM

Capricious Summer (Rozmarné Leto)

(1968, Czech, 75 min)
d Jiri Menzel. *p* Jan Libora, Vladimir Kalina. *sc* Jiri Menzel, Vaclav Nyvlt. *ph* Jaromir Sofr. *ed* Jirina Lukesova. *pd* Oldrich Bosak. *m* Jiri Sust. *cast* Rudolf Hrusínsky, Vlastimil Brodsky, Frantisek Rehák, Jirí Menzel, Jana Drchalová.

● Menzel's second feature is adapted from a novel by Vladislav Vancura, rated alongside *The Good Soldier Schweik* as one of the twin masterpieces of Czech comic literature. Some of the dialogue's subtler social and philosophical relevance may prove elusive, but it hardly matters as three middle-aged friends – priest, retired army officer, and owner of the bathing-station – enjoy some end-of-season bathing in a small provincial watering-place, meanwhile discoursing desultorily on their favourite topics (philosophy, strategy, and fleshly pleasures). Suddenly, like a visitation from another planet, a caravan arrives, bringing a sad, stick-like showman who sets up in the village square. His tacky little tightrope-and-conjuring show is suddenly illuminated by real magic when his wife appears, a delicate, honey-haired vision of beauty in black mask and yellow dress. From that moment, with its glimpse of something lost and forgotten, a kind of autumnal madness invades the trio, until the caravan moves on, leaving them brooding again as the sun goes down on their last Indian summer of romance. Menzel's evocation of place and mood, of soft summer days threatened by winter, of regret for lost youth and opportunity, of hope for things to come, is perfection. TM

Capricorn One

(1977, US, 124 min)
d Peter Hyams. *p* Paul N Lazarus III. *sc* Peter Hyams. *ph* Bill Butler. *ed* James Mitchell. *pd* Albert Brenner. *m* Jerry Goldsmith. *cast* Elliott Gould, James Brolin, Brenda Vaccaro, Sam Waterston, OJ Simpson, Hal Holbrook, Karen Black, Telly Savalas.

● The premise of *Capricorn One* is so intrinsically arresting that it almost saves the film from the sheer incompetence of its script: as a breathless public stands by for the first American flight to Mars, the astronauts are bundled away to a desert location where NASA intends to secretly simulate the whole thing for the TV networks of the world. For a while the film makes the most of the surrealism of this eerie conceit with some effective juxtapositions of illusion and reality as the spacemen play kiddy-cars in their clandestine studio. But pretty soon the project gets bogged down in innumerable difficulties, not helped by the awfulness of most of the dialogue. The climactic introduction of Telly Savalas in a crop-dusting plane must rank as one of the most desperate measures to save a thriller since William Castle hung luminous skeletons from the cinema roof. DP

Captain Blood

(1935, US, 118 min, b/w)
d Michael Curtiz. *p* Harry Joe Brown, Gordon Hollingshead. *sc* Casey Robinson. *ph* Hal Mohr, Ernest Haller. *ed* George Amy. *ad* Anton F Grot. *m* Erich Wolfgang Korngold. *cast* Errol Flynn, Olivia de Havilland, Basil Rathbone, Lionel Atwill, Ross Alexander, Guy Kibbee, Henry Stephenson, Robert Barrat.

● The movie that launched both Flynn and the '30s cycle of swashbucklers. Conceived by Warner Brothers as a rival to MGM's *Mutiny on the Bounty*, it's a straightforward adaptation of Sabatini's adventure novel about a young doctor who starts as a deportee, succeeds as a pirate, and winds up as Governor of Jamaica, with Olivia de Havilland on his arm. Less florid sword-play than in later movies, but the formula is all there. RG

Captain Boycott

(1947, GB, 93 min, b/w)
d Frank Launder. *p* Sidney Gilliat, Frank Launder. *sc* Frank Launder, Wolfgang Wilhelm. *ph* Wilkie Cooper. *ed* Thelma Myers. *ad* Edward Carrick. *m* William Alwyn. *cast* Stewart Granger, Kathleen Ryan, Cecil Parker, Mervyn Johns, Noel Purcell, Niall MacGinnis, Alastair Sim, Robert Donat.

● Lively and intelligent historical drama about the peaceful but spirited battles (in the 19th century) between Irish landowners (led by Boycott, whose name became a synonym for ostracism) and the farmers he tries to evict. Pretty good on period reconstruction, and enlivened no end by a classy cast. GA

Captain Corelli's Mandolin

(2001, US/Fr/GB, 129 min)
d John Madden. *p* Tim Bevan, Eric Fellner, Kevin Loader, Mark Huffam. *sc* Shawn Slovo. *ph* John Toll. *ed* Mick Audsley. *pd* Jim Clay. *m* Stephen Warbeck. *cast* Nicolas Cage, Penélope Cruz, John Hurt, Christian Bale, David Morrissey, Irene Papas, Vicki Maragaki.

● In 1940, on the Greek island of Cephalonia, Pelagia (Cruz) defies the wishes of her father Dr Iannis to become engaged to the fiercely patriotic fisherman Mandras, who enlists to fight the Italians in Albania. Though the letters she writes to her fiancé receive no reply, she firmly resists overtures from Capt Antonio Corelli (Cage), a music-loving bon viveur of sophistication, kindness and charm billeted at Iannis' house when the Italians occupy the island – at least, until attraction gets the better of her. But this is war: loyalty, betrayal and hatred run deep. What fans of Louis de Bernières' bestseller will make of this glossy period romance will depend partly on their reactions to the changes made by Shawn Slovo's screenplay – notably, the elimination of a gay subplot and a lightening of tone. Cage makes a decent stab at the rather implausibly fine Corelli, Hurt is his reliable self as Iannis, and Bale is mostly effective as the troubled Mandras; Cruz, however, neither looks Greek, nor brings much depth to her role. The film's perfectly watchable, but it's never more than that. GA

Captain Horatio Hornblower R.N.

(1950, GB, 117 min)
d/p Raoul Walsh. *sc* Ivan Goff, Ben Roberts, Aeneas MacKenzie. *ph* Guy Green. *ed* Jack Harris. *ad* Tom Morahan. *m* Robert Farnon. *cast* Gregory Peck, Virginia Mayo, Robert Beatty, Denis O'Dea, Terence Morgan, James Robertson Justice, Stanley Baker.

● CS Forester's seafaring epic of the 19th century adapted as a surging tribute to 'bravery', to long-gone 'leaders', and as much a study of the heroic spirit as an action romp. Peck is Hornblower, Mayo the initially ill-fated love interest, and Walsh seems more interested in their inner life and emotional vulnerability, which makes for an oddly limpid (but often quite beautiful) and non-dynamic work from such a primal force. CW

Captain Jack

(1998, GB, 100 min)
d Robert Young. *p* John Goldschmidt. *sc* Jack Rosenthal. *ph* John McGlashan. *ed* Edward Mansell. *pd* Simon Holland. *m* Richard Harvey. *cast* Bob Hoskins, Peter McDonald, Sadie Frost, Anna Massey, Gemma Jones, David Troughton, Maureen Lipman, Patrick Malahide, Michele Dotrice.

● This cosily populist, sentimental comedy of everyday heroism makes those old Ealing fables look comparatively tough, relevant and even contemporary. Hoskins is the ornery, eccentric boat owner who gives up his less than lucrative tourist trips of Whitby harbour to make an epic journey to an uninhabited Arctic island to commemorate his hero, the long dead and neglected Capt Scoresby; his crew, naturally, is a motley selection of misfits and no-hopers who end up – surprise! – redeemed and reconciled by his mad anti-bureaucratic venture. A couple (literally) of funny lines apart, this is tired, tepid and, given the land- and seascape, woefully televisual. GA

Captain January

(1936, US, 75 min, b/w)
d David Butler. *sc* Sam Hellman, Gladys Lehman, Harry Tugend. *ph* John F Seitz. *songs* Louis Silvers, Lew Pollack. *cast* Shirley Temple, Guy Kibbee, Slim Summerville, Buddy Ebsen, June Lang.

● Miss Curly Top, here named Star (yuk!), is orphaned in a shipwreck, brought up by an old lighthouse keeper, hounded by the education authorities, and dazzling in her scholastic prowess. Oh yes, she sings and dances too. Sticky going. TM

Captain Johnno

(1988, Aust, 100 min)
d Mario Andreacchio. *p* Jane Ballantyne. *sc* Rob George. ph Roger Dowling. *ed* Andrew Ellis. *pd* Vicki Niehus. *m* Stephen Mattes. *cast* Damien Walters, John Waters, Joe Petruzzi, Michele Fawdon, Rebecca Sykes.

● A children's tale which illustrates silent life in a world dripping with sound. Quaint, moving, and often humorous, it centres on partially-deaf 12-year-old Johnno (Walters, himself deaf). The setting is a small coastal town where Johnno spends every available moment skin-diving – anything to take his mind off a clumsy, uncaring father (Waters) and taunting classmates. Only his mother (Fawdon) and sister (Sykes) marginally understand his closed world, and new depression comes with his sister's imminent departure for boarding school. Cue the arrival of Italian migrant Tony (Petruzzi) – equally ridiculed for his lack of English – and the start of a close friendship. When father plans his enrolment in a special school, however, Johnno ups and runs… Waters and Fawdon excepted, the performances are quite excellent (Petruzzi especially), and for low-budget film-making, it really drums the message home. DA

Captain Kronos – Vampire Hunter

(1972, GB, 91 min)
d Brian Clemens. *p* Albert Fennell, Brian Clemens. *sc* Brian Clemens. *ph* Ian Wilson. *ed* James Needs. *pd* Robert Jones. *m* Laurie Johnson. *cast* Horst Janson, John Carson, John Cater, Shane Briant, Caroline Munro, Ian Hendry.

● Even by latter-day Hammer standards, writer-director Clemens transfuses movie vampire lore outrageously, and introduces conventions from a host of other pulp forms. Kronos is an unmistakably Germanic comic strip hero with a crusading zeal for his profession (Stan Lee out of Lang's *Siegfried*). By medieval standards he's distinctly cosmopolitan – carries a samurai sword, smokes dope, meditates; is accompanied on his travels by the scholarly Hieronymous Grost as he rescues distressed damsels from pillory or despatches bullies in Falstaffian taverns. Though Clemens manages sly quotes from the likes of *Nosferatu* and *The Seventh Seal*, the film has absolutely no pretensions beyond being a thoroughly endearing entertainment, and succeeds admirably despite the pastiche of incongruous conventions. RM

Captain Nemo and the Underwater City

(1969, GB, 106 min)
d James Hill. *p* Bertram Ostrer. *sc* Pip Baker, Jane Baker, A Wright Campbell. *ph* Alan Hume. *ed* William Lewthwaite. *ad* Bill Andrews. *m* Wally Stott. *cast* Robert Ryan, Chuck Connors, Nanette Newman, John Turner, Luciana Paluzzi, Bill Fraser.

●Jules Verne's Nemo and his undersea kingdom had been the inspiration for numerous special effects work-outs in Hollywood since the silent days, but here it was the MGM-British contingent who were charged with topping the splendours of Disney's *20000 Leagues Under the Sea*, with a recycled yarn of a shipwrecked sextet rescued and then held captive by the venerable captain of the *Nautilus*. Nicely naïve stuff. PT

Captain Ron

(1992, US, 100 min)
d Thom Eberhardt. *p* David Permut, Paige Simpson. *sc* Thom Eberhardt, John Dwyer. *ph* Daryn Okada. *ed* Tina Hirsch. *m* Nicholas Pike. *cast* Kurt Russell, Martin Short, Mary Kay Place, Meadow Sisto, Benjamin Salisbury, Paul Anka.

●Would-be seadog Short inherits old boat and sets sail for adventure in the Caribbean only to have sozzled captain Russell land the whole crew in deep trouble. Queasy ocean-going comedy, not helped by Kurt's Robert Newton impersonation. TJ

Captains Courageous

(1937, US, 116 min, b/w)
d Victor Fleming. *p* Louis D Lighton. *sc* John Lee Mahin, Marc Connelly, Dale Van Every. *ph* Harold Rosson. *ed* Elmo Veron. *ad* Cedric Gibbons. *m* Franz Waxman. *cast* Spencer Tracy, Lionel Barrymore, Freddie Bartholomew, Mickey Rooney, Melvyn Douglas, John Carradine.

●Archetypal MGM family fodder, with rich brat Bartholomew falling overboard from an ocean liner, and getting saved by Portuguese fisherman Tracy, who knocks the stuffing out of the spoilt kid and teaches him a few of the less luxurious lessons of life. Based on a Kipling story, it's hardly great art, but it passes the time. GA

Captains of April (Capitães de Abril/Capitanes d'avril/ aka April Captains)

(2000, Fr/It/Port/Sp, 123 min)
d Maria De Medeiros. *p* Javier Castro, Concha Díaz, Ricardo Evole. *sc* Eve Deboise, Maria De Medeiros. *ph* Michel Abramowicz. *ed* Jacques Witta. *pd* Guy-Claude François. *m* António Vitorino D'Almeida, (song) Zeca Afonso. *cast* Stefano Accorsi, Maria De Medeiros, Joaquim de Almeida, Frédéric Pierrot, Fele Martínez, Manuel João Vieira, Mercanto Del Castro.

●Recognisable to international audiences for her performances in Henry and June and *Pulp Fiction*, De Medeiros' directorial debut is a head-on attempt to record the events of Portugal's 1974 revolution, in which a section of the military, disgusted at domestic repression and bloody colonial conflict, instituted a benign coup. If the history is not familiar, then the opening scenes might be disorienting, as a number of characters and strands are introduced quickly into the preface to the uprising, when the singing of a popular tune on the radio signalled the beginning of the non-violent ousting of dictator Salazar. De Medeiros then focuses exclusively on the first hours, weaving personal stories in among the larger social shifts. She displays real commitment to and pride in what happened, but the dramatic challenge in capturing the energy of a largely unopposed takeover goes unresolved.The relative lack of initial context, meanwhile, suggests this labour of love might deliver most effectively for domestic audiences. GE

Captain's Paradise, The

(1953, GB, 89 min, b/w)
d/p Anthony Kimmins. *sc* Alec Coppel, Nicholas Phipps. *ph* Ted Scaife. *ed* Gerard Turney-Smith. *ad* Paul Sheriff. *m* Malcolm Arnold. *cast* Alec Guinness, Celia Johnson, Yvonne De Carlo, Charles Goldner, Miles Malleson, Peter Bull.

●Lightly likeable farce about a ferryboat captain whose enviable life with two wives – one in Tangier, one in Gibraltar – inevitably begins to come unstuck. Not exactly sophisticated, it benefits from restrained, civilised performances from an excellent cast. GA

Captain's Table, The

(1958, GB)
d Jack Lee. *p* Joseph Janni. *sc* John Whiting, Bryan Forbes, Nicholas Phipps. *ph* Christopher Challis. *ed* Frederick Wilson. *ad* Michael Stringer. *m* Frank Cordell. *cast* John Gregson, Peggy Cummins, Donald Sinden, Nadia Gray, Maurice Denham, Richard Wattis.

●Cargo ship skipper Gregson, having his boorish horizons rapidly widened when he takes command of an ocean liner, is the fulcrum of this class satire co-written by Bryan Forbes. Peggy Cummins, never in British films offered a challenge remotely comparable to that she accepted in *Gun Crazy*, plays one of the shipboard rivals for a status-weighted seat at Gregson's side. PT

Captain Stirrick

(1982, GB, 90 min)
d/p Colin Finbow. *sc* David Scott, Jeremy James Taylor. *ph* Arnos Richardson. *ed* Colin Finbow. *m* David Scott, Jeremy James Taylor. *cast* Julian Silvester, Jason Kemp, Toby Robertson, Christopher Donkin.

●The ballad of *Captain Stirrick* (produced by the Children's Film Unit), to be sung to the tune of 'Oranges and Lemons': Victorian children sit locked up in prison/Telling tales of adventure to keep up their spirits/The newest among them tells a story in his turn/'Bout Captain Stirrick, and his bold gang of kids/Who pick pockets and purses to trade for their supper/At a fair out at Smithfield Captain Ned meets misfortune/ Betrayed by his temper and a friend he's arrested/So much for the plot. The real charm of this film/Is it's the work of children, on both sides of the camera/Dickensian horror and Grange Hill type heroes/Plus rarefied humour, may be too much for parents/For kids it's a treat, it'll keep 'em off the streets. FD

Captive

(1985, GB/Fr, 98 min)
d Paul Mayersberg. *p* Don Boyd. *sc* Paul Mayersberg. *ph* Mike Southon. *ed* Marie Thérèse Boiche. *pd* Voytek. *m* Edge, Michael Berkeley. *cast* Irina Brook, Oliver Reed, Xavier Deluc, Corinne Dacla, Hiro Arai, Nick Reding.

●Mayersberg's first feature is as richly allusive and as teasingly multi-layered as his scripts for Roeg, *The Man Who Fell to Earth* and *Eureka*. The basis is a Patti Hearst-style tale of an heiress, kept more or less secluded in a castle by her doting tycoon father, who is kidnapped by terrorists from equally privileged backgrounds and subjected to a mixture of brain-washing tortures and love until she comes to recognise the sham of her life. It's a film about change, about discovery of self and the rejection of received values. But it is also a fairy-tale, a nightmare, an operatic fantasy (the music is marvellous) in which unreality holds sway right from the spellbound opening evocation of a turreted castle in the moonlight. Thereafter, as the princess is rescued from her ogre-father by the young Japanese terrorist who sets up as her Prince Charming, a complex weave of parallels and mirror images illuminates the path of her discovery that she has escaped one captivity merely to fall into another. Stunningly shot and with a knockout performance from Oliver Reed, it's as strange and magical a movie about childhood as *Les Enfants Terribles*. TM

Captive, La (The Captive)

(2000, Fr/Bel, 118 min)
d Chantal Akerman. *p* Paulo Branco. *sc* Chantal Akerman, Eric de Kuyper. *ph* Sabine Lancelin. *ed* Claire Atherton. *ad* Christian Marti. *cast* Stanislas Merhar, Sylvie Testud, Olivia Bonamy, Liliane Rovère, Françoise Bertin, Aurore Clément, Vanessa Larré.

●Akerman returns to top form with this strange but compelling version of Proust's *La Prisonnière*. Set in (just about) modern-day Paris, it charts the effects of the festering jealousy felt by wealthy young Simon towards his seemingly innocent and defenceless lover Ariane, whom he keeps cooped up in their apartment lest her occasional forays outside for singing lessons tempt her into (improbable) sexual escapades with her girlfriends. Pared in the Bressonian manner, but inflected with an almost operatic intensity, the film transcends/ eschews naturalism to create an almost timeless parable about the deadeningly obsessive/possessive perversities of many male-female relationships. The superb use of Rachmaninov's *Isle of the Dead* is particularly effective. GA

Captive City, The

(1952, US, 90 min, b/w)
d Robert Wise. *p* Theron Warth. *sc* Karl Kamb, Alvin Josephy Jr. *ph* Lee Garmes. *ed* Robert Swink. *m* Jerome Moross. *cast* John Forsythe, Joan Camden, Harold J Kennedy, Marjorie Crosland, Ray Teal, Martin Milner.

●Crime melodrama with crusading small-town newspaper editor Forsythe exposing organised crime, despite collusion of corrupt police force and Mafia threats against his life. The earnest plot is nothing to write home about, but the effective use of documentary-style location shooting and deep-focus photography was innovatory for its day. NF

Captive du Désert, La (Captive of the Desert)

(1990, Fr, 101 min)
d Raymond Depardon. *p* Pascale Dauman, Jean-Luc Ormieres. *sc/ph* Raymond Depardon. *ed* Roger Ikhle, Camille Cotte, Pascale Charolais. *m* Jean-Jacques Lemtre. *cast* Sandrine Bonnaire, Dobi Kor, Fadi Taha, Badei Barka, Dobi Wachink.

●Based on the experience of political kidnappee Françoise Claustre, Depardon's rigorously understated film is short on event but long on presence. The story is rudimentary – a woman lives in captivity with a desert tribe, makes a desultory escape attempt, and is finally released – but the film is extraordinary in its ability to evoke her experience, with its total dislocation of space and time, and above all its fundamental monotony. The image of the desert here is worlds apart from the spuriously mystical dunescape of *The Sheltering Sky*. Depardon's own photography depicts a very material place with its own timetable and demands, the wilderness unfolding prosaically across the screen like some austere colour-field canvas. Acquainting us intimately with the life of the tribe, but without ever coming across as an ethnological document, the film's observation of minutiae is quite transfixing. JRo

Captive Heart, The

(1946, GB, 108 min, b/w)
d Basil Dearden. *p* Michael Balcon. *sc* Angus Macphail, Guy Morgan. *ph* Douglas Slocombe. *ed* Charles Hasse. *ad* Michael Relph. *m* Alan Rawsthorne. *cast* Michael Redgrave, Mervyn Johns, Basil Radford, Jack Warner, Jimmy Hanley, Rachel Kempson, Gordon Jackson.

●Decent, plodding attempt to tell it like it was in a German prisoner of war camp, which still manages to deal almost exclusively in stereotypes (every part comfortably tailored to a familiar character actor) and to wave a flag or two (what with rousing choruses of 'Roll Out the Barrel' drowning out the nasty propaganda emitted by the camp loudspeakers). Redgrave almost makes something of his character as a Czech prisoner who assumes a dead Englishman's identity and is forced for his own protection to write love letters to the widow. But with credibility barely enhanced by establishing shots filmed in occupied Germany, even he is finally swamped by the soap-opera atmosphere. TM

Captive of the Desert

see Captive du Désert, La

Captives

(1994, GB, 100 min)
d Angela Pope. *p* David M Thompson. *sc* Frank Deasy. *ph* Remi Adesfarin. *ed* Dave King. *pd* Stuart Walker. *m* Colin Towns. *cast* Tim Roth, Julia Ormond, Keith Allen, Richard Hawley, Jeff Nuttall, Bill Moody, Peter Capaldi, Siobhan Redmond, Annette Badland.

● Rachel (Ormond) is a dentist who works part-time at an unnamed London prison. An inmate, Philip (Roth), slips her a note asking her to visit him, and she does. They agree to meet in a nearby cafe when Philip's on day-release, and end up making love in the lavatory, but their affair cannot remain secret for long. It's a mark of director Pope's assurance, and the conviction of the performers, that this somewhat far-fetched set-up doesn't overshadow the proceedings. Gripping and economical, this is a romance shot like a thriller. Ormond throws herself into the role, giving a tremendously honest, passionate performance, well matched by a surprisingly sexy Roth. Inevitably, perhaps, the claustrophobia takes on some negative connotations (the film was made for the BBC and that shows round the edges), but at least Pope has the measure of her material: a truly dangerous love story. TCh

Car, The

(1977, US, 98 min)
d Elliot Silverstein. *p* Marvin Birdt, Elliot Silverstein. *sc* Dennis Shryack, Michael Butler, Lane Slate. *ph* Gerald Hirschfeld. *ed* Mary McCroskey. *ad* Loyd S Papez. *m* Leonard Rosenman. *cast* James Brolin, Kathleen Lloyd, John Marley, RG Armstrong, Ronny Cox, John Rubinstein.

● A demonic black limousine, with no driver behind its tinted windows, races around exterminating the inhabitants of a small Californian town. Interminably drawn out, with some good special effects but its characters hauled straight out of the cracker-barrel, it has nowhere near the same minatory charge as Spielberg's *Duel*. TM

Carabiniers, Les (The Riflemen/The Soldiers)

(1963, Fr/It, 80 min, b/w)
d Jean-Luc Godard. *p* Georges de Beauregard. *sc* Roberto Rossellini, Jean Gruault, Jean-Luc Godard. *ph* Raoul Coutard. *ed* Agnes Guillemot. *ad* Jean-Jacques Fabre. *m* Philip Arthuys. *cast* Marino Masè, Albert Juross, Geneviève Galéa, Catherine Ribéro.

● Godard's strangest movie, based on a political play and nurtured along as a project by Rossellini. Two moronic thugs (with ironically 'classical' names) join up as soldiers and pillage the world in a global war; they return home to their equally moronic wives and display their spoils. Godard juxtaposes their mindless exploits with extensive archive footage of warfare. His presentation of the sheer idiocy of war admits moments of grotesque humour (one of the soldiers sees his first-ever movie and tries to enter the screen), but it's mostly a cold and pitiless vision. Perhaps the most usefully extreme film of its kind ever made. TR

Caravaggio

(1986, GB, 93 min)
d Derek Jarman. *p* Sarah Radclyffe. *sc* Derek Jarman. *ph* Gabriel Beristain. *ed* George Akers. *pd* Christopher Hobbs. *m* Simon Fisher Turner. *cast* Nigel Terry, Sean Bean, Tilda Swinton, Nigel Davenport, Robbie Coltrane, Michael Gough.

● As Caravaggio (excellently played by Terry) lies dying at Porto Ercole in 1610, his mind drifts back over a short life of extraordinary passion: his relationship with his model, Ranuccio Thomasoni, who posed perhaps as the muscular assassin in so many 'martyrdom' pictures, and the other apex in the triangle, Lena, who is Ranuccio's mistress and Caravaggio's model for the Magdalene and the dead Virgin. Jarman proposes a murderous intensity as the mainspring for both Caravaggio's love life and for his furious painting, and it certainly carries great weight of conviction. For all the melodrama of the story, however, he has elected a style of grave serenity, composed of looks and glances, long silences in shaded rooms, sudden eruptions of blood. It all works miraculously well, even the conscious use of anachronisms and the street sounds of contemporary Italy. CPea

Caravan of Courage

see Ewok Adventure, The

Caravans

(1978, US/Iran, 123 min)
d James Fargo. *p* Elmo Williams. *sc* Nancy Voyles Crawford, Thomas A McMahon, Lorraine Williams. *ph* Douglas Slocombe. *ed* Richard Marden. *ad* Ted Tester. *m* Mike Batt. *cast* Anthony Quinn, Michael Sarrazin, Jennifer O'Neill, Christopher Lee, Joseph Cotten, Barry Sullivan.

● Quicksand, thirst and sadism: the movies have always traded to good effect on the romantic allure of the Middle East, from Valentino to Peter O'Toole. Unfortunately, this slice of epic schlock has all the seductive power of a syphilitic camel. Lacking enough guts to go for the stops-out treatment suggested by its story-line – the diplomatic pursuit of an American woman gone native – it stutters off into liberal apologetics for Islam's quainter customs (summary executions, their polite reverence for women, and so on). The second half picks up the right note with Slocombe's atmospheric photography of Bedouin thundering around ancient Lost Cities; but Zorba the Arab inevitably spoils it all with spontaneous ethnic dancing of appalling jollity. No great sheiks. CPea

Caravan to Vaccarès

(1974, GB/Fr, 98 min)
d Geoffrey Reeve. *p* Geoffrey Reeve, Richard Morris-Adams. *sc* Paul Wheeler. *ph* Frederic Tammes. *ed* Robert Morgan. *pd* Frank White. *m* Stanley Myers. *cast* Charlotte Rampling, David Birney, Michel Lonsdale, Michael Bryant, Serge Marquand, Marcel Bozzuffi.

● The voices form the most attractive part of this film, which suggests that Alistair MacLean's story would have been better as a radio serial. The plot revolves around a Hungarian professor (Bryant) fleeing ze East vor America vher he can develop hiz infention vor everyvon. With irritatingly smart-ass observations like 'Did you ever see a gypsy wearing Gucci shoes?', it all cries out for a sense of irony that only Lonsdale's performance starts to exploit. Rampling and Birney prove totally incapable of forming a convincing relationship. He makes little of his boorish American hero on the loose and often out of his depth in Europe, while she, looking sadly lost, instead of putting him in his place, climbs into his bed, an event that must go down as one of the most implausible screen moments of the year. CPe

Carbon Copy

(1981, US, 91 min)
d Michael Schultz. *p* Stanley Shapiro, Carter DeHaven. *sc* Stanley Shapiro. *ph* Fred J Koenekamp. *ed* Marion Segal. *pd* Ted Haworth. *m* Bill Conti. *cast* George Segal, Susan Saint James, Jack Warden, Dick Martin, Denzel Washington, Paul Winfield.

● Feeble race comedy, recalling the witlessness and offensiveness of *The Watermelon Man*, in which a secretly Jewish man (Segal secretly Jewish?) makes it big in WASP America until his illegitimate black son shows up and shows him up. Director Schultz is still best known for his funky *Car Wash*, but this marks his decline into MOR movie-making. *Carbon Copy* looks very good, but style doesn't make up for narrative weakness. MA

Card, The (aka The Promoter)

(1952, GB, 91 min, b/w)
d Ronald Neame. *p* John Bryan. *sc* Eric Ambler. *ph* Oswald Morris. *ed* Clive Donner. *ad* T Hopewell Ash. *m* William Alwyn. *cast* Alec Guinness, Glynis Johns, Petula Clark, Valerie Hobson, Edward Chapman, George Devine, Joan Hickson.

● Complacent class-based British comedy, adapted by Eric Ambler from one of Arnold Bennett's Potteries-set novels, charting Guinness' rags-to-riches rise to provincial power with no hint of the sourness underlying the later, ostensibly similar, *Room at the Top*, and even less of the prickly probing of the social texture sustaining a Guinness comedy like *The Man in the White Suit*. PT

Cardinal, The

(1963, US, 175 min)
d/p Otto Preminger. *sc* Robert Dozier. *ph* Leon Shamroy. *ed* Louis R Loeffler. *pd* Lyle Wheeler. *m* Jerome Moross. *cast* Tom Tryon, Romy Schneider, Carol Lynley, Maggie McNamara, John Saxon, John Huston, Dorothy Gish, Burgess Meredith, Cecil Kellaway, Robert Morse, Ossie Davis.

● Interminable trials of an Irish-American boy from seminary to cardinal's hat, taking in some twenty years of history and every problem known to Catholic conscience, from religious intermarriage and abortion to the Ku Klux Klan and the Nazi menace by way of the role of the Man of God. Risible script based on a doorstop novel by Henry Morton Robinson, but handled by Preminger with tremendous panache; worth seeing just for the incredible skill and flair with which he stages the action and moves the camera. TM

Cardinal and the Corpse, The

(1993, GB, 40 min)
d Christopher Petit. *p* Janine Marmot. *sc* Iain Sinclair. *ph* Simon Ffrench. *ed* Robert Hargreaves. *m* Martin Stone, Almost Presley. *with* Driffield, Robin Cook, Alan Moore, Michael Moorcock, Emanuel Litvinoff, Tony Lambrianou.

● Exec-produced by Keith Griffiths, producer of *Radio On*, *The Cardinal and the Corpse* marks the beginning of Petit's loose partnership with writer Iain Sinclair. There's a nod towards narrative here involving a book-search launched by graphic novelist Alan Moore and a dealer (the dapper but barking Driffield), but it's little more than an excuse to showcase a number of authors and other miscreants. Former aristo turned crime writer Robin Cook (aka Derek Raymond) sets the tone ('All life is ultimately about death. It's what I call the general contract') while Michael Moorcock ('Moorcock schmoorcock,' mutters a Charing Cross Road dealer) casts doubt on Driffield's claim that a pulp novel, *The Cardinal and the Corpse* by Stephen Blakesley, is actually the work of Flann O'Brien. Petit and Sinclair's film is a deliberately jarring, oddly engaging rogues' gallery that even makes room for Tony Lambrianou, a former associate of the Krays ('I don't like the word gangster: I feel embarrassed when people use that word'). NRo

Card of Fate

see Grand Jeu, Le

Care Bears Adventure in Wonderland!, The

(1987, Can, 75 min)
d Raymond Jafelice. *p* Michael Hirsh, Patrick Loubert, Clive Smith. *sc* Susan Snooks, John De Klein. *ed* Rob Kirkpatrick. *m* Patricia Cullen. *cast* voices: Bob Dermer, Eva Almos, Dan Hennessy, Jim Henshaw, Colin Fox.

● The Princess of Wonderland has been kidnapped by an evil wizard, so the White Rabbit teams up with a little girl named Alice and (ahem!) the Care Bears to save her. Hemlock to Lewis Carroll fans. TJ

Care Bears Movie, The

(1985, US, 76 min)
d Arna Selznick. *p* Michael Hirsh, Patrick Loubert, Clive Smith. *sc* Peter Sauder. *ph* David Altman, Jim Christianson, Barbara Sachs. *ed* John Broughton, Rob Kirkpatrick. *pd* Charlie Bonifacio, David Brewster, Alan Bunce, John Collins. *m* John Sebastian. *cast* voices: Mickey Rooney, Jackie Burroughs, Georgia Engel, Sunny Besen Thrasher, Harry Dean Stanton.

● Up in the clouds, a bunch of Day-Glo bears (Tenderheart, Funshine, Love-a-Lot, etc) work at keeping the world a happy, caring 'n' sharing place, protecting lonely children from (very mild) evil forces, in this short-lived but lucrative franchise (a TV series was also briefly inescapable). Adults forced to accompany three-year-olds to the movie would have had a little moment of satisfaction when the time came to shovel the Care Bear toys out of the house into landfill sites. Voice talents Mickey Rooney and Harry Dean Stanton are the only distinguished names involved. DO

Career

(1959, US, 105 min, b/w)
d Joseph Anthony. *p* Hal B Wallis. *sc* James Lee. *ph* Joseph LaShelle. *ed* Warren Low. *ad* Hal Pereira, Walter Tyler. *m* Franz Waxman. *cast* Dean Martin, Shirley MacLaine, Anthony Franciosa, Carolyn Jones, Joan Blackman.

● Well-acted version of a Broadway success (by James Lee), has Franciosa in his pre-exploitation days as an aspiring actor going through tough times in New York theatreland. Martin's a bighead director, MacLaine the protagonist's drink-sodden spouse. Low key throughout, it also lacks punch. TJ

Career Girls

(1997, GB, 87 min)
d Mike Leigh. *p* Simon Channing-Williams. *sc* Mike Leigh. *ph* Dick Pope. *ed* Robin Sales. *pd* Eve Stewart. *m* Marianne Jean-Baptiste, Tony Rémy. *cast* Katrin Cartlidge, Lynda Steadman, Mark Benton, Kate Byers, Andy Serkis, Joe Tucker, Margo Stanley, Michael Healy.

●Leigh reverts to type: good news for anyone who feared our harshest caricaturist might be losing his edge, not so good for those who felt *Secrets & Lies* represented a personal breakthrough in its emotional maturity, dramatic coherence and overriding compassion. Presumably, even its admirers would acknowledge that this is a less ambitious piece than its predecessor. The film mirrors Leigh's own development in two contrasting time frames. In the present, Hannah (Cartlidge) and Annie (Steadman) are composed, self-assured young women making their way in society. Ten years earlier, as student flatmates, they were a bundle of nervous tics, inflamed allergies and shrill neuroses. Leigh's eye for detail is precise, but the hysterical, mannered antics of the flashbacks are over-pitched and alienating. Cartlidge, particularly, seems to have angst in her pants. The present tense material comes as some relief, then, with its prevailing mood of calm introspection, the actresses delicately adumbrating the hesitant intimacy of old friends after a long separation. Yet Leigh is at a loss to develop this situation. They drop in on a sexist yuppie for a spot of tired, knee-jerk 'satire', encounter a smarmy estate agent who fails to recognise them with their clothes on, and finally they meet Ricky (Benton), a massive, stammering wreck of a man who may just represent the conscience of this thin, disappointing film. TCh

Carefree

(1938, US, 85 min, b/w)
d Mark Sandrich. *p* Pandro S Berman. *sc* Ernest Pagano, Allan Scott., Dudley Nichols, Hagar Wilde. *ph* Robert de Grasse. *ed* William Hamilton. *ad* Van Nest Polglase, Carroll Clark. *songs* Iving Berlin. *cast* Fred Astaire, Ginger Rogers, Ralph Bellamy, Luella Gear, Jack Carson, Franklin Pangborn.

●Last but one of the RKO Astaire-Rogers series, *Carefree* is the one in which Ginger falls for Fred (rather than the other way round), Fred dances and drives golf-balls at the same time (the title number – it's said the balls fell in a very tight group bang in the middle of the fairway), Ralph Bellamy socks Ginger in the jaw, and Fred and Ginger perform what has been called 'the kiss of the century'. Not quite as unrelievedly marvellous as the earlier films, *Carefree* is short on length and numbers (Berlin's 'Change Partners' is its all-time hit) and on funny supporters and lines. But there can be few better ways of passing the time than watching Fred's psychiatrist hypnotising Ginger's pert patient, or the pair of them doing 'The Yam'. SG

Careful

(1992, Can, 100 min)
d Guy Maddin. *p* Greg Klymkiw, Tracy Traeger. *sc* Guy Maddin, George Toles. *ph/ed/pd* Guy Maddin. *m* John McCulloch. *cast* Gosia Dobrowolska, Kyle McCulloch, Sarah Neville, Paul Cox, Brent Cox, Jackie Burroughs.

●It's time Guy Maddin, the brilliant Winnipeg fabulist who gave us *Tales from the Gimli Hospital* and *Archangel*, was rescued from cult obscurity. Hopefully, this darkly idiosyncratic gem will do the trick. In the 19th century Alpine town of Tolzbad, the puritanical townspeople tread and speak softly, for fear of bringing down an avalanche. But beneath this soft blanket of repression lurk incestuous desires, unspoken fears, and the ever-present threat of violent death. A post-modern silent melodrama, its wry intertitles and colour-tinted images hark back to, and yet cruelly dissect, a lost 'innocence'. Uniquely weird, subtly macabre, and utterly compelling. NF

Careful, He Might Hear You

(1983, Aust, 116 min)
d Carl Schultz. *p* Jill Robb. *sc* Michael Jenkins. *ph* John Seale. *ed* Richard Francis-Bruce. *pd* John Stoddart. *m* Ray Cook. *cast* Wendy Hughes, Robyn Nevin, Nicholas Gledhill, John Hargreaves, Geraldine Turner.

●Schultz presents a knee-high view of the world in this tug-of-love drama, set in the depression, between two sisters fighting for custody of their orphan nephew. Vanessa (Hughes) wants him in order to relive her fantasies about his father; she is rich, snobbish and beautiful, while Lila (Nevin) – poor, kind and asthmatic – is so prim she speaks of his mother being with 'God's angels'. The law settles for Vanessa's wealth, but the film's sympathies lie all too obviously with honest Lila. Sumner Locke Elliott's novel is ill-served by this adaptation: beautiful to look at, it's still a superficial, Gothic costume drama with a romantic score which pounds out the significance of every gesture. JE

Careful, Soft Shoulder

(1942, US, 69 min, b/w)
d Oliver HP Garrett. *p* Walter Morosco. *sc* Oliver HP Garrett. *ph* Charles Clarke. *ed* Nick De Maggio. *ad* Richard Day, Albert Hogsett. *m* Leigh Harline, Emil Newman. *cast* Virginia Bruce, James Ellison, Aubrey Mather, Sheila Ryan, Ralph Byrd, Sigurd Tor.

●Sole directorial credit rung up by screenwriter Garrett (*City Streets*, *Duel in the Sun*, *Dead Reckoning*), this is only a B movie, but one which brings freshness and a touch of reality to tired genre conventions. Set in Washington, it's about a bored socialite, paid a retainer to hang around political and social circles displaying the latest fashions, who gets more than she bargained for when a conversational gambit that she wouldn't mind being a spy is taken seriously by a Nazi (played by the portly Mather in the blandly avuncular Greenstreet manner). Most of it is wisecrackingly light-hearted, gradually shading into Hitchcock territory with a climactic fight in a deserted mill. But the point is that the story is casually told in flashback by the heroine, still offhand and joking about the whole thing, and thereby underlining Garrett's charge of dilettantism about the war (even after Pearl Harbor) aimed against the Washington upper crust at all levels. TM

Care of the Spitfire Grill

see Spitfire Grill, The

Caresses (Carícies)

(1997, Sp, 94 min)
d/p Ventura Pons. *sc* Seri Belbel, Ventura Pons. *ph* Jesús Escosa. *ed* Pere Abadal. *pd* Gloria Marti. *m* Carles Cases. *cast* David Selvas, Laura Conejero, Julieta Serrano, Montserrat Salvador, Augustin González, Sergi López, Mercè Pons, Jordi Dauder.

●A chain of fraught encounters: a husband slaps his wife; his wife attacks her mother; her mother rants at a friend, etc. All the characters, in other words, have two scenes, one in which they soak up vitriol, one in which it sprays out like vomit. Adapted by Catalan director Pons from a play by Sergi Belbel, this stagey film is full of excruciatingly meaningful dialogue. But gradually it picks up momentum. 'Disgusting' is a word that occurs again and again here, but for the audience, as much as for the characters, prejudices are there to be confounded. Each vignette is bleaker than the last. The undernourished visuals help, just so the fine acting. But it's the words which leave the greatest impression, milking the sexual/emotional ambiguities of 'the family' without resorting to melodrama. CO'Su

Caretaker, The (aka The Guest)

(1963, GB, 105 min, b/w)
d Clive Donner. *p* Michael Birkett. *sc* Harold Pinter. *ph* Nicolas Roeg. *ed* Fergus McDonell. *pd* Reece Pemberton. *m* Ron Grainer. *cast* Donald Pleasence, Alan Bates, Robert Shaw.

●Donner's version of Pinter's funniest and most famous play is creditably straight and subdued. Avoiding cinematic intrusions, he allows three of the greatest stage interpretations of Pinter's characters to speak for themselves. Pleasence gives so strong a performance as Davies the tramp that he has never quite been able to escape from it since. Bates and Shaw are both far more restrained than their subsequent careers would lead you to expect. It's rare for a film to rely so heavily on its actors and still be worth watching. DP

Carey Treatment, The

(1972, US, 101 min)
d Blake Edwards. *p* William Belasco. *sc* James P Bonner [Irving Ravetch, Harriet Frank Jr, John DF Black]. *ph* Frank Stanley. *ed* Ralph E Winters. *ad* Alfred Sweeney. *m* Roy Budd. *cast* James Coburn, Jennifer O'Neill, Skye Aubrey, Pat Hingle, Elizabeth Allen, Dan O'Herlihy.

●A bizarre predecessor to *Coma* (in fact based on a pseudonymous novel by Michael Crichton), this hospital thriller sees pathologist Coburn attempting to unravel deaths occurring in connection with abortions and drug pilfering. Oddly balanced between straightforward thriller and semi-parody (towards the end, the body count rises ridiculously), and structured around a nicely complex plot, it nevertheless never examines any of the issues it toys with, and is saddled with incredibly shallow characterisations (O'Neill especially). But for all its faults, at least it's better than the mess of most of Edwards' later efforts. GA

Carla's Song

(1996, GB/Ger/Sp, 125 min)
d Ken Loach. *p* Sally Hibbin. *sc* Paul Laverty. *ph* Barry Ackroyd. *ed* Jonathan Morris. *pd* Martin Johnson. *m* George Fenton. *cast* Robert Carlyle, Oyanka Cabezas, Scott Glenn, Salvador Espinoza, Louise Goodall, Richard Loza. Gary Lewis.

●George (Carlyle), a Glaswegian bus driver, is headstrong and goofy enough to steal his sweetheart away on a diversion around Loch Lomond in his double-decker. The object of his affection, Carla (Cabezas), is a refugee from Nicaragua. Alerted to her suicidal tendencies, George persuades Carla to return with him to Central America, so that she can confront the ghosts of her past, and resolve her relationship with the mysterious Antonio. The year's 1987, and he has no idea what life's really like in a war zone. A film of two halves, this has all Loach's virtues and failings, and in that order. The first hour is sharp and funny, tender and real. George's courtship of an exotic stranger whose pain he can only dimly comprehend rings very true. His attention makes things harder for her, and he's in over his head well before they touch down in Managua. But here the film loses its feet. The focus shifts from foreground to background. George becomes a passive witness – an audience identification figure whose political re-education fits surprisingly neatly into the liberal Hollywood tradition of *Missing* and *Under Fire*. Fair enough, but Loach never looks very comfortable with this formula, Carla is lost in the shuffle, and screenwriter Paul Laverty's belated attempts to graft some suspense on to the proceedings are half-cocked and under-plotted. TCh

Carlito's Way

(1993, US, 145 min)
d Brian De Palma. *p* Martin Bregman, Willi Baer, Michael S Bregman. *sc* David Koepp, Edwin Torres, Leon Ichaso. *ph* Stephen H Burum. *ed* Bill Pankow, Kristina Boden. *pd* Richard Sylbert. *m* Patrick Doyle. *cast* Al Pacino, Sean Penn, Penelope Ann Miller, John Leguizamo, Ingrid Rogers, Luis Guzman, Viggo Mortensen, Paul Mazursky.

●A fairly straightforward '30s-style gangster tragedy about a man doomed to an early grave by his society and his own code. Carlito (Pacino) wants out of the rackets, but to get there he has to 'play Bogart', running a discotheque, and even then he can't escape his friends – lover Miller and lawyer Penn. Just as Carlito can't reconcile who he is and where he came from, so Brian De Palma can't quite craft an anonymous mainstream movie. The picture comes alive in its set-pieces, most notably in the climax at Grand Central Station. It runs long and is ultimately not much more than a showpiece, but Pacino looks every inch a movie star, and De Palma provides a timely reminder of just how impoverished the Hollywood lexicon has become since the glory days of the '70s. TCh

Carlo Giuliani, Ragazzo

(2002, It, 60 min)
d Francesca Comencini. *p* Mauro Berardi. *sc* Francesca Comencini, Luca Bigazzi. *ph* extracts: *A Different World Is Possible* (co-ord Francesco Maselli); sequences: Mario Balsamo, Gianfranco

Fiore, Massimiliano Franceschini, Paolo Pietrangeli, Pasquale Scimeca, Daniele Segre, Carola Spadoni, Fulvio Wetzl. *ed* Linda Taylor.
● An exemplary documentary tracing the events leading to Carlo Giuliani's death during the Genoa anti-globalisation demonstrations of July 2001. Comencini makes persuasive use of archive video footage in her attempt to prove that the police panicked, shot and twice ran over the boy before contriving a cover-up, but what gives the film its emotional power, intellectual weight and dramatic force is having Giuliani's mother – lucid, logical and tearless, despite desolation at her loss and the establishment's secrets and lies – as the sole interviewee, charting Carlo's last hours and carefully assessing the evidence. GA

Carlota Joaquina, Princess of Brazil

(1995, Braz, 101 min)
d Carla Camurati. *p* Carla Camurati, Bianca De Felippes. *sc* Melanie Dimantas, Carla Camurati. *ph* Breno Silveira. *ed* Cezar Migliorim, Marta Luz. *pd* Emilia Duncan, Tadeu Burgos. *cast* Marieta Severo, Marco Nanini, Ludmila Dayer.
● This first feature is like an historically accurate *Carry On* without the camp. In 1785, Carlota (Severo) is married, aged ten, to Portugal's Prince João (Nanini), later Dom João VI. Come 1808 and the Napoleonic invasion, and the Portuguese court relocates to Brazil, its largest colony, at the scheming behest of their English allies, where it remains until 1821. Dom João is a docile, bumbling, sometime idiot who just about manages to run a kingdom; Carlota whiles away her hours having numerous men and babies. The aim may be bawdy comedy, but it ain't funny. All this would be fairly inoffensive, but for the film's flashback structure. In an apparent sop to the international market, the tale is narrated in stultifyingly drawn-out English to a ten-year-old on a Scottish beach: 'She had lots of lovers. L-o-t-s of them. And she could eat any one of them like a crazy animal.' NB

Carl Th. Dreyer: My Work (Carl Th. Dreyer: Min metier)

(1995, Den, 96 min, b/w)
d Torben Skjødt Jensen. *sc* Torben Skjødt Jensen, Parmi Larsen. *ph* Harald Gunnar Paalgard.
● 'Why make a film about me? I'm not interesting, it's my films that are interesting.' This documentary honours Dreyer's conviction that an artist's soul is expressed through his work. The result is an aptly dry but comprehensive tribute to the great Danish director (*The Passion of Joan of Arc, Vampyr*, etc). A steady, narrated progression along the timeline of his life and career is interspersed with plentiful clips from the films themselves (generally austere like most of Dreyer's cinema, these clips aren't going to catch your imagination if you're new to the films), with one of his old actresses offering the summary: 'I think he was the first Zen master I ever met.' NB

Carmen

(1915, US, 77 min, b/w – tinted)
d Cecil B DeMille. *sc* William C de Mille. *ph* Alvin Wyckoff. *ad* Wilfred Buckland. *cast* Geraldine Farrar, Wallace Reid, Pedro de Cordoba, Horace B Carpenter.
● Farrar caught the eye of Jesse Lasky when she sang Carmen at the Met in 1914, and he subsequently persuaded her to collaborate with DeMille on this scaled down version of the opera. The print under review (from George Eastman House) has been restored and tinted to DeMille's specifications (the ethereal blue of the opening sequence with the smugglers on a California hillside is notably striking). It's topped with a montage of stills and some historical notes, and tailed with a number of imperfect recordings of Farrar herself. The result, regrettably, despite the academic documentation, is frankly a mess. There are repeated shots of a breached, theatrical wall, and even the bullfight, staged in Los Angeles 'by special arrangement', is an anti-climax by DeMille standards (where are the 20,000 extras?). Furthermore, to add to the sense of hodge-podge, some modern non-synched arias and duets have been added. All the hand-to-hand fights, however, are staged with that uniquely cheerful, silent screen gusto. JPy

Carmen

(1983, Sp, 101 min)
d Carlos Saura. *p* Emiliano Piedra. *sc* Carlos Saura, Antonio Gades. *ph* Teo Escamilla. *ed* Pedro del Rey. *ad* Felix Murcia. *m* Georges Bizet, Paco de Lucia. *cast* Antonio Gades, Laura del Sol, Paco de Lucia, Cristina Hoyos, Juan Antonio Jimenez.
● Saura's *Carmen* is a Spaniard's examination of the story which did for Spain what the Hovis ads did for Yorkshire. Like his earlier *Blood Wedding*, it explores the legend through various forms of popular Spanish dance and folk-song, entirely transposing Bizet's music. The result is as visually exhilarating as the earlier film, but far more complex in its ambitions and achievements. Mingling dance rehearsals with sexual encounters, real fights with choreographed rumbles, and producing a hilarious pastiche of the dreadful 'March of the Toreadors', *Carmen* is both a new kind of musical and marvellous cinema. NR

Carmen

(1984, Fr/It, 152 min)
d Francesco Rosi. *p* Patrice Ledoux. *sc* Henri Meilhac, Ludovic Halévy (libretto), Francesco Rosi, Tonino Guerra. *ph* Pasqualino De Santis. *ed* Ruggero Mastroianni, Colette Semprun. *pd* Enrico Job. *m* Georges Bizet. *cast* Julia Migenes-Johnson, Placido Domingo, Ruggero Raimondi, Faith Esham, François Le Roux, Jean-Paul Bogart.
● Cameraman Pasqualino De Santis' muted colours provide a suitable frame for Rosi's mixed realistic and balletic treatment of Bizet's opera, which climaxes in the symbolically red-clad Carmen goading her maddened victim into murder on the sun-baked sand. Lorin Maazel, heading the Orchestre National de France, conducts a musically first-rate performance; both leading men are, well, mature, but Domingo's bemused passion as the simple soldier is underpinned by magnificent burnished tones. The warm-voiced Carmen, Migenes-Johnson, fleetingly resembling a de-beaked Streisand, recalls a Broadway background in her engaging bump-and-grind concept of sexuality – a reminder that *Carmen* is simply the best musical ever written. Hugely enjoyable for opera buff and non-buff alike. MHoy

Carmen Jones

(1954, US, 105 min)
d/p Otto Preminger. *sc* Harry Kleiner. *ph* Sam Leavitt. *ed* Louis Loeffler. *ad* Edward L Ilou. *m* Georges Bizet, Oscar Hammerstein (lyrics). *cast* Dorothy Dandridge, Harry Belafonte, Pearl Bailey, Olga James, Roy Glenn, Diahann Carroll, Brock Peters.
● Prosper Mérimée's fine old tale of high passions and low morals gets re-upholstered Hollywood-style in Preminger's all-black musical. The cigarette-maker with a rose instead of a fag between her teeth is transformed into Dandridge's parachute factory worker, whose romance with GI Joe (Belafonte) is interrupted by Harlem's equivalent of the toreador – a boxer. Given such a lushly familiar score as Bizet's, the dis, dats and deys with which Oscar Hammerstein liberally sprinkles his lyrics seem oddly fey, even when handled by the competent voices of Marilyn Horne and Laverne Hutchinson. The somewhat heavy-handed direction and the ultimately two-dimensional characters leave you admiring the workmanship without plucking at the necessary emotional/romantic heart-strings. FL

Carmen Miranda: Bananas Is My Business

(1994, Braz/US, 92 min)
d Helena Solberg. *p* David Meyer, Helena Solberg. *ph* Tomasz Magierski, Amanda Zinoman. *with* Cynthia Adler, Eric Barreto, Leticia Monte. *narrator* Helena Solberg.
● Ae ae ae…at 92 minutes this is more than most people will ever want to know about the Brazilian samba star with the tutti-frutti gimmick. She is clearly a very personal obsession for director/narrator Solberg, though the most interesting material here relates to Miranda's role as a national symbol for Brazilians, and as the embodiment of Roosevelt's Good Neighbor policy during WWII. The exuberant personality comes through loud and clear, but once she made it in Hollywood, Carmen never varied her act, and it's all too obvious why she was crushed under the weight of all those bananas before she reached 50. TCh

Carmin profond

see Deep Crimson

Carnal Knowledge

(1971, US, 97 min)
d/p Mike Nichols. *sc* Jules Feiffer. *ph* Giuseppe Rotunno. *ed* Sam O'Steen. *pd* Richard Sylbert. *cast* Jack Nicholson, Candice Bergen, Art Garfunkel, Ann-Margret, Rita Moreno, Cynthia O'Neal, Carol Kane.
● As a slice of familiar Feiffer cynicism, tracing the arid sex life of two contrasting males from eager college days to drained middle age, this was never quite the major assault on sexism and male chauvinism it set itself up to be. For one thing, Nichols directs with his usual mixture of theatricality and artiness, so that parts (the fumbling triangular courtship at the beginning; the incandescent vulnerability of Ann-Margret; the bleak squalor of Nicholson's slide-show lecture on his conquests) are much better than the whole. For another, Feiffer's arrows, despite some neatly barbed dialogue, mostly seem to fall short of the target. TM

Carné

(1991, Fr, 40 min)
d Gaspar Noé. *ph* Dominique Colin. *ed* Lucile Hadzihalilovic. *ad* Alain Lefebvre. *cast* Philippe Nahon, Blandine Lenoir, Frankye Pain, Hélène Testud.
● The raw power of this disturbing study of an alienated Parisian horsemeat butcher's over-protective, potentially incestuous relationship with his pubescent daughter is contained only by its meticulously framed CinemaScope images. Black humour plays a part too, as Philippe Nahon's coarse, prejudiced butcher tries to cope with the cruel vagaries of life. Noé's bleak social vision is reminiscent of early Fassbinder, but his powerful, visceral imagery is all his own. NF

Carnet de Bal, Un

(1937, Fr, 130 min, b/w)
d Julien Duvivier. *sc* Julien Duvivier, Henri Jeanson, Jean Sarment, Bernard Zimmer. *ph* Michel Kelber. *ed* André Versein. *ad* Serge Pimenoff, Jean Douarinou. *m* Maurice Jaubert. *cast* Marie Bell, Françoise Rosay, Louis Jouvet, Harry Baur, Pierre-Richard Wilm, Raimu, Pierre Blanchar, Fernandel, Robert Lynen.
● A couple of decades on, the list of partners on an old dance card, dating back to when she was 16, excites the curiosity of Bell, a well-heeled widow, who sets off on a quest to discover what became of them all. As if the framework itself wasn't poignant enough, the film's seven episodes plus coda are mostly concerned with death, disappointment and the melancholy of dashed hopes. (Moral: throw stuff away.) Too slick and sentimental to be truly affecting, the film's justification is its extraordinary cast: Jouvet as a rueful but ruthless crook, Raimu a small town mayor conducting his own wedding ceremony, Blanchar a one-eyed abortionist. The actual production is rather skimpy, compared with the resources Duvivier was able to lavish on *Lydia*, his Hollywood remake. BBa

Carne Trémula

see Live Flesh

Carnival

(1946, GB, 93 min, b/w)
d Stanley Haynes. *p* Filippo del Giudice. *sc* Stanley Haynes, Guy Green, Peter Ustinov. *ph* Guy Green. *ed* Ralph Kemplen. *ad* Carmen Dillon. *m* Nicholas Brodszky. *cast* Sally Gray, Michael Wilding, Stanley Holloway, Bernard Miles, Jean Kent, Catherine Lacey, Hazel Court.
● Jenny Pearl, poor but pretty, joins the corps de ballet of the local music hall and has a romance with a posh young sculptor. But he's too weak for her and she marries a chapel-obsessed farmer. It all ends badly, with gunplay on the Cornish sands. This was the third adaptation of Compton Mackenzie's 1912 novel. It's upbeat as regards the lively setting (Edwardian London), but exudes post-war malaise in its view of life as a series of traps – class, religion, marriage. Sally Gray has striking looks, an interesting voice and a presence suggesting brisk common sense – a quality, unfortunately, not much relevant to the character of Jenny Pearl. BBa

Carnival Child, The
see Ivan Mosjoukine, or The Carnival Child

Carnival in Flanders
see Kermesse Héroique, La

Carnival of Souls
(1962, US, 81 min, b/w)
d/p Herk Harvey. *sc* John Clifford. *ph* Maurice Prather. *ed* Dan Palmquist, Bill de Jarnette. *m* Gene Moore. *cast* Candace Hilligoss, Frances Feist, Sidney Berger, Art Ellison, Stan Levitt, Herk Harvey.
● The only survivor when a car plunges into a river, Mary Henry (Hilligoss) emerges on to a sandbank like a sodden sleepwalker. Shortly afterwards, en route to Utah to take up a job as a church organist, Mary is frightened by a ghostly apparition, a white-faced man whose repeated appearances seem mysteriously connected with an abandoned carnival pavilion. Other strange episodes, during which Mary seems to become invisible and inaudible to those around her, exacerbate her feeling that she has no place in this world. With its striking black-and-white compositions, disorienting dream sequences and eerie atmosphere, this has the feel of a silent German expressionist movie. Unfortunately, so does some of the acting, which suffers from exaggerated facial expressions and bizarre gesturing. But the mesmerising power of the carnival and dance-hall sequences far outweighs the corniness of the awkward intimate scenes; and as Mary, caught in limbo between this world and the next, dances to the discordant carnival music of time, the subsequent work of George Romero and David Lynch comes constantly to mind. NF

Carnival of Thieves
see Caper of the Golden Bulls, The

Carny
(1980, US, 106 min)
d Robert Kaylor. *p* Robbie Robertson. *sc* Thomas Baum. *ph* Harry Stradling Jr. *ed* Stuart H Pappé. *pd* William J Cassidy. *m* Alex North. *cast* Gary Busey, Jodie Foster, Robbie Robertson, Meg Foster, Kenneth McMillan, Elisha Cook, Bill McKinney, Bert Remsen.
● A long-cherished project of writer/director Kaylor (hitherto best remembered for *Roller Derby*), packaged on the strength of former Band-leader Robertson's enthusiastic involvement, this caused much unease among its backers with its dark tone and manic moodiness. Set amid the greasepaint and behind-the-canvas graft of a travelling carnival, it features Robertson as the resident con-artist and all-purpose fixer; Busey as the crazed bozo, goading the punters into taking pot-shots at his perch above a water-tank; and Jodie Foster as the runaway who threatens to split their strange bond. The road movie/buddy movie situations and emotions gain an intriguing perverse edge from the setting, with its genuine freaks and sideshow illusionism, as well as from Alex North's wonderfully unsettling score and Harry Stradling's dark cinematography. Better on electric, eccentric ambience than for its final rush of plotting, but such risk-taking movies are a welcome rarity. PT

Caro Diario
see Dear Diary

Carousel
(1956, US, 128 min)
d Henry King. *p* Henry Ephron. *sc* Phoebe Ephron, Henry Ephron. *ph* Charles G Clarke. *ed* William H Reynolds. *ad* Lyle Wheeler, Jack Martin Smith. *songs* Richard Rodgers, Oscar Hammerstein II. *cast* Gordon MacRae, Shirley Jones, Cameron Mitchell, Barbara Ruick, Claramae Turner, Gene Lockhart, Robert Rounseville.
● Ferenc Molnar's play *Liliom* had already been filmed by Fritz Lang (in France) and Frank Borzage (in Hollywood) when Rodgers and Hammerstein adapted it for their Broadway musical, and here Henry King is content to defer to his betters and simply stand back while the schmaltzy material is overwhelmed by Fox opulence. MacRae is the former fairground barker given celestial leave to visit his loved ones on earth for a day, and incidentally revealing the source of a million Kop anthems with 'You'll Never Walk Alone'. PT

Carquake
see Cannonball

Carrie
(1952, US, 118 min, b/w)
d/p William Wyler. *sc* Ruth Goetz, Augustus Goetz. *ph* Victor Milner. *ed* Robert Swink. *ad* Hal Pereira, Roland Anderson. *m* David Raksin. *cast* Jennifer Jones, Laurence Olivier, Miriam Hopkins, Eddie Albert, Ray Teal, Barry Kelley.
● No relation whatever to De Palma's schlock-horror shocker, but a typically grave Wyler adaptation of Theodore Dreiser's dry novel of social criticism, *Sister Carrie*. Depicting the sliding scales of love and money in turn-of-the-century Chicago, the film has Olivier sinking further and further towards ruin with every helping hand he offers to aspiring, ambitious actress Jones. PT

Carrie
(1976, US, 98 min)
d Brian De Palma. *p* Paul Monash. *sc* Lawrence D Cohen. *ph* Mario Tosi. *ed* Paul Hirsch. *ad* William Kenney, Jack Fisk. *m* Pino Donaggio. *cast* Sissy Spacek, Piper Laurie, Amy Irving, William Katt, John Travolta, Nancy Allen.
● Unlike other Hollywood virtuosos, De Palma's central inspiration remains unashamedly the horror film and its thundering techniques of emotional manipulation. *Carrie* is almost an amalgamation of *The Exorcist* and *American Graffiti*, with Spacek as a religious maniac's daughter whose experience of puberty is so harrowing that it develops paranormal aspects. De Palma's ability to combine the romantic and the horrific has never been so pulverising. Here he contrives a wild juxtaposition of Carrie's freakish inner turmoil with the dreamy cruisin' mentality of her high-school colleagues. The style and imagery are strictly primary in the Freudian sense: menstrual blood and spotless ball dresses, Cinderella dressed up for the abattoir. But the fierce sympathy it extends to its unfashionable central character puts the film a million miles above the contemporary line in sick exploitation. DP

Carrie 2
see Rage: Carrie 2, The

Carried Away (aka Acts of Love)
(1995, US, 109 min)
d Bruno Barreto. *p* Lisa M Hansen, Paul Hertzberg. *sc* Ed Jones. *ph* Declan Quinn. *ed* Bruce Cannon. *pd* Peter Paul Raubertas. *m* Bruce Broughton. *cast* Dennis Hopper, Amy Locane, Amy Irving, Julie Harris, Gary Busey, Hal Holbrook.
● A backwoods Texas schoolteacher (Hopper), nearing retirement, is transformed by a relationship with a new 17-year-old pupil (Locane): dodgy territory, given that this is based on a novella by Jim Harrison, author of such 'manly' pseudo-Lawrentian works as *Wolf* and *Legends of the Fall*. Hopper's Joseph Svenden is a likeable, honourable man, consumed by phlegmatic inertia: he describes himself as 'a mediocre teacher', with reluctant plans to return to farming if his small school closes; still lives in the old farm with his dying Ma (Harris); and walks crouched over a stick since a tractor accident. He reacts at first with an almost distant attitude to the forceful, knowing advances of the girl. The movie gets interesting not with his hay-barn sexual encounters, nor when he gazes at her naked form as she does a brazen (and ridiculous) Lady Godiva act, but in later scenes, such as when Joseph talks quietly in a bar with his doctor friend (Holbrook) of his lack of concern at the community's disapproval. Busey is good and authoritative as the girl's menacing father. Hackneyed but dignified. WH

Carrière de Suzanne, La (Suzanne's Profession)
(1963, Fr, 55 min)
d Eric Rohmer. *p* Barbet Schroeder. *sc* Eric Rohmer. *ph* Daniel Lacambre. *ed* Eric Rohmer. *cast* Catherine Sée, Philippe Beuzin, Christian Charrière, Diane Wilkinson, Jean-Claude Biette, Patrick Bauchau, Jean-Louis Comolli.
● The second of the 'Six Moral Tales', and more substantial than the first (*La Boulangère de Monceau*): here the focus is on two young men, Beuzin and Charrière, who take advantage of Catherine Sée's ethereal Suzanne to bum drinks and food off her, but the crunch comes when it's revealed which one she's actually interested in. Although the resources are relatively modest, Rohmer's elegant wordplay and his exquisite attunement to the vagaries of the human psyche are evident even at this early stage in the director's career. TJ

Carriers Are Waiting, The
see Convoyeurs Attendent, Les

Carrington
(1995, GB, 123 min)
d Christopher Hampton. *p* Ronald Shedlo, John McGrath. *sc* Christopher Hampton. *ph* Denis Lenoir. *ed* George Akers. *pd* Caroline Amies. *m* Michael Nyman. *cast* Emma Thompson, Jonathan Pryce, Steven Waddington, Rufus Sewell, Samuel West, Janet McTeer.
● Hampton's solidly performed directorial debut is a tasteful account of the intense, bizarre relationship between the effete author Lytton Strachey (Pryce, particularly good) and the young painter Dora Carrington (Thompson). This devout but chiefly spiritual affair, which eventually drove Carrington into the arms of other members of the bohemian set, should have made for an intriguing, if ironic, study of exploratory eroticism at odds with conventional morals. Instead, Hampton falls into the usual 'heritage movie' traps: the sex scenes are so timid they appear voyeuristic; the seasons in graceful rural England seem always to be late spring or early summer; and in general there's a sense not of a film but of an illustrated book. The few good lines come from Strachey; though you'd hardly know he was a writer, or Carrington an artist, so little attention is paid to their work. GA

Carrington VC (aka Court Martial)
(1954, GB, 106 min, b/w)
d Anthony Asquith. *p* Teddy Baird. *sc* John Hunter. *ph* Desmond Dickinson. *ed* Ralph Kemplen. *ad* Wilfrid Shingleton. *cast* David Niven, Margaret Leighton, Noelle Middleton, Maurice Denham, Laurence Naismith, Mark Dignam, Victor Maddern, Allan Cuthbertson.
● Dorothy and Campbell Christie's stage success was the sort of trusted material to which British stalwart Asquith often turned his skills, and here the result's a typically well-acted courtroom drama lacking only the last ounce of sheer cinematic flair. Niven proves a little more involved than usual as a hard-up army officer, egged on by his unscrupulous wife Leighton, who determines to take the money owed him from the battery safe, then finds himself before a court-martial when his superiors refuse to speak up for him. TJ

Carrosse d'Or, Le
see Golden Coach, The

Carry Greenham Home
(1983, GB, 69 min)
d/ph Beeban Kidron, Amanda Richardson. *ed* Beeban Kidron, Amanda Richardson.
● You don't have to be a woman to watch this documentary by National Film School students, but it certainly helps. Seven months spent sharing the experiences of the peace protesters at Greenham Common has produced a faithful picture, but rarely a compelling one. It is moving to witness the bleak conditions in which the women continue their fight, and solidarity has a way of making you want to participate in its victories. But protests get nowhere by being innocuous, and the film's virtue – it's unflinching honesty – brings about its defects: a bland directorial eye, an assumption that they have your sympathies, and if they don't, they're not worth having. To maintain its momentum, the peace movement needs to make constant inroads on the flagging public consciousness. SMac

Carry Me Back
(1983, NZ, 90 min)
d John Reid. *p* Graeme Cowley. *sc* Derek Morton, Keith Aberdein, John Reid. *ph* Graeme Cowley. *ed* Simon Reece. *ad* Jim Barr. *m* Tim

protagonist. Indeed, the crash is very well staged. The problem is, everyone involved takes it all so seriously as a significant statement about Modern Man, which is why it takes an eternity to end. If I understand this symbol-heavy fable correctly, civilisation hasn't done much for our souls, but if we can only get back to what matters, like worshipping a volleyball as a fire god, maybe we'll see the light. GA

Castaway

(1986, GB, 120 min)
d Nicolas Roeg. *p* Rick McCallum. *sc* Allan Scott. *ph* Harvey Harrison. *ed* Tony Lawson. *pd* Andrew Sanders. *m* Stanley Myers. *cast* Oliver Reed, Amanda Donohue, Georgina Hale, Frances Barber, Tony Rickards, Todd Rippon.

●Given the material he began with – Lucy Irvine's rambling, disconnected, soapy saga of love turned sour in a Pacific paradise – Roeg has produced a remarkably straightforward narrative which, while encapsulating all his previous obsessions and themes (strangers in strange lands, love and hate and the whole damn thing), irons out all the wrinkles and time warps which were the hallmarks of his earlier works. In fact, what we get is surprisingly plain sailing through the Blue Lagoon. Gerald (Reed) is a beer-bellied mcp ('Give me a woman that can cook, sew and put up a tent') who advertises for an island soulmate and winds up with Lucy (Donohue), a frustrated London Inland Revenue clerk up for a voyage of self-discovery. Forced into a marriage of convenience, this ill-matched, ill-equipped couple rapidly becomes a non-item when the Tuin island paradise is reached – she refuses to put out, he refuses to put up the shelter, both refuse to face reality. In fact it's a lifetime of marriage – courtship, estrangement, understanding and separation – condensed into a single year. All of which makes for less than comfortable viewing, but real life rarely is, be it in Tuin or Tooting. DAt.

Castle, The

(1997, Aust, 82 min)
d Rob Sitch. *p* Debra Choate. *sc* Santon Cilauro, Tom Gleisner, Jane Kennedy, Rob Sitch. *ph* Miriana Marusic. *ed* Wayne Hyett. *pd* Carrie Kennedy. *m* Craig Harnath. *cast* Michael Caton, Anne Tenney, Stephen Curry, Sophie Lee, Anthony Simcoe.

●Forget the rudimentary visual style, the Capra-esque plot (against all odds, a family battles the fat cats who slap a compulsory purchase order on their far from prepossessing home), and the very slight possibility that the film could be an allegory about governmental attitudes towards Aboriginal land. This Oz comedy is terrifically funny from start to finish, largely because the relentlessly optimistic Kerrigans are not just the usual wacky eccentrics beloved by cinema – they're downright moronic, under-achievers in almost every imaginable way. (We've heard of stories with unreliable narrators – but cretinous?) Crucially, however, Sitch and his team present them in a sufficiently sympathetic light to make us care about their fate – that is, providing there's time for such considerations between the virtually non-stop laughs. Bonzer indeed. GA

Castle, The (Das Schloss)

(1995, Aus, 123 min)
d Michael Haneke. *p* Veit Heiduschka, Michael Katz. *sc* Michael Haneke. *ph* Jin Stibr. *ed* Andreas Prochaska. *cast* Ulrich Mühe, Susanne Lothar, André Eisermann, Johannes Silberschneider, Paulus Manker, Nikolaus Paryla, Frank Giering, Felix Eitner.

●Haneke's made-for-TV film of Kafka's classic is faithful in letter and spirit to the very end. K, a land surveyor (or is he?), turns up at a village and undergoes endless bewildering, frustrating and demeaning experiences at the hands both of a repressive bureaucracy (the Castle, which we never actually see) and of the strangely complicitous villagers. A strong sense of absurdity imbues the overall atmosphere of guilt, paranoia, misplaced ambition, desire and impotence, and Haneke's cool, characteristically austere direction and the stark design (the village is merely a scattering of smallish houses linked by forever snowy streets) lend the film a strange, mesmerising logic all of its own. GA

Castle Keep

(1969, US, 107 min)
d Sydney Pollack. *p* Martin Ransohoff, John Calley. *sc* Daniel Taradash, David Rayfiel. *ph* Henri Decaë. *ed* Malcolm Cooke. *pd* Rino Mondellini, Max Douy. *m* Michel Legrand. *cast* Burt Lancaster, Patrick O'Neal, Jean-Pierre Aumont, Peter Falk, Al Freeman Jr, Scott Wilson, Astrid Heeren, Tony Bill, Bruce Dern.

●An eccentric endgame allegory based on William Eastlake's novel, critically culted in France but a commercial disaster everywhere, Pollack's war movie contrasts two sets of civilised values (American/European) as Lancaster's platoon fights to hold a medieval castle and its treasures against the German advance, and finds both too retrogressively dogmatic in the face of the holocaust. An ill-omened attempt at likewise fusing an American action genre with Euro art-house 'ideas' ('I didn't intend for people to believe that the castle really existed.'), Pollack's folly remains an intriguing curio in spite of its pretensions. Shot in Yugoslavia by Henri Decaë, with similar sterling French support from art director Max Douy and composer Michel Legrand. PT

Castle on the Hudson (aka Years Without Days)

(1940, US, 77 min, b/w)
d Anatole Litvak. *p* Sam Bischoff. *sc* Seton I Miller, Brown Holmes, Courteney Terrett. *ph* Arthur Edeson. *ed* Thomas Richards. *ad* John Hughes. *m* Adolf Deutsch. *cast* John Garfield, Ann Sheridan, Pat O'Brien, Burgess Meredith, Jerome Cowan, Henry O'Neill.

●Garfield's again made to suffer, this time as an arrogant petty hood who takes the heat when his girlfriend kills a corrupt lawyer. As ever, he brings bravado and pathos in equal measure to a tailor-made role. Pat O'Brien's the righteous prison warder determined to bring him to heel. As usual in Warner Bros pics of the time, there are plenty of swipes at the iniquities of the system. A remake of *20,000 Years in Sing-Sing*. GM

Casual Relations

(1973, US, 80 min)
d Mark Rappaport. *cast* Sis Smith, Mel Austin, Paula Barra, Peter Campus.

●Rappaport's debut feature was an object lesson in turning the limitations of a poverty-row budget to advantage. Various lonely New York neurotics live out their isolated fantasies, fed by cathode-ray glare and memories of movies. It's all pretty funny. A shrink like Lacan might call it a revision of the psychotic subject; the Walker Brothers called their version *In My Room*. TR

Casual Sex?

(1988, US, 97 min)
d Genevieve Robert. *p* Ilona Herzberg, Sheldon Kahn. *sc* Wendy Goldman, Judy Toll. *ph* Rolf Kesterman. *ed* Sheldon Kahn, Donn Cambern. *pd* Randy Ser. *m* Van Dyke Parks. *cast* Lea Thompson, Victoria Jackson, Stephen Shellen, Jerry Levine, Andrew Dice Clay, Mary Gross.

●A sex comedy from the female perspective. Originally a three-song sketch by Wendy Goldman and Judy Toll, it was then worked up into a play, and finally a screenplay, reflecting the new AIDS consciousness. Stacy and Melissa re-evaluate their sexual attitudes, and decide to holiday at an upmarket health spa, where potential partners should at least be in good nick. After a variety of sketchy farcical/romantic complications, the movie settles for a rather sentimental epilogue, but it remains surprisingly engaging. The biggest shock is Andrew Dice Clay – the comedian you love to boycott – whose 'Vin-Man' character gets laughs transforming himself from a macho beast to a caring, sharing New Man via the 'Pretend You're Sensitive Handbook'. TCh

Casualties of War

(1989, US, 113 min)
d Brian De Palma. *p* Art Linson. *sc* David Rabe. *ph* Stephen H Burum. *ed* Bill Pankow. *pd* Wolf Kroeger. *m* Ennio Morricone. *cast* Michael J Fox, Sean Penn, Don Harvey, John C Reilly, John Leguizamo, Thuy Thu Le, Erik King, Ving Rhames, Dale Dye.

●De Palma is not a director one looks to for conscience, and his track record on the issue of rape has been innocent of moral debate. It's odd to find him dealing with both, and the non-sensationalist approach seems to have taken a toll on his energies: *Casualties of War* is dull. Sgt Meserve (Penn) kidnaps a Vietnamese girl to service his squad during a dangerous reconnaisance mission, and only the rookie Eriksson (Fox) opposes him. The quarrel is as static as their characters – Meserve plain nasty, Eriksson a model of decency. They shout at each other lots; when Eriksson reports the crime, Meserve tries to blow him up in the latrine. The official reaction – what's a crime in wartime? – only comes to life when Lt Reilly (Rhames) explains what injustice means to a black Southerner. David Rabe's screenplay is disappointing in the light of his brilliant *Streamers*, and the conclusion in which Eriksson achieves catharsis back home with a Vietnamese girl on a campus is preposterously corny. BC

Cat, The

see Chat, Le

Catamount Killing, The (Lohngelder für Pittsville)

(1974, WGer, 105 min)
d Krzysztof Zanussi. *p* Manfred Durnion. *sc* Julian More, Sheila More, Krzysztof Zanussi. *ph* Witold Sobocinski. *ed* Ilona Wasgint. *pd* Ruffin Barron Bennett. *m* Wojciech Kilar. *cast* Horst Buchholz, Ann Wedgeworth, Louise Clark, Chip Taylor, Patricia Joyce.

●Buchholz plays a bank manager from the big city demoted to the small Vermont town of Catamount. It's not long before he's having a torrid romance with his landlady and both are scheming to relieve the bank of a big payroll delivery. So far, so *noir*. But the film heads off down its own idiosyncratic path, with an absurdist heist, a *Torn Curtain*-like murder of protracted horror, and a finale in which retribution arrives not via greed or mistrust but because the transgressors are unable, finally, to suppress their moral scruples. It's very tentatively handled by Zanussi, who seems ill at ease in his first English-language production, adapted from *I'd Rather Be Poor* by James Hadley Chase. BBa

Cat and the Canary, The

(1927, US, 86 min, b/w)
d Paul Leni. *sc* Robert F Hill, Alfred Cohn. *ph* Gilbert Warrenton. *ed* Lloyd Nosler. *ad* Charles D Hall. *cast* Laura LaPlante, Creighton Hale, Lucien Littlefield, Flora Finch, Arthur Edmund Carewe, Tully Marshall.

●Paul Leni was the first of the great German expressionist directors to split to Hollywood, and this adaptation of John Willard's stage thriller was his American debut. It's the definitive 'haunted house' movie, with the cast gathered for the midnight reading of a bizarre will in a mansion where a maniac is on the loose. Since the plot creaks as much as all the secret passageways, Leni wisely plays it mainly for laughs, but his prowling, Murnau-like camera-work generates a frisson or two on the way. It is, in fact, hugely entertaining, and Laura LaPlante makes a charming victim. TR

Cat and the Canary, The

(1939, US, 72 min, b/w)
d Elliott Nugent. *p* Arthur Hornblow Jr. *sc* Walter de Leon, Lynn Starling. *ph* Charles Lang. *ed* Archie Marshek. *ad* Hans Dreier, Robert Usher. *m* Ernst Toch. *cast* Bob Hope, Paulette Goddard, Gale Sondergaard, John Beal, Douglass Montgomery, George Zucco.

●A remake of Paul Leni's 1927 *Old Dark House* classic, this was Hope's first really big success. The tale of a group of characters gathered for a reading of a will, with spooky goings-on galore, it's a perfect vehicle for Hope's bluff, cowardly persona. Predictable, but surprisingly atmospheric (Sondergaard helps no end) and often very funny. GA

Cat and the Canary, The

(1979, GB, 98 min)
d Radley Metzger. *p* Richard Gordon. *sc* Radley Metzger. *ph* Alex Thomson. *ed* Roger Harrison. *ad* Anthony Pratt, John Hoesli. *m* Steve Cagan. *cast* Honor Blackman, Michael Callan, Edward Fox, Wendy Hiller, Olivia Hussey, Beatrix Lehmann, Carol Lynley, Daniel Massey, Peter McEnery, Wilfrid Hyde-White.

●From the thunderstorm to the old dark house in which no item of furniture can be trusted not to conceal a secret passage, predictability is the keynote to this fifth remake of John Willard's play. It's obvious from the start whodunit; so the cast are much given to eye-rolling and chilling smiles, either to throw one off the scent or to disguise their embarrassment, for this adaptation is so turgidly faithful that one expects the entire lot (mauled bodies and all) to take a bow as the credits roll. FF

Cat Ballou

(1965, US, 96 min)
d Elliot Silverstein. *p* Harold Hecht. *sc* Walter Newman, Frank R Pierson. *ph* Jack Marta. *ed* Charles Nelson. *ad* Malcolm Brown. *m* Frank De Vol. *songs* Mack David, Jerry Livingstone. *cast* Jane Fonda, Lee Marvin, Michael Callan, Dwayne Hickman, Nat King Cole, Stubby Kaye, Tom Nardini, John Marley.

● Western parody, tinged with melancholy for the good old days, in which prim Fonda returns home from school to find her rancher father under threat of eviction or worse, and hires a once-famous gunfighter (Marvin) – who proves to be a drunken bum – as protection against the dreaded hired gunman with the tin nose (also Marvin). The film presents such a mixture of comedy styles that the more lumpen slapstick routines, and the cosy musical interludes from Nat King Cole and Stubby Kaye, may lull you into overlooking some brilliant throwaways. Marvin is consistently brilliant, but the film is patchy. PG

Cat Chaser

(1988, US, 90 min, b/w & col)
d Abel Ferrara. *p* Peter Davis, William Panzer. *sc* Elmore Leonard, Jim Borelli. *ph* Anthony B Richmond. *ed* Anthony Redman. *pd* Dan Leigh. *m* Chick Corea. *cast* Peter Weller, Kelly McGillis, Charles Durning, Frederic Forrest, Tomas Milian, Juan Fernandez, Kelly Jo Minter, Phil Leeds.

● Co-scripted by Elmore Leonard from his own novel, starting out with black-and-white footage of war-torn Santo Domingo before jumping to the palmless tat of a Florida motel, this is a typical Leonard brew: extreme passion and violence interspersed with mature characterisations, wit, and a non-judgemental attitude. Weller leads a splendid cast as George Moran, a laid-back motelier who dreams about his paratrooper past and about the wife (McGillis) of a particularly sadistic Dominican ex-police chief (Milian)who has a thing about testicles and garden shears. On the way, from quirky opening to woozily abrupt climax, we pick up low-life and hustler, big-wig and flunky, as George finds himself tangling not only with the powerful hubby but with the wonderfully decrepit, ruthless figure of Jiggs Scully, played by Charles Durning as if *Blood Simple* had collided with *The Killers*. Jiggs isn't after the lady (perish the thought) but the *generalissimo's* loot. Both Durning and Forrest, as a boozy drifter, excel in a gripping thriller marred only by some precious and unrevealing voice-overs presumably meant to remind us that Leonard is nearer to Hammett and Chandler than *Miami Vice*. SGr

Catchfire

(1989, US, 99 min)
d Alan Smithee [Dennis Hopper]. *p* Dick Clark, Dan Paulson. *sc* Rachel Kronstadt Mann, Ann Louise Bardach. *ph* Ed Lachman. *ed* David Rawlins. *ad* Ron Foreman. *m* Curt Sobel. *cast* Dennis Hopper, Jodie Foster, John Turturro, Joe Pesci, Fred Ward, Dean Stockwell, Vincent Price, Charlie Sheen, Julie Adams, Bob Dylan.

● Dennis Hopper, denying directorial responsibility behind the traditional Alan Smithee credit, has certainly lost a fair amount of plot logic in the editing. Judging by the lady trucker who discusses genital symbolism in Georgia O'Keefe, he may have been shorn of larky disgressions too, as well as the odd guest, though Dylan's walk-on survives. It's a picaresque charade about hit-man Milo (Hopper) who falls for his hit, artist Anne (Foster), kidnaps her and dodges the mob (Price, Pesci, Stockwell) who commissioned him. He has deep, inarticulate feelings of love, despite his underwear fetish and an unfortunate jump-start with rape. Quite why Anne reciprocates has got lost in the wash. Hiding out in the hills, she encourages him to rescue a lamb from a crevasse, but we've already been hipped to his heart since he plays solitary saxophone. Hopper plays a variant on Nicholson in *Prizzi's Honor*, and a finale at the San Pedro oil refinery falls far short of *White Heat*. The nicest idea is the way Milo traces his quarry through her mind, to find her thinking up slogans in an ad agency. BC

Catch Me a Spy (Les Doigts Croisés/aka To Catch a Spy)

(1971, GB/Fr/US, 94 min)
d Dick Clement. *p* Steven Pallos, Pierre Braunberger. *sc* Dick Clement, Ian La Frenais. *ph* Christopher Challis. *ed* John Bloom. *ad* Carmen Dillon. *m* Claude Bolling. *cast* Kirk Douglas, Marlène Jobert, Trevor Howard, Tom Courtenay, Patrick Mower, Bernadette Lafont, Bernard Blier, Sacha Pitoeff, Richard Pearson.

● As befits an espionage story, Clement and La Frenais smuggle in bits of plot from every spy yarn they ever saw, including *The 39 Steps*, hence the otherwise pointless detour to the Scottish highlands. 'Nothing is what it seems' is the watchword in SpyWorld, but here the reverse is true. Recounting the plot (switched suitcase, a waiter who's an agent or vice versa, decoy marriage) would be to imply that anyone might care. DO

Catch My Soul

(1973, US, 95 min)
d Patrick McGoohan. *p* Richard Rosenbloom, Jack Good. *sc* Jack Good. *ph* Conrad Hall. *ed* Sidney Levin. *pd* Tex Reed. *m* Tony Joe White. *songs* Paul Glass, Jack Good. *cast* Richie Havens, Lance LeGault, Season Hubley, Tony Joe White, Susan Tyrrell.

● Lame attempt to film Jack Good's rock opera version of Shakespeare's *Othello*, a folly which started life on the stage. Hampered all the way by McGoohan's languorous direction, which lets each appalling moment of this uncomfortable hybrid of grade-school Shakespeare and grade-school religion sink wincingly in.

Catch-22

(1970, US, 122 min)
d Mike Nichols. *p* John Calley, Martin Ransohoff. *sc* Buck Henry. *ph* David Watkin. *ed* Sam O'Steen. *pd* Richard Sylbert. *cast* Alan Arkin, Martin Balsam, Richard Benjamin, Anthony Perkins, Orson Welles, Jon Voight, Art Garfunkel, Jack Gilford, Buck Henry, Bob Newhart, Paula Prentiss, Martin Sheen.

● Faced with the impossibility of filming Joseph Heller's marvellous novel (the ultimate World War II *purgatorio*), Nichols simply arranges a series of brilliantly funny set pieces around the recurring nightmare that haunts Yossarian (Arkin), the bomber pilot determined to fly no more missions because everyone is trying to murder him out there. Though the vertiginously absurdist logic of the book is hopelessly fractured, some of it does filter through (the mostly superb performances are a great help). Nichols unfortunately grafts on a Meaningful Statement by way of a ponderous Fellini-ish sequence in which Yossarian, on leave in Rome, finds himself wandering the seventh circle of hell. TM

Catch Us If You Can (aka Having a Wild Weekend)

(1965, GB, 91 min, b/w)
d John Boorman. *p* David Deutsch. *sc* Peter Nichols. *ph* Manny Wyn. *ed* Gordon Pilkington. *pd* Tony Woollard. *cast* The Dave Clark Five, Barbara Ferris, David Lodge, Robin Bailey, Yootha Joyce, Clive Swift.

● With this envisaged as a cash-in on the Beatles films, Boorman and playwright Peter Nichols were given a free hand, so long as the group and songs were interwoven into a 'musical'. Taking a landscape Boorman knew from his BBC documentary days – Bath and the west – he was able, in his first feature, to create a cockeyed vision of Britain through the attempt of angry young Clark and determinedly kooky Ferris to escape the fake world of advertising. The film doesn't always avoid glibness in its hedonistic aspirations and obvious satire, but Boorman's passionate eye and his circumscribing of the band's evident lack of acting talent remain impressive. DT

Cat From Outer Space, The

(1978, US, 103 min)
d Norman Tokar. *p* Ron Miller, Norman Tokar. *sc* Ted Key. *ph* Charles F Wheeler. *ed* Cotton Warburton. *ad* John B Mansbridge. *m* Lalo Schifrin. *cast* Ken Berry, Sandy Duncan, Harry Morgan, Roddy McDowall, McLean Stevenson, Hans Conried.

● Disney contribution to the 'we are not alone' syndrome. Billed as a 'Close Encounter of the Furred Kind', it concerns the plight of extra-terrestrial talking cat Jake, when his giant ladybird craft crash-lands on Earth. Despite Jake's paranormal powers, he has to enlist some local boffins to assist in a little spaceship maintenance. Ranged against them is the mighty US Army, and a megalomaniac villain (straight out of *Goldfinger*) bent on collaring the cat. Routine hijinks ensue, mixing strangely with ecology consciousness-raising, pseudo-scientific jargon, and everyday telekinesis. FF

Cat Girl

(1957, GB, 76 min, b/w)
d Alfred Shaughnessy. *p* Herbert Smith, Peter Rogers. *sc* Lou Rusoff. *ph* Peter Hennessy. *ed* Josephine Jackson. *cast* Barbara Shelley, Robert Ayres, Kay Callard, Paddy Webster, Ernest Milton, Jack May.

● Barbara Shelley's first horror film, an extraordinary British pastiche of Jacques Tourneur's *Cat People*, in which she plays a victimised and sexually repressed middle class woman who is suddenly able to channel her repressed emotion and sensuality into a ghostly cheetah which begins by savaging her husband. Tedious in places, and with an obviously low budget, it's still fascinating to witness the Ealing drawing-room tradition merge into that of an RKO-type horror film. DP

Catherine and Co. (Catherine et Cie)

(1975, Fr/It, 99 min)
d Michel Boisrond. *p* Leo L Fuchs. *sc* Catherine Breillat, Leo L Fuchs. *ph* Richard Suzuki. *ed* Jacques Witta. *ad* François de Lamothe. *m* Vladimir Cosma. *cast* Jane Birkin, Patrick Dewaere, Jean-Pierre Aumont, Vittorio Caprioli, Jean-Claude Brialy.

● Not hot enough to be a sexploiter, but not sophisticated enough to be anything better, this never quite finds its feet. Birkin plays a Manchester girl who comes to Paris for some ooh-la-la and ultimately sets up a corporation to accomplish it. She flaunts herself with complete self-confidence, an effect that would be totally horrible if her personality weren't so disarming. The starry actors around her are utterly wasted. GB

Catherine the Great

(1934, GB, 95 min, b/w)
d Paul Czinner. *p* Alexander Korda, Ludovico Toeplitz. *sc* Lajos Biro, Arthur Wimperis, Marjorie Deans, Melchior Lengyel. *ph* Georges Périnal. *ed* Harold Young. *ad* Vincent Korda. *m* Ernst Toch. *cast* Elisabeth Bergner, Douglas Fairbanks Jr, Flora Robson, Gerald du Maurier, Irene Vanbrugh, Griffith Jones.

● Korda's expensive follow-up to *The Private Life of Henry VIII* fared badly against Sternberg's extravaganza *The Scarlet Empress*. Dietrich's siren attractions proved irresistible, and two Catherines in one year was too much for most audiences. Hungarian director Czinner has little of Sternberg's visual flair, but he is well served by Vincent Korda's sets and elicits marvellous performances from his players. Robson, even at 32, has the haggard authority of an old woman; Fairbanks descends into madness with a minimum of cliché; and Bergner, in her first English film, dispenses with her little-girl grotesqueries and is dazzling in her progress from lovelorn child to indomitable empress. RMy

Catholic Boys

see Heaven Help Us

Cathy's Child

(1978, Aust, 89 min)
d Donald Crombie. *p* Pom Oliver, Errol Sullivan. *sc* Ken Quinnell. *ph* Gary Hansen. *ed* Tim Wellburn. *ad* Ross Major. *cast* Michele Fawdon, Alan Cassell, Bryan Brown, Arthur Dignam.

● A turgid tabloid heart-warmer from the director of *Caddie*, in which a hard-drinking hack rediscovers his social concern when he follows a tug-of-love saga through to its happy end. Soft centred for all its crusading zeal against bureaucracy and the baby export trade, it fudges even its rare portrait of the exiled Greek community with its constant recourse to tear-jerk melodramatics. PT

Cathy's Curse (Cauchemars/Une Si Gentille Petite Fille

(1976, Fr/Can, 91 min)
d Eddy Matalon. *p* Nicole M Boisvert. *sc* Alain Sens-Cazenave, Eddy Matalon, Myra Clement.

ph Jean-Jacques Tarbes, Richard Ciupka. *ed* Laurent Quaglio, Pierre Rose, Micheline Thouin. *m* Didier Vasseur. *cast* Alan Scarfe, Randi Allen, Beverley Murray, Roy Witham, Mary Morter.

●One of the many movies puffing along hopefully in the wake of *The Exorcist*. The script places a lot of emphasis on 'possession' special effects, which quite laughably fail to deliver. The direction between these 'climactic' scenes is amateurish. All of which wastes a potentially interesting idea: Cathy's possession begins with a rejection of her female identity. (The writer is credited as 'Eddy Greenwood' on some prints.) VG

Catlow

(1971, GB, 101 min)
d Sam Wanamaker. *p* Euan Lloyd. *sc* Scot Finch, JJ Griffith. *ph* Ted Scaife. *ed* Alan Killick. *ad* Herbert Smith. *m* Roy Budd. *cast* Yul Brynner, Richard Crenna, Leonard Nimoy, Daliah Lavi, Jo Ann Pflug, Jeff Corey, Bessie Love.

●Lowbrow Western shot in Spain, with genial performances from Brynner and Crenna as the roguish outlaw and upright sheriff who remain buddies while trying to do each other down, simultaneously coping with waterless deserts, Mexican soldiers, assorted brands of Indians, and a wildcat girl (Lavi, excellent). Wanamaker's direction, unfortunately, is basic stodge. TM

Cat on a Hot Tin Roof

(1958, US, 108 min)
d Richard Brooks. *p* Lawrence Weingarten. *sc* Richard Brooks, James Poe. *ph* William Daniels. *ed* Ferris Webster. *ad* William A Horning, Urie McCleary. *cast* Elizabeth Taylor, Paul Newman, Burl Ives, Judith Anderson, Jack Carson, Madeleine Sherwood.

●Overheated melodrama, based on Tennessee Williams' play about frustration, greed, lust and impotence wreaking havoc among a wealthy Southern family. Taylor overdoes it as the nagging wife of neurotic Newman, uncertain about his sexuality; Carson connives for the favours of his dying father, hoping to inherit; and Ives is magnificently patriarchal as Big Daddy, ruling the roost with an ego the size of his stomach. As so often with adaptations of Williams, it frequently errs on the side of overstatement and pretension, but still remains immensely enjoyable as a piece of cod-Freudian codswallop. GA

Cat o' Nine Tails, The (Il Gatto a Nove Code)

(1971, It/WGer/Fr, 112 min)
d Dario Argento. *p* Salvatore Argento. *sc* Dario Argento. *ph* Erico Menczer. *ed* Franco Fraticelli. *ad* Carlo Leva. *m* Ennio Morricone. *cast* Karl Malden, James Franciscus, Catherine Spaak, Cinzia De Carolis, Carlo Alighiero.

●Typically over-the-top murder mystery from Argento, neglecting its rather straightforward plot about a series of killings connected with a genetics research institute in favour of gruesome set pieces, bravura camera-work and set design (one character has some truly amazing wallpaper, seemingly spattered with blood), heavy symbolism, and a strong sound-track by Ennio Morricone. Reason doesn't come into it; gorgeous, grisly style is all. GA

Cat People

(1942, US, 73 min, b/w)
d Jacques Tourneur. *p* Val Lewton. *sc* DeWitt Bodeen. *ph* Nick Musuraca. *ed* Mark Robson. *ad* Albert S D'Agostino, Walter E Keller. *m* Roy Webb. *cast* Simone Simon, Kent Smith, Tom Conway, Jane Randolph, Elizabeth Russell, Jack Holt, Alan Napier.

●First in the wondrous series of B movies in which Val Lewton elaborated his principle of horrors imagined rather than seen, with a superbly judged performance from Simon as the young wife ambivalently haunted by sexual frigidity and by a fear that she is metamorphosing into a panther. With its chilling set pieces directed to perfection by Tourneur, it knocks Paul Schrader's remake for six, not least because of the care subtly taken to imbue its cat people (Simon, Russell) with feline mannerisms. Its sober psychological basis is barely shaken by the studio's insistence on introducing, as a stock horror movie ploy, a shot of a black panther during one crucial scene. TM

Cat People

(1982, US, 118 min)
d Paul Schrader. *p* Charles Fries. *sc* Alan Ormsby. *ph* John Bailey. *ed* Jacqueline Cambas. *ad* Edward Richardson. *m* Giorgio Moroder, David Bowie. *cast* Nastassja Kinski, Malcolm McDowell, John Heard, Annette O'Toole, Ruby Dee, Ed Begley Jr.

●Beauty is the beast in Schrader's erotic update of RKO's 1942 horror classic. Kinski's ambivalently bewildered Irena, subject to feline metamorphosis when aroused, is the deadly composite of sex-kitten and *femme fatale*: the virgin who literally develops claws (and more) in bed. Caught between her similarly cursed brother's pleas for incest, and her zoo-keeper boy-friend's ostensibly more natural desires, she's ironically caged as much by current notions of psycho-sexual 'liberation' as by the bars which await her. The seductively exotic surface of this mythically underpinned fantasy might be offset for some by much graphic gore, but if you can buy the romantic metaphors for the primitivisms of sexual obsession, the film delivers down the line. PT

Cats & Dogs

(2001, US/Aust, 90 min)
d Lawrence Guterman. *p* Andrew Lazar, Christopher DeFaria, Warren Zide, Craig Perry. *sc* John Requa, Glenn Ficarra. *ph* Julio Macat. *ed* Michael A Stevenson, Rick W Finney. *pd* James Bissell. *m* John Debney. *cast* Jeff Goldblum, Elizabeth Perkins, Miriam Margolyes, Alexander Pollock, Myron Natwick, Doris Chillcott, Kirsten Robek; voices: Tobey Maguire, Alec Baldwin, Susan Sarandon, Charlton Heston.

●This sentimental tale of an adventurous puppy accidentally drafted into the front line – protecting Prof Goldblum's home from Siamese ninja spies as he perfects his dog-allergy antidote – is astonishingly witless. Originally envisaged as a cartoon, the film emerges as something else, a vaguely reptilian combination of live action and CGI animation. You have to pinch yourself to remember that even quirky actors like Goldblum and Perkins are, after all, human. As for their 'son', the studio claims Alexander Pollock is real flesh and blood, but I don't believe it. TCh

Cat's Eye

(1984, US, 94 min)
d Lewis Teague. *p* Martha Schumacher. *sc* Stephen King. *ph* Jack Cardiff. *ed* Scott Conrad. *pd* Giorgio Postiglione. *m* Alan Silvestri. *cast* Drew Barrymore, James Woods, Alan King, Kenneth McMillan, Robert Hays, Candy Clark, James Naughton, James Rebhorn.

●A trio of moggy-linked Stephen King tales, two of them adapted from his own short stories, the final section a celluloid 'original'. James Woods chooses the wrong method of giving up smoking, when he succumbs to the positively draconian services of 'Quitters, Inc' and suffers bizarre ciggie-filled hallucinations; cuckolded husband McMillan forces his wife's toyboy Hays into a potentially fatal climb around the outside walls of his penthouse; young Barrymore is given a bad time by a demon in the woodwork, while her pet cat takes the blame. In each instance, the limp pay-off undercuts strong performances (manic Woods and sympathetic Drew especially), and the usual caveats about cumulatively unsatisfying portmanteau pictures certainly apply. King's moments of winking self-reference (a ringer for the car in *Christine*, a character reading *Pet Sematary*) hardly seem warranted in the circumstances. TJ

Cat's Meow, The

(2001, Can/Ger/GB, 112 min)
d Peter Bogdanovich. *p* Kim Bieber, Carol Lewis. *sc* Steven Peros. *ph* Bruno Delbonnel. *ed* Edward Norris. *pd* Jean-Vincent Puzos. *cast* Kirsten Dunst, Edward Herrmann, Eddie Izzard, Cary Elwes, Joanna Lumley, Jennifer Tilly.

●Bogdanovich returns to the territory he knows best with this witty, scurrilous account of a vintage Hollywood murder mystery. What really happened on board media magnate William Randolph Hearst's yacht when has-been producer Thomas Ince ended up dead? The starry dramatis personae – Charlie Chaplin (Izzard, a revelation), novelist Elinor Glyn (Lumley, tolerably subdued), Hollywood gossip columnist Louella Parsons and, of course, Marion Davies (Dunst, very good, as usual) – and a nicely barbed script make for an enjoyably colourful and cynical portrait of Tinseltown in its carelessly corrupt, decadent heyday (rather more innocent than nowadays, one suspects). Featherweight but fun. GA

Cat's-Paw, The

(1934, US, 100 min, b/w)
d Sam Taylor. *p* Harold Lloyd. *sc* Sam Taylor. *m* Alfred Newman. *ph* Walter Lundin. *ed* Bernard Burton. *ad* Harry Oliver. *cast* Harold Lloyd, Una Merkel, George Barbier, Grace Bradley, Alan Dinehart, Nat Pendleton.

●Ezekiel Cobb (Lloyd), the only son of missionaries posted to rural China in 1914, returns to Stockport, California, in 1934 to find 'a mother for his children'. He has a letter of introduction to the head of the mission, but the man turns out to be the cat's paw of local tough guys – the man regularly put up against the corrupt mayor of Stockport. During the current mayoral election the cat's paw dies, and Ezekiel agrees to stand in his place, providing he's guaranteed non-election. He is, of course, elected. A ponderous vehicle, for the naive, exact Lloyd (spouting fortune cookie aphorisms), distinguished only by an extended finale in which Ezekiel rounds up the black hats in a dungeon and forces them to confess their crimes by decapitating two of them (with the help of huge Chinese swordsmen) and parading the corpses, complete with bleeding necks and the heads in bowls on their chests. Sixty years on, political incorrectness, in terms of Oriental stereotypes, doesn't come much more incorrect than this. Una Merkel plays the love interest, Petunia Pratt, with a certain dry irony. JPy

Cattle Annie and Little Britches

(1980, US, 98 min)
d Lamont Johnson. *p* Rupert Hitzig, Alan King. *sc* Robert Ward, David Eyre. *ph* Larry Pizer. *ed* Robbe Roberts. *pd* Stan Jolley. *m* Sanh Berti, Tom Slocum. *cast* Burt Lancaster, John Savage, Rod Steiger, Diane Lane, Amanda Plummer, Scott Glenn.

●Uninspired Western about a couple of teenage girls who join the Doolin-Dalton gang, and take to the outlaw life like ducks to water. Highly derivative in its playing with themes about a-changing times and a-shrinking frontiers, it is also plagued by one of those awful cheerful banjo sound-tracks that should have been abandoned back in the days of *Bonnie and Clyde* and *Butch Cassidy*. GA

Cattle Queen of Montana

(1954, US, 88 min)
d Allan Dwan. *p* Benedict Bogeaus. *sc* Robert Blees, Howard Estabrook. *ph* John Alton. *ed* James Leicester, Carlo Lodato. *ad* Van Nest Polglase. *m* Louis Forbes. *cast* Barbara Stanwyck, Ronald Reagan, Gene Evans, Lance Fuller, Anthony Caruso, Jack Elam, Chubby Johnson, Morris Ankrum.

●Despite promising credentials – not just Dwan and Stanwyck, but John Alton on camera – this RKO Western is pretty much a non-starter. The first half is efficient but predictable as Stanwyck and her dad (Ankrum), arriving in Montana after driving a herd up from Texas, are ambushed by a band of renegade Blackfeet secretly in the pay of a would-be cattle baron (Evans) who wants the land on which they plan to build a ranch. Befriended by the Blackfoot chief's college-educated son (Fuller) after her father is killed, Stanwyck stubbornly determines to stay put, though warned off by Evans' hired gunslinger (Reagan, obviously destined to turn good guy). Thereafter, the script starts going in circles, producing plenty of incident (mainly Evans trying to provoke an Indian war, Fuller stoutly fighting for peace) but losing any sense of dramatic progress. Though accused of being an Indian lover, Stanwyck naturally entertains no yearnings for her gallant Blackfoot, but settles for Reagan (working undercover for the army) in what must be one of the most perfunctory love affairs in Western history. TM

Cauchemars

see Cathy's Curse

Caught

(1949, US, 88 min, b/w)
d Max Ophüls. *p* Wolfgang Reinhardt. *sc* Arthur Laurents. *ph* Lee Garmes. *ed* Robert

Parrish. *ad* F Paul Sylos. *m* Frederick Hollander. *cast* Barbara Bel Geddes, Robert Ryan, James Mason, Frank Ferguson, Curt Bois, Natalie Schafer.
● A key American melodrama: draw a line between *Citizen Kane* and *Written on the Wind*, and you'll find Ophuls' *noir* classic at the heady mid-point. A car-hop Cinderella (Bel Geddes) chases a fashion-plate, charm-school dream; a childishly megalomaniac millionaire (Ryan) marries her to spite his analyst. Ophuls holds back his camera to frame the sour domestic nightmare, but gloriously equates motion with emotion when Bel Geddes takes solace with James Mason's virtuous doctor. The alluring web of hearts and dollars has rarely looked so deadly, and only the studio spared us the sight of the kill. PT

Caught in the Act

see Délits Flagrants

Caught Looking

(1992, GB, 35 min, b/w & col)
d Constantine Giannaris. *p* Rebecca Dobbs. *sc* Paul Hallam. *ph* James Welland. *m* John Eacott.
● Commissioned for Channel 4's lesbian and gay series *Out*, this was deemed inappropriate for the mid-evening time slot, which cannot have come as a great shock to Giannaris: with its explicit sex scenes, playful annexation of risqué fantasies, and a tone that veers from weary self-disgust to the enthusiastically debauched, the film positively courts controversy. A man logs on to an inter-active virtual-reality computer game. He has four options, each with a different seduction scenario and a cast of available pick-ups. The first takes place in a (black-and-white) 1940s-style waterfront hotel, another harks back to '50s 'classical' homoerotica (strangely Jarmanesque, this), another zeroes in on cottage trade. It's an original, sly exercise in perversion and subversion, wittily scripted by Paul Hallam, and directed with exquisite poise. TCh

Cause for Alarm!

(1951, US, 74 min, b/w)
d Tay Garnett. *p* Tom Lewis. *sc* Mel Dinelli, Tom Lewis. *ph* Joseph Ruttenberg. *ed* James E Newcom. *ad* Cedric Gibbons, Arthur Lonergan. *m* André Previn. *cast* Loretta Young, Barry Sullivan, Bruce Cowling, Margalo Gillmore, Irving Bacon, Don Haggerty, Richard Anderson.
● A not uninteresting attempt at a suburban film *noir*, with Loretta Young as a housewife whose bed-ridden ex-serviceman husband (Sullivan), consumed with totally unfounded jealousy, concocts a fiendish revenge plot. Having planted evidence indicating that she and her supposed lover were conspiring to poison him, he then proposes to shoot her, but dies of a heart attack. Although rather too fluttery for comfort, Young gives a good account of the woman's panic-stricken dilemma as, left alone with a corpse in the house and her every move adding to the web of suspicious circumstances, she desperately battles red tape to retrieve an incriminating letter posted to the DA. Unfortunately, the script throws in some heavy-handed exposition (notably a 'meeting cute' scene designed to shed light on Sullivan's mental state), betrays its MGM origins by a tiresome insistence on family values (a moppet next door stands in for the child the heroine yearns for), and contrives a risibly arbitrary happy ending. TM

Ça va Barder... (Give 'em Hell/Silenzio...Si Spara!)

(1954, Fr/It, 96 min, b/w)
d John Berry. *sc* John Berry, Henri-François Rey, Jacques Bost, Jacques Nahum. *ph* Jacques Lemare. *ed* Marinette Cadix. *ad* Maurice Colasson, André Guérin. *m* Jeff Davis. *cast* Eddie Constantine, May Britt, Jean Danet, Monique Van Vooren, John Berry, Jess Hahn.
● Such curiosity as this retains is centred on the director, a member of the Hollywood blacklist diaspora. This was his first credited work in Europe, a comedy thriller that features much slapstick along with the scuffling and chasing about expected of an Eddie Constantine vehicle. Although not a Lemmy Caution adventure, the film includes several piquant cross-references to Godard's subsequent *Alphaville*, notably Eddie's arrival in the imaginary Puerto Negro, his luggage consisting of two shirts, a .45 and an attitude of undeceived toughness. But the Constantine style – grinning wolfishly at the crooks before sorting them out and scowling at the dames, ditto – now seems very period. Berry directs himself in a rather masochistic role, getting roughed up by Eddie, dunked in the sea and finally machine gunned to pieces. BBa

Cavafy (Cavafis)

(1997, Greece/Fr, 90 min)
d/sc Iannis Smaragdis. *ph* Nikos Smaragdis. *ed* Iannis Tsitsopoulos. *m* Vangelis. *cast* Dimitris Katalifos, Vassilis Diamandopoulos, Mayia Lyberopoulou, Lazaros Georgakopoulos, Giorgos Moschidis.
● A bio-pic of the great (gay) Greek Alexandrian poet, related with discretion and evident admiration and shot with glissando camera movement and dark, often night-time, hues by cinematographer Nikos Emaragous. The film begins at Cavafy's death bed in 1933, and the episodes – from the waltzes in grand houses in the 1880s to later penury – are told as dream reverie. Cavafy, a passionate, but lonely, secretive and often strangely uncommunicative man, is quoted: 'I've brought to Art desires and sensations, things half-glimpsed, unfulfilled love affairs...' and that's what we're shown. Vangelis, to whom the film is dedicated, provides the emotional if occasionally trivialising score. WH

Cavalcade

(1933, US, 110 min, b/w)
d Frank Lloyd. *sc* Reginald Berkeley, Sonya Levien. *ph* Ernest Palmer. *ed* Margaret Clancy. *ad* William Darling. *m* Louis de Francisco. *cast* Clive Brook, Diana Wynyard, Herbert Mundin, Frank Lawton, Ursula Jeans, Margaret Lindsay, Una O'Connor, Billy Bevan.
● Snobbery, sentimentality and jingoism run riot in Noël Coward's pageant of life as experienced by an 'ordinary' British family (and their comic relief servants) from Boer War and death of the dear old queen to date. Nary a tear-jerking trick is missed (our family loses one son to the Titanic, the other to World War I), and the strangulation is compounded by the staginess since the film, at Coward's insistence, slavishly followed the Drury Lane production. The interpolated war footage was the work of William Cameron Menzies. TM

Caza, La (The Hunt)

(1965, Sp, 87 min, b/w)
d Carlos Saura. *p* Elias Querejeta. *sc* Angelino Fons, Carlos Saura. *ph* Luis Cuadrado. *ed* Pablo G del Amo. *ad* Carlos Ochoa. *m* Luis de Pablo. *cast* Ismael Merlo, Alfredo Mayo, José Maria Prada, Fernando Sanchez, Emilio Guiterrez Caba, Violeta Garcia.
● *La Caza* manages, with very little reading between the lines, a remarkably overt condemnation of Spain's presiding spirit. Three middle-aged men and a youth embark on a day's rabbit hunting. They take with them the trappings of material success, and their prattle places them alongside the status quo. Petty vanities and jealousies lie close to the surface, but it is a deeper-felt, more inarticulate sense of guilt that grows to dominate. Where they hunt had been a battle-ground during the war (and still contains its rotting corpses), half the rabbits they kill are diseased. And as the sun gets hotter, the stare of the camera becomes more relentless, burning into the flesh of ageing men who twitch and grunt in their sleep. Feverish sexuality (linked by implication to repressive politics), outbursts of violence and a sense of foreboding all contribute to the group's self-destruction. Although over-emphatic in its editing, seldom has a film been informed with such crystal hatred for its characters. CPe

CB4

(1993, US, 89 min)
d Tamra Davis. *p* Nelson George. *sc* Bob Locash, Chris Rock, Nelson George. *ph* Karl Walter Lindenlaub. *ed* Earl Watson. *ad* Nelson Coates. *m* John Barnes. *cast* Chris Rock, Allen Payne, Deezer D, Chris Elliott, Phil Hartman, Charlie Murphy.
● A sometimes gross, no-pose-barred rap-culture satire. CB4, aka Cell Block 4, are a trio of hip-hopping young-bloods stage-named Stab Master Arson, Mad Mike and MC Gusto, the last Afrocentric played by the splendid co-writer Chris Rock, who provides most of the threesome's music. CB4 is not, however, in the Spinal Tap league, lacking that film's merciless detail and consistency. But in parts it is hugely, monstrously funny; and with guest cameos from the likes of Ice T, Ice Cube, basketball's Shaquille O'Neal, Eazy E and Flavor Flav, and a first-rate soundtrack from Public Enemy, the Beastie Boys, PM Dawn, MC Ren and CB4 themselves, it will be an undoubted winner with the people who count. SGr

Cease Fire

(1985, US, 98 min)
d David Nutter. *p* William Grefé. *sc* George Fernandez. *ph* Henning Schellerup. *ed* Julio Chavez. *ad* Alan Avchen. *m* Gary Fry. *cast* Don Johnson, Lisa Blount, Robert F Lyons, Richard Chaves, Rick Richards, Chris Noel.
● Tormented by his experiences in Vietnam, Tim (Johnson) finds it increasingly difficult to adjust to everyday life and vents his frustration on his family. The traumatic and insidious aftermath of the 'suckers' war' is a serious subject, but that does not prevent this spasmodic film from being silly. Not only are the war scenes laughable, but there is also a hilarious episode when the flaky veteran reverts to jungle tactics in his own living-room. Lots of acting but little action; worthy but not worth watching. MS

Cecil B. Demented

(2000, US/Fr, 88 min)
d John Waters. *p* Joe Caracciolo Jr, John Fiedler, Mark Tarlov. *sc* John Waters. *ph* Robert Stevens. *ed* Jeffrey Wolf. *pd* Vincent Peranio. *m* Zoë Poledouris, Basil Poledouris. *cast* Melanie Griffith, Stephen Dorff, Alicia Witt, Adrian Grenier, Larry Gillard Jr, Maggie Gyllenhaal, Jack Noseworthy, Mink Stole, Ricki Lake, Patricia Hearst.
● This spirited comic assault on the Hollywood mainstream begins with the visit to Baltimore of pampered Honey Whitlock (Griffith) for the charity premiere of her latest movie, an event which swiftly turns into a riot when the diva is kidnapped by a bunch of celluloid guerillas who force her to star in their own underground flick, under the direction of messianic Cecil B Demented (Dorff). You can't help cheering on these film-obsessive counter-insurgents as they attack their local multiplex and make a stand against Tinseltown mediocrity, but Waters' cause would be better served if the film were faster, funnier and graced with performances which brought more zip to the unfolding lunacy. Likeable, but ultimately disappointing. TJ

Cecilia, La

(1975, It/Fr, 105 min)
d Jean-Louis Comolli. *p* Fanny Berchaux, Pierre-Henri Deleau, Claude Nedjar, Bruno Paolinelli, Georges Richner. *sc* Eduardo de Gregorio, Jean-Louis Comolli, Marianne De Vettimo, Luc Béraud. *ph* Yan Le Masson. *ed* Claudio Biondi. *ad* Carmelo Patrono. *m* Michel Portal. *cast* Massimo Foschi, Maria Carta, Vittorio Mezzogiorno, Biagio Pelligra, Giancarlo Pannese.
● Intelligent and stimulating, *La Cecilia* is based on the story of the colony set up in Brazil in 1890 by a group of Italian anarchists. The colony lasted about three years, and Comolli's account, drawing on original sources, examines its development and eventual collapse. Documenting both external pressures and internal tensions, the film lucidly considers what kind of political organisation is needed in a supposedly collective situation, and the kind of obstacles that occur. Comolli creates no villains to pin the blame on; the fact that one can retain emotional solidarity with the colonists makes the immediate relevance of the questions raised all the more apparent and thought-provoking. AS

Ceddo

(1976, Sen, 117 min)
d/sc Ousmane Sembene. *ph* Georges Caristan. *ed* Florence Eymon, Dominique Blain. *ad* Alpha W Diallo. *m* Manu Dibando. *cast* Tabara N'diaye, Alioune Fall, Moustapha Yade, Mamadou N'diaye Diagne, Ousmane Camara, Nar Sene.
● Banned in Senegal on an absurd technicality which is merely the tip of an iceberg of threats posed by a film which picks at the scab of many of Senegal's current sores. The story concerns an 18th century Senegalese village where the Christian and Islamic faiths are vying with each other and the older African traditions for adher-

ents and power. The Ceddo ('outsiders') who do not wish to be converted take the desperate step of kidnapping the chief's daughter. Within this spare plot, Sembene raises issues of obvious pertinence to modern Senegal, such as the tension between spiritual and temporal power, Princess Dior's renunciation of her role of victim to take decisive action, and village leaders who are only too willing to betray their Africanness to maintain the status quo. Beneath the patina of universally comprehensible motifs lie peculiarly African symbols and meanings which will prove largely inaccessible to an English audience. Still, some of the homilies with which the film is riddled are universally pertinent: 'A man who wears trousers full of fat should not approach the fire'. FD

Ceiling Zero

(1935, US, 95 min, b/w)
d Howard Hawks. *sc* Frank Wead. *ph* Arthur Edeson. *ed* William Holmes. *ad* John Hughes. *m* Leo Forbstein. *cast* James Cagney, Pat O'Brien, June Travis, Stuart Erwin, Isabel Jewell, Barton MacLane.

●Something of a try-out for the later *Only Angels Have Wings*, this adaptation of a stage-play about mail pilots braving not only the elements but their own failing powers may suffer from a certain claustrophobic theatricality of setting, but Hawks keeps both his abiding interests (the tensions and loyalties within an enclosed group, the need for professionalism and a responsibility towards others) and his brisk narrative style to the fore. Cagney is superb as the devil-may-care flier whose womanising imperils the whole operation; O'Brien supplies solid support as the boss who ensures Cagney's belated redemption. Less complex and lyrical than *Angels*, but more than enough to go on with. GA

Cela s'appelle l'Aurore

(1955, Fr/It, 102 min, b/w)
d Luis Buñuel. *sc* Luis Buñuel, Jean Ferry. *ph* Robert le Fèbvre. *ed* Marguerite Renoir. *ad* Max Douy. *m* Joseph Kosma. *cast* Georges Marchal, Lucia Bosé, Nelly Borgeaud, Gianni Esposito, Julien Bertheau, Gaston Modot.

●Highly rated by the director himself, but poorly received and subsequently rarely shown, this is actually a beautifully made parable about commitment, and curiously one of Buñuel's most moving films. The setting is Corsica, where a sympathetic company doctor (Marchal) hides a sacked worker (Esposito) who has murdered their boss in revenge for the death of his sick wife. Typically for Buñuel, he offers no traditional moral structure, but a wealth of complex characters, including a police chief (Bertheau) who dislikes torture, decorates his office with Dali's 'Crucifixion', and reads Claudel. DT

Celebration, The (Festen)

(1998, Den, 105 min)
d Thomas Vinterberg. *p* Brigitte Hald. *sc* Thomas Vinterberg, Mogens Rukov. *ph* Anthony Dod Mantle. *ed* Valdís Óskarsdóttir. *m* Lars Bo Jensen. *cast* Henning Moritzen, Ulrich Thomsen, Thomas Bo Larsen, Paprika Steen, Birthe Neumann.

●Family and friends gather to celebrate the 60th birthday of a wealthy patriarch: after the eldest son, invited to offer a few words in tribute to his recently deceased sister, starts making increasingly serious 'jokes' about his father's horrendously abusive treatment of the family, tensions mount until all hell breaks loose. Played mostly as black anti-bourgeois comedy, this is thoroughly entertaining but rather less outrageous, substantial and original than it thinks it is; imagine Buñuel making a foray into the world of *Fanny and Alexander*, edited by someone determined to impress the younger members of the audience (the style, dictated partly by the back-to-basics 'Dogma 95' manifesto, is somewhat tricksy), and you're almost there. Reservations apart, however, it's an assured, admirably abrasive little movie which never outstays its welcome. GA

Celebrity

(1998, US, 113 min, b/w)
d Woody Allen. *p* Jean Doumanian. *sc* Woody Allen. *ph* Sven Nykvist. *ed* Susan E Morse. *pd* Santo Loquasto. *cast* Hank Azaria, Kenneth Branagh, Melanie Griffith, Judy Davis, Leonardo DiCaprio, Melanie Griffith, Famke Janssen, Michael Lerner, Joe Mantegna, Bebe Neuwirth, Winona Ryder, Charlize Theron, Greg Mottola.

●Robin (Davis) and Lee (Branagh) have recently divorced. Not surprising, since he's a scumbag journo so into fame, fortune and an easy fuck, he'll sell his integrity and ambitions down the line – not to mention the feelings of others – at the drop of a name. Not that Robin's so happy their marriage is over: short on self-confidence, she looks set to crack up, at least until she meets too-good-to-be-true TV producer Tony (Mantegna). Trying to start life anew in their own different ways, the estranged couple keep crossing paths on the ceaseless round of receptions, parties and previews that comprise NY life for those caught in – or keen to share – the hot glare of the limelight. If writer/director Allen's *Deconstructing Harry* was a sour rehash of *Wild Strawberries*, the even more jaundiced *Celebrity* (notwithstanding Sven Nykvist's lustrous b/w camerawork) could be his *La Dolce Vita*. With the exception of neurotic Robin and a handful of others, everyone here is either pathetically shallow and self-deluding in their enjoyment or pursuit of fame, or just pathetically deluded in their adoration of the famous. That said, it's often also very funny, as Allen takes an absurd phenomenon to ever more absurd limits. Agreed, Branagh is a problem – mimicking Woody's inflection and gestures, his Lee is too smug and self-centred to sustain our interest. But most of the others in the unusually large, cameo-packed ensemble (notably Davis, Mantegna, Charlize Theron's self-regarding supermodel, Michael Lerner's cosmetic surgeon, Leonardo DiCaprio's crazily indulged young film star) are cast with expertise and respond accordingly. By no means Allen's best – the humour's a touch too broad, some of the situations too implausible – but a consistently amusing call for help all the same. GA

Céleste

(1981, WGer, 106 min)
d Percy Adlon. *p* Eleonore Adlon. *sc* Percy Adlon. *ph* Jürgen Martin. *ed* Clara Fabry. *ad* Hans Gailling. *m* Cesar Franck. *cast* Eva Mattes, Jürgen Arndt, Norbert Wartha, Wolf Euba.

●An ambitious attempt to film a biography of literature's most celebrated autobiographer, *Céleste* is based on the published memoirs of Céleste Albaret, housekeeper to Marcel Proust from 1914 until his death in 1922. If the movie is only partially successful in making the Proust story cinematic, it may be because, apart from some bold jump-cuts and fastidious camera-work that parallels the writer's sense of precision, Adlon fails to sustain a visual rhetoric that approximates the Proustian style. And although Céleste (finely portrayed by Eva Mattes, matching a peasant woman's restraint and good humour to the dandy's tyranny and dependency) provides the source material, the film's true subject is inescapably Proust himself – his writing, his illness, his occasional sorties into a moribund artistic *demi-monde*. Yet the man remains elusive, almost as if he had died with the 19th century, so that all Céleste was nursing was a 'memory' of Proust. It is this 'emptiness' and Céleste's apparent devotion to it that makes the film at best a half-satisfying experience. MA

Celestine, Maid at Your Service (Célestine, Bonne à Tout Faire)

(1974, Fr, 84 min)
d Clifford Brown [Jesus Franco]. *p* Jacques Garcia. *ph* Howard Vernon. *ed* Gilbert Kikoine. *m* Paul Sennebille. *cast* Lina Romay, Howard Vernon, Jean-Pierre Granet, Pamela Stanford, Olivier Mathot.

●An object lesson in how potentially liberating material (the nominal source is Octave Mirbeau's *Diary of a Chambermaid*) can be manhandled into heavy-handed voyeurism treading an unresolved line between the Pasolini-inspired bawdy romp and Buñuelian subversion. Celestine, fleeing a brothel after a police raid, finds herself in a stately home full of promisingly wan-looking sexual repressives she makes it her task to liberate, while still serving the needs of her fellow-workers (male and female). The print under review is rendered unwatchable by terrible dubbing. VG

Celia

(1988, Aust, 103 min)
d Ann Turner. *p* Timothy White, Gordon Glenn. *sc* Ann Turner. *ph* Geoffrey Simpson. *ed* Ken Sallows. *pd* Peta Lawson. *m* Chris Neal. *cast* Rebecca Smart, Nicholas Eadie, Mary-Anne Fahey, Margaret Ricketts, Victoria Longley, Alexander Hutchinson, Adrian Mitchell, Callie Gray, Martin Sharman.

●A subtly affecting rites-of-passage drama, set in Melbourne in 1957 and charting one summer in the life of nine-year-old Celia (a wonderful performance from Rebecca Smart).Thematic and structural faults expose writer/director Turner's inexperience in her debut: episodes are awkwardly linked, steam runs short towards the end, tenuous links are drawn between political paranoia and legislative attempts to curb an explosion in the rabbit population. But the film beautifully explores the fear which so often informs childhood perception, and focuses on accompanying defensive rituals; superstition (parental discipline is avenged with voodoo) and gang rivalry. The arid Australian landscape is at once banal and mysterious; the hideous creatures stalking Celia's favourite fiction are as real to her as the taunts of an obnoxious cousin. Her imagination is misunderstood by her father, but Celia finds – to his dismay – that the new Communist neighbours encourage flights of fancy and her questioning mind. The central characterisation is the film's strength, striking just the right balance between apprehension and wonder. CM

Céline and Julie Go Boating (Céline et Julie Vont en Bateau: Phantom Ladies Over Paris)

(1974, Fr, 192 min)
d Jacques Rivette. *p* Barbet Schroeder. *sc* Juliet Berto, Dominique Labourier, Bulle Ogier, Marie-France Pisier, Jacques Rivette. *ph* Jacques Renard, Eduardo De Gregorio. *ed* Nicole Lubtchansky. *m* Jean-Marie Sénia. *cast* Juliet Berto, Dominique Labourier, Bulle Ogier, Marie-France Pisier, Barbet Schroeder.

●Favourite films are always the hardest to describe. There are the two pairs of actresses, Berto/Labourier and Ogier/Pisier.The first play a magician and a librarian who meet in Montmartre and wind up sharing the same flat, bed, fiancé, clothes, identity and imagination; the other two are the Phantom Ladies Over Paris, whom Céline and Julie either invent or stumble upon (or both) in a haunted house, along with a man and a child. There's also Rivette's love of cinema – the movies he cherishes – and the childishness of his and our and Céline and Julie's rapt attention as we embark on an adventure together, experiencing a collective form of narrative rape, all spinning a tale that's spinning us. It's scary, evocative, exhilarating and essential. JR

Cell, The

(2000, US/Ger, 109 min)
d Tarsem Singh. *p* Julio Caro, Eric Mcleod. *sc* Mark Protosevich.*ph* Paul Laufer. *ed* Paul Rubell, Robert Duffy. *pd* Tom Foden. *m* Howard Shore.*cast* Jennifer Lopez, Vince Vaughn, Vincent D'Onofrio, Marianne Jean-Baptiste, Jake Weber, Dylan Baker, James Gammon, Tara Subkoff, Patrick Bauchau, Pruitt Taylor Vince.

●Just when you thought that *The Silence of the Lambs* and its anaemic imitators had wrung the last drops of blood out of the serial killer genre, along comes this eyeball-searing, eardrum-punishing variation: a wild, hallucinatory trip inside the damaged mind of murderer Carl Stargher (D'Onofrio). The delirious symbolism and whose extravagant beauty of these surreal mindscapes are not matched, however, by the creaking script's daft contrivances and lack of clock-ticking suspense. Lopez is hard to take as the empathetic psychologist who uses a synaptic transfer machine to penetrate the comatose killer's tortured psyche in hopes of finding his latest victim. That said, victim-to-be Subkoff succeeds against the odds in fleshing out her nightmarish ordeal (trapped in a glass tank filling with water) by capturing the various stages of disbelief, anger and despair. NF

Cellar, The

(1988, US, 90 min)
d Kevin S Tenney. *p* Steve Berman, Patricia Wells. *sc* John Woodward. *cast* Patrick Kilpatrick, Chris Miller, Suzanne Savoy, Ford Rainey.

●Totally pedestrian, directionless dirge concerning a house built upon Indian land whose cellar is home to a living, breathing folk-devil. With over half the running-time spent establishing the existence of the beast in question, the final arrival of a man in a rubber suit walking on all fours is irritatingly laughable. This is really an innocuous Saturday morning kids' movie, complete with a young hero whose father gets angry when his son screams about 'monsters', but who finally realises the error of his ways: 'I was afraid you wouldn't love me if you thought that I was scared,' he opines as the whole family indulges in a wholesome hug. Pass me that bucket, I'm gonna throw up. MK

Celluloid Closet, The

(1995, US, 101 min)
d/p Rob Epstein, Jeffrey Friedman. *sc* Robert Epstein, Jeffrey Friedman, Sharon Wood, Armistead Maupin. *ph* Nancy Schreiber. *ed* Jeffrey Friedman, Arnold Glassman. *ad* Scott Chambliss. *m* Carter Burwell. *with* Tom Hanks, Shirley MacLaine, Gore Vidal, Susan Sarandon, Harvey Fierstein, Armistead Maupin, Richard Dyer, Tony Curtis, Whoopi Goldberg, Antonio Fargas. *narrator* Lily Tomlin.

● A witty, touching study of Hollywood's (mostly on screen) treatment of homosexuality. Epstein and Friedman approach the question chronologically and by type, with astringent comments from an array of unusual suspects, including Gore Vidal (hilarious on how Stephen Boyd played up the gay subtext in *Ben-Hur*, while Heston obliviously rendered his Francis X Bushman impersonation), Tom Hanks, Shirley MacLaine, Armistead Maupin, Richard Dyer and Harvey Fierstein ('I'd rather have visibility than nothing'). There's no great radical agenda here, just an honest assessment of lives relegated to the shadows of the screen. The montage of homophobic slurs from mainstream contemporary movies is especially telling. TCh

Celos

see Jealousy

Cement Garden, The

(1992, GB/Ger/Fr, 105 min)
d Andrew Birkin. *p* Ene Vanaveski, Bee Gilbert. *sc* Andrew Birkin. *ph* Stephen Blackman. *ed* Toby Tremlett. *pd* Bernt Lepel. *m* Edward Shearmur. *cast* Charlotte Gainsbourg, Andrew Robertson, Ned Birkin, Alice Coulthard, Sinead Cusack.

● The film begins with an appropriate oedipal image: surly, spotty, 15-year-old Jack (Robertson) masturbates in front of a mirror, while out in the garden his father keels over and dies. Later, when their mother follows suit, Jack and his older, more pragmatic sister Julie (Gainsbourg) adopt a quasi-parental attitude to their younger siblings. Unusually, they bury Mum in the basement, lest as orphans they be taken into care. Jack longs jealously for Julie. Birkin's film of Ian McEwan's novel soon settles into a claustrophobic mood, the sweltering summer matching the overheated adolescent emotions. Gainsbourg and Coulthard (as sister Sue) give fine performances, the former balanced between bossy provocation and vulnerability; and Birkin keeps it all in line by avoiding sensationalism and showing a tender understanding of youthful confusion. An unusually sensitive and, dare one say, cinematic Brit Lit adaptation. GA

Cemetery Girls

see Velvet Vampire, The

Centennial Summer

(1946, US, 102 min)
d/p Otto Preminger. *sc* Michael Kanin. *ph* Ernest Palmer. *ed* Harry Reynolds. *ad* Lyle Wheeler, Lee Fuller. *songs* Jerome Kern, Oscar Hammerstein II, EY Harburg, Leo Robin. *cast* Jeanne Crain, Cornel Wilde, Linda Darnell, William Eythe, Walter Brennan, Constance Bennett, Dorothy Gish.

● An attempt to recapture the family nostalgia of Minnelli's *Meet Me in St Louis*, made two years earlier, this light musical comedy centres on the Great Exposition of 1876. Sisters Crain and Darnell both drool over dashing Frenchman Cornel Wilde, to the sound of tunes from Oscar Hammerstein II and Jerome Kern, who died shortly before the picture was completed. Director Preminger – best remembered now, perhaps, for such adult pictures as *Anatomy of a Murder* – did a more than adequate job.

Center of the World, The

(2001, US, 88 min)
d Wayne Wang. *p* Peter Newman, Wayne Wang. *sc* Ellen Benjamin Wong [Wayne Wang, Paul Auster, Siri Hustvedt]. *ph* Mauro Fiore. *ed* Lee Percy. *pd* Donald Graham Burt. *cast* Molly Parker, Peter Sarsgaard, Carla Gugino, Shane Edelman, Karry Brown, Alisha Klass, Mel Gorham.

● Dotcom whiz-kid Richard (Sarsgaard) falls for riot grrrl drummer Florence (Parker), a part-time stripper. He persuades her to come to Las Vegas for the weekend, expenses paid, but promises she won't have to sleep with him. The young man repeatedly watches her routine. Then he has the dark side of his sexual obsession exposed (moral: Money Can't Buy You Love). The problem with this po-faced slice of erotica (shot on handheld digital) isn't that the cultural references feel dated, but that the characters are out of time. Wang is desperate to show he's in step with today's crazy mixed-up kids, yet can't work up much enthusiam for young people. Or women. CO'Su

Center Stage

(2000, US/Ger, 116 min)
d Nicholas Hytner. *p* Laurence Mark. *sc* Carol Heikkinen. *ph* Geoffrey Simpson. *ed* Tariq Anwar. *pd* David Gropman. *m* George Fenton. *cast* Amanda Schull, Zoë Saldana, Susan May Pratt, Peter Gallagher, Donna Murphy, Debra Monk, Ethan Stiefel, Sascha Radetsky.

● So the kids from *Fame* did live for ever, and here they are sweatin' all over again, seemingly with the same parents and tutors. Indeed, so many are the clichés in Hytner's film about a group of aspiring young ballet dancers, the script could have been generated by a *Fame*-crazed computer. Sure, a few details are shuffled: the School for the Performing Arts is the American Ballet Academy, the undisciplined but talented Leroy is now a girl called Eva (Saldana), but the hopes and heartache are the same, and boy, do the characters know how to party! Funny thing is, they still do the freestyle stuff to the same lousy rock. SS

Central Do Brasil (Central Station)

(1998, Braz, 115 min)
d Walter Salles. *p* Martine de Clermont Tonnerre, Arthur Cohn. *sc* João Emanuel Carneiro. *ph* Walter Carvalho. *ed* Isabelle Rathéry, Felipe Lacerda. *pd* Cássio Amarante, Carla Caffé. *m* Antônio Pinto, Jaques Morelenbaum. *cast* Fernanda Montenegro, Vincius De Oliveira, Marilia Pera.

● Dora (Montenegro) is a retired schoolteacher eking out an existence by writing letters for illiterate passers-by in Rio's busiest railway station. She never bothers posting the letters. Josue (De Oliveira) is the nine-year-old son of one of the women she deceives. When his mother is killed, Josue is left alone in the big city. Dora takes pity on the boy and reluctantly joins him on an epic cross-country journey in search of his father. Part travelogue, part neo-realist fable, the film works so well because the director refuses to play up the sentimentality. Both the boy and the older woman are hardened and cynical. Only very slowly does their mutual distrust break down. GM

Centre of the World, The

see Center of the World, The

Century

(1993, GB, 112 min)
d Stephen Poliakoff. *p* Thérèse Pickard. *sc* Stephen Poliakoff. *ph* Witold Stok. *ed* Michael Parkinson. *ad* Michael Pickwoad. *m* Michael Gibbs. *cast* Charles Dance, Clive Owen, Miranda Richardson, Robert Stephens, Joan Hickson, Lena Headey.

● Poliakoff's film finds the seeds of two of the 20th century's big ideas present on the cusp of 1900 – eugenics, which led to the Holocaust, and the emancipation of women. Thus Professor Mandry (Dance) sterilises the poor without their consent, and Clara (Richardson) demands control over her own life and no marriage-knot in her relationship with idealistic young doctor Paul Reisner (Owen). But if the plot structure is pleasing, the pacing is not, and the stand-off between the Prof and Doc stalls so badly that it takes an Ealing caricature, philanthropist Joan Hickson, to kick-start the drama again. Paul becomes the Prof's star pupil at the research hospital, hankers after lab assistant Clara, crosses the Prof, turns to Clara for solace, and when he discovers the sterilisation programme, pulls the plug on the entire institution. Dance is elitist arrogance to a nicety, Richardson appropriately spiky, and Stephens turns up in an impersonation of Owen's Romanian Jewish father. A big theme that got away. BC

C'era una Volta

see Cinderella – Italian Style

Cerca de la Frontera

see Close to the Border

Cercle Rouge, Le

see Red Circle, The

Cérémonie, La (A Judgement in Stone)

(1995, Fr, 112 min)
d Claude Chabrol. *p* Marin Karmitz. *sc* Claude Chabrol, Caroline Eliacheff. *ph* Bernard Zitzermann. *ed* Monique Fardoulis. *ad* Daniel Mercier. *m* Mathieu Chabrol. *cast* Sandrine Bonnaire, Isabelle Huppert, Jean-Pierre Cassel, Jacqueline Bisset, Virginie Ledoyen, Valentin Merlet, Julien Roquefort, Dominique Frot.

● When Catherine (Bisset) takes on Sophie (Bonnaire) as housekeeper, her family's impressed by Sophie's aura of quiet responsibility, even though they're not convinced she knows how to serve dinner correctly. Snobbish but liberal, they nevertheless treat her generously. Only when she starts to consort with postmistress Jeanne (Huppert), a gossip whom husband Georges (Cassel) suspects of opening the family mail, do they find real cause for complaint. But by then the women have a secret bond which excludes them from the safe cosseted world of Sophie's employers. Chabrol's adaptation of Ruth Rendell's *A Judgement in Stone* benefits from the director's immaculate sense of social and psychological detail. The film's strong points are not mystery, suspense or even surprise, but Chabrol's flair for characterisation, careful pacing and solid evocation of bourgeois complacency and anti-bourgeois hatred creates a palpable sense of unease that fully justifies the shockingly violent finale. Ledoyen, the daughter of the household, is a discovery; Bisset returns to form; and Huppert, unusually vivacious, is terrific. GA

Ceremony, The (Gishiki)

(1971, Jap, 121 min)
d Nagisa Oshima. *p* Kinshiru Kuzui, Takuji Yamaguchi. *sc* Tsutomo Tamura, Nagisa Oshima, Mamoru Sasaki. *ph* Toichiro Narushima. *ed* Keiichi Uraoka. *ad* Jusho Toda. *m* Toru Takemitsu. *cast* Kenzo Kawarazaki, Atsuo Nakamura, Akiko Koyama, Atsoku Kaku, Kiyoshi Tsuchiya, Kei Sato.

● A thinly disguised commentary on Japan's post-war history, using ceremonial family gatherings (mainly weddings and funerals) as a key to the changes in Japanese society: individual characters represent specific political factions, just as events in the narrative mirror the twists and turns in the country's domestic and foreign policies. However dense the allegory, though, Oshima keeps it very accessible to his audience by stressing individuals' feelings as much as ceremonies; their dreams, aspirations, frustrations and agonies are all too familiar. A significant political film for the time. TR

Cerisaie, La

see Cherry Orchard, The

César

(1936, Fr, 121 min, b/w)
d/p/sc Marcel Pagnol. *ph* Willy. *ed* Suzanne de Troeye, Jeanette Ginestet. *ad* Marius Brouquier. *m* Vincent Scotto. *cast* Raimu, Pierre Fresnay, Orane Demazis, André Fouché, Fernand Charpin, Edouard Delmont.

● Pagnol himself clambered into the director's chair for the final instalment of his trilogy (taking over from Alexander Korda, who directed *Marius*, and Marc Allégret who made Fanny), and things move at a slower, more theatrical pace – luckily entirely suited to events, which are full of remembrances of things past and regrets at the passing of time. A new character stands in the spotlight: Césariot, son of Marius and Fanny, who has to learn the awful truth about his parentage. This is the trilogy's least funny, most affecting, part. 'What a pity that there aren't more of them,' an anonymous critic sighed when it was reissued in 1951; today the modest charms and graces of the Pagnol trilogy seem more precious than ever. GB

César and Rosalie (César et Rosalie)

(1972, Fr/It/WGer, 105 min)
d Claude Sautet. *p* Michelle de Broca. *sc* Jean-Loup Dabadie, Claude Sautet. *ph* Jean Boffety. *ed* Jacqueline Thiédot. *ad* Pierre Guffroy. *m* Philippe Sarde. *cast* Yves Montand, Romy Schneider, Sami Frey, Umberto Orsini, Eva Maria Meincke, Isabelle Huppert.

● One of Sautet's supposedly realistic accounts of French middle-class life, in which a divorcée and her ageing lover battle through an eternal triangle situation with all the romantic agony of *Love Story*, *César and Rosalie* (Lelouch by any other name) is saved from colour supplement chic only by sympathetic performances from Schneider and Montand. TM

C'est arrivé près de chez vous

see Man Bites Dog

C'est la Vie

see La Baule-les pins

C'est la Vie, Ma Cherie (Xin Buliao Qing)

(1993, HK, 105 min)
d Derek Yee [Yee Tung-shing]. *p* Ng Yui-ming. *sc* Derek Yee. *ph* Tam Tsi-wai. *ed* Mei Fung, Kwong Tsi-tseung. *ad* Hai Tsung-man. *m* Peter Pau. *cast* Anita Yuen, Lau Ching-wan, Carina Lau, Sylvia Chang, Carrie Ng.

● Grade-A weepie about a rapturous but doomed affair between a jaded jazz musician and a young woman with health problems who sings in the night market. Just as you're recovering from the shock of a Hong Kong movie made with sincerity, credible emotions, a coherent script and a truly joyous use of music, director Derek Yee delivers an emotional knockout that would make a stone weep. A triumph for independent production (no Hong Kong major wanted to touch it), it made a star of the wonderful Anita Yuen and swept the board at the 1994 HK Film Awards. TR

Cet Obscur Objet du Désir

see That Obscure Object of Desire

Ceux qui m'aiment prendront le train

see Those Who Love Me Will Take the Train

Ce vieux rêve qui bouge

see Real Cool Time

Chac

(1976, Mex, 95 min)
d/sc Rolando Klein. *ph* Alex Phillips Jr. *ed* Harry Keramidas. *m* Victor Forzado, Elizabeth Waldo.*cast* Pablo Cacha Balan, Alonso Mendez Tom.

● Indian villagers are led by charismatic Man of Mountains over a South American lake, through a jungle, across a waterfall and down a cavern to collect a bucket of water used in an elaborate ceremony to the rain-god Chac. Punctuated with unsubtitled Mayan hieroglyphics and the occasional supernatural special effect, *Chac* is probably primarily of interest to students of anthropology. The narrative consists mostly of unrelieved trekking, and remains resolutely free of drama despite a last-minute murder and some initial falling-about comedy involving an ineffective drunken shaman. JPy

Cha-Cha for the Fugitive, A (Gei Taowangzhe de Qiaqia)

(1997, Tai, 85 min)
d Wang Tsai-Sheng. *p* Yang Pao-Fei, Wang Tsai-Sheng. *sc* Wang Tsai-Sheng, Tseng Shu-Mei. *ph* Wang Tsai-Sheng. *ed* Christine Huang. *m* Tseng Seu-Ming. *cast* Julien Chen, Lu Hsin-Yu, Chen Jie-Yi, Liu Shen-Hsin, Ho Tzong-Shian.

● Hard to say if the frenetic visuals are a reaction against most other Taiwanese cinema or merely a reflection of the director's own background in advertising. Either way, this chaotic, enervating first feature has a core of authentic emotion and commitment which makes it impossible to shrug off. A young male dancer with avant-garde leanings dreams of escaping to join a (male) lover in New York, works nights in a sleazy club and spends days failing to relate to his girlfriend in his studio atop a grungy apartment block. His confused thoughts about Taiwan, materialism, corrupt politicians and murderous gangsters hit the screen in shards of splintered imagery. Wang, who wrote, designed and shot the film, as well as directing, doesn't always avoid cliché, but he's definitely on to something real. TR

Chacun cherche son chat

see When the Cat's Away…

Chad Hanna

(1940, US, 86 min)
d Henry King. *p/sc* Nunnally Johnson. *ph* Ernest Palmer, Ray Rennahan. *ed* Barbara McLean. *ad* Richard Day. *m* David Buttolph. *cast* Henry Fonda, Dorothy Lamour, Linda Darnell, Guy Kibbee, John Carradine, Jane Darwell.

● A thin and hardly engrossing story – country boy Fonda joins an upstate New York circus in the 1840s, and falls in love first with bareback rider Lamour, then with runaway Darnell – is decked out by King with lovingly atmospheric details. Attractive to look at, but little more.

Chagrin et la Pitié, Le (The Sorrow and the Pity)

(1969, WGer/Switz, 262 min, b/w)
d Marcel Ophuls. *p* André Harris, Alain de Sedouy. *sc/interviewers* Marcel Ophuls, André Harris. *ph* André Gazut, Jurgen Thieme. *ed* Claude Vajda. *with* Georges Bidault, Maurice Buckmaster, Sir Anthony Eden, Claude Lévy, Pierre Mendès-France, Walter Warlimont.

● An account of the Nazi occupation of France, with particular reference to the town of Clermont-Ferrand, this is an orthodox mixture of contemporary newsreels and present-day interviews. Those questioned include politicians, collaborators, *résistants*, a French admiral, a Wehrmacht captain, a British secret agent – and of course the man and woman in the street who concentrated on just getting through the thing. The mosaic is comprehensive, the documentation overwhelming, particularly regarding the nature and extent of collaboration. In France, of course, the film was dynamite. Other countries, other generations may – or may not – be in sympathy with Anthony Eden, as he firmly declines to condemn those placed in a predicament which he and his compatriots were spared. BBa

Chain, The

(1984, GB, 100 min)
d Jack Gold. *p* Victor Glynn. *sc* Jack Rosenthal. *ph* Wolfgang Suschitzky. *ed* Bill Blunden. *pd* Peter Murton. *m* Stanley Myers. *cast* Bernard Hill, Leo McKern, Billie Whitelaw, Phyllis Logan, Warren Mitchell, Maurice Denham, Anna Massey, Nigel Hawthorne.

● Tracing seven interconnected house moves all scheduled for the same day, this borrows its circular storyline from *La Ronde* while swapping that film's continental obsession with sex for the peculiarly British ones of property and class. The strengths of this old-fashioned, rather parochial picture lie in writer Jack Rosenthal's ear for the absurd undercurrents of everyday speech, and the solid cast of character actors. But its weak links are the grand philosophical pretensions that have each household standing for one of the Seven Deadly Sins, and Mitchell's genial removal man musing benignly on the Great Chain of Being. SJo

Chain of Desire

(1992, US, 107 min)
d Temistocles Lopez. *p* Brian Cox. *sc* Temistocles Lopez. *ph* Nancy Schreiber. *ed* Suzanne Fenn. *pd* Scott Chambliss. *m* Nathan Birnbaum. *cast* Linda Fiorentino, Elias Koteas, Angel Aviles, Patrick Bauchau, Malcolm McDowell, Seymour Cassel.

● Max Ophuls' version of Schnitzler's *La Ronde* epitomised – for all time – world-weary Viennese decadence. The temptations of a remake are obvious. Sex is never off the menu; and what's more, given that the lovers don't stick around, subtleties of characterisation can be dispensed with. Wasting an intriguing cast, this Big Apple bonk-fest drags us on yet another spin on the crotch-level merry-go-round. But when the most noteworthy elements are dire songs and shallow gestures to the spectre of AIDS, the ride's a dull one. Flaccid in every respect. TJ

Chain Reaction, The

(1980, Aust, 92 min)
d Ian Barry. *p* David Elfick. *sc* Ian Barry. *ph* Russell Boyd. *ad* Graham Walker. *m* Andrew Thomas Wilson. *cast* Steve Bisley, Arna-Maria Winchester, Ross Thompson, Ralph Cotterill, Hugh Keays-Byrne.

● A conspiracy thriller based around the increasingly familiar theme of nuclear contamination and corporate cover-up, *Chain Reaction* neatly illustrates the strengths and weaknesses of popular Australian cinema. Its opening is pacy and visually assured, with an effective series of chases and shocks. But once it's necessary to introduce some characters, the script becomes intensely awkward and the whole plot begins to lose its bearings. Only the trappings of apocalypse (radiation suits, zombie-like guards) retain any of the intended impact. DP

Challenge, The

(1982, US, 116 min)
d John Frankenheimer. *p* Robert L Rosen, Ron Beckman. *sc* Richard Maxwell, John Sayles, Ivan Moffatt. *ph* Kozo Okazaki. *ed* Jack Wheeler. *pd* Yoshiyuki Oshida. *m* Jerry Goldsmith. *cast* Scott Glenn, Toshiro Mifune, Donna Kei Benz, Atsuo Nakamura, Calvin Jung.

● Kung-fu action thriller set in Tokyo which pits the samurai tradition of honourable combat against the new westernised Japan of guns and super-capitalism. The elaborate combat will please fans, but anyone not much engaged by martial arts as a genre will soon find themselves pretty bored despite the script's occasional ironies. *The Yakuza* did it all so much better. DP

Chamber, The

(1996, US, 113 min)
d James Foley. *p* John Davis, Brian Grazer, Ron Howard. *sc* William Goldman, Chris Reese. *ph* Ian Baker. *ed* Mark Warner. *pd* David Brisbin. *m* Carter Burwell. *cast* Gene Hackman, Faye Dunaway, Chris O'Donnell, Lela Rochon, Robert Prosky, Raymond Barry, Harve Presnell.

● Opus V from the John Grisham production line is grey, humourless and unimaginative. Alleged killer Sam Cayhill (Hackman) has been on death row in Mississippi since 1967. Now he has a month to live. Sam himself isn't putting much effort into his defence, but legal greenhorn Adam Hill (O'Donnell) can do that. Adam is Sam's grandson, and despite Sam's brush-offs, the young lawyer suspects the black sheep of the family is taking the fall for a racist conspiracy. The occasionally murky character, turning up with some revelation to get things moving, is a relief from O'Donnell's blandness and his earnest delivery of Grisham's lifeless dialogue. NB

Chamber of Horrors

(1966, US, 100 min)
d/p Hy Averback. *sc* Stephen Kandel. *ph* Richard H Kline. *ed* David Wages. *ad* Arthur Loel. *m* William Lava. *cast* Patrick O'Neal, Cesare Danova, Wilfrid Hyde-White, Laura Devon, Patrice Wymore, Philip Bourneuf, Wayne Rogers, Suzy Parker.

● Pilot for a TV series based on *House of Wax* and intended to feature Danova and Hyde-White as owners of a wax museum who dabble in criminology. Judged too gruesome for TV (O'Neal, as the Baltimore Strangler, hacks off his own manacled hand in escaping from the police, later ends up impaled on a hook), it was expanded into a feature, with a *Fear Flasher* and *Horror Horn* as silly gimmicks. Tacky stuff, but it has its luridly bizarre moments and a nice performance from O'Neal as the seemingly indestructible homicidal maniac. TM

Chambre des officiers, La (The Officers' Ward)

(2001, Fr, 135 min)
d François Dupeyron. *p* Michèle Petin, Laurent Petin. *sc* François Dupeyron. *ph* Tetsuo Nagata. *ed* Dominique Faysse. *ad* Patrick Durand. *m* Arvo Pärt. *cast* Eric Caravaca, Denis Podalydes, Grégori Derangere, Sabine Azéma. André Dussollier, Isabelle Renauld, Géraldine Pailhas, Jean-Michel Portal.
●Old-fashioned humanism, certainly, but none the less appealing for all that, Dupeyron's Great War drama (from a novel by Marc Dugain) adopts a slightly unusual narrative policy of proceeding, carefully but rewardingly, from darkness to light. In 1914, after a rather rushed, predatory and desultory erotic encounter that means more to him than us, an officer in the Engineers goes to the Front and has virtually his entire face blown away. The rest of the war he spends in hospital, at first so monstrously disfigured – we don't see his face for a long time – and stricken by pain that life doesn't seem worth living. Slowly, however, with help from medical staff and similarly disfigured patients, his face, faith and sense of identity and personal worth are rebuilt. A few early uncertainties over point of view and a needlessly attenuated ending are mercifully not enough to undermine a marvellously assured film, which is beautifully acted throughout, unexpectedly funny in places, and profoundly moving. And perhaps it's a little more offbeat than it first appears: when did you last hear Arvo Pärt used for a sex scene? GA

Chambre Verte, La (The Green Room)

(1978, Fr, 94 min)
d François Truffaut. *sc* François Truffaut, Jean Grualt. *ph* Nestor Almendros. *ed* Martine Barraque-Curie. *ad* Jean-Pierre Kohut-Svelko. *m* Maurice Jaubert. *cast* François Truffaut, Nathalie Baye, Jean Dasté, Jean-Pierre Moulin, Antoine Vitez.
●Adapted from two Henry James short stories, *The Green Room* stars Truffaut himself as an ageing provincial journalist on a failing periodical, solitary despite his housekeeper and (inexplicably) deaf-mute child, as he looks back from the late 1920s at the two traumas that have shaped his life – the massacre of World War I in which he lost most of his friends and acquaintances, and the death of his beloved wife. A story full of Gothic promise. The similar binding of personal and historical events, of obsessively remembered love and morbid longing for death, were elements that pulsed vitally – if sentimentally – in the earlier *Jules et Jim*. And the failure of *Chambre Verte* is technically all too simple. Truffaut's lack of range as an actor is not helped by the script's purple prose. But one suspects the real problems to be much larger: the human face in this film has become clouded and curiously vague – neither direct enough to stand for itself (as it did in the earlier films), nor sufficiently eloquent to carry as much metaphysical baggage as the script implies. Truffaut has made more than his share of maverick and self-critical films; his later retreat into period pieces and production values becomes all the more regrettable. CA

Chameleon Street

(1991, US, 98 min)
d Wendell B Harris Jr. *p* Dan Lawton. *sc* Wendell B Harris Jr. *ph* Daniel S Noga. *ed/m* Wendell B Harris Jr. *cast* Wendell B Harris Jr, Angela Leslie, Amina Fakir, Paula McGee, Anthony Ennis, David Kiley.
●Virtually a lost film, this picked up a prize at the Sundance festival and earned some critical raves, but when Warners acquired the rights with a view to remaking it, they didn't bother to distribute the shoestring original – according to the writer/director/star, they actively suppressed it (it's never been released in the UK, even on video). It's flawed but often brilliant, one of the most provocative and adventurous American movies of the '90s. Harris is Douglas Street, a kind of professional black Zelig, who successfully passes himself off as a reporter, an exchange student, a lawyer and even a surgeon without any relevant qualifications. Formally adventurous, very funny, and deeply sour. Incredibly, it's based on a true story. TCh

Champ, The

(1979, US, 122 min)
d Franco Zeffirelli. *p* Dyson Lovell. *sc* Walter Newman. *ph* Fred J Koenekamp. *ed* Michael J Sheridan. *pd* Herman A Blumenthal. *m* David Grusin. *cast* Jon Voight, Faye Dunaway, Ricky Schroder, Jack Warden, Arthur Hill, Strother Martin, Joan Blondell, Elisha Cook.
●Syrupy schlock from perhaps the most sentimental of all Italian directors, a pointless update of King Vidor's '30s weepie about a former champion boxer's attempts to hang on to his doting son when his estranged wife reappears on the scene. An all too real and common dilemma treated in tediously glossy fashion. GA

Champagne

(1928, GB, 7,830 ft, b/w)
d Alfred Hitchcock. *sc* Eliot Stannard, Alfred Hitchcock. *ph* Jack Cox. *ad* Wilfred Arnold. *cast* Betty Balfour, Gordon Harker, Ferdinand von Alten, Jack Trevor, Jean Bradin, Marcel Vibert.
●Hitchcock's five not very happy years at Elstree produced a crop of ten films, most of which are now unfairly neglected. Saddled with a clichéd story from studio rival Walter Mycroft and an ebullient, assertive star, he still managed to imbue this light romantic melodrama with an air of sinister menace. The champagne-drinking sophisticate who clouds the destiny of millionaire's daughter Balfour more than makes up for the weak 'cake-hound' hero, and Balfour herself proves remarkably adept at parodying her lost-little-girl image. Hitchcock's sly blend of fantasy, game-playing and frightening lechery, and his continually inventive visuals, make for an intriguing exploration of '20s high-life. RMy

Champagne Charlie

(1944, GB, 107 min, b/w)
d Alberto Cavalcanti. *p* Michael Balcon. *sc* Austin Melford, Angus MacPhail, John Dighton. *ph* Wilkie Cooper, Douglas Slocombe. *ed* Charles Hasse. *ad* Michael Relph. *songs* Una Bart, Frank Eyton, Noel Gay, Billy Mayerl, Ernest Irving, Lord Berners. TEB Clarke. *cast* Tommy Trinder, Stanley Holloway, Betty Warren, Austin Trevor, Jean Kent, Guy Middleton.
●Never did Cavalcanti's misspent avant-garde youth fuse more fascinatingly with his mature flair for melodrama than in this entrancingly flamboyant celebration of the English music hall. Trinder's slyly innocent rendering of 'Everything will be lovely when the pigs begin to fly' is interrupted by a riot and a pair of bizarre female jugglers, Holloway's Great Vance has a luminous vitality which verges on the surreal, and Warren's larger-than-life Bessie Bellwood subversively drowns aristocratic disdain in a sea of sensuous vulgarity. The atmosphere of cosy communality that permeates the film leaves little room for the grim poverty which surrounded the real music halls, but Cavalcanti happily sacrifices realism to create a monument to popular culture. RMy

Champagne Murders, The (Le Scandale)

(1967, Fr, 107 min)
d Claude Chabrol. *p* Raymond Eger. *sc* Claude Brûlé, Derek Prouse. *ph* Jean Rabier. *ed* Jacques Gaillard. *ad* Rino Mondellini. *m* Pierre Jansen. *cast* Anthony Perkins, Maurice Ronet, Stéphane Audran, Yvonne Furneaux, Suzanne Lloyd, Christa Lang.
●The most striking feature of Chabrol's glossy murder mystery is the totally incomprehensible plot, revolving around rivalry for the rights to a family champagne firm: Perkins has said that he took his part solely in order to figure out whodunit. Rather like a pop *Huis Clos*, it turns out that all four parties in the bourgeois household are as intolerable as each other, but who strangled whom and why remains opaque. Made by Chabrol's regular team, it's relentlessly stylish. (A separate English-language version runs 98 minutes.) TR

Champion

(1949, US, 99 min, b/w)
d Mark Robson. *p* Stanley Kramer. *sc* Carl Foreman. *ph* Franz Planer. *ed* Harry Gerstad. *pd* Rudolph Sternad. *m* Dimitri Tiomkin. *cast* Kirk Douglas, Marilyn Maxwell, Arthur Kennedy, Ruth Roman, Lola Albright.
●Given a punchy performance from Douglas and skilful direction, this tale of a boxer's ruthless drive to the top is flashily effective. But it's mostly wind and piss, with the vicious hero of Ring Lardner's story now conventionally excused (he stomps on people because he had an underprivileged childhood and wants to take care of ma). The *Set-Up*, made the same year, is infinitely superior. TM

Champion, The

see Shanghai Lil

Champions

(1983, GB, 115 min)
d John Irwin. *p* Peter Shaw. *sc* Evan Jones. *ph* Ronnie Taylor. *ed* Peter Honess. *ad* Roy Stannard. *m* Carl Davis. *cast* John Hurt, Edward Woodward, Ben Johnson, Jan Francis, Peter Barkworth, Ann Bell, Judy Parfitt, Alison Steadman.
●Into those purple areas where fiction quails to go, Real Life occasionally ventures unabashed. Once launched on its grimly portentous way (in Great Medical Clichés of the Movies, 'That's a nasty cough' has finally been usurped by 'What does your doctor say about that swelling?'), the story of jockey Bob Champion (Hurt), his fight against cancer, and his subsequent ride to glory in the Grand National, steers a careful path between celebration of courage and avoidance of hagiography. Indeed, Champion is portrayed in distinctly unflattering terms: stubborn, bloody-minded, and a rotter to his long-standing girlfriend. It's all efficiently done, and the slow-motion climax can scarcely fail to stuff the requisite frog down the gullet. Nevertheless, one can't help wishing that a director of Irvin's calibre would tackle more testing material than this. JP

Champions

see Mighty Ducks, The

Chance, History, Art...

(1979, GB, 50 min)
d/p/sc James Scott. *ph* Adam Barker-Mill. *ed* AV Mill, Richard White. *m* Simon Brint. *cast* Anne Bean, John McKeon, Rita Donagh, Stuart Brisley, Jamie Reid, Jimmy Boyle, Lusha Kellgren.
●Glaswegian convict Jimmy Boyle pedals a stationary bicycle opposite his prison mural of a disappearing horizon; Sex Pistols designer Jamie Reid offers hints on rip-off art; James Scott's anthology of interviews salutes the practitioners of surrealism (rather than those who mummify it) in an entertainingly provocative film. DMacp

Chance Meeting

see Blind Date

Chance of a Lifetime

(1950, GB, 89 min, b/w)
d/p Bernard Miles. *sc* Walter Greenwood, Bernard Miles. *ph* Eric Cross. *ed* Alan Osbiston, Peter Price. *ad* Don Russell, Joseph Hurley, Michael Stringer. *cast* Basil Radford, Bernard Miles, Niall MacGinnis, Geoffrey Keen, Kenneth More, Josephine Wilson, Julien Mitchell.
●Amiable little film about a small engineering works turning out agricultural equipment whose owner, irritated by disagreements with his workers, stalks out leaving them to get on with it. An independent's answer to the Ealing comedies, it tries (reasonably successfully) to keep its feet more firmly on the ground with locations in a real factory and plausible characters. TM

Chance or Coincidence (Hasards ou coïncidences)

(1998, Fr/Can, 121 min)
d/p/sc Claude Lelouch. *ph* Pierre-William Glenn. *ed* Hélène de Luze. *ad* Jacques Bufnoir. *m* Francis Lai, Claude Bolling. *cast* Alessandra Martines, Pierre Arditi, Marc Hollogne, Laurent Hilaire, Véronique Moreau, Patrick Labbé, Geoffrey Holder.
●Star dancer and single mum, Myriam (Martines), waits for fate to make its next move. Working on a canvas beside a canal in Venice, Pierre Turi (Arditi), an art dealer, happens to forge his 'lost' masterpieces. Myriam and son become part of the frame of his life. Plans are made for a long holiday together, until a yachting accident leaves Martines to make the trip on her own. Camcorder in hand, she creates a video

for those she's lost. Lelouch aims for emotions on a global scale, but only in the first half does the result measure up to his ambitions. Arditi's charisma whisks us along, but once he's off the scene, Martines has a task to carry the picture on numbed grief alone. Furthermore, an intersecting plot strand with Hollogne, a college lecturer and filmed-theatre performer, fails to engage. Without a solid grounding in credibility or emotional involvement, the film's edifice threatens to tumble, but then only a lovable madman such as Lelouch would dare to conjure an epic vision from such ramshackle elements in the first place. TJ

Chances Are

(1989, US, 108 min)
d Emile Ardolino. *p* Mike Lobell. *sc* Perry Howze, Randy Howze. *ph* William A Fraker. *ed* Harry Keramidas. *pd* Dennis Washington. *m* Maurice Jarre. *cast* Cybill Shepherd, Robert Downey Jr, Ryan O'Neal, Mary Stuart Masterson, Christopher McDonald, Josef Sommer.

●This went direct to video in Britain, but as latter-day Hollywood romantic comedies go, it has a bit more style than you might expect. Downey displays a surprising lightness of touch as the teenager who visits his girlfriend's house and gradually comes to the complex oedipal realisation that he himself may be the reincarnated spirit of her mother's late husband. Don't you just hate it when that happens. TJ

Chance to Die, A (Xiang Si Chen Xianzai)

(2000, Tai/Jap, 95 min)
d Chen Yiwen. *p* Kazuyoshi Okuyama, Zhang Huakun, Qiu Shunqing. *sc* Chen Yiwen, Su Zhaobin. *ph* Cai Zhengtai. *ed* Chen Bowen. *ad* Cai Zhaoyi. *m* Yan Zhihong. *cast* Miki Mizuno, Takashi Kashiwabara, Jack Kao, Gao Mingjun, Li Liqun.

●Less 'personal' than *Jam* (Chen wrote it to order for Sino-Japanese producers), this is still much fresher and tastier than the average gangster movie. A team of self-styled mavericks ambushes a drug deal in Taipei, stealing millions in cash from the Japanese buyers and leaving two Japanese dead. While triad bosses fret over the situation, the Japanese – who include the girlfriend of one of the victims – go on the warpath. *Pace* the title, the result is countless violent deaths. It's raised above genre norms by Chen's obvious love for the characters and by the underlying sense that the recklessness of the 'mavericks' is a symptom of a real contemporary malaise. Gao Mingjun, long one of Taiwan's most interesting actors, is terrific as the gang lieutenant who urges calm and caution until the day a hated rival pushes him too far. TR

Chanel Solitaire

(1981, Fr/GB, 124 min)
d George Kaczender. *p* Larry G Spangler. *sc* Julian More. *ph* Ricardo Aronovich. *ed* Georges Klotz. *ad* Jacques Saulnier. *m* Jean Musy. *cast* Marie-France Pisier, Timothy Dalton, Rutger Hauer, Karen Black, Brigitte Fossey.

●Madame Chanel changed the way all women dressed and deserves a better biopic than this. Not that exquisite Pisier is subjected to hours of make-up to achieve the withered beldame of later years. The film simply ends in the '20s, by which time Chanel had made it. But how? When Pisier isn't pouting 'adorably', she's occasionally discovered pinning something, but there's no sign of the hard work that created a huge business empire. Chanel's world apparently revolved round men, and all her intuitive genius is unfortunately attributed to their influence: the bobbed hair is created in pique, and the trademark pearls are a reconciliation gift. A Lesbian affair is treated as an aberration. Worst thing in the film is Dalton as the twit lover. Best thing is a sweaty, corseted Black as a member of the *demi-monde*. Otherwise, chaps, save your money and put it towards that little black dress. JS

Changeling, The

see Middleton's Changeling

Changeling, The

(1979, Can, 109 min)
d Peter Medak. *p* Joel B Michaels, Garth H Drabinsky. *sc* William Gray, Diana Maddox. *ph* John Coquillon. *ed* Lilla Pederson. *pd* Trevor Williams. *m* Rick Wilkins. *cast* George C Scott, Trish Van Devere, Melvyn Douglas, John Colicos, Jean Marsh, Barry Morse.

●Murdered by his father 70 years ago, the outraged spirit of a small boy makes it known through his haunting of Scott, a lonely composer, that his real grudge is not against the killer but The Changeling (now an elderly senator), who took his place and inherited his fortune. In an atmosphere that resembles the electrocardiogram of a corpse, the administration of shocks (murderous wheelchairs, mysterious bangings and firebolts) becomes risible rather than disturbing. And the leaps made by Scott's agile mind in identifying both victim and usurper leave logic and credence on the starting block. FF

Change of Seasons, A

(1980, US, 102 min)
d Richard Lang. *p* Martin Ransohoff. *sc* Erich Segal, Ronni Kern, Fred Segal. *ph* Philip H Lathrop. *ed* Don Zimmerman. *pd* Bill Kenney. *m* Henri Mancini. *cast* Shirley MacLaine, Anthony Hopkins, Bo Derek, Michael Brandon, Mary Beth Hurt.

●Another dull round of middle-class shagging which, twelve years on from *Bob & Carol & Ted & Alice*, still thinks that talking up front about adultery is somehow both daringly honest and funny. Glib trappings (skiing in Vermont, frolics in the hot tub) and witless dialogue sink everything except for the perky intelligence of MacLaine, who clearly deserves better than this, and Derek, who doesn't. Kitsch without conviction, schlock without end. CPea

Chan Is Missing

(1981, US, 80 min, b/w)
d/p Wayne Wang. *sc* Wayne Wang, Isaac Cronin, Terrel Seltzer. *ph* Michael Chin. *ed* Wayne Wang. *m* Robert Kikuchi-Yngojo. *cast* Wood Moy, Marc Hayashi, Laureen Chew, Judi Nihei, Peter Wang.

●A raunchy, sprawling and completely unpredictable panorama of the Chinese-American experience, which opens with Hong Kong pop star Sam Hui's Cantonese version of 'Rock Around the Clock' on the sound-track (he has turned it into a kind of inflation blues, lamenting the rising cost of rice). The plot, such as it is, kicks off with the disappearance of one Chan Hung; the problem is that he had $4,000 in his pocket, belonging to Jo and Steve, two Chinese cab-drivers. Their search for Chan takes them to the heart of the fortune cookie: the tensions between Chinese and American identity (especially when there's a generation gap, as there is between Jo and Steve), the chasm between ABCs (American-Born Chinese) and FOBs (Fresh Off the Boats), the clashes between PRC patriots and renegade Taiwan loyalists… It is sometimes wildly comic, sometimes melancholy, sometimes suspenseful and often strangely touching. The missing Chan – almost certainly a descendant of Charlie Chan, but also a cypher for 'CHinese-americAN' – never turns up, although the missing money does. But the search is the thing, and it goes round all the Chinatown corners you never dared explore for yourself. TR

Chant of Jimmie Blacksmith, The

(1978, Aust, 122 min)
d/p/sc Fred Schepisi. *ph* Ian Baker. *ed* Brian Kavanagh. *pd* Wendy Dickson. *m* Bruce Smeaton. *cast* Tommy Lewis, Freddy Reynolds, Ray Barrett, Jack Thompson, Angela Punch, Steve Dodds.

●Fine adaptation of Thomas Keneally's novel about a half-caste caught between his aboriginal heritage and his mission-bred belief that he has a stake in white society. The setting is New South Wales on the eve of federation between the Australian states in 1900, and when Jimmie discovers the truth of this brave new world ('You'll still have the same rights – none'), he declares war in an orgy of murder. A little too leisurely in its eye for landscapes, but a film of real power. TM

Chantons sous l'Occupation

(1976, Fr, 87 min, b/w)
d/sc André Halimi. *ph* Jean Rouch.

●Brimming with torch songs, boulevard ballads and kitsch dance routines, Halimi's exhaustive documentary compilation is a chronicle of the wartime entertainment scene in Paris, featuring most of the famous names of the period, from Jean Cocteau to Maurice Chevalier. All good French *joie de vivre*…except that Halimi's deadly serious purpose is to expose how eagerly French showbiz collaborated with the Nazis in preserving a public image of 'normality' under the Occupation. Following outraged protests in France, Halimi reportedly added footage showing entertainers who didn't fraternise with the Germans or who actively worked with the Resistance; but his indictment doubtless remains scathing. TR

Chaplin

(1992, GB, 145 min, b/w & col)
d Richard Attenborough. *p* Richard Attenborough, Mario Kassar. *sc* William Boyd, Bryan Forbes, William Goldman. *ph* Sven Nykvist. *ed* Anne V Coates. *pd* Stuart Craig. *m* John Barry. *cast* Robert Downey Jr, Dan Aykroyd, Geraldine Chaplin, Kevin Dunn, Anthony Hopkins, Milla Jovovich, Moira Kelly, Kevin Kline, Diana Lane, Penelope Ann Miller, Paul Rhys, John Thaw, Marisa Tomei, Nancy Travis, James Woods, Bill Paterson.

●Attenborough's very traditional biopic is a disappointment. Going for the whole life has meant an even, plodding, surface treatment, and using the device of an old Chaplin reminiscing to the publisher of his autobiography (Hopkins) lends it an air of Desert Island Discs. The one imaginative stroke misfires: Chaplin's trademark bowler and cane magically presenting themselves to him in the props room like refugees from Industrial Light & Magic. The one conspicuous bit of *mise en scène* – Chaplin and Fairbanks (Kline) clambering about on the Hollywood sign (Hollywoodland: yes, they've done their research) – could have come from a commercial. Downey has captured the idealism and the melancholy, but not the sentimentality of the comic. He has also mastered the pratfalls and the balletics, and there are dazzling demonstrations when he does the drunk in the theatre box and the first impromptu audition for Sennett (Aykroyd), but he isn't funny. This is underlined when clips of the real thing are shown. A bit of a beached whale. BC

Chapman Report, The

(1962, US, 125 min)
d George Cukor. *p* Richard D Zanuck. *sc* Wyatt Cooper, Don M Mankiewicz, Grant Stuart, Gene Allen. *ph* Harold Lipstein. *ed* Robert Simpson. *ad* Gene Allen. *m* Leonard Rosenman. *cast* Efrem Zimbalist Jr, Shelley Winters, Jane Fonda, Claire Bloom, Glynis Johns, Ray Danton, Ty Hardin, Andrew Duggan.

●Cukor at home among the women again, chicly cosseting a quartet of suburbanites as their schematically stereotyped sex lives (frigid Fonda, nympho Bloom, etc) come under the sensationalist investigative eye of Kinsey-style research. With four writers adapting the Irving Wallace novel and numerous hands cutting the result, it's something of a mess; but it's none the less an intriguing staging-post between *Little Women* and *Rich and Famous*. PT

Chappaqua

(1966/1994, US, 82 min, col & b/w)
d/p/sc Conrad Rooks. *ph* Robert Frank. *ed* Kenout Peltier, Cécile Decugis. *ad* Régis Pagniez. *m* Ravi Shankar, The Fugs, JS Bach. *cast* Conrad Rooks, Jean-Louis Barrault, William S Burroughs, Allen Ginsberg, Paula Pritchett, Ornette Coleman, Moondog.

●Recut for video release in 1994, this rich kid's vanity project remains one of the more embarrassing artyfacts from the '60s. Rooks (born in Chappaqua, a sacred burial site for Native Americans) was a teenage alcoholic who turned to stimulants, downers, narcotics and hallucinogens; he spent a month at a Swiss detox clinic in 1962, and uses memories of that attempted cure as the framework for a gibbering mix of 'drama', documentary and fantasy. Counter-culture icons lend misguided support (Barrault as the doctor, Burroughs as the addictive tendency personified) and Rooks gets to cavort with assorted dolly-bird friends in crass 'psychedelic' sequences. Most alarming, it looks as if it could have been a seminal influence on Oliver Stone. TR

Chapter Two

(1979, US, 126 min)
d Robert Moore. *p* Ray Stark. *sc* Neil Simon. *ph* David M Walsh. *ed* Michael A Stevenson. *pd*

Gene Callahan. *m* Marvin Hamlisch. *cast* James Caan, Marsha Mason, Joseph Bologna, Valerie Harper, Alan Fudge.
●The success of Neil Simon movies is dispiriting evidence that most people still watch with their ears. 'Seen one, seen 'em all' quite literally applies to his static exercises in theatrical smart-talk and unfailing wit-under-pressure. *Chapter Two* is no exception: Caan and Mason indulge in a two-hour session of repartee-swapping and painful coming to terms with each other's sense of humour and loss (she's just divo mrced, his wife has just died). Director Moore's ambitions stretch little farther than keeping his actors in frame and earshot, though he occasionally follows them out of chic apartments to chic NY cultural landmarks. The rest is words, words, words – the regular Broadway takeaway. PT

Character

see Karakter

Charade

(1963, US, 113 min)
d/p Stanley Donen. *sc* Peter Stone. *ph* Charles Lang Jr. *ed* James Clark. *ad* Jean d'Eaubonne. *m* Henry Mancini. *cast* Cary Grant, Audrey Hepburn, Walter Matthau, James Coburn, George Kennedy.
●Donen's typically slick comedy thriller, ingeniously scripted by Peter Stone, is a mammoth audience teaser, with a small cast of characters, bursting with multiple identities, caught up in a complicated hunt for a fortune in gold coins seemingly secreted by Hepburn's murdered husband. Grant imparts his ineffable charm, Kennedy (with metal hand) provides comic brutality, while Hepburn is elegantly fraught. There are also smart Parisian settings and smart Mancini music. The result has a chic rating of at least 180; and while hardly as sturdy or provoking an entertainment as *North by Northwest*, say, it remains an entertainment. GB

Charge at Feather River, The

(1953, US, 96 min)
d Gordon Douglas. *p* David Weisbart. *sc* James R Webb. *ph* J Peverell Marley. *ed* Folmar Blangsted. *ad* Stanley Fleischer. *m* Max Steiner. *cast* Guy Madison, Frank Lovejoy, Vera Miles, Helen Westcott, Dick Wesson, Steve Brodie.
●Western originally in 3-D, with the usual hail of arrows and tomahawks hurled at the audience, and here more inventively augmented by a stream of tobacco juice (aimed at a rattlesnake). Actually, directed with great drive and beautifully shot by Peverell Marley, it's much better than you might expect, even though the script (two sisters captured by Cheyennes are rescued five years later, one by force since she has married a chief) serves mainly as an excuse for non-stop Indian fighting. TM

Charge of the Light Brigade, The

(1936, US, 116 min, b/w)
d Michael Curtiz. *p* Hal B Wallis, Sam Bischoff. *sc* Michel Jacoby, Rowland Leigh. *ph* Sol Polito. *ed* George Amy. *ad* John Hughes. *m* Max Steiner. *cast* Errol Flynn, Olivia de Havilland, Patric Knowles, Nigel Bruce, David Niven, Henry Stephenson, Donald Crisp.
●So-so attempt to repeat the success of *Lives of a Bengal Lancer*, with rousing action on the North-West Frontier embedded in much romantic attitudinising from Flynn and Knowles as brothers in love with the same girl. Switching belatedly to the Crimea, the plot finally justifies the title with a bizarre – but beautifully shot – account of the famous charge (the wicked Rajah causing all the trouble in India, it seems, was in command of the Russian guns). TM

Charge of the Light Brigade, The

(1968, GB, 141 min)
d Tony Richardson. *p* Neil Hartley. *sc* Charles Wood. *ph* David Watkin. *ed* Kevin Brownlow, Hugh Raggett. *ad* Edward Marshall. *m* John Addison. *cast* Trevor Howard, Vanessa Redgrave, John Gielgud, Harry Andrews, Jill Bennett, David Hemmings, Peter Bowles, Mark Burns, Howard Marion Crawford, Mark Dignam, Alan Dobie, Willoughby Goddard, TP McKenna, Corin Redgrave, Norman Rossington, Helen Cherry, Rachel Kempson, Donald Wolfit.
●Richardson's shapeless, hapless epic, starring half the British acting profession – the other half having said 'no' or dropped out – in which some stylish touches and a potentially persuasive treatment get buried by the evidence of production difficulties of every conceivable kind. Ironic that, after three years of catastrophes, the animated title sequence by Richard Williams should remain the most memorable element. SG

Chariots of Fire

(1981, GB, 123 min)
d Hugh Hudson. *p* David Puttnam. *sc* Colin Welland. *ph* David Watkin. *ed* Terry Rawlings. *ad* Roger Hall. *m* Vangelis. *cast* Ben Cross, Ian Charleson, Nigel Havers, Cheryl Campbell, Ian Holm, John Gielgud.
●Gosh, aren't the British remarkable? They win Olympic races despite running in slow motion, they castigate old conservatives while revelling in patriotic claptrap, they win Oscars galore while making crappy films. OK, so some of the acting's all right, but really this is an overblown piece of self-congratulatory emotional manipulation perfectly suited for Thatcherite liberals. Pap. And *Greystoke* is no better. GA

Chariots of the Gods (Erinnerungen an die Zukunft)

(1969, WGerm, 98 min)
d/sc Harald Reinl. *ph* Ernst Wild. *ed* Hermann Haller. *m* Wilhelm Roggersdorf.
●Based on Erich von Däniken's books, and heavily cut on release in Britain. A travelogue of 'evidence' that Blue Meanies from deep space got here before us and took time out to knock up the Pyramids, the Easter Island heads and Centre Point. For flat-earthers, people who walk round ladders and get killed by juggernaut lorries, and all those who lie awake fretting about things that go bump and get cut by 46 minutes in the night.

Charisma

(1999, Jap, 103 min)
d Kiyoshi Kurosawa. *p* Satoshi Kanno, Atsuyuki Shimoda. *sc* Kiyoshi Kurosawa. *ph* Junichiro Hayashi. *ed* Junichi Kikuchi. *ad* Tomoyuki Maruo. *m* Gary Ashiya. *cast* Koji Yakusho, Hiroyuki Ikeuchi, Ren Osugi, Yoriko Doguchi, Jun Fubuki.
●Told to 'rest' after a botched hostage rescue attempt, cop Yabuike (Yakusho) sets fire to his car, stumbles into a forest, ingests a strange mushroom – and finds himself in the middle of a guerilla war over a mysterious and supposedly unique tree called Charisma. A woman botanist considers it virulently toxic and wants it destroyed; an eco-activist is determined to save it; thieves try to steal it; and the military has hellish plans of its own for it. The first hour or so of Kurosawa's overtly metaphorical thriller is intriguing and well grounded in eccentric characters, surreal imagery and polemic debate. But then the entire construct falls to pieces in a welter of graphic violence which not only fails to resolve the philosophical issues but also amounts to a slap in the viewer's face for ever taking them seriously to begin with. TR

Charles and Lucie (Charles et Lucie)

(1979, Fr, 98 min)
d Nelly Kaplan. *p* Claude Makovski. *sc* Jean Chapot. *ph* Gilbert Sandoz. *ed* Gérard Le Du. *ad* Didier Massari. *m* Pierre Perret. *cast* Daniel Ceccaldi, Ginette Garcin, Georges Claisse, Nelly Kaplan, Jean-Marie Proslier, Féodor Atkine.
●Whimsical but totally enjoyable romantic comedy from the impressive if erratic Kaplan (*La Fiancée du Pirate*, *Néa*). An elderly couple – a layabout junk merchant and a charlady – take a gamble on gaining fortune and happiness, and find themselves swindled; penniless and pursued by the law through the South of France, they are thrown back on their wits for survival, and finally find their menopausal dissatisfaction with one another replaced by a rebirth of love. Sounds sentimental? It is, but Kaplan's ironic humour, and almost surreal sense of absurdity in her outlandish sequence of narrative events, make for a delightfully off-beat and touching film. GA

Charles Dead or Alive (Charles Mort ou Vif)

(1969, Switz, 93 min)
d/p/sc Alain Tanner. *ph* Renato Berta. *ed* Sylvia Bachmann. *m* Jacques Oliver. *cast* François Simon, Marcel Robert, Marie-Claire Dufour, Maya Simon, André Schmidt.
●Like *The Salamander*, Tanner's first feature takes one person's life and examines it within an environment of ideas as much as within a physical one. Charles is a rich industrialist in complacent old Switzerland who reaches a crisis point in his life – one marked by a TV interview he gives – and walks out. He settles in with a youngish couple (she the daughter of a judge, he a sign painter), and his daughter, a member of a revolutionary student group, visits them. It's an isolated community, at odds with society at large, 'caught in a structure' as Charles says, 'that they can't accept'. As in *The Salamander*, Tanner uses the mechanics of New Wave film-making, but freshly, and is close enough to the unheroic realities of daily life in sad, materialistic, authoritarian Europe to make his film a rewarding experience.

Charles Dickens' David Copperfield

(1993, US, 90 min)
d Don Arioli. *cast* voices: Julian Lennon, Michael York, Kelly LeBrock, Sheena Easton, Joseph Marcell, Andrew Martin.
●The great *Bildungsroman* is animated and set in the mouse community of a cheese factory. Not exactly a tiny tot's best introduction to the Inimitable.

Charles Mingus: Triumph of the Underdog

(1997, US, 78 min)
d Don McGlynn. *p* Don McGlynn, Sue Mingus. *sc* Don McGlynn. Mike Spiller. *ed* Don McGlynn, Christian Moltke-Leth. *cast* Charles Mingus, Eric Dolphy, Gunther Schuller, Sue Mingus, Dannie Richmond, Celia Mingus, John Handy, Jimmy Knepper, Wynton Marsalis, Snookie Young, Eddie Bert, Dorian Mingus.
●Mingus was one of the great jazz composers and bassists; the blend of lyricism, intelligence, soul and fire in his music was also, by all accounts, painfully present in his personality, though this fascinating documentary, complete with rare clips and interviews with those who knew, played and lived with him, tends to soft pedal his more abrasively volatile side. That said, there are treats galore, perhaps most notably footage of Mingus duetting with the equally magnificent Eric Dolphy in 1964 and performing 'Pithecanthropus Erectus' in 1970. GA

Charley-One-Eye

(1972, GB, 107 min)
d Don Chaffey. *p* James Swann. *sc* Keith Leonard. *ph* Ken Talbot. *ed* Mike Campbell. *ad* Maurice Pelling. *m* John Cameron. *cast* Richard Roundtree, Roy Thinnes, Nigel Davenport, Jill Pearson, Aldo Sambrell, Luis Aller.
●Undeniable tendencies to symbolic overkill and messy over-statement mar this Civil War Western polemic on the dispossessed. But Chaffey copes well with the Spanish desert locations, and draws excellent performances from Roundtree and Thinnes as the black Union Army deserter and the Indian outcast who find common ground in oppression (eventually personified by Davenport's ruthless bounty-hunter). VG

Charley Varrick

(1973, US, 111 min)
d/p Don Siegel. *sc* Howard Rodman, Dean Riesner. *ph* Michael Butler. *ed* Frank Morriss. *ad* Fernando Carrere. *m* Lalo Schifrin. *cast* Walter Matthau, Joe Don Baker, Felicia Farr, Andrew Robinson, John Vernon, Sheree North, Benson Fong, Norman Fell.
●Marvellous, toughly eccentric thriller which confirmed that Siegel had more responses to '70s paranoia than a mere Magnum blast, and decisively removed Matthau from the wasteland of Neil Simon wit. Varrick, 'the last of the independents', unwittingly hits a Mafia payroll; staying alive means outwitting Molly (Baker), the Mafia's freak-killer hitman. The defensive odyssey is through sunlit *noir* territory, populated exclusively with cherishably individuated oddballs. Clever, but never cold. PT

Charlie Bubbles

(1967, GB, 89 min)
d Albert Finney. *p* Michael Medwin. *sc* Shelagh Delaney. *ph* Peter Suschitzky. *ed* Fergus McDonnell. *ad* Edward Marshall. *m* Misha Donat. *cast* Albert Finney, Billie Whitelaw, Colin Blakely, Liza Minnelli, Peter Sallis, Timothy Garland, Richard Pearson.

●Finney's sole film to date as director, a *cause célèbre* in its day because it was refused a circuit release, is something of a curio, a movie with a tone and taste all its own. Charlie is a successful writer run dry (Shelagh Delaney, who wrote the script, hasn't exactly been a cataract since 1968). He fools without relish with a pal in a restaurant, watches his female menials on his domestic closed circuit, goes north dutifully to his ex-wife and son, is too tired to care about a come-on from Liza-with-a-Zee en route. The coda, which looked a resonant little fantasy then, may well come across as a thunderous cop-out now. SG

Charlie Chan and the Curse of the Dragon Queen

(1980, US, 97 min)
d Clive Donner. *p* Jerry Sherlock. *sc* Stan Burns, David Axelrod. *ph* Paul Lohmann. *ed* Walter Hannemann, Phil Tucker. *pd* Joel Schiller. *m* Patrick Williams. *cast* Peter Ustinov, Lee Grant, Angie Dickinson, Richard Hatch, Michelle Pfeiffer, Roddy McDowall, Rachel Roberts, Brian Keith.

●A blandoid pastiche in which Ustinov plays the inscrutable detective who has an adoring half-Jewish *klutz* of a grandson, who in turn has an adoring halfwit doll of a girl-friend. Farce, chase sequences and one-liners all fall mirthlessly through the bottomless plot, which has something to do with convoluted family shenanigans, and the whole mess cost a staggering $9 million. Confucius say: 'High time comedies got act together, this one fall apart at scanty seams.' HM

Charlie Chan at the Opera

(1936, US, 66 min, b/w)
d H Bruce Humberstone. *sc* W Scott Darling, Charles Belden. *ph* Lucien Andriot. *ed* Alex Troffey. *ad* Duncan Cramer, Lewis H Creber. *m* Oscar Levant, William Kernell. *cast* Warner Oland, Keye Luke, Boris Karloff, Charlotte Henry, Thomas Beck, William Demarest.

●One of the best in the series featuring Earl Derr Biggers' Chinese detective with the taste for Holmesian deduction and Confucian pearls of wisdom (often acidly apt: 'Bad alibi like dead fish; can't stand test of time'). This was Oland's thirteenth appearance in the role, and the earlier serial-style plotting had given way to subtler whodunitry, here given a considerable boost by atmospheric backstage settings and the inimitable Karloff, who provides a wonderfully sinister red herring as an escaped lunatic, once a famous baritone supposedly burned to death in a fire and vengefully prowling around. Oland – plump, enigmatic, presiding with a barely suppressed air of secret mockery – wasn't the first Charlie Chan (the part had been played once each by George Kuwa, Kamayama Sojin and EL Park between 1926 and 1929); but taking over in 1931 (*Charlie Chan Carries On*) for a run of 16 films, he invariably lent a touch of distinction to the series. Taking over after Oland's death for *Charlie Chan in Honolulu* (1938), Sidney Toler was competent but much less subtle, although the series maintained its standards. Particularly good are *Charlie Chan at Treasure Island* (1939), a spiritedly eerie affair involving murder and blackmail at the San Francisco Fair, where assorted magicians and psychics (one of whom reads the killer's mind to save Charlie's life) get into the act; and the weirdly Gothic *Castle in the Desert* (1942), featuring murder by poison in a Mojave Desert castle built by an eccentric recluse who wears a mask to hide a facial disfigurement and whose wife happens to be a descendant of the Borgias. Toler made 22 films in the series, which began going downhill when Monogram took it over for *Charlie Chan in the Secret Service* (1944). The last six entries (1947–49), with Roland Winters taking over from Toler, are real Poverty Row quickies.

Charlie's Angels

(2000, US/Ger, 98 min)
d McG [Joseph McGinty Nichol]. *p* Leonard Goldberg, Drew Barrymore, Nancy Juvonen. *sc* Ryan Rowe, Ed Solomon, John August. *ph* Russell Carpenter. *ed* Wayne Wahrman, Peter Teschner. *pd* J Michael Riva. *m* Edward Shearmur. *cast* Cameron Diaz, Drew Barrymore, Lucy Liu, Bill Murray, Sam Rockwell, Tim Curry, Kelly Lynch, Crispin Glover, Matt LeBlanc, LLCool J.

●An adaptation of the 'vintage' '70s TV show, in which Murray's droll intermediary, Bosley, adds some comic class to a nominal plot involving the theft of revolutionary voice recognition software from its handsome inventor, Rockwell, and his business partner Lynch. The culprit is tycoon Curry, whose henchman Glover likes to whip out his swordstick whenever the girls are near. Hollywood studios now demand five or six 'trailer moments' – attention-grabbing stunts, explosions or jokes that will draw potential punters. This is nothing but trailer moments. Ex-pop video director McG couldn't organise a pillow fight in a bedding factory. The female leads (Diaz, Barrymore and Liu) let their tacky outfits and buff bodies do the talking, and dozens of pop songs are smeared together on the relentless, pounding soundtrack. NF

Charlotte (La Jeune Fille Assassinée)

(1974, Fr/It/WGer, 103 min)
d/p/sc Roger Vadim. *ph* Pierre-William Glenn. *ed* Victoria Mercanton. *m* Mike Oldfield. *cast* Sirpa Lane, Michel Duchaussoy, Mathieu Carrière, Roger Vadim, Alexandre Astruc.

●Vadim's piece of characteristically humourless comic-strip sexism uses the hoary literary device of revivifying its ex-heroine by patching together a multi-faceted biography from all her previous lovers. It's a predictable chain of *haute-couture* bunk-ups until a wayward playboy takes '*le petit mort*' a shade literally and strangles her at the point of orgasm: she comes and goes. Unlike Damiano's (hardcore) *Story of Joanna* or Roeg's *Bad Timing*, Vadim's film hasn't got the imagination to cope with the large-scale metaphysical implications surrounding sexuality and death. But at least he does have the nerve to confront his fantasies. Where else can you see someone wanking over a Madonna and Child in the Pitti Palace gallery to the strains of Tubular Bells? Or a modern -dress version of Watteau's *The Swing*? Or a pederast film critic quoting Gide in Highgate cemetery? CPea

Charlotte Gray

(2001, GB/Aust/Ger, 121 min)
d Gillian Armstrong. *p* Sarah Curtis, Douglas Rae. *sc* Jeremy Brock. *ph* Dion Beebe. *ed* Nicholas Beauman. *pd* Joseph Bennett. *m* Stephen Warbeck. *cast* Cate Blanchett, Billy Crudup, Michael Gambon, Rupert Penry-Jones, James Fleet, Abigail Cruttenden, Charlotte McDougall, Robert Hands, Gillian Barge, Anton Lesser.

●Sebastian Faulks' romantic fiction has always seemed redolent of cinema, if only because it inhabits worlds we know primarily from old movies – here, London in the Blitz followed by Vichy France and the Resistance. And that's a bit of a problem for Armstrong's film. While it's reasonably absorbing to watch the impeccable Ms Gray join the war effort and fall in love, it hardly feels like uncharted territory. Even after her lover is shot down in France and she's inducted into the mysteries of the undercover operative, the film feels only dourly dutiful. It's more than faintly ridiculous that everyone in Vichy speaks English – so that Charlotte's prime qualification for the job becomes her fluency in Franglais. Nor does the presence of crabby provincial farmer Gambon dispel echoes of TV's Occupation sitcom *'Allo, 'Allo*. Still, you come to accept conventions, and the plot thickens nicely in the second half as Charlotte is forced to rethink her own assumptions of moral cause. Crudup does a creditable job as the angry intellectual Resistance fighter, but it's Blanchett's movie, and she grasps her meatiest role since *Elizabeth* with both hands. Hers is an intelligent, severe and finally very moving performance at the centre of a standard middlebrow drama. TCh

Charlotte's Web

(1972, US, 96 min)
d Charles A Nichols, Iwao Takamoto. *p* Joseph Barbera, William Hanna. *sc* Earl Hamner Jr. *ph* Roy Wade. *ed* Patrick Foley. *ad* Bob Singer. *songs* Richard M Sherman, Robert B Sherman. *cast* voices: Debbie Reynolds, Henry Gibson, Paul Lynde, Agnes Moorehead, Pamelyn Ferdin, Martha Scott.

●Innocuous animated fare (with songs) from Hanna-Barbera, based on EB White's fantasy. About a runt pig who, with some help from unexpected friends, sidesteps the bacon pan forever.

Charme Discret de la Bourgeoisie, Le

see Discreet Charm of the Bourgeoisie, The

Charro!

(1969, US, 98 min)
d/p/sc Charles Marquis Warren. *ph* Ellsworth J Fredricks. *ed* Al Clarke. *ad* James W Sullivan. *m* Hugo Montenegro. *cast* Elvis Presley, Ina Balin, Barbara Werle, Lynn Kellogg, Victor French, James Sikking.

●Turgid Western with Presley (singing only over the titles) wandering expressionlessly through a stock plot as a reformed outlaw framed by his former buddies. All but unwatchable. TM

Chartreuse de Parme, La

(1947, Fr/It, 170 min, b/w)
d Christian-Jaque. *sc* Pierre Véry, Christian-Jaque, Pierre Jany. *ph* Nicolas Hayer. *ed* Jean Desagneaux. *pd* Jean d'Eaubonne. *m* Renzo Rossellini. *cast* Gérard Philipe, Louis Salou, Renée Faure, Maria Casarès, Louis Seigner, Tullio Carminati.

●Fabrizio, Stendhal's hero, contrives to be present at the Battle of Waterloo without really seeing it, which is much the same as Christian-Jaque blithely turning a great novel into a routine swashbuckling vehicle for his willowy leading man. It demonstrates to what degree French *cinéma de qualité* was rather a matter of 'quantity', demanding a complacent accumulation of production values in lieu of the slightest vision or intelligence. GAd

Charulata (The Lonely Wife)

(1964, Ind, 124 min, b/w)
d Satyajit Ray. *p* RD Bansal. *sc* Satyajit Ray. *ph* Subrata Mitra. *ed* Dulal Dutta. *ad* Bansi Chandragupta. *m* Satyajit Ray. *cast* Soumitra Chatterjee, Madhabi Mukherjee, Sailen Mukherjee, Shyamal Ghoshal, Geetali Roy.

●A wonderfully Jamesian study of Victorian India in which a neglected wife, on the point of breaking through to self-awareness, begins to perceive male dominion as a hollow façade of beards, braces and boredom. Immensely funny (with the dialogue peppered by solemn anglicisms and toasts to Gladstone and the Liberals), but also elegant and gracefully moving as the heroine flirts with romance and domestic tragedy on her way to becoming the New Woman. Certainly one of Ray's best films, with a superb music score of his own composition. TM

Chase, The

(1965, US, 133 min)
d Arthur Penn. *p* Sam Spiegel. *sc* Lillian Hellman. *ph* Joseph La Shelle. *ed* Gene Milford. *pd* Richard Day. *m* John Barry. *cast* Marlon Brando, Jane Fonda, Robert Redford, EG Marshall, Angie Dickinson, Janice Rule, James Fox, Miriam Hopkins, Robert Duvall.

●Terror in a Texas town as a prison escapee (Redford), returning home to seek shelter and justice, stirs up a cesspit of hatred, corruption, guilt, lust and racial prejudice. Lillian Hellman's script, based on a novel/play by Horton Foote but emerging as a sort of updated and expanded *Little Foxes*, sometimes fringes absurdity in trying to indict practically everybody in town as a secret sinner, and in its stagy contrivance (the refugee just happens by on the night of a convention when temperatures are running drunkenly high). But it does manage to weave a credible pattern out of the tangled loyalties and enmities, which Penn's direction takes by the scruff and shakes into a firework display of controlled violence. Terrific performances too, although Brando (undergoing his statutory beating up as the sheriff caught in the middle) rather overdoes the broody bit. TM

Chase, The

(1994, US, 94 min)
d Adam Rifkin. *p* Brad Wyman, Cassian Elwes. *sc* Adam Rifkin. *ph* Alan Jones. *ed* Peter Schink. *pd* Sherman Williams. *m* Richard Gibbs. *cast* Charlie Sheen, Kristy Swanson, Ray Wise, Josh Mostel, Wayne Grace, Rocky Carroll, Henry Rollins, Cary Elwes.

●Jack Hammond (Sheen), an escaped, falsely convicted bank-robber, jump starts his romance with unhappy heiress Natalie (Swanson) by abducting her from a gas station. The daughter of Dalton Voss (Wise), the Donald Trump of California, she's none too pleased – even less so when father offers a paltry ransom and turns her live-on-TV kidnap into a travelling media circus. As the ill-matched couple settle their differences and get better acquainted, the growing convoy of cop cars and outside-broadcast vans nears the Mexican border and freedom…or, perhaps, a dead end. Swanson displays fine dental work and a synthetic 'attitude', mostly whining on about what a drag it is to be rich, so only rock'n'roll hardman Henry Rollins, as a standard-issue cop and blasé star of 'reality TV', makes any lasting impression. Unroadworthy. NF

Chase a Crooked Shadow

(1957, GB, 87 min, b/w)
d Michael Anderson. *p* Douglas Fairbanks Jr. *sc* David D Osborn, Charles Sinclair. *ph* Erwin Hillier. *ed* Gordon Pilkington. *ad* Paul Sheriff. *m* Matyas Seiber. *cast* Richard Todd, Anne Baxter, Herbert Lom, Alexander Knox, Faith Brook, Alan Tilvern.

●Hitchcockian thriller with Baxter as an heiress seemingly the victim of a conspiracy of terror involving the family jewels and someone (Todd) turning up claiming to be her supposedly dead brother. Passably suspenseful, but lacking Hitchcock's plausibility (especially the tricksy ending) and saddled with a dreary performance from the dreary Todd. TM

Chasers

(1994, US, 101 min)
d Dennis Hopper. *p* James G Robinson. *sc* Joe Batteer, Dan Gilroy, John Rice. *ph* Ueli Steiger. *ed* Christian Wagner. *pd* Robert Pearson. *m* Dwight Yoakam, Pete Anderson. *cast* Tom Berenger, William McNamara, Erika Eleniak, Dean Stockwell, Gary Busey, Seymour Cassel, Marilu Henner, Dennis Hopper.

●Dennis Hopper's film is a lightweight affair, but amiable enough. It's the story of two naval shore-patrolmen – by-the-book hardass Berenger and slick young McNamara – ordered to escort a prisoner cross-country on the Fourth of July. The catch is the prisoner's a she: Eleniak of *Baywatch* fame. Saddled with such a tired script and a sorely unprepossessing star as McNamara, Hopper amuses himself by doodling in the margins: he's got a wonderful eye for authentic pop-art Americana, truck-stop culture and crazy golf landscapes. He also has a lot of cool friends willing to put in a day's work for the heck of it. Nothing essential, then, but not a total loss either. TCh

Chasing Amy

(1996, US, 113 min)
d Kevin Smith. *p* Scott Mosier. *sc* Kevin Smith. *ph* David Klein. *ed* Kevin Smith, Scott Mosier. *pd* Robert Holtzman. *m* David Pirner. *cast* Ben Affleck, Joey Lauren Adams, Jason Lee, Dwight Ewell, Jason Mewes, Kevin Smith.

●Banky (Lee) and Holden (Affleck) are beginning to make a name for themselves as creators of the cult comic book 'Bluntman & Chronic', but their partnership is threatened when Holden falls for fellow artist Alyssa (Adams). For one thing, Banky – whose attitude to women is at best neanderthal, at worst blatantly misogynist – is jealously proprietorial about his buddy; for another, Alyssa already has a girlfriend. Though Smith's directing talent remains rudimentary, as a writer he's progressed from the basic schtick-and-gags routine of *Clerks*, his gleefully un-PC debut. Again, there's plenty of profanity, but the film scores in its exploration of the social and psychological implications of Alyssa's increasingly tender feelings for Holden. The script moves beyond Smith's customary cataloguing of male adolescent ignorance and idiocy to offer sharp insights into the romanticism and pragmatism, pride and double standards that define the tangled threesome. GA

Chasing Dreams

(1994, GB, 83 min)
d Caleb Lindsay. *p* Therese Conte, David G Brown. *sc* Caleb Lindsay. *ph* Dusan Todorovic, Caleb Lindsay. *ed* Caleb Lindsay, Alexander Victor. *pd* Theo Stossoff. *cast* Ian Prince, Luke Shaw, Adam Russ, Dominic Knutton.

●Something of a gem, writer/director Lindsay's micro-budget independent feature is low on big sets (why worry, if you've got London available), but big on individuality and quirky sensibility. It comes on like a mongrel blend of Jarmusch and Mike Leigh as it traces the lives of a trio of likeable, ever-hopeful non-achievers. Ex-borstal boy Alex tries to make a go of it buying and fixing-up rust-bucket 'motors'; Pat and Dave are struggling with an album (there's an hilarious set-piece with the producer of 'Lucky Records'): all chase girls with a staggering lack of success. Throughout Lindsay shows a real affection for his characters. Often the film is exquisitely inconsequential and disconsolate; it's always stylistically interesting (filters and all); and the ending is great. WH

Chasing the Deer

(1994, GB, 97 min)
d Graham Holloway. *p* Bob Carruthers. *sc* Jerome Vincent, Bob Carruthers, Steve Gillham. *ph* Alan Trow. *ed* Patrick Moore. *m* John Wetton. *cast* Brian Blessed, Iain Cuthbertson, Dominique Carrara, Jake D'Arcy, Dominic Borrelli.

●This bold local production, subtitled 'A Story of the '45', was financed by small investors. The result, regrettably, is not a patch on what Peter Watkins did with a small TV budget in *Culloden*. A handful of beardies in kilts skirl about in the mist of a smoke machine…The best thing in this truly lamentable account of Bonnie Prince Charlie's doomed attempt to regain his throne is bellowing Brian Blessed as an English officer leading a regiment of loyalist Scots. BC

Chat, Le (The Cat)

(1970, Fr, 88 min)
d Pierre Granier-Deferre. sc Pierre Granier-Deferre, Pascal Jardin. *ph* Walter Wottitz. *ad* Jacques Sautier. *m* Philippe Sarde. *cast* Simone Signoret, Jean Gabin, Annie Cordy, Jacques Rispal, Nicole Desailly.

●In this anaemic adaptation of a characteristically sour and sweaty Simenon novel, a long-married couple is sucked into a triangular sado-masochistic relationship with a cat, on which the husband lavishes the suffocatingly possessive affection he once devoted to his once-beautiful, now alcoholically bloated, spouse. Simenon, however, invested her eventual killing of the pet with all the neurotic squalor of a *crime passionnel*; here, given the mutual malignity of Gabin and Signoret, one simply wonders how the cat managed to survive so long. GAd

Chateau, The

(2001, US/Fr, 91 min)
d Jesse Peretz. *p* Robin O'Hara, Scott Macaulay. *sc* Jesse Peretz. *ph* Tom Richmond. *ed* James Lyons, Steve Hamilton. *ad* Christian Marti. *m* Nathan Larson. *cast* Didier Flamand, Donal Logue, Romany Malco, Paul Rudd, Sylvie Testud, Philippe Nahon.

●A half-irritating, half-hilarious blend of comedy and con drama in which two very different American brothers (one black, one white) reunite in the French countryside in order to take over, then sell, a chateau left to them by a long-lost relative. But their naivety about France and their terrible French are only the start of their problems, as the servants prove reluctant to leave the crumbling manse that's housed them for so long – moreover, one staff member is rather attractive. Best when simply going for laughs, it's amiable enough if a mite over-stretched. GA

Château de ma mère, Le (My Mother's Castle)

(1990, Fr, 98 min)
d Yves Robert. *p* Alain Poiré. *sc* Jérôme Tonnerre, Yves Robert, Louis Nucera. *ph* Robert Alazraki. *ed* Pierre Gillette. *ad* Marc Goldstaub, Guy Azzi. *m* Vladimir Cosma. *cast* Philippe Caubère, Nathalie Roussell, Didier Pain, Thérèse Liotard, Julie Timmerman, Paul Crauchet, Jean Rochefort, Jean Carmet, Georges Wilson.

●Unsurprisingly, this sequel to *La Gloire de mon père*, adapted from the second volume of Marcel Pagnol's autobiography, is very similar in tone (though mercifully more sparing with the music). Your attitude to it depends on whether you viewed the first film as a touching evocation of a Provence childhood, or as a tedious travelogue drowning in sentiment. The storyline is enlivened early on by a disillusioning encounter between young Marcel and a most pretentious girl whose father (vividly played by the wonderful Rochefort) is an absinthe-crazed would-be poet who speaks in rhyming couplets *à la* Cyrano. From there on, the tone darkens, with Marcel's father persuaded away from the path of rectitude; and before long the narrator is rounding things off with a solemn roll-call of the dear departed. The coda, in which the adult Pagnol conjures up a vision of his mother as she was in his childhood, is very moving. JMo

Château des singes, Le

see Monkey's Tale, A

Chato's Land

(1971, GB, 100 min)
d/p Michael Winner. *sc* Gerald Wilson. *ph* Bob Paynter. *ed* Frederick Wilson. *ad* Manolo Mampaso. *m* Jerry Fielding. *cast* Charles Bronson, Jack Palance, Richard Basehart, James Whitmore, Richard Jordan, Simon Oakland, Roddy McMillan.

●Bronson and Winner united in their usual sledge-hammer style as Charlie plays a half-breed Apache hunted for murder, and Palance leads a posse in pursuit. They rape his wife, and the Indian plots and watches their downfall. There are attempts in Gerald Wilson's script to say something about racism and violence, and some critics have even suggested parallels with the disastrous American involvement in Vietnam; but in Winner's hands, it's just a rag-bag of muddled clichés. GA

Chattahoochee

(1989, US, 97 min)
d Mick Jackson. *p* Aaron Schwab, Faye Schwab. *sc* James Hicks. *ph* Andrew Dunn. *ed* Don Fairservice. *ad* Patrick Tagliaferro. *m* John Keane. *cast* Gary Oldman, Dennis Hopper, Frances McDormand, Pamela Reed, Ned Beatty, M Emmet Walsh, William De Acutis, Lee Wilkof.

●Florida, 1955. After sniping at his neighbours, Korean war vet Foley (Oldman), depressed by debts, unsuccessfully turns the gun on himself. Committed to the maximum-security Chattahoochee hospital for the criminally insane, he finds himself trapped in a nightmare world of squalor, humiliation and sadism. Life's hell; even his wife (McDormand) deserts him while he's inside. But with help from friends – including his sister (Reed) and Hopper's melancholy rapist – Foley gens up on the law and fights the good fight against institutionalised inhumanity. Coming on like a cross between *Midnight Express*, *One Flew Over the Cuckoo's Nest* and *The Bird Man of Alcatraz*, Jackson's well-meaning but clichéd film staggers towards a predictable climax. Hopper simply does what comes easy, Oldman yields to twitchy histrionics, and it's left to Reed to supply a touch of restraint in a small, relatively thankless part. GA

Che!

(1969, US, 96 min)
d Richard Fleischer. *p* Sy Bartlett. *sc* Michael Wilson, Sy Bartlett. *ph* Charles Wheeler. *ed* Marion Rothman. *ad* Jack Martin Smith, Arthur Lonergan. *m* Lalo Schifrin. *cast* Omar Sharif, Jack Palance, Cesare Danova, Robert Loggia, Woody Strode, Barbara Luna, Frank Silvera.

●One of the bizarre products of Hollywood's brief flirtation with revolution in the '60s, a fence-sitting but occasionally amusing account of Guevara's career. Remarkable for its eccentric casting of Palance as an amphetamine-popping Castro.

Cheap Detective, The

(1978, US, 92 min)
d Robert Moore. *p* Ray Stark. *sc* Neil Simon. *ph* John A Alonzo. *ed* Sidney Levin, Michael A Stevenson. *pd* Robert Luthardt. *m* Patrick Williams. *cast* Peter Falk, Ann-Margret, Eileen Brennan, James Coco, Dom DeLuise, Stockard Channing, John Houseman, Louise Fletcher, Phil Silvers, Sid Caesar, Madeline Kahn.

●Neil Simon-scripted spoof of films based on Chandler/Hammett private eye novels, with *Casablanca* thrown in for bad measure. Designed as a follow-up to the scarcely more successful *Murder by Death*, it's the usual collection of quickfire one-liners punctuated by huge wads of unfunny padding. Buffs may amuse themselves by noting obvious references to *The Maltese Falcon*, *The Big Sleep*, *Farewell My Lovely* and the like. *The Cheap Idea* might have been a better title. NF

Cheaper by the Dozen

(1950, US, 85 min)
d Walter Lang. *p/sc* Lamar Trotti. *ph* Leon Shamroy. *ed* J Watson Webb Jr. *ad* Lyle Wheeler. *m* Cyril J Mockridge. *cast* Clifton Webb, Myrna Loy, Jeanne Crain, Edgar Buchanan, Barbara Bates, Mildred Natwick.

●Webb's spinsterish acidity, so effective in *Laura* and *The Razor's Edge*, was amusing enough when he was elevated to stardom as the waspish baby-sitter in *Sitting Pretty*. But by the time he came to play this paterfamilias of the '20s who organises his twelve children along the same efficiency lines as his business, the act was wearing distinctly thin (and suffering from spots of sentimentality). Only one sequence really takes off, with the delightfully bemused Natwick trying to recruit the mother of twelve as a lecturer on birth control. TM

Cheap Shots

(1988, US, 92 min)
d/p/sc Jeff Ureles, Jerry Stoeffhaas. *ph* Thom Marini. *ed* Ken McIlwaine, Andrew Praskai. *pd* Carl Zollo. *m* Jeff Beal. *cast* Louis Zorich, David Patrick Kelly, Marie Louise Wilson, Clarke Gordon, Patience Moore.

●Middle-aged Latin loser Louie (Zorich) owns a run-down motel, is penniless, fed up with domestic chores, his obnoxious wife, continual promises of help from her wheelchair-bound father, and life in general. Hardly surprising, then, that Louie's eyes should stray in the direction of a blonde guest who arrives with a male companion: a voyeuristic urge shared by young resident Arnold (Kelly). The two decide to instal a newly-acquired video-camera in the couple's cottage in the hope of recording some frisky action, but what they eventually witness is something they rather wish they hadn't... Ureles and Stoeffhaas extract some marvellous performances from an unknown cast, the result being a fine blend of Tati-esque humour, household drama, and mild eroticism, with occasional unexpected dollops of suspenders, sorry, suspense. DA

Checking Out

(1988, GB, 95 min)
d David Leland. *p* Ben Myron. *sc* Joe Eszterhas. *ph* Ian Wilson. *ed* Lee Percy. *pd* Barbara Ling. *m* Carter Burwell. *cast* Jeff Daniels, Melanie Mayron, Michael Tucker, Kathleen York, Ann Magnuson, Allan Havey, Jo Harvey Allen, Ian Wolfe, Billy Beck, John Durbin, Felton Perry.

●You suspect from the first fantasy sequence – hero Ray Macklin (Daniels) in his grave – that things are going to be wild, wacky, raucous and asprawl, and by the time you reach the final fantasy of Heaven as a Howard Hughes desert motel with George Harrison pushing broom, you know it. This 'light-hearted', heavy-handed skit on hypochondria in the suburbs is a miscalculation from start to finish. Macklin's life starts to go wrong when his best friend dies of a heart attack in his prime. Heck, this could happen to him, and he becomes increasingly hysterical and dishevelled, pestering doctors and loading up the household with personal oxygen supplies and pulse monitors until his wife (Mayron) can endure no more of it. There's no real structure to the film, and incidents and meetings – the orgy in the car, or the weirdo junk-food millionaire, for example – are the screenwriter's version of builder's rubble. Desperately unfunny. BC

Cheech & Chong's Next Movie (aka High Encounters of the Ultimate Kind)

(1980, US, 99 min)
d Thomas Chong. *p* Howard Brown. *sc* Tommy Chong, Cheech Marin. *ed* Scott Conrad, Tom Avildsen. *pd* Fred Harpman. *m* Mark Davis. *cast* Richard 'Cheech' Marin, Thomas Chong, Evelyn Guerrero, Betty Kennedy, Sy Kramer, Rikki Marin.

●For a comedy double-act who make their money out of people stoned beyond discrimination, Cheech and Chong are probably better than we deserve. This free-wheeling sequel to their first feature, *Up in Smoke*, has the duo sharing a precarious state of independence in time-warp California. Cheech, the Chicano, charms foxy ladies with his smart line in dirty talk ('I'm serving tube steak covered in underwear. I hope she hasn't eaten yet'). Chong, the dead hippy, deals dope to himself and stays at home awaiting legalisation of the magic weed and laying down Richter-scale solos on his guitar. The plot is, er, like an irrelevant hassle, and the observations on sub-culture work better than the slapstick paced for the brains of the wasted, but there are enough of these – especially a welfare office freak show – to serve as a reminder of how good the high times can be. RP

Cheer Boys Cheer

(1939, GB, 85 min, b/w)
d Walter Forde. *p* Michael Balcon. *sc* Roger MacDougall, Allan MacKinnon. *ph* Ronald Neame. *ed* Ray Pitt. *ad* Wilfrid Shingleton. *cast* Nova Pilbeam, Edmund Gwenn, Jimmy O'Dea, CV France, Peter Coke, Moore Marriott, Graham Moffatt, Alexander Knox.

●The film Charles Barr saw both as an allegory for Ealing's own history and a remarkable precursor of the later Ealing comedies. Unfortunately, Gwenn's fascist brewer (busily trying to take over his rival) is left disappointingly one-dimensional, and the romantic sub-plot wavers precariously as Pilbeam pulls out all the stops to deal with two horribly miscast suitors. As compensation, though, much of the film takes off into glorious comedy as Moore Marriott and Graham Moffatt – surely the most enduring comics of the period – anarchically disrupt each scene they appear in. RMy

Cheetah

(1989, US, 84 min)
d Jeff Blyth. *p* Robert Halmi Sr. *sc* Erik Tarloff, John Cotter, Griff du Rhone. *ph* Thomas Burstyn. *ed* Eric Albertson. *pd* Jane Cavedon. *m* Bruce Rowland. *cast* Keith Coogan, Lucy Deakins, Collin Mothupi, Timothy Landfield, Breon Gorman.

●Disney offering (unreleased in UK cinemas) which sends Californian teenagers Coogan and Deakins to Kenya for a stay in the bush with their parents; there they befriend a Masai boy and look after an abandoned baby cheetah. Decent and old-fashioned. TJ

Chelsea Girls

(1967, US, 215 min, b/w & col)
d/p/ph Andy Warhol. *m* Velvet Underground. *cast* Nico, Ari, Bob 'Ondine' Olivio, Ingrid Superstar, Mario Montez, Marie Menken, Bridget Polk.

●Bits of this shambling mess gave us a big buzz way back when Wendy Arthole flamboyantly (but minimally) gratified curiosity about the then new decadence, while soupcan aesthetic theory glorified its many hours of brain-crushing tat. It's alive while nutty naturals like Menken and Ondine perform. The other 85 per cent is wallpaper, the concept pompous, and zomboidal. View'n doze. RD

Chemins de l'Exil, Les

see Roads of Exile, The

Chère Louise (Louise)

(1972, Fr/It, 105 min)
d Philippe de Broca. *p* Georges Dancigers, Alexandre Mnouchkine. *sc* Jean-Loup Dabadie. *ph* Ricardo Aronovich. *ed* Françoise Javet. *ad* Constantin Mejinsky. *m* Georges Delerue. *cast* Jeanne Moreau, Julian Negulesco, Didi Perego, Yves Robert, Pippos Starnazza, Jill Larsen.

●Moreau is the spinsterly divorcée, taking up a new post as a schoolteacher after the death of her mother, who befriends and then seduces a young, out-of-work Italian in this surprisingly unsentimental, even detached film. However, where in de Broca's comedies the wit of his direction and the speed of his narration are the film's major virtues, here his would-be stylishness has the effect of highlighting rather than camouflaging the thinness of his material. PH

Cherry Falls

(1999, US, 92 min)
d Geoffrey Wright. *p* Marshall Persinger, Eli Selden. *sc* Ken Selden. *ph* Anthony B Richmond. *ed* John F Link. *pd* Marek Dobrowolski. *m* Walter Werzowa. *cast* Brittany Murphy, Michael Biehn, Gabriel Mann, Jesse Bradford, Jay Mohr, Douglas Spain, Keram Malicki-Sánchez, Natalie Ramsey, Candy Clark.

●According to teen slasher movie convention, sexually active girls and boys get diced while good little virgins escape the psycho's knife. So what if there were a killer who targeted only virgins? Faced with a 'hymen holocaust', hitherto chaste teens might reconsider the value of their sexual purity. A potentially subversive scenario is, however, wasted in this half-baked horror movie. Will virginal heroine Murphy opt to save her life by going all the way with boring, horny boyfriend Mann? Sundry characters take a stab at being prime red herring: Brittany's flirtatious, alcoholic mother Clark, her uptight sheriff father Biehn, his slightly butch female deputy, and countless others. But it turns out to be the one you thought it was all along. NF

Cherry Orchard, The (O Visinokipos/La Cerisaie)

(1998, Greece/Cyp/Fr, 141 min)
d/p/sc Michael Cacoyannis. *ph* Aris Stavrou. *ed* Michael Cacoyannis, Takis Hadzis. *pd* Dionysis Fotopoulos. *m* Tchaikovsky. *cast* Charlotte Rampling, Alan Bates, Katrin Cartlidge, Owen Teale, Tushka Bergen, Xander Berkeley, Gerald Butler, Andrew Howard, Melanie Lynskey, Ian McNeice, Frances de la Tour, Michael Gough.

●Chekhov's play submits to a slow, underwhelming adaptation. 1900: a time of social transition in Russia, from feudal past to industrial future. Having been abandoned by her lover, Mme Ranyevskaya (Rampling) returns from Paris, where she fled five years before after the death of her husband and son. Highly strung and melancholic, she's unwilling to confront the reality that the debt ridden family estate will soon be sold at auction. Instead, she spends time reminiscing with her feckless brother Gaev (Bates) about happier days, while her uptight foster-daughter Varya (Cartlidge) continues to run the household as the auction approaches. Despite the auspicious cast and a persuasive period look, Cacoyannis' film doesn't engage, with a lack of momentum or cohesion between scenes constantly distancing the viewer. KW

Cherry 2000

(1988, US, 93 min)
d Steve DeJarnatt. *p* Edward R Pressman, Caldecot Chubb. *sc* Michael Almereyda. *ph* Jacques Haitkin. *ed* Edward Abroms, Duwayne Dunham. *pd* John J Moore. *m* Basil Poledouris. *cast* Melanie Griffith, Ben Johnson, Harry Carey Jr, Tim Thomerson, Pamela Gidley, Jennifer Mayo, David Andrews.

●After a minimal release in the US this tilt at cultish sci-fi wnet straight to video in the UK. Its a post-apocalyptic adventure, from the director of *Miracle Mile*, that plays like a jauntier version of *Mad Max*. Griffith sports bright red hair as the eponymous heroine, a female mercenary charged with breaking into the villains' robot-packed warehouse; and much of the action takes place in striking desert landscapes. Plus marks for the presence of the old-timers, but overall it's a walk on the mild side. TJ

Chess Players, The (Shatranj ke Khilari)

(1977, Ind, 129 min)
d Satyajit Ray. *p* Suresh Jindal. *sc* Satyajit Ray. *ph* Soumendu Roy. *ed* Dulal Dutta. *ad* Bansi Chandragupta. *m* Satyajit Ray. *cast* Sanjeev Kumar, Saeed Jaffrey, Amjad Khan, Richard Attenborough, Shabana Azmi.

●The short-story irony of two nawabs playing interminable games of chess while their domestic domains crumble, and of a king wrapped up in his aesthetic pursuits while his territory is threatened by British expansionism, is decked out opulently enough (notably a lavish recreation of 1856 Lucknow); but it pales beside that of Ray's inability to distinguish a historical film from a mere costume drama. This has its moments as a gentle comedy, with Saeed Jaffrey in good form, but its nudging metaphors on queens and pawns provide a facile analysis of colonial politics. PT

Cheval d'Orgueil, Le (The Proud Ones)

(1980, Fr, 118 min)
d Claude Chabrol. *p* Georges de Beauregard. *sc* Daniel Boulanger, Claude Chabrol. *ph* Jean

Rabier. *ed* Monique Fardoulis. *ad* Hilton Mac Connico. *m* Pierre Jansen. *cast* Jacques Dufilho, Bernadette Lesache, François Cluzet, Paul Le Person, Michel Blanc, Dominique Lavanant.
●This impressionistic account of peasant life in Brittany around the time of World War I is a reminder that Chabrol began his career with a bleak portrayal of the provinces in *Le Beau Serge*. This is a much rosier picture, attractively – perhaps too attractively – shot by Jean Rabier. Stressing the poverty, it caresses the eye with picturesque interiors worthy of any model village, while the peasants decked out in their national costumes look like delegates to a folk-lore congress. Hardly another *Tree of Wooden Clogs*, but it does have charm, sparks of Chabrol clownery, and plenty of intriguing information about superstitions and customs. One problem is that the autobiographical book by Pierre Jakez Hélias on which it is based has obviously been too severely truncated. In the latter half, particularly, attempts to get to grips with the social and cultural implications of being Breton emerge with curious muddlement. TM

Cheyenne Autumn

(1964, US, 170 min)
d John Ford. *p* Bernard Smith, *sc* James R Webb. *ph* William H Clothier. *ed* Otho Lovering. *ad* Richard Day. *m* Alex North. *cast* Richard Widmark, Carroll Baker, Karl Malden, Sal Mineo, Edward G Robinson, James Stewart, Dolores del Rio, Ricardo Montalban, Gilbert Roland, Arthur Kennedy.
●Making amends for his less than sensitive treatment of the Indians in his earlier movies, Ford came up with a sprawling epic illustrating the callous disregard with which the US government treated the Cheyenne in the 1880s, uprooting them from the Yellowstone and resettling them in distant Oklahoma without proper provisions for survival. Over-long, often clichéd and uneven (there are comic interludes complete with cameo performances), but still imbued with moments of true poetry, thanks largely to William Clothier's magnificent Panavision landscapes. GA

Cheyenne Social Club, The

(1970, US, 102 min)
d/p Gene Kelly. *sc* James Lee Barrett. *ph* William H Clothier. *ed* Adrienne Fazan. *pd* Gene Allen. *m* Walter Scharf. *cast* James Stewart, Henry Fonda, Shirley Jones, Sue Ane Langdon, Elaine Devry, Robert Middleton, Arch Johnson.
●Leisurely comedy Western in which Stewart and Fonda, respectively an honest cowpuncher who inherits a brothel and the garrulous friend looking on as he struggles with his moral indignation, cope with their new status as businessmen, their increasing involvement with luscious employees, and the assortment of bad guys who force gunfights on them. Directed very much as it comes by Kelly and utterly undistinguished, but an object lesson by two old masters in the art of conjuring laughs out of nothing. TM

Chicago Joe and the Showgirl

(1989, GB, 103 min)
d Bernard Rose. *p* Tim Bevan. *sc* David Yallop. *ph* Mike Southon. *ed* Dan Rae. *ad* Gemma Jackson. *m* Hans Zimmer, Shirley Walker. *cast* Kiefer Sutherland, Emily Lloyd, Patsy Kensit, Keith Allen, Liz Fraser, Alexandra Pigg, John Lahr, Harry Fowler, Harry Jones.
●It's ironic that each scene seems inspired by movies, rather than life, when the film purports to show wartime England as it was. This cine-literacy may not be writer David Yallop's fault, but the script is hackneyed too, despite the story's (factually-based) potential. In 1944, an American GI (Sutherland) and a local showgirl (Lloyd) met in a Hammersmith café; a week later they were arrested for murder. Nobody ever knew the reason for their crime spree, and Yallop, none too originally, attributes their deeds to a naive faith in movie myth born of economic and cultural deprivation. The film skims the surface of its themes, and it's all poorly executed. Lloyd, like a 12- rather than 18-year-old, offers further evidence of her shortcomings, and Sutherland has no real part to play. Worse still is the 'direction'. Scenes go on far too long; the symbolism is thumpingly obvious; lighting, sets and dodgy London topography all evoke a video-neverworld. GA

Chicken and Duck Talk (Ji tong ya jiang)

(1988, HK, 97 min)
d Clifton Ko. *p* Michael Hui. *sc* Michael Hui, Clifton Ko. *ph* Derek Wan. *ed* Wong Yi-seung. *pd* Hai Tsung-man. *m* Samuel Hui. *cast* Michael Hui, Sylvia Chang, Ricky Hui, Lawrence Ng, Lowell Lo.
●Cantonese comedy generally doesn't travel too well, but Michael Hui's comeback movie (he made a series of Tashlin-esque classics in the '70s) would be a riot in any context. Hui plays the stingy, stupid and backward-looking proprietor of a traditional duck restaurant; his meagre turnover plummets when a bright new fast-food chicken joint opens across the street. He frantically tries to stop his resentful staff from defecting, while dreaming up stunts to win back lost customers; the plot is garnished with everything from inspired slapstick to mother-in-law jokes. You could read it as a sardonic commentary on China's often farcical struggle to 'modernise' – except that you'd be laughing too much to think through the parallels. TR

Chicken Run

(2000, GB/US, 84 min)
d Peter Lord, Nick Park. *p* Peter Lord, David Sproxton, Nick Park. *sc* Karey Kirkpatrick. *ph* (supervising director) Dave Alex Riddett. *ed* Mark Solomon, Robert Francis, Tamsin Parry. *pd* Phil Lewis. *m* John Powell, Harry Gregson-Williams. *cast* voices: Phil Daniels, Lynn Ferguson, Mel Gibson, Tony Haygarth, Jane Horrocks, Miranda Richardson, Julia Sawalha, Timothy Spall, Imelda Staunton, Benjamin Whitrow.
●The last half-hour of Aardman's first feature is pretty much all one might expect. But as far as laughs go, it's slow to take off; and in terms of gags, characters and narrative, it lacks the freshness of some of the earlier films. This is *The Great Escape* with chickens, and herein lie the limitations. First, the fowl are neither as funny nor as well characterised as Gromit and Co. Furthermore, directors Park and Lord are so keen to get the PoW format pat that the film comes across as pastiche not parody. As Ginger tries to persuade Rocky, a Rhode Island Red, to help her fellow egg-layers escape from Tweedy's Farm (where a barbaric pie machine is being built) familiarity with the stereotypes may produce pleasure of recognition, but not consistent laughter. Still, it'd be churlish to carp about this triumph of craftsmanlike technique. GA

Chico

(2001, Hun/Ger/Croatia/Chile, 108 min)
d Ibolya Fekete. *p* Sándor Simó, Hans Kutnewsky, Damir Teresak, JJ Harting. *sc* Ibolya Fekete. *ph* Nyika Jancsó, Mátyás Erdély, Antonio Farias. *ed* Anna Kornis. *pd* Mladen Ozbolt. *cast* Eduardo Rózsa Flores, Sergio Hernández, Richie Varga, Gyula Bodrogi.
●*Bolshe Vita* won Ibolya Fekete a European Young Director of the Year award. His second feature holds much the same empathy for the displaced and itinerant, though with an evidently bigger budget it's much more travelled itself. Presented in a series of flashbacks (elements of the actor/character Flores' own history are incorporated in the story), this traces the ideological journey of a Bolivian-born communist idealist, son of a Jewish Hungarian intellectual and a Spanish Catholic, from nascent Latin American revolutionary, via Soviet-trained Hungarian secret agent and Spanish journalist in Albania and Israel, to resistance fighter battling in early '90s Croatia. The internationalism threatens to get out of hand – the Hungarian scenes are certainly opaque – but it's an idiosyncratic and intrepid film that raises cogent questions of identity and belief. NB

Chicos Ricos

see Rich Kids

Chien Andalou, Un (An Andalusian Dog)

(1928, Fr, 16 min, b/w)
d Luis Buñuel. *sc* Salvador Dali, Luis Buñuel. *ph* Albert Duverger. *ad* Pierre Schildknecht. *cast* Pierre Batcheff, Simone Mareuil, Jaime Miravilles, Jeanne Rucas, Luis Buñuel.
●Prelude: a young woman sits compliantly as Buñuel takes a razor and slices her eye open. What follows is a documentary rendering of the dream state, of dream logic; and/or a surrealist exposition involving, for example, a swarm of ants, underarm hair, a striped box, all addressing each other opaquely; and/or a Freudian sexual smorgasbord, with everything symbolising something else; and/or a contrivance by two ambitious young Spaniards to offer as much outrageousness as an artistic alibi can cover. And so on. Originally a silent, but three soundtrack versions are around, one containing the original (disc) accompaniment of *Tristan and Isolde* plus a tango, the others with specially composed scores by, respectively, Mauricio Kagel and Martin Matalon. BBa

Chienne, La

(1931, Fr, 100 min, b/w)
d Jean Renoir. *p* Pierre Braunberger. *sc* Jean Renoir, André Girard. *ph* Theodore Sparkhuhl. *ed* Marguerite Renoir. *ad* Gabriel Scongnamillo. *cast* Michel Simon, Janie Marèze, Georges Flamant, Magdeleine Bérubet, Gaillard, Jean Gehret.
●M Legrand (Simon), a mild-mannered, middle-aged cashier, uses painting as a means of expression, of escape from his shrewish wife and the tedium of his job. After an accidental encounter with *femme fatale* Lulu (Marèze), he falls madly in love, setting her up in a flat which he fills with his paintings. Lulu, who loves only her pimp Dédé (Flamant), uses Legrand as a milch-cow, and when his money runs short, starts selling his paintings as her own (with the Sunday painter ironically unaware that his work is now much sought after). Freeing himself finally from his wife, Legrand arrives at the flat, only to realise that Lulu is still bedding Dédé... Renoir's first great talkie has been described as 'an insignificant little melodrama, given unexpected vigour and depth by a sense of momentary occasion in the filming'. That is, a glorious experiment in, and exploration of, the nature of cinema. Wonderfully moving, with great performances. Remade by Fritz Lang as *Scarlet Street*. WH

Chiens, Les (The Dogs)

(1978, Fr/Tahiti, 99 min)
d Alain Jessua. *p* Laurent Meyniel. *sc* André Ruellan, Alain Jessua. *ph* Etienne Becker. *ed* Hélène Plemiannikov. *ad* Jean-Louis Poveda. *m* René Koering, Michel Portal. *cast* Gérard Depardieu, Victor Lanoux, Nicole Calfan, Pierre Vernier, Gérard Séty, Pierre Londiche.
●A doctor becomes increasingly disturbed by the number of bite wounds he is treating. The town is a vile new creation in which street crime is rampant, racism abounds, and the local bourgeoisie have taken to keeping Alsatians for pets. But as in *Shock Treatment* (shown here as *Doctor in the Nude*), Jessua is adept at intimating a large political conspiracy from his thriller elements. The finger here seems to point back to Depardieu, who is the local dog-trainer but who when pressed goes a little Fascist around the gills and starts spouting Nietzsche. Considerable ambiguity is lent to it all by the conversion of the doctor's liberal girlfriend from a rape victim into a dog-toting vigilante. There is also the spectre of France's colonial past in the shape of black *gastarbeiter*. A worthwhile, thoughtful film which deals with its large themes with surprising complexity. CPea

Chihwaseon (Strokes of Fire)

(2002, SKor, 117 min)
d Im Kwon-Taek. *p* Lee Tae-Won. *sc* Kim Young-Oak, Im Kwon-Taek. *ph* Jung Il-Sung. *pd* Ju Byoung-Do. *cast* Choi Min-Sik, Ahn Sung-Ki, You Ho-Jeong, Kim Yeo-Jin, Son Ye-Jin, Han Myoung-Gu, Jung Tae-Woo.
●Im's deceptively effortless follow-up to *Chunhyang* is a racy, frequently funny and finally rather moving semi-fictional portrait of a Korean master-painter, Ohwon, who worked, womanised and drank his iconoclastic way through the second half of the 19th century. At first the narrative zips along so briskly that it's hard to do much more than merely keep up – and admire the film's luscious visual elegance. As it proceeds, however, subtle details in the script, coupled with Choi Min-Sik's charismatic performance, lead to a deeper understanding of

Ohwon's personality, of his relationship to the social and political turbulence around him, and of Im's own ideas about art and creativity. In some respects a little like *Five Women Around Utamaro*, but with rather more gags and pep, it's great fun. GA

Chikamatsu Monogatari (The Crucified Lovers)

(1954, Jap, 102 min, b/w)
d Kenji Mizoguchi. *p* Masaichi Nagata. *sc* Yoshikata Yoda. *ph* Kazuo Miyagawa. *ed* Kanji Sugawara. *ad* Hiroshi Mizutani. *m* Fumio Hayasaka. *cast* Kazuo Hasegawa, Kyoko Kagawa, Yoko Minamida, Eitaro Shindo, Sakae Ozawa.

●Straightforward adaptation of a famous kabuki/bunraku play by 16th century master Chikamatsu Monzaemon, about a couple compromised by circumstances who become illicit lovers – and pay the price their society demands. Distinctly pedantic in tone and style compared with *Sansho Dayu*. TR

Chikin Bizniz

(1998, SAf, 103 min)
d Ntshavheni Wa Luruli. *p* Richard Green, Michael Chéze. *sc* Mtutuzeli Matshoba. *ph* Rod Stewart. *m* Shaluza Max Mntambo. *cast* Fats Bookholane, Connie Chiume, Clementine Mosimane, Sello Motloung, Nomsa Nene.

●A light, politics-free, domestic comedy-drama in the vein of the Jamaican-set *Rockers* (1979). Bookholane's Sipho is a middle-aged man at his crossroads. Fed up with years of menial jobs at the Johannesburg stock exchange, he jacks it in, heads back to a fading relationship with his township wife and decides to set up business selling chickens. Along the way he falls foul of chicken rustlers and, later, an irate wife, who discovers he's been having an affair with the girlfriend of possibly the meanest dude in the township. The dialogue sometimes sparks into life, but overall it's somewhat rambling and monotonous. DA

Child and the Soldier, The (Koudak va Sarbaz)

(2000, Iran, 90 min)
d Seyyed Reza Mir-Karimi. *p* Vahid Nikkhah Azad. *sc* Mohammed Rezai-Rad. *ph* Hamid Khozoui Abyane. *ed* Nazanin Mofakham. *ad* Massud Riazi. *cast* Mehdi Lotfi, Rouhollah Hosseini, Mehran Rajabi, Bizhan Soltani.

●The harassed commanding officer of a remote military barracks orders a soldier who's been petitioning for New Year home leave to escort a juvenile offender (he stole some bread) to a reformatory in Tehran. It's a tough mission, not least because every bus in the country seems fully booked for the holiday, but the two set off, handcuffed together. En route, the soldier half-warms to the boy, especially after seeing him reviled and rejected by his family. The turning point is a detour to the soldier's home village, where he consolidates his engagement to a local girl. By the time he's ready to deliver his charge in Tehran, the soldier is more regretful than relieved. Mir-Karimi's debut feature in no way advances Iranian cinema, but its predictable virtues – good non-pro performances, attention to detail, measured pacing and framing, shafts of humour – make it very watchable. TR

Childhood of Maxim Gorki, The (Detstvo Gorkovo)

(1938, USSR, 100 min, b/w)
d Mark Donskoi. *sc* Mark Donskoi, I Grudzev. *ph* Pyotr Yermolov. *ad* I Stepanov. *m* Lev Schwartz. *cast* Alexei Lyarsky, Varvara Massalitinova, Mikhail Troianovski, Daniil Sagal, J Alexieva.

●Donskoi's Gorki Trilogy, completed by *My Apprenticeship* (1939, 98 min, b/w) and *My Universities* (1940, 104 min, b/w) is still widely revered as one of the all-time humanist classics, and it's true that the films' expert balance between guileless simplicity and rustic myth-making (seen to best advantage in *Childhood*) does give them a quality not often found outside the work of John Ford. But it's interesting to note that Dons,m koi's direction couldn't lie further from the mainstream of Russian film culture. Not only is he not very concerned about montage, but his concern with the lyricism of individual images leads him to neglect continuity of almost any sort: at one level, the films play like an anthology of continuity errors. That said, though, all three films do contain images of great strength in the Dovzhenko tradition. And Donskoi's handling of his actors (always encouraging them to play up to emotion, never shy of excess or sentimentality) certainly has the courage of its convictions. TR

Child Is Waiting, A

(1963, US, 102 min. b/w)
d John Cassavetes. *p* Stanley Kramer. *sc* Abby Mann. *ph* Joseph La Shelle. *ed* Gene Fowler. *pd* Rudolph Sternad. *m* Ernest Gold. *cast* Burt Lancaster, Judy Garland, Gena Rowlands, Steven Hill, Bruce Ritchey, Paul Stewart, Lawrence Tierney.

●Disowned by Cassavetes after producer Stanley Kramer edited it against his wishes and made it more sentimental than intended, this is none the less a very affecting study of the plight of mentally retarded children. Shot in semi-documentary style and using (with the exception of Ritchey, the film's central 'case history') actual retarded children, the movie concerns a new teacher (Garland) whose excessive concern with Ritchey's predicament brings her into conflict with her boss (Lancaster). As ever, Cassavetes elicits magnificent performances from his cast, making especially fine use of Garland's tremulous emotionalism, although the occasional drifts into didacticism (the script was by Abby Mann, who wrote *Judgment at Nuremberg* and *Ship of Fools*) entail the sort of special pleading Cassavetes was keen to avoid. Flawed but fascinating. GA

Child of Divorce

(1946, US, 62 min, b/w)
d Richard Fleischer. *p/sc* Lillie Hayward. *ph* Jack Mackenzie. *ed* Samuel E Beetley. *ad* Albert S D'Agostino, Ralph Berger. *m* Leigh Harline. *cast* Sharyn Moffett, Regis Toomey, Madge Meredith, Walter Reed, Doris Merrick, Ann Carter, Una O'Connor.

●Fleischer's modest first feature, about a child's reaction to divorce, is a beauty. Lillie Hayward's script, based on a play (*Wednesday's Child* by Leopold L Atlas), avoids all the pitfalls of special pleading. Both parents (Toomey and Meredith) want what is best for the child; their new partners are genuine in their desire to become friends; but the child herself, partly because of innocent teasing at school, mainly because she just can't understand, remains obstinately unaccommodating. The only solution, therefore, is boarding school: not some Dickensian horror, but a gracious, spacious place in the country boasting every amenity a child could desire. And there, in a nakedly moving final sequence, the child learns, under the sympathetic tutelage of a new friend who has been through the mill, what to expect: a time when presents come thick and fast; a time when visits grow fewer and fewer; and then, just the long, long wait to grow up. Fleischer puts scarcely a foot wrong, and the kids (Sharyn Moffett as the unhappy child, Ann Carter as her friend) are astonishing. TM

Children of a Lesser God

(1986, US, 119 min)
d Randa Haines. *p* Burt Sugarman, Patrick Palmer. *sc* Hesper Anderson, Mark Medoff. *ph* John Seale. *ed* Lisa Fruchtman. *pd* Gene Callahan. *m* Michael Convertino. *cast* William Hurt, Marlee Matlin, Piper Laurie, Philip Bosco, Allison Gompf, John F Cleary.

●Those whom we set free we cannot hope to own. That's the message of Mark Medoff's stage hit, which he and Hesper Anderson have adapted for the screen in a way which opens out its dimensions without ever clouding its intentions or enervating its tensions. Hurt is James, a likeably unorthodox teacher of the hearing-impaired, who becomes attracted by Sarah (Matlin, a stunning debut), a pupil who left the school with little more than a large chip on her shoulder and a knowledge that sex doesn't require too much of a conversational manner. Their relationship is both a genuinely touching love story and a clever gloss on the barriers and extensions of language. It also contains a truly didactic other-dimension which points out some very salutary things about our often unintentional slights towards the deaf, without being either a simple sob or an issue story. SGr

Children of Heaven (Bacheha-Ye aseman)

(1997, Iran, 86 min)
d Majid Majidi. *p* Amir Esfandiari, Mohammad Esfandiari. *sc* Majid Majidi. *ph* Parviz Malekzaade. *ed* Hassan Hassandust.*cast* Mohammad Amir Naji, Amir Farrokh Hashemian, Bahare Seddiqi, Nafise Jafar-Mohammadi, Fereshte Sarabandi, Karnal Mirkarimi, Behzad Rafi.

●One can see why this was the first Iranian title to be Oscar-nominated for Best Foreign Film. The story of two children and a pair of lost shoes leans heavily on plaintive looks and big brown eyes. In a Teheran greengrocer's, a blind rag-and-bone man accidentally makes off with the trainers that nine-year-old Ali has left unattended. The shoes belong to the boy's sister, but when Ali gets home the children agree not to mention the loss to their hard-up dad. Instead, they take it in turns to wear Ali's shoes, an arrangement destined to cause complications. All this promises the sort of junior-quest narrative familiar from Kiarostami's classic *Where Is My Friend's House?*, but the task of recovering the trainers becomes secondary to the notion of weighing material possessions against spiritual worth. The film's storytelling is appealing, but you can't help feeling that the adults are too good to be true, the onrush of tears rather conveniently deployed to ease potential crises. TJ

Children of Lumière, The

see Enfants de Lumière, Les

Children of Nature (Börn Náttúrunnar)

(1991, Ice, 85 min)
d Fridrik Thór Fridriksson. *p* Fridrik Thór Fridriksson, Wolfgang Pfeiffer, Skule Hansen. *sc* Einar Mar Gudmundsson, Fridrik Thór Fridriksson. *ph* Ari R Kristinsson. *ed* Skule Eriksson. *ad* Geir Ottar Geirsson. *m* Hilmar Orn Hilmarsson. *cast* Gisli Halldorsson, Valgerdur Dan, Hallmar Sigurdsson, Sigridur Hagalin, Rurik Haraldsson.

●A worthy film about the elderly – in the style of a road movie with docu-drama trimmings. The protagonist is a taciturn widower (Halldorsson) brought up in the savage northern fjords and mountains, which he abandoned for a lonely sheep farmer's life in the verdant southern pastures. The film starts with him – having shot his old dog – quitting his shack and paying an unannounced visit to his married daughter and family in Reykjavik. They quickly move him into an old people's home, where he meets a fiery old flame. Sympathetic tone but sketchy characters. WH

Children of Paradise

see Enfants du Paradis, Les

Children of Theatre Street, The

(1977, US, 100 min)
d Robert Dornhelm, Earle Mack. *p* Earle Mack. *sc* Beth Gutcheon. *ph* Karl Kofler. *ed* Tina Frese. *m* Igor Stravinsky, Peter Tchaikovsky, Sergei Prokofiev. *with* students and faculty of the Vaganova Choreographic Institute. *narrator* Grace Kelly.

●An affectionate, respectful documentary about the Kirov Ballet School in Leningrad, full of interesting stuff about the school's history, selection of pupils, and teaching techniques. Enjoyable for kids and balletomanes who get misty-eyed over a single *grand jeté*. JS

Children of the Corn

(1984, US, 92 min)
d Fritz Kiersch. *p* Donald P Borchers, Terence Kirby. *sc* George Goldsmith. *ph* Raoul Lomas. *ed* Harry Keramidas. *ad* Craig Stearns. *m* Jonathan Elias. *cast* Peter Horton, Linda Hamilton, RG Armstrong, John Franklin, Courtney Gains, Robby Kiger.

●A dud Stephen King adaptation with a silly creepy cornfield, and a town that time forgot. Entering Nebraska, Burt (Horton) and Vicky (Hamilton) switch on the car radio to hear the holler of fundamentalist preaching. Then their cars hit the body of a young boy. It turns out that he has already been slashed to ribbons by youngsters in thrall to freakboy Isaac (Franklin), their parents all massacred three years past. The couple drive into town, body in the boot, looking for help, but they won t find any in the script, which totters from one cliché to the next, eventually disappearing up its own cornhole in a conflagration of cheap FX. NRo

Children of the Damned

(1963, GB, 90 min, b/w)
d Anton M Leader. *p* Ben Arbeid. *sc* John Briley. *ph* Davis Boulton. *ed* Ernest Walter. *ad* Elliot Scott. *m* Ron Goodwin. *cast* Ian Hendry, Alan Badel, Barbara Ferris, Alfred Burke, Sheila Allen, Ralph Michael, Martin Miller.
● A fairly intriguing and atmospheric exercise in science fiction, made as a sequel to *Village of the Damned* (an adaptation of John Wyndham's novel *The Midwich Cuckoos*). About a race of superchildren who (in the eyes of the authorities, at any rate) threaten to take over the world, it has some good moments, though its surreal beginning promises a generation war of apocalyptic dimensions that is never delivered, and the film finally falls into some unconvincing liberal moralising (one of the persisting curses of SF in the cinema). DP

Children of the Marshland

see Enfants du Marais, Les

Children of the Stork

see Je suis né d'une cigogne

Children's Midsummer Night's Dream, The

(2001, GB, 118 min)
d Christine Edzard. *p* Olivier Stockman. *ph* Joachim Bergamin. *sets* Sands Films. *m* Michel Sanvoisin. *cast* Jamie Peachey, John Heyfron, Danny Bishop, Jessica Fowler, Leane Lyson, Daniel Rouse, David Joyce, Oliver Szczypka, Jack Nottage, Mathew Zelic, Hassan Lahrech, Dominic Haywood-Benge, Rajouana Zalal.
● This opens with a bunch of school kids watching life-size puppets: Egeus is warning daughter Hermia of her fate if she disobeys him and refuses to marry Demetrius. Some spellbound, the children turn into characters with whom they identify, playing out the Dream in an enchanted wood. The cast (with no previous acting experience) conjure up humour and emotion, adding a minx-like quality to the fairies and woodland echoes. A total of 350 children from a range of London schools were involved in this inspired project – some from a school subsequently reported to be 'failed'. JFu

Children Underground

(2000, US, 103 min)
d/p Edet Belzberg. *ph* Wolfgang Held. *ed* Jonathan Oppenheim.
● A documentary on the plight of the estimated 20,000 orphaned, runaway and sometimes disturbed children who live on the streets of Romania. Focusing on five subjects filmed over a year, the director prefers direct observation to commentary. Regrettably, these stagnating lives make torpid viewing. The film coasts for 50 minutes, and only picks up when young Mihai makes a trip to the family house he refuses to regard as home. NB

Child's Play

(1972, US, 100 min)
d Sidney Lumet. *p* David Merrick. *sc* Leon Prochnik. *ph* Gerald Hirschfeld. *ed* Edward A Warschilka, Joanne Burke. *pd* Philip Rosenberg. *m* Michael Small. *cast* James Mason, Robert Preston, Beau Bridges, Ronald Weyand, Charles White, David Rounds.
● Atrocious nonsense set in a Catholic boarding school for boys where melodramatic goings-on suggest that the devil lurks in the person of jolly Joe Dobbs, popular English master and probably closet queen (Preston, looking uncomfortable in a role originally slated for Marlon Brando). With Robert Marasco's play creaking at every joint, not even Mason's carefully tortured performance (he's the master the boys all love to hate, nursing a mum dying of cancer and a drawerful of girlie magazines) can rouse much interest. TM

Child's Play (Kinderspiel)

(1992, Ger, 107 min)
d Wolfgang Becker. *p* Rudi Kaufmann. *sc* Wolfgang Becker, Horst Sczerba. *ph* Martin Kukula. *ed* Wolfgang Becker. *ad* Peter Bausch. *m* Christian Steyer. *cast* Jonas Kipp, Oliver Bröcker, Burghart Klaussner, Angelika Bartsch, Matthias Friedrich.
● This picture of working-class life as seen through the eyes of a depressed child (Kipp) is depressing indeed. Senile Granny spends much of her time on the toilet; Dad is a child-batterer; the lad's contemporaries are bullies; and the only bit of radiance that comes his way is spying on a naked girl through the bathroom keyhole. BC

Child's Play

(1988, US, 87 min)
d Tom Holland. *p* David Kirschner. *sc* Don Mancini, John Lafia, Tom Holland. *ph* Bill Butler. *ed* Edward A Warschilka, Roy Peterson. *pd* Dan Lomino. *m* Joe Renzetti. *cast* Catherine Hicks, Chris Sarandon, Alex Vincent, Brad Dourif, Dinah Manoff, Tommy Swerdlow.
● Faced with the prospect of a movie about a killer doll, you might be forgiven some scepticism; but Holland demonstrates how a well-written script and taut direction can triumph over the silliest premise. When Hicks buys her six-year-old son a talking doll called Chucky for his birthday, she has no idea it's possessed by the malevolent spirit of psychopath Dourif, whom Chicago cop Sarandon blew away in a shootout the day before. So when her babysitting friend (Manoff) takes a dive from her apartment window and the kid says the doll did it, he gets a ticket for the funny farm. Sarandon doesn't buy it either, until vengeful Chucky tries to strangle him while he's driving. While some of the supernatural stuff about witch-doctors and Mojo dolls is a bit daft, Holland's sure handling of the suspense and shock moments lends the film a sharp and scary edge. NF

Child's Play 2

(1990, US, 84 min)
d John Lafia. *p* David Kirschner. *sc* Don Mancini. *ph* Stefan Czapsky. *ed* Edward Warschilka. *pd* Ivo Cristante. *m* Graeme Revell. *cast* Alex Vincent, Jenny Agutter, Gerrit Graham, Christine Elise, Grace Zabriskie, Peter Haskell, Brad Dourif.
● This perfunctory sequel finds the soul of serial killer Charles Lee Ray (voice by Brad Dourif) *still* trapped in the body of a Chucky doll, *still* vainly trying to usurp the more desirable body of sprightly young Andy (Vincent). Conveniently reconstructed from the frazzled ashes of Part One, souped-up Chucky traces Andy to the home of his newly acquired foster parents (Agutter and Graham), spending an inordinate amount of time jumping out of confined spaces, shouting 'Fuck you, bitch!', and slaughtering Andy's nearest and dearest. Since the gaff has long been blown (we know Chucky is alive from the outset), the original's menacing tension is entirely absent. Lafia attempts to compensate by relying heavily on Kevin Yagher's advanced doll animations, but articulated facial features, however clever, are no substitute for thrills. Only in the highly orchestrated, surprisingly gory climax, wherein Chucky's plastic form takes on the sins of the flesh, is there a spark of originality. MK

Child Under a Leaf (aka Love Child)

(1974, Can, 88 min)
d George Bloomfield. *p* Murray Shostak, Robert Bayliss. *sc* George Bloomfield. *ph* Don Wilder. *ed* George Bloomfield. *ad* Jocelyn Joly. *m* Francis Lai. *cast* Dyan Cannon, Donald Pilon, Joseph Campanella, Albert S Waxman, Micheline Lanctôt.
● You've surely seen the prizewinning 'drink and drive' ad where a couple leave a cinema – she muttering that she doesn't know why they make them so sad – and go and get legless before crashing? This might well have been the film they saw: it's a formula two Kleenex movie, and enough to drive anyone to drink. Dyan Cannon is married to the sort of man who'd kill her pet poodle (he does), but she has a beautiful relationship with artist Donald Pilon, who's the father of her newborn child, and they phone each other every day, and regularly zoom off in matching white sports cars for lyrical lovemaking in the fields, and agonise over the husband's violent tendencies. Director Bloomfield's own script veers off into ever more embarrassing melodrama, but his efforts are hardly necessary: Francis Lai's super-lush score tells the whole sorry story. PT

Chill Factor

(1999, US, 102 min)
d Hugh Johnson. *p* James G Robinson. *sc* Drew Gitlin, Mike Cheda. *ph* David Gribble. *ed* Pamela Power. *pd* Jeremy Conway. *m* Hans Zimmer, John Powell. *cast* Cuba Gooding Jr, Skeet Ulrich, Peter Firth, David Paymer, Hudson Leick, Daniel Hugh Kelly, Kevin J O'Connor, Judson Mills, Jordan Mott.
● Pairing Gooding and Ulrich, tyro director Johnson's black/white buddy actioner peddles so much hokum it's a shame that the language and odd bit of gore preclude a younger audience. A vengeful army major (Firth) allows a disastrous last-minute change of formula in a boffin's weapons research, and is sent down for a stretch, only to emerge, satanically lit, announcing: 'I'm ready!' Which is more than the script team was when this got the green light. They make the boffin (Paymer) mentor to Ulrich, a café night-shift worker, and then have him steal his own chemical sample, dying on the café floor with Firth close behind. Johnson served his apprenticeship on Tony Scott movies, so it's a surprise the action scenes are pedestrian. Nor could you say Ulrich and Gooding hit it off. But the atmosphere is winning, with the odd felicity peppering the journey with gags and groans. Montana looks good, too. WH

Chilly Scenes of Winter

see Head Over Heels

Chilsu and Mansu (Chilsu oa Mansu)

(1988, SKor, 109 min)
d Park Kwang-Su. *cast* Ahn Song-Gi, Park Joong-Hun, Bae Chong-Okk.
● Park's first film begins like a buddy movie – it's the story of two billboard painters: Chilsu is a youthful romantic and a bit of a dreamer; Mansu is older, quieter and hard-drinking. The tone shifts subtly with the progress of Chilsu's courtship of a pretty student, and gradually this portrait of a generation obsessed with Western culture takes on a political dimension: when the two friends stand atop one of their own billboards, discussing their frustration with the fledgling democracy down below them, the police mistakenly assume they are staging a protest, with potentially dangerous implications. An estimable film, funny, provocative and very well acted. TCh

Chiltern Hundreds, The (aka The Amazing Mr Beecham)

(1949, GB, 84 min, b/w)
d John Paddy Carstairs. *p* George H Brown. *sc* William Douglas-Home, Patrick Kirwan. *ph* Jack Hildyard. *ed* George Clark. *ad* Ralph Brinton. *m* Benjamin Frankel. *cast* Cecil Parker, AE Matthews, David Tomlinson, Marjorie Fielding, Joyce Carey, Lana Morris, Helen Backlin.
● Adaptation of William Douglas Home's drawing-room comedy about a stuck-up butler (Parker) who puts up for election as Tory candidate when the young master (Tomlinson) proposes to run for Labour and marry the parlourmaid. Needless to say the conservative proprieties are observed at the end, and it all emerges more as domestic farce than political satire, but excellent performances (Parker, Fielding and Matthews in particular) make it really rather engaging. TM

Chimes at Midnight (Campanadas a Medianoche)

(1966, Sp/Switz, 119 min, b/w)
d Orson Welles. *p* Emiliano Piedra, Angel Escolano. *sc* Orson Welles. *ph* Edmond Richard. *ed* Fritz Mueller. *ad* José Antonio de la Guerra, Mario Erdorza. *m* Angelo Francesco Lavagnino. *cast* Orson Welles, Keith Baxter, John Gielgud, Margaret Rutherford, Jeanne Moreau, Norman Rodway, Marina Vlady, Alan Webb, Fernando Rey, Walter Chiari, Andrew Faulds. *narrator* Ralph Richardson.
● The mongrel heritage of *Chimes at Midnight* is hard to credit, given the intensely personal reading of English history and literature that emerges from an incongruous Spanish/Swiss co-production of a life of Falstaff culled from five Shakespearean texts and Holinshed's *Chronicles*. Infused with a politically acute nostalgia for Merrie England, this elegiac tragi-comedy comes over as uncompromisingly modern entertainment,

from its playful ruptures of traditional film grammar to its characterisation of Falstaff as hero at the crossroads of history, a spiritual and thematic precursor of Peckinpah's Cable Hogue. Welles waddles through the foreground with an eye on his own problems of patronage, while behind the camera he conjures a dark masterpiece, shot through with slapstick and sorrow. Magic. PT

China Clipper

(1936, US, 85 min, b/w)
d Ray Enright. *sc* Frank Wead. *ph* Arthur Edeson. *ed* Owen Marks. *ad* Max Parker. *m* Bernard Kaun, W Franke Harling. *cast* Pat O'Brien, Beverly Roberts, Ross Alexander, Humphrey Bogart, Marie Wilson, Joseph Crehan.

● Warner Bros salutes American technology and enterprise in this humdrum but engaging drama about one of the early heroes of aviation. O'Brien, the most solemn star on the lot (he was generally cast as cop or priest), is the hero, an industrious businessman determined to build up a Transpacific air route. Like all such success stories, this one begins in failure. But doughty O'Brien tries and tries again until his vision is made reality. If he neglects his wife and family, that's only because he is in pursuit of the American dream – nothing must stand between him and his manifest destiny. GM

China Girl

(1987, US, 90 min)
d Abel Ferrara. *p* Michael Nozik. *sc* Nicholas St John. *ph* Bojan Bazelli. *ed* Anthony Redman. *pd* Dan Leigh. *m* Joe Delia. *cast* James Russo, Richard Panebianco, Sari Chang, David Caruso, Russell Wong, Joey Chin.

● This superior exploitation picture is a tough, stylish but often painfully misjudged reworking of *Romeo and Juliet*, with rival teenage gangs battling it out, sparked by the inter racial love affair between an Italian (Panebianco) and a Chinese girl (Chang). Ferrara makes excellent use of the Chinatown and Little Italy locations, and delivers the choreographed violence with his usual muscular panache, but his handling of the younger, inexperienced actors is distinctly dodgy. The major strength of the script is its accommodation of three generations: the elders and their aspiring sons are seen to conspire against the warring youngsters, putting money before family. But the bitter taste of this radical undercurrent is ultimately drowned out by saccharine sentiment and histrionic overkill. NF

China Is Near (La Cina è vicina)

(1967, It, 95 min, b/w)
d Marco Bellocchio. *p* Franco Cristaldi. *sc* Marco Bellocchio, Elda Tattoli. *ph* Tonino Delli Colli. *ed* Roberto Perpignani. *ad* Rodolfo Frattaioli, Ugo Novello. *m* Ennio Morricone. *cast* Paulo Graziosi, Glauco Mauri, Elda Tattoli, Daniela Surina, Pierluigi Aprà.

● A stinging political satire which bears the same bizarre hallmarks as *Fists in the Pocket*. Once again the protagonists are a family, and once again they live a secret life as mysteriously inaccessible as that of the epileptics in Bellocchio's earlier film. But this time they are out in the world, with older brother busily pursuing a political career, younger brother touting for Mao in hopes of ruining his brother, and sister squatting at home indulging lazy love affairs. They are upper middle class and the world is theirs; but the day of reckoning is at hand, and in a brilliantly funny series of sexual encounters, elder brother and sister find themselves bemusedly trapped into marriage by a pair of working class secretaries on the make. A dazzling and curiously foreboding comedy of manners, it shares with Godard's *La Chinoise* a sense of May 1968 just around the corner. TM

China Moon

(1994, US, 99 min)
d John Bailey. *p* Barrie M Osborne. *sc* Roy Carlson. *ph* Willy Kurant. *ed* Carol Littleton, Jill Savitt. *ad* Conrad E Angone. *m* George Fenton. *cast* Ed Harris, Madeleine Stowe, Charles Dance, Benicio Del Toro, Pruitt Taylor Vince, Roger Aaron Brown, Patricia Healy.

● Directed by cinematographer John Bailey, and produced by Kevin Costner's TIG company, this neo-noir thriller set in Florida is classier than most UK video premieres, but hardly anything to write home about. The set-up's familiar from *Double Indemnity* and a thousand-and-one other movies: the wife of an abusive millionaire seduces a cop (Harris), and the next thing he knows he's dumping Mr Money's bullet-ridden body in a remote, moonlit lake and watching his whole life go under. The denouement at least produces a novel twist, which it would be churlish to discuss, though that lake would probably be easier to swallow. It's diverting enough, however, with strong performances all round, and it's interesting to see the divine Benicio Del Toro (Fenster in *The Usual Suspects*) in another role, as Harris's partner. No, he doesn't use that voice. TCh

China 9, Liberty 37 (aka Amore, Piomto e Furore/ Clayton & Catherine)

(1978, It/Sp, 102 min)
d Monte Hellman. *p* Gianni Bozzacchi, Valerio De Paolis, Monte Hellman. *sc* Jerry Harvey, Douglas Venturelli. *ph* Giusepe Rotunno. *ed* Cesare D'Amico. *m* Pino Donaggio. *cast* Warren Oates, Fabio Testi, Jenny Agutter, Sam Peckinpah, Isabel Mestres, Franco Interlenghi.

● Hellman's seriously absurdist streak happily finds a comically absurd parallel within the stereotyped framework of the European Western: he revels in the sheer gratuitousness of traditional character-types and plot mechanisms to produce an uproarious genre critique. Fabio Testi, a gunslinger in a Tom Mix hat, alternately stalks, befriends, and is stalked by Warren Oates, holding out against the advancing railroad with his trusty rifle and his less-than-trusty Anglo-Irish wife (Agutter). PT

China Seas

(1935, US, 90 min, b/w)
d Tay Garnett. *p* Albert Lewis. *sc* Jules Furthman, James K McGuinness. *ph* Ray June. *ed* William Le Vanway. *ad* Cedric Gibbons. *m* Herbert Stothart. *cast* Jean Harlow, Clark Gable, Wallace Beery, Lewis Stone, Rosalind Russell, Robert Benchley.

● An implausible but enjoyable tale of sexual rivalry and modern-day piracy aboard a ship *en route* to Hong Kong, this reunites Gable and Harlow, so effective together in the earlier *Red Dust*. The script by James Kevin McGuinness and Jules Furthman (who wrote such exotic masterpieces as *Morocco* and *Only Angels Have Wings*) is tailor-made for its stars, providing Gable with some suitably gruff heroics as the ship's captain, and plenty of snappy innuendo with the remarkable Harlow. It's a typical MGM production – glossy, romantic and far removed from reality – but Garnett keeps the pace going well enough to suspend disbelief. GA

China Syndrome, The

(1978, US, 122 min)
d James Bridges. *p* Michael Douglas. *sc* Mike Gray, TS Cook, James Bridges. *ph* James Crabe. *ed* David Rawlings. *pd* George Jenkins. *cast* Jane Fonda, Jack Lemmon, Michael Douglas, Scott Brady, James Hampton, Peter Donat, Wilford Brimley.

● Largely successful attempt to merge politics with Hollywood mainstream, as Fonda and Douglas play TV news-reporters latching on to a nuclear power scare about falsification and negligence of safety regulations. All a bit too earnest, despite the seriousness of the subject, with Fonda setting her jaw and stepping into father's footsteps as Tinseltown's very own protector of humanity; but it's tightly scripted and directed, and genuinely tense in places. GA

Chinatown 100 (100)

(1974, US, 131 min)
d Roman Polanski. *p* Robert Evans. *sc* Robert Towne. *ph* John A Alonzo. *ed* Sam O'Steen. *pd* Richard Sylbert. *m* Jerry Goldsmith. *cast* Jack Nicholson, Faye Dunaway, John Huston, Perry Lopez, John Hillerman, Darrell Zwerling, Diane Ladd. Roman Polanski.

● Classic detective film, with Nicholson's JJ Gittes moving through the familiar world of the Forties *film noir* uncovering a plot whose enigma lies as much within the people he encounters as within the mystery itself. Gittes' peculiar vulnerability is closer to Chandler's concept of Philip Marlowe than many screen Marlowes, and the sense of time and place (the formation of LA in the '30s) is very strong. Directed by Polanski in bravura style, it is undoubtedly one of the great films of the '70s.

Chinese Box

(1997, US/HK/Fr, 110 min)
d Wayne Wang. *p* Lydia Pilcher, Jean-Louis Piel. *sc* Jean-Claude Carrière, Larry Gross. *ph* Vilko Filac. *ed* Chris Tellefsen. *pd* Chris Wong. *m* Graeme Revell. *cast* Jeremy Irons, Gong Li, Maggie Cheung, Michael Hui, Ruben Blades.

● Designed to reflect the 'drama' of the hand over of Hong Kong, Wang's semi-improvised movie was partly scuppered by the fact that nothing striking happened when China reclaimed its 'Special Administrative Region' on 1 July 1997. But it's hard to imagine that the film would have worked out better if there'd been riots on the streets, despite the big names (Theroux, Carrière) on the credits. Irons plays a foreign correspondent dying in synch with the British administration, obsessed with both Gong Li (manager of a chic bar/cheap hooker – evidently representing China) and Maggie Cheung (a go-getting hustler – evidently representing the confused spirit of HK). Ludicrously contrived incidents are garnished with desultory dialogue; the underlying prostitution and slaughterhouse metaphors were wrung dry last time Wang tackled the city of his birth, in *Life Is Cheap*. Maybe Wang has lived too long in California; the average tourist with a camcorder would see the city more clearly than this. TR

Chinese Boxes

(1984, WGer, 87 min)
d Christopher Petit. *p* Chris Sievernich. *sc* LM Kit Carson, Christopher Petit. *ph* Peter Harvey. *ed* Fred Srp. *ad* Edgar Hinz, Klaus Beiser. *m* Günther Fischer. *cast* Will Patton, Gottfried John, Adelheid Arndt, Robbie Coltrane, Beate Jensen, Christopher Petit.

● Langdon Marsh (an expatriate American played with the charm of early Nicholson by Patton) is trapped in a ghostly, neon-streaked Berlin after the sudden deaths of his heroin-smuggling associate and a teenage girl. A bar-owner friend and a mysterious 'customs' man (Coltrane performing an Orson Welles cameo ahead of his years) both offer Marsh a way out, but only as a pawn in their duplicitous, gun-toting game. With an excess of plot staving off any safe resolution, the reduction of character psychology to a guiltless state of wonder proves a virtue. Despite the contingencies of low-budget filming – bold colour camera-work and blatant post-synchronisation – there is more fun to be had here than in the current British infatuation for the 'Laura Ashley school of film-making'. DT

Chinese Connection, The (Quan Ji/aka Duel of Fists)

(1971, HK, 86 min)
d Chang Cheh. *p* Runme Shaw. *sc* I Kuang. *ph* Kung Mu To. *ed* Kuo Ting-hung. *cast* David Chiang, Ti Lung, Li Ching, Liu Lan-ying, Ku Feng.

● A film from the Shaw Brothers' reliable action unit of director Chang Cheh (obviously relieved to be away from costume heroics) and acting duo Ti Lung and David Chiang, that turns out to be one of the funniest and most invigorating of their output: a spoofy foray into the gangster-controlled world of Thai boxing (it was partly shot in Bangkok), mock heroism, and a sub-Pimpernel search for a missing brother. Good use is made of locations, the ringside boxing sequences, and some well-handled street fighting. VG

Chinese Ghost Story, A (Qiannü Youhun)

(1987, HK, 95 min)
d Ching Siu-Tung. *p* Tsui Hark. *sc* Yuen Kai-Chi. *ph* Poon Hang-Sang, Sander Lee, Tom Lau, Wong Wing-Hang. *pd* Hai Chung-Man. *m* Dai Lemin, James Wong. *cast* Leslie Cheung, Wang Zuxian, Wu Ma, Liu Zhaoming.

● A big hit in Hong Kong, credited to a young director of mildly innovative martial arts films, but showing all the signs of having been gazumped by producer Tsui Hark, director of cult hits *The Butterfly Murders* and *Zu: Warriors from the Magic Mountain*. Many of the ideas and visuals are swiped from recent horror movies like *The Evil Dead*. The storyline is a Ming Dynasty chestnut about a wandering female scholar who falls in love with a glamorous female ghost, only to find the hordes of hell on his tail. Low points include the scenes in town, with market stallholders endlessly rhubarbing warnings about not going near the old house on the lake. High points include the special effects and a rap version of the opening words of 'Tzu's *Tao Te Ching* by a Taoist priest (Wu Ma, himself a director of some talent). TR

Chinese Ghost Story II, A (Qiannü Youhun zhi Renjian Dao)

(1990, HK, 104 min)
d Ching Siu-Tung. *sc* Lau Tai-mok, Lam Kei-to, Leung Yiu-ming. *ph* Arthur Wong. *ed* Mak Chi-sen. *m* James Wong, Romeo Diaz. *cast* Leslie Cheung, Wang Hsu Hsien, Michelle Li, Wu Ma, Jacky Cheung.

●Very much the same formula as last time around: high style, low comedy, classy special effects, rap renditions of classical Taoist poetry, and so on. But the huge international success of the first film has given everyone involved new energy and confidence; sheerly as a ride on a ghost train, the sequel beats the original. The array of demonic foes includes the decomposing corpse of a giant, a lord of hell who poses as the Buddha, and a climactic monster from a William Burroughs nightmare. The only real regret is that the irascible Taoist swordsman (played by Wu Ma) doesn't show up until the last reel. TR

Chinese Ghost Story III, A (Qiannü Youhun III Dao Dao Dao)

(1991, HK, 106 min)
d Ching Siu-Tung. *p* Tsui Hark, Cho King-Man. *sc* Tsui Hark, Roy Szeto. *ph* Lau Moon-Tong. *ed* Mak Chi-Sin. *ad* James Leung. *m* Romeo Diaz, James Wong. *cast* Tony Leung [Leung Chiu-Wai], Jacky Cheung, Joey Wang, Nina Li, Lau Siu-Ming.

●One hundred years later, as promised in Part One, the androgynous tree demon returns, this time to terrorise a timid Buddhist monk (Leung) and his elderly master. Surprisingly enough, history repeats itself almost exactly. Glam wraith Lotus (Wang) tries to snare the virginal prey but complicates matters by falling in love with him. The Taoist end of things is held up by Yin (Cheung), a mercenary swordsman. Anyone who saw the other episodes will find this inexpressibly tedious, despite three plus factors: Tony Leung's performance, a brilliant opening scene (the funniest severed limb gags since *Monty Python and the Holy Grail*) and a great theme song. TR

Chinese Roulette (Chinesisches Roulette)

(1976, WGer/Fr, 86 min)
d/p/sc Rainer Werner Fassbinder. *ph* Michael Ballhaus, Horst Knechtel. *ed* Ila von Hasperg. *ad* Kurt Raab. *m* Peer Raben. *cast* Margit Carstensen, Andrea Schober, Ulli Lommel, Anna Karina, Macha Méril, Alexander Allerson.

●Made after Fassbinder disbanded his 'stock company' of actors, *Chinese Roulette* is quite different from his earlier bourgeois satires. The script is boldly non-naturalistic: a crippled girl connives to get herself, both her parents and their respective lovers to a country house all at the same time, for a weekend of intense embarrassments. And the style, all double reflections and shifting points of view, suspends the cast like flies in an amber of deceptions, neuroses and panics. The humour fits the cruelty as a boot fits a groin. TR

Chinese Vengeance

see Blood Brothers, The

Chino

see Valdez il Messosangue

Chinoise, La (La Chinoise, ou plutôt à la Chinoise)

(1967, Fr, 90 min)
d/sc Jean-Luc Godard. *ph* Raoul Coutard. *ed* Agnès Guillemot, Delphine Desfons. *m* Karlheinz Stockhausen. *cast* Anne Wiazemsky, Jean-Pierre Léaud, Michel Sémeniako, Juliet Berto, Lex de Bruijn, Omar Diop, Francis Jeanson.

●Godard's brilliant dialectical farce, distinctly disquieting as well as gratingly funny, in which five Parisian students, members of a Maoist cell, discuss the implications of the Chinese cultural revolution and the chances of using terrorism to effect a similar upheaval in the West. Dazzlingly designed as a collage of slogans and poster images, it was widely attacked at the time for playing with politics. But Godard was well aware what he was doing creating these 'Robinson Crusoes with Marxism as their Man Friday', and his film stands as a prophetic and remarkably acute analysis of the impulse behind the events of May 1968 in all their desperate sincerity and impossible naïveté. TM

Chin Up!

see Haut les Coeurs

Chi Sei? (Beyond the Door/Devil Within Her)

(1974, It, 109 min)
d Oliver Hellman [Sonia Assonitis]. *p* Ovidio G Assonitis, Giorgio C Rossi. *sc* Sonia Assonitis, Antonio Troisio, Giorgio Marini, Aldo Crudo. *ph* Roberto D'Ettorre Piazzoli. *ed* Angelo Curi. *ad* Piero Filippone, Franco Velchi. *m* Franco Micalizzi. *cast* Juliet Mills, Richard Johnson, Gabriele Lavia, Barbara Fiorini, Elizabeth Turner.

●Ludicrous bastard offspring of *The Exorcist* and *Rosemary's Baby* filmed in English. All-American mum Juliet Mills becomes the victim of a diabolic immaculate conception so that the devil's advocate can take up residence in the baby. Little does he know… IB

Chisum

(1970, US, 110 min)
d Andrew V McLaglen. *p/sc* Andrew J Fenady. *ph* William H Clothier. *ed* Robert Simpson. *ad* Carl Anderson. *m* Dominic Frontiere. *cast* John Wayne, Forrest Tucker, Christopher George, Ben Johnson, Glenn Corbett, Bruce Cabot, Andrew Prine, Patric Knowles, Richard Jaeckel.

●The range wars, Wayne-style; and a piece of Western revisionism to compare with *The Green Berets* for its articulation of the Duke's right-wing ethos. John Chisum here is on the side of the angels, with both Pat Garrett and Billy the Kid riding for him against capitalist competition. No mention of Chisum's own expansionist, monopolistic approach to the land; no mention of his subsequent hiring of the ageing Garrett to kill Billy. Enjoy veteran William Clothier's superb cinematography and wait for the next re-run of Peckinpah's version in *Pat Garrett and Billy the Kid*. PT

Chitty Chitty Bang Bang

(1968, GB, 145 min)
d Ken Hughes. *p* Albert R Broccoli. *sc* Roald Dahl, Ken Hughes. *ph* Christopher Challis. *ed* John Shirley. *pd* Ken Adam. *songs* Robert B Sherman, Richard M Sherman. *cast* Dick Van Dyke, Sally Ann Howes, Lionel Jeffries, Anna Quayle, Benny Hill, James Robertson Justice, Gert Fröbe, Robert Helpmann.

●Nauseatingly cute musical whimsy about an inventor (creations courtesy of Rowland Emmett) and his wonderful magic car. Ken Adam's sets are inventive, but the special effects are shoddy, the songs instantly forgettable, and the leisurely length an exquisite torture. TM

Chocolat

(1988, Fr, 105 min)
d Claire Denis. *sc* Claire Denis, Jean-Pol Fargeau. *ph* Robert Alazraki. *ed* Claudine Merlin. *ad* Thierry Flamand. *m* Abdullah Ibrahim. *cast* Issach de Bankolé, Giulia Boschi, François Cluzet, Cécile Ducasse, Jean-Claude Adelin, Kenneth Cranham, Emmet Judson Williamson, Mireille Perrier.

●A young woman called France (Perrier; Ducasse as a child) returns to the Cameroons, where she recalls (in one long flashback) her childhood as the daughter of a district governor of French West Africa. This idyllic existence is shattered when a plane prangs near her home, forcing the stranded passengers to stay with her parents. The motley crew – all demonstrating various aspects of empire-building – include a white plantation owner and his black concubine, a newly-wed couple on their first visit to the dark continent, and an ex-priest (Adelin) full of Rousseau-esque ideals who turns out to be the worst of the lot. It is his influence that destroys France's friendship with the houseboy (de Bankolé), and prompts her mother (Boschi) to make a pass at the servant. In her amazingly assured debut, Clare Denis draws out the implications of the action with great subtlety. She makes the most of the exotic location, and elicits strong performances from all her cast. Abdullah Ibrahim's excellent score enhances the atmosphere of repression and frustration. MS

Chocolat

(2000, US, 122 min)
d Lasse Hallström. *p* David Brown, Kit Golden, Leslie Holleran. *sc* Robert Nelson Jacobs. *ph* Roger Pratt. *ed* Andrew Mondshein. *pd* David Gropman. *m* Rachel Portman. *cast* Juliette Binoche, Judi Dench, Alfred Molina, Lena Olin, Johnny Depp, Carrie-Anne Moss, Hugh O'Conor, John Wood, Peter Stormare, Victoire Thivosol, Leslie Caron.

●The 1950s. Lent in the Gascony village of Lansquenet. A red-hooded woman (Binoche) and child (Thivosol) boldly set about converting the old bakery into a chocolate shop which offers delights so tempting that hyper-conservative mayor Reynaud (Molina), fearing for the moral and religious health of the villagers, determines to eject her from the community. Well, what with Vianne's witchlike knowledge of their hearts' desires, the effrontery of her fashionable dress, her friendship with the despised 'river rats', led by handsome, Irish-accented Roux (Depp), she does stir some dangerous emotions in this backwater. Even so, the villagers rally to her life-affirming cause. From the start, Hallström's soft adaptation of Joanne Harris's popular novel-cum-magical fable smoothly proceeds to construct a 'feminist' parable about the role of courage, support and pleasure in personal transformation. But, however excellent the performances, their relevance is diminished by the historical bubble in which they're situated. Roger Pratt's 'period' cinematography preserves the whole in aspic. WH

Chocolate Soldier, The

(1941, US, 102 min, b/w)
d Roy Del Ruth. *p* Victor Saville. *sc* Keith Winter, Leonard Lee. *ph* Karl Freund. *ed* James E Newcom. *ad* Cedric Gibbons, John S Detlie. *m* Oscar Straus. *cast* Nelson Eddy, Risë Stevens, Nigel Bruce, Florence Bates, Dorothy Gilmore.

●Confusingly, not the Oscar Straus operetta based on Shaw's *Arms and the Man*, but an operetta using some of the Straus songs to decorate (because Shaw wanted too much money) Molnar's play *The Guardsman*. About a singing duo, with the husband arranging a backfiring plot to test his wife's fidelity, it is pleasant enough (though lethargic) if you can stand that sort of thing and the bovine Eddy. TM

Chocolate War, The

(1988, US, 103 min)
d Keith Gordon. *p* Jonathan D Krane. *sc* Keith Gordon. *ph* Tom Richmond. *ed* Jeff Wishengrad. *ad* David Ensley. *cast* John Glover, Ilan Mitchell-Smith, Wally Ward, Bud Cort, Adam Baldwin, Jenny Wright, Doug Hutchinson.

●Having co-written, co-produced and starred in an outstanding independent film – Mark Romanek's *Static* – Keith Gordon made his directorial debut with this perfectly controlled study of teen tyranny. Every year the pupils of a strict Catholic boys' school are cajoled into selling boxes of chocolates to raise funds for their ailing alma mater. Morale is all-important, so when quiet new boy Jerry (Mitchell-Smith) refuses to participate, the school's principal, Brother Leon (Glover), uses the Vigils (a sadistic elite who terrorise their fellow pupils by giving them devilishly difficult 'assignments' to perform) to bring the rebel into line. But even when the full force of the Vigils is unleashed against him, Jerry continues to resist. A lovingly crafted and superbly acted attack on what Fassbinder used to call 'quiet fascism', this is smooth and rich, but with a delightfully bitter aftertaste. NF

Choice of Weapons, A

see Trial by Combat

Choirboys, The

(1977, US, 120 min)
d Robert Aldrich. *p* Merv Adelson, Lee Rich. *sc* Christopher Knopf. *ph* Joseph Biroc. *ed* Maury Winetrobe. *pd* Bill Kenney. *m* Frank De Vol. *cast* Charles Durning, Lou Gossett, Perry King, Tim McIntire, Randy Quaid, Don Stroud, James Woods, Robert Webber, Burt Young, Charles Haid.

●Sadly, this adaptation of Joseph Wambaugh's bestseller about the LA police plumps entirely for grossly inflating the vulgar 'playfulness' of the dozen-or-so cops in their on and off duty hours, while ignoring the fact that the humour has to be seen in counterpoint to the frightening descriptions of urban horror which the police confront daily. The book's humour was the ribald and understandable explosion of a safety valve; here it is merely an offensive display of stereotyping, sexism and patronising insincerity. A travestied misrepresentation and a notably complete failure. SM

Choke Canyon (aka On Dangerous Ground)

(1986, US, 94 min)
d Chuck Bail. *p* Ovidio G Assonitis. *sc* Sheila Goldberg, Ovidio G Assonitis. *ph* Dante Spinotti. *ed* Robert Silvi. *pd* Frank Vanoris. *m* Sylvester Levay. *cast* Stephen Collins, Janet Julian, Lance Henriksen, Bo Svenson, Victoria Racimo, Nicholas Pryor, Robert Hoy, Walter Robles.

●An agreeable piece of hokum in which a young physicist tries to convert sound waves into a usable form of energy. He believes that the spirits of Choke Canyon and Halley's Comet can help him (I'd advise a trick cyclist). His efforts bring him into conflict with the ruthless Pilgrim Corporation – a nuclear combine – and into the arms of Pilgrim's breathless but beautiful daughter. There are numerous stunts, some of which are quite interesting, and a batty climax in which the comet outshines them all. MS

Choose Me

(1984, US, 106 min)
d Alan Rudolph. *p* Carolyn Pfeiffer, David Blocker. *sc* Alan Rudolph. *ph* Jan Kiesser. *ed* Mia Goldman. *pd* Steven Legler. *m* Luther Vandross. *cast* Keith Carradine, Geneviève Bujold, Lesley Ann Warren, Rae Dawn Chong, Patrick Bauchau, John Larroquette.

●Rudolph here brings his variation on the kaleidoscopic Altman style to perfection with a marvellous gloss on *La Ronde* set in a Los Angeles bar that seems real but serves as a neon-lit dream world where everyone – not least Bujold's agony aunt, solving other people's problems but herself suffering untold miseries of sexual frustration – sooner or later turns up in quest of the partner who will bring emotional fulfilment, only to discover that it isn't necessarily there just for the asking. Often very funny as well as gorgeous to look at in its ineffable blend of realism and rhapsody, it comes on a little like a free jazz improvisation on the vulnerability of the human heart to the ecstasies and disenchantments that attend it in permanent orbit. TM

Chopper

(2000, Aust, 94 min)
d Andrew Dominik. *p* Michele Bennett. *sc* Andrew Dominik. *ph* Geoffrey Hall, Kevin Hayward. *ed* Ken Sallows. *pd* Paddy Reardon. *m* Mick Harvey. *cast* Eric Bana, Simon Lyndon, David Field, Dan Wyllie, Bill Young, Vince Colosimo, Kenny Graham, Kate Beahan.

●Mark Brandon Read earned his nickname by removing his victim's lower digits. Brilliantly portrayed by stand-up comedian Bana, 'Chopper' is one of those boorish Australians who's everyone's best friend until he takes offence: if you're unfortunate enough to tap into his dark side, he'll be sure to blame you for it and the punishment will be twice as severe. With his twinkling grin, his tattoos and beer-bucket frame, he's a plausible heavy, but Bana also shows us his sentimental side. When a cellmate repeatedly stabs him in the chest out of fear and greed, Chopper's hurt by the betrayal, but unfazed by physical pain, as if he's been desensitised to violence of any kind. Later, on the outside, he calls on his treacherous friend and your stomach churns: we know this man is capable of anything. It's funny, too: that commonplace about laughter being a safety valve has never been nearer the knuckle. Writer/director Dominik filters his subject's emotional volatility through colour washes but steps back to expose his fear and loneliness, and the infantile delusions which spur him. TCh

Chorus Line, A

(1985, US, 118 min)
d Richard Attenborough. *p* Cy Feuer, Ernest H Martin. *sc* Arnold Schulman. *ph* Ronnie Taylor. *ed* John Bloom. *pd* Patrizia von Brandenstein. *songs* Marvin Hamlisch, Edward Kleban. *cast* Michael Douglas, Alyson Reed, Terrence Mann, Michael Blevins, Yamil Borges, Jan Gan Boyd.

●Michael Bennett's 1975 Broadway hit was a triumph of edgy nerve and steamroller energy. Attenborough's film version is anything but. The grit and drive of the original have been dissipated into studiously unkempt glitz as empty as plasticised pop. A group of dancers (auditioning for a new show) are put through the hoops of humiliation by the director (Douglas), a mild-mannered sadist who delves into their private parts with voyeuristic enthusiasm, but Attenborough and screenwriter Arnold Schulman fail to justify this guy's nasty Citizen Kane megalomania. It's too corny and unbelievable for words. AR

Chorus of Disapproval, A

(1988, GB, 99 min)
d/p Michael Winner. *sc* Alan Ayckbourn, Michael Winner. *ph* Alan Jones. *ed* Chris Barnes, Michael Winner. *ad* Peter Young. *m* John Du Prez. *cast* Anthony Hopkins, Jeremy Irons, Richard Briers, Gareth Hunt, Patsy Kensit, Alexandra Pigg, Prunella Scales, Jenny Seagrove, Pete Lee-Wilson, Barbara Ferris, Lionel Jeffries, Sylvia Syms.

●Once upon a time there was a stage comedy called *A Chorus of Disapproval*, a clever, multilateral saga about a production of John Gay's *The Beggar's Opera* by a local amateur dramatic society, crawling with a modern suburban version of the twisters, shysters and adulterers presented by Gay with such *brio*. Enter Michael Winner, to take Alan Ayckbourn's vibrant original, ruin its point and its structure, and pour the cold porridge of his filmic imagination all over it. Now we have a great series of visual plugs for the charming seaside town of Scarborough, a very few moments when the humour and poignancy of the original escape unscathed, and a Rolls Royce cast of British actors who, except for Hopkins' ferociously frustrated Dafydd Ap Llewellyn and fine cameos from Briers and Jeffries, can't cope with either the heavily truncated script or Winner's cloddish, half-baked direction. SGr

Chosen, The

see Holocaust 2000

Chosen, The

(1981, US, 108 min)
d Jeremy Paul Kagan. *p* Edie Landau, Ely Landau. *sc* Edwin Gordon. *ph* Arthur J Ornitz. *ed* David Garfield, Howard Smith. *pd* Stuart Wurtzel. *m* Elmer Bernstein. *cast* Maximilian Schell, Rod Steiger, Robby Benson, Barry Miller, Hildy Brooks, Val Avery.

●A worthy but irretrievably dull homily (based on the novel by Chaim Potok) about the conflict between adolescent friendship – two Jewish boys, one orthodox and Zionist, the other a Hasidic – and filial devotion within the demands of the faith. This is post-war New York, and The Issue is the founding of the Jewish state in Palestine, a little-known piece of history but here uncomfortably yoked to a story of heartfelt human relationships, and topped off by Steiger's most mannered performance ever as the Hasidic rabbi. Whispering into his patriarch's beard and rolling his eyes heavenward, Steiger milks the role you suspect he has longed for ever since *The Pawnbroker*, and director Kagan makes little attempt to hold the ham in check. MA

Chosen One, The (Ishanou)

(1991, Ind, 91 min)
d/p Aribam Syam Sharma. *sc* MK Binodini Devi. *ph* Girish Padhiar. *ed* Ujjal Nandi. *m* Aribam Syam Sharma. *cast* Kiranmala, Tomba, Manbi.

●Sharma's film is almost un-Indian in its rapid pacing and tight narrative focus, but it couldn't be more culturally specific in subject. It's set in the Manipur Valley in NE India, and centres on the unique Maibi cult that flourishes in the area. Maibi are women who suddenly respond to some higher call, abandon their normal lives, and join the cult under a guru. The film explores one (fictional) case: a young woman named Tampha who deserts her husband and child and disappears into the cult. Sharma asks all the awkward questions. What does it mean to a mother to abandon her family? And what can a man do when he loses his wife to an impenetrable cult? The film doesn't pretend to explain the cult, but looks at its social repercussions through clear and searching eyes. TR

Choses de la Vie, Les (The Things of Life)

(1969, Fr/It, 89 min)
d Claude Sautet. *sc* Paul Guimard, Jean-Loup Dabadie, Claude Sautet. *ph* Jean Boffety. *ed* Jacqueline Thiédot. *ad* André Piltant. *m* Philippe Sarde. *cast* Michel Piccoli, Romy Schneider, Lea Massari, Gérard Lartigau, Jean Bouise, Henri Nassiet.

●A not uninteresting attempt to make a film about ordinary, everyday minutiae, with Piccoli as an average sensual man, vaguely torn between a demanding mistress (Schneider) and an ex-wife (Massari) to whom he still feels bound. Quietly and deftly, Sautet sketches in the portrait of a man gradually becoming aware that he is coming to a crossroads in his life. But since the opening sequence reveals that he is shortly to die in a car crash, his attempt to make some decision about his life is much ado about nothing – which is precisely the point of the film. Difficult to make a film about banality without being boring in the process, but Sautet all but pulls it off, thanks to a beautifully understated performance from Piccoli which manages to extract a whole lifetime of meaning from a simple gesture like lighting a cigarette, and to illuminate the film's meticulously detailed naturalistic surface. TM

Christiane F. (Christiane F. wir Kinder vom Bahnhof Zoo)

(1981, WGer, 131 min)
d Ulrich Edel. *p* Bernd Eichinger, Hans Weth. *sc* Herman Weigel. *ph* Justus Pankau, Jürgen Jürges. *ed* Jane Seitz. *m* Jürgen Knieper. *cast* Natja Brunckhorst, Thomas Haustein, Jens Kuphal, Rainer Wölk, Jan Georg Effler, Christiane Reichelt.

●A European box-office phenomenon on the strength of aghast multi-media exposure for the true confessions tale of a 13-year-old girl turned hooker to support her heroin habit. As Awful Warnings go, it's way above the *Reefer Madness* class, though its lurid drama-doc sheen – and insistent use of David Bowie's *Heroes* – create some ambivalent tensions between medium and message. Finally, the film's very relentlessness (whether calculated or naive) ensures a 'correct' gut reaction to the spectacle of a near-zomboid alternation of fix and hustle: there's only so much cautionary misery you want rubbed into your face, and this fruitfully goes beyond. Cursory on causes, but devastating on effects. PT

Christie Malry's Own Double-Entry

(2000, Neth/GB/Luxembourg, 92 min)
d Paul Tickell. *p* Kees Kasander. *sc* Simon Bent. *ph* Reinier Van Brummelen. *ed* Chris Wyatt. *pd* Wilbert Van Dorp. *m* Luke Haines. *cast* Nick Moran, Neil Stuke, Kate Ashfield, Mel Raido, Sophie Knijff, Shirley Ann Field, Mattia Sbragia, Salvatore Lazzaro, Sergio Albelli.

●Adapted from the angry novel by experimental novelist BS Johnson, this is an ambitious attempt to capture on film a particularly English strain of frustration, resentment and despair. A strong cast and score (fromAuteurs' Luke Haines) underpin a powerful, politically committed tale of credit and debit, as trainee accountant Christie sets out to balance the books with society, moving from minor transgressions to major urban unrest. Topical and unsettling, it's a vibrant and striking addition to the new wave of leftfield British movies that aim higher than an easy social realism. GE

Christine

(1983, US, 110 min)
d John Carpenter. *p* Richard Kobritz. *sc* Bill Phillips. *ph* Donald M Morgan. *ed* Marion Rothman. *pd* Dan Lomino. *m* John Carpenter. *cast* Keith Gordon, John Stockwell, Alexandra Paul, Robert Prosky, Harry Dean Stanton, Christine Belford.

● Carpenter and novelist Stephen King share not merely a taste for genre horror but a love of '50s teenage culture; and although set in the present, *Christine* reflects the second taste far more effectively than the first. It concerns a demonic 1958 Plymouth Fury which not only suffocates its victims to blasts of Larry Williams' 'Boney Moronie', but also reconstitutes itself before the naked eye like some fetishistic amoeba, incidentally transforming its puny owner from a pimply nonentity into one of the baddest boys on the block. All of this works rather well as black comedy. But from the horror perspective, Carpenter is only the latest in a long line of film-makers who've been seduced by King's sheer plausibility as a writer. Off the page, a 1958 Plymouth is no more scary than the St Bernard which romped through *Cujo*. DP

Christine Jorgensen Story, The

(1970, US, 98 min)
d Irving Rapper. *p* Edward Small. *sc* Robert E Kent, Ellis St Joseph. *ph* Jacques R Marquette. *ed* Grant Whytock. *ad* F Paul Sylos. *m* Paul Sawtell, Bert Shefter. *cast* John Hansen, Joan Tompkins, Quinn Redeker, John W Himes, Ellen Clark, Will Kuluva.

● A well-meaning if somewhat sanctimonious piece of claptrap about the first man to undergo a sex-change operation (in 1952). Although attempting a serious and sympathetic treatment of its subject, it confronts few of the real issues involved, and actor Hansen proves incapable of tackling the female part of his role. DP

Christmas Carol, A

(1984, GB, 101 min)
d Clive Donner. *p* William F Storke, Alfred R Kelman. *sc* Roger O Hirson. *ph* Tony Imi. *ed* Peter Tanner. *pd* Roger Murray-Leach. *m* Nick Bicat. *cast* George C Scott, Frank Finlay, Angela Pleasence, Edward Woodward, Michael Carter, David Warner, Susannah York, Anthony Walters, Roger Rees.

● The only character in Dickens' sentimental tale who never stuck in one's craw was the pre-reformation Scrooge, and so it seems exactly right that Donner's movie should rest entirely on the solid shoulders of George C Scott. His intelligence and quickness at last give us a Scrooge of many dimensions; a man of tortured and forbidding nobility, made cruel by uncaring parentage and a malign fate, rather than the usual thin miser. The fact that he is also one of nature's monetarists does not go unnoticed. As to the rest: Shrewsbury looks well enough under snow; one can enjoy the urge to kick away the crutch of a more than usually repellent Tiny Tim; and only Roger Rees (as Scrooge's nephew) suggests that goodness might be vertebrate. CPea

Christmas Carol – The Movie

(2001, GB/Ger, 81 min)
d Jimmy T Murakami. *p* Iain Harvey. *sc* Piet Kroon, Robert Llewellyn. *ph* (live action) Mike Garfath. *ed* Taylor Grant, (live action) Martin Brinkler. *pd* (live action) Christopher Woods. *m* Julian Nott. *cast* Simon Callow, James Jordan, Tracey O'Flaherty; voices: Simon Callow, Kate Winslet, Nicolas Cage, Jane Horrocks, Michael Gambon, Rhys Ifans, Juliet Stevenson.

● Apart from one or two painterly aerial shots of quintessentially English scenes and one mostly impressive sequence involving the ghosts of Past, Present and Future, much of the animation in this Dickens adaptation is lacking in depth, contrast, fluidity and, above all, colour. The film-makers rarely get a handle on the storytelling and, in a vain effort to inject comedy, have even added two singularly humourless mice. Callow's Scrooge excepted, the voiceovers are uninvolving and personality-free. DA

Christmas Holiday

(1944, US, 93 min, b/w)
d Robert Siodmak. *p* Felix Jackson. *sc* Herman J Mankiewicz. *ph* Woody Bredell. *ed* Ted Kent. *ad* John B Goodman, Robert Clatworthy. *m* Hans J Salter. *cast* Deanna Durbin, Gene Kelly, Gale Sondergaard, Gladys George, Richard Whorf, Dean Harens, David Bruce.

● Scripted by Herman Mankiewicz from Somerset Maugham's novel about a young woman whose illusions come a cropper when she realises that the wealthy charmer she married is a mother-fixated wastrel, this might have been one of Siodmak's best and blackest *noirs* had Deanna Durbin not baulked at portraying a prostitute. Opting for compromise, she appears as a New Orleans nightclub hostess, which makes rather a nonsense of the second half of the plot when the husband, jailed for murder, escapes with the intention of killing her because of 'what she has become'. It also undermines the sense of guilty responsibility for his fate which underlies her claim, as he offers to kill her, that she deliberately hit bottom so that she too should have her prison. A fascinating film nevertheless, tainted with a brooding sense of malaise, and with fine performances from Kelly and Sondergaard which dovetail the suppressed hints of homosexuality and incest. TM

Christmas in August (Pal-Wol ui Christmas)

(1998, SKor, 97 min)
d Hur Jin-Ho. *cast* Han Suk-Kyu, Shim Eun-Ha, Shin Ku, Oh Ji-Hae.

● A likeable, understated movie about facing up to death, from a first time director. Jung-Won (Han, Korea's coolest young actor) is a pro photographer with his own shop in a suburb of Seoul; only he and his immediate relatives know that he has just a few months to live. Nothing 'dramatic' happens. He runs into his childhood sweetheart and regrets that her life hasn't worked out better. He goes to a friend's funeral. He makes a point of seeing other old friends. And he develops a slightly abrasive friendship with a young woman traffic warden, which leaves her wanting to know him better and not understanding why he isn't 'there' for her. Hur conjures up quotidian rhythms very plausibly, and draws fine performances from his whole cast. It was the last film shot by the great Yoo Young-Kil, to whose memory it's dedicated. TR

Christmas in July

(1940, US, 67 min, b/w)
d Preston Sturges. *p* Paul Jones. *sc* Preston Sturges. *ph* Victor Milner. *ed* Ellsworth Hoagland. *ad* Hans Dreier, Earl Hedrick. *cast* Dick Powell, Ellen Drew, Raymond Walburn, William Demarest, Franklin Pangborn, Ernest Truex.

● Minor but delightful Sturges comedy (his second film) about a go-getting clerk who is tricked into believing his truly lousy slogan dreamed up for a contest has won him $25,000, learning the truth only when he has spent the money on credit buying goodies all round. The satire on big business, advertising and the success ethic doesn't amount to much, but the Sturges stock company is rampant, and there is a terrific slapstick escalation when the storeowners, busting in on the ongoing neighbourhood party to repossess their goods, provoke a custard-pie riot (but with fish). TM

Christmas Story, A

(1983, US, 98 min)
d Bob Clark. *p* René Dupont, Bob Clark. *sc* Jean Shepherd, Leigh Brown, Bob Clark. *ph* Reginald Morris. *ed* Stan Cole. *pd* Reuben Freed. *m* Carl Zittrer, Paul Zaza. *cast* Melinda Dillon, Darren McGavin, Peter Billingsley, Ian Petrella, Scott Schwartz, RD Robb.

● Surely everyone remembers how they felt, at primary school, when a literary masterpiece came back marked with a mere C+? This and many other such crimes perpetrated by the adult world on the inhabitants of kid-dom are exposed in this nostalgic mock-epic tale of young Ralphie's quest to ensure that presents assembled under the tree on Christmas morning include a much-coveted BB air-rifle. Delightfully entertaining, with a wryly amusing narration to keep the adults in the audience smirking. DPe

Christopher Columbus

(1949, GB, 104 min)
d David MacDonald. *p* A Frank Bundy. *sc* Muriel Box, Sydney Box, Cyril Roberts. *ph* Stephen Dade. *ed* V Sagovsky. *pd* Maurice Carter. *m* Arthur Bliss. *cast* Fredric March, Florence Eldridge, Francis L Sullivan, Linden Travers, Kathleen Ryan, Derek Bond, James Robertson Justice.

● Gainsborough's flailing attempts to add 'class' and international prestige to their more interestingly low-key 'domestic' output resulted in this expensively mounted dodo, elegantly consigned to the scrapheap of film history by contemporary critic Richard Winnington with the withering opinion that it 'contrives with something like genius neither to inform, excite, entertain, titillate or engage the eye'. PT

Christopher Columbus: The Discovery

(1992, US, 121 min)
d John Glen. *p* Alexander Salkind, Ilya Salkind. *sc* Mario Puzo, John Briley, Cary Bates. *ph* Alec Mills. *ed* Matthew Glen. *m* Cliff Eidelman. *cast* Marlon Brando, Tom Selleck, George Corraface, Rachel Ward, Robert Davi, Catherine Zeta Jones, Oliver Cotton, Benicio Del Toro, Mathieu Carrière.

● Who needs *Carry On Columbus* when you can have the real thing? It's hard to fathom the minds of people who could make this kind of tripe. The film is wretched in most respects (Robert Davi is a ruggedly good Martin Pinzon), but even fine writers like Louis MacNeice and Richard Nelson have been stumped by the intractability of the Columbus story: he came, he saw, he went home. It's boring enough crossing the Atlantic on British Airways, never mind months in a wooden hulk surrounded by exiles from the RSC and the National. Selleck looks suitably embarrassed as King Ferdinand of Aragon, Ward is a head-girl Isabella of Castille, Jones is Columbus' bit on the (quay)side, an unknown Greek with designer stubble (Corraface) is Columbus, and Brando is a completely barmy Torquemada. SGr

Christopher Strong

(1933, US, 77 min, b/w)
d Dorothy Arzner. *p* David O Selznick. *sc* Zoë Akins. *ph* Bert Glennon, Sid Hickox. *ed* Arthur Roberts. *ad* Van Nest Polglase, Charles M Kirk. *m* Max Steiner. *cast* Katharine Hepburn, Colin Clive, Billie Burke, Helen Chandler, Ralph Forbes, Irene Browne, Jack LaRue.

● Early Hollywood movies (re)claimed for feminist film history sometimes require complex analysis to explain their relevance, but this teaming of Arzner and Hepburn is absolutely central to an understanding of women's place within classical Hollywood. Hepburn plays pioneer aviatrix Cynthia Darrington, courted by Christopher Strong (though why the title should bear his name and not hers is a mystery). She plays him along but independently pursues her career, telling Strong 'Don't ever stop me doing what I want', only to fall into typical Hollywood compromise and find herself pregnant by her (married) lover in the last reel. Suicide is offered as the only way out, but even in her dying moments (a high-altitude record-breaking flight) she rebels against society's required sacrifice and tries to replace her oxygen mask. Fascinating precisely for the vacillation of its central (female) character, and for the way in which aviation (itself a uniquely 20th century activity virtually closed to women) is used as a metaphor for film-making and women's attempts to gain a foothold in that male-dominated territory. MA

Christ Stopped at Eboli (Cristo si è Fermato a Eboli)

(1979, It/Fr, 155 min)
d Francesco Rosi. *p* Franco Cristaldi, Nicola Carraro. *sc* Francesco Rosi, Tonino Guerra, Raffaele La Capria. *ph* Pasqualino de Santis. *ed* Ruggero Mastroianni. *ad* Andrea Crisanti. *m* Piero Piccioni. *cast* Gian Maria Volonté, Paolo Bonacelli, Alain Cuny, Lea Massari, Irene Papas, François Simon.

● This adaptation of Carlo Levi's autobiographical book awkwardly bridges the space between Rosi's justly celebrated political dossier thrillers (*The Mattei Affair, Lucky Luciano, Illustrious Corpses*) and his more recent *Three Brothers*, and has to be counted a major disappointment. Covering the period of Levi's Fascist-imposed exile to the southern Italian region of Lucania in the '30s, Rosi ditches analysis to allow the desolate landscapes and faces of a remote peasant culture (seen as somehow beyond ideology) to tell their own tale. An unfortunate tendency to sentimentalise mars even this limited schema, though, and Volonté's suitably humbled Levi is even followed around by a Disneyesque dog. PT

Chronicle of a Death Foretold (Cronaca di una Morte Annunciata)

(1987, It/Fr, 110 min)
d Francesco Rosi. *p* Yves Gasser, Francis von Büren. *sc* Francesco Rosi, Tonino Guerra. *ph* Pasqualino de Santis. *ed* Ruggero Mastroianni. *pd* Andrea Crisanti. *m* Piero Piccioni. *cast* Rupert Everett, Ornella Muti, Gian Maria Volonté, Irene Papas, Lucia Bosé, Alain Cuny.
● Rosi's adaptation of Garcia Márquez's novel is an absorbing and unusual murder mystery set within a tiny South American community. A wealthy and mysterious stranger (Everett, cringingly affected) chooses a local girl (Muti) as his wife. No virgin, she is returned to her family on the wedding night, and the brothers determine to kill her previous lover. They brag their intentions around the village, yet no one intervenes. The tale is narrated, through interviews and flashbacks, by the dead man's best friend, returned home after a long absence to find the villagers still nursing their guilt. The simple facts hold no answers; the real clues lie in a web of tradition and centuries-old conditioning. The omnipresent Catholicism, the empty macho stances of the men, the strains of violence underlying strong familial bonds: these propel the action, giving the film an almost mystical aura. Although occasionally so languorously photographed that it almost grinds to a halt, the film is ultimately memorable. EP

Chronicle of a Love Affair

see Cronaca di un Amore

Chronicle of Anna Magdalena Bach (Chronik der Anna Magdalena Bach)

(1968, It/WGer, 93 min, b/w)
d Jean-Marie Straub. *p* Gian Vittorio Baldi. *sc* Jean-Marie Straub, Danièle Huillet. *ph* Ugo Piccone, Saverio Daimanti, Giovanni Canfarelli. *ed* Danièle Huillet. *m* Johann Sebastian Bach. *cast* Gustav Leonhardt, Christiane Lang, Paolo Carlini, Ernst Castelli, Hans-Peter Boye, Joachim Wolf.
● 'A film about the past which is lucid can help people of the present to achieve that necessary lucidity.' Straub's account of Bach is nothing if not lucid: it documents the last 27 years of its subject's life (through the mediating eyes of his wife) principally in terms of his music. The music itself obviates any need for a 'drama' to present Bach; Straub celebrates its range and complexity while showing it always in performance, to emphasise the nature of Bach's work as musician/conductor. A narration (compiled from contemporary sources) sets the man in his economic and social context. With his minimalist's sensitivity to nuance and inflection, Straub eschews pointless cutting and camera movement. The beautiful result has the air of a crystal-clear meditation. TR

Chronicle of a Summer

see Chronique d'un Eté

Chronique d'un Eté (Chronicle of a Summer)

(1961, Fr, 90 min, b/w)
d Jean Rouch, Edgar Morin. *p* Anatole Dauman, Philippe Lifchitz. *sc* Jean Rouch, Edgar Morin. *ph* Roger Morillère, Raoul Coutard, Jean-Jacques Tarbès, Michel Brault. *ed* Jean Ravel, Néna Baratier, Françoise Colin. *with* Jean Rouch, Edgar Morin, Marceline, Marilù, Angélo.
● The notion of a domestically-based 'ethnological study' dates at least from Montesquieu's *Lettres persanes*. But what distinguishes this attempt by Rouch and the sociologist Edgar Morin to 'bottle' the climate of Paris circa 1960 is their camera's candid assumption of its own disruptively active presence: interviewees are introduced to each other, form groups, and may well (in one case) have got married after shooting was over. In an interesting epilogue, Rouch invites them all to comment on his footage. GAd

Chroniques Marocaines

see Moroccan Chronicles

'Chubby' Down Under and Other Sticky Regions

(1998, GB, 86 min)
d Tom Poole. *p* Harry Storey, Simon Wright. *sc* Roy 'Chubby' Brown. *ph* John Christie, Steve Haskett. *ed* Nigel Williams. *with* Roy 'Chubby' Brown.
● Chubby is a Northern blue comedian and this follows the sex-obsessed lard barrel, in shiny helmet and patchwork suit, as he takes his humour on a 1997 tour from Melbourne to Perth, via Sydney, with a stopover in Hong Kong. It's disturbing to think that this revolting humourist has such an immense and dedicated fan base (each date sold out within four hours) including many women, who shamelessly chortle as he cavorts across the stage with an oversized, blow-up doll. HK

Chu-Chin-Chow

(1934, GB, 103 min, b/w)
d Walter Forde. *p* Michael Balcon. *sc* Edward Knoblock, Sidney Gilliat, L DuGarde Peach. *ph* Max Greene. *ed* Derek Twist. *ad* Ernö Metzner. *songs* Frederick Norton. *cast* George Robey, Fritz Kortner, Anna May Wong, John Garrick, Pearl Argyle, Francis L Sullivan.
● This jolly celebration of Oriental brutality confounds all expectations of restraint and respectability in pre-war British cinema. Bloodcurdling murders, scantily-clad slave-girls, and an atmosphere of delicious terror induced by the ever-present threat of being boiled in oil, fed to the dogs or cut into tiny pieces by the magnetically vindictive villain, come as something of a shock even though they're all part of an unabashedly English pantomime tradition. Filmed with verve and audacity and a lavishness completely untypical of the small Gainsborough Studios, the result is a gutsy melodramatic piece of popular cinema. RMy

Chuck & Buck

(2000, US, 96 min)
d Miguel Arteta. *p* Matthew Greenfield. *sc* Mike White. *ph* Chuy Chávez. *ed* Jeff Betancourt. *pd* Renée Davenport. *m* Joey Waronker, Tony Maxwell, Smokey Hormel. *cast* Mike White, Chris Weitz, Beth Colt, Lupe Ontiveros, Beth Colt, Paul Weitz, Maya Rudolph, Mary Wigmore, Paul Sand, Gino Buccola.
● A comedy about a gay stalker with a mental age of about 12, this is so not-for-everyone! Shot on digital video but looking like Plasticine, it beetles straight for the sexual discomfort zone. Chuck (Weitz) is the straight guy. A record company exec, he lives in an LA villa with his fiancée Carlyn (Colt), but ventures back to the sticks, to pay his respects and offer comfort, when the mother of his former best pal Buck dies. Buck (White) is a strange one. At the funeral, he seems more unhappy about Chuck leaving again than about the death of his mother. He comes on to Chuck in the bathroom: 'Do you remember the games we used to play?' Chuck doesn't – or chooses not to. But Buck doesn't take rejection. He turns up in LA, at Chuck's home and office. When his old friend sends him packing, he writes a play instead, and hires a local theatre to stage it. This deliciously and appropriately odd turn of events lifts the film just when you fear it's about to fold. But it's the insidiously challenging nature of Buck's obsession which makes the movie genuinely unsettling and more than just a goof-off. TCh

Chuka

(1967, US, 105 min)
d Gordon Douglas. *p* Rod Taylor, Jack Jason. *sc* Richard Jessup. *ph* Harold Stine. *ed* Robert Wyman. *ad* Hal Pereira, Tambi Larsen. *m* Leith Stevens. *cast* Rod Taylor, John Mills, Ernest Borgnine, Luciana Paluzzi, James Whitmore, Louis Hayward, Angela Dorian.
● A Western, passably well handled by Gordon Douglas, but scripted (by Richard Jessup from his own novel) along such well-beaten tracks that you can almost sing along to it. Rod Taylor is the roving gunfighter who understands that the Indians are on the warpath only because they're hungry; John Mills is the army officer stubbornly insisting on doing things by the book; the company at the fort he commands, because he has a Fatal Flaw, is composed exclusively of drunks, card-sharps and cut-throats; and of course there is a long-lost love (Paluzzi) conveniently turning up to cover the romantic angle. A cliché is found for every occasion, except perhaps the end, when everybody (with the possible exception of Taylor) gets killed off in the Indian attack. TM

Chump at Oxford, A

(1939, US, 63 min, b/w)
d Alfred Goulding. *p* Hal Roach Jr. *sc* Charles Rogers, Felix Adler, Harry Langdon. *ph* Art Lloyd. *ed* Bert Jordan. *ad* Charles D Hall. *m* Marvin Hatley. *cast* Stan Laurel, Oliver Hardy, Wilfred Lucas, Forrester Harvey, James Finlayson, Anita Garvin, Peter Cushing.
● Not so much a parody of the nonsensically moralising *A Yank at Oxford* as an amiable shaggy-dog romp through the usual Laurel and Hardy routines. It doesn't really matter very much that it takes place at Oxford University (this is not exactly a biting social satire); rather it's the usual collection of slow but delightful set pieces in which the duo are confused by the niceties of normal civilised behaviour. The best moments see Stan and Ollie chaotically in service as butler and maid, and Stan's marvellous transformation, by amnesia, into an aristocratic twit. GA

Chungking Express (100) (Chongqing Senlin)

(1994, HK, 97 min)
d Wong Kar-Wai. *p* Chan Yi-Kan. *sc* Wong Kar-Wai. *ph* Christopher Doyle, Lau Wai Keung. *ed* William Chang, Hai Kit-wai. *m* Frankie Chan, Roel A Garcia. *cast* Brigitte Lin, Tony Leung, Faye Wang, Takeshi Kaneshiro, Valerie Chow.
● Wong Kar-Wai's movie tells two loosely interlinked stories, both about lovelorn cops who get involved with women who are wrong for them. In the first, Takeshi Kaneshiro tries to pick up Brigitte Lin in a late-night bar, unaware she's a big-time heroin smuggler who's spent the evening hunting down some absconding drug couriers. In the second, the boyish Faye Wang (a star is born!) gets a crush on Tony Leung and starts breaking into his apartment to redecorate it while he's out. This is what Godard movies were once like: fast, hand-held, funny and very, very catchy. The year's zingiest visit to Heartbreak Hotel. TR

Chunhyang (Chunhyang Dyeon)

(2000, SKor, 133 min)
d Im Kwon-Taek. *p* Lee Tae-Won. *sc* Kim Myung-Kon. *ph* Jung Il-Sung. *ed* Park Soon-Duk. *pd* Min Un-Ok. *m* Kim Jung-Gil. *cast* Yi Hyo-Jeong, Cho Seung-Woo, Kim Young-Nyo, Lee Jung-Hun, Kim Hak-Yong, Lee Hae-Eun.
● A logical step on from Im's earlier reclamations of Korea's vanishing traditional culture, this frames its retelling of a very well known folk tale as a theatrical performance by *pansori* singer-storyteller Cho Sang-Hyun. (The director's cut dramatises the impact of his performance on sceptical kids in the audience but that's gone from the 121-minute export version.) Chunhyang is the daughter of a *kisaeng* (Korean geisha) in Namwon; the scholar Lee Mong-Ryong woos her doggedly, and the two eventually become lovers. But while he departs for the capital to sit the imperial exam for a civil service post, Chunhyang falls victim to the newly arrived governor, who beats, imprisons and sentences her to death for daring to refuse his advances. Im casts personable newcomers as the young lovers and uses bold colours and compositions to turn the tale into a dark rhapsody. TR

Chuquiago

(1977, Bol, 86 min)
d Antonio Equino. *sc* Oscar Soria. *ph* Antonio Eguino, Julio Lencina. *ed* Deborah Shaffer, Suzanne Fenn. *m* Alberto Villalpando. *cast* Néstor Yujra, Edmundo Villarroel, David Santalla, Tatiana Aponte.
● Equino uses the old neo-realist ploy of overlapping four separate stories, each dealing with a person from a different social stratum, to illustrate the shaping forces, economic and political, of the four lives. A rural Indian boy is sold to a market stallholder in La Paz; a *cholo* boy turns to petty crime; a petit-bourgeois civil servant dies on his Friday night respite from the daily grind; a rich student is torn between radicalism and her

family's wishes. She opts for safety, and is the film's final, most obvious, example of its main topic: the political compromises, knowing and unknowing, by which we undo ourselves. CPea

Chute de la Maison Usher, La (The Fall of the House of Usher)

(1928, Fr, 65 min, b/w & col tinting)
d/sc Jean Epstein. *ph* Georges Lucas, Jean Lucas. *pd* Pierre Kéfer. *cast* Marguerite Abel Gance, Jean Debucourt, Charles Lamy, Fournez-Goffard, Halma, Luc Dartagnan, Pierre Kéfer, Pierre Hot.
● Epstein's stunningly beautiful Poe adaptation has always been notable for its impressionistic approach to narrative and for the brooding, gothic lyricism of its images, but this restored print from the Cinémathèque Royale de Belgique, complete with original colour tinting, may well advance its claim to be one of the most imaginative and entrancing horror movies of the silent era. If its dreamlike strangeness seems faintly surreal, don't forget that Epstein's assistant was none other than the young Luis Buñuel. GA

Ciao Manhattan

(1972, US, 92 min, b/w & col)
d John Palmer, David Weisman. *p* Robert Margouleff, David Weisman. *sc* John Palmer, David Weisman. *ph* John Palmer, Kjell Rostad. *ed* Robert Farnen. *cast* Edie Sedgwick, Wesley Hayes, Isabel Jewell, Jane Holzer, Viva, Roger Vadim, Paul America, Christian Marquand. *with* Edie Sedgwick, Allen Ginsberg.
● Two attempts at a movie spliced uneasily into one. A sort of mystery thriller shot in black-and-white and set in New York in the 1960s with Sedgwick, Holzer, Viva and other 'superstars' of the era, is combined with a colour study of the very deranged and desperate Edie in 1971, living out her last days (she died at 28 soon after the shooting) in her parents' house in California. The result is a mess. On the other hand, the ensuing confusion is in keeping with Edie's own disordered existence in her increasing drug dependency, and the contrasts (and continuities) between the '70s woman with the swollen silicon breasts and the elfin magnetic personality of the '60s are deeply disturbing. MH

Cible émouvante (Wild Target)

(1993, Fr, 88 min)
d Pierre Salvadori. *p* Philippe Martin. *sc* Pierre Salvadori. *ph* Gilles Henry. *ed* Hélène Viard. *ad* Yan Arlaud. *m* Philippe Eidel. *cast* Jean Rochefort, Marie Trintignant, Guillaume Depardieu, Patachou, Charlie Nelson, Wladimir Yordanoff.
● Victor (Rochefort) is a middle-aged hit-man and a self-improver who keeps a fastidiously ordered life. When a naive young messenger (Depardieu) accidentally mixes himself up in Victor's affairs, he keeps him, trains him up, and softens up; enough, at least, to balk at his next assignment (Trintignant), a wanton fellow rogue, art forger and thief. And thus the three are forced to team up to top the man who ordered her killed. Salvadori's debut feature, which he also wrote, is a winning well-directed combination of deadpan black farce, knowing genre comedy and wistful romantic triangle. Anchoring the film is another of Rochefort's superb portrayals of the haut bourgeois whose very inscrutability and repression engender sympathy and amusement in equal portion. As his dignity is eroded in a knockabout farce around the streets of Paris, his emotions begin to unbutton. This situation comedy is fine, but the film's bid for pathos fails, amid sideswipes at sexual manners only the French will ken. But it ends with such ridiculous symmetry that you'll forgive it. WH

Ciclone, Il

see Cyclone, The

Cidade de Deus

see City of God

Cider House Rules, The

(1999, US, 126 min)
d Lasse Hallström. *p* Richard N Gladstein. *sc* John Irving. *ph* Oliver Stapleton. *ed* Lisa Zeno Churgin. *pd* David Gropman. *m* Rachel Portman. *cast* Tobey Maguire, Charlize Theron, Delroy Lindo, Paul Rudd, Michael Caine, Jane Alexander, Kathy Baker, Kieran Culkin, Kate Nelligan.
● With his taste for lengthy melodrama and his idiosyncratic sensibility, John Irving has proved a tricky source for movie-makers; Hallström's film is problematic, but probably the most successful attempt at capturing the tenor, if not the full scope of Irving's vision. Passive and discreet, Maguire is well cast as Homer Wells, the protégé of Dr Larch (Caine, with credible New England accent), who must break free of his mentor to reach full maturity. The first and last acts hold up well enough, with a standout supporting turn from Lindo, but the romantic middle section is less interesting, and Hallström's humanism is possibly a little low key and romantic given such tough themes as abortion and incest. TCh

Ciel est à nous, Le

see Shooting Stars

Ciel, les Oiseaux et... Ta Mère!, Le (Boys on the Beach)

(1998, Fr, 90 min)
d Djamel Bensalah. *p* Didier Creste, Yann Gilbert, Joël Leyendecker, Nicolas Vannier. *sc* Djamel Bensalah, Gilles Laurent. *ph* Martin Legrand. *ed* Fabrice Rouaud. *ad* Gérard Marcireau. *cast* Jamel Debbouze, Julien Courbey, Lorant Deutsch, Stéphane Soo Mongo, Olivia Bonamy, Mariù Roversi, Julia Vaidis Bogard, Jessica Beudaert.
● Four friends from the Paris suburbs (Debbouze, Soo Mongo, Deutsch and Courbey) win a three week holiday to Biarritz. They attack the resort with the simple agenda of 'beach, babes, ass', but they are swiftly thrown on the defensive by the forces of penury, sexual inexperience and inexpedience, and by the fact that they're quite obviously full of shit. Co-written and directed by first-timer Bensalah, this has the flavour of personal reminiscence. The film is punctuated with camcorder footage, as if the boys' own, but the director's five or six years' vantage on his protagonists hasn't given him much on them in terms of human knowledge or film-making know how. Discussions occasionally touch on pertinent issues of race, education, elitism, social exclusion and access to the natural environment, contrasting the boys' confined world view with the life style of Biarritz, but mostly the film sticks with the boys' sexual slang. Debbouze is the most watchable, but he's also a despicable little ball of hate, wantonly indulged by the director. Even teenage boys deserve a better case than this. NB

Cielo Abierto, El

see Ten Days Without Love

Cielo è sempre più blu, Il

see Bits and Pieces

Ciénaga, La (The Swamp)

(2001, Arg/US/Jap/Fr/Switz/Sp/Braz, 100 min)
d Lucrecia Martel. *p* Lita Stantic. *sc* Lucrecia Martel. *ph* Hugo Colace. *ed* Santiago Ricci. *ad* Graciela Oderigo. *cast* Mercedes Morán, Graciela Borges, Martín Adjemián, Sylvia Bayle, Juan Cruz Bordeu, Daniel Venezuela, Sofia Bertolotto.
● Martel's debut is remarkable, a (presumably autobiographical?) slice of life focusing on the households of middle-aged cousins, the kind and sensible Tali (Morán) and the more neurotic and self-centred Mecha (Borges), over the course of a torpid late Argentinian summer. Mostly it's based in and around Mecha's country house. The swimming pool is green and putrid. The electricity keeps cutting out. The phone rings and rings, and no matter how many times you tell them the Indians won't answer it. Cut across the breast after a drunken accident with a tray of glasses, Mecha sticks to her bed, drinks iced wine and vegetates, while her adolescent children negotiate their own tribulations. Although one plot rivulet does involve a cow stuck up to its nostrils in a swamp, the title points to a more general stasis: an inertia and redundancy which creeps up on Mecha and threatens to suffocate her in a quiescent alcoholic haze. Martel's densely layered soundtrack is even more impressive than her distinctive, confident visuals: the scrape of a pool chair against the concrete is enough to set your teeth on edge. It's not that the film lacks compassion, but that Martel's outlook is singularly bleak. TCh

Cimarron

(1960, US, 147 min)
d Anthony Mann. *p* Edmund Grainger. *sc* Arnold Schulman. *ph* Robert Surtees. *ed* John Dunning. *ad* George W Davis, Addison Hehr. *m* Franz Waxman. *cast* Glenn Ford, Maria Schell, Anne Baxter, Arthur O'Connell, Russ Tamblyn, Mercedes McCambridge, David Opatoshu.
● This second screen version of Edna Ferber's frontier saga (1890–1915) marks the transitional point between Mann's '50s cycle of Westerns and the expansive epics which occupied his final years. Ford's hero is a man set on lighting out of Oklahoma territory, but so ambiguous is his relationship with spouse Schell that the producer added new clarifying material without the director's permission. Occasionally spectacular, mostly baggy. TJ

Cina è vicina, La

see China Is Near

Cincinnati Kid, The

(1965, US, 113 min)
d Norman Jewison. *p* Martin Ransohoff. *sc* Ring Lardner Jr, Terry Southern. *ph* Philip H Lathrop. *ed* Hal Ashby. *ad* George W Davis, Edward C Carfagno. *m* Lalo Schifrin. *cast* Steve McQueen, Edward G Robinson, Karl Malden, Tuesday Weld, Ann-Margret, Joan Blondell, Rip Torn, Jack Weston.
● With Jewison replacing Peckinpah as director, nowhere near as strong as it might have been, but Ring Lardner and Terry Southern's script, taken from Richard Jessup's novel about poker-sharks meeting for a big game in '30s New Orleans, is a vivid character study in the tradition of the not dissimilar *The Hustler*. Marvellous performances throughout ensure interest. GA

Cinderella

(1949, US, 74 min)
d Wilfred Jackson, Hamilton Luske, Clyde Geronimi. *sc* William Peed, Ted Sears, Homer Brightman, Kenneth Anderson, Erdman Penner, Winston Hibler, Harry Reeves, Joe Rinaldi. *ed* Donald Halliday. *songs* Mack David, Jerry Livingston, Al Hoffman. *cast* voices: Ilene Woods, William Phipps, Eleanor Audley, Verna Felton.
● From the first tumescent AAaaooooo of the chorus and plig plig of the harp, this is bang-on-course Disney animation. Once you get past the 'storybook' framing and the information that 'a dream is a wish the heart makes' – eat lead, Sigmund – it is played for laughs all the way. Furry creature value is high, and there is an extra-wicked stepmother who is the stuff of infant nightmares. The prince is as wooden as Letraset, and the real moral dramas, battles between good and evil, social conditioning, hygiene, procreation etc. take place among poor Cinders' allies, the mice, and the complacently vicious cat Lucifer. The set pieces, all transformation scenes of some kind, will probably be familiar, the mouse voices rising to operatic heights as they sweatshop together a ball gown in under three minutes. As usual, everything is slightly glossy, soppy and hearty, yet not a string is left untwanged. RP

Cinderella – Italian Style (C'era una Volta)

(1967, It/Fr, 103 min)
d Francesco Rosi. *p* Carlo Ponti. *sc* Tonino Guerra, Raffaele la Capria, Giuseppe Patroni Griffi, Francesco Rosi. *ph* Pasqualino De Santis. *ed* Jolanda Benvenuti. *ad* Piero Poletto. *m* Piero Piccioni. *cast* Sophia Loren, Omar Sharif, Dolores Del Rio, Georges Wilson, Leslie French, Carlo Pisacane.
● This extraordinary fairy-tale couldn't be further from a film like *The Mattei Affair* but it's none the less informed by the same intelligence that Rosi brings to his directly political work. It deals with all its whimsical elements (from Loren to a flying monk) in a wholly non-whimsical way, introduces a strongish undertone of class-consciousness into its comedy, and pushes its plot recklessly into the bizarre. TR

Cinderella Liberty

(1973, US, 117 min)
d/p Mark Rydell. *sc* Darryl Ponicsan. *ph* Vilmos Zsigmond. *ed* Donn Cambern. *pd* Leon Ericksen. *m* John Williams. *cast* James Caan, Eli Wallach, Marsha Mason, Kirk Calloway, Burt Young, Allyn Ann McLerie.

●Uneven semi-comic look at a sailor's romantic adventures while ashore in Seattle, falling in with pool-hustling hooker Mason and her delinquent mulatto son. Based like *The Last Detail* on a novel by Darryl Ponicsan, it starts off well enough, with the offbeat atmosphere and characterisation reminiscent of Altman (Rydell had played Marty Augustine in *The Long Goodbye*), but things steadily turn to mush as crusty exteriors crack to reveal hearts of gold. GA

Cinderfella

(1960, US, 91 min)
d Frank Tashlin. *p* Jerry Lewis. *sc* Frank Tashlin. *ph* Haskell Boggs. *ed* Arthur P Schmidt. *ad* Hal Pereira, Henry Bumstead. *m* Walter Scharf, Jack Brooks, Gene Merritt. *cast* Jerry Lewis, Ed Wynn, Judith Anderson, Anna Maria Alberghetti, Henry Silva, Robert Hutton, Count Basie.

●In a contemporary updating of the fairytale, Lewis plays a male Cinderella, treated as an all-purpose servant by his wicked stepmother and her two greedy sons in a vast mansion belonging to his late father. A hidden secret fortune, a fairy godfather, and a visiting foreign princess complete the mixture; but despite some extremely lavish set design and the occasional good sight gag, the overall effect is glutinous in the extreme. For hardcore fans and soft-centred infants only. DT

Cinema Cinema

(1979, Fr/US, 138 min)
d Krishna Shah. *p* Shahab Ahmed. *sc* Krishna Shah. *ph* KK Mahajan. *ed* Amit Bose. *pd* Ram Mohan. *m* Vijay Raghav Rao. *cast* Hema Malini, Amitabh Bachchan, Dharmendra Aman, Zeenat Aman, Kim Merchant, Mustacq Merchant.

●Subtitled *That's Entertainment – Indian Style*, this is basically a compilation film, substituting Indian epics for MGM musicals. As such, despite the coy introductory comments by well-fed stars, the uncertain grasp of film history, and the interchangeability of most of the extracts, it is not without interest as a helping of 'Madras Curry' (the staple Bombay diet of lavish melodramas packed to inordinate length with interminable songs, dances and comic interludes). Unfortunately it also has semi-sociological pretensions, and assembles a dismal collection of stereotypes (supposedly watching the extracts in a sleazy cinema) in an attempt to demonstrate the screen/audience relationship. Their reactions are, quite literally, the pits. TM

Cinema of Unease

(1995, GB/NZ, 52 min)
d Sam Neill, Judy Rymer. *p* Paula Jalfon, Grant Campbell. *sc* Sam Neill, Judy Rymer. *ph* Alun Bollinger. *ed* Michael Horton. *m* Don McGlashan. *presenter* Sam Neill.

●Neill has been closely involved with New Zealand film-making since it started going places 20 years ago, and his take on this 'uniquely dark and strange film industry' makes for one of the most interesting films in the BFI's 'Century of Cinema' series. He uses clips from movies set in the '50s and '60s (*Heavenly Creatures, An Angel at My Table*) to evoke the strangeness of his own childhood experiences, and goes on to suggest that there's something about the country's landscape which breeds madness and dysfunction, especially in would-be macho men. Maybe Neill overplays NZ's struggle to break away from British cultural domination, but his celebration of the recent arrival of new voices (Maoris, women, gays) provides a genuinely upbeat punchline. TR

Cinema Paradiso (100) (Nuovo Cinema Paradiso)

(1988, It/Fr, 123 min, b/w & col)
d Giuseppe Tornatore. *p* Franco Cristaldi. *sc* Giuseppe Tornatore. *ph* Blasco Giurato. *ed* Mario Morra. *ad* Andrea Crisanti. *m* Ennio Morricone. *cast* Philippe Noiret, Jacques Perrin, Salvatore Cascio, Agnese Nano, Leopoldo Trieste, Nicolo Di Pinto, Tano Cimarosa.

●A successful movie director in his 40s, Salvatore returns home to Sicily after hearing of the death of Alfredo, ex-projectionist at the eponymous village cinema. The greater part of Tornatore's film is a flashback to Salvatore's WWII childhood and adolescence when, obsessed by movies, he is befriended by the wise and gruffly benevolent Alfredo (Noiret), the local priest censors kissing scenes, the whole village is wowed by *Rome, Open City*, a fire caused by nitrate stock blinds Alfredo, and just as Salvatore is shooting his first home movie he falls in love. Warmly nostalgic without (for the most part) falling foul of Felliniesque caricature, the film is too emotionally manipulative for its own good, Noiret's typically professional performance notwithstanding. Alfredo's mystic sagacity is implausible, and the infant Salvatore (Cascio) is too cutely precocious by half. The politics and history, too, are simplified (partly, perhaps, by a 30 minute pruning for export release). But the final montage of censored clips, hoarded by the boy and rediscovered in adult life, is a sweet hymn to the romance of cinema. GA

Cinema Paradiso: The Special Edition (Nuovo Cinema Paradiso)

(1989, It/Fr, 175 min, b/w & col)
d Giuseppe Tornatore. *p* Franco Cristaldi. *sc* Giuseppe Tornatore. *ph* Blasco Giurato. *ed* Mario Morra. *ad* Andrea Crisanti. *m* Ennio Morricone. *cast* Philippe Noiret, Jacques Perrin, Salvatore Cascio, Agnese Nano, Leopoldo Trieste, Nicolo Di Pinto, Tano Cimarosa, Brigitte Fossey.

●This is no mere cash-in, but director Tornatore's original cut, which flopped so badly on its Italian release, was withdrawn, trimmed to 123 minutes, and entered at the 1989 Cannes festival. The rest is cinematic history. Ironically, however, the two-hour version is substantially inferior to the expansive, roundly satisfying original. Largely unaltered is the nostalgic chronicle of Salvatore, a Sicilian youngster's formative relationship with his local movie house and its wise projectionist; still enshrined are the affectionate performances of Cascio and Noiret. The reinstated material follows the much older Salvatore (Perrin) on his traumatic return home, shows what happens when he meets up with his never-forgotten teenage paramour (the previously excised Brigitte Fossey), and alters the tone of the film, darkening it considerably. Here we experience a catalogue of loss, betrayal and regret which renders the paean to celluloid romance a more complex finale, bitter-sweet yet ineffably emotive. A masterpiece restored, Tornatore's film is, literally, a revelation. TJ

Cinq et la Peau

see Five and the Skin

Cinquième Elément, Le

see Fifth Element, The

Cinquième saison

see Season Five

Circle, The (Dayereh)

(2000, Iran, 91 min)
d Jafar Panahi. *p* Jafar Panahi, Mohammad Atebbai. *sc* Kambozia Partovi. *ph* Bahram Badakhshani. *ed* Jafar Panahi. *ad* Iraj Raminfar. *cast* Maryiam Oarvin Almani, Nargess Mamizadeh, Fereshteh Sadr Orafai, Monir Arab, Elham Saboktakin.

●A quantum leap forward from Panahi's films about children, this is a panoramic account of the various ways women are oppressed in present-day Iran. Taking *La Ronde* as its structural model, the narrative passes from one woman to another, finally completing a circle which can only be described as vicious. It opens in a maternity ward with a woman in labour producing a daughter, to the dismay of her in-laws, and ends in a police station, provocatively suggesting an equivalence between the two institutions. The main characters are three women prisoners released on (temporary?) parole; Panahi provides no background for them, the better to see how they cope with a society in which they have virtually no autonomy. Glimpses of Tehran's underworld bespeak a social economy untouched by either the country's ruling clerics or the reformist government. Brave and powerful. TR

Circle of Danger

(1951, GB, 86 min, b/w)
d Jacques Tourneur. *p* Joan Harrison. *sc* Philip MacDonald. *ph* Oswald Morris. *ed* Alan Orbiston. *ad* Duncan Sutherland. *m* Robert Farnon. *cast* Ray Milland, Patricia Roc, Marius Goring, Hugh Sinclair, Naughton Wayne, Dora Bryan.

●An underrated film-maker whose best work (*I Walked with a Zombie, Build My Gallows High*) truly reached the heights, Jacques Tourneur came to Britain for the first time to put together this military conspiracy thriller, adapted by Philip Macdonald from his own novel. It's one of his more routine assignments, however, as Milland returns from the States to investigate his younger brother's death – although the authorities maintain he was killed in action, the testimony of some of his platoon's survivors suggests a very different course of events. Good camerawork by Ossie Morris and fascinating use of the Scottish and Welsh locations. TJ

Circle of Deceit (Die Fälschung)

(1981, WGer/Fr, 109 min)
d Volker Schlöndorff. *p* Eberhard Junkersdorf. *sc* Volker Schlöndorff, Jean-Claude Carrière, Margarethe von Trotta, Kai Hermann. *ph* Igor Luther. *ed* Suzanne Baron. *ad* Alexandre Riachi, Tannous Zougheib. *m* Maurice Jarre. *cast* Bruno Ganz, Hanna Schygulla, Jerzy Skolimowski, Gila von Weitershausen, Jean Carmet, Martin Urtel.

●It's the classic front-line story: Ganz's German war correspondent goes off to Beirut to cover the Lebanese war, and while there suffers a crisis of conscience about whether he should passively observe or actively intervene. So far, so straightforward, except that Schlöndorff actually made his film in Beirut, yards away from the real carnage, which not only gives it an immediacy and power missing from, say, *Missing* or *Under Fire*, but also questions our whole experience of, and attitude towards, 'the pornography of violence' as portrayed by the news media. To complicate things further, Polish director Skolimowski is on hand, playing Ganz's photographer who casually (an)aesthetises the corpses around him as he wanders the streets. A brave film full of danger, and all the more disturbing and provocative for that. GA

Circle of Friends

(1995, Ire/US, 96 min)
d Pat O'Connor. *p* Frank Price, Arlene Sellers, Alex Winitsky. *sc* Andrew Davies. *ph* Kenneth MacMillan. *ed* Kevin Chamberlin. *pd* Jim Clay. *m* Michael Kamen. *cast* Chris O'Donnell, Minnie Driver, Geraldine O'Rawe, Alan Cumming, Saffron Burrows, Colin Firth, Mick Lally, Ciaran Hands.

●Maeve Binchy's novel, adapted by Andrew Davies, whisks us back to rural Ireland, 1957, for a rites-of-passage tale – with the Roman Catholic Church lurking as usual in the wings. Benny (Driver) and her Knockglen chums go to college in Dublin, where she's enraptured by rugby player Jack Foley (O'Donnell, creditable, despite the knitwear) and is dithering about just how fully to give herself when the plot intervenes. Courtesy of father's fatal heart attack, Benny's landed back home and faced with the unwelcome advances of repellent-but-persistent Sean, the prospective shop-owner her parents have long wanted her to marry. The fizzing dialogue gets all the little details right, but the plot's nothing new (cue unwanted pregnancy and Firth's stuffy Anglophile Protestant) and the lingering shots of hibernian greenery aim straight for mid-Atlantic bland-out. While Cumming's turn as the oleaginous Sean offers bravura overstatement, it hardly belongs in the same picture as Minnie Driver's fresh, immensely appealing Benny, one of those rare feature debuts whose palpable inner fire transcends the workaday material. TJ

Circle of Gold

(1988, GB, 52 min)
d/narrator Uday Bhattacharya.

●A first film made almost single-handedly on a tiny budget, this is an admirably ambitious stab at the documentary-essay form familiar from films like Chris Marker's *Sunless*. A brazenly personal response to Calcutta, it attempts to delve beyond the facile notions the West entertains about the city ('an example of wretched over-population'), and combines vivid visuals with a narration that plunges fearlessly into economics, politics, religion, sociology and philosophy. At times the verbal text is too densely literary and abstract, making its often tortuous theses somewhat opaque, but the collision of images and words is generally provocative and telling. Adverts, movie clips, comic strips, stills of the director's mother, footage of religious ritual and street life merge into a complex web of ideas that are neither hackneyed nor obvious. A tantalising effort. GA

Circle of Iron

see Silent Flute, The

Circle of Two

(1980, Can, 105 min)
d Jules Dassin. *p* Henk Van Der Kolk. *sc* Thomas Hedley. *ph* Laszlo George. *ed* David Nicholson. *pd* Claude Bonnière, François de Lucy. *m* Paul Hoffert. *cast* Richard Burton, Tatum O'Neal, Nuala Fitzgerald, Robin Gammell, Patricia Collins, Kate Reid.

● Sarah (O'Neal) is fifteen going on sixteen, and lives at home. Dad's an Egyptologist; Mom refuses to acknowledge any generation gap; boy-friend wants to get her into the sack, but she refuses. Dodging him one day she meets Ashley (Burton), a once-chic artist who's currently light on inspiration. He might be sixty but he's hunky in that experienced way, and he has a Bohemian haven in the country where he plays Vivaldi. The pair get literary and have intense chats in which Sarah learns the difference between the Sistine Chapel and Burger Kings. Sarah tries the physical, but Ashley sagely demurs. Mom and Dad are horrified by the liaison (bye-bye wet liberalism) and imprison her until she sees sense. But Sarah's having none of that… Preposterous serial syrup which should shame everyone involved. IB

Circuito Chiuso

see Closed Circuit

Circumstance, The (La Circostanza)

(1974, It, 97 min)
d/sc/ph/ed Ermanno Olmi. *cast* Ada Savelli, Gaetano Porro, Raffaella Bianchi, Mario Sireci, Massimo Tabak.

● The bourgeois family Olmi observes here is caught in a process of disintegration that hardly requires the promptings of a languid summer's minor crisis. A motorcycle crash, a business reorganisation seminar and a childbirth represent the unlikely-seeming dramatic punctuation in Olmi's mosaic portrait of minimal domestic communication; while the director himself adopts an uncharacteristically elliptical structure and a rare stridency to capture both the frenetic tail-chasing and tentative adaptations to change which criss-cross the dead institutional centre. If the criticism is muted, it's because for Olmi, every new circumstance offers at least a new option. PT

Circus

(2000, US/GB, 95 min)
d Rob Walker. *p* James Gibb, Alan Latham. *sc* David Logan. *ph* Ben Seresin. *ed* Oral Norrie Ottey. *pd* James Merifield. *m* Simon Boswell. *cast* John Hannah, Famke Janssen, Peter Stormare, Brian Conley, Tiny Lister, Amanda Donohoe, Fred Ward, Eddie Izzard, Ian Burfield.

● Some movies are so determined to be different, sexy, stylish and surprising that their countless contrivances become painfully transparent and end up boring. In this British thriller, scripted by much touted up-comer David Logan, the insistent cynicism, the emphatically colourful villains and dialogue, the eye-grabbing Brighton settings, and most of all the relentlessly labyrinthine plotting soon forfeit emotional involvement. When you know for sure there's yet another shock twist coming in a minute, it's no longer unexpected. Moreover, the déjà vu extends beyond the tiresome eventfulness of the narrative to the way it's utterly imitative in the post-Tarantino vein. Hannah is a chess-playing chancer and gambler in with the local mob who agrees to kill Stormare's wife to finance his own dream of a new life abroad with wife Janssen. Things go awry, everyone's at war. Oh, and some of them are lying. GA

Circus, The

(1928, US, 6,500ft, b/w)
d/p/sc Charles Chaplin. *ph* Roland Totheroh. *ed* Charles Chaplin. *ad* Charles D Hall. *cast* Charlie Chaplin, Merna Kennedy, Allan Garcia, Harry Crocker, Henry Bergman.

● Placing screen clowns within congenial environments (as with *The Marx Brothers at the Circus*) is one of the best ways to produce a bummer, but Chaplin manages to work a miracle, exploiting the various circus activities to richly comic effect. Charlie is chased through a hall of mirrors and trapped in a lion's cage the climax comes when he battles along a tightrope hampered by falling trousers and a clinging monkey. The set pieces are linked, none too neatly, by a framing story of disappointed love. GB

Circus Boys (Nijusseiki Shonen Dokuhon)

(1989, Jap, 106 min, b/w)
d Kaizo Hayashi. *p* Mitsuhisa Hida, Yoichi Sakurai. *sc* Kaizo Hayashi. *ph* Yuichi Nagata. *ed* Osamu Tanaka. *ad* Takeo Kimura, Hidemitsu Yamazaki. *m* Hidehiko Urayama, Yoko Kumagai. *cast* Hiroshi Mikami, Moe Kamura, Ken Shu, Michiro Akiyoshi.

● The Japanese title translates as 'The Boy's Own Book of the 20th Century', which gives a good idea of the way it hovers on the brink of allegory without ever quite freezing into pretentiousness. Shot in glittering monochrome, it contrasts the path of two brothers from a circus family: one stays with the circus and tries to renew it, while the other leaves to become a roaming con-man and quack doctor. Between one man's idealism and the other's cynicism, Hayashi traverses a magical terrain of the mind and reaches a conclusion not far off the sublime. TR

Circus of Fear (aka Psycho-Circus)

(1966, GB, 83 min, b/w)
d John Moxey. *p/sc* Harry Alan Towers. *ph* Ernest Steward. *ed* John Trumper. *ad* Frank White. *m* Johnny Douglas. *cast* Leo Genn, Christopher Lee, Anthony Newlands, Klaus Kinski, Suzy Kendall, Cecil Parker, Victor Maddern, Maurice Kauffmann.

● Rarely seen shocker, released in the US as *Psycho-Circus*. Genn plays a dogged, elderly detective investigating an armoured truck robbery. All the evidence points to a local circus, but other suspects include a masked lion tamer (Lee), a jittery knife thrower (Kaufmann) and various other clowns. Worse, the corpses are beginning to stack up. The film-makers never seem quite sure whether they're making a thriller or a horror pic. No wonder Genn looks so confused. GM

Circus of Horrors

(1960, GB, 91 min)
d Sidney Hayers. *p* Julian Wintle, Leslie Parkyn. *sc* George Baxt. *ph* Douglas Slocombe. *ed* Reginald Mills. *ad* Jack Shampan. *m* Franz Reizenstein, Muir Mathieson. *cast* Erika Remberg, Yvonne Monlaur, Donald Pleasence, Jane Hylton, Kenneth Griffith, Yvonne Romain, Anton Diffring.

● A somewhat tacky pendant to *Peeping Tom*, featuring Diffring as a plastic surgeon obsessed by female disfigurement. Obliged to flee after a cosmetic operation goes horribly wrong, he takes to running a travelling circus with his refurbished beauties as performers; there, tangled motives of jealousy and revenge stir up an outlandish bloodbath in which most of the cast are eliminated one by one (incidentally gratifying the sensation-seeking circus audience with a knife-throwing accident, a nosedive from the big top, and a mauling by lion's jaws). Perhaps inspired by *Les Yeux sans Visage*, it misses out on Franju's wild poetry but is undeniably bizarre and bloody. TM

Cisco Kid and the Lady, The

(1939, US, 74 min, b/w)
d Herbert I Leeds. *sc* Frances Hyland. *ph* Barney McGill. *ed* Nick de Maggio. *ad* Richard Day, Chester Gore. *cast* Cesar Romero, Marjorie Weaver, Chris-Pin Martin, George Montgomery, Robert Barrat, Virginia Field, Harry Green, Ward Bond.

● The first of six films in which Cesar Romero took over the O Henry character – now more insouciant lover than ruthless outlaw – from Warner Baxter. Intent on some horse rustling, the Kid finds himself falling heir to an orphaned baby and part of a map to a gold mine, for which the villain (Barrat) had murdered the baby's prospector father. Falling for the new schoolteacher (Weaver), who helps him look after the baby he now regards as his son, the Kid is not displeased when her tight-assed fiancé (Montgomery) misunderstands the situation on arriving from the East. However, realising in the process of routing the villain that the young couple still love each other, the Kid promotes a marriage at gunpoint, presents them with baby and gold mine, and rides off into the sunset with the saloon girl (Field) he intends to marry – to someone else. Unexpectedly, the result has a shaggy-dog charm, with free-wheeling performances (except from the appallingly inept Montgomery) and several sequences benefiting from their air of having been semi-improvised. TM

Cisco Pike

(1972, US, 94 min)
d Bill L Norton. *p* Gerald Ayres. *sc* Bill L Norton. *ph* Vilis Lapenieks. *ed* Robert C Jones. *ad* Alfred Sweeney. *songs* Kris Kristofferson. *cast* Kris Kristofferson, Karen Black, Gene Hackman, Harry Dean Stanton, Viva, Joy Bang, Roscoe Lee Brown, Antonio Fargas.

● Kristofferson gets the title role in his first movie and turns in one of his best performances, as the fading rocker hanging around the LA music scene in the hope of a comeback, but scraping a living as a small time drug dealer. Hackman, on a run of strong pictures at the time, is the conniving cop on his case, who blackmails him into offloading one hundred kilos of marijuana inside three days – or else. Kristofferson conveys the myopic exhilaration of a string of minor scores with the tensile, empty conviction of a man only just holding desperation at bay. TJ

Citadel, The

(1938, GB, 110 min, b/w)
d King Vidor. *p* Victor Saville. *sc* Elizabeth Hill, Ian Dalrymple, Emlyn Williams, Frank Wead. *ph* Harry Stradling. *ed* Charles Frend. *ad* Lazare Meerson, Alfred Junge. *m* Louis Levy. *cast* Robert Donat, Rosalind Russell, Ralph Richardson, Cecil Parker, Rex Harrison, Emlyn Williams.

● Solidly impressive adaptation of AJ Cronin's novel about an idealistic young doctor who, disillusioned by the hostility he encounters while trying to improve slum conditions in the Welsh mining valleys, takes up a Mayfair practice and finds his principles steadily eroded. Sweetened with a happy ending, it's still an effective piece of work, thanks to Donat's typically sturdy performance and Vidor's powerful direction. GA

Citadel, The (El Kalaa)

(1988, Alg, 98 min)
d Mohamed Chouikh. *p* Mohamed Tahar Harhoura. *sc* Mohamed Chouikh. *ph* Allel Yahiaoui. *ed* Yamina Chouikh. *m* Jawad Fasla. *cast* Khaled Barkat, Djillali Ain Tedeles, Fettouma Ousliha, Momo, Fatima Belhadj.

● A sombre portrait of life in a remote Algerian village, with much of the troubled humanity that distinguishes films like the Tavianis' *Padre Padrone*. Through a number of characters – in particular, a rich wool merchant's three wives, and Kaddour (Barkat), an unmarried orphan, shepherd and dogsbody the merchant has adopted – Chouikh dramatises his outrage at the destructive, outmoded workings of the polygamous Muslim marital laws. While the merchant wants to take a fourth wife, the orphan, deemed ineligible for marriage because of his poverty, falls for a married woman. When the community's male elders discover this forbidden liaison, they demand that the merchant find Kaddour a bride within 24 hours to save the village's honour. The film uses powerful, often poetic images to illuminate the iniquities and hypocrisy that produce explosive tensions within the community. But the characterisations are too thin – Chouikh relies heavily on faces – and the sympathies too wide and opaque for the film to work as drama. The result is distanced and confusing, like watching people through a window. WH

Cité des enfants perdus, La (The City of Lost Children)

(1995, Fr, 112 min)
d Jean-Pierre Jeunet, Marc Caro. *p* Claudie Ossard. *sc* Jean-Pierre Jeunet, Marc Caro, Gilles

Adrien. *ph* Darius Khonji. *ed* Hervé Schneid. *m* Angelo Badalamenti. *cast* Ron Perlman, Daniel Emilfork, Judith Vittet, Dominique Pinon, Jean-Claude Dreyfus, Marc Caro.
● A child smiles delightedly in his toy-filled room as Santa emerges from the chimney-piece, but joy turns to terror as the bearded visitor is followed by more of the same; cut to a man screaming in a laboratory where, unable to dream himself, he has stolen the nightmare of a kidnapped orphan. The opening of another of Jeunet and Caro's forays into the *fantastique* is the perfect introduction to what's essentially a hugely inventive blend of dream, fairytale and myth, and to a strange, sinister sea-girt world that functions according to its own crazy logic. After his infant brother is abducted by a gang of semi-robotic Cyclops, kindly strong-man One (Perlman) sets off on a search that will unite him with feisty 9-year-old orphan Miette (Vittet) and lead him to the sea-rig laboratory inhabited by the evil Krank (Emilfork), his six cloned brothers (Pinon), their diminutive 'mother', and Uncle Irvin, a sardonic brain floating in a fish tank. Extraordinary. GA

Citizen Cohn

(1992, US, 115 min)
d Frank Pierson. *p* Doro Bachrach. *sc* David Franzoni. *ph* Paul Elliott. *ed* Peter Zinner. *pd* Stephen Marsh. *m* Thomas Newman. *cast* James Woods, Joe Don Baker, Pat Hingle, Joseph Bologna, Frederic Forrest, Lee Grant, Josef Sommer, Tovah Feldshuh, Allen Garfield.
● In this hard-hitting biopic, renta-scumbag Woods plays Roy Cohn, known during the Communist witch-hunts of the '50s as 'Joe McCarthy's strong right hand'. On his sickbed, dying of AIDS, Cohn is haunted by the ghosts of those he persecuted as a result of his own twisted self-loathing – many of them Jews (like the Rosenbergs) or gays (like himself) – while reflecting on his headline-grabbing victories and behind-the-scenes defeats that 'I had to fight someone to stay strong'. Adapted from Nicholas von Hoffman's biography, the film emphasises Cohn's obsession with loyalty, a lesson learned early from his mother and one which (when he pulled strings to get his rich kid lover out of the army) was to sow the seeds of his destruction. The dialogue-heavy script and claustrophobic, over-dressed interiors betray the film's cable TV origins, but the direction is admirably controlled and the acting first rate, notably Baker's McCarthy and Grant as Cohn's domineering mother. NF

Citizen Kane 100 (100) 10

(1941, US, 119 min, b/w)
d/p Orson Welles. *sc* Herman J Mankiewicz, Orson Welles. *ph* Gregg Toland. *ed* Robert Wise. *ad* Van Nest Polglase. *m* Bernard Herrmann. *cast* Orson Welles, Joseph Cotten, Everett Sloane, Dorothy Comingore, Agnes Moorehead, Ray Collins,Paul Stewart, George Coulouris, Ruth Warrick.
● The source book of Orson Welles, and still a marvellous movie. Thematically less resonant than some of Welles' later meditations on the nature of power, perhaps, but still absolutely riveting as an investigation of a citizen – newspaper tycoon William Randolph Hearst by any other name – under suspicion of having soured the American Dream. Its imagery (not forgetting the oppressive ceilings) as Welles delightedly explores his mastery of a new vocabulary, still amazes and delights, from the opening shot of the forbidding gates of Xanadu to the last glimpse of the vanishing Rosebud (tarnished, maybe, but still a potent symbol). A film that gets better with each renewed acquaintance. TM

Citizen Langlois

(1995, Fr, 67 min, b&w & col)
d Edgardo Cozarinsky. *p* Serge Lalou, Dominique Paini. *sc* Edgardo Cozarinsky. *ph* Jacques Bouquin. *ed* Martine Bouquin. *with* Henri Langlois, Lotte Eisner, Marie Epstein, Mary Meerson, François Truffaut, Eric Rohmer, Georges Franju, Jonas Mekas, Allen Ginsberg. *narrator* Niels Arestrup.
● Cozarinsky's documentary portrait of Henri Langlois, the great film historian, archivist and co-founder (with Georges Franju, seen interviewed here) of the Cinémathèque Française, is respectful, informative but never hagiographic. Langlois had an importance unthinkable in Britain – the French government's attempt to dismiss him from the Cinémathèque was one of the key events in the ferment of 1968 – and his progress from amateur collector to *nouvelle vague* hero and friend of the stars is related with wit and sensitivity, complete with clips from some of the movies he rescued, fascinating interviews and home-movies (Langlois with Mekas and Ginsberg!). GA

Citizens Band

(1977, US, 98 min)
d Jonathan Demme. *p/sc* Paul Brickman. *ph* Jordan Cronenweth. *ed* John F Link Jr. *pd* Bill Malley. *m* Bill Conti. *cast* Paul LeMat, Candy Clark, Ann Wedgeworth, Marcia Rodd, Charles Napier, Roberts Blossom.
● As in *Melvin and Howard*, Demme's genuine curiosity about the eccentricities hidden within the most seemingly ordinary of American lives ensures a largely engaging slab of cinematic graffiti. The populace of script-writer Paul Brickman's small town includes a hooker on wheels, a cattle-truck-driving bigamist whose two wives meet up by accident, and at the centre, the excellent LeMat as a CB vigilante clobbering misusers of the airwaves, his chief misery being a hopeless attachment to a near-gaga father who only comes to life at his radio mike. The film uses the CB craze as a metaphor for lack of human communication, and proceeds in a somewhat elliptical manner, but the alternation of moments of black humour and funny-sad incidents lends it a considerable charm. RM

Città si Difende, La (Four Ways Out)

(1951, It, 85 min, b/w)
d Pietro Germi. *p* Carlo Civallero. *sc* Federico Fellini, Tullio Pinelli, Luigi Comencini, Pietro Germi. *ph* Carlo Montuori. *ed* Rolando Benedetti. *ad* Carlo Egidi. *m* Carlo Rustichelli. *cast* Renato Baldini, Fausto Tozzi, Paul Müller, Enzo Maggio, Gina Lollobrigida, Tamara Lees.
● Four men steal the takings from a football stadium. They split up, and homegrown neo-realism is crossed with Hollywood-style *noir*, as one by one they try and fail to break out of the big, unforgiving city. Germi is so determined to forge ahead from one set-piece to the next that his gallery of femmes fatales, predatory underworld figures and grim-faced police barely register as characters, except via little cameos (a cop's look of distaste as he picks up a discarded bra). Visually exciting, but superficial; few will be able to resist mentally replacing the cast with more familiar Hollywood analogues – the Burt Lancaster dumb ox, the Sal Mineo weakling, etc. BBa

City, The (aka La Ciudad)

(1998, US, 88 min, b/w)
d David Riker. *p* David Riker, Paul S Mezey. *sc* David Riker. *ph* Harlan Bosmajian. *ed* David Riker. *pd* Roshelle Berliner, Arianne Burgess. *m* Tony Adzinikolov. *cast* Anthony Rivera, Joseph Rigano, Miguel Maldonado, Cipriano Garcia, Leticia Herrera, Jose Rabelo.
● The city in question is New York, but could be anywhere in the US with a sizeable Latin American population. Four stories depict telling experiences. 'Bricks' concerns labourers taken off the streets to a site on the edge of town to clean bricks; 'Home' sees a boy new to town strike up a relationship with a girl met at a wedding party; in 'The Puppeteer' an illegal immigrant tries to get his child into school; and in 'Seamstress' a woman working in a sweatshop becomes desperate when she learns her daughter back home is ill. While none of the individual tales in Riker's low budget indie is at all complex in terms of dramaturgy, their uncluttered simplicity makes not only for overall credibility, but for a steady accumulation of emotional power. While the fundamental inhumanity of a system that marginalises the Latins is mercifully never rammed down our throats, it's easy to infer from the lucid narrative, the sturdy performances, and the elegant b/w 'Scope camerawork. GA

City After Dark

see Manila by Night

City Beneath the Sea

(1953, US, 87 min)
d Budd Boetticher. *p* Albert J Cohen. *sc* Jack Harvey, Ramon Romero. *ph* Charles P Boyle. *ed* Edward Curtiss. *ad* Alexander Golitzen, Emrich Nicholson. *m* Joseph Gershenson. *cast* Robert Ryan, Anthony Quinn, Mala Powers, Suzan Ball, Karel Stepanek, Lalo Rios.
● Well below average from Boetticher, whose series of Westerns with Randolph Scott and *The Rise and Fall of Legs Diamond* display a simple but effective B movie intensity. This is far more routine, with Ryan and Quinn as deep-sea divers falling out over sunken treasure. Strong performances from the leads, but little else to hold the interest. GA

City Farm

(1978, GB, 90 min)
d John Davies, Robert Smith. *cast* Peter J Rome, Rosie Tennent, Andy Greenhouse, Chris Charles, Pam Hemmingway.
● The reunion of a sister and two brothers provides Davies and Smith with the basis for an experimentation with, and partial dislocation of, traditional narrative structures. *City Farm* has been compared to a crossword puzzle, but the precision necessary in crossword design is certainly lacking from the film's final shape. A sympathetic tone and worthy ambition do not finally disguise a lack of control over material and direction. SM

City Girl (aka Our Daily Bread)

(1929, US, 88 min, b/w)
d FW Murnau. *sc* Marion Oth, Berthold Viertel. *ph* Ernest Palmer. *ed* Katherine Hilliker, HH Caldwell. *ad* Harry Oliver. *m* Arthur Kay. *cast* Charles Farrell, Mary Duncan, David Torrence, Ivan Linow, Guinn Williams.
● Murnau's final Hollywood film is widely underrated, no doubt because Fox cut it against his wishes and turned the original silent film into a poorly synchronised part-talkie. None the less, the director's visual talents remain evident in the soft lighting and the pastoral landscapes, and the film is of more than passing interest. As in the superior *Sunrise*, Murnau is concerned with the difference between urban and rural life: a wheat-farmer's son marries a waitress who longs to escape the city, but the old man, suspicious of her fidelity, rejects her, turning against his son. If the plot sounds vaguely familiar, that may be because Malick's *Days of Heaven* trod somewhat similar ground. GA

City Hall

(1996, US, 111 min)
d Harold Becker. *p* Edward R Pressman, Ken Lipper, Charles Mulvehill, Harold Becker. *sc* Ken Lipper, Bo Goldman, Paul Schrader, Nichola Pileggi. *ph* Michael Seresin. *ed* Robert C Jones. *pd* Jane Musky. *m* Jerry Goldsmith. *cast* Al Pacino, John Cusack, Bridget Fonda, Danny Aiello, Martin Landau, David Paymer, Tony Franciosa.
● Al Pacino is John Pappas, the best Mayor New York never had. We know because he comes on like Elmer Gantry at every large public gathering, funerals a speciality. But are we're meant to admire his caring-sharing Democrat rabble-rousing? When not being a liberal-conscience drama, or perhaps a political satire (Pappas has presidential ambitions), the film, written by Ken Lipper and Paul Schrader, busies itself being an investigative thriller. Peppy young political strategist Cusack (Pacino's right-hand man) and Detectives' Endowment Association attorney Fonda race for the dark truth behind a Brooklyn street shooting that left a police detective, a small-time mobster and an innocent black child bleeding to death. Confused? The producers obviously were. Five screenwriters are credited, and the end product, despite moments of individual quality from an able cast, pulls in at least as many different directions. There's some attempt to probe the grindings of the Democrat Party machine; there's also a long hard look at the day-to-day workings of the Probation Office. All of this is moderately absorbing, and somehow, somewhere the movie does care; it's just that the notion of corruption being endemic in the US system ain't hot news. TJ

City Heat

(1984, US, 97 min)
d Richard Benjamin. *p* Fritz Manes. *sc* Sam O Brown [Blake Edwards], Joseph C Stinson. *ph* Nick McLean. *ed* Jacqueline Cambas. *pd* Edward C Carfagno. *m* Lennie Niehaus. *cast* Clint Eastwood, Burt Reynolds, Jane Alexander, Madeline Kahn, Rip Torn, Richard Roundtree, Tony Lo Bianco.
● Kansas City in the early '30s: prohibition, mob rule and jumping jazz-joints. Taking on the might of competing gangs are cop Eastwood and seedy

shamus Reynolds, themselves immersed in some pretty ridiculous rivalry since Burt gave up the Department for independent business. This is not only a pleasantly nostalgic mixture of mobster-movie and *noir* thriller; it is also Eastwood's funniest comedy in years. While Reynolds indulges in his usual cheery blend of bluster and craven cowardice, Clint stealthily outdoes him with self-parodic image-knocking; after his lone-ranger walk down a bullet-ridden city street mad with bloody mayhem, his haloed heroics will never seem the same again. It's certainly not a subtle movie, but with memorable performances, ludicrously over-the-top one-liners and amiable zaniness, it qualifies as a lot of fun. GA

City Lights 100

(1931, US, 87 min, b/w)
d/p/sc Charles Chaplin. *ph* Roland Totheroh, Gordon Pollock. *ed* Charles Chaplin. *ad* Charles D Hall. *m* Charles Chaplin. *cast* Charles Chaplin, Virginia Cherrill, Florence Lee, Harry Myers, Allan Garcia, Hank Mann.

● With its plot focusing on Charlie's love for a blind flower-seller and his attempts to get enough money to pay for an eye operation, *City Lights* edges dangerously close to the weepie wonderland of *Magnificent Obsession* and other lace-handkerchief jobs. This horrid fate is narrowly avoided by bracing doses of slapstick (the heroine unravels Charlie's vest thinking it's her ball of wool) and Chaplin's supreme delicacy in conveying all shades of human feeling. Matters aren't helped by the film's structure, which is as tattered and baggy as the tramp's trousers. But there are plenty of great moments, and the occasional comic use of sound (despite its date, the film is silent) is beautifully judged. GB

City of Angels

(1998, US/Ger, 114 min)
d Brad Silberling. *p* Dawn Steel, Charles Roven. *sc* Dana Stevens. *ph* John Seale. *ed* Lynzee Klingman. *pd* Lilly Kilvert. *m* Gabriel Yared. *cast* Nicolas Cage, Meg Ryan, Dennis Franz, André Braugher, Colm Feore, Robin Bartlett.

● A Hollywood remake of *Wings of Desire*, directed by the man who gave us *Casper*. The mind boggles. But elegant direction, luscious camerawork, a mostly unsentimental script, and sterling performances from the stars turns this into be an honourable effort – at least until the last 20 minutes, when the movie goes spectacularly off the rails. Seth (Cage, charismatic) is one of many angels who wander LA listening in to people's thoughts, trying to allay their anxieties, and, when death rears its head, leading them 'home'. He sees heart surgeon Maggie (Ryan) fighting to save a patient: when she fails, he's struck by her sadness, guilt and sense of confusion, and – already wondering what it would be like to experience taste, smell, touch, tears and transient joy – falls so in love that he begins to make himself visible to her. This is funnier than Wenders' version, and it also succeeds in visualising LA as a magical city while dealing intelligently with the themes of mortality, sacrifice, free will, and the mixed blessings of the human condition. GA

City of Fear

(1958, US, 75 min, b/w)
d Irving Lerner. *p* Leon Chooluck. *sc* Steven Ritch, Robert Dillon. *ph* Lucien Ballard. *ed* Robert Lawrence. *ad* Jack Poplin. *m* Jerry Goldsmith. *cast* Vince Edwards, John Archer, Patricia Blair, Steven Ritch, Lyle Talbot, Joe Mell, Sherwood Price.

● Pacy Columbia B-picture from a film-maker who did pretty well on the barest of resources and later won praise from Martin Scorsese (who also hired him as co-editor on *New York, New York*). Edwards escapes from prison with a sealed canister he believes contains $1m worth of heroin. In fact he's toting radioactive cobalt that could contaminate the whole city. The premise is more exciting than the execution, but the movie's strong on seedy atmosphere (notable b/w camerawork from Lucien Ballard) and there's an excellent jazz-tinged score from Jerry Goldsmith. TJ

City of God (Cidade de Deus)

(2002, Braz, 135 min)
d Fernando Meirelles. *p* Andrea Barata Ribeiro, Maurício Andrade Ramos. *sc* Bráulio Mantovani. *ph* César Charlone. *ed* Daniel Rezende. *ad* Tulé Peake. *m* Antônio Pinto, Ed Côrtes. *cast* Matheus Nachtergaele, Seu Jorge, Alexandre Rodrigues, Leandro Firmino da Hora, Phelipe Haagensen, Jonathan Haagensen, Douglas Silva, Roberta Rodriguez Silvia.

● At times a little too hyperkinetic and punchy for its own good, this account of the spread of drug-fuelled crime into Rio's *favelas* from the '60s to the '80s is nevertheless an impressive affair. Centred on a kid keen to keep his nose clean and become a photographer, despite the live-fast-die-young tendencies of those around him, the film blends superb location photography, a pacy but nicely elastic editing style, an ingenious, imaginative approach to narrative, and expertly choreographed action to document the way petty crime and petty rivalries spiral out of control to plunge the neighborhood into murderous gang wars. And the performances, many from non-pros, are terrific. GA

City of Hope

(1991, US, 130 min)
d John Sayles. *p* Sarah Green, Maggi Renzi. *sc* John Sayles. *ph* Robert Richardson. *ed* John Sayles. *pd* Dan Bishop, Dianna Freas. *m* Mason Daring. *cast* Vincent Spano, Joe Morton, Tony Lo Bianco, Barbara Williams, Stephen Mendillo, Chris Cooper, Charlie Yanko, Jace Alexander, Todd Graff, Scott Tiler, John Sayles, David Strathairn, Kevin Tighe, Maggie Renzi, Josh Mostel, Lawrence Tierney, Angela B,massett, Anthony John Denison.

● Building contractor Joe (Lo Bianco) is up to his neck in the scratch-my-back ethics of corrupt property developers and politicians. Son Nick (Spano) has been tempted into petty crime. Idealistic councilman Wynn (Morton) is torn between professional ambition and loyalty to local blacks, who accuse him of having sold them down the line. Black teenagers Tito and Desmond are so fed up with being hassled by racist cops that they mug a college professor... These are only a few of the characters and stories that colour Sayles' masterly account of the everyday workings of a contemporary New Jersey city: a genuinely epic, politically astute, profoundly humanist and dramatically gripping study of the conflicts, compromises and power plays that define life in any community on the verge of economic breakdown. As ever, much enjoyment may be had from both the complex, interwoven threads of Sayles' script and the powerful, naturalistic performances. What really impresses, however, is the confidence of Sayles' fluid direction. GA

City of Industry

(1996, US, 97 min)
d John Irvin. *p* Evzen Kolar, Ken Solarz. *sc* Ken Solarz. *ph* Thomas Burstyn. *ed* Mark Conte. *pd* Michael Novotny. *m* Stephen Endelman. *cast* Harvey Keitel, Stephen Dorff, Famke Janssen, Timothy Hutton, Wade Dominguez, Michael Jai White.

● A derivative, mostly dull contemporary crime movie in which a heist goes wrong and the survivors fight to the death. Wary, honourable, world-weary thief Roy Egan (Keitel) is out for revenge against semi-psychotic, untrustworthy upstart Skip Kovich (Dorff), who betrayed his fellow gang members – including Roy's brother Lee (Hutton) – after a daring diamond snatch. True to formula, the relationship of Roy and the widow of another victim of Skip's deceit (Janssen, not without appeal) shifts from mutually cool to respectful and tender. GA

City of Joy

(1992, GB/Fr, 135 min)
d Roland Joffé. *p* Jake Eberts, Roland Joffé. *sc* Mark Medoff. *ph* Peter Biziou. *ed* Gerry Hambling. *pd* Roy Walker. *m* Ennio Morricone. *cast* Patrick Swayze, Om Puri, Pauline Collins, Shabana Azmi, Ayesha Dharker, Santu Chowdhury, Imran Badsah Khan, Art Malik.

● East and West learn from each other, and it's an interminable seminar. In Calcutta, the fortunes of rickshaw man Hasari (Puri) and American dropout doctor Max (Swayze) intertwine, but the acting styles are so divergent that they may as well be in different films. Max is selfish and suicidally sick of life, while Hasari has to fight for the daily bread to support his family; but Max learns how to care again after delivering a baby, while Hasari learns how to embrace American can-do and reject his Asian acceptance of the system. Together, they stand up to the razor-wielding bad guy (Malik). Presiding over the City of Joy school and clinic is Irish Joan (Collins), pushy, practical, and derived from other movies. It's very old-fashioned stuff, with the impoverished Indian slum-dwellers working like cheerful chipmunks to build a better clinic, and a climactic monsoon on hand to bring out the best in everybody. BC

City of Lost Children, The

see Cité des enfants perdus, La

City of Lost Souls (Hyoryu Gai)

(2000, Jap, 105 min)
d Takashi Miike. *p* Kazunari Hashiguchi, Toshiki Kimura. *sc* Ichiro Ryu. *ph* Naosuke Imaizumi. *ed* Taiji Shimamura. *pd* Akira Ishige. *m* Koji Endo. *cast* Teah, Michele Reis, Koji Kikkawa, Mitsuhiro Oikawa, Terence Yin, Akira Emoto, Eugene Nomura.

● A popular novel by Seishu Hase (the sequel to *Sleepless Town*, filmed in 1998 by Lee Chi-Ngai) gets the full Miike treatment. What's left of the storyline is buried under an avalanche of absurdist comedy, over-ripe action, bent romance and movie parodies. Indeed, the author appears briefly to give the destruction of his book his blessing. Brazilian-Japanese Mario (first-time actor Teah) saves his Chinese girlfriend Kei (Reis) from being deported and then hijacks a ton of cocaine to finance their disappearance. Assorted cops, pervy Chinese triads and ruthless Japanese yakuza get in the way. Not a Miike classic, largely because it takes Mario's boring macho image at face value, but it does have compensations: the heretical vision of Tokyo as a multi-cultural whirl of street parties and ethnic broadcasting, the opening pastiche of Italian Westerns, and the out-of-nowhere sideswipe at *The Matrix*. TR

City of Lost Souls (Stadt der Verlorenen Seelen)

(1983, WGer, 94 min)
d/p/sc Rosa von Praunheim [Holger Mischwitzki]. *ph* Stephan Köster. *ed* Rosa von Praunheim. *ad* Inge Stiborski. *m* Alexander Kraut, Jayne County, Angie Stardust, Holger Münzer. *cast* Angie Stardust, Jayne County, Lorraine Muthke, Wolfgang Schumacher.

● Rosa von Praunheim's fictionalised account of the lives of his expatriate American acquaintances in Berlin. On the surface, a deranged comedy caper; sympathetically observed TVs and TSs, bizarre cabaret artistes, prostitutes, gays, straights, blacks and whites thriving in adversity in a Berlin of hallucinogenic fast-food outlets, lunatic self-improvement cults, cartooned nightclub life and immigration-squad raids. But behind the laughter there are numerous pointed comments on modern-day Germany, on fascism and on sexual, social, political and geographical statelessness. Heavy stuff – but von Praunheim ends up celebrating his friends' lives in a funny, startling and mocking 'punk' musical that even finds time for a Broadway-style happy ending. Jayne County's rise to Iron Curtain pop stardom is debilitatingly funny, and the whole might be described as a Rocky Horror *Gastarbeiter* Problem. JG

City of Pirates (La Ville des Pirates)

(1983, Fr/Port, 121 min)
d Raúl Ruiz. *p* Anne-Marie La Joisin. *sc* Raúl Ruiz. *ph* Acácio de Almeida. *ed* Varleria Sarmiento. *ad* Ze Branco, Isabel Branco. *m* Jorge Arriagada. *cast* Hugues Quester, Anne Alvaro, Melvil Fouqaud, André Engel, Duarte De Almeida.

● Forget the pirates – there aren't any in Ruiz's provocative fairy-tale. But there is a lost boy, who has already massacred his family before he seduces his Wendy, in the shape of a downtrodden servant girl, and transports her to their Neverland (there isn't a city either). If Ruiz's 'free transcription' of *Peter Pan* sounds more like a subtitled *Friday the 13th*, it's because he takes the sexual undercurrent of children's literature as seriously as Angela Carter. The atmosphere is magical, perversely playful and macabre: in a moment of pure, surreal poetry, the boy-murderer sails a fleet of burning paper boats on a tide of his victim's blood. What really distinguishes this is a gripping performance by Alvaro as the haunted lover-cum-mother, and the images that are the very stuff of nightmares. IC

City of Sadness, A (Beiqing Chengshi)

(1989, Tai, 158 min)
d Hou Xiaoxian. *p* Qui Fusheng. *sc* Wu Nianzhen, Zhu Tianwen. *ph* Chien Huai-en. *ed* Liao Ch'ing-sung. *pd* Liu Chi-hua. *m* Chang Hung-yi. *cast* Tony Leung, Xin Shu-fen, Li T'ien-lu, Kao Chieh, Ikuyo Nakamura.
●Loaded with detail and elliptically structured to let viewers make their own connections, Hou's film spans four fateful years of transition in Taiwan, from the defeat of the Japanese colonialists in WWII, when the island was returned to China, to the retreat to Taiwan of Chiang Kai-Shek's Nationalists at the end of the civil war in 1949. The period is shown from the perspective of a single family: a virtually senile widower, his sons (one missing presumed dead, one a gangster, one a deaf-mute photographer, the fourth a former translator for the Japanese) and their wives. As always with Hou, the human dimension is paramount – this is no history lesson – but it's clear that he is reaching for a sense of Taiwan's identity through the family's affairs. Given the panoramic sweep – which focuses particularly on the underworld and the political underground – Hou turns in a masterpiece of small gestures and massive resonance; once you surrender to its spell, the obscurities vanish. TR

City of the Living Dead

see Paura nella Città dei Morti Viventi

City of Women (La Città delle Donne)

(1980, It/Fr, 139 min)
d Federico Fellini. *sc* Federico Fellini, Bernardino Zapponi. *ph* Giuseppe Rotunno. *ed* Ruggero Mastroianni. *ad* Dante Ferretti. *m* Luis Enriquez Bacalov. *cast* Marcello Mastroianni, Anna Prucnal, Bernice Stegers, Iole Silvani, Donatella Damiani, Ettore Manni.
●Will Fellini ever learn to count beyond eight and a half? As Snaporaz (a discreetly ageing Mastroianni, still the alter egoist and flattering mirror image of his director) dozes off in a train to be whisked through a nightmare of ultra-militant feminism, here we are again on that familiar gaudy treadmill of Barnum and ballet, circus and comic strip. Yet if much of it verges on self-parody, a few of the set pieces are superb (the Women's Lib congress, every word of which, swears Fellini, was taken verbatim from feminist literature; the homage to the communal masturbatorium the cinema used to be). In his martyrdom, Snaporaz becomes hardly less poignant a creation than Ophüls' Lola Montès; and only a pinchpenny soul could denigrate the generosity, the sheer fertility of the Maestro's invention in this curate's egg by Fabergé. GAd

City on Fire

(1979, Can/US, 106 min)
d Alvin Rakoff. *p* Claude Héroux. *sc* Jack Hill, David P Lewis, Celine La Freniere. *ph* René Verzier. *ed* Jean-Pol Passet, Jacques Clairoux, John Shirley. *pd* Bill McCrow. *m* Matthew McCauley. *cast* Barry Newman, Susan Clark, Shelley Winters, Leslie Nielsen, James Franciscus, Ava Gardner, Henry Fonda.
●Thoroughly routine disaster movie, about the sweaty travails of a fire-fighting team squirting around a huge inferno after an explosion at an oil-refinery. To make matters worse, there's a hospital in the middle of the holocaust, with babies to deliver and emergency ops to complete. Fonda purses his lips, and the rest of the cast scream, emote and generally irritate. GA

City on Fire (Longhu Fengyun)

(1987, HK, 110 min)
d/p Ringo Lam. *sc* Tommy Sham. *ph* Andrew Lau. *ed* Wong Ming Lam. *ad* Luk Tze Fung. *m* Teddy Robin, Kwan. *cast* Chow Yun Fat, Danny Lee, Sun Yueh, Roy Cheung.
●The inspiration for *Reservoir Dogs*, this 1987 crime movie is a good example of the thriller HK-style ('style' being the operative word). Social and psychological nuance is out. Designer shades are in. Hong Kong's biggest movie star, Chow Yun Fat (*The Killer, A Better Tomorrow, Hard-Boiled*) is the epitome of Esquire cool, more playful than Clint, more intense than Mel, much better looking than Arnie or Sly. Here he's an undercover cop, Ko Chow, who works his way into a gang of jewel thieves at the cost of his fiancée and, perhaps, his own integrity. This is straight-cut, fashion-plate pulp. Tarantino fans will note the familiarity of the set-up. In fact, *Reservoir Dogs* is an elaboration on the the climax of Ringo Lam's film: after the heist goes wrong, the gang hole up in a warehouse, where bullets and recriminations start to fly. There's none of Tarantino's formal inventiveness, none of the finesse or the wit, just a gut-wrenching dramatic situation ready to explode. TCh

City Slickers

(1991, US, 114 min)
d Ron Underwood. *p* Irby Smith. *sc* Lowell Ganz, Babaloo Mandel. *ph* Dean Semler. *ed* O Nicholas Brown. *pd* Lawrence G Paull. *m* Marc Shaiman, Hummie Mann. *cast* Billy Crystal, Daniel Stern, Bruno Kirby, Patricia Wettig, Helen Slater, Jack Palance, Josh Mostel, David Paymer, Noble Willingham, Tracey Walter.
●You've seen it all before: pals approaching mid-life crisis explore the Great Outdoors, rethink values, and by trail's end vow never to complain about putting out the trash. Three married men – bewildered Mitch (Crystal), playboy Ed (Kirby) and unfaithful Phil (Stern) – are pitted against the rigours of a 200-mile cattle drive led by cowpoke Curly (Palance), so tough he lights matches on his face. Crystal's self-pitying character starts out promisingly – an early highlight being his lecture on ageing to schoolchildren – but the constant rapid-fire quips become increasingly predictable. CM

City Slickers II: The Legend of Curly's Gold

(1994, US, 116 min)
d Paul Weiland. *p* Billy Crystal. *sc* Billy Crystal, Babaloo Mandel, Lowell Ganz. *ph* Adrian Biddle. *ed* William Anderson. *pd* Stephen J Lineweaver. *m* Marc Shaiman. *cast* Billy Crystal, Daniel Stern, Jon Lovitz, Jack Palance, Patricia Wettig, Pruitt Taylor Vince, Josh Mostel.
●The original offered an easy-going spin on the fish-out-of-water routine, packing its three suburban menopausal males off into the dusty yonder to be licked into shape by life on the range. This time the chaps head into the desert with a treasure map in the their hands and greed in their hearts. What follows is a jolly blend of zippy dialogue, Western-type action, and lots of spot-on humour about guys being guys together. TJ

City Streets

(1931, US, 75 min, b/w)
d Rouben Mamoulian. *sc* Max Marcin, Oliver HP Garrett. *ph* Lee Garmes. *ed* William Shea. *m* Sidney Cutner. *cast* Gary Cooper, Sylvia Sidney, Paul Lukas, Guy Kibbee, William Boyd, Wynne Gibson, Stanley Fields.
●Strikingly stylised bootlegging yarn, more romance than gangster movie, said to have been an Al Capone favourite because the gang boss (Lukas), far from rampaging Cagney-style with machine-gun in the streets, is always careful to be seen to have clean hands: all deaths take place discreetly off-screen, and a contract to kill drawn up in an offhand line of dialogue ('I'd be willing to do business with you, if anything happened to Blackie') is equally elliptically sealed when the other party lights his cigar, looks at the match, and then pensively snuffs it out. Mamoulian sometimes over-stresses the visual and aural symbolism he experiments with in support of these ellipses, but creates a wonderfully evocative, low-key atmosphere not dissimilar to Sternberg's *Underworld* with terrific camerawork from Lee Garmes, and fine performances from Cooper and Sidney as the young lovers enmeshed in the rackets. TM

City That Never Sleeps

(1953, US, 90 min, b/w)
d John H Auer. *p* Herbert J Yates. *sc* Steve Fisher. *ph* John L Russell. *ed* Fred Allen. *ad* James Sullivan. *m* R Dale Butts. *cast* Gig Young, Mala Powers, Edward Arnold, William Talman, Chill Wills, Marie Windsor, Paula Raymond.
●No, not a satirical documentary about Market Harborough, but a rare example – actually, the only example – of whimsical *noir*. Routinely the film assembles its angst-racked characters: the cop tempted into dishonesty for love of a stripper, the ageing attorney with a bored young wife, the killer who dotes on his pet rabbit, etc. Familiar images recur: a fugitive darting across a railroad yard, headlights slicing down an alley, a sudden sweaty close-up. But then the film tilts towards fantasy with the introduction of Wills as the Spirit of the City, no less, materialising for the night as Young's ghostly patrol car partner, observing the action with Buddha-like understanding. Gig and Chill aside, this is an averagely satisfying thriller, inventively shot on wintry Chicago locations. BBa

City Under the Sea (aka War Gods of the Deep)

(1965, GB/US, 84 min)
d Jacques Tourneur. *p* Daniel Haller. *sc* Charles Bennett, Louis M Heyward. *ph* Stephen Dade. *ed* Gordon Hales. *ad* Frank White. *m* Stanley Black. *cast* Vincent Price, David Tomlinson, Tab Hunter, Susan Hart, John Le Mesurier, Henry Oscar.
●Tacky Jules Verne-ish adventure inspired by Poe's poem 'The City in the Sea', with Price as The Captain (obviously kin to Nemo) kidnapping a girl he takes to be the reincarnation of his dead wife and bringing her to the lost city of Lyonesse under the sea. A sad disappointment as Tourneur's last film, with occasional imaginative touches (but surprisingly little atmosphere) and a dismal cast (Price excepted), although the narrative keeps going perkily enough. TM

Ciudad, La

see City, The

Civil Action, A

(1998, US, 115 min)
d Steven Zaillian. *p* Scott Rudin, Robert Redford, Rachel Pfeffer. *sc* Steven Zaillian. *ph* Conrad L Hall. *ed* Wayne Wahrman. *pd* David Gropman. *m* Danny Elfman. *cast* John Travolta, Robert Duvall, James Gandolfini, Dan Hedaya, John Lithgow, William H Macy, Kathleen Quinlan, Tony Shalhoub, Zeljko Ivanek, Stephen Fry.
●Steven Zaillian scripted *Schindler's List*, and wrote and directed *Searching for Bobby Fischer*. His follow-up is a legal thriller (from a book by Jonathan Harr) which ties itself in knots trying to do justice to a real-life case of toxic dumping. When flash Boston attorney Jan Schlichtmann (Travolta) first hears about the suit brought by eight families whose kids have gone down with leukemia, he dismisses it as a lost cause. It's only when he stumbles across the big corporations behind the contamination that he changes his mind. His subsequent obsession with the case combines his better instincts and a gambler's vain determination to play for the highest stakes. Schlichtmann, then, is not a million miles away from Oskar Schindler, who also sought redemption with a healthy profit margin. Photographed with sober restraint by Conrad Hall, propelled by a literate, reflective voice-over, and expertly played by a first rate cast, the tone here is dispassionate, but sensitive. Zaillian only comes unstuck when he tries to break with the hackneyed showdown: delivering the verdict two thirds into the movie is anti-climactic, while Schlichtmann's belated atonement feels beside the point. Ironically, Duvall steals it with the hokiest role, as the formidable defence attorney. TCh

Civilised People (Civilisées)

(1999, Fr/Switz/Leb, 97 min)
d Randa Chahal Sabbag. *p* Daniel Toscan du Plantier, Frédéric Sichler. *sc* Randa Chahal Sabbag. *ph* Ricardo Jacques Gale, Roby Breidi. *ed* Juliette Welfling. *pd* Sylvain Chauvelot. *m* Ziad Rahbani. *cast* Jalial Baccar, Tamin Chahal, Myrna Maakaron, Carmen Lebbos, Sotigui Kouyate, Renée Dick, Bruno Todeschini, Hassan Farhat.
●Scenes from Lebanon's civil war, sometime around the declaration of its 576th ceasefire. It's a patchwork piece, emphasising the random and rampaging madness of the fragmented remnants

of Beirut civil society, suggestive of greater horrors (a housekeeper holds several children blindly hostage in his cellar in an act of stubborn and senseless vengefulness). Finally, it's because the film never really penetrates the cracked surface of these lives, though it has its share of colourful grotesqueries, a little like Kusturica, but lighter. The Lebanese censor objected to inflammatory language against Christ, the Virgin Mary, Islam and foreigners, and cut some 47 minutes. This is the original version. NB

Claim, The

(2000, GB/Can/Fr, 121 min)
d Michael Winterbottom. *p* Andrew Eaton. *sc* Frank Cottrell Boyce. *ph* Alwin Küchler. *ed* Trevor Waite. *pd* Mark Tildesley, Ken Rempel. *m* Michael Nyman. *cast* Wes Bentley, Milla Jovovich, Nastassja Kinski, Peter Mullan, Sarah Polley, Ron Anderson, Marty Antonini, Randy Birch, Marie Brassard.

●Having already adapted Thomas Hardy's *Jude the Obscure*, Winterbottom plays to his strengths by transporting the heart of *The Mayor of Casterbridge* to the icy mountain wilderness of post-Gold Rush California. From the breathtaking opening panoramas showing the arrival of the determined railroad surveyor Mr Dalglish (a charismatic Bentley) in the remote Sierra Nevada town of Kingdom Come, it's clear this audacious Western was conceived on an epic scale. But what makes this one of the most remarkable British films of recent years is how the use of a heightened visual and aural architecture – the amplified roar of horses, clouds of condensing breath, angular wooden buildings dwarfed by vertiginous mountains – is deepened by a realist approach to acting, costume and design. Its snow settings and gloomy interiors might recall Altman's *McCabe and Mrs Miller*; but the movie is not so much derivative or revisionist as swimming in a sea of cinematic associations and allusions. Its exhilarating, flowing beauty is fittingly scored by Michael Nyman. The often superb performances are marred only by a certain emotional distance which, finally, renders the film marvellous rather than truly moving. WH

Claire Dolan

(1998, Fr/US, 95 min)
d Lodge H Kerrigan. *p* Ann Ruark. *sc* Lodge Kerrigan. *ph* Teodoro Maniaci. *ed* Kristina Boden. *pd* Sharon Lomofsky. *m* Ahrin Mishan, Simon Fisher Turner. *cast* Katrin Cartlidge, Vincent D'Onofrio, Colm Meaney, John Doman, Maryann Plunkett, Miranda Stuart Rhyne, Kate Skinner.

●Writer/director Kerrigan's first film, *Clean, Shaven*, won kudos for its clinical depiction of schizophrenia, but his second is a trickier proposition all round. Cartlidge plays the title role, one of those high-priced call girls so beloved of moviemakers across the spectrum. Claire hustles with a grim relentlessness, presumably to offset the emptiness she feels. The death of her mother is a catalyst for change. Perversely, she keeps her pimp Roland (Meaney) in the dark about it, as she begins to think about getting out of the game, and having a child herself. Kerrigan films all this with a cold, minimalist rigour, as detached and impersonal as the hotel rooms where Claire plies her trade. Dialogue and emotion is pared to a pragmatic base; it's only Roland who expresses compassion. Narrative ellipses creep in with the silence, and with them an ambiguity that's mysterious or just frustratingly obscure, depending on your willingness to adjust to this painstakingly alienated world view. Finally, the film lacks propulsive threat, and its characters come too close to art movie ciphers. Yet the last scene leaves an acrid aftertaste which isn't easily washed away. TCh

Claire's Knee (Le Genou de Claire)

(1970, Fr, 106 min)
d Eric Rohmer. *p* Pierre Cottrell. *sc* Eric Rohmer. *ph* Nestor Almendros. *ed* Cécile Decugis. *cast* Jean-Claude Brialy, Aurora Cornu, Béatrice Romand, Laurence de Monaghan, Michèle Montel, Fabrice Luchini.

●The fifth and most accessible of Rohmer's six 'moral tales', *Claire's Knee* is the story of the temptation of an affianced diplomat (Brialy) while on holiday, and its successful suppression. The film was rapturously received as a cinematic equivalent to Jane Austen at the time of its original release. The comparison is apt, though a better one would be with Joseph L Mankiewicz, a director of similarly literate, talky, classically structured movies, but none the less misses the point. For Brialy is no throwback to the 19th century but rather a Martian, a visitor to this planet discovering the values of his own culture through surveying those of the people he finds himself among, and finally retreating back home. If this makes Rohmer sound like a poet of bourgeois repression (just as Chabrol can be seen as a poet of bourgeois excess), one must also add that the film's self-reflexive structure makes it both more exciting and more ambiguous than such a description allows for. PH

Clairvoyant, The

(1935, GB, 80 min, b/w)
d Maurice Elvey. *p* Michael Balcon. *sc* Edgar Wallace, Charles Bennett, Robert Edmunds. *ph* Glen MacWilliams. ed Paul Capon. *ad* Alfred Junge. *m* Arthur Benjamin. *cast* Claude Rains, Fay Wray, Jane Baxter, Ben Field, Athole Stewart, Mary Clare, Felix Aylmer.

●Enjoyable if unremarkable thriller about a phoney music-hall clairvoyant who suddenly discovers that he has genuine prescience in the presence of a girl (Baxter). Things get fraught when his wife (Wray) disapproves of his involvement, even more so when he predicts a tunnel disaster, it takes place (the authorities wouldn't listen), and he is blamed for causing it by having spread panic. Rains lends a touch of credibility to the far-fetched plot. GA

Clan de los Inmorales, El

see Order to Kill

Clandestine Marriage, The

(1999, GB, 91 min)
d Christopher Miles. *p* Rod Gunner, Johnathan B Stables, Steve Clark-Hall. *sc* Trevor Bentham. *ph* Denis Crossan. *ed* George Akers. *pd* Martin Childs. *m* Stanislas Syrewicz. *cast* Nigel Hawthorne, Joan Collins, Timothy Spall, Tom Hollander, Paul Nicholls, Natasha Little, Cyril Shaps, Mark Burns, Emma Chambers, Hugh Lloyd.

●'Ooh, for a game of *romps*,' avows Hawthorne's Lord Ogleby, a rheumatic fop decades past his prime. Here's a splendid, sympathetic grotesque to set beside Hawthorne's King George: genteel, vain and bankrupt in most ways which count in 18th century England. Hence his sufferance of the marriage between his son, Sir John (Hollander), and the nouveau riche Betsy Sterling (Chambers). The only impediment is that Sir John has his eye on Betsy's beauteous younger sister, Fanny (Little), already secretly married to her father's clerk, Lovewell (Nicholls). Hawthorne and Joan Collins (who share associate producer credits) apparently bailed out the production after its funding collapsed – and the film was worth saving. You can sense the financial problems in the editing (there clearly wasn't enough footage for some sequences) and swathes of post-synched dialogue. Yet it's a droll, elegantly coarse entertainment, a country house farce somewhat reminiscent of *La Règle de Jeu* and *Smiles of a Summer Night*. The ingenues are comparatively bland, but who's watching them when old lechers like Hawthorne and Collins are about? (From the play by George Coleman the elder.) TCh

Clando (Clandestine)

(1996, Cameroon, 98 min)
d/p/sc Jean Marie Téno. *ph* Nurith Aviv. *ed* Aurelie Ricard. *cast* Paulin Fodouop, Caroline Redl, Henriette Fenda, Joseph Momo, Guillaume Nana.

●After an enigmatic opening, this political/psychological drama turns into an arresting portrait of a life thrown into turmoil by the pernicious actions of corrupt authorities. After computer programmer Anatole (Fodouop) is arrested and tortured for helping an anti-government group print leaflets, he becomes impotent both sexually and socially, reduced to working illegally as an unlicensed cab-driver (*clando*); in an attempt to improve his lot, he leaves Cameroon for Cologne, where the life of an exile is a little easier. Occasionally slow and rather clumsily acted, the film nevertheless offers insights into questions of freedom, activism, apathy and responsibility, and as a bonus features a marvellously seductive jazz blues score. GA

Clan of the Cave Bear, The

(1985, US, 98 min)
d Michael Chapman. *p* Gerald I Isenberg. *sc* John Sayles. *ph* Jan de Bont. *ed* Wendy Greene Bricmont. *pd* Anthony Masters. *m* Alan Silvestri. *cast* Daryl Hannah, Pamela Reed, James Remar, Thomas G Waites, John Doolittle, Curtis Armstrong.

●Adopted by the Neanderthal Clan of the Cave Bear, Cro-Magnon Hannah (taking a giant evolutionary leap forward from her previous incarnation in *Splash*) is maligned for her ability to count beyond ten, dexterity with weapons, and disdain for the males' primitive seduction rites (a fist thumped in the palm of the hand as prelude to some vigorous rutting). In the end this primeval feminist rejects miscegenation with nasty, brutish Stone Age bozos, stalking off into the sunset in search of an appropriately Aryan mate. Devotees of John Sayles' witty, literate screenplays will be disappointed by the repartee of subtitled grunts, while beneath the film's apparent plea for tolerance lies the offensive (if quite possibly true) assumption that tall, tanned Californian blondes represent the highest form of human life. Based on a fat novel by Jean Auel (who subsequently sued the producers), this is Reader's Digest prehistory, though at least director Chapman (cameraman on *Raging Bull*) makes sure the murky caves look nice. SJo

Clara's Heart

(1988, US, 108 min)
d Robert Mulligan. *p* Martin Elfand. *sc* Mark Medoff. *ph* Freddie Francis. *ed* Sidney Levin. *pd* Jeffrey Howard. *m* David Grusin. *cast* Whoopi Goldberg, Michael Ontkean, Kathleen Quinlan, Neil Patrick Harris, Spalding Gray, Beverly Todd.

●When Clara (Goldberg) come to America from Jamaica to keep house for an irritating white middle class couple (Ontkean and Quinlan), all does not look well to the couple's little boy: after all Clara is black, cooks weird food, and 'talks funny'. Nevertheless, when his parents' marriage begins to crumble, young David turns to the newcomer, and soon learns that she is the most wonderful human being alive. In no time at all he's 'speaking her language' and generally getting to grips with the real world, while his parents disappear even further up their psychological backsides. Mulligan's adaptation of Joseph Olshan's novel doesn't merely flirt with pathos, it positively marries it. There are moments of genuinely touching comedy; Spalding Gray's nauseatingly condescending psychotherapist is spot on; and Whoopi Goldberg, admirable as always, fights a losing battle against a script which forces her to deliver the most appalling imitation of patois since C Thomas Howell in 'Soul Man'. MK

Clarence and Angel

(1980, US, 75 min)
d/p/sc Robert Gardner. *ph* Doug Harris. *ed* Jonathan Weld. *cast* Darren Brown, Mark Cardova, Izola Armstrong, Janice Jenkins, Lola Langley, Lolita Lewis.

●Clarence, a near-illiterate black teenager, picks up the knack of reading from Angel, a Puerto Rican live wire, during daily sessions together in the school corridor to which both are exiled for misbehaviour. Though lent a superficial 'marginality' by its use of non-professional performers, playground scat songs and dialogue of such authentic (and indecipherable) Harlemese as to give the layman the impression of overhearing rather than hearing it, the film's message – that the resilience of childhood will always win through against the odds – recalls the reactionary softie humanism of a Saroyan. An unassuming little film, nevertheless, touching and droll, and boasting in Cardova (as Angel) a born performer whose flawless timing and diminutive sex appeal suggest that he might grow up to become the American cinema's first Puerto Rican heart-throb. GAd.

Clarence, the Cross-Eyed Lion

(1965, US, 98 min)
d Andrew Marton. *p* Leonard Kaufman. *sc* Alan Caillou, Marshall Thompson, Art Arthur. *ph* Lamar Boren. *ed* Warren H Adams. *m* Shelly Manne. *cast* Marshall Thompson, Betsy Drake, Cheryl Miller, Richard Hayden, Alan Caillou.

●Clarence is a myopic beast who has difficulty focusing on his prey, Thompson is the animal behaviourist who tries to set his vision straight. There are also poachers closing in on the local gorillas. This was the movie which spawned the TV series *Daktari*. Director Marton (once Lubitsch's editor) efficiently blends the human drama with African wildlife footage. GM

Clash By Night

(1952, US, 105 min, b/w)
d Fritz Lang. *p* Harriet Parsons. *sc* Alfred Hayes. *ph* Nick Musuraca. *ed* George Amy. *ad* Albert S D'Agostino, Carroll Clark. *m* Roy Webb. *cast* Barbara Stanwyck, Paul Douglas, Robert Ryan, Marilyn Monroe, Keith Andes, J Carroll Naish.

●Clifford Odets' original play was a hoary item of Broadway neo-realism in the Arthur Miller vein: a 'mature' study of a cynical woman's adultery with an equally cynical man. Lang and his producer Jerry Wald transposed the setting from Staten Island to a small fishing village, and had the brilliant idea of grounding the characters in a documentary on the community industry, giving them a substance never intrinsic in the script. What follows is a very Langian picture of the dangerous undercurrents in emotional relationships, excellently acted by the three principals, interestingly counterpointed by Marilyn Monroe (in her first major role) and Keith Andes as uninhibited young lovers. TR

Clash of the Ash

(1987, Ire, 50 min)
d Fergus Tighe. *p* Jane Gogan. *sc* Fergus Tighe. *ph* Declan Quinn. *ed* Jim Duggan. *pd* Robert Armstrong. *m* Stephen Cooney. *cast* William Heffernan, Vincent Murphy, Gina Moxley, Michael McAuliffe.

●Phil (Heffernan) is in his final year at secondary school. On top of the pressures exerted by the adults around him – from his mother to study and do well at his exams, his father to take a job at the local garage, and his hurling trainer to prove himself on the field – there's the frustration of small-town life with its limited social outlets and air of claustrophobia. Phil's smouldering restlessness pervades this evenly paced and sensitively portrayed slice of provincial life, which manages to tell its yarn with a great deal of humour and compassion. GS

Clash of the Titans

(1981, GB, 118 min)
d Desmond Davis. *p* Charles H Schneer, Ray Harryhausen. *sc* Beverley Cross. *ph* Ted Moore. *ed* Timothy Gee. *pd* Frank White. *m* Laurence Rosenthal. *cast* Harry Hamlin, Judi Bowker, Laurence Olivier, Claire Bloom, Maggie Smith, Burgess Meredith, Ursula Andress, Flora Robson.

●Old style monster-and-mythology movie, made with the entrancing splendour of Ray Harryhausen's visual effects (the Pegasus flights) and the occasional cynicism which results from under-using and abusing a star cast. Perseus (Hamlin) and Andromeda (Bowker) are as boringly lovely as classical hero/ines should be, and even the scaly Kraken looks too dazed to bite Bowker in half. JS

Class

(1983, US, 98 min)
d Lewis John Carlino. *p* Martin Ransohoff. *sc* Jim Kouf, David Greenwalt. *ph* Ric Waite. *ed* Stuart H Pappé, Denis Dolan. *ad* Jack Poplin. *m* Elmer Bernstein. *cast* Jacqueline Bisset, Rob Lowe, Andrew McCarthy, Cliff Robertson, Stuart Margolin, John Cusack.

●Another of those mildly titillating high-school films, soulless and self-satisfied, realising the youthful fantasy of being initiated into the joys of sex by an older woman. Uncritically portraying a group of materialistic pupils (at an expensive academy) for whom education is merely a passport to success, politics don't exist, poverty sucks, and women's panties are collected like trophies, the film has Jonathan and Skip as a couple of pretty little room-mates. Unacceptably still a virgin, Jonathan is packed off to Chicago to bed his first woman, unwittingly meets Skip's 38-year-old mother (Bisset), and is seduced in a glass elevator. Naturally the older, unhappy woman is dumped in favour of male buddyness. JE

Class Action

(1990, US, 109 min)
d Michael Apted. *p* Ted Field, Scott Kroopf, Robert W Cort. *sc* Carolyn Shelby, Christopher Ames, Samantha Shad. *ph* Conrad Hall. *ed* Ian Crafford. *pd* Todd Hallowell. *m* James Horner. *cast* Gene Hackman, Mary Elizabeth Mastrantonio, Colin Friels, Joanna Merlin, Larry Fishburne, Donald Moffat, Jan Rubes, Matt Clark, Fred Dalton Thompson.

●Maggie Ward (Mastrantonio) may have followed her father into the law, but she embodies the kind of values he despises and is embittered about her long-suffering mother. Daddy (the ever reliable Hackman) is a flamboyant civil liberties lawyer who has spent his life championing the underdog and pursuing extra-marital affairs. When a class action lawsuit comes along, involving injured drivers and a car manufacturer accused of producing dangerous vehicles, guess which lawyers decide to take up opposing sides? Apted builds up a combative atmosphere both in and out of the courtroom, but the studied contrivances which work so well before the judge appear more strained during the emotional confrontations, which ambitiously attempt to redress all wrongs. Worthy stuff, most effective during the courtroom theatricals. CM

Classe de neige, La

see Class Trip

Classe Operaia Va in Paradiso, La (Lulu the Tool/The Working Class Go to Heaven)

(1971, It, 117 min)
d Elio Petri. *sc* Ugo Pirro, Elio Petri. *ph* Luigi Kuveiller. *ed* Ruggero Mastroianni. *ad* Dante Ferretti. *m* Ennio Morricone. *cast* Gian Maria Volonté, Mariangela Melato, Mietta Albertini, Salvo Randone.

●Initially the film reprises *Saturday Night and Sunday Morning*, with its hero Lulu at his lathe, churning out the maximum number of gizmos (he's not sure what they're for), contemptuous of bosses, unions and student agitators alike, simply trying to earn enough to maintain a chaotic personal life. Then he loses a finger in an accident. Anticipating the school of Loach, its committed social analysis is leavened with humour and arresting anecdote. What you don't get in Loach is Morricone's aggressive score or Volonté's star turn as the archetype of capitalism's poor bloody infantry. Petri unflinchingly reproduces Lulu's world of earsplitting sound and nothing pleasing to look at. BBa

Classified X (aka Melvin Van Peebles' Classified X)

(1997, Fr/US, 52 min)
d Mark Daniels. *p* Yves Jeanneau, Christine LeGoff. *sc* Melvin Van Peebles. *ph* Mark Daniels. *ed* Catherine Mabilat, Janice Jones. *pd* Patrick Durand. *m* Melvin Van Peebles. *with* (archive) Martin Luther King Jr, Malcolm X. *narrator* Melvin Van Peebles

●Excellent, polemical documentary presented by the director of *Sweet Sweetback's Baadasssss Song* on the history of black cinema from DW Griffith to the 'counter-revolutionary' blaxploitation era and the ghetto gangster genre of the present. Peebles spills his articulate spleen on all and sundry (only Spike Lee, Julie Dash and John Singleton come off lightly) in an elegant rant that scores some scorching points aimed at 'the brothers', but which is pertinent to anyone interested in black representation in the cinema. WH

Class of '44

(1973, US, 95 min)
d/p Paul Bogart. *sc* Herman Raucher. *ph* Andrew Laszlo. *ed* Michael A Hoey. *pd* Ben Edwards. *m* David Shire. *cast* Gary Grimes, Jerry Houser, Oliver Conant, William Atherton, Sam Bottoms, Deborah Winters.

●Little Benjy (remember him?) joins the Marines 'cos of their tradition, while Hermie and Oscy go to college in this follow-up to Robert Mulligan's *Summer of '42*. Looking back to a fat, happy America, from a European point of view very much secure at the end of the rainbow during World War II, it has Oscy thrown out of college for pimping off a 32-year-old whore he installs in his room, while Hermie has girl trouble, feels guilty about not fighting, and is faced with the death of a father he never really knew. A serious analysis of the period might have been interesting, but *Class of '44* just opts for clichés and nostalgia in equal doses.

Class of Miss MacMichael, The

(1978, GB, 99 min)
d Silvio Narizzano. *p/sc* Judd Bernard. *ph* Alex Thomson. *ed* Max Benedict. *ad* Hazel Peiser. *m* Stanley Myers. *cast* Glenda Jackson, Oliver Reed, Michael Murphy, Rosalind Cash, John Standing, Riba Akabusi, Phil Daniels.

●Reed, as the neo-fascist headmaster of a school for delinquents, parodies his boorish film persona to the point of farce, alternately strutting around like a boiled turkey or oiling his way with the school's visitors, while Jackson goes at her role of committed teacher/lone befriender of kids with jaw-forward heartiness. Add to this conflict in styles the film's confused intentions — black comedy, the horrific realities of reform schools, a sentimental belief that understanding will overcome – and you have a mess. HM

Class of 1984

(1981, Can, 98 min)
d Mark L Lester. *p* Arthur Kent. *sc* Mark L Lester, John Saxton, Tom Holland. *ph* Albert Dunk. *ed* Howard Kunin. *ad* Geoff Holmes, Ted Watkins. *m* Lalo Schifrin. *cast* Perry King, Merrie Lynn Ross, Timothy Van Patten, Roddy McDowall, Stefan Arngrim, Michael Fox.

●A stomping reworking of *The Blackboard Jungle* for the '80s, with Perry King – in the part of the well-meaning teacher originally played by Glenn Ford – faced with a bunch of delinquents who make Ford's sulky juveniles look quite angelic by comparison: psychos, pushers and hookers throng the class of '84 carrying a fancy range of weaponry which somehow escapes the metal detector in the hall. And ultimately King wins through not by patience or insight or understanding, but by something more old-fashioned, like ramming them with cars and smashing their brains out on the concrete. While there can be no doubt that in true tabloid style *Class of 1984* feeds on everything it is condemning, as an energetic comic strip it has considerable fascination. DP

Class of Nuke 'Em High

(1986, US, 85 min)
d Richard W Haines, Samuel Weil [Lloyd Kaufman]. *p* Lloyd Kaufman, Michael Herz. *sc* Richard W Haines, Mark Rudnitsky, Lloyd Kaufman, Stuart Strutin. *ph* Michael Mayers. *ed* Richard W Haines. *ad* Art Skopinsky, Arthur Lorenz. *cast* Janelle Brady, Gilbert Brenton, Robert Prichard, RL Ryan, James Nugent Vernon.

●There's a leaky nuclear plant behind the high school, and that's where the local marijuana crop grows in a pool of pulsating green fizz. After one eerily glowing joint, Warren and Chrissie are able to mutate (and de-mutate) at will. Following a bout of protected sex (she keeps her shorts on) Chrissie gives birth through the navel to a giant tadpole that disappears down the loo to grow into a rubber-mask guy, who unerringly spikes, squishes and decapitates bad boys and girls only. To add to this excitement the high school party is bikinis only, and just one radioactive kiss turns the German teacher on to bondage wear. The melting heads and similar consequences of sloppy industrial practices are rendered more expertly than you'd expect, but the cast seem to know they'd better hang on to their day jobs. DO

Class Relations (Klassenverhältnisse)

(1983, WGer/Fr, 127 min, b/w)
d Jean-Marie Straub, Danièle Huillet. p Danièle Huillet. *sc* Jean-Marie Straub. *ph* William Lubtchansky. *ed* Jean-Marie Straub, Danièle Huillet. *ad* Georg Brommer. *cast* Christian Heinisch, Reinald Schnell, Anna Schnell, Klaus Traube, Mario Adorf.

●The Straubs always base their movies on existing texts (novels, poems, essays, plays or operas), choosing material, they say, that 'resists' them in some way. The idea is that their films become battlegrounds where the original author's words are confronted by the rigorous materialism of the Straubs' approach to film-making. In this case the source is Kafka's last novel *Amerika*, and the problem is that it doesn't yield much of a skirmish. This is the closest the Straubs have ever come to a straightforward literary adaptation: young Karl Rossman, newly arrived in a very German America, moves through a series of brutal encounters that destroy his 'New World' idealism and educate him in the verities of power and class difference. This is not to say that the film plays like a BBC 'classic serial', but the axeing of the book's philosophical speculations leaves the Straubs plodding rather than soaring through Kafka's political undercurrents. The stark images none the less have the 'minimalist' beauty that drives some viewers to distraction. TR

Class Trip (La Classe de neige)

(1998, Fr, 98 min)
d Claude Miller. *p* Annie Miller. *sc* Claude Miller, Emmanuel Carrère. *ph* Guillaume Schiffman. *ed* Anne Lafarge. *pd* Jean-Pierre Kohut-Svelko. *m* Henri Texier. *cast* Clément Van Den Bergh, Lokman Nalcakan, François Roy, Yves Verhoeven, Emmanuelle Bercot, Tina Sportolaro, Yves Jacques, Chantal Banlier.
●Sensitively and elegantly made – albeit in a determinedly old-fashioned way – Claude Miller's film is based on a novel by Emmanuel Carrère about the experiences of a shy sheltered boy allowed to go on a school trip to the Alps. A teacher's concern over the lad's behaviour, not to mention his repeated nightmares, convinces him that there's something terribly amiss in his charge's life. You got it: this is another case of sexual abuse (the big issue for serious-minded film-makers in '98, it seems), and while it's hard to fault either the superb performances or Miller's treatment of a tricky subject, the film doesn't ever really work in dramatic terms. It all seems just a bit too obvious. GA

Claudine

(1974, US, 92 min)
d John Berry. *p* Hannah Weinstein. *sc* Tina Pine, Lester Pine. *ph* Gayne Rescher. *ed* Luis San Andres. *pd* Ted Haworth. *m* Curtis Mayfield. *cast* Diahann Carroll, James Earl Jones, Lawrence Hinton-Jacobs, Tamu, David Kruger, Yvette Curtis.
●Black welfare comedy with a catch in its throat that has a beautiful mother of six trying to get her man as well as cope with domestic problems like a militant son and pregnant daughter. Meanwhile her man (a garbage collector) wins the kids over by preaching the virtues of savvy and education. Most of the humour is aware of the blacks' place at the bottom of the heap, and the stream of welfare gags occasionally hit home; but mostly the film is dogged by its middle-of-the road comedy format and its refusal to trade in anything but stereotypes.

Clay Pigeon, The

(1949, US, 63 min, b/w)
d Richard Fleischer. *p* Herman Schlom. *sc* Carl Foreman. *ph* Robert de Grasse. ed Samuel E Beetley. *ad* Albert S D'Agostino, Walter Keller. *m* Paul Sawtell. *cast* Bill Williams, Barbara Hale, Richard Loo, Richard Quine, Frank Fenton, Martha Hyer.
●Williams as an ex-PoW suffering from amnesia (that favourite standby of the *film noir*) and setting out to establish his innocence after being accused of treason and responsibility for the death of a friend in a Jap camp. Directed by Fleischer with tight, spare energy, although the implausible script and bland leading performances (with Hale as the dead friend's wife, initially hostile but soon losing her heart) make it much inferior to *The Narrow Margin*. TM

Clayton & Catherine

see China 9, Liberty 37

Clean and Sober

(1988, US, 124 min)
d Glenn Gordon Caron. *p* Tony Ganz, Deborah Blum. *sc* Tod Carroll. *ph* Jan Kiesser. *ed* Richard Chew. *pd* Joel Schiller. *m* Gabriel Yared. *cast* Michael Keaton, Kathy Baker, Morgan Freeman, M Emmet Walsh, Tate Donovan, Luca Bercovici, Ben Piazza, Henry Judd Baker.
●A film about addiction and redemption which avoids the usual sensationalism. Daryl Poynter (Keaton) doesn't realise how bad he is until he wakes up to find his date dead of an overdose in bed beside him, and embezzlement charges brewing up at his real estate firm. Drink and drugs have eroded all sense of responsibility, and rather than face the music, he takes refuge in a chemical dependency centre without any intention of toeing the line. It takes some tough talk from the councillor (Freeman, excellent) and the shock of enforced abstinence to shape him up. A supportive romance with fellow inmate Charlie (Kathy Baker) nose-dives abruptly, and his rehabilitation is ultimately down to character. The film doesn't cheat at all – Keaton's Poynter is a dislikeable proposition, always ready with a contemptuous crack, his pzazz verging on panic. The cold turkey sequence is devoid of Elmer Bernstein's brass, and the end is no more dramatic than an admission of answerability. A level look at a common problem. BC

Clean, Shaven

(1993, US, 80 min)
d/p/sc Lodge Kerrigan. *ph* Teodoro Maniaci. *ed* Jay Rabinowitz. *pd* Tania Ferrier. *m* Hahn Rowe. *cast* Peter Greene, Molly Castelloe, Megan Owen, Robert Albert, Jennifer MacDonald.
●Kerrigan's feature debut is an edgy, engrossing, intelligent study of schizophrenia, formulated as an impressionistically fragmented variation of the hunter/hunted road thriller. Right from the start, we can see that Peter Winter (Greene) is falling apart at the seams; his reaction to a small girl bouncing a ball against his car, coupled with reports of murder on the radio, suggest that he's probably also homicidal. At any rate, he sets off across a bleak landscape, visiting his far-from-welcoming mother and searching for the daughter whose company he's been denied; meanwhile, a detective is on his trail, checking out murder locations and contacting Winter's estranged wife for clues as to his likely whereabouts and intentions. What lifts the film out of the rut is its use of expressionistic sound design (there's little dialogue, let alone plot) and occasionally disturbing images to reveal Winter's wretched, hallucinatory perceptions of the world around him; few movie portraits of the paranoid experience have been so detailed or, for that matter, so harrowing. GA

Clean Slate (Coup de Torchon)

(1981, Fr, 128 min)
d Bertrand Tavernier. *p* Adolphe Viezzi. *sc* Jean Aurenche, Bertrand Tavernier. *ph* Pierre-William Glenn. *ed* Armand Psenny. *pd* Alexandre Trauner. *songs* Philippe Sarde, Bertrand Tavernier. *cast* Philippe Noiret, Isabelle Huppert, Jean-Pierre Marielle, Stéphane Audran, Eddy Mitchell, Guy Marchand.
●Purists may object to Tavernier's treatment of Jim Thompson's excellent if sordid and sadistic thriller, *Pop.1280*, but this eccentric, darkly comic look at a series of bizarre murders is stylishly well-crafted, and thoroughly entertaining. Transferring the action from the American Deep South to French West Africa in the late '30s, Tavernier elicits a characteristically colourful performance from Noiret as the manic but outwardly easy going slob of a cop who initiates a private vendetta against the town's more obnoxious citizens by resorting to murder. Strange insights into the effects of racism and the complicity of its victims, embellished with black wit and an elegant visual sense. GA

Clear and Present Danger

(1994, US, 141 min)
d Phillip Noyce. *p* Mace Neufeld, Robert Rehme. *sc* Donald Stewart, Steven Zaillian, John Milius. *ph* Donald McAlpine. *ed* Neil Travis. *pd* Terence Marsh. *m* James Horner. *cast* Harrison Ford, Willem Dafoe, Anne Archer, Henry Czerny, Donald Moffat, Harris Yulin, Joaquim de Almeida, Dean Jones, Hope Lange.
●This third, dispiriting screen outing for Tom Clancy's CIA operative Jack Ryan has Ford's rugged protagonist promoted to Deputy Director and swiftly finding himself out of his depth on two fronts: negotiating the treacherous corridors of high office, at the same time as presidential initiative demands improved results in his war against Colombia's drug barons. The elements of the plot can be ticked off: an auto-pilot star; better playing in the subsidiary roles; and a grim determination throughout to impress us with the number of locations, aircraft and warships at the production's disposal. There's a glimmer of interest in the film's ideological contortions, but as a commercial action thriller this is inflated and sluggish. TJ

Cléo de 5 à 7 (Cleo from 5 to 7)

(1961, Fr/It, 90 min, b/w & col)
d Agnès Varda. *p* Bruna Drigo. *sc* Agnès Varda. *ph* Jean Rabier. *ed* Jeanne Verneau. *ad* Bernard Evein. *m* Michel Legrand. *cast* Corinne Marchand, Antoine Bourseiller, Dorothée Blanck, Dominique Davray, Michel Legrand.
●If much of Varda's airy cinema has not lasted well, this classic 'two hours in the life of' still casts a sympathetic spell. Successful pop singer Cleo (Marchand), depressed by the imminent arrival of a doctor's report that could be very serious, quits her secluded, protected world for the Parisian streets and eventually meets up with a young soldier (Bourseiller), finding an unexpected intimacy and renewed hope. The fluid, whited-out photography gives the film a genuine grace, and the music session midway with Michel Legrand is a real joy. There is also a brief burlesque movie, featuring (among others) Godard, Karina and Eddie Constantine. Not every minute is as spirited as Varda would like us to believe, but in the cinema of enchantment this ranks pretty high. DT

Cleopatra

(1934, US, 98 min, b/w)
d/p Cecil B DeMille. *sc* Waldemar Young, Vincent Lawrence, Barlett Cormack. *ph* Victor Milner. *ed* Anne Bauchens. *ad* Hans Dreier, Roland Anderson. *m* Rudolph G Kopp. *cast* Claudette Colbert, Warren William, Henry Wilcoxon, Gertrude Michael, Joseph Schildkraut, C Aubrey Smith.
●Archly silly, but quite fun if you go for DeMille's po-faced blend of titillation and uplift. When you get tired of watching the scantily-clad cuties who seem to go into their dance every few minutes, there are some glitteringly opulent Hans Dreier sets: the burnished barge is a masterpiece of bordello art. TM

Cleopatra

(1963, US, 243 min)
d Joseph L Mankiewicz. *p* Walter Wanger. *sc* Joseph L Mankiewicz, Ranald MacDougall, Sidney Buchman. *ph* Leon Shamroy. *ed* Dorothy Spencer. *pd* John F DeCuir. *m* Alex North. *cast* Elizabeth Taylor, Richard Burton, Rex Harrison, Roddy McDowall, Cesare Danova, Hume Cronyn, Robert Stephens, Kenneth Haigh, George Cole.
●A mess, as you might expect from the disastrous series of stoppages and personnel changes that dogged production. Mankiewicz does his best with a script worked on by so many writers that it never hits any recognisable tone, but the effect is of acres of dreary spectacle (lacking even DeMille's amusing vulgarity) gradually swamping the cast. Harrison, doing his waspish don act as Caesar, alone rises above mediocrity. GA

Cleopatra Jones

(1973, US, 89 min)
d Jack Starrett. *p* William Tennant, Max Julien. *sc* Max Julien, Sheldon Keller. *ph* David M Walsh. *ed* Allan Jacobs. *ad* Peter Wooley. *m* JJ Johnson, Carl Bradt, Shapiro. *cast* Tamara Dobson, Bernie Casey, Brenda Sykes, Antonio Fargas, Bill McKinney, Dan Frazer, Shelley Winters.
●Blaxploitation product in which six-foot-two Agent Tamara Dobson wages war on drugs, rednecks and other social evils. Luckily Starrett played it for laughs: the film stands or falls by the flamboyant comic-strip style of its Cat Woman heroine. VG

Cleopatra Jones and the Casino of Gold

(1975, US/HK, 96 min)
d Chuck Bail. *p* William Tennant, Run Run Shaw. *sc* William Tennant. *ph* Alan Hume. *ed* Willy Kemplen. *ad* Johnson Tsao. *m* Dominic Frontiere. *cast* Tamara Dobson, Stella Stevens, Tanny, Norman Fell, Albert Popwell, Caro Kenyatta.

●This lame follow-up to the less than brilliant Cleopatra Jones has its black special agent combating drug rings in Hong Kong hand-in-glove with the local special branch. Mechanically scripted, incoherently put together. VG

Clerks

(1994, US, 90 min)
d Kevin Smith. *p* Kevin Smith, Scott Mosier. *sc* Kevin Smith. *ph* David Klein. *ed* Scott Mosier, Kevin Smith. *m* Scott Angley. *cast* Brian O'Halloran, Jeff Anderson, Marilyn Ghigliotti, Lisa Spoonauer, Jason Mewes, Kevin Smith.
●Shot in a New Jersey convenience store for $27,575, this talky, scabrous and very funny first feature is a bargain-price comedy. Store clerk Dante (O'Halloran) and his pal Randal (Anderson), who minds the adjacent video shop, use the gaps between awkward customers to discuss their career trajectories, the ending of *Return of the Jedi*, the oral excesses of Dante's current girlfriend, and the impending nuptials of his high-school ex. If it's fancy packaging you want, forget it; if scuzzy talk and laugh-out-loud humour are your bag, check this out. NF

Client, The

(1994, US, 121 min)
d Joel Schumacher. *p* Arnon Milchan, Steven Reuther. *sc* Robert Getchell, Akiva Goldsman. *ph* Tony Pierce-Roberts. *ed* Robert Brown. *m* Howard Shore. *cast* Tommy Lee Jones, Susan Sarandon, Mary-Louise Parker, Anthony LaPaglia, JT Walsh, Brad Renfro, Will Patton.
●When two young brothers find themselves reluctant witnesses to a suicide, at least 11-year-old Mark knows enough to realise that his terrifying conversation with the man immediately before his death will attract the attention of the legal authorities – the Feds, no less, headed by prosecutor Foltrigg (Jones); but he probably didn't expect to hear from the Mob. Trouble is, Mark (Renfro) knows too much. But while lawyer Reggie Love (Sarandon) is canny, caring and tough enough to do her best for the boy, is he man enough to reciprocate her trust? And can the pair of them fend off ruthless law-enforcement types and near-psychotic hitmen? Slick, solid and saddled throughout with hackneyed motivation and implausible moments, Schumacher's film is both the best adaptation of a John Grisham novel to date, and a surprisingly suspenseful slice of escapist entertainment. Efficient fun, no more, no less. GA

Cliffhanger

(1993, US, 112 min)
d Renny Harlin. *p* Alan Marshall, Renny Harlin. *sc* Michael France, Sylvester Stallone. *ph* Alex Thomson. *ed* Frank J Urioste. *pd* John Vallone. *m* Trevor Jones. *cast* Sylvester Stallone, John Lithgow, Michael Rooker, Janine Turner, Rex Linn, Janine Turner.
●There are some things a man just can't walk around. When Gabe Walker (Stallone) fails to stop a girl falling to her death, his nerve is broken and he leaves the Rocky Mountain Rescue Team and his lover Jessie (Turner). But a chance for redemption arises when he and now vengeful colleague Tucker (Rooker) are duped into 'rescuing' a motley gang of villains who have lost three stolen Treasury coffers in an air crash in the high peaks. Director Harlin makes the most of the scenery, but seldom manages to induce a tingling sense of vertigo. Fun for the undemanding, but Stallone's 'comeback' should have been much tighter. GA

Climax (Ich – das Abenteuer heute eine Frau zu sein)

(1972, WGer, 89 min)
d Roswitha vom Bruck. *sc* Denise de Boer, Roswitha vom Bruck. *ph* Werner M Lenz. *ed* Eva Storek. *m* Heinz Kiessling, Cats. *cast* Renate Carol, Frank Glaubrecht, Ingo Baerow, Bert Hochschwarzer.
●Husband Karl is none too good in bed, so Monika's GP advocates masturbation. Friend suggests, 'You'd better get a lover. After all, you can't keep masturbating all your life,' and there's the GP waiting to transport her to full awareness to the accompaniment of a wavering trumpet solo. Not that much to indicate that *Climax* was the first sex film to be directed by a woman. Vom Bruck makes a few jokes at the expense of an expectant male audience, but fights a losing battle against the banality of the acting and a script which comes up with such remarks as 'Any man who makes love to you once would never let you get away,' and so tries to compensate by handling the whole thing with a certain Teutonic relentlessness. CPe

Clinic, The

(1982, Aust, 92 min)
d David Stevens. *p* Robert le Tet, Bob Weis. *sc* Greg Millin. *ph* Ian Baker. *ed* Edward McQueen-Mason. *pd* Tracy Watt. *cast* Chris Haywood, Simon Burke, Gerda Nicolson, Rona McLeod, Suzanne Roylance, Veronica Lang.
●An Australian comedy about the clap is bound to produce premature conclusions. In fact, this is a million kangaroo hops from the chundering humour of Barry McKenzie and similarly broad Ozports. If it weren't for the obviously still taboo nature of the subject matter, the film would be an excellent TV series pilot, a medical cousin to *Barney Miller*. Strong playing from the amiable Haywood as the harassed gay doctor in charge, Burke as his potentially rednecked student trainee. The laughter is infectious, and there aren't too many herpes jokes. GD

Cloak and Dagger

(1946, US, 106 min, b/w)
d Fritz Lang. *p* Milton Sperling. *sc* Albert Maltz, Ring Lardner Jr. *ph* Sol Polito. *ed* Christian Nyby. *ad* Max Parker. *m* Max Steiner. *cast* Gary Cooper, Lilli Palmer, Robert Alda, Vladimir Sokoloff, Helene Thimig, J Edward Bromberg.
●Tolerably exciting, but despite some electric moments (the shockingly casual execution of Thimig, a brutal fight in an alley conducted in death like silence), a conventional World War II espionage thriller and far from Lang at his best. Cooper, morosely miscast as a scientist serving with the OSS, spends most of the time trotting round Europe ensuring that the Nazis don't get the atom bomb and that he gets the girl. The version shot by Lang was considerably more doom-laden, carrying on in a lengthy coda to suggest that Nazi scientists had found the secret of atomic power, and escaped with it to Argentina or parts unknown. Then Warners got into the act, and cut for the happy ending. TM

Clock, The (aka Under the Clock)

(1945, US, 90 min, b/w)
d Vincente Minnelli. *p* Arthur Freed. *sc* Robert Nathan, Joseph Schrank. *ph* George Folsey. *ed* George White. *ad* Cedric Gibbons, William Ferrari. *m* George Bassman. *cast* Judy Garland, Robert Walker, James Gleason, Keenan Wynn, Lucille Gleason, Marshall Thompson.
●Minnelli's charming tale of office girl Garland and soldier Walker (on a two-day leave) meeting at New York's Penn Station and plunging into a whirlwind romance and marriage. Though it might seem a little too heart-warming for modern tastes, it is beautifully designed (with impressive studio sets) and performed, GA

Clockers

(1995, US, 128 min)
d Spike Lee. *p* Martin Scorsese, Spike Lee, Jon Kilik. *sc* Richard Price, Spike Lee. *ph* Malik Sayeed. *ed* Sam Pollard. *pd* Andrew McAlpine. *m* Terence Blanchard. *cast* Harvey Keitel, Mekhi Phifer, Delroy Lindo, John Turturro, Isaiah Washington, Keith David, Pee Wee Love.
●Strike (Phifer) deals crack from the benches in front of the Brooklyn tenement where he grew up. Rodney (Lindo) has his protégé earmarked for big things, but he has to be blooded first: murder is Rodney's only insurance. Strike listens, but when his intended victim turns up dead, it's Strike's straight-arrow brother Victor (Washington) who confesses to the crime. Rodney isn't happy. That goes double for detective Klein (Keitel) who, unlike his partner Mazilli (Turturro), refuses to accept they've put away the real killer. Spike Lee's adaptation of Richard Price's novel cuts back on the cops' perspective but retains the essential overview of a society trapped in a cycle of despair. In an apparent reaction against the plethora of flashy 'hood' movies his success helped spawn, Lee has toned down the snap of his montage, muted his saturated *mise en scène* in favour of streetlight chiaroscuro, and co-opted jerky, handheld zooms from *cinéma vérité*. Scored largely to plaintive soul tracks (Seal, Marc Dorsey), the result is a more sober, mournful and meditative expressionism than you'd expect. That's not to say the film isn't suspenseful, but the director's distaste for the inner city's gun culture is clear to see. Superbly acted. TCh

Clockmaker, The

see Horloger de St Paul, L'

Clockwise

(1985, GB, 96 min)
d Christopher Morahan. *p* Michael Codron. *sc* Michael Frayn. *ph* John Coquillon. *ed* Peter Boyle. *pd* Roger Murray-Leach. *m* George Fenton. *cast* John Cleese, Alison Steadman, Sharon Maiden, Stephen Moore, Chip Sweeney, Penelope Wilton, Joan Hickson.
●Clock-watching comprehensive headmaster Mr Stimpson (Cleese) momentarily boards the wrong train when he sets out for a Headmasters' Conference in Norwich; the result, a never-ending nightmare as he's forced to hijack one of his sixth-formers, complete with her parents' car, and to travel hell-for-leather across the Midlands countryside. Much of Michael Frayn's original screenplay might seem like routine farce, were it not for the furious pace and level of invention in terms of both plot and dialogue. But what finally makes it consistently amusing is, of course, Cleese. GA

Clockwork Mice

(1995, GB, 100 min)
d Vadim Jean. *p* Paul Brooks. *sc* Rod Woodruff. *ph* Gordon Hickie. *ed* Liz Webber. *pd* David Munns. *cast* Ian Hart, Catherine Russell, Joseph Gordon-Levitt, John Alderton, Ruaidhri Conroy, Claire Skinner, Art Malik, James Bolam.
●A novice teacher, Steve (Hart), arrives at a special-needs school just in time to see one of his charges hurtling along a high-wire and dive bombing kamikaze-style some poor teacher's 2CV. Such 'spirited' behaviour turns out to be par for the course at a school, where survival depends on a certain amount of laissez-faire. Steve's thankless attempts to instill a sense of poetry in the kids look doomed, but when he challenges charismatic ne'er-do-well Conrad (Conroy) to a cross-country run he captures the imagination of the school. The film takes 'difficult' raw material and puts it to the service of middlebrow feelgood entertainment. It mostly soft-pedals the trauma of emotional violence and plays the physical variety for (admittedly black) comedy. Hart is a tremendously vigorous, alert screen presence, and Conroy's bruised sensitivity is equally expressive. Prettily photographed and handled with considerable assurance, the film runs up a head of steam, but not much more. TCh

Clockwork Orange, A

(1971, GB, 136 min)
d/p/sc Stanley Kubrick. *ph* John Alcott. *ed* Bill Butler. *pd* John Barry. *cast* Malcolm McDowell, Patrick Magee, Michael Bates, Warren Clarke, John Clive, Adrienne Corri, Carl Duering, Steven Berkoff, David Prowse.
●Kubrick's film exploited the current debate on the validity of aversion therapy in the context of a working lad's freedom to choose violence as his form of self-expression. A sexless, inhuman film, whose power derives from a ruthless subordination of its content to the demands of telling a good story. A glossy, action-packed ritual which is fun to watch but superficial to think about.

Clonus

see Parts: The Clonus Horror

Closed Circuit (Circuito Chiuso)

(1978, It, 105 min)
d Giuliano Montaldo. *sc* Nicola Baldalucco. *ph* Giuseppe Pinori. *m* Egisto Macchi. *cast* Flavio Bucci, Aurore Clément, Ettore Manni, Brizzio Montinaro, Giuliano Gemma, William Berger.
●The central idea of *Closed Circuit* – an audience watches a spaghetti Western in a cinema; as it finishes the gunman on screen shoots and a member of the audience drops dead with a bullet hole in his chest – is just fine. Sadly, the film proceeds to dissipate its generic thriller elements in stodgy

Italian stereotyping and overplaying, while never quite having the courage to fully develop its philosophical pretensions about the spectator and the screen. Unable to resolve its dilemma, it opts for an unsatisfying mish-mash of half-baked notions and presents it as a climax. SM

Closed Doors (El Abwab el Moghalaka)

(1999, Egypt, 105 min)
d/sc Atef Hetata. *ph* Samir Bahzan. *ed* Dalia El Nasser. *pd* Hamed Hemdane. *cast* Mahmoud Hemida, Sawsan Badr, Ahmed Azmi, Manal Afifi, Ahmed Fouad Selim, Seif Abdel Rahman, Salwa Mohamed Ali.

● This excellent first feature from Youssef Chahine's production company is set during the Gulf War and analyses the descent into fundamentalist behaviour of a young Cairo truant. His lone mother, a cleaner, tries hard to keep the boy on the right path, but struggles to afford the extra fees demanded by his teacher, and hopes he won't realise their friendly neighbour is a prostitute. For his part, he tries to keep his mum in the dark about his new friend's identity (he's a street vendor) and the tuition he's receiving at a fundamentalist mosque. Despite an aura of tragic inevitability, this picture of how victims can be produced by poverty, irreconcilable conflicts between traditionalism and modernity, and unresolved psycho-sexual passions brewed in families with absent male figures, displays fine observation, expressive location work and gently nurtured performances. WH

Closed for Family Mourning (Zavreno pro rodinny smutek)

(1991, Czech Rep, 14 min, b/w)
d/sc Sasa Gedeon. *ph* Milos Kabyi. *ed* Petr Turyna. *cast* Renata Becerrova, Barbora Hrzánová, Vácal Polivka, Jakub Spalek, David Vávra.

● Or 'The Hairdresser's Apprentice': menial tyrannies and flights of fancy over a hot summer's day in a Rome barbershop. Sparkier (and of course slighter) than Gedeon's more mature work, this adaptation of an Alberto Moravia short story points to its maker's interest in jejune young romantics learning the reality of love and loyalty the hard way. NB

Close Encounters of the Third Kind

(1977, US, 135 min)
d Steven Spielberg. *p* Julia Phillips, Michael Phillips. *sc* Steven Spielberg. *ph* Vilmos Zsigmond. *ed* Michael Kahn. *pd* Joe Alves. *m* John Williams. *cast* Richard Dreyfuss, François Truffaut, Teri Garr, Melinda Dillon, Bob Balaban, Warren Kemmerling.

● *Close Encounters* takes the favoured dream of every UFO enthusiast (that the US government has been operating a cover-up) and turns it into a majestic and finally unprecedented adventure story. As early references to *The Ten Commandments* and Chuck Jones's Warner cartoons show, the film seems less concerned with science fiction than with recapturing the wonder of a child's first experience of the cinema, and the surprising thing is that Spielberg moves into this territory so effectively. There are some awkward touches (Truffaut never ceases to be Truffaut, while some of the comedy scenes are a little overplayed), but they're small price to pay for the first film in years to give its audiences a tingle of shocked emotion that is not entirely based either on fear or on suspense. DP

Close Encounters of the Third Kind – Special Edition

(1977/80, US, 132 min.)
d Steven Spielberg. *p* Julia Phillips, Michael Phillips. *sc* Steven Spielberg. *ph* Vilmos Zsigmond. *ed* Michael Kahn. *pd* Joe Alves. *m* John Williams. *cast* Richard Dreyfuss, François Truffaut, Teri Garr, Melinda Dillon, Bob Balaban, Warren Kemmerling.

● The years since 1977 have shrunk *Star Wars*, but *Close Encounters* looks more classic than ever, an insane burst of cinematic optimism which somehow combines Disney and '50s SF and the imagery of junk food into the most persuasive (if arrested) version of the American dream yet accomplished. Now Spielberg has added some new special effects, but more importantly, he has cut and altered the central section concerning Dreyfuss' obsession with the image of Devil's Tower, Wyoming. These scenes, formerly hysterical and unconvincing, are now more potent, leaving Truffaut's slightly mannered performance as one of the film's few awkward areas. It is now also easier, following Spielberg's *1941*, to see why *Close Encounters* works so well: the child's bedroom scene where all the toys come alive has more adrenalin in it than a dozen demolitions. DP

Closely Observed Trains (Ostre Sledované Vlaky)

(1966, Czech, 92 min, b/w)
d Jiri Menzel. *p* Zdenek Oves. *sc* Jiri Menzel, Bohumil Hrabal. *ph* Jaromir Sofr. *ed* Jirina Lukesova. *ad* Oldrich Bosak. *m* Jiri Sust. *cast* Václav Neckár, Jitka Bendova, Vladimir Valenta, Josef Somr, Libuse Havelkova, Alois Vachek.

● A real charmer from the heyday of the Czech New Wave, set during the German occupation but totally immersed in the pubescent problems of a youth (as uncannily reminiscent of Buster Keaton as the boy in Olmi's *Il Posto*) taking up his first job as an apprentice railway platform guard with the firmly anti-social resolve to do as little work as possible while others slave. Wonderfully funny observation of the sleepy little backwater depot where nothing ever happens, and he maintains his resolve while hero-worshipping a philandering older guard (who whiles away the time by rubber-stamping the hindquarters of a delighted girl), avoiding the station-master (who emerges now and again to cry Sodom and Gomorrah before returning to his pigeons), and carrying on an unconsummated flirtation with the conductress of a passing train. The Resistance beckons, but *ejaculatio praecox* is still his most pressing problem. An airy pointilliste comedy, but it celebrates a whole universe of frustration, eroticism, adventure and romance. TM

Close My Eyes

(1990, GB, 108 min)
d Stephen Poliakoff. *p* Thérèse Pickard. *sc* Stephen Poliakoff. *ph* Witold Stok. *ed* Michael Parkinson. *pd* Luciana Arrighi. *m* Michael Gibbs. *cast* Alan Rickman, Clive Owen, Saskia Reeves, Karl Johnson, Lesley Sharp, Kate Gartside, Karen Knight.

● Poliakoff's second film as a director marks a distinct change in tone from his rather more languid earlier pieces. It begins in a café full of signals of decay – a ketchup squirter has a rotten tooth inside – and moves forward in time and affluence as brother and sister Richard and Natalie (Owen and Reeves), parted in childhood by divorce, reunite one blistering summer for a torrid, incestuous affair. 'Being single – it's not as simple as it used to be,' declares Richard to his sister one riverside evening. Given that he's rogering her, not only helping her to cheat on husband Rickman (a superbly dynamic performance) but also putting off a visit to his boss who's dying of AIDS, this is some understatement. Despite its obsession with covering up Owen's cock, this is steamy and passionate stuff. As well as the forbidden love theme, the film is also about the end of the '80s, and is full of intelligent insights into physical and moral decay, contrasting the squalor and bathos of the city with the cloistered joys of suburban greenery. SGr

Closer You Get, The

(1999, US/GB/Ire, 92 min)
d Aileen Ritchie. *p* Uberto Paloini. *sc* William Ivory. *ph* Robert Alazraki. *ed* Sue Wyatt. *pd* Tom McCullagh. *m* Rachel Portman. *cast* Ian Hart, Sean McGinley, Niamh Cusack, Ruth McCabe, Ewan Stewart, Pat Short, Cathleen Bradley, Sean McDonagh.

● Kalvara, Co. Donegal, and the menfolk are restive. The pub's the only entertainment, except for the morally uplifting fillums the priest shows once a month in the church, and they want more. More sex, basically. And specifically, sex with the kind of women they see on telly: 'fit and sporty' girls, 'American' girls. And so they place an ad in the *Miami Herald* inviting likely lasses to their summer shindig. Then, of course, they look in the mirror: cue malarky with balding ne'er-do-wells pulling on tracksuits and puffing across the bog. Very *Full Monty*, in other words. In its own mild way, the film scores affectionate points off the vanity and foolishness of men (with Hart coming off worst), and Cusack works up a smidgen of emotional engagement. As notions go, it's amusing enough. But there are few surprises. Instead, it's packed with amusing business too cutely contrived to allow you to relax and enjoy the feel of the place or care about the characters. TCh

Close Shave, A

(1995, GB, 30 min)
d Nick Park. *p* Carla Shelley, Michael Rose. *sc* Bob Baker, Nick Park. *ph* David Alex Riddett. *ed* Helen Garrard. *ad* Phil Lewis. *m* Julian Nott. *cast* voices: Peter Sallis, Anne Reid.

● Park's claymation film follows an Ealing-esque comedy-with-sinister-undertones scenario. The adventure centres on the case of the disappearing sheep. Northern gadget-meister Wallace and his hound Gromit have taken up window-cleaning, and it isn't long before Wallace is swept off his feet by the owner of the local wool shop, Wendolene Ramsbottom. Amateur sleuth Gromit, meanwhile, investigates the mysterious movements of her shifty-looking dog, Preston. Extremely engaging, very funny and perfectly paced (plus nods to *Batman* and *The Terminator*). DA

Closet Land

(1990, US, 89 min)
d Radha Bharadwaj. *p* Janet Meyers. *sc* Radha Bharadwaj. *ph* Bill Pope. *ed* Lisa Churgin. *pd* Eiko Ishioka. *m* Richard Einhorn. *cast* Madeleine Stowe, Alan Rickman.

● This highly stylised drama is resolutely theatrical: with the exception of fleeting flashbacks and fantasy sequences, the action is confined to one austere interior, and revolves around a political interrogation. Stowe plays a bewildered, nameless children's author taken from her bed in the middle of the night to face questioning by a government official (Rickman). She stands accused of 'subliminal indoctrination' in her book 'Closet Land', which explores the liberating force of the imagination. But subversion is far from the writer's mind: under torture, her creations are shown to provide redemption from her traumatised childhood. Writer/director Bharadwaj's debut offers appropriately brutal, intense exchanges, with Rickman's commanding performance quite overshadowing Stowe. But such a stage-bound project demands a stronger script, while the lack of identifiable names and political targets compromises a powerful subject. CM

Close to Eden (A Stranger Among Us)

(1992, US, 109 min)
d Sidney Lumet. *p* Steve Golin, Sigurjon Sighvatsson, Howard Rosenman. *sc* Robert J Averech. *ph* Andrzej Bartkowiak. *ed* Andrew Mondshein. *pd* Philip Rosenberg. *m* Jerry Bock. *cast* Melanie Griffith, Eric Thal, John Pankow, Tracy Polan, Lee Richardson, Mia Sara.

● Detective Emily Eden (Griffith), already chastised for using excessive force, is assigned to investigate the disappearance of a Hasidic jeweller and a fortune in diamonds; when, after finding his corpse in the ceiling of his own office, she concludes that he knew his killer, with the permission of the Rebbe she goes undercover in the Hasidic community. Cue culture clash, romantic yearnings for improbably sensitive Rebbe-to-be Ariel (Thal), and a steadily growing disenchantment with the harsh ways of her own Gentile world. All too obviously influenced by *Witness*, the film fails on all counts. The lackadaisical plotting is frequently implausible, and the depiction of Hasidic warmth and integrity is not only embarrassingly rose-tinted but objectionable in its implied endorsement of the archaically subservient position of women. GA

Close to the Border (Cerca de la Frontera)

(1999, Arg, 90 min)
d/p/sc Rodolfo Durán. *ph* Carlos Torlaschi. *ed* Carla Muzykantski. *pd* Nora Spivak. *m* Gabriel Bajarlia. *cast* Claudio Gallardou, Ulises Dumont, Leonor Manso, Victor Laplace, Alberto Benegas, Mirna Suarez, Paula Pourtale.

● A city journalist discovers the meaning of commitment while in political exile in the country. It's set in 1978 in Argentina, during the military junta, and for some reason it's shot to resemble '70s B-movie schlock, almost as if the writer/

producer/director had learned mise-en-scène from watching the *Airplane* movies. Hitching a ride incognito, our hapless hero claims to be an archeologist. 'Oh, perhaps you can tell me what this is?' says his driver, handing him an old piece of pottery from the glove compartment. Priceless. Regrettably, this unpersuasive take on the familiar theme is framed as a doleful moral drama. TCh

Close to the Wind (Oss Emellan)

(1969, Swe, 110 min)
d Stellan Olsson. *sc* Stellan Olsson, Per Oscarsson. *ph* Jesper Hom, Lasse Dahlqvist. *ed* Ingemar Ejve. *m* Joe Hill, Tage Sivén. *cast* Per Oscarsson, Bärbel Oscarsson, Lina Oscarsson, Boman Oscarsson, Maria Oscarsson, Beppe Wolgers.

●Effectively low-key realism in a naturalistic account of a none-too-successful artist and sculptor who comes into conflict with society at large when his only patrons – a bureaucratic committee commissioning work for a company's centenary – subtly but steadily alter his original conception. It's all pretty thin, and stands or falls by its performances (largely amateur, including Oscarsson's own family), but it does have a certain charm that is never ingratiating. GA

Close-Up (Namayeh Nazdik)

(1989, Iran, 97 min)
d/sc Abbas Kiarostami. *ph* Ali Reza Zarrin-Dast. *ed* Abbas Kiarostami. *cast* Hossain Sabzian, Mohsen Makhmalbaf, Hossain Farazmand, Abdolfazl Ahankhah, Mehrdad Ahankhah, Manoochehr Ahankhah.

●Kiarostami's masterpiece is a rich, multi-layered but beautifully forthright film in which Sabzian (playing himself – a movie fanatic – in a story based on fact) pretends to a middle-class family likewise interested in cinema that he is film director Makhmalbaf (who also appears as himself). As the film alternates between scenes of Sabzian's trial for fraud and reconstructions of his encounters with the family and of a journalist's attempts to discover the truth, Kiarostami constructs a complex (but never complicated) series of interwoven narratives to interrogate notions of fiction and documentary, appearance and reality, truth and falsehood. It's enormously intelligent stuff, witty, poignant and thoroughly engrossing, and ends with one of the sharpest, funniest deconstructions of film form ever shot. Absolutely wonderful. GA

Closing Numbers

(1993, GB, 95 min)
d Stephen Whittaker. *p* Jennifer Howarth. *sc* David Cook. *ph* Nic Knowland. *ed* Max Lemon. *pd* Terry Ackland-Snow. *m* Barrington Pheloung. *cast* Tim Woodward, Jane Asher, Frank Mills, Hazel Douglas, Jamie Glover, Patrick Pearson, Nigel Charnock.

●A comfortable family is thrown in turmoil by infidelity and the spectre of HIV in this Channel 4 movie. Jane Asher's the housewife whose routine existence is ruptured by the shock discovery of husband Woodward's on-going affair with a male lover (Pearson), who in turn is understandably shaken up by caring for his close friend Charnock as he suffers through the advanced stages of full-blown AIDS. Scriptwriter David Cook (who wrote C4's opening night film *Walter*) brings his customary sensitivity to bear on the subject matter, and all concerned tackle their roles with dedication – not least dancer Nigel Charnock in a typically self-lacerating role – but the scale is still one of middle-class chamber drama, however tough-minded and concerned. TJ

Cloud, The (La Nube/ aka Clouds)

(1998, Arg, 116 min)
d Fernando E Solanas. *p* Philippe Cosson, Fernando E Solanas. *sc* Fernando E Solanas. *ph* Juan Diego Solanas. *ed* Luis César D'Angiolillo. *ad* Hoang Thanh At. *m* Gerardo Gandini. *cast* Eduardo Pavlovsky, Angela Correa, Carlos Páez, Leonor Manso, Bernard Le Coq, Christophe Malavoy, Franklin Caicedo, Favio Pocsa.

●This film from the director of *Sur* is strong on atmospherics, but skimpy on plot. The fate of a Buenos Aires theatre (a national treasure, according to the artists) becomes a gloomy microcosm for the state of the nation. Allegory hangs heavy in the air. It has rained for 1,651 days straight and everyone is glued to the TV set. Solanas is a dab hand with smoke and mirrors, running time back and forth at different film speeds, but this exercise in rambling and pretentious nostalgia is unmistakably an old man's movie. TCh

Cloud-capped Star (Meghe Dhaka Tara)

(1960, Ind, 127 min, b/w)
d/p/sc Ritwik Ghatak. *ph* Dinen Gupta. *ed* Ramesh Joshi. *ad* Ravi Chattopadhyay. *m* Jyotirindra Moitra. *cast* Supriya Choudhury, Anil Chatterjee, Bijon Bhattacharya, Guita De, Gita Ghatak, Dwiju Bhawal, Niranjan Roy.

●The Bengali writer/director Ritwik Ghatak has been acclaimed as the most important Indian film-maker after Satyajit Ray. The first part of a trilogy that included *E Flat* and *Subarnarekha*, this is a dark melodrama, set in Calcutta in the late '50s, in which Nita (Choudhury) struggles to keep her refugee family afloat and together. Her father, a teacher, earns a pittance; her elder brother dreams of becoming a famous singer; a younger brother is forced to abandon his studies and work in a factory; and her mother hopes that Sanat, the young scientist her eldest daughter loves, will transfer his affections to the younger Guita. For Western viewers it's perhaps most easily approached as a bitter critique of harsh social and economic conditions, particularly those arising from the 1947 Partition of East Bengal. More interesting cinematically, however, is Ghatak's inventive, not quite naturalistic treatment of the story: in order to underline or undercut certain elements in terms of narrative, theme and characterisation, the performances, images, music and, most especially, sound are given almost expressionist nuances. GA

Clouded Yellow, The

(1950, GB, 96 min, b/w)
d Ralph Thomas. *sc* Janet Green, Eric Ambler. *ph* Geoffrey Unsworth. *ed* Gordon Hales. *ad* Richard Yarrow. *m* Benjamin Frankel. *cast* Jean Simmons, Trevor Howard, Barry Jones, Sonia Desdel, Maxwell Reed, Kenneth More, Geoffrey Keen, Andre Morell, Richard Wattis.

●Eric Ambler had a hand in the script for this unsurprising, but watchable sub-Hitchcock British thriller, which has Howard as a former spy getting himself into hot water after he goes off to catalogue the butterfly collection of the eccentric Jones. When Simmons, his new employer's daughter, is accused of murdering the handyman who's molested her, Howard spirits the girl away and sets about hunting the real killer. TJ

Clouds

see Cloud, The

Clouds of May (Mayis Sikintisi)

(1999, Tur, 130 min)
d/p/sc/ph Nuri Bilge Ceylan. *ed* Ayhan Ergürsel, Nuri Bilge Ceylan. *cast* M Emin Ceylan, Muzzaffer Özdemir, Fatma Ceylan, M Emin Toprak, Muhammed Zimbaoglu, Sadik Inescu, Ebru Yapici.

●A film-maker returns to his home village to prepare his next project, in which his elderly parents and young nephew will play their parts. Life goes on around him; specifically, his father Emin is worried by the threat of the state appropriating his patch of woodland. A still-life portrait of family, landscape and the floating artist, this recalls the self-reflexivity of Kiarostami's *Through the Olive Trees*, but it's a more languid and studious work, and less giving. It's beautifully shot, however, with rich colours and detailed compositions, and it's intermittently very engaging. NB

Clown Must Laugh, A

see Pagliacci

Clowns, The (I Clowns)

(1970, It/Fr/WGer, 92 min)
d Federico Fellini. *p* Elio Scardamaglia, Ugo Guerra, Federico Fellini. *sc* Federico Fellini, Bernardino Zapponi. *ph* Dario di Palma. *ed* Ruggero Mastroianni. *ad* Danilo Donati. *m* Nino Rota. *cast* Riccardo Billi, Tino Scotti, Fanfulla, Carlo Rizzo, Freddo Pistoni, Anita Ekberg.

●Fellini's documentary celebration of the dying art of the clown is his best film in years. As overtly personal as his autobiographical *Roma*, it has little of the self-indulgence of that film, mainly because of Fellini's relentless pursuit of his elusive subject. Made for the RAI TV company, it includes much interview material with once-famous clowns now long forgotten; reconstructions of scenes from Fellini's own childhood, attempting to explain his obsessive fascination with the circus; and a final tribute to the clowns themselves, a slapstick funeral staged in a circus ring. The final image in this funeral sequence, with pathetic trumpet music across an empty ring, is memorably touching. DP

Club, The

(1980, Aust, 99 min)
d Bruce Beresford. *p* Matt Carroll. *sc* David Williamson. *ph* Donald McAlpine. *ed* William Anderson. *ad* David Copping. *m* Mike Brady. *cast* Frank Wilson, Harold Hopkins, Jack Thompson, Alan Cassell, Graham Kennedy, John Howard.

●The Australian cinema in noisy rather than nostalgic mood, indulging a series of lusty bawling bouts (interspersed with *Match of the Day* views of Aussie rules football and its supporters) in a caustic look at the power struggles threatening to disrupt a Melbourne club. Based on a play by David Williamson (who scripted *Don's Party* for Beresford), it's all predictable stuff, but vigorously performed. TM

Club, The (Wuting)

(1981, HK, 90 min)
d Kirk Wong. *p* Dennis Chiu. *sc* Tam Tin-nam. *ph* Johnny Koo. *ed* David Woo. *ad* Raymond Lee. *m* Danny Cheung. *cast* Chan Wai-Man, Tsui Siu-Keung, Mabel Kwong, Miyai Haru.

●This first feature by a young Hong Kong director is an ultra-violent Triad thriller about gang warfare in the sleazier back streets of Kowloon. Characters (macho men and exploited women) are as stereotyped as they come, but plus factors include very stylish visuals, a couple of interesting performances, and a considerable sense of humour. RG

Clubbed to Death

(1997, Fr/Port/Neth, 88 min)
d Yolande Zauberman. *p* Odile Gervais. *sc* Yolande Zauberman, Noémie Lvovsky. *ph* Denis Lenoir. *ed* François Gédigier. *pd* Olivier Radot. *cast* Elodie Bouchez, Roschdy Zem, Béatrice Dalle, Richard Courcet, Alex Descas, Gérald Thomassin, Julie Bataille.

●Lola (Bouchez) falls asleep on a bus and wakes up at the end of the line, in the Parisian 'burbs. She wanders into a cavernous techno club – a barrage of sound and strobing lights – where someone slips her a pill. She becomes involved with a French Arab, Emir (Zem), and returns the next day to look for him in this strange, alien, nocturnal world. The film all but dispenses with dialogue: atmosphere is everything in this minimalist foray into exotic youth culture. This may be full of fascinating insights for sheltered over-40s (if they're interested), but the club scene is hardly uncharted territory for the rest of us. There's something deeply old fashioned about what passes for narrative here, and little else to hold the attention – a tab might relieve the tedium. TCh

Club de Femmes

(1936, Fr, 99 min, b/w)
d/p/sc Jacques Deval. ph Jules Kruger. ad Lucien Aguettand. m Marius-François Gaillard. *cast* Danielle Darrieux, Valentine Tessier, Josette Day, Eve Francis, Elise Argal.

●This French farce suggests that *mesdemoiselles* who sleep around are redeemable, cops a peep at one-and-a-half pairs of breasts, and turns up an unmistakeable lesbian character. Set in a chastely run hotel for women, it traces the fortunes of various young residents of burgeoning sexual impulses: representing the dark side of female sexuality are a student lured into prostitution by the devious hotel telephone operator, and a bookish beauty who kills to avenge a crime against her beloved. But the tale of the spirited dancer (Darrieux), who smuggles her fiancé into the hotel and ends up pregnant, overrides the film's more serious implications to arrive at conclusions of Hollywood-style wholesomeness. Playful, energetic, and sustaining a high level of female hysteria, the movie is certainly camp, often riotously funny, and nostalgically enjoyable, but don't expect feminist leanings just because a lesbian's around. EP

Club Extinction

see Dr M

Clue

(1985, US, 87 min)
d Jonathan Lynn. *p* Debra Hill. *sc* Jonathan Lynn. *ph* Victor J Kemper. *ed* David Bretherton, Richard W Haines. *pd* John J Lloyd. *m* John Morris. *cast* Eileen Brennan, Tim Curry, Madeline Kahn, Christopher Lloyd, Michael McKean, Lesley Ann Warren, Martin Mull, Colleen Camp.

● Years before he cracked it with the likes of Joe Pesci and Eddie Murphy, *Yes, Minister* creator Lynn made an uncertain Hollywood debut with this ill-advised screen adaptation of the sleuthing board game Cluedo (Clue in America). New England, 1954 (!), and a certain Mr Boddy is summarily dispatched as his mansion is filled with suspicious guests, each hiding behind a pseudonym (Col Mustard, Prof Plum, etc), each with a motive for perpetrating the dirty deed. Sadly, however, the characters are less credible than their plastic counterparts, the puerile humour is dispiriting, and the plotting pulled this way and that by the conceit of releasing the film in the US with a trio of alternate endings. On Lynn's insistence, British viewers saw just the one – a small mercy. TJ

Clueless

(1995, US, 98 min)
d Amy Heckerling. *p* Scott Rudin, Robert Lawrence. *sc* Amy Heckerling. *ph* Bill Pope. *ed* Debbie Chiate. *pd* Steve Jordan. *m* David Kitay. *cast* Alicia Silverstone, Stacey Dash, Brittany Murphy, Paul Rudd, Donald Faison, Elisa Donovan, Wallace Shawn, Twink Caplan, Dan Hedaya.

● Heckerling still appears to edit her movies by random select, and, despite reference to Jane Austen's *Emma*, her narrative is anorexic; but this satiric portrait of California rich kids has plenty of charm and wit, and a winning central performance from Silverstone. Cher, 15, is a designer mall rat with a world view several sizes narrower than her vanity mirror, but a heart as big as her dad's bank account. During a typically unexacting term at Beverly Hills High, Cher adopts newcomer Tai (Murphy) and teachers her how to be a 'Betty' (a she-babe), falls for a 'Baldwin' (a he-babe), and learns that "tis a far, far better thing, when you do stuff for other people.' There's something downright perverse about the romantic fade-out Heckerling engineers between Cher and her stepbrother, and the philanthropic message is almost as superficial as the rampant materialism which precedes it, but Silverstone makes Cher's insularity appealingly innocent (even in the midst of crisis, she can't resist checking out the latest fashion lines), and an attempted seduction scene is sweetly hopeless. TCh

Cluny Brown

(1946, US, 100 min, b/w)
d/p Ernst Lubitsch. *sc* Samuel Hoffenstein, Elizabeth Reinhardt. *ph* Joseph LaShelle. *ed* Dorothy Spencer. *ad* Lyle R Wheeler, J Russell Spencer. *m* Cyril Mockridge, Emil Newman. *cast* Charles Boyer, Jennifer Jones, Peter Lawford, Reginald Gardiner, Reginald Owen, Richard Haydn.

● Lubitsch's last film and one of his most engaging comedies, with Jones and Boyer surprisingly well-teamed as the plumber's niece (later housemaid) and the Czech refugee who throw English society into a tizzy with their disregard for conventions, while simultaneously allowing Lubitsch to take a few digs at well-meaning liberals. The satire, though taking in snobbery upstairs, downstairs and in the middle classes, doesn't exactly bite, but is given a jolly run around by a cast comprising most of Hollywood's British stalwarts from Sir C Aubrey Smith to Sara Allgood and Una O'Connor. TM

Coal Face

(1935, GB, 11 min, b/w)
d not credited [Alberto Cavalcanti]. *p* John Grierson. *sc/commentary* not credited [Alberto Cavalcanti, Montagu Slater, WH Auden]. *ed* William Coldstream. *m* Benjamin Britten.

● 'O lurcher-loving collier, black as night…' What the lurcher lovers themselves might have made of Auden's madrigal hardly bears thinking about, but the film itself is genuinely adventurous, giving a brusque, matter of fact account of coal mining ('Principal by-products are… largest fields are to be found in…') matched with Britten's harsh 'industrial' music and the romanticism of Auden's verse. Visually it's merely a bunch of library shots strung together, but the very '30s notion of the teacher and the artist complementing each other is still a powerful one. BBa

Coal Miner's Daughter

(1980, US, 124 min)
d Michael Apted. *p* Bernard Schwartz. *sc* Tom Rickman. *ph* Ralf D Bode. *ed* Arthur Schmidt. *pd* John W Corso. *cast* Sissy Spacek, Tommy Lee Jones, Levon Helm, Phyllis Boyens, Beverly D'Angelo, William Sanderson.

● Beautifully acted (with Spacek winning an Oscar) rags-to-riches biopic of Country & Western singer Loretta Lynn, here working her way from the Kentucky coalfields, via the Grand Ol' Opry, to superstardom. For all the modern gloss, what with poverty and nervous breakdowns it's still highly conventional stuff, but lovingly constructed to produce unremarkable but heart-warming entertainment. GA

Coast to Coast

(1980, US, 94 min)
d Joseph Sargent. *p* Steve Tisch, Jon Avnet. *sc* Stanley Weiser. *ph* Mario Tosi. *ed* George Jay Nicholson, Patrick Kennedy. *ad* Hilyard Brown. *m* Charles Bernstein. *cast* Dyan Cannon, Robert Blake, Quinn Redeker, Michael Lerner, Maxine Stuart, Bill Lucking.

● Dire love-on-the-run frolic in which Cannon flees from the asylum where her nasty husband had her locked up, taking care to whack her shrink with a bust of Freud for his troubles. Hitting the road, she hooks up with trucker Blake, who's got his pedal to the metal because he's worried his rig is about to get repossessed. You'll not be remotely surprised as initial antipathy melts in shared adversity, but you may be disappointed that the two leads, who play off one another rather amiably, didn't have the benefit of more sparkling material. TJ

Coast to Coast

(1986, GB, 96 min)
d Sandy Johnson. *p* Graham Benson. *sc* Stan Hey. *ph* Colin Munn. *ed* Ken Pearce. *pd* Christopher Robbilliard. *cast* Lenny Henry, John Shea, Pete Postlethwaite, George Baker, Peter Vaughan, Cherie Lunghi.

● An often very funny blend of road movie, buddy-buddy comedy and thriller parody, Johnson's film is short on visual delights (it was made for TV) but full of fine performances, strong throwaway lines (courtesy Stan Hey), and deft off-the-wall touches. Shea and Henry make for a good double act as the US air force man and the soul-crazy Liverpudlian DJ who find themselves pursued by cops and murderous mobsters as they travel from Merseyside, via the Lake District, to the Essex coast. Lively, sharp and fast, it also features a wondrous Tamla selection on the soundtrack. TJ

Cobb

(1994, US, 128 min)
d Ron Shelton. *p* David Lester. *sc* Ron Shelton. *ph* Russell Boyd. *ed* Paul Seydor. *pd* Armin Ganz, Scott Ritenaur. *m* Elliot Goldenthal. *cast* Tommy Lee Jones, Robert Wuhl, Lolita Davidovich, Ned Bellamy, Lou Myers, Stephen Mendillo, William Utay.

● In the years surrounding WWI, Ty Cobb was baseball's most successful player, but this dark, probing portrait isn't really a sports movie. It focuses on 1960, when the Georgia Peach had gone sour: a bitter, lonely old man intent on fostering his legend even as he knows that death is upon him. Summoning successful sports writer Al Stump (Wuhl) to write his biography, the egomaniacal, cantankerous Cobb proceeds to dictate a hagiography. The reality is that Cobb's a bully, bigot and woman-beater. Shelton's film is about the nature of truth and popular myth, about the single-minded pursuit of glory, and the horrors within. It's also very funny. Jones gives a grandstand performance – this is his Patton, or even perhaps his Macbeth – as the pistol-packin', pill-poppin' Cobb, a monster who daren't look himself in the face, and refuses to apologise. TCh

Cobra, The

(1925, US, 6,895 ft, b/w)
d Joseph Henabery. *p* JD Williams. *sc* Anthony Coldeway. *ph* Harry Fischbeck, Dev Jennings. *ad* William Cameron Menzies. *cast* Rudolph Valentino, Nita Naldi, Casson Ferguson, Gertrude Olmstead, Hector V Sarno, Henry A Barrows.

● A film which understandably disappeared after being laughed off the screen on its release. As an impoverished Italian count who comes to America to pursue his career as an 'indoor sheik', Valentino initially parodies his image with a nice sense of comic timing. But the script then saddles him with pure love, a best friend to hold camp hands with, and noble self-sacrifice. Thereafter the main amusement in a turgid melodrama is watching Valentino and Naldi (*Queen of the Vampires*) slipping into embarrassingly regulation poses as she plays cobra to his mesmerised lion. TM

Cobra (Le Saut de l'Ange)

(1971, Fr/It, 95 min)
d Yves Boisset. *p* Raymond Danon. *sc* Yves Boisset, Richard Winckler. *ph* Jean Boffety. *ed* Albert Jurgenson. *ad* Théo Meurisse. *m* François de Roubaix. *cast* Jean Yanne, Senta Berger, Sterling Hayden, Giancarlo Sbragia, Gordon Mitchell, Raymond Pellegrin.

● Boisset is a usually reliable second-line French director best known for his conspiracy thrillers *Plot* and *Le Sheriff*. This early policier is pretty rudimentary revenge stuff revolving around electoral gang w ar in Marseilles, perked up by a few neat incidentals. Yanne returns from Laotian retirement when his family is wiped out by Sbragia, accompanied by his comic-reading 'commandos', while American friend Hayden plays piggy in the middle. PT

Cobra

(1986, US, 87 min)
d George Pan Cosmatos. *p* Menahem Golan, Yoram Globus. *sc* Sylvester Stallone. *ph* Ric Waite. *ed* Don Zimmerman, James R Symons. *pd* Bill Kenney. *m* Sylvester LeVay. *cast* Sylvester Stallone, Brigitte Nielsen, Reni Santoni, Andrew Robinson, Brian Thompson, John Herzfeld.

● With Stallone as a *Dirty Harry*-style cop, suffice it to say that there is not nearly enough violence. No one is eviscerated. The villains, all mumblers to a man, are not punished by having their tongues cut out. The body count is only somewhere in the high eighties – and most of these are simply gunned down with a deplorable lack of invention. Very little is done by way of eye-gouging, limb-crushing or tooth-extraction. There are only two points of interest. First, the wimpy liberal cop who wants to do everything by the book is played by Robinson, the man who was once the nastiest killer of the '70s, Scorpio in *Dirty Harry*. Second, Sly has good taste in cars: a chopped '49 Mercury lead-sled with Nitrous Oxide injection. CPea

Cobra Verde

(1988, WGer, 111 min)
d Werner Herzog. *p* Lucki Stipetic. *sc* Werner Herzog. *ph* Viktor Ruzicka. *ed* Maximiliane Mainka. *m* Popol Vuh. *cast* Klaus Kinski, King Ampaw, José Lewgoy, Salvatore Basile, Peter Berling, Guillermo Coronel.

● Based on Bruce Chatwin's *The Viceroy of Ouidah*, this features another of Herzog's doomed outcasts in an alien environment. A farmer-turned bandit in early 19th century Brazil, Cobra Verde (Kinski) is exiled to West Africa to gather slaves while fending off the murderous cohorts of the mad king of Dahomey. Here Herzog's taste for spectacular exotica comes to the fore with extended scenes of mass activity: the restoration of a slave-fortress, tribal processions, a 1,000-strong Amazon army in training, mile after mile of a human telegraph line. Though less apocalyptic than usual, the imagery is as lavish as ever, but the film is wrecked by an underwritten narrative. Certainly, Herzog fulfills his aim of portraying Africa as a cruel, highly civilised continent – the clichés are his own rather than those of conventional movie iconography – but the picture of colonialism is woefully one-dimensional. Finally, however, the film's greatest shortcoming is its inability to stir the emotions. GA

Cobweb, The

(1955, US, 124 min)
d Vincente Minnelli. *p* John Houseman. *sc* John Paxton. *ph* George Folsey. *ed* Harold F Kress. *ad* Cedric Gibbons, Preston Ames. *m* Leonard Rosenman. *cast* Richard Widmark, Lauren Bacall, Gloria Grahame, Charles Boyer, Lillian Gish, John Kerr, Oscar Levant, Susan Strasberg.
● One of the best of Minnelli's 50s dramas, set in an up-market psychiatric clinic with Widmark as the head man, Grahame as the unusually sexual wife and mother, Bacall as the unusually maternal 'other woman'. It is this inversion which disrupts the paternal law and order of the clinic and the home: a worried Widmark appears to be losing his place in both, and only when the two women are back in conventional place can sanity be restored. Don't be put off by the crude surface Freudianism: it's fascinating, with fine performances. JCl

Coca Cola Kid, The

(1985, Aust, 98 min)
d Dusan Makavejev. *p* David Roe. *sc* Frank Moorhouse. *ph* Dean Semler. *ed* John Scott. *ad* Graham 'Grace' Walker. *m* William Motzing. *cast* Eric Roberts, Greta Scacchi, Bill Kerr, Max Gillies, Kris McQuade, Chris Haywood.
● One-time proud sex warrior and anarchist liberator of the libido, Makavejev has lost his bottle on *The Coca Cola Kid*. A Coke missionary arrives in Australia with the intention of ousting the local soft drinks king. Aside from the old man's shotgun methods of dissuasion, there are also the distractions of a rapacious Scacchi, a hotel waiter who thinks he's from the CIA, and the Oz fauna. As usual there are some incidental pleasures (among them a 'roo with its arm in a sling, and Scacchi continuing in her mission to spontaneously combust the male population of the planet). Against these, however, is a plot that goes AWOL in the interests of true love, and Roberts, as the kid from Coke, who is well on his way to becoming the world's worst actor. CPea

Cocaine (Mixed Blood)

(1984, Fr, 99 min)
d Paul Morrissey. *p* Antoine Gannage, Steven Fierberg. *sc* Paul Morrissey. *ph* Stefan Zapasnik. *ed* Scott Vickrey. *ad* Stephen McCabe. *cast* Marilia Pera, Richard Ulacia, Angel David, Geraldine Smith, Ulrich Berr, Marcelino Rivera, Linda Kerridge.
● Briefly celebrated, now long forgotten excursion by Morrissey into the dark world of Lower East Side gangland. Brazil vs Puerto Rico is the grudge match here, featuring the usual drug dealers' turf war as the hard-to-care-about bone of contention. Often taken for black comedy, its lurid visuals, ragbag assortment of performance styles, and the succession of ambushes, escapes and showdowns suggest something closer to Victorian melodrama. DO

Cocaine Fiends, The (aka The Pace That Kills)

(1936, US, 68 min, b/w)
d William A O'Connor. *p* Willis Kent. *ph* Jack Greenhalgh. *ed* Holbrook N Todd. *cast* Lois January, Noel Madison, Sheila Manners, Dean Benton, Lois Lindsay, Eddie Phillips.
● A blatant piece of muck-raking made in obscure conditions in the '30s which delivers its nominal anti-drugs theme with comical relish. A rake's progress of drug-induced degeneracy starts promisingly, but then gets rather bogged down in the banalities of the film's outlook, with the cocaine itself increasingly a side issue.

Cockfighter

(1974, US, 83 min)
d Monte Hellman. *p* Roger Corman. *sc* Charles Willeford. *ph* Nestor Almendros. *ed* Lewis Teague. *ad* Charles Hughes, Pat Mann. *m* Michael Franks. *cast* Warren Oates, Richard B Shull, Harry Dean Stanton, Ed Begley Jr, Laurie Bird, Troy Donahue, Warren Finnerty, Millie Perkins, Charles Willeford.
● Charles Willeford's adaptation of his own novel, shot on authentic locations, with Oates as the obsessive trainer of prize fighting cocks who undertakes a vow of silence after the defeat of his best bird. Even bleaker than *Two Lane Blacktop*, what emerges is what Phil Hardy has called 'one of the most explicit studies of repression that the American cinema has produced' (competitiveness as a substitute for sex). Its commercial failure in the States was hardly surprising. Hellman's films, always terminal in their implications, have been edging closer and closer to self-destruction. *Cockfighter* in many ways carries the stamp of a 'last' movie. Indeed, Hellman has directed only one since. CPe

Cockleshell Heroes

(1955, GB, 97 min)
d José Ferrer. *p* Phil C Samuel. *sc* Bryan Forbes, Richard Maibaum. *ph* John Wilcox, Ted Moore. *ed* Alan Osbiston. *ad* John Box. *m* John Addison. *cast* José Ferrer, Trevor Howard, Victor Maddern, Anthony Newley, David Lodge, Peter Arne, Dora Bryan.
● As the Empire blew away on the winds of change, a spate of films celebrating Britain's heroic achievements in WWII attracted huge box-office success. Bond producer Cubby Broccoli proved adept at finding the right formula: pipe-smoking humanitarian Ferrer battles it out with embittered disciplinarian Howard while tough sergeant-major Maddern licks the bunch of good-for-nothing 'volunteers' into a crack fighting force for a glorious Technicolor finale (breaking the blockade of Bordeaux by limpet-mining German battleships). Fortunately there's more. Ferrer directs with a freshness of vision which cuts through the usual coy clichés, and Howard's magnificently bad-tempered performance lifts the film a degree beyond jingoistic flag-waving. RMy

Cockroach, The (Böcek)

(1995, Tur, 91 min)
d Ümit Elçi. *sc* Ümit Elçi, Erhan Bener. *ph* Colin Mounier. *ed* Aytug Aydin. *m* Cem Idiz. *cast* Halil Ergün, Nurseli Idiz, Füsun Demirel, Meltem Cumbal.
● A cod-Freudian drama (from a novel by Erhan Bener) about an Istanbul police chief who dreams back over his life while dying in an ambulance bound for hospital. His pathological hatred of cockroaches seems to be a metaphor for the fascistic imbalance of his mind. His harsh treatment as a young man and the blame that accrued to him for the fiery death of his sister are presented as the motors for his own brutality. (We see him abusing prisoners, but what is the sequence in which he hunts down Leninist revolutionaries meant to be about?) Less clear are his reasons for marrying a slatternly asthmatic young woman who refuses him sex, love and respect. From the evidence here Istanbul seems in a severe state of run-down, unless that's meant to be another expressionistic device. A far from rosy picture of Turkey. Shame about the grating repetitive piano score. WH

Cocktail

(1988, US, 103 min)
d Roger Donaldson. *p* Ted Field, Robert W Cort. *sc* Heywood Gould. *ph* Dean Semler. *ed* Neil Travis, Barbara Dunning. *pd* Mel Bourne. *m* J Peter Robinson. *cast* Tom Cruise, Bryan Brown, Elisabeth Shue, Lisa Banes, Laurence Luckinbill, Kelly Lynch, Gina Gershon.
● If a visitor from Mars needed a crash course in sexism, this would serve. Freshly demobbed, Brian Flanagan (Cruise) takes a Greyhound to NYC, hell-bent on self-improvement. He enlists in business school, but soon concludes that 'notta goddam thing those professors say makes any difference on the streets'. Brian opts instead to imbibe wisdom (and vast quantities of alcohol) at the feet of grizzled bartender Doug (Brown), a would-be guru of the *in vino veritas* school. Soon Bri is the most dazzling barman on the Upper East Side, and finds that women fall for his bottle-juggling technique and 'killer' smile (permanent rictus is nearer the mark). When he finds his true love (Shue) – no make-up, a 'good' girl – she immediately becomes dependent, cries a lot, and becomes pregnant. Conveniently she's also massively rich. The inevitable occurs, and a long happy future of monogamy, money-making and self-righteousness is in the offing. A tale of cock, signifying nothing. RS

Cocoanuts, The

(1929, US, 96 min, b/w)
d Joseph Santley, Robert Florey. *p* Walter Wanger. *sc* Morrie Ryskind. *ph* George Folsey. *ed* Barney Rogan. *songs* Irving Berlin. *cast* The Marx Brothers, Kay Francis, Oscar Shaw, Mary Eaton, Margaret Dumont.
● The Brothers' first feature, for Paramount, adapted from their 1925 Broadway hit written by George S Kaufman, and set in a Florida hotel running wild with jewel thieves, romantic leads, dancing bellhops, a stately matron (Dumont), a conniving manager (Groucho) and assorted riff-raff (Harpo and Chico). It shows its age, what with indistinct sound, fluffed lines, quaint choreography, quainter songs, a stilted supporting cast and positively arthritic direction. But the Brothers' energy and madness is never in question: when the laughs come, they come loud and long. GB

Cocoon

(1985, US, 117 min)
d Ron Howard. *p* Richard D Zanuck, David Brown, Lili Fini Zanuck. *sc* Tom Benedek. *ph* Don Peterman. *ed* Michael Hill, David Hanley. *pd* Jack T Collis. *m* James Horner. *cast* Don Ameche, Wilford Brimley, Hume Cronyn, Brian Dennehy, Jack Gilford, Maureen Stapleton, Jessica Tandy, Gwen Verdon.
● The cocoons of the title were left in the sea off the Florida coast by aliens. However, the pool of the house the aliens rent when they come back to collect them is regularly used by the occupants of an old folks home next door; when the seniors share the water with the cocoons, they find themselves rejuvenated, youngsters again in spirit. Essentially, this is sci-fi with a heart, albeit one made entirely of cheese. Both director and writer sometimes seem unsure whether to pitch the tale as knockabout comedy (Ameche, who won an Oscar for his turn, breakdances) or sentimental fable. It's to the lasting detriment of the movie that Howard, not for the first or last time, opts for the latter. Resistible. WFJ

Cocoon: The Return

(1988, US, 116 min)
d Daniel Petrie. *p* Richard D Zanuck, David Brown, Lili Fini Zanuck. *sc* Stephen McPherson. *ph* Tak Fujimoto. *ed* Mark Warner. *pd* Lawrence G Paull. *m* James Horner. *cast* Don Ameche, Wilford Brimley, Courtney Cox, Hume Cronyn, Jack Gilford, Steve Guttenberg, Maureen Stapleton, Elaine Stritch, Jessica Tandy, Gwen Verdon, Linda Harrison, Brian Dennehy.
● Not a patch on *Cocoon*; what merit this sequel has comes entirely from the superb cast of veterans, with very little help from a script which seems to have been ghosted by Justice Shallow. The story is so badly recapitulated that anyone not familiar with the situation will wonder why some of the cast seem fitter than others. The rejuvenated leavers return to Earth for a visit, find Bernie (Gilford) suicidal in an old folks' home, and fix him up with a merry widow (Stritch). Ben and Mary (Brimley, Stapleton) start to regret their grandson growing up. Art and Bess (Ameche, Verdon) miraculously conceive a child. Joe and Alma (Cronyn, Tandy) straddle what tension there is, since he will die if he stays. Ameche and Cronyn wring the heartstrings during all the emergency ward scenes. BC

Code Inconnu

see Code Unknown

Codename: The Soldier

see Soldier, The

Code of Silence

(1985, US, 101 min)
d Andrew Davis. *p* Raymond Wagner. *sc* Michael Butler, Dennis Shryack, Mike Gray. *ph* Frank Tidy. *ed* Peter Parasheles, Christopher Holmes. *pd* Maher Amed. *m* David Frank. *cast* Chuck Norris, Henry Silva, Bert Remsen, Mike Genovese, Nathan Davis, Molly Hagan, Dennis Farina, John Mahoney.
● Davis' pacy direction, years before *The Fugitive* pushed him up the Hollywood pecking order, makes this a better than usual entry in the glum Norris filmography, getting good value out of the Chicago locations as big Chuck's no-nonsense cop wipes out warring gangs and cleans up the police department while he's at it. Screenwriters Butler and Shryack penned *The Gauntlet* and *Pale Rider* for Clint Eastwood, and it's possible to imagine the latter's monolithic, taciturn heroism drained of all interesting character in Norris' purely functional presence. The problem is that Norris is such a boring performer, it's hardly edifying watching him waste assorted scumbags. TJ

Code Unknown (Code Inconnu)

(2000, Fr, 117 min)
d Michael Haneke. *p* Marin Karmitz, Alain Sarde. *sc* Michael Haneke. *ph* Jürgen Jürges. *ed* Andreas Prochaska, Karin Hartusch, Nadine Muse. *ad* Manuel de Chauvigny. *m* Giba Gonçalves. *cast* Juliette Binoche, Thierry Neuvic, Sepp Bierbichler, Alexandre Hamidi, Ona Lu Yenke, Luminita Gheorghiu, Hélène Diarra, Arsinée Khanjian.
● Where Haneke's earlier *71 Fragments...* traced a web of seemingly unconnected events leading up to a catastrophe, this takes the reverse tack of following the destinies of diverse characters witness to one seemingly inconsequential action – a disaffected youth tossing a paper wrapper into the lap of a Romanian woman begging on the Boulevard St Germain. It's a rewarding strategy, delving into the lives of an actress, her war-photographer lover, his brother and father, an African music teacher and his family, and the beggar and her compatriots, to produce a multi-perspective portrait of Western Europe as a society predicated on lies, inequality and communication breakdown. Nothing hugely original in that conclusion, perhaps, but the method is both lucid and dramatically compelling. Scenes here like Binoche being terrorised on the Métro while other passengers pretend not to notice are spinechillingly authentic. Moreover, despite the film's Bressonian rigours, its emotional force should finally give the lie to Haneke's reputation as a coldly academic film-maker. GA

Coeur qui bat, Un (Your Beating Heart)

(1991, Fr, 99 min)
d François Dupeyron. *p* René Cleitman. *sc* François Dupeyron. *ph* Yves Angelo. *ed* Françoise Collin. *ad* Carlos Conti. *m* Jean-Pierre Drouet. *cast* Dominique Faysse, Thierry Fortineau, Jean-Marie Winling, Steve Kalfa, Daniel Laloux, Christophe Pichon, Dominique Abel, Roland Amstutz.
● Eyes meet across a crowded Paris metro carriage. She gets out. Percussion builds. He follows her into a bar. 'Do you know a hotel around here?' They leave together. At least this starts with a teasing come-on, but it shares the problem faced by its central couple, Mado (Faysse) and Yves (Fortineau): how to recapture the thrill of that run-up to hot sex with a nameless stranger? Though she's not particularly interested after the deed is done, he gives her his phone number. She's married with a teenage son; husband Jean keeps a little antiques business ticking over, while she earns her crust acting in rather-too-pretentious radio plays. Perhaps that lightning strike of excitement is missing from her life, after all. It's a classic set-up. However, writer/director Dupeyron's flabby, uninspired treatment lets it go for almost nothing. As the couple trawl the Pigalle hotels and agonise over their uncertain future, one hopes for a shard of insight, another angle on the old eternal threesome that would lift the film from its torpor. In vain. TJ

Coeur en hiver, Un (A Heart in Winter)

(1991, Fr, 104 min)
d Claude Sautet. *p* Jean-Louis Livi, Philippe Carcassonne. *sc* Claude Sautet, Jérôme Tonnerre, Jacques Fieschi. *ph* Yves Angelo. *ed* Jacqueline Thiédot. *ad* Christian Marti. *m* Philippe Sarde. *cast* Daniel Auteuil, Emmanuelle Béart, André Dussollier, Elisabeth Bourgine, Brigitte Catillon, Maurice Garrel, Myriam Boyer, Jean-Luc Bideau.
● On the surface, an unassuming, low-key study of a *ménage à trois* that never really takes off physically; dig deeper, however, and it's filled with dark, disturbing emotions and unsettling power-games. Stéphane (Auteuil) and Maxime (Dussollier) are old friends and partners in a violin-making business; Camille (Béart) is a concert violinist and Maxime's lover, who comes increasingly to dominate the taciturn Stéphane's thoughts. As time passes, while she seems to respond to his apparent interest in her, he remains reticent: out of shyness, loyalty to Maxime, or something more perverse? What distinguishes the film is that Sautet and his excellent trio of leads manage to convey complex emotional nuances without resorting to explicit dialogue, plot contrivance, or hackneyed visual metaphor. Everything is underplayed, made manifest through subtle glances, brief but pregnant silences, the rhythms of the editing, the moody qualities of the lighting, and the occasional bursts of Ravel played by Camille. There's not an ounce of fat on this deceptively quiet movie, which at times achieves a real sense of pain and confusion. GA

Coffy

(1973, US, 91 min)
d Jack Hill. *p* Robert A Papazian. *sc* Jack Hill. *ph* Paul Lohmann. *ed* Charles McClelland. *ad* Perry Ferguson. *m* Roy Ayers. *cast* Pam Grier, Booker Bradshaw, Robert DoQui, William Elliott, Allan Arbus, Sid Haig.
● Superficially just another black exploitation film (one of the first to feature a woman in a strong central role), *Coffy* is distinguished by its unremitting moral blackness. With a yellow press feel to the script and a welcome sexual frankness, the world Coffy inhabits is revealed as one where social, sexual and political exploitation are simply the norms. What makes the film is essentially the character of Coffy as played by Pam Grier with increasing alienation: a nurse out to get the men who are responsible for her little sister's addiction, she makes a conscious decision to manipulate the sexual situations which the men around her force her to engage in. It is a performance that defies and subverts the genre. VG

Cohen and Tate

(1988, US, 86 min)
d Eric Red. *p* Anthony Rufus-Isaacs, Jeff Young. *sc* Eric Red. *ph* Victor J Kemper. *ed* Edward Abroms. *pd* David M Haber. *m* Bill Conti. *cast* Roy Scheider, Adam Baldwin, Harley Cross, Cooper Huckabee, Suzanne Savoy.
● Eric Red, scriptwriter of *The Hitcher*, turns his hand to writing and directing for this suspenseful low-budget thriller. Both films revolve around the theme of innocent captured by raving sadist. Travis (Cross) is a nine-year-old boy who has witnessed an underworld killing. Cohen (Scheider) and Tate (Baldwin) are professional killers who must kidnap the boy and transport him from Oklahoma to their bosses in Houston. The nightmarish journey takes place at night, with the jaded taciturn Cohen increasingly angered by the lunatic ramblings of his violent sidekick. Added to this is their young hostage, who sets the men up against each other, and concocts various escape plans. Red does wonders with a simple budget and scenario; the sparsity of props and dialogue enhances the often brutal tension, while balance is struck with hefty doses of black humour. Cohen wears a hearing aid and dreams of retirement, while Tate chews matchsticks and 'has shit for brains': unlikely villains made credible by the context and Scheider's low-key performance. CM

Coilin & Platonida

(1976, GB, 86 min)
d/p/sc James Scott. *cast* Marion Joyce, Seán Bán Breatnach, Katrina Joyce, Bairbre Bolustrom, Bairbre Mac Donncha.
● A transposition of Nikolai Leskov's folk-tale to an Irish setting (refilmed on 16 mm from the original on Super-8), broken up into elusive, ambiguous fragments and using silent movie-type intertitles to convey the dialogue. The result draws a parallel between the act of making a film and the act of picking up and passing on an existing story. Its conceptual challenges are augmented by a harsh, gloomy poetry, crystallised in the Gaelic lament that recurs on the soundtrack. TR

Cold Comfort

(1989, Can, 88 min)
d Vic Sarin. *p* Illana Frank, Ray Sager. *sc* Richard Beattie, Elliot L Sims. *ph* Vic Sarin. *ed* Nick Rotundo. *ad* Jo-Ann Chorney. *m* Jeff Dana. *cast* Maury Chaykin, Margaret Langrick, Paul Gross.
● A disturbed father rescues a businessman (Gross) from a blizzard, then takes him home as a birthday present for his nubile daughter. Apparently based on a cult fringe theatre piece, it's a disquietingly strange offering, powered along by big Maury Chakin's gradually unravelling performance as the wacko paterfamilias. Former cinematographer Sarin sustains the oddball tension; but of interest chiefly to connoisseurs of the bizarre. TJ

Cold Comfort Farm

(1995, GB, 103 min)
d John Schlesinger. *p* Alison Gilby. *sc* Malcolm Bradbury. *ph* Chris Seager. *ed* Mark Day. *pd* Malcolm Thornton. *m* Robert Lockhart. *cast* Kate Beckinsale, Eileen Atkins, Ian McKellen, Sheila Burrell, Rufus Sewell, Joanna Lumley, Freddie Jones, Stephen Fry, Miriam Margolyes.
● England in the '20s. Orphaned at the age of 19, middle-class Flora Poste determines to live off her relatives, rather than do anything so uncivilised as work. The only kin that remotely fit the bill are her distant cousins, the Starkadders, who work a decaying farm in Howling, Sussex, amid sundry yokels seemingly inhabiting another, Hardy-esque era. Made for the BBC, this woeful adaptation of Stella Gibbons' pastoral parody had success with American cinema audiences, who took it, perhaps, as just another British costume drama, rather than a comedy. Mind you, given Malcolm Bradbury's script and John Schlesinger's direction, which between them coarsen, soften and simply lose much of Gibbons' extraordinarily sophisticated, wonderfully funny humour, that's not surprising. The perfromances don't help much either, though that's less the fault of the very broad acting, than of the all-round starry miscasting (Lumley as Mrs Smiling, Fry as Mybug) – Kate Beckinsale in particular is far too sensible as the determined heroine. GA

Cold Dog Soup

(1989, US, 88 min)
d Alan Metter. *p* Richard Gilbert Abramson, Bill McEuen, Thomas Pope. *sc* Thomas Pope. *ph* Frederick Elmes. *ed* Kaja Fehr. *pd* David L Snyder. *m* Michael Kamen, Mark Snow. *cast* Randy Quaid, Frank Whaley, Christine Harnos, Sheree North, Nancy Kwan, Pierre Epstein.
● A lusty young girl (Harnos) promises a wimpy boy (Whaley) that she will be his 'pressure cooker' if he agrees to bury her mother's recently deceased dog in the middle of the night. But his efforts are thwarted by a psychotic cabbie (Quaid), who insists that they sell the dog, and drags the couple on a tour of local nightspots in search of customers. What follows is the cinematic equivalent of water torture, a throbbing migraine of a movie in which our heroes encounter a catalogue of racial stereotypes, all wanting to know 'What's in the bag?' Chinese restaurateur, Jewish furrier, gang of trigger-happy brothers, voodoo coven of frenzied black zombies.. no stone is left unturned by Thomas Pope's horribly repetitive script, or by Alan Metter in his drivelling attempt to create a surreal comic nightmare. Kill yourself rather than endure it. MK

Cold Eye, The

(1980, US, 90 min, b/w)
d/p Babette Mangolte. *sc* James Barth. *ph* Babette Mangolte. *ad* Power Boothe. *cast* Kim Ginsberg, Patricia Caire, Paula Court, Ghislaine Caire, George Deem.
● The New York art world as seen through the 'cold eye' of another of Mangolte's knowing heroines, a thoroughly modern *Manhattan Maisie* whose vision and experiences we're again invited to share. But the distance implied by the choice of this fictional protagonist, the strangeness of having her friends and acquaintances converse direct-to-camera, the opening titles ironically appraising each in turn, all promise a critical perspective that somehow isn't achieved. James Barth's flaccid script has a lot to answer for. One's heart sinks as the voice-over mournfully intones, 'Why am I so alienated?', and after a long ninety minutes of narrative devoted to assorted bores minutely scrutinising their own sensibilities, one feels that it wasn't nearly ironic enough, and wonders whether this is where so-called *avant-garde* cinema really ought to be. SJo

Cold Feet

(1989, US, 94 min)
d Robert Dornhelm. *p* Cassian Elwes. *sc* Jim Harrison, Thomas McGuane. *ph* Brian Duggan. *pd* Bernt Capra. *m* Tom Bahler. *cast* Keith Carradine, Sally Kirkland, Tom Waits, Bill Pullman, Rip Torn, Kathleen York, Macon McCalman, Vincent Schiavelli.
● Thomas McGuane fans are in for a treat with this typically off-the-wall tale of obsessives, oddballs and psychos, set in the New West. Reluctant to marry voracious Maureen (Kirkland) and keen to settle down with his folks in Dead Rock,

Montana, Monte (Carradine) suddenly abandons partner-in-crime Kenny (Waits), a mass-murderer and would-be executive with whom he has smuggled a stallion, its gut full of emeralds, over the Mexican border. The first half, with Maureen and Kenny joining up to hunt down Monte, plays deliciously anarchic variations on road movie clichés; while the second (Sheriff Rip Torn gets suspicious of the three strangers in town) effectively parodies the small town Western. As written by McGuane and Jim Harrison, characters, situations and dialogue are colourfully eccentric *and* strangely plausible: the madness and mayhem are mere matters of detail, while the overview of contemporary outlaw life is surprisingly cogent. That the film is less messy than earlier McGuane adaptations is due partly to the uniformly engaging OTT acting, partly to Dornhelm's firm but light control of the proceedings. Utterly crazed, utterly charming. GA

Cold Fever

(1994, Ice/Ger/Den/US, 107 min)
d Fridrik Thór Fridriksson. *p* Jim Stark. *sc* Jim Stark, Fridrik Thór Fridriksson. *ph* Ari R Kristinsson. *ed* Steingrímur Karlsson. *pd* Arni Poll Johansson. *m* Hilmar Örn Hilmarsson. *cast* Masatoshi Nagase, Gisli Halldórsson, Fisher Stevens, Lili Taylor, Seijun Suzuki, Laura Hughes.

● This Icelandic odyssey reveals Japanese star Nagase (who first came to notice in the West in Jim Jarmusch's *Mystery Train*) to be a screen actor of deceptive skill and enterprise. Here he's stoicism itself, and the core of the picture, as a Tokyo fish-company salaryman who follows the advice of his grandfather (Suzuki) and travels to Iceland to perform authentic funeral rites for his geologist parents, who died there more than a decade ago. He meets all sorts en route – including a kindly local (Halldórsson, most sympathetic) and a bickering American couple (Stevens and Taylor). But in the end, this is a quirky, touching road movie that actually goes somewhere; its culmination is a striking spiritual affirmation and personal epiphany at journey's end. A one-off that lodges in the memory. TJ

Cold Heaven

(1992, US, 105 min.)
d Nicolas Roeg. *p* Allan Scott, Jonathan D Krane. *sc* Allan Scott. *ph* Francis Kenny. *ed* Tony Lawson. *ad* Steven Legler. *m* Stanley Myers. *cast* Theresa Russell, Mark Harmon, James Russo, Talia Shire, Will Patton, Richard Bradford.

● Roeg's adaptation of Brian Moore's novel fuses deeply felt emotions and religious ideas into a gripping metaphysical thriller that is both moving and intellectually challenging. On holiday in South America, Russell tries to tell her husband (Harmon) about her infidelity with Russo; but before she can do so, he is hit by a boat while swimming and declared dead. When Harmon's body subsequently disappears, avowed atheist Russell is plunged into a maelstrom of guilt, self-doubt and confusion. Sadly, for all its technical brilliance and narrative assurance, the film's climactic scenes require an act of faith that no film-maker – Christian, agnostic or atheist – has any right to ask. NF

Colditz Story, The

(1954, GB, 97 min, b/w)
d Guy Hamilton. *p* Ivan Foxwell. *sc* Guy Hamilton, Ivan Foxwell, PR Reid. *ph* Gordon Dines. *ed* Peter Mayhew. *ad* Alex Vetchinsky. *m* Francis Chagrin. *cast* John Mills, Eric Portman, Christopher Rhodes, Lionel Jeffries, Bryan Forbes, Ian Carmichael, Richard Wattis, Frederick Valk.

● The temptation to label this escapist entertainment is just too great. Actually, it's a prosaically inspirational docu-drama on PoW heroism in the notorious World War II fortress, which unambitiously substitutes an obliquely nationalistic self-portrait for the critical resonances of an ostensibly similar film like *La Grande Illusion*. PT

Cold Lands

see Terres Froides, Les

Cold Light of Day, The

(1989, GB, 81 min)
d Fhiona Louise. *p* Richard Bird. *sc* Fhiona Louise. *cast* Bob Flag, Martin Byrne Quinn, Geoffrey Greenhill, Lol Coxhill.

● A very lightly disguised drama-doc on Cranley Gardens serial killer Denis Nielsen (here named Jordan March), who disposed of at least 13 young loners and losers, presumably based on Brian Masters' fine account in his book *Killing for Company*. March (Flag) looks like Roy Orbison wearing a Black-and-White Minstrels wig; the film has the lighting and look of an Andy Warhol home movie – heads cut off, lots of static shots of men on sofas – and a soundtrack composed of deep breathing, the pounding of a demolition ball, and church bells. Little light is thrown by March in the police interrogations on the reasons for his actions ('I didn't mean to. It just happened') or by the film itself. We see March as a boy, presumably traumatised by witnessing the death of his grandfather. Mostly we see strangulations, heads being boiled, viscera being scooped, hands being hacked. Risibility vies with banality; result, objectionability. WH

Cold Nights (Soguk Geceler)

(1995, Tur, 88 min)
d/sc Kadir Sözen. *ph* Ertunc Senkay. *m* Mazlum Cimen. *cast* Menderes Samancilar, Rahim Çakmak, Volkan Pinardag, Levent Elmas, Ferdi Çetinkaya, Engin Inal.

● This gritty tale of child labour in contemporary Turkey, slight but reasonably engaging, follows three junior folk musicians from gig to gig, sleeping indoors or out according to the disposition of their manager Mahmud, who treats them with a combination of concern, cruelty and chicanery. The future looks promising when they incorporate an older blind boy with an ear-catching voice: they tour, and the boys develop plans of their own, but the boss has his own livelihood in mind. If the film has little time for Mahmud, the director shows an unsensational feel for the plight of children forced into employment and adulthood. More perplexing are occasional bizarre nightmare interludes: not only opaque, in visibility and meaning, but also (interrupting the low-key realism) lapsing into hot-blooded melodrama. NB

Cold Sweat (De la Part des Copains)

(1970, Fr/It, 94 min)
d Terence Young. *p* Robert Dorfmann. *sc* Shimon Wincelberg, Albert Simonin. *ph* Jean Rabier. *ed* John Dwyre. *ad* Tony Roman. *m* Michel Magne. *cast* Charles Bronson, Liv Ullmann, James Mason, Michel Constantin, Jill Ireland, Jean Topart.

● Uneasy English language version of a turgid continental thriller. Nominally based on Richard Matheson's very competent early novel *Ride the Nightmare*, which is butchered to yield the usual drearily violent routine about vengeance between crooks. TM

Cold Tracks (Kalde Spor)

(Nor, 1962, 97 min, b/w)
d Arne Skouen. *p* Odd Rohde. *sc* Arne Skouen, Johan Borgen. *ph* Ragnar Sørensen. *ed* Bjorn Breigutu. *ad* HC Hansen. *m* Gunnar Sønstevold. *cast.* Toralv Maurstad, Henny Moan, Alf Malland, Ragnhild Hald, Sverre Holm, Ehil Lorek, Lasse Nœsse, Siv Skjønberg.

● Guilt and sexual jealousy are the main dynamics behind Skouen's gloomy and intense tale about Oddmund, a former Resistance leader who caused the death of 12 refugees during the war. As we learn in flashback, he delayed their escape while he waited for his lover to arrive. By the time she arrived, the weather had worsened. Years later, Oddmund returns to the scene of his crime and comes face to face with his lover and her partner. The location footage is extraordinary. In the height of winter, Skouen and his cameraman spent a month up in the mountains, living in an abandoned hotel, in order to shoot the vicious blizzard sequences which fill the movie.) But the storms are mild by comparison with the recriminations between the guilty man and his former sweetheart. GM

Cold Turkey

(1970, US, 102 min)
d/p/sc Norman Lear. *ph* Charles F Wheeler. *ed* John C Horger. *ad* Arch Bacon. *m* Randy Newman. *cast* Dick Van Dyke, Pippa Scott, Tom Poston, Edward Everett Horton, Bob Newhart, Vincent Gardenia.

● Misbegotten satire of middle American attitudes in which an entire town, coerced by its reverend minister (Van Dyke), gives up smoking to win a $25 million bonanza. Irritation mounts as tiresome running gags run the symptoms of nicotine withdrawal into the ground . TM

Cold Water

see Eau Froide, L'

Collateral Damage

(2001, US, 109 min)
d Andrew Davis. *p* Steven Reuther, David Foster. *sc* David Griffiths, Peter Griffiths. *ph* Adam Greenberg. *ed* Dennis Virkler, Dov Hoenig. *pd* Philip Rosenberg. *m* Graeme Revell. *cast* Arnold Schwarzenegger, Elias Koteas, Francesca Neri, Cliff Curtis, Miguel Sandoval, Harry Lennix, John Leguizamo, John Turturro, Michael Milhoan, Lindsay Frost, Raymond Cruz.

● Schwarzenegger's recidivist grunt-flick returns him to Amazonian *Commando* territory, but with fewer firearms and a greater predilection for taking himself seriously. As LA firefighter and contented family man Gordy Brewer, he's an unassumingly heroic Joe, until Colombian terrorist El Lobo (Curtis) parks a bomb beside his wife and child and leaves him a brooding widower. Finding no redress from the US authorities, he plunges deep into the Colombian jungle to administer some damage of his own. The film's less knee-jerk than it could have been. Brewer may think he's stony set on revenge, but an encounter with a wandering mother (Neri) and her son in the danger zone give pause for thought. That said, it's often daft, whether unveiling the fireman's instinctive bomb-improvising skills, or showing a liberation leader's penchant for shoving snakes down flunkies' throats. Yet a populist American movie that acknowledges a troubled world beyond US borders must be worth flagging, even though the roles and responsibilities of Colombia's guerillas, paramilitaries, army and US 'advisers', and the hierarchy of drugs and politics in its civil war, are all firmly fudged. NB

Collectionneuse, La (The Collector)

(1966, Fr, 90 min)
d Eric Rohmer. *p* Georges de Beauregard, Barbet Schroeder. *sc* Eric Rohmer. *ph* Nestor Almendros. *ed* Jacqueline Raynal. *m* Blossom Toes, Giorgio Gomelsky. *cast* Haydée Politoff, Patrick Bauchau, Daniel Pommereulle, Seymour Hertzberg [Eugene Archer], Mijanou Bardot, Donald Cammell.

● The third of Rohmer's six moral tales, and the first of his films to achieve wide recognition. The collector of the title is a delectable nymphet, footloose in St Tropez, who makes a principle of sleeping with a different man every night until two friends, declining to become specimens, decide to take her moral well-being in hand. In the 18th century game which Rohmer transposes to a contemporary setting, this pair can be seen as intellect trying to dominate instinct, but only succeeding in rousing unwanted passions. Wryly and delightfully witty. TM

Collector, The

(1965, US/GB, 120 min)
d William Wyler. *p* Jud Kinberg, John Kohn. *sc* Stanley Mann, John Kohn. *ph* Robert Surtees, Robert Krasker. *ed* Robert Swink, David Hawkins. *ad* John Stoll. *m* Maurice Jarre. *cast* Terence Stamp, Samantha Eggar, Mona Washbourne, Maurice Dallimore, Kenneth More.

● Wyler's adaptation of John Fowles' excruciatingly cunning first novel maintains a velvet-gloved grip throughout. A psychopathically repressed lepidopterist uses his football pool winnings to abduct a vibrant young art student and pin her down at all costs. Fowles extended the desperate captive-captor relationship into a multi-faceted metaphor, probing into everything from primal sexual politics and the class war to the responsibility of the artist and the dead soul of '60s England.

Collector, The

see Collectionneuse, La

College

(1927, US, 6 reels, b/w)
d James W Horne. *p* Joseph M Schenck. *sc* Carl Harbaugh, Bryan Foy. *ph* Dev Jennings, Bert

Haines. *ed* JS Kell. *cast* Buster Keaton, Anne Cornwall, Harold Goodwin, Snitz Edwards, Florence Turner, Grant Withers.

●Minor Keaton but major almost any other comedian, and notably better than Harold Lloyd's *The Freshman*, whose plot it borrows, with bookworm Buster trying to prove himself a jock to win the girl. There is a marvellous sequence in which he apes – perfectly but disastrously – the tricks of a veteran soda-jerk; an even better one in which he attempts a decathlon of sporting events, but knocks down every single hurdle with metronomic precision, is thrown by the hammer instead of the other way round, etc. Rarely was Keaton's grace and athletic skill demonstrated so clearly, even if he (understandably) had to get a double to perform the great pole vault through a window to rescue the heroine from assault by her jock admirer. TM

Colobane Express

(1999, Fr/Sen, 52 min)
d Khady Sylla. *p* Claude Gilaizeau. *sc* Khady Sylla. *ph* Medaune D'Diaye. *ed* Cécile Fernandez.

●'The Express Bus is like a rainbow, a mad horse on the highway.' This docu-drama provides a glimpse of Dakar through a journey on one of the many buses which provide the city's only public transport. The Express is a microcosm of Senegalese life, from the market women ranting about their feckless husbands to the wealthy businessman unable to pay his fare. The passengers are frustrated and irritated by late buses, short-changing and even a flirtatious conductor, but such episodes are interspersed with impromptu song and strangers sharing food, cigarettes and boundless advice. JFu

Colonel Chabert, Le

(1943, Fr, 102 min, b/w)
d René Le Hénaff. *sc* Pierre Benoit, Maurice Griffe. *ph* Robert Lefebvre. *ed* Marguerite Renoir. *ad* Jacques Colombier. *m* Louis Beydts. *cast* Raimu, Marie Bell, Aimé Clairond, Jacques Baumer.

●Resurfacing in the wake of the Depardieu rendering, this turns out to be a prime example of how the same story can be construed differently, according to time and circumstance. In 1994, Balzac's tale seemed ideologically unexceptionable, with a faded representative of France's military glory denouncing the violence exercised in the name of *la patrie*, and finally withdrawing from a world that has defeated him, to live out a life of quiet resignation. Fifty years before, however, this must have seemed tailor-made for the occupying Nazis; even the flashbacks to the battle of Eylau would have found favour, since that showed a victory over the Russians. Only the film's status as a faithful adaptation of a literary classic mitigates the collaborationist charge. Less urgently, it's fascinating to compare the two Chaberts – Depardieu crashing around like a baffled bull, Raimu all icy disdain and calculated glimpses of pathos. BBa

Colonel Chabert, Le

(1994, Fr, 111 min)
d Yves Angelo. *p* Jean-Louis Livi. *sc* Jean Cosmos, Jean-Louis Livi, Yves Angelo. *ph* Bernard Lutic. *ed* Thierry Derocles. *ad* Bernard Vezat. *cast* Gérard Depardieu, Fanny Ardant, Fabrice Luchini, André Dussollier, Daniel Prevost, Olivier Saladin, Maxime Leroux.

●Cinematographer Yves Angelo marks an auspicious directorial debut with this thoughtful, strongly cast adaptation of a tall tale by Balzac. Depardieu plays a man who's lost everything and left to wonder what life still has to offer: a dishevelled wreck, he wanders into the offices of lawyer Derville (Luchini) to unfold the incredible story of how he was left for dead in the Napoleonic campaigns; how he wandered across Europe for ten years before returning home; how his 'widow' (Ardant) is now a countess after her remarriage to Count Ferraud (Dussollier) – leaving Chabert no option but to reclaim his name and property through the processes of the law. Crackpot or victim of capricious fate? Conniving charlatan or visionary man of principle? It's to Depardieu's immense credit that his grandiloquent Chabert may be all, or any, of these things. Well worth investigating. TJ

Colonel Redl (Redl Ezredes)

(1984, Hun/WGer/Aus, 149 min)
d István Szabó. *p* Manfred Durniok. *sc* Péter Dobai, István Szabó. *ph* Lajos Koltai. *ed* Zsuzsa Csakany. *ad* József Romvari. *m* Zdenkó Tamassy. *cast* Klaus Maria Brandauer, Hans-Christian Blech, Armin Müller-Stahl, Gudrun Landgrebe, Jan Niklas.

●Redl is a man in an iron mask. At the expense of his poverty-stricken family, his Jewishness, homosexuality and friends, he makes a dramatic rise through the ranks of the feuding army of the crumbling Hapsburg Empire, only to discover, under the dyspeptic tutelage of the Archduke, that he will always be a suspicious, disposable intruder into the upper classes. Brandauer's towering performance minutely marks the gradual disintegration of Redl's mask and his final exposure at the point of death. Szabó's film is visually magnificent, shot with a crisp clarity which never succumbs to romantic nostalgia. The suicide of the real-life Redl was the subject of John Osborne's notorious *A Patriot for Me*. But where Osborne revelled in the decadence and debauchery, Szabó gives an extraordinary, chilling, complex account of a man's betrayal of himself. JE

Colorado Territory

(1949, US, 94 min, b/w)
d Raoul Walsh. p Anthony Veiller. *sc* John Twist, Edmund H North. *ph* Sid Hickox. *ed* Owen Marks. *ad* Ted Smith. *m* David Buttolph. *cast* Joel McCrea, Virginia Mayo, Dorothy Malone, Henry Hull, John Archer, Frank Puglia.

●A classic Western, this bleak remake of Walsh's own *High Sierra* substitutes McCrea's weary desperation for Bogart's laconic interpretation of the bandit who wants to go straight but signs up for 'just one more job'. Cinematographer Sid Hickox piles on the black to give it the look of a film *noir*, and writer John Twist creates a fitting atmosphere of doom around McCrea and Mayo, but it is Walsh's direction which brings this darkly romantic Western to life. The *bravura* treatment of landscape is particularly impressive, especially in the final sequence where his ant-sized humans meet their malevolent destiny amid barren mountains. PH

Color Me Blood Red

(1964, US, 74 min)
d Herschell Gordon Lewis. *p* David F Friedman. *sc/ph* Herschel Gordon Lewis. *ed* Robert Sinise. *cast* Don Joseph, Candi Conder, Scott H Hall, Elyn Warner, Patricia Lee.

●The first film to reach Britain made by the notorious Lewis, who shocked the US drive-in audiences of the '60s with some of the goriest films ever made, notably *Blood Feast* and *2000 Maniacs*. If this one is anything to go by, Lewis' films make *Friday the 13th*, etc, look like they were directed by Orson Welles. The narrative – about an artist who paints with human blood – is so token that it verges on abstraction, the acting is unspeakable, even the sound-track sometimes disappears. Set as it is in no kind of context, the mindless, sadistic gore seems all the more depressing, and the film itself becomes unwatchable. DP

Color of Honor, The

(1987, US, 101 min, b/w & col)
d/p/sc Loni Ding. *ph* Tomas Tucker, Michael Chin. *ed* Loni Ding. *pd* James Hamano. *m* Jim McKee, Andy Newell.

●After Pearl Harbor, several hundred thousand Japanese-Americans were incarcerated in concentration camps. Later, young men drafted from these same camps played a key role in US military intelligence and in battle, while their families continued to be imprisoned back home and anti-Jap propaganda raged. Through extensive interviews with victims of the internment policy and war veterans, this thorough and compelling film highlights a previously undocumented injustice. EP

Color of Money, The

(1986, US, 119 min)
d Martin Scorsese. *p* Irving Axelrad, Barbara De Fina. *sc* Richard Price. *ph* Michael Ballhaus. *ed* Thelma Schoonmaker. *pd* Boris Leven. *m* Robbie Robertson. *cast* Paul Newman, Tom Cruise, Mary Elizabeth Mastrantonio, Helen Shaver, John Turturro, Bill Cobbs.

●25 years on, Fast Eddie Felson (Newman, repeating his role in *The Hustler*) is a part-time liquor salesman who keeps his interest in pool and hustling alive by staking players of promise. Enter Vince (Cruise), whose talents Eddie persuasively harnesses to his own experience *en route* to a nine-ball tournament in Atlantic City. Vince is likeable but arrogant, skilful but naïve, and what's more he's accompanied by a precocious girl-friend (Mastrantonio) who spreads her time between flirting with Eddie and massaging young Vince's cue (*Babushka* or otherwise). Anyone looking for a repeat of the immortal *The Hustler* will not only be disappointed but downright stupid: *The Color of Money* is a film for the '80s with many of that decade's strongest preoccupations. The mixture of mutual need and mistrust in the relationship between Vince and Eddie is only one of the motors in a film that sees Scorsese's direction at its most downmarket and upbeat – never have pool tables, balls and cues looked so rich and strange – and has one of the most protean and compelling music soundtracks (Clapton, Charlie Parker, Warren Zevon, Bo Diddley) in ages. As Eddie tells Vince, 'Pool excellence is not about excellent pool'; and in a scene in which Newman recoils from the thought that he is a Frankenstein, trying to recreate his own youth in the person of another, the whole meaning of the hustle, the game of life, becomes spectacularly clear. SGr

Color of Night

(1994, US, 123 min)
d Richard Rush. *p* David Matalon, Buzz Feitshans. *sc* Matthew Chapman, Billy Ray. *ph* Dietrich Lohmann. *ed* Jack Hofstra. *pd* James L L Schoppe. *m* Dominic Frontiere. *cast* Bruce Willis, Jane March, Ruben Blades, Lesley Ann Warren, Scott Bakula, Lance Henriksen, Brad Dourif, Kevin J O'Connor, Jeff Corey.

●This – another of Willis's crimes against celluloid – is a special kind of bad. Connoisseurs of crud, however, will treasure its particular brand of klutzy chemistry. It would be unkind to give away too much of the delirious sequence of events that pass for a plot. Suffice to say that it involves hangdog Willis as a shrink understandably troubled by his patients' habit of jumping out the window during sessions; March as a so-called 'struggling actress' with whom Bruce becomes entangled; sundry scenes of murder, nymphomania, schizophrenia, etc; and, most enjoyably, the likes of Henriksen, Dourif and Warren as game members at a group therapy session, presumably intended for those unfortunates who can't spot a duff script to save their lives. TJ

Color Purple, The

(1985, US, 154 min)
d Steven Spielberg. *p* Steven Spielberg, Kathleen Kennedy, Frank Marshall, Quincy Jones. *sc* Menno Meyjes. *ph* Allen Daviau. *ed* Michael Kahn. *pd* J Michael Riva. *m* Quincy Jones. *cast* Danny Glover, Whoopi Goldberg, Margaret Avery, Oprah Winfrey, Willard Pugh, Akosua Busia, Rae Dawn Chong.

●The adaptation of Alice Walker's Pulitzer Prize-winning novel, about growing up 'poor, female, ugly and black' in the Deep South, by a Middle American movie brat not hitherto noted for his interest in any of the above, could be cynically seen as a blatant (and botched) bid for Oscars. And it's easy – but unfair – to stamp on the Spielberg version of Celie's triumphant pursuit of happiness and self-respect. Example: Walker's clear, lyrical patois has been filmed with, well, purple pomposity, a battering ram of flashy editing and tearful emotion (the brutish husband played by Glover, whom Walker finally allows his own small epiphany, gets especially short shrift as yet another of the big, bad authority figures who stalk Spielberg's world). Nor is it altogether surprising that Spielberg treads delicately round the story's more radical elements, like Celie's lesbian love for free-spirited blues singer Shug (Avery) or the political insights of her sister's African experience. And yet… due in no small measure to a superb cast spearheaded by Whoopi Goldberg, this is a powerful and honourable attempt to wrest an unusual book into the populist Hollywood mainstream. SJo

Colors

(1988, US, 121 min)
d Dennis Hopper. *p* Robert H Solo. *sc* Michael Schiffer. *ph* Haskell Wexler. *ed* Robert Estrin.

pd Ron Foreman. *m* Herbie Hancock. *cast* Sean Penn, Robert Duvall, Maria Conchita Alonso, Randy Brooks, Grand Bush, Don Cheadle, Gerardo Mejia, Glenn Plummer, Sy Richardson, Trinidad Silva.
●Never as eccentric as *The Last Movie* or *Out of the Blue*, *Colors* nevertheless makes most other cop movies look formulary by comparison. Neither its plot – two mismatched cops take on LA's murderous gangs – nor its violence offer anything out of the ordinary. It wins out, rather, with a raw authenticity: gritty location shooting, plausibly inarticulate dialogue, a chaotic episodic narrative, and excellent performances. To a rather predictable master-pupil relationship, Duvall and Penn bring a refreshing lack of buddy-buddy sentimentality, while Hopper avoids sensationalism, rarely condemning or condoning, but providing a stark, even subtle investigation of misplaced loyalties and a moronic sense of honour. He also copes with car chases, stand-offs, and shootouts as efficiently as any director currently working in Hollywood. Finally, however, it's a film with heart; a moving, beautifully acted death scene at the end effortlessly evokes the sense of waste inevitable in a world of such random, unthinkingly violent macho pride. GA

Colossus of New York, The

(1958, US, 70 min, b/w)
d Eugène Lourié. *p* William Alland. *sc* Thelma Schnee. *ph* John F Warren. *ed* Floyd Knudtson. *ad* Hal Pereira, John Goodman. *m* Van Cleave. *cast* John Baragrey, Mala Powers, Otto Kruger, Robert Hutton, Ed Wolff, Ross Martin.
●With the world doomed by over-population, a scientist decides that it's his duty to reanimate the brilliant brain of his dead son in a vast metallic structure. The plot gives out halfway through, but Lourié's visualisation of the monster's metallic agonies – much of them subjective – is cruel and potent. DP

Colossus of Rhodes, The (Il Colosso di Rodi)

(1961, It/Sp/Fr, 127 min)
d Sergio Leone. *p* Michele Scaglione. *sc* Sergio Leone, Ennio de Concini, Luciano Martino, Ageo Gavioli, Cesare Seccia, Luciano Chitarrini, Carlo Gualtieri, Duccio Tessari. *ph* Antonio Lopez Ballesteros, Emilio Foriscot. *ed* Eraldo da Roma. *ad* Ramiro Gomez, Jesús Mateos, Francesco Assensio. *m* Angelo Francesco Lavagnino. *cast* Rory Calhoun, Lea Massari, Georges Marchal, Mabel Karr, Conrado San Martin, Angel Aranda.
●By the time Leone was thirty, he'd worked on well over 50 muscle-and-sweat sagas, including *Helen of Troy*, *Quo Vadis*? and the chariot scene in *Ben Hur*. *The Colossus of Rhodes* was his first attempt at direction, and it was a film remarkable enough, at a time when the peplums had just about reached the end of their particular line, to warrant good notices for its crowd and spectacle scenes. (The Colossus itself is a sophisticated torture chamber hidden behind a persuasively artsy exterior.) After the film's success, Leone turned down attempts to channel him into the manufacture of superman heroics in the Maciste mode, and went back to 2nd Unit work on Aldrich's *Sodom and Gomorrah*.

Colossus of the Stone Age

see Maciste Contro i Mostri

Colossus – The Forbin Project

see Forbin Project, The

Colour of Lies, The (Au Coeur du mensonge)

(1998, Fr, 113 min)
d Claude Chabrol. *p* Marin Karmitz. *sc* Odile Barski, Claude Chabrol. *ph* Eduardo Serra. *ed* Monique Fardoulis. *pd* Françoise Benoit-Fresco. *m* Matthieu Chabrol. *cast* Sandrine Bonnaire, Jacques Gamblin, Antoine de Caunes, Valeria Bruni-Tedeschi, Bulle Ogier, Bernard Verley.
●Chabrol-by-numbers: a female cop (Bruni-Tedeschi) investigates the strangling of a schoolgirl in a Breton village, centring her enquiries on three 'outsiders': an insecure art teacher (Gamblin), his wife/protector (Bonnaire), and a fashionable novelist/TV presenter (de Caunes). All the usual motifs are wheeled out, from guilt-by-thought versus guilt-by-deed to sexual inadequacies and jealousies, but this time the manure lacks nutrients. The denouement comes second to the closing 'meditation' on the deep meaning of lies, as flagged in the title, but most viewers will be too deeply asleep to care. TR

Colour of Love, The (Piel)

(1998, Ven, 90 min)
d Oscar Lucien. *cast* Indhira Serrano, Gabriel Blanco, Eileen Abad, Luke Grande, Andreina Blanco, Sara Sanders, Ana Maria Pagliaci.
●He's a romantic music student from an old, well off Hispanic family; she's a ballet dancer, the daughter of a vet, and black. They meet cute – coy smiles a-plenty– in her mum's surgery after the shell of his tortoise is cracked in an accident (a typical metaphor), but true love runs anything but smooth due to prejudice and snobbery. This racial take on *Romeo and Juliet* might mean something in Caracas (though are Venezuelan bigots really quite so forthright as here?), but it's unsubtle and predictable. The depiction of artistic sensitivity is particularly risible. GA

Colour of Paradise, The (Ranghe Khoda)

(1999, Iran, 90 min)
d Majid Majidi. *p* Mehdi Mahabadi, Ali Ghaem Maghami, Mohsen Sarab. *sc* Majid Majidi. *ph* Hashem Attar. *ed* Hassan Hassandoost. *pd* Masood Madadi. *m* Ali Reza Kohandiri. *cast* Hossein Mahjub, Mohsen Ramezani, Salime Feiza, Farnaz Saffati, Elham Sharifi, Behzad Rafice, Mohamad Rahmani.
●We first encounter the blind Mohammad (Ramezani, extraordinary) at a special school in Teheran, waiting for the arrival of his widower father at the end of term. When the man finally turns up, he tries to persuade the teachers to keep the boy, since the burden of looking after such a child is severely straining his meagre resources. Keen to remarry, the father considers keeping Mohammad out of the picture rather than risk scaring off a prospective bride. Writer/director Majidi shoots the boy with true, clear-eyed matter of factness. The characters' relationship with the divine is the meat of the matter: the father wonders whether the Almighty has deserted him by giving him such a child; the son feels he has spent his whole life reaching out for God without finding him. A considerable advance on Majidi's sugary *Children of Heaven*, this is a passionate investigation of faith tested in adversity, communicated with straightforward eloquence. TJ

Colour of Pomegranates, The (Nran Gouyne) 100

(1969, USSR, 73 min)
d/sc Sergo Paradjanov. *ph* Suren Shakhbazian, M Shakhbazian. *ed* Sergei Paradjanov. *ad* Stepan Andranikian. *m* Tigran Mansurian. *cast* Sofico Chiaureli, M Aleksanian, V Galstian, G Gegechkori.
●Originally refused an export licence, Paradjanov's extraordinary film traces the life of 18th century Armenian poet Sayat Nova ('The King of Song'), but with a series of painterly images strung together to form tableaux corresponding to moments of his life rather than any conventional biographic techniques. Pomegranates bleed their juice into the shape of a map of the old region of Armenia, the poet changes sex at least once in the course of his career, angels descend: the result is a stream of religious, poetic and local iconography which has an arcane and astonishing beauty. Much of its meaning must remain essentially specific to the culture from which the film springs, and no one could pretend that it's all readily accessible, but audiences accustomed to the work of Tarkovsky should have little problem. CPea

Colour of Pomegranates: Director's Cut, The (Nran Gouyne)

(1992, USSR, 73 min)
d/sc Sergo Paradjanov. *ph* Suren Shakhbazian, M Shakhbazian. *ed* Sergei Paradjanov. *ad* Stepan Andranikian. *m* Tigran Mansurian. *cast* Sofico Chiaureli, M Aleksanian, V Galstian, G Gegechkori.
●Paradjanov's most famous film was always a headache for the old Soviet authorities: a queer and obviously dissident paean to the cultures of Armenia and Georgia framed as a spiritual biography of the mysterious 18th century poet Sayat Nova. Paradjanov shot it in 1969. The Kremlin was aghast; it had the film shortened and drastically restructured and didn't allow it out of the country until 1983. Here at last is the director's original *film maudit*, and it's every second the classic of camp/hieratic cinema it promised to be. The film flows uninterrupted from the poet's childhood to his physical death and spiritual resurrection. The 'story' is still told in gorgeously stylised tableaux crammed with Christian and pagan symbols, but the voluptuous psychedelic imagery has a much more organic coherence. It's now much clearer that the poet's ubiquitous muse also represents his female alter ego, and that his inner torments are as much those of the gay icon St Sebastian as those of the Armenian patriotic martyr. And the explicit visual references to Buñuel and Pasolini underline Paradjanov's own ambivalence about the embrace of the church. The film is more profane than sacred, in fact, and all the more magical for it. TR

Colpire al Cuore

see Blow to the Heart

Colt .45 (aka Thundercloud)

(1950, US, 74 min)
d Edwin L Marin. *p* Saul Elkins. *sc* Tom W Blackburn. *ph* Wilfred M Cline. *ed* Frank Magee. *ad* Douglas Bacon. *m* William Lava. *cast* Randolph Scott, Zachary Scott, Ruth Roman, Lloyd Bridges, Chief Thundercloud.
●Fast-paced Technicolor Western, later the basis for a fondly remembered US TV series. R Scott's a gun salesman whose latest consignment of snazzy new pistols falls into the hands of Z Scott and his band of desperados. Unpretentious hokum, and one of the last films of Edwin Marin, a prolific second-feature man, who turned out several Randolph Scott Westerns. TJ

Coma

(1977, US, 113 min)
d Michael Crichton. *p* Martin Erlichman. *sc* Michael Crichton. *ph* Victor J Kemper. *ed* David Bretherton. *pd* Albert Brenner. *m* Jerry Goldsmith. *cast* Genevieve Bujold, Michael Douglas, Elizabeth Ashley, Rip Torn, Richard Widmark, Lois Chiles, Tom Selleck.
●Crichton's excellent adaptation of Robin Cook's novel is one of the most intelligent sci-fi thrillers in years. Bujold is the doctor who, after a series of mysterious and fatal mishaps with patients going into coma for no clear reason, begins to suspect that something evil is being covered up at the hospital. A simple enough story, but one told in such chilling fashion that visitors to hospitals will never feel the same again. Careful to establish an authentic atmosphere, Crichton only slowly lets events spiral off into nightmarish Hitchcockian fantasy, while the fact that nobody will believe Bujold, attributing her suspicions to female hysteria, only serves to point up the patriarchal nature of the medical profession. See it and worry. GA

Comanche Station

(1960, US, 74 min)
d/p Budd Boetticher. *sc* Burt Kennedy. *ph* Charles Lawton Jr. *ed* Edwin Bryant. *ad* Carl Anderson. *m* Mischa Bakaleinikoff. *cast* Randolph Scott, Claude Akins, Skip Homeier, Richard Rust, Nancy Gates, Rand Brooks.
●The last of the marvellous Westerns partnering Boetticher and Scott, beautifully scripted by Burt Kennedy and performed by a solid cast. Scott's the obsessive man, hunting these last ten years for a wife kidnapped by Comanches, who rescues instead another woman, only to find himself up against Akins and his reward-hungry sidekicks as he ferries her back to civilisation. With characters doomed from the start, it's a bleakly pessimistic film that gains warmth from gently ironic humour and a discreetly elegiac tone.

Combat des fauves

see Wild Games

Come and Get It

(1936, US, 99 min, b/w)
d Howard Hawks, William Wyler. *sc* Jane Murfin, Jules Furthman. *ph* Gregg Toland, Rudolph Maté. *ed* Edward Curtiss. *ad* Richard

Day. *m* Alfred Newman. *cast* Edward Arnold, Joel McCrea, Frances Farmer, Walter Brennan, Andrea Leeds.
●Minor Hawks (the last ten minutes were directed by Wyler) in which a 19th century Wisconsin lumber magnate and his son fight for the love of Frances Farmer – daughter of a woman the father once knew. The emphasis on professionalism and definition of character through action (work) is typical Hawks. Good performances all round, especially from Farmer in a dual role. Sadly, the location photography (Gregg Toland, Rudolph Maté) is poorly integrated with the jarringly set-bound dramatic scenes. NF

Come and See (Idi i Smotri)

(1985, USSR, 142 min, b/w & col)
d Elem Klimov. *sc* Ales Adamovich, Elem Klimov. *ph* Alexei Rodionov. *ed* V Belova. *pd* Viktor Petrov. *m* Oleg Yanchenko. *cast* Alexei Kravchenko, Olga Mironova, Liubomiras Laucevicius, Vladas Bagdonas, Victor Lorents, J Lumiste.
●Soviet Belorussia, near the Polish border, 1943. Florya, a young partisan, left behind as his unit moves to prepare for a renewed German advance, returns to his village to find only a mass of bodies, including those of his family, and later witnesses the entire population of a near-by town being machine-gunned and burnt to death. This epic, allegorical and traumatising enactment of the hellish experience of war (especially its effect upon a generation of the Soviet people) is rendered by Klimov – albeit unintentionally – as a disorienting and undifferentiated amalgam of almost lyrical poeticism and expressionist nightmare. WH

Comeback, The

(1977, GB, 100 min)
d/p Pete Walker. *sc* Murray Smith. *ph* Peter Jessop. *ed* Alan Brett. *ad* Michael Pickwoad. *m* Stanley Myers. *cast* Jack Jones, Pamela Stephenson, David Doyle, Bill Owen, Sheila Keith, Holly Palance, Richard Johnson.
●It's sad, 17 years on, to see the British horror film still seeking inspiration from *Psycho*...and still getting it all wrong. But that's not difficult when you confuse horror with the horrible. People don't just die in this film, they decay, slowly and unconvincingly. Unconvincing is the best word for a plot that has a perfectly respectable middle-aged couple driven to heights of murderous passion and lunacy by the filthy songs and lewd gyrations of a singer played by Jack Jones. Not even its brace of transvestite red herrings can help the story stand on its own feet. SM

Come Back Africa

(1959, US, 90 min, b/w)
d/p Lionel Rogosin. *sc* Lionel Rogosin, Lewis N'kosi, Bloke Modisane. *ph* Ernest Artaria, Emil Knebel. *ed* Carl Lerner. *cast* Zachariah Mgabi, Vinah Bendile, Miriam Makeba.
●Rogosin's docudrama was an early exposé of the evils of apartheid, filmed clandestinely and using a non-professional cast who portray a typical township family, separated by law and drifting through a series of menial jobs until a single infringement (i.e. man and wife share a night together) leads to a singularly bleak denouement. Although the film has considerable weaknesses – principally on the narrative level of performance, and the need to spell everything out in the manner of a social science course (this last, an entirely understandable decision for 1959) – its power comes from the location filming of the township, which might have been shot today. This township – Sophiatown – was once the only place in South Africa where blacks could own freehold properties. The area was demolished and became a white suburb called Triumph. ATu

Come Back Charleston Blue

(1972, US, 100 min)
d Mark Warren. *p* Samuel Goldwyn Jr. *sc* Bontche Schweig, Peggy Elliott. *ph* Dick Kratina. *ed* Jerry Greenberg, George Bowers. *pd* Robert Gundlach. *m* Donny Hathaway. *cast* Godfrey Cambridge, Raymond St Jacques, Peter De Anda, Jonelle Allen, Maxwell Glanville, Minnie Gentry.
●Second of two underrated thrillers (the first was *Cotton Comes to Harlem*) inspired by Chester Himes and his ace Harlem detectives, Grave Digger Jones and Coffin Ed Johnson. Black Bogarts with a natty line in upstaged Chandlerisms, the pair tangle here with murders by cut-throat razor, the resurrection of a gangster who died forty years earlier, a regally crazy old lady (wonderful performance by Gentry), and the hijacking of all the heroin in Harlem. No masterpiece, but very funny and full of bizarre touches. TM

Come Back, Little Sheba

(1952, US, 99 min, b/w)
d Daniel Mann. *p* Hal B Wallis. *sc* Ketti Frings. *ph* James Wong Howe. *ed* Warren Low. *ad* Hal Pereira, Henry Bumstead. *m* Franz Waxman. *cast* Burt Lancaster, Shirley Booth, Terry Moore, Richard Jaeckel, Philip Ober, Edwin Max.
●Little Sheba is a dog that's gone AWOL, and its owner, Shirley Booth, has also lost her looks and her love. She's married to a reformed alcoholic (Lancaster), and has a lodger (Moore) whose incessant bonking with Richard Jaeckel drives Burt back to the bottle and Booth into self-pity. Dated now, it's still a classic slice of '50s Americana, based on a play by William Inge and treading gracefully between tragedy and comedy. But unlike *Picnic*, it doesn't score heavily as a movie. Daniel Mann refuses to get off his tripod, and the camera seems transfixed by Booth's screen debut (she had played the part on Broadway), which won her an Oscar and the Cannes prize. ATu

Come Back to the 5 & Dime Jimmy Dean, Jimmy Dean

(1982, US, 110 min)
d Robert Altman. *p* Scott Bushnell. *sc* Ed Graczyk. *ph* Pierre Mignot. *ed* Jason Rosenfield. *pd* David Gropman. *cast* Sandy Dennis, Cher, Karen Black, Sudie Bond, Kathy Bates, Marta Heflin, Mark Patton.
●Startlingly successful translation from one medium to another, with Altman turning the first of his theatrical adaptations into a cinematic tour de force. A group of women, members of a James Dean fan club, reunite in '75 to pay tribute to the death, 20 years earlier, of their hero while shooting *Giant* in the Texan desert nearby. Ed Graczyk's play itself is a humdrum if highly enjoyable affair, gradually proceeding from its comic observations about the way the women aren't quite friends any more to a more serious consideration of shattered dreams and saddened lives, all exposed in a gripping if familiar series of intimate revelations. But beyond the excellent performances and Altman's evident sympathy for his garrulous gathering of beautiful losers, what marks the film is the way he uses both the camera and a wall mirror (which periodically reflects us back to '55) to explore and open up his single dime-store set and the cracks in the masks of his deluded/deluding characters. Stunning stuff. GA

Come Blow Your Horn

(1962, US, 113 min)
d Bud Yorkin. *p* Norman Lear, Bud Yorkin. *sc* Norman Lear. *ph* William H Daniels. *ed* Frank P Keller. *ad* Hal Pereira, Roland Anderson. *m* Nelson Riddle. *cast* Frank Sinatra, Tony Bill, Lee J Cobb, Molly Picon, Barbara Rush, Jill St John.
●Routine comedy fodder – domestic squabbles in a New York Jewish family, with playboy sophisticate Sinatra introducing kid brother Bill to the delights of the high life – from the pen of Neil Simon (his first major success), ploddingly transferred to the screen. A few nice lines and an intriguing cast don't compensate for the over-familiarity of the basic idea. GA

Come, Come, Come Upward (Aje Aje Bara-Aje)

(1989, SKor, 123 min)
d Im Kwon-Taek. *p* Lee Tae-Won. *sc* Han Sung-Won. *cast* Kang Soo-Yeon, Jin Yong-Mi, Yu In-Chon, Jon Moo-Song.
●A female companion-piece to Im's classic *Mandala*, this too rests on a contrast between sacred and profane approaches to Buddhist enlightenment. Sun-Nyo (Kang, superb) runs away from her broken home and her crush on a teacher to become a nun, expecting to pray and meditate. But the convent sends her out into the world, where she mixes with the poor and desperate and forms one sexual attachment after another with rough working-class men. Im compares her self-abasement with the more orthodox asceticism of another young nun, whose retreat from worldly things results in a brutal rape. The drama is rooted in a clear sense of social and psychological realities but lifted above mere social realism by Gu Joong-Mu's sensationally beautiful cinematography, mostly in shades of blue and grey. TR

Comédia Infantil

(1997, Swe/Port/Moz, 92 min)
d/p Solveig Nordlund. *sc* Tommy Karlmark. *ph* Lisa Hagstrand. *ed* Nelly Quettier. *pd* Peter Blävman. *m* Johan Zachrisson. *cast* Ségio Titos, Joao Manja, Adelino Branquinho, Lilia Momplé, Joaquina Odete, Jaime Julio, Avelino Manhica, Francisco Chilengue.
●Children age quickly in Mozambique. At ten, Nelio has already seen his village torched in the civil war and his baby brother mashed under a rifle butt. Parted from his family to fend for himself in the city, he is not alone in his plight, but few of his raggle-taggle chums share his own magic powers, judiciously applied in aid of sick children. Making the most of whatever modest gifts you possess would seem to be the positive message this Swedish-Portuguese-Mozambican co-production wrests from a scenario of potential hopelessness. There is a slight air of wishful thinking, but the director has coaxed unaffected performances from her cast of street children. Piecing the melodramatic plot together from a string of coincidences is where the effort comes in, but the film's fundamentally decency wins us over. TJ

Comedian Harmonists (The Harmonists)

(1997, Ger/Aus, 129 min)
d Joseph Vilsmaier. *p* Hanno Huth, Reinhard Klooss, Danny Krausz. *sc* Klaus Richter, Ulrich Limmer, Alfred Holighaus. *ph* Joseph Vilsmaier. *ed* Peter R Adam. *pd* Rolf Zehetbauer. *m* Harald Kloser. *cast* Ben Becker, Heino Ferch, Ulrich Noethen, Heinrich Schafmeister, Max Tidorf, Kai Wiesinger.
●The Comedian Harmonists were a popular German sextet of the late '20s/early '30s specialising in sentimental or smutty ditties (inventively arranged) with titles like 'My Little Green Cactus'. A showbiz saga with grisly historical trimmings, the film recounts the assembling of the poverty-stricken musicians during the Depression, their initial setbacks and eventual success; followed by personal tensions, exacerbated by the Nazi ascendancy – half the group being Jews – and their final break-up. It ought to be fascinating, and there are intriguing sidelights: their fans, embarrassingly, numbered the prominent anti-Semite Julius Streicher. But it's relentlessly routine, both on the personal and political level, though the director's affection for the Harmonists' music certainly comes across. BBa

Comedians, The

(1967, US/Bermuda/Fr, 156 min)
d/p Peter Glenville. *sc* Graham Greene. *ph* Henri Decaë. *ed* Françoise Javet. *ad* François de Lamothe. *m* Laurence Rosenthal. *cast* Richard Burton, Alec Guinness, Elizabeth Taylor, Peter Ustinov, Paul Ford, Lillian Gish, Raymond St Jacques, Cicely Tyson.
●A sadly inept adaptation of Graham Greene's novel (script by Greene himself) about turmoil in Haiti under Papa Doc, with a group of English-speaking stereotypes going through the usual intrigues, despair and romance. The main problem is that Glenville's lumbering direction concentrates so much on Dick, Liz and trivia. Only the performances of Gish, Ford and Guinness give any relief from the endless battery of clichés. GA

Comédie de l'Innocence

see Fils de Deux Mères ou Comédie de l'Innocence

Comedy of Terrors, The

(1963, US, 88 min)
d Jacques Tourneur. *p* James H Nicholson, Samuel Z Arkoff. *sc* Richard Matheson. *ph* Floyd Crosby. *ed* Anthony Carras. *ad* Daniel Haller. *m* Les Baxter. *cast* Vincent Price, Peter Lorre, Boris Karloff, Basil Rathbone, Joe E Brown, Joyce Jameson, Buddy Mason, Beverley Hills, Linda Rogers.

●Price and Lorre are somewhat over-enthusiastic undertakers in Richard Matheson's disappointingly scripted, self-conscious horror spoof set in New England in the 1890s. With credentials of this calibre, the movie could hardly fail, but it comes perilously close. On the other hand, you've never seen so many scene-stealers together in their natural environment (notably Karloff as Price's senile sleeping partner, and Rathbone as his landlord, a would-be Shakespearean actor with cataleptic tendencies). And Price, of course, deserves a knighthood: Sir Vincent, knight of the long knives. TCh

Come Fill the Cup

(1951, US, 113 min, b/w)
d Gordon Douglas. *p* Henry Blanke. *sc* Ivan Goff, Ben Roberts. *ph* Robert Burks. *ed* Alan Crosland Jr. *ad* Leo K Kuter. *m* Ray Heindorf. *cast* James Cagney, Phyllis Thaxter, Raymond Massey, James Gleason, Gig Young, Selena Royle.

●Despite a not altogether convincing script, a solid piece of entertainment with Cagney as the journalist whose life is almost ruined by alcoholism, until he sees the light and sets about helping to cure others. Gangsters are brought in to contrived effect towards the end, but the whole thing, despite a tub-thumping message, is lent style by a strong cast and Robert Burks' steely photography. GA

Come Next Spring

(1955, US, 92 min)
d RG Springsteen. *sc* Montgomery Pittman. *ph* Jack Marta. *ed* Tony Martinelli. *ad* Frank Arrigo. *m* Max Steiner. *cast* Ann Sheridan, Steve Cochran, Walter Brennan, Sherry Jackson, Richard Eyer, Edgar Buchanan, Sonny Tufts, Mae Clarke.

●Slight but charming slice of rural Americana set in Arkansas and detailing the difficulties facing Cochran (reformed drunkard determined to prove himself) and his wife Sheridan as they try to make a go of their farm. A bit contrived in its incident, and never as tough or as moving as Renoir's superficially similar *The Southerner*, but Sheridan gives her all and breathes life into the proceedings, while Brennan is as reliable as ever. GA

Come on George

(1939, GB, 88 min, b/w)
d Anthony Kimmins. *p* Jack Kitchin. *sc* Anthony Kimmins, Leslie Arliss, Val Valentine. *ph* Ronald Neame. *ed* Ray Pitt. *ad* Wilfrid Shingleton. *songs* George Formby, Fred E Cliffe, Harry Gifford, Allan Nicholson. cast George Formby, Pat Kirkwood, Joss Ambler, Meriel Forbes, Cyril Raymond, Ronald Shiner.

●Once upon a time in a distant land, Formby – the goofy, gormless, ukelele-playing comedian (?) – was a sure-fire box-office success up North. Here he's an ice-cream seller at a racetrack with ambitions to become a jockey, opportunistically employing his natural empathy with a horse, and tangling with a psychiatrist and hordes of performing fleas before he rides to victory. OK if you like that sort of thing. GA

Come Play with Me

(1977, GB, 94 min)
d/p/sc George Harrison Marks. *ph* Terry Maher. *ed* Peter Mayhew. *m* Peter Jeffries. *cast* Irene Handl, Alfie Bass, George Harrison Marks, Ronald Fraser, Ken Parry, Cardew Robinson.

●Truly atrocious sex comedy involving forgers on the run and out-of-work strippers staffing a health farm. Accept an invitation to go swimming in a piranha-infested river rather than play with this lot. SM

Comes a Horseman

(1978, US, 118 min)
d Alan J Pakula. *p* Gene Kirkwood, Dan Paulson. *sc* Dennis Lynton Clark. *ph* Gordon Willis. *ed* Marion Rothman. *pd* George Jenkins. *m* Michael Small. *cast* James Caan, Jane Fonda, Jason Robards, George Grizzard, Richard Farnsworth, Jim Davis.

●From the first, with its graveyard claustrophobically hemmed in by mountains, *Comes a Horseman* is a misfit Western, with Pakula using Jane Fonda's uncanny resemblance to her father to set up a curious tangential relationship, respectful and rebellious, with classic Western mythology. Fonda is the rather uneasy 'banshee woman boss' of a Montana ranch in 1945, fighting off cattle baron (and former incestuous cousin) Robards, assisted only by a Walter Brennan-style old-timer and a reluctant recruit: Anzio veteran Caan. The sparring of veteran and banshee sits uneasily between conviction and irony, the set pieces – stampede, saloon fight – seem token; even the ranchers' conflicts of interest are handled too precisely, too 'politically' for genre material. Only in the later stages, with some appropriate acknowledgments – that the ranches are both mortgaged, that the film is more interested in murder than battle – does conflict come alive. Visually superb, though: a doomed attempt to make Fordian metaphors speak a language of corrupting, intimate anxiety. CA

Come See the Paradise

(1990, US, 133 min)
d Alan Parker. *p* Robert F Colesberry. *sc* Alan Parker. *ph* Michael Seresin. *ed* Gerry Hambling. *pd* Geoffrey Kirkland. *m* Randy Edelman. *cast* Dennis Quaid, Tamlyn Tomita, Sab Shimono, Shizuko Hoshi, Stan Egi, Ronald Yamamoto.

●Parker's movie about the experience of Japanese-Americans immediately after Pearl Harbor characteristically undermines its sociopolitical problems by focusing single-mindedly on the lives of a handful of individuals and resorting to simplistic bombast. The opening sequences bode ill: examining the cultural and racial barriers that divide his would-be lovers – ex-union activist Jack McGurn (Quaid) and Lily (Tomita), the Nisei daughter of Jack's employer – Parker even indulges Quaid with a silly, redundant song-and-dance number. Once Jack is drafted, and Lily and her family are interned in a desert camp with thousands of other victims of US xenophobia, the film plunges headlong into turgid melodrama. Dust, death and disintegrating values are the Kawamuras' lot, as the narrative staggers through an endless series of farewells and reunions, fallings-out and reconciliations; tears flow, the music swells, and Jack, affirming his love for Lily, discovers a poetic articulacy that is quite implausible for this working class hero. Except for the historical data inserted here and there into the dialogue, everything on view derives not from reality but from manipulative movie cliché. GA

Comfort and Joy

(1984, GB, 106 min)
d Bill Forsyth. *p* Davina Belling, Clive Parsons. *sc* Bill Forsyth. *ph* Chris Menges. *ed* Michael Ellis. *pd* Adrienne Atkinson. *m* Mark Knopfler. *cast* Bill Paterson, Eleanor David, CP Grogan, Alex Norton, Patrick Malahide, Rikki Fulton.

●When his girl-friend walks out on him, Alan 'Dicky' Bird (Paterson) grits his teeth and plugs away at his sugar-coated job as a DJ on a Glasgow local radio station. Then by a highly unlikely quirk of fate he finds himself mediating in an ice-cream war between Mr McCool and Mr Bunny, both of them branches of the Scotia Nostra. But while Paterson regains his self-esteem through the injection of seriousness into his life, the film is damaged for the same reason: Forsyth stamps too firmly on the comedy which was his forte, while being apparently too nice to believe that the mafia are anything other than high-spirited boys. The result doesn't go far enough in either direction. Other people make comedy thrillers; this is a whimsical mild-surpriser. CPea

Comfort of Strangers, The (Cortesie per gli ospiti)

(1990, It/GB, 104 min)
d Paul Schrader. *p* Angelo Rizzoli. *sc* Harold Pinter. *ph* Dante Spinotti. *ed* Bill Pankow. *pd* Gianni Quaranta. *m* Angelo Badalamenti. *cast* Christopher Walken, Rupert Everett, Natasha Richardson, Helen Mirren, Manfredi Aliquo.

●Its lush visuals concealing a core of fetid malevolence, Schrader's film of Ian McEwan's novel inhabits a strange, unsettling territory somewhere between art movie and thriller. Colin (Everett) and Mary (Richardson) are second-honeymooning in Venice, warily striving to repair the fissures in their stale relationship. A seemingly fortuitous encounter with the aristocratic Robert (Walken) bemuses them, his evident hospitality sitting uneasily with his unusually frank questions and confessions. But the suave tale-spinner also catalyses what remains of the couple's sexual feelings for each other, and as if mesmerised, they return to the palazzo he shares with his submissive wife (Mirren), only half oblivious to the dangers awaiting them… Adopting an oblique perspective on motivation, Harold Pinter's script sometimes suffers from awkward, even implausible dialogue; but careful pacing and casting make for a film that, while directed with cool discretion, is sensual and shocking in its casual evocation of erotic violence, emotional manipulation and moral torpor. If much of the credit must go to cameraman Dante Spinotti's use of dense, exotic colours and to Gianni Quaranta's elegant sets, it's finally Schrader who deserves praise for the septic, stifling mood. GA

Comic Book Confidential

(1988, Can, 90 min)
d/p Ron Mann. *ph* Robert Fresco, Joan Churchill. *ed* Robert Kennedy, Ron Mann. *ad* Gerlinde Scharinger. *m* Nicholas Stirling. *with* Lynda Barry, Charles Burns, Sue Coe, Robert Crumb, Will Eisner, Al Feldstein, Shary Flenniken, William M Gaines, Bill Griffith, Jaime Hernández, Jack Kirby, Harvey Kurtzman, Stan Lee, Paul Mavrides, Frank Miller, Victor Morosco, Françoise Mouly, Dan O'Neill, Harvey Pekar, Spain Rodriguez, Gilbert Shelton, Art Spiegelman.

●With the comic book industry now enjoying unprecedented respect, Mann's documentary is a timely if unsatisfying look at four decades of comic history, and interviews 22 leading American creators. It opens promisingly with the patriotic '40s and McCarthyite '50s, when comics were burnt and Senate sub-committees investigated questions of depravity and corruption. It's strong, too, on the underground comix of the '60s, but the scope of the film is too broad, and the little time allotted to each writer and artist is further reduced by the fatuous device of having them read out loud their own texts while panels from their comics are shown on the screen. The filming is for the most part an unimaginative and endless succession of talking heads, with narrative links provided by '*Meanwhile*…' – precisely the kind of crass storytelling method modern comics try to avoid. Buffs will no doubt enjoy seeing their heroes, but anyone else will be bored rigid. DW

Comic Magazine (Komikku zasshi nanka iranai)

(1985, Jap, 120 min)
d Yojiro Takita. *p* Yutaka Okada. *sc* Yuya Uchida, Isao Takagi. *ph* Yoichi Suiga. *ed* Masatsugi Kanazawa. *m* Katsuo Ono. *cast* Yuya Uchida, Yumi Asou, Beat Takeshi, Yoshio Harada, Hiromi Go, Taiji Tonoyama.

●The spirit of Paddy Chayefsky unfortunately lives on in this leaden satire of the dubious ethics of the Japanese media. An increasingly ragged TV journalist endures one humiliating setback after another in an unending quest for exclusive celebrity interviews; he tramples on the private feelings of others until his conscience finally asserts itself and he steps in to stop (rather than report) a murder. Hideously protracted, lumberingly obvious, and completely lacking in real bite. TR

Coming Home

(1978, US, 128 min)
d Hal Ashby. *p* Jerome Hellman. *sc* Waldo Salt, Robert C Jones. *ph* Haskell Wexler. *ed* Don Zimmerman. *pd* Michael Haller. *cast* Jane Fonda, Jon Voight, Bruce Dern, Robert Carradine, Penelope Milford, Robert Ginty.

●Hal (*Shampoo*) Ashby takes on (and makes disposable) America's post-Vietnam guilt, with a supremely sentimental tale of war hero's wife (a nurse!) falling for paraplegic war veteran. Cliché piles on cliché to the strains of a garbled '60s soundtrack, but the movie's ending goes some way to recognising its failure. Fonda is magnificent. CA

Coming Out

(1990, Ger, 113 min)
d Heiner Carow. *p* Horst Hartwig. *sc* Wolfram Witt. *ph* Martin Scheslinger. *ed* Evelyn Carow. *m* Stefan Carow. *cast* Matthias Freihof, Dagmar Manzel, Dirk Kummer, Alex Wandtke, Michael Gwisdek, Werner Dissell.

●Hailed as the first East German film to deal with homosexuality, this mixes the romantic yearning, melodrama and self-disgust typical of ground-breaking gay work. The plot is reminiscent of *Nighthawks* and *Taxi zum Klo*: respected schoolteacher leads double life, butch by day, cruising the clubs by night. Philipp (Freihof) makes an enthusiastic stab at heterosexuality with a female colleague (Manzel), only to find himself accidentally wandering into a louche bar full of drag queens that looks like an out-take from *Cabaret*. One night of happiness in the arms of another young man (Kummer) ensues, before fate conspires to separate them and leave Philipp facing loneliness, persecution and alcoholism. So far, so miserable. But the redeeming feature, along with a wonderfully open performance from Freihof, is that, given the social climate of East Germany, this is anything but an exercise in self-pity: when the characters speak of loneliness and persecution, they are *not* posturing. RS

Coming to America

(1988, US, 117 min)
d John Landis. *p* George Folsey Jr, Robert D Wachs. *sc* David Sheffield, Barry W Blaustein. *ph* Woody Omens. *ed* George Folsey Jr. *pd* Richard MacDonald. *m* Nile Rogers. *cast* Eddie Murphy, James Earl Jones, Arsenio Hall, Shari Headley, Madge Sinclair, Calvin Lockhart.
● Murphy plays HRH Akeem, Crown Prince of Zamunda, whose pampered existence extends to molly-coddled privates. But when presented by his father (Jones) with the *fait accompli* of a decreed marriage, Akeem rebels and sets off for New York with his loyal manservant (Hall), where he decides that Queens is the most likely whereabouts of the woman who will love him for himself. Lodging in a run-down tenement, the pair find work as cleaners in a hamburger joint, where Akeem soon encounters elegant, sophisticated Lisa (Headley). Much of the credit for this slick, at times very funny movie must go to Landis, since Murphy's previously wasted talent is here harnessed to reveal a considerable finesse; superb comic timing, a satirical edge, and Murphy's extraordinary gift for mimicry lift it right out of the trough of mediocrity to which it is all but consigned by its utterly predictable storyline. SCu

Coming Up Roses

(1986, GB, 93 min)
d Stephen Bayley. *p* Linda James. *sc* Ruth Carter. *ph* Dick Pope. *ed* Scott Thomas. *pd* Hildegard Bechtler. *m* Michael Story. *cast* Dafydd Hywel, Iola Gregory, Olive Michael, Mari Emlyn, WJ Phillips, Glan Davies.
● In a small Welsh town stands the Rex, an old dog of a cinema showing black-and-white horror pics to an audience of empty seats. Inevitably, the cinema is closed, and the manager Eli, projectionist Trevor, and ice-cream lady Mona are thrown onto the slag-heap of unemployment (this, by the way, is the time of the miners' strike). When Trev's ex-wife needs £700, he borrows the ailing Eli's funeral money, and he and his new love Mona are then faced with the problems of how to pay it back and save the cinema and their jobs. Updating *The Smallest Show on Earth*, this is the second-ever Welsh language movie released in the UK (the first being *Boy Soldier*). Subtitled in English, it's a chuckling good comedy with an edge. 'Take the cinema away from us and what other means of escape is there?' pleads old Eli; none from the grim realities of Thatcher's Britain. CB

Command, The

(1954, US, 94 min)
d David Butler. *p* David Weisbart. *sc* Russell Hughes. *ph* Wilfred M Cline. *ed* Irene Morra. *ad* Bertram Tuttle. *m* Dimitri Tiomkin. *cast* Guy Madison, Joan Weldon, James Whitmore, Carl Benton Reid, Ray Teal, Harvey Lembeck.
● Both the first film in CinemaScope from Warner Bros and the first Western in the widescreen process from any studio. This yarn of a cavalry medical officer inheriting command of a wagon train, and fighting both Indians and smallpox, has its moments; most of them thanks to the script rather than the ponderous direction, although Sam Fuller, credited with the adaptation from a James Warner Bellah novel, disowned the film after screenwriter Russell Hughes' revisions ended up on screen. PT

Command Decision

(1948, US, 112 min, b/w)
d Sam Wood. *p* Sidney Franklin. *sc* William R Laidlaw, George Froeschel. *ph* Harold Rosson. *ed* Harold F Kress. *ad* Cedric Gibbons, Urie McCleary. *m* Miklós Rózsa. *cast* Clark Gable, Walter Pidgeon, Van Johnson, Brian Donlevy, Charles Bickford, Edward Arnold, John Hodiak.
● Talkative but soberly gripping World War II drama about the conflict between Gable, commander of a bomber unit determined to rush through the destruction of German factories producing a new breed of jet fighter, and Pidgeon as his politic superior, well aware that the inevitable heavy losses will reflect badly on his plans for daylight precision bombing. Adapted from a stage play and barely opened out, it isn't as good as *Twelve O'Clock High*, made the following year, but a strong cast pulls it through. TM·

Commando

(1985, US, 90 min)
d Mark L Lester. *p* Joel Silver. *sc* Steven E De Souza. *ph* Matthew F Leonetti. *ed* Mark Goldblatt, John F Link, Glenn Farr. *pd* John Vallone. *m* James Horner. *cast* Arnold Schwarzenegger, Rae Dawn Chong, Dan Hedaya, Vernon Wells, James Olson, David Patrick Kelly, Alyssa Milano, Bill Duke.
● Schwarzenegger went from *The Terminator* to the human equivalent of boys' action figures in this none-too-serious gung-ho adventure, where his former covert agent John Matrix takes the fight back to the reactionary baddies who've kidnapped his daughter and are set on restoring a fascist tyrant to power in the Central American state of 'Val Verde'. Lots of machine-gunfire, explosions and disposable khaki-clad extras, as you'd expect. Occasional suggestions that the tongue might be slightly in cheek include the risible bonding-with-small-daughter fishing trip under the opening credits and pronounced homo-erotic badinage with his final-reel adversary. 'Think of sticking your knife into my flesh – and twisting it,' Arnie hisses at Vernon Wells, the leather-clad, handlebar-moustached heavy, who might just have come from a Village People lookalike contest. TJ

Commare Secca, La (The Grim Reaper)

(1962, It, 100 min, b/w)
d Bernardo Bertolucci. *p* Tonino Cervi. *sc* Bernardo Bertolucci, Sergio Citti, Pier Paolo Pasolini. *ph* Gianni Narzisi. *ed* Nino Baragli. *ad* Adriana Spadaro. *m* Carlo Rustichelli, Piero Piccioni. cast Francesco Ruiu, Giancarlo De Rosa, Alvaro D'Hercole, Romano Labate, Lorenza Benedetti, Vincenzo Ciccora.
● Bertolucci's first feature, a whodunit about a whore's murder, offers more than filmographic interest. The joint passages of time and adolescence are realised in its combination of febrile sexual alertness and the elaborate reconstruction of each defendant's day, always returning to the doomed woman dressing while the same rainstorm rages. Also intriguing are the portraits of the gormless young soldier on leave, accosting literally every female he meets; the ageing prostitute; and the gay witness to the crime. MM

Comment j'ai tué mon père

see Way I Killed My Father, The

Comment je me suis disputé... ('ma vie sexuelle')

see Ma vie sexuelle (Paul Dedalus' Journey)

Comme un Aimant (The Magnet)

(2000, Fr, 100 min)
d Kamel Saleh, Akhénaton. *p* Richard Grandpierre. *sc* Kamel Saleh, Akhénaton. *ph* Denis Rouden. *ed* Fabrice Salinié. *ad* Hassen Saleh. *m* Akhénaton, Bruno Coulais. *cast* Kamel Saleh, Akhénaton, Houari Djerir, Brahim Aimad, Sofiane Madjid Mammeri, Kamel Ferrat, Titoff, Malek Brahimi.
● This clichéd but heartfelt ensemble drama, about a predominantly North African group of twenty-something petty criminals and loose enders living in the Panier region of Marseilles, is co-directed the musician Akhénaton, who also stars. Music is key: the film is well cut to a varied range of rap, soul and international tracks, highlighting themes of alienation, racism, police harassment and generational difficulty. The worse threat, however, comes from the local Mafia; and when retribution is visited on the group following an unpaid loan the response is apocalyptic. Attractive performances and Akhénaton's obvious affection for the subject cover for the script's dramatic deficiencies. WH

Comme un Boomerang

see Boomerang

Commissar, The (Komissar)

(1967, USSR, 108 min, b/w)
d Alexander Askoldov. *p* V Levin, V Grigorev, L Prilutzhakya. *sc* Aleksander Askoldov. *ph* Valery Ginsburg. *ed* V Isayeva, N Loginova, S Lyashinskaya. *ad* Sergei Serebriannikov. *m* Alfred Schnittke. *cast* Nonna Mordyukova, Rolan Bykov, Raisa Niedashkovskaya, Vasily Shukshin, Ludmila Volinskaya.
● Askoldov's movie was sat on after initial screenings in 1967 because it dealt with such unpalatable subjects as anti-Semitism and women's rights. The film, although it enters wholeheartedly into its story and is shot with a certain austere flair, has a hard time engaging the audience. The story, set in 1920, is resolutely stern: Clavdia, a Red Army officer, becomes pregnant by a comrade later executed by the Whites. She is billeted with a poor Jewish family until the birth, by which time her intial racial hostility, and their resentment of her haughty attitude, have worn off, and each side recognises the other's common humanity. Askoldov clearly felt passionately about his subject, but *The Commissar* is a work of promise rather than polish; sadly he was prevented from working again. RS

Commitments, The

(1991, US, 118 min)
d Alan Parker. *p* Lynda Miles, Roger Randall-Cutler. *sc* Dick Clement, Ian La Frenais, Roddy Doyle. *ph* Gale Tattersall. *ed* Gerry Hambling. *pd* Brian Morris. *cast* Robert Arkins, Michael Aherne, Angeline Ball, Maria Doyle, Dave Finnegan, Bronagh Gallagher, Félim Gormley, Glen Hansard, Dick Massey, Johnny Murphy, Kenneth McCluskey, Andrew Strong.
● Foul-mouthed, fast-talking and very funny, this is Parker's best to date. It's an intentionally 'small' movie that treats a familiar subject (kids forming a rock band) with a deft intimacy. But as the young hopefuls from Dublin's working-class Northside go through the round of auditions, rehearsals and gigs, it becomes clear that the film is big in heart. For Parker and his excellent, mostly non-professional cast are indeed committed to characters, milieu and music: classics from Otis, Wilson Pickett, Aretha *et al.* For one thing, the script precisely captures both the witty banter and the modest dreams of the streetwise kids. For another, Parker never over-emphasises the unemployment and poverty, nor does he glamorise the band. The result is a gritty, naturalistic comedy blessed with a wry, affectionate eye for the absurdities of the band's various rivalries and ambitions; and the songs are matchless. GA

Committed

(1983, US, 79 min, b/w)
d/p/sc Sheila McLaughlin, Lynne Tillman. *ph* Heinz Emigholz. *ed* Sheila McLaughlin, Lynne Tillman, Christine Le Goff. *m* Phillip Johnston. *cast* Sheila McLaughlin, Victoria Boothby, Lee Breuer, John Erdman, Heinz Emighol, Lucy Sanger.
● A low-budget independent alternative to the Jessica Lange *Frances* made a couple of years earlier, this sees McLaughlin as Hollywood actress Frances Farmer, reliving her memories while incarcerated in the mental institution to which she has been committed, and employs her as a litmus with which to measure American attitudes to political commitment, mental health, and strong women. It's become fashionable to regard Farmer as something of a martyr, and although she was certainly a talented actress treated abysmally by Hollywood, family and friends, it is hard now to ascertain the truth behind her downfall. That apart, this is an original and stylish movie, austere and bitter. GA

Common Threads: Stories from the Quilt

(1989, US, 75 min)
d Robert Epstein, Jeffrey Friedman. *p* Bill Couturie, Robert Epstein, Jeffrey Friedman. *sc* Robert Epstein, Jeffrey Friedman, Cindy Ruskin. *ph* Frances Reid, Michael Chin, Ed Lachman, Erich Roland. *ed* Robert Epstein,

Jeffrey Friedman. *m* Bobby McFerrin. *with* Sara Lewinstein, Suzi Mandell, David Mandell, Sallie Perryman, Vito Russo, Tracy Torrey. *narrator* Dustin Hoffman.
●Since 1985, the Names Project has based its work around the assembling of a now massive memorial quilt composed of individually-produced squares, each commemorating an AIDS death. In this Oscar-winning documentary, maintaining the high standards of Epstein's earlier *The Times of Harvey Milk*, he and his co-director Friedman have chosen, from the widest possible spectrum, six people who have suffered loss: the wives of an Olympic athlete and a drug addict, the parents of a haemophiliac boy who died at twelve, and a naval commander and a writer, who have both lost lovers and themselves contracted AIDS. Through their moving testimonies, with the aid of photographs and home videos, faces and histories are put to the names on five of the squares. It's a gentle, sensitive film, the fierce anger felt by its makers evident only in the use of statistics and media snippets which build up to a damning indictment of the social and political response to the AIDS crisis. WH

Common Touch, The

(1941, GB, 103 min, b/w)
d/p John Baxter. *sc* Barbara K Emary, Geoffrey Orme. *ph* James Wilson. *ed* Jack Harris. *ad* Holmes Paul. *m* Kennedy Russell. *cast* Geoffrey Hibbert, Harry Welchman, Greta Gynt, Joyce Howard, Edward Rigby, Bransby Williams, Bernard Miles.
● Another of Baxter's sweet-tempered, homely fables proposing a socialist utopia of fairness and freedom from hardship. 'And why not?' says Bransby Williams straight to camera in the last shot of the film. Young company boss Hibbert, with a public school chum for company, takes up lodgings incognito at Charlie's Doss House, to learn how the other half live. The result is less The Road to Wigan Pier than The Street of a Thousand Stereotypes, with Baxter's showbiz instincts as well to the fore as his political ones. Greta Gynt's costumes for her cabaret turns provide the most startling element in the picture. Overall, as hard not to like as it is not to patronise. BBa

Communicants, The

see Nattvardsgästerna

Communion

(1989, US, 101 min)
d Philippe Mora. *p* Philippe Mora, Whitley Strieber, Dan Allingham. *sc* Whitley Strieber. *ph* Louis Irving. *ed* Lee Smith *pd* Linda Pearl. *m* Eric Clapton. *cast* Christopher Walken, Lindsay Crouse, Joel Carlson, Frances Sternhagen, Andreas Katsulas, Terri Hanauer, Basil Hoffman.
●Novelist Whitley Strieber (Walken), taking friends, wife and young son to his country cabin, wakes up to the first of many meetings with 'non-human' creatures. They whisk him off inside their strange craft and subject him to rigorous, painful examination, yet he subsequently remembers nothing. As the encounters become more frequent, his behaviour becomes more erratic, and he agrees to undergo hypnosis sessions, which reveal the ordeals suppressed by his conscious mind. This misjudged adaptation of Strieber's 'true life' experiences (described in his best-seller) eschews his philosophical and scientific theories about the events, offering instead Strieber wielding rifles against the intruders and, in mellower mood, boogying with them. In aiming for the widest popular appeal, the film ends up in no man's land. CM

Communion (aka Holy Terror)

(1976, US, 108 min)
d Alfred Sole. *p* Richard K Rosenberg. *sc* Rosemary Ritvo, Alfred Sole. *ph* John Friberg, Chuck Hall. *ed* Edward Salier. *pd* John Lawless. *m* Stephen Lawrence. *cast* Linda Miller, Mildred Clinton, Paula Sheppard, Niles McMaster, Rudolph Willrich, Jane Lowry.
●Did 12-year-old Alice strangle and set fire to her younger sister during her first communion service? As Robin Wood has noted, the American family film has shifted from the comedy genre to the horror film; in this instance a lot of the humour transfers as well. *Communion* delights in confounding expectations as it conducts three separate enquiries. The plot investigates the murder; the film examines the family's self-destruction; and the film-makers construct a running commentary on the themes of Alfred Hitchcock: against a carefully evoked background of Catholicism emerge twin themes of repression and guilt. Numerous parallels and cross-references neatly bind it all together. The result is far more than a sterile exercise in suspense: *Communion* constantly keeps the audience on its toes with a wealth of incidental detail, excellent set pieces and technical versatility. CPe

Como Agua para Chocolate

see Like Water for Chocolate

Cómo maté a mi padre

see Way I Killed My Father, The

Como ser mujer y no morir en el intento

see How to Be a Woman and Not Die in the Attempt

Companeros (Vamos a Matar, Companeros!)

(1970, It/Sp/WGer, 118 min)
d Sergio Corbucci. *sc* Dino Maiuri, Massimo de Rito, Fritz Ebert, Sergio Corbucci. *ph* Alejandro Ulloa. *ed* Eugenio Alabiso. *ad* Adolfo Cofiño. *m* Ennio Morricone. *cast* Franco Nero, Tomas Milian, Jack Palance, Fernando Rey, Iris Berben, Francisco Bodalo, Karin Schubert.
●A spaghetti Western, and a pretty absurd one. Nero, sporting more costumes than expressions, is a Swedish gunrunner in a straw boater who gets mixed up with hidden treasure and communist revolutionaries down Mexico way. Palance, startlingly like Robert Shaw on a bad day, is a slant-eyed mercenary with a pet hawk and an artificial hand who's pissed at Nero for leaving him nailed to a tree in Cuba. Rey, minus his own voice, is a bespectacled commie professor who advocates Gandhi-esque non-violence but graduates to some serious slaughter by the end. Twangy Morricone score. AO

Company Business

(1991, US, 98 min)
d Nicholas Meyer. *p* Steven-Charles Jaffe. *sc* Nicholas Meyer. *ph* Gerry Fisher. *ed* Ronald Roose. *pd* Ken Adam. *m* Michael Kamen. *cast* Gene Hackman, Mikhail Baryshnikov, Kurtwood Smith, Terry O'Quinn, Daniel Von Bargen, Oleg Rudnick, Geraldine Danon.
●The Cold War is over – or is it? Retired CIA agent Sam Boyd (Hackman) is recalled for one last job: he must travel to Berlin with a former State Department mole (Baryshnikov), plus a briefcase containing $2m to exchange for a captured American pilot. But Sam discovers that he has been betrayed by his own people, and our unlikely duo go on the run with CIA and KGB in hot pursuit. This offers familiar spy movie clichés, and although Meyer's direction creates a moderately menacing atmosphere, his script is at best undemanding, at worst simplistic. Hackman rises above the material, which is more than can be said for Baryshnikov. CM

Company Limited (Seemabaddha)

(1971, Ind, 112 min. b/w)
d Satyajit Ray. *p* Bharat Shamsher Rana. *sc* Satyajit Ray. *ph* Soumendu Roy. *ed* Dulal Dutta. *ad* Ashoke Bose. *m* Satyajit Ray. *cast* Barun Chanda, Sharmila Tagore, Parumita Chowdhary, Harindranath Chattopadhyaya, Haradhan Banerjee, Indira Roy.
●Against a background of neo-imperialist India, and set in Calcutta, a city of severe unemployment and unrest, Ray creates a finely judged satire about the gradual compromise that is the price of ambition. His complacent, but not unlikeable, central character works as a sales manager and possesses sufficient ambition to override any doubts about accepting the privileges remaining from colonial days and the rewards of Westernised industry. But two things undermine his smugness: his provincial but astute sister-in-law pays a visit; and a crisis in the export department forces him to resort to political manipulation in order to further his career. Both events leave him a wiser but lesser man. It's basically an old-fashioned film, but none the worse for that. CPe

Company of Cowards

see Advance to the Rear

Company of Strangers, The

(1990, Can, 100 min)
d Cynthia Scott. *p* David Wilson. *sc* Gloria Demers, Cynthia Scott, David Wilson, Sally Bocher. *ph* David de Volpi. *ed* David Wilson. *ad* Christiane Gagnon. *m* Marie Bernard. *cast* Alice Diabo, Constance Garneau, Winifred Holden, Cissy Meddings, Catherine Roche, Mary Meigs.
●Deftly skirting the dangers of improvisation, this touching and gently humorous film maroons a group of septuagenarian women (and their younger black minder) in an isolated farmhouse, where they while away the time talking about their families, working lives and past loves, and their hopes and fears for an uncertain future. Simple scenes, like one in which a prissy woman is cajoled into removing her wig, or the realisation that one of the women (now deaf) will never again hear birdsong, are suffused with residual strength and intimations of mortality. The only false note is the carefully selected nature of the group (a Navajo woman, a nun, a lesbian, a wacky stroke-survivor), which undercuts the otherwise free-form structure. NF

Company of Wolves, The

(1984, GB, 95 min)
d Neil Jordan. *p* Chris Brown, Stephen Woolley. *sc* Angela Carter, Neil Jordan. *ph* Bryan Loftus. *ed* Rodney Holland. *pd* Anton Furst. *m* George Fenton. *cast* Angela Lansbury, David Warner, Graham Crowden, Brian Glover, Kathryn Pogson, Stephen Rea, Sarah Patterson, Terence Stamp.
●Once upon a time, young Rosaleen was dreaming of an Arcadian past when Granny would tell grim tales of once upon a time when little girls should beware of men whose eyebrows meet in the middle and who are hairy on the inside… And in those dark days, fear accompanied desire and beauty was wed with the beast… The characters in Jordan's film of Angela Carter's story inhabit a magical, mysterious world of cruelty and wonder, rarely seen in cinema. In tales within tales within tales, dream is reality, wolves are human, and vice-versa. Rarely has this Gothic landscape of the imagination been so perfectly conveyed by film; there is simply a precise, resonant portrayal of a young girl's immersion in fantasies where sexuality is both fearful and seductive. Like all the best fairy-tales, the film is purely sensual, irrational, fuelled by an immense joy in story-telling, and totally lucid. It's also a true original, with the most beautiful visual effects to emerge from Britain in years. GA

Company She Keeps, The

(1950, US, 83 min, b/w)
d John Cromwell. *p* John Houseman. *sc* Ketti Frings. *ph* Nick Musuraca. *ed* William Swink. *ad* Albert S D'Agostino, Al Herman. *m* Leigh Harline. *cast* Lizabeth Scott, Jane Greer, Dennis O'Keefe, Fay Baker, John Hoyt, James Bell.
●Dreadful script by Ketti Frings which ties itself up in novelettish knots as a female ex-con (Greer) does battle with her female parole officer (Scott) over the latter's boyfriend. Cromwell does his best in the circumstances, and Greer does wonders. TM

Compartiment Tueurs

see Sleeping Car Murder, The

Competition, The

(1980, US, 129 min)
d Joel Oliansky. *p* William Sackheim. *sc* Joel Oliansky. *ph* Richard H Kline. *ed* David Blewitt. *pd* Dale Hennesy. *m* Lalo Schifrin. *cast* Richard Dreyfuss, Amy Irving, Lee Remick, Sam Wanamaker, Joseph Cali, Ty Henderson.
●Romance in a major key: competitive classical pianists Dreyfuss and Irving spar the sentimental sex war as an inevitable prelude to a four-handed future. The plot's old hat and not half as interesting as any of Michael Ritchie's 'competition' films (*Downhill Racer*, *Smile*, etc), but you

have to admire writer/director Oliansky's confidence in playing it again so straight and so strong to the gallery. The ivories are nicely tinkled, and the vets – Remick and Wanamaker – get most of the saving lines. PT

Completely Pogued

(1989, Ire, 55 min)
d Billy Magra. *p* James Morris. *ph* Eugene McVeigh. *ed* Finola Vereker, Hugh Chaloner. *cast* The Pogues, Kirsty McColl, Joe Strummer, Steve Earle, Lynval Golding.
● 'What we did, right, was we broke open the pop market, right? To trad music, right? Irish trad music, yeah? *Now* what happened after that I don't know…' So confesses toothy, hard-drinkin' Shane McGowan, lead man with punk-folk megastars the Pogues, the band that has taken traditional Irish folk and ramshackle rock to the bright pop lights of Wembley. In this rather haphazard but proud spirit, the documentary, like the Pogues' career itself, continues: the band and the various famous rockers they've jammed with offering opinions and anecdotes in a surprisingly entertaining and often revealing manner. Even if you have absolutely no interest in the music, the vast array of pasty-faced uglies is really quite stunning. LD

Complicity

(2000, UK, 99 min)
d Gavin Millar. *p* Richard Jackson, Neil Dunn. *sc* Bryan Elsley. *ph* David Odd. *ed* Angus Newton. *pd* Jamie Leonard. *m* Colin Towns. *cast* Jonny Lee Miller, Keeley Hawes, Brian Cox, Bill Paterson, Paul Higgins, Jason Hetherington, Samuel West, Rachael Stirling, Valerie Edmond, Paul Young, Andy Gray.
● It says a lot about the British film industry that dross like *Rancid Aluminium* commands a wide theatrical release, while this sensitively judged adaptation of Iain Banks' best novel goes straight to video. In fact, *Complicity* shares many of the virtues of the BBC's excellent 1996 version of *The Crow Road*, among them director Gavin Millar, screenwriter Bryan Elsley and half its cast (including Bill Paterson and Valerie Edmond). Jonny Lee Miller isn't everyone's idea of Cameron Colley – the left-leaning, coke-snorting, sexually deviant Edinburgh hack who finds himself implicated in a series of grisly murders, all of them of corrupt establishment figures – but he's not bad. (Dougray Scott, another *Crow Road* veteran, would have been great.) And although it packs a little too much into its 99 minutes, it has clearly been made with love, as well as respect for the source material. Millar gets Banks' nostalgic, mournful idealism just so. Meanwhile, estimable period-drama queen Keeley Hawes seems to have spent the shoot pondering the question: Why wear a bonnet when you can wear nothing? JO'C

Complot d'Aristote, Le

see Aristotle's Plot

Compromising Positions

(1985, US, 98 min)
d/p Frank Perry. *sc* Susan Isaacs. *ph* Barry Sonnenfeld. *ed* Peter C Frank. *pd* Peter Larkin. *m* Brad Fiedel. *cast* Susan Sarandon, Raul Julia, Edward Herrmann, Judith Ivey, Mary Beth Hurt, Joe Mantegna, Josh Mostel.
● A witty, unbuttoned script by Susan Isaacs, taken from her novel of the same name, puts ex-reporter Sarandon into the middle of a murder scandal that is rocking the well-manicured lawns of commuter-belt New York suburbia. A sleazy dentist, who has been putting more than just his water pick into his female patients' cavities, ends up with one of his own scalpels in the neck. With the help of a *macho simpatico* cop (Julia), Sarandon uncovers a pornography ring, along with some risqué polaroid shots of most of the local female population in various degrees of bondage. What gives her the edge in the investigation is her sympathy with the ladies, and her own wide-eyed innocence. It's all very humorous and engaging, if only for proving that American whodunits don't have to have car chases and brutality; and it has a wicked eye for the vacuity of middle-class good life and what it may conceal. Lots of feelthy girl talk, too. CPea

Compulsion

(1959, US, 103 min, b/w)
d Richard Fleischer. *p* Richard Zanuck. *sc* Richard Murphy. *ph* William C Mellor. *ed* William H Reynolds. *ad* Lyle Wheeler, Mark-Lee Kirk. *m* Lionel Newman. *cast* Dean Stockwell, Bradford Dillman, Orson Welles, Diane Varsi, EG Marshall, Martin Milner.
● Emasculated version of Meyer Levin's novel based on the Leopold-Loeb case, in which two homosexual law students murdered a boy to demonstrate their intellectual superiority. Fine so long as it sticks to the thriller format, but shaky in its period sense (Chicago, 1924) and developing mushy pretensions culminating when Welles is trundled on to deliver an impassioned but hokey boil-down of Clarence Darrow's two-day summation pleading mercy for reasons of insanity. Best performance is Stockwell's, though Dillman and Welles are good value. TM

Comrades

(1986, GB, 183 min)
d Bill Douglas. *p* Simon Relph. *sc* Bill Douglas. *ph* Gale Tattersall. *ed* Mick Audsley. *pd* Michael Pickwoad. *m* Hans Werner Henze, David Graham. *cast* Robin Soans, Alex Norton, William Gaminara, Philip Davis, Robert Stephens, Freddie Jones, Vanessa Redgrave, Michael Hordern, James Fox, Barbara Windsor, Imelda Staunton.
● Douglas' epic and very British film about the Tolpuddle Martyrs – 1830s Dorset farm labourers who formed a union to protest against subsistence wages, only to be deported to Australia – employs a minimum of fussy historical detail to offer a didactic but never dogmatic film of wide-ranging relevance. Politically, it foreshadows modern labour disputes; aesthetically, as 'a lanternist's account', the film is an investigation of different, pre-cinematic modes of story-telling. Fuelling the whole is a deeply humane concern for suffering, coupled with a righteous anger directed against hypocrisy and inequality. Equally importantly, however, it works as often humorous, always intelligently moving spectacle, immaculately performed, structured and shot. GA

Comrades, Almost a Love Story (Tian Mimi)

(1996, HK, 118 min)
d Peter Chan. *p* Raymond Chow, Eric Tsang. *sc* Ivy Ho. *ph* Jingle Ma. *ed* Chan Ki-Hop, Kwong Chi-Leung. *ad* Hai Chung-Man. *m* Chiu Tsang-Hei. *cast* Leon Lai, Maggie Cheung, Eric Tsang, Irene Tsu, Chris Doyle, Kristy Yeung.
● A nine-times winner at the 1997 Hong Kong Film Awards, Chan's film charts the lives of two immigrants to Hong Kong from Mainland China across ten years. Li Xiaojun (Lai) is a naive and gullible northerner with a fiancée back home in Tianjin; Li Chiao (Cheung) is a street-smart southerner from Guangzhou who wants no emotional attachments in her life until she hooks up with a triad boss (Tsang). Both of them receive extended sentimental educations, sometimes together, more often apart. Very well played, the central near-romance serves as a barometer of the social and economic changes in Hong Kong since the mid-1980s. The supporting characters and subplots are far less interesting and credible; a dotty old brothel madam with a thing for William Holden (!) is especially wearisome. TR

Comrade X

(1940, US, 90 min, b/w)
d King Vidor. *p* Gottfried Reinhardt. *sc* Ben Hecht, Charles Lederer. *ph* Joseph Ruttenberg. *ed* Harold F Kress. *ad* Cedric Gibbons. *m* Bronislau Kaper. *cast* Clark Gable, Hedy Lamarr, Felix Bressart, Oscar Homolka, Eve Arden, Sig Rumann.
● By no means classic Vidor: its characters – Gable as an American journalist in Soviet Russia, Lamarr as the source of his scoop stories – are simply too bland to animate the film. Only in the last sequence, where Gable and Lamarr escape from Russia in a tank, closely pursued by virtually the whole of the Russian army, does Vidor successfully visualise (albeit comically: the script is by Ben Hecht and Charles Lederer) the tensions that the characters set in motion. A superb piece of entertainment, none the less. PH

Con Air

(1997, US, 115 min)
d Simon West. *p* Jerry Bruckheimer. *sc* Scott Rosenberg. *ph* David Tattersall. *ed* Chris Lebenzon, Steve Mirkovich, Glenn Scantlebury. *ad* Edward McAvoy, Chris Butcher. *m* Trevor Rabin, Mark Mancina. *cast* Nicolas Cage, John Cusack, John Malkovich, Steve Buscemi, Ving Rhames, Danny Trejo, Colm Meaney, Mykelti Williamson, Rachel Ticotin.
● Led by Cyrus 'The Virus' Grissom (Malkovich), a dozen jailbirds hijack a transport plane. Only parolee Cameron Poe (Cage) – caught up in the middle – stands between the worst of the worst and their freedom. Scott Rosenberg's ingeniously tooled script recalls such vintage entertainments as *The Dirty Dozen* and *The Great Escape*. Dialogue is pared to bullet points, punctuation between spectacular set-pieces, but Rosenberg makes every word count. If it needs strong actors to flesh out the characterisation, so be it: Rhames, Buscemi, Trejo – faces you don't forget in a hurry. Sometimes skin deep is close enough. Commercials director West gives us the hard sell non-stop for 115 ear-splitting minutes. There are misjudgments. He gets off on male flesh rippling against slow motion fireballs, and has no time for women, but throws in a transvestite for cheap jibes. The climax looks like an afterthought, and in trying to top itself, the movie finally goes OTT. Very cool, but also very cold. TCh

Conamara

(2000, Ger/Ire, 107 min)
d Eoin Moore. *p* Ingrid Holzapfel. *sc* Greg Brennan, Eoin Moore. *ph* Michael Hammon. *pd* David Doran. *cast* Ellen Ten Damme, Darragh Kelly, Andreas Schmidt, Maighréad Conneely, Katie Nic Dhonnacha, Maurtin Jajmsie, Rosaleen Linehan.
● Quirky romance set on the West coast of Ireland: an old German boyfriend (Schmidt) unexpectedly and belatedly visits now-married Maria (Ten Damme, vital) and sets off ructions with her placid husband Antaine (Kelly, solid). The crofts and farms of Connemara are shot with a hand-held camera, and the film revels in the idiosyncracies of the local basket weavers and the oddball, bassoon-playing stranger without trespassing too far into cliché. And the ramshackle narrative, about setting up an amphibious tourist tour vehicle, is shored up by uninhibited performances and an overall lack of pomposity. WH

Conan the Barbarian

(1981, US, 129 min)
d John Milius. *p* Buzz Feitshans, Raffaella de Laurentiis. *sc* John Milius, Oliver Stone. *ph* Duke Callaghan. *ed* C Timothy O'Meara. *pd* Ron Cobb. *m* Basil Poledouris. *cast* Arnold Schwarzenegger, James Earl Jones, Max von Sydow, Sandahl Bergman, Ben Davidson, Cassandra Gaviola.
● Big blokes, each seized by some grand costume fetish, hack divots out of each other with big broadswords. Deaths take for ever, years pass in a flash as our muscle-bound hero pursues his Quest for the Father (a villain who, delightfully, transmogrifies into a snake). *Conan the Barbarian* revives the old epics of Steve Reeves, adds some visual sophistication from the Italian Western, and raises a small cheer as a movie for European rather than American illiterates. Milius brags unnecessarily with egghead movie references, manages to lampoon Californian death cults, indulges in some questionable Triumph of the Will stuff, adds an appalling commentary that cries out for O Welles to sell it, and laces the whole thing with intentionally heavy humour that seems to have been misunderstood. Match verdict: no goals, slow build-up, but much absorbing action off the ball. CPe

Conan the Destroyer

(1984, US, 103 min)
d Richard Fleischer. *p* Raffaella De Laurentiis. *sc* Stanley Mann. *ph* Jack Cardiff. *ed* Frank J Urioste. *pd* Pier Luigi Basile. *m* Basil Poledouris. *cast* Arnold Schwarzenegger, Grace Jones, Wilt Chamberlain, Mako, Tracey Walter, Sarah Douglas.
● Shorn of the intellectual pretensions of its predecessor *Conan the Barbarian* (ditto the gratuitous sex), this yarn is far closer to creator Robert E Howard's preference for small minds in big bodies – a requirement Schwarzenegger fills wonderfully. A predictable quest plot is unwound with tremendous verve, and the only real disappointments are some ropey special effects. But Fleischer's zest for action carries it all along splendidly. GD

Concert for Bangladesh, The

(1972, US, 99 min)
d Saul Swimmer. *p* George Harrison, Allen Klein. *sc* Saul Swimmer. *ph* Saul Negrin, Richard Brooks, Fred Hoffman, Tohru Nakamura. *ed* Howard Lester. *with* Eric Clapton, Bob Dylan, George Harrison, Billy Preston, Leon Russell, Ravi Shankar, Ringo Starr.
●The film of the album, distinguished from other roxploitation movies by the fact that it's entirely shot from fixed camera positions, and therefore appears entirely insensitive to both the music and the event as a whole. TR

Concerto of Life

(1997, China, 103 min)
d Xia Gang. *cast* Wang Luoyong.
●A risible melodrama, told in flashback, about a Shanghai piano teacher and his friends who remain devoted to their art (Western classical music) from the '60s to '93. Since the period includes the Cultural Revolution, when foreign music was banned, much secrecy and suffering is involved, but the film often seems perversely apolitical, so that the Revolution registers as a brief, erroneous blip and, as such, part of life's rich tapestry. The tunes, perhaps inevitably, are all popular favourites, the ludicrous, lachrymose finale is overlong and disingenuous ('No regrets' indeed!), and the characterisation facile. Xia Gang should watch some movies by Sirk, who revelled in this kind of tosh, and learn to go with the melodrama, not against it. GA

Concierge, The

see For Love or Money

Concorde – Airport '79, The

see Airport '80 The Concorde

Concrete Jungle, The

see Criminal, The

Condamné à mort s'est échappé, Un (A Man Escaped)

(1956, Fr, 102 min, b/w)
d Robert Bresson. *p* Robert Sussfeld. *sc* Robert Bresson. *ph* Léonce-Henry Burel. *ed* Raymond Lamy. *ad* Pierre Charbonnier. *m* Wolfgang Amadeus Mozart. *cast* François Leterrier, Charles le Clainche, Maurice Beerblock, Roland Monod, Jacques Ertaud, Jean-Paul Delhumeau.
●The true story of a French Resistance worker's escape from imprisonment by the Gestapo in the Montluc fortress at Lyon was the inspiration for *A Man Escaped*: 'The story is true. I give it as it is, without embellishment,' claimed Bresson. However, by pushing through the authentic details into a more transcendental realm, Bresson in fact subtly transforms the simple story into a metaphysical meditation. This he does by introducing an unseen, transcendental force which helps the young man in simple but crucial ways: 'I would like to show this miracle: an invisible hand over the prison, directing what happens and causing such a thing to succeed for one and not another…the film is a mystery…The Spirit breathes where it will.' The kind of film which inspires awe, even in an atheist. NF

Condorman

(1981, US, 90 min)
d Charles Jarrott. *p* Jan Williams. *sc* Marc Stirdivant, Glenn Gordon Caron, Mickey Rose. *ph* Charles F Wheeler. *ed* Gordon D Brenner. *pd* Albert Witherick. *m* Henry Mancini. *cast* Michael Crawford, Oliver Reed, Barbara Carrera, James Hampton, Jean-Pierre Kalfon, Dana Elcar.
●An ideological intervention from the Disney machine: the Cold War re-heated for the kiddies. Lamebrain comic artist Crawford gets to play an American-accented Bond and trash the nasty Reds at their own spy games in approved superhero style. A pathetic shadow of the Frank Tashlin/Jerry Lewis *Artists and Models*. Send the kids to sleep with *How to Read Donald Duck* instead. PT

Conductor

see Maestro, Il

Conductor, The (Dyrygent)

(1979, Pol, 102 min)
d Andrzej Wajda. *sc* Andrzej Kijowski. *ph* Slawomir Idziak. *ed* Halina Prugar. *pd* Allan Starski. *cast* John Gielgud, Krystyna Janda, Andrzej Seweryn, Marysia Seweryn, Jan Ciecierski, Józef Fryzlewicz.
●Culture shocks: Wajda's credit appears over New York; Gielgud's lips move and a disembodied Pole speaks his lines. Such incongruities are never quite integrated within this parable about a prodigal elder's attempted return to the fold. Gielgud is the eponymous international maestro whose encounter with a young violinist stirs memories of a provincial Polish debut – and an old debt – prompting him to celebrate his jubilee with his long-abandoned ain folk. His reception incorporates simmering jealousies and personality clashes (and Wajda's sly digs at the star system of socialist culture), but the film only really lives in fits and starts. PT

Conduct Unbecoming

(1975, GB, 107 min)
d Michael Anderson. *p* Michael Deeley, Barry Spikings. *sc* Robert Enders. *ph* Bob Huke. *ed* John Glen. *ad* Ted Tester. *m* Stanley Myers. *cast* Michael York, Richard Attenborough, Trevor Howard, Stacy Keach, Christopher Plummer, Susannah York, James Faulkner.
●An alarmingly creaky adaptation of Barry England's play about a regimental outpost in India in Victorian times, and the flutterings about honour occasioned when the bounder in the mess attacks a lady. His secret trial by subalterns' court martial reveals unsuspected murky depths in which rigor theatricalis is warded off only by a valiant starry cast giving their all in the big scenes with which each is thoughtfully provided. TM

Confession, The

see Aveu, L'

Confessional, The (Le Confessionnal)

(1995, Can/GB/Fr, 101 min)
d Robert LePage. *p* Denise Robert, David Puttnam, Philippe Carcassonne. *sc* Robert LePage. *ph* Alain Dostie. *ed* Emmanuelle Castro. *ad* François Laplante. *m* Sacha Puttnam. *cast* Lothaire Bluteau, Patrick Goyette, Jean-Louis Millette, Kristin Scott Thomas, Ron Burrage, Richard Fréchette.
●Renowned stage director Robert LePage's debut film is dramatically assured and visually inspired. Returning to Quebec for his father's funeral, Pierre Lamontagne (Bluteau) becomes enmeshed in his adopted brother Marc's obsessive search for roots. The quest takes them back to 1952, when Hitchcock was filming *I Confess* in the city; at that time, Marc's unmarried 16-year-old mother Rachel revealed the father's identity, under the protection of the confessional. Questions of faith and identity are skilfully woven into an entertaining mystery plot. NF

Confessions from a Holiday Camp

(1977, GB, 88 min)
d Norman Cohen. *p* Greg Smith. *sc* Christopher Wood. *ph* Ken Hodges. *ed* Geoffrey Foot. *ad* Harry Pottle. *m* Ed Welch. *cast* Robin Askwith, Anthony Booth, Doris Hare, Bill Maynard, Sheila White, Liz Fraser, Linda Hayden, John Junkin, Lance Percival.
●Cherie's dad Tony (playing one Sid Noggett) buddies the dread Askwith through this excruciating parade of mid-'70s British smut (premise: a holiday camp is taken over by a former prison officer). The title establishment languishes under such grey skies that you feel a twinge of sympathy for the female extras called on to disrobe at regular five-minute intervals. TJ

Confessions of a Bigamist (Warum hab' ich bloss 2 x ja gesagt)

(1969, WGer/It, 89 min)
d François Legrand [Franz Antel]. *p* Gerhard Pöschl. *sc* Kurt Nachman, Günther Ebert, Mario Guerra, Vittorio Vighi. *ph* Hans Matula. *ed* Vincenzo Tamassi, Gertrud Petermann. *ad* Amedeo Mellone. *m* Gianni Ferrio. *cast* Lando Buzzanca, Terry Torday, Raffaella Carrà, Peter Weck, Franco Giacobini, Ann Smyrner.
●The lucky hero is a wagon-lit attendant on the Rome-Munich train, with a wife at each end of the line – boy, does he have fun? Also on hand to raise a snigger in this Teutonic sex-comedy are some blustering bigwigs and a crazy doctor whose speciality is treating impotence. GB

Confessions of a Driving Instructor

(1976, GB, 90 min)
d Norman Cohen. *p* Greg Smith. *sc* Christopher Wood. *ph* Ken Hodges. *ed* Geoffrey Foot. *ad* Albert Witherick. *m* Ed Welch. *cast* Robin Askwith, Anthony Booth, Sheila White, Doris Hare, Bill Maynard, Windsor Davies, Irene Handl.
●This third in the *Confessions* series must be a new low for British comedy, displaying a complete indifference to wit, pacing, timing or observation. Nominally based around the rivalry between two driving instruction schools, it soon bankrupts itself on a series of soft-core gropings, manufactured with awesome clumsiness as women fall for the spectacularly lack-lustre hero.

Confessions of a Nazi Spy

(1939, US, 102 min, b/w)
d Anatole Litvak. *p* Peter Lord. *sc* Milton Krims, John Wexley. *ph* Sol Polito. *ed* Owen Marks. *ad* Carl Jules Weyl. *cast* Edward G Robinson, Francis Lederer, George Sanders, Paul Lukas, Lya Lys, Henry O'Neill, James Stephenson.
●Anti-Nazi propaganda film from Warners, with Robinson (like Cagney, doing an about-face from gangster roles to more respectable characters) as the G-Man ferreting out Nazi fifth columnists working in America. Topically following hard on the heels of several anti-Nazi trials in 1938, the film achieved great popular and critical success in America (though banned in many Latin American and European countries); now, for all its admirable anti-Fascist relevance, it seems weakened by its patriotic flag-waving and the pseudo-documentary approach (sacrificing suspense) taken by Litvak. But the quietly determined Robinson, the sinister Sanders (as a Nazi villain, a role he would later develop in Lang's *Man Hunt*), and Lederer (the man duped into becoming a spy by his vain egocentricity) lend a power to the film that makes it still worth watching. GA

Confessions of a Pop Performer

(1975, GB, 91 min)
d Norman Cohen. *p* Greg Smith. *sc* Christopher Wood. *ph* Alan Hume. *ed* Geoffrey Foot. *pd* Robert Jones. *m* Bugatti Musker. *cast* Robin Askwith, Anthony Booth, Bill Maynard, Doris Hare, Sheila White, Bob Todd.
●No.2 in the *Confessions* series. Although seemingly directed at the lowest common denominator, with nudes sighted every few minutes to revive flagging concentration and plot, glimpses of a time-honoured British comic tradition can occasionally be discerned: good old smut by way of end-of-pier summer shows, What-the-Butlers-Saw and *Carry On* films. It's a world of relentless double entendres, verbal misunderstandings, randy wives and cuckolded husbands, groping couples, snapping braces and perpetual coitus interruptus. All remarkably innocent: no one swears and the family is regarded as sacrosanct (the film, after all, is primarily family entertainment).

Confessions of a Sixth Form Girl (Schulmädchen-Report – Was Eltern nicht für moglich halten)

(1970, WGer, 90 min)
d Ernst Hofbauer. *p* Wolf C Hartwig. *sc* Günther Heller. *ph* Klaus Werner. *ed* Walter Boos, Evelyne Wohlfeiler. *pd* Eberhard Schroeder. *m* Gert Wilden. *cast* Friedrich von Thun, Günter Kieslich, Rolf Harnish, Helga Kruck.
●The rag-bag of confessions (in fact, 'true' case histories) in this poorly graded assembly-line exploiter (the first of a series) are related to the parent-teacher association, with suitable

Teutonic authority, by a sixth-former's portly father who (surprise, surprise) turns out to be a child psychologist. This dismal barrel-scraper induces bottomless gloom and an indefinite loss of sexual appetite. JPy

Confessions of a Suburban Girl

(1992, GB, 50 min)
d Susan Seidelman. *p* Jonathan Brett. *sc* Susan Seidelman. *ph* Maryse Alberti. *ed* Mona Davis. *pd* Jessica Lanier. *m* Joseph S DeBeasi.

●In this slight documentary (commissioned by BBC Scotland) which explores changing sexual attitudes, Seidelman returns to her home town of Huntingdon Valley, just outside Philadelphia, to search out childhood friends. Interspersing interviews with clips from her films, she traces the interest in 'bad girls' which runs through her work to a youth spent in suburbia, when toughnut Italians wore the coolest clothes and looked like being the hottest dates. Bitter-sweet passages contrast youthful expectations with adult reality, but such hopeless Seidelman efforts as *Cookie* and *She-Devil* don't bear up under the weight of this analysis. CM

Confessions of a Trickbaby

see Freeway II: Confessions of a Trickbaby

Confessions of a Window Cleaner

(1974, GB, 90 min)
d Val Guest. *p* Greg Smith. *sc* Christopher Wood, Val Guest. *ph* Norman Warwick. *ed* Bill Lenny. *ad* Robert Jones. *m* Sam Sklair. *cast* Robin Askwith, Anthony Booth, Sheila White, Dandy Nichols, Bill Maynard, John Le Mesurier.

●As dismal as its successors in the brief *Confessions* series, this was covered widely in the trade press at the time. Something to do with the bravery of the producers actually going ahead and making what they all but acknowledged was a whole lot of garbage, on the principle that garbage is better for the British film industry than not making anything at all. VG

Confessions of Winifred Wagner, The (Winifred Wagner und die Geschichte des Hauses Wahnfried 1914–1975)

(1975, WGer, 104 min, b/w)
d/p Hans-Jürgen Syberberg. *ph* Dietrich Lohmann. *ed* Agape Dorstewitz. *with* Winifred Wagner.

●'He had that perfect Austrian warmth and understanding': Winifred Wagner (78-year-old widow of Richard Wagner's son Siegfried) on the human face and personal charm of Adolf Hitler. Hitler's passion for Wagner inevitably led him to Winifred, organiser of the Bayreuth Festival. During their 22-year friendship, to whose memory she is stubbornly faithful, Hitler doted on her family and mentioned nothing of politics: 'I would say he was too easily influenced and gave in to radical demands,' is her only criticism, made apparently without irony. This film features Winifred Wagner's first interview (shot almost entirely in medium close-up) about Hitler as a patron of the arts. It's an extraordinary document – about the role of art in a society, about its relation to politics, and about degrees of unawareness. The original cut ran five hours. CPe

Confidence (Bizalom)

(1979, Hun, 117 min)
d/sc István Szabó. *ph* Lajos Koltai. *ed* Zsuzsa Csakany. *ad* Jozsef Romvary. *cast* Ildikó Bánsági, Péter Andorai, O Gombik, Károly Csáki, Ildikó Kishonti, Lajos Balazsovits.

●*Confidence* may not possess the surface sheen or panache of Szabó's later blockbuster *Mephisto*, but it's a film of near-equivalent substance within its more intimate scope. Acting a role during wartime is again the focus, but here the false identities (as man and wife) of a harmless refugee couple living through the Nazi occupation of Hungary are assumed out of strict necessity. He is a resistance fugitive, she the wife of another underground member, hustled to safety as a net closes on her husband. At first they share only suspicion and insecurity, but they are hemmed by circumstance into an alliance, then an accommodation, then a relationship. Trust is the crucial variable between them; and the more claustrophobic the film becomes, the more it opens out to address the crux of any relationship, sexual or social. Notions of betrayal and commitment resonate far beyond the couple's tenuous haven. This reductionist description may sound dry, but the film isn't: its political-thriller edginess and emotional poignancy intersect absorbingly, and the central performances are flawless. PT

Confidential Agent

(1945, US, 118 min, b/w)
d Herman Shumlin. *p/sc* Robert Buckner. *ph* James Wong Howe. *ed* George Amy. *ad* Leo Kuter. *m* Franz Waxman. *cast* Charles Boyer, Lauren Bacall, Peter Lorre, Katina Paxinou, Victor Francen, Wanda Hendrix.

●Striking, literate adaptation of Graham Greene's novel which takes its tone from Boyer's tired, ageing secret agent (in reality a musician) sent to England in 1937 by the Spanish Loyalists to sabotage a Fascist business deal. Shumlin's direction is inclined to be lethargic (a distinguished stage producer, he made only two movies), but is more than made up for by Wong Howe's moody lighting, which perfectly captures the twilit world of people living constantly in fear. A marvellous cast makes it a must anyway. TM

Confidential Report

see Mr Arkadin

Confirm or Deny

(1941, US, 73 min, b/w)
d Archie Mayo. *p* Len Hammond. *sc* Jo Swerling, Henry Wales, Samuel Fuller. *ph* Leon Shamroy. *ed* Robert Bischoff. *ad* Richard Day, Wiard B Ihnen. *m* David Buttolph. *cast* Don Ameche, Joan Bennett, Roddy McDowall, John Loder, Eric Blore, Arthur Shields, Raymond Walburn.

●Fast-moving if fairly ordinary tribute to the heroism of American war correspondents covering World War II. Much of the film gets bogged down in the growing romance between agency man Ameche and Ministry of Information switchboard girl Bennett, but it's entertaining enough when the bombs drop; and collector-cultists may derive pleasure from a script by former journalist and future genius Sam Fuller. GA

Conflict

(1945, US, 86 min, b/w)
d Curtis Bernhardt. *p* William Jacobs. *sc* Arthur T Horman, Dwight Taylor. *ph* Merritt B Gerstad. *ed* David Weisbart. *ad* Ted Smith. *m* Frederick Hollander. *cast* Humphrey Bogart, Alexis Smith, Sydney Greenstreet, Rose Hobart, Charles Drake, Grant Mitchell.

●Routine *film noir* with Bogart as a murderer disoriented by the mounting evidence that his victim is still alive. Greenstreet, exuding detached benignity, hovers over Bogart's dilemma and has the line which ought to pin down the theme – 'Sometimes a thought can be like a malignant disease and eat away the will power' – but somehow Bernhardt never realises that promise. The dominant irony of the first reel, in which Bogart and wife Hobart are publicly 'the happiest of couples' and privately tearing each other apart (a dichotomy bridged by their theme tune, 'Jealousy'), is dispelled by the patchy development later. Alexis Smith's role remains unfocused, while Bogart suffers defiantly and spits out the odd characteristic line. Robert Siodmak had a hand in the story. SG

Conflict of Wings (aka Fuss Over Feathers)

(1954, GB, 84 min)
d John Eldridge. *p* Herbert Mason. *sc* Don Sharp, John Pudney. *ph* Arthur Grant. *ed* Lito Carruthers. *ad* Ray Simm. *m* Philip Green. *cast* John Gregson, Muriel Pavlow, Kieron Moore, Niall MacGinnis, Guy Middleton, Harry Fowler, Sheila Sweet.

●Produced by Group Three as part of the government's intervention in the British film industry in the '50s. The conflict in question is between birds wings and RAF wings. The Norfolk villagers want to keep their bird sanctuary, and the RAF want a training ground. Needless to say there is a third way: the Great British Compromise. One minor point of interest is that the script is by Don Sharp from his own novel. PH

Conformist, The (Il Conformista)

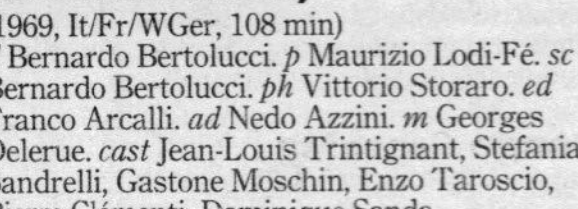

(1969, It/Fr/WGer, 108 min)
d Bernardo Bertolucci. *p* Maurizio Lodi-Fé. *sc* Bernardo Bertolucci. *ph* Vittorio Storaro. *ed* Franco Arcalli. *ad* Nedo Azzini. *m* Georges Delerue. *cast* Jean-Louis Trintignant, Stefania Sandrelli, Gastone Moschin, Enzo Taroscio, Pierre Clémenti, Dominique Sanda.

●Like *The Spider's Stratagem*, a subtle anatomy of Italy's fascist past, but here the playful Borgesian time-travelling is replaced by a more personal drive which heralds the Oedipal preoccupations that haunt Bertolucci's later work. Stripping Moravia's novel of all its psychological annotations except one – as a child, the hero suffered trauma at the hands of a homosexual – Bertolucci presents him simultaneously as a suitably murky protagonist for a *film noir* about political assassination, and as a conformist so anxious to live a normal life that he willingly becomes an anonymous tool of the state. Juggling past and present with the same *bravura* flourish as Welles in *Citizen Kane*, Bertolucci conjures a dazzling historical and personal perspective (the marbled insane asylum where his father is incarcerated; the classical vistas of Mussolini's corridors of power; the dance hall where two women tease in an ambiguous tango; the forest road where the assassination runs horribly counter to expectation), demonstrating how the search for normality ends in the inevitable discovery that there is no such thing. TM

Confrontation, The (Fényes Szelek)

(1968, Hun, 86 min)
d Miklós Jancsó. *sc* Gyula Hernàdi. *ph* Tamás Somlo. *ed* Zoltán Farkas. *cast* Lajos Balázsovits, Andrea Drahota, András Bálint, Kati Kovács, András Kozak, Benedek Toth.

●'What is the role of the individual in history?' asks one of the characters in Jancsó's film, set in the Hungary of 1947 and concerned with the problems of revolutionary tactics, this time posed for a group of students. *The Confrontation* has more talk than is usual in Jancsó's films, precisely because its form is that of a debate on revolutionary tactics, though of course there is the usual recourse to the specifically Hungarian marching, dancing and folk-song rituals which make his movies continually seductive. RM

Confucian Confusion, A (Duli Shidai)

(1994, Tai, 133 min)
d Edward Yang. *p* Yu Weiyen. *sc* Edward Yang. *ph* Arthur Wong, Zhang Zhan, Longyu Li, Hong Wuxiu. *ed* Chen Bowen. *m* Antonio Lee. *cast* Xianggi Chen, Shujun Ni, Weiming Wang, Bosen Wang.

●Yang's brilliantly achieved comedy follows a selection of modern urban types through two fraught days and nights rife with misunderstandings and cross-purposes. The specific focus is on Taipei now, a city torn between me-generation aspirations and age-old Chinese ideas of social conformity, but almost everything here could equally well take place in neo-conservative London: Yang's semi-affectionate caricatures of civil servants, business and PR people and the arts crowd are all too recognisable. The new streamlined version of the film is tighter and more provocative than that which baffled most of the comatose British press corps (TO excepted) at Cannes '94; the creative energies that fired *A Brighter Summer Day* are sparkier than ever. TR

Congo

(1995, US, 108 min)
d Frank Marshall. *p* Kathleen Kennedy, Sam Mercer. *sc* John Patrick Shanley. *ph* Allen Daviau. *ed* Anne V Coates. *pd* J Michael Riva. *m* Jerry Goldsmith. *cast* Dylan Walsh, Laura Linney, Joe Don Baker, Tim Curry, Ernie Hudson, Grant Heslov, Mary Ellen Trainor.

●*Congo* isn't so much a movie as a gigantic theme park, with the name of Michael Crichton (who wrote the original not-half-bad novel) as a flashing attraction. The storylines take in: the return of a talking mountain gorilla to the wilds of central Africa; the discovery of a perfect diamond that can fuel the megalomaniac dreams of Baker's electronics mogul; lots of special effects gadgetry care of explorer-babe Karen Ross (Linney); a grotesquely OTT performance from

Curry as a Translyvanian con-man seeking a lost city; an imminently exploding volcano; jungle disasters and mutant animals; Third World governments in turmoil and nice scenery. Dreadfully muddled, but mildly diverting. SGr

Congo Crossing

(1956, US, 87 min)
d Joseph Pevney. *p* Howard Christie. *sc* Richard Alan Simmons. *ph* Russell Metty. *ed* Sherman Todd. *ad* Alexander Golitzen, Robert Boyle. *cast* George Nader, Peter Lorre, Virginia Mayo, Michael Pate, Rex Ingram.
●Dull and derivative *Casablanca*-type tale of fugitives from the law gathering together in Congotanga, where extradition laws are not practised. The routine goings-on are lit up only by the presence of Lorre and by Russell Metty's elegant Technicolor camerawork. GA

Congo Maisie

(1940, US, 70 min, b/w)
d HC Potter. *p* J Walter Ruden. *sc* Mary McCall Jr. *ph* Charles Lawton. *ed* Frederick Y Smith. *ad* Cedric Gibbons. *m* Edward Ward. *cast* Ann Sothern, John Carroll, Shepperd Strudwick, EE Clive, Rita Johnson, JK Kerrigan.
●Sothern takes the title role for this second entry in the MGM series about big-hearted showgirl Maisie Ravier. In this one she stows away and is shipped off to a strife-torn rubber plantation. Cutprice filler slung together on a quiet corner of the studio backlot. TJ

Congress Dances (Der Kongress tanzt)

(1931, Ger, 92 min, b/w)
d Erik Charell. *p* Erich Pommer. *sc* Norbert Falk, Robert Liebmann. *ph* Carl Hoffmann. *ad* Walter Roehrig, Robert Herlth. *m* Werner Heymann. *cast* Lilian Harvey, Willy Fritsch, Conrad Veidt, Lil Dagover, Adele Sandrock.
●Fluffy Viennese super-operetta: among the most celebrated and sumptuous of the musicals that waltzed all over German screens from the coming of sound to the advent of the 'new' filmmakers in the '60s. Attractions include Karl Hoffmann, one of Germany's great cinematographers; matinée idol Fritsch and his lady-love Harvey; lots of lieder, light comedy, pageantry, dance and romance. Ostrich-like escapism from ominous contemporary events, or dazzling entertainment of the first water to vie with Hollywood's best? SJo

Conman and the Kung Fu Kid (Langbei wei Jian/aka Wits to Wits)

(1974, HK, 107 min)
d Wu Ma. *p* Cony B Sarangawa. *sc* Sitel On. *ed* Mak Chi-Sin. *cast* Henry Yue Young, Wu Ma, Suzy Mang, Shih Kien.
●For fun and profit, this rips off Leone's *Fistful of Dynamite* by translating Coburn's ex-IRA bomber into a compulsive gambling swindler, and Steiger's greedy Mexican thug into a scrofulous oaf on the run from his fiancée. Most Hong Kong action movies as Western-influenced as this wind up as mixtures of lobotomised Chinese popular culture and crass Hollywood plagiarism. This is the happy exception: since it skips all of Leone's more provocative overtones and uses the rambling plot merely to showcase the two lead actors, it retains most of its Chinese identity, and emerges as one of the most genial of its kind. Henry Yue Young and Wu Ma bounce from farce to cynicism and back in the title roles; details are often abrasive or amusing (the swindler severing his 'offending' hand when he's caught cheating in a casino); and the film's anarchic politics keep the physical extravagances on an upswing. TR

Connecticut Yankee in King Arthur's Court, A (aka A Yankee in King Arthur's Court)

(1949, US, 107 min)
d Tay Garnett. *p* Robert Fellows. *sc* Edmund Beloin. *ph* Ray Rennahan. *ed* Archie Marshek. *ad* Hans Dreier, Roland Anderson. *songs* Johnny Burke, James Van Heusen. *cast* Bing Crosby, Rhonda Fleming, William Bendix, Cedric Hardwicke, Henry Wilcoxon.
●A decidedly muted musical version of Mark Twain's story about a 20th century blacksmith transported back into the world of Camelot. It's a highly amiable affair, enlivened by lush Technicolor photography, mindlessly amusing humour, and a marvellous performance by Bendix (at his best singing 'Busy Doin' Nothin'' with Hardwicke and Crosby). GA

Connecting Rooms

(1969, GB, 103 min)
d Franklin Gollings. *p* Harry Field. *sc* Franklin Gollings. *ph* John Wilcox. *ed* Jack Slade. *ad* Herbert Smith, Morley Smith. *m* Joan Shakespeare. *cast* Bette Davis, Michael Redgrave, Alexis Kanner, Kay Walsh, Gabrielle Drake, Olga Georges-Picot, Leo Genn.
●Adapted from a stage play, but still riddled with act and scene pauses. A seedy boarding-house tale, with the inmates' self-constructed illusions protecting their battered souls from bravely borne truths, it's a fairly classic condensation of several fetishistic concerns endemic to British cinema: Redgrave's ex-schoolmaster winces over the painful memory of a sexy little boy with whom he was innocently (of course) involved in a scandal. Davis soldiers through as the musician who turns out to be merely a busker (albeit a remarkably prosperous one), but sadly succumbs.

Connection, The

(1961, US, 110 min, b/w)
d Shirley Clarke. *p* Lewis M Allen, Shirley Clarke. *sc* Jack Gelber. *ph* Arthur J Ornitz. *ad* Richard Sylbert. *m* Freddie Redd. *cast* William Redfield, Warren Finnerty, Garry Goodrow, Jerome Raphael, James Anderson, Roscoe Lee Browne, Carl Lee.
●The gimmicky premise of Jack Gelber's play – that those were real junkies up on the stage waiting for their fix, killing time by improvising jazz and making with street-jive monologues – probably makes more sense as a movie than it ever did in the theatre. Clarke films it as if it were documentary (so that when the cameraman himself takes a fix, the camera-work goes to pieces), and the Living Theatre actors are convincing enough to sustain this close a scrutiny. Some creaky business with a Salvation Army sister recalls the piece's stage origins, but the music and the sense of 'dead time' retain a 'beat' authenticity. TR.

Conqueror, The

(1956, US, 111 min)
d/p Dick Powell. *sc* Oscar Millard. *ph* Joseph La Shelle, Leo Tover, Harry J Wild, William Snyder. *ed* Stuart Gilmore. *ad* Albert S D'Agostino, Carroll Clark. *m* Victor Young. *cast* John Wayne, Susan Hayward, Pedro Armendariz, Agnes Moorehead, Thomas Gomez, William Conrad, John Hoyt, Ted de Corsia, Lee Van Cleef.
●Over-long, very dull epic produced by Howard Hughes, about the territorial and amorous conquests of Genghis Khan. Wayne, who saw the film as an oriental Western, is horribly miscast as the barbaric warrior, drawling lines like 'You're beautiful in your wrath' to the reluctant Hayward, and looking decidedly un-Oriental. GA

Conquest (La Conquista de la Tierra Perdida)

(1983, It/Sp/Mex, 92 min)
d Lucio Fulci. *p* Giovanni di Clemente. *sc* Gino Capone, José Antonio de la Loma, Carlos Vasallo. *ph* Alejandro Alonso Garcia. *ed* Emilio Rodriguez Oses. *ad* Massimo Lentini. *m* Claudio Simonetti. *cast* George Rivero, Andrea Occhipinti, Sabrina Sellers, Corrado San Martin, Violeta Cela.
●An Arthurian quest saga from Mr Eyeball Driller? But don't expect this to mean that heads won't be rolling, in this fragmented nonsense involving a magic bow, shape-shifting demons, wolfmen, an exploding metal-headed witch and, almost from habit, zombies. There's also an impromptu crucifixion, followed by the crucifixee falling into the sea and being rescued by dolphins. Three writers made this up. Did they ever meet? DO

Conquest of Space

(1955, US, 81 min)
d Byron Haskin. *p* George Pal. *sc* James O'Hanlon. *ph* Lionel Lindon. *ed* Everett Douglas. *ad* Hal Pereira, Joseph McMillan Johnson. *m* Van Cleave. *cast* Walter Brooke, Eric Fleming, Mickey Shaughnessy, William Hopper, Ross Martin, Joan Shawlee.
●Totally bizarre sci-fi epic, mounting a 'realistic' attempt at an expedition to Mars, which has some animated segments as pretty as *2001*. This George Pal project tries elaborately (and presumably expensively) for authenticity, and naturally gets it all wrong. But there's something pleasantly loony about the whole thing, from the chicken-pie capsules down to the anti-gravity zip-up boots. At one point the script even has its chief astronaut denouncing the entire mission as a 'cursed abomination' when he gets a touch of religion. A fascinating relic. DP

Conquest of the Air, The

(1940, GB, 71 min, b/w)
d uncredited [Zoltan Korda, William Cameron Menzies, Alexander Esway, Donald Taylor, Alexander Shaw, John Monk Saunders]. *p* Alexander Korda. *sc* John Monk Saunders. *commentary* Peter Bezencenet. *ph* uncredited [Lee Games, Wilkie Cooper, others]. *ed* Charles Frend, Peter Bezencenet. *m* Arthur Bliss. *cast* Valentine Dyall, Alan Wheatley, Hay Petrie, Laurence Olivier, Francis L Sullivan, Michael Rennie. *narrator* Charles Frend.
●Conceived in 1934, shot circa '37 and put together after the outbreak of war, this Korda flying picture is part of a lost genre, from a time when planes still held the thrill of the new. Its first half is a series of sketches – Icarus to the Wright Brothers – about humanity's attempts to outfox gravity. The succession of gaga monks and optimistic daredevils plummeting to earth, plus Olivier as Lunardi the ballooning Neapolitan, is more fun than the second part, a documentary survey of aviation between the wars, as the period had just become known. Alcock and Brown, the Vickers-Vimy, the R101 – it might have seemed quite romantic, but for Frend's posh schoolmaster commentating style. BBa

Conquest of the Earth

(1980, US, 99 min)
d Sidney Hayers, Sigmund Neufeld Jr, Barry Crane. *p* Jeff Freilich, Frank Lupo, Gary B Winter. *sc* Glen A Larson. *ph* Frank P Beascoechea, Mario DiLeo, Ben Colman. *ed* Jean-Jacques Berthelot. *ad* Fred T Tuch. *cast* Kent McCord, Barry Van Dyke, Robyn Douglass, Lorne Greene, John Colicos, Robert Reed, Wolfman Jack.
●The third movie instalment of TV's *Battlestar Galactica*, continuing its sluggish slog in the wake of *Star Wars*. Three directors are credited (presumably three episodes were cobbled), but their efforts are uniformly faceless as the Cylon invaders laboriously make it to Earth. Even Wolfman Jack, making a guest appearance as a disc jockey whose radio transmitter is a prime target for attack, seems under the weather. TM

Conquest of the Planet of the Apes

(1972, US, 85 min)
d J Lee Thompson. *p* Arthur P Jacobs. *sc* Paul Dehn. *ph* Bruce Surtees. *ed* Marjorie Fowler, Allan Jaggs. *ad* Philip M Jefferies. *m* Tom Scott. *cast* Roddy McDowall, Don Murray, Natalie Trundy, Ricardo Montalban, Hari Rhodes, Severn Darden.
●Fourth in the series derived from Pierre Boulle's novel, with the pet apes who have evolved into slaves rebelling against their human masters. Dismally lurid stuff, ham-fistedly directed and low on credibility. TM

Conquest of the South Pole

(1988, GB, 91 min, b/w & col)
d Gillies MacKinnon. *p/sc* Gareth Wardell. *ph* Sean Van Hales. *ed* Stephen Singleton. *ad* Andy Harris. *m* Guy Woolfenden. *cast* Stevan Rimkus, Laura Girling, Leonard O'Malley, Gordon Cameron, Ewen Bremner, Alastair Galbraith, John Michie, Julie-Kate Olivier.
●From the opening credits, featuring archive footage of Amundsen's historic expedition, it's clear that MacKinnon's first feature – a low budget adaptation of Manfred Karge's play – is going to be quite special. Led by the seductive and sinister Sloopianek (Rimkus), a group of unemployed Scottish youngsters decide to fill their time – and fend off fears of failure – by recreating the first

successful trip to the Antarctic in their home town. Almost inevitably, the task takes on epic proportions – glaciers, equipment, huskies and penguins must be found – and the group steadily splinters over strategy and purpose. Shot among the ice-houses, docksides and tenement blocks of Leith, the film is at once faithful to Karge and a visually stimulating piece of cinema. Though endowed with a bleak conclusion, it never lacks wit or tenderness, since MacKinnon celebrates the crucial role played by imagination in the youth's fantastic voyage of self-discovery. With strong performances from a young, largely unknown cast, he explores a broad emotional landscape, never slipping into facile pathos or liberal tub-thumping, so that one is finally left invigorated by what might otherwise have seemed a futile, ludicrous odyssey. GA

Conquista de la Tierra Perdida, La

see Conquest

Conrack

(1974, US, 106 min)
d Martin Ritt. *p* Martin Ritt, Irving Ravetch. *sc* Irving Ravetch, Harriet Frank Jr. *ph* John A Alonzo. *ed* Frank Bracht. *pd* Walter Scott Herndon. *m* John Williams. *cast* Jon Voight, Paul Winfield, Hume Cronyn, Madge Sinclair, Tina Andrews, Antonio Fargas.

● Ritt's taste for significant subjects and some heavy underlining of his themes is confirmed by this tale of a white, hip, long-haired, anti-Vietnam war teacher who takes a backwoods assignment which lands him in a one-room black school where he confronts ignorance and deprivation of a depth he had never dreamed existed. Mercifully, the potentially dubious aspects of the subject are mostly exorcised, in part by a strong script (adapted from the book by real-life teacher Pat Conroy), but largely by the engaging and persuasive performance Ritt draws from Voight (equally convincingly backed by the mainly juvenile cast). *Conrack* treads a line perilously close to Sounder, but avoids that film's mawkish contrivance. VG

Consenting Adults

(1992, US, 99 min)
d Alan J Pakula. *p* Alan J Pakula, David Permut. *sc* Matthew Chapman. *ph* Stephen Goldblatt. *ed* Sam O'Steen. *pd* Carol Spier. *m* Michael Small. *cast* Kevin Kline, Mary Elizabeth Mastrantonio, Kevin Spacey, Rebecca Miller, Forest Whitaker, EG Marshall.

● This faltering addition to Hollywood's yuppies in peril cycle starts better than it finishes. Jingle-writer Richard (Kline, wooden) and his supportive wife Priscilla (Mastrantonio) have every reason to be content with their lifestyle until 'financial adviser' Eddy (Spacey) and his improbably blonde partner Kay (Miller) arrive to upset the balance. Friendly relations are soon established, but 'neath the surface simmer sexual tensions which insurance scam-meister Eddy is all too keen to exploit, suggesting that he and Richard do the not-done thing by sleeping with each other's wives. The following day, police discover semen traces on Kay's battered body, and Richard is suddenly prime suspect in a murder case. His life disintegrates before his very eyes, and the movie follows suit. Twenty years after the taut *Klute*, Pakula's touch has deserted him; the glossy, literalist approach he favours here works firmly against the arrant contrivances in Matthew Chapman's screenplay, rendering already convoluted events even more ridiculous. TJ

Consequence, The (Die Konsequenz)

(1977, WGer, 100 min, b/w)
d Wolfgang Petersen. *p* Bernd Eichinger. *sc* Alexander Ziegler, Wolfgang Petersen. *ph* Jörg-Michael Baldenius. *ed* Johannes Nikel. *ad* O Jochen Schmidt. *m* Nils Sustrate. *cast* Jürgen Prochnow, Ernst Hannawald, Walo Lüönd, Edith Volkmann, Erwin Kohlund, Werner Schwuchow.

● This charts the fraught course of a gay male romance between an actor (who serves time for seducing a minor) and the cherubic son of a prison warden. A contrived story-line erects every obstacle possible along the way, but the overall sincerity and the genuinely sobering ending help make up for the way the dice are loaded. TR

Conspiracy of Hearts

(1960, GB, 113 min, b/w)
d Ralph Thomas. *p* Betty E Box. *sc* Robert Presnell Jr. *ph* Ernest Steward. *ed* Alfred Roome. *ad* Alex Vetchinsky. *m* Angelo Francesco Lavagnino. *cast* Lilli Palmer, Sylvia Syms, Yvonne Mitchell, Ronald Lewis, Albert Lieven, Peter Arne, Nora Swinburne.

● If you want to know what the ultimately synthetic box-office film would look like, then try this weepie. It contains calculated doses of the three magic ingredients guaranteed to gladden all nice old ladies: nuns, animals and children. In fact, it's got Catholic nuns saving Jewish children from naughty Germans. The film conforms to Lawrence's definition of sentimentality as 'working out on yourself feelings you haven't really got'. DP

Conspiracy Theory

(1997, US, 135 min)
d Richard Donner. *p* Joel Silver, Richard Donner. *sc* Brian Helgeland. *ph* John Schwartzman. *ed* Frank J Urioste, Kevin Stitt. *pd* Paul Sylbert. *m* Carter Burwell. *cast* Mel Gibson, Julia Roberts, Patrick Stewart, Cylk Cozart, Stephen Kahan, Terry Alexander, Alex Mcarthur.

● Jabbering Mel Gibson is clearly a Manhattan cabbie with a troubled past, and his pursuit of upper-bracket love interest Julia Roberts, a Justice Department attorney investigating the murder of her judge father, gets the plot rolling on an expansive, glossy thriller that delivers much less than it at first promises. Donner and cameraman John Schwartzman pull out their best stuff early on when unknown assailants tie Mel to a wheelchair and pump him full of truth drugs. Weird colours. Fast-cuts. All very disorienting, until we realise terminally dull Patrick Stewart is the interrogator with the steel-rimmed glasses. Gibson deserves a nod for taking on a character so obviously fractured by military experiments, but despite having the ultimate paranoiac's pad, he too often settles for playing the lovable wacko, and his memory returns at the convenience of screenwriter Brian Helgeland. A series of increasingly desperate chases, and catchy use of the karaoke classic 'Can't Take My Eyes Off You', masks a lack of confidence in a narrative with too few suspects and the same old CIA bad guys behind it. TJ

Conspirators, The

(1944, US, 101 min, b/w)
d Jean Negulesco. *p* Jack Chertok. *sc* Vladimir Pozner, Leo Rosten. *ph* Arthur Edeson. *ed* Rudi Fehr. *ad* Anton F Grot. *m* Max Steiner. *cast* Paul Henried, Hedy Lamarr, Sydney Greenstreet, Peter Lorre, Joseph Calleia, Victor Francen, Eduardo Ciannelli, George Macready.

● In his days at Warners, Negulesco was as polished a perpetrator of pacy, romantic hokum as Michael Curtiz, and he manages to make this *Casablanca*-type tale entertaining and stylish, despite the contrivances and derivativeness of the plot. Henried is again a resistance fighter, turning up in neutral Lisbon to have an affair with Lamarr (who wouldn't?) and to deal with Nazi spies. With such a cast, and wonderfully dark, contrasty camera-work from Arthur Edeson, enjoyment is assured. GA

Conspirators of Pleasure (Spiklenci slasti)

(1996, Czech/Switz/GB, 86 min)
d Jan Svankmajer. *p* Jaromír Kallista. *sc* Jan Svankmajer. *ph* Miloslav Spala. *ed* Marie Zemanova. *ad* Eva Svankmajerova, Jan Svankmajer. *cast* Petr Meissel, Gabriela Wilhelmová, Barbora Hrzánová, Anna Weltlinská.

● Svankmajer, the Czech genius of surrealism, explores the bizarre erotic impulses of various individuals in modern Prague. One man collects porn magazines, chickens and umbrellas to fashion himself a weird creature. His neighbour does similar things with straw. Their newsagent tinkers with anatomical additions to his hi-tech TV set. The newscaster keeps carp in a bowl in her bedroom, while her neglectful husband hears operatic climaxes in his head whenever he encounters saucepan lids, fur, nails and latex fingers. Finally, there's the postwoman, who rolls bread into doughballs for very odd purposes, after delivering to the first man an ominous note simply saying 'Sunday'. Even though there's an inexorable logic to the meticulous preparation of the 'perversions' finally perpetrated by these loners, Svankmajer's humour is as black, sly and subversive as ever. While there's far less animated material here than in his earlier work (and, indeed, no dialogue), there's a marvellously morbid, grotesque sense of absurd sado-masochistic ritual at play. GA

Constance

(1984, NZ, 103 min)
d Bruce Morrison. *p* Larry Parr. *sc* Jonathan Hardy, Bruce Morrison. *ph* Kevin Hayward. *ed* Phillip Howe. *pd* Richard Jeziorny. *m* Dave Fraser, John Charles. *cast* Donogh Rees, Shane Bryant, Judie Douglass, Martin Vaughan, Donald McDonald.

● Imagine that it's 1984 and you go to the cinema dreaming that you're Rita Hayworth, then wake up next morning and find that you are in suburban Auckland, New Zealand – all cheery, scrubbed faces and neat aspirations. A daunting movie subject, which could easily have turned into whimsy and nostalgia; but thanks to a magnificently realised performance by Rees, the film's stab at the tone of the great post-war melodrama is an almost total success. From minor social peccadilloes via debauchery to complete self-abasement, Constance clings to her dream until it destroys her. Combining a real sense of style with some genuine emotion, the film is lush and exhilarating. NR

Constant Factor, The (Constans)

(1980, Pol, 98 min)
d/sc Krzysztof Zanussi. *ph* Slawomir Idziak. *ed* Urszula Sliwinska, Ewa Smal. *ad* Tadeusz Wybult, Maciej Putowski. *m* Wojciech Kilar. *cast* Tadeusz Bradecki, Zofia Mrozowska, Malgorzata Zajaczkowska, Cezary Morawski.

● Putting a youthful idealist under the microscope, Zanussi demonstrates that in a Communist bureaucracy the constant factor is the network of corruption which ensures that some people are more equal than others. Obviously this notion rang out more boldly in its Polish context. Obviously, too, some of the symbolism is pretty basic, with the hero frustrated in his dream of climbing the Himalayas and having to settle for a window-cleaner's cradle. But Zanussi's quasi-scientific approach, building a mosaic of tangential facts and perceptions out of his findings, often manages to turn ordinary life into something extraordinary. Moments of tenderness and surprise abound, especially in a love affair which illuminates the film with shy, sidelong grace. If boredom nevertheless lurks not too far away, it is because the images are too conventionally framed. TM

Consul, The (Konsul)

(1989, Pol, 104 min)
d Miroslav Bork. *sc* Miroslav Bork, Andrzej Jarecki. *ph* Julian Szczerkowski. *ed* Krysztof Osiecki. *ad* Tadeusz Kosarewicz. *m* Zbigniew Karnecki. *cast* Piotr Fronczewski, Maria Pakulnis, Krzysztof Zaleski, Henryk Bista, Jerry Bonczak, Grazyna Kruk.

● A frustratingly dry black comedy which satirises bureaucracy, hypocrisy and greed (what else?) as it follows an ingenious and daring conman around modern Poland. Fronczewski's performance as the eponymous hero is subtly modulated and appropriately charismatic, while the slow-to-start story, which eventually sees him pose as a nonexistent Austrian diplomat, is fascinating enough in a *House of Games* kind of way. But the whole could have benefited from more ebullient direction; as it is, the 'moral' (the swindler couldn't operate successfully if it weren't for the complicity of both his victims and the State) tends to overwhelm any humour or narrative drive. GA

Consuming Passions

(1988, GB/US, 98 min)
d Giles Foster. *p* William P Cartlidge. *sc* Paul D Zimmerman, Andrew Davies. *ph* Roger Pratt. *ed* John Grover. *pd* Peter Lamont. *m* Richard Hartley. *cast* Vanessa Redgrave, Jonathan Pryce, Tyler Butterworth, Freddie Jones, Prunella Scales, Sammi Davis, Thora Hird, Timothy West, William Rushton, Andrew Sachs, Mary Healey, Bryan Pringle.

●Recipe for Chocolate Fudge. Take a half-hour TV play about a traditional family-owned confectionery company, the fortunes of which are miraculously revived when three men fall into the chocolate vats one day, creating an overnight tastebud sensation. Flatten it out until it is about three times the length, being careful to remove all but the most cursory references to the original authors, Michael Palin and Terry Jones. Add an inept Norman Wisdom-style hero (Butterworth), and a salacious subplot about a nymphomaniac Malteser (Redgrave) who blackmails him into having esoteric sex. Add a few drops of Essence of Ealing – small family firm threatened by giant conglomerate whose ruthless axemen (Pryce) puts efficiency and image before quality of product. Stir in some soppy love interest. The consistency should be lumpy and the taste insipid. In America these are known as Soylent Brownies. NF

Contact

(1997, US, 150 min)
d Robert Zemeckis. *p* Robert Zemeckis, Steve Starkey. *sc* James V Hart, Michael Goldenberg. *ph* Don Burgess. *ed* Arthur Schmidt. *pd* Ed Verreaux. *m* Alan Silvestri. *cast* Jodie Foster, Matthew McConaughey, Tom Skerritt, Angela Bassett, John Hurt, David Morse, Rob Lowe, William Fichtner, James Woods.
●Ellie Arroway (Foster) has devoted her scientific career to scanning the cosmos for signs of life. One day she's rewarded with a radio transmission from a distant galaxy, and the world is transfixed. It's clear that the aliens have plans for us, but whether for good or ill defies human understanding. An intergalactic ambassador is called for, and Ellie wants the job. Zemeckis aims for spiritual reverence reminiscent of *Close Encounters*: the scope and scale of his picture are established by the first shot with a brilliantly sustained zoom through space and time. There are two more virtuoso sequences: a climactic space trip and a breathtakingly outrageous piece of post-modern appropriation with the first images broadcast from outer space. Regrettably, these visual coups only point up the inadequacy of a screenplay (from Carl Sagan's novel) which marries profound philosophical questions with hokey melodramatics, shallow characters and infantile conclusions. It's not just that it resorts to an albino Adventist to inject spurious suspense, nor that it foists McConaughey on us as a randy Luddite priest who is, coincidentally, the love interest (the pillow talk is physics vs metaphysics). It also features heavy-handed exposition, repetitive, maudlin flashbacks, uneven performances and endless sermonising. TCh

Contact, The (Jeopsok)

(1997, SKor, 104 min)
d Chang Youn-Hyun. *p* Lee Eun, Shim Bo-Kyung. *sc* Cho Myung-Joo, Chang Youn-Hyun. *ph* Kim Seong-Bok. *ed* Park Gok-Ji. *pd* Shim Bo-Kyung. *cast* Han Suk-Kyu, Chun Doo-Yeon, Chu Sang-Mi, Park Yong-Soo, Kim Tae-Yoo.
●In the late '80s, fresh out of film school in Hungary, Chang led the underground film group Changsan-gotmae away from protests against military government and into Stalinist agit-prop about labour unions. Seven years later this solo debut, a half-arsed romance derived from the Japanese film *Haru*, was a huge commercial hit. Radio producer Dong-Hyun (Han) can't get over an ex-girlfriend and retreats into his own closed world. Home-shopping channel voice Soo-Hyun (Chun) has a crush on her best friend's boyfriend. Brought together by The Velvet Underground's 'Pale Blue Eyes', Dong-Hyun and Soo-Hyun meet in a web chat-room and draw each other out of their shells. But will they dare to meet face to face before he emigrates to Australia? No doubt it's all a searing comment on emotional alienation under capitalism. TR

Contact Man, The

see Alias Nick Beal

Conte d'automne (Autumn Tale, An)

(1998, Fr, 111 min)
d Eric Rohmer. *p* Françoise Etchegaray. *sc* Eric Rohmer. *ph* Diane Baratier. *ed* Mary Stephen. *m* Claude Marti, Gérard Pansanel, Pierre Peyras, Antonello Salis *cast* Marie Rivière, Béatrice Romand, Alain Libolt, Didier Sandre, Alexia Portal, Stéphane Darmon, Aurélia Alcaïs, Mathieu Davette, Yves Alcaïs.
●Rohmer's cinema is unmistakable, dedicated as it is to the art of conversation and the rules of attraction. Still, it's a pleasant surprise to see your quintessential Rohmerian nubile young heroine upstaged here by two formidable women 'of a certain age'. Magali (Romand) is a lonely wine maker whose two best friends are Isabelle (Rivière) and her son's girlfriend Rosine (Portal). The latter wants to fix Megali up with her professor (her own blatantly unsuited ex), while Isabelle secretly places a lonely hearts ad, then auditions the likeliest candidate while masquerading as her friend. It's a leisurely comedy, to be sure, but immensely charming. One to savour. TCh

Conte de printemps (A Tale of Springtime)

(1989, Fr, 112 min)
d Eric Rohmer. *p* Margaret Ménégoz. *sc* Eric Rohmer. *ph* Luc Pages. *ed* Maria-Luisa Garcia. *m* Beethoven, Schumann. *cast* Anne Teyssèdre, Hugues Quester, Florence Darel, Eloise Bennett, Sophie Robin.
●Inaugurating a new Rohmer series (*Tales of the Four Seasons*), this begins with an atypically wordless sequence which effectively introduces the mood of mystery and ambiguity that will recur throughout. Caught between apartments, philosophy graduate Jeanne (Teyssèdre) attends a party, where a young girl, Natasha (Darel), invites her to stay at the flat she shares with her father Igor (Quester). So far so innocent, but presently Jeanne finds herself witness to, then participating in, recriminatory scenes between daughter, father and his youthful lover Eve (Bennett): jealous Natasha detests Eve, accusing her of theft, while Igor – encouraged by Natasha? – seems more than willing to be left alone with Jeanne. As ever, Rohmer examines their hidden motives and analyses the consequences of their actions with great lucidity, repeatedly delving beneath words to uncover, through gesture and intonation, their real meaning; nobody is wholly innocent, no one completely blameless, in the web of intrigue spun between Jeanne and her hosts. Rohmer may not be breaking new ground, but who else could explore his familiar territory so fruitfully? GA

Conte des trois diamants

see Tale of the Three Jewels

Conte d'été (A Summer's Tale)

(1996, Fr, 113 min)
d Eric Rohmer. *p* Françoise Etchegaray. *sc* Eric Rohmer. *ph* Diane Baratier. *ed* Mary Stephen. *m* Philippe Eidel, Sébastien Erms. *cast* Melvil Poupaud, Aurélia Nolin, Amanda Langlet, Gwenaëlle Simon, Aimé Lefèvre, Alain Guellaff, Evelyne Lahana.
●Rohmer's delicious follow-up to *A Tale of Springtime* and *A Winter's Tale* takes the simplest of stories – a young man torn between three women – and conjures up a cornucopia of emotional, philosophical and comic riches. Gaspard (Poupaud), a moody, introspective and seemingly shy student, is lent an apartment in Brittany for the summer; he hopes to be joined by Léna (Nolin), with whom he thinks he's in love. Whiling away the time, he meets Margot (Langlet), an anthropology student and part-time waitress, whose talent as a confidante introduces him to the idea of platonic friendship with a girl; besides, she already has a boyfriend. Gaspard, however, does get involved with her friend Solène (Simon), since Léna still hasn't contacted him. Then, of course, she turns up out of the blue. So who will he end up taking to the isle of Ouessant for a romantic weekend? Funny, perceptive and, in the end, surprisingly suspenseful, Rohmer's characteristically casual but precise exploration of human desire and delusion proceeds with great subtlety from an initial series of what seem to be dramatically inconsequential scenes to a final act so tightly structured it might almost be farce. As the plotting becomes more complex, so does our understanding of the characters' motives. As ever, Rohmer's fecund insights into love, friendship, manipulation, coincidence and chance are backed up by his typically vivid evocation of time and place, and by superb naturalistic performances. GA

Conte d'hiver (A Winter's Tale)

(1992, Fr, 114 min)
d Eric Rohmer. *p* Françoise Etchegaray. *sc* Eric Rohmer. *ph* Luc Pagès, Maurice Giraud. *ed* Mary Stephen. *m* Sébastien Erms. *cast* Charlotte Véry, Frédéric Van Den Driessche, Michel Voletti, Hervé Furic, Ava Loraschi, Christiane Desbois.
●Summer in Brittany: tearfully parting after an idyllic holiday romance with Charles (Van Den Driessche), hairdresser Félicie accidentally gives him an incorrect home address. Four years on, it's Christmas and he still hasn't contacted her; but such is her undying love for him – and the daughter he sired – that she finds it impossible to choose between two adoring suitors: her stolid boss Maxence (Voletti) and intellectual librarian Loïc (Furic). Reluctant to compromise her memories and dreams of true passion, she is hoping against hope for a miracle. In focusing on an often irritatingly indecisive heroine devoted to a barely reasonable romantic ideal, the second of Rohmer's 'Tales of the Four Seasons' is reminiscent of *The Green Ray*, while its wintry study of the varieties of love, faith and religious belief recalls the similarly sublime *My Night with Maud*. This is Rohmer at his very best, effortlessly and unsentimentally charting the absurd complexities of human psychology, while creating a compelling contemporary fairytale firmly rooted in the banality of everyday existence. It has, as ever, enormous compassion, wit and insight, and its ending is exquisitely affecting. GA

Contempt

see Mépris, Le

Contender, The

(2000, Ger/US/GB, 126 min)
d Rod Lurie. *p* Marc Frydman, Douglas Urbanski, Willi Baer, James Spies. *sc* Rod Lurie. *ph* Denis Maloney. *ed* Michael Jablow. *pd* Alexander Hammond. *m* Larry Groupé. *cast* Gary Oldman, Joan Allen, Jeff Bridges, Christian Slater, Sam Elliott, William Petersen, Saul Rubinek, Philip Baker Hall, Mariel Hemingway.
●President Evans (Bridges) needs to appoint a new VP. Aware of the importance of the women's vote, he favours Democrat Senator Hanson (Allen) over Governor Hathaway (Petersen), recently in the news as a heroic would-be lifesaver and himself preferred by Republican congressman Runyon (Oldman). Investigating Hanson's suitability, Runyon obtains photos suggestive of a sexually scandalous past; but insisting on her right to privacy, she refuses to dignify the charge with a denial, thereby setting the scene for all manner of mud-slinging, murky deals and Machiavellian scheming. In the final reels story and characters start turning somersaults so that Hanson and Evans suddenly end up too good to be true, with Runyon a mere villain. This facile endorsement of Clintonian peccadillos is emphasised by some awful sermonising and an embarrassingly heroic score. Until then, however, the performances by a superb cast are uniformly terrific, and the writing is mostly sharp, witty and admirably sceptical about the manoeuvring on all sides. GA

Contes Immoraux

see Immoral Tales

Contraband (aka Blackout)

(1940, GB, 92 min, b/w)
d Michael Powell. *p* John Corfield. *sc* Emeric Pressburger, Michael Powell, Brock Williams. *ph* Freddie Young. *ed* John Seabourne. *ad* Alfred Junge. *m* Richard Addinsell, John Greenwood. *cast* Conrad Veidt, Valerie Hobson, Hay Petrie, Raymond Lovell, Esmond Knight, Charles Victor, Peter Bull.
●Less stylish than *The Spy in Black*, this espionage thriller is more fun, with its tongue-in-cheek plot revelling in Hitchcockian eccentricities. Making atmospheric use of London under the blackout (including a tout hawking electric torches and gas mask cases at Victoria Station), it has its German agents operating from a warehouse packed with patriotic busts of Neville Chamberlain, while hero and heroine tour a series of bizarre nightclubs before rounding up the villains with enthusiastic help from a posse of Danish waiters and carousing rugby players picked up en route. Minor by Powell & Pressburger standards, but most enjoyable. TM

Contract, The (Kontrakt)

(1980, Pol, 111 min)
d/sc Krzysztof Zanussi. *ph* Slawomir Idziak. *ed* Urszula Sliwinska, Ewa Smal. *ad* Tadeusz

Wybult. *m* Wojciech Kilar. *cast* Maja Komorowska, Tadeusz Lomnicki, Leslie Caron, Magda Jaroszówna, Krzysztof Kolberger, Zofia Mrozowska, Beata Tyszkiewicz.
● Written and directed by Zanussi for Polish TV, though with production values hardly inferior to those prevalent in the country's cinema output, *The Contract* has a premise just this side of absurdism: a bride has second thoughts at the altar and dashes from the church, leaving the assembled guests to celebrate as if the wedding had taken place. The resulting party, which occupies most of the film's running time, has more than its share of drunken and embarrassing moments, sexual indiscretions and revelations culminating in the discovery that one of the guests has been pilfering from the others' purses and handbags, all of which Zanussi orchestrates with considerable skill to tragi-comic effect. An illumination of the kind of telling details about contemporary Poland, in fact, that one can hardly begin to glean from newspaper and television reports. RM

Contract Man

see Alias Nick Beal

Contre-allée, La

see Both Sides of the Street

Contre l'Oubli (Against Oblivion)

(1991, Fr, 117 min)
d Michel Deville, Sarah Moon, Jane Birkin, Raymond Depardon, Martine Franck, Jacques Doillon, Patrice Chéreau, Jean-Loup Hubert, Alain Corneau, Jean Becker, Francis Girod, Jean-Michel Carré, Philippe Muyl, Dominique Dante, Jean-Luc Godard/Anne-Marie Miéville, Jacques Deray, Gérard Frot Coutaz, Denis Amar, Patrice Leconte, Claire Denis, René Allio, Romain Goupil, Robert Kramer, Alain Resnais, Chantal Akerman, Nadine Trintignant, Costa-Gavras, Bertrand Tavernier, Coline Serreau, Michel Piccoli. *ph* Yves Angelo, Etienne Becker, Patrick Blossier, others. *m* Philippe Sarde, Philippe Baudoin, others. *cast* Emmanuelle Béart, Sami Frey, Charlotte Gainsbourg, Carole Bouquet, Philippe Noiret, Isabelle Huppert, Guy Bedos, Catherine Deneuve, Anouk Grinberg.
● Produced for the 30th anniversary of Amnesty International, this comprises 30 'film letters' concerning 30 cases of human rights abuse in 30 countries worldwide (though Greece and the UK are the only Europeans in the dock). Even here – especially here – auteur principles apply, and the imaginative minimalism of Depardon (Colombia) or the lucidity of Resnais (Cuba) prove more effective as argument, never mind as cinema, than say the glib Hubert (Greece) or self-conscious Leconte (Russia) segments. Least substantial are the straight-to-camera monologues, though a distraught Anouk Grinberg is moving on the persecution of Aung San Suu Kyi. Biggest impact is made by Martine Franck's piece, in which Henri Cartier-Bresson bears witness to the murdered children of Mauretania. BBa

Convent, The (O Convento)

(1995, Port/Fr, 90 min)
d Manoel de Oliveira. *p* Paulo Branco. *sc* Manoel de Oliveira. *ph* Mario Barroso. *ed* Manoel de Oliveira, Valérie Loiseleux. *pd* Zé Branco, Ana Vaz da Silva. *cast* Catherine Deneuve, John Malkovich, Luis Miguel Cintra, Leonor Silveria, Daniel Auteuil, Duarte de Almeida.
● In which eccentric veteran Oliveira transcends wackiness and achieves utter tosh. US professor Malkovich and wife Deneuve visit a remote Portuguese monastery to research his thesis that Shakespeare was in fact a Spanish Jew, and become embroiled in vaguely sinister sexual shenanigans apparently engineered by the guardian of the place. What might have been an effective horror thriller or psychodrama is turned, by the director's endless erudite allusions to myth, literature and so on, into what looks like a mere blueprint for a more coherent, less tedious meditation on good and evil. GA

Conversa Acabada

see Other One, The

Conversation, The

(1974, US, 113 min)
d/p/sc Francis Coppola. *ph* Bill Butler. *ed* Walter Murch. *pd* Dean Tavoularis. *m* David Shire. *cast* Gene Hackman, John Cazale, Cindy Williams, Allen Garfield, Frederic Forrest, Teri Garr, Robert Duvall.
● An inner rather than outer-directed film about the threat of electronic surveillance, conceived well before the Watergate affair broke. Acknowledged as the king of the buggers, Hackman's surveillance expert is an intensely private man. Living alone in a scrupulously anonymous flat, paying functional visits to a mistress who plays no other part in his life, he is himself a machine; and the point Coppola makes is that this very private man only acquires something to be private about through the exercise of his skill as a voyeur. Projecting his own lonely isolation on to a conversation he painstakingly pieces together (mesmerising stuff as he obsessively plays the tapes over and over, adjusting sound levels until words begin to emerge from the crowd noises), he begins to imagine a story of terror and impending tragedy, and feels impelled to try to circumvent it. In a splendidly Hitchcockian denouement, a tragedy duly takes place, but not the one he foresaw; and he is left shattered not only by the realisation that his soul has been exposed, but by the conviction that someone must have planted a bug on him which he simply cannot find. A bleak and devastatingly brilliant film. TM

Conversation Piece (Gruppo di Famiglia in un Interno)

(1974, It/Fr, 121 min)
d Luchino Visconti. *p* Giovanni Bertolucci. *sc* Luchino Visconti, Suso Cecchi D'Amico, Enrico Medioli. *ph* Pasqualino de Santis. *ed* Ruggero Mastroianni. *pd* Dario Simoni. *m* Franco Mannino. *cast* Burt Lancaster, Helmut Berger, Claudia Marsani, Silvana Mangano, Elvira Cortese, Stefano Patrizi.
● A parable about the approach of death, this centres around a slightly Prospero-like professor (Lancaster incarnating a role similar to the one he played in *The Leopard*) who finds his carefully nurtured, opulent solitude upset by the eruption into his life of a wealthy woman (Mangano) and her chaotic jet-set entourage. Berger, for whom the film on one level seems a valedictory love-song, plays an angel of death figure, to whom a certain mystery attaches. If the *dolce vita*-style intrusion is given distinctly Jacqueline Susann-like overtones by the rather dissociated dialogue in the English language version, *Conversation Piece* nevertheless comes across as a visually rich and resonant mystery, far more fluid and sympathetic than *Death in Venice*. VG

Conversations with Willard Van Dyke

(1981, US, 58 min)
d/p Amalie R Rothschild. *sc* Julie Sloane, Amalie R Rothschild. *ph* Tom McDonough. *ed* Julie Sloane. *m* Amy Rubin. *with* Willard Van Dyke, Cole Weston, Ralph Steiner, Joris Ivens, Donald Richie.
● In the '20s, Willard Van Dyke was a still photographer who apprenticed himself to Edward Weston; in the '30s he moved into socially aware film-making; and during World War II he became an army propagandist. The '50s found him doing personally unsatisfying commercial and documentary work, but the next decade gave him the chance to take over the film department of the Museum of Modern Art, New York, where he introduced the contemporary work of 'downtown' film-makers into the moribund repertory. Now a spry and chipper 76, he has returned to technically pure and richly beautiful still photography; and Rothschild's film allows him to present himself and his career very sympathetically. He is so successful at this, in fact, that subsequent viewing of his famous 1939 documentary, *The City*, is a mite disappointing. The montage is splendid, but the message – that we should abandon squalid cities to live in healthy industrial parks – is embarrassingly naïve, in retrospect at least. MH

Converted, The (Zawrócony)

(1994, Pol, 79 min)
d/sc Kazimierz Kutz. *ph* Wieslaw Zdort. *ed* Zygmunt Dus. *pd* Jacek Osadowski. *m* Jan Kanty Pawluskiewicz. *cast* Zbigniew Zamachowski, Anna Waszczyk, Zofia Rysiowna, Marek Kondrat, Henryk Bista, Marek Kondrat.
● Lugubrious political satire set in a Polish industrial town in 1981. Tomasz is a Party animal who readily agrees to spy on a Solidarity rally for his bosses in return for a promised holiday in Bulgaria. He later finds himself arrested for his subversive activities. Very Eastern European, this. Zamachowski (*Three Colours: White*) plays Tomasz as a benign, bandly-legged buffoon, a kind of post-revolutionary Norman Wisdom. But as for his conversion, and the logic of his superiors, most mystifying. TCh

Convoy

(1978, US, 110 min)
d Sam Peckinpah. *p* Robert M Sherman. *sc* Bill L Norton. *ph* Harry Stradling. *ed* Graeme Clifford. *pd* Fernando Carrere. *m* Chip Davis. *cast* Kris Kristofferson, Ali MacGraw, Ernest Borgnine, Burt Young, Madge Sinclair, Franklyn Ajaye, Seymour Cassel.
● Taking CW McCall's hit single as starting-point, scriptwriter Bill Norton (director of *Cisco Pike*) makes Rubber Duck (Kristofferson) a populist hero of the classic Hollywood kind, leading a group of heavy truckers in their war of independence waged on the highways of America; and Peckinpah's direction places the film in the tongue-in-cheek comic vein of his own earlier *Ballad of Cable Hogue*. Its blatant and impossible artifice is also completely in keeping with Peckinpah's pessimistic streak. Police cars, trucks and bars are destroyed in balletic slow-motion, but none of the characters appears to get hurt (and no one dies – even when you think they do). The narrative goes a bit over the top in the second half, but it's after a large dose of the best kind of escapist good humour. RM

Convoyeurs Attendent, Les (The Carriers Are Waiting)

(1999, Bel/Fr/Switz, 94 min)
d Benoît Mariage. *p* Dominique Janne. *sc* Benoît Mariage. *ph* Philippe Guilbert. *ed* Philippe Bourgueil. *pd* Chris Cornil. *m* Stéphane Huguenin, Yves Sanna. *cast* Benoît Poelvoorde, Morgane Simon, Bouli Lanners, Dominique Baeyens, Philippe Grand'Henry, Jean-François Devigne, Lisa Lacroix, Philippe Nahon.
● In this deadpan comedy, a lowly small town journalist (Poelvoorde, from *Man Bites Dog*) decides to improve his family's lot by training up his understandably reluctant teenage son to break the world record for the number of times a door can be opened in 24 hours. At once gently affectionate and wittily unsentimental about the mundane textures of provincial life – the title refers to a wonderful scene involving racing pigeons – it is sometimes incautiously courageous in touching on darker issues than normally find their way into comedy(death, child abuse, loneliness, unwanted pregnancy). Displaying that genuinely quirky originality often found only in Belgian cinema at its best, the film is sometimes so funny it's quite painful to watch. GA

Coogan's Bluff

(1968, US, 100 min)
d/p Don Siegel. *sc* Herman Miller, Howard Rodman, Dean Riesner. *ph* Bud Thackery. *ed* Sam E Waxman. *ad* Alexander Golitzen, Robert C MacKichan. *m* Lalo Schifrin. *cast* Clint Eastwood, Lee J Cobb, Susan Clark, Tisha Sterling, Don Stroud, Betty Field, Tom Tully.
● The second film in Siegel's rogue cop cycle, this falls between *Madigan* and *Dirty Harry*. It's about an Arizona deputy sent to New York, stetson, boots and all, to escort a prisoner home; the prisoner escapes, and Coogan (Eastwood) roams New York, cowboy in the big city, until he eventually recaptures the hippy prisoner and returns home. Siegel's handling of this conflict between the self-reliant Westerner and the big-city rule book is predictably very funny, and he is aided by a very tight script as well as a mercilessly sarcastic performance from Cobb as Coogan's New York superior. Even Siegel's somehow off-centre treatment of New York hippiedom is intriguingly wry. RM

Cookie

(1989, US, 93 min)
d Susan Seidelman. *p* Laurence Mark. *sc* Nora Ephron, Alice Arlen. *ph* Oliver Stapleton. *ed* Andrew Mondshein. *pd* Michael Haller. *m* Thomas Newman. *cast* Peter Falk, Dianne Wiest, Emily Lloyd, Michael V Gazzo, Brenda Vaccaro, Adrian Pasdar, Lionel Stander, Jerry Lewis, Bob Gunton, Ben Rayson, Ricki Lake, Joe Mantello.

●If this light-hearted account of Mafia mayhem fails to deliver, it's through no fault of the performances. Dino Capisco (Falk) is a labour racketeer on parole after 13 years behind bars; Cookie (Lloyd) is his free-spirited daughter. Despite close surveillance from the law, Dino manages to wrest some prestige and power from old 'business' associates, while his biggest headache concerns his troubled relationship with Cookie. There are moments to savour, notably when Wiest (as Cookie's mother/Dino's mistress), Vacarro (Dino's wife) or Falk are on screen. Lloyd affects a convincing Brooklyn accent, and she does her utmost with limited dialogue. Crucially, the central rift which supposedly exists between father and daughter fails to materialise with any sense of conviction; instead, the film falls back on stereotyping. Seidelman brings visual flair, but given the poorly conceived script, *Cookie* fails to touch female sensibilities in the same way as *Desperately Seeking Susan* and the underrated *Making Mr Right.* CM

Cookie's Fortune

(1998, US, 118 min)
d Robert Altman. *p* Robert Altman, Etchie Stroh. *sc* Anne Rapp. *ph* Toyomichi Kurita. *ed* Abraham Lim. *pd* Stephen Altman. *m* David A Stewart. *cast* Glenn Close, Julianne Moore, Liv Tyler, Chris O'Donnell, Charles S Dutton, Patricia Neal, Ned Beatty, Courtney B Vance, Donald Moffat, Lyle Lovett.

●Holly Springs, Mississippi. Snooty aesthete Camille (Close) is off to rehearse her Easter am-dram production of Wilde's *Salome*. First, however, she and her downtrodden sister Cora (Moore) must drop in on eccentric aunt Cookie (Neal). When Camille finds the old lady dead in bed, she persuades Cora it couldn't possibly be suicide (such disgrace!), steals a necklace to make it look like murder, and then lets Cookie's loyal caretaker/companion Willis (Dutton) take the rap. Not that cop Lester (Beatty) believes his fishing pal should be behind bars, any more than do the town's only lawyer (Moffat) or Cora's rebellious daughter Emma (Tyler). Altman's mercurial film is a mesmerising jewel that works its magic as soon as the faintly shaky opening scenes are over. It may not be 'about' very much (friendship, loyalty, love, self-knowledge), and it'd be too easy just to praise the excellent performances of the typically eccentric cast. Rather, what's so distinctively charming is the easygoing tone, which manages to turn black comedy into a strangely gentle, touching and delicate affair. GA

Cook, the Thief, His Wife & Her Lover, The

(1989, GB/Fr, 124 min)
d Peter Greenaway. *p* Kees Kasander. *sc* Peter Greenaway. *ph* Sacha Vierny. *ed* John Wilson. *pd* Ben van Os, Jan Roelfs. *m* Michael Nyman. *cast* Richard Bohringer, Michael Gambon, Helen Mirren, Alan Howard, Tim Roth, Ciaran Hinds, Gary Olsen, Ewan Stewart, Roger Ashton Griffiths, Ron Cook, Liz Smith, Ian Dury, Diane Langton.

●Greenaway's film begins with a man stripped naked, force-fed shit and pissed on, and it ends in cannibalism. Between, there lies a simple tale of adultery, jealousy and revenge. Wealthy London hoodlum Gambon nightly visits the ritzy restaurant he has bought, humiliating his wife (Mirren), chef (Bohringer) and thugs with his *nouveau riche* vulgarity and threats of violence. Understandably tired of him, his wife embarks on an affair (in the loos, naturally) with another regular customer, the quiet, bookish Howard. It's the details – as in all Greenaway movies, far from incidental – that provide most interest: odd connections made between sex, eating, love and death. Since the characters are here less educated than usual, the witty wordplay of Greenaway's finest work is missing; and though it looks sumptuous enough – with Sacha Vierny's 'Scope camera relishing the reds, golds and greens of the set and Jean-Paul Gaultier's gaudily stylised costumes – shooting in a studio seems to have cramped the director's taste for elegantly surreal symmetries. For a Jacobean-style drama about deadly emotions, the film lacks passion; only in the final half-hour, with Michael Nyman's funereal music supplying a welcome gravity, does it at last exert a stately power. GA

Cool & Crazy (Heftig & begeistret/Häftig och begeistrad)

(2000, Nor/Swe/Fin, 105 min)
d Knut Erik Jensen. *p* Tom Remlov, Jan-Erik Gammleng. *ph* Svein Krøvel, Aslaug Holm. *ed* Aslaug Holm. *m* (producer) Per Oddvar Hildre. *with* The Berlevåg Male Choir.

●Many will enjoy this stunning documentary simply because it's funny and focuses on people who might almost come out of a David Lynch movie: the mostly very elderly male voice choir of the quiet and tiny Norwegian fishing community of Berlevåg. Certainly, the scenes of the old boys braving blizzards as they stand singing outdoors, ice gathering on their eyebrows, verge on the surreal, while some of the interview material – particularly the confessions of womanising – strikes an unexpected note. Finally, however, the film goes much deeper than novelty. it's an affectionate, respectful and subtle study of good people unusually content with their lot, despite the weather, isolation and limitations of life up in the Arctic. GA

Cool Breeze

(1972, US, 102 min)
d Barry Pollack. *p* Gene Corman. *sc* Barry Pollack. *ph* Andrew Davis. *ed* Morton Tubor. *ad* Jack Fisk. *m* Solomon Burke. *cast* Thalmus Rasulala, Judy Pace, Jim Watkins, Raymond St Jacques, Lincoln Kilpatrick, Sam Laws, Pam Grier.

●An updated black remake of *The Asphalt Jungle* becomes formula cops 'n robbers, with all the ethnocentricity needed to turn on those amused by it (usually whites) and those in need of heroes/self images (generally blacks). Having only a few nice touches (like the robbery in which three of the gang wear grotesque masks of Nixon, Agnew and Johnson), the film is most notable for its array of black asses – perhaps the most exploited outfront on the commercial cinema screen. JPi

Cooley High

(1975, US, 107 min)
d Michael Schultz. *p* Steve Krantz. *sc* Eric Monte. *ph* Paul Von Brack. *ed* Christopher Holmes. *ad* William Fosser. *m* Frederick J Perren. *cast* Glynn Turman, Lawrence Hilton-Jacobs, Garrett Morris, Cynthia Davis, Corin Rogers, Maurice Leon Havis.

●An enormous box-office hit in the States, *Cooley High* – a kind of black *American Graffiti* or *Lords of Flatbush* about a group of high school kids in the '60s (hence Motown soundtrack) – is streets ahead of the average blaxploitation effort, yet is still something of a disappointment. Partly the fault lies with the script, and partly with a certain commercial gloss; one or two of the characters nevertheless do come over with some distinctiveness, thanks to OK performances. VG

Cool Hand Luke

(1967, US, 127 min)
d Stuart Rosenberg. *p* Gordon Carroll. *sc* Donn Pearce, Frank R Pierson. *ph* Conrad Hall. *ed* Sam O'Steen. *ad* Cary Odell. *m* Lalo Schifrin. *cast* Paul Newman, George Kennedy, JD Cannon, Lou Antonio, Robert Drivas, Strother Martin, Jo Van Fleet, Clifton James, Dennis Hopper, Harry Dean Stanton.

●A caustically witty look at the American South and its still-surviving chain gangs, with Newman in fine sardonic form as the boss-baiter who refuses to submit and becomes a hero to his fellow-prisoners. Underlying the hard-bitten surface is a slightly uncomfortable allegory which identifies Newman as a Christ figure (and reminds one that Rosenberg once directed the awful, Moral Rearmament-ish *Question 7*). But this scarcely detracts from the brilliantly idiosyncratic script (by Donn Pearce from his own novel) or from Conrad Hall's glittering camerawork (which survives Rosenberg's penchant for the zoom lens and shots reflected in sun-glasses). TM

Cool Runnings

(1993, US, 98 min)
d Jon Turteltaub. *p* Dawn Steel. *sc* Lynn Siefert, Tommy Swerdlow, Michael Goldberg. *ph* Phedon Papamichael. *ed* Bruce Green. *ad* Stephen Marsh. *m* Hans Zimmer. *cast* Leon Robinson, Doug E Doug, Rawle D Lewis, Malik Yoba, John Candy, Raymond J Barry.

●Perhaps the only thing less likely than a Jamaican bobsled team is a Hollywood film inspired by the true story of the crew that competed in the 1988 US Olympics. Not that this sticks closely to the facts; instead, it's another *Rocky*-style sports movie about the underdogs who achieve public recognition and self-respect. Travelogue shots of happy Jamaicans dancing in the sun give way to patronising comedy as slobbish ex-coach Candy is cajoled into teaching four novices. The missing ingredients are snow and ice, but there's plenty of this when the scene shifts to Canada. In his prime, co-writer Michael Ritchie might have turned this into a caustic *Downhill Racer* or *Bad News Bears*-style critique of professional sporting values. Director Turteltaub, on the other hand, patronises both characters and audience with daft knockabout humour, tear-jerking sentiment and racial stereotyping which skates on very thin ice. NF

Cool World

(1992, US, 102 min)
d Ralph Bakshi. *p* Frank Mancuso. *sc* Michael Grais, Mark Victor. *ph* John A Alonzo. *ed* Steve Mirkovich, Annamaria Szanto. *ad* Michael Corenblith. *m* Mark Isham. *cast* Gabriel Byrne, Brad Pitt, Kim Basinger, Michele Abrams, Dierdre O'Connell, Carrie Hamilton.

●Animator Bakshi promises a hipper version of *Who Framed Roger Rabbit*, but delivers a pale imitation. The action shifts between our world and the Cool World, an anarchic cartoon universe where Detective Frank Harris (Pitt) has to stop the only other human (Byrne) from being seduced by voluptuous Holli Would (voiced by Basinger), or for some reason the end of both worlds would be nigh. Bakshi has triumphed before without much plot, happiest when given free rein to be weird, but here you get the impression that the studio got cold feet. Apart from a thumping acid house soundtrack, and one extraordinary shot which takes the 'camera' into a character's mouth, through the guts and out the anus, the chaos is strangely muted. Even the eventual universe-shaking shag is an anti-climax, and by the time all hell rips loose just before the abysmally contrived happy ending, you're well past caring. DW

Cool World, The

(1963, US, 106 min, b/w)
d Shirley Clarke. *p* Frederick Wiseman. *sc* Shirley Clarke, Carl Lee. *ph* Baird Bryant. *ed* Shirley Clarke. *ad* Roger Furman. *m* Mal Waldron. *cast* Hampton Clanton, Yolanda Rodriguez, Carl Lee, Gloria Foster, Bostic Felton, Jerome Raphael.

●*The Cool World* was Frederick Wiseman's first involvement with cinema (he produced it) and Shirley Clarke's second feature as director/writer (after *The Connection*). At heart, it's a not-very-interesting melodrama about a black kid in Harlem learning the hard way that crime is no answer to social problems. But on the surface it's a very much more interesting view of day-to-day life in the ghetto, patterned as a flow of 'insignificant' incidents, variously angry, frightened and defeated characters, and all too credible pressures. Often crudely photographed, but with a brilliantly multi-layered sound-track which integrates some fine jazz. TR

Cop

(1987, US, 110 min)
d James B Harris. *p* James B Harris, James Woods. *sc* James B Harris. *ph* Steve Dubin. *ed* Anthony Spano. *pd* Gene Rudolf. *m* Michel Colombier. *cast* James Woods, Lesley Ann Warren, Charles Durning, Charles Haid, Raymond J Barry, Randi Brooks, Steven Lambert.

●This mean, moody, and muddled *Dirty Harry*-style thriller, adapted from James Ellroy's crime novel *Blood on the Moon*, brutally manhandles its feminist theme and debases Woods' rare talent for portraying sympathetic psychotics. Other than that it's slickly made, violent, and (intentionally and unintentionally) funny. Woods plays a LAPD detective whose idea of communicating with his seven-year-old daughter is sharing sordid tales of his busts. His wife takes exception, the child, and a one-way ticket to San Francisco. Is he sick or merely work obsessed? A call has him fast on the trail of a serial killer. The first mutilated female victim has books on the shelf with titles like *The Womb Has Teeth.* Another call has him rendezvous with a purveyor of sex parties; she's later found trussed up, blood-spattered and dead. Finally, a diary note leads to a feminist bookshop run by a soured romantic Warren, once gang-raped at the very school Woods attended. Could that be the clue? WH

Cop & ½ (aka Cop and a Half)

(1993, US, 97 min)
d Henry Winkler. *p* Paul Maslansky. *sc* Arne Olsen. *ph* Bill Butler. *ed* Daniel Hanley, Roger Tweten, C Timothy O'Meara. *pd* Maria Caso. *m* Alan Silvestri. *cast* Burt Reynolds, Norman D Golden II, Ruby Dee, Holland Taylor, Ray Sharkey, Frank Sivero.

● Eight-year-old Devon (Golden) dreams of being a cop: he watches the TV shows, knows the procedures and has learned the lingo – all he needs is a badge and some cuffs. So when he conveniently witnesses a crime in progress, Devon negotiates a little quid pro quo. He'll spill the beans on the bad guys if the good guys will let him play cop for a day. Cynical, battle-weary plainclothes detective Reynolds, who thinks the only cuffs kids should be given are ones round the ears, gets the assignment. Reynolds' lazy performance combines elements of his tough guy persona and his light comic manner, but is a poor photocopy of his best work. As for the cute, grinning Golden, let's just say Macaulay Culkin can rest easy in his bed. NF

Cop au Vin (Poulet au Vinaigre)

(1984, Fr, 110 min)
d Claude Chabrol. *p* Marin Karmitz. *sc* Dominique Roulet, Claude Chabrol. *ph* Jean Rabier. *ed* Monique Fardoulis. *ad* Françoise Benoit-Fresco. *m* Matthieu Chabrol. *cast* Jean Poiret, Stéphane Audran, Michel Bouquet, Jean Topart, Lucas Belvaux, Pauline Lafont.

● Grotesque murders in a small provincial town; huge meals; a scourging of the bourgeoisie. Where could this be but Chabrol country? The young postboy is investigating the local cartel's murderous business schemes, with the help of his crippled mother (an increasingly uglified Audran) and his girl-friend. But he is no match for the out-of-town cop (*poulet*) wonderfully played by Poiret as an omniscient, genial fellow who transforms into a roughhouse two-fister when occasion demands. And it is all done with the skittishness which Chabrol brings to this kind of policier, but given edge by his very mocking eye. CPea

CopLand

(1997, US, 105 min)
d James Mangold. *p* Cary Woods, Cathy Konrad, Ezra Swerdlow. *sc* James Mangold. *ph* Eric A Edwards. *ed* Craig McKay. *pd* Lester Cohen. *m* Howard Shore. *cast* Sylvester Stallone, Harvey Keitel, Ray Liotta, Robert De Niro, Peter Berg, Janeane Garofolo, Annabella Sciorra, Noah Emmerich, Cathy Moriarty, Deborah Harry.

● When all your citizens are big city cops, NYPD seeking rest in the New Jersey commuter belt, who will police the police? Out of a mixture of complaisance, natural deference and an inferiority complex as big as his middle-age spread, local sheriff Freddy Heflin (Stallone) has let things slide, turning a blind eye to the dubious activities of detective Ray Donlan (Keitel) and his cohorts. Freddy's jerked out of his lethargy when Internal Affairs send Moe Tilden (De Niro) to investigate the apparent suicide of another cop, Donlan's cousin. Writer/director Mangold's latter-day Western is overloaded with good actors, though the bulk of the drama falls on Stallone's broad shoulders. It's effective casting. Stallone's slow, stunted speech patterns mesh well with Freddy's dim realisation that sometimes integrity isn't enough, that you have to put yourself on the line for what you want. His clumsy, unconsummated relationship with Liz (Sciorra) is especially touching – accompanied by scratchy Springsteen records. The mystery suspense elements, however, grind from implausibility (the set-up), to cliché (the climax), with too much back story in between TCh

Cops and Robbers

(1973, US, 89 min)
d Aram Avakian. *p* Elliott Kastner. *sc* Donald E Westlake. *ph* David Quaid. *ed* Barry Malkin. *ad* Gene Rudolf. *m* Michel Legrand. *cast* Cliff Gorman, Joseph Bologna, Dick Ward, Shepperd Strudwick, Ellen Holly, John P Ryan.

● Racy script by Donald Westlake about two of New York's finest who decide that their uniforms and badges give them an ideal camouflage for pursuing extra-legal activities. They proceed to perpetrate one of the most spectacular securities heists Wall Street has ever seen. There's an added twist as the cops also try to rip off the Mafia men to whom they're supposed to fence the proceeds of their crime. An insubstantial film, rather clumsily edited, but pleasant enough, especially for those who dislike violence and love happy endings. MHo

Cop's Honour (Parole de Flic)

(1985, Fr, 98 min)
d José Pinheiro. *p* Jacques Bar. *sc* Philippe Setbon. *ph* Jean-Jacques Tarbès. *ed* Claire Pinheiro. *ad* Théobald Meurisse. *m* Pino Marchèse. *cast* Alain Delon, Jacques Perrin, Fiona Gélin, Vincent Landon, Stéphane Ferrara, Jean-François Stévenin.

● Alain Delon is a man with a mission. An ex-cop ('the best'), his wife and daughter murdered, he returns from playing great white god among the cheery savages of the Congo to avenge his family and rid Lyons of a vigilante group who, dressed like Ninjas, go round town killing petty criminals under orders from a mysterious Mr Big. Not so mysterious, actually, since everything in this atrocious movie is predictable. The women are disposable love objects, the dialogue risible, and the acting wooden in the extreme. Most notable is the appalling sound-track: disco for the sweaty workout, heavy metal for the action, a totally irrelevant use of *Tristan and Isolde* for a car stunt, and Delon himself crooning the end-credits pap. Delon has no excuse; after all, besides 'acting' and 'singing', he also exec produced and had a hand in the script. GA

Copycat

(1995, US, 123 min)
d Jon Amiel. *p* Arnon Milchan, Mark Tarlov. *sc* Ann Biderman, David Madsen. *ph* Laszlo Kovacs. *ed* Alan Heim, Jim Clark. *pd* Jim Clay. *m* Christopher Young. *cast* Sigourney Weaver, Holly Hunter, Harry Connick Jr, Dermot Mulroney, William McNamara, JE Freeman, Will Patton, John Rothman, Shannon O'Hurley.

● Midway through this gimmicky, derivative serial killer thriller, the murderer sends a message to his pursuers, a line from a song by The Police, promising he'll 'turn a murder into Art'. 'Very witty, this guy,' mutters agoraphobic psychologist Sigourney Weaver. 'He wants to dazzle us.' That goes for the film-makers too, of course, who've come up with this peculiarly tasteless, opportunistic conceit: a serial killer who reproduces the murders of notorious serial killers (Bundy, Dahmer, et al). With even less scruple, the screenwriters proceed to replicate the 'feminist' structure from *Silence of the Lambs*, with Weaver and cop Holly Hunter splintering the Clarice Starling role, consulting convicted psycho Harry Connick Jr for the inside dope, and finally coming face to face with their fears in a scary/silly climax. There are flashes of interest between the intriguingly matched stars, and Amiel keeps the tension high, but the film's imagination is circumscribed by the clichés of the genre, so that the name of that Police tune seems relevant: it's 'Murder by Numbers'. It leaves a nasty taste in the mouth. TCh

Coquille et le Clergyman, La

see Seashell and the Clergyman, the

Coraje

see Courage

Coraje del Pueblo, El (The Courage of the People/ The Night of San Juan)

(1971, Bol/It, 94 min)
d Jorge Sanjines. *p* Alberto Luna, Roberto Savio. *sc* Oscar Soria. *ph* Antonia Eguino. *ed* Juan Carlos Macias, Sergio Buzi. *m* Nilo Soruco. *cast* Domitila Chungara, Federico Vallejo, Felicidad Vda. de García, Eusebio Gironda.

● When a talented political film-maker like Sanjines aims a film at a very specific audience (to elucidate that audience's past and present oppression and, hopefully, radicalise its future), then the film may lose much of its impact when transposed to a different culture. So it is with *Courage of the People*, a bleak representation of a 1967 massacre of Bolivian tin miners by the army, reconstructed with the participation of survivors. Introduced by the depiction of a similar event in 1942, the film progresses to the '67 massacre, depicting the workers' growing resistance without analysing the move towards more radical action. SM

Corbeau, Le (The Raven)

(1943, Fr, 93 min, b/w)
d Henri-Georges Clouzot. *sc* Louis Chavance. *ph* Nicolas Hayer. *ed* Marguerite Beaugé. ad André Andréjew. *m* Tony Aubin. *cast* Pierre Fresnay, Pierre Larquey, Micheline Francey, Ginette Leclerc, Louis Seigner, Noël Roquevert, Roger Blin, Héléna Manson.

● David Thomson calls Clouzot's a 'cinema of total disenchantment'. This exposé of a malicious small town in France must be one of the most depressed films to emerge from the period of the German Occupation: everyone speaks badly of everyone else, rumours of abortion and drug addiction are rife, and a flood of poison-pen letters raises the spiteful hysteria to epidemic level. Clouzot's misanthropy concludes in total defeat; his naggingly over-insistent style occasionally achieves a great blackness. CPe

Cornered

(1945, US, 102 min, b/w)
d Edward Dmytryk. *p* Adrian Scott. *sc* John Paxton. *ph* Harry J Wild. *ed* Joseph Noriega. *ad* Albert S D'Agostino, Carroll Clark. *m* Roy Webb. *cast* Dick Powell, Walter Slezak, Micheline Cheirel, Luther Adler, Morris Carnovsky, Nina Vale, Edgar Barrier, Steven Geray.

● Powell's second and definitive attempt to shed his crooner image, as an ex-PoW tracking down the collaborationist responsible for his young French wife's death, is even better than *Murder, My Sweet*. Dispensing with the expressionistic flurries, it concentrates on bleak ambiguity (abetted by a fine cast) as the hunt goes up in Buenos Aires for a villain whom no one – not even his own wife – has ever seen (a telling metaphor for the hidden face of Fascism). As one might expect of a film whose credits carry at least four blacklist victims (Dmytryk, producer Adrian Scott, actors Adler and Carnovsky), the hard-boiled dialogue is studded with political warnings and forebodings in a manner that now looms as pleasantly period, but is in any case effortlessly carried by Harry Wild's superb *noir* camerawork. TM

Correction, Please or how we got into pictures

(1979, GB, 52 min)
d Noël Burch. *p* Margaret Williams. *sc* Noël Burch. *ph* Les Young. *ed* Brand Thumim. *ad* Phoebe de Gaye. *m* John Buller. *cast* Sue Lloyd, Jeff Rawle, Lea Brodie, Jimmy Gardner.

● Using very early archive material and studio-shot footage, Burch – author of *Theory of Film Practice* – contrives a witty re-staging of the tropes of very early silent American cinema: the uses of space, dialogue, design and the camera are seen evolving (degenerating?) into the recognisable form of narrative cinema. CA

Corridors of Blood

(1958, GB, 86 min, b/w)
d Robert Day. *p* John Croydon. *sc* Jean Scott Rogers. *ph* Geoffrey Faithfull. *ed* Peter Mayhew. *ad* Tony Masters. *m* Buxton Orr. *cast* Boris Karloff, Betta St John, Finlay Currie, Francis Matthews, Adrienne Corri, Christopher Lee, Francis de Wolff.

● Despite the presence of Karloff – as a humanitarian doctor of the 1840s whose experiments with anaesthetics lead to drug addiction and involvement with body-snatchers – this often seems to be little more than an excuse for detailed coverage of some utterly gruesome operations and the systematic mutilation of patients on the operating table. There are some compensations, however, notably a cunningly atmospheric recreation of Victorian London from Day (who made the infinitely superior *Grip of the Strangler*), and a brief but superbly stylish appearance by Christopher Lee as a soft-spoken villain. DP

Corrina, Corrina

(1994, US, 116 min)
d Jessie Nelson. *p* Paula Mazur, Steve Tisch, Jessie Nelson. *sc* Jessie Nelson. *ph* Bruce Surtees. *ed* Wayne Wahrman, Lee Percy, Eric McLeod. *pd* Jeannine Claudia Oppewall.

m Rick Cox. *cast* Whoopi Goldberg, Ray Liotta, Tina Majorino, Don Ameche, Wendy Crewson, Joan Cusack, Jennifer Lewis.
● Jessie Nelson's movie is loosely based on his own childhood, and no better for it. The story – little Molly (Majorino) withdraws into a world of silence after her mother's death, causing more grief for her dad (Liotta), until he discovers the perfect nanny (Goldberg), who teaches her to trust her tongue and him his heart again – is stuff you'd stash in a locket. It's a Whoopi vehicle, and the only interest is in Hollywood's tailoring of the race issue to fit the star. Her Corrina is doing the Mary Poppins gig because she can't get a break in the white world. She dreams of writing the sleeve notes to jazz albums and, to illustrate how the system permits blacks to play but not write about jazz, spins Bill Evans' 'Peace Piece' – which is confusing, since Evans was white. Liotta plays Jewish. That's about the level of the debate, but a nearly transparent Don Ameche turns in his last performance, and cinematographer Bruce Surtees gives Rolls-Royce lensing. BC

Corrupt

see Order of Death

Corruptor, The

(1999, US, 110 min)
d James Foley. *p* Dan Halsted. *sc* Robert Pucci. *ph* Juan Ruiz-Anchia. *ed* Howard E Smith. *pd* David Brisbin. *m* Carter Burwell. *cast* Chow Yun-Fat, Mark Wahlberg, Ric Young, Paul Ben-Victor, Andrew Pang, Byron Mann, Elizabeth Lindsey, Brian Cox, Kim Chan, Jon Kit Lee, Tovah Feldshuh.
● 'The end is bullshit. The means is what you live with.' Thus alcoholic ex-cop Cox to son Wahlberg, engaged in undercover double games in New York's Chinatown. You might think the means is bullshit, too, if the NYPD is setting Irish cops to infiltrate the Triads. 'You're worse than white, you're green,' sneers the head of the Asian Gang Unit, Chow Yun-Fat. Yet the newcomer's enthusiasm wins him over – that and his readiness to get his hands dirty if it gets the job done. This is a satisfying, serious reprise of traditional cop-thriller quandaries about ambivalent father figures, integrity and betrayal, public and private moralities. Director Foley frames it in the restless surveillance style of '70s films like *The French Connection* and *Serpico*. On the other hand, the movie is also designed as a star vehicle for Hong Kong action hero Chow, which means that the prevailing naturalism is chained to HK-style eruptions of spectacular gunplay and a death toll in keeping with '90s bloodlust. Affecting a cynicism that's even-handed if hardly progressive, it finds its most compelling culture clash in the John Woo-like play-off between Chow's delicious, extravagant scene-stealing and Wahlberg's fretful, internalised approach. They build up an affection that's only a whisker short of homoerotic. TCh

Corsa dell'innocente, La

see Flight of the Innocent

Cortázar

(1994, Arg, 80 min)
d Tristan Bauer. *sc* Tristan Bauer, Carolina Scaglione. *ph* Marcelo Camorino. *ed* Tristan Bauer, Carolina Scaglione. *pd* Abel Facello. *m* Rodolfo Mederos. *with* Julio Cortazar, Hugo Carrizo, Agustin Goldschmidt.
● A profile of the Argentine writer Julio Cortazar, encompassing his boxing career, literary work, political radicalism, and personal (and cultural) exile in Europe, interspersed with self-penned tangos and various grandiloquent musings on subjects to hand. The film is a montage (Cortazar's own tape recordings, readings from his writings, archive television interviews, filmed reconstructions) shorn of any outside narration. It's a disjointed technique, but one which, given patience, achieves a rare meditative quality that helps to temper some of the film's more drily intellectual aspects. As do the tangos. Even so, its appeal is likely to be confined to those with a prior interest in the man and his work. NB

Corvette K-225 (aka The Nelson Touch)

(1943, US, 99 min, b/w)
d Richard Rosson. *p* Howard Hawks. *sc* John Rhodes Sturdy. *ph* Tony Gaudio. *ed* Edward Curtiss. *ad* John Goodman, Robert Boyle. *m* David Buttolph. *cast* Randolph Scott, James Brown, Ella Raines, Barry Fitzgerald, Andy Devine, Walter Sande, Robert Mitchum.
● Standard, though unusually muted, World War II yarn about the sterling work done by a Canadian commander and his corvette crew on convoy patrol in the Atlantic. As one might expect with Howard Hawks as producer, the accent is on the way things are done, but the result – complete with obligatory romantic interest – is not particularly exhilarating. TM

Corvette Summer (aka The Hot One)

(1978, US, 105 min)
d Matthew Robbins. *p* Hal Barwood. *sc* Hal Barwood, Matthew Robbins. *ph* Frank Stanley. *ed* Amy Jones. *ad* James Schoppe. *m* Craig Safan. *cast* Mark Hamill, Annie Potts, Eugene Roche, Kim Milford, Dick Miller, Richard McKenzie.
● One of Hollywood's better 'growing up' movies, this steers well clear of tear-jerker material by tracking the on-off juvenile romance of car-mad (post-*Star Wars*) Hamill and apprentice hooker Annie Potts through the neon glare of Las Vegas. He's lost his cherished customised Stingray and is gradually losing his illusions too, while she's lost her inhibitions a little too early for safety. 'Life's lessons' are pretty easy to take, though, when delivered in such a stylishly shaggy-dog fashion. PT

Cosh Boy (aka The Slasher)

(1953, GB, 75 min, b/w)
d Lewis Gilbert. *p* Daniel M Angel. *sc* Lewis Gilbert, Vernon Harris. *ph* Jack Asher. *ed* Charles Hasse. *ad* Bernard Robinson. *m* Lambert Williamson. *cast* James Kenney, Joan Collins, Hermione Baddeley, Hermione Gingold, Sean Lynch, Laurence Naismith, Sidney James.
● The first British-made picture to be awarded an 'X' certificate, and much reviled at the time for its sensationalism, Lewis Gilbert's homegrown crime picture looks pretty tame more than 40 years on. Youthful Kenney, who played the role in Bruce Walker's play *Master Crook*, from which the film was adapted, is the kind of hoodlum who steals granny's savings and bashes old ladies over the head, while Collins is the girl he gets pregnant then callously rejects. In fact, it's a reasonably worthy social-conscience effort in the British manner. The resemblance to the Craig/Bentley case (see *Let Him Have It*) didn't go unnoticed, and the BBFC softened some scenes where Kenney wields cosh and razor before letting it pass. TJ

Cosi

(1995, Aust, 100 min)
d Mark Joffe. *p* Richard Brennan. *sc* Louis Nowra. *ph* Ellery Ryan. *ed* Nicholas Beauman. *pd* Chris S Kennedy. *m* Stephen Endelman. *cast* Ben Mendelsohn, Barry Otto, Toni Collette, Rachel Griffiths, Colin Friels, Pamela Raide, Jacki Weaver, Aden Young, Greta Scacchi.
● Ben Mendelsohn is employed as drama therapist at a mental hospital; completely inexperienced, he finds it tough when Otto, ring leader of the patients, insists they stage a production of Mozart's *Cosi fan tutte*... with predictably chaotic results. Though the film is too broadly 'comic' and, in the end, sentimental to live up to director Joffe's earlier *Spotswood*, and while its treatment of mental illness is at the very least dodgy, it does have a quirky vitality, some good lines and likeable performances by many Australian stalwarts (even Greta Scacchi has a nice, uncredited cameo). GA

Costa Brava (Family Album)

(1994, Sp, 92 min)
d/p Marta Balletbò-Coll. *sc* Marta Balletbò-Coll, Ana Simon Cerezo. *ph* Teo López Garcia. *ed* Ignacio Pérez de Olaguer Cordoba. *pd* Gloria Marti-Palanques. *m* Emili Remolins Casas, Xavier Martorell, Miquel Amor. *cast* Desi del Valle, Marta Balletbò-Coll, Montserrat Gausachs, Josep Maria Brugués, Ramon Mari, Sergi Schaaff.
● Shot in English over 14 days, split between Barcelona and the Spanish coast, this witty and gradually affecting study of a lesbian love affair blossoming against the odds is necessarily constrained, the action taking place chiefly in phone booths, an apartment and on a roof. That's not to say though, that the director hasn't made the most of scant resources. Anna (Balletbò-Coll) is forced to make ends meet as a tourist guide; her free time is spent getting her one-woman show, 'Love Thy Neighbour', off the ground. Until, that is, she falls in love with an exasperating Israeli engineer (del Valle) who turns Anna's world (and underwear draw) upside down. Slight, but endearing. FM

Cosy Dens (Pelísky)

(1999, Czech Rep, 115 min)
d Jan Hrebejk. *p* Ondrej Trojan. *sc* Petr Jarchovsk. *ph* Jan Malír. *ed* Vladimír Barák. *pd* Milan Bycek. *m* Ivan Hlas, Ivan Kral. *cast* Miroslav Donutil, Jirí Kodet, Simona Stasová, Emília Vásáryová, Bolek Polívа, Eva Holubová, Marek Morvai, Jaroslav Dusek.
● The pangs of first love may not be radical subject matter for a Czech film, but this family saga, from a novel by Petr Sabach, combines its more intimate sensitivities with a panoramic outlook on the mixed fortunes of three interwoven families swopping ideological and generational ire and occasional goodwill. Set over Christmas 1967 and the first few months of the following year, it was also one of the first Czech films to express the sense of betrayal felt by the nation after the crushing of the Prague Spring, a fact which ensured it was a palpable hit with home audiences. Dramatically and stylistically it's unexceptional, but the performances (especially by the young actors) are convincing, and the overall picture warmly and engagingly detailed. NB

Cottage to Let (aka Bombsight Stolen)

(1941, GB, 90 min, b/w)
d Anthony Asquith. *p* Edward Black. *sc* Anatole de Grunwald, John Orton. *ph* Jack Cox. *ed* RE Dearing. *ad* Alex Vetchinsky. *m* Louis Levy. *cast* Leslie Banks, Alastair Sim, John Mills, George Cole, Jeanne de Casalis, Carla Lehmann, Michael Wilding, Catherine Lacey, Wally Patch.
● Jaunty wartime fare with Cole as a crafty Cockney lad (he'd created the role in Geoffrey Kerr's play) evacuated to rural Scotland in time to stop a Glasgow-based spy ring getting their hands on inventor Banks' revolutionary new bombsight. Mills drops by as a passing parachutist, and Sim makes the most of his role as an *éminence grise*. TJ

Cotton Club, The

(1984, US, 128 min)
d Francis Coppola. *p* Robert Evans. *sc* William Kennedy, Francis Coppola. *ph* Stephen Goldblatt. *ed* Barry Malkin, Robert Q Lovett. *pd* Richard Sylbert. *m* John Barry. *cast* Richard Gere, Gregory Hines, Diane Lane, Lonette McKee, Bob Hoskins, James Remar, Nicolas Cage, Allen Garfield, Fred Gwynne, Gwen Verdon.
● The misconception that sinks this often handsome confection is that revivalism will spread evenly over separate cultures, turning the Prohibition gangsters and backstage romances and old jazz into a winning hand of iconographic flash-cards for the camera. What neck! Neither Ellington's music nor the black dancers will hold still, of course, and fatally detain the emotions while the lovers do not. Gere, with masher's taz and major hair-oil, phones in his performance from the wardrobe department. Hines, his black opposite number, does better with less. Of the hoods, only Hoskins and Fred Gwynne rise above the mundane mayhem, spinning headlines and general dis-dat-doze. The narrative is a mess despite the simplistic twinning of tales, and – worse yet – keeps interrupting the heart-stopping hoofing. BC

Cotton Mary

(1999, GB, 124 min)
d Ismail Merchant, (co-director) Madhur Jaffrey. *p* Nayeem Hafizka, Richard Hawley. *sc* Alexandra Viets. *ph* Pierre Lhomme. *ed* John David Allen. *pd* Alison Riva. *m* Richard Robbins. *cast* Greta Scacchi, Madhur Jaffrey, James Wilby, Sarah Badel, Joanna David, Sakina Jaffrey, Gemma Jones, Prayag Raaj.

●We're back in India in the wake of the Raj, flitting from the bazaars of Kerala to the lush manse of an English family, the Macintoshes, whom we meet as they are inadvisedly adding to their number. The child is premature, the unhappy mother, Lily (Scacchi), won't lactate, and it takes the intervention of Jaffrey's nurse, Cotton Mary, to keep the newborn alive. A proud Anglo-Indian, Mary jumps at Lily's offer of domestic work; and, while her new employers are otherwise distracted, she inveigles her way into the heart of their household. The story might be meant to symbolise the problem of Anglo-Indian identity with the departure of their British patrons, but on the immediate level it's an impenetrable mess. The characters are frustratingly feeble, witless and ill-drawn, and their motivations range from the opaque to the unintelligible. NB

Couch

(1964, US, 40 min)
d Andy Warhol. *cast* Gerard Malanga, Baby Jane Holzer, Ondine, Allen Ginzberg, Jack Kerouac, Peter Orlovsky.

●Pre-*Chelsea Girls* Warhol, which means silent, black-and-white, fixed-angle stares at nothing very much. Actually, *Couch* is action-packed by the standards of most early Warhol: it comprises a series of takes of the couch itself, upon which persons in varying stages of undress enjoy carnal relations with each other in varying permutations. Much of it is gay. The print seen here, a dupe of a dupe, almost totally lacks visual definition: less orgasmic than protoplasmic. TR

Couch in New York, A (Un Divan à New York)

(1996, Bel/Fr/Ger, 106 min)
d Chantal Akerman. *p* Régine Konckier, Jean-Luc Ormières. *sc* Chantal Akerman, Jean-Louis Benoît. *ph* Dietrich Lohmann. *ed* Claire Atherton. *ad* Christian Marti. *m* Sonia Wieder-Atherton. *cast* Juliette Binoche, William Hurt, Paul Guilfoyle, Stephanie Buttle, Richard Jenkins.

●Akerman's most overtly commercial project yet turns out to be a comedy without humour, a romance without affection. She laboriously hauls into place all the items on the specification: wacky premise (dancer Binoche pretending to be a psychiatrist, psychiatrist Hurt pretending to be a patient), best friends to whom the plot can be confided, a big cute dog. But it never begins to come to life. Hurt looks haggard, Binoche flutters prettily, a butterfly in a graveyard. The prevailing gloom is lifted only by some imaginative art direction. BBa

Couch Trip, The

(1987, US, 98 min)
d Michael Ritchie. *p* Lawrence Gordon. *sc* Steve Kampmann, Will Porter, Sean Stein. *ph* Donald Thorin. *ed* Richard A Harris. *pd* Jimmy Bly. *m* Michel Colombier. *cast* Dan Aykroyd, Walter Matthau, Charles Grodin, Donna Dixon, Richard Romanus, Mary Gross, David Clennon.

●When LA celebrity sex therapist George Maitlin (Grodin) succumbs to a nervous breakdown, a London sabbatical is advised. The call to suitably uncharismatic locum Dr Baird is intercepted by lunatic John Burns Jr (Aykroyd). Assuming Baird's identity, Burns duly shows up in Therapy City, where his dotty advice worries the sponsors of Maitlin's popular radio phone-in show but wows the clients. A fellow con-artist (Matthau) rumbles the scam, and wants a piece of the proceeds. Ritchie's irreverent farce won't tip the balance of Hollywood's love/hate relationship with psychiatry, but it does have fun with the mythology. Aykroyd revels in a role tailor-made for his shoot-from-the-lip talent, his exuberant performance illuminating the film's sometimes flabby sentimentality and slack structure. Intermittently hilarious, if rickety, fun. SCu

Counsellor, The (Il Consigliori)

(It/Sp, 1973, 102 min)
d Alberto De Martino. *p* Edmondo Amati. *sc* Adriano Bolzoni, Vincenzo Flamani, Leonardo Martin, Alberto de Martino. *ph* Aristide Massaccesi. *ed* Otello Colangeli. *ad* Emilio Ruiz del Rio. *m* Riz Ortolani. *cast* Martin Balsam, Tomas Milian, Francisco Rabal, Dagmar Lassander, Carlo Tamberlani, Ray K Goman.

●Lame Mafia movie made in San Francisco, but with a predominantly Italian cast dubbed into English. Weighty debts are owed to *Bullitt* (locations and car chases) and *The Godfather* (subject and theme). Balsam excepted, the gangsters are all reduced to wide-screen smiles and hostile eyes, which gives most of the cast the appearance of ventriloquists' dummies; and apart from some amusingly heavy-handed symbolism, there's little of consequence to note.

Count a Lonely Cadence (aka Stockade)

(1990, US, 97 min)
d Martin Sheen. *p* Richard Davis. *sc* Dennis Shryack, Martin Sheen. *ph* Richard Leiterman. *ed* Martin Hunter. *pd* Ian Thomas. *m* Georges Delerue. *cast* Charlie Sheen, Martin Sheen, F Murray Abraham, Larry Fishburne, Blu Mankuma, Michael Beach, Harry Stewart, John Toles-Bey, James Marshall, Ramon Estevez.

●'He's an intelligent enough kid, just lacks discipline'. With these words still ringing in his ears, Charlie Sheen is summarily despatched to the US Army, and before you can say AWOL has taken up a 90-day lease in the stockade. The camp commander, a strict disciplinarian, is Martin Sheen, but this displaced father-son conflict turns out to be only one aspect of the story. The bulk of the screen time is devoted to Charlie and the other five prisoners, all of whom are black. The progression from mutual suspicion to friendship may not be revelatory, but the performances (Fishburne, Stewart, Beach) are lively and Sheen's direction assured. If there's something a mite patronising about the 'colourful' soul-patrol antics, the movie comes as near as dammit to acknowledging, at the close, the gulf that still divides the races, and that's a surprise in this eminently liberal work. On the down side, there's no real feel for period (the mid-'60s), and that dull Sheen psychodrama doesn't go away. TCh

Countdown

(1967, US, 101 min)
d Robert Altman. *p* William Conrad. *sc* Loring Mandel. *ph* William W Spencer. *ed* Gene Milford. *ad* Jack Poplin. *m* Leonard Rosenman. *cast* James Caan, Robert Duvall, Joanna Moore, Barbara Baxley, Michael Murphy, Steve Ihnat.

●Made before *M*A*S*H* (and subjected to re-editing by the studio), Altman's drama about American astronauts being rushed to the moon in an attempt to beat the Russians is a surprisingly human affair, concentrating less on sci-fi hardware than on the emotional crises affecting the men and their families. Slightly soapy in parts, but overall it's an intelligent and taut little film, interesting for the way it foreshadows not only the actual look of the Apollo capsules but also Altman's later style: the lack of interest in 'plot', the overlapping dialogue, and the imaginative use of the 'scope frame are all there, if in embryonic form. GA

Count Dracula (El Conde Dracula)

(1970, Sp/It/WGer, 98 min)
d Jesús Franco. *p/sc* Peter Welbeck [Harry Alan Towers]. *ph* Manuel Marino. *m* Bruno Nicolai. *cast* Christopher Lee, Herbert Lom, Klaus Kinski, Frederick Williams, Maria Rohm, Soledad Miranda.

●With Kinski gibbering away in the padded cell as the puppet-like Renfield, and Lee re-running his seductive Hammer suavity as the Count, this near-forgotten low-budget version seems to have laid much groundwork for later forays into cinematic vampire lore. The script's ambitions (early marked by a not over-extravagant title claim to be illustrating Stoker's novel 'as written') are high and distinctly dead-pan, though perhaps not best served by direction that veers with some consistency to the endearingly inept (or, more charitably, to rigorous anti-illusionism?). Yet the movie emerges as a soberly intelligent reappraisal of a potent and oft-misrepresented mythology. PT

Count Dracula and His Vampire Bride

see Satanic Rites of Dracula, The

Counterfeiters

(1948, US, 73 min, b/w)
d Peter Stewart [Sam Newfield]. *p* Maurice H Conn. *sc* Fred Myton, Barbara Worth. *ph* James S Brown. *ed* Martin G Cohn. *ad* Frank Dexter. *m* Irving Gertz. *cast* John Sutton, Doris Merrick, Hugh Beaumont, Lon Chaney, George O'Hanlon.

●Scotland Yard man Sutton heads for Los Angeles to help the local force bring in a counterfeiting ring. Posing as a confidence trickster, he infiltrates Beaumont's gang, but romance with the alluring Merrick may prove not to be such a good idea after all. Passable support-slot thriller with horror star Chaney as one of the heavies. TJ

Countess Dracula

(1970, GB, 93 min)
d Peter Sasdy. *p* Alexander Paal. *sc* Jeremy Paul. *ph* Ken Talbot. *ed* Henry Richardson. *ad* Philip Harrison. *m* Harry Robinson. *cast* Ingrid Pitt, Nigel Green, Sandor Elès, Maurice Denham, Patience Collier, Lesley-Anne Down, Peter Jeffrey.

●Stiff performances and shoddy sets apart, this late Hammer depiction of the activities of Countess Elisabeth Bathory – who used to bathe in the blood of slain virgins in an attempt to regain her youth – is still intriguing for its emphasis on corruption and decay rather than vampirism. Pitt is excellent as the baleful Countess. GA

Countess from Hong Kong, A

(1966, GB, 120 min)
d Charles Chaplin. *p* Jerome Epstein. *sc* Charles Chaplin. *ph* Arthur Ibbetson. *ed* Gordon Hales. *pd* Don Ashton. *m* Charles Chaplin. *cast* Marlon Brando, Sophia Loren, Sydney Chaplin, Tippi Hedren, Patrick Cargill, Michael Medwin, Margaret Rutherford, Charles Chaplin.

●Everybody wanted to like Chaplin's first film in ten years (and his last, as it turned out), but it just wasn't funny. His direction is antiquated and almost anonymous, and there is a strange stagy atmosphere, almost as if the cast were continually waiting for prompts. Apparently Chaplin worked hard with his actors, but the fact remains that even if Brando weren't hopelessly miscast as a diplomat who finds a Russian émigrée countess (Loren) stowed away in his cabin, it would still have been difficult for anyone to speak Chaplin's stilted lines with conviction. Margaret Rutherford comes off better than most as one of the ship's passengers. DP

Count of Monte-Cristo, The

(1974, GB, 104 min)
d David Greene. *p* Norman Rosemont. *sc* Sidney Carroll. *ph* Aldo Tonti. *ed* Gene Milford. *ad* Walter Patriarca. *m* Allyn Ferguson. *cast* Richard Chamberlain, Tony Curtis, Trevor Howard, Louis Jourdan, Donald Pleasence, Kate Nelligan.

●Shot in Italy and very obviously designed as a TV special (plenty of small gaps for ads, plus a big gap halfway through), this is an above-average piece of junk. The familiar Dumas material is put over with a touch of style (Greene indulges his usual fondness for fancy compositions and loony camera angles), and the equally familiar cast provide good value as they don fancy outfits and parade their clashing mannerisms (Curtis is especially ludicrous, and ends up with a dashing skunk hairdo). The script comes up with the occasional gem as well: 'I didn't know – we'd moved away,' the heroine explains after learning that Chamberlain's dad starved to death. Not very good, in other words, but there are worse ways of wasting time. GB

Count of Monte Cristo, The

(2001, US/GB/Ire, 131 min)
d Kevin Reynolds. *p* Roger Birnbaum, Gary Barber, Jonathan Glickman. *sc* Jay Wolpert. *ph* Andrew Dunn. *ed* Stephen Semel, Chris Womack. *pd* Mark Geraghty. *m* Edward Shearmur. *cast* Jim Caviezel, Guy Pearce, Richard Harris, James Frain, Dagmara Dominczyk, Michael Wincott, Luis Guzmán, Helen McCrory. Freddie Jones, Alex Norton.

●This umpteenth version of Dumas' Napoleonic-era revenge novel makes a preposterous, expansive and self-conscious attempt to resurrect the historical spectacular. As the Count – a dashing but lowly innocent whose years imprisoned at Château d'If only reinforce a cold determination to be revenged on Fernan (Pearce), his treacherous aristocratic pal – the essentially interior Caviezel brings an aura of metaphysical doubt entirely at odds with the psychologically facile narrative drive of the text. Playing the omniscient priest, the hero's fellow prisoner and subsequent tutor and fencing master, Harris knows hokum when he's cast in it, and gives a surprisingly spritely, quietly uproarious turn. Likewise Guzmán, as loyal servant Jacopo, scorns any notion of softening his Hispanic vowels. These are small consolations, however. WH

Country

(1984, US, 109 min)
d Richard Pearce. *p* William Wittliff, Jessica Lange. *sc* William Wittliff. *ph* David M Walsh. *ed* Bill Yahraus. *pd* Ron Hobbs. *m* Charles Gross. *cast* Jessica Lange, Sam Shepard, Wilford Brimley, Matt Clark, Therese Graham, Levi L Knebel.

● A gritty examination of the way that Reaganite economics is squeezing the life out of the small farmer. Shepard is very fine as the farmer, who, with Lange as his land-owning wife, faces foreclosure by the loan company. The scenes of the hard life are becoming familiar from the down-home type of film, but what sets this one apart is the emphasis placed upon Lange, who becomes the mainstay of family and farm. It's not a comfortable film, nor even a very optimistic one, but its power lies in a very truthful depiction of the men and women that the movies tend to forget. CPea

Country

(2000, Ire, 92 min)
d Kevin Liddy. *p* Jack Armstrong. *sc* Kevin Liddy. *ph* Donal Gilligan. *ed* Ben Yeates. *pd* Clodagh Conroy. *m* Niall Byrne. *cast* Lisa Harrow, Des Cave, Gary Lydon, Marcella Plunkett, Pat Laffan, Laurence Kinlan, Dean Pritchard.

● A well told if conventional tale of rural bigotry, narrow horizons and pointless feuds, this steady, painstaking movie centres on a a farmer's household in Co. Down – belt-wielding father Frank (Cave, first rate), resentful son Con (Lydon) and young Jack (Pritchard) – into which comes emotional/dramatic catalyst Miriam (Harrow, struggling with the accent). The villain is Mike Clifford, a hater of wide-ranging appetite, and an agent of corruption/destruction with regard to the innocence and hopes of the entire Murphy family. Writer/director Liddy favours gently heightened imagery (rather overdoing the rhapsodic barley-field landscapes) and seems unashamed of his allegiance to the Ladybird Book of Cinematic Symbolism. But his trust in the impact of patiently rendered universal emotions more than pays off. WH

Country Dance (aka Brotherly Love)

(1969, GB, 112 min)
d J Lee Thompson. *p* Robert Emmett Ginna. *sc* James Kennaway. *ph* Ted Moore. *ed* Willy Kemplen. *ad* Maurice Fowler. *m* John Addison. *cast* Peter O'Toole, Susannah York, Michael Craig, Harry Andrews, Cyril Cusack, Brian Blessed, Robert Urquhart.

● The US release title, *Brotherly Love*, better signalled the incestuous relationship at the core of this quirkily comic melodrama of emotional Highland flings (scripted by James Kennaway from his own novel). O'Toole's Scots aristocrat, obsessively possessive of married sister York, comes across as an outline first draft for his later role in *The Ruling Class*. The use of Irish landscapes as a stand-in for all the pastoral bits doesn't help much. PT

Country Girls, The

(1983, GB, 108 min)
d Desmond Davis. *p* Aida Young. *sc* Edna O'Brien. *ph* Denis Lewiston. *ed* Timothy Gee. *ad* Arden Gantly. *m* Francis Shaw. *cast* Sam Neill, Maeve Germaine, Jill Doyle, John Olohan, Britta Smith, Patricia Martin.

● Clever Kate and naughty Baba are ingenuous heroines typical of novelist Edna O'Brien's shamrock imaginings. Growing together in leaps and bounds, the girls progress honourably from village to convent school, propelled from there by the boot of notoriety to Dublin. Maeve Germaine and Jill Doyle are splendid, cutting an irreverent swath through this lyrical romance, transforming guilty pleasures into innocent delights. And Sam Neill deserves a mention for recreating yet again a character of urbane charm and simian morals with no discernible sign of boredom. But it is finally director Davis' verdant vision of southern Ireland that opens out O'Brien's novel of '50s mores and manners to something that, although essentially a TV film, plays gracefully on the cinema screen. FD

Country Life

(1994, Aust, 117 min)
d Michael Blakemore. *p* Robin Dalton. *sc* Michael Blakemore. *ph* Stephen Windon. *ed* Nicholas Beauman. *m* Peter Best. *cast* Kerry Fox, Greta Scacchi, Sam Neill, Michael Blakemore, John Hargreaves, Googie Withers, Patricia Kennedy.

● Blakemore's 'quality' riff on *Uncle Vanya* is set down under in 1919. Deborah (Scacchi) is the object of desire, the frustrated younger wife of a pompous theatre critic (Blakemore). Returning from London to his stepfamily's ornate ancestral pile in New South Wales, the pair, respectively, spark ardour and resentment in the Anglophile household: Dr Askey (Neill), drinker, pacificist and conservationist, is smitten with Deborah, as is his rival, the nervous, artistic and generous master of the house, Uncle Jack (Hargreaves). Meanwhile, fresh and self-effacing as the critic's abandoned daughter, Fox steals the acting honours. Blakemore introduces some intriguing reflections on colonial coming-of-age, but they are sketched in such bald, symbolic strokes, it feels easy to be ahead of the game. For the rest, there's a lot of the camera gazing on impressive Hunter Valley locations, and a working over of small snobberies, racism and manners in candle-lit dinner scenes. Neill takes Scacchi for a walk in the bush among the rutting 'roos, where he gets – 'Hadn't we better get back!' – to unbuckle her shoe. Well-dressed, entirely respectable drama, but with little cinematic frisson. WH

Countryman

(1982, GB, 100 min)
d Dickie Jobson. *p* Chris Blackwell. *sc* Dickie Jobson, Michael Thomas. *ph* Dominique Chapuis. *ed* John Victor Smith, Peter Boyle. *ad* Bernard Leonard. *cast* Countryman, Hiram Keller, Carl Bradshaw, Basil Keane, Freshey Richardson, Kristina St Clair.

● First production from Island Pictures, whose parent record company did so much to introduce reggae to a white audience, but *The Harder They Come* it ain't. An underworked script by writer/director Jobson has Countryman, a Jamaican village fisherman, rescuing two Americans whose small plane has crashed, then sheltering them as they become the quarry of a national man-hunt conducted to disgrace the opposition party during a national election. Unfortunately, the film never works out its political confusions. But even more problematic are the supernatural powers with which its innocent protagonist is endowed, probably the sticking point for wide audience acceptance. An excellent sampler-style soundtrack – Marley, Toots, Scratch Perry, Aswad – isn't enough to paper over the deficiencies. Nor is the film's superbly lush landscape cinematography. RM

Count Yorga, Vampire

(1970, US, 90 min)
d Bob Kelljan. *p* Michael Macready. *sc* Bob Kelljan. *ph* Arch Archambault. *ed* Tony de Zarraga. *ad* Bob Wilder. *m* William Marx. *cast* Robert Quarry, Roger Perry, Michael Murphy, Michael Macready, Donna Anders, Judith Lang, Edward Walsh.

● This low-budget modern-day vampire movie is primitive but not unimaginative. Robert Quarry is the Count, a new arrival in California who knows a superstitious state when he sees it. He soon enlists a series of genuinely disgusting vampire brides (one of them tucks into her pet cat), despite the efforts of their mortal husbands. The flip humour and gruesome effects have lost the novelty value that appealed to cult audiences in 1970, but Yorga remains an intriguing offshoot to the vampire family tree. TCh

Coup de Foudre (At First Sight/Entre Nous)

(1983, Fr, 111 min)
d Diane Kurys. *p* Ariel Zeitoun. *sc* Diane Kurys. *ph* Bernard Lutic. *ed* Joële van Effenterre. *pd* Jacques Bufnoir. *m* Luis Enriquez Bacalov. *cast* Miou-Miou, Isabelle Huppert, Guy Marchand, Jean-Pierre Bacri, Robin Renucci, Patrick Bauchau.

● After dealing with the growing pangs of being a teenager during the '60s in *Diabolo Menthe*, Diane Kurys here turns to the problems of her parents' generation. In 1942, Huppert buys her way out of a camp for Jews in occupied France by marrying an ex-Legionnaire who proposes in a *coup de foudre*. Ten years later, a prosperous bourgeoise in Lyon, she meets an artist (Miou-Miou) who is equally disaffected with her marriage to a good-natured no-hoper. Their developing relationship, 'a little more than friendship and a little less than passion', is the core of the film, enabling them to kick against the pricks. It's all very much in line with the sort of 'Women's Picture' at which Dorothy Arzner was once adept in Hollywood: hardly likely to stretch or threaten the system, but showing – without resorting to melodrama – the desire and heartbreak of everyday life. CPea

Coup de Grâce (Der Fangschuss)

(1976, WGer/Fr, 95 min, b/w)
d Volker Schlöndorff. *p* Eberhard Jukersdorf. *sc* Geneviève Dorman, Margarethe von Trotta, Jutta Brückner. *ph* Igor Luther. *ed* Jane Sperr. *ad* Hans-Jürgen Kiebach. *m* Stanley Myers. *cast* Margarethe von Trotta, Matthias Habich, Rüdiger Kirschstein, Mathieu Carrière, Valeska Gert.

● Of all Schlöndorff's many literary adaptations, this sombre movie from Marguerite Yourcenar's novel is probably the best. It's set in a Baltic country house in 1919, surrounded by echoes and traces of the war, and the meat of it is a gay/straight triangle: Communist sympathiser Sophie (von Trotta) loves German officer Erich (Habich), who seems to be repressing a passion for her brother (Kirschstein). But it's drained of (melo)drama: Schlöndorff films it with eerie detachment, like a *noir Effi Briest*, the better to underline the politics. One memorable indulgence is a squawking performance from Valeska Gert as a crazed aunt. TR

Coup de Menhir, Le

see Asterix and the Big Fight

Coup de Torchon

see Clean Slate

Coupe de Ville

(1990, US, 99 min)
d Joe Roth. *p* Larry Brezner, Paul Schiff. *sc* Mike Binder. *ph* Reynaldo Villalobos. *ed* Paul Hirsch. *pd* Angelo Graham. *m* James Newton Howard. *cast* Patrick Dempsey, Arye Gross, Daniel Stern, Annabeth Gish, Rita Taggart, Joseph Bologna, Alan Arkin, James Gammon.

● Roth's low-budget comedy bottles sibling rivalry inside a vintage Cadillac on a cross-country journey, shakes it up, fuels on '60s rock, quarrels and caring, and proves to be a sweetheart of a film. Three dissimilar brothers – a bully in uniform (Stern), a dreamer (Gross) and a teenage rebel (Dempsey) – are directed by their father (Arkin) to deliver the car intact and without a scratch for their mother's birthday. The assignment proves tricky, but along the way the boys learn about co-existence and family loyalty, which was dad's idea in the first place. Nothing spectacularly original about the plot, but the playing throughout is so juicy and the writing so idiosyncratic that it feels like hot news. Fans of major chromium and the white-wall tyre will go through hell with the title vehicle. BC

Coup pour Coup (Blow for Blow)

(1972, Fr/WGer, 90 min)
d Marin Karmitz. *sc* cast and crew. *ph* André Dubreuil. *m* Jacky Moreau. *cast* Anne-Marie Bacquier, Danielle Chinsky, Eva Damien, Jean Hébert, Annick Fougéry.

● For anyone who has suffered a boring, meaningless job and wasted hours planning exquisite revenge on domineering officials, *Coup pour Coup* – a fictional reconstruction of the successful occupation by women of a French textile factory – is the stuff that dreams are made of. At one stage, a group of seamstresses do in fact subject their boss to some of the treatment normally accorded them. More important, the film is a study of the general conditions of many working class women in France, and the suppression they endure both at work and at home. An often exhilarating film, based on actual events, it was made as a collective effort: all the workers in the cast are genuine, but actors were called on to play the management 'heavies'. Its momentum should be enough to dispel any doubts you might have about its naïveté.

Courage (Coraje)

(1998, Peru, 110 min)
d Alberto Durant. *p* Alberto Durant, Beatriz de la Gándara. *sc* Alberto Durant, Ana Caridad Sanchez. *ph* Mario Garcia Joya. *ed* Miguel Angel Santamaria. *m* Juan Bardem. *cast* Olenka Cepeda, Salvador del Solar, Rosana Pastor, Martin Abriqueta, Jorge Chiarella.

● Solid but unremarkable account of the last months of Peru's martyred María Elena Moyano (Cepeda), from the first appearance of the Shining Path in her home town of Villa Salvador to the height of its fear and her assassination, which galvanised national resistance to the terrorists. Portrayed as a campaigner for a new spirit of participation and solidarity at odds with a reactionary government and a tyrannical insurrection, her story is as sympathetic and disturbing as you'd expect, never sensationalised. María herself is given an ordinary human warmth and range of attachments. Her flights from and back to her home town become dramatically repetitive, though, and the film lacks the sort of attention to detail that would really engage the viewer. NB

Courage Fuyons (Courage – Let's Run)

(1979, Fr, 98 min)
d/p Yves Robert. *sc* Jean-Loup Dabadie, Yves Robert. *ph* Yves Lafaye. *ed* Pierre Gillette. *ad* Jean-Pierre Kohut-Svelko. *m* Vladimir Cosma. *cast* Jean Rochefort, Catherine Deneuve, Philippe Leroy-Beaulieu, Robert Webber, Michel Aumont.

● One would have thought that the subversive ironies of *Préparez vos Mouchoirs* might have trashed the current run of lightweight French comedies of adultery, but *Courage Fuyons* proves to be yet another bastard offspring of *Pardon Mon Affaire*. In its favour it does have the lugubrious Rochefort, a congenital coward given to such acts as stoning his own car rather than irritate some like-minded students (May 1968), and the ever-watchable Deneuve as the *chanteuse* for whom he forsakes all. But the main theme of cowardice and its toxic effects soon loses its impetus: incidental humour shrinks to a brittle misanthropy, and the underlying suggestion that true love is best contained in the realms of deceit is no more than boulevard comedy has been proclaiming for centuries. CPea

Courage Mountain

(1989, US, 98 min)
d Christopher Leitch. *p* Stephen Ujlaki. *sc* Weaver Webb. *ph* Jacques Steyn. *ed* Martin Walsh. *pd* Robb Wilson King. *m* Sylvester Levay. *cast* Juliette Caton, Charlie Sheen, Leslie Caron, Yorgo Voyagis, Laura Betti, Jan Rubes, Joanna Clarke, Jade Magri, Nicola Stapleton, Kathryn Ludlow.

● Since Shirley Temple's *Heidi* of 1937, numerous rehashes have ensued. In this innocuous sequel, set in October 1915, 14-year-old Heidi (Caton) is despatched to school in Italy by her loveable grandfather (Rubes), leaving behind her 'best friend' and prospective lover (Sheen). When the school is commandeered by the Italian army, Heidi and three chums are separated from their guardian (Caron) and fall into the clutches of a fiendish, child-exploiting workhouse owner (Voyagis). Will the girls escape and make it back across the Alps for Christmas? Will Heidi's rustic charm sustain the city-bred cissies through their ordeal? Will Sheen's astonishingly square jaw save the day? Cynical exploitation aside, this is actually an amiable rites-of-passage movie for pre-pubescent audiences. MK

Courage of the People, The

see Coraje del Pueblo, El

Courage Under Fire

(1996, US, 116 min)
d Edward Zwick. *p* John Davis, Joseph M Singer, David T Friendly. *sc* Patrick Sheane Duncan. *ph* Roger Deakins. *ed* Steven Rosenblum. *pd* John Graysmark. *m* James Horner. *cast* Denzel Washington, Meg Ryan, Lou Diamond Phillips, Michael Moriarty, Scott Glenn, Matt Damon, Bronson Pinchot.

● The Gulf War. In a night engagement, Lt Col Nathaniel Serling (Washington) gives the order to fire on one of his own tanks and kills his best friend. Later, having taken a desk job under Gen Hershberg (Moriarty), he's detailed to investigate helicopter pilot Karen Walden (Ryan), who's been recommended for the Medal of Honor. He discovers conflicting testimonies in Walden's case, and also that his own guilt can no longer be hidden. Will the combination of absence from his family, drink, the promptings of journalist Tony Gartner (Glenn), and the conflicting pulls of 'truth' and 'honour' take away his moral courage to deliver the right report? Zwick's second movie with Washington, following his Civil War epic *Glory*, is a rolling campaign. It starts well, with an opening 'fog-of-war' sequence of old-fashioned panache. And as the detective-story flashback structure gets under way, what initially seemed adherence to dramatic and moral cliché becomes more complex and interesting. But having set up the pins and knocked 'em down, Zwick disappointingly starts standing them up again – to demonstrate the compromising nature of his 'liberal' values. WH

Courier, The

(1987, Ire, 85 min)
d Joe Lee, Frank Deasy. *p* Hilary McLoughlin. *sc* Frank Deasy. *ph* Gabriel Beristain. *ed* Derek Trigg, Annette D'Alton. *ad* David Wilson. *m* Elvis Costello [Declan McManus]. *cast* Gabriel Byrne, Ian Bannen, Cait O'Riordan, Kevin Doyle, Mary Ryan, Michelle Houlden, Padraig O'Loingsigh.

● This independent Irish thriller has Mark (O'Loingsigh), a young dispatch rider, becoming embroiled in the nefarious network of horse-trading controlled by Val, a vicious video-dealer played with great malignancy by Byrne. When druggy Danny, an old buddy, is set up by the police and snuffs it sniffing strychnine, Mark determines to get the whole lot of them, and in so doing win the heart of Colette (ex-Pogue O'Riordan). The film's lovey-dovey scenes degenerate into a photo-romance, but the frequent violence is handled with an often distressing realism, and the suspense is generally kept taut. Gabriel Beristain photographs the Dublin locations with a seedy stylishness, and it is clear that Deasy and Lee will one day be directors of flair. Never mind if the flaws provide the odd giggle, this is a work of imagination and ambition. MS

Courtesans of Bombay, The

(1982, GB, 75 min)
d/p Ismail Merchant. *sc* Ismail Merchant, James Ivory, Ruth Prawer Jhabvala. *ph* Vishnu Mathur. *ed* Amit Bose. *cast* Saeed Jaffrey, Zohra Segal, Kareem Samar.

● Docu-drama set in the huge Bombay tenement of Pavanpul, where scores of dancing girls go through their paces in a warren of tiny, squalid rooms for the benefit of rapt, occasionally lecherous, male audiences. A fascinating subject, ill-served by Merchant's strangely coy approach, and his device of interspersing reportage with the fictional reminiscences of imaginary habituées. The effect is confusing as well as extremely irritating, and casts a pall of artifice over the whole proceedings. Devotees of Indian dancing will no doubt find much of interest, but those who attempt to follow the recipe for lime pickle are likely to end up scratching their heads, as instructions have been severely truncated in the cutting-room. JP

Court Jester, The

(1955, US, 101 min)
d/p/sc Norman Panama, Melvin Frank. *ph* Ray June. *ed* Tom McAdoo. *ad* Hal Pereira, Roland Anderson. *songs*. Sylvia Fine, Sammy Cahn. *cast* Danny Kaye, Glynis Johns, Basil Rathbone, Angela Lansbury, Cecil Parker, Mildred Natwick, John Carradine, Robert Middleton.

● Spasmodically effective spoof of Robin Hood-style adventures, with Kaye as the former circus clown joining up with a band of outlaws to overcome a tyrannical usurper king. Whether it's really watchable depends on what you feel about the charmless Kaye, whose vehicle this is from start to finish. GA

Court Martial

see Carrington VC

Court-Martial of Billy Mitchell, The (aka One Man Mutiny)

(1955, US, 100 min)
d Otto Preminger. *p* Milton Sperling. *sc* Milton Sperling, Emmet Lavery. *ph* Sam Leavitt. *ed* Folmar Blangsted. *ad* Malcolm Bert. *m* Dimitri Tiomkin. *cast* Gary Cooper, Charles Bickford, Ralph Bellamy, Rod Steiger, Elizabeth Montgomery, Darren McGavin.

● Based on fact, Preminger's impressively low-key film is about an American general who, in 1925, accused the military of incompetence and criminal negligence for their lack of interest in building up an air force, and was court-martialled for his views. With Cooper as the crusading officer, one is never in any doubt as to the correctness and sincerity of his views (Mitchell was posthumously rehabilitated in 1947), while Steiger puts in one of his inimitably flashy performances as the prosecuting attorney. GA

Courtneys of Curzon Street, The (aka The Courtney Affair)

(1947, GB, 120 min, b/w)
d/p Herbert Wilcox. *sc* Nicholas Phipps. *ph* Max Greene. *ed* Flora Newton, Vera Campbell. *ad* William C Andrews. *m* Anthony Collins. *cast* Anna Neagle, Michael Wilding, Gladys Young, Coral Browne, Michael Medwin, Daphne Slater, Jack Watling.

● Tedious family soaper stretching over three generations, starting with romance between a parlourmaid and a baronet's son, and gradually moving on to the working classes. With the once popular but wimpy pairing of Neagle and Wilding, it's emotionally restrained in that typically frustrating British cinema fashion. GA

Cousin, Le

(1997, Fr, 112 min)
d Alain Corneau. *p* Alain Sarde. *sc* Michel Alexandre, Alain Corneau. *ph* Michel Amathieu. *ed* Thierry Derocles. *ad* Dan Weil. *cast* Alain Chabat, Patrick Timsit, Agnès Jaoui, Marie Trintignant, Samuel Le Bihan, Caroline Proust.

● While not stinting on hold-ups, bungled drug busts and so on, this has its heart in the relationship between glum detective Chabat and his snitch (Timsit), a dope-pusher of Pesci-like volatility. (*Cousin* is *flic*-speak for a cop's personal informer.) Their part of the movie is plausible and unpredictable. The generic aspects (the edgy camaraderie of the squadroom, the motorway car chase, the neglected family) is okay-ish, and there's an agreeably low body count; but we've been there so often before. BBa

Cousin Bette

(1997, US/GB, 108 min)
d Des McAnuff. *p* Sarah Radclyffe. *sc* Lynn Siefert, Susan Tarr. *ph* Andrzej Sekula. *ed* Tariq Anwar, Barry Alexander-Brown. *pd* Hugo Luczyc-Wyhowski. *cast* Jessica Lange, Geraldine Chaplin, John Benfield, Hugh Laurie, Kelly MacDonald, Aden Young, Elisabeth Shue, John Sessions, Bob Hoskins.

● Paris, 1846; decadence and corruption among the aristocracy. Oft spurned in love, Bette (Lange) attempts to live at a remove from the romantic duplicity and boorishness of her cousins the Hulots and their world, especially after she takes under her wing a penurious but ravishing artist, Wenceslas (Young). Alas, once back on his feet Wenceslas forms a clandestine liaison with young Hortense Hulot (MacDonald), and Bette resolves to wreak revenge, by exploiting the various involved parties' sexual, financial and professional weaknesses with Machiavellian ease. So what's new? This Balzac adaptation steers a cheerfully populist course through the familiar romantic intrigue, with the tone firmly one of bawdy sarcasm. The assorted cast mostly play along with this, and once in a while the farce hits a right note. Mostly, though, McAnuff renders the whole show flat, simple and thumpingly obvious, fluffs much of the comedy, and over-eggs it with camera gimmicks. NB

Cousin Bobby

(1992, US, 69 min)
d Jonathan Demme. *p* Edward Saxon. *ph* Ernest Dickerson, Craig Haagensen, Tony Jannelli, Jacek Laskus, Declan Quinn. *ed* David Greenwald. *m* Anton Sanko. *with* Robert Castle.

● It's perhaps characteristic of Demme's quirky integrity that he should follow *The Silence of the Lambs* with a low-key, 16mm documentary about a long-lost relative. Typical, too, that the film, for all its seeming amateurishness, ends up being far more than a home movie. For the Reverend Robert Castle, the cousin Demme hasn't seen for over 30 years, is not only a colourful figure – a politically radical Episcopalian minister battling against the poverty, racism and drugs that blight Harlem – but a welcome reminder that even in Bush's America the Left has just about managed to survive. If the film's loose structure means it occasionally lacks focus, Demme's relaxed, open narrative style allows him to paint a wide-ranging portrait of America. GA

Cousin Cousine

(1975, Fr, 95 min)
d Jean-Charles Tacchella. *p* Bertrand Javal. *sc* Jean-Charles Tacchella. *ph* Georges Lendi. *ed* Agnès Guillemot. *m* Gérard Anfosso. *cast* Marie-Christine Barrault, Victor Lanoux, Marie-France Pisier, Guy Marchand, Ginette Garcin, Sybil Maas.

● Two families become united by marriage, and a slightly bored wife finds herself falling for one of her new relatives. A sardonic look at family life in France, with winning performances, well handled peripheral details and characters, all as tasty and insubstantial as a marshmallow. GB

Cousins

(1989, US, 113 min)
d Joel Schumacher. *p* William Allyn. *sc* Stephen Metcalfe. *ph* Ralf D Bode. *ed* Robert Brown. *pd* Mark Freeborn. *m* Angelo Badalamenti. *cast* Ted Danson, Isabella Rossellini, Sean Young, William Petersen, Lloyd Bridges, Norma Aleandro, Keith Coogan, Gina De Angelis, George Coe.

● In this uninspired remake of the 1975 French film *Cousin Cousine*, dance instructor Larry (Danson) and flirtatious wife Tish (Young) become, through complications attendant upon a marriage, distant relatives of some sort to aggressive car rep Tom (Petersen) and his dithering spouse Maria (Rossellini). Celebrations hardly begin before Tish is openly attaching herself to Tom. Confiding their mutual sense of an impending collapse of family ties, Larry and Maria find themselves platonically drawn to one another. Tom, being aware of his wife's growing relationship, does what any butch hypocritical chauvinist would do, and thumps Larry. Will Tom and Tish and Larry and Maria find total happiness, or just go back to being odd couples? The answer's sadly obvious. The film's failure lies in its characterisation: far too many folk have been flung in from all directions, allowing little chance for the central figures to emerge, let alone gell. A ragged, unfunny affair. DA

Cousins, Les (The Cousins)

(1959, Fr, 103 min, b/w)
d/p/sc Claude Chabrol. *ph* Henri Decaë. *ed* Jacques Gaillard. *ad* Jacques Saulnier, Bernard Evein. *m* Paul Misraki. *cast* Gérard Blain, Jean-Claude Brialy, Juliette Mayniel, Claude Cerval, Guy Decomble, Corrado Guarducci, Stéphane Audran.

● The town mouse and his country cousin. Or, the story of two students, one who was very, very good, and one who was very, very bad; but the bad one passed his exams, got the girl (when he wanted her), and survived to live profitably ever after. A fine, richly detailed tableau of student life in Paris, and Chabrol's first statement (in his second film) of his sardonic view of life as a matter of the survival of the fittest. The centrepiece, as so often in the early days of the *nouvelle vague*, is an orgiastic party climaxed, as the guest sleeps it off next morning, by a sublimely cruel and characteristic 'joke' by the bad cousin (Brialy) when he performs an eerie Wagnerian charade with candelabra and Gestapo cap to wake a Jewish student into nightmare. TM

Cousins in Love (Tendres Cousines)

(1980, Fr/WGer, 91 min)
d David Hamilton. *p* Linda Gutenberg, Georg M Reuther. *sc* Pascal Lainé. *ph* Bernard Daillencourt. *ed* Jean-Bernard Bonis. *ad* Eric Simon. *m* Jean-Marie Sénia, Karinne Trow. *cast* Thierry Tevini, Jean Rougerie, Catherine Rouvel, Anja Shute, Valerie Dumas, Laure Dechasnel.

● Feeble sexploiter set in the French countryside at the start of World War II. A male lead with the build of a nine-year-old (and a dubbed voice like Dustin Hoffman circa *The Graduate*) beds an almost endless queue of palpitating teenage girls. The oily-lensed soft-focus of 'respectable' erotica merchant Hamilton more often looks like a badly processed Super-8 home movie, with playing and dialogue to match, and all the sexuality of a stale meringue. GD

Cover Girl

(1944, US, 107 min)
d Charles Vidor. *p* Arthur Schwartz. *sc* Virginia Van Upp. *ph* Rudolph Maté, Allen M Davey. *ed* Viola Lawrence. *ad* Lionel Banks, Cary Odell. *songs* Jerome Kern, Ira Gershwin. *cast* Rita Hayworth, Gene Kelly, Phil Silvers, Lee Bowman, Eve Arden, Jinx Falkenburg, Otto Kruger.

● Cliché-ridden as it follows Hayworth's rise to fame as a magazine model, this musical nevertheless offers plenty of style: Kelly dances up a dream, Hayworth is elegance incarnate, the Jerome Kern/Ira Gershwin score – including the marvellous 'Long Ago and Far Away' – is tuneful throughout, and the whole thing, especially the comic stuff from Silvers and Arden, is executed with considerable brio. And Rudolph Maté's Technicolor photography is faultless.

Cover Girl Killer

(1959, GB, 61 min, b/w)
d Terry Bishop. *p* Jack Parsons. *sc* Terry Bishop. *ph* Gerald Gibbs. *ed* John Trumper. *ad* Peter Proud. *m* William Davies. *cast* Harry H Corbett, Felicity Young, Spencer Teakle, Victor Brooks, Tony Doonan, Bernadette Milnes, Dermot Kelly, Charles Lloyd Pack.

● Compact British filler set against the background of pin-up publishing which pits have-a-go Spencer Teakle, a young Canadian who inherits 'Wow' magazine, against the crazed slayer of a string of glamour models, Harry H Corbett no less. TJ

Cow, The (Gav)

(1968, Iran, 101 min, b/w)
d/p Daryush Mehrjui. *sc* Daryush Mehrjui, Gholam-Hosayn Sa'edi. *ph* Fereydun Ghovanlu. *ed* Daryush Mehrjui. *m* Hormoz Farhat. *cast* Ezat Entezami, Ali Nasirian, Jamshid Mashayekhi.

● Beguilingly bizarre tale of a peasant who so adores his cow, the only one in the village, that he is driven insane by suspicion when it dies and he is told (in an attempt to lessen the blow) it has disappeared. Basically the film is designed as a naturalistic portrait of village life, with its sense of community, its petty intrigues and rivalries, its primitive ways and means. But over it, quite literally, hangs the dark of the moon as the bereaved hero sits on the roof of his stable, staring out into the night before descending to take the cow's place, terrified of being stolen in his turn. The man's delusion (or is it a self-protecting magic?) boils up into a dark, demonic possession which suddenly bursts like a star-shell in an ending which speaks volumes about the failure to understand which turns some men into beasts. Truly fascinating, even if Mehrjui occasionally loses his way. TM

Cow and I, The

see Vache et le Prisonnier, La

Cowboy

(1958, US, 92 min)
d Delmer Daves. *p* Julian Blaustein. *sc* Edmund H North. *ph* Charles Lawton Jr. *ed* William A Lyon, Al Clark. *ad* Cary Odell. *m* George Duning. *cast* Glenn Ford, Jack Lemmon, Anna Kashfi, Brian Donlevy, Dick York, Richard Jaeckel.

● Likeable attempt to show what life was really like in the old West (ironically based on reminiscences by the notoriously mendacious Frank Harris), with Lemmon as the hotel clerk who joins a 2,000 mile cattle drive from Chicago to the Rio Grande in the 1870s. The episodic narrative, taking in an Indian attack, a Mexican fiesta and a cattle stampede, is more romantic than realistic; but it remains consistently atmospheric and enjoyable, with the striking use of landscape characteristic of Daves. TM

Cowboys, The

(1971, US, 127 min)
d/p Mark Rydell. *sc* Irving Ravetch, Harriet Frank Jr, William Dale Jennings. *ph* Robert Surtees. *ed* Robert Swink. *pd* Philip M Jefferies. *m* John Williams. *cast* John Wayne, Roscoe Lee Browne, Bruce Dern, Slim Pickens, Colleen Dewhurst, Slim Pickens.

● Offbeat and intriguing Western, with Wayne as a cattle driver who, deserted when his cowhands head off to a gold-rush, gathers together eleven schoolboys to help him get his herd to market. En route they are easy prey for villains; meanwhile, Wayne introduces them to the joys of shooting, drinking, whoring and killing. Although the film is well performed and beautifully shot by Robert Surtees, its ideology is highly objectionable, celebrating as it does the turning of the boys into hardened killers. Interesting to compare to *The Shootist*, in which young Ron Howard's desire to emulate the skills of his hero, an ageing gunfighter (Wayne again) is criticised at every turn. GA

Cows

see Vacas

Coyote Ugly

(2000, US, 101 min)
d David McNally. *p* Jerry Bruckheimer, Chad Oman. *sc* Gina Wendkos. *ph* Amir Mokri. *ed* William Goldenberg. *pd* Jon Hutman. *m* Trevor Horn. *cast* Piper Perabo, Adam Garcia, John Goodman, Maria Bello, Izabella Miko, Tyra Banks, Bridget Moynahan, Melanie Lynskey, Bud Cort.

● A romantic comedy set in NY: beautiful songwriter, Violet (Perabo), finds fame and everything she ever dreamed of despite her disapproving daddy (Goodman), working class background and all the odds in the world multiplied tenfold. But only after she learns to conquer stage fright by singing karaoke half-naked to crowds of sweaty drunks, one of several happy events to take place at a bar run by women. It could be argued that the constant stream of self-mocking touches makes for a less manipulative experience than many a Hollywood confection, though it's doubtful whether anyone familiar with producer Bruckheimer's record would consider him a misunderstood satirist. SS

Crackers

(1983, US, 91 min)
d Louis Malle. *p* Edward Lewis, Robert Cortes. *sc* Jeffrey Fiskin. *ph* Laszlo Kovacs. *ed* Suzanne Baron. *pd* John J Lloyd. *m* Paul Chihara. *cast* Donald Sutherland, Jack Warden, Sean Penn, Wallace Shawn, Larry Riley, Trinidad Silva.

● Whatever your opinions of the art-house gloss that used to varnish Malle's films from *Lacombe Lucien* to *Atlantic City*, they did at least suggest a beating heart at work. This thin concoction, based on a 1958 Roman comedy, *I Soliti Ignoti*, has a gang of villains gathering around Warden's rickety pawnshop, mostly to avoid the mean backstreets of San Francisco. Spurred on by poverty and frustration, they decide to crack his safe, only to botch the whole caper in a welter of escalating cack-handedness. There's a nice cameo from Shawn, doing nothing but eat dinner without André, but Sutherland is uncharacteristically null. Cardiac arrest finally seizes the film, after a long case of terminal whimsy. CPea

Crack in the Mirror

(1988, US, 94 min)
d Robby Benson. *p* Fred Berner, Jubran Jubran. *sc* Robert Madero. *ph* Neil Smith. *ed* Craig McKay. *pd* Reuben Freed. *m* Nile Rodgers,

Philippe Saisse. *cast* Robby Benson, Tawny Kitaen, Danny Aiello, Kevin Gray, Cliff Bemis, Tony Levine, Paul Herman.
● Yes, this is about drug-taking in New York. The movie wants to do two things: to attract a lucrative young audience, and to deliver a heavy anti-drugs message. The two, unfortunately, are mutually exclusive in this case. Scott (Benson) and Vanessa (Kitaen) are young, beautiful, and upwardly mobile. To look at their Park Avenue apartment and trendy attire, you'd never believe they were short of dosh, but they are; so short that preppy, clean-living Scott goes AWOL to take over a drugs empire for a villain he hardly knows. Unlikely? Well, get this. While the dealer is hiding from the mob, Scott settles into his employer's high-tech penthouse, and within days has taken to coke-dealing and crack manufacturing like a duck to water. The downward spiral of self-debasement begins as Vanessa gets into crack in a big way, and Scott discovers that, when high, he'll sleep with any old beautiful girl, but will come too quickly. It ends in tragedy. Score by Nile Rodgers (funky); fashion by Rosemary Ponzo (tacky); moral (missed opportunities); drugs (uncredited). Gross movie. EP

Crack in the World

(1965, US, 96 min)
d Andrew Marton. *p* Bernard Glasser, Lester A Sansom. *sc* Jon Manchip White, Julian Halevy [Julian Zimet]. *ph* Manuel Berenguer. *ed* Derek Parsons. *ad* Eugène Lourié. *m* John Douglas. *cast* Dana Andrews, Janette Scott, Kieron Moore, Alexander Knox, Peter Damon, Gary Lasdun.
● Infinitely better than the appalling *Day the Earth Caught Fire*, which developed along similar lines. A team of scientists are attempting to harness the energy at the earth's core, and explode some nuclear bombs underground in order to speed up their probe. The result is a nightmarish rupture in the earth's crust, which begins to have apocalyptic consequences in terms of climate, earthquakes and human devastation. The theme often seems awesomely credible and the special effects are excellent, although the usual character conflicts in the scientific team become trying at times. The images of chaos at the end are particularly disturbing. DP

Cracksman, The

(1963, GB, 112 min)
d Peter Graham Scott. *p* WA Whittaker. *sc* Lewis Schwarz, Charlie Drake. *ph* Harry Waxman. *ed* Richard Best. *ad* Tony Masters. *m* Ron Goodwin. *cast* Charlie Drake, George Sanders, Dennis Price, Nyree Dawn Porter, Eddie Byrne, Finlay Currie.
● Charlie Drake, like many British comedians, was never able to transfer his style of humour to the screen. All his films were much of a muchness, and this one – in which he's a locksmith shanghaied into big-time crime – is merely funny in parts. Co-star Sanders looks embarrassed. DP

Crack-Up

(1936, US, 70 min, b/w)
d Malcolm St Clair. *sc* Charles Kenyon, Sam Mintz. *ph* Barney McGill. *ed* Fred Allen. *ad* Duncan Cramer, Lewis Creber. *m* Harry Akst. *cast* Peter Lorre, Brian Donlevy, Helen Wood, Ralph Morgan, Thomas Beck.
● Basically B movie espionage hokum, but with ideas behind both script (Charles Kenyon and Sam Mintz) and direction as Donlevy, an arrogant test pilot disgruntled because he feels (justifiably) he has been cheated over a new patent, decides to recoup his losses by selling the plans to a foreign power. When things seem on the verge of falling into routine, Lorre emerges from his disguise as an amiable half-wit, tolerated around the airport as a harmless mascot, to reveal himself – inimitably – as the ruthless spymaster. The final sequence, in which their escape plane crash-lands in the sea and the prospect of imminent death prompts both Lorre and Donlevy to a wry re-examination of the masks they have assumed, is contrived but bizarrely effective. TM

Crack-Up

(1946, US, 93 min, b/w)
d Irving Reis. *sc* John Paxton, Ben Bengal, Ray Spencer. *ph* Robert de Grasse. *ed* Frederick Knudtson. *ad* Albert S D'Agostino, Jack Okey. *m* Leigh Harline. *cast* Pat O'Brien, Claire Trevor, Herbert Marshall, Ray Collins, Wallace Ford, Dean Harens, Erskine Sanford.
● A modest but gripping little thriller set in and around a big New York art gallery, with O'Brien as the expert on forgeries who is dismissed when his erratic conduct – due, he claims, to having been in a train crash of which there proves to be no record – is put down to drunkenness. Setting out to clear his name through a fog of amnesia (in fact the train wreck was an illusion produced by way of an injection of sodium pentothal), he uncovers a vast, ramifying plot to substitute forgeries for masterpieces on loan to the museum. Marginally intriguing for its view of art (pro populist, anti élitist stuff like surrealism), it's made as a thriller by the excellent supporting cast and fine, *noir*-ish camerawork from Robert de Grasse. TM

Cradle Will Rock

(1999, US, 133 min)
d Tim Robbins. *p* Jon Kilik, Lydia Dean Pilcher. *sc* Tim Robbins. *ph* Jean-Yves Escoffier. *ed* Geraldine Peroni. pd Richard Hoover. *m* David Robbins. *cast* Emily Watson, John Turturro, Hank Azaria, Susan Sarandon, John Cusack, Angus MacFadyen, Cary Elwes, Vanessa Redgrave, Bill Murray, Joan Cusack.
● Writer/director Robbins' lightly fictionalised recreation of the events leading up to Welles and Houseman's historic staging of Marc Blitzstein's Federal Theater Project musical is perhaps a little too long and (inevitably) theatrical for its own good, but it makes a very decent stab at evoking the social, political and artistic fervour of mid-'30s New York. The script cleverly integrates the numerous plot strands – Rockefeller becoming an unlikely bedfellow of Diego Rivera, an Italian diplomat selling Da Vincis to rich Manhattanites to gain funds for Mussolini, Blitzstein haunted by his dead wife and the spirit of Brecht – while never losing sight of the central themes of idealism and prostitution, loyalty and betrayal; moreover, Robbins elicits some very affecting performances from his expertly cast ensemble, so that the final, short-lived triumph is authentically stirring. GA

Craft, The

(1996, US, 101 min)
d Andrew Fleming. *p* Douglas Wick. *sc* Peter Filardi, Andrew Fleming. *ph* Alexander Gruszynski. *ed* Jeff Freeman. *pd* Marek Dobrowolski. *m* Graeme Revell. *cast* Fairuza Balk, Neve Campbell, Rachel True, Robin Tunney, Christine Taylor, Skeet Ulrich, Cliff De Young, Helen Shaver.
● A tale of supernatural LA high-school high jinks featuring the three members of a teenage 'coven' – 'The Bitches of Eastwick'. Outsiders all – Nancy (Balk), the punk with an alcoholic single parent; Bonnie (Campbell) with facial scars from a childhood car crash; and Rochelle (True) who's, well, black – they're in need of a fourth to complete their empowered circle. When new girl Sarah (Tunney) arrives, her brooding demeanour and telekinetic powers announce her as the natural candidate. The school's a hothouse of resentment, conflict and hurt, and the girls' experiments in spellcraft are regarded as deliciously dangerous excursions into adolescent self-discovery. There are some fine set-pieces, including a magical release of butterflies and a disturbing dream sequence, but the end opts disappointingly for standard horror-house effects. WH

Craic, The

(1999, Aust, 89 min)
d Ted Emery. *p* Jimeoin McKeown, Marc Gracie. *sc* Jimeoin McKeown. *ph* John Wheeler. *ed* Michael Collins. *pd* Penny Southgate. *m* Ricky Edwards. *cast* Jimeoin McKeown, Alan McKee, Colin Hay, Bob Franklin, Robert Morgan, Nicholas Bell, Jane Hall, Catherine Arena.
● Following a kerfuffle with the IRA, two likeable Irish bods leave Northern Ireland for what they hope will be a more relaxed lifestyle down under. They wish. Emery's plotless fish-out-of-water road movie moves along at a fair lick. At times it's very funny and elicits an endearing performance from Irish comedian Jimeoin McKeown, who also wrote the script. DA

Craig's Wife

(1936, US, 75 min, b/w)
d Dorothy Arzner. *p* Edward Chodorov. *sc* Mary C McCall Jr. *ph* Lucien Ballard. *ed* Viola Lawrence. *ad* Stephen Goosson. *m* Morris Stoloff. *cast* Rosalind Russell, John Boles, Billie Burke, Jane Darwell, Dorothy Wilson, Alma Kruger, Thomas Mitchell.
● A '30s rarity: a Hollywood picture written and directed by women. Russell is a strong-willed but glacial spouse determined to rule both husband Boles and their home. She comes to regret her intransigence, however, when she becomes meshed in a murder case and finds there are few friends around to help out. Arzner gives Mary C McCall Jr's adaptation of a play by George Kelly a remarkably austere tone. TJ

Crane World (Mundo Grúa)

(1999, Arg, 89 min, b/w & col)
d Pablo Trapero. *p* Lita Stanic, Pablo Trapero. *sc* Pablo Trapero. *ed* Nicolas Golbart. *pd* Andres Tambornino. *m* Francisco Canaro. *cast* Luis Margani, Daniel Valenzuela, Adriana Aizenberg, Graciana Chironi, Federico Esquerro, Luis Margani, Rollo Serrano, Daniel Valenzuela.
● This tale of an unemployed crane driver is a potent and moving depiction of contemporary survival. If it's specific to Argentinian society, it's also a general take on maintaining hope in the face of various forms of despair. Avoiding crude oppositions, it's a subtle and reasoned response to an unfortunately everyday occurrence, invested with real humanity. With its luminous monochrome camerawork reminiscent in places of the still photography of the great Brazilian Salgado, it's also equally committed to a truthful depiction of labour and its changing nature. It joins a select few films made recently that have successfully played personal dramas off against the huge forces of international capital and consequent social upheaval. GE

Crash

(1976, US, 78 min)
d Alan Gibson. *p* Fred Weintraub, Paul Heller. *sc* Michael Allin. *ph* Alan Hume. *ed* Alan Holzman. *ad* William Sandell. *m* Art Freeman. *cast* Joe Don Baker, Susan Sarandon, Larry Hagman, Alan Vint, Parnelli Jones.
● Gibson, a former employee of BBC TV, attempts to enter his low-budget rally movie in the mini-disaster stakes. Motorists and motorcyclists roar round Manila, while sweaty promoter (Hagman) strives to drum up excitement at base, dealing with a string of implausible catastrophes. Documentary footage of floods and car crashes constitute the film's most spectacular moments. A hilarious song ('Checkered flag or crash/Going for the heavy green/There ain't no in between/So do me right, you damned machine') momentarily enlivens an otherwise thoroughly moribund venture. JPy

Crash

(1996, Can, 100 min)
d/p/sc David Cronenberg. *ph* Peter Suschitzky. *ed* Ron Sanders. *pd* Carol Spier. *m* Howard Shore. *cast* James Spader, Holly Hunter, Elias Koteas, Deborah Kara Unger, Rosanna Arquette.
● Arguably the closest commercial Western cinema has come to Oshima's *Ai No Corrida* – what 'story' there is consists chiefly of a series of obsessive, claustrophobic, transgressive sex-scenes – Cronenberg's film of JG Ballard's novel is both imaginative and, notwithstanding its 'scandalous' content, strangely 'respectable' (in terms of fidelity and finding appropriate solutions to problems of adaptation). Basically, it's about a couple (Spader and Unger), already so disenchanted by notions of conventional sex that they tell each other in detail about their various other liaisons, who are further aroused when they encounter Hunter (widowed victim of a car collision with Spader) and Koteas, a near-crazy car-crash freak who introduces them to the perverse erotica of scars, wrecked debris and the threat of violent death itself. It's a dark, disturbing, languorous movie, as ludicrous, hermetic and repetitive, perhaps, as Ballard's original, but admirably assured and true to itself. GA

Crash of Silence

see Mandy

Craze

(1973, GB, 95 min)
d Freddie Francis. *p* Herman Cohen. *sc* Aben Kandel, Herman Cohen. *ph* John Wilcox. *ed* Henry Richardson. *ad* George Provis. *m* John Scott. *cast* Jack Palance, Diana Dors, Julie Ege, Edith Evans, Hugh Griffith, Trevor Howard, Michael Jayston, Suzy Kendall.

●London antique shop owner Palance becomes enslaved to an African idol which demands female sacrifices in return for worldly goods. But with such a poor and perfunctory script which quickly establishes Palance as nutty as they come and reduces him to uttering every line as though it had been dragged out of him only after half-an-hour's torture, we're left depending on the numerous cameo roles. At least Evans, Howard, Griffith and Dors ensure that the film is in safe hands, but ultimately their brief appearances can't compensate for the yawning gaps elsewhere. Francis does little to make it atmospheric, so it's soon down to the staple diet of sex'n'murder. CPe

Crazies, The

(1973, US, 103 min)
d George A Romero. *p* AC Croft. *sc* George A Romero. *ph* S William Hinzman. *ed* George A Romero. *m* Bruce Roberts. *cast* Lane Carroll, WG McMillan, Harold Wayne Jones, Lloyd Hollar, Richard Liberty, Lynn Lowry.

●*Night of the Living Dead* suggested that Romero was an unusual if none too clearly defined talent; two non-horror movies later, *The Crazies* proved it. The main plot premise echoes *The Andromeda Strain*: an accident with a virus creates a terrifying civil emergency, and incidentally reveals that the US government is working towards germ warfare. Romero, however, is more interested in effect than cause. First, he brilliantly updates the riddle Don Siegel posed in *Invasion of the Body Snatchers*: how can one tell who is infected and who isn't? The virus drives its victims mad before killing them, but what is the line between 'normal' hysteria and actual insanity? Second, and equally brilliantly, he demonstrates the difficulty in imposing martial law on a community of gun-owners, thereby creating a highly feasible vision of social collapse. Good dialogue and performances, too. Altogether, enough plusses to excuse weak plotting and occasional lapses into cliché. TR

Crazy

(1999, Ger, 95 min)
d Hans-Christian Schmid. *p* Thomas Wöbke, Jakob Klaussen. *sc* Hans-Christian Schmid, Michael Gutman. *ph* Sonja Rom. *ed* Hansjörg Weissbrich. *m* Christoph M Kaiser. *cast* Robert Stadlober, Tom Schilling, Oona-Devi Liebich, Julia Hummer, Can Taylanlar, Willy Rachow.

●A skilful adaptation of Benjamin Lebert's autobiographical account of his boarding school experiences. 'My name is Benjamin and I'm a cripple,' is the new boy's frank introduction to his classmates. Ben (Stadlober, excellent) is gradually accepted and, together with Janosch (Schilling) and his gang, learns about friendship and relationships through boyish antics. The characters in this tragi-comic rites-of-passage are connected by their respective adolescent difficulties – lonely, fat, silent, dumb – but as the optimistic Janosch observes: 'Chicks go for fringe groups.' Ben's irrefutable 'difference' separates him from his friends and is captured in a wordless scene where he stands alone on a pontoon after his friends have swum away. JFu

Crazy/Beautiful

(2001, US, 99 min)
d John Stockwell. *p* Mary Jane Ufland, Harry J Ufland, Rachel Pfeffer. *sc* Phil Hay, Matt Manfredi. *ph* Shane Hurlbut. *ed* Melissa Kent. *pd* Maia Javan. *m* Paul Haslinger. *cast* Kirsten Dunst, Jay Hernandez, Lucinda Jenney, Taryn Manning, Rolando Molina, Bruce Davison, Hernan Osorio, Miguel Castro.

●The first time Latino student Carlos Nuñez (Hernandez) hangs with troubled rich girl Nicole Oakley (Dunst) and her directionless friends, he gets a detention. He's not amused: it takes two hours on the bus from his home in East LA to the Pacific Palisades school they both attend. Nevertheless the relationship blossoms into a reckless, exquisitely teenage romance. Nicole's stepmom and Congressman father don't care what she does. But Carlos' family are furious. What's he doing, throwing away hard-won opportunities – and over a white girl? When even Mr Oakley (Davison) advises caution, on the ground that Nicole will drag him off the rails after her, Carlos wonders if his dream of becoming a USAF pilot isn't more important. Affectingly directed, this takes every cliché in the teen-romdram book – and squeezes some life out of them. All credit to the leads, especially Dunst, whose raw, egoless performance betokens great things. The ending, of course, is a cornball cop-out, but otherwise, for a Hollywood genre movie this feels wonderfully real. JO'C

Crazy English (Fengkuang Yingyu)

(1999, China, 92 min)
d Zhang Yuan. *p* Chen Ziqiu, Zhang Yuan. *ph* Zhang Yuan. *ed* Xu Hong. *m* Li Xiaolong. *with* Li Yang.

●Zhang's first government-approved film in nearly a decade is a documentary about a bizarre social/cultural/political phenomenon. In 1988, Li Yang was a mechanical engineering student with poor grades when he came up with a self-help strategy which he has parlayed into a lucrative business empire. He now tours China exhorting stadium-sized crowds to learn English as he did – by shouting it at the tops of their voices. He charges admission to his rallies and sells teaching aids; 'Crazy English' T-shirts, beer and other merchandise will follow soon. He clears the way politically for his enterprise by playing every 'patriotic' card in the deck. The film has no commentary and offers no explanation. Zhang simply reports what Li does and leaves viewers to draw their own conclusions. TR

Crazy Family (Gyakufunsha Kazoku)

(1984, Jap, 107 min)
d Sogo Ishii. *p* Banmei Takahashi. *sc* Yoshinori Kobayashi, Fumio Konami, Sogo Ishii. *ph* Masaki Tamura. *ed* Junichi Kikuchi. *ad* Terumi Hosoishi. *m* 1984. *cast* Katsuya Kobayashi, Mitsuko Baisho, Yoshiki Arizono, Yuki Kudo, Hitoshi Ueki, Kazuhiko Kishino.

●On the surface, Ishii's 'crazy family' is as normal as you or me: husband, wife and two pretty, healthy teenage kids, living in the suburban house of their dreams. But Ishii rips aside this bourgeois façade to show the horror festering beneath. Dad's mind is a seething can of paranoid worms, convinced that his 'love' is the only cure for the 'sickness' he detects in the others, and well before the end he's trying to trick them into a painless group suicide with a stout dose of insecticide in the coffee. The problems come to a head when his senile father (disgusting as only the elderly know how to be) visits and outstays his welcome, forcing Dad to take a chainsaw to the living-room floor with the perfectly reasonable intention of digging a cellar-cum-fallout shelter to accommodate the old misery. But that's when he strikes the nest of white ants… Seeing Ishii's film is a bit like rediscovering the thrill of your first encounter with Monty Python all those years ago: black humour at its most vicious (ie. funniest), paced like a commuter express and spiked with a dash of science fiction to keep even the most microchipped viewer unsure where he, she or it is going. TR

Crazy for Love

see Trou Normand, Le

Crazy for You

see Vision Quest

Crazy Horse of Paris, The (Crazy Horse de Paris)

(1977, Fr, 95 min)
d/sc Alain Bernardin. *ph* Roland Pontoizeau. *ed* Yvonne Martin. *m* Jacques Morali. *cast* John Lennox, Dickie Henderson, Alain Bernardin, George Carl, Senor Wences.

●A sort of concert film of the naughty show at the Crazy Horse Saloon in Paris, with a backstage 'story' concocted around the arrival of a repulsive hack who claims to come from the *Dundee Chronicle* to do a story on 'the girls'. The acts are wholesome and lifeless – on-the-spot dancing and strips which take one from next-to-nothing to absolutely nothing. The guy who runs the joint seems on the level, but a dirty-old-man note creeps into his voice when asked to describe the qualities he looks for in a prospective chorine. Out comes stuff about *poitrines agressives* and thighs being the pillars of temples. It's just a clean, old-fashioned peep-show, really, tedious beyond belief. JS

Crazy in Alabama

(1999, US, 104 min)
d Antonio Banderas. *p* Meir Teper, Linda Goldstein Knowlton, Debra Hill, Diane Sillan Isaacs. *sc* Mark Childress. *ph* Julio Macat. *ed* Maysie Hoy, Robert C Jones. *pd* Cecilia Montiel. *m* Mark Snow. *cast* Melanie Griffith, David Morse, Lucas Black, Cathy Moriarty, Robert Wagner, Meatloaf Aday, Rod Steiger, Richard Schiff, John Beasley, Paul Mazursky.

●Much is wrong and plain embarrassing about director Banderas' first feature, yet it's also likeable, sincere and eye catching. The tone, however, is dismayingly up and down (Almodóvar may get away with this, but Banderas doesn't). It's a nostalgic coming of age yarn about a boy growing up in the racist South in the mid-'60s, and his wacky aunt (Griffith), who chops off her husband's head and scoots off to Hollywood, where she makes an implausible starlet. Magic realism and black comedy sit uncertainly beside liberal platitudes, but it has some fine, high moments. (Adapted by Mark Childress from his own novel.) TCh

Crazy Joe

(1973, US/It, 99 min)
d Carlo Lizzani. *p* Dino de Laurentiis. *sc* Lewis John Carlino. *ph* Aldo Tonti. *ed* Vanio Amici. *ad* Robert Gundlach. *m* Giancarlo Chiaramello. *cast* Peter Boyle, Paula Prentiss, Fred Williamson, Charles Cioffi, Rip Torn, Luther Adler, Fausto Tozzi, Eli Wallach, Henry Winkler.

●*Crazy Joe* sprawls, but for the most part it sprawls with a certain style. The film opens with four hoods singing opera while driving to make a killing, and goes on to a 10-year retrospective on the history of the New York Mafia. Not content with that, Lizzani throws in a good 20 minutes' worth of prison movie (including a riot), a bit about the gangster as existentialist and his relationships to the media. And that's topped off by Peter Boyle doing imitations of Bogart and Widmark for his mates. The film is at its best when examining the Mafia power structure. It encompasses the farce of the Italian-American Federation (no more than a PR whitewash by the Mafia, which succeeded only in drawing attention to itself); deals with Mafia-Negro relations; and generally boasts an awareness that few recent Mafia movies have had. It does, in fact, emerge as something of a B picture epic. CPe

Crazy Love

(1987, Bel, 87 min)
d Dominique Deruddere. *p* Erwin Provoost. *sc* Marc Didden, Dominique Deruddere. *ph* Willy Stassen. *ed* Ludo Troch, Guido Henderickx. *pd* Hubert Pouillé, Erik van Belleghem. *m* Raymond van het Groenewoud. *cast* Josse De Pauw, Geert Hunaerts, Michaël Pas, Gène Bervoets, Amid Chakir, François Beukelaers.

●It's easy to see why Charles Bukowski loves this interpretation of his work. The linking of three Bukowski short stories shows one boy/youth/ man's progression from one carefree, fairytale pre-pubescence, through a sexual education which starts conventionally (and wittily) enough but which is derailed in the second episode by the development of the most heart-rendingly grotesque case of acne. De Pauw, as the older Harry Voss, proves a startlingly good actor, leading us gently and sadly from the standpoint of the youth's growing alienation from love and women, down a strange path to an awful place typically reeking of Bukowskian angst, spunk, death, booze, and loneliness. Norra lorra laffs? Untrue. The film is mordantly funny, stunningly designed, exquisitely photographed, quirkily directed, and all too brief. This director, in his debut, knows how to tell a story. Bizarre and beautiful. TC

Crazy Mama

(1975, US, 82 min)
d Jonathan Demme. *p* Julie Corman. *sc* Robert Thom. *ph* Bruce Logan. *ed* Allan Holzman, Lewis Teague. *ad* Peter Jamison. *m* Snotty Scotty and the Hankies. *cast* Cloris Leachman, Stuart Whitman, Jim Backus, Ann Sothern, Donny Most, Linda Purl, Bryan Englund, Merie Earle, Dick Miller.

●Not so much a sequel to Corman's *Bloody Mama*, more a good-natured parody of the *Bonnie and Clyde* family gangster genre, scripted by Robert Thom. Demme took on this riotous

Corman production at very short notice, and played up the laughs rather than the violence. Set in the '50s, the story centres on Depression child Melba Stokes (Leachman) and her journey from West to East coast along with mom (Sothern) and daughter (Purl), gathering together en route a motley band united in their sufferance at the hands of the law. Demme brings to the sly social commentary his usual deft choice of rock'n'roll standards, and draws enthusiastic performances from his wacky cast. DT

Crazy People

(1990, US, 92 min)
d Tony Bill. *p* Tom Barad. *sc* Mitch Markowitch. *ph* Victor J Kemper. *ed* Mia Goldman. *ad* John J Lloyd. *m* Cliff Eidelman. *cast* Dudley Moore, Daryl Hannah, Paul Reiser, JT Walsh, Bill Smitrovich, Alan North, David Paymer, Mercedes Ruehl.
● Dudley Moore plays a jaded copywriter who ends up in a sanatorium after he decides to produce ads devoid of hype. His fellow patients suffer from a variety of stereotypes, the worst case being Daryl Hannah, who harbours a dangerous penchant for loose dresses and baggy cardigans. Everyone feels much better once spurred into writing ads; and the agency snaps up their copy when consumers become hungry for truth. This is a lazy, obvious film, functionally directed and crudely characterised, which testifies to, rather than criticises, the power and influence of advertising. John Malkovich, originally cast, walked out on the project. Now *there's* an actor who knows when to make an exit. CM

Crazy Ray, The

see Paris qui Dort

Crazy Stranger, The

see Gadjo Dilo

Creator

(1985, US, 107 min)
d Ivan Passer. *p* Stephen J Friedman. *sc* Jeremy Leven. *ph* Robbie Greenberg. *ed* Richard Chew. *ad* Josan F Russo. *m* Sylvester Levay. *cast* Peter O'Toole, Mariel Hemingway, Vincent Spano, Virginia Madsen, David Ogden Stiers, John Dehner, Jeff Corey.
● A not unlikeable dog's dinner of a campus comedy, centring on Nobel prize-winning professor O'Toole's attempts to recreate his dead darling wife in his garden shed. Despite workaday direction, a slightly forced optimism, and the centrifugal force of Jeremy Leven's untogether script (adapted from his own novel), the cheeriness and enthusiasm of the playing carries it through. The film comes on like a dumb 1970s version of a Shaw play, with O'Toole running his University Research Department like a happy Captain Shotover, appropriating funds and equipment with carefree abandon and forever inviting his assistants to search for the 'Big Picture'. Hemingway plays the 'Life Force', a free spirit with a permanent orgasm who agrees to provide an egg for O'Toole's experiment. Spano's gadget-obsessed assistant gives outline to O'Toole's paternal qualities, and David Ogden Stiers' small-minded colleague provides the foil for O'Toole's flamboyant irresistability. It's a Peter O'Toole show, and it's worth it for his craggy-stoned face alone. WH

Creature

see Titan Find, The

Creature from the Black Lagoon

(1954, US, 79 min, b/w)
d Jack Arnold. *p* William Alland. *sc* Harry Essex, Arthur A Ross. *ph* William Snyder. *ed* Ted J Kent. *ad* Bernard Herzbrun, Hilyard Brown. *m* Joseph Gershenson. *cast* Richard Carlson, Julia Adams, Richard Denning, Antonio Moreno, Whit Bissell, Nestor Paiva, Ricou Browning.
● The routine story – members of a scientific expedition exploring the Amazon discover and are menaced by an amphibious gill man – is mightily improved by Arnold's sure sense of atmospheric locations and by the often sympathetic portrait of the monster. Interestingly, the threat is perceived as partly sexual (notably in the scene where the creature swims mesmerised beneath the tightly swimsuited Adams), and thus the film can be seen as a precursor of *Jaws*. GA

Créatures, Les

(1966, Fr/Swe, 93 min, b/w)
d Agnès Varda. *p* Mag Bodard. *sc* Agnès Varda. *ph* Willy Kurant. *ed* Janine Verneau. *ad* Claude Pignot. *m* Pierre Barbaud. *cast* Michel Piccoli, Catherine Deneuve, Eva Dahlbeck, Nino Castelnuovo, Jacques Charrier.
● 'Losing the plot' is more than a metaphor in this metaphor-strewn illustration of the creative process in action. Edgar (Piccoli) is in the throes of writing a novel. He plays dice games with his grumpy Muse and co-opts assorted shopkeepers and neighbours into his shifting narrative. A couple of sinister jokers dash about undermining attempts at order. Meanwhile the novelist's pregnant wife (Deneuve) undergoes her own process of creation. Finally both baby and book are safely delivered. It's an audacious concept with, in the background, a characteristically sharp documentary on the island of Noirmoutier, Varda's home at the time. But it's too whimsical to be very enlightening, and by the end you probably won't feel much urge to tackle old Edgar's doubtless quite unreadable tome. BBa

Creatures the World Forgot

(1970, GB, 95 min)
d Don Chaffey. *p/sc* Michael Carreras. *ph* Vincent G Cox. *ed* Chris Barnes. *pd* John Stoll. *m* Mario Nascimbene. *cast* Julie Ege, Brian O'Shaugnessy, Tony Bonner, Robert John, Marcia Fox, Rosalie Crutchley.
● Actually, it was Hammer who forgot the creatures, for this sequel to the money-spinning *One Million Years BC* is a resolutely dinosaur-free zone. Instead, there's a lot of grunting, a daft plot involving a tribe of cave-dwellers on a trek across the desert to a new home, and enough of trash icon Julie Ege in (and out of) a fur bikini to earn the thing an 'X' certificate . Despite so much cult potential, however, one abiding problem remains: it's unbelievably tedious. TJ

Creature Walks Among Us, The

(1956, US, 78 min, b/w)
d John Sherwood. *p* William Alland. *sc* Arthur A Ross. *ph* Maury Gertsman. *ed* Edward Curtiss. *ad* Alexander Golitzen, Robert E Smith. *m* Joseph Gershenson. *cast* Jeff Morrow, Rex Reason, Leigh Snowden, Gregg Palmer, Ricou Browning, Don Megowan.
● Third outing for the creature from the black lagoon, a dim affair in which the amphibious man is subjected to laboratory experiment (and is naturally cross). Jack Arnold's guiding hand is sorely missed. TM

Creepers (Phenomena)

(1984, It, 110 min)
d/p Dario Argento. *sc* Dario Argento, Franco Ferrini. *ph* Romano Albani. *ed* Franco Fraticelli. *pd* Maurizio Garrone, Nello Giorgetti, Luciano Spadoni, Umberto Turco. *m* Bill Wyman, Iron Maiden, Motorhead, Andy Sex Gang, Simon Boswell. *cast* Jennifer Connelly, Daria Nicolodi, Dalila Di Lazzaro, Patrick Bauchau, Donald Pleasence, Fiore Argento.
● Swiss Transylvania: Jennifer (Connelly), insect fancier and daughter of an American actor, arrives at a Swiss girls' school. A killer is loose. Entomologist McGregor (Pleasence, a Scot, it seems) decides that Jennifer should save the land of the cuckoo clock from itself. Where Inspector Geiger (Bauchau) has so far failed – in tracking down the psychopath – a young girl and a sympathetic Great Sarcophagus Fly will succeed. Between shots of stunning mountain scenery there are paranormal breezes, unfeasibly bright night-lighting and buckets and buckets of maggots. NRo

Creeping Flesh, The

(1972, GB, 91 min)
d Freddie Francis. *p* Michael Redbourn. *sc* Peter Spenceley, Jonathan Rumbold. *ph* Norman Warwick. *ed* Oswald Hafenrichter. *ad* George Provis. *m* Paul Ferris. *cast* Christopher Lee, Peter Cushing, Lorna Heilbron, George Benson, Kenneth J Warren, Duncan Lamont.
● Above-average horror, positively crammed with Gothic themes and put together with some care, with Freddie Francis' camera recapturing that crystal-sharp quality which he understandably abandoned for *Tales from the Crypt*. The sheer multiplication of ideas sometimes becomes contrived, but Cushing is right back on form as a Wilhelm Reich-like scientist who is convinced that he has detected 'the principle of evil' under the microscope. This intrinsically fascinating theme (which implies a liaison between the rational and the mystical) is never properly developed, but does give rise to good moments, especially when Cushing injects the 'evil' into his prim little daughter (Heilbron) and she is transformed into a wildly sensual image of female libido. DP

Creepshow

(1982, US, 120 min)
d George A Romero. *p* Richard P Rubinstein. *sc* Stephen King. *ph* Michael Gornick. *ed* Michael Spolan, Pasquale Buba, George A Romero, Paul Hirsch. *pd* Cletus Anderson. *m* John Harrison. *cast* Hal Holbrook, Leslie Nielsen, Adrienne Barbeau, Fritz Weaver, Viveca Lindfors, Carrie Nye, Stephen King, EG Marshall.
● 'I waanntt myy caaakkkeee!' gurgles the decaying birthday revenant of the first segment of this well-dressed and frequently beautifully framed tribute to the graveyard hoots of Bill Gaines's EC horror comics, complete with links in the original cartoon style. Sadly, the combined talents of King and Romero fail to sustain the opener's deft mesh of blood-letting and black humour. King himself is excellent as a bumpkin with fungus-from-space problems, but the other stories – a watery re-run of *Cask of Amontillado*, EG Marshall as a Howard Hughes type overrun by cockroaches during a power failure, etc. – are simply too long for anybody's comfort. The old Amicus movies used EC originals to better effect and with more brevity, for all their cardboard sets. GD

Creepshow 2

(1987, US, 90 min)
d Michael Gornick. *p* David Ball. *sc* George A Romero. *ph* Richard Hart, Tom Hurwitz. *ed* Peter Weatherley. *pd* Bruce Miller. *m* Les Reed. *cast* George Kennedy, Dorothy Lamour, Lois Chiles, Tom Wright, Stephen King, Tom Savini.
● Just as you can't judge a '50s comic book by its lurid cover, so you can't judge a cheapo, three-part film by its sources: in this case, original stories by Stephen King and a screenplay by George Romero. The linking animation sequences featuring a young comic reader are reasonably effective, but first-timer Gornick's direction is so painfully inept that not one of the episodes is even slightly scary, let alone horrifying. See a wooden cigar-store Indian come to life and bump off even more wooden teenage delinquents in *Old Chief Wood'nhead!* See dope-smoking teenage swimmers terrorised by a floating bin-liner in *The Raft!* See a sexually-active married woman, who has just enjoyed six orgasms ('count 'em') with a paid stud, terrorised by the indestructible *Hitch-hiker!* Marvel at the film's hypocritical moralising! The only terrifying thing about *Creepshow 2* is the thought of *Creepshow 3*. NF

Cremaster 5

(1997, US, 55 min)
d Matthew Barney. *p* Matthew Barney, Barbara Gladstone. *sc* Matthew Barney. *ph* Peter Strietmann. *m* Jonathan Bepler. *cast* Matthew Barney, Ursula Andress, Joanne Rha, Susan Rha.
● Fifth in the series of weird films by Californian artist Barney, this consists of stunning visuals that are like animated paintings – Greenaway without the narrative flow. Andress plays the Queen of Chains. Overlooking the empty stage, she sings mournful arias to her dead lover – the black knight (Barney). Flashbacks recall his bizarre end. Throwing off his cloak, he reveals his nakedness. He perches on the balustrade of the bridge, peering down into the dark waters of the Danube. He topples down to a watery grave and comes to rest among white lilies. In a sequence shot in Budapest's famous Gellért baths, Barney also appears as an exotic satyr with a glass head-dress, fungoid ear and beard extensions, hooves and frilled red waders. The water nymphs who inhabit the pool are blessed with decorative genital growths and marbled skin resembling porcelain. In a catalogue accompanying the film you can study these exotica, but on screen many of the gorgeous details are lost, especially as your attention is occupied in trying to unravel the symbolism of these strange and beautiful sights. SK

Cremator, The (Spalovac Mrtvol)

(1968, Czech, 102 min, b/w)
d Juraj Herz. *sc* Juraj Herz, Ladislav Fuks. *ph* Stanislav Milota. *ad* Zbynek Hloch. *m* Zdenek Liska. *cast* Rudolf Hrusinsky, Vlasta Chramostová, Jana Stehnová, Milos Vognic, Jiri Menzel.

●A promising idea for a black comedy about a mild-mannered family man who runs a crematorium, this works well enough for a while as he fusses simultaneously over the details of his trade and matters of personal hygiene, gradually becoming obsessed with the notion that his ovens are a last defence against earthly torments. The trouble is that the time is the late 1930s, and Herz makes such heavy allegorical weather of his tale that one is giving absolutely nothing away by revealing that the hero and his ovens eventually find fulfilment the Nazis. TM

Crescendo

(1969, GB, 95 min)
d Alan Gibson. *p* Michael Carreras. *sc* Jimmy Sangster, Alfred Shaughnessy. *ph* Paul Beeson. *ed* Chris Barnes. *ad* Scott MacGregor. *m* Malcolm Williamson. *cast* Stephanie Powers, James Olson, Margaretta Scott, Jane Lapotaire, Joss Ackland.

●This lazy variation on script-writer Jimmy Sangster's *Taste of Fear* (1961) is further crippled by the lack of Seth Holt's assured direction. At a villa in southern France, American heroine Powers gets mixed up with a strange widow (Scott), her invalid, heroin-addicted son (Olson), and their attentive maid (Lapotaire). When the maid is murdered, Powers is drawn into a conspiracy by the scheming widow, while the son drives himself crazy with nightmares about being murdered himself. Some cursory soft-core sex scenes fail to enliven the mechanical plot, and the contrived ending never rises to the promised crescendo. NF

Cría Cuervos (Raise Ravens)

(1975, Sp, 110 min)
d Carlos Saura. *p* Elias Querejeta. *sc* Carlos Saura. *ph* Teo Escamilla. *ed* Pablo G del Amo. *ad* Rafael Palmero. *m* Federico Mompoll. *cast* Geraldine Chaplin, Ana Torrent, Conchi Perez, Maite Sanchez, Héctor Alterio, Germán Cobos.

●A mesmerising film which conflates the drive to wish-fulfilment – a young girl, after watching the death of her father, comes to believe she holds the key to life and death – with a partial account of the last days of Fascism in Spain. At the root of both strands of Saura's elliptical script lies the idea of repression as the motor force behind the strange goings-on in the isolated (yet in the middle of Madrid) house of the Anselmo family. Intriguingly, the film suggests that the spirit of the dusty surrealism of Buñuel lives on in his native Spain. PH

Cri du Coeur, Le

(1994, Fr, 86 min)
d Idrissa Ouedraogo. *p* Sophie Salbot. *sc* Robert Gardner, Idrissa Ouedraogo, Jacques Achoti. *ph* Jean Monsigny. *ed* Luc Barnier. *ad* Olivier Paultre, Alain Poirot. *m* Henri Texler. *cast* Richard Bohringer, Saïd Diarra, Félicité Wouassi, Alex Descas, Clémentin Célarié.

●Writer/director Ouedraogo, maker of the acclaimed *Yaaba*, travelled to Paris from his native Burkina Faso to shoot this intriguing tale of an African boy adjusting to life in France, where he's troubled by memories and visions of his homeland. Although the overall feel isn't as idiomatic as the film-maker's previous work, Bohringer is on mercurial form as the former truckdriver who befriends the child, and the blend of the experiences of two worlds and cultures is arresting, if not fully achieved. TJ

Cri du Hibou, Le (The Cry of the Owl)

(1987, Fr/It, 108 min)
d Claude Chabrol. *p* Antonio Passala. *sc* Odile Barski, Claude Chabrol. *ph* Jean Rabier. *ed* Monique Fardoulis. *m* Matthieu Chabrol. *cast* Christophe Malavoy, Mathilda May, Jacques Penot, Jean-Pierre Kalfon, Virginie Thévenet, Patrice Kerbrat.

●A young woman moves around her isolated house. Outside in the dark, among the trees, a man watches her – is he smiling? From this equivocal opening there unfolds a tale, unpredictable but of rather precarious credibility, that takes in rage, persecution and several violent deaths. Actually the plot is unpredictable only if you haven't read the Patricia Highsmith novel of which this is a doggedly faithful adaptation. Since Highsmith and Chabrol have so much in common, both as regards tone and preoccupations, it's surprising it took so long for their paths to cross. But maybe it's precisely this lack of reciprocity which explains why the movie is somewhat disappointing. Author and director in this case are not complementary so much as tautological. BBa

Cries and Whispers (Viskingar och Rop)

(1972, Swe, 91 min)
d/p/sc Ingmar Bergman. *ph* Sven Nykvist. *ed* Siv Lundgren. *ad* Marik Vos. *cast* Harriet Andersson, Kari Sylwan, Ingrid Thulin, Liv Ullmann, Erland Josephson, Henning Moritzen.

●You can interpret *Cries and Whispers* through a whole religious metaphysic, and no doubt Bergman himself would; but latterly this has been something of a red herring for a director whose talent lies more in straight psychodrama. None of the films immediately preceding have been more visually seductive than *Cries*, so much so that form, repeatedly, gets the better of content. Mostly Bergman is able to regain control, which is where the scenes that make the film come in: for instance, the short sequence where Thulin, in period costume, is undressed by her maid, which says all there is to say about clothes, disguise, repression. *Cries* is about bodies, female bodies, in extremity of pain, isolation or neglect (the cards are heavily stacked). Karin (Thulin) mutilates her cunt with a piece of broken glass and, stretched out on her marital bed, smiles through the blood she's smeared across her mouth at her husband in celebration of a marriage that's a 'tissue of lies'. Maria (Ullman) finds herself lacking a thread that would tie her irreversibly to life. Bergman's hour remains resolutely that of the wolf. VG

Crime and Punishment

(1935, US, 88 min, b/w)
d Josef von Sternberg. *p* BP Schulberg. *sc* SK Lauren, Joseph Anthony. *ph* Lucien Ballard. *ed* Richard Cahoon. *ad* Stephen Goosson. *m* Louis Silvers. *cast* Edward Arnold, Peter Lorre, Marian Marsh, Tala Birell, Elisabeth Risdon, Mrs Patrick Campbell.

●Far from Sternberg's best, but still a fairly impressive, if overly condensed, adaptation of Dostoevsky's novel. Lorre is highly effective as the arrogant Raskolnikov, committing a murder and then battling it out both with his conscience and with police inspector Arnold. The strongest scenes, in fact, are those dealing with the cat-and-mouse games between the two men, although the whole thing benefits from Lucien Ballard's characteristically fine photography. Of course it falls a long way short of the book in terms of philosophical import and characterisation, but it's pretty compelling nevertheless. GA

Crime + Punishment in Suburbia

(2000, US, 98 min)
d Rob Schmidt. *p* Pamela Koffler, Larry Gross, Christine Vachon. *sc* Larry Gross. *ph* Bobby Bukowski. *ed* Gabriel Wrye. *pd* Ruth Ammon. *m* Michael Brook. *cast* Monica Keena, Vincent Kartheiser, Jeffrey Wright, James DeBello, Michael Ironside, Christian Payne, Conchata Ferrell, Ellen Barkin.

●A rare disappointment from maverick indie producer Christine Vachon, this story of festering psychosis beneath the placid surface of everyday US suburbia looks familiar coming so soon after *American Beauty*. Director Schmidt coaxes assured performances from Keena's good-girl-gone-bad and Kartheiser's black-clad loner, with Barkin suitably ravaged as the unhappy mom, and Ironside playing on his usual villainous screen image as the violent dad. One waits in vain for genuine revelations as the plot spirals into murder and remorse, since the artful visuals and supercool soundtrack (Sleater-Kinney, Joey Santiago of The Pixies) make the film seem more cutting edge than it actually is. TJ

Crime and Punishment (Rikos ja Rangaistus)

(1983, Fin, 93 min)
d Aki Kaurismäki. *sc* Aki Kaurismäki, Pauli Pentti. *ph* Timo Salminen. *cast* Markku Toikka, Aino Seppo, Esko Nikkari, Olli Tuominen, Hannu Lauri.

●Kaurismäki does Dostoevsky, and though it's not exactly a straight adaptation, the gloom and foreboding are authentic. Here Raskolnikov is Rahikainen, a Helsinki slaughterhouse worker who shoots the man responsible for killing his wife in a hit-and-run incident three years earlier. At the victim's house, however, he meets a young woman with whom he gets into a relationship, and she, for the moment, withholds his name from the police. TJ

Crime Busters (Due Superpiedi quasi Piatti)

(1976, It, 115 min)
d/sc EB Clucher [Enzo Barboni]. *ph* Claudio Cirillo. *ed* Eugenio Alabiso. *ad* Enzo Bulgarelli. *m* Guido de Angelis, Maurizio de Angelis. *cast* Terence Hill, Bud Spencer, David Huddleston, Luciano Catenacci, Laura Gemser, Luciano Rossi.

●Laurel and Hardy become first Starsky and Hutch, then Robin Hood and Little John, as lovable layabouts Hill and Spencer fetch up in Miami, try to rob a supermarket, and stumble by accident into a police recruiting parade. This is Italian hybrid at its most tiresome, covering up a threadbare second-hand plot with thick slapstick and sentiment. AN

Crime de Monsieur Lange, Le (The Crime of Monsieur Lange)

(1935, Fr, 85 min, b/w)
d Jean Renoir. *p* André Halley des Fontaines. *sc* Jacques Prévert. *ph* Jean Bachelet. *ed* Marguerite Renoir. *ad* Jean Castanier, Robert Gys. *m* Jean Wiener. *cast* René Lefèvre, Jules Berry, Odette Florelle, Nadia Sibirskaïa, Sylvia Bataille, Marcel Levesque.

●One of Renoir's most completely delightful movies (scripted by Jacques Prévert in the euphoria of the Popular Front days), a comedy-thriller-romance about employees of a publishing firm setting up a glorious collective when their lecherous and oppressive boss suddenly goes missing. Chaos sets in when he unexpectedly reappears to reap the fruit of their success, built on the imaginative efforts of a writer of Westerns who also finds a way out of the predicament by using a gun. Fantasy, politics and gentle naturalism combine to perfection, while Renoir's sympathies for his domestic revolutionaries are so infectious as to make the film genuinely uplifting. GA

Crime in the Streets

(1956, US, 91 min, b/w)
d Don Siegel. *p* Vincent M Fennelly. *sc* Reginald Rose. *ph* Sam Leavitt. *ed* Richard C Meyer. *ad* Serge Krizman. *m* Franz Waxman. *cast* James Whitmore, John Cassavetes, Sal Mineo, Mark Rydell, Virginia Gregg, Peter Votrian.

●A rain-slicked wharf, a foghorn sounds, and the rumble starts. With just a single back-alley set and a five-and-ten cent script, Siegel's early B gang picture can make 'the street' more real than all the stylisations of later efforts like *The Wanderers*. There's a street-corner girl who dances with her mouth, and there's Cassavetes as Frankie, the leader who can't bear to be touched, dripping all the bug-eyed surliness of his grown-up movies and hiding all the dirty little secrets that each family contains. Coil-spring tension is supplied by the long run-in to the first test of manhood – the big kill. If it's a shade heavy on the psychodrama at the expense of the action, at least the confrontations have spine; and if the ending is necessarily happy, at least it's due to a kid brother rather than the earnest social worker. Like a zip-gun, cheap and effective. CPea

Crime Kings (Sua...Jone Pan Sua)

(1998, Thai, 130 min)
d Thanit 'Pued' Jitnukul. *p* Charoen Iamphungporn, Somsak Payapdaechachai. *sc* Thanit Jitnukul. *ph* Wichien

Reungwichayakul. *ed* Mahasak Tassanapayak. *ad* Tekayu Tummanitkul, Sathit Pradirsarn, Kwanlada Lim. *m* Jumras Saewataporn. *cast* Amphon Lumpoon, Dom Hetrakul, Supakorn Kijsuwan, Sanantinee Punchuchit.
● Macho-romantic biopic about a real life outlaw, Sua Bai, who was Lopburi's answer to Robin Hood in the lawless years after the Japanese defeat in 1945, stealing from the rich and corrupt and sharing the proceeds with the villagers who sheltered him. Historiography takes second place to the relationship between the bandit and his nemesis, police captain Ying, who eventually drove him into hiding on a rubber plantation in the south. The surprise is that it's framed less as a cops-and-robbers movie than as a Leone-esque Western. The casting is interesting (swoonsomely handsome leads and dozens of politicians, artists and celebrities in cameo roles) and the whole, though overlong, is executed with a certain zest. TR

Crime of Monsieur Lange, The

see Crime de Monsieur Lange, Le

Crime of Passion

(1956, US, 86 min, b/w)
d Gerd Oswald. *p* Herman Cohen. *sc* Jo Eisinger. *ph* Joseph LaShelle. *ed* Marjorie Fowler. *ad* Leslie Thomas. *m* Paul Dunlap. *cast* Barbara Stanwyck, Sterling Hayden, Raymond Burr, Fay Wray, Royal Dano, Virginia Grey.
● 'Behind every successful man...': the old cliché gets full-bloodedly melodramatic illustration as Stanwyck takes detective husband Hayden's prospects for LAPD promotion into her own hands (soon bloodied). Oswald, son of German director Richard and responsible for one of the most visually arresting and thematically over-the-top episodes of *The Outer Limits* (*Shape of Things Unknown*), could usually be relied on to turn budgetary constraints to energetic advantage. PT

Crime of the Century

(1996, US, 120 min)
d Mark Rydell. *p* Mike Moder. *sc* William Nicholson. *ph* Toyomichi Kurita. *ed* Antony Gibbs. *pd* Steven Legler. *m* John Frizzell. *cast* Stephen Rea, Isabella Rossellini, JT Walsh, Michael Moriarty, David Paymer, John Harkins, Allen Garfield, Barry Primus.
● An impressive cast weigh in for this HBO period drama, a re-creation of the Lindbergh kidnap case based on Ludovic Kennedy's *The Airman and the Carpenter*. Richard Hauptmann (Rea) was picked up with marked ransom notes and charged with the murder of the famous aviator's baby. America was baying for blood, and Hauptmann, a German immigrant, fitted the bill. The limited budget makes for so-so production work and competent, but severely constrained direction by old pro Mark Rydell. The upside is an eloquent, thoughtful screenplay by William Nicholson and some juicy character acting by the likes of Harkins (as an alcoholic defence lawyer), Moriarty (the concerned local Governor), Paymer (the prosecuting attorney) and Walsh (the police chief). It takes a while to get used to Rea talking with an aksent lak dis, but he comes through with a couple of burning speeches. TCh

Crimes and Misdemeanors

(1989, US, 104 min)
d Woody Allen. *p* Robert Greenhut. *sc* Woody Allen. *ph* Sven Nykvist. *ed* Susan E Morse. *pd* Santo Loquasto. *cast* Caroline Aaron, Alan Alda, Woody Allen, Claire Bloom, Mia Farrow, Joanna Gleason, Anjelica Huston, Martin Landau, Jenny Nichols, Jerry Orbach, Stephanie Roth, Sam Waterston.
● In the first of two loosely interwoven stories, rich, philanthropic ophthalmologist Judah Rosenthal (Landau), afraid his lover (Huston) will reveal all to his wife (Bloom), decides to dispose of the former with the help of a hit-man friend of his brother. In the second, more comic story, earnest, impoverished documentarist Clifford Stern (Allen), falls for the producer (Farrow) of a TV tribute he has reluctantly agreed to make about the brother-in-law he hates (Alda), a conceited, successful maker of sitcoms. Judah and Clifford meet only in the final scene: what links them throughout is guilt, stemming from an obsessive interest in matters of faith and ethics. It's an extremely ambitious film, most akin perhaps to Hannah and her Sisters, the narrative and tonal coherence of which it sadly lacks, though the assured direction and typically fine ensemble acting manage partly to conceal the seams. Dramatically, the film seldom fulfils its promise, and its pessimistic 'moral' – that good and evil do not always meet with their just deserts – looks contrived and hollow. Intriguing and patchily effective, nevertheless. GA

Crimes at the Dark House

(1940, GB, 69 min, b/w)
d George King. *p* Odette King. *sc* Edward Dryhurst. *ph* Hone Glendining. *ed* Jack Harris. *ad* Bernard Robinson. *m* Jack Beaver. *cast* Tod Slaughter, Sylvia Marriott, Hilary Eaves, Hay Petrie, Geoffrey Wardwell, David Horne.
● Cheap, cheerful and none too faithful adaptation of Wilkie Collins' *The Woman in White*, with the barnstorming Slaughter purveying prime ham as the murderous opportunist wreaking havoc at the mansion of an impoverished aristocratic family. Juicy stuff, entertaining enough if not taken at all seriously. GA

Crimes of Passion

(1984, US, 107 min)
d Ken Russell. *p/sc* Barry Sandler. *ph* Dick Bush. *ed* Brian Tagg. *pd* Richard MacDonald. *m* Rick Wakeman. *cast* Kathleen Turner, Anthony Perkins, John Laughlin, Annie Potts, Bruce Davison, John G Scanlon.
● First and foremost, an extremely uninhibited satire on American sexual dreams and nightmares. Turner, a career woman who doubles by night as the ultra-hooker China Blue, acts out every male fantasy in the book until she picks up a cop, sees him turn into a piece of meat beneath her, and gets carried away with her stiletto heels and his nightstick. She meets her Baudelairean match in Perkins, a deranged fundamentalist consumed by lust and slowly mustering the energy to act out his own dark fantasies. In between, the film lays into an 'average' suburban couple, living a sexual fantasy of their own – of marital fulfilment. It relies on sheer pace and stylistic bravura, and talks dirty more wittily than anything since Bogart and Bacall. There are lapses, but this is in the main a comedy so black that it recaptures some of the cinema's long-lost power to shock. TR

Crimes of the Future

(1970, Can, 65 min)
d/p/sc/ph/ed David Cronenberg. *cast* Ronald Mlodzik, Jon Lidolt, Tania Zolty, Jack Messinger, Paul Mulholland.
● *Crimes of the Future* explores a world of genetic mutations, in which all adult women have died from the use of cosmetics and the surviving men keep finding themselves reverting to more primitive forms. The mainspring of Cronenberg's humour is the discrepancy between theory and actual experience; as with the earlier *Stereo*, the movie is dominated by an 'absent' theorist (in this case the mad dermatologist Antoine Rouge), whose hapless disciple struggles to uphold his master's teachings in situations of escalating absurdity and anarchy. The humour couldn't be blacker, and the quality of invention is outrageously high. TR

Crimes of the Heart

(1986, US, 105 min)
d Bruce Beresford. *p* Freddie Fields. *sc* Beth Henley. *ph* Dante Spinotti. *ed* Anne Goursaud. *pd* Ken Adam. *m* Georges Delerue. *cast* Diane Keaton, Jessica Lange, Sissy Spacek, Sam Shepard, Tess Harper, Hurd Hatfield, David Carpenter.
● When Meg (Lange) steps off the Greyhound bus, trailing behind her a blown-out singing career and a series of failed relationships, Babe (Spacek) has just emptied a gunful of lead into her noxious senator husband, and buttoned-up, neurotic Lenny (Keaton) is singing herself 'Happy Birthday' all alone in the kitchen. The stage is set for an escalating black farce on the theme of broken dreams; but all we get, sadly, is a meandering display of half-hearted Mississippi drawl as these three dizzy sisters wander from room to room trading reminiscence and recrimination. Symptomatically, it is only when Meg and her old flame (Shepard) take off to the bayou that the movie starts to sing. Elsewhere, Beresford fails to generate sufficient chemistry to bind the performances. Occasional bursts of delicious tragic humour nevertheless make this a not unlikeable 'feminist' mood piece. WH

Crime Story (Zhong'an Zu)

(1993, HK, 106 min)
d Kirk Wong. *p* Leonard Ho. *sc* Cheun Tin-Nam, Chan Man-Keung, Cheung Lai-Ling. *ph* Leu Wai-Keung. *ed* Peter Cheung. *m* James Wong. *cast* Jackie Chan, Kent Cheng, Law Kar-Ying, Ko Shou-Liang, Ng Wing-Mei.
● Kirk Wong's determination to play this straight (there's no space for any of Jackie Chan's comedy schticks, and not much for set-piece stunts either) makes this the best pure thriller Chan has ever starred in. He plays a cop assigned to rescue a wealthy but morally dubious property developer (Law) from the gang which is holding him to ransom. But even his most ingenious efforts to trick the kidnappers go awry – because his corrupt superior Inspector Hung (Cheng) is secretly behind the whole thing. Moody visuals, expertly paced montages and climactic sequences aboard a rusting sea-tanker and in a burning slum tenement all deliver above and beyond genre norms. TR

Crimetime

(1996, GB/US/Ger, 118 min)
d George Sluizer. *p* David Pupkewitz. *sc* Brendan Somers. *ph* Jules van den Steenhoven. *ed* Fabienne Rawley. *pd* Bernd Lepel. *m* David Stewart, Marianne Faithfull. *cast* Stephen Baldwin, Pete Postlethwaite, Sadie Frost, Geraldine Chaplin, Karen Black, James Faulkner, Philip Davis, Marianne Faithfull.
● A struggling actor (Baldwin) gets a job on 'Crimetime', a TV show reconstructing hideous recent killings. But when the murderer (Postlethwaite) arrives at a hiatus in his activities, it's a decisive moment for his small-screen counterpart: lose a nice little earner, or kill to continue the mayhem. A worthless London-set shocker purporting to comment on the values of the media. TJ

Crimewave

(1985, US, 86 min)
d Sam Raimi. *p* Robert Tapert. *sc* Ethan Coen, Joel Coen, Sam Raimi. *ph* Robert Primes. *ed* Michael Kelly. *ad* Gary Papierski. *m* Arlon Ober. *cast* Louise Lasser, Paul Smith, Brion James, Sheree J Wilson, Edward R Pressman, Reed Birney.
● Despite its ambition and a Coen Brothers script credit, Raimi's second film was a disappointment after his astonishing debut *The Evil Dead*. Exterminators Crush and Coddish wipe out more than just bugs, but don't end up carrying the can, hence Vic Ajax is languishing on Death Row for a crime he didn't commit. There are some accomplished set pieces, but the film remains interesting, perhaps, mainly for the hindsight view it offers of the career trajectory – *The Evil Dead*, *Crimewave*, *Darkman* – that led to Raimi finally getting his hands a cartoon-inspired blockbuster in *Spider-man*. NRo

Criminal

(1994, Ger, 80 min, b/w)
d/p/sc David Jacobson. *ph* Wolfgang Held. *ed* David Jacobson. *pd* Manuel Wilhelm. *cast* Ralph Feliciello, Liz Sherman, Sheila York, Eric Reid, Gianfranco Piras, Tim Miller.
● Shot in English, and in grainy high-contrast b/w in the US, this reflective, stylish but heavy-handed blend of muted realism, melodrama and *film noir* focuses on a gentle businessman who embezzles a fortune to buy his nagging wife her dream house, only to find that she's been cheating on him. As he takes to the road, meeting up with a disenchanted damsel in distress, the film begins to exert a strange, poetic power not unlike that of, say, *Detour* – but far more tender. Bleak, crude even, but decked out with fine performances and a good use of music ('50s kitsch and John Adams' *Shaker Loops*). GA

Criminal, The (aka The Concrete Jungle)

(1960, GB, 97 min, b/w)
d Joseph Losey. *p* Jack Greenwood. *sc* Alun Owen. *ph* Robert Krasker. *ed* Reginald Mills. *ad* Scott MacGregor. *m* John Dankworth. *cast*

Stanley Baker, Sam Wanamaker, Margit Saad, Patrick Magee, Grégoire Aslan, Jill Bennett, Rupert Davies, Laurence Naismith.
● Terrific performance from Baker as the criminal, an existential loner whose violence is essentially self-destructive as, literally trapped within the bars of a prison, he finds himself metaphorically caught between two complementary systems: one represented by the sadistic chief warder (Magee), who feeds his sense of power by fomenting a dog-eat-dog code in the cells, the other by the underworld kingpin (Wanamaker) waiting outside to kill Baker and hijack his stashed loot. Losey's American eye and expertise make it jaggedly explosive and visually brilliant, a million miles beyond other British crime movies. TM

Criminal, The

(1999, GB, 98 min)
d Julian Simpson. *p* Christopher Johnson, Mark Aarons, David Chapman. *sc* Juliam Simpson. *ph* Nic Morris. *ed* Mark Aarons. *pd* Martyn John. *m* The Music Sculptors, Tolga Kashif, Mark Sayer Wade. *cast* Steve Mackintosh, Eddie Izzard, Bernard Hill, Natasha Little, Holly Aird, Yvan Attal, Andrew Tiernan, Jana Carpenter, Justin Shelvin, Barry Stearn.
● Like *Lock, Stock and Two Smoking Barrels*, this impressive British debut feature is a comic (rather than comedy) thriller, but Mackintosh has exchanged a mannered performance for one of assured complexity. He plays J, a musician whose life takes a turn after he meets Sarah (Little) in a bar. Soon he's caught in a web of murder and conspiracy spun by a powerful criminal elite. From the imaginative opening (with its excruciatingly funny chat-up banter), this is a sophisticated drama marked by fresh ideas, economic and highly entertaining dialogue, and visual flair. And Bernard Hill should get a gong for his support role as a foul mouthed detective. EPe

Criminal Code, The

(1930, US, 97 min, b/w)
d Howard Hawks. *p* Harry Cohn. *sc* Fred Niblo Jr, Seton I Miller. *ph* Ted Tetzlaff, James Wong Howe. *ed* Edward Curtiss. *ad* Edward Jewell. *cast* Walter Huston, Phillips Holmes, Constance Cummings, Mary Doran, Boris Karloff, De Witt Jennings, John Sheehan.
● Detailing the conflict between a cynical prosecuting attorney turned warden (Huston) and a green young killer (Holmes), whose stretch in the slammer threatens to destroy not only his faith in life but also his sanity, the taut, unsentimental plot about betrayal and revenge proposes that the convicts' sense of honour and justice is not so very different from that of the authorities: 'Someone's gotta pay' lies all too easily on the lips of both vengeful hard-asses like Karloff and self-righteous perpetrators of the law such as Huston. But there's no facile moralising here; rather, the fast pacing, grimly realistic atmosphere, and superb performances summon up a tragic battle of wits and power in which both sides are equally right and wrong, forced to do what their position in life requires them to, and from which the only way out is death. Hawks' later concerns are in full bloom here – pride in professionalism, loyalty and betrayal within the group, the difficulties facing men forced to live without women, responsibility and respect – and his totally assured style is reflected in the quick, naturalistic dialogue, quirky black humour, and the ability to turn potentially risible set pieces – like Huston's first confrontation with a yard full of riotous cons – into electrifying suspense. GA

Criminal Face

see Ho!

Criminal Law

(1989, US, 118 min)
d Martin Campbell. *p* Robert Maclean, Hilary Heath. *sc* Mark Kasdan. *ph* Philip Meheux. *ed* Chris Wimble. *ad* Curtis Schnell. *m* Jerry Goldsmith. *cast* Gary Oldman, Kevin Bacon, Karen Young, Joe Don Baker, Tess Harper, Ron Lea, Karen Woolridge, Elizabeth Sheppard.
● After winning an acquittal for wealthy client Martin Thiel (Bacon), defence attorney Ben Chase (Oldman) discovers that he is in fact guilty of rape and murder. Will the attorney follow the advice of his fellow professional – 'Justice is for God' – or use privileged knowledge to expose Thiel? Given the basic plot, behind-camera talent and cast, the film should be better than it is. Martin Campbell (who directed the superb *Edge of Darkness* for television) uses tight frames and a sense of restlessness to convey tension, but this makes for uneasy viewing when combined with Mark Kasdan's overwrought script. A crude, confused psychology operates here: Thiel blames everything on Mother, and a conscience-stricken Chase turns homicidal while his old mentor offers quiet advice from the death-bed. CM

Criminal Life of Archibaldo de la Cruz, The (Ensayo de un Crimen/La Vida Criminal de Archibaldo de la Cruz)

(1955, Mex, 91 min, b/w)
d Luis Buñuel. *p* Alfonso Patiño Gomez. *sc* Luis Buñuel, E Ugarte Pages. *ph* Augusto Jimenez. *ed* Jorge Bustos. *ad* Jesús Bracho. *cast* Ernesto Alonso, Miroslava Stern, Ariadna Welter, Rita Macedo, José Maria Linares Rivas.
● Buñuel marshals all of his characteristic amoral wit in this tale of a would-be murderer frustrated at every turn in his efforts to get his kicks from a successful sex killing. As usual, the master eschews the visual fussiness of 'style', opting for the straightforward camera set-up at all times. The use of props like the toy music box from his childhood which triggers off Archibaldo's lust, and the wax dummy burned after one of his attempts is thwarted, is all the more stunning (and hilarious) as a result. RM

Criminal Lovers (Les Amants Criminels)

(1999, Fr, 90 min)
d François Ozon. *p* Marc Missonnier, Olivier Delbosc. *sc* François Ozon. *ph* Pierre Stoeber. *ed* Dominique Petrot. *pd* Arnaud de Moleron. *m* Philippe Rombi. *cast* Natacha Régnier, Jérémie Renier, Miki Manojlovic, Salim Kechiouche, Yasmine Belmadi.
● Alice (Régnier, from *Dream Life of Angels*) is a provocative bitch, toying with the vulnerable affections of Luc (Renier), who loves her, he thinks, even if he can't get it up. After she manipulates the murder of another boy, they go on the run in the woods, and the movie turns into a macabre gay fairytale, with nods to everthing from the Brothers Grimm through *Night of the Hunter* to *Texas Chain Saw Massacre*. The flashback structure maintains the intrigue, but the movie never rouses much sympathy for its protagonists, and you sense that on some sick level Ozon finds it funny. Accomplished it may be, but it's just too knowing to be truly involving. TCh

Crimson Blade, The

see Scarlet Blade, The

Crimson Cult, The

see Curse of the Crimson Altar

Crimson Kimono, The

(1959, US, 82 min, b/w)
d/p/sc Samuel Fuller. *ph* Sam Leavitt. *ed* Jerome Thoms. *ad* William Flannery, Robert Boyle. *m* Harry Sukman. *cast* Victoria Shaw, Glenn Corbett, James Shigeta, Anna Lee, Paul Dubov, Jaclynne Greene.
● Fuller developing his theme of urban alienation: landscape, culture and sexual confusion are all juxtaposed, forcing the Japanese-born detective (who, along with his buddy, is on the hunt for a burlesque queen murderer) into a nightmare of isolation and jealousy. Some fine set pieces – like the disciplined Kendo fight that degenerates into sadistic anarchy – and thoughtful camerawork serve to illustrate Fuller's gift for weaving a poetic nihilism out of his journalistic vision of urban crime. GSa

Crimson Pirate, The

(1952, GB, 104 min)
d Robert Siodmak. *p* Harold Hecht. *sc* Roland Kibbee. *ph* Otto Heller. *ed* Jack Harris. *ad* Paul Sheriff. *m* William Alwyn. *cast* Burt Lancaster, Nick Cravat, Eva Bartok, Torin Thatcher, James Hayter, Noel Purcell, Margot Grahame.
● Marvellous semi-serious swashbuckler, with Lancaster and Cravat – his diminutive acrobat colleague – taking on a tyrant in the 18th century Mediterranean. Racily but elegantly directed by Siodmak, it effortlessly merges thrills and spoofery to produce entertainment that really is, for once, suitable for 'kids of all ages'. But the film's strongest point is the opportunity it offers to watch its stars' relaxed, energetic stunt-work: never has Burt looked so graceful. GA

Crimson Rivers, The (Les Rivières Pourpres)

(2000, Fr, 106 min)
d Mathieu Kassovitz. *p* Alain Goldman. *sc* Jean-Christophe Grangé, Mathieu Kassovitz. *ph* Thierry Arbogast. *ed* Maryline Monthieux. *ad* Thierry Flamand. *m* Bruno Coulias. *cast* Jean Réno, Vincent Cassel, Nadia Farès, Jean-Pierre Cassel, Karim Belkhadra, Didier Flamand, François Levantal, Francine Bergé, Dominique Sanda.
● Commissaire Niémans (Réno) is a gruff, taciturn 'one-man vice squad', Lt Kerkerian (Cassel) a spunky smalltime cop who cadges spliffs off old car thief pals. Plotted like a clammy alpine thriller crossed with aspects of *The Name of the Rose* and *Cliffhanger*, the movie keeps them apart for an hour before bringing them together for the bare minimum of character friction. Adapted by Jean-Christophe Grangé from his own bestseller, the film pushes a heap of plot information so convoluted it effaces the characters and bores the baffled viewer. A demeaning mainstream effort from the director of *La Haine*. NB

Crimson Tide

(1995, US, 116 min)
d Tony Scott. *p* Don Simpson, Jerry Bruckheimer. *sc* Michael Schiffer. *ph* Dariusz Wolski. *ed* Chris Lebenzon. *pd* Michael White. *m* Hans Zimmer. *cast* Gene Hackman, Denzel Washington, George Dzundza, Viggo Mortensen, Matt Craven, James Gandolfini, Rocky Carroll, Jaime P Gomez.
● The crisis in the former Soviet Union has intensified. With a nuclear base in the hands of nationalist rebels, the world is waking up to another Cuban missile crisis, and the USS 'Alabama' is dispatched to deep waters within striking distance of Moscow. Only executive officer Hunter (Washington) stands between hawkish Captain Ramsey (Hackman) and a pre-emptive strike. Conceived as a post-Cold War update on *Fail Safe*, this tense, lucid brinksmanship drama also incorporates elements from *The Caine Mutiny*, *A Few Good Men*, and every submarine movie you've ever seen. There's no disguising the braggadocio with which director Scott plays cat-and-mouse with nuclear holocaust, cranking up the excitement with crazy angles, hot reds and greens, and Dariusz Wolski's hyper, heat-seeking camera. The screenplay may be credited to Michael Schiffer, but the punchy dialogue has Quentin Tarantino written all over it. The cast has a ball. Hackman, especially, brings immense reserves of humour, dignity and conviction to his meatiest role since *Unforgiven*. TCh

Crise, La

(1992, Fr, 95 min)
d Coline Serreau. *p* Alain Sarde. *sc* Coline Serreau. *ph* Robert Alazraki. *ed* Catherine Renault. *pd* Guy-Claude François. *m* Sonia Wieder-Atherton. *cast* Vincent Lindon, Patrick Timsit, Annik Alane, Valérie Alane, Gilles Privat, Zabou.
● Serreau, who made *Romuald et Juliette* and *Trois Hommes et un Couffin*, is determined to bring her troubled male protagonist around to a more feminine, even feminist, understanding of the world. Like *Romuald*, this begins with a harassed but apparently successful businessman losing both job and wife. As one might expect, however, *La Crise* has a less romantic, more coruscating edge: Romuald had his Juliette after all. But when Victor (Lindon) turns loser, he's stuck with Michou (Timsit), a kind, if slow-witted social outcast. This is a black comedy which takes itself very seriously. There's a pervasive sense of bankruptcy and malaise as Victor rebounds from one rejection to the next. Every couple is breaking up, racism is rife, politicians are hypocrites. The shrill opening is probably intentionally aggravating, but it ebbs into affecting, melancholy moments of transcendence and a more gently droll, if still spiky, sentimental education. There are problems: Michou's 'holy fool' takes some swallowing, and Serreau would do better to refrain from sermonising. Nevertheless, this is urgent, scalding satire, with a terrific performance from Lindon. TCh

Crisis

(1950, US, 96 min, b/w)
d Richard Brooks. *p* Arthur Freed. *sc* Richard Brooks. *ph* Ray June. *ed* Robert J Kern. *ad* Cedric Gibbons, Preston Ames. *m* Miklós Rózsa. *cast* Cary Grant, José Ferrer, Signe Hasso, Paula Raymond, Ramon Novarro, Gilbert Roland.

●Screenwriter Richard Brooks kicked off a largely distinguished directorial career with this highly charged political melodrama. Grant plays an American doctor forced to perform a brain tumour operation on South American dictator Ferrer (based, it seems, on Peron). The success of the endeavour places the medic and his wife Raymond in even greater danger themselves. Although the storyline bears a strong resemblance to the British thriller *State Secret*, also made in 1950, Brooks is adept at maintaining the tension. Grant looks as though he'd rather be holding a dry martini than a scalpel. TJ

Criss Cross

(1948, US, 88 min, b/w)
d Robert Siodmak. *p* Michel Kraike. *sc* Daniel Fuchs. *ph* Franz Planer. *ed* Ted J Kent. *ad* Bernard Herzbrun, Boris Leven. *m* Miklós Rózsa. *cast* Burt Lancaster, Yvonne De Carlo, Dan Duryea, Stephen McNally, Richard Long.

●Wonderfully seedy tale of betrayal and obsession from superb *noir*-thriller stylist Siodmak. Beautifully shot (Franz Planer) and scripted (Daniel Fuchs), it bears more than a slight resemblance to the same director's *The Killers*. Again Lancaster is the fall guy, an armoured-car payroll guard still brooding over his ex-wife (De Carlo), who has taken up with gangster Slim Dundee (Duryea) but leads Lancaster to believe that they can make a new start with booty gained from a daring heist if he will go through with it. As always with Siodmak, the suspense is maintained throughout by taut pacing, visual precision, and excellent characterisation. GA

Critic, The

(1962, US, 6 min)
d/p Ernest Pintoff. *sc* Mel Brooks. *pd/animation* Bob Heath. *ed* Harry Chang. *m* JS Bach. *cast* voice: Mel Brooks.

●Uninteresting shapes and colour combinations lumber across the screen to the accompaniment of Bach. 'What da hell is dis?' demands a rude New York voice. The tedious animated abstractions of Hans Richter, Oscar Fischinger and their ilk defy parody, and Pintoff/Heath simply reproduce the style. On the soundtrack Mel Brooks' robust philistine assesses the visuals ('Doit and filt') and suggests alternative work for the artist ('make a shoe or somepn'). A potshot that needed taking, ideally 30 years sooner. BBa

Critters

(1986, US, 86 min)
d Stephen Herek. *p* Rupert Harvey. *sc* Stephen Herek, Dominic Muir, Don Opper. *ph* Tim Suhrstedt. *ed* Larry Bock. *pd* Gregg Fonseca. *m* David Newman. *cast* Dee Wallace Stone, M Emmet Walsh, Billy Green Bush, Scott Grimes, Nadine Van Der Velde, Don Opper.

●The Critters in question, aliens escaping from a space prison, are rolling amok in the small town of Grovers Bend, Kansas, where they've penned up Farmer Brown's family. They've cut the phone lines, killed the electricity, and eaten his goldfish. Now they want him. Judging from the title, Spielberg's *Gremlins* would be the immediate target, and indeed *Critters* does share a sardonic similarity. In fact, *Critters* looks like several dozen films without looking like any one of them, the action and characters lifted whole from a dissimilar plethora of cinematic sources and underscored with a sizzling sarcasm which elevates it from its source material. As a local puts it when he encounters the outer-space bounty hunters who've come to save humanity dressed in what look like worn-out Flash Gordon pyjamas (the locals wear bowling shirts with a *Ghostbusters* logo), 'They must be from Los Angeles.' No they don't make 'em like they used to, they make 'em exactly like they used to, only with a bit more bite. SGo

Critters 2: The Main Course

(1988, US, 87 min)
d Mick Garris. *p* Barry Opper. *sc* David N Twohy, Mick Garris. *ph* Russell Carpenter. *ed* Charles Bornstein. *pd* Philip Dean Foreman. *m* Nicholas Pike. *cast* Scott Grimes, Liane Curtis, Don Opper, Barry Corbin, Terrence Mann, Cynthia Garris.

●*Critters*, you may remember, concerned a group of oversized mothballs from space who landed on Earth and ate everybody, until some intergalactic bounty hunters turned up and fried them. The 'Krites', however, had the good business sense to lay some eggs before getting splattered, so now Grover's Bend is up to its neck in the little buggers again, and the space-borne pest control are back on the job. Garris plays it for laughs, and despite dull moments (and the obvious plagiarisation of *Gremlins*), does a pretty good job. Massive guns go KABOOM! everywhere as one gribbly after another gets stiffed, each exploding in a fountain of what looks strangely like the green gunk Linda Blair spewed over von Sydow in *The Exorcist*. The superimposure (particularly at the end when the hero meets his double) is diabolical, and the Chiodo brothers' creations are, as before, both spectacularly silly and disconcertingly vicious as they munch people's vital organs. The effect is perhaps not unlike watching Sooty in a video nasty. MK

Crocodile Dundee

(1986, Aust, 98 min)
d Peter Faiman. *p* John Cornell. *sc* Paul Hogan, Ken Shadie, John Cornell. *ph* Russell Boyd. *ed* David Stiven. *pd* Graham (Grace) Walker. *m* Peter Best. *cast* Paul Hogan, Linda Kozlowski, John Meillon, David Gulpilil, Ritchie Singer, Mark Blum, Michael Lombard, Irving Metzman.

●Another hick hits another big city. Having shown our hero to be master of life in the outback, the film whisks him off to New York, which he takes in his easy stride mainly by refusing to notice it's all that different from what he's used to back at Walkabout Creek. Permanently unfazed, overcoming all adversity with casual efficiency, Dundee wards off audience displeasure by intimating that although he may be the real thing he's also a bit of a con-man. A canny construct is old Crocky, and a star-maker of a role for bronzed, wiry Hogan. BBa

Crocodile Dundee II

(1988, Aust, 112 min)
d John Cornell. *p* John Cornell, Jane Scott. *sc* Paul Hogan, Brett Hogan. *ph* Russell Boyd. *ed* David Stiven. *pd* Larry Eastwood. *m* Peter Best. *cast* Paul Hogan, Linda Kozlowski, Charles Dutton, Mark Blum, John Meillon, Hechter Ubarry.

●In the mega-hit series league, the trick is to keep the bits that went down well. Thus writer/producer/star Hogan has retained instances of the naive Natural Man in the metropolis: he falls off a ledge on learning that a would-be suicide is driven by unrequited gay love, and fishes with dynamite off New York's Battery. Back home in the outback, he repeats the sophisticated Aborigines stuff – 'It needs garlic', comments one, crouching over some unspeakable tucker. But there's little time for character in this standard issue plot about a rascally coke baron (Ubarry) trying to recover incriminating evidence from Dundee's sheila (Kozlowski). The violence is still pleasantly paddling-pool stuff, but the disarming G'day factor has been pasteurised away. BC

Crocodile Dundee in Los Angeles

(2001, US/Aust, 95 min)
d Simon Wincer. *p* Lance Hool, Paul Hogan. *sc* Matthew Berry, Eric Abrams. *ph* David Burr. *ed* Terry Blythe. *pd* Leslie Binns. *m* Basil Poledouris. *cast* Paul Hogan, Linda Kozlowski, Jere Burns, Jonathan Banks, Alec Wilson, Serge Cockburn, Gerry Skilton, Steve Rackman, David Ngoombujarra, Aida Turturro.

●Dundee's blunt charisma was already fading in his second crime-bustin' outing. Thirteen years on, talk about flogging a dead croc. Living in unwed bliss with Sue (Kozlowski), Mick is proud pa of squeakily precocious Mikey (Cockburn). The outback, he realises, has become a tourist trap. So all head for LA, where Sue has an editing job on her father's newspaper. It isn't Mick's first stateside trip, but he's still clueless about technology and exotic enough to wow high society, besides going undercover to investigate film folk who – and here's the irony – make tacky sequels to conceal international corruption scams. AHa

Croix de Bois, Les (Wooden Crosses)

(Fr, 107 min, b/w)
d Raymond Bernard. *sc* André Lang, Raymond Bernard. *ph* Jules Kruger, René Ribault. *ed* Lucienne Grumberg. *ad* Jean Perrier. *cast* Pierre Blanchar, Charles Vanel, Antonin Artaud, Aimos, Raymond Cordy, Paul Azaïs.

●An adaptation of Roland Dorgelès' celebrated (back then) WWI novel, this differs from its near contemporaries *All Quiet* and *Westfront 1918* by having no explicit pacifist message. The intended audience were probably the veterans themselves, the movie being a necessarily circumspect but reasonably honest-seeming account of their collective experience. It's set throughout at the front, eschewing the customary 'home on leave' episode and concentrating remorselessly on the process of attrition, culminating in Blanchar's lonely calvary, as he slowly dies of a stomach wound in no man's land. The combat scenes, which go on and on, are filmed conventionally but sensibly with the camera, static or tracking, at ground level except when – unusually for the time – it seems to be hand-held. The sequence where the *poilus* listen nervously in their dugout to the sound of the Germans mining below them has the excitement of the newly feasible, characteristic of such early talkies. BBa

Cromwell

(1970, GB, 141 min)
d Ken Hughes. *p* Irving Allen. *sc* Ken Hughes. *ph* Geoffrey Unsworth. *ed* Bill Lenny. *pd* John Stoll. *m* Frank Cordell. *cast* Richard Harris, Alec Guinness, Robert Morley, Dorothy Tutin, Frank Finlay, Timothy Dalton, Patrick Magee.

●Turgid history lesson which never quite makes up its mind whether it means to be subtle or spectacular, and eventually compromises on both counts. Fact is considerably fictionalised in order to present Cromwell (loudly played by Harris) as a blameless champion of the underprivileged. The battle scenes are staged vigorously enough, but also play havoc with history. TM

Cronaca di un Amore (Chronicle of a Love Affair)

(1950, It, 100 min)
d Michelangelo Antonioni. *sc* Michelangelo Antonioni, Daniele d'Anza, Silvio Giovanietti, Francesco Maselli, Piero Tellini. *ph* Enzo Serafin. *ad* Piero Filippone. *m* Giovanni Fusco. *cast* Lucia Bosè, Massimo Girotti, Ferdinando Sarmi, Gino Rossi, Franco Fabrizi.

●Antonioni's early work has been overshadowed by the international acclaim which greeted *L'Avventura* and *L'Eclisse* (though David Thomson for one celebrates the 'triumphant' vitality and 'tender rigour' which characterise the director's first films). It's difficult to watch his feature debut, *Cronaca di un Amore*, without looking ahead to the elliptical masterpieces which grew out of it. The film might as well be called *Identification of a Woman*: a detective is hired to investigate the past of an industrialist's wife, but the assignment only precipitates further loss and disappointment. If the form is more conventional than what was to follow, the mood of decadent ennui, alienation and anguish is instantly recognisable. TCh

Cronos

(1993, Mex, 92 min)
d Guillermo Del Toro. *p* Berta Navarro, Arthur H Gorson. *sc* Guillermo Del Toro. *ph* Guillermo Navarro. *ed* Raul Davalos. *m* Javier Alvarez. *cast* Federico Luppi, Ron Perlman, Claudio Brook, Margarita Isabel, Claudio Brook, Tamara Shanath.

●Luppi, an elderly antiques dealer, discovers a gold gizmo which a mysterious alchemist had hidden inside a statue centuries before. The old man becomes immortal, his body undergoes a bizarre transformation, and he develops a thirst for blood. Resisting the efforts of dying businessman Brook and his henchman Perlman to get hold of the so-called Cronos device (it has strange body-piercing abilities), Luppi struggles to hold on to his humanity even beyond the grave. Del Toro gives an intriguing spin to the time-honoured vampire pic. Out goes gratuitous blood letting, in comes dry wit, a sombre pace and a substantial emotional kick, as Luppi seeks to maintain the powerful bond with his wife and young granddaughter, even though he looks, well, like something from a horror movie. A most startling genre piece: tender, imaginative and wholly its own. TJ

Crooklyn

(1994, US, 114 min)
d/p Spike Lee. *sc* Spike Lee, Joie Lee, Cinqué Lee. *ph* Arthur Jafa. *ed* Barry Alexander Brown. *pd* Wynn Thomas. *m* Terence Blanchard. *cast* Alfred Woodard, Delroy Lindo, David Patrick Kelly, Zelda Harris, Carlton Williams, Sharif Rashed, Tse-Mach Washington.

●This semi-comic look at middle-class family life in Brooklyn, New York, in the mid-'70s was written by Spike Lee and his siblings Joie and Cinqué. As well as hanging out on the stoop and battling with four idle brothers, ten-year-old Troy (Harris) – from whose point of view the story is told – witnesses the tensions between her mother (Woodard) and father (Lindo). While Lee's customary visual style and sense of street vitality are much in evidence, it's easy to see why this fond, semi-autobiographical evocation of a largely vanished lifestyle bombed in the US. It's not just the misjudgment of depicting Troy's lengthy visit to an aunt in Virginia through the squeezed perspective of an anamorphic lens, nor even the final scenes in which the story lurches from comedy to half-hearted melodrama: the key problem is that the film is simply a ragged series of anecdotal sketches. GA

Crook's Tour

(1940, GB, 84 min. b/w)
d John Baxter. *p* John Corfield. *sc* John Watt, Max Kester. *ph* James Wilson. *ed* Michael C Chorlton. *ad* Duncan Sutherland. *m* Kennedy Russell. *cast* Basil Radford, Naunton Wayne, Greta Gynt, Abraham Sofaer, Charles Oliver, Gordon McLeod.

●A relic from the days of radio spin-offs, this genially rickety comedy features Caldicott and Charters, the two amiable asses from the old boy network – impersonated by Radford and Wayne – who enlivened *The Lady Vanishes* and *Night Train to Munich*, then graduated to a radio series. The stock plot has them stranded in an Arabian desert while on a package tour, being mistakenly entrusted with secret information in a Baghdad nightclub, and then pursued all over the place by Nazi agents. Uninspiring stuff, but the patter remains endearingly funny. Rescued from a nasty fate in the desert by a sheik who also proves to be a member of the old boy network and invites them to dinner (sheep's eyes, of course), Wayne remains distraught: 'But we haven't got dinner jackets,' he protests. TM

Cross, The (La Cruz)

(1997, Arg, 90 min)
d Alejandro Agresti. *p* Alejandro Agresti, Pascual Condito. *sc* Alejandro Agresti. *ph* Mauricio Rubinstein. *ed* Alejandro Brodersohn. *cast* Norman Briski, Mirta Busnelli, Carlos Roffe, Laura Melillo.

●After the delightful *Buenos Aires Vice Versa*, this is a disappointment. It starts well, with Briski's drunkard film critic arguing vehemently with the editors who find his reviews too negative. But as the film goes on to chart his mid-life crisis born of his drinking and his wife's departure for another man, it turns into an indulgent rant, enlivened only by the critic's ludicrous attempts to impersonate his wife's lover in order to discredit the man's sexual past. Strong performances, but the drama ends up going nowhere. GA

Cross and Passion

(1981, GB, 60 min)
d/sc Claire Pollak, Kim Longinotto. *ph/ed* Kim Longinotto.

●A film documenting how the Troubles affect the Catholic women living on and around a cheerless, battle-scarred Belfast estate. A schoolgirl, a housewife, a nun speak fluently (though in accents often elusive to an English ear) of the forces shaping their daily lives. British soldiers are shown only as distant figures in khaki squatting by house corners, rifles cocked, next to kids who imperviously continue their games. The film's title (the name of a Catholic girls' school) proposes as more immediate, more powerful a source of oppression the papist catechism of chastity and sexual guilt passed on through generations of Irish women. The nuns also preach meekness and resignation in the face of the God-sent Troubles, but the implied connections between Church and occupying forces are never fully explored. SJo

Cross and the Switchblade, The

(1970, US, 105 min)
d Don Murray. *p* Dick Ross. *sc* Don Murray, James Bonnet. *ph* Julian C Townsend. *ed* Angelo Ross. *ad* Charles Bailey. *m* Ralph Carmichael. *cast* Pat Boone, Erik Estrada, Jackie Giroux, Jo-Ann Robinson, Dino DeFilippi.

●Trash has a certain attractiveness, especially when it's the sort that claims to be based on fact and at the same time pits Pat Boone against a ghetto full of black and Puerto Rican kids. A preacher from Pennsylvania launching into reform work in New York, Boone comes out with phrases like 'God'll get you high, but he won't let you down', and there's layings-on of sweaty palms, a lady on heroin reclaimed, bible handouts, gang fights out of *West Side Story*, betrayals, young love, even light forming an unmistakable cross on the screen at a crucial moment. The best thing about it, this being one of those movies that seem unconscious of what they're really about, is that Boone's motivations are never less than equivocal, so that the switchblade wins hands down over God-is-loveism.

Cross Creek

(1983, US, 122 min)
d Martin Ritt. *p* Robert B Radnitz. *sc* Dalene Young. *ph* John A Alonzo. *ed* Sidney Levin. *pd* Walter Scott Henderson. *m* Leonard Rosenman. *cast* Mary Steenburgen, Rip Torn, Peter Coyote, Dana Hill, Alfre Woodard, Joanna Miles.

●Sporting a fancy line in hats and a dangerously overripe sensibility, writer Marjorie Kinnan Rawlings (Steenburgen) abandons her husband and journeys south to grapple with The Great American Gothic Novel. Stuck in a renovated backwoods shack, the local colour soon proves far more vivid than anything her imagination can conjure up. There's the suave hotelier who gets her jalopy back on the road, the doting black maid with an errant lover, and punting through the swampweed cackling balefully here's Torn as the resident rustic loon. Never one to stint himself when it comes to romantic overkill, Ritt piles on the slush with even more gusto than usual. Broadly – and self-consciously – signposted as The Stirring Story of a Woman's Struggle to Find Herself, the result suffers from a bad case of the cutes and a quite intolerable smugness. JP

Crossfire

(1947, US, 85 min, b/w)
d Edward Dmytryk. *p* Adrian Scott. *sc* John Paxton. *ph* J Roy Hunt. *ed* Harry Gerstad. *ad* Albert S D'Agostino, Al Herman. *m* Roy Webb. *cast* Robert Ryan, Robert Young, Robert Mitchum, Gloria Grahame, Sam Levene, Paul Kelly, Jacqueline White, Steve Brodie.

●This ultra-low-budget thriller did what all great B movies do: it broached a subject that 'respectable' movies wouldn't touch. In this case, the racist murder of a Jew (although it was a homosexual in Richard Brooks' source novel, *The Brick Foxhole*), and the exposure of the murderer's fanatical anti-Semitism. Dmytryk exploits the poverty-row sets for their claustrophobic quality, and introduces 'expressionist' lighting and distorted angles to dramatise the tensions that simmer and finally explode between the characters, GIs back from the war in Europe but not yet discharged. This was the kind of movie that provoked the McCarthy witch-hunt in Hollywood. TR

Cross-Harbour Tunnel (Guo Hai Suidao)

(1999, HK, 93 min)
d Lawrence Wong. *p* Karen Chu, Ken Wong, Lawrence Wong, Carly Wong. *sc* Lawrence Wong, GC Goo Bi. *ph* Ng Yuet-Fung, Ah Wai. *ed* Chan Chi-Wai. *ad* Kim Lo, So Au. *m* Anthony Teoh. *cast* Syna Lee, Martin Kam, Anthony Teoh, Pauline Yam, GC Goo Bi, Kwan Lung.

●Wong's no-budget indie (dreamt up in a night, shot in a week) tells four distinct stories which intersect in the manner of *Mystery Train*. They range from character-based comedy (a young couple nervously venture into a 'love hotel' for the first time) to Grand Guignol melodrama (a Filipina maid seeks revenge on her two-timing lover – the actress being the director's mother's real-life maid). The best strand is the wicked parody of Tsai Ming-Liang's *Vive l'amour*: a young guy finds a key to someone else's apartment, starts using it as his own and falls in love with its temporarily absent owner – who turns out to be another boy. Often unashamedly flip and juvenile, the film has enough sparks of invention and wit to keep most people watching. TR

Crossing Delancey

(1988, US, 97 min)
d Joan Micklin Silver. *p* Michael Nozik. *sc* Susan Sandler. *ph* Theo van de Sande. *ed* Rick Shaine. *pd* Dan Leigh. *m* Paul Chichara. *cast* Amy Irving, Peter Riegert, Reizl Bozyk, Jeroen Krabbé, Sylvia Miles, George Martin, John Bedford Lloyd.

●Izzy Grossman (Irving) is a NY Upper West Sider, managing a bookstore, arranging readings and literary soirées, whose grandmother Bubbie Kantor (Bozyk) decides that, at 33, she should be married to a nice Jewish man. So she employs the matchmaking services of the overbearing Mrs Mandelbaum (Miles), who introduces Izzy to Sam Posner (Riegert), the pickle man. Meanwhile, Izzy is flirting with egocentric novelist Anton Maes (Krabbé). Her dilemma begins: should she opt for Posner's peck of pickles – dull, reliable, and resistable – or for Maes' seductive sophistication? Some poignant and charming moments undercut the Munchkin aspect of the ethnic elderly portrayed here, but on the whole Silver's direction spoon-feeds chicken soup covered in a slightly unpalatable patina of schmaltz. JGl

Crossing Guard, The

(1995, US, 114 min)
d Sean Penn. *p* Sean Penn, David Hamburger. *sc* Sean Penn. *ph* Vilmos Zsigmond. *ed* Jay Cassidy. *pd* Michael Haller. *m* Jack Nitzsche. *cast* Jack Nicholson, David Morse, Robin Wright, Anjelica Huston, Piper Laurie, Richard Bradford.

●After six years of desperate, unrelieved mourning, Freddy Gale (Nicholson) feels his life has just one terminus: the murder of John Booth (Morse) who killed his daughter in a drunk-driving accident. Writer/director Penn cuts between Gale's impotent, pent-up rage, aimed also at his ex-wife (Huston), and Booth's equally consuming remorse after his release from prison. Only a hesitant affair with a painter (Wright) proffers hope. This is a naive film. Very evidently the work of an actor, it follows the performances with a dogged faith which lands you in all sorts of nooks and crannies, some no more than dead ends. Yet Nicholson delivers his most committed, penetrating work in years. Penn is at his best simply pointing a camera at lonely men in anonymous rooms, choking for air in emotional vacuums of their own devising. TCh

Crossing the Bridge

(1992, US, 103 min)
d Mike Binder. *p* Jeffrey Silver, Robert Newmyer. *sc* Mike Binder. *ph* Tom Sigel. *ed* Adam Weiss. *m* Peter Himmelman. *cast* Josh Charles, Jason Gedrick, Stephen Baldwin, Cheryl Pollak, Jeffrey Tambor, Rita Taggart.

●Mike Binder's directorial debut (he previously scripted the superior teen comedy *Coupe de Ville*) is a self-consciously wrought portrait of the artist as a young man; a series of comic and melancholy vignettes in the vein of *Stand by Me* and *Diner*. It's a likeable, engagingly woolly affair, the story of three friends dragging their feet after high school, pondering whether they should grow up and go to college or run drugs over the bridge from Canada and make some money – or both. This is one of those movies where a rough-and-ready game of football is endowed with near-metaphysical significance. But that's how middle-aged lads like to remember their youth, and there's usually a well-turned gag to undercut the nostalgia. Charles is good as the aspiring writer, but Threesome co-star Baldwin steals the movie from him all over again. TCh

Crossmaheart

(1998, GB, 93 min)
d Henry Herbert. *p* Don Boyd, Stephanie Mills. *sc* Colin Bateman. *ph* Peter Butler. *ed* Adam

Ross. *pd* Shane Bunting. *m* Gary Kemp, Edward Shearmur. *cast* Gerard Rooney, Maria Lennon, Enda Oates, Des Cave, Seamus Ball.
● Adapted by Ulster novelist Colin Bateman from one of his own books (*A Cycle of Violence*), this features a smart-lipped journalist wise-cracking his way through Northern Ireland's moral turmoil. The plot inches towards the thriller angle, but unfortunately someone forgot to bring the thrills. Rooney is the latest correspondent to be sent from Belfast to the border bandit country of Crossmaheart, where the previous incumbent in the post has gone missing. The plot adds dark sexual secrets to the usual Troubles paranoia, and features a guess-the-villain device so obvious it beggars belief. (Far inferior to 1998's other Bateman adaptation, *Divorcing Jack*.) TJ

Cross My Heart

see Fracture du myocarde, La

Cross My Heart and Hope to Die (Ti Kniver I Hjertet)

(1994, Nor, 96 min)
d Marius Holst. *p* Petter Borgli. *sc* Lars Saabye Christiensen. *ph* Philip Ogaard. *ed* Hakon Overas. *pd* Billy Johansson. *m* Magne Furuholmen, Kjetil Bjerkestrand. *cast* Martin Dahl Garfalk, Jan 'Devo' Kornstad, Kjersti Holmen, Reidar Sørensen.
● An intriguing but not wholly successful coming-of-age saga which blends mystery, comedy and Oedipal drama as Otto, a teenager abandoned by his friends for the summer holidays, strikes up a love-hate relationship with an enigmatic older kid who seems to exert a strange, malign influence (largely sexual) over the local women, including Otto's mother. The quiet small-town '60s setting is well conveyed, but the mystery is finally a somewhat annoying red herring. GA

Cross of Iron

(1977, GB/WGer, 133 min)
d Sam Peckinpah. *p* Wolf C Hartwig. *sc* Julius Epstein, Walter Kelly, James Hamilton. *ph* John Coquillon. *ed* Tony Lawson, Michael Ellis. *pd* Ted Haworth, Brian Ackland-Snow. *m* Ernest Gold. *cast* James Coburn, Maximilian Schell, James Mason, David Warner, Klaus Löwitsch, Senta Berger.
● Peckinpah's only war film, based on a novel by Willi Heinrich, displays his familiar preoccupation with the individual confronted by events beyond his control. Dealing with a German platoon involved in the 1943 retreat on the Russian front, the film reveals a special feeling for the universalities of war: lives in the balance, the single-suppression of emotion. Sombre and claustrophobic photography, an intelligent script, and Peckinpah's clear understanding of a working platoon of men, are all far removed from the monotonous simplicity of most big-budget war films. CPe

Crossover Dreams

(1985, US, 86 min)
d Leon Ichaso. *p* Manuel Arce. *sc* Manuel Arce, Rubén Blades, Leon Ichaso. *ph* Claudio Chea. *ed* Gary Karr. *pd* Octavio Soler. *m* Mauricio Smith. *cast* Rubén Blades, Shawn Elliot, Elizabeth Peña, Tom Signorelli, Virgilio Marti, Frank Robles.
● Despite the boil-in-the-bag plot – struggling musician (*salsa* superstar Blades) hits big time and goes off the rails – this has lots going for it. It's the story of countless jazz and rock musicals, and the song remains the same, that rich whites in their 5th Avenue eyries still run and ruin people's lives. But this deals with the new leisure marginals: the *salsa* musicians of America's massive *barrio* populations. Barring one set piece, the music is subordinate to the narrative, sometimes annoyingly so. That said, the soundtrack remains a powerful cultural, er, signifier, and Blades and cast turn in strong, unsentimental performances. Apart from some choc-boxy scenes, Ichaso films New York with a hard-edged realism, presenting the mixed Latin communities cusping on their own social crossover. JG

Crossroads

(1942, US, 84 min)
d Jack Conway. *p* Edwin Knopf. *sc* Guy Trosper. *ph* Joseph Ruttenberg. *ed* George Boemler. *ad* Cedric Gibbons, John S Detlie. *m* Bronislau Kaper. *cast* William Powell, Hedy Lamarr, Basil Rathbone, Claire Trevor, Margaret Wycherly, Felix Bressart.
● Hollywood's cannibalisation of the 1939 French psychological thriller *Carrefour*, here developed along lighter lines to match Powell's *Thin Man* image. He plays a happily married diplomat who, on the eve of an ambassadorial appointment, finds himself being blackmailed as a supposed former crook (amnesia has conveniently left a hole in his memory), and confronted by proof in the form of a confederate, a mistress and a mother. It emerges as a typical MGM confection, but the cast remains very watchable. TM

Crossroads

(1986, US, 96 min)
d Walter Hill. *p* Mark Carliner. *sc* John Fusco. *ph* John Bailey. *ed* Freeman Davies. *pd* Jack T Collis. *m* Ry Cooder. *cast* Ralph Macchio, Joe Seneca, Jami Gertz, Joe Morton, Robert Judd, Harry Carey Jr.
● While it begins as a variation of sorts on *The Karate Kid*, with young Macchio learning life lessons and string-picking from an old bluesman (Seneca) he rescues from a New York nursing-home, when their odyssey on the road reaches the Mississippi Delta this atypical Walter Hill movie develops into a strange fantasy mingling the legends of Faust and Robert Johnson. The latter element works better than the Devil business, and the script, by John (*Young Guns*) Fusco, might have had more resonance than the finished film, which is too slick for its own good. But Seneca is worth watching, Ry Cooder's score is among his best work, and this certainly isn't sequel fodder. TCh

Crossroads

(2001, US, 93 min)
d Tamra Davis. *p* Ann Carli. *sc* Shonda Rhimes. *ph* Eric Edwards. *ed* Melissa Kent. *pd* Waldemar Kalinowski. *m* Trevor Jones. *cast* Britney Spears, Anson Mount, Zoë Saldana, Taryn Manning, Dan Aykroyd, Kim Cattrall, Justin Long, Beverly Johnson, Bahni Turpin.
● Britney Spears plays preppy Lucy, whose yearning for her absent mother reunites her with childhood friends for a road trip: bitchy high-school queen Kit has signed on to visit her boyfriend, and pregnant trailer-park chick Mimi wants to enter a singing competition in LA. And they're travelling cross-country in style, thanks to enigmatic beefcake musician Ben (Mount) and his cool convertible. As kitschy escapism it's passably entertaining with the girls packing enough costume changes for the radiant open road to resemble a fashion shoot. A successful karaoke set hauls in a fortune, and 'real' adults barely surface. However, it's also riddled with leaden Hollywood clichés: geeky girls transform, geeky guys don't get laid, and during a love scene, the camera tastefully pans away to crashing waves. Britney is slick and confident, with everything pushing her centrestage. Which means that more emotive players, such as Mimi (Manning), suffer insensitively handled storylines. What could have been a fabulous pop fantasy becomes a one-track star vehicle that tramples down its own potential. AHa

Crossup

see Tiger by the Tail

Crossways (Jujiro)

(1928, Jap, 5,841 ft, b/w)
d/sc Teinosuke Kinugasa. *ph* Kohei Sugiyama. *ad* Bonji Taira. *cast* Junosuke Bando, Akiko Chihaya, Yukiko Ogawa, J Soma.
● Kinugasa's second film with his experimental theatre company, made two years after the better-known *Page of Madness*. At root, it's a simple melodrama about a young man's infatuation with a geisha, and his sister's frantic attempts to save him from himself. As such, it may seem too slow and over-emphatic for some tastes. But its imagery, lighting and montage effects are at least as daring as those in the earlier film, and fully the equal of anything done in the West at the time. Kinugasa's fidelity to physical realities (like breath misting in the freezing air and steam rising from sodden clothing) is often chilling, but his vision of the Yoshiwara pleasure district as a 'hell' of lights, shadows and frenetic movement also brings out his remarkable gifts as an expressionist. Certainly much more than an archive curiosity. TR

Crouching Tiger, Hidden Dragon (Wo Hu Zang Long) (100)

(2000, China/Tai/US, 120 min)
d Ang Lee. *p* Bill Kong, Hsu Li-Kong, Ang Lee. *sc* James Schamus, Wang Hui-Ling, Tsai Kuo-Jung. *ph* Peter Pau. *ed* Tim Squyres. *pd* Tim Yip. *m* Tan Dun. *cast* Chow Yun-Fat, Michelle Yeoh, Zhang Ziyi, Chang Chen, Lung Sihung, Cheng Pei-Pei.
● A rich, romantic take on the *wuxia*, China's heroic swordsman genre, from the eclectic Ang Lee. The first ten minutes or so offer dense exposition, introducing the legendary and righteous swordsman Li Mu Bai (Chow Yun-Fat), his esteemed partner Yu Shu Lien (Michelle Yeoh) and the wilful young aristocrat Jen (Zhang Ziyi), who enjoys a double life as a thief under the malign tutelage of her governess (Cheng Pei-Pei). They clash over the Green Destiny, a priceless sword which Jen steals as a mark of defiance. Yu gives chase in a brilliantly modulated set-piece across the roof-tops, the women defying gravity in exhilarating leaps and bounds. Once it takes flight the movie never touches the ground, spinning myriad duels of the body and spirit. Ang Lee has always been a director of finesse and fine feeling, but his touch is just as deft even as he extends his grasp to reveal the breathtaking vistas of mythic China, then relaxes enough to stage the demolition of a tavern with slapstick aplomb. Inventively choreographed by Yeun Wo-Ping – of *The Matrix* fame – the film imbues every look, every gesture with resonance and grace. Sexy and sublime, it's a feast for the senses and 100 per cent sheer cinema. TCh

Croupier

(1997, GB/Ire/Ger/Fr, 94 min)
d Mike Hodges. *p* Jonathan Cavendish. *sc* Paul Mayersberg. *ph* Mike Garfath. *ed* Les Healey. *pd* Jon Bunker. *m* Simon Fisher Turner. *cast* Clive Owen, Kate Hardie, Alex Kingston, Gina McKee, Nicholas Ball, Nick Reding, Alexander Morton.
● It's pitiful that no British distributor had the imagination to give Mike Hodges' 1997 film a proper release. An interior thriller set in the seductive nocturnal world of London's casinos and after-hours drinking clubs, it's every bit as compelling as the fashionable *Get Carter*. Jack (Clive Owen) wants to be a writer, but it's only when he falls back on his old skills as a croupier and accepts a job at the Golden Lion that the novel starts to write itself. A wideboy colleague suggests a theme ('I wanna fuck over the world'); and a beautiful gambler (Kingston) initiates a plot when she propositions him outside the casino. Only the central character presents problems: Jack's girlfriend Marion (McKee) is horrified that the fictional 'Jake' is such a callous operator. *Croupier* is as much about writing as it is about gambling. It bills itself, quite properly, as 'a film by Mike Hodges and Paul Mayersberg' – the man who wrote *The Man Who Fell to Earth*. Almost every exchange of dialogue is punctuated with Jack's internal commentary: 'In life there is a choice: be a gambler or a croupier,' he muses. 'I was hooked on watching punters lose.' Not since *Casino* has a film leaned so heavily on voice-over, but in many ways Mayersberg and Hodges use it more inventively than Scorsese, not only to draw parallels between the dealer (who must never gamble) and the author (who also looks down on his subjects), but as an integral element in an unravelling game of karma, conscience and duplicity. Superbly played – Owen has never been better – and directed with a mature, imperturbable calm, this is cinema worth seeking out. TCh

Crow, The

(1994, US, 101 min)
d Alex Proyas. *p* Edward R Pressman, Jeff Most. *sc* David Schow, John Shirley. *ph* Dariusz Wolski. *ed* Dov Hoenig, Scott Smith. *pd* Alex McDowell. *m* Graeme Revell. *cast* Brandon Lee, Michael Wincott, Rochelle Davis, Ernie Hudson, David Patrick Kelly, Angel David.
● Lee died making this supernatural rock-star revenge movie, and, after the lawsuits, recriminations and distribution problems, it has mopped up at the US box office. Lee had almost completed filming, so the thrust of the story (from James O'Barr's graphic novel) is intact. The footage has been bumped up with flashbacks, stand-in shots, and hi-tech tweaking whereby Lee was extracted from spare scenes and installed in new ones. It's unobtrusively done, but makes the action a

touch repetitive. More radically, the sicko storyline has been softened, becoming an elegiac, not to say maudlin, portrait of lost love. This has, sadly, worked to the advantage of the film: what was once slick, vacuous and trashy is now shot through with a terrible post-production irony. This is a most morbid film, a twisted Gothic romance with shards of the original black wisecracking splintering through the portentousness. Visually, it's a treat; characterisation is sharp, particularly the nicely defined villains; and the action scenes, though soft-pedalled, still pack a satisfying crunch. SFe

Crow: City of Angels, The

(1996, US/GB, 86 min)
d Tim Pope. *p* Edward R Pressman, Jeff Most. *sc* David S Goyer. *ph* Jean-Yves Escoffier. *ed* Michael N Knue, Anthony Redman. *pd* Alex McDowell. *m* Graeme Revell. *cast* Richard Brooks, Vincent Perez, Mia Kirshner, Vincent Castellanos, Ian Dury, Iggy Pop.

● Following Brandon Lee's death in an on-set accident, the producers of the first *Crow* movie completed it using computer graphics, thus proving that there's no limit to Hollywood's cynical exploitation of a star's box-office appeal. This necrophiliac sequel, the first feature of a British pop promo-maker, tries to sidestep the Lee issue by resurrecting the cathartic purity of James O'Barr's original comic book. Sadly, like its unfortunate protagonist, it's very soon dead in the water. Although the setting has moved from Detroit to LA, the stylised urban wasteland, morbid atmosphere and basic plot remain the same: gunned down by Judah (Brooks) and his gang of low-lifes, Ashe (Perez) returns from the dead, inheriting the dark mantle of the first film's Eric Draven. On the plus side, legendary rock survivor Iggy Pop exudes raw power as Judah's search-and-destroy sidekick. NF

Crowd, The

(1927, US, 130 min, b/w)
d King Vidor. *sc* King Vidor, John VA Weaver, Harry Behn. *ph* Henry Sharp. *ed* Hugh Wynn. *ad* Cedric Gibbons, A Arnold Gillespie. *cast* James Murray, Eleanor Boardman, Bert Roach, Estelle Clark, Daniel G Tomlinson, Dell Henderson.

● Certainly one of Vidor's best films, a silent masterpiece which turns a realistically caustic eye on the illusionism of the American dream. A young man ('born on America's 124th birthday') arrives in the big city convinced that he is going to set the world on fire, only to find that life isn't quite like that. A humble but steady job leads to love, marriage, kids and a happiness arbitrarily cut short by an accident (one of the children is run over and killed) which leads to the loss of his job, despairing unemployment, and impossible tensions starting to erode the marriage. The performances are absolutely flawless, and astonishing location work in the busy New York streets (including a giddy tour of Coney Island on a blind date) lends a gritty ring of truth to his intensely human odyssey, bounded by his eager arrival among the skyscrapers (the camera slowly panning up the side of a vast office block to discover him at work, lost in a sea of identical desks), and the last shot that has him merging as just another face in the crowd. Simple but superb. TM

Crows (Wrony)

(1994, Pol, 66 min)
d/sc Dorota Kedzierzawska. *ph* Artur Reinhart. *ed* Dorota Kedzierzawska, Artur Reinhart. *pd* Magdalena Kujszczyk. *m* Wlodzimierz Pawlik. *cast* Karolina Ostrozona, Kasia Szczepanik, Anna Prucnal, Malgorzata Hajewska-Krzysztofik, Ewa Bukowska, Krzysztof Grabarczyk.

● A charming if sad film about a ten-year-old girl – mischievous, brave, isolated at school, and hungry for the love denied by her mother – who decides to run away 'to the end of the world', abducting a four-year-old with whom she recreates a kind of mother-daughter relationship. Beautifully shot, the film might seem a little too studiously poetic were it not for young Karolina Ostrozona's performance: vibrant, touching, natural, and totally free of sentimentality. GA

Crows and Sparrows (Wuya yu Maque)

(1949, China, 112 min, b/w)
d Zheng Junli. *p* Xia Yunhu, Ren Zongde. *sc* Chen Baichen and others. *ph* Miao Zhenhua, Hu Zhenhua. *ed* Wu Tingfang. *pd* Niu Baorong, Xu Xing. *m* Wang Yunjie. *cast* Zhao Dan, Wu Yin, Wei Heling, Sun Daolin, Ouyang Yunzhu, Huang Zongying, Li Tianji.

● An unsung classic made in Shanghai as the KMT prepared to flee to Taiwan and the communist army approached the city – events which the film daringly uses as cornerstones of its narrative. The downtrodden tenants in a Shanghai boarding house (a teacher, a pedlar and a newspaper subeditor, the latter the real owner of the building) face eviction when their 'landlord', the KMT official who seized the premises, announces that he is selling up and moving to Taiwan. Amid rising crime and social panic, the 'little people' realise that they can stand up to tyranny by banding together. Thanks to terrific ensemble work from the cast and a talented director who keeps his foot off the 'melodrama' pedal, this is very different from the propaganda vehicles which all concerned found themselves making a few years later. The best of all Peak Film Industries productions of the late 1940s – which is saying a lot. TR

Crucible, The

(1996, US, 123 min)
d Nicholas Hytner. *p* Robert A Miller, David V Picker. *sc* Arthur Miller. *ph* Andrew Dunn. *ed* Tariq Anwar. *pd* Lilly Kilvert. *m* George Fenton. *cast* Daniel Day-Lewis, Winona Ryder, Paul Scofield, Joan Allen, Bruce Davison, Rob Campbell, Jeffrey Jones, Peter Vaughan, Charlayne Woodard.

● Salem, Massachusetts, 1692. The town tears itself apart during the investigations testing the claims of a group of young girls that their nocturnal forest gatherings were the result of satanic possession. At the root of the hysteria is the sexual and emotional turmoil of Abigail Williams (Ryder), bent on vengeance against Elizabeth Proctor (Allen) who put a stop to Abigail's affair with her husband John (Day-Lewis); but that particular power struggle, with its deceit, suspicion and resentment, is as nothing to the deadly vortex that consumes Salem when Judge Danforth (Scofield) arrives to take control with trials and hangings. The ironies of the piece, adapted by Arthur Miller from his own 1953 play on the perils of McCarthyism, are savage and well served by a top-notch cast perfectly attuned to the poetry of the dialogue and the parable's fiery passions. Hytner holds the action together with solid, unflashy, well-paced direction, ensuring that this is no mere period piece but a compelling, pertinent account of human fear, frailty and cold ambition. GA

Crucible of Terror

(1971, GB, 91 min)
d Ted Hooker. *p* Tom Parkinson. *sc* Ted Hooker, Tom Parkinson. *ph* Peter Newbrook. *ed* Maxine Julius. *ad* Arnold Chapkis. *m* Paris Rutherford. *cast* Mike Raven, Mary Maude, James Bolam, Ronald Lacey, Betty Alberge, Melissa Stribling.

● A modest but quite enjoyable variation on the *House of Wax* theme, which has some well-used location footage of Cornwall and a couple of good scenes to make up for the trite script, obviously low budget, and total miscasting of Mike Raven as the psychotic sculptor. DP

Crucified Lovers, The

see Chikamatsu Monogatari

Cruel Intentions

(1999, US, 97 min)
d Roger Kumble. *p* Neal H Moritz. *sc* Roger Kumble. *ph* Theo Van de Sande. *ed* Jeff Freeman. *pd* Jon Gary Steele. *m* Edward Shearmur. *cast* Sarah Michelle Gellar, Ryan Phillippe, Reese Witherspoon, Selma Blair, Louise Fletcher, Joshua Jackson, Eric Mabius, Sean Patrick Thomas, Swoosie Kurtz, Christine Baranski.

● An update of *Les Liaisons Dangereuses* to the decadent world of whitebread Manhattan preppies. Hiding behind step-brother Sebastian (Phillippe), a notorious seducer, the equally corrupt but infinitely more subtle Kathryn (Gellar) schemes to avenge herself on the ex who's dumped her for the innocent Cecile (Blair). Kathryn wants Sebastian to deflower her rival, but he's more interested in the challenge of the new headmaster's daughter, a proselytising virgin (Witherspoon). A wager is struck, Seb's antique Jag against Kat's body – but the consequences go deeper than that. There's a certain frisson in seeing an American teen pic so louche and worldly about all manner of debaucheries (Kumble is an old associate of those taboo-busting Farrelly brothers), but the movie's aristo sensibility doesn't really connect, while the redemptive volte face can't help but feel false – and The Verve's 'Bittersweet Symphony' doesn't help. For all that, it's an assured piece of work. Lascivious blackmailers and inveterate immoralists, these characters behave despicably, but the movie affects a tone of urbane detachment which puts sex in its proper perspective. Once Gellar has revealed both her faces there's not much more to know about Kathryn, and Witherspoon has even less to show, but Ryan Philippe is simply irresistible in the John Malkovich role. TCh

Cruel Passion

(1977, GB, 97 min)
d/p Chris Boger. *sc* Ian Cullen. *ph* Roger Deakins. *ed* Peter Delfgou. *pd* Tony Curtis. *cast* Koo Stark, Lydia Lisle, Martin Potter, Hope Jackman, Katherine Kath, Maggie Petersen.

● The improbabilities of this awkward period sexploiter (which vainly attempts to emulate the look of *Barry Lyndon*) are compounded by a strain of casual nastiness which would be thoroughly offensive were it not so carelessly handled. Two sisters are expelled from a nunnery; one takes to harlotry, the other hangs on to her virginity, only to be raped in the last reel prior to being torn to pieces by Doberman Pinschers. Drawn from Sade, the film is veneered with a spurious morality which supposedly made its catchpenny cruelty somehow acceptable to the censor. JPy

Cruel Sea, The

(1952, GB, 126 min, b/w)
d Charles Frend. *p* Leslie Norman. *sc* Eric Ambler. *ph* Gordon Dines. *ed* Peter Tanner. *ad* Jim Morahan. *m* Alan Rawsthorne. *cast* Jack Hawkins, Donald Sinden, Stanley Baker, John Stratton, Denholm Elliott, Virginia McKenna, Moira Lister, Liam Redmond, Alec McCowen.

● A sterling, old-fashioned war film of the type too readily devalued these days. Jack Hawkins gives perhaps his most notable performance as the captain of a Royal Navy corvette, suggesting as much life above as below that stiff upper lip, while Eric Ambler's adaptation of Nicholas Monsarrat's book gives the minnows their due as the enlisted men face storms and German U-boats with more courage than experience. Best of all, Frend's documentary style puts us smack in the middle of the Atlantic – the cruel sea indeed. TCh

Cruel Story of the Shogunate's Downfall (Bakumatsu Zankoku Monogatari)

(1964, Jap, 99 min, b/w)
d Tai Kato. *p* Hiroshi Okawa. *sc* Takeo Kunihiro. *ph* Juhei Suzuki. *ed* Katsumi Kawai. *cast* Hashizo Okawa, Junko Fuji, Ryuhei Uchida, Choichiro Kawarazaki, Akira Nishimura.

● Made as a genre quickie, this shatteringly violent movie has entered Japanese film history as a classic anatomy of militarism – and, incidentally, the first movie to be frank about homosexual relations between samurai. Fresh from the countryside, a wide-eyed young man (Okawa, excellent) arrives in Kyoto in 1864 and manages to join the elite Shinsen-gumi. Brutalised physically and mentally during his training but sustained by an illicit liaison with a servant girl (Fuji), he survives to expose the truth about the way the force is run and the very dark secrets in its history. More radical in its way than contemporary 'new wave movies' by the likes of Oshima and Shinoda. TR

Cruise, The

(1998, US, 76 min, b/w)
d/p/sc/ph Bennett Miller. *ed* Michael Levine. *m* Marty Beller. *with* Timothy 'Speed' Levitch.

● This unclassifiable indie feature (a winner on the fest circuit) evidently started out as a performance documentary capturing the spiels and routines of Timothy 'Speed' Levitch, an ineffably camp (but self-proclaimed straight) New York City tour guide. He approaches each bus ride through the metropolis as a new situationist experiment in psycho-geography, treating bemused tourists alternately to waspish putdowns of buildings and their former residents and floods of free association between his own (sad) life and the universe. Some of his patter is pretty droll, so it's understandable that Miller periodically takes off from it into visual fantasias rather like the little 'city poems' underground film-makers used to churn out in the 1950s. Ultimately, though, your response to the movie depends on your response to Levitch himself. TR

Cruising

(1980, US, 106 min)
d William Friedkin. *p* Jerry Weintraub. *sc* William Friedkin. *ph* James A Contner. *ed* Bud Smith. *pd* Bruce Weintraub. *m* Jack Nitzsche. *cast* Al Pacino, Paul Sorvino, Karen Allen, Richard Cox, Don Scardino, Joe Spinell.

● Starting from a classic undercover premise (Pacino descends into Manhattan's SM gay underworld to track a psychopathic killer), and opening with some powerful moments, Cruising soon drifts into bloody Village People-type caricature, with Pacino overplaying his nameless angst as the script patently refuses to tackle the central issue – its hero's sexual ambivalence. The structure continues to loosen, and although Friedkin – like Coppola – has always had difficulty with endings, this one is so arbitrary it's as if he just gave up. DP

Crumb

(1995, US, 120 min)
d Terry Zwigoff. *p* Lynn O'Donnell, Terry Zwigoff. *ph* Maryse Alberti. *ed* Victor Livingston. *with* Robert Crumb, Aline Kominsky, Charles Crumb, Maxon Crumb, Robert Hughes, Martin Muller, Don Donaghue, Dana Crumb, Trina Robbins, Spain Rodriguez.

● At four, Robert Crumb would hump his mother's cowboy boots while singing 'Jesus Loves Me'. At six, he developed a sexual attraction to Bugs Bunny. At 17, he became driven by an obsession: to take his revenge on the alpha-males of his school by going down in history as a great artist. Crumb was an unlikely hero of the '60s counterculture, but strips like *Fritz the Cat*, *Mr Natural* and *Keep on Truckin'* made him the toast of Haight-Ashbury. More interesting still is his later, confessional work, analysed and berated in the film by a series of female comic pundits and ex-girlfriends. So far, so good, but when focusing on Crumb's relationship with his two brothers the documentary occasionally goes off the rails to become a prurient, though undeniably fascinating, freakshow. Still, it remains an outstandingly interesting portrait of obsession and genius. DW

Crush

see Kung Fu Fighting

Crush

(1992, NZ, 97 min)
d Alison Maclean. *p* Bridget Ikin. *sc* Alison Maclean, Anne Kennedy. *ph* Dion Beebe. *ed* John Gilbert. *pd* Meryl Cronin. *m* JPS Experience, Antony Partos. *cast* Marcia Gay Harden, Donogh Rees, Caitlin Bossley, William Zappa, Pete Smith.

● An intriguing and often impressive debut feature in which, following a car crash, the driver (Harden) – a predatory young American – takes the place of her injured literary critic friend (Rees), then insinuates herself into the home and hearts of a famous writer (Zappa) and his teenage daughter (Bossley). A study in deceit, manipulation, obsession and awakening awareness, Maclean's film starts unsteadily – the narrative a mite too elliptical and enigmatic for its own good – but slowly resolves itself into a powerful if faintly overheated melodrama. Beautifully performed, however, and shot with a great deal of dramatic resonance in a bleak, dank New Zealand countryside full of glooping geysers and precarious footholds. GA

Crush, The

(1993, US, 89 min)
d Alan Shapiro. *p* James G Robinson. *sc* Alan Shapiro. *ph* Bruce Surtees, Ian Crafford. *ed* Ian Crafford. *pd* Michael Bolton. *m* Graeme Revell. *cast* Cary Elwes, Alicia Silverstone, Jennifer Rubin, Amber Benson, Kurtwood Smith, Gwynyth Walsh.

● A harmless sex-teaser, from a first-time writer/director, which develops into a confused, cynical and third-rate exploitationer. Upcoming journalist Nick Eliot (Elwes) cruises into Seattle in his bashed-up jalopy to take up a job at *Pique* magazine. Fortune finds him accommodation with a wealthy family whose 14-year-old daughter Darian (Silverstone), a would-be Lolita, soon despatches her mate to check him out. Leaves much to be desired. WH

Crush Proof

(1998, GB/Neth/Ire, 93 min)
d Paul Tickell. *p* Kees Kasander. *sc* James Mathers. *ph* Reinier van Brummelen. *ed* Catherine Creed, Chris Wyatt. *pd* Tom Conroy. *m* Attie Bauw, Alen Svetopetric, Aleksandar Radojcic. *cast* Darren Healy, Viviana Verveen, Jeff O'Toole, Mark Dunne, Michael McElhatton, Lisa Fleming, Mary Murray, Fiona Glascott.

● Just out of the Dublin slammer, Neal (Healy) has reincarceration snapping at his heels, no matter where he bolts. His ex-girl calls the cops when he tries to break down her door for a first sight of his son; a righteous copper harasses him over the mobile phone Neal then steals from a passer-by; and by nightfall he's at the centre of a manhunt after a punishment mock hanging of the boy who betrayed him goes wrong. At least his gang, pony kids living around a sink estate on the city's fringes, rally round as he contemplates quitting his hometown – though his best friend Liam (O'Toole) choosing this moment to take up with sassy stable lass Nuala (Verveen), Neal's deeply estranged half-sister and ex-lover, certainly complicates matters. Despite the in-your-face semi-vérité style, with an epileptic selection of urgently modern audio pyrotechnics obtruding from the soundtrack, the working class Irish setting is used merely as picturesque milieu. The myriad relationships often seem impenetrably inbred, actions range from implausible to inexplicable, and the plot is fraught with undirected bombast and melodramatic contrivance. NB

Crusoe

(1988, US, 94 min)
d Caleb Deschanel. *p* Andrew Braunsberg. *sc* Walon Green, Christopher Logue. *ph* Tomislav Pinter. *ed* Humphrey Dixon. *pd* Viejko Despotovic. *m* Michael Kamen. *cast* Aidan Quinn, Ade Sapara, Warren Clarke, Hepburn Graham, Shane Rimmer, Elvis Payne, Jimmy Nail, Timothy Spall.

● Deschanel's intriguing variation on Defoe's novel employs a clever if contrived anti-colonial twist. After a storm, ruthless slave-trader Crusoe (Quinn) is washed up on a desert island, where he develops survival skills and a capacity for solitude. The footsteps in the sand and the obsequious Friday, however, are nowhere to be found; instead, he saves a black slave (Graham) intended for human sacrifice by fearsome cannibals, arrogantly christening him Lucky ('I have no one to sell you to'). But the next day he wakes to find himself sharing the island with Lucky's headless corpse and a physically and intellectually superior warrior (Sapara) who is clearly unimpressed by Crusoe's efforts to impose the white man's language, table manners and 'civilised' lifestyle on his own sophisticated culture. On the back foot from the outset, Crusoe is forced to endure various indignities and re-examine his own racist elitism. The film works best when dialogue is kept to a minimum, partly because much of it is embarrassingly bad, partly because the island's exotic beauty and the dynamics of the pair's relationship are best conveyed through Deschanel's meticulous attention to telling visual minutiae. NF

Cruz, La

see Cross, The

Cry-Baby

(1990, US, 85 min)
d John Waters. *p* Rachel Talalay. *sc* John Waters. *ph* David Insley. *ed* Janice Hampton. *ad* Vincent Peranio. *m* Patrick Williams. *cast* Johnny Depp, Amy Locane, Susan Tyrell, Iggy Pop, Traci Lords, Patty Hearst, Polly Bergen, Troy Donahue, Mink Stole, Joe Dallesandro, Joey Heatherton, Willem Dafoe.

● An energetic and hyperactively hormonal romp through '50s kitsch from trash-master Waters. In Baltimore, 1954, the town's youth are divided into Squares and Drapes, the latter presided over by gang-leader Wade 'Cry Baby' Walker (Depp), orphaned son of the electrocuted Alphabet bomber. When Cry Baby ('That's *Mister* Baby to you!') falls for lithesome daughter-of-wealth Allison Vernon-Williams (Locane), she is sucked into a world of 'coloured' music, skin-tight slacks and reckless driving, from which her erstwhile companions seek to extract her forthwith. Replete with a thumpingly good soundtrack mixing old standards with modern pastiches, this is Waters' finest film to date, a worthy successor to *Hairspray* which exudes teen angst and young lust from every pore. Cameos from notable degenerates Iggy Pop and Traci Lords beautifully complement Depp's spunkily hollow-cheeked performance, while Patty Hearst plays the American middle class nightmare to a tee. Seriously sexy stuff. MK

Cry Danger

(1951, US, 79 min, b/w)
d Robert Parrish. *p* Sam Wiesenthal, WR Frank. *sc* Robert Parrish, William Bowers. *ph* Joseph Biroc. *ed* Bernard W Burton. *ad* Richard Day. *m* Emil Newman, Paul Dunlap. *cast* Dick Powell, Rhonda Fleming, Richard Erdman, William Conrad, Jean Porter, Regis Toomey, Jay Adler.

● A former child actor (*City Lights*) and celebrated editor (for Ford; an Oscar-winner for *Body and Soul*), Parrish directed one masterpiece (*The Wonderful Country*), one almost-masterpiece (*The Purple Plain*) and a gallery of engaging, civilised movies before getting tangled in the shoals of the swinging British '60s. His major theme is of a man seeking not so much an identity as a place to belong, and here, in his directorial debut, the theme lurks behind a low-budget thriller framework as ex-bookie Powell exits the slammer to get revenge on the bad guys who put him there. Shot in 22 days (Parrish rewrote the script with William Bowers), it's the kind of movie in which, told to expect someone extra for dinner, delicious Fleming smiles 'OK, I'll put more water in the soup'. With excellent support players like a young, thin (for him) William Conrad and Jay Adler, this is a fast, crisp and laconic delight. CW

Cry Freedom

(1987, GB, 158 min)
d/p Richard Attenborough. *sc* John Briley. *ph* Ronnie Taylor. *ed* Lesley Walker. *pd* Stuart Craig. *m* George Fenton, Jonas Gwangwa. *cast* Kevin Kline, Penelope Wilton, Denzel Washington, John Hargreaves, Alec McCowen, Kevin McNally, Zakes Moke, Ian Richardson.

● Donald Woods (Kline), editor of the *Daily Dispatch*, following the publication of a critical article on black activist Steve Biko (Washington), is challenged to meet him, and is won over. After Biko's brutal murder by the South African police, Woods refuses to accept the official cause of death (hunger strike) and campaigns for a full public enquiry. Viciously persecuted along with his wife and family, he finds that flight is the only answer. The initial stages of this epic movie are somewhat stodgy, but once Attenborough achieves his momentum there's no holding him. The performances are excellent, the crowd scenes astonishing, and the climax truly nerve-wracking. An implacable work of authority and compassion, Cry Freedom is political cinema at its best. MS

Cry from the Grave, A

see Srebrenica: A Cry from the Grave

Cry from the Mountain

(1986, US, 90 min)
d James F Collier. *p* William F Brown. *sc* Daniel L Quick. *ph* Gary D Baker. *ed/pd* J Michael Hooser. *m* JAC Redford. *cast* James Cavan, Wes Parker, Rita Walter, Chris Kidd, Coleen Gray, Jerry Ballew.

● When Parker takes his ten-year-old son on a canoeing trip in the Alaskan wilderness to break the news of his impending divorce, he bashes his head when their kayak collapses. An old mountain dweller (Cavan) comes to the rescue, and – he's an ardent evangelist – accompanies the pair home, where he convinces the wife (Walter) to go to a Billy Graham crusade. The sermon convinces her, like her hospitalised husband, that there is a way to solve their problems. She and her son are born again, the old man is born again, and the viewer is invited by Graham's voice to follow suit. It's a well-worn weepie formula, but there's little in the simplistic working out of the plot or the idea of salvation as an all-round happy ending to move sceptics very far. EP

Crying Freeman

(1995, Fr/Can/US/Jap, 102 min)
d Christophe Gans. *p* Samuel Hadida, Brian Yuzna. *sc* Christopher Gans, Thierry Cazals. *ph* Thomas Burstyn. *ed* Christopher Roth. *pd* Douglas Higgins, Alex McDowell. *m* Patrick O'Hearn. *cast* Mark Dacascos, Julie Condra, Rae Dawn Chong, Byron Mann, Tcheky Karyo, Masaya Kato.

●Based on an epic Japanese comic book of rare intelligence and detail, this is almost too reverential towards its source material: several sequences inspire déjà vu, having literally been story-boarded in the original manga; and both Dacascos, as the eponymous Chinese assassin who cries when he makes a hit, and Condra, as the virgin who falls for the soft-hearted hard man, look the part uncannily. Director Gans tries honourably to put the Art into martial arts, but comes fatally unstuck. Though slo-mo fight sequences distance the action from your traditional Jackie Chan beat-'em-ups, you find yourself longing for some good, old-fashioned shit-kicking. When we finally get it, and discover that Dacascos not only looks like Johnny Depp on steroids, but that he could whup Jean-Claude Van Damme's sorry ass as Hollywood's next action hero, you just wonder what took him so long. DW

Crying Game, The

(1992, GB, 112 min)
d Neil Jordan. *p* Stephen Woolley. *sc* Neil Jordan. *ph* Ian Wilson. *ed* Kant Pan. *m* Anne Dudley. *cast* Forest Whitaker, Miranda Richardson, Stephen Rea, Adrian Dunbar, Jaye Davidson, Breffini McKenna, Joe Savino, Birdie Sweeney, Jim Broadbent, Tony Slattery.

●Drunk at a South Armagh fairground, black British soldier Jody (Whitaker) is abducted by the IRA and held hostage on a farm. His jailer Fergus (Rea) comes to respect and understand his prisoner, and after an army raid, heads for London to seek out Jody's lover, hairdresser and chanteuse Dil (Davidson)... It's perhaps surprising that Jordan's thriller hangs together at all. After the opening carnival scene, it virtually turns into a statically theatrical two-hander; then, when Fergus reaches London, both locations and focus become more diffuse as the narrative steadily winds itself up for a bloody finale. There's a problem not only in the clumsy structure, but in Jordan's determination to keep surprising us with twists. Even though the whole is never more than the sum of its parts, the film does work, raises a plethora of questions concerning loyalty, violence and the nature of desire, and is in some respects a summation of the various themes that have emerged from Jordan's work. GA

Cry in the Dark, A

(1988, Aust, 121 min)
d Fred Schepisi. *p* Verity Lambert. *sc* Robert Caswell, Fred Schepisi. *ph* Ian Baker. *ed* Jill Bilcock. *pd* Wendy Dickson, George Liddle. *m* Bruce Smeaton. *cast* Meryl Streep, Sam Neill, Charles Tingwell, Kevin Miles, Jim Holt, Nick Tate.

●On a family camping trip, Lindy Chamberlain (Streep) sees a dingo emerge from the tent and finds her baby gone. A torchlight search ensues, and a bloody baby suit is discovered. Lindy and her husband Michael (Neill) go on TV, and seize the opportunity to plug their Seventh Day Adventist faith, which does not go down well. They don't seem to be grieving. Australia takes against this unnervingly self-contained victim of disaster. The press go for the jugular, the Australian public ridicule the dingo story, and the couple go on trial for murder. Schepisi's matter-of-fact direction and the rather undernourished screenplay don't mine much beyond the lousiness of the press and the unknowableness of the victims, but Streep (the best thing she has done in ages) carries it along. BC.

Cry of the Banshee

(1970, GB, 87 min)
d/p Gordon Hessler. *sc* Tim Kelly, Christopher Wicking. *ph* John Coquillon. *ed* Oswald Hafenrichter. *ad* George Provis. *m* Les Baxter. *cast* Vincent Price, Elisabeth Bergner, Essy Persson, Hugh Griffith, Sally Geeson, Patrick Mower, Hilary Dwyer.

●Screenwriter Chris Wicking's third collaboration with director Hessler is set in 16th century England, where evil spirit Mower exacts revenge on witch-hunting magistrate Price. Despite authentic location work and rather opportunistic flashes of graphic mayhem, this has none of the narrative concision, thematic richness or overall conviction of Michael Reeves' *Witchfinder General*, in which Price and Dwyer also appeared, two years earlier. TJ

Cry of the City

(1948, US, 96 min, b/w)
d Robert Siodmak. *p* Sol C Siegel. *sc* Richard Murphy. *ph* Lloyd Ahern. *ed* Harmon Jones. *ad* Lyle Wheeler, Albert Hogsett. *m* Alfred Newman. *cast* Victor Mature, Richard Conte, Shelley Winters, Fred Clark, Debra Paget, Hope Emerson, Betty Garde.

●Riveting example of Siodmak's skill not only in transforming indifferent material, but in giving the feel of studio *noir* to location shooting. The familiar '30s theme (cop and criminal sharing the same deprived background in New York's Little Italy) acquires an almost metaphysical ring in being displaced by what turns into a literal cry of the city as the wounded gangster (Conte, terrific) goes on the run for the last few hours of his life, leaving behind him a dark trail of murder, pain and betrayal. Rarely has the cruel, lived-in squalor of the city been presented in such telling detail, both in the vivid portrayal of ghetto life and in the astonishing parade of corruption uncovered in the night (a slug-like shyster; a monstrous, sadistic masseuse; a sleazy refugee abortionist, etc). TM

Cry of the Hunted

(1953, US, 95 min, b/w)
d Joseph H Lewis. *p* William Grady Jr. *sc* Jack Leonard. *ph* Harold Lipstein. *ed* Conrad A Nervig. *ad* Cedric Gibbons, Malcolm Brown. *cast* Vittorio Gassman, Barry Sullivan, Polly Bergen, William Conrad, Mary Zavian, Robert Burton.

●Far from Lewis' best, this chase thriller is nevertheless an engagingly taut affair, its various visual flourishes climaxing in a characteristically atmospheric swamp shoot-out (one of several in his work). Gassman is the escaped con who, for none too clear reasons, heads back home to his beloved Louisiana bayous, Sullivan the pursuing lawman with whom he shares a strange bond. Hardly original, but highly enjoyable. GA

Cry of the Owl, The

see Cri du Hibou, Le

Cry of the Penguins

see Mr Forbush and the Penguins

Cry Onion (Cipolla Colt)

(1975, It/Sp/WGer, 91 min)
d Enzo Castellari. *p* Carlo Ponti. *sc* Luciano Vincenzoni, Sergio Donati. *ph* Alejandro Ulloa. *ed* Gianfranco Amicucci. *ad* Alberto Boccianti. *m* Guido de Angelis. *cast* Franco Nero, Martin Balsam, Sterling Hayden. Emma Cohen, Duilio Cruciani.

●Attempting to spice up this lamentable slapstick Western, those responsible for the dubbing have foisted an inappropriate James Stewart drawl on freckle-faced Franco Nero (a gormless, onion-eating fanatic who refuses to sell a patch of land to Balsam, an oil baron with a dart-firing mechanical hand), while his juvenile sidesick spouts Al Pacino Brooklynese. Nero spends most of the movie throwing onions at the baddies, or rendering them unconscious with his malodorous breath. JPy

Crystal Gazing

(1982, GB, 92 min)
d/sc Laura Mulvey, Peter Wollen. *ph* Diane Tammes. *ed* Larry Sider. *ad* Mick Hurd. *cast* Gavin Richards, Lora Logic, Mary Maddox, Jeff Rawle, Alan Porter, Patrick Bauchau.

●Wollen and Mulvey's most narrative feature to date marks time in London during the Thatcher recession as it follows (and digresses from) the paths of two men who have less of a future than the two women who make up the centre of the film. The main object of its makers is to make connections, placed somewhere between Brecht and Breton, in a city where the wires are either crossed or the lines down and things are falling apart under Thatcher, leaving only isolated pockets of activity. If the subject matter is dour, tragic even according to Wollen and Mulvey, they take pains to disrupt the sombreness with deliberate levities, and their playfulness in establishing connections recalls early Godard. Its achievements are to show how life proceeds at different rhythms, not often caught in fiction, and to make everything in the film so clearly recognisable – for once the title says it all. CPe

Crystal Voyager

(1974, US, 78 min)
d George Greenough. *p* David Elfick. *sc* George Greenough. *ph* George Greenough, Albert Falzon. *m* Pink Floyd. *narrator* George Greenough.

●Boring surfing film saved by the last twenty minutes, the only segment with music by Pink Floyd and actually shot from a surfboard.

Cry Uncle (aka Super Dick)

(1971, US, 87 min)
d John G Avildsen. *p* David Jay Disick. *sc* David Odell. *ph/ed* John G Avildsen. *ad* Henry Shrady. *m* Harper MacKay. *cast* Allen Garfield, Madeleine Le Roux, David Kirk, Devin Goldenberg, Deborah Morgan, Nancy Salmon

●Perhaps the least likely candidate ever for the 'extended version' trend is Avildsen's early cheapo feature: a contemporary of *Joe*, but made before the respectability of *Save the Tiger*, the bankability of *Rocky*, or the honour of removal from *Saturday Night Fever*. First released here as *Super Dick*, in deference to Garfield's private eye/cocksman role, it re-emerged with its original US title and ten minutes of footage restored to its choppy continuity. A bizarre soft-core comedy-thriller, its frantically parodic sexual anarchism is of a pretty reactionary species, and even the guilty guffaws sometimes obstinately refuse to come; though Garfield's gargoyle slob is definitely one for the Divine crowd to savour. PT

Cry Wolf

(1947, US, 83 min, b/w)
d Peter Godfrey. *p* Henry Blanke. *sc* Catherine Turney. *ph* Carl Guthrie. *ed* Folmar Blangstead. *ad* Carl Jules Weyl. *m* Franz Waxman. *cast* Barbara Stanwyck, Errol Flynn, Geraldine Brooks, Richard Basehart, John Ridgely, Jerome Cowan.

●Stanwyck makes a brave attempt as the woman in peril in this old dark house thriller with its creaky plot about her coming to claim the inheritance of her recently deceased husband and suspecting that his uncle (Flynn) may have murdered him. The twists in the plot don't really improve matters much, but the cast is generally watchable, if wasted. GA

Cry-Woman (Kuqi Nüren)

(2002, Can/SKor/Fr, 91 min)
d Liu Bingjian. *p* Deng Ye, Ellen Kim, Michel Reilhac, Jason Chae. *sc* Liu Bingjian, Deng Ye. *ph* Xu Wei. *ed* Zhou Ying. *ad* Liu Liguo. *m* Dong Liqiang. *cast* Liao Qin, Wei Xingkun, Li Longjun, Wen Jing, Wu Wengli, Zhou Yihui.

●Illegally resident in Beijing, Wang Guixiang (Liao) scratches a living hawking pirated VCDs until everything goes wrong: the cops confiscate her stock, her husband (Li) is imprisoned for assault and the neighbours do a bunk, leaving her literally holding their baby. Sent back to her country-town home by the authorities, she runs into a former boyfriend (Wei) who suggests that she'd make a good 'cry-woman' – a professional mourner who sings and wails for hire at funerals. Liu tried to set this up as a legal production, but when the China Film Bureau vetoed the script made it as a foreign-financed underground indie. The approach (non-pro cast, semi-improvised scenes, protracted wide-angle shots) and the small town setting make it very 'school of Jia Zhangke', and some narrative elisions seem more clumsy than inspired. But the central idea – a woman expresses her own pain only by performing at strangers' funerals – is a good one, and Liao's hard-as-nails performance as Guixiang is up there with Alia's in *Ermo* as an icon of female strength, will and resilience. TR

CS Blues

(1972, US, 95 min)
d Robert Frank, Daniel Seymour. *with* The Rolling Stones, Dick Cavett, Lee Radziwill, Truman Capote, Stevie Wonder, Andy Warhol.

●It's *Cocksucker Blues* of course, a film made of the Rolling Stones on tour in North America, 1972 (at the time of their excellent *Exile On Main Street* LP). It has acquired considerable cult status, largely on account of the group's reluctance to have it shown – whether because they are portrayed as Satanic Majesties, or just an above-average rock group, is not altogether clear. There is some intravenous use of heroin, not by the principal characters, natch, and some mucking about with groupies. There are also some well composed and shot concert sequences, but what the film does best is present a picture of the mini-society that attached itself to the group at its peak. A pretty dismal society it is, too. For fans this is practically unmissable, but less partisan voyeurs are likely to concur with guitarist Mick Taylor's observation on one of the many dreary drug-taking scenes: 'I've never seen a hotel room filled with such Olympian ecstasy.' He's joking. MC

Cuba

(1979, US, 122 min)
d Richard Lester. *p* Alex Winitsky, Arlene Sellers. *sc* Charles Wood. *ph* David Watkin. *ed* John Victor Smith. *pd* Gil Parrondo, Philip Harrison. *m* Patrick Williams. *cast* Sean Connery, Brooke Adams, Jack Weston, Hector Elizondo, Denholm Elliott, Martin Balsam, Chris Sarandon, Lonette McKee.

●'Havana, Cuba, 1959'. Lucky they print this on the screen, as it's the first and last coherent piece of information you can glean from Lester's political love story, which mentions neither politics nor love but plays out its actions against a background of both. Confused? So, it would seem, was Lester, for his indecision over making either element dominant produces a central love affair which is hollow, and a revolution which is just so much local colour. Ultimately, it's about corruption, apathy and crumbling values, in all their seedy splendour. Everyone is on the lam: Connery, a mercenary for Batista; Adams, a female cuckold with her eyes wide open, but wedded to wealth and power; Elliott, a crop-sprayer turned gunrunner. Not so much 'Cuba Si' as Cuba…what? FF

Cuba Libre – Velocipedi ai Tropici

(1996, It/Cuba, 88 min)
d David Riondino. *sc* David Riondino, Roberto Duiz, Francesco Bruni, Paolo Virzi. *ph* Federico Schatter. *ed* Mauro Bonanni. *m* David Riondino. *cast* David Riondino, Sabina Guzzanti, Antonio Catania, Dario Cassini, Bjliana Bosniakovic, Remo Remotti.

●This putative update of *Bicycle Thieves* is full of rambling but seductive incident. It focuses on the arrival in Havana of a plane load of Italians: a venal promo director seeking revolutionary posters and poverty as a backdrop to shoe commercials; a bossy 'capitalist' setting up a restaurant; a self-obsessed 50-year-old poet forever declaiming his verse from the rooftops; a student come to research Zavattini's Cuban period, who fails to notice a real-life version of the De Sica tale re-run before his eyes. Writer/director Riondino, who also stars, may not turn tourist clichés about Cuba on their heads, but he leads them a merry, salsa seasoned dance. WH

Cube

(1997, Can, 90 min)
d Vincenzo Natali. *p* Mehra Meh, Betty Orr. *sc* Andre Bijelic, Vincenzo Natali, Graeme Manson. *ph* Derek Rogers. *ed* John Sanders. *pd* Jasna Stepfanovic. *m* Mark Korven. *cast* Nicole deBoer, Nicky Guadagni, David Hewlett, Andrew Miller, Julian Richings, Wayne Robson, Maurice Dean Wint.

●Spatially confined but intellectually expansive, this micro budget sci-fi movie is driven by conceptual ideas and narrative tension rather than breathless action and gratuitous explosions. Six apparently unconnected individuals wake up inside a three-dimensional maze of interlocking cubes. None of them knows how they got there, why they have been chosen, or whether they will get out alive. Building tension through skilful use of narrative rhythm and tonal shifts, Natali preserves the underlying enigma of who is behind this deadly conundrum. Is it some deranged scientist, a sinister government agency, or perhaps aliens from outer space? Instead of providing answers, the ingenious script focuses on the seldom altruistic behaviour of those trapped within the maze, revealing that their greatest enemy is not the lethal maze itself, but each other. The absorbing mathematical puzzles, understated allegory, nail-biting suspense and strategic gore more than compensate for some variable acting. NF

Cuerpo en el Bosque

see Body in the Forest, A

Cugini Carnali

see Visitor, The

Cugino Americano, Il

see Blood Ties

Cujo

(1983, US, 91 min)
d Lewis Teague. *p* Daniel H Blatt, Robert Singer. *sc* Don Carlos Dunaway, Lauren Currier. *ph* Jan de Bont. *ed* Neil Travis. *pd* Guy Comtois. *m* Charles Bernstein. *cast* Dee Wallace, Daniel Hugh-Kelly, Danny Pintauro, Christopher Stone, Ed Lauter, Kaiulani Lee.

●This adaptation on a modest budget from Stephen King's bestseller about a rabid St Bernard is a pleasing illustration of the filmic simplicity at the heart of King's better writing. Any old pulp writer can trap heroine and child in a broken-down car menaced by a vicious dog, but it takes a King to spot the enormous advantage of keeping them there for two-thirds of the book. Fortunately Teague follows his lead, making considerable visual and narrative mileage out of the struggle between dog and car, as his actors scream and cry their way through the movie with commendably little shame. But for all its ingenuity, *Cujo* does lose an awful lot of ground from the fact that rabid St Bernards tend to evoke pity rather than terror. Perhaps that explains why the film's US earnings would buy few dog biscuits. DP

Cul-de-Sac

(1966, GB, 111 min, b/w)
d Roman Polanski. *p* Gene Gutowski. *sc* Roman Polanski, Gérard Brach. *ph* Gilbert Taylor. *ed* Alastair McIntyre. *pd* Voytek Roman. *m* Krzysztof Komeda. *cast* Donald Pleasence, Françoise Dorléac, Lionel Stander, Jack MacGowran, Robert Dorning, Iain Quarrier, Jacqueline Bisset.

●Shot through with the same surreal, absurdist wit as Polanski's shorts, this bizarre variation on a classic theme – a couple who have withdrawn from the world (Pleasence and Dorléac) to live on an isolated island are visited by gangsters on the run (Stander and MacGowran) – centres around the director's abiding concerns: sexual perversity, insecurity and humiliation, the eruption of nightmarish chaos into a seemingly ordered world, human betrayal, corruptibility and self-destruction. If the subject matter is bleak and bitterly serious, the tone throughout is darkly comic, while the precise imagery effortlessly conveys the tension, the claustrophobia, and the madness of the situation. GA

Culloden

(1964, GB, 71 min, b/w)
d/p/sc Peter Watkins. *ph* Dick Bush. *ed* Michael Bradsell. *pd* Anne Davey, Brendan Woods, Colin MacLeod, John Shaw. *cast* George McBean, Alan Pope, the people of Inverness.

●Watkins' films are compulsively interesting almost in spite of themselves. His *oeuvre* may be characterised as a progression from polemical hysteria towards formal paranoia, yet it is impossible to deny his films their emotive, affective power, derived from an innovatory manipulation of technique. *Culloden* (made for TV) exhibits Watkins' virtues and vices in about equal proportions, but takes on a critical centrality as an initiator of the 'drama-doc' strain of British TV. These quasi-newsreels of the past and future, feeding off the documentary tradition to bolster the 'realism' of their speculative fictions, and usurping the medium's primary resources for capturing 'actuality' to present reconstructions, effectively efface their artifice by playing on the 'integrity' of certain strategies of representation. Yet Watkins must still here rely on an omniscient/propagandist commentary to convey the contextual discourses around his 'horror movies': a problem superseded in his later, similar, but increasingly worrying work. PT

Culpepper Cattle Co., The

(1972, US, 92 min)
d Dick Richards. *p* Paul Helmick. *sc* Eric Bercovici, Gregory Prentiss. *ph* Lawrence Edward Williams, Ralph Woolsey. *ed* John F Burnett. *ad* Jack Martin Smith, Carl Anderson. *m* Tom Scott, Jerry Goldsmith. *cast* Gary Grimes, Billy Green Bush, Luke Askew, Bo Hopkins, Geoffrey Lewis, Wayne Sutherlin, Matt Clark.

●Engaging 'demythologising' Western, with Grimes as the naive young Texan who joins a cattle drive with romantic dreams of the cowboy life, only to have them dashed as he encounters death, crime and compromise. Deliberately downbeat, aided no end in its aims at authenticity by the excellent photography (Lawrence Edward Williams and Ralph Woolsey). GA

Culture Club – A Kiss Across the Ocean

(1984, GB, 64 min)
d Keith MacMillan. *with* Culture Club: Boy George, Jon Moss, Ron Hay, Mikey Craig.

●Filmed in December 1983 at the band's Hammersmith Odeon gig (and first released on video), this features all their singles and material from both albums. The picture quality is superb, due no doubt to the special equipment used in the filming, but that's more than can be said for the digital-sound mix. The drums dominate most of the time (probably because drummer Jon Moss mixed it), with George and Helen Terry's vocals often lost in the sea of scream from adoring fans. Other than that, a tight, well-paced show. DA

Cumbres borrascosas

see Abismos de pasión

Cup, The (Phörpa)

(1999, Aust, 94 min)
d Khyentse Norbu. *p* Malcolm Watson, Raymond Steiner. *sc* Khyentse Norbu. *ph* Paul Warren. *ed* John Scott. *pd* Raymond Steiner. *m* Douglas Mills. *cast* Kunsang Nyima, Pema Tshundup, Jamyang Lodro, Neten Chokling, Orgyen Tobgyal, Lama Chonjor.

●Writer/director Norbu is Bhutanese and this, his first feature, is an affecting story about football and Buddhism. Shot at an Indian monastery, the film uses only monks as actors. Fearful of the Chinese regime in Tibet, a family sends its boys Palden (Nyima) and Nyima (Tshundup) to a Buddhist monastery-in-exile in the Himalayan foothills. The boys are distracted from their studies, however, by their room-mates, the football mad Orgyen (Lodro) and his sidekick Lodo (Chokling). The World Cup is on in France. The opening 20 minutes are slow, but matters picks up with the appearance of Orgyen. His single minded efforts to secure a screen on which to watch the cup final, along with his relaxed interpretation of the monastery's rules, breathe life into the story. TH

Cup Final

(1991, Isr, 107 min)
d Eran Riklis. *p* Michael Sharfstein. *sc* Eyal Halfon. *ph* Amnon Salomon. *ed* Anat Lubarsky. *m* Raviv Gazit. *cast* Moshe Ivgi, Muhamad Bacri, Salim Dau, Basam Zuamut, Salim Daou, Yussuf Abu-Warda.

●June, 1982. Israel invades Lebanon. When his squad is ambushed, Sergeant Cohen (Ivgi) is captured by a retreating PLO foot patrol. As the patrol pick their way through the unmarked minefield their country has become, back towards the dubious safety of Beirut, Cohen tries to reach out to his captors. English provides the means, but the real common language proves to be a shared passion for football: Palestinian and Israeli alike are stunned to learn of West Germany's defeat by Algeria in the World Cup finals in Spain, while Cohen's passionate support for Italy commends him to the patrol-leader Ziad (Bacri). Although his gripping, fundamentally humanist movie doesn't break any new ground, Riklis doesn't shirk from the complexity of the Arab-Israeli conflict, maintaining an admirably even-handed political stance as Cohen and Ziad gravitate from mutual incomprehension to grudging respect, with the tension between them never far away. After a slightly stilted opening, Riklis steers confidently between irony, menace and warmth, helped by a uniformly excellent cast. NF

Curdled

(1996, US, 88 min)
d Reb Braddock. *p* John Maass, Raul Puig. *sc* Reb Braddock, John Maass. *ph* Steve Bernstein. *ed* Mallory Gottlieb. *pd* Sherman Williams. *m* Joseph Julian Gonzalez. *cast* Angela Jones, William Baldwin, Bruce Ramsay, Mel Gorham, Lois Chiles, Daisy Fuentes.
●In 1992, while doing the rounds with *Reservoir Dogs*, Tarantino saw a short which he later encouraged director Reb Braddock to expand to a feature. The result is this smart, over-stretched black comedy about a young Latino woman, Gabriela (Jones), who gratifies her morbid obsession with murder by working for a cleaning company that specialises in mopping up its gruesome aftermath. The childlike quality of Gabriela's macabre fascination is deftly sketched, as she pores over her collection of newspaper cuttings or tries to recreate the choreography of death suggested by the chalk marks, bullet holes and blood stains. Fantasy and reality finally merge when she comes face to face with the Blue Blood Killer, a smooth sociopath (played with icy charm by Baldwin) who preys on wealthy women. In a confrontation filmed as a single four-and-a-half-minute shot, the killer forces her to re-enact the dance of death implied by the murder scene, from both the victim's and the assailant's point of view. This bravura sequence virtually justifies the price of admission, but elsewhere the congealed blood is spread a little too thinly, a deficiency only partly made up for by a catchy, Spanish-influenced soundtrack. NF

Cure

(1997, Jap, 115 min)
d Kiyoshi Kurosawa. *p* Tetsuya Ikeda, Satoshi Kanno. *sc* Kiyoshi Kurosawa. *ph* Tokusho Kikumura. *ed* Kan Suzuki. *pd* Tomoyuki Maruo. *m* Gary Ashiya. *cast* Koji Yakusho, Tsuyoshi Ujiki, Masato Hagiwara, Anna Nakagawa.
●Rumpled cop Takabe (Yakusho), whose wife is cracking up, investigates a rash of inexplicable murders; in each case the murderer can't say why he or she did it – or why it was necessary to carve a large 'X' on the victim's body. The common factor turns out to be contact with Mamiya (Hagiwara), a drop-out from med school, now a seemingly helpless drifter. And when Mamiya is brought in for questioning, Takabe seems next in line to fall under his malign spell. Kurosawa's dark thriller owes too much to other recent movies (the murderous mind games from *Angel Dust*, the police-procedural blues from *MARKS*) and the metaphysical climax doesn't convince. But it's well enough acted and directed to advance Kurosawa's claim to be taken as an important new voice in Japanese cinema. TR

Cure, The

(1995, US, 97 min)
d Peter Horton. *p* Mark Burg, Eric Eisner. *sc* Robert Kuhn. *ph* Andrew Dintenfass. *ed* Anthony Sherin. *pd* Armin Ganz. *m* David Grusin. *cast* Brad Renfro, Diana Scarwid, Joseph Mazzello, Bruce Davison, Aeryk Egan.
●Stillwater, Minnesota: Erik (Renfro) lives alone with his sourpuss mom Gail (Scarwid). He's bored. Next door is Dexter (Mazzello), who has AIDS. The two 11-year-olds have never met – Gail's too bigoted – but that doesn't stop the lads at school from dubbing Erik 'homo' and generally cramping his social options. So he figures, what the hell, may as well jump over the fence and strike up a friendship; next thing, the pair are inseparable. Gail finds out, threatens to take Erik away, and so the boys board a raft for a wholly irresponsible escapade, heading downriver to New Orleans where, claims a *National Examiner* headline, a Dr Fishburne has found a miracle cure for AIDS. A first feature from a 'thirty-something' actor: well played, lots of jaunty episodes, unobtrusively squidgy emotions, a good cry at the end. The real weakness arises from the weepie format itself. There's never any ambition here to delve into those more interesting facets of the story littered around its edges. Avoids the worst excesses of mawkishness, but essentially just the usual mix of life-affirming, flabby humanist hogwash. NB

Cure in Orange, The

(1987, GB, 114 min)
d Tim Pope. *p* Gordon Lewis. *ph* Chris Ashbrook. *ed* Peter Goddard. *songs* The Cure. *with* The Cure: Robert Smith, Laurence Tolhurst, Simon Gallup, Porl Thompson, Boris Williams.
●An astonishingly lavish production number for one of the world's less dynamic live bands, rendered noteworthy by its setting against the magnificent backdrop of an ancient amphitheatre (the Théâtre Antique d'Orange in France). Smith, in a non-stop run through their best-known numbers, proves that he is not one of the world's great frontmen, but for Cure fans this is as perfect and cinematographically compelling a record of a gig as could be asked for. For the rest of us, it's a bit of a yawn. DPe

Cure Show, The

(1993, GB, 96 min, b/w & col)
d Aubrey Powell, Leroy Bennett. *with* The Cure.
●The Cure have spent 15 years championing the ultimate shoe-shuffling indie music for staying in to, so it's perhaps strange that this is their *second* live film. Mumbling into the microphone from behind a guitar and tumbleweed haircut, leadman Robert Smith carries these huge concerts surprisingly well, and this is an attractive, well-shot movie of a colourful (if not imaginatively) staged concert (Palace Stadium, Detroit, July 1992). The songs range from 'Let's Go to Bed' to 'Never Enough'. Even fans of trendy bands, it seems, get their lighters out for the slowies. LD

Curly Sue

(1991, US, 102 min)
d/p/sc John Hughes. *ph* Jeffrey Kimball. *ed* Peck Prior, Harvey Rosenstock. *pd* Doug Kraner. *m* Georges Delerue. *cast* James Belushi, Kelly Lynch, Alisan Porter, John Getz, Fred Dalton Thompson, Cameron Thor.
●Tousle-haired orphan Curly Sue (Porter) and her down-and-out guardian Bill (Belushi), are carrying out a tried-and-tested scam which involves deliberately colliding with an expensive car to elicit favours from the remorseful driver. As luck would have it, their latest victim is a posh, high-powered lawyer (Lynch). The first collision brings free grub, but a second, unintentional encounter also brings accommodation in her apartment, new wardrobes for both, and – bingo! – romance. From the opening montage of childhood moments through to the contrived resolution, this is utterly formulaic. Hughes' leaden direction and script give no hint of the skill that distinguishes his best work. CM

Curse of Frankenstein, The

(1957, GB, 82 min)
d Terence Fisher. *p* Anthony Hinds. *sc* James Sangster. *ph* Jack Asher. *ed* James Needs. *ad* Edward Marshall. *m* James Bernard. *cast* Peter Cushing, Christopher Lee, Hazel Court, Robert Urquhart, Valerie Gaunt, Noel Hood.
●The first of the Hammer Frankensteins, bringing blood and amputated limbs to the story but cursed with an inept make-up for Lee's monster (Jack Pierce's Karloff creation was copyright). The whole thing in fact looks surprisingly tacky for a film which sparked a box-office bonanza. Fisher's voluptuous use of colour was much more assured in the following year's *Dracula*. TM

Curse of Greed, The

see Twin Pawns

Curse of the Cat People, The

(1944, US, 70 min, b/w)
d Robert Wise, Gunther von Fritsch. *p* Val Lewton. *sc* DeWitt Bodeen, Val Lewton. *ph* Nick Musuraca. *ed* Jack Whittredge. *ad* Albert S D'Agostino, Walter Keller. *m* Roy Webb. *cast* Simone Simon, Ann Carter, Kent Smith, Elizabeth Russell, Julia Dean, Jane Randolph, Sir Lancelot.
●Though very different in purpose and tone to *Cat People*, Val Lewton's 'sequel' is far more closely tied to its predecessor than is commonly believed. For one thing, all the main characters remain very much the same as they were in the earlier film, to which there are many specific references; for another, both films concern the way that guilt, fear and fantasy can arise from isolation and misunderstanding. In this case, it's a small girl, lonely and repeatedly scolded by her parents and shunned by her friends for indulging in day-dreaming; when she populates her solitary world with the ghost of her father's dead first wife (Simon, heroine of *Cat People*), her imagination (or is it?) gets her into serious trouble. Far from being a horror film, it's a touching, perceptive and lyrical film about childhood, psychologically astute and occasionally disturbing as it focuses entirely on the child's-eye view of a sad, cruel world. GA

Curse of the Crimson Altar (aka The Crimson Cult)

(1968, GB, 89 min)
d Vernon Sewell. *p* Louis M Heyward. *sc* Mervyn Haisman, Henry Lincoln. *ph* John Coquillon. *ed* Howard Lanning. *ad* Derek Barrington. *m* Peter Knight. *cast* Boris Karloff, Christopher Lee, Mark Eden, Virginia Wetherell, Barbara Steele, Rupert Davies, Michael Gough.
●A shoddy horror pic, notable only as the 81-year-old Karloff's last completed feature. Robert Manning (Eden) traces his vanished brother to Craxted Lodge in the village of Greymarsh, but the owner (Lee) – in fact taking revenge against the Manning family on behalf of a witch ancestor, Lavinia (Steele), burned in the 17th century – denies all knowledge of him. Robert has strange dreams featuring Steele, her face painted green, her lips blood-red, and wearing a ram's horn headpiece; but he and his girlfriend (Wetherell) are ultimately saved by a wheelchair-bound witchcraft expert (Karloff). The story has (uncredited) similarities to HP Lovecraft's *Dream in the Witch House*, but director Sewell never gets to grips with the muddled script. NF

Curse of the Demon

see Night of the Demon

Curse of the Mummy's Tomb, The

(1964, GB, 80 min)
d/p/sc Michael Carreras. *ph* Otto Heller. *ed* Eric Boyd-Perkins. *ad* Bernard Robinson. *m* Carlo Martelli. *cast* Ronald Howard, Terence Morgan, Fred Clark, Jeanne Roland, George Pastell, Jack Gwillim, Dickie Owen.
●Limp Hammer sequel to *The Mummy*, with the bandaged one (Owen) escaping from his Pharaoh's sarcophagus when it is excavated and exhibited on tour, going on the rampage in London and ending up in the sewers. Resolutely unimaginative. GA

Curse of the Pink Panther

(1983, GB, 110 min)
d Blake Edwards. *p* Blake Edwards, Tony Adams. *sc* Blake Edwards, Geoffrey Edwards. *ph* Dick Bush. *ed* Ralph E Winters. *pd* Peter Mullins. *m* Henry Mancini. *cast* David Niven, Robert Wagner, Herbert Lom, Joanna Lumley, Capucine, Robert Loggia, Harvey Korman, Burt Kwouk, Ted Wass, Leslie Ash.
●An abysmal cash-in from a bunch of people who really ought to have known better. The Pink Panther diamond has been stolen again, and with Inspector Clouseau missing (Peter Sellers was deceased), a computer conducts a search to find a detective skilled enough to track him down. Twitchy former boss Lom has nobbled the technology, however, so that the world's worst sleuth is selected, whereupon Wass makes the transition from TV's *Soap* for a charisma-free turn as bumbling NYPD man Clifton Sleigh. Intrigue continues apace, with tedious complications and flat slapstick taking in a roster of the series' former stars doing tired cameos. A frail Niven made a last screen appearance. TJ

Curse of the Werewolf, The

(1961 GB, 91 min)
d Terence Fisher. *p* Anthony Hinds. *sc* John Elder [Anthony Hinds]. *ph* Arthur Grant. *ed* James Needs, Alfred Cox. *ad* Bernard Robinson, Tom Goswell. *m* Benjamin Frankel. *cast* Oliver Reed, Yvonne Romain, Catherine Feller, Clifford Evans, Anthony Dawson, Richard Wordsworth, Warren Mitchell.
●The life and times of a lycanthrope down in sunny but sinister Spain, developing the story from the mutant's conception (when a beggar rapes a deaf-mute servant girl), through his early years when he causes church fonts to bubble, to his final death at the hands of a lynch mob incensed by his murders. Sex, naturally, is the catalyst that sets Reed off on his homicidal binges. More ambitious and complex than most Hammer films in its investigation of the opposing forces that rule the life of the monster (though

still a drastic simplification of Guy Endore's marvellous source novel, *The Werewolf of Paris*), but badly lacking in dramatic tension. GA

Curse of the Wraydons, The (aka Stranglers Morgue)

(1946, GB, 94 min, b/w)
d Victor M Gover. *p* Gilbert Church. *sc* Owen George. *ph* SD Onions. *ed* Victor Gover. *m* DeWolfe. *cast* Tod Slaughter, Bruce Seton, Gabriel Toyne, Andrew Lawrence, Lorraine Clewes, Pearl Cameron.

● Adapted by director Gover from the play *Springheeled Jack, the Terror of London*, this is a ridiculously overcooked period melodrama. Slaughter (b. 1885), not as young or nimble as in his Sweeney Todd days, looks a little out of breath as the villain of the piece, a murderous Napoleonic spy with a hatred of all things British. Watching him wobble and roar his way through the film, you can only regret he was never given the chance to work with Ed Wood Jr, the one director who would surely have cherished his pantomime style. GM

Curtain Call

(1997, US, 94 min)
d Peter Yates. *p* Andrew Karsch. *sc* Todd Alcott. *ph* Sven Nykvist. *ed* Hughes Winborne. *pd* Stuart Wurtzel. *m* Richard Hartley. *cast* James Spader, Michael Caine, Maggie Smith, Polly Walker, Buck Henry, Sam Shepard, Marcia Gay Harden, Frances Sternhagen, Valerie Perrine.

● Spader, a publisher with job trouble and a nervous love life, moves into an old house, which, he soon discovers, he's sharing with a couple of bickering ghosts (Caine and Smith). Not a lot happens. Plotting is unadventurous, the dialogue contains about a million words, none of them amusing or clever, and the film curls up and dies in the pauses for laughter which the actors have optimistically allowed after each feeble rally. Spader, lacking the practised insouciance of his co-stars, makes heavy weather of the hero. BBa

Curtain Up

(1952, GB, 82 min, b/w)
d Ralph Smart. *p* Robert Garrett. *sc* Michael Pertwee, Jack Davies. *ph* Stan Pavey. *ed* Douglas Robertson. *ad* Geoffrey Drake. *m* Malcolm Arnold. *cast* Robert Morley, Margaret Rutherford, Olive Sloane, Kay Kendall, Michael Medwin, Liam Gaffney, Joan Rice.

● Intriguing potboiler set in the world of seaside rep (adapted from Philip King's play *On Monday Next*): Morley and Rutherford, two of the dottiest character actors in the British movie firmament, are given rare leading roles. He's a hectoring director, she's the equally stubborn playwright whose latest, quite atrocious work the company's mounting for purely mercenary reasons. GM

Curtis's Charm

(1995, Can, 75 min)
d John L'Ecuyer. *p* Sandra Cunningham. *sc* John L'Ecuyer. *ph* Harald Bachmann. *ed* Craig Webster. *pd* John Dondertman. *m* Mark Korven. *cast* Maurice Dean Wint, Callum Keith Rennie, Rachael Crawford, Barbara Barnes-Hopkins, Hugh Dillon.

● Small but beguiling movie, based on a story by Jim Carroll. A recovering heroin addict runs into an old comrade-in-arms in the park, but Curtis is crawling the bench with fright: he thinks he's being followed by a squirrel. His voodoo juju mother-in-law has put a spell on him, he explains. The man needs a talisman to protect him. Even at 75 minutes this feels over-extended, and the budget evidently didn't stretch to New York locations, but it's a cool, off-the-wall conversation piece, snappily put together with a darkly humorous sense of the metaphysical. TCh

Custard Boys, The

(1979, GB, 82 min)
d/p Colin Finbow. *sc* Kiran Garcha, Colin Finbow. *ph* Colin Finbow. *ad* Jenny Clennell. *m* David Hewson. *cast* Tony Collins, Chris Chescoe, Les Scott, Glenn Dunderdale, Eric Milliet, Peter Setram.

● An Indian summer, 1942: 'When I was thirteen, all I wanted to be was a hero.' A young evacuee's response to the surrounding war-obsessed adult world seems the only one available to him, until he forms 'a particular friendship' with another boy, a Jewish refugee. This threatens the stability of his gang (who also mirror the racist/jingoist attitudes of adulthood), and he is caught in Forster's great liberal crux: your country or your friend? A celebration of all that is lost and found in the process of growth, all the more remarkable for the performances of the boys involved, who act the adults into the ground. CPea

Custer of the West

(1966, US/Sp, 146 min)
d Robert Siodmak. *p* Louis Dolivet, Philip Yordan. *sc* Bernard Gordon, Julian Halevy [Julian Zimet]. *ph* Cecilio Paniagua. *ed* Maurice Rootes. *ad* Jean d'Eaubonne, Eugène Lourié, Julio Molina. *m* Bernardo Segall. *cast* Robert Shaw, Mary Ure, Jeffrey Hunter, Ty Hardin, Robert Ryan, Lawrence Tierney, Kieron Moore, Marc Lawrence.

● Siodmak's penultimate movie which, as an epic Cinerama Western lumbered with the need for irrelevant spectacle, manages to be far less affecting than his less expensive *noir* thrillers of the '40s. Nevertheless, it's an ambitious and occasionally stylish work, expertly crafted but let down by a script which doesn't quite decide what angle to take on its controversial protagonist. Shaw's erratic American accent doesn't help either, though some of the supporting performances (Ryan especially) are very watchable. GA

Custodian, The

(1993, Aust, 109 min)
d John Dingwall. *p* Adrienne Read. *sc* John Dingwall. *ph* Steve Mason. *ed* Mike Honey. *m* Philip Houghton. *cast* Barry Otto, Anthony LaPaglia, Hugo Weaving, Kelly Dingwall, Essie Davis, Gosia Dobrowolska.

● Quinlan (LaPaglia) is a cop on the verge of a nervous breakdown. He is separating from his drunken wife, who hates that he's honest but poor, and suspicious of his best mate Church (Weaving), who's dishonest but rich. After a bout on the bottle, which gets him passed over for promotion and suspended, Quinlan goes in with Church, but simultaneously dishes the dirt to crusading journalist Reynolds (Kelly Dingwall) who passes on the info to nice guy Ferguson (Otto) of Internal Affairs. A somewhat involving but on the whole rather heavy-handed thriller on the theme, 'Who will watch over our protectors?' AO

Cut Above, A

see Gross Anatomy

Cutter and Bone

see Cutter's Way

Cutter's Way (aka Cutter and Bone)

(1981, US, 109 min)
d Ivan Passer. *p* Paul R Gurian. *sc* Jeffrey Alan Fiskin. *ph* Jordan Cronenweth. *ed* Caroline Ferriol. *ad* Josan F Russo. *m* Jack Nitzsche. *cast* Jeff Bridges, John Heard, Lisa Eichhorn, Ann Dusenberry, Stephen Elliott, Nina Van Pallandt, Arthur Rosenberg, Patricia Donahue.

● A dazzling *film noir* out of the same paranoiac mould as *Klute*. It begins with classic murder as a girl's body is stuffed into a trash-can one stormy night. When the killer is tentatively identified as a fat-cat oil tycoon, stern retribution against the powers who never pay for their sins is demanded by Cutter (Heard), a horribly mutilated Vietnam veteran who hounds the tycoon to his doom, guilty or not. But the quixotic Cutter is gradually transformed into an Ahab pursuing his Moby Dick, and the hallucinatory quality of the film comes from its view of California as a paradise turned into a hunting-ground for the leviathans of speculation. As three minnows threshing desperately to avoid being engulfed, Cutter, his drunken wife (Eichhorn), and his beach-bum best friend (Bridges) are caught in a nightmarish personal triangle of extraordinary, constantly shifting complexity, rippling with secrecies and ambivalent emotions that escape easy definition. Amazing performances from Heard, Bridges and Eichhorn in one of the key films of the decade. TM

CutThroat Island

(1995, US, 125 min)
d Renny Harlin. *p* Renny Harlin, Joel B Michaels, Laurence Mark, James Gorman. *sc* Robert King, Marc Norman. *ph* Peter Levy. *ed* Frank J Urioste, Ralph E Winters. *pd* Norman Garwood. *m* John Debney. *cast* Geena Davis, Matthew Modine, Patrick Malahide, Frank Langella, Maury Chaykin, Stan Shaw, Rex Linn, Harris Yulin.

● The pirate movie requires a dashing male star and a dose of lightly self-deprecating humour. In this $90m revisionist swashbuckler, we get Geena Davis doing the all-action honours, and a hotchpotch script that seems to think pirate movies are so funny in themselves the need for more humour is superfluous. The plot's well worn: a treasure map is sought by the star, her ill-matched cohort Modine, dully rhubarbing villain Langella, and others. On screen the money has bought yards of 17th century Jamaican fixtures and fittings, a couple of attractive galleons, and a warehouse of Semtex. Harlin is never a man to shy away from the lure of Very Big Explosions, and, on a technical level, the spectacle's impressive. The only actor to make much of an impact is Malahide's colonial officer, who extracts tart irony from the merest crumbs. TJ

Cutting Edge, The

(1992, US, 102 min)
d Paul Michael Glaser. *p* Robert Colt, Karen Murphy, Ted Field. *sc* Tony Gilroy. *ph* Elliot Davis. *ed* Michael Polakow. *m* Patrick Williams. *cast* DB Sweeney, Moira Kelly, Roy Dotrice, Terry O'Quinn, Dwier Brown, Chris Benson.

● When a collision on the ice robs Olympic ice hockey player Doug Dorsey (Sweeney) of his peripheral vision, his life falls apart. Kate Moseley (Kelly) is one of the most talented and temperamental figure-skaters in the world, her sights fixed firmly on winning gold at the 1992 Winter Olympics. Her only problem is that she can't get a regular partner. In desperation her trainer turns to Dorsey, but can the former sportsman forget his old ways, acquire a new skating style, overcome his natural loathing for his new partner, *and* win gold at the Olympics? What do you think? A lobotomised ice-skating obsessive (since many of the skating sequences are choreographed by former Olympic gold medallist Robin Cousins) *might* find something praiseworthy in all this predictable, ham-fisted, romantic tosh. NKe

Cutting It Short (Postrizini)

(1980, Czech, 98 min)
d Jiri Menzel. *sc* Bohumil Hrabal, Jiri Menzel. *ph* Jaromir Sofr. *ed* Jiri Brozek. *ad* Zbynek Hloch. *m* Jiri Sust. *cast* Jiri Schmitzer, Magda Vasáryová, Jaromír Hanzlik, Rudolf Hrusínsky, Oldrich Vlach, Frantisek Rehak.

● Caution was obviously still the watchword for Menzel after his political troubles. Charming but desperately thin, like *Those Wonderful Movie Cranks* this is a period comedy, set in a provincial brewery and working very hard to extract some fun out of the local dignitaries who serve on the board. A gorgeous performance from Vasáryová, as a local beauty delighting in her bounteous sensuality, lends a welcome touch of Maupassant to the rustic frolics. TM

Cyberworld 3D

(1999, US, 48 min)
d Colin Davies, Elaine Despins; (segment directors) Brummbaer, Jerzy Kular, Satoshi Kitahara, Noriaki Kaneko, Howard Greenhalgh, Paul Sidlo, Peter Spans, Eric Darnell, Tim Johnson, Bob Anderson. *p* Steve Hoban, Hugh Murray, Sally Dundas. *sc* Hugh Murray, Charlie Rubin, Steve Hoban. *m* Hummie Mann. *cast* voices: Jenna Elfman, Matt Frewer, Robert Smith, Dave Foley.

● This mesmerising spectacle of contemporary 3-D animation is a laudable effort, despite its resemblance to a computer game. The collaborators have pulled in a couple of TV and movie moments recognisable from the past, namely Homer and Bart Simpson and the dance sequence from *Antz*, and thrust them into the third dimension. And although the two USPs are supremely rendered – Bart, especially, looks very cuddly in the round – neither can hold a candle to the fantastic dreamlike fantasy sequence British team Eye Animation have made for the Pet Shop Boys 'Liberation' single; nor, for that matter, Sony Pictures' dark, surreal segment, 'Monkey Brain Sushi'. Introductory host of the show is a fiesty CGI-generated femme named Phig (voiced by Elfman). Sadly her ensuing battle with a trio of dimwitted computer 'bugs' slightly hampers the flow of what is an otherwise astounding and visually arresting 3-D showcase. DA

Cycle, The (Dayereh Mina)

(1974, Iran, 102 min)
d Daryush Mehrjui. *sc* Daryush Mehrjui, Gholam-Hosayn Sa'edi. *ph* Hushang Baharlu. *ed* Talat Mirfendereski. *cast* Ezat Entezami, Ali Nassiriane, Frouzan, Said Kangarani, Bahman Forssi, Esmail Mohamadi.
● A surprisingly eloquent piece of poetic neorealism. A young man accompanies his dour old father to hospital in Tehran; while waiting there, both become enmeshed in the corrupt business cycle which surrounds it. It's arty but articulate, a social allegory in which the hospital's contaminated blood supply poisons exactly those people (the urban poor) who are also its desperate donors. This cyclical logic of exploitation unfortunately yields moral rather than political conclusions, and produces some heavy-handed thematic oppositions – honesty versus corruption, country versus city. But with its overwhelming intuitions of visual truth (the luminous hospital, the dusty waste of an industrial hinterland), the central drama of lost hope and tyrannical poverty in the Shah's 'free' market state retains considerable force; you can see why it was banned for three years. CA

Cyclist, The

(1989, Iran, 85 min)
d/sc Mohsen Makhmalbaf. *ph* Alireza Zarrindast. *m* Majid Entezami. *cast* Moharram Zeynalzadeh, Esmail Soltanian, Mohamad Reza Maleki.
● An Afghani immigrant worker rides in a circle for a week to raise money for his sick wife. Mohsen Makhmalbaf's output is distinctly variable, with a tendency to convoluted intellectualism, but in this case (a variation on *They Shoot Horses, Don't They?*) the prevailing ponderousness is only exacerbated by the crudeness of his technique. Well-meaning, maybe, but an alienatingly opaque and clumsy effort. NB

Cyclo (Xich Lo)

(1995, Fr/Vietnam, 129 min)
d Tran Anh Hung. *p* Christophe Rossignon. *sc* Tran Anh Hung. *ph* Benoit Delhomme. *ed* Nicole Dedieu, Claude Ronzeau. *pd* Daniel Zalay. *m* Ton That Tiet. *cast* Le Van Loc, Tran Nu Yen Khe, Tony Leung, Nguyen Nhu Quynh, Nguyen Hoang Phuc.
● The story's set in motion by the theft of a pedal cab essential to the economic survival of an 18-year-old Vietnamese. But forget *Bicycle Thieves*, and forget, too, writer/director Tran Anh Hung's debut feature, *The Scent of Green Papaya*. When the 'cyclo' (Le Van Loc) tells his boss that his vehicle's been stolen by professional rivals, he finds himself at the mercy of the Poet (Tony Leung), a taciturn gangster who diverts the boy from self-improvement (as advised by his late father) and into a life of crime. What the boy doesn't know, however, is that the Poet has also lured his sister (Tran Nu Yen Khe) into prostitution: in the desperate, hustling world of Ho Chi Minh City, it seems, innocence is unprotected. With its dazzling camerawork, feverish energy and dark, visceral power, this admirably unsentimental film paints a compelling portrait of moral derailment and salvation in a city in social and spiritual turmoil. The plot's packed with absent, uncaring or malign father figures; the tone is alternately tender or brutally violent; and the use of water and fire as symbols of purification and destruction gives rise to vivid dreamlike imagery. It'll have you reeling. GA

Cyclone, The (Il Ciclone)

(1996, It, 94 min)
d Leonardo Pieraccioni. *p* Alessandro Calosci, Vittorio Cecchi Gori, Rita Cecchi Gori. *sc* Leonardo Pieraccioni, Giovanni Veronesi. *ph* Roberto Forza. *ed* Mirco Garrone. *ad* Francesco Frigeri. *m* Claudio Guidetti. *cast* Leonardo Pieraccioni, Lorena Forteza, Barbara Enrichi, Massimo Ceccherini, Mario Monicelli, Sergio Froconi.
● A huge hit in Italy (indeed, the biggest local box office smash ever), this simply doesn't travel. The 'cyclone' is a touring flamenco dance company whose bus breaks down in an insular Tuscan town. Our accountant hero, a flustered romantic, puts them up in the family barn. He has an idiot brother who sleeps in a coffin, a butch lesbian sister, and a sex mad friend – he doesn't seem to know anyone who isn't a stereotype. The endless stream of avuncular ribaldry occasionally hits paydirt, but only if you have the patience for it. TCh

Cyrano de Bergerac

(1990, Fr, 138 min)
d Jean-Paul Rappeneau. *p* Michel Seydoux, René Cleitman. *sc* Jean-Paul Rappeneau, Jean-Claude Carrière. *ph* Pierre Lhomme. *ed* Noëlle Boisson. *ad* Ezio Frigerio. *m* Jean-Claude Petit. *cast* Gérard Depardieu, Jacques Weber, Anne Brochet, Vincent Perez, Roland Bertin, Philippe Morier-Genoud, Philippe Volter.
● Rappeneau's version of Rostand's theatrical warhorse never puts a foot wrong. Much of the credit goes to Depardieu, perfect as the 17th century Gascon swordsman and braggart whose unsightly nose prevents him from confessing his love for his cousin Roxane. The text, cut, reworked and still in alexandrine verse, exudes all the grace and pace of a deftly orchestrated *rondo* (admirably served by Anthony Burgess' English subtitling), and this almost musical sense of meaning reinforced by rhythm extends throughout: the camera swoops at moments of ebullience, the performers' gestures, movements and delivery of lines seem almost choreographed. Everything has been fleshed out to its full potential; the entire scale of the piece, too, is augmented, so that landscapes, sets, battles and countless extras reflect the enormity of the poet Cyrano's unspoken torment. Rappeneau's movie-making demonstrates an unshowy confidence in itself and its subject that is wholly justifiable. GA

d

Dracula (1931)

Da

(1988, US, 102 min)
d Matt Clark. *p* Julie Corman. *sc* Hugh Leonard. *ph* Alar Kivilo. *ed* Nancy Nuttal Beyda. *pd* Frank Conway. *m* Elmer Bernstein. *cast* Barnard Hughes, Martin Sheen, William Hickey, Doreen Hepburn, Karl Hayden, Hugh O'Conor.
●Hugh Leonard's stage play translates dully to the screen in this valentine to a dead Dublin father. Da (Hughes) is dead and buried but comes back to exasperate his son Charlie (Sheen), now a successful playwright in New York. The ghost device releases a flood of flashbacks from Charlie's boyhood and young manhood, in all of which ineffectual Da plays the spoiler's part. His prospect of certain sex, for instance, is banjaxed when Da approaches the park bench and, by dint of garrulity, unearths the girl's family history and queers the lad's pitch. Any hope of presenting an emotional exorcism, as Charlie wins through to the realisation that his Da loves him, is shafted by the sheer obviousness of the old man's affection from the start. Mildly entertaining. BC

Daan (Don)

(1997, Iran, 90 min)
d/p/sc Abolfazl Jalili. *ph* Farzad Judat. *ed* Abolfazl Jalili. *cast* Farhad Bahremand, Bakhtiyar Bahremand, Farzad Halili, Tayebeh Soori.
●More linear and less obviously poetic than Jalili's likewise impressive *Dance of Dust*, this affecting docu-drama concerns a nine-year-old unable to hold down a job because his drug addict parents never properly registered his birth or got him an ID. Meanwhile the family of a girl – the boy's friend – plans to take her out of school and marry her to a much older man. An intelligent, heartfelt indictment not only of how adult worlds wreck childhood, but of the Catch-22 situations fostered by excessive bureaucracy. A tough, deeply humane film. GA

Dad

(1989, US, 118 min)
d Gary David Goldberg. *p* Joseph Stern, Gary David Goldberg. *sc* Gary David Goldberg. *ph* Jan Kiesser. *ed* Eric Sears. Jack De Govia. *m* James Horner. *cast* Jack Lemmon, Ted Danson, Olympia Dukakis, Kathy Baker, Kevin Spacey, Ethan Hawke, Zakes Mokae, JT Walsh.
●Sharp, successful businessman John (Danson), out of step with his folks, grudgingly comes home to help care for his confused and helpless father Jake (Lemmon) while his indomitable mom Bette (Dukakis) is in hospital. Roles are reversed as son coaxes father from his childlike state, and John's success leads him to reassess his failed relationship with his own teen son (Hawke). Lemmon wrings genuine pathos from his role, as does Dukakis as shrewish, sardonic Bette. It's Danson in sincere mode who makes the film difficult to endure, especially in the later learning, caring and sharing scenes. Eventually, Jake falls foul of the Big C. He's sick! He gets better! He has a relapse! He rallies! This is called milking it. The film does assert there are some things positive thinking won't conquer, like sickness, senility and death. But it smothers any serious intent in cheap homily, modern mythology and sickly sentimentality. SFe

Daddy

(1972, GB/Switz, 90 min)
d Peter Whitehead *cast* Niki de St Phalle, Gwynne Rivers, Mia Martin; ballet: Clarisse Rivers, Rainer von Dietz.
●What began as a documentary on sculptress Niki de St Phalle finished up as a fantasy about a woman's attempts to exorcise the influence of her sexually domineering father. It provides an excuse for a whole ragbag of Freudian neuroses, six-foot phalluses in coffins, nubile girls in nun's habits stripping in front of altars, masturbation, some obvious jokes, pretty photography, abysmal acting, and a commentary that reads and sounds like a Home Service children's story for adults. Still, with father looking like a hangover from vaudeville and mother coming on like Jean Harlow, along with a laughably insistent piano score thumping away in the background, any girl would have her problems. CPe

Daddy Long Legs

(1955, US, 126 min)
d Jean Negulesco. *p* Samuel G Engel. *sc* Phoebe Ephron, Henry Ephron. *ph* Leon Shamroy. *ed* William Reynolds. *ad* Lyle Wheeler, John F DeCuir. *songs* Johnny Mercer. *m* (ballet) Alex North. *cast* Fred Astaire, Leslie Caron, Thelma Ritter, Fred Clark, Terry Moore, Larry Keating.
●This third film version (fourth if you count Shirley Temple and *Curly Top*) of Jean Webster's novel/play, about an orphaned waif who falls for a playboy sophisticate who has become her anonymous benefactor, is for the most part an unusually flaccid Astaire musical, despite sterling efforts from the two leads plus Clark and Ritter (as, respectively, Fred's manager and secretary). The chief problem is the story's utter predictability, although the score and choreography (with the single exception of 'Something's Got to Give') are also uninspired. Shot to no apparent advantage in 'Scope, this is Hollywood escapism at its most mediocre. GA

Daddy Nostalgie

see These Foolish Things

Daddy's Dyin' – Who's Got the Will?

(1990, US, 95 min)
d Jack Fisk. *p* Sigurjon Sighvatsson, Steve Golin, Monty Montgomery. *sc* Del Shores. *ph* Paul Elliot. *ed* Edward A Warschilka Jr. *pd* Michelle Minch. *m* David McHugh. *cast* Beau Bridges, Beverly D'Angelo, Tess Harper, Judge Reinhold, Amy Wright, Patrika Darbo, Bert Remsen, Molly McClure, Keith Carradine.
●A flaccid adaptation by Del Shores of his own play in which the title tells all: while Texan patriarch Bert Remsen lies on his death-bed, his offspring assemble for a binge of bickering greed. Beer-swilling Beau Bridges and six-times divorced C&W singer Beverly D'Angelo are only concerned with who gets what; older sister (Wright) is into that old-time religion, while the other (Harper) is worried fiancé Keith Carradine will fall prey to the promiscuous charms of D'Angelo, whose neglected hippy lover (Reinhold) seems to be mighty fond of Bridges' dumpy wife (Darbo). Meanwhile grandmomma (McClure) strives to invest Remsen's last days with a modicum of peace and dignity. Dull, dated and displaying its stage origins at every turn, this clichéd account of sibling strife convinces neither as black comedy nor in its dim final hymn to family unity. Worse, a largely superior cast is let down by Fisk's stolid direction. GA

Daddy's Girl

(2001, GB, 9 min)
d Irvine Allan. *p* Carolyne Sinclair Kidd. *sc* John Maley. *ph* Mark Raeburn. *ed* Bert Eeles. *cast* John Joseph Campbell, Annie George, Daniel Heally, Russell Hunter, Heather Keenan.
●Excellent Cannes prize-winning short about a young girl left by her dad outside a Glasgow pub in the sheeting rain. Beautifully written, shot and played, this small stunner is poignant but never maudlin. Furthermore, it's infinitely more relevant than most features currently being made in the UK. GA

Dadetown

(1995, US, 93 min)
d Russ Hexter. *p* Jim Carden. *sc* Russ Hexter, John Housley. *ph* Bill Gorman. *ed* David Kirkman. *m* Tom Carden. *cast* Bill Garrison, David Phelps, Pete Nagler, Tom Nickenback, Ed Hubble, Jim Pryor.
●The film's crew sets out to make a documentary about an archetypal small town, and realises it's on the brink of breakdown. The antagonism between the town's older inhabitants (mostly employed at a factory going out of business) and newcomers who've moved on to smart new estates in order to work at an obscure but powerful communications company looks set to turn horribly violent. Hexter's involving analysis of the social, economic, political and technological factors undermining a once happy community is absolutely persuasive – and entirely false, for this is a dazzlingly authentic bogus documentary, whose status as a forgery is admitted only in a few hilarious, faintly absurdist gags. A brilliant debut, perfectly shot, scripted and performed; the tragedy is that Hexter died, still in his mid-30s, soon after it was made. GA

Dad's Army

(1971, GB, 95 min)
d Norman Cohen. *p* John R Sloan. *sc* Jimmy Perry, David Croft. *ph* Terry Maher. *ed* Willy Kemplen. *ad* Terence Knight. *m* Wilfred Burns. *cast* Arthur Lowe, John Le Mesurier, Clive Dunn, John Laurie, James Beck, Ian Lavender, Arnold Ridley, Liz Fraser.
●Since the original was one of the few TV series which successfully resisted the temptation to broaden its effects as time went by, one might have expected this spinoff to translate painlessly to the big screen. Lowe (sublimely unaware as he barks 'I must ask you to keep your hands off my privates') and the rest of the regulars are as irresistible as ever. But the script digs several pits for itself by needlessly recapitulating the history of the platoon, by foregrounding details best left to the imagination (like Sgt Wilson's relationship to Pike's mother), and worst of all by offering a climax involving real Germans. Surely only an invisible enemy, never materialising but ineffably menacing, can exist in the same world as this moonshine Home Guard crew. TM

Dad Savage

(1997, GB, 104 min)
d Betsan Morris Evans. *p* Gwynneth Lloyd, Robert Jones. *sc* Steven Williams. *ph* Gavin Finney. *ed* Guy Bensley. *pd* Michael Carlin. *cast* Patrick Stewart, Kevin McKidd, Helen McCrory, Joe McFadden, Marc Warren, Jake Wood.
●This first feature – a Fen country heist drama knee-deep in illicit banknotes, callous youths, betrayal, confusion and general bellicosity – evidently takes *Shallow Grave* as its inspiration. But it's a hash job, a blank, tiresome muddle of vapid characters and threadbare plotting. The one distinction is the show-role provided for senior actor Patrick Stewart as tulip farmer Dad Savage, known just as 'D' to his boys: son Sav (Wood) and his buddies H (McKidd), Vic (Warren) and Bob (McFadden), D's recently hired hands. This being (supposedly) an East Anglian Western, Dad wears a stetson and cowboy boots, enjoys Country and Western line dancing, and has scant regard for the law and a stash of loot buried in the woods. Likewise, the boys get off on guns, killing and blood – as a brief introductory montage informs us – and evince just enough wherewithal to hatch a half-baked scheme which instantly unravels for the duration of the film. NB

Daemon

(1986, GB, 71 min)
d/p Colin Finbow. *sc* Colin Finbow, Children's Film Unit. *ph* Titus Bicknell, Rory MacFarquhar, Orlando Wells, Leigh Melrose, Jason Wulfsohn. *ed* Ben Timberlake, Arnaud Morell, Orlando Swayne, Colin Finbow. *ad* Bec Knight. *m* David Hewson. *cast* Arnaud Morell, Susannah York, Bert Parnaby, Sadie Herlighy, Donna Glaser, Orlando Swayne.
●This Children's Film Unit production is bound to grip young audiences: a horror story told from a child's point of view, the new kid in town who's convinced he's possessed by the devil. In all, a remarkable achievement from a production crew whose average age is twelve, highlighted by a warm performance from Susannah York, who neither steals the show from the featured young performers nor from the young audiences it will undoubtedly entertain. SGo

Daens

(1993, Bel/Fr/Neth, 138 min)
d Stijn Coninx. *p* Dirk Impens. *sc* François Chevallier, Stijn Coninx. *ph* Walther van den Ende. *ed* Ludo Troch. *pd* Allan Starski. *m* Dirk Brossé. *cast* Jan Decleir, Gérard Desarthe, Antje De Boeck, Michael Pas, Johan Leysen, Idwig Stéphane.
●A Belgian chronicle of a notorious 'red' priest and the formative years of his country's democratic process. During the closing decades of the 19th century, Aalst has become a thriving provincial mill town, a boon for the wealthy owners of the textile factories, less happy for the workers toiling for subsistence pay. The poor find a champion in Father Adolf Daens (Decleir), who is elected against opposition to represent the Christian People's Party in Belgium's new assembly. It's not long, however, before the establishment closes ranks to protect its interests. Without Decleir's gruff authority, the film would probably go for very little. As it is, the combination of stirring

music, rippling indignation and plenty of idealistic speechifying marks it down as earnest, decent, middlebrow viewing. TJ

Daisies (Sedmikrásky)

(1966, Czech, 76 min, b/w &w)
d Vera Chytilová. *p* Bohumil Smida, Ladislav Fikar. *sc* Vera Chytilova, Ester Krumbachova. *ph* Jaroslav Kucera. *ed* Miroslav Hajek. *ad* Karel Lier. *m* Jiri Slitr, Jiri Sust. *cast* Jitka Cerhová, Ivana Karbanová, Julius Albert, Jan Klusák, Marie Ceskova, Jirina Ceskova.

● Visually hideous, tiresomely gimmicky satire on materialism, with two bored girls, both named Marie, who spend the entire movie causing havoc in restaurants and nightclubs, ripping off unsuspecting men and generally eating and behaving like pigs. As an allegory it lacks any resonance, as a movie it stinks. ATu

Daisy Kenyon

(1947, US, 99 min, b/w)
d/p Otto Preminger. *sc* David Hertz. *ph* Leon Shamroy. *ed* Louis Loeffler. *ad* Lyle Wheeler, George Davis. *m* David Raksin. *cast* Joan Crawford, Dana Andrews, Henry Fonda, Ruth Warrick, Martha Stewart, Peggy Ann Garner, Connie Marshall.

● Fascinating melodrama (from the novel by Elizabeth Janeway) which has anguished Crawford torn between the two men in her life, army sergeant Fonda and married lawyer Andrews. She's a fashion designer (cue costume changes); as always with Crawford, though, it's her gaunt, angular face that dominates the screen. She may only have agreed to do the film on condition that Andrews and Fonda were her co-stars, but fine actors though they are, they can't match her pitch of intensity. GM

Daisy Miller

(1974, US, 92 min)
d/p Peter Bogdanovich. *sc* Frederic Raphael. *ph* Alberto Spagnoli. *ed* Verna Fields. *ad* Ferdinando Scarfiotti. *cast* Cybill Shepherd, Barry Brown, Cloris Leachman, Mildred Natwick, Eileen Brennan, Duilio Del Prete.

● Bogdanovich's nervous essay in the troubled waters of Henry James, where American innocence and naiveté are in perpetual conflict with European decadence and charm, reveals him to be less an interpreter of James than a translator of him into the brusquer world of Howard Hawks. The violence done James in this is forgiveable – indeed, Cybill Shepherd's transformation of Daisy into a Hawks heroine is strangely successful – but as a result there is no real social conflict in the film, and it becomes just a period variant on *The Last Picture Show*, without the vigour of that film or the irony of the original James novel. PH

Dakota Incident

(1956, US, 88 min)
d Lewis R Foster. *p* Michael Baird. *sc* Frederic Louis Fox. *ph* Ernest Haller. *ed* Howard Smith. *ad* Walter Keller. *m* R Dale Butts. *cast* Linda Darnell, Dale Robertson, Ward Bond, John Lund, Regis Toomey, Skip Homeier.

● The stagecoach breaks down in the desert, the Indians attack, but bad girl Darnell and bad boy Robertson survive (in best *Stagecoach* tradition) to walk into the sunset. Usually slagged off as routine, it is in fact beautifully shot (by Ernest Haller), vividly characterised, and surprisingly well written. Frederic Louis Fox's script functions as a sort of parable, with Robertson's bank robber, dogged on the one hand by a bank clerk blamed for one of his exploits and hoping somehow to win his good name back, and on the other by a senator preaching peace with the red man, cynically maintaining his belief in the power of the gun. Both these good people are killed, and the 'miracle' of Robertson's redemption is a complex mix arising out of their deaths, his own unexpected inability to kill the last surviving Indian with his bare hands, and the arrival of a storm out of a clear sky just as death from thirst seems imminent. Superbly embroidered in and around the characters, the 'message' is much less naive than it sounds when spelled out. TM

Dakota Road

(1991, GB, 88 min)
d Nick Ward. *p* Donna Grey. *sc* Nick Ward. *ph* Ian Wilson. *ed* William Diver. *pd* Careen Hertzog. *m* Paul Stacey. *cast* Charlotte Chatton, Amelda Brown, Alan Howard, Jason Carter, Rachel Scott, Matthew Scurfield, David Warrilow.

● Ward, an experienced writer/director of stage, radio and TV, displays a talent for literate cinema in his first film. Bored by her existence in rural Norfolk, 15-year-old Jen Cross (Chatton), daughter of a farm labourer, dreams of reaching the heights of passion with a pilot from the local American air base. Brought down to earth by fumbling sex with orphaned signalman Raif (Carter), Jen is later caught in the act by the Reverend Stonea (Warrilow). Her father Bernard (Scurfield), already angry at being sacked by landowner Alan Brandon (Howard) – a frustrated widower who adds to the indignity by employing Bernard's wife (Brown) as a cleaning woman – now sinks into a smouldering, jealous rage which hints at some darker family secret… Framing both the wide vistas and the claustrophobic interiors with a painterly eye, Ward coaxes sympathetic performances from a good cast. Occasionally, the inertia that afflicts the characters also arrests the flow of the narrative; but for the most part, Ward's direction and Ian Wilson's sublime photography capture the feel of a bleak fen country with just a glimmer of hope on the distant horizon. NF

Dak van de Walvis, Het

see On Top of the Whale

Daleks – Invasion Earth 2150 A.D.

(1966, GB, 84 min)
d Gordon Flemyng. *p* Max J Rosenberg, Milton Subotsky. *sc* Milton Subotsky. *ph* John Wilcox. *ed* Ann Chegwidden. *ad* George Provis. *m* Bill McGuffie. *cast* Peter Cushing, Bernard Cribbins, Ray Brooks, Andrew Keir, Roberta Tovey, Jill Curzon, Godfrey Quigley.

● Second and last to date of the big screen *Dr Who* spinoffs. Very tame but marginally better than the first, with the Daleks unsurprisingly coming to grief after invading a ruined London of the future and robotising the inhabitants. Very variable special effects and often excruciatingly cheapo sets. TM

Dallas

(1950, US, 94 min)
d Stuart Heisler. *p* Anthony Veiller. *sc* John Twist. *ph* Ernest Haller. *ed* Clarence Kolster. *ad* Douglas Bacon. *m* Max Steiner. *cast* Gary Cooper, Ruth Roman, Raymond Massey, Steve Cochran, Antonio Moreno, Barbara Payton, Leif Erickson.

● Civil War renegade Cooper fakes death in a shoot-out with Wyatt Earp and heads for Texas to revenge himself on the brothers who massacred his family. A routine plot, but plenty of diversions on the trail – Coop pretending to be a danified US marshall in frock coat and top hat, horseback chases, furtive romance. The star sleepwalks, though since he's supposed to be the laconic outsider-type, this doesn't matter at all. Impressive production values and blazing Technicolor camerawork by Ernest Haller. Basically a B-Western though. GM

Dallas Doll

(1994, US, 104 min)
d Ann Turner. *p* Ross Matthews. *sc* Ann Turner. *ph* Paul Murphy. *ed* Mike Honey. *pd* Marcus North. *m* David Hirschfelder. *cast* Sandra Bernhard, Victoria Longley, Frank Gallagher, Jake Blundell, Rose Byrne, Jonathon Leahy.

● US golf pro Bernhard is invited to enliven an Australian club in suburban Sydney and ends up staying with a nice, normal family. Only the young daughter and the dog are suspicious of her seductive, go-getting character; nevertheless, the family is duly transformed. Bernhard is boringly herself, and Longley's born-again housewife steals the film from her. Occasionally coming on like a satirical update of Theorem, it's neither funny nor frightening; indeed, it's hard to fathom what it's really meant to be about, though its attitude to both America and Japan lay it open to charges of xenophobia (which might, of course, be part of the satire). Oddly unsatisfying. GA

Dal Polo all'Equatore

see From Pole to Equator

Dama do cine Shanghai, A

see Lady from the Shanghai Cinema, The

Damage

(1992, GB/Fr, 111 min)
d/p Louis Malle. *sc* David Hare. *ph* Peter Biziou. *ed* John Bloom. *pd* Brian Morris. *m* Zbigniew Preisner. *cast* Jeremy Irons, Juliette Binoche, Miranda Richardson, Rupert Graves, Leslie Caron, Ian Bannen, Gemma Clarke.

● This good-looking version of Josephine Hart's bestseller – a cautionary tale of *amour fou*, risqué sex and power play 'twixt a married Tory minister and an enigmatic young French-born auctioneer – is a dull affair. We follow Irons' MP to a crowded cocktail party, where he falls in lust at first glance with his son's girlfriend (Binoche), and soon we're motoring through one ritzy London postal district after another, along a predictable road to disaster – but for whom? The acting strays in different directions. Binoche is reduced to an elegant-chic clothes-horse; Irons, to point up the explosive, mysterious nature of erotic attraction, has to stress ordinariness, which strangely makes his motivation seem mysterious and the erotic attraction ordinary. Richardson, as the wife, gives a shuddering, raging howl of a breakdown, which stuns the movie into silence. The sex scenes make you consider the acting. Boredom is maybe the clue: Malle has been charting this territory since the late '50s, and co-scriptwriter David Hare said it all before in *Paris by Night*. WH

Dam Busters, The

(1954, GB, 124 min, b/w)
d Michael Anderson. *p* Robert Clark. *sc* RC Sherriff. *ph* Erwin Hillier. *ed* Richard Best. *ad* Robert Jones. *m* Leighton Lucas, Eric Coates. *cast* Michael Redgrave, Richard Todd, Ursula Jeans, Derek Farr, Patrick Barr, John Fraser, George Baker, Brewster Mason, Basil Sydney.

● At one time seemingly up as a candidate for culting by those who found the surrounding footage of *Pink Floyd: The Wall* to taste (this was the movie playing incessantly on Pink's TV). Anderson and RC Sherriff's tribute to Barnes Wallis (inventor of World War II's bouncing bomb) and Wingco Guy Gibson (who spearheaded their use in destroying strategically-important Ruhr dams) slips some thoughtful reservations and some gross sentimentality into its bouncing bombast. With its final cost-counting, it contorts the stiff upper lip into something like a deathly grimace. PT

Dame aux Camélias, La

(1981, Fr/It, 121 min)
d Mauro Bolognini. *p* Margaret Ménégoz, Manolo Bolognini. *sc* Jean Aurenche, Vladimir Pozner, Enrico Medioli. *ph* Ennio Guarnieri. *ed* Nino Baragli. *ad* Mario Garbuglia. *m* Ennio Morricone. *cast* Isabelle Huppert, Gian Maria Volonté, Fabrizio Bentivoglio, Fernando Rey, Jann Babilée, Bruno Ganz.

● Not based on the play or novel, but on the real-life romance that inspired the tearful tale of Marguerite Gautier. But the unhappy love of Dumas *fils* for Marie Duplessis is turned into hoary melodrama, as lavishly tatty as any rep performance of the play. Matters are not improved by a very choppy narrative, adapted from a longer TV version. TM

Dame dans l'auto avec des lunettes et un fusil, La

see Lady in the Car with Glasses and a Gun, The

Dames

(1934, US, 90 min, b/w)
d Ray Enright. *sc* Delmer Daves. *ph* Sid Hickox, George Barnes, Sol Polito. *ed* Harold McLernon. *ad* Robert M Haas, Willy Pogany. *songs* Harry Warren, Al Dubin, Sammy Fain, Irving Kahal, Mort Dixon, Allie Wrubel. *cast* Joan Blondell, Dick Powell, Ruby Keeler, ZaSu Pitts, Hugh Herbert, Guy Kibbee.

● A predictable puttin'-on-a-show plot is basically a superfluous framework for some bright comic acting from the likes of Blondell and Pitts, and for typically ornamental musical scenes staged by Berkeley, with dozens of girls waving their legs around while lying on their backs (and they call that dancing?). GA

Dames du Bois de Boulogne, Les

(1945, Fr, 90 min, b/w)
d Robert Bresson. *sc* Robert Bresson, Jean Cocteau. *ph* Philippe Agostini. *ed* Jean Feyte. *ad* Max Douy. *m* Jean-Jacques Grünenwald. *cast* Maria Casarès, Elina Labourdette, Paul Bernard, Lucienne Bogaërt, Paul Bernard, Jean Marchat.
●Like *Les Anges du Péché*, Bresson's second feature, based on a self-contained anecdote in Diderot's novel *Jacques le Fataliste*, is in many ways atypical of his oeuvre. He uses, quite brilliantly, professional actors. The visual texture is not muted grey, but sharp and contrasty. The camera is constantly prowling and tracking. The dialogue (by Cocteau) is brilliantly jewelled, literary to the point of preciousness, the very antithesis of the later monosyllabics. Yet as one watches the elegant socialite (played by Casarès with superbly steely venom) spin a cold-blooded plot to destroy her rival after being humiliatingly spurned in a liaison in the interests of true love, one could hardly be anywhere but in Bresson's world. Sexuality takes precedence over salvation, but there is the same interiority, the same intensity, the same rigorous exclusion of all inessentials. TM

Damien – Omen II

(1978, US, 109 min)
d Don Taylor. *p* Harvey Bernhard. *sc* Stanley Mann, Michael Hodges. *ph* Bill Butler. *ed* Robert Brown Jr. *pd* Philip M Jefferies, Fred Harpman. *m* Jerry Goldsmith. *cast* William Holden, Lee Grant, Jonathan Scott-Taylor, Robert Foxworth, Nicholas Pryor, Lew Ayres, Sylvia Sidney.
●This sequel lacks the bravura pacing of the original, and though it tries to maintain the biblical tone in following the adolescence of its antichrist anti-hero, immense problems emerge. Murderous adolescents are much more routine movie material than murderous five-year-olds, and making Damien vaguely unhappy about his identity only serves to make him more irritating. The number of surrogate demons is also vastly inflated, thereby stacking the decks against the angels from the beginning and undermining any real tension. DP

Damnation (Kárhozat)

(1988, Hun, 116 min, b/w)
d Béla Tarr. *p* József Marx. *sc* László Krasznahorkai, Béla Tarr. *ph* Gábor Medvigy. *ed* Agnes Hranitzky. *ad* Gyula Pauer. *m* Mihály Víg. *cast* Miklós B Székely, Vali Kerekes, Hédi Temessy, Gyula Pauer, György Cserhalmi.
●Béla Tarr is acclaimed a maestro not only in his native Hungary, but in France, North America and by festival directors worldwide. This is a serious art movie, with the accent on all three words. Most definitely it moves, and the art is serious, albeit tinged with black comedy. In a rainy, rundown mining town, the introverted and listless Karrer (Székely) brightens (somewhat) his regular visits to the Titanic Bar by sinking into a desultory, obsessive on-off affair with the bar's singer (Kerekes), whose husband alternates between hostile warnings and drunken banter. Keen to keep his lover to himself, Karrer devises a scheme to get his rival out of the way. It would be easy, but unfair, to dismiss this slow, solemn, somewhat oblique monochrome study of suspicion, corruption, betrayal and revenge as pretentious miserabilism. If its grey aura of despair sometimes hangs a mite heavily, it's certainly worth persevering with for a pay-off that is as perverse as it is powerful; the film's subject, finally, would appear to be the diminution not only of a human soul, but of a society; of the world, perhaps. But it's the absolutely assured direction that's most impressive. GA

Damnation Alley

(1977, US, 91 min)
d Jack Smight. *p* Jerome M Zeitman, Paul Maslansky. *sc* Alan Sharp, Lukas Heller. *ph* Harry Stradling Jr. *ed* Frank J Urioste. *pd* Preston Ames. *m* Jerry Goldsmith. *cast* Jan-Michael Vincent, George Peppard, Dominique Sanda, Paul Winfield, Jackie Earle Haley, Kip Niven.
●Insanely jettisoning the Hell's Angel protagonist of Roger Zelazny's cult novel of a post-holocaust odyssey, this dire slice of uninspired sci-fi tracks an amphibious armoured truck from a California missile base cross-country towards the source of taped signs of life in Albany, NY. Military redneck Peppard and rebel Vincent gather a model post-nuclear family (one black, one woman, one kid) like tokens en route, hampered by appalling process work and by derivative confrontations with mutant mountain men and man-eating cockroaches. A real mess. PT

Damned, The (aka These Are the Damned)

(1961, GB, 87 min, b/w)
d Jospeh Losey. *p* Anthony Hinds. *sc* Evan Jones. *ph* Arthur Grant. *ed* Reginald Mills. *pd* Bernard Robinson. *m* James Bernard. *cast* MacDonald Carey, Shirley Ann Field, Alexander Knox, Viveca Lindfors, Oliver Reed, James Villiers.
●Certainly the strangest Hammer film ever made, this combines apocalyptic sci-fi, teen rebellion, and portentous philosophising to awkward but riveting effect. Set, strangely but successfully, in Weymouth, it begins as a rather mundane romance, with Carey and Field threatened by local Teddy Boys, before spiralling into a dour mystery about a scientist's experiments with radioactive kids. The performances are universally weak, and Losey's clearly ambivalent attitude towards the demands of the genre ensures that the film is never exciting. But as an ambitious oddity, it exerts not a little fascination. GA

Damned, The (La Caduta degli Dei/Götterdämmerung)

(1969, It/WGer, 164 min)
d Luchino Visconti. *p* Alfredo Levy, Ever Haggiag. *sc* Nicola Badalucco, Enrico Medioli, Luchino Visconti. *ph* Armando Nannuzzi, Pasqualino de Santis. *ed* Ruggero Mastroianni. *ad* Pasquale Romano, Enzo Del Prato. *m* Maurice Jarre. *cast* Dirk Bogarde, Ingrid Thulin, Helmut Griem, Helmut Berger, Renaud Verley, Umberto Orsini, Charlotte Rampling, Florinda Bolkan.
●Visconti on the rise of Nazism as reflected within a German industrialist family in the '30s is as operatic and overblown as you'd expect, often to extremely impressive effect. But the overall languorousness finally swamps even the carefully elaborated decadence, making heavy going of otherwise interesting performances from Bogarde and Rampling. And the indulgence of Helmut Berger (who debuts in drag, impersonating Dietrich) is already unmistakeable. TR

Damn the Defiant

see HMS Defiant

Damn Yankees (aka What Lola Wants)

(1958, US, 110 min)
d/p George Abbott, Stanley Donen. *sc* George Abbott. *ph* Harold Lipstein. *ed* Frank Bracht. *ad* William Eckart, Jean Eckart, Stanley Fleischer. *songs* Richard Adler, Jerry Ross. *cast* Tab Hunter, Gwen Verdon, Ray Walston, Russ Brown, Shannon Bolin, Rae Allen, Bob Fosse.
●A musical lumbered with too much plot and tiresome Walston as the Devil who tempts an ageing baseball fan into rejuvenation for a year (in the person of Tab Hunter). But it also has scintillating choreography by Bob Fosse (his duet with Verdon, 'Who's Got the Pain?' is an eye-opener), and an equally brilliant score by Richard Adler and Jerry Ross (a songwriting team also responsible for the marvellous *The Pajama Game*, and only prevented from becoming the best on Broadway by the latter's untimely death). TM

Damsel in Distress, A

(1937, US, 101 min, b/w)
d George Stevens. *p* Pandro S Berman. *sc* PG Wodehouse, Ernest Pagano, SK Lauren. *ph* Joseph August. *ed* Henry Berman. *ad* Van Nest Polglase. *songs* George Gershwin, Ira Gershwin. cast Fred Astaire, Joan Fontaine, George Burns, Gracie Allen, Reginald Gardiner, Constance Collier, Montagu Love.
●Temporary parting of the ways for Fred and Ginger, with Astaire (in hopes of avoiding comparisons) saddled with a non-dancing partner plus Burns & Allen for comic relief. Nicely directed but a bit on the twee side with its Wodehouse plot and mock Englishisms, the result would be questionable but for a rich Gershwin score. Though shackled to Fontaine for 'Things Are Looking Up', Astaire has some sparkling solos, notably the beautiful 'A Foggy Day' and his intermezzo with percussion instruments to 'Nice Work if You Can Get It'. TM

Dan Candy's Law

see Alien Thunder

Dance Craze

(1981, GB, 91 min)
d Joe Massot. *p* Gavrik Losey. *ph* Joe Dunton. *ed* Anthony Sloman. *m/cast* Bad Manners, The Beat, The Bodysnatchers, Madness, The Selecter, The Specials.
●As a blueprint for an investigation of rock's 2-Tone phenomenon, *Dance Craze* works well. Not only does Joe Dunton's photography make the movie look sumptuous, but the music catches the genre's brittle beat and loose-limbed spontaneity. However, if you're over 14 and have seen any of the bands, the experience soon becomes relentlessly dull. Despite scattered wakey-wakey devices (like Pathé News footage from the '50s and '60s), the catalogue of live footage is devoid of any context that might explain the origins, development and effects of the movement. Pity. IB

Dance, Girl, Dance

(1940, US, 90 min, b/w)
d Dorothy Arzner. *p* Erich Pommer. *sc* Tess Slesinger, Frank Davis. *ph* Russell Metty. *ed* Robert Wise. *ad* Van Nest Polglase. *m* Edward Ward. *cast* Maureen O'Hara, Lucille Ball, Louis Hayward, Ralph Bellamy, Virginia Field, Maria Ouspenskaya.
●Arzner's internal critique of Hollywood ideology (woman as silent object of male scrutiny). It works within the confines of a stock vaudevillian golddiggers comedy-drama, tagging along with the old vamp/virgin dichotomy between dancers Ball and O'Hara until the latter upsets the spectacular equation by turning on her (the) audience of leering males with her observations. PT

Dance Hall

(1950, GB, 80 min, b/w)
d Charles Crichton. *p* Michael Balcon. *sc* EVH Emmett, Diana Morgan, Alexander Mackendrick. *ph* Douglas Slocombe. *ed* Seth Holt. *ad* Norman Arnold. *m* Joyce Cochran. *cast* Natasha Parry, Diana Dors, Petula Clark, Jane Hylton, Donald Houston, Sydney Tafler, Kay Kendall, Bonar Colleano, Geraldo, Ted Heath.
●Perhaps the closest the British cinema of its period came to a neo-realist fresco: a matrix of low-key melodramatic narratives converging on the communal (rather than institutional) core of the local palais, and on an upcoming dance contest. The diffuse focus on working-class women marks it as a welcome rarity (presumably to the credit of unsung Ealing screenwriter Diana Morgan), and even the domestic cliché situations communicate a lively sense of resistance to dominant social and economic austerity. Director Crichton moved on to some of the cosier Ealing comedies, but working on *Dance Hall*, as co-writer and editor respectively, were more abrasive talents Alexander Mackendrick and Seth Holt. PT

Dance Little Lady

(1954, GB, 87 min)
d Val Guest. *p* George Minter. *sc* Val Guest, Doreen Montgomery. *ph* Wilkie Cooper. *ed* John Pomeroy. *ad* Fred Pusey. *m* Ronald Binge. *cast* Terence Morgan, Mai Zetterling, Guy Rolfe, Mandy Miller, Eunice Gayson, Reginald Beckwith, Richard O'Sullivan.
●Tepid British melodrama which reunites Terence Morgan and child actress Mandy Miller (they first appeared together in *Mandy* – Ealing's outstanding 'serious' picture – in 1952). Morgan's again a tyrannical bullying father, this time determined to make Mandy into a Hollywood star. Estranged wife Mai Zetterling, a former ballerina, is set against the idea. GM

Dance Me to My Song

(1998, Aust, 102 min)
d Rolf de Heer. *p* Domenico Procacci, Rolf de Heer, Giuseppe Pedersoli. *sc* Heather Rose, Rolf de Heer, Frederick Stahl. *ph* Tony Clark.

ed Tania Nehme. *pd* Beverley Freeman. *m* Graham Tardif. *cast* Heather Rose, Joey Kennedy, John Brumpton, Rena Owen.
● Julia (Rose, persuasive) is bound to a wheelchair and her carer Madeleine (Kennedy) is a man chasing bitch pushed by frustration and jealousy towards violence against her vulnerable charge; Eddie (Brumpton) is the faintly mysterious but ultimately angelic local guy who, much to Mad's jealous annoyance, takes a shine to Julia. The third film in de Heer's loose trilogy dealing with the fraught relationship of the marginalised with the world is his bravest yet (it was scripted by Rose, who is herself confined to a wheelchair); often, however, it resorts to fairytale coincidence and contrivance, while the characterisation is cartoon thin and the message heavy handed. GA

Dance of Dust (Raghs-e-Khak)

(1998, Iran, 73 min)
d Abolfazl Jalili. *p* Mohammad Mehdi Dadgu. *sc* Abolfazl Jalili. *ph* Atta Hayati. *ed* Abolfazl Jalili. *m* Nezamoodin Kia'ie. *cast* Mahmood Khosravi, Limua Rahi.
● There's scant plot (what little there is concerns the blossoming, unspoken friendship between two child labourers) and even less dialogue in this determinedly poetic semi-documentary account of life in a remote, windswept desert village whose economy and very survival depends on brick making. Instead, the fragmented sequence of vivid, extraordinarily beautiful, sometimes surreal images focuses on a number of repeated leitmotifs – most notably human faces and the elements – to create an impressionistic portrait of hardship, spiritual strength and human solidarity. At first it all seems a little too self-consciously arty, but after a while it does weave a mesmerising spell; indeed, admirers of Vigo's *A Propos de Nice*, Herzog's *Fata Morgana*, or the more abstract flights of fancy by Pasolini or Paradjanov will probably succumb to its strange magic. GA

Dance of Love (Reigen)

(1973, WGer, 122 min)
d/p/sc Otto Schenk. *ph* Wolfgang Treu. *ed* Anneliese Artelt. *ad* Herta Hareiter. *m* Francis Lai. *cast* Senta Berger, Maria Schneider, Helmuth Lohner, Sydney Rome, Peter Weck, Helmut Berger.
● Described as 'delightfully mischievous' by its distributors, Schenk's film – not so much a remake of Max Ophüls' classic *La Ronde* as a return to Arthur Schnitzler's more sardonic play – takes full advantage of relaxing censorship attitudes. Predictably, all the visual richness and stylish elegance of the Ophüls version has given way to bumbling sexual romps. Censorship at least had the positive value of forcing directors to be imaginative in the way they presented Eros on the screen. GSa

Dance of the Vampires (aka The Fearless Vampire Killers)

(1967, US, 107 min)
d Roman Polanski. *p* Gene Gutowski. *sc* Gérard Brach, Roman Polanski. *ph* Douglas Slocombe. *ed* Alastair McIntyre. *pd* Wilfred Shingleton. *m* Krzysztof Komeda. *cast* Jack MacGowran, Roman Polanski, Alfie Bass, Jessie Robbins, Sharon Tate, Ferdy Mayne, Iain Quarrier, Terry Downes.
● Messy vampire spoof-cum-homage to Hammer, which doesn't really come off on either count. On the other hand, no film can be all bad which has a screen credit reading 'Fangs by Dr Ludwig von Krankheit'; and Polanski does pull out some gems, like the very Jewish monster menaced with a crucifix who cheerfully gloats, 'You got the wrong vampire, girl!' Other pluses include very attractive sets and Douglas Slocombe's camerawork, Krzysztof Komeda's bat-winged musical score, and the marvellous sequence of the great vampire ball, in which the guests rise from their graves to embark on a stately minuet that ends in front of a vast mirror reflecting only the three human interlopers. With all its faults, an engaging oddity. TM

Dance of the Wind (Wara Mandel)

(1997, GB/Fr/Ger/Neth, 85min)
d Rajan Khosa. *p* Karl Baumgartner. *sc* Robin Mukherjee. *ph* Piyush Shah. *ed* Emma Matthews. *pd* Amardeep Behl. *m* Shubha Mudgal. *cast* Kitu Gidwani, Bhaveen Gosain, Roshan Bano, BC Sanyal, Roshan Bano, Kapila Vatsyayan.
● Though visually arresting and making beautiful use of classical Indian music, this film by British-based Rajan Khosa never opts for a picture postcard view of life in contemporary Delhi. It centres on an acclaimed singer who finds herself unable to perfom after the death of her mother and mentor. The loss affects her career, and her relationship with her students and her husband. Lyrical and meditative it may be, but the film shows us things seldom depicted in Indian cinema (the heroine vomiting in the lavatory) and firmly contextualises the singer's life, steeped in art, tradition and taste, within a world that also includes poverty, violence, injustice and bhangra. Simple, elegant and as resonant as the lovely sounds heard throughout. GA

Dancer in the Dark

(2000, Den/Swe, 139 min)
d Lars von Trier. *p* Vibeke Windeløv. *sc* Lars von Trier. *ph* Robby Müller. *ed* Molly Malene Stensgaard, François Gedigier. *pd* Karl Juliusson. *m* Björk. *cast* Björk, Catherine Deneuve, David Morse, Peter Stormare, Joel Grey, Vincent Paterson, Cara Seymour, Jean-Marc Barr, Udo Kier.
● After the rigours of *The Idiots*, von Trier returns to *Breaking the Waves* territory with another emotionally upfront, somewhat hollow tale of self-sacrificing, saintly womanhood. In rural America, Czech single mother Björk keeps quiet about her rapidly deteriorating sight so that she can retain her factory job and pay for an op to prevent her son from going blind. After she accidentally kills her neighbour (Morse), who has stolen her savings, her continuing refusal to keep the truth from her child makes for 'tragedy' (or so the director would define it). What makes the film a little unusual is that every so often it jolts into dance-musical sequences, illustrating the optimistic fantasies into which our brave heroine escapes. The trouble is, all the cameras in the world (and a 100 were reportedly used for some scenes), coupled with MTV-style editing, can't conceal the imaginative poverty of von Trier's response to the (admittedly ho-hum) choreography, nor the disingenuous contrivances of the plot. Whether one finds Björk's angelic attempts to console fellow Death Row inmates with a song deeply moving or offensive, trivial and tasteless is a matter of personal sensibility (I gagged!), but, Deneuve's under-used presence as Bjork's workmate notwithstanding, there's no denying that this can't hold a candle to the best work by Demy, let alone von Trier's beloved Dreyer. GA

Dancers

(1987, US, 99 min)
d Herbert Ross. *p* Menahem Golan, Yoram Globus. *sc* Sarah Kernochan. *ph* Ennio Guarnieri. *ed* William H Reynolds. *pd* Gianni Quaranta. *m* Pino Donaggio. *cast* Mikhail Baryshnikov, Alessandra Ferri, Leslie Browne, Thomas Rall, Lynn Seymour, Victor Barbee, Julie Kent.
● A lot of ballet nonsense with Baryshnikov as a celebrated dancer who likes to play hide the salami with his leading ladies, but has for the moment lost contact with his creative muse. Naive American teenager Lisa (Kent) arrives in Southern Italy to join his production of Giselle. Their brief liaison fans Baryshnikov's creative spark, allowing him to dance with new passion while Lisa weeps in the wings. Predictably, the off-screen entanglements are echoed by the on-stage action, in which the rake is haunted by the ghosts of his wronged lovers. Ross stages the extended dance sequences with considerable flair, and it's a treat to see the graceful Alessandra Ferri stealing the show. However, in a terpsichorean turkey stuffed with silliness, the pliés and pirouettes are a long time coming. NF

Dances with Wolves

(1990, US, 180 min)
d Kevin Costner. *p* Kevin Costner, Jim Wilson. *sc* Michael Blake. *ph* Dean Semler. *ed* Neil Travis. *pd* Jeffrey Beecroft. *m* John Barry. *cast* Kevin Costner, Mary McDonnell, Graham Greene, Rodney A Grant, Floyd Red Crow Westerman, Tantoo Cardinal, Robert Pastorelli, Maury Chaykin.
● Disenchanted after being wounded in the American Civil War, Lt Dunbar (Costner) is assigned to a frontier outpost. Finding nothing but a deserted fort and left to his own devices, Dunbar gradually gains the friendship and trust of both a wolf and the Sioux Indians. Won over by the native Americans' love of the land, the honourable soldier joins in their buffalo hunt, courts a white woman the tribe adopted in childhood, transfers allegiance from predatory white man to peaceful Indian, and discovers en route his true self. At three hours long, and with a largely Indian cast delivering (subtitled) Lakota dialogue, Costner's debut as a director is a genuinely, impressively epic Western. It may lack complexity and political sophistication – the Sioux are a mite sentimentalised, the US Cavalry too obviously ignorant bigots, and Costner's two-dimensional hero too prone to cute pratfalls – but its sentiments are conspicuously sincere and its dramatic sweep hugely confident. Historical and cultural authenticity is virtually an end in itself, and although the last half-hour founders in repeated farewells, it looks great. Once you're sucked into the leisurely narrative, it's hard to resist. GA

Dances with Wolves – Special Edition

(1990/91, US, 236 min)
d Kevin Costner. *p* Kevin Costner, Jim Wilson. *sc* Michael Blake. *ph* Dean Semler. *ed* Neil Travis. *pd* Jeffrey Beecroft. *m* John Barry. *cast* Kevin Costner, Mary McDonnell, Graham Greene, Rodney A Grant, Floyd Red Crow Westerman, Tantoo Cardinal, Robert Pastorelli, Maury Chaykin.
● The additional footage in this extended version of Costner's Western epic is basically more of the same, fleshing out relationships but making no radical difference to the film. Splendid panoramas abound, but a couple of extra sequences do serve to enhance understanding and motivation: notably, the battered state of Fort Sedgwick (with its caves and wreckage), and a scene in which an unsettled Lt Dunbar watches Sioux celebrate their slaughter of white settlers. CM

Dance With a Stranger

(1984, GB, 102 min)
d Mike Newell. *p* Roger Randall-Cutler. *sc* Shelagh Delaney. *ph* Peter Hannan. *ed* Mick Audsley. *pd* Andrew Mollo. *m* Richard Hartley. *cast* Miranda Richardson, Rupert Everett, Ian Holm, Matthew Carroll, Tom Chadbon, Jane Bertish, Stratford Johns, Joanne Whalley-Kilmer.
● Newcomer Richardson is Ruth Ellis, peroxided 'hostess' in a Soho drinking club and the last woman to be hanged in Britain for the murder of her upper middle class lover. Not so much star-crossed as class-crossed, the affair has all the charm of fingernails on a blackboard, and it's filmed with a merciless eye for the sort of bad behaviour that Fassbinder made his own. But what the movie captures perfectly is the seedy mood of repression, so characteristic of austerity Britain in the '50s. Richardson gives full rein to the two things that British cinema has hardly ever had the guts to face: sexual obsession and bad manners. And, since this is England, it's the latter that finally sends her to the scaffold. It's shot, designed and acted with an imaginative grasp that puts it straight into the international class. CPea

Dance with Me

(1998, US, 126 min)
d Randa Haines. *p* Lauren C Weissman, Shinya Egawa, Randa Haines. *sc* Daryl Matthews. *ph* Fred Murphy. *ed* Lisa Fruchtman. *pd* Waldemar Kalinowski. *m* Michael Convertino. *cast* Vanessa L Williams, Chayanne, Kris Kristofferson, Jane Krakowski, Beth Grant, Harry Groener, William Marquez, Scott Paetty, Joan Plowright.
● Rafael (Chayanne), a young Cuban, comes to America in search of his American father (Kristofferson) and winds up falling in love with dancer Ruby (Williams). With his bouffant hair-do and matronly hips, Chayanne looks like he has been beamed down from the '50s. Compared to street savvy Williams (surprisingly good), he's just not cool. And certainly not sexy. This works well because ballroom dancing is somewhat cheesy. But since when did Hollywood prefer grit to glitter? About halfway through, director

Haines panics, and decides to sell our awkward hero as an old-fashioned heart throb. The dancing, too, is forced into a glamour suit, with a stock finale at the World Open Dance Championships. Here the film takes a dive, first because Chayanne isn't a natural dancer, and second because the moves themselves, though well choreographed, necessarily appeal to a limited market. Meanwhile, the use of Plowright as a middle-aged frump wanting to get in on the sexy action is deeply patronising. CO'Su

Dancing at Lughnasa

(1998, Ire/GB/US, 95 min)
d Pat O'Connor. *p* Noel Pearson. *sc* Frank McGuinness. *ph* Kenneth MacMillan. *ed* Humphrey Dixon. *pd* Mark Geraghty. *m* Bill Whelan. *cast* Meryl Streep, Michael Gambon, Catherine McCormack, Kathy Burke, Brid Brennan, Sophie Thompson, Rhys Ifans.

●Donegal, 1936. The Mundy sisters – five of them, none married – welcome home their brother Jack, a missionary (Gambon). But whatever their private hopes, the bewildered Jack proves just another burden to carry. The eldest, Kate (Streep), is a schoolteacher, but her wage is barely enough to feed them all. Agnes (Brennan) and the simple-minded Rose (Thompson) help out with their knitting, while Maggie (Burke) keeps house and Christina (McCormack) cares for her young son Michael. Framed as the grown boy's wistful evocation of his childhood, Brian Friel's luminous play presents more than the usual problems attendant on 'opening out' for the cinema. A magical reverie in which a crackled radio broadcast can conjure its own special epiphany, ghosts of pagan gods and a heartbreaking sense of home and family, this might have been ideal material for Terence Davies. But O'Connor is altogether too literal a director, his costume drama naturalism sitting oddly with the play's more nebulous sense of reality. Nevertheless, it looks ravishing, Frank McGuinness's adaptation retains the play's subtle sibling interaction, and Streep's virtuosity of expression is as spectacular as ever. TCh

Dancing Bull (Wuniu)

(1990, HK, 116 min)
d Allen Fong. *p* Willy Tsao, Allen Fong. *sc* Chi-Sing Cheung. *ph* George Chan. *ed* Kwok Keung. *pd* Kwan Pak-hyn. *m* Eugene Pao, Ric Halstead, Violet Lam. *cast* Cora Miao, Lindzay Chan, Anthony Wong, Fung Kin-Chung.

●The strains of running a modern-dance company in the Thatcherite cultural climate of Hong Kong cause a marriage to break up: the choreographer husband lapses into inertia with a new girlfriend, while the dancer wife becomes a cultural mover. Not much of a storyline to support a movie that aims to take the temperature of present-day Hong Kong (in the aftermath of the Beijing massacre), and it must be said that the film is neither as impassioned nor as incisive as it thinks it is. But it does sustain interest at several levels, and Cora Miao (the first *bona fide* star to appear in an Allen Fong movie) copes with the director's improvisational methods as if born to them. TR

Dancing in the Dark

(1985, Can, 99 min)
d Leon Marr. *p* Anthony Kramreither. *sc* Leon Marr. *ph* Vic Sarin. *ed* Tom Berner. *pd* Lillian Sarafinchan. *cast* Martha Henry, Neil Munro, Rosemary Dunsmore, Richard Monette, Elena Kudaba.

●Marr's first feature offers a tunneled vision of the 20-year marriage of Edna and Harry in their small suburban home (not just the centre of Edna's world, but her entire universe), where the camera catches the woman like a grub burrowing its way in the soil. Edna's story is told in flashback: sitting in her white dressing-gown in a psychiatric hospital, she examines her notebook (the diary of a mad housewife?) and proceeds to reveal the details of a 20-year career of cleaning, screwing and cooking for her mate before one day deciding to sharpen a kitchen knife against the bones of his ribcage. This murderous act of 'liberation' becomes, in a sense, Edna's birth, where the grub finally asserts its identity after a life led solely to complement that of her boorish husband. Unfortunately it is difficult to base a feature-length film on a character who has no character. Inevitably it makes for a rather tedious and highly non-moving use of exposed silver nitrate on plastic. SGo

Dancin' Thru the Dark

(1989, GB, 95 min)
d Mike Ockrent. *p* Andrée Molyneux, Annie Russell. *sc* Willy Russell. *ph* Philip Bonham-Carter. *ed* John Stodhart. *pd* Paul Joel. *m* Willy Russell. *cast* Claire Hackett, Con O'Neill, Angela Clarke, Julia Deakin, Louise Duprey, Sandy Hendrickse, Andrew Naylor, Conrad Nelson, Simon O'Brien, Peter Watts, Mark Womack, Colin Welland.

●'It's raised more misery than all the wars and revolutions put together', mutters a jaded soul on the subject of marriage. Certainly Willy Russell's adaptation of his own play *Stags and Hens* is unequivocal about tying the knot too soon. The action takes place the night before Linda and Dave's wedding: Linda (Hackett) is out with the girls for a hen night, Dave (Nelson) is carousing with the boys. Both parties unwittingly converge on the same nightclub, where Linda has gone to see her almost-famous ex-boyfriend (O'Neill) perform with his group. Emotions run high when Linda is overwhelmed by second thoughts… It's a straightforward tale about a well-worn theme – it has no pretensions to be otherwise – but the frequent moralising about marriage tends towards excess. The more obvious jokes (I'm gregarious' –'Pleased to meet you, Greg') hold far less humour than the trenchant observations of disco politics: from early-evening boogies around handbags to booze-fuelled advances. Overall, with a solid cast, Ockrent makes an assured and lively film debut. CM

Dancing With Crime

(1947, GB, 83 min, b/w)
d John Paddy Carstairs. *p* James Carter. *sc* Brock Williams, Peter Fraser. *ph* Reginald Wyer. *ed* Eily Boland. *ad* Harry Moore. *m* Benjamn Frankel. *cast* Richard Attenborough, Sheila Sim, Barry K Barnes, Barry Jones, Garry Marsh, Bill Owen.

●Attenborough as an earnest young taxi-driver, recently demobbed, who, though headed for marriage on a shoestring, stoutly refuses the temptation to come in on a mysterious black market deal with an ex-army pal (Owen). Setting out to investigate when he finds the dead pal dumped in his taxi, he tracks the villains to a local dance hall they use as a front, and – with his girl (Sim) intrepidly going undercover on his behalf – brings them to justice. Strictly conventional all the way, but not unlikeable, despite some clumsily staged fisticuffs for the climax. TM

Dandy (La Bande du Drugstore)

(Fr, 2001, 98 min)
d François Armanet. *p* Jean Bréhat, Rachid Bouchareb. *sc* François Armanet, Jean Helpert. *ph* Guillaume Schiffman. *ed* Sandrine Degeen. *ad* Jean-Marc Tran Tan Ba. *cast* Mathieu Simonet, Cécile Cassel, Aurélien Wiik, Alice Taglioni, Matthias Van Khache, Laurent Pialet.

●While British mods were listening to The Who and roaring around Brighton on their scooters, their Parisian equivalents – or so Armanet's entertaining debut feature suggests – were discussing Sartre, preening themselves in the sun and working out how best to seduce as many women as possible. The protagonists here, the floppy-haired aesthete Philippe (Simonet) and his rugged Belmondo-like pal Marc (Wiik), are rich kids who certainly don't have to put up with any of the daily humiliations that Phil Daniels and Co endured in *Quadrophenia*. What might have been a tiresome exercise in narcissism and nostalgia is rescued by its self-mocking humour and attractive performances from Simonet and Cécile Cassel (as the dark-haired beauty who throws into question his chauvinistic assumptions about life and love). Writer/director Armanet is the editor of *Libération*, one of France's best-known newspapers. Whatever his journalistic credentials, he shows considerable promise as a film-maker. GM

Dandy in Aspic, A

(1968, GB, 107 min)
d/p Anthony Mann. *sc* Derek Marlowe. *ph* Christopher Challis. *ed* Thelma Connell. *ad* Carmen Dillon. *m* Quincy Jones. *cast* Laurence Harvey, Tom Courtenay, Mia Farrow, Lionel Stander, Harry Andrews, Peter Cook, Per Oscarsson, Barbara Murray, John Bird.

●Scripted by Derek Marlowe from his own novel, Anthony Mann's last film (he died during shooting and was replaced as director by Laurence Harvey) is the story of a Russian double agent, Krasnevin (Harvey), given a difficult mission by the British secret service: to hunt down and eliminate himself. Driven by a byzantine plot that would turn out to be characteristic of the writer (compare Stuart Cooper's *The Disappearance*, adapted from Marlowe's *Echoes of Celandine*), the film is strong on Cold War atmospherics and notable for its superior cast. NRo

Dandy, the All-American Girl (aka Sweet Revenge)

(1976, US, 90 min)
d/p Jerry Schatzberg. *sc* BJ Perla, Marilyn Goldin. *ph* Vilmos Zsigmond. *ed* Evan Lottman, Richard Fetterman. *ad* Bill Kenney. *m* Paul Chihara. *cast* Stockard Channing, Sam Waterston, Franklyn Ajaye, Richard Doughty, Norman Matlock.

●Determinedly offbeat comedy, with Channing as a slightly crazy car-thief, stealing and selling a variety of autos as she attempts to gain enough cash to buy herself a Ferrari. Meanwhile, she plays a complex romantic game with three very different male admirers. Schatzberg, forsaking the serious and muddled statements of films like *Scarecrow* and *Puzzle of a Downfall Child*, here comes up with a relaxed and meandering study of eccentric characters on the fringes of society, as messy and occasionally likeable as Henry Jaglom's far more garrulous efforts. Indulgent, directionless, but well-performed and often witty. GA

Dang Bireley's and the Young Gangsters (2499 Antapan Krong Muang)

(1997, Thai, 110 min)
d Nonzee Nimibutr. *p* Visute Poolvoralaks. *sc* Wisit Sasnatiang. *ph* Winai Patomboon. *ed* Sunit Ussavinikul. *pd* Ek Lemchuen. *cast* Jesdaporn Pholdee, Noppachai Muttaweevong, Attaporn Teemakorn, Suppakorn Kitsuwan.

●Ths stylish and assured first feature is based on the true story of a '50s gangster, who modelled himself on Dean and Elvis, and became famous in Bangkok after killing two men by the age of 18. The film charts his rise to power, his exile in the countryside after a martial law clampdown, and his battles with two friends turned hothead thugs. Told in flashback, from the day he's ordained a monk (to please his mum), the film seldom moralises, but never glamorises the violence either. Clearly influenced by the early work of John Woo, it's best seen as a tale of honour, loyalty and love among hoodlums. GA

Danger by My Side

(1962, GB, 63 min, b/w)
d Charles Saunders. *p* John I Phillips. *sc* Ronald C Liles, Aubrey Cash. *ph* Walter J Harvey. *ed* Jim Connock. *ad* Harold Watson. *m* Martin Slavin. *cast* Maureen Connell, Anthony Oliver, Alan Tilvern, Bill Nagy, Tom Naylor, Brandon Brady.

●Plucky Connell gets a job in a shady nightclub to follow up her hunch that the sleazy proprietor was involved in her detective brother's murder. An unexceptional British B-thriller with an anonymous cast and a risible striptease which even in 1962 can't have set many hearts aflutter. TJ

Danger: Diabolik (Diabolik)

(1967, It/Fr, 105 min)
d Mario Bava. *p* Dino de Laurentiis. *sc* Mario Bava, Dino Maiuri. *ph* Antonio Rinaldi. *ed* Romana Fortini. *ad* Flavio Mogherini. *m* Ennio Morricone. *cast* John Phillip Law, Marisa Mell, Michel Piccoli, Adolfo Celi, Terry-Thomas, Claudio Gora.

●A delightfully outlandish comic strip directed by the master of the Italian B movie, a former cameraman who could always be relied on to ravish the eye with wonderfully bizarre imagery. Part James Bond parody, part Feuillade serial, it sends itself up as cheerfully as anything else as its hero dallies with his beloved under a snowfall of banknotes or prowls about his nefarious (but always chivalrous) purposes in black leotards, armed with suction pads that turn him into a human fly. But from time to time it also hits a high note of fantasy worthy of Cocteau, notably in a scene where Diabolik, encased in plumes of molten gold, is transformed into a living statue by his arch-enemy. TM

Danger – Love at Work

(1937, US, 81 min, b/w)
d Otto Preminger. *sc* James Edward Grant, Ben Markson. *ph* Virgil Miller. *ed* Jack Murray. *ad* Duncan Cramer. *m* David Buttolph. *cast* Ann Sothern, Jack Haley, Edward Everett Horton, Mary Boland, John Carradine, Walter Catlett, Elisha Cook Jr.

●Uncle Goliath warms his pan of snail soup, the child prodigy rehearses his Ancient Egyptian vocables, while the artist wrestles with his masterwork, 'The Sublimation of the Inanimate': just the average members of your average screwball-comedy family. Haley is the lawyer tasked with getting the signatures of the entire bunch on some McGuffin of a property deed. Preminger, in one of his early assignments, directs efficiently, but with little feeling for screwball form; with hindsight it was hardly his sort of thing. Amiable enough, but, as ever, a little loveable eccentricity goes a very long way. BBa

Dangerous

(1935, US, 78 min, b/w)
d Alfred E Green. *p* Harry Joe Brown. *sc* Laird Doyle. *ph* Ernest Haller. *ed* Thomas Richards. *ad* Hugh Reticker. *m* Bernhard Kaun. *cast* Bette Davis, Franchot Tone, Margaret Lindsay, Alison Skipworth, John Eldredge.

●Davis, as a former star actress now wallowing in the gutter and self-pity, is rehabilitated by Tone's handsome young architect. Even Davis says she found the script maudlin and mawkish, though she won an Oscar for her performance.

Dangerous Beauty (aka The Honest Courtesan)

(1997, US, 112 min)
d Marshall Herskovitz. *p* Marshall Herskovitz, Edward Zwick, Arnon Milchan, Sarah Caplan. *sc* Jeaninine Dominy. *ph* Bojan Bazelli. *ed* Steven Rosenblum, Arthur Coburn. pd Norman Garwood. *m* George Fenton. *cast* Catherine McCormack, Rufus Sewell, Oliver Platt, Moira Kelly, Fred Ward, Jacqueline Bisset, Peter Eyre, Naomi Watts, Jeroen Krabbé.

●This lengthy 16th century romp detailing the life of Venetian courtesan Veronica Franco (McCormack) is so awash in '60s costume kitsch, old-fashioned sexual banter and feeble innuendo as to make a mockery of its putative celebration of the self-emancipating efforts of its low born heroine. Poetry loving Veronica can't wed her dashing aristo Marco Venier (Sewell), since he's bound for a marriage of convenience. Her mother Paola (Bisset) steps in to announce, shockingly, 'You will be a courtesan, like your *mother*!', proceeding to teach her the ropes. Before you know it, this gifted student is jousting with verses against court poet Maffio Venier (Platt), and bedding Doges, cardinals, cabbages and kings, while outside the pox, the plague and puritanism rage. There are few traces of irony, intended fun, or *Casanova*-style exoticism here: the director may intened a feminist Visconti, but he ends up with a Zalman King *Red Shoe Diary* crossed with a Dick Lester Dumas adaptation. Only the finale, a preposterous trial with Veronica caught in a bitter war between church and state, raises the spirits. WH

Dangerous Female

see Maltese Falcon, The

Dangerous Game

see Snake Eyes

Dangerous Ground

(1996, SAf/US, 95 min)
d Darrell James Roodt. *p* Gillian Gorfil, Darrell Roodt. *sc* Greg Latter, Darrell Roodt. *ph* Paul Gilpin. *ed* David Heitner. *pd* Dimitri Repanis. *m* Stanley Clarke. *cast* Ice Cube, Elizabeth Hurley, Sechaba Morojele, Eric 'Waku' Miyeni, Ving Rhames.

●Feisty South African academic Vusi (Ice Cube) was thrown into America's 'fugee-loving arms at 14, but now, with the death of his father, it's time to pop home. Thanks to an inability to stick big knives into squirming goats, he finds himself at odds with his family. Nevertheless, as first-born, he's the one sent to find an errant brother in Johannesburg, where he teams up with his brother's girlfriend Karen (Hurley), a crack-addled stripper. Directed by Darrell Roodt, a white South African, this set-up promises some interesting conflicts: 'sophisticated' America vs 'authentic' Africa; the old apartheid South Africa vs the new. But you get the feeling there was a kerfuffle about who the film was aimed at, and that someone plumped for adolescent boys weaned on *Beverly Hills Cop*. The doom and gloom surrounding South Africa's future merely serves as an excuse for America's finest to take matters in hand. Why, you might ask, can't the South Africans do it for themselves? Because, according to this film, they're ineffectual kaftan-wearers or effete junkies. CO'Su

Dangerous Liaisons

(1988, US, 120 min)
d Stephen Frears. *p* Norman Heyman, Hank Moonjean. *sc* Christopher Hampton. *ph* Philippe Rousselot. *ed* Mick Audsley. *pd* Stuart Craig. George Fenton. *m* George Fenton. *cast* Glenn Close, John Malkovich, Michelle Pfeiffer, Swoosie Kurtz, Keanu Reeves, Mildred Natwick, Uma Thurman, Peter Capaldi.

●Choderlos de Laclos' 18th century novel is a monument to lust, guilt and duplicity, written in letter form. One of the film's enormous strengths is scriptwriter Christopher Hampton's decision to go back to the novel, and save only the best from his play. Frears, under commercial pressure but also determined to start afresh, has chosen American actors for the main roles: Malkovich as the professional philanderer Valmont; Close as the sadistic aristocrat with whom he plots to ruin both a social union and a virtuous woman (Pfeiffer, splendid). The result is a sombre, manipulative affair in which the décor is never allowed to usurp our interest. Broader, nastier even than the play, it uses recurring epistolary motifs, shadow and close-up to convey the themes of the piece: the relationships between pleasure and pain, our inability to control others, our endless desire to do so. Malkovich's final demise, run through, wasted and resigned, recalls the misty-eyed days of Fairbanks and Flynn; while Close, all eye-contact, front, and self-possession, ends the film unforgettably as a sacrificial lamb on the altar of decency. SGr

Dangerously They Live

(1942, US, 77 min, b/w)
d Robert Florey. *p* Ben Stoloff. *sc* Marion Parsonnet. *ph* William O'Connell. *ed* Harold McLernon. *ad* Hugh Reticker. *cast* John Garfield, Nancy Coleman, Raymond Massey, Moroni Olsen, Lee Patrick, Esther Dale, Christian Rub.

●Creaky spy melodrama in which Coleman, working for British intelligence, is abducted in New York by Nazi sympathisers intent on gaining access to a message she has memorised concerning the route to be taken by a big convoy. When the car crashes, she lands in hospital, and confides in a young intern (Garfield) after recovering from temporary amnesia. Garfield's doubts about her story are confirmed when the man she insists *isn't* her father (Olsen) summons a distinguished psychiatrist (Massey) under whom Garfield had once studied. Florey can't do much about the lumbering script or about Coleman's inept performance. But once the girl has been taken 'home' – a large, lonely mansion where she and Garfield (brought along to lull lingering suspicions) find themselves held prisoner while Massey and his Nazi cohorts do their dirty work – Florey seems more interested, bringing off some nice semi-Gothic atmospherics. The ending, alas, reverts to routine histrionics and heroics. TM

Dangerous Minds

(1994, US, 99 min)
d John N Smith. *p* Don Simpson, Jerry Bruckheimer. *sc* Ronald Bass. *ph* Pierre Letarte. *ed* Tom Rolf. *pd* Donald Graham Burt. *m* Wendy and Lisa. *cast* Michelle Pfeiffer, George Dzundza, Courtney B Vance, Robin Bartlett, Bruklin Harris, Renoly Santiago.

●A surprise hit at the US box office, this is a standard 'inspirational' foray into the blackboard jungle, a place where over-age ethnic actors vye for the attention of the camera and pay no heed to their English teacher until she gets relevant by quoting Bob Dylan. Actually it's quite a respectable piece of work, with an impressive tough-love performance from Pfeiffer, but Ronald Bass's hackneyed screenplay is all carrot and no stick. TCh

Dangerous Mission

(1954, US, 75 min)
d Louis King. *p* Irwin Allen. *sc* Horace McCoy, WR Burnett, Charles Bennett. *ph* William Snyder. *ed* Gene Palmer. *ad* Albert S D'Agostino, Walter Keller. *m* Roy Webb. *cast* Victor Mature, Piper Laurie, Vincent Price, William Bendix, Betta St John, Dennis Weaver.

●A thriller which opens resonantly with a man being gunned down as he sits at the piano in a dark, deserted nightclub. But despite good performances, the presence of Horace McCoy, WR Burnett and Charles Bennett among the credited writers, and a potentially workable story – detective Mature sets out in pursuit of a girl who witnessed the murder, ostensibly to protect her from the Mob – this never really takes off. Mature is so nudgingly pointed up as the killer that it's painfully obvious he isn't, and the supposedly nail-biting climax among the treacherous mountain crevasses (shot in the Glacier National Park, Montana, with excessive attention to scenic grandeur) is absurdly hamfisted. TM

Dangerous Moonlight

(1941, GB, 98 min, b/w)
d Brian Desmond Hurst. *p* William Sistrom. *sc* Terence Young. *ph* Georges Périnal. *ed* Alan L Jaggs. *ad* John Bryan. *m* Richard Addinsell. *cast* Anton Walbrook, Sally Gray, Derrick de Marney, Cecil Parker, Keneth Kent, Guy Middleton.

●Splendidly slushy World War II melodrama, with Walbrook an angst-ridden Polish pianist torn between success in America and death in the skies above beleaguered Britain. Hurst, the wild Irishman of British cinema, proves surprisingly proficient at investing his slight, improbable story with power and resonance. The issues may be tritely resolved – only a miracle allows us a final encore of the Warsaw Concerto – but in taking the myth of the great artist and subordinating it to the more immediately relevant one of the do-or-die fighter-pilot hero, Hurst conjures up a satisfying concoction of fantasy and propaganda. RMy

Dangerous Moves (La Diagonale du Fou)

(1983, Switz, 110 min)
d Richard Dembo. *p* Arthur Cohn. *sc* Richard Dembo. *ph* Raoul Coutard. *ed* Agnès Guillemot. *ad* Ivan Maussion. *m* Gabriel Yared. *cast* Michel Piccoli, Alexandre Arbatt, Liv Ullmann, Leslie Caron, Daniel Olbrychski, Michel Aumont.

●Set during the World Chess Championship, and focusing on the intense rivalry between ageing, ailing Soviet champion Liebskind (Piccoli) and his former pupil, the unorthodox young rebel Fromm (Arbatt) – himself a Russian defector whom the Soviet authorities wish to humiliate – the film's fascination lies partly in the bizarre, underhanded tactics employed to distract keyed-up competitors, partly in the vivid characterisations. Also of interest, however, is the wider context which reveals the rivals as reluctant pawns in political power struggles. Expertly performed (particularly by Piccoli), and shot through with moments of memorably absurd humour, Dembo's miniature thriller is an unusual delight. GA

Dangerous Summer, A

(1981, Aust, 100 min)
d Quentin Masters. *p* Jim McElroy. *sc* David Ambrose, Quentin Masters. *ph* Peter Hannam. *ed* Ted Otton. *ad* John Carroll, Bob Hilditch. *m* Groove Myers. *cast* Tom Skerritt, Ian Gilmour, Wendy Hughes, Ray Barrett, James Mason, Guy Doleman.

●Ludicrous conspiracy thriller set in the Blue Mountains during the bush fire season, with the plot huffing and puffing round attempts to sabotage a multi-million dollar resort project. Made the same year as Phillip Noyce's skilful but slightly tub-thumping *Heatwave*, which looks like a masterpiece of subtlety and discretion by comparison. TM

Dangerous When Wet

(1953, US, 95 min)
d Charles Walters. *p* George Wells. *sc* Dorothy Kingsley. *ph* Harold Rosson. *ed* John McSweeney. *ad* Cedric Gibbons, Jack Martin Smith. *songs* Arthur Schwarz, Johnny Mercer. *cast* Esther Williams, Charlotte Greenwood, William Demarest, Fernando Lamas, Jack Carson, Denise Darcel.

●A ludicrous plot, designed to cash in on Williams' rather specialised talent, sees her and her Arkansas family preparing for a cross-channel swim. Arthur Schwartz and Johnny Mercer's songs are pleasant enough, as are the performances; but the highlight of the humdrum proceedings is the sequence in which Esther swims with Tom and Jerry. GA

Dangerous Woman, A

(1993, US. 101 min)
d Stephen Gyllenhaal. *p/sc* Naomi Foner. *ph* Robert Elswit. *ed* Harvey Rosenstock. *pd* David Brisbin. *m* Carter Burwell. *cast* Debra Winger, Barbara Hershey, Gabriel Byrne, Chloe Webb, David Strathairn, Laurie Metcalf.

●Gyllenhaal's third feature (from a script by his wife Naomi Foner) is happily less hackneyed than one might anticipate. The cast are a great help: Debra Winger as Martha, a gauche social and emotional misfit whose naive insistence on telling the truth gets her into trouble with those around her; Barbara Hershey as her attractive aunt Frances, who finds that looking after Martha is taking its toll on her affair with a married politician; Chloe Webb as Martha's friend Birdy, and the ever-excellent David Strathairn as Birdy's lover Getso; and Gabriel Byrne as Mackey, the drunken handyman who's taken on to repair Frances and Martha's home, only to upset the already precarious applecart. Much here may be routine, in the lyrical small-town genre, but now and then a welcome sense of pain, confusion and frustrated desire erupts from the well-honed narrative. GA

Danger Route

(1967, GB, 92 min)
d Seth Holt. *p* Max J Rosenberg, Milton Subotsky. *sc* Meade Roberts. *ph* Harry Waxman. *ed* Oswald Hafenrichter. *pd* William Constable. *m* John Mayer. *cast* Richard Johnson, Carol Lynley, Barbara Bouchet, Sylvia Syms, Gordon Jackson, Diana Dors, Sam Wanamaker.

●The late British director Seth Holt has something of a cult reputation, although even his supporters would probably admit that his was a frustrated and frustrating career, being full of films that are half-impressive, half-banal. This espionage thriller, with Johnson as a hired assassin caught in a complex web of betrayal and violence when he's commissioned to murder a Czech scientist, is typical; the narrative is confused and fragmented, but the tension is taut, especially when Johnson is called upon to kill his own girlfriend. GA

Daniel

(1983, US, 129 min)
d Sidney Lumet. *p* Burtt Harris. *sc* EL Doctorow. *ph* Andrzei Bartkowiak. *ed* Peter C Frank. *pd* Philip Rosenberg. *m* Bob James. *cast* Timothy Hutton, Mandy Patinkin, Lindsay Crouse, Edward Asner, Ellen Barkin, Julie Bovasso, Tovah Feldshuh, Joseph Leon, Amanda Plummer.

●Adapted by EL Doctorow from his own novel, *The Book of Daniel*, this fictional telling of the story of the Rosenbergs (executed in the 1950s in Chicago for Soviet espionage concerning the atom bomb) jerks every tear, rehearses every cliché, and obscures every insight that the perspective of thirty years might grant us. Hutton plays the son of the Rosenbergs (called here the Isaacsons), who becomes a hippy in the '60s and is convinced that if he can find the truth about his parents' guilt or innocence he will be able to free his schizophrenic sister from her madness. Unfortunately, Doctorow and Lumet mix this story up with a polemic about capital punishment. They also destroy their focus by never coming clean about what they think the Rosenbergs actually did. This leaves *Daniel* as just a psycho-political melodrama. MH

Daniel and the Devil

see All That Money Can Buy

Daniel Takes a Train (Szerencsés Dániel)

(1983, Hun, 92 min)
d Pál Sándor. *sc* Zsuzsa Toth. *ph* Elemér Ragalyi. *ed* A Karmento. *pd* Attila Kovacs. *m* György Selmeczy. *cast* Péter Rudolf, Sándor Zsótér, Kati Szerb, Mari Töröcsik, Dezsö Garas, Gyula Bodrogi.

●In 1956 two teenage boys, one an army deserter whose unit turned against the government when the Russians rolled in, the other an apolitical youth called Daniel who aims to follow his girlfriend and her family to the West, take one of the last, overcrowded trains from Budapest to Vienna during the brief period when emigration was allowed. The atmosphere of panic and moral dilemma (whether to stay loyal to Hungary or escape to 'freedom') is keenly sustained, and the period reconstruction well bolstered by Elemér Ragályi's clever camerawork. But apart from the buddy relationship of the two fugitives, characterisation is thin, and there's almost too much plot incident to keep it on the rails. Still, it rattles along and is by turns amusing and heartstopping. (The conflict between the generations is more than touched on, but the implications – of the ending in particular – might have emerged more clearly had censorship not eliminated the information that Daniel has in fact killed his father). MA

Danny Jones

(1971, GB, 91 min)
d Jules Bricken. *p* Donald Getz. *sc* Alene Bricken, Jules Bricken. *ph* Davis Boulton. *ed* Barry Peters. *ad* Bruce Grimes. *m* David Whitaker. *cast* Frank Finlay, Jane Carr, Len Jones, Jenny Hanley, Nigel Humphreys.

●Some nice shots of the Welsh countryside, but mostly a cliché story about a Welsh carpenter, his apprentice son, and a posh bint who comes between them. The father learns that the boy must have his independence; the boy figures out that women who see themselves as sex objects can be used as such; and the posh bint ends up happy to have someone whom she thinks loves her in spite of her weight problem. Visit Wales instead. JK

Danny the Champion of the World

(1989, GB, 99 min)
d Gavin Millar. *p* Eric Abraham. *sc* John Goldsmith. *ph* Oliver Stapleton. *ed* Peter Tanner, Angus Newton. *pd* Don Homfray. *m* Stanley Myers. *cast* Jeremy Irons, Robbie Coltrane, Samuel Irons, Cyril Cusack, Michael Hordern, Lionel Jeffries, Ronald Pickup, Jean Marsh, Jimmy Nail, William Armstrong, John Woodvine, Jonathan Davis.

●Roald Dahl takes on green politics in this adaptation of his children's book: screenwriter John Goldsmith introduces the theme of rural conservation and injects topicality into a tale of post-war village life. But the basic conflict is more personal: between loveable poacher William (Irons) and crass, *nouveau riche* lord of the manor Hazell (Coltrane). Widower William runs a garage and lives in a caravan with his nine-year old son Danny (Samuel Irons). One day their peace is shattered when Hazell decides that all he surveys should become a housing estate, but his plans are thwarted by the fact that William's patch of land is smack in the middle of the estate. In the ensuing battle of wills, we can thrill to the dangers of poaching, and hiss at Hazell's dastardly schemes. Millar directs with authority and loving attention to period detail. There's also a pleasing ring of truth about the relationship built up between real-life father and son Jeremy and Samuel Irons. Family entertainment: cosy, intimate, a touch cloying. CM

Dans le Ventre du dragon

see In the Belly of the Dragon

Dante's Inferno

(1935, US, 88 min, b/w)
d Harry Lachman. *p* Sol Wurtzel. *sc* Philip Klein, Robert Yost. *ph* Rudolph Maté. *ed* Alfred DeGaetano. *ad* Duncan Cramer, David Hall, Willy Pogany. *m* Samuel Kaylin. *cast* Spencer Tracy, Claire Trevor, Henry B Walthall, Alan Dinehart, Scotty Beckett, Rita Hayworth.

●Despite the rather over-the-top moralising of the finale, which posits a dramatic comeuppance for Tracy, the ambitious and cynical showman who has built himself into a wealthy carnival- and ship-owner by exploiting and manipulating people, this is still a very enjoyable film. Partly for its bizarre, pre-*Nightmare Alley* Gothic vision of circus life, partly for Tracy's admirably tough performance, and partly for the spectacular insertion of the famous 'hell' sequence (later re-used in Ken Russell's *Altered States*). The allegory may be banal, the vision pure kitsch, but it's hard to deny the sheer fun of seeing so many scantily-clad extras cavorting wildly amid such architecturally extravagant sets. GA

Dante's Peak

(1997, US, 108 min)
d Roger Donaldson. *p* Gale Anne Hurd, Joseph M Singer. *sc* Leslie Bohem. *ph* Andrzej Bartkowiak. *ed* Howard Smith, Conrad Buff, Tina Hirsch. *pd* J Dennis Washington. *m* John Frizzell. *cast* Pierce Brosnan, Linda Hamilton, Jamie Renée Smith, Jeremy Foley, Elizabeth Hoffman, Charles Hallahan.

●The first of 1997's two volcano movies acquits itself well in the spectacle department, but its colourless characters, dwarfed from the outset by a computer-generated peak, finally get lost among the deadly emissions. There's a familiar feel to the film's *Jaws*-like set-up, with Brosnan's intuitive volcanologist predicting imminent catastrophe while local councillors insist there's no need for panic. As an exercise in disaster-movie logistics, this is on a par with *Twister*, although the jaw-dropping SFX are far more varied and genuinely terrifying. NF

Danton

(1982, Fr/Pol, 136 min)
d Andrzej Wajda. *sc* Jean-Claude Carrière. *ph* Igor Luther. *ed* Halina Prugar. *ad* Allan Starski. *m* Jean Prodomidès. *cast* Gérard Depardieu, Wojciech Pszoniak, Anne Alvaro, Patrice Chéreau, Roger Planchon, Alain Mace.

●Despite Wajda's denials, it's hard to resist the superficial comparison between Robespierre and Danton, Jaruzelski and Lech Walesa. Granted there are huge distinctions in ideology, but on the level of political personalities, Robespierre's ruthless dedication to the Revolution and Danton's man-of-the-people charisma carry potent contemporary resonance. Maybe history does repeat itself, and to some extent Wajda does too, here fleshing-out a costume drama with the kind of historical details that work in favour of the film's meaning rather than just prettifying it. OK, it's a message movie with a predictable punchline, but as Depardieu cries on the scaffold: 'Show them my head. It will be worth it'. It is. MA

Danzón

(1991, Mex, 96 min)
d María Novaro. *p* Jorge Sanchez. *sc* Maria Novaro, Beatriz Novaro. *ph* Rodrigo Garcia. *ed* Nelson Rodriguez, Maria Novaro. *ad* Marisa Pecarlins, Noberto Sanchez-Mejorada. *cast* María Rojo, Carmen Salinas, Blanca Guerra, Tito Vasconcelos, Victor Carpinteiro, Márgarita Isabel.

●Danzón is the name of a dance and its music: a style particularly attractive to Julia (Rojo) a 40-year-old single mother, telephonist and star of the local *salon de baile* in Mexico City. When her white-suited Danzón partner of 20 years standing – a real *caballero* – disappears one day, Julia is thrown into crisis and embarks on a trip to the coastal port of Vera Cruz in search not only of him but of herself too. Described as 'hot and spicy' in the programme for London's 1992 Latin American Film Festival, it is anything but. Instead, it is a gentle, affirmative and honest depiction of a particular culture (what the Danzón expresses about the emotional and sexual longings of its adherents) from the woman's point of view, which uses song to structure the narrative. It is directed by Novaro with non-obtrusive sensitivity. WH

Darby O'Gill and the Little People

(1959, US, 90 min)
d Robert Stevenson. *sc* Lawrence E Watkin. *ph* Winton C Hoch. *ed* Stanley Johnson. *ad* Carroll Clark. *m* Oliver Wallace. *cast* Albert Sharpe, Jimmy O'Dea, Sean Connery, Janet Munro, Kieron Moore, Walter Fitzgerald, Jack MacGowran.

●Walt Disney had wanted to make this Oirish fantasy (suggested by HT Kavanagh's stories) for more than 20 years and even visited Ireland to do the research, acknowledging the co-operation of 'King Brian of Knocknasheega', lord of the little people, on the final credits. Forty years on, with M'Lord Fitzpatrick's caretaker Darby O'Gill (Sharpe) falling down a well and landing in the realm of the leprechauns where he's given three wishes, it registers as a pretty hokey entertainment. But Peter Ellenshaw and Eustace Wallace's effects are put together with the studio's customary care – and there's even a banshee sequence with flame throwers to put the wind up the kids, begorrah begob. For those of a sentimental turn, there is the delight of watching young Connery romancing the ineffably wholesome Janet Munro, a couple of years before things turned nasty for Commander Bond at Crab Key with the somewhat more knowing Ursula Andress.

Dark Angel

(1990, US, 91 min)
d Craig R Baxley. *p* Jeff Young. *sc* Jonathan Tydor, Leonard Maas, Leonard Maas Jr. *ph* Mark Irwin. *ed* Mark Helfrich. *pd* Phillip M Leonard. *m* Jan Hammer. *cast* Dolph Lundgren, Brian Benben, Betsy Brantley, Matthias Hues, David Ackroyd, Michael J Pollard, Jesse Vint, Jay Bilas, Sherman Howard.

●An unpretentious sci-fi action pic in which Lundgren does battle with extra-terrestrial drug-dealers armed with lethal space-age flying CDs. Caine (Lundgren) is a conventionally 'unconventional' Houston vice cop, who works on instinct and would rather die than break his word. When his buddy is blown away infiltrating a local drug ring, Caine finds himself forced into partnership with strait-laced, by-the-book Laurence Smith (Benben, nicely irritating). Relations between the two are strained to breaking point as Caine announces his belief that a spate of peculiarly vampiric killings are being carried out by drug-fiends from outer space. But Smith's incredulity naturally turns to awed acceptance as the corpse-count rises. With an upbeat script and a healthy sense of humour, this is an unashamedly ridiculous affair with moderate ambitions and matching success. MK

Dark Angel, The

(1935, US, 110 min, b/w)
d Sidney A Franklin. *sc* Lillian Hellman, Mordaunt Shairp. *ph* Gregg Toland. *ed* Sherman Todd. *ad* Richard Day. *m* Alfred Newman. *cast* Fredric March, Merle Oberon, Herbert Marshall, Janet Beecher, John Halliday, Claud Allister.

●Lush Goldwyn weepie, based on a Guy Bolton play previously filmed by George Fitzmaurice in 1925, with Ronald Colman and Vilma Banky. Man loves woman who turns to his equally smitten cousin when he's reported killed in the war, but finds (gulp) that he's only blinded and living in self-sacrificial hiding. Irredeemable tosh (with a distinctly tepid performance from Oberon), despite Lillian Hellman script and sleek Gregg Toland camerawork. TM

Dark at the Top of the Stairs, The

(1960, US, 123 min)
d Delbert Mann. *p* Michael Garrison. *sc* Harriet Frank Jr, Irving Ravetch. *ph* Harry Stradling. *ed* Folmar Blangsted. *ad* Leo K Kuter. *m* Max Steiner. *cast* Robert Preston, Dorothy McGuire, Eve Arden, Angela Lansbury, Shirley Knight, Lee Kinsolving.

●A Pulitzer Prize winner in its Broadway version, William Inge's play based on memories of his Oklahoman youth in the '20s suffers here from undue reverence from both Mann and screenwriters Irving Ravetch and Harriet Frank – usually much sharper with oddball Westerns or liberal dramas for Martin Ritt – and undue hamming from a wildly disparate cast. Small-town domestic intrigues push one way, sub-plots about adolescent fears and anti-Semitism pull another. PT

Dark Avenger, The (aka The Warriors)

(1955, GB, 85 min)
d Henry Levin. *p* Vaughan N Dean. *sc* Daniel B Ullman, Phil Park. *ph* Guy Green. *ed* EB Jarvis. *ad* Terence Verity. *m* Cedric Thorpe Davie. *cast* Errol Flynn, Joanne Dru, Peter Finch, Yvonne Furneaux, Patrick Holt, Michael Hordern, Moultrie Kelsall, Robert Urquhart.

●The sets left at Borehamwood after MGM's *Ivanhoe* provided the excuse for this rather more modest production to nip in and show that even a 46-year-old Flynn still had a modicum of swash and buckle left in him – and if he didn't, there was always the stunt double. The Black Prince (Flynn) must subdue the restless nobles in English-held Aquitaine and defeat the machinations of duplicitous count Finch. Unpretentious hokum, and any movie that casts Michael Hordern as Errol Flynn's dad has to raise a smile, especially since he was two years the star's junior. TJ

Dark Blue World (Tmavomodry svet)

(2001, Czech Rep/GB/Ger/Den/It, 112 min)
d Jan Sverák. *p* Eric Abraham, Jan Sverák. *sc* Zdenek Sverák. *ph* Vladimir Smutny. *ed* Alois Fisárek. *pd* Jan Vlasák. *m* Ondrej Soukup. *cast* Ondrej Vetchy, Krystof Hádek, Tara Fitzgerald, Oldrich Kaiser, Hans Jorg Assmann, Charles Dance, David Novotny.

●Sverak is certainly a technically polished filmmaker; but he's also a shameless manipulator of easy emotions and – judging by the way he drastically changed tack from his early films to *Kolya* and this likewise mushy melodrama – perhaps none too committed to serious art. A shame, because one can imagine there being a very fine movie about Czech pilots flying missions out of Britain, only to be incarcerated by the Commies after the war. But this isn't the one. It offers a predictable, soppily romantic tale of male friendship undermined by the love of a woman, heroics overcoming culture clash, and so on. The dogfighs are mostly terrific, however, and the authentically grim '50s scenes hint at what might have been. GA

Dark Circle

(1982, US, 81 min)
d Chris Beaver, Judy Irving, Ruth Landy. *p* Chris Beaver, Judy Irving, Ruth Landy. *sc/ph/ed* Chris Beaver, Judy Irving. *m* Gary S Remal.

●A well done, preaching-to-the-converted anti-nuclear documentary. An intense, low-key production which shows up the flashy decontextualising of *Atomic Café*, it ranges from Nagasaki survivors, through neighbours of a plutonium plant near Denver, to the fiasco of Diablo, the Californian nuclear power plant described as 'the most analysed building in the world' which, at the last minute, turned out to have been built back to front. JCo

Dark City

(1950, US, 88 min, b/w)
d William Dieterle. *sc* John Meredyth Lucas, Lawrence B Marcus. *ph* Victor Milner. *ed* Warren Low. *ad* Hans Dreier, Franz Bachelin. *m* Franz Waxman. *cast* Charlton Heston, Lizabeth Scott, Viveca Lindfors, Dean Jagger, Jack Webb, Don Defore, Ed Begley, Henry Morgan, Mike Mazurki.

●Given that Heston spent most of his career playing monumental heroes, it's a surprise to find him cast as a petty hood in this, his Hollywood debut. He's a war hero fallen on tough times who makes a living hustling at poker. There's a homicidal maniac on his heels, out to avenge the death of his brother who committed suicide after losing a fortune to Heston at the table. As the title makes clear, we're in the realm of *film noir*. A plaintive score from Franz Waxman and moody camerawork from Victor Milner ensure the picture scores on atmosphere, but veteran director Dieterle hasn't been dealt much of a hand by his scriptwriters. GM

Dark City

(1997, US/Aust, 100 min)
d Alex Proyas. *p* Andrew Mason. *sc* Alex Proyas, Lem Dobbs, David S Goyer. *ph* Dariusz Wolski. *ed* Dov Hoenig. *pd* George Liddle, Patrick Tatopolous. *m* Trevor Jones. *cast* Rufus Sewell, Kiefer Sutherland, Jennifer Connelly, Richard O'Brien, Ian Richardson, Colin Friels, William Hurt.

●At midnight the city stops. Citizens black out, transfixed in whatever activity they're engaged in, while all around them 'The Strangers' modify the urban environment, transforming streets and buildings, the fabric of people's lives. When the clock starts again, collective amnesia shrouds the general unease. John Murdoch (Sewell) wakes up to face a murder rap he knows makes no sense. Tipped off by the mysterious Dr Schreber (Sutherland), he evades captures and sets about unearthing his apparently metaphysical pursuers. Proyas' overwrought MTV camera jitters tend to highlight characterisation that's two dimensional even by comic book standards, and the film can't stand the inevitable comparisons with *Blade Runner* or *Brazil*. Nevertheless, Murdoch's quandary proves surprisingly engrossing, the art direction is always striking, and unlike most contemporary sci-fi, the movie does risk a cerebral approach, tapping a vein of postmodern paranoia. TCh

Dark Corner, The

(1946, US, 99 min, b/w)
d Henry Hathaway. *p* Fred Kohlmar. *sc* Jay Dratler, Bernard C Schoenfeld. *ph* Joseph MacDonald. *ed* J Watson Webb Jr. *ad* James Basevi, Leland Fuller. *m* Cyril J Mockridge. *cast* Mark Stevens, Lucille Ball, Clifton Webb, William Bendix, Constance Collier, Kurt Kreuger, Cathy Downs, Reed Hadley.

●Fine *noir* thriller, superbly paced by Hathaway, equally superbly shot by Joe MacDonald, and benefiting from the Fox trademark (at this time) of location shooting. Stevens is the private eye just released from jail after being framed for murder, only to find a sinister thug tailing him and gradually driving him into a nightmare which ends with him wanted for murder all over again. Although Webb's suave villain is carried over virtually intact from *Laura* (complete with the manic possessiveness about beautiful women), *The Dark Corner* manages its own note of individuality by casting the vulnerable Stevens as a tough Sam Spade whose façade is systematically cracked ('I'm backed up in a dark corner and I don't know who's hitting me') until his devoted, wisecracking secretary (Ball) has to mother him through. Terrific performances, not least from Bendix as the thug in a white suit, Downs as the dark angel of the piece, and Kreuger as a Teutonic snake. TM

Dark Crystal, The

(1982, GB, 93 min)
d Jim Henson, Frank Oz. *p* Jim Henson, Gary Kurtz. *sc* David Odell. *ph* Oswald Morris. *ed* Ralph Kemplen. *pd* Harry Lange. *m* Trevor Jones. *cast* character performers: Jim Henson, Kathryn Mullen, Frank Oz, Dave Goelz, Brian Muehll.

●Every attempt to film in the epic fantasy style of *The Lord of the Rings* has foundered on the technical difficulties involved, particularly Equity's failure to produce trolls, orks and hobbits in sufficient quantities. Henson, creator of the Muppets, has put all his energies into creating a spectacular range of live-action creatures who prance and gobble their way across the screen with an unprecedented conviction. Given this enormous advantage, it is therefore disappointing that this $26 million film should restrict itself to a very basic pulp fantasy plot – the hero's quest to free his world from the ravages of an evil race – when there are superior models available in any bookshop. Monstrous characterisations, and the relish with which the strange rituals of evil creatures are portrayed, make up for this deficiency. Desiccated, clawing villains feasting on rotting food in a castle as unprepossessing as the crashed spaceship in *Alien* have a splendour that is almost operatic. DP

Dark Days

(2000, US, 82 min, b/w)
d/p/ph Marc Singer. *ed* Melissa Neidich. *m* DJ Shadow. *with* Rick Rubell, Mike Harris, Tommy, Tito, Ralph, Greg, Henry, Ronnie, Clarence, Dee, Julio, Lee, Brian.

●A novice documentarist mixes with the 'mole people' of Manhattan's train tunnels. Marc Singer is not interested, however, in displacing the denizens of this unlikely habitat, but in documenting the simple fact of them – their way of life and their outlook. The film records a Hadean vision of the city's genuine underground. HG Wells foresaw the dispossessed living something like this in the year 802,701, but his Morlocks were creatures of the night, picking off the powerless above ground. As Singer swiftly clarifies, the men and women who fall into this particular chasm are society's truly vulnerable. The film's deference to its subjects' reality is such that it eschews drama and style, preferring a spare, to-camera intimacy. Hence the surprise when Singer turns to describing the eviction of the mole people by Amtrak and their resettlement overground: a happy ending that leaves a raft of questions begging. NB

Dark Enemy

(1984, GB, 97 min)
d/p Colin Finbow. *ph* Andrew Fleury. *ed* Matthew Landauer, Charles Robertson. *m* David Hewson. *cast* David Haig, Douglas Storm, Rory MacFarquhar, Martin Laing, Chris Chescoe, Jennifer Harrisson.

● Finbow set up the Children's Film Unit in 1981 in order to encourage youngsters to participate in all aspects of film-making, and it looks to be paying off. This, the unit's third film, is centered around a group of children who are living in a post-nuclear world, unaware of the civilisation before them. Only two Most Elders remain, the rest were either too young or not yet born at the time of the holocaust. And now the time has come for a new leader to be elected. Apart from a rather slow start, the film encompasses some excellent acting, a great music score, and a haunting underlying moral. DA

Darker Than Amber

(1970, US, 96 min)
d Robert Clouse. *p* Walter Seltzer, Jack Reeves. *sc* Ed Waters. *ph* Frank Phillips. *ed* Fred Chulack. *ad* Jack T Collis. *m* John Parker. *cast* Rod Taylor, Suzy Kendall, Theodore Bikel, Jane Russell, James Booth, Janet McLachlan, William Smith.

● An attempt to crash the then popular *Tony Rome* market with John D Macdonald's seedy eye Travis McGee – Kendall's first appearance is as a 'lady in cement' – that flounders around confusedly in the Florida underground. Russell here made her final appearance, while Kendall gets two roles, one hideously dubbed. PT

Darkest Light, The

(1999, GB/Fr, 94 min)
d Simon Beaufoy, Bille Eltringham. *p* Mark Blaney. *sc* Simon Beaufoy. *ph* Mary Farbrother. *ed* Ewa J Lind. *pd* Chris Townsend. *m* Adrian Johnston. *cast* Stephen Dillane, Kerry Fox, Keri Arnold, Kavita Sungha, Jason Walton, Nisha K Nayer, Nicholas Hope.

● Farm life in the Yorkshire Dales isn't easy at the best of times, but things are exceptionally tough for Tom (Dillane) and Sue (Fox). Their eight-year-old son (Walton) has leukaemia, and the doctors aren't making headway. Meanwhile, Catherine (Arnold), ten, feels lonely and neglected; befriending Uma (Sungha), the first Hindu at the village school, she takes her to the Moors. Something strange happens, which Catherine interprets as a vision of the Virgin Mary, and a sign her brother will be all right. Uma, though, is terrified by the implications of what they've seen. Co-directed from Beaufoy's screenplay, this is the latest installment in the writer's project to carve out a distinctive Yorkshire cinema. The directors pick up on the exoticism of a terrain incorporating both ancient limestone pavements and wind farms, but these flourishes sit uncomfortably with a subdued aesthetic that wouldn't look out of place in the British TV soap *Emmerdale*. A good actor, Dillane is nevertheless an unlikely Dalesman. On the plus side, young Arnold works wonders, and you can hardly fail to be moved by the end. TCh

Dark Eyes (Oci Ciornie)

(1987, It, 118 min)
d Nikita Mikhalkov. *p* Silvia d'Amico Bendico, Carlo Cucchi. *sc* Alexander Adabashian, Nikita Mikhalkov. *ph* Franco di Giacomo. *ed* Enzo Meniconi. *pd* Mario Garbuglia, Alexander Adabashian. *m* Francis Lai. *cast* Marcello Mastroianni, Silvana Mangano, Marthe Keller, Elena Sofonova, Pina Cei, Innokenti Smoktunovski.

● Mikhalkov's adaptation of several of Chekhov's short stories makes for bland viewing indeed. Mastroianni is in fine form as the fickle, philandering and finally irritatingly spineless Romano, a wealthy Italian whose dismay at the imminent bankruptcy of his wife's bank takes him away from family and mistress to the distracting lassitudes of a health spa, where he encounters and seduces the shy, reluctant Anna (Sofonova). When Anna returns to Russia and husband, Romano follows, but will he do the honourable thing and tell his wife (Mangano) the truth? Mikhalkov manages, remarkably, to render the harrowing dilemmas thrown up by problems of adultery, commitment, disillusionment and solitude woefully shallow. Mastroianni apart, the film is a glossy, unprepossessing example of the mainstream art movie. GA

Dark Eyes of London (aka The Human Monster)

(1939, GB, 76 min, b/w)
d Walter Summers. *p* John F Argyle. *sc* John Argyle, Walter Summers, Patrick Kirwan. *ph* Brian Langley. *ed* EG Richards. *ad* Duncan Sutherland. *m* Guy Jones. *cast* Bela Lugosi, Hugh Williams, Greta Gynt, Wilfred Walter, Arthur Owen, May Hallatt.

● Engaging chiller based on an Edgar Wallace novel, with Lugosi giving one of his better performances as the director of an insurance company and (incognito) of a home for the blind where the newly-insured are drowned in a tank and disposed of in the Thames. Let down by extremely conventional characterisation of the intrepid hero and heroine (Williams and Gynt), but weirdly atmospheric, with good use made of the Thames mudflats and a splendidly macabre denouement involving two blind henchmen, one of them a hulking Frankenstein monster (Walter). TM

Dark Habits (Entre Tinieblas)

(1983, Sp, 116 min)
d Pedro Almodóvar. *p* Luis Calco. *sc* Pedro Almodóvar. *ph* Angel L Ferndandez. *ed* José Salcedo. *pd* Pin Morales, Roman Arango. *m* Cam España. *cast* Cristina S Pascual, Marisa Paredes, Mari Carrillo, Lina Canalejas, Manuel Zarzo, Carmen Maura, Chus Lampreave.

● Almodóvar's third feature is slapdash, occasionally slow-moving, haphazardly plotted. That it's also wildly funny, bitchy, affecting and surreal is a tribute to his perennial warmth and wit. Nightclub singer Yolanda (Pascual) is impelled, via a bit of drug trouble, into the arms of the Mother Superior of the Convent of Humble Redeemers. Lying low in a spacious cell, decked with the trappings of Catholic kitsch, she finds the demands of the religious life needn't cramp her style too much: Sister Rat (the wonderful Lampreave) pens bodice-rippers, the Mother Superior jacks off in the privacy of her office, Sister Manure has LSD-fuelled religious ecstasies, and Sister Sin (Maura, radiant) is spotted from a bedroom window wrestling with a tiger. The whole thing winds up with the inevitable scandal and is almost completely silly; but as ever, Almodóvar's adoration of his female stars is heart-warming, and his visual style a delight. SFe

Dark Half, The

(1991, US, 121 min)
d George A Romero. *p* Declan Baldwin. *sc* George A Romero. *ph* Tony Pierce-Roberts. *ed* Pasquale Buba. *pd* Cletus Anderson. *m* Christopher Young. *cast* Timothy Hutton, Amy Madigan, Michael Rooker, Julie Harris, Roger Joy, Kent Broadhurst, Rutanya Alda.

● Proof that not all films derived from Stephen King's books need be intellectually banal and cinematically dull. Romero's movie centres on Thad Beaumont (Hutton), a small-town author and creative-writing tutor, who, threatened with exposure, decides to kill off his literary doppelgänger, crime novelist George Stark. Soon afterwards, Thad's friends and colleagues start meeting violent deaths, apparently at the hands of the late Stark. Thad's wife Liz (Madigan) is frightened for the children, but although the local lawman (Rooker) is sympathetic, he refuses to believe that Thad's fictional alter ego is the razor wielding culprit. It's a strong conceit, but precisely how it's linked to a feather-brained subplot about the black-outs and aural hallucinations Thad suffered as a child remains obscure. This one-paced psychological horror movie delivers its share of visual shocks, but relies mainly on a controlled build-up of tension. NF

Dark Journey

(1937, GB, 82 min, b/w)
d/p Victor Saville. *sc* Arthur Wimperis. *ph* Harry Stradling. *ed* William Hornbeck, Hugh Stewart. *ad* André Andréjew. *m* Richard Addinsell. *cast* Vivien Leigh, Conrad Veidt, Joan Gardner, Anthony Bushell, Ursula Jeans, Austin Trevor.

● An amiable melodrama in which two World War I spies (witty Leigh, icy Veidt) fall for each other in high society Stockholm (treated by the movie as some Nordic Casablanca!). The film ultimately bears the stamp of its director less than of its producer (Korda) and studio, and a certain blandness pervades. Fascinating, though, for the date it was made and its appropriately confused sympathies (pacifist? militarist? continental? British? – hard to say). CA

Darklands

(1996, GB, 91 min)
d Julian Richards. *p* Paul Brooks. *sc* Julian Richards. *ph* Zoran Djordjevic. *ed* Mark Talbot-Butler. *pd* Hayden Pearce. *m* John Murphy, David Hughes. *cast* Craig Fairbrass, Rowena King, Jon Finch, David Duffy, Roger Nott, Richard Lynch, Nicola Branson.

● This £500k first feature has been called the Welsh *Wicker Man*. Writer/director Richards readily acknowledges his debt to the 1973 horror classic – partly out of fanboy respect, partly, one suspects, to defuse accusations of plagiarism. In his least action-oriented role to date, Fairbrass plays Frazer Truick, a Welsh-born, London-raised journo whose investigations into the death of a young steelworker suggest links between the industrial 'accident', fervent nationalist politician David Keller (Finch), and an uppity group of Celtic neo-pagans. Truick's nose for a story and lust for the dead youth's beautiful sister, cub reporter Rachel (King), soon have him knee-deep in desecrated churches, slaughtered pigs, crazy priests and a revivalist political conspiracy. The confident direction and Zoran Djordevic's atmospheric visuals are complemented by a score that effectively blends Test Department's percussive industrial noise with gentler Welsh folk songs. NF

Darkman

(1990, US, 91 min)
d Sam Raimi. p Robert Tapert. sc Daniel Goldin, Chuck Pfarrer, Sam Raimi, Ivan Raimi, Joshua Goldin. ph Bill Pope. ed David Stiven. pd Randy Ser. m Danny Elfman. cast Liam Neeson, Frances McDormand, Colin Friels, Larry Drake, Nelson Mashita, Jesse Lawrence Ferguson.

● Dr Westlake (Neeson) is on the verge of perfecting a synthetic skin which conceals disfigurements; the problem is, the skin dissolves in sunlight after 99 minutes. When his laboratory is ransacked and blown up by gangster Durant (Drake), Westlake is left for dead, face down in a vat of caustic chemicals. But he survives (*sans visage*) as Darkman, an avenging angel who uses temporary masks to impersonate and destroy his enemies, while simultaneously attempting to win back his estranged love (McDormand). Drawing self-consciously on the 'misunderstood monster' tradition of Universal's golden age, Raimi's major studio debut abounds with conflicting ambitions, juggling pathos, horror and incongruous slapstick as it attempts to meld (with variable success) an archaic narrative structure with a kinetic, modern visual style. Neeson's performance encapsulates these contradictions, mixing camp histrionics with moments of touching precision. But the breathtaking action sequences find Raimi in his element: wild, woolly and occasionally wondrous, *Darkman* has the chaotic charm of untrammelled, undisciplined talent. MK

Dark Mirror, The

(1946, US, 85 min, b/w)
d Robert Siodmak. *p/sc* Nunnally Johnson. *ph* Milton Krasner. *ed* Ernest Nims. *pd* Duncan Cramer. *m* Dimitri Tiomkin. *cast* Olivia de Havilland, Lew Ayres, Thomas Mitchell, Richard Long, Charles Evans, Gary Owens.

● Impressively unusual thriller with typically simplistic Freudian elements as psychiatrist Ayres is called in by the police to help investigate a murder committed by one of two identical twins…but which one? Intriguing cat-and-mouse games and perverse power struggles as both he and we try to fathom which of the sisters is the warped psycho, with de Havilland (in the dual role) and Siodmak managing admirably to counteract the contrived plot. What really makes it work, though, is

Siodmak's firm grasp of mood and suspense; the opening scene, in which the camera prowls a darkened room until it finds a corpse, sets the tone perfectly for the sense of uncertainty and chaos that follows. GA

Darkness and Light (Heian zhi Guang)

(1999, Tai, 102 min)
d Chang Tso-Chi. *p* Chen Xisheng, Lu Shih-Yuan. *sc* Chang Tso-Chi. *ph* Chang Tsang. *ed* Chen Bo-Wen. *ad* Lee Fu-Hsiung, He Kuen-Chuan. *m* Hugo Pandaputra. *cast* Lee Kang-Yi, Tsai Ming-Shiou, Hsieh Bau-Huei, He Huang-Ji, Fan Zhenwei.

● A girl student comes home for the holidays (her father, blinded in an accident, runs a traditional blind-massage clinic in the port of Keelung) and falls for a new boy in town – thereby infuriating the local gangster kid who considers her his girlfriend. With his brilliantly chosen non-professional actors, some of them genuinely blind and one genuinely retarded, Chang constructs achingly plausible accounts of both small town life and volatile teenage passions. An extraordinary wish-dream ending seems anomalous until you realise that the film's realism is primarily psychological, not social. A former assistant to Hou Xiaoxian, Chang might make films that fit a certain template for Taiwan cinema, but they are quite different from other Taiwanese movies in tone, form and approach to performance. TR

Darkness Falls

(1998, GB, 91 min)
d Gerry Lively. *p* Alan Latham, Clifford Haydn-Tovey. *sc* John Howlett. *ph* Adam Santelli. *ed* David Spiers. *pd* Edward Thomas. *m* Guy Farley. *cast* Sherilyn Fenn, Ray Winstone, Tim Dutton, Anita Dobson, Bryan Pringle, Robin McCaffrey, Michael Praed, Oliver Tobias.

● Obnoxious Dutton (£10m in debt) and brittle, childless wife Fenn live in a big house (paid for with her money) on the Isle of Man. Mysterious Winstone calls at the house, holds them hostage, and Dutton's secret is exposed. Knowing the bank manager's coming round, Dutton tells Fenn to wear one of her short dresses, 'tight around the breasts, you know what he likes'. As he says with a sneer, 'I'm in the shit with the wrong people.' Winstone can't save the day. In fact, he adds to our woes, with a brand of trembling, ordinary-bloke psychosis. Fenn is more interesting – her spoilt, controlled facade is full of tiny, unhappy cracks – but she spends most of her time undressing (or rather her body double does). Meanwhile, the music digs you in the ribs until you're black and blue, obtuse flashbacks spread like a rash, and for all the attempts at glamour, everything looks cheap. Even peerlessly camp appearances by Tobias and Dobson fail to bring cheer. CO'Su

Darkness in Tallinn (Tallinn pimeduses/ Tallinnan pimeys)

(1993, Fin/US/Swe/Estonia, 99 min, b/w & col)
d Ilkka Järvilaturi. *p* Lasse Saarinen. *sc* Paul Kolsby. *ph* Rein Kotov. *ed* Chris Tellefsen. *pd* Toomas Hörak. *m* Mader. *cast* Ivo Uukkivi, Milena Gulbe, Monika Mäger, Enn Klooren, Väinö Laes, Yuri Järvet.

● This ultra-black comedy by Finnish film-maker Järvilaturi is an unexpected joy. It begins, almost disconcertingly, with Estonia's newly re-established independence being marked by a secret gathering of criminals, who plan to nab the country's massive bullion reserves when they're brought from Paris back to Tallinn. Thus is Toivo (Uukkivi), a small-time caviar smuggler and electrician, advised by his very pregnant wife Maria (Gulbe) to abandon ideals for the promise of money, brought in on a daring night hold-up. True to form, the scheme hits the skids with in-fighting among the ill-matched hoods. Ingeniously written (by Paul Kolsby), tautly paced with b/w photography that never fails to surprise, this is *noir* at its blackest. The characters, too, are pleasingly quirky, but never contrived. A funny, suspenseful heist movie with a properly sharp moral/political edge. GA

Dark of the Sun

see Mercenaries, The

Dark Passage

(1947, US, 106 min, b/w)
d Delmer Daves. *p* Jerry Wald. *sc* Delmer Daves. *ph* Sid Hickox. *ed* David Weisbart. *ad* Charles H Clarke. *m* Franz Waxman. *cast* Humphrey Bogart, Lauren Bacall, Bruce Bennett, Agnes Moorehead, Tom D'Andrea, Clifton Young, Douglas Kennedy.

● Classic thriller based on the David Goodis novel about a man wrongly convicted of murder who escapes, has his face changed by plastic surgery, and clears his name with the aid of a girl whose father was similarly framed. Brilliantly atmospheric San Francisco settings, memorably bizarre supporting performances, a superb use of subjective camera (much more effective than in *Lady in the Lake*) throughout the entire first third of the film. The only flaw is the momentary absurdity when the bandages are finally unwrapped to reveal the 'new' face as dear old Bogart's (although prepared for by the use of his distinctive voice from the start). TM

Dark Past, The

(1948, US, 75 min, b/w)
d Rudolph Maté. *p* Buddy Adler. *sc* Philip MacDonald, Michael Blankfort, Albert Duffy. *ph* Joseph Walker. *ed* Viola Lawrence. *ad* Cary Odell. *m* George Duning. *cast* Lee J Cobb, William Holden, Nina Foch, Adele Jergens, Stephen Dunne, Lois Maxwell.

● Cast against type, Holden's the ringleader of a gang which takes over shrink Cobb's lakeside retreat while they await their getaway in this competent remake of the 1939 Chester Morris picture *Blind Alley*. The twist, and it's not altogether convincing, is that Cobb uses his professional insights into his captor's personality profile to turn the tables, with much pop pyschology along the way. One's not absolutely flabbergasted to learn that it all started life as a stage play. TJ

Dark Star

(1974, US, 83 min)
d/p John Carpenter. *sc* John Carpenter, Dan O'Bannon. *ph* Douglas Knapp. *ed/pd* Dan O'Bannon. *m* John Carpenter. *cast* Brian Narelle, Dre Pahich, Cal Kuniholm, Dan O'Bannon, Joe Saunders, Miles Watkins.

● Carpenter's fondly remembered first feature, which the director himself described as 'One big optical – *Waiting for Godot* in space'. Four bombed-out astronauts journey endlessly through the galaxy, whiling away the time with jokes, sunlamp treatment, personal diaries on videotape, and games with their own pet alien. Arguably the last great hippy movie with its jokey references to drugs, the Absurd and California surfing (one crew member makes it back to earth on an improvised board), it also anticipates the sci-fi vogue of the '70s (*Alien* and Carpenter's own gem *The Fog*) as well as taking a healthy sideswipe at the pretensions of *2001*. Sheer delight. MA

Dark Summer

(1994, GB, 85 min)
d/p/sc/ph/ed Charles Teton. *pd* Elouise Attwood. *m* Clive Chin. *cast* Joeline Garner Joel, Steve Ako, Chris Darwin, Bernie Deasy, Sylvia Amoo, Wayne Oko.

● The skanking reggae heard over shots of a decaying Liverpool seems promising. Abe and Jess exchange glances over the rubble when Jess starts working for her Dad on site. They're young and in love (we must assume it's that old 'chemistry', since there's little dialogue or emotional build-up), but her Dad is appalled, though whether it's because Abe's black or an employee isn't clear. Jess moves out to be with Abe, which is fine until the heartbreak begins. The five years writer/director Teton spent in advertising do not seem to have given him a grip on the basics of dramatic film-making. A self-financed first feature which fails to take flight. EPe

Dark Victory

(1939, US, 106 min, b/w)
d Edmund Goulding. *sc* Casey Robinson. *ph* Ernest Haller. *ed* William Holmes. *ad* Robert M Haas. *m* Max Steiner. *cast* Bette Davis, George Brent, Humphrey Bogart, Geraldine Fitzgerald, Ronald Reagan, Cora Witherspoon.

● Davis has a field day as the petulant Long Island heiress who wields her riding-crop to humble the Irish chauffeur (Bogart, no less, badly miscast), then learns she has only months to live and spends the rest of her time discovering resignation and romantically dying (partnered, alas, by the soggy Brent). She and Goulding almost transform the soap into style; a Rolls-Royce of the weepie world. TM

Dark Waters

(1944, US, 90 min, b/w)
d André De Toth. *p* Benedict Bogeaus. *sc* Joan Harrison, Marian Cockrell. *ph* John Mescall, Archie Stout. *ed* James Smith. *ad* Charles Odds. *m* Miklos Rozsa. *cast* Merle Oberon, Franchot Tone, Thomas Mitchell, Fay Bainter, John Qualen, Elisha Cook Jr, Rex Ingram.

● Woman-in-peril thriller with Oberon, orphaned and left a nervous wreck by a World War II torpedoing, recuperating with relatives living in Louisiana (in an old dark house, naturally) who conspire to have her declared insane so that they can claim her fortune. Oberon is tiresomely tremulous, and the script almost as shaky; but the sterling efforts of De Toth and cameraman John Mescall (whose lighting invests the bayou swamplands surrounding the house with a magically eerie mystery) combine to turn dross into a wonderfully mean and moody slice of Southern Gothic. TM

Dark Wind, The

(1991, US, 111 min)
d Errol Morris. *p* Patrick Markey. *sc* Neal Jimenez, Mark Horowitz, Eric Bergren. *ph* Stefan Czapsky. *ed* Susan Crutcher, Freeman Davies. *pd* Ted Bafaloukos. *m* Michel Colombier. *cast* Lou Diamond Phillips, Gary Farmer, Fred Ward, Guy Boyd, John Karlen, Jane Loranger, Gary Basaraba.

● Produced by Robert Redford, this was the first in a proposed series of films based on Tony Hillerman's contemporary Navajo thrillers. Phillips stars as Tribal Policeman Jim Chee, embroiled in four complicated cases ranging from vandalism to drugs and murder – or are they all the same case? It seems appropriate that Errol Morris, the film-maker/detective whose documentary *The Thin Blue Line* freed a convicted murderer, should make his first fiction feature about a shaman/cop. Evidently, he shares Hillerman's respect for Native American culture, but this is a less distinctive film than might have been anticipated (Redford might almost have directed it). What we get is an engrossing, thoughtful and unusual mystery which arguably tips us the wink too early. It's very faithful to the novel – perhaps that's the problem. TCh

Darling

(1965, GB, 127 min, b/w)
d John Schlesinger. *p* Joseph Janni. *sc* Frederic Raphael. *ph* Ken Higgins. *ed* Jim Clark. *ad* Ray Simm. *m* John Dankworth. *cast* Dirk Bogarde, Laurence Harvey, Julie Christie, Roland Curram, Alex Scott, Basil Henson.

● No one need look further than *Darling* for a succinct guide to the reasons for the rapid decline of the British 'New Wave' in the '60s: the film supports the argument that the movement was stillborn. Frederic Raphael's script tramples its own studied issues (Third World poverty, corrupt Western values, jet-set alienation) under its equally studied Sophisticated Characterisation. Schlesinger's direction is a leaden rehash of ideas from Godard, Antonioni and Bergman, which nonetheless contrives to remain firmly rooted in British theatre of the Royal Court school. Excruciatingly embarrassing at the time, it now looks grotesquely pretentious and pathetically out of touch with the realities of the life-styles that it purports to represent. TR

Darling Lili

(1969, US, 136 min)
d Blake Edwards. *sc* Blake Edwards, William Peter Blatty. *ph* Russell Harlan. *ed* Peter Zinner. *pd* Fernando Carrere. *m* Henry Mancini. *cast* Julie Andrews, Rock Hudson, Jeremy Kemp, Lance Percival, Michael Witney, Jacques Marin.

● A commercial failure that was savaged and ridiculed at the time, *Darling Lili* is a glorious film. Edwards' wedding present to Julie Andrews, it is yet another instalment of his ongoing celebration of innocence as the great virtue of life. To understand the film, a simple enough love/spy story set in World War I, one simply has to accept that love (and jealousy) is more important than winning wars. That done, the seemingly bizarre emotional switches of the film stand revealed as the perfect pivots around which Edwards has carefully constructed one of the most satisfying lyrical films in years. PH

Dársena Sur

see South Dock

D'Artagnan's Daughter

see Fille de D'Artagnan, La

Darwin Adventure, The

(1971, GB, 91 min)
d Jack Couffer. *p* Joseph Strick. *sc* William Fairchild. *ph* Denys Coop. *ed* Bob Dearberg. *ad* John Stoll. *m* Marc Wilkinson. *cast* Nicholas Clay, Susan Macready, Ian Richardson, Christopher Martin, Robert Flemyng.

●About Darwin's journey to the Galapagos Islands, and the evidence he found there for evolution rather than individual creation of each species. The film refuses to go into the implications in the realm of ideas of Darwin's discovery, and suffers through the innate ambiguity of Hollywood-type movie-making towards its thinking characters. A good subject spoilt through unimaginative handling of both animal and human sequences.

D.A.R.Y.L.

(1985, GB, 100 min)
d Simon Wincer. *p* John Heyman. *sc* David Ambrose, Allan Scott, Jeffrey Ellis. *ph* Frank Watts. *ed* Adrian Carr. *pd* Alan Cassie. *m* Marvin Hamlisch. *cast* Mary Beth Hurt, Michael McKean, Kathryn Walker, Colleen Camp, Josef Sommer, Ron Frazier, Barret Oliver.

●He's smart, nice, liked by all, so why make a film about this boring little jerk? The first half is somewhat short on drama as the new boy in town (Oliver) establishes himself as a wiz at advanced calculus, brill at baseball, and insufferably cute. Eventually, however, the heavies arrive: this microchip marvel (Data Analysing Robot Youth Lifeform) is the Pentagon's most powerful secret weapon since Cruise, and now the army wants it back, please. Oz director Wincer has produced a bland slice of ersatz Americana that's about as folksy as MacDonalds apple pie; a filming-by-numbers mix of small-town nostalgia, soapy family drama and high-tech sfx, this Dreary Android Runaway Yarn Lags way behind the Spielberg thoroughbreds it tries so hard to ape. SJo

Daughter of Rosie O'Grady, The

(1950, US, 104 min)
d David Butler. *p* William Jacobs. *sc* Melville Shavelson, Jack Rose, Peter Milne. *ph* Wilfred M Cline. *ed* Irene Morra. *ad* Douglas Bacon. *songs* MK Jerome, Jack Scholl. *cast* June Haver, Gordon MacRae, Debbie Reynolds, Gene Nelson, James Barton, SZ Sakall, Jane Darwell.

●Nowhere near as satisfying as *Stage Door* as a backstage epic, this period musical attempts to evoke the good old days of vaudeville, an era for which Hollywood had an extravagant, irrational affection. June Haver plays an ingenue who hits the boards against her father's wishes; the ensuing drama tends towards wide-eyed sentimentalism. Still, it's worth watching if only to witness the struggle to get into the next big musical number, and for a sterling performance from SZ 'Cuddles' Sakall, the rotund, white-haired comedian who duplicated this bumbling, fatherly role in dozens of films, including *Casablanca*. ATu

Daughter of the Nile (Niluohe Nüer)

(1987, Tai, 91 min)
d Hou Xiaoxian. *p* Li Xianchang, Zhang Huakun. *sc* Zhu Tianwen. *ph* Chen Huai'en. *ed* Liao Qingsong, Chen Liyu. *ad* Liu Zhihua, Lin Ju. *m* Chen Zhiyuan, Zhang Hongyi. *cast* Yang Lin, Gao Jie, Yang Fan, Xin Shufen, Li Tianlu, Cui Fusheng.

●At first sight, you wouldn't clock this as a film from the director of *A Summer at Grandpa's* and *The Time to Live and the Time to Die*. But despite the shift from his usual rural settings to the extremely mean streets of present-day Taipei, this is another of Hou's haunting accounts of the joys and terrors of adolescence. The central character is a young woman struggling to keep her father and elder brother (cop and thief respectively) from each other's throats, while nursing a distant crush on one of her brother's friends, a too-pretty gigolo who gets into trouble when he starts dating a gangster's moll. The tangled relationships resolve themselves into a mesh of disappointments and frustrations, but despite the downbeat mood there are charming eruptions of humour, and the sheer eloquence of Hou's mellow visual style makes the film a lot more life-enhancing than most. TR

Daughter of the Puma, The

(1994, Guatemala/Den/Swe, 85 min)
d Ulf Hultberg, Asa Faringer. *p* Peter Ringgaard. *sc* Bob Foss, Asa Faringer, Ulf Hultberg. *ph* Dirk Brüel. *ed* Leif Axel Kjeldsen. *m* Jacob Groth. *cast* Angela Cruz, Gerardo Taracena, Alfonso Lopez, Dolores Heredia, Elpdia Carillo, Nora Aguirre.

●Deceptively simple, moving tale, set in the aftermath of the 1982 San Francisco massacre, of a Mexico-exiled Amero-Indian girl's search across 'the border of death' for her 'disappeared' brother (partly financed by the Danish and Swedish Save the Children fund and supported by the Nobel Peace Prize-winner Rigoberta Menchu). At its heart is the fine, almost wordless performance of Angela Cruz as the girl, the horrific re-enactment of the massacre of her village, and the finely crafted scenes of personal intimacy, as the family members attempt to live their lives torn between the irreconcilable demands of the murderous military and the guerrillas, whom the girl's brother joins. WH

Daughters of Darkness (Les Lèvres Rouges)

(1970, Bel/Fr/WGer/It, 96 min)
d Harry Kümel. *p* Alain Guilleaume, Paul Collet. *sc* Harry Kümel, Pierre Drouot. *ph* Edward van der Enden. *ed* Gust Verschueren, Denis Bonan, Fima Noveck. *ad* Françoise Hardy. *m* François de Roubaix. *cast* Delphine Seyrig, Danièle Ouimet, John Karlen, Andréa Rau, Paul Esser, Georges Jamin, Fons Rademakers.

●Stranded in a palatial seafront resort hotel in out-of-season Ostend, newlyweds Stefan (Karlen) and Valerie (Ouimet) find themselves in thrall to the hotel's only other guests, the Countess Elisabeth Bathory (Seyrig) and her surly but sultry companion Ilone (Rau). Tension within the young couple – Valerie is pressurising Stefan to inform his disapproving mother of their marriage – is exploited by the countess when she rouses Stefan to ecstasy with an account of her ancestor's unquenchable thirst for blood. Three young women, meanwhile, have been found murdered in nearby Bruges, their bodies drained, and the hotel concierge (Esser) can't get past the fact he remembers the countess staying at the hotel 40 years previously, and she hasn't aged a day. There are neither fangs nor longueurs in this sumptuous blend of lesbian vampire flick and European art movie. The casting of Seyrig, trailing memories of Marienbad, is inspired, and her swooning performance bewitches the entire cast. Kümel casts his own spells with alternating blue washes and red dissolves, and skilful location work that doesn't allow you to see the join between hotel exteriors and interiors – in Ostend and Brussels respectively. NRo

Daughters of Satan

(1972, US, 96 min)
d Hollingsworth Morse. *p* Aubrey Schenck. *sc* John C Higgins. *ph* Nonong Rasca. *ed* Tony di Marco. *ad* Hernando Balon. *m* Richard La Salle. *cast* Tom Selleck, Barra Grant, Tani Phelps Guthrie, Paraluman, Vic Diaz. Vic Silayan.

●Made in the Philippines back-to-back with *Superbeast*, only it doesn't look like there was very much money left. Selleck buys an old painting of witches being burned at the stake, fascinated because one of them closely resembles his wife. The witches are out for revenge, the wife starts going into murderous trances, and it's a fiendishly boring plod all the way. TM

Daughters of the Dust

(1991, US, 112 min)
d/p/sc Julie Dash. *ph* A Jaffa Fielder. *ed* Amy Carey, Joseph Burton. *pd* Kerry Marshall. *m* John Barnes. *cast* Cora Lee Day, Alva Rogers, Barbara-O, Trula Hoosier, Umar Abdurrahamn.

●Set in 1902, on a barrier island off Georgia, this first feature is an impressionistic portrait of the ritual last supper of the Peazant family before migrating to the mainland. The younger generations are leaving the matriarch Nana (Day) and the insulated traditional life she symbolises. Tensions are raised by the return of family members Viola, a Baptist missionary, and Yellow Mary (Barbara-O), a proud whore, and by Eli's apprehension that his wife Eula (Rogers) is carrying the child of a rapist. Nana fears these rifts will destroy her family when they leave the home of their African ancestors and calls on the spirit of Eula's unborn child to heal them. Steeped in symbolism, superstition and myth, this disconcertingly original film is structured in tableaux which jump through time. The characters speak in the islanders' Gullah dialect and little is explained; however, Dash's universal message about holding on to tradition in face of change rings clear. CO'S

Dave

(1993, US, 110 min)
d Ivan Reitman. *p* Lauren Shuler Donner, Ivan Reitman. *sc* Gary Ross. *ph* Adam Greenberg. *ed* Sheldon Kahn. *pd* J Michael Riva. *m* James Newton Howard. *cast* Kevin Kline, Sigourney Weaver, Frank Langella, Kevin Dunn, Ben Kingsley, Charles Grodin.

●This warm-hearted film casts the copiously talented but still underrated Kline in the double role of Dave Kovic, nice, unassuming, uncoordinated but helpful Mr Nobody, and Bill Mitchell, unpleasant, cynical and adulterous incumbent of the White House. Kline is magnificent as the man who moves in when the President goes down with a sex-induced stroke, and the supporting cast are first rate, with Weaver as Mitchell's estranged, increasingly baffled consort, and Kingsley as the idealistic Vice President. Politicians such as Tip O'Neill supply celebrity cameos. A buoyant comedy in the Capra tradition. SGr

David Copperfield

(1935, US, 132 min, b/w)
d George Cukor. *p* David O Selznick. *sc* Hugh Walpole, Howard Estabrook. *ph* Oliver T Marsh. *ed* Robert J Kern. *ad* Cedric Gibbons. *m* Herbert Stothart. *cast* Freddie Bartholomew, Frank Lawton, WC Fields, Roland Young, Edna May Oliver, Basil Rathbone, Maureen O'Sullivan, Lionel Barrymore, Lewis Stone, Lennox Pawle, Elsa Lanchester.

●As one might expect from Cukor, an exemplary adaptation of Dickens' classic, condensing the novel's sprawl with careful clarity, and yielding up a host of terrific performances from its superb cast. Pride of place, of course, goes to Fields as Micawber, refusing to conceal his American accent, relishing the verbal gems, and for once allowing us to inspect the heart of tarnished gold that lay beneath his crusty exterior. One of those rare things: a blend of Art and Hollywood that actually works. GA

David Copperfield

see Charles Dickens' David Copperfield

David Holzman's Diary

(1967, US, 73 min, b/w)
d Jim McBride. *sc* Jim McBride. *ph* Michael Wadleigh. *ed* Jim McBride. *cast* LM Kit Carson, Penny Wohl, Louise Levine, Fern McBride, Eileen Dietz, Mike Levine.

●An enduring delight from the Underground era, cleverly sowing arrant lies at the then-sacred 24 fps. McBride's good-humoured gag on 'personal cinema' and the diary genre casts a wry sidelight on a generation's self-obsession and cinephilia. David Holzman commits his life (film-making) to film – directing and starring in the film we're watching, his home-movie autobiography. So far, so faddish. But 'David' is actor Kit Carson, behind the camera he's apparently twiddling is Michael Wadleigh, and the auto-vérité amounts to as much of McBride's script as could be filmed before his $2,500 ran out. Retrospective ironies pile up with interim career leaps: Carson shot a documentary on Dennis Hopper, married Karen Black, and is now a Hollywood screenwriter; Wadleigh tripped through *Woodstock* to *Wolfen*; and McBride has limped through sci fi and softcore satire to the added narration credit for *The Big Red One* and the remake of *Breathless*. The illusion is complete. PT

Dawn!

(1979, Aust, 120 min)
d Ken Hannam. *p/sc* Joy Cavill. *ph* Russell Boyd. *ed* Max Lemon. *pd* Ross Major. *m* Michael Carlos. *cast* Bronwyn Mackay-Payne, Tom Richards, John Diedrich, Bunney Brooke.
●One might have expected Ken Hannam, who made one of Australia's breakthrough movies in *Sunday Too Far Away*, to have brought a bit more bite to this bland biopic of swimming ace Dawn Fraser, the Olympic gold medallist whose clashes with authority culminated in a flag-stealing incident at the 1964 Tokyo games that saw her banned from competition for ten years. Mackay-Payne, a swimmer herself, looks more confident in the pool than out of it. TJ

Dawn, The (To Harama)

(1994, Greece, 110 min)
d Alexis Bistiskas. *p* Panagiotis Papahadzis. *sc* Alexis Bistikas. *ph* Ian Dodds. *ed* Takis Koumoundouros. *m* Christos Nikolopoulos. *cast* Katerina Kouka, Stavros Zalmas, Smaragda Karydi.
●A conventional tale of a rake's downward progress and his ingenue's rise from rags to riches. An Athens clothes shop assistant Vasso (Kouka, fine) befriends (it turns out) a selfish, drunken night-club singer (Zalmas) and ends up taking the limelight herself. Of interest mainly for its mild feminism and the extended sequences of Greek ballad singing. WH

Dawning, The

(1988, GB, 97 min)
d Robert Knights. *p* Sarah Lawson. *sc* Moira Williams. *ph* Adrian Biddle. *ed* Max Lemon. *pd* Mike Porter. *m* Simon May. *cast* Rebecca Pidgeon, Anthony Hopkins, Jean Simmons, Trevor Howard, Tara MacGowran, Hugh Grant.
●This modest period drama, set in the south of Ireland before partition in 1921, successfully avoids most of the pratfalls and preciousness inherent in the genre. Based on Jennifer Johnston's elegant and expressive novel *The Old Jest*, it mirrors the events of the mounting IRA terrorist campaign in the maturing mind and soul of an 18-year-old girl. The setting is the world of fading grandeur of the old Anglo-Irish ascendancy. Independent-minded Nancy (Pidgeon) lives in a great house presided over by her aunt (Simmons) and wheelchair-ridden ex-General grandfather (Howard, visibly his last role). Wilful and arty, she thinks herself enamoured of a strait-laced ex-army stockbroker (Grant), but with the arrival of a mysterious stranger (Hopkins), events take a tragic turn; a crisis is triggered, and Nancy is forced to examine her loyalties. Knights' film is solidly crafted, but its main strength lies in the performances. Rebecca Pidgeon makes a remarkable debut, exhibiting a rare ability to externalise thought and feeling. WH

Dawn of the Dead (aka Zombies)

(1978, US, 126 min)
d George A Romero. *p* Richard P Rubinstein. *sc* George A Romero. *ph* Michael Gornick. *ed* George A Romero. *ad* Josie Caruso, Barbara Lifsher. *m* Goblins, Dario Argento. *cast* David Emge, Ken Foree, Scott H Reininger, Gaylen Ross, David Crawford, David Early.
●Undoubtedly the zombie movie to end 'em all, *Dawn of the Dead* starts roughly where *Night of the Living Dead* ended, and then proceeds to build mercilessly on its vision of a USA engulfed and decimated by murderous flesh-eating corpses. The horror/suspense content is brilliant enough to satisfy the most demanding fan, and the film uses superb locations like a huge shopping mall to further its Bosch-like vision of a society consumed by its own appetites. But take no munchies. DP

Dawn Patrol, The

(1930, US, 103 min, b/w)
d Howard Hawks. *sc* Dan Totheroh, Seton I Miller. *ph* Ernest Haller. *ed* Ray Curtiss. *ad* Jack Okey. *m* Etrno Rapée. *cast* Richard Barthelmess, Douglas Fairbanks Jr, Neil Hamilton, William Janney, Gardner James, Clyde Cook, James Finlayson, Frank McHugh.
●A group of men doing what men have to do during World War One, with a characteristically Hawksian emphasis on professionalism, self-respect and loyalty: Brit pilots Barthelmess and Fairbanks respond to German taunts about their flying prowess by massacring a squadron, thus incurring the displeasure of commander Hamilton, who points out the need to act more responsibly. If the early recording techniques in Hawks' first talkie entail a stiltedness in dialogue and performance, he compensates by contrasting the claustrophobic psychological tension of the interior scenes with the liberating, expertly shot action of the aerial footage (so good that it was used again in Goulding's 1938 remake). GA

Dawn Patrol, The

(1938, US, 103 min, b/w)
d Edmund Goulding. *sc* Seton I Miller, Dan Totheroh. *ph* Tony Gaudio. *ed* Ralph Dawson. *ad* John Hughes. *m* Max Steiner. *cast* Errol Flynn, Basil Rathbone, David Niven, Donald Crisp, Melville Cooper, Barry Fitzgerald.
●Remake of the 1930 Howard Hawks film, from which it borrows its fine aerial footage (mostly shot by Elmer Dyer). Neither version (pace Hawks fans) is exactly a masterpiece, since the dialogue scenes in the first version are stiff and stodgily directed, while Goulding gets smoother performances (Flynn in particular is excellent), but has doctored dialogue more suited to bellicose times: not altering the thematic concern with the psychological stresses of combat leadership, but discreetly stressing the heroism of the young World War I flyers rather than the terrible waste of their deaths. TM

Day After Day (Yom Yom)

(1998, Fr/Isr, 97 min)
d Amos Gitai. *p* Laurent Truchot, Eyal Shiray. *sc* Amos Gitai, Jacky Cukier. *ph* Renato Berta. *ed* Nili Richter, Ruben Korenfeld. *pd* Thierry François, Miguel Markin. *m* Philippe Eidel, Josef Bardanshvilly. *cast* Moshe Ivgi, Hannah Maron, Yussup Abu-Warda, Keren Mor.
●With its mood of disconsolate philosophising and sexual/romantic unfulfilment against a background of generalised political malaise, Gitai's movie plays like a hetero Israeli version of Alea's *Memories of Underdevelopment*. Hyper-tense Moshe (Ivgi) desultorily goes through the motions as an army reservist (he seems to have no other employ), while fending off advice from his overcaring mother and arguing about the pointlessness of having children with his wife, who is on the verge of departure. Built loosely around the tale of the possible sale of the old family home, the film presents a three-layered portrait, of Moshe's family and friends, of the changing city, Haifa, and of the state of the state of Israel. Only slowly do we realise Moshe's is a family of mixed Israeli/Palestinian descent. It's a movie about becoming old as a new state itself grows into complex maturity, but it's too diffuse and parsimonious with its insights. WH

Day After Trinity, The

(1980, US, 89 min, b/w & col)
d/p Jon Else. *sc* David Peoples, Janet Peoples, Jon Else. *ph* Tom McDonough, David Espar, Stephen Lighthill, Jon Else. *ed* David Peoples, Ralph Wikke. *m* Martin Bresnick. *with* Frank Oppenheimer, II Rabi, Robert Wilson, Jane Wilson, Dorothy McKibbin, Stirling Colgate, Robert Oppenheimer . *narrator* Paul Frees.
●Los Alamos, 1941. A boom town (literally) where some of the best and brightest minds of the age, summoned by J Robert Oppenheimer, fabricated America's first atomic bomb. In this documentary they recall how the initial win-the-war fervour, and euphoria that their contraption actually worked, faded fast when they realised they'd replaced one Final Solution with another. Awe-inspiring footage of the Bomb in action, though the film's tiresome obsession with moral anguish and reliance on anecdote, sometimes revealing but often rambling, makes the film less than explosive. SJo

Day a Pig Fell into the Well, The (Daijiga Umule Pajinnal)

(1996, SKor, 115 min)
d Hong Sang-Soo. *sc* Hong Sang-soo, Chung Dae-song, Yeo Hae-young, Alah Kim, Seo Shin-hae. *ph* Jo Dong-kwan. *ed* Park Kok-li. *pd* Cho Yungsao. *m* Ok Kil-sung. *cast* Kim Eui-Sung, Park Jin-Sung, Jo Eun-Sook, Lee Eun-Kyung.
●No pigs or wells in sight in Hong's justly acclaimed first feature, which looks at the lives of five very recognisable urban types as if all of them were witnesses at the scene of some freak accident. These men and women make mistakes and suffer frustrations in the ways we all do: a failed novelist blames everyone but himself for his inability to keep a relationship going; a woman dreams of divorcing her husband and pins her hopes on a lover who has already moved on; a generally faithful husband impulsively rents a hooker while on a business trip and catches an STD. Part of the pleasure here comes from the skill with which Hong interweaves these seemingly unconnected lives; the rest comes from the excellence of the images, sounds and performances and from Hong's warm but unsentimental engagement with his characters. TR

Day at the Races, A

(1937, US, 111 min, b&w)
d Sam Wood. *sc* Robert Pirosh, George Seaton, George Oppenheimer. *ph* Joseph Ruttenberg. *ed* Frank Hull. *ad* Cedric Gibbons, Stan Rogers. *cast* The Marx Brothers, Allan Jones, Maureen O'Sullivan, Margaret Dumont, Douglass Dumbrille, Sig Ruman.
●The Brothers' second film for MGM should be retitled 'A Week at the Races' at least: it's overlong, overweight, overplotted. Even the comedy scenes are often played to excess, with too much raucous slapstick (like Harpo's destruction of Chico's piano). The plot formula established in *Opera* is repeated, but the script and characterisations are shallow: who'd have thought to find the Brothers fighting to save a sanatorium when there's a nice racetrack alongside? Still, worth seeing for its good stretches; you can always stock up with refreshments when anyone starts singing. GB

Daybreak

see Jour se lève, Le

Daydream Believer

(1991, Aust, 86 min)
d Kathy Mueller. *p* Ben Gannon. *sc* Saturday Rosenberg. *ph* Andrew Lesnie. *ed* Robert Gibson. *pd* Roger Ford. *m* Todd Hunter, Johanna Pigott. *cast* Miranda Otto, Martin Kemp, Anne Looby, Alister Smart, Gia Carides, Bruce Venables, Howard Vernon.
●Australian schoolgirl Nell (Otto) thinks she is a horse, whinnying her way through conflict until a shrink tells her that 'deep down in all of us, there lurks an animal'. Flash forward. Now an adult, she trades hay for acting and self-help, still communing with horses but reverting to their lingo only during moments of acute stress. There's plenty of *that* about after she drives into the flash sports-car belonging to Digby (Kemp), one-time London orphan turned wealthy theatrical producer/horse-breeder, who juggles attempts to raise backing for a musical with efforts to find a stallion to impregnate his prize mare. This is where Nell comes in handy: can she get the name of the mare's mate during a session of horse-talk? An involving premise, which sees parental abuse giving rise to Nell's escapism, is wasted on a ludicrous romantic comedy full of signposted jokes and pratfalls. CM

Day for Night (La Nuit Américaine)

(1973, Fr/It, 116 min)
d François Truffaut. *sc* François Truffaut, Jean-Louis Richard, Suzanne Schiffman. *ph* Pierre-William Glenn. *ed* Yann Dedet, Martine Barraque-Curie. *ad* Damien Lanfranchi. *m* Georges Delerue. *cast* Jacqueline Bisset, Valentina Cortese, Jean-Pierre Aumont, Jean-Pierre Léaud, Dani, Alexandra Stewart, Jean Champion, François Truffaut.
●One of Truffaut's most captivating sentimental comedies, built around his obvious love for cinematic illusionism. What story there is concerns the various emotional upsets, logistical difficulties, and moments of sheer elation during the shooting of a rather silly-looking feature called *Meet Pamela*. Basically it's all just an excuse for a marvellous series of delicately observed gags about how things are really done behind the scenes on a film set: grande dame Cortese infuriates everyone by forgetting her lines, a cat awkwardly refuses to drink its milk, Léaud throws adolescent fits every few hours. Coupled with Georges Delerue's uplifting score and some superb performances (none more so than the director himself), it's a must for anyone besotten with the glamorous trivialities of the cinematic medium. GA

Day I Became a Woman, The (Roozi Keh Zan Shodam)

(2000, Iran, 78 min)
d Marziyeh Meshkini. *p/sc* Mohsen Makhmalbaf. *ph* Ebrahim Ghafori, Mohammad Ahmadi. *ed* Maysam Makhmalbaf, Shahrzad Poya. *ad* Akbar Meshkini. *m* Ahmad Reza Darvishi. *cast* Fatemeh Cherag Akhar, Shabnam Toloui, Azizeh Sedighi.

● An allegory of 'the three ages of woman' set on the free trade island of Kish. Part one: a girl reaches her ninth birthday, the age she officially becomes a woman; but she doesn't want to wear a *chador* or stop playing with the boy next door. Part two: a young woman participates in a cycle race with other women, deaf to demands from her husband and other men that she stop disporting in public. Part three: an elderly woman on a shopping spree, buys herself all the mod cons she always wanted and sets them up in an imaginary home on the beach. The overall escalation into fantasy points up the limitations of the allegories: this offers a very arm's length feminist protest, with too much attention to surreal visuals. Still, it announces Meshkini (Mohsen's wife, Samira's stepmother/aunt) as another asset for Makhmalbaf Film House, the family's production company. TR

Daylight

(1996, US, 114 min)
d Rob Cohen. *p* John Davis, Joseph M Singer, David T Friendly. *sc* Leslie Bohem. *ph* David Eggby. *ed* Peter Amundson. *pd* Benjamin Fernandez. *m* Randy Edelman. *cast* Sylvester Stallone, Amy Brenneman, Jay O Sanders, Viggo Mortensen, Dan Hedaya, Karen Young, Claire Bloom.

● The disaster movie returns. Manhattan: a motley group – including a lonesome gal (Brenneman) and a dog – is trapped in an tunnel beneath the Hudson. After a garbled mishap involving joyriders and trucks carrying nitroglycerine, they face further explosions, flood water and panic-induced bickering. Their survival depends on the heroic efforts of Stallone; they're lucky to have him, since he trod this line of work before, until taking the rap for an earlier fatal incident. Director Cohen keeps the vehicle cruising in fourth gear, hoping the audience won't get too impatient with the familiar scenery. Big, efficient, mindless entertainment. NB

Day of the Animals

(1976, US, 98 min)
d William Girdler. *p* Edward L Montoro. *sc* William Norton, Eleanor E Norton. *ph* Robert Sorrentino. *ed* Henry Asman, James Mitchell. *m* Lalo Schifrin. *cast* Christopher George, Leslie Nielsen, Lynda Day George, Richard Jaeckel, Michael Ansara, Ruth Roman.

● Twelve ill-assorted people (and twelve low-voltage performers) on a survival trek in the High Sierras are attacked by bears, wolves, birds, snakes, dogs – all of whom aren't feeling quite themselves. The cause of their unease is ultra-violet rays, seeping through an atmosphere polluted with aerosol sprays. The result is the most routine kind of thrills, packed with all the lack of imagination Girdler lavished on *Grizzly*. GB

Day of the Beast, The (El día de la bestia)

(1995, Sp/It, 104 min)
d Alex de la Iglesia. *p* Antonio Saura, Claudio Gaeta. *sc* Alejandro de la Iglesia, Jorge Guerricaechevarria. *ph* Flavio Martinez Labiano. *ed* Teresa Font. *pd* José Luis Arrizabalaga, Biaffra. *m* Battista Lena. *cast* Alex Angulo, Armando De Razza, Santiago Segura, Terele Pávez, Nathalie Seseña, Jaime Blanch.

● Alex de la Iglesia's clever, more assured follow-up to *Acción Mutante* is a devilishly funny horror-comedy in which Angulo's priest becomes convinced that the Antichrist will be born in Madrid on Christmas Day. Immersing himself in evil, he searches for clues among the city's human detritus and in the lyrics of 'death metal' songs, before kidnapping, with the help of a gonzoid record-shop assistant (Segura), a famous TV para-psychologist (De Razza). Meanwhile, somewhere out there, El Diablo is waiting to be born. This is essentially a black comedy about two hapless individuals caught up in an impending cataclysm way beyond their understanding. Responding to the robust humour and underlying seriousness of the script, Angulo brings an engaging subtlety to his theologically inspired madman, Segura's HM fan is likewise bonkers yet oddly loveable. NF

Day of the Dead

(1985, US, 102 min)
d George A Romero. *p* Richard P Rubinstein. *sc* George A Romero. *ph* Michael Gornick. *ed* Pasquale Buba. *pd* Cletus Anderson. *m* John Harrison. *cast* Lori Cardille, Terry Alexander, Joseph Pilato, Jarlath Conroy, Antone DiLeo, Gary Howard Klar, Ralph Marrero, John Amplas, Richard Liberty.

● The final instalment in Romero's Living Dead trilogy somehow failed to replicate the impact of *Night of the Living Dead* (1968) or *Dawn of the Dead* (1978), although not through any fault of its own. Some months after their emergence, the zombies are everywhere in the ascendant. A depleting scientific research team conducts experiments on captured zombies in a cavernous Florida bunker under increasingly despotic military protection. There's no radio contact with the outside world, and the pressure is taking its toll: the soldiers are impatient for results that Dr Logan's social conditioning tests just aren't going to meet. Tense rather than terrifying, and with a strong black comic undercurrent, it rests on the mordant observation that zombies or no zombies, chances are the living will tear each other apart. A fitting conclusion to a remarkably astute series, a landmark in the horror genre. TCh

Day of the Dolphin, The

(1973, US, 104 min)
d Mike Nichols. *p* Robert E Relyea. *sc* Buck Henry. *ph* William A Fraker. *ed* Sam O'Steen. *pd* Richard Sylbert. *m* Georges Delerue. *cast* George C Scott, Trish Van Devere, Paul Sorvino, Fritz Weaver, Jon Korkes, Edward Herrmann.

● Having taught his beloved marine playmate to speak (i.e. to say 'Fa, Ma, Pa' and other fascinating gems), scientist Scott discovers that the creature's intelligence is being exploited by horrible humans in a plot to kill the president. A bizarre and often ridiculous attempt to merge documentary, suspense and comedy that is marginally less silly than Nichols' best-loved film, *The Graduate*. GA

Day of the Evil Gun

(1968, US, 93 min)
d/p Jerry Thorpe. *sc* Charles Marquis Warren, Eric Bercovici. *ph* W Wallace Kelley. *ed* Alex Beaton. *ad* George W Davis, Marvin Summerfield. *m* Jeff Alexander. *cast* Glenn Ford, Arthur Kennedy, Dean Jagger, John Anderson, Paul Fix, Harry Dean Stanton, Parley Baer, Royal Dano, Ross Elliott.

● A Western directed with lazy assurance, and scripted by Charles Marquis Warren as something like a cross between *The Searchers* and Peckinpah's *The Deadly Companions*. Glenn Ford is an ageing gunfighter, tired of the macho kick, who returns home after three years only to learn from a neighbouring farmer (Kennedy) that his wife and two small daughters have been carried off by Apaches. Kennedy claims that the wife intended to marry him, presuming her husband dead; and in uneasy alliance the two men set out on the trail. Their odyssey, with the two men subtly changing places as the farmer begins to revel in the hunt and the gunfighter leaves him to get on with the killing, is studded with pleasingly bizarre encounters: a minister's wife brooding in a darkened room over her experiences as an Apache captive; Indians who disarm them with lassoes and stake them out to die from buzzard's beak; a cluster of burning shacks that turns out to be a town in the death-throes of cholera; a Mormon ghost town that harbours a sinister band of Confederate deserters. No masterpiece, but distinctly effective. TM

Day of the Jackal, The

(1973, GB/Fr, 142 min)
d Fred Zinnemann. *p* John Woolf. *sc* Kenneth Ross. *ph* Jean Tournier. *ed* Ralph Kemplen. *ad* Willy Holt, Ernest Archer. *m* Georges Delerue. *cast* Edward Fox, Michel Lonsdale, Alan Badel, Eric Porter, Jean Martin, Cyril Cusack, Delphine Seyrig, Donald Sinden.

● Inherently suspenseless (history would give us several more years of assassination-target De Gaulle), this adaptation of Frederick Forsyth's bestseller yet provides an occasionally satisfying core of tension that owes less to Zinnemann's penchant for *High Noon*-ish clock-watching than to his schematic opposition of a cold, chameleonic lone killer (Fox, the OAS's hired pro) with a messy, though equally ruthless, bureaucracy of 'democratic' defence. Low on documentary conviction and political context, but an intriguing exercise in concealing the obvious. PT

Day of the Locust, The

(1974, US, 143 min)
d John Schlesinger. *p* Jerome Hellman. *sc* Waldo Salt. *ph* Conrad Hall. *ed* Jim Clark. *pd* Richard MacDonald. *m* John Barry. *cast* Donald Sutherland, Karen Black, Burgess Meredith, William Atherton, Geraldine Page, Richard A Dysart, Bo Hopkins, Jackie Earle Haley.

● Schlesinger's misguided version of Nathanael West's cynical classic about a tormented Tinseltown, peopled by no-hopers trying in vain to work their way into the glamorous, starry life of the Hollywood studios. Admittedly the book, an elusive, mesmeric work of associated images and ideas, surreal and analytical, would present problems for the most talented of film-makers. But Schlesinger really blows it. West's thin plot is stretched out to excessive length, with little sense of pace or the significance of events; the characters are cut down, stranded without pasts and motivations; images are emphasised with no sense of context; the narrative is often confused and confusing. Only the hysterical holocaust at the end of the film gives any idea of West's conception, and even then the power of the scene is betrayed by a pathetic, superfluous coda. GA

Day of the Outlaw

(1959, 96 min, b/w)
d André De Toth. *p* Sidney Harmon. *sc* Philip Yordan. *ph* Russell Harlan. *ed* Robert Lawrence. *ad* Jack Poplin. *m* Alexander Courage. *cast* Robert Ryan, Burl Ives, Tina Louise, Nehemiah Persoff, Jack Lambert, Alan Marshal.

● *Day of the Outlaw* carries further (and further inward) the viciousness of *The Indian Fighter*, with its claustrophobic tensions coiled tight in a snowbound township when the arrival of a murderous renegade cavalry unit interrupts Ryan's attempt to reclaim his woman and his land. The incisive bleakness of Philip Yordan's script finds its perfect complement in the absurdist violence of De Toth's direction.

Day of the Premiere of 'Close Up'

see Giorno della prima di 'Close Up', Il

Day of the Triffids, The

(1962, GB, 94 min)
d Steve Sekely. *p* George Pitcher. *sc* Bernard Gordon [actual], Philip Yordan [credited]. *ph* Ted Moore. *ed* Spencer Reeve. *ad* Cedric Dawe. *m* Ron Goodwin. *cast* Howard Keel, Nicole Maurey, Janette Scott, Kieron Moore, Mervyn Johns.

● Not a particularly faithful adaptation of John Wyndham's novel, though it sticks to the basic theme about a world epidemic of blindness followed by the attack of strange plant-like creatures called 'triffids'. The film shows signs of having been put together rather patchily, with several uncertain performances and some rather dodgy process work. But quite a few of Wyndham's ideas do translate to the screen most effectively, like the airliner whose crew and passengers are suddenly struck blind, and the electric fortress surrounded for miles and miles around by invading triffids. Sometimes unintentionally funny, and it could have done without the customary moralising. DP

Day of Wrath (Vredens Dag)

(1943, Den, 105 min, b/w)
d Carl Dreyer. *sc* Carl Dreyer, Poul Knudsen, Mogens Skot-Hansen. *ph* Carl Andersson. *ed* Erik Ases, Lis Fribert, Edith Schlüssel, Anne-Marie Petersen. *ad* Erik Aaes. *m* Poul Schierbeck. *cast* Thorkild Roose, Lisbeth Movin, Sigrid Neiiendam, Preben Lerdorff Rye, Anna Svierkier, Albert Hoeberg.

● Often seen as an allegory on the Nazi occupation of Denmark, this austere and very sombre account of the persecution of witches in 17th century Denmark is arguably Dreyer's most pessimistic film. When a pious elderly parson sends an old woman to the stake, she curses him. His young wife (the daughter of a woman suspected of witchcraft) falls in love with her stepson; the affair induces the parson's death. Is the wife, then, herself a witch? Dreyer remains wisely ambivalent, preferring instead to focus on the powerful, earthly emotions of fear and love: the grim, grey confession chambers – location of perhaps the most discreet yet horrific torture scenes in cinema – embody the former, rippling streams and sun-dappled meadows the latter. Almost paradoxically, Dreyer evokes the soul through the physical world; the result is a masterpiece, its slow, measured pace and stark visuals achieving an almost unbearable emotional intensity. GA

Days, The (Dong-Chun de Rizi)

(1993, China, 75 min, b/w)
d Wang Xiaoshuai. *p* Wang Yao, Zhang Hongtao. *sc* Jin Jin [Wang Xiaoshuai]. *ph* Liu Jie. *ed* Wang Xiaoshuai. *m* Liang Heping. *cast* Yu Hong, Liu Xiaodong, Lou Ye.

● To those whose experience of Chinese cinema has been limited to the visually exotic films of Chen Kaige and Zhang Yimou, this rather wonderful movie by young independent Wang Xiaoshuai may come as a surprise. Shot in lyrical, melancholy b/w, it begins with a sensual, languorous scene of a couple making love in a Beijing bedsit, before proceeding to chart the slow, inexorable break-up of their relationship. Dong and Chun are both unsuccessful artists-turned-tutors, but shared interests and sexual passion haven't managed to stave off boredom and petty domestic tensions, with the result that she now wants to go to America, and he hasn't the fire left in his soul to tell her he'd rather she didn't. The days pass, and Chun's proposed departure gets even closer. What makes the movie so compelling is Wang's subtle control of mood: the stark, elegant visuals, the music, the elliptical approach to narrative, the long takes, and the taciturn but telling performances – all work together to produce a hauntingly poetic elegy to the transience of love. GA

Days and Nights in the Forest (Aranyer din Ratri)

(1969, Ind, 115 min, b/w)
d Satyajit Ray. *p* Nepal Dutta, Ashim Dutta. *sc* Satyajit Ray. *ph* Soumendu Roy. *ed* Dulal Dutta. *ad* Bansi Chandragupta. *m* Satyajit Ray. *cast* Soumitra Chatterjee, Sharmila Tagore, Subhendu Chatterjee, Samit Bhanja, Robi Ghose, Pahari Sanyal, Kaberi Bose.

● Ray's most overtly Renoir-ish film, this might almost be a remake of *Une Partie de Campagne*, transposed to another time and place and through another sensibility. Instead of the French bourgeois family setting off for a picnic, four young men leave Calcutta for a few days in the country, trailing their westernised careerist attitudes, a middle class indifference to the lower orders, a self-satisfaction that leaves them closed to experience. Out of a series of delightfully funny mishaps as the visitors eagerly try to pursue acquaintance with their two promisingly attractive neighbours, Ray gradually distils a magical world of absolute stasis: a shimmering summer's day, a tranquil forest clearing, the two women strolling in a shady avenue, wistful yearnings as love and the need for love echo plangently. Elsewhere jobs have to be won or lost, problems faced and solved, but not here; an illusion of course, revealed as time lifts its suspension but leaves one of the quartet a changed man, the other three assailed by tiny waves of self-doubt. Beautifully shot and acted, it's probably Ray's masterpiece. TM

Days in London (Ayam fi London)

(1977, Leb, 97 min, b/w)
d Samir Al Ghosaini. *sc* Mahmoud Al Tokhi, Shaker Barikhan. *ph* Mohammed Al Rawas, Paul Atkinson. *ed* Marwan Akkawi. *cast* Samira Tawfeek, Yossif Shaaban, Rafeek Al Soubeiy, Khaled Taja.

● On this evidence, Arab musical escapism is directly comparable with the Bombay variety, but it is to be hoped that the film industries of the Middle East can boast some writers and directors better capable of stringing images and characters together than those responsible for this pathetic comedy-thriller. The leading lady, as a gaudily dressed shepherdess stranded in tourist London, is required to register confusion and mime three songs; reputed to be a big star in her home market, she is not, by any European definition of the word, an actress. TR

Days of Being Wild (A-Fei Zhengchuan)

(1990, HK, 94 min)
d Wong Kar-Wai. *p* Rover Tang. *sc* Wong Kar-Wai. *ph* Christopher Doyle. *ed* Kai Kit Wai. *pd* William Chang. *m* Chan Do-ming. *cast* Leslie Cheung, Andy Lau, Maggie Cheung, Carina Lau, Tony Leung, Jacky Cheung.

● Wong Kar-Wai's second feature is a brilliant dream of Hong Kong life in 1960. A young man of Shanghainese descent drifts through a series of casual friendships and uncommitted affairs, unconsciously pining for a relationship with his mother, who has started a new life in Manila. He finally takes off for the Philippines, where he sets himself up for the ultimate fall... The terrific, all-star cast enacts this as a series of emotionally unresolved encounters; the swooningly beautiful camera and design work takes its hallucinatory tone from the protagonist's own uncertainties. The mysterious appearance of Tony Leung only in the closing scene heralds a sequel that will sadly never be made. But this is already some kind of masterpiece. TR

Days of Glory

(1944, US, 86 min, b/w)
d Jacques Tourneur. *p/sc* Casey Robinson. *ph* Tony Gaudio. *ed* Joseph Noriega. *ad* Albert S D'Agostino, Carroll Clarke. *m* Daniele Amfitheatrof. *cast* Gregory Peck, Alan Reed, Maria Palmer, Lowell Gilmore, Tamara Toumanova, Hugo Haas.

● Peck making his debut as a Russian guerrilla in one of those World War II tributes to our gallant Soviet allies which caused so much embarrassment later on. Actually, while making no bones about the fact that the protagonists are Communists, Casey Robinson's script is much more concerned with their doggedly gallant resistance under siege than with any political or propagandist purpose. No one had much to say for the film at the time, but it's sober and surprisingly convincing, even making the romantic interludes with Toumanova (a Catholic ballerina who joins the godless guerillas in their fight) unforced and natural. Quite beautifully directed by Tourneur. TM

Days of Heaven

(1978, US, 94 min)
d Terrence Malick. *p* Bert Schneider, Harold Schneider. *sc* Terrence Malick. *ph* Nestor Almendros. *ed* Billy Weber. *ad* Jack Fisk. *m* Ennio Morricone. *cast* Richard Gere, Brooke Adams, Sam Shepard, Linda Manz, Robert Wilke, Jackie Shultis, Stuart Margolin.

● Wide-eyed, streetwise Abby (Adams) and her lover come (amidst thousands of other croppers from the industrial north) to the startlingly fertile harvest landscape of World War I Texas. Once there, they are caught up in a diffident, ultimately fatal triangle with their ailing young landowner-boss (Shepard): these are the surreal, idyllic, numbered *Days of Heaven*. This strange fusion of love story, social portrait and allegorical epic, by the director of *Badlands*, is rooted like that film in recent history, and held together only by its voice-over commentary and staggering visual sense. Where it goes further is in a profound chilling of romantic style, which treats lovers and insects alike as they flit through the vast wheat fields at dusk. Eventually (with a plague-of-locusts climax and the lovers' flight) the narrative collapses, leaving its audience breathlessly suspended between a 90-minute proof that all the bustling activity in the world means nothing, and the perfection of Malick's own perverse desire to catalogue it nonetheless. Compulsive. CA

Days of Hope

see Espoir

Days of Thunder

(1990, US, 107 min)
d Tony Scott. *p* Don Simpson, Jerry Bruckheimer. *sc* Robert Towne. *ph* Ward Russell. *ed* Billy Weber, Chris Lebenzon. *ad* Tom Sanders, Benjamin Fernandez. *m* Hans Zimmer. *cast* Tom Cruise, Robert Duvall, Nicole Kidman, Randy Quaid, Cary Elwes, Michael Rooker, Fred Dalton Thompson, JC Quinn.

● A flashy, pre-packaged racing picture featuring stock cars and stock situations. Veteran crew chief Duvall's efforts to get the naturally gifted Cruise to drive within the mechanical limits of the car provide the character-building father/son conflict. Kidman meanwhile provides the obligatory love interest as an improbably young doctor who offers TLC and a little more besides after Cruise is involved in a near-fatal crash. The plot's driving momentum is lost when Cruise's arch-rival (played with quiet intensity by Rooker) is badly injured in the same crash, to be replaced by insipid Val Kilmer-lookalike Cary Elwes. The resulting tedium is relieved only by Kidman's spirited berating of Cruise for his infantile macho desire to control his unruly emotions, and by yet another sterling performance from the ever-excellent Duvall. NF

Days of Water, The (Los Dias del Agua)

(1971, Cuba, 110 min)
d Manuel Octavio Gómez. *sc* Manuel Octavio Gomez Gomex, Bernadé Hernandez, Julio Garcia Espinoza. *ph* Jorge Herrera. *ed* Nelson Rodriguez. *m* Leo Brouwer. *cast* Idalia Anreus, Raúl Pomares, Adolfo Llaurado, Mario Balmaseda, Omar Valdés.

● Based round the true case of a woman who became a saint and 'miracle' worker in 1936 Cuba, *The Days of Water*, with its restless camerawork, offers broad and sweeping intimations of the popular revolution to come: the exploited and pent-up energies of an oppressed peasantry will eventually transform themselves into revolutionary forces (symbolised towards the end by the firing of the first shot of defiance). Appropriately, the atmosphere is near hysteria, culminating with the wish fulfilment of the final carnage. Huge crowds harangued by a commercial conman wait to be blessed or healed; the Church rails impotently while a fantasy sequence reveals that its Virgin Mary has a malevolent face; decadent and opportunist politicians exploit the 'saint's' popularity with typically gangsterish methods. Voodoo and Catholicism combine to produce what can only be described as primitive baroque – an array of startling images, often as crude as they are effective. CPe

Days of Wine and Roses

(1962, US, 116 min, b/w)
d Blake Edwards. *p* Martin Manulis. *sc* JP Miller. *ph* Philip H Lathrop. *ed* Patrick McCormack. *ad* Joseph C Wright. *m* Henry Mancini. *cast* Jack Lemmon, Lee Remick, Charles Bickford, Jack Klugman, Alan Hewitt, Tom Palmer, Debbie Megowan, Jack Albertson.

● A heartrending saga of alcoholic dependency, adapted by JP Miller from his own teleplay. Cast heavily against type, Lemmon plays a San Francisco PR man uneasy about his job (which involves procuring women for business parties) and covering it by convivial drinking. When he marries Remick, they drink to celebrate. They drink to everything else, too. And then they start drinking simply to drink. The couple's battle to get off the bottle is harrowingly chronicled, so much so that you almost forget it's a Blake Edwards picture – his best by some margin, with a touching score by Henry Mancini. TJ

Day the Earth Caught Fire, The

(1961, GB, 99 min, b/w)
d/p Val Guest. *sc* Wolf Mankowitz, Val Guest. *ph* Harry Waxman. *ed* Bill Lenny. *ad* Tony Masters. *m* Monty Norman. *cast* Edward Judd, Janet Munro, Leo McKern, Michael Goodliffe, Bernard Braden, Reginald Beckwith, Arthur Christiansen.

● Thoroughly old-fashioned disaster film about a *Daily Express* reporter who learns that the earth has been tilted off its axis by the impact of two simultaneous H-bomb tests. Its 'authentic' newspaper setting looks quaint now, but there's some effective atmospheric build-up to the big one as London swelters in fog and heat. Perhaps inevitably, given the period and the film's medium budget, the ending is a cop-out. DP

Day the Earth Stood Still, The

(1951, US, 92 min, b/w)
d Robert Wise. *p* Julian Blaustein. *sc* Edmund H North. *ph* Leo Tover. *ed* William H Reynolds. *ad* Lyle Wheeler, Addison Hehr. *m* Bernard Herrmann. *cast* Michael Rennie, Patricia Neal, Hugh Marlowe, Sam Jaffe, Billy Gray.
● A classic science fiction fable, its ambitious storyline conveying a surprising pacifist message. A flying saucer lands in Washington DC, and the humanoid alien which emerges is immediately shot and wounded by nervous state troopers. A ten-foot tall robot, Gort, emerges and disintegrates guns and tanks, before being deactivated by the wounded alien (Rennie). Rennie later delivers an ultimatum to the world's leaders: stop these senseless wars or face the awesome consequences – demonstrated by a period of one hour in which all the world's power is stopped. The scenes in which the fugitive Rennie learns about life on Earth by living incognito in a boarding-house with a young widow (Neal) and her son (Gray) are particularly effective, and it is telling that it is the widow who prevents Gort from destroying the world by uttering the immortal line, 'Gort! Klaatu barada nikto'. Edmund H North's intelligent script and Wise's smooth direction are serious without being solemn, while Bernard Herrmann's effectively alien-sounding score reinforces the atmosphere of strangeness and potential menace. NF

Day the Fish Came Out, The

(1967, Greece/GB, 109 min)
d/p/sc Michael Cacoyannis. *ph* Walter Lassally. *ed* Vassilis Syropoulos. *ad* Spyros Vassiliou. *m* Mikis Theodorakis. *cast* Tom Courtenay, Colin Blakely, Sam Wanamaker, Candice Bergen, Ian Ogilvy, Patricia Burke.
● In 1972, a military aircraft crashes near a tiny Greek island after jettisoning its nuclear load, and a team of experts is sent to conduct a discreet search for the missing bombs. Their presence, supposedly as representatives of a hotel development company, turns the island into a thriving tourist resort, and the beaches are packed with holidaymakers by the time the fish start mysteriously dying. Directing with an eye to Dr Strangelove, Cacoyannis turns it all into hideously lumbering farce, so unconvincing that one is heartily glad when the unprepossessing characters at last seem likely to be overwhelmed by radiation. TM

Day the Sun Turned Cold, The (Tianguo Niezi)

(1994, HK, 100 min)
d/p Yim Ho. *sc* Wang Xing Dong, Wang Zhe Bin. *ph* Hou Yong, Shang Yong. *ed* Wong Yee-Shun, Zhou Ying Wu, Yun Jiang Chun. *ad* Gong Ming Hui. *m* Otomo Yoshihide, Na Bing Chen. *cast* Siqin Gaowa, Tao Chung-Hua, Ma Jingwu, Wei Zhi, Shu Ziong, Li Hu.
● Yim Ho's sober, engrossing and finely observed film is based on actual events in China, but it's not an exercise in docu-drama. A young man goes to the police in Changchun to confide his fear that his mother murdered his father in their village home ten years earlier; the cops don't take him too seriously, but his persistence forces them to launch an investigation. The core issue, though, is not whether or not murder was done, but the love/hate relationship between a mother and son, and casting of the extraordinary Mongolian actress Siqin Gaowa as the mother gives full play to the Oedipal implications. The mix of realist detail and psychological insight takes the film way beyond the limitations of traditional Chinese melodrama. TR

Day the World Ended, The

(1955, US, 81 min, b/w)
d/p Roger Corman. *sc* Lou Rusoff. *ph* Arthur Feindel. *ed* Ronald Sinclair. *m* Ronald Stein. *cast* Richard Denning, Adele Jergens, Lori Nelson, Mike Connors, Paul Birch, Raymond Hatton, Paul Dubov.
● An early Corman sci-fi movie (his first, in fact, as a director) which has survivors of the holocaust fending off an unfriendly mutant, and is engaging (almost convincing, even) in its pervasive seediness. The use of locations and the interplay between the desperate characters is surprisingly ambitious. TR

Day Time Ended, The

(1979, US, 80 min)
d John 'Bud' Cardos. *p* Wayne Schmidt. *sc* Wayne Schmidt, J Larry Carroll, David Schmoeller. *ph* John Morrill. *ed* Ted Nicolaou. *ad* Rusty Rosene. *m* Richard Band. *cast* Jim Davis, Chris Mitchum, Dorothy Malone, Marcey Lafferty, Natasha Ryan, Scott Kolden.
● Targeted at a family audience in the wake of Spielberg and *Close Encounters*, but the narrative won't hold any child's attention as it wanders incoherently around the cosmic chaos caused by – wait for it! – a trinary supernova. And the crucial special effects are zilch, although a pixie-sized alien scores simply because of its cow-eyed charm. IB

Daytrippers, The

(1995, US, 88 min)
d Gregg Mottola. *p* Nancy Tenebaum, Steven Soderbergh. *sc* Greg Mottola. *ph* John Inwood. *ed* Anne McCabe. *pd* Bonnie Brinkley. *m* Richard Martinez. *cast* Hope Davis, Parker Posey, Anne Meara, Stanley Tucci, Liev Schreiber, Pat McNamara, Campbell Scott, Marcia Gay Harden.
● Loving wife Davis finds a love letter in husband Tucci's pocket. He's a publisher, so it may be more innocent than it seems, but then, mysteriously, he's not at the office. The wife, her parents, her sister and the sister's boyfriend cram into the car and drive into the city to confront him. Mottola's dysfunctional family comedy is a bit arch, but sometimes sharp. Indie cinema and Neil Simon intersect on the corner of pathos and farce. TCh

Dazed and Confused

(1993, US, 102 min)
d Richard Linklater. *p* Richard Linklater, Sean Daniel, Jim Jacks. *sc* Richard Linklater. *ph* Lee Daniel. *ed* Sandra Adair. *ad* Jenny C Patrick. *cast* Jason London, Joey Lauren Adams, Milla Jovovich, Shawn Andrews, Rory Cochrane, Adam Goldberg.
● School's breaking up for the summer of '76. The seniors debate party politics while next term's freshmen run the gauntlet of brutal initiation rites, barely comforted by the knowledge that they'll wield the stick one day. No one's looking much farther ahead than that. This has a free-wheeling, 'day-in-the-life-of' structure which allows writer/director Linklater, in his second feature, to eavesdrop on an ensemble cast without much in the way of dramatic contrivance. There's a quirky counter-cultural intelligence at work: sympathy for those on the sidelines, and a dead-pan pop irony which places this among the hippest teenage movies. While the camera flits between some two dozen youngsters (played by uniformly excellent unknowns), Linklater allows himself to develop a handful of stories. Seriously funny, and shorn of any hint of nostalgia or wish-fulfilment, this is pretty much where it's at. TCh

D.C. Cab (aka Street Fleet)

(1983, US, 99 min)
d Joel Schumacher. p Topper Carew. sc Joel Schumacher. ph Dean Cundey, Ron Van Nostrand. ed David Blewitt. pd John J Lloyd. m Giorgio Moroder. cast Max Gail, Adam Baldwin, Mr T, Charlie Barnett, Gary Busey, DeWayne Jessie, Gloria Gifford.
● Fast-rappin' hi-jinks with the staff of the lowliest cab company in Washington DC. Basically a cross between TV's *Taxi* and the Schumacher-scripted *Car Wash*. Unfortunately, the sharp one-liners and quickie situation-jokes stop about halfway through, when an attempt at a plot is introduced. Ironically, despite a Keystone chase sequence, all this does is slow things down. Still, most of the jokes are a hoot (even Mr T parodies himself), and the soundtrack really frizzles. If this screen debut is anything to go by, Charlie Barnett should give Eddie Murphy a run for his money in the New Richard Pryor race – a Black Power Harpo, no less. GD

Dead, The

(1987, US/GB, 83 min)
d John Huston. *p* Wieland Schulz-Keil, Chris Sievernich. *sc* Tony Huston. *ph* Fred Murphy. *ed* Roberto Silvi. *pd* Stephen Grimes. *m* Alex North. *cast* Anjelica Huston, Donal McCann, Helena Carroll, Cathleen Delany, Ingrid Craigie, Rachel Dowling, Dan O'Herlihy, Donal Donnelly, Marie Kean.
● John Huston's last film is a small masterpiece on the order of Welles' *The Immortal Story*, perfectly achieved and unapologetic towards its literary antecedents. Joyce's novella is extraordinary for – among other virtues – the seamless flow from the mosaic approach to a dinner party into an anguished examination of the varieties of love, and the director delicately captures this musical movement. 'Is love worse living?' Joyce joked elsewhere, but at this stage allows the deceived husband (McCann) to make his peace with a shattered dream. His wife (Anjelica Huston) is moved by a song to remember a long-ago suitor who died for love – an impossible card for her decent, conventional husband to trump, and in turn leading him to reflect upon the transience of human lives. The closing shots of falling snow carry a complex emotional charge and a sort of resolution. The married couple get the lion's share of the drama and are wonderfully moving, while the rest of the cast – Donnelly, in particular, as Freddy the loveable drunk – are perfect. Tony Huston's script adds only the masterly stroke of the reading of a poem, and leaves the import of hope-achieved-at-a-cost intact. BC

Dead Again

(1991, US, 108 min)
d Kenneth Branagh. *p* Lindsay Doran, Charles H Maguire. *sc* Scott Frank. *ph* Matthew F Leonetti. *ed* Peter E Berger. *pd* Tim Hervey. *m* Patrick Doyle. *cast* Kenneth Branagh, Andy Garcia, Emma Thompson, Derek Jacobi, Wayne Knight, Hanna Schygulla, Robin Williams, Campbell Scott, Richard Easton.
● Branagh's lame stab at a romantic psychological thriller makes no sense. Sloppily constructed and cut, riddled with clichés and cant, it tells the old tale of a tough, wisecrackin' LA private eye (Branagh) hired to discover the identity of a mute, amnesiac woman (inevitably Thompson). Her nightmares derive from a violent past, from which, it seems, only an eccentric hypnotist (Jacobi) can free her. The none-too-plausible and unexplained twist is that Em's flashbacks are to a previous life (1949) when she was a famous pianist and Ken was her famous composer hubby, who was executed for her murder. The leads are dreadful, and Garcia as a news-hack who fires the muso's jealousy, Schygulla as the muso's loyal German housekeeper, and Williams as the dick's defrocked shrink pal are all awfully misused. Could it be that nothing – not the over-bearingly 'Hitchcockian' score, nor the OTT art direction – must distract our attention from the subtext: that Ken and Em are destined to dance through eternity together? GA

Dead and Buried

(1981, US, 95 min)
d Gary A Sherman. *p* Ronald Shusett, Robert Fentress. *sc* Ronald Shusett, Dan O'Bannon. *ph* Steve Poster. *ed* Alan Balsam. *ad* William Sandell, Joe Aubel. *m* Joe Renzetti. *cast* James Farentino, Melody Anderson, Jack Albertson, Dennis Redfield, Nancy Locke Hauser, Lisa Blount.
● Establishing shots of a bleak, colourless Atlantic seaboard fishing town, and the presence of *Alien* scriptwriter Dan O'Bannon on the credits, combine to make one expect a more adult-aimed variation on Carpenter's *The Fog*. Unfortunately a series of progressively grisly murders intervenes, suggesting a mere overtime-earner for the chaps at SFX; but after some irritating meanderings, the film picks up momentum and, via a splendidly staged confrontation in a Mabuse-style lab, progresses to a 'surprise' climax which, even if anticipated, must still rank a close second to the false ending of *Carrie*. Gruesome almost to a fault, but not quite, it emerges as an efficient shocker. GD

Dead Babies

(2000, GB, 101 min)
d William Marsh. *p* Richard Holmes, Neil Peplow. *sc* William Marsh. *ph* Danny Cohen. *ed* Eddie Hamilton. *pd* Mark Tanner. *m* Mark 'Meat Katie' Pember, Marvin Beaver. *cast* Paul Bettany, Katy Carmichael, Hayley Carr, Charlie Condou, Alexandra Gilbreath, William Marsh, Kris Marshall, Andy Nyman, Cristian Solimeno, Olivia Williams.
● Long before Martin Amis' mid-'70s novel reached the screen, the shock value masking a country house whodunit in the Agatha Christie

mould was already dated. Admittedly, there's rather more sexual and chemical mayhem, but the basic outline provides assorted English toffs, sundry visiting Yanks, and a mystery assailant in their midst. Writer/director Marsh's update on the material to a post-millennial near-future adds the Conceptualists, an anarchic terror group who advertise their atrocities on the Web, and whose deadly graffiti signature, 'Johnny', signals imminent danger for the drug-fuelled revellers at Appleseed Rectory. If 'Johnny' doesn't get them first, acid guru Marvel's pharmaceutical cocktails just might pitch them all over the edge. Presumably there's a satirical intent: the path of youthful excess leading not to free-wheeling hedonism but further psychological turmoil. Yet the film hardly encourages us to engage with its woolly debate on how we pursue our freedoms when it's so gruellingly tiresome to sit through. TJ

Dead Bang

(1989, US, 102 min)
d John Frankenheimer. *p* Steve Roth. *sc* Robert Foster. *ph* Gerry Fisher. *ed* Robert F Shugrue. *pd* Ken Adam. *m* Gary Chang. *cast* Don Johnson, Penelope Ann Miller, William Forsythe, Bob Balaban, Frank Military, Tate Donovan.

● Based on the career of a real-life homicide cop, this is a vehicle for the still-pending big screen launch of Johnson, the casual fashion-plate from *Miami Vice*. To show his range, this time he looks like shit, with specs held together by tape, and Hoke Moseley-style personal problems. He vomits on a suspect, too, but don't think the camera doesn't love him, right down to the freeze-frame finish. Popeye Doyle he ain't. Having Johnson aboard entails a certain amount of tailored scenario that doesn't drive the story. The brief affair with cop's widow Miller is unconvincing, and the scene with the psychiatrist seems to be there to show the star getting the giggles. The plot begins with race murders, leads to a cross-country pursuit, and ends daftly with neo-Nazis in underground caverns. Routine stuff. BC

Dead Beat

(1994, US, 93 min)
d Adam Dubov. *p* George Moffly, Christophe Lambert. *sc* Adam Dubov, Janice Shapiro. *ph* Nancy Schrieber. *ed* Lorraine Salk. *m* Anton Sanko. *cast* Bruce Ramsay, Natasha Wagner, Balthazar Getty, Meredith Salenger, Alex Cox, Deborah Harry.

● Produced by Christopher Lambert, this is a quirky US indie about a rock'n'roll rebel stuck in a Midwestern hole in the early '60s. He wears cowboy boots, make-up, and models himself on Elvis. He's a real ladykiller. Literally. Dubov's debut has plenty of zip, but it doesn't entirely come off, perhaps because it shows its hand too soon, perhaps because the hip amoral tone just doesn't gel with the bozo narrator young Balthazar Getty provides. Intriguing all the same, with cameos from Alex Cox and Deborah Harry, and a ticklish, narcissistic turn from Ramsay. TCh

Deadbeat at Dawn

(1987, US, 80 min)
d Jim Van Bebber. *p* Michael King. *sc* Jim Van Bebber. *ph* Michael King. *ed* Jim Van Bebber. *m* Ned Folkerth, Mike Pierry. *cast* Paul Harper, Jim Van Bebber, Megan Murphy, Ric Walker, Marc Pitman, Maureen Gentner, Tom Burns.

● Can't say I took to this wanton disarray of guns, guts and splattered brains (at least behind the camera) when I watched it on video – a planned release since scotched by the BBFC, which objects to the film's explicit depiction of nunchakus – so it might be more charitable to quote the box blurb's synopsis: 'Goose (Van Bebber) decides to quit his street gang The Ravens and plans to settle down when he's made enough money selling junk. But other members of The Ravens aren't too hot on his career plans and brutally murder his girlfriend. When rival gang The Spiders hook up with The Ravens in order to pull off a big bank heist, Goose decides to join the action once more. However, his motives are personal and of the violent retribution kind.' *The Psychotronic Video Guide* calls it 'one of the most downbeat, unpretentious, independent action movies I've seen.' Chas Balun of Deep Red says it 'hits like a jackboot to the nuts'. Fans of *The Warriors*, Abel Ferrara and inchoate B-movie-making technique might find something of interest. NB

Dead Calm

(1988, Aust, 96 min)
d Phillip Noyce. *p* Terry Hayes, Doug Mitchell, George Miller. *sc* Terry Hayes. *ph* Dean Semler. *ed* Richard Francis-Bruce. *pd* Graham Walker. *m* Graeme Revell. *cast* Nichole Kidman, Sam Neill, Billy Zane, Rod Mulliner, Joshua Tilden, George Shevtsov, Michael Long.

● Recuperating from a family tragedy, a seasoned seaman (Neill) and his young wife (Kidman) sail their yacht, the Saracen, off the coast of Australia. Spotting a stricken boat, the Orpheus, they are amazed when a terrified young man (Zane) rows towards them, climbs aboard, and tells a horrifying story about an attack of food poisoning which he alone survived. But when Neill rows to the Orpheus to investigate, he is astonished to see his yacht, complete with wife and dog, sail off in the opposite direction with Zane at the wheel. Aboard the sinking Orpheus, Neill finds evidence of the marine hitchiker's lunacy; meanwhile, on the Saracen, Kidman is learning the hard way. A classic piece of pared-down genre film-making is lent extra depth by an emotional subtext stressing Kidman's transition from dependent wife to resourceful individual. Director Noyce's bravura camerawork conspires with Terry Hayes' spare script (adapted from the novel by Charles Williams) and some edgy cutting to exploit every ounce of tension, right down to a killer ending. NF

Dead Can't Lie, The

(1988, US, 98 min.)
d Lloyd Fonvielle. *p* David J Latt. *sc* Lloyd Fonvielle. *ph* Michael Chapman. *ed* Evan Lottman. *pd* Carol Spier. *m* George Clinton. *cast* Tommy Lee Jones, Virginia Madsen, Colin Bruce, Kevin Jarre, Denise Stephenson, Frederic Forrest, Michael Chapman.

● Eddie Mallard (Jones) is a piss-poor PI hired by Charlie, a very rich man, to find his wife Rachel (Madsen), whom he buried 10 years ago. She asked to be entombed naked except for her priceless jewels, and her husband obliged, but later had second thoughts, dug her up, and retrieved the rocks. Now she has returned to the land of the living to get them back. Soon Rachel and Eddie are power-showering away, Eddie convinced that Rachel is real, which she ain't. She's a succubus using him for her own evil ends, which entails quite a bit of nudity: Mr Jones is too old for this kind of thing. There's one good joke, albeit an old and sexist one. It might have been possible to view this catalogue of clichés as a tongue-in-cheek tribute to cornball cinema if irony hadn't been wholly absent. Mallard's movie is just a dead duck. MS

Dead Cert.

(1974, GB, 99 min)
d Tony Richardson. *p* Neil Hartley. *sc* Tony Richardson, John Oaksey. *ph* Freddie Cooper. *ed* John Glen. *ad* David Brockhurst. *m* John Addison. *cast* Scott Antony, Judi Dench, Michael Williams, Nina Thomas, Mark Dignam, Julian Glover.

● A film about racing from Richardson, who made *The Charge of the Light Brigade* so he must know all about horses. An amateur jockey (well, none of them professionals can speak proper) tries to discover who is nobbling the favourite for the National (well, they do say that racing attracts the worst of every class). Seems he's having an affair with the wife of a racehorse owner and getting a bit on the side with a masseuse. But it's OK. They both help him to go and win the Grand National. Despite a few concessions to our times, and a potentially promising subject, the film manages nothing in the way of suspense, insight or entertainment. There ought to be a steward's enquiry. CPe

Dead End

(1937, US, 93 min, b/w)
d William Wyler. *sc* Lillian Hellman. *ph* Greg Toland. *ed* Daniel Mandell. *ad* Richard Day. *m* Alfred Newman. *cast* Sylvia Sidney, Joel McCrea, Humphrey Bogart, Wendy Barrie, Claire Trevor, Marjorie Main, Allen Jenkins, the Dead End Kids.

● A muscle-bound Goldwyn production with an inflated reputation, interesting now chiefly in that, transposed virtually intact from the stage, it lets you see what the original Broadway production of Sidney Kingsley's play must have been like; particularly fascinating is the composite set which makes a metaphor of the rich man's terraces overhanging the slums. The social thesis (deprived backgrounds may make criminals, but they can make good guys and padres too) is familiar from countless problem pictures of the period, and the Dead End Kids are about as menacingly streetwise as Shirley Temple in her naughtier moods. Cruising along like a well-oiled machine tended by an excellent cast, it remains highly watchable, even if the basic mawkishness – in evidence everywhere from the rhyming of Sidney's dewy-eyed good girl with Trevor's ravaged bad one, down to the fact that Bogart's gangster is risking his neck to see mom one more time (she slaps him and sends him packing, true, but that just adds to the pity of it all) – keeps sticking in the craw. TM

Deadfall

(1968, GB, 120 min)
d Bryan Forbes. *p* Paul Monash. *sc* Bryan Forbes. *ph* Gerry Turpin. *ed* John Jympson. *ad* Ray Simm. *m* John Barry. *cast* Michael Caine, Giovanna Ralli, Eric Portman, Nanette Newman, David Buck, Carlos Pierre, Leonard Rossiter, Vladek Sheybal.

● Question: When is a thriller not a thriller? Answer: When it's a Forbes. A jewel thief (Caine) falls in love with the wife (Ralli) of his homosexual accomplice (Portman). She has been mentally scarred by her father's membership of the Gestapo, and her husband, a former French resistance fighter, is buggering a gigolo. And then, bugger *moi*, it transpires that the wife is also her husband's daughter, and they all commit suicide happily ever after. Replete with a Shirley Bassey theme tune and a 20-minute John Barry guitar concerto to accompany the robbery, this isn't a Freudian *Rififi*. It's rubbish. ATu

Dead Forest (Mrtvy Les)

(1990, Czech Rep, 40 min)
d/sc Pavel Marek. *cast* Tomás Hanák, Jiri Skala.

● A mushroom hunter wanders the wilderness of a morning while his wife cavorts with her spaghetti. A naked boy in the chicken shed advises him on 'something obviously fowl-like in your movements'; vacuum cleaner hounds pursue him across the landscape; and a man chopping wood in a swamp pool gives cryptic directions. 'I don't understand you.' 'I don't understand you either.' Wacky? NB

Dead Funny

(1994, US, 96 min)
d John Feldman. *p* David Hannay, Richard Abramowitz. *sc* John Feldman, Cindy Oswin. *ph* Todd Crockett. *ed* Einar Westerlund. *pd* Michael Shaw. *m* Sheila Silver. *cast* Elizabeth Peña, Andrew McCarthy, Paige Turco.

● It's hard to fathom what Feldman intended with this smug, excessively 'smart' tale, related largely in flashback, of the rise and fall of a passionate but shallow New York love affair between Peña and the resistible McCarthy. She returns home from work one day to find him in the kitchen stabbed with a samurai sword. (They are practical jokers.) How did it happen? Who did it? Who cares? Probably not Feldman who seems more interested in shooting his actresses' naked thighs. GA

Dead Heart

(1996, Aust, 105 min)
d Nick Parsons. *p* Bryan Brown, Helen Watts. *sc* Nick Parsons. *ph* James Bartle. *ed* Henry Dangar. *pd* Brian Edmonds. *m* Stephen Rae. *cast* Bryan Brown, Angie Milliken, Ernie Dingo, Aaron Pedersen, Gnarnayarrahe Waitaire, Lewis Fitzgerald.

● When a young Aborigine is found dead in a police cell, the local cop (Brown, who also produced) finds that his rule-bending ways of keeping the peace in a remote Aboriginal settlement are no longer sufficient to prevent racial conflict and violence. Not without appeal as a culture-clash thriller, this suffers from an occasional lack of narrative clarity, perhaps inevitably given the magical beliefs held by the older Aborigines whose notions of justice fuel the plot. That said, there are nice touches here (notably some scenes featuring white liberal documentarists), and strong performances from Brown and Milliken. GA

Dead Knot (Si Jie)

(1969, HK, 16 min, b/w)
d Wong Chi-Keung, John Woo. *p* John Woo. *sc* John Woo, Wong Chi-Keung. *ph* Chiu Tak-Hark. *ed* John Woo, Wong Chi-Keung. *cast* John Woo, Tso Chung-Lan, Chan Kai-Yat.
● Rescued by the Hong Kong Film Archive, this is the earliest surviving trace of John Woo's beginnings as an indie film-maker. A psychodrama in the vein of Anger's *Fireworks*, it's divided into eight short chapters. A young man (Woo) tries to escape from a gay sado-masochist relationship into a 'normal' relationship – with a girl! – but ends up back where he started, unable to buck his deepest desires. Whatever light this may shed on Woo's later work, it's fascinating for teasing out the subtext from the perverse swordplay bloodbaths which Chang Cheh was making at the time (*Golden Swallow*, etc). Co-director Wong is now better known as Sek Kei, a leading film critic. The HKFA print is a 35mm blow-up from a damaged 16mm original. TR

Dead Letter Office

(1998, Aust, 93 min)
d John Ruane. *p* Denise Patience. *sc* Deb Cox. *ph* Ellery Ryan. *ed* Denise Haratzis. *pd* Chris Kennedy. *m* Roger Mason. *cast* Miranda Otto, Georgina Naidu, George Delhoyo, Nicholas Bell, Syd Brisbane, Jane Hall.
● Twenty-something Alice (Otto) has, since childhood, written umpteen letters to her estranged father in an attempt to make contact, all to no avail. Still desperate after all these years, she manages to land a job at a dead letter office, and soon begins to snoop through the 'special cases' drawers and ask pertinent questions of her colleagues, most notably her Chilean boss to whom she takes a bit of a shine. This touching Australian film (from the director of *Death in Brunswick*) comes with a roster of fine performances, a well-tailored script and an unobtrusive but thoroughly likeable soundtrack. A film about loneliness, pure and simple, and wholly engaging with it. DA

Deadline at Dawn

(1946, US, 83 min, b/w)
d Harold Clurman. *p* Adrian Scott. *sc* Clifford Odets. *ph* Nick Musuraca. *ed* Roland Gross. *ad* Albert S D'Agostino, Jack Okey. *m* Hanns Eisler. *cast* Susan Hayward, Bill Williams, Paul Lukas, Joseph Calleia, Osa Massen, Lola Lane, Jerome Cowan, Marvin Miller, Roman Bohnen, Steve Geray.
● 'Golly, the misery that walks around in this pretty, quiet night!' murmurs Hayward's vibrant dance-hall dame, chasing round Manhattan trying to get her sailor pal off a murder rap. Golly, indeed, for the script by playwright Clifford Odets never lets up for a moment. Terse and flowery by turns, it elaborates the plot of Cornell Woolrich's novel almost to the point of incomprehension, yet movingly enhances the notion of New York as a fateful presence, teeming with the homeless and unhappy. Clurman, moonlighting in Hollywood after the collapse of his Group Theatre in New York, later dismissed it as just 'a run-of-the-mill RKO movie', but take no notice: it's made with cockeyed artistry from beginning to end, and shouldn't be missed. GB

Deadline – USA (aka Deadline)

(1952, US, 87 min, b/w)
d Richard Brooks. *p* Sol C Siegel. *sc* Richard Brooks. *ph* Milton Krasner. *ed* William B Murphy. *ad* Lyle Wheeler, George Patrick. *m* Cyril J Mockridge. *cast* Humphrey Bogart, Ethel Barrymore, Kim Hunter, Martin Gabel, Ed Begley, Paul Stewart, Jim Backus.
● Former newspaperman Brooks made a good fist of this media drama. He has Bogey in his favour as the crusading editor of a New York daily, battling to expose crime kingpin Gabel, while at the same time persuading owner Barrymore from selling the whole operation. Tautly scripted and put over with a feeling for authenticity (it was shot in the offices of the *New York Daily News*), it's one of those films where Brooks' liberal sympathies and no-nonsense storytelling is squarely on target. TJ

Dead Liqueur

(1992, Greece, 91 min)
d Georges Karypides. *sc* Yiannis Xanthoulis, Georges Karypides. *ph* Andreas Sinanos. *ed* Pavlos Philippou. *ad* Michalis Sdougos. *m* Nikos Kypourgos. *cast* Yiannis Karabellas, Costas Karabellas, Vaso Youlielmaki, Spyros Fokas.
● A remembrance of a '50s bourgeois childhood in a major Greek city, with something of the 'forbidden games' mystery tale about it, Karypides' film follows the life of two younger boys (one the narrator) who undergo a secret double marriage rite to their adolescent sister in the memory-laden cellar of their house. The basement is a place of mysteries – including a strange story that their father may have murdered a girl in a vat in the liqueur still – that need to be exorcised. Much of the tale is obscure, full of intimations of a class and society struggling to survive past its time, and doing so in the absence of a strong male presence. The pace is slow, and the film is shot with a restrained cinematic style. Odd, moody but intriguing. WH

Deadly

(1991, Aust, 101 min)
d Esben Storm. *p* Richard Moir. *sc* Esben Storm. *ph* Geoffrey Simpson. *ed* Ralph Strasser. *pd* Peta Lawson. *m* Graeme Revell. *cast* Jerome Ehlers, Frank Gallagher, John Moore.
● This competent, moderately nail-biting feature belongs to that uneasy genre, the investigative thriller with a political point to make. As often happens, the point (here, the brutal treatment meted out to Australia's aboriginal community) is driven home with hammerhead subtlety and at the same time obscured by hard-guy shenanigans. Ehlers is a Sydney cop sent to the outback to investigate the apparent suicide of an Aboriginal in police custody. Predictably, he's required to rubber-stamp a cover-up, but his maverick tendencies get the better of the situation… Director-writer Storm is good at setting the scene, and the sense of the outback town as a bastion of apartheid and entrenched hatred is the film's strongest point. But the jaw-clenched heroics are pedestrian and the mystery too transparent to hold interest. JRo

Deadly Advice

(1994, GB, 91 min)
d Mandie Fletcher. *p* Nigel Stafford-Clark. *sc* Glenn Chandler. *ph* Richard Greatrex. *ed* John Jarvis. *pd* Christopher Hobbs. *m* Richard Harvey. *cast* Jane Horrocks, Brenda Fricker, Imelda Staunton, Jonathan Pryce, Edward Woodward, Ian Abbey, Billie Whitelaw, Hywel Bennett, John Mills, Eleanor Bron.
● Set in Hay-on-Wye, infamous locally as the home of 1920s poisoner Major Herbert Armstrong, this competent, intermittently funny film casts Horrocks as Jodie, a mother-dominated shrew for whom life is anything but sweet. While her sister Beth (Staunton) is out and about with male stripper Bunny (Abbey), Jodie is stuck at home with her lazy, oppressive mother (Fricker). Inspired by a book about Armstrong's exploits, Jodie decides to bump her off, receiving unexpected help when the Major (Woodward) slides into reality from the pages of the book. Soon Jodie's bedroom is crammed with veteran British character actors playing real-life killers with conflicting advice on how best to dispose of the troublesome mother. Horrocks easily holds her own in this distinguished company, while Fricker is far more terrifying than any of the genteel killers. Mandie Fletcher's handling of Glenn Chandler's script is, however, sketchy and hurried, a legacy perhaps of her background in formula TV (*Blackadder*, *Only Fools and Horses*). NKe

Deadly Affair, The

(1966, GB, 107 min)
d/p Sidney Lumet. *sc* Paul Dehn. *ph* Freddie Young. *ed* Thelma Connell. *ad* John Howell. *m* Quincy Jones. *cast* James Mason, Simone Signoret, Maximilian Schell, Harriet Andersson, Harry Andrews, Kenneth Haigh, Roy Kinnear, Max Adrian, Lynn Redgrave.
● The usual John Le Carré net of intrigue, betrayal and death (based on his *Call for the Dead*) as Mason's Foreign Office security inspector investigates a colleague's suicide and finds himself under threat from an espionage ring. Lumet handles the atmosphere and performances with solid professionalism, and manages to tease out emotional strands from the knotty plotting; but there's no denying it's all been done before and since, even if rarely so efficiently. GA

Deadly Blessing

(1981, US, 102 min)
d Wes Craven. *p* Micheline Keller, Max A Keller, Pat Herskovic. *sc* Glenn M Benest, Matthew Barr, Wes Craven. *ph* Robert Jessup. *ed* Richard Bracken. *pd* Jack Marty. *m* James Horner. *cast* Maren Jensen, Susan Buckner, Sharon Stone, Jeff East, Lisa Hartman, Lois Nettleton, Ernest Borgnine.
● An excellent example of a mundane project elevated into quite a palatable genre movie by its director. Craven (who previously made *The Hills Have Eyes*) faced a script with one laborious idea in which a woman is terrorised by a rural religious sect. Realising the limitations, Craven has to keep audience interest alive with some desperate but occasionally inspired strategies: several unpredictable plot twists have been added, as well as an atmospheric sub-theme involving the heroine's nightmares. The shock sequences are punchy and varied, including one disturbingly Freudian horror of a snake in a bathtub, while the visual style is a deliberate attempt to make Texas look as lonely and lost as an Andrew Wyeth painting. Best of all, the impudent ending seeks to imply that all the sect's demonic imaginings are literally true. *Deadly Blessing* isn't a very good movie, but it holds out distinct promise that Craven will soon be in the front rank of horror film-makers. DP

Deadly Companions, The

(1961, US, 90 min)
d Sam Peckinpah. *p* Charles B Fitzsimons. *sc* Sid Fleischman. *ph* William H Clothier. *ed* Stanley Rabjohn. *m* Marlin Skiles. *cast* Brian Keith, Maureen O'Sullivan, Chill Wills, Steve Cochran, Strother Martin, Will Wright.
● Peckinpah's first film, a not altogether characteristic but nevertheless quirky Western which sees Keith's ex-army sergeant making amends for killing a boy by ferrying his corpse and his mother on a funeral procession through Apache territory. Routine in places, but enlivened by the sardonic characterisation (reminiscent in some ways of Faulkner's superficially similar *As I Lay Dying*) and by odd moments of visual bravura. GA

Deadly Eyes

see Rats, The

Deadly Females, The

(1976, GB, 105 min)
d/p/sc Donovan Winter. *ph* Austin Parkinson. *ed* Donovan Winter. *cast* Tracy Reed, Bernard Holley, Scott Fredericks, Heather Chasen, Brian Jackson, Roy Purcell, Rula Lenska.
● 'Tart I may be, thanks to you, but cheap I am not!' someone bawls at her boorish hubby before summoning one of Tracy Reed's gang of Kensington hit-women to dispose of him. Writer/producer/director/editor Winter strives to make exactly the same distinction in this sex-and-crime potboiler with classy notions ('you' in his case would be the impecunious, short-sighted British film industry). The film's nasty goings-on are supposedly a comment on the 'Savage Seventies'; but it takes more than close-ups of newspaper headlines screaming about IRA attacks and Bunny Girl murders to establish a fruitful connection, and the film's inept pretensions make it even more pernicious than your straightforward sexploiter. Reed's Godmother figure is cool enough to win the respect of any praying mantis, but the only glimmer of style Winter shows is to shoot one set-up through the back of a wicker chair. GB

Deadly Friend

(1986, US, 90 min)
d Wes Craven. *p* Robert M Sherman. *sc* Bruce Joel Rubin. *ph* Philip H Lathrop. *ed* Michael Eliot. *pd* Daniel Lomino. *m* Charles Bernstein. *cast* Matthew Laborteaux, Kristy Swanson, Michael Sharrett, Anne Twomey, Anne Ramsey, Richard Marcus.
● Teenage boffin Paul has developed a robot, BB, that can think for itself but it still has a silly voice. It suddenly starts seeing red, but no matter – Elvira, a paranoid neighbour, blows it away. Samantha, though, is a nice neighbour, and Paul is off his rocker when her kooky father kills her. But love will find a way: Paul implants BB's brain into Samantha's. She jerks into action. She is set on revenge… Although the prevailing

tone is comic, there is plenty of grue and gore; the heart stops several times. This may be Craven at his crummiest, but the resulting sick still ranks higher than anything his imitators can come up with. MS

Deadly Maria

see Tödliche Maria, Die

Deadly Pursuit

see Shoot to Kill

Deadly Run (Mortelle Randonnée)

(1982, Fr, 120 min)
d Claude Miller. *sc* Michel Audiard, Jacques Audiard. *ph* Pierre Lhomme. *m* Carla Bley. *cast* Michel Serrault, Isabelle Adjani, Guy Marchand, Stéphane Audran, Macha Méril, Genevieve Page, Sami Frey.

●Miller in Chabrol territory with an intriguing thriller, based on Marc Behm's novel *The Eye of the Beholder*, in which Serrault's somewhat eccentric private eye is given a case following a young runaway couple. When the woman (Adjani) murders the man, Serrault simply follows her through a series of further killings, suspecting (or wishing) she might be his long-lost daughter. A colourful if not altogether successful study in obsession and guilt transference, it features excellent performances all round (Serrault is magnificent, as always) and a surprisingly appropriate score by Carla Bley. GA

Deadly Strangers

(1974, GB, 93 min)
d Sidney Hayers. *p* Peter Miller. *sc* Philip Levene. *ph* Graham Edgar. *ed* Barry Peters. *ad* Ken Jones. *m* Ron Goodwin. *cast* Hayley Mills, Simon Ward, Sterling Hayden, Ken Hutchison, Peter Jeffrey, Hubert Tucker.

●Old-fashioned psychopathic goings-on in the West Country. Ward, a travelling salesman, shoe fetishist and voyeur, gives a lift to nice Hayley Mills while we're left to guess which one's the nutter escaped from the local funny farm. The script disastrously lumbers itself with this cumbersome suspense mechanism at the expense of developing more profitable themes, and the camerawork stresses the obvious with its movements. Sole redeeming feature is Hayley Mills, who suggests an actress capable of much better things than she has been offered recently. Hayers, to his credit, does exploit her best quality – an insolent, slightly offhand sex appeal. CPe

Deadly Trackers, The

(1973, US, 110 min)
d Barry Shear. *p* Fouad Said. *sc* Lukas Heller. *ph* Gabriel Torres. *ed* Michael Economou, Carl Pingitore. *ad* Javier Torres Torija. *cast* Richard Harris, Rod Taylor, Al Lettieri, Neville Brand, William Smith, Paul Benjamin, Pedro Armendariz Jr.

●Primarily a vehicle for Richard man-called-horse-lost-in-the-wilderness Harris. It's a formula pursuit Western, Harris starting out as reason-loving, gun-hating sheriff, ending up seeking revenge for his wife and son killed in a bank hold-up. Once south of the border, the excuses are all set for what the film's really about: a comedy of cruelty for us, seemingly a masochistic indulgence for Harris. He's beaten by a mob, almost lynched, and temporarily blinded before he exacts his revenge. The perfunctory questioning of the morality of revenge lacks any real conviction; Taylor as the villainous bandit leads an uninspired wild bunch; and the film never more than plods along under the weight of Harris' long-suffering performance. RM

Deadly Trap, The (La Maison sous les Arbres)

(1971, Fr/It, 100 min)
d René Clément. *p* Robert Dorfmann, Georges Casati. *sc* Sidney Buchman, Eleanor Perry. *ph* Andréas Winding. *ed* Françoise Javet. *ad* Jean André. *m* Gilbert Bécaud. *cast* Faye Dunaway, Frank Langella, Barbara Parkins, Michèle Lourié, Patrick Vincent, Karen Blanguernon, Maurice Ronet.

●A leisurely but cunningly paced story which starts off looking like a *Woman's Own* romance, and by the time it's finished has somehow involved you in domestic drama, murder, kidnapping and espionage intrigue. The ending has an impact similar to the punchline of a shaggy dog story, but the lead-up is always interesting thanks to Clément's nice Hitchcockian-flavoured style and deft use of menacingly 'ordinary' locations. VG

Deadly Weapons

(1974, US, 73 min)
d/p Doris Wishman. *sc* JJ Kendall. *ph* Joao Fernandez. *ed* Lou Burdi. *cast* Zsa Zsa, Harry Reems, Greg Reynolds, Saul Meth, Philip Stahl, Mitchell Fredericks.

●Wishman directs a lady boasting a 73-inch bust, and variously known as Zsa Zsa or Chesty Morgan, in a bizarre softcore sex movie in which she ultimately takes to suffocating mobsters between her mammaries. The whole thing is put together with such amateurishness that it almost seems as though the director is consciously rebelling against every convention of narrative cinema: close-ups of carpets, tracking shots of the sky, technicians weaving in and out of vision. But (just in case you're wondering) it hasn't enough unintentional humour or erotic content to make a visit worthwhile.

Dead Man

(1995, US/Ger, 120 min, b/w)
d Jim Jarmusch. *p* Demetra J MacBride. *sc* Jim Jarmusch. *ph* Robby Müller. *ed* Jay Rabinowitz. *pd* Bob Ziembicki. *m* Neil Young. *cast* Johnny Depp, Gary Farmer, Robert Mitchum, Lance Henriksen, Gabriel Byrne, John Hurt, Alfred Molina, Crispin Glover, Iggy Pop.

●A bizarre, funny, almost mystical take on the Western, Jarmusch's film charts the sentimental education of a clerk, William Blake (Depp), when he travels out West and finds himself, after an unexpected violent incident, pursued by vicious bounty hunters and taken up by a decidedly eccentric Indian (Farmer) who believes his new friend is the English visionary poet. Looser in structure than the director's earlier work, but pervaded with the same deadpan humour and superb imagery (cameraman,Robby Müller), this is an original and very weird account of the American wilderness. Haunting electric guitar score by Neil Young. GA

Deadman, The

(1989, US, 40 min, b/w)
d Peggy Ahwesh, Keith Sanborn. *cast* Jennifer Montgomery, Ramon Quanta la Gusta, Dianne Torr.

●A woman leaves her dead lover and staggers through torrential rain to a dingy bar where she fucks, sucks and pisses on the assembled staff and clientèle. Based on a story by Georges Bataille, high-priest of Erotico-Necro Theory, *The Deadman* is a joyless exercise in the transgressive imagination that gets its kicks defiling the mouldering body of silent cinema. Shot through monochrome drizzle with an exaggeratedly raw soundtrack that makes every cough a thunderous eruption, every urinary trickle a sonic deluge, the story is framed as a fragment from some apocryphal silent era, the libertine visuals intercut with funereally solemn, wryly redundant intertitles. As a dour exercise in 'anti-porn', liberating excess from the titillating rhetoric of 'erotic' cinema, you can see where it's aiming, but it never really engages the viewer in any interrogation of the viewing process, largely because it's dull. JRo

Dead Man's Curve

(1997, US, 91 min)
d Dan Rosen. *p* Michael Amato, Theodore Schipper, Jeremy Lew. *sc* Dan Rosen. *ph* Joey Forsyte. *ed* Glenn Garland. *pd* Robert Harbour. *m* Shark. *cast* Matthew Lillard, Michael Vartan, Randall Batinkoff, Keri Russell, Tamara Craig Thomas, Anthony Griffith. Bo Dietl.

●A roommate's suicide, it seems, guarantees top grades, so two college students, rich sociopath Tim (Lillard) and ambitious scholarship boy Chris (Vartan), conspire to push their moody, under-achieving pal Rand (Batinkoff) over the edge, literally. Distressed by news that his drippy girlfriend Natalie (Thomas) is pregnant, Rand is easy prey, but just to be sure, Tim laces the victim's farewell bottle of tequila with rat poison. But when the body can't be found, and the police start sniffing around, the plot begins to unravel… A shade too clever for its own good, Rosen's wordy script operates on two levels. On one hand, Tim and Chris are students involved in an elaborate conspiracy; on the other, they're also actors playing roles in their own script. The interchange between these levels is the key: most of the dialogue is meant to be overheard and acted on by the other parties. The characters are deeply unsympathetic, but the interplay of shifting alliances draws us in, while simultaneously undermining our confidence in any of them. And the 'sucker punch' ending, which some find too glib, is a killer blow, reinforcing the film's clever, heartless misanthropy. NF

Dead Man Walking

(1995, US, 122 min)
d Tim Robbins. *p* Jon Kilik, Rudd Simmons, Tim Robbins. *sc* Tim Robbins. *ph* Roger Deakins. *ed* Lisa Churgin. *ad* Richard Hoover. *m* David Robbins. *cast* Sean Penn, Susan Sarandon, Robert Prosky, Scott Wilson, R Lee Ermey, Raymond J Barry, Celia Weston, Lois Smith, Roberta Maxwell, Margo Martindale.

●Sister Helen Prejean (Sarandon) is a nun who works with the mainly black poor. When she first visits the Louisiana State Penitentiary, however, she's unprepared for the ethical, emotional and spiritual turmoil which follows. Inmate Matthew Poncelet has requested her help in his appeal against execution. With politicians and radio fundamentalists advocating tougher measures, the chances of a stay of execution are slim for an unrepentant white-trash racist who insists he only watched, rather than participated in, the rape and murder of a teenage couple. If his appeal fails, will Helen have the strength not merely to continue as his spiritual adviser, but to guide her arrogant, hate-filled charge towards some sort of redemption? Though it finally takes a firm stand against institutionalised murder, director Robbins' tough, balanced script (from an autobiographical book) never succumbs to special pleading. Poncelet is a very nasty piece of work (superbly played by Penn with bouffant hair and goatee), while the vengeful grief of the victims' families is depicted with sympathy and respect. Though the message is underlined by the questions raised (whose pain, exactly, is the 'humane' method of lethal injection finally intended to diminish?), this brave, intelligent and very moving film is no dry thesis – thanks principally to the vivid excellence of the performances. GA

Dead Men Don't Die

(1991, US, 94 min)
d Malcolm Marmorstein. *p* Wayne Marmorstein. *sc* Malcolm Marmorstein. *ph* Tom Fraser. *ed* Michael Ornstein. *pd* Phillip Vasels, Diane Hughes. *m* Daivd Williams. *cast* Elliott Gould, Melissa Anderson, Mark Moses, Mabel King, Jack Betts, Philip Bruns.

●A TV newsman who stumbles on a major scoop is wiped out by the Mob, resurrected by a voodoo priestess and, in zombified state, sets out to track down his killers. Not good. TJ

Dead Men Don't Wear Plaid

(1982, US, 88 min, b/w)
d Carl Reiner. *p* David V Picker, William E McEuen. *sc* Carl Reiner, George Gipe, Steve Martin. *ph* Michael Chapman. *ed* Bud Molin. *pd* John F DeCuir. *m* Miklós Rozsa. *cast* Steve Martin, Rachel Ward, Carl Reiner, Reni Santoni, George Gaynes.

●Not the first movie to be built around cameo performances, but these are somewhat novel. Forties stars (Bergman, Bogart, Cagney, etc.) are exhumed from the Hollywood vaults to live again in a new mystery comedy whose convolutions stem not least from forcing various clips from old thrillers to look as though they belong together. Some amusement is derived from watching a film that so obviously had to be worked out backwards. The bits in between feature likeable Martin as a keen but clumsy detective – with all the good lines, which is no bad thing because he's the best part of this fairly amusing, clever exercise in editing. CPe

Dead of Night

(1945, GB, 102 min, b/w)
d Robert Hamer, Basil Dearden, Charles Crichton, Alberto Cavalcanti. *p* Michael

Balcon. *sc* John Baines, Angus MacPhail. *ph* Douglas Slocombe, Stan Pavey. *ed* Charles Hasse. *ad* Michael Relph. *m* Georges Auric. *cast* Mervyn Johns, Michael Redgrave, Frederick Valk, Googie Withers, Sally Ann Howes, Basil Radford, Naunton Wayne, Roland Culver.

●Nearly 60 years on, Ealing's compendium of spooky tales remains scary as hell. The best of the five stories, which we see enacted as they're related in turn by guests at a country house, are Cavalcanti's 'The Ventriloquist's Dummy', with Redgrave possessed by his deceptively lifeless little partner, and Hamer's 'The Haunted Mirror', with the splendid Withers a reluctant participant as history repeats itself; least frightening, but amusing, are Radford and Wayne as typically obsessive sporting coves in Crichton's 'Golfing Story'. Best of all, however, is the overall narrative arc, with the framing story finally taking a headlong rush into a nightmarish realm almost surreal in its weird clarity and familiarity. GA

Dead of Night (aka Deathdream)

(1972, Can, 90 min)
d/p Bob Clark. *sc* Alan Ormsby. *ph* Jack McGowan. *ed* Ronald Sinclair. *ad* Forest Carpenter. *m* Carl Zittrer. *cast* John Marley, Lynn Carlin, Henderson Forsythe, Richard Backus, Anya Ormsby.

●Modest and reasonably intriguing horror film. Andy (Backus) is reported killed in action, but returns from the grave to seek retribution from the family and small-town society that drove him to enlist in the first place. The film's novelty lies in its observation of Andy's home life; notably the tensions between Mom (impressively played by Carlin) and Dad which degenerate from minor squalls to major sores. Andy emerges as the hapless problem child forced into a vampiric blood habit through the sins of his parents. The film plunges in the final chase sequence, however, where Clark's artless direction strains against almost comic strip events. IB

Dead of Winter

(1987, US, 100 min)
d Arthur Penn. *p* John Bloomgarden, Marc Shmuger. *sc* Marc Schmuger, Mark Malone. *ph* Jan Weincke. *ed* Rick Shaine. *pd* Bill Brodie. *m* Richard Einhorn. *cast* Mary Steenburgen, Roddy McDowall, Jan Rubes, William Russ, Ken Pogue, Wayne Robson.

●Struggling actress Katie (Steenburgen) auditions for a part that entails travelling upstate to a rambling country house inhabited by crippled Dr Lewis (Rubes) and his amanuensis (McDowall). She should, however, be less concerned about her acting prospects than about the missing actress she is to replace, Julie Rose. Were she a thriller fan, she'd realise that her life is in danger; after all, she's the pawn in a game reminiscent of Joseph H Lewis' *My Name Is Julia Ross*. While beautifully shot, admirably old-fashioned (sexual violence and explicit gore are absent), and endowed with pleasing plot twists, the film is too formulaic and offers little opportunity for Penn to display his prodigious talents. GA

Dead or Alive

(1999, Jap, 105 min)
d Takashi Miike. *p* Katsumi Ono, Makoto Okada, Toshiki Kimura. *sc* Ichiro Ryu. *ph* Hideo Yamamoto. *ed* Taiji Shimamura. *pd* Akira Ishige. *m* Koji Endo. *cast* Riki Takeuchi, Sho Aikawa, Renji Ishibashi, Hitoshi Ozawa, Susumu Terajima, Ren Osugi.

●Handed a tedious script about a turf war in Shinjuku's Kabuki-cho entertainment district (a maverick Chinese gang pulls a robbery which upsets organised crime; a care-worn cop lumbers towards a showdown with the troublemakers), Miike threw away half of it and used the rest as a springboard to amazing inventions. The exposition scenes are boiled down to an entire reel of 'abstract' action – a cataclysmic restaurant ambush, a gay man killed while sodomising a kid, the world's longest line of coke, a homo-erotic knife-throwing act in a girlie bar – while the unrevealable ending is turned into the ultimate blast. In between, Miike offers a series of electrifyingly sad vignettes of death, failure and loss, including what must be the most disturbing stoned murder scene the genre has ever known. A future classic. TR

Dead or Alive 2 – Birds

(2000, Jap, 97 min)
d Takashi Miike. *p* Ken Takeuchi. *sc* Masa Nakamura. *ph* Kazu Tanaka. *ed* Yasushi Shimamura. *m* Chu Ishikawa. *cast* Riki Takeuchi, Sho Aikawa, Edison Chen, Masato, Teah, Shinya Tsukamoto, Tomoro Taguchi, Ren Osugi.

●Was the end of the world in the first *Dead or Alive* all a dream? Maybe not, because this time Aikawa and Takeuchi are back as angels. More exactly, they're boyhood friends and rival hitmen who run into each when both are hired to kill one racketeer. They figure it's time to retire from the yakuza fray and take a slow boat back to the island where they were both raised in an orphanage, reminiscing about the good times, the bad times and their favourite noodles. The only narrative issue of any consequence is how and where they will die this time. Miike's film (this time written to order) parodies its own predecessor, rhymes gunplay with conjuring tricks, considers the morality of Christian retribution and ponders the exhaustion of the yakuza genre. It might be best to file it under 'avant-garde'. TR

Dead Pigeon on Beethovenstrasse (Kressin und die tote Taube in der Beethovenstrasse)

(1972, WGer, 103 min)
d Samuel Fuller. *p* Joachim von Mengershausen. *sc* Samuel Fuller. *ph* Jerzy Lipman. *ed* Liesgret Schmitt-Klink. *ad* Lothar Kirchem. *m* Can. *cast* Glenn Corbett, Christa Lang, Anton Diffring, Eric P Caspar, Sieghart Rupp, Anthony Chin, Alex D'Arcy.

●Those misguided individuals who didn't like *White Dog* had better stay clear of this, Fuller's most bizarre film. Made for German TV, it's a complex crime thriller about an American agent visiting Bonn to find the killer of his partner, and getting involved in a treacherous world of blackmail, drugs, nude photography and murder. In conventional terms it's ruined by wooden acting (notably Fuller's wife Lang as femme fatale) and a wayward plot. But its great attraction lies not only in the typically vigorous direction (pacy action scenes accompanied by the music of Can), but in the madcap humour which turns the entire film into a parody of thuggish thrillers. Add to that the wicked movie references (*Alphaville* is presented as a skinflick, *Rio Bravo* is shown with a German Dean Martin ordering schnapps), and the startling, even surreal use of locations, not to mention a weird credits sequence, and you have what is virtually a professional home movie that delights by its sheer sense of fun and absurdity. GA

Dead Poets Society

(1989, US, 129 min)
d Peter Weir. *p* Steven Haft, Paul Junger Witt, Tony Thomas. *sc* Tom Schulman. *ph* John Seale. *ed* William Anderson, Lee Smith, Priscilla Nedd. *pd* Wendy Weir. *m* Maurice Jarre. *cast* Robin Williams, Robert Sean Leonard, Ethan Hawke, Josh Charles, Gale Hansen, Dylan Kussman, Allelon Ruggiero, James Waterston, Norman Lloyd, Kurtwood Smith, Alexandra Powers.

●With Tom Schulman's script scrutinising educational conformity, the casting of Robin Williams as English teacher John Keating is inspired. Keating's eccentric teaching methods, exhorting his students with cries of 'Carpe Diem', promote spontaneity and idealism. But in the prestigious Welton Academy circa 1959, these male offspring are put on the same career path as their fathers, and face stern opposition from the educational establishment when they choose to indulge their imaginations. Keating's gospel breeds hope for some, frustration and despair for others. To a large degree, Schulman avoids cliché by focusing almost exclusively on entrenched paternal prejudice against artistic pursuits. Weir infuses the film with his customary mysticism, but more importantly, draws sensitive performances from his largely inexperienced cast (Leonard is particularly impressive). Williams does wonders with a role that tends to be reduced to one of catalyst. CM

Dead Pool, The

(1988, US, 91 min)
d Buddy Van Horn. *p* David Valdes. *sc* Steve Sharon. *ph* Jack N Green. *ed* Ron Spang. *pd* Edward C Carfagno. *m* Lalo Schifrin. *cast* Clint Eastwood, Patricia Clarkson, Liam Neeson, Evan C Kim, David Hunt, Michael Currie, Michael Goodwin.

●*Dirty Harry* part five ain't much cop. True, the morgues and breakers' yards are filled to brimming, but the sight of Lt Callahan (Eastwood) and new partner Lt Quan (Kim) trying to look scared as they are chased through San Francisco by a 6-inch remote-controlled model car quickly un-suspends disbelief. Down in Chinatown there are murderous thugs flying through windows into his lap; worse, now that he's hit the headlines and has go-getter newscaster Samantha Walker (Clarkson) on his back, Harry fears he may become a victim in a series of psychopathic murders of local celebrities. So many ethical debates later, a prolonged burst of Uzi machine-gun fire forces Walker into his arms and his way of thinking; and the anonymously sent hit-list – the eponymous dead pool – is traced to sicko horror film director Peter Swan (Neeson). Eastwood still manages to run about almost energetically, and there are occasional flashes of the old laconic wit; but the direction is woefully loose, and can't marry the parody with the thrills. WH

Dead Presidents

(1995, US, 121 min)
d/p Allen Hughes, Albert Hughes. *sc* Michael Henry Brown. *ph* Lisa Rinzler. *ed* Dan Lebental. *pd* David Brisbin. *m* Danny Elfman. *cast* Larenz Tate, Rose Jackson, Freddy Rodriguez, Chris Tucker, N'Brushe Wright, Bookeem Woodbine.

●The twins' follow-up to *Menace II Society* is essentially a classic gangster movie (*The Roaring Twenties*, say) revamped and remoulded for a new context: black experience in the late '60s and early '70s. The war this time is Vietnam, but Anthony Curtis (Tate) comes back to face the age-old problems: unemployment and a woman he hasn't seen for too long. There are intriguing aspects to this yarn, and the brothers can choreograph a scene, but you get the impression that they learned all they know from other movies, the blood and guts is gratuitous, and the episodic narrative takes an awful long time to get nowhere very rewarding. Great heist sequence though. TCh

Dead Reckoning

(1947, US, 100 min, b/w)
d John Cromwell. *p* Sidney Biddell. *sc* Oliver HP Garrett, Steve Fisher, Allen Rivkin. *ph* Leo Tover. *ed* Gene Havlick. *ad* Stephen Goosson, Rudolph Sternad. *m* Marlin Skiles. *cast* Humphrey Bogart, Lizabeth Scott, Morris Carnovsky, Charles Cane, William Prince, Marvin Miller, Wallace Ford.

●Faced with the synthetic Scott instead of genuine Bacall, Bogart reacts with a hint of self-parody. Or maybe it's just that the film, cast in flashback form with a guilt-ridden narration by Bogart, tries too hard to maintain its note of doomed *noir* romance. Excellent hardboiled shenanigans as Bogart's ex-paratrooper sets out with a 'Geronimo!' on his lips to investigate the disappearance of his buddy, uncovering a web of duplicities at the centre of which is the alluringly equivocal Scott. But the relationship never quite convinces, leading to a faintly embarrassing emotional climax as death conjures one last 'Geronimo!' Highly enjoyable all the same. TM

Dead Ringers

(1988, Can, 115 min)
d David Cronenberg. *p* David Cronenberg, Marc Boyman. *sc* David Cronenberg, Norman Sinder. *ph* Peter Suschitzky. *ed* Ron Sanders. *pd* Carol Spier. *m* Howard Shore. *cast* Jeremy Irons, Genevieve Bujold, Heidi von Palleske, Jonathan Haley, Nicholas Haley.

●Cronenberg's emotionally devastating study of the perverse relationship between identical twin gynaecologists, Beverly and Elliot Mantle, is an intense psychological drama which confronts his familiar preoccupations – fear of physical and mental disintegration, mortality, the power struggle between the sexes – without the paradoxical protection of visceral disgust. Instead, the abstract, expressionist imagery synthesises the physical and the mental. Courtesy of clever, unobtrusive trick camerawork, Irons gives a superlative performance as both twins. The delicate symbiotic balance between the brothers is suddenly upset by the eruption into their lives of hedonistic actress Claire (Bujold). As always, they share everything, including Claire, until Beverly realises that he has at last found something he does not want to share, and he is plunged into a whirlpool of emotional confusion; when Elliot tries to help, he too is sucked into the vortex of pain and despair. Likewise, Cronenberg pulls us deeper and deeper into his harrowing tale of separation and loss, the disturbing, cathartic power of which leaves one drained but exhilarated. NF

Dead Zone, The

(1983, US, 103 min)
d David Cronenberg. *p* Debra Hill. *sc* Jeffrey Boam. *ph* Mark Irwin. *ed* Ronald Sanders. *pd* Carol Spier. *m* Michael Kamen. *cast* Christopher Walken, Brooke Adams, Tom Skerritt, Herbert Lom, Anthony Zerbe, Colleen Dewhurst, Martin Sheen, Nicholas Campbell, Sean Sullivan.

●After a long coma, school teacher Walken wakes up with psychic powers (but no girlfriend). Depending on your point of view, this is either Cronenberg's most progressive, humanist movie (*pace* Robin Wood), or one of his least personal, most conventional pictures. Adapted from a Stephen King novel, and produced by Dino De Laurentiis, it's well crafted and atmospheric, with an arresting central character (Walken in one of his most sympathetic and controlled performances), but the episodic plot strands don't really mesh. In the most striking, the teacher unmasks a serial killer; in another he prevents a young boy from drowning; and in yet another his path crosses with a single-minded politician (Sheen). Cronenberg pulls it off, but you can't help feeling it's a movie in search of a TV series. TCh

Deaf and Mute Heroine, The (Longya Jian)

(1971, HK, 102 min)
d Wu Ma. *p* Wong Toh. *sc* Wan Tong, Hui Ho Chiang. *ph* Wah San. *ed* Kwok Hung. *cast* Helen Ma, Tang Dic, Shirley Wong, Tang Ching, Lee Ying.

●A superbly rendered fantasy, dominated by brilliantly handled tussles of sheer wit and ingenuity (rather than muscle power) as the heroine of the title disorientates and confounds assailant after assailant. Wu Ma sustains his idealised world with almost as many visual sleights-of-hand as his heroine, having his camera actively recoil from the entrance of a giant knight (whose face remains unseen for a whole sequence, and who has attained the state of weightlessness) to perch somewhere near the ceiling, or filling the screen with a diffuse flood of red which, for a moment, the eye is unable to interpret: is it a pool of blood or merely a floating scarf? The climactic conflict, too, is fought out in a genuinely dreamlike atmosphere. VG

Deaf Smith & Johnny Ears (Los Amigos)

(1972, It, 92 min)
d Paolo Cavara. *p* Joseph Janni, Luciano Perugia. *sc* Harry Essex, Oscar Saul, Paolo Cavara, Lucia Drudi, Augusto Finocchi. *ph* Tonino Delli Colli. *ed* Mario Morra. *ad* Francesco Calabrese. *m* Daniele Patucchi. *cast* Anthony Quinn, Franco Nero, Pamela Tiffin, Ira Furstenberg, Franco Graziosi, Adolfo Lastretti.

●An unmemorable Italian Western spoilt by an over-complicated, over 'historical' plot (about the Republic of Texas in 1834 and its entry into the Union); not to mention some some very unfunny business between Quinn, in his nature man guise as a deaf mute, and Nero as his would-be engaging 'ears'.

Dealer

(1998, Ger, 74 min)
d/sc Thomas Arslan. *ph* Michael Wieswag. *ed* Bettina Blickwede. *pd* Gabriella Ansonio. *cast* Tamer Yigit, Idil Üner, Birol Ünel, Hussi Kutlucan, Lea Stefanel, Baki Davrak.

●If plot won't knock anyone off their seat, this intimate diary portrait of a young Turkish drug pusher caught between family (his young wife and child), mob patron, cops and the daily grind is a stunning and assured piece of work. Clean, clear and concise, it watches the impassive protagonist's inexorable slide with dramatic restraint, his failure of will punished by some brutally abrupt turns of fate. Hard not to see the influence of Bresson in Arslan's taste for understatement and uninflected imagery – there's the same introspective austerity, if not the same depth of insight The writer/director loves shooting the blank profile of his dark,chiselled lead against moody backdrops of the Berlin streets by night. Very impressive. NB

Dealers

(1989, GB, 91 min)
d Colin Bucksey. *p* William P Cartlidge. *sc* Andrew MacLear. *ph* Peter Sinclair. *ed* Jon Costelloe. *pd* Peter J Hampton. *m* Richard Hartley. *cast* Paul McGann, Rebecca De Mornay, Derrick O'Connor, John Castle, Paul Guilfoyle, Rosalind Bennett, Adrian Dunbar, Nicholas Hewetson, Sara Sugarman.

●This strangely dated City drama is set, they suggest, in the near future, even though it notches up all those mid-'80s obsessions: need, greed, gratification. Daniel Pascoe (McGann), bad boy of the dealer room, takes insane risks but does nicely, ta very much: lord of the manor lifestyle, seaplane, portable phone, vintage sportscar. We get a glimpse of other values as a sexy girlfriend (Bennett) gives him the shove for being money-driven, though she's soon shown to be as pretentious and self-indulgent as every other character. The top trader has offed himself, and the job's been given to stuck-up, by-the-book Anna (De Mornay, surprisingly convincing). Anna just ain't got that flair, so bad boy and good girl have to cooperate to win back the lost millions. You know the scenario: it's loathe at first sight, but soon they're allies, and she hangs back admiringly while he pulls off the big one. The climax comes in the dealer room as the cast all stare mesmerised at flashing green numbers. The most likeable performance is O'Connor's Robby Barrell, a dire warning of what happens when you stay in the mythic City over the age of 35: coke-snuffing, booze-sloshing, graven with lines, emotionally undisciplined. Poetic, really. SFe

Dealers Among Dealers

(1995, US, 77 min)
d Gaylen Ross.

●An engrossing fly-on-the-wall study of New York's Jewish jewellery trade. As Orthodox cutters sing Yiddish songs, and their bosses buy and sell stones for millions, we become privy to a profoundly conservative society devoted equally to craftsmanship and capitalism, and determined to perpetuate social and economic transactions built on notions of honour, hierarchy and tradition endlessly passed from father to son. Throughout the film runs a keen sense of history – whether of the pogroms, when owning a diamond could make the difference between life and death, or of the early '90s recession, when hitherto successful dealers might be reduced to working as chauffeurs. GA

Dear America: Letters Home from Vietnam

(1987, US, 87 min)
d Bill Couturie. *p* Bill Couterie, Thomas Bird. *sc* Richard Dewhurst, Bill Couterie. *ph* Michael Chin. *ed* Stephen Stept, Gary Weinberg. *m* Todd Boekelhide. *cast* voices: Tom Berenger, Ellen Burstyn, William Defore, Robert De Niro, Brian Dennehy, Matt Dillon, Robert Downey Jr, Michael J Fox, John Heard, Harvey Keitel, Sean Penn, Randy Quaid, Martin Sheen, Kathleen Turner, Robin Williams.

●This beautifully crafted documentary brings home the tragedy of the Vietnam war in ways well out of the reach of feature films. Nothing is re-enacted, and the interweaving of newsreel and amateur footage puts you right there next to the bloody stumps and the booby-traps in the elephant grass. The letters home – read by Robert De Niro, Martin Sheen, Sean Penn, Tom Berenger, Robin Williams among others – range from family ordinary to the staring horror of Joseph Conrad's Kurtz. Tears and fear are a constant refrain. An intensely moving and disturbing experience. BC

Dear Boys (Lieve Jongens)

(1980, Neth, 88 min)
d Paul de Lussanet. *sc* Chiem van Houweninge, Paul de Lussanet. *ph* Paul van de Bos. *ed* Hans van Dongen. *ad* Gebr Goedemans. *m* Laurens van Rooyen. *cast* Hugo Metsers, Hans Dagelet, Bill van Dijk, Albert Mol, Pleuni Touw, Marina de Graaf.

●Writer Wolf lures Tiger and Beaver to his country home, ditching Beaver's wrinkled old sugar daddy so that the Pinteresque games can start. Wolf's only currency in the bargain is the fantasies he weaves for Beaver: sweet boys, fast cars, romance. His own fantasy, it seems, is of marrying both boys in church, but he's faced with the same problem as the banished old lover – no one loves an ageing queen. The trio, with the axe-wielding ex- in tow, pass through a series of bizarre tableaux, erotic, humorous, surreal, pathetic, occasionally firing off intellectual squibs. But ultimately *Dear Boys* hovers unsatisfactorily between contrived wank literature and the inspired narrative conceits of Roeg, Resnais, et al. A gay *Providence* it is not. JG

Dear Diary (Caro Diario)

(1994, It/Fr, 100 min)
d Nanni Moretti. *p* Nanni Moretti, Angelo Barbagallo, Nella Banfi. *sc* Nanni Moretti. *ph* Giuseppe Lanci. *ed* Mirco Garrone. *pd* Marta Maffucci. *m* Nicola Piovani. *cast* Nanni Moretti, Renato Carpentieri, Antonio Neiwiller, Jennifer Beals, Alexandre Rockwell, Carol Mazzacurati.

●Moretti's three-part movie-essay is structured as a wry, affectionate and very funny odyssey through the Roman suburbs, the Aeolian Isles, and the Italian health system. Relaxed and leisurely, it's an effortless blend of documentary and fiction, part road movie, part sociological satire, part polemical reminiscence. As Moretti travels around, investigating and commenting, he manages to provoke not only laughter, but the sense that we are seeing Italy anew. Accordingly, just as he includes offbeat gags about, say, movie critics being fed a taste of their own medicine, so when he drives to the site of Pasolini's murder, he forces us simply to look and listen, to take in light, space, shape, movement and music; in other words, to recognise the essence of cinema shorn of story and superfluous stylistic tropes. That's no mean achievement in these days of narrative and technological overkill, though the movie is too modest to insist even on its own quirkiness, let alone its more serious subtextual concerns. GA

Dearest Love

see Souffle au Coeur, Le

Dear Inspector (Tendre Poulet)

(1977, Fr, 105 min)
d Philippe de Broca. *p* Alexandre Mnouchkine. *sc* Michel Audiard, Philippe de Broca. *ph* Jean-Paul Schwartz. *ed* Françoise Javet. *ad* François de Lamothe. *m* Georges Delerue. *cast* Annie Girardot, Philippe Noiret, Catherine Alric, Hubert Deschamps, Paulette Dubost, Roger Dumas.

●De Broca hit gold regularly with entertainments like *That Man from Rio* and *King of Hearts*, but for the witty panache of the former and the cultish whimsy of the latter *Dear Inspector* substitutes a tired, slapdash soufflé of middle-aged romance and comedy-thriller. Ex-Sorbonne classmates, bearded Greek professor Noiret and female cop Girardot meet cute. She keeps quiet about her job, until the strains of hunting the murderer of a lengthening list of Deputies prove too much. They part, she resigns, turns to spring-cleaning. They reunite in scenic Honfleur; she solves the case, he gets involved; they limp off towards bliss. Routine froth. PT

Dear Mother, I'm All Right (Liebe Mutter, mir geht es gut)

(1972, WGer, 87 min)
d Christian Ziewer. *p* Regina Otto-Gundelach, Max Willutzki. *sc* Klaus Wiese, Christian Ziewer. *ph* Jörg-Michael Baldenius. *ed* Stephanie Wilke. *ad* Edwin Wengoborski. *cast* Claus Eberth, Nikolaus Dutsch, Heinz Herrmann, Ernest Lenart, Kurt Michler, Horst Pinnow.

●If *Tout va Bien* was a movie about industrial relations for a middle class audience, then this is the equivalent movie for workers themselves. Shot with guileless simplicity, it analyses the situation of workers at a West Berlin factory where cutbacks are proposed; a strike is called, but it proves difficult to maintain solidarity. It's seen mainly from the point of view of one 'average' employee, but there are also glimpses of management machinations. The links between general economic policies and such facts of life as workers' problems with accommodation are made absolutely explicit. The approach has the immediacy of a good comic strip, naive in the best, non-patronising sense. It looks exemplary. TR

Dear Summer Sister (Natsu no Imoto)

(1972, Jap, 95 min)
d Nagisa Oshima. *sc* Tsutomu Tamura, Mamoru Sasaki, Nagisa Oshima. *ph* Yashuhiro Yoshioka. *ed* Keiichi Uraoka. *ad* Jusho Toda. *m* Toru Takemitsu. *cast* Hosei Komatsu, Hiromi Kurita, Lily, Akiko Koyama, Shoji Ishibashi, Rokko Toura.

●A film in which Oshima tackles Japan's 'Okinawa problem'. The Japanese today treat Okinawa as a holiday resort, and so this begins as a light, summery dream of sun, sand and teenage flirtation. But the underlying thread (a girl's search for her long-missing brother) conjures up darker spectres, and before long the entire idyll has been effectively undercut by guilt-ridden memories of the past – and especially the atrocities perpetrated on the island during the war. TR

Death and the Maiden

(1994, GB/US/Fr, 103 min)
d Roman Polanski. *p* Thom Mount, Josh Kramer. *sc* Raphael Iglesias, Ariel Dorfman. *ph* Tonino Delli Colli. *ed* Hervé de Luze. *pd* Pierre Guffroy. *m* Wojciech Kilar. *cast* Sigourney Weaver, Ben Kingsley, Stuart Wilson, Krystia Mova.

●In a newly democratised South American country, Escobar (Wilson) heads a commission investigating the abuse of political prisoners. One such prisoner was his wife Paulina (Weaver). When one night Escobar comes home late, having been given a lift by seemingly liberal Dr Miranda (Kingsley), Paulina is convinced that their guest is the tormentor who 15 year ago subjected her to sexual humiliation and violence. Escobar feels duty-bound to defend the stranger from the woman he loves, but who may be lying, even insane. In filming Ariel Dorfman's adaptation of his own stage hit, Polanski wisely never opens out the action from the remote clifftop house. In keeping things claustrophobic, close-up and ambivalent, he heightens the suspense (not to mention the sexual tension) and allows for a fluent, lucid exploration of notions of justice, responsibility, forgiveness, and corruption by power. At the same time, the three powerful, sensitively nuanced performances ensure that the characters never become mere mouthpieces for an ethical enquiry. GA

Death at Broadcasting House

(1934, GB, 74 min, b/w)
d Reginald Denham. *p* Hugh Perceval. *sc* Basil Mason. *ph* Günther Krampf. *ed* Reginald Beck. *ad* R Holmes Paul. *m* Ord Hamilton. *cast* Ian Hunter, Donald Wolfit, Henry Kendall, Austin Trevor, Mary Newland, Jack Hawkins, Val Gielgud, Betty Ann Davies.

●'Thirty-five million people hear actor strangled on the air', scream the headlines. Radio producer Val Gielgud had the intriguing idea of making one of those quaintly melodramatic BBC murder mysteries the fulcrum for an archetypically English whodunit, with everyone apart from Sir Herbert Farquharson (homage to Sir John Reith!) likely suspects. This may be a low-budget quickie, but with efficient direction and a very knowledgeable script, the film becomes an evocative reminder of the seminal influence the BBC – with its Blattnerphones and sound-FX men and toffee-nosed producers – must have exercised on the cultural life of the 30s. You'll never guess whodunit, either. RMy

Death Becomes Her

(1992, US, 104 min)
d Robert Zemeckis. *p* Steve Starkey, Robert Zemeckis. *sc* David Koepp, Martin Donovan. *ph* Dean Cundey. *ed* Arthur Schmidt. *pd* Rick Carter. *m* Alan Silvestri. *cast* Meryl Streep, Bruce Willis, Goldie Hawn, Isabella Rossellini, Ian Ogilvy, Adam Storke, Nancy Fish, Alaina Reed Hall, Michelle Johnson.

●Zemeckis' black comedy seems oddly old-fashioned, reminiscent less of *Roger Rabbit* and *Back to the Future* than of '40s screwball and horror spoofs. When fading star Madeline (Streep) finds that Ernest (Willis), the plastic surgeon fiancé of her friend Helen (Hawn), is besotted by her tarnished glamour, her vanity demands that she marry this wimp who can restore her looks. Years later, 'Hell' plots revenge, and all is set for a bitching battle of Baby Jane proportions; but what finally drags the murderous trio into a maelstrom is the Faustian pact Madeline makes with Lisle Van Rhuman (Rossellini) in return for an elixir of eternal youth. Sporadically very funny indeed, the script features some nicely wicked one-liners, which are well complemented by Zemeckis' sight gags and by performances of great gusto. Far from sophisticated in its satire of narcissism, but enormous fun. GA

Death by Hanging (Koshikei)

(1968, Jap, 117 min, b/w)
d Nagisa Oshima. *p* Masayuki Nakajima, Takuji Yamaguchi, Nagisa Oshima. *sc* Tsutomu Tamura, Mamoru Sasaki, Michinori Faukao, Nagisa Oshima. *ph* Yashuhiro Yoshioka. *ed* Sueko Shiraishi. *ad* Jusho Toda. *m* Hikaru Hayashi. *cast* Yun-Do Yun, Kei Sato, Fumio Watanabe, Toshiro Ishido, Masao Adachi, Mutsuhiro Toura.

●All of Oshima's films deal in a challenging and committed way with specifically Japanese questions and problems. *Death by Hanging* is an 'absurd' comedy about the situation of Korean immigrants in Japan, centering on a state execution that goes wrong, mounted as a sort of witty Brechtian argument. TR

Death Collector

(1975, US, 85 min)
d Ralph De Vito. *p* William N Panzer. *sc* Ralph De Vito. *ph* Bob Bailin. *ed* Dominique Milbank. *m* Media Counterpoint. *cast* Joseph Cortese, Lou Criscuola, Joe Pesci, Bobby Alto, Frank Vincent, Keith Davis.

●A tarted-up Mafia morality tale, redeemed by Joseph Cortese's striking central performance as a bad-tempered small-town hoodlum down on his luck (yet icy in his resolution). Routinely 'picturesque' butchery is punctuated by memorable details, incidental observations of character, underworld jargon, oafish bravado. Effective, but flawed. AC

Deathdream

see Dead of Night

Death in a French Garden (Péril en la Demeure)

(1985, Fr, 101 min)
d Michel Deville. *p* Emmanuel Schlumberger. *sc* Michel Deville, Rosalinde Damamme. *ph* Martial Thury. *ed* Raymonde Guyot. *ad* Philippe Combastel. *m* Brahms, Schubert, Granados. *cast* Michel Piccoli, Nicole Garcia, Anemone, Christophe Malavoy, Richard Bohringer, Anaïs Jeanneret.

●A handsome young man arrives at a suburban mansion to give guitar lessons to an attractive teenage girl, and before you can say plectrum her mother launches into a grand seduction. But does her formidable husband know? Is their curious neighbour sane? Who is video-taping their affair? And who is the man following the guitarist? An elegant, teasing narrative unfolds, complete with elliptical dialogue, sleight-of-hand editing, and poised performances all round. A sophisticated entertainment from French stylist Deville, whose films have been little seen here since the '60s period romp *Benjamin.* DT

Death in Brunswick

(1990, Aust, 109 min)
d John Ruane. *p* Timothy White. *sc* John Ruane, Boyd Oxlade. *ph* Ellery Ryan. *ed* Neil Thumpston. *pd* Chris Kennedy. *cast* Zoe Carides, Sam Neill, John Clarke, Yvonne Lawley, Nico Lathouris, Nicholas Papademetriou.

●Drinking heavily, stuck as the cook for a trendy rock club, and nagged by his visiting mother, Sam Neill desperately hopes that a romance with Sophie (Carides), a Greek-Cypriot barmaid, will alter his luck. Instead, the death of his drug-dealing Turkish washer-up embroils him in a black comic nightmare involving an inconvenient body, a sadistic bouncer, and Sophie's club-owner fiancé. This being a comedy, though, Neill eventually 'sees the light' and resolves to change his life. A likeably offbeat and often surprisingly dark comedy thriller, set amid a seldom acknowledged working class ethnic community. NF

Death in the Seine

(1989, GB/Fr, 44 min)
d Peter Greenaway. *ph* Jean Penzer. *ed* Patrick Tornare, Benoit Majean. *pd* Jan Roelfs. *m* Michael Nyman. *cast* Jean-Michel Dagory, Jim van der Woude, Hans Verbrugge, Denis Verkroese, Roos Peters.

●Made for TV and the French Bicentennial celebrations, this is an extreme case of Peter Greenaway's obsession with cataloguing and classification. Comprising 23 case histories of corpses fished out of the Seine between 1795 and 1801, it forms a kind of micro-reprise of his monumental *The Falls*, piling up its narratives, Holmesian speculations and slow, clinical tracking shots over corpses, in a rigidly uniform structure. But within this forbidding system, Greenaway breaks up the frame, much as in *Prospero's Books*, using Paintbox graphics to play on the comparative textures of television and paper. *Death in the Seine* is a pedantic film, because it's about pedantry and the systematic collecting of facts which might or might not constitute evidence. It wasn't taken up by British TV, which considering the film's sign-off comments about the transience of memory and recorded knowledge, is a rather sour irony. JRo

Death in the Sun (Der Flüsternde Tod)

(1975, WGer, 96 min)
d/p Jürgen Goslar. *sc* Scot Finch. *ph* Wolfgang Treu. *ed* Richard C Meyer. *ad* Tony Sutherland. *m* Erich Ferstl. *cast* Christopher Lee, James Faulkner, Trevor Howard, Sibyle Danning, Erik Schumann, Sam Williams.

●Rape and revenge in the African veldt. What matters more than the plot are the assumptions that the movie (made in Rhodesia) parades up front: Lee's police chief is eminently humane (under crusty exterior), Howard's white settler eminently soft-hearted (under crusty exterior), the blacks sorely in need of the white man's guiding hand, and the terrorist leader an albino sexual pervert. CPe

Death in Venice (Morte a Venezia)

(1971, It, 128 min)
d/p Luchino Visconti. *sc* Luchino Visconti, Nicola Badalucco. *ph* Pasqualino de Santis. *ed* Ruggero Mastroianni. *ad* Ferdinando Scarfiotti. *m* Gustav Mahler. *cast* Dirk Bogarde, Björn Andresen, Silvana Mangano, Marisa Berenson, Mark Burns, Romolo Valli.

●Dire adaptation of Thomas Mann's novella, which turns the writer of the original into a composer, simply so that Visconti can flood his luscious, soft-focus images of Venice with the sombre sounds of Mahler, thus attempting to give a heartfelt emotional core to the hollow, camped-up goings-on. Bogarde is more than a little mannered as the ageing pederast whose obsession with a beautiful young boy staying at the same hotel (Andresen in sailor-suit and blond locks) leads him to outstay his welcome in the plague-ridden city. Everything is slowed down to a funereal (some might claim magisterial) pace, Mann's metaphysical musings on art and beauty are jettisoned in favour of pathetic scenes of runny mascara, and the whole thing is so overblown as to become entirely risible. GA

Death Is Child's Play

see Quién Puede Matar a un Niño?

Death Is My Trade (Aus einem deutschen Leben)

(1977, WGer, 145 min)
d Theodor Kotulla. *p* Fred Ilgner. *sc* Theodor Kotulla. *ph* Dieter Naujeck. *ed* Wolfgang Richter, Gabriele Friedrichs. *ad* Wolfgang Schünke. *m* Eberhard Weber. *cast* Götz George, Elisabeth Schwarz, Kurt Hübner, Kai Taschner, Sigurd Fitzek, Peter Franke.

●Though the fundamental sincerity of *Death Is My Trade* is unchallengeable, one gags on it nevertheless. With explicative chapter headings and a visual texture so grainily sepia as to make the film look as if it's being projected on sandpaper, Kotulla traces the gradual transformation of an earnest young World War I hero into the commandant at Auschwitz, mulling over plans to step up the 'output' in the crematoria and finally confessing to his baffled American captor that he is 'physically incapable' of disobeying an order. But that arresting admission only exposes the film's inadequacy: the intimate contingency of the holocaust on an individual (or national) psyche is cited rather than dramatised, and we are confronted yet again with the obscene aping of concentration camp victims by bony old extras in striped pyjamas. GAd

Death Japanese Style

see Ososhiki

Death Kick (Huang Feihong/ aka The Master of Kung Fu)

(1973, HK, 100 min)
d Ho Menghua. *p* Run Run Shaw. *sc* I Kuang. *ph* Tsao Hui Chi, Kuang Han Yeh. *ed* Chiang Hsing Lung. *ad* Chen Ching Shen. *m* Chen Yung Yu. *cast* Chen Ping, Gu Feng, Wang Xie, Lin Weidu, Xu Shaoxiong.

●Set in '20s China and based around the life of the famous Cantonese boxer/martial arts master Huang Fei-hong, *Death Kick* doesn't really manage to surmount the drawback of its over-complicated plot to convey much of the feeling of the period, or much of its latent theme either. Perhaps surprisingly, its strong points are its humour, some engaging if broad characterisations, and its sly view of the activities of the opium- and jade-dealing Europeans who ran China's concessions at the time. Amiable enough, but its fight sequences lack the style to make them more than competent. VG

Death Line (aka Raw Meat)

(1972, GB, 87 min)
d Gary Sherman. *p* Paul Maslansky. *sc* Ceri Jones. *ph* Alex Thomson. *ed* Geoffrey Foot. *ad* Denis Gordon-Orr. *m* Jeremy Rose, Wil Malone. *cast* Donald Pleasence, Norman Rossington, David Ladd, Sharon Gurney, Christopher Lee, Hugh Armstrong.

●One of the great British horror films, *Death Line* is a classic example of what *Hellraiser* director Clive Barker calls 'embracing the monstrous'. The film's basic premise is a gruesome one: following a cave-in during the construction of an underground tunnel in 1892, successive generations of plague-ridden cannibals have survived and developed their own subterranean culture. Forced out of hiding by the death of his wife, the sole surviving cannibal begins abducting passengers from Russell Square tube station. The disgust provoked by the corpse-filled underground world inhabited by the cannibal is offset by the tenderness with which he treats his dying wife, and by the unutterable sadness of his lonely plight. The film's great achievement is in eliciting sympathy for a creature whose residual capacity for human feeling amid such terrible degradation is ultimately more moving than horrifying. NF

Death of a Bureaucrat (Muerte de un Burocrata)

(1966, Cuba, 85 min)
d Tomás Gutiérrez Alea. *sc* Alfredo del Cueto, Tomás Gutiérrez Alea. *ph* Ramón F Suarez. *ed* Mario Gonzalez. *ad* Luis Marquez. *m* Leo Brouwer. *cast* Salvador Wood, Silvia Planas, Manuel Estanillo, Gaspar de Santelices, Carlos Ruiz de la Tejera.

●This arresting early work by one of Cuba's foremost film-makers is a black comedy about institutionalised bureaucracy at its most pedantic. After a model factory worker is killed in an accident at work, he's buried with his union card as a mark of eternal solidarity; trouble is, when his wife applies for a pension, she's told she must present the card before she can get any money – and there's a law forbidding exhumation within the first two years of burial. It's a surprising piece to have been made in the Cuba of the mid-'60s, but the laughs come as much from a Buñuelian sense of absurdity as they do from any outright criticism of Castro's regime. TJ

Death of a Cameraman (Morte di un Operatore)

(1978, It, 65 min)
d Faliero Rosati. *cast* Daniele Griggio, Remo Remotti.

●Attempting dubious homage to his former mentor Antonioni, Rosati merely succeeds in evoking tinny echoes of *The Passenger* with this debut feature. His journalist in the desert is retracing with the aid of video equipment and a surviving tape the final journey through Sinai of a 10-years-dead cameraman colleague – whose surname just happens to be an anagram of his own. Such glibly suggestive 'profundity' props up a boringly arty succession of arid compositions and 'enigmatic' silences, betraying little more than a director with nothing to say. PT

Death of a Gunfighter

(1969, US, 100 min)
d Allen Smithee [Robert Totten, Don Siegel]. *p* Richard E Lyons. *sc* Joseph Calvelli. *ph* Andrew Jackson. *ed* Robert F Shugrue. *ad* Alexander Golitzen. *m* Oliver Nelson. *cast* Richard Widmark, Lena Horne, John Saxon, Michael McGreevey, Darleen Carr, Carroll O'Connor, Kent Smith.

●A fringe Siegel Western (he spent two weeks finishing it off). The theme of a law and order marshal who has tamed a frontier town, only to become an embarrassment to the 'civilised' community, is sufficiently interesting for one to wonder what it would have been like if Siegel had done the whole thing.

Death of a Salesman

(1985, US, 136 min)
d Volker Schlöndorff. *p* Robert F Colesberry. *sc* Arthur Miller. *ph* Michael Ballhaus. *ed* David Ray. *pd* Tony Walton. *m* Alex North. *cast* Dustin Hoffman, Kate Reid, John Malkovich, Stephen Lang, Charles Durning, Louis Zorich.

●The setting is awful: sludgy indoors and sunsets on painted backdrops in the yard. That apart, all that's wrong with this version of the 1984 Broadway revival of Arthur Miller's play is the salesman himself. Dustin Hoffman's Willy Loman is a hard-working actor playing old; it's a technical performance, starting at such a pitch of sound and fury that it has nowhere to go when the humiliations really clock in. Loman is a complex character, pompous, self-deluding, bullying, laughable, pitiable, and ultimately tragic – this last never tapped by the actor. It isn't until the salesman's wife (Reid) lays into her sons (Malkovich and Lang) that you feel the dynamic of this family, the power of the play, and what acting can do to the emotions. This trio is terrific, trapped in the hell of the unattainable American Dream, and tearing into each other. Hoffman hadn't been on the stage for 17 years, and it shows. BC

Death of a Soldier

(1985, Aust, 96 min)
d Philippe Mora. *p* David Hannay, William Nagle. *sc* William Nagle. *ph* Louis Irving. *ed* John Scott. *ad* Geoff Richardson. *m* Allan Zavod. *cast* James Coburn, Reb Brown, Bill Hunter, Maurie Fields, Belinda Davey, Max Fairchild.

●Edward Leonski (Brown) was the first American soldier to be sentenced to death by a US military tribunal in World War II, convicted for the murder of three women while stationed in Australia. His motive, as he told his defence counsellor Major Dannenberg (Coburn) was a need to possess the women's 'voices'. The American military, seeking to defend their reputation, responded to public outcry by prosecuting Leonski themselves, while Dannenberg pushed to save the soldier's life with an insanity plea. Mora uses the trial in an attempt to examine the fragile relationship that existed between Americans and Australians during the war, and to demonstrate the need for due process of law. But sadly for any intelligent treatment of these issues, the film concentrates on the depiction of the murders and the manhunt which ensued, with Melbourne presented as an outrageous Frat party for the GIs, while Coburn struggles with stilted dialogue and what would seem to be an inordinate amount of starch in his jockeys. SGo

Death of Maria Malibran, The (Der Tod der Maria Malibran)

(1972, WGer, 104 min)
d/p/sc/ph/ed Werner Schroeter. *cast* Magdalena Montezuma, Christine Kaufmann,Candy Darling, Anette Tissier, Ingrid Caven.

●A series of tableaux illustrating the life and death of a celebrated 19th century German opera singer. Each tableau has a different motif, and each comes across with a decadent romanticism that lies somewhere between the Pre-Raphaelites and a quick flick through the pages of a '40s copy of Vogue. Schroeter's film is a delight to the eye – rich, strange and perverse.

Death of Mario Ricci, The (La Mort de Mario Ricci)

(1983, Switz/Fr/WGer, 101 min)
d Claude Goretta. *p* Yves Peyrot, Norbert Sada. *sc* Claude Goretta, Georges Haldas. *ph* Hans Liechti. *ed* Joële van Effenterre. *pd* Yanko Hodjis. *m* Arié Dzierlatka. *cast* Gian Maria Volonté, Magali Noël, Heinz Bennent, Mimsy Farmer, Jean-Michel Dupuis, Michel Robin.

●A country road glimpsed through a dirty windscreen…a mangled car wreck on a garage forecourt…Volonté blowing up an inflatable coat hanger and reminding his assistant that 'it's the details that count'. And so they clearly do in Goretta's film, although quite what they add up to is never sharply defined. A crippled TV journalist (Volonté) arrives in a Swiss village to interview a specialist in world food shortages disillusioned by the non-application of his theories. But he soon becomes embroiled in a web of local intrigue resulting from the death of a young immigrant worker. Goretta counterpoints his two stories with deft assurance, letting them strike subdued ironies off one another; there are thematic strands galore here, clearly signposted but seemingly left deliberately smudged. Yet there is no shortage of delights either: fine atmospherics, immaculately fluid camerawork, and a towering performance from Volonté, sympathy and disdain flickering back and forth across those marvellously expressive features. JP

Death of the Flea Circus Director, The (Der Tod des Flohzirkusdirektors)

(1973, Switz, 111 min, b/w)
d/p Thomas Koerfer. *sc* Dieter Feldhausen. *ph* Renato Berta. *ed* Heinz Berner. *ad* Toutschka von Goldschmidt. *m* Ernst Kolz. *cast* François Simon, Paul Gogel, Norbert Schwientek, Janine Weill, Gotthard Dietrich, Gerhard Dorfer.

●Fleas, like the Swiss, operate a risky balancing act of neutrality: in part this political comedy of the absurd revolves around the problems of radical action in that stolid, prosperous, complacent country. After losing his flea circus in a pesticide accident, Ottocaro Weiss (Simon) tries to seek compensation from the authorities, undergoes a ritual death during an anniversary ceremony for the plague, and rises again, with two assistants and a mysterious financial backer, to unleash his theatre of the plague upon the public. Starkly comic and distanced, the film explores the symbolic significances of this theatre from various perspectives, wryly noting the paradoxes thrown up and how polar arguments often in fact overlap: ideas are as infectious as diseases. And until the final scene, Weiss' dreams of a new political liberty are part of a terrifying grand design of which he knows nothing. In that sense, the film seems to offer little hope, the humour of the first half a reflex action against what is to come. CPe

Death on a Full Moon Day (Purahanda Kaluwara)

(1997, Sri Lanka/Jap, 75 min)
d Prasanna Vithanage. *p* Makota Ueda, Prasanna Vithanage. *sc* Tony Ranasinghe. *ph* MD Mahindapala. *ed* E Sreekar Prasad. *pd* KA Milton Perera. *cast* Joe Abeywickrama, Priyanka Samaraweera, Linton Semage, Mahendra Perera, Nayanna Hettiarachchi, Kumara Karunananda, KA Milton Perera.

●The face of Abeywickrama (playing the blind father) represents the soul of a nation suffering 20 years of civil strife as the state and Tamil fighters continue their war of attrition. His son, a state soldier, returns home in a casket (he's too disfigured to be recognisable), but the father receives a letter and refuses to believe his son is dead, to the annoyance of a local landowner who wants the man's compensation money. It's an observational, impassioned and impartial neo-realist movie, vaguely in the Satyajit Ray mould, which uses a spare, medium shot style and little music outside of natural sound, focusing instead on the excellent performances and the pathos and understanding of Tony Ranasinghe's script. WH

Death on the Nile

(1978, GB, 140 min)
d John Guillermin. *p* John Brabourne, Richard Goodwin. *sc* Anthony Shaffer. *ph* Jack Cardiff. *ed* Malcolm Cooke. *pd* Peter Murton. *m* Nino Rota. *cast* Peter Ustinov, Bette Davis, Mia Farrow, Jane Birkin, David Niven, Jack Warden, Angela Lansbury, Maggie Smith, George Kennedy, Lois Chiles.
●Over-extended and sloppily characterised Agatha Christie whodunit, with Ustinov's Poirot investigating the murder of an heiress aboard a steamer in the 30s. Nostalgic period recreation is everything, with the cast reduced to a gallery of stylish eccentrics and the whole film slavishly modelled on the earlier *Murder on the Orient Express*. GA

Death Race 2000

(1975, US, 79 min)
d Paul Bartel. *p* Roger Corman. *sc* Robert Thom, Charles B Griffith. *ph* Tak Fujimoto. *ed* Tina Hirsch. *ad* Robinson Royce, BB Neel. *m* Paul Chihara. cast David Carradine, Simone Griffeth, Sylvester Stallone, Mary Woronov, Roberta Collins, Joyce Jameson.
●The perfect example of a 'corporation' movie; dreamed up as a quickie rival to Rollerball, it follows its big brother in playing for bust on its basic concept – here, a coast-to-coast road race in which drivers score points by mowing down pedestrians. It could have been made by anybody; the fact that it was actually produced by Corman and directed by Bartel is so much icing on the cake. Corman's involvement doubtless accounts for the general vigour and the careful attention to exploitation values; Bartel was probably behind most of the quirky incidental humour and the unexpected casting (including Warhol's Chelsea girl Mary Woronov as the driver Calamity Jane). Overall the movie isn't as synchromeshed as it might be; the rivalry between champions Carradine and Stallone isn't very interesting, and some of the gags aren't sick or funny enough. But it's a great audience film. TR

Death Sentence (Mrityudand)

(1997, Ind, 115 min)
d/p Prakash Jha. *sc* Prakash Jha, Anil Ajitabh, Rajan Kothari. *ph* Rajan Kothari. *ed* Prakash Jha. *ad* Sharmishtha Roy. *m* Anand-Milind, Raghunath Seth. *cast* Shabana Azmi, Madhuri Dixit, Om Puri, Ayub Khan, Shipla Shirodkar, Mohan Joshi.
●This conspiracy thriller kicks like a frenzied mule. After an introduction in the style of a news report, on the sponsored village murder of a 22-year-old widow, it turns abruptly into a convoluted *faux* political documentary, detailing the networks of business, religious and familial ties that form the dense mass of upper caste politics in Bilaspur. It's a world rife with corruption, avarice, sabotage – and misogyny. New recruit Vinay tries to play the game, using his bride Ketki's dowry to sign a quarry contract with local government businessmen, despite Ketki's pleas that they won't play fair. So the bride (Dixit) and her sister-in-law Chandravati (Azmi, commanding) take a stand, whereupon all the weight of entrenched male power mobilises against them. NB

Death Ship

(1980, Can/GB, 91 min)
d Alvin Rakoff. *p* Derek Gibson, Harold Greenberg. *sc* John Robins. *ph* René Verzier. *ed* Mike Campbell. *pd* Chris Burke. *m* Ivor Slaney. *cast* George Kennedy, Richard Crenna, Nick Mancuso, Sally Ann Howes, Kate Reid, Victoria Burgoyne.
●A crewless Nazi torture-ship malevolently hunts down and sinks Caribbean pleasure cruisers. Good enough. But a *Ten Little Indians* plot soon takes over which is as rusty as the evil vessel. Kennedy gradually, but without much conviction, becomes the demented embodiment of the Third Reich as the corpses pile up; the *Psycho* shower murder is 'borrowed' again; the direction never moves beyond endless zooms to mirror pumping engines. SJ

Deaths in Tokimeki (Tokimeki ni Shisu)

(1984, Jap, 105 min)
d/sc Yoshimitsu Morita. *ph* Yonezo Maeda. *pd* Katsumi Nakazawa. *m* Osama Shiomura. *cast* Kenji Sawada, Kanaka Higuchi, Naoki Sugiura.
●The man who fell to earth this time is an unnamed hit-man cloistered in a seaside villa, awaiting the arrival of his victim, the leader of a new religious cult. Morita (young director of *Family Game*) structures the movie like a computer game, in which unexpected new information is required to move on to the next phase; he exerts vice-like control over the images and moods, juggling moments of eroticism, inner violence, misogyny and black humour. It all works like a pacemaker with induced hiccups. TR

Deathsport

(1978, US, 83 min)
d Henry Suso [Nicholas Niciphor], Allan Arkush. *p* Roger Corman. *sc* Henry Suso, Donald Stewart. *ph* Gary Graver. *ed* Larry Bock. *ad* Sharon Compton. *m* Andrew Stein. *cast* David Carradine, Claudia Jennings, Richard Lynch, William Smithers, Will Walker, Jesse Vint.
●Mutant offspring of the *Death Race 2000* line of cheapo sci-fi. The inhabitants of its post-holocaust society are familiar enough: cannibal freaks, sadist overlords of the fascist city-states, and the samurai-like 'Range Guides' gladiatorially pitched against the death-machines (dressed-up trail bikes). The plot, however, soon escalates into a frenzied biker chase pic, embracing both Kung-fu mysticism and the heavy pyrotechnics which push it to its most effective level. If it never quite rises to the kind of parable one half expects from the Corman factory, it's still OK. CPea

Deathtrap

(1982, US, 116 min)
d Sidney Lumet. *p* Burtt Harris. *sc* Jay Presson Allen. *ph* Andrzej Bartkowiak. *ed* John J Fitzstephens. *pd* Tony Walton. *m* Johnny Mandel. *cast* Michael Caine, Christopher Reeve, Dyan Cannon, Irene Worth, Henry Jones, Joe Silver.
●Undeterred by the resistance to translation from the stage of *Sleuth* and its parlour murder game, Michael Caine tries again, this time as a harassed Broadway playwright, a one-time master of the mystery thriller now driven to plot murder as a way of getting round his writer's block. Beautifully played (especially by Cannon, listening with increasing unease as her husband expounds his death trap), this adaptation of Ira Levin's play is witty, edgy and teasingly compelling until about the end of act one. Then, with the ingenious groundwork laid, all reality is tossed overboard as the multiplication of Chinese boxes begins, revealing murder within murder, play within play. Turned into puppets arbitrarily shunted round at the service of a plot much too clever for its own good, the characters are soon creaking as loudly as the stage machinery. TM

Death Trap (aka Eaten Alive)

(1976, US, 96 min)
d Tobe Hooper. *p* Mardi Rustam, Alvin L Fast. *sc* Alvin L Fast, Mardi Rustam. *ph* Bob Carmico. *ed* Michael Brown. *ad* Marshall Reed. *m* Tobe Hooper, Wayne Bell. *cast* Neville Brand, Mel Ferrer, Carolyn Jones, Marilyn Burns, William Finley, Stuart Whitman, Roberta Collins.
●Hooper's follow-up to *The Texas Chain Saw Massacre* is a further exploration of American rural degeneracy, about a senile swamp dweller (Brand) with a hook arm who likes to feed tourists and their children to his alligator. At its best, the film's lurid tone matches the evocative gloom of the EC horror comics of the '50s, in particular the amazing swamp stories drawn by 'Ghastly' Graham Inglis. Otherwise, it's trite and unconvincing. DP

Death Valley

(1981, US, 88 min)
d Dick Richards. *p* Elliott Kastner. *sc* Richard Rothstein. *ph* Stephen H Burum. *ed* Joel Cox. *ad* Allen H Jones. *m* Dana Kaproff. *cast* Paul Le Mat, Catherine Hicks, Stephen McHattie, Wilford Brimley, Peter Billingsley, Edward Herrmann.
●An achingly average low-rent slasher. Noisome kid (Billingsley), on vacation in Arizona with his mom and her new boyfriend to establish the seeds of familial love, stumbles across a clue to what appears to be a novel way of (literally) cutting down the tourist trade, and spends the rest of the movie getting the adults into tight corners. A touch of the Spielbergs in that the action is seen from the kid's viewpoint, but the plot's predictability is well-matched by short measures in both acting and direction. The obnoxious kid becomes the slasher's target, and one feels rather cut up when he isn't. FL

Death Vengeance

see Fighting Back

Death Watch (La Mort en Direct)

(1979, Fr/WGer, 130 min)
d Bertrand Tavernier. *p* Gabriel Boustani, janine Rubiez. *sc* David Rayfiel, Bertrand Tavernier. *ph* Pierre-William Glenn. *ed* Armand Psenny, Michael Ellis. *pd* Anthony Pratt. *m* Antoine Duhamel. *cast* Romy Schneider, Harvey Keitel, Harry Dean Stanton, Max von Sydow, Thérèse Liotard, Caroline Langrishe, Robbie Coltrane.
●As so often with Tavernier, a film that promises more than it delivers. Science fiction set in a near future, it starts from the intriguing premise that, in a society from which death has been effectively banished or at least tucked out of sight, a TV network plans to transmit a real-life soap opera for the benefit of curious viewers. A network employee (Keitel) has a miniature camera planted in his brain to record everything he sees, and the subject of his death watch (Schneider) is told she has an incurable disease. But as rebellious emotions begin to rage in both parties, the humanist in Tavernier gets the better of his fantasy, leading to some windy preachment and loss of credibility. A film to be seen, nevertheless, strikingly cast and with Glasgow lending its persuasive presence as a city of the future. TM

Death Weekend (aka The House by the Lake)

(1976, Can, 94 min)
d William Fruet. *p* Ivan Reitman. *sc* William Fruet. *ph* Robert Saad. *ed* Jean Lafleur, Debbie Karjala. *ad* Roy Forge Smith. *cast* Brenda Vaccaro, Don Stroud, Chuck Shamata, Richard Ayres, Kyle Edwards, Don Granberry.
●Inordinately wealthy dentist takes incredulous date for dirty weekend at his secluded mock-Tudor mansion. Fun (which doesn't look like materialising anyway) is spoiled by the arrival of four irate middle-aged greasers (led by Stroud in best bovine form). They take their time smashing the place up, killing the dentist and raping the girl. Spunky Vaccaro fights back (slitting the throat of smallest psycho at moment of orgasm), and at this point matters begin to pick up. Moderately exciting manhunt wraps up this excessively violent exploiter. Uneasy performances all round, however, don't help the tediously unbelievable premise of Fruet's dog-eared script. JPy

Death Wish

(1974, US, 94 min)
d Michael Winner. *p* Hal Landers, Bobby Roberts, Michael Winner. *sc* Wendell Mayes. *ph* Arthur J Ornitz. *ed* Bernard Gribble. *pd* Robert Gundlach. *m* Herbie Hancock. *cast* Charles Bronson, Hope Lange, Vincent Gardenia, Stuart Margolin, Steven Keats, William Redfield, Jeff Goldblum.
●Objectionable vigilante trash from the objectionable Winner, with the stony Bronson taking the law into his own vengeful hands when his wife is killed and his daughter turned into a traumatic vegetable after an attack by muggers. The sense of location is strong, emphasising a hostile, nightmarish terrain; but Winner's recourse to caricature when dealing with police and thugs, and his virtually overt sympathies with the confused, violent Bronson, make for uncritical, simplistic viewing. GA

Death Wish II

(1981, US, 95 min)
d Michael Winner. *p* Menahem Golan, Yoram Globus. *sc* David Engelbach. *ph* Richard L Kline, Thomas Del Ruth. *ed* Arnold Crust [Michael Winner], Julian Semilian. *pd* William M Hiney. *m* Jimmy Page. *cast* Charles Bronson, Jill Ireland, Vincent Gardenia, JD Cannon, Anthony Franciosa, Ben Frank.
●It's difficult to decide here which appeals to the nastier of audience instincts, the rape or the retribution. But what is clear about this sequel is that its attitude to its death-dealing urban

vigilante is now much less ambivalent. Where *Death Wish* 'persuaded' it s audience that its protagonist might be justified in his crusade, this takes popular support for granted, and even allows the stoic Bronson a certain relish in blowing away the LA street gang responsible for the rape and death of his teenage daughter (still recovering from the trauma of the 1974 story). Overall, it's as unstylish as anything Winner has put his name to. RM

Death Wish 3

(1985, US, 90 min)
d Michael Winner. *p* Menahem Golan, Yoram Globus. *sc* Michael Edmonds. *ph* John Stanier. *ed* Arnold Crust [Michael Winner]. *pd* Peter Mullins. *m* Jimmy Page. *cast* Charles Bronson, Deborah Raffin, Ed Lauter, Martin Balsam, Gavan O'Herlihy, Kirk Taylor.

● An ageing Bronson is released from gaol to clear the local territory of human trash. The mugger-slugger shows Brooklyn how to fight back, and provides much ammunition for anti-liberals: warfare not welfare. Initial excitement at the welter of violence soon palls into boredom, only intermittently relieved by the preposterousness of the action. With the strong element of fantasy, the frenetic attempts to create an end-product, and the squandering of resources, this is nothing more than cinematic masturbation. MS

Death Wish 4: The Crackdown

(1987, US, 99 min)
d J Lee Thompson. *p* Pancho Kohner. *sc* Gail Morgan Hickman. *ph* Gideon Porath. *ed* Peter Lee Thompson *ad* Whitney Brooke Wheeler. *m* Paul McCallum, Valentine McCallum, John Bisharat. *cast* Charles Bronson, Kay Lenz, John P Ryan, Perry Lopez, George Dickerson, Soon-Teck Oh.

● When his girlfriend's daughter dies of a coke overdose, semi-retired vigilante Bronson deals out some summary justice to the pusher who sold the stuff. Shortly afterwards, he is summoned by businessman Ryan, who encourages Old Stone Face to take on the gang controlling 90 percent of the LA drugs trade. Director Thompson ignores the thick-ear dialogue and wooden acting, and blows up every car and building in sight. Gail Morgan Hickman's complicated script manages a couple of nice twists, but it's too formulary to pursue the ambiguities it reveals. Most enjoyable is the clear thread of self-parody, which keeps the laughs and bullets coming thick and fast. NF

Debt Collector, The

(1999, GB, 110 min)
d Anthony Neilson. *p* Graham Broadbent, Damian Jones. *sc* Anthony Neilson. *ph* Dick Pope. ed John Wilson. *pd* Mark Geraghty. *m* Adrian Johnston. *cast* Billy Connolly, Ken Stott, Francesca Annis, Iain Robertson, Annette Crosbie, Alastair Galbraith, Shauna MacDonald.

● After serving 17 years for a murder rap that ended his fearsome reign as an Edinburgh loan shark, Nickie Dryden (Connolly) leaves jail as a lauded writer and sculptor. Though Nickie believes he's discharged his debt to society, his former arresting officer Gary Keltie (Stott) thinks otherwise, and will remind anyone who cares to listen, especially Nickie's wife (Annis). Coming from theatre, first-time drirector Neilson promises a suspenseful revenge drama, turning on the compelling theme of Nickie's culpability against atonement and reform, contrasted with Keltie's obsessive crusade. Solid performances go some way to mitigate Nielson's technical unsteadiness. But when it becomes clear that the director can't illuminate his characters' motivations beyond dropping clues about Keltie's professional and personal disappointments, the film fetches up in the primal revenge territory of *Cape Fear* in reverse: a repentant, reformed ex-convict is harassed by a brooding, bitter and vengerful cop. An unlikely proposition. NB

Decadence

(1993, GB, 108 min)
d Steven Berkoff. *p* Lance Reynolds, Christoph Meyer-Wiel. *sc* Steven Berkoff. *ph* Denis Lenoir. *ed* John Wilson. *ad* Yolande Sonnabend, Simon Holland. *m* Stewart Copeland. *cast* Joan Collins, Steven Berkoff, Christopher Biggins, Michael Winner, Marc Sinden, Edward Duke.

● Berkoff is the sneering adulterer, Collins the snooty aristo – and the parallel characters, scuzzbag private dick and arriviste housewife. The fringe play (from which this is drawn) usually delivers a short, sharp shock, but here Berkoff's stagy direction dissipates most of the scathing wit and pleasing vulgarity. The film resembles a video shot from the front row of the audience. She romps on silk sheets; he writhes at the crack of a riding crop. Dreadful. ACh

Décade Prodigieuse, La

see Ten Days' Wonder

Decameron, The (Il Decamerone)

(1970, It/Fr/WGer, 111 min)
d Pier Paolo Pasolini. *p* Alberto Grimaldi. *sc* Pier Paolo Pasolini. *ph* Tonino Delli Colli. *ed* Enzo Ocone. *pd* Dante Ferretti. *m* Pier Paolo Pasolini, Ennio Morricone. *cast* Franco Citti, Ninetto Davoli, Angela Luce, Patrizia Capparelli, Pier Paolo Pasolini.

● Pasolini manages in his uninhibited fashion to capture the anarchic comic spirit of Boccaccio's bawdy tales in this episodic romp; but the sight of the endless assembly of seemingly toothless proles Pasolini picked up as extras can be a bit intimidating.

Deceived

(1991, US, 108 min)
d Damian Harris. *p* Michael Finnell, Wendy Dozoretz, Ellen Collett. *sc* Mary Agnes Donoghue, Derek Saunders. *ph* Jack N Green. *ed* Neil Travis. *pd* Andrew McAlpine. *m* Thomas Newman. *cast* Goldie Hawn, John Heard, Ashley Peldon, Robin Bartlett, Tom Irwin, Amy Wright, Jan Rubes, Kate Reid, Beatrice Straight.

● After the comedy fiasco of Bird on a Wire, Hawn gets serious for this psychological thriller, only to find herself immured in an equally preposterous plot. She plays Adrienne, whose seemingly blissful life with museum curator Jack (Heard) conceals all manner of horrors. After six happy years of marriage, Jack's apparent death in a car crash leaves his grieving wife to unravel the mystery of why he assumed a false identity sixteen years earlier. With increasingly macabre/laughable developments in the story, poor Goldie is left stomping around, convincingly distraught as she vacillates between threats and toe-curling terror. Too bad, because slick direction and rich textures created by long-time Eastwood cinematographer Jack Green prove enticing, as does a strong performance from Heard. CM

Deceivers, The

(1988, GB, 103 min)
d Nicholas Meyer. *p* Ismail Merchant. *sc* Michael Hirst. *ph* Walter Lassally. *ed* Richard Trevor. *pd* Ken Adam. *m* John Scott. *cast* Pierce Brosnan, Saeed Jaffrey, Shashi Kapoor, Helen Michell, Keith Michell, David Robb, Tariq Yunus.

● Insecure young Englishman Savage (Brosnan) breaks colonial taboos by dyeing his skin to infiltrate the 'thuggees', a band of murderers dedicated to the goddess Kali. John Masters' novel is a great story, but the movie misses much of it. The opening set of clichés – a tiger hunt, a *Gone With the Wind* dance, a regimental wedding – give way to better film-making as the bizarre thuggery gets under way, but it's a case of too little too late for this shock-horror costume caper. Actors as powerful as Kapoor, Jaffrey and Keith Michell are reduced to hackneyed cameos, India looks like something out of a travel brochure, and blasting Hollywood-Viennese music ensures that we know it's a major motion picture. PHo

December Bride

(1990, GB, 88 min)
d Thaddeus O'Sullivan. *p* Jonathan Cavendish. *sc* David Rudkin. *ph* Bruno de Keyser. *ed* Rodney Holland. *pd* Adrian Smith. *m* Jurgen Kneiper. *cast* Donal McCann, Saskia Reeves, Ciaran Hinds, Patrick Malahide, Brenda Bruce, Michael McKnight, Dervla Kirwan, Peter Capaldi, Geoffrey Golden.

● In turn-of-the-century Ireland, Sarah (Reeves) and her mother (Bruce) are servants in the Echlin household; but after the old master's death, the remote Presbyterian community is shocked when Sarah starts having sexual relations with both Echlin brothers (McCann and Hinds), all three resisting overtures from the minister (Malahide) to join his flock. Sarah becomes pregnant: unsure which man is the father, reluctant to marry and embrace the hypocrisies of the church, she chooses to let both share in the child's upbringing. David Rudkin's intelligent adaptation of Sam Hanna Bell's novel explores national conflicts within the context of the community's intense divisions. 'The three curses of Ireland: England, religion and the drink' muses the elder brother as he strives to maintain equilibrium between the enraged locals and his defiant family. O'Sullivan's careful compositions and Bruno de Keyzer's exquisite cinematography lend the film a stark, simple grandeur, which in turn emphasises the harsh, physical nature of the characters' lives. The measured pace – beautifully sustained by the performances – ensures a film of sharp insight and striking clarity. CM

Deception

see Reindeer Games

Deception

(1946, US, 112 min, b/w)
d Irving Rapper. *p* Henry Blanke. *sc* John Collier, Joseph Tuan. *ph* Ernest Haller. *ed* Alan Crosland. *ad* Anton Grot. *m* Erich Wolfgang Korngold. *cast* Bette Davis, Claude Rains, Paul Henreid, John Abbott, Benson Fong.

● Four years after *Now Voyager*, *Deception* resurrects the same team for another grand emotional wallow – the 'woman's picture' at its historical zenith. Here, though, the passions are even more overblown, with Rains, excellent as a mad, bad composer, exerting a Svengali-like influence over Davis, his duplicitous pupil, and Henreid, as the master cellist who needs Rains' new composition to make his reputation but needs Davis even more. As she lies her way out of Rains' clutches and into marriage with Henreid, so the effects of her 'deceptions' become more corrosive. Blazing histrionics in the concert hall, *crime passionel* in the salon, and outside on the streets of Manhattan it's always raining. CPea

Decline and Fall...of a Birdwatcher!

(1968, GB, 113 min)
d John Krish. *p/sc* Ivan Foxwell. *ph* Desmond Dickinson. *ed* Archie Ludski. *ad* Jonathan Barry. *m* Ron Goodwin. *cast* Robin Phillips, Genevieve Page, Donald Wolfit, Colin Blakely, Robert Harris, Leo McKern, Patience Collier, Felix Aylmer, Griffith Jones.

● Rather softened adaptation of Evelyn Waugh's first novel satirising the mores of decadent wealthy Britain, with Phillips as the innocent undergraduate being sent down from Oxford and suffering a sentimental education (while teaching in a seedy Welsh boarding-school) at the hands of various darkly comic characters. Faithful to the letter if not quite the spirit of Waugh (it lacks the novel's bite, and is also unwisely updated), it's nevertheless endowed with strong performances all round and civilised, if literary, direction by Krish. GA

Decline of the American Empire, The (Le Déclin de l'Empire Américain)

(1986, Can, 101 min)
d Denys Arcand. *p* Pierre Gendron. *sc* Denys Arcand. *ph* Guy Dufaux. *ed* Monique Fortier. *ad* Gaudeline Sauriol. *m* François Dompierre. *cast* Dominique Michel, Dorothée Berryman, Louise Portal, Geneviève Rioux, Pierre Curzi, Rémy Girard, Yves Jacques, Daniel Brière.

● Four university history professors, three married and one gay, gather at a country retreat and prepare a large meal for the evening. They talk about their sex lives. Meanwhile their wives are at a health club. They too trade dirty secrets. Finally they all converge for the big dinner and the knives come out… Arcand has assembled a band of middle class professionals, sinking onto that middle-age plateau of resignation, and with little to occupy their minds but the pursuit of personal pleasure. His achievement is to make the subject appear by turns black and satiric, without ever falling out of love with his characters. A penetrating, discomforting study; recommended for all those who worry about feeling too smug about their private lives. CPea

Decline of Western Civilization, The

(1980, US, 100 min)
d/p/sc Penelope Spheeris. *ph* Steve Conant. *ed* Charles Mullin, Peter Wiehl. *m/cast* Black Flag, Germs, Catholic Discipline, X, Circle Jerks, Alice Bag Band, Fear.

● By far the most noteworthy aspect of Penelope Spheeris' LA punk movie is its timing, late on two counts. To her credit, she is keen neither to bury nor to champion the movement; and if that means throwing the appalling bands in with the talented, and the dodo interviewees in with the perceptive, then so be it. Hence, of the seven bands featured heavily, one can be grateful for the lasting hardcore beatings of John Doe's X, the grim all-or-nothing mania of the Germs' singer Darby Crash, and the hugely insulting spewings of John Belushi's faves Fear. Memories to squeal at, on the other hand, are the Alice Bag Band and critic Claude Bessy's Catholic Discipline – both wholly disastrous shots of pea-brains with amps meet social realism. The interviews are mostly very funny, probably not always intentionally so. It's far from unmissable, but it's valuable rock history with some great noise. SGa

Decline of Western Civilization Part II: The Metal Years, The

(1988, US, 93 min)
d Penelope Spheeris. *p* Jonathan Dayton, Valerie Faris. *ph* Jeff Zimmerman. *ed* Earl Ghaffari. *m/cast* Aerosmith, Alice Cooper, Kiss, Motorhead, Ozzy Osbourne, Chris Holmes, Poison, Lizzy Borden, Faster Pussycat, Seduce, Odin, London, Megadeth.

● Spheeris' second look at what the sweet young things of the City of Angels get up to when they're not free-basing and setting fire to classrooms or their hair. She puts a camera in front of a number of kids and Heavy Metal 'stars', and lets them talk about their music and their lives – both ultimately worthless. There are musical interludes from the likes of Faster Pussycat, London, and other almost indistinguishable crap acts, all wanting and waiting to be as big and bigoted as Guns'n'Roses, who wanted too much money to appear. Osbourne is the greatest walking example of just how stupid the HM creed of drugs, booze and macho sexism really is: fat and funny at first, sickening after a while. Holmes is pathetic, Alice Cooper is sad, Paul Stanley displays amazing penis envy, and Aerosmith are simply stupid. The regular HM girlfriends are tough and strangely feminist, the groupies singularly ugly and dumb. The boys all brag about sex but look like Mother Fist is their main mistress. The values stink, the music stinks, and Lemmy from Motorhead is a dickhead, but the movie is totally compelling. Rather like watching a car wreck on the opposite side of a motorway. MPe

Deconstructing Harry

(1997, US, 96 min)
d Woody Allen. *p* Jean Doumanian. *sc* Woody Allen. *ph* Carlo Di Palma. *ed* Susan E Morse. *pd* Santo Loquasto. *cast* Woody Allen, Kirstie Alley, Bob Balaban, Richard Benjamin, Billy Crystal, Judy Davis, Hazelle Goodman, Mariel Hemingway, Amy Irving, Julie Kavner, Elisabeth Shue, Stanley Tucci, Robin Williams.

● Harry Block (Allen) is a priapic foul-mouthed author whose ex-wives and lovers, family and friends object to his philandering and unreliability, and his habit of using them, thinly disguised, as fodder for his work. He goes to receive a fellowship at his alma mater with his nine-year-old son, his best friend and a black hooker in tow, and you'd think – this being Woody's *Wild Strawberries* – that Harry will learn something. But will he? Thankfully, despite many similarities to Bergman's film, this is not one of Allen's arty efforts (though the jump cuts are tiresome). As it alternates events from Harry's life with their fictionalised versions, proceeding towards a meeting of art and reality, the film is mainly very funny – most memorably in a vignette with Robin Williams as an actor who literally lacks focus. The sour take on artistic endeavour makes a welcome change from Allen's earlier work (as, indeed, does the inclusion of a significant black character – albeit a whore). But whether the idea of a man able to live and love only through his art is original or deep is another matter entirely. GA

Décroches les étoiles

see Unhook the Stars

Deep, The

(1977, US/GB, 124 min)
d Peter Yates. *p* Peter Guber. *sc* Peter Benchley, Tracy Keenan Wynn. *ph* Christopher Challis. *ed* David Berlatsky. *pd* Tony Masters. *m* John Barry. *cast* Jacqueline Bisset, Nick Nolte, Robert Shaw, Dick Anthony Williams, Earl Maynard, Louis Gossett, Eli Wallach.

● If *Star Wars* is basically a movie for people who like to play amusement arcades, then *The Deep* (adapted by Peter Benchley from his own novel) is the ultimate disco experience. It unerringly evokes all those misspent hours: it has sex objects for all tastes, instant fun, danger and boredom in unequal proportions, strobe-light climaxes, and Donna Summer in stereo. Furthermore, it does away with a storyline and dances on the spot for two hours, taking voodoo, buried treasure, violence and sea monsters in its stride. The Bermuda locations conjure up adverts for rum, but nothing much else has anything to do with the cinema. TR

Deep Blue Sea

(1999, US, 105 min)
d Renny Harlin. *p* Akiva Goldsman, Tony Ludwig, Alan Riche. *sc* Duncan Kennedy, Donna Powers, Wayne Powers. *ph* Stephen Windon. *ed* Frank J Urioste, Derek G Brechin, Dallas S Puett. *pd* William Sandell, Joseph Bennett. *m* Trevor Rabin. *cast* Thomas Jane, Saffron Burrows, LL Cool J, Jacqueline McKenzie, Michael Rapaport, Stellan Skarsgård, Aida Turturro, Samuel L Jackson.

● Buoyed by borrowings from *The Poseidon Adventure*, *Alien* and *The Abyss*, the leaky old aqua-thriller has weathered all the storms and doldrums which have beset the horror genre over the decades, and this is the best effort for some time. Harlin's movie may have a routine plot, but check out that gleaming marine research facility. Think hi-tech *Titanic*, and try not to worry about the practicalities. Burrows provides the unwitting comedy relief as a high minded scientist driven to cut corners in her quest to cure Alzheimer's by experimenting on (live) shark brains – the rationale being they don't age, or some such. This business about genetically modified 'smart sharks' with brains the size of a V-8 is priceless (maybe they should have had a go at the script), especially when the digital fx guys get carried away and work up a synchronised attack routine that would wow any Olympic committee. But if we're laughing at the movie: there's something very gratifying about the regularity with which Harlin cuts his cheesy characters down to size. And as a piece of cinematic engineering, it's nothing if not efficient. TCh

Deep Cover

(1992, US, 112 min)
d Bill Duke. *p* Pierre David. *sc* Michael Tolkin, Henry Bean. *ph* Bojan Bazelli. *ed* John Carter. *pd* Pam Warner. *m* Michel Colombier. *cast* Larry Fishburne, Jeff Goldblum, Victoria Dillard, Charles Martin Smith, Sydney Lassick, Clarence Williams III, Gregory Sierra, Roger Guenveur Smith.

● Fishburne, sensational in his first starring role, is a mid-West undercover cop brought in to infiltrate a West coast drugs ring whose members stretch up to the Latin American diplomatic corps. In a stunning opening sequence, we see a ten-year-old boy (who grows up to be Fishburne's John Q Hull) cradling his junkie father as the latter dies on a doomed Christmas attempt to rob a liquor store for dope money. Twenty years later, Hull is a cop with an attitude problem, a man who obeyed his father's order never to touch drugs but still has all the animal instincts of the dark side of the street. In the course of his work, Hull has to feign indifference to scenes of hideous violence, and gradually becomes embroiled with Goldblum's on-the-edge lawyer/user/dealer. Eventually, biting on a little more than it can chew, the film reverts to type. But in addition to Fishburne, it gives us a first-rate soundtrack, a clutch of splendid cameos, fine, grainy direction from Duke, and much pointed stuff about the hypocrisy behind the USA's so-called war against drugs. SGr

Deep Crimson (Profundo carmesí/Carmin profond)

(1996, Mex, 115 min)
d Arturo Ripstein. *p* Miguel Necoechea, Pablo Barbachano. *sc* Paz Alicia Garciadiego. *ph* Guillermo Granillo. *ed* Rafael Castenedo. *ad* Monica Chirinos, Patricia Nava, Marisa Pecanins, Macarene Folache. *m* David Mansfield. *cast* Regina Orozco, Daniel Giménez Cacho, Marisa Paredes, Verónica Merchant, Julieta Egurrola, Patricia Reyes Spindola.

● This version of the true story that inspired Leonard Kastle's *The Honeymoon Killers* (1969) is set in Mexico in 1949. Black comedy informs both films, but where Kastle's was notable for its grim austerity, Ripstein opts for a sumptuous yet strangely detached variation on the traditional Mexican melodrama. For all their protestations of undying love, Coral (Orozco) and Nicolás (Giménez Cacho) are hardly the most sympathetic of protagonists. Besides murdering a series of widows, Coral, an obese, slatternly, Charles Boyer-obsessed nurse, dumps her kids at the first opportunity, while her beloved Nicolás is a deceitful gigolo con-man. The sickly, overheated emotions are reflected in the ornate, even gaudy decor and lighting, while Ripstein's grasp of the couple's cowardice and cruelty and of the social, sexual and psychological circumstances which render their victims gullible and vulnerable is evident both in his matter-of-fact depiction of the killings, and in the subtly ironic tone of the dialogue and performances. Imagine late Fassbinder filtered through a Latin sensibility and you're only halfway there. GA

Deep End

(1970, WGer/US, 88 min)
d Jerzy Skolimowski. *p* Lutz Hengst. *sc* Jerzy Skolimowski, Jerzy Gruza, Boleslaw Sulik. *ph* Charly Steinberger. *ed* Barrie Vince. *ad* Anthony Pratt, Mac Ott Jr. *m* Cat Stevens, Can. *cast* Jane Asher, John Moulder-Brown, Diana Dors, Karl Michael Vogler, Christopher Sandford.

● Set in a decidedly unglamorous and unswinging London, Skolimowski's sex comedy posits a beautifully bizarre and totally unsentimental education for his adolescent hero, employed at a rundown swimming baths and obsessively pining for colleague Asher. Often very funny, tainted perhaps by a whiff of misogyny, and blessed with a thudding soundtrack from early Can, it's a brief and highly original delight. GA

Deep End, The

(2001, US, 100 min)
d/p/sc Scott McGehee, David Siegel. *ph* Giles Nuttgens. *ed* Lauren Zuckerman. *ad* Kelly McGehee. *m* Peter Nashel. *cast* Tilda Swinton, Goran Visnjic, Jonathan Tucker.

● Perhaps inevitably, this suffers in comparison both with McGehee and Siegel's extraordinary debut *Suture* and with Max Ophuls' *The Reckless Moment*, of which this is an intelligent, gay-inflected remake. Swinton gives one of her finest performances yet as the woman whose teenage son gets involved with a gay hustler; when she finds the man's corpse, she tries to hide it, but soon finds herself being blackmailed. Changing the gender of her offspring spices and thickens the brew, rather than creating a whole new flavour, but the film-makers have succeeded in translating the story for the present without the melodrama becoming merely hysterical or camp. Giles Nuttgens' cool, sumptuous shots of the Lake Tahoe settings fit the mood admirably. GA

Deep End of the Ocean, The

(1999, US, 107 min)
d Ulu Grosbard. *p* Kate Guinzburg, Steve Nicolaides. *sc* Stephen Schiff. *ph* Stephen Goldblatt. *ed* John Bloom. *pd* Dan Davis. *m* Elmer Bernstein. *cast* Michelle Pfeiffer, Treat Williams, Jonathan Jackson, John Kapelos, Whoopi Goldberg, Ryan Merriman.

● Jacquelyn Mitchard's novel hangs on so implausible a twist, that it's easy to mistake it for real life. Beth Cappadora (Pfeiffer) is a professional photographer and mother of three. Attending a high school reunion with kids in tow (baby Kerry, three-year-old Ben, older brother Vincent), Beth turns her back for just a minute or two, and Ben disappears from her life. Then, out of the blue, after nine years of bereavement, she recognises her missing son in the face of some kid down the road who wants to mow her lawn. This

Pfeiffer vehicle made no impact at the US box office, but despite the TV movie subject matter, it's surprisingly absorbing. Director Grosbard's restraint holds sentimentality off screen, recognising that grief is most poignantly an intimate, internalised affair, even within the closest families. The film gains its interest from that troubling question about what constitutes a family: if this is Ben, oblivious to his real identity, should his blood parents uproot him once again? For his sake – or theirs? Pfeiffer has never been afraid to relinquish glamour on screen; now she's also confident enough to relinquish centre stage in the last act to Vincent (Jackson, excellent) and Ben (Merriman, irritating). Worth a detour. TCh

Deep Impact

(1998, US, 121 min)
d Mimi Leder. *p* Richard D Zanuck, David Brown. *sc* Bruce Joel Rubin, Michael Tolkin. *ph* Dietrich Lohmann. *ed* David Rosenbloom. *pd* Leslie Dilley. *m* James Horner. *cast* Robert Duvall, Téa Leoni, Elijah Wood, Vanessa Redgrave, Maximilliam Schell, Morgan Freeman, James Cromwell.

● A meteor is heading for Earth. The first 40 minutes are the least bad. Astronomers are caught napping when schoolboy Wood spots something strange coming this way. Washington keeps a lid on it, until TV reporter Leoni stumbles across 'the biggest story in history'. A year hence, we will be destroyed, unless the US-Soviet space mission Messiah can deflect the asteroid's course by detonating nuclear explosions deep in its core. It's at this point – when the President (Freeman) places the fate of the world into the hands of astronaut Duvall and his crew – that the movie really goes into under-drive. They learn the value of self-sacrifice and togetherness. If director Leder fails to make the personal stories come to life, she's even sketchier on the big picture – her idea of social breakdown begins and ends with a traffic jam. TCh

Deep in the Heart

see Handgun

Deep Rising

(1998, US, 106 min)
d Stephen Sommers. *p* Laurence Mark, John Baldecchi. *sc* Stephen Sommers. *ph* Howard Atherton. *ed* Bob Ducsay, John Wright. *pd* Holger Gross. *m* Jerry Goldsmith. *cast* Treat Williams, Famke Janssen, Anthony Heald, Kevin J O'Connor, Wes Studi.

● Plumbing unfathomable depths of stupidity, this rushes headlong through the expected scenes of carnage towards a suitably dumb climax to reveal the mother of all sea monsters. During her maiden voyage, the cruise liner *Argonautica* becomes a virtual 'ghost ship' when passengers and crew are attacked by giant serpentine sea creatures. The few survivors are later joined by mercenary captain-for-hire Williams, his crazy engineer O'Connor, and their human cargo – sundry seafaring scumbags lead by Studi. A little gruesome light relief from the risible dialogue is provided by those scenes in which victims with 'Eat Me' tattooed on their foreheads are duly dispatched and digested. Monstrously bad, yet undeniably enjoyable. NF

DeepStar Six

(1988, US, 99 min)
d Sean S Cunningham. *p* Sean S Cunningham, Patrick Markey. *sc* Lewis Abernathy, Geof Miller. *ph* Mac Ahlberg. *ed* David Handman. *pd* John Reinhart. *m* Harry Manfredini. *cast* Taurean Blacque, Nancy Everhard, Greg Evigan, Miguel Ferrer, Nia Peeples, Matt McCoy, Cindy Pickett, Marius Weyers, Elya Baskin, Thom Bray, Ronn Carroll.

● The 11-strong crew of the DeepStar Six are wrapping up their six month research project on the ocean floor when a mysterious blip appears on their radar screens: an unidentified swimming object! What follows is a particularly messy game of sardines, the only rule being that no one attemps anything remotely unpredictable. The actors put up a good fight, but the cod technobabble is so unremitting ('Stabilise stabilisers' – 'Stabilisers stabilised') that it is tempting to cheer when they are finally shut up. The only inventive aspects of the movie are the variously contrived fatalities, and a sea monster so ugly it makes Jaws look like a tadpole. Cunningham apes Ridley Scott and James Cameron competently enough, and there are scary moments, but he has not got the 'vision thing'. This simply rehashes the phony trappings of countless TV shows, to baldly go where we have been before. TCh

Deep Throat

(1972, US, 61 min)
d Jerry Gerard [Gerard Damiano]. *p* Lou Perry [Lou Periano]. *sc* Jerry Gerard [Gerard Damiano]. *ph* Harry Flecks. *ed/m* Gerard Damiano. *cast* Linda Lovelace, Harry Reems, Dolly Sharp, Bill Harrison, William Love, Carol Connors, Bob Phillips, Ted Street, Gerard Damiano.

● This notorious porn movie was originally released in 1972. Its sole intention is to arouse with close-ups of fellatio. One of three principal women, Lovelace, discovers that her clitoris is in the wrong place – in her throat. Cue close-ups of one dick-swallowing trick after another. Stilted performances, dud production values and a thrashy, hilariously cheesy '70s soundtrack. DA

Deer Hunter, The (100)

(1978, US, 182 min)
d Michael Cimino. *p* Barry Spikings, Michael Deeley, Michael Cimino, John Peverall. *sc* Deric Washburn. *ph* Vilmos Zsigmond. *ed* Peter Zinner. *ad* Ron Hobbs, Kim Swados. *m* Stanley Myers. *cast* Robert De Niro, John Cazale, John Savage, Christopher Walken, Meryl Streep, George Dzundza, Chuck Aspegren.

● This is probably one of the few great films of the decade. It's the tale of three Pennsylvanian steelworkers, their life at work, at play (deer-hunting), at war (as volunteers in Vietnam). Running against the grain of liberal guilt and substituting Fordian patriotism, it proposes De Niro as a Ulyssean hero tested to the limit by war. Moral imperatives replace historical analysis, social rituals become religious sacraments, and the sadomasochism of the central (male) love affair is icing on a Nietzschean cake. Ideally, though, it should prove as gruelling a test of its audience's moral and political conscience as it seems to have been for its makers. CA

De eso no se habla

see We Don't Want to Talk About It

DEF by Temptation

(1990, US, 95 min)
d/p/sc James Bond III. *ph* Ernest Dickerson. *ed* Li-Shin Yu. *pd* David Carrington. *m* Paul Laurence. *cast* James Bond III, Kadeem Hardison, Bill Nunn, Samuel L Jackson, Cynthia Bond.

● Mixing singles bar seduction with bestial blood-sucking, this all-black horror movie offers a vampiric variation on Spike Lee's She's Gotta Have It. Drawn to New York by strange dreams, religious country boy Joel (Bond) competes with his streetwise brother K (Hardison) for a bad sexual temptress who prefers Bloody Marys to screwdrivers. The sexist overtones of Cynthia Bond's predatory vampire leave a nasty taste in the mouth, the special effects are poor, and the plot sags badly in the middle. Nevertheless, the stylish visuals, sharp dialogue and incidental humour make this an unusually classy Troma release. The production values are B negative, but actor/producer/ director Bond's debut feature rates a B plus. NF

Defence Counsel Sedov

(1988, USSR, 45 min, b/w & col)
d Yevgeny Tsymbal. *cast* Vladimir Ilyin, Tamara Chernova, Tatiana Rogozina, Natalia Schukina.

● Just when you thought *glasnost* had allowed Soviet film-makers to say all there was to say about the horrors of the Stalin years, along comes this astonishing short feature (based on fact) to peel away more layers of the onion. Harassed, middle-aged Sedov is the only lawyer in Moscow willing to take on the defence of four farmers accused of sabotaging their commune and tortured into making false confessions. His dogged persistence against the state's legal and political bureaucracy gets the men off, but results in his own canonisation as a Stalinist zealot – and in the execution of dozens of other men. A genuinely shocking parable of the biter bit, it incorporates some staggering newsreel footage from the '30s, never seen before. TR

Defence of the Realm

(1985, GB, 96 min)
d David Drury. *p* Robin Douet, Lynda Myles. *sc* Martin Stellman. *ph* Roger Deakins. *ed* Michael Bradsell. *pd* Roger Murray-Leach. *m* Richard Harvey. *cast* Gabriel Byrne, Greta Scacchi, Denholm Elliott, Ian Bannen, Fulton Mackay, Bill Paterson.

● A conspiracy yarn which looks to the tradition of Buchan as well as the more recent one of *Three Days of the Condor*. A far from crusading hack uncovers a mystery behind a political scandal and feels impelled to investigate. What's going on? Something not very nice at all involving nuclear weapons, that's what. Drury coaxes an excellent performance from newcomer Byrne, and directs with a style and sense of location rarely present in homegrown cinema. The Fenland scenes and those in London by night are notably atmospheric, and while the ending isn't entirely satisfactory, there is no questioning the quality and pedigree of the film. RR

Defending Your Life

(1991, US, 111 min)
d Albert Brooks. *p* Michael Grillo. *sc* Albert Brooks. *ph* Allen Daviau. *ed* David Finfer. *ad* Ira Random. *m* Michael Gore. *cast* Albert Brooks, Meryl Streep, Rip Torn, Lee Grant, Buck Henry, Michael Durrell, James Eckhouse, Gary Beach.

● Although gentle and sentimental, Brooks' satire is better by far than most Hollywood movies about the afterlife. As LA advertising man Daniel, killed in a car crash, Brooks brings his familiar neuroses to bear on a pristine purgatory where self-acceptance, as opposed to goodness, determines one's progress through infinity. Nervy and self-centred, Daniel is clearly ill-qualified for promotion to a higher plane, but with help from brave, becalmed Julia (Streep) and his celestial advocate (Torn), he might just make it through the official review of his sojourn on earth to emerge as something more than a lowly amphibian. Much of the comedy centres around life in Judgement City, where American obsessions are indulged to a utopian degree; if there's something a tad New Age about the emphasis on feeling good, at least that ol' time religion is mercifully absent, while the satire hits target more often than not. The film is finally too soft, but the performances are uniformly strong, the humour intelligently adult, and Brooks once again proves a pleasing alternative to Woody Allen. GA

Defiance

(1979, US, 102 min)
d John Flynn. *p* William S Gilmore Jr, Jerry Bruckheimer. *sc* Thomas Michael Donnelly. *ph* Ric Waite. *ed* David Finfer. *pd* Bill Malley. *m* Basil Poledouris. *cast* Jan-Michael Vincent, Theresa Saldana, Fernando Lopez, Danny Aiello, Santos Morales, Rudy Ramos, Art Carney.

● A nasty and simplistic urban-Western parable for Reagan's America. Stranger-in-town Vincent takes it from a marauding Puerto Rican street gang 'til he can't take no more, then comes on like a righteous Cruise missile to trash the bad guys on a wave of populist reaction. Objectionable. PT

Defiant Ones, The

(1958, US, 96 min, b/w)
d/p Stanley Kramer. *sc* Harold Jacob Smith, [Ned Young]. *ph* Sam Leavitt. *ed* Frederick Knudtson. *ad* Fernando Carrere. *m* Ernest Gold. *cast* Tony Curtis, Sidney Poitier, Theodore Bikel, Charles McGraw, Lon Chaney, King Donovan, Cara Williams.

● Typical piece of liberal pleading from Kramer in which two escaped cons (Curtis and Poitier) go on the run manacled together in an oh-so-obvious metaphor for racial hatred. The suspense of the manhunt in the swamps never really overcomes the dead weight of Kramer's 'message', but pleasures are to be found in the supporting roles of McGraw and Chaney. MA

Def Jam's How to Be a Player

(1997, US, 94 min)
d Lionel C Martin. *p* Mark Burg, Todd Baker, Russell Simmons, Preston Holmes. *sc* Mark Brown, Demetria Johnson. *ph* Ross Berryman. *ed* William Young. *pd* Bruce Curtis. *m* Darren Floyd. *cast* Bill Bellamy, Natalie Desselle, Lark Voorhies, Mari Morrow, Max Julien, Beverly Johnson.

●A ponderous, compromised essay in misogyny. Dray Jackson (insipid MTV comic Bellamy) has a loyal if jealous girlfriend Lisa (Voorhies) but remains an incorrigible Don Juan. Sister Jenny (Desselle) and sexy Katrina (Morrow) decide to teach him a lesson. Dray's visits to his well-heeled women, for all the attempted glamour, seem essentially the rounds of a high-class male prostitute. CO'Su

De Grands Evénements et des Gens Ordinaires

see Of Great Events and Ordinary People

Degree of Murder, A (Mord und Totschlag)

(1966, WGer, 87 min)
d Volker Schlöndorff. *p* Rob Houwer. *sc* Volker Schlöndorff. *ph* Franz Rath. *ed* Claus von Boro. *ad* Wolfgang Hundhammer. *m* Brian Jones. *cast* Anita Pallenberg, Hans P Hallwachs, Manfred Fischbeck, Werner Enke, Angel Hillebrecht, Sonja Karzau.

●Schlöndorff's second film. Pallenberg plays a Munich waitress who shoots her ex-boyfriend in a quarrel, and then ropes in two strangers to help her dispose of the body. She sleeps with both of them, but nothing much else happens on the way to the open ending. Schlöndorff presents it all as a detached observer, and accompanies it with a score by the soon-to-be-late Brian Jones.

Déjà Vu

(1997, US/GB, 117 min)
d Henry Jaglom. *p* John Goldstone. *sc* Victoria Foyt, Henry Jaglom. *ph* Hanania Baer. *ed* Henry Jaglom. *pd* Helen Scott. *m* Gaili Schoen. *cast* Stephen Dillane, Victoria Foyt, Vanessa Redgrave, Glynis Barber, Michael Brandon, Rachel Kempson, Anna Massey.

●Engaged for six years to Alex (Brandon), an American importer of objets d'art, Dana (Foyt) is on the brink of marriage when she meets a woman in Israel who tells her of lost love for an American soldier. He gave her a keepsake brooch, which she inadvertently leaves with Dana. In London, Dana falls for painter Sean (Dillane) but nevertheless returns to the US with Alex to continue preparations for the big day. But is her heart still in it? Jaglom's self-absorbed, ad hoc romantic drama written with his partner Foyt, tries embarrassingly hard to conjure up the wistful ways of love with a mixture of mild social comedy and pseudo-philosophical speculation. Matters aren't helped by Foyt's insular, distracted performance. The tone is, thankfully, less acidic than is usual in Jaglom's work; and things are enlivened somewhat by a series of engaging cameos. WH

Déjeuner sur l'Herbe, Le (Lunch on the Grass/Picnic on the Grass)

(1959, Fr, 92 min)
d/p/sc Jean Renoir. *ph* Georges Leclerc. *ed* Renée Lichtig. *ad* Marcel-Louis Dieulot. *m* Joseph Kosma. *cast* Paul Meurisse, Catherine Rouvel, Jacqueline Morane, Fernand Sardou, Jean-Pierre Granval, Ingrid Nordine.

●Often seen as a paean to Nature (and Renoir père – it was shot at Auguste Renoir's house at Les Collettes). With its odd tale of a future bureaucrat liberated from glacial rationalism through enforced submission to Nature's whims, *Le Déjeuner sur l'Herbe* is one of Renoir's most ravishing, and simultaneously most irritating films. Again and again, sumptuous photography collapses into cold argument. PH

Dekalog 1: 'I am the Lord thy God, Thou shalt have no other God but me'

(1988, Pol, 53 min)
d Krzysztof Kieslowski. *p* Ryszard Chutkowski. *sc* Krzysztof Kieslowski, Krzysztof Piesiewicz. *ph* Wieslaw Zdort. *ed* Ewa Smal. *m* Zbigniew Preisner. *cast* Henryk Baranowski, Wojciech Klata, Maja Komorowska.

●It's a freezing early winter morning on the Warsaw estate where Pavel (Klata), an intelligent boy approaching teenage, and his lecturer father (Baranowski) are playing with computers. Using a scientific formula, they input the recent ground temperatures, which confirms the safety of the ice on the nearby ponds; and thus reassured, father allows Pavel to have his Christmas present (a pair of ice skates) early. That day, Pavel's pleasure in his intellectual accomplishments is tempered by the sadness he feels about a dead dog; and prompted by the Catholic talk of his beloved aunt (Komorowska), he is moved to question his father on the nature of the soul. 'Why' he asks, 'do people have to die at all?'. Kieslowski's moving drama unfolds with all the force of a metaphysical ghost story as the father, having heard that three children are feared dead on the ponds, begins a frenetic search to locate his son. The performances and direction are calibrated to perfection; the result is a film of shattering insight, laced with black humour and savage irony. WH

Dekalog 2: 'Thou shalt not take the name of the Lord thy God in vain'

(1988, Pol, 57 min)
d Krzysztof Kieslowski. *p* Ryszard Chutkowski. *sc* Krzysztof Kieslowski, Krzysztof Piesiewicz. *ph* Edward Klosinski. *ed* Ewa Smal. *m* Zbigniew Preisner. *cast* Krystyna Janda, Aleksander Bardini, Olgierd Lukaszwicz.

●Bardini plays a consultant at the local hospital, a lonely, diffident man in his sixties, who has just begun to relate, in weekly instalments, the sad story of his life (his wife and children were killed during the war). A neighbour (Janda), a chain-smoker, knocks insistently on his door, much to his annoyance, demanding news of her husband, a patient of his who may be dying of cancer. Her problem, it transpires, is that she is pregnant (by another), and the decision whether she has an abortion or not is dependent on the survival or otherwise of her husband. The consultant refuses to play God by saying whether the husband will live or die. As he says, 'I have a God, but it's only enough for me'. As in Dekalog 1, the film's power comes from the precise, economic delineation of character and circumstance. WH

Dekalog 3: 'Honour the Sabbath Day'

(1988, Pol, 56 min)
d Krzysztof Kieslowski. *p* Ryszard Chutkowski. *sc* Krzysztof Kieslowski, Krzysztof Piesiewicz. *ph* Piotr Sobocinski. *ed* Ewa Smal. *m* Zbigniew Preisner. *cast* Daniel Olbrychski, Maria Pakulnis, Joanna Szczepkowska.

●Taxi-driver Janusz, his mother, wife and two kids leave a chair free, in the traditional manner, at their Christmas Eve dinner-table. At midnight mass, Janusz spots a familiar-looking woman looking at him, and later, back at his flat, receives a call from her and meets her in the street. Her husband is missing; he must help find him. He reluctantly agrees, and having lied to his wife about his taxi being stolen, embarks with the woman – with whom it becomes clear he has had an affair – on a search through the lonely city and its hospitals, dry-out clinics and railway terminuses. A film of enormous compassion, this long night's journey into day says more in under an hour about the suffering consequent on exclusion (the film is full of closing doors), infidelity and the absence of charity than a life-time of sermons. WH

Dekalog 4: 'Honour thy father and thy mother'

(1988, Pol, 55 min)
d Krzysztof Kieslowski. *p* Ryszard Chutkowski. *sc* Krzysztof Kieslowski, Krzysztof Piesiewicz. *ph* Krzysztof Pakulski. *ed* Ewa Smal. *ad* Halina Dobrowolska. *m* Zbigniew Preisner. *cast* Adrianna Biedrzynska, Janusz Gajos, Artur Barcis.

●Easter. Young acting student Anka (Biedrzynska) lives with her architect father, as she has since her mother's death in childbirth. They have a close relationship, and josh each other with the easy intimacy of lovers. Her relationship with her boyfriend, on the other hand, she finds far more difficult. Her father leaves for a trip abroad, and asks her to attend to some unpaid bills. Looking in a drawer for them, she finds an old envelope marked in her father's hand, 'To be opened in the event of my death', and inside it another envelope addressed, presumably in her mother's writing, to 'My darling Anka'. What truth can it contain? When her father returns, they drink vodka and she challenges him to a game of Truth or Dare... Kieslowski's masterly film addresses the question of incest – more properly, incestuous impulses and their roots – and has all the discomforting compulsion of watching open-heart surgery. The performances by Biedrzynska and Gajos as the father are astounding. WH

Dekalog 5: 'Thou shalt not kill'

(1988, Pol, 57 min)
d Krzysztof Kieslowski. *p* Ryszard Chutkowski. *sc* Krzysztof Kieslowski, Krzysztof Piesiewicz. *ph* Slawomir Idziak. *ed* Ewa Smal. *ad* Halina Dobrowolska. *m* Zbigniew Preisner. *cast* Miroslaw Baka, Krzysztof Globisz, Jan Tesarz.

●Kieslowski's extraordinary film depicts two acts of slaughter. Pimply country kid Yatzek (Baka) unexplainedly kills a taxi-driver. The State then kills him. Both are deaths by hanging, of different kinds, both shown in graphic detail and in real time, shocking in itself. The effect is deeply unsettling. Kieslowski shoots in a calm, heightened-realist style, using multiple filters to bleed and darken the colours of the dour locations, and gets to the heart of our inability to obey the edict 'Thou shalt not kill', thus suggesting the mystery of our deepest motives, without preaching or simplification. A raw, edgy, challenging work originally made, like the rest of the *Dekalog*, for TV; Kieslowski himself expanded it into an 85-minute theatrical version entitled *A Short Film About Killing*. WH

Dekalog 6: 'Thou shalt not commit adultery'

(1988, Pol, 58 min)
d Krzysztof Kieslowski. *p* Ryszard Chutkowski. *sc* Krzysztof Kieslowski, Krzysztof Piesiewicz. *ph* Witold Adamek. *ed* Ewa Smal. *ad* Halina Dobrowolska. *m* Zbigniew Preisner. *cast* Grazyna Szapolowska, Olaf Lubaszenko, Stefania Iwinska, Piotr Machalica.

●Hints of a *Rear Window*-style thriller give way to an unorthodox love story when teenage postal clerk Tomek (Lubaszenko) confesses to spying on artist Magda (Szapolowska). The older woman's interest is piqued, and though initially angry, she draws him into a tremulous, ultimately humiliating love affair. Kieslowski maintains a dispassionate objectivity, and presents the simplest gestures, expressions and words with calculated restraint, allowing the audience to bring their own compassion to bear on the ill-fated relationship. Mature and profoundly moving. Expanded to 87 minutes, the theatrical version was called *A Short Film About Love*. NF

Dekalog 7: 'Thou shalt not steal'

(1988, Pol, 55 min)
d Krzysztof Kieslowski. *p* Ryszard Chutkowski. *sc* Krzysztof Kieslowski, Krzysztof Piesiewicz. *ph* Dariusz Kus. *ed* Ewa Smal. *ad* Halina Dobrowolska. *m* Zbigniew Preisner. *cast* Anna Polony, Maja Barelkowska, Wladyslaw Kowalski, Boguslaw Linda.

●Kieslowski's camera roves past the windows of a Warsaw housing estate and looks in on a family of four. Majka (Barelkowska), a sad-faced woman in her early twenties, is having trouble comforting four-year-old Anka – screaming from nightmares about wolves – when she is roughly pushed aside by a 50-year-old woman. Majka herself takes comfort from her father, a gentle organ-pipe maker. What are the relationships between these four? And what is the cause of the awful tension in the air? *Dekalog 7* is only nominally about stealing (Majka kidnaps Anka and takes the child to her teddy-bear-making ex-boyfriend's cabin in the Josefow woods). It is really a questioning – and insightful – examination of the difficulty of growing up (for all generations), and the true meaning and implications of fathering and mothering. WH

Dekalog 8: 'Thou shalt not bear false witness'

(1988, Pol, 55 min)
d Krzysztof Kieslowski. *p* Ryszard Chutkowski. *sc* Krzysztof Kieslowski, Krzysztof Piesiewicz. *ph* Andrzej Jaroszewicz. *ed* Ewa Smal. *ad* Halina Dobrowolska. *m* Zbigniew Preisner. *cast* Maria Koscialkowska, Teresa Marczewska, Artur Barcis, Tadeusz Lomnicki.

● One of the more schematic – though no less fascinating, nor less acute – of the series, this concerns the question of choice 'in a moral hell'. An elderly female university professor of ethics is introduced to an American academic who is researching the fate of Jews after WW2. Sitting in on the professor's lectures, the American offers a story – which has personal significance both for her and the professor – for the students to analyse. A Jewish child, during the Nazi occupation of Warsaw, is offered sanctuary on condition that she obtain a certificate of baptism. The Catholic couple who have promised to help refuse on the grounds that they will not bear false witness, thus condemning the child to almost certain death. But, of course, that is not the whole story… WH

Dekalog 9: 'Thou shalt not covet thy neighbour's wife'

(1988, Pol, 58 min)
d Krzysztof Kieslowski. *p* Ryszard Chutkowski. *sc* Krzysztof Kieslowski, Krzysztof Piesiewicz. *ph* Piotr Sobocinski. *ed* Ewa Smal. *ad* Halina Dobrowolska. *m* Zbigniew Preisner. *cast* Ewa Blaszczyk, Piotr Machalica.

● Promiscuous surgeon Roman (Machalica) is told by his doctor that he can no longer have children, nor sex. He tells his airport-receptionist wife Hanka, who replies that there are more things in a relationship than five minutes of panting in bed once a week. The unspoken things count – but what are they? They cuddle. Soon, however, his curiosity and nascent jealousy aroused by mysterious phone calls, Roman begins to suspect her of having a lover. He takes to spying on her, a process that threatens to destroy his spirit… A complex, unsettling movie (Roman's diagnosis could be AIDS) that digs deep to find the 'irreducible' in people, but offers no simplistic answers (save that of Love, the subject and object of all ten of the *Dekalog* series). WH

Dekalog 10: 'Thou shalt not covet thy neighbour's goods'

(1988, Pol, 57 min)
d Krzysztof Kieslowski. *p* Ryszard Chutkowski. *sc* Krzysztof Kieslowski, Krzysztof Piesiewicz. *ph* Jacek Blawut. *ed* Ewa Smal. *ad* Halina Dobrowolska. *m* Zbigniew Preisner. *cast* Jerzy Stuhr, Zbigniew Zamachowski, Henryk Bista.

● Kieslowski lightens up somewhat in the last of the series, a black comedy on the potentially destructive effect of material wealth. Two brothers, one a singer in punk band 'City Death', the other older and married, discover a stamp collection in their dead athlete father's flat. As the collection's significance (and value) dawns on them, they are forced to turn the flat into a mini Fort Knox, replete with security systems, Rottweilers and window bars. But are they guards or prisoners? Zamachowski and Stuhr are perfect as the brothers, moving and comic at the same time. The film plays like a version of Bresson's *L'Argent* directed by Bertrand Blier. WH

De l'Autre Côté du Périph' (From the Other Side of the Tracks)

(1997, Fr, (*Le Coeur de la Cité*) 85 min /(*Le Meilleur de l'Ame*) 63 min)
d Bertrand Tavernier, Nils Tavernier. *p* Frederic Bourboulon, Denis Poncet. *sc* Bertrand Tavernier. *ph* Nils Tavernier, Eric Philbert. *ed* Luce Grunenwaldt. *narrator* Bertrand Tavernier.

● Bertrand Tavernier was challenged by a right-wing minister to test his liberal ideas about integration and unemployment by spending time in a densely populated housing project in Montreuil, a paradigm of racially mixed joblessness. The ensuing reportage, a two-parter for TV, is more cheering than disheartening; many of the people the Taverniers meet prove generous, optimistic and impressively clear-sighted. As ever, generalisations crumble before complex, idiosyncratic individuals: the delinquent rehabilitated by an interest in glass blowing; the Malians with a round-the-clock bazaar in their building's vestibule; the '50s leftie, mellowed with age, whose death during the filming elicits a most moving tribute. Tavernier ends with a quotation from Thoreau about abject humanity living in fine, dignified palaces, commenting that Thoreau got it precisely the wrong way round. BBa

Delbaran

(2001, Iran/Jap/Neth, 97 min
d Abolfazl Jalili. *p* Abolfazl Jalili, Shozo Ichiyama. *sc* Abolfazl Jalili. *ph* Mohammad Ahmadi. *ed* Abolfazl Jalili. *cast* Kaeem Alizadeh, Rahmatoallah Ebrahami, Hosein Hashemian, Ahmad Mahdavi.

● Kalim, 14, does odd-jobs at Khan's truckstop near the Afghan border. He shouldn't; he's a refugee, and there's a cop always on the lookout for the Afghans he suspects pass through into Iran with a little help from cunning old Khan. Kalim's got by so far, but there are few hiding places in the desert while he's helping out with the countless vehicles that break down. How long can he remain at liberty? Several contemporary Iranian films have centred on Afghans. But this has less in common with *Kandahar* than with *Djomeh*, and not only because it concerns refugees. It displays a lighter touch than that exercised by Makhmalbaf père. Jalili may specialise in tough stories about the perilous plight of children, but he eschews melodrama, message-mongering and maudlin simplification, and sometimes favours an elliptical, impressionistic, allusive narrative over a conventional linear structure. Not that Jalili's work is unduly obscure; allow a little time for the establishment of character, milieu and situation, and his finest films attain a poetic lucidity unique to themselves. GA

Delicate Balance, A

(1974, US/GB, 134 min)
d Tony Richardson. *p* Ely Landau. *sc* Edward Albee. *ph* David Watkin. *ed* John Victor Smith. *ad* David Brockhurst. *cast* Katharine Hepburn, Paul Scofield, Lee Remick, Kate Reid, Joseph Cotten, Betsy Blair.

● Albee's powerful, coruscatingly brilliant study of tribal rites among the New England jet set. It is also first and foremost a stage play, utterly dependent on direct confrontation between actors and audience, verbal in origins, drawing-room in setting and, on the surface, eminently static. Richardson (as is the norm in this American Film Theatre series) settles for 'filming' the proceedings, and only succeeds in evaporating the tension and the clarity of the original. That said, the cast on show is unbeatable. They make the whole grinding affair bearable, but you'll still get a stiff neck. SGr

Delicate Delinquent, The

(1956, US, 100 min, b/w)
d Don McGuire. *p* Jerry Lewis. *sc* Don McGuire. *ph* Haskell Boggs. *ed* Howard Smith. *ad* Hal Pereira, Earl Hedrick. *m* Buddy Bregman. *cast* Jerry Lewis, Martha Hyer, Darren McGavin, Horace McMahon, Milton Frome, Robert Ivers.

● Jerry's first solo pic after his split-up with Dino sends up the '50s 'problem' teenflick something rotten. Lewis is the odd kid out in a gang of urban ruffians, so kindly cop McGavin takes him under his wing – and before long he wants to join the force too. Excessive physical slapstick, gooey sentiment, plain dumbness. TJ

Delicatessen (100)

(1990, Fr, 99 min)
d Jean-Pierre Jeunet, Marc Caro. *p* Claude Ossard. *sc* Marc Caro, Jean-Pierre Jeunet, Gilles Adrien. *ph* Darius Khondji. *ed* Hervé Schneid. *ad* Marc Caro. *m* Carlos D'Alessio. *cast* Dominique Pinon, Marie-Laure Dougnac, Jean-Claude Dreyfus, Karin Viard, Ticky Holgado, Anne-Marie Pisani, Jacques Mathou, Rufus, Howard Vernon.

● The near future: taking a job and a bedsit at a shabby rooming-house above a butcher's shop, ex-clown Louison (Pinon) falls for the butcher's daughter. But her father, unhappy about the blossoming romance, deals in human flesh: will Louison fall victim, or will the Troglodistes, an underground group of vegetarian fanatics, come to his rescue? On to this slim story, writer-directors Jeunet and Caro pile a wealth of delicious comic detail. Each grotesquely larger-than-life inhabitant of the scrofulous tenement has his own little story; visually, the film evokes Gilliam, Lynch, the Coens and Carné, but the allusions never get in the way of the nightmarish humour. The sets, special effects, photography, pace and performances all contribute to the brash comic-strip vivacity, and even the fairytale romance avoids sentimentality. Increasingly inventive as it progresses, Jeunet and Caro's fast, funny feature debut entertains from sinister start to frantic finish. GA

Delinquents, The

(1989, Aust, 105 min)
d Chris Thomson. *p* Alex Cutler, Michael Wilcox. *sc* Clay Frohman, Mac Gudgeon. *ph* Andrew Lesnie. *ed* John Scott. *pd* Laurence Eastwood. *m* Miles Goodman. *cast* Kylie Minogue, Charlie Schlatter, Angela Punch McGregor, Bruno Lawrence, Todd Boyce, Desiree Smith, Melissa Jaffer, Lynette Curran, Jonathon Hardy.

● Lola (Minogue, winsome and wimpy) and American Brownie (Schlatter, presumably cast because he looks like a young Mel Gibson) share so very, very much: they both love books, rock-'n'roll and lolling around in their underwear, and are both entirely lacking in charisma or acting ability. Small wonder, then, that the adults, who are all bastards, *just don't understand*; small wonder, too, that when this small-town Australian Romeo and Juliet decide to make a go of it alone in the big city, they find it bloody hard. After all, Lola and Brownie are not very bright, even allowing that it is 1957. For one thing, despite forever professing their romantic spirit of adventure, all they really want to do is chuck away their lives by producing a brat at the age of 15; for another, they shack up with a couple of squatters, one of whom is a brainless, Pythonish parody of a DH Lawrence Yorkshireman. Retards flock together, apparently. The acting is universally atrocious, the direction flat and tedious, and the script, which cuts a dash through every cliché in the book, risible. GA

Delinquent School Girls (aka Sizzlers)

(1975, US, 83 min)
d Gregory Corarito. *p* Maurice Smith. *sc* Gregory Corarito, John Lamb, Maurice Smith. *ph* Louis Horvath. *ed* Rick Beck-Meyer. *ad* Roger Pancake. *m* Fred Selden, Randy Johnson. *cast* Michael Pataki, Bob Minor, Stephen Stucker, Sharon Kelly, Brenda Miller, Ralph Campbell.

● An insipid dilution of the women's prison movie. Three male convicts (a black rapist, a gay dress designer, and a relentless mimic whom *Opportunity Knocks* would have had difficulty in presenting) escape from a State Asylum for the Criminally Insane. They accidentally hit upon a Corrective Institute for girls, and the results are obvious. A snail's pace, lumbering direction, lame script, and performances that keep caricature one-dimensional and top-heavy, make this well worth avoiding. IB

Delirious

(1991, US, 96 min)
d Tom Mankiewicz. *p* Lawrence J Cohen, Fred Freeman, Doug Claybourne. *sc* Lawrence J Cohen, Fred Freeman. *ph* Robert Stevens. *ed* William Gordean, Tina Freeman. *ad* Angelo Graham. *m* Cliff Eidelman. *cast* John Candy, Mariel Hemingway, Emma Samms, David Rasche, Charles Rocket, Raymond Burr, Dylan Baker, Jerry Orbach.

● The idea of a writer finding himself within the fictional world he creates (after a bang on the head) is here developed with jokes so obvious they don't need to be made. Candy plays the scriptwriter of an American daytime soap. A fat fool, in reality he's a failure, abused by the soulless producers of *Beyond Our Dreams*, used by the leading bitch (Samms, who acts as if *Dynasty* had never been axed), and blind to the only woman worth caring for (Hemingway). In Ashford Falls, the world of his creation, he is transformed into a hero. After an hour of high farce, he finally sees Samms and Hemingway for what they are. His still being able to sit down at the typewriter and play God is used to drive home the moral – which Capra conveyed with far more charm in *It's a Wonderful Life* – that if you stop trying so hard happiness will find you. Old jokes are piled on top of incomprehensible plot development until you feel truly delirious. CO'S

Délits Flagrants (Caught in the Act)

(1994, Fr, 113 min)
d Raymond Depardon. *p* Pascale Dauman. *ph* Nathalie Crédon. *ed* Roger Ikhle, Camille Cotte, Georges-Henri Mauchant.

●In France, criminals caught red-handed are first interviewed by a public prosecutor to determine how to proceed. Of the 86 such interviews Depardon filmed, he shows us 14. Conventional TV fare, except here it's up on the big screen in 35mm 'Scope. Shot from a fixed position with set focus and no cuts (save for legal reasons: what on earth did those three editors do?) the footage is gripping, funny, hair-raising. Depardon is non-manipulative, leaving us free to muse on anything from the officials' archaic fountain pens to the Oliver Hardy associations of those exasperated, appealing looks to camera. Curiously, from the deaf Arab up for petty larceny at the start, to the HIV+ prostitute on a car theft charge at the end, no one seems vicious or even unpleasant, making you wonder by what criteria those other 72 were excluded. BBa

Delitto in pieno sole

see Plein Soleil

Deliverance

(1972, US, 109 min)
d/p John Boorman. *sc* James Dickey. *ph* Vilmos Zsigmond. *ed* Tom Priestley. *ad* Fred Harpman. *m* Eric Weissberg. *cast* Jon Voight, Burt Reynolds, Ned Beatty, Ronny Cox, Billy McKinney, James Dickey.

●Four Atlanta businessmen decide to prove that the frontier spirit is not dead by spending a canoeing weekend shooting the rapids of a river high in the Appalachians. Terrific boy's own adventure stuff with adult ingredients of graphic mutilation and buggery, but Boorman is never content either to leave it at that or to subscribe to the ecological concerns of James Dickey's novel (where man's return to nature becomes vital because 'the machines are going to fail, and then – survival'). Instead, he adds a dark twist of his own by suggesting that concern is too late. From the quartet's first strange encounter with the deformed albino child in a mountain community almost Dickensian in its squalor, down to the last scene where Voight watches coffins being unearthed and removed to safety before the new dam floods the valley, their trip down the river becomes an odyssey through a land that is already dead, killed by civilisation and peopled by alien creatures rather than human beings. Signposted by the extraordinary shot of a corpse, surfaced from the water with one arm grotesquely wrapped round its neck and the other pointing nowhere, it's a haunting, nightmarish vision. TM

Delta, The

(1996, US, 85 min)
d Ira Sachs. *p* Margot Bridger. *sc* Ira Sachs. *ph* Ben Speth. *ed* Affonso Gonçalves. *m* Michael Rohatyn. *cast* Shayne Gray, Thang Chan, Rachel Zan Huss, Colonious Davis.

●No less striking than Gus Van Sant's debut *Mala Noche*, this low-budget first feature by the assistant director of *Longtime Companion* offers a completely fresh perspective on life in Memphis, Tennessee. Lincoln (Gray) is a cute, 17-year-old kid from a good Jewish family with a nice girlfriend and plenty of straight buddies. But something draws him to the city's gay subculture – and into a dangerous relationship with the disturbed and unreliable Minh (Chan), child of a Vietnamese mother and a black GI, victim of every prejudice going. Sachs allowed his actors to develop situations and dialogue through improvisation, giving the film a meandering, naturalistic feel. When plot does assert itself, in the abrupt closing scenes, the effect is truly disconcerting. TR

Delta Force, The

(1986, US, 129 min)
d Menahem Golan. *p* Menahem Golan, Yoram Globus. *sc* James Bruner, Menahem Golan. *ph* David Gurfinkel. *ed* Alain Jakubowicz. *pd* Luciano Spadoni. *m* Alan Silvestri. *cast* Chuck Norris, Lee Marvin, Martin Balsam, Joey Bishop, Robert Forster, Lainie Kazan, George Kennedy, Hanna Schygulla, Susan Strasberg, Bo Svenson, Robert Vaughn, Shelley Winters.

●Once more the dream machine rewrites US foreign policy; after Rambo, we now get their Delta Force. Amid all the pyrotechnics of airport hijackings, blown over stunt men, rackety chases through bazaars, all of it quite competently handled, there are a few asides of interest. Students of minimal acting techniques can compare Marvin and Norris: impassivity versus vacancy. Students of the disaster film should write a short thesis on why George Kennedy is ubiquitous. Everyone else might wonder why the film is so virulently anti-Arab. CPea

Deluge, The (Potop)

(1974, Pol, 183 mins)
d Jerzy Hoffman. *sc* Wojciech Zukrowski, Jerzy Hoffman, Adam Kersten. *ph* Jerzy Wojcik. *ad* Wojciech Krysztofiak. *m* Kazimierz Serocki. *cast* Daniel Olbrychski, Malgorzata Braunek, Tadeusz Lomnicki, Wladyslaw Hancza, Leszek Teleszynski, Kazimierz Wichniarz.

●A bum-shifting 17th century war epic drawn from a highly popular Henryk Sienkiewicz novel. Formations march through impressive countryside, finally battling it out with a flurry of horses, cannon fire, wounded bodies and spurting blood – none of which comes over visually with the force one might expect, despite nice colour photography in shades of brown. Worming his way through it all, miraculously unscathed, is the courageous adventurer (Olbrychski) who also finds time for a little routine romancing. A long trek at three hours, though it does pick up its heels towards the end, but in Poland, presented in two parts, it ran for 312 minutes. GB

Delusion

(1990, US, 100 min)
d Carl Colpaert. *p* Daniel Hassid. *sc* Carl Colpaert, Kurt Voss. *ph* Geza Sinkovics. *ed* Mark Allan Kaplan. *pd* Ildiko Toth. *m* Barry Adamson. *cast* Jim Metzler, Jennifer Rubin, Kyle Secor, Jerry Orbach, Robert Costanzo, Tracey Walter.

●When computer exec Metzler embezzles half a million dollars or so and heads off for Reno, he thinks he's got it made, but that's before he picks up showgirl Rubin and boyfriend Secor. Obviously, he hasn't watched many *films noirs*, because we're talking Big Mistake here in an unsung little picture that's got pace and a handful of diverting twists, but not quite the requisite star power. TJ

Dementia

(1953, US, 60 min, b/w)
d/p/sc John Parker. *ph* William C Thompson. *ed* Joseph Gluck. *pd* Ben Roseman. *m* George Antheil. *cast* Adrienne Barrett, Bruno VeSota, Richard Barron, Ben Roseman, Ed Hinkle, Debbie VeSota.

●This genuinely bizarre oddity seems to have been masterminded by Bruno VeSota (later a Corman associate), who acted as associate producer and plays the Orson Welles part as the villain; the director, Parker, is obscure to the point that his name is missing from the print under review. The movie spends an hour exploring a lonely woman's sexual paranoia through a torrent of expressionist distortions which would look avant-garde if the vulgar Freudian 'message' weren't so reminiscent of '50s B features. Still, parts of it anticipate Welles' *Touch of Evil*. TR

Dementia 13 (aka The Haunted and the Hunted)

(1963, US/Eire, 81 min, b/w)
d Francis Ford Coppola. *p* Roger Corman. *sc* Francis Ford Coppola. *ph* Charles Hanawalt. *ed* Stewart O'Brien. *ad* Al Locatelli. *m* Ronald Stein. *cast* William Campbell, Luana Anders, Bart Patton, Mary Mitchell, Patrick Magee, Eithne Dunn.

●Produced by Roger Corman, and evidently made under his presiding spirit, this runs briskly through one of those family reunion plots in which the challenge is to guess which seemingly benign member of the family is the mad axe-murderer who's steadily picking off the rest. The location (an Irish castle) is used imaginatively, the Gothic atmosphere is suitably potent, and there's a wonderfully sharp cameo from Patrick Magee as the family doctor. TR

Demetrius and the Gladiators

(1954, US, 101 min)
d Delmer Daves. *p* Frank Ross. *sc* Philip Dunne. *ph* Milton Krasner. *ed* Dorothy Spencer, Robert Fritch. *ad* Lyle Wheeler, George W Davis. *m* Franz Waxman. *cast* Victor Mature, Susan Hayward, Michael Rennie, Debra Paget, Anne Bancroft, Ernest Borgnine, Richard Egan.

●Sequel to *The Robe* and just as absurd, with Christ's garment now the object of a quest by Caligula. But the pieties have gone, to be replaced by the tortuous court machinations of Caligula, Messalina and Claudius; there are some spiffing gladiatorial combats; and with Daves showing much more ease in the CinemaScope format than Henry Koster, it's a lot of fun. TM

Demi-Paradise, The (aka Adventure for Two)

(1943, GB, 115 min, b/w)
d Anthony Asquith. *p/sc* Anatole de Grunwald. *ph* Bernard Knowles. *ed* Renee Woods. *ad* Carmen Dillon. *m* Nicholas Brodszky. *cast* Laurence Olivier, Penelope Dudley Ward, Marjorie Fielding, Margaret Rutherford, Miles Malleson, George Cole.

●Russian engineer Olivier invents a special propeller for ice-breakers and comes to England to supervise the building of a new ship in this pro-Soviet propaganda piece. A stranger in a strange land comes to understand our funny ways. Says a lot about how homefront film-makers thought Britain should be represented in 1943 – very cosy it all is, too. TJ

Demoiselles de Rochefort, Les (The Young Girls of Rochefort)

(1967, Fr, 126 min)
d Jacques Demy. *p* Mag Bodard, Gilbert de Goldschmidt. *sc* Jacques Demy. *ph* Ghislain Cloquet. *ed* Jean Hamon. *ad* Bernard Evein. *m* Michel Legrand. *cast* Catherine Deneuve, Françoise Dorléac, George Chakiris, Grover Dale, Danielle Darrieux, Michel Piccoli, Gene Kelly, Jacques Perrin, Henri Crémieux.

●Jolliest of the Demy-Michel Legrand operettas, sometimes wholly entrancing (especially the ecstatic Darrieux-Piccoli celebration of long lost love), but also foolishly inviting comparison with the Hollywood musical by borrowing Gene Kelly (painfully awkward in toupee and dubbed voice) and a couple of alumni from *West Side Story* (accompanied by a good deal of pastiche Jerome Robbins choreography). The result lacks the delicate purity of *The Umbrellas of Cherbourg*, but makes up for it with boundless vitality and the ravishing spectacle of Rochefort itself, with the town square freshly repainted as a pastel-coloured dreamscape. TM

Demolition Man

(1993, US, 115 min)
d Marco Brambilla. *p* Joel Silver, Michael Levy, Howard G Kazanjian. *sc* Peter M Lenkov, Daniel Waters, Robert Reneau. *ph* Alex Thomson. *ed* Stuart Baird. *pd* David L Snyder. *m* Elliot Goldenthal. *cast* Sylvester Stallone, Wesley Snipes, Sandra Bullock, Nigel Hawthorne, André Gregory, Benjamin Bratt.

●This state-of-the-art action comedy is a cruel satire on a PC society where sex, smoking, swearing and salt are banned, and violence has been eradicated. Cryogenically frozen in 1996, psychotic criminal Phoenix (Snipes) and LA cop Spartan (Stallone) are defrosted in 2036: the former to sort out sewer-dwelling eco-terrorists, the latter to clear up the mess left by his old arch-enemy. In sprawling 21st century San Angeles, under benevolent dictator Dr Cocteau (Hawthorne), the only weapons are in a museum. Phoenix escapes and heads straight for them, and the duplicitous Cocteau admits that Spartan's ultra violent methods may be necessary to restore boring normality. First-time director Brambilla stages the senseless violence with skill and relish, aided by producer Joel Silver's trademark mega-explosions. Forget your preconceptions, but not your brain cells and sense of irony. NF

Demon

see God Told Me To

Demon Lover Diary

(1980, US, 90 min)
d/p/sc/ph/ed Joel DeMott. *cast* Joel DeMott, Don Jackson, Jerry Youngkins, Jeff Kreines, Carol Lasowsky.

●A documentary about the filming of *The Demon Lover* (1976), a movie/dream realised by two factory workers who sacrificed security (mortgaged home) and a finger (industrial 'accident') to raise the funds. But amateurs and professionals don't mix, and the non-communication between producers and crew leads to disturbing outbursts of frustration, filmed – and in part caused by – this film-within-a-film. FF

Demons (Demoni)

(1985, It, 93 min)
d Lamberto Bava. *p* Dario Argento. *sc* Dario Argento, Lamberto Bava, Dardano Sacchetti, Franco Ferrini. *ph* Gianlorenzo Battaglia. *ed* Franco Fraticelli. *pd* David Bassan. *m* Claudio Simonetti. *cast* Urbano Barberini, Natasha Hovey, Karl Zinny, Fiore Argento, Paolo Cozzo, Nicoletta Elmi.

● Years before *Scream*, Italian horror came over all self-referential in this niftily nasty slice 'n' dice. The setting is one of those casually plush Roman cinemas that resemble nothing so much as a small opera house – sadly an exotic antique to the multiplex generation. Here teenage couples assemble to watch a creakily gothic Nostradamus flick, suck face and play pranks. And here it is they turn into cannabalistic demons, wreaking havoc worse than any exhibitor's grisliest nightmare. If great ideas made for great movies, this would be an all-time classic. Regrettably, it's a mediocre slasher with a terrific gimmick. The post-modernity extends off-screen: Dario Argento produced, and the director is the son of Mario (*Black Sabbath*) Bava. An inferior sequel followed. TCh

Demons 2 (Demoni 2)

(1986, It, 91 min)
d Lamberto Bava. *p* Dario Argento. *sc* Dario Argento, Lamberto Bava, Franco Ferrini, Dardano Sacchetti. *ph* Gianlorenzo Battaglia. *ed* Franco Fraticelli. *ad* David Bassan. *m* Simon Boswell, Smiths, Cult, Art of Noise, Peter Murphy, Dead Can Dance. *cast* David Knight, Nancy Brilli, Coralina Cataldi Tassoni, Bobby Rhodes, Asia Argento.

● Accidentally reanimated, the Demons killed off in the original invade a tower block through the TV screens. Cue the obligatory party full of bright young things who bop till they drop dead, then, transformed, rampage about the building like Hooray Henries with a dental hygiene problem. The cliché meter keeps pace with the body count as Argento and Bava throw in the old claustrophobic-trapped-in-lift chestnut, the cute kid all alone with toy ray gun, and the pregnant woman terrorised by same when a plastic Gremlin bursts from his stomach. Only a gym full of demon-bashing body-builders provides any real spark, and even the gore isn't in sufficient abundance to satisfy the diehards. DW.

Demons (Pangarap ng Puso)

(2000, Phil, 102 min)
d Mario O'Hara. *p* Lily Monteverde, Joey Gosiengfiao, Allan Santos. *sc* Mario O'Hara, Rey De Castro. *ph* Johnny Araojo. *ed* Reggie Gulle, Fiona Barres. *ad* Judy Lou del Pio, John Portugal. *m* Blitz Padua, Corintha. *cast* Hilda Koronel, Leo Rabago, Anita Linda, Matet De Leon, Alex Alano, Mike Magat, Lucita Soriano.

● One-time Lino Brocka protégé O'Hara is not shy of traditional melodrama, still the lifeblood of most Filipino cinema, but *Demons* fits no established genre template. Part social history, part ghost horror story, part romance, part quasi-Marxist parable, it has no obvious antecedent except parts of *Night of the Hunter*. Set on Negros Island, the action spans nearly 20 years in the lives of Nena (De Leon), daughter of a fish-farmer, and Jose (Alano), the son of casual labourers. As they move through puberty and try to bridge the class gap, the island is riven by terrorist actions and military reprisals (echoing assassinations and political turmoil in faraway Manila), giving new meaning to the local mythology of jungle demons. O'Hara balances the narrative between drama and elegy, between occasionally shocking images and the poetry of Amado Hernandez and Florentino Collantes. Often wonderful. TR

Demon Seed

(1977, US, 95 min)
d Donald Cammell. *p* Herb Jaffe. *sc* Robert Jaffe, Roger O Hirson. *ph* Bill Butler. *ed* Frank Mazzola. *pd* Edward C Carfagno. *m* Jerry Fielding. *cast* Julie Christie, Fritz Weaver, Gerrit Graham, Berry Kroeger, Lisa Lu, Larry Blake; voice: Robert Vaughn.

● Back from the post-*Performance* wilderness, Cammell was offered the thankless task of spinning a cripplingly restrictive premise – Christie trapped, menaced and impregnated by a super-computer desperate to produce a 'brain-child' offspring before its plugs are pulled – to feature length. A few of his labyrinthine concerns and much advanced animation work (plus optical assistance from once-celebrated avant-gardist Jordan Belson) spice the thin conceit, but it's a doomed project. PT

Demons of the Mind

(1971, GB, 89 min)
d Peter Sykes. *p* Frank Godwin. *sc* Christopher Wicking. *ph* Arthur Grant. *ed* Chris Barnes. *ad* Michael Stringer. *m* Harry Robinson. *cast* Paul Jones, Gillian Hills, Robert Hardy, Michael Hordern, Patrick Magee, Shane Briant, Yvonne Mitchell.

● Sykes' first feature, an exotic Wildean horror story, visually as extravagant and tantalising as a decadent painting: rose petals drop lightly over corpses, an emaciated and incestuous brother and sister communicate through a keyhole dividing their sickrooms, a father hunts and shoots his children in the woods. These are some of the surreal fragments around which the plot revolves, and the script by Christopher Wicking is a striking attempt to introduce new themes and ideas to British horror. Badly let down, though, by some grotesque overacting, notably from Hardy, who sabotages a key role by playing it as cod Shakespeare. DP

Denise Calls Up

(1995, US, 80 min)
d Hal Salwen. *p* J Todd Harris. *sc* Hal Salwen. *ph* Michael Mayers. *ed* Gary Sharfin. *pd* Susan Bolles. *m* Lynn Geller. *cast* Alanna Ubach, Tim Daly, Caroleen Feeney, Dan Gunther, Dana Wheeler Nicholson, Liev Schreiber, Aida Turturro, Sylvia Miles.

● It's the morning after the night before, and Linda's clearing up. Lots of food's still on the table because nobody turned up. Gail calls up to check how things went and apologise for being too busy to come. Afterwards she calls Frank who calls Jerry. None of them made it either. We're talking to New York's home office set here, laptops à go-go, busy busy busy. Still there's something which might drag them away from their keyboards. Gail wants to set up Jerry with her friend Barbara, but she needs Frank to call Jerry to get them together. Oh yes, and Denise calls up Martin, because she found out he made a donation to the sperm bank, and she's having his child. Maybe they could meet up, if he can get out the door, or even get off the phone. And so it goes on and on. Seventy minutes of phone conversations, cordless and mobile, call-waiting and 'Call you right back.' After about three minutes, though, the joke runs dry, the gimmickry (death on the phone, a birth on the phone) grates, the irony flattens out, and the constant yabbering of a bunch of thespian also-rans is enough to set you screaming. TJ

Dennis the Menace (aka Dennis)

(1993, US, 96 min)
d Nick Castle. *p* John Hughes, Richard Vane. *sc* John Hughes. *ph* Thomas Ackerman. *ed* Alan Heim. *pd* James Bissell. *m* Jerry Goldsmith. *cast* Walter Matthau, Mason Gamble, Joan Plowright, Christopher Lloyd, Paul Winfield, Lea Thompson.

● John (*Home Alone*) Hughes is a dab hand at reconstituted family comedies. The script for this one he based on characters from Hank Ketcham's comic strip. Cherubic blond moppet Dennis (Gamble) – not to be confused with the *Beano*'s tousle-haired anarchist – is about as naughty as a choirboy on a Sunday school outing, and in terms of mischief only half as imaginative. Abandoned by his parents to the care of grouchy Mr Wilson (Matthau) and his childless wife (Plowright), Dennis runs amok. Wilson rashly prepares to exhibit his ultra-rare Moon Plant at the local horticultural society's annual beanfeast… A smooth blend of sentiment and slapstick. NF

Dentellière, La (The Lacemaker)

(1977, Fr/Switz/WGer, 107 min)
d Claude Goretta. *p* Yves Gasser. *sc* Pascal Lainé, Claude Goretta. *ph* Jean Boffety. *ed* Joële van Effenterre, Nelly Meunier, Martine Charasson. *ad* Serge Etter, Claude Chevant. *m* Pierre Jansen. *cast* Isabelle Huppert, Yves Beneyton, Florence Giorgetti, Anne Marie Düringer, Renata Schroeter, Michel de Ré.

● As much as anything, it's probably the intriguing ambivalence of a narrative in which connections are never overtly made that turned this into an unexpected box-office hit. Where *A Girl from Lorraine* treads a clearcut feminist path, *The Lacemaker* lurks in more shady byways. Its heroine (beautifully played by Huppert as a passive object) seems less a candidate for women's lib than a helpless prisoner of the incommunicability Goretta had in mind when he defined the film as being about the problem between two people 'who are unable to love each other because they do not express themselves in the same way'. The refreshing quality of the film, as one listens to the expressive eloquence of its silences, is that it cannot be reduced to ideological terms. The heroine may be a victim of both social convention and a suave though sympathetic seducer, but with a mysterious inner radiance glowing behind her patient suffering, she is also much, much more. TM

Denti

see Teeth

Dentist in the Chair

(1960, GB, 88 min, b/w)
d Val Guest. *p* Bertram Ostrer. *sc* Val Guest. *ph* Reginald Wyer. *ed* Bill Lenny. *ad* Bill Andrews. *m* Ken Jones. *cast* Bob Monkhouse, Peggy Cummins, Kenneth Connor, Eric Barker, Ronnie Stevens, Eleanor Summerfield, Reginald Beckwith.

● Stock up on the laughing gas, you'll need it to get through this farce involving student driller killer Monkhouse, dodgy petty crook Connor and a vanload of 'hot' dental instruments. The storyline may be full of cavities, but at least it's funnier than *Marathon Man*. TJ

Départ, Le

(1966, Bel, 91 min, b/w)
d Jerzy Skolimowski. *p* Bronka Ricquier. *sc* Jerzy Skolimowski, Andrzej Kostenko. *ph* Willy Kurant. *ed* Bob Wade. *m* Krzysztof Komeda. *cast* Jean-Pierre Léaud, Catherine Duport, Jacqueline Bir, Paul Roland, Léon Dony.

● Skolimowski's first film made outside Poland, this perhaps laid the seeds for the later troubles and misunderstandings of his years in the wilderness with its sharp contrast between surface visual excitements and the shallow substance underneath. The hero (Léaud, hot from Godard's *Masculin Féminin*, along with Catherine Duport) is as much of a firecracker as the director, playing a Brussels hairdresser who gets up to crazy, startling tricks in order to secure a Porsche for a weekend racing rally. His obsessive quest allows Skolimowski to score some points about Capitalist excess and isolation, but not enough to keep the film properly balanced. Still, if you feel in the mood for frenzied hijinks, you'll get your money's worth. GB

Deranged

(1974, US, 82 min)
d Jeff Gillen, Alan Ormsby. *p* Tom Karr. *sc* Alan Ormsby. *ph* Jack McGowan. *ad* Albert Fischer. *m* Carl Zittrer. *cast* Roberts Blossom, Cosette Lee, Robert Warner, Marcia Diamond, Brian Sneagle.

● This dark, stark account of the murderous activities of Wisconsin necrophile Ed Gein (the real-life character who inspired *Psycho* and *The Texas Chain Saw Massacre*) impresses not only through its occasional flashes of black humour (Gein, distressed by his beloved mother's death, exhumes her, and when she proves a little taciturn at the dinner-table, kills various women to keep her company), but by the sheer austerity of the direction. The more sensationalist aspects of the story are admirably underplayed, and Blossom's nicely gauged performance lends the film surprising conviction. GA

Derby (aka Roller Derby)

(1970, US, 96 min)
d Robert Kaylor. *p* William Richert. *ph* Robert Kaylor. *ed* Anthony Potenza. *cast* Mike Snell, Charlie O'Connell, Butch Snell, Christina Snell, Eddie Krebs, Lydia Gray.

● A documentary which follows one Mike Snell through his decision to leave his job and become a derby skater, incorporating interviews with his family, friends, and team members. The derby itself is a natural for film: violent, colourful, full of great sweeping movements. In practice it seems all but devoid of rules. Everyone very definitely stomps hard on everyone else. Kaylor, formerly a still photographer, makes full use of the sport's spectacular aspects (filming from high up over Madison Square Gardens, for instance, so that the skaters become a blur of colour in a small ring of light), and delights in tracing the rituals that separate the game from the mainstream of life. He also allows people and events to explain themselves; the result is a remarkably lucid exposition of the roller derby at all points (not least its appeal to violent and masochistic instincts). VG

Derby Day (aka Four Against Fate)

(1952, GB, 84 min, b/w)
d Herbert Wilcox. *p* Maurice Cowan. *sc* John Baines. *ph* Max Greene. *ed* William Lewthwaite. *ad* William C Andrews. *m* Anthony Collins. *cast* Anna Neagle, Michael Wilding, Googie Withers, John McCallum, Nigel Stock, Ralph Reader, Alfie Bass.

●Deeply unchallenging portmanteau of stories, from the Wilcox-Neagle stable, following the comic and dramatic adventures that befall visitors to Epsom's biggest race day, these include a taxi driver, a French maid and a murderer. Retitled for its US release, just in case it caused confusion in Kentucky. TJ

Dernier Combat, Le

see Last Battle, The

Dernières Vacances, Les

(1947, Fr, 95 min, b/w)
d Roger Leenhardt. *sc* Roger Breuil, Roger Leenhardt. *ph* Philippe Agostini. *ed* Myriam Borsoutzky. *ad* Léon Barsacq. *m* Guy Bernard. *cast* Odile Versois, Michel François, Berthe Bovy, Pierre Dux, Renée Devillers, Jean d'Yd.

●Modest, unassuming and tremblingly fresh, this is the kind of miracle that will always pass unnoticed. If its theme (the end of adolescence), period (the '20s) and mood (elegiac) have all become clichés of contemporary cinema, it only confirms how much the dilettante Leenhardt, a critic, documentarist and *éminence grise* of the New Wave, was ahead of his time. Not to be missed – honestly. GAd

Dernier Harem, Le

see Harem Suare

Dernier Mélodrame, Le

see Last Melodrama, The

Dernier Métro, Le

see Last Metro, The

Dernier Milliardaire, Le

(1934, Fr, 100 min, b/w)
d/sc René Clair. *ph* Rudolph Maté, Louis Née. *ed* Jean Pouzet. *ad* Lucien Aguettand, Lucien Carré. *m* Maurice Jaubert. *cast* Max Dearly, Renée Saint-Cyr, Marthe Mellot, Raymond Cordy, José Nogueiro, Aimos.

●Turning his patrician gaze for a moment on the real world (in the squalid aftermath of the Stavisky affair), Clair characteristically set this comedy on political chicanery in a Mediterranean Ruritania of Monte Carlo dimensions. Feeble as satire, and only occasionally amusing, it can best be described as a cross between *The Merry Widow* (without Lehar) and *Duck Soup* (without the Marx Brothers). GAd

Dernier Tournant, Le

(1939, Fr, 90 min, b/w)
d Pierre Chenal. *sc* Charles Spaak, Henry Torrès, Jacques Brunius, Pierre Chenal, André Chenal. *ph* Christian Matras. *ed* Boris Lewin. *ad* Georges Wakhévitch. *m* Jean Wiener. *cast* Fernand Gravey, Michel Simon, Corinne Luchaire, Robert Le Vigan, Florence Marly, Marcel Vallée.

●When it comes to *noir*, we Anglos may have appropriated the word, but the *thing* was the result of the most delicate Franco-American reciprocity, well illustrated here. Preceding Visconti (*Ossessione*), Garnett and Rafelson, this is the first adaptation of James M Cain's 1934 novel *The Postman Always Rings Twice*, with its triangle of slobbish husband/bored wife/tough drifter. Apart from an accommodation with Michel Simon's star status, which required the husband to live longer, it's a faithful transposition of the novel's tone and content. But it's the style of the actors – Gravey's soulful eyes and mournful presence, Luchaire's other worldly beauty and air of resignation – which makes the difference, nudging the distinctively French world of 'poetic realism' and that of American pulp finally and irrevocably into alignment. (Luchaire's career stopped in 1940; she was the daughter of pro-Nazi writer Jean Luchaire, shot after the Liberation, and she herself was dead at 29.) BBa

Dérobade, La (The Life)

(1979, Fr, 113 min)
d Daniel Duval. *p* Benjamin Simon, Gérard Lorin. *sc* Christopher Frank. *ph* Michel Cenet. *ed* Jean-Bernard Bonis. *pd* François Chanut. *m* Vladimir Cosma. *cast* Miou-Miou, Maria Schneider, Daniel Duval, Niels Arestrup, Brigitte Ariel, Jean Benguigui.

●Based on a book by a French ex-prostitute, this is the extremely unpleasant story of a woman (Miou-Miou) dominated, despised and frequently beaten up by her pimp (played by the director). Perhaps seen in a French social context there might be an excuse to make for the film: it is in part set up to attack their very vicious system of pimps. However, it remains fetishistic, voyeuristic and racist, with its arty camera lingering over bodies, kinky outfits, and scenes of stomach-turning brutality perpetrated for the most part by swarthy men. HM

Dersu Uzala

(1975, USSR/Jap, 141 min)
d Akira Kurosawa. *p* Eiti Mattsue. *sc* Akira Kurosawa, Yuri Nagibin. *ph* Asakazu Nakai, Yuri Gantman, Fyodor Dobronravov. *ed* V Stepanovoi. *ad* Yuri Raksha. *m* Isaak Shvartz. *cast* Maksim Munzuk, Yuri Solomin, M. Bichkov, V. Khrulev.

●Kurosawa went to Russia because he'd found it impossible to get work in Japan, but sadly he succumbed almost completely to the Mosfilm line in crude spectacle and simplistic, lumbering drama. Drawn from the autobiographical novels of a military explorer who encounters an elderly Goldi forest-dweller at the turn of the century, what emerges is a transparently sincere but entirely predictable account of the friendship between 'civilised' urban Russian and 'primitive' Oriental man of nature. TR

Der var engang en Krig

see Once There Was a War

Des Chambres et des Couloirs

see Bedrooms and Hallways

Des Enfants Gâtés (Spoiled Children)

(1977, Fr, 113 min)
d Bertrand Tavernier. *p* Alain Sarde. *sc* Bertrand Tavernier, Christine Pascal, Charlotte Dubreuil. *ph* Alain Levent. *ed* Armand Psenny, Arlane Beoglin. *m* Philippe Sarde. *cast* Michel Piccoli, Christine Pascal, Michel Aumont, Gérard Jugnot, Arlette Bonnard, Gérard Zimmerman, Isabelle Huppert.

●Only partly autobiographical, this account of a film director's brief affair with a young neighbour, and his involvement in the social and political ramifications of a tenancy dispute in an apartment block, still carries the weight of Tavernier's convictions about the injustices everyone (including film-makers) is forced to contest, domestically and at work. A striking performance from Pascal and the familiar leonine one from Piccoli. More 'parochial' than most Tavernier, but worth catching up with. MA

Desert Bloom

(1985, US, 106 min)
d Eugene Corr. *p* Michael Hausman. *sc* Eugene Corr. *ph* Reynaldo Villalobos. *ed* David Garfield, John Currin, Cari Coughlin. *ad* Lawrence Miller. *m* Brad Fiedel. *cast* Annabeth Gish, Jon Voight, Jobeth Williams, Ellen Barkin, Jay D Underwood, Allen Garfield.

●A near flawless mood piece. It is the '50s and nuclear testing is about to begin in the Nevadan wastes, but back in Las Vegas 13-year-old Rose (Gish) finds family life quite volatile enough. Her alcoholic stepfather (Voight), a traumatised World War II military-freak, seems to hate her but love her glam-puss aunt (Barkin). Written and directed by Corr, the film's main strength is its humorous understatement: it may take a little time to exert its considerable power, but once achieved its control never slips. The performances all round are excellent, avoiding histrionics and conveying with total authenticity the terrifying naivety of the mushrooming atomic age: 'Rise and shine, it's A-bomb time!' MS

Désert des Tartares, Le

(1976, Fr/It/WGer, 148 min)
d Valerio Zurlini. *p* Jacques Perrin. *sc* André G Brunelin, Jean-Louis Bertucelli. *ph* Luciano Tovoli. *ed* Raimondo Garbini. *ad* Giancarlo Bartoloni-Salimberi. *m* Ennio Morricone. *cast* Jacques Perrin, Max von Sydow, Philippe Noiret, Vittorio Gassman, Laurent Terzieff, Jean-Louis Trintignant, Fernando Rey, Francisco Rabal.

●Something nasty is lurking on the steppes outside the fort, while inside the years pass and the occupying garrison sits around brooding. Is it the dread Tartars, the vengeance of God, or simply a figment of the uneasy military imagination? Difficult to care much, since portentousness hangs heavy over this handsome but hamfisted adaption of Dino Buzzati's Kafkaesque novel, abstracted in time, place and almost everything else way beyond the reach of a fine cast. TM

Deserter and the Nomads, The (Zbehovia a Poutnici)

(1968, Czech/It, 102 min)
d Juro Jakubisko. *p* Moris Ergas. *sc* Juraj Jakubisko, Karol Sidon. *ph* Juraj Jakubisko. *ed* Maximilian Remen. *ad* Ivan Vanicek. *m* Stepán Konicek. *cast* Stefan Ladizinsky, August Kubán, Gejza Ferenc, Jana Stehnová.

●Three tales of war, the first being by far the best. A young WWI soldier flees from the battlefield carnage and returns to the native village he has dreamed of as a haven of peace. But his return sparks off violent dissensions; he is betrayed to the Hussars as a deserter; and soon the whole village is a welter of brutal killings. With colour and images guided by folk art and a tang of surrealism, Jakubisko shapes his material into a sort of medieval death's jest-book, with Death himself – a grinning, skull-like refugee from a Bergman film – eagerly waiting to reap his harvest. Technique unfortunately begins to run rather wild in the rest of the film, all zooms, filters, distortions and wild arabesques. But the main problem is that the two remaining stories (WWII and a future nuclear holocaust) tend to ram home the message about the continuing horrors of war with a dull thud. An extraordinary, offbeat movie all the same. TM

Desert Fox, The (aka Rommel – Desert Fox)

(1951, US, 88 min, b/w)
d Henry Hathaway. *p/sc* Nunnally Johnson. *ph* Norbert Brodine. *ed* James B Clark. *ad* Lyle Wheeler, Maurice Ransford. *m* Daniele Amfitheatrof. *cast* James Mason, Cedric Hardwicke, Jessica Tandy, Luther Adler, Everett Sloane, Leo G Carroll, George Macready, Richard Boone.

●Considered daring at the time for its sympathetic view of a World War II enemy general as tragic hero. A whitewashed Rommel, returning to Germany disillusioned after the African defeat, becomes involved in the abortive Operation Valkyrie plot to assassinate Hitler, and opts for suicide rather than stand trial. Not really persuasive, despite careful performances and the journalistic flair of Hathaway's direction. TM

Desert Hearts

(1985, US, 93 min)
d/p Donna Deitch. *sc* Natalie Cooper. *ph* Robert Elswit. *ed* Robert Estrin. *pd* Jeannine C Oppewall. *cast* Helen Shaver, Patricia Charbonneau, Audra Lindley, Andra Akers, Dean Butler, Gwen Welles, James Staley.

●To Reno (in 1959) comes a mid-thirtyish New York teacher, her hair in a bun and her nerves in shreds, in search of a divorce from a stultified marriage. She puts up at a local ranch, and it's not long before she is succumbing to the advances of a much younger woman, though not without resistance. Suspicions that the film will simply be a period piece, viewed through the modern lens of post-feminist wishful thinking, are soon allayed however. Redneck Reno might still adhere to the old frontier notions of anything-goes morality, but it still harbours enough of the puritan spirit to make life uncomfortable for lesbians. Moreover, the ranch is more of an emotional snake-pit than first appears. Deitch is well served by Shaver as the teacher and Charbonneau as the young seducer. Best of all, however, is the way the movie dignifies all its characters. There is also an incendiary consummation of the affair, and Patsy Cline on the soundtrack; two features which had this paleneck by the throat. CPea

Desert Mice

(1959, GB, 83 min, b/w)
d Michael Relph. *p* Michael Relph, Basil Dearden. *sc* David Climie. *ph* Ken Hodges. *ed* Reginald Beck. *ad* Peter Proud. *m* Philip Green. *cast* Alfred Marks, Sidney James, Dick Bentley, Patricia Bredin, Dora Bryan, Irene Handl, Kenneth Fortescue, Reginald Beckwith, Joan Benham, Marius Goring, Liz Fraser.
●Groundbreaking melodrama about the love that dare not squeak its name... No, no, just taking the mickey. Africa, 1941: a third-rate ENSA concert party captures German officer (Goring) masquerading as one of ours. Strong odour of mouldy cheese. GM

Deserto Rosso

see Red Desert, The

Desert Song, The

(1953, US, 110 min)
d H Bruce Humberstone. *p* Rudi Fehr. *sc* Roland Kibbee. *ph* Robert Burks. *ed* William Ziegler. *ad* Stanley Fleischer. *songs* Sigmund Romberg, Oscar Hammerstein II. *cast* Gordon MacRae, Kathryn Grayson, Steve Cochran, Raymond Massey, William Conrad, Ray Collins.
●The third movie of Sigmund Romberg's operetta in three decades – and if the result (adapted by Max Steiner) is utter tosh, at least it's utter tosh done dead straight. Full-throated Kathryn Grayson is the general's daughter who takes her time in realising gentleman anthropologist Gordon MacRae, the object of her affections, is also moonlighting as El Khobar, daring leader of North Africa's rebel contingent. TJ

Desert Trail, The

(1935, US, 54 min, b/w)
d Cullen Lewis [Lewis D Collins]. *p* Paul Malvern. *sc* Lindsley Parsons. *ph* Archie Stout. *ed* Carl Pierson. *cast* John Wayne, Mary Kornman, Paul Fix, Eddy Chandler, Carmen LaRoux, Lafe McKee, Al Ferguson, Henry Hall.
●Larky, no-account Western: rodeo rider John Scott (Wayne, unusually talkative), and his gambling buddy Kansas Charlie (Fix) are framed for murder, but John's girl, orphan Anne (Kornman), saves the day, after many a double-cross, when her mortally wounded brother admits to the crime. The stock rodeo footage suggests the two-horse town of Rattlesnake Gulch has a population of fifty thousand. The title's a mystery. JPy

Desert Victory

(1943, GB, 60 min, b/w)
d Roy Boulting. *p* David MacDonald. *ed* Roy Boulting. *m* William Alwyn.
●The full story of Montgomery's World War II campaign in North Africa as recorded by 26 combat cameramen attached to the 8th Army. Boulting's role as director and supervising editor kept him in London, cutting the footage as it was rushed from the front. The result is a classic wartime propaganda job, refreshingly soft in the commentary and unflinching in its visuals. GA

Designated Mourner, The

(1996, GB, 94 min)
d David Hare. *p* Donna Grey, David Hare. *sc* Wallace Shawn. *ph* Oliver Stapleton. *ed* George Akers. *pd* Bob Crowley. *m* Richard Hartley. *cast* Miranda Richardson, Mike Nichols, David de Keyser.
●Three people sit behind a desk: an old man (de Keyser), his daughter (Richardson), and his son-in-law (Nichols). They talk, not to each other, but to us, the audience. They reminisce about Judy's relationship with her father, a poet and dissident, and her husband Jack, who wilts under his own sense of intellectual inferiority. Gradually Jack takes centre stage to trace the contours of a narrative, the story of his failed marriage, his political and moral cowardice, his increasing alienation from the world of words and ideas. Hare's subtle, artful film of Wallace Shawn's play exists purely in that abstract, literary world – it is, defiantly, a piece of theatre, pared and minimalist. The film has something of the intimate quality of an actors' read through: what you lose in action, you gain in concentration and insight. Hare says the play is about 'the death of culture, the danger of culture becoming a minority pursuit', which obviously reflects his conviction that 'Keats is better than Dylan', highbrow better than lowbrow; certainly the film fulfils his own elitist criteria. Me? I could barely keep my eyes open. TCh

Design for Living

(1933, US, 90 min, b/w)
d/p Ernst Lubitsch. *sc* Ben Hecht. *ph* Victor Milner. *ed* Frances Marsh. *ad* Hans Dreier. *m* Nathaniel Finston. *cast* Gary Cooper, Fredric March, Miriam Hopkins, Edward Everett Horton, Franklin Pangborn, Isabel Jewell.
●Noël Coward's teacup wit and elegance hardly suits the beer glass temperament of his screen adaptor Ben Hecht, who later complained of the author's 'vaudeville patter with an English accent', not to mention a 'superiority complex that went over big with sofa-cushion menders'. The script galumphs when it should glide, and neither the director nor the stellar cast can bring this would-be soufflé about a bohemian ménage-à-trois (Cooper paints, March writers, Hopkins flits between them) to the right fluffy consistency. GB

Designing Woman

(1957, US, 118 min)
d Vincente Minnelli. *p* Dore Schary. *sc* George Wells. *ph* John Alton. *ed* Adrienne Fazan. *ad* William A Horning, Preston Ames. *m* André Previn. *cast* Gregory Peck, Lauren Bacall, Dolores Gray, Sam Levene, Chuck Connors, Mickey Shauhnessy, Ed Platt.
●A bubbly comedy in the best plush MGM style, following a fashion designer's amiable clash of interests with her sports journo husband. Peck however, is not an actor with the featherweight comic touch, and Bacall, herself a late replacement for the Monaco-bound Grace Kelly, had to get through the death of partner Bogart during production. A misfire. TJ

Desire

(1936, US, 96 min, b/w)
d Frank Borzage. *p* Ernst Lubitsch. *sc* Edwin Justus Mayer, Waldemar Young, Samuel Hoffenstein. *ph* Charles Lang Jr, Victor Milner. *ed* William Shea. *ad* Hans Dreier, Robert Usher. *m* Frederick Hollander. *cast* Marlene Dietrich, Gary Cooper, John Halliday, Akim Tamiroff, William Frawley, Alan Mowbray.
●Elegant romantic comedy in the style of Lubitsch (who produced), but lacking his nudging innuendo thanks to Borzage's less cynical romanticism. Dietrich is the spritely, sophisticated jewel thief who uses naive young Cooper to smuggle a necklace from France into Spain, only for love to bloom despite the difference in their moral outlooks. Marlene's best movie away from Sternberg, it's relaxed, funny and charming. GA

Desire Under the Elms

(1958, US, 114 min, b/w)
d Delbert Mann. *p* Don Hartman. *sc* Irwin Shaw. *ph* Daniel L Fapp. *ed* George Boemler. *ad* Hal Pereira, Joseph McMillan Johnson. *m* Elmer Bernstein. *cast* Sophia Loren, Anthony Perkins, Burl Ives, Frank Overton, Pernell Roberts, Anne Seymour.
●Surprisingly faithful to the play, but still a leaden travesty. Director and cast (Loren especially) are hopelessly at sea with Eugene O'Neill's tragedy of familial lust (for land as much as for the body), which is a loose transposition to 19th century New England of Euripides' *Hippolytus*. TM

Desk Set (aka His Other Woman)

(1957, US, 103 min)
d Walter Lang. *p* Henry Ephron. *sc* Phoebe Ephron, Henry Ephron. *ph* Leon Shamroy. *ed* Robert Simpson. *ad* Lyle Wheeler, Maurice Ransford. *m* Cyril J Mockridge. *cast* Spencer Tracy, Katharine Hepburn, Joan Blondell, Gig Young, Dina Merrill, Neva Patterson.
●Most reviewers agreed at the time that Hepburn got far more out of this mere bauble of a sex comedy than the 1955 Broadway play by William Marchant deserved. In it she plays the leader of an all-female TV network research team fearful of being rendered redundant by the arrival of an electronics expert's computer, with Tracy wooing her into acceptance. If Tracy was never quite as interesting as Hepburn's best comic foil, Cary Grant, he always allowed his offscreen lover ample scope. The results are some splendidly crisp exchanges between the pair, and the inevitable scene of embarrassment where he is literally 'caught with his pants down'. RM

Des Nouvelles du Bon Dieu (News from the Good Lord)

(1996, Fr, 110 min)
d Didier Le Pêcheur. *p* Fabrice Coat. *sc* Didier Le Pêcheur, Artus de Penguern. *ph* Gérard Simon. *ed* Sylvie Landra. *cast* Marie Trintignant, Maria de Medeiros, Christian Charmetant, Isabelle Candelier, Michel Vuillermoz, Jean Yann, Mathieu Kassovitz.
●A superbly inventive and witty first feature charting the effects of a trendy philosopher's suicide on his widow, a priest with shaky faith, and a near incestuous brother and sister who are the writer's greatest fans. The plot is driven by the siblings' belief that they're living out a novel written by God, and since the story's lousy they want to line up a chat with Him. If it all sounds weird, it is – but also rather wonderful. The Pope gets his, cops and mediums join in the search, the increasingly outrageous black comedy is seamlessly mixed with proper (if parodied) metaphysical ideas, and the plotline has enough surprises for several features. Subversive, sexy, thought-provoking. GA

Despair

(1978, WGer/Fr, 119 min)
d Rainer Werner Fassbinder. *p* Peter Märthesheimer. *sc* Tom Stoppard. *ph* Michael Ballhaus. *ed* Reginald Beck. *pd* Rolf Zehetbauer. *m* Peer Raben. *cast* Dirk Bogarde, Andrea Ferreol, Volker Spengler, Klaus Löwitsch, Alexander Allerson, Bernhard Wicki.
●This generally ill-received assault (in both senses) on the art house market, filmed in English, toys perversely with its signifiers of 'class' (Nabokov novel, Stoppard script, Bogarde performance) to both plainly outrageous and oddly hermetic effect. The novel's surprises are merrily given away half way through (when distressed chocolate manufacturer Hermann Hermann decides to opt out of proto-Nazi Germany by murdering a 'double' who in fact looks nothing like him), and Fassbinder increasingly aligns the material with his more personal studies in schizophrenia like *Satan's Brew* or *World on a Wire*, while matching his own concerns with illusionism to Nabokov's with delusion. Bold, garish and obsessive, but more than a little irritating. PT

Desperado

(1995, US, 105 min)
d Robert Rodriguez. *p* Robert Rodriguez, Bill Borden. *sc* Robert Rodriguez. *ph* Guillermo Navarro. *ed* Robert Rodriguez. *pd* Cecilia Montiel. *m* Los Lobos. *cast* Antonio Banderas, Salma Hayek, Joaquim De Almeida, Steve Buscemi, Cheech Marin, Quentin Tarantino.
●Less a sequel than a loose, bigger-budget remake of *El Mariachi*, Rodriguez's second feature may be a rambling, derivative exercise in gratuitous violence, but its determination to proceed as if the word 'restraint' never existed makes for gleeful entertainment. The story takes off from and rehashes the first film. Out to avenge his girlfriend's death, the mariachi (Banderas) turns up in a lawless border town, determined, against the advice of his buddy Buscemi (Steve, that is), to kill drug-lord Bucho (De Almeida). There's a hitch: Bucho knows he's targeted, and orders his myriad henchmen to waste anybody new in town.

Happily, after a run-in with one such thug, the mariachi falls in with bookstore proprietor Carolina (Hayek), who offers him shelter from the storm of bullets. Humour comes mainly via Buscemi, De Almeida and, in a pleasingly curtailed cameo, a mugging Tarantino. If the irony and invention lacks the light touch of *El Mariachi*, there's more than enough preposterous pleasure to be had from Rodriguez's expertise with the action set-pieces and absurdist approach to the story's mythical aspirations. Bloody good fun. GA

Desperate

(1947, US, 73 min, b/w)
d Anthony Mann. *p* Michel Kraike. *sc* Harry Essex. *ph* George E Diskant. *ed* Marston Fay. *ad* Albert S D'Agostino, Walter Keller. *m* Paul Sawtell. *cast* Steve Brodie, Audrey Long, Raymond Burr, Douglas Fowley, William Challee, Jason Robards Sr, Freddie Steele.
●Mann's B thrillers are as tough and harshly stylised as they come. Here Steve Brodie and wife flee both the mob fingering him for murder and the law. Burr is a superb gangleader, and one scene – a beating-up in a dark basement lit by a single swinging light – is essence of *noir*. SJ

Desperate

(1991, US, 90 min, b/w)
d Rico Martinez. *cast* Kimberli Ghee, Elvis Christ.
●So hip it hurts, the first film from Martinez, 'a Chinese-Filipino/Mexican-American', chronicles the desperate lives and times of Troy and Tan-Yah: fame-fetishists, losers hooked on bogus dreams, desperate for success. When we first meet them, Tan-Yah (Ghee) is Tina Toilet, a would-be punk singer with pseudo-English accent and attitude to match, while Troy (Christ) is desperately over-extended in an investment pyramid that's about to crash. It's 1979, a desperate year. Cut to 1984 – a desperate year – and Tan-Yah Tempter's Heavy Metal thing doesn't happen. The 'Big New Hair' is a washout, the record deal a bust. Troy's acting career climaxes at the bottom: porno, steroids, liposuction, collagen injections. Both know that making it is murder. It's 1989, a desperate year... At 90 minutes, this is exactly 75 minutes too long (we all deserve 15 minutes, okay?). For a film about 'now', it is laboured, repetitive, derivative. In a word, desperate. TCh

Desperate Hours

(1990, US, 105 min)
d Michael Cimino. *p* Dino De Laurentiis, Michael Cimino. *sc* Lawrence Konner, Mark Rosenthal, Joseph Hayes. *ph* Douglas Milsome. *ed* Peter Hunt. *pd* Victoria Paul. *m* David Mansfield. *cast* Mickey Rourke, Anthony Hopkins, Mimi Rogers, Lindsay Crouse, Kelly Lynch, Elias Koteas, David Morse, Shawnee Smith.
●From its two opening scenes – scenic and sensational(ist) respectively – it's pretty clear that Cimino's film of Joseph Hayes' thriller (a virtual remake of William Wyler's 1955 version) will be strong on visuals, weak on continuity and characterisation. Three hoodlums (Rourke, Koteas, Morse) randomly choose the Cornell home as a hideaway, and hold the family (Rogers, estranged husband Hopkins, and two kids) hostage. But where Wyler was content to wind up the claustrophobic tension, and focus on getting the best out of Bogart and Fredric March, Cimino appears distinctly frustrated by the scale of his materials. He does, however, manage to keep Rourke's escaped con – a volatile mix of charm and menace – under control, while Hopkins is dependably solid, if miscast as a Vietvet. Mostly, however, the impression is of Cimino trying to prove he can behave himself, and deserting his cast in the process. Not desperate, but disappointingly ordinary. GA

Desperate Hours, The

(1955, US, 112 min, b/w)
d/p William Wyler. *sc* Joseph Hayes. *ph* Lee Garmes. *ed* Robert Swink. *ad* Hal Pereira, Joseph McMillan Johnson. *m* Gail Kubik. *cast* Humphrey Bogart, Fredric March, Arthur Kennedy, Martha Scott, Dewey Martin, Gig Young, Mary Murphy, Robert Middleton.
●From a Broadway play, with Bogart giving his penultimate performance as the desperate fugitive, a role played on stage by Paul Newman. A trio of convicts on the run terrorise an average American suburban family headed by March. One of a number of '50s films which revealed the paranoia lurking under the facade of the American dream, this time the respectability and security of the family being disrupted with a vengeance. Bogart clearly enjoys himself as a man with no redeeming features, and he's well supported by the other two (Martin, Middleton). Wyler directs efficiently, if somewhat mechanically. CPe

Desperate Journey

(1942, US, 107 min, b/w)
d Raoul Walsh. *p* Hal B Wallis. *sc* Arthur Horman. *ph* Bert Glennon. *ed* Rudi Fehr. *ad* Carl Jules Weyl. *m* Max Steiner. *cast* Errol Flynn, Raymond Massey, Ronald Reagan, Nancy Coleman, Arthur Kennedy, Alan Hale.
●Boy's Own adventure as Flynn and his World War II bomber crew (RAF courtesy of Hollywood) escape from Nazis sneeringly led by Massey after being shot down over the Black Forest. Aside from some expendable propaganda heroics, rousingly handled by Walsh. TM

Desperate Living

(1977, US, 91 min)
d/p/sc John Waters. *ph* Thomas Loizeaux, John Waters. *ed* Charles Roggero. *ad* Vincent Peranio. *m* Chris Lobinger. *cast* Liz Renay, Mink Stole, Susan Lowe, Edith Massey, Mary Vivian Pearce, Jean Hill.
●Revelling in the travesty of carnal excess, *Desperate Living* transforms the standard elements of fairytale into a pastiche of dominant sexual mores. The wicked queen is an omnivorous barracuda-mother with a predilection for leather boys, who devours her empire's sub-lumpen populace with an appetite that is tempered only by perverse sadism. Her princess daughter, trapped in the heterosexual pursuit of a Love Story, is finally saved by a rebellious uprising of lesbian transsexual heroines who bring about the collapse of the maternal dictatorship. Single-mindedly tracing the limits where hedonism becomes revulsion, this is a celebration of the flesh, a revindication of marginalised sexualities, of desire as artifice, which is a lot less misogynist than the tasteful aestheticism of 'natural' sexuality in softcore porn. CPa

Desperately Seeking Susan

(1985, US, 103 min)
d Susan Seidelman. *p* Sarah Pillsbury, Midge Sanford. *sc* Leora Barish. *ph* Ed Lachman. *ed* Andrew Mondshein. *pd* Santo Loquasto. *m* Thomas Newman. *cast* Rosanna Arquette, Madonna, Aidan Quinn, Mark Blum, Robert Joy, Will Patton, Steven Wright, John Turturro, Rockets Redglare, Ann Magnuson, John Lurie.
●Mired in suburban wedlock Roberta (Arquette) turns to the personal ads for vicarious romance, with unexpected results. Seidelman brings a hip '80s SoHo sensibility to this emancipated screwball comedy, even if the plotting (a mistaken identity farce involving that old chestnut, amnesia brought on by a bump to the head) is square as a square peg. Madonna has never found a better fit than the role of Susan, a thrift-store free spirit – and even then Arquette gives as good as she gets with a deliciously kooky comic turn. Followers of indepedent American cinema should keep an eye out for John Turturro, Richard Edson, John Lurie, Giancarlo Esposito, Anne Carlisle, Victor Argo, Richard Hell and Rockets Redglare, among others. TCh

Desperate Measures

(1998, US, 100 min)
d Barbet Schroeder. *p* Barbara Schroeder, Susan Hoffman, Gary Foster, Lee Rich. *sc* David Klass. *ph* Luciano Tovoli. *ed* Lee Percy. *pd* Geoffrey Kirkland. *m* Trevor Jones. *cast* Michael Keaton, Andy Garcia, Brian Cox, Marcia Gay Harden, Erik King, Efrain Figueroa.
●Frank Connor, a lone parent cop, competes with the police force on a manhunt for escaped con McCabe, and finds himself in a no man's land between hunter and prey. The cops want the fugitive dead, and Frank wants his bone marrow to save his little boy. The title describes the film's strategy of victimising the child, a leukaemia patient whose pre-op vulnerability is exploited first to enable McCabe's escape, and then later as he becomes a hostage to the latter's fortunes. Keaton plays the con like Hannibal Lecter: a multiple murderer who can outwit his captors, unblinking, droll and occasionally vicious. Garcia is a rather dull embodiment of earnest persistence, and Harden flits in and out in an underexplored role as the boy's surgeon. NB

Desperate Remedies

(1993, NZ, 93 min)
d Stewart Main, Peter Wells. *p* James Wallace. *sc* Stewart Main, Peter Wells. *ph* Leon Narbey. *ed* David Coulson. *pd* Michael Kane. *m* Peter Scholes. *cast* Jennifer Ward-Lealand, Kevin Smith, Lisa Chappell, Cliff Curtis, Michael Hurst.
●This preposterous 19th century bodice-ripper is set Down Under in a raunchy harbour town periodically injected with fresh blood in the form of grimy transportees. One such is Hayes (Smith) who is enlisted by an opulent but penniless dressmaker (Ward-Lealand) to save her opium-addicted sister from a callous fop (Curtis). Stagy, set-bound, and dazzling enough to trigger a migraine. A film that dares to be bad, and succeeds quite splendidly. SFe

Desperate Search

(1952, US, 73 min, b/w)
d Joseph H Lewis. *p* Matthew Rapf. *sc* Walter Doniger. *ph* Harold Lipstein. *ed* Joseph Dervin. *ad* Cedric Gibbons, Eddie Imazu. *m* Rudolph G Kopp. *cast* Howard Keel, Jane Greer, Patricia Medina, Keenan Wynn, Robert Burton, Lee Aaker.
●Not much dramatic fat on Lewis's involving open-air suspense picture about the search for a couple of children who have survived an air crash somewhere in the mountains of British Columbia. A familiar set-up brings professional and personal rivalries between Keel's reformed alcoholic father, his iron-willed ex-wife, pilot Patricia Medina, and latest (non-airborne) flame Jane Greer, but there's little sentiment in the handling of the children's plight and good-egg support from moustachioed Keenan Wynn. A minor thing perhaps, but they did a sound job with what they had. TJ

Desperate Siege

see Rawhide

Des Terroristes à la retraite

see Terrorists in Retirement

Destination Gobi

(1953, US, 89 min)
d Robert Wise. *p* Stanley Rubin. *sc* Everett Freeman. *ph* Charles G Clarke. *ed* Robert Fritch. *ad* Lyle Wheeler, Lewis H Creber. *m* Sol Kaplan. *cast* Richard Widmark, Don Taylor, Casey Adams, Murvyn Vye, Darryl Hickman, Martin Milner.
●A WWII action movie with a difference, this somewhat implausible adventure has US Navy officer Widmark seconded to the Gobi desert to take charge of a group of American meteorologists at a remote weather station. Ambitiously, he tries to engage local Mongol tribesmen to attack the Japanese, who respond by bombing the station, leaving Widmark and company alone in the wilderness to fend for themselves. TJ

Destination Moon

(1950, US, 91 min)
d Irving Pichel. *p* George Pal. *sc* Rip Van Ronkel, Robert Heinlein, James O'Hanlon. *ph* Lionel Lindon. *ed* Duke Goldstone. *ad* Ernst Fegté. *m* Leith Stevens. *cast* John Archer, Warner Anderson, Tom Powers, Dick Wesson, Erin O'Brien Moore.
●One of the George Pal-produced series of sci-fi movies from the '50s, this is characteristically thin on plot and characterisation, high on patriotism, and impressive in its colour photography and special effects; a true precursor to *Star Wars*, in fact. A group of scientists defy the familiar bunch of superstitious and unadventurous philistines (politicians, businessmen) and take off in their new rocket to beat the Russians to the moon. GA

Destinées Sentimentales, Les

(2000, Fr, 180 min)
d Olivier Assayas. *p* Bruno Pesery. *sc* Jacques Fieschi, Olivier Assayas. *ph* Eric Gautier. *ed* Luc Barnier. *ad* Katia Wyszkop. *cast* Charles Berling, Emmanuelle Béart, Isabelle Huppert, Olivier Perrier, Dominique Reymond, André Marcon, Alexandra London, Julie Depardieu.

●Assayas' adaptation of Jacques Chardonne's novel – about the heir (Berling) to a devoutly Protestant porcelain dynasty in Charente, and his life-changing encounter in 1900 with the non-conformist niece (Béart) of a family friend – is typically intelligent, elliptical, and beautifully acted. It's also, perhaps a little surprisingly given Assayas' earlier work, a little dull and banal, rounding off its survey of some four decades of personal and societal change with an over-extended, trite conclusion that love is all important, and never quite letting us forget that the protagonist is for the most part a selfish, sanctimonious bore – even his embittered but absurdly faithful ex-wife, immaculately played by Huppert, is more sympathetic. (Is the protagonist's eventual devotion to the ceramic arts an apology for cinematic obsession and craftsmanship on Assayas' part? Who knows? The character's still a bore.) Ambitious, efficient, sensitive, but a little disappointing. GA

Destin Fabuleux de Désirée Clary, Le

(1942, Fr, 112 min, b/w)
d Sacha Guitry. *p* Edouard Harispuru. *sc* Sacha Guitry. *ph* Jean Bachelet. *ed* René Le Hénaff. *ad* Jacques Colombier. *m* Adolphe Borchard. *cast* Gaby Morlay, Geneviève Guitry, Sacha Guitry, Jean-Louis Barrault, Lise Delamare, Yvette Lebon, Jacques Varennes, Aimé Clariond.

●Désirée Clary met Napoleon when he was an obscure general. There was evidently a romance but, in the outcome, Désirée's sister married Napoleon's brother, while she went on to marry the prickly General Bernadotte, ending up years later as Queen of Sweden. The Hollywood melodrama *Désirée*, directed by Henry Koster in 1954 with Brando and Jean Simmons, makes an amusing comparison with this characteristically clever, ironic account. Guitry's prosaic camerawork contrasts with his audacious approach to storytelling: the movie's credits, 50 minutes in, are especially cheeky. Barrault, as the young Napoleon, looks so much like Kenneth Williams, you half expect to spot Sid James slouching around the Tuileries. BBa

Destiny (Al Massir)

(1997, Egypt/Fr, 135 min)
d Youssef Chahine. *p* Humbert Balsan, Gabriel Khoury. *sc* Youssef Chahine, Khaled Youssef. *ph* Mohsen Nasr. *ed* Rachida Abdel-Salam. *pd* Hamed Hemdane. *m* Kamal El-Tawil, Yohia El-Mougy. *cast* Nour El-Cherif, Laila Eloui, Mahmoud Hemeida, Safia El-Amary, Mohamed Mounir.

●Its occasional dramatic longueurs notwithstanding, Chahine's film about the 12th century Moorish philosopher Averroës is a brave, engrossing attack on Islamic fundamentalist dogma and oppression. Averroës and his followers are shown as free-thinking liberals, the Caliph (who ordered his work burnt) a mere political pawn, but secondary to the narrative itself is the glorious, stirring (and generically traditional) use of song and dance – frowned on by the philosopher's enemies – as an energising, liberating force which embodies Chahine's notion that 'thought has wings'. Common sense and sensuality merge in the intelligent script and vibrant, colourful mise en scène to often exhilarating effect. GA

Destiny (Der Müde Tod)

(1921, Ger, 7,566 ft, b/w)
d Fritz Lang. *p* Erich Pommer. *sc* Fritz Lang, Thea Von Harbou. *ph* Erich Nitzschmann, Fritz Arno Wagner, Hermann Saalfrank. *ad* Walter Röhrig, Hermann Warm, Robert Herlth. *m* Peter Schirman. *cast* Bernhard Goetzke, Lil Dagover, Walter Janssen, Rudolph Klein-Rogge, Georg John, Eduard Von Winterstein, Karl Huszar.

●Lang's first major success was inspired by the *Intolerance* device of mixing parallel settings and cultures. Death gives a young girl three chances to save her lover's life, in old Baghdad, in 17th century Venice, and in mythical China. The tone ranges from baroque melodrama to eccentric whimsy, and the plotting is full of digressions and asides, but Lang's design sense and use of architectural space gives the film a basic consistency. And the plentiful special effects still look amazingly inventive. TR

Destiny Turns on the Radio

(1995, US, 102 min)
d Jack Baran. *p* Gloria Zimmerman. *sc* Matthew Stone, Robert Ramsey. *ph* James L Carter. ed Raúl Davalos. pd Jean-Philippe Carp. m Steve Soles. *cast* Dylan McDermott, Nancy Travis, James Belushi, Quentin Tarantino, James LeGros, Allen Garfield.

●This naff comedy-romance has McDermott's escaped con pitch up in Vegas looking for his heist loot and his beloved (Travis). The news is poor. Torch singer Travis is shacked up with Belushi's casino boss, and partner-in-crime LeGros explains his empty pockets with an incredible yarn. Cue a flashback to Tarantino's Johnny Destiny rising like Neptune from the hotel swimming pool, naked amidst thunderbolts and flashing neon light. No wonder he lost consciousness! And there's more. The guy who stole the booty was the same guy who gave McDermott a lift into Vegas. It's sad when deliberately self-mocking films backfire. This whimsical morass is a genuine trip to Palookaville. McDermott is no romantic hero, and the script is a woeful hash of *Bus Stop*, *Repo Man* and the musical sequences of *The Fabulous Baker Boys*. WH

Destroy All Monsters (Kaiju Soshingeki)

(1968, Jap, 89 min)
d Inoshiro Honda. *sc* Kaoru Mabuchi, Inoshiro Honda. *ph* Taiichi Kankura. *ed* Ryohei Fujii. *ad* Takeo Kita. *m* Akira Ifukube. *cast* Akira Kubo, Jun Tazaki, Yoshio Tsuchiya, Kyoko Ai, Yukiko Kobayashi, Kenji Sahara.

●A romping Japanese monster rally, the 20th production in this vein from Toho studios, who have energetically devastated Japan on film virtually every year since 1954. Their output is graphic and witty, with a weird gladiatorial style which has emerged under the guidance of Honda since his first *Godzilla*. In some ways these features are more like sporting events than fantasies, with a radio commentary ('It's Godzilla leading the attack') as the monsters of this world rally to protect it from extraterrestrial invasion.

Destry Rides Again

(1939, US, 94 min, b/w)
d George Marshall. *p* Joe Pasternak. *sc* Felix Jackson, Gertrude Purcell, Henry Myers. *ph* Hal Mohr. *ed* Milton Carruth. *ad* Jack Otterson. *m* Frank Skinner. *songs* Frank Loesser, Frederick Hollander. *cast* James Stewart, Marlene Dietrich, Charles Winninger, Brian Donlevy, Una Merkel, Mischa Auer, Samuel S Hinds, Jack Carson, Billy Gilbert.

●Marvellous comedy Western, with Stewart's pacifist, reputedly wimpy marshal taming the lawless town of Bottleneck by means of words and jokes rather than the gun Donlevy's villain repeatedly provokes him to use. What is remarkable about the film is the way it combines humour, romance, suspense and action so seamlessly (with individual scenes – Dietrich singing 'See What the Boys in the Back Room Will Have', Stewart's delicious parable about a homicidal orphan, Mischa Auer losing his pants – indelibly printed in the memory). Flawless performances, pacy direction and a snappy script place it head and shoulders above virtually any other spoof oater. GA

Desvio al Paraiso (Shortcut to Paradise)

(1994, Sp, 97 min)
d Gerardo Herrero. *p* Gerardo Herrero, Juan Gerard, Letvia Arza-Goderich, Juan Gerard Gonzalez. *sc* Santiago Tabernero, Daniel Monzon. *ph* Alfredo Mayo. *ed* Carmen Frias. *m* José Nieto. *cast* Charles Dance, Assumpta Serna, Morgan Weisser, Katrina Gibson, Louise Strasenburgh, Gladys Rodriguez.

●To a backwoods Puerto Rican apartment complex comes Dance's Quinn, who lies his way into a job as janitor, befriends a tenant's ten-year-old daughter, and becomes murderously heavy with anyone who gets in his way. Much of this is nonsense of the OTT sort, but Herrero certainly gives it a patina of style, and here and there it almost works. Indeed, as a schlocky psycho-thriller, it's not unwatchable, helped out by some decent performances and a nice sense of milieu. Trashy but, for the most part, fun. GA

Détective

(1985, Fr, 98 min)
d Jean-Luc Godard. *p* Alain Sarde. *sc* Jean-Luc Godard, Anne-Marie Miéville. *ph* Bruno Nuytten. *ed* Marilyne Dubreuil. *cast* Nathalie Baye, Claude Brasseur, Johnny Hallyday, Jean-Pierre Léaud, Alain Cuny, Laurent Terzieff.

●The trouble with Godard films is the weight of expectation brought to them: sometimes they're strained and serious (*Passion*), sometimes they're megabores (*Hail Mary*), and sometimes mini-masterpieces like *Détective*. This is a cross between a *Grand Hotel* for the 1980s and *film noir*: a crumbling Paris hotel houses four groups of people whose paths occasionally cross. One is the group around house-detective Terzieff, still trying to solve a murder of years ago; another is the entourage of boxer Tiger Jones, in training under the eye of his manager (Hallyday); another is a couple on the verge of breaking up; and the last is the Mafia. Much of it, especially Léaud (Terzieff's nephew-aide) and Cuny as a Godfather who judges men by their toilet habits, is riotously funny. Built on the charisma of its stars and on memories of the great thrillers of the 40s, tenuously held together by Godard's romantic pessimism, curiosity and sense of humour, it's co-dedicated, sensibly, to Clint Eastwood. TR

Detective, The

(1968, US, 114 min)
d Gordon Douglas. *p* Aaron Rosenberg. *sc* Abby Mann. *ph* Joseph Biroc. ed Robert Simpson. *ad* Jack Martin Smith, William J Creber. *m* Jerry Goldsmith. *ca st* Frank Sinatra, Lee Remick, Jacqueline Bisset, Ralph Meeker, Jack Klugman, Horace McMahon, Lloyd Bochner, Robert Duvall.

●Fairly strong follow-up to the Sinatra/Douglas private eye caper *Tony Rome*, with the former now a New York cop fighting crime and corruption in a determinedly sleazy environment. Well acted and directed, though Abby Mann's script is an uneasy mixture of toughness and preachiness, while the succession of gays and man-hungry women looks badly dated. GA

Detective Story

(1951, US, 103 min, b/w)
d/p William Wyler. *sc* Philip Yordan, Robert Wyler. *ph* Lee Garmes. *ed* Robert Swink. *ad* Hal Pereira, Earl Hedrick. *cast* Kirk Douglas, Eleanor Parker, William Bendix, Horace McMahon, Cathy O'Donnell, George Macready, Joseph Wiseman, Lee Grant.

●Twenty-four hours in the life of a precinct station, just another day during which Douglas' jutting-jawed cop uses sadistic strong-arm tactics on a variety of suspects, discovers that his wife has had dealings with a slimy abortionist, throws a hysterical tantrum or two, and runs accidentally on purpose into a hoodlum's bullet. Underlying it all is a morality about the good man driven over the edge by the evil all around him, not made any less stagy by the way several characters come on as though auditioning for a Method class. It has a certain compulsiveness, but as with *Dead End* (also based on a play by Sidney Kingsley), the main interest lies in the admirable set. TM

Detenuto in Attesa di Giudizio

see Why?

Det Means Girl (Det, Yani Dokhtar)

(1994, Iran, 86 min)
d Abolfazl Jalili. *p* I Alai. *sc* Abolfazl Jalili. *ph* Mehdi Majd-Vaziri. *ed* Abolfazl Jalili. *cast* Hossein Saki. Zeinab Barbandi, Nabi Jalilian, Massomeh Kordi.

●Jalili's fourth completed feature typically deals with the plight of the young (here, a teenager working in a Tehran workers' hostel, struggling to find cash for medical treatment for his mysteriously paralysed little sister) in a style that's at once realistic and impressionistic. The surreal aural collage over the opening credits presages the poetic evocation of the world's myriad sights, sounds, opinions, remedies, etc, while the lucid account of the conflict between ancient and modern, science and superstition, city and country, faith and despair, ensures that this moving story never descends into mawkish melodrama. GA

Detour

(1945, US, 68 min, b/w)
d Edgar G Ulmer. *p* Leon Fromkess. *sc* Martin Goldsmith. *ph* Benjamin Kline. *ed* George McGuire. *ad* Edward C Jewell. *m* Leo Erdody. *cast* Tom Neal, Ann Savage, Claudia Drake, Edmund MacDonald, Tim Ryan, Esther Howard.
●The kind of film (made in six days, almost entirely in a Poverty Row studio, its extensive road scenes shot with back projection) that would be impossible to make today, even as a TV movie. Now it would require 100% locations (the 'art' of studio shooting having been discredited and thus lost), and the minimal narrative would never justify a go-ahead (pianist Neal is bumming from New York to rejoin his girl in California until tripped by hostile fate and the literally amazing femme fatale Savage). Neither pure thriller nor pure melodrama (though it has its true complement of doomed lovers, dead bodies, and a cruel sexual undertow), on an emotional level it most resembles the wonderful purple-pulp fiction of David Goodis. Passion joins with folly to produce termite art *par excellence*. CW

Détour, Le (The Detour)

(2000, Fr, 71 min)
d Pierre Salvadori. *p* Philippe Martin, Gilles Sandoz. *sc* Pierre Salvadori, Nicolas Saada. *ph* Gilles Henry. *ed* Isabelle de Winck. *pd* Yan Arlaud, Sandrine Jarron. *m* Camille Baz Baz. *cast* Robert Castel, Mathieu Demy, Guillaume Depardieu, Serge Riaboukine, Marina Golovine.
●This TV cut of Salvadori's *Les Marchands de Sable* – a tortuous thriller charting a barman and a girl's search for the killer of the latter's brother, set among drug dealers, petty thieves and protection racketeers in modern Paris – benefits from a running time so short the plot turns skeletal and feels like quasi-abstract play with genre tropes. No depth of meaning or characterisation, but the script avoids modishness while delivering plenty of surprises, ironic twists and pleasurable moments. GA

Detroit Rock City

(1999, US, 95 min)
d Adam Rifkin. *p* Gene Simmons, Barry Levine, Kathleen Haase. *sc* Carl V Dupré. *ph* John R Leonetti. *ed* Mark Goldblatt. *pd* Steve Hardie. *m* J Peter Robinson. *cast* Edward Furlong, Giuseppe Andrews, James DeBello, Sam Huntington, Kiss, Melanie Lynskey, Nick Scotti, Shannon Tweed.
●It's 1978 and middle America is split in twain by disco fever and Kiss mania. Furlong (the cool one), Andrews (big lug), DeBello (resident pothead), and Huntington (shy boy) knock out painful Kiss covers in the garage and throb with excitement over their tickets for their heroes' forthcoming gig in Chicago. Until, that is, Huntington's godfearing parent consigns said priceless items to the flames. The day looks lost until they win four top seats in a radio competition. Given that it's a comedy aimed at adolescent males of all ages, we get gags involving drugged pizza and volcanic vomiting. Thankfully, though, the movie never relies on the big gross out, opting instead for an *American Graffiti*-style rites of passage, in which our callow youths learn about love, sex and how not to pass for a roadie. This is a bit undercooked, though enjoyable none the less, stretching to give each of its central quartet enough to do, but never patronising their cause. Only when Kiss themselves pop up in the final reel does the heart sink, but they're put through their paces briskly enough. TJ

Deuce Bigalow: Male Gigolo

(1999, US, 88 min)
d Mike Mitchell. *p* Sid Ganis, Barry Bernardi. *sc* Harris Goldberg, Rob Schneider. *ph* Peter Lyons Collister. *ed* George Bowers, Lawrence Jordan. *pd* Alan Au. *m* Teddy Castellucci. *cast* Rob Schneider, William Forsythe, Eddie Griffin, Arija Bareikis, Oded Fehr, Gail O'Grady, Richard Riehle, Jacqueline Obradors.
●If you're a fan of heaving breasts, dick jokes and scatology, you've won the lottery. When gigolo Antonio goes out of town he entrusts Deuce Bigalow (Schneider), a goofy, out-of-work aquarium cleaner, with his $6,000 state-of-the-art aquarium and Malibu pad. But the tank gets smashed, leaving Deuce in urgent need of fast cash. Enter TJ, Antonio's pimp, who reckons Deuce could be a high-earning 'man-whore' too. A little strategic waxing, a dodgy perm, and he's all ready for the laydees. Proving a hit, he's soon raking it in. He didn't reckon on falling in love though. First-timer Mike Mitchell directs, but this has Adam Sandler's production stamped all over it. He's clearly still trapped in the mind of a 13-year-old boy. Spectacularly crass. KW

Deus, Patria e Autoridade (God, Fatherland and Authority)

(1976, Port, 120 min)
d Rui Simoes.
●For this documentary about Portugal's political explosion, Simoes had access to the archives of Portuguese TV, but he has cut the material together in a very different way from its original presentation (most of the archive footage predates the April 1974 coup). In addition, he includes filmed interviews with workers about their conditions, and with others about their own and the Portuguese colonies' part in the downfall of the Caetano regime. The film is less a history than a statement about class realities, and how political power in Lisbon never left the hands of the bourgeoisie.

Deutsche Kettensagenmassaker, Das

see German Chainsaw Massacre, The

Deutschland, Erwache! (Germany, Awake!)

(1966, WGer, 90 min, b/w)
d/p/sc Erwin Leiser. *ed* René Martinet.
●A look at the propaganda content of entertainment films in the Third Reich. Leiser keeps his commentary brief, letting the extracts, plus his arrangement of them, speak for themselves. He identifies a number of themes: Dying for Germany, The Hitler Prototype and No Entitlement to Life (anti-Semitic stories) are some of the labels he uses. The common fantasy though is of noble Us being oppressed by malignant Them. And the appeal – belonging, shared victimhood, the promise of revenge under the great leader – is consistent and chilling. Leiser has done a service by marshalling this stuff so the rest of us don't have to sit through the whole of *Hitlerjunge Quex* (1935), *Jud Süss* ('40) or *Stukas* ('41), with its Luftwaffe pilots harmonising lustily and patriotically as they head for London. BBa

Deux Anglaises et le Continent, Les (Anne and Muriel/Two English Girls)

(1971, Fr, 132 min)
d François Truffaut. *sc* Jean Gruault, François Truffaut. *ph* Nestor Almendros. *ed* Yann Dedet. *ad* Michel de Broin. *m* Georges Delerue. *cast* Jean-Pierre Léaud, Kika Markham, Stacy Tendeter, Sylvia Marriott, Philippe Léotard.
●One of Truffaut's most tantalising romances, a discreet *ménage à trois* involving a French writer of the *belle époque* and two sisters living on the romantic Welsh coast. It's a tale of art born from emotional sacrifice as – all in love with one another and reluctant to cause hurt – the three withdraw from any final conflict or consummation of their feelings. As such, it's as much about what doesn't happen as about what does, and the form employed by Truffaut and Henri Pierre Roché's source novel (he also wrote *Jules et Jim*) – a literary narration – is thus entirely appropriate to the film's detached, gently nostalgic mood. Concerned not so much with feelings as with feelings about feelings, the film is simultaneously introspective and passionate, a perfect complement to the artistic era it portrays. Originally released in both Britain and America in a cut version. GA

Deux Hommes dans Manhattan

(1958, Fr, 84 min, b/w)
d/p/sc Jean-Pierre Melville. *ph* Nicolas Hayer. *ed* Monique Bonnot. *ad* Daniel Guéret. *m* Martial Solal, Christian Chevallier. *cast* Pierre Grasset, Jean-Pierre Melville, Christiane Eudès, Ginger Hall, Monique Hennessy, Jean Darcante, Jerry Mengo.
●If *Bob le Flambeur* was Melville's love letter to Paris, *Deux Hommes* is his billet-doux to New York. The chief pleasure from this fast, laconic movie is in the appearance of Melville himself, playing one of two journalists who are sent to Manhattan to trace the French UN delegate, only to discover that he died in his mistress' arms, thus creating possible scandal. The New York scenes were shot on the run, and mainly consist of Melville racing from a cab and into the entrances of famous buildings, which are then matched with suspiciously Parisian-looking interiors. A well-sustained, cheeky joke, full of life and a love for all things American, indispensable for an overview of the man. CPea

Deuxième Souffle, Le (Second Breath)

(1966, Fr, 150 min, b/w)
d Jean-Pierre Melville. *p* Charles Lumbroso, André Labay. *sc* Jean-Pierre Melville. *ph* Marcel Combes. *ed* Michel Boehm. *ad* Jean-Jacques Fabre. *m* Bernard Gérard. *cast* Lino Ventura, Paul Meurisse, Raymond Pellegrin, Christina Fabrega, Pierre Zimmer, Michel Constantin, Denis Manuel.
●Made after three years 'in the wilderness' for Melville, this is his most elaborate and intricately plotted *film noir*, a labyrinthine exploration of loyalties and betrayals in the French underworld. It centres on an ageing gangster (Ventura at his most gnarled), in hiding after escaping from jail, who involves himself in a daring highway robbery while waiting to be smuggled out of the country. The steely location photography gives the action a veneer of realism, but the film's real energies are subterranean, and suffused with Melville's typical poetry: the bizarre interdependence of cop and criminal here is seen with the same eyes as the passionate love/hate of the brother and sister in *Les Enfants Terribles*. TR

Deux ou Trois Choses que Je Sais d'Elle (Two or Three Things I Know About Her)

(1966, Fr, 95 min)
d Jean-Luc Godard. *p* Philippe Senné. *sc* Jean-Luc Godard. *ph* Raoul Coutard. *ed* Françoise Collin, Chantal Delattre. *m* Ludwig van Beethoven. *cast* Marina Vlady, Anny Duperey, Roger Montsoret, Jean Narboni, Christophe Bourseiller, Marie Bourseiller, Raoul Lévy.
●Despite some time-bound concerns and irritating conceits, the sheer energy of Godard's dazzling sociological fable is enough to commend it. Paris and prostitution, seen through 24 hours in the life of a housewife-prostitute (Vlady), tell a story of selling yourself to buy happiness, but getting paid in bad dreams. A fictional documentary of *Alphaville*'s nightmare, its virtuoso display of confession and analysis, the sublime and ridiculous, show Godard's deft grasp of the subversive nature of laughter and passions. Too good to miss. DMacp

Deveeri

(1999, Ind, 100 min)
d Kavitha Lankesh. *p* Bharathi Gowda, Arathi Gadasalli, Hanumanth Reddy, Kavitha Lankesh. *sc* Kavitha Lankesh. *ph* S Ramachandra. *ed* MN Swamy. *pd* Shashidar Adapa. *m* Isaac Thomas, Kotakapally. *cast* Manja, Nandita Das, Bhavana, Bhavana, Kashi, B Jaishree, Asif Farooqi.
●Adapted from a novel by P Lankesh, in the Kannada dialect, this first feature is an arresting, lower depths portrait of the Bangalore slums during elections for the provincial governor. It follows 12-year-old Kyatha (Manja), a lively lad, who skips school, runs errands and lives in a government 'sponsored' shack under the watchful eye of older sister Deveeri (Das) whose innocence he comes to suspect (she says she 'carries bricks by night', but is in fact a prostitute). Fine location work and rich colour tones, with a non-strident, unsentimental but passionate take on the material, add up to a powerful condemnation of 'socialist' hypocrisy, corruption and male domination, tempered only by writer/director Lankesh's uncertain control of dramatics. Essentially, though, she builds immense sympathy for her young protagonist. WH

Devi (The Goddess)

(1960, India, 93 min, b/w)
d/p/sc Satyajit Ray. *ph* Subrata Mitra. *ed* Dulal Dutta. *ad* Bansi Chandragupta. *m* Ali Akbar Khan. *cast* Chabi Biswas, Sharmila Tagore, Soumitra Chatterjee, Karuna Bannejee.

●Less obviously a work of humanist realism than the Apu trilogy, Ray's film is nevertheless a carefully nuanced study in religious obsession, with Biswas convinced that his daughter-in-law (Tagore) is in fact the goddess Kali reincarnated. Comparatively baroque and melodramatic in terms of its images and story, it manages to mount a lucid, finally very moving argument against the destructive nature of fanaticism and superstition, with Tagore gradually losing all sense of her own individuality. Without a doubt, it is impressive film making; but whether its very Indian concerns are of widespread interest remains a moot point. GA.

Devil and Daniel Webster, The

see All That Money Can Buy

Devil and Max Devlin, The

(1981, US, 95 min)
d Steven Hilliard Stern. *p* Jerome Courtland. *sc* Mary Rodgers. *ph* Howard Schwartz. *ed* Ramond A deLeuw. *ad* John B Mansbridge, Leon Harris. *m* Buddy Baker. *cast* Elliott Gould, Bill Cosby, Susan Anspach, Adam Rich, Julie Budd, David Knell.

●This inspiring story of how an out-and-out slob makes a pact with the Devil but is finally converted to the Disney organisation would make better entertainment if the studio hadn't thrown so many disparate elements together in an attempt to grab their audience. We get one played out anti-hero, one winsome child actor, one Streisand clone who keeps belting out the same song, one wry black comic; the wonder is that there's no cute dolphin chortling in the swimming-pool. The script has its moments, especially when Cosby is around as the Devil's aide, but the film finally subsides in a welter of structural flaws and heartwarming sentiment. GB

Devil and Miss Jones, The

(1941, US, 92 min, b/w)
d Sam Wood. *p* Frank Ross. *sc* Norman Krasna. *ph* Harry Stradling. *ed* Sherman Todd. *pd* William Cameron Menzies. *m* Roy Webb. *cast* Jean Arthur, Robert Cummings, Charles Coburn, Edmund Gwenn, Spring Byington, SZ Sakall, William Demarest.

●A pleasant enough script by Norman Krasna lends sparkle to a Capra-corn style comedy about a cantankerous department store tycoon seeing the light when, in an attempt to put down a labour dispute, he disguises himself as a worker. Coburn is fine as the converted boss, Arthur is her usual professional self as the committed shopgirl with a heart of gold, but Cummings' wooden performance and Wood's stolid direction are something of a let-down. GA

Devil at 4 O'Clock, The

(1961, US, 126 min)
d Mervyn LeRoy. *p* Fred Kohlmar. *sc* Liam O'Brien. *ph* Joseph Biroc. *ed* Charles Nelson. *ad* John Beckman. *m* George Duning. *cast* Spencer Tracy, Frank Sinatra, Jean-Pierre Aumont, Kerwin Mathews, Barbara Luna, Grégoire Aslan, Alexander Scourby.

●Spencer Tracy plays Ingrid Bergman in this hideous Polynesian variation on *The Inn of the Sixth Happiness*. He is a drunken and soul-searching missionary on an island about to be fire and brimstoned by a volcano, and can't save the leper children on his own. Enter three escaped convicts whose souls need saving. Everyone goes toheaven. ATu

Devil Commands, The

(1941, US, 65 min, b/w)
d Edward Dmytryk. *sc* Robert Hardy Andrews, ML Gunzburg. *ph* Allen Siegler. *ed* Al Clark. *ad* Lionel Banks. *m* MW Stoloff. *cast* Boris Karloff, Richard Fiske, Anne Revere, Amanda Duff, Ralph Penney, Dorothy Adams.

●Boris Karloff, at the time in the middle of a mad scientist rut that threatened to bog him down completely, is here attempting to contact his dead wife with weird machinery (involving Frankensteinian electricity, metallic space suits and hijacked bodies) and predictably disastrous results. Basically, it's a thick-ear version of a fine novel by William Sloane (*The Edge of Running Water*), but Karloff's performance is as reliable as ever, and Dmytryk injects what style he can on the budget, notably an atmospheric opening sequence more than reminiscent of the beginning of *Rebecca*. TM

Devil-Doll, The

(1936, US, 79 min, b/w)
d Tod Browning. *sc* Garrett Fort, Guy Endore, Erich von Stroheim. *ph* Leonard Smith. *ed* Frederick Y Smith. *ad* Cedric Gibbons. *m* Franz Waxman. *cast* Lionel Barrymore, Maureen O'Sullivan, Frank Lawton, Robert Greig, Lucy Beaumont, Henry B Walthall, Rafaela Ottiano.

●Anticipating *Dr Cyclops* and *The Incredible Shrinking Man* in its miniaturisation effects, this was co-scripted by Erich von Stroheim from an excellent novel, *Burn Witch Burn!*, by A Merritt. Barrymore is an escaped convict who masquerades as the proprietress of a toy shop. The dolls he sells are actually real people reduced in size; and much of the film shows them – charmingly and only occasionally disturbingly – coping with giant furniture, evading their schoolgirl owners, and carrying out Barrymore's murderous revenge on those who sent him to Devil's Island. Browning had made *Freaks* at MGM, much to Mayer's disgust, and in working out his contract he had to lighten his uniquely dark vision, though the scene of a doll climbing out of a Christmas tree is effectively chilling. ATu

Devil in a Blue Dress

(1995, US, 101 min)
d Carl Franklin. *p* Gary Goetzman, Jesse Beaton. *sc* Carl Franklin. *ph* Tak Fujimoto. *ed* Carole Kravetz. *pd* Gary Frutkoff. *m* Elmer Bernstein. *cast* Denzel Washington, Tom Sizemore, Jennifer Beals, Don Cheadle, Maury Chaykin, Lisa Nicole Carson, Terry Kinney, Mel Winkler.

●Recently fired and desperate to keep up the payments on his beloved home, WWII veteran Easy Rawlins (Washington) is offered a job by the shady Dewitt Albright (Sizemore): to discover the whereabouts of one Daphne Monet (Beals), a politician's fiancée scandalously rumoured to hang out in black bars. Assured that there's nothing illegal involved, Easy accepts. Pretty soon, however, he finds himself suspected of murdering a friend's girl (Carson) and under threat from both the cops and Albright's thuggish henchmen. Reluctantly, he puts in a call to Mouse (Cheadle), an old friend from his native Texas – reluctantly, because while Mouse has guts and loyalty to spare, he's also a volatile psychopath. Franklin's follow-up to *One False Move* is an impressively complex, polished and intelligent adaptation of Walter Mosley's thriller. It not only shows us an immaculately recreated world hitherto ignored by the movies (the black neighbourhoods of late '40s LA), but locates race, alongside more familiar elements like money and power, as a central motivating force for the various characters' actions. Mercifully, however, Franklin never preaches but allows the racial theme to emerge naturally from story and situation. Everything – the performances, Tak Fujimoto's elegant camerawork, the jazz and blues soundtrack, the snappy script – slots neatly into his overall design. Sheer pleasure. GA

Devil in Miss Jones, The

(1973, US, 67 min)
d/p/sc Gerard Damiano. *ph* Harry Flecks. *ed* Gerard Damiano. *m* Alden Shuman. *cast* Georgina Spelvin, Harry Reems, John Clemens, Marc Stevens, Rick Livermore, Albert Gork [Gerard Damiano].

●The late Justine Jones (Spelvin, non-glamorous, the most striking presence in hardcore) finds herself facing eternal damnation for slitting her wrist and negotiates a stay of execution so that she can sample all the lusts she never indulged in while alive. The episodes she goes through are standard for hardcore of the period (a lesson in blowjobbing from the hirsute Harry Reems, lesbian massage, masturbation games and assorted threesomes), but the pay-off is straight outta Sartre's *Huis Clos*: she's locked in a cell with a helpless paranoid who refuses to gratify her – played by Damiano himself under the name 'Albert Gork'. The film's modest ambitions once seemed phenomenal for the genre, but the only elements of lasting interest are Spelvin's performance and the climactic 'sandwich' scene, in which Miss Jones enquires of the two men taking her whether they can feel their cocks rubbing together inside her. TR

Devil in Miss Jones Part II, The

(1982, US, 84 min)
d Henri Pachard. *p* James Bochis. *sc* Ellie Howard, Henri Pachard. *ph* Larry Revene. *ed* Ted Ryan. *ad* Eddie Heath. *m* Barry Levitt. *cast* Georgina Spelvin, Jack Wrangler, Jacqueline Lorians, Joanna Storm, Anna Ventura, Samantha Fox.

●Spelvin lends her name and, briefly, her presence to this ten-years-on sequel. She's still in porno hell, but clearly getting a little too mature for comfort so far as the producers are concerned. Their solution is a plot whereby Miss J's lustful soul is sent back to earth and shuffled through a selection of nubile starlets: cue standard (softcore on this occasion) action. Hell's preferable, at least for the viewer, who's allowed to glimpse Cleopatra coming on strong with Marie-Antoinette. BBa

Devil in the Flesh

see Diable au corps, Le

Devil in the Flesh

see Diavolo in Corpo, Il

Devil Is a Woman, The

(1935, US, 83 min, b/w)
d Josef von Sternberg. *p* Adolph Zukor. *sc* John Dos Passos. *ph* Josef von Sternberg. *ed* Sam Winston. *ad* Hans Dreier. *m* Rimsky-Korsakoff. *cast* Marlene Dietrich, Lionel Atwill, Cesar Romero, Edward Everett Horton, Alison Skipworth.

●Sternberg's final film with Dietrich, as precisely aimed as a whiplash to the coccyx. Marlene is Concha Perez, cigarette factory girl, sailing serenely through a comic-opera Spain in a steely, deeply-felt analysis of male masochism. Sternberg adapts the same Pierre Louys novel as Buñuel did for *That Obscure Object of Desire*, but he does it from the inside, centreing on the experience of two men (a young revolutionary and an older military man) who love Marlene and compulsively submit to the agonies of being rejected by her. Even those who go only for the Dietrich glamour can't miss these underlying tensions, since the stoic acceptance of emotional pain undermines all the surface frivolity. Some will find the glittering cruelty sublime. Unique now, as it was then. TR

Devil Never Sleeps, The

see Satan Never Sleeps

Devil, Probably, The

see Diable Probablement, Le

Devil Rides Out, The (aka The Devil's Bride)

(1967, GB, 95 min)
d Terence Fisher. *p* Anthony Nelson Keys. *sc* Richard Matheson. *ph* Arthur Grant. *ed* Spencer Reeve. *ad* Bernard Robinson. *m* James Bernard. *cast* Christopher Lee, Charles Gray, Nike Arrighi, Leon Greene, Patrick Mower, Gwen Ffrangcon-Davies, Sarah Lawson, Paul Eddington.

●Over the years, this film's reputation has grown enormously, and its cult status must be as high as any horror movie. Richard Matheson, who scripted it, was able to improve immeasurably on Dennis Wheatley's ponderous novel, and it is consequently the best film that Fisher and Hammer ever made, an almost perfect example of the kind of thing that can happen when melodrama is achieved so completely and so imaginatively that it ceases to be melodrama at all and becomes a full-scale allegorical vision. Christopher Lee has never been better than as the grim opponent of Satanism, and the night in the pentacle during which the forces of evil mobilise an epic series of cinematic temptations rediscovers aspects of mythology which the cinema had completely overlooked. DP

Devils, The

(1971, GB, 111 min)
d Ken Russell. *p* Robert H Solo, Ken Russell. *sc* Ken Russell. *ph* David Watkin. *ed* Michael Bradsell. *ad* Robert Cartwright. *m* Peter Maxwell-Davies. *cast* Oliver Reed, Vanessa Redgrave, Dudley Sutton, Max Adrian, Gemma Jones, Murray Melvin, Georgina Hale.

●Russell's overwrought adaptation of John Whiting's play and Aldous Huxley's book *The Devils of Loudun*, full of much spiritual and physical writhing, is best approached as a diabolical comedy. No matter how thickly Russell piles on the masturbating nuns, tortured priests and dissolute dauphins, there's no getting round the fact that it's all more redolent of a camp revue than a cathartic vision. Derek Jarman's sets, however, still look terrific. TR

Devil's Accordion, The (El Acordéon del Diablo)

(2000, Switz/Ger, 90 min)
d Stefan Schwietert. *p* Thomas Kufus. *sc* Stefan Schwietert. *ph* Ciro Capellari. *ed* Tania Stöcklin. *with* Francisco 'Pacho' Rada, Alfredo Gutierrez, Manuel Rada Oviedo, Rafael Valencia, Israel Romero, José 'Morre' Romero, Antonio Jaramillo, 'El Perro Negro', José Villadiego Ospino, 'Mambo', Petrona Martinez.

●Slick documentary about the (then) 92-year-old Colombian accordionist, singer and songwriter Pacho Rada. He not only invented the musical style *son*, he also purportedly survived a legendary encounter with Satan himself. The latter claim points both to a (justifiable) sense of pride and self-satisfaction in the old man, and to the odd mix of Christianity and pagan superstition in Colombian village life. But having touched on this cultural factor, the film largely ignores it. Ditto its treatment of Colombia's drug barons. Mainly the film shows elderly men playing, singing and smiling at each other while others listen and dance; many clumsily staged scenes (forlornly meant to evoke 'actuality') suggest the European film-makers, maybe hoping to emulate the success of *Buena Vista Social Club*, are resorting to 'we're poor but happy 'cos we got rhythm' stereotypes. GA

Devil's Advocate, The (Des Teufels Advokat)

(1977, WGer, 109 min)
d Guy Green. *p* Helmut Jedele. *sc* Morris West. *ph* Billy Williams. *ed* Stefan Arnsten. *pd* Rolf Zehetbauer. *m* Bert Grund. *cast* John Mills, Stéphane Audran, Jason Miller, Paola Pitagora, Daniel Massey, Leigh Lawson, Timothy West, Patrick Mower.

●Spiritual torment is written all over this excruciating adaptation of Morris West's best-selling tale of betrayal and redemption, with Mills as the monsignor investigating a dubious case for canonisation, and having a torrid time (quite apart from dying of cancer) as he uncovers evidence of a murky story. Filmed in English, peopled entirely by caricatures, risibly righteous in its attitude to homosexuality, the film rivals *The Hiding Place* as an example of misplaced religiosity. JPy

Devil's Advocate, The

(1997, US, 144 min)
d Taylor Hackford. *p* Arnon Milchan, Arnold Kopelson, Anne Kopelson. *sc* Jonathan Lemkin, Tony Gilroy. *ph* Andrzej Bartkowiak. *ed* Mark Warner. *pd* Bruno Rubeo. *m* James Newton Howard. *cast* Keanu Reeves, Al Pacino, Charlize Theron, Jeffrey Jones, Judith Ivey, Craig T Nelson, Connie Nielsen, Tamara Tunie, Delroy Lindo.

●In this enjoyably daft legal thriller, fromde a novel by Andrew Neiderman, Reeves is a small time Florida defense attorney corrupted by ambition, greed and vanity. At one point, Al Pacino, impressive head of the multinational law firm that's lured him to New York with promises of fame and fortune, takes Reeves to the top of a high building, and promises to make him lord of all he surveys. But what does it profit a man to gain the whole world, if he loses his sexy girlfriend (Theron) and quaint, church-going mother? As the epitome of charismatic evil, Pacino is perversely attractive, his seductive performance making Reeves' temptation all the more believable. For his part, Keanu never quite convinces that he has the brain power necessary for exacting legal work. Tongue planted gently in his cheek, director Hackford makes his anti-materialist points without ever taking things too seriously. Regrettably, an overblown finale and redundant trick ending undercut the mild subversiveness of what's gone before. NF

Devil's Backbone, The (El Espinazo del Diablo)

(2001, Sp/Mex, 108 min)
d Guillermo del Toro. *p* Augustín Almodóvar, Bertha Navarro. *sc* Guillermo del Toro, Antonio Trashorras, David Muñoz. *ph* Guillermo Navarro. *ed* Luis De La Madrid. *ad* César Macarrón. *m* Javier Navarrete. *cast* Marisa Paredes, Eduardo Noriega, Federico Luppi, Fernando Tielve, Iñigo Garcés, Irene Visedo, Berta Ojea.

●A classy Hispanic horror pic written and directed by the Mexican cinephile who made *Cronos* and *Mimic*. Like many Spanish movies about the Civil War, it filters that traumatic conflict through the partly comprehending eyes of a child. After his Republican father dies in battle, 10-year-old Carlos (Tielve) is left in a desert orphanage, where crippled widow Carmen (Paredes) and kindly Professor Casares (Luppi) hope to protect their charges from advancing Fascists. But danger exists inside the fragile sanctuary, too – not only does Carlos clash with older bully Jaime, but there's surly, self-serving janitor Jacinto (Noriega) to worry about, not to mention chilling rumours about a kid who went missing. If only for its technical aspects, this would rate as a pleasurably superior supernatural psychological thriller, with polished but subtle special effects, painterly, atmospheric cinematography and vivid performances from a top-notch cast. What lifts it, however, is an adept use of generic elements as a poetic/metaphorical gloss on political and historical realities. Hence a ghost mystery becomes a tale of opposing forces building to a deadly, explosive denouement in which concealed passions finally burst forth. GA

Devil's Brigade, The

(1968, US, 130 min)
d Andrew V McLaglen. *p* David L Wolper. *sc* William Roberts. *ph* William Clothier. *ed* William Cartwright. *ad* Alfred Sweeney Jr. *m* Alex North. *cast* William Holden, Cliff Robertson, Vince Edwards, Andrew Prine, Claude Akins, Carroll O'Connor, Richard Jaeckel, Jack Watson, Harry Carey, Dana Andrews, Michael Rennie, Patric Knowles.

●Apparently based on fact, this emerges as a pretty slavish reprise of Aldrich's *The Dirty Dozen*. This time round, Holden is the unconventional officer assigned the task of knocking a bunch of thugs and misfits into shape for a special do-or-die mission. Appealing to their pride by pitting them against a crack Canadian regiment, he naturally succeeds. Thereafter, while not behaving impeccably on the battlefield, they sing 'For He's a Jolly Good Fellow' and hold birthday celebrations for the man who showed them the path to glory. The characterisations are strictly cardboard and the direction sluggish. TM

Devils, Devils (Diably, Diably)

(1991, Pol, 86 min)
d/sc Dorota Kedzierzawska. *ph* Zdzislaw Najda. *ed* Wanda Zeman. *ad* Wojciech Jaworski. *m* Magdalena Sliwa. *cast* Justyna Ciemny, Pawel Chwedoruk, Grzegorz Karabin.

●This is rather like everyone's idea of the Polish art film – slow-moving, shadow-laden, practically silent, and packed with significant close-ups and baleful looks. There's not much narrative either: gypsies come to a gloom-laden small town and small-minded souls rail at their alien ways, while a young girl finds the presence of the Other curiously in synch with her (you guessed it) burgeoning sexuality. At times soporific in its drowsy pace, it's nevertheless strangely seductive, not least for its tendency to dissolve into formalism. The occasional gypsies' knees-ups seem to have wandered in from another film entirely, but overall this is a curious, extremely atmospheric exercise. JRo

¡Devils Don't Dream! Research on Jacobo Arbenz Guzmán (¡Devils don't dream! Nachforschungen über Jacobo Arbenz Guzmán)

(1995, Switz, 80 min)
d Andreas Hoessli. *p* Isabella Huser. *sc* Andreas Hoessli. *ph* Matthias Kälin. *ed* Fee Lichti. *with* Maria Vilanova de Arbenz, Howard E Hunt, Pio Quinto Hernandez, Richard Nixon, Winston Churchill.

●Documentary on the '40 years of war' that have troubled and haunted Guatemala since the US-executed coup against the liberal regime of Jacobo Arbenz Guzmán – a young army officer who himself led a coup against the prevailing right-wing dictatorship and, on being elected president, instituted a programme of progressive reforms. The absence of witnesses willing to talk (with the exception of Arbenz's widow) betokens the climate of fear that still obtains in Guatemala, and also limits the scope of the documentary. On the other hand, writer/director Hoessli has located much footage long thought lost in the private archives of a contemporary news cameraman. CIA-man Howard Hunt, chief of propaganda and political action in 1954, gives first-hand testimony of the arrogance of the US towards this one-time 'banana republic'. WH

Devil's Doorway

(1950, US, 84 min, b/w)
d Anthony Mann. *p* Nicholas Nayfack. *sc* Guy Trosper. *ph* John Alton. *ed* Conrad A Nervig. *ad* Cedric Gibbons, Leonard Vasian. *m* Daniele Amfitheatrof. *cast* Robert Taylor, Louis Calhern, Paula Raymond, Marshall Thompson, Edgar Buchanan.

●Actually made before *Broken Arrow*, but held up by a nervous MGM so that the Delmer Daves film reaped all the kudos for spearheading the pro-Indian cycle of Westerns. Taylor is the Indian who, having fought for the North in the war between the states, returns to his homelands only to find that the war against racism has still not been won. Mann's first Western, which he shoots as if it were a *film noir* and makes into a tough, bleak and cynical tragedy. CW

Devil's Envoys, The

see Visiteurs du Soir, Les

Devil's Eye, The (Djävulens Öga)

(1960, Swe, 90 min, b/w)
d Ingmar Bergman. *p* Allan Ekelund. *sc* Ingmar Bergman. *ph* Gunnar Fischer. *ed* Oscar Rosander. *ad* PA Lundgren. *m* Domenico Scarlatti. *cast* Jarl Kulle, Bibi Andersson, Nils Poppe, Sture Lagerwall, Stig Järrel, Gunnar Björnstrand.

●Bergman's first earnest attempt to grapple with the question of theatricality in cinema. It retells the key incidents in the life of Don Juan, but its account of the seducer's shallow bravado and inner angst and his final despatch to hell is like Fellini's *Casanova* to the power of ten: a 'comedy' from which the laughs have all been drained. It's mounted as an overtly theatrical performance throughout: the episodes are introduced by Bergman veteran Björnstrand, who lectures the audience on what they're seeing and instructs them to view it as comedy. The episodes themselves are highly stylised, with (non-musical) hints of *Don Giovanni* foreshadowing Bergman's declared passion for Mozart opera. The dominant impression, though, as in so many early Bergman movies, is of a deep pessimism that is imposed rather than felt as necessary or productive. TR

Devil's Island

(1939, US, 62 min, b/w)
d William Clemens. *sc* Kenneth Gamet, Don Ryan. *ph* George Barnes. *ed* Frank Magee. *ad* Max Parker. *cast* Boris Karloff, Nedda Harrigan, James Stephenson, Adia Kuznetzoff, Will Stanton, Robert Warwick.

●B movie variation on *The Prisoner of Shark Island*, with Karloff as a French doctor sentenced to ten years on Devil's Island after tending an escaped prisoner convicted of treason. The predictable exposé of barbaric conditions is leavened by some nice touches (a mini-guillotine used for clipping cigars by Stephenson's corrupt governor), but falls apart latterly in a flurry of sentimental contrivance: Karloff performs delicate brain operation on governor's injured child; grateful mother helps him escape with evidence of governor's evildoings; he's recaptured, but saved from guillotine by arrival of *deus-ex-machina*. Karloff's sobering presence (he's excellent throughout) keeps it watchable. TM

Devil's Island (Djöflaeyjan)

(1996, Ice/Nor/Ger/Den, 103 min)
d Fridrik Thór Fridriksson. *p* Fridrik Thór

Fridriksson, Egil Ödegård, Peter Rommel. *sc* Einar Karason. *ph* Ari R Kristinsson. *ed* Steingrímur Karlsson, Skule Eriksen. *pd* Arni Páll Johansson. *m* Hilmar Orn Hilmarsson. *cast* Baltasar Kormákur, Gísli Halldórsson, Sigurveig Jónsdóttir, Halldóra Geirhardsdóttir, Sveinn Geirsson, Gudmundur Olafsson.
● A decade after WWII, the Americans abandon Camp Thule, Iceland – bestowing makeshift homes on the slum dwellers of Reykjavik. Gógó departs with them, but leaves behind her three grown kids – Baddi, Danni and Dolli, who live with their grandparents, Tommi (Halldórsson) and Karolína (Jónsdóttir). At first glance, Fridriksson's charmer looks studiedly eccentric. There's something cartoonish about the motley bunch of ne'er-do-wells. They may be out of it, but they're not immune to the world, in fact they're peculiarly vulnerable to change. Baddi (a stellar performance from Kormákur) visits his mother in the States, and comes back a rock'n'roll hound dog who rules the roost with his Cadillac, hep talk and cocksure moves. It's soon obvious there's nothing for him in Iceland any more. This is a bright, tangy, highly engaging account of the old world trying to get to grips with the new. The incidental structure gives the extended cast plenty of room to make their mark, and despite the sometimes harrowing circumstances, Fridriksson always keeps the energy up. TCh

Devils on the Doorstep (Guizi Lai-le)

(2000, China, 162 min, b/w)
d Jiang Wen. *p* Jiang Wen, Dong Ping, Zheng Quangang. *sc* You Fengwei, Shi Jianquan, Shu Ping, Jiang Wen. *ph* Gu Changwei. *ed* Zhang Yifan, Folmer Weisinger. *pd* Tang Shiyun. *m* Cui Jian, Liu Xing, Li Haiying. *cast* Jiang Wen, Jiang Hongbo, Teruyuki Kagawa, Yuan Ding, Chen Qiang, Cong Zhijun.
● Jiang's second film as director echoes the structure of *Red Sorghum*, the film which launched him as a star: a broadly comic story of peasant cowardice, heroism and rivalry is abruptly curtailed by a Japanese army massacre. *Devils*, though, adds a smart, sardonic coda. Set in 1944/45, on the eve of Japan's defeat, it centres on a North China villager (Jiang) who is dismayed to have foisted on him two prisoners: a Japanese soldier and a Chinese collaborator. The resistance never turns up to reclaim them and he eventually hits on the idea of ransoming them back to the local Japanese garrison. Framed as a gallery of human weaknesses, the film darkens its tone to suggest that fear and paranoia can make *anyone* capable of being a 'devil'. This sprawling version won a major prize in Cannes; a shorter export cut is promised. TR

Devil's Own, The

(1997, US, 111 min)
d Alan J Pakula. *p* Lawrence Gordon, Robert F Colesberry. *sc* David Aaron Cohen, Vincent Patrick, Kevin Jarre. *ph* Gordon Willis. *ed* Tom Rolf, Dennis Virkler. *pd* Jane Musky. *m* James Horner. *cast* Harrison Ford, Brad Pitt, Margaret Colin, Rubén Blades, Treat Williams, George Hearn, Mitchell Ryan, Natascha McElhone.
● A Hollywood blockbuster in which Northern Ireland comes over as the usual assemblage of gentle natives, scheming Brits, down-home knitwear, and gunfire stilling the plaintive sound of the uileann pipes. His fisherman dad a victim of the 'security forces', IRA man Pitt takes the battle to the sanctuary of the US, where he plots a missile shipment from a safe house set up by republican sympathisers. His unwitting host, decent Irish-American cop Ford, is kind enough to offer shelter to the young man from a troubled homeland, but as the visitor settles in, an ominous shadow is already looming over his Transatlantic sojourn. The tension between the dedicated terrorist and the family nest that might yet redeem him proves the piece's strongest dramatic suit, buoyed by Ford's believable performance as the hard-pressed NYPD man trying to do the decent thing against the odds. Otherwise, lacking the adrenalin of an out-and-out action movie, and without the intelligence to be much of anything else, the film has nowhere to go. Pitt's accent, most convincing when he says 'aye', is somewhat tested by whole sentences. TJ

Devil's Playground, The

(1976, Aust, 107 min)
d/p/sc Fred Schepisi. *ph* Ian Baker. *ed* Brian Kavanagh. *ad* Trevor Ling. *m* Bruce Smeaton. *cast* Arthur Dignam, Nick Tate, Simon Burke, Charles McCallum, John Frawley, Jonathan Hardy.
● Stirrings of style in this semi-autobiographical first feature (Schepisi matured markedly in *The Chant of Jimmie Blacksmith* and *Barbarosa*). But its tale of troubles in a Catholic boys' school follows the familiar catechism of crises of faith and puberty, told in the impressionistic manner that was the quality hallmark of the 'new' Australian cinema. TM

Devil's Rain, The

(1975, US, 86 min)
d Robert Fuest. *p* James V Cullen, Michael S Glick. *sc* Gabe Essoe, James Ashton, Gerald Hopman. *ph* Alex Phillips. *ed* Michael Kahn. *pd* Nikita Knatz. *m* Al DeLory. *cast* Ernest Borgnine, Eddie Albert, Ida Lupino, William Shatner, Keenan Wynn, Tom Skerritt, Joan Prather, John Travolta, Claudio Brook.
● After a luxuriant Bosch credit sequence, we plunge into thirty minutes of bewildering but entertaining events that revolve around a dissolving dad, a satanic register, a protective amulet, a Mansonesque coven of dead-eyed converts led by a reincarnated witch, plus an expert in the fields of ESP and demonology. When the explanations begin (mainly a flashback to 17th century ancestors), things become heavy-handed, revealing the ragged direction, a dire script, and performances which range from the bemused (Albert) to the awful (Borgnine). Fuest butters on the special effects, which culminate in a tediously extended final splurge when almost the whole cast dissolves into a puddle of green slime. IB

Devil's Wheel, The (Chyortovo Koleso)

(1926, USSR, 8,695 ft, b/w)
d Grigori Kozintsev, Leonid Trauberg. *sc* Piotrovsky. *ph* Andrei Moskvin, Sviatislav Belayev. *ad* Yevgeni Enei. *cast* Ludmila Semyonova, N Foregger, Pyotr Sobolevsky, Sergei Gerasimov, Emil Gal.
● Typically of the heady days of early Soviet cinema, this is constructed according to the fast, sharp editing principles advocated by Eisenstein, complete with symbolic inserts; but in terms of subject matter, it's much less explicitly political than most movies emerging from Russia in the '20s. Chronicling a young sailor's descent into a murky, treacherous underworld of pimps and thieves, after having encountered a Louise Brooks lookalike at a fairground and missed his departing boat, it's a lively moral fable that delights in vivid visual effects and quirky characterisations. If the plot occasionally reveals gaping holes, and the tacked-on ending urging the clearance of the Leningrad slums seems to be rather gratuitous, there's enough going on to keep one attentive and amused. GA

Devil Within Her

see Chi Sei?

Devil Within Her

see I Don't Want to be Born

Devotion

(1946, US, 107 min, b/w)
d Curtis Bernhardt. *p* Robert Buckner. *sc* Keith Winter. *ph* Ernest Haller. *ed* Rudi Fehr. *ad* Robert M Haas. *m* Erich Wolfgang Korngold. *cast* Ida Lupino, Olivia de Havilland, Nancy Coleman, Paul Henreid, Sydney Greenstreet, Arthur Kennedy, Montagu Love.
● Pure hokum. In a studio-recreated Haworth parsonage, Charlotte (bitchy de Havilland) and Emily (dreamy Lupino) indulge in various highly romantic intrigues and passions, overshadowing the quieter Anne (Coleman) even before they set to writing and become the famous Brontë sisters. Silly even to the point of having the beloved curate inexplicably played by Austrian Henried, but endowed with a charm and conviction all its own, helped enormously by Bernhardt's swooning direction and Ernest Haller's photography. Enjoyably absurd. GA

Diable au corps, Le

see Diavolo in Corpo, Il (1986)

Diable au corps, Le (Devil in the Flesh)

(1947, Fr, 112 min, b/w)
d Claude Autant-Lara. *sc* Jean Aurenche, Pierre Bost. *ph* Michel Kelber. *ed* Madeleine Gug. *ad* Max Douy. *m* René Cloerec. *cast* Gérard Philipe, Micheline Presle, Jean Debucourt, Germaine Ledoyen, Denise Grey, Jacques Tati.
● One of the cornerstones of the *cinéma de papa* so opportunistically maligned by Truffaut, this solid adaptation (by Aurenche and Bost) of the Raymond Radiguet novel hasn't lost its power to move. While all around celebrate the end of the war in 1918, a schoolboy (Philipe) remembers his impossible affair with an older married woman (Presle), from whose funeral he is barred. Autant-Lara unfortunately overplays some of his stylistic devices (such as the slowed-down sound that announces each flashback), but for the main part he elicits sensitive performances from his leads, and the smoky photography and sets evoke a unique period atmosphere. DT

Diable Probablement, Le (The Devil, Probably)

(1977, Fr, 95 min)
d Robert Bresson. *p* Stéphane Tchalgadjieff. *sc* Robert Bresson. *ph* Pasqualino De Santis. *ed* Germaine Lamy. *pd* Eric Simon. *m* Philippe Sarde. *cast* Antoine Monnier, Tina Irissari, Henri de Maublanc, Laetitia Carcano, Régis Hanrion, Nicolas Deguy.
● Bresson observes his Parisian student protagonist in numb recoil from a culture, almost a species, compromised beyond recall. As so often in Bresson, the process of detachment ends in deliberately sought death. Here Charles' proxy suicide stands, as Jan Dawson has perceptively noted, both as an affirmation of a purity no longer possible within society, and 'as a portent of the millions of deaths, not self-willed, which must inevitably follow', given the ruthless course of society's crimes. Charles and the two women in his life are offered less as convincing portrayals of life on the student fringe than as indices of a particular state of consciousness. Beside the toughness of *Pickpocket*, the depth of feeling of *Une Femme Douce*, the rigour of *Lancelot du Lac*, *The Devil, Probably* has a certain opaque quality. Its case is presented rather than argued: one buys its cosmic bleakness or one doesn't, but there is no doubt about the conviction with which it is put. VG

Diabolik

see Danger Diabolik

Diabolique

see Diaboliques, Les

Diabolique

(1996, US, 107 min)
d Jeremiah Chechik. *p* Marvin Worth, James G Robinson. *sc* Don Roos. *ph* Peter James. *ed* Carol Littleton. *pd* Leslie Dilley. *m* Randy Edelman. *cast* Sharon Stone, Isabelle Adjani, Chazz Palminteri, Kathy Bates, Spalding Gray, Shirley Knight, Allen Garfield.
● Remake of Clouzot's 1954 chiller with an arty veneer. Stone's the hard-bitten mistress and Adjani the fearful, ailing wife of Palminteri, sadistic head of a Philadelphia boarding school. Bates is the sassy private eye who smells something fishy after Palminteri's reported missing. We, of course, have already seen the ladies drown him in the bath, so how come it seems he may still be alive or, at the very least, haunting his killers? Working from a rickety script, Chechik coughs up a string of Grand Guignol clichés and attempts to give a 'modern' twist to a plot over-familiar from inferior imitations. The cast is wasted: Adjani, suitably vulnerable in the Véra Clouzot role, has little scope to deliver the raw emotions she's so good at; Stone is two-dimensionally terse and tough; Bates is lumbered with some dubious gags about mastectomy; and Palminteri mugs as the sneering ogre. Not scary. GA

Diaboliques, Les (Diabolique/The Fiends)

(Fr, 1954, 114 min, b/w)
d/p Henri-Georges Clouzot. *sc* Henri-Georges Clouzot, Jérôme Géronimi, René Masson, Frédéric Grendel. *ph* Armand Thirard. *ed*

Madeleine Gug. *ad* Léon Barsacq. *m* Georges Van Parys. *cast* Simone Signoret, Véra Clouzot, Paul Meurisse, Charles Vanel, Pierre Larquey, Michel Serrault, Jean Brochard.
● Headstrong mistress (Signoret) and retiring wife (Clouzot) conspire to murder the man they share, a tyrannical headmaster of a seedy boarding-school whose curriculum offers nothing but stagnation and decay. But in this black world (where, ironically, only the dead comes to life) everyone is in the end a victim, and their actions operate like snares setting traps that leave them grasping for survival. The camera watches these clammy proceedings with a cold precision that relishes its neutrality. At least one source claims that all Clouzot's films were shot in an atmosphere of bitterness and recrimination. It shows. But in this case it makes for a great piece of Guignol misanthropy. CPe

Diabolo Menthe (Peppermint Soda)

(1977, Fr, 101 min)
d Diane Kurys. *p* Armand Barbault. *sc* Diane Kurys. *ph* Philippe Rousselot. *ed* Joële van Effenterre, Nelly Meunier, Marie-Dominique Fournier. *ad* Bernard Madelenat, Laurent Janet, Tony Egry. *m* Yves Simon. *cast* Eléonore Klarwein, Odile Michel, Anouk Ferjac, Michel Puterflam, Yves Rénier, Robert Rimbaud.
● Kurys' impressive feature debut, based in autobiography, is a sensitive account of a year in the lives of two sisters – 13-year-old, introverted Anne, and outgoing 15-year-old Frédérique – in the early '60s. Without ever lapsing into melodrama, the film adopts a decidely un-nostalgic tone, lucidly charting the everyday oppressions of school life and the girls' difficult relationships with their parents – a separated Jewish couple – their friends and each other. Indeed, it's a harsh, unsentimental look at adolescence, with the '60s setting serving primarily to define the social and political context of the girls' rites of passage; at the same time, however, the film is invested with great warmth through Kurys' assured, sympathetic handling of her cast. GA

Día de la bestia, El

see Day of the Beast, The

Diagnosis: Murder

(1974, GB, 90 min)
d Sidney Hayers. *p* Peter Miller. *sc* Philip Levene. *ph* Bob Edwards. *ed* Barry Peters. *ad* Ken Jones. *m* Laurie Johnson. *cast* Jon Finch, Judy Geeson, Christopher Lee, Tony Beckley, Dilys Hamlett, Jane Merrow, Colin Jeavons.
● A lumbering, shakily scripted essay in the kind of emotional area (actions stemming from hatred, greed and possessiveness) that Chabrol effortlessly activates into his fraught and loving critiques of the bourgeoisie. Consultant psychiatrist Lee's wife disappears; notes appear blaming him for her murder. Enter Finch's police inspector, dragging with him an ambitous but awkward subplot involving his girlfriend and her crippled husband (not only is the poor guy confined to a wheelchair, he is also given the most unspeakable lines in the script). Hayers' pedantic, explanatory style, and failure to sustain any very revealing mood or to probe his characters with the necessary relentlessness, makes the going grim. VG

Diagonale du Fou, La

see Dangerous Moves

Dial M for Murder

(1953, US, 105 min)
d Alfred Hitchcock. *sc* Frederick Knott. *ph* Robert Burks. *ed* Rudi Fehr. *ad* Edward Carrere. *m* Dimitri Tiomkin. *cast* Ray Milland, Grace Kelly, Robert Cummings, Anthony Dawson, John Williams, Anthony Dawson.
● Shot in 3-D – which resulted in some rather strained and awkward compositions – this nevertheless remains one of Hitchcock's very stagiest films. Milland is the has-been tennis star who decides to have his wife killed in order to lay his hands on her fortune; Kelly is the potential victim who cannot, at first, work out why a stranger should enter her house and try to murder her. It all moves along in a rather efficient if lifeless fashion, with only John Williams shining as a canny police detective, and only the murder scene itself breaking the tedium induced by Hitchcock's decision to shoot on a single apartment set. GA

Dialogue des Carmélites, Le

(1959, Fr/It, 113 min, b/w)
d RL Bruckberger, Philippe Agostini. *p* Jules Borkon. *sc* RL Bruckberger, Philippe Agostini. *ph* André Bac. *ed* Gilbert Natot. *ad* Maurice Colasson. *m* Jean Françaix. *cast* Jeanne Moreau, Alida Valli, Pascale Audret, Madeleine Renaud, Pierre Brasseur, Georges Wilson, Jean-Louis Barrault, Claude Laydu.
● Only Bresson, perhaps, could have done justice to Gertrud von le Fort's novel of Carmelite martyrdom during the French Revolution (already adapted for the stage by Bernanos and opera house by Poulenc). What it got instead was the ultra-static co-direction of Bresson's cinematographer (Agostini) and a fashionable 'literary' priest (Bruckberger). Though a potentially moving study of grace (in the most literal, theological sense) under pressure, neither of these qualities is very conspicuous in this pallid Sunday school picnic of a film. GAd

Dialogues With Madwomen

(1993, US, 90 min)
d Allie Light.
● Seven articulate women speak about manic depression, schizophrenia and multiple-personality disorders. Director Allie Light, who adds her own experience of depression, offsets the interviews with experimental montage sequences. Archive footage and reconstructed images illuminate the darkest corners of the psyche: a keyhole drips blood; a silhouette dances in front of the moon; an interviewee walks into the sea with a suitcase; horrific photographs of self-mutilation. The material draws heavily on early childhood, the reasons for insanity being attributed to life-experience rather than biochemistry; and abuse at the hands of fathers and stepfathers features strongly. JBa

Dial Rat for Terror

see Bone

Diamond Mercenaries, The

(1975, Switz, 101 min)
d Val Guest. *p* Nat Wachsberger, Patrick Wachsberger. *sc* Michael Winder, Val Guest, Gerald Sanford. *ph* David Millin. *ed* Bill Butler. *ad* Peter Church. *m* Georges Garvarentz. *cast* Telly Savalas, Peter Fonda, OJ Simpson, Maude Adams, Hugh O'Brian, Christopher Lee.
● 'Is that Miss or Ms?' Savalas asks of Adams. 'That depends on the man,' she replies. In other words, we have here an old-fashioned adventure given the veneer of modernity. The crooks planning the desert heist are Vietnam veterans rather than league of gentlemen; but in other respects we're back in the world of Val Guest hokum (Savalas wanders about showing off his wardrobe, you don't quite get to see anything in the bed scene, all the interiors are in medium-shot). Still, the robbery is a smart piece of editing, the desert looks handsome, and Christopher Lee staggers around in it wearing khaki – a rare delight. AN

Diamonds

(1975, US, 108 min)
d/p Menahem Golan. *sc* David Paulsen, Menahem Golan. *ph* Adam Greenberg. *ed* Dov Hoenig. *ad* Kuli Sander. *m* Roy Budd. *cast* Robert Shaw, Richard Roundtree, Barbara Hershey, Shelley Winters, Shai K Ophir.
● All jokes about a boy's best friend aside, this is an irredeemable disaster of a caper movie. Shot in Israel, it has Shaw in an embarrassing double role as both security head of the Tel Aviv Diamond Exchange and his playboy brother, out to outwit him with a pair of love-bird thieves. PT

Diamonds Are Forever

(1971, GB, 120 min)
d Guy Hamilton. *p* Harry Saltzman, Albert R Broccoli. *sc* Richard Maibaum, Tom Mankiewicz. *ph* Ted Moore. *ed* Bert Bates, John W Holmes. *pd* Ken Adam, Bill Kenney. *m* John Barry. *cast* Sean Connery, Jill St John, Charles Gray, Lana Wood, Jimmy Dean, Bruce Cabot, Joseph Furst.
● Apart from a clumsy climax, a wry and exhilarating bit of entertainment. The film's virtues stem mainly from a sense of self-parody, an intelligent script, the deft handling of the Las Vegas locations, and the presence of Jill St John instead of the usual array of pneumatic androids that super-bureaucrat Bond preys upon. Although the Bond films have succeeded in referring only to themselves, *Diamonds* achieves somewhat of a breakthrough by being set in a kind of socio-political reality: the Howard Hughes-type recluse in his Vegas empire; the implications of the nuclear blackmail game; the peculiarly Californian obsession with mortuaries; right down to the fey but villainous homosexuals and the pair of beautiful killer-karate female bodyguards who initiate 007 into contemporary femininity. On the debit side, the plot is about as watertight as a sieve, and the unwillingness of Bond's enemies to fill him with lead – instead opting for elaborate and ludicrous devices from which he escapes far too easily – has become tiresome. PG

Diamond Skulls

(1989, GB, 87 min)
d Nick Broomfield. *p* Tim Bevan. *sc* Tim Rose Price. *ph* Michael Coulter. *ed* Rodney Holland. *pd* Jocelyn James. *m* Hans Zimmer. *cast* Gabriel Byrne, Amanda Donohoe, Michael Hordern, Judy Parfitt, Ian Carmichael, Sadie Frost.
● 'It begins as if it's going to be a film about class, which is obviously what people expect from the British cinema'. Nick Broomfield goes on to protest that his film deals with the murkier subject of obsession, but in fact it dabbles with both themes – and neither satisfactorily. Lord Hugo Buckton (Byrne), the exceptionally jealous husband of ex-model Ginny (Donohoe), thinks she's having an affair with her publishing colleague. After a heavy night wining and dining, Buckton gets behind the wheel of a car, while fellow officers from his former regiment pile into the back. A woman is run down. After momentary dithering, they decide to close ranks, and so leave her fatally injured. One of the group, noting the victim's strong resemblance to Buckton's wife, suffers from a pricked conscience. But will he run squealing to the police? In documentarist Broomfield's transition to fiction, the camera lingers over Byrne's sculptured features and captures each careful gesture from Donohoe. The controlled technique echoes the theme of domination, but combined with the largely unsympathetic characters, results in a film that affects emotion and remains curiously hollow. CM

Diane

(1955, US, 110 min)
d David Miller. *p* Edwin H Knopf. *sc* Christopher Isherwood. *ph* Robert Planck. *ed* John McSweeney Jr. *ad* Cedric Gibbons, Hans Peters. *m* Miklós Rozsa. *cast* Lana Turner, Pedro Armendariz, Roger Moore, Marisa Pavan, Cedric Hardwicke, Henry Daniell.
● A 16th century romp: young Roger Moore is the king's son, Lana Turner the French countess who falls for him – but he can't reciprocate since Dad wants him to marry Catherine de Medici. Despite a script from Christopher Isherwood and one of Miklos Rosza's ludicrously overblown scores, this is stodgy, soporific stuff. Turner's ridiculously miscast while Moore hadn't yet mastered the let's-raise-my-eyebrows style of acting he later used to show off to Miss Moneypenny. GM

Diaries

(1981, US, 200 min)
d Ed Pincus. *cast* Jane, Sami, Ben and Ed Pincus, David Neuman, David Hancock.
● If you set out to make a film diary of your family and friends over five years – births, deaths, break-ups, etc. – would you wish it on the public? Ed Pincus does. Hailed by some as a remarkable piece of cinéma-vérité validated by the film-maker's disarming honesty, *Diaries* comes across to anyone not living among the artistic elite of Cambridge Mass. as a self-indulgent suffering-Seventies bore. MA

Diary for My Children (Napló Gyermekeimnek)

(1982, Hun, 107 min, b/w)
d/sc Martá Mészáros. *ph* Miklós Jancsó. *ed* Éva Karmentö. *pd* Éva Martin. *m* Zsolt Döme. *cast* Zsuzsa Czinkóczi, Anna Polony, Jan Nowicki, Tamás Tóth, Mari Szemes, Pál Zolnay.
● After the war, teenage Juli and her grandparents return from exile in Russia to Budapest. But Juli's hopes of happiness in her homeland are gradually eroded by the strictures of a disciplinarian society; her guardian offers love but no freedom; a free-thinking older man who befriends Juli is incarcerated. The fact that the film is based

on Mészáros' own experiences makes for a certain veracity about life in Hungary during the Stalinist era, and certainly one is struck by its sincerity, intelligence and strong performances. But the film is so coldly directed, and the portrait of period and place so resolutely joyless that it is hard to care in any real way about the grim fates of its characters. GA

Diary for My Loves (Napló Szerelmeimnek)

(1987, Hun, 130 min, b/w & col)
d Martá Mészáros. *sc* Martá Mészáros, Éva Pataki. *ph* Nyika Jancso. *ed* Éva Karmentö. *pd* Éva Martin. *m* Zsolt Döme. *cast* Zsuzsa Czinkóczi, Anna Polony, Jan Nowicki, Irina Kouberskaya, Mari Szemes.
●Mészáros' second semi-autobiographical film diary picks up where *Diary for My Children* left off in the Hungary of 1953. Alter-ego Juli, still played by the frosty but winningly resolute Czinkóczi, is now 18, has lost her lover in the Stalinist purges, and is placed in the care of her party-puppet foster mother. Juli's dream of becoming a film director comes true in Moscow, but her adherence to documentary truths troubles the comrades back in Budapest, even after the death of Bad Father Joe. Taking us up to the '56 Uprising, Mészáros creates a superbly confident portrait of her country's traumatic past, painted through individual passions and more than a touch of psychoanalysis. Sometimes her points may miss their mark without a crash course in East European history, official and more especially unofficial; but her integrity binds the mixture of psychodrama and newsreel, monochrome and colour, novelette and history lesson. DT

Diary of a Chambermaid, The

(1945, US, 86 min, b/w)
d Jean Renoir. *p* Benedict Bogeaus, Burgess Meredith. *sc* Burgess Meredith. *ph* Lucien Andriot. *ed* James Smith. *pd* Eugène Lourié. *m* Michel Michelet. *cast* Paulette Goddard, Hurd Hatfield, Francis Lederer, Burgess Meredith, Judith Anderson, Reginald Owen, Florence Bates, Irene Ryan.
●In its own strange way, even more genuinely surreal than Buñuel's later version of Mirbeau's novel about a keyhole-peeking chambermaid whose arrival in the household of a decadent and eccentric aristocratic family wreaks havoc. What's so bizarre about Renoir's adaptation (scripted and produced by Meredith, then husband of Goddard) is the sheer artificiality of both setting and performances, emphasising the power struggles that develop as a theatre of deceit and delusion. Less bitterly savage than Buñuel, but equally sharp in its satire, it stands on an otherwise uncharted point between *La Règle du Jeu* and, say, *The Golden Coach*. GA

Diary of a Chambermaid, The (Le Journal d'une Femme de Chambre)

(1964, Fr/It, 98 min, b/w)
d Luis Buñuel. *p* Serge Silberman, Michel Safra. *sc* Luis Buñuel, Jean-Claude Carrière. *ph* Roger Fellous. *ed* Louisette Hautecoeur. *ad* Georges Wakhevitch. *cast* Jeanne Moreau, Georges Géret, Michel Piccoli, Françoise Lugagne, Daniel Ivernel, Jean Ozenne, Gilberte Géniat.
●Moreau as the beautiful, ambitious Célestine makes it from Downstairs to Upstairs by manipulating her right-wing boss (Piccoli), his leftish neighbour (Ivernel), and his fascist gamekeeper (Géret). Octave Mirbeau's muckraking 1900 novel has abiding insight into the deep structures of French political instability. Buñuel shifts the story to the rise of Fascism in the '30s. He digs right down to that spiritual gunge which links political, sexual and social positions (and impositions) as equal perversions of human desires (in turn perversions of animal desires). Like most Buñuel heroines, Célestine is intuitively a feminist, but before her time, and blows it by her egoism and ambivalence before male ruthlessness. Moreau's baleful charisma complements Buñuel's sardonic sadness. It's his greyest film since *Nazarin*, and all the more troubling for its impassive flow, which successive explosions of strange desire can never quite disturb. RD

Diary of a Country Priest (Journal d'un Curé de Campagne)

(1950, Fr, 120 min, b/w)
d Robert Bresson. *p* Léon Carre. *sc* Robert Bresson. *ph* Léonce-Henry Burel. *ed* Paulette Robert. *pd* Pierre Charbonnier. *m* Jean-Jacques Grünenwald. *cast* Claude Laydu, Marie-Monique Arkell, André Guibert, Jean Riveyre, Nicole Ladmiral, Nicole Maurey.
●Alone and dying of cancer, a young curate faces the mortal torment of failure in his task of saving souls. What he finds in the ultimate victory over self is that mysterious touch of grace which remains one of the immutable signs of a Bresson film. Watching this spiritual odyssey is almost a religious experience in itself, but one which has nothing to do with faith or dogma, everything to do with Bresson's unique ability to exteriorise an interior world. TM

Diary of a Lost Girl (Das Tagebuch einer Verlorenen)

(1929, Ger, 9,393 ft, b/w)
d/p Georg Wilhelm Pabst. *sc* Rudolf Leonhardt. *ph* Sepp Allgeier. *ad* Ernö Metzner, Emil Hasler. *cast* Louise Brooks, Edith Meinhardt, Vera Pawlowa, Josef Rovensky, Fritz Rasp, André Roanne, Arnold Korff.
●An elegant narrative of moral musical chairs, Pabst's last silent film not only plays on who holds what kind of legitimate place in society, but is also a starkly direct view of inter-war Germany. Feasting the camera on Brooks' radiant beauty, Pabst follows the adventures of innocence led astray in the shape of Thymian, a pharmacist's daughter. Her progress from apple of her father's eye, through sexual lapse and approved school, to darling of an expensive brothel and finally to dowager countess, gives Pabst the opportunity to measure the Germany of the Weimar republic against Brooks' embodiment of a vitality so exuberant that it equals innocence. However damning, though, Pabst's indictment of the bourgeoisie as torn between powerless compassion, greed and scandal-lust, his alternatives – the brothel as the one place of true friendship, or the aristocratic father-figure who puts everything right in the end – smack very much of a cop-out, allowing him to both revel in decadence and enjoy the moral superiority of denouncing it. RB

Diary of a Mad Housewife

(1970, US, 95 min)
d/p Frank Perry. *sc* Eleanor Perry. *ph* Gerald Hirschfeld. *ed* Sidney Katz. *ad* Peter Dohanos. *cast* Richard Benjamin, Frank Langella, Carrie Snodgress, Lorraine Cullen, Frannie Michel, Peter Boyle.
●Perry and his scriptwriter-wife Eleanor have consistently made provocative, offbeat films about mental and spiritual reawakening (until the disastrous *Mommie Dearest*, that is). Some of them, like the allegorical *The Swimmer*, have been intriguing catastrophes; this is one of the more successful. Bored New York housewife Snodgress tires of smug, over-ambitious husband Benjamin and his persistent nagging, and decides to gamble on an affair with narcissistic writer Langella, only to find that relationship equally dissatisfying. Often very funny in its acerbic swipes at American success-orientated society (as revealed at a camp art preview and an unsuccessful party), imaginatively scripted and acted (Benjamin is superbly repellent), it's an entertaining satire that disappoints only in the stereotypically limited choices it offers to the woman. GA

Diary of Anne Frank, The

(1959, US, 170 min, b/w)
d/p George Stevens. *sc* Frances Goodrich, Albert Hackett. *ph* William C Mellor, Jack Cardiff. *ed* David Bretherton, Robert Swink, William Mace. *ad* Lyle Wheeler, George W Davis. *m* Alfred Newman. *cast* Millie Perkins, Joseph Schildkraut, Shelley Winters, Richard Beymer, Lou Jacobi, Diane Baker.
●One of those extremely long and well-meaning adaptations of plays, this doesn't really amount to very much, despite its intrinsically moving subject matter. The story of a Jewish family, who had to hide in a concealed attic for two years before they were captured by the Nazis, is poignantly true, but remains a little too theatrical in this production. Millie Perkins looks good as Anne (though her personality seems wrong), while Shelley Winters' hysterical performance as Mrs Van Daan won her an Oscar as best supporting actress. DP

Diary of a Shinjuku Thief (Shinjuku Dorobo Nikki)

(1968, Jap, 94 min, b/w & col)
d Nagisa Oshima. *p* Masayuki Nakajima. *sc* Tsutomu Tamura, Mamoru Sasaki, Masao Adachi, Nagisa Oshima. *ph* Yashuhiro Yoshioka, Seizo Sengen. *ed* Nagisa Oshima. *ad* Jusho Toda. *cast* Tadanori Yokoo, Rie Yokoyama, Moichi Tanabe, Tetsu Takahashi, Kei Sato, Fumio Watanabe.
●One of Oshima's most teasing and provocative collages, inspired by the student riots of '68 and contemporary 'youth culture' generally. The main thread running through it is the relationship between a passive and vaguely effeminate young man and an aggressive and vaguely masculine young woman. They meet when he steals books and she poses as a shop assistant who catches him in the act; they spend the rest of the movie trying to reach satisfactory orgasms with each other. Their route takes them through a dizzying mixture of fact and fiction, from an encounter with a real-life sexologist to involvement in a 'fringe' performance of a neo-primitive kabuki show. The logical connections are there, but they're deliberately submerged in a welter of contrasting moods, styles and lines of thought. TR

Diary of Lady M, The

see Journal de Lady M, Le

Días Contados (Running Out of Time)

(1994, Sp, 93 min)
d Imanol Uribe. *p* Imanol Uribe, Andres Santana. *sc* Imanol Uribe. *ph* Javier Aguirresarobe. *ed* Teresa Font. *pd* Felix Murcia. *m* José Nieto. *cast* Carmelo Gomez, Ruth Gabriel, Javier Bardem, Candela Peña, Karra Elejalde, Elvira Minguez.
●A slick contemporary thriller loosely inspired by *Carmen* (really very loosely: Gomez is an ETA terrorist and part-time photographer, Gabriel a junkie prostitute). Uribe keeps threatening to take it somewhere interesting, but never really gets there – the terrorist background feels opportunistic and the characters don't have lives of their own. What's more, the director's penchant for photographing women naked from the waist down is unalloyed voyeurism. TCh

Diavolo in Corpo, Il (Le Diable au corps/ Devil in the Flesh)

(1986, It/Fr, 110 min)
d Marco Bellocchio. *sc* Marco Bellocchio, Enrico Palandri, Ennio De Concini. *ph* Giuseppe Lanci. *ed* Mirco Garrone. *ad* Andrea Crisanti. *m* Carlo Crivelli. *cast* Maruschka Detmers, Federico Pitzalis, Anita Laurenzi, Alberto Di Stasio, Riccardo De Torrebruna.
●Bellocchio further extends his rap sheet on the stultifying bourgeoisie via an update of the Raymond Radiguet novel and its 1947 Autant-Lara adaptation. But he has a job trying to find any equivalent in the contemporary scene for the offence against Family and Country which Radiguet's lovers presented. The student hero (Pitzalis – no Gérard Philipe) embarks on an affair with Detmers, patient of his psychiatrist father and girlfriend of a left-wing extremist facing trial on terrorist charges. The familiar Bellocchio problem – the sense that his characters are being marshalled mainly in the service of some generalising thesis – is aggravated by the flat *mise-en-scène*. More likely to be remembered for the headline-making on-camera blow job nonchalantly administered by Detmers, than for its polemics, such as they are. BBa

Dick

(1989, US, 14 min, b/w)
d Jo Menell, B Moell. *p* Jo Menell. *ph* Paul Latoures. *m* John Cale.
●Comprising b/w stills of several hundred adult penises at rest, this occupies a place between *La Jetée* (except here, nothing whatever moves) and Yoko Ono's *Film No. 4*, which

filled the screen with bare backsides. On the soundtrack, women's voices (American, Australian, British) discuss such topics as resemblances ('sort of a… duckbilled platypus'), experiences ('this big thing coming at me') and what it might be like to have one ('I'd definitely wank a lot'). Fifty years ago this might have seemed wonderfully liberating for men and women alike. Fifty years ahead it's probably going to seem quite eerie. For the present, if you can find a taped version, try fast forwarding it for a visual experience you probably never expected to have. BBa

Dick Barton – Special Agent

(1948, GB, 70 min, b/w)
d Alfred Goulding. *p* Henry Halstead. *sc* Alfred Goulding, Alan Stranks. *ph* Stanley Clinton. *ed* Eta Simpson. *ad* James A Marchant. *m* John Bath. *cast* Don Stannard, Jack Shaw, George Ford, Gillian Maude, Colin Douglas, Geoffrey Wincott.

● The ace radio 'tec and his faithful sidekicks Jock and Snowy made their film debut in this cheap programmer (the first of three) that pitted them against dastardly foreign saboteurs tampering with the water system. Elementary stuff – the nostalgist's equivalent of steam cinema. PT

Dick Deadeye, or Duty Done

(1975, GB, 81 min)
d Bill Melendez. *p* Steven Cuitlahuac Melendez. *sc* Robin Miller, Leo Rost. *ed* Steven Cuitlahuac Melendez, Babette Monteil. *ad* Ronald Searle. *songs* Gilbert and Sullivan. *cast* voices: Victor Spinetti, Peter Reeves, George A Cooper, Miriam Karlin.

● An animated feature designed by Ronald Searle and based on the plots, characters and songs of Gilbert and Sullivan. Those in love with G & S may find the narrative line stupid, the new lyrics silly, and the reggae accompaniment sedate (compared, that is, with the rollicking *Black Mikado*). Animation fans will no doubt moan that Melendez' movie is hardly animated at all – just a series of grandly designed backgrounds and characters who are jerked about like puppets. But those with a taste for Searle's ornately grotesque style will find much pleasure, both in the elaborate settings and in the hideous array of barmaids, whores, pirates, policemen, rear admirals, sisters, cousins and aunts (with not a well-formed human body among them). GB

Dick Down Under

see True Story of Eskimo Nell, The

Dick Tracy

(1990, US, 105 min)
d/p Warren Beatty. *sc* Jim Cash, Jack Epps Jr. *ph* Vittorio Storaro. *ed* Richard Marks. *pd* Richard Sylbert. *m* Danny Elfman, Stephen Sondheim. *cast* Warren Beatty, Al Pacino, Madonna, Glenne Headly, Charlie Korsmo, Charles Durning, Paul Sorvino, Dustin Hoffman, James Caan, Mandy Patinkin, Dick Van Dyke, Michael J Pollard, Estelle Parsons, William Forsythe, Henry Silva, Allen Garfield, John Schuck, Seymour Cassel, Ed O'Ross, RG Armstrong, Bert Remsen, Mike Mazurki.

● Set in the '30s, Beatty's film culls its villains – a gallery of grotesques with names like Pruneface, Flattop and The Brow – from the later '40s strips. As Tracy (Beatty) sets about foiling the plans of Big Boy and The Blank to take over the city, Breathless Mahoney (Madonna) introduces emotional conflict for the careerist detective, whose long-standing relationship with Tess Trueheart (Headly) is going nowhere fast. Beatty has rejected 'psychology and behaviour' (read complexity) in characterisation; this is old-fashioned, clearly defined morality, with literally no shades of grey (the use of colour is wonderfully imaginative and carefully modulated). Pleasing restraint is evident in the way Beatty allows his character to be outshone by his adversaries. As mobster Big Boy, a brash thug fond of misquoting Lincoln, Nietzsche and Plato, Pacino is virtually unrecognisable and hugely enjoyable; and Madonna gives confident renditions of the Stephen Sondheim numbers. A spectacular movie whose technical achievements – notably the sharp editing – will surely provide a gauge by which subsequent comic strip films are judged. CM

Didn't You Kill My Brother?

(1987, GB, 52 min)
d Bob Spiers. *sc* Alexei Sayle, Pauline Melville, David Stafford. *cast* Alexei Sayle, Beryl Reid, Graham Crowden, Pauline Melville, Peter Richardson, David Stafford.

● Comic Strip's radical remake of *Bicycle Thieves* has Alexei Sayle as twins: Sterling Moss is bad and ignorant, Carl Moss is good and prison-educated. Carl makes bikes with the help of a gang of dole-ites; Sterling, with their help, nicks them. Their murder-mad mum (Beryl Reid, as wonderful as ever: 'You should always put a dead badger on a head wound…') encourages the sibling rivalry with lethal results. Sayle's 'satirical' script takes social awareness to new shallows: the charges of a horribly realistic social worker are called Laura and Ashley. You'll laugh. MS

Die Artisten in der Kirkuskuppel: Ratlos

see Artistes at the Top of the Big Top: Disoriented

Die Bad (Juk Gona Ho Gun Napun Gona)

(2000, SKor, 98 min, b/w & col)
d Ryoo Seung-Wan. *p* Kim Sung-Jae. *sc* Ryoo Seung-Wan. *ph* Cho Yong-Kyu, Choi Young-Whan. *ed* Ahn Byung-Kun. *m* Kim Dong-Kyu. *cast* Park Sung-Bin, Ryoo Seung-Wan, Bae Jong-Sik, Ryoo Seung-Bom.

● Sparky indie feature in four chapters, two previously shown as shorts in their own right. The chapters are deliberately varied in style (cinéma-vérité, horror-*noir*, etc), but linked into a loose narrative. Seok-Hwan (Ryoo himself) provokes a pool hall fight between rival student gangs in which one guy dies. Seven years later he's become a cop and his kid brother is drifting into crime. Meanwhile the accidental murderer Sung-Bin (Park) is released from jail and universally ostracised. Haunted by the ghost of the boy he killed, he becomes a crimelord's enforcer and eventually revenges himself on Seok-Hwan by putting his brother in danger. By the end everyone is dead, dying or merely irredeemable. Basically an excuse for Ryoo and friends to show off their stunt action skills, it says all the obvious things about macho values and delinquency, but comes up fresh and watchable thanks to its play with form. A version trimmed by 3 to 4 minutes was a surprise hit in Korea. TR

Die! Die! My Darling

see Fanatic

Die Hard

(1988, US, 132 min)
d John McTiernan. *p* Lawrence Gordon, Joel Silver. *sc* Jeb Stuart, Steven E De Souza. *ph* Jan De Bont. *ed* Frank J Urioste, John F Link. *pd* Jackson De Govia. *m* Michael Kamen. *cast* Bruce Willis, Alan Rickman, Alexander Godunov, Bonnie Bedelia, Reginald Veljohnson, William Atherton, Paul Gleason, James Shigeta.

● A hi-tech thriller with a human heart, offering slam-bang entertainment on a par with *Lethal Weapon* or *Aliens*. On Christmas Eve, visiting New York cop McClane (Willis) enters the high-rise LA office block where his estranged wife works, not realising that it has already being taken over by sadistic smoothie Hans Gruber (Rickman) and his ruthless terrorists. Inside the building, having taken wife (Bedelia) and celebrating colleagues hostage, the gang tries to crack open the Nakotomi corporation's computerised vault; outside, LA cops and FBI agents squabble over jurisdiction, while opportunistic TV reporters gather like jackals; it's up to McClane, having established a chance radio link with a passing patrolman (Veljohnson), to use the building's 39 empty floors, lift shafts, and heating ducts to improvise diversionary tactics. McTiernan excels in the adrenalin-inducing action scenes, staging the murderous mayhem and state-of-the-art violence as if he were born with a camera in one hand and a rocket launcher in the other. NF

Die Hard 2

(1990, US, 123 min)
d Renny Harlin. *p* Lawrence Gordon, Joel Silver, Charles Gordon. *sc* Steven E De Souza, Doug Richardson. *ph* Oliver Wood. *ed* Stuart Baird. *pd* John Vallone. *m* Michael Kamen. *cast* Bruce Willis, Bonnie Bedelia, William Atherton, Reginald Veljohnson, Franco Nero, William Sadler, John Amos, Dennis Franz, Sheila McCarthy.

● Yet again, humble detective John McClane (Willis) stumbles into a terrorist plot, this time to hijack a whole airport. Yet again, the authorities dismiss him as a jerk, and he must save the day single-handedly. 'Man, I can't believe this,' he moans. 'How can shit like this happen to the same guy twice?' This kind of self-referential irony, stopping just short of full-blown parody, saves the film; no one carries a one-liner better than Willis. He's also unusual among Hollywood's Action Men in seeming vulnerable at the same time as being invincible. Harlin fails to bring out the claustrophobic tension between the terrorists that made the original a masterpiece among blockbusters, but more than compensates in timing, speed and sheer *volume*. So what if there are reservations? We're talking action not art, and on that level *Die Hard 2* succeeds magnificently. DW

Die Hard with a Vengeance

(1995, US, 128 min)
d John McTiernan. *p* Michael Tadross, John McTiernan. *sc* Jonathan Hensleigh. *ph* Peter Menzies. *ed* John Wright. *pd* Jackson De Govia. *m* Michael Kamen. *cast* Bruce Willis, Samuel L Jackson, Jeremy Irons, Graham Greene, Colleen Camp, Nick Wyman, Sam Phillips, Larry Bryggman.

● The first (entertaining) *Die Hard* film put an ordinary Joe in an extraordinary situation – namely, saving an office block from terrorists. The second just squeaked by on the same formula – saving an airport from terrorists – with the ironic line, 'How can shit like this happen to the same guy twice?' But you can only suspend disbelief so far, and by the third in the series – saving a city from terrorists (led by Irons) – the joke wears thin. With Willis's John McClane transformed by his previous experiences into a more traditional action superman, it's left to sidekick Jackson to play vulnerable. As the racist, Caucasian-hating Harlem store-owner Zeus, he provides some of the best moments with his inversion of 48 HRS, as well as the incidental pleasure of seeing two disparate characters from *Pulp Fiction* united at last: 'What have you been doing all this time?' the drunken ex-cop McClane is asked at the outset. 'Smoking cigarettes and watching Captain Kangaroo,' he replies cryptically – a line recognisable to Taranteenies as coming from the song which played while Marcellus was being buggered. Apart from that, there's little wit or originality on offer, just the familiar escalation of car chases and big bangs. DW

Die, Monster, Die!

see Monster of Terror

Different for Girls

(1996, GB, 97 min)
d Richard Spence. *p* John Chapman. *sc* Tony Marchant. *ph* Sean Van Hales. *ed* David Gamble. *pd* Grenville Horner. *m* Stephen Warbeck. *cast* Steven MacKintosh, Rupert Graves, Miriam Margoyles, Saskia Reeves, Charlotte Coleman, Neil Dudgeon.

● When a traffic accident brings together laddish biker Paul and greetings card versifier Kim, it takes a while for them to realise they're acquainted. True, it's nearly two decades since they left school, but Kim has changed – after all, before her operation, she used to be Paul's best mate Karl. As they try tentatively to revive their friendship, Kim (MacKintosh) finds herself attracted to Paul (Graves), whose own emotions are a confused blend of protectiveness, curiosity and ill-repressed desire. But wary of attracting unwanted attention, Kim prefers a life of tidy tranquil conformity, which Paul's hot headedness threatens to disrupt. While Tony Marchant's script and Spence's direction suffer from a certain stolid inevitability, the movie never degenerates into mere worthiness, and in narrative terms, special pleading about the plight of transsexuals is kept low. Crucial to the slim story is MacKintosh's extraordinarily subtle performance: every expression, gesture, glance and vocal nuance rings true. It's a performance, in fact, as frank, sensitive and brave as the troubled character he plays, and affecting enough even to triumph over the film's final predictability. GA

Different Story, A

(1978, US, 108 min)
d Paul Aaron. *p* Alan Belkin. *sc* Henry Olek. *ph* Philip H Lathrop. *ed* Lynn McCallon. *ad* Lee Poll. *m* David Frank, Bob Wahler. *cast* Perry King, Meg Foster, Valerie Curtin, Peter Donat, Richard Bull, Barbara Collentine.

● Actually, the same old schlock, except that the first thirty minutes are in drag: a sort of *Touch of Class* screwball comedy which has been uneasily welded to a homosexual subject. Albert (King) wears aprons, designs frocks, and shacks up with Stella (likeable Meg Foster, playing a happily adjusted lesbian). But when Albert starts staying out nights, it looks like he's backsliding… A glossily persuasive film which presents its 'real' gays as neurotics or gangsters, and offers us so many clichés about role reversal, marriage and pregnancy that it makes *An Unmarried Woman* look like an intelligent study of divorce. SHi

Digby – the Biggest Dog in the World

(1973, GB, 88 min)
d Joseph McGrath. *p* Walter Shenson. *sc* Michael Pertwee. *ph* Harry Waxman. *ed* Jim Connock. *ad* Maurice Fowler. *m* Edwin T Astley. *cast* Jim Dale, Spike Milligan, Angela Douglas, John Bluthal, Norman Rossington, Milo O'Shea.

● Surprisingly, this attraction for all the family isn't at all bad. McGrath has taken a rather thin and unimaginative children's fantasy (dog drinks Project X and grows thirty feet high) and developed it into a cross between a spoof horror film and a gag show for his mates. A pity the special effects are so shoddy. DMcG

Diggstown (aka Midnight Sting)

(1992, US, 98 min)
d Michael Ritchie. *p* Robert Schaffel. *sc* Steven McKay *ph* Gerry Fisher. *ed* Don Zimmerman. *pd* Stephen Hendrickson. *m* James Newton Howard. *cast* James Woods, Louis Gossett Jr, Bruce Dern, Oliver Platt, Heather Graham, Randall 'Tex' Cobb, Thomas Wilson Brown, Duane Davis.

● Ritchie's scam movie, based on a Leonard Wise novel, is about a backwoods community famous as the 'rural capital of cash fighting'. The town is named after a fallen hero called Charles Macum Diggs, who was set up so nastily by the town's current boss, Gillon (Dern), that Diggs now sits in a wheelchair. So what better than to con the con-man? Enter Caine (supercool Woods), just out of jail, and his sidekick Fitz (the brilliant Platt), who aim to take Gillon to the cleaners by setting up a huge bet that Caine's ageing protégé, 'Honey' Roy Palmer (Gossett) can beat ten consecutive opponents in 24 hours. Of course, there's more to it than this: old-fashioned racism, Mafia involvement, killings, copious side-bets, and all the chicanery that goes on when big bucks are at stake. Though the blood flows copiously, the film is mainly a mass of punchy one-liners, sight gags, sporting and heroic fantasies, and champion performances. Naturally the film bears no relation to the physical laws of bodily damage, but in the end, who cares? SGr

Digimon Digital Monsters – The Movie

(1999/2000, Jap/US, 88 min)
d Mamoru Hosada, Shigeyasu Yamauchi. *p* Terry-Lei O'Malley, (Japan) Hiromi Seki. *sc* Reiko Yoshida, (English adaptation) Jeff Nimoy, Bob Buchholz. *ed* Douglas Purgason, Gary A Friedman. *m* Udi Harpaz, Amotz Plessner. *cast* voices: Lara Jill Miller, Joshua Seth, Bob Papenbrook, David Lodge, Dorothy Elias-Fahn, Jeff Nimoy, Bob Buchholz.

● Despite being another sub-standard TV merchandising tie-in, this *animé* monster movie is, if anything, a little more endurable than both *Pokémon* flicks. Obviously, the level of animation won't set the world on fire – it's fuzzy and flat – but there are occasional flourishes from the design team. The action takes place mostly in cyberspace, where an evil Digimon (digital monster) is messing with the Internet and the world's email systems. Time for the technically literate DigiDestined (eight spikey-haired kids) to summon their own friendly Digimons and do what they gotta do. Good to see a kids' movie address a few bang up to date issues. Indeed, some of Jeff Nimoy's translated dialogue is rather witty. The peppy soundtrack, too, is ripe for the Internet generation. But the film's still poppycock. (The US version consists of three Japanese *Dejimon* shorts.) DA

Dillinger

(1945, US, 70 min, b/w)
d Max Nosseck. *p* Frank King, Maurice King. *sc* Philip Yordan. *ph* Jackson Rose. ed Edward Mann. *ad* Frank P Sylos. *m* Dimitri Tiomkin. *cast* Lawrence Tierney, Edmund Lowe, Anne Jeffreys, Eduardo Ciannelli, Elisha Cook Jr, Marc Lawrence.

● Dubbed 'the first conceptual gangster epic', this unmoralistic, detached portrayal of Public Enemy Number One is a fine example of a sensational story, cheaply produced with stock footage, that gets away with artistic murder. Tierney is the glum psychopath, a skilled professional hitting the headlines with his dubious talent. Unemotional and rough at the edges, it's a sobering inventory of a fabulous myth. DMacp

Dillinger

(1973, US, 107 min)
d John Milius. *p* Buzz Fietshans. *sc* John Milius. *ph* Jules Brenner. *ed* Fred R Fietshans. *ad* Trevor Williams. *m* Barry DeVorzon. *cast* Warren Oates, Ben Johnson, Michelle Phillips, Cloris Leachman, Harry Dean Stanton, Steve Kanaly, Richard Dreyfuss, Geoffrey Lewis, John Ryan.

● Against a background of Depression America, where legendary status is bestowed on anyone who can beat the System, Dillinger and his gang rob banks with one eye already on posterity. Milius rightly makes no apology for endorsing the mythic qualities of his characters and setting his film firmly in the roots of American folklore. Bonnie and Clyde are dismissed as two-bit hoodlums, while the film's style condemns the knowing chic of Penn's film. Rather, it's closer in spirit to standard Western myths, or as if Corman had got his hands on Peckinpah's 'Pat Garrett and Billy the Kid'. Milius filters his story through countless B movies and detective stories, indirectly paying homage to all the different media that have contributed to the Dillinger legend, but keeps things the right side of nostalgia. Good to see AIP delivering the goods and producing movies like this. CPe

Dimanche à la Campagne, Un

see Sunday in the Country

Dimenticare Venezia (Forget Venice/To Forget Venice)

(1979, It/Fr, 110 min)
d Franco Brusati. *p* Claudio Grassetti. *sc* Franco Brusati, Jaja Fiastri. *ph* Romano Albani. *ed* Ruggero Mastroianni. *ad* Luigi Scaccianoce. *m* Benedetto Ghiglia. *cast* Erland Josephson, Mariangela Melato, Eleonora Giorgi, David Pontremoli, Hella Petri, Fred Personne.

● Bergman's icy world of guilts and repression transposed wholesale to sunnier Italian climes in Brusati's curiously allusive Art Movie (a surprise Oscar contender). An extended family reunion becomes (inevitably) an exorcism of childhood for its reticent participants, two discreetly gay couples spellbound by an operatic matriarch; while the eternal abstracts – sex, death, religion and art – provide a hermetic seal of 'class', only pierced by a few sharp edges of pain and a single shaft of optimism. PT

Dimples

(1936, US, 78 min, b/w)
d William A Seiter. *p* Darryl F Zanuck, Nunnally Johnson. *sc* Arthur Sheekman, Nat Perrin. *ph* Bert Glennon. *ed* Herbert Levy. *ad* William Darling. *m* Louis Silvers. *songs* Jimmy McHugh, Ted Koehler. *cast* Shirley Temple, Frank Morgan, Helen Westley, Robert Kent, Stepin Fetchit.

● Dimples you want, Shirley Temple you get, in this unstoppably cute vehicle for 1936's top attraction at the US box office. Even sceptics have to admit that Shirley's instinctive abilities acted most of her co-stars off the screen, but here loveable Morgan gives as good as he gets as the kindly grandfather who battles to keep custody of the dear little brat when rich socialite Helen Westley tries to adopt her. The tug-of-love plot is followed by the moppet's success on Broadway. TJ

Dim Sum – A Little Bit of Heart

(1985, US, 87 min)
d Wayne Wang. *p* Tom Sternberg, Wayne Wang, Danny Yung. *sc* Terrel Seltzer. *ph* Michael Chin. *ed* Ralph Wikke. *ad* Danny Yung. *m* Todd Boekelheide. *cast* Laureen Chew, Kim Chew, Victor Wong, Ida FO Chung, Cora Miao, John Nishio.

● A wonderful film about a more-or-less westernised Chinese family in San Francisco. Geraldine is perfectly happy going steady with her long-standing boyfriend, and she doesn't want to leave her widowed mother alone. But Mrs Tam is convinced that she will die soon, and she's determined to see Geraldine married. It's hard to say what makes this modest, undramatic story so extremely appealing. Maybe it's because Wang uses one family's experience as a key to a larger picture of the Chinese immigrant experience. Maybe because he's learned from Ozu and Allen Fong how to structure scenes that faithfully record the chaotic sprawl of everyday life. Or maybe it's just because of the great sense of humour. A real treat. TR

Diner

(1982, US, 110 min)
d Barry Levinson. *p* Jerry Weintraub. *sc* Barry Levinson. *ph* Peter Sova. *ed* Stu Linder. *ad* Leon Harris. *m* Bruce Brody, Ival Kral. *cast* Steve Guttenberg, Daniel Stern, Mickey Rourke, Kevin Bacon, Timothy Daly, Ellen Barkin, Paul Reiser, Kathryn Dowling.

● Directing from his own script, Levinson revels in detailed observation in this rites-of-passage movie about a college student returning home to Baltimore for the Christmas holidays in 1959, and picking up with the old gang as they try to fend off adulthood and marriage by hanging out at the local diner and talking about football, women, cars and rock'n'roll (Stern is particularly fine as the R&B buff, memorising record label serial numbers with religious awe). Not a lot to it, but the sense of period is acute, the script witty without falling into the crude pitfalls that beset other adolescent comedies, and the performances are spot-on. GA

Dîner de cons, Le

(1998, Fr, 80 min)
d Francis Veber. *p* Alain Poiré. *sc* Francis Veber. *ph* Luciano Tovoli. *ed* Georges Klotz. *ad* Hugues Tissandier. *m* Vladimir Cosma. *cast* Jacques Villeret, Thierry Lhermitte, Francis Huster, Alexandra Vandernoot, Daniel Prévost, Catherine Frot, Edgar Givry.

● Supercilious publisher Brochant (Lhermitte) needs a buffoon for his dining circle's 'idiot's dinner' party. Whoever sports the most exceptional idiot goes home triumphant, so Brochant can barely contain his pleasure at meeting slug-witted Pignon (Villeret), a well meaning but decidedly inane minion accountant blessed only with a gift for ornate matchstick modelmaking. As any fule might guess, Brochant won't be making it to the dinner; back strain leaves him stranded with his now unwanted guest in his Paris flat, just when his wife has decided to walk out in protest at his cruel games. A lowbrow French farce of the sort rarely exported to these shores, Veber's adaptation of his own stage comedy has nothing to offer by way of surprise or provocation, but it's deft as basic burlesque. The leads fill out their archetypes comfortably, the timing's well pitched, and the narrative moves busily enough. Cinematically, though, there's little of interest. NB

Dinner at Eight

(1933, US, 113 min, b/w)
d George Cukor. *p* David O Selznick. *sc* Frances Marion, Herman J Mankiewicz, Donald Ogden Stewart. *ph* William Daniels. *ed* Ben Lewis. *ad* Leon Harris. *m* William Axt. *cast* Marie Dressler, John Barrymore, Wallace Beery, Jean Harlow, Lionel Barrymore, Billie Burke, Lee Tracy, Edmund Lowe, Jean Hersholt.

● Edna Ferber/George Kaufman play about sophisticated New York society, adapted for the screen by Frances Marion and Herman J Mankiewicz and perfect material for Cukor's satirical touch, despite his forebodings that Marie Dressler, starring as a haughtily impoverished Broadway star, 'looked like a cook and had never played this kind of part'. The laughs are mainly at the expense of the *nouveau riche* couple, a comedy of manners in which Harlow reveals her natural gift for humour and Beery confirms his status as the definitive boor. But the film also reflects the vagaries of the 1930s social scene, and John Barrymore virtually plays himself as the all-time lush. Perfect viewing for a wet Saturday afternoon. MA

Dinner Rush

(2000, US, 98 min)
d Bob Giraldi. *p* Lou Digiamo, Patty Greaney. *sc* Rick Shaughnessy, Brian Kalata. *ph* Tim Ives. *ed* Allyson C Johnson. *pd* Andrew Bernard. *m* Alexander Lasarenko. *cast* Danny Aiello, Edoardo Ballerini, Kirk Acevedo, Vivian Wu, Mike McGlone, Summer Phoenix, Sandra Bernhard.

●Cumulatively enjoyable, this restuarant-set entertainment blends mobster thriller, ensemble chamber piece and subtly affecting dynastic social drama. Aiello gives one of his graceful yet quietly formidable performances as the owner of an Italian eatery in NY's Tribeca that has recently gone 'nouvelle' under the influence of his son, an arrogant celebrity chef. 'When did eating dinner become a Broadway show?' drawls bigshot food writer Bernhard, as director Giraldi speeds expertly from the kitchens to the covers, perfectly capturing the dynamism and diversity of a busy evening through a string of colourful vignettes, paced to a good jazz, opera and fast beat score. Aiello is the anchor, surveying the business from his table like a benevolent lord, dispensing advice both culinary and personal – not least to his other, dangerously impecunious gambler son. If it's finally a little too neat, that's a small price to pay for such a smorgasbord of small delights. WH

Dinosaur

(2000, US, 82 min)
d Ralph Zondag, Eric Leighton. *p* Pam Marsden. *sc* John Harrison, Robert Nelson Jacobs. *ed* H Lee Peterson. *pd* Walter P Martishius. *m* James Newton Howard. *cast* voices: DB Sweeney, Alfre Woodard, Ossie Davis, Max Casella, Hayden Panettiere, Samuel E Wright, Julianna Margulies, Peter Siragusa, Joan Plowright.

●The breathtaking opening of Disney's computer-generated family entertainment – a swooping bird's eye view of Earth's fauna and flora 65 million years ago – knocks spots off earlier CGI movies, but must have eaten so much of the budget that the rest looks strangely pedestrian. That's a shame, because aurally and visually this creature feature is a treat, no matter that it's a palaeontological/climatalogical/geological pick 'n' mix. The script nods towards the meteorite theory of dinosaur extinction, but allows little iguanodon Aladar to survive among a cutesy lemur community. The dull plot concerns a cross-species dinosaur drive through the desert to fresh breeding grounds and sees ideological battle between nasty down-mouthed Kron and young Aladar. Kron's sister, meanwhile, is caught between the two. Disney has gained a lot from its relationship with the smaller more adventurous Pixar, which shows in the marvellous point-of-view shots, backgrounds and surface textures. WH

Dinosaurus!

(1960, US, 85 min)
d Irvin S Yeaworth Jr. *p* Jack H Harris. *sc* Jean Yeaworth, Dan E Weisburd. *ph* Stanley Cortez. *ed* John Bushelman. *ad* Jack Senter. *m* Ronald Stein. *cast* Ward Ramsey, Paul Lukayher, Kristina Hanson, Gregg Martell, Fred Engelberg, Alan Roberts.

●A tropical island that time has half forgotten. Thanks to some very contrived plotting (freak flashes of lightning and the like), various animals of Jurassic vintage are brought back to life. There's a bizarre sub-plot about the friendship between all-American teenager Alan Roberts and caveman Gregg Martell, and a surprising vein of sentimentality. Ludicrous but mildly more engaging than the customary Killer-B. GM

Diplomat, The

(2000, Aust, 81 min, b/w & col)
d Tom Zubrycki. *p* Sally Browning, Wilson Da Silva. *sc* Wilson Da Silva, Tom Zubrycki. *ph* Robert Humphreys, Tom Zubrycki, Jo Parker, Joel Peterson. *ed* Ray Thomas. *m* Jan Preston. *with* José Ramos Horta.

●After the fall of Indonesia's President Suharto comes a timely documentary portrait of Nobel Peace prizewinner José Ramos Horta. East Timor, the former Portuguese colony, experienced a brief taste of freedom before the Indonesian invasion of 1975 forced Ramos Horta into a 24-year exile. The film shows both the public and private face of a man who gave up the gun for an ambassador's suit, intercutting his tireless campaigning with b/w footage of military atrocities. While the film doesn't examine reasons for the invasion, or the political and commercial motivation for the world's apparent apathy, it gives insight into the character of this tenacious and charismatic diplomat as well a being a paean to his eventual success in securing the freedom of his homeland. JFu

Diplomatic Courier

(1952, US, 97 min, b/w)
d Henry Hathaway. *p* Casey Robinson. *sc* Casey Robinson, Liam O'Brien. *ph* Lucien Ballard. *ed* James B Clark. *ad* Lyle Wheeler, John F DeCuir. *m* Sol Kaplan. *cast* Tyrone Power, Patricia Neal, Stephen McNally, Hildegard Knef, Karl Malden, James Millican.

●Neat, taut espionage thriller, with Power out to avenge a friend's death and finding himself on the trail of a secret document which will alert America to Soviet plans for the invasion of Yugoslavia. Cold War simplistics rule, as always in the early '50s. But the plot, adapted from a Peter Cheyney novel (*Sinister Errand*) runs mainly to fast-moving action, and with Trieste as the principal location, it's beautifully shot by Lucien Ballard in a globe-trotting equivalent to the semi-documentary style Hathaway evolved in *The House on 92nd Street*, *13 Rue Madeleine* and *Call Northside 777*. TM

Diplomatic Immunity

(1991, Can, 94 min)
d Sturla Gunnarsson. *p* Sturla Gunnarsson, Steve Lucas. *sc* Steve Lucas. *ph* Harald Ortenburger. *ed* Jeff Warren. *ad* Therese Wachter. *m* Jonathan Goldsmith. *cast* Wendel Meldrum, Michael Hogan, Michael Riley, Ofelia Medina, Pedro Armendariz Jr, Salvador Sanchez.

An Ottawa diplomat arrives in El Salvador after a coup to find that the Canadian housing project for the homeless has been taken over by soldiers and prostitutes. Though it doesn't shrink from the brutalities of civil war, this is not an action movie, but an intelligent investigation of the nature of Western aid, the hidden political agendas that control its distribution, and the desire of these 'victims' to determine their own future rather than just gratefully accept hand-outs. DW

Directed by Andrei Tarkovsky (Regi – Andrej Tarkovskij)

(1988, Swe, 101 min)
d Michal Leszczylowski. *p* Lisbet Gabrielsson. *sc* Michal Leszczylowski. *ph* Arne Carlsson. *ed* Michal Leszczylowski, Lasse Summanen. *with* Andrei Tarkovsky, Larissa Tarkovsky, Sven Nykvist, Tommy Kjellqvist.

●As documentaries on film-makers go, this is exemplary. The late Russian director's style and creative methods are illustrated, respectively, by clips from *The Sacrifice* and by shots of him on location in Sweden for that film; rehearsing his actors, functioning as his own camera operator during practice shots, discussing points of design and lighting with ace lensman Sven Nykvist, and most endearingly, revealing himself to be possessed of an easy sense of humour. But Tarkovsky is most widely revered for his spirituality and his ideas, which are manifested here in readings from his own book *Sculpting in Time*, and in excerpts from a lecture delivered to adoring students and fans. Indeed, where Leszczylowski comes up trumps is in the way he shows Tarkovsky turning theory into practice. Inevitably, given the man, the accent is on Art and Poetry, and it's arguable that there are too many shots of him in characteristic 'great director' pose, framing a scene with his hands and looking suitably intense. But overall, the film is to be commended for its objectivity. GA

Directed by William Wyler

(1986, US, 58 min, b/w & col)
d Aviva Slesin. *p* Catherine Tatge. *sc* A Scott Berg (narration). *ph* Robert Leacock. *ed* Aviva Slesin. *m* Roger Englander. *with* William Wyler, Bette Davis, Laurence Olivier, Lillian Hellman, Terence Stamp. *narrator* Harry S Murphy.

●Any biographical documentary that wheels on La Streisand as the first witness to genius is hardly likely to be profoundly critical or analytical, and this film rarely rises above the factual and sycophantic. That said, it's a watchable enough account of the career of one of Hollywood's most craftsmanlike directors, and with testimonies from Bette Davis, Billy Wilder, Lillian Hellman et al, does occasionally come up with unfamiliar information. Wyler's own contributions (recorded three days before his death) reveal a likeable, intelligent man. And the clips – from his debut A feature *Counsellor-at-Law*, through Goldwyn classics like *Wuthering Heights*, *The Letter* and *The Best Years of Our Lives*, to the final mess of *Funny Girl*, are well chosen. GA

Dirigible

(1931, US, 102 min, b/w)
d Frank Capra. *sc* Jo Swerling, Dorothy Howell. *ph* Joe Wilbur, Elmer Dyer. *ed* Maurice Wright. *cast* Jack Holt, Ralph Graves, Fay Wray, Hobart Bosworth, Clarence Muse, Roscoe Karns.

●Two Navy pilots testing dirigibles for use in antarctic regions; one crashes, and the other, off to the rescue, covets his wife. Actually, it isn't quite so sappy as it sounds, thanks to good performances and careful pacing, but the triangle still creaks a little in a strangled, peculiarly British way: Wray tires of hubby Graves never being home, since he's always swashbuckling off to risk his neck and keep his name in the news; Holt loves her in quiet, strong-jawed self-abnegation; but he knows where her true love lies, even when she proposes to divorce Graves to marry him, and so bows out gracefully. There's compensation in some fine special effects involving the irresistibly photogenic dirigibles. TM

Dirnentragödie (Tragedy of the Street)

(1927, Ger, 85 min approx, b/w)
d Bruno Rahn. *sc* Ruth Goetz, Leo Heller. *ph* Guido Seeber. *ad* Carl Ludwig Kirmse. *cast* Asta Nielsen, Werner Pittschau, Oscar Homolka, Hilde Jennings.

●Before road movies there were street films, a distinct cycle within German silent cinema. The essential ingredient – misalliance between bourgeois and slum dweller – is present here, though somewhat displaced by Asta Nielsen's star persona. She plays an aging hooker who falls for handsome Felix, a student who has rowed with his parents and ventured into the lower depths. Dreaming of a new life, she ejects her pimp and invests her savings in a cake shop. Even without that title, though, you wouldn't bet on a happy ending. Nielsen is a quite restrained sort of diva, and Rahn likewise soft pedals the melodrama, except for the grand finale. He died soon after making this, his contemporaries regretting the masterworks the cinema was thus denied. Well, maybe. BBa

Dirt

(2001, US, 102 min)
d Michael Covert, Trace Fraim. *p* Trudi Callon, Kirk Hassig. *sc* Michael Covert. *ph* Seo Mutarevic. *ed* Rod Dean, William Fletcher. *pd* Cody Rogers. *m* Tommy Coster. *cast* Trace Fraim, Michael Covert, Jack Kehler, Tara Chocol, Shirley A Williams, Bethany 'Rose' Hill, Patrick Warburton, Jennifer Tilly, Angel, Sandra Horse, Fiona Curtis, Michael Horse.

●Quirky US indie fare, with cultish aspirations and more than a nod to both David Lynch and the Coen brothers. We're down Texas way for an everyday tale of kidnappings and bank robbery, when simple brothers Junior and Scooter need to replace their deceased mother in the care stakes. Things inevitably spiral. There's not enough going on beyond the reasonably amusing set-up to warrant major attention, but it's diverting enough, nicely played and generally understated. GE

Dirt for Dinner (Dreckfresser)

(2000, Ger, 75 min)
d/sc Branwen Okpako. *ph* Susanne Schüle. *ed* Calle Overweg, Gilda Rosskamp, Bettina Blickwede. *with* Sam Meffire.

●Sam Meffire is one of those documentary subjects crying out for movie treatment. To begin at the end, he's currently serving ten years for a number of armed robberies committed with his partners in a security firm. Only a year or two earlier – in his early 20s – he'd been Saxony's most famous policeman, held up as a model of East German multiculturalism and integration in a national advertising campaign, interviewed by reporters at home and abroad. See, Meffire is the son of a (white) German and a (black) Cameroon – a Cameroon, moreoever, who died claiming he had been poisoned by his fellow students. Okpako's TV doc interviews friends and reporters (often one and the same, as everyone he met seems to have befriended him) and exposes the intolerable pressures on a young man growing up German and black without parental support. TCh

Dirty Dancing

(1987, US, 100 min)
d Emile Ardolino. *p* Linda Gottlieb. *sc* Eleanor Bergstein. *ph* Jeff Jur. *ed* Peter C Frank. *pd* David Chapman, Stephen Lineweaver. *m* John Morris. *cast* Jennifer Grey, Patrick Swayze, Jerry Orbach, Cynthia Rhodes, Jack Weston, Jane Bruckner.

●In many ways, a routine teen-flick with its '60s setting, sex, rock'n'roll and interfering stereotypical adults; but after so many movies trading on the oats-sowing traumas of male adolescence, here's one that looks at a young girl's sexual adventures in a serious and self-effacing manner. College-bound Baby (Grey), on holiday with her parents at a Borscht-Belt hotel, finds her way to a party where the resort's resident dance partners (Swayze and Rhodes) are feeling each other up and rubbing crotches in time to the music. Baby is shocked and thrilled, and when Rhodes is put out of action by an abortion, jumps at the chance to partner Swayze. This involves being coached to professional standard in just a few days, which stretches credibility but allows for some movingly coy scenes as the two fall in love and into bed, with none of the incumbent fretting about loss of respect, integrity or virginity on Baby's part. A safe combination of laughs, tears and an improbably happy ending, but sensitive performances, a burning rock'n'soul soundtrack and sleazy choreography carry the day. EP

Dirty Dozen, The

(1967, US/GB, 150 min)
d Robert Aldrich. *p* Kenneth Hyman. *sc* Nunnally Johnson, Lukas Heller. *ph* Ted Scaife. *ed* Michael Luciano. *ad* William Hutchinson. *m* Frank De Vol. *cast* Lee Marvin, Ernest Borgnine, Richard Jaeckel, Robert Ryan, George Kennedy, (and The Dirty Dozen) Charles Bronson, John Cassavetes, Telly Savalas, Donald Sutherland, Jim Brown, Trini Lopez, Ben Carruthers, Clint Walker, Stuart Cooper, Al Mancini, Colin Maitland, Tom Busby.

●Over the years, *The Dirty Dozen* has taken its place alongside that other commercial classic, *The Magnificent Seven*. The violence which liberal critics found so offensive has survived intact. Aldrich sets up dispensable characters with no past and no future, as Marvin reprieves a bunch of death row prisoners, forges them into a tough fighting unit, and leads them on a suicide mission into Nazi France. Apart from the values of team spirit, cudgeled by Marvin into his dropout group, Aldrich appears to be against everything: anti-military, anti-Establishment, anti-women, anti-religion, anti-culture, anti-life ('We got enough here to blow up the whole world'). Overriding such nihilism is the super-crudity of Aldrich's energy and his humour, sufficiently cynical to suggest that the whole thing is a game anyway, a spectacle that demands an audience. (*The Mean Machine* offers the reverse: American football as total war). The then-unknown Donald Sutherland's moronic performance is a treat. CPe

Dirty Harry

(1971, US, 101 min)
d/p Don Siegel. *sc* Harry Julian Fink, Rita M Fink, Dean Riesner. *ph* Bruce Surtees. *ed* Carl Pingitore. *ad* Dale Hennesy. *m* Lalo Schifrin. *cast* Clint Eastwood, Harry Guardino, Reni Santoni, John Vernon, Andy Robinson, John Larch, John Mitchum.

●Uncredited writer John Milius was thinking of Kurosawa's detective movies, and of outrageous antagonists differentiated only by the badge one wears; director Siegel was thinking of bigotry and, as ever, in terms of questions rather than answers. Critics were immediately thinking of effects ('Every frame votes Nixon'). Siegel's ambiguity wins out, as it had done with *Invasion of the Body Snatchers* (anti-Red? anti-McCarthy?). Seminal law-and-order cinema, and the site of revival for the oldest cine-political argument of all: does an articulated theme necessarily constitute an ideological position, especially when it's so transparent (cop Callahan's fascism) that it's noticed by everyone who's ever written about the film? It's more than a little embarrassing when critics trust audiences less than film-makers do. PT

Dirty Ho (Lantou He)

(1979, HK, 99 min)
d Lau Kar-Leung aka Liu Jialiang. *p* Run Run Shaw. *cast* Gordon Liu, Wong Yu, Lo Lieh, Hui Yinghong, Wang Longwei.

●Marking the very highest point ever reached by the kung fu genre, Lau's masterpiece concerns an imperial prince (Liu) travelling incognito in South China who 'enslaves' the petty thief Ho (Wong) by wounding him with a poison to which he alone possesses the antidote. When the prince is summoned back to Beijing for an urgent meeting about the imperial succession, the thief has no choice but to tag along; there are daily traps and ambushes on the road because a rival wants the prince out of the way. The film lovingly exploits the ambiguity of the central relationship: does the prince pick up the thief because he lusts after his body, because he wants to improve him morally or simply because he needs a bodyguard? Working with two of his own most brilliant pupils, Lau constructs several of the genre's most intricately choreographed set-pieces: the 'disguised' fight conducted while examining priceless antiques is in the Gene Kelly class. The UK video release of this 'Scope film is correctly letterboxed but poorly dubbed – because Shaw Brothers refused to supply a Chinese-language master. TR

Dirty Knight's Work

see Trial by Combat

Dirty Laundry

(1996, US, 92 min)
d Michael Normand, Robert Sherwin. *p* Robert Sherwin, Robert E Dimilia. *sc* Michael Norman. *ph* John Newby. *ed* Andrew Morreale. *pd* John Paino. *m* James Legg. *cast* Jay Thomas, Tess Harper, Tresa Hughes, Michael Marcus, Stanley Earl Harrison.

●Worried about his dry-cleaning business and unduly concerned about hair loss, Thomas finds himself unable to respond sexually to his wife Tess Harper. A shrink's advice that infidelity might buck him up backfires, and soon Harper's gone off with her chiropractor. This black marital comedy is in many ways a conventional, even predictable affair, though it's enlivened by neat one-liners and occasionally transmits a genuine sense of pain, confusion and absurdity. Minor but watchable. GA

Dirty Little Billy

(1972, US, 100 min)
d Stan Dragoti. *p* Jack L Warner. *sc* Charles Moss, Stan Dragoti. *ph* Ralph Woolsey. *ed* David Wages. *ad* Malcolm Bert. *m* Sascha Burland. *cast* Michael J Pollard, Lee Purcell, Richard Evans, Charles Aidman, Dran Hamilton, Willard Sage, Gary Busey.

●A surreally realistic account of the pre-fame days of Billy the Kid (characterised by Pollard as the mental retard of history) that culminates in the first of his many killings. A film full of contradictions: Dragoti's vision of the West is truly unromantic, Coffeyville, Kansas, being seen as a mudbath with the saloon as a womb no one wants to leave, yet at the same time the visuals are breathtakingly beautiful. Well worth a look. PH

Dirty Mary

see Fiancée du Pirate, La

Dirty Mary, Crazy Larry

(1974, US, 92 min)
d John Hough. *p* Norman T Herman. *sc* Leigh Chapman, Antonio Santean. *ph* Michael D Margulies. *ed* Christopher Holmes. *m* Jimmie Haskell. *cast* Peter Fonda, Susan George, Adam Roarke, Vic Morrow, Kenneth Tobey, Eugene Daniels, Roddy McDowall.

●B road-movie that serves only to underline how much Monte Hellman transformed the genre with *Two-Lane Blacktop*. This outing offers little more than plastic, would-be superstars playing at being kooky people as Fonda holds up a supermarket and drives around furiously, the police in pursuit, with his mechanic and girl-along-for-the-ride in tow (yes, another fashionable three-way relationship). The script, about small-timers who wished they were bigger, is soon totally undermined by Fonda's most complacent performance to date and Susan George's sub-Goldie Hawn antics. By way of compensation, the locations are quite pretty and the car stunts are handled with a certain verve. CPe

Dirty Money

see Flic, Un

Dirty Pictures

(2000, US, 104 min)
d Frank Pierson. *p* Michael Manheim, Vicky Herman. *sc* Ilene Chaiken. *ph* Hiro Narita. *ed* Peter Zinner. *pd* Alicia Keywan. *m* Mark Snow. *cast* Ann Marin, James Woods, Craig T Nelson, Diana Scarwid, Leon Pownall, David Huband, Judah Katz, RD Reid.

●Reality meets genre in a pacy exploration of events surrounding the Robert Mapplethorpe's posthumous 1990 exhibition. Notorious for his frank depiction of children and gay SM practices, the American photographer was admired and reviled. When Dennis Barrie (Woods), director of the Cincinnati Contemporary Arts Center, goes ahead with the show, despite pressure from his Board and right-wing campaigners, obscenity charges are brought. The trial tests Barrie's family ties, while shaping as a key battle in the struggle for freedom of expression. So far, so worthy (and worthwhile), but the film lifts off from its factual origins to deliver a major plea for tolerance and minority understanding, and against political censorship in culture generally. Coming over at times like a radical left-field essay film, it weaves talking heads (Salman Rushdie, William Buckley Jr, politicos and creatives) with archive and news footage to build a profound argument about the ramifications for the entire community of such 'slippery slope' behaviour. GE

Dirty Rice

(1997, US, 87 min)
d Pat Mire. *p* Pat Mire, Susan Levitas, Susannah MacMillan, Alan Durand. *sc* Pat Mire. *ph* Randy Walsh. *ed* Kyle Curry. *pd* Randall LaBry. *m* Gerry McGee. *cast* Ben Mouton, Myriam Cyr, Gerry McGee, Mary Ann Boudreaux, David Petitjean, Bob Edmundson.

●City lad inherits father's rundown rice farm, and with just days to go before the banks close in, he chances on the old man's groundbreaking recipe for rice wine. Documentary maker Mire's first feature may well be an accurate depiction of rural Cajun life, but its quaint little *Field of Dreams*-style tale unwinds so slowly and with so little dramatic intrigue that you're left longing for something – anything – to inject a little gumbo into the proceedings. Matters aren't helped by an ensemble of mostly bland performances. Fortunately, McGee's evocative soundtrack – a spicey mix of traditional Cajun foot-stompin' tunes and Ry Cooder-esque bottleneck geetar – keeps one tuned through to the predictable coda. DA

Dirty Rotten Scoundrels

(1988, US, 110 min)
d Frank Oz. *p* Bernard Williams. *sc* Dale Launer, Stanley Shapiro, Paul Henning. *ph* Michael Ballhaus. *ed* Stephen A Rotter, William Scharf. *pd* Roy Walker. *m* Miles Goodman. *cast* Steve Martin, Michael Caine, Glenne Headly, Anton Rodgers, Barbara Harris, Ian McDiarmid.

●Two con men working the Riviera town of Beaumont-sur-mer set a wager to decide which of them should have the rights to the patch. In standard 'odd couple' style, our heroes' credentials are diametrically opposed: Caine is all textbook sophistication, posing as a prince in exile; Martin is a two-bit hustler whose party-piece involves a bedridden granny about to pop her clogs. The wager involves screwing the first available woman for $50,000, although the money becomes secondary as the boys' hearts are set aflame by Headly's physical charms.

Since the film's publicity tells you that there's a 'delightful final twist', you'd have to be a bit dippy not to figure out that the lads are themselves being soft-soaped. There's little enough to keep you occupied as Caine and Martin go through their comic set pieces in workaday fashion while the film moves mechanically from one contrived situation to the next. A remake of *Bedtime Story*, 1946, with Brando and Niven in the leading roles. MK

Dirty Weekend

(1992, GB, 103 min)
d Michael Winner. *p* Michael Winner, Robert Earl. *sc* Michael Winner. *ph* Alan Jones. *ed* Arnold Crust [Michael Winner]. *pd* Crispian Sallis. *m* David Fanshawe. *cast* Lia Williams, Rufus Sewell, Michael Cule, David McCallum, Sean Pertwee, Ian Richardson.

●Is it too easy to say that Winner's version of Helen Zahavi's brutal feminist best-seller resembles the shoddier end of the Death Wish series? Could the director, perhaps, be playing a deeper game? Winner has cunningly shot whole tracts to resemble out-takes from local cinema advertising, which distances the audience from the material and indeed from wakefulness itself. The story is pie simple. Bella (Williams), sick of gropers and peeping toms, visits an Iranian clairvoyant (Richardson in cocoa butter) who advises her to join the predators – and donates his flick knife. Over a weekend in Brighton, she dispatches chaps with a hammer, a polythene bag, a car, a gun and the knife. Fans of the gross will savour the bondage freak and the forced blow-job with vomiting. Pretty rotten. BC

Disappearance, The

(1977, GB/Can, 102 min)
d Stuart Cooper. *p* David Hemmings. *sc* Paul Mayersberg. *ph* John Alcott. *ed* Eric Boyd-Perkins. *pd* Anne Pritchard. *m* Robert Farnon. *cast* Donald Sutherland, Francine Racette, David Hemmings, John Hurt, David Warner, Peter Bowles, Virginia McKenna, Christopher Plummer.

●Impressive and glossy thriller, scripted by Paul Mayersberg from Derek Marlowe's novel *Echoes of Celandine*, about a hired killer forced to take on an assignment in England even though his wife has mysteriously disappeared. Although the direction is occasionally a little precious – with studiedly stylish tableaux accompanied by Ravel – Sutherland is suitably haunted and cold as the confused assassin, and John Alcott's superb camerawork, on location in an icy Canada and a leafy Suffolk, is a definite bonus. And there are some fine supporting performances, particularly from Warner, Hurt and, most memorably, McKenna. GA

Disappearance of Finbar, The

(1996, Ire/GB/Swe/Fr, 105 min)
d Sue Clayton. *p* Bertil Ohlsson, Martin Bruce-Clayton. *sc* Sue Clayton, Dermot Bolger. *ph* Eduardo Serra *ed* J Patrick Duffner. *ad* Ned McLoughlin, Connor Devlin, Bengt Fröderberg. *m* Davy Spillane. *cast* Jonathan Rhys Meyers, Luke Griffin, Sean Lawlor, Sean McGinley, Fanny Risberg.

●Bored by life on a Dublin housing estate, rebellious teen Finbar Flynn (Rhys Meyers) is used to disappointing the everyone's expectations of him, but not to the extent of vanishing without trace, leaving only the unanswered question: did he jump, fall, or was he even pushed from that unfinished motorway flyover? The mystery of whether he's dead or alive haunts the community, his mum cracks up and his best friend, Danny (Griffin), can't seem to get on with living his own life. Then, one night three years later, Danny hears from Finbar, berating him about a pop video commemorating his disappearance. The call is from Stockholm, and Danny leaves on a search that will lead to the snowy wastes of Lapland. This quirky comedy-drama is hard to categorise, but extremely watchable. For one thing, Danny's odyssey involves encounters with a variety of engagingly eccentric, deftly drawn characters resulting in deadpan, off-the-wall humour reminiscent of Jarmusch or Kaurismäki. The performances are appealing, too, with Griffin's mix of innocence and indignation holding the rambling story together, and Rhys Meyers oozing cool, feckless charisma. GA

Disappearance of Kevin Johnson, The

(1995, US, 106 min)
d Francis Megahy. *p* Scott Richard Wolf. *sc* Francis Megahy. *ph* John Newby. *ed* Hudson LeGrand. *ad* Sandy Grass. *m* John Coda, Keely Sims. *cast* Pierce Brosnan, James Coburn, Dudley Moore, Alexander Folk, Bridget Baiss, Ian Ogilvy, Richard Beymer.

●A British documentary crew, making a feature about Hollywood Brits, wants to interview prospective mogul Kevin Johnson. Then Johnson's announced missing. No one's perturbed, so the film-makers start to investigate, interviewing studio execs and estate agents, screenwriters and gardeners, girlfriends, starlets, models and waitresses. This 'mockumentary' (from a former BBC documentarist) is structured like *Spinal Tap*, looks like *Heidi Fleiss – Hollywood Madam*, and appears to have broadly scandalous (if light hearted) ambitions in the vein of *The Player*. With its enigmatic central figure set against the hermetic, shallow and guileful ways of LA's movie-making class, the movie recalls diverse examples of great American art: *Gatsby, Kane, Sunset Boulevard, The Long Goodbye*. Deliberate or not, this multiplicity of reference points fails the film, since essentially it's never anything more than slight, diverting entertainment. NB

Disciple of Death

(1972, GB, 84 min)
d Tom Parkinson. *p/sc* Tom Parkinson, Mike Raven. *ph* William Brayne. *ed* Richard Key. *ad* Denys Pavitt. *m* Johann Sebastian Bach. *cast* Mike Raven, Ronald Lacey, Stephen Bradley, Marguerite Hardiman, Virginia Weatherell, Rusty Goff.

●Words cannot convey the awfulness of this Grand Guignol about a revivified corpse vampirising maidens in 18th century Cornwall. It might well have been made over a weekend. The watchword was obviously one take of everything: people fluff lines and mess up entrances (particularly on the horses, which nobody can ride), and close-ups reveal the gauze holding wigs, beards and eyebrows together. The acting is preposterous, and towards the end, the appearance of a Jewish magician ('Trinity schminity') heralds an irrationally jokey (but quite unfunny) climax which is either an indication that the whole thing is a leg-pull or a last-ditch attempt to pump some life into the proceedings (it's difficult to tell).

Discipline for the Left-Handed (Hidari Chokyo)

(1999, Jap, 57 min)
d Koji Shirakawa. *collaborators/cast* Shirakawa Toshiko, Jonoichi Akira, Ishii Kenichiro, Shinohara Ryuichi, Matsubara Toyo, Hayashiyama Kiyomi.

●Disturbed and disturbing punk art memento as the director addresses his mother's suicide from the confines of the mental institution where she worked. How much of this can be read as autobiographical 'truth' is difficult to imagine, but the assault of primal imagery, loops, samples, and alienation effects speaks volumes. TCh

Disclosure

(1994, US, 128 min)
d Barry Levinson. *p* Barry Levinson, Michael Crichton. *sc* Paul Attanasio. *ph* Tony Pierce-Roberts. *ed* Stu Liner. *pd* Neil Spisak. *m* Ennio Morricone. *cast* Michael Douglas, Demi Moore, Donald Sutherland, Caroline Goodall, Dennis Miller, Roma Maffia, Dylan Baker.

●DigiCom executive Tom Sanders (Douglas) expects a promotion. Instead he gets shafted: first, an old flame, Meredith Johnson (Moore), gets the job, then she attempts to seduce him in the office. He resists her advances, and next day finds himself accused of sexual harassment. When he counter-sues, DigiCom close ranks against him. This slick Michael Crichton adaptation certainly knows its business. It's glossy, suspenseful, and features what – for a mainstream movie – must be the most explicit unconsummated sex scene in years. Screenwriter Paul Attanasio has effectively neutralised Crichton's meretricious sexism with a string of impressive, independent female roles, and a surprisingly sophisticated take on gender discrimination, even if the casting of Douglas and Moore suggests a more reductive reading. Hokey and classy in equal measure, this is better than it ought to be. TCh

Disco Pigs

(2000, GB/Ire, 93 min)
d Kirsten Sheridan. *p* Ed Guiney. *sc* Enda Walsh. *ph* Igor Jadue-Lillo. *ed* Ben Yeates. *pd* Zoë MacLeod. *m* Gavin Friday, Maurice Seezer. *cast* Elaine Cassidy, Cillian Murphy, Brian O'Byrne, Eleanor Methven, Geraldine O'Rawe, Darren Healy.

●Born only moments apart, next door neighbours Pig (Murphy) and Runt (Cassidy) have been inseparable ever since, their unique bond expressed by a private language somewhere between infant gurgling and sixth form poetry. The secondary school reckons it's unhealthy and tries to prise them apart, but while Runt herself is starting to experience a few hormonal tingles over classmate Marky (Healy), Pig is intent on taking their relationship 'to a new level'. The end of innocence is shaping up to be rather messy. Sheridan's adaptation of Enda Walsh's play is marked by the decision to retain Walsh's heightened theatrical dialogue, which invites the performers to deliver a commensurate full-on emotionalism. Some may be spellbound, others will want to spit. With his spookily blue eyes, Murphy is a unique, forceful presence among young leading men, Cassidy deftly shades the progression from wide-eyed pixie to complicated adult complete with fears and longings, while Sheridan displays an unerring feel for the build-up of tension within scenes, despite the overall predictability of the 'fairytale goes sour' outline. TJ

Discreet Charm of the Bourgeoisie, The (Le Charme Discret de la Bourgeoisie)

(1972, Fr, 105 min)
d Luis Buñuel. *p* Serge Silberman. *sc* Luis Buñuel, Jean-Claude Carrière. *ph* Edmond Richard. *ed* Hélène Plemiannikov. *ad* Pierre Guffroy. *cast* Fernando Rey, Delphine Seyrig, Stéphane Audran, Bulle Ogier, Jean-Pierre Cassel, Paul Frankeur, Julien Bertheau.

●Delightful if overrated comedy from Buñuel, flitting about from frustrating situation to frustrating situation as six characters in search of a meal never manage actually to eat it. Are they prevented by their own fantasies? by their lack of purpose? by their discreet charm? Buñuel never really lets us know, while managing to skip through some very funny scenes en route. But it does lack the savage bite and genuinely nightmarish feel of his earlier work (comparison with *The Exterminating Angel* shows up the later film's complacency), while the chic stylishness of the characters comes over as overbearing rather than satirically revealing. GA

Discrète, La

(1990, Fr, 95 min)
d Christian Vincent. *p* Alain Rocca. *sc* Christian Vincent, Jean-Pierre Ronssin. *ph* Romain Winding. *ed* François Ceppi. *m* Jay Gottlieb. *cast* Fabrice Luchini, Judith Henry, Maurice Garrel.

●In this very Rohmer-esque film, Rohmer alumnus Fabrice Luchini is wonderfully cringesome as a literary dilettante who revenges himself on womankind by writing a seduction diary at the expense of a randomly chosen victim. The interest lies not so much in the predictable intrigue – it almost reads like a commonplace seduction comedy – as in the treatment of a particularly unpalatable strain of French amorous discourse. Seen from the perspective of Old World *libertinage* – the film drops its eighteenth century references liberally enough to tip you off – it takes issue with a tradition of socially-sanctioned nastiness. It is also perilously balanced on the quality of its performances: idiosyncratic new name Judith Henry, and Luchini displaying a fabulous repertoire of prissy tics and moues. If nothing else, see it for the way he answers the telephone. JRo

Diseurs de Vérité, Les (Speakers of the Truth)

(2000, Neth, 70 mins)
d/sc Karim Traïdia. *ph* Jacques Laureys. *ed* Chris Teerink. *pd* Jany Temime, Anne Winterink. *m* Fons Merkies. *cast* Sid Ahmed Agoumi, Monique Hendrickx, Mireille Perrier, Jaap Spijkers.

●Algerian journalist Sahafi (Agoumi) is faced with an awful dilemma. If he returns to Algeria, he's almost certain to be assassinated. If he takes political asylum in the Netherlands, he faces a bleak existence in a country where he knows no one and is treated like a pariah. Writer/director Traïdia (who emigrated to Holland from Algeria in the late 1970s) explores both options. It's as if Sahafi is leading parallel lives. In one strand of the story, we see him fighting a forlorn battle for freedom of speech in Algeria. In the other, he runs aground against an implacable Dutch bureaucracy. Sombre, heavy on talk, this is a probing and intelligent political drama. Agoumi, one of Algeria's best known stage actors, brings dignity and pathos to his role as the conscience-torn journalist. GM

Dish, The

(2000, Aust, 101 min)
d Rob Sitch. *p* Santo Cilauro, Tom Gleisner, Jane Kennedy, Rob Sitch, Michael Hirsh. *sc* Santo Cilauro, Tom Gleisner, Jane Kennedy, Rob Sitch. *ph* Graeme Wood. *ed* Jill Bilcock. *pd* Carrie Kennedy. *m* Edmund Choi. *cast* Sam Neill, Kevin Harrington, Tom Long, Patrick Warburton, Genevieve Mooy, Tayler Kane, Billie Brown, Roy Billing.

●Sitch and company follow their bonzer Aussie comedy *The Castle* with a wry and gently patriotic retelling of how a satellite dish in the middle of a sheep paddock and its small team of operators broadcast the first Moon landing to the watching world. The story is slight, a mishap with the power supply and an unexpected gale providing the only notes of tension. But the warmth and breadth of the characterisation, which extends from Neill and his team to a NASA interpolator, half the local community and the Australian PM, certainly commends it, and the throwaway comic detail is very endearing. NB

Dishonored

(1931, US, 91 min, b/w)
d Josef von Sternberg. *sc* Daniel N Rubin. *ph* Lee Garmes. *ad* Hans Dreier. *m* Karl Hajos. *cast* Marlene Dietrich, Victor McLaglen, Lew Cody, Warner Oland, Gustav von Seyffertitz, Barry Norton.

●'1915…Strange figures emerge from the rubble of the Austrian Empire': among them X-27 (Dietrich) and H-14 (McLaglen), military spies and best-loving enemies. Sternberg's absurd espionage melodrama is just one more peg on which to hang his familiar, outrageous pictorial stylistics and to extend his fetishisation of Marlene – yet the result is amazing. Beyond improbability lies another of Sternberg's systematic examinations of the feminine mystique, and the tragedy of a woman sacrificed on the altar of her sexualty. Right on the surface lies the inevitable patina of telling innuendo; in one deliciously transparent scene, Marlene is betrayed by her own pussy(cat), which eventually lands up safe in the arms of the church as Marlene is shot for her sins. PT

Disney's The Kid

(2000, US, 104 min)
d Jon Turteltaub. *p* Jon Turteltaub, Christina Steinberg, Hunt Lowry. *sc* Audrey Wells. *ph* Peter Menzies Jr. *ed* Peter Honess, David Rennie. *pd* Garreth Stover. *m* Marc Shaiman. *cast* Bruce Willis, Spencer Breslin, Emily Mortimer, Lily Tomlin, Chi McBride, Jean Smart, Dana Ivey, Daniel Von Bargen.

●If you had a chance to meet yourself as an eight-year-old, would that kid be happy with who you turned out to be? That's the premise, according to the blurb, of this Disney's offering. How it ever got beyond the pitch is a mystery. Willis is Russ Duritz, a cynical, short-tempered but successful image consultant who's missing something in life – and doesn't even realise it. That's when the kid (Breslin) arrives: a rambunctious klutz called Rusty who wheedles himself into Russ's life. Rusty, as it happens, is Russ as a youngster, and has unwittingly tripped back in time to help Russ, er, find himself. Sentimental moments are signposted by Marc Shaiman's typically bombastic score, but there's little to touch the heart here, since Russ and Rusty's predicament is completely nonsensical. Besides, how can we root for a smug workaholic who has everything and seems happy with it? Willis alone makes it just about endurable. DA

Disorderly Orderly, The

(1964, US, 89 min)
d Frank Tashlin. *p* Paul Jones. *sc* Frank Tashlin. *ph* W Wallace Kelley. *ed* John Woodcock. *ad* Hal Pereira, Tambi Larsen. *m* Joseph J Lilley. *cast* Jerry Lewis, Glenda Farrell, Everett Sloane, Karen Sharpe, Kathleen Freeman, Susan Oliver, Alice Pearce.

●Some longueurs, but also wonderful gags in Tashlin's best cartoon style (ranging from Lewis helping an astonished patient to brush the teeth he isn't wearing yet, or furtively sweeping dust away under a corner of artificial lawn, to the mathematically precise demolition of a supermarket by runaway stretcher). How much you enjoy the film probably depends on the extent to which you can stomach the Lewis sentimentality, here given fulsome rein since he is not only forlornly in love but practically canonised in his desire to help suffering humanity. There is also, alas, plenty of opportunity for characteristic Lewis mugging each time his would-be doctor, afflicted with a severe case of squeamishness, meets his nemesis in the shape of a patient (the inimitable Pearce) with an inexhaustible supply of ghastly symptoms on tap. TM

Disparen a Matar (Shoot to Kill)

(1992, Ven, 90 min)
d Carlos Azpurúa. *p* Adolfo López Sojo. *sc* David Suarez. *ph* Adriano Moreno. *ed* Sergio Curiel. *cast* Amalia Pérez Díaz, Jeancarlo Simancas, Daniel Alvarado.

●A minister's son is killed passing a troubled working-class estate on the outskirts of the Venezuelan capital, Caracas. A woman from the estate (whose husband was killed by dictatorship forces 30 years before) witnesses her son being beaten up by the police in a reprisal attack. He later dies, and she approaches journalist Santiago, insisting that he expose the injustice, a course of action which brings him into conflict with his editor, the corrupt police and security forces, and his own political conscience. This first fiction film by veteran documentarist Azpurúa is a hard-hitting, deeply felt attack on the mechanics of political corruption, injustice and repression, made into a stylish thriller in the Costa-Gavras mould. WH

Disparus de Saint-Agil, Les

(1938, Fr, 102 min, b/w)
d Christian-Jaque. *sc* Jean-Henri Blanchon. *ph* Marcel Lucien. *ed* Claude Nicole. *ad* Pierre Schild. *m* Henri Verdun. *cast* Michel Simon, Erich von Stroheim, Aimé Clariond, Serge Grave, Armand Bernard, Robert le Vigan, Marcel Mouloudji.

●Odd that a charming, facile and wholly unmemorable journeyman like Christian-Jaque (the Vadim of Martine Carol) should have excelled in that most problematic of genres: the children's film. An almost surrealistically creepy thriller set in a boys' school (with faint echoes of *Zéro de Conduite*) and boasting a cast that would have done credit to a more heavyweight movie, *Les Disparus* can be recommended to all grown-ups from eight to eighty. GAd

Distance

(2001, Jap, 132 min)
d Hirokazu Kore-eda. *p* Masayuki Akieda. *sc* Hirokazu Kore-eda. *ph* Yutaka Yamazaki. *ed* Hirokazu Kore-eda. *ad* Toshihiro Isomi. *cast* Arata, Susumu Terajima, Yusuke Iseya, Yui Natsukawa, Tadanobu Asano, Ryo.

●It's admirable that Kore-eda sets himself new challenges each time he makes a film, but the attempt to conjure substance from conversations improvised around a complicated and obscure back-story in *Distance* proves fairly unrewarding. Opening scenes sketch the domestic lives of four very disparate individuals; only when they converge and drive into a forest together is it revealed that they're all relatives of cult members whose terrorist action in Tokyo caused many deaths three years earlier. The cult executed the culprits, and these protagonists are visiting the site to commemorate the deaths. Along the way they meet a cult member (Asano), who leads them to an old cabin in the woods; a night is spent reminiscing and soul searching. Kore-eda must be searching for something banal and everyday which explains why people join cults and perpetrate atrocities in their name. Whatever the answer, it proves elusive – which must be why he suddenly introduces an anomalous hint of melodrama in the closing scenes, questioning the real identity of Atsushi (Arata), one of the mourners. TR

Distant Drums

(1951, US, 101 min)
d Raoul Walsh. *p* Milton Sperling. *sc* Niven Busch, Martin Rackin. *ph* Sid Hickox. *ed* Folmar Blangsted. *ad* Douglas Bacon, William Morris. *m* Max Steiner. *cast* Gary Cooper, Mari Aldon, Richard Webb, Arthur Hunnicutt, Ray Teal, Robert Barrat.

●A reworking of *Objective Burma!* in Western terms, with Seminoles replacing the Japanese as Cooper's veteran scout leads a motley group through jungle swamplands during an Indian uprising. The characters are fairly basic, but marvellous use is made of the Florida Everglades, and the set pieces (the nocturnal attack on the fort garrisoned by Indians and their renegade gunrunners, Coop's underwater duel with the Seminole chief) are terrific. TM

Distant Thunder (Ashani Sanket)

(1973, Ind, 101 min)
d Satyajit Ray. *p* Sarbani Bhattacharya. *sc* Satyajit Ray. *ph* Soumendu Roy. *ed* Dulala Dutt. *m* Satyajit Ray. *cast* Soumitra Chatterjee, Babita, Romesh Mukerji, Chitra Bannerji, Gobinda Chakravarty, Sandhya Roy, Noni Ganguly, Sheli Pal, Suchita Roy, Anil Ganguly, Debatosh Ghosh.

●Middle period Ray in that its political theme is powerfully evident, yet remains filtered through a prime concern with the characters. The setting is Bengal in 1942, with millions threatened by man-made famine (food is diverted for military use; prices rise; profiteers profit). Against this background, Ray delicately sketches the coming of age of a young Brahmin (an endearingly funny and tender performance by Soumitra Chatterjee); from a caste traditionally acting as priest, teacher and doctor, supported by his village as a mark of respect, the Brahmin first has to learn – mainly through the agency of his strong-minded and sensitive wife (Babita) – not only just what he is supposed to be preaching, teaching and prescribing, but how to earn the respect he is accorded. The crux for these two good people comes when, faced by their own hunger as well as the starving beggars by now omnipresent, an untouchable dies outside their house. The Brahmin's decision (tacitly approved by his wife) to break taboo by touching the body (to bury it, safe from the jackals) rings out in Indian terms as a call to revolution. Distant thunder, indeed; a superb film. TM

Distant Thunder

(1988, US/Can, 114 min)
d Rick Rosenthal. *p* Robert Schaffel. *sc* Robert Stitzel, Deedee Wehle. *ph* Ralf Bode. *ed* Dennis Virkler. *m* Maurice Jarre. *cast* John Lithgow, Ralph Macchio, Kerrie Keane, Reb Brown, Janet Margolin, Dennis Arndt.

●The dependable Lithgow is a Vietnam vet who's taken to the wilderness to be alone with his psychological wounds, while Macchio tries his best as the son he hasn't seen in more than 15 years. A putative reunion is the motor for this drearily uninvolving offering: a very well-troden trail. Not for Satyajit Ray fans. TJ

Distant Trumpet, A

(1964, US, 116 min)
d Raoul Walsh. *p* William H Wright. *sc* John Twist. *ph* William H Clothier. *ed* David Wages. *ad* William Campbell. *m* Max Steiner. *cast* Troy Donahue, Suzanne Pleshette, James Gregory, Diane McBain, William Reynolds, Claude Akins, Judson Pratt, Bartlett Robinson, Bobby Bare, Richard X Slattery, Larry Ward, Kent Smith.

●Walsh's last film, saddled with an average script and a colourless lead performance from Donahue, but nevertheless emerging as a majestically simple, sweeping cavalry Western, a little reminiscent of Ford in mood and manner. Brilliantly shot by William Clothier, it tends to have its cake and eat it by indulging in a spectacular massacre before introducing the liberal message, but still goes further than most in according respect to the Indian by letting him speak his own language (with subtitles). The laconic mastery here belies the accusations of decline levelled at Walsh, even if many of his later films were disappointing. TM

Distant Voices, Still Lives

(1988, GB, 84 min)
d Terence Davies. *p* Jennifer Howarth. *sc* Terence Davies. *ph* William Diver, Patrick Duval. *ed* William Diver. *ad* Miki van Zwanenberg, Jocelyn James. *cast* Freda Dowie, Peter Postlethwaite, Angela Walsh, Dean Williams, Lorraine Ashbourne, Sally Davies, Nathan Walsh, Susan Flanagan, Michael Starke, Vincent Maguire, Antonia Mallen, Jean Boht, Pauline Quirke.
●Through a fragmented series of almost ritualistic gatherings drawn from his own family's memories of the '40s and '50s, Davies paints a vivid picture of the painfully restrictive knots bound round a working class family by a stern, unforgiving patriarch who lords it over wife, son and daughters with mute menace and brute force. These stark, impressionistic vignettes are explained, deepened, counterpointed and savagely undercut by the popular songs of the period that fuel the narrative: never have 'Taking a Chance on Love', 'O Mein Papa' and 'Up a Lazy River' been heard to such ironic and emotionally devastating effect. Music is crucial to Davies' decidedly neo-realist method, partly as a self-protective strategy adopted by his downtrodden creatures. If this sounds unbearably cerebral or excruciatingly melancholy, fear not. It all looks superb, the largely unknown cast performs to perfection, and the entire movie works beautifully, both as an unprecedentedly honest, unpatronising account of British working class life, and as a tribute to the human spirit's capacity to survive immense setbacks with dignity. Ambitious, intelligent, profoundly moving, it thrills with passion, integrity and imagination unseen in British cinema since Powell and Pressburger. GA

Distinguished Gentleman, The

(1992, US, 112 min)
d Jonathan Lynn. *p* Leonard Goldberg, Michael Peyser. *sc* Marty Kaplan. *ph* Gabriel Beristain. *ed* Tony Lombardo, Barry B Leirer. *pd* Leslie Dilley. *m* Randy Edelman. *cast* Eddie Murphy, Lane Smith, Sheryl Lee Ralph, Joe Don Baker, Victoria Rowell, Grant Shaud, Kevin McCarthy, Charles S Dutton, James Garner.
●Murphy makes a partial return to form as a con-artist in this *Trading Places*-style comedy. After Senator Jeff Johnson (Garner) dies while giving job satisfaction to his attractive female researcher, Thomas Jefferson Johnson (Murphy) shortens his name, lengthens his CV, and breezes into Congress on the strength of misplaced 'name recognition'. Once elected, abetted by a political wheeler-dealer (Smith) and a power lobbyist (Baker), he wastes no time in greasing the right palms, making the best social connections, and getting on to financially advantageous committees. The film's credibility takes a sudden dive, though, when Murphy, confronted by a young female constituent whose cancer *may* have been caused by her school's proximity to high-voltage power lines, instantly abandons avarice and cynicism. Lynn handles the set-ups and verbal fencing deftly, but there is only so much he can do with former political speech-writer Marty Kaplan's crass script, which aims at easy targets, lacks momentum, and ultimately fails to pay off. NF

Disturbed

(1990, US, 96 min)
d Charles Winkler. *p* Brad Wyman. *sc* Charles Winkler, Emerson Bixby. *ph* Bernd Heinl. *ed* David Handman. *pd* Marek Dobrowolski. *m* Stephen Scott. *cast* Malcolm McDowell, Geoffrey Lewis, Priscilla Pointer, Pamela Gidley, Irwin Keyes, Deep Roy, Clint Howard, Kim McGuire.
●A black comic tale of medical madness, Winkler's debut feature stars McDowell as Dr Russell, a perverted psychiatrist whose past misdemeanours come back to haunt him. Ten years ago, Russell drove a patient to suicide with his forced sexual attentions. But when he tries it again with Sandy Ramirez (Gidley), it all goes wrong. Drugged into submission like the last victim, Sandy is seized by spasms and apparently dies; but the following day her body has vanished. Soon Russell starts getting nightmares, hallucinations, and pertinent singing telegrams from beyond the grave. McDowell gives a gloriously deranged performance, while the beautiful Gidley gets strong support from Lewis (as a sympathetic fellow-patient) and Pointer (a professionally compromised nurse). Who could resist a film which contains this pithy exchange: Nurse Francine to the wigged-out Dr Russell, 'You need professional help'; Russell, 'I am professional help!' NF

Disturbing Behavior

(1998, US/Aust, 84 min)
d David Nutter. *p* Armyan Bernstein, John Shestack. *sc* Scott Rosenberg. *ph* John S Bartley. *ed* Randy Jon Morgan. *pd* Nelson Coates. *m* Mark Snow. *cast* James Marsden, Katie Holmes, Nick Stahl, Steve Railsback, Bruce Greenwood, William Sadler, Chad E Donella, Ethan Embry.
●Traumatised by the suicide of his brother, Steve (Marsden) and his family start a new life in the seemingly idyllic small town of Cradle Bay. Steve finds the local high school divided into familiar groups – jocks, geeks, skateboarders, etc – but soon he, sultry Rachel (Holmes) and geeky Gavin (Stahl) uncover a dastardly plot to iron out all the students' differences and turn them into jocks. How this is achieved is never adequately explained in this attempted cash-in on the high school horror cycle. A vaguely offensive cautionary thriller. TH

Dita Saxová

(1967, Czech, 112 min, b/w)
d Antonín Moskalyk. *sc* Arnost Lustig, Antonín Moskalyk. *ph* Jaroslav Kucera. *ed* Zdenek Stehlík. *ad* Vladimír Labsky. *m* Lubos Fiser. *cast* Krystyna Mikolajewska, Bohus Záhorsky, Karel Höger, Martin Ruzck, Noemi Sixtova, Jaroslava Obermaierová, Yvonne Prenosilová, Dana Syslová.
●Set in 1947, in a Jewish hostel for orphans of the concentration camps, this is a lyrical, humanist examination of the inevitable cost of loss. Dita, a striking young woman who works in the shelter, is barely present in her own life. Courted by numerous men, she's unable to make decisions about her future. Repeating the observation that 'life is not what we wish to have, but what we have,' she decides against emigration, and resigns herself to the drift of days. The quiet inevitability of her story's conclusion, coming as it does in the snow-capped mountains, adds a scale and grandeur to a struggle already given up, among dark interiors and the weary decadence of post-war parties and reconstruction. The b/w visuals, the almost Persian tableaux and Krystyna Mikolajewska's haunting looks all underline the nature of this personal journey, while staying cognizant of the huge social forces that have precipitated it. GE

Dites-lui que Je l'aime

see This Sweet Sickness

Diva (100)

(1981, Fr, 123 min)
d Jean-Jacques Beineix. *p* Irène Silberman. *sc* Jean-Jacques Beineix, Jean van Hamme. *ph* Philippe Rousselot. *ed* Marie-JosèpheYoyotte, Monique Prim. *pd* Hilton McConnico. *m* Vladimir Cosma. *cast* Frédéric Andrei, Richard Bohringer, Wilhelmenia Wiggins Fernandez, Thuy An Luu, Chantal Deruaz, Jacques Fabbri, Gérard Darmon.
●Marvellous amalgam of sadistic thriller and fairytale romance, drawing on a wild diversity of genres from *film noir* to Feuillade serial. The deliriously offhand plot, cheekily parodying Watergates and French Connections, has switched tapes setting a pair of psychopathic hoods on the trail of a young postal messenger, turning his obsessive dream – of romance with a beautiful black opera singer whose performance on stage he has secretly recorded – into a nightmare from which he is rescued by a timely *deus-ex-machina* (clearly a descendant of the great Judex). The most exciting debut in years, it is unified by the extraordinary decor – colour supplement chic meets pop art surrealism – which creates a world of totally fantastic reality situated four-square in contemporary Paris. TM

Divan à New York, Un

see Couch in New York, A

Dive Bomber

(1941, US, 133 min)
d Michael Curtiz. *p* Hal B Wallis. *sc* Frank 'Spig' Wead, Robert Buckner. *ph* Bert Glennon, Winton C Hoch. *ed* George Amy. *ad* Robert Haas. *m* Max Steiner. *cast* Errol Flynn, Fred MacMurray, Ralph Bellamy, Alexis Smith, Robert Armstrong, Regis Toomey.
●Released just months before the Japanese attack on Pearl Harbor, this isn't the wartime propaganda effort you'd expect from the title and star, but a tautly handled study of flying-related medical problems in which doc Flynn puts a few hours in the cockpit so he can discover exactly what it is that makes his fellow pilots blackout when they go into a dive. A surefire bet for plane nuts, only moderately engrossing for the rest of us. Rich camerawork courtesy of Technicolor specialists Bert Glennon and Winton C Hoch. TJ

Divided Heart, The

(1954, GB, 89 min, b/w)
d Charles Crichton. *p* Michael Truman. *sc* Jack Whittingham, Richard Hughes. *ph* Otto Heller. *ed* Peter Bezencenet. *ad* Edward Carrick. *m* Georges Auric. *cast* Cornell Borchers, Yvonne Mitchell, Armin Dahlen, Michel Ray, Alexander Knox, Geoffrey Keen, Theodore Bikel, Alec McCowen.
●A change of tack for comedy specialist Crichton in Ealing's true-life tug-of-love saga (written by Jack Whittingham and Richard Hughes) about a Bavarian couple, Borchers and Dahlen, who raise war orphan Ray as their own, then have to face the difficult consequences when the boy's real mother, a survivor of Auschwitz, is traced back in Yugoslavia. Mitchell is impressive as the distraught genuine mum trying to win back her child's affection through the language barrier that's grown up between them, and producer Michael Balcon rated this stolid, earnest drama one of the best films made at Ealing. TJ

Divided We Fall (Musíme si Pomáhat)

(2000, Czech Rep, 122 min)
d Jan Hrebejk. *p* Ondrej Trojan, Pavel Borovan. *sc* Petr Jarchovsky. *ph* Jan Malír. *ed* Vladimír Barák. *pd* Milan Bycek. *m* Ales Brezina. *cast* Boleslav Polívka, Anna Sisková, Jaroslav Dusek, Csongor Kassai. Jiri Pecha, Simona Stasova, Martin Huba.
●Czechoslovakia, a summer's day, 1937: three friends travel a deserted road and share a joke. Several years later, their relationship is incontrovertibly altered and their lives reveal in microcosm the destructiveness of war. David, a Jew, escapes from a concentration camp and is sheltered by Josef and his wife Marie in their pantry – while Horst, now a Nazi collaborator, is a dangerously regular visitor. Events take a bizarre turn when the only way of saving themselves is for David to father Marie's child. Like Benigni's *Life Is Beautiful*, this handsome, well acted and exemplary film allows humour and humanity to commingle with the full horror of war. JFu

Dividing Line, The

see Lawless, The

Divine (El Evangelio de las maravillas)

(1997, Mex, 112 min)
d Arturo Ripstein. *p* Jorge Sánche, Laura Imperiale. *sc* Paz Alicia García Diego. *ph* Guillermo Granillo. *ed* Ximena Cuevas. *ad* Mónica Chirinos. *m* David Mansfield. *cast* Paco Rabal, Katy Jurado, Carolina Papaleo, Flor Edwarda Gurrola, Bruno Bichir, Patricia Reyes Spíndola, Rafael Inclán.
●Those who enjoyed *Deep Crimson* will surely be disappointed by Ripstein's follow-up, an infuriatingly obscure parable about the millennium, religious faith, deception and God knows what. A bizarre sect wanders around the Mexican plains and indulges in in-fighting, but that's about all this viewer got out of it, notwithstanding the venerable presence of Rabal and Jurado. GA

Divine Body (Divine Carcasse)

(1998, Bel/Benin, 88 min)
d/p/sc Dominique Loreau. *ph* Etienne Degrammont. *ed* André Delvaux. *m* Philippe Woitchik. *cast* Szymon Zaleski, Alphonse Atacolodjou, Simonet Biokou.

● This debut feature by a Belgian woman director traces the trajectory of a battered old Peugeot exported from Belgium to Benin (West Africa), where its white owner, an economic development adviser, hands it on to his black houseboy. Frequently in for repairs, the car is run into the ground as a makeshift taxi and eventually left to be scavenged for its parts by the roadside – whereupon its remains are recycled by an artist who has been asked to fashion a sculpture of the god of nightwatchmen. The vague air of portentousness that hangs over a mainly lightweight film is offset by the modest charm of its glimpses of village life and people. But the overriding sense of 'us' and 'them' leaves it uncomfortably close to Jamie Uys territory. TR

Divine Emma, The (Bozká Ema)

(1979, Czech, 111 min)
d Jirí Krejcík. *sc* Zdenek Mahler, Jirí Krejcík. *ph* Miroslav Ondricek. *ed* Miroslav Hajek. *ad* Jindrich Goetz. *m* Zdenek Liska. *cast* Bozidara Turzonovová, Juraj Kukura, Milos Kopecky, Jirí Adamíra, Josef Somr, Cestmír Randa.

● An old-fashioned, slow-moving biopic, redeemed by some luscious photography and the gorgeous singing of Gabriela Benacková as the off-screen voice of Emma Destinn, opera singer and Czech nationalist at a time when Bohemia was submerged in the Austro-Hungarian Empire. Turning her back on fortune and fans in America at the start of WWI, Destinn rashly returned home carrying a cape with a concealed decoding device, to be arrested at the border and interned in her own stately home. Spurned by the opera houses, with only a deteriorating relationship with her estate manager and lover to sustain her, she rejected opportunities to escape and held hugely popular open-air concerts, to the severe embarrassment of her imprisoners. The film glories in her courage and talent, and she emerges as a sad, passionate woman. JE

Divine Intervention (Yadon Ilaheyya)

(2002, Fr/Ger/Morocco, 92 min)
d Elia Suleiman. *p* Humbert Balsan. *sc* Elia Suleiman. *ph* Marc-André Batigne. *ed* Véronique Lange. *ad* Miguel Markin, Denis Renault. *cast* Elia Suleiman, Manal Khader, Nayef Fahoum Daher.

● An engagingly offbeat if hit-and-miss Palestinian response to how Israeli checkpoints impose damaging barriers on the lives of ordinary individuals, this starts impressively with a deadpan comic sequence involving neighbourly neuroses, rivalries and vengeful rage in Nazareth. Then there's a shift as Suleiman arrives to take care of his hospitalised dad, while indulging in tricky trysts down by the watchtower with a girl from Ramallah. The gags range from the obvious and the attenuated, to the inspired, while Suleiman's blank Keatonesque stare is so overused that it soon becomes irritating. But there's an intelligence and freshness to the film's mostly wordless comic style (reminiscent of Tati and Iosseliani) that is undeniably appealing. GA

Divine Madness

(1980, US, 93 min)
d/p Michael Ritchie. *sc* Jerry Blatt, Bette Midler, Bruce Vilanch. *ph* William A Fraker. *ed* Glenn Farr. *pd* Albert Brenner. *cast* Bette Midler, 'The Harlettes' (Jocelyn Brown, Ula Hedwig, Diva Gray).

● Wearing what looks like an old dressing-gown, hair shoved up any old how, pouring sweat and mascara, Bette Midler closes her stage show a heaving wreck, and the audience love it. As 'The Divine Miss M', 'Sophie Tucker' and 'Dolores DeLago, the Toast of Chicago', she has cracked the dirtiest jokes, sung the raunchiest songs, derided the audience ('You'll laugh at any old thing'), belittled the Royals, the French, the Germans, herself, strutted, gone through her bump and grind routine, and yet at the end of it all manages to convince you with that tremulous smile that she is as insecure as any little girl from the Bronx just starting out in showbiz. It is the precise dash of self-mockery that she adds to even her crudest stories and gestures that takes the sting from the tail, that makes the wonderfully slaggy Greek chorus ('The Harlettes') her partners and not just a titillating sideshow, and that raises the 'smutty joke' from the gutter to the flyover. Unsullied, despite her efforts, Bette triumphs. FF

Divorce American Style

(1967, US, 108 min)
d Bud Yorkin. *p/sc* Norman Lear. *ph* Conrad Hall. *ed* Ferris Webster. *pd* Edward Stephenson. *m* David Grusin. *cast* Dick Van Dyke, Debbie Reynolds, Jason Robards, Jean Simmons, Van Johnson, Shelley Berman, Joe Flynn, Martin Gabel, Tom Bosley, Lee Grant, Eileen Brennan.

● 'When was the last time you had relations, Mr Harmon?' With this question, put by a marriage counsellor to Dick Van Dyke – who is of course excused from answering – Norman Lear's script toys uneasily with the realities of marital life but carefully preserves the conventions. Despite the trappings of hard-boiled satire – a couple breaking up in a welter of money-grubbing ill-temper, children facing up to broken homes, other divorcees hovering in hopes of snaring a remarriage that will get them off the alimony hook – this is in fact divorce Hollywood style. Li'l ol' love wins out, with Dick and Debbie coming together again like the beautiful people they are. Two or three very funny scenes, all the same, and a first-rate batch of supporting performances. TM

Divorce of Lady X, The

(1938, GB, 91 min)
d Tim Whelan. *p* Alexander Korda. *sc* Ian Dalrymple, Arthur Wimperis, Lajos Biro. *ph* Harry Stradling. *ed* LJW Stockviss, William Hornbeck. *ad* Lazare Meerson, Paul Sheriff. *m* Miklos Rozsa. *cast* Merle Oberon, Laurence Olivier, Binnie Barnes, Ralph Richardson, Morton Selten, JH Roberts.

● Korda lavished an expensive Technicolor production job on this wafer-thin comedy, a remake of the 1933 quota quickie *Counsel's Opinion*. Unable to find a room at a top London hotel, Oberon spends an innocent night in stranger Olivier's bed under the pretence that they're a married couple. Next day the latter is visited by Lord Richardson, ready to divorce his wife on the ground that she'd been in another gentleman's room the night before. Major-league thesps in their fresh-faced youth. TJ

Divorcing Jack

(1998, GB/Fr, 110 min)
d David Caffrey. *p* Robert Cooper. *sc* Colin Bateman. *ph* James Welland. *ed* Nick Moore. *pd* Claire Kenny. *m* Adrian Johnston. *cast* David Thewlis, Rachel Griffiths, Jason Isaacs, Laura Fraser, Richard Grant, Robert Lindsay.

● If a madcap comedy-thriller about Northern Ireland sounds like a dubious proposition, think again. Ulsterman Colin Bateman's screenplay from his own novel is the first to capture Northern Ireland's pitch black sense of humour fully on screen. Thewlis plays boozy newspaper columnist Dan Starkey, used to shit-stirring on both sides of the political divide, but not to landing in the thick of it himself when murder pitches up at his door. On the run from gunmen of unknown persuasion, he hooks up with nurse and part-time Nun-o-Gram Griffiths, as the trail leads back to Robert Lindsay's slick prime ministerial candidate, who promises to heal the sectarian rift forever. This first feature impressively sidesteps the old questions of Orange or Green affiliation, so we can enjoy its whirl of sarky remarks, killer plot twists and genuine Belfast locations. TJ

Dixie

(1943, US, 89 min)
d A Edward Sutherland. *p* Paul Jones. *sc* Karl Tunberg, Darrell Ware, Claude Binyon. *ph* William C Mellor. *ed* William Shea. *ad* Hans Dreier, William Flannery. *songs* Johnny Burke, Jimmy van Heusen. cast Bing Crosby, Dorothy Lamour, Billy De Wolfe, Marjorie Reynolds, Lynne Overman, Raymond Walburn, Eddie Foy Jr.

● Routinely whitewashed biopic of blackface minstrel Daniel Decatur Emmett, finding fame, fortune and love in 19th century New Orleans, and managing to turn the title song into the Confederate battle hymn en route. A surprisingly attractive film, nevertheless, with the impressive period reconstructions – shot in glowing colours – helping to flesh out a desperately manufactured plot. Above all, it's directed by Sutherland with a care and affection that shows, relying on nostalgic, old-fashioned groupings that cunningly echo the quaintly formalised stage groupings of the resurrected minstrel show acts. Excellent cast, too. TM

Dixie Dynamite

(1976, US, 88 min)
d Lee Frost. *p* Wes Bishop. *sc* Lee Frost, Wes Bishop. *ph* Lee Frost. *ed* Igo Kantor. *songs* Jerry Styner, Porter Jordan. cast Warren Oates, Jane Anne Johnstone, Kathy McHaley, Christopher George, Wes Bishop, Stanley Adams, RG Armstrong.

● After the ramshackle delights of *Race with the Devil* and *The Thing with Two Heads*, this is a disappointing addition to the Lee Frost/Wes Bishop collection. Though the story – sisters Patsy and Dixie enlist the help of motor-cycling drunk Warren Oates in a campaign of explosive revenge after the death of their pa in a moonshine war – is told with its authors' usual exuberance in both action and dialogue, there's no disguising how humdrum the basic material is. It's time Lee and Wes graduated to more ambitious budgets. AN

17 rue Bleue

see 17 rue Bleue [as 'Seventeen rue Blue']

Django

(1966, It/Sp, 95 min)
d Sergio Corbucci. *p* Manolo Bolognini, Sergio Corbucci. *sc* Sergio Corbucci, Bruno Corbucci. *ph* Enzo Barboni. *ed* Nino Baragli, Sergio Montanari. *ad* Giancarlo Simi. *m* Luis Enriquez Bacalov. *cast* Franco Nero, Eduardo Fajardo, Loredana Nusciak, José Bodalo, Angel Alvarez, Rafael Vaquero.

● Originally banned in Britain for its comic-strip iconoclasm and graphic violence, this rates alongside Leone's 'Dollars' trilogy as one of the daddies of the spaghetti/paella Western. It's a clean-up-and-paint-the-town-blood-red revenge drama with a difference. Nero's mud-spattered ex-Yankee soldier, first seen squelching towards a US-Mexican border ghost town, a coffin forever in tow, has every Western hero's quality *in extremis*. His speed-of-light gunslinger outlaw has a romantic heart – his wife was killed by one of Major Jackson's KKK-like henchmen – and an enigmatic morality. He solves the war between Jackson's men and General Rodríguez' bandidos by dispensing death to all, but his sympathies are shown when he later teams up with Rodríguez for a gold heist. Corbucci's style is a mix of social realism, highly decorative visuals, and finely mounted action sequences. For the rest, there are enough mud-wrestling prostitutes, whippings, ear-loppings, explosions and scenes of wholesale slaughter to keep any *muchacho* happy. Funny, visceral, bloody, no-nonsense entertainment with a touch of class. WH

Django Kill (Se Sei Vivo, Spara)

(1967, It/Sp, 120 min)
d Giulio Questi. *p* Alex J Rascal. *sc* Giulio Questi, Franco Arcalli. *ph* Franco Delli Colli. *ed* Franco Arcalli. *m* Ivan Vandor. *cast* Tomas Milian, Piero Lulli, Milo Quesada, Paco Sanz, Roberto Camardiel, Marilù Tolo.

● Giulio Questi (a former associate of Fellini) and Franco Arcalli (later Bertolucci's regular writing partner) devised this dour, notoriously excessive spaghetti Western, which pushes the brutality of the genre to almost surreal ends. Milian's the double-crossed Mexican gang leader out for revenge on his former partner (Lulli). The film begins promisingly but then loses its way in a succession of melodramatic grotesqueries, including suffocation by molten gold, roastings on a spit, and the killing of children. The Italian version runs two hours – 19 minutes longer than the original international release print. Not for the squeamish. TJ

Djomeh (aka Djomeh, L'Histoire du garçon qui tombait amoreux)

(2000, Fr/Iran, 94 min)
d/sc Hassan Yektapanah. *ph* Ali Loghmani. *ed/pd* Hassan Yektapanah. *cast* Jalil Nazari, Mahmoud Behraznia, Rashid Akbari, Mahbobeh Khalili, Valiollah Beta.

● Another subtle, resonant, utterly engrossing Iranian film. A young Afghani working on a dairy farm tries to overcome the wariness of the local villagers and, more significantly, the grocer's daughter he forlornly woos. Again, it's a quest story, but one whose exact import is often oblique (the 'message' is nicely understated) and whose tone is less sentimental or earnest than a wry blend of compassion and irony. Add to that its lovely, lucid, off-kilter imagery, and it sometimes echoes Kiarostami's *The Wind Will Carry Us* – on which Yektapanah worked as assistant. GA

D.O.A.

(1949, US, 83 min, b/w)
d Rudolph Maté. *p* Leo Popkin. *sc* Russell Rouse, Clarence Greene. *ph* Ernest Laszlo. *ed* Arthur H Nadel. *ad* Duncan Cramer. *m* Dimitri Tiomkin. *cast* Edmond O'Brien, Pamela Britton, Luther Adler, Beverly Campbell, Lynn Baggett, Willing Ching, Neville Brand.

● Delirious descent into the maelstrom of '40s *film noir* as a small town businessman trades dull days and a loyal lover for a fling in the jazz nights of San Francisco. How he becomes enmeshed in the crueller, deadlier corruption of LA, solving the case of his own murder, involves a succession of ingenious twists too good to give away. Maté shoots fast and always to the point as he drives his protagonist through endless doorways and rooms which are like trapdoors and boxes in an accelerating nightmare. Maté, whose credits as cameraman include *Vampyr*, *Foreign Correspondent* and *Gilda*, holds it all together with no trouble, and without the slightest appeal to art gives the images the intensity of a dying man's last story. Breathless, indeed. CPe

D.O.A.

(1988, US, 97 min, b/w & col)
d Rocky Morton, Annabel Jankel. *p* Ian Sander, Laura Ziskin. *sc* Charles Edward Pogue. *ph* Yuri Neyman. *ed* Michael R Miller, Raja Gosnell. *pd* Richard Amend. *m* Chas Jankel. *cast* Dennis Quaid, Meg Ryan, Charlotte Rampling, Daniel Stern, Jane Kaczmarek, Christopher Neame, Robin Johnson, Rob Knepper.

● A remake of the 1950 *film noir*, presumably attracted by the lure of that implacable opening in which the hero staggers into the precinct house to report a murder: his own. Morton and Jankel's version likes that enough to re-stage it in black and white, and to issue the hero, boozy, disillusioned Eng Lit prof Dexter Cornell (Quaid), with a bellyful of slow-acting poison which gives him a day or so to find his murderer. Aided by adoring student Sydney (Ryan), to whom he attaches himself (literally) with superglue, Cornell batters against an impenetrable nighttown of red herrings. After a welter of murders, suicides, adulteries, buried birthrights, and a struggle with a tar-pit, Cornell learns the real meaning of publish or die on the campus. Borrowings apart, the plot is a muddle, and further confused by the Max Headroom team's mania for angle shots and distortions. Quaid is miles better than his material. BC

Dobermann

(1997, Fr, 103 min)
d Jan Kounen. *p* Frédérique Dumas, Eric Névé. *sc* Joël Houssin, Jan Kounen. *ph* Michel Amathieu. *ed* Bénédicte Brunet. *pd* Michel Barthélémy. *m* Schyzomaniac. *cast* Vincent Cassel, Monica Bellucci, Tchéky Karyo, Antoine Basler, Dominique Bettenfeld, Romain Duris.

● This is a film disconcertingly at ease with the hyper-charged squalor of its dog-eat-dog criminal netherland. The attraction is obvious – guns'n'goons here mean sex, drugs and rock'n'roll, at high speed and volume – and obviously limited. Either you get off on this cartoon nihilism or you get out. There's an end, a middle, and at least three beginnings to announce the director's intentions: a swaggeringly animated dog pisses over the opening credits; a baptismal benediction ends with the baby united with a gun in his cot; and the now grown Dobermann (Cassel) and moll (Bellucci) get hard and wet playing highway robbers with a rocket launcher. Thereafter, there's an extended sequence in which the Dobermann and his 'kennel' of depraved hard cases pull off a Paris bank heist under the noses of their police watchdogs, followed by another in which an extremely renegade police inspector (Karyo) attempts to trump his nemesis by taking the law and its arsenal into his own brutal hands. NB

Doc

(1971, US, 96 min)
d/p Frank Perry. *sc* Pete Hamill. *ph* Gerald Hirschfeld. *ed* Juan Serra. *pd* Gene Callahan. *m* Jimmy Webb. *cast* Stacy Keach, Faye Dunaway, Harris Yulin, Mike Witney, Denver John Collins, Dan Greenberg.

● A stab at the Doc Holliday/Wyatt Earp/OK Corral story which has pretensions towards 'stripping away the myth', but there are still the narrowed eyes, the staccato demands for whisky, and lines like 'One hand of five-card stud; my horse against your woman'. In return we have constant reminders of Doc's TB, and pregnant pauses which, in eschewing the tongue-in-cheek intensity of the Italian Westerns, are simply empty. The result is very downbeat, and ultimately fails to replace the excitement of total involvement in the myth with any deeper understanding of the real West. JC

Doc Hollywood

(1991, US, 103 min)
d Michael Caton-Jones. *p* Susan Solt, Deborah D Johnson. *sc* Jeffrey Price, Peter S Seaman, Daniel Pyne. *ph* Michael Chapman. *ed* Priscilla Nedd-Friendly. *ad* Lawrence Miller. *m* Carter Burwell. *cast* Michael J Fox, Julie Warner, Barnard Hughes, Woody Harrelson, David Ogden Stiers, Frances Sternhagen, George Hamilton, Bridget Fonda, Mel Winkler, Helen Martin, Roberts Blossom.

● Washington intern Ben Stone (Fox at his frenetic best) nurses hopes of fun, sun, bimbos and bucks from cosmetic surgery in California. Setting off for an interview in Beverly Hills, he loses his way in the Bible Belt and crashes his car in Grady, 'Squash Capital of the South'. The town seems stuck in the '50s. The natives initially resent the squirt from the city; also unwelcome are the manipulatory moves by man-hungry Nancy Lee (Fonda), and by the town elders who want a replacement for old Dr Hogue. But from the moment Stone sees ambulance-woman Lou (Warner) emerge from a lake naked, love raises its head. Will the charms of Grady and the independent Lou erode his determination before the car is rebuilt? Caton-Jones views all the characters with undisguised affection; the whole thing bubbles along nicely in a fresh, witty, unselfconscious manner, making you forget the dated Capra-corn message. WH

Doc Savage – The Man of Bronze

(1975, US, 100 min)
d Michael Anderson. *p* George Pal. *sc* George Pal, Joseph Morhaim. *ph* Fred J Koenekamp. *ed* Thomas J McCarthy. *ad* Fred Harpman. *m* John Philip Sousa. *cast* Ron Ely, Paul Gleason, Bill Lucking, Michael Miller, Eldon Quick, Darrell Zwerling, Paul Wexler.

● George Pal's last effort is a gargantuanly awful visualisation of the first in Kenneth Robeson's popular '30s pulp series, with Ron Ely (TV's Tarzan) as the superhuman leader of 'The Amazing Five' world experts as they track down the murderer of his father in South America. The special effects are pretty grim (unusual for a Pal production), but Anderson's direction is even grimmer, adopting the now obligatory (in the wake of Batman and Flash Gordon) camp attitude towards its pre-war fantasy subject. It's almost as though America is taunting itself for ever having taken its superheroes seriously. PM

Doc's Kingdom

(1987, Port/Fr/GB, 90 min)
d/p/sc [Robert] Kramer. *ph* Richard Copans. *ed* Sandrine Cavafian. *m* Barre Phillips. *cast* Paul McIsaac, Vincent Gallo, Ruy Furtado, Cesar Monteiro, Roslyn Payne.

● James 'Doc' Matter (McIsaac) might be a character from *Milestones*, Kramer's *cinéma-vérité* documentary-fiction about '60s activism in the US. Doc finds himself in a shack on the Lisbon waterfront. He's put his time in the political underground behind him, and he's survived (so we're told) a stint in a 'permanent war zone' in Africa and a disease which was never diagnosed. The writer/director, who credits himself simply 'Kramer', as though, like his anti-hero, he's mislaid his personal identity, takes a very long time reaching his point. Jimmy, the son Doc's never seen (he was conceived in the office of a prison chaplain while Doc was doing time), comes from America bringing news of his mother's death. Their meeting settles only that they need never meet again. JPy

Docteur Jekyll et les Femmes (The Blood of Doctor Jekyll/ Doctor Jekyll and Miss Osbourne)

(1981, Fr, 92 min)
d Walerian Borowczyk. *p* Robert Kuperberg, Jean-Pierre Labrande. *sc* Walerian Borowczyk. *ph* Noël Véry. *ed* Khadicha Bariha. *ad* Walerian Borowczyk. *m* Bernard Parmeggiani. *cast* Udo Kier, Marina Pierro, Patrick Magee, Howard Vernon, Clément Harari, Gérard Zalcberg.

● Borowczyk brings to this the same bizarre, poetic sensibility which made *Goto, Island of Love* and *Blanche* such outlandish wonders, but which forced him into working in the margins of the sex-film industry. He takes the traditional elements of the Stevenson story and turns them to his own surreal ends: the good doctor is transformed into a ravening beast and then stalks the corridors of a rambling Victorian house; the inhabitants find themselves under siege from within, and the threat is largely sexual. As usual Borowczyk exercises his immaculate, painterly eye for unusual objects and settings, and a fetishist's delight in costume (especially shoes). God knows what the raincoat trade makes of it: a film of strange and outrageous beauty which seems to emanate from that place where our fears are also desires. CPea

Docteur Petiot

(1990, Fr, 102 min, b/w & col)
d Christian de Chalonge. *p* Alain Sarde, Philippe Chapelier-Dehesdin. *sc* Dominique Garnier, Christian de Chalonge. *ph* Patrick Blossier. *ed* Anita Fernandez. *ad* Yves Brover. *m* Michel Portal. *cast* Michel Serrault, Pierre Romans, Zbigniew Horoks, Berangère Bonvoisin, Aurore Prieto, André Chaumeau, Axel Bogousslavski.

● De Chalonge's true story of mass murder in Occupied Paris has Dr Petiot stalking the city like a Nosferatu reborn, surrounding his murders with an obsessive theatrical ritual to a scratchy tango accompaniment. Self-conscious cinematic trickery – all expressionist *chiaroscuro* and silent-era iris shots – makes an unsettling frame for Petiot's career. The factual part is that Petiot ran a roaring trade persuading Jews that he could ship them safely to Argentina; after handing over their possessions, they ended up in his oven rather than Hitler's. Grisly as the tale is, de Chalonge gives it an almost comic air of Grand Guignol. A hideously flamboyant Serrault plays the killer as a Demon King with kohled eyes and flapping coat-tails. Yet there's a real sense of history, of the emergence from the night of Occupation into the tainted daylight of Liberation. This is a powerfully idiosyncratic shadow-show, an inventively cold-blooded inquiry into the way war breeds monsters – and an unqualified marrow-chiller to boot. JRo

Docteur Popaul (High Heels/ Scoundrel in White)

(1972, Fr/It, 101 min)
d Claude Chabrol. *p* André Génoves. *sc* Paul Gégauff. *ph* Jean Rabier. *ed* Jacques Gaillard. *ad* Guy Littaye. *m* Pierre Jansen. *cast* Jean-Paul Belmondo, Mia Farrow, Laura Antonelli, Daniel Ivernel, Daniel Lecourtois, Dominique Zardi, Henri Attal.

● The project on which Chabrol first gave his cynicism full rein and took his mordant playfulness to outrageous lengths. This coarse farce, hardly worth the vitriol poured on its apparent misogyny, always looked more like the director's revenge on the French mass audience, who had consistently ignored his good movies, but would accept anything with Belmondo, and in this case did. Ironic inversions of the star's image, charming ugly women for their 'moral beauty', or 'unmanned' as his schemes rebound, ring pretty hollow. PT

Doctor, The

(1991, US, 123 min)
d Randa Haines. *p* Laura Ziskin. *sc* Robert Caswell. *ph* John Seale. *ed* Bruce Seth Green, Lisa Fruchtman. *pd* Ken Adam. *m* Michael Convertino. *cast* William Hurt, Christine Lahti, Elizabeth Perkins, Mandy Patinkin, Adam Arkin, Charlie Korsmo, Wendy Crewson, Bill Macy.

●Reunited five years after *Children of a Lesser God*, Haines and Hurt are trapped here by a trite, predictable script. Jack McKee is a brilliant, happily married surgeon who lacks compassion for his patients. Only when he himself develops cancer does he start to appreciate the trials and terrors of being under the knife. McKee's search for inner goodness is guided by June (Perkins), a terminally ill fellow-patient. Can he right the wrongs of his thoughtless past and become a kinder, gentler man? Of course he can. This is American sitcom morality writ large: a lesson to be learned the hard way, but everyone comes out smiling at the end. Both Hurt and Lahti as his wife struggle valiantly with the material, but you can't help but wonder why they took it on in the first place. NKe

Doctor and the Devils, The

(1985, GB, 92 min)
d Freddie Francis. *p* Jonathan Sanger. *sc* Ronald Harwood. *ph* Gerry Turpin, Norman Warwick. *ed* Laurence Méry-Clark. *pd* Robert Laing. *m* John Morris, In Tua Nua. *cast* Timothy Dalton, Jonathan Pryce, Twiggy, Julian Sands, Stephen Rea, Phyllis Logan, Lewis Fiander, Beryl Reid, TP McKenna.
●Based on a screenplay by Dylan Thomas, this thinly disguised story of the notorious 'resurrectionists' Burke and Hare, supplying freshly killed bodies to a Victorian surgeon, comes across as watered-down Hammer Gothic, complete with trite metaphysical meditations. The depiction of the huddled Victorian whores, hags, beggars, drunks, idiots and street-pedlars forever rhubarbing in the grimy gloom is risible. The cast is as wooden as the three admittedly elegant studio sets. Twiggy's Cockney prostitute takes the Golden Stiff Award for sheer ineptitude, but surely even she didn't deserve the random, irrelevant inclusion of her tuneless tavern song spot? GA

Doctor Blood's Coffin

(1960, GB, 91 min)
d Sidney J Furie. *p* George Fowler. *sc* Jerry Juran. *ph* Stephen Dade. *ed* Antony Gibbs. *ad* Scott MacGregor. *m* Buxton Orr. *cast* Kieron Moore, Ian Hunter, Hazel Court, Gerald C Lawson, Kenneth J Warren, Fred Johnson, Paul Hardtmuth, Paul Stockman.
●Surprisingly grisly low-budget British exploitation effort in which surgeon Hunter and son Moore attempt to cheer up their widowed receptionist by exhuming her late husband and performing a primitive heart transplant. TJ

Dr Cyclops

(1940, US, 75 min)
d Ernest B Schoedsack. *p* Dale Van Every. *sc* Tom Kilpatrick. *ph* Henry Sharp, Winton Hoch. *ed* Ellsworth Hoagland. *ad* Hans Dreier, Earl Hedrick. *m* Ernst Toch. *cast* Albert Dekker, Thomas Coley, Janice Logan, Victor Kilian, Charles Halton.
●Marvellous performance by Dekker as the villainous Dr Cyclops – as bald as Lorre's Dr Gogol and going blind behind his pebble glasses, hence the echo of Homer's Polyphemus in his name and his ultimate fate – who lurks in the Amazonian jungle conducting experiments in which he shrinks people to manikin size. An engaging fantasy with brilliantly executed (though mostly rather unimaginative) special effects which look back to *The Devil Doll* and forward to *The Incredible Shrinking Man*. Let down by a dull supporting cast, but retrieved by the attractively pale, tremulous Technicolor. Based on a fine story by Henry Kuttner, writing under the pseudonym of Will Garth; beware the novelisation, also published as by 'Garth' but unmistakably the work of a hack. TM

Doctor Death: Seeker of Souls

(1973, US, 89 min)
d/p Eddie Saeta. *sc* Sal Ponti. *ph* Kent Wakeford, Emil Oster. *ed* Tony DiMarco. *ad* Ed Graves. *m* Richard La Salle. *cast* John Considine, Barry Coe, Cheryl Miller, Stewart Moss, Leon Askin, Jo Morrow, Moe Howard.
●Ludicrous hokum apparently completely recut at one stage in its history, about one Doctor Death who transplants souls. It all turns completely hilarious when the good doctor repeatedly fails to implant another soul in our hero's recently dead wife. The amateurishness of the proceedings give the whole thing the appearance of a pantomime, or maybe a stray episode from the *TV Batman* series. VG

Doctor Dolittle

(1998, US, 85 min)
d Betty Thomas. *p* John Davis, Joseph M Singer, David T Friendly. *sc* Nat Mauldin, Larry Levin. *ph* Russell Boyd. *ed* Peter Teschner. *pd* William Elliott. *m* Richard Gibbs. *cast* Eddie Murphy, Ossie Davis, Oliver Platt, Peter Boyle, Richard Schiff, Kristen Wilson, Jeffrey Tambor.
●John Dolittle (Murphy) has a way with animals. His childhood was spent chatting to dogs – his father put it down to an overactive imagination – but by the time he'd married, fathered kids and become a physician, he'd forgotten his unusual gift. Then, one evening, he narrowly misses running over a dog. The disgruntled hound proceeds to give the quack a piece of his mind, and before he knows it, Dolittle's hearing voices from trees, dustbins and café tables. Much to his chagrin, he can still communicate with the animal world. Everyone else, of course, thinks he's lost his marbles. Not surprisingly, Thomas's anthropomorphic comedy is as far from Hugh Lofting's sing-song original as it's possible to get. The thin storyline is a sideshow to some of the most realistic animatronic and computer effects to date. Not all the animal characters ring true, though, and some of the humour strays into crude, buttsniffin' territory. But Murphy's likeable, the script's laden with a gaggle of one-liners, and there's even a vague message nestling beneath the zoological chaos. DA

Dr Dolittle 2

(2001, US, 87 min)
d Steve Carr. *p* John Davis. *sc* Larry Levin. *ph* Daryn Okada. *ed* Craig P Herring. *pd* William Sandell. *m* David Newman. *cast* Eddie Murphy, Kristen Wilson, Jeffrey Jones, Kevin Pollak, Kyla Pratt, Raven-Symoné, Lil' Zane, James L Avery; voices: Steve Zahn, Lisa Kudrow, Jacob Vargas, Michael Rapaport, Isaac Hayes.
●This adolescent claptrap, complete with basement humour and barrel-scraping dialogue, treads a path similar to that of its predecessor. A raccoon insists that Dr D (Murphy) meet head honcho the Beaver. Their forest is about to be cleared by ruthless loggers, and nothing can save the furry folk except a preservation order. A rare Pacific Western bear provides an incentive for Dolittle to solve the crisis. The creatures are mostly irritating, Murphy is in cruise mode, and a subplot involving the doctor's family plays like an afterthought. DA

Dr Ehrlich's Magic Bullet

(1940, US, 103 min, b/w)
d William Dieterle. *p* Wolfgang Reinhardt. *sc* John Huston, Heinz Herald, Norman Burnside. *ph* James Wong Howe. *ed* Warren Low. *ad* Carl Jules Weyl. *m* Max Steiner. *cast* Edward G Robinson, Ruth Gordon, Otto Kruger, Donald Crisp, Maria Ouspenskaya, Sig Ruman.
●Misleadingly titled biopic of a doctor (Robinson) whose dedication to research brings him into conflict with the staid late-19th century German hospital in which he works. His subsequent discovery of a cure for syphilis vindicates his methods and earns him a wealthy patron. The screenplay – by John Huston (shortly to begin directing), Heinz Harald and Norman Burnside – earned a deserved Oscar nomination. NF

Doctor in the House

(1954, GB, 91 min)
d Ralph Thomas. *p* Betty E Box. *sc* Nicholas Phipps, Ronald Wilkinson. *ph* Ernest Steward. *ed* Gerald Thomas. *ad* Carmen Dillon. *m* Bruce Mongomery. *cast* Dirk Bogarde, Kenneth More, Donald Sinden, Donald Houston, Kay Kendall, Muriel Pavlow, James Robertson Justice.
●First in the Doctor series spawned by Richard Gordon's novels, a steady slog through the medical student joke-and-jape book, made bearable by the amiable (if somewhat over-age) cast. The sequel, Doctor at Sea, took Dr Simon Sparrow (Bogarde) on his first job as medical officer on a cargo steamer, starting the steady degeneration into mechanical farce that accelerated as the series progressed. Basically a slightly more sophisticated variation on the *Carry On* films, subtler in innuendo but even more predictable in situations, the series produced five more films up to 1970 (*Doctor at Large, Doctor in Love, Doctor in Distress, Doctor in Clover, Doctor in Trouble*), but found a more welcome refuge as a TV sitcom.

Doctor in the Nude, The

see Traitement de Choc

Doctor Jekyll and Miss Osbourne

see Docteur Jekyll et les Femmes

Dr Jekyll and Mr Hyde

(1920, US, 5,670 ft, b/w)
d John S Robertson. *p* Adolph Zukor. *sc* Clara S Beranger. *ph* Roy Overbaugh. *ad* Robert M Haas, Charles O Sessel. *cast* John Barrymore, Brandon Hurst, Martha Mansfield, Charles Lane, Nita Naldi, Louis Wolheim.
●Dominated by Barrymore's stagy bravura, and especially by the celebrated transformation scenes, this early adaptation of Stevenson's story elsewhere rarely rises above the routine, despite the efforts of cinematographer Roy Overbough to shadow the squalid streets of London expressionistically. PT

Dr Jekyll and Mr Hyde

(1931, US, 98 min, b/w)
d/p Rouben Mamoulian. *sc* Samuel Hoffenstein, Percy Heath. *ph* Karl Struss. *ed* William Shea. *ad* Hans Dreier. *cast* Fredric March, Miriam Hopkins, Rose Hobart, Holmes Herbert, Halliwell Hobbes, Edgar Norton.
●Still the best version of Stevenson's novella, shot in pre-Hayes Code days and therefore able to trace Jekyll's troubles to their source in sexual repression. Jekyll's frustration over the enforced delay in his marriage becomes a reiterated motif in the dialogue, and just in case anyone misses the point, it is underlined by diagonal wipes linking him to his fiancée at moments of stress preceding transformation. Cunningly, Mamoulian opens the film with a lengthy subjective sequence, so that our first real view of Jekyll (an admirable performance from March) is when he embarks on his lecture on the possibility of separating the two natures of man: a ploy which simultaneously arouses curiosity about this man, indicates his soaring intellectual arrogance, and divorces him from society as represented by his distinguished, disapproving audience. The rest, stunningly shot by Karl Strauss as a visual tour de force, is both superb and slyly subversive. TM

Dr Jekyll and Mr Hyde

(1941, US, 127 min, b/w)
d Victor Fleming. *p* Victor Saville, Victor Fleming. *sc* John Lee Mahin. *ph* Joseph Ruttenberg. *ed* Harold F Kress. *ad* Cedric Gibbons, Daniel B Cathcart. *m* Franz Waxman. *cast* Spencer Tracy, Ingrid Bergman, Lana Turner, Donald Crisp, Ian Hunter, Barton MacLane, C Aubrey Smith.
●Glossy MGM version of Stevenson's horror classic about the good and ambitious doctor whose experiments on himself turn him into a raving homicidal beast. Not a patch on Mamoulian's 1932 version, since it jettisons the overt sexuality (which saw repression as the reason for Jekyll's experiments), and never really allows us to identify with the demonic protagonist, thus forfeiting the opportunity to make the audience complicitous in his guilt. Furthermore, though Bergman (admittedly a little too fresh-faced for a prostitute, even if MGM had allowed such a thing) makes a reasonable barmaid, Turner is badly miscast as the upmarket fiancée. Well shot by Joseph Ruttenberg, and the transformations are effectively handled, but it's generally shallow and anaemic. GA

Dr Jekyll and Ms Hyde

(1995, US, 90 min)
d David F Price. *p* Jerry Leider, Robert Shapiro. *sc* Tim John, Oliver Butler, William Osbourne, William Davies. *ph* Tom Priestley. *ed* Tony Lombardo. *ad* Gregory Melton. *m* Mark McKenzie. *cast* Sean Young, Tim Daly, Lysette Anthony, Stephen Tobolowsky, Harvey Fierstein, Polly Bergen.
●The old yarn gets a gender-bending twist in this crass comedy (not to be confused with the enjoyably imaginative *Dr Jekyll and Sister Hyde*). Using Victorian journals belonging to his grandfather, perfume developer Richard Jacks (Daly) discovers a formula which transforms him into his female alter ego, Helen Hyde (Young). Suddenly sprouting breasts in public can be a little embarrassing, but there are beneficial side effects: instead of an

ineffectual male dork, he/she is now a self-confident, go-getting woman. In a lead role intended for the frenetic Jim Carrey, the anonymous Daly seems trapped in a state of suspended animation. As the ballsy Helen, Young looks a million dollars, but acts like she's being paid loose change. Yves DuBois, a token gay (Fierstein), gets one of the few mildly amusing pieces of comic dialogue: mightily perplexed by his desire for Helen, he exclaims, 'Twenty years in therapy and I start liking girls! That's malpractice.' NF

Dr Jekyll and Sister Hyde

(1971, GB, 97 min)
d Roy Ward Baker. *p* Albert Fennell, Brian Clemens. *sc* Brian Clemens. *ph* Norman Warwick. *ed* James Needs. *ad* Robert Jones. *m* David Whitaker. *cast* Ralph Bates, Martine Beswick, Gerald Sim, Lewis Fiander, Dorothy Alison.

●Admirably successful attempt to ring new changes on an old theme, with the good doctor turning himself into a beautiful femme fatale who lures prostitutes to their death in an East End in panic at the Jack the Ripper killings. The transgression thus being sexual as well as moral, the already rich story takes on a wealth of new meanings, while Brian (*Avengers*) Clemens' script is both witty and imaginative. Enormous fun. GA

Dr M (aka Club Extinction)

(1990, Ger/It/Fr, 116 min)
d Claude Chabrol. *p* Ingrid Windisch. *sc* Sollace Mitchell, Claude Chabrol. *ph* Jean Rabier. *ed* Monique Fardoulis. *pd* Wolfgang Hundhammer, Dante Ferretti. *m* Paul Hindemith. *cast* Alan Bates, Jennifer Beals, Jan Niklas, Hanns Zischler, Benoît Régent, William Berger.

●Chabrol's futuristic thriller, set in a still divided Berlin, turns out to be something of a *folie de grandeur*, flawed but fascinating. Dr Marsfeldt (Bates, playing like a Bond villain) is head of the omnipotent Mater Media corporation, and has his headquarters in a technology-filled back room of the 'Death' nightclub, where youngsters dance while mushroom clouds blossom on screens. Screens also fill the streets, the thousand faces of Sonja Vogler (Beals) inviting an increasingly suicidal populace to get away from it all at Theratos holiday camp. Detective Hartmann (Niklas) pads the mean polluted streets to fathom the rash of self-destruction. Chabrol's film, intended as a loose homage/reworking of Fritz Lang's proto-fascist master criminal Dr Mabuse, is at heart a sombre, timely meditation on our millenial, self-destructive instincts. Retained from Lang is the use of overawing architectural compositions, and his mix of silent serial, comic strip melodrama and expressionism. Less rewarding are a hopelessly difficult exposition, and the dial-a-country casting exigencies of the new Euro-productions. WH

Dr Mabuse, the Gambler (Dr Mabuse, der Spieler)

(1922, Ger, 116 min)
d Fritz Lang. *p* Erich Pommer. *sc* Fritz Lang, Thea von Harbou. *ph* Carl Hoffmann. *ad* Otto Hunte, Stahl-Urach, Erich Kettelhut, Karl Vollbrecht. *cast* Rudolf Klein-Rogge, Alfred Abel, Aud Egede Nissen, Gertrude Welcker, Bernhard Goetzke, Paul Richter.
Part I, 11,470 ft; Part II ('Inferno'), 8,399 ft. b/w.

●Lang's introduction to Mabuse is typical of his early work in being disorganised and erratically paced as a narrative, but shot through with flashes of inspiration. The master criminal (taken from a pulp novel by Norbert Jacques) is presented as an overlord of the contemporardr noy social chaos in Berlin: he profits from the ills of the time, and adopts countless disguises to instigate new varieties of exploitation. Lang has said that he intended the film as a kind of social criticism, and his sprawling plot does take glimpses of night-life decadence and themes like economic inflation in its stride. But overall the grasp of social reality is as shaky as the plotting, and the film's interest – certainly by comparison with the later *Testament of Dr Mabuse* – remains basically historical. TR

Dr No

(1962, GB, 105 min)
d Terence Young. *p* Harry Saltzman, Albert R Broccoli. *sc* Richard Maibaum, Johanna Harwood, Berkely Mather. *ph* Ted Moore. *ed* Peter Hunt. *ad* Syd Cain, Ken Adam. *m* Monty Norman. *cast* Sean Connery, Ursula Andress, Joseph Wiseman, Jack Lord, Anthony Dawson, John Kitzmiller, Zena Marshall.

●The first Bond film, made comparatively cheaply but effectively establishing a formula for the series – basically a high-tech gloss repackaging of the old serials – and setting up a box-office bonanza with its gleeful blend of sex, violence and wit. As memorable as anything in the series (the arteries hadn't hardened yet) are modest highlights like Bond's encounter with a tarantula, Honeychile's first appearance as a nymph from the sea, the perils of Dr No's assault course of pain. Looking back with hindsight, one realises the extent to which the later films got bigger but not better, relying on expertise rather than creativity, and reducing film-making to committee decisions. One Bond film can be tighter, wittier, better cast, more outrageous than the next, but basically soulless, they remain as individually unmemorable as computer printouts.

Dr Phibes Rises Again

(1972, GB, 89 min)
d Robert Fuest. *p* Louis M Heyward. *sc* Robert Fuest, Robert Blees. *ph* Alex Thomson. *ed* Tristam Cones. *ad* Brian Eatwell. *m* John Gale. *cast* Vincent Price, Robert Quarry, Valli Kemp, Fiona Lewis, Peter Cushing, Beryl Reid, Terry-Thomas, Hugh Griffith.

●Dull, witless rehash of *The Abominable Dr Phibes*, with Price murderously buckling down to the task of securing the ancient Egyptian elixir which will resurrect his wife. The same wasted opportunities with art deco sets, a scattering of pointless guest appearances, and only one death scene with balls (murder by scorpion). Pity it wasn't given to a director who could exploit the real possibilities. TR

Dr Rhythm

(1938, US, 80 min, b/w)
d Frank Tuttle. *p* Emanuel Choen. *sc* Jo Swerling, Richard Connell. *ph* Charles Lang. *ed* Alex Troffey. *ad* Wiard Ihnen. *songs* Johnny Burke, James V Monaco. *cast* Bing Crosby, Mary Carlisle, Beatrice Lillie, Andy Devine, Laura Hope Crews, Sterling Holloway, Franklin Pangborn, Louis Armstrong.

●Lamebrained musical which makes a hash of O Henry's story *The Badge of Policeman O'Roon*, about a hungover doctor who takes over bodyguard duties (falling for the heiress, naturally) from a policeman friend unable to work because he was bitten by a recalcitrant seal. Enlivened (although even she seems under the weather) by the marvellous Bea Lillie, who unleashes a wild gypsy dance, and entraps a bemused Franklin Pangborn as recipient of her famous 'Two dozen double damask dinner napkins' routine. TM

Dr Seuss' How the Grinch Stole Christmas (aka The Grinch)

(2000, US, 105 min)
d Ron Howard. *p* Brian Grazer, Ron Howard. *sc* Jeffrey Price, Peter S Seaman. *ph* Don Peterman. *ed* Dan Hanley, Mike Hill. *pd* Michael Corenblith. *m* James Horner. *cast* Jim Carrey, Jeffrey Tambor, Christine Baranski, Bill Irwin, Molly Shannon, Clint Howard, Taylor Momsen, Anthony Hopkins.

●Dr Seuss's squiggly sketches and early learning doggerel appear to have come straight off the top of his head. This Hollywood version captures precisely that endearing spirit of imaginative doodling, at least when Carrey's anti-hero is on screen. A shaggy, potbellied green yeti with an attitude problem, the Grinch lives in the rubbish dump and casts a baleful eye over the ersatz yuletide 'Who-bilation' of the rodent featured Whos in their suburban Shangri-La, Whoville. This toyshop grotto society is a caricature of consumerism, a town embodying such a level of superficiality that only a child, Cindy Lou, can see through it. She doesn't understand why the Grinch is excluded from the party, and even gets him nominated for 'Holiday Cheermeister'. Big mistake. Howard's film develops the story with ingenuity, subverting acceptable sentiment with lashings of sardonic wit. Smartly melding cartoon backdrops and kitsch carnivalesque production design, this cinematic candy floss honours the Seussian universe by satirising our own. And Carrey's comic tornado of a performance is a triumph. TCh

Dr Seuss's How the Grinch Stole Christmas!

see How the Grinch Stole Christmas!

Dr Strangelove: or, How I Learned to Stop Worrying and Love the Bomb 100 (100)

(1963, GB, 94 min, b/w)
d/p Stanley Kubrick. *sc* Stanley Kubrick, Terry Southern, Peter George. *ph* Gilbert Taylor. *ed* Anthony Harvey. *pd* Ken Adam. *m* Laurie Johnson. *cast* Peter Sellers, George C Scott, Sterling Hayden, Keenan Wynn, Slim Pickens, Peter Bull, Tracy Reed, James Earl Jones.

●Perhaps Kubrick's most perfectly realised film, simply because his cynical vision of the progress of technology and human stupidity is wedded with comedy, in this case Terry Southern's sparkling script in which the world comes to an end thanks to a mad US general's paranoia about women and commies. Sellers' three roles are something of an indulgent showcase, though as the tight-lipped RAF officer and the US president he gives excellent performances. Better, however, are Scott as the gung-ho military man frustrated by political soft-pedalling, and – especially – Hayden as the beleaguered lunatic who presses the button. Kubrick wanted to have the antics end up with a custard-pie finale, but thank heavens he didn't; the result is scary, hilarious, and nightmarishly beautiful, far more effective in its portrait of insanity and call for disarmament than any number of worthy anti-nuke documentaries. GA

Dr Syn, Alias the Scarecrow

(1963, GB, 98 min)
d James Neilson. *p* Walt Disney. *sc* Robert Westerby. *ph* Paul Beeson. *ed* Peter Boita. *ad* Michael Stringer. *m* Gerard Schurmann. *cast* Patrick McGoohan, George Cole, Tony Britton, Michael Hordern, Geoffrey Keen, Kay Walsh, Eric Pohlmann.

●Conventional adventure yarn with a mysterious smuggler (actually the Vicar of Dymchurch) performing deeds of derring-do up and down the Kent coast during the reign of George III. It's a Disney production, so naturally the piratical vicar (previously incarnated by George Arliss in 1937) takes on tiresomely po-faced Robin Hood traits. The cast is exceedingly British, so many minutes can be whiled away spotting familiar figures in side-whiskers and breeches. GB

Dr T & the Women

(2000, US, 122 min)
d Robert Altman. *p* Robert Altman, James McLindon. *sc* Anne Rapp. *ph* Jan Kiesser; (desert unit) Ed Lachman. *ed* Geraldine Peroni. *pd* Stephen Altman. *m* Lyle Lovett. *cast* Richard Gere, Helen Hunt, Farrah Fawcett, Laura Dern, Shelley Long, Tara Reid, Kate Hudson, Liv Tyler, Robert Hays, Matt Malloy, Lee Grant.

●Sullivan Travis (Gere) is Dallas's most successful gynaecologist. Maybe it's his medical skill, maybe it's because he listens well, maybe it's because he not only loves women, but regards each individual as so special as to be worthy of worship. But if that's so, why is his wife Kate (Fawcett) cracking up? Is it due merely to the imminent wedding of their youngest, Dee Dee (Hudson), or to the visit of her sister Peggy (Dern)? And how will Dr T cope with all this? No wonder he spends more and more time on the fairway, often in the company of the new assistant pro – yet another female, Bree (Hunt). Though Altman's film, another large ensemble piece, has been knocked as shrill and misogynistic, it's considerably more complex than that. It's certainly not woman-hating: unlike the good doctor, whose adulation of all females is deluded, perhaps even deleterious, Altman and writer Anne Rapp prefer their women warts and all. It's the absurd (man's?) world they live in that's at fault. If the babble in some group scenes gets a bit much, it's countered by moments of genuine tenderness, neat observation and astute insights into love. GA

Dr Terror's House of Horrors

(1964, GB, 98 min)
d Freddie Francis. *p* Milton Subotsky, Max J Rosenberg. *sc* Milton Subotsky. *ph* Alan Hume. *ed* Thelma Connell. *ad* William Constable. *m* Elisabeth Lutyens. *cast* Peter Cushing,

Christopher Lee, Donald Sutherland, Max Adrian, Roy Castle, Neil McCallum, Michael Gough, Ursula Howells, Alan Freeman.
●The first Amicus portmanteau film, which combines five stories comprising a vampire, a severed hand, a man-eating plant, a voodoo curse and a werewolf. The production suffers from some weak moments (notably the feeble voodoo story with even feebler comedy relief from Roy Castle), but two of the episodes are good; and who can resist the spectacle of Alan Freeman being engulfed by a man-eating plant?

Dr Who and the Daleks

(1965, GB, 83 min)
d Gordon Flemyng. *p* Milton Subotsky, Max J Rosenberg. *sc* Milton Subotsky. *ph* John Wilcox. *ed* Oswald Hafenrichter. *ad* William Constable. *m* Malcolm Lockyer. *cast* Peter Cushing, Roy Castle, Jennie Linden, Roberta Tovey, Barrie Ingham, Michael Coles, Geoffrey Toone.
●The first big-screen spinoff from the TV series, plodding through a shopworn plot in which the good Doctor helps an outcast tribe (a singularly camp crew they are too) against their Dalek oppressors. The settings are moderately imaginative in a tacky sort of way; even tackier comedy on the side from Castle; OK for undemanding kids. TM

Doctor X

(1932, US, 80 min)
d Michael Curtiz. *sc* Robert Tasker, Earl Baldwin. *ph* Richard Towers, Ray Rennahan. *ed* George Amy. *ad* Anton F Grot. *m* Bernard Kaun. *cast* Lionel Atwill, Lee Tracy, Fay Wray, Preston Foster, Mae Busch, John Wray.
●Despite its high reputation, a disappointing movie that dithers somewhere between horror and whodunit, never quite coming good on either and further crippling itself with some horrendous comic relief. The mystery concerns a moon murderer who cannibalises his victims and a one-armed scientist (Foster) working on a synthetic flesh substitute (and if you don't guess the killer's identity way ahead of time, your head needs examining). Stylish sets, though, and Curtiz adds some nice expressionistic flourishes, plus a bizarrely stilted but effective re-enactment of the crimes. It looks better if you're lucky enough to catch one of the rare two-colour Technicolor prints. TM

Doctor Zhivago

(1965, US, 193 min)
d David Lean. *p* Carlo Ponti. *sc* Robert Bolt. *ph* Freddie Young. *ed* Norman Savage. *pd* John Box. *m* Maurice Jarre. *cast* Omar Sharif, Julie Christie, Geraldine Chaplin, Rod Steiger, Alec Guinness, Tom Courtenay, Ralph Richardson, Siobhan McKenna, Rita Tushingham.
●Visually impressive in a picture postcard sort of way. Otherwise an interminable emasculation of Pasternak's novel, seemingly trying to emulate *Gone With the Wind* in romantic vacuity as Russia is torn by revolution and Sharif's Zhivago moons on about the elusive love of his life. Steiger and Courtenay excepted, all the performances are very uncomfortable. TM

Dodes'ka-den

(1970, Jap, 140 min)
d Akira Kurosawa. *p* Akira Kurosawa, Keisuke Kinoshita, Kon Ichikawa, Masaki Kobayashi. *sc* Akira Kurosawa, Hideo Oguni, Shinobu Hashimoto. *ph* Takao Saito, Yasumichi Fukusawa. *ed* Reiko Keneko. *ad* Yoshiro Muraki, Shinobu Muraki. *m* Toru Takemitsu. *cast* Zuchi Yoshitaka, Kin Sugai, Kazou Kato, Junzaburo Ban, Kiyoko Tange.
●A highly ambitious social panorama, with the shanty dwellers of a contemporary Tokyo rubbish dump serving as a microcosm for Kurosawa's Gorki-style celebration of the human condition through the triumph of loyalty and the imagination. Many of the threatened shortcomings of earlier Kurosawa films here reach fruition: extremely crude psychological characterisation of the gallery of down-and-outs, lushly melodramatic score, explicit statement of themes by several of the characters for anyone who's missed the point, grossly stylised acting and design (particularly the use of colour symbolism, this being Kurosawa's first film in colour). Nevertheless, there's a laudable fluidity in the way the characters are knitted together into a cyclical narrative, and some of them have moments of quiet poignancy. RM

Dodge City

(1939, US, 105 min)
d Michael Curtiz. *sc* Robert Buckner. *ph* Sol Polito, Ray Rennahan. *ed* George Amy. *ad* Ted Smith. *m* Max Steiner. *cast* Errol Flynn, Olivia de Havilland, Ann Sheridan, Bruce Cabot, Alan Hale, Victor Jory, John Litel, Frank McHugh, Guinn Williams.
●A leisurely 'epic' Western, hugely enjoyable in its skilful marshalling of stock ingredients as Flynn, wagonmaster turned sheriff, tames the rumbustious cattle town at the end of the railroad line with the aid of the crusading newspaper editor's daughter (de Havilland). Nothing here you haven't seen before (in fact the marathon saloon brawl turns up all over the place as stock footage), but it's put together with great freshness and skill. Ann Sheridan, though given little enough screen time as the saloon girl, is as usual a standout. TM

Does, The

see Biches, Les

Dog Day Afternoon

(1975, US, 130 min)
d Sidney Lumet. *p* Martin Bregman, Martin Elfand. *sc* Frank R Pierson. *ph* Victor J Kemper. *ed* Dede Allen. *pd* Charles Bailey. *cast* Al Pacino, John Cazale, Sully Boyar, Penelope Allen, Beulah Garrick, Carol Kane, Charles Durning, James Broderick, Chris Sarandon.
●At first sight, a film with large, self-conscious ambitions where a bank siege (the film is based on a real incident that occurred in the summer of '72) seems a metaphor for Attica and other scenes of American overkill and victimisation. But it turns into something smaller and less pretentious: a richly detailed, meandering portrait of an incompetent, anxiety-ridden, homosexual bank robber (played with ferocious and self-destructive energy by Pacino) who wants money to finance a sex-change operation for his lover. The film's strength lies in its depiction of surfaces, lacking the visual or intellectual imagination to go beyond its shrewd social and psychological observations and its moments of absurdist humour. LQ

Dog Days (Hundstage)

(2001, Aus, 121 min)
d Ulrich Seidl. *p* Helmut Grasser. *sc* Ulrich Seidl, Veronika Franz. *ph* Wolfgang Thaler. *ed* Andrea Wagner. *cast* Alfred Mrva, Maria Hofstätter, Georg Friedrich, Christine Jirku, Viktor Hennemann.
●Lord knows what they're putting in the water in Austria these days, but it ain't happy pills! Like Michael Haneke's *Code Unknown*, Seidl's first fiction film cuts back and forth between half-a-dozen characters who may occasionally cross paths. There's the mental girl who hitches rides from the supermarket and proceeds to provoke and insult her benefactors; the security advisor plying for trade; the sexist asshole insanely jealous of his girl; the divorcee still living with her alienated husband. Seidl has a couple of controversial documentaries to his name (Werner Herzog is a big fan) and he apparently used an improvisational method here, although it's framed with careful ironic poise. Seidl himself is a lot like the crazy hitcher: pushing and humiliating his characters and his audience alike. There are a couple of extremely explicit orgy scenes, one featuring the Austrian National Anthem. They're probably meant as shock therapy. TCh

Dog Eat Dog

(2000, GB, 93 min)
d Moody Shoaibi. *p* Amanda Davis. *sc* Mark Tonderai, Moody Shoaibi. *ph* John Daly. *ed* Luke Dunkley. *pd* Greg Shaw. *m* Mark Hinton Stewart. *cast* Mark Tonderai, Nathan Constance, David Oyelowo, Crunski, Alan Davies, Melanie Blatt, Gary Kemp, Geff Francis.
●London lads Rooster, Changarcy, CJ and Jess have dead-end jobs and heady dreams of stardom. In serious debt and never on the A list, they embark on a series of screwy 'get rich quick' scams – and in timid Jess's case, a romance with rich kid Mina. Meanwhile, Rooster has inherited his grandmother's habit of quoting '80s pop lyrics as adages. And, naturally, the trouble just escalates. Writers Moody Shoaibi (also directing) and Tonderai (playing Rooster) share a TV comedy background, and their debut feature basically resembles an extended sitcom. Various cameo roles are fun to spot, although the abundance of minor characters and subplots distracts from the core action. While our heroes are hapless in a winsome kind of way, the baddies they're attempting to outwit are feebly formed: puritanical crime baron Jesus (Kemp in seasonal panto mode) and dubious African porn enthusiast Tunde (Francis). The film's gross-out humour actually smacks of the Farrelly Brothers' sloppy seconds, right down to the compulsory semen gag. AHa

Dogfight

(1991, US, 93 min)
d Nancy Savoca. *p* Peter Newman, Richard Guay. *sc* Bob Comfort. *ph* Bobby Bukowski. *ed* John Tintori. *pd* Lester W Cohen. *m* Mason Daring. *cast* River Phoenix, Lili Taylor, Richard Panebianco, Anthony Clark, Mitchell Whitfeld, Holly Near.
●Savoca skilfully negotiates the nastiness of the opening scenes: four Marines organise a party, the object of which is to see who can bring along the most unattractive date. She is almost as successful with the potentially maudlin central section, after Phoenix has picked up Taylor, and remorse segues into affection and tenderness. But the opening title – 'November 1963' – signals certain inevitable moments: the news from Dallas, the reference to the Marines' next posting ('some little country near India, called Vietnam'). A 1966 coda represents America feeling very sorry for itself, and is unlikely to tug many heartstrings outside the family. BBa

Dogma

(1999, US, 128 min)
d Kevin Smith. *p* Scott Mosier. *sc* Kevin Smith. *ph* Robert Yeoman. *ed* Kevin Smith, Scott Mosier. *pd* Robert 'Ratface' Holtzman. *m* Howard Shore. *cast* Ben Affleck, Matt Damon, Linda Fiorentino, Salma Hayek, Jason Lee, Alan Rickman, Chris Rock, Kevin Smith, Jason Mewes.
●Smith takes an ambitious step sideways to introduce theological debate into his now familiar world of profanely garrulous New Jersey no-hopers, and, after a promising if confusing first few minutes, falls flat on his face. Essentially, it's a 'race against time' comedy, with disillusioned Fiorentino reluctantly persuaded by 'Voice of God' Rickman to travel to New Jersey in the company of two unlikely prophets (Jason Mewes' Jay and Smith's Silent Bob from the earlier films) in order to stop vengeful fallen angels Affleck and Damon destroying existence as we know it. Too talky, too fond of in-jokes, too caught up (especially during the dismally weak climax) in its crass comic-strip ethos, and not, finally, as funny, subversive or thought-provoking as it would like to be. Nor, despite the hype, is it outrageous – it's no surprise to learn Smith is a practising Catholic. GA

Dog of Flanders, A

(1959, US, 96 min)
d James B Clark. *p* Robert B Radnitz. *sc* Ted Sherdeman. *ph* Otto Heller. *ed* Benjamin Laird. *ad* Nico AV Baarle. *m* Paul Sawtell, Bert Shefter. *cast* David Ladd, Donald Crisp, Theodore Bikel, Max Croiset, Monique Ahrens.
●Less about a dog than a boy of (19th century) Flanders: Nelo, who lives in poverty with his grandfather and wants to become an artist. His progress towards this ambition is helped by a painter who befriends him and, in the happy ending, takes him as an apprentice. But the film is really about the kind of life led by Nelo and his grandfather, blending attractive images of the Flemish countryside with a story of personal and social values (Nelo is forbidden by the well-off miller to play with his daughter; the priest won't let him see the Rubens in the cathedral because he can't pay). An old-fashioned tearjerker for kids (the grandfather dies), it's pretty, but not pretty-pretty. JWi

Dogpound Shuffle (aka Spot)

(1974, Can, 97 min)
d/p/sc Jeffery Bloom. *ph* Gerry Fisher. *ed* Peter Weatherley. *ad* Anthony Pratt. *m* David White. *cast* Ron Moody, David Soul, Pamela McMyler, Ray Stricklyn, Raymond Sutton, Robert Ruth.

●In Vancouver, rasping Irish bum (Moody) loses his little old terrier Spot, and can't fork up the thirty dollars to get the mutt out of the dog-pound, but eventually raises the money in a rather enchanting way. Despite this gooey storyline, the movie has a good bit of guts, and the director/producer/writer shows a nice talent for wittily depicting life's seamier side: there's a brief moment in a rock-bottom café where Moody digs into a cesspit masquerading as a bowl of soup, and a hearty off-screen cougher turns out to be the cook; scenes in the dog-pound bristle with well-modulated violence and general unpleasantness. Moody's acting is agreeably restrained, as is the dog's. GB

Dogs

(1976, US, 90 min)
d Burt Brinckerhoff. *p* Allan F Bodoh, Bruce Cohn. *sc* O'Brian Tomalin. *ph* Robert Steadman. *ed* John Wright. *m* Alan Oldfield. *cast* David McCallum, George Wyner, Eric Server, Sandra McCabe, Sterling Swanson, Holly Harris.

●Bearded, be-jeaned and sporting a Beatle cut, McCallum's biology professor stumbles through the movie – usually accompanied by beercan – mumbling his disgust over the idiocy of his students and cynicism about his dilettante colleagues at a small, isolated college campus. The local dogs seem to share his view that the planet could do without this particular bunch of morons, and proceed to dispose of them with much slavering and gnashing of teeth. McCallum suspects that olfactory stimuli can cause mass behaviour in animals, and he just manages to survive; perhaps it was his resemblance to an Old English Sheepdog that fooled 'em. FF

Dogs, The

see Chiens, Les

Dogs in Space

(1986, Aust, 109 min)
d Richard Lowenstein. *p* Glenys Rowe. *sc* Richard Lowenstein. *ph* Andrew De Groot. *ed* Jill Bilcock. *ad* Jody Borland. *m* Iggy Pop, Dogs in Space, others. *cast* Michael Hutchence, Saskia Post, Nique Needles, Deanna Bond, Tony Helou, Chris Haywood, Peter Walsh.

●A squat in Melbourne, 1978: discernible among the roaches, mouldering cans of beans, Eno albums and the odd sheep, are the truly terrible punk band Dogs in Space, a gaggle of hippies, students and nurses, and sundry visitors including a chainsaw fanatic and two strangely amiable cops. Into this seething heap drifts the Girl, a taciturn waif whose perceptions of the house's giggling, garrulous grotesques form the narrative springboard for Lowenstein's admirably adventurous film. No mere rock movie, it is a remarkably rich portrait both of a much-maligned subculture and of the end of an era: story, for the most part, is held at bay, with the vividly realised fragments as apparently chaotic yet as tautly structured as *Nashville*. Lowenstein generously but unsentimentally allows his initially irritating, immature characters to become interesting and sympathetic. A funny, elegiac, uplifting, and deliciously different movie. GA

Dogs of War, The

(1980, GB, 118 min)
d John Irvin. *p* Larry De Waay. *sc* Gary DeVore, George Malko. *ph* Jack Cardiff. *ed* Antony Gibbs. *pd* Peter Mullins. *m* Geoffrey Burgon. *cast* Christopher Walken, Tom Berenger, Colin Blakely, Hugh Millais, Paul Freeman, Jean-François Stévenin, JoBeth Williams, Roberet Urquhart.

●If you thought *The Deer Hunter* was racist, then get your eyes round this: Frederick Forsyth's novel about a mercenary coup in a small African dictatorship adapted with all the lost-empire sentimentality that the book avoided. And, given Irvin's reputation after directing *Tinker, Tailor, Soldier, Spy* for the BBC, it's odd to find a film which muffs locations (New York, London, 'the tropics') and themes (solitude, the joy of action) with such indifference. Ten out of ten to Colin Blakely for his cameo (as an itinerant o'booze), but otherwise this is just another weary hack job from a rootless British film industry in decline. CA

Dog Soldiers

see Who'll Stop the Rain?

Dog Soldiers

(2001, GB/Luxembourg, 105 min)
d Neil Marshall. *p* Christopher Figg, Tom Reeve, David E Allen. *sc* Neil Marshall. *ph* Sam McCurdy. *ed* Neil Marshall. *pd* Simon Bowles. *m* Mark Thomas. *cast* Sean Pertwee, Kevin McKidd, Emma Cleasby, Liam Cunningham, Thomas Lockyer, Darren Morfitt, Chris Robson, Leslie Simpson.

●The lost patrol meets the werewolf movie. Sgt Harry Wells (Pertwee) is leading his squad on manoeuvres in the Scottish Highlands when the training exercise unexpectedly turns nasty. Happening across the remains of a butchered Special Forces unit, they are rescued just in time by environmental researcher Megan (Cleasby), and shelter in the only farmhouse within 50 miles. It's deserted, the moon is high, the wolves are baying. Directing his first feature, Marshall allows his cast to overplay the squaddies' hard-nosed attitude in the opening section; but he's on surer footing when it comes to action and suspense. The werewolves are impressively realised, and the damage they inflict will put you right off your sausages. The farmhouse siege is intelligently constructed to shut off idle hope, and what's left of the cast strike the right pitch of bleeding machismo. It may be barking, but this British underdog has teeth. TCh

Dog Star Man

(1964, US, 83 min, b/w)
d/p/sc/ph/ed/with Stan Brakhage.

●Brakhage revitalises the Romantic concept of the artist as heroic protagonist, struggling with Nature, the seasons, life, death, and above all with his own developing consciousness. This work introduced to the '60s avant-garde a new use of visual analogy and metaphor, in a language based on wild camera movement, hand painting, superimposition, and the reconstruction and recapitulation of series of images and whole sequences. DC

Dogtown and Z-Boys

(2001, US, 91 min)
d Stacy Peralta. *p* Agi Orsi, *sc* Stacy Peralta, Craig Stecyk. *ph* Pete Pilafian, (additional) Modi, Paul Stukin, Kevin Roberts. *ed* Paul Crowder. *pd* Craig Stecyk. *with* Zephyr Skateboard Team, Jay Adams, Tony Alva, Bob Biniak, Paul Constantineau, Shogo Kubo, Jim Muir, Peggy Oki, Stacy Peralta, Nathan Pratt, Wentzle Ruml, Allen Sarlo. *narrator* Sean Penn.

●Infectiously exuberant documentary chronicling the '70s golden age of US skateboarding. Director Peralta, a member of the legendary Z-Boys team operating out of LA's Zephyr surf/skate shop, cuts between terrific archive footage and interviews with the survivors, chubbier and balder, 25 years on. While the gang might have been as seminal and cool as everyone keeps telling us, the relentlessly uncritical tone gives the project a distinct feel of blowing their own trumpets. Modesty, of course, had no part in this aggressively renegade subculture, and neither, it seems, did loyalty – Sean Penn's drawling narration blithely tells how the ingrate crew cut their Zephyr ties at the first whiff of fame and fortune. It's never less than compulsively watchable, as it unfolds to a soundtrack of suitably kickass contemporary rock, but Peralta's approach falls a little short of his dynamite material – like *Almost Famous*, the movie's MOR line on sex and drugs is prissily evasive, and the package ends up a little too MTV for comfort: conventionally unconventional. NY

Doigts Croisés, Les

see Catch Me a Spy

Doing Time for Patsy Cline

(1996, Aust, 95 min)
d Chris Kennedy. *p* Chris Kennedy, Patrick Fitzgerald, John Winter. *sc* Chris Kennedy. *ph* Andrew Lesnie. *ed* Ken Sallows. *pd* Roger Ford. *m* Peter Best. *cast* Richard Roxburgh, Miranda Otto, Matt Day.

●Ralph (Day), a teenager, dreams of leaving the Australian outback and seeking fame in Nashville. Hitching to Sydney, with his guitar under his arm, he's picked up by the flamboyant Boyd (Roxburgh) and his girl Patsy (Otto), and yep, you guessed, an adventure of an entirely different nature begins. Ralph falls in love with the pallid, breathy Patsy, while being dragged into Boyd's tangle of lies and crime. It's a slight affair, retreading familiar territory, albeit against the photogenic Australian skyline, with the help of a handful of country tunes. Otto and Roxburgh do their own singing, which in Otto's case is fine. FM

Dolce Vita, La 100 (100) (The Sweet Life)

(1960, It/Fr, 176 min, b/w)
d Federico Fellini. *p* Giuseppe Amato, Angelo Rizzoli. *sc* Federico Fellini, Tullio Pinelli, Ennio Flaiano, Brunello Rondi. *ph* Otello Martelli. *ed* Leo Catozzo. *ad* Piero Gherardi. *m* Nino Rota. *cast* Marcello Mastroianni, Yvonne Furneaux, Anouk Aimée, Anita Ekberg, Alain Cuny, Annibale Ninchi, Magali Noël, Lex Barker.

●The opening shot shows a helicopter lifting a statue of Christ into the skies and out of Rome. God departs and paves the way for Fellini's extraordinarily prophetic vision of a generation's spiritual and moral decay. The depravity is gauged against the exploits of Marcello (Mastroianni), a playboy hack who seeks out sensationalist stories by bedding socialites and going to parties. Marcello is both repelled by and drawn to the lifestyles he records: he becomes besotted with a fleshy, dimwit starlet (Ekberg), he joins in the media hysteria surrounding a child's alleged sighting of the Virgin Mary, yet he longs for the bohemian life of his intellectual friend Steiner (Cuny). There are perhaps a couple of party scenes too many, and the peripheral characters can be unconvincing, but the stylish cinematography and Fellini's bizarre, extravagant visuals are absolutely riveting. EP

Dôlé (L'Argent)

(2001, Gabon/Fr, 88 min)
d/sc Imunga Ivanga. *ph* Dominique Fausset. *ed* Patricia Ardouin. *pd* Didier M'Boutsoux. *m* François N'Gwa, Emile Mepango. *cast* David N'Guema, N'Koghe, Emile Mepango, Roland Nkeyi, Evrard Elle Okoué.

●In this spirited if somewhat muddled and maudlin cautionary tale, a group of rap-obsessed kids in Libreville, capital of Gabon, take to petty crime to further their plans to get a ghetto-blaster and find fame, one of them meanwhile neglecting his ailing mother and going through girl problems. Inevitably, given the humble resources, the movie could have benefited from better performances. A tighter story would have helped too. Better for effort than achievement, but engaging in its generally amoral attitude. GA

Doll, The (Gudia)

(1997, Ind, 107 min)
d Goutam Ghose. *p* Amit Khanna. *sc* Ain Rashid Khan. *ph* Gautam Ghose. *ed* Moloy Banerjee. *pd* Ashoke Bose. *m* Gautam Ghose. *cast* Pran Sikand, Mithun Chakraborty, Nandana Dev Sen, Avtaar Gill, Masood Akhtar.

●This quietly subversive Indian drama in Bollywood garb, adapted from a novel by the Bengali writer Mahashweta Devi, does well by its central metaphor. Johnny Mendes (Chakraborty) is a young musician under an ageing master ventriloquist who passes on his prize lifesize female dummy. To the dismay of his would-be girlfriend, Johnny's new act blends pop music with sharp social comment from the doll's lips, swiftly gaining mass popularity that local politicos seek to exploit. Images of Indian femininity, the lack of genuine political debate and the corruption of the system come in for searching examination, though the frequent stops for musical numbers may inhibit the involvement of a Western audience. TJ

Doll, The (Lalka)

(1968, Pol, 159 min)
d/sc Wojciech Has. *ph* Stefan Matyaskiewicz. *ad* Jerzy Skarzynski, Adam Nowakowski, Tadeusz Kosarewicz. *m* Wojciech Kilar. *cast* Beata Tyszkiewicz, Mariusz Dmochowski, Jan Kreczmar, Tadeusz Fijewski, Janina Romanówna.

●A handsomely mounted Polish marathon based on a celebrated 19th century novel set in Warsaw about a merchant who falls in love with a beautiful aristocrat. For the first half-hour or so the going is pretty heavy, but after that, although the numerous characters remain confusing, it begins to mesmerise. The acting is persuasive, and the scope of the production is quite vast, with

Has' camera sweeping through 19th century Warsaw, setting up a satirical portrait of social decadence as the obsessional love of the wealthy merchant, scorned by the aristocracy behind his back, is meticulously probed. DP

$ (aka The Heist)

(1971, US, 121 min)
d Richard Brooks. *p* MJ Frankovich. *sc* Richard Brooks. *ph* Petrus Schloemp. *ed* George Grenville. *ad* Guy Sheppard, Olaf Ivens. *m* Quincy Jones. *cast* Warren Beatty, Goldie Hawn, Gert Fröbe, Robert Webber, Scott Brady, Arthur Brauss.

● Detailing in meticulous fashion a perfect bank robbery, committed by Beatty and Hawn after he, as a security expert, has installed an apparently impenetrable safe in a Hamburg bank. The comedy sits uneasily with the admittedly efficient action scenes, although at least here we have none of the usual Brooks sermonising to dilute the brew. It's all a bit flashy – lots of emphasis on technology, and shot in a mosaic of short, snappy scenes that seem to converge only after a while – but entertaining if you can stand the pace. GA

Dollar Mambo

(1993, Mex, 80 min)
d Paul Leduc. *p* Arturo Whaley, Angel Amigo. *sc* Paul Leduc, Jaimes Alives, José Joaquin Blanco. *ph* Guillermo Navarro. *ed* Guillermo S Maldonado. *pd* Arturo Nava. *m* Eugenio Toussaint Uththoff. *cast* Dolores Pedro, Roberto Sosa, Raul Medina, Litico Rodriguez, Olga de la Caridad Diaz, Gabino Diego.

● The third part of Leduc's loose trilogy (after *Barocco* and *Latino Bar*) is a kind of Mambo-ballet, a more or less wordless series of dance cabaret sequences, intercut with short narrative sections, centred around the 'Panama Saloon' in a small town on the Canal Zone in the period leading up to the American invasion. One of the group of entertainers, a mime artist, warns about the penalty of silence over this sad episode of Panamanian history; and certainly the last part of the movie (as soldiers descend on the club and then have sex and snort cocaine with their masks still on) enacts events that are nasty in the extreme. A weird entertainment. WH

Dollmaker, The

(1983, US, 104 min)
d Daniel Petrie. *p* Bill Finnegan. *sc* Susan Cooper, Hume Cronyn. *ph* Paul Lohmann. *ed* Rita Roland, George Jenkins. *m* John Rubinstein. *cast* Jane Fonda, Levon Helm, Amanda Plummer, Geraldine Page.

● A film which failed to go out on release, and it doesn't take long to discover why. Fonda (and she's one of the producers) is grossly miscast as a hillbilly farmer's wife, fighting the world on behalf of her children and her land, and disastrously uprooted from wartime Kentucky to Detroit where to her horror the women wear flashy underwear and the men go on strike. Sophisticated Fonda is hardly the sacrificial earth mother type, given to whittling in her spare time surrounded by angelic children. She would have had the farmers' wives doing aerobics to improve their figures. Sentimental nonsense. JE

Doll's Eye

(1982, GB, 75 min)
d Jan Worth. *p* Jill Pack. *sc* Jan Worth, Annie Brown, Anne Cottringer. *ph* Mike Tomlinson. *ed* Christine Booth, Jan Worth, Alan MacKay. *ad* Gemma Jackson. *m* Ben Mason. *cast* Sandy Ratcliff, Bernice Stegers, Lynne Worth, Paul Copley, Nick Ellsworth, Richard Tolan.

● This examines contradictory male attitudes to women as they affect a researcher, a prostitute and a switchboard operator. Documentary evidence and fictionalised scenes are interwoven to produce a daunting picture of incomprehension and abuse. But in its apparent determination to be non-didactic, the film ends up a victim of its own honesty, constantly undercutting its arguments. Nevertheless, if it ultimately bites off rather more than it can chew, there are plenty of incidental pleasures along the way; not least Worth's sharp eye for absurdity, and her resolve to forge a style of British political cinema that is daring and informative as well as entertaining. JP

Doll's House, A

(1973, GB, 95 min)
d Patrick Garland. *p* Hillard Elkins. *sc* Christopher Hampton. *ph* Arthur Ibbetson. *ed* John Glen. *ad* Elliot Scott. *m* John Barry. *cast* Claire Bloom, Anthony Hopkins, Ralph Richardson, Denholm Elliott, Anna Massey, Edith Evans, Helen Blatch.

● Ibsen's discussion of marriage is so strong, so contemporary, so close to the bone that it can survive even being submitted to the uncomfortable stylistic hybrid of filmed theatre. If the production wanders a little and suffers through the declamatory acting style, then the acuteness of the play itself is there to compensate. Money and the attendant charade of security confront the unexpected miracle of change. It is absurd how little progress we have made, how little of the play sounds redundant, and how tenacious the situation of Ibsen's heroine (for that's what she turns out to be) is. The crippling love of the patriarchal society rides on, strong as ever. Richardson makes a completely credible Dr. Rank, Hopkins is solid as Torvald, and when Bloom forgets about performing she manages to speak with something like conviction.

Doll's House, A

(1973, GB/Fr, 106 min)
d/p Joseph Losey. *sc* David Mercer. *ph* Gerrry Fisher. *ed* Reginald Beck. *ad* Eileen Diss. *m* Michel Legrand. *cast* Jane Fonda, David Warner, Trevor Howard, Delphine Seyrig, Edward Fox, Anna Wing.

● Here we are no longer in the realm of a play brought to the screen with marginal concessions, as was the case with Patrick Garland's version, but in that of film. Losey has deliberately cooled the 'dramatic' confrontations of the play, and drawn them out so that they form a complex emotional tapestry against which his superb floating camera movements, his ominous shots of skating figures and his long vistas through ornate rooms, serve to diffuse the spotlight from Nora herself to those around her. Her husband, as played by Warner, is no longer the dry pedant of Garland's version; he ends up less dismissable, and therefore more dangerous. By, in a sense, playing devil's advocate to Fonda's Nora, Losey has assured her feminist metamorphosis a strength (helped by echoes of the actress' own evolution) not found in a simple interpretation. Both versions are worth seeing, but this one shades it. VG

Dolores Claiborne

(1995, US, 131 min)
d Taylor Hackford. *p* Charles Mulvehill, Taylor Hackford. *sc* Tony Gilroy. *ph* Gabriel Beristain. *ed* Mark Warner. *pd* Bruno Rubeo. *m* Danny Elfman. *cast* Kathy Bates, Jennifer Jason Leigh, David Strathairn, Judy Parfitt, Christopher Plummer, Vernon Bogosian.

● Reporter Selena (Leigh) returns home to a remote island off the Maine coast for the first time in 15 years. Her mother Dolores (Bates) has been charged with the murder of her wealthy employer (Parfitt). She's shocked at the dilapidated state of their lonely old house, but her mother is even more shocked at how much Selena has blanked out from the past, about Dolores's husband Joe (Strathairn), and about his death. A melodrama with Grand Guignol trappings, adapted from a first-person novel by Stephen King, Hackford's film invites comparison not only with *Misery*, but a whole sub-genre of movies, including *What Ever Happened to Baby Jane?* and *Marnie*, which cast a beady eye over the 'Monstrous Feminine'. In terms of suspense, it becomes wrapped up in itself in a series of long and overwrought flashbacks, but there's a strong, pervasive sense of barely contained dementia, and it's a rare movie which presents three formidable female roles. No classic, but a real kettle of fish. TCh

Dolphins

(2000, US, 45 min)
d/p Greg MacGillivray. *sc* Tim Cahill, Stephen Judson. *ph* Greg MacGillivray, Brad Ohlund. *ed* Stephen Judson. *m* Sting, Steve Wood. *with* Alejandro Acevedo-Gutiérrez, Dean Bernal, Kathleen Dudzinski, Dr Louis Herman, Bernd Würsig. *narrator* Pierce Brosnan.

● Without getting soppy or anthropomorphic, there's something about images of bottlenose dolphins that brings a lump to the throat. That beautiful domed head, the permanent smile, those tiny teeth, the mammal's complex language, and, above all, the dolphin's seemingly instinctive desire to interact with human beings. This sensational 2-D IMAX documentary (produced by the *Everest* and *The Living Sea* team) whisks us to the West Indies and Patagonia where its subjects are filmed in the wild, or while entertaining tourists at various research-based institutions. The documentary follows several marine biologists at work: Kathleen Dudzinski studies dolphin communication in the wild; Alejandro Acevedo-Gutiérrez monitors their feeding habits off Costa Rica; Bernd Würsig tracks migratory movements; while naturalist Dean Bernal takes a dip with his unusual companion, JoJo. It is ably narrated by Pierce Brosnan and aptly scored by Sting who has rearranged many of his Police songs for the occasion. DA

Domenica

(2001, It, 95 min)
d Wilma Labate. *p* Maurizio Tini. *sc* Sandro Petraglia, Wilma Labate. *ph* Alessandro Pesci. *ed* Enzo Meniconi, Daniel C Hoffman. *pd* Marta Maria Maffucci. *m* Paolino Dalla Porta. *cast* Claudio Amendola, Domenica Giuliano, Valerio Binasco, Peppe Servillo, Rosalinda Celentano, Annabella Sciorra.

● Offering panoramas of Naples, effective performances, traces of Pasolini-like realism and occasional flashes of poignancy, this tale of the friendship that develops between an angst-ridden cop and an orphan girl being brought up by the nuns is nevertheless too sentimental and emotionally self-conscious to satisfy. Giuliano is good as the girl, capturing her blend of saintliness, resourcefulness and idiosyncratic morality, as she assiduously collects money for the convent while pocketing a percentage for her own good works. It's the cop's job to prevail upon her to identify the man who raped her. Their link is the cop's old girlfriend, who runs a café, a regular stop-off point for the girl. In the process, the film takes an askance look at an outsider Italian family. WH

Domésticas

see Maids

Domestic Disturbance

(2001, US, 89 min)
d Harold Becker. *p* Donald De Line, Jonathan D Krane. *sc* Lewis Colick. *ph* Michael Seresin. *ed* Peter Honess; Beth Jochem. *pd* Clay A Griffith. *m* Mark Mancina. *cast* John Travolta, Vince Vaughn, Teri Polo, Matt O'Leary, Steve Buscemi, James Lashly, Rebecca Tilney, Debra Mooney.

● Boat-builder Travolta battles to protect his son Danny (O'Leary) from the machinations of a psychopath masquerading as the his charming new stepfather. 'Rick' (Vaughn) is a stranger in town who has no friends, family or connections with the past, the only (uninvited) guest at his wedding being an embittered weirdo recently released from prison. He's also possessed of a mysteriously earned fortune, which not only enables him to revive the failing local economy, but, more importantly, ingratiate himself with police bigwigs, naturally disinclining them to give a damn when the aforementioned wedding guest is dispatched to an incinerator. The kid has witnessed the murder, but being 'a notorious liar' discovers nobody will believe him. Cue Travolta: 'He doesn't lie to me!' Meanwhile, you're left with these bare mechanics of suspense: stalking behind doors, cut phonelines, a face reflected in the bathroom mirror. To be fair, Travolta isn't all bad in the role of ex-alcoholic, virtual bankrupt, loving father and magnanimous divorcee. But the script mocks his every attempt at sincerity. SS

Domestic Violence

(2001, US, 196 min)
d/p Frederick Wiseman. *ph* John Davey. *ed* Frederick Wiseman.

● Wiseman takes a typically lengthy, penetrating look at wife-battering and related matters, focusing on the work and inmates of The Spring, a shelter in Tampa, Florida. As ever, we get a sense of what the institution is trying to do and how, as well as a vivid portrait of the fear, courage, confusion, revenge, rage and complicity of victims, staff, cops and culprits. The final sequence, of two cops trying to calm down a couple seemingly bent on self/mutual destruction, is extraordinary, and the perfect summation to a fine film. GA

Domicile Conjugal (Bed and Board)

(1970, Fr/It, 97 min)
d François Truffaut. *p* Marcel Berbert. *sc* François Truffaut, Claude de Givray, Bernard Revon. *ph* Nestor Almendros. *ed* Agnès Guillemot. *ad* Jean Mandaroux. *m* Antoine Duhamel. *cast* Jean-Pierre Léaud, Claude Jade, Hiroko Berghauer, Daniel Ceccaldi, Claire Duhamel, Barbara Laage.

● For those who found Truffaut's later work becoming flaccid, this fourth instalment in the continuing saga of Antoine Doinel provides plenty of critical ammunition. The early years of marriage for Truffaut's quasi-autobiographical character involve estrangement from his wife, an affair with a Japanese mistress (ending in long silences and cramp in the legs for Doinel), reunion with his wife, fatherhood, and acceptance of his lot. Truffaut takes immense pains to keep his characters interesting, scenes being built around elaborate (and often very funny) sight gags and running jokes, but ultimately they only serve to remind us what a pompous and self-regarding bore Doinel has become. Funny enough, if that's all you want. RM

Dominick and Eugene (aka Nicky and Gino)

(1988, US, 109 min)
d Robert M Young. *p* Marvin Minoff, Mike Farrell. *sc* Alvin Sargent, Corey Blechman. *ph* Curtis Clark. *ed* Arthur Coburn. *pd* Douglas Kraner. *m* Trevor Jones. *cast* Tom Hulce, Ray Liotta, Jamie Lee Curtis, Todd Graff, Bill Cobbs, David Strathairn, Mimi Cecchini.

● Pittsburgh trash collector Nicky Luciano (Hulce), dropped on his head as a boy (the truth about that event is held over for a last-reel revelation), is all misguided good intentions, easily led (he runs drugs unknowingly for neighbourhood hoods), and clearly a considerable burden to his brother Gino (Liotta). Constantly having to fend off Nicky's fears of abandonment, Gino also has guilt of his own: Nicky's wages pay for his medical schooling (and his internship will call him to Stanford for two years), while his efforts to have a life and a girlfriend (Curtis) of his own cause irreconcilable jealousy. Coming in the wake of *Rain Man*, Young's socially-concerned drama is unafraid of tackling complex emotional issues, but what few patronising and hackneyed insights it offers are waved like red flags. Unsophisticated. WH

Dominique

(1978, GB, 100 min)
d Michael Anderson. *p* Milton Subotsky, Andrew Donally. *sc* Edward Abraham, Valerie Abraham. *ph* Ted Moore. *ed* Richard Best. *ad* David Minty. *m* David Whitaker. *cast* Cliff Robertson, Jean Simmons, Jenny Agutter, Simon Ward, Ron Moody, Judy Geeson, Michael Jayston, Flora Robson.

● Convoluted and comatose psychological horror film. Tap your toes and twiddle your thumbs while the weary cast fumble around trying to hide from you who is trying to drive who mad and for which implausible reason. All is explained in one Niagara Falls-velocity speech, but only after the zomboid stars have made at least eleven snail-paced trips through the mansion down to the conservatory to discover who's hanging from the creaking beam again. Definitely for the Will-the-Real-Criminal-Please-Sit-Down category. CR

Domino Killings, The

see Domino Principle, The

Domino Principle, The (aka The Domino Killings)

(1977, US, 100 min)
d/p Stanley Kramer. *sc* Adam Kennedy. *ph* Fred J Koenekamp, Ernest Laszlo. *ed* John F Burnett. *pd* William J Creber. *m* Billy Goldenberg. *cast* Gene Hackman, Candice Bergen, Richard Widmark, Mickey Rooney, Edward Albert, Eli Wallach.

● Paranoid conspiracy thriller with Hackman as a crackshot Viet vet sprung from prison by unidentified government agencies for a sniping mission. With a lame script and the leaden hand of Kramer's direction, it blows most of its chances: dreadful clichés in the reunion scenes between Hackman and loyal waiting wife (Bergen); waste of interesting guest stars like Widmark and Rooney; dull use of establishing long shots for atmosphere; pretentious exchanges like 'Did you ever hear of Franz Kafka?' – 'Who's he?' – 'Nobody. Just a guy'. Worst of all – and unforgiveable in an action thriller – is that it simply fails to thrill. RM

Don

see Daan

Doña Flor and Her Two Husbands (Doña Flor e Seus Dois Maridos)

(1976, Braz, 110 min)
d Bruno Barreto. *p* Luis Carlos Barreto, Newton Rique, Cia Serrador. *sc* Bruno Barreto. *ph* Maurilo Salles. *ed* Raimundo Higino. *ad* Anisio Mederios. *m* Chico Buarque de Holanda. *cast* Sonia Braga, José Wilker, Mauro Mendonça, Dinorah Brillanti, Nelson Xavier, Arthur Costa Filho.

● An occasionally engaging Brazilian comedy, taken from a novel by Jorge Amado, about a woman whose irresponsible husband Vadinho drops dead dancing in a carnival. She subsequently remarries the respectable but, alas, not-so-sexy pharmacist Teodoro. The comedy format allows a neat reconciliation of her conflicting urges for sex and security: she simply calls up Vadinho as a ghost, and lives happily with both husbands. Unfortunately, the film tries to get it both ways too, by marrying arty satire with *Carry On* innuendo. JM

Doña Herlinda and Her Son (Doña Herlinda y su Hijo)

(1986, Mex, 91 min)
d Jaime Humberto Hermosillo. *p* Manuel Barbachano Ponce. *sc* Jaime Humberto Hermosillo. *ph* Miguel Ehrenberg. *ed* Luis Kelly. *pd* Daniel Varela. *cast* Arturo Meza, Marco Antonio Treviño, Leticia Lupercio, Guadalupe del Toro, Angelica Guerrero.

● Doña Herlinda, despite her indulgent front, is a woman of implacable will. She wants her son to marry, produce children, and be happy, but Rodolfo is gay. She proceeds to take charge of his love life. Ramón, Rodolfo's lover, is moved into the family house, and drops his taco in shock when she suggests adjoining beds. 'What if you need something in the middle of the night?' she says, without innuendo. The film has some of the subversive charm of Agnès Varda's 'Le Bonheur', and adds a new dimension to the concept of extended family. Serenaders appear with small guitars at the drop of a sombrero, camping key moments with their sentimental songs – just one amusing detail in this nicely judged satire. BC

Donald Cammell: The Ultimate Performance

(1998, GB, 75 min)
d Chris Rodley, Kevin Macdonald. *with* James Fox, Mick Jagger, Nicolas Roeg, Kenneth Anger, Cathy Moriarty, Barbara Steele, Johnny Shannon.

● For Cammell, the ultimate performance, of course, was to shoot himself (only to remain lucid for some while as he spoke to his wife China before dying): a shocking but strangely appropriate end for the writer/co-director of *Performance*. He had led a dramatic life – a precocious painter, a charismatic sexual adventurer and a member of fashionable/arty sets in Paris and London during the Swinging '60s, a reclusive exile in LA occasionally hanging out with the likes of Kenneth Anger and (less happily) Brando – but was he, finally, an underachiever? Post-*Performance*, his career was littered with uneven or unmade films, and perhaps one can't blame others for being wary of his artistic risk-taking, his abiding interest in sexuality, violence and death, Crowley and Borges, and some of his near mystical ideas. He may have had a dissociative personality, someone says here. This excellent documentary is enthusiastic but never hagiographic. At its core lies the fascinating history of Performance – a movie that looks even more insanely uncompromising now than when it first appeared. GA

Donald Cammell's Wild Side

see Wild Side

Donato and Daughter

(1993, US, 90 min)
d Rod Holcomb. *p* Marian Brayton, Anne Carlucci. *sc* Robert Roy Pool. *ph* Thomas Del Ruth. *ed* Christopher Nelson. *pd* Richard Sherman. *m* Sylvester Levay. *cast* Charles Bronson, Dana Delaney, Xander Berkeley.

● After its *Death Wish* heyday, Bronson's career has slowly faded. He still has one of the most gloom-ridden faces in contemporary US cinema, but given most of his recent material, it's not surprising he looks so miserable. He's in typically saturnine form in this routine police thriller about a father and daughter in the LAPD. They're on the trail of a serial killer. The killer's also preying on them. Not much cop. GM

Don Giovanni

(1979, It/Fr/WGer, 176 min)
d Joseph Losey. *p* Luciano De Feo, Michel Seydoux, Robert Nador. *sc* Joseph Losey, Patricia Losey, Frantz Salieri. *ph* Gerry Fisher, Carlo Poletti. *ed* Reginald Beck, Emma Menenti, Marie Castro Vasquez. *ad* Alexandre Trauner. *m* Mozart. *cast* Ruggero Raimondi, John Macurdy, Edda Moser, Kiri Te Kanawa, Kenneth Riegel, José van Dam.

● Losey's *Don Giovanni* is a social study out of Brecht, who once argued: 'We find the glamour of this parasite less interesting than the parasitic aspects of his glamour'. As the orchestra strikes up the Overture, the Don is touring his glass factory, suspended on a single plank above the fires which will finally consume him. Here labour vies with leisure, license with liberty, in a production mindful of Mozart's (and Sade's) era: the opera antedated the French Revolution by a mere two years. Filmed largely in formal long shot against Palladian Vicenza, Losey's cinematic version is a conscious attempt to 'make the unreal tangible'. Mostly – despite the odd Zeffirelli-ism and occasional 'motivation' – it succeeds. Appropriately histrionic performances from an excellent opera cast (notably Raimondi's vampiric Don and Kiri Te Kanawa's hysterical harlequin Elvira) and a very vocal mix which displeases record reviewers, but clarifies the libretto, combine with autumnal colours out of Masaccio and Giorgione to map the declining empire of the ancien regime. MM

Don Is Dead, The

(1973, US, 117 min)
d Richard Fleischer. *p* Hal B Wallis. *sc* Marvin H Albert. *ph* Richard H Kline. *ed* Edward A Biery. *ad* Preston Ames. *m* Jerry Goldsmith. *cast* Anthony Quinn, Frederic Forrest, Robert Forster, Al Lettieri, Charles Cioffi, Angel Tompkins.

● All too obviously trying to cash in on the success of *The Godfather*, this tale of Mafiosi dividing up Las Vegas between themselves, and then resorting to doublecross to get more than their fair share, still manages to hold the interest. Quinn is surprisingly subdued and effective as the big boss, Forrest turns in a nice performance as a young member of the family wanting out, and Fleischer handles the material in pleasantly forthright fashion. GA

Don Juan DeMarco

(1995, US, 90 min)
d Jeremy Leven. *p* Francis Ford Coppola, Fredric S Fuchs, Patrick Palmer. *sc* Jeremy Leven. *ph* Ralph D Bode. *ed* Antony Gibbs. *pd* Sharon Seymour. *m* Michael Kamen. *cast* Marlon Brando, Johnny Depp, Faye Dunaway, Rachel Ticotin, Bob Dishy, Geraldine Pailhas, Richard Sarafian.

● Depp is Don Juan. Or is he? He claims to be the world's greatest lover – at 21, to have seduced more than a thousand women – but in his cape and mask, he looks more like the world's greatest loony tune. Retiring psychiatrist Jack Mickler (Brando) has ten days to figure the kid out, to commit him or recommend his release. Juan is a charmer, but how do his picaresque tales of love in Mexico and the East square with the few known facts: the father who died in an auto accident, the mother who turned to religion in her grief? Mickler isn't sure, but his patient's romantic vision of the world proves highly infectious. Written and directed by novelist and former psychiatrist Leven, this is a slight, likeable comedy (despite inelegant camerawork and a somewhat slack pace) trading heavily on the emotional pull of its stars. It's a joy to see Brando throwing himself into the spirit of the thing, ardently courting his perplexed wife of 30 years, a ravished Dunaway (they share a lovely five-minute bed scene – in one, uninterrupted take). And not many young actors would (or could) have played the purity and innocence of Don Juan with Depp's sensitivity (especially as such obvious centrefold-types are cast as his conquests). His soft, Castillian lilt and natural elegance are well-nigh irresistible. TCh

Don Juan or If Don Juan Were a Woman (Don Juan, ou Et si Don Juan était une Femme)

(1973, Fr/It, 94 min)
d Roger Vadim. *sc* Jean Cau, Roger Vadim, Jean-Pierre Petrolacci. *ph* Henri Decaë, Andréas Winding. *ed* Victoria Spiri-Mercanton. *ad* Jean André. *m* Michel Magne. *cast* Brigitte Bardot, Jane Birkin, Maurice Ronet, Mathieu Carrière, Robert Hossein, Michèle Sand, Robert Walker Jr.

● Nearly forty, and Bardot's facade is still intact, but the films don't get any better. She makes a good enough feminine incarnation of Don Juan, but the three stories of her lethal prowess look as though they were designed as some form of tortuous revenge by her ex-husband, director Vadim. VG

Don King: Only in America

(1997, US, 118 min)
d John Herzfeld. *p* David Blocker, Thomas Carter. *sc* Kario Salem. *ph* Bill Butler. *ed* Steven Cohen. *m* Anthony Marinelli.*cast* Ving Rhames, Vondie Curtis-Hall, Jeremy Piven, Darius McCrary, Keith David, Bernie Mac, Loretta Devine, Lou Rawls.

● HBO biopic of the larger than life boxing promoter, from the book by Jack Newfield. Starting in the late '50s, when the young Don first killed a man (in self-defence), taking in his petty criminal career running numbers ('selling hope', he calls it) through the '60s, then settling down to business after a prison revelation that boxing is where a black man can make it big, the movie is episodic but pretty lively. The most notable device is to have King commenting on the action as it unfolds, railing against the hypocritical HBO motherfuckers (there's a wonderful scene explaining the potency of that word) for what is anything but a whitewash. It feels too rushed to land a really heavy punch, and the Ali lookalike doesn't, but slick direction by John (*Two Days in the Valley*) Herzfeld and Rhames' Emmy-winning performance ensure this comes out a winner on points. TCh

Donnie Brasco

(1997, US, 126 min)
d Mike Newell. *p* Mark Johnson, Barry Levinson, Louis Di Giaimo, Gail Mutrux. *sc* Paul Attanasio. *ph* Peter Sova. *ed* Jon Gregory. *pd* Donald Graham Burt. *m* Patrick Doyle. *cast* Al Pacino, Johnny Depp, Michael Madsen, Bruno Kirby, James Russo, Anne Heche, Zeljko Ivanek, Gerry Becker.

● A small-time operator specialising in stolen jewellery, Donnie Brasco knows a 'fugazi' – a fake – when he sees one. So he should, because he's fugazi himself, an FBI undercover agent working his way into the good graces of the Mob by way of Lefty Ruggiero, a wiseguy who takes him under his wing. Brasco's so successful, the operation becomes open-ended: for months, even years, he amasses evidence reaching throughout the Mafia – but his wife and kids never see him, and his friendship with Lefty goes beyond the parameters of the job. When push comes to shove, which way will he jump? A tense, sharp and compelling character study, Newell's film is a worthy addition to the Mob-movie canon. Comparison with *GoodFellas* is inevitable, though these wiseguys are no high-rollers, and the tone is much more measured; low-key, even. While Depp is admirably controlled in the necessarily passive, contained title role, Donnie is rather overshadowed by his more sympathetic mentor. Even when he's scrupulously underplaying, Pacino's Lefty dominates every scene he's in: relishing the comic foibles supplied by Paul Attanasio's witty script, the gruff, coded vocabulary and a strong element of pathos. TCh

Donnie Darko

(2001, US, 122 min)
d Richard Kelly. *p* Sean McKittrick, Nancy Juvonen, Adam Fields. *sc* Richard Kelly. *ph* Steven Poster. *ed* Sam Bauer, Eric Strand. *pd* Alexander Hammond. *m* Michael Andrews. *cast* Jake Gyllenhaal, Holmes Osborne, Mary McDonnell, Jena Malone, James Duval, Drew Barrymore, Katharine Ross, Patrick Swayze, Noah Wyle.

● This flawed but promising debut from writer/director Kelly is like *The Ice Storm* with a surreal psychological twist. It's 1988, and the title character (Gyllenhaal) is a moody adolescent in small town America. After a near fatal incident in which a jet engine falls on his house, Donnie suffers schizophrenic hallucinations of a spooky figure warning of imminent apocalypse. Kelly's script is an over-ambitious mess, dragging in time travel, high school politics, premonition and the presidential chances of Michael Dukakis, but his assured direction compensates. The tone alternates nimbly between comedy and horror, and two early sequences combine music (Echo and the Bunnymen's 'Killing Moon' and 'Tears for Fears') and image to stunning effect. NY

Do Not Disturb

(1965, US, 102 min)
d Ralph Levy. *p* Aaron Rosenberg, Martin Melcher. *sc* Milt Rosen, Richard L Breen. *ph* Leon Shamroy. *ed* Robert Simpson. *ad* Jack Martin Smith, Robert Boyle. *m* Lionel Newman. *cast* Doris Day, Rod Taylor, Sergio Fantoni, Hermione Baddeley, Reginald Gardiner, Maura McGiveney, Leon Askin.

● An American woollen executive (Taylor) is transferred to England: at home in the big country house, spouse Day wring her hands over her husband's imagined infidelity with his London secretary, then gets back at him by dallying with sultry antique dealer Fantoni. An inane comedy of marital complications, from a play by William Fairchild, with the usual off-beam Hollywood views of London and Paris. TJ

Donovan's Brain

(1953, US, 81 min, b/w)
d Felix Feist. *p* Tom Gries. *sc* Felix E Feist. *ph* Joseph Biroc. *ed* Herbert L Strock. *pd* Boris Leven. *m* Eddie Dunstedter. *cast* Lew Ayres, Gene Evans, Nancy Davis (Reagan), Steve Brodie, Lisa K Howard.

● Curt Siodmak's neat horror/sci-fi novel, about a human brain which is brought back to life after an air crash, was first filmed by George Sherman in 1944 as *The Lady and the Monster*, and remade by Freddie Francis as *Vengeance* in 1962. This version (sticking closest to the novel), scripted and directed by a rather obscure film-maker who subsequently went into television, is modest but effective, distinguished by an excellent performance from Ayres as the well-meaning scientist taken over by the vengeful brain.

Donovan's Reef

(1963, US, 108 min)
d/p John Ford. *sc* Frank S Nugent, James Edward Grant. *ph* William H Clothier. *ed* Otho Lothering. *ad* Hal Pereira, Eddie Imazu. *m* Cyril J Mockridge. *cast* John Wayne, Lee Marvin, Jack Warden, Elizabeth Allen, Cesar Romero, Dorothy Lamour, Jacqueline Mazurki, Mike Mazurki, Marcel Dalio.

● Most critics agree that *Donovan's Reef* is a fun film – 'A couple of Navy men who have retired to a South Sea island now spend most of their time raising hell', runs one brief description of the film – but beneath the fun lies one of Ford's most desperate films. Set on an idyllic island, the film seemingly depicts a 'natural' (semi-feudal) society in which Ford's wandering heroes (Wayne, Marvin and Warden) can at last settle down and find peace. However, the arrival of Warden's Boston-reared daughter (Allen) reveals that, like the town in *The Sun Shines Bright*, the island of Ailakaowa is a paradise built on ritual and racial division. In short, a very bleak – but very funny – comedy. PH

Don Quichotte

(1932, Fr, 63 min, orig 85 min approx, b/w)
d Georg-Wilhelm Pabst. *sc* Paul Morand, Jean de Limur Alexandre Arnoux. *ph* Nicolas Farkas, Paul Portier. *ad* André Andréjew. *m* Jacques Ibert. *cast* Fedor Chaliapin, Dorville, Renée Vallier, Mireille Balin, Mady Berry, Jean de Limur, Vladimir Sokoloff.

● Along with an English-language doppelgänger, shot concurrently, this has long been a hard film to find, so we should be grateful for even an abridged, disjointed version (all that remains?). The film's commercial wash-out is easy to understand. This is a bleak, comfortless adaptation, emphasising madness (Chaliapin is grotesque, though not inappositely so), failure and death. But as an evocation of period (sets by Andrejew) and of sun-baked Iberian languor, it shows how stylish a film-maker Pabst could be. The ending is pure despair: Quixote dead, the police burning his books, and long, long slow-motion shots (reprised by Truffaut in *Fahrenheit 451*) of pages curling up in agony, accompanied by Ibert's vigorous score. (Students of the composer's work will be best placed to identify such songs as have been excised in this copy.) BBa

Don Quixote

(1957, USSR, 105 min)
d/p Grigori Kozintsev. *sc* E Schwartz. *ph* Andrei Moskvin, Appolinari Dudko. *ed* E Manhankov. *ad* Yevgeny Yenei. *m* Kara-Karayev. *cast* Nikolai Cherkassov, Yuri Tolubeyev, Serafima Birman, T Agamirova, V Friendlich, L Vertinskaya.

● Like Kozintsev's *Hamlet* and *King Lear*, this is a marvellously sensitive adaptation of a notoriously difficult classic text. Of course, Cervantes' epic has been curtailed and condensed so that it focuses on the picaresque odyssey of Quixote and Sancho Panza, rather than on the countless tales with which the author parodied chivalric literature. But it's absolutely faithful in spirit: not only are the arid Spanish plains admirably evoked by the Crimean locations (with Moskvin's masterly 'Scope camerawork weaving its own magic spell), but Cherkassov (Eisenstein's Nevsky and Ivan) and Tolubeyev are magnificent, respectively, as the gangly, naive and idealistic knight errant and his loyal friend and servant. Witty, elegant and touching. GA

Don Quixote

(1973, Aust, 111 min)
d Rudolf Nureyev, Robert Helpmann. *p* John L Hargreaves. *sc* Rudolf Nureyev. *ph* Geoffrey Unsworth. *ed* Anthony Buckley. *pd* Barry Kay. *m* Ludwig Minkus. *cast* Robert Helpmann, Ray Powell, Rudolf Nureyev, Francis Croese, Lucette Aldous, Colin Peasley.

● A film of Petipa's 19th century Russian ballet, publicised as being produced with 'full film techniques' rather than as a straightforward record of a stage performance. It nevertheless falls into the trap of theatre conventions (heavy make-up, even heavier hamming, unvarying lighting for each separate scene, crude blackouts to indicate changes of locale, identical dress for the populace) without taking advantage of the fluidity and mystery possible in film. The one sequence that works is a moonlit *pas de deux* for Nureyev as the jolly Barber of Barcelona (a more suitable title, as the ballet bears no resemblance to Cervantes' masterpiece) and coquettish Lucette Aldous of the steely feet and spiky eyelashes. Otherwise it's unremitting dancing, enthusiastically performed by members of the Australian Ballet. For Rudi-watchers and balletomanes only. JMu

Don's Party

(1976, Aust, 90 min)
d Bruce Beresford. *p* Phillip Adams. *sc* David Williamson. *ph* Donald McAlpine. *ed* William Anderson. *ad* Rhoisin Harrison. *cast* Ray Barrett, John Hargreaves, Jeanie Drynan, Graham Kennedy, Graeme Blundell, Clare Binney.

● An adaptation of leading Aussie playwright David Williamson's stage hit about a suburban 1969 Sydney election telly party predominantly attended by about-to-be-disappointed-yet-again Labour supporters. The play crackled with a nice line in witty, scatological abuse as characters tore strips off each other's psyches, marital infidelities were unmasked, and sexual vanities (particularly masculine ones) were deflated. Beresford's clumsy direction blows much of the carefully orchestrated gag timing in the text, leaving it mostly up to the (good) actors. Otherwise, it's a moderately successful statement about the marginality of politics in the lives of the philistines, who profess socialism but are completely preoccupied with booze and birds. RM

Don't Answer the Phone!

(1979, US, 95 min)
d Robert Hammer. *p/sc* Robert Hammer, Michael D Castle. *ph* James L Carter. *ed* Joe Fineman. *ad* Kathy Cahill, Elliot Nachbar. *m* Bryan Allred. *cast* James Westmoreland, Flo Gerrish, Ben Frank, Nicholas Worth, Pamela Bryant, Paula Warner.

●This routinely mindless sickie – identikit psycho on the loose; women in peril; macho cop to the rescue – crept out shamefacedly over Christmas without the dubious benefit of either press screening or poster campaign. An encouraging sign that Wardour Street might be getting just a wee bit perturbed by the feminist backlash? PT

Don't Bother to Knock

(1952, US, 76 min, b/w)
d Roy Baker. *p* Julia Blaustein. *sc* Daniel Taradash. *ph* Lucien Ballard. *ed* George A Gittens. *ad* Lyle Wheeler, Richard Irvine. *m* Lionel Newman. *cast* Richard Widmark, Marilyn Monroe, Anne Bancroft, Jeanne Cagney, Elisha Cook Jr, Jim Backus.

●This psychodrama takes place in a hotel, and the feel of the film is dominated by the sense of both distance and closeness between things happening in different parts of it. Bancroft is the singer in the hotel bar, who breaks up with Widmark's airline pilot because he doesn't have 'an understanding heart'. Encountering the mentally disturbed Monroe babysitting in a guest's bedroom, Widmark goes through rapid (!) personal growth (he *cares*), which makes him ultimately worthy of his girlfriend. The plot is so simple that psychological interest is needed to sustain it, and this would require stronger performances than those Widmark and Monroe give. The film's most powerful effect is the play-off between sound and image in hotel geography (Monroe and Widmark speak on the phone across a courtyard; Bancroft's singing is switched on via internal radio, in counterpoint with visual cuts to the bar), which provides a coherence lacking in the emotional drama. JWi

Don't Bother to Knock (aka Why Bother to Knock)

(1961, GB, 89 min)
d Cyril Frankel. *p* Frank Godwin. *sc* Denis Cannan, Frederic Gotfurt, Frederic Raphael. *ph* Geoffrey Unsworth. *ed* Anne V Coates. *ad* Tony Masters. *m* Elisabeth Lutyens. *cast* Richard Todd, Elke Sommer, June Thorburn, Nicole Maurey, Eleanor Summerfield, Judith Anderson.

●Surprisingly, Frederic Raphael had a hand in this limp attempt at a sophisticated sex farce, about a philandering Edinburgh travel agent who hands out numerous keys to his flat to different girls. Of course they all turn up just when he gets together again with an old flame (Thorburn) he seriously wants. The sort of thing that a few years later Leslie Phillips would make his own dire speciality. GA

Don't Call Me Frankie

(1993, US, 70 min)
d/sc Thomas A Fucci. *ph* Barbu Marioan, Barbod Taheri. *ed* Jackie French. *pd* Silvana Alfonso. *m* Virginia Ellsworth. *cast* Peter van Norden, Elizabeth Ann Bowen, Martin Beck, Nan Moog.

●Frank Connally is holed up in a truly sleazy California hotel with a gun in his hand. A week ago his wife walked out with the kids, pausing only to empty the bank account and sell Frank's beloved record collection. Now he just wants to end it all. Trouble is, his eccentric neighbour-tenants keep getting in the way. Fucci (producer of *Purple Haze* and *Nightsongs*) piles on the West Coast clichés and stereotypes in his debut feature, which looks and plays like off-Hollywood fringe theatre. Good soundtrack, though. TR

Don't Cry for Me Little Mother (aka Little Mother)

(1972, WGer/Yugo, 100 min)
d/p Radley Metzger. *sc* Brian Phelan. *ph* Hans Jura. *ed* Amedeo Salfa. *m* George Craig. *cast* Christiane Kruger, Siegfried Rauch, Ivan Desny, Mark Damon, Anton Diffring, Elga Sorbas.

●Metzger's commercially disastrous attempt to get away from the framework of orthodox sexploitation. Filmed in English, it's a direct rehash of the Eva Peron story, using an exceedingly tricksy flashback structure to follow its 'heroine' from her illegitimate birth in the slums, through a lifetime of whoring, torturing and backstabbing, to a planned martyrdom by public assassination. There are only two scenes that aim to titillate; the rest is played for 'drama', complete with theatrical repartee and a generous quota of recrimination scenes. But the flash shooting and cutting cannot disguise the sheer dinginess of the Yugoslav locations, any more than they can compensate for a script and performances of hopeless banality. TR

Don't Forget You're Going to Die

see N'oublie pas que tu vas mourir

Don't Get Me Started (aka Psychotherapy)

(1994, GB/Ger, 76 min)
d Arthur Ellis. *p* Steve Clark-Hall, Michael Smeaton. *sc* Arthur Ellis. *ph* Gilbert Taylor. *ed* Michael Bradsell. *pd* Caroline Amies. *m* Roger Bolton. *cast* Trevor Eve, Steve Waddington, Marion Bailey, Ralph Brown, Nathan Grower, Marcia Warren.

●First shown at Cannes under the title *Psychotherapy*, this British Film Institute fiasco has been trimmed (mainly at the beginning and end), recut and retitled. Sure, the awkward mix of black comedy and psychological thriller – it's about a quiet insurance salesman whose taste for murder is awakened by the tensions of his giving up smoking – never quite plumbs the absurd depths of the earlier version, but the stilted dialogue, wooden performances, ugly visuals, and overall wrongheadedness, still make it a clinker. A shame, since the director's short films have been a joy. GA

Don't Go Breaking My Heart

(1998, GB, 94 min)
d Willi Patterson. *p* Bill Kenwright. *sc* Geoff Morrow. *ph* Vernon Layton. *ed* Peter Beston. *pd* Tony Noble. *m* Rolfe Kent. *cast* Anthony Edwards, Jenny Seagrove, Charles Dance, Jane Leeves, Tom Conti, Linford Christie, Ben Reynolds.

●Seagrove is a grieving widow and mother of two, whose eldest (Reynolds) is having a hard time at his London school. She and Edwards (an unconventional American sports therapist recently sacked by Christie) get it together and he trains her son for sports day and a finale which passes with barely a flicker of interest. Perfect viewing for those who don't like surprises, this contrives to make heavy weather of the numbingly predictable. Plotwise, Dance is the spanner in the works as a philandering hypno-dentist, and there's an excruciating cameo from Conti in sub-Peter Sellers mode as a loopy Viennese shrink. TJ

Don't Just Lie There, Say Something!

(1973, GB, 91 min)
d Bob Kellett. *p* Andrew Mitchell. *sc* Michael Pertwee. *ph* Jack Atcheler. *ed* Al Gell. *ad* Ken Court. *m* Peter Greenwell. *cast* Leslie Phillips, Brian Rix, Joan Sims, Joanna Lumley, Derek Royle, Peter Bland, Katy Manning.

●Sir William Mainwaring-Brown (Phillips) is the spokesman for a Government anti-porn Bill; Under Secretary Ovis (Rix) is kidnapped, on his way to to be married, by hippies opposed to the legislation; Sir William gets in a muddle with his mistress and his secretary (Lumley, then in bimbo mode); the leader of the Opposition (Royle) turns out to be the grandfather of the leader of the hippies (Katy Manning). Based on a play by Michael Pertwee: farcical political 'sleaze' from the era of Edward Heath – dire and very stagebound.

Don't Knock the Rock

(1956, US, 84 min, b/w)
d Fred F Sears. *p* Sam Katzman. *sc* Robert E Kent, James B Gordon. *ph* Benjamin Kline. *ed* Edwin Bryant, Paul Borofsky. *ad* Paul Palmentola. *cast* Alan Dale, Bill Haley and His Comets, Alan Freed, Little Richard, The Treniers.

●A swift follow-up to *Rock Around the Clock* from producer Sam Katzman resulted in this rudimentary teenflick, in which singing sensation Alan Dale returns to his hometown to convince the fuddy-duddy mayor that rock'n'roll is no threat to civilisation, merely the Charleston of its day. Witnesses for the defence: Bill Haley, who does 'Hook, Line and Sinker', and Little Richard, who clinches the argument with 'Tutti Frutti' and 'Long Tall Sally'. TJ

Don't Look Back

(1967, US, 96 min, b/w)
d DA Pennebaker. *p* Albert Grossman, John Court. *sc* DA Pennebaker. *ph* Jones Alk, Howard Alk. *ed* DA Pennebaker. *cast* Bob Dylan, Joan Baez, Donovan, Alan Price, Allen Ginsberg.

●1965. Bob Dylan's Yankee caravan moves through a dreary, unswinging Britain. The attendant press and entourage look to the beautiful Mr D for answers ('Do you read the Bible?') which he doesn't provide, being too busy with his metamorphosis from nice folkie to withdrawn rockstar. His mask slips, fascinatingly, as he struggles between affection and disaffection. Only the wardrobe is definitely set: shades, leather jacket, tight pants and raked back hair (a rocker, no less) set him aside from the denim and fringes, dating him less than his surroundings. While Dylan plays a part and apart, nearly all the others, drawn like moths to his flame, appear in the grip of some great masochism. The abiding memories of *Don't Look Back* are lack of privacy, dull cliques, stumble-drunkenness, very insecure British artists (Price, Donovan), and Dylan's bored, amused sparring with anyone trying to point him in the direction of Damascus. The restless hand-held camera is the main disadvantage of a fascinating document: a sore sight for the eyes, with enough whip-pans to defeat the most determined self-flagellant. CPe

Don't Look Now 100 (100)

(1973, GB/It, 110 min)
d Nicolas Roeg. *p* Peter Katz. *sc* Allan Scott, Chris Bryant. *ph* Anthony B Richmond. *ed* Graeme Clifford. *ad* Giovanni Soccol. *m* Pino Donaggio. *cast* Donald Sutherland, Julie Christie, Hilary Mason, Clelia Matania, Massimo Serrato, Renato Scarpa.

●A superbly chilling essay in the supernatural, adapted from Daphne du Maurier's short story about a couple, shattered by the death of their small daughter, who go to Venice to forget. There, amid the hostile silences of an off-season resort, they are approached by a blind woman with a message of warning from the dead child; and half-hoping, half-resisting, they are sucked into a terrifying vortex of time where disaster may be foretold but not forestalled. Conceived in Roeg's usual imagistic style and predicated upon a series of ominous associations (water, darkness, red, shattering glass), it's hypnotically brilliant as it works remorselessly toward a sense of dislocation in time; an undermining of all the senses, in fact, perfectly exemplified by Sutherland's marvellous Hitchcockian walk through a dark alley where a banging shutter, a hoarse cry, a light extinguished at a window, all recur as in a dream, escalating into terror the second time round because a hint of something seen, a mere shadow, may have been the dead child. TM

Don't Make Waves

(1967, US, 97 min)
d Alexander Mackendrick. *p* John Calley, Martin Ransohoff. *sc* Ira Wallach, George Kirgo. *ph* Philip H Lathrop. *ed* Rita Roland, Thomas Stanford. *ad* George W Davis, Edward C Carfagno. *m* Vic Mizzy. *cast* Tony Curtis, Claudia Cardinale, Robert Webber, Joanna Barnes, Sharon Tate, David Draper, Mort Sahl, Edgar Bergen, Jim Backus, Dub Taylor.

●Mackendrick's last film is a determinedly hip and wacky '60s comedy drawn from Ira Wallach's novel *Muscle Beach*. Curtis plays Carlo, a little like the Sidney Falco of *Sweet Smell of Success* gone West, whose accident-strewn introduction to California leads him to sell swimming pools to the rich and famous. A range of women cross his path – including a rather one-note Cardinale and, in her first role, Sharon Tate – in a fitful satire on spaced-out beach folk and greedy businessmen. Mackendrick's customary visual elegance and sense of timing lead to occasional highlights, and he at least delivers a good finale with a house sliding into the sea, reminiscent of *The Gold Rush*. But the tasteless hand of producer Marty Ransohoff results in much awkward cutting and dodgy script turns, making the film barely eligible for cult status. DT

Don't Move, Die and Rise Again! (Zamri, Umri, Voskresni!)

(1989, USSR, 103 min, b/w)
d/sc Vitaly Kanevsky. *ph* Vladimir Brylyakov. *ed* Galina Kornilova. *pd* Yuri Pashigorev. *m* Sergei Banevich. *cast* Dinara Drukarova, Pavel Nazarov, Elena Popova, Valery Ivchenko, Vyacheslav Bambushek.

●This unrelentingly severe autobiographical nightmare is probably the dourest memoir of childhood ever made. Twelve-year-old Valerka (Nazarov) lives in a far-flung corner of Soviet Asia in 1946, in a mining town partly inhabited by Japanese PoWs. His tense hustle of an existence is relieved only by Galia (Drukarova), a rival tea-vendor in the market. Rarely was a film so single-mindedly devoted to the proposition that life is hell, but Kanevsky's philosophy is rather less compelling than his way of conveying it. Jerky camera movements and monochrome photography so grainy it's better described as grubby – these trademarks of high *vérité* pall quickly. It's the often baffling cuts and jumps that let the story breathe. Kanevsky ends his thorough dramatic drubbing by pulling out a Brechtian 'only-a-movie' twist that whiffs somewhat of bad faith. This apart, the film has an undeniable authority, though with the best will in the world you couldn't call it life-enhancing. JRo

Don't Play With Fire (Diyi Leixing Weixian/aka Dangerous Encounter – First Kind)

(1980, HK, 95 min)
d Tsui Hark. *cast* Lo Lieh, Lin Chen-Chi, Albert Au, Paul Che.

●An extraordinary thriller in which Tsui Hark matches the graphic horror-comic violence of his narrative – involving arms-dealing Vietnam vets, Triad gangsters, and a dash of anarchic urban terrorism – with an equally 'violent' sense of character and *mise en scène*. As genre limits are stretched in an atmosphere of seemingly constant hysteria, the security of even the most cynical viewer will crumble. SJ

Don't Say a Word

(2001, US/Aust, 113 min)
d Gary Fleder. *p* Arnon Milchan, Arnold Kopelson, Anne Kopelson. *sc* Anthony Peckham, Patrick Smith Kelly. *ph* Amir Mokri. *ed* William Steinkamp, Armen Minasian. *pd* Nelson Coates. *m* Mark Isham. *cast* Michael Douglas, Sean Bean, Brittany Murphy, Skye McCole Bartusiak, Guy Torry, Jennifer Esposito, Shawn Doyle, Victor Argo, Famke Janssen.

●Douglas is a dish best served cold. Irritation, contempt and fake bonhomie are the emotions that make his clownish face gripping. Tragically, as uptown psychiatrist Nathan Conrad in this noisy New York thriller, he's in cosy mode – the doting husband and father thrown into turmoil when a downtown colleague asks for help with a disturbed and apparently catatonic teen, Elizabeth (Murphy). What Nathan doesn't know is that jewel thieves, done out of their booty ten years before, also need Elizabeth to open up – she's got a vital number trapped inside her head. And when these Desperate Dans kidnap Nathan's daughter, he's forced to start picking the vulnerable girl's brain. Meanwhile, stroppy cop Sandra Cassidy (Esposito) knows there's something fishy here. Sandra is the film's only plausible presence and she's hardly in it. Far more time is spent with the dough-faced Murphy, usually excellent, but here caught in a 24-hour pout vortex and forced to sing Ophelia-like ditties. Janssen also gets too much exposure as Nathan's wife. As for Bean – the requisite British nasty – he makes Vinnie Jones look subtle. And Douglas? Well, he's the smug liberal to the last. CO'Su

Don't Take It To Heart

(1944, GB, 91 min, b/w)
d Jeffrey Dell. *p* Sydney Box. *sc* Jeffrey Dell. *ph* Eric Cross. *ed* Frederick Wilson. *ad* Alex Vetchinsky. *m* Mischa Spoliansky. *cast* Richard Greene, Patricia Medina, Alfred Drayton, Edward Rigby, Richard Bird, Wylie Watson, Moore Marriott, Brefni O'Rorke.

●Dell, a novelist/screenwriter here making his writer-director debut, reveals a pleasing lightness of touch in this whimsical comedy in the manner of *The Ghost Goes West* (restless spirit, stirred up by bomb, helps to settle ruffled village politics). Stuffed to the brim with quaint characters, it is occasionally guilty of milking its jokes (Rigby's delightfully crumbling butler does his arthritic patter through the castle corridors, with accompanying theme, just once too often). On the other hand there are nicely offhand jokes like the village high street with shopfronts all indicating ownership by members of the Bucket family except for one interloping Pail; and the resolution, with the squire (O'Rorke) happily looking forward to life as a poacher when it turns out that he owes his position to an ancestral usurpation, is perfectly in keeping with the spirit of gently anarchic satire. TM

Don't Tell Anyone (No se lo digas a nadie)

(1998, Peru, 114 min)
d Francisco J Lombardi. *sc* Giovanna Pollarolo. *cast* Santiago Magill, Lucia Jimenez, Christian Meier, Lucía Jiménez, Giovanni Ciccia, Vanessa Robbiano, Carlos Fuentes, Carmen Elias, Hernán Romero, Lita Baluarte.

●A coming-out, coming-of-age tale (from a novel by Jaime Bayly) set within a predominantly homophobic religious Peruvian society, this is by turns sensitive, touching, funny, alarming and, for the most part, very enjoyable. For just under two hours, we witness all the ups and downs of a young man, Joaquin (Magill), struggling to come to terms with his sexuality in a country where being gay is akin to being a leper, and violence towards gays is an almost daily occurrence. Joaquin's mother is overbearingly protective and very religious, while his father just wants to see his lad grow up to be a huntin', shootin', drinkin' type. Joaquin, though, is unsure of whether he's gay or het, and this dilemma stays with him right from the moment he leaves home, through his off-the-rails period as a coked-out dope fiend right up to the – admittedly, mostly unfulfilling – final reel. DA

Don't Tell Her It's Me (aka The Boyfriend School)

(1990, US, 102 min)
d Malcolm Mowbray. *p* George G Braunstein, Ron Hamady. *sc* Sarah Bird. *ph* Reed Smoot. *ed* Marshall Harvey. *pd* Linda Pearl, Daryl Kerrigan. *m* Michael Gore. *cast* Shelley Long, Steve Guttenberg, Jami Gertz, Kyle MacLachlan, Madchen Amick, Kevin Scannell, Perry Anzilotti.

●Guttenberg is cartoonist Gus, bald, bloated and bitter after a course of chemotherapy; Long is his busybody sister Lizzie, aka romantic novelist Vivica Lamoureaux. Lizzie determines to fix Gus up with Ms Right in the shape of rag journo Emily (Gertz); and by the miracle of modern workout techniques, Gus is transformed into Lobo, a lone-wolf macho bike boy. It would take a virulently mean-minded director to make anything of this gruesome plot, but Mowbray turns in a very mawkish piece of work. He's not helped by Gertz, and especially not by Long. Guttenberg just about musters interest as a dryly charming nebbish; but as a variant on the ever popular wimp-into-lovegod scam (pay-off: she prefers the wimp), it's a poor second to *The Nutty Professor*. JRo

Don't Tell Mom the Babysitter's Dead

(1991, US, 105 min)
d Stephen Herek. *p* Robert Newmyer, Brian Reilly, Jeffrey Silver. *sc* Neil Landau, Tara Ison. *ph* Tim Suhrstedt. *ed* Larry Bock. *pd* Stephen Marsh. *m* David Newman, Brian Nazarian. *cast* Applegate, Joanna Cassidy, John Getz, Josh Charles, Keith Coogan, Concetta Tomei, Kimmy Robertson, Eda Reiss Merin.

●This isn't just another teen movie. Mom is notable only for her absence, packed off for two months to Australia. That leaves 17-year -old Sue 'Swell' Ellen, her brothers Kenny, Zach and Walter, 6-year-old Melissa, and a little old lady who is clearly some sort of serial babysitter. 'TV rots your brain' she wheezes menacingly, before Kenny's satanic bedroom brings on a coronary. Once the 'sitter' has snuffed it, the kids opt to fend for themselves, and elect Swell as their breadwinner. So far, so predictable. But this is a sassy little comedy of wit and intelligence from the director of *Bill and Ted's Excellent Adventure*. As Swell, Applegate is appealing and resourceful, while Coogan's dope-head Kenny contributes to a wonderfully dry, on-going marital spoof. Getz is the unctuous boardroom chauvinist to a tee, and Cassidy rounds off the picture's relaxed *Cosmo*-feminism as Swell's scatty boss. TCh

Don't Touch the White Woman

see Touche pas à la femme blanche

Doomed Cargo

see Seven Sinners

Doom Generation, The

(1995, Fr/US, 85 min)
d Gregg Araki. *p* Andrea Sperling, Gregg Araki. *sc* Gregg Araki. *ph* Jim Fealy. *ed* Gregg Araki. *pd* Thérèse DePrez. *m* Dan Gatto. *cast* James Duval, Rose McGowan, Johnathon Schaech, Cress Williams, Heidi Fleiss.

●'Welcome to Hell': this 'heterosexual movie' by Gregg Araki is not for the faint-hearted. A couple-on-the-road movie, with a sexually voracious third party along for the ride, this is a highly stylised, luridly coloured provocation, aimed squarely at the moral majority (not that they'd be seen dead at a flick like this). Firing on all cylinders for the first time, Araki throws in decapitation, spunk munching, outrageous visual and structural puns, Hollywood madam Heidi Fleiss, and a running 666 gag, all in the service of American sexual liberation. Imagine *Natural Born Killers* with a sense of humour. TCh

Doomwatch

(1972, GB, 92 min)
d Peter Sasdy. *p* Tony Tenser. *sc* Clive Exton. *ph* Ken Talbot. *ed* Keith Palmer. *ad* Colin Grimes. *m* John Scott. *cast* Ian Bannen, Judy Geeson, John Paul, Simon Oates, George Sanders, Percy Herbert.

●Spinoff from the muddled ecological teleseries, with the gang of scientists here investigating the effects of a sunken oil tanker on the inhabitants of a remote island off the Cornish coast. Predictably, the serious intentions of the original series have been forsaken on the big screen for a half-baked horror thriller. GA

Doors, The

(1991, US, 140 mins)
d Oliver Stone. *p* Sasha Harari, Bill Graham, A Kitman Ho. *sc* Oliver Stone, J Randal Johnson. *ph* Robert Richardson. *ed* David Brenner, Joe Hutching. *pd* Barbara Ling. *cast* Val Kilmer, Frank Whaley, Kevin Dillon, Meg Ryan, Kyle MacLachlan, Kathleen Quinlan, Billy Idol, Dennis Burkley.

●It's one of several compensatory surprises in this foray into the '60s that, as Jim Morrison, erstwhile paperweight Val Kilmer almost does for screwed-up rock stars what De Niro did for hapless middleweights; and less so that Stone all but manages to save his biopic of the hazy, crazy days of yore from becoming just another well-worn variation on the theme of self-destructive cock-rock and self-styled shamanism. This swirling dervish of a film charts the Doors' rise from avant-gardists to pop sensations to notoriety symbols, with Morrison rapidly alienating his less visionary and far less pretentious colleagues, led by MacLachlan's pragmatic Ray Manzarek. Stone sometimes loads the narrative with too much sub-Freudian baggage about Morrison's childhood, but the music, the excess and the excitement come across well; there are splendid cameos of the likes of Warhol and the Velvet Underground's Nico (giving Jim good head in a New York elevator); and Meg Ryan (as Jim's 'lady') shows commendable patience in the role of band ornament. SGr

Doppelganger: The Evil Within

(1992, US, 100 min)
d Avi Nesher. *p* Donald P Borchers. *sc* Avi Nesher. *ph* Vance Burberry. *ed* Tatiana S Riegel. *m* Jan Kaczmarek. *cast* Drew Barrymore, George Newbern, Dennis Christopher, Leslie Hope, Sally Kellerman, Luana Anders.

●Barrymore proves she's grown into a mature, talented actress in this psychological horror movie about a young woman haunted by a lethal, ghostly double. Following the brutal murder of her mother in New York, Holly Gooding (Barrymore) leaves Los Angeles, moving into a shared apartment with aspiring screenwriter Patrick Highsmith (Newbern), who can't believe his luck. But Holly's confusing mood swings leave him wondering whether he's dealing with a volatile nymphomaniac or a vulnerable child-woman. The answer, of course, is both. Nesher's direction never does justice to his own script, which moves forward smoothly without neglecting emotional texture: the spiky exchanges between Patrick and his jealous old flame/writing partner Elizabeth (Hope) are especially good. NF

Dora-Heita

(1999, Jap, 110 min)
d Kon Ichikawa. *p* Yoshinobu Nishioka. *sc* Akira Kurosawa, Keisuke Kinoshita, Kon Ichikawa, Masaki Kobayashi. *ph* Yukio Isohata. *ed* Chizuko Osada. *ad* Yoshinobu Nishioka. *m* Kensaku Tanikawa. *cast* Koji Yakusho, Yuko Asano, Bunta Sugawara, Ryudo Uzaki, Tsurutaro Kataoka, Saburo Ishikura, Renji Ishibashi.

● Ichikawa's 74th film was planned 30 years earlier as a collective project for Yonki-no-Kai, the partnership of four veterans led by Kurosawa. But *Dodes'kaden* bankrupted the company and the script was forgotten until Ichikawa dusted it off as a vehicle for Yakusho. 'Dora-Heita' is the louche nickname of Koheita Mochizuki, a magistrate sent to clean up the small fief which contains the Horisoto enclave, a hotbed of prostitution, gambling and smuggling. He poses as dissolute to disarm the crimelords and their allies in local government, then pounces. But he still has a clinging geisha and a traitorous 'friend' to deal with. Less an exercise in nostalgia than a film with the authentic charm, humour and excitement of the likes of *Yojimbo*. TR

Dossier 51, Le

(1978, Fr/WGer, 108 min)
d Michel Deville. *p* Philippe dussart. *sc* Michel Deville, Gilles perrault. *ph* Claude Lecomte. *ed* Raymonde Guyot. *ad* Noëlle Galland. *m* Jean Schwarz, Schubert. *cast* François Marthouret, Claude Mercault, Roger Planchon, Nathalie Juvet, Philippe Rouleau, Françoise Lugagne.

● An effectively sinister paranoid thriller, an exercise in voyeuristic point-of-view which consists almost entirely of the detailed surveillance file constructed by a foreign intelligence agency in an attempt to 'turn' a totally unwitting minor French diplomat. A sleek technocratic nightmare of the impossibility of maintaining privacy, it plays fearfully ambiguous games with its audience, inviting complicity in piecing together manipulatable 'evidence', while advising the wisdom of an over-the-shoulder glance, and reveals even such ostensibly healing techniques as psychoanalysis to be easily amenable to annexation to the impersonal mechanics of espionage. Compelling ammunition for the 'information is power' anti-databank lobby. PT

Do the Right Thing

(1989, US, 120 min)
d/p/sc Spike Lee. *ph* Ernest Dickerson. *ed* Barry Alexander Brown. *pd* Wynn Thomas. *m* Bill Lee. *cast* Danny Aiello, Ossie Davis, Ruby Dee, Giancarlo Esposito, Spike Lee, Bill Nunn, John Turturro, Paul Benjamin, John Savage, Rosie Perez, Samuel L Jackson.

● After the dismally miscalculated *School Daze,* Spike Lee returns to splendid form with a pacy, punchy ensemble piece set in Brooklyn during one stiflingly hot 24 hours. Lee himself plays Mookie, pizza delivery-man for Sal (Aiello) and his two sons; though selfishly neglectful of his Hispanic lover and child, Mookie is mostly Mr Nice Guy, ever ready to lend his calming influence to the storm of insults that fly between the local blacks, Italians, Koreans and white cops. Eventually, however, the heat takes its toll, and petty disagreements escalate into a full-scale riot. Effortlessly moving from comedy to serious social comment, eliciting excellent performances from a large and perfectly selected cast, and making superb use of music both to create mood and comment on the action, Lee contrives to see both sides of each conflict without falling prey to simplistic sentimentality. Best of all, the film – at once stylised and realistic – buzzes throughout with the sheer, edgy bravado that comes from living one's life on the streets. It looks, sounds, and feels *right*: sure proof that Lee's virtuoso technique and righteous anger are tempered by real humanity. GA

Double Agent 73

(1974, US, 72 min)
d/p Doris Wishman. *sc* Judy J Kushner. *ph* Yuri Haviv. *ed* Louis Burdi. *m* Cine-Top. *cast* Chesty Morgan, Frank Silvano, Saul Meth, Jill Harris, Louis Burdi.

● Another cheapo epic from the director and star of *Deadly Weapons*, with 'Chesty' this time playing a Bond-style secret agent chosen to root out a heroin gang because her 73-inch physical attributes enable her to have a camera embedded in her left breast – an excuse to let it all hang out. With the plot to all intents and purposes out of commission, we are left with a series of grotesquely filmed, weird, almost symbolic acts. A kind of cryptic, distorted meditation on femaleness develops, given the obvious alienation 'Chesty' experiences from her body, with breasts as objects of fear to be operated on and deployed in the context of various phallic objects. Despite maternal connotations, she is associated totally with death and loneliness, and the film becomes a monument to pathological male fantasies. VG

Double Cross

see Triple Cross, The

Double Game

see Maestro, Il

Double Headed Eagle, The

(1973, GB, 93 min, b/w)
d Lutz Becker. *p* Sandy Lieberson, David Puttnam. *sc* Lutz Becker, Philippe Mora. *ed* David Mingay. *m* Walter Gronostay, Frederick Hollander, Ernst Krenek, Theo Mackeben, Kurt Weill.

● A documentary in which Becker uses contemporary footage, some of it extremely rare, to trace the rise of the Nazis up to Hitler's first speech as Chancellor in 1933. As a study it's anthropological rather than historical, discarding the tortuous intrigues of the scrabble for power in favour of a broader survey that shows the tacit acquiescence of a people. The film is best on gradual development: the transformation of the ill-kempt party gatherings, watched by a few amused villagers, into the half-baked symbolism and phrase-mongering of the mass rallies. It also implies that against such a background, moral stands were not as easy as we might assume. Einstein and Thomas Mann slip away, supposedly for their holidays, leaving the club-foot dwarf Goebbels to tell the nation that one day patience towards the Jew will come to an end. A chilling moment. CPe

Double Impact

(1991, US, 118 min)
d Sheldon Lettich. *p* Ashok Amritraj, Jean-Claude Van Damme. *sc* Sheldon Lettich, Jean-Claude Van Damme. *ph* Richard H Kline. *ed* Mark Conte. *pd* John Jay Moore. *m* Arthur Kempel. *cast* Jean-Claude Van Damme, Geoffrey Lewis, Alan Scarfe, Alonna Shaw, Cory Everson, Philip Chan Yan Kin, Bolo Young.

● Hong Kong: two babes-in-arms, present when Mater and Pater are shot to noodles by Triad hitmen, are so traumatised they both grow up to be Van Damme. Chad is a kickboxing LA aerobics instructor and something of a fop; twin brother Alex is a strong, mean, silent headbutt merchant with a cigar grafted to his lower lip. Chad's Vietvet Uncle Frank (Lewis) reunites the boys, who swiftly set about the sibling snarling, but soon team up to kick the baddies. Lettich directs with the limpness you associate with the vegetable he's very nearly named after. The idea of two Van Dammes must have seemed workable on paper, but both exude the charisma of a packet of Cup-a-Soup, and not even Van Damme seems able to tell himselves apart. JRo

Double Indemnity 100 *(100)*

(1944, US, 106 min, b/w)
d Billy Wilder. *p* Joseph Sistrom. *sc* Billy Wilder, Raymond Chandler. *ph* John F Seitz. *ed* Doane Harrison. *ad* Hans Dreier, Hal Pereira. *m* Miklós Rozsa. *cast* Barbara Stanwyck, Fred MacMurray, Edward G Robinson, Porter Hall, Jean Heather, Tom Powers, Fortunio Bonanova.

● Before he settled down to being an ultra-cynical connoisseur of vulgarity, Wilder helped (as much as any of his fellow Austro-German émigrés in Hollywood) to define the mood of brooding pessimism that laced so many American movies in the '40s. Adapted from James M Cain's novel, *Double Indemnity* is certainly one of the darkest thrillers of its time: Wilder presents Stanwyck and MacMurray's attempt at an elaborate insurance fraud as a labyrinth of sexual dominance, guilt, suspicion and sweaty duplicity. Chandler gave the dialogue a sprinkling of characteristic wit, without mitigating any of the overall sense of oppression. TR

Double Jeopardy

(1999, US/Ger, 105 min)
d Bruce Beresford. *p* Leonard Goldberg. *sc* David Weisberg, Douglas S Cook. *ph* Peter James. *ed* Mark Warner. *pd* Howard Cummings. *m* Norman Corbeil. *cast* Tommy Lee Jones, Ashley Judd, Bruce Greenwood, Annabeth Gish, Benjamin Weir, Jay Brazeau, John MacLaren, Edward Evanko, Betsy Brantley.

● Libby Parsons (Judd) is in prison, wrongly convicted of killing her husband (Greenwood). She's just discovered, however, that he's not dead but making hay under an assumed identity, whereupon one of her fellow inmates – an ex-lawyer who's offed her other half – gives her the legal scoop: 'double jeopardy,' meaning you can't be tried for the same crime twice. Theoretically, then, Libby can serve her time, track the scoundrel down, and blow his brains out while the law stands and looks at its toes. To set her plan in motion, though, she has to break the strictures of her parole, and there's no way her hard-nut supervisor (Jones) is about to let that happen. What follows is an occasionally slick but mostly stupid vehicle for Tommy Lee to play his usual Mr Gruff, and a right old showcase for Judd to show vulnerability, get mad, shoot guns, run around a bit, all with a touch of the maternal thrown in. TJ

Double Life, A

(1947, US, 104 min, b/w)
d George Cukor. *p* Michael Kanin. *sc* Garson Kanin, Ruth Gordon. *ph* Milton Krasner. *ed* Robert Parrish. *pd* Harry Horner. *m* Miklós Rozsa. *cast* Ronald Colman, Signe Hasso, Edmond O'Brien, Shelley Winters, Ray Collins, Millard Mitchell.

● The first of Cukor's string of fruitful collaborations with screenwriters Garson Kanin and Ruth Gordon, a curious melodrama about a Broadway matinée idol who so loses himself in his role as Othello that he carries it over, murderously, into a backstreet affair with a waitress. The theatre scenes are so brilliantly observed, so rich in the sort of affectionate detail that made *The Actress* a small masterpiece, that the film seems to grind gears uncomfortably when venturing into the grey and shabby B movie world of the murder. All the more so in that it then returns to its happier idiom for a grand finale of on-stage retribution. Flawed, undoubtedly, but fascinating. TM

Double Life of Véronique, The

see Double Vie de Véronique, La

Double Man, The

(1967, GB, 105 min)
d Franklin J Schaffner. *p* Hal E Chester. *sc* Frank Tarloff, Alfred Hayes. *ph* Denys Coop. *ed* Richard Best. *ad* Arthur Lawson. *m* Ernie Freeman. *cast* Yul Brynner, Britt Ekland, Clive Revill, Anton Diffring, Moira Lister, Lloyd Nolan.

● Barely passable spy thriller in which Brynner's CIA agent is lured to Europe in search of his son (reported dead) and finds himself abducted by the Commies, who replace him with his double (Brynner again). The cast do their best (Brynner, Revill and Lister especially) to enliven the routine spy larks, while Denys Coop's camerawork makes an elegant picture postcard spread of the Tyrolean Alps. GA

Double Suicide (Shinju Ten no Amijima)

(1969, Jap, 106 min, b/w)
d Masahiro Shinoda. *p* Masayuki Nakajima,

Masahiro Shinoda. *sc* Taeko Tomioka, Masahiro Shinoda, Toru Takemitsu. *ph* Toshiro Narushima. *ad* Kiyoshi Awaza. *m* Toru Takemitsu. *cast* Kichiemon Nakamura, Shima Iwashita, Hosei Komatsu, Yusuke Takita, Kamatari Fujiwara, Yoshi Kato.
● Shinoda's interesting film is a generally faithful adaptation of a play by Chikamatsu, preserving all the theatrical conventions of the puppet theatre original, and even trumping that level of artifice with bizarre devices of his own: eccentric framing, ultra-formal compositions, and a very stylised use of black-and-white. The trouble is that the very simple plot (a married man's fateful love for a courtesan) sometimes gets lost amid all the stylistic bustle: the formal beauty comes dangerously close to sheer formalism, and the 'fantastic' elements risk degenerating into Fellini-esque excess. TR

Double Team

(1997, US, 93 min)
d Tsui Hark. *p* Moshe Diamant. *sc* Don Jakoby, Paul Mones. *ph* Peter Pau. *ed* Bill Pankow. *pd* Marek Dobrowolski. *m* Gary Chang. *cast* Jean-Claude Van Damme, Dennis Rodman, Paul Freeman, Mickey Rourke, Natacha Lindinger, Valeria Cavalli.
● More than just another action director, Tsui Hark is one of world cinema's great fantasists, with *The Butterfly Murders* and *Once Upon a Time in China* among his many credits. But this is rubbish: an incoherent James Bond-ish yarn distinguished only by its formal decadence and the presence of basketball's Dennis Rodman. He looks like a punk, but has a disarmingly fey, debonair manner which gives his scenes a fillip. In contrast, Van Damme is puny and square as a CIA operative press-ganged into The Colony, a secret think-tank for 'retired' international agents. After that, the film-makers can't think of anything more interesting for him to do than the rescue of wife and new-born child from the clutches of villain Stavros (Rourke). Directing on autopilot-gone-haywire, Tsui rips off that old HK gag of the shoot-out in a baby ward, throws in a tiger for the gladiatorial climax, and blows up the Coliseum as an afterthought. TCh

Double Trouble

(1966, US, 92 min)
d Norman Taurog. *p* Judd Bernard, Irwin Winkler. *sc* Jo Heims. *ph* Daniel L Fapp. *ed* John McSweeney. *ad* George W Davis, Merrill Pye. *m* Jeff Alexander. *songs* Doc Pomus, Mort Shuman. *cast* Elvis Presley, Annette Day, John Williams, Yvonne Romain, Chips Rafferty, Norman Rossington, The Wiere Brothers.
● Presley, well into his descent towards celluloid oblivion, tours a Europe which a mere gust of wind would have dislodged, pursued by comical policemen, oafish villains, and girls, girls, girls. AC

Double Vie de Véronique, La (The Double Life of Véronique)

(1991, Pol, 98 min)
d Krzysztof Kieslowski. *p* Leonardo De La Fuente. *sc* Krzysztof Kieslowski, Krzysztof Piesiewicz. *ph* Slawomir Idziak. *ed* Jacques Witta. *ad* Patrice Mercier, Halina Dobrowolska. *m* Zbigniew Preisner. *cast* Irène Jacob, Halina Gryglaszewska, Kalina Jedrusik, Aleksander Bardini, Wladyslaw Kowalski, Jerzy Gudejko.
● Two physically identical girls, living in Poland and France, are mysteriously linked in numerous respects. Each has a talent for music, each entertains doubts about her current lover, and each has a weak heart. And although they have never met, when Veronika collapses on stage during a recital, Véronique immediately feels that her life has changed in a profound way. Kieslowski may not proffer the lucid moral insights of his earlier *Dekalog* series, but it's hard to imagine anyone else making a more mesmerising study of spiritual disquiet. If the story is simplicity itself, this is certainly not an easy film, but coherence is assured by Irène Jacob's luminous double performance, by Kieslowski's effortless control of mood, and by his subtle use of repeated motifs. Whether you swallow what seems to be Kieslowski's thesis (if we can recognise our affinities with some obscure soul-twin, we may learn from their suffering) comes down to a matter of faith; but there's no denying his compassion or ability to invest places, objects and passing moments with an almost numinous power. GA

Double Vue

see Afraid of the Dark

Double X

(1991, GB, 97 min)
d/p/sc Shani S Grewal. *ph* Dominique Grosz. *ed* Michael Johns. *pd* Colin Pocock. *m* Raf Ravenscroft. *cast* Simon Ward, William Katt, Norman Wisdom, Bernard Hill, Gemma Craven, Leon Herbert, Chloe Annett, Derren Nesbitt, Vladek Sheybal.
● The brainchild of its director, this is an unspeakably dreadful, amateurish affair which shows, if nothing else, the desperate straits the British film industry has come to. What possessed actors of the calibre of Ward, Hill and Craven to consider this clueless cheapo about British organised (or rather, unorganised) crime is a matter only for speculation; Wisdom was presumably resurrecting his ambitions to be a serious actor in the part of a bank robber who tries to protect himself and his young daughter from a band of vicious crooks. There is absolutely no level – not even in the realms of self-parody – on which the film works. Inauspiciously, it's the first product of the Business Enterprise scheme. SGr

Douce

(1943, Fr, 111 min, b/w)
d Claude Autant-Lara. *sc* Jean Aurenche, Pierre Bost. *ph* Philippe Agostini. *ed* Madeleine Gug. *ad* Jacques Krauss. *m* René Cloerec. *cast* Odette Joyeux, Roger Pigaut, Marguerite Moréno, Jean Debucourt, Madeleine Robinson.
● If Harold Robbins had been alive and well in Paris under the German Occupation, he might have produced something like *Douce*: a story that follows the conflicting passions of a young girl and her governess in a stately Parisian home in 1887. What he would have missed is the delicately detailed charm, the burning class antagonisms, and a handsome young spectre who appears out of nowhere to wreak destruction upon all. In short, it wouldn't be what it is: enchanting. Melancholic melodrama at its best, knocking the soapbox out from under the legs of upperclass landlords, the ambitious bourgeoisie who seek to usurp their position, even Cupid himself. SGo

Dougal and the Blue Cat (Pollux et le Chat Bleu)

(1970, Fr, 82 min)
d Serge Danot. *p* L Danot, L Auclin. *sc* Serge Danot, Jacques Josselin. *ph* C Giresse. *ed* S Gerstemberg. *m* Joss Basselli. *cast* voices (English version): Eric Thompson, Fenella Fielding.
● When blue-furred Buxton turns up in the Magic Garden, Dougal suspects that all is not well. The new feline friend's habit of hanging around in the nearby deserted glue factory and talking to the disembodied 'Blue Voice' (Fenella Fielding) doesn't increase his confidence one jot. And indeed in no time at all our hero's worst fears are realised: Zebedee's moustache is hijacked, the chums are chucked in a dungeon, and Dougal himself gets sent to the moon by Madame Blue. It's a tribute to Eric Thompson's superb voice-overs that this remains a quite inspiring animation movie, by turns witty, satirical, and occasionally downright weird. Kids will love it, adults go bananas over it, and spaced-out acid casualties think they've astrally projected on to another planet. (The English version was written and directed by Gavrick Losey and Joyce Herlihy.) MK

Doug's 1st Movie

(1999, US, 77 min)
d Maurice Joyce. *p* Jim Jinkins, David Campbell, Jack Spillum, Melanie Grisanti. *sc* Ken Scarborough. *ed* Alysha Nadine Cohen, Christopher K Gee. *pd* Freya Tanz, Pete List, Eugene Salandra. *m* Mark Watters. *cast* voices: Thomas McHugh, Fred Newman, Chris Phillips, Constance Schulman, Frank Welker, Doug Preis.
● As befits its hero, this feature spin-off from TV's *Doug*, the Disney-ABC cartoon series, is gentle and politically correct. Doug, a mild seventh-grader (year seven, to Brits), has something of Tin-Tin about him (note the bright Hergé-inspired graphics and the designers' acute angle perspectives). But the screenplay never lets him stray far beyond the home and high school axis, playing a juvenile riff on Capra-esque concerns. Happily, though, this is not just another disguised musical: no irksome da-da-da songs, even if Mark Watters' music lacks variation and zest. These spin-offs remain animation on the cheap, and none yet – straitjacketed by fidelity to its respective series – has attained the density of image and kineticism of design of the art form's true originals. WH

Doulos, Le (The Finger Man)

(1962, Fr/It, 108 min, b/w)
d/sc Jean-Pierre Melville. *ph* Nicolas Hayer. *ed* Monique Bonnot. *ad* Daniel Guéret. *m* Paul Misraki. *cast* Jean-Paul Belmondo, Serge Reggiani, Jean Desailly, René Lefèvre, Fabienne Dali, Michel Piccoli, Marcel Cuvelier, Monique Hennessy, Daniel Crohem.
● Darker than *Bob le Flambeur*, Melville's second foray into the Parisian underworld borrows its epigraph from Céline: 'One must choose: die… or lie?' Appropriately, in a film devoted to the principle of duplicity, Melville teases the spectator by reproducing the police station from Mamoulian's *City Streets*, while his Paris features American lampposts, call-boxes, subway entrances. At the heart of this ambiguous world is Silien (Belmondo), by repute a professional informer, who juggles twin friendships with a police inspector (Crohem) and a burglar (Reggiani). Just out of jail, afraid he can't cut it in the underworld any more, involved in an act of revenge that leaves him with a nasty taste in his mouth, Reggiani finds Crohem lurking in ambush when he undertakes his next job. The images point unequivocally to Belmondo as the informer, until Melville skims through them again to reveal a different story; but either way, the doubt conjures disaster. Terrific performances, and equally terrific camerawork from Nicolas Hayer – more *gris* than *noir* – conjure a rivetingly treacherous, twilit world. TM

Dove, The

(1974, US, 104 min)
d Charles Jarrott. *p* Gregory Peck. *sc* Peter Beagle, Adam Kennedy. *ph* Sven Nykvist. *ed* John Jympson. *ad* Peter Lamont. *m* John Barry. *cast* Joseph Bottoms, Deborah Raffin, John McLiam, Dabney Coleman, John Meillon, Colby Chester.
● The five-year, round-the-world voyage of teenage Californian yachtsman ('I just had to get out and see what else was going on') Robin Lee Graham, produced by Gregory Peck as a chaste romance in picturesque locations for the family film market. Boring as hell, with even cinematographer Sven Nykvist's invention sorely taxed by the tedious succession of seascapes. PT

Down Among the Z Men

(1952, GB, 71 min, b/w)
d Maclean Rogers. *p* EJ Fancey. *sc* Jimmy Grafton, Francis Charles. *ph* Geoffrey Faithfull. *ed* Peter Mayhew. *ad* Don Russell. *m* Jack Jordan. *cast* Michael Bentine, Spike Milligan, Peter Sellers, Harry Secombe, Carole Carr, Robert Cawdron.
● The sole feature film with all four original Goons, going their own sweet way through an absurd plot about foiling crooks who are after an obscure atomic formula. Rickety and pretty juvenile, though Sellers' Major Bloodnok, played more or less straight, is nice. Bentine, as the mad professor, does his stage act with the all-purpose chair-back as part of a show at the army camp. Milligan does his gormless Eccles as a private. Secombe is straight man. GA

Down and Dirty

see Brutti, sporchi e cattivi

Down and Out in Beverly Hills

(1986, US, 103 min)
d/p Paul Mazursky. *sc* Paul Mazursky, Leon Capetanos. *ph* Donald McAlpine. *ed* Richard Halsey. *pd* Pato Guzman. *m* Andy Summers. *cast* Nick Nolte, Bette Midler, Richard Dreyfuss, Little Richard, Tracy Nelson, Elizabeth Peña, Evan Richards.
● When Nolte's gentleman of the road tries to drown himself in a Beverly Hills swimming-pool, coathanger baron Dreyfuss welcomes him into a

family riddled with the whole gamut of late 20th century neuroses. Another of Mazursky's looks at the pursuit of happiness, this update of Renoir's *Boudu Saved from Drowning* starts life as a satire on the tribal rites of the new and filthy rich, but goes badly wrong somewhere down the line. Renoir's anarchic hobo romantically ditched bourgeois bliss for the open road; Mazursky presents his bag people as pathetic basket cases, with Nolte's upwardly mobile tramp only too happy to take up permanent residence in Lotusland. And it betokens some kind of desperation (or perhaps the fact that this was produced by Disney's adult offshoot) that the comedy rests increasingly on the cute antics of the family dog. As one of David Mamet's characters would say, money talks and bullshit walks. SJo

Down by Law

(1986, US, 107 min, b/w)
d Jim Jarmusch. *p* Alan Kleinberg. *sc* Jim Jarmusch. *ph* Robby Müller. *ed* Melody London. *m* John Lurie, Tom Waits. *cast* Tom Waits, John Lurie, Roberto Benigni, Nicoletta Braschi, Ellen Barkin, Billie Neal.

●Jack (Lurie) and Zack (Waits), super-cool no-hopers, meet up in a New Orleans jail. Initially at odds with one another, they are soon distracted by the arrival of Roberto (Benigni), whose pidgin English, memories of old movies, and quotations from Robert Frost in his native Italian keep them both irritated and amused. Finally, however, it is this garrulous and eternally optimistic little man who leads the two self-appointed tough guys to freedom. Jarmusch's fairytale amalgam of prison movie, *noir* thriller and offbeat comedy bears some resemblance to his earlier Stranger than Paradise: both are in three parts; both concern jaded Americans transformed by contact with a foreign innocent; both are shot in stunning, sharp black-and-white. And again music (by Waits and Lurie) and mood are essential components to Jarmusch's poetry. But what makes this more accessible (and perhaps less ambitious) is the emphasis on humour; after the initial establishment of character and atmosphere, the laughs come thick and fast, most notably from the marvellous Benigni. For all the wit and style, however, the film's most delightful triumph is to demonstrate that 'Ees a sad an' beautiful world'. GA

Down from the Mountain

(2000, US, 98 min)
d Nick Doob, Chris Hegedus, DA Pennebaker. *p* Bob Neuwirth, Frazer Pennebaker. *ph* Joan Churchill, Jim Desmond, Nick Doob, Chris Hegedus, Bob Neuwirth, Jehane Noujaim, DA Pennebaker, John Paul Pennebaker. *ed* Nick Doob, DA Pennebaker. *with* The Cox Family, Fairfield Four, John Hartford, Emmylou Harris, Chris Thomas King, Alison Krauss and Union Station, Colin Linden, The Nashville Bluegrass Band, The Peasall Sisters, Ralph Stanley, Gillian Welch, David Rawlings, The Whites.

●Just before *O Brother, Where Art Thou?* premiered at Cannes, Pennebaker (*Monterey Pop*, *Don't Look Back*) and his crew went to Nashville to film a gala concert featuring the musicians who had played and sung on the Coens' soundtrack. In the event, the film's success spawned a surprise million-selling hit for the accompanying CD, thus helping to broaden the audience for bluegrass, gospel and American traditional music, a process this movie can only continue. Following a modicum of backstage chat as bonhomie and mutual respect flow between the assembled performers, it proceeds as wry MC John Hartford ushers on both those artists you may well have heard of (Emmylou Harris, Gillian Welch, Alison Krauss) and those who were certainly a discovery for this relative newcomer (authentic vocals and pickin' courtesy of The Cox Family and The Whites, timeless gospelling from the Fairfield Four). The keening melodies, lyrics of love, death and hard-earned wisdom, not to mention ace banjo and guitar work, connect back to roots from which blues and soul also sprang. TJ

Downhill

(1927, GB, 95 min approx, b/w)
d Alfred Hitchcock. *p* CM Woolf, Michael Balcon. *sc* Eliot Stannard. *ph* Claude McDonnell. *ed* Lionel Rich. *ad* Bert Evans. *cast* Ivor Novello, Isabel Jeans, Ian Hunter, Annette Benson, Norman McKinnel, Lilian Braithwaite.

●Ivor Novello, public school sixth-former, loyally takes the blame when a chum impregnates Mabel, the tuck shop temptress. Cast out of the family circle, he becomes a chorus boy in the West End, inherits some money, marries a gold-digger, goes broke again and works as a taxi dancer-cum-gigolo in Paris. Finally he is (or hallucinates that he is) transported back to London and into the apologetic arms of his family. The author of the source play – 'David L'Estrange' – was a pseudonym for Novello and Constance Collier, and this adaptation abounds in Novello-esque gay motifs: brutish father, voluptuous victimhood, bloody women. It's directed by Hitchcock with imagination and, especially in the first half, much comedy. Essentially though, this should be filed under 'Novello'. BBa

Downhill Racer

(1969, US, 101 min)
d Michael Ritchie. *p* Richard Gregson. *sc* James Salter. *ph* Brian Probyn. *ed* Nick Archer. *ad* Ian Whittaker. *m* Kenyon Hopkins. *cast* Robert Redford, Gene Hackman, Camilla Sparv, Joe Jay Jalbert, Timothy Kirk, Dabney Coleman, Karl Michael Vogler.

●Fine first feature from the once wonderful Ritchie, concentrating – as in so much of his work (*The Candidate, Smile, Semi-Tough*) – on the cost and rewards of winning. Redford is the ambitious skier, out to break all records, and contemptuous of the teamwork advocated by the coach (Hackman) when he goes to Europe for the Olympics. The understated performances and reluctance to emphasise plot result in convincing characterisations, to such an extent that the often narcissistic Redford actually allows himself to come across as a dislikeably selfish, arrogant and icy man. And the location skiing sequences, revealing Ritchie's background and interest in documentary styles, are simply astounding, even for those with little interest in the sport. GA

Down Memory Lane

(1949, US, 72 min, b/w)
d Phil Karlson. *p* Mack Sennett. *sc* Steve Allen. *ph* Walter Strenge. *ed* Fred Allen. *m* Sol Kaplan. *cast* Steve Allen, Franklin Pangborn, Mack Sennett, Frank Nelson, Bing Crosby, Gloria Swanson, WC Fields.

●A Steve Allen TV show provides a pretty dumb frame for re-runs of some cherishable Sennett material: silent clips and longer extracts from WC Fields' *The Dentist* and Bing Crosby's *Blue of the Night*. An oddball credit for tough-guy director Karlson, who knocked it out, with his radio discovery Allen, in a mere two days at Eagle-Lion. PT

Down Periscope

(1996, US, 93 min)
d David S Ward. *p* Robert Lawrence. *sc* Hugh Wilson, Andrew Kurtzman, Eliot Wald. *ph* Victor Hammer. *ed* William Anderson, Armen Minasian. *pd* Michael Corenblith. *m* Randy Edelman. *cast* Kelsey Grammer, Lauren Holly, Bruce Dern, Rob Schneider, Harry Dean Stanton, William H Macy, Ken Hudson Campbell, Rip Torn.

●The Navy doesn't know what to do with Tom Dodge – he's due his own command, but he's such an impulsive maverick, he has more enemies among the top brass than most officers face in wartime. That's how he finds himself at the helm of a rusty diesel-powered submarine that should have been junked decades ago, with a crew of no-hopers to match. His mission impossible: a war game pitting the technology of yesteryear against the nuclear powered might of today's US Navy. Grammer's first major feature after his TV success with *Frasier* finds him embracing a new persona. Out goes the intellectual cold fish, in comes the intuitive, warm, fun-loving leader of men. The role looks good on him, but it's a shame that he's also jettisoned the sophisticated dry wit which has been his hallmark in favour of a much broader, wetter humour. But what would you expect of a movie directed by Ward and co-written by Hugh (*Police Academy*) Wilson? The funniest bit plumbs the depths for a silent-running gag which could seriously damage any future submarine picture. The construction is so ramshackle (or the mood so PC) that the film-makers put a woman (Holly) on board, then can't find a thing to do with her. TCh

Down the Ancient Stairs (Per le Antiche Scala)

(1975, It/Fr, 102 min)
d Mauro Bolognini. *p* Fulvio Lucisano. *sc* Raffaele Andreassi, Mario Arosio, Tullio Pinelli, Bernardino Zapponi, Sinko Solleville Marie. *ph* Ennio Guarnieri. *ed* Nino Baragli. *ad* Piero Tosi. *m* Ennio Morricone. *cast* Marcello Mastroianni, Françoise Fabian, Marthe Keller, Barbara Bouchet, Pierre Blaise, Lucia Bosè.

●A film that hardly deserves the outright dismissal it has generally received; it at least shows evidence of an intelligent awareness of the issues it broaches, and a loving attention to period detail (Italy in the '30s). Its biggest handicap is probably its central metaphor, ultimately too facile, which has the mental asylum in which most of the action takes place, dominated by an all-powerful and supposedly much-loved Professor, standing as a microcosm of the fascist state. But Françoise Fabian's rational and sensitive performance, as the young doctor come to investigate the professor's methods, is a major plus; and Mastroianni is totally credible as the self-deluding professor who finds the veiled tyranny he has practised within the walls reproducing itself frighteningly outside. VG

Down Three Dark Streets

(1954, US, 85 min, b/w)
d Arnold Laven. *p* Arthur Gardner, Jules V Levy. *sc* The Gordons, Bernard C Schoenfeld. *ph* Joseph Biroc. *ed* Grant Whytock. *pd* Ted Haworth. *m* Paul Sawtell. *cast* Broderick Crawford, Ruth Roman, Martha Hyer, Marisa Pavan, Kenneth Tobey, Gene Reynolds.

●Watchable enough, thanks to the performances, despite an overblown finale. But with its commentary and backstage glimpses of new detection techniques as Crawford's FBI agent unravels three cases on which his buddy was working when killed, it looks like a slightly sheepish echo of *Dragnet* (whose first movie spinoff also appeared in 1954). TM

Downtime

(1997, GB/Fr, 91 min)
d Bharat Nalluri. *p* Richard Johns. *sc* Caspar Berry. *ph* Tony Imi. *ed* Leslie Healey. *pd* Chris Townsend. *m* Simon Boswell. *cast* Paul McGann, Susan Lynch, Tom Georgeson, David Roper, Denise Bryson, Adam Johnston, David Horsefield.

●Imagine Ken Loach remaking *Die Hard*. Police shrink McGann talks single mum Lynch out of jumping off the tower block that's home to her and her small son, but the place also has a vandalism problem and a creaking old lift – where the three end up, dangling and fighting for their lives. Director Nalluri makes the best of this, but can do little about the script's tin ear for would-be hard boiled dialogue, and Georgeson's overheated performance as the unemployed dad who's not going to take it anymore. Credibility doesn't really come into it. TJ

Down to Earth

(1947, US, 101 min)
d Alexander Hall. *p* Don Hartman. *sc* Edwin Blum, Don Hartman. *ph* Rudolph Maté. *ed* Viola Lawrence. *ad* Stephen Goosson, Rudolph Sternad. *m* Heinz Roemheld. *cast* Rita Hayworth, Larry Parks, Marc Platt, Roland Culver, James Gleason, Edward Everett Horton.

●Terpsichore, Muse of the Dance (Hayworth), is sent to terra firma to help Broadway producer Parks with his latest musical extravaganza. The result, however, never quite gleams as bright as Rudolph Maté's Technicolor photography, despite the return of Culver and Horton as the helpful angelic types from the earlier and superior *Here Comes Mr Jordan*. TJ

Down to Earth

(2001, US/Ger/Aust, 87 min)
d Chris Weitz, Paul Weitz. *p* Sean Daniel, Michael Rotenberg, James Jacks. *sc* Chris Rock, Lance Crouther, Ali Le Roi, Louis CK. *ph* Richard Crudo. *ed* Priscilla Nedd Friendly. *pd* Paul Peters. *m* Jamshied Sharifi. *cast* Chris Rock, Regina King, Mark Addy, Eugene Levy, Frankie Faison, Greg Germann, Jennifer Coolidge, Chazz Palminteri.

●After eye-catching supporting roles in *Lethal Weapon 4* and *Dogma*, stand-up comic Chris Rock falls from grace in his first star vehicle. What possessed the edgy, subversive Rock to remake Warren Beatty's corny celestial comedy, *Heaven Can Wait*, is a puzzler. Prematurely whisked off to Heaven, the glitzy Pearly Gates nightclub fronted by Italian wise guy Mr King (Palminteri), bike messenger and would-be stand-up Lance Barton (Rock) is given a second chance in a new body. He returns to Earth as Charles Wellington, a white, middle-aged business magnate recently murdered by his scheming wife and weasely personal assistant. Except that Rock still looks to us, the audience, like a slim, cool black man. It's only the characters in the film who see him as a corpulent, balding and terminally unhip white man. Confused? He sure is. And we are too. Apart from odd flashes, Rock never appears in his white incarnation. So all the best jokes go for nothing. NF

Downtown 81 (aka Glenn O'Brien's New York Beat Movie)

(1981/2000, US/Switz/Bel, 75 min)
d Edo Bertoglio. *p* Maripol Fauque, Glenn O'Brien. *sc* Glenn O'Brien. *ph* John McNulty. *ed* Pamela French. *pd* Maripol Fauque. *ed* Pamela French. *songs* (performed by) Gray, John Lurie, DNA, Tuxedo Moon, Melle Mel, Lydia Lunch, Suicide. *cast* Jean-Michel Basquiat, Anna Schroeder, Giorgio Giomelsky, Marshall Chess, Deborah Harry, Arto Lindsay, DNA, Kid Creole and the Coconuts, James White and the Blacks. *narrator* Saul Williams.

●Years before Jeffrey Wright starred in Julian Schnabel's posthumous biopic, ill-fated NY artist Jean-Michel Basquiat more or less played himself in this ramshackle portrait of the city's intermingling art and music scene, c. 1981. Basquiat was 19 at the time, yet to have his first show, but he did have his own band Gray (with one Vincent Gallo in the line-up) and he was already using the city streets as a canvas for his graffiti-related art. As he trudges the city sidewalks, Basquiat's an undeniably charismatic figure, the trouble is that this flimsy slice of celluloid hipness doesn't really give him a chance to do an awful lot else. Although shot in 1980–81 by fashion photographer Edo Bertoglio, much of the footage was lost until 1998, when post-production included adding a voice-over for the Basquiat character (courtesy of *Slam* star Saul Williams). Despite some pretentious narration, there's significant archival interest in the musical contributions from New York No Wavers Arto Lindsay's DNA and punk-funky James White and the Blacks, plus Japanese electro-popsters The Plastics, and prime-time Kid Creole and the Coconuts. It gives good cameo too, with Debbie Harry as a bag lady and some very early rapping from Fab Five Freddie. TJ

Down to You

(2000, US, 92 min)
d Kris Isacsson. *p* Jason Kliot, Joana Vicente. *sc* Kris Isacsson. *ph* Robert Yeoman. *ed* Stephen A Rotter. *pd* Kevin Thompson. *m* Edmund Choi. *cast* Freddie Prinze Jr, Julia Stiles, Selma Blair, Shawn Hatosy, Zak Orth, Ashton Kutcher, Rosario Dawson, Lucie Arnaz, Henry Winkler.

●Al (Prinze) and Imogen (Stiles) are 19-year-olds tackling New York college life. The course of their relationship is charted in numbing detail and interspersed with the antics of their quirky friends. Prinze is unimpressive; Stiles – promising in *10 Things I Hate About You* – is better, but in the end unable to do much with the toe-curling script. Straight to camera monologues and dated split-screen and fantasy sequences don't help. KW

Drachenfutter

see Spicy Rice

Dracula

(1931, US, 85 min, b/w)
d Tod Browning. *p* Carl Laemmle Jr. *sc* Garrett Fort, Dudley Murphy. *ph* Karl Freund. *ed* Milton Carruth, Maurice Pivar. *ad* Charles D Hall. *m* Peter Tchaikovsky, Richard Wagner. *cast* Bela Lugosi, Helen Chandler, David Manners, Dwight Frye, Edward Van Sloan, Herbert Bunston.

●Not by any means the masterpiece of fond memory or reputation, although the first twenty minutes are astonishingly fluid and brilliantly shot by Karl Freund, despite the intrusive painted backdrops. Innumerable imaginative touches here: the sinister emphasis of Lugosi's first words ('I...am...Dracula') and the sonorous poetry of his invocation to the children of the night; the moment when Dracula leads the way up his castle stairway behind a vast cobweb through which Renfield has to struggle as he follows; the vampire women, driven off by Dracula, reluctantly backing away from the camera while it continues hungrily tracking in to Renfield's fallen body. Thereafter the pace falters, and with the London scenes growing in verbosity and staginess, the hammy limitations of Lugosi's performance are cruelly exposed. But the brilliant moments continue (Renfield's frenzy in his cell, for instance), and Freund's camerawork rarely falters. TM

Dracula (aka Horror of Dracula)

(1958, GB, 82 min)
d Terence Fisher. *p* Anthony Hinds. *sc* Jimmy Sangster. *ph* Jack Asher. *ed* James Needs, Bill Lenny. *ad* Bernard Robinson. *m* James Bernard. *cast* Peter Cushing, Christopher Lee, Michael Gough, Melissa Stribling, Carol Marsh, Valerie Gaunt.

●This was the first Hammer remake of *Dracula*, and it is by now more or less established as a classic. The film is perhaps typified by its beautiful opening sequence in which Christopher Lee appears, a menacing shadow between pillars at the top of a staircase, then glides down the stairs in a prolonged take to reveal not the grotesque figure that Lugosi portrayed but, on the contrary, a crisply charming aristocrat 'with pale face and unforgettable eyes'. Other parts, however, have worn less well. DP

Dracula

(1973, GB, 98 min)
d/p Dan Curtis. *sc* Richard Matheson. *ed* Richard A Harris, Tony Palk. *pd* Trevor Williams. *m* Robert Cobert. *cast* Jack Palance, Simon Ward, Nigel Davenport, Pamela Brown, Fiona Lewis, Penelope Horner, Murray Brown.

●A TV movie theatrically released in Britain. Despite traditionally atmospheric touches in the direction, a disappointing adaptation which boasted of going back to source in Bram Stoker's novel but lets Richard Matheson's script stray into silly infidelities and inventions. Radically miscast, Palance does have his moments as a Dracula mourning his lost love, but misses out on the chance to be romantically Byronic since, with his love reincarnated as Lucy Westenra (Lewis), he is mostly required to rage because she is killed again. TM

Dracula

(1979, US, 112 min)
d John Badham. *p* Walter Mirisch. *sc* WD Richter. *ph* Gilbert Taylor. *ed* John Bloom. *pd* Peter Murton. *m* John Williams. *cast* Frank Langella, Laurence Olivier, Donald Pleasence, Kate Nelligan, Trevor Eve, Jan Francis, Tony Haygarth.

●Langella offers the best interpretation of Stoker's villain since Christopher Lee, and Badham's film, shot in England, gives him a classy environment to devastate. But the decision to create such a sympathetic vampire (especially alongside Olivier's hammy Van Helsing) leaves the film short of suspense, and so romance has to take most of the weight. As a result, it begins to drift badly at the climax.

Dracula (aka Bram Stoker's Dracula)

(1992, US, 127 min)
d Francis Ford Coppola. *p* Fredric S Fuchs, Francis Ford Coppola, Charles Mulvehill. *sc* James V Hart. *ph* Michael Ballhaus. *ed* Nicholas C Smith, Glen Scantlebury, Anne Goursaud. *pd* Tom Sanders. *m* Wojciech Kilar. *cast* Gary Oldman, Winona Ryder, Anthony Hopkins, Keanu Reeves, Richard E Grant, Cary Elwes, Bill Campbell, Sadie Frost, Tom Waits, Jay Robinson.

●From the moment Dracula (Oldman) trails a bloodied razor across his tongue with a look of ecstasy, you know that this version, going back to source in Stoker's novel, isn't going to offer a silver-tongued bloodsucker hovering over swooning damsels. In the opening sequences, Dracula's soul-mate Elisabeta (Ryder) commits suicide in the mistaken belief that he had died in battle. Forsaking God, he seems doomed to an endless existence of guilt and loneliness, until lawyer Jonathan Harker (Reeves) shows him a picture of his fiancée, who just happens to be the spitting image of Elisabeta. A gorgeous, stylised adaptation, full of visual tricks and dazzling camerawork, this places the emphasis firmly on perverse, rampant eroticism. Equally forceful is Oldman's extraordinary performance, especially in his older guise, complete with bouffant hairdo and elongated fingers. In contrast to Hopkins' aggressive performance as vampire-hunter Van Helsing, a stupefied Reeves puts in a hopeless show of defiance. This lack of a convincing central dynamic leads to the occasional sense that the film is little more than a spectacular edifice, but you'll be too spellbound to resist seduction. CM

Dracula A.D. 1972

(1972, GB, 98 min)
d Alan Gibson. *p* Josephine Douglas. *sc* Don Houghton. *ph* Dick Bush. *ed* James Needs. *pd* Don Mingaye. *m* Michael Vickers. *cast* Christopher Lee, Peter Cushing, Stephanie Beacham, Michael Coles, Christopher Neame, Marsha Hunt.

●Feeblest of the early 1970s cycle of Dracula revivals, set in contemporary London and decorated with scantily-clad female victims. Plot revolves around a trendy party-goer, Johnny Alucard (geddit?), who suggests livening up a party with a spot of devil worship. Guess who materialises, ludicrously rigged out in traditional period garb? Crass Hammer trash. MA

Dracula: Dead and Loving It

(1995, US, 90 min)
d/p Mel Brooks. *sc* Mel Brooks, Rudy DeLuca, Stever Haberman. *ph* Michael O'Shea. *ed* Adam Weiss. *pd* Roy Forge Smith. *m* Hummie Mann. *cast* Leslie Nielsen, Peter MacNicol, Steven Weber, Amy Yasbeck, Lysette Anthony, Harvey Korman, Mel Brooks, Clive Revill, Anne Bancroft.

●Brooks has always grounded his humour on high production values, a practice admirers claim achieves satirical effect and fond *hommage*. Certainly, this is as lavish as ever, and the narrative likewise takes care to keep up with both Stoker's original and the Coppola facsimile. There are some slight shortcuts. Renfield (MacNicol), not Jonathan Harker, travels to Transylvania, where Dracula (Nielsen) entrances and enslaves him, thus securing food (the crew of the *Demeter*) and shelter (Carfax Abbey). The Count provides the clothing himself – a Gary Oldman-esque bouffant wig, for instance, which he takes off indoors (one of the surviving jokes). Coppola had trouble stuffing the book into two hours, and this hasty hour-and-a-half feels perfunctory in the extreme. Brooks, as Van Helsing, is one of the more successful aspects, but he hasn't imbued in his stock company a similar ability to rise above their underwritten roles. NB

Dracula Has Risen from the Grave

(1968, GB, 92 min)
d Freddie Francis. *p* Aida Young. *sc* Anthony Hinds [John Elder]. *ph* Arthur Grant. *ed* James Needs. *ad* Bernard Robinson. *m* James Bernard. *cast* Christopher Lee, Rupert Davies, Veronica Carlson, Barbara Ewing, Barry Andrews, Ewan Hooper.

●With the exception of Peter Sasdy, none of the Hammer directors who followed Terence Fisher into the Dracula series have been able to relate the atmosphere and poetry of vampirism to the rest of the plot. Here, Freddie Francis creates some admirable atmosphere and tension in the first half-hour, but ultimately reduces the film to an inconsequential splurge of arbitrary religious and sexual motifs. DP

Dracula, Prince of Darkness

(1965, GB, 90 min)
d Terence Fisher. *p* Anthony Nelson Keys. *sc* John Sansom. *ph* Michael Reed. *ed* James Needs. *pd* Bernard Robinson. *m* James Bernard. *cast* Christopher Lee, Andrew Keir, Barbara Shelley, Francis Matthews, Suzan Farmer, Thorley Walters.

●Full of the sensual mysteriousness which Hammer used to achieve so effortlessly during their long occupation of Bray Studios. Starting with a re-run of the Count's dusty demise at the hands of Van Helsing, this was the official sequel to *Dracula*, and – though it tails off – the first hour has real grandeur as Dracula's servant uses a prudish Victorian couple to effect his master's restoration. DP

Dracula's Daughter

(1936, US, 72 min, b/w)
d Lambert Hillyer. *sc* Garrett Fort. *ph* George Robinson. *ed* Milton Carruth. *ad* Albert S D'Agostino. *m* Heinz Roemheld. *cast* Gloria Holden, Otto Kruger, Marguerite Churchill, Irving Pichel, Edward Van Sloan, Nan Grey.
●A genuine sequel to Tod Browning's *Dracula* (based on Bram Stoker's story *Dracula's Guest*), Universal's low-budget shocker finds Van Helsing placed under arrest for the murder of the Count, only for a mysterious woman (Holden) to turn up and take away Dracula's body for ritual consignment to a funeral pyre. Though she has inherited the vampic urge from her father, this princess of darkness desperately seeks release from her condition through an understanding psychologist (Kruger). Apart from its haunting, low-key mood, the film is also notable for its subtle suggestion (hardly expected from a former director of B Westerns) of the lesbian nature of the female vampire. DT

Dracula 2000 (aka Dracula 2001)

(2000, US, 99 min)
d Patrick Lussier. *p* WK Border, Joel Soisson. *sc* Joel Soisson. *ph* Peter Pau. *ed* Patrick Lussier, Peter Devaney Flanagan. *pd* Carol Spier. *m* Marco Beltrami. *cast* Jonny Lee Miller, Justine Waddell, Gerard Butler, Colleen Ann Fitzpatrick, Jennifer Esposito, Danny Masterson, Omar Epps, Christopher Plummer.
●After stealing a vacuum-sealed coffin from the vault of London antiques dealer Van Helsing (Plummer), American crooks flee by private plane, open the casket, find Count Dracula, and crash land in a Louisiana swamp – just in time for Mardi Gras. Van Helsing has kept himself alive leeching the immortal one's body; the old man's infected bloodline continues with estranged daughter Mary (Waddell), who has erotic nightmares about a tall, dark, swishy stranger. When Van Helsing's assistant Simon (Miller) follows his boss to New Orleans, one half-expects a sexually subversive, blood-soaked gay carnival. Instead, Simon makes the effete Dracula (Butler) suck on some abuse, firing silver stakes from an ancient crossbow, and delivering such arch kiss-off lines as: 'Never, ever fuck with an antiques dealer.' NF

Dragnet

(1987, US, 106 min)
d Tom Mankiewicz. *p* David Permut, Robert K Weiss. *sc* Dan Aykroyd, Alan Zweibel, Tom Mankiewicz. *ph* Matthew F Leonetti. *ed* Richard Halsey, William Gordean. *pd* Robert Boyle. *m* Ira Newborn. *cast* Dan Aykroyd, Tom Hanks, Christopher Plummer, Harry Morgan, Alexandra Paul, Jack O'Halloran, Elizabeth Ashley, Dabney Coleman.
●The contemporary perspective is even less kind to '50s TV's sententious Sergeant Joe Friday than to Elliot Ness. Aykroyd really has the character down, too – the stolidly purposeful walk, the endless uninflected speeches about decency and proper procedure, punctuated with time checks – but where Jack Webb was little more than the Mount Rushmore of public service, Aykroyd's big soft nellie features and prissy mien trawl for laughs. All of which is wonderful, but little else is. Friday's new partner, Hanks, is not so much a character as an unnecessary intermediary between us and the joke. He is here to point up the risibility of the procedural rule book, so he's been issued with instinct and major dishevellment. Porn king Coleman and evangelist Plummer plan to rig the struggle of good against evil for profit, which somehow involves sacrificing an Orange County virgin on the altar. Entertaining enough, but a pity they didn't draft in more of the Eisenhower context. BC

Dragon Dies Hard, The (aka The Bruce Lee Story)

(1974, US, 90 min)
d Shih Ti. *p* Chien Hsiao-Fu. *sc* Lu Pin-Chung. *cast* Li Hsiao-Lung, Tang Pei, Yamada, Na Yin-Hsiu, Ko Li-Ssu, Li Ching-Kuan.
●Produced by Chinese businessmen in the States and withdrawn there as libellous, this fictionalised biography of Bruce Lee has its heart firmly in the dirt-digging world of Hong Kong movie gossip. Very rough and perfunctory, it's nonetheless diverting as a curiosity. VG

DragonHeart

(1996, US, 103 min)
d Rob Cohen. *p* Raffaella De Laurentiis. *sc* Charles Edward Pogue. *ph* David Eggby, Buzz Feitshans IV. *ed* Peter Amundson. *pd* Benjamin Fernandez. *m* Randy Edelman. *cast* Dennis Quaid, David Thewlis, Dina Meyer, Julie Christie, Peter Postlethwaite, Jason Isaacs.
●Brave knight-turned-bounty-hunter Bowen (Quaid) teams up with Draco, an 18 by 43ft last-surviving dragon (voice by Sean Connery). They go from village to village, faking the dragon's capture and pocketing the reward. Thus Bowen is kept in turnips, while Draco escapes extinction. Being a medieval Hollywood romp for the '90s (notable computer-generated effects), the film has a villainous king played by an English actor – here, the wonderful Thewlis, who distracts attention from Quaid's obvious inability to match the technology. When he finds out his mother the Queen (Christie) has tried to have him killed, he pauses before muttering, 'How unmotherly of you.' Engaging fare: part Dungeons and Dragons, part buddy movie – in the style of 'The Good, the Bad and the Very Ugly' – and, finally, a tale of redemption. Connery's dragon doesn't baulk at chatting up the leading lady. SGr

Dragonslayer

(1981, US, 110 min)
d Matthew Robbins. *p* Hal Barwood. *sc* Hal Barwood, Matthew Robbins. *ph* Derek Vanlint. *ed* Tony Lawson. *pd* Elliot Scott. *m* Alex North. *cast* Peter MacNicol, Caitlin Clarke, Ralph Richardson, John Hallam, Peter Eyre, Albert Salmi, Sydney Bromley.
●The saga is simple enough in this hybrid sword-and-sorcery fantasy: Dark Ages necromancer, summoned to conquer tyrannical dragon, inconveniently dies testing his powers; Sorcerer's Apprentice takes over, falls foul of virgin-sacrificing king; eventually takes on the impressively monstrous 'Vermithrax Pejorative' with a little help from the beyond. But it's the universal resonance of myth and legend that works against the film despite its creditable packaging: Richardson's 'last sorcerer' is inevitably close kin to the Merlin of *Excalibur*, while the callow youth with an ambitious half-grasp of his mentor's magic comes to us ready-filtered through the likes of Luke Skywalker. Verges on the nasty for the nippers; sails close to déjà vu for fantasy fans; fated, probably, to damnation by faint praise. PT

Dragon: The Bruce Lee Story

(1993, US, 120 min)
d Rob Cohen. *p* Raffaella De Laurentiis. *sc* Rob Cohen, Edward Khmara, John Raffo. *ph* David Eggby. *ed* Peter Amundson. *pd* Robert Ziembicki. *m* Randy Edelman. *cast* Jason Scott Lee, Lauren Holly, Robert Wagner, Nancy Kwan, Michael Learned.
●In this lively if inevitably compromised biopic of the charismatic Hong Kong martial arts star, Jason Scott Lee (no relation) looks good and moves well as the Chinese street kid who came to America, set up his own martial arts school, landed a supporting role in the *Green Hornet* TV series, then returned to Hong Kong to find he had become a national celebrity. Unlike most film star biopics, this is especially strong on the films themselves, with skilful re-creations from *Fists of Fury* and *Enter the Dragon*. Less successful is the subplot in which Lee faces up to his inner demons, depicted as a fantastical giant samurai figure. NF

Dragon Town Story (Long cheng Zheng Yue)

(1997, HK, 94 min)
d Yang Feng Liang. *cast* Wu Chien-Lien, Yaoyong.
●The Hong Kong Film Festival brochure erroneously attributes this to Zhang Yimou, who in fact signs on as executive producer (Yang Feng Liang reportedly got a co-director credit on *Red Sorghum*, though not in the West). Any fan of Zhang's will spot the mistake within the first hundred frames – this is a resolutely ordinary looking movie. That disappointment aside, it's still highly watchable. Wu Chien-Lien is the only survivor of a blood bath on her wedding day. Having sworn vengeance on the warlord who wiped out her family, she eventually persuades an assassin-for-hire to take up her cause. They get close to the warlord by pretending to be man and wife – too close, perhaps. It's a good yarn, with strong performances and some nice touches, but it never achieves the tragic resonance it's aiming for. TCh

Dragonwyck

(1946, US, 103 min, b/w)
d Joseph L Mankiewicz. *p* Darryl F Zanuck. *sc* Joseph L Mankiewicz. *ph* Arthur Miller. *ed* Dorothy Spencer. *ad* Lyle R Wheeler, J Russell Spencer. *m* Alfred Newman. *cast* Gene Tierney, Vincent Price, Glenn Langan, Walter Huston, Anne Revere, Henry Morgan, Jessica Tandy.
●Mankiewicz's directing debut is a far cry from the acerbically scripted satires – *A Letter to Three Wives*, *All About Eve* – for which he is best known; indeed, though it inhabits basically the same Gothic territory as his later *The Ghost and Mrs Muir*, it lacks that film's charm, easy wit and ambivalent psychological insights. Still, it's an efficient enough drama in the tradition of Rebecca, with innocent young Tierney leaving her rural home to stay with wealthy and sophisticated cousin Price. Needless to say, she marries him only to discover that he's a cruel, brooding tyrant who maltreats his workers and has a sinister skeleton in his closet. Few surprises, but the performances are vivid and the recreation of the 1840s setting is subtly plausible. GA

Dragoon Wells Massacre

(1957, US, 97 min)
d Harold Schuster. *p* Lindsley Parsons Sr. *sc* Warren Douglas. *ph* William H Clothier. *ed* Maurice Wright. *m* Paul Dunlap. *cast* Barry Sullivan, Dennis O'Keefe, Mona Freeman, Katy Jurado, Sebastian Cabot, Jack Elam.
●A motley group – it includes a cavalry officer, a sheriff, two convicts, two women (one haughtily respectable, one not), a renegade gun-and-whisky runner – fight a desperate rearguard battle as they trek across the Arizona desert with Apaches on their tail. It's a stock Western situation but a highly enjoyable film, magnificently shot by William Clothier and with a surprisingly tight, inventive script by Warren Douglas (the Apaches need the renegade alive for future use, for example, so they merely pick off the horses as the first stage in a war of attrition) which is particularly strong on characterisation (with the good/bad balances subtly shifting under pressure). Excellent performances, too, with Elam especially memorable as a man so accustomed to being pigeonholed as an ugly desperado that he is doggily abashed by an orphaned child's unhesitating acceptance of him as a trustworthy protector. TM

Drama of the Rich (Fatti di Gente Perbene)

(1974, It/Fr, 115 min)
d Mauro Bolognini. *p* Gianni Di Clemente. *sc* Sergio Bazzini, Mauro Bolognini. *ph* Ennio Guarnieri. *ed* Nino Baragli. *ad* Guido Iosia. *m* Ennio Morricone. *cast* Giancarlo Giannini, Catherine Deneuve, Fernando Rey, Marcel Bozzuffi, Corrado Pani, Tina Aumont.
●In late 19th century Italy, the Murri family caused a scandal. Bolognini's reconstruction of their story looks like nothing so much as a Visconti sub-text: a slowly unfurled melodrama full of weighty but unexplored themes (political power, incest, science, religion) whose passion is almost entirely spent on the aristocratic stylishness of its looks. At least Morricone's resonant score lends emotional life. HM

Dramma della Gelosia (Jealousy, Italian Style/ The Pizza Triangle)

(1970, It/Sp, 106 min)
d Ettore Scola. *p* Pio Angeletti, Adriano De Micheli. *sc* Agenore Incrocci, Furio Scarpelli,

Ettore Scola. *ph* Carlo Di Palma. *ed* Alberto Gallitti. *ad* Luciano Ricceri. *m* Armando Trovaioli. *cast* Marcello Mastroianni, Monica Vitti, Giancarlo Giannini, Manolo Zarzo, Marisa Merlini, Hercules Cortez.
●Scola's satire on screaming, gesticulating, Italian romantic dramas inevitably and unfortunately falls into the trap of indulging in the same overheated histrionics that it attacks. But, as it tells its melodramatic story of a beautiful florist torn between her two jealous lovers – a pizza-cook and a bricklayer – it still manages to be intelligently entertaining, with its eclectic humour (parody, social satire, and a nice line in cool, throwaway dialogue counterbalancing the boiling emotions) and polished performances. GA

Draughtsman's Contract, The

(1982, GB, 108 min)
d Peter Greenaway. *p* David Payne. *sc* Peter Greenaway. *ph* Curtis Clark. *ed* John Wilson. *ad* Bob Ringwood. *m* Michael Nyman. *cast* Anthony Higgins, Janet Suzman, Anne Louise Lambert, Neil Cunningham, Hugh Fraser, Dave Hill, David Gant.
●Although set in an English country house in 1694, this is essentially science fiction of the most dazzling kind, being a far more vivid exploration of an alien world than 99 per cent of big budget Hollywood films. The story about a painter who undertakes to draw an estate is as intriguing as the culture it displays. Greenaway's 17th century is a place of ribald honesty as well as unfathomable mystery, and it revels in the spoken word. Of course this is non-genre, low-budget cinema, and some people will be irritated by its singlemindedness; but for others it's proof that wit can sometimes carry a film to places special effects just don't reach. DP

Draws

see American Tickler or The Winner of 10 Academy Awards

Dreamchild

(1985, GB, 94 min)
d Gavin Miller. *p* Rick McCallum, Kenith Trodd. *sc* Dennis Potter. *ph* Billy Williams. *ed* Angus Newton. *pd* Roger Hall. *m* Stanley Myers. *cast* Coral Browne, Ian Holm, Peter Gallagher, Caris Corfman, Nicola Cowper, Jane Asher.
●At eighty, Alice Liddell is met in New York in 1932 by intrusive hacks who thrust a pink nylon bunny in her arms and demand a message for the children of America. Confronted with these alien surroundings, the hoity-toity and terribly British Alice is forced to unbend a little and piece together the fragments of her life. Dennis Potter's screenplay contrasts sassy New York with Alice's recollections, both of an idyllic youth in Oxford with the stammering Dodgson (Holm), and of Carroll's classic dominated by Jim Henson's ferocious puppets. An imaginative tour de force which is more than matched by Millar's direction of his first feature film. JE

Dream Demon

(1988, GB, 89 min)
d Harley Cokliss. *p* Paul Webster. *sc* Christopher Wicking, Harley Cokliss. *ph* Ian Wilson. *ed* Ian Crafford, David Martin. *pd* Hugo Luczyc-Wyhowski. *m* Bill Nelson. *cast* Jemma Redgrave, Kathleen Wilhoite, Timothy Spall, Jimmy Nail, Mark Greenstreet, Susan Fleetwood.
●A fantasy thriller with an intricate dream-within-a-dream structure, low on budget but high on ambition, this offers a breathless run down the corridors of the unconscious mind. As her wedding to a Falklands hero approaches, virgin Diana (Redgrave) suffers disturbing nightmares. When wacky Jenny (Wilhoite) turns up claiming to have lived in Diana's house during a childhood since blotted from her mind, their fates become intertwined. Catalysed by her memories, Jenny's repressed past also surfaces as a recurring nightmare. Blurring the line between reality and dream, the film keeps the audience off-balance, while the effects are employed sparingly but to good effect. With more time and money, Cokliss might have sorted out the shaky plot and made more of some intriguing ideas. Still, stylish photography, excellent sets, and Bill Nelson's jagged soundtrack ensure scariness. NF

Dreamer

(1979, US, 86 min)
d Noel Nosseck. *p* Mike Lobell. *sc* James Proctor, Larry Bischof. *ph* Bruce Surtees. *ed* Fred Chulack. *ad* Archie Sharp. *m* Bill Conti. *cast* Tim Matheson, Susan Blakely, Richard B Shull, Jack Warden, Barbara Stuart, Pedro Gonzalez-Gonzalez.
●Matheson's the dewy-eyed idealist of the title, a handsome lad who hopes to make it big on the professional bowling circuit. Craggy old-timer Warden (who seems to be doing an impersonation of Burgess Meredith in *Rocky*) offers to coach him. Tim's girlfriend, Blakely, is dead set against his choice of career, but if he knocks down enough skittles, he's sure to win her round. Not much polish on this particular ball. GM

Dream Flights (Polioty Vo Sne Naiavou)

(1983, USSR, 90 min)
d Roman Balayan. *sc* Victor Merezhko. *ph* Vilen Kaliuta. *ad* Vitaly Volynsky. *m* Vadim Khrapachev. *cast* Oleg Yankovsky, Liudmila Gurchenko, Oleg Tabakov, Liudmila Ivanovna, Liudmila Zorina, Elena Kostina.
●Clowning his way through life, 40-year-old Seryozha feels infinitely superior to his far more staid and steady colleagues and friends; he's ambitious, attractive and, it seems, free. But beneath the wayward liveliness lies a sad reality of loneliness, insecurity and despair; when his wife and mistress meet each other, they both leave him; when he accuses his fellow workers of moral hypocrisy, he loses his job. Balayan's film, a subtle, sensitive tragicomedy, traces its charismatic but dislikeable hero's picaresque odyssey from complacency to confusion with an admirable ambivalence of attitude. On the one hand, a petulant, selfish prankster who's never grown up; on the other, someone who refuses to play by the rules of conformist society. Central to the film's ability not only to hold interest but also to convince is Tarkovsky's leading man Yankovsky's remarkable performance, as edgy, exciting, charming and suggestive of vulnerability as De Niro at his best. GA

Dreaming of Joseph Lees

(1998, US/GB, 92 min)
d Eric Styles. *p* Christopher Milburn. *sc* Catherine Linstrum. *ph* Jimmy Dibling. *ed* Caroline Limmer. *pd* Humphrey Jaeger. *m* Zbigniew Preisner. *cast* Samantha Morton, Lee Ross, Miriam Margolyes, Frank Finlay, Nick Woodeson, Holly Aird, Rupert Graves, Lauren Richardson.
●Catherine Linstrum's original screenplay, a melodrama set in the '50s, is something of a pot-boiler – Somerset mill lass Eva (Morton) nurses a deep fancy for Joseph Lees, her absent geologist cousin (Graves), but succumbs to stolid, persistent Harry (Ross), only to be impaled on a dilemma when Joseph returns unexpectedly. Graves' character, a minor counties English Patient, with his scarred history and amputated leg, is standard Mills & Boon; and there are extravagant developments which make you gawp or check your neighbour. The director, however, treats the story with seriousness, intensity and commitment, and Graves brings a sadness and decency to his part. But the reality and sheer freshness that Morton brings to a role – see her smiling and admiring witty teenage sister Janie (Richardson, a natural) – makes the movie. WH

Dreaming of Rita (Drömmen om Rita)

(1993, Swe, 108 min)
d Jon Lindström. *p* Börje Hansson. *sc* Jon Lindström, Rita Holst. *ph* Kjell Lageroos. *ed* Martin Jordan. *ad* Staffan Erstam. *cast* Per Oscarsson, Marika Lagercrantz, Philip Zandén, Yaba Holst, Patrik Ersgard, Lise Ringheim.
●Having recently buried his wife, Oscarsson goes in search of an old flame who reminds him of his beloved Rita Hayworth; trouble is, he's far from young and healthy himself, so his daughter sets off in pursuit, leaving her workaholic husband behind, and meeting a more appreciative hitcher en route. Cue for a romantic farce-cum-road movie endowed with engaging twists, but not exactly startling or original – indeed, the end is a disappointing cop-out. The landscape is a bonus, as is the charismatically beautiful Lagercrantz. GA

Dream Life (La Vie Rêvée)

(1972, Can, 90 min)
d Mireille Dansereau. *sc* Mireille Dansereau, Patrick Auzepy. *ph* François Gill, Louis de Ernsted, Richard Rodrigue. *ed* Danielle Gagné. *ad* Michèle Cournoyer. *m* Emmanuel Charpentier. *cast* Liliane Lemaître-Auger, Véronique Le Flaguais, Jean-François Guité, Guy Foucault.
●A film about sexism and women's liberation which is ideologically clear and cohesive, uncompromising, and well made. Two young girls, one working class, the other middle class, meet at work and become friends. Finding it hard to live in the present, and that their fantasies bear no relation to the way they experience men's attitudes to them, they lure one of their dream lovers to act out 'his' reality; he fails, and the grip is broken; they have proved that the real men they know are peripheral to their lives, and thus are no longer dependent on their own fantasies. Filmed as a punctuated story – with narrative, fantasy, flashback and slow-motion – it's a superbly rounded and sensual presentation of ideas. MV

Dream Life of Angels, The

see Vie Rêvée des Anges, La

Dream Lover

(1986, US, 104 min)
d Alan J Pakula. *p* Alan J Pakula, Jon Boorstin. *sc* Jon Boorstin. *ph* Sven Nykvist. *ed* Trudy Ship, Angelo Corrao, Norman Cole. *pd* George Jenkins. *m* Michael Small. *cast* Kristy McNichol, Ben Masters, Paul Shenar, Justin Deas, John McMartin, Gayle Hunnicutt.
●McNichol plays a tyro musician plagued by nightmares after fatally stabbing an assailant in her apartment; but the 'dream therapy' she undertakes to shake off the shock brings with it new traumas. Pakula treats all this as a Bergmanesque case study, but the male figures besieging the heroine's mind aren't drawn with sufficient firmness. Intriguing idea; ramshackle plotting. TJ

Dream Lover

(1994, US, 103 min)
d Nicholas Kazan. *p* Wallis Nicita, Lauren Lloyd, Sigurjon Sighvatsson. *sc* Nicholas Kazan. *ph* Jean-Yves Escoffier. *ed* Jill Savitt, Susan Crutcher. *ad* Richard Hoover. *m* Christopher Young. *cast* James Spader, Mädchen Amick, Fredric Lehne, Bess Armstrong, Larry Miller, Kathleen York.
●Spader is high-earning yuppie-type Ray Reardon who thinks, having gone through one divorce, that he's found the ideal mate in alluring Lena (Amick). But after several years of apparent happiness, her increasingly erratic behaviour strikes doubt in his heart. Here's the person he should know best – but is she the woman he thought she was? Promising material, disappointingly frittered away. TJ

Dream of Kings, A

(1969, US, 110 min)
d Daniel Mann. *p* Jules Schermer. *sc* Harry Mark Petrakis, Ian Hunter. *ph* Richard H Kline. *ed* Walter Hannemann, Ray Daniels. *ad* Boris Leven. *m* Alex North. *cast* Anthony Quinn, Irene Papas, Inger Stevens, Sam Levene, Val Avery, Tamara Daykarhanova.
●Quinn doing his Zorba act as a cheerful Chicago loafer who despises money and spends his days brightening the neighbourhood (not to mention a sex-starved widow) with his life-giving presence. Insisting ad nauseam that as a Greek he belongs to a race of kings, he is brought down to earth only when he discovers that his small son is dying. Dripping with ludicrously overblown dialogue to match the performance. TM

Dream of Passion, A

(1978, Switz/Greece, 110 min)
d/p/sc Jules Dassin. *ph* Yorgos Arvanitis. *ed* Georges Klotz. *ad* Dionysis Fotopoulos. *m* Yiannis Markopoulos. *cast* Melina Mercouri, Ellen Burstyn, Andreas Voutsinas, Despo Diamantidou, Dimitris Papamichael, Yannis Voglis.
●This disastrous blend of Euripides, Bergman (credited inspiration) and sub-Cassavetes role-confusion glibly juxtaposes the theatrical angst of Mercouri, grappling with her interpretation of Medea for a new production of the play,

alongside the cold religious fanaticism of Burstyn, jailed for a triple infanticide in response to her husband's infidelity, and fails miserably in attempting to invoke 'Persona-I' correspondences between them. A hammer-blow insistence on the 'relevance' of Greek tragedy, a modish 'distancing' of the creative process, and a token exploration of feminist implications conspire to produce a nightmare of pretension. Filmed (basically) in English. PT

Dream On

(1991, GB, 115 min)
d Amber Production Team. *sc* Kitty Fitzgerald, Ellin Hare, Lorna Powell. *cast* Amber Styles, Maureen Harold, Anna-Marie Gascoigne, Pat Leavy, Niall Toibin, Art Davies.

● There's something remarkable about the low-budget work of North Shields' Amber Collective. *Seacoal* was politically sharp Loachian realism; *In Fading Light* saw a growth in confident technique and a flair for the epic; here, they move still further from the documentary naturalism of their beginnings, with an engaging, coherent, continually surprising blend of realism and fantasy, witty comedy and serious social comment. It depicts the problems faced by three women (alcoholism, anorexia, abuse and battering) with honesty, depth of feeling and an unexpected touch of magic. As ever, the performances are highly convincing (even the men – however stupid or nasty – are never reduced to stereotypes), the politics are spot-on, and the finale, firmly rooted in the gritty reality of a celebration dance after the women's darts-night, is wholly moving. GA

Dreams

see Kvinnodröm

Dreams

see Akira Kurosawa's Dreams

Dreamscape

(1983, US, 99 min)
d Joseph Ruben. *p* Bruce Cohn Curtis. *sc* David Loughery, Chuck Russell, Joseph Ruben. *ph* Brian Tufano. *ed* Richard Halsey. *ad* Jeff Staggs. *m* Maurice Jarre. *cast* Dennis Quaid, Max von Sydow, Christopher Plummer, Eddie Albert, Kate Capshaw, David Patrick Kelly, George Wendt.

● Quaid is a gambler with psychic powers. To pay off debts, he is persuaded to take part in an experiment where he links up with sleepers and tours through their dreams, solving a neurosis here, dealing with a demon there. Some of the dreams are funny (one middle-aged man's fidelity nightmare is hysterical); most are pretty nasty, though, especially a trip through an 8-year-old's primal fears. In the end, things get a bit silly: Quaid has to save the USA by fighting off the forces of evil in the President's nightmares. But as a night out this is as good a piece of solid, down-the-line schlock as anything to come along since *Halloween III*. NR

Dreams That Money Can Buy

(1946, US, 90 min)
d Hans Richter, Max Ernst, Fernand Léger, Man Ray, Marcel Duchamp, Alexander Calder. *p* Hans Richter, Peggy Guggenheim, Kenneth Macpherson. *sc* Hans Richter, Max Ernst, Fernand Léger, Man Ray, Marcel Duchamp, Alexander Calder, Hans Richter. *ph* Arnold Eagle. *ed/pd* Hans Richter. *m* Paul Bowles, Darius Milhaud, John Cage, David Diamond, Louis Applebaum. *cast* Jack Bittner, Dorothy Griffith, Lauren Denny, Peter Glushanok, Julie Levy, Roth Sobotka.

● The movie's artistic credentials couldn't be more imposing (in addition to the various expatriate Surrealists/Dadaists who contributed episodes, there is music by John Cage and Darius Milhaud, among others), but that makes its manifest failure all the more striking. Richter has created a feeble pastiche of the contemporary *film noir* as the framing story, centring on a man with the power to generate dreams; other contributions are therefore integrated as dream sequences. The movie quickly degenerates into a series of party pieces: Duchamp rehashes his 'roto-reliefs' of 1927, Léger animates dolls, Calder animates his mobiles, and so on. Only Ernst, who recreates an image-sequence from his collage-novel *La Semaine de la Bonté* in live action terms, emerges with much credit. TR

Dream Team, The

(1989, US, 113 min)
d Howard Zieff. *p* Christopher W Knight. *sc* Jon Connolly, David Loucka. *ph* Adam Holdender. *ed* C Timothy O'Meara. *pd* Todd Hallowell. *m* David McHugh. *cast* Michael Keaton, Christopher Lloyd, Peter Boyle, Stephen Furst, Dennis Boutsikaris, Lorraine Bracco, Milo O'Shea, Philip Bosco, James Remar, Jack Giplin.

● The Dream Team is a collection of fruitcakes, locked away because they're just too annoying for polite society. Only Billy (Keaton), with his violent temper, poses any threat, but even this is a symptom of his being too in tune with his emotions. Of the others, Albert (Furst), after 12 years of institutionalised TV viewing, can communicate only in telespeak; Jack (Boyle) thinks he's Christ; and Henry (Lloyd) thinks he's a doctor. These open-hearted innocents are misunderstood but not mistreated: *One Flew Over the Cuckoo's Nest* is acknowledged and dismissed in an inspired opening scene. Caring psychiatrist Dr. Weitzman (Boutsikaris) escorts the Team on a day out to the Yankee Stadium, and is separated from his charges in the heart of Manhattan. Abandoned in the madness of the urban jungle, they are forced to overcome their mental handicaps in order to trace the missing doctor and foil a murder plot. Halfway through, the plot settles into an obvious stride, but by then we're hooked into each character's personal voyage of self-discovery. Despite the barrage of one-liners and almost farcial plot twists, Zieff's light touch and some unselfish ensemble acting make this team genuinely endearing. EP

Dream with the Fishes

(1997, US, 97 min)
d Finn Taylor. *p* Johnny Wow, Mitchell Stein. *sc* Finn Taylor. *ph* Barry Stone. *ed* Rick LeCompte. *pd* Justin McCartney. *m* Tito Larriva. *cast* David Arquette, Brad Hunt, Cathy Moriarty, Patrick McGaw, Kathryn Erbe, EJ Freeman.

● This arresting semi-autobiographical debut is a latter-day *On the Road*. Suicidal, voyeuristic 'suit' Terry (Arquette) is talked down from his perch on the Golden Gate Bridge by cool, gun-toting dude Nick (Hunt) who persuades him to take sleeping pills instead, which Nick will provide as long as he can watch Terry die. It turns out Nick himself is dying of leukaemia, the pills are vitamins, and when Terry recovers at the hospital, fighting mad, they have a set-to that ends in a bargain: Terry will bankroll a go-for-it trip for the pair of them; Nick can live out his fantasies and then kill Terry in return. The celebratory laddish episodes – getting it on with prostitutes, a robbery at a pharmacy, yelling hell from a church bell tower – are mostly undercut by these guys' pain, confusion and shortness of time. In this regard, Hunt's more understated performance is essential. Arquette grates as, presumably, the auteur stand-in, and the women don't get much of a look in. It's finely shot though and moves along crisply to the beat of its atmospheric modern blues and indie soundtrack. WH

Dreckfresser

see Dirt for Dinner

Dreigroschenoper, Die (The Threepenny Opera)

(1931, Ger, 111 min, b/w)
d GW Pabst. *p* Seymour Nebenzal. *sc* Leon Lania, Belá Balasz, Ladislao Vajda. *ph* Fritz Arno Wagner. *ed* Jean Oser. *ad* Andre Andrejew. *m* Kurt Weill. *cast* Rudolf Forster, Carola Neher, Reinhold Schunzel, Fritz Rasp, Lotte Lenya, Valeska Gert.

● Brecht and Weill may have sued Pabst over what they considered his manhandling of their musical (the director rewrote Brecht's script and dropped several songs), but the social satire remains thankfully intact. The story itself is preserved: in Victorian London, womanising gentleman thief Mack the Knife joins, through marriage, both the king of the beggars and the chief of police in setting up a bank. If Brecht's anti-capitalist sentiments are muted by Pabst's heavily stylised lyricism, there is no denying either the sheer visual eloquence of the sets and photography or the charismatic power of the performances, most notably, perhaps, Lenya as the whore Jenny. GA

Drei Sterne

see Mostly Martha

Dressed to Kill

(1980, US, 104 min)
d Brian De Palma. *p* George Litto. *sc* Brian De Palma. *ph* Ralf D Bode. *ed* Jerry Greenberg. *pd* Gary Weist. *m* Pino Donaggio. *cast* Michael Caine, Angie Dickinson, Nancy Allen, Keith Gordon, Dennis Franz, David Margulies.

● Beginning and ending with a pair of shower frissons, this brazen reworking of *Psycho* is most striking for its sheer audacity, and actually lifts that film's most shattering device. But having achieved this coup, the film degenerates into near-farce, punctuated by a number of hollow audience-grabbing moments which hang together not at all. Ultimately, the film amounts to little more than a consummate study of suspense technique, all dressed up with nowhere to go. DP

Dresser, The

(1983, GB, 118 min)
d/p Peter Yates. *sc* Ronald Harwood. *ph* Kelvin Pike. *ed* Ray Lovejoy. *pd* Stephen Grimes. *m* James Horner. *cast* Albert Finney, Tom Courtenay, Edward Fox, Zena Walker, Eileen Atkins, Michael Gough.

● An accomplished film of Ronald Harwood's theatrical two-hander, animated by two gigantic performances. Finney, grossly Shakespearean as Sir, the imperious, declamatory actor-manager with a Moses-like command of his company and inanimate objects ('St-o-o-p th-a-a-a-t tr-ai-ai-n!' he bawls, bringing British Rail to its knees), is fully matched by Courtenay's pantomime poof Norman, Sir's devoted dresser: mincing, nagging, but the only one able to reach to the furthest depths of Sir's hair-tearing madness and coax him into the costumes and roles that have by wicked irony destroyed him. Especially pleasing, then, that in the final act it is the quiet craft of an actress – Atkins as the long-suffering, love-lorn stage manageress – that rises above constrictions of plot and thankless part to upstage them. FD

Dressmaker, The

(1988, GB, 91 min)
d Jim O'Brien. *p* Ronald Shedlo. *sc* John McGrath. *ph* Michael Coulter. *ed* William Diver. *pd* Caroline Amies. *m* George Fenton. *cast* Joan Plowright, Billie Whitelaw, Jane Horrocks, Tim Ransom, Peter Postlethwaite, Pippa Hinchley, Tony Haygarth.

● Liverpool, 1944. Nellie (Plowright), elderly dressmaker to her upper-working-class neighbourhood, has a scatty, sexually-active younger sister Margo (Whitelaw), and rules with a Victorian rod of iron over their repressed niece Rita (Horrocks). Nellie is not amused to disocer that Margo and Rita attended a raucous bonking bash with GIs stationed locally; still less, that Rita had fallen in love with boring Southern GI Wesley (Ransom). But Rita fails to meet the horny GI halfway, thereby ensuring an early end to the romance…and subsequently plunging the family into unexpected tragedy. In his first feature O'Brien admirably conveys an atmosphere of arsenic and old lace through realistic period sets, claustrophobic camerawork, and dim lighting, while John McGrath's wittily scripted adaptation of Beryl Bainbridge's novel is played with stylish gusto by all concerned. Horrocks plays the innocent so well that you feel like strangling her; Plowright and Whitelaw are a joy throughout. DA

Drifting Clouds (Kauas Pilvet Karkaavat/Au loin s'en vont les nuages)

(1996, Fin/Ger/Fr, 97 min)
d/p/sc Aki Kaurismäki. *ph* Timo Salminen. *ed* Aki Kaurismäki. *ad* Markku Pätilä, Jukka Salmi. *cast* Kati Outinen, Kari Väänänen, Elina Salo, Sakari Kuosmanen, Markku Peltola, Matti Onnismaa.

● When the Helsinki restaurant where Ilona (Outinen) works is taken over, the new owners decide not to retain the existing staff. To make matters worse, Ilona's tram-driver husband Lauri (Väänänen) is made redundant. There are a few jobs around and the couple are no longer in the bloom of youth. Will their marriage survive the belt-tightening and the blows to dignity that unemployment brings? The potentially depressing subject matter is superbly offset by Kaurismäki's customary deadpan brand of gently absurdist comedy, by the use of primary colours in the set designs, and by the quiet yet real sense of supportiveness that imbues Ilona and Lauri's relationship not only with each other but with their friends and colleagues. As ever, the performances from Kaurismäki regulars are understated to the point of minimalism, but the writer/director treats the lives, aspirations and anxieties of his less-than-beautiful losers with such unsentimental affection that we care about every one of them (Ilona and Lauri's magnificently solemn mutt Pietari included). As ever, too, the semi-ironic use of music (Tchaikovsky, old-fashioned tango), Timo Salminen's subdued, precise camerawork, and Kaurismäki's miniaturist's eye for the telling detail yield rewards aplenty. GA

Drifting Life, A (Chunhua Menglu)

(1996, Tai, 123 min)
d Lin Cheng-Sheng. *p* Hsu Li-Kong. *sc* Lin Cheng-Sheng, Ko Su-ching. *ph* Tsai Cheng-tai. *ed* Chen Po-wen. *cast* Lee Kang-Sheng, Vicky Wei, Grace Chen, Chen Shi-Huang, Wang Yu-Wen, Lang Jing.

● An intensely moving directorial debut from Lin, hitherto best known as a comic actor in movies like *Buddha Bless America*. A family in rural Taiwan starts to break up when the son's young wife dies giving birth to her second child. The son Kun-Cheng (Lee) leaves home and drifts into another sexual relationship, but tries to be a good father to his kids and a tolerant, filial son to his parents, both of whom irritate the hell out of him. The storyline is minimal, but Lin builds up a commanding picture of the ways parents influence children and children resist parents. It's a film about cutting ties and mending ties, acted with total conviction and directed with light-handed control. TR

Driftwood

(1947, US, 90 min, b/w)
d Allan Dwan. *sc* Mary Loos, Richard Sale. *ph* John Alton. *ed* Arthur Roberts. *ad* Frank Arrigo. *m* Nathan Scott. *cast* Natalie Wood, Dean Jagger, Walter Brennan, Ruth Warrick, Charlotte Greenwood, Jerome Cowan.

● Fascinating and unusual movie about a young, orphaned girl found wandering in the wilderness by an idealistic doctor, and taken back to be cared for at his village, a hothouse of political intrigue where the authorities refuse him full medical facilities, and where the girl herself provokes outrage among the locals with her outspoken honesty and strange, biblical morality. At times the religious allegory is pushed a bit too far, and there's a certain amount of sentimentality about a dog the girl finds. But generally, it's an admirably dreamlike and often dark conjuring up of the way the adult world is viewed by children, in its own way almost as effective as *Curse of the Cat People*, made three years earlier. GA

Driftwood

(1996, Ire/GB, 100 min)
d Ronan O'Leary. *p* Mary Breen-Farrelly. *sc* Richard Waring. *ph* Billy Williams. *ed* Malcolm Cooke. *pd* Tim Hutchinson. *m* John Cameron. *cast* James Spader, Anne Brochet, Barry McGovern, Anna Massey, Aiden Grenell, Kevin McHugh.

● Man washes up, wounded and without memory, on windswept Irish shore. Woman takes Man back to remote cottage, tending his crippled leg, and telling him she's the island's sole inhabitant and he can't leave till the boat brings supplies in three months' time. Weeks pass. Man, attracted and grateful, sleeps with Woman, but still plans to leave; Woman, between sculpting naked Men and having intense conversations with her dead mum, plans otherwise. This determinedly arty, allegorical and anaemic look at the emotional and psychological power plays that constitute male-female interaction comes across as a lame rip-off of such female-fruitcake fare as *Misery*, *Images* and *Repulsion*. At best it's gynophobic, at worst misogynistic – though Spader's amnesiac noname seems incapable of committing, that's peanuts compared to the neurotic disorders displayed by Anne Brochet's Sarah, whose smothering, possessive obsession pushes her from simple repeated deceits to deadly violence. GA

Driller Killer, The

(1979, US, 85 min)
d Abel Ferrara. *sc* NG St John. *ph* Ken Kelsch. *ed* Orlando Gallini, Bonnie Constant, Michael Constant, Abel Ferrara. *ad* Louis Mascolo. *m* Joe Delia. *songs* Douglas Anthony Metro, Abel Ferrara. *cast* Jimmy Laine [Abel Ferrara], Carolyn Marz, Harry Schultz, Baybi Day, Richard Howorth.

● Reno, a painter, is driven to distraction by financial troubles, the punk band rehearsing next door, and the city squalor he sees all around him. Picking up a power tool, he vents his fury on the homeless, bit by bit. Ferrara's first film coincided with John Sayles' *Return of the Secaucus Seven* at the onset of the American indie scene – though, like nearly all Ferrara's work, this feels more at home on the exploitation fringe than the art-house circuit. (There's even a gratuitous lesbian shower scene.) Notorious in Britain as one of the much-cited, little-seen 'video nasties' that ushered in the censorious Video Recordings Act of 1984, this reappeared in 1999 in a version six minutes longer than previously (though still shorn of its goriest moments), basking in the retrospective glow of such hard-won auteurist credibility as Ferrara has mustered. The very first image sees Laine (aka Ferrara) approaching an altar, for all the world like Harvey Keitel in *Bad Lieutenant*. We even get glimpses of Ferrara's own paintings on the walls. Take out the killings, and you're left with an anguished (even somewhat boring) stab at urban ennui, heavily influenced by *Repulsion* and *Taxi Driver*. TCh

Dritte Generation, Die

see Third Generation, The

Drive, The (Saigo no Drive)

(1992, Jap, 93 min)
d Shunichi Nagasaki. *cast* Koji Tamaki, Shigeru Muroi, Yoko Nogiwa, Takeshi Naito, Kaori Mizushima, Tatsuo Yamada, Tomoko Otahara.

● This is more restrained and less spectacular than Nagasaki's subversive thriller *The Enchantment*, but ultimately just as chilling . A divorced single mother (Muroi) is desperate to keep her married lover and business partner (Tamaki). With loan sharks circling, she picks up a schoolgirl, murders her, and tries to extract a ransom from the child's senile grandfather, while enticing her 'innocent' partner into a weekend on the lam. An anguished, misplaced love story, with a wrenching performance from Muroi, and no cop-outs. TCh

Drive, He Said

(1970, US, 90 min)
d Jack Nicholson. *p* Steve Blauner, Jack Nicholson. *sc* Jeremy Larner, Jack Nicholson. *ph* Bill Butler. *ed* Pat Somerset, Donn Cambern, Christopher Holmes, Robert L Wolfe. *ad* Harry Gittes. *m* David Shire. *cast* William Tepper, Karen Black, Michael Margotta, Bruce Dern, Robert Towne, Henry Jaglom.

● It's strange that while *Easy Rider* has often been credited with opening up Hollywood, its prime movers should subsequently have had such a hard time. But Hopper, Fonda and Nicholson all overreached next time out, and the fascinating *Last Movie*, *Hired Hand* and *Drive, He Said* each got pigeonholed – or shelved – as 'failures'. Nicholson's movie was nothing less than his own variant on *W.R.– Mysteries of the Organism*: a boldly-shot campus yarn of basketball and revolution turning on notions of Reichian sex-pol. No way can it be said to work, despite the cast's cultish distinction, but it still knocks most of its quasi-radical contemporaries sideways as an index of doomed '60s/'70s causes and confusions. PT

Drive-In

(1976, US, 96 min)
d Rod Amateau. *p* Alex-Rose, Tamara Asseyev. *sc* Bob Peete. *ph* Robert Jessup. *ed* Bernard Caputo, Guy Scarpitta. *cast* Lisa Lemole, Glenn Morshower, Gary Cavagnaro, Billy Milliken, Lee Newsom, Regan Kee.

● Frantic goings-on during a performance of *Disaster '76*, a movie showing at a Texas drive-in theatre (The Alamo), are the promising ingredients of this cod catastrophe movie. That they constitute no more than an unsatisfying hodgepodge is less the fault of Bob Peete's indulgent, idiosyncratic story (two engaging amateur crooks bungle hold-up in theatre concession stand), than the frenetic pace of its execution and Amateau's overriding concern with busy narrative mechanics. A successful directorial debut demands more than incidental charms and a string of formulary sight gags in a by now thoroughly overworked parodic style. JPy

Drive Me Crazy

(1999, US, 91 min)
d John Schultz. *p* Amy Robinson, Nancy Paloian-Breznikar. *sc* Rob Thomas. *ph* Kees van Oostrum. *ed* John Pace. *pd* Aaron Osborne. *m* Greg Kendall. *cast* Melissa Joan Hart, Adrian Grenier, Stephen Collins, Susan May Pratt, Mark Webber, Kris Park, Gabriel Carpenter.

● A teen flick: the question – cool or lame? This one concerns two high school seniors who think they've nothing in common beyond mutual unresolved prom date issues. Nicole (Hart) is a well-scrubbed blonde who serves on the prom committee, listens to bubblegum pop and fancies a fickle basketball jock; her neighbour Chase (Grenier) is a tousled rebel into alt-rock, subversion-lite and his rent-a-cause girlfriend, until she dumps him. The title of the source novel (*How I Created My Perfect Prom Date* by Todd Strasser) and the film's working title (*Girl Gives Birth to Prom Date*) suggest what unfolds, but obscure the film's relatively even-handedness, which tries ingenuously to broach the sensibilities of both parties and their peers. The plot lurches, the script's peg-legged, and the acting hits notes of staggering clumsiness. Not, like, totally lame, perhaps, but pretty sappy all the same. NB

Driven

(2001, US, 117 min)
d Renny Harlin. *p* Elie Samaha, Sylvester Stallone, Renny Harlin. *sc* Sylvester Stallone. *ph* Mauro Fiore. *ed* Stuart Levy, Steve Gilson. *pd* Charles Wood. *m* BT. *cast* Sylvester Stallone, Burt Reynolds, Kip Pardue, Til Schweiger, Gina Gershon, Estella Warren, Christián de la Fuente, Stacy Edwards, Brent Briscoe, Robert Sean Leonard.

● Scripted by and starring Stallone, this is ostensibly about a battle for the Formula One championship between German automaton Beau Brandenburg (Schweiger) and American tyro Jimmy Bly (Pardue), but by the end director Harlin has managed to cram in one comeback tale, two extraneous bits of love interest, a host of petrolhead cameos from the likes of Jean Alesi and Jacques Villeneuve, the most ridiculous car chase of the year, and one burning head to head between Stallone and Reynolds. This is PlayStation cinema, popcorn porn crammed with so many ludicrous/ breathtaking SFX sequences that you almost forget the comic storyline, cartoon characters and crass leaps in plot logic. It also takes liberties with motor racing which even non-believers might consider diabolical. PW

Driver, The

(1978, US, 91 min)
d Walter Hill. *p* Lawrence Gordon. *sc* Walter Hill. *ph* Philip H Lathrop. *ed* Tina Hirsch, Robert K Lambert. *pd* Harry Horner. *m* Michael Small. *cast* Ryan O'Neal, Bruce Dern, Isabelle Adjani, Ronee Blakley, Matt Clark, Felice Orlandi.

● Scriptwriter-turned-director Walter Hill's *Hard Times* (retitled *The Streetfighter* in Britain) received deservedly excellent reviews when it opened a few years back. His second feature is even better, a combination of brilliantly edited car chases and existential thriller which recalls the sombreness of Melville and the spareness of Leone in a context which is the 'classical' economy of directors like Hawks and Walsh. A brilliant plot of cross and double-cross, with cop Dern out to nail ace getaway driver O'Neal, unravels with a tautness to put it on a par with the same year's action hit, *Assault on Precinct 13*. RM

Driving Licence, The

see Permis de Conduire, Le

Driving Me Crazy

(1988, GB, 81 min)
d Nick Broomfield. *p* Andrew Braunsberg. *ph* Robert S Levi. *ed* John Mister. *with* André Heller, Andrew Braunsberg, Nick Broomfield, Joe Hindy, Edek Bartz, Roy Lichtenstein.

●A hilarious cautionary tale tracing documentarist Broomfield's efforts to film the genesis of a glitzy stage show, to be produced in Munich by singer/impresario André Heller, reflecting the diversity of black musical experience. The budget for the associated documentary film is slashed from $1.4 million to $300,000, and a fictional subplot is introduced against Broomfield's will. Efforts to salvage the *Fame*-style feature founder, and fearing the collapse of the whole project, Broomfield continues on the understanding that he is allowed to film *everything*. The New York auditions give a first hint of the show's likely quality, a synthetic showbiz extravaganza incorporating a mish-mash of calypso, gospel, rap, tap, ballet and breakdance. More captivating by far are the off-stage machinations, including surreal conversations with neurotic scriptwriter Joe Hindy, a clandestine meeting between Broomfield and his producer in a broom cupboard, and crisis discussions conducted in financial double-speak. Several memorable characters emerge as Broomfield struggles to keep things in focus, his intrusive camera revealing artistic compromise, fragile egos, and a great deal of unintentional humour. NF

Driving Me Crazy

see Dutch

Driving Miss Daisy

(1989, US, 99 min)
d Bruce Beresford. *p* Richard D Zanuck, Lili Zanuck. *sc* Alfred Uhry. *ph* Peter James. *ed* Mark Warner. *pd* Bruno Rubeo. *m* Hans Zimmer. *cast* Morgan Freeman, Jessica Tandy, Dan Aykroyd, Patti Lupone, Esther Rolle, Joann Havrilla, William Hall Jr, Alvin M Sugarman.

●Beresford and writer Alfred Uhry have produced a polished adaptation of the latter's play, but it's the sharp performances from Freeman and Tandy which save it from being overwhelmed by hazy filters and a surfeit of gleaming low-angle shots of period cars. Tandy plays a spirited Jewish matron who takes on black chauffeur Freeman; and the story, set in Atlanta against the social changes of the American South, charts their relationship over 25 years as they progress from caution to affection. Real events in the city's history are pinpointed (the bombing of the synagogue in 1958, the 1965 hotel reception in honour of Martin Luther King), with Tandy refusing to acknowledge prejudice, Freeman all too painfully aware of its consequences. Far too cosy to serve as an effective social or political metaphor; better to regard it as a solid ensemble piece. CM

Drôle de Drame (Bizarre, Bizarre)

(1937, Fr, 97 min, b/w)
d. Marcel Carné. *sc* Jacques Prévert. *ph* Eugene Schüfftan. *ed* Marthe Poncin. *pd* Alexandre Trauner. *m* Maurice Jaubert. *cast* Louis Jouvet, Michel Simon, Françoise Rosay, Jean-Louis Barrault, Jean-Pierre Aumont, Nadine Vogel, Alcover.

●At the centre of a farcical plot, scripted by Jacques Prévert from a novel by J Storer Clouston and supposedly set in London, is a mild, bumbling botanist (Simon), secretly the author of murder stories and accused of murdering his wife by the Bishop of Beckford (Jouvet), who disappears, reappears in disguise as a detective, and turns a table or two. Meanwhile a real killer goes happily about his business (Barrault, who murders butchers because he loves animals). Carné isn't renowned for his wacky temperament, and he fails to extract all the fun possible from such rich material. But there are plenty of piquant absurdities, from the proliferating milk bottles delivered by Aumont's lovelorn Express Dairy milkman, to the gents in Limehouse robbed of the flowers in their buttonholes (a typical Prévert touch). And Simon is marvellous. GB

Drôle de Félix

(1999, Fr, 95 min)
d Olivier Ducastel, Jacques Martineau. *p* Philippe Martin. *sc* Olivier Ducastel, Jacques Martineau. *ph* Matthieu Poirot-Delpech. *ed* Sabine Mamou. *ad* Louis Soubrier. *cast* Sami Bouajila, Patachou, Ariane Ascaride, Pierre-Loup Rajot, Charly Sergue, Maurice Bénichou.

●Félix (Bouajila, life affirming) cycles along the docks at Dieppe, a nice song, an air of easy, unforced naturalism. He decides to hitch to Marseilles and confront the man who fathered and then abandoned him. All he packs is a kite. So: it's a road movie. Albeit at a gentle pace. En route he stumbles on a racist murder, and is beaten for his trouble. He picks up an art student, and they steal a car just for fun; an old woman press gangs him into carrying her shopping; and the mother of a multitude gives him a lift as she drops off her brood with their various fathers for weekend visits. Chapter headings underscore the obvious: that these encounters supply Félix with his own surrogate family: a younger brother; a grandmother; wife and children. The journey may not be 'that original' as Félix concedes, but it's suffused with tenderness and warmth. TCh

Drôle d'Endroit pour une rencontre

see Strange Place to Meet, A

Drop Dead Fred

(1991, US, 99 min)
d Ate De Jong. *p* Paul Webster. *sc* Carlos Davis, Anthony Fingleton. *ph* Peter Deming. *ed* Marshall Harvey. *pd* Joseph T Garrity. *m* Randy Edelman. *cast* Phoebe Cates, Rik Mayall, Marsha Mason, Tim Matheson, Bridget Fonda, Carrie Fisher, Keith Charles, Ashley Peldon.

●This boisterous comedy allows Mayall to be completely naughty, to shock, to offend…and to exasperate beyond belief. Elizabeth (Cates) reverts to youthful fantasies in a bid to escape the trauma of losing both her husband and her job. Tucked up in her own bed back home with Mom, she revives her imaginary childhood friend Fred (Mayall), and together they make sweet music. Too bad for adult viewers that this entails smearing dog shit on the living-room carpet, concocting mud pie for dinner, destroying a houseboat, etc; while Elizabeth's desperate attempts to get back together with her husband and to exorcise childhood demons aren't likely to appeal to younger viewers. Mason (as Elizabeth's domineering mother) and Fisher (as her best friend) lend strong support. But Cates appears strangely resigned to each life-shattering episode; even the goggle-eyed, frantic Mayall fails to galvanise her. CM

Drop Dead Gorgeous

(1999, US/Ger, 98 min)
d Michael Patrick Jann. *p* Gavin Polone, Judy Hofflund. *sc* Lona Williams. *ph* Michael Spiller. *ed* David Codron, Janice Hampton. *pd* Ruth Ammon. *m* Mark Mothersbaugh. *cast* Kirstie Alley, Ellen Barkin, Kirsten Dunst, Denise Richards, Allison Janney, Will Sasso, Mindy Sterling, Sam McMurray.

●This sicko spin on Michael Ritchie's *Smile* is tailor made for modern audiences who feel free to laugh at violent death, mutilation, fat people and the mentally retarded because they know it's all terribly ironic. At Mount Rose, Minnesota, preparations for a heat of the Miss Teen America beauty pageant proceed under the supervision of former winner Alley, confident that daughter Richards will follow in her footsteps. Nearly everyone reckons the result's a foregone conclusion, but that doesn't deter trailer park siren Dunst and sundry misguided contestants eager to unleash their party pieces. Competition is intense. Indeed untimely fatality is visited on one contender after another, and an explosive act of trailer sabotage leaves Dunst's sozzled mom Barkin with a beer can fused to her hand. The first appearance of the mutant mitt is effective, but further sightings less amusing. Decidedly patchy, the film gains from the supporting talent of Janney as Barkin's mutton-dressed-as-lamb pal, another perceptive turn from a comedienne who deserves a movie of her own. TJ

Drop Zone

(1994, US, 102 min)
d John Badham. *p* DJ Caruso, Wallis Nicita, Lauren Lloyd. *sc* Peter Barsocchini, John Bishop. *ph* Roy H Wagner. *ed* Frank Morriss. *pd* Joe Alves. *m* Hans Zimmer. *cast* Wesley Snipes, Gary Busey, Yancy Butler, Michael Jeter, Corin Nemec, Kyle Secor, Luca Bercovici.

●After *Demolition Man* and *Sugar Hill*, action hero Snipes plummets to earth in this sky-diving picture. Busey is characteristically out of order as the leader of an aerial team that swoops into Drug Enforcement Agency offices and downloads information about their undercover agents. The crooks then sells the information to drug barons, who in turn arrange for the exposed DEA agents to disappear. So US Marshal Snipes and his fearless partner (Butler) take to the skies in pursuit of the bad guys. Some spectacular sky-diving sequences, but a very unpersuasive story. NF

Drowning by Numbers

(1988, GB, 119 min)
d Peter Greenaway. *p* Kees Kasander, Denis Wigman. *sc* Peter Greenaway. *ph* Sacha Vierny. *ed* John Wilson. *pd* Ben van Os, Jan Roelfs. *m* Michael Nyman. *cast* Bernard Hill, Joan Plowright, Juliet Stevenson, Joely Richardson, Jason Edwards, Bryan Pringle, Trevor Cooper.

●Obsessed with obscure English folk games and father to corpse-collecting Smut, coroner Madgett becomes involved with three generations of women all named Cissie Colpitts. Unsurprisingly, his amorously optimistic agreement to keep mum about the aquatic deaths of their husbands lands him in deep water. Greenaway returns to the playful punning, ludicrous lists, and quizzical conundrums of his earlier work: opening with a girl counting a hundred stars, the 'plot' then proceeds with those same numbers appearing either in the dialogue or in suitably bizarre images. Equally teasing is the film's complex web of absurdly interlocking allusions to games, sex and mortality: famous last words, Samson and Delilah, Breughel, circumcision, etc. Elegantly scored and luminously shot, it's a modernist black comedy filled with arcane, archaic and apocryphal lore, and hugely enjoyable. GA

Drowning Man, A (Oboreru Hito)

(2000, Jap, 82 min)
d Naoki Ichio. *p* Keiko Kusakabe, Naoki Ichio. *sc* Naoki Ichio. *ph* Noriaki Yamazaki. *ed* Naoki Ichio. *m* Azusa Minamio, Emotional Awa. *cast* Shinya Tsukamoto, Reiko Kataoka, Senko Hida, Takehiro Uebaba, Hiromi Unakami.

●One evening Yumiko (Kataoka) drowns in her bath. Her husband Tokiyo (Tsukamoto, director of *Tetsuo*) notices, but doesn't know what to do. He makes coffee, drains the tub, carries Yumiko to the couch and begs her to revive. Meanwhile, Yumiko herself dreams of being dead and traversing scrubland. Next day, things are nearly normal: Yumiko makes dinner, Tokiyo has a hangover. Soon, though, Yumiko starts piling on the air-freshener to camouflage the very dodgy smell permeating the apartment. Ichio says his debut feature was inspired by his own divorce, and his script has an originality and impact that suggest authentically felt emotional pain. Sadly, the film is let down by rather dull *mise-en-scène* and visuals. But the actors are terrific and the slide towards emotional breakdown is quite moving. A love story, then, but with a dripping tap and a nagging bad smell. TR

Drowning Pool, The

(1975, US, 108 min)
d Stuart Rosenberg. *p* Lawrence Turman, David Foster. *sc* Tracy Keenan Wynn, Lorenzo Semple Jr, Walter Hill. *ph* Gordon Willis. *ed* John C Howard. *pd* Paul Sylbert. *m* Michael Small. *cast* Paul Newman, Joanne Woodward, Tony Franciosa, Murray Hamilton, Gail Strickland, Melanie Griffith, Coral Browne, Richard Jaeckel.

●Newman, playing Ross Macdonald's private eye for the second time (the first was in *Harper*), embarks on a Deep South excursion through broads, nymphet daughters, twitchy cops, hookers, hoods, and gangsters of a more refined but dangerous sort. As so often with Macdonald, it's the corruption of rich families that is exposed: dominated by a grotesque mother figure (Browne) who is at least morally responsible for their sins, both weak and strong are warped by perversions. What matters in this type of film is not so much the plot as the way in which an atmosphere is created. Unfortunately, Rosenberg directs flatly, hopping from one set piece to the next, disjointedly throwing characters of varying interest across Newman's path, while the latter – in his coarsest performance yet – remains content to wisecrack and ham outrageously. Murray Hamilton scores as the villain, however, and the title sequence offers some sort of compensation. CPe

Drugstore Cowboy

(1989, US, 101 min)
d Gus Van Sant. *p* Nick Wechsler, Karen Murphy. *sc* Gus Van Sant, Daniel Yost. *ph* Robert Yeoman. *ed* Curtiss Clayton, Mary Bauer. *pd* David Brisbin. *m* Elliot Goldenthal. *cast* Matt Dillon, Kelly Lynch, James Le Gros, Heather Graham, Beah Richards, Grace Zabriskie, Max Perlich, William S Burroughs, James Remar.

● Bob (Dillon), his wife Dianne (Lynch), Rich (Le Gros) and Nadine (Graham) are junkies who survive by robbing pharmacies in Portland, Oregon, in 1971. The natural leader of the gang, Bob decides they had better leave town after one too many scrapes with the law. It's Bob, too, who finally elects to straighten out after one of their number ODs. Though hardly earth-shakingly original, Van Sant's low-budget movie takes a cool, contemplative and sometimes comic look at American drug-culture, manages for the most part to dispense with easy moralising, and comes close to grasping *why* the addiction to chemicals of every kind ('A dope fiend always knows how he's gonna feel'). Despite some Coppola-esque touches with speeding clouds, the stark simplicity of Bob's fantasies suitably complements the overall gritty realism. But it's the acting that carries the day: Dillon's wildly obsessive and sporadically articulate Bob avoids the usual bratpack mannerisms, Remar makes a plausibly boorish cop, and William Burroughs brings a raddled, fragile integrity to the role of a junkie ex-priest Bob meets at a detox hostel. GA

Drum

(1976, US, 110 min)
d Steve Carver. *p* Ralph Serpe. *sc* Norman Wexler. *ph* Lucien Ballard. *ed* Carl Kress. *pd* Stan Jolley. *m* Charlie Smalls. *cast* Warren Oates, Isela Vega, Ken Norton, Pamela Grier, Yaphet Kotto, John Colicos, Fiona Lewis.

● 'Niggers fornicating's what Falconhurst's all about,' growls Warren Oates in this dire sequel to Richard Fleischer's magnificent *Mandingo*. Likewise the movie itself, except that even this aspect remains unfocused. Much of the blame rests with the chaotic and clumsy script fashioned from Kyle Onstott's potboiling bestseller: an incoherent introductory sequence takes the Onstott cruderies, which Fleischer was scrupulous in making a function of the characters themselves, and gives them the status of a voice-over, thereby fatally altering the audience's relationship to what is on the screen. VG

Drum, The (aka Drums)

(1938, GB, 104 min)
d Zoltan Korda. *p* Alexander Korda. *sc* Lajos Biro, Arthur Wimperis, Patrick Kirwan, Hugh Gray. *ph* Georges Périnal, Osmond Borradaile. *ed* Henry Cornelius, William Hornbeck. *ad* Vincent Korda. *m* John Greenwood. *cast* Sabu, Raymond Massey, Roger Livesey, Valerie Hobson, Desmond Tester, Francis L Sullivan.

● Korda's lively slice of imperialist adventure set on the Northwest Frontier during the days of the Raj, with true blue Brit officer Livesey helping out young prince Sabu against the machinations of his evil uncle, the snarling Massey. Good fun, brimful of action and Boy's Own heroics, given a touch of class by Georges Périnal's Technicolor camerawork. GA

Drums

see Drum, The

Drums Along the Mohawk

(1939, US, 103 min)
d John Ford. *p* Raymond Griffith. *sc* Lamar Trotti, Sonya Levien. *ph* Bert Glennon, Ray Rennahan. *ed* Robert Simpson. *ad* Richard Day, Mark-Lee Kirk. *m* Alfred Newman. *cast* Claudette Colbert, Henry Fonda, Edna May Oliver, John Carradine, Arthur Shields, Robert Lowery, Ward Bond.

● A typical Ford hymn to the pioneer spirit, his first film in colour and absolutely stunning to look at. Set on the eve of the Revolutionary War, it's a stirring account of the trials of a young couple setting up home in an isolated farming community, particularly memorable for the sequence in which Fonda outdoes Rod Steiger's 'run of the arrow', racing two Mohawks in a fantastic cross-country marathon to bring help to the beleaguered fort. Very funny too, on occasion, as witness the redoubtable Edna May Oliver's confrontation with a band of marauding Indians. TM

Dry Rot

(1956, GB, 87 min, b/w)
d Maurice Elvey. *p* Jack Clayton. *sc* John Chapman. *ph* Arthur Grant. *ed* Gerry Hambling. *ad* Norman Arnold. *m* Peter Akister. *cast* Ronald Shiner, Brian Rix, Peggy Mount, Lee Patterson, Sidney James, Joan Sims, Heather Sears, Miles Malleson.

● John Chapman's stage farce opened in London in the summer of 1954 and was still running to full houses when this film version came out. Here, however, it all begins to creak. Bent bookies Shiner, Rix and James plan a killing at the races by switching their decrepit nag for a so-called French wonder horse, but, unsurprisingly, things don't exactly go to plan. TJ

Dry White Season, A

(1989, US, 107 min)
d Euzhan Palcy. *p* Paula Weinstein. *sc* Colin Welland, Euzhan Palcy. *ph* Kevin Pike, Pierre-William Glenn. *ed* Sam O'Steen, Glenn Cunningham. *pd* John Fenner. *m* David Grusin. *cast* Donald Sutherland, Janet Suzman, Zakes Mokae, Jürgen Prochnow, Susan Sarandon, Marlon Brando, Winston Ntshona, Thoko Ntshinga, Leonard Maguire.

● Behind the credits, two boys play happily together. Within minutes, the black boy is caught up in the Soweto uprising, the murderous violence of which is cross-cut with the white boy's family sitting on a manicured lawn to the strains of classical music. That, unfortunately, is the end of the film. Oh, there's business to clear up over the next 100 minutes, as Afrikaaner Ben du Toit (Sutherland) sees that Something Is Wrong in South Africa and that Something Should Be Done. There's Brando's star turn as a lawyer jaded by the realisation that justice cannot exist in matters of race, puffing, pausing, snorting, looking like he's wandered in from another movie. There's Prochnow's nicely understated Special Branch officer, and Suzman playing the bitch again; horrific tortures in police custody; and a sub-plot, not in André Brink's novel, designed to include a few black faces (South African exile Zakes Mokae is particularly good). But like *Cry Freedom*, it's still whites debating racial injustice: fine for a book published in Afrikaans a decade ago, but a poor premise for a message movie. DW

D-Tox (D-Tox Im Auge der Angst)

(2001, US/Ger/Can, 96 min)
d Jim Gillespie. *p* Ric Kidney. *sc* Ron L Brinkerhoff. *ph* Dean Semler. *ed* Steve Mirkovich, Tim Alverson. *pd* Gary Wissner. *m* John Powell. *cast* Sylvester Stallone, Tom Berenger, Charles S Dutton, Sean Patrick Flanery, Christopher Fulford, Stephen Lang, Dina Meyer, Courtney B Vance, Polly Walker, Jeffrey Wright, Rance Howard, Kris Kristofferson.

● This killer-chiller isn't preposterous enough for laughs and is too sloppily directed and scripted to scare or surprise. The lead, Stallone, comes off lightly, however; he's the alcoholic FBI enforcer who takes the advice of his superior Charlie (Dutton) to go to a snowy Wyoming detox centre run by ex-cop Doc (Kristofferson) as the only way to recover from the gruesome murder of his girlfriend Mary. It ain't no ordinary clinic we have here, guys. The defunct nuclear command and control post is only accessible by snow-mobile; it's staffed by bitter and sneering loonies; the ex-cop patients vary from paranoid, through suicidal, to psychotically aggressive; the power generator's on the blink; the medication goes missing; and, worse, it seems there's a killer on the loose. The early action sequences prove the athleticism of Stallone's double; the man himself, falling to his knees in inarticulate suffering, could challenge German silent star Emil Jannings in the realm of gigantic pathos. The gratuitous violence is predictable; but so is the plot. Any student of American xenophobia will spot the villain as soon as he opens his mouth. Cinematographer Dean Semler's good eye is wasted on this hokum. WH

D2: The Mighty Ducks

(1994, US, 107 min)
d Sam Weisman. *p* Jordan Kerner, Jon Avnet. *sc* Steve Brill. *ph* Mark Irwin. *ed* Eric A Sears, John F Link. *pd* Gary Frutkoff. *m* JAC Redford. *cast* Emilio Estevez, Kathryn Erbe, Michael Tucker, Jan Rubes, Carsten Norgaard, Maria Ellingsen, Wayne Gretzky.

● Weisman's sequel to *The Mighty Ducks* is the formula again, and probably mandatory for fans of juvenile ice hockey. Gordon Bombay (Estevez) is grounded from the minor leagues and returns to coaching the Mighty Ducks. This time, however, they are entered in the Junior Goodwill Games as Team USA and sponsored to the hilt. Weakling that he is, Bombay prefers a penthouse overlooking the sea to the team barracks, gets his hair swept back like the evil coach of the opposing Icelandic team, Wolf (Norgaard), and stops using the beloved duck whistle. Iceland wipes the ice with the tiny multi-ethnic Yanks until…but one's lips must remain sealed. There's a spark of interest when Estevez renders the Michael Moriarty speech from *The Deadliest Season*, invoking duck-pond memories of the lost touchstone of integrity. Sports moralists will faint at the ease with which the introduction of a goon element into a children's team is accepted by all, not to mention the business with the lasso. Puck off. BC

DuBarry Was a Lady

(1943, US, 101 min)
d Roy Del Ruth. *p* Arthur Freed. *sc* Irving Brecher, Wilkie Mahoney, Nancy Hamilton. *ph* Karl Freund. *ed* Blanche Sewell. *ad* Cedric Gibbons, Edwin B Willis, Henry Grace. *songs* Cole Porter. cast Red Skelton, Lucille Ball, Gene Kelly, Virginia O'Brien, Zero Mostel, Rags Ragland, Douglas Dumbrille, Donald Meek, Tommy Dorsey and his Orchestra.

● Produced by Arthur Freed, who should have known better, this adaptation of the Cole Porter musical ditches most of the songs – and the lusty bawdiness that went with them – to fashion a vehicle for Skelton and Ball, in the process interpolating more 'suitable' numbers (including a dismal girlie calendar item). It begins well with Ball (dubbed by Martha Mears) singing the title song with suitably costumed chorus, exquisitely shot by Karl Freund in delicate pastels. The colour then glossies up, and acres of unfunny comic business are expended on Skelton, a nightclub cloakroom attendant loved by the cigarette girl (O'Brien) but smitten by singer Ball. Ball loves an aspiring songwriter (Kelly), but has set her sights on a millionaire, and settles for Skelton when he wins a sweepstake. Hit with a Mickey Finn, Skelton imagines the situation transposed to 18th century France: 30 minutes of witless parody which supposedly sorts out the romantic tangle. Kelly has a good song-and-dance solo (staged by Charles Walters) to one of the surviving Porter songs, 'Do I Love You'; another, 'Friendship' is perfunctorily sung by the cast to bring the curtain down. TM

Dubious Business, A

see Pas três Catholique

Duchess and the Dirtwater Fox, The

(1976, US, 104 min)
d/p Melvin Frank. *sc* Melvin Frank, Barry Sandler, Jack Rose. *ph* Joseph Biroc. *ed* Frank Bracht, William Butler. *ad* Trevor Williams, Robert Emmet Smith. *m* Charles Fox. *cast* George Segal, Goldie Hawn, Conrad Janis, Thayer David, Roy Jenson.

● Segal and Hawn, card sharp and happy hooker respectively, form an uneasy alliance for this amiable if calculated comedy Western. Some sharp Jewish humour displays an eye for the bawdy and profane, but finally the rest of the film falls behind the one-liner jokes as the comedy becomes increasingly contrived. CPe

Duck Soup (100)

(1933, US, 70 min, b/w)
d Leo McCarey. *sc* Bert Kalmar, Harry Ruby. *ph* Henry Sharp. *ed* LeRoy Stone. *ad* Hans Dreier, Wiard B Ihnen. *songs* Bert Kalmar, Harry Ruby. *cast* The Marx Brothers, Margaret Dumont, Louis Calhern, Edgar Kennedy.

● The greatest of the surreally anarchic threesome's films (foursome here), this is a breathtakingly funny and imaginative spoof of war movie heroics, with a couple of Ruritanian states going to war because someone calls President Groucho an upstart (anyway, he's paid a month's advance rent on the battlefield). Totally irreverent towards patriotism, religion (a song proclaims 'We Got Guns, They Got Guns, All God's Chillun Got Guns'), diplomacy, courtroom justice, and anything even vaguely respectable, it also includes what is perhaps the Brothers' funniest scene ever: an immaculately timed and performed sequence with a broken mirror in which Groucho, Chico and Harpo look absolutely identical. A masterpiece. GA

Duck, You Sucker

see Giù la Testa

Dudes

(1987, US, 97 min)
d Penelope Spheeris. *p* Herb Jaffe, Tejada Flores. *sc* John Randall Johnson. *ph* Robert Richardson. *ed* Andy Horvitch. *pd* Bob Ziembicki. *m* Charles Bernstein. *cast* Jon Cryer, Catherine Mary Stewart, Daniel Roebuck, Lee Ving, Flea, Pete Willcox, Read Morgan.

●Continuing her preoccupation with terminal punks, Spheeris mines unexpected humour by relocating the sub-culture Way Out West, neatly combining random savagery and whimsy. 'Looking for exit signs', the despairing Grant (Cryer) leads his spiky band out of New York, but doesn't discover a 'reason to live' until one of them is murdered in the desert by bad guy Missoula (Ving). Ghost riders in the sky in the shape of the Marlboro Cowboy and a tribe of Indians appear to the surviving punks during a night of bootleg whisky, but more practical help is offered by a gunslinging girl gas-station owner (Stewart) and an Elvis impersonator (Willcox). It's all pretty daft, but there are felicities – Elvis transfixing a bull at a rodeo with a golden oldie, punk Biscuit (Roebuck) requesting 'Holidays in Cambodia' by the Dead Kennedys from the drunk in the sheriff's lockup, and a genuine shoot-up in a cinema showing *Jesse James*. Visually it's a good deal more inventive and accomplished than the sketchy material. BC

Dude, Where's My Car?

(2000, US, 83 min)
d Danny Leiner. *p* Wayne Rice, Broderick Johnson, Andrew Kosove, Gil Netter. *sc* Philip Stark. *ph* Robert Stevens. *ed* Kimberly Ray. *pd* Charles Breen. *m* David Kitay. *cast* Ashton Kutcher, Seann William Scott, Kristy Swanson, Jennifer Garner, Marla Sokoloff, David Herman, Hal Sparks.

●Car-less and amnesiac the day after a pardee, stoners Jesse (Kutcher) and Chester (Scott) set about retracing their steps in order to find some gifts they hope will tempt their girlfriends into bed. The gifts are in the car: cue endless repetitions of the title. So where is it? 'Dude' and 'Sweet' are soon mixed up with, in no particular order, 'dressing up box' aliens, spiteful ostriches, a murderous transvestite and a posse of 'black-clad sluts and bitches' who keep promising them oral sex in exchange for something called a continuum transfunctioner, capable of blowing up the universe. Whaddever. Fine, the ambitions are low brow and the characters so artificially dumb they bear no relation to human beings – and we're not talking about the aliens here. The real problem with the shoddy looking, rabidly heterosexual and relentlessly sexist movie is that it hasn't a scrap of goodwill towards anyone. SS

Duel

(1971, US, 90 min)
d Steven Spielberg. *p* George Eckstein. *sc* Richard Matheson. *ph* Jack Marta. *ed* Frank Morriss. *ad* Robert S Smith. *m* Billy Goldenberg. *cast* Dennis Weaver, Jacqueline Scott, Eddie Firestone, Lou Frizzell, Gene Dynarski, Lucille Benson, Tim Herbert.

●Spielberg's first film, superbly scripted by Richard Matheson, made for TV but booking its own place on the big screen: an absolute cracker about a salesman driving along the highway who gradually realises that the huge petrol tanker playfully snapping at his heels – apparently driverless – has more sinister designs. There are no explanations and no motivations, except perhaps for a hint of allegory in the script (the motorist's name is Mann) and an intriguing visual suggestion that this is the old, old battle between the shining, prancing, vulnerable knight and the impervious, lumbering dragon. Simply a rivetingly murderous game of cat and mouse that keeps you on the edge of your seat. TM

Duel at Diablo

(1965, US, 102 min)
d Ralph Nelson. *p* Ralph Nelson, Fred Engel. *sc* Marvin H Albert, Michael M Grilikhes. *ph* Charles F Wheeler. *ed* Fredric Steinkamp. *ad* Alfred Ybarra. *m* Neal Hefti. *cast* James Garner, Sidney Poitier, Bibi Andersson, Bill Travers, Dennis Weaver, William Redfield, John Hoyt, John Crawford.

●Not as suggestive as Nelson's subsequent Vietnam Western, *Soldier Blue*, this is an action-packed oater with racial overtones. Garner hankers after revenge as his Indian wife has been murdered and scalped by Bibi Andersson's soldier boy husband (Weaver); for her part, Andersson has been kidnapped and held captive by Indians. Poitier is the only one without a racial hang-up. The story unravels itself with bouts of vicious bloodletting, Garner is his usual excellent self, and Neal Hefti contributes an especially good score. ATu

Duel at Silver Creek, The

(1952, US, 77 min)
d Don Siegel. *p* Leonard Goldstein. *sc* Gerald Drayson Adams, Joseph Hoffman. *ph* Irving Glassberg. *ed* Russell Schoengarth. *ad* Bernard Herzbrun, Alexander Golitzen. *m* Hans J Salter. *cast* Audie Murphy, Stephen McNally, Faith Domergue, Susan Cabot, Gerald Mohr, Lee Marvin.

●Siegel's first Western and his first film in colour (very nicely shot by Irving Glassberg). Statutory stuff about wicked claim-jumpers and the quick-draw artiste who sees justice done. But it's handled with great verve and more than a suspicion of tongue-in-cheek by Siegel, who rewrote as much as he could, giving the characters outrageous names (Silver Kid, Lightning Tyrone, Opal Lacy, Tinhorn Burgess), stretching the amorous complications and the villainies into near-absurdity, and building up a special explosive bit for Marvin in one of his earliest roles. TM

Duel in the Sun

(1946, US, 138 min)
d King Vidor. *p/sc* David O Selznick, Oliver HP Garrett. *ph* Lee Garmes, Harold Rosson, Ray Rennahan. *ed* Hal C Kern, William Ziegler, John D Faure, Charles Freeman. *pd* Joseph McMillan Johnson. *m* Dimitri Tiomkin. *cast* Jennifer Jones, Gregory Peck, Joseph Cotten, Lionel Barrymore, Lillian Gish, Walter Huston, Charles Bickford, Herbert Marshall, Harry Carey.

●If ever a Western deserved the title of horse opera, this is it: a soaring extravaganza variously described as 'Lust in the Dust' and 'Liebestod Among the Cactus' as two brothers play Cain and Abel in rivalry for a steamy halfbreed sexpot while their father broods over his crumbling empire. Luridly beautiful, with stunning passages jostling near-bathos in a patchiness not surprising since Selznick went through three cameramen and half-a-dozen directors in his vaulting ambition to outdo *Gone With the Wind*, it has rare power and a great supporting cast. The climax, which has Peck and Jones consummating their tempestuous passion by orgasmically shooting each other to bits has an absurdist magnificence that defies criticism. TM

Duell – Enemy at the Gates

see Enemy at the Gates

Duellists, The

(1977, GB, 101 min)
d Ridley Scott. *p* David Puttnam. *sc* Gerald Vaughan-Hughes. *ph* Frank Tidy. *ed* Michael Bradsell. *pd* Peter J Hampton. *m* Howard Blake. *cast* Keith Carradine, Harvey Keitel, Albert Finney, Edward Fox, Cristina Raines, Robert Stephens, Tom Conti, John McEnery, Diana Quick.

●A curious mixture. This British film, based on a Conrad story, received heavy US financial backing and stars two Americans conspicuously at odds with their British supporting cast. The film-makers dubiously opt for a kind of Napoleonic Western: a tale of honour and obsession with one French officer pursued down the years by another. Keitel struggles gamely against a wooden Carradine, but the American influences further dislocate a script that delivers little observation, psychological or social, on their running feud. Instead, the film concentrates on the look of things, backed up by heavy research into contemporary French fashions. Scott, a name in TV commercials making his first feature, brings little overall thrust, working instead in short bursts. CPe

Duet for One

(1986, US, 107 min)
d Andrei Konchalovsky. *p* Menahem Golan, Yoram Globus. *sc* Tom Kempinski, Jeremy Lipp, Andrei Konchalovsky. *ph* Alex Thomson. *ed* Henry Richardson. *pd* John Graysmark. *cast* Julie Andrews, Alan Bates, Max von Sydow, Rupert Everett, Margaret Courtenay, Cathryn Harrison.

●In this sensitive adaptation of Tom Kempinski's play, Andrews, as the internationally acclaimed concert violinist whose career, marriage and life are shattered by the onset of multiple sclerosis, is as professional as ever; the supporting cast – Bates as the surly, selfish composer husband, Everett as a rebellious protégé, von Sydow as the psychotherapist whose seemingly callous attitude conceals his own fear of dying – is equally solid. And, except for a couple of scenes concerning sexual jealousy, Konchalovsky's direction is reliable and unsentimental. But the use of the sugary slow movement from Bruch's Violin Concerto – a real family favourite – to accompany the crucial moments of Andrews' dark night of the soul is symbolic of the film's limited achievement: to confront anxiety, illness and the realisation of life's meaninglessness without ever exuding a real sense of pain. GA

Due to an Act of God (Im Zeichen des Kreuzes)

(1983, WGer, 106 min)
d Rainer Boldt. *p* Hermann Wolf. *sc* Hans-Rüdiger Minow. *ph* Karl Kases. *ed* Elke Boisch. *ad* Winfried Hennig. *m* Jens-Peter Ostendorf. *cast* Renate Schroeter, Wigand Witting, Johanna Rudolph, Mathias Nitschke, Antje Hagen, Karl-Heinz von Hassel.

●Detailing the effects that a collision between juggernauts transporting liquid nitrogen and radioactive waste has on the area surrounding a quiet and tidy German village, Boldt paints a grim and unsentimental picture. The nightmare lies not merely in the atrocious physical aftermath (though there are no *Day After Nosferatu* lookalikes here), but in the way the faceless and culpable authorities deal with the situation: to prevent panic, a massive cover-up is implemented, contagious victims are incarcerated like criminals, martial law is imposed, and the most seriously contaminated are left to die without any real aid. Tense without being melodramatic, tough but fuelled by a passionate concern for human life, it's a fine, intelligent film that offers little hope and plenty of cause for worry. And as a thriller, it takes an honourable place in the tradition best represented by Romero's *The Crazies*. GA

Duets

(2000, US, 114 min)
d Bruce Paltrow. *p* Kevin Jones, Bruce Paltrow, John Byrum. *sc* John Byrum. *ph* Paul Sarossy. *ed* Jerry Greenberg. *pd* Sharon Seymour. *m* David Newman. *cast* Maria Bello, André Braugher, Paul Giamatti, Huey Lewis, Gwyneth Paltrow, Scott Speedman, Marian Seldes, Kiersten Warren.

●Three odd couples are headed for a $5,000 Grand Prize Karaoke Contest in Omaha, Nebraska: an estranged father and daughter (Lewis and Paltrow); milksop cabbie and ballsy waitress (Speedman and Bello); disillusioned businessman and ex-con (Giamatti and Braugher). The film aims for the fragmented, kooky sharpness of *Short Cuts* but quickly dissolves into offensive mush. As for the cast, they're overstretched. Lewis looks uncomfortable in the acting scenes, while Braugher is made to appear foolish by a singing voice that's clearly been enhanced. Giamatti also deserves better: a delightful cross between Nicolas Cage and Mr Magoo, he jitters for America but can't make sense of his character's ludicrous mood swings. Only Gwyneth is left looking smug. The headgirl of ick, she makes an implausible showgirl. But she can carry a tune and, if this were karaoke night, she'd cart off any medals going. CO'Su

Duffer

(1971, GB, 75 min, b/w)
d Joseph Despins, William Dumaresq. *sc* William Durmaresq. *ph* Jorge Guerra. *ed* Joseph Despins. *m* Galt MacDermot. *cast* Kit Gleave, Erna May, James Roberts [William Dumaresq], Lisa Doran, Marcelle McHardy.
● A first feature by two expatriate Canadians, this tells the mock-ingenuous tale of a passably attractive lad who spends most of his life submitting to a homosexual sadist but occasionally scurries to a golden-hearted whore for relief. Duffer's account of himself in a voice-over narration starts out ultra-subversive ('I didn't much enjoy the things that Louis-Jack did to me, but they seemed to give him pleasure, and there really isn't much of that around') and gets more and more Joycean. The plot gets rather lost in musings on fantasy versus reality, but the imagery remains funny and, when needed, tough; the mood is predominantly wistful, well caught by Galt MacDermot's simple piano score. TR

Duffy

(1968, GB, 101 min)
d Robert Parrish. *p* Martin Manulis. *sc* Donald Cammell, Harry Joe Brown Jr. *ph* Otto Heller. *ed* Willy Kemplen. *ad* Philip Harrison. *m* Ernie Freeman. *cast* James Coburn, James Mason, James Fox, Susannah York, John Alderton, Guy Deghy.
● Parrish, it has been observed, was a director happiest when dealing with outsider figures, but above all in need of a good scriptwriter. Donald Cammell, who co-directed *Performance*, looked to be just the person to provide him with his best opportunity since *Wonderful Country*, made ten years earlier. The script promisingly featured a dropout ex-criminal, enlisted to aid two English boys in robbing their own millionaire father; and an excellent cast was assembled. The results were woeful: the last word in modishness, and the final nail in the coffin of '60s pop. CPe

Dulce Olor a Muerte, Un

see Sweet Scent of Death, A

Dulces Horas

see Tender Hours

Dulcima

(1971, GB, 98 min)
d Frank Nesbitt. *p* Basil Rayburn. *sc* Frank Nesbitt. *ph* Tony Imi. *ed* William Lewthwaite. *ad* Ray Sim. *m* Johnny Douglas. *cast* Carol White, John Mills, Stuart Wilson, Bernard Lee, Sheila Raynor, Dudley Foster.
● Product of Bryan Forbes' uneasy reign at EMI Film Productions. An adaptation of an HE Bates story about a randy, miserly old farmer and the golddigging girl who comes to work for him. Nothing more than a *Woman's Own* story, with one point of interest: it deals with a sort of society rarely thought interesting enough for movies, and therefore the Gloucestershire locations and bits of 'country lore' are refreshing. It's neat, but nothing.

Dulcimer Street

see London Belongs to Me

Dumb & Dumber

(1994, US, 107 min)
d Peter Farrelly. *p* Charles Wessler, Brad Krevoy, Steven Stabler. *sc* Bob Farrelly, Bennett Yellin, Peter Farrelly. *ph* Mark Irwin. *ed* Chris Greenbury. *pd* Sidney Bartholomew Jr. *m* Todd Rundgren. *cast* Jim Carrey, Jeff Daniels, Lauren Holly, Teri Garr, Karen Duffy, Charles Rocket.
● Notes on a motion picture recollected in tranquillity. Story: the two dumbest guys in the world drive across America to return a lady's briefcase. Inside the case is a $1m ransom. Complications ensue. Character: Carrey and Daniels. The lady is blonde (Holly). Un film de: Farrelly, who previously worked on rewrites for *Wagons East!* Both *Wagons East!* and *Dumb & Dumber* feature sequences where a minor character unwittingly drinks piss. Carrey: he's trying too hard to please (no one has mugged this much since Steve Martin's *The Jerk*), but the force is with him. He's like Jerry Lewis, but less recherché. Less sentimental, too. Context: given American cinema's current obsession with innocence and ignorance (*Forrest Gump*, *Nell*, *I.Q.*), at least this never romanticises its protagonists. They are genuinely, irredeemably, 100 per cent no-hopers. They are not kind to strangers (except wealthy blondes), they are lousy conversationalists, they have no social graces – no grace at all in fact – and terrible haircuts. Economics: they paid Carrey $7 million. The entire budget totalled $15m. In the US to date [1995], the film has grossed $117m. TCh

Dumbo

(1941, US, 64 min)
d Ben Sharpsteen. *sc* Joe Grant, Dick Huemer. *ph* Chuck Wheeler. *ad* Herb Ryman, Ken O'Connor, Terrell Stamp, Don Da Gradi, Al Zinnen, Ernest Nordli, Dick Kelsey, Charles Payzand. *songs* Oliver Wallace, Frank Churchill. *cast* voices: Edward Brophy, Herman Bing, Sterling Holloway, Cliff Edwards, Verna Felton.
● One of the best of Disney's animated features. An ugly duckling variation, lifted by those unforgettable characters: the ancient, haywire stork who delivers Dumbo late, the circus train reminiscent of the Tin Man, the irrepressible mouse who befriends the rejected hero, the bitchy old elephant troupe ('Hey girls, have I got a trunkful of dirt…'), and the beautifully characterised crows – stolen by Bakshi for *Fritz the Cat* – who sing the classic 'When I See A' Elephant Fly'. The artwork, of course, is magisterial: aerial views of the States, the erecting of the big top in a storm, and the brilliant drunken vision of pink elephants. Magic. SG

Dumb Die Fast, the Smart Die Slow, The (Galok Bang Tai Cha, Galok Na Tai Gon)

(1991, Thai, 123 min)
d Manop Udomdej. *cast* Sorasak Wongthai, Khachonsak Ratana-nidsai, Aungkana Timdee, Manop Aswathep.
● The hard-boiled thriller, Thai-style – obviously indebted to *The Postman Always Rings Twice* and other models, but irreducibly Thai in its plotting and characterisations. The kindly owner of a gas station with a no-good wife takes on a hitchhiker as a handyman, unaware that he's on the run. The wife learns the newcomer's secret, and tries to blackmail him into robbing her husband. Manop started out as an 'underground' political film-maker, which doubtless explains the hints of social comment here. Mostly, though, he has fun in the plot's moral quicksand. Very entertaining, and very novel to see these conventions through Thai eyes. TR

Dune

(1984, US 137 min)
d David Lynch. *p* Raffaella De Laurentiis. *sc* David Lynch. *ph* Freddie Francis. *ed* Antony Gibbs. *pd* Anthony Masters. *m* Toto, (prophecy theme) Brian Eno, Daniel Lanois, Roger Eno, (addit) Marty Paich. *cast* Kyle MacLachlan, Francesca Annis, Sting, Jurgen Prochnow, Brad Dourif, José Ferrer, Kenneth McMillan, Linda Hunt, Max von Sydow, Silvana Mangano, Freddie Jones, Dean Stockwell.
● Lynch has toiled to condense Frank Herbert's mammoth SF novel into two hours twenty: the life-and-death struggle between the Atreides and Harkonnens for the vital spice *melange* takes place on a third planet – Arrakis, the desert planet, home to the Fremen, dune dwellers with vivid blue eyes. Fremen legend tells of a messiah who will be able to drink the water of life, previous tasters having tried and died. That Paul Atreides (MacLachlan) knows how to fit his desert survival suit is taken as a promising early sign that now, perhaps, the time has come. Lynch's third feature may have been a commercial disaster, but it gets under your skin and is marked by unforgettable images and an extraordinary soundtrack. The sets and props – from steaming machinery to dimly lit interiors, via personal bug-juice extractors – are reminiscent of *Eraserhead*, and also recall *Metropolis* and *Blade Runner*. There's a ton of exposition, but consider the source material. The constant whispered thoughts may be expositionally expedient, but they also help to establish a much-needed intimacy in a film of this epic scale. NRo

Dungeons & Dragons

(2000, US, 108 min)
d Courtney Solomon. *p* Courtney Solomon, Kia Jam, Tom Hammel. *sc* Topper Lilien, Carroll Cartwright. *ph* Doug Milsome. *ed* Caroline Ross. *pd* Bryce Perrin. *m* Justin Caine Burnett. *cast* Justin Whalin, Marlon Wayans, Zoe McLellan, Thora Birch, Kristen Wilson, Richard O'Brien, Tom Baker, Jeremy Irons.
● Now concentrate, there are a lot of funny names to take in. The Empire of Izmer, ruled by young Empress Savina (Birch), carrier of the magical Royal Sceptre and commander of a fleet of gold dragons, is in grave danger. Savina's Archmage, Profion (Irons), would like to take over this land of incredibly tall buildings, but he's going to need the Rod of Savrille, another magical sceptre-like thingy that enables its holder to command a fleet of red dragons. What Profion hasn't banked on is a couple of petty thieves, Ridley Freeborn (Whalin) and Snails (Wayans), getting in the way. Warning bells sound during the opening scene, which features, believe it or not, a dragon … in a dungeon. Irons adopts a maniacal grin that suggests his character has taken an overdose of angel dust and spews forth some of the most risible dialogue you've ever heard. The other performances, too, are from another world. DA

Dunkirk

(1958, GB, 134 min, b/w)
d Leslie Norman. *p* Michael Balcon. *sc* David Divine, WP Lipscomb. *ph* Paul Beeson. *ed* Gordon Stone. *ad* Jim Morahan. *m* Malcolm Arnold. *cast* John Mills, Richard Attenborough, Bernard Lee, Robert Urquhart, Patricia Plunkett, Maxine Audley.
● Overlong, stolid account of the famous World War II rescue operation from the Normandy beaches in 1940, reconstructed by Ealing with exactly the sort of cast you would expect, doing their plucky Brit acts as they portray a small group separated from the main force. The usual quiet heroics, dressed up with a semi-documentary atmosphere. GA

Dunston Checks In

(1996, Can, 88 min)
d Ken Kwapis. *p* Joe Wizan, Todd Black. *sc* John Hopkins, Bruce Graham. *ph* Peter Collister. *ed* Jon Pol. *pd* Rusty Smith. *m* Miles Goodman. *cast* Jason Alexander, Faye Dunaway, Eric Lloyd, Rupert Everett, Graham Sack, Glenn Shadix, Nathan Davis.
● An unruly orang-utan plus an opulent hotel setting equals a natural disaster, or in this case a kids' movie. Robert (Alexander) manages the Majestic Hotel, New York, owned by avaricious Mrs Dubrow (Dunaway). She's convinced that the so-called Lord Rutledge (Everett) is really a hotel critic, and insists that everything runs extra smoothly. But Robert's sons discover that the lord's a jewel thief with an anthropoid accomplice. When the gangly one, Dunston, finally escapes Rutledge's clutches, the kids spend the rest of the film trying to conceal him. The children we took adored the cheerful scenario and sad-cum-happy signposted climax. Adults, on the other hand, will probably be stupefied by Everett's unrecognisable twit, complete with lip-distorting gum guard, and Dunaway's raging Ivana Trump turn. Alexander, though, is a likeable comic player in the Charles Grodin manner, and younger sibling Lloyd makes for a more loveable character than Macaulay Culkin. The film's admirably bereft of realistic violence, but then the makers blow it by slipping in a scene featuring Dunston innocently puffing on a cigarette. DA

Durante l'Estate

see During the Summer

Durian, Durian (Liulian Piaopiao)

(2000, HK/Fr, 117 min)
d Fruit Chan. *p* Doris Yang. *sc* Fruit Chan. *ph* Lam Wah Chuen. *ed* Tin Sam Fat. *pd* Tin Muk. *m* Lam Wah Chuen, Chu Hing Cheung. *cast* Qin Hailu, Mak Wai-Fan, Bai Xiao Ming, Yung Wai Yiu, Mak Suet-Man.
● The durian is a popular but sickly smelling fruit which plays a small but pivotal role in this improvised drama – a companion piece to the director's *Little Cheung* – about a young woman

from northern China who makes a mint during a brief spell as a prostitute in Hong Kong, then returns home sure she'll never return. The film's casual naturalistic style is enlivened by a couple of quirky montage sequences. TCh

Du Rififi à Paname (Rififi in Paris/The Upper Hand)

(1965, Fr/It/WGer, 98 min)
d Denys de la Patellière. *p* Maurice Jacquin. *sc* Alphonse Boudard, Denys de la Patelliere. *ph* Walter Wottitz. *ed* Claude Durand. *ad* Robert Clavel. *m* Georges Garvarentz. *cast* Jean Gabin, Claudio Brook, Gert Fröbe, Nadja Tiller, George Raft, Claude Brasseur, Mireille Darc, Daniel Ceccaldi.

●One of those latter-day vehicles in which, portly and white-haired, Gabin brushes importunate girls aside to lavish attentions on his pet Boxer, meanwhile masterminding a series of unenterprising crimes which win him the usual admiring accolade: 'He's a real man!' Thoroughly routine stuff, it mixes some passable action sequences with statutory travelogue footage (London, Munich, Tokyo), allows Gabin to coast through without exerting himself, and finds time for George Raft to do his coin-flipping act. But Claudio Brook, taking time off from Buñuel (he was the major-domo in *The Exterminating Angel* and the nutty saint in *Simon of the Desert*) makes a refreshingly unstereotyped hero, and Gert Fröbe steals his scenes as a crook with leftist leanings. TM

Du Rififi chez les Hommes (Rififi)

(1955, Fr, 117 min, b/w)
d Jules Dassin. *sc* Jules Dassin, René Wheeler, Auguste Le Breton. *ph* Philippe Agostini. *ed* Roger Dwyre. *ad* Auguste Capelier. *m* Georges Auric. *cast* Jean Servais, Carl Möhner, Robert Manuel, Perlo Vita [Jules Dassin], Magali Noël, Pierre Grasset, Robert Hossein.

●Archetypal heist thriller, with a group of thieves banding together for a daring jewel robbery and falling out afterwards. Highly acclaimed for the 35-minute robbery sequence, conducted without a word being spoken, and for the generally downbeat atmosphere, it's actually rather overrated, lacking the tension, profundity, and vivid characterisation of similar films by, say, Becker and Melville. Like even the best of Dassin's work, in fact, it never penetrates beneath its fashionable, self-conscious surface. GA

During the Summer (Durante l'Estate)

(1971, It, 105 min)
d Ermanno Olmi. *p* Gaspare Palumbo. *sc* Ermanno Olmi, Fortunato Pasqualino. *ph* Ermanno Olmi. *m* Bruno Lauzi. *cast* Renato Parracchi, Rosanna Callegari.

●The marvellously quaint and funny tale of a timid, unprepossessing little man – self-styled as The Professor – who busies himself with designing coats-of-arms, and presenting them to anyone who matches up to his private assessment of nobility. Recipients include an old man patiently waiting on a railway station for the son who doesn't turn up, a hall porter who brings a cup of coffee when he hurts his leg, a girl with whom he embarks on a sidelong little romance, and who proves that she deserves his accolade of 'Princess' when the law finally catches up and he is jailed for his 'malpractices'. Stunningly shot in colour, with a non-professional cast and very much the same wryly observant sense of humour as *Il Posto*, it has a touch of real Olmi magic to it. TM

Du Soleil pour les Gueux (Sunshine for the Scoundrels)

(2000, Fr, 55 min)
d/sc Alain Guiraudie. *ph* Antoine Héberlé. *ed* Anne-Marie Groscolas. *cast* Isabelle Girardet, Michel Turquin, Jean-Paul Jourdan, Alain Guiraudie.

●Judging by this and the later *Real Cool Time*, Guiraudie is a mercurial talent with a penchant for creating strange worlds. This, far more than its successor, is genuinely eccentric: set on the *causses* of Languedoc (the region's dry windswept grazing plateaux), it's an absurdist fable about a woman in search of a shepherd who, when she finds him, has lost his improbably dangerous flock; meanwhile, they keep meeting a bandit unable to flee the region despite being pursued by a merciless bounty hunter. There's much running hither and thither, much digressive sophistry and frequent sight-gags – but what it's finally all about is up for grabs. Engrossing and funny, though, and reminiscent of *Candide*, Jarry and Beckett, with a little Keaton thrown in for good measure. GA

Dust

(1985, Bel/Fr, 88 min)
d Marion Hänsel. *p* Marion Hänsel, Jean Daskalidès. *sc* Marion Hänsel. *ph* Walther van den Ende. *ed* Susana Rossberg. *ad* Pierre Thévenet. *m* Martin St Pierre. *cast* Jane Birkin, Trevor Howard, John Matshikiza, Nadine Uwampa, Lourdes Christina Sayo Momobok, René Diaz.

●Cape Province, South Africa. In a remote farmhouse, spinsterly Magda tends to her stern, imperious father. Life might continue this way forever, were it not for an intrusion into the household by a new maid that arouses a maelstrom (or Magda's dreams) of seduction, jealousy, murder and rape. Hänsel's stark adaptation (shot in English) of JM Coetzee's *In the Heart of the Country* is a strangely interior film, viewed through the lonely eyes of the repressed Magda (Birkin). As the film somewhat uneasily blends reality and fantasy, family bonds are twisted, master-servant roles are reversed, and 'the work of generations falls to ruins'. But for all its admirable evocation of Magda's mounting hatred and hysteria, Hänsel's approach is finally flawed by its careful adherence to introspective, literary qualities. GA

Dust

(2001, GB/Ger/It/Macedonia/US/Sp/Switz, 124 min)
d Milcho Manchevski. *p* Chris Auty, Vesna Jovanoska, Domenico Procacci. *sc* Milcho Manchevski. *ph* Barry Ackroyd. *ed* Nic Gaster. *pd* David Munns. *m* Kiril Dzajkovski. *cast* Joseph Fiennes, David Wenham, Adrian Lester, Anne Brochet, Nikolina Kujaca, Rosemary Murphy, Vlado Jovanovski, Salaetin Bilal, Vera Farmiga, Matthew Ross, Meg Gibson.

●This very wild eastern Western bears an uncanny resemblance to that supposedly extinguished early-'90s entity, the Euro-pudding. Biblical in scope, Babel-like in execution, it's a sprawling revenge saga starring Wenham and Fiennes as Luke and Elijah, sharp-shooting brothers from the old American West who fall out over a woman and high-tail it in turn to the post-Ottoman turmoil of Macedonia. Luke finds his calling as a brutal bounty hunter; Elijah shows but rarely, solemnly hunting Luke. Already distended by a dearth of sensible explication and an excess of editing interventions, this muffled tale is further fractured by its failing narrator, a present-day Ancient Mariner called Angela (Murphy) whose New York apartment Edge (Lester) makes the mistake of trying to burgle. The ambition might be a magical layering and merging of stories, lives and eras, but the effect is a bewildering crush. NB

Dust Devil

(1992, GB, 103 min)
d Richard Stanley. *p* JoAnne Sellar. *sc* Richard Stanley. *ph* Steven Chivers. *ed* Derek Twigg, (Final Cut) Paul Carlin. *pd* Joseph Bennett. *m* Simon Boswell. *cast* Robert Burke, Chelsea Field, Zakes Mokae, Marianne Sägebrecht, William Hootkins, Rufus Swart.

●More personal and ambitious than Stanley's killer-android debut *Hardware*, this boldly juxtaposes murder, magic and South African politics. A near-wordless opening reel leads us into a nightmarish world of mysticism and ritual slaughter. Drawn to the drought-ridden town of Bethany by the smell of death, shape-shifting 'Hitcher with No Name' (Burke) kills and dismembers a lonely young woman who picks him up. While the hitcher feeds off the despair of others, including fugitive wife Field, local policeman Mokae enlists the help of a half-mad, half-blind cinema projectionist in his search for a suspected serial killer. The non-linear storyline relies more on atmosphere than forward momentum, and the tone veers wildly between dream-like mysteriousness and indulgent incomprehensibility. A sidewinder snaking across a dune, hazy desertscapes, and an extraordinary scene in a sand-filled cinema are evidence of a visionary talent. But Field's vacant performance, some poorly realised dream sequences, the leaden dialogue, and a mortuary scene with Sägebrecht are grim. NF

Dust in the Wind (Lian Lian Feng Chen)

(1987, Tai, 110 min)
d Hou Xiaoxien. *p* Zhang Huakun, Li Xianchang. *sc* Wu Nianzhen, Zhu Tianwen. *ph* Li Ping-pin. *ed* Liao Ch'ing-sung. *pd* Zhao Qi Bin. *m* Ch'en Ming-chang. *cast* Wang Ching-wen, Hsing Shu-fen, Ch'en Shu-fang, Li Tien-lu, Lin Yang, Mei Fang.

●Faintly disappointing by Hou's own very high standards, this story of teenage love and betrayal (framed by a move from village to city) is notable for its sociological precision and its oblique criticism of Taiwanese militarism. As often in Hou's movies, mainland China is a huge off-screen presence, here briefly stumbling on-screen in the person of a terrified fisherman whose boat has sailed off-course. Performances and technical standards are both superb, but there's a nagging sense that the director is marking time rather than moving forward. TR

Dutch (aka Driving Me Crazy)

(1991, US, 107 min)
d Peter Faiman. *p* John Hughes, Richard Vane. *sc* John Hughes. *ph* Charles Minsky. *ed* Paul Hirsch, Adam Bernardi. *pd* Stan Jolley. *m* Alan Silvestri. *cast* Ed O'Neill, Ethan Randall, JoBeth Williams, Christopher McDonald, Ari Meyers, EG Daily, L Scott Caldwell, Kathleen Freeman.

●Little positive to report on this John Hughes production (he also scripted, and must therefore carry the can for the below-par dialogue). The rite-of-passage here is a car ride, from school in Atlanta to Thanksgiving dinner in Chicago, undertaken under protest by adolescent rich kid Doyle (Randall) in the company of Dutch (O'Neill), his separated mother's working-class boyfriend. Doyle is superior sonofabitch personified, his only rival in loathsomeness Doyle's absentee father (McDonald). O'Neill displays lazy charm, a Matthau-like rambling bear of a man-child with a grin set somewhere between gormless and amiable. The set pieces, involving fireworks, a walk in the cold, a car crash and a pair of prostitutes who turn Doyle's cheeks cherry red, are the milestones on the path to friendship and respect. It's all assembly-line stuff. WH

Dutchman

(1966, GB, 56 min, b/w)
d Anthony Harvey. *p* Gene Persson. *sc* LeRoi Jones. *ph* Gerry Turpin. *ed* Anthony Harvey. *ad* Herbert Smith. *m* John Barry. *cast* Shirley Knight, Al Freeman Jr, Howard Bennett, Robert Calvert.

●Harvey's transition from editor to director is a brilliantly spare, edgy adaptation of LeRoi Jones' play, basically a two-hander set on a New York subway train: a grim duel between cat and mouse as a rangily sexy white woman circles a young black sitting alone, deliberately teasing, taunting, flaunting herself in a perverse attempt to break his control. Resentment and attraction crackle through the dialogue (and the superb performances) in an almost orgiastic expression of provocation and desire, until she wins and the black is goaded into retaliation. It ends, of course, in violence: a devastating acknowledgment that this is just about the only ground on which black and white can meet. The film's one minor flaw is when the camera eventually pulls back from the duo to reveal that the carriage has filled with commuters studiously minding their own business; true to life, perhaps, but it comes over as a facile trick. TM

Dybbuk, The

(1938, Pol, 125 min, b/w)
d Michael Waszynski. *cast* Abram Morewski, Lilli Liliana, Dina Halpern, Leon Liebgold.

●In this Yiddish language version of Ansky's play, the immersion in the traditional culture of the Eastern European 'shtetl' (Jewish village) is complete, and even heightened by the expressionistic style of acting and filming amid fairly realistic sets and costuming. From the initial shots in the synagogue to the marvellous singing and dancing at peak moments of the plot, this supernatural tale of the tragic possession of a bride by the soul of her true loved one is as weird and wonderful as an Isaac Bashevis Singer story. The Jewish absorption in the inexplicable suffering of humanity is made almost unbearably poignant by the knowledge that not only the traditional culture of the Polish Jews, but even the lives of the makers d actors of this film, were to be utterly destroyed over the next few years by an evil beyond even the imagination of a society that could produce irrational, tragic tales as remorseless as *The Dybbuk*. MH

Dying Swan, The (Umirajuseij lebed)

(1917, Rus, 1,078 metres, b/w)
d Evgenij Bauer. *cast* Vera Karalli, V Polanskij, A Gromov, I Perestiani.

●Bauer was one of the two leading figures in pre-Soviet Russian cinema; he trained in fine arts and made films prolifically for only five years before dying in an accident. This lugubrious melodrama, evidently quite representative of his output, suggests that he was a big fan of *Dorian Gray*, *Salome* and other Wilde perversities. The mute Gizella Raccio, raised in the countryside, longs to dance in Moscow. Her father (a dead ringer for Boris Yeltsin) persuades an impresario to give her a break, and she becomes a star as the Dying Swan. This attracts the attention of painter Valerian Gliiniski, a talentless psychotic who believes that perfect beauty is found only in death. Gizella innocently poses for him. She later has recurrent nightmares, but a reunion with her first love Viktor helps her to shake them. Valerian, however, is enraged by the new light in her eyes. He lures her back to his studio. Within the limiting conventions of the period, Bauer's staging and the performances remain valid and in some ways surprisingly fresh. Vera Karalli, an Imperial Theatre ballerina, is even quite touching as Gizella. But it's the necrophilia motif – developed in the skull-strewn design of Valerian's studio and the starkly Freudian dream scene, not to mention the no-concessions ending – which gives the film its lasting interest. TR

Dying Young

(1991, US, 111 min)
d Joel Schumacher. *p* Sally Field, Kevin McCormick. *sc* Richard Freidenberg. *ph* Juan Ruiz-Anchia. *ed* Robert Brown, Jim Prior. *pd* Guy J Comtois, Richard Johnson. *m* James Newton Howard. *cast* Julia Roberts, Campbell Scott, Vincent D'Onofrio, Colleen Dewhurst, David Selby, Ellen Burstyn, Dion Anderson, George Martin.

●Shamateurishly directed, this Roberts vehicle traversing the clichéd class-clash/love story territory of *Pretty Woman* is a dog. Working-class, Catholic, unemployed and single, Hilary (Roberts) applies for a job as live-in carer for Victor Geddes (Scott), a millionaire's son suffering from leukemia, but is given the thumbs-down by Geddes *père*. Soon, however, she is summoned to the basement flat where Victor lives in splendid social isolation, surrounded by the morbid works of Klimt and Rossetti. Sadly, down at the disco where Hilary gets her kicks, nobody told her about art history… The surprising thing is the film's coyness. As their relationship grows and we finally get to sex – after all the business of her helping him through frightening post-chemotherapy attacks – the camera pulls away ashamedly to view their contact through mirrors. Judy Holliday and Jean Hagen would have sent the script back. WH

Dynamite Chicken

(1971, US, 76 min, b/w & col)
d/p/sc Ernest Pintoff. *ph* Guy Fraumeni, Amran Nowak, David Hoffman, Bob Godfrey, Irene Trivas, Bob Silverstein. *ed* Tom Pagnotta. *m* Jimi Hendrix, Nina Simone, Rhinoceros, Groupies, Cat Mother and the All Night Newsboys. *cast* Richard Pryor, Paul Krassner.

●Pryor's gags and monologues, mostly delivered while toying with a basketball on the site of a derelict building, link a series of archive clips of marginal hippies being really free, man, and politically didactic. 'Stars' such as Warhol and Lennon and Yoko appear fleetingly and to no great effect. Sketches by the Ace Trucking Co are mildly amusing. Are there better ways to spend 76 minutes? Only about 26,958. Yep, *Dynamite Chicken* lays egg. GB

Dynamite Women

see Great Texas Dynamite Chase, The

Dyn Amo

(1972, GB, 120 min)
d Stephen Dwoskin. *p* Michael Armitage, Maggie Pinhorn. *sc/ph/ed* Stephen Dwoskin. *m* Gavin Bryars. *cast* Jenny Runacre, Pat Ford, Catherine Kessler, Linda Marlowe, John Grillo, Derek Paget.

●From (a long way apparently) Chris Wilkinson's play of the same name. The film is set in a strip club. The girls go through their routines to shreds of Zippety-doo-dah and Sweet Dream Baby on the pocket-sized stage amid the usual cheap tinsel and glitter tat, acting out sour fantasies that point to a painful divorce from self – woman as servant, as little girl, as programmed seductress – each more grotesque than the last. It's typical Dwoskin, examining faces, gestures, half-movements. Rewarding unless you're after a good story.

Dynasty (Qian Dao Wan Li Zhui)

(1977, Tai/HK, 95 min)
d Zhang Meijun. *p* Wang Dafu. *sc* Liu Guoxiong. *ph* Chen Rongshu. *ad* Zou Zhiliang. *cast* Bobby Ming, Pai Ying, Tang Wei, Jin Gang, Jin Yongxiang, Lin Dadian.

●A very average swordplay/martial arts movie, enlivened by proficient 3-D photography in the Polaroid process. The plot (vengeful young monk has seven days to kill wicked Imperial Court eunuch) is rehashed from a 1966 King Hu film called *Dragon Gate Inn*, and Pai Ying – one of the heroes in *A Touch of Zen* – reprises his role as the eunuch from that film. The rest is typical '70s kung-fu stunts. Reasonably engaging exposition, very flat climax, feeble gestures towards the Ming Dynasty historiography. Best 3-D effect: arrows fired directly into the audience. TR

e

Educating Rita

Each Dawn I Die

(1939, US, 92 min, b/w)
d William Keighley. *sc* Norman Reilly Raine, Warren Duff, Charles Perry. *ph* Arthur Edeson. *ed* Thomas Richards. *ad* Max Parker. *m* Max Steiner. *cast* James Cagney, George Raft, George Bancroft, Jane Bryan, Stanley Ridges, Maxie Rosenbloom, Alan Baxter.

●Somewhat routine Warner Brothers social-conscience movie, with Cagney as the crusading reporter fighting political corruption and getting framed for murder; in prison he meets up with gangster Raft, becomes a hardened victim of the tough system, and eventually becomes involved in a riot. Theoretically interestingly bleak, in that Cagney, already disillusioned about justice, also loses his faith in friendship (thinking himself betrayed by Raft) and goes round the bend in solitary. But the muddled script ties itself up in knots, and the broody direction is unremarkable. Cagney's fiery presence gives the whole thing a much-needed lift. GA

Eadweard Muybridge, Zoopraxographer

(1974, US, 59 min, b/w & col)
d/p Thom Andersen. *ph* (anim) Thom Andersen, Don Baker, Rocco Damiano, Alan Harding, Marilyn O'Connor, (live action) Doug Ryan. *ed* Morgan Fisher. *m* Michael Cohen. *narrator* Dean Stockwell.

●There are many pleasures in this film about the 19th century photographic pioneer, not least that of seeing a complicated subject laid out with crystal clarity. With the aid of multiple cameras, Muybridge made tiny strips of film containing consecutive shots of humans and animals in motion – embryonic moving pictures, in fact. Andersen dwells on all angles of interest, from the technical through to the philosophical and the sociological. Muybridge himself had many personal quirks, too: he shot his wife's lover (but was acquitted of murder), and he documents his animal models with more care than the humans (excepting some of the women). Andersen, previously a sly parodist of underground styles, brings to the material the ironist's penchant for brevity and suggestive implication; his film is a delight. GB

Eagle, The

(1925, US, 6,900 ft, b/w)
d Clarence Brown. *p* John W Considine Jr. *sc* Hans Kraly. *ph* George Barnes, Dev Jennings. *ed* Hal C Kern. *ad* William Cameron Menzies. *cast* Rudolph Valentino, Vilma Banky, Louise Dresser, Albert Conti, James Marcus, George Nichols.

●Clarence Brown was better than most of his contemporaries at handling the kernel of human interest at the heart of large-scale action dramas; his direction here serves Valentino unusually well, bringing equal intensity to the romantic intrigue and the set-piece thrills. This was Valentino's penultimate film (made a year before his death), and is probably the best surviving key to an understanding of the death-cult that swept the world in 1926. Bonus: William Cameron Menzies' sets are astounding. TR

Eagle Has Landed, The

(1976, GB, 135 min)
d John Sturges. *p* Jack Wiener, David Niven Jr. *sc* Tom Mankiewicz. *ph* Anthony B Richmond. *ed* Anne V Coates. *pd* Peter Murton. *m* Lalo Schifrin. *cast* Michael Caine, Donald Sutherland, Robert Duvall, Jenny Agutter, Donald Pleasence, Anthony Quayle, Jean Marsh, Judy Geeson, Treat Williams.

●Plodding time-passer about a Nazi plot to kidnap Churchill from his Norfolk retreat in 1943. Tom Mankiewicz, adapting Jack Higgins' bet-hedging bestseller ('at least half documented historical fact'), goes for an examination of good/bad German motivations that cuts across the sub-*Jackal* suspense; Sturges turns in a tired study of Cherman and Oirish accents, and little else. There's not one iota of the two-way menace of a partly similar Germans-in-Britain picture like *Went the Day Well?* PT

Eagle Has Two Heads, The

see Aigle à Deux Têtes, L'

Eagle With Two Heads

see Aigle à Deux Têtes, L'

Eagle's Wing

(1978, GB, 111 min)
d Anthony Harvey. *p* Ben Arbeid. *sc* John Briley. *ph* Billy Williams. *ed* Lesley Walker. *pd* Herbert Westbrook. *m* Marc Wilkinson. *cast* Martin Sheen, Sam Waterston, Harvey Keitel, Stéphane Audran, Caroline Langrishe, John Castle, Jorge Luke.

●Set in the as yet untamed American wilderness 'long before the myths', this is unusual not only as a first-class Western made by a British director, but in being virtually a silent movie as an Indian and a white man (Waterston and Sheen), each a failure in his own world and determined to prove otherwise, pursue a strange, obsessive duel for possession of the glorious white stallion that gives the film its title. Quirkishly funny as the duel evolves into a sort of medieval quest attended by its own rituals and chivalries, the film gradually weaves its concentric subplots (various other parties tag along behind, driven by their own passions) into a plaintively spiralling lament for lost illusions. Marvellously shot by Billy Williams, it's weird, hypnotic and magical. TM

Ear, The (Ucho)

(1969, Czech, 93 min, b/w)
d Karel Kachyna. *sc* Jan Prochazka. *ph* Joseph Ilik. *ed* Miroslav Hájek. *ad* Oldrich Okác. *m* Svatopluk Havelka. *cast* Jirina Bohdalová, Radoslav Brzobohaty, Gustav Opocensky, Miloslav Holub, Lubor Tokos, Gustav Opocensky.

●By far the best of the Czech movies banned when Dubcek was toppled in 1969, this uses a flashback structure to explore a crucial night in the lives of Ludvik, a high-ranking bureaucrat, and his semi-estranged wife Anna. They come home from a reception (at which Ludvik learns that his boss and other government officials have just been arrested in a political purge) to find that their home has been comprehensively bugged. During the long and sleepless night, they tear each other apart with Albee-like ferocity while imagining the worst that the future may hold for them. The dawn brings a twist ending that makes Kachyna's film the bitterest and most scathing account of what it takes to get ahead in a Communist bureaucracy. TR

Early Bird, The

(1965, GB, 98 min)
d Robert Asher. *p* Hugh Stewart. *sc* Jack Davies, Norman Wisdom, Eddie Leslie, Henry Blyth. *ph* Jack Asher. *ed* Gerry Hambling. *ad* Bill Andrews. *m* Ron Goodwin. *cast* Norman Wisdom, Edward Chapman, Jerry Desmonde, Paddie O'Neil, Bryan Pringle, Richard Vernon.

●Norman Wisdom, like much of Jerry Lewis, should perhaps be reserved exclusively for kids. The continual emphasis on slapstick, the sentimental celebration of the downtrodden but happy moron, and the total inability to rise above the invariably banal plots, tend to induce teeth-gritting agony for the adult viewer. This 'comedy' sees the staggering cretin as a milkman for a small firm whose inept antics save his unappreciative employers from a takeover. GA

Early Spring (Soshun)

(1956, Jap, 149 min, b/w)
d Yasujiro Ozu. *p* Shizuo Yamanouchi. *sc* Yasujiro Ozu, Kogo Noda. *ph* Yuharu Atsuta. *ed* Yoshiyasu Hamamura. *ad* Tatsuo Hamada. *m* Takanori Saito. *cast* Ryo Ikebe, Chikage Awashima, Keiko Kishi, Chishu Ryu, Daisuke Kato, So Yamamura.

●A typically low-key domestic drama in Ozu's mournful, defeatist vein: it deals with the break-up between an office-worker and his wife when the husband embarks on a tentative affair, and surrounds both partners with extensive webs of friends, relatives, acquaintances and colleagues. It's shot and edited in Ozu's characteristic 'minimalist' style, with hardly any camera movement, a carefully circumscribed syntax, and an editing method that's as unconventional by Japanese standards as it is remote from the Western norm. Ozu's pessimism is deeply reactionary, and the idiosyncrasy of his methods is more interesting for its exoticism than anything else; but anyone who finds the socio-psychological problems of post-war Japan engaging will find the movie both fascinating and rather moving, simply as evidence. TR

Early Summer (Bakushu)

(1951, Jap, 125 min, b/w)
d Yasujiro Ozu. *p* Takeshi Yamamoto. *sc* Kogo Noda, Yasujiro Ozu. *ph* Yuharu Atsuta. *ed* Yoshiyasu Hamamura. *ad* Tatsuo Hamada. *m* Senji Ito. *cast* Setsuko Hara, Chishu Ryu, Chikage Awajima, Kuniko Miyake, Ichiro Sugai, Chieko Higashiyama, Haruko Sugimura, Shuji Sano.

●Another of Ozu's poignant dramas concerning the marrying off of an 'old maid' daughter (Setsuko Hara, superb as ever), though here (unlike in *Late Spring* and *An Autumn Afternoon*) she's subjected to pressure from the whole family, not just a widowed father. That's about it plotwise. Typically, Ozu seems more interested in the texture of family life in the immediate post-war years (with Western influences affecting a woman's right to choose), in the opportunities for gentle comedy (particularly involving a couple of kids), and in the film's formal qualities. The camera is surprisingly mobile at times, but what really impresses is the use of omission and repetition. Intriguingly, we're kept in the dark as to what Hara is missing out on, while a simple shot of the sky, devoid of a balloon seen earlier, speaks volumes about loss, tolerance and resignation. GA

Earrings of Madame de..., The

see Madame de...

Earth

see Tierra

Earth

(1998, Ind/Can, 115 min)
d Deepa Mehta. *p* Deepa Mehta, Anne Masson, Dilip Mehta. *sc* Deepa Mehta. *ph* Giles Nuttgens. *ed* Barry Farrell. *pd* Aradhana Seth. *m* AR Rahman. *cast* Aamir Khan, Nandita Das, Rahul Khanna, Kitu Gidwani, Maia Sethna.

●This powerful and impressive drama from the director of *Fire* (an Indian film-maker now resident in Canada) is based on Bapsi Sidhwa's autobiographical novel *Cracking India* and is set against the background of Partition. Eight-year-old Lenny-Baby is a Parsee growing up in Lahore, but her nanny Shantu (Das) is Hindu, and her beaus Ice Candy Man and Hasan are both Muslim. This schematic melodrama functions both as a credible historical explanation of the India/Pakistan political fault line (the Parsees remained unaligned), and as a chilling exploration of how ordinary people are sucked into religious and sectarian hatred. TCh

Earth (Zemlya) 100

(1930, USSR, 73 min, b/w)
d/sc Alexander Dovzhenko. *ph* Danylo Demutsky. *ed* Alexander Dovzhenko. *ad* Vassili Krichevsky. *cast* Semyon Svashenko, Stepan Shkurat, Mikola Nademsky, Yelena Maximova, Yulia Solntzeva.

●One of the last of the silents, and though increasingly an absentee from Ten Best lists, a very great film indeed. The director's trademarks – a field of sunflowers all waving goodbye, a lowering sky filling three-quarters of the frame – remained well nigh constant throughout his career, but he seldom recaptured the pantheistic phosphoresence of this hymn both to nature and to the gleaming new tractors and ploughs which aimed to transform it. Such is the authenticity of its pictorialism, in fact, that one has to remind oneself that it was actually shot like other films. GAd

Earth Girls Are Easy

(1988, US, 100 min)
d Julien Temple. *p* Tony Garnett. *sc* Julie Brown, Charlie Coffey, Terrence McNally. *ph* Oliver Stapleton. *ed* Richard Halsey. *pd* Dennis Gassner. *m* Nile Rodgers. *cast* Geena Davis, Jeff Goldblum, Jim Carrey, Damon Wayans, Julie Brown, Michael McKean, Charles Rocket, Larry Linville, Rick Overton, Diane Stillwell.

●Crass, silly, tacky: it's not easy to depict the complexities of being a Valley Girl, but in this zany musical, director Temple and co-writer/star Julie Brown have a go. The plot is about a day in the lives of three aliens (led by Goldblum) who, after crash-landing in LA, set off to explore the hot-spots in the company of a lovelorn manicurist (Davis). But first they're introduced to beauty salon owner Candy (Brown), who transforms the furry freaks into human-looking specimens capable of partying and falling in love. The plot ain't much, nor is it supposed to be. This is deliberately, gleefully vacuous entertainment, and any satirical edge is blunted by the film's obvious affection for its subject. But there are excesses, as when Brown, in a beach-movie parody, kicks up sand and warbles about the virtues of being blonde. It's one of several redundant moments, aimed at patently dated, soft targets. But by the time the aliens are shaved and shimmying in the beauty parlour, you'll either be shamelessly hooked or hopelessly bored. CM

Earth Is a Sinful Song (Maa on Syntinen Laulau)

(1973, Fin, 102 min)
d/p Rauni Mollberg. *sc* Rauni Mollberg, Pirjo Honkasalo, Panu Rajala. *ph* Kari Sohlberg, Hannu Peltomaa. *ed* Marjatta Leporinne. *ad* Ensio Suominen, Seppo Heinonen. *m* Hannu Sinnemäki. *cast* Maritta Viitamäki, Pauli Jauhojärvi, Aimo Säukko, Milja Hiltunen, Niiles-Jouni Aikio, Maija-Liisa Ahlgren.

●Set in a remote rural Lapp community, economically deprived, culturally backward and repressed. A spirited young girl is broken by her family and friends as they discourage her relationship with a nomadic herdsman whose loose reputation they despise and envy. For the villagers, escape comes from drink, bouts of joyless sex, or through the hysteria of the occasional church meeting. Mollberg infuses his film with a gloomy sensuality, sodden colours, virtually no music and little relief. In between the feverish action, he groups his characters in painterly tableaux in which they look more than usually stunned. The film works best at placing its figures in landscapes, less so with characterisation and momentum. The melodramatic ending lacks impact for all its cyclical neatness. CPe

Earthquake

(1974, US, 123 min)
d/p Mark Robson. *sc* George Fox, Mario Puzo. *ph* Philip H Lathrop. *ed* Dorothy Spencer. *pd* Alexander Golitzen. *m* John Williams. *cast* Charlton Heston, Ava Gardner, George Kennedy, Lorne Greene, Genevieve Bujold, Richard Roundtree, Marjoe Gortner, Barry Sullivan, Lloyd Nolan, Walter Matthau.

●Lovers of bizarre cinematic gimmickry will find much to enjoy thanks to an ingenious aural device known as Sensurround which induces a minor tremor in the cinema during climactic sequences. The special effects are of a high order as Los Angeles is razed, so it is unfortunate that the same intelligent attention is not extended to either script or direction. Both settle for flat, generally laughable hokum, and the film ends up nowhere near as interesting a comment on the psychological aspects of disaster as *Juggernaut*. DP

Earth vs the Flying Saucers (aka Invasion of the Flying Saucers)

(1956, US, 81 min, b/w)
d Fred F Sears. *p* Charles H Schneer. *sc* George Worthing Yates, Raymond T Marcus [Bernard Gordon]. *ph* Fred Jackman Jr. *ed* Danny B Landres. *ad* Paul Palmentola. *m* Mischa Bakaleinikoff. *cast* Joan Taylor, Hugh Marlowe, Harry Lauter, Morris Ankrum, Donald Curtis, John Zaremba.

●Androids in flying saucers give the Earth sixty days in which to surrender. Scientist Hugh Marlowe sets about devising a sonic gun which will show 'em who's boss. Despite a mundane script, this works quite effectively by adopting a dry, documentary tone and splurging the budget on Ray Harryhausen's spectacular special effects. Check out the wholesale destruction of Washington, DC's most famous landmarks. TCh

Earth vs the Spider (aka The Spider)

(1958, US, 73 min, b/w)
d/p Bert I Gordon. *sc* Laszlo Gorog, George Wothing Yates. *ph* Jack Marta. *ed* Ronald Sinclair. *m* Albert Glasser. *cast* Ed Kemmer, June Kenney, Gene Persson, Gene Roth, Hal Torey, June Jocelyn, Mickey Finn.

●Routine creature feature in which a small town teenage couple, looking for the girl's missing father, stumble on a giant spider lurking in a network of caves and narrowly escape its trampoline-style web (dad, of course, is already a victim). A sheriff's posse manages to knock the creature out with DDT; and supposedly dead, it is parked in the school gym to await shipment for scientific study. Cue for teenagers to break in for some rock'n'roll larks, while the monster revives and goes on the rampage before being finally electrocuted. The special effects are nothing to write home about, with the spider fitting comfortably into the gym, but once outside, towering over two- and three-storey buildings. The Carlsbad Caverns in New Mexico provide a spectacular setting used to remarkably little effect. Altogether inferior to its obvious model, Jack Arnold's *Tarantula*. TM

Easter Parade

(1948, US, 103 min)
d Charles Walters. *p* Arthur Freed. *sc* Sidney Sheldon, Frances Goodrich, Albert Hackett. *ph* Harry Stradling. *ed* Albert Akst. *ad* Cedric Gibbons, Jack Martin Smith. *songs* Irving Berlin. *cast* Fred Astaire, Judy Garland, Peter Lawford, Ann Miller, Jules Munshin, Clinton Sundberg.

●The only time the two greatest Hollywood musical stars teamed up was an accident – Gene Kelly had broken his ankle and suggested the initially reluctant Fred as his replacement. In the event, it's not an ideal coupling, a stylistic unease between them – save in the legendary novelty song 'A Couple of Swells' – being often apparent. Nevertheless, *Easter Parade* is the sort of musical to put your feet up for, lifted by three bursts of dynamism: Fred's show number 'Steppin' Out with My Baby', his brilliantly inventive 'Drum Crazy', and Ann Miller's knock-down broadside 'Shakin' the Blues Away'. The story is *Pygmalion*-esque, the songs vintage Irving Berlin. And if you think they can't sing in 'At Long Last Love', bend an ear to Peter Lawford wrestling with 'A Fella with an Umbrella'. SG

East Is East

(1999, GB, 96 min)
d Damien O'Donnell. *p* Leslee Udwin. *sc* Ayub Khan-Din. *ph* Brian Tufano. *ed* Michael Parker. *pd* Tom Conroy. *m* Deborah Mollison. *cast* Om Puri, Linda Bassett, Jordan Routledge, Archie Panjabi, Emil Marwa, Chris Bisson, Jimi Mistry, Raji James.

●In focusing on the experiences and conflicting hopes of Asians living in the north of England, Ayub Khan-Din's serio-comic script bears some resemblance to *My Son the Fanatic*. Set in Salford in 1971, it tells of a family mustering forces to rebel against their sternly patriarchal father and his insistence they submit to traditional arranged marriages. While some of the humour is considerably broader than that in the Kureishi adaptation, and while director O'Donnell never matches the tenderness Prayad brought to the scenes between Puri and Rachel Griffiths, this is a very decent debut indeed, full of neat insights into '70s Britain, endowed with engagingly profane dialogue, and blessed with another terrific turn from Puri. GA

East LA

see My Family

East of Eden

(1955, US, 115 min)
d/p Elia Kazan. *sc* Paul Osborn. *ph* Ted McCord. *ed* Owen Marks. *ad* James Basevi, Malcolm Bert. *m* Leonard Rosenman. *cast* James Dean, Raymond Massey, Julie Harris, Richard Davalos, Jo Van Fleet, Burl Ives, Albert Dekker.

●Notable mainly for the electrically emotional scenes between Massey as the stiff, stern patriarch, and Dean as the rejected 'bad' son, Kazan's adaptation of Steinbeck's novel, about the rivalry between two teenage boys for the love of their father, is as long-winded and bloated with biblical allegory as the original. That said, it's a film of great performances, atmospheric photography, and a sure sense of period and place (the California farmlands at the time of World War I). A pity, however, about Leonard Rosenman's dreary score, which goes way over the top in attempting to underline the intensity of the various familial conflicts. GA

East of Elephant Rock

(1976, GB, 92 min)
d Don Boyd. *p* Don Boyd, Gerry Harrison, Richard Boyle. *sc* Don Boyd. *ph* Keith Goddard. *ed* Humphrey Dixon. *m* Peter Skellern. *cast* John Hurt, Jeremy Kemp, Judi Bowker, Christopher Cazenove, Anton Rodgers, Tariq Yunus, Vajira.

●Old Hollywood traditions hang heavy and ridiculous over this depressingly redundant sample of British independent cinema. It's a colonial romantic tragedy, set somewhere in South East Asia during 1948. In place of people like Gable, Harlow or Bette Davis, a cast of British stalwarts gamely beat their breasts over sexual and racial problems brought to the boil by the philandering of Embassy secretary Hurt, whose mistresses include a native girl and the far from native wife of a plantation owner. Boyd's direction revives antique clichés like newspaper headlines spinning into close-up to pull the plot forward, but nothing seems likely to pull the audience out of its slumbers. Peter Skellern's score provides a parallel musical pastiche, and the photography recalls ads for Bacardi and Coke. GB

East of Sumatra

(1953, US, 82 min)
d Budd Boetticher. *p* Albert J Cohen. *sc* Frank Gill Jr. *ph* Clifford Stine. *ed* Virgil W Vogel. *ad* Bernard Herzbrun, Robert Boyle. *m* Joseph Gershenson. *cast* Jeff Chandler, Marilyn Maxwell, Anthony Quinn, Suzan Ball, Peter Graves, John Sutton.

●A striking opening sequence has Chandler, a ruthlessly efficient mining engineer, summarily shoot a member of his crew for turning up drunk and endangering lives on the site by playing silly games with dynamite. When the crew is packed off to prospect on a remote Pacific island, budget limitations begin to show in the terrible backdrop of rocks and jungle as their plane lands; and before too long, box-office considerations loom large in the curvaceous shape of a jungle princess disporting herself in a rock pool. The Hawksian theme nevertheless survives, sporadically taking fire in the mutually respectful relationship between Chandler and the island's king (Quinn), a man of honour and some civilisation, who has ceded the mineral rights against a promise of medical supplies for his people. When the penny-pinching head office decides to palm off some tacky trade goods instead, the jungle drums naturally begin to throb and poisoned darts to fly. It's a typical concoction, in other words, not without its moments thanks to Boetticher, with excellent performances from Chandler and Quinn. TM

East of the Rising Sun

see Malaya

East Palace, West Palace (Dong Gong Xi Gong)

(1996, China, 94 min)
d/p Zhang Yuan. *sc* Wang Xiaobo, Zhang Yuan. *ph* Zhang Jian. *ed* Vincent Levy. *pd* An Bing. *m* Xiang Min. *cast* Hu Jun, Si Han, Liu Yuxiao, Lu Rong, Ma Wen, Wang Quan.

●The most daring and achieved of all the 'illegal' independent films made in China in the '90s – and quite probably the last, since it prompted the Film Bureau to formally outlaw unauthorised production and confiscate Zhang Yuan's passport. A-Lan, a young gay man, is arrested in a Beijing cruising park and held for overnight interrogation by Shi, a macho but latently ambivalent cop. As he describes his life since childhood and his sexual history, it becomes clear that his stories are actually expressions of his desire for the cop. This realisation makes Shi more aggressive. The film is an intense chamber drama with large resonances: its ultimate implication is that the bond between the people and the authorities in China is essentially a sado-masochist one. This is the closest cinema has ever come to the spirit of Jean Genet, closer even than Genet's own *Chant d'amour*. TR

East Side Story

(1997, Ger/US/Fr, 80 min)
d Dana Ranga. *p* Andrew Horn. *sc* Andrew Horn, Dana Ranga. *ph* Mark Daniels. *ed* Guido Krajewski. *with* Erich Gusko, Karin Schröder, Brigitte Ulbrich, Helmut Hanke.

●Romanian Dana Ranga and American Andrew Horn's documentary on the little known story of socialist musicals casts a colourful light on screen life behind the Iron Curtain, a place and time where the pressure on film-makers was to deliver didactic propaganda in the Socialist Realist vein, while light entertainment was frowned on as expensive decadence. Yet it was Stalin, an avid if unpredictable cinephile, who first championed the cause of Soviet musicals, promoting former Eisenstein assistant Grigori Alexandrov's musical comedy *The Jolly Fellows* over the work of frowning ideologues and apparatchiks. Later, East German audiences lapped up such '60s divertissements as *My Wife Wants to Sing* and *Hot Summer*. All in all, though, producing such trifles proved an uphill, thankless task, faced with technical, economic and official constraints, critical disregard and instant oblivion. Ranga and Horn approach their subject with a light, self-effacing touch. NB

East-West (Est-Ouest)

(1999, Fr/Rus/Bulg/Sp, 125 min)
d Régis Wargnier. *p* Yves Marmion. *sc* Sergueï Bodrov, Roustam Ibraguimbekov, Louis Gardel, Régis Wargnier. *ph* Laurent Dailland. *ed* (supervising) Hervé Schneid. *pd* Vladimir Svetozarov, Alexeï Levtchenko. *m* Patrick Doyle. *cast* Sandrine Bonnaire, Oleg Menchikov, Sergei Bodrov Jr, Catherine Deneuve, Tatiana Doguileva, René Feret, Grigori Manoukov, Atanass Atanassov.

●In 1946 Russian emigrants flock back to the USSR, answering Stalin's invitation to help rebuild the ravaged motherland. Docking at Odessa, Dr Alexei (Menchikov) and his French wife Marie (Bonnaire) find, however, that many fellow returnees are sent to labour camps. Alexei's professional status wins the couple and their son a room in a Kiev apartment, but as the grimness of their new lives sinks in, the confiscation of their passports makes return to the West an apparent impossibility. Then a chance encounter with a touring French actress (Deneuve) offers a chink of hope. After the colonial gloss of *Indochine* and *Une Femme Française*, it's a surprise to find director Wargnier shivering under the grey skies of the former Soviet Union; but with this tale of love and betrayal offset by a dark political backdrop, accompanied by Patrick Doyle's grandiose score, it's evident he's taking *Doctor Zhivago* as his new model. If you expect a credible historical drama, this falls short, but as an old-fashioned Hollywood wallow it works rather well. TJ

Easy Living

(1937, US, 91 min, b/w)
d Mitchell Leisen. *p* Arthur Hornblow Jr. *sc* Preston Sturges. *ph* Ted Tetzlaff. *ed* Doane Harrison. *ad* Hans Dreier, Ernst Fegté. *m* Boris Morros. *cast* Jean Arthur, Edward Arnold, Ray Milland, Franklin Pangborn, William Demarest, Luis Alberni.

●Unmistakably scripted by Preston Sturges (stout tycoon falls down stairs; 'I see you're down early today, sir' remarks the imperturbable butler), this irresistible screwball comedy with a dash of Wall Street satire has the penniless Arthur and the pompous Arnold meet cute when his wife's fur coat (thrown out of the window in a marital spat) falls on her head. Subsequently assumed to be the tycoon's mistress and encouraged to live on credit in an extravagance beyond anyone's wildest dreams, she is brought down from her cloud by falling for the poor boy met in an automat diner (Milland), who ironically turns out in best fairytale tradition to be the tycoon's son. Directed by Leisen with his airy elegance, his infallible eye for decor (the outrageous splendours of the hotel suite in which Arthur is installed have to be seen to be believed), and injections of slapstick which must have given Sturges ideas when he came to direct his own movies (in particular the custard-pie food riot in the automat), it is a delight. TM

Easy Living

(1949, US, 77 min, b/w)
d Jacques Tourneur. *p* Robert Sparks. *sc* Charles Schnee. *ph* Harry J Wild. *ed* Frederick Knudtson. *ad* Albert S D'Agostino, Al Herman. *m* Roy Webb. *cast* Victor Mature, Lucille Ball, Lizabeth Scott, Sonny Tufts, Lloyd Nolan, Paul Stewart, Jeff Donnell.

●Scripted by Charles Schnee (*The Bad and the Beautiful, Two Weeks in Another Town*) from an Irwin Shaw story, this might have been another *Sweet Smell of Success* with a lowdown angle on professional sport. Tourneur does his best (always concisely, sometimes brilliantly) as Mature's ageing football star gambles his life to ensure security while his wife (Scott) turns the screw on his troubles by ruthlessly pursuing fame as a designer. But studio interference and script compromises (notably in begging the question of whether the wife screws her way to success, and in treating her ambitions with routine bias) sugar the sourness. TM

Easy Money

(1983, US, 95 min)
d Jim Signorelli. *p* John Nicolella. *sc* Rodney Dangerfield, Michael Endler, PJ O'Rourke, Dennis Blair. *ph* Fred Schuler. *ed* Ronald Roose. *pd* Eugene Lee. *m* Laurence Rosenthal. *cast* Rodney Dangerfield, Joe Pesci, Geraldine Fitzgerald, Candy Azzara, Tom Ewell, Taylor Negron, Jennifer Jason Lee.

●The tale of an all-American slobbo (Dangerfield) who spends his days photographing overweight babies and nights swilling beer, guzzling pizza, gambling, doping and generally whooping it up with his 'regular guy' buddies. When his mother-in-law (cue 1001 ancient jokes) leaves him a fortune, it's with the proviso that he gives up these little pleasures for a whole year. If one fails to give a toss for his ensuing sufferings, it's largely because he is a character so repellent he makes Alf Garnett look like a Salvatian Army sergeant. The fact that it took four writers (among them *National Lampoon*'s PJ O'Rourke) to concoct this pile of doggy-doo riddled with sexism and racism doesn't make it any funnier than woodworm in a cripple's crutch. FL

Easy Rider

(1969, US, 95 min)
d Dennis Hopper. *p* Peter Fonda. *sc* Peter Fonda, Dennis Hopper, Terry Southern. *ph* Laszlo Kovacs. *ed* Donn Cambern. *ad* Jerry Kay. *cast* Peter Fonda, Dennis Hopper, Antonio Mendoza, Phil Spector, Jack Nicholson, Warren Finnerty.

●'Some day I'd like to see some of this country we're travelling through' says one of the fugitive couple in *They Live By Night*. Two decades later, their spiritual children had gone 'underground', discovered dope, rock and road... and a preference for male friendships. In this simplistic amalgam of travelogue and the zoom lens, a beatific Fonda and his mumbling St John go looking for America, financed courtesy of a coke deal with Phil Spector. The film was right about one thing at least: the advent of cocaine as the drug. CPe

Easy Virtue

(1927, GB, 7,300 ft, b/w)
d Alfred Hitchcock. *p* Michael Balcon. *sc* Eliot Stannard. *ph* Claude McDonnell. *ed* Ivor Montagu. *ad* Clifford Pember. *cast* Isabel Jeans, Franklin Dyall, Eric Bransby Williams, Ian Hunter, Robin Irvine, Violet Farebrother.

●Based on a Noël Coward play about the effects of scandal and gossip on a young woman after a much-publicised divorce by her brutal and jealous husband. Though occasional acerbic touches remain, the sections that are drawn directly from the original remain hampered by the loss of Coward's dialogue. But the first half of the film, an addition detailing events only described in the play, is pure Hitchcock, its combination of conciseness and idiosyncrasy demonstrating his mastery of silent narration. A typically bold example is the scene where a proposal of marriage is both made and accepted by telephone without either speaker being shown: Hitchcock traces the conversation via the reactions of the switchboard operator who's eavesdropping on the call. But he's almost certainly right about the final title, which he describes as being the worst he ever wrote. AS

Eat a Bowl of Tea

(1989, US, 103 min)
d Wayne Wang. *p* Tom Sternberg. *sc* Judith Rascoe. *ph* Amir Mokri. *ed* Richard Candib. *pd* Bob Ziembick. *m* Mark Adler. *cast* Victor Wong, Russell Wong, Cora Miao, Eric Tsang Chi Wai, Lau Siu Ming, Wu Ming Yu, Hui Fun.

●New York, in the late '40s: Ben Loy (Russell Wong) is a loyal Chinese-American son, and when he visits his mother in China after the war, he takes advantage of the recently changed US immigration laws and returns to New York with a wife, Mei Oi (Miao), to live in a closed Chinese community almost entirely made up of men (until the end of the war, America forbade male Asian immigrants to bring wives and daughters with them). Their fathers want the couple to be both prosperous and parents, but Ben Loy works so hard he becomes impotent; meanwhile, understandably bored, Mei Oi encounters temptation in the form of a smooth womaniser. Wang's semi-comic romance is a light-hearted account of the problems faced by young lovers in a displaced and oppressively watchful society. It's a charming rather than probing film, with Wang successfully focusing attention on performances and period atmosphere rather than on moral nuance. Although rather more emotional pain would not have gone amiss, the result is enjoyable, assured and stylish. GA

Eat Drink Man Woman (Yinshi Nan Nu)

(1994, Tai, 124 min)
d Ang Lee. *p* Hsu Li-Kong. *sc* Hui-Ling Wang, Ang Lee, James Schamus. *ph* Jong Lin. *ed* Tim Squyres. *pd* Fu-Hsiung. *m* Mader. *cast* Sihung Lung, Kuei-Mei Tang, Yu-Wen Wang, Chien-Lien Wu, Winston Chao, Sylvia Chang, Ah-Leh Gua.

●Comedy drama about a widower and his three unmarried daughters. Mr Chu, a retired Taipei chef, would like his girls to leave home, but is too repressed and stubborn to communicate frankly with them, relying instead on the ritual Sunday dinners he serves up to preserve a sense of family. They, however, feel guilty about their own needs: Jia-Jen, a Christian teacher, nursing a broken heart and covert desire for the sports coach; Jia-Chien, a career woman into casual sex with her ex; and the youngest, Jia-Ning who works in a burger-joint and gets on uncomfortably well with a friend's boyfriend. Which daughter, if any, will stay with Dad? Or will he succumb to predatory widow Mrs Liang – if his health holds out? Tasty ingredients (Sihung Lung's Mr Chu and Chien-Lien Wu's Jia-Chien are especially good), but the food metaphor never carries weight, and the characterisations are too shallow to lend the film emotional punch. GA

Eaten Alive

see Death Trap

Eating Air (Zhi Feng)

(1999, Singapore, 100 min)
d Kelvin Tong, Jasmine Ng. *p* Loraine Frugniet, Mabelyn Ow. *sc* Kelvin Tong, Jasmine Ng. *ph* Lucas Jodogne, Mary Van Kets. *ed* Jasmine Ng. *cast* Benjamin Heng, Alvina Toh, Joseph Cheong, Andy Chang, Ferris Yeo.

●Another valiant attempt to kickstart Singaporean film culture, focused (like Eric Khoo's films) on characters who aren't exactly model citizens of the nanny state. This lot smoke, get drunk, wear tattoos, trade in pirated porno VCDs, drive dangerously on motorbikes and, in one case, fantasise about slaughtering parents. Amid the flow of juvenile delinquent pranks, a shy girl stuck in a boring shopping mall job makes friends with a boy who rides a second-hand 125cc – simply because she likes racing through the night on his pillion. Both the performances and the direction have a rough and ready charm. It's a gusty, physical movie, in no way as constipated as the city it describes. And it's cut to a quite tasty alt-rock beat. TR

Eating Raoul

(1982, US, 83 min)
d Paul Bartel. *p* Anne Kimmel. *sc* Richard Blackburn, Paul Bartel. *ph* Gary Thieltges. *ed* Alan Toomayan. *pd* Robert Schulenberg. *cast* Paul Bartel, Mary Woronov, Robert Beltran, Susan Saiger, Ed Begley Jr, Buck Henry.

●The most delicious blackly comic collision of sex, food and murder, Bartel's film arrives as a delightful surprise from the former court jester of Roger Corman's exploitation stable. Featuring Bartel himself and his frequent B-queen, Woronov, as the Blands, innocently stranded amid the hedonist detritus of LA, dreaming (like their Hollywood forebears, the Blandings) of rural retreat, Paul and Mary's

Country Kitchen. And dreaming vainly, until 'accidental' homicide propels them into a scheme to exploit carnal as well as culinary appetites, luring disposable perverts to a deadpan doom with the haphazard help and hindrance of such figures as Doris the Dominatrix and Hispanic hustler Raoul. The style stays straight-faced, the more to crease ours with the disparity between sick joke frenetics and a gentle, unruffled sitcom sensibility. A genuine treat for civilised cannibals. PT

Eat My Dust!

(1976, US, 89 min)
d Charles B Griffith. *p* Roger Corman. *sc* Charles B Griffith. *ph* Eric Saarinen. *ed* Tina Hirsch. *ad* Peter Jamison. *m* David Grisman. *cast* Ron Howard, Christopher Norris, Warren Kemmerling, Dave Madden, Robert Broyles, Evelyn Russell.

●With the camera on the bumper and David Grisman's country swing on the soundtrack, the opening sequence of this movie raises false hopes that it will offer some sort of distillation of the 'hot-car' cycle put out by exploitation studio New World. Griffith's directorial debut – after 20 years of scripting for Corman – does deliver the expected race/chase/demolition derby mayhem, but every time the focus switches to Ron Howard's adolescent romantic worries, it stalls. Strange that a writer's movie should rely so heavily on stunting and second unit work; sad that it does so little new with its regulation good ol' boys and dumb cops. PT

Eat the Peach

(1986, Ire, 95 min)
d Peter Ormrod. *p* John Kelleher. *sc* Peter Ormrod, John Kelleher. *ph* Arthur G Wooster. *ed* J Patrick Duffner. *pd* David Wilson. *m* Donal Lunny. *cast* Stephen Brennan, Eamon Morrissey, Catherine Byrne, Niall Toibin, Joe Lynch, Tony Doyle.

●When their Japanese employers decide to up sticks and take their jobs with them, are brothers-in-law Arthur (Morrissey) and Vinnie (Brennan) the type to sit and mope? Nope! It takes only a viewing of Elvis risking life and limb motorcycling around the Wall of Death in *Roustabout* for them to decide to employ their idle hours erecting their very own Wall (on Arthur's wife's vegetable plot). Money's the problem (not to mention Arthur's wife, who ups sticks and legs it too), so there's nothing to it but a stint of bootlegging across the nearby border to raise the readies, finish the job, and wait for the crowds we know will never come. Within the modest dimensions of his small budget, Ormrod succeeds remarkably well, with a deft touch, a light heart, and not a trace of patronising, to give a true human measure to the dreams and ambitions, failures and disappointments of this collection of likeable loonies. Eat the peach and hear the mermaids sing. WH

Eat the Rich

(1987, GB, 98 min)
d Peter Richardson. *p* Tim Van Rellim. *sc* Peter Richardson, Pete Richens. *ph* Witold Stok. *ed* Chris Ridsdale. *ad* Caroline Amies. *m* Simon Brint, Roland Rivron. *cast* Ronald Allen, Sandra Dorne, Jimmy Fagg, Lemmy, Lanah Pellay, Nosher Powell, Fiona Richmond, Ron Tarr, Robbie Coltrane, Paul McCartney, Ruby Wax, Jennifer Saunders.

●In this second feature from the Comic Strip team (following *The Supergrass*), genderless black waiter Pellay takes to the road to lead a People's Revolution, while arch-adversary Powell, a fascistic East End tough turned Home Secretary, bids for top office through headlines in the *Sun*. True to *Comic Strip* form, the film lampoons the lunacy of every social group it touches (political extremists, civil servants, the press, the royals, the rich, the poor); make what you will of the politics, as a series of sketches it delivers the laughs. Powell turns in one of the funniest performances of the year, and Pellay's transformation of a swank London restaurant into an eatery on the lines of a pie shop is not to be missed. SGo

Eau Froide, L' (Cold Water)

(1994, Fr, 92 min)
d Olivier Assayas. *p* Georges Benayoun, Paul Rozenberg. *sc* Olivier Assayas. *ph* Denis Lenoir. *ed* Luc Barnier. *ad* Gilbert Gagneux. *cast* Virginie Ledoyen, Cyprien Fouquet, Laszlo Szabo, Jean-Pierre Darroussin.

●Commissioned as part of a series in which directors went back to their adolescence, this is a brave, moving film, set in the outskirts of Paris in 1972. It's a portrait of two delinquents, both from broken homes, and both about to be packed off to institutional care. Christine is on the verge of a mental breakdown, and Gilles, who buys dynamite for kicks, is headed for boarding school. Assayas shoots with a hand-held camera and favours cold, blue lighting and diagetic sound. He's rewarded with two resolutely natural, unshowy performances by Ledoyen and Fouquet, and a tremendous emotional pull. The centrepiece is a marvellously sustained midnight party sequence (a requirement of the series), where a horde of teens group, groove and get off to the sounds of Janis Joplin, Creedence Clearwater Revival, Leonard Cohen and Alice Cooper. Recommended. TCh

Ebirah – Terror of the Deep (Nankai no Daiketto)

(1966, Jap, 86 min)
d Jun Fukuda. *sc* Shinichi Sekizawa. *ph* Kazuo Yamada. *ad* Takeo Kita. *m* Masaru Sato. *cast* Akira Takarada, Toru Watanabe, Hideo Sunazuka, Kumi Mizuno, Jun Tazaki.

●The film's title notwithstanding, the real star of this Toho production is Godzilla, who – with the aid of another friendly monster, Mothra – puts paid to Ebirah ('an enormous crab' that looks very much like a boiled lobster) and the hordes of The Red Bamboo, a SMERSH-like organisation intent on world domination, and rescues various humans in distress. PH

Echo Park

(1985, Aus, 89 min)
d Robert Dornhelm. *p* Walter Shenson. *sc* Michael Ventura. *ph* Karl Kofler. *ed* Ingrid Koller. *ad* Bernt Capra. *m* David Ricketts. *cast* Susan Dey, Tom Hulce, Michael Bowen, Christopher Walker, Shirley Jo Finney, Heinrich Schweiger.

●An aspirant actress turned stripagrammer, her songwriting pizza-delivery-boy lodger, and the Austrian body-builder neighbour (not a hundred umlauts from one Arnold S) bid fair to become the *Jules et Jim* of the seedy clapboard milieu of suburban LA. Romanian-born, Vienna-trained Dornhelm has the quirky mitteleuropäisch eye (cf Milos Forman) for the freaks and oddities of American life. Tom Hulce, a long way from *Amadeus,* reveals a splendidly individual comic presence; and the hopes, shocks, sulks and loyalties of this free-wheeling trio are a small but real delight. MHoy

Eclipse

(1976, GB, 85 min)
d Simon Perry. *p* David Munro. *sc* Simon Perry. *ph* Mike Berwick. *ed* Norman Wanstall. *ad* Humphrey Jaeger. *m* Adrian Wagner. *cast* Tom Conti, Gay Hamilton, Gavin Wallace, Paul Kermack, David Steuart, Jennie Paul, Patrick Cadell.

●Twin brothers take a small boat out into the Atlantic to watch a lunar eclipse. The body of one is subsequently found on the beach. Showing a fine eye for domestic detail (the main action occurs over Christmas in an isolated cliffside house occupied by the dead brother's widow, where the surviving brother broods over his twin and their relationship), Simon Perry's palpably well-crafted first feature leaves the viewer to decide whether the death was murder or an accident. Despite occasional over-strong symbols, the result is an intelligent attempt to breach the philistine bastions of British commercial cinema. JPy

Eclipse

(1994, Can, 95 min, col & b/w)
d Jeremy Podeswa. *p* Camelia Frieberg, Jeremy Podeswa. *sc* Jeremy Podeswa. *ph* Miroslaw Baszak. *ed* Susan Maggi. *ad* Tamara Deverell. *m* Ernie Tollar. *cast* Von Flores, John Gilbert, Pascale Monpetit, Manuel Aranguiz, Maria Del Mar, Greg Ellwand, Matthew Ferguson.

●This debut feature updates the La Ronde idea of a chain of lovers, but with a multi-cultural mix of straight, bi and gay characters and without the focus on the etiquettes of romance and seduction. From the opening financial transaction between a middle-aged businessman and an Asian rent boy, it's clear that the characters will all be more or less up-front about their sex drives. What's difficult for them is not the quick squelch of the sex act itself, but the feelings that follow: the fears, the insecurities, the expectations that the encounter will be either forgotten or parlayed into something more substantial and durable. The same anxieties that haunt *La Ronde*, in fact. Each of the ten sexual encounters is credible and superbly acted, but the film really takes off around halfway with the episode involving a nervous immigration lawyer and an angelic boy student. This and subsequent scenes combine novelistic depth with short-story concision: entire lifetimes of unspoken longings and unthought assumptions are laid bare with remarkable skill. The acute wit of the sex scenes isn't, however, always present in the linking material, which tries to conjure an impending solar eclipse into a grand metaphor, but doesn't really make it stick. TR

Eclipse, The (L'Eclisse)

(1962, It/Fr, 125 min, b/w)
d Michelangelo Antonioni. *p* Robert Hakim, Raymond Hakim. *sc* Michaelangelo Antonioni, Tonino Guerra, Elio Bartolini, Ottiero Ottieri. *ph* Gianni Di Venanzo. *ed* Eraldo Da Roma. *ad* Piero Poletto. *m* Giovanni Fusco. *cast* Monica Vitti, Alain Delon, Francisco Rabal, Lilla Brignone, Rossana Rory, Louis Seigner.

●With *L'Avventura* and *La Notte*, *L'Eclisse* completes an Antonioni trilogy on doomed relationships in a fractured world. This time, Vitti has a traumatic bust-up with the bookish Rabal, and apathetically lets herself get involved with brash young stockbroker Delon. At first glance it's a more formally innovative movie than its predecessors (witness the ending: a long montage that doesn't show the principal characters), but it's underpinned by the same hackneyed symbolism: dawn and nightfall, construction sites, the Bomb, 'ethnic' spontaneity and the rest. Anyone disenchanted with the vacuity of later Antonioni will find the seeds of their dissatisfaction well-rooted in the mannerism and facile anguish evident here. TR

Ecole de la Chair, L' (The School of Flesh)

(1998, Fr/Bel, 101 min)
d Benoît Jacquot. *p* Fabienne Vonier. *sc* Jacques Fiéschi. *ph* Caroline Champetier. *ed* Luc Barnier. *ad* Katia Wyszkop. *cast* Isabelle Huppert, Vincent Martinez, Vincent Lindon, Marthe Keller, François Berléand, Jean-Claude Dauphin, Jean-Louis Richard.

●Huppert's gaze of amused but benevolent appraisal is also the director's in this adaptation of a Mishima novel concerning the relationship between a well-to-do woman in her 40s and a callow young hustler. Soap addicts looking to have their nerves jangled by a sex 'n' rows opus will be disappointed. What interests Jacquot is the complex of power play and genuine affection between the two characters, which he documents in a cool, thoroughly adult manner. Huppert is formidable. BBa

Ecole des Facteurs, L' (School for Postmen)

(1947, Fr, 15 min, b/w)
d Jacques Tati. *p* Fred Orain. *sc* Jacques Tati. *ph* Louis Félix. *ed* Marcel Moreau. *m* Jean Yatove. *cast* Jacques Tati, Paul Demange.

●Tati took no chances with his first feature, *Jour de Fête*. He'd developed his rural postman character in cabaret, fine-tuning the choreography of all those bike-and-satchel routines; and, as we see here, he even contrived a preliminary draft in the comparative privacy of a short film. No doubt something was learned, but his caricature of self-absorption, his vividly absurd miming of determination, pleasure, puzzlement and so on are already down pat; only the postman's dance in the café works better in this version, perhaps because here he dances alone. Tati deserved the happy accident whereby an extra dimension was added to the farce, with that towering frame and broad backside irresistibly recalling General de Gaulle. BBa

Ecoute Voir... (See Here My Love)

(1978, Fr, 110 min)
d Hugo Santiago. *sc* Claude Ollier, Hugo Santiago. *ph* Ricardo Aronovich, Philippe Brun. *ed* Alberto Yaccelini. *ad* Emilio Carcano. *m* Michel Portal. *cast* Catherine Deneuve, Sami Frey, Florence Delay, Anne Parillaud, Didier Haudepin, Antoine Vitez, Jean-François Stévenin.

● A weird political thriller, this features Deneuve as a private eye (part Emma Peel, part Bogart), investigating a group practising thought control via doctored radio waves, shuffling trench-coated through a country house mystery. Not entirely free of the metaphysical riddles that swamped the earlier work of Argentinian exile and Borges enthusiast Santiago, this hit-and-miss effort is at least shot with flair and works the senses (particularly by way of its complex stereo soundtrack) without ever quite making sense itself. PT

Ecstasy

see Extase

Eddie

(1996, US, 101 min)
d Steve Rash. *p* David Permut, Mark Burg. *sc* Jon Connolly, David Louka, Eric Champnella, Keith Mitchell, Steve Zacharias, Jeff Buhai. *ph* Victor J Kemper. *ed* Richard Halsey. *pd* Dan Davis. *m* Stanley Clarke. *cast* Whoopi Goldberg, Frank Langella, Dennis Farina, Richard Jenkins, Lisa Ann Walter, John Benjamin Hickey, Malik Sealy.

● Trying to add bounce to her well worn flounce, Whoopi's the eponymous, mouthy basketball fan who's caught up in the machinations of rhinestone cowboy Wild Bill (Langella). Bill has been brought in to save New York's ailing basketball team, the Knicks, and plucks Eddie from the crowd to act as a rinky-dink mascot coach. But she's the real thing – grabs a'hold of those NBA boys, shakes 'em up and you can guess the rest. They're all present and correct, the elements of a Goldberg vehicle we've come to know and dread. What saves the film from abomination is the basketball. It may not look good (TV values reign), but the floor pounding games are edited to create real rushes of glee. The NBA stars, too, are superb, particularly real-life hoop-dreamer Sealy as arrogant golden boy Stacy Patton. CO'Su

Eddie and the Cruisers

(1983, US, 95 min)
d Martin Davidson. *p* Joseph Brooks, Robert K Lifton. *sc* Martin Davidson, Arlene Davidson. *ph* Fred Murphy. *ed* Priscilla Nedd. *ad* Gary Weist. *m* John Cafferty. *cast* Tom Berenger, Michael Paré, Joe Pantoliano, Matthew Laurance, Helen Schneider, Ellen Barkin.

● 1964. The band are poised for national success when singer Eddie drives his car off a bridge. His body is never found… cue, 20 years later, the inevitable Cruisers revival, and a rock'n'roll mystery ensues with renewed speculation over the singer's fate. Overlong live sequences of the band threaten to take over from the fairly reasonable storyline, and relationships don't have the chance to develop. Add to this the fact that the band sound more like Springsteen than Del Shannon, and it all seems a little unrealistic. Clothes and settings, too, seem strangely anonymous. Where it works is in the present, and a sharper look at how various band members had made out 20 years on would have made it still more interesting. Low key and, despite the music, rather likeable. GO

Eddie Murphy Raw

(1987, US, 90 min)
d Robert Townsend. *p* Robert D Wachs, Keenen Ivory Wayans. *ph* Ernest Dickerson. *ed* Lisa Day. *pd* Wynn Thomas. *with* Eddie Murphy.

● In an immaculate record of his one-man show, the self-appointed superstud levels his sights against anyone who isn't black, male or Murphy. Women come in for more than their fair share of the offensive, as castrating bitches whose duty is to fuck husbands and cook burgers for hungry sons; the predatory infidelities of men, however, would seem excusable through Nature, Destiny, or simply because it's Okay with Eddie. Lisping gays, *Rocky*-obsessed Italians, whites in general, and Murphy's rivals are also subject to the foul-mouthed brew of complaint and contempt. It's impossible to deny the virtuosity of his non-stop delivery, but the relentless macho onslaught sadly lacks the saving grace of Richard Pryor's self-irony. Even if Murphy doesn't mean what he says (and he probably does), laughs are forestalled by the feeling that it's all too mechanically manipulative. GA

Eden Valley

(1994, GB, 95 min)
d/p/sc Richard Grassick, Ellin Hare, Sirkka-Liisa Konttinen, Murray Martin, Pat McCarthy, Lorna Powell, Peter Roberts. *m* Richard Grassick, Ellin Hare, Sirkka-Liisa Konttinen, Murray Martin, Pat McCarthy, Lorna Powell, Peter Roberts, Aladair Robertson, Graham Raine. *cast* Brian Hogg, Darren Bell, Mike Elliott, Jimmy Killeen, Mo Harold, Amber Styles.

● When Billy (Bell), a listless, disaffected teenager from a neglected housing estate, is put on probation for stealing drugs from a chemist's, his mother sends him to the country to stay with his dad Hoggy (Brian Hogg), who left the family some ten years earlier to live in a caravan and raise horses for harness-racing. Interested only in raves, drugs and music, Billy remains resolutely unimpressed by his dad's home, his passion for racing, and the working-class sense of honour that impels him to work on, however cold the wind that blows over the snowy hills of Co Durham. But is this harsh new life better than serving time? Once again, the Amber Production Team has produced a film notable for its authenticity, its muscular, naturalistic performances, and its lack of sentimentality. The film is marked by a droll humour, a celebratory sense of community, and a responsiveness to nature and landscape. A British film made with limited resources standing foursquare on its own ground. GA

Edge, The

(1997, US, 117 min)
d Lee Tamahori. *p* Art Linson. *sc* David Mamet. *ph* Donald McAlpine. *ed* Neil Travis. *pd* Wolf Kroeger. *m* Jerry Goldsmith. *cast* Anthony Hopkins, Alec Baldwin, Elle Macpherson, Harold Perrineau, LQ Jones, Kathleen Wilhoite.

● Getting back to nature in the Alaskan hinterland, billionaire Charles Morse (Hopkins) peruses a tattered book, *Lost in the Wild*. Soon a plane crash allows him to show off his encyclopedic memory, coping with shame, fear, hunger and the elements, plus a smarmy photographer (Baldwin) and his wounded assistant (Perrineau, who should have 'Dead Meat' tattooed on his forehead). Moreover, there's a Kodiak bear on their trail. This boasts an original screenplay by David Mamet and enough outdoor pursuit to fill a men's monthly for a year. They've even worked in a cameo by Elle Macpherson as the wife who may or may not be fooling around behind Morse's back. This last plot wrinkle gives the boys something to thrash out. The movie's on stronger ground with the rudiments of survivalism, in particular the long central battle with the bear, so exciting it makes everything afterwards seem anti-climactic. Hopkins keeps his hamminess in check, and Baldwin finds layers of insidious charm, frailty and menace. TCh

Ed Gein

(2000, US, 89 min)
d Chuck Parello. *p* Michael Muscal, Hamish McAlpine. *sc* Stephen Johnston. *ph* Vanja Cernjul. *ed* Elena Maganini. *pd* Mark Harper. *m* Robert McNaughton. *cast* Steve Railsback, Carrie Snodgress, Carol Mansell, Sally Champlin, Steve Blackwood, Nancy Lineham Charles, Bill Cross, Ryan Thomas Brockington, Austin James Peck.

● Ever since 'Wisconsin necrophile' Ed Gein first made the news at the time of his arrest in 1957, he's remained a figure of such grisly fascination that film-makers have felt it viable to revisit his memorably macabre exploits at regular intervals. *Psycho* is merely the finest, most famous film to use his crimes for inspiration; others include *The Texas Chain Saw Massacre*, *Deranged* (until now most faithful to the facts) and *The Silence of the Lambs*. Here the director never flinches from providing the requisite disturbing images, but his is a surprisingly sober response to a potentially salacious subject. After shy, gentle Ed (Railsback – Charlie Manson in *Helter Skelter*) disinters a woman from the local cemetery, we proceed, via key encounters (friendly barmaid, sympathetic shopkeeper) and flashbacks and fantasies mostly featuring his nine-years-dead but still dangerously influential religious-nut mom (Snodgress), to the cops' discovery of the mausoleum, abattoir, ossuary, offbeat eatery, eccentric furniture warehouse and walk-in wardrobe that the decrepit family farmhouse had become. As with the best scenes of *Deranged*, the conjunction of colourful case history, odd impulses, gallows humour, low budget austerity and genuinely grotesque iconography produces a felicitous and engaging variant of American Gothic. GA

Edge of Darkness

(1943, US, 120 min. b/w)
d Lewis Milestone. *p* Henry Blanke. *sc* Robert Rossen. *ph* Sid Hickcox. *ed* David Weisbart. *ad* Robert M Haas. *m* Franz Waxman. *cast* Errol Flynn, Ann Sheridan, Walter Huston, Nancy Coleman, Helmut Dantine, Judith Anderson, Rutgh Gordon.

● WWII propaganda piece, scripted by Robert Rossen, paying tribute to the Norwegian resistance movement, which now appears too worthy for even the most die-hard action fancier. Flynn was then getting over the scandal surrounding his trial for statutory rape, so it's not surprising, perhaps, that he looks as though he'd rather be elsewhere.

Edge of Doom (aka Stronger Than Fear)

(1950, US, 96 min, b/w)
d Mark Robson. *p* Samuel Goldwyn. *sc* Philip Yordan. *ph* Harry Stradling. *ed* Daniel Mandell. *ad* Richard Day. *m* Hugo Friedhofer. *cast* Farley Granger, Dana Andrews, Joan Evans, Robert Keith, Paul Stewart, Mala Powers, Adele Jergens, Mabel Paige.

● Goldwyn-produced religious trumpery, with Granger indulging heavily sulky histrionics as a young man driven to murder a priest when, with dad already refused consecrated burial as a suicide, he can't raise the money (or persuade the church) to bury mom with suitably ostentatious solemnity. Beautifully shot in *noir* terms by Harry Stradling as Granger wanders the seamy side of the city on his dark night of the soul, it might have been more effective had Goldwyn not hired Ben Hecht to expand Andrews' role (as the priest who realises that Granger did the killing, and tries to persuade him to relieve his torment by confessing) after the New York opening. Now saddled with prologue and epilogue in which Andrews tells the story in flashback to a young priest with 'doubts' (by way of restoring his faith, as it did his own, though why remains a mystery), the whole thing is impossibly sententious. TM

Edge of Night (Afti i Nighita Meni)

(2000, Greece, 117 min)
d/p Nikos Panagiotopoulos. *sc* Nikos Panagiotopoulos, Thanos Alexandris. *ph* Aris Stavrou. *ed* Giannis Tsitsopoulos. *ad* Giorgos Andritsogiannis. *m* Stamatis Kraounakis. *cast* Nikos Kouris, Athina Maximou, Zoe Nalbanti.

● The primary image of this drama is that of the planes arriving at and departing from Athens airport. 'Yogurt' salesman Andreas, ever offering classical quotes gleaned from alcoholic customer, 'The Professor', knows the destination of every one, but is wise enough to know these are destinations he may never visit. Love-of-his -life Stella, on the other hand, is determined to become a singer even if it means hiking off to godforsaken night clubs in the back of beyond. Do these two have a future? Elegantly shot, atmospheric, on the whole, and clearly half in love with the sleazy night club milieu, this makes up for its occasional indulgence and melodramatic posturing, with a nice dramatisation of the two-way tussle of convention and adventure for the hearts of the new generation of young Greeks, both male and female. Songs are by Hadjidakis, Spanos and Kraounakis. WH

Edge of Sanity

(1988, US, 90 min)
d Gerard Kikoine. *p* Edward Simons, Harry Alan Towers. *sc* JP Felix, Ron Haley. *ph* Tony Spratling. *ed* Malcolm Cooke. *pd* Jean Charles Dedieu. *m* Frederick Talgorn. *cast* Anthony Perkins, Glynis Barber, Sarah Maur-Thorp, David Lodge, Ben Cole, Ray Jewers.

● Although allegedly based on Stevenson's classic horror tale, *The Strange Case of Dr Jekyll and Mr Hyde*, this tawdry slasher pic seems more like an attempt to cash in on 1988's Jack the Ripper centenary. After inhaling the fumes from a substance he has been using on a laboratory monkey, Dr Jekyll is transformed into his baser alter ego, though he looks more a seasick Dr Caligari than a bestial Mr Hyde. Perkins doesn't so much chew up the cardboard scenery as swallow it whole, as his debauched Hyde stalks the dark streets and lurid brothels in search of sensual pleasures and potential victims. The tarts all wear fetishistic underwear, and there is some blasphemous stuff involving a crucified client and a writhing nun, but Stevenson's underlying allegory is itself tortured to death by the atrocious dialogue, wooden acting, and inept direction. NF

Edge of Terror

see Wind, The

Edge of the City (aka A Man Is Ten Feet Tall)

(1957, US, 85 min, b/w)
d Martin Ritt. *p* David Susskind. *sc* Robert Alan Aurthur. *ph* Joseph Brun. *ed* Sidney Meyers. *ad* Richard Sylbert. *m* Leonard Rosenman. *cast* John Cassavetes, Sidney Poitier, Jack Warden, Kathleen Maguire, Ruby Dee, Ruth White, Robert Simon.

●Ritt's first feature, scripted by Robert Alan Aurthur from his own teleplay *A Man is Ten Feet Tall*. Cassavetes and Poitier become friends down on the waterfront. Cassavetes is the mixed-up, insecure white boy picked on by the brutal, bigoted foreman/union racketeer (Warden); Poitier the wiser, maturer black who defends him (at the cost of his life) in an attempt to teach him to stand up for the right thing. A worthy enough piece, well acted and making excellent use of locations on the New York docks; but when you get down to it, no less dramatically artificial than *On the Town*, and this boy Poitier is whiter than white. TCh

Edge of the World, The

(1937, GB, 81 min, b/w)
d Michael Powell. *p* Joe Rock. *sc* Michael Powell. *ph* Ernest Palmer, Skeets Kelly, Monty Berman. *ed* Derek Twist. *m* WL Williamson. *cast* Niall MacGinnis, John Laurie, Belle Chrystall, Finlay Currie, Eric Berry, Grant Sutherland.

●Powell's first major movie, shot on location and as much an account of the harshness of life on the isolated Shetland Isles as the story of two friends torn apart by the elements they struggle against for sustenance. In an interesting move in 1978, Powell was commissioned by BBC TV to return to the island of Foula and film a new introduction and epilogue to his original film. The resulting 'bookends', in colour, give *Edge of the World* (retitled *Return to the Edge of the World*) even greater strength, pushing the story further back and emphasising the mysterious and frightening poetry that Powell captures in his search for images that define the waywardness of nature. (The film was later recut by Powell to 65 minutes.) PH

Edie & Pen

(1996, US, 97 min)
d Matthew Irmas. *p* Matthew Irmas, Victoria Tennant. *sc* Victoria Tennant. *ph* Alicia Weber. *ed* Michael Ruscio. *pd* Jon Gary Steele. *m* Shawn Colvin. *cast* Stockard Channing, Jennifer Tilly, Scott Glenn, Stuart Wilson, Chris Sarandon, Randy Travis, Michael McKean, Beverly D'Angelo, Louise Fletcher, Martin Mull.

●Edie (Tilly) and Pen (Channing) meet in Reno. They're both getting divorced, but Edie's marriage lasted only a fortnight, and she's planning to remarry the very next day, while Pen's still in love with her husband of ten years. Together, they embark on an ill-advised nocturnal adventure with Harry, a womanising cowboy (Glenn). This post-romantic comedy has a lot of charm. The direction leaves something to be desired, but Victoria Tennant's script is witty and well structured without seeming mechanical, and cameos from the likes of McKean, D'Angelo, Mull and Travis keep things ticking over nicely. Channing and Glenn work up an easy rapport, and it's another notch in Tilly's promising career. TCh

Edipo Re

see Oedipus Rex

Edison the Man

(1940, US, 107 min, b/w)
d Clarence Brown. *p* John W Considine Jr. *sc* Talbot Jennings, Bradbury Foote, Hugo Butler, Dore Schary. *ph* Harold Rosson. *ed* Frederick Y Smith. *ad* Cedric Gibbons. *m* Herbert Stothart. *cast* Spencer Tracy, Rita Johnson, Lynne Overman, Charles Coburn, Gene Lockhart, Henry Travers.

●Glossily polished biopic made as a sequel to *Young Tom Edison*, with Tracy in suitably earnest form, struggling through the trials and tribulations of poverty and neglect en route to inventing the light bulb. Something of a whitewash job, it never begins to suggest the stubborn and sometimes shortsighted side to the inventor's character that led him, for example, first to fail to recognise the potential of his invention of the movie camera and projector, and secondly, to hang so firmly on to his patent that the movie medium was in thrall to him for many years. GA

Edith and Marcel (Edith et Marcel)

(1983, Fr, 140 min)
d Claude Lelouch. *p* Tania Zazulinsky. *sc* Claude Lelouch. *ph* Jean Boffety. *ed* Hugues Darmois, Sandrine Péry. *ad* Jaques Bufnoir. *m* Francis Lai.*cast* Evelyne Bouix, Jacques Villeret, Francis Huster, Jean-Claude Brialy, Jean Bouise, Marcel Cerdan Jr, Charles Aznavour, Jacques Villeret, Francis Huster.

●The story of France's celebrated ill-fated lovers – Piaf the tremulous songbird and Cerdan the world welterweight boxing champ – is obviously ripe movie material, but not for Lelouch the conventional biopic. With characteristic lateral thinking, he intercuts the couple's stormy relationship (the boxer's own son a last-minute replacement for the late Patrick Dewaere) with the fictional romance between a shy country girl (Bouix plays both the key female roles) and a podgy soldier, who follow Piaf and Cerdan's fortunes through the media like millions of their countryfolk. Lelouch's whirling camera leads them all a merry dance, Aznavour keeps popping up as songwriter delivering his newest ditties, while Piaf's original recordings supply much-needed emotional underpinning. It verges on the cherishably daft, but Piaf's heart-rending rendition of 'Hymne à l'Amour', recorded in 1950 the year after Cerdan's death, tells you all you need to know about the couple's passion in a couple of minutes. TJ

EDtv

(1999, US, 123 min)
d Ron Howard. *p* Brian Grazer, Ron Howard. *sc* Lowell Ganz, Babaloo Mandel. *ph* John Schwartzman. *ed* Mike Hill, Dan Hanley. *pd* Michael Corenblith. *m* Randy Edelman. *cast* Matthew McConaughey, Jenna Elfman, Woody Harrelson, Sally Kirkland, Martin Landau, Ellen DeGeneres, Rob Reiner, Dennis Hopper, Elizabeth Hurley.

●Ed (McConaughey) is a big-grinned lunk, overshadowed by his loud brother (Harrelson). But when Ed's chosen to star on a 'live' 24-hour TV soap, he's faced with a new problem: as the centre of attention, he loses all control. Shadowy media figures will do anything to increase ratings, and his bids for freedom only increase the viewers' oppressive interest. Forever doomed to be mentioned in the same breath as *The Truman Show*, what this most obviously lacks is the cruel suspicion at the heart of Weir's comedy that it's the hero, not the world, who has the problem; that his revelations about 'being watched' may well be the result of paranoid meltdown. Ed never doubts himself to the same extent and thus our emotions aren't quite as engaged. On the plus side, there's Ed's bristling, white trash family (Hopper makes a great appearance as his long lost dad). Even better, we have crunchy, plausible Elfman as the love interest whom audiences initially warm to, then reject a few weeks down the line. Unfortunately, this isn't pushed far enough. Having wined and one-lined us on *Simpsons*-style savvy, the film turns a touch hypocritical. CO'Su

Educating Rita

(1983, GB, 110 min)
d/p Lewis Gilbert. *sc* Willy Russell. *ph* Frank Watts. *ed* Garth Craven. *ad* Maurice Fowler. *m* David Hentschel. *cast* Michael Caine, Julie Walters, Michael Williams, Maureen Lipman, Jeananne Crowley, Malcolm Douglas.

●Willy Russell's adaptation of his own slick theatrical two-hander pits Liverpudlian housewife Walters, in pursuit of true learning via the Open University, against alcoholic academic hack Caine. Apart from the odd cinematic in-joke (Caine's booze concealed behind a copy of *The Lost Weekend*), Gilbert's direction remains serviceable but stolid: the film's faults – and merits – are mostly those of the play. A few flashes of wit and insight lie embedded in a morass of prejudice, cliché and evasion. Only Walters' ebullient movie debut as the chirpy working class sparrow wanting to 'sing a different song' (the role she created on stage) almost succeeds in infusing the exercise with infectious life. SJo

Edvard Munch

(1976, Nor/Swe, 173 min)
d/sc Peter Watkins. *ph* Odd Geir Saether. *ed* Peter Watkins. *pd* Grethe Heijer. *cast* Geir Westby, Gro Fraas, Iselin von Hanno Bart, Kjersti Allum, Erik Allum, Susan Troldmyr. *narrator* Peter Watkins.

●Watkins' biography of the formative years of the pioneer Expressionist easily vindicates its running time. As Munch moves through his youth, quiet and alienated, we realise that he too was eluded by any lasting intimacy: a long, abortive affair with an older woman joins the ubiquitous ghosts of a childhood scarred by sickness and death. In the end it's the paintings which do Munch's talking for him, both directly and through the prefigurations and echoes in the film's set pieces, a fuzzed, mutely anguished procession of half-profiles and silently helpless groups with numb, naked eyes. A remarkable film. GD

Edward II

(1991, GB, 90 min)
d Derek Jarman. *p* Steve Clark-Hall, Antony Root. *sc* Derek Jarman, Stephen Mcbride, Ken Butler. *ph* Ian Wilson. *ed* George Akers. *pd* Christopher Hobbs. *m* Simon Fisher Turner. *cast* Steven Waddington, Kevin Collins, Andrew Tiernan, John Lynch, Dudley Sutton, Tilda Swinton, Jerome Flynn, Nigel Terry, Roger Hammond, Annie Lennox.

●This modern dress adaptation of Marlowe's play excites through its sheer guts and combativeness. Despite the visual lyricism, the mood is raw and angry. Jarman re-uses his sub-Brechtian clothes-as-class characterisation: scheming Mortimer (Terry) in army officer kit; nobles in business suits; Isabella (Swinton) in a *Vogue*'s gallery of designer dresses; Edward's supporters as gay Outrage activists. Jarman rips from Marlowe what is relevant to our times, to comment on the repressive nature of the British state; but this is problematic. The tragic, idealistic love of Edward (Waddington) for lowly-born, upstart Gaveston (Tiernan) speaks volumes about gay relationships in repressive, class-conscious societies, but Isabella's relationship with Mortimer is shown in images redolent of horror movies. This ambivalence, however, does not deny the film's power. Central to its pleasures are the performances; it isn't Jarman's best film, but it's his most accessible. WH

Edward Scissorhands

(1990, US, 105 min)
d Tim Burton. *p* Denise DiNovi, Tim Burton. *sc* Caroline Thompson. *ph* Stefan Czapsky. *ed* Richard Halsey. *pd* Bo Welch. *m* Danny Elfman. *cast* Johnny Depp, Winona Ryder, Dianne Wiest, Anthony Michael Hall, Kathy Baker, Vincent Price, Alan Arkin, Robert Oliveri, Conchata Ferrell.

●With his electric-shock hairdo and kinky black gear, Edward (Depp) is a model of trendy respectability – except for one thing. This man-made creature has got shears instead of hands, because his creator (Price) died mid-project. He sits lonely and lethal in his gloomy mansion, until the Avon Lady (Wiest) comes to call. She invites him home, and he proceeds to dazzle her family and neighbours with his flair for topiary and surreal hair-styling. With its skewed vision of suburbia, Burton's film bears comparison with his earlier *Pee-Wee's Big Adventure*. It's a visual treat, complete with pastel bungalows, surreal shrubbery and grotesque outfits, but it remains curiously hollow. CM

Ed Wood

(1994, US, 127 min, b/w)
d Tim Burton. *p* Denise DiNovi, Tim Burton. *sc* Scott Alexander, Larry Karaszewski. *ph* Stefan Czapsky. *ed* Chris Lebenzon. *pd* Tom Duffield. *m* Howard Shore. *cast* Johnny Depp, Martin Landau, Sarah Jessica Parker, Patricia Arquette, Jeffrey Jones, Vincent D'Onofrio,

GD Spradlin, Lisa Marie, Juliet Landau, Bill Murray, George 'The Animal' Steele, Mike Starr, Max Casella, Brent Hinkley.
● Burton's biopic of the man often described as the world's worst film-maker (*Glen or Glenda*, *Plan Nine from Outer Space*, etc) may offer a somewhat favourably distorted account of the man and his films – it ends before his slide into porn, penury and alcoholism and, while recreating certain scenes from Wood's work with astonishing accuracy, manages to avoid showing his most tiresomely nonsensical sequences – but it certainly succeeds as a funny, touching tribute to tenacity, energy, ambition and friendship. Affection shines through warm and bright, aided no end by Stefan Czapsky's evocative b/w camerawork, and by a host of spot-on lookalike performances. Landau, especially, is superb, bringing fire, acid, pathos, wit and real dignity to the role of the pitiful, occasionally deranged former horror hero Bela Lugosi; and, in the film's most conspicuous, outrageous but surprisingly appropriate bit of fictionalisation, Vincent D'Onofrio makes a notably beleaguered Welles. Depp himself, all innocence, bright-eyed zeal and itchy obsession, never really lets us get beneath Wood's skin, but gives such a good-natured performance that it's hard not to end up rooting for someone who was talentless, naive and misguided in virtually everything he did. GA

Eel, The (Unagi)

(1996, Jap, 121 min)
d Shohei Imamura. *p* Hisa Ino. *sc* Shohei Imamura, Motofumi Tomikawa, Dasuke Tengai. *ph* Shigeru Komatsubara. *ed* Hajime Okayasu. *pd* Hsiao Inagaki. *m* Shinichiro Ikebe. *cast* Koji Yakusho, Misa Shimizu, Fujio Tsuneta, Mitsuko Baisho, Akira Emoto, Sho Aikawa.
● After a deceptively dark, brutal beginning in which Yakusho murders his adulterous wife, Imamura's Palme d'Or winner lightens up quite considerably to present an offbeat, occasionally even comic account of his reintegration into the world after eight years in prison. Unusually, it's the protagonist's own hesitancy and introversion that makes rehabilitation difficult, rather than society; indeed, the eccentric folk who frequent his remote barber's shop, and especially a young woman he saves from suicide, are mostly very supportive and helpful. Still, the past catches up with him, leading to a climax as violent, farcical and ultimately affecting as Imamura's cool, clear direction is subtle and assured. GA

Eeny Meeny (Ene Bene)

(2000, Czech Rep, 107 min)
d Alice Nellis. *p* Pavel Sodomka. *sc* Alice Nellis. *ph* Ramunas Greicius. *ed* Josef Valusiak. *pd* Petr Fort. *m* Tomás Polák. *cast* Iva Janzurová, Theodora Remundová, Leos Sucharípa, Vladimír Javorsky, Eva Holubová.
● A story of discord, disaffection and torpor among a committee of ballot-box monitors in a small Czech town on election day, this first feature offers a gently poignant glimpse of familial and political growing pains and generational torch passing. It centres on a daughter-mother-father triangle. Student Jana (Remundová) is home from her first term at college, and surreptitiously stuck on James Joyce and her tutor; her faithful mother (Janzurová) is meanwhile battling to maintain her slightly naive commitment to the niceties of democratic participation despite the demands and disdain of Jana's infirm father. Funny and unforced, the film itself is democratic in spirit, tolerant of and engaged with all its characters; it's also, finally, a touching portrait of the mother-daughter bond. NB

Efecto Mariposa, El

see Butterfly Effect, The

Effect of Gamma Rays on Man-in-the-Moon Marigolds, The

(1972, US, 101 min)
d/p Paul Newman. *sc* Alvin Sargent. *ph* Adam Holender. *ed* Evan Lottman. *pd* Gene Callahan. *m* Maurice Jarre. *cast* Joanne Woodward, Nell Potts, Roberta Wallach, Judith Lowry, Richard Venture.
● An engaging adaptation of Paul Zindel's Pulitzer Prize-winning play, which sees Paul Newman's cool, lucid direction transforming what could have been a pretentious domestic drama into a touching account of small joys in sad and stunted lives. Woodward is excellent as the slatternly mother of two daughters, one introverted and hiding a tenacious interest in science (the title refers to her school project), the other a boy-chasing cheerleader destined to follow in her mother's unsuccessful footsteps. Newman and Woodward's daughter Potts steals the movie, but what makes it so watchable is Newman's reluctance to sentimentalise. GA

Effi Briest

(1974, WGer, 140 min, b/w)
d/p/sc Rainer Werner Fassbinder. *ph* Jürgen Jürges, Dietrich Lohmann. *ed* Thea Eymesz. *ad* Kurt Raab. *m* Camille Saint-Sens. *cast* Hanna Schygulla, Wolfgang Schenck, Ulli Lommel, Karl-Heinz Böhm, Ursula Strätz, Irm Hermann.
● Late 19th century Germany. A wholly inexperienced teenage girl is pushed into a marriage with a minor aristocrat many years her senior. She bears him a child, but her first knowledge of emotional warmth is gained when a neighbour makes moves to seduce her. Fassbinder's *Effi Briest* is quite literally a film of Theodor Fontane's novel: everything about the way it's conceived and structured draws attention back to the literary source. As a result, Effi is not just another Fassbinder victim-figure, but (true to Fontane) an index of her society's morality; she is exploited in various ways by everyone around her, but she suffers only because she hasn't the strength to challenge the social codes that bind her. Schygulla plays her with absolute conviction. Filmed in black and white, with extraordinary delicacy and reserve, this is one of Fassbinder's best films. TR

Effrontée, L'

see Impudent Girl, An

Egyptian Story, An (Hadduta Misriya)

(1982, Egypt, 130 min)
d/p/sc Youssef Chahine. *ph* Mohsen Nasr. *ed* Rashida Abdel-Salam. *pd* Gaby Karraze. *m* Gamal Salama. *cast* Nour El-Sherif, Yusra, Ussama Nadir, Magda-El-Khatib, Leila Hamada, Mohsen Mohieddin.
● Boldly blending personal and political histories, intercutting its fast-moving fictional scenes with documentary footage, this sort of sequel to *Alexandria – Why?* follows the fortunes of Chahine's charismatic film-maker hero and alter ego, forced to review his past and learn to love himself by a critical open-heart operation. The occasionally clumsy central conceit – Yehia/Chahine standing trial for his life during surgery – is amply offset by the energy and style of this indulgent, exuberant, and immensely likeable self-portrait. SJo

Ehe der Maria Braun, Die

see Marriage of Maria Braun, The

Eiger Sanction, The

(1975, US, 125 min)
d Clint Eastwood. *p* Robert Daley. *sc* Warren B Murphy, Hal Dresner, Rod Whitaker. *ph* Frank Stanley. *ed* Ferris Webster. *ad* George Webb, Aurelio Crugnola. *m* John Williams. *cast* Clint Eastwood, George Kennedy, Vonetta McGee, Jack Cassidy, Heidi Bruhl, Thayer David.
● The most puzzling of Eastwood's self-directed films, lacking the ironic detachment that characterised his long journey from the Man with No Name to *Bronco Billy*. Shot in a straightforward adventure style, with Eastwood as the art lecturer cum cold-blooded assassin hired to kill his victim while climbing the North face of the Eiger, the movie is little but a series of nice panoramas and clichéd action sequences. PH

8½ 100 (100) 10 (Otto e Mezzo)

(1963, It, 138 min, b/w)
d Federico Fellini. *p* Angelo Rizzoli. *sc* Federico Fellini, Tullio Pinelli, Ennio Flaiano, Brunello Rondi. *ph* Gianni Di Venanzo. *ed* Leo Catozzo. *ad* Piero Gherardi. *m* Nino Rota. *cast* Marcello Mastroianni, Claudia Cardinale, Anouk Aimée, Sandra Milo, Rossella Falk, Barbara Steele, Guido Alberti.
● The passage of time has not been kind to what many view as Fellini's masterpiece. Certainly Di Venanzo's high-key images and the director's flash-card approach place *8½* firmly in its early '60s context. As a self-referential work it lacks the layering and the profundity of, for example, *Tristram Shandy*, and the central character, the stalled director (Mastroianni), seems less in torment than doodling. And yet… The bathing of Guido sequence is a study extract for filmmakers, and La Saraghina's rumba for the seminary is a gift to pop video. Amiably spiking all criticism through a gloomy scriptwriter mouthpiece, Fellini pulls a multitude of rabbits out of the showman's hat. BC

8½ Women

(1999, Neth/GB/Ger/Luxembourg, 120 min)
d Peter Greenaway. *p* Kees Kasander. *sc* Peter Greenaway. *ph* Sacha Vierny. *ed* Elmer Leupen. *pd* Wilbert Van Dorp, (Japan) Emi Wada. *cast* John Standing, Matthew Delamere, Vivian Wu, Shizuka Inoh, Barbara Sarafian, Kirina Mano, Toni Collette, Amanda Plummer, Natacha Amal, Manna Fujiwara, Polly Walker.
● A Swiss businessman, rich with property in Japan, is so distraught with grief at his wife's death that his grown son tries to console him by setting up a harem of women, inspired by Fellini's *8½*. (The half-woman introduced into their private bordello, incidentally, is not mutilated but a dwarf – so much for taste!) Cue various liaisons, experiments and emotional intrigues, as Peter Greenaway's lacklustre narrative meanders towards its predictable and banal conclusion. The film's the usual collage of lists, perverse conceits, strange images, arcane allusions and nudity, but far more lazily assembled than previously. The writing is without wit, the pacing clumsy, the 'surrealism' forced and clumsy, the whole pretty pointless. And only Polly Walker gives anything approaching a decent performance. GA

8-Diagram Pole Fighter, The (Wulang Bagua Gun/aka The Invincible Pole Fighters)

(1983, HK, 99 min)
d Lau Kar-Leung aka Liu Jialiang. *cast* Fu Sheng, Gordon Liu, Lily Li, Hui Yinghong, Lau Kar-Leung, Ke Ming, Gao Fei.
● Turned upside down during production by the death of Fu Sheng in a car crash, this is by far Lau's most sombre and serious minded film. It set out to retell the famous Song Dynasty legend of the Yang family, massacred by Mongol invaders with the connivance of a Chinese traitor. In the film, Yang's 5th and 6th sons (Liu and Fu respectively) survive the massacre: 6 returns home deranged to be nursed by his mother and sisters (but, due to Fu's death, never to fight again), while 5 eventually finds his way to a temple where he learns to use his now bladeless spear as a weapon, mastering the art of 8-Diagram pole fighting. The many scenes of combat, choreographed to Lau's usual high standard, are relentlessly grim and bloody; the monks who back up 5 in his climactic revenge respect their Buddhist principles by disabling rather than killing their enemies – by knocking out all their teeth. The dubbed UK video release is a horrible pan-and-scan job. TR

18 Again!

(1988, US, 100 min)
d Paul Flaherty. *p* Walter Coblenz. *sc* Josh Goldstein, Jonathan Prince. *ph* Stephen M Katz. *ed* Danford B Greene. *pd* Dena Roth. *m* Billy Goldenberg. *cast* George Burns, Charlie Schlatter, Tony Roberts, Anita Morris, Miriam Flynn, Jennifer Runyon, Red Buttons.
● This production-line vehicle for nonagenarian comic Burns is notable in that he plays a younger man: 81-year-old company director Jack Watson, a dictatorial and lecherous pain-in-the-ass, who makes a birthday wish to be 18 again which – no really? – comes true. Shy grandson David (Schlatter), bullied by the frat jocks, has a near-fatal car accident at the very moment Jack has a heart-attack, and bodies and souls swop partners. For two weeks, David wanders around in Jazz Age gear, fisting a cigar and cocktail, cracks vaudeville jokes, and stuns the girl of his dreams (Runyon, the usual blonde with piano-keyboard teeth) by his prowess on track and field, skills courtesy of grandpa. Meanwhile, newly humanised, Jack boots out parasitic playmate Madelyn

(Morris struggling womanfully with an ugly role) and recognises the neglected talents of son Arnold (Roberts). A ramshackle, uninspiring enterprise, full of vaguely objectionable humour and gags of pensionable age. WH

1871

(1989, GB, 100 min)
d Ken McMullen. *p* Stewart Richards. *sc* Terry James, James Leahy, Ken McMullen. *ph* Elso Roque. *ed* William Diver. *pd* Paul Cheetham. *m* Barrie Guard. *cast* Roshan Seth, John Lynch, Timothy Spall, Alexandre de Sousa, Maria de Medeiros, Ian McNeice, Ana Padrao, Jack Klaff, Dominique Pinon, Med Hondo, Lutz Becker.

●McMullen's film about the Paris Commune offers a stirring rendition of the 'Internationale' sung, at a moment of seeming defeat, by the actors in Ramborde's Theatre in Paris, as reactionary government forces close in to remove, as it were, the masses from the stage of history. McMullen depicts the events of those heady days – from the assassination of Emperor Maximilian of Mexico in 1867, through the crazy Franco-Prussian war, to the crushing of the communards – as a farcical theatrical event, taking his cue, no doubt, from Marx's famous remarks about how history repeats itself (his words themselves repeated imperiously by a black Marx played by director Med Hondo). In and out of Ramborde's Theatre or the nearby Café Anglais, a gallery of historical cut-outs impersonates the various mighty forces at work in society. It's a grand, ambitious, three-act, sub-Brechtian affair, which exhibits the McMullen trademarks: a painterly eye, an unashamed taste for Big Ideas and allusive puns, and a tendency to lapse into obscurity and pretentiousness. WH

Eighteen Springs (Ban Sheng Yuan)

(1997, HK, 126 min)
d Ann Hui. *p* Raymond Wong, Leung Fung-Yee. *sc* John Chan. *ph* Li Ping-Bin. *ed* Wong Yee-Shun, Poon Hung-Yiu. *ad* Yu Jia'an, Yank Wong. *m* Yeh Xiaogang. *cast* Leon Lai, Wu Chien-Lien, Anita Mui, Ge You, Wang Lei, Annie Wu, Wang Zhiwen.

●A sublime melodrama by Hong Kong's most highly respected female director, based on a novel by the late Eileen Chang (whose *Red Rose, White Rose* was filmed by Stanley Kwan). Set in Shanghai in the '30s, the film chronicles the heartbreaking love affair of two office workers (Leon Lai and Wu Chien-Lin) whose romance is doomed by the forces of social and sexual hypocrisy, and by Wu's sister Anita Mui's chilling act of betrayal. Visually lush and beautifully layered – Hui's use of retrospective voice-overs recalls Wong Kar-Wai – this is a lyrical, poignant souvenir. TCh

Eighth Day, The (Le Huitième Jour)

(1996, Fr/Bel/GB, 118 min)
d Jaco Van Dormael. *p* Philippe Godeau. *sc* Jaco Van Dormael. *ph* Walther van den Ende. *ed* Susana Rossberg. *ad* Hubert Pouillé. *m* Pierre Van Dormael. *cast* Daniel Auteuil, Pascal Duquenne, Miou-Miou, Henri Garcin, Isabelle Sadoyan.

●For sales executive Harry (Auteuil), life has gone terribly wrong: he's so caught up in the system, his wife (Miou-Miou) and kids have left, and happiness eludes him. One rainy night, he closes his eyes, takes his hands off the steering wheel – and runs over a dog belonging to Georges (Duquenne), a Down's syndrome fugitive from an institution who's searching for his (dead) mother. As Harry searches for somewhere suitable to dump the chaotically unpredictable Georges, his initial grumpiness and prejudice turns to understanding and affection, revived by his charge's spontaneity, innocence and warmth. After a visually gorgeous, brilliantly executed opening, which evokes through a bizarre creation myth Georges' skewed but beautiful perceptions of the world, Van Dormael's follow-up to *Toto the Hero* slowly but surely turns into something altogether more conventional, simplistic and, regrettably, sentimental. The contrast between the emotional riches of Georges' life and the dessicated orderliness of Harry's world is often trite, and the plotting frequently implausible. Clearly Van Dormael has a huge heart and a fertile imagination, but here he seems too close to his subject for the film's good. GA

8 Heads in a Duffel Bag

(1997, US/GB, 95 min)
d Tom Schulman. *p* Brad Krevoy, Steve Stabler, John Bertolli. *sc* Tom Schulman. *ph* Adam Holender. *ed* David Holden. *pd* Paul Peters. *m* Andrew Gross. *cast* Joe Pesci, Andy Comeau, Kristy Swanson, Todd Louise, George Hamilton, Dyan Cannon.

●Two identical duffel bags: one belongs to cocky mobster Tommy Spinelli (Pesci), the other to meek medical student Charlie (Comeau). Charlie's bound for a holiday in Mexico with girlfriend Laurie (Swanson) and her parents, smarmy Dick and neurotic Annette (Hamilton and Cannon). Spinelli's bag contains eight human heads, grisly 'proof' of a Mob hit. If Spinelli fails to deliver all the evidence to his boss, his head will roll too. But then the bags get mixed up at the airport, and, worse, some of the heads go missing. The black humour's shovelled on in the first ten minutes, giving the impression that we're in for a swell bit of dark bad-taste comedy. But when Cannon lunges into frame, having discovered the contents of Charlie's bag, all becomes clear: the film's actually several shades lighter than Hamilton's tan and better suited to TV. DA

Eight Men Out

(1988, US, 120 min)
d John Sayles. *p* Sarah Pillsbury, Midge Sanford. *sc* John Sayles. *ph* Robert Richardson. *ed* John Tintori. *pd* Nora Chavooshian. *m* Mason Daring. *cast* John Cusack, Clifton James, Michael Lerner, Christopher Lloyd, Charlie Sheen, David Strathairn, DB Sweeney, John Mahoney, Michael Rooker, Perry Lang, Don Harvey, Kevin Tighe, Maggie Renzi, Studs Terkel, John Sayles.

●Sayles tells the story of the 1919 World Series baseball scandal as an allegory of the way the uneducated poor can be manipulated, corrupted and destroyed by the rich and powerful. The Chicago White Sox were tempted, thanks to the paltry salaries paid by their penny-pinching boss, to take bribes from a group of gambling hoodlums (Arnold Rothstein included) in return for throwing the World Series to the Cincinnati Reds. The affair rocked America; and Sayles' movie, sticking close to the known facts, reflects the disillusionment that came with the realisation that these heroic figures were merely weak, corruptible humans. At the same time, however, his use of a near-legendary story to comment on the economic and social factors which made such corruption possible pushes him into a black-and-white polarisation of the characters which is only partly redeemed by the overall excellence of the acting. Given the inevitably knotty plotting, the message is oddly unrevealing, although the film features more than enough intelligently, wittily scripted moments to remain a fascinating insight into a crucial episode in the souring of that old American Dream. GA

8 Million Ways to Die

(1986, US, 115 min)
d Hal Ashby. *p* Steve Roth. *sc* Oliver Stone, David Lee Henry. *ph* Stephen H Burum. *ed* Robert Lawrence, Stuart Pappe. *ad* Michael Haller. *m* James Newton Howard. *cast* Jeff Bridges, Rosanna Arquette, Alexandra Paul, Randy Brooks, Andy Garcia.

●What happened? With Ashby, Bridges, Arquette and a script co-written by Oliver Stone, you expect the result to be better than a long drawn-out episode of *The Equalizer*. Bridges plays a dipso cop who gets dropped from the force for blowing away a man going berserk with a baseball bat. When an unhappy hooker comes to him for protection, she ends up in a storm drain, and our decrepit hero determines to get even with her killer, a pigtailed drug-dealer. People say 'shit' and 'fuck' a lot; the spurts of action are too few and far between to hold the interest. However, there are a couple of things that make you sit up. Firstly, a fanny-flaunting floozie says 'Streetlight makes my pussy-hair glow in the dark'. And second, Arquette pukes over Bridges' groin. No wonder. MS

8MM

(1998, US/Ger, 123 min)
d Joel Schumacher. *p* Gavin Polone, Judy Hofflund, Joel Schumacher. *sc* Andrew Kevin Walker. *ph* Robert Elswit. *ed* Mark Stevens. *pd* Gary Wissner. *m* Mychael Danna. *cast* Nicolas Cage, Joaquin Phoenix, James Gandolfini, Peter Stormare, Anthony Heald, Chris Bauer, Catherine Keener, Myra Carter.

●Despite a script by *Seven* writer Andrew Kevin Walker, this shines only the faintest of lights on the darker side of the human psyche. Summoned by wealthy widow Mrs Christian and her lawyer (Heald), ambitious PI Tom Welles (Cage) is asked to establish whether the 8mm 'snuff movie' found in the dead husband's safe is real or fake. This starts like a hetero reprise of *Cruising*, with Welles neglecting wife and child to immerse himself in LA's porno underworld, guided by Max (Phoenix), an assistant in an adult bookshop. Once he homes in on the film-makers, however, the emphasis shifts from challenging ambivalence to the crudest knee-jerk vigilantism. And by the time we get to the climactic confrontation with masked sadist 'Machine', it's clear that, whereas Walker's collaboration with David Fincher on *Seven* was a successful meeting of minds, *8MM* was born out of a serious clash of sensibilities. There's no faulting Cage's committed, intense performance, but his slide from professional, internalised concern into personal, self-righteous rage still leaves a nasty aftertaste. NF

Eight O'Clock Walk

(1953, GB, 87 min, b/w)
d Lance Comfort. *p* George King. *sc* Katherine Strueby, Guy Morgan. *ph* Brendan J Stafford. *ed* Francis Bieber. *ad* Norman Arnold. *m* George Melachrino. *cast* Richard Attenborough, Cathy O'Donnell, Derek Farr, Maurice Denham, Lily Kann, Ian Hunter.

●Taxi driver Attenborough's the chief suspect in the killing of an eight-year-old girl, and though spouse O'Donnell never doubts his innocence, circumstantial evidence seems damning. Led by an effectively squirming Attenborough, the performers are more credible than the creaking screenplay. TJ

8 Seconds

(1994, US, 105 min)
d John G Avildsen. *p* Michael Shamberg. *sc* Monte Merrick, Larry Brothers. *ph* Victor Hammer. *ed* J Douglas Seelig. *pd* William J Cassidy. *m* Bill Conti. *cast* Luke Perry, Cynthia Geary, Stephen Baldwin, James Rebhorn, Red Mitchell, Ronnie Claire Edwards, Carrie Snodgress, George Michael.

●Perry stars as a demon rodeo rider Lane Frost. From the moment tiny tot Frost is hoisted on to a baby bull, charges 20 feet and falls off on his head, his path to fame is assured. It's a true story, so the plot is perfunctory – is Frost too common for cute rodeo gal Kellie (Geary)? Next thing you know he's married and buckling on the World Championship belt. But soon he's canoodling with the 'buckle bunnies', neglecting doe-eyed Kellie and proving his inability to tame too unridden monsters, the wild bull Red Rock and his marriage. Perry is too petulant to convince us of Frost's dark side; while Avildsen remains a proponent of the point-and-shoot school of direction. The film redeems itself somewhat by its downbeat ending. SFe

80th Step, The (80. Adim)

(1996, Tur, 105 min)
d Tomris Giritlioglu. *cast* Zuhal Olcay, Levent Ülgen, Haluk Bilginer.

●Korkut Laçin lies in hospital, arguably in a coma, certainly with three bullets inside him. Who put them there, and why? And just who is this man? With an idiosyncratic flashback structure involving both the reminiscences of state investigators' interviewees and Korkut's own memories, we painstakingly unravel a history involving childhood at an orphanage, a 1975 burnt-down chemistry lab, flight abroad, 1978 capture in Bangkok, protracted torture by the Turkish military authorities, and various unexplained phenomena. The net result is unexpectedly wacky: partly because of the impenetrability of the drama, partly because of the strange fascination of its enigmatic central figure, a man 'just more ordinary than others', says his ex-lover, but also hard and lonely, a man who alienates his old friends with his deadpan fearlessness, but who seems to have picked up an inscrutable chip on his shoulder somewhere along the way. NB

Eight Taels of Gold (Ba Liang Jin)

(1989, HK, 119 min)
d Cheung Yeun Ting [Mabel Cheung]. *p* John Sham, John Chan. *sc* Cheung Yeun

Ting. *ph* Bill Wong. *ed* Yu Shun, Kwok Chi-leung. *pd* Alex Law. *m* Lo Ta-yu, Richard Lo. *cast* Sammo Hung, Sylvia Chang, Gu Hui, Liu Guoping.

● Mabel Cheung's previous movie was a bitter-sweet romance set in New York: stuffy middle class Chinese girl meets working class Chinese layabout. This one reverses the formula: working class achiever from New York's Chinatown visits China and falls for a glamorous peasant girl who is already engaged to someone else. Conspicuously lacking in depth, and all too ready to go for easy laughs and pathos, this is partially redeemed by the strength of its two lead performances. Sylvia Chang and Sammo Hung, both cast somewhat against type, relish the chance to play off each other, and both are highly watchable. Hard to forgive the endlessly dragged-out unhappy ending, though. TR

8,000 Li Under the Clouds and Moon (Baqian Li Lu Yun he Yue)

(1947, China, 124 min, b/w)
d Shi Dongshan, (associate) Wang Weiyi. *p* Xia Yunhu, Tao Boxun, Zhou Boxun. *sc* Shi Dongshan. *ph* Han Zhongliang. *ed* Wu Tingfang. *ad* Niu Baorong. *cast* Bai Yang, Tao Jin, Gao Zheng, Zhou Feng, Huang Chen.

● Two members of a wartime travelling theatre group fall in love while slogging through the Chinese hinterlands promoting resistance against the invading Japanese. At war's end, they marry and settle in Shanghai – only to be worn down by poverty and the pervasive sense of defeat. The early scenes of Shi's seminal melodrama, crammed with colourful incidents and underpinned by newsreel inserts, are based on his own experiences in a wartime theatre troupe. The rest of the film, blending romantic realism with a polemic attack on social and moral ills, testifies to the enduring influence of Borzage's melodramas on China's left-leaning directors. Glamorously cast, indelibly performed and capably directed, this film launched the Peak Film Industries Corp (aka Kunlun Film Company), one of the two great Shanghai studios of the late 1940s. TR

Eight-Tray Gangster: The Making of a Crip

(1993, US, 65 min)
d/p/sc Thomas Lee Wright. *ph* Jean de Segonzac. *ed* Patrick Barber. *cast* Kershaun Scott.

● This documentary gives the camera over to LA gang members – of whom there are an estimated 80,000 – and a community activist, Kershaun 'Lil Monster' Scott, a member of the CRIPs (Common Resources for an Independent People). His is not a savoury tale. We follow Scott through the neighbourhoods and up into the hills for gun practice, as he explains what he sees as the inevitable process of initiation into gang membership: the need for self-defence and survival. The other interviewees are his brother 'Kody Monster', jailed aged 14 for first-degree murder, filmed in prison, and their mother. Director Wright offers no analysis, little distance, and regrettably, in the end, little genuine insight. The most moving scene is in the casualty department of the Daniel Freeman Hospital, which resembles a WWI first-aid post: mothers sit with heads bowed and nurses are left, literally, to pick up the pieces. WH

8-Wheel Beast, The (Il Bestione)

(1974, It/Fr, 102 min)
d Sergio Corbucci. *p* Carlo Ponti. *sc* Luciano Vincenzoni, Sergio Donati. *ph* Giuseppe Rotunno. *ed* Eugenio Alabiso. *ad* Giantito Burchiellaro. *m* Guido De Angelis, Maurizio De Angelis. *cast* Giancarlo Giannini, Michel Constantin, Giuseppe Maffioli, Giuliana Calandra, Dalila Di Lazzaro, Giuliana Calandra.

● A truck-driving movie with pretensions towards social realism. Events start unpromisingly with an utterly predictable conflict between the cool old hand and the hothead novice. Things turn lukewarm with some background detail. Then the last third raises questions about going independent, and the ensuing problems with the unions and the Mafia. It ends up with more than a nod in the direction of *The Wages of Fear*. That the film improves on its atrocious beginnings is more a matter for relief than any indication of quality.

8 Women (8 Femmes)

(2001, Fr, 103 min)
d François Ozon. *p* Olivier Delbosc, Marc Missonier. *sc* François Ozon, Marina de Van. *ph* Jeanne Lapoirie. *ed* Laurence Bawedin. *ad* Arnaud de Moléron. *m* Krishna Levy. *cast* Catherine Deneuve, Isabelle Huppert, Emmanuelle Béart, Fanny Ardant, Virginie Ledoyen, Danielle Darrieux, Ludivine Sagnier, Firmine Richard.

● Ozon couldn't get the rights to remake Cukor's *The Women*, and so he fell upon a forgotten boulevard-theatre mystery by one Robert Thomas as a vehicle for divas of all ages. The play is an Agatha Christie knock-off set in the 1950s: all eight women stuck in a snowbound country house had motives for killing the patriarch Marcel, whose corpse lies upstairs. Ozon reruns all his strategies from *Water Drops on Burning Rocks*: he wallows in homages to Hollywood melodramas, plays up the theatricality of all, and gives each diva one vintage French pop song to perform, to express her character's inner feelings. It's never boring, and sometimes quite bracing: the moment when Deneuve hits Darrieux over the head with a bottle lingers in the memory. But the material is hopelessly thin and the package is too obviously calculated to hit box-office gold. And this is a style of camp so broad that even the most bovine straight can get it. TR

80 Blocks from Tiffany's

(1980, US, 60 min)
d Gary Weis.

● Bring 'em back alive documentary for which the crew ventured into the wilds of the South Bronx street-gang territory to talk to members of the Savage Skulls and Savage Nomads. Picturesque shots of the natives posing with steel helmets and swastikas, muttering darkly about dastardly deeds and codes of honour. Muddled and messy, the film is as inarticulate as its heroes. TM

84 Charing Cross Road

(1986, US, 99 min)
d David Jones. *p* Geoffrey Helman. *sc* Hugh Whitemore. *ph* Brian West. *ed* Chris Wimble. *pd* Eileen Diss, Edward Pisoni. *m* George Fenton. *cast* Anne Bancroft, Anthony Hopkins, Judi Dench, Jean De Baer, Maurice Denham, Eleanor David.

● David Jones' film of Helene Hanff's book, recording the bizarre transatlantic relationship between a New York bibilophile and a London bookseller, comes as a pleasant surprise. Though inevitably literary in tone – the letters between Hanff and the Marks employees structure the narrative – it is never less than intelligent, touching, humorous. Central to this success is the subtle contrast between the austerity of postwar London and the comparatively bright affluence of Hanff's New York; also rewarding is the way images wittily counterpoint and comment on the lovingly intoned letters. And the film somehow manages to convey Hanff's almost sensual passion for pages bound in leather and still resounding with the pleasurable reactions of previous readers. None of which qualities would be evident were it not for the performances: Hopkins as the staid, shy family man Frank P Doel, and the marvellous Bancroft, relishing the vagaries of English pronunciation, as the headstrong Ms Hanff. Thankfully, the film has nothing to do with easy nostalgia; it's about real, credible people, and as such finally becomes very moving. GA

84 Charlie Mopic

(1988, US, 95 min)
d Patrick Duncan. *p* Michael Nolin. *sc* Patrick Duncan. *ph* Alan Casco. *ed* Stephen Purvis. *ad* Douglas Dick. *m* Donovan. *cast* Jonathan Emerson, Nicholas Cascone, Jason Tomlins, Christopher Burgard, Glenn Morshower, Richard Brooks, Byron Thomas.

● This independently produced Vietnam film presents an unusual perspective on the familiar platoon movie scenario. '84 Charlie Mopic' is a two-man army documentary film crew assigned to accompany an average platoon and 'record procedures peculiar to this combat situation'. Black leader OD and his mixed-bag platoon – joker Easy, tough guy Hammer, hillbilly Cracker etc – are therefore filmed and interviewed, on the job and at rest, as they hump the boonies in search of 'Charlie'. The dense slang, attention to detail and ensemble acting lend an air of immediacy and authenticity, although the use of handheld camera throughout is hard on the eyes. One short scene gives an intimation of what's in store: cameraman Mopic talks about developing reels of film that have come back from the front line, minus their cameraman – 'You never knew what you were gonna see', he says ominously. A shade too worthy, perhaps, but quietly effective. NF

Eijanaika

(1981, Jap, 151 min)
d Shohei Imamura. *p* Shoichi Ozawa, Jiro Tomoda, Shigemi Sugisaki. *sc* Shohei Imamura, Ken Miyamoto. *ph* Masahisa Himeda. *ed* Keiichi Uraoka. *ad* Akiyoshi Satani. *m* Shirichiro Ikebe. *cast* Kaori Momoi, Shigeru Izumiya, Ken Ogata, Shigeru Tsuyuguchi, Masao Kusakari, Minori Terada.

● Picking his way through the anarchy and absurdity of a society in violent transition like some oriental Makavejev, Imamura breathes bawdy life into the bones of Japanese history with this mosaic portrait of the political chaos preceding the Imperial Meiji Restoration. A confusing welter of factions and mercenary figures flit through a complex of allegiances and relationships, but as the title translates – echoing the rioters' cries – 'What the hell'. The canvas is vivid enough to impress the most Eurocentric of spectators. PT

Eika Katappa

(1969, WGer, 144 min)
d Werner Schroeter. *cast* Magdalena Montezuma, Gisela Trowe, Rosa von Praunheim, Carla Aulaulu, Rosy-Rosy.

● Any adjectives that you might (with reasonable objectivity) apply to grand opera, apply just as much to Schroeter's hysterical celebration of the form. *Eika Katappa* is interminably long, highly repetitive, commitedly clichéd, and very camp indeed. It is also, at times, extremely funny. It begins with a preview of coming attractions (a skinny Siegfried, a battleaxe Brunhilde) and ends with a survey of past highlights; in between lies a vast melting pot of scenes, situations and characters from your best and least loved operas, shifting restlessly in and out of narratives like an addict on overdrive. Just when it appears to be drawing its threads together, it launches into a tragic gay love story likely to cause a massive increase in Kleenex sales. Those hardy souls who stay the course are lavishly rewarded. TR

Einmal Ku'damm und Zurück

see Girl in a Boot

Ek Baar Phir (Once Again)

(1979, GB, 125 min)
d Vinod Pande. *cast* Deepti Naval, Suresh Oberoi, Pradeep Varma, Saeed Jaffrey.

● The first Hindi film to be shot in London (with English subtitles), *Ek Baar Phir* should provide students of the genre with enough material to keep them distracted (unusual locations, heroine demanding a divorce from husband over the phone). Non-Hindi filmgoers might find other elements of interest – Saeed Jaffrey playing himself; an intriguing account of rupee black market finance – but are more likely to be deterred by the inordinate length, eccentric use of song, and heavy emotional underlining. Something like reading 2,000 pages of Mills & Boon romance. CPea

El

(1952, Mex, 91 min, b/w)
d Luis Buñuel. *p* Oscar Dancigers. *sc* Luis Buñuel, Luis Alcoriza. *ph* Gabriel Figueroa. *ed* Carlos Savage. *ad* Edward Fitzgerald. *m* Luis Hernandez Breton. *cast* Arturo de Córdova, Delia Garcés, Luis Beristáin, José Pidal, Aurora Walker, Carlos Martinez Baena.

● Why would a fanatically jealous husband creep up on his sleeping wife clutching a bottle of anaesthetic and a needle and thread? In the gospel according to Buñuel, it's because he's a typical bourgeois male, terrified of female sexuality, projecting his own heavily repressed lusts on to every other male in sight. Buñuel examines him dispassionately, as a victim of himself and of the society that formed him; his story is neither a tragedy nor a comedy, but a necessary working out of certain moral and psychological tensions that are intrinsic in his class. The tone couldn't be further from the self-congratulation of an exercise like *The Discreet Charm of the Bourgeoisie*. TR

E la Nave Va

see And the Ship Sails On

El Cid

(1961, US/Sp, 184 min)
d Anthony Mann. *p* Samuel Bronston, Robert Haggiag. *sc* Philip Yordan, Fredric M Frank, (uncredited) Ben Barzman. *ph* Robert Krasker. *ed* Robert Lawrence. *ad* Veniero Colasanti, John Moore. *m* Miklós Rozsa. *cast* Charlton Heston, Sophia Loren, Raf Vallone, Geraldine Page, John Fraser, Hurd Hatfield, Herbert Lom, Michael Hordern, Douglas Wilmer, Frank Thring.

● One of the very finest epics produced by Samuel Bronston, equally impressive in terms of script (by Philip Yordan, who mercifully steers clear of florid archaisms) and spectacle. Heston is aptly heroic as the 11th-century patriot destined to die in the fight for a Moor-less Spain, Mann's direction is stately and thrilling, and Miklos Rosza's superb score perfectly complements the crisp and simple widescreen images. Sobriety and restraint, in fact, are perhaps the keynotes of the film's success, with the result that a potentially risible finale (in which Cid's corpse is borne into the realm of legend, strapped to his horse as it leads his men to battle) becomes genuinely stirring. GA

El Condor

(1970, US, 102 min)
d John Guillermin. *p* André de Toth. *sc* Larry Cohen, Steven Carabatsos. *ph* Henri Persin. *ed* William Ziegler, Walter Hanneman. *ad* Julio Molina Juanes. *m* Maurice Jarre. *cast* Jim Brown, Lee Van Cleef, Patrick O'Neal, Mariana Hill, Iron Eyes Cody, Imogen Hassall, Elisha Cook Jr.

● A real hotch-potch, this: an American spaghetti Western, shot in Spain, set in Mexico, directed by British expatriate Guillermin, produced by the Hungarian Andre De Toth (who would probably have made a better job of directing it), and written by Steven Carabatsos and Larry (*It's Alive, Demon*) Cohen. Plus, its story features a black chaingang fugitive, a Yankee conman and an Apache, hunting down buried gold in a desert fortress. Unfortunately, too many cooks spoil the unappetising broth; the film is emptily flashy, fashionably violent, and totally lacking in subtlety or real tension. GA

El Dorado

(1921, Fr, 100 min appx, b/w)
d Marcel L'Herbier. *sc* Marcel L'Herbier, Dimitri Dragomir. *ph* Georges Lucas, Georges Specht. *ed* Marcel L'Herbier. *ad* Louis Le Bertre, Robert-Jules Garnier, Jaque Catelain. *m* (1995 restoration) Marius François Gaillard. *cast* Eve Francis, Jaque Catelain, Marcelle Pradot, Georges Pallais, Philippe Hériat.

● 'Sibilla is troubled by conflicting emotions,' reads one inter-title. Audiences may feel likewise, faced with a movie in which the spirit of 1920s avant-garde is brought to bear on a tale of deepest Victorian bathos. Sibilla is a dancer at the El Dorado, a penurious single mum with an infant wasting away in the back room. Also figuring are a sensitive artist, a clown who loves her from afar, and a cad who behaves despicably simply because he's the story's designated villain. L'Herbier gives every scene the works – subliminal cut-ins, subjective distortions, split screen – effects which lack any consistency but which cumulatively achieve considerable intensity by the blood-spattered finale. BBa

El Dorado

(1966, US, 127 min)
d/p Howard Hawks. *sc* Leigh Brackett. *ph* Harold Rosson. *ed* John Woodcock. *ad* Hal Pereira, Carl Anderson. *m* Nelson Riddle. *cast* John Wayne, Robert Mitchum, James Caan, Charlene Holt, Michele Carey, Arthur Hunnicutt, RG Armstrong, Edward Asner.

● Hawks' effortless Western gathers together a gunfighter, a drunken sheriff, a young hopeful, a couple of tough women, and sets them up in a jail, fighting for their lives against a cattle baron and his hired killers. Sounds familiar? In many ways the plot resembles Hawks' earlier *Rio Bravo*, and several of the themes are again present: the importance of group solidarity, self-respect, professionalism, and acceptance of others' faults. But the tone here is transformed by the emphasis on his two central heroes' infirmity: not only is Mitchum a drunk, but Wayne suffers badly from age and a gun wound. Seemingly a lazy, leisurely coast towards the final shootout, it is in fact an elegy on lost youth assuaged by friendship, moving from lush pastures to dusty township, from light to darkness. This is an old man's movie only in the sense that it deals with the problems of approaching the valley of death. In other words, it's a witty, exciting and deeply moving masterpiece. GA

El Dorado

(1988, Sp/Fr, 123 min)
d Carlos Saura. *p* Victor Albarran. *sc* Carlos Saura. *ph* Teo Escamilla. *ed* Pedro del Rey. *ad* Terry Pritchard. *cast* Omero Antonutti, Eusebio Poncela, Lambert Wilson, Gabriela Roel, José Sancho, Feodor Atkine, Inés Sastre.

● Saura's account of Spain's quest for Peruvian gold differs from Herzog's *Aguirre, Wrath of God* in intention and budget. Loopy Lope de Aguirre and his conquistadors sail themselves up a creek without gold or paddle, decimated by unseen assailants, hostile environs, exhausted provisions, and mad, merciless self-slaughter. Aguirre (the excellent Antonutti) is a tired 50-year-old way down the military pecking order; if voiceovers suggest he sees himself as God's instrument, Saura portrays his murderous deeds as a product of the clashing forces of Spanish society. His attempt to demythologise this *folie de grandeur* within the conventions of the big budget epic (at $9 million, Spain's most expensive film to date) excels in evoking the destructive effects of sexual jealousy, envy, greed and the Spanish obsession with death. But despite lush 'Scope photography and the meticulous display of authentic armour and finery, the film is often oppressive, and too dependent on faces to communicate meaning, adding obscurity to something already complex and ambiguous. Not Saura's best, perhaps, but a fascinating attempt to get to the heart of myths, men and history. WH

Election

(1999, US, 103 min)
d Alexander Payne. *p* Albert Berger, Ron Yerxa, David Gale, Keith Samples. *sc* Alexander Payne, Jim Taylor. *ph* James Glennon. *ed* Kevin Tent. *pd* Jane Ann Stewart. *m* Rolfe Kent. *cast* Matthew Broderick, Reese Witherspoon, Chris Klein, Jessica Campbell, Mark Harelik, Delaney Driscoll, Molly Hagan, Colleen Camp.

● This remarkable film may be set in high school, but its satiric take on moral corruption, political chicanery, adultery and seduction is anything but juvenile. In a smart role reversal, Ferris Bueller (aka Broderick) plays Mr McAllister, a responsible, concerned teacher worn thin by long years at George Washington Carver High, by his sexless marriage, and by the plight of his best friend, sacked for sleeping with the redoubtable but under age Tracy Flick (Witherspoon). Come elections for student council president, Tracy is far and away the front runner, but Mr McAllister, terrified by the prospect of working so closely with this closet Lolita, and charged with overseeing the proceedings, discreetly sponsors a rival candidate, gormless jock Paul (Klein). Things hot up when Paul's lesbian younger sister joins the race. Granted, McAllister's narration has a sour, misogynist aftertaste, even if director/co-writer Payne affects a certain balance by giving Tracy her say. There's more than a whiff of Monica Lewinsky about Ms Flick. With her clipped diction, prim demeanour and blinkered ability to see only her side of every issue, she makes a frighteningly credible proto despot. This may not be politically correct, but as a microcosm of the malaise creeping through Western democracies, the apathy, vote rigging, and character assassination manifest at Carver High serve all too well. TCh

Elective Affinities (Die Wahlverwandtschaften)

(1974, EGer, 101 min)
d Siegfried Kühn. *p* Bernd Gerwien. *sc* Régine Kühn. *ph* Claus Neumann. *ed* Renate Bade, Helga Krause. *ad* Reinhart Zimmermann. *m* Karl-Ernst Sasse. *cast* Beata Tyszkiewicz, Hilmar Thate, Magda Vasary, Gerry Wolff.

● Goethe can't be much read recreationally these days, and this characteristic East German production is unlikely to spark much fresh interest. The novel's central analogy – chemical processes representing human relations, one nature calling to another, being repelled by a third – is no more helpful in this version, and the plot Goethe devised by way of illustration must be an adaptor's nightmare. The Kühns negotiate the more implausible moments by omission and ambiguity; and the four principals are skilled attention-holders. But the sense is that the movie originated not in any urgent personal engagement, but in the compulsion of the GDR film industry to adapt the country's literary classics, one by one. BBa

Elective Affinities (Le Affinità Elettive)

(1996, It/Fr, 98 min)
d Paolo Taviani, Vittorio Taviani. *p* Grazia Volpi. *sc* Paolo Taviani, Vittorio Taviani. *ph* Giuseppe Lanci. *ed* Roberto Perpignani. *m* Carol Crivelli. *cast* Isabelle Huppert, Fabrizio Bentivoglio, Jean-Hugues Anglade, Marie Gillain, Massimo Popolizio, Laura Marinoni.

● The Tavianis' adaptation of Goethe's novel may seem strangely restrained compared to their other fables, but it's still a work of exquisite elegance and precision. Set in Tuscany during the Napoleonic era, it charts the forces of attraction and repulsion that shape the complex relationships between a happily married baron and his wife (Anglade, Huppert), the baron's architect friend (Bentivoglio) and the wife's goddaughter (Gillain). If the story itself (engrossing enough) never seems very much more than an unusually formal period romance, the immaculate performances and the Tavianis' masterly control of colour, composition and music (a poignant but unexpectedly modernist score from Carlo Crivelli) make for absorbing viewing. GA

Electra Glide in Blue

(1973, US, 113 min)
d/p James William Guercio. *sc* Robert Boris. *ph* Conrad Hall. *ed* Jim Benson, John F Link II, Jerry Greenberg. *m* James William Guercio. cast Robert Blake, Billy Green Bush, Mitchell Ryan, Jeannine Riley, Elisha Cook, Royal Dano.

● Striking one-off by a former record producer. A weirdly funny black comedy about an undersized cop, barely five feet tall but nursing a dream of becoming a Clint Eastwood hero. He makes the grade (after a fashion, since the dream turns sour) by way of an alarmingly funny echo of *Dr Strangelove* (his mentor in detection has no use for evidence, preferring instead to stand in the moonlight listening to his inner voices) and some spiky mockery of police methods. The message may be a little naïve when he finally opts for humanity rather than authoritarianism, but the film has an extraordinary texture, peeling away layer after layer to reveal dark depths of loneliness and despair as this cop Candide learns that he isn't living in the best of all possible worlds. And Conrad Hall's photography, especially of the Monument Valley landscapes, is a joy. TM

Electric Dragon 80,000

(2000, Jap, 53 min, b/w)
d Sogo Ishii. *p* Takenori Sento. *d* Sogo Iishi. *ph* Norimichi Kasamatsu. *ed* Shuichi Kakesu. *pd* Toshihiro Isomi. *m* Hiroyuki Onogawa. *cast* Tadanobu Asano, Masatoshi Nagase.

● A tidal wave of white noise and black arts, Ishii's live-action cartoon is inspired (improbably) by the form of silent movies: it cranks up visual expression to the max and relegates what little dialogue there is to intertitles in punk graffiti style. Dragon-Eye Morrison (Asano) was electrocuted as a kid, stimulating the saurian rage-centre in his brain.He now plays deafening electric guitar to express his anger and locks himself in bed at night to avoid hurting others. But along comes the Thunderbolt Buddha (Nagase) to challenge him to a high voltage showdown. Its sheer kinetic attack is, if nothing else, admirably singleminded, but the sad fact is that much of this was done many years earlier (at a fraction of the budget) in the first *Tetsuo* movie. TR

Electric Dreams

(1984, GB/US, 112 min)
d Steve Barron. *p* Rusty Lemorande, Larry De Waay. *sc* Rusty Lemorande. *ph* Alex Thomson. *ed* Peter Honess. *pd* Richard MacDonald. *m* Giorgio Moroder. *cast* Lenny

Von Dohlen, Virginia Madsen, Maxwell Caulfield, Don Fellows, Alan Polonsky, Miriam Margolyes; voice: Bud Cort.
● A further reworking of the sci-fi stand-by about an item of hardware that takes on a human personality. In this one, Edgar the computer becomes jealous of his owner's romance with the pretty cellist upstairs. Exec produced by Richard Branson for Virgin (Films) Ltd, the picture seems more a vehicle for Virgin-related rockery and poppery than for storytelling. Photographically busy, though to no meaningful purpose, mildly amusing at best, the piece finally expires with what could be, but probably isn't, a parody of a feel-good ending. BBa

Electric Horseman, The

(1979, US, 120 min)
d Sydney Pollack. *p* Ray Stark. *sc* Robert Garland. *ph* Owen Roizman. *ed* Sheldon Kahn. *pd* Stephen Grimes. *m* David Grusin. *cast* Robert Redford, Jane Fonda, Valerie Perrine, Willie Nelson, John Saxon, Nicolas Coster, Allan Arbus, Wilford Brimley.
● Simple-minded tract disguised as a romantic comedy in which Redford's has-been rodeo cowboy, condemned to star in breakfast food commercials, takes off for the wide open spaces to stage a protest when he finds that his horse is being kept drugged. Beguilingly sharp at first, but the later stages, with Fonda's toughie reporter tagging along for a story but going all mushy inside, wallow in sentimentality about integrity, ecology and all that jazz. TM

Electric Man, The

see Man-Made Monster

Electric Moon

(1991, GB, 103 min)
d Pradip Krishen. *p* Sundeep Singh Bedi. *sc* Arundhati Roy. *ph* Giles Nuttgens. *ed* Pradip Krishen. *pd* Arundhati Roy. *m* Basaya Khan, Zakab Khan, Deepak Castelino, Sanjee Saith. *cast* Roshan Seth, Naseeruddin Shah, Leela Naidu, Gerson Da Cunha, Raghubir Yadav, Alice Spivak, Frances Holm, James Fleet, Barbara Lott.
● A former Maharajah (Da Cunha), known as Bubbles to his friends, spends his advancing years running the Machan holiday lodge in the forests of central India. And while his sister (Naidu) shares his weary resignation at the disruption caused by tourists, their go-getting brother (the wonderful Seth) is keen to package his culture for Western consumption. But the mean-minded bureaucrat who oversees the national park seems determined to hinder the enterprise. Writer Arundhati Roy relies far too heavily on comic stereotype, from the women who lust after Bubbles to the patronising Brit harbouring memories of Empire; while director Krishen fails to control the rambling narrative. As a comedy, the film lacks pace; as a serious look at cultural and social exploitation, it lacks edge. CM

Eleftherios Venizelos

(1980, Greece, 150 min)
d Pantelis Voulgaris. *p* Yannis Horn. *sc* Vangelis Raptopoulos. *ph* Yorgos Arvanitis. *ed* Takis Yannopoulos. *ad* Yannis Flery. *m* Lucianos Kiaidonis. *cast* Minas Christidis, Yannis Voglis, Manos Katrakis, Dimitris Myrat, Olga Carlatou, Vassilis Andronidis, Andreas Filipidis, Anna Calouta.
● This lengthy non-didactic chronicle covers the years 1909–22; from the arrival in Athens of the progressive, if expansionist Cretan politician Venizelos (Christidis, authoritative), his premiership through the Balkan Wars (1910–12), his conflict with the German-leaning King, to the loss of the 1920 election. He was to be recalled in 1928 and led Greece till his death which was followed by the Metaxas military takeover. It's an episodic story, expensively mounted and finely shot, and intercut with contemporary political revues which summarise, Brecht-style, the unfolding events. Voulgaris lays winning emphasis on the human dimension, even as Venizelos remains an enigmatic, if sympathetic figure, but there's probably a surfeit of unexplained historical detail for non-Greek specialists. WH

Elektreia (Szerelmem, Elektra)

(1975, Hun, 74 min)
d Miklós Jancsó. *p* József Bajusz. *sc* László Gyurko, Gyula Gernadi. *ph* János Kende. *ed* Zoltán Farkas. *ad* Éva Martin, Tamás Banovich. *m* Tamás Cseh. *cast* Mari Töröcsik, Jozsef Madaras, György Cserhalmi, Mária Bajcsay, Lajos Balázsovits, Gabi Jobba.
● There are two main levels in Jancsó's enthralling reinvention of the Elektra myth as a fable of permanent revolution. One is the troubling analysis of people's capacity for submission to tyranny; the other is the triumphant celebration of the 'firebird' of revolution, reborn daily with the rising sun. Grounding the political fable in the story of Elektra and Orestes' revenge on their father's murderer, Aegisthus, gives it an implicit psychoanalytical dimension of a kind new in Jancsó's work. The film's balletic and musical elements are even more central than they are in *Red Psalm*: the rhapsody of song and dance replaces conventional dramatic exposition, leaving Jancsó free to explore the dialectical cross-currents of his subject. It's mesmerising. TR

Element of Crime, The (Forbrydelsens Element)

(1984, Den, 104 min)
d Lars von Trier. *sc* Niels Vorsel. *ph* Tom Elling. *ed* Tómas Gislason. *pd* Peter Hoimark. *m* Bo Holten. *cast* Michael Elphick, Esmond Knight, Me Me Lai, Jerold Wells, Ahmed El Shenawi, Astrid Henning-Jensen.
● Von Trier's first feature, and it shows: all the stops are pulled out in this operatic horror-thriller, filmed in English and set in the blitzed-out, rain-lashed hinterlands of Northern Europe, steeped in a sulphurous yellow light. Bogart meets Borges as battered detective Elphick agonises over the mad mathematical computations behind the diabolical 'lotto murders' under the baleful gaze of his mentor (mesmerisingly played by Knight), whose method involves entering the criminal mind. A cinephile's film, stuffed with influences and allusions which, together with the precocious brilliance of every single image, can become numbing at times rather than stunning; but the absolute assurance and ingenuity make this a debut as startling as *Eraserhead* and every bit as spectacular. SJo

Eléna et les Hommes (Paris Does Strange Things)

(1956, Fr/It, 95 min)
d Jean Renoir. *sc* Jean Renoir, Jean Serge. *ph* Claude Renoir. *ed* Boris Lewin. *ad* Jean André. *m* Joseph Kosma. *cast* Ingrid Bergman, Jean Marais, Mel Ferrer, Pierre Bertin, Jean Richard, Juliette Greco, Magali Noël, Gaston Modot.
● With Renoir at the height of his later artifice, this completes what was effectively a trilogy begun by *The Golden Coach* and *French Cancan*, exploring both the glorious innocence of the past and the power of theatrical illusion. A prancing ballet of love's surprises, set amid the military manoeuvres and Quatorze Juillet carnivals of France in the 1880s, it is sheer delight as Bergman's entrancing Polish princess (or goddess from Olympus) weaves her spell over destiny to inspire men to fame and fortune until – in a magnificent *coup de théâtre* – she is herself finally trapped and rendered human by love. Fantasy, yes, but hardly escapist in the astonishing pertinence with which it reduces the hawkish military and political ambitions of the day to derisory farce while demonstrating the infallibility with which love goes on making the world go round. TM

Eleni

(1985, US, 117 min)
d Peter Yates. *p* Nick Vanoff, Mark Pick, Nicholas Gage. *sc* Steve Tesich. *ph* Billy Williams. *ed* Ray Lovejoy. *pd* Roy Walker. *m* Bruce Smeaton. *cast* Kate Nelligan, John Malkovich, Linda Hunt, Ronald Pickup, Oliver Cotton, Rosalie Crutchley.
● After the considerable delights of *Breaking Away* and *The Janitor*, Yates and writer Steve Tesich are clearly floundering with this adaptation of Nicholas Gage's book. A *New York Times* reporter (Malkovich) gets himself transferred to the Athens office on the pretext of investigating atrocities committed during the Greek Civil War of the '40s. There, he traces the events that led to his mother Eleni's execution at the hands of the Commie 'liberators'. Bent on revenge, he tracks down the main culprit... As an obsessive vengeance thriller, this is strangely flat, flawed by a cool performance from the usually reliable Malkovich. Worse, however, are the flashbacks to the peasant village of Lia, an arena of endless betrayal and self-sacrifice among the black-clad womenfolk. Nelligan's eponymous martyr is both a paragon of maternal virtue and a caricature of Hellenic emotionalism, while life in Lia is portrayed in shallow fashion as picturesquely primitive and poverty-stricken. Worst of all is Cotton's villain, an unmotivated sadistic oppressor with all the subtle characteristics of a '40s Hollywood Nazi. GA

Elenya

(1992, GB, 82 min)
d Steve Gough. *p* Heidi Ulmke. *sc* Steve Gough. *ph* Patrick Duval. *ed* Alan Smithee [William Diver]. *pd* Hayden Pearce. *m* Simon Fisher Turner. *cast* Pascale Delafouge Jones, Klaus Behrendt, Margaret John, Seiriol Tomes, Sue Jones Davies, Iago Wynn Jones.
● An all-too-familiar tale of a lonely young Welsh girl who, ostracised during WW2 because her mother was Italian, cares for a wounded German pilot who has crashed in the local woods, keeping him a secret from both the aunt she lives with and the cruelly jingoistic villagers. Rather like a cross between *Whistle Down the Wind* and *Another Time, Another Place*, the film is elegantly shot, nicely acted, worthy in its liberal sentiments, and almost entirely predictable. GA

Elephant Boy

(1937, GB, 80 min, b/w)
d Robert Flaherty, Zoltan Korda. *p* Alexander Korda. *sc* John Collier. *ph* Osmond Borradaile. *ed* William Hornbeck, Charles Crichton. *ad* Vincent Korda. *m* John Greenwood. *cast* Sabu, Walter Hudd, Allan Jeayes, WE Holloway, Bruce Gordon, Wilfrid Hyde-White.
● Amiable but dated version of Kipling's tale about a boy who has a way with elephants helping out government hunters in their transportation of a herd through the jungle. Fiction and documentary footage rub shoulders uneasily, but the latter (shot by Flaherty in India) is vividly watchable. GA

Eléphant ça trompe énormément, Un

see Pardon Mon Affaire

Elephant Man, The

(1980, US, 124 min, b/w)
d David Lynch. *p* Jonathan Sanger. *sc* Christopher De Vore, Eric Bergren, David Lynch. *ph* Freddie Francis. *ed* Anne V Coates. *pd* Stuart Craig. *m* John Morris. *cast* John Hurt, Anthony Hopkins, Anne Bancroft, John Gielgud, Wendy Hiller, Freddie Jones, Michael Elphick, Hannah Gordon.
● More accessible than Lynch's enigmatically disturbing *Eraserhead*, *The Elephant Man* has much the same limpidly moving humanism as Truffaut's *L'Enfant Sauvage* in describing how the unfortunate John Merrick, brutalised by a childhood in which he was hideously abused as an inhuman freak, was gradually coaxed into revealing a soul of such delicacy and refinement that he became a lion of Victorian society. But that is only half the story the film tells. The darker side, underpinned by an evocation of the steamy, smoky hell that still underlies a London facelifted by the Industrial Revolution, is crystallised by the wonderful sequence in which Merrick is persuaded by a celebrated actress to read Romeo to her Juliet. A tender, touching scene ('Oh, Mr Merrick, you're not an elephant man at all. No, you're Romeo'), it nevertheless begs the question of what passions, inevitably doomed to frustration, have been roused in this presumably normally-sexed Elephant Man. Appearances are all, and like the proverbial Victorian piano, he can make the social grade only if his ruder appendages are hidden from sensitive eyes; hence what is effectively, at his time of greatest happiness, his suicide. A marvellous movie, shot in stunning black-and-white by Freddie Francis. TM

Elephant Song

(1994, Jap, 60 min)
d Go Riju. *cast* Miyuki Matsuda, Seiichiro Shimotsuki, Susumu Terajima, Yuki Takamura.

●A small, perfectly formed gem. Coffee-shop waitress Kanako, divorced with a young son, finds herself obliged to honour a rash promise she made to a long-time customer. He always wanted to be buried in the land rather than a cemetery, so that his body would be 'useful' – and now he's dead. Kanako and her boy enlist the help of a friendly florist with a small truck (Terajima, a regular in Takeshi Kitano's films), steal the corpse, and head for the mountains. All three learn a lot on the trip: about death, about friendship, about self-esteem and about keeping promises. Funny and touching, and probably more than a little profound. TR

Elevator (Asansör)

(1999, Tur, 90 min)
d Mustafa Altioklar. *ph* Omer Faruk Sorak. *ed* Must Presheva. *cast* Arzu Yanardag, Mustafa Ugurlu, Demetiener, Funda Barin.

●This starts in *Kika* territory, with a garish TV sexposé and videotaped revenge-murder spree, before settling down into more claustrophobic territory it wants you to associate with Malle's *Lift to the Scaffold.* The show's brash, womanising producer is lured into a broken lift by a blonde-wigged femme fatale and in effect held hostage for four days. That he doesn't escape comes down partly to lack of enterprise, partly to his fascination with his kidnapper (tantalising, agreed), but a whole lot to the fact that he enjoys remonstrating with himself in front of a mirror – though he's also occasionally treated to glimpses of his hunt on TV. It half comes off. Determined chiefly by Yanardag's performance, the tone's more maniacal than minimalist, and sometimes pretty crude, but the film doesn't feel too overextended, and there's perhaps some sort of censure of modern urban Turkish braggadocio lurking here if you want it. NB

Elève doué, Un

see Apt Pupil

11 Harrowhouse

(1974, GB, 108 min)
d Aram Avakian. *p* Elliott Kastner. *sc* Jeffrey Bloom. *ph* Arthur Ibbetson. *ed* Anne V Coates. *ad* Peter Mullins. *m* Michael J Lewis. *cast* Charles Grodin, Candice Bergen, John Gielgud, Trevor Howard, James Mason, Peter Vaughan, Helen Cherry.

●Engaging caper movie which manages to breathe some new life into the old formula: American outsider (Grodin) grappling with a bland wall of English bowlers, brollies and phlegm as he becomes involved in an elaborate plan to rob a London diamond house. Some pleasingly fantastical notions (painted cockroaches used to blaze a trail to the target vault), and witty use made of Grodin's offscreen commentary to spoof the usual genre heroics. But the last quarter of the film, already undercut by the fact that the amateur thieves suddenly and inexplicably develop professional skills, degenerates into direly facetious knockabout. TM

Eline Vere

(1991, Bel/Fr/Neth, 132 min)
d Harry Kümel. *p* Matthijs van Heijningen. *sc* Jan Blokker, Patrick Pesnot. *ph* Eduard van der Enden. *ed* Ludo Troch. *pd* Ben van Os, Jan Roelfs. *m* Laurens van Rooyen. *cast* Marianne Basler, Monique van de Ven, Johan Leysen, Thom Hoffman, Aurore Clément, Bernard Kruysen, Michael York.

●In this re-creation of Brussels and The Hague at the turn of the century, Kümel returns to the formula of his debut, *Monsieur Hawarden*, the period adaptation of an established literary work. *Eline Vere* (1899) was a first novel by Louis Couperus, regarded by many as the Netherlands' greatest novelist. A young woman is rejected in love and then has a series of encounters that fail to meet her expectations. The source material offers no opportunity for the director to indulge his taste for the bizarre or surreal, as in *Daughters of Darkness* or *Malpertuis*, but most of his output has, in fact, been costume drama of one sort or another. Even those who don't particularly relish this kind of thing will find much to entertain the eye in this sumptuously designed and beautifully lit film. The camera of Eduard van der Enden, who has worked with Kümel on and off since 1968, swoops and glides like a dancer across the sound-stage, to the near constant accompaniment of van Rooyen's syrupy score. Kümel's choreography of the different disciplines is assured. A director's cut version added 29 minutes to the running time. NRo

Elisa

(1994, Fr, 114 min)
d Jean Becker. *p* Henri Brichetti. *sc* Fabrice Carazo, Jean Becker. *ph* Etienne Becker. *ed* Jacques Witta. *ad* Thérèse Ripaux. *m* Zbigniew Preisner, Serge Gainsbourg, Michel Colombier. *cast* Vanessa Paradis, Gérard Depardieu, Clothilde Courau, Sekkou Sall, Florence Thomassin, Michel Bouquet, Philippe Léotard, Catherine Rouvel.

●This vehicle for the gamine pop-star/actress Vanessa Paradis is by Jean Becker, a director who has done, and should know, better. Here, she prances her hot-panted way as an ex-children's home rebel who leaves her surrogate 'family' (Courau's fellow home-girl Solange, Sall's Arab sidekick Ahmed) to wreak emotional revenge for her mother's suicide on both her suburban grandparents and her 'real' father. The first half is a series of loosely linked scenes of posturing 'rebellion'. Older men figure strongly. She twists a late-middle-aged bookseller around her little finger, seduces an older man in the (mistaken) belief he may have been her mother's lover, and (at last!) tracks down her father, who turns out to be Depardieu. Thrown in, for good measure, is a bemusing scene with Léotard doing a Serge Gainsbourg impression at the piano as 'the Gitanes Smoker'. The final sequence is more diverting. She finds Depardieu brawling and boozing among the matelots in a port-side bistro, and strips for him on the sands before slowly realising that redemption is a game two must play. WH

Elizabeth

(1998, GB, 123 min)
d Shekhar Kapur. *p* Alison Owen, Eric Fellner, Tim Bevan. *sc* Michael Hirst. *ph* Remi Adefarasin. *ed* Jill Bilcock. *pd* John Myhre. *m* David Hirschfelder. *cast* Cate Blanchett, Geoffrey Rush, Christopher Eccleston, Joseph Fiennes, Richard Attenborough, Fanny Ardant, Kathy Burke, Eric Cantona, James Frain, Vincent Cassel, John Gielgud.

●The costume drama escapes its mothballs in this labyrinthine conspiracy movie, which opens on the fiery persecution of Bloody Mary's reign. When young, skittish Elizabeth (Blanchett) succeeds, one can well understand the misgivings of the court. Cecil (Attenborough) would have her marry a foreign prince to shore up the country's parlous state, but the new queen prefers the company of the charming Lord Dudley (Fiennes). Elizabeth's pragmatic Protestantism makes her the target for numerous Catholic intrigues, drawing in the Duke of Norfolk (Eccleston), Mary of Guise (Ardant) and her nephew Anjou (Cassel), the French and Spanish ambassadors (Cantona and Frain), and even the Pope himself (Gielgud). Best known for the revenge saga *Bandit Queen*, Kapur is a bold, intuitive director with a taste for melodrama and an aversion towards the staid. hence this eclectic and electric cast. The film plays fast and loose with history but creates a sweeping portrait of her early life and times. It's a mark of how thoroughly Blanchett makes the role her own that we're reminded more of Diana and Thatcher than Glenda Jackson or Bette Davis. Kapur cunningly confuses gender roles, equates sex with death, and rattles through dark, stony passions with some considerable panache. TCh

Elles n'oublient pas

see Love in the Strangest Way

El Mariachi

(1992, US, 80 min)
d Robert Rodriguez. *p/sc* Robert Rodriguez, Carlos Gallardo. *ph/ed* Robert Rodriguez. *m* Marc Trujillo, Alvaro Rodriguez, Chris Knudson, Cecilio Rodriguez, Eric Guthrie. *cast* Carlos Gallardo, Consuelo Gomez, Peter Marquardt, Jaime de Hoyos, Reinol Martinez, Ramiro Gomez.

●In terms of plot, there's little remarkable about Rodriguez's debut feature: the tale of a loner mistaken for a killer and hounded by all manner of vengeful furies has blessed countless movies. But it's not the story, or the low budget, which makes this polished foray into mythic conflict so deliciously fresh; it's the sheer joy taken in the medium of film. As the hobo musician of the title (Gallardo) drifts into a small, dusty Mexican township – only to find himself the target of armed gangs in search of a hitman – Rodriguez goes for broke with a breakneck pace, swarms of bullets, cinematic tricks, and a tone as playful as it is knowing of genre conventions. The director's light touch is all his own; and this unpretentious offering delivers in all departments. GA

Elmer Gantry

(1960, US, 145 min)
d Richard Brooks. *p* Bernard Smith. *sc* Richard Brooks. *ph* John Alton. *ed* Marjorie Fowler. *ad* Edward Carrere. *m* André Previn. *cast* Burt Lancaster, Jean Simmons, Arthur Kennedy, Shirley Jones, Dean Jagger, Edward Andrews, Hugh Marlowe, Rex Ingram.

●A 'controversial' look at revivalist religion which, with the passing of the years, is unlikely to raise many eyebrows. That said, it's still an entertaining, intelligent movie, thanks largely to the magnetic presence of Lancaster. As the charming charlatan with the powerfully persuasive tongue who joins up with Sister Simmons' touring grass-roots evangelist circus during the depressed '20s, he has only to flash that silvery smile for us to believe that it's not the good will of the Good Lord he's after, but a rather more carnal acquaintance with the Bible-spouting glamour girl who employs him. Brooks' script and direction never really delve beneath the surface, leaving the relationship between faith, corruption, sex and money largely unexplored (one would have loved to see this filmed by Sirk or Minnelli); but with a host of fine performances, and a strong sense of period and place conveyed by John Alton's lush camerawork, there's still plenty to enjoy. GA

Elmore Leonard's Gold Coast

see Gold Coast

El Norte

(1983, US, 140 min)
d Gregory Nava. *p* Anna Thomas. *sc* Gregory Nava, Anna Thomas. *ph* James Glennon. *ed* Betsy Blankett. *m* Folkloristas, Melecio Martinez, Emil Richards. *cast* Ernesto Gomez Cruz, David Villalpando, Zaide Silvia Gutierrez, Alicia Del Lago, Miguel Gomez Giron.

●After a military massacre of labourers in Guatemala, which leaves his father's head dangling from a tree, Enrique takes his sister Rosa and heads off for the fabled land of opportunity, *El Norte* or North America, where every house has running water, every man a job. Unfortunately Mexico, with its border guards and illegal operators who smuggle wetback labour, stands in the way; but after crawling several miles through a sewage pipe full of rats, Los Angeles is within sight. Life there without a permit, however, proves harder than down among the rats. Traditional immigrant films from Hollywood (*The Godfather*?) end in fame, money and beautiful women for the inheritors of the new found land's promise; but El Norte gives us a vision of the downside of the American dream. The film's concentration on the plight of its young hopefuls, however, is done with much humour and compassion, so that the tragedy of its message is very bracing. CPea

Eloge de l'amour (In Praise of Love)

(2001, Fr, 97 min, b/w & col)
d Jean-Luc Godard. *presented by* Alain Sarde, Ruth Waldburger. *sc* Jean-Luc Godard. *ph* Christophe Pollock, Julien Hirsch. *ed* Raphaële Urtin. *m* Ketil Bjornstad, David Darling, Georges Van Parys, Maurice Jaubert, Karl Amadeus Hartmann, Arvo Pärt. *cast* Bruno Putzulu, Cécile Camp, Claude Baignères, Remo Forlani, Philippe Loyrette, Audrey Klebaner, Mark Hunter, Jérémy Lippmann, Jean Davy, Françoise Verny.

●The wilful difficulty of Godard lost him his English audience with 1987's *King Lear.* Though hardly a conventional narrative – passages of sombre grandeur vie with sequences of irritating obscurity – this offers evidence of a desire to communicate, which may recommend it to a new audience. Autobiography appears to play a part.

In *Lear* he cast a director (Carax) to play Edgar – a name given to the director (Putzulu) at the centre of *Eloge*. To summarise: in the first half (shot memorably in b/w), Edgar muses in voiceover about a project he wishes to make (a play, a movie or an opera); three couples are profiled, as is the young actress he hopes to cast. The second half, in colour-drenched DV, flashes back two years to describe a conflict between a Hollywood producer and an elderly couple whose Resistance story he wants to film; their granddaughter (Camp) is the young actress. How these parts comment on each other is unclear. What is clear is that Godard's obsessions (anti-globalisation, the role of art and cinema in life, etc) are as passionately held as ever, though their precise meaning remains elusive. WH

El Salvador: Another Vietnam

(1981, US, 50 min)
d/p Glenn Silber, Tete Vasconcellos. *ph* Tom Sigel. *ed* Deborah Shaffer. *m* Wendy Blackstone, Bernardo Palombo.
● Next wobbly domino in Central America after Nicaragua was El Salvador, whose progress from banana republic to flashpoint for Cold War paranoia is traced in this documentary. American military support for the Duarte dictatorship and the suppression of popular dissent are recorded in footage from diverse sources; US public protest and consternation in Congress swell; and the Vietnam parallels become ever more apparent. A companion piece (and ominous sequel) to Silber's record of the anti-Nam movement, *The War at Home*, it's more urgent and cogent than that neat historical package. SJo

El Salvador – Decision to Win (El Salvador – La Decision de Vencer)

(1981, El S, 67 min)
d 'Ceró a la Izquierda' Film Collective.
● This documentary catalogues largely non-violent images of the continuing internecine guerilla war, in which everyday tasks become part of the revolution and politically precocious children cry 'the last one's a fascist' as they race. It's all in accordance with FMLN hero Farabundo Marti's 1932 scheme for 'mass organisation in cities and countryside to establish an effective rearguard'. Sadly, the film is as valid but uninspiring as these words, and does little to revive deflected world interest in El Salvador. FD

El Salvador – Portrait of a Liberated Zone

(1981, GB, 61 min)
d Michael Chanan, Peter Chappell. *p/ph* Peter Chappell. *ed* Michael Chanan.
● In January 1981, the Farabundo Marti Liberation Front launched a General Offensive represented as a failure by the US and international press. However, this film, shot after the offensive in the liberated zone east of the capital, presents a highly organised guerilla army with high morale and the overwhelming support of the peasant population. The interview format allows time for peasant fighters to speak not only of the current situation, but of the years of poverty and daily oppression motivating the war. JWi

El Salvador – The People Will Win (El Salvador – El Pueblo Vencerà)

(1980, El S, 80 min)
d Diego de la Texera. *p* Carlos Alvarez. *sc/ph* Diego de la Texera. *ed* Antonio Iglesias, Deborah Shaffer, Roberto Bravo, Luis Fuentes.
● In a forest clearing, a freedom fighter carrying a movie camera approaches a peasant woman with a large basket. She produces a rifle from her basket, he gives her the camera to hide. Guerilla war means guerilla cinema. Both weapons are equally vital in the struggle against a barbarous US-backed junta and a pernicious US-mediated TV account of the two-year-old civil war. This documentary collates material from European TV and clandestine film crews to update the account of the war already lost in Vietnam being re-fought by America's new warlords. MA

Elstree Calling

(1930, GB, 86 min, b/w & col)
d Adrian Brunel, Alfred Hitchcock, André Charlot, Jack Hulbert, Paul Murray. *sc* Val Valentine. *ph* Claude Friese-Greene. *ed* AC Hammond, Emile de Ruelle. *m* Ivor Novello, Reg Casson, Vivian Ellis, Chick Endor, Jack Strachey. *lyrics* Douglas Furber, Rowland Leigh, Donovan Parsons. *cast* Will Fyffe, Cicely Courtneidge, Jack Hulbert, Tommy Handley, Lily Morris, Gordon Harker, Anna May Wong, Donald Calthrop.
● Brunel's 'revolutionary plans for camera and editing treatment' for Britain's first musical were thwarted by the Elstree establishment, but the film's display of revue artists and music hall stars of another age has a hypnotic quality hardly affected by its primitive technique. Worth seeing, if only as a belated guide to 'What's On in London, 1930'. In the print under review, the stencil-coloured dancing girls have been restored. Brunel served as supervising director; Hitchcock directed the sketches; Charlot, Hulbert and Murray the ensemble numbers. RMy

El Topo

see Topo, El

Elusive Corporal, The

see Caporal Epinglé, Le

Elusive Pimpernel, The

(1950, GB, 109 min)
d/p/sc Michael Powell, Emeric Pressburger. *ph* Christopher Challis. *ed* Reginald Mills. *pd* Hein Heckroth. *m* Brian Easdale. *cast* David Niven, Margaret Leighton, Jack Hawkins, Cyril Cusack, Robert Coote, Edmond Audran, Charles Victor, Danielle Godet.
● A reasonably faithful adaptation of Baroness Orczy's tale of the French Revolution and the debonair Englishman who spirited aristos out of reach of the Terror. Somewhat over-elaborated, especially in the lavish court sequences, it contrives to get bogged down in a marshy area somewhere between straightforward boy's adventure and classic P & P territory. Powell's original intention was to make it a musical, but Korda and Goldwyn objected; with relics of this conception surviving in the return to Orczy's adventure yarn, the result was that, as Powell commented, 'it really was a terrible mess'. Not terrible, since it is characteristically vivid and colourful, and sparked by bright flashes of sardonic humour. TM

Elvira Madigan

(1967, Swe, 95 min)
d/sc Bo Widerberg. *ph* Jörgen Persson. *ed* Bo Widerberg. *m* Mozart. *cast* Pia Degermark, Thommy Berggren, Lennart Malmer, Nina Widerberg, Cleo Jensen.
● Candidate for the prettiest pic ever award. A lyrical elegy about a circus tightrope walker and a soldier who elope in 19th century Sweden, and eventually commit suicide. Beautifully photographed and set to a Mozart piano concerto; you may be enchanted by it if you don't laugh yourself sick.

Elvira, Mistress of the Dark

(1988, US, 96 min)
d James Signorelli. *p* Eric Gardner, Mark Pierson. *sc* Sam Egan, John Paragon, Cassandra Peterson. *ph* Hanania Baer. *ed* Battle Davis. *pd* John DeCuir Jr. *m* James Campbell. *cast* Cassandra Peterson, W Morgan Sheppard, Daniel Greene, Susan Kellerman, Jeff Conway, Edie McClurg.
● Elvira (Peterson), a camp vamp modelled on Morticia Addams and all other screen vampires, is fired from her job with an LA TV station. A telegram arrives telling her a great aunt has died and she is named in the will, which could mean the $50,000 she needs to appear in Vegas. Hotpedalling it to Massachusetts to collect her loot in her vampmobile, she upsets puritan locals with her appearance and outgoing charms, gains a house, a recipe book, and a familiar in the shape of a poodle called Algonquin, and falls foul of her great uncle, the warlock (Sheppard). Elvira realises that she, like her mother, has Powers, nearly ends up being burned at the stake, inherits more money, and opens in Vegas. A predictable plot and cheapskate effects deaden Elvira's occasional witty lines, while references to the horror genre make the film busy without going anywhere. Vamp high camp, where Elvira is more mistress of the dork. JGl

Elvis (aka Elvis – The Movie)

(1979, US, 150 min)
d John Carpenter. *p* Anthony Lawrence. *ph* Donald M Morgan. *ed* Tom Walls. *ad* Tracy Bousman, James William Newport. *m* Joe Renzetti. *cast* Kurt Russell, Shelley Winters, Pat Hingle, Season Hubley, Bing Russell, Robert Gray.
● The TV movie trimmed by half-an-hour and with *The Movie* added to the title when released theatrically in Britain in 1979. A biopic ending in 1969 (and framed by Elvis' triumphant return to Las Vegas in July of that year), it alternates periods of brash psychologising with creditable re-enactments of some legendary performances. Carpenter copes best with the minutiae of a star at tenuous leisure, but wasn't around for the post-production overseen by Dick Clark. The result is inevitably compromised, but compulsive. (Presley vocals by Ronnie McDowell.) PT

Elvis! Elvis!

(1977, Swe, 100 min)
d Kay Pollak. *p* Bert Sundberg. *sc* Maria Gripe, Kay Pollak. *ph* Mikael Salomon. *ed* Lasse Lundberg. *m* Ralph Lundsten. *cast* Lele Dorazio, Lena-Pia Bernhardsson, Fed Gunnarsson, Elisaveta, Allan Adwall.
● A smart, slightly lonely 7-year-old finds that growing up in Sweden isn't made any easier when mother has named you after Swivel-Hips. Occasionally diverting, mostly over-familiar rites- of-passage story, from a novel by Maria Gripe. TJ

Elvis on Tour

(1972, US, 93 min)
d/p/sc Pierre Adidge, Robert Abel. *ph* Robert Thomas. *ed* Ken Zemke. *with* Elvis Presley, Vernon Presley, Jackie Kahane, James Burton, Charlie Hodge.
● An unrevealing portrait of the Presley army on tour – Colonel Parker forever hovers around, just offscreen as it were – *Elvis on Tour* is none the less eminently watchable, if only for the sight and sound of James Burton's incredible guitar-playing and the re-run of an early Presley performance on the Ed Sullivan show. The history of Elvis' montage at the end – the film is basically directionless and veers from subject to subject – was 'supervised' by Martin Scorsese. PH

Elvis – That's the Way It Is

(1970, US, 108 min)
d Denis Sanders. *p/sc* Denis Sanders. *ph* Lucien Ballard. *ed* Henry Berman. *ad* John DG Wilson. *with* Elvis Presley.
● A documentary chronicling Presley's second Las Vegas season following his welcome return to the stage in 1969. Its concern with underlining the obsessive zeal of his followers leads to too many irritating interviews; but the off-stage material is curiously revealing, and the performance itself enjoyable if only occasionally exciting. AC

Emanuelle and the Last Cannibals (Emanuelle e gli Ultimi Cannibali)

(1977, It, 87 min)
d Joe D'Amato [Aristide Massaccesi]. *p* Gianfranco Couyoumdjian. *sc* Romano Scandariato, Aristide Massaccesi. *ph* Aristide Massaccesi. *ed* Alberto Moriani. *ad* Carlo Ferri. *m* Nico Ficenco. *cast* Laura Gemser, Gabriele Tinti, Susan Scott, Donald O'Brien, Percy Hogan, Monica Zanchi.
● Deeply involved in her journalist career, and glowing with the earnest nobility of a sixth form prefect, black Emanuelle (descended from the French softcore heroine but with only one 'm' to her name) finds little time for sex in this hilariously gruesome tale set in the Amazon jungles.

Embrujo, Un

see Under a Spell

Emerald Forest, The

(1985, GB, 114 min)
d/p John Boorman. *sc* Rospo Pallenberg. *ph* Philippe Rousselot. *ed* Ian Crafford. *pd* Simon Holland. *m* Junior Homrich, Brian Gascoigne. *cast* Powers Boothe, Meg Foster, William Rodriquez, Yara Vaneau, Estee Chandler, Charley Boorman.

●An American engineer working on a dam project in Brazil loses his seven-year-old son in the rain forest to an isolated Indian tribe, and spends the next ten years in a tireless search. The film's ultimate message – that we continue to destroy this hot house at our peril –is the uncomfortable truth to which he returns in a final caption. What lies between is a half-fantasised view of Indian tribal culture, with its peculiar codes of existence and bewildering intimacy with nature. For despite some flamboyant violence, this is less the despairing Boorman of *Deliverance* than the unabashed visionary who twisted *The Exorcist* into its over-ambitious sequel. The forest scenery is ravishingly photographed, and the sheer visual sweep more than compensates for some occasionally shaky acting. Full marks, too, for giving us subtitles for the Indian language; as an ethnographic adventure, there is more to these decorated natives than Mad Max Factor. A rare delight. DT

Emergency

(1962, GB, 63 min, b/w)
d/p Francis Searle. *sc* Don Nicholl, Jim O'Connolly. *ph* Ken Hodges. *ed* Jim Connock. *ad* Duncan Sutherland. *m* John Veale. *cast* Glyn Houston, Zena Walker, Dermot Walsh, Colin Tapley, Anthony Dawes, Garard Green.
●Dim little drama about an injured child awaiting a blood transfusion (rare blood group, naturally) and the police round-up of donors – including, would you believe it, a convicted killer and an atomic scientist in jeopardy – who save her life. Meanwhile, of course, the anguished parents patch up their marital problems. Any resemblance to *Emergency Call* of 1952 is hardly coincidental, since both films were produced by British B movie specialists Butcher's. TM

Emergency Call

(1952, GB, 90 min, b/w)
d Lewis Gilbert. *p* Ernest G Roy. *sc* Vernon Harris, Lewis Gilbert. *ph* Wilkie Cooper. *ed* Charles Hasse. *ad* Bernard Robinson. *m* Wilfred Burns. *cast* Jack Warner, Anthony Steel, Joy Shelton, Sidney James, Earl Cameron, Freddie Mills, Sydney Tafler, Dandy Nichols.
●Three pints from a rare blood group are desperately sought to save a child's life. Slick enough as a thriller, but the script – with the potential donors a black with a chip on his shoulder, a boxer about to throw a fight, and a murderer on the run – is pure novelettish crap. TM

Emigrants, The (Utvandrarna)

(1970, Swe, 191 min)
d Jan Troell. *p* Bengt Forslund. *sc* Jan Troell, Bengt Forslund. *ph/ed* Jan Troell. *ad* PA Lundgren. *m* Erik Nordgren. *cast* Max von Sydow, Liv Ullmann, Eddie Axberg, Svenolof Bern, Aina Alfredsson, Allan Edwall.
●First half of a two-film adaptation of a quartet of novels by Vilhelm Moberg: an austere, long, and picturesque recreation of the hardships which led Swedish farmers in the 1850s to leave home and travel in search of a better life in America. It's very slow, subtly acted, and if you can last the course, quite moving. Troell not only directed, but also photographed, co-scripted and edited the film, which becomes something of an assertion of human courage, determination and dignity. The second part, *The New Land*, deals with the pioneers' arrival and settlement in America. GA

Emil & the Detectives (Emil & die Detektive)

(2001, Ger, 110 min)
d Franziska Buch. *p* Uschi Reich, Peter Zenk. *sc* Franziska Buch. *ph* Hannes Hubach. *ed* Patricia Rommel. *pd* Albrecht Konrad. *m* Biber Gullatz, Eckes Malz. *cast* Tobias Retzlaff, Anja Sommavilla, Jürgen Vogel, Maria Schrader, Kai Wiesinger, Florian Lukas.
●Life has not been good for 10-year-old Emil's father since his wife left; he's broke, jobless and without a driving licence. So when young Emil (Retzlaff) goes to Berlin to visit a family friend, he plans on using his savings to buy his dad a forged licence. But his money's stolen on the train by 'rotten pig' Max Grundeis (Vogel), who turns out to be more than just a common adult thief. By chance, Emil bumps into the plucky Pony Hütchen (Sommavilla), head of a seven-strong kids' gang, and together they set about getting his money back, and more besides. This mostly fresh Bavarian spin on Erich Kästner's story is moderately enjoyable and well cast, if at times a mite tedious. DA

Emily – Third Party Speculation

(1979, GB, 60 min)
d/p/sc Malcolm Le Grice. *ph* Jack Murray. *ed* Malcolm Le Grice. *cast* Malcolm Le Grice, Judith Le Grice, Margaret Murray.
●Le Grice's *Blackbird Descending* the previous year signalled such witty potential for exploring narrative and perpetual time and space that this retread disappoints by its ponderousness and unrelieved seriousness. Constructed around a repeating 'neutral' domestic scene, the film examines its material elements in relation to point-of-view, first in the conventional sense of the film-maker's objectivity and subjectivity, then by an assumption of the spectator's perception. But the visual/verbal punning is so strained, and the focused narrative fragment so barren, that the opening image, of the film-maker-cum-spectator sitting blankly in front of a screen, transfers all too easily to the 'real' – and bored – viewer. PT

Emitaï

(1972, Sen, 103 min)
d Ousmane Sembene. *p* Paulin Soumanou Vieya. *sc* Ousmane Sembene. *ph* Michel Remaudeau. *ed* Gilbert Kikoine. *cast* Robert Fontaine, Michel Remaudeau, Pierre Blanchard, Ibou Camara, Ousmane Camara, Joseph Diatta.
●A strong statement from Sembene about the forms of oppression practised by the French in West Africa. Set during World War II, it deals with the staggered annihilation of a small tribe that attempts to resist the exploitation of its labour and resources. The initial part of the film presents the theft of their labour, conscripted into the White Man's War. The French quash resistance by separating the village into groups that can be held hostage against the others. Allowing the separation, the village elders bemuse themselves with their unhelpful gods, losing the last chance to organise themselves into militant resistance. Sembene makes his point with a humour all the more powerful for the anger it induces at the genocidal antics of the whites. A conventional film, but it succeeds in its aim, clarifying the logic of the colonial struggle through a specific example. JDuC

Emma

(1996, GB/US, 120 min)
d Douglas McGrath. *p* Steven Haft, Patrick Cassavetti. *sc* Douglas McGrath. *ph* Ian Wilson. *ed* Lesley Walker. *pd* Michael Howells. *m* Rachel Portman. *cast* Gwyneth Paltrow, Toni Collette, Juliet Stevenson, Alan Cumming, Ewan McGregor, Jeremy Northam, Sophie Thompson, Greta Scacchi, Polly Walker, Phyllida Law.
●Paltrow looks the part as pretty, wealthy, would-be social engineer Emma Woodhouse, doesn't alienate our sympathies in her patronising attempt to find a match for orphan Harriet Smith (Collette), and pulls off an affecting arc into chastened self-knowledge when circumstances turn her machinations back on herself. Throughout, the acting's the thing, with Cumming's oleaginous cleric vying to outdo Stevenson's screeching harridan, McGregor's modern charmer, and the smooth voice of reason from the agreeably understated Northam – though they all give way to Sophie Thompson as bespectacled Miss Bates. Indeed if the performers catch the eye, it's largely because McGrath (an American screenwriter here directing his first feature) has given them substantial chunks of Austen's dialogue and more or less left them to it, since the background's generic period-England adds little but the usual breeches, bonnets and gauzy soft-focus. Sadly, when the going gets tougher the film doesn't have many answers, and the odd unsettling surge of over-emphasis betrays an eye on the American market. TJ

Emmanuelle

(1974, Fr, 94 min)
d Just Jaeckin. *p* Yves Rousset-Rouard. *sc* Jean-Louis Richard. *ph* Richard Suzuki, Marie Saunier. *ed* Claudine Bouché. *ad* Baptiste Poirot. *m* Pierre Bachelet. *cast* Sylvia Kristel, Marika Green, Daniel Sarky, Alain Cuny, Jeanne Colletin, Christine Boisson.
●Very glossy, very French voyage into sexual discovery that mingles cliché and elegant posturing with an attempt to broaden the horizons of the sex film. As such, it looks like a softcore version of *The Story of O* commissioned by *Vogue* magazine. CPe

Emmanuelle 2 (Emmanuelle II, L'Anti-Vierge)

(F1975, Fr, 92 min)
d Francis Giacobetti. *p* Yves Rousset-Rouard. *sc* Francis Giacobetti, Bob Elia, Patrick Aubrée. *ph* Robert Fraisse. *ed* Marie-Sophie Dubus. *ad* François de Lamothe. *m* Francis Lai. *cast* Sylvia Kristel, Umberto Orsini, Catherine Rivet, Frédéric Lagache, Caroline Laurence, Florence Lafuma.
●Unashamedly endorses all the clichés of *Emmanuelle*, particularly the lure of the Orient. The camera moves smugly through spacious colonial rooms, occasionally padding things out with ethnic travelogue footage. Plotting is marginal and characterisation zero, lacking even its predecessor's pretence of a voyage into sexual discovery. CPe

Emmanuelle in Tokyo (Tokyo Emmanuelle Fujin)

(1975, Jap, 91 min)
d Akira Kato. *p* Kei Ichizi, Koji Okumuva. *sc* Kensho Nakano. *ph* Masahisa Himeda. *ed* Shinichi Yamada. *ad* Hiroshi Tokuda. *cast* Kumi Taguchi, Mitsuyasu Maeno, Katsunori Hirose, Midori Otani, Fujio Murakami, Mitsuko Aoi.
●The first example of the genre known as Nikkatsu roman-porno (romantic porn) to have reached British distribution. Since Japanese censorship is much stricter in sexual matters than our own, it didn't get cut here. It is, of course, both sexist and idiotic, but genre specialists might find comparisons between the underlying attitudes and those of European sexploitation instructive. TR

Emma's War

(1985, Aust, 96 min)
d Clytie Jessop. *p* Clytie Jessop, Andrena Finlay. *sc* Peter Smalley, Clytie Jessop. *ph* Tom Cowan. *ed* Sonia Hofmann. *ad* Jane Norris. *m* John Williams. *cast* Lee Remick, Miranda Otto, Mark Lee, Terence Donovan, Donal Gibson, Bridey Lee.
●Yet another Australian period drama in which an independent woman suffers from Life and a surfeit of syrupy sentiment. With husband away at the war, Anne Grange (Remick) has taken to drinking and dancing with cushions. Meanwhile, daughters Emma and Laurel thrive under the eccentric tuition of stout Miss Arnott, until their panicky mother packs them off to the country to avoid the threatened Japanese bombing raids. Striking a distinctly autobiographical note, and prey therefore to the unwieldy nature of personal recollection, Jessop's film has a disjointed, episodic quality. It also contorts itself to include the pacifist sentiments and puberty blues of 14-year-old Emma's friendship with a young, poetry-reading conscientious objector. As the dipso, Remick reprises her most famous role, but in more ways than one these are not *The Days of Wine and Roses*. NF

Emmène-moi (Last Chance Hotel)

(1994, Fr, 86 min)
d Michel Spinosa. *sc* Michel Spinosa, Gilles Bourdos. *ph* Antoine Roch. *ed* Stephanie Mahe. *m* Peter Hammill. *cast* Karin Viard, Antoine Basler, Ines de Medeiros, Didier Bénureau.
●Authentically painful study (with a Peter Hammill string score) of an ill-matched couple's forlorn attempts to revive their relationship after a two-year break. Sophie is headstrong, dominant, irresponsible, and incapable of finishing what she starts; Vincent, her deserted hotel-receptionist lover, is resentful, cautious and a mite dull. Though the film sometimes seems a little too self-consciously sordid, it's generally a fine effort, beautifully acted, shot through with real sexual passion and torment, and astute on the psychology of self-destruction. GA

Emmerdeur, L' (A Pain in the A**)

(1973, Fr/It, 84 min)
d Edouard Molinaro. *p* Georges Dancigers. *sc* Edouard Molinaro, Francis Weber. *ph* Raoul Coutard. *ed* Robert Isnardon, Monique Isnardon. *ad* Jacques Brizzio. *m* Jacques Brel, François Gabuber. *cast* Lino Ventura, Jacques Brel, Caroline Cellier, Nino Castelnuovo, Jean-Pierre Darras.

● Good crazy comedies are few and far between these days. This one (disappointingly remade by Billy Wilder as *Buddy Buddy* in 1981) takes off nicely after about twenty minutes thanks to the solid presence of Ventura, an unwordy script, and a deceptively deadpan beginning. Ventura, a hired killer with one shooting already under his belt, takes a hotel room from which he plans a political assassination. Meanwhile, in the next room, the pain in the arse of the title attempts to hang himself. Ventura's calm exterior slowly shatters as the incompetent idiot slowly latches onto him; he ends up driving pregnant women to hospital, falling off ledges, getting drugged in a case of mistaken identity, looking for a garage distributing free plastic saints, and finally sharing a cell with the amiable idiot, the possessor of a mammoth persecution complex. Ventura's slow disintegration is a delight to watch, and Brel manages well at being extremely irritating. CPe

Emperor and the Assassin, The (Jing Ke Ci Qin Wang)

(1999, China/Jap/Fr, 160 min)
d Chen Kaige. *p* Chen Kaige, Shirley Kao, Satoru Iseki. *sc* Chen Kaige, Wang Peigong. *ph* Zhao Fei. *ed* Zhou Xinxia. *pd* Tu Juhua. *m* Zhao Jiping. *cast* Gong Li, Zhang Fengyi, Li Xuejian, Chen Kaige, Sun Zhou, Wang Zhiwen.

● 'Chen Kaige thinks the reason *The Emperor's Shadow* was a flop is that Chen Kaige didn't direct it.' The cruel joke which did the rounds of Beijing's film circles in the summer of 1998 proved all too prescient: Chen's rehash of the attempt on the life of China's first emperor is longer and much heavier than Zhou Xiaowen's film but did no better commercially at home or abroad. (Worse, most experts agree that Zhou's film was sharper, smarter and generally richer.) Chen goes for 'epic' compositions, 'monumental' performances, mannerist framing and imagery and dubious political parallels with more recent times. Ironically the best thing in it may be his own cameo as the prime minister, the man who may or may not be the emperor's real father. TR

Emperor of the North Pole, The (aka Emperor of the North)

(1973, US, 119 min)
d Robert Aldrich. *p* Stan Hough. *sc* Christopher Knopf. *ph* Joseph Biroc. *ed* Michael Luciano. *ad* Jack Martin Smith. *m* Frank De Vol. *cast* Lee Marvin, Ernest Borgnine, Keith Carradine, Charles Tyner, Simon Oakland, Matt Clark, Elisha Cook.

● Set during the Depression, Aldrich's film starts out from a lovely gamesmanship premise derived from the legendary enmity between railwaymen and the hoboes who rode the rails. It's a duel to the death, developed with dark humour and nail-biting excitement, between Borgnine's sadistic guard – up to all the tricks and armed with a fearsome array of sledgehammers and steel chains – and Marvin's laconically contrary hobo, who cannot resist the challenge of making a lie of Borgnine's boast that no one has ever jumped his train and lived to tell the tale. A pity, perhaps, that the script pursues a vague political allegory instead of exploring its characters more deeply, but the vivid background detail (including a Baptist river-dunking which is the occasion for a cheeky theft of clothes) is brilliantly realised. TM

Emperor's Naked Army Marches On, The (Yuki Yukite Shingun)

(1987, Jap, 123 min)
d Kazuo Hara. *p* Sachiko Kobayashi. *sc/ph* Kazuo Hara. *ed* Jun Nabeshima. *m* Shigeru Yamakawa. *cast* Kenzo Okuzaki, Shizumi Okuzaki, Kichitaro Yamada, Iseko Shimamoto.

● A documentary portrait of Kenzo Okuzaki, a 62-year-old WWII veteran who acquired a prison record (for killing a man and for firing *pachinko* balls at the Emperor) in the course of his fanatical campaign to lay the blame for Japan's conduct of the war on the Emperor. Here the self-proclaimed messenger of God seeks to uncover what truly happened in New Guinea in 1945, 23 days after the war ended, when two Japanese soldiers were killed by their colleagues in very mysterious circumstances. The outcome of his investigations is gruesomely weird (cannibalism figures heavily), but stranger still is his style of interrogation, a volatile mix of apologetic politeness, deceit (his wife and anarchist friend pose as victims' relatives), and sudden violence, so relentless that one of his many ageing interviewees, fresh from hospital, ends up in an ambulance. Kazuo Hara's fly-on-the-wall documentary fascinates both for its bizarre protagonist, and for its brutally frank portrait of a society constrained by notions of shame rather than guilt. Jigsaw-like in construction, alleviated by mad wit, the film is unlike any other: rough, raw and sometimes surprisingly moving, it's absolutely compelling. GA

Emperor's New Groove, The

(2000, US, 78 min)
d Mark Dindal. *p* Randy Fullmer. *sc* David Reynolds. *ed* Pamela Ziegenhagen-Shefland. *pd* Paul Felix. *m* Sting, John Debney. *songs* Sting. *cast* voices: David Spade, John Goodman, Eartha Kitt, Patrick Warburton, Wendie Malick, Eli Russell Linnetz.

● This Disney comedy makes a self-conscious and largely successful attempt to modernise the studio's format with a jive-ass sensibility. Not that the customary caution has been jettisoned wholesale. The tradition of appropriating as backdrop either a 'classic' children's text or a classical culture – here the arrogant young Emperor reigns over a pre-Columbian culture comprising three parts Inca, two parts Aztec and one part Disney – is naturally upheld. Musically, although efforts have been made to give the production contemporary snap, rhythm and soul, enlisting Tom Jones to sing the theme tune and Sting to write the songs ensures the groove is cheekily adaptive rather than threatening. Nasty imperial advisor Yzma turns newly enthroned emperor Kuzco into a helpless talking llama, who's befriended and aided in retaking his throne by herdsman Pacha in return for promises not to redevelop the latter's idyllic mountain village. But knowing anachronisms, witticisms and one-liners, allied with a tongue in cheek attitude to storytelling convention and Dindal's easygoing direction, make for an entertaining change of tone. WH

Emperor's Shadow, The (Qin Song)

(1996, HK/China, 116 min)
d Zhou Xiaowen. *p* Jimmy Tan. *sc* Lu Wei. *ph* Lu Gengxin. *ed* Zhong Furong. *ad* Cao Jiuping, Zhang Daqian, Dou Guoxiang. *m* Zhao Jiping. *cast* Jiang Wen, Ge You, Xu Qing.

● Although designed and staged on a fairly spectacular scale, this Qin Dynasty epic is at heart a chamber tragedy centred on the love-hate bond between Ying Zheng, China's first emperor, and his one-time blood brother, a musician named Gao Jianli. The unapologetic modernity of Jiang Wen's great performance as the emperor suggests that Zhou Xiaowen is less concerned with history than with present-day relations between the artist and the Chinese state. But the film feels more like an aesthetic adventure than a political commentary, and Zhou (director of *Ermo*) makes it all the more extraordinary by stressing the homo-erotic feelings which run just beneath the surface of the central relationship. TR

Emperor Waltz, The

(1947, US, 106 min)
d Billy Wilder. *p* Charles Brackett. *sc* Charles Brackett, Billy Wilder. *ph* George Barnes. *ed* Doane Harrison. *ad* Hans Dreier, Franz Bachelin. *m* Victor Young. *cast* Bing Crosby, Joan Fontaine, Richard Haydn, Roland Culver, Lucile Watson, Sig Ruman.

● Generally reckoned to be Wilder's worst movie, as thick a slice of *sachertorte* as ever served – even Lubitsch would have thrown up. One of Wilder's favourite themes – the confrontation between New and Old World values – is given an early airing with Crosby's phonograph salesman washing up in a mythical mittel-European kingdom, where he sets about usurping Strauss with a clambake. Fontaine is a countess and there's a dodgy romance as well. There are acres of wasted space, yet occasionally this movie bursts into life, and the whole thing is tinged with a postwar nostalgia for a Europe that has been snuffed out. Oh yes, Wilder prefigured Antonioni by having the hills dyed a nicer shade of green. ATu

Empire des Sens, L'

see Ai No Corrida

Empire of Passion (L'Empire de la Passion/Ai no Borei)

(1978, Fr/Jap, 105 min)
d Nagisa Oshima. *p* Anatole Dauman. *sc* Nagisa Oshima. *ph* Yoshio Miyajima. *ed* Keiichi Uraoka. *ad* Jusho Toda. *m* Toru Takemitsu. *cast* Kazuko Yoshiyuki, Tatsuya Fuji, Takahiro Tamura, Takuzo Kawatani, Akiko Koyama.

● At once a companion film to *Ai no Corrida* and a compulsive reaction against it: the dominant themes here are guilt, repression and censorship. It's set in rural Japan, around the turn of the century, and it centres on a crime passionel: the murder of an elderly rickshaw-man by his wife and her lover, a soldier recently discharged from the army. But the couple are literally haunted by their crime (in the person of the old man's ghost), cannot separate themselves from their own society, and finally pay for their crime at the hands of a grotesquely cruel policeman. It now seems obvious that the film expressed Oshima's reaction to the worldwide 'scandal' generated by *Ai no Corrida*, but it's worth remembering that while he made it, Oshima was undergoing a prosecution in Japan for publishing the script of his previous film. His hatred of the 'authority' figure here reaches heights unseen since *Death by Hanging*. TR

Empire of the Ants

(1977, US, 89 min)
d/p Bert I Gordon. *sc* Jack Turley. *ph* Reginald Morris. *ed* Michael Luciano. *ad* Charles Rosen. *m* Dana Kaproff. *cast* Joan Collins, Robert Lansing, John David Carson, Albert Salmi, Jacqueline Scott.

● 'Have you ever taken a close look at what the ant is all about?' a voice harangues us in the opening minutes of this flat-footed piece of stupidity, supposedly derived (like the same director's *Food of the Gods*) from HG Wells. Thanks to Gordon's special effects, a close look reveals that the ant is really an incredibly hairy octopus and about as frightening as a muppet. The plot hardly grabs one either: the giant ants (fed on spilled atomic waste) attack a motley bunch of dithering idiots being taken round an isolated spot of Florida swamp by fraudulent land developer Joan Collins. The sleekly mature Joan acts as though she's always about to say 'Look at me, I'm still sexy!' What she does say, however, is things like 'Oh my God', as does everybody else. It's all drastically boring. GB

Empire of the Sun

(1987, US, 152 min)
d Steven Spielberg. *p* Steven Spielberg, Kathleen Kennedy, Frank Marshall. *sc* Tom Stoppard. *ph* Allen Daviau. *ed* Michael Kahn. *pd* Norman Reynolds. *m* John Williams. *cast* Christian Bale, John Malkovich, Miranda Richardson, Nigel Havers, Joe Pantoliano, Leslie Phillips, Masato Ibu, Emily Richard, Rupert Frazer.

● JG Ballard's autobiographical novel, about his experiences in the WWII Japanese concentration camps in China, is a mild version of the events he witnessed; Spielberg's is milder still. young Jim Graham (Bale) is Ballard, an obnoxious expat brat separated from his parents as the war overwhelms Shanghai. His world of balsa-wood models and servants is blown apart and replaced by prison camp brutality. Stripped of its sci-fi trappings, Ballard's text is about what shits we may become in order to survive. Spielberg includes a strand of populist heroism, yet even this fails to dent the awful message. And the budget makes itself seen, as does Bale's superlative Jim. JG

Empire Records

(1995, US, 89 min)
d Allan Moyle. *p* Arnon Milchan, Michael Nathanson, Alan Riche, Tony Ludwig.

sc Carol Heikkinen. *ph* Walt Lloyd. *ed* Michael Chandler. *pd* Peter Jamison. *m* Mitchell Leib. *cast* Anthony LaPaglia, Liv Tyler, Rory Cochrane, Maxwell Caulfield, Robin Tunney, Debi Mazar.

● Twenty-four incident-packed hours in a groovy New Jersey record store. This Hollywood attempt to plug into 'Generation X' mixes together all those things twenty-somethings are meant to care about: top sounds past and present, the uncertainties of the future, the problems of self-esteem, and how to get off with other twenty-somethings. Pile in lots of bright young talent plus a jukebox soundtrack, and you'd think hipster status was guaranteed, were it not for that Carol Heikkinen's screenplay resolves all its dilemmas with cornball tidiness. Remember those old movies where the kids put the show on in a barn and save the day? Well, the Oldest Living Plot Device shakes an elderly hoof in the big finale here, too, scuppering the film's nose-diving cred for good. Still, even if it's not as cool as the execs would like to hope, Moyle's movie is not unenjoyable in a synthetic kind of way. Tyler confirms her star status as the ill-advised lass who decides to lose her virginity with has-been teen idol Caulfield (admirably self-satirising), while the rest of the junior cast hold their own. Overall, fatally ersatz but good natured at heart. TJ

Empire State

(1987, GB, 102 min)
d Ron Peck. *p* Norma Heyman. *sc* Ron Peck, Mark Ayres. *ph* Tony Imi. *ed* Christopher Kelly. *pd* Adrian Smith. *m* Steve Parsons. *cast* Ray McAnally, Cathryn Harrison, Martin Landau, Emily Bolton, Lee Drysdale, Elizabeth Hickling, Ian Sears.

● Outside the futuristic Empire State nightclub in London's docklands, yuppie housing developments and fly-by-night warehousing projects are rapidly replacing the old working class communities. Wide boy Paul (Sears) tries to set up a deal with American businessman Chuck (Landau), but his plans to cut former boss Frank (McAnally) out of the game seriously underestimate the strength of old East End money. The fates of a chorus of minor characters criss-cross one another before finally converging on the club, where the rivalry between Paul and Frank explodes into primitive bare knuckles pugilism. For all its stylised images and electro muzak, the film's two-dimensional characters are simply static figures in what wants to be a hard-edged Hollywood-style thriller, but is in fact a cold hi-tech design. A brave but flawed attempt to escape the strait-jacket of British realism. NF

Empire Strikes Back, The (100)

(1980, US, 124 min)
d Irvin Kershner. *p* Gary Kurtz. *sc* Leigh Brackett, Lawrence Kasdan. *ph* Peter Suschitzky. *ed* Paul Hirsch. *pd* Norman Reynolds. *m* John Williams. *cast* Mark Hamill, Harrison Ford, Carrie Fisher, Billy Dee Williams, Anthony Daniels, David Prowse, Kenny Baker, Alec Guinness.

● Familiarity breeds content; from the corny 'droids to the tired and emotional Wookie, the events, recognitions and revelations of the sequel have the rhythm of *Soap* in 70 mm – and we love it, it makes us better people. As it appears that the plot is now infinitely extendable, a li'l oedipal confidence works in; there's more passion, more pain and more riddles in this family plot. With a goddam muppet as its spiritual guide, '*Star Wars*: Episode V' is an impressive indulgence in Hollywood style for the TV generation. RP

Empire Strikes Back: Special Edition, The

(1980, US, 124 min)
d Irvin Kershner. *p* Gary Kurtz. *sc* Leigh Brackett, Lawrence Kasdan. *ph* Peter Suschitzky. *ed* Paul Hirsch. *pd* Norman Reynolds. *m* John Williams. *cast* Mark Hamill, Harrison Ford, Carrie Fisher.

● This second instalment of the 'Star Wars' series, directed not by George Lucas but by his former USC tutor Irvin Kershner, is the tautest – an extended ricochet from one incendiary set-piece battle to another which still finds time to attend to plot, pace and character. After the destruction of the Rebel base on icy Hoth, Han (Ford), Leia (Fisher), et al, escape in the Millennium Falcon, eventually finding dubious sanctuary in the city of Bespin. Meanwhile, Luke (Hamill) heads for the Degobah system to be schooled in Jedi lore by Yoda. These two plot strands dovetail in the final quarter, when Luke rushes to Bespin to save his friends and confront Darth Vader, ignoring Yoda's pleas that he finish his training and risking his own helpless conversion to the Dark Side. The 'special edition' restoration work is impressive, though there's barely a minute's worth of extra footage this time round. In fact, the film's reliance on stop-frame animation means that, visually at least, it hasn't dated quite as well as *Star Wars*. The dialogue, too, will have you chewing your fist in places. Fisher and Hamill are clearly relishing the challenge to Be More Feisty and the robot comedy, driven by an outrageously camp Threepio, is almost funny. JO'C

Emploi du temps, L'

see Time Out

Empress Yang Kwei Fei, The (Yokihi)

(1955, Jap/HK, 98 min)
d Kenji Mizoguchi. *p* Masaichi Nagata, Run Run Shaw. *sc* Yoshikata Yoda, Matsutaro Kawaguchi, Masashige Narusawa, Tao Jin. *ph* Kohei Sugiyama. *ad* Hiroshi Mizutani. *m* Fumio Hayasaka. *cast* Machiko Kyo, Masayuki Mori, So Yamamura, Eitaro Shindo, Sakae Ozawa, .

● Mizoguchi's first film in colour is set in 8th century China during the latter years of the T'ang dynasty, and contrasts the 'pure' love story of Emperor Huan Tsung and his mistress Yang Kwei Fei with the corruption and opportunism rife in the imperial court. Those who find Mizoguchi's later films guilty of arid formulism will find fuel for their arguments here. The director's lifelong preoccupation with the position of women in feudal society is undoubtedly diminished by the idealised treatment of his heroine, while the depiction of members of her family seeking preferment and promotion within the court often borders on caricature. On the other hand, there are sequences of stunning beauty, notably Yang Kwei Fei's execution scene (accompanied by some terrific music). RM

Empty Days

see Rien à Faire

Empty Table, The (Shokutaku no Nai ie)

(1985, Jap, 142 min)
d Masaki Kobayashi. *p* Ginichi Kishimoto, Kyoto Oshima. *sc* Masaki Kobayashi. *ph* Kozo Okazaki. *ed* Nobuo Ogawa. *pd* Shigemasa Toda. *m* Toru Takemitsu. *cast* Tatsuya Nakadai, Mayumi Ogawa, Kie Nakai, Kiichi Nakai, Takeyuki Takemoto.

● When a student is arrested for his part in a terrorist siege, his apparently cool, callous father resists the customary Japanese social pressures to resign from his job (or even kill himself), and instead stands firm in his refusal to take the blame for his son's criminal acts. Result: virtually total breakdown of the family's stability. Glossily stylish, with impeccably composed visuals, the film focuses throughout on the dilemmas facing the unbending, outwardly unfeeling father (played with stoic taciturnity by Nakadai), charting the conflict between individual needs and emotions and the demands of society at large. Overlong and overschematic, it would benefit from a more total immersion in the hysterical conventions of melodrama to bring it to life, but admirers of vaguely politicised psychodramas may find much to enjoy. GA

Enamorada (Woman in Love)

(1946, Mex, 99 min, b/w)
d Emilio Fernández. *p* Benito Alazraki. *sc* Emilio Fernández, Inigo de Martino, Benito Alazraki. *ph* Gabriel Figueroa. *ed* Gloria Schoemann. *ad* Manuel Fontanels. *m* Eduardo Hernández Moncada. *cast* María Félix, Pedro Armendáriz, Fernando Fernández, José Morcillo.

● A deliriously romantic reworking of *The Taming of the Shrew*, set during the Juarez Revolution. When general Armendáriz seizes the town of Cholula, he immediately falls for the beautiful but volatile Félix, daughter of a wealthy landowner; unsympathetic to the revolutionary cause, she treats his attempts at courtship with fiery contempt. Acted and directed with wit, verve and passion, the film also benefits from Gabriel Figueroa's stunning b/w photography; see it, too, for the overwhelmingly lovely scene when Armendáriz finally begins to win over the stubborn Félix with a heart-rending serenade. GA

En avoir (ou pas)

(1995, Fr, 90 min)
d Laetitia Masson. *p* François Cuel. *sc* Laetitia Masson. *ph* Caroline Champetier. *ed* Yan Dedet. *cast* Sandrine Kiberlain, Arnaud Giovaninetti, Roschdy Zem, Claire Denis.

● Despite a certain predictability in the ending, Masson's film is an unusually bleak 'meeting of misfits' drama, in which Kiderlain's sacked Boulogne fish-packer – she dreams, vaguely, of becoming a singer – moves virtually at random to Lyon, and meets Giovaninetti's terminally depressive labourer, just dumped by his girl because he's scared of women. Determinedly downbeat in its raw realism (the soundtrack includes Marianne Faithfull and Nick Drake!), and packed with strong performances from various young stalwarts of the New French Cinema, it's well observed, intelligently written, and finally quite moving. GA

En Cas de Malheur (La Ragazza del Peccato/ Love Is My Profession)

(1958, Fr/It, 122 min, b/w)
d Claude Autant-Lara. *sc* Jean Aurenche, Pierre Bost. *ph* Jacques Natteau. *ed* Madeleine Gug. *ad* Max Douy. *m* René Cloerec. *cast* Brigitte Bardot, Jean Gabin, Edwige Feuillère, Franco Interlenghi, Nicole Berger, Madeleine Barbulée.

● Considering she was operating at a time of such constraint, when 24 frames of exposed nipple constituted at least a month's ration of cinematic erotica, it's surprising how potent a sexual presence the vintage Bardot remains 40 years on. She's offset here by Gabin at his most world-weary and Autant-Lara at his most sardonic: when the director finally permits the audience to ogle BB's bare breasts, they're soaked in blood, after she's been butchered by a deranged ex-lover (a shot widely censored at the time). Essentially this is bourgeois nightmare – successful lawyer seduced away from marriage and career by proletarian pussy – but presented non-judgementally and with icy control. BBa

Enchanted April

(1991, GB, 99 min)
d Mike Newell. *p* Ann Scott. *sc* Peter Barnes. *ph* Rex Maidment. *ed* Dick Allen, George Akers. *pd* Malcolm Thornton. *m* Richard Rodney Bennett. *cast* Josie Lawrence, Miranda Richardson, Alfred Molina, Jim Broadbent, Michael Kitchen, Joan Plowright, Polly Walker.

● London, 1922. Lottie (Lawrence) is fed up: her fuddy-duddy husband (Molina) is the sort who says cut flowers are 'extravagant', and the weather is miserable. She decides to rent a small Italian castle for a month-long holiday, minus spouse. Joining her plans for temporary escape are a writer's disgruntled wife (Richardson), a snobbish widow (Plowright), and an aloof aristocrat (Walker). Period is tastefully evoked, and loving care has gone into the visuals; but crucially, a weak script (based on Elizabeth von Arnim's novel) lets down any spirit of adventure. Personalities clash but are cheerfully reconciled, and marital tensions are swiftly resolved. Newell does manage to draw out fine performances (although Lawrence struggles with an impossibly simplistic role), but this is a sentimental journey you'd be wise to avoid. CM

Enchanted Cottage, The

(1945, US, 91 min, b/w)
d John Cromwell. *p* Harriet Parsons. *sc* De Witt Bodeen, Herman J Mankiewicz. *ph* Ted Tetzlaff. *ed* Joseph Noriega. *ad* Albert S D'Agostino, Carroll Clark. *m* Roy Webb. *cast* Dorothy McGuire, Robert Young, Herbert Marshall, Mildred Natwick, Spring Byington, Hillary Brooke.

● Icky romantic whimsy adapted from Pinero's play about a honeymoon cottage which waves the magic wand of love to transform a pair of uglies into an ideal couple. Full of sanctimonious guff, and not made any more palatable by the glamour convention whereby Young's war wounds give him Frankensteinian facial scars (nobody thinks of plastic surgery) while McGuire's blemishes just need a touch of the hairdos to set right. Ted Tetzlaff's clean camerawork comes out of it with distinction, but Herbert Marshall (as the blind pianist who composes a tone poem to the lovers) wins the yuk of the year award. TM

Enchantment, The (Yuwakusha)

(1989, Jap, 109 min)
d Shunichi Nagasaki. *p* Toshiro Kamata, Kei Sasaki, Shinya Kawai. *sc* Goro Nakajima. *ph* Makoto Watanabe. *m* Satoshi Kadokura. *cast* Kumiko Akiyoshi, Masao Kusakari, Kiwako Harada, Takeshi Naito, Tsutomu Isobe.

● Nagasaki's assured teaser produces several surprises. As it begins, with Tokyo shrink Dr Sotomura being visited by Miyako, a beautiful young woman claiming to suffer beatings from her flatmate (who may be a lesbian lover), the film looks set to be an intelligent if faintly formulary psychodrama on the theme of sexual jealousy. Within minutes, however, another patient is discovered dead with a knife in his back, and as the good doctor becomes increasingly besotted with Miyako, the film shifts into moody *femme fatale* territory. So far, so intriguing, but by the film's end Nagasaki has repeatedly pulled the rug from under our feet, so that our assumptions, like Sotomura's, are shaken by a truly subversive conclusion. This seductively cunning movie, whose preposterous twists contain a provocative questioning of traditional ideas on sex, sanity and masculine authority, should appeal not only to feminists of every hue, but to anyone looking for crisp visuals, subtle suspense and inventive direction. GA

Encino Man (aka California Man)

(1992, US, 88 min)
d Les Mayfield. *p* George Zaloom. *sc* Shawn Schepps. *ph* Robert Brinkmann. *ed* Eric A Sears. *pd* James Allen. *m* J Peter Robinson. *cast* Sean Astin, Brendan Fraser, Pauly Shore, Megan Ward, Robin Tunney, Mariette Hartley, Richard Masur, Michael DeLuise.

● This depressingly witless teen comedy continues the revenge-of-the-nerds theme popularised by Bill, Ted, Wayne and Garth. 'It's not enough to be a geek from Encino,' Harold (Astin) tells spaced-out friend Dave (Shore), 'I'm gonna be Prom King'. The message of these films is not just that the last shall be first, but that it's cool to be a dweeb. What's striking is that the underdogs are not transformed by their experiences – the ugly ducklings don't become swans – but their values are completely vindicated, and the world (Wayne's world) remade in their image. Here, Dave and Harold dig up a frozen caveman in their back yard, defrost and groom him, and in no time 'Link' (Fraser) is all but indistinguishable from the other high school neanderthals. That Link's makeover proves so painless – so devoid of comic or dramatic situations – suggests that this high-concept movie forgot what it was about. TCh

En Compagnie d'Antonin Artaud (My Life and Times with Antonin Artaud)

(1993, Fr, 90 min, b/w)
d Gérard Mordillat. *p* Denis Freyd. *sc* Gérard Mordillat, Jérôme Prieur. *ph* François Catonné. *ed* Sophie Rouffio. *ad* Jean-Pierre Clech. *m* Jean-Jacques Petit. *cast* Sami Frey, Marc Barbé, Julie Jézéquel, Valérie Jeannet, Clothilde de Bayser, Charlotte Valandrey.

● A fascinating re-creation of post-war bohemian Paris and the relationship between the dying and paranoid theatre polemicist Antonin Artaud and the young poet Jacques Prevel who kept the cultural titan in drugs. Superb performances by Frey as Artaud, whose Theatre of Cruelty was a great influence on Brook, Berkoff, Marowitz and Grotowski, and by Barbé as Prevel looking like a young Chet Baker. SGr

En Construcción

see Work in Progress

Encore

(1951, GB, 86 min, b/w)
d Pat Jackson, Anthony Pélissier, Harold French. *p* Antony Darnborough. *sc* TEB Clarke, Arthur MacRae, Eric Ambler. *ph* Desmond Dickinson. *ed* Alfred Roome. *ad* Maurice Carter. *m* Richard Addinsell. *cast* Nigel Patrick, Roland Culver, Alison Leggatt, Kay Walsh, Noel Purcell, John Laurie; Glynis Johns, Terence Morgan, Ferdy Mayne.

● After the success of *Dead of Night* in the mid-1940s, portmanteau pictures enjoyed a vogue in British cinema. This is the third film adapted from Somerset Maugham's short stories. It starts brightly enough with 'The Ant and the Grasshopper' (script, TEB Clarke). A typically English variation on *The Rake's Progress*, this follows an upper-class ne'er-do-well who sponges mercilessly off his brother. 'Winter Cruise' (Arthur MacRae), set on an ocean liner, and 'Gigolo and Gigolette' (Eric Ambler), about a circus performer who loses her nerve, are less convincing, if only because their endings seem so contrived. Maugham introduces the stories himself. GM

Encounter at Raven's Gate

(1988, Aust, 89 min)
d Rolf de Heer. *p* Rolf de Heer, Marc Rosenberg. *sc* James Michael Vernon. *ph* Richard Michalak. *ed* Suresh Ayyar. *pd* Judith Russell. *m* Graham Tardif, Roman Kronen. *cast* Steven Vidler, Celine Griffin, Ritchie Singer, Max Cullen, Vince Gil, Saturday Rosenberg, Terry Camilleri.

● Arriving to investigate the smouldering wreckage of an outback property, Special Branch agent Hemmings (Camilleri) seems disconcerted to find local police sergeant Taylor (Cullen) already at the scene. Taylor senses that he has stumbled on Something Big, and as the two men piece together the events leading up to the disappearance of the house's three inhabitants, he begins to suspect a government cover-up. In flasback, we observe the fraught triangular relationship between paroled car-thief Eddie (Vidler), his responsible older brother Richard (Singer), and Richard's frustrated artist wife Rachel (Griffin). Meanwhile, cars grind to a halt, wells dry up, dead sheep and birds litter the sun-parched earth. De Heer's disconcerting images suggest not only an intangible link between the seething emotions and the unexplained physical events, but also an invisible, all-seeing alien presence. The original screenplay apparently explained the strange occurences; the film itself is more enigmatic and open-ended, using an elliptical narrative and bizarre camera angles to reinforce the prevailing mood of mystery and unease. NF

End, The

(1978, US, 100 min)
d Burt Reynolds. *p* Lawrence Gordon. *sc* Jerry Belson. *ph* Bobby Byrne. *ed* Donn Cambern. *pd* Joan Scott. *m* Paul Williams. *cast* Burt Reynolds, Dom DeLuise, Sally Field, Strother Martin, David Steinberg, Joanne Woodward, Norman Fell, Myrna Loy, Kristy McNichol, Pat O'Brien, Carl Reiner.

● Reynolds' second film as director, casting himself as a man learning that he is terminally ill, is an engaging attempt to take the piss out of the crocodile tears that have been gleefully exploited since *Love Story*. The early sequences are by far the best, teasing a wry black comedy out of the revelations of inadequacy and failure of communication as the condemned man sets out to seek comfort and take leave of his loved ones. Strain shows later on as his frenzied attempts to achieve suicide, both aided and hindered by a genial lunatic (the direly mugging DeLuise), veer into Mel Brooks slapstick. Pretty funny, all the same. TM

Endangered Species

(1982, US, 97 min)
d Alan Rudolph. *p* Carolyn Pfeiffer. *sc* Alan Rudolph, John Binder. *ph* Paul Lohmann. *ed* Tom Walls. *pd* Trevor Williams. *m* Gary Wright. *cast* Robert Urich, JoBeth Williams, Paul Dooley, Hoyt Axton, Peter Coyote, Marin Kanter, Dan Hedaya, Harry Carey Jr.

● A strange, stylish, bizarrely eclectic conspiracy thriller. Out in the rural American Midwest, cows are found slaughtered and mutilated, the crimes having been perpetrated by UFO-like flashing lights in the sky. Purportedly based on facts connected with regular illegal tests conducted into the effectiveness of germ and chemical warfare, Rudolph's film fascinates partly by its oddball characterisation – the investigators include a juvenile delinquent, her drunken detective father, and a raunchy woman sheriff – and partly by the enigmatic, almost impressionistic structure of the narrative, which throws up weird, thought-provoking connections and correspondences. For all its occasional pretensions, a film that offers many rewards, thanks largely to its firm alliance with the sci-fi genre: a strategy that entails rather more intelligence and emotional power than a superficially similar exercise like *Silkwood*. GA

End as a Man

see Strange One, The

Endless Love

(1981, US, 115 min)
d Franco Zeffirelli. *p* Dyson Lovell. *sc* Judith Rascoe. *ph* David Watkin. *ed* Michael J Sheridan. *pd* Ed Wittstein. *m* Jonathan Tunick. *cast* Brooke Shields, Martin Hewitt, Shirley Knight, Don Murray, Richard Kiley, Beatrice Straight, Jimmy Spader, Tom Cruise.

● Almost fifteen years after *Romeo and Juliet*, Zeffirelli delivered yet another film about star-crossed young lovers. Endless? It's interminable – a tale of consummated puppy love between two high school kids, at first sanctioned by parents and then frustrated by them, whereupon the male partner burns down their house, is committed for psychiatric care, and from then on pursues his obsession of sexual reunion. Pitched at an audience of teenagers, it's of no interest to anyone else, except for a peculiar undertow of incest, intergenerational sex and giant death wishes. As excruciating as the Diana Ross/Lionel Richie title tune. RM

Endless Night

(1971, GB, 99 min)
d Sidney Gilliat. *p* Leslie Gilliat. *sc* Sidney Gilliat. *ph* Harry Waxman. *ed* Thelma Connell. *pd* Wilfrid Shingleton. *m* Allan McKeown. *cast* Hayley Mills, Hywel Bennett, Britt Ekland, George Sanders, Per Oscarsson, Peter Bowles, Lois Maxwell.

● Based on the novel by Agatha Christie. An Olde English mystery developing (eventually) from Bennett's marriage to the sixth richest girl in the world (Mills). An example of the sort of thing Christie was writing in her later years: moody psychological studies very different from, and not so much fun as, her early thrillers.

End of an Era (Telos Epochis)

(1994, Greece, 98 min)
d/p Antonis Kokkinos. *sc* Antonis Kokkinos, Alexandros Kakavas. *ph* Stavros Hassapis. *ed* Ioanna Spiliopoulou. pd Yioula Ziopoulou. m Yiannis Spyropoulous. *cast* Demosthenes Papadopoulos, Costas Kazanas, Giorgis Pyrpassopoulos, Peggy Trikalioti, Despina Kourti.

● This rites-of-passage movie set in late-'60s Athens (the musical references are somewhat misdated) is not exactly gripping, but gets by on fair performances, as Christos, shy, intelligent son of a Patras workman determined that his boy study medicine, begins to make friends at his new school. Not much happens – they discuss music, date girls, stage *Rhinoceros*, and the father of one of them is arrested (this is the era of the Colonels) – but at least it avoids the usual macho adolescent pitfalls. GA

End of August, The

(1981, US, 107 min)
d Bob Graham. *p* Warren Jacobson, Sally Sharp. *sc* Eula Seaton, Leon Heller. *ph* Robert Elswit. *ed* Jay Lash Cassidy. *pd* Warren Jacobson, Erin Jo Jurow, Fred Baldwin. *m* Shirley Walker. *cast* Sally Sharp, Lilia Skala, David Marshall Grant, Kathleen Widdoes, Paul Roebling, Paul Shenar.

● Another earnest attempt by film-makers gripped by that proselytising zeal which affects those who read good novels (in this case, Kate Chopin's *The Awakening*). After some years of married restraint in turn-of-the-century New Orleans Creole society, Edna (Sharp) abandons propriety and exchanges her life of comfort, dependence and 2.4 kids for the Bohemian Way. More vitally (and shockingly), she rejects the duty of the conjugal bed in order to find sensual and sexual fulfilment between the sheets with the charismatic Arobin (Shenar), and on a more cerebral plane with the callow Robert (Grant). Regrettably, the film finds no satisfactory substitute for reflective insights into the female mind, condemning the well-acted characters to a two-dimensional existence and inadvertently relegating Chopin's work to the genre of 'local colourist' from which she endeavoured to escape. A potboiler. FD

End of Days

(1999, US, 122 min)
d Peter Hyams. *p* Armyan Bernstein, Bill Borden. *sc* Andrew W Marlowe. *ph* Peter Hyams. *ed* Steven Kemper, Jeff Gullo. *pd* Richard Holland. *m* John Debney. *cast* Arnold Schwarzenegger, Gabriel Byrne, Kevin Pollak, Robin Tunney, CCH Pounder, Rod Steiger, Derrick O'Connor, Miriam Margolyes, Udo Kier, Victor Varnado.

● Schwarzenegger looks like yesterday's man in this solemn, silly theological Apocalypse thriller, an overblown rehash of *The Terminator* movies, *The Omen*, *Seven*, *The Usual Suspects* and what have you. A few days before the millennium, Satan returns as the libidinous Byrne to make a baby and kick start Armageddon. His chosen bride, Christine (Tunney), is an orphan, earmarked from birth for this service. The Roman Catholic Church is split between those who would murder her for the greater good and those who would protect her. Either way, suicidal ex-cop Jericho Cane (Schwarzenegger) keeps getting in the way. Murkily shot by director Peter Hyams, and scored to the inevitable, portentous choral music, this seems all the more risible for taking itself so seriously. No killer quips here, though screenwriter Andrew (*Air Force One*) Marlowe's conception of the Prince of Darkness resembles nothing so much as a supernatural Bond villain. TCh

End of St Petersburg, The (Konyets Sankt-Peterburga)

(1927, USSR, 8,202 ft, b/w)
d Vsevolod Pudovkin. *sc* Nathan Zarkhi. *ph* Anatoli Golovnya, K Vents. *ad* S Kozlovsky. *cast* AP Chistyakov, Vera Baranovskaya, Ivan Chuvelyov, V Chuvelyov, V Obolensky.

● Pudovkin's account of the 1917 Revolution is less celebrated than Eisenstein's *October*, and will be (for a while at least) than Warren Beatty's *Reds*. Not entirely without justification, for this is textbook cinema (the film was mapped out in advance, not with a storyboard, but with a kind of 'montage-board') which, unlike *October*, relies on a prototypical worker hero to embody the soul of the masses. Ironically, it's the power of the images themselves rather than the way they are edited that has kept it alive. GAd

End of the Affair, The

(1999, US/Ger, 108 min)
d Neil Jordan. *p* Stephen Woolley, Neil Jordan. *sc* Neil Jordan. *ph* Roger Pratt. *ed* Tony Lawson. *pd* Anthony Pratt. *m* Michael Nyman. *cast* Ralph Fiennes, Julianne Moore, Stephen Rea, Ian Hart, Jason Isaacs, James Bolam, Samuel Bould, Heather Jay Jones.

● Maurice Bendrix (Fiennes) is a well regarded English novelist – Graham Greene's unflattering self-portrait – whose passionate love affair with the married Sarah (Moore) leads him into a fatal duel, not with her husband, the quiescent civil servant Henry Miles (Rea), but with God Himself. If ever an actor was born to play Greene, it was surely Fiennes. So English, so civilised, and so terribly anguished. Writer/director Jordan, too, makes a good match: another glumly romantic Catholic, another fatalistic Cavalier. The film retraces the novel's looped time structure, starting in 1946, two years after the end of the affair, when Maurice takes it upon himself to have Sarah followed, on his friend Henry's behalf, of course. As his investigation proceeds (through the services of Hart's Cockney dick, Parkis), and meeting Sarah again, Maurice becomes consumed with jealousy, obsessed with the idea of uncovering evidence of his ex-lover's duplicity – instead, he finds a saint. Watered down from the novel, the metaphysics are still perilously heady stuff, but it's as a poison pen love letter that the movie compels: a torrid confession of sexual passion, delving into those tweeds and suspenders, and the rancorous diatribe of a jilted man. The performances, too, are all pitch perfect. TCh

End of the Day, The

see Fin du Jour, La

End of the Golden Weather, The

(1992, NZ, 103 min)
d Ian Mune. *p* Christina Milligan. *sc* Ian Mune, Bruce Mason. *ph* Alun Bollinger. *ed* Michael Horton. *pd* Ron Highfield. *m* Stephen McCurdy. *cast* Stephen Fulford, Stephen Papps, Paul Gittins, Gabrielle Hammond, David Taylor, Alexandra Marshall.

● Co-writer/director Mune's adaptation of Bruce Mason's one-man show is full of the sort of frantic hamming which makes for bad theatre and bad cinema. Set against the unspoilt beaches of Auckland, the cluttered plot revolves around the imaginings of 12-year-old Geoff Crome (Fulford): the gallery of eccentrics on offer include an athlete who carries boulders while he trains, an overweight matron, and a lonely loony with a parasol. But Geoff reserves his affection and support for crazy Firpo (Papps), whose oft-repeated mantra of 'made-man' alludes to his ambition to run in the Olympics. The domestic tension between the budding Walter Mitty and his father is clichéd and laboured; but most maddening of all is Firpo, whose wide-eyed tantrums evoke memories of nails scraped against blackboards. Pee-wee kiwi. CM

End of the Road

(1969, US, 110 min)
d Aram Avakian. *p* Terry Southern, Stephen F Kesten. *sc* Dennis McGuire, Terry Southern, Aram Avakian. *ph* Gordon Willis. *ed* Robert O Lovett. *pd* John K Wright III. *m* Teo Macero, Tchaikovsky, Bach. *cast* Stacy Keach, Harris Yulin, Dorothy Tristan, James Earl Jones, Grayson Hall, Ray Brock, James Coco.

● First feature as director from Avakian, a former editor, this adaptation of John Barth's black comedy deals somewhat incoherently with the problems of operating 'normally' amid the aberrations and monstrosities of middle class America. Tracing the progress of college graduate Jake Horner (Keach) from mental hospital (ie. 'normal' society as nightmare) to life outside – spent undermining the marriage of a teacher colleague – the film holds the attention despite its mess of styles: a mixture of incisive black comedy (Terry Southern had a hand in the script), inarticulate rage and self-indulgence. The main problem is a lack of perspective: the implications of issues, like the roles of psychiatry and women, for example, are virtually ignored. Muddled but interesting, the strengths and weaknesses of its nihilism are summarised by the pointed quote from Shakespeare: 'A tale told by an idiot, full of sound and fury, signifying nothing.' CPe

End of Violence, The (Am Ende der Gewalt)

(1997, US/Fr/Ger, 122 min)
d Wim Wenders. *p* Deepak Nayar, Wim Wenders, Nicholas Klein. *sc* Nicholas Klein. *ph* Pascal Rabaud. *ed* Peter Przygodda. *pd* Patricia Norris. *m* Ry Cooder. *cast* Bill Pullman, Andie MacDowell, Gabriel Byrne, Loren Dean, Traci Lind, Daniel Benzali, Marisol Padilla Sanchez, K Todd Freeman, Pruitt Taylor-Vince, Udo Kier, Frederic Forrest, Sam Fuller.

● At once infuriatingly solemn and the best thing from Wenders in a decade, this visually resplendent LA 'thriller' concerns Mike Max (Pullman), a wealthy producer of violent movies who goes to ground with a group of Mexican gardeners after escaping an attempt on his life, and the movie-obsessed cop Doc Block (Dean) and the surveillance expert Ray (Byrne) who search, separately, for a solution to the crime. It's a complicated affair, involving – or does it? – Max's wife (MacDowell); stuntwoman Cat (Lind); a refugee from El Salvador (Sanchez) hired by Ray's boss (Benzali); rap poet Six (Freeman); and expat European film-maker Zoltan (Kier). As the film explores links between life and the movies, politics and power, venality and violence, crime and new technology, it occasionally slips into mediocre comedy and smug self-reflexiveness, but for the most part it's stylish and intelligent. As a love-hate letter to the movie-making capital, it's superbly designed and shot; as a contemporary *film noir* expressing a European unease at the future of the world as presaged by this blessed/damned city on the Western edge, it's strangely compelling. GA

End Play

(1975, Aust, 114 min)
d/p/sc Tim Burstall. *ph* Robin Copping. *ed* David Bilcock. *ad* Bill Hutchinson. *cast* John Waters, George Mallaby, Belinda Giblin, Ken Goodlet, Robert Hewett, Delvene Delaney, Charles Tingwell.

● Absolutely appalling dross. Two brothers – one on shore leave, one paraplegic – play theatrical cat and mouse with each other and the witless police over who's been knocking off hot-panted hitchhikers and dramatically dumping their bodies. It could all take place on amateur dramatics night at the local village hall, and would probably come across with more conviction. PT

Endstation Freiheit

see Slow Attack

Enemies, a Love Story

(1989, US, 120 min)
d Paul Mazursky. *p* Paul Mazursky, Irby Smith, Pato Guzman. *sc* Paul Mazursky, Roger L Simon. *ph* Fred Murphy. *ed* Stuart Pappe. *pd* Pato Guzman. *m* Maurice Jarre. *cast* Anjelica Huston, Ron Silver, Lena Olin, Margaret Sophie Stein, Judith Malina, Alan King, Rita Karin, Paul Mazursky.

● The war is over, but for Herman (Silver) conflict continues. It's New York, 1949; Herman is an educated Jew married to the gentile peasant girl (Stein) who saved him from the Nazis. Life gets complicated. He's carrying on a turbulent affair with Masha (Olin), a deeply troubled survivor of the camps. Enter his first wife Tamara (Huston), long presumed dead. 'Ten enemies can't harm a man as much as he can harm himself': in its reference to the Yiddish saying, Isaac Bashevis Singer's novel sums up Herman's predicament. A 'fatalistic hedonist' makes for a seemingly unsympathetic lead character, but in this intelligent adaptation, Mazursky (co-scripting with Roger L Simon) conveys emotion without manipulation, sensitively distilling despair and self-hatred, but lifting the mood with dark humour. Philosophical issues are brought into focus rather than generated by the Holocaust, and are examined within the realm of relationships rather than intellectual debate. The performances (from Lena Olin in particular) are perfectly suited to the mood, while period is beautifully evoked in subdued tones and subtly lit interiors. CM

Enemy, The (Düsman)

(1980, Tur, 160 min)
d Zeki Ökten. *sc* Yilmaz Güney. *ph* Cetin Tunca. *ed* Zeki Ökten. *m* Yavuz Top. *cast* Aytaç Arman, Güngör Bayrak, Güven Sengil, Kâmil Sönmez.

● Written from jail by Yilmaz Güney, as was *The Herd*, this is a gritty, atmospheric story of the struggle for survival in Third World urban poverty, and its impact on a marriage. Overlaid with symbolism, some of which is inevitably lost in the culture gap (the dog poisoning, one gathers, is specially meaningful to Turks), its style is at once compelling and disturbing. Regrettably, in the interests of low Western attention spans, some 20 minutes have been cut, and the loss of one arguably crucial scene reduces the ending to a deus-ex-machina resolution rather than the narrative progression of the original. JCo

Enemy at the Gates (Duell – Enemy at the Gates)

(2000, Ger/GB/Ire/US, 131 min)
d Jean-Jacques Annaud. *p* Jean-Jacques Annaud, John D Schofield. *sc* Alain Godard, Jean-Jacques Annaud. *ph* Robert Fraisse. *ed* Noëlle Boisson, Humphrey Dixon. *pd* Wolf Kroeger. *m* James Horner. *cast* Jude Law, Joseph Fiennes, Rachel Weisz, Ed Harris, Ron Perlman, Eva Mattes, Gabriel Marshall-Thomson, Matthias Habich.

● A turning point of World War II, the siege of Stalingrad cost the lives of an estimated 800,000 Axis troops and 1.1m Soviet soldiers, as well as decimating the city's population: a saga recounted with great dignity and care in Antony Beevor's bestseller. And so one approaches Annaud's film with some hope and even expectation of intensity, scale, and gravity. Then you remember that Annaud's 'best' films are *Quest for Fire* and *The Bear*: dialogue is not his forte. This begins as it means to go on, somewhere under the shadow of *Saving Private Ryan*. Law is Vassili Zaitsev, a sharpshooter from the Urals, fed into the meat grinder that is Stalingrad by Uncle Joe's war machine. His introduction to this hell-zone is the best thing in the film. Making what is reportedly the most expensive European production ever, Annaud hasn't stinted on the mud, the rubble or the corpses. An unerring shot, Zaitsev becomes a banner hero with the help of Fiennes' army press attaché. Set-pieces get you so far (and Annaud delights in blowing this set to pieces), but the script's shortcomings aren't camouflaged by the decision to adopt Home Counties' accents as the film's lingua franca. To offset the drama's necessarily remote snipers' duel (Harris is the German officer drafted in to get rid of this upstart Russian morale-booster), the film contrives an underwritten love triangle between Fiennes, Law and Weisz, which can't help but seem like a sop to box office considerations. TCh

Enemy Below, The

(1957, US, 98 min)
d/p Dick Powell. *sc* Wendell Mayes. *ph* Harold Rosson. *ed* Stuart Gilmore. *ad* Lyle Wheeler, Albert Hogsett. *m* Leigh Harline. *cast* Robert Mitchum, Curt Jurgens, David Hedison, Theodore Bikel, Doug McClure, Kurt Kreuger.
●Powell's subaquatic suspense picture follows war-weary US destroyer captain Mitchum as he tracks Jurgens' U-boat across the Atlantic, hoping to stop the vessel before she joins up with other German subs. The psychology of personal confrontation and the mechanics of marine combat are the focus here, rather than flagwaving, so we're allowed some sympathy for Jurgens, an old hand from the Great War who loves his country but despises the Nazis. Mitchum holds up the American end with his customary stoic reserve. Shot in CinemaScope. TJ

Enemy Mine

(1985, US, 108 min)
d Wolfgang Petersen. *p* Stephen J Friedman. *sc* Edward Khmara. *ph* Tony Imi. *ed* Hannes Nikel. *pd* Rolf Zehetbauer. *m* Maurice Jarre. *cast* Dennis Quaid, Louis Gossett Jr, Brion James, Richard Marcus, Carolyn McCormick, Bumper Robinson.
●Little more than a buddy movie set in space which, sadly, relies like Wolfgang Petersen's earlier *Neverending Story* more upon special effects than storyline. Earth warrior Quaid shoots it out with 'Drac' warrior Gossett, then both man and creature crash-land on the deserted Fyrine IV. The gloomy planet, with its meteor storms and bug-eyed monsters, soon draws the combatants together as they realise that the greatest threat to their survival is not each other, but the planet itself. *Enemy Mine* then mutates into a story of friendship, understanding and eventual love between the two Robinson Crusoes in space. Both Quaid and Gossett, the latter doing a passable imitation of a fish, perform like troopers, and one special effect in particular, where Gossett gives birth to a Drac-brat, is impressively moving. What the film lacks, however, is the epic vision to match its epic pretensions, something to bind together the action and the ideas. CB

Enemy of the People, An

(1977, US, 107 min)
d/p George Schaefer. *sc* Alexander Jacobs. *ph* Paul Lohmann. *ed* Sheldon Kahn. *pd* Eugène Lourié. *m* Leonard Rosenman. *cast* Steve McQueen, Bibi Andersson, Charles Durning, Richard A Dysart, Michael Cristofer, Michael Higgins.
●The casting of Steve McQueen as the hero of Ibsen's play (a scientist determined to expose the pollution of a prosperous small town's water supply) threatens the worst. But his performance, together with Durning's as his brother the mayor (equally determined to put the lid on any scandal) make it fairly creditable. Sure, it's stage-bound. But decent production values, and direction that preserves the suspense of Ibsen's exposition, ensure that it remains watchable until the play's own unsatisfactory last act. The only really offensive aspects are the denunciation scene, and the degeneration of the hero into an increasingly sentimentalised Christ-like martyrdom, as much the fault of the text as of McQueen's interpretation. RM

Enemy of the People, An (Ganashatru)

(1989, Ind, 100 min)
d Satyajit Ray. *p* Anil Gupta. *sc* Satyajit Ray. *ph* Barun Raha. *ed* Dulal Dutta. *ad* Ashoke Bose. *m* Satyajit Ray. *cast* Soumitra Chatterjee, Ruma Guhathakurta, Dhritiman Chatterjee, Mamata Shankar, Dipankar Dey, Subhendu Chatterjee, Vischwa Guhthakurta, Manoj Mitra.
●This transplant of Ibsen's play to present-day Bengal, with Soumitra Chatterjee as the doctor foiled by vested interests in his fight to secure a costly overhaul of the town's polluted water supply, has to get everyone's sympathy vote: it was Ray's first movie since his heart attack, and doctor's orders limited him to a studio shoot. Sadly, the film needs all the sympathy it can get. Ray's own script remains locked in a 19th century sense of 'dramatics', reducing the characters to mouthpieces for positions, and the plot to a thin and unconvincing set of political manoeuvres. The actors struggle gamely to breathe life into it, but their efforts are hopeless. And the ludicrously optimistic ending is blatantly imposed from above; nothing in the preceeding 95 minutes earns or justifies it. TR

Enemy of the State

(1998, US, 132 min)
d Tony Scott. *p* Jerry Bruckheimer. *sc* David Marconi. *ph* Dan Mindel. *ed* Chris Lebenzon. *pd* Benjamin Fernandez. *m* Trevor Rabin, Harry Gregson-Williams. *cast* Will Smith, Gene Hackman, Jon Voight, Regina King, Loren Dean, Jason Lee, Gabriel Byrne, Lisa Bonet, Ian Hart.
●Fort Mead, Maryland, is home to the National Security Agency (NSA), a workforce with 18 underground acres of computers capable of tapping two million phone calls an hour. As a conspiracy thriller, produced by Jerry (*Armageddon*) Bruckheimer, this strives for the techno significance of *The Conversation*, although given the standard chase narrative, a closer model is *North by Northwest*. The MacGuffin is spelt out: to neutralise his opposition to the Telecommunications Security and Privacy Bill, a senior Senator is bumped off by rogue NSA agents. The deed is caught on amateur CCTV, and the evidence leads to the innocent pockets of attorney Will Smith. Hackman plays the grizzled recluse who talks us through the contemporary surveillance scene. Add Smith's lippy innocent and a host of subcontracted indie fresh faces, and you have the Bruckheimer formula: loud, lavish, seemingly efficient; over-large, over-long, over-plotted. Safe and sorry. NB

Enfance nue, L' (Naked Childhood/Me)

(1968, Fr, 90 min)
d Maurice Pialat. *p* Mag Bodard, François Truffaut, Claude Berri, Jo Siritzky, Samy Siritzky. *sc* Maurice Pialat. *ph* Claude Beausoleil. *ed* Arlette Langmann. *m* Richard Wagner. *cast* Michel Terrazon, Marie-Louise Thierry, René Thierry, Marie Marc, Pierrette Deplanque, Henri Puff.
●Pialat's first feature is a wonderfully delicate study of a ten-year-old boy and his decline into delinquency when boarded out with foster parents after being abandoned by his mother. With Truffaut as co-producer, comparisons with *Les Quatre Cents Coups* are inevitable, but there is really little resemblance between the two films except in theme and refusal to sentimentalise. Instead of focusing on the child, Pialat concentrates on the adults: the foster parents puzzled by the boy's delinquency since he so clearly responds to their affection; the ancient grandmother with whom he breaks through to a special relationship (very warm and funny); the welfare and adoption officers, carrying out their jobs with weary patience, but tending to treat the children as pets rather than as human beings. It's a film in which nuance is everything; amazingly, given that Pialat was working exclusively with non-professionals, the performances are stunning. TM

Enfant Sauvage, L' (The Wild Child)

(1969, Fr, 84 min, b/w)
d François Truffaut. *p* Marcel Berbert. *sc* François Truffaut, Jean Gruault. *ph* Nestor Almendros. *ed* Agnès Guillemot. *ad* Jean Mandaroux. *m* Antonio Vivaldi. *cast* Jean-Pierre Cargol, François Truffaut, Jean Dasté, Françoise Seigner, Paul Villé, Claude Miller.
●The story, based on fact, of a late 18th century behavioural scientist's attempts to condition a wild boy found in the woods in the ways of 'civilisation'. The confrontation of Rousseau's noble savage with Western scientific rationalism makes for a film with enormous philosophical implications: emotional subjectivity versus scientific objectivity, nature versus nurture, society versus the individual. Given the semi-documentary treatment and the subject itself, the film could have been excruciatingly dull in lesser hands. In fact it's as lucid and wryly witty a film as you could wish for, uncluttered by superfluous period detail. A beautiful use of simple techniques – black-and-white photography, Vivaldi music, even devices as outmoded as the iris – give it a very refreshing quality. The use of much voice-over from Dr Itard's original journals, set against images patently contradicting the scientist's detached assumptions, make for some pretty ironies, and fundamentally question the morality of much scientific investigation, as well as attempting to evaluate the worth of many of our social constructs (such as education). A deeply moving film, dedicated to Jean-Pierre Léaud, the actor who plays Truffaut's semi-autobiographical hero, Antoine Doinel. RM

Enfants de Lumière, Les (The Children of Lumière)

(1995, Fr, 102 min, b/w & col)
d André Asseo, Pierre Billard, Pierre Phillippe, Alain Corneau, Claude Miller, Claude Sautet. *p* Jacques Perrin. *ed* Jacques Perrin, Christophe Barratier, Olivier Barrot, Pierre Phillippe, Jean-Claude Romer. *m* Michel Legrand. *narrator* Jacques Perrin.
●A delicious sprint leading us through about 300 sensitively chosen and juxtaposed clips from 100 years of French cinema, from the Lumières' *Workers Leaving the Factory* to the latest version of *Les Misérables* starring an aged Belmondo. Loosely structured around various topics (history, fantasy, crime, war, love, travel, food) and featuring a mercifully unwordy narration from Jacques Perrin, it's a joyous, uplifting tribute to a national industry whose major achievements are countless – impossible, indeed, to imagine a British equivalent. GA

Enfants du Marais, Les (Children of the Marshland)

(1998, Fr, 115 min)
d Jean Becker. *p* Hervé Truffaut. *sc* Sébastien Japrisot. *ph* Jean-Marie Dreujou. *ed* Jacques Witta. *pd* Thérèse Ripaud. *m* Pierre Bachelet. *cast* Jacques Villeret, Jacques Gamblin, André Dussollier, Michel Serrault, Isabelle Carré, Eric Cantona, Suzanne Flon, Jacques Dufilho, Gisèle Casadesus, Jacques Boudet.
●This 'gentle' yarn set in the Loire valley in the 1930s, follows an odd couple of odd-jobbers – Riton (Villeret) and Garris (Gamblin), muddling through life in relative poverty – and their friendships with various locals. Thus we meet middle-aged bachelor and dandy Amédée (Dussollier), who grins boyishly and introduces them to jazz on his gramophone; Tane (Boudet), who drives a train, so isn't around much; and bored self-made industrialist Pépé (Serrault), who finds his priggish family stultifying. Riton is an idler who waxes alcoholic on the marvels of his long-lost first wife, while his straight friend Garris secretly nurses a footloose spirit. The tone is lyrical and bittersweet – Garris develops a crush on a local girl (Carré) who heads elsewhere; Pépé rediscovers the rustic joys of his childhood – which is, perhaps, poignant, supposing you can rouse yourself to care a hoot. It's narrated by Riton's little daughter, who takes a shine to Pépé's grandson, and falls ill somewhere along the story; and, lest there seem a dearth of dramatic tension, there's an imprisoned ex-champion boxer (Cantona) who blames Riton for his misfortunes and swears revenge. NB

Enfants du Paradis, Les (Children of Paradise) (100)

(1945, Fr, 187 min, b/w)
d Marcel Carné. *sc* Jacques Prévert. *ph* Roger Hubert. *ed* Henri Rust. *ad* Léon Barsacq, Raymond Gabutti, Alexandre Trauner. *m* Maurice Thiriet, Joseph Kosma. *cast* Pierre Brasseur, Arletty, Jean-Louis Barrault, Marcel Herrand, Maria Casarès, Louis Salou, Pierre Renoir, Fabien Loris, Jane Marken.

● A marvellously witty, ineffably graceful rondo of passions and perversities animating the Boulevard du Crime, home of Parisian popular theatre in the early 19th century, and an astonishing anthill of activity in which mimes and mountebanks rub shoulders with aristocrats and assassins. Animating Jacques Prévert's script is a multi-layered meditation on the nature of performance, ranging from a vivid illustration of contrasting dramatic modes (Barrault's mime needing only gestures, Brasseur's Shakespearean actor relishing the music of words) and a consideration of the interchangeability of theatre and life (as Herrand's frustrated playwright Lacenaire elects to channel his genius into crime), to a wry acknowledgment of the social relevance of performance (all three men are captivated by Arletty's insouciant whore, who acts herself out of their depth to achieve the protection of a Count, establishing a social barrier which Lacenaire promptly breaches in his elaborate stage management of the Count's murder). Flawlessly executed and with a peerless cast, this is one of the great French movies, so perfectly at home in its period that it never seems like a costume picture, and at over three hours not a moment too long. Amazing to recall that it was produced in difficult circumstances towards the end of the German Occupation during World War II. TM

Enfants du siècle, Les

(1999, Fr/GB, 137 min)
d/p Diane Kurys. *sc* François-Olivier Rousseau, Murray Head, Diane Kurys. *ph* Vilko Filac. *ed* Joële van Effenterre. *pd* Bernard Vezat. *m* Luis Bacalov. *cast* Juliette Binoche, Benoît Magimel, Stefano Dionisi, Robin Renucci, Karin Viard, Isabelle Carré, Patrick Chesnais, Victoire Thivisol.

● At the start of Kurys' tale of high romantic pride and passion in 1830s Paris and Venice, a textural preamble solemnly relates the cultural conditions that held sway at the time of the film's setting. Post-Napoleon, the young have grown up rebellious but lost. Kurys' children of the century are the writer George Sand, née Aurore Dupin (Binoche), and the poet and playwright Alfred de Musset (Magimel), who met and spent a torrid 18 months together. A separated mother of two, Sand had already scandalised Paris with her essays on male sexual chauvinism and female frigidity. After one ill-received reading, the flamboyant Musset comes to her with support and advice, observing for instance that she's too pure to understand the perversity of a perfidious lover. The film describes a brief, picturesque courtship, and has Musset stab his meddling brother with a fork, whereupon the lovers' road together turns rocky. Kurys recreates every capricious twist of their affair with reverential detail, without ever illuminating their hearts, and the impression of abridgement – 19 minutes have been shorn from the original French release – only redoubles the effect of unguided bustle. Well upholstered amour fou. NB

Enfants Terribles, Les (The Strange Ones)

(1949, Fr, 107 min, b/w)
d/p Jean-Pierre Melville. *sc* Jean-Pierre Melville, Jean Cocteau. *ph* Henri Decaë. *ed* Monique Bonnot. *ad* Mathys. *m* Johann Sebastian Bach, Antonio Vivaldi. *cast* Nicole Stéphane, Edouard Dhermitte, Jacques Bernard, Renée Cosima, Roger Gaillard, Mel Martin.

● One of Cocteau's most satisfying contributions to the cinema, largely because of Melville's lucid interpretation of the writer's poetic vision. Essence and myth lie at the centre of Cocteau's story of a young sister (a startling performance from Nicole Stéphane) and brother who retreat into their private world to play out their erotically charged games. It is easy to see why the film was so influential with subsequent French film-makers, especially in the way it anticipates the self-obsessiveness of an adolescent culture that grew up in the '50s. How Melville achieved its lightness of touch – a quality much admired by Cocteau – remains a small mystery, given Cocteau's constant interference and a wooden male lead (Cocteau's protégé, not Melville's choice). CPe

Enfer, L' (Torment)

(1993, Fr, 103 min)
d Claude Chabrol. *p* Marin Karmitz. *sc* Henri-Georges Clouzot. *ph* Bernard Zitzermann. *ed* Monique Fardoulis. *ad* Emile Ghigo. *m* Matthieu Chabrol. *cast* Emmanuelle Béart, François Cluzet, Nathalie Cardone, André Wilms, Marc Lavoine, Dora Doll, Jean-Pierre Cassel.

● Paul (Cluzet) is charming, attractive, hardworking; Nelly (Béart) is beautiful and carefree, devoted to her husband and more than happy to help him make a success of his Edenic lakeside hotel. They're madly in love. Nelly has a baby. Paul has trouble sleeping; he can't shake off a nagging inner voice which needs to know what Nelly's up to every minute of the day. Little by little his suspicions take shape, and jealousy plunges him into an unfathomable purgatory of doubt and dementia. Chabrol's film is a relentlessly bleak, gripping study of pathological jealousy which finds the director more thoroughly engaged than he's been for some while. Based on a rediscovered screenplay by Henri-Georges Clouzot (whose 1964 production was abandoned after six days' shooting), this is a black comedy which evolves into a long dark night of the soul. The nihilistic vision may be Clouzot's, but the economy, concentration and oppressive atmosphere are ure Chabrol, as is the eruption of the suppressed into the public arena. A work of enthralling virtuosity. TCh

Enforcer, The (aka Murder, Inc.)

(1951, US, 88 min, b/w)
d Bretaigne Windust, [Raoul Walsh]. *p* Milton Sperling. *sc* Martin Rackin. *ph* Robert Burks. *ed* Fred Allen. *ad* Charles H Clarke. *m* David Buttolph. *cast* Humphrey Bogart, Everett Sloane, Zero Mostel, Ted de Corsia, Roy Roberts, Bob Steele, King Donovan.

● Based on the 1940 revelations of Abe Reles as to the existence of an organisation called Murder Inc, but prompted by the Kefauver Committee investigations of 1950, this is very much a transitional film between the *noir* Forties and the syndicate Fifties. Unveiling the argot of the murder business for the first time (eg. 'contract', 'hit', 'finger'), it scored another notable first by using its intricate web of flashbacks, conjured by the interrogations of Bogart's crusading assistant DA, to explore the mysterious structures of organised crime. Bathed in a typically *noir* aura of fear, shot by Robert Burks in a semi-documentary style, and with a laconically witty script by Martin Rackin, it only occasionally reveals the cracks one might expect given that part of the footage had to be restaged by Walsh (who contributed, most notably, the climactic shootout with the killer finally nailed in a doorway). TM

Enforcer, The

(1976, US, 96 min)
d James Fargo. Robert Daley. *sc* Stirling Silliphant, Dean Riesner. *ph* Charles W Short. *ed* Ferris Webster, Joel Cox. *ad* Allen Smith. *m* Jerry Fielding. *cast* Clint Eastwood, Tyne Daly, Harry Guardino, Bradford Dillman, John Mitchum, DeVeren Brookwalter.

● *Dirty Harry* part three doggedly revives the formula of its predecessors, with Eastwood again the tough San Francisco cop, at odds with his liberal superiors, stalking psychopaths, this time a supposedly revolutionary group of kill-crazy kids. Whereas the earlier films went some way to exploring the political and personal tensions of operating as a modern lawman, this simplifies to the point of crudity – 'It's a war, isn't it?' – and misuses Eastwood's monolithic presence, primarily as a butt for gags like lumbering him with a female partner. This last could have worked, especially with Eastwood tiring of his image (cf. *The Outlaw Josey Wales*), but the scriptwriters fail dismally to develop the relationship, opting instead for a predictable one-note comedy of encumbrance. Yet despite inferior contributions from most departments, Eastwood carries the picture, and Tyne Daly does well as the female cop against very stacked odds. CPe

Engelchen

see Little Angel

England Made Me

(1972, GB, 100 min)
d Peter Duffell. *p* Jack Levin. *sc* Desmond Cory, Peter Duffell. *ph* Ray Parslow. *ed* Malcolm Cooke. *pd* Tony Woollard. *m* John Scott. *cast* Peter Finch, Michael York, Hildegard Neil, Michael Hordern, Joss Ackland, Tessa Wyatt.

● Duffell's adaptation of Graham Greene's novel retreads the path of both *Cabaret* and *The Damned*, but comes far closer to the spirit of Isherwood's *Goodbye to Berlin*. The film never allows its characters to be dwarfed by set pieces, and instead concentrates on conveying the ingenuous and ineffectual charm of a young Englishman (York) caught between the decadence and encroaching violence of Nazi Germany and a potentially incestuous twin sister (Neil). It's a pity that the film was unfairly neglected at the time, thereby throwing a hitch into Duffell's promising career. DP

Englishman Who Went Up a Hill, But Came Down a Mountain, The

(1995, GB, 95 min)
d Christopher Monger. *p* Sarah Curtis. *sc* Christopher Monger. *ph* Vernon Layton. *ed* David Martin. *pd* Charles Garrad. *m* Stephen Endelman. *cast* Hugh Grant, Ian McNeice, Colm Meaney, Tara Fitzgerald, Ian Hart, Tudor Vaughn, Kenneth Griffith.

● English cartographer Reginald Anson (Grant, blinking and stammering) and his colleague George (McNeice) arrive at a quiet Welsh village in 1917 to measure Ffynnon Garw – the 'first mountain in Wales', the locals boast. The Englishmen's findings dismay them. At 984 ft the summit is 15 ft short of a mountain. Led by the landlord, Morgan the Goat (Meaney), and his arch-rival, the Rev Jones (Griffith), the villagers determine that the surveyors will not leave until the hill has become a mountain. Monger (*Just Like a Woman, Waiting for the Light*) heard this yarn from his father and his father's father, but the film owes as much to the parochial charm of the Ealing comedies of the 1940s, and that obsession with size which runs through much British film humour (*The Mouse That Roared, The Smallest Show on Earth*, etc). It's a gentle, indulgent celebration of community values, heart and home, with a sprinkling of Welsh nationalist propaganda. Well crafted as it is, and hard to dislike, it's harder still to shake the suspicion that Monger is making a mountain out of a molehill. TCh

English Patient, The

(1996, US, 162 min)
d Anthony Minghella. *p* Saul Zaentz. *sc* Anthony Minghella. *ph* John Seale. *ed* Walter Murch. *pd* Stuart Craig. *m* Gabriel Yared. *cast* Ralph Fiennes, Juliette Binoche, Willem Dafoe, Kristin Scott Thomas, Naveen Andrews, Colin Firth, Julian Wadham, Jürgen Prochnow, Kevin Whately, Clive Merison.

● Tuscany, as the Allies pursue the Germans north at the end of WWII: traumatised by loss and carnage, Canadian nurse Hana (Binoche) decides to stay behind in an abandoned, bombed monastery and care for her dying patient (Fiennes). He seems to recall little of his life, but when Caravaggio (Dafoe), a vengeful, morphine-addicted thief, turns up and quizzes him over past dark secrets, and as Hana reads from his beloved Herodotos, memories return of the pre-war years when, as an archaeologist/cartographer in the Sahara, he had a passionate affair with Katharine (Scott Thomas), wife of a British colleague. Though Anthony Minghella's adaptation of Michael Ondaatje's novel simplifies, jettisons and changes certain elements of the original story, it remains a rich, complex, entrancing piece of work. Part poignant romance, part suspenseful adventure, part enigmatic mystery, it's essentially a study in different responses to love and war, honour and betrayal, nationality and identity, falsehood and forgiveness, which sounds subtle echoes as the narrative flashes to and fro between two main time frames. Needless to say, the performances are flawless; more surprising is the fluency, poetry and scale of Minghella's direction (John Seale's sensuous desert photography is superb), equally eloquent whether depicting boudoir intimacies, bomb-disposal skills, drunken dementia or a deadly sandstorm. GA

Enid Is Sleeping (aka Over Her Dead Body)

(1989, US, 102 min)
d Maurice Phillips. *p* John A Davis, Howard Malin. *sc* AJ Tipping, James Whaley, Maurice Phillips. *ph* Affonso Beato. *ed* Malcolm Campbell. *pd* Paul Peters. *m* Craig Safan. *cast* Elizabeth Perkins, Judge Reinhold, Jeffrey Jones, Maureen Mueller, Rhea Perlman, Brion James, Charles Tyner, Henry Jones, Michael J Pollard.
●Enid (Mueller) catches her cop husband (Reinhold) in bed with her sister (Perkins), and in the ensuing fracas is killed. What to do with the body? Everything goes wildly wrong… The troublesome corpse as a comic theme is usually a bit of a flounder. Even Hitchcock couldn't do much with it in *The Trouble with Harry*, and Phillips does even less, though he's noisier about it. In fact, the cast shout a lot to make things funnier, or stand about mugging to give the gag a chance to go down. Pity, since Reinhold and Perkins are accomplished comic players when they get the material. BC

Enigma

(1982, GB/Fr, 122 min)
d Jeannot Szwarc. *p* Peter Shaw. *sc* John Briley. *ph* Jean-Louis Picavet. *ed* Peter Weatherley. *pd* François Comtet. *m* Marc Wilkinson, Douglas Gamley. *cast* Martin Sheen, Sam Neill, Brigitte Fossey, Michel Lonsdale, Derek Jacobi, Frank Finlay.
●In this disastrous mid-Atlantic spy thriller, Sheen plays an expatriate American who grew up behind the Iron Curtain and now makes propaganda broadcasts for Free World Radio in Paris. Learning that the KGB has a plan to assassinate five leading Soviet dissidents now living in Europe, the CIA recruit Sheen to obtain a crucial scrambling device fitted to a Communist word processor in East Berlin. Sheen changes his appearance almost as often as John Briley's script changes its mind (about every five minutes), and both of them are forever rushing down blind alleys in search of an excitement which continually eludes them. NF

Enigma

(2001, Neth/US/GB/Ger, 119 min)
d Michael Apted. *p* Lorne Michaels, Mick Jagger. *sc* Tom Stoppard. *ph* Seamus McGarvey. *ed* Rick Shaine. *pd* John Beard. *m* John Barry. *cast* Dougray Scott, Kate Winslet, Jeremy Northam, Saffron Burrows, Nikolaj Coster Waldau, Tom Hollander, Corin Redgrave, Matthew Macfayden.
●Bletchley Park WWII code-breakers Scott and Winslet battle to save the world. The cracking of the German Enigma machine and the diversity and oddity of the personnel involved should have provided for a fascinating and relevant story. Regrettably, Apted's film, from Robert Harris' romantic thriller, gets caught between the demands of crowd-thrilling adventure and psychologically compelling history, and satisfies neither. The director, his design team and cameraman have ably recreated the ruddy, grey surface tones of 1943 Britain. But the stress is on surface. Psychological authenticity is, perhaps, too alienating for modern audiences, though it was a bold move to render Winslet so plain while giving all the glamour to the Veronica Lake-like femme fatale Burrows. Equally bold is the fractured playing of Scott's genius don. However, his late conversion to all-action hero strips the film of credibility. WH

Enigma of Kaspar Hauser, The

see Jeder für sich und Gott gegen alle

Enigma Rosso

see Red Rings of Fear

Ensayo de un Crimen

see Criminal Life of Archibaldo de la Cruz, The

Ennui, L'

(1998, Fr, 122 min)
d Cédric Kahn. *p* Paulo Branco. *sc* Cédric Kahn, Laurence Ferreira Barbosa. *ph* Pascal Marti. *ed* Yann Dedet. *ad* François Abelanet. *cast* Charles Berling, Sophie Guillemin, Arielle Dombasle, Robert Kramer, Alice Grey, Maurice Antoni, Tom Ouedraogo.
●Jaded after the failure of his marriage, Martin (Berling) has 'given up love', and taken to his car. On one voyeuristic drive around Paris he sees something spark between a girl and a grave older man. Drawn in, he tracks the man to a bar, and later, to his studio, only to find him dead of a heart attack and the girl, Cécilia (Guillemin, a revelation) – his muse – collecting her belongings. Martin interrogates, accosts and couples with her, a dance he performs as an increasingly frantic ritual over the following months, compelled and confounded by this docile and wholly unremarkable girl's casual availability and calm impenetrability. It's like banging a brick wall. Sex and ennui make strange but apt cinematic bedfellows. Kahn's adaptation of Alberto Moravia's *Boredom* bears a close resemblance to Godard's treatment of the same author's *Le Mépris* – thematically more than cinematically – with its fateful study of an incompatible, inscrutable relationship. Moravia's clinical, obsessive analysis of the pitfalls of sexual attraction and rejection offers potentially gloomy going, and the narrative here certainly spins round and round nowhere. But Kahn enlivens the drama by comically spiking Martin's mono-maniacal self-absorbtion, and counterposes Berling's restless neurotic and Guillemin's unflappable, unyielding enigma to dynamic and fascinating effect. NB

En plein coeur

see In All Innocence

Ensign Pulver

(1964, US, 104 min)
d/p Joshua Logan. *sc* Joshua Logan, Peter S Feibleman. *ph* Charles Lawton. *ed* William Reynolds. *ad* Leo Kuter. *m* George Duning. *cast* Robert Walker Jr, Burl Ives, Walter Matthau, Tommy Sands, Millie Perkins, Kay Medford.
●Sequel to Thomas Heggen's long-running play *Mister Roberts* which, in the film version at least, coasted along largely on the strength of fine performances from Cagney, Lemmon and William Powell. The substitute cast taking over here is competent enough, but the script has nothing whatsoever to add, and soon runs out of invention in trying to prolong the feud between the ship's crew and its martinet captain. TM

Entebbe: Operation Thunderbolt

see Operation Thunderbolt

Entertainer, The

(1960, GB, 96 min, b/w)
d Tony Richardson. *p* Harry Saltzman. *sc* John Osborne, Nigel Kneale. *ph* Oswald Morris. *ed* Alan Osbiston. *ad* Ralph Brinton. *m* John Addison. *cast* Laurence Olivier, Brenda de Banzie, Albert Finney, Joan Plowright, Roger Livesey, Alan Bates, Shirley Anne Field, Thora Hird, Daniel Massey.
●John Osborne's quirky indictment of '50s stagnation still looks stagebound, despite extensive location shooting and the cool, inventive photography of Oswald Morris. Too many words, too many tantrums, too much kitchen-sink sentimentality; yet there are moments when this looks like a good film. The performances are remarkable: Plowright and de Banzie beating desperately against the bars of the mad male family; Livesey, a resurrected Colonel Blimp, inspiring the OAPs with 'Don't Let Them Scrap the British Navy'; and Olivier, throwing Shakespearean dignity to the winds to play Archie Rice, the epitome of '50s tattiness with his gratifyingly awful theme song, 'Thank God We're Normal'. RMy

Entertaining Angels: The Dorothy Day Story

(1996, US, 111 min)
d Michael Ray Rhodes. *p* Ellwood Kieser. *sc* John Wells. *ph* Mike Fash. *ed* George Folsey Jr, Geoffrey Rowland. *pd* Charles Rosen. *m* Bill Conti, Ashley Irwin. *cast* Moira Kelly, Heather Graham, Melinda Dillon, Lenny Von Dohlen, Martin Sheen, Brian Keith.
●An evangelical biography of the firebrand reporter, feminist and philanthropist Dorothy Day (Kelly, persuasive): in 1933, following her conversion, she co-founded *The Catholic Worker* with Peter Maurin (Sheen), an eccentric philosopher. The film opens in Greenwich Village, 1917, where Dorothy boozes with anarchists, communists and Eugene O'Neill, and argues journalistic priorities at *The Call*. But as the opening credit ('A Paulist Picture') and the end-list of 'thank-yous' (including the Conrad Hilton Foundation) testify, the makers are more interested in her later mission to bring Christ into the lives of the poorest and most dejected of New York's Lower East Side. The first hour, 1917-33, rushes through too much placard-waving social history, rendered in nicely composed but familiar umbra washes. The second deals at tedious length with Day's conflicting commitment to the poor, her daughter and the paper. WH

Entertaining Mr Sloane

(1969, GB, 94 min)
d Douglas Hickox. *p* Douglas Kentish. *sc* Clive Exton. *ph* Wolfgang Suschitzky. *ed* John Trumper. *pd* Michael Seymour. *m* Georgie Fame. *cast* Beryl Reid, Harry Andrews, Peter McEnery, Alan Webb.
●Joe Orton's four-hander about a sister and brother (nympho and queer respectively) vying for the favours of a desirable stud (under the eyes of their ancient dadda) loses much of its savoury charm in this movie version. Clive Exton's script opens out the play conventionally, to little effect, and Hickox's direction shows little flair for farce in general or Orton in particular. The cast are good enough for the original, though. RG

Enter the Dragon

(1973, US/HK, 98 min)
d Robert Clouse. *p* Fred Weintraub, Paul Heller. *sc* Michael Allin. *ph* Gil Hubbs. *ed* Kurt Hirschler, George Watters. *ad* James Wong Sun. *m* Lalo Schifrin. *cast* Bruce Lee, John Saxon, Shih Kien, Jim Kelly, Bob Wall, Yang Sze, Ahna Capri.
●The first of a burgeoning series of American film industry attempts to colonise the kung-fu market, this manages to be inferior to even the weakest of Bruce Lee's *echt*-Chinese movies. A sorry mixture of James Bond and Fu Manchu, it tacks together the exploits of a multi-national crew of martial artists converging on Hong Kong for a tournament, infiltrated by Lee – fresh from his Shaolin temple – on an assignment to bust an opium racket. Worth seeing for Lee, but still unforgivably wasteful of his talents.

Enter the Ninja

(1981, US, 99 min)
d Menahem Golan. *p* Judd Bernard, Yoram Globus. *sc* Dick Desmond. *ph* David Gurfinkel. *ed* Mark Goldblatt, Michael J Duthie. *ad* Robert Lee. *m* W Michael Lewis, Laurin Rinder. *cast* Franco Nero, Susan George, Sho Kosugi, Alex Courtney, Will Hare, Zachi Noy, Christopher George.
●A Z-grade international cast fumbles its way through a tiresome series of action movie clichés (impotent wealthy farmer and his frustrated wife ask their Ninja friend to defend them from ruthless oil baron and his incompetent hoods), with the characters mouthing appallingly clumsy lines in a startling variety of post-dubbed accents ('Why is Hasegawa so frustrated?' – 'Because it's the twentieth century'). With monotonous regularity the story pauses for graceless and unexciting fight scenes, complete with incessant death gurgles and bone-creaking, or for banal cod-Zen philosophising and rituals. Even on the level of unintentional humour this fails to entertain: the mark of a truly dreadful movie. GA

Enter the 7 Virgins (aka Virgins of the Seven Seas)

(1974, HK/WGer, 92 min)
d Kuei Chih-Hung, Ernst Hofbauer. *p* Runme Shaw, Wolf C Hartwig. *sc* Chen I Hsin. *ph* Yu Chi. *ed* Chiang Hsing Lung, Chang Shao Hsi. *ad* Johnson Tsao. *m* Wang Fu Ling. *cast* Yueh Hua, Tamara Elliot, Gillian Bray, Sonja Jeanine, Diana Drube, Deborah Rulls, Wang Hsieh, Liu Hui-Ling.
●Kuei Chih-Hung's magnificently atmospheric direction (making consummate use of the Shaw sets), and supremely dignified playing by Yueh Hua and Liu Hui-Ling, go for nothing in this

co-production. Some idiot has seen fit to burden the film with intensely degrading, not to say racist dubbing into joke Chinese full of 'vellys' and 'walkee plankees' (the story starts on board ship). There is also a liberal sprinkling of hip Americanisms of the 'Man, I'm really into kung-fu' variety. The appalling Hofbauer, veteran of innumberable leaden sex farces, presumably contributed the derisory sex scenes. VG

Enthusiasm (El Entusiasmo)

(1998, Chile, 120 min)
d/p Ricardo Larrain. *sc* Jorge Goldenberg, Ricardo Larrain. *ph* Esteban Courtalón. *ed* Danièle Fillois. *ad* Patricio Aguilar. *m* Jorge Arriagada. *cast* Maribel Verdu, Alvaro Escobar, Alvaro Rudolphi, Carmen Maura.
● This slightly rambling parable, by the director of *La Frontera*, on the commercialisation and loss of identity of his native country describes a love triangle formed by three friends. Guillermo (Rudolphi) dreams of a truly independent republic for Chile, but is nevertheless a pragmatist; Fernado (Escobar) is a poet who compromises his vision building a tourist development in the desert; Isabel (Verdu), is the woman they both love and who further functions in the film as an embodiment of the soul of the mother country. Nicely directed, good if sometimes overly moody performances, with some fine landscape photography. Shame about the faint cast of xenophobia. WH

Entity, The

(1981, US, 125 min)
d Sidney J Furie. *p* Harold Schneider. *sc* Frank De Felitta. *ph* Stephen H Burum. *ed* Frank J Urioste. *pd* Charles Rosen. *m* Charles Bernstein. *cast* Barbara Hershey, Ron Silver, David Labiosa, George Coe, Margeret Blye, Jacqueline Brooks.
● Perhaps any movie with such a wretched central idea (woman sexually assaulted by an invisible demon), supposedly based on fact or not, deserved the feminist picket-line which attended its West End screening. But for reasons that may be fortuitous, *The Entity* doesn't emerge quite as one-dimensionally nasty as its synopsis suggests. The film's men are so uniformly creepy, and its heroine so strong and sympathetic, that apart from a couple of unpleasant moments the story often seems less like horror than feminist parable, especially when Hershey (giving a fine performance) is reduced to a laboratory object with her home recreated in the psychology department. None of this may be intended, of course, but it goes to show that commercial movies sometimes hit spots that more intentionally didactic efforts can't reach. DP

Entrapment

(1999, US/Ger, 113 min)
d Jon Amiel. *p* Sean Connery, Michael Hertzberg, Rhonda Tollefson. *sc* Ron Bass, William Broyles. *ph* Phil Meheux. *ed* Terry Rawlings. *pd* Norman Garwood. *m* Christopher Young. *cast* Sean Connery, Catherine Zeta-Jones, Ving Rhames, Will Patton, Maury Chakin, Kevin McNally, Terry O'Neill, Madhav Sharma, David Yip.
● Connery plays Robert 'Mac' MacDougal, the world's wisest master thief, which is more or less the character he played in *Rising Sun* and *Just Cause*, the sexy *éminence grise* who's still surprisingly light on his feet. His performance is not the only secondhand item on display. There are shades of *To Catch a Thief* in the climactic robbery-with-fireworks and the age difference between the stars, Connery and Zeta-Jones as the insurance investigator on his trail. It's no surprise that they're not quite what they seem, but the plot throws up so many double-crosses you hardly believe a word of it. Instead, it tries to dazzle us with James Bondish set-pieces, while hoping that pure star power will fill in the blanks. Unfortunately, Amiel's bob-a-job direction fails to excite, Connery's coasting, and Zeta-Jones is pretty plasticky. TJ

Entre Nous

see Coup de Foudre

Entre Nous

(2001, Fr, 82 min)
d Serge Lalou. *p* Patrick Sobelman, Gilles Sandoz. *sc* Serge Lalou, Chantal Pelletier. *ph* Katel Djian. *ed* Catherine Gouze. *ad* Emmanuelle Daverton, Judith Gouze. *cast* Bruno Putzulu, Emmanuelle Grangé, Emilie Lafarge, Philippe Fabbri, Célia Mabille, Elizabeth Vitali, Thierry Bosc, Fauwzi Saichi, Thomas Roux.
● This first feature from producer and documentarist Lalou is an intriguing, if finally frustrating study of a family isolated on a small island and attempting to come to terms with their variously bewildering emotions after the father drowns while swimming back to the mainland. It's a film of few words and often enigmatic gestures, as the children – ranging from about eight to 30 – struggle against their mother's determination to stay true to the family's intentions of removing themselves from the rest of the harsh world. Too insistently 'poetic' to hold the attention, but enhanced with some eye-catching digital camerawork. GA

Entre Tinieblas

see Dark Habits

Entusiasmo, El

see Enthusiasm

Enzo, Domani a Palermo!

(1999, It, 70 min, b/w)
d Daniele Cipri, Franco Maresco. *p* Tea Nova. *sc/ph/ed* Daniele Cipri, Franco Maresco. *with* Enzo Castagna, Carlo Giordano, Mario Salmeri.
● Cipri and Maresco's delicious documentary portrays Sicilian super-agent Enzo Castagna, a man with some 20,000 extras on his books, who has worked with the likes of Loren, Pasolini, Rosi, Coppola and Cimino (indeed, virtually anyone who's ever chosen to film in Palermo). It's typically weird, witty and wonderful, partly due to its subject, a self-styled 'little big man' who consents to be described as 'almighty' and 'the greatest contributor to Italian cinema in the last 35 years'. The local favourite has also done time for bribery, but refuses to comment on Cosa Nostra. The film is as astonishing as its subject. Shot in luscious b/w, it's driven forward by an offscreen interrogator who alternates between ludicrously hyperbolic flattery and forthright questions about corruption and crime. It also serves as a study of the way ethics get abandoned in the unending pursuit of fame, wealth and self-esteem. GA

Epoque formidable..., Une (Incredible Times...)

(1991, Fr, 90 min)
d Gérard Jugnot. *p* Alain Depardieu. *sc* Gérard Jugnot, Philippe Lopès Curval. *ph* Gérard de Batista. *ed* Catherine Kelber. *ad* Geoffroy Larcher. *m* Francis Cabrel. *cast* Gérard Jugnot, Richard Bohringer, Victoria Abril, Ticky Holgado, Chick Ortéga, Roland Blanche.
● Jugnot's dream of drowning anticipates his social downfall in this comedy of misfortune. In quick succession he loses his job, home, family, car and finally even his shoes. Shuffling around Paris with a couple of plastic bags tied to his feet, he falls in with Bohringer's little band of bums, who introduce him to a life of sleeping in métro stations, begging and petty thievery. Eventually his luck turns and he escapes from what is never presented as a particularly desperate existence: the rosé spirit of René Clair moves in the picture. Full marks to Jugnot for never trying to make his own character sympathetic. But his opposition of lovable outsiders vs. a flint-hearted society of traffic wardens and civil servants is facile. BBa

Equilibristes, Les (Walking a Tightrope)

(1991, Fr, 128 min)
d Nico Papatakis. *p* Hubert Balsan. *sc* Nico Papatakis. *ph* William Lubtchansky. *ed* Delphine Desfons. *cast* Michel Piccoli, Lilah Dadi, Polly Walker, Doris Kunstmann, Patrick Mille, Juliette Degenne.
● Based on an episode in the life of Jean Genet – but possessing none of the depth of play with sex and power in his writing – this features Piccoli as a supposedly great poet, playwright and all-round manipulator who falls for a young German-Algerian sweeper-up at the circus (Dadi), and resolves to make him a great tightrope-walker. Needless to say, the young man is soon tossed aside for a sexy would-be racing driver, and retreats for histrionic hair-tearing sessions with his beer-sodden mother. Ludicrously overwrought, and with a positively 19th-century notion of gay sex – all ageing Svengalis and gamy young Ganymedes – this wears its symbolism heavily, to say the least; and worst of all, it's stultifyingly dull, right up to the daft apocalyptic climax. Polly Walker, as Piccoli's confidante and 'cock-catcher', is mysteriously got up as a dead ringer for Grace Kelly. JRo

Equinox

(1992, US, 115 min)
d Alan Rudolph. *p* David Blocker. *sc* Alan Rudolph. *ph* Elliot Davis. *ed* Michael Ruscio. *pd* Steven Legler. *cast* Matthew Modine, Lara Flynn Boyle, Tyra Ferrel, M Emmet Walsh, Fred Ward, Marisa Tomei, Lori Singer.
● After a dip into the mainstream with *Mortal Thoughts*, the wildest card in American cinema is back on his own bizarre terrain. This modern urban fairytale is a beautifully ambivalent retelling of *The Prince and the Pauper*. Modine is the separated-at-birth twins (both of them), one a hood whose dream life – moppet children, a cooing fashion-plate wife (Singer) – is coupled with violent megalomania, the other a cringing wimp who can't bring himself to date his best friend's anguished, poetry-reading sister (Boyle). The whole is held together with a plot about an aspiring writer (Ferrel) on the track of her first real-life drama, and by an atmospheric soundtrack (Terje Rydal, Ali Farka Toure) that accompanies the characters' hypnotically crazed manoeuvres. M Emmet Walsh steals the show as a garage boss in a drolly choreographed homage to Jacques Demy. Delirious stuff. JRo

Equus

(1977, GB, 137 min)
d Sidney Lumet. *p* Elliott Kastner, Lester Persky. *sc* Peter Shaffer. *ph* Oswald Morris. *ed* John Victor Smith. *pd* Tony Walton. *m* Richard Rodney Bennett. *cast* Richard Burton, Peter Firth, Colin Blakely, Joan Plowright, Harry Andrews, Eileen Atkins, Jenny Agutter, Kate Reid.
● Lumet's reverential adaptation of Peter Shaffer's play all but defies sane comment: the sub-Lawrentian pretensions that theatre audiences took so seriously stand revealed in all their Pythonesque absurdity when transposed to the screen. The problem is very basic: theatrical symbolism just isn't the same as filmic realism. Add to this that Burton lacks even a shred of credibility as the psychiatrist, and that Firth's performance – technically faultless – is periodically interrupted by scenes in which the awe-struck camera simply observes him undressed, and you begin to comprehend the film's true wretchedness. TR

Era Notte a Roma

(1960, It/Fr, 120 min, b/w)
d Roberto Rossellini. *sc* Robert Rossellini, Sergio Amidei, Diego Fabbri, Brunello Rondi. *ph* Carlo Carlini. *ed* Roberto Cinquini. *ad* Flavio Mogherini. *m* Renzo Rossellini. *cast* Leo Genn, Giovanna Ralli, Sergei Bondarchuk, Hannes Messemer, Peter Baldwin, Sergio Fantoni, Enrico Maria Salerno, Paolo Stoppa, Renato Salvatori, Laura Betti, Rosalba Neri.
● Stylistically an intriguing (and not wholly successful) mixture of Rossellini's early 'realism', Bergman-period melodrama, and the contemplative didacticism of his later films, this return to the milieu of Nazi-occupied Rome may not have the raw power of *Rome, Open City*, but is immensely affecting all the same. Three escaped Allied PoWs – a Brit, an American and a Russian – take refuge in the home of Roman black marketeer Ralli, whose Communist lover (Salvatori) is executed when they are betrayed by a corrupt, Nazi-collaborator priest. On one level, it's a fairly straightforward suspense movie, detailing the countless threats to the safety of the fugitives and the woman who provides sanctuary; on another, it's an unsentimental, *Paisà*-like celebration of the shared humanity that allows the various characters to communicate with one another despite linguistic differences and the wariness born of perilous circumstance. An uneven, flawed, but very intelligent work of enormous humanity. GA

Eraser

(1996, US, 114 min)
d Charles Russell. *p* Arnold Kopelson, Anne Kopelson. *sc* Tony Puryear, Walon Green. *ph* Adam Greenberg. *ed* Michael Tronick. *pd* Bill Kenney. *m* Alan Silvestri. *cast* Arnold

Schwarzenegger, James Caan, Vanessa Williams, James Coburn, Robert Pastorelli, Andy Romano.
●A cumbersome, resolutely formula thriller of the kind that Arnie made before he *was* Arnie (think of *Commando* or *Raw Deal*). Still, it intermittently takes off into the realms of comic fantasy hyper-drive, with our hero leaping from burning jets at 11,000 feet, grappling with alligators in the New York Zoo ('You're luggage!'), and trading lead with the latest hi-tech X-ray weaponry – the influence of John Woo, perhaps, or simply the result of the current fetish for digital effects. Schwarzenegger is Kruger, the government's best agent in the federal witness protection programme. When a mole in the organisation seeks to wipe out his latest charge (Williams), Kruger only has his old clients to turn to. It's a movie constructed around three or four self-consciously 'cool' episodes, and passably entertaining as such, but there's also an awful lot of uncool contrivance, coincidence and contempt for the audience. TCh

Eraserhead

(1976, US, 89 min, b/w)
d/p/sc David Lynch. *ph* Frederick Elmes, Herbert Cardwell. *ed/pd* David Lynch. *m* Fats Waller. *cast* Jack Nance, Charlotte Stewart, Allen Joseph, Jeanne Bates, Judith Anna Roberts, Laurel Near.
●Lynch's remarkable first feature is a true original. There's little in the way of a coherent story: nervy Henry, living in a sordid industrial city of smoke, steam and shadows, is forced to marry his girlfriend when she pronounces herself pregnant, and finds himself the father of an all-devouring, inhuman monster. But, almost like a surrealist movie, it has its own weird logic, mixing black comedy (concerning nuclear families and urban life), horror and sci-conventions, and pure fantasy. Best seen as a dark nightmare about sexuality, parenthood and commitment in relationships, it astounds through its expressionist sets and photography, the startling, sinister soundtrack, and relentlessly imaginative fluency. Only the sequence that gives the film its name – a dream within the dream about Henry's head being lopped off and turned into a pencil-eraser – fails to work, and that's a small reservation for a film with so many cinematic coups. GA

Ercole alla conquista di Atlantide (Hercules and the Captive Women/Hercules Conquers Atlantis)

(1961, It/Fr, 101 min)
d Vittorio Cottafavi. *p* Achille Piazzi. *sc* Alessandro Continenza, Vittorio Cottafavi, Duccio Tessari. *ph* Carlo Carlini. *ed* Maurizio Lucidi. *ad* Franco Lolli. *m* Gino Marinuzzi. *cast* Reg Park, Fay Spain, Ettore Manni, Luciano Marin, Laura Altan, Enrico Maria Salerno, Ivo Garrani, Gian Maria Volonté.
●Some extreme claims have been made for Cottafavi's sword and sandal epics, but essentially this example impresses by its simplicity and excellent pictorial values. Reluctant hero Hercules (Park) is hoodwinked into serving the Greek cause by quashing the scheme of the Queen of Atlantis (Spain) who, under the influence of the god Uranus, is producing a race of supermen. The knockabout comedy is unexceptional and most of the cast only adequate, though Spain delivers a high camp performance as the arrogant queen, letting off coloured puffs of smoke for her pleasure. Best of all is the dynamic design: deep and mysterious hallways, a team of white horses flying through subterranean tunnels, and a wholly identical super-race revealed from beneath their equally identical armoured visors. DT

Eredità Ferramonti, L'

see Inheritance, The

Erendira

(1982, Fr/Mex/WGer, 105 min)
d Ruy Guerra. *p* Alain Quéffélean. *sc* Gabriel Garcia Márquez. *ph* Denys Clerval. *ed* Kénout Peltier. *ad* Pierre Cadiou, Rainer Chaper. *m* Maurice Lecoeur. *cast* Irene Papas, Claudia Ohana, Michel Lonsdale, Oliver Wehe, Rufus, Blanca Guerra, Pierre Vaneck.
●Once upon a time there was a comely maiden who lived with a tame baby ostrich and her wicked granny in a windswept hacienda dripping with alabaster and gilt and paper flowers. But the foolish girl forgot to snuff out the candles one night, and the magnificent palace blazed into ashes. 'My poor darling,' murmured the grandmother gently, 'your life will not be long enough to repay me', and she set the virgin to work as a courtesan. And admirers came from far and wide to follow their exotic progress through the Mexican desert and to lie with Erendira... This febrile fairytale, adapted by Gabriel García Márquez from his own novella, is handsome to behold and laden with symbols, though of what it's difficult to say. Only Irene Papas, as the imperious, peacock-plumed beldame, brings a touch of mad comic grandeur to brighten the portentous solemnity. SJo

Eric Clapton and His Rolling Hotel

(1980, GB, 70 min)
d/p/sc Rex Pyke. *ph* John Metcalf. *ed* Philip McDonald. *with* Eric Clapton, Muddy Waters, George Harrison, Elton John.
●The Rolling Hotel, which carried the Clapton entourage on their 1979 European tour, is a luxury train originally built by Goering and usually reserved for the German chancellor. On board, and on various European stages, Pyke shot what, surprisingly, was the first documentary footage about this veteran rock guitarist. The film gives space to the man as well as his music, and treats his talents with the seriousness they deserve. SWo

Erik the Viking

(1989, GB, 108 min)
d Terry Jones. *p* John Goldstone. *sc* Terry Jones. *ph* Ian Wilson. *ed* George Akers. *pd* John Beard. *m* Neil Innes. *cast* Tim Robbins, Mickey Rooney, Eartha Kitt, Terry Jones, Imogen Stubbs, John Cleese, Tsutomu Sekine, Antony Sher, Gary Cady, Charles McKeown, Tim McInnerny, John Gordon Sinclair, Freddie Jones.
●Terry Jones' post-Python frolic, inspired by his own Norse saga children's book, is not a funny film, and neither well-directed nor exciting. Robbins plays a kind of lovelorn gentle giant, dismayed by the daily drudgery of conquest, pillage and rape, who seeks enlightenment from a cave-dwelling seer/hag (Kitt). This is the Dark Age of Ragnarok, she tells him, which will end in an orgy of fighting and destructiveness. He thus sets out with a long-ship full of squabbling warriors with names like Sven the Berserk and Thorfinn Skullsplitter, to awaken the gods with the Horn Resounding so that they may usher in the new era of peace and light. In pursuit are snivelling Loki (Sher), maker of weapons, and the very-evil-indeed Halfdan the Black (Cleese). There's a certain precocious schoolboy mentality at work in the film: an indulgent delight in making fantasies come to life. Its disarming mix of blood-and-muck realism, researched detail, and soaring wish-fulfillment, wonder and irreverence, does provide lots of small incidental pleasures. WH

Erin Brockovich

(2000, US, 133 min)
d Steven Soderbergh. *p* Danny DeVito, Michael Shamberg, Stacey Sher. *sc* Susannah Grant. *ph* Ed Lachman. *ed* Anne V Coates. *pd* Philip Messina. *m* Thomas Newman. *cast* Julia Roberts, Albert Finney, Aaron Eckhart, Marg Helgenberger, Cherry Jones, Veanne Cox, Conchata Ferrell, Tracey Walter, Peter Coyote.
●Being the true story of a struggling single mother's exposé of a water poisoning case, implicating the giant utility Pacific Gas and Electric, the film has obvious antecedents in the likes of *The Rainmaker* and *A Civil Action*. As with *Out of Sight* and *The Limey*, though, the pleasure of Soderbergh's approach lies not in the familiarity of the storyline, but in his fresh, intelligent reconstruction of it. Where the film differs from, and marks a maturation on, his earlier work is in its humanist rather than formalist inclinations: while the glowing cinematography and bluesy soundtrack maintain the sheen of the previous films, the focus here is on Erin (Roberts, in her best performance to date) and her relations with her family, lover (Eckhart), colleagues and some of the plaintiffs whose cause she trumpets. It's a credible, magnificent characterisation. As the brisk, concise storytelling excises the fat, so Erin cuts through the crap. The film steers past every potential cliché, finally redeeming not only Erin but the true life genre. Perhaps not as purely enjoyable as the director's last two films, but a deeply satisfying achievement. NB

Erl King, The

see Roi des Aulnes, Le

Ermo

(1994, China, 98 min)
d Zhou Xiaowen. *p* Chen Kunming, Jimmy Tan. *sc* Lang Yun. *ph* Lu Gengxin. *ed* Zhong Furong. *ad* Zhang Daqian. *m* Zhoi Xiaowen. *cast* Alia, Liu Pieqi, Zhang Haiyan, Ge Zhijun.
●This highly entertaining tragi-comedy is the best film yet about the ups and downs of 'modernisation' in the Chinese countryside. The heroine Ermo is a doughty noodle-maker bent on regaining her social status in the village; she sets her heart on earning and saving enough to buy the largest TV set in the country, even if it kills her – which it begins to look like doing. Wry, sexy and very wittily observed, the film sees China now as a tangle of materialism, amorality and left-overs from both feudalism and communism. Buñuel himself couldn't have come up with a more devastating account of stone-ground passions or preservative-free desires. TR

Ernest Saves Christmas

(1988, US, 91 min)
d John Cherry. *p* Stacy Williams, Doug Claybourne. *sc* B Kline, Ed Turner. *ph* Peter Stein. *ed* Sharyn L Ross. *ad* Ian Thomas. *m* Mark Snow. *cast* Jim Varney, Douglas Seale, Oliver Clark, Noëlle Parker, Gailard Sartain, Billie Bird, Robert Lesser.
●What can you expect from a cheap seasonal movie directed by an advertising executive and starring a character devised as a vehicle for selling American couch-potatoes anything from milk to financial services? Santa Claus (Seale) arrives in America (by plane) in search of Joe Carruthers (Clark), unemployed children's entertainer and heir apparent to Father Christmas' throne. Not surpisingly, everyone thinks Mr Claus is a fruitcake, but with the help of a 'wacky' cab-driver and a 'streetwise' runaway girl, rampant festivity triumphs. At the centre of the film is the said taxi-driver, Ernest P Worrell (Varney), a twisted, cheap imitation of the young Jerry Lewis, whose comic turns make Paul Hogan's repertoire seem a galaxy of creativity. This, combined with Cherry's staggeringly inept direction, is not unlike watching 91 solid minutes of commercials, with Varney's resolutely unfunny zaniness interspersed with tooth-rottingly saccharine messages from the sponsor (Christmas is nice, children are nice, etc). MK

Erotic Quartet (aka The Lickerish Quartet)

(1970, US/WGer/It, 90 min)
d/p Radley Metzger. *sc* Michael De Forrest. *ph* Hans Jura. *ed* Amedeo Salfa. *ad* Enrico Sabbatini. *m* Stelvio Cipriani. *cast* Sylvana Venturelli, Frank Wolff, Erika Remberg, Karl Otto Alberty, Paolo Turco.
●The brash, all-American certainties of Russ Meyer's sexploiters find their exact opposites in the work of Metzger, whose stylishly shot and designed movies are riddled with 'European' ambiguities of mood, theme and sexual identity. *Erotic Quartet* is his most ambitious and 'personal' film: a study of an Italian bourgeois family's involvement with a girl who might or might not be a star in one of the 8mm blue movies they like to run at home. The films-within-the-film generate some almost Pirandellian games with appearance and reality, but the movie's real claims to distinction in its field are its balanced sensitivity to male and female sexuality, and its bravura set pieces (notably the library set, decorated with blown-up dictionary definitions of erotic terms). TR

Erotikon

(1929, Czech, 87 min approx, b/w)
d/sc Gustav Machaty. *ph* Václav Vích. *ad* Julius von Borsody, Alexander Hackenschmied. *m* Jan Klusák. *cast* Ita Rina, Olaf Fjord, Karel Schliechert, Theodor Pistek, Charlotte Susa, Luigi Serventi.
●Machaty's silent second feature takes a simple, linear, fable-like story – a young woman's passage from girlhood to knowledge, from countryside to

city, and from sentimental gullibility to a more level-headed, prudent sensibility – and invests it with a tumult of emotions: lust, longing, shame, jealousy, despair, courage and confusion. The plot might be knottier melodrama than Machaty's *Extase*, but its potentially sensational aspects remain subservient to the director's themes of emotional conflict and compromise. The daughter of a railway station guard, having run away after being seduced and left her pregnant, finds shelter with a gallant (if not so captivating) rescuer who has saved her from rape. But what really distinguishes the film is its wealth of poetic detail (merging raindrops, charging trains), and its bold, frank eroticism, most notably in the opening sequence of the girl's sexual initiation, with its luminous whites and ecstatic throes set almost in abstraction from her world hitherto. The film was censored, of course. This is the near-complete restoration made in 1993, and comes accompanied by Jan Klusák's score, performed by five members of the Czech Film Symphony Orchestra. NB

Erotique

(1994, US/Ger/HK, 90 min)
d Lizzie Borden, Monika Treut, Clara Law. *p* Christopher Wood, Vicky Herman, Monika Treut, Michael Sombetzki, Teddy Robin Kwan, Eddie Fong. *sc* Eddie Fong, Monika Treut, Lizzie Borden. *ph* Larry Banks, Elfi Mikesch, Arthur Wong. *ed* Steve Brown, Richard Fields. *cast* Kamala Lopez-Dawson, Bryan Cranston, Priscilla Barnes, Camilla Soeberg, Ron Orbach, Marianne Sägebrecht.

● Three feminist stories confront and subvert the standard porn movie (up to a point). Borden and Treut are comfortable with the brief, allowing their central characters fantasy, force and passion, but Law's cinematic concerns lie in cultural rather than gender differences, and she opts (out) for humour. 'Let's Talk About Sex', Borden's tale of phone sex worker Rosie (Lopez-Dawson), reworks themes from *Working Girls*. It's a sometimes steamy little affair, though Borden does well to question Rosie's own fantasy which slips easily into stereotype. Treut's deadly lesbian vignette, 'Taboo Parlour', plays hard ball. Her dildo-wearing heroine works out a variation of the *Black Widow* scenario – an uncompromising gender power game likely to alienate any man hoping for titillation. Law's meditation on the future of Hong Kong, 'Wonton Soup', ends the film with a soft-core wimper as a couple explore a version of the Kama Sutra. FM

Escalier C

(1985, Fr, 101 min)
d Jean-Charles Tacchella. *p* Marie-Dominique Girodet. *sc* Jean-Charles Tacchella, Elvire Murail. *ph* Jacques Assuérus. *ed* Agnès Guillemot. *ad* Georges Lévy. *m* Raymond Alessandrini. *cast* Robin Renucci, Jean-Pierre Bacri, Catherine Leprince, Jacques Bonnaffé, Jacques Weber, Claude Rich, Michel Aumont.

● Tacchella's film centres on the inhabitants of one staircase in a 14th arrondissement apartment block. A dipso, a widow and a novelist *manqué* all take second place to a lugubriously handsome art critic (Renucci), who is cynical, obnoxious and very rude to women. It takes the death of a neighbour to effect his moral reawakening, whereupon he declares his intention to move in with a caring gay and makes a pilgrimage to Jerusalem. Even if the fact that the film treats indulgence in all its manifestations doesn't quite excuse its total implausibility,it's superbly acted and contrives to be both amusing and affecting. MS

Escape!

(1930, GB, 70 min, b/w)
d/p Basil Dean. *sc* Basil Dean, John Galsworthy. *ph* Jack MacKenzie, Robert G Martin. *ed* CD Milner Kitchin. *ad* Clifford Pember. *m* Ernest Irving. *cast* Gerald du Maurier, Edna Best, Gordon Harker, Madeleine Carroll, Austin Trevor, Lewis Casson, Ian Hunter, Nigel Bruce.

● 'Do you know how I spend most of my time in prison? Holding imaginary conversations with the Respectable'. Dean's early talkie (from a play by John Galsworthy) is interesting not only for its innovatory location shooting, but for its charmingly archaic concern for the upper class outcast. Killing a policeman in defence of a lady of the streets, our officer and gentleman hero finds himself breaking rocks on Dartmoor and 'treated like a dog'. With a 'By gosh I'll do it!' he's away, and before being caught by a gaggle of policemen, warders, bell-ringers and peasants, encounters genuine class solidarity among the local gentry. 'I can't bear to see a man like that chased by a lot of yokels', exclaims one of his genteel admirers. Quite so. RMy

Escape

(1940, US, 104 min, b/w)
d Mervyn LeRoy. *p* Lawrence Weingarten. *sc* Arch Oboler, Marguerite Roberts. *ph* Robert Planck. *ed* George Boemler. *ad* Cedric Gibbons, Urie McCleary. *m* Franz Waxman. *cast* Norma Shearer, Robert Taylor, Conrad Veidt, Alla Nazimova, Felix Bressart, Albert Basserman, Elsa Basserman.

● Glossy wartime sentiment from MGM, as American widow Shearer turns against her German lover (Veidt in his Hollywood debut) to help a young compatriot artist (Taylor) rescue his mother from a pre-war Nazi concentration camp. Adapting from a bestselling novel by Ethel Vance, LeRoy forsakes the hard-nosed 'realism' learned during his days with Warners, and goes all out for a well-crafted, controlled, but finally rather bland weepie. Supporting roles are performed by the usual group of stock European actors – Bressart, the Bassermans, all highly watchable – and there's an added bonus in Taylor's incarcerated mother being played by Nazimova, exotic temptress of silent movies, here returning to the screen after an absence of 15 years. But lacking the romantic conviction of Borzage, LeRoy all too often seems stranded in a smooth, unruffled sea of MGM banality. GA

Escape (Szökés)

(1997, Hun, 92 min)
d Livia Gyarmathy. *p* Zsuzsa Böszörményi. *sc* Géza Böszörményi. *ph* Gabor Balogh. *ed* Gabriella Koncz. *pd* Zsolt Juhász Buday. *m* Ferenc Darvas. *cast* Daniel Olbrychski, Artur Zmijewski, Krzysztof Kolberger, Ádám Schnell, Zsolt László, Barbara Hengyi.

● Hungary, just a few years on from the country's liberation from fascism, and the new Communist regime is settling in nicely, filling the prisons with political dissenters. This is the true story of one such innocent, as he spends two years in a secret labour camp before effecting a daring escape. He has memorised the names of his fellow internees in the hope of bringing the story to the outside world, but half the Hungarian army seems to be on his trail. Not unexpectedly, a fairly dour piece of film-making, but it does tell its story with a certain gritty urgency, and there's a fine performance from Olbrychski as the steely camp commandant. TJ

Escape from Alcatraz

(1979, US, 112 min)
d/p Don Siegel. *sc* Richard Tuggle. *ph* Bruce Surtees. *ed* Ferris Webster. *pd* Allen Smith. *m* Jerry Fielding. *cast* Clint Eastwood, Patrick McGoohan, Roberts Blossom, Jack Thibeau, Fred Ward, Paul Benjamin, Larry Hankin.

● Siegel's finest film since *The Shootist*, this tells the story of the one successful escape ever believed to have been made from the island penitentiary of Alcatraz. It's not an action film: there's little in the way of exciting set pieces, and Eastwood's restrained performance is low-key almost to the point of minimalism. Rather, as he slowly tries to tunnel out with a pair of nail-clippers, it's an austere depiction of the tedious routines of prison life, and of the courage and strength of spirit needed in coping with unpleasant warders, tough fellow-inmates, and a life sentence. As such, it's closer to Bresson's *A Man Escaped* (although obviously without the Catholic theme of redemption) than to the Hollywood prison escape movie. GA

Escape from Fort Bravo

(1953, US, 98 min)
d John Sturges. *p* Nicholas Nayfack. *sc* Frank Fenton. *ph* Robert Surtees. *ed* George Boemler. *ad* Cedric Gibbons, Malcolm Brown. *m* Jeff Alexander. *cast* William Holden, Eleanor Parker, John Forsythe, Polly Bergen, William Demarest, William Demarest.

● Western set in Arizona during the Civil War, neatly sustained from a familiar set of ingredients. Femme fatale Parker helps some Confederate soldiers escape their Union captors, whose efforts to recapture them are hindered by hostile Indians. Holden's suitably steel-jawed as the cavalry captain leading the boys in blue. Photographed by Robert Surtees. TJ

Escape from L.A.

see John Carpenter's Escape from L.A.

Escape from New York

(1981, US, 99 min)
d John Carpenter. *p* Larry Franco, Debra Hill. *sc* John Carpenter, Nick Castle. *ph* Dean Cundey. *ed* Todd Ramsay. *pd* Joe Alves. *m* John Carpenter, Alan Howarth. *cast* Kurt Russell, Lee Van Cleef, Ernest Borgnine, Donald Pleasence, Isaac Hayes, Season Hubley, Tom Atkins, Harry Dean Stanton, Adrienne Barbeau.

● Sporting a black eye-patch and a mutinous sneer, anti-hero Snake Plissken (Russell) prepares to invade the Manhattan of 1997, sealed off as a self-regulating maximum security prison following a 400% rise in the crime rate, and ruled over by a black drug-dealing Prospero (Hayes) attended by his punk Ariel. Victim of a Catch-22 situation and primed to self-destruct if he fails, Snake's task is to rescue the hijacked US president (Pleasence) from this ominous underworld; and for about half the film, Carpenter's narrative economy and explosive visual style (incorporating some marvellous model work of the new Manhattan skyline) promise wonders. The trouble is that his characters neither develop nor interact dynamically, so the plot gradually winds down into predictable though highly enoyable histrionics. TM

Escape from the Dark (aka The Littlest Horse Thieves)

(1975, US, 104 min)
d Charles Jarrott. *p* Ron Miller. *sc* Rosemary Anne Sisson. *ph* Paul Beeson. *ed* Richard Marden. *ad* Robert Laing. *m* Ron Goodwin. *cast* Alastair Sim, Peter Barkworth, Maurice Colbourne, Susan Tebbs, Geraldine McEwan, Prunella Scales, Leslie Sands, Joe Gladwin.

● A loathsome Disney attempt to foist the standards of *Upstairs Downstairs* on a turn-of-the-century Yorkshire colliery: anyone taking children to see it will have to put up with 'Can I go down a mine, too?' for the rest of the week. In a daringly flagrant disregard for the Industrial Revolution, our story shows how humble pit-ponies can beat new-fangled mechanisation every time, and how honest colliers only want to get on with their job without interference from The Bosses. 'Them ponies belong in the pit, same as us' is the line of the film: it's as if Lawrence and Orwell, let alone *Kes*, had never existed. England's class-ridden society of acting talent (Sim as crusty earl, beaming Joe Gladwin down t'pit) does its duty, but all are on a hiding to nothing. AN

Escape from the 'Liberty' Cinema (Ucieczka z Kina 'Wolnosc')

(1990, Pol, 92 min)
d/sc Wojciech Marczewski. *ph* Jerzy Zielinski. *ed* Elzbieta Kurkowska. *m* Zygmunt Konieczny. *cast* Janusz Gajos, Zbigniew Zamachowski, Teresa Marczewska, Wladyslaw Kowalski, Jerzy Binczycki, Piotr Fronczewski.

● A complex, allusive and deeply-felt examination of the nature and effects of censorship, directed by one of Poland's leading intellectual – and much censored – film-makers. It employs a rich mixture of dark political satire and poetic allegory as it details the life of the head of an unnamed town's District Censorship Office, a divorced ex-poet, journalist and literary critic suffering from psychosomatic headaches and heart palpitations. There are ructions outside his local cinema, the Liberty: the actors on screen stage a strike (shades of *The Purple Rose of Cairo*), refuse their allotted lines and roles, and begin to assert their freedom to make demands on the audience. The pressure on the head censor becomes unbearable, so when the local political bosses get involved and his vodka bottle runs out, he decides on extraordinary action... WH

Escape from the Planet of the Apes

(1971, US, 97 min)
d Don Taylor. *p* Arthur P Jacobs. *sc* Paul Dehn. *ph* Joseph Biroc. *ed* Marion Rothman. *ad* Jack Martin Smith, William J Creber. *m* Jerry Goldsmith. *cast* Roddy McDowall, Kim

Hunter, Bradford Dillman, Ricardo Montalban, Natalie Trundy, Sal Mineo, Albert Salmi, M Emmet Walsh.
● The third in the series. Quite a cheat, really, as Cornelius, Zira and Milo slip through a bend of time and avoid the holocaust. They find themselves back on human-dominated earth. Which is good for the budget as there is hardly a space device in sight. Instead, all we get is hysterical reactions from the local US Gov. fascist, Zira lecturing to the Women's Institute, a friendly circus owner…But the pessimism of the earlier two films remains, as well as another loophole, for the follow-up. It's a long way down from even the second in the series.

Escape from Zahrain

(1961, US, 93 min)
d/p Ronald Neame. *sc* Robin Estridge. *ph* Ellsworth J Fredricks. *ed* Eda Warren. *ad* Eddie Imazu. *m* Lyn Murray. *cast* Yul Brynner, Sal Mineo, Jack Warden, Madlyn Rhue, Tony Caruso, James Mason, Jay Novello.
● Turgid desert-trek drama, featuring Brynner and various bottle-tanned cohorts as escapee political prisoners in an Arab oil state. A predictable combination of the woeful exotic urges of both director Neame (*Mister Moses*) and screenwriter Robin Estridge (the dire Frankie Avalon-starring *Drums of Africa*). PT

Escape of The Amethyst

see Yangtse Incident

Escape Route to Marseilles (Fluchtweg nach Marseilles)

(1977, WGer, 210 min)
d Ingemo Engström, Gerhard Theuring. *p* Ingemo Engström, Gerhard Theuring, Christhart Burgmann, Annelen Kranefuss. *sc* Ingemo Engström, Gerhard Theuring. *ph* Axel Block, Melanie Walz. ed Heidi Murero, Elke Hager. *with* Katharina Thalbach, Rüdiger Vogler, Ruth Fabian, Peter Gingold, Alfred Kantorowicz. *narrator* Reinhart Firchow, Hildegard Schmahl.
● Studies of Germany's recent fascist past – especially from film-makers on the left – are notorious for their length (e.g. *Confessions of Winifred Wagner*), but this would put even Hans-Jürgen Syberberg to the test. Basically, it's an analysis of how people escaped from Occupied France through the so-called Free Zone to Marseilles and, with a lot of luck, abroad by sea. But the film also aims to point the significance of these events for all those involved in resistance activities today. Mixing documentary, interview and newsreel footage, but deliberately avoiding the 'dramatic' aspects of the mass exodus, this quasi-documentary is comprehensive to the point of pedantry and sober to the point of solemnity, lacking the essential irony that made Kluge's *The Patriot* such an entertaining yet progressive treatise on 20th century German history. Overburdened by a sense of expiation, and unrelieved by any feeling for accessible film-making. MA

Escape to Athena

(1979, GB, 117 min)
d George P Cosmatos. *p* David Niven Jr, Jack Wiener. *sc* Edward Anhalt, Richard S Lochte. *ph* Gilbert Taylor. *ed* Ralph Kemplen. *pd* Michael Stringer. *m* Lalo Schifrin. *cast* Roger Moore, Telly Savalas, David Niven, Claudia Cardinale, Stefanie Powers, Richard Roundtree, Sonny Bono, Elliott Gould, Anthony Valentine.
● Planning a summer holiday? *Escape to Athena* suffers from that tourist brochure look, with bouzouki music throbbing as we skim across the Aegean back to the sun-soaked days of 1944 and a PoW Camp *Méditerranée* on an idyllic isle, frequented by film stars like Moore, Niven and Gould. Take a drop of ouzo with colourful local characters like Savalas (as the island's big, sensitive Resistance leader) and Cardinale (the island's patriotic madame). The plot is like something knocked together by Alistair MacLean in his sleep, but was actually devised by the director. Awful. JS

Escape to Burma

(1955, US, 88 min)
d Allan Dwan. *p* Benedict Bogeaus. *sc* Talbot Jennings, Hobart Donovan. *ph* John Alton. *ed* James Leicester. *ad* Van Nest Polglase. *m* Louis Forbes. *cast* Barbara Stanwyck, Robert Ryan, David Farrar, Robert Warwick, Murvyn Vye, Lisa Montell, Reginald Denny, Peter Coe.
● Pure hokum in which Ryan goes on the run through the Burmese jungle after supposedly murdering the local ruler's son, pursued by a British police officer (Farrar) intent on bringing him back for trial, and by the ruler's underlings, bent on summary justice. He finds succour and romance in the unlikely person of Stanwyck, who runs her late father's teak plantation, rules the natives with matriarchal benevolence (they call her Gwen Ma), and has a special soft spot for her labour force of elephants. Dwan does his best with a script which doesn't miss a potboiling ingredient: a ravening tiger for Ryan to save Stanwyck from, a baby elephant that performs cute tricks, a bagful of rubies to incite a roving gang of bandits to thoughts of robbery and murder. The three leads give good performances, but the film's sole distinction is John Alton's brilliantly lucid Technicolor/Superscope camerawork. TM

Escape to Happiness

see Intermezzo

Escape to Victory

see Victory

Escape to Witch Mountain

(1974, US, 97 min)
d John Hough. *p* Jerome Courtland. *sc* Robert M Young. *ph* Frank Phillips. *ed* Robert Stafford. *ad* John B Mansbridge, Al Roelofs. *m* Johnny Mandel. *cast* Eddie Albert, Ray Milland, Donald Pleasence, Kim Richards, Ike Eisenmann, Walter Barnes.
● A Disney adventure with quite a lot going for it, even if it does end up spreading itself too wide for the sakes of the entire family. Two orphans, gifted with extra-terrestrial powers, get sidetracked in their search for their origins by an unscrupulous Milland, who hopes to use their clairvoyance to increase his own wealth. What emerges is a chase film – with the kids aided by a gruff but friendly Eddie Albert – which employs fast cars and a helicopter in much the same manner as Hough's earlier *Dirty Mary, Crazy Larry*. Most of the credit must rest with the adult actors, who refuse to patronise their material; interestingly, the film's underlying themes ('Our planet was dying. The only industry left was the manufacture of spaceships') are both topical and quite serious. CPe

Escort, The

see Scorta, La

Escort, The (Mauvaise Passe)

(1999, Fr/GB, 106 min)
d Michel Blanc. *p* Claude Berri. *sc* Michel Blanc. *ph* Barry Ackroyd. *ed* Marilyne Monthieux. *pd* Gary Williamson. *m* Barry Adamson. *cast* Daniel Auteuil, Stuart Townsend, Liza Walker, Noah Taylor, Frances Barber, Claire Skinner, Béatrice Agenin, Keith Allen, Barbara Flynn, Heathcote Williams.
● Pierre (Auteuil) is AWOL in London. A middle-aged university lecturer with a wife and teenage son, he's run away from the trappings of conformity to write that long talked about novel which will give meaning to his life. Instead, he winds up bruised and beaten outside a Soho sex club – which is how Tom (Townsend) finds him, takes pity and offers him a room. Young and handsome, Tom invites his new friend to a party. Turns out that their dates are paying for the privilege. Pierre is surprised, and flattered, to discover the gigolo within. Hanif Kureishi is credited with the seed for this not terribly original 'male crisis' drama, but writer/director Blanc must take the lion's share of blame for its banal development and perverse disinclination to exploit the set-up's obvious erotic, comic or suspense potential. Here we have a meagre parade of sour and dishonest relationships: between Pierre and his family back in France; with his new prostitute girlfriend (Walker); a client (Skinner); and of course Tom, who becomes increasingly alarmed at the heroin-guzzling monster he's created. TCh

Eskiya

see Bandit, The

Espalda del Mundo, La

see Back of the World, The

Esperando al Mesias

see Waiting for the Messiah

Esperanza & Sardinas

(1996, Sp, 92 min, b/w)
d Roberto Romeo. *p* Julia Romero Lopez. *sc* Jean-Luc Cambier. *ph* Yves Cape. *ed* Anita Fernandez Diaz. *m* Juan Reina, Pedro Esparza. *cast* Manuel de Blas, Paulina Gálvez, Luis Beviá, Juan Antonio Blasco.
● Shot quite stylishly in b/w on a very low budget, this example of the new Spanish cinema is formless, meandering and inconsequential. Set in an Alicante village, it simply observes the not particularly arresting relationships between sundry unsavoury characters – the men are mostly braggarts and brawlers into drink, drugs and sex talk, the women objects of their desire. GA

Espinazo del Diablo, El

see Devil's Backbone, The

Espion Lève-toi

(1982, Fr, 98 min)
d Yves Boisset. *p* Norbert Saada. *sc* Michel Audiard, Claude Veillot, Yves Boisset. *ph* Jean Boffety. *ed* Albert Jurgenson. *ad* Serge Dony. *m* Ennio Morricone. *cast* Lino Ventura, Michel Piccoli, Krystyna Janda, Bruno Crémer, Heinz Bennent, Bernard Fresson.
● Here's a belated digest of mid-'60s espionage clichés, from the bandstand rendezvous at the start (*The Ipcress File*) to the perforated hero and heroine at the end (*The Spy Who Came In From the Cold*). Once again government agencies and their creatures are characterised as ruthless, cynical and devious beyond comprehension, crushing the innocent in the interests of some great obscure McGuffin. The setting (Zurich, with all its Franco-German confusions) might have stimulated some originality, but no: this is all cold-eyed hitmen, spot the traitor and shoot-outs on the funicular. Ventura, Piccoli and the composer Morricone in their different ways keep their heads below the parapet, but Janda unwisely charges forth, acting away as though all this might mean something. From George Markstein's novel *Chance Awakening*. BBa

Espions, Les

(1957, Fr, 125 min, b/w)
d/p Henri-Georges Clouzot. *p* L de Mazure. *sc* Henri-Georges Clouzot, Jérôme Géronimi. *ph* Christian Matras. *ed* Madeleine Gug. *ad* René Renoux. *m* Georges Auric. *cast* Curd Jurgens, Peter Ustinov, Gérard Séty, Sam Jaffe, Paul Carpenter, Martita Hunt.
● A lunatic asylum in remote countryside, a top secret patient smuggled on to the premises at dead of night, the arrival in the village of a flock of sinister strangers. Turns out the Secret Service has invented a pretend spy to fox the foe and this is all in aid of spinning out the deception. The fiction-about-a-fiction idea aside, this bears no resemblance to Hitchcock's similar set up *North by Northwest*, and it's hard to know whether the wildly fluctuating tone was a matter of accident or design. The multi-national casting doesn't help, with the humourless Jurgens apparently suffering the agonies of the damned, and Peter Ustinov's very presence shifting all his scenes into waggishness. Beginning as Gothic horror, ending as cynical shaggy dog story, this is one of the more peculiar contributions to the '50s Cold War cycle. BBa

Espoir (Days of Hope/Man's Hope)

(1939, Fr/Sp, 78 min, b/w)
d André Malraux. *p* Edouard Corniglion-Molinier. *sc* André Malraux. *ph* Louis Page. *ed* Georges Grace. *m* Darius Milhaud. *cast* José Sempere, Andres Mejuto, Nicolas Rodriguez, Pedro Codina, José Lado.
● Begun in 1938 in Barcelona, but interrupted by the arrival of Franco's troops, Malraux's crudely made but historically fascinating film only drew on one episode from his novel of the same title. Basically an assemblage of memories of the anti-Fascist fighting during the Civil War, the dialogue scenes now look very inadequate. What are extraordinary, however, are the sequences of

combat, a bombing raid filmed from the air, and the film's climactic set piece, a procession of over 2,000 carrying dead and wounded pilots down the mountain of the Sierra de Teruel to the music of Darius Milhaud. DT

Esprit de Mopti, L'

see Spirit of Mopti, The

Essex Boys

(1999, GB, 102 min)
d Terry Winsor. *p* Jeff Pope. *sc* Jeff Pope, Terry Winsor. *ph* John Daly. *ed* Edward Mansell. *pd* Chris Edwards. *m* Colin Towns. *cast* Sean Bean, Alex Kingston, Charlie Creed-Miles, Tom Wilkinson, Larry Lamb, Gareth Milne, Amelia Lowdell, Michael McKell, Holly Davidson.

● A hardcore criminal fraternity peddles drugs, brute sex and violence amid Norfolk's farms and marshes and the neon nightlife of Southend. Adopting the perspective of Billy (Creed-Miles), a local lad whose curiosity and driving skills outweigh his better sense, it follows the attempt of his new employer, ex-con Jason Locke (Bean), to pick up the pieces with his pre-prison contacts and girlfriend (Kingston). When a drug consignment proves disastrously spiked, the recriminations fly. 'Inspired' by a real event which left three men dead, two sentenced to life imprisonment and another living under an assumed identity, the basics are certainly credible, even quite effectively cinematic. The locale is rendered compellingly with crisp photography and moody compositions; but the construction is botched by disjointed editing and plotting often so opaque that, despite an amenable cast, you struggle to comprehend or care about the characters' predicaments. NB

Esther Kahn

(2000, Fr/GB, 157 min)
d Arnaud Desplechin. *p* Pascal Caucheteux, Grégoire Sorlat, Chris Curling. *sc* Arnaud Desplechin, Emmanuel Bourdieu. *ph* Eric Gautier. *ed* Hervé de Luze, Martine Girodano. *pd* Jon Henson. *m* Howard Shore. *cast* Summer Phoenix, Ian Holm, Fabrice Desplechin, Frances Barber, László Szabó, Emmanuelle Devos.

● A distinct disappointment after Desplechin's earlier work, this is an ambitious but misguided adaptation of a novel about a young and wholly unremarkable Jewish girl, emerging from London's East End towards the close of the 19th century to become, through sheer determination, a celebrated actress. The film founders mainly on Desplechin's shaky grasp of English: the dialogue is full of implausible profanity, the director's brother is less than convincing as a theatre critic, while Summer Phoenix, shaky accent, awkward intonation, shallow performance and all, never convinces for a moment, let alone as a triumphant Hedda Gabler. Holm and Barber, and Howard Shore's score briefly counteract the overall clumsiness, but in the end that's nowhere near enough to save a doomed project. GA

Esther Waters

(1948, GB, 109 min, b/w)
d/p Ian Dalrymple, Peter Proud. *sc* William Rose. *ph* CM Pennington-Richards, HE Fowle. *ed* Brereton Porter. *ad* Fred Pusey. *m* Gordon Jacob. *cast* Kathleen Ryan, Dirk Bogarde, Cyril Cusack, Fay Compton, Ivor Barnard, Mary Clare, Julian d'Albie, Morland Graham, Shelagh Fraser.

● Having made her mark in Reed's *Odd Man Out*, Irish actress Ryan got herself a real showcase in this period melodrama, from the novel by George Moore (1894), suffering nobly and at length as the honest serving wench in a country house who gets herself pregnant by rapscallion groom Bogarde (in his second screen appearance). He, on the other hand, is more interested in horse racing, and there'll be a fortune won and lost before the day is done. The actors win our sympathy despite the hoary subject matter, though the well-staged racecourse sequences almost convince you the movie's a lot better than it actually is. TJ

Est-Ouest

see East-West

Estratagia del Caracol, La

see Strategy of the Snail, The

Etat de Siège

see State of Siege

Et Dieu Créa la Femme (And God Created Woman/ And Woman...Was Created)

(1956, Fr, 91 min)
d Roger Vadim. *p* Raoul J Lévy. *sc* Roger Vadim, Raoul Lévy. *ph* Armand Thirard. *ed* Victoria Mercanton. *ad* Jean André. *m* Paul Misraki. *cast* Curd Jürgens, Brigitte Bardot, Christian Marquand, Jean-Louis Trintignant, Georges Poujouly.

● Cautiously titled *And Woman... Was Created* for its British release, this was the film that started the Bardot thing. Basically a clever piece of pre-New Wave programming with its St Tropez locations, 'daring' sex and amoral youth, it adds up to little more than a series of semi-nude posturings as the sex kitten flits nymphomaniacally from man to man and back again. But the lively characterisations and wry wit make the first half a good deal more watchable than most of Vadim's abject later creations.

Eté à La Goulette, Un

see Summer in La Goulette, A

Eté inoubliable, Un

see Unforgettable Summer, An

Eté Meurtrier, L'

see One Deadly Summer

Eternal Love

see Eternel Retour, L'

Eternel Retour, L' (Eternal Love/Love Eternal)

(1943, Fr, 111 min, b/w)
d Jean Delannoy. *p* André Paulvé. *sc* Jean Cocteau. *ph* Roger Hubert. *ed* Suzanne Fauvel. *ad* Georges Wakhévich. *m* Georges Auric. *cast* Madeleine Sologne, Jean Marais, Jean Murat, Yvonne de Bray, Pierre Pieral, Jane Marken.

● Made during the German Occupation in World War II, Cocteau's updating of the Tristan and Isolde legend remains a sadly neglected film, largely because postwar critics jumped on the Aryan blondness of the two leads to tag it as collaborationist. Actually the pair look more like a tribute to camp chic, drifting photogenically but sexlessly through the grand passion that unites the lovers in death. But the film itself, broodingly set in an ancient castle overhanging the sea, has a rare, dreamlike beauty that captures the quality of legend almost as successfully as *La Belle et la Bête*. Some stunning performances, too, not least from Pieral as the malevolent dwarf and de Bray as his horribly complacent mother. TM

Eternity and a Day (Mia Eoniotita Ke Mia Mera)

(1998, Greece/Fr/It/Ger, 130 min)
d Theo Angelopoulo. *p* Fibi Ikonomopoulou. *sc* Theo Angelopoulos. *ph* Giorgos Arvanitis, Andreas Sinanos. *ed* Giannis Tsitsopoulos. *pd* Giorgos Ziakas, Kostas Dimitriadis. *m* Eleni Karaindrou. *cast* Bruno Ganz, Isabelle Renauld, Achileas Skevis, Despina Bebedeli.

● A dying author (Ganz) prepares to leave his beloved family home by the sea, and settle things with his daughter; his feelings of despair are interrupted, complicated and finally, to some extent, banished by memories of happier times with his wife (Renauld) and by an encounter with a young Albanian orphan. Angelopoulos' film, a deserving winner of the Palme d'Or at Cannes '98, is a characteristically elegant, eloquent and idiosyncratic meditation on the relationships between personal and political histories, and between life and art. More intimate than, say, *The Travelling Players* or *Ulysses' Gaze*, the film nevertheless reaches out, as its long, fluid takes escort us through space and time, to universal themes and broader topicalities, effortlessly fending off charges of hermetic aestheticism. GA

Ethan Frome

(1993, US, 99 min)
d John Madden. *p* Stan Wlodkowski. *sc* Richard Nelson. *ph* Bobby Bukowski. *ed* Katherine Wenning. *pd* Andrew Jackness. *m* Rachel Portman. *cast* Liam Neeson, Patricia Arquette, Joan Allen, Tate Donovan, Katharine Houghton, Stephen Mendillo.

● The landscapes of winter mirror the emotions in this adaptation of Edith Wharton's 1911 novel. Ethan Frome (Neeson), the New England farmer struggling to make ends meet, is one side of an eternal triangle, the others are his sickly cousin Zeena (Allen) and his fragile relative Mattie (Arquette). Their story is related by Mrs Hale (Houghton), the sexton's wife, to Rev Smith (Donovan), the new minister, who wants to help the Fromes. Although the dutiful husband, the bed-ridden wife and the poor relation are staples of melodrama, audiences should be able to identify with characters who see their hopes crushed, revivified and crushed again. Plainly filmed this tale may be – it is an 'American Playhouse' theatrical release – but it is honestly played and deeply felt. Bobby Bukowski's bleak cinematography and Rachel Portman's mournful score make the pain palpable. AO

Et là-bas quelle heure est-il?

see What Time Is It There?

Etoile du Nord, L' (The Northern Star)

(1982, Fr, 124 min)
d Pierre Granier-Deferre. *p* Alain Sarde. *sc* Jean Aurenche, Michel Grisolia, Pierre Granier-Deferre. *ph* Pierre-William Glenn. *ed* Jean Ravel. *ad* Dominique André. *m* Philippe Sarde. *cast* Simone Signoret, Philippe Noiret, Fanny Cottençon, Julie Jezequel, Liliana Gérace, Gamil Ratib.

● Clearly borrowing both inspiration and key personnel from the Bertrand Tavernier school of eccentric thrillers, Granier-Deferre teases this Simenon adaptation towards irresistible absurdity. The brilliant Noiret is a forgetful killer on the lam, spinning exotic yarns to fend off compound disappointments and derangements (prompting the film to incongruous cross-fades between the Belgian boarding-house where he's staying and his previous home in Egypt), stirring in his ageing landlady (Signoret) the memory of her own long-abandoned dreams of 'escape', and cueing several nice black ironies about travel broadening the mind. There's a flighty femme fatale, a murder on a train, dirty money burnt – but all the conventions of the genre make scant impression on Noiret's fantastic fakir act. Which, however you look at it, is the only conceivable abiding impression of this incoherent, oddball joy. PT

Etoile sans Lumière (Star Without Light)

(1945, Fr, 86 min, b/w)
d Marcel Blistène. *p* Eugène Tuscherer. *sc* Marcel Blistène, A-P Antoine. *ph* Paul Cotteret. *ed* Ginou Bretoneiche. *ad* A (Jean) d'Eaubonne. *m* Guy Luypaerts. *songs* Marguerite Monnot, Henri Contet. *cast* Edith Piaf, Serge Reggiani, Marcel Herrand, Mila Parély, Jules Berry, Yves Montand.

● This would make a good double bill with *Singin' in the Rain*: same premise, opposite treatments. The setting is the dawn of the talkies, with Piaf playing the Debbie Reynolds part, an unknown brought in secretly to dub the unsatisfactory voice of a popular but obnoxious star of the silents. It's primarily a Piaf vehicle, her persona in the line of Giulietta Masina and Gracie Fields: sparky, resilient, endlessly put upon, always falling in love with unattainables (Reggiani as a kindly sound recordist). It's as gloomy overall as *SITR* is sunny, but Piaf's vanity gave rise to one twist: the role of the dull hometown sweetheart patiently waiting for this film business to blow over is taken by a young, extravagantly handsome Yves Montand. BBa

Etrange Monsieur Victor, L'

(1938, Fr, 91 min, b/w)
d Jean Grémillon. *sc* Albert Valentin, Charles Spaak, Marcel Achard. *ph* Werner Krien. *ad* Willy Schiller, Otto Hunte. *m* Roland Manuel. *cast* Raimu, Madeleine Renaud, Pierre Blanchar, Viviane Romance, Marcelle Géniat, Andrex.

● Or the strange Monsieur Grémillon... Though unquestionably a major film-maker, Grémillon – also an accomplished musician, painter and documentarist – has remained a marginal figure even in his native land, a French Humphrey Jennings, perhaps. In this bleak study of malevolence, an example of his painterly rather than poetic realism, Raimu plays (magnificently) a modest clerk whose mousy respectability conceals the psychology of a monster. GAd

E.T. The Extra-Terrestrial (100)

(1982, US, 115 min)
d Steven Spielberg. *p* Steven Spielberg, Kathleen Kennedy. *sc* Melissa Mathison. *ph* Allen Daviau. *ed* Carol Littleton. *pd* James D Bissell. *m* John Williams. *cast* Dee Wallace, Henry Thomas, Peter Coyote, Robert MacNaughton, Drew Barrymore.

● Returning to the rich pastures of American suburbia, Spielberg takes the utterly commonplace story of a lonely kid befriending an alien from outer space, and invests it with exactly the same kind of fierce and naive magic that pushed Disney's major masterpieces like *Pinocchio* into a central place in 20th century popular culture. Moreover, with its Nativity-like opening and its final revelation, the plot of *E.T.* has parallels in religious mythology that help to explain its electric effect on audiences. But although conclusively demonstrating Spielberg's preeminence as the popular artist of his time, *E.T.* finally seems a less impressive film than *Close Encounters*. This is partly because its first half contains a couple of comedy sequences as vulgar as a Brooke Bond TV chimps commercial, but more because in reducing the unknowable to the easily loveable, the film sacrifices a little too much truth in favour of its huge emotional punch. DP

Eureka

(1982, GB/US, 129 min)
d Nicolas Roeg. *p* Jeremy Thomas. *sc* Paul Mayersberg. *ph* Alex Thomson. *ed* Tony Lawson. *pd* Michael Seymour. *m* Stanley Myers. *cast* Gene Hackman, Theresa Russell, Rutger Hauer, Jane Lapotaire, Mickey Rourke, Ed Lauter, Helena Kallianiotes, Joe Pesci.

● The usual nervy Roeg cross-cutting has almost vanished in favour of a cleaner but just as distanced narrative, in two plain parts: a prospector (Hackman) in Canada in the '20s finally strikes it lucky, engulfed in a river of gold; and then the rest of his life, immured in his house ('Eureka') in the Bahamas and wondering what on earth there is left. While the weight of Roeg's success is usually stylistic, this is more of a harkback to the cosmic scale of *The Man Who Fell to Earth*, with enormous themes streaming through a strange tale. Alongside the bass-line of a man who 'once had it all, and now just owns everything', there are games of knowledge and power (voodoo, cabbalahs, magick), a devouring relationship with his daughter (Russell), and a nebulous running battle with business competitors who want their own share of the planet. The man who raped the earth and lost his demon is finally the victim of 'business interests' in the same way that Jagger was in *Performance*. It's a great, *Kane*-like notion – the price we pay for gaining what we want – and overflowing with awkward ideas and strange emotion. CPea

Eureka

(2000, Jap, 217 min, b/w)
d Shinji Aoyama. *p* Takenori Sento. *sc* Shinji Aoyama. *ph* Masaki Tamra. *ed* Shinji Aoyama. *pd* Takeshi Shimizu. *m* Isao Yamada, Shinji Aoyama. *cast* Koji Yakusho, Aoi Miyazaki, Masaru Miyazaki, Yohichiroh Saitoh, Sayuri Kokusho, Ken Mitsuishi.

● A bus is hijacked; only the driver (Yakusho, from *The Eel* and *Shall We Dance?*) and two school-age passengers survive the bloodbath. Two years later, the driver returns from his mysterious wanderings, finds life with his family awkward, and moves in with the brother and sister, by now utterly speechless and living alone (at least until their student cousin also comes to stay). Meanwhile, a number of local women are murdered. The slightly bogus serial killer subplot notwithstanding, Aoyama's lengthy, but never over-long study of psychological trauma and regeneration is beautifully shot (in monochrome 'Scope), acted, and directed; at least until the last two shots, an elegant understatement holds sway, even allowing for wry, gentle humour to be slowly but surely introduced into the otherwise serious proceedings. Like his superb lead actor, Aoyama achieves a lot with a little, proving that one needn't shout to be heard. Ozu, one feels, would have approved. GA

Europa

(1991, Den, 114 min, b/w & col)
d Lars von Trier. *p* Peter Aalbaek Jensen, Bo Christensen. *sc* Lars von Trier, Niels Vørsel, Tómas Gislason. *ph* Henning Bendtsen, Jean-Paul Meurisse, Edward Klosinski. *ed* Hervé Schneid. *pd* Henning Bahs. *m* Joakim Holbek. *cast* Jean-Marc Barr, Barbara Sukowa, Udo Kier, Ernst-Hugo Järegård, Erik Mark, Jergen Reenberg, Henning Jensen, Eddie Constantine.

● Von Trier's *Element of Crime* was one of the great love-it-or-hate-it films, and this divided opinions even more furiously. Portentous but hypnotic, it's a mannered delve into postwar history: an American German (Barr) returns to work on the German railways after WWII, only to get entangled in underground politics and the dark machinations of a railway dynasty. The grandiose scale and visual pyrotechnics paradoxically combine to claustrophobic effect (imagine something between Fassbinder and Lynch's *Dune)*; and like the constantly shuttling sleeping car in which much of the film is set, where it's going is hard to say. Max von Sydow's ominously mesmeric opening voice-over makes for a wind-up from the outset, but if you can stay awake through that, you're in for a highly idiosyncratic mystery tour. JRo

Europa, Europa

(1991, Fr/Ger, 112 min)
d Agnieszka Holland. *p* Margaret Ménégoz, Artur Brauner. *sc* Agnieszka Holland. *ph* Jacek Petrycki. *ed* Ewa Smal, Isabelle Lorente. *pd* Allan Starski. *m* Zbigniew Preisner. *cast* Marco Hofschneider, Julie Delpy, Hanns Zischler, André Wilms, Andrzej Mastalerz, Delphine Forest.

● Although both look and subject matter are familiar – from *Mephisto* and *The Tin Drum* – Agnieska Holland's war story is all the more unsettling for being true. Salomon Perel (Hofschneider) is a young German Jew who flees eastwards as the Nazis move in. Fate ensures his survival by landing him first in a Soviet Komsomol school, where he learns to be a fervent young Stalinist, then in a German front-line detachment where he passes as the flower of pure Aryan youth. Enrolled in an élite Hitler Youth academy, he falls for lovely Jew-hating Leni (Delpy); but by this point the effort of hiding behind so many masks, not to mention hiding the most physical evidence of his Jewishness, is beginning to take its toll... The story is so absurd that it could have made a grotesque historical burlesque of the Günter Grass variety. Holland takes a more prosaic approach, but the ironies bite hard, and occasional farcical moments add an unsettling edge to Perel's fortunes. Holland plays on the paradox of role-playing with moderation, but the moral uncertainties of Perel's survival are no less dizzying for all that. JRo

Europe After the Rain

(1978, GB, 88 min, b/w & col)
d/sc Mick Gold. *ph* Nic Knowland, Derek Waterman. *ed* Barry Beckett. *m* JS Bach, Stéphane Grappelli, Bartok, Schoenberg, Mahler. *songs* Georges Auric, Tristan Tzara. *with* Marcel Duchamp, Max Ernst. *cast* Nickolas Grace, Michael Harbour, Dennis Clinton.

● As an idiosyncratic anthology of Dadaist and Surrealist artifacts and attitudes, Gold's film for the Arts Council is fine. A chock-full collage of texts, reproduced artworks, actual footage and dramatised reconstructions, it constantly unearths delights, both visual and aural (some strictly tangential, such as Joan Bakewell interviewing Marcel Duchamp). But as an analysis of the movements' aesthetic ideas, aims and achievements, it flounders: by reducing the 20th century historical and cultural context to two world wars, plus the thought of Freud and Trotsky; and by crucially failing to make adequate distinction between 'authentic' surrealism and its latter-day manifestations in, for instance, cigarette advertising and TV comedy. PT

Europeans, The

(1979, GB, 83 min)
d James Ivory. *p* Ismail Merchant. *sc* Ruth Prawer Jhabvala. *ph* Larry Pizer. *ed* Humphrey Dixon. *ad* Jeremiah Rusconi. *m* Richard Robbins. *cast* Lee Remick, Robin Ellis, Tim Woodward, Wesley Addy, Lisa Eichhorn, Nancy New, Tim Choate, Kristin Griffith.

● A wonderfully elegant adaptation of Henry James' early novel about the impact of a sophisticated but impecunious European countess and her brother on their wealthy country cousins in America. Staged with affection, insight, a whole fistful of superb performances and exquisite settings. Odd, though, that Ruth Prawer Jhabvala's otherwise excellent script fails to note James' distinction between the Countess, who is a fortune-hunter, and her brother who is not; without it, the subtlest irony of this comedy of manners goes by the board. TM

Eu Tu Eles

see Me You Them

Evangelio de las maravillas, El

see Divine

Eve

(1962, Fr/It, 135 min, b/w)
d Joseph Losey. *p* Robert Hakim, Raymond Hakim. *sc* Hugo Butler, Evan Jones. *ph* Gianni Di Venanzo. *ed* Reginald Beck, Franca Silvi. *ad* Richard MacDonald, Luigi Scaccianoce. *m* Michel Legrand. *cast* Jeanne Moreau, Stanley Baker, Virna Lisi, Giorgio Albertazzi, James Villiers, Riccardo Garrone, Lisa Gastoni

● The film is set in Venice, in the season that most suits that city (winter), shot in Losey's characteristic baroque style of the period, and features Baker as the upstart Welsh novelist, engaged to an empty marriage but gradually ensnared into an *amour fou* by the ferocious, loose temptress Eve. Love hardly enters into it; it is corruption by power, money and bad faith that are Losey's obsessions, and they are dwelt upon insistently with more sheerly scathing disaste than he allowed himself subsequently. The film undoubtedly belongs to Moreau who, in one of her finest performances, gives a portrait of terrifying honesty – the heartless self-possession of a woman who does nothing unless for money or whim. The figures of alienation wandering through an elegant landscape may be familiar from the Antonioni trilogy of the period, but the pessimism, energetic misanthropy and disenchantment with the world are all Losey's own. CPea

Evel Knievel

(1971, US, 90 min)
d Marvin Chomsky. *p* George Hamilton. *sc* Alan Caillou, John Milius. *ph* David M Walsh. *ed* Jack McSweeney. *ad* Norman Houle. *m* Patrick Williams. *cast* George Hamilton, Sue Lyon, Bert Freed, Rod Cameron, Dub Taylor, Ron Masak.

● A fascinating and enjoyable film about the daredevil motorcyclist-stuntman (played ebulliently by Hamilton, although the spectacular stunt scenes are documentary footage of Knievel himself). Piecing together events in his life – his early delinquent driving, an attempted safe-cracking career, and the increasing audacity of his legendary rides – it portrays something of an egomaniac, basking in the light of his own fame while privately racked by neuroses. Chomsky's seemingly nonchalant direction, from a script by John Milius and Alan Caillou, sensibly refuses neat psychological explanations, and instead opens out to provide a finely detailed portrait of middle America. GA

Even Cowgirls Get the Blues

(1993, US, 96 min)
d Gus Van Sant. *p* Laurie Parker. *sc* Gus Van Sant. *ph* John Campbell, Eric Edwards. *ed* Curtiss Clayton. *pd* Missy Stewart. *m* kd Lang, Benjamin Mink. *cast* Uma Thurman, John Hurt, Rain Phoenix, Keanu Reeves, Lorraine Bracco, Angie Dickinson, Carol Kane, Roseanne Arnold, Ken Kesey, Buck Henry, William Burroughs.

● This adaptation of Tom Robbins' cult novel finally emerges as an embarrassing miscalculation. Thurman is Sissy Hankshaw, a model by profession and hitch-hiker by vocation. On a photo-shoot at a Dakota beauty ranch, Sissy is caught in the middle of a cowgirl sexual revolution against the feminine hygiene regimen of the Countess (Hurt). The film is a sour comedy and a curiously inert road movie. Mostly, though, it's a wacky allegory of the kind in vogue in the '70s, which is roughly when this sort of material might have had some sort of relevance. It's actually more like a time capsule: anyone nostalgic for woolly women's lib metaphors, feckless counter-culturalism, hippy-dippy rhetoric and bird symbolism, this is the trip you've been waiting for. TCh

Even Dwarfs Started Small (Auch Zwerge haben klein angefangen)

(1970, WGer, 96 min, b/w)
d/p/sc Werner Herzog. *ph* Thomas Mauch. *ed* Beate Mainka-Jellinghaus. *m* Florian Flicke. *cast* Helmut Döring, Gerd Gickel, Paul Glauer, Erna Gschwnedtner, Gisela Hartwig, Gergard Marz.

●A film about man's relation to the world of objects he surrounds himself with. Dwarfs are used to emphasise the extent to which objects dominate our personal relations: their alienation from the institution and its products is ours too. The anarchist uprising is a beautiful negation of bourgeois values, sometimes savage, but usually compassionate and amusing. The dwarfs are great, and the tribal music superb.

Evénement le plus Important depuis que l'Homme a Marché sur la Lune, L'

see Slighty Pregnant Man, The

Evening Dress

see Tenue de Soirée

Evening Performance (Función de Noche)

(1981, Sp, 90 min)
d Josefina Molina Reig. *p* José Sámano. *sc* Josefina Molina, José Sámano. *ph* Teo Escamilla. *ed* Nieves Martin. *ad* Rafael Palermo. *m* Alejandro Massó, Luis E Aute. *cast* Lola Herrera, Daniel Dicenta, Natalia Dicenta Herrera, Luis Rodriguez Olivares.

●Intensely private, largely improvised, this portrait of a middle-aged actress struggling with a role that propels her into personal crisis (echoes of Cassavetes' *Opening Night*) consists mainly of an emotional confrontation between Lola Herrera and her ex-husband Dicenta. But the brief moments showing her with friends, children and doctor aren't enough to open up a painfully introverted central scene into the promised analysis of 'machismo'; and although it's impossible not to admire Herrera's honesty, as the endless hysterics/histrionics mount, so unfortunately does the spectator's tedium. SJo

Evening Star, The

(1996, US, 129 min)
d Robert Harling. *p* David Kirkpatrick, Polly Platt, Keith Samples. *sc* Robert Harling. *ph* Don Burgess. *ed* Priscilla Nedd-Friendly, David Moritz. *pd* Bruno Rubeo. *m* William Ross. *cast* Shirley MacLaine, Miranda Richardson, Bill Paxton, Juliette Lewis, Ben Johnson, Scott Wolf, Jack Nicholson.

●Fifteen years after the death of her daughter (and 14 years after *Terms of Endearment*), the sun's setting on Aurora Greenway (MacLaine). She's fighting with her grandchildren, feuding with her neighbour Patsy (Richardson) and succumbing to a shrink with a mother complex (Paxton). While Lewis is convincingly cast as Debra Winger's daughter, and you can always look to Richardson for poised bitchery, writer/director Harling ensures that everyone is but further grist to Aurora's already monstrous ego: even the ubiquitous Jack Nicholson pops in to pay tribute. This isn't so much a movie as a memorial service. MacLaine, though, is still very much alive and kicking, more than able to take a scene by the scruff of the neck. If there's no edge, at least there's a centre. Harling is best known for his play *Steel Magnolias*, and he also had a hand in the scripts for *Soapdish* and *First Wives Club*, so it's no surprise that the film's female characters have more going on than their feckless partners, but this adaptation of Larry McMurtry's novel irons out depth without tightening up a baggy shapeless narrative. TCh

E Venne un Uomo

see Man Named John, A

Evensong

(1934, GB, 84 min, b/w)
d Victor Saville. *p* Graham Cutts. *sc* Edward Knoblock, Dorothy Farnum. *ph* Max Greene. *ed* Otto Ludwig. *ad* Alfred Junge. *songs* Alfred Nathan, George Oppenheimer, Edward Knoblock, Mischa Spoliansky. *cast* Evelyn Laye, Fritz Kortner, Conchita Supervia, Emlyn Williams, Alice Delysia, Carl Esmond.

●Irish diva (Laye) is moulded by Viennese impresario (Kortner) into a top opera star and romancer of the Austrian nobility, but refusal to acknowledge the approach of her twilight years leads to an inevitable fall from grace. A touch more sophisticated than the usual run of home-grown '30s musicals, genre specialist Saville's film benefits no end from the commanding and courageous central performance. TJ

Event Horizon

(1997, US/GB, 96 min)
d Paul Anderson. *p* Lawrence Gordon, Lloyd Levin, Jeremy Bolt. *sc* Philip Eisner. *ph* Adrian Biddle. *ed* Martin Hunter. *pd* Joseph Bennett. *m* Michael Kamen. *cast* Laurence Fishburne, Sam Neill, Kathleen Quinlan, Joely Richardson, Jack Noseworthy, Richard T Jones, Jason Isaacs, Sean Pertwee.

●After 35 years lost in the cosmos, the spaceship 'Event Horizon' re-establishes contact. A team of crack astronauts, led by Fishburne and accompanied by scientist Neill, is sent from Earth to salvage the vessel and pick up survivors. When they arrive, they get more than they bargained for. For all its big budget effects and scenery, Brit director Anderson's third feature – after *Shopping* and *Mortal Kombat* – is less sci-fi spectacular than old fashioned ghost-cum-horror yarn, set 56 days away from Earth. Walls drip blood and shapeless evil hovers. Horror piles on horror without much intervening suspense. Even the fine supporting cast (Pertwee, Richardson and Quinlan) fails to raise the ghost of a smile to ease the tension. But, despite its shortcomings, this is never dull. The movie avoids Alien space monster clichés brilliantly and the soundtrack contains more of the 'Boo!' effects than I've heard since *Halloween*. NKe

Eve of Destruction

(1991, US, 98 min)
d Duncan Gibbins. *p* David Madden. *sc* Duncan Gibbins, Yale Udoff. *ph* Alan Hume. *ed* Caroline Biggerstaff. *pd* Peter Lamont. *m* Philippe Sarde. *cast* Renee Soutendijk, Gregory Hines, Michael Greene, Kurt Fuller, John M Jackson, Loren Haynes, Ross Malinger.

●In her American debut, Soutendijk plays Dr Eve Simmons, a beautiful research scientist who creates a cyborg in her own image. A military robot endowed with her body, brains and emotional hang-ups, it turns into a super-destructive, castrating, father-hating RoboSlut. Sadly, too little is made of the premise that Soutendijk's damaged doppelgänger is giving vent to her own repressed urges. Also, the bursts of explosive action are punctuated by turgid, talky scenes in which angry cop Hines harangues Soutendijk about the ethics of military science. In short, an attention-catching idea in search of a movie. NF

Eve of St Mark, The

(1944, US, 96 min, b/w)
d John M Stahl. *p* William Perlberg. *sc* George Seaton. *ph* Joseph La Shelle. *ed* Louis Sackin. *ad* James Basevi, Russell Spencer. *m* Cyril J Mockridge. *cast* Anne Baxter, William Eythe, Michael O'Shea, Vincent Price, Dickie Moore, Ruth Nelson.

●Maxwell Anderson's blank verse play, a Broadway hit, comes over on screen as a slightly artsy WWII flag-waver, as GI Eythe survives conditions in the Pacific campaign with the help of Midwestern sweetheart Baxter. The treatment of familiar material is more sensitive than usual, but some of the ambitious dialogue sticks in the craw. TJ

Ever After

(1998, US, 121 min)
d Andy Tennant. *p* Mirieille Soria, Tracey Trench. *sc* Susannah Grant, Andy Tennant, Rick Parks. *ph* Andrew Dunn. *ed* Roger Bondelli. *pd* Michael Howells. *m* George Fenton. *cast* Drew Barrymore, Anjelica Huston, Dougray Scott, Patrick Godfrey, Megan Dodds, Timothy West, Judy Parfitt, Jeroen Krabbé, Jeanne Moreau.

●Barrymore manages just fine in carrying this Cinderella update – updated, that is, in terms of feistied-up characterisation rather than period, which is 16th century France. This Cinderella, named Danielle, is a daddy's girl, jealously guarding the copy of More's *Utopia* her father (Krabbé) gave her before his death reduced her to wench/farm labourer under an envious stepmother (Huston) and self-deluding stepsisters. She's something of a Renaissance woman, too, in her independent way, knowledgeable in arts both martial and liberal. And something of a paragon: loyal, stoic and true. Given that this is adolescent romance, never straying far from traditional stereotypes, its 'progressive' feel-good aura is mainly down to Barrymore, whose limitations are only exposed in big love scenes. WH

Everest

(1997, US, 43 min)
d David Breashears.

●The Himalayan vistas viewed from the world's tallest mountain on an IMAX screen 'seven storeys' high is breathtaking. Cameraman Rob Schauer and the rest of the team clearly went through hell: the crew (including the son of Sherpa Tenzing who accompanied Hillary on the first ascent) was required to cart more than 100lb of IMAX stock across crevasses and over unpredictably ice boulders. They witnessed the misfortune of eight climbers from another expedition perishing on the same slopes. And then there was the frost bite and altitude sickness. George Harrison provides the swirling soundtrack, Liam Neeson the sincere commentary. DA

Evergreen

(1934, GB, 91 min, b/w)
d Victor Saville. *p* Michael Balcon. *sc* Marjorie Gaffney, Emlyn Williams. *ph* Glen MacWilliams. *ed* Ian Dalrymple. *ad* Alfred Junge, Peter Proud. *songs* Richard Rodgers, Lorenz Hart. *cast* Jessie Matthews, Barry Mackay, Sonnie Hale, Betty Balfour, Ivor McLaren, Patrick Ludlow.

●Matthews, the stallholder's daughter from Berwick Street, paid heavily for the acclaim she won as Britain's leading musical star. Despite Saville's sympathetic direction, she suffered horrifying nervous rashes and temporary mental breakdown during the making of this, her most famous film. She nevertheless gives a dazzling performance in the dual role of a famous music hall star and the daughter, an unemployed chorus-girl, who impersonates her in a desperate bid for fame and fortune. If Saville fails to explore the sexual undertones of the story, the exciting *post-Metropolis* sets designed by Alfred Junge provide an impressive showcase for Jessie's elfin beauty and superb dancing (to a Rodgers and Hart score). RMy

Everlasting Piece, An

(2000, US, 103 min)
d Barry Levinson. *p* Mark Johnson, Louis DiGiaimo, Jerome O'Connor, Barry Levinson, Paula Weinstein. *sc* Barry McEvoy. *ph* Seamus Deasy. *ed* Stu Linder. *pd* Nathan Crowley. *m* Hans Zimmer. *cast* Barry McEvoy, Brian F O'Byrne, Anna Friel, Pauline McLynn, Ruth McCabe, Laurence Kinlan, Billy Connolly, Des McAleer.

●Belfast, the 1980s, and in the midst of the province's political strife, barber Colm (screenwriter McEvoy) lands himself a job as the token Catholic in a mental asylum, cutting hair alongside lugubrious Protestant and would-be poet George (O'Byrne). Fortune smiles on them when they encounter The Scalper (Connolly), a purported serial killer who once ran Northern Ireland's only wig-selling operation. Acquiring his list of local baldies presents a golden opportunity to Colm and George, who set themselves up as 'The Piece People', but soon find that any non-sectarian operation faces its difficulties in a society beset with such bitter divisions. How do you stay friends with your Protestant partner when the IRA offers you a deal to become official hairpiece suppliers to the armed struggle? At first glance, this is unlikely material for a Levinson picture, but to give the Yanks some credit they haven't turned it into Oirish whimsy. Instead, the humour's authentically black, McEvoy's dialogue the genuine craic. Levinson's slightly bemused handling sometimes gives the shaggy dog interplay a little too much slack, but you can forgive the occasional scrappiness when the overall combination of daft jokes and a determined statement of reconciliation produces such a disarming one-off. TJ

Everlasting Secret Family, The

(1987, Aust, 93 min)
d/p Michael Thornhill. *sc* Frank Moorhouse. *ph* Julian Penney. *ed* Pamela Barnetta. *ad* Peta Lawson. *m* Tony Bremner. *cast* Arthur Dignam, Mark Lee, Heather Mitchell, Dennis Miller, Paul Goddard, Beth Child, John Clayton.

●Sports day at an exclusive Australian boys' school. One of the gorgeous youths, watched by a sinister black-clad figure, is whisked off to a hotel room, divested of clothes and ravished. As he doesn't object, he is taken to a party and seduced by a Japanese gent who insists on doing things to him with a large live crab. Next, he undergoes an initiation ceremony à la Knights Templar and joins 'the family', an ancient sex-ring which wreaks terrible punishment on those who blab. From then on, it's a confused tale of the boy's attempts to flee, his search for eternal youth, and his burgeoning relationship with his master's son, with lots of male nudity and some fairly explicit sex. All the gay characters are 'elderly pervert' stereotypes, cruel, calculating and vampirish; yet, for a film that takes so rigidly homophobic a stance, an awful lot of time is spent dwelling on youthful tanned muscles, taut buttocks, and the like. Revolting, ludicrous, infuriating, and (blush) often very erotic, it is about nothing but self-hatred. RS

Everybody Dance

(1936, GB, 75 min, b/w)
d Charles Reisner. *sc* Leslie Arliss, Ralph Spence. *ph* Jack Cox. *ed* RE Dearing, Terence Fisher. *ad* Vetchinsky. *songs* Mack Gordon, Harry Revel. *cast* Cicely Courtneidge, Ernest Truex, Charles Reisner, Billie de la Volta, Kathleen Harrison, Peter Gawthorne, Roland Culver.

●Misleading title. This is a comedy with only three songs and hardly any dancing – or dahncing, and very British, despite imported American personnel on both sides of the camera. Conflicting agendas are in evidence, with the studio (Gainsborough) pushing to compete with Hollywood, the director trying to promote his namesake son into a film star, and Courtneidge, whose persona combined an upperclass manner with lowbrow knockabout, determined that no one else is going to get a look in. She plays a notorious nightclubber masquerading as a straitlaced member of the county set, as part of her scheme to adopt two American teenagers (Reisner and the splendidly named Billie de la Volta). A museum piece, still affording some residual entertainment value. BBa

Everybody Does It

(1949, US, 98 min, b/w)
d Edmund Goulding. *p/sc* Nunnally Johnson. *ph* Joseph La Shelle. *ed* Robert Fritch. *ad* Lyle Wheeler, Richard Irvine. *m* Mario Castelnuovo-Tedesco. *cast* Paul Douglas, Linda Darnell, Celeste Holm, Charles Coburn, Millard Mitchell, Lucille Watson.

●A typically Hollywoodised version of James M Cain's fine novella (*Career in C Major*, previously filmed in 1939 as *Wife, Husband, and Friend*) about a rough-diamond building contractor whose life is made a misery by the socialite wife he adores. Intent, like Charles Foster Kane's beloved, on parlaying a tiny talent into a career as a concert singer, she loses no opportunity to walk over her husband's supposed cultural inferiority. Her comeuppance is neatly contrived when a celebrated diva, sought for an opinion of her voice, discovers not only that the despised husband has the sensational voice in the family, but that his body is desirably hunky. Shorn of most of Cain's acid social and sexual overtones, the script turns into a routine romantic comedy. Given elegantly sharpish direction, plus fine performances by the leads (Douglas as the husband, Holm as the wife, Darnell as the diva), it makes for pleasantly civilised viewing all the same. TM

Everybody's All-American (aka When I Fall in Love)

(1988, US, 127 min)
d Taylor Hackford. *p* Taylor Hackford, Laura Ziskin, Ian Sander. *sc* Tom Rickman. *ph* Stephen Goldblatt. *ed* Don Zimmerman. *pd* Joe Alves. *m* James Newton Howard. *cast* Jessica Lange, Dennis Quaid, Timothy Hutton, John Goodman, Carl Lumbly, Ray Baker, Savannah Smith Boucher, Patricia Clarkson.

●Based on the novel by Frank Deford, this spans 25 years in the lives of three characters: Gavin Grey (Quaid), Babs (Lange), and Gavin's nephew Donnie (Hutton). Everybody loves Gavin. Revered as a footballer, he leaves college to go professional and marries Babs, while peripheral Donnie – juggling his naive regard for Gavin alongside a latent passion for Babs – heads for an academic career. Typically of such scenarios, the story charts the trials which beset the golden couple, and the self-realisation which comes with hardship and maturity. The idolatry which surrounds Gavin verges on the absurd, making it nearly impossible to establish sympathy for him or those who adore him. Given the material, the performances are competent enough; but Hackford and cinematographer Stephen Goldblatt are too indulgent in creating a near-religion out of the characters' self-absorption. CM

Everybody's Cheering

see Take Me Out to the Ball Game

Everybody's Fine (Stanno tutti bene)

(1990, It/Fr, 126 min)
d Giuseppe Tornatore. *p* Angelo Rizzoli. *sc* Giuseppe Tornatore, Tonino Guerra, Massimo De Rita. *ph* Blasco Giurato. *ed* Mario Morra. *ad* Andrea Crisanti. *m* Ennio Morricone. *cast* Marcello Mastroianni, Michèle Morgan, Salvatore Cascio, Valeria Cavalli, Marino Cenna, Roberto Nobile.

●Tornatore's follow-up to *Cinema Paradiso* isn't quite so dewy-eyed, but will still have cynics retching into their popcorn. Amiable old buffer Matteo (Mastroianni) lives a lonely life in Sicily. On a whim, he ups sticks and travels to the mainland; his aim, to reunite his family round a dinner table. But his children seem strangely embarrassed by him. Contrasted with the highly unsatisfactory behaviour of his adult offspring are his vivid memories of them as kids. His son Alvaro remains absent, and as the old man camps miserably on the doorstep, young Alvaro (the terminally cute Cascio) shimmers into view. There is a melodramatic plot lurch, a haunting dream sequence, a well-handled autumnal love affair, and a neat twist at the end. Like *Cinema Paradiso*, it's expertly manipulative and good-looking, though a tad darker. Mastroianni gambols through it. SFe

Everybody Wins

(1990, GB, 97 min)
d Karel Reisz. *p* Jeremy Thomas. *sc* Arthur Miller. *ph* Ian Baker. *ed* John Bloom. *pd* Peter Larkin. *m* Leon Redbone. *cast* Debra Winger, Nick Nolte, Will Patton, Judith Ivey, Jack Warden, Kathleen Wilhoite, Frank Converse, Frank Military.

●Arthur Miller's play, *Some Kind of Love Story*, was a black comedy on the themes of fantasy and corruption played out over a film noir framework, exciting speculation as to how far marriage to Marilyn Monroe had been source material. Expanded into film, it's a tantalising, brave failure. Here, the central relationship between private investigator Tom O'Toole (Nolte), variously encouraged by *femme fatale* Angela Crispini (Winger) to dig into the false conviction of a lad for murder, is significantly altered. On stage, their relationship has been going on for years; but film being film and stasis meaning stalled, they've been issued with a beginning and an end. This weakens a symmetry of compromised interdependence between the lovers, and between cops, judges and crooks in society at large. Everywhere is Chinatown; the town could be Hammett's Poisonville, USA. The film also introduces a biker cult of a weirdness that at times touches *Twin Peaks*. With infinitely changeable Angela on the strength, and viewed by her amazingly credulous gumshoe, human behaviour is unfathomable enough already. He looks Amish and plays patsy for his Cleopatra, who turns in an outstanding performance despite a difficult script, while Karel Reisz negotiates most of the shoals like a master. BC

Every Day God Kisses Us on the Mouth (In fiecare zi Dumnezeu ne saruta pe gura)

(2001, Romania, 93 min, b/w)
d/sc Sinisa Dragin. *ph* Alexandru Solomon. *ed* Cristina Ionescu. *ad* Anca Raduta, Daniël Raduta. *cast* Dan Condurache, Ana Ciontea, Horatiu Malaele, Dan Astilean, Valer Delakeza.

●A little like Béla Tarr on speed, Dragin's second feature charts the corpse-strewn path undertaken by an habitual killer after he's released from prison and returns to his village, family and butcher's job. Dumitru (the delightfully hangdog Condurache) sometimes puts up with all kinds of affronts; at others, he just loses it – killings apart, however, he's basically a good sort. Bible-black humour, flashes of lyrical fantasy, elegant b/w digital camerawork, lovely performances, and Dragin's confident handling of the elliptical narrative make for a fine movie, at its most charming in depicting the friendship between Dumitru and a boozy cop. GA

Every Little Crook and Nanny

(1972, US, 92 min)
d Cy Howard. *p* Leonard J Ackerman. *sc* Cy Howard, Jonathan Axelrod, Robert Klane. *ph* Philip H Lathrop. *ed* Henry Berman. *pd* Philip M Jefferies. *m* Fred Karlin. *cast* Lynn Redgrave, Victor Mature, Paul Sand, Maggie Blye, Austin Pendleton, John Astin, Dom DeLuise.

●It had to come – the Mafia Family comedy. Plus the English nanny gag. Plus a hamfisted script routine around a kidnapped son. Gee whizz…Victor Mature points his profile and doesa-da-dago accent. (From a novel by Evan Hunter.)

Every Little Thing (La Moindre des Choses)

(1996, Fr, 104 min)
d Nicolas Philibert. *p* Serge Lalou. *ph* Nicolas Philibert, Katell Dijan. *ed* Nicolas Philibert, Julietta Roulet. *m* André Giroud.

●The La Borde clinic, a stately chateau surrounded by forest, takes an unorthodox approach to psychiatric care. The clinic's regime resembles that of a laidback boarding school for eccentrics, with pills – although there's no introduction to or analysis of such matters. Rather, we're straight in to an intimate documentary record of the several months the patients and staff take to prepare their summer theatrical production. Sometimes the patients talk – to each other or the camera; other times they just watch, or whistle, or walk slowly across the gravel…or we see trees blowing in the wind. The play (briefly excerpted) looks interesting, but the film as a whole doesn't repay one's patience. NB

Every Man for Himself

see Sauve Qui Peut – la Vie

Every Man for Himself and God Against All

see Jeder für sich und Gott gegen alle

Everyone Says I Love You

(1996, US, 101 min)
d Woody Allen. *p* Robert Greenhut. *sc* Woody Allen. *ph* Carlo Di Palma. *ed* Susan E Morse. *pd* Santo Loquasto. *m* Dick Hyman. *cast* Alan Alda, Woody Allen, Drew Barrymore, Lukas Haas, Goldie Hawn, Gaby Hoffmann, Natasha Lyonne, Edward Norton, Natalie Portman, Julia Roberts, Tim Roth, David Ogden Stiers, Billy Crudup.

●Springtime in New York. Norton and Barrymore stroll hand in hand around a fountain, then burst into a deliciously sloppy rendition of 'Just You, Just Me', and immediately we're right into it, and you can't imagine why it's taken Woody Allen so long to get round to reviving the musical. Romantic, nostalgic and decadent as Fred Astaire, this might as well be an old movie, for all its relevance to the '90s or Allen's on-going problems. In some ways, it's not like a Woody Allen film at all. The plot – a frippery about the affairs of an extended upper-class family – transports us from Manhattan to Venice and Paris; there are black faces about the edges, a female, teenage narrator; even some fancy special effects work. Yet it never feels cynical or self-serving; indeed, it feels like the work of a younger, more open-hearted man. Unlike *Mighty Aphrodite*, in which Allen's on-screen character is apparently irresistible to Mira Sorvino, here his courtship of Roberts is accomplished only through underhand means, and the joke's ultimately on him. The musical standards are beautifully orchestrated, staged with wit and invention, and enthusiastically performed, particularly by Norton, Tim Roth and Hawn, three stand-outs in a charming, sweet-natured *divertissement*. Enjoy yourself (it's later than you think). TCh

Everyone's Happy

(2001, GB, 60 min)
d Frances Lea. *p* Mark Blaney. *sc* Simon Beaufoy. *ph* Sam McCurdy. *ed* Søren Ebbe, Carol Salter. *pd* Jude Walton. *m* Andrew Blaney. *cast* Alit Kreiz, Anton Mirto, Holly de Jong, Mark Vegh, David Taylor.

●Simon Beaufoy (*Among Giants*, *The Darkest Light* and, uhh, *The Full Monty*) developed this script working with director Lea, the actors, and students from the Bournemouth Film School, who helped out on the ten-day shoot. It involves two couples camping on the hills above Swanage. By some measure the most interesting character is Mike, a gambling addict trying to go cold turkey, but unable to help himself when one of the girls in the tent next door proves obliging. 'My whole life is a system of odds,' he tells her. 'Is that a good way to live?' His wife, meanwhile, is plucking up courage to visit the son she put up for adoption when he was a baby, and is none too thrilled that he seems on the point of sleeping with their other neighbour, a performance artist. Shot in that fashionable jerky, jumpy DV-TV style, and bolstered with a drum 'n' bass soundtrack, it's a lively calling card of a picture which wouldn't look out of place on the small screen, but there's no ending to speak of. TCh

Every Picture Tells a Story

(1984, GB, 83 min)
d James Scott. *p* Christine Oestreicher. *sc* Shane Connaughton. *ph* Adam Barker-Mill. *ed* Chris Kelly. *pd* Louise Stjernsward. *m* Michael Storey. *cast* Phyllis Logan, Alex Norton, Leonard O'Malley, Mark Airlie, John Docherty, Melanie Fleming.

●Scott reaches back into his family history to describe the adolescence of his father, painter William Scott. The film traces William's life from his childhood in an Irish Catholic family in Scotland to his teenage years in Enniskillen and Belfast. The fundamental theme is the emergence of the boy's talent as an artist, part rooted in his harsh childhood experiences and part born of his need to break away from those roots. Handsomely stylised images and performances of unassailable authority make it very beautiful, and sometimes very moving. TR

Everything for Sale (Wszystko na Sprzedaz)

(1968, Pol, 105 min)
d Andrzej Wajda. *p* Jerzy Bossak, Ernest Bryll, Jozef Krakowski. *sc* Andrzej Wajda. *ph* Witold Sobocinski. *ed* Halina Prugar. *ad* Wieslaw Sniadecki. *m* Andrzej Korzynski. *cast* Andrzej Lapicki, Beata Tyszkiewicz, Elzbieta Czyzewska, Daniel Olbrychski, Witold Holtz.

●Here they are again, our old friends illusion and reality, battling it out to unsettling effect in a film with more layers than an onion and umpteen references to Wajda's own career. A film director called Andrzej tries to continue shooting after his lead (clearly modelled on Zbigniew Cybulski, the actor who became the personification of postwar Polish cinema through his work with Wajda, and who had recently died in tragic circumstances) has disappeared. The result is stylistically and emotionally overwrought, but Wajda's technical assurance helps enormously in maintaining tension. GB

Everything's Gonna Be Great (Hersey Çok Güzel Olacak)

(1999, Tur, 107 min)
d Omer Vargi. *p* Mine Vargi. *sc* Omer Vargi, Cem Yilmaz, Hakan Haksun. *ph* Gary Turnbull. *ed* Istvan Sipos. *pd* Zeynep Tercan. *m* Mazhar Alanson. *cast* Mazhar Alanson, Cem Yilmaz, Selim Nasit Ozcam, Ceyda Duvenci, Mustafa Uzunyilmaz.

●A charming, if reckless buffoon, Altan (Yilmaz) is the sort of character the movies have been in love with since De Niro's Johnny Boy, or perhaps Phil Harris's Baloo the Bear. He runs into his straitlaced big brother Nuri (Alanson, in the Baghera role) after two years four months out of touch, and sticks to him long enough to break into his boss's safe and swipe the prescription drugs whose sale he hopes will be the making of his dream bar. It's a slap-happy jaunt, goofy and determinedly upbeat. Psychological realism is not its strong suit, and there's not much originality on show, but then the film-makers' only ambition seems to be to please. The beautiful impressionistic opening credits of street life by night might have dropped out of a different film. NB

Everything You Always Wanted to Know About Sex, But Were Afraid to Ask

(1972, US, 87 min)
d Woody Allen. *p* Charles H Joffe. *sc* Woody Allen. *ph* David M Walsh. *ed* James T Heckert. *pd* Dale Hennesy. *m* Mundell Lowe. *cast* Woody Allen, Lynn Redgrave, John Carradine, Burt Reynolds, Anthony Quayle, Gene Wilder, Lou Jacobi, Tony Randall, Louise Lasser.

●Seven sketches parodying a sex manual, in which Allen – before trying to change his name to Fellini-Bergman – strung together 'every funny idea I've ever had about sex, including several that led to my own divorce'. Some dross, but the parodies of Antonioni (all angst and alienation of a wife who can achieve orgasm only in public places) and of TV panel games ('What's My Perversion?') are brilliantly accurate and very funny. Best of all is the sci-fi parody entitled 'What Happens During Ejaculation?', which has the miniaturised scientists of *Fantastic Voyage* inside a life-sized male robot, busily checking data and providing the necessary bodily reactions by hand-turned winch as the robot wines, dines and seduces a real-life woman. Allen achieves his finest hour here, dressed as one of the sperm, poised anxiously with parachute by the escape hatch and crying 'Gung ho!' as he jumps, 'We're gonna make babies!' TM

Every Time We Say Goodbye

(1986, US, 98 min)
d Moshe Mizrahi. *p* Jacob Kotzky, Sharon Harel. *sc* Moshe Mizrahi, Rachel Fabien, Leah Appet. *ph* Giuseppe Lanci. *ed* Mark Burns. *ad* Micky Zahar. *m* Philippe Sarde. *cast* Tom Hanks, Cristina Marsillach, Benedict Taylor, Anat Atzmon, Gila Almagor, Monny Moshanov.

●Hanks' aptitude for romantic comedy can do nothing for this corny World War II love story, which has a script so sugary it goes for your fillings. A heavily American-accented RAF officer, he meets a beautiful young Jewish girl (Marsillach) in Jerusalem. While she is as fresh and pure as her little white underslips, with smouldering eyes and a 180 degree wiggle that he finds irresistible, she is also a Sephardim, a branch of Jewry which permits marriage only within the faith. True love is in for a rocky ride. She fights her feelings for him, saying no a lot when she means yes. 'I'll wait a hundred years for you' she wails as her dashing flight lieutenant departs to do his bit for the desert campaign. Strictly for addicts of Mills & Boon. EP

Every Which Way But Loose

(1978, US, 114 min)
d James Fargo. *p* Robert Daley. *sc* Jeremy Joe Kronsberg. *ph* Rexford Metz. *ed* Ferris Webster, Joel Cox. *ad* Elayne Ceder. *cast* Clint Eastwood, Sondra Locke, Ruth Gordon, Geoffrey Lewis, Beverly D'Angelo, Walter Barnes.

●A huge disappointment after *The Outlaw Josey Wales* and *The Gauntlet*, this rambling comedy forsakes the subtle, self-deprecating humour of those films and opts for a far rowdier and broader comedy that never really goes anywhere or says anything. Clint is the somewhat dumb prizefighter who wins an orangoutan and sets off with his new buddy in pursuit of hard-to-get C&W singer Locke. The attempt to counter his apparent superiority over other men with his gauche reactions to the woman makes no interesting points, and the whole thing seems like an indulgent, expensive home movie created by and for Eastwood's customary stock company of actors. GA

Eve's Bayou

(1997, US, 108 min)
d Kasi Lemmons. *p* Caldecot Chubb, Samuel L Jackson. *sc* Kasi Lemmons. *ph* Amy Vincent. *ed* Terilyn A Shropshire. *pd* Jeff Howard. *m* Terence Blanchard. *cast* Samuel L Jackson, Lynn Whitfield, Debbi Morgan, Vondie Curtis Hall, Branford Marsalis, Lisa Nicole Carson, Jurnee Smollett.

●'Memory is a selection of images – some elusive, others printed indelibly on the brain. The summer I killed my father, I was ten years old...' Thus Eve, at the beginning of this rich, assured directorial debut, set in a Louisiana backwater. Eve Batiste (Smollett) is second daughter to the elegant Roz (Whitfield) and her husband Louis (Jackson), the popular local doctor. Louis is an effortless charmer, debonair and handsome – that's his trouble. When Eve catches him kissing a woman in the shed, she does her best to block out the memory of this betrayal, but the past is not so easily contained. The film is suffused in a lovely amber light, whence the material slips easily into a spirit world of ghosts, fancy and voodoo curses. Yet the languid air and lazy ambience defuses these 'excessive' elements and keep the focus squarely on character. The female competition for Louis' affections is movingly played out from the youngster's perspective. Writer/director Kasi Lemmons shows sweet judgment here, doesn't caricature or demonise the errant father, and elicits a host of nuanced performances from women of all ages. TCh

Evictors, The

(1979, US, 92 min)
d/p/sc Charles B Pierce. *ph* Chuck Bryant. *ed* Shirak Khojayan. *ad* John Ball. *m* Jaime Mendoza-Nava. *cast* Vic Morrow, Michael Parks, Jessica Harper, Sue Ane Langdon, Dennis Fimple, Bill Thurman.

●'Let 'em have it!' yells a G-Man behind the credits, initiating a chain of mayhem that will continue unabated for 90 minutes. Pierce toiled unspectacularly in the low-budget mills for several years, but scored a bullseye with this energetically ghoulish exploiter which relocates the Old Dark House on Bonnie and Clyde terrain. The plot (city couple buy a lonely farm whose massacred former owners refuse to stay dead) may be perfunctory, but there are likeable performances, nice period details, and terrific set pieces, as well as a final twist incredible enough to be mildly surprising. TP

Evil

see Mal

Evil Dead, The

(1982, US, 86 min)
d Sam Raimi. *p* Robert Tapert. *sc* Sam Raimi. *ph* Tim Philo. *ed* Edna Ruth Paul. *m* Joseph LoDuca. *cast* Bruce Campbell, Ellen Sandweiss, Betsy Baker, Hal Delrich, Sarah York.

●Raimi's first feature, a sensationally bad-taste effort which narrates the rapid decline into demonic mental and physical possession of a clean-cut, all-American holiday party holed up in a mountain Tennessee retreat. The woods come alive, devils possess the living, and Tom Sullivan's amazing make-up effects climax with a final fiery exorcism which makes George Romero look like *Playschool*. Short on characterisation and plot but strong on atmospheric horror and visual churns, this movie blends comic fantasy (EC Tales) with recent genre gems like *Carrie* and *Texas Chain Saw Massacre* to impressive effect. SGr

Evil Dead II

(1987, US, 84 min)
d Sam Raimi. *p* Robert Tapert. *sc* Sam Raimi, Scott Spiegel. *ph* Peter Deming. *ed* Kaye Davis. *ad* Philip Duffin, Randy Bennett. *m* Joseph Lo Duca. *cast* Bruce Campbell, Sarah Berry, Dan Hicks, Kassie Wesley, Theodore Raimi, Denise Bixler.

●Not so much a sequel, more a self-parodic reprise, like some black comic nightmare in the damaged brain of sole survivor Ash (Campbell). This time though, tired of cowering in the corner, Ash gets tooled up with a shotgun and a chainsaw, and lets the monsters suck on some abuse. Meanwhile, four other victims – none of whom has ever seen a horror movie – arrive at the shack and start settling in, unaware that they'll be dead by dawn. The dialogue has been pared to the bone, the on-screen gore toned down, and the maniacal laughter cranked up to full volume. Using the same breathless pacing, rushing camera movements and nerve-jangling sound effects as before, Raimi drags us screaming into his cinematic funhouse. Delirious, demented and diabolically funny. NF

Evil Eden

see Mort en ce Jardin, La

Evil That Men Do, The

(1983, US, 90 min)
d J Lee Thompson. *p* Pancho Kohner. *sc* David Lee Henry, John Crowther. *ph* Javier Rubalcava Cruz. *ed* Peter Lee-Thompson. *ad* Enrique Estevez. *m* Ken Thorne. *cast* Charles Bronson, Theresa Saldana, Joseph Maher, José Ferrer, René Enriquez, John Glover, Raymond St Jacques.

● Bronson as a hit man persuaded out of retirement to terminate a sadistic professional torturer in the pay of an oppressive South American government. Right from the opening sequence the film is a clumsy catalogue of pain and death, from the mutilated victims of the torturer to the trail of wasted baddies who were foolish enough to incur Bronson's wrath. The title openly declares a moral stance, but with the film quite happy to accept the assassin as a meter of justice, its ethics are as muddled and erratic as the editing and camerawork. There's only one lesson that comes through loud and clear: don't mess with Charles Bronson. DPe

Evil Trap, The

see Folle à Tuer

Evil Under the Sun

(1981, GB, 117 min)
d Guy Hamilton. *p* John Brabourne, Richard Goodwin. *sc* Anthony Shaffer. *ph* Christopher Challis. *ed* Richard Marden. *pd* Elliot Scott. *m* Cole Porter. *cast* Peter Ustinov, Jane Birkin, Colin Blakely, Nicholas Clay, Maggie Smith, Roddy McDowall, James Mason, Sylvia Miles, Denis Quilley, Diana Rigg.

● With Ustinov's energetic impersonation of Poirot and Anthony Shaffer's traditionally structured script, *Death on the Nile* offered a fair recreation of Agatha Christie's world, but this time Christie herself would rightly have disowned the film. It's not just that her novel's English coastal setting has been switched to an Adriatic island; for some reason, Shaffer and Hamilton have swopped the elegant English-style menace for a splurge of theatrical camp. The emphasis on gaudy costumes and bitchy back-biting is hideously amplified by a composite Cole Porter score, and it is only in the last section that Shaffer finally drops the double entendres and allows the golden-age-of-detection feel to reassert itself. DP

Evil Woman

see Saving Silverman

Evita

(1996, US, 134 min)
d Alan Parker. *p* Robert Stigwood, Alan Parker, Andrew Vajna. *sc* Alan Parker, Oliver Stone. *ph* Darius Khondji. *ed* Gerry Hambling. *pd* Brian Morris. *songs* Andrew Lloyd-Webber, Tim Rice. *cast* Madonna, Antonio Banderas, Jonathan Pryce, Jimmy Nail, Victoria Sus, Julian Littman, Peter Polycarpou.

● The most significant Hollywood musical in 15 years (virtually the only Hollywood musical in 15 years) turns on the dubious political integrity of one Eva Duarte, 1930s actress, working-class heroine, and consort of Argentina's fascist leader Col Juan Perón. Born into poverty, Eva worked her way up a ladder of men, then hitched her star to the military dictator to become the self-appointed 'spiritual leader of the nation'. Her socialist rhetoric may have been at odds with her glamorous lifestyle, but her death in 1952 caused an outpouring of grief. Is the musical still a credible genre in these cynical times? On the basis of this film, the answer's a qualified yes. Parker has no embarrassment when it comes to putting over a song, and he's assembled a strong cast in Madonna, Pryce (Perón) and a fiercely brow-beating Banderas as the ubiquitous narrator. Unfortunately, for all its popularity on stage, the Andrew Lloyd Webber/Tim Rice show makes an unlikely movie. Parker does his best to disguise the fact with extensive cross-cutting and plentiful crowd scenes, but there's no real dynamic to the story, no sense of movement. The film cries out for the liberation of choreography to supplement the thin, repetitive score. An unholy cocktail of Emiliano Zapata, Eva Braun, and Princess Di, Evita's politics are intriguing; presumably that's what attracted Parker and co-screenwriter Oliver Stone to the material, but the movie's so seriously weighty, the bombast rather tips the balance against Evita charisma. Despite Madonna's impressive performance, we're never remotely tempted to cry for her – and, in the end, that must make the film a failure. TCh

Evolution

(2001, US, 102 min)
d Ivan Reitman. *p* Ivan Reitman, Daniel Goldberg, Joe Medjuck. *sc* David Diamond, David Weissman, Don Jakoby. *ph* Michael Chapman. *ed* Sheldon Kahn, Wendy Greene Bricmont. *pd* J Michael Riva. *m* John Powell. *cast* David Duchovny, Orlando Jones, Seann William Scott, Julianne Moore, Ted Levine, Ethan Suplee, Michael Ray Bower, Pat Kilbane.

● A meteor crashes in the Arizona desert and, to the consternation of local college professors Duchovny and Jones, begins to ooze. They've stumbled across the most exciting scientific discovery of the new millennium: alien plankton. That's only the beginning. These suckers evolve 800 million years in a few hours; by mid-week they're growing legs, lungs and appetites. By Sunday the professors realise their tenure is at stake, along with the rest of mankind's. On the face of it, the film is a sloppy, catch-all conflation of *Independence Day* and *Ghostbusters*. Fun, though. Director Reitman obviously doesn't hold with the stereotype of the earnest, dry, dedicated scientist: his heroes are cynical, immoral and only fractionally smarter than the petty bureaucrats and pompous military officers with whom they must contend. It would be stretching a point to call this 'satire' – Reitman's comedy is pitched squarely to the libertarian right. It's anti-establishment, anti-Other, and mind-bogglingly obsessed with anal sex. Whatever possessed Moore to demean herself as a sexy klutz government scientist, who falls flat on her face repeatedly, and Scott is also highly resistible in a part shoe-horned in for teen audiences; at least Duchovny is agreeably mild-mannered, allowing Jones to milk the black-sidekick role for many more laughs than it's worth. But of course the real eye candy comes in the CGI work. TCh

Ewok Adventure, The (aka Caravan of Courage)

(1984, US, 100 min)
d John Korty. *p* Thomas G Smith. *sc* Bob Carrau. *ph* John Korty. *ed* John Nutt. *pd* Joe Johnston. *m* Peter Bernstein. *cast* Eric Walker, Warwick Davis, Fionnula Flanagan, Guy Boyd, Aubree Miller, Dan Frishman.

● Ewoks (first seen in *Return of the Jedi*) have lifeless eyes, nuclear families, short fuses, clean bums, hang-gliders, priestesses, wise men and rhythm. They look like short, furry Colin Wellands, and sound like David Rappaport clearing his throat in a subway. They live on Endor, which is like California with rocky bits painted in front of the lens. The caravan is a vehicle for a kiddy-quest for lost parents – young, curly-top cutie and big, bolshie brother coming to terms with his inner obnoxiousness via confrontation with alien culture. Short on action by Lucasfilm standards, stuffed with toothy teddies which lack the charm of Phase One Gremlins, or the wit of any muppet… I blame Thatcher. RP

Excalibur

(1981, US, 140 min)
d/p John Boorman. *sc* Rospo Pallenberg, John Boorman. *ph* Alex Thomson. *ed* John Merritt. *pd* Anthony Pratt. *m* Trevor Jones. *cast* Nigel Terry, Helen Mirren, Nicholas Clay, Cherie Lunghi, Paul Geoffrey, Nicol Williamson, Robert Addie, Gabriel Byrne.

● Visually impressive but generally muddled and uneven adaptation of Malory's *Morte d'Arthur*, both overlong and incoherent as it follows the quest for the Holy Grail and the climactic battle between Arthur and Mordred. Almost determinedly bizarre (or stupid?) in some of its characterisation – most notably Williamson's eccentric Merlin – it also adds a dash of gore and a touch of sex for good modernist measure. Nothing, however, can counter the film's inability to sway the emotions. For all its audacity, a misguided folly. GA

Excess Baggage

see Bulto, El

Excess Baggage

(1997, US, 101 min)
d Marco Brambilla. *p* Bill Borden, Carolyn Kessler. *sc* Max Adams, Dick Clement, Ian La Frenais. *ph* Jean-Yves Escoffier. *ed* Stephen Rivkin. *pd* Missy Stewart. *m* John Lurie. *cast* Alicia Silverstone, Benicio Del Toro, Christopher Walken, Jack Thompson, Nicholas Turturro, Michael Bowen, Sally Kirkland, Harry Connick Jr.

● Rich girl Emily (Silverstone, irritating) kidnaps herself and demands a ransom from neglectful father. But then car thief Del Toro unwittingly steals the vehicle in which she's locked herself. Emily takes charge of the abduction. Pursued by the cops, two incompetent hoods, and a cool ex-CIA agent (Walken), the couple flee across country and fall in love. Del Toro, so brilliant as the vowel-gargling felon in *The Usual Suspects*, is just too weird to convince as a romantic lead. The action covers 72 hours and, despite some classy visuals, it sometimes feels like it. NF

Executioner, The

see Verdugo, El

Executioners from Shaolin (Hong Xiguan)

(1977, HK, 103 min)
d Lau Kar-Leung [Liu Jialiang]. *cast* Chen Guantai, Wong Yu, Lo Lieh, Lily Li, Gordon Liu, Cheng Kang Yeh.

● Not as finely crafted as Lau's later Shaw Brothers films, but this reframing of one of the key Shaolin legends in explicitly sexual terms is an amazing achievement. After the sack of the Shaolin Temple, monk Hong Xiguan (Chen) goes into hiding and marries; but he neglects his wife and son because he's set on fighting the eunuch Bai Mei (Lo), who destroyed Shaolin. His macho 'Tiger Stance' cannot equal the eunuch's quasi-mystical power, and he dies in the duel. His widow (Li) trains their son Wending (Wong) in the feminine 'Crane' style, which is all she knows, and the boy is ridiculed as a sissy by his schoolmates. Wending eventually picks up scraps of his father's techniques from a worm-eaten training manual and confronts his father's killer as a 'bi-sexual' fighter: half male, half female. The eunuch, conversely, is a sexual 'black hole' who can suck opponents into his body through the void where his genitals once were. If only Freud could have seen it. The UK video release of this 'Scope film is panned-and-scanned and wretchedly dubbed. TR

Executioner's Song, The

(1982, US, 135 min)
d/p Lawrence Schiller. *sc* Norman Mailer. *ph* Freddie Francis. *ed* Richard A Harris, Tom Rolf. *pd* Jac McAnelly. *m* John Cacavas. *cast* Tommy Lee Jones, Christine Lahti, Rosanna Arquette, Steven Keats, Jordan Clarke, Richard Venture, Eli Wallach.

● Schiller and Norman Mailer's docu-drama – about double-killer Gary Gilmore, who demanded to be executed – exists in a curiously harsh netherworld beyond traditional genre, skirting the realm of the clinical dossier. Sensation (crimes and punishment: two murders and a firing squad) and incongruity (Gilmore as media event) produce a troubled, quizzical analysis of background and context, but seem as displaced from being the movie's elusive subject as does Gilmore himself. Jones (playing Gilmore) goes his own fascinating route to the loser's nirvana without recourse to psycho-style tics, while strong character performances from Arquette and Lahti constantly shift the focus back towards the everyday straitjacket of Utah underdogs. In all, easier to recommend than to define. This is an edited version of the 2-part TV movie, running 200 minutes. PT

Execution in Autumn (Qiu Jue)

(1971, Tai, 99 min)
d Li Xing. *p* Chen Ju Lin. *sc* Chang Yung-Hsing. *ph* Lai Cheng-Ying. *ed* Chen Hung-Min. *ad* Chou Chih-Liang. *m* Icharo Saito. *cast* Ou Wei, Tang Pao-Yun, Ko Hsiang-Ting, Fu Pi-Hui, Wu Chia-Chi, Chen Hui-Lou.

● It's hard to pinpoint why a film apparently as simple as this should be so extraordinarily moving. The story couldn't be more direct: in Han Dynasty China, executions are confined to the autumn, and the selfish, brutal Pei finds himself in prison for eleven months, waiting for his sentence to be carried out. During that period he is inveigled into marrying, so that his wife can bear him an heir, and his character gradually begins to mellow. The film's real richness seems to lie in its web of undercurrents; the tangle of hopes, dreams, memories and desires that enmeshes the characters, sometimes almost tangible, sometimes elusive.

Execution Protocol, The

(1992, GB, 90 min)
d Stephen Trombley. *p* Stephen Trombley, Mitch Wood. *ph* Paul Gibson. *ed* Peter Miller. *m* Robert Lockhart.

● The Potosi Correctional Center is the showcase maximum security prison for Missouri's 'most dangerous criminals'; every inmate has been convicted of capital murder, and sentenced either to 50 years or life without parole, or to death by lethal injection. Trombley's exemplary film focuses not only on the ethics of capital punishment, with officials and prisoners alike allowed to give their opinions on the issue, but on the minutiae of who does what and how whenever an execution takes place. The prisoners (including one whose execution was stayed with just three hours to go) are especially articulate in their condemnation of the centre's 'humane' methods; and Trombley's cool tone, sharp images, and use of a superb modern jazz score, make for powerful viewing. One complaint only: we never learn what the prisoners actually did, which – while it doesn't alter the fact that the State is committing institutionalised murder – rather weakens the force of the film's argument. GA

Executive Action

(1973, US, 91 min)
d David Miller. *p* Edward Lewis. *sc* Dalton Trumbo. *ph* Robert Steadman. *ed* George Grenville, Irving Lerner. *ad* Kirk Axtell. *m* Randy Edelman. *cast* Burt Lancaster, Robert Ryan, Will Geer, Gilbert Green, John Anderson, Ed Lauter.

● A compelling dramatic hypothesis constructed by Dalton Trumbo from the conspiracy theories advanced by persistent Kennedy assassination investigator Mark Lane, in turn based on evidence the Warren Commission refused to hear. Fudged slightly towards tidy fictional coherence by an unwillingness to acknowledge the very discrepancies that Lane had earlier illustrated with Emile de Antonio in the documentary *Rush to Judgement*, but a plausible enough attempt to weld the 'political thriller' style of Costa-Gavras on to Hollywood. Producer Edward Lewis, nine years later, was responsible for setting up Costa-Gavras' Hollywood debut with *Missing*. PT

Executive Decision

(1995, US, 132 min)
d Stuart Baird. *p* Joel Silver, Jim Thomas, John Thomas. *sc* Jim Thomas, John Thomas. *ph* Alex Thomson. *ed* Dallas Puett, Frank J Urioste, Stuart Baird, Kevin Stitt, Derek Brechin. *pd* Terence Marsh. *m* Jerry Goldsmith. *cast* Steven Seagal, David Suchet, Kurt Russell, Oliver Platt, John Leguizano, Halle Berry, Joe Morton, JT Walsh, Marla Maples Trump.

● This 'bomb on a plane' action-thriller takes off smoothly, hits some terrorist turbulence at cruising altitude, and doesn't come down until the palm-sweating finale. Koran-quoting Arab Nagi Hassan (Suchet) and his team take over a 747 bound for Washington, DC, and threaten to kill all on board if their imprisoned leader isn't freed. But intelligence analyst David Grant (Russell) senses that Hassan has a more heinous plan: to land the plane, release its (supposed) payload of lethal nerve toxin, and wipe out the Eastern seaboard. So, while on the ground the military men and politicians decide whether to down the plane and cut their losses, an anti-terrorist unit led by Lt Col Austin Travis (Seagal) uses a prototype 'sleeve' to board the aircraft in midair. Providing high-altitude intelligence back-up are pencil-pusher Grant and the sleeve's designer Cahill (Platt), both way out of their depth. As befits an editor-turned-director, Baird has a strong sense of pace and suspense, but even his cross-cutting skills are no match for a plot that fragments the action and blurs the narrative focus. Even so, the escalating tension largely compensates for the lack of character involvement, and the climax will have you reaching for your safety belt. NF

Executive Suite

(1954, US, 104 min, b/w)
d Robert Wise. *p* John Houseman. *sc* Ernest Lehman. *ph* George Folsey. *ed* Ralph E Winters. *ad* Cedric Gibbons, Edward C Carfagno. *cast* William Holden, June Allyson, Barbara Stanwyck, Fredric March, Walter Pidgeon, Louis Calhern, Shelley Winters, Paul Douglas, Nina Foch, Dean Jagger.

● Slick MGM account of intrigues that take place among five viciously opportunistic company executives, jostling for position when their president dies. Taut and gripping, its chief strengths are a finely structured script by Ernest Lehman, and top-notch acting by the starry ensemble. March is particularly memorable, cast against the grain as a devious, maliciously selfish company controller. For all its sheerly entertaining wallowing in spiritual corruption, however, it never approaches the acerbic pungency of Lehman's collaboration with Clifford Odets on *Sweet Smell of Success*. GA

Exhibited, The (De Udstillede)

(2000, Den, 81 min)
d Jesper Jargil. *p* Vinca Wiedemann. *sc* Jesper Jargil, Niels Vørsel, Lars von Trier. *ph* Jesper Jargil. *ed* Janus Billeskov-Jansen, Camilla Schyberg. *m* Joachim Holbek. *cast* Carsten Bjørnlund, Regitze Estrup, Lotte Aske Fredskov, Betina Henriette Grove, Niels Peter Johansen, Karoline Lieberkind, Klaus Løwert, Luis Mesonero, Bo Overgaard.

● Dogme docu about a bizarre theatrical stunt dreamed up Lars von Trier: 'Psychomobile 1: The World Clock'. Essentially, this boiled down to sticking 53 actors in a large house, giving them a quick character sketch, and letting them improvise for two months. Oh yes, and then there are lights in each room. Any change in colour must trigger a change in the mood of the scene. And the lights are linked to the to and fro within a colony of ants in New Mexico. A metaphor for the random pull of human destiny, perhaps. Jargil gets some amusing insights from the cast, but the film doesn't merit its running time, especially as the omniscient LvT remains offscreen. Agnostics are unlikely to be converted. TCh

Exile, The

(1947, US, 95 min, b/w)
d Max Ophüls. *p/sc* Douglas Fairbanks Jr. *ph* Franz Planer. *ed* Ted J Kent. *pd* Howard Baye. *m* Frank Skinner. *cast* Douglas Fairbanks Jr, Maria Montez, Paule Croset [Rita Corday], Henry Daniell, Nigel Bruce, Robert Coote.

● Fairbanks Jr may have written and produced *The Exile*, but thankfully Ophüls' camera performs more gymnastics than he does as Charles II, the escapee king tiptoeing through the tulip fields of Holland. The obligatory swashbuckling is held well in check in Ophüls' first American movie, and an essentially lightweight, star-oriented period piece is transformed into a pertinent series of reflections on love and duty, on identity and role, and on destiny. PT

eXistenZ

(1999, Can/GB, 97 min)
d David Cronenberg. *p* Robert Lantos, András Hámori, David Cronenberg. *sc* David Cronenberg. *ph* Peter Suschitzky. *ed* Ronald Sanders. *pd* Carol Spier. *m* Howard Shore. *cast* Jennifer Jason Leigh, Jude Law, Ian Holm, Don McKellar, Callum Keith Rennie, Sarah Polley, Robert A Silverman, Christopher Eccleston, Willem Dafoe.

● *eXistenZ* is a virtual reality game where players, their nervous systems linked to a techno-biological pod via a plug in the spinal column, enter hallucinatory worlds/stories fuelled by their fears, needs and desires. At the game's launch, cultish, controversial creator Allegra (Leigh) survives an assassination attempt by an anti-games fanatic. Fleeing from a 'fatwa' with the game company's trainee marketing man Ted (Law), she soon persuades him to join her in playing her invention, both to assess the damage done to her pod, and to share the vicarious pleasures to which she's addicted. But how can they tell which of the bizarre scenarios they find themselves in is imagined or real? And do they have any control over them? While weaving fresh variations on familiar Cronenberg themes, the film also proffers intriguing metaphors about the role of the artist in a consumer-driven world, and the ambivalent effects of fetishised, thrill-based entertainment. Most welcome, however, is the playful wit – unprecedented for Cronenberg – and the pacy, tortuous narrative, a series of Chinese boxes which leave fugitives and viewers alike wondering where in hell they are and what could possibly happen next. Dark, delirious fun. GA

Exit to Eden

(1994, US, 114 min)
d Garry Marshall. *p* Garry Marshall, Alex Rose. *sc* Deborah Amelon, Bob Brunner. *ph* Theo van de Sande. *ed* David Finfer. *pd* Peter Jamison. *m* Patrick Doyle. *cast* Dana Delany, Paul Mercurio, Rosie O'Donnell, Dan Aykroyd, Hector Elizondo, Stuart Wilson, Iman.

● Garry (*Pretty Woman*) Marshall's sexploiter makes Zalman King's 'women's fantasy' movies seem sophisticated and daring. His film begs the question – how humiliatingly it begs! – 'What do women really want?' On this issue, dominatrix Delany, unbending mistress of the SM sex ranch island 'Eden', takes a while to accept the missionary position: lots of foreplay and a straight 'kindness and cute butt' pay-off in the form of Paul (*Strictly Ballroom*) Mercurio's photographer, here mostly naked and canine-collared. Given the film is such a foolish exercise (you have to accept O'Donnell in bondage attire and Aykroyd's dumb-klutz maintenance man as a pair of LA cops investigating a jewel heist in deep cover), you'd expect excess or a camp romp à la Russ Meyer at least. But no such luck. There's certainly plenty of tits'n'ass, male and female, scantily adorned in *Fellini-Satyricon*-style gold lamé Roman chic, but it's not an erotic show. There are a few in-jokes and droll moments, but otherwise you wouldn't know it was a Garry Marshall movie. Neither bad enough for cult status, nor good enough for vicarious thrills. WH

Exit Wounds

(2001, US/Aust, 100 min)
d Andrzej Bartkowiak. *p* Joel Silver, Dan Cracchiolo. *sc* Ed Horowitz, Richard D'Ovidio. *ph* Glen MacPherson. *ed* Derek G Brechin. *pd* Paul Denham Austerberry. *m* Jeff Rona, Damon 'Grease' Blackman. *cast* Steven Seagal, DMX, Isaiah Washington, Anthony Anderson, Michael Jai White, Bill Duke, Jill Hennessy, Tom Arnold.

● Seagal, the po-faced eco-warrior turned self-mocking action hero, plays a loose cannon detective who's busted to street cop in Detroit's toughest precinct. His improbably beautiful boss (Hennessy) warns him against any 'Lone Ranger stuff', but he's no team player. Meanwhile, $5m worth of heroin has been lifted from the precinct's property vaults and there are more suspects than he can shake a nightstick at. Bartkowiak directs with the same flashy, kinetic energy he brought to *Romeo Must Die*, rendering the overplotted storyline virtually incomprehensible. On the plus side, Seagal's role as the underdog keeps him on a tighter lead. This Joel Silver-produced package frontlines handsome HipHop artist DMX as a cool nightclub owner, with strong support from Anderson as his comic sidekick and Washington as Seagal's partner. Sadly, the corrupt cops and one-dimensional villains bring new meaning to the phrase 'as thick as thieves'. NF

Exodus

(1960, US, 220 min)
d/p Otto Preminger. *sc* Dalton Trumbo. *ph* Sam Leavitt. *ed* Louis Loeffler. *ad* Richard Day, Bill Hutchinson. *m* Ernest Gold. *cast* Paul Newman, Eva Marie

Saint, Ralph Richardson, Peter Lawford, Lee J Cobb, Sal Mineo, John Derek, Hugh Griffith, Felix Aylmer, Jill Hayworth.
●Touted as a masterpiece by stout Preminger-ites; but with one eye on the box-office, the other on avoiding giving offence, this adaptation of Leon Uris' blockbusting novel about the founding of modern Israel could hardly be anything but a compromise. Moral issues are raised, only to be forgotten in urgent deluges of action or romance; characters are all fashioned strictly to stereotype; and for all its caution, it finally comes across (especially in view of subsequent history) as a pretty objectionably blinkered slice of Zionist propaganda. Watchable mainly for the sheer skill and drive of Preminger's direction, although at 220 minutes even that long outstays its welcome. TM

Exodus – Bob Marley Live

(1978, GB, 74 min)
d Keith Macmillan. *with* Bob Marley and the Wailers.
●An excellent low-key high fidelity record of a stage set (at the Rainbow Theatre, North London, in June 1977) welds musical restraint to wild exuberance. It catches all Marley's moments and moods – angry, jiving, teasing, wasted – a great antidote to the rock-machine calculations and reverence of *The Last Waltz*. Only the exclusion of the audience disappoints. The climactic high is irresistible: Marley in the spotlight, a chalk-blue bird hovering in the dark, reaching out to the howling crowd – 'Don't give up your rights...' CA

Exorcist, The

(1973, US, 122 min)
d William Friedkin. *p/sc* William Peter Blatty. *ph* Owen Roizman. *ed* Jordan Leondopoulos. *pd* Bill Malley. *m* Jack Nitzsche. *cast* Ellen Burstyn, Max von Sydow, Lee J Cobb, Kitty Winn, Jack MacGowran, Jason Miller, Linda Blair.
●Friedkin's film about the possession of a 12-year-old girl works as an essay in suspension of disbelief and on the level of titillatory exploitation. Although harrowing, its effects depend entirely on technical manipulation, and with Friedkin's pedestrian handling of background story and supporting characters, we're left more or less willing the film towards its climax. Sure enough, during the act of exorcism the girl obliges with a spectacular levitation. It would all be forgiveable, somehow, if the film was at all likely to alter anyone's perceptions one jot. But all *The Exorcist* does is take its audience for a ride, spewing it out the other end, shaken up but none the wiser. CPe

Exorcist – Director's Cut, The

(1973, US, 132 min)
d William Friedkin. *p/sc* William Peter Blatty. *ph* Owen Roizman. *ed* Jordan Leondopoulos. *pd* Bill Malley. *m* Jack Nitzsche. *cast* Ellen Burstyn, Max von Sydow, Lee J Cobb, Kitty Winn, Jack MacGowran, Jason Miller, Linda Blair.
●A re-release with an impeccable digital soundtrack and ten minutes of extra footage, including the notorious 'spider walk' (which lasts about 3 seconds) and a longer coda with corny banter between the cop and Father Dyer. As any aficionado will tell you, this is not a 'director's cut' in any real sense (Friedkin's version was released in 1973), but it's probably closer to how writer/ producer Blatty might have edited the film. As well as new subliminal demon imagery, it also includes a scene between Chris and Regan's first doctor, and an expanded role for von Sydow's Father Merrin, most notably a key speech about why the demon has picked on this little girl: to make us despair for humanity. In other words it's now more than ever a faithful Catholic treatise on Evil, even if the film's shock effects remain at least half the story. Either way it's rigged, but it certainly puts you through an emotional grinder. TCh

Exorcist II: The Heretic

(1977, US, 117 min.)
d John Boorman. *p* Richard Lederer, John Boorman. *sc* William Goodhart. *ph* William A Fraker. *ed* Tom Priestley. *pd* Richard MacDonald. *m* Ennio Morricone. *cast* Linda Blair, Richard Burton, Louise Fletcher, Max von Sydow, Kitty Winn, Paul Henried, James Earl Jones, Ned Beatty.
●Substantially recut by Boorman after his original version was derided in America, but it's still easy to see why New Yorkers jeered. Boorman completely avoids gore and obscenity, treating the original as a kind of sacred good-versus-evil text, and weaving its sets and characters into a highly traditional confrontation of occult forces. The theme is attacked with engaging intensity, and Boorman brings off more than one visual coup (notably the ingenious locust photography in the African sequences). Dennis Wheatley fans, at least, will love it. DP

Exorcist III, The

(1990, US, 110 min)
d William Peter Blatty. *p* Carter DeHaven. *sc* William Peter Blatty. *ph* Gerry Fisher. *ed* Tom Ramsey. *pd* Leslie Dilley. *m* Barry DeVorzon. *cast* George C Scott, Ed Flanders, Brad Dourif, Jason Miller, Nicol Williamson, Scott Wilson, Nancy Fish, Viveca Lindfors, Zohra Lampert, Barbara Baxley.
●Fifteen years after the execution of the Gemini killer, Georgetown falls prey to grisly serial slayings bearing the Gemini's trademark mutilations. Meanwhile, deep in the bowels of the town's psychiatric institution, a patient emerges from catatonia, claiming to be the Gemini and demanding recognition. Investigating the case is Lt Kinderman (Scott), whose world-weary scepticism is challenged not only by the patient's exact knowledge of the crimes, but by his uncanny resemblance to Father Damien Karras, who fell to his death fifteen years earlier while performing an exorcism. Blatty's sequel eschews the visceral effects of its predecessor (it ignores Boorman's *The Heretic*) to rely instead on the chilling power of suggestion. The excessively wordy dialogue is interrupted by intervals of brooding malevolence, and by a couple of contrived but startlingly effective shocks. The real terror, however, comes from Dourif's straight-to-camera serial killer monologues, which breathe eerie life into the script. With the exception of an unnecessary spectacular climax, this is a restrained, haunting chiller which stimulates the adrenalin and intellect alike. MK

Exotica

(1994, Can, 103 min)
d Atom Egoyan. *p* Atom Egoyan, Camelia Frieberg. *sc* Atom Egoyan. *ph* Paul Sarossy. *ed* Susan Shipton. *pd* Linda del Rosario, Richard Paris. *m* Mychael Danna. *cast* Don McKellar, Mia Kirshner, Arsinée Khanjian, Elias Koteas, Bruce Greenwood, Sarah Polley.
●Characteristically stylish, intriguing film from Atom Egoyan, heavy on the eroticism and mystification as it delves into the lives of a number of characters connected by their relationship to the strip joint of the title: the owner and MC; a table-dancer; a taxman obsessed with the dancer; and a pet-shop proprietor, whose business the taxman is auditing. It's another excursion into projected fantasies, anxiety, exploitation and secret needs; the elegant camerawork and intense performances sustain interest, although the fragmentation of the plot sometimes seems unnecessarily obscurantist – finally, the mystery is not so very startling or significant. Fascinating, though, and without the pretensions that have marred some of Egoyan's earlier work. GA

Experience Preferred But Not Essential

(1982, GB , 75 min)
d Peter Duffell. *p* Chris Griffin. *sc* June Roberts. *ph* Phil Méheux. *ed* John Shirley. *ad* Jane Martin. *m* Rachel Portman. *cast* Elizabeth Edmonds, Sue Wallace, Geraldine Griffiths, Karen Meagher, Maggie Wilkinson, Ron Bain.
●Small, basically honest, very English film, made for 'Film on Four' by David Puttnam's Goldcrest, about a girl from Cleveland filling in the summer before college with a job as a maid at a Welsh seaside hotel. The chef, an ex-seaman from Paisley, lays siege to the girl's virginity. This is the Campaign for Nuclear Disarmament '60s. Nothing particularly surprising here (Ivan the wine waiter sleepwalks naked; backstairs life is uncarpeted, cheerful and over-emotional), but the sentiment is notably unforced. Found particular favour in America. JPy

Experiment, The (Das Experiment)

(2001, Ger, 115 min)
d Oliver Hirschbiegel. *p* Norbert Preuss, Marc Conrad, Fritz Wildfeuer, (Typhoon Film) Ulrike Leibfried. *sc* Mario Giordano, Christoph Darnstädt, Don Bohlinger. *ph* Rainer Klausmann. *ed* Hans Funck. *pd* Uli Hanisch. *m* Alexander van Bubenheim. *cast* Moritz Bleibtreu, Christian Berkel, Oliver Stokowski, Wotan Wilke Möhring, Stephan Szasz, Polat Dal, Justus von Dohnányi, Nicki von Tempelhoff, Timo Dierkes, Edgar Selge, Andrea Sawatzki, Maren Eggert
●This slick, occasionally disturbing German thriller (adapted from Mario Giordano's novel *Black Box*) was inspired directly by the notorious Stanford University prison psychology studies of the early '70s. Filmically, it borrows from *Shock Corridor* in sending undercover a journalist, Tarek Fahd (Bleibtreu) as an inmate participating in a university-administered exploration of prisoner-guard relations, where volunteers adopt roles in a lab environment of punishment and humiliation. What starts as a challenging investigative model soon slides out of control as peer pressure, dehumanisation and sadism threaten the lives of the participants. Given extra resonance by Germany's history, the film works effectively enough both as a psycho-social critique of the limits of behavioural safeguards and in the suspense stakes. The tension is grounded in character relations and their shifts under pressure as much as in the cranking of the narrative. By the climax, this develops into a standard shoot-out and clean-up operation, but there still remains a disquieting sense of the film-makers' initial intentions. GE

Experiment in Evil

see Testament du Docteur Cordelier, Le

Experiment in Terror (aka The Grip of Fear)

(1962, US, 122 min, b/w)
d/p Blake Edwards. *sc* The Gordons. *ph* Philip H Lathrop. *ed* Patrick McCormack. *ad* Robert Peterson. *m* Henry Mancini. *cast* Glenn Ford, Lee Remick, Stefanie Powers, Roy Poole, Ned Glass, Ross Martin, Clifton James.
●After seven lightish comedies and dramas, and directly following *Breakfast at Tiffany's*, Edwards launched himself in a new direction with this thriller: an experiment for him (although he had trodden thick-ear territory with his TV series, such as the legendary *Peter Gunn*) and also for the genre. Years before John Carpenter and other movie brats began to play with audience expectations and memories, Edwards constructed his film – about an asthmatic psycho pursuing Lee Remick – around precisely similar attitudes. Gone was the whodunit mystery formula; gone the need for psychological explanations; in their place, an exercise in steely style, with the audience split between its concern for the victim and its fascination with the psycho's activities. After Carpenter and De Palma, it may seem a little dated; yet Edwards' classical feel for pure cinema remains unalloyed. CW

Experiment Perilous

(1944, US, 91 min, b/w)
d Jacques Tourneur. *p/sc* Warren Duff. *ph* Tony Gaudio. *ed* Ralph Dawson. *ad* Albert S D'Agostino, Jack Okey. *m* Roy Webb. *cast* Hedy Lamarr, George Brent, Paul Lukas, Albert Dekker, Margaret Wycherly, Julia Dean.
●A comparatively minor but characteristically elegant Tourneur costume melodrama-cum-psychological thriller in the vein of *Rebecca* and *Gaslight*, this features Lamarr as the wife of a wealthy philanthropist; inevitably, she comes to fear not only for her own sanity, but also for that of her genuinely dangerous husband, a manic authoritarian patriarch whose violence is the product of a troubled, traumatic childhood. Equally inevitably, doctor/detective Brent is there to save her and supply romantic interest, but Tourneur manages to overcome the formulaic plotting and cod-Freudian characterisations through carefully controlled performances and Tony Gaudio's fine camerawork. GA

Experts, The

(1989, US, 83 min)
d Dave Thomas. *p* James Keach. *sc* Nick Thile, Steven Greene, Eric Alter. *ph* Robbie Taylor. *ed* Bud Molin. *pd* David Fischer. *m* Marvin Hamlisch. *cast* John Travolta, Arye Gross, Charles Martin Smith, Kelly Preston, Deborah Foreman, James Keach, Jan Rubes, Brian Doyle Murray.

● A lame-brain Cold War comedy. New York trendies Travolta and Gross are hired to open a disco in a small Midwestern town – or so they think. In fact, they have been flown in to a top-secret KGB installation modelled on a supposedly average American burgh. The Russkies hope these innocents abroad will authenticate and update their project. In terms of the Super Powers, this is very thin stuff. Fractionally more interesting is the implicit contrast between the pure '50s Americana the Soviets have reproduced, and the '80s values (Japanese hardware, *et al*) Travolta brings to it. TCh

Explorers

(1985, US, 109 min)
d Joe Dante. *p* Edward S Feldman, David Bombyk. *sc* Eric Luke. *ph* John Hora. *ed* Tina Hirsch. *pd* Robert Boyle. *m* Jerry Goldsmith. *cast* Ethan Hawke, River Phoenix, Jason Presson, Amanda Peterson, Dick Miller, Robert Picardo.

● Three kids are inspired by strange nightmares and a stroke of scientific luck to build their own spaceship, but suddenly find themselves out of control, yanked towards an encounter with some extremely oddball aliens. What really lifts this into the stratosphere of heady entertainment is its dizzy wit and intelligence. The dialogue is deliriously deadpan, the story surreal but surprisingly convincing, and the wealth of references to movie and TV classics hilarious rather than mere smartass posing. Dante's wacky comedy-thriller never degenerates into Spielbergian sentimentality, but mixes its inventive originality with a winning self-deprecating irony. It looks terrific, moves along at a gallop, and is marvellously good-natured. GA

Exposé

(1975, GB, 82 min)
d James Kenelm Clarke. *p* Brian Smedley-Aston. *sc* James Kenelm Clarke. *ph* Denis Lewiston. *ed* Jim Connock. *m* Steve Grey. *cast* Udo Kier, Linda Hayden, Fiona Richmond, Patsy Smart, Vic Armstrong, Karl Howman.

● This follow-up to Clarke's *Man Alive* TV report on sexploitation movies ran into censorship troubles with its explicit links between sex and violence. A paranoid author (Kier) living in an isolated country house hires a secretary (Hayden) to help him complete an overblown but potentially successful sex novel. The secretary turns out to be a psychopath who, before exposing the author as bogus, blasts two rapists with a shotgun, cuts the throat of an elderly woman, and then kills the author's girlfriend (Richmond) in the bath with the same knife. Clarke directs this derivative screenplay (a diluted solution of *Psycho* and *Straw Dogs*) with more economy than one expects from the genre. But Richmond demonstrates little of her renowned sexual athleticism, and the decorous, carefully placed sexual encounters are as predictable and passionless as ever. JPy

Exposed

(1983, US, 99 min)
d/p/sc James Toback. *ph* Henri Decaë. *ed* Robert Lawrence. *pd* Brian Eatwell. *m* Georges Delerue. *cast* Nastassja Kinski, Rudolf Nureyev, Harvey Keitel, Ian McShane, Bibi Andersson, Ron Randell, Pierre Clémenti, James Toback.

● An eccentric thriller meandering an uneasy route between jet-set melodrama – Kinski quits small town college to become top model – and terrorist activities, with Keitel not really at his most convincing as terrorism's Paris kingpin. Toback's earlier *Fingers* won some critical support, and his script here is not without philosophical moments concerning the ambiguities of the 'look' and the 'self'; but *Exposed* does not entirely have the courage of its frequently heady high art absurdities, despite moments like the one in which Nureyev (cast as a renowned violinist) literally attempts to play Kinski's body like a violin. For this kind of material the temperature must not be allowed to drop, but it frequently does. VG

Exposure

(1978, Ire, 48 min)
d Kieran Hickey. *cast* Catherine Schell, TP McKenna, Bosco Hogan, Niall O'Brien, Mairin O'Sullivan, Leslie Lalor.

● Alongside his excellent and chilling short *A Child's Voice*, *Exposure* demonstrates that Hickey is an Irish director of considerable power and assurance who seems intent on making the most of the tradition in Celtic fiction for quiet and subtle terror. Set on the desolate west coast of Ireland, the film explores a Polanski-like plot in which three surveyors find themselves stuck in a remote hotel with a French girl photographer. There are a few unsuccessful moments (notably a jarring beach-montage sequence), but in general the tone is deft and sharp, and the use of the tiny hotel bar to convey accumulating tension is masterly. DP

Expresso Bongo

(1959, GB, 111 min, b/w)
d/p Val Guest. *sc* Wolf Mankowitz. *ph* John Wilcox. *ed* Bill Lenny. *ad* Tony Masters. *songs* Robert Farnon, Val Guest, Norrie Paramor, Bunny Lewis, Paddy Roberts, Julian More, Monty Norman, David Henneker. *cast* Laurence Harvey, Cliff Richard, Sylvia Syms, Yolande Donlan, Kenneth Griffith, Meier Tzelniker, Hermione Baddeley, Wilfrid Lawson.

● An adaptation of Wolf Mankowitz's 1958 showbiz musical, bristling with period flavour, from the cast's brylcreemed coiffures and snazzy ties to the presence of Gilbert Harding playing himself. More surprisingly, it also bristles with energy and wit, and even survives the presence of the 19-year-old Cliff Richard as the bongo-thumping boy pushed up to stardom by Harvey's impeccably smarmy agent. The result is probably Britain's most abrasive and entertaining film musical. GB

Exquisite Tenderness

(1995, US/Ger, 100 min)
d Carl Schenke. *p* Alan Beattie, Chris Chesser, Willi Baer. *sc* Bernard Sloane, Patrick Cirillo. *ph* Thomas Burstyn. *ed* Jimmy B Frazier. *pd* Douglas Higgins. *m* Christopher Franke. *cast* Isabel Glasser, James Remar, Malcolm McDowell, Peter Boyle, Charles Dance, Sean Haberle.

● Schenkel handles this medical chiller with the sledge-hammer subtlety he brought to *Knight Moves*. Ironically, although he expressed reservations about the gore quotient, the set-piece nastiness is the one element that works. A giant syringe being shoved up someone's nostril is guaranteed to provoke a response. By contrast, attempts at suspense fail dismally, due to lack of narrative control and a surfeit of flashy camerawork. A monochrome pre-credits sequence in which a boy witnesses the blood-spattered demise of his sick brother explains the killer's psychological trauma. We then flash forward to the present, where Dr McCann (Glasser), desperate to clear her name after the gruesome death of a dialysis patient, enlists the help of an ambitious toxicologist (Remar). As the mystery unfolds, it becomes clear that someone with a grudge is bumping off the hospital's patients, in order to disgrace the medical staff and further his own Frankensteinian research into tissue and bone regeneration. The presence of McDowell as the fanatical Dr Stein offers a glimmer of hope, but when he dies, the film dies with him. Schenkel's reputation rests on his tense, lift-bound suspenser *Out of Order*, but on this evidence he's never going to get past the first floor. NF

Extase (Ecstasy/aka Symphony of Love)

(1932, Czech, 81 min, b/w)
d Gustav Machaty. *p* Frantisek Horky, Moriz Grunhut. *sc* Vitezslav Nezval, Gustav Machaty, Jacques A Koerpel, Frantisek Horky. *ph* Jan Stallich, Hans Androschin. *ad* Bohumil Hes. *m* Giuseppe Becce. *cast* Hedy Kiesler [Hedy Lamarr], Aribert Mog, Zvonimir Rogoz, Leopold Kramer.

● Opening with an exquisite image of a groom carrying his bride over the threshold of their conjugal abode, Machaty's film immediately unravels this romantic ideal, with the seemingly urbane husband proving an impotent dilettante unable to give his wife any attention. Sympathy lies strongly with the woman's plight, but not to the exclusion of other characters' feelings; and when the now abandoned husband comes across the farm labourer his wife has fallen in love with, his tragedy again intercepts her happiness. The simplicity of the story couches some stunning visual coups: a wry, idyllic pastoralism when the woman retreats from the town to her father's horse farm; and the famous sequence of Hedy Kiesler (later Lamarr) bathing nude, with its suggestion of a return to prelapsarian innocence (Vatican censure helped bring the film to a wider audience); the detailed attention to the play of light and shadow, animal and plant life and imagery (from flowers to fly paper); and a magical coda, turning a montage of static machinery into a reflective ode to love and labour. NB

Extasis

(1996, Sp, 93 min)
d Mariano Barroso. *p* Gerardo Herrero. *sc* Joaquin Oristrell, Mariano Barroso. *ph* Flavio Martinez Laviano. *ed* Fernando Pardo. *pd* Ion Arretxe. *m* Bingen Mendizabal, Kike Suarez Alba. *cast* Javier Bardem, Federico Luppi, Silvia Munt, Daniel Guzmán, Leire Berrocal, Alfonso Lusson, Guillermo Rodriguez.

● Disaffected rebels who dream of opening their own bar, Bardem, Guzmán and Berrocal are firm friends who even rob their own families to get the cash together. But when Bardem impersonates Guzmán in order to trick the latter's wealthy, long-estranged theatre-director father (Luppi), the trio's plans start to fall apart: seduced by Luppi's affections and fortune, not to mention the fame he offers in trying to turn the boy into a star, Bardem begins to enjoy bourgeois society. Though a little too chic and overwrought (all that symbolism and metaphor!), this succeeds thanks to a nicely ambiguous take on Bardem and Luppi's motives and an assured control of mood and pace. GA

Extension du domaine de la lutte

see Whatever

Exterminating Angel, The (El Angel Exterminador)

(1962, Mex, 93 min, b/w)
d Luis Buñuel. *p* Gustavo Alatriste. *sc* Luis Buñuel, Luis Alcoriza. *ph* Gabriel Figueroa. *ed* Carlos Savage Jr. *ad* Jesús Bracho. *cast* Silvia Pinal, Enrique Rambal, Lucy Gallardo, Claudio Brook, Tito Junco, Bertha Moss.

● In the best surrealist tradition, Buñuel claimed that his brilliant, disconcertingly funny joke – after an upper class dinner party, the guests find some mysterious compulsion making it impossible for them to leave the premises – has no rational explanation. True enough, but there are meanings aplenty in his powerful central image of decay as the vast, magnificently appointed bourgeois salon is gradually reduced to a sordid rubbish-heap where the once elegant guests squat and gnaw at bones. Significantly, the whole thing takes place under the sign of the church, but what still delights about the film is the way it refuses to be pigeonholed. Devastatingly funny, illuminated by unexpected shafts of generosity and tenderness, it remains one of Bunuel's very best. TM

Exterminator 2

(1984, US, 90 min)
d Mark Buntzman. *p/sc* Mark Buntzman, William Sachs. *ph* Robert Baldwin, Joe Mangine. *ed* George Norris, Marcus Mantron. *ad* Mischa Petrow, Virginia Field. *m* David Spear. *cast* Robert Ginty, Deborah Geffner, Mario van Peebles, Frankie Faison, Scott Randolph, John Turturro.

● Established in the parent *Exterminator* as a vigilante Vietnam vet whose gimmick is wielding a blow torch as weapon of choice, the unprepossessing Ginty is back with more of the same. This time he has a mean adversary in Mario (son-of-Melvin) van Peebles, which means that Robert had sure better have a black buddy in tow. Luckily, BG the garbage collector wants to make the streets safe for low budget, low ambition film-makers too. When Ginty's all-dancin', all-strippin' girlfriend exits the film in messy fashion, there's nothing for it but to fire up the old blow torch. But she's got nothing to complain about: the movie's over for her a lot quicker than it is for us. DO

Extraordinary Adventures of Mister West in the Land of the Bolsheviks, The (Neobychainye Prikliucheniya Mistera Vesta v Stanye Bolshevikov)

(1924, USSR, 80 min, b/w)
d Lev Kuleshov. *sc* Nikolai Aseyev, Lev Kuleshov, Vsevolod Pudovkin. *ph* Alexander

Levitzky. *ad* Vsevolod Pudovkin, Boris Barnet, Sergei Komarov, ALexander Khokholova.
●Satircal look at Western versus Soviet manners, politics and relaities with a high-fur-coated American tourist first casting a superficial eye over the new Moscow, only to be taken off by a bunch of abductors, and then escaping their clutches and glimpsing the 'real essence' of the Soviet Union.

Extreme Close-Up

(1972, US, 82 min)
d Jeannot Szwarc. *p* Paul N Lazarus III. *sc* Michael Crichton. *ph* Paul Lohmann. *ad* Mary Ann Newfield. *m* Basil Poledouris. *cast* James McMullan, James A Watson Jr, Kate Woodville, Bara Byrnes, Al Checco, Anthony Carbone.
●The idle fantasies provoked by watching a pretty girl become rather more concrete for a young TV reporter (McMullan), conducting a series on invasion of privacy ('Privacy is not clearly a legal right'), when he gets his hands on the latest bugging devices. From lazily scanning the block opposite, through some more dedicated spying, his voyeurism culminates with a self-appraisal in the mirror while his wife reaches orgasm beneath him. Because the central character is given little motivation (he's ordinary, personable, reasonably married), the audience is forced into an examination of its own condoning of the voyeur's actions. Unfortunately, with the sex scenes so routinely softcore, this investigation doesn't necessarily go very deep. As scripted by Michael Crichton, however, the pitfalls of peeping are well accounted for: the fear of being found out, the mixture of fear and elation, and above all, the lengths to which people are prepared to go. As our reporter says on TV, 'If someone wants to spy badly enough, he'll find a way to do it.' Even if it means squatting behind a tree in the pitch black with an infra-red scanner. CPe

Extreme Measures

(1996, US/GB, 118 min)
d Michael Apted. *p* Elizabeth Hurley. *sc* Tony Gilroy. *ph* John Bailey. *ed* Rick Shaine. *pd* Douglas Kraner. *m* Danny Elfman. *cast* Hugh Grant, Gene Hackman, Sarah Jessica Parker, David Morse, Bill Nunn, John Toles-Bey, Paul Guilfoyle, Debra Monk.
●A promising start for Hugh Grant and Liz Hurley's Simian Films. Grant's a junior doctor in the A&E department of a NY teaching hospital who's intrigued by the perplexing symptoms of a fatally disturbed mystery patient. The disappearance of the body spurs him to dig deeper into the case. With nurse Parker on hand to lend support and romantic involvement, Grant doesn't realise he's getting into dark conspiratorial waters, which will threaten his life and livelihood, implicate revered neurologist Hackman, and take him to parts of the city he didn't even know existed. Grant has just the right amount of offhand decency to sustain the film's moralising impetus and bring an emotional relevance to its spiralling plot reversals. Perhaps screenwriter Tony Gilroy's adaptation of Michael Palmer's novel slightly labours the discussion of medical ethics, but Hackman's involving performance, as the researcher bending the rules in the treatment of spinal injuries, never leaves the arguments cut and dried. An effective crowd-pleaser which never goes dumb on you. TJ

Extreme Prejudice

(1987, US, 104 min)
d Walter Hill. *p* Buzz Feitshans. *sc* Deric Washburn, Harry Kleiner. *ph* Matthew F Leonetti. *ed* Freeman Davies, Carmel Davies, David Holden, Billy Weber. *pd* Albert Heschong. *m* Jerry Goldsmith. *cast* Nick Nolte, Powers Boothe, Michael Ironside, Maria Conchita Alonso, Rip Torn, Clancy Brown, William Forsythe.
●A thinly disguised remake of Sam Peckinpah's *The Wild Bunch*, set on the US/Mexico border, updated to include a CIA team of Vietnam veterans trained in the use of sophisticated hi-tech weaponry. The central conflict between Texas Ranger Nolte and his former buddy turned drug baron (Boothe) is textbook Western stuff, complete with the standard rivalry over the love interest (Alonso). Covert CIA team leader Ironside asks Nolte for help in recovering secret government documents allegedly in Boothe's possession, thus forcing the ranger to choose between old loyalties and the demands of duty. The action is lean and tough, the body count huge, and the final shootout an obvious reprise of Peckinpah's finale. But where the latter's vision transformed *The Wild Bunch* into a savage elegy for the passing of the Old West, Hill can only duplicate its choreographed violence. NF

Extremities

(1986, US, 89 min)
d Robert M Young. *p* Burt Sugarman. *sc* William Mastrosimone. *ph* Curtis Clark. *ed* Arthur Coburn. *pd* Chester Kaczenski. *m* JAC Redford. *cast* Farrah Fawcett, James Russo, Diana Scarwid, Alfre Woodard, Sandy Martin, Eddie Vélez.
●Attacked by a masked would-be rapist (Russo), Fawcett manages to escape but leaves her ID behind. The police ('Ever been picked up for prostitution before?') are less than sympathetic, and her two flatmates are kind enough to take her car with them when they leave her alone to face, as she and we know, her assailant's inevitable return. What follows is an hour of violent and voyeuristically relished confrontation as Fawcett, initially stripped, humiliated and terrorised, manages to turn the tables to blind and cage her 'animal' aggressor. This offensive adaptation of William Mastrosimone's controversial play suggests that there was never much question of making any serious attempt to deal with the important subjects raised. The use of subjective camera and meaningless circling shots cannot disguise either the essential abuse of cinematic technique or the crippling lack of psychological insight and detail. Under the restrictive hand of Young's direction, Russo's moronic 'Method' maniac and Fawcett's grimy avenger are equated as mere beasts in this one-room zoo. WH

Eye for an Eye

(1995, US, 101 min)
d John Schlesinger. *p* Michael I Levy. *sc* Amanda Silver, Rick Jaffa. *ph* Amir Mokri. *ed* Peter Honess. *pd* Stephen Hendrickson. *m* James Newton Howard. *cast* Sally Field, Kiefer Sutherland, Ed Harris, Olivia Burnette, Alexandra Kyle, Joe Mantegna, Beverly D'Angelo.
●A virulent throwback to the vigilante movies of the '70s. Field is a respectable middle-class wife and mother who turns into a gun toting suburban Rambette after her daughter's raped and murdered before her very ears (she's on the phone). The police have an airtight case, but a technicality allows the killer to walk free, and Sally takes to following him. What she sees confirms her already low opinion: not only is he bearded, tattooed and Sutherland, he's also rude and unrepentant, tortures animals, and pisses on the sidewalk. For this, he must die. Vigilante thrillers are by nature contrived and manipulative, but Schlesinger's reactionary film knows no bounds when it comes to emotional blackmail. Does it make the crime more terrible that it's committed on the victim's birthday? Are such judicial miscarriages so prevalent that a victim support group could shield a summary execution agency? While assorted authority figures pay lip service to law and order, compassion and forgiveness, their words ring hollow: the film operates as propaganda for capital punishment. Mercifully, it's not very effective propaganda. The characterisation is so thin, and the plotting so crude, it's only the violence which sets this apart from the banalities of TV fare – that and the novelty of seeing Sally Field come on like Travis Bickle. TCh

Eye for an Eye, An

(1981, US, 104 min)
d Steve Carver. *p* Frank Capra Jr. *sc* William Grey, James Bruner. *ph* Roger Shearman. *ed* Anthony Redman. *ad* Vance Lorenzini. *m* William Goldstein. *cast* Chuck Norris, Christopher Lee, Richard Roundtree, Matt Clark, Mako, Maggie Cooper, Rosalind Chao.
●Norris, the Great White Hope of the Hollywood martial arts movie, beefcakes his way through an Oriental Connection drug ring with a bullet-proof spiritual aura and a dated fantasy line in abode, wardrobe and transportation. An undercover narc who quits the San Francisco force when his buddy is set up and blown away, his lone-wolf biblical revenge gets further prompts from the ravages of a mammoth Mongolian henchman and such minor irritants as a machine-gun helicopter raid by boiler-suited Triad lackeys. His facial muscles twitch for love or laughter; otherwise it's a frozen-frown, feet first routine all the way to the signposted Bad Guy. PT

Eye of the Beholder

(1998, Can/GB/US/Aust, 110 min)
d Stephan Elliott. *p* Tony Smith, Nicolas Clermont, Al Clark. *sc* Stephan Elliott. *ph* Guy Dufaux. *ed* Sue Blainey. *pd* Jean-Baptiste Tard. m Marius De Vries. *cast* Ashley Judd, Ewan McGregor, Patrick Bergin, KD Lang, Jason Priestley, Geneviève Bujold.
●Ewan McGregor plays the Eye, a surveillance operative in British Intelligence. Investigating blackmail, he witnesses murder. The killer is a blonde – or is she brunette? – who disappears into metropolitan anonymity; yet the Eye will not let it go, and hearing about a suspiciously familiar-sounding crime some months later, he picks up the trail, gradually closing in on Joanna (Judd) even as he loses the plot. The Eye, you see, is an unreliable witness, whose only human interaction is with the voices in his head, and who comes to believe that Joanna and his missing daughter are one and the same. A change of tack for Aussie auteur Elliott, formerly a purveyor of garish, misanthropic camp (most famously *The Adventures of Priscilla Queen of the Desert*), this swaps bad taste comedy for bad taste romance: it's a love story for sociopaths. Marc Behm's post-modern *noir* novel – *Lolita* with a body count – has been filmed before: most hauntingly by Claude Miller as *Mortelle Randonnée*, with Isabelle Adjani and Michel Serrault; then, unacknowledged and with a gender twist, by Bob Rafelson as *Black Widow*. Elliott's flamboyantly surreal version is undone by the central miscasting of McGregor – at least a decade too young to be fixated on a long-lost daughter. Judd is more murderous mannequin than 'Marnie', but then the real star is Elliott's inventive mise-en-scène. Staking a claim as the heir apparent to ageing stylists Brian De Palma and Dario Argento, he drives the voyeurism theme to hi-tech distraction. The result is compellingly bonkers. TCh

Eye of the Cat

(1969, US, 102 min)
d David Lowell Rich. *p* Bernard Schwartz, Phillip Hazelton. *sc* Joseph Stefano. *ph* Russell Metty, Ellsworth J Fredricks. *ed* J Terry Williams. *ad* Alexander Golitzen, William DeCinces. *m* Lalo Schifrin. *cast* Michael Sarrazin, Gayle Hunnicutt, Eleanor Parker, Tim Henry, Laurence Naismith, Jennifer Leak.
●A nicely extravagant tale of horror in which an army of cats protect a rich invalid (Parker) from her two-faced hairdresser-confidante (Hunnicutt), who has set a nephew with a phobia about cats (Sarrazin) to scheming for her money. Its success can be largely attibuted to two of Hitchcock's collaborators: writer Joseph Stefano, who turned in the script for *Psycho*, and Ray Berwick, who trained the birds for *The Birds*. CPe

Eye of the Needle

(1981, GB, 113 min)
d Richard Marquand. *p* Stephen J Friedman. *sc* Stanley Mann. *ph* Alan Hume. *ed* Sean Barton. *pd* Wilfrid Shingleton. *m* Miklós Rozsa. *cast* Donald Sutherland, Kate Nelligan, Christopher Cazenove, Ian Bannen, Alex McCrindle, Stephen MacKenna.
●Sutherland, a Canadian, plays a German who is pretending to be an Englishman, and makes a convincing job of it. At the outset seeming to be an old-fashioned World War II spy thriller, with its steam trains, fog, lacquered advertisements and Bulldog Spirit, this keeps up with the times by also offering a string of sudden 'necessary' murders, a half-severed hand, a ration of naked top-half bed-thrashing, and a hopeless, vicious triangle relationship. The war is ultimately reduced to three people, stranded on a rain-soaked Scottish island. But the drama remains strangely unengaging: we soon realise that the legless (in both senses) ex-Spitfire pilot is going to have to go, and though the hysterical, bullet-ridden climax is impressive, we know that there can be only one survivor. On an afternoon as wet as those on the island, the film would pass the time agreeably, nothing more. JC

Eyes in the Night

(1942, US, 80 min, b/w)
d Fred Zinnemann. *p* Jack Chertok. *sc* Guy Trosper, Howard Emmett Rogers. *ph* Robert

Planck, Charles Lawton Jr. *ed* Ralph E Winters. *ad* Cedric Gibbons. *m* Lennie Hayton. *cast* Edward Arnold, Ann Harding, Donna Reed, John Emery, Allen Jenkins, Stephen McNally, Reginald Denny, Mantan Moreland.

●Zinnemann's second film, from Baynard Kendrick's novel *Odor of Violets*, is a minor but jolly slice of ingenious sleuthery with Arnold as a blind detective whose dog Friday helps him clear up the mystery that may connect the death of Harding's old flame Emery, a Nazi spy ring and the involvement of her scientist husband. The result's a spruce little MGM second feature, neatly worked out within its limits. TJ

Eyes of a Stranger

(1980, US, 85 min)
d Ken Wiederhorn. *p* Ronald Zerra. *sc* Mark Jackson, Eric L Bloom. *ph* Mini Rojas. *ed* Rick Shaine. *ad* Jessica Sack. *m* Richard Einhorn. *cast* Lauren Tewes, Jennifer Jason Leigh, John DiSanti, Peter DuPré, Gwen Lewis, Kitty Lunn.

●A muddled piece of misogynistic violence, which tries to offset its all too common tale of a murderous rapist by having a Fonda-style newscaster (Tewes) bravely investigate while confronted by apathy and accusations of hysteria from boyfriend, police and male colleagues at work. This promising (?) aspect, however, is betrayed both by the repeatedly voyeuristic assaults, and by the objectionable climax in which the newscaster's younger sister (Leigh), made deaf, dumb and blind by a childhood rape, is 'cured' by the killer's attack. GA

Eyes of Hell, The

see Mask, The

Eyes of Laura Mars

(1978, US, 103 min)
d Irvin Kershner. *p* Jon Peters. *sc* John Carpenter, David Zelag Goodman. *ph* Victor J Kemper. *ed* Michael Kahn. *pd* Gene Callahan. *m* Artie Kane. *cast* Faye Dunaway, Tommy Lee Jones, Brad Dourif, Rene Auberjonois, Raúl Julia, Frank Adonis.

●John Carpenter's intriguing original script, about a woman telepathically keyed-in to the sight of a murderer, underwent a cautionary transformation before its final emergence on screen as a glossily gimmicky murder mystery, featuring Dunaway as a female Helmut Newton. Carpenter baled out after nine months' work for producer Jon Peters, trying to soften his conception into a possible Streisand vehicle; and co-credited David Zelag Goodman was but the last of eight or nine scriptwriters subsequently employed to turn it into a shallow, chic confusion of eyes, camera lenses, and saleable images of violence of the sort it now purports to question as an 'issue'. Almost incidentally, it no longer works as a thriller, with a final revelation that one would have thought *Psycho* rendered impossible to re-use. PT

Eyes Wide Shut

(1999, US/GB, 159 min)
d/p Stanley Kubrick. *sc* Stanley Kubrick, Frederic Raphael. *ph* Larry Smith. *ed* Nigel Galt. *pd* Les Tomkins, Roy Walker. *m* Jocelyn Pook. *cast* Tom Cruise, Nicole Kidman, Sydney Pollack, Marie Richardson, Rade Sherbedgia, Todd Field, Vanessa Shaw, Alan Cumming, LeeLee Sobiesky.

●After a swanky Manhattan party, Alice (Kidman), wife of well-to-do doctor William Harford (Cruise), confesses to fantasising about a naval officer. Haunted by visions of Alice with another man, William embarks on a long dark night of the soul during which he's repeatedly confronted by sexual temptation. Kubrick's final film is perfectly watchable but neither shocking, erotic nor profound. Actually, it's rather silly. It's not just that the sex party sequence is both tame (the film plays as if *Last Tango* had never been made) and portentous, the main flaw lies in the script which rehashes plotline, chunks of dialogue and social and sexual mores from Schnitzler's *Traumnovelle* – a story set in early 20th-century Vienna. What starts as a study of a marriage threatened by complacency becomes a murky conspiracy mystery that's barely suspenseful or credible. That said, despite often overstretched scenes, it is entertaining. Cruise is stretched, but Kidman, when she's in it, is excellent, and Larry Smith's camerawork is never less than handsome. Finally, however, it's just a cautionary tale about some very mild, old-fashioned erotic fantasies. GA

Eyes Without a Face

see Yeux sans Visage, Les

Eyewitness (aka Sudden Terror)

(1970, GB, 91 min)
d John Hough. *p* Paul Maslansky. *sc* Ronald Harwood. *ph* David Holmes. *ed* Geoffrey Foot. *pd* Herbert Westbrook. *m* Fairfield Parlour, David Whitaker. *cast* Mark Lester, Lionel Jeffries, Susan George, Tony Bonner, Jeremy Kemp, Peter Vaughn, Peter Bowles, Betty Marsden.

●Scripted by Ronald Harwood from the novel by Mark Hebden, this runs a lame variation on *The Window*. Lester is the eleven-year-old who witnesses a murder (in fact of the wrong man), isn't believed because he's always spinning yarns, and can't go to the cops because the killers are two policemen (Vaughn and Bowles). The Maltese locations are unusual and attractive, but the plot blows up into an absurd mayhem of chases and corpses. With credibility low, watchability gets even lower thanks to Hough's hideously mannered efforts at style (zooms, distortions, weird angles, images reflected in spectacle lenses, etc). TM

Eyewitness (aka The Janitor)

(1981, US, 108 min)
d/p Peter Yates. *sc* Steve Tesich. *ph* Matthew F Leonetti. *ed* Cynthia Scheider. *pd* Philip Rosenberg. *m* Stanley Silverman. *cast* William Hurt, Sigourney Weaver, Christopher Plummer, James Woods, Irene Worth, Kenneth McMillan, Pamela Reed, Albert Paulsen.

●It's easy to say that this is much less than the sum of its parts – part fairytale love story, in which a poor boy loves and wins rich TV reporter, part soufflé of New York paranoia, which involves a murder (with a Vietnamese background) in the building where the poor boy works as a janitor. However, it is rare to find an American film these days that manipulates its plot to accommodate the relationships (and there are lots of them – friends, families, dogs), and whose characters are at least interesting. Steve Tesich's script sometimes smacks of screenwriting classes, but Yates (who worked with Tesich on *Breaking Away*) easily accommodates these lapses with his unfussy, medium-fast direction. Indeed, he guides his cast around the furniture better than most. The result is an enjoyable entertainment whose box-office failure was thoroughly undeserved. CPe

f

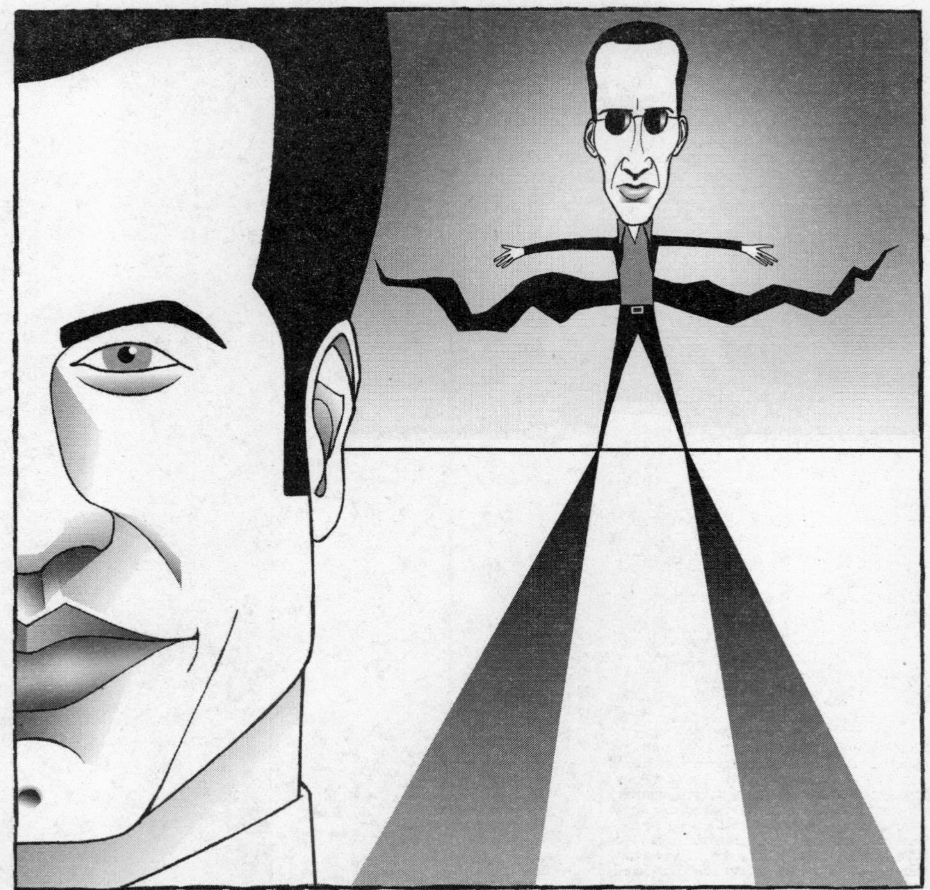

Face/Off

Fabelhafte Welt der Amélie, Die

see Amélie

Fabiola (aka Fighting Gladiator)

(1948, It/Fr, 166 min, b/w)
d Alessandro Blasetti. *sc* Alessandro Blasetti, Jean-Georges Auriol, Antonio Pietrangeli, Diego Fabbri, Cesare Zavattini, Emilio Cecchi, Vitaliano Brancati, Corrado Parolini, Mario Chiari. *ph* Mario Craveri, Osvaldo Civirani. *ed* Mario Serandrei. *ad* Arnaldo Foschini, Aldo Tomassini, Franco Lolli. *m* Enzo Masetti. *cast* Michèle Morgan, Henri Vidal, Michel Simon, Louis Salou, Massimo Girotti, Gino Cervi, Paolo Stoppa, Franco Interlenghi.

● Ancient Rome, slavery, senatorial intrigue, the spread of Christianity, the Colosseum's circus of horrors – but Blasetti's credo of 'historical realism' founders on the proselytising melodrama of Cardinal Wiseman's source novel, and the result is awfully dull, until the spectacular violence of the climax. In her form-hugging costumes, Michèle Morgan (Fabiola) looks good enough to eat, a proposition almost put to the test by those Colosseum lions. Michel Simon as her dad, the genial Senator Fabius, is murdered far too soon for the film's own good: the appreciative way he eyes Fabiola is about all the picture has to offer by way of Roman decadence. An American dubbed version cut to 97 minutes is also around. BBa

Fabuleux Destin d'Amélie Poulain, Le

see Amélie

Fabulous Baker Boys, The

(1989, US, 113 min)
d Steve Kloves. *p* Paula Weinstein, Mark Rosenberg. *sc* Steve Kloves. *ph* Michael Ballhaus. *ed* Bill Steinkamp. *pd* Jeffrey Townsend. *m* David Grusin. *cast* Jeff Bridges, Michelle Pfeiffer, Beau Bridges, Wendy Girard, Ellie Raab, Jennifer Tilly, Xander Berkeley, Dakin Matthews.

● Piano duo Jack and Frank Baker (Jeff and Beau Bridges) have been gigging so long that their act has become a stale routine of schmaltzy intros and cocktail favourites. Auditioning for a singer to spice up the brew, they land themselves with Susie Diamond (Pfeiffer), a tough cookie if ever there was one. The new act is a success, but Susie's intrusion into the brothers' settled ways causes complications: family-man Frank, half-preferring things the way they were, is worried that womaniser Jack will seduce and drop Susie, while she wants a say in shaping the musical repertoire. If Steve Kloves' directing debut, from his own script, is hardly original, it does play fresh variations on an old theme. Much of the credit must go to the actors, with the Bridges brothers making a superb double act. Jeff, especially, manages with very sparse dialogue to convey a wealth of information about a less than sympathetic character; indeed, understatement is crucial to the script's success, keeping us puzzled about characters and situation for longer than one might hope. Sadly, Susie doesn't fully escape stereotyping (though Pfeiffer proves she can belt out a song). Otherwise, with more than enough witty, well-observed details, it's a little charmer. GA

Face

(1997, GB, 105 min)
d Antonia Bird. *p* David M Thompson, Elinor Day. *sc* Ronan Bennett. *ph* Fred Tammes. *ed* St John O'Rorke. *pd* Chris Townsend. *m* Andy Roberts, Paul Conboy, Adrian Corker. *cast* Robert Carlyle, Ray Winstone, Steven Waddington, Phil Davis, Damon Albarn, Lena Headey, Peter Vaughn, Gerry Conlon, Arthur Whybrow.

● Ray (Carlyle), a lapsed East End communist, has long since given up the common good for private gain. Still, even he's shocked when his brothers-in-arms turn their guns on each other after persons unknown steal the stash from their latest raid. The suspects are limited: there are five in the gang, and Ray knows at least he's staunch. After Antonia Bird's unhappy Hollywood venture, *Mad Love*, this heist-gone-wrong picture reclaims lost ground on home turf, and shares with Bird's BBC films *Safe* and *Priest* a determination to get in where the action is. It's muscular, raw, and aggressive. These un-English qualities make for rough edges, but also for vividly authentic popular cinema and plenty to argue about in the pub afterwards. Ronan Bennett's hard-boiled script keeps the tension simmering, the excellent Carlyle and a knockout cast somehow make you care, and there's a palpable sense of London in the dark days of winter, dog eat dog, and time running out. TCh

Face (Kao)

(2000, Jap, 124 min)
d Junji Sakamoto. *p* Yukiko Shii. *sc* Isamu Uno, Junji Sakamoto. *ph* Norimichi Kasamatsu. *ed* Toshihide Fukano. *ad* Mitsuo Harada. *m* Coba. *cast* Naomi Fujiyama, Etsushi Toyokawa, Michio Ookusu, Kankuro Nakamura, Ittoku Kishibe.

● Overweight and pushing forty, the virginal Masako (stage star Fujiyama, making a brilliant, belated film debut) has endured life-long put-downs from her mother and sister. Then her mother dies suddenly. Masako skips the funeral and responds to her sister's criticisms by strangling her and doing a bunk with the funeral donations. One step ahead of the police, she sets out to catch up on everything she's missed in life. She meets both kindness and cruelty and spends much of the time fending off (or succumbing to) sexual predators – including kabuki star Nakamura in a cameo as a rapist. Ultimately her journey is a quest to break free of the prison of her own self-image. As such it's hearteningly vulgar, funny and poignant. Not only Sakamoto's best film to date, but also the best Imamura film that Imamura never made. TR

Face, The

see Ansiktet

Face at the Window, The

(1939, GB, 65 min, b/w)
d/p George King. *sc* AR Rawlinson, Randall Faye. *ph* Hone Glendining. *ed* Jack Harris. *ad* Philip Bawcombe. *m* Jack Beaver. *cast* Tod Slaughter, Marjorie Taylor, John Warwick, Leonard Henry, Aubrey Mallalieu, Robert Adair.

● The last of the great theatrical barnstormers, particularly famed for his lusty impersonation of the Demon Barber of Fleet Street, Slaughter generally disappoints on film, not only because the movies themselves tend to be creaky reproductions of stage performances, but because his speciality – the hissable villains of Victorian melodrama – really requires live audience participation to complete its larger-than-life mockery. *The Face at the Window,* closer to Grand Guignol in its tale of a mysterious killer who terrorises Paris in the 1880s, stabbing his victims while their attention is claimed by a bestial face at the window, is probably the best of them. The plot, statically but effectively staged as a series of tableaux, and filled out by a mad scientist who revives corpses by electricity (and proposes to assist the police by reviving a victim to finger the killer), is agreeably dotty. But Slaughter's performance, stylised in movement and gesture to an almost Brechtian degree, as self-parodic as a pantomime demon yet oddly chilling in its assumption of a sadism gleefully shared with the audience, is extraordinary. TM

Face Behind the Mask, The

(1941, US, 69 min, b/w)
d Robert Florey. *p* Wallace MacDonald. *sc* Allen Vincent, Paul Jarrico. *ph* Franz Planer. *ed* Charles Nelson. *ad* Lionel Banks. *m* Sidney Cutner. *cast* Peter Lorre, Evelyn Keyes, Don Beddoe, George E Stone, John Tyrell

● Lorre is superlative as an immigrant watchmaker who arrives in America full of beaming enthusiasm for the promised land (his scenes with Beddoe, as the neighbourhood cop totally disarmed by his naive friendliness, are a joy), but whose reward is horrible disfigurement in a tenement fire. Forced to turn to crime to pay for the expensive facial mask without which he is unemployable, suicidally distressed by the betrayal of his own ideals, he is redeemed by the love of a blind girl (Keyes)…a tender, totally unsentimental idyll ended when her death by violence leaves him to plot a cold-blooded, self-immolating revenge. With Lorre's own sensitive features serving miraculously as the expressionless 'mask', while Florey's direction and Franz Planer's camerawork put scarcely a foot wrong, the film effortlessly transcends its B horror status to become a bleak, plangently poetic little tragedy. TM

Face in the Crowd, A

(1957, US, 126 min, b/w)
d/p Elia Kazan. *sc* Budd Schulberg. *ph* Harry Stradling, Gayne Rescher. *ed* Gene Milford. *ad* Richard Sylbert, Paul Sylbert. *songs* Tom Glazer, Budd Schulberg. *cast* Andy Griffith, Patricia Neal, Anthony Franciosa, Lee Remick, Walter Matthau, Kay Medford, Burl Ives, Rip Torn.

● When radio producer Neal discovers the homespun philosophy and musical talents of Griffith's Lonesome Rhodes in an Arkansas jail, she little knows that the hobo she's about to launch on a massively successful television career is going to turn into a monstrous national demagogue, not only cherished by his public but listened to by politicians. In the opening scenes of Kazan and writer Budd Schulberg's satire on the dangers of television and advertising, Griffith's virtuoso, likeably irreverent performance makes for genuinely amusing viewing; but once he's mixing with the bigwigs, the film-makers' political messages start flying thick and fast, and the drama soon becomes overheated and unconvincing. Nor is it politically sophisticated: as in late-'30s Capracorn, the ordinary 'little people' are presented as being so gullible that what starts out as a seemingly liberal tract rapidly becomes a smug, cynical exercise in misanthropy. GA

Face of Darkness, The

(1976, GB, 58 min)
d Ian FH Lloyd. *cast* Lennard Pearce, John Bennett, David Allister, Gwyneth Powell, Roger Bizley.

● After an uncertain start (through over-use of close-up), this feature debut settles into an interesting occult thriller that treats its subject with some intelligence. Concentrating on an MP's extremist ambitions, it deals with his recruitment of (and, unwittingly, by) the powers of evil, and his raising of one of the undead to further his totalitarian plans. Although inexperience sometimes shows in both plotting and direction, Lloyd manages his set pieces with conviction and a talent for bringing out the uneasy sexual undertones of necromancy. CPe

Face/Off

(1997, US, 139 min)
d John Woo. *p* David Permut, Barrie Osborne, Terence Chang, Christopher Godsick. *sc* Mike Werb, Michael Colleary. *ph* Oliver Wood. *ed* Christian Wagner, Steven Kemper. *pd* Neil Spisak. *m* John Powell. *cast* John Travolta, Nicolas Cage, Joan Allen, Alessandro Nivola, Gina Gershon, Dominique Swain, Nick Cassavetes, Harve Presnell, CCH Pounder.

● Pay attention, none of this makes much sense. Five years after the murder of his son, FBI agent Sean Archer (Travolta) finally has the drop on terrorist Castor Troy (Cage) – but with Castor comatose and a bomb ticking somewhere in LA, Archer's persuaded to undergo facial surgery, swapping Castor's features for his own. In this way, Archer-as-Troy (Cage) hopes to trick the location out of Castor's brother Pollux (Nivola). Unfortunately, Castor wakes up, and makes off with Archer's face, killing everyone who's in on the secret, and moving into his enemy's office. Woo's poetic-kinetic style has evolved, if not to the point of abstraction, then to delirium: he makes a virtue of incredulity. With two of Hollywood's most flamboyant actors playing each other, the movie becomes a kind of pop *Heat*, an elaborate self-parody and quasi-serious examination of the art of film acting. Yet there's an authentic subversive frisson as Travolta (as-Troy-as-Archer) sizes up his rebellious teenage daughter, puts the sizzle back into a stale marriage, and generally carries on with the air of a sociopath getting the most out of life. 'Are we having any fun yet?' he demands. Twice over. TCh

Face of Fu Manchu, The

(1965, GB, 94 min)
d Don Sharp. *p/sc* Peter Welbeck [Harry Alan Towers]. *ph* Ernest Steward. *ed* John Trumper. *ad* Frank White. *m* Christopher Whelen. *cast* Christopher Lee, Nigel Green, Joachim Fuchsberger, Karin Dor, Tsai Chin, Howard Marion Crawford, Walter Rilla.

●Sax Rohmer's fiendish Yellow Peril revived and played straight in a beautifully designed, perfectly paced and genuinely exciting thriller, with terrific performances from Lee (Fu Manchu) and Green (a magnificently imperturbable Nayland Smith). The Chinoiserie sets are gorgeous; even better are the locations, so carefully chosen for their period possibilities that the spirit of Feuillade hovers benignly over sequences like the great chase with rattletrap cars speeding along cobbled alleys while the pilot of a pursuing aeroplane leans, entrancingly, over the side to drop his squat, fin-tailed bombs by hand. Stylish, witty and a treat to watch. TM

Faces

(1968, US, 130 min, b/w)
d John Cassavetes. *p* Maurice McEndree. *sc* John Cassavetes. *ph* Al Ruban. *ed* Al Ruban, Maurice McEndree. *ad* Phedon Papamichael. *m* Jack Ackerman. *cast* John Marley, Gena Rowlands, Lynn Carlin, Fred Draper, Seymour Cassel, Val Avery.

●Cassavetes' first independent film since *Shadows* – made after the severely compromised, if fascinating, studio movies *Too Late Blues* and *A Child Is Waiting* – is a compelling, sometimes harrowing account of the seemingly random and inconsequential events leading to marital breakdown. As always, the excellent, nervy performances are the thing, and the result – a classic of modern realism – is a convincingly bleak precursor to *Husbands* and *A Woman Under the Influence*. GA

Faces of Women (Visages de Femmes)

(1985, Ivory C, 105 min)
d/sc Désiré Ecaré. *ph* François Migeat, Dominique Gentil. *ed* Giselle Miski. *cast* Eugénie Cissé Roland, Albertine Guéssan, Véronique Mahile, Alexis Leatche, Désiré Bamba.

●A wonderfully unpredictable and lively triptych on the financial, sexual and emotional emancipation of African women, pieced together over twelve years by a film-maker who hasn't a single dull thought in his head. Traditional choruses and dances link the episodes and comment on the action, lending the film a structure that owes no debts to colonial models. The middle episode, about a woman who tires of her possessive husband and goes out to get herself a lover, is a real eye-opener: an extremely naked scene of seduction in and around a river lays a hundred puritan ghosts. TR

Face to Face (Ansikte mot Ansikte)

(1975, Swe, 136 min)
d Ingmar Bergman. *p* Ingmar Bergman, Lars-Owe Carlberg. *sc* Ingmar Bergman. *ph* Sven Nykvist. *ed* Siv Lundgren. *ad* Anne Terselius-Hagegord, Anna Asp, Maggie Strindberg. *m* Wolfgang Amadeus Mozart. *cast* Liv Ullmann, Erland Josephson, Gunnar Björnstrand, Aino Taube-Henrikson, Kari Sylwan, Sif Ruud, Sven Lindberg.

●Try to catch the original four-part TV series rather than this truncation for cinema release (especially the hideously dubbed English version); it emerges as Bergman's most potent psychodrama from the cycle that began with *Cries and Whispers* and ended with *Autumn Sonata*. The story concerns the gradual and agonising breakdown of a successful psychiatrist (Ullmann, married to another shrink played by Lindberg), who returns to her family home and becomes overwhelmed by memories of the past. The acting is intense, as you would expect from Ullmann and Josephson, working under a director who was coming to terms with his own breakdown in this film; and the nightmare imagery (washed-out backgrounds clashing vividly with stark colours) delivers a strong jolt to the subconscious. Laugh if you like, but check your dreams over the next few weeks after seeing it and you'll find fragments of this film corroding your conscience. MA

Facts of Murder, The

see Maledetto Imbroglio, Un

Faculty, The

(1998, US, 104 min)
d Robert Rodriguez. *p* Elizabeth Avellan. *sc* Kevin Williamson. *ph* Enrique Chediak. *ed* Robert Rodriguez. *pd* Cary White. *m* Marco Beltrami. *cast* Jordana Brewster, Clea Duvall, Laura Harris, Josh Hartnett, Shawn Hatosy, Salma Hayek, Famke Janssen, Piper Laurie, Bebe Neuwirth, Elijah Wood.

●This smart, involving sci-fi picture, set in an Ohio high school, pays homage to several genre faves, notably *Invasion of the Body Snatchers* and *The Thing*. But more surprising is the nod to *The Breakfast Club*, with peer group pressure, disaffected teens rebelling against 'alien' adult authority figures, and Duvall's miserablist Goth, Stokely, a dead ringer for Ally Sheedy's shy, neurotic Allison. The neatly worked scenario pits a disparate group of Herrington High students against teachers who've been transformed by an alien parasite into smily, emotionless drones. Forced to work together, the kids put aside their differences, using their newly discovered collective strength to fight the common alien foe. But since affected humans show no outward signs of having been 'turned', even this tightknit group is riven by suspicion and paranoia. Rodriguez opts for a slow build-up, using John Carpenter style framing and fluid camera movements to generate creepy suspense, before pushing in close to engage with the threatened teens. NF

Fade to Black

(1980, US, 102 min)
d Vernon Zimmerman. *p* George G Braunstein, Ron Hamady. *sc* Vernon Zimmerman. *ph* Alex Phillips. *ed* Howard Kunin. *ad* Robert E Lowy. *m* Craig Safan. *cast* Dennis Christopher, Tim Thomerson, Gwynne Gilford, Normann Burton, Linda Kerridge, Morgan Paull.

●Christopher's teenage angst-ridden movie addict with the nervous pre-murder giggle is a darker cousin of *Billy Liar*. But what promises to be sublime turns gradually to ridiculous as the young antihero's banes – wheelchaired ma, teasing workmates, boss – are obliterated in a mess of gore and nostalgia as he turns Dracula (marvellous), Mummy, Hopalong Cassidy etc. The film aspires to hommage, it's true, but its references are altogether too obvious. That said, there's a *Psycho* bathroom pastiche that's almost worth the price of a ticket all by itself; and no collector of movie mush will want to miss it for its good bits, which are more than a few. GD

Fading Memories (Las Huellas Borradas)

(1999, Sp/Arg, 95 min)
d Enrique Gabriel. *p* Tomás Cimadevilla, Enrique González Macho. *sc* Enrique Gabriel, Lucía Lipschutz. *ph* Raúl Pérez Cubero. *ed* Julio Peña. *pd* Jaime Pérez Cubero. *m* Ramón Paus. *cast* Federico Luppi, Mercedes Sampietro, Elena Anaya, Héctor Alterio, Asunción Balaguer, Marivi Bilbao, Armando Del Rio, Sergi Calleja.

●After 20 years of exile in Argentina, journalist/poet Manuel (Luppi) returns to Spain to find his small town, Higueras, packing up in preparation for the flooding of the valley for a new reservoir. The difficult emotional and financial stocktaking undertaken by the town's inhabitants intensifies his own – not least in regard to his relationships with his dead brother's wife (an old flame), and idiosyncratic town elder Don José (Alterio). The film works familiar material to self-conscious effect. The excellent performances are undermined somewhat by over-emphatic and sometimes clumsy direction, with elements of farce or tragedy concerning minor characters reduced to histrionics. Undoubtedly a sincere lament for the abrogative effect on relationships and notions of belonging by change and the passage of time, but the poetry is missing and the emotions are stifled. WH

Fahrenheit 451

(1966, GB, 112 min)
d François Truffaut. *p* Lewis M Allen. *sc* François Truffaut, Jean-Louis Richard. *ph* Nicolas Roeg. *ed* Thom Noble. *ad* Syd Cain. *m* Bernard Herrmann. *cast* Oskar Werner, Julie Christie, Cyril Cusack, Anton Diffring, Bee Duffell, Jeremy Spenser.

●An underrated film, perhaps because it is less science fiction than a tale of 'once upon a time'. Where Ray Bradbury's novel posited a strange, terrifyingly mechanised society which has banned books in the interests of material well-being, Truffaut presents a cosy world not so very different from our own, with television a universal father-figure pouring out reassuring messages, and the only element of menace a fire-engine tearing down the road. A bright, gleaming childhood red, the engine is like a reminder of toyhood days; and as Werner's fireman hero goes about his task of destroying literature, his growing awareness of the almost human way in which books curl up and die in the flames gradually assumes the dimensions of a quest for a legendary lost treasure – movingly glimpsed as he slowly and painfully deciphers the title-page of *David Copperfield*. Here the rich, nostalgic pull of the past wins out over technocracy, and the film ends, as it began, with a scene lifted right out of time: a wonderful shot of the rebels – each dedicated to the preservation of a literary masterpiece by committing it to memory – wandering in contented, idyllic exile by the edge of a glitteringly icy lake. TM

Faille, La

see Quarry, The

Fail Safe

(1964, US, 112 min, b/w)
d Sidney Lumet. *p* Max E Youngstein. *sc* Walter Bernstein. *ph* Gerald Hirschfeld. *ed* Ralph Rosenblum. *ad* Albert Brenner. *cast* Henry Fonda, Dan O'Herlihy, Walter Matthau, Frank Overton, Edward Binns, Fritz Weaver, Larry Hagman.

●Eclipsed by its contemporary, *Dr Strangelove*, *Fail Safe* eschews the former's black humour and opts for a deadly serious mix of cold-war melodrama and rampant psychosis. Creeping unease builds up to terminal paranoia as the machines run away from their masters, the 'fail safe' fails, and the unstoppable 'Vindicator' bomber homes in on Moscow – all by accident. Lumet sensibly avoids pyrotechnics in favour of tightening the psychological screws, as Larry Hagman (the president's translator – nice looking kid) does nervy trade-offs on the hot-line, and everyone, from President Fonda down, starts drowning in a sea of cold sweat. CPea

Fair Game (Mamba)

(1988, It, 81 min)
d/p Mario Orfini. *sc* Lidia Ravera, Mario Orfinin. *ph* Dante Spinotti. *ed* Claudio Cutry. *pd* Ferdinando Scarfiotti. *m* Giorgio Moroder. *cast* Trudie Styler, Gregg Henry, Bill Mosley.

●I'm slithering around on my belly in a chic warehouse flat with no windows and a jammed front door, *Psycho* shower scene sound effects shrieking in my ears, injected with a fatal overdose of sex hormone that only gives me 30 minutes to sink my teeth into 150 pounds of thirty something-ish designer flesh while squinting through an 8am fish-eye lens. What am I? Right. I'm a bemused black mamba with a schizophrenic libido (a randy poisonous snake to you) chasing Trudie Styler around because her rich ex-husband can't deal with the business parties on his own, nor with the fact that she hates his designer gadgets and executive toys. Welcome to the flip side of *Fatal Attraction*: 7,287 feet of 'serious' camera work with a plot worthy of a third-rate acid trip. The heavy mythological pointers (Styler plays Eva) are completely subverted by Orfini's insistence on fondling Styler's bum from as many obscure angles as possible. JCh

Fair Game

(1995, US, 90 min)
d Andrew Sipes. *p* Joel Silver. *sc* Charles Fletcher. *ph* Richard Bowen. *ed* David Finfur. *pd* James Spencer. *m* Mark Mancina. *cast* William Baldwin, Cindy Crawford, Steven Berkoff, Christopher McDonald, Miguel Sandoval, Johann Carlo, Salma Hayek, John Bedford Lloyd.

●Miami lawyer Crawford, whose life is threatened by Berkoff and his team of over-armed baddies (she knows not why), finds detective Baldwin her only salvation. Cue shoot-out, car chase, explosions, repeated ad nauseam. One of her alimony cases is (somehow) connected to ex-KGB agents looking to transfer savings from Cold War-era Swiss bank accounts. But who cares, since no one lets either her or us in on the secret. Dire in all departments. NB

FairyTale – A True Story

(1997, US, 98 min)
d Charles Sturridge. *p* Wendy Finerman, Bruce Davey. *sc* Ernie Contreras. *ph* Michael Coulter. *ed* Peter Coulson. *pd* Michael Howells.

m Zbigniew Preisner. *cast* Florence Hoath, Elizabeth Earl, Paul McGann, Phoebe Nicholls, Bob Peck, Harvey Keitel, Peter O'Toole, Anton Lesser, Mel Gibson.

● One of two 1997 films inspired by Elsie Wright and Frances Griffiths' photographs of the fairies resident at the bottom of their Cottingley garden. While Nick Willing's *Photographing Fairies* used the hullabaloo surrounding the pics to spin a distinctly ambivalent, adult story about bereavement, imagined realities and the post-WWI national psyche, Sturridge's film takes up the same issues in the children's film format, proclaims a whole hearted, affirmative response to the Fairy Question, and induces a more ambiguous reaction. Despite the high production values, however, the glitzy cast and several tried-and-tested storytellers, I never truly believed that the film-makers believed. Children, on the other hand, may not be so cynical. It's a respectable tale, but there's too much baggage for the fancy fully to take flight. NB

Faithful Narrative of the Capture, Sufferings and Miraculous Escape of Eliza Fraser, A

see Rollicking Adventures of Eliza Fraser, The

Faithless (Trolösa)

(2000, Swe, 155 min)
d Liv Ullmann. *p* Kaj Larsen. *sc* Ingmar Bergman. *ph* Jörgen Persson. *ed* Sylvia Ingemarsson. *ad* Göran Wassberg. *cast* Lena Enore, Erland Josephson, Krister Henriksson, Tomas Hanzon, Michelle Gylemo, Juni Dahr.

● Alone in an isolated coastal cottage, elderly dramatist Josephson (a clumsy, obvious stand-in for Bergman, who wrote the semi-autobiographical script) summons up his conscience/muse (Enore), an actress who relates in painstaking, painful detail her story of adultery, jealousy, guilt and punishment. The lucid, steady, inexorable progression to cruel catharsis is reminiscent of such '70s Bergman psycho-dramas as *Scenes from a Marriage* and *Face to Face*, and Ullmann clearly respects her mentor. She trusts in the performances (Enore's protagonist is superb and charismatic, the lover and husband less so), explores every moral and emotional nuance, and inadvertently courts charges of solipsistic indulgence. The shifts in season, weather and setting are hackneyed, and the film as a whole is astonishingly old-fashioned, but somehow, against the odds, it still manages to pack a real punch. GA

Fakebook

see American Blue Note

Falbalas

(1944, Fr, 111 min, b/w)
d Jacques Becker. *p* André H des Fontaines. *sc* Maurice Aubergé, Jacques Becker, Maurice Griffe. *ph* Nicolas Hayer. *ed* Marguerite Houllé-Renoir. *ad* Max Douy. *m* Jean-Jacques Grünenwald. *cast* Raymond Rouleau, Micheline Presle, Jean Chevrier, Gabrielle Dorziat.

● Becker spent years as Jean Renoir's assistant, and the influence is plain, even in this novelettish tale of a philanderer's downfall. Characters are presented warmly but objectively, so that the fashion designer hero, M. Clarence, is at once a childish manipulator who spins out of control when denied his own way, and a helpless victim in the grip of an infatuation. The object of his desire – his best friend's fiancée – is a careless flirt and a kind woman trying her best not to hurt anyone. Also Renoir-like is the absorbing picture of a fashion house at work. Becker probably had no choice, though, except to go for a big finish, with suicides galore (well, two) as Maison Clarence unveils its autumn collection. BBa

Falcon and the Co-eds, The

(1943, US, 68 min, b/w)
d William Clemens. *p* Maurice Geraghty. *sc* Ardel Wray, Gerald Geraghty. *ph* J Roy Hunt. *ed* Theron Warth. *ad* Albert S D'Agostino. *m* C Bakaleinikoff. *cast* Tom Conway, Jean Brooks, Rita Corday, Amelita Ward, Isabel Jewell, George Givot, Cliff Clark.

● Despite the off-putting title, an attractive little thriller in which the Falcon investigates murder in a girl's school, where an atmosphere of fear and loathing centres on a girl with second sight, while she herself is driven to suicidal despair by her predictions of murder. Scripted by Ardel Wray, who worked regularly with Val Lewton (*I Walked with a Zombie, Leopard Man, Isle of the Dead*), it is beautifully characterised and has some vividly eerie touches (better exploited in Roy Hunt's camerawork than by Clemens' direction). It's one of the best in a series which took over from *The Saint* after RKO tired of paying Leslie Charteris for rights, and turned instead to a Michael Arlen story (*The Gay Falcon*, retained as the title of the first film in 1941). George Sanders, with five appearances as the Saint behind him, was clearly bored playing virtually the same character (less ruthless, more honest); and after three appearances, he was killed off by Nazi assassins in *The Falcon's Brother* (1942), leaving his real-life brother Conway to succeed him. Of the four Sanders films, *The Falcon Takes Over* (1942) is distinguished as the first adaptation of a Raymond Chandler novel: a breathless scurry through the plot of *Farewell My Lovely* with an excellent performance from Ward Bond as the moronically lovelorn Moose Malloy, it finds the suave Sanders distinctly anomalous in Chandler territory. Conway, bringing a lighter touch to the series (which managed its comic relief better than most), starred in nine films after *The Falcon's Brother,* most of them deft and surprisingly enjoyable. *The Falcon Strikes Back* (1943), for instance, though saddled with a dull plot about missing war bonds, is directed by Edward Dmytryk with strikingly elliptical economy, and has the bonus of Edgar Kennedy as a mad puppeteer villain. *The Falcon in Hollywood* (1944) is a lively studio murder mystery directed by Gordon Douglas, with RKO itself serving as the set. *The Falcon in San Francisco*, vividly directed by Joseph H Lewis (particularly the opening sequence with the little girl on the train), makes excellent use of locations. *The Falcon in Mexico* enlivens a stock plot with some elaborate location footage clearly not shot on a B movie budget: could it possibly be errant footage from Welles' abortive *It's All True*? TM

Falcon and the Snowman, The

(1985, US, 131 min)
d John Schlesinger. *p* Gabriel Katzka, John Schlesinger. *sc* Steven Zaillian. *ph* Allen Daviau. *ed* Richard Marden. *pd* James D Bissell. *m* Pat Metheny, Lyle Mays. *cast* Timothy Hutton, Sean Penn, Pat Hingle, Joyce Van Patten, David Suchet, Lori Singer, Richard Dysart.

● Seminary drop-out Hutton fetches up in a job deep in the heart of the CIA telex circuit; sick with his country, he persuades his ex-altar boy buddy and current dope dealer, Penn, to peddle secrets to the Russians in Mexico City. Much is made of the mechanics of the business, and in this area the movie belongs to Penn, his eyebrow-pencil moustache dissolving in cocaine as he keeps up a front of jittery bravado. Hutton succumbs firstly to a thin role, and secondly to the film's lack of any strong viewpoint about its leading men. As usual Schlesinger is more than half in love with what he might be satirising. CPea

Falconer, The

(1998, GB, 56 mins)
d Chris Petit, Iain Sinclair. *p* Keith Griffiths. *ph* Chris Petit, Iain Sinclair. *ed* Emma Matthews. *with* Peter Whitehead, Françoise Lacroix, Francis Stewart, Stewart Home, Olga Utechina, Howard Marks, Kathy Acker.

● This documentary investigation into the lives and careers of Peter Lorrimer Whitehead, treads the uncertain border country between fact and fiction. Film-maker, novelist, falconer, Whitehead seems an ideal subject for the quasi-mythologising approach that directors Petit and Sinclair first hinted at in *The Cardinal and the Corpse*. Here they go at it in full-blooded fashion, assisted to superb effect by digital artist Dave McKean and the sound design of Bruce Gilbert. We are warned that this is a film 'in which nothing is true and everything is permitted.' A researcher (Lacroix) is hired, but Whitehead is drawn to her because she reminds him of his daughter. Lacroix, too, is drawn in, for a while, and finds listening to his voice like 'being stroked along the spine with a feather dipped in formaldehyde.' When she later quits, editor Matthews is sent in to reinterrogate Lacroix's interviewees (among them Stewart Home anticipating the ritual slaughter of Prince Charles on Millennium eve) and track down the missing researcher. The directors combine footage from security cameras with digital video and film clips. Superficial dazzle repels interpretation, which the cunning play of imagery then reinvites. Whitehead himself, boasting on Swedish TV about copulating with falcons, is as mesmerising as you would expect of someone who both looks and sounds like a genetic splice of Rutger Hauer and Anthony Hopkins. NRo

Fallen

(1998, US, 127 min)
d Gregory Hoblit. *p* Charles Roven, Dawn Steel. *sc* Nicholas Kazan. *ph* Newton Thomas Sigel. *ed* Lawrence Jordan. *pd* Terence Marsh. *m* Tan Dun. *cast* Denzel Washington, John Goodman, Donald Sutherland, Embeth Davidtz, James Gandolfini, Elias Koteas, Robert Joy.

● Super-clean cop John Hobbes (Washington) unleashes evil spirit 'Azazel' when he sends a serial killer (Koteas) to the chair. Unlike Morgan Freeman's learned sleuth in *Seven*, the parochial Hobbes is convinced that cops are 'the chosen people'. Having captured the killer, he appears on TV smug and smiling. Things turn intriguing, however, when later his attention is drawn to the biblical injunction 'Hide your good works.' His consequent fear that the whole city is against him is straddled between paranoia and intuition. Azazel's spirit is passed along by touch: in a crowded, aggressive city (Philadelphia), anyone can turn nasty. On a metaphorical level, this makes sense – AIDS and a fear of the city are central to the '90s. But God (or the Devil) is in the detail: every time a fluid is taken into the body, the fidgety camera zooms in, fascinated, suspicious. Excellent support from Davidtz, Goodman, and Joy, as Hobbes' brother, though as the plot twists take precedence over character, much of the film's nuance trickles away and, along with it, the tension. CO'Su

Fallen Angel

(1945, US, 97 min, b/w)
d/p Otto Preminger. *sc* Harry Kleiner. *ph* Joseph LaShelle. *ed* Harry Reynolds. *ad* Lyle R Wheeler, Leland Fuller. *m* David Raksin. *cast* Alice Faye, Dana Andrews, Linda Darnell, Charles Bickford, Anne Revere, Bruce Cabot, John Carradine.

● Dana Andrews marries sweet little Alice Faye for her money in order to keep his waitress mistress (Darnell) in the style to which she would like to be accustomed. But things go wrong when the waitress is murdered. A sharp, small town melodrama, with the contrasts between the two ends of town well observed: the suburban houses and the seedy roadhouse with its run-down rooms. CPe

Fallen Angels (Duoluo Tianshi)

(1995, HK, 96 min)
d Wong Kar-Wai. *p* Jeff Lau. *sc* Won Kar-Wai. *ph* Christopher Doyle. *ed* William Chang, Wong Ming-Lam. *pd* William Chang. *m* Frankie Chan, Roel A Garcia. *cast* Leon Lai, Michele Reis, Takeshi Kaneshiro, Karen Mong, Charlie Young, Chan Fai-Hung.

● Tired of the wounds incurred at work, Hong Kong hitman Wong Chi-Ming (Lai) decides to break his partnership with the agent (Reis) who hires and secretly loves him; when he meets the punkish Baby (Mong), there's a small chance his loneliness will come to an end, but the agent's still keen to revive their relationship. Meanwhile, mute ex-con He Zhiwu (Kaneshiro), who makes a living by re-opening shops closed for the night, meets up with Charlie (Young). Helping her hunt down her ex-boyfriend's new lover, He Zhiwu falls for Charlie himself, but after she disappears, he fills his time shooting videos of his flophouse-proprietor father. As stylish and audacious as *Days of Being Wild* and *Chungking Express*, Wong Kar-Wai's film is another poignant but occasionally playful study of forlorn romance and melancholy solitude. Good-looking twenty-somethings struggle to make it through the night in the neon-lit streets, bars and diners of a Hong Kong rendered magically moody by the extreme wide-angle lens of Chris Doyle's fluid camera. Exhilarating and, in the end, unexpectedly touching. GA

Fallen Idol, The

(1948, GB, 95 min, b/w)
d/p Carol Reed. *sc* Graham Greene. *ph* Georges Périnal. *ed* Oswald Hafenrichter. *ad* Vincent Korda, James Sawyer. *m* William Alwyn. *cast* Ralph Richardson, Michèle Morgan, Bobby Henrey, Sonia Dresdel, Denis O'Dea, Jack Hawkins, Dora Bryan.
● A perfect example of the respectable quality film which achieved its apotheosis in late '40s Britain: tasteful, restrained, carefully crafted, but in the long run a little anaemic. Reed, once considered the great British director, had his clay feet mercilessly exposed by the *auteur*ist critics of the '60s. Now stripped of his inflated reputation, it is possible to appreciate his virtues: an ability to elicit remarkable performances from his actors – here an engaging Anglo-French child and an admirably controlled Richardson – and a fine skill for exploring psychological depths without sacrificing narrative coherence. Taking Graham Greene's story of the relationship between an (upper class) boy and his (working class) hero, he expands it into a sophisticated analysis of the intersections between the separate realities of children and adults. RMy

Falling Down

(1992, US, 115 min)
d Joel Schumacher. *p* Arnold Kopelson, Herschel Weingrod, Timothy Harris. *sc* Ebbe Roe Smith. *ph* Andrzej Bartkowiak. *ed* Paul Hirsch. *pd* Barbara Ling. *m* James Newton Howard. *cast* Michael Douglas, Robert Duvall, Barbara Hershey, Frederic Forrest, Tuesday Weld, Lois Smith.
● Schumacher's film goes beyond the confines of vigilante films like *Death Wish* whose concerns stop at the criminal justice system. 'D-Fens' (Douglas), named after his own car number plate and his now redundant job as a bastion of America's nuclear defence industry, is a one-man terrorist in the Los Angeles jungle. Forced by a traffic jam to make his way 'home' on foot, Douglas strikes at various targets: rude car drivers, obstructive fast-food workers, violent gangs, overcharging Korean shopkeepers, snobby golf-course wrinklies. However, the only person he directly murders is a disgusting, homophobic neo-Nazi. The scumbag is played by the invariably excellent Forrest who, along with Duvall as a speak-softly cop and Hershey as Douglas's estranged wife, gives the cast an air of huge respectability. There are reservations: too many plot and moral loose-ends, while the film veers giddily between Douglas the psycho-menace and Douglas the sad sympathy-object. Sometimes funny, sometimes touching, and certainly unnerving. SGr

Falling For You

(1933, GB, 78 min, b/w)
d Robert Stevenson, Jack Hulbert. *p* Michael Balcon. *sc* Jack Hulbert, Douglas Furber, Robert Stevenson. *ph* Bernard Knowles. *ed* RE Dearing. *ad* Alex Vetchinsky. *songs* Vivian Ellis, Jack Furber. *cast* Jack Hulbert, Cicely Courtneidge, Tamara Desni, Garry Marsh, Alfred Drayton, OB Clarence.
● Patchy vehicle for West End revue darlings Courtneidge and Hulbert. As rival journalists on the trail of Ruritanian heiress Desni, they tangle with haunted castles, irate editors, runaway sleighs, a ghost called Stephen and a villain called Sausage. Hulbert's snow and ice slapstick is embarrassingly unfunny, but the film is saved by the bit-part players and the exuberantly inventive Courtneidge. Disguised as a twitching rabbit-toothed hypochondriac, as 'onest, affable and 'elpful ladies 'elp Hettie Bartholomew, and finally as a kangaroo leading her bemused adversaries in a chorus of 'Why Has a Cow Got Four Legs?', she is absurdly magnificent. RMy

Falling in Love

(1984, US, 106 min)
d Ulu Grosbard. *p* Marvin Worth. *sc* Michael Cristofer. *ph* Peter Suschitzky. *ed* Michael Kahn. *pd* Santo Loquasto. *m* David Grusin. *cast* Robert De Niro, Meryl Streep, Harvey Keitel, Jane Kaczmarek, George Martin, David Clennon.
● De Niro and Streep play two Manhattan commuters who fall in love, *Brief Encounter* style; but to invoke Coward and Lean's film is to realise just how thin and unsatisfying this one is. Coincidences are difficult to get right in any romantic movie, yet here they are piled on without regard for sense or subtlety, while the script is so concerned to give its big names equal screen time that it fails to establish an innocuous but hardly compelling love story of the old school. De Niro merely coasts, while Streep's woman-at-the-emotional-crossroads now seems as familiar as a stale variety turn. DP

Fall of the House of Usher, The

see Chute de la Maison Usher, La

Fall of the House of Usher, The

see House of Usher, The

Fall of the Roman Empire, The

(1964, US, 187 min)
d Anthony Mann. *p* Samuel Bronston. *sc* Ben Barzman, Basilio Franchina, Philip Yordan. *ph* Robert Krasker. *ed* Robert Lawrence. *pd* Veniero Colasanti, John Moore. *m* Dimitri Tiomkin. *cast* Sophia Loren, Stephen Boyd, James Mason, Christopher Plummer, Alec Guinness, Anthony Quayle, John Ireland, Mel Ferrer, Omar Sharif, Eric Porter.
● Though lacking the mythic clarity of *El Cid* – Mann's other epic for Samuel Bronston – this is a superior example of the genre. Deserting the usual conflict of Christians and Romans, the story moves to a later era and charts the intrigues surrounding the Imperial throne, held by Marcus Aurelius and coveted by the corrupt Commodus, that led to the Romans' downfall at the hands of the Barbarians. Largely accurate in historical terms, thanks to a wordy but intelligent script by Philip Yordan (a master of the epic style), it is surprisingly restrained, both in terms of action and acting. But the atmosphere is consistently convincing: darkness holds sway on the fringes of the Empire, where the armies are struggling to repel the invading hordes, while Rome is presented as a magnificent but decadent monument to the unimaginative pragmatism of the Roman mind. Terrific sets, a stirring score by Dimitri Tiomkin and the overall quality of the production values manage to counteract the film's excessive length. GA

Fall of the Romanov Dynasty, The (Padenie Dinasti Romanovikh)

(1927, USSR, 5,578 ft, b/w)
d/sc/ed Esther Shub.
● In 1927, when Eisenstein was making *October*, Esther Shub was working on neglected newsreel footage from the Moscow archives to create a dramatic 'montage of film document' spanning 1913-1917. In 1967, Mosfilm re-produced the film, adding an introduction and a soundtrack of classical piano music to counterpoint and underline her juxtaposition of images and terse intertitles. The result is a highly entertaining and visually interesting history lesson, which charts in succinct and often amusing terms the decline of the Tsars (the Romanov dynasty) and the rise of the masses. HM

Falls, The

(1980, GB, 185 min)
d/sc Peter Greenaway. *ph* Mike Coles, John Rosenberg. *ed* Peter Greenaway. *m* Michael Nyman, Brian Eno, John Hyde, Keith Pendlebury. *cast* Peter Westley, Aad Wirtz, Michael Murray, Lorna Poulter, Patricia Carr, Adam Leys.
● Greenaway's fantasy expands enormously the same obsessions as his earlier *A Walk Through H* and *Vertical Features Remake*: a cross between Alice after the Holocaust and the ramblings of a deranged film librarian. Set in a strangely serene future – after a Violent Unexplained Event which has irrevocably changed Life as We Know It – *The Falls* sets out to document the biographies of 92 victims of the event, all selected on the basis that their names begin with the letters 'Fall'. The strategy is ingenious, substituting an amazing excess of 'content' for the formalism that has (usually) defined the avant-garde. Not recommended to people who like one story, two characters, and a happy ending. But for those who like riddles, acrostics, sudden excursions, romantic insights, and the eerie music of Michael Nyman (plus bits of Brian Eno)…come to Xanadu. CA

Fall Time

(1994, US, 88 min)
d Paul Warner. *p* Edward Bates. *sc* Steve Alden, Paul Skemp. *ph* Mark Gordon. *ed* Steve Nevius. *pd* Andrew Precht. *m* Hummie Mann. *cast* Stephen Baldwin, Mickey Rourke, Jason London, David Arquette, Jonah Blechman, Sheryl Lee, J Michael Hunter.
● High-school grads London, Arquette and Blechman plan a play-acted 'murder' in front of the bank which major sleazo Rourke and psychotic accomplice Baldwin just happen to be holding up. The dear young chaps find themselves sucked into a miasma of paranoia, violence, muddled scripting and drearily mannered turns from the two hoods. The plot delivers up a ludicrous roadside sex scene involving harassed female hostage Lee, before crumbling to a grandiose and deeply bathetic conclusion. A singularly unpromising first feature. TJ

Falsche Bewegung

see Wrong Movement

Fälschung, Die

see Circle of Deceit

Fame

(1980, US, 133 min)
d Alan Parker. *p* David De Silva, Alan Marshall. *sc* Christopher Gore. *ph* Michael Seresin. *ed* Gerry Hambling. *pd* Geoffrey Kirkland. *m* Michael Gore. *cast* Irene Cara, Lee Curreri, Laura Dean, Antonia Franceschi, Paul McCrane, Barry Miller, Gene Anthony Ray, Maureen Teefy.
● A British-directed, New-York based musical which follows the heartbreak-and-success story of a group of youngsters as they're put through their paces at the High School of Performing Arts. The main characters, all lightly sketched in, offer a brief showcase for just about every kind of performing talent from classical ballet to stand-up comedy; the song'n'dance numbers are edited to an unstoppable disco beat; and the brazen jokes (Jews, blacks, women, gays, etc.) keep coming to show that we're all part of the same pie in the sky. It's a crack at the American Dream which carries all the exhilaration and depth of a 133-minute commercial break. HM

Fame Is the Spur

(1947, GB, 116 min, b/w)
d Roy Boulting. *p* John Boulting. *sc* Nigel Balchin. *ph* Gunther Krampf. *ed* Richard Best. *ad* John Howell. *m* John Wooldridge. *cast* Michael Redgrave, Rosamund John, Hugh Burden, Bernard Miles, Carla Lehmann, Seymour Hicks, Milton Rosmer.
● We meet Hamer Radshaw in the 1870s, a socialist firebrand, his anger over injustice and inequality fuelled by his grandfather's tales of the Peterloo Massacre. We take our leave of him in the 1930s, a doddering member of the peerage, his principles having been picked off one by one over the years. This adaptation of Howard Spring's novel is no Tory satire, but a Labour-committed inveighing against the dangers of demagoguery and of succumbing to the lure of the Establishment. Its interest is mostly socio-political rather than dramatic or cinematic, though individual scenes are quite powerful, notably the force feeding of a suffragette, shot appropriately like something out of a horror film. BBa

Family Album

see Costa Brava

Family Business

(1982, US, 87 min)
d/p Tom Cohen. *ph* Tom Hurwitz. *ed* Bob Brady. *with* Howard Snider, Judy Snider, the Snider children.
● A fly-on-the-wall documentary examining the dodgy finances of a pizza parlour in Muncie, Indiana, and the strain on the family who run it. Howard Snyder is Mr Shakey, the pizza man who hasn't made it to Hamburger Row. He embraces the American way of life with zest as he serves his mouthwateringly massive pizzas, sings to the customers, records his own radio ads, and works enormously long hours; but beneath the 'have a nice day' exterior, he is struggling to retain his franchise and to balance his books. Wrong orders, bickering and dating take place against a background of mounting anxiety which

culminates in an emotional family meeting. They are all extraordinarily unselfconscious in front of the camera, but in the end one longs for a little less vérité and rather more creativity. JE

Family Business

(1989, US, 113 min)
d Sidney Lumet. *p* Lawrence Gordon. *sc* Vincent Patrick. *ph* Andrzej Bartkowiak. *ed* Andrew Mondshein. *pd* Philip Rosenberg. *m* Cy Coleman. *cast* Sean Connery, Dustin Hoffman, Matthew Broderick, Rosana DeSoto, Janet Carroll, Victoria Jackson, Bill McCutcheon, Deborah Rush, BD Wong.
● The credits imply class; but while everyone is proficient, this uneasy mix of comedy, thriller and melodrama fumbles its way through a forest of clichés and contrivances. Vito (Hoffman) is a respectable New York meat-trader who has renounced the criminal ways of his roguish dad Jesse (Connery). But in giving son Adam (Broderick) the best education money can buy, Vito has alienated himself from both, driving them into conspiratorial buddydom. When Adam plans a million-dollar scam involving the theft of plasma from a low-security lab, Jesse wants in, but Vito is co-opted only when he realises that the only way to protect his son is to be there. The heist goes awry, and a vaguely light-hearted romp enters the register Emotional. This being Lumet, issues are broached – genes and generational conflict, the relationship between morality and law, the purpose of life – but meaningful dialogues do not a good movie make: the battle lines, clear from the start, proceed with the inevitability of a computer game towards weepy reconciliation. Worse, it's hard to like or care for the characters; and since writer Vincent Patrick (adapting his own novel) stacks the odds to favour Jesse's selfish anarchy, the end result is at best morally confused, at worst devious. GA

Family Game (Kazoku Game)

(1983, Jap, 107 min)
d Yoshimitsu Morita. *p* Shiro Sasaki, Yu Okada. *sc* Yoshimitsu Morita. *ph* Yonezo Maeda. *ed* Akimasa Kawashima. *pd* Katsumi Nakazawa. *cast* Yusaku Matsuda, Ichirota Miyagawa, Junichi Tsujita, Juzo Itami, Saori Yuki.
● A subtly cruel satire on the Japanese obsession with corporate and academic success which blends striking visual compositions, pithy dialogue and absurdist humour. Matsuda plays a young private tutor hired by ambitious parents to cram their youngest son into the 'right' school. The father works all the hours God sends, while the wife busies herself with obsessive cleaning. Both are alienated from their sons, for whose benefit they are supposedly making these sacrifices, and the presence of the tutor opens up the cracks which the formalities of parental love and filial duty are meant to paper over. The juxtaposition of meticulously framed images with terse, ironic dialogue and explosions of slapstick violence exposes the frustrations generated by an unhealthy preoccupation with material aspiration and social status. Sogo Ishii ripped into similar issues with a chainsaw in *Crazy Family*, but Morita dissects equally tellingly with a scalpel. NF

Family Jewels, The

(1965, US, 100 min)
d/p Jerry Lewis. *sc* Jerry Lewis, Bill Richmond. *ph* W Wallace Kelley. *ed* Arthur P Schmidt. *ad* Hal Pereira, Jack Poplin. *m* Pete King. *cast* Jerry Lewis, Sebastian Cabot, Donna Butterworth, Gene Baylos, Robert Strauss, Anne Baxter.
● Lewis could never be a father, but here he plays seven uncles from whom a rich industrialist's orphaned daughter must pick a daddy. Parodying a gangster film, it's a tour de force of Lewisian disguise, slowly unfolding gags, and monstrous sentimentality. A morose clown, a Terry-Thomas style pilot, a gaga photographer, and an incomprehensible old sea captain all figure; but nothing so funny as when the gangster uncle sheds his 'funny mask' disguise to reveal a worse real face beneath. Ups and downs on the laughter scale, perhaps, but there's more than meets the eye. DMacp

Family Life

(1971, GB, 108 min)
d Ken Loach. *p* Tony Garnett. *sc* David Mercer. *ph* Charles Stewart. *ed* Roy Watts. *ad* Bill McCrow. *m* Marc Wilkinson. *cast* Sandy Ratcliff, Bill Dean, Grace Cave, Malcolm Tierney, Hilary Martyn, Michael Riddall, Alan Macnaughtan.
● A fictional documentary (scripted by David Mercer) that charts the influence of family relations on a young girl's deteriorating ability to handle her environment. It presents a highly biased attack against the techniques of drug and electro-convulsive therapy, in favour of a more personal approach that takes into account the complexities of the individual's social context. As propaganda, the film tends to distort and oversimplify the issues, with a method disturbingly similar to that which it is attacking. *Family Life* continues Loach's examination of class exploitation, and because its purpose and function are clearer than *Poor Cow* or even *Kes*, it's arguably a better film, even if remaining limited by its TV-derived visual puritanism. JDuC

Family Life (Zycie Rodzinne)

(1970, Pol, 93 min)
d Krzysztof Zanussi. *p* Janina Krassowska. *sc* Krzysztof Zanussi. *ph* Witold Sobocinski. *ed* Urszula Sliwinska. *ad* Tadeusz Wybult. *m* Wojciech Kilar. *cast* Daniel Olbrychski, Maja Komorowska, Jan Nowicki, Jan Kreczmar, Halina Mikolajska, Anne Mikolajska.
● Tricked into returning home for the first time in six years, a successful young Polish engineer is forced to decide whether or not to take responsibility for the destructive lifestyle of his estranged, alcoholic father, bitter that the family's wealth has gone, his furniture is being sold, and his grandfather's glass factory is now state-owned. Despite the laconic passivity of Olbrychski's performance as the engineer, *Family Life* compels attention by its richly detailed evocation of the family's crumbling mansion, its overgrown garden under siege from modern apartment buildings, and the precision with which Zanussi develops the engineer's struggle to accept, and finally to free himself from, the tentacles of his father's capitalist past. A neatly dismissive coda wraps up this taut, supremely well-made example of formal Polish film-making. JPy

Family Man, The

(2000, US, 126 min)
d Brett Ratner. *p* Zvi Howard Rosenman, Tony Ludwig, Alan Riche, Marc Abraham. *sc* David Diamond, David Weissman. *ph* Dante Spinotti. *ed* Mark Helfrich. *pd* Kristi Zea. *m* Danny Elfman. *cast* Nicolas Cage, Téa Leoni, Jeremy Piven, Josef Sommer, Saul Rubinek, Don Cheadle, Mary Beth Hurt, Harve Presnell, Tom McGowan, Lisa Thornhill.
● Cage is mega-successful Wall Street banker Jack Campbell. He's filthy rich, enjoys the high life, gets off on power. Then he does a good deed, talking down a crazy black dude with a gun (Cheadle in a role so patronising it reeks), and before you can say 'the Ghost of Christmas Yet to Come', Jack's waking up to the life he might have had: married ten years to college girlfriend Kate (Leoni), a couple of kids screaming, deadend job selling tyres. Yup, they're poor. And it seems Jack's stuck with it. Now, this first third of the movie is the most enjoyable – which is to concede that there's mild entertainment in seeing a rich man brought down to earth with a bump. Not one to do things by halves, Cage almost chokes on the ratty furniture, check shirts, and the dubious pleasures of bowling with the guys. It's rare that an American movie lets slip such a snobbish distaste for the humdrum lives of its blue-collar audience base, but of course it doesn't last. Fearful lest we get the deluded idea that it may actually be easier to enjoy life with tons of money, director Ratner takes enormous pains to assure us that nothing could be further from the truth – and then has the gall to contrive a happy ending promising love *and* money. TCh

Family Plot

(1976, US, 120 min)
d/p Alfred Hitchcock. *sc* Ernest Lehman. *ph* Leonard South. *ed* J Terry Williams. *pd* Henry Bumstead. *m* John Williams. *cast* Karen Black, Bruce Dern, Barbara Harris, William Devane, Ed Lauter, Cathleen Nesbitt, Katherine Helmond.
● With his last film, Hitchcock made a triumphant return to form in the comic thriller. His most relaxed, witty and urbane movie since *North by Northwest* (also scripted by Ernest Lehman), it's a dense but extremely entertaining collection of symmetric patterns, doubles and rhymes. One couple (Dern/Harris) are amiable fakes, dealing in bogus spiritualism; another (Black/Devane) are sinister fakes, trading in the physical merchandise of kidnapped diplomats and ransomed jewels. Linking these two pairs is an illegitimate child, an empty grave, and a mountain of misunderstandings. Hitchcock ties together the complex strands in a delightful way, with a series of symbols and set pieces which demonstrate that the Old Master had lost his touch not one jot. Beneath all the fun, there's a vision of humans as essentially greedy and dishonest, presented with a gorgeously amoral wink from Hitchcock, and performed to perfection by an excellent cast. GA

Family Portrait (Sishi Buhuo)

(1992, China, 90 min)
d Li Shaohong. *p* Cheng Zhiu. *sc* Liu Heng. *ph* Zeng Nieping. *ed* Zhou Xinxia. *ad* Lin Chaoxiang. *m* Hou Muren. *cast* Li Xuejian, Song Dandan, Ye Jing, Yang Guixiang, Ding Ding.
● After laying bare backward village mentalities in *Bloody Morning*, Li Shaohong turns her attention to China's urban middle class. Cao is a photographer, married to an opera singer and with an infant son, caught in the usual professional morass of political compromise. His life starts to fall apart when he learns that his ex-wife also bore him a son some months after their divorce – and when the boy turns up looking for his father. Nothing wildly dramatic, just believable people in believable situations. If the ending seems a touch forced, this is nevertheless a sign that 'Fifth Generation' cinema is changing and coming to terms with up-to-date realities. TR

Family Resemblances

see Air de Famille, Un

Family Viewing

(1987, Can, 86 min)
d/p/sc Atom Egoyan. *ph* Robert MacDonald. *ed* Atom Egoyan, Bruce McDonald. *ad* Linda Del Rosario. *m* Mychael Danna. *cast* David Hemblem, Aidan Tierney, Gabrielle Rose, Arsinée Khanjian, Selma Keklikian, Jeanne Sabourin.
● Dad seems like a regular, middle class guy, but his penchants for mild sado-masochism and phone sex have driven his wife to leave him. He packes his senile mother-in-law off to a low-rent old people's home, and instals a charming, sit-com-style bimbo to meet his domestic and sexual needs. His son, meanwhile, spends all his free time visiting Granny in the home, where he strikes up a friendship with a young woman who happens to work for the phone-sex business patronised by his father. Egoyan's movie offers a rare – in 1988, unique – blend of black comedy, parody, formal fun-and-games, and emotive drama, and finally proves to have a remarkable range and maturity, giving equal weight to everything from the implications of video surveillance to the plight of elderly ethnic immigrants. You laugh one minute, gasp the next, and grope for the Kleenex moments later. TR

Fan, The

(1981, US, 95 min)
d Edward Bianchi. *p* Robert Stigwood. *sc* Priscilla Chapman, John Hartwell. *ph* Dick Bush. *ed* Alan Heim. *pd* Santo Loquasto. *m* Pino Donaggio. *cast* Lauren Bacall, James Garner, Maureen Stapleton, Hector Elizondo, Michael Biehn, Anna Maria Horsford, Griffin Dunne.
● Tacky adaptation of Bob Randall's novel in which (prefiguring the Jodie Foster case) a Broadway star's youthful fan (Biehn) graduates from epistolary devotion to homicidal mania when his overtures receive increasingly curt responses. Since impending shocks are loudly telegraphed in advance, and mainly comprise a series of virtually identical slasher attacks with open razor, the result is crude, nasty and predictable. Sole reason for watching the film is the wonderful Bacall as the toast of Broadway, currently celebrating yet another forty-ninth birthday, curling her basso purr round lines to make their banality sound like wit, and rehearsing a musical (songs by Marvin Hamlisch) that gives her the chance to strut her stuff as a song-and-dancer. TM

Fan, The

(1996, US, 115 min)
d Tony Scott. *p* Wendy Finerman. *sc* Phoef Sutton. *ph* Dariusz Wolski. *ed* Christian Wagner, Claire Simpson. *pd* Ida Random. *m* Hans Zimmer. *cast* Robert De Niro, Wesley Snipes, Benicio del Toro, Ellen Barkin, John Leguizamo, Patti D'Arbanville-Quinn, Chris Mulkey.

●It's hard to imagine what De Niro saw in this crass 'study' of a delusional stalker, which merely requires him to reprise, in cruder form, two of his best-known roles, Rupert Pupkin and Travis Bickle. Alienated from his job as a hunting-knife salesman, and separated from a wife who resents any time he spends with their young son, Gil Renard (De Niro) hones his obsession with the San Francisco Giants baseball team and their classy new signing Bobby Rayburn (Snipes). When Rayburn hits a slump, Renard focuses his resentment on usurper Juan Primo (del Toro), whose winning streak he brings to a sudden, brutal end. Facile pop psychology, hysterical performances, frenetic editing and a deafening, aggressive soundtrack. NF

Fanatic (aka Die! Die! My Darling!)

(1965, GB, 96 min)
d Silvio Narizzano. *p* Anthony Hinds. *sc* Richard Matheson. *ph* Arthur Ibbetson. *ed* James Needs. *pd* Peter Proud. *m* Wilfred Josephs. *cast* Tallulah Bankhead, Stefanie Powers, Peter Vaughan, Maurice Kaufman, Yootha Joyce, Donald Sutherland, Robert Dorning.

●One of the best of Hammer's psychological thrillers, mainly thanks to Richard Matheson's ingenious and terrifying script (adapted from a novel by Anne Blaisdell) about a religious crank who gradually becomes homicidal. There are plenty of *Psycho* rip-offs – notably at the climax – but Tallulah Bankhead is great in the title role, and for once the basis of the plot seems disturbingly credible. Admittedly Narizzano (who made the awful *Georgy Girl*) has little to offer in the way of direction, but then Matheson's scripts tend to be able to look after themselves. DP

Fancy Dance

(1990, Jap, 102 min)
d Masayuki Suo. *p* Shoji Masui. *sc* Masayuki Suo. *ph* Yuichi Nagata. *ed* Junichi Kikuchi. *ad* Minoru Ohashi. *m* Yoshikazu Suo. *cast* Masahiro Motoki, Honami Suzuki, Ken Osawa, Hiromasa Taguchi, Naoto Takenaka, Akira Emoto.

●Suo escaped from the purgatory of doing 'Making of...' documentaries for the appalling Juzo Itami into the relative bliss of this evident prototype for *Shall We Dance?* Successful punk-rock vocalist Yohei (Motoki) happens to come from a long line of Buddhist priests and is expected to serve a year as a novice monk. He reluctantly submits, shaving the half of his head which wasn't already shaved, and resigns himself to a life of asceticism and discipline in a mountain temple. But he and three fellow novices soon learn that some monks are more equal than others. The gay almoner monk secretly hoards chocolates and the disciplinarian monk likes to don a wig and hit karaoke bars. And then Yohei's girlfriend (Suzuki) shows up. The mix of belly laughs, slapstick, sex jokes and satire pushes towards a predictably serene, spiritual conclusion. TR

Fandango

(1985, US, 91 min)
d Kevin Reynolds. *p* Tim Zinnemann. *sc* Kevin Reynolds. *ph* Thomas Del Ruth. *ed* Arthur Schmidt, Stephen Semel. *ad* Peter Lansdown Smith. *m* Alan Silvestri. *cast* Kevin Costner, Judd Nelson, Sam Robards, Chuck Bush, Brian Cesak, Marvin J McIntyre, Suzy Amis.

●Five college friends strike out on one last fling – and the buddy buddy coming of age road movie is born. Despite patronage from Steven Spielberg, *Fandango* made no box-office impact. There is a sense of *déjà vu* all right, but this is an extremely attractive valediction to youth, with farcical underpinnings ably handled by Reynolds. His potential as a film-maker has since been confirmed (check out *The Beast*), and his pal Costner (surely the most important star to emerge from the '80s: Howard Hawks would have loved him) holds this one together. As a consequence, the picture's jumpy tone is safely grounded in character. BC

Fanny

(1932, Fr, 126 min, b/w)
d Marc Allégret. *p/sc* Marcel Pagnol. *ph* Nicolas Toporkoff. *ed* Raymond Lamy. *m* Vincent Scotto. *cast* Raimu, Pierre Fresnay, Orane Demazis, Alida Rouffe, Fernand Charpin, Robert Vattier, Milly Mathis.

●Part two of Marcel Pagnol's Marseilles trilogy, which began with *Marius*. The story so far: Marius, eager-beaver son of choleric but loveable César, has deserted Fanny, the love of his life, for the other love of his life, the sea – leaving Fanny bearing his child. Panisse, a middle-aged old fool, offers to solve all problems by marrying the girl himself, thus securing the son he longs for. However, when Marius returns... But plots are the last thing to worry about in the trilogy; one's best bet is to savour instead the finely drawn character studies, the triumphant acting, the warmth, humanity, and tightly-reined sentimentality of Pagnol's whole outlook. Allégret's direction is notably neater than Korda's in the first part or Pagnol's own for *César*. GB

Fanny

(1960, US, 133 min)
d/p Joshua Logan. *sc* Julius J Epstein. *ph* Jack Cardiff. *ed* William H Reynolds. *ad* Rino Mondellini. *m* Harold J Rome. *cast* Leslie Caron, Maurice Chevalier, Charles Boyer, Horst Buchholz, Salvatore Baccaloni, Lionel Jeffries.

●Curious adaptation of the 1954 Broadway musical (book by SN Behrman and Logan) which cavalierly cut out the excellent Harold Rome score, leaving only the title song for background orchestrations. What's left, clumsily compressed from Pagnol's Marseilles trilogy so as to play up the romantic complications, is both dire and dull. Jack Cardiff's pretty Technicolor photography is some compensation. TM

Fanny and Alexander (Fanny och Alexander) 100

(1982, Swe, 189 min)
d Ingmar Bergman. *p* Jörn Donner. *sc* Ingmar Bergman. *ph* Sven Nykvist. *ed* Sylvia Ingermarsson. *ad* Anna Asp. *m* Daniel Bell. *cast* Gunn Wållgren, Jarl Kulle, Erland Josephson, Jan Malmsjö, Harriet Andersson, Bertil Guve, Allan Edwall, Mats Bergman, Gunnar Björnstrand.

●Bergman's magisterial turn-of-the-century family saga, largely seen through the eyes of a small boy and carrying tantalising overtones of autobiography. Perhaps more accurately described as an anthology of personal reference points, designed as an auto-critique analysing his repertoire of artistic tricks. Years ago, in *The Face*, Bergman was agonising over the humiliations of the artist caught out in his deceptions and manipulations; but *Fanny and Alexander* cheerfully acknowledges his role as a charlatan conjuring his own life into dreams and nightmares for the edification or jollification of humanity. Here again are the smiles of a summer night (transferred to a dazzling evocation of traditional Christmas celebrations), the terror of the small boy harried by a sternly puritanical father, the crisis of religious doubt, the apocalyptic materialisation of God through a glass darkly (but seen this time to be only a marionette). Pulling his own creations apart to show how they tick, Bergman demonstrates the role of art and artifice, ocassionally slipping in a stunning new trick to show that the old magic still works. Certainly the most illuminating and most entertaining slice of Bergman criticism around, even better in the uncut TV version which clocks in at 300 minutes. TM

Fanny & Elvis

(1999, GB/fr, 111 min)
d Kay Mellor. *p* Laurie Borg. *sc* Kay Mellor. *ph* John Daly. *ed* Christopher Blunden. *pd* Maria Djurkovic. *m* Stephen Warbeck. *cast* Kerry Fox, Ray Winstone, Ben Daniels, David Morrissey, Jennifer Saunders, Colin Salmon, Gaynor Faye, Michael Medwin.

●Angered when his Jag is pranged by aspiring romantic novelist Kate (Fox), Dave (Winstone), a Cockney Hebden Bridge 'motor' salesman, moves into her spare room in lieu of compensation. His wife (Faye) has left him. Kate's biological clock is ringing alarm bells, and IVF and lonely hearts dates offer no solution. Dave looks virile. This witty first feature from TV writer Mellor motors safely between the deep and the trivial, passing through many amusing scenes, handled in TV sitcom mode. If the tart language and occasional delight in brassy crudity ground the film on the cobbles of feelgood Northern comedy, the trite West Yorkshire exteriors reveal a movie anxious for the applause of international audiences. WH

Fanny Hill

(1983, GB, 92 min)
d Gerry O'Hara. *p* Harry Benn. *sc* Stephen Chesley. *ph* Tony Spratling. *ed* Peter Boyle. *ad* Geoffrey Tozer. *m* Paul Hoffert. *cast* Lisa Raines, Oliver Reed, Wilfrid Hyde-White, Shelley Winters, Alfred Marks, Jonathan York, Paddie O'Neil.

●A relatively large budget and some respectable names in the cast list, but this is still limp soft-core flummery sold on the half-remembered notoriety of its purported 18th century source. Raines disrobes with efficiency, but she's not really earthy enough as the simple country lass who proceeds via sundry London brothels to woman-of-pleasure status and unlikely true love. Lawyer Reed and madam Winters, meanwhile, seem as though they have their teeth gritted in the hope that it will all be over soon. TJ

Fantasia

(1940, US, 120 min)
d Ben Sharpsteen (supervisor). *sc* Joe Grant, Dick Huemer. *ed* Stephen Csillag. *m* Bach, Tchaikovsky, Dukas, Stravinsky, Beethoven, Ponchielli, Moussorgsky, Schubert. *presenter* Deems Taylor.

●Renowned abstract film-maker Oskar Fischinger, employed in a distant capacity on the Bach sequence, called this Disney effort a 'conglomeration of tastelessness'. He wasn't kidding. Only the Dukas *Sorcerer's Apprentice* sequence, with Mickey Mouse, where the storyboard is effectively provided by the composer, achieves a respectable kind of success. For the rest, Disney's attempts at the visual illustration of Beethoven and Co – a dubious exercise anyway – produce Klassical Kitsch of the highest degree. Awesomely embarrassing; but some great sequences for all that, and certainly not to be missed. GB

Fantasia/2000 (aka Fantasia 2000)

(1999, US, 75 min)
d James Algar ('The Sorceror's Apprentice'), Gaëtan Brizzi, Paul Brizzi ('Firebird Suite'), Hendel Butoy ('Pines of Rome', 'The Steadfast Tin Soldier'), Francis Glebas ('Pomp and Circumstance'), Eric Goldberg ('Rhapsody in Blue', 'Carnival of the Animals'), Dohn Hahn (host sequences), Pixote Hunt (Beethoven's Fifth). *p* Donald W Ernst. *sc* Hans Christian Andersen ('The Steadfast Tin Soldier'), Don Hahn, Irene Mecchi, David Reynolds (host sequences). *ph* Tim Suhrstedt. *ed* Jessica Ambinder-Rojas, Lois Freeman-Fox, Julia Gray, Craig Paulsen, Greg Plotts. *pd* Pixote Hunt. *m* Dukas, Elgar, Gershwin, Respighi, Saint-Saëns, Shostakovich, Stravinsky, Beethoven. *with* Penn Jillette, James Earl Jones, Quincy Jones, Angela Lansbury, James Levine, Steve Martin, Bette Midler, Itzhak Perlman, (archive footage) Leopold Stokowski.

●This must be the most belated sequel the movies have produced. It features seven new animations, plus the stand-out from the original, Mickey Mouse as 'The Sorceror's Apprentice'. The recipe is much the same, with eclectic visual styles and a penchant for the strident end of the classical repertoire. It gets off to a dreadful high kitsch start with a pastel abstract and Beethoven's Fifth, then Respighi's 'Pines of Rome' with a herd of flying whales under the aurora borealis – an Athena poster brought to life. Just as you abandon hope, director Goldberg pulls out something special with a caricature of 1930s New York in the linear style of illustrator Al Hirschfeld, a vivid compliment to Gershwin's 'Rhapsody in Blue'. A CGI combination of Hans Christian Andersen's 'The Steadfast Tin Soldier' and Shostakovich's 'Piano Concerto No 2' also works quite well, with a nasty jack-in-the-box providing welcome villainy. And so it veers on, culminating in Stravinsky's 'Firebird Suite', and a spritely allegory about the renewal of nature. It's still not clear who the audience might be, except perhaps the hopeful parents of potential musical prodigies, but it's surely an inspired marketing idea to release the film on IMAX screens, where sight can match sound for scale, and competition is limited to *National Geographic* documentaries. TCh

Fantasist, The

(1986, Eire, 98 min)
d Robin Hardy. *p* Mark Forstater. *sc* Robin Hardy. *ph* Frank Gell. *ed* Thomas Schwalm. *ad* John Lucas. *m* Stanislas Syrewicz. *cast* Moira Harris, Christopher Cazenove, Timothy Bottoms, John Kavanagh, Mick Lally, Bairbre Ni Chaoimh.

●Down Dublin's mean streets stalks a psychopath who, before pouncing for the kill, mesmerises his victims-to-be with lengthy telephone monologues that blend blarney, threats and pure poetry. Armed only with a strange mixture of canny courage and coy innocence, Patricia – a young Southern Irish farmgirl leaving home to try her luck teaching in the city – is simultaneously attracted to and terrified by three admiring males, each of whom might turn out to be her saviour or her slayer. Hardy's thriller is often as offbeat as his earlier *The Wicker Man*, embellishing its suspense with oddball characters, intimations of magic and the polarities of innocence and experience, country and city, dream and reality. Attempting to investigate different aspects of sexual/romantic fantasy (all four central characters might lay claim to the film's title), Hardy nevertheless remains constricted by both the narrative formulas and the moral conventions of the woman-in-peril film: too often, Patricia, as played by Moira Harris, seems not just foolhardy but actually compliant in her dangerous predicament. That said, however, Hardy deserves praise for his very evident ambitions. GA

Fantastic Disappearing Man, The

see Return of Dracula, The

Fantasticks, The

(1995/2000, US, 86 min)
d Michael Ritchie. *p* Michael Ritchie, Linne Radmin. *sc* Tom Jones, Harvey Schmidt. *ph* Fred Murphy. *ed* William Scharf. *pd* Douglas W Schmidt. *m/songs* Harvey Schmidt, Tom Jones. *cast* Joel Grey, Barnard Hughes, Jean Louisa Kelly, Jonathon Morris, Brad Sullivan.

●One of several oddities redeeming the latter part of Ritchie's switchback career, this plays like the last 1950s musical – fittingly, since the Broadway show from which it derives, an adaptation of Rostand's *Les Romantiques*, actually opened in 1960. Ritchie enthusiastically embraces the unfashionableness both of the narrative (innocent boy/girl romance offset by comic parental scheming) and of the songs (the wistful 'Try to Remember' being the most familiar). The intervention of a Bradbury-esque sinister/magical carnival gives Ritchie the opportunity for some lively staging. But the film's double copyright notation, the abbreviated running time and various loose ends indicate that the suits reacted to this celebration of the passé with dither and dismay. BBa

Fantastic Night, The

see Nuit fantastique, La

Fantastic Planet (La Planète Sauvage)

(1973, Fr/Czech, 71 min.)
d René Laloux. *p* Simon Damiani, André Valio-Cavaglione. *sc* René Laloux, Roland Topor. *ph* Lubomir Rejthar, Boris Baromykin. *ed* Hélène Arnal, Marta Latalova. *pd* Roland Topor. *m* Alain Goraguer. *cast* voices: (English-language version) Barry Bostwick, Cynthia Alder, Mark Gruner, Nora Heflin, Marvin Miller, Monika Ramirez.

●Are you ready for the struggle of the Oms against their oppressive masters, the 40-foot Draags? Something of a revelation to anyone who thinks animation extends only as far as *Fritz the Cat*, Roland Topor's graphics create a world reminiscent of two of the greatest artists of the fantastic, Bosch and Odilon Redon. He sketches a menacing landscape full of womb-like passages, intestinal plants, strange phallic and vaginal shapes, and extraordinary posthistoric monsters. CPe

Fantastic Voyage

(1966, US, 100 min)
d Richard Fleischer. *p* Saul David. *sc* Harry Kleiner. *ph* Ernest Laszlo. *ed* William B Murphy. *ad* Jack Martin Smith, Dale Hennesy. *m* Leonard Rosenman. *cast* Stephen Boyd, Raquel Welch, Donald Pleasence, Edmond O'Brien, Arthur Kennedy, Arthur O'Connell.

●Very nearly a corking sci-fi lark, kicking off from the premise that when a top scientist defecting to the West suffers brain damage in an assassination attempt, the only answer is to inject a miniaturised submarine and medical team through his bloodstream to deal with the clot on his brain. The voyage through the fantastic landscapes of the body is brilliantly imagined, with the heart a cavernous vault, tidal waves menacing the canals of the inner ear (caused when a nurse drops an instrument in the operating theatre), cyclonic winds tossing the sub helplessly about as the lungs are reached. The script, alas, is pretty basic, expending half its energies on delivering a gee-whiz medical lecture, the other on whipping up suspense around the mysterious saboteur who lurks aboard (and is so sweatily shifty-eyed that there isn't much mystery). An opportunity missed, therefore – especially as the imaginative sets are slightly tackily realised – but fun all the same. TM

Fantômas

(1913/14, Fr, 332 min)
d/p/sc Louis Feuillade. *ph* Georges Guérin, Albert Sorgius. *cast* René Navarre, Edmond Bréon, Georges Melchior, Renée Carl, Jane Faber, André Luguet, Fabienne Fabrèges.

●Feuillade's legendary Fantômas cycle, based on pulp novels by Pierre Souvestre and Marcel Allain, comprises five episodes, each divided into between three and six chapters: *Fantômas* (54 min), *Juve versus Fantômas* (59 min), *The Death Which Kills* (90 min), *Fantômas versus Fantômas* (59 min) and *The False Magistrate* (70 min). All of them concern the unending duel of wits between Inspector Juve of the Sûreté (Bréon) and the protean jewel thief Fantômas (Navarre), a master of disguise who exults in wrecking a train or dynamiting a villa to eliminate individual enemies. Because Feuillade filmed mostly on the streets of Paris and, melodramatic climaxes aside, got broadly naturalistic performances from his actors, his best work is the only cinema from the 1910s which still feels startlingly immediate and 'real'. And because he rooted the magical, the dangerous and the perverse in the everyday, he not only fathered the Lang-Hitchcock-Lynch current in cinema but also predicted a century of moral mazes, art terrorism and justified paranoia. The French DVD release offers Jacques Champreux' 1998 restoration (with captions to summarise lost footage), plus clips from a 1966 Franju interview with the elderly Marcel Allain. TR

Fantômas contre Fantômas

(1948, Fr, 91 min, b/w)
d Robert Vernay. *sc* Solange Térac, Robert Vernay, Pierre Laroche. *ph* Maurice Barry. *ed* Marthe Poncin. *ad* Raymond Gabutti. *m* Joë Hajos. *cast* Yves Furet, Alexandre Rignault, Maurice Teynac, Marcelle Chantal, Odile Versois.

●Here's another example of an obscure work by a disregarded director turning out to have worn better than many of the official key movies of the day. Blithely transcending all concepts of period and genre, this deploys the hooded master criminal from the Belle Epoque alongside a berserk brain surgeon intent on creating an army of killer zombies (the backlog of Universal horrors must just have hit France), a gang of comic black marketeers, and an abandoned Gestapo torture centre with handy pool of sulphuric acid. It's hectic and ruthless, shot in self-conscious deep-focus (the Gregg Toland backlog…) and incorporates so much location film to render the director an accidental documentarist of Paris, summer of '48. It may not be Feuillade, it may not add up to anything very coherent, but it would certainly have been a waste had this uninhibited fever dream been left in the vaults. BBa

Fantôme de la Liberté, Le (The Phantom of Liberty)

(1974, Fr, 104 min)
d Luis Buñuel. *p* Serge Silberman. *sc* Luis Buñuel, Jean-Claude Carrière. *ph* Edmond Richard. *ed* Hélène Plemiannikov. *ad* Pierre Guffroy. *cast* Bernard Verley, Jean-Claude Brialy, Monica Vitti, Milena Vukotic, Michel Lonsdale, Jean Rochefort, Claude Piéplu, Julien Bertheau, Michel Piccoli, Adriana Asti.

●As a good Surrealist who aimed to disturb rather than to please, Buñuel must have felt that the Oscar which crowned the worldwide success of *The Discreet Charm of the Bourgeoisie* was the last straw. At any rate, he made sure that this isn't such an easy pill to digest, though its delightful humour goes down just as easily. The Chinese box structure, with a series of bizarre episodes never quite reaching the point of resolution, is exactly the same as in the earlier film. But where *The Discreet Charm* used the interrupted dinner-party as a comfortably recognisable motif, *The Phantom of Liberty* works more disconcertingly by stringing its episodes on an invisible thread woven by the prologue (where Spanish patriots welcome the firing-squad with cries of 'Long live chains!', and a Captain of Dragoons falls in love with a statue of a saint). Thereafter, beneath the surface, the film busily explores the process whereby the human mind, burying itself ostrich-like in convention, invariably fails to recognise the true nature of freedom and sexuality. TM

Fantôme du Moulin Rouge, Le

(1924, Fr, 6,900 ft, b/w)
d René Clair. *p* René Fernand. *ph* Jimmy Berliet, Louis Chaixet. *sc* René Clair. *ad* Robert Gys. *cast* Albert Préjean, Sandra Milovanoff, Georges Vaultier, José Davert, Maurice Schutz, Paul Olivier.

●Made immediately after the experimental short *Entr'acte*, this uses many of the same devices – superimposition, trick effects, comic occurrences caused by 'magic' – but harnesses them to a much more conventional narrative. A young man, unsuccessful in love, manages to leave his body and tours Paris, disembodied and invisible, playing practical jokes: a row of coats walks off from a hotel cloakroom; an unattended taxi drives itself away; a row of top hats appears on the pavement. This reconciliation of romantic comedy and surrealist gags, using fantasy to present avant-garde motifs, is typical of Clair, as is the largely irrelevant but utterly inspired 'Eccentrics' Bar' sequence. AS

Fantômes du Chapelier, Les (The Hatter's Ghosts)

(1982, Fr, 120 min)
d Claude Chabrol. *p* Philippe Grumbach. *sc* Claude Chabrol. *ph* Jean Rabier. *ed* Monique Fardoulis. *ad* Jean-Louis Povéda. *m* Matthieu Chabrol. *cast* Michel Serrault, Charles Aznavour, Monique Chaumette, Isabelle Sadoyan, François Cluzet, Aurore Clément, Mario David.

●The hatter (Serrault) is a mass strangler who allows his secret to be discovered by hangdog Cachoudas (Aznavour), the tubercular Armenian tailor opposite. The ensuing relationship seems unbelievably reckless, even with a mad hatter involved, and manifestly it's the Hitchcocko-Jesuitical theology about shared guilt which animates the picture. If it's all a bit exclusive, it's redeemed by Serrault's baroque performance – shaking with secret mirth, letting slip snippets of the mysterious conversations running on in his head. Though based on a 1956 Simenon novel (*The Judge and the Hatter*) Chabrol locates his adaptation in an off-kilter time zone – little bit '30s, little bit '50s – that some may find the most intriguing aspect of the movie. BBa

Far and Away

(1992, US, 140 min)
d Ron Howard. *p* Ron Howard, Brian Grazer. *sc* Ron Howard. *ph* Mikael Salomon. *ed* Michael Hill, Daniel Hanley. *pd* Jack T Collis, Allan Cameron. *m* John Williams. *cast* Tom Cruise, Nicole Kidman, Thomas Gibson, Robert Prosky, Barbara Babcock, Cyril Cusack, Eileen Pollock, Colm Meaney, Michelle Johnson.

●A change of pace for Cruise and Kidman, after the dismal *Days of Thunder*, with this old-fashioned period romance. In 19th century Ireland, tenant farmer Joseph Donelly (Cruise) sets his handsome face against injustice, planning to avenge his father's death at the hands of unscrupulous landowners. Instead, he falls in with Shannon (Kidman), his intended victim's daughter, who persuades him to travel to America as her servant-companion. Once in

Boston, Joseph makes good with bouts of bare-knuckle fighting, Shannon sweats and fumes in a chicken-plucking factory, and the pair feud and tease. Howard's lifelong ambition to make a film about his Irish ancestry results in a light confection, full of sweeping overhead shots and predictable pulp-fiction intrigue. CM

Far Away (Loin)

(2001, Fr/Sp, 120 min)
d André Téchiné. *p* Philippe Carcassonne, Saïd Bensaïd. *sc* André Téchiné, Faouzi Bensaïdi. *ph* Germain Desmoulins. *ed* Hervé de Luze. *pd* Maria-José Branco. *m* Juliette Garrigues. *cast* Stéphane Rideau, Lubna Azabal, Mohamed Hamaïdi, Gaël Morel, Yasmina Reza, Jack Taylor.

● One of Téchiné's better efforts, this digitally shot drama centres on Serge, a Tangier-based truck driver who crosses the strait to Spain so often that the authorities barely check if there are illegal immigrants hidden in or beneath his vehicle. Not that he's entirely clean in such regards, but he refuses to smuggle his pal Saïd across, even though the boy, desperate to go to Europe, helps him meet up again with his beloved Jewish ex, Sarah. An engrossing portrait of a multicultural city in a state of flux, with deftly drawn characters, and a narrative that manages never to feel stale. GA

Faraway, So Close (In weiter Ferne, so nah!)

(1993, Ger, 144 min, b/w & col)
d/p Wim Wenders. *sc* Wim Wenders, Ulrich Zieger, Richard Reitinger. *ph* Jürgen Jürges. *ed* Peter Przygodda. *pd* Albrecht Konrad. *m* Laurent Petitgand. *cast* Otto Sander, Peter Falk, Horst Buchholz, Nastassja Kinski, Heinz Rühmann, Bruno Ganz, Solveig Dommartin, Lou Reed, Willem Dafoe, Mikhail Gorbachev.

● Wenders' follow-up to *Wings of Desire* is a considerable disappointment, a sprawling metaphysical caper movie which has much in common with his previous picture, *Until the End of the World*. Beginning a few years after Damiel (Ganz) hung up his wings to settle down with Marion (Dommartin), the film follows the angel Cassiel (Sander) as he too becomes mortal. Life doesn't throw him any great romance, however – instead, he finds himself in an extraordinary convoluted (and extremely tedious) mystery thriller. We get jokes, whimsy, hijinks and escapades; we get Lou Reed strumming a new song; we even get bungee-jumping at the climax. What's lacking is any sense of form. The movie meanders for two and a half hours, has glaring continuity gaps, and repeatedly confuses self-consciousness with irony, sincerity with significance. There are grace notes here, but Wenders' ambitions seem far, far away. TCh

Far Country, The

(1954, US, 97 min)
d Anthony Mann. *p* Aaron Rosenerg. *sc* Borden Chase. *ph* William H Daniels. *ed* Russell Schoengarth. *ad* Bernard Herzbrun, Alexander Golitzen. *m* Joseph Gershenson. *cast* James Stewart, Walter Brennan, Ruth Roman, Corinne Calvet, John McIntire, Jay C Flippen, Harry Morgan.

● A strange, almost self-conscious Western written, like *Where the River Bends*, by Borden Chase. Stewart travels north to the Oregon territory with old-timer Brennan and a herd of cattle, only to be cheated out of the steers by corrupt judge McIntire. Signing up with saloon owner Roman's wagon-train to the gold-mining camps, ostensibly to earn some money, Stewart in fact plans to steal back his cattle and take his revenge. Stewart again plays the driven, vengeful loner, and the emphasis is again on his eventual acceptance of a social rather than an individual sense of justice. What distinguishes this from *Where the River Bends*, though, is Mann's use of painted backdrops, rear-projections and other artificial devices which tend – like the odd, cryptic dialogue – to undermine any sense of realism. NF

Farewell (Abschied)

(2000, Ger, 88 min)
d Jan Schütte. *p* Gesche Carstens, Henryk Romanowski, Jan Schütte. *sc* Klaus Pohl. *ph* Edward Klosinski. *ed* Renate Merck. *pd* Katharina Wöppermann. *m* John Cale. *cast* Josef Bierbichler, Monica Bleibtreu, Jeanette Hain, Elfriede Irrall, Margit Rogall, Samuel Fintzi.

● August 1956: the ailing Bertolt Brecht is with his wife, staff and various guests at his lakeside villa, alternating his time writing, chasing after new lovers, avoiding old lovers, and generally feeling rotten, curmudgeonly and tyrannical; meanwhile, unbeknown to him, the authorities want a couple of his guests for 'treason'. This is nothing if not earnest and arty: taciturn, elegiac, measured, oblique, allusive, elegant. It's also, unfortunately, a touch dull and somewhat insubstantial. The themes – compromise, creativity, self-awareness and deception, power, loyalty and betrayal – are all present and correct, but aren't developed in any particularly interesting way. GA

Farewell (Proshchanie)

(1981, USSR, 126 min)
d Elem Klimov. *p* A Rasskazov, G Sokolova. *sc* Larissa Shepitko, Rudolf Tyurin, German Klimov. *ph* Alexei Rodionov, Yuri Skhirtladze, Sergei Taraskin. *ed* V Byelova. *ad* V Petrov. *m* V Artyomov, Alfred Schnittke. *cast* Stefaniya Stayuta, Lev Durov, Alexei Petrenko, Leonid Kryuk, Vadim Yakovenko, Yuri Katin-Yartsev.

● This monitors the dying gasps of a remote Siberian village, its vibrant peasant culture threatened by a government hydro-electric scheme, and examines the conflict – desire for individual happiness versus pragmatic plans for the greater good of society – in balanced, fruitful terms. What really distinguishes the movie, however, and offers allegories for the asking, is the resonant, mystical nature of Klimov's images: Mother Earth, symbolised most notably by a gigantic, seemingly indestructible tree, is imbued with a primitive, pantheistic power, while the engineers sent to raze the island first appear as hazy angels of death emerging from the mists of the lake. As guilt and recrimination, fear and confusion take grip of the villagers, who prepare for evacuation with a mixture of melancholia and bawdy celebration, Klimov paints a haunting picture of the onset of death that culminates in a stunning sequence located in a fearful limbo. All of which suggests Russian ruminations of an impenetrably joyless kind; nevertheless, despite the stately pace and excessive length, the film's assured, elegiac evocation of a virtually pagan world, both defined and doomed by its traditions, exerts considerable fascination. GA

Farewell Again (aka Troopship)

(1937, GB, 85 min, b/w)
d Tim Whelan. *p* Erich Pommer. *sc* Clemence Dane, Patrick Kirwan. *ph* James Wong Howe, Hans Schneeburger. *ed* Jack Dennis. *ad* Fred Pusey. *m* Richard Addinsell. *cast* Leslie Banks, Flora Robson, Patricia Hilliard, Sebastian Shaw, René Ray, Anthony Bushell, Robert Newton, Edward Lexy, Wally Patch.

● Carrying the same call to preparedness as *Fire Over England* (both were produced by Erich Pommer and scripted by Clemence Dane), this is a prototype *In Which We Serve* about a troopship bringing men home on leave after five years army service in India. Trouble stirs when orders require an immediate return to duty, but – after six hours in port during which all the carefully planted domestic problems and heartbreaks get a cursory airing – everybody nobly buckles to. Quite warmly praised at the time, but the class attitudes accepted as perfectly normal – the officers, suffering stoically, soothe other-rank grumbles with a patronising pat on the head; the gentry cavort over cocktails and dancing in the saloon while the lower orders huddle like squalid sardines below decks – are positively cringe-making. No wonder Churchill and the Conservatives were elected out after World War II. TM

Farewell, Home Sweet Home (Adieu, Plancher des Vaches!)

(1999, Fr/Switz/It, 117 min)
d Otar Iosseliani. *p* Martine Marignac. *sc* Otar Iosseliani. *ph* William Lubtchansky. *ed* Otar Iosseliani, Ewa Lenkiewicz. *pd* Manu de Chauvigny. *m* Nicolas Zourabichvili. *cast* Nico Tarielashvili, Lily Lavina, Philippe Bas, Stéphanie Hainque, Amiran Amiranachvili, Otar Iosseliani.

● Iosseliani's wholly delightful, assured and typically idiosyncratic fable tells of the various reversals of fortune that affect a well to do 19-year-old, who rebels against his culture-vulture business-woman mother and boozily indolent father. He forsakes the family chateau for café 'society, preferring the company of its denizens – Parisian dropouts, immigrants, barstaff – to home life. As ever, the jigsaw narrative slowly pieces itself together, and the overall dearth of dialogue means that the audience has to work for its pleasures. But it's a hugely charming piece, wondrously inventive, consistently witty, engaging in its devotion to the joys of wine, women and song, and somewhat deeper than it first appears. GA

Farewell My Concubine (Ba Wang Bie Ji)

(1993, HK/China, 156 min)
d Chen Kaige. *p* Hsu Feng. *sc* Lilian Lee, Lu Wei. *ph* Gu Changwei. *ed* Pei Xiaonan. *pd* Chen Huaikai. *m* Zhao Jiping. *cast* Leslie Cheung, Zhang Fengyi, Gong Li, Lu Qi, Ying Da, Ge You, Li Chun, Lei Han.

● Hitherto, Chen Kaige's films have specialised in poetic, allusive allegory: in *King of the Children* and *Life on a String*, especially, socio-political content was conveyed by elliptical narratives and vivid but often enigmatic images. Here, however, Chen adopts a direct and less personal approach to his country's troubled history as he charts the similarly troubled relationship, from 1925 to 1977, of two Peking Opera actors. Their boyhood friendship arises in protective reaction to the disciplines of the Academy; but by the time they've become stars, Dieyi (Cheung) has fallen for his friend Xiaolou (Zhang Fengyi), mirroring the on-stage devotion of the concubine he plays for Xiaolou's King of Chu. Inevitably, he is distraught when Xiaolou marries a prostitute, Juxian (Gong Li), who is more than a match for Dieyi's jealous hysteria; but the trio are also caught up in bigger events so that over the decades their mutual suspicion, deceits, divided loyalties, betrayals and acts of desperate support for one another chime with the mood of China itself. Appropriately operatic, Chen's visually spectacular epic is sumptuous in every respect. Intelligent, enthralling, rhapsodic. GA

Farewell My Darling (Haksaeng Bukunshinwi)

(1996, SKor, 124 min)
d Park Chul-Soo. *cast* Park Chul-Soo, Choi Sung, Kwon Sung-Duk, Moon Jung-Sook, Jung Ha-Hyun, Bang Eun-Jin.

● A very old man dies in his home village and the members of his family – now scattered far and wide – converge for the three-day funeral. The eldest son happens to be a Seoul-based film director (guess who plays him), who neglects his duties as chief mourner and stands to one side to watch – as film directors do – the tensions build and elements of grotesquerie multiply. Before long skeletons are tumbling out of family closets. Park marshals a huge cast and episodic narrative with assurance and delivers a very filmic tragi-comedy. TR

Farewell, My Lovely

(1975, US, 95 min)
d Dick Richards. *p* George Pappas, Jerry Bruckheimer. *sc* David Zelag Goodman. *ph* John A Alonzo. *ed* Walter Thompson, Joel Cox. *pd* Dean Tavoularis. *m* David Shire. *cast* Robert Mitchum, Charlotte Rampling, John Ireland, Sylvia Miles, Anthony Zerbe, Harry Dean Stanton, Jack O'Halloran, Sylvester Stallone, Jim Thompson.

● After Altman's intensive analysis of Philip Marlowe in *The Long Goodbye*, it's hard to imagine another straightforward adaptation. Yet *Farewell, My Lovely* deliberately courts nostalgia with lovingly recreated '40s settings and film techniques recalling the thrillers of the time, besides the casting of Mitchum, who made his name in just such films. As such, it lies alongside the successful 1944 adaptation rather than the current Californian detective pictures, whose troubled introspections it lacks. The film's triumph is Mitchum's definitive Marlowe, which captures perfectly the character's down-at-heel integrity and erratic emotional involvement with his cases. Purists may find the script's tinkering with Marlowe's character irritating. But there are plenty of compensations: strong supporting performances, moody renderings of the underbelly of Los Angeles nightlife, and a jigsaw plot with Marlowe's chase through seven homicides to find an ex-nightclub singer, six years disappeared. CPe

Farewell, My Lovely (aka Murder My Sweet)

(1944, US, 95 min, b/w)
d Edward Dmytryk. *p* Adrian Scott. *sc* John Paxton. *ph* Harry J Wild. *ed* Joseph Noriega. *ad* Albert S D'Agostino, Carroll Clark. *m* Roy Webb. *cast* Dick Powell, Claire Trevor, Anne Shirley, Otto Kruger, Mike Mazurki, Miles Mander, Esther Howard.

●Fine adaptation of Chandler's novel (which had served as plot fodder for *The Falcon Takes Over* only two years earlier), evocatively creating a seedy, sordid world of shifting loyalties and unseen evil as Marlowe goes in search of the young and missing Velma at the urgent behest of Moose Malloy (Mazurki in fine form), a brutish ex-con unaware that the girl he left behind when he went to jail has metamorphosed into the dangerously duplicitous Claire Trevor (another marvellous performance). Powell is surprisingly good as Marlowe, certainly more faithful to the writer's conception than Bogart was in *The Big Sleep*, while the supporting cast make the most of John Paxton's superb dialogue. And Harry Wild's chiaroscuro camerawork is the true stuff of *noir*. Although released in America as *Murder My Sweet*, the film was in fact originally screened there as *Farewell, My Lovely*. GA

Farewell, Stranger (Lebewohl Fremde)

(1991, Ger, 100 min)
d Tevfik Baser. *p* Jan Michael Brand, Helga Bähr. *sc* Tevfik Baser, Achim Haag, Thomas Strittmatter. *ed* Helga Borsche. *pd* Wolf Sesselberg. *m* Claus Bantzer. *cast* Grazyna Szapoloska, Musfik Kenter.

●Sensitive if familiar romantic drama, from a Turkish director, set on a remote German island (Langeness), with a 40-year-old. woman forming a relationship with an exiled Turkish writer and poet in the absence of her husband and daughter. The closed community's response is deftly handled, and the couple's courting watched with tenderness. The cinematography is fine too – lovely night-time vistas against cold blue light. It's a film that stresses common humanity rather than political outrage, but it's none the less for that. Tevfik Baser relies on rather obvious symbolism (storms, floods, fires), but otherwise directs with confidence and emotional restraint. WH

Farewell to Arms, A

(1932, US, 88 min, b/w)
d/p Frank Borzage. *sc* Benjamin F Glazer, Oliver HP Garrett. *ph* Charles Lang Jr. *ed* Otto Lovering. *ad* Hans Dreier, Roland Anderson. *m* W Franke Harling. *cast* Gary Cooper, Helen Hayes, Adolphe Menjou, Mary Philips, Jack LaRue, Blanche Frederici, Henry Armetta.

●Not only the best film version of a Hemingway novel, but also one of the most thrilling visions of the power of sexual love that even Borzage ever made. An American ambulanceman, serving in Italy in World War I, falls in love with an English nurse; he finally goes AWOL to rejoin her, only to find her carrying his child and dying of hunger and loneliness. No other director got performances like these: Cooper at his youngest and sexiest, moving from drunkenness to intoxication; moon-faced Hayes, at once a mother-figure and a lover; and Menjou as Cooper's repressed homosexual friend, jealously coming between the lovers. And no other director created images like these, using light and movement like brushstrokes, integrating naturalism and a daring expressionism in the same shot. This is romantic melodrama raised to its highest degree, fittingly set to the music of Wagner's 'Liebestod'. TR

Farewell to Arms, A

(1957, US, 152 min)
d Charles Vidor. *p* David O Selznick. *sc* Ben Hecht. *ph* Piero Portalupi, Oswald Morris. *ed* Gerard J Wilson, John M Foley. *pd* Alfred Junge. *m* Mario Nascimbene. *cast* Rock Hudson, Jennifer Jones, Vittorio De Sica, Alberto Sordi, Mercedes McCambridge, Elaine Stritch, Oscar Homolka, Victor Francen.

●Inflated remake of Frank Borzage's classic 1932 adaptation of the Hemingway novel (almost literally twice the length), with Hudson as the US ambulance driver and Jones the British nurse finding their World War I romance crushed beneath surplus production values and spectacle. A padded Ben Hecht script and Selznick's invariable tendency to overkill are equally to blame. PT

Farewell to False Paradise (Abschied vom Falschen Paradies/Yalanci Cennete Elveda)

(1989, WGer/Tur, 92 min)
d Tevfik Baser. *p* Ottakar Runze. *sc* Tevfik Baser. *ph* Izzet Akay. *ed* Klaus Bassine. *m* Claus Bantzer. *cast* Zuhal Olcay, Brigite Janner, Ruth Olafsdottir, Barbara Morawiecz, Ayse Altan, Serpil Inanc.

●Baser's film describes the emotional journey of a woman who, sentenced to six years in a German prison for murdering her cruel husband, finds that the friendship of her fellow female cellmates serves to renew her spirit, until she hears that on release she will be deported to Turkey and retrial... WH

Farewell to the King

(1988, US, 117 mins)
d John Milius. *p* Albert S Ruddy, André Morgan. *sc* John Milius. *ph* Dean Semler. *ed* John W Wheeler. *pd* Gil Parrondo. *m* Basil Poledouris. *cast* Nick Nolte, Nigel Havers, Frank McRae, James Fox, Marilyn Tokudo, Marius Weyers.

●Or *Apocalypse Now* revisited. When, in a World War II mission to mobilise resistance against the Japs, plucky Brit officer (Havers) and his black radioman (McRae) parachute into Borneo, they find the tribes united in peace under US Army deserter-turned-king Nolte. This Great White God proves reluctant to fall in with the fork-tongued Allied forces until a surprise Jap attack on his village. Persuaded that he 'can't avoid History', Nolte leads his men into war against the brutal, oddly honourable enemy, and thus enters the dominion of Myth. Havers and Nolte proceed from initial suspicion, through wary respect, to the kind of unspoken love between men that remains a matter of adoring glances; and Havers braves the top brass in an effort to guarantee post-war freedom for Nolte's Noble Savages. Despite the craftsmanlike visual bravura, entire scenes verge on incoherence, and the portentous script serves only to expose how vague and misplaced is Milius' faith in anarchism. Where once he seemed an original, now he merely regurgitates his own woolly, vacuous clichés. GA

Far from Home: The Adventures of Yellow Dog

(1994, US, 81 min)
d Phillip Borsos. *p* Peter O'Brian. *sc* Philliip Borsos. *ph* James Gardner. *ed* Sidney Wolinsky. *pd* Mark Freeborn. *m* John Scott. *cast* Bruce Davison, Mimi Rogers, Jesse Bradford, Tom Bower, Josh Wannamaker, Margot Finley, Dakotah.

●This movie about a lad and his dog surviving in the British Columbian wilderness is better than the formula might suggest. Playing the parents is normally a thankless gig, but Davison and Rogers bring a believability to the frantic pair: their 14-year-old son, Angus (Bradford), hasn't emerged from the tall timbers after three weeks. Parted from his father when their boat sinks in a storm, the boy and the dog survive on fish, grubs, berries and confection, and traverse the Book of Genesis terrain despite attacks by wolves. As usual, Angus is stuck in ravines every time the air-rescue helicopter goes over. As usual, the dog supplies resolution in the darkest hour. Yellow Dog (Dakotah) is a splendidly trained labrador who brings off a brilliant leap into a lineful of washing that had at least one junior audience cheering. Simple, effective stuff. BC

Far from the Barbarians

see Loin des Barbares

Far From the Madding Crowd

(1967, GB, 168 min)
d John Schlesinger. *p* Joseph Janni. *sc* Frederic Raphael. *ph* Nicolas Roeg. *ed* Malcolm Cooke. *pd* Richard MacDonald. *m* Richard Rodney Bennett. *cast* Julie Christie, Terence Stamp, Peter Finch, Alan Bates, Fiona Walker, Prunella Ransome, Alison Leggatt, Freddie Jones.

●Another classic bites the dust. Thomas Hardy's Bathsheba, a country girl who attempts to better her station and find true love, miscast Julie Christie just as effectively as did *Dr Zhivago*; for some mysterious reason, the notion that she should play classic roles was one that persisted for several years. Nicolas Roeg's evocative photography of the West Country dominates the film, and shows up the characters as just going through the motions. PH

Far from Vietnam (Loin du Viêt-nam)

(1967, US, 115 min, b/w & col)
d Alain Resnais, William Klein, Joris Ivens, Agnès Varda, Claude Lelouch, Jean-Luc Godard. *sc* Michèle Ray, Roger Pic, KS Karol, Marceline Loridan, François Maspero, Chris Marker, Jacques Sternberg, Jean Lacouture, François. *ph* Willy Kurant, Jean Bofferty, Kien Tham, Denys Clerval, Ghislain Cloquet, Bernard Zitzermann, Alain Levent, Theo Robichet. *ed* Chris Marker, Jean Ravel, Colette Leloup, Eric Pluet, Albert Jurgenson. cast (Resnais episode) Bernard Fresson, Karen Blanguernon. *with* Fidel Castro, Jean-Luc Godard.

●Necessarily dated but still a fascinating document, this collective protest against the Vietnam war begins with a graceful ballet of bomb-loading and take-off preparations aboard an American carrier, contrasted with shots of civilians in Hanoi hurrying to pathetically inadequate improvised shelters. Suspected Vietcong sympathisers are beaten up; peace marchers in America are confronted by counter-demonstrators shouting 'Bomb Hanoi!'; General Westmoreland appears reassuringly on TV to state that 'Civilian casualties do not result from our firepower; they result from mechanical errors'. All good, stirring stuff, edited into a remarkably coherent whole by Chris Marker. But the film goes on to probe the ambiguity behind the protest. Inherent throughout (but explicitly explored in fictional interludes directed by Renais and Godard) is the dilemma that, although this was 'the first war everyone can watch' and all of us were involved, the very remoteness (in every sense) of the conflict carried inevitable obfuscations. There is a certain amount of navel-gazing here, but at least the film acknowledges the sense of impotent frustration shared by many in trying to decide what to *do*. TM

Fargo (100)

(1995, US, 98 min)
d Joel Coen. *p* Ethan Coen. *sc* Ethan Coen, Joel Coen. *ph* Roger Deakins. *ed* Roderick Jay [Joel Coen, Ethan Coen]. *pd* Rick Heinrichs. *m* Carter Burwell. *cast* Frances McDormand, Steve Buscemi, Peter Stormare, William H Macy, Harve Presnell, Kristin Rudrüd.

●Car salesman Jerry Lundegaard (Macy) hires low-lifes Carl and Gaear (Buscemi and Stormare) to kidnap his wife, hoping that her wealthy father will pay a ransom from which Jerry can cream a share. The abduction goes according to plan, but the kidnappers commit three murders as they drive by night through the snowy Minnesota wastes. Police chief Marge Gunderson (McDormand), a slow-talkin', smart-thinkin', pregnant housewife, investigates. Joel and Ethan Coen's beguiling film is both very funny and, finally, very moving. Performed to perfection by an imaginatively assembled cast, it displays the customary Coen virtues, at the same time providing a robust emotional core unaffected by the taint of mere technical virtuosity. The talk is more leisurely than usual, the camera largely static, the focus firmly on relationships, character, ethics. However banal the lives and aspirations of the leading figures, there's nothing condescending about the humour. Marge and her husband are genuinely good, ordinary people caught up in extraordinary events of, to them, unfathomable evil. Suspense, satire, mystery, horror, comedy and keen (if faintly surreal) social observation combine to prove yet again that (bar very few) the Coens remain effortlessly ahead of the American field. GA

Farinelli Il Castrato

(1994, It/Bel, 111 min)
d Gérard Corbiau. *p* Véra Belmont. *sc* André Corbiau, Gérard Corbiau, Marcel Beaulieu. *ph* Walther Vanden Ende. *ed* Joelle Hache. *pd* Gianni Quaranta. *cast* Stéfano Dionisi, Enrico

Lo Verso, Elsa Zylberstein, Caroline Cellier, Marianne Basler, Jacques Boudet, Omero Antonutti, Jeroen Krabbe.
●Today the average opera isn't over till the diva trills her high notes, but in the 18th century the major stars were the male castrati. The film is soon ripping bodices and bunging three in a bed, allowing the angel-voiced Farinelli (Dionisi) and his composer sibling Riccardo (Lo Verso) to display their perfected love-making routine. Physiological queries thus answered, we can get on with the musical meat of a substantially true story. The castrato voice powered baroque opera through exquisite ornamentation and long-breathed melody, and here the dramatic conflict sparks between the brothers' loyalty to each other and the demanding presence of composer Handel (Krabbe) who wants to write for Farinelli, but ditch Riccardo. Corbiau's film gives convincing attention to the process of musical creation, but complicates itself with a tricksy narrative framework and an underwritten romantic subplot (Zylberstein wasted as the woman who flits between the brothers). Lavish sets and costumes make a colourful impression, the unusual material compels attention in its own way, but it's the vocal and authentic instrumental performances that raise the film momentarily towards the sublime. (The castrato voice was created by the IRCAM synthesis of soprano and countertenor voices.) TJ

Farm, The (aka The Farm: Angola, USA)

(1997, US, 91 min)
d/p Liz Garbus, Jonathan Stack. *ph* Samuel Henriques, Bob Perrin. *ed* Mona Davis, Mary Manhardt *m* Curtis Lundy. *narrator* Bernard Addison.
●Angola State Penitentiary, Louisiana, is the oldest, largest and perhaps toughest prison in the US. Given a high preponderance of lifers and a packed Death Row, more than two thirds of its inmates are going to die within its walls. The directors were granted unprecedented access to the facility, but instead of concentrating on the violence, drugs and brutal warders – the standard view of life in the pen – they choose to examine the iron mindset of prisoners who know they may never be released. How do you stay motivated when it takes ten years to get a parole hearing? How do you keep going when you've spent four decades of you life on a trumped-up charge and the State Governor can't be bothered to sign the pardon form that'll get you released? How do you have the discipline not to walk away when trustee status allows you unsupervised outside assignments? Forget Tarantino, this is where the real hard men are. TJ

Farmer's Wife, The

(1928, GB, 67 min, b/w)
d Alfred Hitchcock. *p* John Maxwell. *sc* Eliot Stannard. *ph* Jack Cox. *ed* Alfred Booth. *ad* Wilfred Arnold. *cast* Jameson Thomas, Lillian Hall-Davies, Maud Gill, Gordon Harker, Louise Pounds, Olga Slade.
●Charming comedy of rural manners, about a morose middle-aged farmer, having recently lost his wife, making inept and irascible attempts to find himself a new spouse. His final humble discovery of true love is signalled far too early in the film, but that doesn't destroy the effects of a great deal of subtle slapstick and witty caricature, especially in a marvellously sustained sequence at a tea-party.

Far North

(1988, US, 89 min)
d Sam Shepard. *p* Malcolm R Harding, Carolyn Pfeiffer. *sc* Sam Shepard. *ph* Robbie Greenberg. *ed* Bill Yahraus. *pd* Peter Jamison. *m* The Red Clay Ramblers, JA Deane. *cast* Jessica Lange, Charles Durning, Tess Harper, Donald Moffat, Ann Wedgeworth, Patricia Arquette, Nina Draxten.
●Save us from Renaissance men. Shepard writes plays, directs them, acts in plays and movies, and now wants to direct movies. Think again, Sam. This opens promisingly, with wonderfully gritty acoustic music from the Red Clay Ramblers on the soundtrack, and Durning slowly losing control of his horse and coming to grief. Cut to a big close-up of the offending beast's dark, mysterious eye. Later, the music turns synthetic and so do the emotions. Citified daughter Lange gets the job of shooting the nag ('While it still knows why' rumbles the hospitalised Durning) and returns to the homestead, somewhere near the Great Lakes. Will she do it? Or will she be prevented by her older sister (Harper) and the sister's fun-loving daughter (Arquette)? What does barmy mother (Wedgeworth) think? Will Sam lose interest in all this women's stuff and concentrate on the boring, boorish double act of Durning and his brother Moffat as they drink their way out of hospital and into the wild woods? The characters wander around emoting and shouting at one another, but saying nothing; and Shepard's cod-Eisensteinian montage effects (jump cuts between women and owls, most notably) belong in a film museum. JMo

Far Off Place, A

(1993, US, 116 min)
d Mikael Salomon. *p* Eva Monley, Elaine Sperber. *sc* Jonathan Hensleigh, Sally Robinson, Robert Caswell. *ph* Juan Ruiz-Anchia. *ed* Ray Lovejoy. *pd* Gemma Jackson. *m* James Horner. *cast* Reese Witherspoon, Ethan Randall, Jack Thompson, Sarel Bok, Maximilian Schell, Robert Burke.
●An updated but old-fashioned eco-adventure (from Laurens van der Post's *A Story Like the Wind* and *A Far Off Place*), with the accent on the adventure. Teens Witherspoon and Randall don't get on at the start but end up in love. The elements include ruthless poachers; a craggy game warden (Schell), irate at the villains for slaughtering not only elephants but the teens' parents; a wise African guide (Bok); and a trek across the Kalahari. A cameraman's directorial debut; handsome and quite sincere. AO

Farrebique

(1947, Fr, 85 min, b/w)
d Georges Rouquier. *p* Etienne Lallier. *sc* Georges Rouquier. *ph* André Dantan. *ed* Madeleine Gug. *m* Henri Sauguet.
●Shot between 1944 and '46 in the Aveyrand area of the rugged Massif Central, this documentary milestone called on three generations of a peasant family to act out their lives for the camera. It charts cycles of birth, death and work, and records the coming of electrification. The protagonists sometimes appear slightly stiff (to modern eyes), but there's compact storytelling in the way Rouquier binds our sympathies to their on-going grind, and an exquisite moment of lyricism (despite the superfluous voice-over) when stop-motion photography catches the turn of the seasons. TJ

Fast and the Furious, The

(2001, Ger/US, 107 min)
d Rob Cohen. *p* Neal H Moritz. *sc* Gary Scott Thompson, Erik Bergquist, David Ayer. *ph* Ericson Core. *ed* Peter Honess. *pd* Waldemar Kalinowski. *m* BT. *cast* Paul Walker, Vin Diesel, Michelle Rodriguez, Jordana Brewster, Rick Yune, Chad Lindberg, Johnny Strong, Matt Schulze, Ja Rule.
●A surprise hit at the US box office, Cohen's teen hotrod flick revives fond memories of Roger Corman's B-movie thrills, the kind of unpretentious drive-in fodder directors like Demme and Scorsese cut their teeth on. Walker plays Brian, the good-looking young auto-fiend who none too subtly insinuates himself into the circle of Dom Toretto (Diesel) and his street-racing gang. Brian's an undercover cop, but he has more on his mind than speeding tickets: someone's been jacking trucks in daredevil stunt-driving fashion, and Dom is suspect numero uno. The twists are well signposted. Brian finds an alternate family among the desperadoes and falls hard for Dom's sister; when the time comes to do his duty, it feels like betrayal. It doesn't matter that we know where it's going, what counts is that Cohen keeps his pedal to the floor and that his actors gun their lines with absolute conviction. Loud cars, fast music: this movie knows exactly what it's about. TCh

Fast Charlie, the Moonbeam Rider

(1978, US, 99 min)
d Steve Carver. *p* Roger Corman. *sc* Michael Gleason. *ph* Bill Birch. *ed* Tony Redman, Eric Orner. *ad* William Sandell, J Michael Riva. *m* Stu Phillips. *cast* David Carradine, Brenda Vaccaro, LQ Jones, RG Armstrong, Terry Kiser, Jesse Vint, Noble Willingham.
●Corman and Carradine teamed up again for yet another version of the coast-to-coast race with no holds barred. This time it's 1919 and motorcycles, not cars as in *Death Race 2000.* Not just a straightforward win-or-bust movie, it often goes for laughs with its miraculously injury-free carnage, and demonstrates how the scorn of a good woman can make an honest man out of free-wheelin' Charlie, ex-army dispatch rider and con-man extraordinaire. FF

Fast, Cheap & Out of Control

(1997, US, 82 min)
d/p Errol Morris. *ph* Robert Richardson. *ed* Karen Schmeer, Shondra Merril. *pd* Ted Basaloukos*m* Caleb Sampson.
●One of the finest movies of the '90s, as unforgettable as it is improbable. And it is improbable – in fact it sounds more like a gag than a putative masterpiece: Morris takes a lion tamer, a robot inventor, a topiarist and an expert on the mole rat, cutting between these self-confessed obsessives (and clips from old B serials) with a juggler's flamboyant skill. The carnivalesque score and Robert Richardson's characteristically eye-popping cinematography make it all the more disorienting. Entertaining as it is, you have to wonder how Morris can possibly draw it all together. When he does, it's on the most profound philosophical level, as the film engages with questions of what it is that distinguishes human consciousness from animal and artificial (and vegetable) varieties. Dazzling. TCh

Fast Company

(1978, Can, 92 min)
d David Cronenberg. *p* Michael Lebowitz, Peter O'Brian, Courtney Smith. *sc* Phil Savath, Courtney Smith, David Cronenberg. *ph* Mark Irwin. *ed* Ron Sanders. *ad* Carol Spier. *m* Fred Mollin. *cast* William Smith, Claudia Jennings, John Saxon, Nicholas Campbell, Cedric Smith, Judy Foster.
●Drag racing may seem an aberrant subject for the Carl Dreyer of Splatter, but the sport is the man's secret passion, and it shows. The hokey plot is strictly off the peg: when soft-hearted hairy-arse drag racers are shit-sandwiched between corrupt team manager (Saxon at his most reptilian) and the mean-minded neanderthal opposition, they come up smelling like roses. But Cronenberg's obsessive attention to the detail of preparing the machines, mixing the fuel, armour-plating the drivers and theical skills of winning, makes the track sequences enthralling. The weakness (in line with every other racetrack saga) is that once off the track, the picture hits the skids. Instead of following through the ruthless drive of the drag strip, it indulges in ill-advised sidetracks into softcore sex, gags and rock-'n'roll, a brand of exploitation the late Claudia Jennings (here in her last screen role) made her own in the likes of *Truck Stop Women.* But at the beginning, middle and end, there are still the races, staged amid the racket and the razzmatazz with Cronenberg's customary skill. AT

Faster, Pussycat! Kill! Kill!

(1965, US, 83 min, b/w)
d Russ Meyer. *p* Russ Meyer, Eve Meyer. *sc* Jack Moran. *ph* Walter Schenk. *ed* Russ Meyer. *m* Paul Sawtell, Bert Shefter. *cast* Tura Satana, Haji, Lori Williams, Susan Bernard, Stuart Lancaster, Paul Trinka.
●This shows Meyer to be a fine action director as well as America's best-known tit man. Though decorated with the usual array of top-heavy starlets – a trio of homicidal disco dancers on rest-and-recreation in the Californian desert (which means fast cars and whatever kinky thrills come their way) – it was in fact made as an exploiter for the Southern states' undemanding drive-in market. A cheap and efficient comic horror movie, it's funniest when its dialogue and characters' behaviour are at their most non sequitur. The twaddlesome plot about the cover-up of a man's murder by the (lesbian) leader of this girlie gang is helped enormously by a brooding music score which sounds as if it had walked in from a paranoid Cold War sci-fi film; and the weirdo desert farmhouse family the trio happen upon pre-dates *The Texas Chain Saw Massacre* by almost a decade. RM

Fastest Gun Alive, The

(1956, US, 88 min, b/w)
d Russell Rouse. *p* Clarence Greene. *sc* Frank D Gilroy, Russell Rouse. *ph* George Folsey. *ed* Ferris Webster, Harry V Knapp. *ad* Cedric

Gibbons, Merrill Pye. *m* André Previn. *cast* Glenn Ford, Jeanne Crain, Broderick Crawford, Russ Tamblyn, Allyn Joslyn, Leif Erickson, John Dehner, Noah Beery Jr, JM Kerrigan, Rhys Williams.

●Similar in theme to Henry King's *The Gunfighter*, this begins impressively, with Crawford riding into town to challenge a complete stranger ('They say you're faster than me') and triumphantly out-drawing him ('Get him a headstone to say he was killed by the fastest gun alive'), only to be faced by a blind man's prophetic warning ('No matter how fast you are, there's always someone faster'). Meanwhile, mild storekeeper Ford wrestles with his promise to his wife (Crain) to forget about his prowess with a gun. Unfortunately, having set up the inevitability of confrontation, the script loses its ballad-like directness, meandering through a bank robbery, taking in a dance number for Tamblyn, and providing yards of psychological explanation (Ford, afraid of guns, is obsessed with his failure to avenge his father's death; Crawford, whose wife left him for another man, is out to prove he is mucho macho). That said, the reactions of the townsfolk are detailed with some complexity, the key scenes are extremely well staged, and the performances are excellent. TM

Fast, Fast (Deprisa, Deprisa)

(1980, Sp, 98 min)
d Carlos Saura. *p* Elias Querejeta. *sc* Carlos Saura. *ph* Teo Escamilla. *ed* Pablo G del Amo. *ad* Antonio Belizon. *cast* Berta Socuéllamos Zarco, José Antonio Valdelomar, José Maria Hervas Roldan, Jesus Arias Aranzeque, Maria del Mar Serrano.

●Meandering through the suburbs of Madrid and its empty hinterlands, an episodic plot follows the sex, drugs and crime life-style of four felonious but likeable punks (played by real-life delinquents, two of whom were later apprehended for robbing banks). A teen-gang movie, and in many ways an unassuming genre piece, but mercifully free of moralising. Distinguished by an inventive soundtrack and stirring flamenco music score, and a mobile, intimate camera that follows its characters like a shadow, closely capturing not only action but reaction, ephemeral moments of camaraderie, friction and a perfidious 'freedom': fast living, leisurely observed. SJo

Fast Food

(1998, GB, 98 min)
d Stewart Sugg. *p* Phil Hunt. *sc* Stewart Sugg. *ph* Simon Reeves. *ed* Jeremy Gibbs. *pd* Katie Franklyn-Thompson. *m* Ben Lee-Delisle. *cast* Douglas Henshall, Emily Woof, Miles Anderson, Stephen Lord, Gerard Butler, Sean Hughes, David Yip.

●This moody city drama (it's clearly London but has a generic feel) sees returning telephone engineer Benny (Henshall, superb) reluctantly reacquaint himself with his gang of old pals, who are now firmly set on criminal endeavours as the only way out of dead end lives. Dragged into a nightmare of conflicting loyalties, he's torn between protecting deaf, airhead phone-sex prostitute Letitia (Woof, in a misconceived role) from her pimp and saving his old friends from themselves. Writer/director Sugg provides some sharp, witty dialogue, and manages to thrust the movie forward through the ups and downs of philosophic introspection, and uncertain, self-parodic small-time gangster scenes. Too post-modern for its own good, but often droll, and enthusiastically directed. WH

Fast Food, Fast Women

(2000, US, 96 min)
d Amos Kollek. *p* Hengameh Panahi. *sc* Amos Kollek. *ph* Jean-Marc Fabre. *ed* Sheri Bylander. *pd* Stacey Tanner. *m* David Carbonara. *cast* Anna Thomson, Jamie Harris, Robert Modica, Louise Lasser, Austin Pendleton, Victor Argo.

●In this dismally indulgent male-fantasy romantic comedy, a selection of New York Jews of various ages go through the usual troubled rites and rituals of meeting cute. At the centre, waitress Thomson dates even less appealing taxi driver Harris, and they have a misunderstanding over their respective attitudes to kids; meanwhile shy widower Modica courts widow Lasser, and curmudgeonly Argo falls for a peepshow stripper. A handful of funny lines aside, this is an awkward, reactionary and ugly movie. Henry Jaglom fans may like it; others should probably avoid. GA

Fast Forward

(1984, US, 110 min)
d Sidney Poitier. *p* John Patrick Veitch. *sc* Richard Wesley. *ph* Matthew F Leonetti. *ed* Harry Keller. *ad* Michael Baugh. *m* Tom Scott, Jack Hayes. *cast* John Scott Clough, Don Franklin, Tamara Mark, Tracy Silver, Cindy McGee, Constance Towers, Irene Worth.

●Wish fulfilment on a grandiose scale with the cotton candy saga of eight alarmingly attractive teenagers from Ohio. Convinced of their own dance talents, they storm the Big Apple, and in a mere three weeks have the rock world knocked for a loop. Poitier's direction is earnest, and the four-square camerawork comes from someone who never heard of Bob Fosse. Still, there is some high energy performing going on – notably from Franklin, a proud and sexy black who could go far. It's all too sanitised, and has nothing to do with rock reality, but it's always fun to see the underdog triumph over the moguls. AR

Fast Lady, The

(1962, GB, 95 min)
d Ken Annakin. *p* Julian Wintle, Leslie Parkyn. *sc* Jack Davies, Henry Blyth. *ph* Reginald Wyer. *ed* Ralph Sheldon. *ad* Harry Pottle. *m* Norrie Paramor. *cast* James Robertson Justice, Stanley Baxter, Leslie Phillips, Kathleen Harrison, Julie Christie, Dick Emery, Frankie Howerd, Monsewer Eddie Gray.

●Mercurial Scots TV comedian Baxter plays a cycling enthusiast determined to win the heart of roadhog Robertson Justice's daughter (Julie Christie, in her second movie, again with Baxter) by impressing her with a vintage Bentley acquired expressly for the purpose. Amiable but faddish, with Phillips in splendidly slimy form as a used car salesman. TJ

Fast Talking

(1983, Aust, 95 min)
d Ken Cameron. *p* Ross Matthews. *sc* Ken Cameron. *ph* David Gribble. *ed* David Hugget. *pd* Neil Angwin. *m* Sharon Calcraft. *cast* Rod Zuanic, Toni Allaylis, Chris Truswell, Gail Sweeny, Steve Bisley, Tracy Mann.

●Comedy about a delinquent dope-dealing 15-year-old with a quick-thinking scam for every possible occasion. Of course he's got problems, with an alcoholic father and teachers out to get him, but he always has the last laugh, until one day... The acting is superb, and Cameron makes his characters even more believable through some swift, sure touches: a teacher obsessed with gardening, a classmate with a bad line in Frank Spencer impersonations. A sharp, entertaining portrait of teenage life based around the admirable idea that there's far more to happiness and dignity than simply doing what you're told. CS.

Fast Times at Ridgemont High (aka Fast Times)

(1982, US, 92 min)
d Amy Heckerling. *p* Art Linson, Irving Azoff. *sc* Cameron Crowe. *ph* Matthew F Leonetti. *ed* Eric Jenkins. *ad* Dan Lomino. *cast* Sean Penn, Jennifer Jason Leigh, Judge Reinhold, Phoebe Cates, Brian Backer, Ray Walston.

●Although nominally based on journalist Cameron Crowe's investigative study of high school kids, this is essentially a straight sex'n'-fun exploitation movie. There's the usual array of school stereotypes (the lecher, the stoned surfer, the hustler), a rock score, and endless attention to the rituals of dating and mating. Taken purely on this level, it's a relatively witty example of its kind, with an enjoyable performance from Penn as the stoned surfer, and some good lines. But it lacks the frenzied energy which allowed *Porky's* to beat all competitors in its field. DP

Fast Trip, Long Drop

(1993, US, 54 min)
d Gregg Bordowitz. *cast* Gregg Bordowitz, Bob Huff.

●In 1988, Gregg Bordowitz, a New York video-maker, tested HIV positive, and set about making an autobiographical documentary. It's a freewheeling, funny, irate, provocative look at attitudes – his, ours, the media's – towards AIDS; at how one might 'live' with such an immediate, persistent awareness of imminent mortality. On one level, the film's 'documentary' aspects are conventional: Bordowitz speaks confessionally and straight-to-camera about his sex life and Jewish heritage, discusses his illness and his assumption of gay identity with his mother and stepfather, and mulls over the impossibility of hope with his support group. All this, however, is intercut not only with archive footage of various risky activities (car stunts, a man juggling a baby atop a skyscraper) and with sour satirical sketches featuring Borodowitz's surly Alter Allesman and various broadcasters, doctors and activists played by one Bob Huff. The resulting *mélange*, faintly reminiscent of early Makavejev, is troubled and troubling, occasionally exhilarating, and admirably honest; more surprisingly, against the odds, Bordowitz finally steers us towards some sort of gentle hope. GA

Fast-Walking

(1981, US, 115 min)
d/p/sc James B Harris. *ph* King Baggot. *ed* Douglas Stewart. *ad* Richard Y Haman. *m* Lalo Schifrin. *cast* James Woods, Tim McIntire, Kay Lenz, Robert Hooks, M Emmet Walsh, Timothy Carey, Susan Tyrrell.

●A characteristic, off-beam offering from James B Harris, a former Kubrick collaborator, this starts out as a straightforward prison movie but soon splinters into a wayward character study of morally irredeemable individuals. Woods' prison warden, 'Fast-Walking' Miniver, is up to every scam in the book, but his trade in pimping and the like is disrupted by the rumpus over the arrival of black political activist Hooks and the growing megalomania of trustee inmate McIntire. Downbeat, greasy and with a genuinely eccentric sense of humour. TJ

Fatal Attraction

see Head On

Fatal Attraction

(1987, US, 120 min)
d Adrian Lyne. *p* Stanley R Jaffe, Sherry Lansing. *sc* James Dearden. *ph* Howard Atherton. *ed* Michael Kahn, Peter E Berger. *pd* Mel Bourne. *m* Maurice Jarre. *cast* Michael Douglas, Glenn Close, Anne Archer, Ellen Hamilton Latzen, Stuart Pankin, Ellen Foley, Fred Gwynne.

●A glossy, Hitchcock-by-numbers thriller, with Douglas as a happily married New York attorney whose clandestine weekend of passion with business associate Close provokes the wrath of a woman scorned when he tries to give her the brush-off. Angered by his insensitive chauvinism, Close becomes increasingly unhinged, progressing from insistent phone calls to acid attacks on Douglas' car, and finally to physical attacks on his family. Lyne employs the same flashy imagery as in *Nine ½ Weeks*, but his overheated visual style seems curiously inappropriate to James Dearden's tepid script. The film finally comes to the boil in the brilliantly staged, crowd-pleasing finale – a nail-biting showdown between a knife-wielding Close, a frightened wife and an enraged Douglas. A predictable dog's dinner of Pavlovian thriller clichés, this will appeal strongly to those who think women should be kept on a short lead. NF

Fatal Beauty

(1987, US, 104 min)
d Tom Holland. *p* Leonard Kroll. *sc* Hilary Henkin, Dean Riesner. *ph* David M Walsh. *ed* Don Zimmerman. *pd* James William Newport. *m* Harold Faltermeyer. *cast* Whoopi Goldberg, Sam Elliott, Rubén Blades, Harris Yulin, John P Ryan, Jennifer Warren, Brad Dourif, Mike Jolly, Charles Hallahan, David Harris, Cheech Marin.

●A designed-by-committee vehicle for Whoopi Goldberg, allowing her to keep her comedy act and extend her range into territory staked out by Eddie Murphy, with risible – therefore enjoyable – results. Unorthodox undercover cops Rita Rizzoli – a Dirty Harriet with an MA in wisecracks – is a mean fatherfucker dedicated to keeping 'snow' off the streets of LA. Down in Chinatown, nude coolies are adulterating cocaine with lethal proportions of Ventonol; she figures one Conrad Kroll (Yulin) for the villain of the piece, but it takes days and nights of padding the streets in disguise – hobbling heels, leopard-skin, and Tina Turner rup – before the breaks come. Meanwhile, a trio of giggling psychopaths muscle in (Brad Douril's staring-eyed Leo Nova is a gem), and all is set for a 15-minute showdown in a shopping mall. Sam Elliott's love interest takes too long warming up, but a confused plot and plenty of poor taste leave Whoopi relatively unscathed. WH

Fatal Bond

(1991, Aust, 90 min)
d Vincent Morton. *p/sc* Phil Avalon. *ph* Ray Henman. *ed* Ted Otten. *ad* Keith Holloway. *m* Art Phillips. *cast* Linda Blair, Jerome Ehlers, Stephen Leeder, Donal Gibson, Caz Lederman, Joe Bugner.
● Blair heads down under in search of a decent part and winds up in this so-so thriller playing an American-born hairdresser who drifts across Australia with boyfriend Ehlers, and discovers too late that a trail of murders seems to follow them wherever they go. No prizes for guessing who's the next victim. TJ

Fatal Reaction: Singapore

(1996, Neth, 78 min)
d Marijke Jongbloed.
● Documentaries about dating agencies are scarcely original, but this foray into the genre (the second part of a series about the problems single women face finding suitable partners) has a novel twist: the dating agency in question is a government organisation. As we hear the ex-leader Lee Kuan Yew proclaim, Singapore needs to boost its population to compete in the world market. The director follows a handful of Singaporeans as they attend various 'dating' events, including a love cruise. Men and women have very different expectations. The grimmest, most poignant moment comes as a die-hard chauvinist, used to bullying his mother, tells the young woman he hopes to marry what he expects in terms of obedience and housework. As he gorges himself on a pizza, she breaks down in tears. GM

Fata Morgana

(1971, WGer, 78 min)
d/p/sc Werner Herzog. *ph* Jörg Schmidt-Reitwein. *ed* Beate Mainka-Jellinghaus.
● Herzog's completely non-narrative movie is cast in the mock-heroic form of an epic poem, each of its chapter headings ('Creation', 'Paradise', 'The Golden Age') being more ironic than the one before. Shot in and around the Sahara, its images evoke the idea of the desert as a terminal beach, littered with colonial debris, spanning extremes of poverty and misery, peopled with the dispossessed and the eccentric, haunted by mirages. It's the nearest thing yet to a genuine political science-fiction movie. Brilliantly original, utterly haunting. TR

Fat City

(1972, US, 96 min)
d John Huston. *p* Ray Stark. *sc* Leonard Gardner. *ph* Conrad Hall. *ed* Margaret Booth. *pd* Richard Sylbert. *m* Marvin Hamlisch. *cast* Stacy Keach, Jeff Bridges, Susan Tyrrell, Candy Clark, Nicholas Colasanto, Art Aragon.
● Marvellous, grimly downbeat study of desperate lives and the escape routes people construct for themselves, stunningly shot by Conrad Hall. The setting is Stockton, California, a dreary wasteland of smoky bars and sunbleached streets where the lives of two boxers briefly meet, one on the way up, one on the way down. Neither, you sense instantly, for all their talk of past successes and future glories, will ever know any other world than the back-street gymnasiums and cheap boxing-rings where battered trainers and managers exchange confidences about their ailments, disappointments and dreams, and where in a sad and sobering climax two sick men beat each other half to death for a few dollars and a pint of glory. Huston directs with the same puritanical rigour he brought to *Wise Blood*. Beautifully summed up by Paul Taylor as a 'masterpiece of skid row poetry'. TM

Fate (Verhängnis)

(1994, Ger, 76 min)
d Fred Kelemen. *p* Christian Hohoff. *sc* Fred Kelemen. *ph* Fred Kelemen, Ann-Katrin Schaffner. *ed* Fred Kelemen. *cast* Sanja Spengler, Valerij Fedorenko.
● The title is grimly apt: Fred Kelemen's is a stark, singular, often oppressively determined cinema. Susan Sontag, among others, has lauded the film as a rare example of modern visionary film-making, comparing the director with the likes of Alexandr Sokurov. *Fate* is a vision of a *mittel*-European neo-Dark Age – a life of filth, squalor and desperation, cheaply blown up from video, giving it the same corrupted, grimy hue Thomas Vinterberg exploited for *Festen*'s dark night of the soul. Here, though, without any allusive or reflective wherewithal, the stripped down, unremittingly bleak narrative – following first a man, then his woman, through a nocturnal waste of alcoholic and sexual violence and alienation – seems just so much tendentious angst, hollow high-browbeating from a Pained Artist. NB

Fate of Lee Khan, The (Ying-chun-ge zhi Fengbo)

(1973, HK, 105 min)
d/p King Hu. *sc* King Hu, Wang Chung. *ph* Chen Chao-Yung. *ed* Liang Yung Tsan. *m* Joseph Ku. *cast* Li Li Hua, Angela Mao, Hsu Feng, Hu Chin, Tien Feng, Pai Ying.
● *The Fate of Lee Khan* is to the Chinese martial arts movie what *Once Upon a Time in the West* in to the Italian Western: a brilliant anthology of its genre's theme and styles, yielding an exhilaratingly original vision. It's set in the Yuan Dynasty, when China was under Mongol rule, and centres on the efforts of a band of Chinese patriots (mostly women) to retrieve a map that has fallen into the hands of Mongol baron Lee Khan. A lighthearted exposition (especially witty in its handling of the sexual politics) leads up to a tense stalemate, with the patriots posing as manager and staff of an inn where their enemy is lodging, but unable to follow through their original plan. King Hu's mastery of pace, humour, colour and design makes most other movies around look tatty. TR

Father

(1990, Aust, 100 min)
d John Power. *p* Damien Parer, Tony Cavanaugh, Paul Barron. *sc* Tony Cavanaugh, Graham Hartley. *ph* Dan Burstall. *ed* Kerry Regan. *pd* Phil Peters. *m* Peter Best. *cast* Max Von Sydow, Carole Drinkwater, Julia Blake, Steve Jacobs, Tim Robertson.
● Drinkwater's world is upended when her elderly father, Von Sydow, is identified as a concentration camp functionary by Holocaust survivor Blake. The difficult material needed firmer handling than it gets here, however, for the film fudges the central issue of Von Sydow's culpability and turns the victim of injustice into a batty neurotic scheming for revenge. (See also Costa-Gavras' *Music Box*, 1989.) TJ

Father (Baba)

(1996, China, 96 min)
d Wang Shuo, Lao Yun. *p* Han Sanping, Wang Weijing. *sc* Wang Shuo, Feng Xiaogang. *ph* Yang Xiaoxiong. *ed* Zhou Ying. *ad* Feng Xiaogang. *m* Shi Wanchun. *cast* Feng Xiaogang, Hu Xiaopei, Xu Fan, Qin Yan, Wang Weining.
● 'Bad-boy' novelist Wang Shuo ran headlong into the brick wall of Film Bureau censorship with this adaptation of his own 1991 novel *I'm Your Dad*. The film was not seen anywhere until an English subtitled print was smuggled to Europe in 2000 for festival screenings. Ma Linsheng (Feng, also the co-writer and designer) is a minor Party functionary, a recent widower sharing his old Beijing courtyard apartment with his schoolboy son Ma Che (Hu). The first hour explores the generation gap, attitude gap and emotional tensions between father and son with a fair degree of wit and sympathy for both sides. But everything falls apart after the boy pushes his father into a second marriage. The film loses touch with recognisable realities and lapses into over-heated rhetoric and fantasy. Still, some of the satire bites. TR

Father, The (Fadern)

(1969, Swe, 100 min)
d/sc Alf Sjöberg. *ph* Lasse Björne. *ed* Wic Kjellin. *ad* Bib Lindström. *m* Torbjörn Lundqvist. *cast* Georg Rydeberg, Gunnel Lindblom, Lena Nyman, Jan-Olof Strandberg, Tord Stål, Sif Ruud, Axel Düberg.
● A battle between a retired army captain and his wife for dominance and possession of their only daughter ends in madness and death. The dice are probably loaded from the start in Strindberg's play, but a rather too engaging Rydeberg, as the father, isolates the much stronger performance of the wife to a point where the conflict does not mesh, and at the end emerges as more melodramatic than tragic. Matters aren't helped by some curious technical effects altogether more appropriate to Disney (writing appears as if by magic on a page), along with obtrusive and often unnecessary use of flashback. Too often the attempts to find a visual metaphor for Strindberg's imagery are so literal (hallucinatory sequences to illustrate the captain's madness) that they must detract from the original. A pity that Sjöberg didn't extend his treatment of the background to the central drama. There he successfully portrays a twilight world of sombre colours, full of eavesdroppers, a world where the central drama is played out in front of, and constantly interrupted and inhibited by, servants who say nothing but know everything. Straight theatre, in other words. CPe

Father, The (Pedar)

(1996, Iran, 92 min)
d Majid Majidi. *sc* Mehdi Shojai, Majid Majidi. *ph* Mohsen Zolanvar. *ed* Hassan Hassandoost. *pd* Behzad Kazazi. *m* Mohammed-Reza Aligholi. *cast* Mohammad Kasebi, Parivash Nazarieh, Hassan Sadeghi, Hossein Abedini.
● 'I know of no other world than a child's world,' director Majid Majidi has said. 'A small and simple world, yet vast and magnificent. Blue like the sky, clear like the river, and upright like the mountains.' This statement captures Majidi's style: its child-like directness sidesteps naivety to achieve singular emotional clarity. Following the death of his father, a 14-year-old Iranian boy, Mehrollah (Sadeghi), travels south to find work, returning later to find that the local policeman is now a domineering presence in his mother's house. Fleeing from his occupied home, he's pursued and caught by his new father, but the journey back is longer and harder than either of them could have imagined. NF

Father and Son (Fuzi Qing)

(1981, HK, 96 min)
d Allen Fong. *p* Wong Kai-Chuen. *sc* Chan Chiu, Lilian Lee, Cheung Kin-Ting. *ph* Patrick Wong. *ed* Sammy Chow. *ad* Wong Kwai-Ping, Wong Hok-Sun. *m* Violet Lam. *cast* Shek Lui, Lee Yu-Tin, Cheng Yu-Or, Chan Sun, Leslie Cheung, Kung Yee.
● A boy from a poor family struggles to survive in a shanty town suburb of Hong Kong, clashing with his father and with a society that denies him almost every opportunity to realise his dream of making movies. The boy is an autobiographical portrait by Fong, who finally broke into film, making martial arts adventures for Hong Kong Television. Even then, when he went independent, he had to hassle with producers to get the freedom to make this personal film, which satirises the traditional Chinese notion of self-improvement through education. Warmly understated in its central performances, it's replete with humour and sympathy for the father as much as for the son. MA

Father Brown

(1954, GB, 91 min, b/w)
d Robert Hamer. *p* Vivian A Cox. *sc* Thelma Schnee, Robert Hamer. *ph* Harry Waxman. *ed* Gordon Hales. *ad* John Hawkesworth. *m* Georges Auric. *cast* Alec Guinness, Peter Finch, Joan Greenwood, Cecil Parker, Bernard Lee, Sidney James, Ernest Thesiger.
● Far from Hamer at his best, but still a stylishly civilised comedy thriller, with an engagingly sly (if occasionally too ingratiating) performance from Guinness as GK Chesterton's sleuthing priest, here calmly countering the suave criminal mastermind Flambeau (played by Finch with a fine touch of sardonic melancholy) in his attempt to purloin the priceless Cross of St Augustine. One of the most attractive things about the film is the way Hamer manages to update the story to a contemporary setting without losing any of its quintessential period flavour. Basically the performances are the thing, although there are two outstanding sequences: the Hitchcockian auction set up as a trap for Flambeau, and the delightfully eccentric encounter between Father Brown and the ancient Vicomte de Verdigris (Thesiger), a veritable ballet of misadventures which ends in two sets of broken spectacles. TM

Father Goose

(1964, US, 116 min)
d Ralph Nelson. *p* Robert Arthur. *sc* Peter Stone, Frank Tarloff. *ph* Charles Lang Jr. *ed* Ted J Kent. *ad* Alexander Golitzen, Henry Bumstead. *m* Cy Coleman. *cast* Cary Grant, Leslie Caron, Trevor Howard, Jack Good, Stephanie Berrington, Jennifer Berrington.
●It's a shame that Grant, one of the finest actors ever to grace a cinema screen, should have logged this sentimental claptrap as his penultimate film. He plays an irascible South Pacific beachcomber who becomes a military observer for the island during World War II, and finds his independence softened by a French schoolmarm and her seven cloyingly sweet girl pupils. Admittedly, Grant frequently looks as if he really didn't want to be there, wading lost in a sludge of turgid drama and pallid comedy. GA

Fatherland

(1986, GB/WGer/Fr, 107 min)
d Kenneth Loach. *p* Raymond Day. *sc* Trevor Griffiths. *ph* Chris Menges. *ed* Jonathan Morris. *pd* Martin Johnson. *m* Christian Kunert, Gerulf Pannach. *cast* Gerulf Pannach, Fabienne Babe, Cristine Rose, Sigfrit Steiner, Robert Dietl, Heike Schrotter.
●An intriguing departure for Loach, scripted by Trevor Griffiths, this concerns the voluntary exile of an East German Liedermacher (a kind of radical singer/songwriter) to West Berlin, where his worst fears are confirmed: he has swopped intimidation and censorship for the kind of 'repressive tolerance' that only American record executives and progressive GDR capitalists can convey in all its seductive horror. So far, so good. Superbly composed and cleverly paced, this story of one man's unillusioned exile gives way to a second half in which a thriller-style subplot concerning the singer's vanished father (tracked down to England) takes over, but fails to match the tension and interest of what has gone before. A flawed but always stimulating and intelligent film, with fine performances from Pannach (debuting as the exile) and Steiner (as his father). SGr

Father of the Bride

(1950, US, 93 min. b/w)
d Vincente Minnelli. *p* Pandro S Berman. *sc* Albert Hackett, Frances Goodrich. *ph* John Alton. *ed* Ferris Webster. *ad* Cedric Gibbons, Leonard Vazian. *m* Adolph Deutsch. *cast* Spencer Tracy, Joan Bennett, Elizabeth Taylor, Don Taylor, Billie Burke, Leo G Carroll.
●Thoroughly enchanting comedy about the trials and tribulations a middle-aged family man faces when the daughter he dotes on decides to get married. As one might expect, Tracy is superb, and while the film is never as impressive as Minnelli's all-out melodramas (*Some Came Running*, *Two Weeks in Another Town*), it's still fascinating for the rather bleak undercurrents coursing beneath the many laughs: the father's problems are engendered by his own jealousy, insecurity and fears about getting old. A less effective sequel, *Father's Little Dividend* (1951), had Tracy facing the trial of becoming a grandfather. GA

Father of the Bride

(1991, US, 105 min)
d Charles Shyer. *p* Nancy Meyers, Carol Baum, Howard Rosenman. *sc* Frances Goodrich, Albert Hackett, Nancy Meyers, Charles Shyer. *ph* John Lindley. *ed* Richard Marks. *pd* Sandy Veneziano. *m* Alan Silvestri. *cast* Steve Martin, Diane Keaton, Kimberley Williams, Kieran Culkin, George Newborn, Martin Short, BD Wong, Peter Michael Goetz.
●Minnelli's 1950 comedy about wedding-day horrors is updated for the '90s, but is tamer stuff than the original. Co-writer/co-producer Nancy Meyers and co-writer/director Shyer go for broad laughs; the closest they come to recreating Minnelli's dark, disturbing nightmare sequence is a scene in which the bride's father fantasises about a cut-price reception. Martin is the harassed dad, wrestling with ever-escalating costs and rapidly diminishing pride; mom (Keaton) is the voice of moderation. Some sequences and dialogue are lifted directly from the original, but in the wider context, this merely serves to underline the remake's comparative lack of tenderness and subtlety. CM

Father of the Bride Part II

(1995, US, 106 min)
d Charles Shyer. *p/sc* Charles Shyer, Nancy Meyers. *ph* William A Fraker. *ed* Stephen A Rotter. *pd* Linda DeScenna. *m* Alan Silvestri. *cast* Steve Martin, Diane Keaton, Kimberly Williams, Martin Short, George Newbern, Kieran Culkin.
●Having scored an unexpected hit with their bland update of the Minnelli classic *Father of the Bride* (1950), the production team of Charles Shyer and Nancy Meyers knew where to go for inspiration for the sequel: *Father's Little Dividend* (1951), wherein pa becomes a granddaddy. The result's a collection of feelgood clichés advertising the benefits of a massive house, children and grandchildren, beige furnishings and a racing green sportster. The narrative has to conjure up obstacles to Martin's happiness (a nastily caricatured Arab buys the family nest, then spouse Keaton and daughter Williams fall pregnant at the same time) before resolving them all in a multiple-childbirth finale. Martin has nothing to work with, and mugs away thoughtlessly; Keaton strains credibility in the cushion-up-the-jumper role; while the ill-used Short is the family's design adviser, an egregious camp stereotype, vowel-strangler and master of Viennese frippery. Very unexciting. TJ

Fathers' Day

(1997, US, 99 min)
d Ivan Reitman. *p* Joel Silver, Ivan Reitman. *sc* Lowell Ganz, Babaloo Mandel. *ph* Stephen H Burum. *ed* Sheldon Kahn, Wendy Greene Bricmont. *pd* Tom Sanders. *m* James Newton Howard. *cast* Robin Williams, Billy Crystal, Julia Louis-Dreyfus, Nastassja Kinski, Charlie Hofheimer, Patti D'Arbanville, Jared Harris, Mel Gibson.
●Kinski's teenage son runs away from home in LA, after yet another row with dad. She calls old boyfriend Crystal, informs him he has a son, and suggests he go find the kid. Then she calls old boyfriend Williams, and informs him that he has a son, etc. Crystal's the relatively straight guy, a self-centred lawyer with a taste for time-saving social shortcuts, Williams – somewhat restrained – his goofier accomplice, a wimpy failed writer who flaps and emotes. Writers Ganz and Mandell (*Parenthood*, *City Slickers*) go pleasingly light on the syrup and sentimentality. A remake of Francis Verber's *Les Compères* (1983). NB

Father-to-Be

see Jag Är Med Barn

Fathom

(1967, GB, 99 min)
d Leslie Martinson. *p* John Kohn. *sc* Lorenzo Semple Jr. *ph* Douglas Slocombe. *ed* Max Benedict. *ad* Maurice Carter. *m* John Dankworth. *cast* Tony Franciosa, Raquel Welch, Ronald Fraser, Greta Chi, Richard Briers, Clive Revill, Tom Adams.
●Raquel Welch as an amateur sky-diver who turns Modesty Blaise to recover a missing nuclear device which isn't what it seems. The mind boggles, but she is really sweet and funny in an 007 parody which maintains a remarkably light touch, and also offers the admirable Revill as a sinister, fish-blooded villain. Low on surprises, but strong on sunny good humour. TM

Fatma

(2001, Tun/Fr, 124 min)
d Khaled Ghorbal. *p* Lofti Layouni, Francine Jean-Baptiste. *sc* Khaled Ghorbal. *ph* Jean-Luc L'Huillier. *ed* Andrée Davanture. *m* Foued Ghorbal. *cast* Awatef Jendoubi, Nabila Guider, Bagdadi Aoum, Amel Afta.
●After Fatma, aged 17, is assaulted by her cousin, off-camera in the opening scenes, writer/director Ghorbal explores the implications of rape in modern Tunisian society. Pressured into angry silence, Fatma (Jendoubi) goes on to study at Tunis University (not without a struggle) and then teaches in a village primary school, where she meets a young doctor. Their marriage is to prove her entrance into the educated middle-classes. Ghorbal places emphasis on modernity and liberality to highlight the universal pertinence of this deep, often hidden social problem, ably dramatising the selfishness and self-serving which sexism allows. Though the script is schematic, the performances and direction are lucid, balanced and effective. WH

Fat Man and Little Boy (aka Shadow Makers)

(1989, US, 127 min)
d Roland Joffé. *p* Tony Garnett. *sc* Bruce Robinson, Roland Joffé. *ph* Vilmos Zsigmond. *ed* Françoise Bonnot. *pd* Gregg Fonseca. *m* Ennio Morricone. *cast* Paul Newman, Dwight Schultz, Bonnie Bedelia, John Cusack, Laura Dern, Ron Frazier, John McGinley, Natasha Richardson, Ron Vawter.
●Co-scripted by Bruce Robinson, Joffé's film explores the wartime race between America and Germany to develop the atom bomb. Even when it transpires that the enemy is not seriously beavering away on such a project, the American military, under the guidance of General Groves (Newman) continue with development. J Robert Oppenheimer (Schultz) is the tortured genius heading the project, his public litany about scientific objectivity at odds with private agony over ethics. Groves and Oppenheimer strike an uneasy pact of sorts; their conflict makes the moral issues manifest and is well played. Other characters, however, remain half-realised and functional: Oppenheimer's neglected wife (Bedelia) and mistress (Richardson); an idealistic young physicist (Cusack) and his nurse girlfriend (Dern). On one level, the film compels through force of intellect, but ultimately it lacks the cohesive emotional force, the ferocity, to consistently nurture its conviction over two hours. CM

Fat World (Fette Welt)

(1998, Ger, 90 min)
d Jan Schütte. *p* Gerhard Hegele, Andreas Bareiss, Hanno Huth. *sc* Jan Schütte, Klaus Richter. *ph* Thomas Plenert. *ed* Renate Merck.*cast* Jürgen Vogel, Stefan Dietrich, Julia Filimonow, Sibylle Canonica, Lars Rudolph, Thomas Thieme, Ursula Strätz.
●A sympathetic portrait of the Munich homeless, from a novel by Helmut Krausser. Taciturn, permanently pissed but basically 'together' Hagen (Vogel, excellent) shares an abandoned urine-filled concrete building with a gallery of drifters, druggies, alkies and the emotionally vulnerable. He finds some kind of redemption through his slowly burgeoning love for a 15-year-old Berlin runaway (Filimonov), despite the intervention of the police. Keeping stylisation to a minimum (he's evidently beguiled by realist absurdity), Schütte charts a confident course between the destructive rocks of indulgent gutter poetry and mawkish care-junkie semi-documentaryism. Softer emotionally, but as intelligent and observant, this encouraging, involving drama comes close to the class of MacKinnon's *The Grass Arena*. WH

Faust

(1926, Ger, 7,875 ft, b/w)
d FW Murnau. *sc* Hans Kyser. *ph* Carl Hoffmann. *ad* Walter Rohrig, Robert Herlth. *cast* Emil Jannings, Gösta Ekman, Camilla Horn, Wilhelm Dieterle, Yvette Guilbert, Frieda Ricard.
●Murnau's version of the story of the man who sold his soul to the Devil (Jannings) in return for youth is visually extraordinary but dismally uneven in terms of its dramatic effect. Certainly, its opening scenes (the prologue between an Angel and Satan, and the temptation of Faust, after which Mephistopheles takes him on an astonishing, beautiful journey through the skies) easily hold the attention, but a long, tedious central section, portraying in farcical detail Faust's courtship of Marguerite, sits awkwardly with what has preceded it. The finale finds Murnau returning to form, but too late: one is left merely marvelling at the way he and cameraman Carl Hoffman have imitated the old Dutch, German and Italian masters, and the German romanticists. GA

Faust (Lekce Faust)

(1994, Czech Rep/Fr, 87 min)
d Jan Svankmajer. *p* Jaromír Kallista. *sc* Jan Svankmajer. *ph* Svatopluk Maly. *ed* Marie Zemanova, Alan Brett. *cast* Peter Cepek, Jiri Suchy, Antonin Zacpal; voices: Andrew Sachs, Jan Kraus, Vladimir Kudla.
●Opening in a determinedly familiar contemporary milieu – a man emerging from a crowded Prague subway is handed a map – this film by the Czech surrealist Jan Svankmajer soon moves into stranger, darker territory. The man visits the

spot on the map marked 'X' – a courtyard and a theatre dressing-room complete with costumes, make-up and a copy of Goethe's *Faust*. Reading the book, he becomes embroiled in a world of obscure spells, alchemy and deals with the Devil. On to this the director grafts a wealth of themes, motifs, allusions and gags, his method an expertly executed, profoundly imaginative combination of live action, claymation, puppet theatre, stop-motion animation and special effects. There are a couple of dramatically flat moments, when one feels Svankmajer hasn't quite got the measure of the feature-length narrative, but for the most part this is a film which galvanises the mind and astonishes the eye. In a word, magic. GA

Fausto

(1992, Fr, 82 min)
d Rémy Duchemin. *p* Joël Foulon, Daniel Daujon. *sc* Richard Morgiève, Rémy Duchemin. *ph* Yves Lafaye. *ed* Marilyne Monthieux. *m* Denis Barbier. *cast* Jean Yanne, Ken Higelin, Florence Darel, François Hauteserre, Maurice Bénichou, Bruce Myers.
● Teenage orphan Fausto Barbarico (Higelin) gets a gig as an apprentice tailor with old-school tradesman Mietek (Yanne). Under his mentor's guidance and support, Fausto lets his imagination run free on a series of fantastical couture designs that bring him fame and fortune, cement his relationship with flatulent pal Raymond (Hauteserre), and win the heart of winsome lass Tonie (Darel). And that's pretty much it. Just when you're ready for some conflict to rear its head and give the narrative some ballast, up come the credits and you're out in the street again pondering the undeniable but slight charm of a movie that dares to be so cheerily wistful. Fausto's creations are fun at the time, and Yanne does a really warm turn as the hunchback bespoke tailor learning to change his ways. But there's just so little to it; only the most desperate fantasist could be borne away on the gossamer wings of this fixed smile fairy-tale. TJ

Fausto 5.0

(2001, Sp, 93 min)
d Isidro Ortíz, Alex Ollé, Carlos Padrissa. *p* Ramón Vidal, Eduardo Campoy. *sc* Fernado León De Aranda. *ph* Pedro Del Rey. *ed* Manuel J Frasquiel. *pd* Leo Casamitjana. *m* Josep M Sanou, Toni Mir. *cast* Miguel Ángel Solá, Eduard Fernández, Najwa Nimri, Juan Fernández, Raquel González, Irene Montalá.
● This modern-day Spanish re-working of Goethe's *Faust* is the final part of a Faustian trilogy which also includes a play and an opera. Miguel Ángel Solá is Fausto, a brilliant but mentally unstable doctor whose speciality is saving terminal cases. He's a cold and vain man whose emotional life seems to have frozen. Santos Vella (Fernández), the ex-patient he meets (seemingly by chance) while at a medical conference in a far-away town, is gregarious, even aggressively friendly. At its best, this is eerie and ingenious, with an undertow of macabre humour. Shot in desaturated colours, it makes conventional cityscapes appear threatening. As Fausto's sanity begins to crack, he sees evil everywhere. Even the little old lady sitting next him on a train is not to be trusted. The three directors who collaborated on the film delight in such an arrogant and self-obsessed man's fall from grace. The one grating note is struck by Santos Vella himself. Bearded, grinning, gaudily dressed, he looks more like an egregious 1970s DJ than the incarnation of evil. GM

Faustrecht der Freiheit (Fox/Fox and His Friends)

(1975, WGer, 123 min)
d/p Rainer Werner Fassbinder. *sc* Rainer Werner Fassbinder, Christian Hohoff. *ph* Michael Ballhaus. *ed* Thea Eymesz. *ad* Kurt Raab. *m* Peer Raben. *cast* Rainer Werner Fassbinder, Peter Chatel, Karl-Heinz Böhm, Harry Bär, Adrian Hoven, Ulla Jacobsen, Kurt Raab.
● One of Fassbinder's excellent melodramas focusing on the manipulation and destruction of a working-class victim-figure, in this case a surly fairground worker who is taken up by effete bourgeois gays when he wins a small fortune on a lottery. It's the usual vision of exploitation and complicity hidden under the deceiving mantle of love, but Fassbinder's precision, assured sense of milieu, and cool but human compassion for his characters, make it a work of brilliant intelligence. And the director himself is superb as the none-too-intelligent hero. GA

Faute à Voltaire, La (Blame It on Voltaire)

(2000, Fr, 130 min)
d Abdellatif Kechiche. *p* Jean-François Lepetit. *sc* Abdellatif Kechiche. *ph* Dominique Brenguier, Marie-Emmanuelle Spencer. *ed* Annick Baly, Tina Baz-Legal, Amina Mazani. *pd* Quentin Prévost. *ad* Catherine D'Halluin. *cast* Sami Bouajla, Elodie Bouchez, Bruno Lochet, Aure Atika, Virginie Darmon, Olivier Loustau, François Gentry, Sami Zitouni.
● A touch too long, perhaps, but otherwise this account of the experiences of a young North African illegal immigrant in Paris is a very impressive first feature. Dealing with authorities suspicious about his papers, poverty, unemployment, racism, and a couple of tempestuous relationships – the first with a single mum wary of men, the second with an emotionally unstable obsessive (Bouchez in mannered but finally very affecting form) – he struggles to survive in a land that often pays mere lip service to Voltaire's ideals. The acting is great, the gritty social realism compelling but mercifully peppered with humour and vibrant energy, the whole all too credible. GA

Faute de l'Abbé Mouret, La (The Sin of Father Mouret)

(1970, Fr/It, 93 min)
d Georges Franju. *p* Véra Belmont. *sc* Jean Ferry, Georges Franju. *ph* Marcel Fradetal. *ed* Gilbert Natot. *ad* Théo Meurisse. *m* Jean Wiener. *cast* Francis Huster, Gillian Hills, Tino Carrero, André Lacombe, Margo Lion, Lucien Barjon.
● An adaptation of Zola's novel by one of the world's most idiosyncratic and fascinating directors. As always, Franju finds fantasy and surreal images in the everyday world, and taking a 'naturalistic' anti-clerical novel – in which a young priest, obsessed with the Madonna, is led to a far more openly physical passion for a young girl – he creates an amoral, poetic vision of a world where religious dogma and fanaticism are imbued with a sense of Gothic expressionism. Faithful to Zola, the film is nevertheless recognisably a creation of Franju: beautiful, bizarre and lucid. GA

Faute de Soleil (For Want of Sun)

(1995, Fr, 57 min)
d Christophe Blanc. *cast* Jean-Jacques Benhamou, Sarah Hazaire.
● When lonely Lucie makes her debut dancing at a strip joint, she meets and falls for Jean, brother of the show's compere. Trouble is, he's blind from an accident, and given to drunken binges, bitter self-pity and fits of rage. A bleak variation on the meeting-cute theme, with an accent on the roles played by need and acceptance in the development of love. Downbeat, but the performances punch home. GA

Favourites of the Moon (Les Favoris de la Lune)

(1984, Fr, 102 min)
d Otar Iosseliani. *p* Philippe Dussart. *sc* Otar Iosseliani, Gérard Brach. *ph* Philippe Theaudière. *ed* Dominique Bellfort. *pd* Claude Sune. *m* Nicolas Zourabichvili. *cast* Katia Rupe, Hans Peter Cloos, Alix De Montaigu, Maïté Nahyr, François Michel.
● The lunatic dance which constitutes the action need trouble no one who remembers the pool-table ploy of *Nashville* by which an endless supply of characters are cannoned off each other. More difficult is the remoteness and enigma which mark many of the episodes; the moods are fragile and often shifting. The tale woven by the crossing paths of these thieves and lovers may be about the way that, as the price of a work of art increases, so art itself is devalued, but this is pursued tenuously, allowing many crazed asides. What unifies the episodes is a patient moral scourging of our greed and futile desires; but where the British would use satire, this opts for the French form of Tatiesque anarchy and fun. And fun it certainly is. CPea

Favour, the Watch and the Very Big Fish, The (Rue Saint-Sulpice)

(1991, Fr/GB, 89 min)
d Ben Lewin. *p* Michelle de Broca. *sc* Ben Lewin. *ph* Bernard Zitzermann. *ed* John Grover. *pd* Carlos Conti. *m* Vladimir Cosma. *cast* Bob Hoskins, Jeff Goldblum, Natasha Richardson, Michel Blanc, Jacques Villeret, Angela Pleasence, Jean-Pierre Cassel.
● Louis (Hoskins) earns his crust photographing devotional pictures in Paris, but his tyrannical boss (Blanc) has threatened the sack unless he can find the perfect model for Christ. All appears lost until he meets actress Sybil (Richardson), who sweeps him off his feet and straight into her muddled life: she's traumatised by an abortive affair with a grumpy pianist (Goldblum), who attempted to set fire to the last rival for her affections. Now released from prison, he's a changed man – morose, vengeful, and a dead ringer for Christ. Based on a Marcel Aymé short story, this 'surreal romantic comedy' stretches its ideas too far. Writer-director Lewin heightens language and gesture until the central relationship is rendered absurd; Goldblum broods menacingly and deludes himself that he really is Christ. The effect is dislocating. CM

Fear (La Paura)

(1954, It/WGer, 81 min, b/w)
d Roberto Rossellini. *sc* Franz Treuberg, Sergio Amidei. *ph* Carlo Carlini, Heinz Schnackertz. *ed* Jolanda Benvenuti, Walter Boos. *m* Renzo Rossellini. *cast* Ingrid Bergman, Mathias Wiedman, Renate Manhardt, Kurt Kreuger, Elise Aulinger.
● Pretty much passed over at the time, Rossellini's Bergman films are now being touted, not always too convincingly, as supremely personal masterpieces. This one, the last in the series, has a fine central idea: a woman, driven to infidelity and then suicidal angst by her husband's hostility, is viewed as yet another victim of his vivisectional experiments. But the sense of moral preachment that so often marred Rossellini's work remains inescapable. TM

Fear

(1989, US, 95 min)
d/sc Rockne S O'Bannon. *ph* Robert Stevens. *ed* Ket Beyda. *pd* Joseph Nemec III. *m* Henry Mancini. *cast* Ally Sheedy, Pruitt Taylor Vince, Lauren Hutton, Michael O'Keefe, Stan Shaw, Dina Merrill, Keone Young, John Agar.
● Despite its attention-grabbing opening and intriguing central conceit – a psychic 'detective' capable of entering the minds of serial killers – this erratic thriller never lives up to its initial promise. Egged on by her manager (Hutton), successful author and media celebrity Cayce Bridges (Sheedy) teams up with a pair of sceptical LA detectives to track down a ruthless murderer. She soon realises, however, that the Shadow Man (Vince) has tuned into her psychic wavelength and is drawing her into his sick scenario, not only by forcing her to see through his eyes but by sending her telepathic messages. One or two scenes do achieve a genuine *frisson*. But a poorly integrated romance with a hunky neighbour (O'Keefe) serves only to introduce tedious red herrings, and eventually the unsettling switchback logic of the early scenes gives way to the cheap thrills of a fairground finale. NF

Fear

(1996, US, 97 min)
d James Foley. *p* Brian Grazer, Ric Kidney. *sc* Christopher Crowe. *ph* Thomas Kloss. *ed* David Brenner. *pd* Alex McDowell. *m* Carter Burwell. *cast* Mark Wahlberg, Reese Witherspoon, William Petersen, Amy Brenneman, Alyssa Milano.
● A replay of *Cape Fear* for a teenage audience. Wahlberg takes the De Niro role seducing both the virginal 16-year-old Nicole (Witherspoon), and, at least metaphorically, her stepmother (Brenneman). He's a charmer on the surface, but big trouble underneath, as Nicole's father (Petersen) quickly recognises. Trying to keep them apart, he only makes things much, much worse. The film, set in Seattle, begins very gloomily and ends well off the rails in *Straw Dogs* territory. There's just enough play on the idea of paternal jealousy to merit the term 'subtext', but

the text itself is hackneyed, and the invitation to take this macho pissing contest seriously is all too resistible. TCh

Fear and Loathing in Las Vegas

(1998, US, 118 min)
d Terry Gilliam. *p* Leila Nabulsi. Patrick Casavetti, Stephen Nemeth. *sc* Terry Gilliam, Tony Grisoni, Tod Davies, Alex Cox. *ph* Nicola Pecorini. *ed* Lesley Walker. *pd* Alex McDowell. *m* Ray Cooper. *cast* Johnny Depp, Benicio Del Toro, Christina Ricci, Ellen Barkin, Cameron Diaz, Gary Busey, Harry Dean Stanton.

●Everyone tries so hard at getting this adaptation of Hunter S Thompson's gonzo classic just right that one would love to like it more. Certainly, Gilliam pulls out the stops with the hallucinatory madness – the film does at least look good – and Depp and Del Toro, as the drug deranged heroes exploring the darkest excesses of the American Dream in 1971 Vegas, give their energetic all. The trouble is, they end up mugging like mad, and it's all too relentlessly weird, wacky and tacky: it takes an hour before the pace calms down sufficiently to let in a few laughs, and only Barkin, in a brief (and superior) scene towards the end anchors the manic antics in some sort of human reality. A film of brilliant moments, but sadly less coherent – and, on senses, rather less personal – than most of Gilliam's work. GA

Fear Eats the Soul (Angst essen Seele auf)

(1973, WGer, 92 min)
d Rainer Werner Fassbinder. *p* Christian Hohoff. *sc* Rainer Werner Fassbinder. *ph* Jürgen Jürges. *ed* Thea Eymesz. *pd* Rainer Werner Fassbinder. *cast* Brigitte Mira, El Hedi Ben Salem, Barbara Valentin, Irm Hermann, Rainer Werner Fassbinder, Karl Scheydt.

●A deceptively simple tale of the doomed love affair between an ageing cleaner (Mira) and a young Moroccan *gastarbeiter* (immigrant worker) which exposes the racial prejudice and moral hypocrisy at the heart of modern West German society. Drawing upon the conventions of Hollywood melodrama (the film has many similarities to Douglas Sirk's *All That Heaven Allows*), Fassbinder uses dramatic and visual excess to push everyday events to extremes, achieving a degree of political and psychological truth not accessible through mere social realism. Watch for Fassbinder himself as the reptilian son-in-law, and relish the scene in which Mira's son kicks in the television to demonstrate his disgust at the idea of her marrying an Arab. NF

Fear in the Night

(1947, US, 72 min, b/w)
d Maxwell Shane. *p* William H Pine, William C Thomas. *sc* Maxwell Shane. *ph* Jack Greenhalgh. *ed* Howard Smith. *ad* F Paul Sylos. *m* Rudy Schrager. *cast* DeForest Kelley, Paul Kelly, Ann Doran, Kay Scott, Robert Emmett Keane.

●A remarkable thriller about a young man's torture by nightmare when he dreams he committed a murder, and then finds himself in possession of tangible evidence proving that somehow, somewhere, he actually did kill. An adaptation of Cornell Woolrich's story *Nightmare*, it's a real poverty row quickie produced by the Pine-Thomas team. Admirably acted in a raw-boned way, tricked out with a barrage of cheap but surprisingly effective expressionistic tricks, above all using a subjective narration which orchestrates the hero's terrors with Bressonian intensity, it creates (almost by accident, it would seem) a hauntingly exact visualisation of the dark, seedy world of Woolrich's imagination that made him the patron saint of *film noir*. Shane remade the film in 1956 as *Nightmare*, with twice the budget and half the effect. TM

Fear in the Night

(1972, GB, 85 min)
d/p Jimmy Sangster. *sc* Jimmy Sangster, Michael Syson. *ph* Arthur Grant. *ed* Peter Weatherley. *ad* Don Picton. *m* John McCabe. *cast* Judy Geeson, Joan Collins, Ralph Bates, Peter Cushing, Gillian Lind, James Cossins.

●One of those neatly constructed but slightly mechanical psycho-thrillers which make you feel as if someone is pushing buttons connected to electrodes in your brain. Geeson plays a young woman recovering from a nervous breakdown who is terrorised into wanting to kill the aged, deranged headmaster of the prep school where her husband (Bates) teaches. What she doesn't know is that Bates is in league with the headmaster's wife (Collins). There is a sporadically effective use of prowling camera movements and atmospheric sounds, but Hammer fans will soon recognise the plot as a thinly disguised reworking of *A Taste of Fear*, which Sangster scripted for Seth Holt back in 1961. GA

Fear Is the Key

(1972, GB, 108 min)
d Michael Tuchner. *p* Alan Ladd Jr, Jay Kanter. *sc* Robert Carrington. *ph* Alex Thomson. *ed* Ray Lovejoy. *pd* Syd Cain, Maurice Carter. *m* Roy Budd. *cast* Barry Newman, Suzy Kendall, John Vernon, Dolph Sweet, Ben Kingsley, Ray McAnally.

●Slightly obscure plot from Alistair MacLean's novel about a gang of thugs out to hijack a planeload of gold and jewels. The hero's wife, brother and kid are on the plane, which is shot down into the sea. So he (Newman) vengefully sets out to infiltrate his way into the organisation, as salvage expert to retrieve the loot, by means of spectacular car chases and assorted killings. A sexless, insubstantial movie, but it's fast and clean, with a reasonable line in suspense.

Fearless

(1993, US, 122 min)
d Peter Weir. *p* Paula Weinstein, Mark Rosenberg. *sc* Rafael Yglesias. *ph* Allen Daviau. *ed* William Anderson. *pd* John Stoddart. *m* Maurice Jarre. *cast* Jeff Bridges, Isabella Rossellini, Rosie Perez, Tom Hulce, John Turturro, Benicio Del Toro.

●By the time Max Klein (Bridges) has grabbed Carla (Perez) for a quick liberating fandango in downtown Oakland, Weir's ambitious movie has already hit the skids. Having survived a terrible air crash, Max goes AWOL before returning to his devoted wife (Rossellini) and their son – reborn, as it were, afraid of nothing. Is he in shock, or has his near-death experience given him special insight, power even, as Max feels? After an intriguing, laconic first half hour, the film sinks into portentous solemnity. One problem is that Weir and writer Rafael Yglesias can't make up their minds about Max's status and state of mind; moreover, the director's much-advertised 'mysticism' often results in spasms of incoherence, not to mention tedium. As often with Weir, there's considerably less here than meets the eye. GA

Fearless Vampire Killers, The

see Dance of the Vampires

Fear of a Black Hat

(1992, US, 88 min)
d Rusty Cundieff. *p* Darin Scott. *sc* Rusty Cundieff. *ph* John Demps. *ed* Karen Horn. *pd* Stuart Blatt. *cast* Mark Christopher Lawrence, Larry B Scott, Rusty Cundieff, Kasi Lemmons, Howie Gold.

●A derivative, sporadically funny comedy that chronicles a year in the life of rap band Niggaz with Hats, and tries to do for rap what *This Is Spinal Tap* did for heavy metal. Given the lyrical and sartorial excesses of rap luminaries such as Ice T, Public Enemy and Niggaz with Attitude, the idea has potential. But while individual interviews, pop-video parodies and album titles hit the mark, the film as a whole is insufficiently clear-cut in its satire of the bands' dubious antics and attitudes. NF

Fear Strikes Out

(1956, US, 101 min, b/w)
d Robert Mulligan. *p* Alan Pakula. *sc* Ted Berkman, Raphael Blau. *ph* Haskell Boggs. *ed* Aaron Stell. *ad* Hal Pereira. *m* Elmer Bernstein. *cast* Anthony Perkins, Karl Malden, Norma Moore, Adam Williams, Brian G Hutton.

●In his autobiography, baseball star Jim Piersall described his childhood (Depression-era poverty, Catholicism, aggressive father, mentally unstable mother), his career with the Boston Red Sox and his years of battling with schizophrenia. The film is in effect a psychoanalysis of the book, concluding (big surprise) that Jim's breakdown was all Dad's fault. The '50s-style confrontations between autocratic Malden and sensitive Perkins draw quite entertainingly on the precepts of Freud and the conventions of melodrama. It's a little poky and tentative, but a promising start by the Pakula-Mulligan team. BBa

Feast at Midnight, A

(1994, GB, 106 min)
d Justin Hardy. *p* Yoshi Nishio. *sc* Justin Hardy, Yoshi Nishio. *ph* Tim Maurice-Jones. *ed* Michael Johns. *ad* Christiane Ewing. *m* David Hughes, John Murphy. *cast* Freddie Findlay, Christopher Lee, Robert Hardy, Edward Fox, Lisa Faulkner, Samuel West, Aled Roberts, Andrew Lusher.

●A throwback to the days of the Children's Film Foundation: well-spoken kids teach a few bumbling adults a thing or two and sort everything out in time for a happy ending. Arriving at bleak Dryden Park prep school, new boy Magnus (Findlay) starts a secret food club to win over his classmates, tangles with a variety of public school types (Lee, Hardy, West), and falls in puppy love with a master's daughter (Faulkner). All the while, he writes to his sick father (Fox), honorary chairman of the Scoffers, and upper-class dispenser of culinary and life-related wisdom. There's the germ of a good family movie here but neither the script nor the production values are of a very high order. AO

Feast of July

(1995, GB, 118 min)
d Christopher Menaul. *p* Henry Herbert, Christopher Neame. *sc* Christopher Neame. *ph* Peter Sova. *ed* Chris Wimble. *pd* Christopher Robilliard. *m* Zbigniew Preisner. *cast* Greg Wise, Embeth Davidtz, Ben Chaplin, Tom Bell, James Purefoy, Kenneth Anderson, Jemma Jones.

●Dismissed from her job when she's found to be pregnant, and subsequently miscarrying, young Bella Ford (Davidtz) is in a parlous way when she arrives, cold and alone, in an unfamiliar late-Victorian town in search of Arch Wilson (Wise), the cad who promised to marry her. She's taken in for the night by Pa Wainwright (Bell) and next day Ma Wainwright (Jones) offers her food and board alongside their three sons – Jed (Purefoy), a brash, cocksure soldier home on leave, Matty (Anderson), a more retiring shoemaker, and dark horse Con (Chaplin), slow of mind, hot of temper. Inevitably, Bella's presence stirs up rivalry between the three. Moreover, her past may yet return. This is another landscape- and costume-driven piece, a lavishly designed, earnestly acted period drama which risks smothering its characters' emotions under their bonnets and livery. Closer examination reveals the problem to be less the props than Christopher Neame's screenplay, which troubles neither to develop the characters nor to allow the drama respite from a raft of narrative clichés. It's no disaster, but grand and ultimately tragic goings-on like these ought to inspire more than a raised eyebrow. NB

Fedora

(1978, WGer, 113 min)
d/p Billy Wilder. *sc* Billy Wilder, IAL Diamond. *ph* Gerry Fisher. *ed* Fredric Steinkamp, Stefan Arnsten. *pd* Alexandre Trauner. *m* Miklós Rózsa. *cast* Marthe Keller, William Holden, Hildegard Knef, Jose Ferrer, Mario Adorf, Frances Sternhagen, Michael York, Henry Fonda.

●A shamefully underrated film, *Fedora* is Wilder's testament and one of the most sublime achievements of the '70s. Only superficially does it resemble *Sunset Blvd.*, since time has moved on; appropriately, *Fedora* is about a star's disastrous attempt to make time stop, and a washed-up producer's efforts to cope with Hollywood's inexorable new generation. Atmospherically set on Corfu, it explores the basis of cinema: realism, illusion, romance and tragedy – in a word, emotion. It's not a flashy film, let alone a cynical one, and it has a narrative assurance beyond the grasp of most directors nowadays: finely acted, mysterious, witty, moving and magnificent. ATu

Feds

(1988, US, 91 min)
d Dan Goldberg. *p* Ilona Herzberg, Len Blum. *sc* Len Blum, Dan Goldberg. *ph* Timothy Suhrstedt. *ed* Donn Cambern. *pd* Randy Ser. *m* Randy Edelman. *cast* Rebecca De Mornay,

Mary Gross, Fred Dalton Thompson, Ken Marshall, Larry Cedar, Raymond Singer.
●Two young women try to make the grade at the FBI Training Academy. They're given a predictably hard time by their male colleagues, a leering, chauvinist bunch of halfwits and bullies who seem to have strayed out of a National Lampoon movie, but the feisty lasses prove their mettle by the final reel. Director Goldberg seems uncertain whether he should be aiming for slapstick or an earnest docu-drama about sexism in the FBI. Despite an engaging Goldie Hawn-style performance from De Mornay, the end result is bland, toothless satire with neither the gusto of *Police Academy*, nor the charm of *Private Benjamin*. GM

Feedback

(1978, US, 90 mins)
d Bill Doukas. *cast* Bill Doukas, Myriam Gibril, Denise Gordon, Taylor Mead, Olie Armstead.
●Shades of Kafka and the '60s cinema of narcissism haunt this rambling film in which the actor-*auteur* wanders blankly through both comic-strip New York street life and the intricacies of plea-bargaining after receiving a summons on a mysterious conspiracy charge. Though fitfully encouraging speculation on the relativity of guilt, it's essentially a movie of moments. Some, such as Taylor Mead's characteristically quirky cameo as a judge, are definitely worth waiting for; but finally there aren't quite enough to sustain the feature length. PT

Feeling Minnesota

(1996, US, 99 min)
d Steven Baigelman. *p* Danny DeVito, Michael Shamberg, Stacey Sher. *sc* Steven Baigelman. *ph* Walt Lloyd. *ed* Martin Walsh. *pd* Naomi Shohan. *cast* Keanu Reeves, Cameron Diaz, Vincent D'Onofrio, Delroy Lindo, Courtney Love, Tuesday Weld, Dan Aykroyd, Levon Helm.
●The title comes from a Soundgarden song: 'I'm looking California and feeling Minnesota.' Unfortunately, the movie pretty much looks Minnesota too: drab, flat, and overcast (in both senses). There are germs of interest in director Baigelman's screenplay: a shotgun wedding in which Diaz is forcibly married off to accountant D'Onofrio by the local mob bigwig (Lindo) as a kind of incentive payment – she ends up humping her husband's tearaway brother (Reeves) during the reception. They take to the road, but foolishly come back for the money. The movie strains for cool, but the result's something of a mess. TCh

Feelings

(1975, GB, 92 min)
d Gerry O'Hara. *p* Basil Appleby. *sc* James Stevens. *ph* Ken Hodges. *ed* Tony Lenny. *ad* Bernard Sarron. *m* Pierre Dutour. *cast* Kate O'Mara, Paul Freeman, Edward Judd, David Markham, Bob Sherman, Frances Kearney.
●Learning of his sterility, a prosperous record producer (Freeman) reluctantly agrees that his wife (O'Mara) should be artificially inseminated. Nothing happens. A distinguished sexologist (Markham) suggests her chances of conception will improve if she submits to normal sexual intercourse. A physiotherapy student obliges. A child is born which in due course inherits a fortune from a great uncle. The student attempts blackmail to get his hands on the cash. Ludicrous yarn based on clinical balderdash about AI, with an unsavoury attitude to miscegenation and lesbian mothers. JPy

Feeling Sexy

(1999, Aust, 50 min)
d Davida Allen. *p* Glenys Rowe. *sc* Davida Allen. *ph* Garry Phillips. *ed* Heidi Kennessey. *pd* Hillary M Austin. *m* Claire Jordan. *cast* Susie Porter, Tamblyn Lord, Amanda Muggleton, John Donatiu, George Neumann, Simone Dumbleton.
●At 50 minutes this is more a long short than a short feature. Aussie painter Davida Allen has a lot of fun with her (presumably) autobiographical tale of a frustrated wife and mother whose healthy sex drive leads her to take a lover, but who doesn't find fulfilment until she picks up a paint brush. It's brash, honest and haphazardly inventive. TCh

Feet First

(1930, US, 70 min, b/w)
d Clyde Bruckman. *sc* Felix Adler, Lex Neal, Paul Gerard Smith. *ph* Walter Lundin, Henry N Kohler. *ed* Bernard W Burton. *cast* Harold Lloyd, Barbara Kent, Robert McWade, Lillian Leighton, Henry Hall, Noah Young, Sleep 'n' Eat, Willie Best.
●Harold Horne (Lloyd), a not very practised Honolulu shoe salesman, falls for the boss's 'daughter' (in reality his far more accessible secretary) and having pursued his loved one on to an oceangoing liner finds himself tied up in a mail sack with an important business bid in his pocket. All of which tedious business takes up the first two-thirds of the picture. However, once the mail sack lands on a rising builder's hoist outside a skyscraper, the acrobatic fun begins in earnest. A familiar reprise, to be sure, of *Safety Last*, but none the worse for that. The high spot has Lloyd flailing halfway down the building at the end of a gushing high-pressure fire hose. Be warned, there's a lot of prehistoric business in the skyscraper with a slow, barely verbal Negro servant (Best), played to the *n*-th degree of dumbness and then some. JPy

Felice... Felice...

(1998, Neth, 99 min)
d Peter Delpeut. *p* Pieter van Huystee, Suzanne van Voorst. *sc* Peter Delpeut. *ph* Walther Vanden Ende. *ed* Menno Boerema. *pd* Vincent de Pater. *m* Loek Dikker *cast* Johan Leysen, Toshie Ogura, Rina Yasima, Noriko Sasaki, Kumi Nakamura, Yoshi Oida.
●Delpeut's exquisitely crafted drama is at once a travelogue, a love story, a tribute to Mizoguchi, and a gentle satire about Western attitudes toward Japan. Felice (Leysen) is a nineteenth century photographer and explorer who returns to Japan after an absence of six years in search of O-kiku, his former wife. Delpeut, a film historian and archivist, uses old photographs to bring Felice's journey to life. Felice is an observer who always seems to be looking in on life. Delpeut's approach likewise veers toward the academic. Nevertheless, the final encounter between the traveller and the woman he lost is all the more affecting because it is handled with such detached, understatment. GM

Felicia's Journey

(1999, US/Can, 116 min)
d Atom Egoyan. *p* Bruce Davey. *sc* Atom Egoyan. *ph* Paul Sarossy. *ed* Susan Shipton. *pd* Jim Clay. *m* Mychael Danna. *cast* Bob Hoskins, Elaine Cassidy, Arsinée Khanjian, Sheila Reid, Peter McDonald, Gerard McSorley, Brid Brennan, Claire Benedict.
●Egoyan's adaptation of William Trevor's novel is a genuinely unsettling affair that benefits immensely from the director's ability to show both the Midlands and Hoskins' face as unfamiliar, faintly sinister landscapes. The film centres on the charged encounter between innocent Irish colleen Cassidy, searching for her errant boyfriend in and around Birmingham, and factory catering-manager Hoskins, a kindly, yet lonely bachelor deeply disturbed by fantasies inspired by his own childhood. The flashbacks to Ireland are too often underlined by pastoral folk music (whereas those to Hoskins' youth, with Khanjian as a Fanny Craddock-style TV chef, are delightfully witty), and Hoskins' accent is occasionally a little wobbly, but mostly this is a beautifully crafted affair, with Egoyan's script making the most of various dark ironies while his typically confident direction creates an intense mood. GA

Felix the Cat: The Movie

(1989, US, 82 min)
d Tibor Hernádi. *p* Don Oriolo, Christian Schneider, Janos Schenk. *sc* Don Oriolo, Pete Brown. *ph* Laszlo Radocsay. *pd* Tibor A Belay, Tibor Hernadi. *cast* voices: Chris Phillips, Maureen O'Connell, Peter Neuman, Alice Playton, Susan Montanaro.
●Felix made his screen debut as an animated short in 1919, passing through newspaper strips to become a major TV star in the '50s and '60s. Unfortunately, updating him for today's kids seems to mean ripping off *Star Wars*. A beautiful princess sends off a hologrammatic plea for help when she is captured and relieved of her kingdom by an evil duke. There follows a Quest through an alternative dimension inhabited by all manner of hybrid creatures (beasts with detachable heads, carnivorous marsh gas, rampaging robots), in which Felix fills in for Luke Skywalker (with the same combination of wide-eyed innocence and happy-go-lucky optimism that set him apart from more scurrilous cartoon cats like Sylvester, Top Cat and Fritz). Felix always had a surrealist slant, but this inane fantasy lacks the motor of good plot or dialogue. True, the animation is consistently inventive and the voicing good, but the end result is a TV cartoon padded out to feature length. DW

Fellini A Director's Notebook (Block-Notes di un Regista)

(1969, US/It, 53 min)
d Federico Fellini. *p* Peter Goldfarb. *sc* Federico Fellini, Bernardino Zapponi. *ph* Pasqualino De Santis. *ed* Ruggero Mastroianni. *m* Nino Rota. *with* Federico Fellini, Giulietta Masina, Marcello Mastroianni, Caterina Boratto.
●Fellini revisits the weatherworn sets of his abandoned *Il Viaggio di G Mastorna*; scours Rome while preparing *Satyricon* looking for continuities (a slaughterhouse, hookers on the Appian Way) between Now and Then; auditions assorted oddballs to play gladiators, senators and whatnot. He drops in on a Mastroianni beset by fans and journalists, while Giulietta Masina introduces a deleted sequence from *Notti di Cabiria*. And much more. This is hardly a documentary since clearly it's all scripted and staged, down to the way Fellini covers his bald patch when the camera gets behind him. Disinterested viewers should find it all haphazardly diverting; for Fellini-philes it's ambrosia. Made for NBC, which entails Fellini having to nag everyone please to talk in English. BBa

Fellini's Casanova (Il Casanova di Federico Fellini)

(1976, It, 163 min)
d Federico Fellini. *p* Alberto Grimaldi. *sc* Federico Fellini, Bernardino Zapponi. *ph* Giuseppe Rotunno. *ed* Ruggero Mastroianni. *pd* Danilo Donati, Federico Fellini. *m* Nino Rota. *cast* Donald Sutherland, Tina Aumont, Cicely Browne, Carmen Scarpitta, Clara Algranti.
●Imbued with an air of funereal solemnity and elegance, this forsakes realism in favour of a stylised romantic pessimism which confronts impotence, failure, sexuality and exploitation as fully as Pasolini's *Salò*. Although teetering at times dangerously close to Ken Russell, the visual daring and pure imagination of every image leave it as an elegiac farewell to an era of Italian cinema; and Sutherland's performance is the most astonishing piece of screen acting since Brando's in *Last Tango in Paris*. SM

Fellini's Roma (Roma)

(1972, It/Fr, 128 min)
d Federico Fellini. *p* Turi Vasile. *sc* Federico Fellini, Bernardino Zapponi. *ph* Giuseppe Rotunno. *ed* Ruggero Mastroianni. *pd* Danilo Donati. *m* Nino Rota. *cast* Peter Gonzales, Fiona Florence, Marne Maitland, Britta Barnes, Anna Magnani, Federico Fellini, Gore Vidal.
●Fellini in the self-indulgent mood that mars so much of his later work, taking us on an extravagantly sentimental and grotesque tour of 'his' Rome. The lack of any structural organisation of his 'insights' and 'memories' – though flaccid fantasies would be a better description – and the familiar gallery of obese, noisome stereotypes quickly become tiresome. But there is no denying that the man still has the capacity to pull off startling visual coups. GA

Fellini-Satyricon

(1969, It/Fr, 129 min)
d Federico Fellini. *p* Alberto Grimaldi. *sc* Federico Fellini, Bernardino Zapponi. *ph* Giuseppe Rotunno. *ed* Ruggero Mastroianni. *pd* Danilo Donati. *m* Nino Rota, Ilhan Mimaroglu, Tod Dockstader, Andrew Rudin. *cast* Martin Potter, Hiram Keller, Salvo Randone, Max Born, Fanfulla, Capucine, Alain Cuny, Lucia Bosè.
●Sprawling and conspicuously undisciplined, this is less an adaptation of Petronius than a free-form fantasia on his themes. Fellini's characteristic delirium is in fact anchored in a precise,

psychological schema: under the matrix of bisexuality, he explores the complexes of castration, impotence, paranoia and libidinal release. And he pays homage to Pasolini's ethnographic readings of myths. It's among his most considerable achievements. TR

Fellow Traveller

(1989, GB/US, 97 min)
d Philip Saville. *p* Michael Wearing. *sc* Mick Eaton. *ph* John Kenway. *ed* Greg Miller. *pd* Gavin Davies. *m* Colin Towns. *cast* Ron Silver, Imogen Stubbs, Hart Bochner, Daniel J Travanti, Katherine Borowitz, Julian Fellowes, Richard Wilson, Doreen Mantle.

●1954: blacklisted Hollywood screenwriter Asa Kaufman (Silver) arrives in London to work anonymously on scripts for the new independent television series 'Robin Hood'. Shattered by the news of the Hollywood suicide of his actor friend Cliff Byrne (Bochner) but unable to return home (he faces a HUAC subpoena), Asa enlists the reluctant help of Cliff's ex-lover Sarah (Stubbs), and dredges through his dreams and memories in search of clues to Cliff's death. As scripted by Michael Eaton, this McCarthy-period thriller interweaves numerous themes: guilt, confession and repression; privacy, paranoia and betrayal; the difference between America and Britain in the '50s; the role played by obsession in artistic creativity; the conflict between Marxist and freudian concepts of socio-political change. But it's also a moody, gripping suspense drama, reminiscent of classic film noir, its tortuous narrative full of mysterious flashbacks and dream sequences. Saville elicits some very fine performances, notably from Silver, and Travanti as a 'pink shrink' who treats Hollywood's Left; but finally it's the sheer wealth of detail and the uncommonly intelligent ambitions of the script that carry the day. GA

Feluettes, ou La Répétition d'un drama romantique

see Lilies

Female Company (Thiliki Etairia)

(2000, Greece, 90 min)
d Nikos Perakis. *p* Manos Krezias, Nikos Perakis, Dionyssis Samiotis, Antonis Vassiliou. *sc* Katerina Bei, Nikos Perakis. *ph* Yorgos Argiroiliopoulos. *ed* Yorgos Mavropsaridis. *ad* Olga Leontiadou. *m* Nikos Mamangakis. *cast* Maria Georgiadou, Smaragda Diamantidou, Sophie Zaninou, Christina Theodoropoulou, Katia Nikolaidou, Tania Kapsali, Nikos Kalogeropoulos.

●Five middle class women – politician's wife Eva, heiress Kiki, Anna-Maria, Electra and Ritsa – convene at the backroom of their friend/hairdresser Lia to discuss, in bald terms, their sex lives. They decide to make use of a spare apartment to widen their sexual horizons. Meanwhile, seedy surveillance engineer and mother's boy Lambrou sets up cameras to film their indiscretions and sexual encounters. If he blows their story on the 75th anniversary of their local paper, 'The Liberal', what repercussions may follow? Who cares? Certainly not director Perakis, who makes clear in this frothy, fast-talking, camera-swinging satire, his intention is to enjoy making some broad swipes at provincial patriarchal sexual and religious attitudes, not least by showing an unrepentant, sexually active Archimandrite priest. Unsophisticated, but lively. WH

Female Jungle, The

(1956, US, 69 min, b/w)
d Bruno Ve Sota. *p* Burt Kaiser. *sc* Burt Kaiser, Bruno Ve Sota. *ph* Woody Bredell. *ed* Carl Pingitore. *pd* Ben Roseman. *m* Nicholas Carras. *cast* Lawrence Tierney, John Carradine, Jayne Mansfield, Kathleen Crowley, Rex Thorsen, Bruno Ve Sota.

●When a Hollywood actress is found dead, drunken cop Tierney (the heist organiser in *Reservoir Dogs* some decades later) has an obvious murder suspect in Carradine's gossip columnist, but a further killing gives him second thoughts. Murky B melodrama with a cult value cast. After her screen debut as a passing good-time girl, Mansfield went back to selling popcorn at a cinema, but not for long. TJ

Female Perversions

(1996, US/Ger, 113 min)
d Susan Streitfeld. *p* Mindy Affrime. *sc* Julie Herbert, Susan Streitfeld. *ph* Teresa Medina. *ed* Curtiss Clayton, Leo Trombetta. *pd* Missy Stewart. *m* Debbie Wiseman. *cast* Tilda Swinton, Amy Madigan, Karen Sillas, Frances Fisher, Clancy Brown, Laila Robins.

●Adapted from an academic tome by US feminist Louise J Kaplan, this first feature centres on the crimes and misdemeanours of two thirty-something sisters. It's a fiery polemic/sex romp/watery Mamet soap. Tilda Swinton is a successful attorney, Eve, a brittle beast forever candying over her 'masculine' ambition with lipstick, lingerie and high heels. Politically correct Madelyn (Madigan) is attempting to hide 'femaleness' (she steals frilly underwear). Events focus on Eve's interview for the post of judge and Madelyn's arrest for theft. As family secrets unravel, the question becomes which side of the law should women want to be on? The film totters under the weight of its earnest symbolism (an ageing, overweight woman, for instance, struggling on a tightrope). Moreover, for all director/co-writer Streitfeld's desire to explode our culture's fascination with beauty, she herself seems besotted with Swinton, fixating on her perfect, scrubbed-with-nails aesthetic; the more homely Madigan, wonderfully restrained in her dead-eyed lunacy, just doesn't attract the same attention. Among the po-faced dross, however, there's much that's stunning. Interminable and flawed though the film is, the images that work grip like ivy. CO'Su

Female Trouble

(1974, US, 95 min)
d/p/sc/ph John Waters. *ed* Charles Roggero, John Waters. *ad* Vincent Peranio. *m* Bob Harvey. *cast* Divine, David Lochary, Mary Vivian Pearce, Mink Stole, Edith Massey, Cookie Mueller.

●Waters scrapes the bottom of the flash/trash barrel as artlessly as he did in *Pink Flamingos.* Again starring the wonder wobble Divine, *Female Trouble* documents the winsome life of one Dawn Davenport, from the moment she mashes Mum under the Christmas tree (having failed to receive her coveted cha-cha heels from Santa) to her shocking end in the electric chair. In between, accepted notions of beauty get flipped over on their bum as the sublime Divine sails through her various guises (loving mother, mugger, model and mass murderer), taking time out to double as her own deflowerer. Hilarious moments pockmark the movie like a bad case of acne, but like the person with only one joke to tell, it soon loses its appeal and laughter is replaced by lethargy. FL

Female Vampires

(1973, Fr, 94 min)
d Jess Franco. *p* Marius Lesoeur. *sc* Jess Franco. *ph* Joan Vincent. *ed* P Querut [Jess Franco]. *m* Daniel White. *cast* Lina Romay, Alice Arno, Jack Taylor, Monica Swin.

●A wretched soft-porn piece which substitutes oral sex for blood-sucking. For Lina Romay vampirism manifests itself mainly as a lack of make-up and a surly expression. Even the genre's sartorial elegance has passed her by as she mooches round the woods in nothing but a pair of boots, cape and belt. Plenty of below-the-belt sex. SFe

Femi Kuti: What's Going On

(2001, Nigeria/Fr, 52 min)
d Jacques Goldstein. *m/cast* Femi Kuti.

●Absorbing fly-on-the-wall portrait of the Nigerian singer Femi Kuti – son of the late, great Fela. Goldstein follows him recording in Paris, London and New York, then back to Lagos, where he maintains his home, and is building a club called Shrine, dedicated to his father's memory and to the popular democratic struggle. Fans won't find much new here, and it doesn't dig deep enough either into the memory of Fela or Femi's more pragmatic politics, but it's still a good introduction to the sound and fury of Afro-beat. TCh

Femme d'à côté, La

see Woman Next Door, The

Femme Défendue, La (The Forbidden Woman)

(1997, Fr, 100 min)
d Philippe Harel. *p* Michel Guilloux. *sc* Philippe Harel, Eric Assous. *ph* Gilles Henry. Bénédicte Teiger. *pd* François Emmanuelli. *cast* Isabelle Carré, Philippe Harel, Nathalie Conio, Sophie Niedergang, Julien Niedergang.

●An intriguing if flawed experiment in cinematic storytelling. A 22-year-old woman (Carré) hesitantly enters into an affair with a 39-year-old man (Harel), who's married with a kid. The film's a shrewd analysis of an adulterous relationship, but what lifts it out of the ordinary is that it's shot with a subjective camera from the man's PoV (Harel appears only briefly in reflection). The narrative is limited to the man's conversations with his lover, so that what we see is almost entirely Carré (who carries the film impressively). More than a gimmick, this device puts the viewer in a complex position – somewhere between contempt and complicity – with regard to the weak-willed, manipulative seducer. Regrettably, the story sometimes lacks the dramatic drive to match this potentially interesting conceit. GA

Femme de l'Aviateur, La

see Aviator's Wife, The

Femme de Mon Pote, La

see My Best Friend's Girl

Femme Douce, Une (A Gentle Creature)

(1969, Fr, 88 min)
d Robert Bresson. *p* Mag Bodard. *sc* Robert Bresson. *ph* Ghislain Cloquet. *ed* Raymond Lamy. *ad* Pierre Charbonnier. *m* Jean Wiener. *cast* Dominique Sanda, Guy Frangin, Jane Lobre.

●Bresson's first film in colour, a wonderfully lucid adaptation of Dostoievsky's enigmatic short story about a young woman who kills herself for no apparent reason. An elliptical intimation of the suicide; a shot of the husband staring at his dead wife's face in an attempt to understand; then in a flat, even monotone, his voice embarks on its voyage of exploration – part confession, part accusation – and a series of heart-rendingly non-committal flashbacks fill in the details of their story. By the end, in a sense, one is no wiser than before. Was it because he loved her too much or too little, because he gave her too little money or too much, because he felt she was too good for him or not good enough? The extraordinary thing about the film is that any or all of these interpretations can be read into it, still leaving, undisturbed at the bottom of the pool, an indefinable sense of despair. Time was when Bresson's characters could look forward to salvation as a reward for their tribulations; but around this time the grace notes disappeared, his world grew darker, and the people in it – like this haplessly unhappy husband and wife – seemed doomed to a pilgrim's progress in quest of the secret which would allow the human race to belong again. TM

Femme du Boulanger, La (The Baker's Wife)

(1938, Fr, 116 min, b/w)
d/p/sc Marcel Pagnol. *ph* Georges Benoit. *ed* Suzanne de Troeye. *m* Vincent Scotto. *cast* Raimu, Ginette Leclerc, Charles Moulin, Fernand Charpin, Robert Vattier, Robert Bassac, Charles Blavette.

●'Lucky people who will be seeing *La Femme du Boulanger* for the first time', said the *New Statesman*'s William Whitebait when Pagnol's movie was on one of its periodic reissues in 1944. One only hopes that today's audiences will feel equally lucky: if they've no objections to seeing something flagrantly unfashionable, but bursting with bucolic vigour and sly satirical wit, they ought to be happy enough. Raimu, a French clown *sans pareil*, plays a baker in Provence who refuses to bake another loaf until his flighty wife (currently in the arms of a local shepherd) is returned to him. Pagnol's direction has been described as 'elaborately unobtrusive', whatever that means. GB

Femme entre Chien et Loup, Une (Woman In a Twilight Garden)

(1978, Bel/Fr, 111 min)
d André Delvaux. *sc* Ivo Michels, André Delvaux. *ph* Charlie van Damme. *ed* Pierre

Gillette. *ad* Claude Pignot, Françoise Hardy, Philippe Graff. *m* Etienne Verschueren. *cast* Marie-Christine Barrault, Roger Van Hool, Rutger Hauer, Bert André, Raf Reyman, Senne Rouffaer, Mathieu Carrière.
● Elliptical tale of a World War II triangle (and its aftermath) in which a Belgian woman falls for a French-speaking Resistance leader while her husband, an idealistic Flemish-speaking nationalist, is serving on the eastern front as a volunteer with the German SS. Delicately shaded and much less schematic than it sounds, it still emerges as little more than a specifically Belgian/Flemish rehash of the usual traumas. Exquisitely shot, but a disappointment from the usually evocative and subtle Delvaux. TM

Femme est une Femme, Une (A Woman Is a Woman)

(1961, Fr, 84 min)
d Jeanne-Luc Godard. *p* Georges de Beauregard. *sc* Jean-Luc Godard. *ph* Raoul Coutard. *ed* Agnès Guillemot, Lila Herman. *ad* Bernard Evein. *m* Michel Legrand. *cast* Anna Karina, Jean-Paul Belmondo, Jean-Claude Brialy, Marie Dubois, Nicole Paquin, Marion Sarraut, Jeanne Moreau, Catherine Demongeot.
● Most of Godard's early movies are so much of their particular time that they'll need explanatory footnotes before long. This was the first of his colour/cinemascope tributes to the changing moods of Karina (his then wife); the film's own soundtrack notes that it might equally be a comedy or a tragedy because it's certainly a masterpiece. It has a thin thread of plot about Karina's desire to get pregnant, it flanks her with the pragmatic Brialy on one side and the romantic Belmondo on the other, then stands all of them in the shadow of MGM musical stars of the '40s and '50s, and it collages these elements together with sundry gags, worries, contradictions and asides into a kind of movie that nobody had seen before. The result is brash, defiant, gaudy and infinitely fragile. TR

Femme Fatale

(1991, US, 96 min)
d André Guttfreund. *p* Andrew Lane, Nancy Rae Stone. *sc* John Brancato, Michael Ferris. *ph* Joey Forsyte. *ed* Richard Candib. *pd* Pam Warner. *m* Parmer Fuller. *cast* Colin Firth, Lisa Zane, Billy Zane, Scott Wilson, Lisa Blount, Carmine Caridi.
● Joseph (Firth) meets enigmatic Cynthia (Lisa Zane) at his nature centre. A brief courtship and marriage follow, but when Cynthia walks out on the eve of their honeymoon, the distraught groom embarks on a search of her old Los Angeles neighbourhood, and discovers that she is not who he thought she was. The path to discovery is difficult – not so much for Joseph as for the weary viewer. The camera roves around a landscape scattered with affected sycophants and wide-eyed drug dealers before jolting on, periodically, into flashbacks of life in the countryside. With each bizarre revelation, the film descends further into hysterical nonsense. CM

Femme française, Une (Eine Französische Frau)

(1994, Fr/GB/Ger, 98 min)
d Régis Wargnier. *p* Yves Marmion. *sc* Régis Wargnier. *ph* François Catonné. *ed* Geneviève Winding, Agnès Schwab. *pd* Jacques Bufnoir. *m* Patrick Doyle. *cast* Emmanuelle Béart, Daniel Auteuil, Gabriel Barylli, Jean-Claude Brialy, Geneviève Casile, Michel Etcheverry, Heinz Bennent.
● After bathing Deneuve in exotic colonial finery for the dull *Indochine*, writer/director Wargnier reserves a worse fate for Béart in this bathetic, absurdly misjudged trawl through the emotional wreckage of an army marriage. Summer 1939 brings the union of Jeanne (Béart) and youthful lieutenant Louis (Auteuil) and fleeting bliss before he spends the next five years in a German PoW camp. Release finds him returning home to a wife who's scandalised the family by having an affair, and the couple are only just reconciled before the next set of orders sends them to Berlin, where Louis joins the Allied occupation force. Jeanne finds herself irresistibly drawn to her German landlord's son Mathias (Barylli), a passion that causes intolerable tensions. Pushed hither and thither, Auteuil is right to look ill at ease, but Béart is sadly reduced to an empty repertoire of stamping mini-*mélo*, swaths of *décolletage* and sheer pouty desperation. The star chemistry (the leads split off-screen during production) is pure corrosion, while Patrick Doyle's overblown score merely expands the agony. TJ

Femme Infidèle, La (Unfaithful Wife)

(1968, Fr/It, 98 min)
d Claude Chabrol. *p* André Génoves. *sc* Claude Chabrol. *ph* Jean Rabier. *ed* Jacques Gaillard. *ad* Guy Littaye. *m* Pierre Jansen. *cast* Stéphane Audran, Michel Bouquet, Maurice Ronet, Serge Bento, Michel Duchaussoy, Guy Marly.
● One of Chabrol's mid-period masterpieces, a brilliantly ambivalent scrutiny of bourgeois marriage and murder that juggles compassion and cynicism in a way that makes Hitchcock look obvious. The obligatory cross-references are still there (blood in the sink; the exactly appropriate final use of simultaneous backtrack and forward zoom adapted from *Vertigo*), but they're no longer there to legitimise a vision now mature. Audran and Bouquet, as the first of Chabrol's recurring Charles/Hélène couples, are superb in discovering 'secret' parts of each other denied as much by complacency as convention. PT

Femme Mariée, Une (A Married Woman)

(1964, Fr, 98 min, b/w)
d/sc Jean-Luc Godard. *ph* Raoul Coutard. *ed* Agnès Guillemot, Françoise Collin. *m* Ludwig van Beethoven, Claude Nougaro. *cast* Macha Méril, Bernard Noël, Philippe Leroy, Roger Leenhardt, Rita Maiden.
● Relatively minor Godard which, characteristically, plays off fictional form (a day in the life of an adulterous wife) against documentary moments (face-on interviews in which characters lecture on abstracts like 'Memory' and 'Childhood'). Another of his socio-sexual fables, in fact, curious for the way it was censored. Outraged by its mockery of Marriage and Family, the authorities insisted that the title be changed – from *La Femme Mariée* (*Married Woman*, a collectivity, a condition) to *Une Femme Mariée* (*A Married Woman*, an individual, unrepresentative case). CA

Femme ou Deux, Une

see Woman or Two, A

Fencing Master, The (El Maestro de Esgrima)

(1992, Sp, 88 min)
d Pedro Olea. *p* Pedro Olea, Antonio Cardenal. *sc* Antonio Larreta, Francisco Prada, Arturo Pérez Reverte, Pedro Olea. *ph* Alfredo Mayo. *ed* José Salcedo. *ad* Luis Valles. *m* José Nieto. *cast* Omero Antonutti, Assumpta Serna, Joaquim de Almeida, José Luis Lopez Vazquez, Alberto Closas, Miguel Rellan.
● Madrid, 1868: Queen Isabel's regime is crumbling, and Don Jaime de Astarloa (Antonutti) lives only for fencing. When the beautiful Adela de Otero (Serna) asks him to teach her, he refuses to instruct a lady. A demonstration of her skill, however, has him curling his moustache. Soon he's infatuated, but Adela has a more prominent partner in mind. Olea's adaptation of Arturo Pérez Reverte's novel begins in a solemn register, but just as you're about to write it off as a museum piece, it abruptly changes tack and develops into a lively old-fashioned melodrama: Don Jaime is duped in love, a friend is murdered, a woman's corpse is fished out of the river. This intrigue has enough cut and thrust to tickle all but the most jaded palate, while Serna makes a fine foil for Antonutti's crafty performance. Only Olea's wider socio-historical pretensions seem a mite sketchy. TCh

Fengriffen

see And Now the Screaming Starts!

FernGully: The Last Rainforest

(1992, Aust, 76 min)
d Bill Kroyer. *p* Wayne Young, Peter Faiman. *sc* Jim Cox. *ed* Gillian Hutshing. *ad* Susan Kroyer. *m* Alan Silvestri. *cast* voices: Tim Curry, Samantha Mathis, Christian Slater, Jonathan Ward, Robin Williams, Grace Zabriskie, Cheech Marin, Tommy Chong.
● The FernGully of this animation feature is a pretty, pastel-coloured glade in the middle of a rainforest where animals and plants live in harmony, tended by Magi Lune and her gentle nature-spirits. 'Everything in Creation is connected by the delicate web of life,' says the aptly named Ms Lune. As if to put this theory to the test, Crysta flies out to the smoke at the edge of the rainforest. It is her first encounter with Man. Impetuously, she saves the life of Zak, a particularly cute specimen, and shrinks him to her size. Alas, Zak's colleagues at the logging operation are possessed by the evil spirit Hexxus, and the whole forest is imperilled. *FernGully* is black and white and Green all over. Aimed squarely at the under-12s, it won't displease most parents, if only for the welcome absence of marketable accessories. TCh

Ferris Bueller's Day Off

(1986, US, 103 min)
d John Hughes. *p* John Hughes, Tom Jacobson. *sc* John Hughes. *ph* Tak Fujimoto. *ed* Paul Hirsch. *pd* John W Corso. *m* Ira Newborn. *cast* Matthew Broderick, Alan Ruck, Mia Sara, Jeffrey Jones, Jennifer Grey, Cindy Pickett.
● Ferris (Broderick) is a boy who gets anything he wants, screws over anyone who gets in his way, and gets patted on the back for doing so. Gathering his best friend (Ruck) and his best girlfriend (Sara), he skips school for the day out in Chicago. Hughes revels in Ferris' ingenuity, then neatly adds dimension after a ninety-minute parade of hubris and material wealth by telling us that people count more than their possessions. Ferris is an admittedly entertaining, at times delightful fellow. How unfortunate that no one got to wring the little bastard's neck. SGo

Ferroviere, Il (Man of Iron/The Railroad Man)

(1956, It, 116 min, b/w)
d Pietro Germi. *p* Carlo Ponti. *sc* Pietro Germi, Alfredo Giannetti, Luciano Vincenzoni, Ennio De Concini, Carlo Musso. *ph* Leonida Barboni. *ed* Dolores Tamburini. *ad* Carlo Egidi. *m* Carlo Rustichelli. *cast* Pietro Germi, Luisa Della Noce, Sylva Koscina, Edoardo Nevola, Saro Urzi.
● The director himself plays a boozy, autocratic engine driver who severs relations with his daughter over her love life and chases away his elder son, who's immersed in the usual teenage troubles. A suicide dies under his train, his drinking increases. He refuses to join a strike and is ostracised. Eight-year-old Sandrino, a chubby charmer, hovers on the periphery, half-understanding, but more concerned with not letting dad see his poor school reports. It all ends in a warm Dickensian bath of Christmas Eve reconciliation. The blend of sharp observation and slick sentimentality is characteristic of the neorealist cycle, of which this is a late, quite entertaining example. BBa

Ferry Cross the Mersey

(1964, GB, 85 min, b/w)
d Jeremy Summers. *p* Michael Holden. *ph* Gilbert Taylor. *ed* John Victor Smith. *ad* Tony Masters. *cast* Gerry Marsden, Fred Marsden, Les Chadwick, Les Maguire, Julie Samuel, Eric Barker, Deryck Guyler.
● Grotesquely inept and dated pop musical featuring Gerry and the Pacemakers which is so bad that it doesn't even make it as nostalgia. Shot in a very short space of time to cash in on the Liverpool sound; the other pop personalities involved are Cilla Black, Jimmy Savile and the Fourmost. Ken Tynan, whose film reviewing was not always so succinct and penetrating, gave it the most accurate five-word review ever in *The Observer* when he called it 'a little glimpse into hell'. DP

Ferry to Hong Kong

(1958, GB, 113 min)
d Lewis Gilbert. *p* George Maynard. *sc* Vernon Harris, Lewis Gilbert. *ph* Otto Heller. *ed* Peter Hunt. *pd* John Stoll. *m* Kenneth Jones. *cast* Curd Jürgens, Sylvia Syms, Orson Welles, Jeremy Spenser, Noel Purcell, Milton Reid.
● The first of Rank's clueless strikes at the international market is a moronic male melodrama-cum-adventure movie with Curd Jürgens as a shiftless Austrian drifter who's in his element when Orson Welles' ferry is threatened by a typhoon off Macao. All at sea away from his

favoured British subject matter, Lewis Gilbert tries to navigate by the stars, but he's duly scuppered by his own rocky script. Filmed in CinemaScope. TCh

Festen

see Celebration, The

Festival (Chukje)

(1996, SKor, 108 min)
d Im Kwon-Taek. *p* Lee Tae-Won. *sc* Yook Sang-Hyo. *ph* Park Seoung-Bai. *ed* Park Soon-duk. *m* Kim Su-Chul. *cast* Ahn Song-Gi, Oh Jung-Hae, Han Eun-Jin, Chung Kyung-Soon, Park Seung-Tae, Lee Kem-Joo.

●Odd there should be two major Korean films centred on funerals in the same year, but this one is very different in form, tone and style from *Farewell My Darling*, even if it also shows a family at risk of tearing itself apart. Im directs with his usual classical restraint and places great weight on the many rituals that form part of the ceremonies; the beauty and serenity of these customs ultimately see the mourners through the parade of bad behaviour, drunken outbursts and hitherto unvoiced resentments. One element marks it as Im's most experimental film in some time: the story is filtered through glimpses of a child's picture-book vision of the death of her grandma – arresting, stylised sequences whose meaning falls into place only at the very end. TR

Festival

(1996, It, 95 min)
d Pupi Avati. *p* Antonio Avati, Aurelio De Laurentiis. *sc* Pupi Avati, Antonio Avati, Giorgio Gosetti, Doriano Fasoli. *ph* Chicca Ungaro. *ed* Amedeo Salfa. *m* Pino Donaggio. *cast* Massimo Boldi, Isabelle Pasco, Gianni Cavina, Margaret Mazzantini, Lorenzo Flaherty, Andrea Scorzoni.

●An over-the-hill comic, scrambling for bookings on the provincial club circuit, Franco (Boldi) cuts a sad figure. His only prospect is the release of a low-budget film by a first-time director – a hateful experience for a star of Franco's former stature. Then, a miracle! The film's invited to the Venice festival, in competition. The critics start buzzing, and suddenly Franco is tipped for the Golden Lion. Avati's melancholy answer to *The King of Comedy* is sour and unfunny. Chiefly shot at the Venice fest in 1995, and screened there in '96, the film holds up a mirror to the vanity of the event, but echoes with empty laughter. TCh

Fetishes

(1996, US, 84 min)
d Nick Broomfield. *p* Nick Broomfield, Michele D'Acosta. *ph* Christoph Lanzenberg. *ed* Betty Burkhart. *m* Jamie Muhoberac. *cast* Mistresses Raven, Catherine, Beatrice and Delilah, Goddess Natasha.

●Pandora's Box, downtown Manhattan, caters to a niche market. They do sadism, the clientele provide the masochism. If you're into bondage, rubber, female wrestling or toilet-licking, this is your place. Of course there are two fetishes being explored here: SM and voyeurism. Perhaps that's why Broomfield plays a less aggressively upfront role than usual – though we do see him flirting with the mistresses and sticking his microphone in some unexpected places. TCh

Fette Welt

see Fat World

Feu Follet, Le (A Time to Live and a Time to Die/ The Fire Within/Fox Fire/ Will o'the Wisp)

(1963, Fr, 110 min, b/w)
d Louis Malle. *p* Jean Pieuchot. *sc* Louis Malle. *ph* Ghislain Cloquet. *ed* Suzanne Baron. *ad* Bernard Evein. *m* Erik Satie. *cast* Maurice Ronet, Lena Skerla, Yvonne Clech, Hubert Deschamps, Jeanne Moreau, Alexandra Stewart.

●Arguably the finest of Malle's early films, this is a calmly objective but profoundly compassionate account of the last 24 hours in the life of a suicide. Ronet gives a remarkable, quietly assured performance as the alcoholic who, upon leaving a clinic, visits old friends in the hope that they will provide him with a reason to live. They don't, and Malle's achievement lies not only in his subtle but clear delineation of his protagonist's emotions but in his grasp of life's compromises; his portrait of Parisian society is astringent, never facile. A small gem, polished to perfection by an unassuming professional. GA

Feverhouse

(1984, GB, 46 min, b/w)
d Howard Walmesley. *sc* Ken Hollings. *cast* Joanne Hill, Graham Massey, Patrick Nyland.

●Scripted by Ken Hollings, this short feature might better be considered as a poem: something out of Baudelaire's *Fleurs du Mal* via the French Surrealist cinema and Throbbing Gristle's brutalist chic. Shot in expressionist monochrome, it roams the rooms and corridors of what might be the titular hospital, a grim Victorian edifice where bodies lie untended on trolleys, nurses murder inmates, a nurse-patient love affair flutters in the shadows, the sick and blind stumble in Beckettian repetition, and the oblique, disturbing narrative only hints at larger horrors. Given all that, it hovers dangerously close to pretension, sometimes teetering over the edge, but still remains a darkly individual visual essay, despite its precedents. It's also blessed with an exciting score, a brew of metal gamelan and junkyard bebop from Biting Tongues. JG

Fever Pitch

(1985, US, 96 min)
d Richard Brooks. *p* Freddie Fields. *sc* Richard Brooks. *ph* William A Fraker. *ed* Jeff Jones. *pd* Ray Storey. *m* Thomas Dolby. *cast* Ryan O'Neal, Catherine Hicks, Giancarlo Giannini, Bridgette Andersen, Chad Everett, John Saxon.

●Hollywood old-stager Brooks' last completed feature to date (1996) is an old-fashioned and numbingly predicable problem pic of the kind that he used to do rather better (*The Blackboard Jungle*, for instance). Here the horror of gambling comes under the microscope as ace reporter O'Neal sets out to write an exposé of Las Vegas, but (surprise, surprise) ends up a slave to the gaming table. TJ

Fever Pitch

(1996, GB, 102 min)
d David Evans. *p* Amanda Posey. *sc* Nick Hornby. *ph* Chris Seager. *ed* Scott Thomas. *pd* Michael Carlin. *cast* Colin Firth, Ruth Gemmell, Neil Pearson, Lorraine Ashbourne, Mark Strong, Holly Aird, Ken Stott, Stephen Rea.

●Nick Hornby's done a clever thing. While a Hollywood studio has bought the rights to his best-seller *High Fidelity*, and are trying to work out how to Americanise it, he's transposed the battle of the sexes scenario on to this most parochial of romantic comedies – only he's passing it off as *Fever Pitch*, an adaptation of his first, strictly unfilmable book. Firth is Paul, an English teacher with an unhealthy obsession for Arsenal Football Club. Gemmell is Sarah, a starchy colleague who despises the game and the hooligans who follow it – Paul, especially. You don't need a crystal ball to predict the result. Mercifully dispensing with the best part of 25 seasons of Highbury inaction, the film concentrates on the championship hopes of 1988-9, with brief, explanatory flashbacks to Paul's childhood. The focus is a kind of reverse angle on conventional soccer coverage, with the camera trained on the fans, not the players. Director Evans doesn't catch the psychological acuity of Hornby's prose, but he brings the push and pull of that fateful season to life even for non-Arsenal fans, and scores early on with a very funny seduction scene. Gradually, though, the energy sags. It's so much more in love with football than heterosexual relationships. The mismatched couple is a staple of screwball comedy, but these characters are fundamentally dislikeable – he's an arrested adolescent with a one-track mind, she's got nothing going for her at all. TCh

Few Good Men, A

(1992, US, 138 min)
d Rob Reiner. *p* Andrew Scheinman, David Brown, Rob Reiner. *sc* Aaron Sorkin. *ph* Robert Richardson. *ed* Robert Leighton. *pd* J Michael Riva. *m* Marc Shaiman. *cast* Tom Cruise, Jack Nicholson, Demi Moore, Kevin Bacon, Kiefer Sutherland, Kevin Pollak, James Marshall, JT Walsh, Wolfgang Bodison.

●Scripted by Aaron Sorkin from his own play, considerably less interesting than *A Soldier's Story*, this centres on a fatal case of bullying in the US Marines and the ensuing trial. The intellectual cut-and-thrust of the courtroom is largely absent here, and the denouement seems slick, arbitrary, and derived from the Captain Queeg catalogue. Even worse, Cruise is cast as the dilettante Navy lawyer with a brilliant legal brain, and jives about in much the same manner as he did in *Top Gun*. Lieutenant Commander Demi Moore wants him to get serious, praises his brain repeatedly in case we missed it, and finally gets him shouting idealistically in court. The pair of them are useless in uniform, and shown up by the highly professional Bacon, who gives a layered performance as the opposing counsel. Unfortunately, the most interesting character is little more than a cameo for Nicholson, but he does give an alarming sketch of the élitist military mind. BC

F for Fake (Vérités et Mensonges)

(1975, Fr/Iran/WGer, 85 min)
d Orson Welles. *p* Dominique Antoine, François Reichenbach. *sc* Orson Welles, Oja Kodar [Olga Palinkas]. *ph* Christian Odasso, Gary Graver. *ed* Marie-Sophie Dubus, Dominique Engerer. *m* Michel Legrand. *cast* Orson Welles, Oja Kodar, Elmyr de Hory, Clifford Irving, Edith Irving, François Reichenbach, Joseph Cotten, Laurence Harvey, Richard Wilson.

●A triumphantly self-amused, self-aware reflection on the verities of art and creativity and the lies that sustain them, Welles' quizzical homage to forgery and illusionism is both a self-portrait and a wry refutation of the *auteur* principle, a labyrinthine play of paradoxes and ironies that comes off as the cinematic equivalent of an Escher painting. Starting with some 'found' footage of art forger Elmyr de Hory shot by documentarist François Reichenbach, Welles manipulates it into a mock inquisition on the mysteries of authorship, autonomy, attribution and associative editing, arriving back at *Kane* and the *War of the Worlds* broadcast via Howard Hughes and his hoax biographer Clifford Irving. Alongside the films of Jacques Rivette, the epitome of cinema-as-play. PT

Fiancée du Pirate, La (Dirty Mary/A Very Curious Girl)

(1969, Fr, 106 min)
d Nelly Kaplan. *sc* Nelly Kaplan, Claude Makovski. *ph* Jean Badal. *ed* Gérard Pollicand, Nelly Kaplan, Noëlle Boisson, Suzanne Lang-Willar. *ad* Michel Landi, Patrick Lafarge, Jean-Claude Landi. *m* Georges Moustaki. *cast* Bernadette Lafont, Georges Géret, Michel Constantin, Julien Guiomar, Jean Parédès, Francis Lax, Claire Maurier.

●Kaplan's first feature is a cruel inversion of the Cinderella fable: the story of a 'pirate' woman, social outcast of a backbiting, bigoted provincial village, who takes her revenge by turning prostitute in order to seduce and blackmail her clients and oppressors into ruin. The mockery is harsh, despite the bright colours and playful tone: greed, malice and bigotry are satirised with merciless, atheistic scorn, and the final blow for sexual and social revenge is struck in the hamlet's church. Piggy eyes, once popping out of their sockets with lust, burn with hatred, while the heroine (the marvellous Lafont) dances off down the open road, leaving behind only a strange abstract sculpture of fridges, showers and bric-a-brac, as though thumbing her nose at the very possibility of marriage and homely virtue. CA

Fiddler on the Roof

(1971, US, 180 min)
d/p Norman Jewison. *sc* Joseph Stein. *ph* Oswald Morris. *ed* Antony Gibbs, Robert Lawrence. *pd* Robert Boyle. *songs* Jerry Bock, Sheldon Harnick. *cast* Chaim Topol, Norma Crane, Leonard Frey, Molly Picon, Paul Mann, Rosalind Harris, Michael Glaser.

●Jewison fairly wallows in ethnic roots in this adaptation of the Sheldon Harnick/Jerry Bock musical, set in a Jewish village community in the pre-Revolutionary Ukraine: three hours of pure schmalz, buried up to its neck in noisy national traditions as the hero marries off three daughters in turn, pausing each time to unload buckets of song, sentiment and homespun philosophy. Very hard to take with the film sitting up and practically slobbering in its eagerness to prove how loveable it is. A pity, because the score isn't half bad (the show-stopping 'If I Were a Rich Man' almost gets lost), the choreography has possibilities, and Topol is distinctly personable. TM

Fiddlers Three

(1944, GB, 88 min, b/w)
d Harry Watt. *p* Michael Balcon. *sc* Angus MacPhail, Diana Morgan. *ph* Wilkie Cooper. *ed* Eily Boland. *ad* Duncan Sutherland. *songs* Mischa Spoliansky, Harry Jacobson, Geoffrey Wright, Diana Morgan, Robert Hamer, Roland Blackburn. cast Tommy Trinder, Frances Day, Sonnie Hale, Francis L Sullivan, Diana Decker, Elisabeth Welch, James Robertson Justice.

●Sailors Trinder and Hale plus plucky Wren Frances Day are struck by lightning on Salisbury Plain and transported back to Ancient Rome, where they're acclaimed as powerful seers and outwit Sullivan's cheerily debauched Nero. Cheeky wartime British comedy with odd imaginative touch (associate producer Robert Hamer reshot a good deal of it). James Robertson Justice appears as a young centurion. TJ

Fidélité, La (Fidelity)

(2000, Fr, 166 min)
d Andrzej Zulawski. *p* Paulo Branco. *sc* Andrzej Zulawski. *ph* Patrick Blossier. *ed* Marie-Sophie Dubus. *ad* Jean-Pierre Puzos. *m* Andrzej Korzynski. *cast* Sophie Marceau, Pascal Greggory, Guillaume Canet, Magali Noël, Michel Subor, Edith Scob, Manuel Lelièvre, Aurélien Recoing, Jean-Charles Dumay.

●Apart from the Isabelle Adjani shocker *Possession*, the films of French-based Polish maverick Zulawski have rarely crossed the Channel, and it's hard to give this elephantine romantic folly much of a welcome. Marceau never convinces as a photographer so consumed by her art she shoots everything, from piles of rubbish to ice hockey matches, while the rivalry between her eccentric publisher husband Greggory and smouldering fellow lensman Canet never achieves psychological credibility. Worse is the director's misguided confidence in his own artistry, mixing Marceau's artfully blurred prints with quoted chunks of Auden's poetry, John Woo-style shoot-outs, and a hideous piano score uncomfortably reminiscent of Richard Clayderman. (From *La Princesse de Clèves* by the Mme de La Fayette.) TJ

Fidelity

see Fidélité, La

Field, The

(1990, GB, 110 min)
d Jim Sheridan. *p* Noel Pearson. *sc* Jim Sheridan. *ph* Jack Conroy. *ed* J Patrick Duffner. *ad* Frank Hallinan Flood. *pd* Frank Conway. *m* Elmer Bernstein. *cast* Richard Harris, John Hurt, Tom Berenger, Sean Bean, Frances Tomelty, Brenda Fricker, John Cowley, Ruth McCabe, Sean McGinley.

●John B Keane's play takes on some of the resonances of an Irish *Lear* in Jim Sheridan's adaptation. West Coast tenant farmer Bull McCabe (Harris) has lavished all his love upon a rented field which he hopes to leave to his weak son (Bean), in the belief that a man is nothing without land. His dream is shattered when the widowed owner puts it up for auction, and he is outbid by an outsider, an American (Berenger) with plans to modernise the area. Following the American's murder, Bull cracks apart, driving wilfully ever deeper into tragedy. Some of the ingredients are given – Bull's wife (Fricker) hasn't spoken to him in a decade, his second son killed himself – but most of the burden of developing a tragic character is down to Harris, and he layers it richly without too much thespian tilting of the beard into the elements. His Bull is a spectrum of patience, violence, parsimony and ceilidh, intimidating to his son and awesome to his fawning creature Bird O'Donnell (Hurt, also at his peak). Sense of place, time and custom are faultless, and despite a few narrative lurches, it's a moving experience. BC

Field of Dreams

(1989, US, 106 min)
d Phil Alden Robinson. *p* Lawrence Gordon, Charles Gordon. *sc* Phil Alden Robinson. *ph* John Lindley. *ed* Ian Crafford. *pd* Dennis Gassner. *m* James Horner. *cast* Kevin Costner, Amy Madigan, James Earl Jones, Timothy Busfield, Ray Liotta, Burt Lancaster, Gaby Hoffmann, Frank Whaley, Dwier Brown.

●Despite a happy family life, Iowa farmer Ray Kinsella (Costner) is left musing over lost idealism and a squandered relationship with his father, a former baseball player now dead. Hearing a disembodied voice urging 'If you build it, he will come', he is propelled on a quest which initially involves putting a baseball pitch in the middle of his crop. This in turn heralds the arrival of ghostly baseball players – including the infamous Shoeless Joe Jackson, implicated in the fixing of the 1919 World Series. Taken in bare outline, the plot may appear faintly ridiculous; but this often beautiful film (John Lindley's cinematography is breathtaking) – using baseball as a metaphor for other issues, namely the bonding or lack of it between father and son – embraces qualities which are skilfully amplified and *not* sentimentalised. Writer/director Robinson has embellished WP Kinsella's novel to examine the ideological conflict between the '60s and the '80s; together with moments of dry humour and fine performances, the political element lends the film gravity sufficient to counterbalance any sense of whimsy. Pure magic. CM

Fiendish Plot of Dr Fu Manchu, The

(1980, US, 108 min)
d Piers Haggard. *p* Zev Braun, Leland Noan. *sc* Jim Moloney, Rudy Dochtermann. *ph* Jean Tournier. *ed* Russell Lloyd, Claudine Bouché. *pd* Alexandre Trauner. *m* Marc Wilkinson. *cast* Peter Sellers, Helen Mirren, David Tomlinson, Sid Caesar, Simon Williams, Steve Franken, Stratford Johns, John Le Mesurier, Burt Kwouk.

●Sadly, this final movie from Sellers is also one of his worst. Most of the jokes one anticipates seconds before they occur; many are of the ethnic stereotype sort; the visual running gag palls at its second appearance. Co-star Helen Mirren continues her determined bid to give up acting for the role of ripest screen-tease sex object of the '80s. RM

Fiends, The

see Diaboliques, Les

Fiend Without a Face

(1958, GB, 74 min, b/w)
d Arthur Crabtree. *p* John Croydon. *sc* Herbert J Leder. *ph* Lionel Banes. *ed* Richard Q McNaughton. *ad* John Elphick. *m* Buxton Orr. *cast* Marshall Thompson, Kim Parker, Terence Kilburn, Kynaston Reeves, Stanley Maxted, Michael Balfour.

●Close by a US Army base in a remote corner of Canada, a trail of corpses leads Thompson to uncover a hideous experiment gone wrong. A familiar plot right down to the atomic mutation premise, but the special effects – killer brains that propel themselves through the air with a whip of the spinal cord and latch onto the backs of their victims' necks – are among the most memorable in the eco-horror genre. Crabtree (a former cinematographer who graduated to Gainsborough melodramas and also made the bizarre *Horrors of the Black Museum*) is one of the unsung *auteurs* of the pre-*Outer Limits* era. This may be his finest hour and a bit. MA

Fierce Creatures

(1997, US/GB, 93 min)
d Robert Young, Fred Schepisi. *p* Michael Shamberg, John Cleese. *sc* John Cleese, Iain Johnstone. *ph* Adrian Biddle, Ian Baker. *ed* Robert Gibson. *pd* Roger Murray-Leach. *m* Jerry Goldsmith. *cast* John Cleese, Kevin Kline, Jamie Lee Curtis, Michael Palin, Ronnie Corbett, Carey Lowell, Robert Lindsay, Maria Aitken.

●Not a sequel, but a belated reunion for Cleese and his co-stars from *A Fish Called Wanda*, and as strained as such occasions tend to be. The set-up's silly. Rollo Lee (Cleese) runs a small British zoo, a surprisingly prominent blip on Aussie tycoon Rod McCain's plans for global conglomeration. Obsessed with profit margins, Rollo decides only dangerous animals pay – the rest will have to go. The staff are appalled, but things get even worse when McCain (Kline) drafts in corporate hotshot Willa (Curtis) and his no-good son Vince (Kline again), who embark on a crass sponsorship scheme. There's some funny business with the zoo-keepers pretending that meerkats are the most vicious beasts on four legs, and Cleese briefly reminds us of Python's cutting edge when he dispatches a handful of the cutest creatures with a shotgun, but the movie soon settles for dismally obvious running gags about bestiality, Curtis's body, and Cleese's sexual charisma. Just about musters enough laughs to cover up the cracks. TCh

Fièvre Monte à El Pao, La (Republic of Sin)

(1959, Fr/Mex, 100 min, b/w)
d Luis Buñuel. *p* Raymond Borderie. *sc* Luis Buñuel, Luis Alcoriza, Charles Dorat, Louis Sapin. *ph* Gabriel Figueroa. *ed* James Cuenet. *ad* Jorge Fernandez. *m* Paul Misraki. *cast* Gérard Philipe, Maria Félix, Jean Servais, Miguel Angel Ferriz, Raúl Dantés, Domingo Soler.

●Philippe's last role before his death from cancer, playing a small-time government administrator – the setting is a South American dictator-state – whose time comes when the governor is assassinated and he temporarily takes over until a successor is appointed. The film is a study in the futility of liberal sentimentality when it refuses to acknowledge the fascist mechanism for what it is: Philippe's few attempts to improve the lot of political prisoners prove useless in face of a stronger rival and his own desire for security and power. It's hardly major Buñuel – he himself blamed its shortcomings on the inevitable compromises of a co-production – but his view of greed, hypocrisy and cruelty is as lucidly sardonic as ever, and the portrait of the dangers of trying to improve a totalitarian regime from the inside remains as relevant today as when the film was made. GA

15 Amore

(2000, Aust, 92 min)
d Maurice Murphy. *p* Maurice Murphy, Brooke Wilson. *sc* Maurice Murphy. *ph* John Brock. *ed* Dana Hughes. *pd* Kate Walker. *m* Carlo Giacco. *cast* Lisa Hensley, Steve Bastoni, Domenic Galati, Tara Jakszewicz, Gertrude Ingeborg, Rhianna Griffith, Bill Hunter.

●Likeable period drama with the wife (Hensley) of an officer serving overseas taking on four PoWs – two handsome Italians and a Jewish mother and daughter. Filmed as a kid's remembrance by writer/director Murphy, this tale of surrogate fatherhood and sexual spice takes place in a kind of Eden composed of the nearby lakes and fields. Good performances all round, and accurate period detail make for a pleasant, sunny and thoughtful little picture. WH

15 Minutes

(2001, US/Ger, 121 min)
d John Herzfeld. *p* Nick Wechsler, Keith Addis, David Blocker, John Herzfeld. *ph* Jean Yves Escoffier. *ed* Steven Cohen. *pd* Mayne Berke. *m* Anthony Marinelli, J Peter Robinson. *cast* Robert De Niro, Edward Burns, Kelsey Grammer, Avery Brooks, Melina Kanakaredes, Karel Roden, Oleg Taktarov, Vera Farmiga, Charlize Theron, Kim Cattrall.

●When Oleg and Emil arrive in New York from Eastern Europe, their first act is to steal a digicam. Then they murder the couple who ripped off their loot, torch the place and check in to a fleapit under the name 'Frank Capra'. Then they review the rushes. Already homicide cop Eddie Fleming (De Niro), arson investigator Jordy Warsaw (Burns) and tabloid TV reporter Robert Hawkins (Grammer) are vying for jurisdiction, but all the boys really want is a movie deal. Writer/director Herzfeld is best known for the stylish thriller *Two Days in the Valley*. His follow-up aspires to the hard-boiled satire of novelist Carl Hiaasen, but it's a total misfire, a reactionary revenge thriller with the American Dream as the sacrificial victim. Herzfeld works hard to bring in unusual textures and disrupt the predictable patterns of the tired buddy cop genre. He does muster a few surprises, but neither the director nor his actors seem at all sure of the tone they're after. It's too broad to engender any credible suspense, too violent to be more than fitfully funny – and too half-baked for its assault on tabloid irresponsibility to stand up in court. TCh

5th Avenue Girl

(1939, US, 83 min, b/w)
d/p Gregory LaCava. *sc* Allan Scott. *ph* Robert de Grasse. *ed* William Hamilton, Robert Wise. *ad* Van Nest Polglase, Perry Ferguson. *m* Russell Bennett. *cast* Ginger Rogers, Walter Connolly, Verree Teasdale, James Ellison, Tim Holt, Franklin Pangborn, Kathryn Adams.

● LaCava seems to have lost his touch, usually good for some sharpish social satire, in this comedy about a jobless and homeless girl taken into his stately mansion by a despondent millionaire, mainly with a view to shaking up his money-grubbing family by having her come on as a golddigger. The family duly fulminate while the millionaire happily plays with his pet pigeons instead of attending to business, and true love predictably looms to provide a happy resolution for his protégée. Even Rogers seems curiously listless. TM

Fifth Element, The (Le Cinquième Elément)

(1997, Fr, 126 min)
d Luc Besson. *p* Patrice Ledoux. *sc* Luc Bresson, Robert Mark Kamen. *ph* Thierry Arbogast. *ed* Sylvie Landra. *pd* Dan Weil. *m* Eric Serra. *cast* Bruce Willis, Gary Oldman, Milla Jovovich, Ian Holm, Chris Tucker, Luke Perry, John Neville, Mathieu Kassovitz, Julie T Wallace.

● The 23rd century: Earth's being threatened by a fireball – Absolute Evil – and our only hope lies with the Fifth Element, sent by friendly aliens and given human form as the waifish Leeloo (Jovovich), who's rescued from a suspicious militia by Korben Dallas, spacefighter turned Brooklyn air-cabbie (Willis). Until he takes her to the priest Cornelius (Holm), who alone understands the ancient mysteries, Dallas has no idea of his charge's role in the scheme of things – though her exceptional powers and the unwelcome attentions of Zorg (Oldman), a power maniac aligned with Evil, soon convince him she's something special. While there's enjoyment to be had from Willis's amiably tongue-in-cheek performance, Dan Weil's production design, Jean-Paul Gaultier's outlandish costumes and Digital Domain's special effects, Besson's futuristic fable is flawed by a messy narrative which strains to incorporate far too many grotesque and eccentric characters. Leeloo's sorrowing horror at humanity's propensity for violence and war is a bit rich in a movie that delights in, and depends for effect on, firepower, explosions and loudly destructive mayhem. GA

Fifth Horseman Is Fear, The

see Fifth Rider Is Fear, The

Fifth Monkey, The

(1990, US, 93 min)
d Eric Rochat. *p* Menahem Golan. *sc* Eric Rochat. *ph* Gideon Porath. *ed* Alin Jakubowicz, Fabien D Tordjmann. *ad* Pedro Nanni. *m* Robert O Ragland. *cast* Ben Kingsley, Mika Lins, Vera Fischer, Silvia De Carvalho, Vera Fischer, Carlos Kroeber.

● A poor Brazilian trapper sees the lucrative sale of four rare chimpanzees as his pathway to marital happiness with high maintenance widow De Carvalho, but after a perilous journey to the city to find a buyer he realises he's formed a stronger relationship with his primate pals than he's ever had with his would-be bride. Modest but not unpleasing tropical adventure with a strong eco-friendly message and eye-catching location work. TJ

Fifth Rider Is Fear, The (...a páty jezdec je Strach/aka The Fifth Horseman Is Fear)

(1964, Czech, 93 min, b/w)
d Zbynek Brynych. *sc* Hana Belohradska, Zbynek Brynych, Ota Koval, Ester Krumbachová. *ph* Jan Kalis. *ed* Miroslav Hájek. *pd* Milan Nejedly. *cast* Miroslav Machácek, Olga Scheinpflugová, Jirí Adamíra, Slávka Budínová, Bohuslav Dodek, Ivo Gubel, Zdenek Hodr.

● Made during the onset of the Czech New Wave, this powerful tale of personal responsibility is informed as much by Cold War paranoia – and Czech resistance to Soviet impositions – as it is by the torments of the Nazi era. Unquestionably of the '60s in design and scoring, and set chiefly in a single apartment block, the film details the attempts of a Jewish doctor to obtain morphine for an injured resistance figure under police investigation. His internal discussions about when and how one is compelled to help, given his own imminent difficulties, are profoundly moving. Stylised and in places absurdist, with visits to an asylum and a decadent party, it's a striking portayal of a society in moral meltdown, where 'hate's terribly contagious'. The doctor's final act is an absolute attempt to draw a line in the sand against this, and a final measure of commitment to the greater good. GE

51st State, The

(2001, Can/GB, 92 min)
d Ronny Yu. *p* David Pupkewitz, Malcolm Kohll, András Hamori, Seaton McLean, Jonathan Debin. *sc* Stel Pavlou. *ph* Poon Hang Sang. *ed* David Wu. *pd* Alan MacDonald. *m* Headrillaz: Casper Kedros, Darius Kedros. *cast* Samuel L Jackson, Robert Carlyle, Emily Mortimer, Sean Pertwee, Ricky Tomlinson, Stephen Walters, Anna Keaveney, Rhys Ifans, Meatloaf.

● Stev Pavlou was working in a wine merchants until he struck gold with this screenplay, a fanboy action comedy drawing on *True Romance* and cynical Jerry Bruckheimer gunfests like *The Last Boy Scout* – but set in Liverpool, and laced with a distinctly British sense of humour. Momentum Pictures put up more than $20m, cast Jackson as the Californian chemist Elmo McElroy and brought in HK's Ronny Yu to direct. Here's the plot: Elmo has concocted a new mega brainblaster of a recreational drug; he does the dirty on his boss Lizard (Meatloaf) to sell it to a Scouse kingpin (Tomlinson). Lizard hires hitwoman Dakota (Mortimer) to dispense with the competition, which she readily manages, sparing only Elmo and local guide Felix (Carlyle) – who happens to be Dakota's ex. And so the scene is set for further flash action choreography, reams of bad taste jokes, and due homage to Liverpool FC. It's slapdash, but generates enough eccentric energy to excuse its baser elements. TCh

55 Days at Peking

(1962, US, 154 min)
d Nicholas Ray. *p* Samuel Bronston. *sc* Philip Yordan, Bernard Gordon. *ph* Jack Hildyard. *ed* Robert Lawrence, Magdalena Paradell. *ad* John Moore, Veniero Colasanti. *m* Dimitri Tiomkin. *cast* Charlton Heston, David Niven, Ava Gardner, Robert Helpmann, Flora Robson, Leo Genn, John Ireland, Kurt Kasznar, Paul Lukas, Harry Andrews.

● From its marvellous opening – in the Legation compound at Peking, the troops of eight foreign powers raise their national flags to the accompaniment of a cacophony of national anthems – to the final relief of the diplomats to whom the Boxers have laid siege in the compound, Ray almost transcends the spectacular world of international co-production film deals. He carefully orchestrates the big action sequences (the sine qua non of the Epic) so that they form a mere background to the unfolding drama of the awkward love affair between Heston and Gardner. The result, Ray's farewell to Hollywood, is admittedly a broken-backed movie – producer Samuel Bronston re-cut it – but one full of delicious moments as Ray's camera cranes and swoops around his protagonists, almost taking us back to the nervous grandeur of *Johnny Guitar* on occasion. A magnificent failure. PH

54

(1998, US, 93 min)
d Mark Christopher. *p* Richard N Gladstein. Dolly Hall, Ira Deutchman. *sc* Mark Christopher. *ph* Alexander Gruszynski. *ed* Lee Percy. *pd* Kevin Thompson. *m* Marco Beltrami. *cast* Mike Myers, Ryan Phillippe, Neve Campbell, Breckin Meyer, Salma Hayek, Sherry Stringfield.

● It's 1979, and naive adonis Shane O'Shea (Phillippe) is sick of his grey New Jersey existence. Entranced by a photo of soap star Julie Black (Campbell), he visits her New York hangout, Studio 54. Club boss Steve Rubell (Myers) takes a fancy to him, and soon Shane's a busboy, enjoying a new life with sexy couple Anita (Hayek) and Greg (Meyer). He thinks things can only get better, but... The strange truth about *54* is that it's almost great; its best moments have a bleak, blasted energy reminiscent of *Boogie Nights* and *Blue Collar*. There's a political sensibility at work here. Ultimate exclusionist Rubell provides the perfect means to study America's race and class divisions, and Myers exploits every vicious, self-hating line that comes his way. All Rubell's scenes are beguiling. The problem is, the other characters – straight in every way, their highs and lows come over like the twitterings of *Fame*. CO'Su

52 Pick-up

(1986, US, 110 min)
d John Frankenheimer. *p* Menahem Golan, Yoram Globus. *sc* Elmore Leonard, John Steppling. *ph* Jost Vacano. *ed* Robert F Shugrue. *pd* Philip Harrison. *m* Gary Chang. *cast* Roy Scheider, Ann-Margret, Vanity, John Glover, Robert Trebor, Clarence Williams III, Lonny Chapman.

● This is the one Elmore Leonard fans were waiting for, the one that lost least on the swings and roundabouts of translation to the screen. It has, damagingly, exchanged the precise economic placing of Detroit for impersonal LA, fiddled a bit with the plot, but courageously sticks by the unheroic tone of the book. Married Harry's passing fling with a young 'model' places him in the hands of a trio of extortionists. They show him the evidence on video, and when he refuses to pay up, execute his mistress with his gun, and play him the subsequent snuff movie. Harry's survival depends upon his ability to play the unstable trio off against each other. Excellent performances. Best of all is the casting of Williams as Bobby Shy – as shamblingly conspicuous as the brother from another planet, golliwog hair and a too-tight raincoat that clings like a hobo's fart, this is a guy who wants a good leaving alone. BC

Fight Club (100)

(1999, US/Ger, 139 min)
d David Fincher. *p* Art Linson, Ceán Chaffin, Ross Grayson Bell. *sc* Jim Uhls. *ph* Jeff Cronenweth. *ed* James Haygood. *pd* Alex McDowell. *m* The Dust Brothers. *cast* Brad Pitt, Edward Norton, Helena Bonham Carter, Meat Loaf Aday, Jared Leto, Zach Grenier, Richmond Arquette.

● This is not an action movie, but a cerebral comedy – which is to say, an ideas movie. Some of those ideas are startling, provocative, transgressive, even subversive. They're also pretty funny. It goes like this: Norton used to be an upwardly mobile urban professional; now, he's pallid, neurotic and unhappy. Then he bumps into Tyler Durden (Pitt), his apartment blows up, and everything changes. Gaudy and amoral, Tyler's an id kind of guy: living on the edge is the only way he knows to feel alive. Pitt's raw physical grace embodies everything his alter ego has lost touch with; they trade body blows for fun, and you can sense the gain in the pain. Their 'club' draws emasculates from across the city; under Tyler's subtle guidance, the group evolves into an anarchist movement. The film wobbles alarmingly at this point, then rallies for the kind of coup de grâce that sends you reeling. Jim Uhls' cold, clever screenplay, from Chuck Palahniuk's novel, is a millennial mantra of seditious agit prop. Shot in a convulsive, stream-of-unconsciousness style, with disruptive subliminals, freeze frames and fantasy cutaways, the film does everything short of rattling your seat to get a reaction. You can call that irresponsible. Or you can call it the only essential Hollywood film of 1999. TCh

Fighting Back

(1982, Aust, 100 min)
d Michael Caulfield. *p* Sue Milliken, Tom Jeffrey. *sc* Tom Jeffrey, Michael Cove. *ph* John Seale. *ed* Ron Williams. *ad* Christopher Webstser. *m* Colin Stead. *cast* Lewis Fitz-Gerald, Kris McQuade, Caroline Gillmer, Paul Smith, Robyn Nevin, Wyn Roberts, Ben Gabriel.

● After much frustrated head-banging, a troublesome boy (Smith) finds a friend (brother, mentor, father figure, etc.) in a well-meaning teacher (Fitz-Gerald) whose revolutionary methods stretch to playing AC/DC in class. Caught between developing the individual relationship of pupil to teacher and exposing the injustices of the educational system, the film opts for an unhelpful sentimentality. The teacher's lack of sexual definition, and the film's refusal to raise the question of sex in general – strange, as its real subject is puberty – makes the subtext of the relationship decidedly odd. Analysts will have a field day, others needn't bother. CPe

Fighting Back (aka Death Vengeance)

(1982, US, 98 min)
d Lewis Teague. *p* D Constantine Conte. *sc* Tom Hedley, David Zelag Goodman. *ph* Franco De Giacomo. *ed* John J Fitzstephens, Nicholas Smith. *ad* Robert Gundlach. *m* Piero Piccioni. *cast* Tom Skerritt, Patti LuPone, Michael Sarrazin, Yaphet Kotto, David Rasche, Donna DeVarona.

●'We gotta go out and scare some respect into these punks.' It's urban vigilante time again, though here more of a clean-streets variant on the current craze for survivalism. Skerritt plays an Italian-American deli owner who organises his People's Neighbourhood Patrol along textbook paramilitary lines, and mounts a violent campaign to stomp all 'deviants' and restore the local park to his kids. There's political conscience somewhere in the script which places its hero as a blood-lust racist and an opportunist politico, but it's all too easily drowned by the crowd-pleaser set pieces of 'righteous' revenge. PT

Fighting Elegy (Kenka Elegy)

(1966, Jap, 86 min, b/w)
d Seijun Suzuki. *cast* Hideki Takahashi.

●Suzuki made more than his share of genre classics, but this (his penultimate film for Nikkatsu) is something else: a completely original anatomy of young male hormones that shows how repressed violence can be channelled into fascism. Being the director he is, Suzuki films it as comedy. It's set in the militarist 1930s, and the 'hero' is a high-school student who finds that a good rumble beats a cold shower. The film has none of Suzuki's usual florid visuals, and doesn't need them. It catches the tone of adolescent fumblings precisely, and its cool 'Scope images give it the contours of a masterpiece. TR

Fighting Gladiator

see Fabiola

Fighting Justice

see True Believer

Fighting Mad

(1976, US, 90 min)
d Jonathan Demme. *p* Roger Corman. *sc* Johnathan Demme. *ph* Michael Watkins. *ed* Anthony Magro. *m* Bruce Langhorne. *cast* Peter Fonda, Lynn Lowry, John Doucette, Philip Carey, Scott Glen, Kathleen Miller.

●Engaging piece of exploitation that manages to both paint in broad colours and pay attention to detail at the same time. It's rednecks vs yellow hardhats as Arkansas farmers find themselves bulldozed off their property by the unscrupulous mining corporation. Into this conflict comes Fonda, who has got scruples, and a bow-and-arrow. Once his brother and sister-in-law and father have been murdered, he wreaks his own vengeance, blowing up, and maiming, and adjusting his liberal spectacles after every killing. Where writer/director Demme scores is in extracting maximum story value from his cast and location, so that every scrap of sex and violence is highly realistic, and advances the plot. Altogether, another winner from the House of Corman. AN

Fighting Seabees, The

(1944, US, 100 min, b/w)
d Edward Ludwig. *p* Albert J Cohen. *sc* Borden Chase, Aeneas Mackenzie. *ph* William Bradford. *ed* Richard Van Enger. *ad* Duncan Cramer. *m* Walter Scharf. *cast* John Wayne, Susan Hayward, Dennis O'Keefe, William Frawley, Grant Withers, Duncan Renaldo.

●Standard World War II flagwaver in which Wayne, having fought for the principle that a non-combatant pioneer corps should nevertheless be armed, spends his time wiping out loads of brutish Japs in between bouts of romancing the pretty (and pretty unbelievable) war correspondent who happens to be on hand in the person of Susan Hayward. TM

Fighting 69th, The

(1940, US, 90 min, b/w)
d William Keighley. *sc* Norman Reilly Raine, Fred Niblo Jr, Dean Franklin. *ph* Tony Gaudio. *ed* Owen Marks. *ad* Ted Smith. *m* Adolph Deutsch. *cast* James Cagney, Pat O'Brien, George Brent, Jeffrey Lynn, Alan Hale, Dennis Morgan, Frank McHugh.

●Sentimental propagandist claptrap recounting the heroic adventures of New York's famous Irish regiment during World War I. With distinct echoes of *Angels With Dirty Faces* – Cagney's the brash punk knocking the company's traditions until he discovers patriotism, O'Brien's the pious priest giving him guidance – the film is one of its star's most sugary, and therefore most disappointing efforts. Still, he does make the film come alive during a couple of hysterical screaming scenes. GA

Figures in a Landscape

(1970, GB, 110 min)
d Joseph Losey. *p* John Kohn. *sc* Robert Shaw. *ph* Henri Alekan. *ed* Reginald Beck. *ad* Ted Tester. *m* Richard Rodney Bennett. *cast* Robert Shaw, Malcolm McDowell, Henry Woolf, Christopher Malcolm, Andy Bradford, Warwick Sims.

●A misguided adaptation of Barry England's excellent novel about two Englishmen on the run from an unspecified prison camp in the Far East (Burma, Korea, Vietnam, take your pick). Relocated in Europe, with Robert Shaw's script still harping insistently on their nationality, one is left wondering bemusedly what military authority two evidently apolitical Englishmen can be running from in fear of instant annihilation. A Kafka nightmare of totalitarianism seems to be the answer, alas. But if you can forget the pretensions and the clumsy characterisations, Losey's direction is a dazzling example of pure mise en scène, with every shot perfectly calculated to frame the theme of two figures caged in a landscape. The sequences in which they are stalked by a helicopter playing cat-and-mouse are good enough to suspend disbelief in the game. TM

File of the Golden Goose, The

(1969, GB, 109 min)
d Sam Wanamaker. *p* David E Rose. *sc* John C Higgins, James B Gordon. *ph* Ken Hodges. *ed* Oswald Hafenrichter. *ad* George Provis. *m* Harry Robinson. *cast* Yul Brynner, Edward Woodward, Charles Gray, John Barrie, Bernard Archard, Adrienne Corri.

●Lots of red London buses and telephone boxes in this touristy-looking thriller from the scrag end of the Swinging London scene. Brynner's the American agent who hits Blighty in search of the gang of murderous counterfeiters who killed his girl, while Woodward is the decent British copper Scotland Yard insist on having in on the case. The movie's a bit of a plod too, though Gray enjoys himself as the chief villain. TJ

File on Thelma Jordon, The

(1949, US, 100 min, b/w)
d Robert Siodmak. *p* Hal B Wallis. *sc* Ketti Frings. *ph* George Barnes. *ed* Warren Low. *ad* Hans Dreier, Earl Hedrick. *m* Victor Young. *cast* Barbara Stanwyck, Wendell Corey, Paul Kelly, Joan Tetzel, Stanley Ridges, Richard Rober, Barry Kelley.

●A fine *film noir* which works an ingenious, intricate variation on the situation in *Double Indemnity*, but which takes its tone, unlike Wilder's film, not from Stanwyck's glittering siren who courts her own comeuppance ('Judgement day, Jordon!'), but from the nondescript assistant DA she drives to the brink of destruction. The part is played (remarkably well) by Corey, whose haunted, hangdog persona as a perennial loser is echoed so perfectly by the deliberately slow, inexorable tempo of Siodmak's direction (not to mention George Barnes' superbly bleak lighting) that the film emerges with a quality akin to Lang's dark, romantic despair. TM

Fille de D'Artagnan, La (D'Artagnan's Daughter)

(1994, Fr, 130 min)
d Bertrand Tavernier. p Véronique Bourboulon. *sc* Michel Leviant, Riccardo Freda, Jean Cosmos, Bertrand Tavernier. *ph* Patrick Blossier. *ed* Ariane Boeglin. *m* Philippe Sarde. *cast* Sophie Marceau, Philippe Noiret, Claude Rich, Charlotte Kady, Sami Frey, Jean-Luc Bideau, Raoul Billerey, Nils Tavernier.

●1654, the South of France. When horsemen follow a runaway black slave into the convent where he's taken sanctuary and kill both the fugitive and the Mother Superior, they little realise that one of the novices is Eloïse (Marceau), spirited sprog of retired musketeer D'Artagnan (Noiret). Suspecting that the murders are somehow linked to a plot against Louis XIV, the girl dons buckskins and sword and rides off, accompanied by an adoring poet (Tavernier) acquired en route, to ask her dad to protect the boy king. Only when the headstrong Eloïse seems set to fall into the hands of the villainous Duc de Crassac (Rich) and his scarlet mistress (Kady) does D'Artagnan return to the fray. Tavernier's swashbuckler never quite turns into parody and never quite plays it straight. Sadly, it never quite takes off, either. Yes, it's as good-natured and elegant to look at as one might expect, but the leisurely pace sags at times, and the two main conceits – centring the film on a feisty female and stressing the way age has affected the musketeers' skills and ideals – are hardly original. Good swordplay, but a bit too much breezy banter. GA

Fille de l'Air, La

(1992, Fr, 107 min)
d Maroun Bagdadi. *p* Farid Chaouche, Michel Vandestein. *sc* Florence Quentin, Dan Franck, Maroun Bagdadi. *ph* Thierry Arbogast. *ed* Luc Barnier. *ad* Michael Vandestien. *m* Gabriel Yared. *cast* Béatrice Dalle, Thierry Fortineau, Hippolyte Girardot, Roland Bertin, Liliane Rovère.

●This big-screen treatment of a notorious 1986 French prison breakout plays rather like an extended TV 'reconstruction'. It's based on the autobiography of Nadine Vaujour (Dalle), a secretary who fell for fugitive armed robber Michel (Fortineau), when her petty-crook brother asked her to shelter him. After a doomed attempt to go straight, Michel was recaptured and given a heavy sentence, while Nadine served several months on a complicity charge – during which time the couple married and she gave birth to a son. On release, distressed by Michel's mental deterioration, this determined woman learned to fly a helicopter and successfully freed her husband from prison. Lebanese director Bagdadi handles the physical details with visceral aplomb (a raid on the Vaujour household is, for example, absolutely terrifying), but neglects the contextualising niceties of characterisation. It's one thing to allow the audience room to consider their own moral perspective, another, surely, to leave the motivations of these real-life people so frustratingly opaque. A stellar cast can do little but look scruffy and hope the narrative's factual interest gets them through. It does (just), but the psychological grit of the story is clearly elsewhere. TJ

Fille de l'Eau, La (The Whirlpool of Fate)

(1924, Fr, 85 min approx, b/w)
d/p Jean Renoir. *sc* Pierre Lestringuez. *ph* Alphonse Gibory, Jean Bachelet. *cast* Catherine Hessling, Pierre Philippe, Harold Livingston, Pierre Champagne, Maurice Touzé, André Derain.

●Virginie lives on a barge with her father and uncle. Papa accidentally drowns, uncle develops an incestuous itch and Virginie flees into a series of adventures with a gypsy poacher, a brutal farmer and, for hero, a handsome young landowner. This was Renoir's first feature, and various influences are discernible: a dash of Stroheim here, a streak of Surrealism there. But the naturalistic settings, sensuously rendered (with very few interiors), contrasted with the theatricality of the narrative and an eccentric attitude to performance (especially that of the clown-like Hessling), already reveal a quite recognisable Renoir. BBa

Filles Perdues, Cheveux Gras

see Hypnotised and Hysterical (Hairstylist Wanted)

Fille sur le Pont, La

see Girl on the Bridge, The

Fillmore

(1972, US, 106 min)
d Richard T Heffron. *p* Claude Jarman, Herbert F Decker. *ph* Alan Capps, Al Kihn, Paul Lohmann, Eric Saarinen. *ed* Eli F Streich, Richard Clarke, Daniel Halas, Charles Titone. *with* The Grateful Dead, Jefferson Airplane, Hot Tuna, NRPS, Quicksilver Messenger Service, Santana, Cold Blood and Lamb, Bill Graham.

●A clumsy, cluttered, grainy tribute to San Francisco's former music Vatican, shot during the venue's final week. The views of promoter Bill Graham (a manic, chest-thumping telephone thug) quickly cease to amuse as he's allowed to thunder one-dimensionally onwards, volume constantly on the up. In between times, a motley selection of performers deliver predominantly lacklustre material to an unimaginative film crew. A still splendidly gritty Box Scaggs is the easy victor, while only the most fervent Jefferson Airplane fans are advised to wade through the surrounding swamp for the measly minute or so of 'Up Against the Wall' offered here. Cinephiles may be able to squeeze an odd laugh from the cretinous use of split screen, but that's pitiful compensation for one of the worst music films of the past decade. GD

Film

(1965, US, 22 min, b/w)
d Alan Schneider. *sc* Samuel Beckett. *ph* Boris Kaufman. *ed* Sidney Meyers. *ad* Burr Smidt. *cast* Buster Keaton.

●A man scrambles through a silent grey landscape to his sparsely decorated room, where he systematically rids himself of every possible witness to his existence: pets, mirror, a picture of a staring ancient god, photos of his own past. But also watching him is someone else, embodied by the gaze of the camera, which remains behind the man virtually throughout the film. There is a profound philosophical theme in Beckett's sole foray into cinema, based on the idea to be/exist is to be perceived. But perhaps more intriguing than Beckett's largely successful attempt to examine an abstract epistemological concept through the materialist medium of film, is the wholly appropriate casting of Keaton who, in the classic comedies of the '20s, envisaged a universe notable for its cruel, arbitrary absurdity, and who, perhaps, anticipated Beckett's thesis on perception (and cinema) in *Sherlock Junior*. Dark, witty and fascinating.

Film About a Woman Who...

(1974, US, 105 min, b/w & col)
d/sc Yvonne Rainer. *ph* Babette Mangolte. *ed* Yvonne Rainer, Babette Mangolte. *cast* Dempster Leech, Shirley Soffer, John Erdman, Renfreu Neff, James Barth, Yvonne Rainer.

●Rainer's second feature takes 'performing' as a central theme and metaphor. The protagonists are at once dancers, actors and lovers – for others, for an audience. The context they are set in constitutes a remarkable juxtaposition of visual and verbal descriptive methods: inter-titles, written texts, voices off, dance, slides and acted sequences. Insight, irony and wit are marvellously combined, reaching a height in the appropriately labelled central section, 'An Emotional Accretion in 48 Steps'. SF

Film from the Clyde

(1977, GB, 83 min)
d/p/ph/ed Cinema Action.

●Halfway through this documentary study of the work-in at Upper Clyde Shipbuilders in 1971, one of the workers says, 'This is a group of workers who are not going to grovel, tugging their forelocks, to the labour exchange'. Such clarity of expression and considered determination to participate in the political process powerfully highlights the platitudinous gobbledegook of declared official policy: 'to keep what is in the long term keepable'. The film serves as an enlightening view of exactly how workers can help determine their own future by refusing to be sacrificed to the forces of capitalism (albeit in the name of economic expediency). SM

Filofax

see Taking Care of Business

Fils, Le

see Son, The

Fils de Deux Mères ou Comédie de l'Innocence

(2000, Fr, 103 min)
d Raul Ruiz. *p* Martine de Clermont-Tonnerre. *sc* Françoise Dumas, Raul Ruiz. *ph* Jacques Bouquin. *ed* Mireille Hannon. *ad* Bruno Beaugé. *m* Jorge Arriagada. *cast* Isabelle Huppert, Jeanne Balibar, Charles Berling, Nils Hugon, Edith Scob, Denis Podalydès.

●After his inspired *Time Regained*, Ruiz returns with this brittle, rather drab-looking Buñuelian 'comedy' (from a novel by Massimo Bontempelli) about a nine-year-old boy, Camille (Hugon), who announces to his bewildered mother (Huppert) that his name is Paul and he'd like to go home, now, please. He takes her to an apartment on the other side of Paris, claims to recognise 'his' room, and what's more, the woman who lives there (Balibar) seems to recognise him as the child she lost two years before. Ruiz presents this surreal conceit with matter-of-fact dispassion (and suspense chords on the soundtrack), even as the boy's family go to pieces. TCh

Fils du Requin, Le

see Shark's Son

Filth and the Fury, The

(1999, GB/US, 107 min)
d Julien Temple. *p* Anita Camarata, Amanda Temple. *ed* Niven Howie. *with* Paul Cook, Steve Jones, Glen Matlock, John Lydon, Sid Vicious.

●2000 would have marked the Sex Pistols' silver jubilee, if the band hadn't self-destructed after 26 months of creative chaos unparalleled even in the annals of rock'n'roll. Director Temple was there from the beginning and stayed to document their rise from underground heroes to media bogeymen and beyond. He has already told the story once, as *The Great Rock'n'Roll Swindle*, which he now admits was very much Malcolm McLaren's version of events. This answers McLaren's entrepreneurial cynicism with John Lydon's still seething wit. Collaging Temple's original footage and contemporary broadcast material, the film has the sniff of '70s Britain all right: London swung out to dry, rubbish on the streets, nothing worth working at. Lydon's angry prole rhetoric has an element of rationalisation, but Temple captures Johnny Rotten in all his camp glory. Interviews with the surviving band members are conducted (rather feyly) in silhouette, presumably to preserve the integrity of their younger images. Fortunately, the guys themselves harbour no such inhibitions. Their recollections are frank, funny, compassionate and damning. TCh

Final Analysis

(1992, US, 124 min)
d Phil Joanou. *p* Paul Junger Witt, Tony Thomas, Charles Roven. *sc* Wesley Strick. *ph* Jordan Cronenweth. *ed* Thom Noble. *pd* Dean Tavoularis. *m* George Fenton. *cast* Richard Gere, Kim Basinger, Uma Thurman, Eric Roberts, Paul Guilfoyle, Keith David, Robert Harper, Harris Yulin.

●It's not clear whether this film's genesis is Hitchcock homage or an attempt to build on the success of *Prime Suspect* and *Jagged Edge*. The result is an overlong, hardly believable psychological thriller in which Gere plays a San Francisco shrink involved with the older sister of one of his more disturbed patients. Gere (who spends much of his time testifying in court for the defence) becomes embroiled with Basinger in no time at all. After a heady trip to a very obviously phallic lighthouse, the 'double jeopardy' plot spins off into the blue yonder when she bumps off her fashionable but sadistic American-Greek gangster husband (Roberts, acting with his muscles). While Basinger has the projection, it's Thurman as her younger sister who has most of the real allure, though much of the film's latter half is taken up with a rather tedious game to decide which sis is the psycho. It's hard to care in the end. SGr

Final Combination

(1993, US, 93 min)
d Nigel Dick. *p* Steve Golin, Gregg Fienberg. *sc* Larry Golin. *ph* David Bridges. *ed* Jonathan Shaw, Henry Richardson. *pd* Gary Steele. *m* Rolfe Kent. *cast* Michael Madsen, Lisa Bonet, Gary Stretch, Tim Russ, Damian Chapa, Carmen Argenziano.

●Detective Madsen teams up with reporter Bonet to track down serial killer Stretch. Cop falls for scribe, scribe knows something about the nutcase, nutcase has things in common with cop, etc. Very ordinary. AO

Final Conflict, The

(1981, US, 108 min)
d Graham Baker. *p* Harvey Bernhard. *sc* Andrew Birkin. *ph* Bob Paynter, Philip Meheux. *ed* Alan Strachan. *pd* Herbert Westbrook. *m* Jerry Goldsmith. *cast* Sam Neill, Rossano Brazzi, Don Gordon, Lisa Harrow, Barnaby Holm, Mason Adams, Robert Arden,

●The third part of *The Omen* trilogy is contrived as a series of set pieces whose point is the grisliest possible end for the Antichrist's victims. Damien is now head of the world's largest multinational corporation, a powerful and charismatic man in his early thirties, and the eventual corpses are a band of seven Italian monks armed with sacred daggers, out to stop Damien from preventing the Second Coming (by slaughtering all first-born males). If these elements make it a suitable entrant in the cinema's long blood sports lists, it must be said that the non-delivery of Satan's promised reign is something of a letdown. Still, it does mark a return of sorts to the stylishness of *The Omen* after the tackiness of *Damien – Omen II*. RM

Final Countdown, The

(1980, US, 105 min)
d Don Taylor. *p* Peter Douglas. *sc* David Ambrose, Gerry Davis, Thomas Hunter, Peter Powell. *ph* Victor J Kemper. *ed* Robert K Lambert. *pd* Fernando Carrere. *m* John Scott. *cast* Kirk Douglas, Martin Sheen, Katharine Ross, James Farentino, Ron O'Neal, Charles Durning.

●What happens when the mighty US aircraft carrier 'Nimitz' is carried through a timewarp to find itself off Pearl Harbor minutes before the Japs attack in 1941? An idea worthy of Harlan Ellison, but disappointingly fumbled. Taylor handles most of the aircraft carrier material like a recruiting film, and though the script manages a few deft twists and turns, and even a neat final frisson, it ultimately works more on the tease level of a TV episode than as a movie. Sheen's performance, as always, is engagingly low-key. DP

Final Cut

(1998, GB, 93 min)
d/p/sc Dominic Anciano, Ray Burdis. *ph* John Ward. *ed* Sam Sneade. *pd* Sabrina Sattar. *m* John Beckett. *cast* Ray Winstone, Jude Law, Sadie Frost, Holly Davidson, Lisa Marsh, John Beckett, Mark Burdis.

●The lines between indie experimentation and aggrandised home movie self-indulgence are getting harder to draw. Digital video is on the verge of democratising cinema. Case in point: this mischievous little jape from actors turned producers, writers and directors, Anciano and Burdis. Shot quickly and cheaply in the fashionable fake documentary style, this has a dozen mates gathering at the wake of late lamented Jude (Law), where they're the first audience to see the film à clef he'd been shooting up to his death: a hidden-camera portrait of his marriage to Sadie (Frost – Law's offscreen wife), and all their friends. What begins as a bit of a prank quickly turns nasty as Jude's camera reveals the extent to which his 'friends' moan about, steal from and cheat on their nearest and dearest. Having stuck themselves with a fixed camera and improvisation for Jude's film within the film (the bulk of the running time), the directors are unusually dependent on their cast to nail the tone. The emotional pitch is often so high, they look stranded before this cold, unflinching gaze. Still, such appalling behaviour exerts a certain fascination. It just about works as an insidious home movie – on video. TCh

Final Destination

(2000, US, 98 min)
d James Wong. *p* Warren Zide, Craig Perry, Glen Morgan. *sc* Glen Morgan, James Wong, Jeffrey Reddick. *ph* Robert McLachlan. *ed* James Coblentz. *pd* John Willett. *m* Shirley Walker. *cast* Devon Sawa, Ali Larter, Kerr Smith, Kristen Cloke, Seann William Scott, Chad E Donella, Amanda Detmer, Daniel Roebuck, Roger Guenveur Smith.

●Ominous: 17-year-old Alex (Sawa) is excited to be flying to Paris with his high school French class, but seven of the party miss the flight, and watch in horror as the plane explodes above the airport. It seems Alex has got one over on Death – but the Grim Reaper isn't about to let him and his pals off that easily. This portentous chiller is a nasty piece of work. It's not that the idea is unserviceable, more that the film-makers are contemptuous of both the teenagers the movie is about and the teen audience at which it is aimed. It's difficult to say which is more offensive: an uninspired cast struggling with lines about 'Death's design', or the callousness of the characters, who bury their pals without a hint of remembrance or regret. Here death is a mere special effect, the ultimate gross-out spectacle. TCh

Final Fantasy: The Spirits Within

(2001, US, 120 min)
d Hironobu Sakaguchi. *p* Hironobu Sakaguchi, Jun Aida, Chris Lee. *sc* Al Reinert, Jeff Vintar. *ed* Christopher S Capp. *m* Elliot Goldenthal. *cast* voices: Ming-Na, Alec Baldwin, Ving Rhames, Steve Buscemi, Peri Gilpin, Donald Sutherland, James Woods, Jean Simmons.

●A computer-generated story of earthlings battling wraithlike alien invaders. It's 2065; lithe scientist Dr Aki Ross (voiced by Ming-Na) is trying to harness the spiritual power of near extinct plants and animals to overcome the extra-terrestrials' grip on the planet. Protecting her are square-jawed trooper Gary Edwards (Baldwin) and his assault team, but the project faces an uncertain future: hawkish General Hein (Woods) favours a space-launched raygun aimed at the aliens' nerve centre – putting the Earth itself at risk. It's hard not to be impressed by writer/director Sakaguchi's visualisation of military hardware and squishy monsters. The human figure, however, remains a challenge to current CGI technology, since the detailing of hair and freckles, for instance, proves rather more credible than the marionette-like impression created by cold eyes and oddly unconvincing body movements. TJ

Finally Sunday!

see Vivement Dimanche!

Final Programme, The (aka The Last Days of Man on Earth)

(1973, GB, 89 min)
d Robert Fuest. *p* John Goldstone, Sandy Lieberson. *sc* Robert Fuest. *ph* Norman Warwick. *ed* Barrie Vince. *pd* Robert Fuest. *m* Paul Beaver, Bernard Krause. *cast* Jon Finch, Jenny Runacre, Sterling Hayden, Harry Andrews, Hugh Griffith, Julie Ege, Patrick Magee, Graham Crowden, George Coulouris.

●Read Michael Moorcock's novel first and you might make sense of this garbled sci-fi fantasy about scientists trying to breed a self-reproducing hermaphrodite as the end of the world approaches. Concentrating as always on giving his work a chic gloss, Fuest (acting as his own set designer) simply lets things drift from muddle to muddle while a few moments of black comedy surface. TM

Final Terror (aka Campsite Massacre)

(1981, US, 84 min)
d Andrew Davis. *p* Joe Roth. *sc* Jon George, Neill Hicks, Ronald Shusett. *ph* Andreas Da Videscu [Andrew Davis]. *ed* Paul Rubell, Erica Flaum. *ad* Aleka Corwin. *m* Susan Justin. *cast* John Friedrich, Adrian Zmed, Daryl Hannah, Rachel Ward, Ernest Harden Jr, Mark Metcalf, Joe Pantoliano.

●Something sinister in the woods. Isn't there always? But apart from a couple of minutes of mayhem at beginning and end, the nearest the movie gets to dealing with the deranged slasher plot is to have it told, midway, as a campfire spook story. Undermining genre expectations, Davis reveals an affectionate respect for the woods, and likes his characters enough not to line them up as Slasher Victims 1 to 8. Surprisingly few citizens get carved up, and the women aren't on board to be decorative rape victims. *Deliverance* is the inspiration, but finally this movie rafted down a different stream. DO

Finances of the Grand Duke, The (Die Finanzen des Grossherzogs)

(1924, Ger, 85 min approx, b/w)
d FW Murnau. *p* Erich Pommer. *sc* Thea von Harbou. *ph* Karl Freund, Franz Planer. *ad* Rochus Gliese, Erich Czerwonski. *cast* Harry Liedtke, Alfred Abel, Mady Christians, Adolphe Engers, Max Schreck, Walter Rilla.

●The 1994 restoration confirms that this is indeed a *farce* by FW Murnau, featuring such uncharacteristic ingredients as a madcap Russian princess, a happy go lucky duke, stolen letters, disguises and the like; and featuring Max Schreck, Nosferatu himself, as a comic revolutionary. Murnau takes it all at a fast clip, combining extensive location shooting with a couple of elaborate studio sets, and bringing off two or three shots which, independent of context, are as haunting as any in the canon. Agreeable yet quite forgettable, except for collectors of directorial anomalies, and Murnau-ites on the hunt for correspondences, gay subtexts, etc. BBa

Finanzen des Grossherzogs, Die

see Finances of the Grand Duke, The

Fin août, début septembre

see Late August, Early September

Finders Keepers

(1984, US, 96 min)
d Richard Lester. *p* Sandra Marsh, Terence Marsh. *sc* Ronny Graham, Terence Marsh, Charles Dennis. *ph* Brian West. *ed* John Victor Smith. *pd* Terence Marsh. *m* Ken Thorne. *cast* Michael O'Keefe, Beverly D'Angelo, Louis Gossett Jr, Pamela Stephenson, Ed Lauter, David Wayne, Brian Dennehy, John Schuck.

●While Lester's variable output has been a lot more variable than most, nothing in his assorted canon quite prepares one for the full ghastliness here. Apparently starting from the assumption that *Honky Tonk Freeway* was one of the major movies of our time, this sets off in hot emulation, by rail this time rather than road. The plot has the luckless O'Keefe teaming up with D'Angelo (doing her by now depressingly familiar screwball kookie routine) on the trail of the usual cache of stolen goodies. Lester, whose soft spot for particularly witless capers has been well documented, tries to shore things up with as much trickery as he can muster, but it's a doomed exercise. JP

Finding Forrester

(2000, US/Can, 137 min)
d Gus Van Sant. *p* Laurence Mark, Sean Connery, Rhonda Tollefson. *sc* Mike Rich. *ph* Harris Savides. *ed* Valdís Óskarsdóttir. *pd* Jane Musky. *cast* Sean Connery, F Murray Abraham, Anna Paquin, Busta Rhymes, April Grace, Michael Pitt, Michael Nouri, Rob Brown, Matt Damon.

●What is it with Gus Van Sant and remakes? First he Xeroxed *Psycho*; here he rehashes one of his own films. Jamal (Brown) is an exceptionally bright, black 16-year-old and nifty basketballer who leaves the Bronx for the WASP-ish confines of an exclusive prep school. A quiet, literary whiz kid, he bristles at attempts to belittle his off-court talent, and falls under the tutelage of local recluse William Forrester (Connery), a Salinger-esque figure burdened with having written the Great American Novel in his youth and not much else. In short: take *Good Will Hunting*, swap English for maths, and add a dash of race and a smidgen of Caledonian élan. The leaden screenplay can be fingered for many of the film's faults. But what happened to the off-kilter film-maker last seen at work in *To Die For*? Van Sant shoots and paces Jamal's developing relationship with Forrester as generically as it's scripted; a weakness all the more apparent when compared with Curtis Hanson's far saltier treatment of similar themes in *Wonder Boys*. Sift through the remains, and all that emerges is the strong central performances: Brown impresses in his first film role, while Connery, for once, reveals a vulnerability commensurate with his age. MHi

Finding Graceland

(1998, US, 96 min)
d David Winkler. *p* Cary Brokaw. *sc* Jason Horwitch. *ph* Elliot Davis. *ed* Robert K Lambert, Luis Colina. *pd* Jeffrey Townsend. *m* Stephen Endelman. *cast* Harvey Keitel, Johnathon Schaech, Bridget Fonda, John Aylward, Susan Traylor, Gretchen Mol.

●'The name's Elvis. I'm trying to find my way to Memphis.' Yes, the King has come amongst us again, to improve our souls and do good works. In this uncommonly whimsical picture, Keitel plays either a businessman deranged by the death of his family, or the repository of Elvis's spirit, up and about after a 20-year lay-off. As he heads home to Graceland, he's joined by Schaech (robotic) who nurses a secret grief, and by Fonda as a cheery Marilyn impersonator. The platitudes, the soggy symbolism and cop-out ending are mitigated by Keitel's hardboiled charisma, which survives even a scene where, got up in a jumpsuit and a little cape, he tears into a rendition of 'Suspicious Minds'. Co-exec produced by Priscilla Presley. BBa

Finding North

(1997, US, 95 min)
d Tanya Wexler. *p* Steven A Jones, Stephen Dyer. *sc* Kim Powers. *ph* Michael Barrett. *ed* Thom Zimny. *pd* James B Smythe. *m* Café Noir. *cast* Wendy Makkena, John Benjamin Hickey, Anne Bobby, Rebecca Creskoff, Angela Pietropinto, Freddie Roman, Molly McClure.

●For all its bold, comic treatment of gay issues, simple staging and quirky yet predictable ending, this tale of friendship, self-discovery and small town life holds few surprises. It starts in New York, with kooky Jewish-Italian bank clerk Ronda Portelli (Makkena) spotting a naked Travis Furlong (Hickey) as he contemplates jumping off the Brooklyn Bridge. Two days later, he enters her bank; convinced fate has orchestrated their meeting, Rhonda becomes infatuated, unaware that he's gay and mourning the death of his lover. To Travis's horror, she gatecrashes the wake and pursues him to Texas. While the narrative is signposted in the first 15 minutes, debut director Wexler's depiction of Travis and Rhonda as polar opposites, through character detail and vignettes of their daily lives, is genuinely affecting. Once in Texas, however, the film descends into eager to please humour, overworking the stale 'mismatched duo on a mission' scenario. HK

Fin du Jour, La (The End of the Day)

(1939, Fr, 108 min, b/w)
d Julien Duvivier. *sc* Charles Spaak, Julien Duvivier. *ph* Christian Matras, Armand Thirard. *ed* Marthe Poncin. *ad* Jacques Krauss. *m* Maurice Jaubert. *cast* Louis Jouvet, Michel Simon, Victor Francen, Madeleine Ozeray, Gabrielle Dorziat, François Périer, Sylvie.

●Set in an abbey that serves as a retirement home for actors, rife with squabbles, jealousies and remembrances of past glory, to which a threat of closure adds waves of despairing self-pity, *La Fin du Jour* once rated highly as a biting depictment (like *La Règle du Jeu* though in a different key) of the decadence of France just before World War II. Despite its dark edges, it hasn't worn nearly so well as Renoir's masterpiece, with a complacently whimsical sentimentality constantly threatening to break through. The performances, though, are terrific: Jouvet as the suave ladykiller determined to maintain his image at all costs; Simon as the hopeless ham who lived out a marginal career as the eternal understudy; Francen as the classical artist too proud to court popular success and still regretting it. TM

Fine Day, A (Der Schöne Tag)

(2000, Ger, 74 min)
d Thomas Arslan. *p* Thomas Arslan, Martin Hagemann. *sc* Thomas Arslan. *ph* Michael Wiesweg. *ed* Bettina Blickwede. *pd* Ulrika Anderson. *m* Selda Kaya, Morton Feldman, Saul Williams. *cast* Serpil Turhan, Bilge Bingül, Florian Stetter, Selda Kaya, Hafize Üner, Hanns Zischler, Elke Schmitter.

●Arslan's previous feature *Dealer* suggested a poised talent, a sure eye and a composed sensibility brought to bear on a 'still waters run deep' portrait surely inspired by Bresson. His follow-up maintains the promise, though the template has shifted towards Rohmer, with a meandering female protagonist (shown dubbing *A Summer's Tale*), a good bit of talk and some string-pulling.

A 'day in the life' snapshot, it's likewise reminiscent of prime Richard Linklater, in both its episodic linearity and its deployment of lop-sided set piece dialogue – as Deniz (Turhan) leaves her lover, surveys romantic plights with old family and friends, submits to a curiously sparse job audition, shares ideas with strangers and eyes up boys. It's a study of the proverbial hungry heart, profiled mostly through speech but also through Deniz's roving eye and the daily pattern of her peregrination. Not as substantial as the aforementioned models, mind, but lucid and definitely intriguing. NB

Fine Madness, A

(1966, US, 104 min)
d Irvin Kershner. *p* Jerome Hellman. *sc* Elliott Baker. *ph* Ted McCord. *ed* William Ziegler. *ad* Jack Poplin. *m* John Addison. *cast* Sean Connery, Joanne Woodward, Jean Seberg, Patrick O'Neal, Clive Revill, Jackie Coogan.
● An engaging, sharply scripted comedy (Elliott Baker, from his own novel), with Connery oddly but not inaptly cast as a poet driven berserk by the frustrations of wage-earning in New York. Perceptive, persuasive and often very funny, especially in a sequence where Connery, forced to address a staid group of female culture-vultures because he needs the fee, gets drunk and proceeds to relieve his feelings ('Open your corsets and bloom…let the metaphors creep above your knees'). Silly farce takes over latterly as a doctor he has cuckolded vengefully prescribes a pre-frontal lobotomy (which has no effect). Ted McCord's location camerawork, and Woodward's performance as the poet's harassed, embarrassed wife, are outstanding. TM

Fine Mess, A

(1986, US, 90 min)
d Blake Edwards. *p* Tony Adams. *sc* Blake Edwards. *ph* Harry Stradling Jr. *ed* John F Burnett, Robert Pergament. *pd* Rodger Maus. *m* Henry Mancini. *cast* Ted Danson, Howie Mandel, Richard Mulligan, Stuart Margolin, Maria Conchita Alonso, Jennifer Edwards, Paul Sorvino.
● Clever of Blake Edwards to review his frenetic comedy in the title, but after that it's downhill all the way to the tune of screeching tires, the jabber of gibberish, and a hysteria count likely to leave audiences gasping like goldfish. What plot there is has movie extra Danson blundering into a race-horse-nobbling racket, and attempting to stay one car chase ahead of the cops, the mob and a string of irate old flames long enough to collect his ill-gotten winnings. This involves more crashes than the M1 on a Bank Holiday, a host of throwaway jokes which should all have been thrown away, and wild overacting all round. The biggest disappointment is Danson, who created an exquisite satire on the American superstud in TV's *Cheers*; his extension of the role here, as Sex Machine Spence, is a downright embarrassment. DAt

Finger Man, The

see Doulos, Le

Finger of Guilt

see Intimate Stranger, The

Fingers

(1978, US, 91 min)
d James Toback. *p* George Barrie. *sc* James Toback. *ph* Michael Chapman. *ed* Robert Lawrence. *pd* Gene Rudolf. *cast* Harvey Keitel, Jim Brown, Tisa Farrow, Michael V Gazzo, Tanya Roberts, Georgette Muir.
● Bearing not a little resemblance to Scorsese's *Mean Streets*, not to mention Toback's earlier script for Karel Reisz's *The Gambler*, this is a raw thriller-cum-psychodrama about a split personality: Keitel plays an aspiring concert pianist strangely fascinated by the violence he encounters while enforcing the payment of 'debts' owed to his criminal father. The idea is none too original, and the film can certainly be faulted for its macho posturing and unquestioning misogyny. Nonetheless, Toback, making his directing debut, is clearly exorcising – or indulging – a few personal demons, and the perverse conviction of Keitel's tormented performance, reinforced by restless, sometimes volatile visuals, prevents the overheated plot from becoming entirely risible. It's not exactly pleasant, but it is compelling. GA

Finian's Rainbow

(1968, US, 144 min)
d Francis Ford Coppola. *p* Joseph Landon. *sc* EY Harburg, Fred Saidy. *ph* Philip H Lathrop. *ed* Melvin Shapiro. *pd* Hilyard Brown. *m* Burton Lane. *cast* Fred Astaire, Petula Clark, Tommy Steele, Don Francks, Barbara Hancock, Keenan Wynn, Al Freeman Jr.
● An underrated musical, admittedly a little dated in the social comment (on labour exploitation and race relations) which probably seemed quite daring on the original's Broadway debut in 1947. But Burton Lane's score – intact save for the curious omission of the marvellous 'Necessity' – is still first rate, and Coppola steers his motley cast through it with an instinct for rhythm and movement which shows that the choreographic preoccupation which surfaced in his work starting with 'One From The Heart' was nothing new. Certainly the best of the latter-day musicals in the tradition of Minnelli and MGM. TM

Finnegans Wake (aka Passages from James Joyce's Finnegans Wake)

(1965, US, 97 min, b/w)
d/p Mary Ellen Bute. *sc* Mary Manning, Mary Ellen Bute. *ph* Ted Nemeth. *ed* Mary Ellen Bute, Yoshio Kishi, Paul Ronder, Thelma Schoonmaker, Catherine Pichonnier. *m* Elliot Kaplan. *cast* Martin J Kelly, Jane Reilly, Peter Haskell, Page Johnson, John V Kelleher, Ray Flanagan.
● A surprisingly successful attempt to bring Joyce's gargantuan novel to the screen – especially surprising considering Mary Ellen Bute's previous work for the cinema (some very footling animation à la McLaren). The reason probably lies in her use of the play adaptation by Mary Manning, which transforms much of the original's humour and verbal fireworks into stunning theatre. The film isn't stunning cinema, but it's consistently entertaining and far more Joycean than Joseph Strick's pedantic efforts. GB

Finyé (The Wind)

(1982, Mali, 105 min)
d/p/sc Souleymane Cissé. *ph* Etienne Corton de Grammont. *ed* Andrée Davanture. *ad* Malick Guisse. *m* Pierre Gorse. *cast* Fousseyni Sissoko, Goundo Guisse, Balla Moussa Keita, Ismaila Sarr, Oumou Diarra.
● A campus protest movie, complete with drugs, generation gaps, fascistic policing and boy-girl problems. Cissé's students actually are living under a military dictatorship and trying to come to terms with a patriarchal society still weighed down with hundreds of superstitions. No one is caricatured, and the film develops its conflicts with splendid directness, shifting easily between realism and fantasy. It boils down to a fairly simple argument for liberal democracy, but the specifics of the setting give it an immediacy that an equivalent western film could never approach. TR

Fiore delle Mille e una Notte, Il

see Arabian Nights

Fiorile

(1993, It/Fr/Ger, 122 min)
d Paolo Taviani, Vittorio Taviani. *p* Grazia Volpi. *sc* Sandro Petraglia, Vittorio Taviani. *ph* Giuseppe Lanci. *ed* Roberto Perpignani. *ad* Gianni Sbarra. *m* Nicola Piovani. *cast* Claudio Bigagli, Galatea Ranzi, Michael Vartan, Lino Capolicchio, Constanza Engelbrecht.
● The Tavianis' film recounts the changing fortunes of a Tuscan family – the Benedetti ('blessed'), later known as the Maledetti ('cursed') – from the time of the Napoleonic Wars, when a young girl's love for a French soldier is thwarted by her brother's theft of gold from the invading army's coffers, to the present day, when one of the girl's descendants returns from France with his children to introduce them to their disillusioned, reclusive grandfather. In the intervening years, even when the family was at its wealthiest at the start of the 20th century, ambition, guilt, power and desire for vengeance dominated the Benedettis' lives – but what of the future? Will the children at last be able to shake off the 200-year-old 'curse'? A film of immense elegance, the Tuscan landscape ravishingly photographed by Giuseppe Lanci, the poignant emotions subtly underscored by Nicola Piovani's characteristically lovely music. GA

Fire

(1977, US, 100 min)
d Earl Bellamy. *p* Irwin Allen. *sc* Norman Katkov, Arthur Weiss. *ph* Dennis Dalzell. *ed* Bill Brame. *ad* Ward Preston. *m* Richard La Salle. *cast* Ernest Borgnine, Vera Miles, Patty Duke Astin, Alex Cord, Donna Mills, Lloyd Nolan, Neville Brand, Ty Hardin, Gene Evans.
● Spectacularly ham-fisted disaster movie (made for TV). The disaster this time is a forest fire, ignited by convict Neville Brand as part of an elaborate escape plan. Bellamy's sluggish direction dampens every opportunity for suspense as he brings together groups of gruff rangers, public-spirited prisoners, an anguished teacher and her cosmetic schoolchildren, an incredibly silly couple of doctors whose marriage is on the rocks, and two ageing sweethearts. Curdled sentiment predominates, the performances are uniformly awful, and the script ('Any psychiatrist would tell us that our real problem is your father') is stilted in the extreme. IB

Fire

(1996, Can, 104 min)
d Deepa Mehta. *p* Deepa Mehta, Bobby Bedi. *sc* Deepa Mehta. *ph* Giles Nuttgens. *ed* Barry Farrell. *pd* Aradhana Seth. *m* AR Rahman. *cast* Shabana Azmi, Nandita Das, Kulbushan Kharbanda, Jaaved Jaaferi, Ranjit Chowdhury, Kushal Rekhi.
● Adultery, masturbation and lesbianism…this taboo-breaking Indian film from the producer of *Bandit Queen* has 'em all. Significantly, perhaps, it's in English, but otherwise the portrait of a New Delhi household caught between the contradictory impulses of duty and desire rings reasonably true (though the emancipated new bride Sita may be a somewhat idealised figure). It's a courageous picture that never gets too pompous – writer/director Mehta isn't above interjecting a parodic fantasy sequence or a song – very attractively photographed by Giles Nuttgens, with radiant performances from Azmi and Das. TCh

Fire and Ice

(1982, US, 82 min)
d Ralph Bakshi. *p* Ralph Bakshi, Frank Frazetta. *sc* Roy Thomas, Gerry Conway. *ph* Francis Grumman. *ed* A David Marshall. *m* William Kraft. *cast* voices: Randy Norton, Cynthia Leake, Steve Sandor, Sean Hannon, Leo Gordon.
● More cut-ups from Bakshi's animated cut-outs. Here his collaborator is Frank Frazetta, dean of Sword'n'Sorcery illustration – and with predictable results. It's all Chas Atlas heroes slicing one another to bits in order to win ladies with more curves than a bunch of grapes. Complete with sub-Wagnerian score and just a hint of subliminal racism – the disposable 'sub-humans' are dusky chaps, the hero an Aryan blond – it may well satisfy a low IQ, pubescent (probably) male Iron Maiden fan, but the rest of us are poorly served. GD

Firebirds (aka Wings of the Apache)

(1990, US, 86 min)
d David Green. *p* Bill Badalato. *sc* Nick Thiel, Paul F Edwards. *ph* Tony Imi. *ed* Jon Poll, Norman Buckley, Dennis O'Connor. *ad* Joseph T Garrity. *m* David Newman. *cast* Nicolas Cage, Tommy Lee Jones, Sean Young, Bryan Kestner, Dale Dye, Mary Ellen Trainor, JA Preston, Peter Onorati.
● When the American military decides to wade in against Latin American drug cartel terrorism, young pilot Jake Preston (Cage) joins the task force, and undergoes training by Brad Little (Jones) on the wonder attack-helicopter known as the Apache. Brad can spot a soul-mate: 'I joined the army to kick ass' he tells Jake, 'and so did you'. Problems with his sight and ex-girl-friend/fellow pilot Billie Lee (Young) ruffle Jake's plans. Inevitable comparisons with *Top Gun* leave this action adventure wanting. With a gung ho script, sometimes rudimentary editing and uninvolving relationships, the whole effect is rather flat. None of the aerial sequences boast the visual thrills of *Top Gun*, while even the attempt to inject controversy in the shape of Hollywood's first female combatant is

half-realised. In mid-battle, a pursued Billie Lee pleads, 'Oh Jake, save my ass'. She should have heard his reason for enlisting. CM

Firebrand

see Affairs of Cellini, The

Fire Festival (Himatsuri)

(1984, Jap, 120 min)
d Mitsuo Yanagimachi. *p* Kazuo Shimizu. *sc* Kenji Nakagami. *ph* Masaki Tamura. *ed* Sachiko Yamaji. *ad* Takeo Kimura. *m* Toru Takemitsu. *cast* Kinya Kitaoji, Kiwako Taichi, Ryota Nakamoto, Norihei Miki, Rikiya Yasuoka.

●This deals with Grand Themes – mankind versus nature, the immanence of the divine – without seeming either stupid or pretentious. Yanagimachi starts from a brilliant location (a small coastal town ringed by mountains), and then tells an extraordinary tale. An ultra-macho lumberjack identifies completely with the forests he pillages. He is sexually unfulfilled by his marriage, by an old flame, and by the vaguely gay thing he has going with the teenage boy on his team; his sexual energies, nurtured by the pantheist tradition of shinto, are focused on the goddesses of the place. His mind finally snaps during the town's annual fire festival, leading to a truly shattering climax. Ecological and social issues resonate in the background, and the haunting sounds and images will leave most audiences shaken, stirred and awed. TR

Firefox

(1982, US, 136 min)
d/p Clint Eastwood. *sc* Alex Lasker, Wendell Wellman. *ph* Bruce Surtees. *ed* Ferris Webster, Ron Spang. *ad* John Graysmark, Elayne Ceder. *m* Maurice Jarre. *cast* Clint Eastwood, Freddie Jones, David Huffman, Warren Clarke, Ronald Lacey, Kenneth Colley.

●Ex-Vietnam flier with poor nerves (and bad case of flashbacks) is ordered to steal deadly Russian jet from behind 'enemy' lines. The simple storyline is quickly grounded by flying chunks of exposition that director/actor Eastwood tries to ignore. Eastwood the director disregards many Cold War possibilities, preferring to dawdle over a first hour that mooches along while Eastwood the actor enjoyably dons various disguises, playing a man who can't act (or so everyone tells him) and is happiest left alone with his gippy nerves. Only in the airborne climax – a prolonged chase of modest ability – does he achieve solitary ecstasy, while, with a touch so perverse as to be admirable, the wordy finale is left to a foreign actor whose English is actually incomprehensible. CPe

Fire in the Sky

(1993, US, 109 min)
d Robert Lieberman. *p* Joe Wizan, Todd Black. *sc* Tracy Tormé. *ph* Bill Pope. *ed* Steve Mirkovich. *pd* Laurence Bennett. *m* Mark Isham. *cast* DB Sweeney, Robert Patrick, James Garner, Craig Sheffer, Peter Berg, Henry Thomas.

●This modest sci-fi movie treads the same ground as *Communion*, but more purposefully. The small community of Snowflake, Arizona, is thrown into confusion when loggers return from the forest claiming one of their number has been taken away in a spacecraft. A sceptical special investigator (Garner) shares the locals' doubts, believing the story is a cover for murder…until the missing man (Sweeney) turns up with his own incredible story. The imagery is familiar: scientific experiments in which orifices are penetrated, and womblike interiors representing primal fears about the integrity of the body. Surely this is inner, not outer space. Even so, the handling of the small-town social dynamics, the media circus and the scary special effects provide an engrossing build-up and satisfying pay-off. NF

Firelight

(1997, US/GB, 103 min)
d William Nicholson. *p* Brian Eastman. *sc* William Nicolson. *ph* Nick Morris. *ed* Chris Wimble. *pd* Rob Harris. *m* Chris Gunning.*cast* Sophie Marceau, Stephen Dillane, Kevin Anderson, Lia Williams, Dominique Belcourt, Joss Ackland, Emma Amos, Wolf Kahler. Annabel Giles.

●To defend her debt-hounded father, Swiss governess Elisabeth (Marceau) accepts a financial proposition from an anonymous English aristocrat. She spends three nights with him in a quiet Normandy hotel and delivers a child nine months later. Seven years later fate brings them together again. Charles (Dillane) has since moved to Sussex with 'their' daughter Louisa (Belcourt), a rebellious girl who has seen off a string of governesses. Elisabeth, the latest incumbent, enters a strange household where Charles' wife remains a bedridden invalid, and Louisa spends hours of lonely reverie in a water-surrounded outhouse. First time director William (*Shadowlands*) Nicholson fails to disguise the air of contrivance hanging over this 19th century saga of thwarted maternal love. While young Belcourt makes an effectively moody contribution, the two central performances are less well-balanced. Dillane is as remote as he was in *Welcome to Sarajevo*; and Marceau, while showing characteristic determination, is never an actress to win much emotional empathy from the audience. Christopher Gunning's music over-compensates for their reticence and nearly drowns the lot in genteel syrup. TJ

Firemen's Ball, The (Horí, má Panenko)

(1967, Czech/It, 73 min)
d Milos Forman. *p* Carlo Ponti. *sc* Milos Forman, Ivan Passer, Jaroslav Papousek. *ph* Miroslav Ondricek. *ed* Miroslav Hajek. *ad* Karel Cerny. *m* Karel Mares. *cast* Jan Vostrcil, Josef Kolb, Josef Svet, Frantisek Debelka, Josef Sebánek.

●The scene is the annual firemen's ball in a small Czech town. The action, characteristically tenuous but packed with detail, concerns the committee's efforts to round up girls for a beauty contest, the winner to make the presentation of a golden hatchet to their 86-year-old retiring president. As the ball proceeds, a patchwork of comic incident unfolds: the committee, finding girls too shy and mothers too ferocious, are busily trying to hijack *any* girl, pretty or not; an anxious official watches as the lottery prizes mysteriously vanish one by one; and the ancient president, desperate to slip away for a pee, is kept forcibly waiting and waiting. Quietly, irresistibly funny in the early Forman manner (this was his first film in colour); but the belated switch to allegorical satire (in the closing sequences, an elderly peasant's house burns down while the firemen revel; a sympathetic whip-round nets the now worthless lottery tickets for him) seems altogether too sour in the context. TM

Fire Monsters Against the Son of Hercules

see Maciste contro i Mostri

Fire Over England

(1936, GB, 92 min, b/w)
d William K Howard. *p* Erich Pommer. *sc* Clemence Dane, Sergei Nolbandov. *ph* James Wong Howe. *ed* Jack Dennis. *ad* Lazare Meerson, Frank Wells. *m* Richard Addinsell. *cast* Flora Robson, Laurence Olivier, Leslie Banks, Raymond Massey, Vivien Leigh, Tamara Desni, James Mason.

●Lavish Korda production designed partly as a coronation year spectacular, partly as a call to arms against the Nazi threat. The script is the usual historico-romantico bunk, tricked out with some literary frills and providing some mild swashbuckling for Olivier, playing a young man seeking revenge for his father's death at the hands of the Spanish Inquisition, and simultaneously serving Queen and Country by obtaining advance news of the Armada. Directed stylishly enough, but it gets by mainly on the handsome sets, superb camerawork (Wong Howe), and some sterling performances (notably Robson's pawky Queen Elizabeth and Massey as the villainous Philip of Spain). Pity the climactic burning of the Armada is so obviously tank-bound. TM

Firepower

(1979, GB, 104 min)
d/p Michael Winner. *sc* Gerald Wilson. *ph* Bob Paynter, Dick Kratina. *ed* Arnold Crust [Michael Winner]. *pd* John Stoll, John Blezard. *m* Gato Barbieri. *cast* Sophia Loren, James Coburn, OJ Simpson, Eli Wallach, Anthony Franciosa, George Grizzard, Vincent Gardenia.

●Typically brash and lurid thriller from Winner, which starts off with Loren's chemist husband being blown up as he's on the point of exposing a racket in contaminated drugs. As Loren and an ex-lover (Coburn) try to track down the killers, the film turns into an endless series of noisy, colourful explosions and crashes in glossily picturesque locations. Tiresome. GA

Firestarter

(1984, US, 114 min)
d Mark L Lester. *p* Frank Capra Jr. *sc* Stanley Mann. *ph* Giuseppe Ruzzolini. *ed* David Rawlins. *ad* Giorgio Postiglione. *m* Tangerine Dream. *cast* David Keith, Drew Barrymore, Freddie Jones, Heather Locklear, Martin Sheen, George C Scott, Art Carney, Louise Fletcher, Moses Gunn, Antonio Fargas.

●Stephen King's novel not only concerns that most awkward of all combinations, the CIA and paranormal psychology, it has the episodic quality that is a hallmark of King's less filmable fiction. Barrymore (the sister in *ET*) plays a girl with telekinetic powers who is eventually captured and shoved into a government laboratory. Lester manages to maintain a fair level of suspense, and he is greatly helped by Scott, giving his best performance in years as the demonic CIA man sporting a sneer and a pony tail, but King's supernatural ideas need a human focus or they seem nearly idiotic. And, unlike the central figures in *Carrie* or *The Shining*, the heroine of *Firestarter* is just a rather wet little girl who happens to throw fireballs. DP

Fires Were Started (aka I Was a Fireman)

(1943, GB, 74 min, b/w)
d Humphrey Jennings. *p* Ian Dalrymple. *sc* Humphrey Jennings. *ph* C Pennington-Richards. *ed* Stewart McAllister. *ad* Edward Carrick. *m* William Alwyn. *cast* George Gravett, Philip Dickson, Fred Griffiths, Loris Rey, Johnny Houghton, William Sansom.

●Jennings' one venture into feature-length drama-documentary narrowly escaped being brutally chopped down by the publicity men at the Ministry of Information. Certainly it lacks the tight narrative structure common in good commercial films, but Jennings is a strong enough film-maker to ignore formulae and conventions to build his own unique structures. Here he used real firemen and real fires – kindled among the blitzed warehouses of London's dockland – but with the aim of creating something more than documentary realism. It is the epic quality of the firemen's struggle that excites Jennings, and his celebration of the courage and dignity of ordinary people working together in the shadow of disaster makes the film extraordinarily impressive. RMy

Fire with Fire

(1986, US, 103 min)
d Duncan Gibbins. *p* Gary Nardino. *sc* Bill Phillips, Warren Skaaren, Paul Boorstin, Sharon Boorstin. *ph* Hiro Narita. *ed* Peter E Berger. *pd* Norman Newberry. *m* Howard Shore. *cast* Virginia Madsen, Craig Sheffer, Jon Polito, Jeffrey Jay Cohen, DB Sweeney, Kate Reid, Jean Smart, Ann Savage.

●It's romance across the tracks time as reform school kid Sheffer goes on the run with Catholic schoolgirl Madsen in this time-passer which went straight-to-video in Britain. Trivia fans will tick the presence of *Detour*'s Ann Savage in a small role as one of the nuns. The title conceals a tragic irony: Duncan Gibbins, the British-born writer/director, perished when a forest inferno swallowed up his Los Angeles home in 1994. TJ

Fire Within, The

see Feu Follet, Le

Fire Within, The (Onibi)

(1997, Jap, 101 min)
d Rokuro Mochizuki. *p* Yoshi Chiba, Toshiki Kimura. *sc* Toshiyuki Morioka. *ph* Nao'aki I,aizumi. *ed* Yashushi Shimamura. *pd* Hirohid Shibata. *m* Ken-ichi Kamio. *cast* Yoshio Harada, Reiko Kataoka, Sho Aikawa, Yashushi Kitamura, Noriko Hayami, Eiji Okuda.

●There's nothing startlingly original about this tale of a gangster trying to go straight on his release from prison (no, he doesn't succeed for long), but Mochizuki finds a fresh, sidelong slant on even the most hackneyed situations. Yoshio Harada – a laconic tough guy in the Takeshi Kitano mould – makes Kuni a decent, if impatient man. His actions carry real weight, allowing the director to develop an unexpectedly romantic tone. TCh

Fireworks

see Anger Magick Lantern Cycle, The

Firm, The

(1993, US, 154 min)
d Sydney Pollack. *p* Scott Rudin, John Davis, Sydney Pollack. *sc* David Rabe, Robert Towne, Dvid Rayfiel. *ph* John Seale. *ed* Fredric Steinkamp, William Steinkamp. *pd* Richard Macdonald. *m* David Grusin. *cast* Cruise, Gene Hackman, Gary Busey, Holly Hunter, Jeanne Tripplehorn, Hal Holbrook, Ed Harris, Toibin Bell.

● Pollack's conventional race-against-time version of John Grisham's best-seller soft pedals on the novel's conspiracy-paranoia atmosphere, makes goons of the Mob, and shows signs of having been rewritten. But it does have Cruise as the go-for-it law graduate, whose now rather faded physical charm takes nothing from his dumb-but-earnest ingénu appeal. The plot has Cruise scorn the advances of the big Eastern law firms for a small 'family'-oriented outfit in Memphis, only to find rottenness at the heart and hearth of the New South. Adorning the film, in supporting roles, are its saving graces: Hackman's moving and dissolute *consigliere*/ father-figure; madcap investigator Busey and floozy helpmeet Hunter; and Bell's eerily engaging white-haired psychopath. WH

First a Girl

(1935, GB. 94 min, b/w)
d Victor Saville. *p* Michael Balcon. *sc* Marjorie Gaffney. *ph* Glen MacWilliams. *ed* Al Barnes. *ad* Oscar Werndorff. *songs* Maurice Sigler, Al Goodhart. *cast* Jessie Matthews, Sonnie Hale, Griffith Jones, Anna Lee, Alfred Drayton, Martita Hunt.

● The last in a series of German musicals transposed into English (and later remade with Julie Andrews as *Victor/Victoria*). Matthews is, as usual, an aspiring seamstress whose singing and dancing ambitions are fulfilled only after a sequence of sexual shenanigans. In *Evergreen* she won fame and fortune by impersonating her granny. Here, doing a *Tootsie* in reverse, she resorts to playing a female impersonator – with understandably convincing results. Saville doesn't quite get his Busby Berkeley act together, and an aura of inane innocence keeps at bay the interesting undertones of the plot. But for an English musical, this is tight, professional and unpretentious, and Matthews has a winsome vitality which is irresistible. RMy

First Blood

(1982, US, 93 min)
d Ted Kotcheff. *p* Buzz Feitshans. *sc* Michael Kozoll, William Sackheim, Sylvester Stallone. *ph* Andrew Laszlo. *ed* Joan Chapman. *pd* Wolf Kroeger. *m* Jerry Goldsmith. *cast* Sylvester Stallone, Richard Crenna, Brian Dennehy, David Caruso, Jack Starrett, Michael Talbott.

● A long-haired undesirable, run off-limits by a small town sheriff, turns right around and comes back. Taken to the police station for a spot of persuasion, he suffers flash recalls of torture in Vietnam. Going momentarily berserk, and hounded like a mad dog, he leads his pursuers a frightening dance through the woods before returning to give the town its comeuppance. As a Stallone vehicle this is sleek, slick and not unexciting, but crassly castrates the David Morrell novel on which it is based. Read the book: tough, provocative, savagely ironical and infinitely more complex, it's much better value. TM

First Deadly Sin, The

(1980, US, 112 min)
d Brian G Hutton. *p* George Pappas, Mark Shanker. *sc* Mann Rubin. *ph* Jack Priestley. *ed* Eric Albertson. *ad* Woods MacKintosh. *m* Gordon Jenkins. *cast* Frank Sinatra, Faye Dunaway, David Dukes, George Coe, Brenda Vaccaro, Martin Gabel, Anthony Zerbe, James Whitmore.

● Dull, confused thriller, with cop Sinatra tracking down an apparently motiveless murderer, meanwhile worrying about his wife becoming increasingly unhealthy after a kidney operation. Totally superfluous religious imagery haunts the plot, the relationship between Sinatra and Dunaway seems to have been inserted entirely for sentimental reasons, and the whole thing fails to convince throughout. GA

First Effort (Opera Prima)

(1979, Sp, 92 min)
d Fernando Trueba. *p* Fernando Colomo. *sc* Oscar Ladoire, Fernando Trueba. *ph* Angel Luis Fernandez. *ed* Miguel Santamaria. *m* Fernando Ember. *cast* Oscar Ladoire, Paula Molina, Antonio Resines, Kitty Manver, Marisa Paredes, Luis Gonzalez Regueral.

● Romantic comedy of manners manqué, set in the post-Franco Swinging '70s and centred on a super-conventional Antoine Doinel clone and his encounters: with a sweet young thing and her swain; his waspish ex-spouse; one Belch, nihilist author of *Dried Shit* (subtle humour this isn't); Zoila, blue movie-maker who gets off on bestiality and ball-breaking fornication; and a bizarrely incongruous Ingmar Bergman, who luckily never appears. Well-liked in New York ('a new Woody Allen') and France ('neo-Truffaut'), this peevish and impatient portrait of Spain's late-blossoming flower generation has the generosity and incisiveness of neither. SJo

First Great Train Robbery, The (aka The Great Train Robbery)

(1978, GB, 111 min)
d Michael Crichton. *p* John Foreman. *sc* Michael Crichton. *ph* Geoffrey Unsworth. *ed* David Bretherton. *pd* Maurice Carter. *m* Jerry Goldsmith. *cast* Sean Connery, Donald Sutherland, Lesley-Anne Down, Alan Webb, Malcolm Terris, Robert Lang, Michael Elphick.

● Connery and Sutherland as a pair of free-wheeling Victorian criminals in the Butch and Sundance mould who attempt to rob a bullion train. Crichton's adaptation of his own novel falls badly between genres, never quite making up its mind whether it's aiming for comedy or suspense, and not succeeding very conclusively at either. The characters stay largely undeveloped, while – despite superficially peculiar features – the robbery is stripped of the ingenious exposition of the novel to become just another heist. There are some excellent sequences, notably those built around the search for the bullion keys; but in general this odd hybrid cuts through the crap of much period melodrama without finding anything very substantial to put in its place. DP

First Knight

(1995, US, 134 min)
d Jerry Zucker. *p* Jerry Zucker, Hunt Lowry. *sc* William Nicholson. *ph* Adam Greenberg. *ed* Walter Murch. *pd* John Box. *m* Jerry Goldsmith. *cast* Richard Gere, Sean Connery, Julia Ormond, Ben Cross, Liam Cunningham, Christopher Villiers, Valentine Pelka, Colin McCormack, John Gielgud.

● This expensive, star-heavy retake on the Arthurian legend works well enough as Hollywood Gothic hokum: Connery is his usual reliable self as the renowned first among equals; Ormond is quite excellent as a thoroughly modern maiden torn between love and duty; and Gere's fearless Lancelot may be about as medieval as a roller disco but still has charm and athleticism (less Lancelot du Lac than Lancelot du Lacquer). William Nicholson's script produces a few dud lines, but the big scenes are spaciously put together and the final sequence in which Arthur is launched towards Avalon on a raft ignited by a lone arrow is genuinely touching. There's even a cameo by Gielgud and the semblance of a happy ending to a story that is usually shrouded in mist and tears. No Merlin, no Holy Grail, and no Lady of the Lake. Lots of lovely torches though and some really neat crossbows. SGr

First Legion, The

(1950, US, 86 min, b/w)
d/p Douglas Sirk. *sc* Emmet Lavery. *ph* Robert De Grasse. *ed* Francis D Lyon. *m* Hans Sommer. *cast* Charles Boyer, William Demarest, Lyle Bettger, Barbara Rush, Leo G Carroll, HB Warner, George Zucco.

● Something of an oddity in the Sirk canon, in that it was shot on location and is unusually static and talky. It concerns various crises of religious faith suffered by a number of priests in a Jesuit seminary; Sirk admitted that he wanted to push it towards comedy, since the subject as he saw it related religion to the absurd, namely a bogus 'miracle', performed by an atheist doctor on a crippled priest, which revives belief among the brotherhood. The film, it must be said, is not one of the director's best; his interest in his material seems academic rather than inspired, and there's scant evidence of the irony that informs his finest work. Even so, the performances are generally very impressive (perhaps most notably Demarest, cast against type) and the film is for the most part free of the winsome pieties commonly found in Hollywood films dealing with devotion and divine mystery. GA

First Light of Dawn (Prime luci dell'alba)

(2000, It, 86 min)
d Lucio Gaudino. *p* Andrea De Liberato, Antonio Fusco. *sc* Nicola Molino. *ph* Felice de Maria. *ed* Patrizio Marone. *ad* Alfonso Rastelli. *m* Andrea Guerra. *cast* Gianmarco Tognazzi, Francesco Giuffrida, Laura Morante, Roberto Nobile, Turi Scalia, Vittorio Ciorcalo.

● This elegantly shot, sensitive and admirably modest drama concerns a successful engineer torn away from his globetrotting existence to return to Palermo and care for his disabled, clearly disturbed younger brother after their parents are murdered by mafiosi. Mainly, it's the tale of the older man's gradual transition from duty to commitment, from alienation to belonging. For a virtual two-hander it manages to hold the attention pretty well. That said, patience is tested by the overall talkiness and by the fact that the younger brother, for all his problems, still comes across as a petulant, irritating whinger. The maudlin score doesn't help. GA

First Love

(1977, US, 92 min)
d Joan Darling. *p* Lawrence Turman, David Foster. *sc* Jane Stanton Hitchcock, David Freeman. *ph* Bobby Bryne. *ed* Frank Morriss. *pd* Robert Luthardt. *m* John Barry. *cast* William Katt, Susan Dey, John Heard, Beverly D'Angelo, Robert Loggia, Tom Lacy, Swoosie Kurtz.

● College romance set in an unspecified American institution. Katt, alternately called 'sweet' or 'a very special person', takes love seriously and loses his marbles over Dey. He describes her as 'fragile', but she seems surprisingly resilient, having been involved with a charmless older man (Loggia) for three years, no doubt a surrogate for the father who shot himself. Through this ogre the relationship sours, but they adapt and life goes on. Not a bad story, but a pity that director Darling spends so much time setting up such a condescending approximation of contemporary college life, full of merry japes, poignant incoherence, and all those clichés about sex for the under 21s. Don't rate Cat Stevens' mood music much either. JS

First Love (Chut Sarang)

(1992, SKor, 108 min)
d Lee Myung-Se. *p* Park Hyo-Sung. *sc* Lee Myung-Se, Yang Sun-Hee. *ph* Yu Young-Gil. *ed* Kim Hyun. *m* Song Byung-Jun. *cast* Kim Hae-Soo, Song Young-Chang, Cho Min-Gi, Choi Jong-Won.

● Shot almost entirely on the studio lot, Lee's extraordinary vision of a shy 19-year-old student's unrequited love for her drama teacher unfolds in the run-up to a college production of Thornton Wilder's *Our Town*. The film's own tonal emphasis balances the touching romantic innocence of the girl with the knowing by-play of florid fantasy and down-home reality surrounding her. There's humour and deft observation here; but it's rare to find a movie deep-hearted enough to give touching consideration to the purity of a love untainted by bitter experience, or indeed to view the loss of these illusions with such warm compassion. Unexpectedly impressive. TJ

First Love, Last Rites

(1997, US, 101 min)
d Jesse Peretz. *p* Scott Macaulay, Robin O'Hara, Herbert Beigel. *sc* David Ryan. *ph* Tom Richmond. *ed* James Lyons. *pd* Dan Estabrook. *m* Nathan Larson, Craig Wedren. *cast* Natasha Gregson Wagner, Giovanni Ribisi, Robert John Burke, Jeanetta Arnette, Donal Logue, Eli Marienthal.

●Transposing the English seaside town of Ian McEwan's original story to the Louisiana Bayou without undue difficulty, Peretz's film has a tougher time fleshing out the material to feature length. Joey (Ribisi) and Sissel (Wagner) spend most of their time making out in a hot, stinky cabin – a spectacle which palls soon enough. He's a Northern college boy on vacation, she's the unlikeliest Cajun you ever heard. Things perk up when her crazy, scary father (Burke) talks Joey into an eel-catching scheme, despite zero market demand. Sissel, meanwhile, takes to boiling his vinyl. There's oodles of atmosphere, but you have to be very very good to get away with this little. Ultimately enervating. TCh

First Love – The Litter on the Breeze (Chu Chanlian Hou de Liang Ren Shijie)

(1997, HK, 102 min)
d Eric Kot. *p* Wong Kar-Wai, Yokichi Osato. *sc* Eric Kot, Ocean Chan, Yip Lim-Sum. *ph* Chris Doyle. *ed* Chan Ki-Hop. *ad* Man Lim-Chung. *m* Grasshopper. *cast* Eric Kot, Karen Mok, Takeshi Kaneshiro, Lee Wei-Wei.
●Ex-DJ/rap star Kot's first feature is the only attempt to 'do' Wong Kar-Wai which was actually produced by Wong Kar-Wai. Framed as an enquiry into the true nature of 'first love', it comprises five sketchy episodes interrupted by directorial voice-overs ('Isn't Chris Doyle's hand-held camerawork amazing? Got anything for a headache?') and to-camera pieces by Kot posing as a big time director. The only sustained episode is the last one, in which a grocer, fearing a long delayed retribution from the fiancée he jilted ten years earlier, imagines himself the victim in an urban remake of *Ashes of Time*. The generally childish humour is fairly wearying, but it never quite cancels out the naked sincerity which underpins the whole thing. TR

First Man into Tokyo

see First Yank into Tokyo

First Men in the Moon

(1964, GB, 103 min)
d Nathan Juran. *p* Charles H Schneer. *sc* Nigel Kneale, Jan Read. *ph* Wilkie Cooper. *ed* Maurice Rootes. *ad* John Blezard. *m* Laurie Johnson. *cast* Lionel Jeffries, Martha Hyer, Edward Judd, Miles Malleson, Peter Finch, Betty McDowall, Marne Maitland.
●Nigel Kneale was presumably responsible for the Quatermass-like opening: astronauts on the moon find a faded Union Jack and a note dated 1899, while back on Earth, an old man in a nursing home babbles about terrible dangers. But then this HG Wells adaptation turns very tame indeed, with the principals rendered as bumbling Victorian comics by a serviceable if not very exciting cast, and Juran taking it all far too slowly. Once on the moon ('colour by Lunacolor') things perk up, though Ray Harryhausen has mixed success with his monsters. The giant centipede isn't bad, but the belligerent beetles are too obviously chaps in rubber suits. No poetic effusions, incidentally, for Lionel Jeffries, on taking that pioneering small step. 'Hello, moon,' he says brightly. BBa

First Monday in October

(1981, US, 99 min)
d Ronald Neame. *p* Paul Heller, Martha Scott. *sc* Jerome Lawrence, Robert E Lee. *ph* Fred J Koenekmap. *ed* Peter E Berger. *pd* Philip M Jefferies. *m* Ian Fraser. *cast* Walter Matthau, Jill Clayburgh, Barnard Hughes, Jan Sterling, James Stephens, Joshua Bryant, Wiley Harker.
●In which the rule is disproved that any film starring Walter Matthau can't be all bad. The date of the title marks the opening session of the US Supreme Court, when liberal Justice Snow (Matthau) discovers to his disgust that the first woman Justice is to be the dread conservative, Judge Loomis (Clayburgh). A half-heartedly serious script about integrity in high places is further degraded by Neame to a lifeless comedy about professional antagonism conquered by grudging affection. The pair confront each other in a series of private debates about matters judicial/ethical, which are about as intellectually bracing as Snow-White-meets-Grumpy. The scene where Matthau rises from the coronary unit to Right a Wrong, and marches into the Supreme Court hand-in-hand with the Widow Loomis, simply confirms that we're in fairyland Washington. JS

First Name: Carmen (Prénom Carmen)

(1983, Fr/Switz, 84 min)
d Jean-Luc Godard. *p* Alain Sarde. *sc* Anne-Marie Miéville. *ph* Raoul Coutard. *ed* Suzanne Lang-Willar. *m* Ludwig van Beethoven. *cast* Maruschka Detmers, Jacques Bonnaffé, Myriem Roussel, Jean-Luc Godard, Hyppolite Girardot, Christophe Odent.
●Something like a remake of *Pierrot le Fou* in its cosmic despair, doom-laden romanticism, and stinging, insolent wit. Replacing Bizet with Beethoven and recasting the operatic cigarette girl as a cheapo terrorist, this is really an intimate journal musing about three movies in one. As in *Passion*, there is a bleak acknowledgement of the difficulty of making films (with the string quartet's Beethoven rehearsals indicating how the film-maker is going astray in the tone and tempo of his attempts to communicate). Then there is the story of Carmen and Don José, which obstinately refuses to get off the ground, grinding into a grim stasis where *l'amour fou* dies miserably as the naked lovers take sexual stock. And finally there is Godard himself, drawing all the threads together in a confessional performance as a burnt-out film-maker languishing in a lunatic asylum, out of which he is tempted only to suffer both professional and personal betrayal by Carmen (last name Karina?). Not for nothing does the film carry a nostalgic dedication 'in memoriam small movies'. This, throwaway jokes and all, is Godard back at his most nouvelle vague in years. TM

First of the Few, The (aka Spitfire)

(1942, GB, 118 min, b/w)
d Leslie Howard. *p* Leslie Howard, George King, John Stafford, Adrian Brunel. *sc* Miles Malleson, Anatole De Grunwald. *ph* Georges Périnal. *ed* Douglas Myers. *ad* Paul Sheriff. *m* William Walton. *cast* Leslie Howard, David Niven, Rosamund John, Roland Culver, Anne Firth, Cyril Raymond, Bernard Miles, Miles Malleson.
●Detailed and assured chronicle of RJ Mitchell's trials and triumphs in designing and building the Spitfire, the fighter plane whose aerial superiority won the Battle of Britain. Director/star Howard – who died on an RAF mission in 1943 – brings appropriate dedication to his final screen role, while Niven is suitably chummy as his test-pilot pal. Stirring score by William Walton. TJ

First Power, The

(1990, US, 98 min)
d Robert Resnikoff. *p* David Madden. *sc* Robert Resnikoff. *ph* Theo van de Sande. *ed* Michael Bloecher. *pd* Joseph T Garrity. *cast* Lou Diamond Phillips, Tracy Griffith, Jeff Kober, Mykel T Williamson, Elizabeth Arlen, Dennis Lipscomb.
●Before Gary Gilmore was executed, he announced his belief in reincarnation and his intention of coming back. Inspired by this, writer-director Resnikoff's silly thriller has LA detective Logan (Phillips), who headed the successful investigation, up against the evil soul of an executed serial killer, Channing (Kober). Logan's nightmares begin as he is terrorised by a disembodied voice, lurid graffiti, and a resumption of the killings. He recruits the services of a psychic (Griffith) and the local convent, where a nun recognises Satan's handiwork. Resnikoff fails to sustain the tension established in the opening sequences, and the plot quickly degenerates into a repetitive pattern of possession and exorcism for the victims requisitioned by Channing's soul to do its bidding. With the exception of Phillips, the performances are remarkably unconvincing. CM

First Strike (Jingcha Gushi 4 zhi Jiandan Renwu)

(1996, HK, 107 min)
d Stanley Tong. *p* Barbie Tun. *sc* Stanley Tong, Nick Tramontane, Greg Mellott, Elliot Tong. *ph* Jingle Ma. *ed* Peter Cheung, Chi Wai Ya. *pd* Oliver Wong. *m* J Peter Robinson. *cast* Jackie Chan, Jackson Lau, Annie Wu, Bill Tung, Jouri Petrov, Grishajeva Nonna.
●A lot more fun than the Bond movies it gets into bed with, this sprawling action-adventure (nominally No 4 in Jackie Chan's *Police Story* series) shuttles from Hong Kong to the Ukraine and on to Australia for a climactic fight under water amid real live sharks. The McGuffin is the usual stolen nuclear warhead, but the stunts are the movie's raison d'être: a chase/shoot-out up a snowy mountain, immersion in an icy lake, a tussle on the outside of a tall building, a fight with improvised weapons including an aluminium step-ladder. The highpoint is Chan singing 'I Will Follow Him' while stripping at gunpoint. Watch out for substantial differences between the original Chinese version and the re-edited, dubbed US version. TR

First Time with Feeling (Vous Intéressez-vous à la Chose?)

(1973, Fr/WGer, 82 min)
d Jacques Baratier. *p* Francis Cosne, Raymond Eger. *sc* Claude Eymouche, Stéphane Jourat, Jean-Michel Ribes, Jacques Baratier, Ludwig Spitaler. *ph* Daniel Gaudry. *ed* Hélène Plemiannikov. *m* Yani Spanos. *cast* Nathalie Delon, Muriel Catala, Didier Haudepin, Bernard Jeantet, Renée Saint-Cyr, Joachim Hansen.
●If Eric Rohmer ever went crackers and plunged into porno, the results could be something like this. The hero – suffering, need one say, from awful inhibitions – spends one of those idyllic French summers where everyone talks, drinks, writes journals, drinks, and gives their personal codes a good shake. By the end of it all he is able to treat his heart's desire – a lovely cousin – in the style she deserves. Baratier has seen better days: time was when he wowed the critics with a New Wave/cinéma-vérité send-up called *Dragées au Poivre*. GB

First Wives Club, The

(1996, US, 103 min)
d Hugh Wilson. *p* Scott Rudin. *sc* Robert Harling. *ph* Donald Thorin. *ed* John Bloom. *pd* Peter Larkin. *m* Marc Shaiman. *cast* Goldie Hawn, Bette Midler, Diane Keaton, Stockard Channing, Maggie Smith, Dan Hedaya, Eileen Heckhart, Philip Bosco.
●It's 1969 and four young women, full of peace, love and ambition, are about to graduate. Cut to present-day New York, and the bleary spectacle of Cynthia (Channing), the gang's leading light, thrown over by her husband for pert-breasted wife number two. Lonely as hell, she takes a short walk off a tall building. At her funeral, superstar Elise (Hawn), mouthy frump Brenda (Midler) and doormat Annie (Keaton) realise they too are dizzyingly close to the edge; now saggy and a bit loose at the seams, they've been turned in for younger models. What to do? You've got it – revenge: they're going to kick those badfellas where it hurts – in the pocket. This comedy finds all three stars in wryly cartoonish form, with Keaton particularly charming/irritating. One-liners aside, however, there's no disguising the film's social smugness or predictability. CO'Su

First Yank into Tokyo (aka First Man into Tokyo/Mask of Fury)

(1945, US, 83 min, b/w)
d Gordon Douglas. *p/sc* J Robert Bren. *ph* Harry J Wild. *ed* Philip Martin Jr. *ad* Albert S D'Agostino, Walter Keller. *m* Leigh Harline. *cast* Tom Neal, Barbara Hale, Marc Cramer, Richard Loo, Keye Luke, Benson Fong, Leonard Strong.
●A wartime potboiler in which a Japanese-speaking US pilot (Neal), his features orientalised by plastic surgery, is smuggled into Japan to retrieve vital data from a scientist (Cramer) captured while testing a component for the A-Bomb. Desperate plotting ensures that the commandant (Loo) of the PoW camp was once Neal's college room-mate, while a US nurse (Hale) playing Florence Nightingale to the prisoners is his long-lost sweetheart. Will either penetrate his inscrutable disguise when he worms his way in as a guard? The mission is accomplished with the aid of more plot contrivances, and Neal – his plastic surgery irreversible – elects to die while killing innumerable Japs rather than force his new features on his beloved. Skilful direction and camerawork (Harry Wild) just about keep things going. The A-Bomb theme and a gloating commentary ('Hiroshima destroyed! Nagasaki devastated!') were added when the war's abrupt end caught up with the film's release. TM

Fish and Elephant (Yu he Daxiang/aka Jin Nian Xiatian)

(2001, China, 106 min)
d Li Yu. *p* Lao Ge, Cheng Yong, Li Yu. *sc* Li Yu. *ph* Fei Xiaoping. *ed* Jiang Jianwei, Anna. *cast* Pan Yi, Shitou, Zhang Jilian, Zhang Qianqian, Xi Wei, So Pengcheng.
● A favourite on the lesbian-and-gay festival circuit, Li Yu's underground feature (her debut) has a tangible gust of reality blowing through it. Xiao Qun is an elephant keeper at Beijing Zoo and her lover Xiao Ling flogs clothes in an indoor market. Their stable relationship hits two obstacles: the arrival of Qun's divorced mother, who has no idea her daughter is lesbian and foists on her a string of prospective husbands, and the reappearance of Qun's ex-girlfriend Junjun, on the run from the cops after killing her abusive father. Nothing here to surprise western viewers used to frank treatment of gay issues, but plenty to enjoy in the way Li uses locations and integrates the plot and characters in shrewd observation of Beijing's street-life. TR

Fish Called Wanda, A

(1988, GB, 108 min)
d Charles Crichton. *p* Michael Shamberg. *sc* John Cleese. *ph* Alan Hume. *ed* John Jympson. *pd* Roger Murray-Leach. *m* John Du Prez. *cast* John Cleese, Jamie Lee Curtis, Kevin Kline, Michael Palin, Maria Aitken, Tom Georgeson, Patricia Hayes, Geoffrey Palmer, Stephen Fry.
● A perfectly old-fashioned romantic comedy, big on caper, generous on Ealing, and heavy on the twisted stereotypes. Cleese scripts and stars as London barrister Archie Leach, hired to defend a gem thief, and earning a much-vaunted 'sex symbol' tag with the affections of gangster's moll Wanda Gershwitz (Curtis). It's a plot too jagged to document in full – Where are the gems? Who has the safe-deposit key? Who's betraying whom? Is the London Underground really a political movement? – but the interest lies less in outcome than in character: Palin as a madly stuttering, animal-loving dog-murderer, Kline as a maybe-CIA cruel paranoid pseud who's intermittently Wanda's lover/gay brother, and Cleese and Curtis as the most unlikely rug-tearers since Miller and Monroe. There's nothing deep, nothing groundbreaking, but it's a never-dull, tightly scripted yarn with some very funny gags. SGa

Fisher King, The

(1991, US, 137 min)
d Terry Gilliam. *p* Debra Hill, Lynda Obst. *sc* Richard LaGravenese. *ph* Roger Pratt. *ed* Lesley Walker. *pd* Mel Bourne. *m* George Fenton. *cast* Robin Williams, Jeff Bridges, Amanda Plummer, Mercedes Ruehl, Michael Jeter, Harry Shearer.
● When New York radio DJ Jack Lucas (Bridges) inadvertently drives a listener to commit mass murder, his confidence and career crumble. Three years on, he's rescued from suicide and muggers by Parry (Williams), a deranged hobo whose wife died in the massacre. A former professor of medieval history, Parry has two dreams: to retrieve the Holy Grail, and to win the heart of the fair Lydia (Plummer). Consumed by guilt, doubtful about his future with his lover Anne (Ruehl), Lucas concludes he can redeem himself if only he can bring Parry and Lydia together. The plot may be wayward, but Gilliam's film is mostly funny and exhilarating: at once nightmarish and deeply romantic, a partly fantastic study in loneliness, lunacy, despair and violence, it's also spectacularly visual (despite the atypical dearth of special effects). Moreover, Gilliam allows his actors unprecedented space, and they respond admirably (Bridges and Plummer especially). Scary, touching, often hilarious, this modern fairytale is surprisingly enchanting. GA

F.I.S.T.

(1978, US, 145 min)
d/p Norman Jewison. *sc* Joe Eszterhas, Sylvester Stallone. *ph* Laszlo Kovacs. *ed* Antony Gibbs. *pd* Richard MacDonald. *m* Bill Conti. *cast* Sylvester Stallone, Rod Steiger, Peter Boyle, Melinda Dillon, David Huffman, Tony Lo Bianco.
● Despite its Watergate scars, *F.I.S.T.*, with its marches on Washington and its attacks on conspiracy and monopoly, is a striking reaffirmation of traditional populism. Stallone, the all-American *auteur*/contender of *Rocky* (and how much of this film too?), plays an industrial worker in Depression Ohio who makes good as the boss of the (thinly disguised) Teamsters Union. With few exceptions, Hollywood has proved consistently unwilling to treat questions of labour, and the political drama here remains substantially conventional, anchoring the issues in violence, romance and righteous individualism. Stallone's performance is a superb blend of stubborn-jawed gravity and ironic hamming as he heads, Godfather-like, for a confrontation with the Senate. It, and a curious historical leap in the narrative from 1930 to 1960, together push the film beyond the point where it can supply a traditional conclusion or a sufficient hero. The climactic murder of the Union boss by his Mafia backers is a puzzled attempt to resolve the contradiction between individualist demands (Law & Order, enterprise: Capital) and social needs (subsistence, justice: Labour). CA

Fistful of Dollars, A (Per un Pugno di Dollari)

(1964, It/WGer/Sp, 100 min)
d Sergio Leone. *p* Arrigo Colombo, Giorgio Papi. *sc* Sergio Leone, Duccio Tessari. *ph* Massimo Dallamano. *ed* Roberto Cinquini. *ad* Carlo Simi. *m* Ennio Morricone. *cast* Clint Eastwood, Gian Maria Volonté, Marianne Koch, Pepe Calvo, Wolfgang Lukschy.
● Though far less operatic and satisfying than Leone's later work, his first spaghetti Western with Eastwood still looks stylish, if a little rough at the edges. Based on Kurosawa's *Yojimbo*, it set a fashion in surly, laconic, supercool heroes with Eastwood's amoral gunslinger, who plays off two gangs against one another in a deadly feud. All the classic Leone ingredients were there – the atonal score, the graphic violence, the horrendous dubbing – and the film's Stateside success changed the face of a genre. GA

Fistful of Dynamite, A

see Giù la Testa

Fistful of Fingers, A

(1995, GB, 81 min)
d Edgar Wright. *p* Daniel Figuero. *sc* Edgar Wright. *ph* Alvin Leong. *ed* Giles Harding. *pd* Simon Bowles. *m* François Evans. *cast* Graham Low, Oliver Evans, Martin Curtis, Quentin Green, William Cornes, Neil Mullarkey, Nicola Stapleton.
● This is a homemade spaghetti Western (budget £10,000, cardboard horses and a handful of sixth-formers) which parodies itself along with the genre archetypes. The moving story of a bounty hunter's love for his murdered horse is a ragbag of the surreal, the satiric and the plain lame in the tradition of *Hot Shots! Part Deux*, with one Graham Low, a tour guide at Wookey Hole Caves, doing an uncanny impersonation of Eastwood's 'No Name'. Wright may not be in the class of Robert (*El Mariachi*) Rodriguez, but he has talent. Best seen after a couple of beers. TCh

Fistful of Flies

(1996, Aust, 85 min)
d Monica Pellizzari. *p* Julia Overton. *sc* Monica Pellizzari. *ph* Jane Castle. *ed* James Manché. *pd* Lissa Coote. *m* Felicity Fox. *cast* Dina Panozzo, Tasma Walton, John Lucantonio, Anna Volska, Maria Venuti, Rachael Maza, Giordano Gangl.
● Here's the angle, in the words of the heroine's mother: 'Men are all like toilets: all engaged, all pissed-off or all full of shit!' Sixteen-year-old refusenik Mars (Walton) finds growing up is hard to do in the repressive, racist, hypocritical, male-dominated Italian-Australian Catholic community she has the privilege to live in. This is daughter-of-Jane-Campion stuff, an off-kilter, suburban surrealist drama, shot in primary colours, with its broad satirical swipes accompanied with droll social observation, brutal episodes of domestic cruelty and an ending of male-vanquishing wish-fulfilment. The performances are in the farce-meets-realist tradition of *Sweetie*, with Walton giving an especially brave one as the Girl on the Road to Empowerment. Great fun, and all power to the sisters. WH

Fist of Fury (Jingwu Men/ aka The Chinese Connection)

(1972, HK, 106 min)
d Lo Wei. *p* Raymond Chow. *sc* Lo Wei. *ph* Chen Ching-chu. *ed* Chang Yao Chung. *pd* Lo Wei. *m* Joseph Koo. *cast* Bruce Lee, Nora Miao, James Tien, Robert Baker, Maria Yi, Tien Feng.
● One of the best of the Chinese chop sock dramas. It has a basically serious story: the inmates of one kung-fu school have poisoned the teacher of a rival school, and our devoted hero sets out on a course of revenge. But a potential revenge tragedy turns into a film of comic strip outrageousness as Bruce Lee tries, but fails, to reconcile his natural thirst for revenge with his desire to keep the name of his school clean. The result is a patently absurd and funny movie, involving a series of spectacular fight routines, often filmed in slow motion, which are highly acrobatic and exciting.

Fist of Fury Part II (Jingwu Men Xuji)

(1976, Tai, 104 min)
d Li Zuonan. *p* Jimmy Shaw, RP Shah. *sc* Chang Hsin-Yi. *ph* Yip Ching-Bui. *ed* Leung Wing-Chai. *ad* Wu Shui-Ping. *m* Chow Fuk-Leung. *cast* Bruce Li, Lo Lieh, Tien Feng, Lee Quinn, Shikamura Yasuyoshi, Nan Kuan-Hsun.
● One of a flood of Bruce Lee spin-offs, this purports to be a sequel to the Lee vehicle *Fist of Fury* (but is in fact an ultra-low-budget rehash of its script), and it stars Lee lookalike Ho Tsung-Tao (whom it bills as 'Bruce Li'). It's not the worst of its kind, but it is unremittingly feeble, both as a drama and as a kung-fu exploiter. Only the final duel is given set piece status; the rest is so much scrappy action and emoting. TR

Fist of the North Star

(1990, Jap, 112 min)
d Toyoo Ashida. *sc* Susumu Takahisa. *cast* voices: Wally Burr, John Vickery, Melodee Spivack, Michael McConnohie, Holly Sidell.
● If you thought *Akira* was strange, violent and hard to understand, get a load of this animated feature, based on the comic available in translation from specialist shops. Like many Japanese *manga*, it's set in a barren, post-apocalyptic world where only men's muscles can grow. The plot is the usual fantasy rubbish about fraternal betrayal and maiden-rescuing; but what distinguishes it is the stylised visuals, the existentialist landscapes, and the quite exceptional levels of violence perpetrated by the martial arts supermen. Heads bulge and explode, arms fall to the ground, blood gushes skywards, torsos are severed, bodies are crushed to pulp. If Sam Peckinpah had murdered Walt Disney and disembowelled Bambi, the result would have been tame in comparison. DW

Fists in the Pocket (I Pugni in Tasca)

(1965, It, 113 min, b/w)
d Marco Bellocchio. *p* Enzo Doria. *sc* Marco Bellocchio. *ph* Alberto Marrama. *ed* Silvano Agosti. *ad* Gisella Longo. *m* Ennio Morricone. *cast* Lou Castel, Paola Pitagora, Marino Masè, Liliana Gerace, Pier Luigi Troglio, Jenny MacNeil.
● A synopsis of Bellocchio's amazing first film might suggest an Italian version of US TV's *Soap*, with its story of a family variously plagued by epilepsy, blindness, low IQs and raging frustration. But Bellocchio orders his material and directs his actors with such verve and passion that audiences have little time and less inclination to giggle. In particular, Lou Castel's performance as Alessandro, a teenage epileptic ultimately driven to frenzied acts of violence, seethes with a hateful energy rarely seen on the screen. Both Castel and Bellocchio have been simmering down quietly ever since. A stunning film, literally. GB

Fists of Fury

see Big Boss, The

Fit to Be Untied (Matti da Slegare)

(1975, It, 120 min)
d/p/sc Marco Bellocchio, Silvano Agosti, Sandro Petreglia, Stefano Rulli. *ph* Dimitri Nicolau, Ezio Bellani. *m* Nicola Piovani.
● For a tale of misery, woe and black despair, a surprisingly optimistic film. Focusing on Parma, this documentary (really two, put together by a collective) claims insanity as a social disease, the predictable result of compounding

poverty with ignorance, and banishing the halt and lame to secretive (often church-run) institutions where they are beaten and tormented. The film's unspoken question is who is really insane, the inmates or their cruel keepers. Certainly Paolo, the youngest of the cases studied, does not seem mad. Although oblivious to the discipline of parents or school, and forever tugging at jumper, hat or hair, Paolo's discussion of his problem shows a reasoning unclouded by naivety or insanity. He's not looking for a miracle, but he knows what would help – a job. And as Part Two shows, the effects of just this upon the truly mentally handicapped can be miraculous when the job comes complete with fellow-workers who offer friendship as well as instruction. FD

Fitzcarraldo

(1982, WGer, 158 min)
d Werner Herzog. *p* Werner Herzog, Lucki Stipetic. *sc* Werner Herzog. *ph* Thomas Mauch. *ed* Beate Mainka-Jellinghaus. *ad* Henning von Gierke, Ulrich Bergfelder. *m* Popol Vuh. *cast* Klaus Kinski, Claudia Cardinale, José Lewgoy, Miguel Angel Fuentes, Paul Hittscher, Grande Otélo.

● Though there was a distinct possibility that the much-publicised and characteristically fraught production saga of Herzog's movie would overshadow the completed film itself, it turned out to be some kind of appropriately eccentric and monumental marvel. Operatic excess is both the subject and the keynote, as Kinski's visionary Irish adventurer obsessively hatches grandiose schemes to finance a dream of bringing Caruso and the strains of Verdi to an Amazon trading-post. Staked by loving Molly, a madam (Cardinale), he pilots the resurrected tub 'Molly-Aida' down an uncharted tributary in search of untapped rubber, wooing the fierce natives with gramophone arias before securing their inexplicable collaboration in the ludicrous task of hauling the ship manually over a hill towards a parallel waterway. Overcoming his own disparaged image as an inspired madman, Herzog charts an ironically circular course around an indulged, benevolent Aguirre; perversely illuminates colonialism with surrealism; and demonstrates once again in his always suspect yet somehow irresistible way that 'only dreamers move mountains'. PT

Five

(1951, US, 89 min, b/w)
d/p/sc Arch Oboler. *ph* Louis Clyde Stoumen. *ed* John Hoffman. *pd* Arch Oboler. *m* Henry Russell. *cast* William Phipps, Susan Douglas, James Anderson, Charles Lampkin, Earl Lee.

● A quintet of survivors – idealist, pregnant woman, black doorman, hunk and wimp – debate mankind's future in this naive post-apocalyptic drama, set mainly in the writer/director's Frank Lloyd Wright-designed apartment. Earnest and not very pacy. TJ

Five and the Skin (Cinq et la Peau)

(1982, Fr/Phil, 97 min)
d Pierre Rissient. *sc* Pierre Rissient, Eugène Guillevic, Lucie Albertini, Alain Archambault. *ph* Alain Derobe, Daniel Vogel, Romeo Vitug. *ed* Bob Wade, Marie-Josée Chauvel, Schéhérazade Saadi, Mounira Mihirsi. *m* Benôit Charvet, Claude Danu. *cast* Feodor Atkine, Eiko Matsuda, Gloria Diaz, Rafael Roco, Phillip Salvador, Louie Pascua, Roberto Padua. *narrator* Roger Blin.

● A completely unclassifiable feature from Frenchman-about-cinema Rissient, but clearly autobiographical at heart. The images show a Frenchman in Manila, and explore his movements, his meetings, his enthusiasms, and his sexual fantasies. There is synch-sound, but no dialo.gue; instead, his thoughts and reflections are heard in an exquisitely literary voice-over. The blend of specifics and abstracts is mesmerising. RG

Five Came Back

(1939, US, 75 min, b/w)
d John Farrow. *p* Robert Sisk. *sc* Jerry Cady, Dalton Trumbo, Nathanael West. *ph* Nick Musuraca. *ed* Harry Marker. *ad* Van Nest Polglase, Albert S D'Agostino. *m* Roy Webb. *cast* Chester Morris, Lucille Ball, Wendy Barrie, John Carradine, Joseph Calleia, C Aubrey Smith, Patric Knowles, Allen Jenkins, Elizabeth Risdon, Kent Taylor.

● If the plot sounds familiar, that's partly because Farrow himself remade this film in 1956 as *Back from Eternity* (also for RKO), partly because it's the old warhorse about air passengers crash-landed in a hostile wilderness that has left its mark on everything from Buñuel's *La Mort en ce jardin* and Aldrich's *The Flight of the Phoenix* to the *Airport* sagas and *Alive*. But despite what now seem clichés – the headhunters, the cowardly braggart, the tart with a heart, the noble revolutionary – this one still comes up fresh, thanks to a taut, economic script (by Jerry Cady, Dalton Trumbo and Nathanael West!) full of twists and vivid characters, and to Farrow's eminently civilised handling of his material. (A devout Catholic, he even manages to make the scenes of redemption and sacrifice both plausible and remarkably unsentimental.) And Nick Musuraca's photography is as atmospheric as in his later *films noirs*. GA

5 Card Stud

(1968, US, 103 min)
d Henry Hathaway. *p* Hal B Wallis. *sc* Marguerite Roberts. *ph* Daniel L Fapp. *ed* Warren Low. *pd* Walter Tyler. *m* Maurice Jarre. *cast* Dean Martin, Robert Mitchum, Roddy McDowall, Inger Stevens, Katherine Justice, John Anderson, Yaphet Kotto, Denver Pyle.

● A card-sharp caught palming an ace is lynched by six of the seven men he was playing poker with (Martin protests in vain); and panic spreads through the small Colorado town as the lynchers begin to die one by one, killed in gruesome parodies of the hanging. Hathaway directs this Western *Ten Little Indians* with a sort of weary authority, alternating patches of boredom with fresh, striking detail. What chiefly keeps it afloat is the excellent cast, headed by Martin as the gambler who turns Sherlock Holmes to solve the mystery, and Mitchum – in a variation on his performance in *Night of the Hunter* – as the mysterious hellfire preacher who rides into town with a secret and a faster draw than anyone else. TM

Five Corners

(1987, US, 94 min)
d Tony Bill. *p* Forrest Murray, Tony Bill. *sc* John Patrick Shanley. *ph* Fred Murphy. *ed* Andy Blumenthal. *pd* Adrianne Lobel. *m* James Newton Howard. *cast* Jodie Foster, Tim Robbins, Todd Graff, John Turturro, Elizabeth Berridge, Rose Gregoria, Gregory Rozakis, John Seitz, Cathryn de Prume.

● The teenage Bronx in '64 was divided into the concerned and the heads. Harry (Robbins) is on the brink of joining civil rights Down South. Melanie (Berridge) and Brita (de Prume) sniff from bags and play yo-yo on top of elevators. Linda (Foster) works in a pet store and is preoccupied with stopping psychotic Heinz (Turturro) from attempting rape again now that he's out of the slammer. The latter's courtship is unconventional. Unbidden, he steals a pair of penguins for her from the zoo, and when she demurs, clubs one to death. Like *American Graffiti*, all these teenie tales take place against a specific historical time, with TV and electioneering vans everywhere on the go to remind us. Some tales work better than others, with the mysterious killings by bow-and-arrow convenient but low on credibility. The investigating cop duo (Rozakis and Seitz) could have strayed in from Chabrol at his daftest; Linda's crippled boyfriend (Graff) is a curdler; Turturro's Heinz, however, is rivetingly over the top. Lots of good ideas and memorable scenes, but it's a bit of a mess. BC

Five Days One Summer

(1982, US, 108 min)
d/p Fred Zinnemann. *sc* Michael Austin. *ph* Giuseppe Rotunno. *ed* Stuart Baird. *pd* Willy Holt. *m* Elmer Bernstein. *cast* Sean Connery, Betsy Brantley, Lambert Wilson, Jennifer Hilary, Isabel Dean, Gerard Buhr, Anna Massey.

● A film which creates drama more out of gesture and nuance than dialogue, and employs a lush setting which overwhelms instead of pointing up the characters' emotions. Older, married doctor takes his young niece for a dirty week in the Swiss Alps in the 1930s. The mountain climbing footage is remarkable, but the plot gathers so little pace that when the girl runs to find out whether the doctor she loves or the handsome young guide she fancies has been killed in an avalanche, our interest in her dilemma is academic. MB

Five Easy Pieces

(1970, US, 98 min)
d Bob Rafelson. *p* Bob Rafelson, Richard Wechsler. *sc* Adrien Joyce [Carole Eastman]. *ph* Laszlo Kovacs. *ed* Christopher Holmes, Gerald Sheppard. *ad* Toby Carr Rafelson. *cast* Jack Nicholson, Karen Black, Lois Smith, Susan Anspach, Billy Green Bush, Helena Kallianiotes, William Challee.

● Rafelson's second film – in which Jack Nicholson, seemingly a redneck oil-rigger, turns out to be a fugitive from a musical career inherited from a family of classical musicians – is a considered examination of the middle-class patrician American way of family life. Centreing on Nicholson's drifter, the film unswervingly brings him into confrontations with his past as he equally unswervingly attempts to evade everything, preferring to make gestures rather than act consistently. The result is less a story and more a collection of incidents and character studies, all of which inform each other and extend our understanding of Nicholson's mode of survival: flight. PH

Five Evenings (Pyat Vecherov)

(1980, USSR, 101 min, b/w & col)
d Nikita Mikhalkov. *sc* Alexander Adabashian, Nikita Mikhalkov. *ph* Pavel Lebeshev. *ed* E Praksinoi. *songs* Yu Mikhailov. *cast* Liudmila Gurchenko, Stanislav Liubshin, Valentina Telichkina, Larisa Kuznetsova, Igor Nefedov.

● Taken from a theatrical text, filmed in grimy, tinted black-and-white, the minimal narrative tracks the prosaic interaction of four characters, young/old, male/female, through the interiors of urban Russia a generation or so ago. Mikhalkov transforms these unpromising ingredients with consummate skill into a film quite unlike the heroic or prestigious bombast prevalent in Russian cinema. At worst, a delightful, meticulous tour de force, and at least, a resonant and revealing miniature. SH

5 Fingers

(1952, US, 108 min, b/w)
d Joseph L Mankiewicz. *p* Otto Lang. *sc* Michael Wilson. *ph* Norbert Brodine. *ed* James B Clark. *ad* Lyle Wheeler, George W Davis. *m* Bernard Herrmann. *cast* James Mason, Danielle Darrieux, Michael Rennie, Walter Hampden, Oscar Karlweis, Herbert Berghof.

● An elegantly witty espionage movie, founded on fact but no slave to the facts as recounted by German military attaché LZ Moyzisch in his account (*Operation Cicero*) of an Albanian-born valet to the British ambassador in Turkey in 1944 who hawked top secret allied documents to the Germans. In Mankiewicz's hands, characteristically elaborated into a teasing rondo of political and sexual intrigue where each new doublecrossing move is mated by a totally unexpected irony of fate, the tale becomes an irresistibly dry, cynical comedy of manners in which the crafty gentleman's gentleman (a marvellous performance from Mason), scheming to secure the means to promote himself as a member of the leisured classes, falls victim to his own pretensions when a beautiful but unprincipled refugee Countess (the equally marvellous Darrieux) trails a heady promise of romance across his path. An irresistible treat. TM

Five Fingers of Death

see King Boxer

5:48, The

(1979, US, 58 min)
d James Ivory. *p* Peter Weinberg. *sc* Terrence McNally. *ph* Andrzej Bartkowiak. *ad* John Wright Stevens. *ed* David McKenna. *m* Jonathan Tunick. *cast* Mary Beth Hurt, Laurence Luckinbill, Laurinda Barrett, John DeVries, Robert Hitt, Ann McDonough.

● Ivory's only feature film to date (1999) not produced by his business partner Ismail Merchant, this short suspense picture was adapted by the playwright Terrence McNally from a story by John Cheever and commissioned by New York's Channel 13 TV. Hypocrites abound in Merchant Ivory's work, but the unvarnished cruelty which runs through the character of John Blake (Luckinbill), the ad-man held at gunpoint on his train journey home to Shady Hill, Westchester

County, by his wronged secretary (Hurt), may come as a shock to those who've grown accustomed to the elegant subtleties of Ruth Jhabvala's MIP scripts. Made back-to-back with *The Europeans*. JPy

Five Graves to Cairo

(1943, US, 91 min, b/w)
d Billy Wilder. *sc* Billy Wilder, Charles Brackett. *ph* John Seitz. *ed* Doane Harrison. *pd* Hans Dreier, Ernst Fegté. *m* Miklos Rozsa. *cast* Franchot Tone, Anne Baxter, Akim Tamiroff, Erich von Stroheim, Peter Van Eyck, Fortunio Bonanova, Konstantin Shayne.

● An impressive wartime espionage thriller, with Tone as a British corporal holed up in a Nazi-controlled hotel in the North African desert, and posing as a German in an attempt to discover the whereabouts of Rommel's secret fuel dumps. The script by Wilder and his long-term associate Charles Brackett is taut and intelligent, but the film's real strengths are John Seitz's superb photography of the desert and hotel, and von Stroheim's resumption of his 'man you love to hate' persona as Rommel. Lajos Biro's source play had been filmed twice before as *Hotel Imperial* (1927 and 1939), and in 1951 resurfaced in an engaging parody version as *Hotel Sahara*. GA

Five Heartbeats, The

(1991, US, 121 min)
d Robert Townsend. *p* Loretha Jones. *sc* Robert Townsend, Keenen Ivory Wayans. *ph* Bill Dill. *ed* John Carter. *pd* Wynn Thomas. *m* Stanley Clarke. *cast* Robert Townsend, Michael Wright, Leon, Harry J Lennix, Tice Wells, Diahann Carroll, Harold Nicholas, Chuck Patterson.

● The year is 1965, and five young guys aim for fame with a sloppy but impassioned vocal group. They're a bit Four Tops, a bit Temptations, and a lot Smokey Robinson and the Miracles, since starstruck songwriter 'Duck' (Townsend) seems conceived as an adoring homage to the acknowledged laureate of soul. The film stands mainly on its characterisations, and the band itself is fairly flawlessly cast: not so much the rather listless Townsend, but certainly Duck's Casanova brother JT (Leon), the virtuous Choirboy (Wells), and lead singer Eddie (Wright), whose fate is blatantly a Dire Warning. For all the specificity of the soul background, Townsend gives us a retread illustration of the familiar pitfalls of fame; while some of the broader music biz gags seem left over from his earlier *Hollywood Shuffle*, as do the strictly 2D female characterisations. By the time it ends in a heartwarming nuclear family hoedown, we've learned nothing new. JRo

Five Seconds to Spare

(2000, GB, 98 min)
d Tom Connolly. *p* Amanda Posey. *sc* Jonathan Coe, Tom Connolly. *ph* Ashley Rowe. *ed* Caroline Biggerstaff. *pd* Mark Tildesley. *m* Ben Pope. *cast* Max Beesley, Ray Winstone, Anastasia Hille, Valentina Cervi, Andy Serkis, Sarah Jane Potts, John Light, Lee Ross, John Peel, Sean Pertwee.

● Keyboard player William Small (Beesley) moves to London to make a go of it with his group, the Alaska Factory. Success does not happen overnight. Playing gold lamé boogie woogie in a shopping mall to make ends meet, he encounters Madeleine (Cervi), with whom he falls in love. The Alaska Factory play a pub gig and Madeleine turns up with another man (Pertwee), prompting William to seek solace in the arms of lonely barmaid Karla (Hille). It's only when he witnesses a murderous assault on a fellow musician by two hooded dwarves that William begins to wish he'd stayed in Macclesfield. In its adaptation, Jonathan Coe's story (from his novel *The Dwarves of Death*) has become darker but retains much of its sparky comedy. The new title seems arbitary: while the Dwarves of Death are a recurrent motif, 'Five Seconds to Spare' comes from a throwaway line that perhaps should have been. First time director Connolly draws fine performances all round, with particular respect due to Winstone for his foul-tempered recording studio boss and Light for a wonderfully twitchy dopehead muso. John Peel's charming cameo is a bonus. NRo

Five Senses, The

(1999, Can, 105 min)
d Jeremy Podeswa. *p* Camelia Frieberg, Jeremy Podeswa. *sc* Jeremy Podeswa. *ph* Gregory Middleton. *ed* Wiebke Von Carolsfeld. *pd* Taavo Soodor. *m* Alexina Louie, Alex Pauk. *cast* Mary Louise Parker, Pascale Bussières, Richard Clarkin, Brendan Fletcher, Daniel MacIvor, Gabrielle Rose, Philippe Volter.

● The central conceit of this Canadian drama is so simple, you wonder why nobody's ever tried it before: a movie based around the five senses. So, among the residents of a Toronto apartment block, we find a massage therapist (Rose) out of touch with her emotions, a cake decorator (Parker) who rarely tastes her own creations, a cleaner (MacIvor) who believes romance has a smell, an eye doctor (Volter) losing his hearing, and a prostitute (Bussières) who teaches him the delights of a soundless world. Various senses appropriately ticked off, the story's weave of destinies begins to exert its spell as the traumatic disappearance of a young girl in a park affects the precarious emotional balance of all concerned. Writer/director Podeswa presides over unfolding events with benign confidence, artfully concealing the narrative stitching which holds the piece together. Partly, it's due to the measured tone he adopts, giving the film a wise, cultured feel in place of rollercoaster melodrama, but it's also in casting players requiring little screen-time to convince us of a vivid inner life. TJ

Five Star Final

(1931, US, 88 min, b/w)
d Mervyn LeRoy. *sc* Byron Morgan, Robert Lord. *ph* Sol Polito. *ed* Frank Ware. *ad* Jack Okey. *cast* Edward G Robinson, Marian Marsh, HB Warner, Anthony Bushell, Boris Karloff, George E Stone, Ona Munson, Aline MacMahon.

● Much praised in its day as a biting attack on gutter journalism (one of dozens trotted out during the first years of sound), this early entry in the Warner 'social protest' cycle hasn't worn nearly so well as Hecht-Milestone's much less solemn and self-righteous *The Front Page*. Robinson is more than adequate as the editor persuaded to boost circulation by reviving an old scandal, with tragic results ending in a double suicide. But with the victims coming on like characters in a Victorian melodrama, and LeRoy's direction accentuating the plot's origins (from the play by Louis Weitzenkorn) with its graceless gestures towards 'cinema' (including a clumsy attempt at split screen), the film hovers more than once on the brink of risibility. Worth seeing mainly for Karloff's wonderfully Uriah Heep-ish performance as a reporter ('the most blasphemous thing I've ever seen,' his editor drily observes) formerly expelled from divinity school for some evident but unspecified sexual misdemeanour. TM

5000 Fingers of Dr T, The

(1953, US, 88 min)
d Roy Rowland. *p* Stanley Kramer. *sc* Allan Scott, Dr Seuss [Ted Geisel]. *ph* Franz Planer. *ed* Harry Gerstad. *pd* Rudolph Sternad. *m* Frederick Hollander. *cast* Tommy Rettig, Hans Conried, Peter Lind Hayes, Mary Healy, John Heasley, Robert Heasley.

● *The 5000 Fingers of Dr T* can barely contain its multiple fascinations within the 'kids' movie' format, attempting as it does to make explicit the connections between dreams, surrealism and psychoanalysis. Using the child's fantasy structure of *The Wizard of Oz*, it's the tale of nine-year-old Bart (Rettig), who resents his piano lessons and projects teacher Terwilliker (Conried) as an authoritarian madman bent on mesmerising his mother, killing the friendly plumber, imprisoning all other musicians, and enslaving 500 little boys at a giant keyboard to rehearse his own masterpiece for eternity. There's enough colourful whimsy here to divert a young audience; but also enough pop Freud and political allegory to keep even the most compulsively note-taking adults happy. And with a couple of musical routines that come close to defining camp, this awesome entertainment really does have something for everyone. PT

Five Women Around Utamaro (Utamaro o Meguru Go-nin no Onna)

(1946, Jap, 94 min, b/w)
d Kenji Mizoguchi. *sc* Yoshikata Yoda. *ph* Minoru Miki. *ed* Shintaro Miyamoto. *ad* Isamu Motoki. *m* Hisato Osawa, Tamexo Mochizuki. *cast* Minosuke Bando, Kotaro Bando, Kinuyo Tanaka, Hiroko Kawasaki, Toshiko Iizuka, Aizo Tamashima.

● Made immediately after the war, despite continuous opposition from the Occupation Forces, this remarkable film about the late 18th century artist marks the beginning of Mizoguchi's commitment to the theme of female emancipation: Utamaro himself is seen as the 'neutral' centre of a series of emotional intrigues which illustrate the corruption of Edo period morals and highlight the particular vulnerability of women. The film is also something of a meditation on the status of the artist; scriptwriter Yoshikata Yoda is on record as saying that he intended it as a reflection on Mizoguchi himself. In style it's much like Mizoguchi's later work, but less emotional, more formalised, more mysterious, and a great deal more daring aesthetically. TR

Fixed Bayonets!

(1951, US, 92 min, b/w)
d Samuel Fuller. *p* Jules Buck. *sc* Samuel Fuller. *ph* Lucien Ballard. *ed* Nick De Maggio. *ad* Lyle Wheeler, George Patrick. *m* Roy Webb. *cast* Richard Basehart, Gene Evans, Michael O'Shea, Richard Hylton, Craig Hill, Skip Homeier, Henry Kulky.

● 'His films are like scenarios made from communities of rats, the camera itself a king rat,' David Thomson wrote of Fuller. The rat trap is the Korean war, in a studio set of fake rock and fake snow, literally a theatre of war. The constantly moving camera isolates the tensions within an American platoon fighting a rearguard action. As the leaders are picked off by the 'alien' reds, one sensitive corporal's struggle with the responsibilities of leadership drags the plot in a slow dance of death; only to be blasted apart by a typical cigar-chewing affirmation of good old Yankee guts. From John Brophy's novel *Immortal Sergeant* (previously filmed in 1943). RP

Fixer, The

(1968, US, 130 min)
d John Frankenheimer. *p* Edward Lewis. *sc* Dalton Trumbo. *ph* Marcel Grignon. *ed* Henry Berman. *ad* Béla Zeichan. *m* Maurice Jarre. *cast* Alan Bates, Dirk Bogarde, Georgia Brown, Jack Gilford, Hugh Griffith, Elizabeth Hartman, Ian Holm, David Warner, Murray Melvin, Peter Jeffrey.

● Blacklisted screenwriter Dalton Trumbo adapted Bernard Malamud's heavyweight novel, a tale of injustice set in pre-revolutionary Russia, but despite obvious effort all round this remains one of those worthy responsible movies trading on its self-proclaimed prestige. Bates suffers his way to an Oscar nomination as Yakov Bok, the Jew who refuses to confess to a crime (the ritual murder of a child) of which he's innocent and is imprisoned without trial. Bogarde, on the other hand, as the melancholy lawyer, who's murdered for attempting to help Bok, has a touch more charisma. Not a patch on the director's earlier *Bird Man of Alcatraz*. GM

Flambierte Frau, Die

see Woman in Flames, A

Flame (aka Slade in Flame)

(1974, GB, 91 min)
d Richard Loncraine. *p* Gavrik Losey. *sc* Andrew Birkin. *ph* Peter Hannon. *ed* Michael Bradsell. *ad* Brian Morris. *cast* Slade, Tom Conti, Johnny Shannon, Kenneth Colley, Alan Lake.

● A straightforward account of the rise and ultimate disillusionment of a typical teenage rave band, tightly scripted and directed. The seediness of the behind-the-scenes machinations runs through the story: they are seedy whether perpetrated by a third-rate Midlands agent or by the suave director of a London management and investment company. The film (which isn't a moment too long, a welcome rarity) doesn't say much that you don't know already; good performances, though, from Shannon, Conti, and Lake as the all-time loser vocalist. JC

Flame

(1996, Zim/Fr/Namibia, 90 min)
d Ingrid Sinclair. *p* Simon Bright. *sc* Ingrid Sinclair, Barbara Jago. *ph* Joao (Funcho) Costa. *ed* Carine Tredgold. *m* Keith Goddard, Philip Roberts, Dick Chingaira. *cast* Marian Kunonga, Ulla Mahaka, Norman Madawo, Moise Matura.

● The war that transformed Rhodesia into Zimbabwe is shown through the experiences of two young women freedom fighters, one dedicated to improvement through study, the other a more robust type with a tendency to fall for the wrong man. An intelligent, sympathetic first feature, but a tad predictable and so rushed in places that it slides into less than persuasive melodrama. 'Flame' (Kunonga) finds she's pregnant, gives birth in a truck and loses the baby in an air raid, all in about five minutes. GA

Flame and the Arrow, The

(1950, US, 88 min)
d Jacques Tourneur. *p* Harold Hecht, Frank Ross. *sc* Waldo Salt. *ph* Ernest Haller. *ed* Alan Crosland Jr. *ad* Edward Carrere. *m* Max Steiner. *cast* Burt Lancaster, Virginia Mayo, Robert Douglas, Aline MacMahon, Nick Cravat.

● The first of Burt Lancaster's attempts to revive the swashbuckling spirit of Douglas Fairbanks Senior. Perhaps not quite so irresistibly ebullient as *The Crimson Pirate*, but also less arch in its use of verbal anachronisms. Great fun, at any rate, beautifully paced by Tourneur, as Lancaster and Cravat romp through their incredible gymnastic stunts while rescuing medieval Lombardy from wicked oppressors. TM

Flame in My Heart, A (Une Flamme dans Mon Coeur)

(1987, Fr/Switz, 110 min)
d Alain Tanner. *sc* Myriam Mézières, Alain Tanner. *ph* Acácio de Almeida. *ed* Laurent Uhler. *cast* Myriam Mézières, Aziz Kabouche, Benoît Régent, Biana, Jean-Yves Berthelot, André Marcon.

● A folly from Tanner, scripted by its heavily emoting star Mézières, this tells the ludicrous tale of a woman who can never get what she wants, whether she's rehearsing Racine on stage or stripping in an immigrants' bar in Paris. She spends the first half of the movie trying to shake off an exceptionally persistent Arab lover, then picks up a journalist on the Métro and launches into an affair that takes her to Egypt. Ms Mézières' overheated performance would not be out of place in a Rosa von Praunheim movie; the embarrassment quotient is off the scale. TR

Flame in the Streets

(1961, GB, 93 min)
d/p Roy Baker. *sc* Ted Willis. *ph* Christopher Challis. *ed* Roger Cherrill. *ad* Alex Vetchinsky. *m* Philip Green. *cast* John Mills, Brenda de Banzie, Sylvia Syms, Earl Cameron, Johnny Sekka, Ann Lynn, Wilfrid Brambell.

● A relatively early attempt to come to terms – in melodramatic form – with racism and the aspirations of black immigrants in Britain. Mills owns a furniture factory and is proud of his tolerance, endorsing a Jamaican's candidacy as shop steward. However, enlightened shop floor attitudes are one thing; his daughter marrying a black is quite another. It's a bit like a social thesis – Discuss – but its background of poor housing and gangs of teddy boys roving the streets like the Ku Klux Klan is convincing enough. ATu

Flamenco

(1995, Sp, 102 min)
d Carlos Saura. *p* Juan Lebrón. *sc* Carlos Saura. *ph* Vittorio Storaro. *ed* Pablo de Amo. *ad* Rafael Palmero. *cast* La Paquera de Jerez, Merche Esmeralda, Manolo Sanlucar, Joaquín Cortés, Manuel Moneo, Agujeta, Mario Maya, Paco Toronjo, Antonio Toscano, Fernando de Utrera, José Menese, and others.

● Showcasing different styles and generations, and featuring 500 dancers, singers and guitarists from all walks of flamenco life (from Joaquín Cortés down), Saura's film is both an exciting document of a thriving Spanish art form and a boring documentary. Technically, it's dazzling. The setting, Seville's Plaza de Armas (a converted station), is revealed through Vittorio Storaro's cool, translucent rays of orange light suggesting the movement from dusk to dawn; there are mirrors, white panels, silhouettes. Surprising, then, that a film celebrating flamenco as a popular affair should offer so little contextualisation – and no subtitles – to a non-Spanish-speaking audience. Who are these people? What is this dance about? It's a valid artistic decision and preferable to cockeyed translation, but what it gains in purity over most of Saura's other films, it loses in accessibility. SS

Flame of New Orleans, The

(1941, US, 78 min, b/w)
d René Clair. *p* Joe Pasternak. *sc* Norman Krasna. *ph* Rudolph Maté. *ed* Frank Gross. *ad* Jack Otterson. *m* Frank Skinner. *cast* Marlene Dietrich, Bruce Cabot, Roland Young, Mischa Auer, Andy Devine, Laura Hope Crews, Franklin Pangborn.

● After the end of her partnership with Josef von Sternberg, Dietrich didn't regain her professional stride until 1939, when she was cast as a roistering bar hostess in the spoof Western, *Destry Rides Again*. Here, two films later, she's playing a variation on the role: an émigré adventuress with a dubious past in St Petersburg, trying to pose as a countess in New Orleans, torn between a 'sensible' marriage and her wild passion for the butch young captain of a Mississippi steamer. This was the first of the four films that Clair directed in Hollywood during his wartime exile from France, and he was clearly content to swim with the tide: he simply films the formulary but entertaining script, with a minimum of directorial touches. It is, of course, Dietrich who carries it. TR

Flame Over India

see North West Frontier

Flame Top (Tulipää)

(1980, Fin, 141 min)
d Pirjo Honkasalo, Pekka Lehto. *cast* Asko Sarkola, Rea Mauranen, Kari Franck, Esko Salminen, Ritva Juhanto, Markku Blomqvist.

● Finnish epic about a celebrated national hero, Maiju Lassila: novelist, revolutionary and wealthy businessman. From his poor, rural childhood, through his arrival in St Petersburg in 1900, his success as a writer, his exile in the Finnish forests, and his eventual imprisonment and death, the film charts Lassila's political development – his terrorist activities against the Russians, and his part in the 1918 Finnish Civil War. Shot on location not only in Finland but also in Leningrad, the film is well-crafted and authentic, but the slow pace and broodingly melancholic atmosphere make it generally heavy-going. GA

Flaming Creatures

(1962, US, 43 min. b/w)
d Jack Smith. *cast* Mario Montez.

● One of the legendary *maudit* films, Smith's extravaganza of underground pleasure(ing)s doesn't quite stand up to its chequered fame. Shot in murky black-and-white, it visibly belongs to the early '60s, but nevertheless appears to originate from some arcane time pocket of the '20s, populated by vampy drag queens and draggy vampires, guests at a boisterous but strangely innocent orgy orchestrated with pulpy pop ditties and flapper anthems. Admittedly, it now comes across as an archive piece, and proves that boredom has always been a factor in the avant-garde's articulation of perverse desire. But as a missing link between prehistoric cine-camp and the dazed excesses of Warhol and the infinitely more trenchant George Kuchar, it is of academic interest at the very least. JRo

Flaming Ears

(1991, Aus, 83 min)
d/p Angela Hans Schierl, Dietmar Schipek, Ursula Pürrer. *ph* Margarete Neumann, Curd Duca, Hermann Lewetz, Manfred Neuwirth. *cast* Susanna Heilmayr, Angela Hans Schierl, Ursula Pürrer, Margarethe Neumann, Gabriele Szekatsch, Anthony Escott.

● It's safe to say that this apocalyptic lesbian fantasy is one of a kind, but that's as far as it goes. Set in 2700 in the mouldering city of Asche, it chronicles the star-crossed amours of a group of women: Volley (Pürrer), a roller-skating pyromaniac; her plastic-suited, possibly extraterrestrial lover Nun (Schierl); and Spy (Heilmayr), a comics artist who vows revenge on Volley for burning down her printing press. There's little coherent narrative; the directors are more concerned with elaborating a wild and woolly style, comprising daft decor, lurid colours and free-floating camerawork. They merrily cut corners with the futurism, knocking up a passable *Alphaville* world from table-top Meccano and leaving the rest to creaky stop-motion animation. Despite oddball gags seemingly beamed in from another dimension, the feel is leadenly Teutonic. JRo

Flamingo Kid, The

(1984, US, 100 min)
d Garry Marshall. *p* Michael Phillips. *sc* Neal Marshall, Garry Marshall. *ph* James A Contner. *ed* Priscilla Nedd. *pd* Lawrence Miller. *m* Curt Sobel. *cast* Matt Dillon, Hector Elizondo, Molly McCarthy, Martha Gehman, Richard Crenna, Jessica Walter, Fisher Stevens.

● In 1963, Brooklyn-born Jeffrey (Dillon) takes a summer job at the El Flamingo beach club on Long Island, and receives an education in the art of making money; his family, however, is dismayed by the boy's dreams of speedy upward mobility. Hardly original stuff, and morally the film wants to have its cake and eat it, celebrating working-class simplicity while revelling in the luxuriance of beach club life. But the performances compensate, with Dillon turning in a light and touching portrait of confused ambitions. GA

Flaming Star

(1960, US, 101 min)
d Don Siegel. *p* David Weisbart. *sc* Clair Huffaker, Nunnally Johnson. *ph* Charles G Clarke. *ed* Hugh S Fowler. *ad* Duncan Cramer, Walter M Simonds. *m* Cyril J Mockridge. *cast* Elvis Presley, Barbara Eden, Steve Forrest, Dolores Del Rio, John McIntire, Rodolfo Acosta.

● By far and away Presley's best film, in which he sings only one song (apart from the title number), and is used emblematically rather than required to act as the half-breed son in a mixed race family which is gradually torn apart as the Kiowas go on the rampage against white settlers and both sides draw up their racist lines. Despite the stolid liberal intentions behind the script, Siegel keeps the tensions finely balanced on a knife edge, with the inevitable violence threatening to explode at every moment and the tortured emotions cutting surprisingly deep. A fine Western. TM

Flap (aka The Last Warrior)

(1970, US, 106 min)
d Carol Reed. *p* Jerry Adler. *sc* Clair Huffaker. *ph* Fred J Koenekamp. *ed* Frank Bracht. *pd* Arthur Loel. *m* Marvin Hamlisch. *cast* Anthony Quinn, Claude Akins, Tony Bill, Victor Jory, Don Collier, Shelley Winters, Rodolfo Acosta.

● A feeble comedy. Quinn reprises his primitive savage-with-savvy bit as the drunken Indian who inaugurates a public relations war for Indian rights, Red Power. Reed's leaden direction and the script's poetry-as-prose language trivialise every issue the film touches upon. Even the wonderful idea of lassooing a helicopter is thrown away. PH

Flashback

(1990, US, 108 min)
d Franco Amurri. *p* David Loughery, Marvin Worth. *sc* David Loughery. *ph* Stefan Czapsky. *ed* C Timothy O'Meara. *pd* Vincent Cresciman. *m* Barry Goldberg. *cast* Kiefer Sutherland, Dennis Hopper, Carol Kane, Cliff De Young, Paul Dooley, Michael McKean, Richard Masur.

● Hopper gives a strong performance as a '60s radical who came near to murdering Vice-President Spiro Agnew back in 1969. After emerging from two decades in hiding, he finds himself being escorted to face trial in Washington state by reactionary FBI man Sutherland. He manages to change clothes with his minder and both land in trouble with a local sheriff. The main pleasure here is the repartee between the stars. Lots of appeal for ageing hippies, too. TJ

Flashdance

(1983, US, 98 min)
d Adrian Lyne. *p* Don Simpson, Jerry Bruckheimer. *sc* Tom Hedley, Joe Eszterhas. *ph* Don Peterman. *ed* Bud Smith, Walt Mulconery. *pd* Charles Rosen. *m* Giorgio Moroder. *cast* Jennifer Beals, Michael Nouri, Lilia Skala, Sunny Johnson, Kyle T Heffner, Belinda Bauer.

● Depressing to think that this was a huge hit on the back of the Irene Cara hit single, since there's absolutely nothing to it, beyond Ms Beals cavorting in a leotard, lots of sheeny backgrounds courtesy of Lyne the former adman, and a Joe

Eszterhas screenplay mixed through with cliché concentrate as female blue-collar worker proceeds from showgirl at a men's club to the big audition for the Pittsburgh ballet school. The star, it has to be said, is not at her most convincing as a welder (how does she afford an apartment the size of an aircraft hangar?), nor should we forget that most of the serious terpsichorean gymnastics were done by uncredited French dancer Marine Jahan. The snappily edited pop-video for the title tune renders the rest of this guff surplus to requirements. TJ

Flash Gordon

(1980, GB, 115 min)
d Michael Hodges. *p* Dino De Laurentiis. *sc* Lorenzo Semple Jr. *ph* Gilbert Taylor. *ed* Malcolm Cooke. *pd* Danilo Donati. *m* Queen. *cast* Sam J Jones, Melody Anderson, Chaim Topol, Max von Sydow, Ornella Muti, Timothy Dalton, Brian Blessed, Peter Wyngarde, Mariangela Melato, John Osborne.

● Forget the hi-tech droidery of the current strain of sci-fi, *Flash Gordon* time warps us thirty years back into the baroque world of wedding-cake sky castles, crystal swords, hawk-men, and chaps who have just twelve hours to save the world, armed only with a lantern jaw and a clean pair of tights. The narrative is a little plodding, but adult punters will soon slip back into a reverie for the lost visions of Saturday morning cinema, and their kids can get off on the extraordinary undercurrent of febrile sexuality. Acting honours go to von Sydow as Ming the Merciless and Mariangela Melato as his dark-eyed henchperson. Flash himself is as thick as a brick, but will no doubt appeal to gentlemen who prefer blonds. CPea

Flatliners

(1990, US, 114 min)
d Joel Schumacher. *p* Michael Douglas, Rick Bieber. *sc* Peter Filardi. *ph* Jan de Bont. *ed* Robert Brown. *pd* Eugenio Zanetti. *m* James Newton Howard. *cast* Kiefer Sutherland, Julia Roberts, Kevin Bacon, William Baldwin, Oliver Platt, Kimberly Scott.

● Medical school student Nelson Wright (Sutherland) is so obsessed with research into the near-death experience that he recruits four friends, and they take turns at stopping their hearts until the monitors reading their vital signs indicate nothing but flat lines. Once revived by other members of the team, armed with their new-found knowledge they set about rectifying past misdeeds. Schumacher's aggressive direction sweeps across weird panoramas and dives headlong into terrifying memories. We're in mystical territory here, hence the flamboyant visuals; but that's no excuse for Peter Filardi's affected script, which culminates in Bacon railing against the heavens, fists and feet flying. There's also a sorry lack of restraint from production designer Eugenio Zanetti, whose other-worldly atmosphere reaches its apotheosis in Sutherland's all-white apartment, which contains only one piece of furniture (a bed, of course). CM

Flat Tyre (Po Luntai)

(1999, Tai, 72 min)
d Huang Mingchuan. *p* Shell Wang. *sc* Huang Mingchuan. *ph* Zeng Bodo *ed* Huang Mingchuan. *m* TIP. *cast* Ding Ning, Yang Mingxiong, Zeng Bodo, Liu Jixiong.

● A photographer noted for b/w landscapes grows obsessed with filming immobile subjects: the statues, most of them religious or political, which litter Taiwan. He treks around the island with his cynical cameraman, from mountain peaks to village squares, shooting representations of Buddha, Guanyin and Chiang Kai-Shek. Meanwhile the young woman fan who moved in with him starts working on a vacuous commercial movie as a location scout/actress and gets drawn into an abrasive sexual relationship with the lead actor. Taiwan's foremost indie filmmaker uses a project with obvious roots in documentary to perform surgery on the island's damaged heart; few directors would see the link between a failing relationship and the motive for putting up a statue, and fewer would posit that link with such dream-like wit. TR

Flavia la Monaca Musulmana

see Rebel Nun, The

Flavour of Green Tea Over Rice, The (Ochazuke no aji)

(1952, Jap, 115 min, b/w)
d Yasujiro Ozu. *sc* Yasujiro Ozu, Kogo Noda. *ph* Yoshun Atsuta. *m* Senji Ito. *cast* Shin Saburi, Michiyo Kogure, Koji Tsuruta, Chishu Ryu, Chikage Awajima, Keiko Ksujima.

● Beginning in light-hearted mood with four women deceiving their husbands to go drinking at a spa, this exquisite Ozu film gradually turns dark as it charts the marital crisis of one of the women and her taciturn husband. At once a study of the shortcomings and strengths of the arranged marriage, and an exploration of what constitutes deceit, and an understated celebration of love tentatively rekindled (one might almost call it Ozu's *Viaggio in Italia*), this is also one of the director's most 'active' films; the camera frequently moves, there are car rides, train journeys and planes taking off, as well as scenes at baseball games and cycle races. Very funny and very moving. GA

Flawless

(1999, US, 111 min)
d Joel Schumacher. *p* Joel Schumacher, Jane Rosenthal. *sc* Joel Schumacher. *ph* Declan Quinn. *ed* Mark Stevens. *pd* Jan Roelfs. *m* Bruce Roberts. *cast* Robert De Niro, Philip Seymour Hoffman, Barry Miller, Chris Bauer, Skipp Sudduth, Wilson Jermaine Heredia, Nashom Benjamin. Scott Allen Cooper.

● For what it's worth, this could be Schumacher's best film. There's no stylised-to-oblivion cartoon sensationalism, none of the knee-jerk politics of *Falling Down*; just two lonely men in a big bad city (New York, natch), and a couple of involved performances from De Niro and Hoffman, one bearing a speech impediment, the other wearing a dress. The story's an opposites-repel number, a chaste male love story charting the reluctant meeting of minds of homophobic cop Walt and ballsy drag diva Rusty, tenement-block neighbours who spend their spare time squabbling across the courtyard that separates them. An uninvolving mob-loot plot, which mostly keeps itself in the background, intercedes to leave the policeman crippled by a stroke. Too ashamed to seek help from his friends, he grudgingly shuffles upstairs and supplicates Rusty for singing lessons by way of therapy. A palatably mainstream critique of pride, prejudice and identity barriers, it's unexceptional material; indeed, it might seem drab were it not for the leads. De Niro pulls out a couple of stops, and Hoffman has a ball. NB

Fled

(1996, US, 98 min)
d Kevin Hooks. *p* Frank Mancuso Jr. *sc* Preston A Whitmore. *ph* Matthew F Leonetti. *ed* Richard Nord, Joe Gutowski. *pd* Charles Bennett. *m* Graeme Revell. *cast* Stephen Baldwin, Laurence Fishburne, Will Patton, Robert John Burke, Victor Rivers, David Dukes, Ken Jenkins, Salma Hayek.

● A disgraced cop (Fishburne) and a hacker-with-a-heart (Baldwin) go on the lam in Georgia – first from jail-house nasties, then from cops and crims alike – while trading (witless) insults and punches. There's an intrepid local sheriff (Patton) who won't accept the official line; sinister expat Cubans with slicked hair and shades; a double-dealing superior (Burke) in the witness protection programme; and an accommodating driver (Hayek) whose car the boys co-opt, and who has to stop falling for cops. Add in elusive computer disks with vital info, regular soft-core violence, a baddy who won't stay dead, chases on foot, by car, truck, motorbike, and a cable-car finale. Lots of physical energy, but little else. NB

Flesh

(1968, US, 105 min)
d Paul Morrissey. *p* Andy Warhol. *sc/ph* Paul Morrissey. *cast* Joe Dallesandro, Geraldine Smith, Maurice Bradell, Louis Waldon, Geri Miller, Candy Darling, Jackie Curtis, Patti Darbanville.

● About a hustler who goes to work to earn money for his wife's girlfriend's abortion. Self-consciously analytical, self-consciously beautiful. Visually always fine, persuasive, flattering, curious, and occasionally blatantly sociological. A product of the Warhol factory, it keeps the non-edited appearance of Warhol's own films. VG

Flesh & Blood

(1985, US/Neth, 127 min)
d Paul Verhoeven. *p* Gys Versluys. *sc* Gerard Soeteman, Paul Verhoeven. *ph* Jan De Bont. *ed* Ine Schenkkan. *ad* Félix Murcia. *m* Basil Poledouris. *cast* Rutger Hauer, Jennifer Jason Leigh, Tom Burlinson, Jack Thompson, Fernando Hillbeck, Susan Tyrrell, Ronald Lacey.

● Although shot in Spain, this was Verhoeven's first English-language movie and a stepping stone to Hollywood (Orion put up half the budget). Not that the Dutchman seems to have borne American sensibilities in mind: a medieval anti-romance about a virginal heiress (Leigh) who falls into the grip of a rapacious band of superstitious mercenaries led by the brutal Martin (Hauer), the film overflows with pestilence, plague and pillage. The girl's fondness for her rapist won't commend the film to feminists either. It's hamstrung by leaden dialogue and the motley international cast – Python and the Grail are never that far away – but it's admirably unsentimental and by no means stupid. TCh

Flesh and Bone

(1993, US, 124 min)
d Steve Kloves. *p* Mark Rosenberg, Paul Weinstein. *sc* Steve Kloves. *ph* Philippe Rousselot. *ed* Mia Goldman. *pd* John Hutman. *m* Thomas Newman. *cast* Dennis Quaid, James Caan, Meg Ryan, Gwyneth Paltrow, Scott Wilson, Christopher Rydell.

● When Arlis Sweeney (Quaid) was a kid, he saw his dad Roy (Caan) kill an entire farmstead family, except the screaming baby. Thirty years on, Arlis is content to drift around Texas fixing candy and condom machines; at least until he meets Kay Davies (Ryan), a volatile young woman keen to escape an unhappy marriage. Their hesitant relationship blooms – then, one night, the past catches up with Arlis in the shape of his father, for whom blood ties override all other considerations. Writer/director Kloves seems preoccupied with character and milieu. The performances are sound, but for much of the time the film seems undecided whether it's a mystery, a romance, a social document or an art movie. And that indecision is fatal, stifling the life out of what might have been an effective little thriller. GA

Flesh and Fantasy

(1943, US, 94 min, b/w)
d Julien Duvivier. *p* Charles Boyer, Julien Duvivier. *sc* Ernest Pascal, Samuel Hoffenstein, Ellis St Joseph. *ph* Paul Ivano, Stanley Cortez. *ed* Arthur Hilton. *ad* John B Goodman, Richard Riedel, Robert Boyle. *m* Alexandre Tansman. *cast* Charles Boyer, Edward G Robinson, Barbara Stanwyck, Betty Field, Robert Cummings, Thomas Mitchell, Robert Benchley.

● Three tales of the supernatural, rather tiresomely linked by reflections on superstition from Benchley and his clubmen friends. A wonderfully atmospheric shot, with Mardi Gras revellers huddling on the riverbank, suddenly hushed as the body of a drowned girl is retrieved from the water, introduces the charming but slightly icky tale of a plain and embittered Cinderella (Field) who is given a mask of beauty to wear at the ball by a mysterious old man in a novelty shop, thereby precariously ensnaring the heart of the student prince (Cummings) who has hitherto ignored her. The second and best episode adapts Wilde's *Lord Arthur Savile's Crime*, with Robinson as the distraught man told by a fortune-teller (Mitchell) that he's going to commit murder, deciding to get it over with, and finding that fate is not so easily cheated. Superb throughout, the camerawork (Paul Ivano and Stanley Cortez) excels itself here. The third tale (Boyer as a tightrope walker haunted by visions of Stanwyck) is negligible, despite excellent performances. TM

Flesh and the Devil

(1927, US, 9 reels, b/w)
d Clarence Brown. *sc* Benjamin F Glazer. *ph* William H Daniels. *ed* Lloyd Nosler. *ad* Cedric Gibbons, Fredric Hope. *cast* John Gilbert, Greta Garbo, Lars Hanson, Barbara Kent, William Orlamond, Marc MacDermott.

● Renowned for its electric love scenes between Garbo and Gilbert (though these days they don't seem that torrid), this is an elegant bit of melodramatic fluff, with Garbo in swooning form as the adulterous Countess coming between her soldier lover (Gilbert) and his best buddy (Hanson), who marries her after the count (MacDermott) is killed in a duel. Much ado about nothing, really, but Garbo is as luminous as ever, thanks to William Daniels' camerawork. GA

Flesh and the Fiends, The (aka Mania/Psycho Killers/ The Fiendish Ghouls)

(1959, GB, 97 min. b/w)
d John Gilling. *p* Robert Baker, Monty Berman. *sc* Leon Griffiths, John Gilling. *ph* Monty Berman. *ed* Jack Slade. *ad* John Elphick. *m* Stanley Black. *cast* Peter Cushing, Donald Pleasence, George Rose, Billie Whitelaw, June Laverick, Renee Houston, Dermot Walsh, Melvyn Hayes.

● A somewhat rickety old chiller (to the back-door of Dr Knox's Edinburgh medical academy come the 'Resurrectionists') not helped by the stiff second leads, Laverick and Walsh, but much enlivened by the black-comic caperings of Pleasence (Ulster accent and rolling eyes) and Rose (a very simple-minded killer) as the body-snatchers Hare and Burke. The film, written by John Gilling and Leon Griffiths, is notably cold-hearted when it comes to the off-hand murders, young 'Daft' Jamie (Hayes), for instance, being strangled in a pig pen, amid the squealing of the porkers. Incidental pleasures include Billie Whitelaw, as a noisy trollop, and Renee Houston, as Mrs Burke, a most businesslike murderess. JPy

Flesh for Frankenstein (Carne per Frankenstein)

(1973, It/Fr, 95 min)
d Paul Morrissey. *p* Andrew Braunsberg. *sc* Paul Morrissey. *ph* Luigi Kuveiller. *ed* Franca Silvi, Jed Johnson. *pd* Enrico Job. *m* Claudio Gizzi. *cast* Joe Dallesandro, Monique Van Vooren, Udo Kier, Carla Mancini, Srdjan Zelenovic.

● Here Morrissey stops pretending that he's making Warhol movies and sets his sights on the US drive-in market, which takes its sex softcore but its violence unbridled. The plot boils down to Baroness Frankenstein entertaining the local stud in her boudoir, while hubby Victor chops up the rest of the peasant population in the lab downstairs. Trouble is, Morrissey just doesn't cut it as a 'real' director: there's no way that he can conjure even a sickie horror comedy from one over-played concept (yards of bursting entrails), a three-page script, a bunch of game but mostly talentless players, and a few decorative sets. Well aware of his problems, he stakes everything on a gimmick and films in a 3-D process. Somehow, it's not enough. TR

Flesh Gordon

(1974, US, 90 min)
d Michael Benveniste, Howard Ziehm. *p* Howard Ziehm, William Osco. *sc* Michael Benveniste. *ph* Howard Ziehm. *ed* Abbas Amin. *ad* Donald Harris. *m* Ralph Ferraro. *cast* Jason Williams, Suzanne Fields, Joseph Hudgins, William Hunt, John Hoyt, Candy Samples.

● Flesh Gordon, to save the world from a Sex-Ray attack, takes on the evil Wang, ruler of the planet Porno. Unsatisfying as a sex film, not much cop as anything else, this sci-fi ski-fli manages to be visually compulsive and dully unimaginative at the same time. AN

Flesh Is Hot, The

see Pigs and Battleships

Fletch

(1985, US, 98 min)
d Michael Ritchie. *p* Alan Greisman, Peter Douglas. *sc* Phil Alden Robinson, Andrew Bergman. *ph* Fred Schuler. *ed* Richard A Harris. *pd* Boris Leven. *m* Harold Faltermeyer. *cast* Chevy Chase, Joe Don Baker, Dana Wheeler-Nicholson, Richard Libertini, Tim Matheson, M Emmet Walsh, George Wendt, Kenneth Mars, Geena Davis.

● Two fairly routine plots (who is the Mr Big in the drug supply chain and Lady from Shanghai's 'I want you to murder me please') are neatly interwoven in a film that depends heavily on how we feel about Chevy Chase and his delivery of wisecracks. This could be Bob Hope material c1942 and Chase does acquit himself well (though with cool reserve) in the gags-to-plot transitions. What dulls the enterprise is that Ritchie so keeps his distance from every character that we seldom give a damn. Subdued performances by Mars and Baker are hard to imagine, but here they are. From Gregory McDonald's novel. DO

Fletch Lives

(1989, US, 95 mins)
d Michael Ritchie. *p* Alan Greisman, Peter Douglas. *sc* Leon Capetanos. *ph* John McPherson. *ed* Richard A Harris. *ad* Cameron Birnie, Jimmy Bly, W Steven Graham, Don Woodruff. *m* Harold Faltermeyer. *cast* Chevy Chase, Hal Holbrook, Julianne Phillips, R Lee Ermey, Richard Libertini, Randall 'Tex' Cobb, Cleavon Little, Patricia Kalember.

● Bequeathed an 80-acre plantation in the Deep South, Fletch (Chase) jets off to his new-found ancestral home. Surprise, surprise, the mansion turns out to be a ruin, but Fletch decidesd to hang around just long enough to get his end away with a 'lovely local lawyer' (Kalember), who promptly drops dead. Chase makes *fnar fnar* jokes about her death being a result of his sexual prowess, but a more likely explanation would be that Ms Kalember had read the script and decided it was a good time to get out. The ensuing plot, in which Chase gets tangled up in murder, mystery, intrigue, and derring-do, isn't worth describing since it serves only as a vehicle for Fletch to don various disguises and deliver his own 'inimitable' comic patter. The humour throughout is alternately mindless, sexist, racist, and homophobic, and would probably offend if you managed to stay awake. MK

Flic, Un (Dirty Money)

(1972, Fr/It, 98 min)
d Jean-Pierre Melville. *p* Robert Dorfman. *sc* Jean-Pierre Melville. *ph* Walter Wottitz. *ed* Patricia Renaut. *pd* Théo Meurisse. *song* Michel Colombier, Charles Aznavour. *cast* Alain Delon, Catherine Deneuve, Richard Crenna, Ricardo Cucciolla, Michael Conrad, Simone Valère, Jean Desailly.

● The great Melville's thirteenth and last film – another French gangster thriller filtered through American hard-nosed conventions – is stylistically his most pared-down. Aside from the two set-piece heists, as ingeniously planned and meticulously shot as ever, the connecting storyline of an increasingly inept 'flic' (Delon) pursuing his alter ego across a darkening urban landscape has a near psychotic disregard for place, time or even plot, but total coherence in terms of mood – more blue than *noir*. A bitter meditation on disenchantment and defeat, as glacial and hermetic as Deneuve's face. CPea

Flickering Roads (Asphaltflimmern)

(1994, Ger, 80 min)
d Johannes Hebendanz. *p* Bernd Medek, Elke Müller. *sc* Johannes Hebendanz. *ph* Peter Krause. *ed* Johannes Henendanz. *pd* Stephanie Wirth. *m* Wolfgang von Henko. *cast* Fäti Sengul, Thorsten Schatz, Oda Pretschner, Sergej Gritsai, Utz Krause.

● An unpretentious road movie through the underside of contemporary Germany. Swaggering delinquent teenager Micka and abandoned Rumanian immigrant Gena try to steal the same car. When they subsequently swindle café waitress Phillipa out of their bill and her job, all three find themselves on the lam, estranged from society and hounded by the police. Despite losing his way in places, director Hebendanz treats his several subjects in a light and determinedly balanced fashion, forgoing both judgment and cliché. The open ending leaves one rather more optimistic about the prospects for this makeshift family than for the society they finally abandon. NB

Flight from Ashiya

(1963, US/Jap, 102 min)
d Michael Anderson. *p* Harold Hecht. *sc* Elliott Arnold, Waldo Salt. *ph* Joseph MacDonald, Burnett Guffey. *ed* Gordon Pilkington. *pd* Eugène Lourié. *m* Frank Cordell. *cast* Yul Brynner, Richard Widmark, George Chakiris, Suzy Parker, Shirley Knight, Danièle Gaubert, Eiko Taki.

● Tepid adventure movie, with an American Air-Sea Rescue Service team flying to save the crew of a ship sunk off the Japanese coast in a typhoon. The lumbering action scenes are further deflated by flashbacks to previous disasters the heroes have experienced; and Anderson, master of the overblown twaddle-movie (*Around the World in 80 Days, Logan's Run*), miraculously even manages to waste the photographic talents of Burnett Guffey and Joe MacDonald. GA

Flight of the Bee, The (Parvozi Zanbur/aka Bee-Fly)

(1998, Tajikistan, 90 min, b/w)
d Jamshed Usmonov, Min Boung-Hun. *p* Min Boung-Hun, Kim Tae-Hun, Yoo Jun-Sang. *sc* Jamshed Usmonov. *ph* Min Boung-Hun. *ed* Min Boung-Hun, Jamshed Usmonov. *m* Satyajit Ray. *cast* Muhammadjon Shodi, Mastura Ortiq, Tagmoimurod Roziq, Fakhriddin Fathiddin.

● Usmonov (Tajik) and Min (Korean) were fellow film students in Moscow who teamed up to make this remarkable film, a social fable which deals obliquely with the root causes of the Tajik civil war but has the elemental simplicity of a legend. Schoolteacher Anor is outraged by the behaviour of his nouveau riche neighbour, who stares lustfully at Anor's wife and builds a stinking toilet next to Anor's wall. When the corrupt local magistrate (pressured by the neighbour) fails to intervene, Anor vengefully buys land next to the magistrate's home and begins digging out what he says will be a public toilet. Kiarostami comparisons are in order: the blend of earthy plainness, conceptual sophistication and muscular mise en scène is that beautiful. TR

Flight of the Doves

(1971, GB, 101 min)
d/p Ralph Nelson. *sc* Frank Gabrielson, Ralph Nelson. *ph* Harry Waxman. *ed* John Jympson. *ad* Frank Arrigo. *m* Roy Budd. *cast* Ron Moody, Jack Wild, Dorothy McGuire, Stanley Holloway, Helen Raye, William Rushton.

● Having perpetrated a repellent mixture of bloody violence, pacifist plea and spoony romance in *Soldier Blue*, Nelson followed up with this equally odious whimsy about two Liverpudlian moppets who take flight from a cruel stepfather and head for Ireland, where a loving granny (McGuire) waits with open arms in a little thatched cottage. Various grotesques met along the way, plus Moody as a wicked uncle with an eye to their inheritance (and adopting a series of wild disguises as he gives chase), provide some laborious relief from the maudlin sentiment. Nelson produced and co-scripted as well as directing, so the sorry mess is all his. TM

Flight of the Innocent (La Corsa dell'innocente)

(1993, It, 100 min)
d Carlo Carlei. *p* Franco Cristaldi, Domenico Procacci. *sc* Carlo Carlei, Gualtiero Rosella. *ph* Raffaele Mertes. *ed* Claudio Di Mauro, Carl Fontana. *pd* Franco Ceraolo. *m* Carlo Siliotto. *cast* Manuel Colao, Francesca Neri, Jacques Perrin, Federico Pacifici, Sal Borgese, Lucio Zagaria.

● Deep in the Calabrian countryside, young Vito (Colao) stumbles across a shooting, the bleeding victim fleeing before an unknown assailant. When Vito returns home, his father is marked as the killer by a red blot on his shoes – and further shocks are to come. Later that evening, gunmen break into the farmhouse and slaughter the family. Pitched into the stuff of nightmares, Vito barely escapes with his life. Writer/director Carlei constructs a bravura, killer opening, but later – as angelic Colao imagines himself a surrogate son to the wealthy parents (Neri and Perrin) of an abducted boy – the plot becomes mired in sentimentality and wish-fulfilment. TJ

Flight of the Intruder

(1991, US, 113 min)
d John Milius. *p* Mace Neufeld. *sc* Robert Dillon, David Shaber. *ph* Fred J Koenekamp. *ed* C Timothy O'Meara, Steve Mirkovich, Peck Prior. *pd* Jack T Collis. *m* Basil Poledouris. *cast* Danny Glover, Willem Dafoe, Brad Johnson, Rosanna Arquette, Tom Sizemore, J Kenneth Campbell, Dann Florek, Madison Mason, Ving Rhames.

●'My politics are strange,' John Milius has said, 'I'm so far to the right, I'm almost an anarchist'. *Almost?* Judging by this gung-ho tale of a pair of frustrated Navy fliers – vengeful, disillusioned pilot Brad Johnson, and jaded, cynical bombardier Willem Dafoe – flying an unauthorised two-man mission to knock out a Vietcong missile dump in Hanoi, he's gone beyond good and evil. Sadly, his direction is as muddled as his ideology, stodgy exchanges of dialogue punctuating the disappointingly dull action sequences, which are long on military hardware but short on adrenalin. Even a diehard Milius fan would be hard-pressed to find anything of merit in this leaden, macho nonsense. NF

Flight of the Navigator

(1986, US, 89 min)
d Randal Kleiser. *p* Robby Wald, Dimitri Villard. *sc* Michael Burton, Matt MacManus. *ph* James Glennon. *ed* Jeff Gourson. *pd* William J Creber. *m* Alan Silvestri. *cast* Joey Cramer, Veronica Cartwright, Cliff De Young, Sarah Jessica Parker, Matt Adler, Howard Hesseman.
●One dark night, 12-year-old David goes looking for his younger brother Jeff. Falling into a ditch, he knocks himself out. Moments later he awakens and walks home, only to find that his family have moved. Not only that, for the past eight years he's been missing, presumed dead. It's a pity the film can't quite live up to the promise of this opening: the boy's confusion is nicely handled, and the reaction on his face when he discovers that the revolting Jeff is now four years older than he and twice his size is one of the high spots of the movie. But as the answer to this strange little riddle unfolds, with NASA scientists discovering that his head is full of space charts and that he can communicate with computers, we're back on familiar Hollywood hi-tech territory. One for the none too discerning youngster. CB

Flight of the Phoenix, The

(1965, US, 149 min)
d/p Robert Aldrich. *sc* Lukas Heller. *ph* Joseph Biroc. *ed* Michael Luciano. *ad* William Glasgow. *m* Frank De Vol. *cast* James Stewart, Richard Attenborough, Peter Finch, Hardy Kruger, Ernest Borgnine, Ian Bannen, Ronald Fraser, Christian Marquand, Dan Duryea, George Kennedy.
●Basically a disaster movie about survival problems when a cargo-passenger plane crashes miles from anywhere in the Arabian desert. The pilot (Stewart), conscious of his responsibility for the lives of all concerned, suffers doubts; his navigator (Attenborough), a man accustomed to relying on the bottle for his courage, starts shaping up; a regular army officer (Finch) courts suicide because he blindly insists on playing by regulations...So far, so conventional, although beautifully characterised and directed by Aldrich with a grip that keeps tension high and heroics low. What takes the film right out of the rut is the gradual emergence of the group's saviour: a youthful German designer of model aircraft (Kruger), who develops a strain of pure Nazi fanaticism in his determination to prove that he can build a plane which will fly from bits of the wreck. He does it, too, although his only previous experience has been in toy-making; and in doing so, he raises spiky questions about leadership (democratic/dictatorial) and the survival of the fittest. A fadeout handshake of mutual congratulation finally shoves those questions aside – this is a Hollywood movie, after all – but not before they've achieved their abrasive task. TM

Flight to Berlin (Fluchtpunkt Berlin)

(1983, WGer, 90 min)
d Christopher Petit. *p* Chris Sievernich. *sc* Christopher Petit, Hugo Williams. *ph* Martin Schäfer. *ed* Peter Przygodda. *ad* Rainer Schaper. *m* Irmin Schmidt. *cast* Tusse Silberg, Paul Freeman, Lisa Kreuzer, Jean-François Stévenin, Ewan Stewart, Eddie Constantine, Tatjana Blacher.
●A mysterious death, a dissatisfied loner who may or may not be somehow guilty, a journey, introspection all round...where else but in Petit territory? As the film throws up plentiful questions regarding Tusse Silberg's relation to a dead woman, her sister, and the strange city of the title, Petit films in a terse, thought-provoking but oddly classical style, sounding echoes not merely of Godard, Rivette and Wenders, but also of older masters like Lang. Whether it works or not depends on your attitude towards the script's hesitantly elliptical way with narrative, but there's no denying that Petit is one of Britain's most ambitious film-makers. Infuriating or inspired, either way it's still worth a look. GA

Flim-Flam Man, The (aka One Born Every Minute)

(1967, US, 115 min)
d Irvin Kershner. *p* Lawrence Turman. *sc* William Rose. *ph* Charles Lang Jr. *ed* Robert Swink. *ad* Jack Martin Smith, Robert E Smith, Lewis H Creber. *m* Jerry Goldsmith. *cast* George C Scott, Michael Sarrazin, Sue Lyon, Harry Morgan, Jack Albertson, Alice Ghostley, Albert Salmi, Slim Pickens, Strother Martin.
●Aside from a long and outrageously destructive car chase, this is mainly a matter of mild charm and much cracker-barrel philosophy as an ageing confidence trickster (Scott) sardonically undertakes to instruct a youthful army deserter (Sarrazin) in the ways of the world. Good performances all round, but it's a long haul before the boy, having proven himself an apt pupil but deciding to do the right thing, teaches his mentor that there is at least one honest person in the world. TM

Flintstones, The

(1994, US, 92 min)
d Brian Levant. *p* Bruce Cohen. *sc* Tom S Parker, Jim Jennewein, Steven E de Souza. *ph* Dean Cundey. *ed* Kent Beyda. *pd* William Sandell. *m* David Newman. *cast* John Goodman, Elizabeth Perkins, Rick Moranis, Rosie O'Donnell, Kyle MacLachlan, Halle Berry, Elizabeth Taylor.
●This 'Spielrock' production is faithful to the original in everything but scale. The trick was not to stray too far from the cartoon simplicity of the Hanna-Barbera TV series, so the movie is a spectacular celebration of the superficial and the reassuring. The town of Bedrock is a genuine foam- design wonder: the bustling quarry, the monumental high street with its stone-roller cars. The exploited Jurassic-era fauna, from Dino the pet dinosaur to the lobster lawnmowers, all courtesy of Henson puppet technology and enhanced computer animatronics are so sympathetic you wish they'd organise a 'toon union. The actors, on the other hand – Goodman's Fred, Moranis's Barney, Perkins' Wilma – replicate the voices, manners, tics and tropes of the originals so accurately, they seem like programmed automatons. WH

Flintstones in Viva Rock Vegas, The

(2000, US, 90 min)
d Brian Levant. *p* Bruce Cohen. *sc* Deborah Kaplan, Harry Elfont, Jim Cash, Jack Epps Jr. *ph* Jamie Anderson. *ed* Kent Beyda. *pd* Christopher Burian-Mohr. *m* David Newman. *cast* Mark Addy, Stephen Baldwin, Kristen Johnston, Jane Krakowski, Thomas Gibson, Alan Cumming, Harvey Korman, Joan Collins.
●Six years on from the dull thud of the first live-action Flintstones movie, comes this belated attempt to turn the Bedrock crew into a big screen franchise. This time though, the bets have been hedged, with a second-rank cast and more obvious targeting of the children's audience. Addy is no John Goodman, but he makes a personable Fred, irrepressible without overplaying his hand; Baldwin's worryingly persuasive as the semi-troglodytic Barney Rubble; while Johnston proves an energetic Wilma, and Krakowski's a good egg Betty. Cumming tenuously frames the story as a sly-witted, bright green alien visiting Earth to study primitive mating habits. The cast put a lot of spirit into the workaday material and returning director Levant emerges with a somewhat livelier movie. The succession of prehistoric puns, fun cartoonish sets and comic dinosaur effects are all colourful enough to divert the very young. TJ

Flipper

(1963, US, 90 min)
d James B Clark. *p* Ivan Tors. *sc* Arthur Weiss. *ph* Lamar Boren, Joseph Brun. ed Warren Adams. *m* Henry Vars. *cast* Chuck Connors, Luke Halpin, Kathleen Maguire, Connie Scott, Jane Rose, Joe Higgins.
●Straightforward tale of a boy and a dolphin which proved popular enough to merit a movie sequel and launch a fondly remembered '60s TV series. You know the score by now: young Halpin nurses the dolphin back from injury, then has to persuade a grouchy old pop to let him keep his new-found pal as a pet. Will pacify small children. TJ

Flipper

(1996, US, 96 min)
d Alan Shapiro. *p* James J McNamara, Perry Katz. *sc* Alan Shapiro. *ph* Bill Butler. *ed* Peck Prior. *pd* Tom Walsh. *m* Joel McNeely. *cast* Paul Hogan, Elijah Wood, Chelsea Field, Jessica Wesson, Isaac Hayes, Jonathan Banks, Jason Fuchs.
●Amiable yarn based on the mid-'60s TV series about a growing youngster and an 'orphan' dolphin. Wood is the diffident single-parent child, Sandy, who vacations in a Caribbean backwater with his uncle Porter (Hogan), an ex-Beach Boys roadie turned salty sea dog (plus Hemingway cap and parrot). It's something of a muted comeback for Hogan, waltzing through his role as the eccentric but straight-arrow father-substitute with a pared version of his real man 'Dundee' persona. Writer/director Shapiro blends the elements of romance, adventure and comedy with easy if anonymous competence. Sandy trysts with bright-eyed Kim (Wesson), Porter romances marine biologist Cathy (Field); no wonder the dolphin keep springing into the air as if to protest he's been forgotten. Excellent technical credits, notably Bill Butler's camerawork, but the best stuff is the kid's lingo – 'Gotta jet, here comes the hippy.' WH

Flirt

(1995, US/GB/Jap, 84 min)
d Hal Hartley. *p* Ted Hope. *sc* Hal Hartley. *ph* Michael Spiller. *ed* Hal Hartley, Steve Hamilton *pd* Steve Rosenzweig. *m* Hal Hartley, Jeffrey Taylor. *cast* Bill Sage, Parker Posey, Martin Donovan, Robert Burke, Karen Sillas, Dwight Ewell, Dominik Bender, Geno Lechner, Elina Lowensöhn, Miho Nikaido, Toshio Fujiwara, Chikako Hara, Hal Hartley, Masatoshi Nagase.
●Hartley's jeu d'esprit starts from an intriguing premise: the same script is delivered three times, by three different casts, thus allowing local cultural differences and the viewer's cumulative knowledge to influence various shifts in tone and treatment. Shot first as a stand alone short, 'New York, February 1993' brings the tart romantic confusions familiar from the director's earlier work, as Bill Sage gives himself 90 minutes to decide if his future lies with partner Posey, and has his decision shaped by barfly Donovan's suicidal response to rejection by Sage's other lover. In 'Berlin, October 1994' black American Dwight Ewell hesitates over his affair with art dealer Bender, and a chorus of refreshingly straightforward workmen explain the film's self-reflexive strategies. 'Tokyo, March 1995' sets down with *butoh* performer Nikaido (Hartley's off-screen wife) and visiting American film-maker 'Hal', played with quizzical self-consciousness by the writer/director himself. Although the aphoristic dialogue and sly wit are by now a given, the structure allows Hartley to jettison more and more of the narrative exposition as he goes along, creating a Godardian sense of playfulness and also renewing the director's interest in purely choreographic nuance. TJ

Flirting

(1989, Aust, 99 min)
d John Duigan. *p* George Miller, Doug Mitchell, Terry Hayes. *sc* John Duigan. *ph* Geoff Burton. *ed* Robert Gibson. *pd* Roger Ford. *cast* Noah Taylor, Thandie Newton, Nicole Kidman, Bartholomew Rose, Felix Nobis, Josh Picker, Kiri Paramore.
●The second part of a trilogy which began with *The Year My Voice Broke*. Teenage student Danny (Taylor) divides his time between being bullied for his stutter and being bewitched by Thandiwe (Newton), a Ugandan pupil from a nearby girls' school. Both misfits, the two find solace in each other's affection, crossing the lake in search of adulthood. Beautifully written and directed by Duigan, the film maintains a delicate balance between wry satire, childish laughter, and dark, brooding malevolence. Not since Bill Forsyth's *Gregory's Girl* has a movie so precisely captured the goose-bumps, grunts, giggles and gorgeous rapture of teenage love. Taylor is a jowly delight,

while 16-year-old newcomer Newton throws savage glances and sensuous smiles with the assured air of a seasoned professional. Electrifying and heartbreaking; cherish it. MK

Flirting with Disaster

(1996, US, 92 min)
d David O Russell. *p* Dean Silvers. *sc* David O Russell. *ph* Eric A Edwards. *ed* Chris Tellefsen. *pd* Kevin Thompson. *m* Stephen Endelman. *cast* Ben Stiller, Patricia Arquette, Téa Leoni, Mary Tyler Moore, George Segal, Alan Alda, Lily Tomlin.

● Mel (Stiller) has a wife, Nancy (Arquette), an as yet unnamed baby, and a 'psychic need' to track down his biological parents. An adoption agency provides him with information so efficiently that he readily agrees to let research psychologist Tina (Leoni) witness the reunion. Besides, she's an attractive ex-dancer and he and Nancy aren't exactly back up to speed in the bedroom. Unfortunately, there's been a mix-up in the records, and the next 'father' he checks out isn't legitimate either; so the threesome – plus baby – work their way across the country, picking up a couple of gay federal agents en route. Writer/director Russell's follow-up to the incest comedy *Spanking the Monkey* confirms his gift for acute mischief-making. The neurotic frenzy threatens to annoy, but Russell's edgy, abbreviated style generates farcical comic friction without sacrificing character. When, early on, that icon of wholesomeness Mary Tyler Moore flashes her support bra, it's clear that, henceforth, nothing's sacred. It must be excruciatingly embarrassing to be related to this film-maker, but he's fast becoming a favourite son to the rest of us. TCh

Floating Life

(1996, Aust, 95 min)
d Clara Law. *p* Bridget Ikin. *sc* Clara Law, Eddie Fong. *ph* Dion Beebe. *ed* Suresh Ayyar. *pd* Hai Chung-Man. *m* Davood A Tabrizi. *cast* Annette Shun Wah, Annie Yip, Anthony Wong, Edwin Pang, Cecilia Fong Sing Lee, Toby Wong.

● A fascinating if flawed tale of a Hong Kong family who emigrate to Australia, where the bossy, largely Westernised second daughter's warnings about pit-bulls, killer wasps and skin cancer only add to the difficulties of adjustment; meanwhile, the eldest sister tries to persuade her husband that they should leave Germany, and the womanising eldest son wonders whether he too should see in 1997 or join his family. Shifting steadily from gentle comedy to something more poignant, the film never quite adds up to anything very compelling or cohesive. Watchable, none the less. GA

Flor di me Secreto, La

see Flower of My Secret, The

Florentine Dagger, The

(1935, US, 69 min, b/w)
d Robert Florey. *p* Harry Joe Brown. *sc* Brown Holmes, Tom Reed. *ph* Arthur L Todd. *ed* Thomas Pratt. *ad* Anton Grot, Carl Jules Weyl. *cast* Donald Woods, Margaret Lindsay, C Aubrey Smith, Robert Barrat, Henry O'Neill, Eily Malyon.

● Genuinely bizarre thriller about a young man, tormented by his heritage as 'the last of the Borgias', who tries to commit suicide to put an end to his impulse to kill. Advised by a psychiatrist to sublimate his fears, he writes a successful play about the Borgias, only to come to fear that his leading lady, who has problems of her own – a mother horribly burned in a theatrical fire, an amorous stepfather who is found stabbed with a Florentine dagger – may be being taken over by the personality of Lucretia. Over-compressed from Ben Hecht's novel, the script emerges as a bit of a ragbag, meandering from a classically stylish horror movie opening into conventional whodunit and back again to Grand Guignol. It is held together a trifle uncertainly by some Freudian analysis (the setting is Vienna), and rather more securely by Florey's consistently inventive, moodily evocative direction. Acting honours go to Barrat for his marvellously witty performance as the susceptibly gallant police chief. TM

Flower Island (Kkot Seom)

(2001, SKor/Fr, 126 min)
d Song Il-Gon. *p* Ahn Hoon-Chan. *sc* Song Il-Gon. *ph* Kim Myong-Joon. *ed* Moon In-Dae. *ad* Yoo Seong-Hee. *m* Noh Young-Shim. *cast* Seo Joo-Hee, Im Yoo-Jin, Kim Hye-Na, Son Byong-Ho, Choi Ji-Yeon.

● Three damaged women (a teen who's just given herself an abortion, a prostitute sick of her job, and an opera singer with throat cancer) meet by chance in mid-winter, deter each other from suicide and form a tenuous bond as they travel across Korea in search of a magic island where pain and sorrow can be exorcised. The highlight of the trip is running into an underground rock band (played by the actual band Uh-Uh-Boo), whose flamboyantly gay singer is the most credible character on screen. Song, a graduate from the Lodz Film School who won the Cannes Palme d'Or for his short *Picnic*, has gone for the kind of psycho-drama that excites extreme reactions, pro and con. But his decision to centre it on women (because they express pain better?) seems suspect, and there's a fundamental mismatch between the improvisational methods and the rigid conceptual framework. TR

Flower of My Secret, The (La Flor di me Secreto/La Fleur de mon secret)

(1995, Sp/Fr, 107 min)
d Pedro Almodóvar. *p* Esther Garcia. *sc* Pedro Almodóvar. *ph* Affonso Beato. *ed* José Salcedo. *ad* Wolfgang Burmann. *m* Alberto Iglesias. *cast* Marisa Paredes, Chus Lampreave, Rossy de Palma, Juan Echanove, Imanol Aria, Carmen Elias.

● Here we have Almodóvar's most open, unadorned, emotive and maybe even courageous film to date, an intimate portrait of pain and regeneration that strikes the heart without trickery. Gone are the chic excesses of *Kika* and the uneasy balance between superficial sensationalism and pocket melodrama that's marked the director's work since *Women on the Verge*. Paredes is immensely sympathetic as Leo, a forty-something writer of romantic fiction who hits crisis point when she's rejected by her absentee husband and finds she's trapped by her reputation when she tries to expand her literary horizons. Although she's supported by Angel (Echanove), cultural editor of *El Pais*, the constant bickering between her mother and sister doesn't help matters (Lampreave and de Palma, in a double-act to treasure); a trip home to her native village in La Mancha proves, however, an unlikely source of solace. Rarely has Almodóvar focused so closely on a single character, and the challenge of developing an individual portrait has reconnected him with the emotional realities of an everyday damaged life, where loneliness, professional frustration and the irritation and commitment that permeate family relationships are observed with perceptiveness, honesty and the usual incisive humour. TJ

Flowers in the Attic

(1987, US, 92 min)
d Jeffrey Bloom. *p* Sy Levin, Thomas Fries. *sc* Jeffrey Bloom. *ph* Frank Byers, Gil Hubbs. *ed* Gregory F Plotts. *pd* John Muto. *m* Christopher Young. *cast* Louise Fletcher, Victoria Tennant, Kristy Swanson, Jeb Stuart Adams, Ben Ganger, Lindsay Parker.

● Tennant is the perfect little mother whose husband dies in a car crash, and who puts herself and her four children at the mercy of her dying father and sadistic mother. Daddy never approved of her marriage and wrote her out of his will, and her unforgiving mother (Fletcher) insists that the children be kept locked in the attic to prevent him ever discovering their existence. Months pass, and the children, suffering from exhaustion and poisoned cookies, realise that their loving mother is just as deranged as their granny, and plot their escape. Incestuous desires run rampant in the original novel by VC Andrews, but all the movie has to offer is soft-focus innuendo. As fantasy stripped of all its metaphorical trimmings, the sublimely ridiculous plot is more likely to reduce an audience to laughter than to tears. TRi

Flowers of Shanghai (Hai Shang Hua)

(1998, Tai/Jap, 125 min)
d Hou Xiaoxian. *p* Yang Teng-kuei, Shozo Ichyama. *sc* Chu Tien-wen. *ph* Lee Ping-ben. *ed* Liao Ching-song. *pd* Hurang Wern-ying. *m* Yoshiro Hanno. *cast* Tony Leung Chiu-Wai, Michelle Reis, Jack Gao, Carina Lau.

● Entirely studio shot, Hou's most formally daring film to date is less an adaptation of a century old novel by Han Ziyun than a distillation of the lost world it describes. The 'flower houses' of old Shanghai were technically brothels, but not primarily places for sex; at a time when arranged marriages were the norm, China's male elite patronised them to get an *éducation sentimentale*. Hou organises the film around two strands of narrative. In one, Cantonese civil servant Wang (Leung) turns his back on his favourite 'flower girl' after catching her with another lover. In the other, a 'gentleman caller' and a cynical 'flower girl' conspire to profit from arranging to cover up the scandal of an attempted suicide. Each scene is a continuous take, bracketed by fades up from and back to black; the one (crucial) exception is the insert of Wang's point-of-view as he witnesses Ms Crimson's unfaithfulness. Hauntingly sad, the film elegantly deranges the viewer's sense of time: this seemingly unchanging world is in fact riven by off-screen incidents – which change everything. TR

Flubber

(1997, US, 94 min)
d Les Mayfield. *p* John Hughes, Ricardo Mestres. *sc* John Hughes, Bill Walsh. *ph* Dean Cundey. *ed* Harvey Rosenstock, Michael A Stevenson. *pd* Andrew McAlpine. *m* Danny Elfman. *cast* Robin Williams, Marcia Gay Harden, Christopher McDonald, Raymond J Barry, Clancy Brown.

● 'Flubber' – Prof Brainard (Williams) informs us, pseudo-scientifically – is an elastomer, ductile and elastic. All we really really need to know, however, is that the Professor's flying rubber superballs cause spectacular destruction. Top honours in this Disney remake of *The Absent-Minded Professor* go to cameraman Dean Cundey and the effects and design teams: to the whizzing balls, flying cars, aerial simulations, the 'Time Machine' laboratories and the Heath Robinson-style domestic aids. Williams produces another of his strangely sympathetic cartoons, an arrested adult so forgetful he's three times missed his own wedding (to Harden). He wears the same bow ties as Fred MacMurray, but dispenses with any residual traces of maturity. The script (by John Hughes and Bill Walsh) has Brainard selling the flubber to save the college. He's frustrated by fiancée-stealing McDonald, and the henchmen of entrepreneur Barry, who, naturally enough, want to exploit the green goo. WH

Fluchtweg nach Marseilles

see Escape Route to Marseilles

Fluffer, The

(2000, US, 94 min)
d Richard Glatzer, Wash West. *p* Victoria Robinson, John R Sylla. *sc* Wash West. *ph* Mark Putnam. *ed* John Binninger. *pd* Devorah Herbert. *m* The Bowling Green, John Vaughn. *cast* Scott Gurney, Michael Cunio, Roxanne Day, Taylor Negron, Richard Riehle, Tim Bagley, Adina Porter, Ruben Madera, Josh Holland, Deborah Harry.

● A fluffer is primarily an ego reinforcer, the provider of stimulation before a porn shoot. It's a role new kid in LA Sean McGinnis (Cunio) finds himself occupying when a mistaken video rental ('Citizen Cum') kick-starts his obsession with the film's star, 'gay for pay' Johnny Rebel (Gurney). Securing work as a cameraman at the films production company, Men of Janus, he's soon on his knees before the man, but watches powerless as Johnny, blind to all needs except his own and shaken by his lapdancer girlfriend's pregnancy, proceeds to lose the plot bigtime. Fortunately, the film doesn't, offering a surprisingly coy, occasionally parodic, but knowing take on a world where innocence, addiction and destruction all come into play. Beneath the surface there's a fair slice of Queer Theory at work and the overall intention is certainly serious minded, but as a modest riff on insecurity, longing and the patina of celebrity, this delivers enjoyably enough. A light touch keeps it pacy and with a Debbie Harry cameo and Buzzcocks on the soundtrack, it's got a fair shot in the cult stakes as well. GE

Fly, The

(1958, US, 94 min)
d/p Kurt Neumann. *sc* James Clavell. *ph* Karl Struss. *ed* Merrill G White. *ad* Lyle Wheeler, Theobold Holsopple. *m* Paul Sawtell. *cast* David Hedison, Patricia Owens, Vincent Price, Herbert Marshall, Kathleen Freeman, Charles Herbert.

● Differing greatly from David Cronenberg's very loose remake, this sci-fi classic is equally entertaining in its love of the grotesque. When scientist Hedison's matter-transference experiment goes wrong, he ends up with a fly's head and wing, while the insect in question is lumbered with his head and arm. His attempts to reverse the process inevitably fail, and he gradually goes insane, leading to a pleasingly bleak finale in which his wife crushes his head in a steam press and the fly gets trapped in a spider's web. Ludicrous stuff, of course, but Price lends his own inimitable and delightful brand of bravura to the role of Hedison's concerned brother, while James (*Shogun*) Clavell's script successfully treads a fine line between black comedy and po-faced seriousness. GA

Fly, The

(1986, US, 100 min)
d David Cronenberg. *p* Stuart Cornfeld. *sc* Charles Edward Pogue, David Cronenberg. *ph* Mark Irwin. *ed* Ron Sanders. *pd* Carol Spier. *m* Howard Shore. *cast* Jeff Goldblum, Geena Davis, John Getz, Joy Boushel, Les Carlson, George Chuvalo, David Cronenberg.

● 'What am I working on? I'm working on something that will change the world and human life as we know it!' So Seth Brundle (Goldblum) promises in the opening line of Cronenberg's inspired remake. Sure, he wants to get science reporter Davis into bed, but he means it too. Not that Cronenberg evinces any interest in teleportation – Brundle's hokey invention. Nor does he hang his scientist for Frankensteinian hubris. Rather, this is a film about fusion. That of man and insect, of course; but also the emotional and physical fusion between man and woman – liberating and painful as that may be. The playful, quirky chemistry between Goldblum and Davis in the first half of the movie ensures that this gothic horror is heartbreaking as well as stomach-churning (the special effects by Chris Walas are still staggering, 16 years on). TCh

Fly II, The

(1989, US, 104 min)
d Chris Walas. *p* Steven-Charles Jaffe. *sc* Mick Garris, Jim Wheat, Ken Wheat, Frank Darabont. *ph* Robin Vidgeon. *ed* Sean Barton. *pd* Michael Bolton. *m* Christopher Young. *cast* Eric Stoltz, Daphne Zuniga, Lee Richardson, John Getz, Frank Turner, Anne Marie Lee, Gary Chalk, Saffron Henderson.

● With the original director and leads having nothing to do with this sequel, we suffer a nasty opening scene in which an unconvincing Geena Davis lookalike gives birth to a crusty chrysalis, whence emerges Seth Brundle's son, Martin (Stoltz). He looks normal on the outside, but inside his genetic wiring is seriously crossed. Growing up under the clinical eyes of the sinister Bartok industries, Martin zips from boyhood to manhood in a ridiculously short period, and in no time at all is getting it together with Beth Logan (Zuniga), who doesn't know about his dad being a creepy-crawly. But when Martin's skin starts falling off, she begins to suspect that it's more than just a case for Clearasil, and resolves to help her loved one sort out his confused chromosomes – too late to avoid the onslaught of latex and squishy special effects for which we've all been waiting, and which is indeed the movie's only interesting commodity. Other than that, it's standard directionless fare. MK

Fly a Flag for Poplar

(1974, GB, 81 min, b/w & col)
d Roger Buck, Caroline Goldie, Ron Orders, Geoff Richman, Marie Richman, Tony Wickert. *ph* Ivan Strasburg. *ed* Roger Buck. *m* Misha Donat. *with* Alice Mahoney, John Mahoney, Andrew Tuck, Joe Mitchell, Bill Pyne.

● Those convinced that the proper translation of cinéma-vérité is cinema boredom will have their belief confirmed by this documentary tribute to Poplar's community spirit. Large, inert slabs of it are devoted to the day-to-day doings of its people, particularly those organising a neighbourhood festival: mums prepare meals, a clergyman greets passers-by, a Ford worker drives to Dagenham, someone performs on the spoons. The fragmentary reconstruction of Poplar's past, using newsreels and photographs, is far more interesting; and the print quality is often better, too. GB

Fly Away Home

(1996, US, 107 min)
d Carroll Ballard. *p* John Veitch, Carol Baum. *sc* Robert Rodat, Vince McKewin. *ph* Caleb Deschanel. *ed* Nicholas C Smith. *pd* Seamus Flannery. *m* Mark Isham. *cast* Jeff Daniels, Anna Paquin, Dana Delany, Terry Kinney, Holter Graham, Jeremy Ratchford.

● An inspirational movie from the director of *The Black Stallion*. The shock opening, however, sets a tone of emotional realism unusual for a children's film. (A car crash leaves 13-year-old Amy traumatised and her mother dead.) The ostensible (true-life) adventure – Amy is shipped to backwoods Canada to live with her eccentric sculptor/inventor father (Daniels), learns to fly a microlight aircraft in order to reach the breeding grounds of the orphaned geese she's raised – is made a metaphor for the girl's empowerment thanks to the enabling support of her parent. It's a common enough image, but it's realised here without strain. Caleb Deschanel's cinematography is as arresting as Mark Isham's score is discreet. But the performances are key: as Amy, Anna Paquin proves again what an expressive, soulful actress she is, and Daniels' madcap dad is a winning study in hippy ingenuity and indefatigability. WH

Flying Camel, The (Hagamal Hameofef)

(1994, Isr, 93 min)
d Rami Na'aman. *p* Marek Rozenbaum. *sc* Rami Na'aman. *ph* Yoav Kosh. *ed* Tova Asher. *ad* Ariel Roshko. *m* Shem Tov Levi. *cast* Gideon Singer, Salim Dau, Laurence Bonard, Gilat Ankori, Roy Scheider, Sonia Braga.

● Slight Israeli comedy in which an ageing Jewish professor (determined to stop the city council's demolition of Bauhaus buildings) and an Arab garbage collector (whose father owned an orange grove on the site of the Jew's shack) first lock horns and then, predictably, join forces. Focused on questions of land, tradition and cultural difference, the film is easy to read, but too broad to provoke more than the odd chortle. GA

Flying Down to Rio

(1933, US, 89 min, b/w)
d Thornton Freeland. *sc* Cyril Hume, HW Hanemann, Erwin Gelsey. *ph* J Roy Hunt. *ed* Jack Kitchin. *ad* Van Nest Polglase, Carroll Clark. *songs* Vincent Youmans, Edward Eliscu, Gus Kahn. *cast* Dolores Del Rio, Gene Raymond, Raul Roulien, Ginger Rogers, Fred Astaire, Blanche Frederici, Franklin Pangborn, Eric Blore.

● Fred and Ginger teamed for the first time as featured artists in the big production number, 'The Carioca': 'I'd like to try this thing just once' says Fred, launching the movies' greatest partnership. Otherwise notable mainly for the non-stop opticals which turn the film into a series of animated postcards. The nominal star, the wooden Raymond, is swept off his feet by the exotic Del Rio (one of those actresses who age only ten years in forty-odd), of whom a Yankee girl cries, 'What have these South Americans got below the equator that we haven't?'. The Berkeleyesque aerial ballet is a gas. SG

Flying Fool, The

(1931, GB, 76 min, b/w)
d/sc Walter Summers. *ph* Claude Friese-Greene, Stanley Rodwell, James Wilson, Joe Rosenthal, AL Fisher. *ed* Walter Stokvis. *pd* Clarence Elder, John Mead. *cast* Henry Kendall, Benita Hume, Wallace Geoffrey, Ursula Jeans, Martin Walker.

● One of the 'thick-ear' melodramas which made up the bulk of British B movies, with Kendall as a pilot assigned by the Secret Service to unmask a killer. Not quite up to *Dark Eyes of London* or *Traitor Spy*, but old maestro Summers, structuring his cardboard story around low-life Paris and Croydon airport, manages some marvellous moments. An airsick passenger swearing never again to cross the Channel, a villain rising Dracula-like from his coffin, some superbly seedy can-can dancers, even an Antonioni-ish car/plane duel. Maybe not great cinema, but for those with happy memories of Saturday morning pictures, an essential part of life. RMy

Flying Leathernecks

(1951, US, 102 min)
d Nicholas Ray. *p* Edmund Grainger. *sc* James Edward Grant. *ph* William Snyder. *ed* Sherman Todd. *ad* Albert S D'Agostino, James W Sullivan. *m* Roy Webb. *cast* John Wayne, Robert Ryan, Don Taylor, Janis Carter, Jay C Flippen, William Harrigan, James Bell, Barry Kelley.

● Made between the marvellous *In a Lonely Place* and *On Dangerous Ground*, this is arguably Ray's least distinguished film, a relatively conventional, anonymous WWII drama made for RKO mogul Howard Hughes – hence the authentic, Technicolor aerial footage of fighters in combat, as a Marine Corps squadron fight the Japs at Guadalcanal. Rather more interesting, perhaps, is the private conflict between Wayne's sternly no-nonsense disciplinarian CO and Ryan's more openly compassionate executive officer, who is afflicted with several of the neuroses commonly found in Ray's protagonists. Finally, however, it's all very predictable, even culminating in a flag-waving endorsement of traditional heroism. Thanks to the solid performances and fine camerawork, the film is not bad, merely professional. GA

Flying Tigers

(1942, US, 102 min, b/w)
d David Miller. *sc* Kenneth Gamet, Barry Trivers. *ph* Jack Marta. *ed* Ernest Nims. *ad* Russell Kimball. *m* Victor Young. *cast* John Wayne, Anna Lee, John Carroll, Paul Kelly, Mae Clarke, Tom Neal.

● This has elements of a '30s-style aviation picture (e.g. *Only Angels Have Wings*) and a WWII air force morale booster. Before Pearl Harbor, a bunch of American civilian pilots in China operate their own squadron, flying for Chiang Kai-shek. Cowards redeem themselves, cynics see the light; sidearms are worn as routinely as in a Dodge City saloon, about the only detail that strikes one as authentic. *Did* this sort of thing boost morale? Did the sight of the Duke in his fake cockpit, smiling grimly at some interpolated newsreel carnage, really offer aid and comfort, except to schoolkids? Remarkable, if so. BBa

Fly Low (Ha Woo Deung)

(1998, SKor, 95 min)
d Kim Si-On. *p* Kim Si-On, Jason Chae. *sc* Kim Si-On. *ph* Hong Kyong-Pyo. *ed* Kang Myung-Wan. *ad* Lee Jin-Ho. *m* Kim Sae-Chan. *cast* Kang Tae-Young, Lee Jong-Woo, Jung Jae-Wook, Lim Ji-Eun, Lee Ah-Young, Jang Ga-Hyun.

● In late summer, after the rains, three young men hide out from the police in an abandoned schoolhouse. Some months earlier, three young women had come to the same building to remember their own schooldays there and a classmate who has died. Kim's indie feature, made on a shoestring, crosscuts between the boys and the girls, the present and the recent past, to construct a pattern of parallels and contrasts. Generally understated but shot through with moments of humour and suspense and the occasional spasm of violence, it creates strong moods and a palpable sense of place. It was the first 16mm feature to win theatrical release in Korea. TR

FM

(1978, US, 104 min)
d John A Alonzo. *p* Rand Holston. *sc* Ezra Sacks. *ph* David Myers. *ed* Jeff Gourson. *pd* Lawrence G Paull. *m* Barry Fasman. *cast* Michael Brandon, Eileen Brennan, Alex Karras, Cleavon Little, Martin Mull, Cassie Yates, Norman Lloyd, James Keach.

● Set in a slick little LA music station, QSKY (7.11 on your FM dial), *FM* barely concerns itself with the daily business of radio. Really it's the story of a group of hip (but nice) dedicated broadcasters, led by sexy, buddy-hugging Jeff Dugan

(Brandon), out to combat the interfering idiocy of the indentured slaves of the network corporation. Dugan, who's heavily into the music biz, is against commercials on commercial radio (but since QSKY pumps out an endless stream of Ronstadt, the Eagles and Queen, wouldn't a few mindless jingles go unnoticed?) The crunch comes when Dugan is forced to resign after refusing to broadcast a recruiting ad from the army. His crew of husky-voiced neurotics pull themselves together and start a sit-in. Much solidarity and hugs. Deus-ex-machina, the head of the corporation flies into LA, and as you might guess, he admires guts…A lot of Pie in the QSKY. JS

[Focus]

(1996, Jap, 73 min)
d Satoshi Isaka. *p* Junji Akai, Nobutsugu Tsubomi. *sc* Kazuo Shin. *ph* Tetsuo Sano. *pd* Tomoyuki Maruo. *m* Hiroshi Mizuide. *cast* Tadanobu Asano, Keiko Unno, Akira Shirai, Tetsuro Sano.

●Despite an escalation into melodrama as it heads towards its climax, this is an almost completely believable fake documentary. A TV current affairs crew is interviewing a shy, repressed nerd about his addiction to listening in on short-wave radio and mobile phone conversations. But the director is a scuzzy opportunist whose sole ambition is to land a sensational scoop; an overheard call about a gun in a coin-locker starts them on a descent into hysteria and disaster. The casting of the film's actual cameraman as the TV crew's off-screen cameraman gives the overall credibility a huge boost. It's also extremely well acted (Asano, who plays the nerd, is currently Japan's hottest young star) and executed with considerable skill and welcome shafts of humour. In sum, it's as good as 'social-conscience' movies ever get. TR

Fog, The

(1979, US, 91 min)
d John Carpenter. *p* Debra Hill. *sc* John Carpenter, Debra Hill. *ph* Dean Cundey. *ed* Tommy Lee Wallace, Charles Bornstein. *pd* Tommy Lee Wallace. *m* John Carpenter. *cast* Adrienne Barbeau, Hal Holbrook, Janet Leigh, Jamie Lee Curtis, John Houseman, Tom Atkins, Nancy Loomis.

● *The Fog* will disappoint those expecting a rerun of the creepy scares from *Halloween*. Instead, expanding enormously on the fantasy elements of his earlier films, Carpenter has turned in a full-scale thriller of the supernatural, as a sinister fog bank comes rolling in off the sea to take revenge on the smug little town of Antonio Bay, N.Calif. No shotguns pumping; no prowling of dark corners; no tricksy dry-ice chills. Instead you'll find a masterful simplicity of style, a lonely and determined group of characters under siege, and a childlike sense of brooding fear that almost disappeared in the '70s. Carpenter's confidence is outrageous; the range of his models even more so (from Poe to RKO); and the achievement is all his own, despite ragged moments and occasional hesitations. CA

Fog Over Frisco

(1934, US, 67 min, b/w)
d William Dieterle. *p* Henry Blanke. *sc* Robert N Lee. *ph* Tony Gaudio. *ed* Harold McLernon. *ad* Jack Okey. *cast* Bette Davis, Lyle Talbot, Margaret Lindsay, Donald Woods, Henry O'Neill, Hugh Herbert, Robert Barrat.

●No masterpiece, but a fascinatingly brisk thriller about a journalist (Woods, living up to his name) and a young heiress (Lindsay) searching for the kidnappers of her wayward, irresponsible sister (Davis). The plot is complex enough to hold the attention, the performances by and large passable (Davis unfortunately disappears after about twenty minutes), though the injections of comedy with Hugh Herbert's inept photographer are excruciating. But Dieterle directs for all he's worth, moving the plot along at a furious pace and making excellent use of Tony Gaudio's chiaroscuro camerawork. GA

Folies Bergère

(1935, US, 84 min, b/w)
d Roy Del Ruth. *p* William Goetz, Raymond Griffith. *sc* Bess Meredyth, Hal Long. *ph* Barney McGill, Peverell Marley. *ed* Allen McNeil. *ad* Richard Day. *songs* Jack Meskill, Jack Stern, others. *cast* Maurice Chevalier, Ann Sothern, Merle Oberon, Eric Blore, Walter Byron, Ferdinand Munier.

●A real Chevalier show as he demonstrates his saucy Gallic charm in two roles: as a wealthy Baron in financial straits, and as a Folies comedian the Baron employs to impersonate him to help him out of an awkward scrape. The comedy that arises from mistaken identities and complications with wife and girlfriend is brisk enough, though the musical numbers – even the one starring Chevalier's trademark straw hat – hardly match the Warners Busby Berkeley style that Fox's Zanuck was so keen to emulate. GA

Folks!

(1992, US, 106 min)
d Ted Kotcheff. *p* Victor Drai, Malcolm R Harding. *sc* Robert Klane. *ph* Larry Pizer. *ed* Joan E Chapman. *pd* William J Creber. *m* Michel Colombier. *cast* Tom Selleck, Don Ameche, Anne Jackson, Christine Ebersole, Wendy Crewson, Robert Pastorelli, Michael Murphy.

●Jon Aldrich (Selleck) has a solid job on the Chicago Stock Exchange, a spacious home, lovely wife (Crewson), two kids and a dog. Then, one day, his perfect life is thrown into chaos: while he's visiting his sick mother (Jackson) in Florida, the FBI invades his office to investigate insider trading, freezing his private account in the process. No money means no nursing care for Mom, but worse is to come when Jon visits his senile father (Ameche), who burns down his own home in a fit of forgetfulness. All Mom and Dad want is a swift journey to that trailer park in the sky, and when Jon is enlisted to help their (abortive) suicide attempts, a series of signposted accidents leaves him *sans* sight, toe and testicle. Masquerading as a commentary on the greedy '80s, this is clearly the sort of moronic comedy beloved of the *Weekend at Bernie's* team of Kotcheff and writer Robert Klane. CM

Folk Tales of Lu Ban (Lu Ban de Chuanshuo)

(1958, China, min, b/w)
d Sun Yu. *sc* Zhu Xin. *ph* Yao Shiguan. *ed* Sun Yu. *ad* Ge Shuaicheng. *m* Ji Ming. *cast* Wei Heling, Li Baoluo, Mao Lu, Feng Ji, Er Lin, Qiao Zhi.

●Like many veterans from the Shanghai film industry of the 1930s, Sun had endless political problems once the communists took power; he made few films after 1949 and none which recaptured the sexy, exuberant qualities of his pre-war classics. *Lu Ban* (his penultimate film) is the best of them, a celebration of the legendary father of Chinese architecture as a self-effacing man of the people. It imagines three episodes from Lu Ban's wanderings around China two millennia ago. In each, he comes upon a building or design problem in the making, obliquely provides the craftsmen with the solution and then slips away without waiting for credit or thanks. Devoid of Maoist propaganda, the film is enjoyable for Sun's simple, elegant mise en scène and for its historical naturalism. Wei (the prostitute's lover in *Street Angel*, twenty years earlier) plays Lu Ban with real charm and grace. TR

Folle à Tuer (The Evil Trap)

(1975, Fr/It, 95 min)
d Yves Boisset. *p* Raymond Danon, Ralph Baum. *sc* Yves Boisset, Sébastien Japrisot. *ph* Jean Boffety. *ed* Albert Jurgenson. *ad* Maurice Sergent. *m* Philippe Sarde. *cast* Marlène Jobert, Tomas Milian, Victor Lanoux, Michel Lonsdale, Jean Bouix.

●A fair thriller that begins with one of WC Fields' anti-kid quotes, and promisingly looks like despatching one averagely noxious brat quite early on, but settles instead for making his survival a condition of its heroine's redemption. Having just been released from a mental clinic and hired as a governess, Jobert finds herself at the centre of a kidnap-and-murder conspiracy hatched by her apparent benefactor, and involving a studiedly vicious Milian as its agent. On the run from both killer and media-fanned frame-up, she's perhaps just a little too much the bastion of resourceful sanity in a mad world, but Boisset conjures a pleasing momentum for her flight, and allows some of the absurd humour of her plight to seep blackly out. Based on the gloriously titled *série noire* novel *O Dingos, O Châteaux* by Jean-Patrick Manchette (*Aggression, Nada*), it leans surprisingly little on modish paranoia, and pleases most for its essential modesty. PT

Follow a Star

(1959, GB, 104 min, b/w)
d Robert Asher. *p* Hugh Stewart. *sc* Jack Davies, Henry Blyth, Norman Wisdom. *ph* Jack Asher. *ed* Roger Cherrill. *ad* Maurice Carter. *m* Philip Green. *cast* Norman Wisdom, June Laverick, Jerry Desmonde, Hattie Jacques, Eddie Leslie, Richard Wattis, John Le Mesurier, Fenella Fielding, Ron Moody, Sydney Tafler, Joe Melia.

●His old producer, Hugh Stewart, used to reckon Wisdom was as close British cinema had come to a comedian in the mould of Harold Lloyd or Buster Keaton. It's certainly true that Wisdom was in his heyday a consummate acrobat with a knack for slapstick. But little Norman had a fatal flaw: he always sugared his comedy with spoonfuls of outrageous, cloying sentiment. This picture (which he co-scripted) is a case in point. He's a tailor's assistant with a beautiful singing voice. Unflappable straightman Desmonde is the faltering crooner who gets Wisdom to stand offstage and sing while he mimes. There are plenty of laughs, but the script again relies on making us feel sorry for our poor mistreated hero. GM

Following

(1998, GB, 70 min, b/w)
d Christopher Nolan. *p* Emma Thomas, Christopher Nolan, Jeremy Theobald. *sc/ph* Christopher Nolan. *cast* Jeremy Theobald, Alex Haw, Lucy Russell, John Nolan.

●Shot at weekends on a shoestring, Nolan's 16mm b/w feature is more *Shallow Grave* than Shane Meadows. Blocked writer Bill (Theobald) takes to following strangers through the streets of Soho, ostensibly to kickstart his fiction. One day, one of his 'targets' bites back: Cobb (Haw) introduces himself as a burglar skilled at 'reading' people's identities from rifling through their possessions, and he insists that Bill should tag along to experience the thrill for himself. A complicated time structure (the film flashes backwards and forwards) signals that more is going on here than meets the eye. Sure enough, the denouement involves two double crosses, a femme fatale, a murder and a crowning triple cross. The generic pay off is a little disappointing after the edgy, character based scenes of exposition, but the film is acted and directed confidently enough to work well as a wry mystery thriller. TR

Follow That Dream

(1962, US, 109 min)
d Gordon Douglas. *p* David Weisbart. *sc* Charles Lederer. *ph* Leo Tover. *ed* William B Murphy. *ad* Malcolm Bert. *songs* Jay Livingston, Mack David, Sid Tepper, others. *cast* Elvis Presley, Arthur O'Connell, Anne Helm, Joanna Moore, Jack Kruschen, Simon Oakland.

●Presley made 33 films, and at least 30 were considered duds by the critics. However, they all made money, and they're still a fixture on TV. Here, he's a homeless army veteran who heads south to Florida with his father and four orphans (songs include 'Home Is Where the Heart Is'). Opportunities for sneering and hip-swivelling are limited. One of Hollywood's most celebrated (and cynical) screenwriters, Charles Lederer, provided the script (from the novel *Pioneer Go Home* by Richard Powell), but it's such a feeble, mawkish affair that you half suspect he wrote it tongue-in-cheek. Or perhaps he thought Perry Como was the star. GM

Follow the Fleet

(1936, US, 109 min, b/w)
d Mark Sandrich. *p* Pandro S Berman. *sc* Dwight Taylor, Allan Scott. *ph* David Abel. *ed* Henry Berman. *ad* Van Nest Polglase, Carroll Clark. *songs* Irving Berlin. *cast* Fred Astaire, Ginger Rogers, Randolph Scott, Harriet Hilliard, Astrid Allwyn, Lucille Ball, Betty Grable.

●Fred plays an ex-exponent of 'genteel dancing' who became a gob when Ginger wouldn't marry him. They meet up again at the Paradise Club and, in this revamp of *Hit the Deck*, put on a show and save a floundering romance between four-square Scott and awful-pain Hilliard. The numbers, being by Irving Berlin, are top-hole. 'I'm Putting All My Eggs in One Basket' gets a hilarious sparring dance routine, 'Let Yourself Go' is a marvellous piece of showing off, and 'Let's Face the Music and Dance' the most beautifully integrated of any of their evening dress jobs. Fred's piano-playing and typing turn out just like his dancing – no surprise: his hands always danced as much as his feet. SG

Folly To Be Wise

(1952, GB, 91 min, b/w)
d Frank Launder. *sc* Frank Launder, John Dighton. *ph* Jack Hildyard. *ed* Thelma Connell. *ad* Arthur Lawson. *m* Temple Abady. *cast* Alastair Sim, Roland Culver, Elizabeth Allan, Martita Hunt, Colin Gordon, Janet Brown, Miles Malleson.

●National Service and Launder & Gilliat comedies are such clearly marked symptoms of the '50s that one might expect their combination to distil the very essence of that dreary decade. Indeed, Launder brings James Bridie's play to the screen with a minimum of flair and ingenuity, but the themes the film deals with are intriguing. Bumbling entertainments officer Sim attempts to come to terms with youth and modernism by dispensing with the services of the local lady violinists and giving the masses what they want. That it should be a 'brains trust' of local celebrities that draws the crowds in is highly implausible, but the resulting display of middle class moral bankruptcy and celebration of working class common sense is extraordinary. RMy

Fong Sai-Yuk (aka Fang Shiyu)

(1993, HK, 100 min)
d Yuan Kwai. *p* Li-Young Zhong. *sc* Jeff Lau, Chai Kung-Yung. *ph* Ma-Tsu Cheng. *ed* Angie Lam. ad Benjamin Lau. *m* James Wong, Romeo Diaz, Mark Lui. *cast* Jet Li, Josephine Siao, Adam Cheng, Chen Songyonh.

●Fast action comedy in period costume. The cobbled script uses real characters and organisations, but whips up an entirely fictitious froth of martial arts tournaments, undeclared passions and underground resistance movements. It centres less on the nominal star Jet Li than on the sublime Josephine Siao, in and out of drag as the hero's protective mother, her performance a show-stopping culmination of three decades of fine work in the Hong Kong cinema. TR

Food of Love

(1997, GB/Fr, 109 min)
d Stephen Poliakoff. *p* Karin Bamborough. *sc* Stephen Poliakoff. *ph* Wit Dabal. *ed* Anne Sopel. *pd* Michael Pickwoad. *m* Adrian Johnston. *cast* Richard E Grant, Nathalie Baye, Joe McGann, Juliet Aubrey, Lorcan Cranitch, Penny Downie, Holly Davidson, Mark Tandy, Sylia Syms.

●Alex (Grant) is a fogeyish assistant bank manager who, in an attempt to stave off the depredations of an increasingly wired world, retreats to the countryside to stage – as he did in the same village a decade before – an am-dram *Twelfth Night*. With him he takes a trio of rough kids from the acting class he teaches and the cast of the original production, now a collective indictment of the thirty-something treadmill. The Pimm's soaked idyll of memory, however, resembles nothing so much as the urban jungle they've escaped. The natives are just as hostile, and you can't see the rose beds for the satellite dishes. Poliakoff's jaded yuppy schtick has a lineage stretching back to *Close My Eyes*. However, once the film leaves the sinister metropolis, the writer/director is clearly straying from home ground. The village harridans intent on stymying the play, for instance, are merely crass, headscarfed stereotypes. Grant and company, though, are hardly better served by the screenplay, which spreads itself too thin in trying to address the concerns of each and every character. MHi

Food of the Gods, The

(1976, US, 88 min)
d/p/sc Bert I Gordon. *ph* Reginald Morris. *ed* Corky Ehlers. *ad* Graeme Murray. *m* Elliot Kaplan. *cast* Marjoe Gortner, Pamela Franklin, Ralph Meeker, Ida Lupino, Jon Cypher, Tom Stovall.

●Gordon's reworking of his *Village of the Giants* (1965), replacing the giant teenagers with amazing colossal chickens, wasps and (especially) rats, all of whom have gorged themselves on a vile fluid found bubbling on the ground near Lupino's farm and put into bottles helpfully labelled FOTG. It's a piece of low-budget rubbish (based on a portion of HG Wells' 1904 fantasy) featuring all the genre's well-loved ingredients: a frightful script, variable special effects, and a weird bunch of actors who manage to look just a little less ludicrous than the giant rats. Unfortunately, the film's attractions pall about half way through: Gordon can't muster the lunatic verve necessary to bind things together, and one marauding rodent soon begins to look like any other, no matter what its size. GB

Fool, The

(1990, GB, 140 min)
d Christine Edzard. *p* Richard Goodwin, Christine Edzard. *sc* Christine Edzard, Olivier Stockman. *ph* Robin Vidgeon. *ed* Olivier Stockman. *m* Michael Sanvoisin. *cast* Derek Jacobi, Cyril Cusack, Ruth Mitchell, Maria Aitken, Irina Brook, Paul Brooke, Jim Carter, Rosalie Crutchley, Patricia Hayes, Don Henderson, Michael Hordern, Stratford Johns, Miriam Margolyes, John McEnery, Michael Medwin, Murray Melvin, Miranda Richardson, Joan Sims.

●Edzard's *Little Dorrit* was rightly acclaimed for its impeccable attention to detail; the same care, if not the literary pedigree, has gone into this successor, co-written by Edzard with her editor Olivier Stockman, but owing its inspiration to the more prosaic if equally socially-conscious work of Henry Mayhew. She has again produced an authentic period feel, but what the film lacks is a strong narrative. The confusing premise lies in the fact that Jacobi is leading a double life: first as Mr Frederick, a lowly theatrical booking clerk of humble means and charisma; then as Sir John, the effortless darling of polite Victorian society, able almost to create money out of the air, and accepted not because of who he is but how he behaves. Much has been made of the parallels between the ebullience of 1857 and the stock market scandals of today, but more intriguing is a fine theatrical climax in which Jacobi turns on the representatives of True-Brit greed, tearing their selfishness to bits – much to their seeming incomprehension. Jacobi is as usual superb, well supported by a galaxy of British actors. SGr

Fool for Love

(1985, US, 108 min)
d Robert Altman. *p* Menahem Golan, Yoram Globus. *sc* Sam Shepard. *ph* Pierre Mignot. *ed* Luce Grunenwaldt, Stephen P Dunn. *pd* Stephen Altman. *m* George Burt. *cast* Sam Shepard, Kim Basinger, Harry Dean Stanton, Randy Quaid, Martha Crawford.

●Sam Shepard's play was a short, Strindbergian chamber piece, in which a semi-incestuous affair between half-brother and sister was enacted largely by them hurling each other off the walls of their small motel room. While maintaining the claustrophobia, Altman's adaptation is much more leisurely in approach, allowing a good half-hour for the arrival of Eddie (Shepard himself) at the motel in the Mojave desert, before getting down to the hurting match between the two obsessive would-be lovers. The play had a ghostly figure, the Old Man, who hovered in the wings, breaking into occasional monologue to comment on the affair, in which it was revealed that he was in fact their father. The film successfully weaves him into the action, still standing slightly apart as a Greek chorus, but nonetheless integrated: Stanton is his usual excellent self as the man who may be a spirit from the past. Shepard is perfect as the dumb hick in cowboy gear who likes lassoing the bedpost; and Basinger, as the faded girl in a red dress, brings a curious, tatty dignity to the role, and proves at last that she can act when not required to pout in her underwear. It's the best of Altman's series of theatre adaptations, capturing the original's dreamlike musings on the nature of inherited guilt; what one misses is the sexual ferocity. CPea

Foolish Wives

(1921, US, 13,800 ft, b/w)
d/sc Erich von Stroheim. *ph* Ben Reynolds, William H Daniels. *ed* Erich von Stroheim. *ad* Erich von Stroheim, Richard Day. *cast* Erich von Stroheim, Maude George, Mae Busch, Cesare Gravina, Malvine Polo, Dale Fuller.

●The first full-scale working-out of Stroheim's explorations of the ground between high society manners and terminal squalor and depravity. The plot centres on the sexual and criminal activities of Count Karamzin (Stroheim). The sumptuous visual style continually invites the viewer to indulge Karamzin's fantasies, only to undercut them with 'real life' details designed to shake the whole edifice. TR

Fools of Fortune

(1990, GB, 109 min)
d Pat O'Connor. *p* Sarah Radclyffe. *sc* Michael Hirst. *ph* Jerzy Zielinski. *ed* Michael Bradsell. *pd* Jamie Leonard. *m* Hans Zimmer. *cast* Julie Christie, Iain Glen, Mary Elizabeth Mastrantonio, Michael Kitchen, Niamh Cusack, Tom Hickey, Neil Dudgeon.

●An adaptation of the novel by William Trevor (whose *Ballroom of Romance* O'Connor adapted for TV a few years back), following the fortunes of a wealthy middle class Irish family during the violent period of revolutionary Republicanism and British military repression in the 1920s and '30s, this is made with such loving care that one can easily forgive its minor weaknesses. The tranquil life of the Quinton family is shattered when an attack on their rural home by the notorious 'Black and Tans' leaves young Willie's father and two sisters dead. Five years later, his mother (Christie) is a drunken wreck, and not even a tender love affair with his childhood friend Marianne (Mastrantonio) can free Willie (Glen) from his morbid obsession with the man (Dudgeon) who destroyed his family. O'Connor's assured direction effortlessly evokes the historical period without detracting from the emotional core of the unfolding drama; only some puzzling flashes forward and Iain Glen's over-pitched grimacing seem out of key. There are times too, when Hans Zimmer's musical score seems to be straining for a dramatic impact that the quietly engrossing emotional drama can't always match. Special praise, though, for Julie Christie, who is equally convincing as the vivacious young wife and as the dipsomaniac widow. NF

Fools Rush In

(1997, US, 109 min)
d Andy Tennant. *p* Doug Draizin. *sc* Katherine Reback. *ph* Robbie Greenberg. *ed* Roger Bondelli. *pd* Edward Pisoni. *m* Alan Silvestri. *cast* Matthew Perry, Salma Hayek, Jon Tenney, Carlos Gomez, Tomas Milian, John Bennett Perry, Jill Clayburgh.

●A nervy NY exec (Perry) has a fling in Las Vegas with a Mexican photographer (Hayek). Result, pregnancy. His stern New England poetry, however, is at odds with her vibrant magic realism (literally, a battle of the books). Playing a smart alec terrified by his own lack of substance, Perry seems genuinely in need, as helpless in his own way as old stars like Grant or Stewart. Hayek is also impressive, endowing the photographer with an unaffected moral strength. The scenes with Alex's WASPish parents are amusingly jagged: reactionary in-laws are usually 'brought round', but these two (Perry and Clayburgh) remain politely vile throughout. Scriptwriter Katherine Reback rather takes her time answering all the old questions. CO'Su

Footlight Parade

(1933, US, 101 min, b/w)
d Lloyd Bacon. *sc* Manuel Seff, James Seymour. *ph* George Barnes. *ed* George Amy. *ad* Anton F Grot, Jack Okey. *songs* Harry Warren, Al Dubin, Sammy Fain, Irving Kahal. *cast* James Cagney, Joan Blondell, Ruby Keeler, Dick Powell, Frank McHugh, Guy Kibbee, Ruth Donnelly, Hugh Herbert.

●The third of Warners' major backstage musicals to appear in 1933, unlike *42nd Street* and *Gold Diggers of 1933* in that it deals not so much with putting on a Broadway show as with combating the threat of talking pictures; unlike them, too, in that it pins its atmospheric faith less on the Depression than on Roosevelt optimism as personified by Cagney's irrepressibly bouncy choreographer. It ends with a string of three grandiose numbers by Busby Berkeley, that kitschy darling of current fashion, two of which (*Honeymoon Hotel* and *By a Waterfall*) are well suited to the wimpish personalities of Powell and Keeler; but the third, *Shanghai Lil*, is given a terrific boost by Cagney and by a camera raptly tracking through smoky Chinese bars, nightclubs and opium dens. But by far the best part of the film is its first hour, fast, furious and funny as Cagney sets out to convince his nervous backers that his idea for live prologues to accompany talkies can be made to work. TM

Footloose

(1984, US, 107 min)
d Herbert Ross. *p* Lewis J Rachmil, Craig Zadan. *sc* Dean Pitchford. *ph* Ric Waite. *ed* Paul Hirsch. *pd* Ron Hobbs. *cast* Kevin Bacon, Lori Singer, John Lithgow, Dianne Wiest, Christopher Penn, Sarah Jessica Parker.
● Twenty years on, Herbert Ross's teen yarn is already a period piece. It's set at that moment in the mid-1980s when musical sequences in studio films began to be filmed like pop promos. The premise wouldn't pass muster in a Cliff Richard movie. Bacon is the clean-cut but rebellious big city boy adrift in a white, Protestant backwater town where (absurdly) rock'n'roll is banned. He's pitted against the neurotic town preacher (Lithgow), whose daughter (Singer) he promptly falls in love with. Ross, who began his career as a dancer and choreographer, brings plenty of gusto to the material and the performances are ebullient, but this is still a cynical and manipulative exercise with little feel for the teen culture it purports to celebrate. GM

Footman, The (Il Portaborse)

(1991, It, 95 min)
d Daniele Luchetti. *sc* Sandro Petraglia, Stefano Rulli, Daniele Luchetti. *ph* Alessandro Pesci. *ed* Mirco Garrone. *m* Dario Lucantoni. *cast* Silvio Orlando, Nanni Moretti, Giulio Brogi, Anne Roussel, Angela Finocchiaro, Graziano Giusti.
● A dry satire on corruption and compromise in contemporary Italian politics. A schoolteacher obsessed with poetry and experienced in ghost-writing is hired by an ambitious young minister to write his speeches and tend to the credibility of his image. Occasionally contrived, even obvious, and never quite as funny as it would like to be, it's nevertheless an agreeably adult film, far more telling than what generally passes for political satire in British and American movies. GA

Footsteps in the Fog

(1955, GB, 90 min)
d Arthur Lubin. *p* Maxwell Setton, MJ Frankovich. *sc* Dorothy Reid, Lenore J Coffee. *ph* Christopher Challis. *ed* Alan Osbiston. *ad* Wilfrid Shingleton. *m* Benjamin Frankel. *cast* Stewart Granger, Jean Simmons, Bill Travers, Ronald Squire, Finlay Currie, Belinda Lee, William Hartnell, Peter Bull, Victor Maddern.
● Granger and Simmons, husband-and-wife team of the time, are well matched in this florid Edwardian thriller (from WW Jacobs' *The Interruption*), in which he's the master of the house and she's the maid hoping to blackmail her way up the pecking order by threatening to reveal that he's just done away with his wife. The twisty plot stretches credibility here and there, but the film's gusto is infectious and Granger's limited range is much suited to period caddishness. TJ

For a Few Dollars More (Per Qualche Dollari in più)

(1965, It/Sp/WGer, 130 min)
d Sergio Leone. *p* Alberto Grimaldi. *sc* Sergio Leone, Luciano Vincenzoni. *ph* Massimo Dallamano. *ed* Alabiso Serralonga, Giorgio Serralonga. *ad* Carlo Simi. *m* Ennio Morricone. *cast* Clint Eastwood, Lee Van Cleef, Gian Maria Volonté, Klaus Kinski, Mara Krup, Aldo Sambrell, Mario Brega.
● The one in which Eastwood and Van Cleef, bounty hunters both, reluctantly join forces to take on psychotic bandit Volonté and his gang (which includes Kinski as a hunchback). Not as stylish as *The Good, the Bad and the Ugly*, but a significant step forward from *A Fistful of Dollars*, with the usual terrific compositions, Morricone score, and taciturn performances, not to mention the ubiquitous flashback disease. GA

For All Mankind

(1989, US, 90 min, b/w & col)
d/p Al Reinert. *ed* Susan Korda, Goran Milutinovic, Erick Jenkins, Chuck Weiss. *m* Brian Eno, Daniel Lanois.
● Between 1968 and 1972, NASA sent 24 astronauts into space as part of its Apollo Space Program. All nine missions (six of which involved lunar landings) were accompanied by a plethora of on-board cameras. It was left to producer-director Reinert to sift through a staggering six million feet of footage and over 90 hours of interviews in order to arrive at this fascinating record. The footage is astonishingly good. It begins with an early launch filmed from every conceivable angle, and in such fine detail that you'd be forgiven for thinking George Lucas and his effects team had a hand in the making. From those fierce images of the launch blast, the tone then shifts to the serenity of space… There is no commentary as such. Instead, Reinert allows the stunning slo-mo images and the many conversations between the astronauts and mission control to speak for themselves. It works a treat, as does the accompanying sound track by atmospheric soundsmiths Brian Eno and Daniel Lanois. DA

For Better, For Worse

see Zandy's Bride

Forbidden

(1932, US, 81 min, b/w)
d Frank Capra. *sc* Frank Capra, Jo Swerling. *ph* Joseph Walker. *ed* Maurice Wright. *cast* Barbara Stanwyck, Adolphe Menjou, Ralph Bellamy, Dorothy Peterson, Henry Armeta.
● This early Capra melodrama plays as a tear-jerker. Stanwyck has an illegitimate child by politician Menjou, whose refusal to leave his invalid wife forces the single mother into a marriage of convenience with the unscrupulous Bellamy. He in turn threatens to ruin Menjou by revealing his infidelities, bullish tactics that prove no match for Stanwyck's obsessive love. Unsophisticated and hammy, it's a soap opera that hasn't stood the test of time. TJ

Forbidden

(1984, GB/WGer, 114 min)
d Anthony Page. *p* Mark Forstater. *sc* Leonard Gross. *ph* Wolfgang Treu. *ed* Thomas Schwalm. *pd* Toni Lüdi. *m* Tangerine Dream. *cast* Jacqueline Bisset, Jürgen Prochnow, Irene Worth, Peter Vaughan, Robert Dietl, Avis Bunnage.
● Set in Nazi infested Berlin, a ploddingly dull World War II Resistance drama, based on a true story. Bisset plays a German countess as good as she is beautiful, who studies veterinary medicine, joins the underground, saves hundreds of lives, and falls in love with the equally nice Prochnow who, being Jewish, is forced to play Anne Frank in the dark corners of Bisset's cramped apartments. Fassbinder would soon have set the lovers at each other's throats, but here they behave with unimpeachable forbearance and nobility. SJo

Forbidden Games

see Jeux Interdits

Forbidden Planet

(1956, US, 98 min)
d Fred M Wilcox. *p* Nicholas Nayfack. *sc* Cyril Hume. *ph* George Folsey. *ed* Ferris Webster. *ad* Cedric Gibbons, Arthur Lonergan. *m* Louise Barron, Bebe Barron. *cast* Walter Pidgeon, Anne Francis, Leslie Nielsen, Warren Stevens, Jack Kelly, Richard Anderson, Earl Holliman, James Drury.
● Classic '50s sci-fi, surprisingly but effectively based on *The Tempest*, with Nielsen's US spaceship coming across a remote planet, deserted except for Pidgeon's world-wearied Dr Morbius (read Prospero), his daughter (Miranda) and their robot Robby (Ariel). Something, it transpires, has destroyed the planet's other inhabitants, and now, as Bard and Freud merge, a monster mind-thing Caliban begins to pick on the spaceship's crew. An ingenious script, excellent special effects and photography, and superior acting (with the exception of Francis), make it an endearing winner. GA

Forbidden Relations (Visszaesök)

(1982, Hun, 92 min)
d/sc Zsolt Kézdi-Kovács. *ph* János Kende. *ed* Andrásné Karmentö. *ad* Tamás Banovich. *cast* Lili Monori, Miklós B Székely, Mari Töröcsik, József Horváth, József Tóth, Tibor Molnar.
● It opens with a suicide and ends with a birth – the second child of a brother-sister love affair. So *Forbidden Relations* is a film of illicit passions haunted by fears of insanity and the strictures of state morality. But don't expect high melodrama, or indeed a panting, prettified art house parable: this is spare social realism from Hungary, with a young widow falling for a returning ex-con whom she later learns is her half-brother. Feckless in the eyes of their rural community but obstinately faithful to their *amour fou*, the couple wind up in jail, despite the compassion of police and magistrates required to implement the law. Controversial and courageous in its home country, largely because of the humanist warmth Kézdi-Kovács brings to the subject; but despite the vigorous earthiness of the sexuality on display, this is a rather too muted, meandering attack on the ancient taboo. MA

Forbidden Woman, The

see Femme Défendue, La

Forbidden World (aka Mutant)

(1982, US, 77 min)
d Allan Holzman. *p* Roger Corman. *sc* Tim Curnen. *ph* Tim Suhrstedt. *ed* Allan Hozman. *pd* Christopher Horner. *m* Susan Justin. *cast* Jesse Vint, Dawn Dunlap, June Chadwick, Linden Chiles, Fox Harris, Raymond Oliver, Scott Paulin.
● Instead of killing off the ghastly by-product of an off-world genetic engineering project, the B-picture scientists decide to keep the slimy little splodge under observation. So it escapes, gets bigger and comes back to snack. While the writer conjured up everything he could remember about *Alien*, the rest of the New World crew were working out how to reproduce Scott's film for about 50 bucks. The barely seen mutant, a kind of metal spider-thing, is finally disposed of by feeding it a freshly available cancerous tumour. The involvement of Corman alumnus Aaron Lipstadt (directing second unit) portends nothing of interest. DO

Forbin Project, The (aka Colossus – The Forbin Project)

(1969, US, 100 min)
d Joseph Sargent. *p* Stanley Chase. *sc* James Bridges. *ph* Gene Polito. *ed* Folmar Blangsted. *ad* Alexander Golitzen, John J Lloyd. *m* Michel Colombier. *cast* Eric Braeden, Susan Clark, Gordon Pinsent, William Schallert, Leonid Rostoff.
● Two giant defence plan computers, distrustful of man's eternal stupidity, link terminals across the Iron Curtain to hold an agitated world in thrall. After an excellent beginning, the craven script (based on DF Jones' novel *Colossus*) develops cold feet, injects some tiresome comic relief, and gradually begins to drag the whole thing down to *Dr Who* level. A pity, since the first half is chillingly persuasive. TM

Force: Five

(1981, US, 96 min)
d Robert Clouse. *p* Fred Weintraub. *sc* Robert Clouse. *ph* Gil Hibbs. *ed* Bob Bring. *ad* Richard Lawrence. *m* William Goldstein. *cast* Joe Lewis, Bong Soo Han, Sonny Barnes, Richard Norton, Benny Urquidez, Ron Hayden, Pam Huntington, Mandy Wyss.
● Potentially interesting martial arts caper of battle against a Rajneesh-like guru, allowed to stagnate in a mire of sickening gore, endless destruction, and simplistic, humourless sermonising. As the stereotypically mixed *Force: Five* – a black, a Chicano, a woman, a psychotic, and a Handsome Leader – sets out to save gullible disciples from the wicked Reverend Rhee's Palace of Celestial Tranquillity (a minotaur's labyrinth of torture and carnage), it becomes increasingly difficult to distinguish morally between the opposing sides. All the breathtaking brutality makes for tiresome viewing. GA

Force More Powerful, A

(1999, Aust, 115 min)
d Steve York. *p* Peter Ackerman, Steve York. *sc* Steve York. *ph* Giulio Biccari, Peter Pearce, Dilip Varma. *ed* Anny Lowery Meza, Joseph Wiedenmayer. *m* John D Keltonic. *with* Janet Cherry, Mkhuseli Jack, Tango Lamani, James Lawson, Diane Nash, Alyque Padamsee, Davavrat Pathak, Desmond Tutu. *narrator* Ben Kingsley.
● This two-hour documentary traces the infectious proliferation of non-violent popular movements for change over the course of the last

century, from Gandhi's civil disobedience campaign against the Raj, through Jim Lawson's Nashville sit-ins against segregation, to Mkhuseli Jack's boycott's of apartheid business in Port Elizabeth. The film's a bit of a history lesson – there have been fleeter expositions of people power. It also begs questions of context and comparison, but the evidence it marshals of effective methods for defeating oppression – Gandhi's principle of satyagraha ('holding to truth'), Lawson and Jack's flair for dramatising issues and thereby raising awareness, and the ever potent strategy of making life costly and controversial for those holding the purse strings – is certainly absorbing. NB

Force of Evil

(1948, US, 78 min, b/w)
d Abraham Polonsky. *p* Bob Roberts. *sc* Abraham Polonsky, Ira Wolfert. *ph* George Barnes. *ed* Art Seid. *ad* Richard Day. *m* David Raksin. *m* David Raksin. *cast* John Garfield, Beatrice Pearson, Thomas Gomez, Howland Chamberlain, Roy Roberts, Marie Windsor.

●One of the key films of the '40s. From a novel by Ira Wolfert (*Tucker's People*), it extracts a clinical analysis of the social, moral and physical evils attending on the numbers racket, centering this on a remarkably complex portrayal of the mutual guilt of two brothers caught at opposite ends of the same rat trap: one (Garfield) torn by the realisation that his corruption means the destruction of his brother, the other (Gomez) by his awareness that he was responsible for that corruption in the first place. If their conflict has the authentic ring of tragedy, it is partly because Polonsky uses the iconography of the underworld thriller so skilfully that his touches of allegory and symbolism – like Garfield's last bleak descent down a stairway to discover the reality of his personal hell – are natural outcroppings rather than artificial injections; and partly because the dialogue, terse and unpretentious but given an incantatory quality by its calculated hesitations and repetitions, has an unmistakable tang of gritty urban poetry that floods the entire film. Like no other film of the period, it stands as a testament, its mood – as Polonsky has confessed – being compounded on the one hand by fear of the McCarthy witch-hunts, and on the other by conflict in potential victims doubting the absolute justice of their cause. TM

Force of One, A

(1978, US, 91 min)
d Paul Aaron. *p* Alan Belkin. *sc* Ernest Tidyman. *ph* Roger Shearman. *ed* Bert Lovitt, Anne Goursaud. *ad* Norman Baron. *m* Dick Halligan. *cast* Jennifer O'Neill, Chuck Norris, Clu Gulager, Ron O'Neal, Bill Wallace, Eric Laneuville, James Whitmore.

●With a dope epidemic on the streets and a karate cop-killer on the loose, undercover narc Jennifer O'Neill enlists the martial artistry of (real-life champ) Norris to help stomp the bad guys. A typically plot-heavy script from Ernest Tidyman survives unimaginative direction to deliver that current rarity, an unpretentious action movie. A bit out of its depth at the top of a bill, but vastly superior to the ostensibly similar *Jaguar Lives*. PT

Forces of Nature

(1999, US, 106 min)
d Bronwen Hughes. *p* Susan Arnold, Donna Arkoff Roth, Ian Bryce. *sc* Marc Lawrence. *ph* Elliot Davis. *ed* Craig Wood. *pd* Lester Cohen. *m* John Powell. *cast* Sandra Bullock, Ben Affleck, Maura Tierney, Steve Zahn, Blythe Danner, Ronny Cox. Michael Fairman, Janet Carroll, Bert Remsen.

●A bumbling and typically charmless latter-day studio screwball comedy. Ben (Affleck) is flying to Savannah, Georgia, to marry Bridget (Tierney). He's evidently too stiff backed for happy marriage, because he won't admit he's apprehensive. Thus the screenplay throws a seagull in the plane's works and packs him off cross-country with a fellow passenger, kooky, emotionally battered Sarah (Bullock), to test his heart. To compensate for the lack of chemistry between the leads and in the script, director Hughes adds a spattering of vapid sunsets, loud hail and high storms to suggest some sort of elemental struggle. The various contemporary pop songs plastered over the soundtrack are equally pointlessly. Anyway, beyond the fumbled technique, Tierney is so patently the better bet that Ben's problem really looks like one of transport. NB

Force 10 from Navarone

(1978, GB, 118 min)
d Guy Hamilton. *p* Oliver A Unger. *sc* Robin Chapman. *ph* Christopher Challis. *ed* Raymond Poulton. *pd* Geoffrey Drake. *m* Ron Goodwin. *cast* Robert Shaw, Harrison Ford, Barbara Bach, Edward Fox, Franco Nero, Carl Weathers, Richard Kiel, Alan Badel.

●Survivors of *The Guns of Navarone* mission return to deal with the spy who betrayed them. Under Hamilton's moribund direction, this becomes a Bond-in-uniform saga, with a can-they-spike-the-Kraut-guns-in-time plot. All the potentially exciting set pieces (traitor in our midst, whose side are the Gucci-clad partisans on?) are thrown away with a disregard for the basic mechanics of suspense, and the climax is literally cardboard thin. Edward Fox is consistently watchable, but on the whole a damned poor show from the chaps down at EMI HQ. CPea

Fords on Water

(1983, GB, 83 min)
d Barry Bliss. *p* Nita Amy, Jill Pack. *sc* Barry Bliss, Billy Colvill. *ph* Russell Murray. *ed* Neil Thomson. *ad* Ian Watson, Caroline Amies. *m* Keith Donald. *cast* Elvis Payne, Mark Wingett, Kathryn Apanowicz, Jason Rose, Allister Bain, David Ryall.

●Two London kids, one black, one white, are cast into the outer darkness of the dole. But as this duo leave behind the night-locked city, speeding northwards in a stolen motor, it's soon clear that Bliss' first feature celebrates resistance not resignation; and that with its lustrous, colourful images and laconic screenplay, its jump cuts and jazzy score, it owes less to drab naturalism than to the moody poetry of Neil Jordan's *Angel*, spiked with *Nouvelle Vague* verve and nerve. There is much to enjoy: an irreverent sense of humour, a great saxy soundtrack by *Angel* composer Keith Donald, and above all an upbeat ending that has Thatcher's flotsam cheekily waving, not drowning. SJo

Foreign Affair, A

(1948, US, 116 min, b/w)
d Billy Wilder. *p* Charles Brackett. *sc* Charles Brackett, Billy Wilder, Richard L Breen. *ph* Charles Lang Jr. *ed* Doane Harrison. *ad* Hans Dreier, Walter Tyler. *m* Frederick Hollander. *cast* Jean Arthur, Marlene Dietrich, John Lund, Millard Mitchell, Bill Murphy, Stanley Prager, Peter von Zerneck.

●Shot amid the ruins of Berlin, Wilder's satire on the corruption among GIs fraternising with the locals did not go down too well with the Defence Department. Arthur plays a prim congresswoman investigating an army officer (Lund), and when she realises she really has fallen for her man, she has to win him away from the exotic charms of chanteuse Dietrich. This may not be Wilder at his best – the story develops along fairly predictable lines, with Arthur switching her starchy uniform for a glistening evening gown – but there are some precious set pieces, notably a seduction among a row of filing cabinets and Dietrich's club act, not to mention a crackling script. DT

Foreign Body

(1986, GB, 111 min)
d Ronald Neame. *p* Colin Brewer. *sc* Celine La Freniere. *ph* Ronnie Taylor. *ed* Andrew Nelson. *pd* Roy Stannard. *m* Ken Howard. *cast* Victor Banerjee, Warren Mitchell, Geraldine McEwan, Denis Quilley, Amanda Donohoe, Eve Ferret, Anna Massey, Stratford Johns, Trevor Howard.

●The major problem here is determining the most offensive performance. Is it Banerjee as Indian immigrant Ram Das, or Mitchell in blackface as his scheming cousin IQ? The comedy centres on the daydreaming Das, who comes to England in '75 after losing his job as night porter in a Calcutta brothel. He takes a job as bus conductor until IQ – a toilet attendant at Heathrow – persuades him to pose as a Harley Street chiropractor. Das attends to wealthy female patients in need of attention rather than medical advice, bowing and gesticulating his way into the hearts of the English aristocracy. Despite the make-up, Mitchell charms, his comedy based in character rather than the rabbit punchlines. It's Banerjee, the wide-eyed fool, whose antics are not only less than entertaining, but also alarming. SGo

Foreign Correspondent

(1940, US, 120 min, b/w)
d Alfred Hitchcock. *p* Walter Wanger. *sc* Charles Bennett, Joan Harrison, James Hilton, Robert Benchley. *ph* Rudolph Maté. *ed* Otho Lovering, Dorothy Spencer. *pd* William Cameron Menzies. *m* Alfred Newman. *cast* Joel McCrea, Laraine Day, Herbert Marshall, George Sanders, Albert Basserman, Edmund Gwenn, Eduardo Ciannelli, Robert Benchley.

●Despite the now rather embarrassing propagandistic finale, with McCrea urging an increase in the war effort against the Nazis, Hitchcock's espionage thriller is a thoroughly enjoyable affair, complete with some of his most memorable set pieces. McCrea and Day are the lovers searching out Nazi agents in London and Holland after the disappearance of a peace-seeking diplomat, while Sanders, Gwenn amd the normally wooden Marshall lend fine support. Something of a predecessor of the picaresque chase thrillers like *Saboteur* and *North by Northwest*, its main source of suspense comes from the fact that little is what it seems to be: a camera hides an assassin's gun, sails of a windmill conceal a sinister secret, and the sanctuary of Westminster Cathedral provides an opportunity for murder. Not one of the director's greatest – there's little of his characteristic cruelty or moral pessimism – but still eminently watchable. GA

Foreigners (Jag Heter Stelius)

(1972, Swe, 113 min)
d Johan Bergenstråhle. *p* Bengt Forslund. *sc* Johan Bergenstråhle. *ph* Petter Davidsson, Walter Hirsch. *ad* Eva Linnman. *m* Bengt Ernryd. *cast* Konstantinos Papageorgiou, Anastasios Margetis, Savas Tzanetakis, Andreas Bellis, Maria Antipa, Despina Tomazani.

●A worthy, sometimes telling film about the experiences of Greek immigrants in egalitarian Sweden, scripted from a novel based on the (Greek) author's own experiences. Sadly, though, the processing from life-to-book-to-film hasn't made for conviction, and the film's fictionalised aspects tend to be more intrusive than revealing. Oddly memorable, though. VG

Foreign Land

(1995, Braz, 100 min, b/w)
d Walter Salles, Daniela Thomas. *p* Flávio Tambellini. *sc* Walter Salles, Daniela Thomas, Marcos Bernstein. *ph* Walter Carvalho. *ed* Walter Salles, Felipe Lacerda. *pd* Daniela Thomas. *m* Jose Miguel Wisnik. *cast* Fernanda Torres, Fernando Pinto, Laura Cardosa, Luis Mello, Alexandre Borges, Joao Lagarto.

●Salles' second feature, fluently shot in b/w, focuses on Brazilian youth torn between the hardships of the newly democratic homeland and exile in the corrupted émigré sub-culture of Lisbon. The story eventually settles on a young man on a bungled smuggling operation to Portugal, who finds himself on the run with a disenchanted Brazilian woman. Their sudden plunge into violence and romance, as well as their struggle for identity, is reminiscent of Antonioni's *The Passenger*. Despite not quite steering clear of road movie clichés, the film's stylistic bravura, occasional moments of real humour and excellent performances are pretty invigorating. DT

Foreign Moon

(1995, GB/HK, 90 min)
d Zhang Zeming. *p* Ma Fung-kwok, Jane Caldwell. *sc* Zhang Zeming. *ph* Lu Lik. *ed* Xu Juan Ping. *pd* Haibo Yu. *cast* Chen Hsiao Hsuan, Harrison Liu, Chen Daming, David Tse.

●Deeply unconvincing from the start, this loose assemblage of clichés about émigré Chinese has only its London setting to distinguish it from a dozen predecessors set in New York. The three central characters (impossibly naive girl, sad ex-radical and muscle-queen wide-boy) plod through a highly predictable teaming-up and falling-out; there's no psychological depth, sociological insight or even credible emotion. Maybe the excellent *Swan Song* was the only real film that Zhang Zeming had in him. TR

Foreman Went to France, The

(1941, GB, 87 min, b/w)
d Charles Frend. *p* Michael Balcon. *sc* Angus MacPhail, John Dighton, Leslie Arliss. *ph*

Wilkie Cooper. *ed* Robert Hamer. *ad* Tom Morahan. *m* William Walton. *cast* Tommy Trinder, Constance Cummings, Clifford Evans, Robert Morley, Gordon Jackson, Francis L Sullivan.
●Preceding Ealing's marvellous *Went the Day Well?*, this contribution to the war effort is less imaginative but almost as effective in its more conventional way. Based on fact, it has Evans as a factory foreman sent to France in 1940 and, aided by two soldiers (Trinder, Jackson) and an American girl (Cummings), contriving to spirit vital machinery away from the advancing Germans. Beautifully dovetailing comedy and drama, it is remarkably discreet in its patriotics, aside from a final scene where French refugees nobly give up their possessions to make room for the machines on the last boat out. A pity the efforts of some of the cast – notably Morley – to pass as Frenchmen are disastrous. TM

Forest of Bliss

(1986, US, 90 min)
d Robert Gardner. *p* Robert Gardner, Akos Oster. *ph/ed* Robert Gardner.
●Basically, a documentary day in the life of the Ganges riverbank at Benares. Well shot, but it has all been seen before in countless variations from Ray's *Aparajito* to Malle's *Phantom India*, except that here the stress is on the jostling extremes of sacred and profane: worshippers standing absorbed in their rituals while dogs gnaw hungrily at corpses floating by. Oddly, though made for the Harvard Film Study Center, it is presented as an impressionistic travelogue without either commentary or subtitles. Several of the rites and customs, and at least one dialogue scene, demand elucidation. TM

Forever Amber

(1947, US, 140 min)
d Otto Preminger. *p* William Perlberg. *sc* Philip Dunne, Ring Lardner Jr, Jerome Cady. *ph* Leon Shamroy. *ed* Louis Loeffler. *ad* Lyle Wheeler. *m* David Raksin. *cast* Linda Darnell, Cornel Wilde, Richard Greene, George Sanders, Richard Haydn, Jessica Tandy, Anne Revere, Glenn Langan.
●A cleaned-up adaptation of Kathleen Winsor's novel about a peasant wench's rise to riches – by means of sexual favours – during the reign of Charles II, this was originally planned as a John Stahl film, with Peggy Cummins in the role of the opportunistic Amber. Stahl, in fact, would probably have been better suited to the lurid emotional melodrama than Preminger, though Darnell – blonde for once but as sultrily sensuous as ever – is fine in the central role, while the supporting cast (notably Sanders as the king) is excellent. It's all lavish enough, beautifully shot in Technicolor by Leon Shamroy, but Preminger's direction lacks the sophisticated lightness of touch that Mitchell Leisen brought to the in some ways similar *Kitty*. GA

Forever England (aka Born for Glory/ Brown on Resolution)

(1935, GB, 80 min, b/w)
d Walter Forde. *p* Michael Balcon. *sc* John Orton, Michael Hogan Gerard Fairlie. *ph* Bernard Knowles. *ed* Otto Ludwig. *pd* Alfred Junge. *cast* Betty Balfour, John Mills, Jimmy Hanley, Barry McKay, Felix Aylmer, Howard Marion-Crawford.
●This Michael Balcon production is a rather creaky adaptation of CS Forester's WWI nautical novel *Brown on Resolution*. Mills is bright-eyed and full of pluck as an ordinary seaman whose bravery in German captivity leads single-handedly to the sinking of an enemy vessel. The rest of the movie only just passes muster, but you can see the young star was clearly destined to move up the ranks. The island sequences were directed by Anthony Asquith. TJ

Forever in Love

see Pride of the Marines

Forever Mary (Mery per sempre)

(1988, It, 100 min)
d Marco Risi. *p* Claudio Bonivento. *sc* Sandro Petraglia, Stefano Rulli. *ph* Mauro Marchetti. *ed* Claudio Di Mauro. *ad* Massimo Spano. *m* Giancarlo Bigazzi. *cast* Michele Placido, Claudio Amendola, Francesco Benigno, Alessandro Di Sanzo, Tony Sperandeo.
●Teacher Marco Terzi (Placido) deliberately picks the short straw in the Italian educational lottery and chooses a posting to the Rosaspina reform school, home to Palermo's toughest delinquent youth. There he wins these hard nuts' hearts by setting them essays on love, letting them draw on him with felt tip pen, and snogging Mary the class transvestite to prove he's a real man. Before long, the boys are eating out of his hand; the authorities are, naturally, less enamoured. This is a fairly standard exercise in the boys-behind-bars genre, with all the usual ingredients – cruelty, camaraderie, and a surprisingly teasing attitude to the sodomy that never quite takes place. The main appeal lies in the honest, unshowy performances of the non-professional cast of real reform school alumni. JRo

For Ever Mozart

(1996, Fr, 82 min)
d/sc Jean-Luc Godard. *ph* Christoph Pollock. *ed* Jean-Luc Godard. *pd* Ivan Niclass. *m* David Darling. *cast* Madeleine Assas, Bérangère Allaux, Ghalya Lacroix, Vicky Messica, Frédéric Pierrot, Harry Cleven.
●Godard (director/writer/editor) casts a quizzical eye on Sarajevo, art and the cinema: in the first half, a group of naive youngsters drive to Bosnia to perform Alfred de Musset's play *On ne badine pas avec l'amour*; in the second, a film-maker strives to get 'Fatal Bolero' in the can. The two parts are linked by Godard's insistence on a cinema of the intellect (dis-chord; absurdism; quotation; provocation), and by his recognition of the futility of the exercise ('Cinema substitutes our gaze with a world in harmony with our desires…something essential is renounced'). TCh

Forever Young

(1983, GB, 84 min)
d David Drury. *p* Chris Griffin. *sc* Ray Connolly. *ph* Norman Langley. *ed* Max Lemon. *ad* Jeffrey Woodbridge. *cast* James Aubrey, Nicholas Gecks, Karen Archer, Alec McCowen, Liam Holt, Jane Forster, Ruth Davies.
●On stage a trendy curate strums his way through 'Donna', while a long-lost friend looks on in amazement to see his one-time singing partner still reliving his teenage memories 20 years on. It's Ray Connolly parading his '50s fantasies once more, but this time with a more ironic gloss than usual, since his script is about the way both friends are still trapped by unresolved problems. As a series of flashbacks shows, they used to be inseparable – testing each other's pop knowledge in the school showers, chatting up girls, performing their Everly Brothers-style act – until in their different ways they betrayed each other…a treachery which is about to repeat itself 20 years on. Made as a TV movie in Channel 4's *First Love* series, *Forever Young* catches well the psychology of the relationship, but it also has the cosiness and soft nostalgia one has come to expect from executive producer David Puttnam. Basically, a night out for the middle-aged. CS

Forever Young

(1992, US, 101 min)
d Steve Miner. *p* Bruce Davey. *sc* Jeffrey Abrams. *ph* Russell Boyd. *ed* Jon Poll. *pd* Gregg Fonseca. *m* Jerry Goldsmith. *cast* Mel Gibson, Jamie Lee Curtis, Elijah Wood, Isabel Glasser, George Wendt, Joe Morton, Nicolas Surovy.
●In 1939, test pilot Daniel McCormick (Gibson) finds his courage deserting him whenever it comes to proposing to his childhood sweetheart (Glasser). Overwhelmed by grief when she is hit by a truck and rendered comatose, he agrees to be cryogenically frozen by a scientist pal (Wendt); but when he wakes up, it is 1992. Fortunately, single mother Claire (Curtis) and her young son (Wood) are on hand to help him adjust to modern living and piece together his lost past. Jeffrey Abrams' script gets the tone just right, playing everything straight and never lapsing into knowing irony; while Miner, content to let the storyline unfold, leaves it to the actors to flesh out the sometimes touching, sometimes comic collision between Daniel's old-fashioned gallantry and modern-day cynicism. Looked at with a jaundiced eye, the scenario is slushy and full of holes; surrendered to in a spirit of careless romanticism, it works. NF

Forever Yours

see Forget-Me-Not

Forfaiture (Obligation)

(1937, Fr, 99 min, b/w)
d Marcel L'Herbier. *p* Pierre Braunberger, Michel Salkind. *sc* Jacques Companeez, Jean-Georges Auriol, Herbert Juttke, Jacques Natanson. *ph* Eugen Schuftan. *ed* Pierre de Hérain. *ad* Robert Gys. *m* Michel Levine. *cast* Sessue Hayakawa, Lise Delamare, Louis Jouvet, Victor Francen, Sylvia Bataille.
●A remake, in another time, another place, of Cecil B DeMille's 1915 *The Cheat* (written by Hector Turnbull) with Hayakawa repeating his role of the wealthy Oriental who literally puts his brand on the fair-skinned heroine – evidently a deliciously horrifying moment for WASP audiences of the day. It would be instructive, if a bit tedious, to list all the alterations the story has undergone. It's essentially a matter of tone, with the fastidious, sophisticated L'Herbier about the polar opposite of full-steam-ahead DeMille. The most significant embellishments involve a private secretary played by Jouvet on a darkly enigmatic note which does much to deflect Turnbull's compendium of unexamined prejudices. BBa

For Freedom

(1940, GB, 84 min, b/w)
d Maurice Elvey, Castleton Knight. *p* Edward Black. *sc* Leslie Arliss, Miles Malleson. *ph* Arthur Crabtree. *ed* RE Dearing, Alfred Roome. *m* George Walter. *cast* Will Fyffe, Anthony Hulme, EVH Emmett, Guy Middleton, Albert Lieven, Hugh McDermott, Terry-Thomas, Robert Beatty.
●1938: newsreel chief Fyffe compiles a movie explaining the genesis of the war that's about to break out; then the Munich agreement is signed. 1939: he's now working on a picture about world peace; the Nazi/Soviet pact is signed (the censor allows Fyffe to say 'God damn', unheard of licence at the time) and war starts a week later. Quite an ingenious format for propaganda, this, permitting more comedy than usual, but the film then forgets about Fyffe in favour of a re-enactment of the destruction of the Graf Spee (cf. *The Battle of the River Plate*). A speech by Churchill rounds off the proceedings. For the cinephile this is all pretty negligible. For the historian it's worth a look, as an artefact from the momentous summer of 1940. BBa

For Fun (Zhao Le)

(1993, HK/China, 97 min)
d Ning Ying. *p* Liu Yuansheng, Cheng Zhigu. *sc* Ning Dai, Ning Ying. *ph* Xiao Feng, Wu Di. *ed* Zhou Weidon. *ad* Yang Xiaowen. *m* Meng Weidong. *cast* Huang Zongluo, Huang Wenjie, Han Shanxu, He Ming.
●Ning Ying hit the jackpot with this her second feature, financed from Hong Kong but shot entirely in Beijing. The story, about retired old codgers who team up to form an amateur Peking Opera troupe and enter a talent contest, is warm, funny and extremely likeable. It's also quite sharp politically, since it pricks the bubble of pomposity associated with Chinese officialdom – incarnated in the story by a former stage-doorman who sees himself as a natural leader. Wonderful performances from the two queens in the troupe, and from Huang Zongluo as the petty tyrant. TR

Forget Me Not (aka Forever Yours)

(1936, GB, 72 min, b/w)
d [Zoltan Korda, Augusto Genina]. *p* Alberto Giacolone, Alexander Korda. *sc* Hugh Gray, Arthur Wimperis. *ph* Hans Schneeberger. *ed* OH Cornelius. *m* Mischa Spoliansky. *cast* Beniamino Gigli, Joan Gardner, Ivan Brandt, Hugh Wakefield, Jeanne Stuart, Allan Jeayes.
●Majestic Italian tenor Gigli was the raison d'être for this soppy sea-going romance, made by the Kordas in simultaneous English and Italian (*Non Ti Scordar de Me*) versions. Having lost his wife, Gigli is much taken with fellow passenger Gardner and resolves to marry, though the reappearance of her former fiancé is to test their love. Undistinguished elsewhere, but whenever the big man sings you'll understand why he's reckoned one of the greats. Best approached as an addendum to the records for interested fans. TJ

Forget Paris

(1995, US, 101 min)
d/p Billy Crystal. *sc* Billy Crystal, Babaloo Mandel, Lowell Ganz. *ph* Don Burgess. *ed* Kent Beyda. *pd* Terence Marsh. *m* Marc Shaiman. *cast* Billy Crystal, Debra Winger, Joe Mantegna, Cynthia Stevenson, Richard Masur, Julie Kavner, Cathy Moriarty.
● Waiting for friends to arrive at their engagement party, Andy (Mantegna) tells Liz (Stevenson) about the bizarre romance between his pal Mickey (Crystal) and Ellen (Winger): how the airline she worked for in Paris mislaid the coffin carrying Mickey's father, and how despite this inauspicious beginning (and her rich husband) they fell in love, married and lived happily…for a while. Craig (Masur) and Lucy (Kavner) take up the story: Mickey, a basketball referee, was always on the road, and Ellen started climbing the walls of their suburban LA home. She'd given up everything for the marriage; what would Mickey give up? We've been this way before. An alternative title might be 'When Mickey Met Ellen'. Produced, directed and co-written by Crystal, the film has a generous number of acerbic asides and some memorable slapschtick, but as Ellen discovers, laughs aren't enough, and, like the relationship it depicts, everything goes terribly slack in the middle. TCh

Forget Venice

see Dimenticare Venezia

Forgotten Silver

(1995, NZ, 55 min, b/w & col)
d Peter Jackson, Costa Botes. *p* Sue Rogers. *sc* Peter Jackson, Costa Botes. *ph* Alun Bollinger, Gerry Vasbenter. *ed* Eric De Beus, Mike Horton. *pd* John Girdlestone. *m* Dave Donaldson, Steve Roche, Janet Roddick. *with* Peter Jackson, Costa Botes, Leonard Maltin, Sam Neill, Harvey Weinstein.
● A lovingly produced tribute to obscure Kiwi film-maker Colin Mackenzie (1888–1937). Highlights include snippets from the feature length 1908 *Warrior Season*, with its pioneering sound recording, and rare footage of the Spanish Civil War in which Mackenzie met his end. The centrepiece is the restored version of the 'lost' *Salome* and the discovery of its dilapidated outdoor set, still standing decades on. Such authorities as Leonard Maltin and Sam Neill attest to Mackenzie's importance, though it's a pity that, for copyright reasons, the directors were obliged to omit all mention of his 1931 Himalayan project and of the controversial Yeti footage he secured. BBa

For Keeps (aka Maybe Baby)

(1987, US, 98 min)
d John G Avildsen. *p* Jerry Belson, Walter Coblenz. *sc* Tim Kazurinsky, Denise DeClue. *ph* James Crabe. *ed* John G Avildsen. *pd* William J Cassidy. *m* Bill Conti. *cast* Molly Ringwald, Randall Batinkoff, Kenneth Mars, Miriam Flynn, Conchata Ferrell, Sharon Brown, Jack Ong.
● The main claim to fame of Kenosha, Wisconsin, is that it was the birthplace of Orson Welles; the fact that the town is also now the setting of Avildsen's film is unlikely to increase its reputation. High school kids Darcy (Ringwald) and Stan (Batinkoff) are very much in lerv, but when Darcy becomes pregnant all hell breaks loose: their folks argue over adoption and abortion, the kids get spliced, and the sacrifices demanded by parenthood (Darcy's future in journalism, Stan's in architecture) temporarily threaten to split the pair asunder. Though the film finally opts for ear-bashing histrionics, its prevailingly pedagogic tone is both coy and tricksy. The dialogue is relentless in its banality, the stereotype characters unattractive and poorly motivated, the plot protracted and predictable. GA

For Love of the Game

(1999, US, 138 min)
d Sam Raimi. *p* Armyan Bernstein, Amy Robinson. *sc* Dana Stevens. *ph* John Bailey. *ed* Eric L Beason, Arthur Coburn. *pd* Neil Spisak. *m* Basil Poledouris. *cast* Kevin Costner, Kelly Preston, John C Reilly, Jena Malone, Brian Cox, JK Simmons, Vin Scully, Steve Lyons, Carmine D Giovinazzo.
● From a novel by Michael Shaara, this rehashes a story that's so familiar it's beyond cliché. Costner is Billy Chapel, the Detroit Tigers' star pitcher. He is reaching the end of his career: time for reassessment. His team has been sold, and the new owners are thinking of trading the ageing star. Plus his on-off girlfriend (Preston) has called time on their relationship. Now he has to play what may well be the last game of his career. That game stretches over most of the film, but any anticipated suspense is undercut by the sepia-tinted inserts charting the couple's bumpy uninvolving five-year romance from first meeting to acrimonious split(s). WI

For Love or Money

(1983, Aust, 109 min)
d Megan McMurchy, Jeni Thornley. *p/sc* Megan McMurchy, Margot Oliver, Jeni Thornley. *ph* Erika Addis. *ed* Margot Nash. *m* Elizabeth Drake. *cast* Jane Clifton, Diane Craig, Nick Enright, Vivienne Garrett.
● Documentaries probably don't come more ambitious than this: co-produced by an Australian women's collective, its subject matter is little less than a feminist analysis of Australian women's fortunes in (and out of) the work force – where Australian includes Aborigine and migrant women – across a 200-year sweep from the arrival of the first women convicts to the present day. To document this huge and diverse subject, the film-makers use a dense montage of footage – archive material, clips from feature films, TV ads, even donated home movies – which is complemented or ironically counterpointed with a medley of narrative voices and incidental music. In more crudely didactic hands, the material could have been unpalatable, but agile editing, some grimly humorous footage, and a prevailing sense of conviction keep it moving along, while the strength of the analysis it develops justifies its exhausting means. HH

For Love or Money (aka The Concierge)

(1993, US, 96 min)
d Barry Sonnenfeld. *p* Brian Grazer. *sc* Lawrence Konner, Mark Rosenthal. *ph* Oliver Wood. *ed* Jim Miller. *pd* Oliver Wood. *m* Bruce Broughton. *cast* Michael J Fox, Gabrielle Anwar, Anthony Higgins, Michael Tucker, Bob Balaban, Udo Kier.
● Michael J Fox was the acceptable face of '80s yuppiedom: the little guy who thinks big, the all-American optimist who believes in profit without loss. Mercenary he may be, but the manners are impeccable. Here, as concierge in New York's elite Bradbury Hotel, he's a one-man service industry who'll do anything for a tip. This supposedly romantic comedy is every bit as hackneyed as it sounds. TCh

For Me and My Gal

(1942, US, 104 min, b/w)
d Busby Berkeley. *p* Arthur Freed. *sc* Richard Sherman, Fred F Finklehoffe, Sid Silvers. *ph* William Daniels. *ed* Ben Lewis. *ad* Cedric Gibbons, Gabriel Siognamillo. *songs* Gus Kahn, Joseph McCarthy, Fred Fisher, others. *cast* Judy Garland, Gene Kelly, George Murphy, Stephen McNally, Marta Eggerth, Keenan Wynn, Ben Blue, Richard Quine.
● Set just before World War I, this corny musical introduced 30-year-old debutant Gene Kelly in the intially unsympathetic role of an ambitious hoofer who joins up with fellow vaudevillians Garland and Murphy in the, hope of fulfilling his/their dream of playing at the famous Palace Theatre. Their plans are complicated by Kelly's selfish scheming to avoid the draft, and by a romantic triangle in which Murphy loves Garland, Garland loves Kelly, and Kelly loves, besides himself, the idea of being famous. Kelly's contrived transformation from ruthless heel to self-effacing war hero is totally unconvincing, but the excellent numbers – including the title song, 'When You Wore a Tulip' and 'Ballin' the Jack' – may help to numb the pain. NF

Formula, The

(1980, US, 117 min)
d John G Avildsen. *p/sc* Steve Shagan. *ph* James Crabe. *ed* John G Avildsen, John Carter. *pd* Herman A Blumenthal. *m* Bill Conti. *cast* George C Scott, Marlon Brando, Marthe Keller, John Gielgud, GD Spradlin, Beatrice Straight, Richard Lynch.
● Laborious thriller about a formula for synthetic fuel which reaches back to the Nazi past and forward to contemporary terrorism. Avildsen and Steve Shagan (scripting from his own novel) go wildly astray in trying to mine some more of the breast-beating vein they opened up in *Save the Tiger*, with Brando playing some particularly loony tunes as the tycoon who orates in defence of big business and power games. TM

For Pete's Sake

(1974, US, 90 min)
d Peter Yates. *p* Martin Erlichman, Stanley Shapiro. *sc* Stanley Shapiro, Maurice Richlin. *ph* Laszlo Kovacs. *ed* Frank P Keller. *pd* Gene Callahan. *m* Artie Butler. *cast* Barbra Streisand, Michael Sarrazin, Estelle Parsons, William Redfield, Molly Picon, Louis Zorich.
● Yates sure is an erratic talent. *Bullitt* made one think he was only good with action scenes. *The Friends of Eddie Coyle, Breaking Away* and *The Janitor* suggested that he could indeed handle strong characterisation and droll humour. Everything else makes him look almost totally talentless. Here he's adrift in a sea of poor performances and bad comic timing, as Streisand gets farcically involved with loan sharks and others in an attempt to supplement the income of herself and her student-cum-cab driver hubbie Sarrazin. GA

For Queen and Country

(1988, GB/US, 106 min)
d Martin Stellman. *p* Tim Bevan. *sc* Martin Stellman, Trix Worrell. *ph* Richard Greatrex. *ed* Stephen Singleton. *pd* Andrew McAlpine. *m* Michael Kamen. *cast* Denzel Washington, Dorian Healy, Amanda Redman, Sean Chapman, Bruce Payne, George Baker.
● For his debut as a director, Stellman (scriptwriter on *Quadrophenia, Babylon* and *Defence of the Realm*) has produced an ambitious but disappointing piece about class and race in 'Thatcher's Britain'. His storyline concerns Reuben, a Falklands war hero whose return to a dreadfuly run-down South London council block is marked by rejection from white cops and the blacks with whom he grew up. When the immigration authorities inform Reuben, who was born in St Lucia, that he's no longer officially a British citizen, something snaps. Stellman's script contains an intelligent appraisal of a country divided more subtly by loyalty and habit than the media often realise. But the choice of Washington doesn't help: he isn't bad in the part, but his accent strays absurdly. More worrying is the often corny plotting, the by now tired-looking exploitation of Broadwater violence, and a preposterous shootout ending. Stellman's direction is often as sluggish as the daily routines of his protagonists. SGr

Forrest Gump (100)

(1994, US, 142 min)
d Robert Zemeckis. *p* Wendy Finerman, Steve Tisch, Steve Starkey. *sc* Eric Roth. *ph* Don Burgess. *ed* Arthur Schmidt. *pd* Rick Carter. *m* Alan Silvestri. *cast* Tom Hanks, Robin Wright, Gary Sinise, Mykelti Williamson, Sally Field, Michael Conner Humphreys.
● Played by Hanks with a sing-song Southern drawl and an evangelical earnestness, Gump is the quintessential simpleton, his only characteristic the inert righteousness instilled in him by his mama (Field). Gump's story is as extraordinary as he is banal. He conducts us on what amounts to a virtual-reality tour of late twentieth century American history. Beneath its babyboomer soundtrack, its restive feel-good aesthetic and conventional liberal veneer, this is a dismayingly reactionary work. Consider Forrest's one true love, Jenny (Wright), a 'nice' girl who takes a wrong turn when she abandons home for showbusiness. Throughout director Zemeckis contrasts Gump's charmed progress with Jenny's unhappy engagement with the counter culture. It's only when she's dying that Jenny realises she should have stayed with Forrest all along. He's asexual, square and a tedious conversationalist, but God knows he loves his mother – as this mawkish conservative movie ultimately goes to prove: ignorance is bliss. Winner of a raft of Oscars. TCh

For Roseanna

see Roseanna's Grave

Forsaken, The

(2001, US, 91 min)
d JS Cardone. *p* Carol Kottenbrook, Scott Einbinder. *sc* JS Cardone. *ph* Steven Bernstein. *ed* Norman Buckley. *pd* Martina Buckley. *m* Johnny Lee Schell, Tim Jones. *cast* Kerr Smith, Brendan Fehr, Izabella Miko, Phina Oruche, Simon Rex, Carrie Snodgress, Johnathon Schaech, Alexis Thorpe.

●Stealing its set-up from *The Hitcher* and its itinerant bloodsuckers from *Near Dark*, this tawdry exploitation pic establishes its credentials with an opening shot of a naked woman lubriciously washing her blood-smeared breasts. Filmed cheaply, mostly on desert locations, it relies heavily on nudity, gore and violence – often all at once. When LA-based schlock-movie editor Sean (Smith) picks up the drive-away Mercedes in which he plans to cruise across country to his sister's wedding in Miami, he's expressly told, 'No hitchers'. But after losing his wallet, he picks up the seemingly drug-addicted Nick (Fehr), who turns out to be a bitten but not yet turned vampire hunter with a soft spot for other strung-out victims, such as Megan (Miko). For Nick and Megan it's a case of 'Once bitten, forever smitten.' Unless they can kill the source of the virus coursing through their veins – vampire gang leader Kit (Schaech) – they are doomed to join the blood-craving undead. This starts promisingly, with an unusual variation on vampire mythology. The writer/director then squanders his wayward energies on repetitive, ham-fisted action and boring violence. Pretty boy actors Smith and Fehr fared better in *Final Destination*; the mostly mute Miko lets her body do the talking; the sharp cheekboned Schaech and his striking black sidekick, Phina Oruche, exude the louche, sexless appeal of slumming fashion models. NF

Fort Apache

(1948, US, 127 min, b/w)
d John Ford. *p* John Ford, Merian C Cooper. *sc* Frank S Nugent. *ph* Archie J Stout. *ed* Jack Murray. *ad* James Basevi. *m* Richard Hageman. *cast* Henry Fonda, John Wayne, Shirley Temple, Pedro Armendariz, John Agar, George O'Brien, Ward Bond, Victor McLaglen, Anna Lee.

●The first of Ford's cavalry trilogy (to be followed by *She Wore a Yellow Ribbon* and *Rio Grande*), and an intriguing development of questions of leadership, responsibility, heroism and legend, first raised in the muted officers' conflict of *They Were Expendable*. West Point stiffness (the Custer-like Fonda) meets the more organic Western community of an isolated Arizona outpost, and inflexible notions of 'duty' lead inexorably to disaster, historically rewritten as glory. Not for the last time, Ford gives us telling evidence of tragic ambiguity, but none the less decides to 'print the legend'. PT

Fort Apache, the Bronx

(1981, US, 123 min)
d Daniel Petrie. *p* Martin Richards, Tom Fiorello. *sc* Heywood Gould. *ph* John Alcott. *ed* Rita Roland. *pd* Ben Edwards. *m* Jonathan Tunick. *cast* Paul Newman, Edward Asner, Ken Wahl, Danny Aiello, Rachel Ticotin, Pam Grier, Kathleen Beller.

●It's not that Newman turns in anything less than his customarily diligent performance as a greying career cop, nor that his affair with a Puerto Rican nurse played by an actress who must be 30 years his junior strains credibility (since that blue-eyed sex appeal remains intact). But the material strung together in a script about urban police work is so familiar from countless cop shows that it's difficult to see who needs this movie. The litany of routine duties includes disarming crazy knifers, saving gays from suicide, delivering babies, chasing muggers, preventing pimps from beating their whores, all depicted in ramblingly episodic fashion and without a shred of street credibility. RM

For the Boys

(1991, US, 140 min)
d Mark Rydell. *p* Bette Midler, Bonnie Bruckheimer, Margaret South. *sc* Marshall Brickman, Neal Jimenez, Lindy Laub. *ph* Stephen Goldblatt. *ed* Jerry Greenberg, Jere Huggins. *pd* Assheton Gorton. *m* David Grusin. *cast* Bette Midler, James Caan, George Segal, Patrick O'Neal, Christopher Rydell, Arye Gross, Norman Fell, Rosemary Murphy, Bud Yorkin, Jack Sheldon.

●A drama spanning three wars and professional/emotional skirmishes over two generations. Dixie (Midler) is to be awarded a medal for a career spent entertaining US troops, an honour she shares with her one-time partner Eddie (Caan). A television ceremony is planned, but at the last minute, she won't budge from her house. A long-standing grudge against Eddie is to blame, and it's up to a sweet-talking studio minion to coax an explanation. Cue a flashback to her life story, complete with battle footage and the occasional tune... Rydell charts the decline in American values: good-natured soldiers of WWII give way to druggies in Vietnam, and quick-witted writer Art (Segal) enjoys fame and fortune before falling victim to McCarthyism. Marshall Brickman's script is full of marvellous one-liners, but despite its aspirations, this sentimental Midler road-show is hopelessly unrestrained. CM

For Them That Trespass

(1948, GB, 96 min, b/w)
d Alberto Cavalcanti. *p* Victor Skutezky. *sc* J Lee-Thompson, William Douglas Home. *ph* Derick Williams. *ed* Margery Saunders. *ad* Peter Proud. *m* Philip Green. *cast* Richard Todd, Stephen Murray, Patricia Plunkett, Joan Dowling, Michael Laurence, Rosalyn Boulter.

●*For Them That Trespass*, scripted by J Lee Thompson of all people, is notable for the way Cavalcanti transforms his story, of how Richard Todd, wrongly imprisoned for murder, clears his name, into a bleak account of guilt. Shot so as to bring out both the poetry and the squalor of working class life, it was one of the postwar British films that presaged the arrival of *Room at the Top* and *Saturday Night and Sunday Morning* a decade later. PH

Fortini/Cani

(1976, It/Fr/WGer/GB/US, 85 min)
d/p/sc Jean-Marie Straub, Danièle Huillet. *ph* Renato Berta, Emilio Bestetti. *ed* Jean-Marie Straub, Danièle Huillet. *with* Franco Fortini, Luciana Nissi, Adriano Aprà.

●The film essay is a fairly recondite genre, but it's safe to say that there has never been an example like this. It's a film of a book: the Italian writer Franco Fortini is seen and heard reading sections from his book *The Dogs of Sinai*, in which he attacks Italian reactions to the war in Palestine in the light of his own part-Jewish upbringing. Although Straub completely respects the integrity of Fortini's words, he 'contexts' the argument in a number of provocative ways. A haunting image of a seashore at night, or a brief extract from Schoenberg's *Moses and Aaron*, are enough to underline the element of melodrama in Fortini's autobiography; a placid study of the hills where Nazis massacred the Italian resistance is enough to generate a meditation on the meaning of Fortini's anti-fascism. The film draws attention to issues of frightening relevance, and yet allows the viewer plenty of space to think and feel. TR

Fortress

(1992, US/Aust, 89 min)
d Stuart Gordon. *p* John A Davis, John Flock. *sc* Troy Neighbours, Steven Feinberg, Terry Fox. *ph* David Eggby. *ed* Tim Wellburn. *pd* David Copping. *m* Frederic Talghorn. *cast* Christopher Lambert, Kurtwood Smith, Loryn Locklin, Lincoln Kilpatrick, Jeffrey Combs, Tom Towles.

●Stuart Gordon calls this prison movie 'a sort of science-fiction version of *The Great Escape*'. Regrettably, Lambert, imprisoned because his pregnant wife is about to exceed the government limit of children allowed a married couple, is no Steve McQueen. Built 30 storeys below ground, the state-of-the-art prison features laser bars, robot guards and a nasty device called the Intestinator. While confined to the futuristic prison interiors, the film works reasonably well; but once Lambert springs his wife from the women's section and escapes, the limitations of budget and narrative imagination start to show. As it moves away from the ensemble feel of the early scenes, this quickly degenerates into a part explosive, part sentimental star vehicle. NF

Fortress II: Re-entry

(1999, US/Luxembourg, 93 min)
d Geoff Murphy. *p* John Flock. *sc* John Flock, Peter Doyle. *ph* Hiro Narita. *ed* James R Symons. *pd* Rod Stratfold. *m* Christopher Franke. *cast* Christopher Lambert, Patrick Malahide, Liz May Brice, Willie Garson, Yuki Okumoto, Fredric Lane, Nick Brimble, David Roberson, Aidan Rea.

●Recaptured by Men-Tel after ten years on the run, 'multiple-breeder' John Brennick (Lambert) is plotting escape from a high tech prison 26,000 miles up in space. But enough complicated analysis. Buckle up, keep up, shut up and buy into this, or you're gonna get lost. Hey you! Need a video recorder to bypass the surveillance apparatus wired to your optic nerve? Just 'stitch one together' from a few bits of wire! Watch out! Meteorite shower! That was close, need a shuttle? No worries! There's one arriving in about 30 seconds! No matter that the villains are as confused by the Men-Tel gibberish blaring out of TV screens as the Brennick-led dopes they're supposed to be guarding. Coherence is hardly the point of a movie in which men in shiny boiler suits go about muttering 'This is some real bullshit.' Anyway, the question isn't who's in charge here, but how any of these headless chickens ever managed to build Skycell in the first place. SS

Fortunat

(1960, Fr/It, 120 min, b/w)
d Alex Joffé. *p* Robert Dorfmann. *sc* Alex Joffé, Pierre Corti. *ph* Pierre Petit. *ed* Eric Pluet. *ad* Henri Schmitt. *m* Denis Kieffer. *cast* Michèle Morgan, Bourvil, Teddy Bilis, Rosy Varte, Gaby Morlay, Jacques Harden, Alan Scott.

●Alex Joffé, who he? Truffaut thought well of him, calling his films 'messages of love and benevolence' and giving him a role in *Shoot the Pianist*. Joffé's handling of his child characters suggests some affinity, but Truffaut never manipulated his audience as crudely as the director of this film. It's the Occupation again, with upper class fugitive Morgan obliged to spend the war pretending to be the wife of boozy layabout Bourvil. He shapes up, she unbends, one thing leads to another. But then peace comes, her real husband returns, and poor old Bourvil sadly hits the road. The tone is so rosy, Joffé might as well have shot it in colour, with a few songs by Michel Legrand. BBa

Fortune, The

(1974, US, 88 min)
d Mike Nichols. *p* Mike Nichols, Don Devlin. *sc* Adrien Joyce [Carole Eastman]. *ph* John A Alonzo. *ed* Stu Linder. *pd* Richard Sylbert. *m* David Shire. *cast* Jack Nicholson, Warren Beatty, Stockard Channing, Florence Stanley, Richard B Shull, Tom Newman, Scatman Crothers, Dub Taylor.

●This starts promisingly as a sardonic comedy about an absurd ménage-à-trois, the mechanics of sex in the '20s, and the men's bewilderment about matters female. Beatty and Nicholson, as the sleazy lounge lizard and halfwit accomplice who conspire to run away with an heiress, send up their own images as though indulging a private joke, but still manage a couple of delirious moments. Their flight west (incognito, but with Nicholson constantly drawing attention to them) throws away its gags shamelessly, but once in California lethargy settles in. The film becomes almost static, a series of stagy, glossy tableaux: such lack of momentum may be an adequate assessment of the characters' limited capacity for development, but it has a disastrous effect on the film's pacing. Events degenerate into miscalculated farce and underline Nichols' continuing slick superficiality. Adrien Joyce's much hacked-about script sounds as though it was once excellent: a pity everyone treats it so off-handedly. CPe

Fortune and Men's Eyes

(1971, Can/US, 102 min)
d Harvey Hart. *p* Lester Persky, Lewis M Allen. *sc* John Herbert. *ph* Georges Dufaux. *ed* Douglas Robertson. *ad* Earl Preston. *m* Galt MacDermot. *cast* Wendell Burton, Michael Greer, Zooey Hall, Danny Freedman, Larry Perkins, James Barron.

●Clumsy adaptation of John Herbert's play (he scripted himself) about homosexual brutalisation in men's prisons. If you believe in a prison that tolerates Michael Greer's flamboyant queen, then you'll probably also believe in Wendell Burton's progress from cute/butch innocence to rapist in the showers. TR

Fortune Cookie, The (aka Meet Whiplash Willie)

(1966, US, 124 min, b/w)
d/p Billy Wilder. *sc* Billy Wilder, IAL Diamond. *ph* Joseph La Shelle. *ed* Daniel Mandell. *ad* Robert Luthardt. *m* André Previn. *cast* Jack Lemmon, Walter Matthau, Ron Rich, Cliff Osmond, Judi West, Lurene Tuttle, Harry Holcombe.

●Wilder's first match of Matthau and Lemmon pushes the idea of role-playing even further than *Some Like It Hot*: TV cameraman Lemmon gets knocked out accidentally during a football game, and his shyster attorney-cum-brother-in-law Matthau gets him to feign partial paralysis in order to claim huge damages. On the surface it's a complete delight, with Matthau's relentlessly funny lines taking most of the honours, but underneath lies a disenchantment as bleak as *The Apartment*: amoral, misogynist characters (in Lemmon's case, literally spineless) racing through ever more futile efforts to outmanoeuvre each other. The friction between the laughs and the cynicism generates more heat than most Hollywood comedies even aim at, including Wilder's later *The Front Page* with the same stars. TR

48 HRS

(1982, US, 97 min)
d Walter Hill. *p* Lawrence Gordon, Joel Silver. *sc* Roger Spottiswoode, Walter Hill, Larry Gross, Steve E De Souza. *ph* Ric Waite. *ed* Freeman Davies, Mark Warner, Billy Weber. *pd* John Vallone. *m* James Horner. *cast* Nick Nolte, Eddie Murphy, Annette O'Toole, Frank McRae, James Remar, David Patrick Kelly.

●Having built a creditable reputation by standing slightly to one side of his action material and looking at it from a different angle, Hill finally comes clean and delivers a down-the-line thriller, plain, fast and efficient. After losing his gun to some low-life, cop Nolte springs a black ex-member of the gang (Murphy) from jail to help him, and has just *48 HRS* in which to recover his piece and wrap up the case. Superfly Murphy proves the perfect foil for the gruff, shambling Nolte; together they shoot it out with what looks suspiciously like the remnants of the street gangs from *The Warriors*, while thankfully sidestepping most of the old buddy-buddy pitfalls. For the first time, Hill gives himself enough time to allow a fair amount of fast-talk dialogue through his usually gritted teeth, and enough space to pay his respects to such sources as Peckinpah and Siegel. It takes an honourable place in a line of San Francisco thrillers from *Point Blank* through *Bullitt* and *Dirty Harry* to *Killer Elite*. CPea

40 Graves for 40 Guns (aka The Great Gundown)

(1971, US, 100 min)
d Paul Hunt. *sc* Ron Garcia, Paul Hunt. *ph* Ron Garcia. *ed* Paul Hunt, Ron Garcia, Mike Bennett. *ad* Rahn Vickery. *m* Jack Preisner. *cast* Robert Padilla, Richard Rust, Malila St Duval, Steven Oliver, David Eastman, Stanley Adams.

●Sombre half-breed robs train, is betrayed by gang, returns to deserted wife, loses her, assembles new bunch of misfits, then bloodily offs old gang. Borrowing heavily from Peckinpah for his themes (conflicting allegiances, the lore of machismo, the letting of blood, etc), Hunt never attains the former's understanding, control or grace, with the result that his film degenerates into a series of random slaughters which lack even sufficient cruelty to be interesting. CPea

Forty Guns

(1957, US, 80 min, b/w)
d/p/sc Samuel Fuller. *ph* Joseph Biroc. *ed* Gene Fowler Jr. *ad* John Mansbridge. *m* Harry Sukman. *cast* Barbara Stanwyck, Barry Sullivan, Dean Jagger, John Ericson, Gene Barry, Robert Dix, Jidge Carroll.

●Possessed of a gun-crazy sting all its own, Fuller's near-legendary B Western still excites dazed amazement and still resists critical shorthand. As an explicitly sexual range-war yarn, you'd automatically dub it a Freudian Western, except that the good doctor's shade could never cope with dreams like Fuller's: vivid, abstract, brutal affairs of naked emotion and violence. So you're left cataloguing the movie's startlingly pleasurable elements – the daring, darting camera style; the keynote performances from Stanwyck as a sensual autocrat and Sullivan as a tired, Earp-like killer; the radical jettisoning of comfortable myth – until you happily concede that essences are irreducible. And this is the essence of American action cinema. Just watch, and be stunned speechless yourself. PT

40 Metre Square Germany (40 Metrekare Almanya)

(1986, WGer, 80 min)
d/p/sc Teufik Baser. *ph* Izzet Akay. *ed* Renate Merck. *pd* Wolf Sesselberg. *m* Claus Bantzer. *cast* Özay Fecht, Yaman Okay, Demir Gökgöl, Mustafa Gülpinar.

●This makes a pair with Baser's *Farewell to False Paradise* (1989). Both are prison films, one literal, the other domestic, and both describe the travails of Turkish women brought to Hamburg by guest-worker husbands. Here a young 'bride', Turna (first seen trying to light an electric stove), is virtually imprisoned in the dingy apartment she shares with a factory worker. 'Why did you lock me in, I'm not an animal!' she screams, which doesn't stop him having sex with her as if she were one. The flashbacks to the 'old country' aren't, however, vaseline-lensed, as they were in *Farewell to False Paradise*: Turna is going to have to make her own way in Germany. WH

49th Parallel

(1941, GB, 124 min, b/w)
d/p Michael Powell. *sc* Emeric Pressburger, Rodney Ackland. *ph* Freddie Young. *ed* David Lean. *ad* David Rawnsley. *m* Ralph Vaughan Williams. *cast* Eric Portman, Anton Walbrook, Leslie Howard, Raymond Massey, Laurence Olivier, Finlay Currie, Niall MacGinnis, Glynis Johns.

●Commissioned by the Ministry of Information in hopes of swaying public opinion in favour of America's entry into the war, this now seems a little dated in patches, with the characterisations all too self-consciously tailored to the propaganda notion of providing a cross-section of ethnic types united in their resistance to Nazism (Leslie Howard's stereotypically laconic Englishman suffers most). But the episodic account of a stranded U-Boat crew's brutal foray into Canada still grips (Emeric Pressburger's script is beautifully structured), and the running debate on democracy versus dictatorship is conducted in terms far from simplistic. What really lifts the film, though, is what David Thomson calls 'a primitive feeling for endangered civilisation': a feeling very much akin to the passionate concern for England's green and pleasant land which flowered in the marvellous *A Canterbury Tale* three years later. TM

42nd Street

(1933, US, 89 min, b/w)
d Lloyd Bacon. *p* Darryl F Zanuck. *sc* James Seymour, Rian James. *ph* Sol Polito. *ed* Thomas Pratt, Frank Ware. *ad* Jack Okey. *songs* Al Dubin, Harry Warren. *cast* Warner Baxter, Ruby Keeler, Bebe Daniels, Dick Powell, Guy Kibbee, George Brent, Ginger Rogers, Una Merkel.

●Reviving the musical's fortunes in one fell swoop, Bacon and Busby Berkeley's backstage saga set the benchmark for the putting-on-a-show subgenre not by means of plot (a thin and hackneyed affair about a young understudy finding stardom when she covers for the temperamental diva) but through sassy songs and dialogue and dazzling *mise-en-scène*. A grand cast makes the most of numbers like 'You're Getting to Be a Habit with Me', 'Shuffle Off to Buffalo' and 'Young and Healthy', while Berkeley choreographs chorines and camera with mischievous dexterity. GA

For Valour

(1937, GB, 94 min, b/w)
d Tom Walls. *p* Max Schach. *sc* Ben Travers. *ph* Philip Tannura. *ed* EB Jarvis. *ad* OF Werndorff. *cast* Tom Walls, Ralph Lynn, Veronica Rose, Joan Marion, Henry Longhurst.

●Aldwych farce from the pen of Ben Travers. Walls is the private who saves his compatriot's life in the Boer War and Lynn the soldier who nominates his rescuer for a VC and unwittingly reveals that he's an escaped con. Later, the plot whips into overdrive with the pair playing their own sons, but it doesn't raise much laughter these days. TJ

For Want of Sun

see Faute de Soleil

For Whom the Bell Tolls

(1943, US, 168 min)
d/p Sam Wood. *sc* Dudley Nichols. *ph* Ray Rennahan. *ed* Sherman Todd, John F Link. *ad* Hans Dreier, Haldane Douglas. *m* Victor Young. *cast* Gary Cooper, Ingrid Bergman, Akim Tamiroff, Katina Paxinou, Joseph Calleia, Arturo de Cordova, Vladimir Sokoloff, Mikhail Rasumny, Fortunio Bonanova.

●One of Paramount's prestige pictures in 1943, when Katina Paxinou won an Oscar for best supporting actress, and the film picked up nominations in virtually every major category – but not in writing and in direction, and that's the *tell*. As an American fighting with the partisans in the Spanish Civil War, Cooper makes a perfect Hemingway hero, robust and romantic in equal measures. Falling in love with Ingrid Bergman's peasant guerilla makes a lot of sense too, but the film's a mess dramatically. Wood approaches the material with kid gloves, when Hemingway was always a bare-knuckle fighter. Most later prints were tightened dramatically by being reduced to 130 minutes. TCh

For Your Eyes Only

(1981, GB, 127 min)
d John Glen. *p* Albert R Broccoli. *sc* Richard Maibaum, Michael Wilson. *ph* Alan Hume. *ed* John Grover. *pd* Peter Lamont. *m* Bill Conti, Michael Leeson. *cast* Roger Moore, Carole Bouquet, Chaim Topol, Lynn-Holly Johnson, Julian Glover, Cassandra Harris, Jill Bennett, Michael Gothard, Lois Maxwell, Desmond Llwelyn.

●An inflation-fighter Bond dumps the giant sets and mechanical gizmos of recent years in favour of stunts galore, courtesy of John Glen, who was second unit director on earlier 007s. Worth a try, but without his Art Dept clothes on, Bond is like the naked Emperor. Look, Ma, no plot and poor dialogue, and Moore really is old enough to be the uncle of those girls. MB

Foul King, The (Ban-Chik Wang)

(1999, SKor, 112 min)
d Kim Jee-Woon. *p* Oh Jung-Wan, Lee Mi-Yeon. *sc* Kim Jee-Woon. *ph* Alex Hong. *ed* Ko Im-Pyo. *pd* Hwang In-Jun. *m* Chang Young-Kyu, Uh-Uh-Boo Band. *cast* Song Kang-Ho, Chang Jin-Young, Park Sang-Myun, Jung Woong-In, Kim Ka-Yeon.

●Always late for work at the bank and routinely humiliated by his tyrannical manager, Daeho (Song) is physically large, clumsy, none too smart and deeply insecure. Thanks to a chain of accidents, he finds himself spending his free time training to become a masked villain in the wrestling ring under the name The Foul King; he naively expects his increasingly successful alter ego to give his everyday life a boost, but… The best thing about Kim's accomplished and funny movie (a huge hit in Korea) is its ability throughout to see humour through melancholy and vice versa – sometimes within single shots. It helps that everything from the slapstick gags to the comedy of embarrassment is rooted in a kind of realism, and that Song gives a quite phenomenal performance in the lead. TR

Foul Play

(1978, US, 116 min)
d Colin Higgins. *p* Thomas L Miller, Edward K Milkis. *sc* Colin Higgins. *ph* David M Walsh. *ed* Pembroke J Herring. *pd* Alfred Sweeney. *m* Charles Fox. *cast* Goldie Hawn, Chevy Chase, Burgess Meredith, Rachel Roberts, Eugene Roche, Dudley Moore, Brian Dennehy, Marc Lawrence.

●A big budget, San Francisco-set comedy thriller, with Goldie Hawn playing self-contained kook Gloria Mundy. A significant name, since the deliberately ridiculous plot involves an attempt to murder the pontiff. (Or is it because Hawn's a little too well-worn in this kind of role, sic transit Gloria Mundy?) Unsatisfactory as a whole, the film is hilarious and tense in bits. For while writer/director Higgins uses almost every stock thriller device – sinister dwarf, albino, scarfaced man, moving shower curtain, disappearing corpses, a chase, an escape or two, even the identical twin wheeze – he approaches this semi-parody with more zest and originality than is common, and careers from farce to thrills before you can say 'Spot the hommage'. JS

Fountain, The (Fontan)

(1988, USSR, 101 min)
d Yuri Mamin. *sc* Vladimir Vardounas. *ph* Anatoli Lapshow. *ed* O Adrianova. *ad* Yuri Pugach. *m* Aleksei Zalivalov. *cast* Asankul Kuttubaev, Sergei Dontsov, Zhanna Kerimtaeva, Viktor Mikhailov, Anatoli Kalmikov.

●Mamin's film is already a historical record of a certain phase of *perestroika*. But as an extremely broad social comedy, as well as a swingeing critique of personal and bureaucratic (ir)responsibility, it's little short of irresistible. Kazakhstan herdsman Kerbabaev moves to Moscow to live with his daughter and her husband Peter, the harassed maintenance official of a rancid, crumbling apartment block beset by constant disasters. With its catalogue of accumulating mishaps, *The Fountain* fires off its barbs in ample salvos, some of them perhaps too obviously allegorical of Russia's woes. But as an adeptly choreographed ensemble piece, and for its fairly pullulating sense of place, the film gushes with anarchic pleasures. JRo

Fountainhead, The

(1949, US, 114 min, b/w)
d King Vidor. *p* Henry Blanke. *sc* Ayn Rand. *ph* Robert Burks. *ed* David Weisbart. *ad* Edward Carrere. *m* Max Steiner. *cast* Gary Cooper, Patricia Neal, Raymond Massey, Kent Smith, Robert Douglas, Henry Hull, Ray Collins.

●The most bizarre movie in both Vidor's and Cooper's filmographies, this adaptation of Ayn Rand's first novel mutes Ms Rand's neo-Nietzschean philosophy of 'Objectivism' but lays on the expressionist symbolism with a 'free enterprise' trowel. Cooper plays the up-and-coming architect with unorthodox ideas who dynamites a building that doesn't conform with his plans, marries wealthy heiress Neal, and winds up building the world's tallest tombstone as a memorial to a friend who committed suicide. As berserk as it sounds, although handsomely shot by Robert Burks and directed with enthusiasm. TR

4 Adventures of Reinette & Mirabelle (4 Aventures de Reinette & Mirabelle)

(1986, Fr, 99 min)
d/p/sc Eric Rohmer. *ph* Sophie Maintigneux. *ed* Maria-Luisa Garcia. *m* Ronan Girre, Jean-Louis Valero. *cast* Joëlle Miquel, Jessica Forde, Philippe Laudenbach, Yasmine Haury, Marie Rivière, Fabrice Luchini.

●In Rohmer's slight but delightful low-key account of the up-and-down friendship between two teenage girls, the naturalistic performances are, as ever, supremely credible, with unknowns Miquel and Forde stealing the honours as the eponymous heroines. Reinette is a charming if changeable country girl longing to become a successful painter, Mirabelle the Parisian student who offers to share her flat in town. The four largely un-dramatic adventures, first in the remote countryside, then in Paris, concentrate on their different reactions to the world: nature, social injustice, money, and in the wonderful final sequence, the familiar Rohmeresque problem of too much talk. It's all inescapably French (in the best sense) and concerned with the joys not only of good conversation but of seeing. Finally, for all its deliciously light humour and anecdotal quality, the film is essentially about people. Which other film-maker loves us, warts and all, so perceptively or so generously? Therein lies Rohmer's abiding genius. GA

Four Against Fate

see Derby Day

Four Bags Full

see Traversée de Paris, La

Four Days in July

(1985, GB, 95 min)
d Mike Leigh. *p* Kenith Trodd. *sc* Mike Leigh. *ph* Remi Adefarasin. *ed* Robin Sales. *ad* Jim Clay. *m* Rachel Portman. *cast* Des McAleer, Stephen Rea, Shane Connaughton, Brid Brennan, Charles Lawson, BJ Hogg.

●Commissioned by producer Kenith Trodd and shown by the BBC in 1985, this is deviser/director Leigh's Northern Ireland film. This is alien territory for Leigh, who had some difficulty getting used to the grubby terrain of working-class Belfast and hanging a storyline on characters taken from both sides of the sectarian divide. Another departure for the now internationally established director is that the film has none of those people whom Leigh just can't portray properly: the English middle or upper classes. The result is a low-key but intriguing film which depicts the relations and friends of two families, Catholic and Protestant, linked by the arrival of babies in the month of the Orange marches. There are no shoot-outs or killings, even if the impact of the Troubles is exemplified by the crippled Eugene (McAleer, superb and understated) and ex-internees Brendan and Dixie, who swap yarns about using the prison lavatory system to distil poteen. Although strongly cast, the film has its longueurs (plus a Catholic bias), but it's sometimes very funny and tinged with sadness, even tragedy, throughout. A miserable man in hospital whose wife is expecting their first child asks: 'Three hours she's been in there. What does she think she's playing at?' SGr

Four Days in September (O Que é Isso, Companheiro?)

(1997, Braz, 105 min)
d Bruno Barreto. *p* Lucy Barreto. *sc* Leopoldo Serran. *ph* Felix Monti. *ed* Isabelle Rathéry. *pd* Marcos Flaksman. *m* Stewart Copeland. *cast* Alan Arkin, Pedro Cardoso, Fernanda Torres, Luiz Fernando Guimaraes, Claudi Abreu, Nelson Dantas.

●1969: a little known revolutionary group kidnaps US ambassador Charles Burke Elbrick in order to spotlight Brazil's military dictatorship. The kidnappers demand the release of political prisoners and, more importantly, air time. The authorities track them down – but dare they endanger the ambassador? The film (from a book by Fernando Gabeira, a journalist who'd participated in the abduction) is somewhat reminiscent of Costa-Gavras, but without the ideological programme. Indeed, Bruno Barreto goes out of his way both to round out the ambassador (Arkin, excellent as usual), and to humanise one of the official torturers. Nor are the radicals romanticised: they're young, naive, and in over their heads. A tense, absorbing, character piece – and a clear, balanced, historical study. TCh

Four Days of Snow and Blood (226)

(1989, Jap, 114 min)
d Hideo Gosha. *p* Yoshinobu Nishioka. *sc* Kazuo Kasahara. *ph* Fujio Morita. *ed* Isamu Ichida. *ad* Yoshinobu Nishioka. *m* Akira Senju. *cast* Kenichi Hagiwara, Tomokazu Miura, Masahiro Motoki, Naoto Takenaka, Daisuke Ryu, Kaho Minami.

●Based on Kazuo Kasahara's book *226*, Gosha's turgid and hopelessly undramatic movie reconstructs the failed military coup of 26 February 1936, when a group of emperor-worshipping army officers tried to overthrow the civilian government. Dozens of earlier Japanese movies have dealt with these events, but few have been so wrong-footed: Gosha devotes most of two hours to the political and ethical debates that followed the assassinations, pausing only to weep along with the officers' long-suffering wives. A wretched dog of a movie. TR

4 Faces of Eve (4 [Si] Mian Xiawa)

(1996, HK, 91 min)
d Jan Lamb, Eric Kot, Kam Kwok-Leung. *cast* Sandra Ng, Eric Kot, Jan Lamb, Karen Mok, Wyman Wong.

●Four-episode vehicle for comedienne Sandra Ng, designed both to show off her versatility and to give some of the orthodoxies of Hong Kong film production a kick in the arse. Sadly, despite Ng's obvious talent, most of it is neither fresh nor funny. The second episode, played in a guttural invented language, is almost unwatchable (she's a Mainland Chinese wife ministering to her husband's every cruel need) and the final episode, in which she's a housewife winning prizes on a TV game show for exposing the full misery of her marriage, pales beside such realities as *The Jerry Springer Show*. But the first and third episodes have their moments, and Chris Doyle's anarchic cinematography is, to say the least, unpredictable. TR

Four Faces West

see They Passed This Way

Four Feathers, The

(1939, GB, 130 min)
d Zoltan Korda. *p* Alexander Korda. *sc* RC Sherriff, Lajos Biro, Arthur Wimperis. *ph* Georges Périnal, Osmond Borradaile, Jack Cardiff. *ed* William Hornbeck, Henry Cornelius. *ad* Vincent Korda. *m* Miklós Rozsa. *cast* John Clements, June Duprez, Ralph Richardson, C Aubrey Smith, Allan Jeayes, Jack Allen, Donald Gray.

●Classic British imperialist adventure, about a man accused of cowardice and redeeming himself through lofty heroics during the Sudan campaign of the 1890s. Produced by Alexander Korda, and directed by his brother Zoltan with flair and imagination, it's a typically polished vehicle for saluting a certain British mythology, with a rousing score by Miklos Rosza, superb Technicolor camerawork by a crew that included Périnal and Jack Cardiff, and solid performances all round. The fourth (and best) version of AEW Mason's ripping yarn, previously filmed in 1915, 1921 and 1929. GA

Four Feathers, The

(1978, GB, 105 min)
d Don Sharp. *p* Norman Rosemont. *sc* Gerald DiPego. *ph* John Coquillon. *ed* Eric Boyd-Perkins, Bill Blunden. *ad* Herbert Westbrook. *m* Allyn Ferguson. *cast* Beau Bridges, Robert Powell, Simon Ward, Jane Seymour, Harry Andrews, Richard Johnson.

●Redundant sixth version of the Mason yarn aimed squarely at the US TV audience who lapped it up shortly after its royal premiere here, complete with episodic structure (climaxes before commercials) and insistence on close-ups. Hardly worth a giggle, even over Bridges' 'English' accent, Ward's *Monty Python* beard, or Johnson in blackface. Harry Andrews gets to articulate the Boy's Own ethos: 'I doubt if a woman could understand'. PT

Four Flies on Grey Velvet (Quattro Mosche di Velluto Grigio)

(1971, It/Fr, 105 min)
d Dario Argento. *p* Salvatore Argento. *sc* Dario Argento. *ph* Franco Di Giacomo. *ed* Franco Fraticelli. *ad* Enrico Sabbatini. *m* Ennio Morricone. *cast* Michael Brandon, Mimsy Farmer, Jean-Pierre Marielle, Francine Racette, Calisto Calisti.

●Rock drummer Brandon finds himself at the centre of a blackmail murder mystery in Rome. The script remains a distinct handicap, but Argento's handling of set pieces (mainly a series of elaborate murders) shows flair. A pity that he doesn't spend more time concentrating on heightening the atmosphere of hysteria and menace. DP

Four Friends (aka Georgia's Friends)

(1981, US, 115 min)
d Arthur Penn. *p* Arthur Penn, Gene Lasko. *sc* Steve Tesich. *ph* Ghislain Cloquet. *ed* Barry Malkin, Marc Laub. *pd* David Chapman. *m* Elizabeth Swados. *cast* Craig Wasson, Jodi Thelen, Michael Huddleston, Jim Metzler, Reed Birney, Julia Murray, James Leo Herlihy.

●To some extent drawing on the experiences of its scriptwriter Steve Tesich, this traces key moments in the life of Yugoslav immigrant Danny (Wasson), from his arrival in the States as a boy to the time when, thirty years later, his parents return to the old country. Although its episodic narrative entails a certain lack of unity, it's nevertheless an ambitious and impressive work that deals intelligently with a number of themes: the way time and distance play havoc with relationships, particularly with Danny's beloved Georgia, a lively, infuriating and generous girl whom he shyly rejects with saddening results; the way personal lives often rhyme with wider history; and most of all, the difficulties romantic Danny faces in trying to come to terms with the many contradictions and polarities – poverty and wealth, rural simplicity and urban sophistication – inherent in his adopted homeland. A dense but never pretentious film that manages to convey the atmosphere of the '50s and '60s succinctly, it offers delights galore, not least a light, perceptive wit and an unsentimental ability to touch the emotions. GA

400 Blows, The

see Quatre Cents Coups, Les

Four Just Men, The

(1939, GB, 85 min, b/w)
d Walter Forde. *p* Michael Balcon. *sc* Sergei Nolbandov, Angus MacPhail, Ronald Pertwee. *ph* Ronald Neame. *ed* Charles Saunders. *ad* Wilfrid Shingleton. *m* Ernest Irving. *cast* Hugh Sinclair, Griffith Jones, Francis L Sullivan, Frank Lawton, Anna Lee, Basil Sydney.

●Edgar Wallace's vigilante quartet save the Empire from foreign agents plotting to block the Suez Canal. Ludicrously jingoistic (even remembering 1956), and further blemished by a bland romance between an intrepid girl reporter (Lee) and the most handsomely boyish of the four (Jones). But still quite fun thanks to Forde's Hitchcockian flair for everyday menace (murder by poisoned suitcase at Victoria Station, by electrocution in a bathroom, by empty lift-shaft). TM

4 Little Girls

(1997, US, 102 min, b/w & col)
d Spike Lee. *p* Spike Lee, Sam Pollard. *ph* Ellen Kuras. *ed* Sam Pollard. *m* Terence Blanchard. *with* Bill Cosby, Walter Cronkite, Ossie Davis, Jesse Jackson, George Wallace.

●The dynamiting in September 1963 of a Baptist church in Birmingham, Alabama was a specially horrible addition to the litany of racist horrors of the time, since it took place during Sunday school and the victims were children. The big part of Lee's film commemorates the lives of the '4 little girls' who died, through the memories of parents, siblings and friends. A number of public figures, including a gaga George Wallace, recall the wider civil rights struggle. A final section describes the conviction, years later, of one of the killers, a merry-looking mannikin, clearly out of his mind. Lee's tough decision to include photos of the victims' smashed-up bodies was probably correct, but adding 'soulful' music to some of the interviews was more questionable. BBa

Four Men and a Prayer

(1938, US, 85 min, b/w)
d John Ford. *p* Kenneth MacGowan. *sc* Richard Sherman, Sonya Levien, Walter Ferris. *ph* Ernest Palmer. *ed* Louis R Loeffler. *ad* Bernard Herzbrun, Rudolph Sternad. *m* Ernst Toch. *cast* Loretta Young, Richard Greene, George Sanders, David Niven, Sir C Aubrey Smith, J Edward Bromberg, William Henry, Alan Hale, John Carradine, Reginald Denny, Barry Fitzgerald, Berton Churchill.

●A ripping yarn in which Colonel Sir C Aubrey Smith is cashiered on the Northwest Frontier for conduct unbecoming that resulted in a massacre. His four sons (Sanders, Greene, Niven and Henry) rally round in London, and have time to learn that the old boy was framed by a munitions syndicate before he is murdered. Determined to clear the family name, the sons disperse to India, South America and Egypt. Once the preliminaries are over, their adventures are more enjoyable than they have any right to be, given that Ford directs with pace, wit, and tongue firmly in cheek. Clichés are exaggerated to the point of absurdity; Niven is given a good deal of subversively funny business as the flightiest brother; and pomposities (like the royal vindication at the end) are deflated by the malice with which they are staged. Loretta Young is particularly cleverly used: a wealthy socialite in love with Greene, she keeps popping up wherever the action is, downgrading it into a romantic comedy, and making the point that heroics solve nothing (her father is the armaments king the sons unmask, but he *isn't* the villain). TM

Four Musketeers: The Revenge of Milady, The

(1974, Pan/Sp, 106 min)
d Richard Lester. *p* Alexander Salkind, Michael Salkind. *sc* George MacDonald Fraser. *ph* David Watkin. *ed* John Victor Smith. *pd* Brian Eatwell, Fernando Gonzalez. *m* Lalo Schifrin. *cast* Oliver Reed, Raquel Welch, Richard Chamberlain, Michael York, Frank Finlay, Simon Ward, Christopher Lee, Faye Dunaway, Charlton Heston, Geraldine Chaplin, Jean-Pierre Cassel.

●The second half of Lester's brilliant *The Three Musketeers* is a reasonably beguiling, if noticeably padded coda, with the best bits containing in abundance that quality of penetrating period wit which made its predecessor such a delight. The tone is darker and more oppressive; there are sequences that lapse into boredom; but the scenes involving Dunaway – whether she's lobbing poisoned darts at her lovers or busily seducing her English warder – have a lushly ironic fairytale quality that the movies capture all too rarely. DP

Four Nights of a Dreamer (Quatre Nuits d'un Rêveur)

(1971, Fr/It, 82 min)
d/sc Robert Bresson. *ph* Pierre Lhomme. *ed* Raymond Lamy, Geneviève Billo. *ad* Pierre Charbonnier, Arakel Araquelian. *m* Michel Magne, Groupe Batuki, Christopher Hayward, Louis Guitar, FR David. *cast* Isabelle Weingarten, Guillaume des Forêts, Jean-Maurice Monnoyer, Jérôme Massart, Patrick Jouanné, Lidia Biondi.

●Adapted from Dostoevsky's story of a couple's chance encounter and the advance of their parallel obsessions over four successive nights. The hallucinatory light and colour of Paris at night act as both mirror and landscape for their fragile relationship. Shot through with a mystical, almost frosty compassion, the film is rescued from occasional moments of pretension by the gentle eroticism and absolute conviction with which it is made. The Dostoevsky story, *White Nights*, was filmed under that title by Luchino Visconti in 1957. CA

Four Rooms

(1995, US, 97 min)
d Allison Anders, Alexandre Rockwell, Robert Rodriguez, Quentin Tarantino. *p* Lawrence Bender. *sc* Allison Anders, Alexandre Rockwell, Robert Rodriguez, Quentin Tarantino. *ph* Rodrigo Garcia, Phil Parmet, Guillermo Navarro, Andrzej Sekula. *ed* Margaret Goodspeed, Elena Maganini, Robert Rodriguez, Sally Menke. *pd* Gary Frutkof. *m* Combustible Edison. *cast* Tim Roth, Marisa Tomei, Sammi Davis, Valeria Golino, Madonna, Jennifer Beals, David Proval, Antonio Banderas, Lana McKissack, Quentin Tarantino.

●It's New Year's Eve in a Hollywood hotel; Ted the bellboy (Roth) is on his own. In Anders' episode, a witches' coven is after his semen; in Rockwell's he stumbles into a SM marital nightmare; Rodriguez has him looking after two mischievous children; and Tarantino reruns an 'Alfred Hitchcock Presents...' yarn involving a machete, a drunken wager, and a pinkie. Ted is the lynchpin, but Roth's is a gibbering, fidgeting, nervous breakdown of a performance. Only Rodriguez paces and shapes the material; his virtuoso story has the authentic black comic lunacy of a Tom and Jerry cartoon brought to life. And Tarantino? Unwisely holding court as a Hollywood star, he offers further proof of his own acting limitations, with dialogue so patently Tarantino-esque it might be intentional self-parody. Most worryingly, his self-conscious, meandering takes raise doubts about his hitherto infallible cinematic intuition. They should have called this 'One Room' and released it as a Rodriguez short. TCh

Four Seasons, The

(1981, US, 108 min)
d Alan Alda. *p* Martin Bregman. *sc* Alan Alda. *ph* Victor J Kemper. *ed* Michael Economou. *pd* Jack T Collis. *m* Antonio Vivaldi. *cast* Alan Alda, Carol Burnett, Len Cariou, Sandy Dennis, Rita Moreno, Jack Weston, Bess Armstrong.

●The dialogue written by Alda for his directorial debut has the cut and thrust, but not the edge, of his script for *The Seduction of Joe Tynan*. Three married couples, friends of long standing, have their complacency challenged when one of their number replaces his wife with a younger woman. The camerawork is unadventurous (the only variation on static observation of the characters being the nature footage signalling the seasonal changes), but the performances Alda elicits from his co-actors almost justifies this. Within the characterisations, most of the fears and foibles of middle class, middle-aged America may be found. Amusing and worth a look. FD

Four Seasons of the Law, The (I Earini Synaxis ton Agrofylakon)

(1999, Greece, 177 min)
d/p/sc Demos Avdeliodis. *ph* ('Summer') Odysseas Pavlopoulos, ('Autumn') Alekos Giannaros, ('Winter') Linos Meitanos, ('Spring') Sotiris Perreas. *ed* Kostas Iordanidis. *ad* Nikos Hatzis. *m* Vivaldi. *cast* Angeliki Malamati, Panayotis Louros, Ilias Petropouleas, Markellos Poupalos; ('Summer') Takis Agoris, ('Autumn') Yannis Tsoubariotis, ('Winter') Stelios Makrias, ('Spring') Angelos Pantelaras.

●This droll leisurely parable shows how realist cinema and mythological storytelling can produce intriguing art when combined with the director's restraint and gnomic professionalism. Set on the island of Chios in 1960, the tale is simple and cyclic: four 'Field Guards' are employed in a village, in the island's south, that has a fearsome reputation for awkwardness, superstitiousness and pagan magic. At once a celebration of the idiosyncracy of pre-industrial community, a paean to nature (ramified by the judicious musical accompaniment of Vivaldi's 'Four Seasons') and a deadpan comedy, this unclassifiable film is a compulsive, surprising and slowly rewarding delight. WH

Four Sons

(1940, US, 89 min, b/w)
d Archie Mayo. *p* Darryl F Zanuck. *sc* John Howard Lawson, Milton Sperling. *ph* Leon Shamroy. *ed* Francis D Lyon. *ad* Richard Day, Albert Hogsett. *m* David Buttolph. *cast* Don Ameche, Eugenie Leontovich, Mary Beth Hughes, Alan Curtis, George Ernest, Robert Lowery.

●Solid propaganda effort demonstrating the effects of the German invasion of Czechoslovakia on an ordinary family, with Ameche standing firm to fight the good fight and brother Curtis embracing the Nazi cause. Schematic but not ineffective melodrama responding to the crisis in Europe. A remake of a 1928 John Ford silent about a German family surviving the horrors of WWI. TJ

Fourteen Hours

(1951, US, 92 min, b/w)
d Henry Hathaway. *p* Sol C Siegel. *sc* John Paxton. *ph* Joseph MacDonald. *ed* Dorothy Spencer. *ad* Lyle Wheeler, Leland Fuller. *m* Alfred Newman. *cast* Richard Basehart, Paul Douglas, Barbara Bel Geddes, Debra Paget, Agnes Moorehead, Robert Keith, Howard da Silva, Jeffrey Hunter, Grace Kelly, Jeff Corey.

●Back in 1938, John Warde perched on a ledge 17 floors up a skyscraper, and, for 14 hours, threatened to jump. This vertiginous melodrama recounts the event in professional low-key journalistic fashion. As in *Ace in the Hole*, the emphasis is as much on the reaction of bystanders as on the plight of the would-be suicide. Cab-drivers take bets, while cops and psychiatrists try to talk him down. Grace Kelly, in her debut, appears among the onlookers. GM

1492: Conquest of Paradise

(1992, US, 155 min)
d Ridley Scott. *p* Ridley Scott, Alain Goldman. *sc* Roselyne Bosch. *ph* Adrian Biddle. *ed* William Anderson, Françoise Bonnot. *pd* Norris Spencer. *m* Vangelis. *cast* Gérard Depardieu, Armand Assante, Sigourney Weaver, Loren Dean, Angela Molina, Fernando Rey, Michael Wincott, Tchéky Karyo, Kevin Dunn, Frank Langella, Mark Margolis.

●Christopher Columbus: hero, or villain paving the way for genocide? Scott straddles the quincentenary controversy, painting him as a rebellious sort who finds reality at variance with his dreams. The film covers 20 years, from his early efforts to raise backing to his ensuing triumphs and, ultimately, the disillusionment of seeing Eden turning into Hell. It was a shrewd move to cast Depardieu in the role: few actors could so skilfully reconcile the necessary qualities of enthusiasm, vulnerability and arrogance. As Queen Isabel, Weaver proves a good foil, while spectacular visuals convey the brutality and grandeur of the age. But in attempting to explore the man, Roselyne Bosch's script also embraces the myth, most obviously in some initial exchanges laden with significance. Vangelis' thunderous, intrusive score doesn't help; even more tedious is foppish villain Wincott, fashion victim and confirmed sadist.

Fourth Man, The (De Vierde Man)

(1983, Neth, 102 min)
d Paul Verhoeven. *p* Rob Houwer. *sc* Gerard Soeteman. *ph* Jan De Bont. *ed* Ine Schenkkan. *ad* Roland de Groot. *m* Loek Dikker. *cast* Jeroen Krabbé, Renée Soutendijk, Thom Hoffman, Dolf De Vries, Geert De Jong, Hans Veerman.

● Verhoeven's last Dutch movie is a deliciously overripe male melodrama based on a novel by Gerard Reve and packed with ostentatious, tongue-in-cheek symbolism. Krabbé is entirely persuasive as a feverish, manic-depressive Catholic homosexual novelist (!) who beds a female fan though it's her fella he really fancies (in one sexy sacrilegious fantasy he imagines him crucified). Christine, proprietress of the Sphinx beauty parlour, washes his hair with Delilah shampoo, and it may be that she's dangerous – her track record with men leaves a lot to be desired. A hot, florid, outrageously funny film that nevertheless plays at a dreamy, trance-like pace, this earned Verhoeven his best ever notices – an anomaly he attributes to its slow, arty camera moves. TCh

Fourth Protocol, The

(1987, GB, 119 min)
d John MacKenzie. *p* Timothy Burrill. *sc* Frederick Forsyth, George Axelrod. *ph* Philip Meheux. *ed* Graham Walker. *pd* Allan Cameron. *m* Lalo Schifrin. *cast* Michael Caine, Pierce Brosnan, Ned Beatty, Joanna Cassidy, Julian Glover, Michael Gough, Ray McAnally, Ian Richardson.

● This adaptation of Frederick Forsyth's espionage thriller is neither fish nor fowl. Brosnan, who plays the ice-cool and ruthless Soviet undercover agent sent to an East Anglian American airbase to execute a 'devastating' plan to destabilise Anglo-American nuclear cooperation, poses and pouts so much that there are hopes of the film developing into a Bond-like spoof. No such luck. Still, Caine – a kind of middle-aged Harry Palmer – is at his shambling best as the no-nonsense spycatcher overcoming the deviousness or incompetence of his Intelligence bosses; and MacKenzie gives this home-grown blockbuster the requisite glossy, if predictable finish. What is missing is any real tension or psychological detail that might lend plausibility to all the hocus-pocus about East-West political and military intrigue. WH

Fourth War, The

(1990, US, 90 min)
d John Frankenheimer. *p* Wolf Schmidt. *sc* Stephen Peters, Kenneth Ross. *ph* Gerry Fisher. *ed* Robert F Shugrue. *pd* Alan Manzer. *m* Bill Conti. *cast* Roy Scheider, Harry Dean Stanton, Jürgen Prochnow, Tim Reid, Lara Harris, Dale Dye.

● When asked what kind of weapons would be used in the third world war, Einstein replied that he didn't know, but that the fourth war would be fought with stones. Nothing in this rather old-fashioned thriller has the bite of this remark. Scheider plays the clichéd military hardass, a veteran of Vietnam, divorced, disenchanted. 'A warrior', says his old comrade General Harry Dean Stanton, who intuitively installs him as a base commander on the German-Czech border. Soon Scheider is mounting one-man nocturnal sorties behind the Iron Curtain, partying with Soviet patrols and incurring the wrath of his Russian counterpart (Prochnow). The latter is Scheider's kind of guy; he was in Afghanistan. As Stanton puts it, in a rare animated moment, these are two 'disillusioned, pissed-off malcontents', and when the inevitable macho stand-off develops, it's to hell with the consequences. *The Fourth War* may have been conceived as the thinking person's *Rambo*, but in the event it isn't a patch on *First Blood*; for a simple story, it's quite a mess, the very dubious voice-over hardly clarifying a clumsy sense of chronology. With the twists in the intrigue all too blatant, the climactic fight is a relief when it comes. TCh

Four Times That Night

see Quante Volte…Quella Notte

Four Ways Out

see Città si Difende, La

Four Weddings and a Funeral (100)

(1993, GB, 117 min)
d Mike Newell. *p* Duncan Kenworthy. *sc* Richard Curtis. *ph* Michael Coulter. *ed* Jon Gregory. *pd* Maggie Grey. *m* Richard Rodney Bennett. *cast* Hugh Grant, Andie MacDowell, Kristin Scott Thomas, James Fleet, Simon Callow, John Hannah, David Bower, Corin Redgrave, Rowan Atkinson, Charlotte Coleman.

● A British comedy that's classy and commercial – and, most important, very, very funny. Admittedly, as it charts the social, sexual and romantic fortunes of thirty-something Charles (Grant), a self-confessed serial monogamist, and the friends, old flames and potential lovers (notably MacDowell's rather enigmatic American beauty), who are his fellow guests at one wedding after another, the film's focus on well-heeled jovial oafs and its conventional attitude to modern relationships hardly make for 'radical romantic comedy'. But that's quibbling. Newell's direction switches smoothly between affecting intimacy and sequences of rowdy chaos; perhaps the film's trump card, however, is its emotional honesty, particularly in the poignant and sobering funeral scene. Genuine feel-good entertainment. GA

Fox

see Faustrecht der Freiheit

Fox, The

(1967, US, 110 min)
d Mark Rydell. *p* Raymond Stross. *sc* Lewis John Carlino, Howard Koch. *ph* William A Fraker. *ed* Thomas Stanford. *ad* Charles Bailey. *m* Lalo Schifrin. *cast* Sandy Dennis, Anne Heywood, Keir Dullea, Glen Morris.

● Overdone adaptation of DH Lawrence's novella, making explicit everything that was implicit in his study of two women living together on an isolated poultry farm (menaced by a marauding fox), and the opposition of one to the marriage of the other. Dullea and Dennis, two of the worst overactors in the business, don't help any; but most of the blame must go to Rydell for his heavily emphatic direction. CPe

Fox and His Friends

see Faustrecht der Freiheit

Fox and the Hound, The

(1981, US, 83 min)
d Art Stevens, Ted Berman, Richard Rich. *p* Wolfgang Reitherman, Art Stevens. *sc* Larry Clemmons, Peter Young, Steve Hulett, Dave Michener, Burny Mattinson, Earl Kress, Vance Gerry. *ed* James Melton, Jim Kofrod. *ad* Don Griffith. *m* Buddy Baker. *cast* voices: Mickey Rooney, Kurt Russell, Pearl Bailey, Jack Albertson, Jeanette Nolan, Sandy Duncan.

● One of the more homely Disney animated features, neither hip like *The Jungle Book* nor (pardon the expression) trippy like *Fantasia*. We're back in that serene Disney woodland where bright flowers dot heavily shaded glades and snow plops off branches like ice-cream. Here female creatures bat long eyelashes and kindly old Widow Tweed lives in a cosy cabin. She domesticates Tod, an orphaned fox cub who plays happily with a puppy hound until they grow up (and Tod acquires Mickey Rooney's voice). 'Two friends who didn't know they were supposed to be enemies', runs the catch-line. But the moral aimed at the children is a very conservative one: duty to your kind must come before personal friendship, that's nature's way. JS

Foxes

(1979, US, 105 min)
d Adrian Lyne. *p* David Puttnam, Gerald Ayres. *sc* Gerald Ayres. *ph* Leon Bijou. *ed* James Coblentz. *ad* Michel Levesque. *m* Giorgio Moroder. *cast* Jodie Foster, Cherie Currie, Marilyn Kagan, Kandice Stroh, Scott Baio, Sally Kellerman, Randy Quaid, Adam Faith.

● Almost like an inverted *Saturday Night Fever*, *Foxes* follows four LA teenage girls who seduce, humiliate, adore and befriend various men, but whose primary loyalties are always to each other. The first half, unfortunately, is poor: the producers (Casablanca Record) have lumbered it with undigested lumps from the company rock catalogue; there is some pretty variable comedy, dreary travelogue footage, and a very ugly use of filters and soft focus. But gradually a much more interesting film takes over. The tone becomes darker and more moralistic, concentrating on the relationship between Foster (looking uncannily old) and her impossible, dope-happy friend (a fine performance from ex-Runaway Cherie Currie), both contemplating with real hurt the certainty of separation. The ending takes this feeling to its logical conclusion, and works a hell of a lot better as post-'60s tragedy than *The Rose*. DP

Fox Fire

see Feu Follet, Le

Foxy Brown

(1974, US, 91 min)
d Jack Hill. *p* Buzz Feitshans. *sc* Jack Hill. *ph* Brick Marquand. *ed* Chuck McClelland. *ad* Kirk Axtell. *m* Willie Hutch. *cast* Pam Grier, Antonio Fargas, Kathryn Loder, Peter Brown, Terry Carter, Sid Haig.

● Grier's follow-up to *Coffy*, also scripted and directed by Hill, lacks all the fine, subversive qualities she lent that film. She continues the avenger role, but in much diluted form, simply exacting retribution for the murder of her narcotics officer boyfriend (gone is *Coffy*'s environment of all-pervasive and over-weening corruption); and in any case this is subsumed in a general racial tone, with every white within spitting distance made a bigot, for the sole purpose of milking audience reactions in the most blatant way possible. Grier is an actress able to convey an amazing and unflinching strength, and she reveals the film for the dross it is. VG

F.P.1 antwortet nicht

see No Answer from F.P.1

Fracture du myocarde, La (Cross My Heart)

(1990, Fr, 105 min)
d Jacques Fansten. *p* Ludi Boeken, Jacques Fansten. *sc* Jacques Fansten. *ph* Jean-Claude Saillier. *ed* Colette Farruggia. *pd* Gilbert Gagneux. *m* Jean-Marie Sénia. *cast* Sylvain Copans, Nicolas Parodi, Cécilia Rouaud, Delphine Gouttman, Olivier Montiège, Lucie Blossier.

● Snapped up by Hollywood for a remake by Spielberg, this is the best story about kids since *Stand by Me*. 12-year-old Martin (Copans), terrified that he will be sent to an orphanage, conceals the fact that his mother has died. His classmates band together to keep the secret and outwit the authorities. The burial of the corpse in baking foil with a grandfather clock as a coffin is funny, touching, and memorably surreal. Martin's friends steal food from home for him, learn to forge his mother's signature, and devise scams at school to derail parent meetings. The adult world – and the usual sexual rites of passage – are seen as largely irrelevant. Social workers are useless, teachers have forgotten what it was like to be a child, and there are no villains. Neither sentimental nor melodramatic, the film earns its tragic ending. Collective playing by the large cast of kids is excellent. BC

Fragments de Vies

see Fragments of Life

Fragments of Isabella

(1989, Ire, 79 min)
d/sc Ronan O'Leary. *ph* Walter Lassally. *m* Carl Davis. *cast* Gabrielle Reidy.

● O'Leary's film is a transposition of a stage play based on a book written by Holocaust survivor Isabella Leitner. As a teenager, Leitner was taken from the Hungarian Jewish ghetto of Kisvarda to Auschwitz, thence to Birnbaumel. On the death march to Bergen-Belsen, she escaped with two of her sisters. The horrors and atrocities she witnessed on that darkest of journeys – including the deaths of her mother and two young sisters – are related here in the form of a long monologue by

Reidy. Her performance is hard to fault, not least because of its restraint. The monologue is interspersed with newsreel footage, but no shots of horror. If the film's power derives essentially from the word, it is a compliment to the unobtrusive sensitivity of O'Leary's direction – the film is staged on simple sets, carefully lit by Walter Lassally, and incorporates a very subtle use of music (by Carl Davis) and sound – that nothing gets in the way of our hearing it. WH

Fragments of Life (Fragments de Vies)

(1999, Cameroon/Bel/Ger/Fr, 87 min)
d/p/sc François L Woukoache. *ph* Bonaventure Takoukam. *ed* Jean Thomé. *m* Sébastian Buchholz. *cast* Tshilombo Lubambu, Deneuve Djobong, Jean Bediebe, Jérôme Bolo, Thérèse Ngo Ngambi, Hélène Beleck, Salomon Tatmfo.
●The title tells all: three vignettes, apparently unconnected, save that they take place in a large city in equatorial Africa in the late '90s, and each is marked by hardship, injustice, exploitation and struggle. An unemployed man tries to resist temptation offered by criminal acquaintances; a young woman plots vengeance on a tormentor from the past; a barmaid/prostitute encounters an old flame who vanished years before. The storytelling is elliptical, discursive, intriguing, taking its time to make its points; but the performances and camerawork have an immediacy which renders this unsentimental portrait of modern Africa vivid and engrossing. GA

Framed

(1974, US, 106 min)
d Phil Karlson. *p* Mort Briskin, Joel Briskin. *sc* Mort Briskin. *ph* Jack Marta. *ed* Harry Gerstad. *pd* Stan Jolley. *m* Patrick Williams. *cast* Joe Don Baker, Conny Van Dyke, Gabriel Dell, John Marley, Brock Peters, John Larch, Warren Kemmerling, Paul Mantee.
●Everything about this film is ugly and elephantine. A barely audible Joe Don Baker becomes the victim of a baffling frame-up involving people in 'high places', does a spell in jail, then sets out full of vengeful bitterness to unravel the whys and wherefores. The fragmented direction, which persists in spotlighting the irrelevant, is not even within shouting distance of creating any suspense or intrigue; one violent act merely mindlessly succeeds another. The performances are tediously one-dimensional: Joe snarls, Conny breaks down, while the various legal guardians bully. The final twist loses any power it might have had when the one vaguely sympathetic cop, leafing through evidence of top-level corruption, passionately declares, 'Oh no, not him!' IB

Franc, Le

(1995, Switz/Fr/Senegal, 44 min)
d Djibril Diop-Mambéty. *p* Silvia Voser. *sc* Djibril Diop-Mambéty. *ph/ed* Stéphan Oriach. *m* Dieye Ma Dieye, Issa Cissokho. *cast* Dieye Ma Dieye, Aminta Fall, Demba Bâ.
●Diop-Mambéty's short final part of the trilogy he began way back when with the acclaimed *Touki Bouki* is a winning cautionary tale about a poor Senegalese congoma player who wins the lottery. Shot (in beautiful colour) in a lively composite style that brings to mind the experimental freshness of '20s Soviet cinema, it veers easily and joyfully between realist, surrealist and almost-documentary modes, with jangling camera angles and a foot-tapping soundtrack featuring music in French, English and Arabic (including a delightful Tom Waits-like, deep-toned vocalist). It's a satire, of course, on Senegal's economic and social contradictions (the S. Franc has recently devalued, the lottery's an irrelevant fantasy), delivered as the sweetest of pills. WH

Frances

(1982, US, 140 min
d Graeme Clifford. *p* Jonathan Sanger. *sc* Eric Bergren, Christopher De Vore, Nicholas Kazan. *ph* Laszlo Kovacs. *ed* John Wright. *pd* Richard Sylbert. *m* John Barry. *cast* Jessica Lange, Sam Shepard, Kim Stanley, Bart Burns, Christopher Pennock, James Karen, Kevin Kostner.
●The sad life of '30s and '40s actress Frances Farmer is surely the stuff of melodrama: the story of an intelligent, uncompromising young actress with strong radical political opinions, who fell or was pushed from grace in Hollywood and ended up undergoing a lobotomy in an asylum. But in this version the vein becomes increasingly American Gothic; the potential romantic exploration of the American Left is abandoned in favour of a concentration on the star's incarceration in a series of increasingly Hogarthian asylums. Indeed, Farmer, as scripted here and played by Lange, unsurprisingly remains something of a cypher. VG

Francesco, giullare di Dio (Francis, God's Jester)

(1950, It, 83 min, b/w)
d Roberto Rossellini. *p* Angelo Rizzoli. *sc* Roberto Rossellini, Federico Fellini. *ph* Otello Martelli. *ed* Jolanta Benvenuti. *ad* Virgilio Marchi. *m* Renzo Rossellini. *cast* Aldo Fabrizi, Brother Nazario, Arabelle Lemaître, the monks of Nocere Inferiore Monastery.
●Like *Rome, Open City* and *Paisà*, this was co-written by Federico Fellini. Inspired by the *Little Flowers of St Francis*, it's the story of Francis of Assisi and his acolytes, the first Franciscans. They're a motley crew – simple, humble, joyful – quite prepared to give away anything they have (even their cassocks!) if it is required. Rossellini's film shares their qualities. How you react to it probably depends on your own state of grace… or your sense of humour. TCh

Franchesca Page

(1997, US, 92 min)
d Kelley Sane. *p* Pietro Cuevas, Mark E Downie. *sc* Kelley Sane. *ph* Chris Norr. *ed* Maddy Shirazi, Thomas Ostuni. *pd* Ronald L Norsworthy. *m* Jeff Roberson, Ken Compton, Pietro Cuevas, Kelley Sane. *cast* Varla Jean Merman, Rossy de Palma, Tara Leon, Mark Dendy, Linda Smith, Leigh Rose, Marc Cunningham.
●The *faux* Almodóvar opening credits are pretty fab, but from then on this cross-dressing NY frolic entertains only fitfully. The problem isn't in Jeff Robertson's central turn as fun-sized drag queen Varla Jean Merman, who makes the late Divine look like a wilting flower. It's in the plot line spun around her (romance, ambition and murder behind the scenes of an off-off-off-Broadway disco extravaganza, 'The Lady Does It All'), the director's timing of the sundry catty one-liners, and the enthusiastic, but distinctly amateur-hour supporting cast. For indulgent connoisseurs of high camp. TJ

Franchise Affair, The

(1950, GB, 88 min, b/w)
d Lawrence Huntington. *p* Robert Hall. *sc* Robert Hall, Lawrence Huntington. *ph* Günther Krampf. *ed* Cliff Boote. *ad* Terence Verity. *m* Philip Green. *cast* Michael Denison, Dulcie Gray, Anthony Nicholls, Marjorie Fielding, Athene Seyler, Peter Jones, John Bailey, Ann Stephens, Hy Hazell, Kenneth More.
●A strangled adaptation of Josephine Tey's mystery (itself based on the 18th century Elizabeth Canning case). Denison is the country solicitor retained by two women new to the area (Gray as the distressed daughter, Fielding as her battleaxe mother) accused of sequestering, starving and beating a local girl (Stephens) in an attempt to make her their servant. In the novel, the solicitor is shaken out of his complacency by what transpires, but you would never guess as much from Denison's wooden performance in a context – the direction consists largely of posing the actors in static groupings – which looks very much like a repertory company matinée, with risible 'opening out' attempts to portray the town's mounting harassment of the interlopers. All tension is soon dissipated, with Gray so palpitatingly innocent, and her accuser so clearly a lying minx, that the lengthy trial sequence becomes tiresomely redundant (except to explain the plot). TM

Francis

(1949, US, 91 min, b/w)
d Arthur Lubin. *p* Robert Arthur. *sc* David Stern. *ph* Irving Glassberg. *ed* Milton Carruth. *ad* Bernard Herzbrun, Richard H Riedel. *m* Frank Skinner. *cast* Donald O'Connor, Patricia Medina, ZaSu Pitts, Ray Collins, John McIntire, Tony Curtis.
●First of Lubin's sextet of Universal comedies 'starring' Francis the Talking Mule alongside Donald O'Connor. With information culled (as near as dammit) from the horse's mouth, raw second lieutenant O'Connor becomes a hero of the Burma campaign and, not unnaturally, a candidate for the funny farm. The series pegged out when Charles Lamont and Mickey Rooney replaced Lubin and O'Connor in 1955. Chill Wills provided Francis' voice. PT

Francis, God's Jester

see Francesco, giullare di Dio

François Truffaut, Portraits Volés (François Truffaut, Stolen Portraits)

(1992, Fr, 93 min)
d Serge Toubiana, Michel Pascal. *p* Monique Annaud. *ph* Maurice Fellous, Jean-Yves Le Mener, Michel Sourioux. *ed* Dominique B Martin. *with* Eric Rohmer, Claude Chabrol, Bertrand Tavernier, Olivier Assayas, Fanny Ardant.
●It's not hard to guess why people like Jean-Pierre Léaud and Jean-Luc Godard wouldn't participate in this autopsy of Truffaut's reputation as a man and as a film-maker, but it's harder to understand why the directors pass over their absence in silence. In essence, this is a clips-and-talking-heads documentary, notably mainly for prying into some of the darker corners of Truffaut's psyche, including the ruthlessness with which he craved attention during his days as a young critic. Both fans and non-fans will come away with their prejudices confirmed. TR

Frank Capra's American Dream

(1997, US, 109 min, b/w & col)
d Kenneth Bowser. *p* Charles A Duncombe Jr. *sc* Kenneth Bowser. *ph* Richard Pendleton. *ed* Arnold Glassman. *m* John Hodian. *cast* Robert Altman, André De Toth, John Milius, Martin Scorsese, Richard Schickel, Fay Wray, Edward Zwick.
●An expansive, sympathetic and well-illustrated survey of Capra's career, this bio-doc by-passes archive interviews with the garrulous and self-centred director, but then sometimes dwells too long on celebrity gush. Concentrating on the golden '30s and '40s, and skipping over Capra's decline in the '50s, the film gives due weight to such significant collaborators as screenwriter Robert Riskin. Especially piquant is the loyal sound man (sole survivor of the team) declaring his exasperation over Capra's indulgences on *Lost Horizon*. DT

Frankenhooker

(1990, US, 90 min)
d Frank Henenlotter. *p* Edgar Ievins. *sc* Robert Martin, Frank Henenlotter. *ph* Robert Baldwin. *ed* Kevin Tent. *m* Joe Renzetti. *cast* James Lorinz, Patty Mullen, Charlotte Helmkamp, Shirley Stoler, Joe Gonzales.
●'Jesus Christ, this could get ugly', says Jeffrey, nerdy would-be Frankenstein, as a laboratory guinea pig explodes after inhaling fumes from his patented Super-Crack. And it does. When his bride-to-be is turned into a tossed salad by a runaway lawnmower, Jeffrey salvages her head and reconstructs her with limbs, breasts and torsos gleaned from hookers he has tricked into 'cracking up' in similar fashion. Revived by the obligatory bolt of lightning, Elizabeth is not quite her old self; even her clients find her too hot to handle. Henenlotter indulges his penchant for sleaze to the max, throwing in a few bad-taste puns and a little therapeutic head-drilling for laughs. The resulting fragmented mess will no doubt keep some in stitches, but it is definitely less than the sum of its body parts. NF

Frankenstein

(1931, US, 71 min, b/w)
d James Whale. *p* Carl Laemmle Jr. *sc* Garrett Fort, Francis Edwards Faragoh, John L Balderston. *ph* Arthur Edeson. *ed* Maurice Pivar, Clarence Kolster. *ad* Charles D Hall. *m* David Broekman. *cast* Boris Karloff, Colin Clive, Mae Clarke, John Boles, Edward Van Sloan, Dwight Frye, Frederick Kerr.
●A stark, solid, impressively stylish film, overshadowed (a little unfairly) by the later explosion of Whale's wit in the delirious *Bride of Frankenstein*. Karloff gives one of the great performances of all time as the monster whose mutation from candour to chill savagery is mirrored only through his limpid eyes. The film's

great imaginative coup is to show the monster 'growing up' in all too human terms. First he is the innocent baby, reaching up to grasp the sunlight that filters through the skylight. Then the joyous child, playing at throwing flowers into the lake with a little girl whom he delightedly imagines to be another flower. And finally, as he finds himself progressively misjudged by the society that created him, the savage killer as whom he has been typecast. The film is unique in Whale's work in that the horror is played absolutely straight, and it has a weird fairytale beauty not matched until Cocteau made *La Belle et la Bête.* TM

Frankenstein

see Mary Shelley's Frankenstein

Frankenstein and the Monster from Hell

(1973, GB, 99 min)
d Terence Fisher. *p* Roy Skeggs. *sc* John Elder [Anthony Hinds]. *ph* Brian Probyn. *ed* James Needs. *ad* Scott MacGregor. James Bernard. *m* J Bernard. *cast* Peter Cushing, Shane Briant, Madeline Smith, John Stratton, Bernard Lee, Dave Prowse, Patrick Troughton.

●Fisher's last film is a disappointment. Using the already well-proven formula, it offers the Baron this time as a doctor in a criminal asylum for the insane, secretly working with his assistant towards creating yet another life. Things begin well, with Fisher adding some atmospheric touches and Cushing suggesting a man undermined by his excessive rationality. Unfortunately the script, which treads a wavering line between jerky comedy and seriousness, soon dissipates anyone else's better intentions. Things are further weakened by a listless assistant, a monster that looks as if it has strayed from some never-realised 'Apes' project, and a gratuitously unpleasant brain transplant. CPe

Frankenstein Created Woman

(1966, GB, 86 min)
d Terence Fisher. *p* Anthony Nelson-Keys. *sc* Anthony Hinds. *ph* Arthur Grant. *ed* James Needs. *pd* Bernard Robinson. *m* James Bernard. *cast* Peter Cushing, Susan Denberg, Thorley Walters, Robert Morris, Duncan Lamont, Alan Macnaughtan.

●Fisher's third film in the Hammer *Frankenstein* series is a subtly decadent reworking of the *Bride of Frankenstein* theme (although it bears absolutely no relation to the Universal picture), about a Lamia-like seductress who returns from the grave to seduce and slaughter her former tormentors. It's full of cloying Keatsian imagery, which somehow transcends the more idiotic aspects of the plot. DP

Frankenstein Meets the Wolf Man

(1943, US, 72 min, b/w)
d Roy William Neill. *sc* Curt Siodmak. *ph* George Robinson. *ed* Edward Curtiss. *ad* John Goodman. *m* Hans Salter. *cast* Lon Chaney Jr, Bela Lugosi, Lionel Atwill, Ilona Massey, Patrick Knowles, Maria Ouspenskaya, Dwight Frye.

●The first of Universal's frantic attempts to halt falling box-office receipts by doubling up on its monsters, with Chaney's despairing Wolf Man coming to consult Dr Frankenstein in the hope of finding cure or release. The good doctor is dead, but another overweening scientist (Knowles) is on hand to be tempted to revive the monster, found frozen in ice, for a last-reel showdown with the Wolf Man in which both are swept away when the villagers blow up a dam. Fast-paced and quite atmospheric in its tacky way, but definitively sabotaged by Lugosi as the monster; at last getting to play the role he missed out on in 1931, he gives a performance of excruciatingly embarrassing inadequacy. TM

Frankenstein Must Be Destroyed

(1969, GB, 97 min)
d Terence Fisher. *p* Anthony Nelson-Keys. *sc* Bert Batt. *ph* Arthur Grant. *ed* Gordon Hales. *ad* Bernard Robinson. *m* James Bernard. *cast* Peter Cushing, Veronica Carlson, Simon Ward, Freddie Jones, Thorley Walters, Maxine Audley, George Pravda.

●Hammer's fifth Frankenstein film shifts the horror from the Monster, now a sad and pathetic victim, to the Baron (Cushing), now an embittered and ruthless tyrant. Abducting his former assistant Dr Brandt (Pravda) from a lunatic asylum, the Baron transplants his brain into the body of Dr Richter (Jones). Restored to sanity but with his brain trapped within an alien body, the heavily bandaged Brandt/Richter monster is able to talk to his grief-stricken wife (Audley) but unable to understand or explain the transformation that has 'cured' him. Fisher taps a rich vein of Romanticism here, making this the high point of a series that afterwards degenerated into the sloppy self-parody of Jimmy Sangster's *The Horror of Frankenstein.* NF

Frankenstein: The True Story

(1973, GB, 123 min)
d Jack Smight. *p* Hunt Stromberg Jr. *sc* Christopher Isherwood, Don Bachardy. *ph* Arthur Ibbetson. *ed* Richard Marden. *pd* Wilfrid Shingleton. *m* Gil Mellé. *cast* James Mason, Leonard Whiting, David McCallum, Jane Seymour, Nicola Paget, Michael Sarrazin, Michael Wilding, Agnes Moorehead, Margaret Leighton, Ralph Richardson, John Gielgud.

●Scripted by Christopher Isherwood and Don Bachardy, this is not exactly a faithful rendering of Mary Shelley's novel, although it deserves full marks for using the magnificent Arctic ending so long ignored by the cinema. Difficult to assess properly, since the feature is a boil-down from the 200-minute version shown on American TV, although a misogynistic reading is clearly intended (with the two brides, Frankenstein's and the monster's, emerging as more treacherously villainous than either of their mates). For a while it comes on like bad Hammer, until the arrival of the monster – a handsome lad, but the process is reverting – perks things up considerably. Particularly memorable is a scene where the monster's demurely virginal Bride sings 'I Love Little Pussy, Her Coat Is So Warm', before gleefully attempting to strangle a sleepy persian and lasciviously licking a drop of mauve blood from her scratched arm; and a glorious moment of delirium when the monster disrupts a society ball to collect his bride, ripping off her pearl choker to reveal the stitched neck, then annexing her head as his property. Whiting is a weak Frankenstein, but more than made up for by Sarrazin (the monster), Seymour (his bride), Richardson (the hermit) and Mason (first cousin to Fu Manchu as Polidori). TM

Frankie & Johnny

(1991, US, 118 min)
d/p Garry Marshall. *sc* Terrence McNally. *ph* Dante Spinotti. *ed* Battle Davis, Jacqueline Cambas. *pd* Albert Brenner. *m* Marvin Hamlisch. *cast* Al Pacino, Michelle Pfeiffer, Hector Elizondo, Nathan Lane, Jane Morris, Kate Nelligan, Greg Lewis, Al Fann, Glenn Plummer.

●Adapted by Terrence McNally from his own play *Frankie and Johnny in the Clair de Lune,* this shares the squashiness of Neil Simon. Against a klaxon background of New York, Frankie (Pfeiffer), a waitress at the Apollo Café, has problems responding to the courting of Johnny (Pacino), the short-order cook. She's withdrawn, wants a VCR, and seems content to observe her neighbours' relationships through the window. But Johnny, after a mousy one-night stand with another waitress (Nelligan), won't take no for an answer. He gatecrashes her bowling night, they go to bed, she supplies the condom, and this time he lets rip with an orgasmic cry. Quaint cameos from Morris as a species of Dandy Nichols waitress, and Elizondo as the loveably cheap Greek cafe-owner. Pacino wears a vest and bandanna and moons through the part. Pfeiffer plays dowdy. Marshall directs as if *Marty* had never happened. BC

Frankie Starlight

(1995, US/Ire, 101 min)
d Michael Lindsay-Hogg. *p* Noel Pearson. *sc* Chet Raymo, Ronan O'Leary. *ph* Paul Laufer. *ed* Ruth Foster. *pd* Frank Conway. *m* Elmer Bernstein. *cast* Anne Parillaud, Matt Dillon, Gabriel Byrne, Rudi Davies, Georgina Cates, Alan Pentony, Corban Walker.

●This tale of a physically impaired Irishman (a dwarf) and the literary success of his family reminiscences does itself no favours by courting comparison with producer Noel Pearson's *My Left Foot.* Frankie's mam Bernadette (Parillaud) lands in Ireland by accident after WWII (she's discovered stowing away on a ship from France with homebound GIs). In Cork, naval officer Jack Kelly (Byrne) sees her alone and pregnant and becomes a father figure to young François (Pentony). Later, Frankie takes a shine to one of Jack's daughters, Emma, until the Kellys are transferred elsewhere. Next, from Texas, comes biker Terry Klout (Dillon), who whisks Bernsie and Frank to the States. Meanwhile, the adult Frank (Walker) is selling his life story to a publisher, reading the reviews, attending book-signings, crossing paths once more with Emma. Alas, the effect of these episodes is feeble. Whereas *My Left Foot* built up around the formidable figure of Christy Brown, here there's a void. The diffuseness is central to the star-gazing metaphor, but more than a tight plot is needed to entrance the audience, and director Lindsay-Hogg's picture postcard naturalism isn't it. The film does, however, have some charm, and the performances help it amble along pleasantly. NB

Frantic

see Ascenseur pour l'Echafaud

Frantic

(1988, US, 120 min)
d Roman Polanski. *p* Thom Mount, Tim Hampton. *sc* Roman Polanski, Gérard Brach. *ph* Witold Sobocinski. *ed* Sam O'Steen. *pd* Pierre Guffroy. *m* Ennio Morricone. *cast* Harrison Ford, Betty Buckley, Emmanuelle Seigner, Alexandra Stewart, David Huddleston, Robert Barr, Boll Boyer.

●Polanski's thriller boasts several superb set pieces, even if it doesn't quite snap shut on the mind the way *Chinatown* did. Dr Walker (Ford) checks into a Paris hotel with his wife (Buckley) to attend a conference. She has collected the wrong suitcase at the airport, their problems escalate, and to watch how Polanski calibrates the build-up of disquiet in a standard hotel suite until the wife disappears is deeply satisfying. Walker is suddenly alone with the unimaginable in alien territory, asking for help. Officialdom won't take him seriously and he resorts to clues lit by match flares. We are in *film noir* territory. The wrong suitcase leads him to a corpse, and then to Michelle (Seigner), a swinging chick who attaches herself to his quest. Polanski's penchant for the surreal goes adrift on one dislocation involving the Statue of Liberty through a porthole, but scores heavily with Ford's increasingly disreputable returns to base, a discreet, tiptoe hotel into which he creeps shoeless, and with a bubblegum punkette in tow. Funny and unsettling. BC

Frantz Fanon: Black Skin, White Mask

(1996, GB/Fr, 70 min)
d Isaac Julien. *p* Mark Nash. *sc* Isaac Julien, Mark Nash. *ph* Nina Kellgren. *ed* Justin Krish, Nick Thompson, Robert Hargreaves. *ad* Mick Hurd. *m* Paul Gladstone-Reid, Tunde Jegede. *cast* Colin Salmon, Al Nedjari, John Wilson, Ana Ramalho, Noirín Ní Dubhgaill; Homi Bhabha, Stuart Hall, Françoise Vergès.

●A fine introduction to the life and work of the Frantz Fanon (1925-61), the Martinican-born, Paris-educated author, intellectual and activist. Isaac Julien and co-writer Mark Nash's study shows the influence of Derek Jarman's similar work on Wittgenstein. Mixing the talking heads (notably Stuart Hall), interviews with relatives, co-workers and friends, and archive footage, clips and reconstructions, they have produced a clear résumé of Fanon's ideas, but also something rarer, a strong, affecting sense of the man's complex personality. With his interest in violence, black identity and psychiatry (it was Fanon's professional work with war-damaged 'natives' and French soldiers in early '50s Algeria that was to revolutionise his politics, leading him later to join the FLN), Fanon is in many ways a perfect subject for Julien, enabling him to pursue themes that have figured in his work since *Territories* in the early '80s. In many ways this is the director's most mature film and not without the lyricism of his earlier discursive documentaries. Fanon died young (of leukaemia), just before the publication of *The Wretched of the Earth,* the analytical manifesto which became the freedom fighter's bible. WH

Französische Frau, Eine

see Femme française, Une

Fraternally Yours

see Sons of the Desert

Frauds

(1992, Aust, 94 min)
d Stephan Elliott. *p* Stuart Quin, Andrena Finlay. *sc* Stephan Elliott. *ph* Geoff Burton. *ed* Frans Vandenburg. *pd* Brian Thomson. *m* Guy Cross. *cast* Phil Collins, Hugo Weaving, Josephine Byrnes, Peter Mochrie, Helen O'Connor, Colleen Clifford.

●Phil Collins as an insurance investigator? Unctuous, supercilious, insidious, Roland Copping is surely the part he was born to play. A pair of dice always in hand, he allows Lady Luck to rule his destiny – which is bad news for ill-fated middle-class couple Jonathan and Beth Wheats (Weaving and Byrnes), vulnerable to blackmail after their opportunistic insurance claim. Copping tempts the couple into a spiral of defiance and defeat, his brinkmanship taking them ever closer to disaster; and as the stakes get higher, the movie gets wilder, mutating into a surreal black comedy with a brash carnivalesque tone. Copping's apartment looks like a spare set from *Toys*, while acute camera angles ensure that any semblance of reality is purely coincidental. But while this movie may be different, it's not *that* different; actually, it resembles an extended episode of *The Avengers*. Elliott's thesis is that all men are children at heart – and that children are malicious, vindictive beasts. It's hardly an edifying conceit, and the movie has an over-insistent, meretricious feel about it. TCh

Frau im Mond

see Woman in the Moon

Freaked

(1993, US, 79 min)
d Tom Stern, Alex Winter. *p* Harry J Ufland, Mary Jane Ufland. *sc* Tom Stern, Alex Winter, Tim Burns. *ph* Jamie Thompson. *ed* Malcolm Campbell. *pd* Catherine Hardwicke. *m* Kevin Kiner. *cast* Alex Winter, Randy Quaid, Megan Ward, Michael Stoyanov, Brooke Shields, Keanu Reeves, Mr T, Bobcat Goldthwait.

●Clearly a labour of love for co-writer, co-director and star Alex Winter (the other one in the *Bill and Ted* movies), this freewheeling, anarchic, gross-out comedy should satisfy the six-pack post-pub crowd, but it can't really stand up to sober viewing. It's the vaguely satirical story of a spoiled young movie star (Winter) whose South American product endorsement tour turns sour when he's waylaid in Quaid's bizarre jungle-freak circus and given a dose of the truly evil medicine he's been pushing. The wit is all in the casting: Mr T as the bearded lady (you got a problem with that?), Bobcat Goldthwait as 'Sockhead', Brooke Shields as a TV presenter, and Keanu Reeves behind layers of hair as 'Ortiz the Dog Boy'. Brian (*Society*) Yuzna's surreal make-up effects are also worth a look – check out those gun-toting Rasta eyeballs! – but the sum is less than its (very ugly) parts. TCh

Freaks

(1932, US, 64 min, b/w)
d/p Tod Browning. *sc* Willis Goldbeck, Leon Gordon, Al Boasberg. *ph* Merritt B Gerstad. *ed* Basil Wrangell. *ad* Cedric Gibbons. *cast* Harry Earles, Olga Baclanova, Wallace Ford, Leila Hyams, Henry Victor, Daisy Earles.

●A superb and unique film from that master of the morbid, masochistic and macabre, Tod Browning. Set in a travelling circus – a milieu Browning knew and loved from his own experience – it shows the revenge taken by a group of circus freaks on a beautiful trapeze artist and her strongman lover after they have tried to kill a midget (the marvellous Harry Earles, one of the stars of Browning's *The Unholy Three*) for his fortune. The basic themes of the film are the strength in solidarity of the individually weak freaks, and the inner beauty of the physically malformed as compared to the greed and deceit of the physically resplendent. Although using real freaks, Browning's treatment is never voyeuristic or condescending, but sympathetic in such a way that after a few minutes we almost cease to perceive them as in any way abnormal. There is a strong, black humour that, remarkably, lacks cruelty, and a real sense of terror in the awful revenge the wronged freaks exact. MGM never knew what hit them with this film; they virtually disowned it, and it remained unseen in Britain until the '60s. It has now achieved deserved recognition as a masterpiece. GA

Freaky Friday

(1976, US, 100 min)
d Gary Nelson. *p* Ron Miller. *sc* Mary Rodgers. *ph* Charles F Wheeler. *ed* Cotton Warburton. *ad* John B Mansbridge, Jack Senter. *m* Johnny Mandel. *cast* Barbara Harris, Jodie Foster, John Astin, Patsy Kelly, Dick Van Patten, Vicki Schreck, Sorrell Booke, Ruth Buzzi, Marie Windsor.

●'I wish I could swop places with her for just one day', is the mutual cry of suburban mom and teenage daughter. And sure enough, Jodie Foster duly informs the audience, 'Mom's body has got my mind in it!' But in some ways nothing changes: Barbara Harris merely becomes her usual scatty self, while Foster adds another display of unbridled precocity to her credits. This being a Disney comedy, nothing too drastic happens; and attendant adults can rest assured that, because Dad is so dithering and ineffectual, awkward questions about potentially incestuous relations, sadly, do not arise. Good performances struggle gamely to overcome the increasingly predictable plot. CPe

Freddie as F.R.0.7.

(1992, GB, 91 min)
d Jon Acevski. *p* Jon Acevski, Norman Priggen. *sc* Jon Acevski, David Ashton. *ph* Rex Neville. *ed* Alex Rayment. *ad* Paul Shardlow. *m* David Dundas, Rick Wentworth. *cast* voices: Ben Kingsley, Jenny Agutter, Brian Blessed, Nigel Hawthorne, Michael Hordern, Jonathan Pryce, Prunella Scales, Billie Whitelaw, John Sessions.

●Prince Frederic is transformed into a magical frog by his wicked aunt in a fairytale preamble to this animation feature. Bizarrely, we cut to the modern day, where he is the pride of the French secret service. Meanwhile, Blighty is losing its heritage at an alarming rate. Nelson's Column has vanished. The Tower of London disappears overnight. With 007 in Hollywood, MI6 turn in desperation to F.R.0.7. Billed as 'An Amazing Fantasy of a New Kind', the movie is a hotchpotch of half-baked ideas ransacked from Disney, Bond and, at a guess, cult shows like *The Avengers* and *Dr Who*. The most intriguing notion is that by stealing historic monuments, the Snake Queen hopes to extract the country's life force and plunge the population into inertia. The rest is lame jokes and outmoded stereotypes. TCh

Freddy's Dead: The Final Nightmare

(1991, US, 90 min)
d Rachel Talalay. *p* Aron Warner, Robert Shaye. *sc* Michael De Luca. *ph* Declan Quinn. *ed* Janice Hampton. *pd* CJ Strawn. *m* Brian May. *cast* Robert Englund, Lisa Zane, Shon Greenblatt, Lezlie Deane, Ricky Dean Logan, Breckin Meyer, Yaphet Kotto.

●Once again, a spurious piece of Freddy mythology – involving an adopted daughter – provides the excuse for some not-so-special effects sequences and flip one-liners in this terminally boring conclusion to the *Nightmare on Elm Street* series. An amnesiac teenager, christened 'John Doe' (Greenblatt), lands up at the centre for disturbed adolescents run by child psychologist Maggie Burroughs (Zane). Apparently providing the link Freddy needs to get at rich runaway Spencer (Meyer), bellicose martial arts expert Tracy (Deane) and aurally impaired Carlos (Logan), 'John' is also drawn into Freddy's nightmare world. All that remains, therefore, is for Freddy to bump off each of the disposable teens in turn, by exploiting their psychological weaknesses. Plus, of course, the long overdue demise of Freddy himself. Even the much-heralded 3-D finale is murky and unimaginative. NF

Freebie and the Bean

(1974, US, 113 min)
d/p Richard Rush. *sc* Richard Kaufman. *ph* Laszlo Kovacs. *ed* Fredric Steinkamp, Michael McLean. *ad* Hilyard Brown. *m* Dominic Frontiere. *cast* Alan Arkin, James Caan, Loretta Swit, Jack Kruschen, Mike Kellin, Paul Koslo, Valerie Harper.

●Not the latest Disney, as the title implies, but yet another cop movie, a strangely callous exercise that divides its time between comic destruction of *It's a Mad World* proportions, and a super-violence that makes no distinction between the people and the machinery that it destroys. Caan and Arkin manage just enough to justify the presence of yet another wisecracking male duo, but the general feeling is of an attempt at audience manipulation, assembled by computer, apart from the truly bizarre final confrontation that looks like something strayed from another movie. On the whole, a film one can live without. CPe

Freedom

see Libertad, La

Freedom

(2000, Fr/Lithuania/Port, 96 min)
d Sharunas Bartas. *p* Paulo Branco. *sc* Sharunas Bartas. *ph* Sharunas Bartas, Rimvydas Leipus. *ed* Mingaile Murmulaitiene. *pd* Jirij Grigorovic. *m* Kipras Masanauskas. *cast* Valentinas Masalskis, Fatima Ennaflaoui, Axel Neumann.

●Insofar as this slow, visually stunning, determinedly 'poetic' film has a story, it concerns two men and a girl who alight on the empty and windswept Moroccan coast after a drug trafficking operation goes wrong. Separately and together they wander the desert, trying to survive. It would be easy to dismiss this almost dialogue-free, enigmatic piece as pretentious nonsense. Certainly, the portentous title suggests that writer/director Bartas has allegorical aspirations with regard to the human condition, but the film simply cannot sustain them. It's also arguable that the pictorialism and miserabilist tone are self-conscious and studied. Disregard this unfortunate touch of the Tarkovskys, however, and you may just succumb to the mesmerising mood, in which case there are epiphanies here – gulls, waves, crabs and flamingos – to savour. GA

Freedom for Us

see A Nous la Liberté

Freedom Is Paradise (SER)

(1989, USSR, 75 min)
d Sergei Bodrov. *p* Victor Trakhtenberg. *sc* Sergei Bodrov. *ph* Yuri Skirtladze. *ed* Valentina Kulagnina. *pd* Valery Kostrin. *m* Alexander Raskatov. *cast* Volodya Kozyrev, Alexander Bureyev, Svetlana Gaitan, Vitautas Tomkus.

●Bodrov's excellent movie has no more flab than its young hero, a tough but doe-eyed teenager in a black-leather jacket who escapes from reform school and traverses the USSR in search of his father, also in prison. The title really ought to be *FIP* since, like the other kids in the reform school, 13-year-old Sasha has the acronym *SER* (*'svoboda eto rai'*) tattooed on his arm as a kind of badge of hope. His quest takes him from Alma Ata (the city where Bodrov got his own first break) all the way to Archangel (site of Lenin's first gulag): an ideal itinerary for a road movie, full of regional and ethnic variety and rich in political associations. Bodrov, a one-time satirical journalist, starts from the assumption that almost everyone in the USSR is conditioned to think and behave like a prisoner. But his focus is squarely on Sasha's resilience, imagination and emotional needs. As a picture of childhood's end, it's strong enough to stand alongside genre classics like *My Life as a Dog* and *A Summer at Grandpa's*; and the fluency and simplicity of Bodrov's film language makes it a pleasure to watch. TR

Freedom Road

(1979, US, 100 min)
d Ján Kadár. *p* Zev Braun. *sc* David Zelag Goodman. *ph* Charles Correll. *ed* George Folsey Jr. *pd* Dan Lomino. *m* Coleridge-Taylor Perkinson, Terrence James. *cast* Muhammad Ali, Kris Kristofferson, Ron O'Neal, Edward Herrmann, Barbara-O Jones, Sonny Jim Gaines.

●Originally a four-hour tele-drama in the States, but mercifully trimmed to feature length here, *Freedom Road* marks a sad close to the career of the late expatriate Czech director, Kadár. Howard Fast's bulky novel is transposed with all the numbing insistence and impeccable stacked-deck liberalism of an old Stanley Kramer message-movie, with Muhammad Ali struggling to portray a quiet black Spartacus in the midst of the fight for post-Civil War emancipation. Flashbacks span 13 years' shallow history of 'the story so far', while former slave niggers and poor white trash together prepare for martyrdom in battle with the baby-burning Klan. The sentiments are fine; the sermonising's not. PT

Freejack

(1992, US, 109 min)
d Geoff Murphy. *p* Ronald Shusett, Stuart Oken. *sc* Ronald Shusett, Steven Pressfield, Dan Gilroy. *ph* Amir Mokri. *ed* Dennis Virkler. *pd* Joe Alves. *m* Trevor Jones. *cast* Emilio Estevez, Mick Jagger, Rene Russo, Anthony Hopkins, Jonathan Banks, David Johansen, Amanda Plummer.

●Catapulted into the future a split second before a motor-racing accident, Alex Furlong (Estevez) wakes up in 2009, just in time to avoid a lobotomy. Dazed and confused, he flees across a polluted New York divided between the rich, powerful executives of the McCandless Corporation and the poor who live on the streets. Monosyllabic 'Bonejacker' Vacendak (Jagger) is despatched to capture Alex, a 'Freejack' intended for a mind-transplant that will allow an ailing client to transfer to his youthful body. The central idea is never explored, despite the obvious potential of a scenario in which Alex is confronted with old flame Julie (Russo), now a high-flying executive with the Corporation owned by her love-struck but unrequited boss (Hopkins). Whenever things get boring, which is often, the double-crossing factor is increased, which complicates the plot without adding substance to the two-dimensional characters or to the mechanical suspense. NF

Freelance

(1970, GB, 81 min)
d/p Francis Megahy. *sc* Bernie Cooper, Francis Megahy. *ph* Norman Langley. *ed* Arthur Solomon. *ad* Philip Harrison. *m* Basil Kirchin. *cast* Ian McShane, Gayle Hunnicutt, Keith Barron, Alan Lake, Peter Gilmore, Charles Hyatt.

●Kept on the shelf for five years, this surfaced for one week in London as a supporting feature, then disappeared. In fact, it's a very straightforward, serviceable thriller about a small-time con man who is trapped into graduating to bigger crime. Filmed essentially as a chase, the film boasts a couple of good action sequences and some nicely low-key location shooting. CPe

Freelancers, The

see Cachetonneurs, Les

Freeway

(1996, US, 98 min)
d Matthew Bright. *p* Matthew Bright, Chris Hanley, Brad Wyman. *sc* Matthew Bright. *ph* John Thomas. *ed* Maysie Hoy. *pd* Pam Warner. *m* Danny Elfman, Tito Larriva. *cast* Reece Witherspoon, Kiefer Sutherland, Dan Hedaya, Amanda Plummer, Brooke Shields.

●The directorial debut for *Guncrazy* screenwriter Matthew Bright, this enthusiastically grotesque exploitation flick turns out to be Little Red Riding Hood transposed to '90s California. In her most engaging performance to date, Witherspoon is a polite, affectionate, shit-kicking teen stuck with a fuck-up mom, an abusive stepdad, and all the bad luck in the world. Fleeing welfare officers for Grandma's house, she breaks down on the freeway, and gets a lift from a concerned psychologist – Sutherland – who isn't all he appears to be. There's not much edification in store, and Bright cruises over some bumpy plot holes, but the teen's perspective does put a black comic spotlight on wider social hypocrisies. Danny Elfman contributes a rusty, rollicking carnival-esque theme tune. TCh

Freeway II: Confessions of a Trickbaby (aka Confessions of a Trickbaby)

(2000, US/Fr/Can, 97 min)
d Matthew Bright. *p* Brad Wyman, Chris Hanley. *sc* Matthew Bright. *ph* Joel Ransom. *ed* Suzanne Hines. *pd* Brian Davie. *m* Kennard Ramsey. *cast* Natasha Lyonne, Maria Celedonio, Vincent Gallo, David Alan Grier, Michael T Weiss, John Landis, Max Perlich, Bob Dawson.

●Lyonne, a bulimic career junkie, and Celedonio, a lesbian psycho murderer, are on the lam from the iniquities of the juvenile detention system. They believe sanctuary awaits in Tijuana with one Sister Gomez. A no holds barred assault on received notions of taste, decency, righteousness and good film-making, this doesn't even begin on the rails. Picking up the perspective of Lyonne's White Girl as she's sent down for 25 years for dealing, prostitution and armed robbery, it mainlines for a while on her group bingeing and purging parties. Her evidently crazy cellmate Cyclona (Celedonio) makes a few passes, but it's not until their first snack break-cum-bloodbath as fugitives that Cyclona shows her truly disturbed colours. So they rampage down to Mexico. Perhaps for the better, it gets worse. Come the gruesome, purgatorial finale and an astoundingly degenerate turn from Gallo, the film really lets its guts hang out, and you finally get the measure of its black hysterical horror. NB

Free Willy

(1993, US, 112 min)
d Simon Wincer. *p* Lauren Shuler Donner, Jennie Lew Tugend. *sc* Keith Walker, Corey Blechman. *ph* Robbie Greenberg. *ed* O Nicholas Brown. *pd* Charles Rosen. *m* Basil Poledouris. *cast* Jason James Richter, Lori Petty, Jayne Atkinson, August Schellenberg, Michael Madsen, Michael Ironside.

●Sweeping strings accompany the opening sequence of balletic whales cavorting in brilliant blue sea, changing abruptly to a cacophony as the bad guys with nets chug up in their tugs. Willy is trapped and his family swims mournfully away. Cut to an angelic street-kid, Jesse (Richter), caught graffiti-ing Willy's tank; the only way to escape 'baby jail' he discovers is to go to well-meaning but stiffo foster parents and clean up the tank under the tutelage of Haida Indian whale-trainer Randolph (Schellenberg). Willy, meanwhile, has turned ornery. Soon, however, Jesse's mouth organ is echoing Willy's whalesong and the message is spelt out: boy and whale get on because they're both looking for a family. This well-acted film has a straight-faced tone which is hard to resist. SFe

Free Willy 2

(1995, US, 97 min)
d Dwight Little. *p* Lauren Shuler Donner, Jennie Lew Tugend. *sc* Corey Blechman, Karen Janszen, John Mattson. *ph* Laszlo Kovacs. *ed* Robert Brown. *pd* Paul Sylbert. *m* Basil Poledouris. *cast* Jason James Richter, Jon Tenny, Michael Madsen, Jayne Atkinson, Elizabeth Peña, August Schellenberg.

●Maybe it takes time to mix the formula, but this is tons better entertainment than the original. Dwight Little has understood the visual appeal of these black-and-white killer whales in open, chromium sea and cinematographer Laszlo Kovacs has done them proud. Last time, the threat to Willy was continued imprisonment in the aquarium, but here, more excitingly, it's an oil slick down the blowhole, plus an oil explosion at sea, and another threat of imprisonment in the aquarium to make up the weight. Disturbed teenager Jesse (Richter) is issued with an even more disturbed younger half-brother Elvis, who lies all the time, but they make common cause on the plight of the whale. Their foster father (Madsen) has reconciled himself to the role, and Randolph the Native American (Schellenberg) gets to mix some magic herbs and chant healingly over the waters. BC

Free Willy 3: The Rescue

(1997, US, 86 min)
d Sam Pillsbury. *p* Jennie Lew Tugend. *sc* John Mattson. *ph* Tobias Schliesser. *ed* Margaret Goodspeed. *pd* Brent Thomas. *m* Cliff Eidelman. *cast* Jason James Richter, August Schellenberg, Annie Corley, Vincent Berry, Patrick Kilpatrick.

●Jesse, now 17, and Max, aged ten, team up to gather evidence needed by the authorities to clamp down on the illegal trade in whale meat. The film tactfully brings home the cruelty of the whaling industry (a U certificate notwithstanding), and declines to treat Max's dad (himself a whaling captain) as a black-hearted monster. A satisfying family movie, with plenty of aquatic frolicking, and not too preachy. TJ

French Cancan

(1955, Fr, 102 min)
d/sc Jean Renoir. *ph* Michel Kelber. *ed* Boris Lewyn. *ad* Max Douy. *m* George Van Parys. *cast* Jean Gabin, Françoise Arnoul, Maria Félix, Gianni Esposito, Philippe Clay, Michel Piccoli, Edith Piaf, Dora Doll, Patachou.

●Renoir's return to film-making in France after an absence of fifteen years is a nostalgic studio reconstruction of the Paris of his painter father. Despite its artificiality and meandering plot construction – with Renoir falling in love with some of his minor characters – it brilliantly evokes the world of the French Impressionists, building into a comic riot of colour and movement. The story is a backstage musical on the founding of the Moulin Rouge and the training of the famous cancan dancers. The climactic cancan scene is one of the finest dance sequences ever filmed, and worth the price of a ticket on its own. RM

French Connection, The

(1971, US, 104 min)
d William Friedkin. *p* Philip D'Antoni. *sc* Ernest Tidyman. *ph* Owen Roizman. *ed* Jerry Greenberg. *ad* Ben Kazaskow. *m* Don Ellis. *cast* Gene Hackman, Fernando Rey, Roy Scheider, Tony Lo Bianco, Marcel Bozzuffi, Frédéric de Pasquale.

●An urban crime thriller which won undeserved acclaim for its efficient but unremarkable elevated-railway chase and its clumsy, showy emphasis on grainy, sordid realism. The performances are strong, although Hackman has done far better than this portrayal of a hard-nosed cop obsessively tracking down a narcotics ring in New York, using methods disapproved of by his superiors. The real problems, however, are that Friedkin's nervy, noisy, undisciplined pseudo-realism sits uneasily with his suspense-motivated shock editing; and that compared to (say) Siegel's *Dirty Harry*, the film maintains no critical distance from (indeed, rather relishes) its 'loveable' hero's brutal vigilante psychology. GA

French Connection II

(1975, US, 119 min)
d John Frankenheimer. *p* Robert L Rosen. *sc* Robert Dillon, Laurie Dillon, Alexander Jacobs. *ph* Claude Renoir. *ed* Tom Rolf. *pd* Jacques Saulnier. *m* Don Ellis. *cast* Gene Hackman, Fernando Rey, Bernard Fresson, Jean-Pierre Castaldi, Charles Millot, Cathleen Nesbitt, Ed Lauter.

●Far superior to Friedkin's original, simply because Robert Dillon's script is much more critical in its probing of the Popeye Doyle character. As Doyle visits Marseilles to track the drugs ring to its source, his natural, bigoted arrogance and sense of superiority are undermined, not merely by being a stranger in a strange land, but also by being shot full of heroin and forced to suffer the terrors of cold turkey. Hackman takes the enlarged role by the scruff of the neck and delivers yet another fine performance of doubt and the dawning awareness of his own weakness. Frankenheimer directs in taut, pacy fashion to keep the suspense high. GA.

French Kiss

(1995, US, 111 min)
d Lawrence Kasdan. *p* Tim Bevan, Eric Fellner, Meg Ryan, Kathryn Galan. *sc* Adam Brooks. *ph* Owen Roizman. *ed* Joe Hutshing. *pd* John Hutman. *m* James Newton Howard. *cast* Meg Ryan, Kevin Kline, Timothy Hutton, Jean Reno, François Cluzet, Susan Anbeh, Renee Humphrey.

●This is a tissue-thin affair tarted up with phoney continental charm. Kate, a skittish control freak (Ryan), follows her fiancé to Paris when he tells her he's fallen in love with another woman. En route, she meets Gallic con-man Luc (Kline), who stows his contraband in her valise for customs, and reluctantly stands by when it's promptly stolen. Directed by Kasdan, this plays like a lighter version of *The Accidental Tourist* – there's the same cautious exhortation to open yourself to life's risks. Like the wine Luc treasures, the film wants to be sophisticated but not pretentious, cynical yet sincere. In other words, it wants it both ways. There's farce, slapstick, Kline's Clouseau accent, gibes at American puritanism and French driving, and then there's the desultory pacing, the plaintive life-enhancing sentiments and the travelogue cinematography. TCh

French Lieutenant's Woman, The

(1981, GB, 123 min)
d Karel Reisz. *p* Leon Clore. *sc* Harold Pinter. *ph* Freddie Francis. *ed* John Bloom. *pd* Assheton Gorton. *m* Carl Davis. *cast* Meryl Streep, Jeremy Irons, Hilton McRae, Emily Morgan, Charlotte Mitchell, Lynsey Baxter, Leo McKern.
●John Fowles' novel is a full-blooded 19th century romance, but written in 1969 and addressed to the intellectual vanity of the modern reader by means of confidential asides, footnotes which titillate while purporting to add documentary authority (all that absurdly solemn stuff about sausage skins and condoms), and frequent recourse to passwords like Darwin, Marx and (just once) Freud. As a result it places that easy target – repressed Victorian sexuality – well within our drooling sights. Harold Pinter's screenplay gives flesh to this 20th century perspective with a parallel story: not only do Streep and Irons play the 19th century lovers, they are also cast as a pair of adulterous sophisticates, swotting up on Victorian social history between takes during filming of *The French Lieutenant's Woman.* As a solution to the almost impossible problem of adapting the book, this film-within-a-film idea is an honourable failure, providing a modest, nearly redundant framework since the Victorian sequences stand on their own merits, with performances (the pre-Raphaelite Streep is outstanding), exquisite photography (Freddie Francis) and Reisz's direction combining to deliver a powerful and persuasive anatomy of passion. JS

French Line, The

(1953, US, 102 min)
d Lloyd Bacon. *p* Edmund Grainger. *sc* Mary Loos, Richard Sale. *ph* Harry J Wild. *ed* Robert Ford. *ad* Albert S D'Agostino, Carroll Clark. *songs* Josef Myrow, Robert Wells, Ralph Blane. *cast* Jane Russell, Gilbert Roland, Arthur Hunnicutt, Mary McCarty, Craig Stevens, Steven Geray.
●Jane Russell shown 'flat' is perhaps an anatomical impossibility, but the film was originally made in 3-D, and most screenings nowadays will unfortunately prevent you from testing the accuracy of RKO's publicity teaser: 'It'll knock both your eyes out!' The woman who once gave Howard Hughes his greatest technical challenge plays a Texan tycoon who disguises herself as a model and goes to Paris to find a man unaware of her vast fortune. Enter Gilbert Roland as a French musical comedy star and the excuse for some song-and-dance routines that look like outtakes from *Gentlemen Prefer Blondes* and *How to Marry a Millionaire.* ATu

Frenchman's Creek

(1944, US, 112 min)
d Mitchell Leisen. *p* BG De Sylva. *sc* Talbot Jennings. *ph* George Barnes. *ed* Alma Macrorie. *ad* Hans Dreier, Ernst Fegté. *m* Victor Young. *cast* Joan Fontaine, Arturo de Cordova, Basil Rathbone, Nigel Bruce, Cecil Kellaway, Ralph Forbes.
●Captivatingly extravagant piece of escapism from the much underrated Leisen: an adaptation of a Daphne du Maurier story about a 17th century aristocratic woman who leaves London for Cornwall with her children – mainly to escape pressingly unwelcome attentions from her complaisant husband's best friend (Rathbone) – and there falls in love with a swashbuckling French pirate. Fontaine is a little too prissy to enter fully into the spirit of things (although this brings dividends when she is faced with the heartbreaking problem of her children), but the combination of exquisite colour, sets and location photography with Leisen's light touch is a winning formula. GA

French Mistress, A

(1960, GB, 98 min, b/w)
d Roy Boulting. *p* John Boulting. *sc* Roy Boulting, Jeffrey Dell. *ph* Max Greene. *ed* John Jympson. *ad* Albert Witherick. *m* John Addison. *cast* James Robertson Justice, Cecil Parker, Raymond Huntley, Ian Bannen, Agnès Laurent, Irene Handl, Kenneth Griffith, Thorley Walters.
●One of the great disappointments in post-war British film history is the decline of the Boulting Brothers. It's a mystery how film-makers capable of turning out thrillers as accomplished as *Brighton Rock* and *Seven Days to Noon* spent the latter half of their career churning out flaccid satirical comedies. This effort, set in an English public school, is typical late Boulting nonsense, a prurient yarn about how excited teachers and students alike become when a glamorous new female teacher arrives on their doorstep. There's a certain pleasure in seeing warhorses like Justice and Parker try to out-ham one another, but no hiding the feebleness of the material (from a play by Robert Munro) or the Boultings' approach to it. GM

French Mustard (La Moutarde Me Monte au Nez)

(1974, Fr, 98 min)
d Claude Zidi. *p* Christian Fechner. *sc* Claude Zidi, Pierre Richard, Michel Fabre. *ph* Henri Decaë. *ed* Robert Isnardon, Monique Isnardon. *ad* Michel de Broin, Jacques Bufnoir. *m* Vladimir Cosma. *cast* Pierre Richard, Jane Birkin, Claude Piéplu, Jean Martin, Danou Minazzoli, Vittorio Caprioli.
●Generally insufferable farce which steers an unhappy course between odd moments of style, heavy Gallic charm, and tasteless bursts of visceral slapstick. Harmless enough to have been seen on BBC TV, it shows not very much of Birkin as scandalous starlet Jackie Logan, who gets repeatedly embroiled with the mayor's son. Here and there among all the falling about there are swipes at spaghetti Westerns, anti-pornographers, and Henry Kissinger. Sometimes the chapter of accidents befalling the mayor's son snowballs to good nutty effect; mostly not though. AN

French Twist

see Gazon maudit

French Without Tears

(1939, GB, 85 min, b/w)
d Anthony Asquith. *p* Mario Zampi. *sc* Anatole De Grunwald, Ian Dalrymple, Terence Rattigan. *ph* Bernard Knowles. *ed* David Lean. *ad* Paul Sheriff. *m* Nicholas Brodszky. *cast* Ray Milland, Roland Culver, Guy Middleton, Ellen Drew, David Tree, Janine Darcy, Jim Gérald.
●In an idyllic little French language school, trainee diplomats and a sex-starved naval commander lose their hearts and minds to a winsome, gooey adventuress. Terence Rattigan's 'well made play' – a mixture of sophisticated badinage and schoolboy misogyny – now looks utterly inconsequential, redolent only of the anaemic '30s complacency which led to Munich. PM's son 'Puffin' Asquith struggles valiantly but in vain to turn it into something cinematic, and even Culver's nicely judged performance as the stoically lovesick sailor fails to life the film beyond being simply a historical curiosity. Needless to say the critics at the time thought it was wonderful. RMy

Frenzy

(1972, GB, 116 min)
d/p Alfred Hitchcock. *sc* Anthony Shaffer. *ph* Gilbert Taylor. *ed* John Jympson. *pd* Syd Cain. *m* Ron Goodwin. *cast* Jon Finch, Alec McCowen, Barry Foster, Barbara Leigh-Hunt, Anna Massey, Vivien Merchant, Billie Whitelaw.
●Hitchcock's return to Covent Garden, 'wrong man' plotting, the neuroses of sexual immaturity, and black-humoured slapstick ironies, tied up neatly in Anthony Shaffer's screenplay from the novel by Arthur Le Bern about the panic wrought by the 'necktie murderer', and glossed with the usual quota of stand-out sequences: the camera's descending recoil from a murderer's first-floor flat; a grisly wrestling match with a corpse in a lorry-load of potatoes; the inspector's mealtimes (almost a reverse homage to Chabrol); the one extended, disturbing seduction/rape/ murder scene. A series of variations on themes of excess, surplus and waste from the most fastidious of directors. PT

Frenzy

see Hets

Frequency

(2000, US, 118 min)
d Gregory Hoblit. *p* Hawk Koch, Gregory Hoblit, Bill Carraro, Toby Emmerich. *sc* Toby Emmerich. *ph* Alar Kivilo. *ed* David Rosenbloom. *pd* Paul Eads. *m* Michael Kamen. *cast* Dennis Quaid, Jim Caviezel, André Braugher, Elizabeth Mitchell, Noah Emmerich, Shawn Doyle, Jordan Bridges, Melissa Errico.
●This ambitious but frustrating timeshift thriller never quite manages to jam together two distinct stories. In 1999, freak weather and an old ham radio allow Queens cop John Sullivan to communicate with his fireman dad, Frank (Quaid), dead these 30 years. Coincidentally, a murder mystery from 1969 is revived after John (Caviezel) and his partner Satch (Braugher) discover new evidence. Things get weird when John tells his much missed father how to escape the warehouse fire that killed him. The effects are unpredictable and frightening, especially when father and son try to prevent the '69 murders. Their efforts repeatedly place Frank at the scene of the crime, eventually making him prime suspect. And who was the investigating officer back then? Why, a much younger Satch. With me so far? The script's original concept opens up fascinating possibilities, then disappointingly plumps for the boring serial killer option. NF

Fresa y Chocolate

see Strawberry and Chocolate

Fresh

(1994, US/Fr, 112 min)
d Boaz Yakin. *p* Lawrence Bender, Randy Ostrow. *sc* Boaz Yakin. *ph* Adam Holender. *ed* Dorian Harris. *pd* Dan Leigh. *m* Stewart Copeland. *cast* Sean Nelson, Giancarlo Esposito, Samuel L Jackson, N'Bushe Wright, Ron Brice, Jean LaMarre, Luis Lantigua.
●A stylish, affecting, ingeniously plotted first feature in which a 12-year-old black kid, beset by drug-dealers, a junkie sister, and his clean-living aunt, struggles to put his life in order by means of lessons he's learned from his chess-playing dad. Yakin never settles for the easy, last-minute moralising and macho posturing that has afflicted much of the otherwise intriguing new black cinema; here, story and character take priority, helped no end by Nelson's quiet, riveting central performance. GA

Fresh Horses

(1988, US, 105 min)
d David Anspaugh. *p* Dick Berg. *sc* Larry Ketron. *ph* Fred Murphy. *ed* David Rosenbloom. *pd* Paul Sylbert. *m* David Foster, Patrick Williams. *cast* Molly Ringwald, Andrew McCarthy, Patti D'Arbanville, Ben Stiller, Leon Russom, Molly Hagan, Viggo Mortensen, Chiara Peacock.
●We know things aren't right between lovebirds Matt (McCarthy) and Alice (Peacock) when he turns up late for his engagement party. A conventional guy, training for a conventional career, Matt is having a crisis of faith, and only bourbon-drinking, dishevelled Jewel (Ringwald) can help him. While Alice talks about wedding china, Matt enjoys secret assignations with Jewel in a trackside shack. She's lower class, been abused, a high school dropout. Matt is appalled, attracted, confused, and has an uncontrollable urge to correct her syntax. Wordily scripted by Larry Ketron from his own play, this tortured attempt to sustain the bratpack formula fails dismally. Ringwald's performance is fine, but McCarthy suffers unconvincingly, with exaggerated looks and pauses to convey inner torment; the contrast between urban and rustic values is forced; and there's no real emotional depth in the lead character's tedious, muddled excesses. CM

Freshman, The

(1990, US, 103 min)
d Andrew Bergman. *p* Mike Lobell. *sc* Andrew Bergman. *ph* William A Fraker. *ed* Barry Malkin. *ad* Ken Adam. *m* David Newman. *cast* Marlon Brando, Matthew Broderick, Bruno Kirby, Penelope Ann Miller, Frank Whaley, Jon Polito, Paul Benedict, Richard Gant, Maximilian Schell.
●Film student Clark Kellogg (Broderick) arrives in New York ready to start his first term, but within minutes smooth-talking hustler Victor Ray (Kirby) has relieved him of money and luggage. When Kellogg later chances across Ray, the latter makes amends by offering the distraught teen a part-time job with his uncle Carmine Sabatini (Brando) who, seen sprawled behind his desk at an Italian 'social club', looks every inch the Godfather. Kellogg's first assignment seems fraught with hazards… Writer/director

Bergman's good-natured comedy makes light of gangster genre conventions, and humorously under- cuts some of the more portentous aspects of film academia: Kellogg's plight is rendered farcical when, at a seminar on Coppola's *The Godfather*, he begins to find disturbing similarities between his life and the movie. The casting, needless to say, is perfect, and Bergman keeps the various escalating intrigues clipping along at a brisk pace. CM

Freud

(1962, US, 140 min, b/w)
d John Huston. *p* Wolfgang Reinhardt. *sc* Charles A Kaufman, Wolfgang Reinhardt. *ph* Douglas Slocombe. *ed* Ralph Kemplen. *ad* Stephen Grimes. *m* Jerry Goldsmith. *cast* Montgomery Clift, Susannah York, Larry Parks, Susan Kohner, Eileen Herlie, Fernand Ledoux, David McCallum, Rosalie Crutchley, Eric Portman.

● Huston concentrates on the young Freud, driven by a pathological desire to 'know', discovering the existence of the unconscious. The narrative suggests similarities between Freud and other Huston heroes who are inexorably compelled to acknowledge the unacceptable faces of the self. But the banal misconceptions about psychoanalysis repeated in the film are contradicted by the force of the *mise en scène*, with its narrative dislocations and the excessive pictorialism of the image track making 'Freud' an extraordinary, uncanny *film noir*. As if the telling of this particular tale could not but reinscribe into the text what the trivialisation of psychoanalysis seeks to repress. Together with *The Asphalt Jungle*, *Freud* is Huston's most remarkable film.

Freudlose Gasse, Die

see Joyless Street, The

Friday

(1995, US, 92 min)
d F Gary Gray. *p* Pat Charbonnet. *sc* Ice Cube, DJ Pooh. *ph* Gerry Lively. *ed* John Carter. *pd* Bruce Bellamy. *m* Hidden Faces. *cast* Ice Cube, Chris Tucker, John Witherspoon, Anna Maria Horsford, Tiny 'Zeus' Lister Jr, Nia Long.

● 'It's Friday – let's get high!' pretty much sums up this so-so 'hood comedy. Craig (Ice Cube, motionless) is a soft-natured teen who still resides with his parents. His best buddy is quick-talking Smokey (Tucker, OTT), a drug-dealing dopefiend with a cash-loan problem. What action there is rarely shifts beyond the parents' porch. Director Gray tries (unsuccessfully) to create a '90s Cheech and Chong with inane lavatory humour, manic facial expressions, and plenty of close-ups of a tokin' Smokey. Passé the spliff. DA

Friday the 13th

(1980, US, 95 min)
d/p Sean S Cunningham. *sc* Victor Miller. *ph* Barry Abrams. *ed* Bill Freda. *ad* Virginia Field. *m* Harry Manfredini. *cast* Betsy Palmer, Adrienne King, Jeannine Taylor, Robbi Morgan, Kevin Bacon, Harry Crosby.

● A motley crew of teenagers whose idea of relaxation is a game of strip Monopoly take jobs at a run-down summer camp, but get gorily hacked and sliced to death by a local nutter almost before they've had time to unpack. A tame, poorly plotted serving of schlock, less horrific for its ketchup-smeared murders than for the bare-faced fashion in which it tries and fails to rip off Carpenter's *Halloween* in matters of style and construction. TP

Friday the 13th Part 2

(1981, US, 87 min)
d Steve Miner. *p* Dennis Murphy, Steve Miner. *sc* Ron Kurz. *ph* Peter Stein. *ed* Susan E Cunningham. *pd* Virginia Field. *m* Harry Manfredini. *cast* Amy Steel, John Furey, Adrienne King, Kirsten Baker, Stu Charno, Warrington Gillette.

● This first sequel to *Friday the 13th* opens with mild panache when a summary recapitulation of the story so far ends with the sole survivor of the previous massacre being unexpectedly despatched by a new killer (the grief-crazed woman's supposedly dead son). The script then jumps five years, assembles a new set of victims at the summer camp, and repeats the gory carnage as before. The formula reached Part VIII by 1989. Cynically manipulative, stultifying in their sameness, they require no comment except that Part III was shot in 3-D, Part V (*A New Beginning*) toyed with being tongue in cheek, and Part VI (*Jason Lives*) took the rather desperate step of resurrecting its psycho like Frankenstein's monster.

Friday the 13th Part VIII: Jason Takes Manhattan

(1989, US, 100 min)
d Rob Hedden. *p* Randolph Cheveldave. *sc* Rob Hedden. *ph* Bryan England. *ed* Steve Mirkovich. *ad* David Fischer. *m* Fred Mollin. *cast* Jensen Daggett, Kane Hodder, Scott Reeves, Peter Mark Richman, Barbara Bingham, Vincent Craig Dupree.

● For what it's worth (very little), probably the best in the series. Human threshing-machine Jason is scraped up from the bottom of Crystal Lake by the anchor of a passing pleasure boat and soon finds himself on a cruise to New York with a bunch of eminently scythable high school students. With more flair and less gore than the other eight, *Jason Goes to Hell: The Final Friday* brought matters to a grim conclusion four years later. TJ

Frieda

(1947, GB, 98 min, b/w)
d Basil Dearden. *p* Michael Balcon. *sc* Angus MacPhail, Ronald Millar. *ph* Gordon Dines. *ed* Leslie Norman. *pd* Michael Relph. *m* John Greenwood. *cast* Mai Zetterling, David Farrar, Glynis Johns, Flora Robson, Albert Lieven, Barbara Everest, Gladys Henson.

● With World War II hostilities just over, RAF officer Farrar brings home a German bride (Zetterling), having married her in gratitude for her part in helping him to escape from a PoW camp (unaware that Johns, whom he loved but who married his brother, is now a widow). 'It's a pleasant, peaceful spot…like any town in England', he tells her as he looks out of the train taking them home. Cue for one of those comfortable slices of social criticism in which rabid prejudice is gradually broken down by sweet reasonableness. But with Farrar and Zetterling doing their respective glowering and cowering acts, he treating her with increasing callousness as she becomes increasingly unnerved by her hostile reception, the whole thing begins to shape up as a melodramatic thriller. Highly watchable, perhaps for the wrong reasons. TM

Fried Green Tomatoes at the Whistle Stop Café

(1991, US, 130 min)
d Jon Avnet. *p* Jon Avnet, Jordan Kerner. *sc* Jon Avnet, Fannie Flagg, Carol Sobieski. *ph* Geoffrey Simpson. *ed* Debbie Neil. *ad* Barbara Ling. *m* Thomas Newman. *cast* Kathy Bates, Jessica Tandy, Mary Stuart Masterson, Mary Louise Parker, Gailard Sartain, Stan Shaw, Cicely Tyson, Gary Basaraba, Lois Smith, Grace Zabriskie.

● Southern housewife Evelyn (Bates) has had enough of her couch-potato husband (Sartain). Their sex life is dying, and even wrapping her naked body in cling-wrap merely provokes further apathy. Then, at a nursing-home, she meets old-timer Ninny (Tandy), who launches into a rambling recollection of long-gone friends and family: tales of feisty Idgie (Masterson) and Ruth (Parker) who once ran a café in Ninny's small Alabama home town. Gradually, Evelyn finds strength in the bravery of these two, and solace in Ninny's evocation of simpler times. With director Avnet, Fannie Flagg co-scripted this adaptation of her novel; but while the book deftly juggles separate narratives, the device proves clumsy on screen. More dizzying than the jumps between past and present is the speed with which consciousness-raised Evelyn swaps caricatures, evolving from Frump to Fighter. Essentially, the film is about fine performances – with Tandy securing an Oscar nomination – but it wins no prizes for subtlety. CM

Friend (Chingu)

(2001, SKor, 117 min)
d Kwak Kyung-Taek. *p* Vicki Kyung-Lim Hyun, Cho Won-Jang. *sc* Kwak Kyung-Taek. *ph* Ki S Hwang. *ed* Park Gok-Ji. *ad* Oh Sang-Man. *m* Choi Man-Shik. *cast* Yoo Oh-Sung, Jang Dong-Gun, Suh Tae-Hwa, Jung Woon-Taek.

● More than 8m Koreans bought tickets to see it, but Kwak's autobiographical film is not your average Korean blockbuster. It traces the relationships between four young men across 20 years, from schooldays in the '70s to an adulthood in the mid-'90s which sees one dead, another in jail for ordering his murder, another happily married and the fourth just back from the US and poised to begin a career in the film industry. Shooting impressionistically and draining most of the colour from the images to stress how remote in time these relatively recent memories seem, Kwak focuses squarely on questions of trust, honour and loyalty. There are some large-canvas action sequences (a gang fight which takes over an entire cinema) and some moments of intense violence, but the core of the film is an account of the joys and terrors of male bonding, rendered with a raw immediacy. TR

Friendly Fire (Ação entre Amigos)

(1998, Braz, 76 min)
d/sc Beto Brant. *ph* Marcelo Durst. *m* Andre Abujamra. *cast* Leonardo Villar, Zé Carlos Machado, Leonardo Villar, Cacá Amaral, Genesio de Barros, Carlos Meceni, Sergio Cavalcante, José Mayer.

● Beto Brant, director of *Belly Up*, tackles the theme of revenge – a double edged sword – in this tense but facile drama. Miguel (Machado) recognises a face on a postcard as that of one Correia, São Paulo's chief torturer in the days of the dictatorship 25 years ago. Correia was the man responsible for the murder of Miguel's pregnant girlfriend and fellow freedom fighter, and Miguel sets out, with the help of three ex-'brothers', to kill him. A worthwhile cautionary tale is marred by a crude script, over-acting and flashy camerawork – even if the 'Scope format is sometimes striking. WH

Friendly Persuasion

(1956, US, 140 min)
d/p William Wyler. [*sc* Michael Wilson.] *ph* Ellsworth J Fredricks. *ed* Robert Swink, Edward Biery Jr, Robert Belcher. *ad* Ted Haworth. *m* Dimitri Tiomkin. *cast* Gary Cooper, Dorothy McGuire, Marjorie Main, Anthony Perkins, Richard Eyer, Robert Middleton, Walter Catlett.

● Wyler in characteristically earnest form with a Western-style story of a family of Quakers whose faith in a non-violent way of life is sorely tried by the outbreak of the Civil War. Solid performances, particularly from Perkins as the anguished son, and odd touches of humour (which might, ironically, offend Quakers, since their way of life is presented as eccentrically old-fashioned); but the basic dilemma – whether to take up arms or not – is presented in simplistic and predictable fashion. From a novel by Jessamyn Wess. GA

Friends

(1971, GB, 102 min)
d/p Lewis Gilbert. *sc* Jack Russell, Vernon Harris. *ph* Andréas Winding. *ed* Anne V Coates. *ad* Marc Frédérix. *m* Elton John. *cast* Sean Bury, Anicée Alvina, Ronald Lewis, Toby Robins, Joan Hickson, Pascale Roberts.

● Hideous schmaltz, all lyrical slow motion and soft focus, in which a fourteen-year-old French girl (Alvina) and a fifteen-year-old English boy (Bury) run away from their respective unhappy homes to the Camargue (complete with wild horses). There, in a cosy cottage, they play at marriage, have a baby, and *almost* manage to live happily ever after in their Garden of Eden. Complete with Elton John on the soundtrack. Yuck. TM

Friends

(1993, GB/Fr, 109 min)
d Elaine Proctor. *p* Judith Hunt. *sc* Elaine Proctor. *ph* Dominique Chapuis. *ed* Tony Lawson. *pd* Carmel Collins. *m* Rachel Portman. *cast* Kerry Fox, Dambisa Kente, Michele Burgers, Marius Weyers, Tertius Meintjes.

● Set in South Africa just before the release of Nelson Mandela, this film focuses on three representative women who meet at university: Sophie (Fox) comes from an affluent white Johannesburg suburb; Thoko (Kente) is a Zulu teacher; Aninka (Burgers) a working-class Afrikaner. They live together, defiantly, but their friendship is tested when Sophie, an anti-apartheid activist, plants a bomb, with bloody consequences. This fiction film, by a South African-born documentary-maker, rather labours its points. Powerful prison scenes, though, and convincing snapshots of Johannesburg social life. JBa

Friends and Husbands (Heller Wahn)

(1982, WGer/Fr, 106 min)
d Margarethe von Trotta. *p* Eberhard Junkersdorf. *sc* Margarethe von Trotta. *ph* Michael Ballhaus. *ed* Dagmar Hirtz. *ad* Jürgen Henze, Werner Mink. *m* Nicolas Economou. *cast* Hanna Schygulla, Angela Winkler, Peter Striebeck, Christine Fersen, Franz Buchrieser, Wladimir Yordanoff.
●Something of a disappointment after *The German Sisters*. Von Trotta's theme – the obsessive interdependence of two women, one (Schygulla) assured and outgoing, the other (Winkler) timid and reclusive – resembles her earlier chamber piece, *Sisters, or the Balance of Happiness*. But here her more ambitious scope opens up glaring weaknesses in the minor roles, particularly the husbands, and the story rambles furiously, with little added by location shooting in Cairo and Provence. And a heavy pall of Teutonic neuroticism sits over the whole thing, stemming not from Hitler's legacy as in *The German Sisters*, but more diffusely from the German Romantics, whose suicides and madmen and women exercise a highly ambivalent fascination. But von Trotta does extract excellent performances from her two leads, making this a delicate and penetrating study of (platonic) love between women. SJo

Friendship's Death

(1987, GB, 78 min)
d Peter Wollen. *p* Rebecca O'Brien. *sc* Peter Wollen. *ph* Witold Stok. *ed* Robert Hargreaves. *pd* Gemma Jackson. *m* Barrington Pheloung. *cast* Bill Paterson, Tilda Swinton, Patrick Bauchau, Ruby Baker, Joumana Gill.
●In September 1970, a British war correspondent (Paterson) is distracted from his coverage of the bloody conflict between Palestinians and Jordanians when he rescues a young lady (Swinton) from a PLO patrol. Simply named Friendship, she claims to be an extraterrestrial robot sent to Earth on a peace mission and accidentally diverted from her original destination, the Massachusetts Institute of Technology. Is she insane, a spy, or telling the truth? Wollen's film comes across as a two-set *Dr Who* for adults, complete with political, philosophical and more pettily personal problems; the use of the alien outsider's way of seeing the world is perceptive and provocative, the plentiful ideas counterbalance the lack of extravagant spectacle. Best of all, the film displays a droll wit (Friendship viewing a typewriter as a distant cousin, or concocting a surreal thesis on the big toe's importance in the oppression of women) and a surprising ability to touch the heart. With two impressive central performances, Wollen at last proves himself able to direct actors, and has made by far his most rewarding movie to date. GA

Friends of Eddie Coyle, The

(1973, US, 102 min)
d Peter Yates. *p/sc* Paul Monash. *ph* Victor J Kemper. *ed* Patricia Jaffe. *pd* Gene Callahan. *m* Dave Grusin. *cast* Robert Mitchum, Peter Boyle, Richard Jordan, Steven Keats, Alex Rocco, Joe Santos, Mitchell Ryan.
●Yates' downbeat dissection of Boston's underworld, based on the novel by George V Higgins, revolves around the dilemma of Mitchum's weary small-time mobster and all-time loser Eddie 'Fingers' Coyle (somebody shut a drawer on his hand), under pressure to turn stoolie in the wake of a couple of murderous bank heists. The cast lend the film an authority that Yates' curiously pedestrian approach fails to provide, and Mitchum's agonies over codes of underworld honour segue perfectly into his subsequent explorations of loyalty and obligation in *The Yakuza*. PT

Frightened City, The

(1961, GB, 98 min, b/w)
d John Lemont. *p* John Lemont, Leigh Vance. *sc* Leigh Vance. *ph* Desmond Dickinson. *ed* Bernard Gribble. *ad* Maurice Carter. *m* Norrie Paramor. *cast* Herbert Lom, John Gregson, Sean Connery, Alfred Marks, Ruth Romain, David Davies, Olive McFarland, Kenneth Griffith, Bruce Seton.
●When dodgy accountant Waldo Zhernikov (Lom) convenes a meeting of London's top racketeers, the craggy, grandfatherly characters who turn up seem more like grocers than gangsters. At least Connery, pre-Bond, brings a little muscle to the proceedings; but Gregson, as Insp Sayers, is simply too wholesome a cop for the protection-busting job in hand. GM

Frighteners, The

(1996, NZ/US, 110 min)
d Peter Jackson. *p* Jamie Selkirk, Peter Jackson. *sc* Fran Walsh, Peter Jackson. *ph* Alun Bollinger, John Blick. *ed* Jamie Selkirk. *pd* Grant Major. *m* Danny Elfman. *cast* Michael J Fox, Trini Alvarado, Peter Dobson, John Astin, Jeffrey Combs, Chi McBride, Jim Fyfe, Jake Busey, Dee Wallace Stone, R Lee Ermey.
●Jackson's follow-up to *Heavenly Creatures* is an sfx-heavy scarefest that looks at first like a return to the slapstick horror-comedy of *Braindead*. Later, however, it flips into a grim, disturbing horror movie about the malevolent spirit of a serial killer back from the grave to increase his body count. Fake para-psychologist Frank Bannister (Fox) is in cahoots with a trio of tortured souls – hip dude Cyrus (McBride), creaky-boned old-timer The Judge (Astin), and nerdy bookworm Stuart (Fyfe): they scare the shit out of Fairwater's inhabitants while Frank cleans up the mess. A series of unexplained deaths heralds the arrival of a Grim Reaper-like spirit that Frank alone can see. This may be connected to a thrill-kill case in which Patricia Bradley (Stone), now a middle-aged, mother-dominated recluse, and her hospital orderly boyfriend Johnny Bartlett (Busey) massacred a dozen patients and hospital staff. Though funded by Hollywood, this New Zealand-shot movie was creatively controlled by Jackson and co-writer Fran Walsh. So while the on-screen violence is toned down, there's no soft-pedalling the ugliness of mass murder or the obscenity of ill-deserved media celebrity. At times the relentless special effects and tangled plotting veer towards visual and narrative overkill, but the final tonal swerve is shocking and effective. NF

Frightmare

(1974, GB, 86 min)
d/p Pete Walker. *sc* David McGillivray. *ph* Peter Jessop. *ed* Bob Dearberg. *ad* Chris Burke. *m* Stanley Myers. *cast* Rupert Davies, Sheila Keith, Deborah Fairfax, Paul Greenwood, Kim Butcher, Fiona Curzon.
●With *Frightmare* following on *House of Whipcord*, David McGillivray's scriptwriting is undoubtedly having a marked effect on Walker's exploitation pictures. Where he used to settle for routine plots, his films now teem with demonic life, plus vicious and genuinely disturbing shock effects. *Frightmare* is about a psychopathic mum (Keith) who has the nasty habit of going at her victims with an electric drill before devouring them raw. It is far better written and acted than you might expect, and Walker's direction is on another level altogether from *Cool It Carol!* or *The Flesh and Blood Show*. The problem is that there is absolutely no exposition or analysis, no flexibility about the theme; still contained within a basic formula, it tends to leave a highly unpleasant aftertaste. DP

Fright Night

(1985, US, 106 min)
d Tom Holland. *p* Herb Jaffe. *sc* Tom Holland. *ph* Jan Kiesser. *ed* Kent Beyda. *pd* John F DeCuir Jr. *m* Brad Fiedel. *cast* Chris Sarandon, William Ragsdale, Amanda Bearse, Roddy McDowall, Stephen Geoffreys, Jonathan Stark.
●Charley (Ragsdale) has seen a coffin being carried into the house next door and a corpse being dragged out, but no one will take him seriously. In desperation he enlists a TV vampire killer, who's initially charmed by neighbour-from-hell Jerry (Sarandon), before noticing the absence of his reflection in a mirror. A farrago of cartoonish exaggeration (mouthfuls of fangs, razor-sharp talons and eyes like burning coals), knowing humour and '80s camp, it shouldn't even begin to work, and yet, strangely, it does, sort of, thanks to the assured handling of writer/director Holland, and two performances in particular – Geoffreys as Charley's pal Evil, and McDowall as the timid vampire killer. The music helps, covering an ambitious range from piano-murdering suspense-raisers, through disco fodder, to a Sparks tune, 'Armies of the Night', by Ron and Russell Mael. NRo

Fright Night Part 2

(1988, US, 104 min)
d Tommy Lee Wallace. *p* Herb Jaffe, Mort Engelberg. *sc* Tim Metcalfe, Miguel Tejada-Flores, Tommy Lee Wallace. *ph* Mark Irwin. *ed* Jay Lash Cassidy, Jonathan Shaw. *pd* Dean Tschetter. *m* Brad Fiedel. *cast* Roddy McDowall, William Ragsdale, Traci Lin, Julie Carmen, Jonathan Gries, Russell Clark.
●Another stop-me-if-you've-heard-this sequel, with young Ragsdale emerging from three years of psychotherapy to find that the vampires he's been persuaded are imaginary really do exist. Having convinced TV horror-show host McDowall that the fanged ones are back in business, Ragsdale confronts the deliciously dangerous Carmen, sister of suave bloodsucker Chris Sarandon whom they stalked in Part 1. With Carmen's fatal allure substituted for Sarandon's sexually ambiguous charm, the intriguing homoerotic overtones of the original give way to a more blatant equation of hunger and desire. What few innovations there are – notably Carmen's spectacular usurpation of McDowall's show – go for nothing. Wallace's direction lacks the flair and intelligence that Tom Holland brought to *Fright Night*. NF

Fringe Dwellers, The

(1986, Aust, 98 min)
d Bruce Beresford. *p* Sue Milliken. *sc* Bruce Beresford, Rhoisin Beresford. *ph* Donald McAlpine. *ed* Tim Wellburn. *pd* Herbert Pinter. *m* George Dreyfus. *cast* Kristina Nehm, Justine Saunders, Bob Maza, Kylie Belling, Denis Walker, Ernie Dingo.
●This adaptation of Nene Gar's novel about contemporary life among the Aborigines of Australia shows them as outcasts in their own country, despised by the whites, disinclined to work at what menial jobs they can get, and with a big partiality for hitting the booze. The Comeaway family is persuaded by their 15-year-old daughter Trilby (Nehm) to move from the shantytown where they live to a new estate. She is determined not to fall into the same over-breeding, underachieving trap as the women around her, but finds that events seem constantly to be conspiring against her. Beresford evidently feels considerable sympathy with the Aborigines, but this is tinged with despair at their apparent penchant for self-destruction. The film never really jells, but is notable for an engaging performance from Nehm. JP

Frisk

(1995, US, 83 min)
d Todd Verow. *p* Marcus Hu, Jon Gerrans. *sc* Jim Dwyer, George LaVoo, Todd Verow. *ph* Greg Watkins. *ed* Joseph Hoffman. *pd* Jennifer Graber. *m* Coil, Lee Ranaldo, Elph, New E-Z Devils, Octarine. *cast* Michael Gunter, Craig Chester, Parker Posey, James Lyons, Alexis Arquette, Raoul O'Connell.
●Dennis (Gunter) begins to explore his violent homosexual fantasies when he meets Henry (Chester), a masochist who's also a necrophiliac pin-up. His friends are alarmed, but sceptical, when Dennis begins to write confessional letters describing acts of murder. The dubious equation of homosexuality, perversity and murder made in mainstream Hollywood thrillers like *Basic Instinct* or *Cruising* has outraged the gay community. Is it a sign of decadence or maturity that gays can now exploit gay-on-gay violence? And is it for edification or entertainment? Neither, probably. Verow made his mark as cameraman on Gregg Araki's *Totally F***ed Up* and MTV's *Real World* series. His first film as director (from a cult novel by Dennis Cooper) boasts occasional bursts of flashy editing, lousy performances (exception: Parker Posey in a ten-minute cameo as a fag hag only too happy to participate in a spot of orgiastic murder), and a sour sensibility quite in keeping with the characters. TCh

Frisson des Vampires, Le (Sex and the Vampire/ Vampire Thrills)

(1970, Fr, 90 min)
d Jean Rollin. *p* Jacques Prayer. *sc* Jean Rollin. *ph* Jean-Jacques Renon. *ed* Olivier Gregoire. *ad* Michel Delesalles. *m* Acanthus. *cast* Sandra Julien, Dominique, Nicole Nancel, Michel Delahaye, Jacques Robiolles, Jean Marie Durand.

●An involved vampire story, badly acted and with an idiotic plot, but visually a feast. It features a fantastic gaunt lady vampire in vermilion make-up who materialises at one stage out of a grandfather clock, and at another comes down the chimney. Also two gentlemen in Carnaby Street evening gear. Quite sexy. Great curiosity value.

Fritz the Cat

(1971, US, 78 min)
d Ralph Bakshi. *p* Steve Krantz. *sc* Ralph Bakshi. *ph* Gene Borghi, Ted C Bemiller. *ed* Renn Reynolds. *m* Ed Bogas, Ray Shanklin, BB King. *cast* voices: Skip Hinnant, Rosetta Le Noire, John McCurry, Judy Engles, Phil Seuling.
●Animated feature based on Robert Crumb's comic strip, detailing a young hipster cat's exploits with dope, Harlem, the police, the Angels, etc. Despite some ingenious effects, a generally trivial exercise that never matches the punch of the original.

Frog Dreaming

(1985, Aust, 93 min)
d Brian Trenchard-Smith. *p* Barbi Taylor. *sc* Everett De Roche. *ph* John McLean. *ed* Brian Kavanagh. *pd* Jon Dowding. *m* Brian May. *cast* Henry Thomas, Tony Barry, Rachel Friend, Tamsin West, Dempsey Knight, John Ewart.
●Something's alive at the bottom of an uncharted pond, and 10-year-old adventurer Cody (Henry Thomas of *ET*) is determined to find it. Director Trenchard-Smith sets the action of this children's movie (involving aboriginal magic) in a remote town in southern Australia, constructing the parallel worlds of doting adults and their irrepressible children as a foundation for his adventure in minutiae. The real adventure, however, is Trenchard-Smith's rediscovery of boyhood, with all its inventiveness, innocence and independent, fearless strength. SGo

Frog Prince, The

(1984, GB, 90 min)
d Brian Gilbert. *p* Iain Smith. *sc* Posy Simmonds. *ph* Clive Tickner. *ed* Jim Clark. *pd* Anton Furst. *m* Enya Ni Bhraonain. *cast* Jane Snowden, Alexandre Sterling, Jacqueline Doyen, Raoul Delfosse, Jeanne Herviale, Françoise Brion.
●Paris, 1960: a wicked city where English ingénue Snowden, sent to polish her French, acquires a sentimental education, fending off lecherous frogs with varying degrees of Gallic smarm. The film, with David Puttnam as executive producer, has a nostalgic *Film on Four* blandness about it, although Posy Simmonds' semi-autobiographical screenplay adds a little spice with its sharp ear for dialogue and its broadly farcical slant, indulging much humour at the expense of those funny French. SJo

Frogs

(1972, US, 90 min)
d George McCowan. *p* Peter Thomas, George Edwards. *sc* Robert Hutchison, Robert Blees. *ph* Mario Tosi. *ed* Fred R Feitshans. *m* Les Baxter. *cast* Ray Milland, Sam Elliott, Joan Van Ark, Adam Roarke, Judy Pace, Lynn Borden.
●A 'nature strikes back' eco-drama built on sturdy, if predictable, *Ten Little Nigger* lines. Elliott plays an ecological photographer snapping wildlife and garbage around the private island home of a millionaire family with nasty habits like spraying insecticide, collecting hunting trophies, catching butterflies. They gather annually for birthday celebrations under the iron fist of patriarch Milland; multiplying and mutating into giant (but not unbelievable) species as a result of the pollution, the reptiles become malevolent, causing the deaths of one after another of the family. Two good points: no revenge-on-frog scenes after they climactically overwhelm Milland in the abandoned house; and apart from some manipulation by cross-cutting, all the reptiles behave fairly normally. Filmed in the usual crisp AIP style, with dazzling sunlight and ominous shadows.

From Beyond

(1986, US, 85 min)
d Stuart Gordon. *p* Brian Yuzna. *sc* Dennis Paoli. *ph* Mac Ahlberg. *ed* Lee Percy. *pd* Giovanni Natalucci. *m* Richard Band. *cast* Jeffrey Combs, Barbara Crampton, Ken Foree, Ted Sorel, Carolyn Purdy-Gordon, Bunny Summers.
●A horror movie from beyond the pale. While experimenting with a sound resonator, mad scientist Dr Edward Pretorius (Sorel) has his head bitten off by an eel which swims in the air. Arrested and charged with his boss' murder, Crawford Tillinghurst (Combs), released into the care of a psychiatrist, later repeats the experiment to prove his innocence. This opens up another can of worms, to improbable results. NF

From Beyond the Grave

(1973, GB, 98 min)
d Kevin Connor. *p* Max J Rosenberg, Milton Subotsky. *sc* Robin Clarke, Raymond Christodoulou. *ph* Alan Hume. *ed* John Ireland. *pd* Maurice Carter. *m* Douglas Gamley. *cast* Peter Cushing, David Warner, Donald Pleasence, Ian Bannen, Diana Dors, Angela Pleasence, Margaret Leighton, Nyree Dawn Porter, Ian Carmichael, Ian Ogilvy, Lesley-Anne Down.
●Although a vast improvement on the derisory *Vault of Horror*, this seventh Amicus horror omnibus, using stories by R Chetwynd-Hayes, suffers from much the same faults as its immediate predecessors. As usual there's one really good episode (a remarkable sub-Pinter piece on witchcraft with a stunning performance from Angela Pleasence), but the others are at best average. And the linking story, with Cushing manning an antique shop, is feeble even by *Vault of Horror* standards. The script's concentration on suspense and visual effects, with a minimum of dialogue, should be a virtue; but the Amicus budgets are so low (with name casts a priority) that the technique frequently results in sequences of cramping boredom. DP

From Dusk till Dawn

(1995, US, 107 min)
d Robert Rodriguez. *p* Gianni Nunnari, Meir Teper. *sc* Quentin Tarantino. *ph* Guillermo Navarro. *ed* Robert Rodriguez. *pd* Cecilia Montiel. *m* Graeme Revell. *cast* Harvey Keitel, George Clooney, Quentin Tarantino, Juliette Lewis, Cheech Marin, Fred Williamson, Salma Hayek, John Saxon.
●It might be more interesting to watch this Tarantino/Rodriguez film without knowing what's in store, in which case, skip this review and take your chances. But don't come running back to me if double-barrelled schizophrenic gun-crazy gut-shot evangelical sleaze, incendiary, popcorn-blowing macho mayhem, slinky, soul-searching zombie strippers, and vampiric cult-infested cinemania don't light your pipe. Tarantino and Clooney are the Gecko brothers, sick and ruthless killers, respectively. They commandeer the motor home of the Rev Fuller (Keitel) to evade the cops en route to a midnight rendezvous at the Titty Twister, hottest whorehouse in all Mexico. Along for the ride are Fuller's teen kids, and the Reverend himself, who has most definitely picked the wrong day to lose his faith. Written by Tarantino in 1990 on a commission from a special effects company, the film is aimed squarely at (male) horror movie fans who appreciate the nuances of impalement by pool cue, pencil and table leg. Rodriguez has a lot of fun dreaming up cool ways to kill people (he's making this his life's work), but he also gets something resembling a performance from Tarantino and transforms Clooney into a full-fledged movie star. Bikers, head-bangers and film geeks will rave to the grave. TCh

From Hell

(2001, US/Czech Rep, 123 min)
d The Hughes Brothers [Albert Hughes, Allen Hughes]. *p* Don Murphy, Jane Hamsher. *sc* Terry Hayes, Rafael Yglesias. *ph* Peter Deming. *ed* Dan Lebental, George Bowers. *pd* Martin Childs. *m* Trevor Jones. *cast* Johnny Depp, Heather Graham, Ian Holm, Robbie Coltrane, Ian Richardson, Jason Flemyng, Katrin Cartlidge, Terence Harvey, Susan Lynch, Paul Rhys, Lesley Sharp.
●With the help of the producers of *Natural Born Killers*, American ghetto blasters the Hughes Brothers (*Menace II Society*, *Dead Presidents*) jack up the Ripper. The first 20 minutes are grim. One prostitute after another is assaulted with gruesome relish – the Brothers' camera honing in for the kill, slicing through the Whitechapel fog. One fancies it's not just the Ripper who is getting off on this. Then there's Graham's Mary Kelly struggling wanly with an alleged Irish accent and Depp's Inspector Fred Abberline, with his soft south London sting and predilections for absinthe and laudanum – shades of Sherlock Holmes. Depp gives a typically studious performance, though locals may require a period of readjustment to understand him. This is not for sensitive souls. But then sensitive souls probably wouldn't be caught dead at a Ripper movie. How foolish, then, that Twentieth Century Fox should have insisted on a trite romance – the Brothers' disinterest is palpable – to weigh down what is otherwise a surprisingly compelling conspiracy yarn. Here is one costume movie that doesn't allow its period atmospherics to clog up the works, while the Hughes' kinetic style heightens the script's attack on endemic class issues, snobbery, racism and sexual hypocrisy. Fitfully arresting late night entertainment. TCh

From Hell It Came

(1957, US, 71 min, b/w)
d Dan Milner. *p* Jack Milner. *sc* Richard Bernstein. *ph* Brydon Baker. *ed* Jack Milner. *ad* Rudi Field. *m* Darrell Calker. *cast* Tod Andrews, Tina Carver, Linda Watkins, John McNamara, Gregg Palmer, Robert Swan.
●'And to hell it can go!' A South Sea island prince is put to death by the tribal elders for fraternising with scientists. He returns as Tabanga…the people-eating tree.

From Hell to Texas (aka Manhunt)

(1958, US, 100 min)
d Henry Hathaway. *p* Robert Buckner. *sc* Robert Buckner, Wendell Mayes. *ph* Wilfred M Cline. *ed* Johnny Ehrin. *ad* Lyle Wheeler, Walter M Simonds. *m* Daniele Amfitheatrof. *cast* Don Murray, Diane Varsi, Chill Wills, Dennis Hopper, RG Armstrong, Jay C Flippen.
●When cowboy Murray accidentally murders one of the sons of powerful rancher Armstrong, the old man despatches his other boy Hopper at the head of a posse to hunt down the killer. Meanwhile, Murray finds refuge with kindly farmer Wills and falls for his daughter, but trouble won't remain far away for long. Capably handled (in 'Scope) by Hathaway, with Murray and young Hopper particularly striking, and the script achieving a timeless resonance by focusing on the morality of vengeance and the power of forgiveness. TJ

From Hell to Victory (De l'Enfer à la Victoire)

(1979, Fr/It/Sp, 102 min)
d Hank Milestone [Umberto Lenzi]. *p* Edmondo Amati. *sc* Umberto Lenzi, Gianfranco Clerici, José Luis Martinez Molla. *ph* José Luis Alcaine. *ed* Vincenzo Tomasi. *ad* Giuseppe Bassan. *m* Riz Ortolani. *cast* George Peppard, George Hamilton, Horst Buchholz, Jean-Pierre Cassel, Capucine, Sam Wanamaker, Anny Duperey.
●As the title suggests, a large slice of epic schlock, which criss-crosses the cosmopolitan cast of second-string heavies through the fortunes of war and the woman they love. Some make it, some don't. In spite of Euro-computer dialogue and a general makeshift air, it's still hard to dislike the awesome nerve of a movie which has incidentals like a shootout on the Eiffel Tower and George Hamilton wasting a Panzer Brigade single-handed. *Merde*! CPea

From Here to Eternity

(1953, US, 118 min, b/w)
d Fred Zinnemann. *p* Buddy Adler. *sc* Daniel Taradash. *ph* Burnett Guffey. *ed* William A Lyon. *ad* Cary Odell. *m* George Duning. *cast* Burt Lancaster, Deborah Kerr, Frank Sinatra, Montgomery Clift, Donna Reed, Ernest Borgnine, Philip Ober, Jack Warden.
●Bowdlerised version of James Jones' novel about physical passion, jealousy and anti-semitism in a Honolulu barracks immediately prior to Pearl Harbor. Best known for Lancaster and Kerr's adulterous romp in the surf, but besides Burnett Guffey's crisp monochrome camerawork and Daniel Taradash's taut screenplay, it's the performances that stay in the memory, particularly those of Clift and Sinatra. Zinnemann's flat direction does produce its dull moments, though; one can only dream of what Minnelli, say, might have made of the steamy melodrama. GA

From Mao to Mozart: Isaac Stern in China

(1980, US, 83 min)
d/p Murray Lerner. *ph* Nic Knowland, Nick Doob, David Bridges. *ed* Tom Haneke. *with* Isaac Stern, David Golub, Tan Shuzhen.
●Far more than a tribute to the man and his music; as well as virtuoso violinist Stern on his 1979 tour of China, we also see a China eager to hear and learn about Western music. Chinese conservatory students' technically superb renditions of Sibelius and Brahms understandably lack the nuances of emotion customary in the West, but playing their own music, or in action at the Peking Opera and the gymnasium, they display dazzling talents. The enthusiastic, amiable Stern occasionally offers paternalistic judgments on Chinese musical abilities, and is thoroughly confused when asked to consider Mozart in a socio-political context. But he's a musician, and his violin sings passionately. Most remarkable, however, are a Shanghai professor's account of his incarceration during the Cultural Revolution, and some truly amazing child prodigies. An uplifting film, made with intelligence and love. GA

From Noon Till Three

(1975, US, 99 min)
d Frank D Gilroy. *p* MJ Frankovich, William Self. *sc* Frank D Gilroy. *ph* Lucien Ballard. *ed* Maury Winetrobe. *pd* Robert Clatworthy. *m* Elmer Bernstein. *cast* Charles Bronson, Jill Ireland, Douglas V Fowley, Stan Haze, Damon Douglas, Hector Morales.
●A Western, adapted by Gilroy from his own novel, whose ideas are executed with an uncertainty that makes whole chunks of the film virtually unwatchable. After a premonition, Bronson sends his gang to their deaths while he passes the afternoon conning a rich widow (Ireland) into bed. Later, thinking he has died a heroic death, she turns the memorabilia of their relationship into a flourishing tourist industry; and when he finally turns up again (after an ignoble spell in jail), she safeguards the legend by ensuring that no one will heed his attempts to reclaim his identity. In its unfolding, the story becomes distinctly uncomfortable, an unhappy mixture of light romantic comedy and something altogether darker (after all, it begins with a nightmare and ends in madness). On top of this, there's the added torture of watching Bronson trying to struggle out of the acting straitjacket that he has worn for some years.

From Pole to Equator (Dal Polo all'Equatore)

(1986, It/WGer, 96 min, tinted)
d/p Yervant Gianikian, Angela Ricci Lucchi. *ph* Angela Ricci Lucchi. *m* Keith Ullrich, Charles Anderson.
●Archivalism was never like this. The film-makers have explored a mass of 'travelogue' footage shot by the Italian explorer-cameraman Luca Comerio in the early years of this century, and turned it into a magical, terrifying journey through inner space. The original images have been stretch-printed and colour-tinted, giving them a fragile surface beauty, but also creating a crucial distance from the original content: the slaughter of big game, the taming of colonised peoples in Africa and Asia, the glorification of imperial conquest. There's no moralising commentary to point up the contradictions; each viewer is left to dream his/her way through a phantasmagoria that extends the definition of Empire-building to the act of photography itself. *Sauve qui peut.* TR

From Russia to Hollywood: The 100-Year Odyssey of Chekhov and Shdanoff

(1999, US, 66 min)
d Frederick Keeve. *p* Frederick Keeve, Lisa Dalton, Charles X Block, Peter Spirer. *sc* Frederick Keeve. *ph* Peter Bonilla. *ed* Robert Gordon. *m* Frederick Keeve. *with* Anthony Quinn, Leslie Caron, Patricia Neal, Robert Stack, Lloyd Bridges, John Berry, Craig Sheffer, Hurd Hatfield, Sharon Gless, Beatrice Straight, Richard Schickel, Ford Rainey. *narrator* Gregory Peck.
●Yes, it's good to set the record straight by documenting the work and influence of people like Russian émigré actors turned drama coaches Michael Chekhov and George Shdanoff, who have too little recognition in proportion to their true importance in the movie industry; and yes, it's pleasant enough to see and hear the likes of Robert Stack, Patricia Neal, Leslie Caron and Anthony Quinn testify to their importance while delivering anecdotal reminiscences and thoughts about what they learned. That said, this is hagiographic, slick and predictable, assembled with no real sense of style or pace, and somehow exuding smugness. But that's Hollywood for you. GA

From Russia With Love

(1963, GB, 116 min)
d Terence Young. *p* Harry Saltzman, Albert R Broccoli. *sc* Richard Maibaum, Johanna Harwood. *ph* Ted Moore. *ed* Peter Hunt. *ad* Syd Cain. *m* John Barry. *cast* Sean Connery, Daniela Bianchi, Pedro Armendariz, Lotte Lenya, Robert Shaw, Bernard Lee, Eunice Gayson.
●Bond number two and probably the best of the lot, with a remarkably gritty, wittily exciting plot in which the international crime organisation SPECTRE implements a diabolically complex scheme, hatched by a chess grand master, designed to cause terminal deterioration in Cold War relations. Memorable for the brilliant pre-credits stalk, Lenya's lesbo sadist, Shaw's psycho assassin, the cat-and-mouse game on the Orient Express, and – by no means least – the enchanting Daniela Bianchi, so vividly alive by comparison with the plastic dollies later Bonds toyed with. To see the film again now is to see all too vividly the abject depths of mechanical mindlessness into which the series has been sinking. TM

From Russia with Rock (Sirppi ja Kitara)

(1988, Fin, 108 min)
d Mafjaana Mykkanen. *p* Pauli Pentti, Aki Kaurismäki. *sc* Mafjaana Mykkanen. *ph* Heikki Ortamo, Christian Valdes, Olli Varja. *ed* Veikko Aaltonen. *with* Alliance Aquarium, Avia, Bravo, Brigada K Cruise, Mister Twister, Nuance, Televizor, Nautilius Pompilius, Va Bank, Uriah Heep.
●In December 1987, a seven-day rock festival was staged in Moscow, the first ever such event in the Soviet Union. Mykkanen and her crew were there to cover the festival, a mixture of state-sanctioned pop and 'underground' Soviet bands, many of whom belong to a Moscow-based collection, Rock Laboratory. One band, Nautilius Pompilius from Siberia, shot into the charts as a result of their festival appearance, and the last third of the film records their reactions to fame and final retreat to Siberia. Throughout, there is a sense of the importance of rock music to young Russians, their enthusiastic embrace of perestroika, and, sadly, a sense that the medium is totally played out in the West. RS

From Saturday to Sunday (Ze Soboty na Nedeli)

(1931, Czech, 69 min, b/w)
d Gustav Machaty. *sc* Vitezslav Nezval, Gustav Machaty. *ph* Václav Vích. *ed* Gustav Machaty. *ad* Alexander Hackenschmied. *m* Jaroslav Jezek. *cast* Magda Maderová, LH Struna, Jirína Sejbalová, Karel Jicinsky, RA Dvorsky.
●Slighter than either *Erotikon* or *Extase*, Machaty's first sound film remains typical in its technical and stylistic elan, its transcendence of a potentially banal narrative, and its thematic focus on female innocence and experience in love. Two working women go out on a Saturday night double date with a pair of prospective sugar daddies. Unlike her more knowing friend, shy Mary (Maderová) proves out of her depth, and eventually takes flight into a humbler watering hole, where she meets a man after her own heart. It's a sweet yarn, bolstered by some gentle discursive comedy (the girl surreptitiously returning the skin of her coffee to her host's mug; a delightfully odd cut-away to the corpulent physique behind the voice of a morning radio exercise programme), and an unforced attention to differences of class, character, moral habit and expectation. NB

From South to South

see South of a Passion, The

From the Cloud to the Resistance (Nube alla Resistenza)

(1979, It/Fr/WGer/GB, 103 min)
d/sc Jean-Marie Straub, Danièle Huillet. *ph* Saverio Diamanti, Gianni Canfarelli. *ed* Jean-Marie Straub, Danièle Huillet. *cast* Olimpia Carlisi, Walter Pardini, Mauro Monni, Carmelo Lacorte, Luigi Giordanello, Guido Lombardi.
●Straub and Huillet expand their concerns with dazzling scope and beauty: the struggle between gods and men, the eruption of the past into the present. From the first shots of a goddess seated in a tree, through a long debate between mythological characters, to the exploration of a village's fascist past, the film constantly startles by its imaginative and historical leaps. Operatic and documentary in approach, the film carefully juxtaposes two texts by Cesare Pavese, one a series of dialogues on fate and destiny, the other an elliptical narrative about the search for memories in an Italian village after the Liberation. A work of provocation which strips ornament and leaves essences, and whose integrity gives it a distinct sense of the sublime. DMacp

From the Edge of the City (Apo tin Akri tis Polis)

(1998, Greece, 93 min)
d Konstantinos Giannaris. *p* Dionysis Samiotis, Anastasios Vasiliou. *sc* Konstantinos Giannaris. *ph* Giorgos Argyroiliopoulos. *ed* Ioanna Spiliopoulou. *pd* Roula Nikolaou. *m* Akis Daoutis. *cast* Stathis Papadopoulos, Kostas Kotsianidis, Panagiotis Chartomatsidis, Dimitris Papoulidis, Theodora Tzimou.
●In the immigrant ghettos outside Athens, kids seek kicks fast and furiously. Sasha from Kazakhstan like sex, drugs and lying in. He quits his job on a construction site to spend more time with his girlfriends and hang out with his mates – one of whom, Giorgos, wants to sell him a Russian prostitute, Natasia, for safe keeping. The others are too out of it to offer him any better advice. Giannaris, a Greek-born director now based in Britain, propels the film forward on the back of pulsating dance music and a busy montage of action, dream tableaux and reflective interviews to camera with his inscrutable protagonist (Papadopoulos). There's an urgency here that well describes these kids' outlook; equally, a symptomatic bravado and bluster. But the restless jumpcutting never adds up to much and the roles themselves elicit minimal sympathy or interest. NB

From the Hip

(1987, US, 112 min)
d Bob Clark. *p* René Dupont, Bob Clark. *sc* David E Kelley, Bob Clark. *ph* Dante Spinotti. *ed* Stan Cole. *pd* Michael Stringer. *m* Paul Zaza. *cast* Judd Nelson, Elizabeth Perkins, John Hurt, Darren McGavin, Ray Walston, Dan Monahan, David Alan Grier, Allan Arbus.
●Judd Nelson – the 'rebel' in *The Breakfast Club* – perfects his impersonation of a wild bronco in this flashy drama from the director of *Porky's*. The only trouble is, he's supposed to be playing ambitious yuppie lawyer Robin Weathers (nickname: 'Stormy'). Assigned to defend John Hurt on a murder rap, he loses his cool when he figures out his client may in fact be guilty of some greater evil. Cue self-righteous moralising and a contrived courtroom denouement. A trial, for sure. TCh

From the Journals of Jean Seberg

(1995, US, 97 min)
d/sc Mark Rappaport. *ph* Mark Daniels. *ed* Mark Rappaport. *cast* Mary Beth Hurt.
●Rappaport's remarkable documentary works through Seberg's life, from her Midwest school days, through her much-publicised debut in Preminger's *Saint Joan* and her success in *A Bout de Souffle*, to her nightmarish marriage to Romain Gary, her involvement with the Black Panthers, and her eventual suicide in 1979. But it also uses the actress's experiences as a starting point for the exploration of an array of subjects. Hurt's Seberg is impressive as she reminisces straight to camera from beyond the grave, but what makes the film so extraordinary is the way

Rappaport weaves illuminating connections between the threads of his densely informative thesis. This is intertextuality at its most accessible, provocative and surprising: a scene in *Saint Joan*, for example, leads to observations on Jane Fonda that take in *Klute*, Vadim, Vietnam, Josh Logan, workout tapes, Ted Turner, Lev Kuleshov and the opportunities afforded ageing actresses – even as Fonda is rhymed with Falconetti, Vanessa Redgrave and Seberg herself. Entertaining, moving, intellectually sharp and imaginatively brilliant. GA

From the Life of the Marionettes (Aus dem Leben der Marionetten)

(1980, WGer, 104 min, b/w & col)
d Ingmar Bergman. *p* Horst Wendlandt, Ingrid Bergman. *sc* Ingmar Bergman. *ph* Sven Nykvist. *ed* Petra von Oelffen, Geri Ashur. *pd* Rolf Zehetbauer. *m* Rolf Wilhelm. *cast* Robert Atzorn, Christine Buchegger, Martin Benrath, Rita Russek, Lola Müthel.

● Bergman's not exactly successful examination of the events and warped psychology leading up to a bourgeois businessman's murder of a prostitute. Laden with sexual traumas, fading marriages and nightmare death wishes, it's a trip through Bergman territory that we've all taken before. But Sven Nykvist's camerawork is as usual impeccable, and a certain curiosity value is afforded by the spectacle of Swedish angst filtered, as through a glass darkly, by way of an entirely German cast. TM

From the Other Side of the Tracks

see De l'Autre Côté du Périph'

From the Queen to the Chief Executive (Denghou Dong Jianhua Faluo)

(2001, HK, 106 min)
d Herman Yau. *p* Nam Yin, Tiffany Chen. *sc* Elsa Chan. *ph* Joe Chan. *ed* Chan Ki-Hop. *ad* Fung Yuen-Chi. *m* Brother Hung. *cast* Stephen Tang, Ai Jing, David Lee, Sam Wong, Alson Wong, Jeffrey Lam, Mercy Wong.

● Recently Hong Kong's most prolific director, Yau has quite often found an interesting social dimension in schlock genre material. Here he does the exact opposite, spiking a serious-minded social protest movie with steroid-like injections of genre-movie style. From the opening newsreel (Tung Chee-Hwa taking his oath of office as the new Chief Executive in 1997), overlaid with noisy alt-rock from the resettlement estates, the effect is quite bracing. Around ten years before the handover, five Chinese teenagers were arrested for the rape and murder of two English schoolchildren and – being juveniles – detained 'at Her Majesty's pleasure'. Chief Executive Tung inherited the problem when he took over, and still hasn't resolved it: now older and wiser, the perpetrators are still in jail with no hope of parole. The film reconstructs the campaign to get defined sentences for the teenagers. It centres on the efforts of a tireless Urban Councillor (Tang) and the young woman (mainland singer Ai Jing in her acting debut) who has fallen for one of the boys in jail. Terrific. TR

From the Terrace

(1960, US, 144 min)
d/p Mark Robson. *sc* Ernest Lehman. *ph* Leo Tover. *ed* Dorothy Spencer. *ad* Lyle Wheeler, Maurice Ransford, Howard Richman. *m* Elmer Bernstein. *cast* Paul Newman, Joanne Woodward, Myrna Loy, Ina Balin, Leon Ames, Felix Aylmer, George Grizzard, Patrick O'Neal, Elizabeth Allen, Barbara Eden, Mae Marsh.

● An adaptation of John O'Hara's bestseller which settles for soapy melodrama instead of the novel's more sardonic perspective on a young ex-serviceman's rise to success among the idle rich of Pennsylvania. Robson's film is still highly watchable, with Paul and Joanne pretending their marriage is on the rocks, and all sorts of machinations in the boardroom and the bedroom. It's an American cousin to *Room at the Top*, shot in CinemaScope and DeLuxe colour, with an Elmer Bernstein score and plenty of histrionics. TCh

From This Day Forward

(1946, US, 95 min, b/w)
d John Berry. *p* William L Pereira. *sc* Hugo Butler, Garson Kanin, Edith Sommer, Charles Schnee. *ph* George Barnes. *ed* Frank Doyle. *ad* Albert S D'Agostino, Alfred Herman. *m* Leigh Harline. *cast* Joan Fontaine, Mark Stevens, Rosemary DeCamp, Henry Morgan, Arline Judge, Bobby Driscoll.

● As Sgt Stevens endures the bureaucracy of demobilisation he remembers the '30s – privation, unemployment, insecurity – the past which must never return. Such strands as post-war optimism, the impact of neo-realism, the socialist convictions of director and chief writer (Butler), both blacklist-bound, can easily be picked out. But as ever when Hollywood tried to engage with everyday realities, the trade off came in glamourisation – syrupy music, Fontaine (as Stevens' wife) never looking less than a film star, and an idea of poverty that must have irritated many audiences on home ground, never mind in Europe. It's surprisingly vigorous but you do have to keep making allowances. From the novel *All Brides Are Beautiful* by Thomas Bell. BBa

Front, The

(1976, US, 95 min)
d/p Martin Ritt. *sc* Walter Bernstein. *ph* Michael Chapman. *ed* Sidney Levin. *ad* Charles Bailey. *m* David Grusin. *cast* Woody Allen, Zero Mostel, Herschel Bernardi, Michael Murphy, Andrea Marcovicci, Remak Ramsay, Lloyd Gough.

● Woody Allen, miscast in his first straight role (as a schnook who lends his name to blacklisted writers for ten percent of the take, eventually coming under scrutiny himself), struggles through a reenactment of the communist witch-hunting of the '50s. Although made by those who suffered blacklisting at first hand, the film pulls all its political punches, settling instead for sentimental narrative. Its suggestion that each individual can buck the brutality of political oppression by standing up against the bullies lies squarely in the great reactionary tradition: 'a man's gotta do what a man's gotta do' replaces political analysis, and turns the film into an empty monument to the senility of American liberalism. SM

Frontera, La

(1991, Chile/Sp, 115 min)
d Ricardo Larrain. *p* Eduardo Larrain, Mara Sanchez, Alvaro Corvera, Sebastian Penna, Dolores Soler. *sc* Ricardo Larrain, Jorge Goldenberg. *ph* Hector Rios. *ed* Claudio Martinez. *ad* Juan Carlos Castillo. *m* Jaime De Aguirre. *cast* Patricio Contreras, Gloria Laso, Aldo Bernales, Hector Noguera, Alonso Venegas, Grisela Nuñez 'La Batacuna'.

● This absorbing first feature explores one man's internal exile in a country whose recent history has known the worst of political repression. Ramiro (Contreras), a Santiago teacher, is banished to a remote coastal community for putting his name to a public denunciation of the military authorities' abduction of one of his colleagues. His enforced sojourn leaves him under the restrictive care of the local police; yet the unexpected resonance of his encounters with the locals – Maite (Laso), a fugitive from Franco's Spain with her own troubled past, and Buzo (Bernales), a half-crazed diver – prompts him to rethink his life and his political commitment. With its wry treatment of the prisoner's bumbling captors and an uplifting climactic coup to savour, we witness a journey of discovery from a national cinema where the term 'political film' still means something. TJ

Front Page (Xin Ban Jin Ba Liang)

(1990, HK, 92 min)
d Philip Chan. *sc* Philip Chan, Michael Hui. *ph* Lam Kwok-wah. *ed* Ma Chang-yiu, Tsu San-kit. *pd* David Chan. *m* Cheu Kai-sang. *cast* Michael Hui, Samuel Hui, Ricky Hui, Catherine Hung.

● Although it does feature a sub-text criticising tabloid journalism in Hong Kong, this is first and foremost a Michael Hui comedy – the first in many years to reunite him with his brothers Sam and Ricky, young hero and eternal fall guy respectively. It's not as funny as Hui's *Chicken and Duck Talk*, but the patchwork script has a satisfying integrity of structure, the performances are terrific, and there are plenty of droll situations and sight gags. Michael Hui himself shines in his usual role as the would-be tyrant unable to sustain his tyranny; this time the character is a news magazine editor trying to stave off the official receiver. TR

Front Page, The

(1931, US, 101 min, b/w)
d Lewis Milestone. *p* Howard Hughes *sc* Barlett Hughes, Charles Lederer. *ph* Glen McWilliams. *ed* Duncan Mansfield. *ad* Richard Day. *cast* Adolphe Menjou, Pat O'Brien, Mary Brian, Walter Catlett, Edward Everett Horton, Mae Clarke, George E Stone.

● The first screen version of Hecht and MacArthur's fast-talking play set in a cynical newspaper world is, not surprisingly, rather less hilarious than Hawks' definitive *His Girl Friday* or Wilder's '70s vulgarisation. The main problem is that O'Brien, as Hildy Johnson, torn between his obsession for journalism's glamour and his desire to marry, never actually looks very interested in committing himself to either life; thus the dilemma at the heart of the drama barely seems to matter, and it's left to Menjou, suave, hard and mendacious, to bring the film alive during his regrettably brief appearances as Walter Burns, the editor lacking all human qualities except ambition. Milestone's direction, veering between stagey two-shots and extravagant but purposeless camera movements, doesn't help either. But it's still worth seeing, if only to hear the jokes which the Hays Code later put an end to. GA

Front Page, The

(1974, US, 105 min)
d Billy Wilder. *p* Paul Monash. *sc* Billy Wilder, IAL Diamond. *ph* Jordan Cronenweth. *ed* Ralph E Winters. *ad* Henry Bumstead, Henry Larrecq. *m* Billy May. *cast* Jack Lemmon, Walter Matthau, Carol Burnett, Allen Garfield, David Wayne, Vincent Gardenia, Herbert Edelman, Charles Durning, Susan Sarandon, Austin Pendleton, Martin Gabel.

● Third and least of the movie versions of Hecht and MacArthur's classic stage comedy about a manic editor's attempts to win back his star reporter – on the eve of the latter's marriage – by means of working up a hysterical storm about the forthcoming execution of an insane killer. Quite simply vulgar in comparison to its predecessors (especially Hawks' brilliant *His Girl Friday*), it relies too much on foul language, inappropriate slapstick, and superficial cynicism. That said, the cast – particularly the Gentlemen of the Press, acting as a profane Greek chorus to the battle between Walter Burns and Hildy Johnson (Matthau and Lemmon in usual form) – is impressive. GA

Front Page Woman

(1935, US, 82 min, b/w)
d Michael Curtiz. *p* Samuel Bischoff. *sc* Laird Doyle. *ph* Tony Gaudio. *ed* Terry Morse. *ad* John Hughes. *m* Heinz Roemheld. *cast* Bette Davis, George Brent, June Martel, Joseph Crehan, Roscoe Karns, Winifred Shaw.

● Not exactly a proto-feminist text (despite being based on a story called *Women Are Born Newspapermen*), nor for that matter an at all accurate picture of journalism, but still a vivid comedy-drama with Davis and Brent in fine form as the wisecracking couple working for rival papers and trying to better each other in following up a murder story. Absurd at times, with the two papers at one point printing absolutely identical stories, but directed and acted with sparkle and speed. GA

Frost

(1998, Ger, 203 min)
d Fred Kelemen. *p* Björn Koll. *sc/ph* Fred Kelemen. *ed* Fred Kelemen, Anna Schuchardt, *pd* Fred Kelemen. *m* Charles Mori. *cast* Paul Blumberg, Mario Gericke, Anna Schmidt, Harry Baer, Isolde Barth, Adolfo Assor, Thomas Baumann.

● The first film invited to the 1998 London Film Festival, Kelemen's stark epic presently looks like the cinema's latest lost cause: its producer refuses Kelemen access to his negative, and the director's own cutting copy, while it lasts, is all that can be screened. A mammoth, excoriating vision of a barren, forbidding German geography, it is variously reminiscent of Fassbinder, Sokurov, Angelopoulos and sundry young French realists, yet for the most part it's a singular, unforgettable experience. The story is deceptively simple – mother and son leave her abusive partner at Christmas and trudge toward New Year across interminably empty vistas in search of her East German childhood home. At half the length the film would be entirely accessible. As it is, the camera's endless gaze and grindingly cyclical narrative test patience to the absolute limit. NB

Frozen (Jidu Hanleng)

(1997, China, 90 min)
d Wu Ming [Wang Xiaoshuai]. *p* Shu Kei, Xu Wei. *sc* Pang Ming, Wu Ming. *ph* Yang Shu. *ed* Qing Qing. *pd* Li Yanxiu. *m* Roland Dol. *cast* Jia Hongshen, Ma Xiaoqing.

●Shot in 1994 and reflecting the dark mood in Beijing's 'underground' art circles at that time, this was an independent production – hence illegal in the eyes of the Film Bureau. The subsequent outlawing of unauthorised film-making in China forced the director to hide behind the pseudonym 'Wu Ming' (No Name). A young performance artist decides to trump the nihilism and self-destructive theatrics prevailing among the avant-garde crowd by staging a series of four symbolic deaths for himself, each coinciding with an equinox. He appears to die during the last, frozen to death on midsummer's day. But this 'death' was as much a fake as the others. A wry, semi-detached narration expresses a precise ambivalence about the protagonist and his friends, mocking their pretensions but respecting their helpless feelings of impotence in the China of the 1990s. TR

Fruit Machine, The

(1988, GB, 108 min)
d Philip Saville. *p* Steve Morrison. *sc* Frank Clarke. *ph* Dick Pope. *ed* Richard Bedford. *pd* David Brockhurst. *m* Hans Zimmer. *cast* Emile Charles, Tony Forsyth, Robert Stephens, Clare Higgins, Bruce Payne, Robbie Coltrane, Carsten Norgaard.

●Eddie (Charles) is a chubby 17-year old dreamer who loves scoffing chocs and watching old movies with his blowsy mum. Dad thinks he's a nancy boy, so when his mate Michael (Forsyth) calls for help the two scousers take off in search of adventure, and find it in a nightclub called 'The Fruit Machine', presided over by Annabelle (Coltrane, marvellous), an outsize drag queen whom they witness receiving too close a shave from a sicko called Echo (Payne). Running for their lives, the pair fall in with an opera singer (Stevens) and his agent (Higgins), who takes them to Brighton. Michael pays for their fares by horizontally dancing with both of them. Eddie remains oblivious to all this – he's too involved with a dripping dolphin man (Norgaard) who keeps appearing in front of him...Saville films Frank Clarke's script in a mishmash of styles, and the pace sometimes flags. But what the hell, it's as camp as Christmas, and if it rarely hits the jackpot, playing along with it is wildly enjoyable. MS

Fruits of Passion, The (Les Fruits de la Passion)

(1981, Fr/Jap, 83 min)
d Shuji Terayama. *p* Anatole Dauman, Hiroko Govaers. *sc* Shuji Terayama. *ph* Tatsuo Suzuki. *ed* Michel Valio. *ad* Hiroshi Yamashita. *m* JA Seazer. *cast* Klaus Kinski, Isabelle Illiers, Arielle Dombasle, Peter, Kenichi Nakamura, Takeshi Wakamatsu.

●Terayama supposedly knocked off this piece of arse-with-class to finance his theatre work. Certainly it's a highly dispiriting plunge into latter-day Borowczyk territory: softcore gropings dished up with arty trappings and fetishistic gloss to guarantee French box-office action. The narrative (based on the sequel to *The Story of O*) has Kinski testing his young love's affection in an Oriental brothel. Lashings of surrealist 'touches', so male culture-hunters needn't feel guilty when aroused. SJ

F.T.A.

(1972, US, 94 min)
d Francine Parker. *p* Francine Parker, Jane Fonda, Donald Sutherland. *ph* Juliana Wang, Eric Saarinen, John Weidman. *ed* Joel Moorwood, Michael Beaudry. *m* Aminadav Aloni. *with* Jane Fonda, Donald Sutherland, Len Chandler, Holly Near, Pamela Donegan.

●A documentary inevitably dated by the very success of the cause of which it was part. The title's an acronym for the Free Theatre of America revue's slogan 'Free the Army/Fuck the Army', and the film records performances by the group at US military bases on the Pacific Rim – Hawaii, Okinawa, the Philippines – in an openly subversive attempt to motivate sentiment within the rank-and-file of the US forces against the war in Vietnam. It's pretty conventional stuff, comprising footage of the revue in performance (campus-style anti-war sketches, protest songs) and interviews with soldiers. Even more so than when it was made, it will be of interest mostly to fans intrigued by the prospect of Fonda and Sutherland hoofing their way through song'n'dance routines. RM

F.T.W.

(1994, US, 97 min)
d Michael Karbelnikoff. *p* Tom Mickel. *sc* Mari Kornhauser. *ph* James L Carter. *ed* Joe D'Augustine. *ad* JK Reinhart. *m* Gary Chang. *cast* Mickey Rourke, Lori Singer, Brion James, Rodney Grant, Peter Berg.

●Either 'Fuck the War', which is tattooed across Lori Singer's knuckles, or Frank T Wells – being the name of Mickey Rourke's ex-con rodeo rider. She's on the run from the law after the death of her psychotic brother (Berg), and he's the gentle loser who tries to straighten her out. Rourke's face has become fascinating. He's aged quickly, and that dimple is now surrounded by the craggy features of a real cowboy. He gives a strong performance in a very capable little movie: a melancholy love story with bloody bookends. TCh

Fucking Åmål

see Show Me Love

Fuckland

(2000, Arg, 85 min)
d José Luis Marquès. *p* Edi Flehner, Mariano Suez. *sc* José Luis Marquès. *ph* Fabian Stratas, José Luis Marquès, Alejandro Hartman, Guillermo Naistat. *ed* Pipo Bonamino. *m* Sergio Figueroa. *cast* Fabian Stratas, Camilla Heaney.

●That's 'Falklands', to you and me. An Argentine with a hidden camera and a curious attitude, Fabian Stratas arrives in the Malvinas in the run-up to Christmas 1999. He wants to get to know his enemy and lay some ghosts – and at first his reportage seems like a straight video diary, recording his impressions of a wintery outcrop where dim drinking holes boast defiant names like the Colony and the Victory Bar, and the natives view Latin interlopers with well-mannered suspicion. As well they might. For Stratas is a man with a plan. His mission: to take back the islands by instigating a population explosion of Argentine bastards. Improvised by the actors, conceived and directed by Marquès, and certified by the Dogme brethren, this is a borderline political provocation which can be read as a further covert and undignified assault on sovereign territory, or – more plausibly – as a satire on rampant Argentine machismo. TCh

Fufu the Worldweary (Ensei Fufu)

(1998, Jap, 153 min)
d Yuri Obitani. *p/sc* Yuri Obitani, Yukie Saito. *ph/ed* Yuri Obitani. *m* 'wholly unidentified'. *cast* Takao Murase, Yuri Obitani, Sora Kawamura, Kim Miryeo, Daisuke Akai, Fuyume, Yukie Saito, Richard Williams.

●Shot on video, Obitani's amazing *magnum opus* covers a huge amount of ground: car theft, lesbianism, Japanese nationalism and racism, animist cults, Anglo-Irish conflicts, war crimes, scooter crashes and much besides. Obitani himself plays a right-wing leather boy whose only real friend is Hajime, a poet of Korean descent. Their former girlfriends (now a twosome) become disciples of a mysteriously silent guru, who soon adds Hajime to his flock. Fufu, meanwhile, is missing. His elder sister Kayo is scouring Japan for him; her only leads are that he plays the piano and might be waiting on a bridge. Obitani says that the film (which took four years to complete) originated in dreams and acid trips during the hot summer of 1995, and it's true that its experimentalism sometimes verges on the chaotic. But it's also formally rigorous, funny, sexy and politically astute – not to mention conceptually brilliant. TR

Fugitif, Le

see Pierre dans la Bouche, Une

Fugitive, The

(1947, US, 104 min, b/w)
d John Ford. *p* John Ford, Merian C Cooper. *sc* Dudley Nichols. *ph* Gabriel Figueroa. *ed* Jack Murray. *ad* Alfred Ybarra. *m* Richard Hageman. *cast* Henry Fonda, Dolores Del Rio, J Carrol Naish, Pedro Armendariz, Ward Bond, Leo Carrillo, Robert Armstrong, John Qualen.

●Graham Greene's *The Power and the Glory* given typically Fordian treatment, in that the moral complexities of the novel have been replaced by simplicity, picturesque poetry, and emotional power. Fonda plays the priest pursued by police and informers in an anti-clerical Latin American country, wandering the countryside in search of sanctuary and someone to understand him. It's generally one of Ford's most turgid efforts, slow, overstated, and with an annoying tendency towards obvious religious symbolism. But one cannot deny the beauty of Gabriel Figueroa's glowing photography. GA

Fugitive, The

(1993, US, 130 min)
d Andrew Davis. *p* Arnold Kopelson. *sc* Robert Mark Kamen, Jeb Stuart, David N Twohy. *ph* Michael Chapman. *ed* Dennis Virkler. *pd* Dennis Washington. *m* James Newton Howard. *cast* Harrison Ford, Tommy Lee Jones, Sela Ward, Julianne Moore, Jeroen Krabbé, Andreas Katsulas.

●A glossy, formula chase movie with the requisite number of extravagant action sequences (most notably a massive train crash). Brilliant doctor Richard Kimble (Ford) flees death row after wrongful conviction for his wife's murder. He vaguely recalls what the culprit looked like, but can he evade the authorities long enough to track him down? More or less as soon as you see him you know who the villain is. Ford is up to par for the strenuous stuff, but falls short on the grief, anxiety and compassion, allowing Tommy Lee Jones to walk away with the show as the wise-cracking marshal on Kimble's trail. GA

Fugitive Kind, The

(1959, US, 121 min, b/w)
d Sidney Lumet. *p* Martin Jurow, Richard A Shepherd. *sc* Tennessee Williams, Meade Roberts. *ph* Boris Kaufman. *ed* Carl Lerner. *ad* Richard Sylbert. *m* Kenyon Hopkins. *cast* Marlon Brando, Anna Magnani, Joanne Woodward, Maureen Stapleton, Victor Jory, RG Armstrong.

●Despite its stellar credentials, just about everything is wrong with this adaptation of Tennessee Williams' play *Orpheus Descending*. Brando plays a mysterious drifter who ignores a local tramp (Woodward doing her well-practised degenerate shtick) in favour of a lady of maturer years with a cancer-ridden husband. Magnani, with her unintelligible English, is not much worse than Brando, who undergoes the ultimate indignity of having to sing through another man's voice (for this role he became the first actor to be offered a million dollars, which he needed badly to cover his debts on *One-Eyed Jacks*). Lumet's direction is either ponderous or pretentious, and he failed to crack the problem of the florid stage dialogue and a dangerously weak role for Brando. DT

Full Body Massage

(1995, US, 93 min)
d Nicolas Roeg. *p* Julie Bilson Ahlberg, Robert Littman, Michael Nolin. *sc* Dan Gurskis. *ph* Anthony B Richmond. *ed* Louise Rubacky. *pd* Jeffrey Tex Schell. *m* Harry Gregson-Williams. *cast* Mimi Rogers, Bryan Brown, Christopher Burgard.

●Wealthy art dealer Nina (Rogers) is expecting her regular masseur Douglas (Burgard), but new guy Fitch (Brown) turns up in his place. Fitch has been around the block and picked up spiritual wisdom, but his approach to massage is more confrontational than that of Douglas, who was quite happy to press the right buttons to keep his client happy. 'There's more to happiness than just being happy,' Fitch tells Nina. But there's sadness in his own past. The script is all crystals, auras and Hopi Indian philosophy. It's as disconcerting watching Roeg become a born again Californian as it was witnessing the heady Catholicism of *Cold Heaven*.

There are some signature touches – slow zooms on to inanimate objects that invest them with mystical significance; the clash of old and new cultures (Hopi/Western); the unselfconscious nudity, which Roeg handles like no other British director – but the film lacks intrigue, depth and narrative drive. Less Full Body Massage, more damp flannel. Still, it's worth it for the line, 'It's a shiatsu thumb for when I get tired.' NRo

Full Circle (aka The Haunting of Julia)

(1976, GB/Can, 97 min)
d Richard Loncraine. *p* Peter Fetterman, Alfred Pariser. *sc* Dave Humphries. *ph* Peter Hannan. *ed* Ron Wisman. *ad* Brian Morris. *m* Colin Towns. *cast* Mia Farrow, Keir Dullea, Tom Conti, Jill Bennett, Robin Gammell, Cathleen Nesbitt, Mary Morris.

●Mia Farrow's fragile air of neurotic self-possession equips her well for the central role as a woman slowly destroyed by the ghost of an evil child. The narrative, from a story by Peter Straub, juggles ambiguously – if not carelessly – with themes thrown up and better developed in *The Turn of the Screw*, *Don't Look Now* and *Rosemary's Baby*: corrupted innocence, dead children, obsession with the past, introversion, possession, guilt, the haunted house, etc. But there is much to commend in Farrow's performance, complemented by Colin Towns' softly chilling score, which is more than can be said for Conti and Dullea. JS

Full Confession

(1939, US, 73 min, b/w)
d John Farrow. *sc* Jerry Cady. *ph* J Roy Hunt. *ed* Harry Marker. *m* Roy Webb. *cast* Victor McLaglen, Joseph Calleia, Sally Eilers, Barry Fitzgerald, Elisabeth Risdon.

●McLaglen as a dumb-ox killer, Calleia the priest forced to respect the sanctity of the confessional. Heavy echoes of *The Informer* as McLaglen is hounded by the voice of conscience. Much capering Irishry, too, from Barry Fitzgerald as the wrong man awaiting execution. Calleia is remarkably good, while Farrow does his best, steering a smoothly moody course between the twin reefs of McLaglen and Fitzgerald. TM

Full Contact (Xia Dao Gao Fei)

(1992, HK, 97 min)
d/p Ringo Lam. *sc* Nam Yin. *ph* Lau Hung-Chuen, Joe Chan, Ngau Chi-Gwan. *ed* Tony Chow. *ad* Ray Lam. *m* Teddy Robin Kwan. *cast* Chow Yun-Fat, Simon Yam, Bonnie Fu, Ann Bridgewater, Anthony Wong, Chris Lee.

●Jeff (Chow Yun-Fat), a tough guy with a sense of honour, saves his debt-ridden friend Sam from loan sharks. Hooking up with gay gangster Judge (Simon Yam) and his dubious henchmen, the friends are double-crossed in a violent heist. Sam saves his own skin, while Jeff is left for dead. Big mistake. When Jeff comes back, he's mad. Ringo Lam is like John Woo, but lapsed – there are none of those spiritual affectations to clog up the works; he'll pay lip service to macho codes, but that's as far as it goes. Super-slick, making opportune use of Bangkok locations, and relishing every violent episode, the film's unquestionably good of its type, but also sleazy and soulless. TCh

Full House

see O. Henry's Full House

Full Metal Jacket

(1987, GB, 116 min)
d/p Stanley Kubrick. *sc* Stanley Kubrick, Michael Herr, Gustav Hasford. *ph* Douglas Milsome. *ed* Martin Hunter. *pd* Anton Furst. *m* Abigail Mead [Vivian Kubrick]. *cast* Matthew Modine, Adam Baldwin, Vincent D'Onofrio, Lee Ermey, Dorian Harewood, Arliss Howard.

●The first half of Kubrick's movie steers clear of South East Asia altogether, focusing on the dehumanising training programme undergone by a group of novice US Marines. Then, after a suitably melodramatic bloodbath, the action switches to 'Nam, where star recruit Pvt Joker (Modine) soon tires of his behind-the-lines job as military journalist and provokes his CO into sending him forth into the shit. Black but obvious irony abounds, madness and racist bigotry are rampant, and a muddled moral message arises from the mire of a sprawling second half when the cynical, nominally heroic Joker finally learns to kill. None of which is to suggest that the film is bad; despite a certain stereotyping and predictability there are moments of gripping interest. Finally, however, Kubrick's direction is as steely cold and manipulative as the régime it depicts, and we never really get to know, let alone care about, the hapless recruits on view. GA

Full Moon (Denj Polnoluniya)

(1998, Rus, 92 min)
d Karen Shakhnazarov. *p* Vladimir Dostal. *sc* Karen Shakhnazarov, Alexander Borodyansky. *ph* Gennady Karjuk. *ed* Lidia Milioti. *pd* Ludmila Kusakova. *m* Anatoly Kroll. *cast* Elena Koreneva, Vladimir Iljin, Filipp Yankovsky, Valery Priemykhov, Valery Storozhik.

●This detailed but ultimately unrewarding portrait of the tragic, comic and romantic aspects of contemporary Moscow life follows a decathlon of loosely connected narratives. A man sits opposite a plump girl on the metro and fantasises about having sex with her; an ageing dog, basking in the sun, remembers his hunting days; and a young prostitute dreams of a medieval Prince visiting her grave. While Shakhnazarov successfully strives for an evocative balance of fantasy and reality, the film is let down by primitive camerawork and flaccid performances. HK

Full Monty, The

(1997, US/GB, 91 min)
d Peter Cattaneo. *p* Uberto Pasolini. *sc* Simon Beaufoy. *ph* John de Borman. *ed* Nick Moore, David Freeman. *pd* Max Gottlieb. *m* Anne Dudley. *cast* Robert Carlyle, Tom Wilkinson, Mark Addy, Lesley Sharp, Emily Woof, Steve Huison, Paul Barber, Hugo Speer, Deirdre Costello, Bruce Jones.

●Sheffield. Unemployment. Men battling for their self-respect in a post-industrial waste land. Like *Brassed Off*, this turns feel-bad clichés on their head. The men here don't make a sentimental stand by blowing their own trumpets: their shot at self-respect involves stripping to the bare essentials – out-raunching the Chippendales before a horde of noisy local lasses. Carlyle's assured with the self-deprecating humour of the unlikely bump 'n' grind, and the understated, but still palpable desperation underlining the men's plight – and his able cohorts have enough problems of their own to stop matters developing into out-and-out farce. With the women virtual bystanders, there's some attempt at addressing manhood-in-crisis – squaring loss-of-breadwinner status with the finale's cheering reassertion of sexual identity. Along the way, screenwriter Simon Beaufoy slips in an affectionate gay sub-plot, makes things awkward for himself by exposing Carlyle's pubescent son to the chaps' developing routines, and never quite manages to convince the head as much as the heart. Still, director Cattaneo thrives on the sheer incongruity of it all. TJ

Full Moon in Blue Water

(1988, US, 95 min)
d Peter Masterson. *p* Lawrence Turman, David Foster, John Turman. *sc* Bill Bozzone. *ph* Fred Murphy. *ed* Jill Savitt. *pd* Jeanette Scott. *m* Phil Marshall. *cast* Gene Hackman, Teri Garr, Burgess Meredith, Elias Koteas, Kevin Cooney, David Doty,

●A low-budget comedy-drama, slow to start, in which Masterson's uncinematic direction, and first-time screenwriter Bill Bozzone's reliance on characterisation, reveal their shared theatrical backgrounds. Hackman helps no end with a strong performance as the self-pitying, cynical owner of a poky bar on the Texas Gulf Coast. Mounting debts, combined with the disappearance of his wife, lead him to the verge of selling out to unscrupulous land-grabbers. But that same day he also has to contend with the muddled kidnapping of his wheelchair-bound father-in-law (Meredith), a hold-up, and a bust-up with his casual girlfriend (Garr). Low-key stuff with an assortment of eccentric rednecks, probably better suited to the small screen.

Full Moon in New York (Ren zai Niu-Yue)

(1989, HK, 89 min)
d Stanley Kwan. *p* Henry Fong. *sc* Zhong Acheng. *ph* Bill Wong, Fred Murphy. *ed* Jill Savitt. *m* Phil Marshall. *cast* Maggie Cheung, Sylvia Chang, Siqin Gaowa, Josephine Koo, Richard Hsiung.

●Kwan's New York feature overcomes a spurious 'political' subtext (women from Hong Kong, Taiwan and Mainland China must figure out how to get along) thanks to some fairly trenchant observations about the émigré Chinese experience. Chang is the would-be Shakespearean actress from Taiwan, stuck playing horses in off-off-Broadway clinkers; Cheung is the Hong Kong restaurateur/property magnate coming to the end of a lesbian affair; and Siqin Gaowa is the bride from China, barely coping with strange Western ways. Richer and more imaginative than most Chinatown movies, persuasive enough as a sketch of female bonding, and superbly shot by Bill Wong. TR

Full Moon in Paris (Les Nuits de la Pleine Lune)

(1984, Fr, 101 min)
d Eric Rohmer. *p* Margaret Ménégoz. *sc* Eric Rohmer. *ph* Renato Berta. *ed* Cécile Decugis. *ad* Pascale Ogier. *m* Elli, Jacno. *cast* Pascale Ogier, Tchéky Karyo, Fabrice Luchini, Virginie Thévenet, Christian Vadim, Laszlo Szabo.

●Ogier and Karyo are an ill-matched couple; she longs for freedom, love and excitement, and moves out into her own Parisian pied-à-terre in order to see him only at weekends. But rumours, misunderstandings and flirtations hold sway with such vengeance that Ogier's double life backfires. It's as elegant and incisive a comedy of manners as ever from Rohmer, deriving much wit and subtlety from the simplest of plots, merely by concentrating on conversations and the mixed-up motives that fuel them. But accusations that the film is too literary or verbal miss the point entirely: performance, decor and composition – not to mention narrative structure – are all at the service of the film's meaning, perhaps most notably in a marvellous party scene where the body language of dancing and glances speaks volumes. GA

Full of Life

(1956, US, 91 min, b/w)
d Richard Quine. *p* Fred Kohlmar. *sc* John Fante. *ph* Charles Lawton Jr. *ed* Charles Nelson. *ad* William Flannery. *m* George Duning. *cast* Judy Holliday, Richard Conte, Salvatore Baccaloni, Esther Minciotti, Joe De Santis, Silvio Minciotti.

●Breezy comedy, with gargantuan Baccaloni (a popular New York opera singer of the '50s) pissing off Italian-American couple Holliday and Conte by interfering in the birth of their child. Holliday has no special religious convictions but her boozy father-in-law-to-be insists she confirm her faith before the sprog is born. Holliday is vivacity itself; Baccaloni is a roly-poly firecracker; and the script by cult author John Fante (from his own novel) strikes just the right note. NF

Full Speed

see A Toute Vitesse

Full Tilt Boogie

(1997, US, 81 min)
d Sarah Kelly. *p* Rana Joy Glickman. *ph* Christopher Gallo. *ed* Lauren Zuckerman. *m* Cary Berger, Dominic Kelly. *with* Lawrence Bender, George Clooney, Harvey Keitel, Juliette Lewis, Cecilia Montiel, Michael Parks, Robert Rodriguez, Quentin Tarantino.

●A documentary on the industrial process known as film-making, specifically on the manufacture of a product called *From Dusk to Dawn*. Kelly chats to assistants, grips, drivers, extras, the paparazzi. We get unshutuppable Tarantino, comically intense Keitel and Rodriguez strumming his guitar while issuing bits of direction. Though *From Dusk to Dawn* was shot with a non-union crew, the feared hordes of protesting Teamsters never materialised. The big impression is of everyone taking their cue from the juvenile nature of the script they're filming and having a great time even when they're having a lousy time. Engrossing enough, but it's a pity the questioning didn't extend to broader issues than George Clooney's sex life. BBa

Fun

(1994, US, 105 min)
d/p Rafal Zielinski. *sc* James Bosley. *ph* Jens Sturup. *ed* Monika Lightstone. *ad* Vally Mestroni. *m* Mark Tschanz. *cast* Renee Humphrey, Alicia Witt, Leslie Hope, William R Moses, Leslie Hope, Ania Suli.

● Two teenage girlfriends murder an old lady – for fun. The film unfolds in flashbacks as a court psychiatrist and a reporter probe the girls' motives (past in colour, present in grainy blue and white). The girls keep talking about the TV movie they'll inspire ('Is that how you expect to see yourself: Drew Barrymore?'), and that's exactly what this feels like: a TV movie. There's even a *Pretty Woman*-type pop promo in the middle. There is one big plus though – two arresting, naturalistic performances from Humphrey and Witt. TCh

Fun Bar Karaoke

(1997, Thai, 100 min)
d Pen-ek Ratanaruang [Tom Pannet]. *p* Dhiranan Sukwibul. *sc* Pen-ek Ratanaruang. *ph* Chankit Chamnivikaipong. *ed* Pattamanadda Yukol, Adrian Brady. *ad* Pen-ek Ratanaruang. *cast* Fay Asavase, Paiboonkiat Keawkaew, Ray MacDonald.

● With its racked up soundtrack, fancy dissolves, slo-mo camera and moments of Tarantino-like casual violence, this dreamy tale of a young commercials film-assistant (or is she a check-out girl?) seems more an exercise in style than an exploration of modern Bangkok. Young Pu lives with her dad, who forgets her birthday, more concerned, it seems, with the femme fatale down at the karaoke bar. He's beaten up by a gang of bouncers including a cool young hitman whom Pu fancies. Pu goes to the swimming pool a lot and visits a fortune teller who predicts her father's death. The director, whose debut this is, comes from commercials, so maybe he's fed up with unmistakable meanings. WH

Fun Down There

(1989, US, 85 min)
d/p/ed/ad Roger Stigliano. *sc* Roger Stigliano, Michael Waite. *ph* Peggy Ahwesh. *m* James Baker, Wayne Hammond. *cast* Michael Waite, Nickolas B Nagourney, Martin Goldin, Jeanne Smith, Gretschen Somerville, Roger Stigliano.

● Stigliano takes the grainy docu-drama angle in following the fortunes of Buddy (Waite) a young gay man from upstate New York who leaves home for the Big Apple. He soon finds himself involved with a group of typical urban bohemians, with whose help he loses his virginity, makes friends, and gets a job. It's all shot with dispassionate detatchment, by means of fixed camera angles that record party small talk and sexual acts without comment or sensationalism. Occasionally the home movie mood is annoying: one feels the cast are allowed to do their party pieces a little too much (they're just not interesting enough to hold attention). But in general it's an engaging piece, with a central performance by Waite that radiates a convincing innocence and an electric sexuality. RS

Funeral, The

(1996, US, 99 min)
d Abel Ferrara. *p* Mary Kane. *sc* Nicholas St John. *ph* Ken Kelsch. *ed* Bill Pankow, Mayin Lo. *pd* Charles M Lagola. *m* Joe Delia. *cast* Christopher Walken, Isabella Rossellini, Vincent Gallo, Annabella Sciorra, Chris Penn, Benicio del Toro, Gretchen Mol.

● Walken, Penn and Gallo are brothers in 1930s New York. When one is killed, the lives of the other two quickly unravel. This stylishly shot mobster comedy-thriller has a flashback structure of such complexity – it starts with the funeral and works backwards – that the makers themselves seem confused by it. There are some distracting plot strands (for instance, Gallo's sudden embrace of workers' rights) and a few too many nods to *The Godfather*, but this is still a brilliant, very visceral piece of film-making with an infectious strain of morbid humour. GM

Funeral in Berlin

(1966, GB, 102 min)
d Guy Hamilton. *p* Charles Kasher. *sc* Evan Jones. *ph* Otto Heller. *ed* John Bloom. *pd* Ken Adam. *m* Konrad Elfers. *cast* Michael Caine, Eva Renzi, Paul Hubschmid,Oscar Homolka, Guy Doleman, Rachel Gurney, Hugh Burden.

● Second outing for Caine and Len Deighton (after *The Ipcress File*). This time the plot thickens almost to the point of congealing, with everybody seemingly tailing everybody else (you soon give up caring why) as Harry Palmer is despatched to Berlin to get the real story when a Russian intelligence colonel, chief of security on the Wall, is reported to be anxious to defect. Left to twiddle your thumbs while the plot gradually strangles, you can relish some nice location photography, two straightforward action sequences, and a lovely performance from Homolka as the bluffly sinister defector. TM

Funeral Parade of Roses (Bara no Soretsu)

(1969, Jap, 105 min, b/w)
d Toshio Matsumoto. *p* Mitsuru Kudo. *sc* Toshio Matsumoto. *ph* Tatsuo Suzuki. *ed* Toshie Iwasa. *ad* Setsu Asakura. *m* Joji Yuasa. *cast* Peter, Osamu Ogasawara, Toyosaburo Uchiyama, Don Madrid, Emiko Azuma.

● Like Oshima's contemporary *Diary of a Shinjuku Thief*, this still extraordinary film was a response to the 1968 student riots. But Matsumoto goes further than Oshima – into Shinjuku 2-chome, Tokyo's gay ghetto, to enact a queer revamp of the Oedipus myth. Popular young trannie Eddie (Peter, later the Fool in *Ran*) throws himself into affairs with a black GI and a Japanese hippie to drown out his memories of killing his mother when he caught her in flagrante with a stranger. Then he shacks up with Gonda, manager of the gay bar Genet, only to find out that the man is his long-lost father. Matsumoto splinters the story's time-frame, splashes captions across the frame and cuts in bits of *ciné vérité* and interviews with the cast – making it one of the most formally advanced films of the psychedelic decade. TR

Funeral Rites

see Ososhiki

Funhouse, The

(1981, US, 96 min)
d Tobe Hooper. *p* Derek Power, Steven Bernhardt. *sc* Larry Block. *ph* Andrew Laszlo. *ed* Jack Hofstra. *pd* Morton Rabinowitz. *m* John Beal. *cast* Elizabeth Berridge, Cooper Huckabee, Miles Chapin, Largo Woodruff, Shawn Carson, Sylvia Miles, Wayne Doba, William Finley.

● Which is socially acceptable – to love Tobe Hooper movies for their perverse but stubborn puritanism, or to love them for the incredible way they decoy your attention with stylish homages to other horror classics, then spring on you new and inventive means of scaring you out of your seat? *The Funhouse*, a story of two amorous young couples who arbitrarily enter the sleazoid world of a sinister travelling carnival (despite warnings) and Find They Are Not Alone, is a little too long, but what the hell? It's not every day the fright genre produces a film capable of commenting on epic subjects like the ties that bind and the disintegration of the modern family, the foolishness of dabbling voyeuristically in others' pain, and the possible detrimental effect of the Polaroid Instamatic on American moral fibre (a theme touched upon also in *The Texas Chainsaw Massacre*, Hooper's extreme pro-vegetarianism tract), while doing its proper job providing plenty of cheap thrills. Not that taste is nesessarily involved here, but it's rare that any film follows through its chosen themes with such attention to detail, much less leavening the package with a truly anarchic blend of black humour. CR

Funny About Love

(1990, US, 101 min)
d Leonard Nimoy. *p* Jon Avnet, Jordan Kerner. *sc* Norman Steinberg, David Frankel. *ph* Fred Murphy. *ed* Peter E Berger. *pd* Stephen Storer. *m* Miles Goodman. *cast* Gene Wilder, Christine Lahti, Mary Stuart Masterson, Robert Prosky, Stephen Tobolowsky, Anne Jackson, Susan Ruttan, David Margulies.

● As interminably cute as its title suggests, Nimoy's film strains for a sophisticated view of adult relationships, while in reality taking the director's obsession with babies to new depths. Wilder plays Duffy, a satirical cartoonist – so we're told, though on the evidence presented he seems no more than a rather pathetic chauvinist in mid-life crisis. Be that as it may, he can boast good taste in women. First, he woos the wonderful Christine Lahti in double quick time; then, when she has failed to reproduce and been put aside, he turns to the young, spunky Masterson. A stronger actor than Wilder – a cabbage patch doll of a man – might have persuaded us that he is more than a sentimental sexist. As it is, the movie drowns in a maudlin sea of sickly sentiment. TCh

Funny Bones

(1994, US/GB, 126 min)
d Peter Chelsom. *p/sc* Simon Fields, Peter Chelsom. *ph* Eduardo Serra. *ed* Martin Walsh. *pd* Caroline Hanania. *m* John Altman. *cast* Oliver Platt, Jerry Lewis, Lee Evans, Leslie Caron, Richard Griffiths, Oliver Reed, Ian McNeice, Gavin Millar, Terence Rigby.

● Writer/director Chelsom's follow-up to *Hear My Song* throws plenty of comic ideas around, but only one or two stick. Platt stars as Tommy Fawkes, a stand-up comic overshadowed by his father (Lewis), whose Las Vegas show falls so flat he takes off to relearn his trade – in Blackpool. There he comes across Jack Parker (Evans), a natural-born comedian with a talent so pure it's positively dangerous. This paternalistic yarn inhabits a curiously nostalgic neverland where sentimental whimsy and showbiz escapism ultimately drown out acute psychological trauma. Evans is okay in his cinema debut, but his role seems to have been emasculated in large-scale cuts which play havoc with what was evidently an undeveloped script (it still runs over two hours). What any of this has to do with Oliver Reed, French smugglers and an ancient immortality drug we may never know. TCh

Funny Dirty Little War, A (No Habrá más Penas ni Olvido)

(1983, Arg, 79 min)
d Héctor Olivera. *p* Fernando Ayala, Luis Osvaldo Repetto. *sc* Roberto Cossa, Héctor Olivera. *ph* Leonardo Rodriguez Solis. *ed* Eduardo Lopez. *ad* Emilio Basaldua, Maria Julia Bertotto. *m* Oscar Cardoza Ocampo. *cast* Federico Luppi, Héctor Bidonde, Victor Laplace, Rodolfo Ranni, Miguel Angel Sola, Julio de Grazia.

● A profound, aptly titled insight into the madness of recent Argentinian political history. Set in a fictional town near Buenos Aires, the year is 1974: an aged Peron has been returned to power and is encouraging a purge of the leftist forces (his original supporters in the '40s) by the same right wing opportunists who brought about his exile in 1955. Mayor, Secretary General and Police Chief each pass down the responsibility of removing a 'Peronist' administrator and his 'subversive' assistant from the town hall. Verbal banter and threats escalate into a full-scale bloody siege when the building itself becomes a refuge to those who cling to a position variously labelled Marxist or even apolitical. Olivera's skill is to proceed from a farcical opening to a dramatic and black conclusion without losing sight of the appalling reality behind the jokes: torture here is casually enacted in a schoolroom where physical agony is juxtaposed with portraits of national heroes and the naive drawings of children. Wittily scripted, furiously paced, deftly performed, this is explosive political comedy that demonstrates the absurd division of groups who believed in some sort of salvation through Peron. Don't die for me, Argentina – but they did. DT

Funny Face

(1956, US, 103 min)
d Stanley Donen. *p* Roger Edens. *sc* Leonard Gershe. *ph* Ray June. *ed* Frank Bracht. *ad* Hal Pereira, George W Davis. *songs* George Gershwin, Ira Gershwin. *cast* Fred Astaire, Audrey Hepburn, Kay Thompson, Michel Auclair, Suzy Parker, Robert Flemyng.

● The musical that dares to rhyme Sartre with Montmartre, *Funny Face* – surprisingly from Paramount rather than MGM – knocks most other musicals off the screen for its visual beauty, its witty panache, and its totally uncalculating charm. The beauty is most irresistible in the sylvan scene, shimmering through gauze, when Astaire and Hepburn find they 'empathise', to use the film's joke. The panache is most sustained in the 'Clap Yo' Hands' number, in which Astaire and Thompson shuffle on as a couple of beats and develop a dazzlingly inventive send-up. The charm is everywhere. Love triumphs over capitalist exploitation, joyless intellectualisation, and all things phony; and the thesis persuades because of the commitment and skill of the team and the lightness of the underrated Donen's touch. SG

Funny Games

(1997, Aus, 108 min)
d Michael Haneke. *p* Veit Heiduschka. *sc* Michael Haneke. *ph* Jürgen Jürges. *ed* Andreas Prochaska. *pd* Christoph Kanter. *cast* Susanne Lothar, Ulrich Mühe, Frank Giering, Arno Frisch, Stefan Clapczynski, Doris Kunstmann.
●Continuing the fascination with violence and its representation evident in his earlier films, Haneke's movie may be shocking, but it's also entirely serious. A couple and their young son arrive at their lakeside holiday home, only to have it invaded by two strange, ultra-polite young men who turn out to be sadistic, homicidal psychopaths. No facile explanations are offered for the killers' behaviour; rather, through their regular asides to the camera, and by occasionally disrupting the otherwise 'realist' narrative, Haneke explores both the emotional and physical effects of violence, and interrogates our own motives in consuming violent stories. Amazingly, very little violence is actually seen; we hear its perpetration and witness its aftermath, which (though no less disturbing) is absolutely crucial to the responsible treatment of such a horrific subject. Brilliant, radical, provocative, it's a masterpiece that is at times barely watchable. GA

Funny Girl

(1968, US, 147 min)
d William Wyler. *p* Ray Stark. *sc* Isobel Lennart. *ph* Harry Stradling. *ed* Maury Winetrobe, William Sands. *pd* Gene Callahan. *songs* Jule Styne, Bob Merrill. *cast* Barbra Streisand, Omar Sharif, Kay Medford, Anne Francis, Walter Pidgeon, Lee Allen, Gerald Mohr.
●Wyler's only musical, *Funny Girl* is the fictionalised biography of Fanny Brice (Streisand), the ugly duckling who became a glamorous Ziegfeld star and achieved fame as a comic, so puncturing the mythic public eroticism of the *Ziegfeld Follies*. The film's central irony is not the usual one of public success at the expense of private pain, but the complex one of success at the expense of personal knowledge. Streisand never looks into the mirrors that Wyler surrounds her with. Well worth watching, even if most later Streisand movies aren't. PH

Funny Lady

(1975, US, 138 min)
d Herbert Ross. *p* Ray Stark. *sc* Jay Presson Allen, Arnold Schulman. *ph* James Wong Howe. *ed* Marion Rothman. *pd* George Jenkins. *songs* John Kander, Fred Ebb, Harry Warren, Harold Arlen, others. *cast* Barbra Streisand, James Caan, Omar Sharif, Roddy McDowall, Ben Vereen, Carole Wells.
●Funny Girl becomes Funny Lady as Streisand completes the tragi-comic tale of Fanny Brice in a curate's egg of a musical blockbuster. The opening is good, with Streisand taking off Brice again with astounding ease and the plausible Billy Rose soon established by Caan. But the inexorable slide into stodge begins early with merely efficient numbers, and the unspeakable flash-forward at the end brings it flatulently to earth. Ben Vereen goes some in 'Clap Hands, Here Comes Charley'; while Streisand and the dancers doing 'Great Day' is one for the anthologies. The lady can still turn a one-liner with sweet malevolence – 'when you're a star, everything you do is magic' as she falls over in the wardrobe – but she can't save a galumpher any more than she could save the (far worse) *Hello Dolly*. Neither can the glowing cinematography of James Wong Howe. SG

Funny Man

(1994, GB, 93 min)
d Simon Sprackling. *p* Nigel Odell. *sc* Simon Sprackling. *ph* Tom Ingle Jr. *ed* Ryan Driscoll. *pd* David Endley. *cast* Tim James, Christopher Lee, Benny Young, Matthew Devitt, Pauline Black, Ingrid Lacey.
●Christopher Lee appears at the start of this farrago as a suave aristo who on the turn of a card loses his beloved ancestral home to a sleazy record producer, but neglects to warn the new owner that his des res comes complete with an evil jester who slaughters unwelcome visitors. Lee subsequently pops up chuckling from the madhouse, as the sick and sad jester disposes of the cast in various repellent ways. There's the threat of a sequel. AO

Funny Money

(1982, GB, 97 min)
d James Kenelm Clarke. *p* Greg Smith. *sc* James Kenelm Clarke. *ph* John Wyatt. *ed* Bill Lennie. *pd* Harry Pottle. *cast* Gregg Henry, Elizabeth Daily, Gareth Hunt, Derren Nesbitt, Annie Ross, Joe Praml.
●A love-on-the-lam movie about credit card fraud, with guest zombies and second-rate leads playing out a totally charmless fiction in one and a half locations. The money is plastic but the love, eventually, is true: he (Henry) is a balding cocktail pianist with deeply hidden talent, she (Daily) is an irrepressible (ha!), elfin American, fresh in town with a tote-bag full of stolen cards. In the seamless sleaze of a Park Lane hotel, the couple turn their tricks and discover the piles of pathos on the jet set bum. If it had in any critical way been about this grubby little criminal sub-culture it just might have been watchable. RP

Funny Thing Happened on the Way to the Forum, A

(1966, US, 98 min)
d Richard Lester. *p* Melvin Frank. *sc* Melvin Frank, Michael Pertwee. *ph* Nicolas Roeg. *ed* John Victor Smith. *pd* Tony Walton. *m* Stephen Sondheim. *cast* Zero Mostel, Phil Silvers, Jack Gilford, Buster Keaton, Michael Crawford, Annette Andre, Patricia Jessel, Michael Hordern.
●Mix a bawdy story in the style of the Roman satirist Plautus with modern New York humour and the flashy direction of Lester, and what have you got? Not surprisingly, a spasmodically successful farce taken along at breakneck pace so that half of the good gags don't have time to sink in, and half of the bad ones fortunately disappear in the mêlée. All in all, a middling affair, with the overrated Mostel playing the slave on the lookout for freedom, and many of Stephen Sondheim's songs from the original Broadway musical thrown out in the rush. GA

Fun With Dick and Jane

(1976, US, 100 min)
d Ted Kotcheff. *p* Peter Bart, Max Palevsky. *sc* David Giler, Jerry Belson, Mordecai Richler. *ph* Fred J Koenekamp. *ed* Danford B Greene. *pd* James Hulsey. *m* Ernest Gold. *cast* George Segal, Jane Fonda, Ed McMahon, Dick Gautier, Allan Miller, John Dehner, Hank Garcia.
●Aerospace engineer Segal's redundancy puts his and acquisitive wife Fonda's one-up materialism on the line for some incongruous satire; but the easy option lure of crazy comedy soon has them turning ineptly to crime, and the attack on the values they incarnate and so desperately cling to peters out into fuzzy independent/corporate criminal contrasts. Compromised intentions mean that the cynical premise leaks all its acid as we're actually asked to sympathise with the artificial 'poverty' of the executive class. It's the sort of thing that would undoubtedly amuse Norman Tebbitt. PT

Für

(1993, Braz, 95 min)
d Paulo Thiago. *cast* Norma Bengell, Maria Zilda Bethlem.
●Focused on the relationship between three very different women who share an apartment, this meandering, allegorical movie may be intended as some sort of statement on the female condition, but with the trio (wary, promiscuous and neurotic respectively) all defined exclusively by their attitudes to men, it's certainly not feminist. GA

Furies, The

(1950, US, 109 min, b/w)
d Anthony Mann. *p* Hal B Wallis. *sc* Charles Schnee. *ph* Victor Milner. *ed* Archie Marshek. *ad* Hans Dreier, Henry Bumstead. *m* Franz Waxman. *cast* Barbara Stanwyck, Walter Huston, Wendell Corey, Gilbert Roland, Judith Anderson, Beulah Bondi, Thomas Gomez, Albert Dekker, Wallace Ford, Blanche Yurka.
●A fraught, violent Freudianism stampedes through Charles Schnee's script (adapted from Niven Busch's novel) for Anthony Mann's intense Western – only his second stab at the genre which would bring out his very best qualities: his gritty treatment of physical and mental conflict, his classical intelligence and expressive use of landscape. In comparison, *The Furies* smacks of primitivism, its central feud between Stanwyck and her cattle baron father Walter Huston being both overwritten and underdeveloped. That said, these two performers are so compelling in their own right that Mann could get away with murder with them on the screen together. TCh

Further and Particular

(1988, GB, 112 min)
d Steve Dwoskin. *p* Simon Hartog. *cast* Richard Butler, Bruce Cooper, Jean Fennell, Irene Marot, Julie Righton, Nicola Warren, Carola Regnier.
●This film dovetails two obsessions: a man's with woman's sexuality, and a film director's with the nature of the camera's gaze. Needless to say, there is a lot of repetition. The camera approximates Memory, first that of a young boy, and of the sexual encounters arranged for him by his mother, and eventually that of an old man, with corresponding fragmentation. Many of the images of sexual stereotypes, and the games they play, are arresting if over-long, but too much of the film is taken up with commonplace profundities ('Truth is change') and doubtful maxims ('Love is reality transformed into a sport') spoken directly into the camera. References to Hitchcock's *Rope* and Welles' *The Lady from Shanghai* serve mainly to highlight the discrepancy between what the film demands of the viewer and what it gives back in the way of ideas and entertainment. MC

Further Gesture, A (aka The Break)

(1996, GB/Ger/Jap/Ire, 101 min)
d Robert Dornhelm. *p* Chris Curling. *sc* Ronan Bennett. *ph* Andrzej Sekula. *ed* Masahiro Hirakubo. *pd* Kalina Ivanov, Tom McCullagh. *m* John Keane. *cast* Stephen Rea, Alfred Molina, Rosana Pastor, Brendan Gleeson, Pruitt Taylor Vince, Maria Doyle Kennedy.
●Dowd (Rea), an IRA prisoner in the H-blocks, is gloomily facing his sentence, until he spontaneously joins a comrade (Gleeson) in a risky escape. Dowd begins a new life in New York, but he might as well be in prison again – until he strikes up a friendship with co-worker Tulio (Molina) and gets to know his close group of Guatemalan exiles. A bond with Monica (Rosana Pastor) seals his acceptance among the exiles, and Dowd learns the dark truth behind their presence in the US. Ronan Bennett's screenplay, based on an idea by Rea, is free from special pleading: there's no turning back, for instance, once you've used violence in the service of ideology. Director Dornhelm peaks in the opening burst of action, but keeps control of a narrative that asks spectators to assess their own sympathies. In trying to combine action thriller, love story and political think piece, the film bites off more than it can chew, but Rea and Gleeson are absolutely credible, and there's black Ulster humour in abundance. TJ

Furtivos

see Poachers

Fury

(1936, US, 94 min, b/w)
d Fritz Lang. *p* Joseph L Mankiewicz. *sc* Barlett Cormack, Fritz Lang. *ph* Joseph Ruttenberg. *ed* Frank Sullivan. *ad* Cedric Gibbons. *m* Franz Waxman. *cast* Spencer Tracy, Sylvia Sidney, Walter Abel, Bruce Cabot, Edward Ellis, Walter Brennan.
●Lang's first American film, with Tracy as the man wrongly accused of a kidnapping who escapes summary justice by lynch mob as the jail burns down, then goes into hiding, plants evidence to suggest he died, and sits back gloatingly as his 'killers' are brought to trial. Softened along pious lines at the end (what else from MGM, who tinkered cravenly with the script all down the line?), so not quite the masterpiece of reputation: Lang later made much better, much less touted films. Still impressive, all the same, especially in the build-up to the lynching sequence. TM

Fury (Il Giorno del Furore)

(1973, It/GB, 118 min)
d Antonio Calenda. *p* Marcello Danon, Harry Saltzman. *sc* Edward Bond, Antonio Calenda, Ugo Pirro. *ph* Alfio Contini. *ed* Sergio

Montanari. *pd* Franco Ninnis. *m* Riz Ortolani. *cast* Oliver Reed, John McEnery, Raymond Lovelock, Carol André, Claudia Cardinale, Zora Valcova.
● An adaptation of Lermontov's novel *Vadim* which must rate as one of the crassest ventures in years, so God knows how Edward Bond, respected playwright, got himself muddled up with it. Presumably the director, who also has a hand in the script, must shoulder most of the blame; if his writing is anything like his direction, then it must have represented the kiss of death to Bond's contribution. As for the film, it has Reed as an 18th century Russian landowner, given to telling his dog that he's the only one he can trust, and to fondling girls' nighties while one of his peasants is flogged half to death outside. Meanwhile, Vadim (McEnery), a strange new servant bent on avenging the death of his parents at the hands of the tyrannical Reed, incites the masses to agitate. Agitation is likely to be already rife in the audience. CPe

Fury, The

(1978, US, 118 min)
d Brian De Palma. *p* Frank Yablans. *sc* John Farris. *ph* Richard H Kline. *ed* Paul Hirsch. *pd* Bill Malley. *m* John Williams. *cast* Kirk Douglas, John Cassavetes, Carrie Snodgress, Charles Durning, Amy Irving, Fiona Lewis, Andrew Stevens.
● Here De Palma poses the burning question: is there still commercial mileage in demonic possession? But this attempted follow-up to *Carrie* almost entirely lacks its predecessor's narrative thrust and suspense. At centre it's another common-or-garden story of children screwed up by their own telekinetic powers, but there are several distracting subplots: one about secret US government research into psychic phenomena (masterminded by Evil Incarnate in the person of Cassavetes), more on the hero's paternal angsts as he approaches the male menopause. Stylistic pretensions further defuse whatever punch the original script might have had. In so far as the film lives at all, it's in its shock effects, which are adequately cruel if too thin on the ground – although the heartwarming sight of Cassavetes getting his just deserts compensates for a lot. TR

Fuss Over Feathers

see Conflict of Wings

Future Cop

see Trancers

Future Is Woman, The (Il Futuro è Donna)

(1984, It/Fr/WGer, 100 min)
d Marco Ferreri. *sc* Marco Ferreri, Dacia Maraini, Piera Degli Esposti. *ph* Tonino Delli Colli. *ed* Ruggero Mastroianni. *ad* Dante Ferretti. *m* Carlo Savina. *cast* Ornella Muti, Hanna Schygulla, Niels Arestrup, Maurizio Donadoni, Michèle Bovenzi.
● Once upon a time Ferreri made sprightly little sexual fables with a tasty black humour. Then the shock factor took over, culminating in Ferreri's beloved phallocracy capitulating to feminism with Depardieu chopping off his dong in *The Last Woman* Now Ferreri seems to have gone soft in this uninspiring tale of an attempted New Deal in relationships, in which a bored bourgeois couple take in a pregnant *femme maudite* and squabble over her body and baby. Terrific design and loud disco music are no compensation for the spectacle of this tiresome trio, who weep, pout and beat each other up, giving little hope for the result of Ornella Muti's (real-life) pregnancy. DT

Future of Emily, The (L'Avenir d'Emilie)

(1984, Fr/WGer, 116 min)
d Helma Sanders-Brahms. *p* Nicole Flipo, Hildegard Westbeld. *sc* Helma Sanders-Brahms. *ph* Sacha Vierny. *ed* Ursula West. *ad* Jean-Michel Vierny, Rainer Schaper. *m* Jürgen Knieper. *cast* Brigitte Fossey, Hildegard Knef, Ivan Desny, Herman Treusch, Camille Raymond.
● Sanders-Brahms' films are not for the faint-hearted. Compared to *No Mercy, No Future*, her coruscating study of schizophrenia, this is almost a joyride, a long day's journey into O'Neill territory with three generations of mothers and daughters at each other's throats. Fossey, successful actress and single mother, returns home to Normandy to visit daughter and parents. Recriminations multiply, with Fossey and Knef (her mother) living through a dark night of the soul, each balancing the family/career equation and baring her passionate obsession with the other. Strong meat, but the actresses sink their teeth into it with consummate relish. SJo

Futureworld

(1976, US, 107 min)
d Richard T Heffron. *p* Paul N Lazarus III, James Aubrey. *sc* Mayo Simon, George Schenck. *ph* Howard Schwartz, George Schenck. *ed* James Mitchell. *ad* Trevor Williams. *m* Fred Karlin. *cast* Peter Fonda, Blythe Danner, Arthur Hill, Yul Brynner, John Ryan, Stuart Margolin.
● Set in 1985, this sequel to the pithy *Westworld* is all gloss and no substance. *Westworld's* vast pleasure centre, where any and every fantasy could be fulfilled by means of highly sophisticated humanoid robots, is rebuilt on an even more lavish and supposedly fail-safe scale. Leading diplomats plus the press are invited to sample the goods, and only one intrepid newshound (Fonda) suspects that all is not well. Instead of expanding the possibilities, the film opts for a guided tour of the various simulated marvels, from a Cape Kennedy blast-off and a chess game with holograms as the pieces to a ski-race down a Martian hillside. At one point there is an asinine dream sequence whose only relevance seems to be as a reminder that Yul Brynner played the lead resurgent robot in the parent film. The script, which labours under polysyllabic mumbo-jumbo at times, is infantile, while the performances, apart from a sprightly Danner as Fonda's TV cohort, are spineless. IB

F/X (aka F/X – Murder by Illusion)

(1985, US, 108 min)
d Robert Mandel. *p* Dodi Fayed, Jackie Wiener. *sc* Robert T Megginson, Gregory Freeman. *ph* Miroslav Ondricek. *ed* Terry Rawlings. *pd* Mel Bourne. *m* Bill Conti. *cast* Bryan Brown, Brian Dennehy, Diane Venora, Cliff De Young, Mason Adams, Jerry Orbach.
● The Justice Department invites effects maestro Rollie Tyler (Brown) to stage the murder of a Mob informer. He declines the job, but then changes his mind rather than see it go to his industry rival. Lured into pulling the trigger himself, Tyler dives into the getaway car and wonders why they covered the back seat in plastic. Man with gun in front seat turns round. So begins Tyler's own personal witness relocation programme, a soft-boiled crime caper stuffed with latex masks, stick-on beards and smoke bombs. Dennehy is charming and entertaining as the maverick cop who turns out to be Tyler's best bet. The action sequences are efficiently handled, but look elsewhere for psychological or emotional insight. Dead girlfriends and murdered bystanders are collateral damage in the war against serious film-making. NRo

F/X2 (aka F/X2 – The Deadly Art of Illusion)

(1991, US, 108 min)
d Richard Franklin. *p* Dodi Fayed, Jack Wiener. *sc* Bill Condon. *ph* Victor J Kemper. *ed* Andrew London. *pd* John Jay Moore. *m* Lalo Schifrin. *cast* Bryan Brown, Brian Dennehy, Rachel Ticotin, Joanna Gleason, Philip Bosco, Kevin J O'Connor, Tom Mason, Dominic Zamprogna, Josie DeGuzman, John Walsh.
● Six years after part one, special effects ain't what they used to be. While *F/X – Murder by Illusion* relied heavily on explosions and smoke for excitement, here we're offered a 'telemetry' suit (enabling the wearer to control a robot's movements via remote control) and advanced video technology. But certain things remain constant: Rollie (Brown) and Leo (Dennehy) are still at odds with a corrupt system. After the traumatic events which left his girlfriend dead, special effects wizard Rollie has settled for a peaceful life as a toymaker. But when he is recruited to help the police on a case, he becomes embroiled in an intrigue involving the Vatican, the Mafia and precious gold medallions. Although this sequel spends more time developing the friendship between the crime-busting buddies, it remains rather flat and uninvolving. CM

g

Gosford Park

Gabbeh

(1996, Iran/Fr, 74 min)
d Mohsen Makhmalbaf. *p* Khalil Daroudchi, Khalil Mahmoudi. *sc* Mohsen Makhmalbaf. *ph* Mahmud Kalari. *ed* Mohsen Makhmalbaf. *m* Hussein Alizadeh. *cast* Shaghayegh Djodat, Hossein Moharami, Abbas Sayahi, Rogheih Moharami, Parvaneh Ghalandari, Hassen Kermi.

●In Iran, a *gabbeh* is a colourful woollen carpet woven by the women of sheep-herding nomadic tribes. In this visually gorgeous film, Gabbeh (Djodat) is also a young woman prevented from marrying her horseman suitor by her father, who keeps coming up with lame excuses about her uncle needing to find a bride first, or his own wife having to give birth to their latest child. On one level, the film functions as fascinating ethnographic semi-documentary; on another, as a study in storytelling, both traditional and modern(-ist). Gabbeh, herself a figure depicted in a carpet, relates her tale of love and frustration to an ancient, bickering couple who may just be her future self and her lover. The tone is at once lyrical and epic, charming and whimsical. GA

Gable and Lombard

(1976, US, 131 min)
d Sidney J Furie. *p* Harry Korshak. *sc* Barry Sandler. *ph* Jordan Cronenweth. *ed* Argyle Nelson. *pd* Edward C Carfagno. *m* Michel Legrand. *cast* James Brolin, Jill Clayburgh, Allen Garfield, Red Buttons, Joanne Linville, Melanie Mayron.

●A disastrous example of a short-lived mid-'70s cycle of Lives of the Stars (see also *WC Fields and Me*), *Gable and Lombard* gets neither the history nor the glamour right. The film seems as insulated and remote from the 'real' Hollywood as Hollywood vehicles of the time were from the 'real' world. Allen Garfield does a reasonable turn as Louis Mayer, but Brolin is a wax dummy and Clayburgh produces a very modern version of the Lombard larkishness. Furie completes the pretence by presenting the Gable and Lombard story as if it were one of the crazy comedies they appeared in. MA

Gabriela

(1983, Braz, 99 min)
d Bruno Barreto. *p* Harold Nebenzal, Ibrahim Moussa. *sc* Leopoldo Serran, Bruno Barreto. *ph* Carlo Di Palma, (addit) Pedro Farkas, Carlos Egberto. *ed* Emmanuelle Castro. *ad* Hélio Eichbauer. *m* Antônio Carlos Jobim. *cast* Sonia Braga, Marcello Mastroianni, Antonio Cantáfora, Paulo Goulart, Nelson Xavier, Nuno Leal Maia, Fernando Ramos, Nicole Puzzi.

●This was a Jorge Amado novel that became a TV soap, then a movie – the rock opera we still await, but sexy, free-spirited Gabriela has certainly struck a chord with Brazilians. The throng of characters and plotlines jostling for position – it's all to do with romantic/political manoeuvrings in a coastal town in the 1920s – are presumably an attempt to accommodate favourite bits from earlier manifestations. Number one item on the agenda, however, is the camera's on-going perusal of the Braga bod. Mastroianni as Gabriela's main man lends an air of consequence to the proceedings. BBa

Gabriel & Me

(2001, GB, 87 min)
d Udayan Prasad. *p* Marc Samuelson, Peter Samuelson. *sc* Lee Hall. *ph* Alan Almond. *ed* Barrie Vince. *pd* Andy Harris. *m* Stephen Warbeck. *cast* Iain Glen, David Bradley, Sean Landless, Rosie Rowell, Billy Connolly, Ian Cullen, Sean Foley, Trevor Fox.

●Director Prasad made us laugh with *My Son the Fanatic*, but Lee Hall's adaptation of his own play *I Luv You Jimmy Spud* goes for more transcendent pay-offs. The emotional breastbaring Hall displayed in *Billy Elliot* is upped here, as is his muscular symbolism. Jimmy (Landless), a working-class lad from Newcastle, talks to an angel, Gabriel (Connolly). Looking to join the ranks, Jimmy makes his own wings and takes fledgling flights, at one point diving to save an Asian boy scout from drowning. Glen is effective and moving as Jimmy's redundant shipworker father, whose sufferings are the wellspring for the boy's imaginative leap into the world of the miraculous. There are also nicely turned performances from Rowell as mam and Bradley as the gentle, politically aware grandparent. As father's illness progresses, Jimmy sings to him in a sweet scene that exposes, by contrast, a tendency to dissipation in many others. No complaints about Landless (okay, maybe the boy could do with a few more rough edges), but visually, the film is a little disappointing, though it sticks to its broadly democratic appeal. WH

Gabriel Over the White House

(1933, US, 87 min, b/w)
d Gregory La Cava. *p* Walter Wanger. *sc* Carey Wilson, Bertram Bloch. *ph* Bert Glennon. *ed* Basil Wrangell. *ad* Cedric Gibbons. *m* William Axt. *cast* Walter Huston, Karen Morley, Franchot Tone, Arthur Byron, C Henry Gordon, Samuel S Hinds, Jean Parker.

●A party stooge in the pockets of 'special interests', the newly elected US President, Hammond (Huston), has no intention of squaring up to the Great Depression…until he wakes up from a car accident a changed man: a visionary leader. What distinguishes La Cava's political fable from ostensibly similar populist fantasies by Frank Capra is not so much ideology as urgency. Where John Doe preached neighbourliness and Mr Smith talked boys' camps, Hammond sidesteps Congress to declare a state of emergency, establishes an 'Army of Construction' (a prototype for Workfare), pits the military against the mob, and instigates World Disarmament. His 'divine madness' smacks of fascism, though La Cava might have enlisted Plato in his support as well as Lincoln; and in any case, American movies are as paradoxical as American politics: Louis B Mayer – a staunch Republican – held up the film's release because he saw it as an insult to ex-President Hoover and a boost for Franklin Roosevelt's New Deal. Any similarities with Messrs Bush and Clinton are *entirely* coincidental. TCh

Gadael Lenin

see Leaving Lenin

Gadjo Dilo (The Crazy Stranger)

(1997, Fr, 100 min)
d Tony Gatlif. *p* Guy Marignane. *sc* Tony Gatlif. *ph* Eric Guichard. *ed* Monique Dartonne. *ad* Brigitte Brassart. *m* Tony Gatlif. *cast* Romain Duris, Rona Hartner, Izidor Serban, Florin Moldovan, Ovidiu Balan, Dan Astileanu.

●Tony Gatlif, a Rom himself, continues his exploration of gypsy culture with this tale of a young Parisian (Duris) who travels to Romania in search of a gypsy singer. Slowly accepted by a clan suspicious of the outside world, he witnesses the joys and heartbreaks of Romany experience. This funny, bawdy, moving blend of gritty drama, glorious music and dance, and ethnographic semi-documentary never romanticises the characters: while they're lively, lusty, talented and passionate, they also have a tendency towards drunkenness, theft, xenophobia and foul-mouthed aggression – the result, probably, of being treated as unwanted outsiders by the world around them. Simultaneously stirring and illuminating, and as well worth catching as Gatlif's earlier *Les Princes* and *Lacho Drom*. GA

Gaea Girls

(2000, GB, 106 min)
d/p/sc Kim Longinotto, Jano Williams. *ph* Kim Longinotto. *ed* Brian Tagg. *with* Chigusa Nagaya, Meiko Satomura, Yuka Sugiyama, Saika Takeuchi.

●This fascinating documentary is based around the Japanese wrestling organisation Gaea's rural training camp, and traces, in the main, the careers of four hopefuls. In charge are two magnificent specimens, the butch champion Chigusa Nagaya, still venting her hurt at the hands of her army father as she tries to whip her surrogate daughters through the pain and commitment barriers; and her sophisticated and slightly menacing Chairman. It's a gruelling, physical film, as you would expect, but the makers don't make heavy weather of it. And it certainly disposes of any idea that the game is faked. WH

Gai Savoir, Le

(1968, Fr/WGer, 91 min)
d/sc Jean-Luc Godard. *ph* Jean Leclerc. *cast* Juliet Berto, Jean-Pierre Léaud, Chantal Jeanson.

●Commissioned (in a moment of exceptional naiveté) by French TV, *Le Gai Savoir* was Godard's first 'radical' break with established methods of exhibition and distribution; the film was never televised, and has been seen only by political groups and film societies. Two militants meet in a darkened film studio to educate themselves in the ideological meanings of specific sounds and images: their work is essentially 'deconstructive', and it represents an important step in Godard's own return to a 'degree zero' of cinema. In Godard's own terms, the film is not at all revolutionary: it's a confused, idiosyncratic attempt at an analysis of the way things are, not yet a committed attempt to construct the way they should be. TR

Galahad of Everest

(1991, GB, 90 min)
d John-Paul Davidson. *cast* Brian Blessed, Chris Bonnington.

●This spectacular but extremely bizarre BBC documentary recounts the madcap efforts of actor Brian Blessed to exorcise an obsession that has dogged him since childhood: to follow the footsteps of mountaineers George Leigh Mallory and Andrew Irving's fated 1924 attempt on Everest. It charts his preparation in England, the trip to India, a blessing by the Dalai Lama, to a final assault on the summit, kitted out *à la* Mallory in '20s plus-fours and umbrella. Davidson intercuts archive footage of Mallory's original expedition with a snow-blasted Blessed reading Mallory's last letters from five miles high. If this sounds like your average 'climbing movie', it isn't. It adds up to a hilarious study in English eccentricity. WH

Galaxy of Terror

(1981, US, 80 min)
d Bruce Clark. *p* Roger Corman. *sc* Mark Siegler, Bruce Clark. *ph* Jacques Haitkin. *ed* RJ Kizer, Larry Boch, Barry Zetlin. *m* Barry Schrader. *cast* Edward Albert, Erin Moran, Ray Walston, Bernard Behrens, Zalman King, Sig Haig.

●A Roger Corman tummy-ripper on the *Alien* theme, involving a rescue mission's dash into deep space to discover the whereabouts of one of their craft. However, they soon end up wishing they hadn't, as one crew member after another is exterminated by those nasty slimy things that usually inhabit such desolate places. Forget the story, 'cause there isn't one, but see it for the gory bits and marvellous gutsy make-up. Yech! DA

Galaxy Quest

(1999, US, 102 min)
d Dean Parisot. *p* Mark Johnson, Charles Newirth. *sc* David Howard, Robert Gordon. *ph* Jerzy Zielinski. *ed* Don Zimmerman. *pd* Linda Descenna. *m* David Newman. *cast* Tim Allen, Sigourney Weaver, Alan Rickman, Tony Shalhoub, Sam Rockwell, Daryl Mitchell, Enrico Colantoni, Robin Sachs, Patrick Breen, Missy Pyle.

●The series only ran from '79 to '82, but the cast of 'Galaxy Quest' are making a living of sorts on the fan convention circuit. Facing yet more dorky devotees hardly enthuses the show's alien and science officer, Alexander Dane (Rickman), communications officer Gwen DeMarco (Weaver), and commander Jason Nesmith (Allen). Still, they need the money, so they tag along when a dweeby-looking bunch inveigles them into visiting their mock-up of the programme's old vessel, the 'Protector'. But the twist is, this time the ship was actually crafted on a distant planet, where transmissions of 'Galaxy Quest' have been mistaken for historical documents, and the misguided extra-terrestrials have gambled on recruiting heroic Allen and crew to save their world from interstellar rivals. The actors have played this script before, but now it's for real. Gently satirising the Trekkie phenomenon, Parisot's movie works a treat because it's sufficiently knowing to have the references down pat, but affectionate enough to have a soft spot for just about everyone. Effects and production design are also splendidly integrated into the overall enterprise, which is even more enjoyable for being so unexpected. TJ

Galileo

(1968, It/Bulg, 108 min)
d Liliana Cavani. *p* Leonardo Pescarolo. *sc* Liliana Cavani, Tullio Pinelli, Fabrizio Onofri.

ph Alfio Contini. *ed* Nino Baragli. *ad* Ezio Frigerio. *m* Ennio Morricone. *cast* Cyril Cusack, Gheorghi Kolaiancev, Irene Kokonova, Lou Castel, Gigi Ballista.
●Cavani's second feature, a film that makes an impassioned plea for the primacy of the evidence of the senses as against a seemingly undentable wall of dogma and passively accepted consensus opinion. And the plea is articulated in the early part of the film with real urgency, fervour and individuality. The impenetrable, monolithic quality of state-authenticated truth is wittily rendered in the rigid curlicues and ostentatious grandeur of Papal architecture, and the argument is convincingly developed around the person of Giordano Bruno (Kolaiancev), Galileo's fellow scientist and martyr. The film, however, becomes a lot more conventional and less passionate on Bruno's death, and Cavani is unable to solve the perennial Galileo problem: he (played here by Cusack) turns by degrees into an unastonishing symbol. VG

Galileo

(1974, GB/Can, 145 min)
d Joseph Losey. *p* Ely Landau. *sc* Barbara Bray, Joseph Losey. *ph* Michael Reed. *ed* Reginald Beck. *pd* Richard MacDonald. *m* Hanns Eisler, Richard Hartley. *cast* Chaim Topol, Edward Fox, Michel Lonsdale, Richard O'Callaghan, Tom Conti, Mary Larkin, Judy Parfitt, John McEnery, Patrick Magee.
●Maybe Losey simply lived too long with a project he had been trying to get off the ground ever since he first directed Laughton in Brecht's play in 1947, and which emerges here as a curiously academic exercise. For one thing, giving a likeable but lightweight performance, Topol is allowed to get away with presenting Galileo as a hero, which makes nonsense of Brecht's condemnation of him as a coward for his betrayal of science (the crucial carnival scene now becomes just a jolly romp). For another, Losey hedges uncertainly between theatre and cinema, so that Brecht's linking songs and captions are retained, but rendered in 'cinematic' ways that make them both clumsy and tautological. By far the most striking sequence is also the most purely theatrical (Galileo's daughter and disciples waiting anxiously to hear whether he has recanted, shot on a bare stage with stark, theatrical groupings and spotlights projecting a shadow-play of their emotions on the cyclorama behind). Elsewhere, smooth theatrical continuity tends to blunt the raw edges of Brecht's distancing effects. TM

Gallery Murders, The

see Uccello dalle Piume di Cristallo, L'

Gallipoli

(1981, Aust, 111 min)
d Peter Weir. *p* Robert Stigwood, Patricia Lovell. *sc* David Williamson. *ph* Russell Boyd. *ed* William Anderson. *ad* Herbert Pinter. *m* Brian May. *cast* Mark Lee, Mel Gibson, Bill Hunter, Robert Grubb, Tim McKenzie, David Argue, Bill Kerr, Ron Graham.
●Australia's answer to *Chariots of Fire*, similarly buoyed up by a fulsome nationalistic fervour, and coincidentally also featuring two sprinters whose friendly rivalry leads not to the Olympic track but to the World War I battlefront of Gallipoli. Expensively and handsomely shot, the Gallipoli reconstructions (complete with conventional message about the waste of war) are impressively done. Much less appealing, the central section devoted to training in Egypt sags badly through its crass buddy antics and its crude caricatures of wogs and pommies. TM

Gallivant

(1996, GB, 100 min)
d Andrew Kötting. *p* Ben Woolford. *sc* Andrew Kötting. *ph* Nick Gordon-Smith. *ed* Clifford West. *m* David Burnand. *cast* Andrew Kötting, Gladys Morris, Eden Kötting.
●A delightfully offbeat road movie in which the oddball director Andrew Kötting, his grandmother Gladys, and his daughter Eden, who has learning difficulties and communicates by sign language, travel around the coast of Britain. If the camerawork occasionally veers towards the tricksy, this first feature is still a warm, enlightening and often very funny look at Britain and what it means to be British. GA

Gal Young 'Un

(1979, US, 105 min)
d/p/sc Victor Nuñez. *ph* Victor Nuñez, Greg Garner. *ed* Victor Nuñez. *ad* Pat Garner, Greg Garner. *m* Charles Engstrom. *cast* Dana Preu, David Peck, J Smith, Gene Densmore, Jennie Stringfellow, Tim McCormack.
●Florida, 1930s. Mattie Siles (Preu) tolerates everything her bootlegging lover throws at her (stealing her money, flaunting a rival young gal) rather than lose him. Nuñez is one of the gentlest souls active in cinema – hence perhaps the long pauses between realised projects – and he persists in finding the humanity in even the most heartless of characters. Not much of a budget is in evidence, but it wouldn't be a step closer to perfection with money to burn. From the story by Marjorie Kinnan Rawlings. DO

Gambit

(1966, US, 108 min)
d Ronald Neame. *p* Leo L Fuchs. *sc* Jack Davies, Alvin Sargent. *ph* Clifford Stine. *ed* Alma Macrorie. *ad* Alexander Golitzen, George Webb. *m* Maurice Jarre. *cast* Shirley MacLaine, Michael Caine, Herbert Lom, Roger C Carmel, John Abbott, Arnold Moss.
●Likeable performances from Caine and MacLaine as the Cockney con-man and the Eurasian showgirl in Hong Kong who conspire to steal a priceless statue from Lom. But it's all pretty thin as the conventionally unconventional caper, involving cross and double-cross, veers erratically from comedy to thriller and back again to romance. GA

Gambler, The

(1974, US, 111 min.)
d Karel Reisz. *p* Irwin Winkler, Robert Chartoff. *sc* James Toback. *ph* Victor J Kemper. *ed* Roger Spottiswoode. *pd* Philip Rosenberg. *m* Jerry Fielding. *cast* James Caan, Paul Sorvino, Lauren Hutton, Morris Carnovsky, Jacqueline Brookes, Burt Young, Vic Tayback, M Emmet Walsh, James Woods.
●Caan's gambler (a fine performance) is a university lecturer who gets into hot water with the mobsters over his debts, and uses Dostoievsky to intellectualise his weakness into tragic compulsion. Predictably, his increasingly desperate measures are at the expense of those closest to him, and are accompanied by a deepening masochistic streak. In keeping with this definition of classic impulses, Reisz's direction is panoramic, with aspirations towards the epic, when it should have been closer in and faster. The result is a highly melodramatic and romantic film, for all the veneer of disillusion, whose weighty statement too often swamps the potentially strong suspense. *The Gambler* looks all the more old-fashioned for coming in the wake of Altman's systematic demythology of the subject in *California Split*; and James Toback showed how his script might perhaps have been tackled when he came to make his own directing debut with *Fingers*. CPe

Gambler, The

(1997, GB/Neth/Hun, 97 min)
d Károly Makk. *p* Charles Cohen, Marc Vlessing. *sc* Katherine Ogden, Charles Cohen, Nick Dear. *ph* Jules van den Steenhoven. *ed* Kevin Whelan. *pd* Ben van Os. *m* Brian Lock. *cast* Michael Gambon, Jodhi May, Polly Walker, Dominic West, John Wood, Johan Leysen, Angeline Bell, Luise Rainer.
●St Petersburg, 1866: debt-ridden Dostoevsky (Gambon) has struck a deal with his publisher – in exchange for an advance, he must meet the deadline for his next book, or forfeit the rights to all his published work. With a month to go, doom looks inevitable, unless stenographer Anna Snitkina (May) can channel the author's violent mood swings into sustained creativity. Yet, as he unfolds an autobiographical story of obsessive desire and self-destruction around the roulette wheel, this prim naive girl begins to experience unexpected feelings for the much troubled artist. Gambon has the dissolute look down pat, but earns our compassion as a man shaped for good and ill by the contours of his own weakness. In a less obviously showy role, May deftly suggests a woman coming to terms with desires she never knew she had, and her underplaying blends nicely with the larger-than-life contributions from Walker's voluptuous femme fatale and Rainer's marvellously vibrant grandmother. Makk balances dramatic interest across the twin-track narrative and delivers an absorbing venture into the psychology of addiction. TJ

Game, The

(1997, US, 128 min)
d David Fincher. *p* Steve Golin, Ceán Chaffin. *sc* John Brancato, Michael Ferris. *ph* Harris Savides. *ed* James Haygood. *pd* Jeffrey Beecroft. *m* Howard Shore. *cast* Michael Douglas, Sean Penn, James Rebhorn, Deborah Kara Unger, Peter Donat, Carroll Baker, Armin Mueller-Stahl.
●San Francisco. Ruthless financier Nicholas Van Orton (Douglas) is a control freak who no longer knows the meaning of fun or friendship. When his estranged, addictive brother Conrad (Penn) enrolls him with Consumer Recreation Services for his birthday, his curiosity's aroused by the offer of a mysterious 'game' tailored to the needs of each participant. At first his application is rejected, but when, on TV, a newscaster starts talking directly to him, Nicholas realises the game's already begun and that his actions are being monitored and manipulated. As his privacy is progressively invaded and the situations in which he finds himself become ever more life-threatening, Van Orton tries to pull out of the game, but too late. Though the film's 'message' about complacency transformed by chaos and uncertainty is hackneyed, the alarming twists of the witty, ingenious script (by John Brancato and Michael Ferris) hold the attention throughout. GA

Game for Vultures

(1979, GB, 106 min)
d James Fargo. *p* Hazel Adair. *sc* Phillip Baird. *ph* Alex Thomson. *ed* Peter Tanner. *ad* Herbert Smith. *m* John Field, Tony Duhig. *cast* Richard Harris, Richard Roundtree, Joan Collins, Ray Milland, Sven-Bertil Taube, Denholm Elliott.
●Rhodesia…1979…guerilla warfare in the bush…arms smuggling in the Hilton…torrid passion (Collins + Harris) between the bedsheets. If this attempt to cash in on international news (made in South Africa, incidentally) were a little more reactionary and a little less 'responsible', it might have made a decent action film and turned its images of men at war (platoons skirmishing hopelessly in the bush) to some use. As it is, the plot meanders in desperation, and the increasing archness of Joan Collins in her usual role becomes just another dead-weight irrelevance. If white Rhodesia feels as dispirited as this movie looks, the war of black liberation has already been won. CA

Gamekeeper, The

(1978, GB, 80 min)
d Kenneth Loach. *sc* Barry Hines. *ph* Chris Menger, Charles Stewart. *ed* Roger James. *ad* Martin Johnson, Graham Tew. *cast* Phil Askham, Rita May, Andrew Grubb, Peter Steels, Michael Hinchcliffe, Philip Firth.
●Loach's adaptation for TV of a script by Barry (*Kes*) Hines is a superb study of a year in the life of a gamekeeper working on an aristocrat's Northern estate, subtly examining his relationships with his family, his employer, his dog, and the land itself. Avoiding didactic simplifications, beautifully shot by Chris Menges, and superbly acted, it's the type of totally honest social document that shows up a film like *Begging the Ring* for the half-baked idea it is. GA

Game of Danger

see Bang! You're Dead

Gamera: The Guardian of the Universe (Gamera Daikaiju Kuchu Kessen)

(1995, Jap, 92 min)
d Shusuke Kaneko. *p* Tsutomu Tsuchikawa. *sc* Kazunori Ito. *ph* Junichi Tozawa, Kenji Takama. *ed* Shizuo Arakawa. *pd* Hajime Oikawa. *m* Ko Otani. *cast* Tsuyoshi Ihara, Akira Onodera, Ayako Fujitani, Shinobu Nakayama, Hirotaro Honda, Yukijiro Hotaru.
●'How do you explain a life form which flies, spinning like a flying saucer?' Obviously, it's a 10,000-year-old, manmade giant turtle, Gamera, originally the final desperate creation of the people of Atlantis before that civilisation was

destroyed by its prior invention, Gyaos, 'the shadow of evil'. Gyaos would be those giant, fanged birds currently storming Tokyo, then, which grow more powerful as they feed on people. But how do you explain why the Japanese political establishment now want to protect Gyaos and shoot down the resurrected turtle? More to the point, why do these beasts all look and sound like plastic toys stomping around a miniature balsa-wood set? The product of an earlier age, Shusuke Kaneko's film relies on special effects and a script that are clearly the products of human beings, rather than computers. And while it's hardly original, the cheap, zippy comic-book sensibility leaves the film cheerfully free of bombast. NB

Gandhi

(1982, GB, 188 min)
d/p Richard Attenborough. *sc* John Briley. *ph* Billy Williams, Ronnie Taylor. *ed* John Bloom. *pd* Stuart Craig. *m* Ravi Shankar. *cast* Ben Kingsley, Candice Bergen, Edward Fox, John Gielgud, Trevor Howard, John Mills, Martin Sheen, Ian Charleson, Athol Fugard.

●By virtue of its subject matter, and of the prodigious effort that has gone into its production, *Gandhi* has to be considered one of the major British films of the year. Its subject is an Indian spiritual leader almost unknown to today's Western youth, who not only preached a more sophisticated and forceful version of the pacifist ethic than ever flowered in the '60s, but succeeded in using it to help liberate his country and change its political history. Of course the film raises more questions than it comes near to answering, but its faults rather pale beside the epic nature of its theme, and Kingsley's performance in the central role is outstanding. FD

Gang, Le

(1976, Fr/It, 103 min)
d Jacques Deray. *p* Henri Jaquillard. *sc* Alphonse Boudard, Jean-Claude Carrière. *ph* Silvano Ippoliti. *ed* Henri Lanoe. *ad* Théo Meurisse. *m* Carlo Rustichelli. *cast* Alain Delon, Maurice Barrier, Roland Bertin, Adalberto Maria Merli, Xavier Depraz, Raymond Bussières, Nicole Calfan, Laura Betti.

●Old-fashioned, simple-minded stuff, with a bewigged Delon leading the notorious but effortlessly elusive 'front-wheel-drive gang' in a not too serious succession of hold-ups in postwar France. Deray periodically clobbers the audience with second-hand chunks of morality, but for the most part is content to move the action along with a minimum of violence and the occasional pastoral interlude evocative of a simpler age when crooks – however psychopathic – all had hearts of gold and faithful molls. The gendarmes, we are told, are busy purging their ranks of collaborators; it falls, therefore, to a jeweller's comely wife to despatch our hero (his demise coming as no surprise, since the movie is one long flashback). JPy

Gang Related

(1997, US, 111 min)
d Jim Kouf. *p* Brad Krevoy, Steve Stabler, John Bertolli. *sc* Jim Kouf. *ph* Brian J Reynolds. *ed* Todd Ramsay. *pd* Charles Breen *m* Mickey Hart. *cast* James Belushi, Tupac Shakur, Lela Rochon, Dennis Quaid, James Earl Jones, David Paymer, Wendy Crewson, Gary Cole.

●Street cops Divinci (Belushi) and Rodriguez (Shakur) have a scam going, fake drug deals in which they sell the dope, dispose of the customer in a drive-by execution, retrieve the drugs and record the shooting as gang related. A nice little earner, this also helps clean the streets of dealers, or so justifies Divinci, whose ethics on the job have stretched as wide as his waistline. The plot unravels when one victim proves to have been an undercover DEA agent, his boss now baying for answers. Short of the usual scapegoats, Divinci lines up an alcoholic tramp (Quaid) to take the fall, ropes in his girlfriend (Rochon) to stand witness, and borrows the odd item of evidence from a concurrent murder trial. Despite a vaguely interesting premise – something like a chaos theory of police karma, the two partners precipitating their own downfall via a series of triggered repercussions – this never rises above the functional. NB

Gang's All Here, The (aka The Girls He Left Behind)

(1943, US, 103 min)
d Busby Berkeley. *p* William LeBaron. *sc* Walter Bullock. *ph* Edward Cronjager. *ed* Ray Curtiss. *ad* James Basevi, Joseph C Wright. *songs* Leo Robin, Harry Warren. *cast* Alice Faye, Carmen Miranda, Phil Baker, James Ellison, Charlotte Greenwood, Eugene Pallette, Edward Everett Horton, Sheila Ryan.

●Busby Berkeley's first in colour, reaching some sort of apotheosis in vulgarity with Carmen Miranda's 'Lady in the Tutti-Frutti Hat' accompanied by a parade of chorines manipulating outsize bananas. Basically terrible, although Berkeley fans get some bizarre eyefuls and Benny Goodman provides some bland Big Band swing. But Alice Faye does get to sing two terrific Harry Warren numbers, 'No Love, No Nothing' and 'A Journey to a Star'. TM

Gangster No. 1

(2000, GB/Ger/Ire, 103 min)
d Paul McGuigan. *p* Norma Heyman, Jonathan Cavendish. *sc* Johnny Ferguson *ph* Peter Sova. *ed* Andrew Hulme. *pd* Richard Bridgland. *m* John Dankworth. *cast* Malcom McDowell, David Thewlis, Paul Bettany, Saffron Burrows, Kenneth Cranham, Jamie Foreman, Razaaq Adoti, Doug Allen, Eddie Marsan.

●The structure of this British gangster picture, from a play by Louis Mellis and David Scinto, harks back to classics of the genre, *Little Caesar* and *Scarface*. It's the story of a thug who rises through the ranks to become a gang boss through brute will and cunning; like *Once Upon a Time in America*, it doubles back over the decades to assume a deeper emotional timbre. The anonymous 'Gangster' is played by McDowell in his old age, reflecting on his nefarious '60s heyday, when – played by the newcomer Bettany – he became right-hand man to the 'Butcher of Mayfair', Freddie Mays (Thewlis). Mays exudes charm and class; Gangster's Iago-like enmity is part working class envy, part repressed homosexual attraction – and then he's psychotic, which clinches it. The treatment here is full-on and relentless, taking precise period detail and transforming it into the stuff of Expressionist nightmare. Gangster is a monster worthy of a horror movie – Bettany gives great hard stare ('Look at me,' he commands a stoolie repeatedly, and the man's fear has a stench); when things get tense, he's given to a startling subconscious scream (the soundscape designed by Simon Fisher Turner is also impressive). So, with all due respect, it has to be added there's something repellent and self-serving about this film's beady sadism and calculated moral fixing. Belated attempts to squeeze tragic pathos from this very nasty piece of work ring like tin. TCh

Ganja and Hess

(1973, US, 110 min)
d Bill Gunn. *p* Chiz Schultz. *sc* Bill Gunn. *ph* James E Hinton. *ed* Victor Kanefsky. *pd* Tom John. *m* Sam Waymon. *cast* Duane Jones, Marlene Clark, Bill Gunn, Sam Waymon, Leonard Jackson, Richard Harrow.

●Gunn's *film maudit* was the most ambitious 'black movie' of its day and a milestone for indie film-making in the US. Opening captions explain that academic Dr Hess Green (Jones, *Night of the Living Dead*) has been invulnerable and addicted to blood since being stabbed (in a parody of Catholic dogma) with a dagger from 'the ancient Black civilisation of Myrthia'. Affluent and (thanks to discreet raids on a local blood-bank) comfortable, he avoids murdering for sustenance until stuck with a new assistant (Gunn), who turns out to be a suicidal alcoholic. Deliberately fragmented and punctuated with disquieting cutaways to art works, the film charts his growing sense that he is afflicted with a curse, across his marriage to his assistant's widow Ganja (Clark) and his provision of a stud-victim to feed her 'hunger'. Theological musings jostle with sexual-visceral imagery in a mix which is still very potent. TR

Garage Olimpo

(1999, Arg/It, 98 min)
d Marco Bechis. *p* Amedeo Pagani. *sc* Marco Bechis, Lara Fremder. *ph* Ramiro Civita. *ed* Jacopo Quadri. *pd* Rómulo Abad. *m* Jacques Lederlin. *cast* Antonella Costa, Carlos Echeverría, Dominique Sanda, Chiara Caselli, Enrique Pineyro, Pablo Razuk.

●Maria (Costa) teaches literacy to the Buenos Aires poor, belongs to an anti-junta political cell, and lives with her Italian immigrant mother in a grand old house with a shy lodger, Felix (Echeverria), whose tentative advances faintly tickle her. One day the goon squad abducts her to the Garage Olimpo, an anonymous metal shuttered workshop which contains a hive of concrete torture chambers; it'll be several long weeks in hell before Maria sees daylight again. Felix is employed here. He's good at his job, too, and works over Maria, but afterwards, and around the edges of her torment, a bond is forged between them. This dramatisation of the mass 'disappearances' under the military dictatorship of the late '70s induces appropriate queasiness. The psychological dynamic between torturer and victim isn't as strongly realised as that in *Death and the Maiden*, but the power of deceptive appearances and unthinkable realities – authoritarianism underground – certainly leaves its mark. NB

Garde à Vue (The Inquisitor)

(1981, Fr, 88 min)
d Claude Miller. *p* Georges Dancigers, Alexandre Mnouchkine. *sc* Claude Miller, Jean Vautrin. *ph* Bruno Nuytten. *ed* Albert Jurgenson. *ad* Eric Moulard. *m* Georges Delerue. *cast* Lino Ventura, Michel Serrault, Guy Marchand, Romy Schneider, Didier Agostini, Patrick Depeyrat.

●A fine psychological thriller, adapted from an English mystery novel (John Wainwright's *Brainwash*) already accented by a *Série Noire* translation. The potential staginess of the material – a New Year's Eve interrogation in a provincial police station – is admirably shaken by inspired adaptation, *mise en scène* and editing as cop Ventura turns 'witness' Serrault (an attorney obsessed with his own mediocrity) into a suspected rapist and murderer. No descent to glib cat-and-mouse cleverness, and no recourse to actorly fireworks: Miller's confidence in dialogue and an ever more tightly twisting plot is simply a gripping joy. PT

Garde du Corps, Le (The Bodyguard)

(1984, Fr, 89 min)
d François Leterrier. *sc* Didier Kaminka, François Leterrier. *ph* Eduardo Serra. *ed* Claudine Bouché, Loula Morin. *m* Jean-Pierre Sabar. *cast* Jane Birkin, Sami Frey, Gérard Jugnot, Didier Kaminka, Evelyne Didi, Nicole Jamet.

●A light comic variation on the Bluebeard scenario: personable, plausible Sami Frey keeps his safari park solvent by bumping off the rich women he marries. The setting is Morocco, Birkin his latest victim-to-be, and Jugnot her hound-like suitor, who sees through Frey and is determined to thwart him. With her air of good-natured vacuity, Birkin beams her way through a series of murderous assaults ('Ugh, a crab,' she murmurs, crunching Frey's scorpion underfoot). The problem is Letterier, who seems more attracted by the unpleasantness of the situation than by such humour as may derive from it, and some bits are quite startlingly cruel. BBa

Garden, The

(1990, GB, 92 min)
d Derek Jarman. *p* James Mackay. *sc* Derek Jarman. *ph* Christopher Hughes. *ed* Peter Cartwright. *ad* Derek Brown. *m* Simon Fisher Turner. *cast* Tilda Swinton, Johnny Mills, Kevin Collins, Pete Lee-Wilson, Spencer Leigh, Jody Graber, Roger Cook, Michael Gough.

●At first this looks like *The Last of England 2*, but there's a crucial difference: this time, there's no pretension to objectivity. Jarman's own presence is central, and everything else on the screen is presented as his subjective dreams. Hence Jarman looks at his own garden near the sea in Dungeness, and imagines that it's the Garden of Eden or Garden of Gethsemane; Jarman reads about the government passing Section 28 and about the Synod witch-hunting gay priests, and imagines that Christ died for downcast gays; Jarman contemplates his own mortality (he is HIV-positive), and imagines that the end of the world is nigh. Touching, intense, sometimes unexpectedly amusing, sometimes agonising, and always achingly sincere. TR

Garden, The (Záhrada)

(1995, Slovakia, 99 min)
d Martin Sulik. *p* Rudolf Biermann. *sc* Martin Sulik, Martin Lescak, Ondrej Sulaj. *ph* Martin Strba. *ed* Dusan Milko. *m* Vladimir Godnar. *cast* Roman Luknar, Marian Labuda, Zuzana Sulajova, Jana Svandova, Katarina Vrzalova.

● There are a few amusing moments (notably the drunken reunion between the teacher hero and his generally hostile father) in this offbeat tale of spiritual renewal, but most of the time it's too oblique, allegorical and, perhaps, tinged with misogyny for its own good. Jakub, asked to leave his tailor dad's flat, goes to live in and tidy up his late grandfather's rundown rural cottage and garden; while there, he meets saintly and philosophical types, not to mention a teenage girl ('The Virgin Miraculous') whose mother beats her. Sadly, the film never lives up to its 14 intriguing chapter headings. GA

Garden of Allah, The

(1936, US, 80 min)
d Richard Boleslawski. *p* David O Selznick. *sc* WP Lipscomb, Lynn Riggs. *ph* W Howard Green, Harold Rosson. *ed* Hal C Kern, Anson Stevenson. *ad* Sturges Carne, Lyle Wheeler, Edward Boyle. *m* Max Steiner. *cast* Marlene Dietrich, Charles Boyer, Basil Rathbone, Tilly Losch, C Aubrey Smith, Joseph Schildkraut, John Carradine.

● Selznick's first colour production, a load of lush tosh about the complicated romance in the Algerian desert between disillusioned socialite Dietrich (grieving after her father's death) and Boyer's deserting Trappist monk. Based on a hideously dated Robert Hichens novel, complete with absurdly portentous dialogue, it's all pretty dull as well as silly, despite the rich Technicolor camerawork and sturdy attempts by Dietrich and Boyer to breathe life into the turgid story. GA

Garden of Eden, The

see Jardin del Eden, El

Garden of the Finzi-Continis, The (Il Giardino dei Finzi-Contini)

(1970, It/WGer, 95 min)
d Vittorio De Sica. *p* Gianni Hecht Lucari, Arthur Cohn. *sc* Tullio Pinelli, Valerio Zurlini, Franco Brusati, Ugo Pirro, Vittorio Bonicelli, Alain Katz. *ph* Ennio Guarnieri. *ed* Adriana Novelli. *ad* Giancarlo Bartolini-Salimbeni, Maurizio Chiari. *m* Manuel de Sica. *cast* Dominique Sanda, Lino Capolicchio, Helmut Berger, Romolo Valli, Fabio Testi, Camillo Cesarei, Inna Alexeief.

● De Sica's most watchable film in years of crude farces and coarse melodramas. Based on the novel by Giorgio Bassani and set in Ferrera in 1938, it deals with the net of persecution that gradually closes in on Italian Jews as Mussolini models his state ever more closely on Hitler's Germany. External events hold the film in a vice-like grip, while its dreamy evocation of a doomed way of life ambivalently records the placidity with which the aristocratically wealthy Finzi-Continis – retreating within their walled estate when they are no longer welcome outside – simply wait for fate to overtake them. Formally beautiful, sometimes moving, it's ultimately rather hollow. TM

Gardens of Stone

(1987, US, 112 min)
d Francis Ford Coppola. *p* Michael I Levy, Francis Ford Coppola. *sc* Ronald Bass. *ph* Jordan Cronenweth. *ed* Barry Malkin. *pd* Dean Tavoularis. *m* Carmine Coppola. *cast* James Caan, Anjelica Huston, James Earl Jones, DB Sweeney, Dean Stockwell, Mary Stuart Masterson, Dick Anthony Williams, Lonette McKee, Sam Bottoms.

● Coppola's oblique, muted and curiously revisionist drama of life on the home front during the Vietnam war. Sgt Hazard (Caan), a battle-seasoned veteran frustrated by his present role in the 'toy soldier' regiment guarding the Arlington military cemetery, is shaken out of his self-pitying cynicism by his love affair with an anti-war journalist (Huston) and a spiky father/son relationship with a gung-ho rookie (Sweeney). Caan is against the war – 'It's not even a war. There's nothing to win, and no way to win it' – but for the military; he won't go back to Vietnam, but desperately wants a transfer to Fort Benning, where he can train young recruits to die valiantly. Meanwhile, the bodies arrive daily, to be boxed up and buried with full military honours. While Ronald Bass' subtly understated dialogue, Coppola's meticulous direction, and some exceptional acting (especially from Caan) never fail to rivet the attention, there's a pervasive and worrying sense of the central issues being gently but undeniably fudged. NF

Garlic Is as Good as Ten Mothers

(1980, US, 54 min)
d/p/sc/ph Les Blank. *ed* Maureen Gosling.

● Better than any dry martini as an aperitif, even in the non-Smellaround version, this documentary eulogy to garlic sure gets the juices going. Featuring such eccentrics as the Chief Garlic Head, and tabling the many and varied delights of the 'stinking rose', this is a real breath of fresh air. Will repeat and repeat. FF

Garment Jungle, The

(1957, US, 88 min, b/w)
d Vincent Sherman, [Robert Aldrich]. *p/sc* Harry Kleiner. *ph* Joesph Biroc. *ed* William A Lyon. *ad* Robert E Peterson. *m* Leith Stevens. *cast* Lee J Cobb, Kerwin Mathews, Gia Scala, Richard Boone, Valerie French, Robert Loggia, Joseph Wiseman, Wesley Addy.

● Cut from familiar *noir* cloth – all eerie ceiling fans and empty elevator shafts expressionistically shot and lit – *The Garment Jungle's* off-the-peg plot concerns a coming-home Korean war veteran's discovery of foul play in the family firm and political gangsterism on either side. It's a sort of 'pro-labour' (Aldrich's term) On the Fashion Front, a radical retort to *On the Waterfront*'s anti-union allegory three years earlier (both films were Columbia releases, both were set in New York, and both cast Cobb as a proto-capitalist patriarch). Uncredited director Robert Aldrich was replaced by Sherman only one week before shooting ended for his refusal to tone down a tough screenplay. In spite of Sherman's efforts, though, *The Garment Jungle* makes latter-day labour films like *F.I.S.T.*, *Norma Rae* and *Blue Collar* look comparatively unstarched. PK

Gasbags

(1941, GB, 77 min, b/w)
d Marcel Varnel. *p* Edward Black. *sc* Val Valentine, Marriot Edgar, Val Guest. *ph* Arthur Crabtree. *ed* RE Dearing. *ad* Alex Vetchinsky. *cast* The Crazy Gang, Moore Marriott, Wally Patch, Peter Gawthorne, Carl Jaffe, Irene Handl, Billy Russell.

● Moore Marriott, grizzled, knobbly-kneed, and looking old enough to be Wilfrid Brambell's great-grandfather, steals the picture from under the very noses of the Crazy Gang – no small feat, considering this is probably the Gang's finest comedy. He plays a venerable PoW who just happens to have the plans of a secret weapon drawn on his back. The plot is set in motion by a flying fish-and-chip stall, no less, and barminess prevails throughout. Ranks with *The Goose Steps Out* as one of Britain's funniest wartime films. GM

Gas Food Lodging

(1991, US, 101 min)
d Allison Anders. *p* Bill Ewart, Dan Hassid, Seth Willenson. *sc* Allison Anders. *ph* Dean Lent. *ed* Tracy S Granger. *pd* Jane Ann Stewart. *m* J Mascis. *cast* Brooke Adams, Ione Skye, Fairuza Balk, James Brolin, Robert Knepper, David Landsbury, Jacob Vargas, Donovan Leitch.

● Nora (Adams) waits tables and scrapes by, single-handedly raising two teenage daughters in a clapped-out trailer. Romance seems as scarce as rain in her New Mexico backwater: Nora and elder daughter Trudi (Skye) know what it means to be left high and dry, and even young Shade (Balk) suffers rejection at the hands of dreamy Darius (Leitch). But hopes of love die hard, and there's escapism to be found at the local Spanish fleapit. Shade decides to go father-hunting, but an attempt at match-making and the hunt for her long-absent dad (Brolin) yield decidedly mixed results. Far from gloomy fare, this debut from an American independent offers humour, wry observation and sympathetic characterisation. Without patronising her characters, writer-director Anders captures the frustrations of both generations, and the concluding optimistic note isn't forced. Delightfully oddball and strangely sane. CM

Gaslight

(1940, GB, 88 min, b/w)
d Thorold Dickinson. *p* John Corfield. *sc* AR Rawlinson, Bridget Boland. *ph* Bernard Knowles. *ed* Sidney Cole. *ad* Duncan Sutherland. *m* Richard Addinsell. *cast* Anton Walbrook, Diana Wynyard, Frank Pettingell, Robert Newton, Jimmy Hanley, Cathleen Cordell.

● The first film version of Patrick Hamilton's stage play about a Victorian criminal who tries to drive his wife mad in order to prevent her from discovering his guilty secret while he searches their house for a stash of precious rubies. Nothing like as lavish as the later MGM version with Charles Boyer and Ingrid Bergman, but in its own small-scale way a superior film by far. Lurking menace hangs in the air like a fog, the atmosphere is electric, and Wynyard suffers exquisitely as she struggles to keep dementia at bay. It's hardly surprising that MGM tried to destroy the negative of this version when they made their own five years later. NF

Gaslight (aka The Murder in Thornton Square)

(1944, US, 114 min, b/w)
d George Cukor. *p* Arthur Hornblow Jr. *sc* John Van Druten, Walter Reisch, John L Balderston. *ph* Joseph Ruttenberg. *ed* Ralph E Winters. *ad* Cedric Gibbons, William Ferrari. *m* Bronislau Kaper. *cast* Ingrid Bergman, Charles Boyer, Joseph Cotten, Angela Lansbury, Dame May Whitty, Terry Moore, Barbara Everest.

● Lusher and less resonant than the 1939 British version of Patrick Hamilton's moody period melodrama, which had a much surer sense of background (in particular the English class thing, trailing an inbred distrust of the smarmy foreigner), and mined a chilling vein of psychosis in Walbrook's performance. Directed with consummate skill, all the same, as Cukor plants an indefinable sense of unease during the sunnily romantic Italian honeymoon (a lengthy addition in this version), then gradually orchestrates it into a genuinely harrowing crescendo of terror in the claustrophobically cluttered house in fogbound London where the husband is methodically driving his wife insane. One of Bergman's best performances, with Boyer not too far behind, and Lansbury unforgettable as the sulkily insolent parlourmaid whom the husband cunningly uses to add insult to his wife's injury. TM

Gas-s-s-s, or it became necessary to destroy the world in order to save it

(1970, US, 79 min)
d/p Roger Corman. *sc* George Armitage. *ph* Ron Dexter. *ed* George Van Noy. *ad* David Nichols. *m* Country Joe and the Fish. *cast* Robert Corff, Elaine Giftos, Pat Patterson, George Armitage, Alex Wilson, Alan Braunstein, Ben Vereen, Bud Cort.

● This started life as a serious science fiction movie, but relatively late in the day Corman decided to transform it into a wacky comedy. He dispenses with his usual tight construction, and the almost non-existent plot chronicles the activities of America's youth after the adult population has been wiped out, with many of the themes and characters from his earlier movies turning up in a caricatured form. It may sound promising, but thanks to Country Joe's tedious score and an endless succession of feeble jokes, it is likely to be of more interest to Cormanologists than anyone else. DP

Gate, The

(1986, Can, 86 min)
d Tibor Takacs. *p* John Kemeny. *sc* Michael Nankin. *ph* Támas Vamos. *ed* Rit Wallis. *pd* William Beeton. *m* Michael Hoenig, J Peter Robinson. *cast* Stephen Dorff, Christa Denton, Louis Tripp, Kelly Rowan, Jennifer Irwin, Deborah Grover.

● Glenn (Dorff), a Canadian in his early teens, has a thing about rockets, a 16-year-old sister who cares, an HM-loving demonologist buddy, and parents who make untimely decisions to go away for the weekend. As such, this spunky, diminutive

Everyman is clearly well equipped to deal with the Forces of Darkness when, for no apparent reason, they come steaming out of a hole in his back garden. After an eventful but soporific first half, the plot, as full of holes as the Albert Hall, takes off into surreal nonsense that is almost delightful: inappropriately cute and beautifully animated SFX monsters thrown up from Hell; a hand stigmatised with a functionless eye; and a dead workman who never existed in the first place arriving zombie-like to wreak revenge for nothing in particular. The lunacy on view is strangely dreamlike, and no bad thing. It's only a pity the film actually tries to make sense. More abandon all round, and the result could have been a Z-grade cult classic. GA

Gate of Flesh (Nikutai No Mon)

(1965, Jap, 90 min)
d Seijun Suzuki. *sc* Goro Tanada. *ph* Shigeyoshi Mine. *cast* Jo Shishido, Satako Kasai, Yumiko Nogowa, Kayo Matsuo, Tomiko Ishi.

●A deliciously torrid melo in which the solidarity of a group of prostitutes – based on mutual anarchy, and the threat of torture and humiliation for anyone who offers a freebie – disintegrates when they shelter a criminal whom they all fall for. Fascinating for its lurid colour-coding, theatrical lighting, quirky editing, and the overall artifice of design, which revels in both the dog-eat-dog decrepitude of post-war Tokyo and the bitter, sweaty mood of sado-masochistic cruelty. GA

Gate of Lilacs

see Porte des Lilas

Gates of Heaven

(1978, US)
d/p/sc Errol Morris. *ph* Neg Burgess. *ed* Charles Laurence Silver. *cast* Floyd McClure, Joe Allen, Martin Hall, Mike Koewler.

●Is the canine after-life a concept sufficiently dear to the heart of California to form an exploitable basis for corporate capitalist credibility? Well, it may seem a dumb question, but at least two family concerns profiled in this winningly absurdist documentary think the answer is yes. For it's the unpredictable market economy of pet cemeteries over which Morris' subjects wax both lyrical and hymnal, as they affirm in endearingly ludicrous detail their earnest commitment to dead doggies and the dollar, and insistently hard-sell alternative routes through the eponymous portals. Morris respects the manic integrity of his interviewees, and handles his Great American Metaphors with the lightest of touches; incidentally winning a bet that saw Werner Herzog eat his shoe (having wagered that the film would never get made), he ultimately achieves a real treat of everyday surrealism. PT

Gates of Hell

see Paura nella Città dei Morti Viventi

Gates of Paris

see Porte des Lilas

Gates of the Night

see Portes de la Nuit, Les

Gathering of Eagles, A

(1962, US, 115 min)
d Delbert Mann. *p* Sy Bartlett. *sc* Robert Pirosh. *ph* Russell Harlan. *ed* Russell Schoengarth. *ad* Alexander Golitzen, Henry Bumstead. *m* Jerry Goldsmith. *cast* Rock Hudson, Mary Peach, Rod Taylor, Barry Sullivan, Kevin McCarthy, Henry Silva,Leora Dana.

●This loose remake, transposed to a peacetime setting, of producer Sy Bartlett's script for the much superior *Twelve O'Clock High* sees Rock Hudson struggling vainly to imitate the former version's Gregory Peck, as a colonel determined to improve the alertness and efficiency of a Strategic Air Command base. The conflict that arises from his ruthlessness – and the rumours surrounding his relationship with another officer's wife – are a pale shadow of the desperate strain evoked by Peck's wartime predicament. The flying footage, however, with its impressive if disturbingly hawkish shots of B-52 bombers, gives the film a sense of life; hardly surprising, since Bartlett and his director were both former fliers themselves. GA

Gathering of Old Men, A

(1987, US/GB/WGer, 91 min)
d Volker Schlöndorff. *p* Gower Frost. *sc* Charles Fuller. *ph* Edward Lachman. *ed* Nancy Baker. *pd* Thomas A Walsh. *m* Ron Carter. *cast* Louis Gossett Jr, Richard Widmark, Holly Hunter, Joe Seneca, Julius Harris, Will Patton, Woody Strode, Tiger Haynes.

●A murderous white Louisiana farmer chases a black man and is killed for his trouble by an anonymous shotgun blast. Plantation owner Hunter rounds up all her retired hands (Gossett, Seneca, Harris, Strode), each bringing with him a discharged shotgun. All confess to the shooting. Sheriff Widmark parks his car and awaits developments. A hot day with nothing to do but go fishing, and a stand-off in front of a shack where a white man of no great consequence lies spreadeagled on his back, slowly unfolds. Taken from a novel by Ernest J Gaines, an affecting moralist, this TV film has a dry tone and an appropriate lack of display, but the old stars, for all their impassivity, rather overwhelm the proceedings. JPy

Gatica

(1993, Arg, 136 min)
d Leonardo Favio. *cast* Edgardo Nievas, Juan Costa, Cristina Child, Horacio Taicher.

●A wearisome boxing picture about the rise and fall of lightweight boxing champ Gatica set in Argentina during the Peronist period of the 1940s and '50s: very, very derivative of *Raging Bull*. TJ

Gator

(1976, US, 116 min)
d Burt Reynolds. *p* Jules V Levy, Arthur Gardner. *sc* William Norton. *ph* William A Fraker. *ed* Harold F Kress. *ad* Kirk Axtell. *m* Charles Bernstein. *cast* Burt Reynolds, Jack Weston, Lauren Hutton, Jerry Reed, Alice Ghostley, Dub Taylor, Mike Douglas.

●A sequel to the thick-eared *White Lightning*, this offers marginal interest as Burt Reynolds' directorial debut. The plot is formula pulp – Reynolds is blackmailed into exposing a former buddy, now a big-shot Southern crook – but it takes far too long to tell. Much of the two hours rather quaintly concerns Reynolds' star image. After a tongue-in-cheek he-man opening, and between further bouts of action, things dawdle to a standstill while Reynolds projects his sensitivity, lazy singalong good nature, and old-fashioned romanticism; he even expresses doubts about his 'style' and inability to cope with independent women. Too much of this is tedious, rather like off-cuts from his recent movies, but the reasonable photography and good action material help. Country singer Jerry Reed makes a good heavy, and when Reynolds keeps it simple, his direction suggests the makings of a modest craftsman. CPe

'Gator Bait (aka Swamp Bait)

(1974, US, 88 min)
d/p Ferd Sebastian, Beverly Sebastian. *sc* Beverly Sebastian. *ph* Ferd Sebastian. *ed* Ron Johnson. *m* Ferd Sebastian. *cast* Claudia Jennings, Sam Gilman, Doug Dirkson, Don Baldwin, Ben Sebastian, Bill Thurman, Clyde Ventura.

●Despite the tantalising title, this exploiter is a woefully sodden, Z-grade fusion of *Deliverance* and *Gator*. In the Louisiana swamplands, the local sheriff's boy (Ventura) frees swamp Valkyrie (Jennings) for what was an accidental killing. The film is devoted to the lumbering efforts of the demented family of the deceased, together with the lapsed forces of law and order, to track down the 'wildcat'. The directors manage to blow every opportunity of the pulp genre. The location is totally wasted (were alligators out of season?), the script and performances devoid of any real energy or brash humour. Sadly, even Claudia Jennings, heroine of the excellent *Truck Stop Women*, doesn't deliver as she catches snakes with her bare hands and leads her male pursuers a merry dance. IB

Gattaca

(1997, US, 106 min)
d Andrew Niccol. *p* Danny DeVito, Michael Shamberg, Stacey Sher. *sc* Andrew Niccol. *ph* Slawomir Idziak. *ed* Lisa Churgin. *pd* Jan Roelfs. *m* Michael Nyman. *cast* Ethan Hawke, Uma Thurman, Alan Arkin, Jude Law, Loren Dean, Gore Vidal, Ernest Borgnine, Blair Underwood, Tony Shalhoub, Elias Koteas.

●In the future, geneticists will design test-tube babies to be disease-free. Physical perfection will become the norm, and those flawed specimens born the old-fashioned way will form the new underclass – the 'in-valids'. Vincent Freeman (Hawke), an in-valid with a heart defect, is only taken seriously in the powerful Gattaca space programme when he assumes the identity of Jerome (Law), a 'valid' who supplies blood, tissue and urine samples in return for shelter (he himself having been crippled in a car accident). The subterfuge is successful – until a murder draws unwelcome scrutiny from the authorities. Self-consciously at a remove from the trashy B-movie sensibilities which have dominated science-fantasy movies in recent times, this harks back to the vacuum-packed, classically alienated dystopia of *Brave New World* and *Fahrenheit 451*. Chilly, elegant, and a little bloodless. TCh

Gattopardo, Il

see Leopard, The

Gauntlet, The

(1977, US, 109 min)
d Clint Eastwood. *p* Robert Daly. *sc* Michael Butler, Denis Shryack. *ph* Rexford Metz. *ed* Ferris Webster, Joel Cox. *ad* Allen Smith. *m* Jerry Fielding. *cast* Clint Eastwood, Sondra Locke, Pat Hingle, William Prince, Bill McKinney, Michael Cavanaugh, Carole Cook, Mara Corday.

●'Big .45 calibre fruit! Macho mentality!' – Eastwood under siege as Sondra Locke leads the assault on his monolithic image. As much comedy as action picture, *The Gauntlet* mines the vein of humour discovered in *The Outlaw Josey Wales*: again most of the laughs are at Eastwood's expense. In his most mellow cop role yet, he plays a long-suffering, rather dumb officer who extradites a smart, fast-talking hooker, but ends up hiking her cross country, pursued by mob and cops alike (more identical than alike). The well paced script is an effective mixture of worldliness and naïveté: despite the couple's graphic sparring scenes, in which Eastwood more than meets his match, their relationship remains curiously innocent; a kind of fugitive romanticism pervades. A major source of amusement is watching Eastwood the director leaving Eastwood the actor barely in control throughout. Eastwood's *Annie Hall*? CPe

Gaunt Stranger, The (aka The Phantom Strikes)

(1938, GB, 73 min, b/w)
d Walter Forde. *p* Michael Balcon. *sc* Sidney Gilliat. *ph* Ronald Neame. *ed* Charles Saunders. *ad* OF Werndorff. *m* Ernest Irving. *cast* Wilfrid Lawson, John Longden, Alexander Knox, Sonnie Hale, Louise Henry, Patrick Barr, Patricia Roc.

●Michael Balcon's experiment in independent production, an adaptation of Edgar Wallace's *The Ringer*, still looks good despite its low budget. An intelligent script by Sidney Gilliat effectively tightens up the typical Wallace tale of a master of disguise who outwits the police to carry out his errand of righteous vengeance. From nervy opening to unexpectedly upbeat ending, Forde copes in bold, workmanlike fashion with the convoluted plot, and Ronald Neame's moody photography is adequate compensation for the limited studio setting. Splendidly slimy Lawson gives a virtuoso performance as the degenerate miscreant who doggedly refuses to face his doom, Patricia Roc – the darling of the '40s – makes her debut as a snootily wrong-headed secretary, and Hale proves surprisingly proficient at providing comic relief. All in all, a classic British thriller. RMy

Gawain and the Green Knight

(1973, GB, 93 min)
d Stephen Weeks. *p* Philip M Breen. *sc* Philip M Breen, Stephen Weeks. *ph* Ian Wilson. *ed* John Shirley. *ad* Tony Woollard. *m* Ron Goodwin. *cast* Murray Head, Ciaran Madden, Nigel Green, Anthony Sharp, Robert Hardy, David Leland, Murray Melvin, Ronald Lacey.

●Ye olde Englishe poem, filtered through Mallory, Weeks, and United Artists (who tampered with the director's original cut). It's an only just watchable tale of the Arthurian gallant having a go at the grass-coloured magical being, which never makes it as a serious attempt to film the original text, nor as an out-and-out fantasy. Weeks had another try ten years later, remaking it as *Sword of the Valiant*, with very little more success.

Gawin

(1991, Fr, 91 min)
d Arnaud Selignac. *p* Gérard Louvin. *sc* Arnaud Selignac, Alexandre Jardin. *ph* Jean-Claude Larrieu. *ed* Emmanuelle Castro. *pd* Thomas Chevalier. *m* Jérôme Soligny. *cast* Jean-Hugues Anglade, Wojtek Pszoniak, Catherine Samie, Bruno.

● Making ET look like a right hard bastard, Gawin is the winsome space-hopping chum of little Felix, sci-fi crazy and suffering from leukaemia. When Felix's doctor starts to mutter balefully that medicine can do no more, stricken widowed Papa (Anglade) decides it's time for extra-terrestrial forces to take a hand... They seem to have taken a hand in the script as well, since *Gawin* proceeds with a blithe disregard for plausibility. Clearly conceived as a three Kleenex-box movie, it's guaranteed to leave you dry-eyed, not to say slack-jawed with disbelief. Give or take a couple of flash Beineixian gliding shots in the first minute, it's unmitigated astro-piffle. JRo

Gay Divorcee, The

(1934, US, 107 min, b/w)
d Mark Sandrich. *p* Pandro S Berman. *sc* George Marion Jr, Dorothy Yost, Edward Kaufman. *ph* David Abel. *ed* William Hamilton. *ad* Van Nest Polglase, Carroll Clark. *songs* Cole Porter, Con Conrad, Mack Gordon, Harry Revel, Herb Magidson. *cast* Fred Astaire, Ginger Rogers, Alice Brady, Edward Everett Horton, Eric Blore, Erik Rhodes, Betty Grable.

● Having insured Fred's legs for the equivalent of £200,000, RKO producer Pandro S Berman launched the Astaire-Rogers musicals with this extensive revamp of Cole Porter's famous stage show. Only the classic 'Night and Day' was retained in the score, with an archetypal dance duet set to it; new songs included 'Let's K-nock K-neez' for the divine Horton and a starlet called Betty Grable. A big, brash production number, 'The Continental', tries to cap the similar item from *Flying Down to Rio* ('The Carioca'). SG

Gazebo, The

(1959, US, 102 min, b/w)
d George Marshall. *p* Lawrence Weingarten. *sc* George Wells. *ph* Paul C Vogel. *ed* Adrienne Fazan. *ad* George W Davis, Paul Groesse. *m* Jeff Alexander. *cast* Glenn Ford, Debbie Reynolds, Carl Reiner, John McGiver, Mabel Albertson, Doro Merande, Bert Freed, Martin Landau.

● An amiable black comedy, adapted from Alec Coppel's play, in which Ford plays a TV writer-director, on the verge of the big time (a script commission from Hitchcock), who decides in desperation to murder the blackmailer who is bleeding him white over an amorous indiscretion, afterwards disposing of the body under the gazebo being erected in the garden. It's much too long and leisurely, needlessly incorporating a routine song-and-dance number for Reynolds (as Ford's showbiz wife), and belabouring the plot to show that Ford didn't actually kill anyone. But the central sequence in which Ford (excellent throughout) nervously executes his perfect murder, only to find *everything* going wrong except the murder itself, is hilarious, and perfectly capped by a call from Hitchcock to ask how his script is coming on, whereupon the despairing Ford asks the Maestro how he would solve the dilemma of a killer with a body to bury and no shovel to do it with. Nice supporting cast, too. TM

Gaze of Ulysses, The

see Ulysses' Gaze

Gazon maudit (French Twist)

(1995, Fr, 107 min)
d Josiane Balasko. *p* Claude Berri. *sc* Josiane Balasko. *ph* Gérard de Battista. *ed* Claudine Merlin. *ad* Carlos Conti. *m* Manuel Malou. *cast* Victoria Abril, Josiane Balasko, Alain Chabat, Ticky Holgado, Miguel Bosé, Catherine Hiegel, Catherine Samie, Telsche Boorman, Katrine Boorman.

● Serial adulterer Laurent (Chabat) has all the women he wants, and in Loli (Abril), a beautiful, blissfully ignorant wife. At first the intrusion of butch, cigar-smoking Marijo (Balasko) seems no more than a minor irritation (her van breaks down outside their home, and Loli immediately takes a shine to her), but when she puts the moves on his wife, Laurent cannot contain his shock and revulsion. His reaction sends the women into each other's arms, and soon he's negotiating for equal conjugal rights. An astute, modern spin on the ménage-à-trois farce, this begins like one of Bertrand Blier's tongue-in-cheek intellectual provocations, with Balasko reprising her unlikely seductress role from *Trop belle pour toi!* Unlike Blier, however, Balasko (who also wrote and directed) actually seems to like her characters, even as she accentuates their foibles: Laurent's chauvinist hypocrisy, Loli's naive pride and jealousy, and Marijo's domineering self-confidence. These stereotypes are endowed with rather more dignity than their circumstances allow, and most of the playing is marvellously sympathetic. A very funny and expertly timed farce. TCh

Gebroken Spiegels

see Broken Mirrors

Geburt der Nation, Die

see Birth of a Nation, The

Geheimnisse einer Seele

see Secrets of a Soul

Geisha, A

see Gion Festival Music

Geisha Boy, The

(1958, US, 98 min)
d Frank Tashlin. *p* Jerry Lewis. *sc* Frank Tashlin. *ph* Haskell Boggs. *ed* Alma Macrorie. *ad* Hal Pereira, Tambi Larsen. *m* Walter Scharf. *cast* Jerry Lewis, Marie McDonald, Sessue Hayakawa, Nobu McCarthy, Barton MacLane, Suzanne Pleshette.

● One of Jerry Lewis' first comedies away from former partner Dean Martin, this rather flaccid vehicle reveals the mawkish side that would arise more often in his solo efforts. Lewis plays an unsuccessful magician who takes a job entertaining the troops in the Far East. In Japan, a young orphan (as he's euphemistically labelled) becomes attached to this goofy surrogate father. Fortunately, Tashlin's direction supplies some great visual jokes, principally with a live rabbit that is made to seem more of an animated human character. DT

General, The 100

(1926, US, 7,500 ft, b/w)
d Buster Keaton, Clyde Bruckman. *p* Joseph M Schenck. *sc* Buster Keaton, Clyde Bruckman, Al Boasberg, Charles Smith. *ph* Dev Jennings, Bert Haines. *ed* Sherman Kell. *ad* Fred Gabourie. *cast* Buster Keaton, Marian Mack, Glen Cavender, Jim Farley, Frederick Vroom, Joe Keaton.

● Keaton's best, and arguably the greatest screen comedy ever made. Against a meticulously evoked Civil War background, Buster risks life, limb and love as he pursues his beloved railway engine, hijacked by Northern spies up to no good for the Southern cause. The result is everything one could wish for: witty, dramatic, visually stunning, full of subtle, delightful human insights, and constantly hilarious. GA

General, The

(1998, Ire/GB, 124 min, b/w)
d/p/sc John Boorman. *ph* Seamus Deasy. *ed* Ron Davis. *pd* Derek Wallace. *m* Richard Buckley. *cast* Brendan Gleeson, Adrian Dunbar, Sean McGinley, Maria Doyle Kennedy, Angelina Ball, Jon Voight.

● Dublin, the 1980s and '90s. Martin Cahill (Gleeson) is forever a few steps ahead of the police, cocking a snook at all the authority figures he's detested since a childhood in the slums, defined by poverty, petty crime and priestly abuse. Determined to get his man, Inspector Ned Kenny (Voight) nevertheless views him with grudging respect, but it's only when he arranges full time surveillance that Cahill's loyal gang begin to buckle under pressure; even then, the self-styled Godfather can probably count on the support of his wife (Kennedy), her sister (Ball), his right-hand man Noel (Dunbar), and an amused, hero-hungry public, so that his pranks and perversions of justice go unpunished. But how long can he get away with refusing to hand over a portion of his spoils to the IRA? Boorman's energetic account of Cahill's real-life escapades (from the book by Paul Williams) is notable for its deft characterisations and authenticity: while Cahill's sentiments and actions are appreciated as the exploits of a canny born rebel, we're never allowed to forget that he's also volatile, violent and, whatever his feelings for his family, ultimately self-obsessed. All the performances are impressive, but Gleeson and Voight are especially memorable, lending an almost tragic air of inexorability to Cahill and Kenny's cat-and-mouse games. GA

General Amin (Général Idi Amin Dada: Autoportrait)

(1974, Fr, 90 min)
d Barbet Schroeder. *p* Jean-François Chauvel. *sc* Barbet Schroeder. *ph* Nestor Almendros. *ed* Denise de Casabianca. *m* Idi Amin Dada. *with* Idi Amin Dada.

● The only moment of real insight in a rambling and overlong documentary comes at its climax: 'After a century of colonialism' the commentary asks, 'isn't it in fact a deformed image of ourselves that Amin reflects?' It's a highly pertinent question, and one that a film-maker like Godard could have used to shattering effect. Here, however, it arrives as a postscript to a patchy assemblage of footage. The facts presented are disturbing, but Amin himself emerges as a dumber, more naïve, and more boring version of countless Western politicians. Occasionally, and surprisingly, the man seems prepared to laugh at himself: one of the few unexpected features in an otherwise profoundly depressing and exploitative film. DP

General Line, The (Staroye i Novoye/aka Old and New)

(1929, USSR, 8,102 ft, b/w)
d Sergei Eisenstein. *sc* Sergei Eisenstein, Grigori V Aleksandrov. *ph* Eduard Tissé. *ed* Sergei Eisenstein. *ad* Vladimir Kovrigin, Vasili Rakhals. *cast* Marfa Lapkina, Vasya Buzenkov, Kostya Vasiliev, I Yudin, E Sukhareva, G Matvei.

● *The General Line* was the project Eisenstein interrupted to make *October*, the epic commissioned to mark the tenth anniversary of the USSR. Neither of these two celebrations of his theory of 'associative montage' (which remain among his most powerful and innovative movies) met with official approval or popular success; Eisenstein was condemned as a 'formalist'; and began the world travels that eventually led him to Mexico. *The General Line* is a comprehensive account of Soviet agricultural policies, showing the struggle for collectivisation of the farms, distinguished (like *October*) by Eduard Tissé's phenomenal photography, by Eisenstein's muscular homo-erotic poetry, and by extraordinary sado-masochistic undercurrents. Fans of Kenneth Anger's *Eaux d'Artifice* should not miss the daringly erethistic cream-separator sequence in *The General Line* on which it is based. TR

General Sahib

see Burra Sahib

General's Daughter, The

(1999, US/Ger, 116 min)
d Simon West. *p* Mace Neufeld. *sc* Christopher Bertolini, William Goldman. *ph* Peter Menzies Jr. *ed* Glen Scantlebury. *pd* Dennis Washington. *m* Carter Burwell. *cast* John Travolta, Madeleine Stowe, James Cromwell, Timothy Hutton, Clarence Williams III, James Woods, Leslie Stefanson.

● The general's daughter, a US Army instructor in psychological warfare, is found naked, strangled and staked to the ground at a Florida military base. Only hours before, she'd stopped by the road to help undercover army cop Travolta with a flat tyre. He'd been staking out an illicit arms sale operation, but his assignment soon switches to the murder investigation, on which he's teamed with fellow MP Stowe, specialist in sexually motivated cases, and Travolta's old flame. Pressure builds to clear it all up 'the army way', so the victim's war hero father (Cromwell) can proceed with his political ambitions – but the discovery that his daughter had been indulging in S&M with a string of male officers does little to shorten the list of suspects. This is intended, presumably, as a hardhitting exposé of sexual misconduct in the military; there's little room for sensitivity, however, in the context of a button pushing Hollywood thriller. The scenes of rape, and the salacious bondage asides, are as much part of the spectacle as the massed helicopters that the budget so indulges. Only when Travolta gets together with Woods (slick psy-ops boss with a secret to hide) does the movie's grasp on its characters kick in. TJ

Generation, A (Pokolenie)

(1954, Pol, 91 min, b/w)
d Andrzej Wajda. *sc* Bohdan Czeszko. *ph* Jerzy Lipman. *ed* Czeslaw Raniszewski. *pd* Roman Mann. *m* Andrzej Markowski. *cast* Tadeusz Lomnicki, Urszula Modrzynska, Tadeusz Janczar, Roman Polanski, Zbigniew Cybulski.

●First part of Wajda's trilogy, completed by *Kanal* and *Ashes and Diamonds*. Those were exciting times for Polish cinema: 'In Poland art fulfils a special function…it carries a certain burden of tradition through the fact that for a hundred years the state did not exist, or it existed only in literature, in art, to which everyone could refer'. Cinema, sometimes laboriously, had to carry the Polish identity. In the '50s, Wajda processed great public events (later too, perforce through analogy), and the trilogy covers the Resistance in Warsaw. *A Generation*, set in occupied Warsaw in 1942 and revolving around the setting up of a youth resistance group, was his first feature, and hews to the Socialist Realist line. Courage, honour and self-sacrifice inform the actions of his hero, who discovers a sense of purpose in unity, the collective and the Party. Hope opens the trilogy, disillusionment closes it, and the final part centres on an individual crisis and a great star performance fit to rank beside James Dean from Zbigniew Cybulski, here featured in a supporting part. One from the heart. BC

Genesis (Génésis)

(1986, Fr/Ind/Bel/Switz, 109 min)
d/sc Mrinal Sen. *ph* Carlo Varini. *ed* Elisabeth Waelchli, Nadine Muse. *ad* Nitish Roy. *m* Ravi Shankar. *cast* Shabana Azmi, Naseeruddin Shah, Om Puri, MK Raina.

●In the past, Mrinal Sen's leftist films have eschewed mystical visions of an India outside history; here he focuses on the collapse of just such an escapist dream. Two men, the Farmer and the Weaver (Shah and Puri) have abandoned the poverty of contemporary India to start life anew in the sprawling ruins of a long lost village. Their only tie with the outside world is the Merchant (Raina), who provides the raw materials and markets for their product; their only connection with the 20th century is the roar of the odd plane jetting across the desert. Alone in their world, the pair build a new society, and their land begins to bloom…until harmony is shattered with the arrival of the Woman (Azmi), a refugee from recent floods. Though Sen's sexual politics may strike western eyes as dubious, the simplistic power of the film is unquestionable. The fifth character is the landscape which comes to bloom, beautifully complemented by a score from Ravi Shankar. GA

Genevieve

(1953, GB, 86 min)
d/p Henry Cornelius. *sc* William Rose. *ph* Christopher Challis. *ed* Clive Donner. *ad* Michael Stringer. *m* Larry Adler. *cast* Dinah Sheridan, John Gregson, Kay Kendall, Kenneth More, Geoffrey Keen, Joyce Grenfell.

●Everyone seems to remember this gentle comedy – about two couples entering the London to Brighton veteran car race, and indulging in friendly rivalry – with great affection. But with the exception of the delectable Kay Kendall, gorgeously belting out jazz on the trumpet, it just isn't very funny any more; and Larry Adler's whining harmonica score only makes things worse. GA

Genghis Cohn

(1993, GB, 80 min)
d Elijah Moshinsky. *p* Ruth Caleb. *sc* Stanley Price. *ph* John Daly. *ed* Ken Pearce. *pd* Tony Burrough. *m* Carl Davis. *cast* Anthony Sher, Robert Lindsay, Diana Rigg, John Wells.

●Twelve years on, Jewish stand-up comic Cohn (Sher) returns to haunt the SS officer (Lindsay) – now a successful Bavarian police commissioner – who commanded the firing squad which executed him. At the same time, the town is beset by a series of bizarre murders of lovers caught in flagrante, and rumour, intrigue and ambition tip the community into self-destructive chaos. Not a bad idea (from a novel by Romain Gary), and not exactly a bad film – but the black comedy would be far blacker and funnier if the direction and acting weren't so awfully, awfully theatrical. GA

Genou de Claire, Le

see Claire's Knee

Gens de la rizière, Les (Rice People)

(1994, Cambodia/Fr, 130 min)
d Rithy Panh. *p* Jacques Bidou. *sc* Rithy Panh, Eve Deboise. *ph* Jacques Bouquin. *ed* Andrée Davanture, Marie-Christine Rougerie. *pd* Nhean Chamnaul. *m* Marc Marder. *cast* Peng Phan, Mom Soth, Chhim Naline, Va Simorn, Sophy Sodany, Meas Daniel.

●Paris-resident Rithy Panh's first feature (he was previously a documentarist) is an elegaic, unsentimental tribute to his native Cambodia (in 1979, he escaped, aged 16, from a Khmer Rouge camp), and its peasant people, the farmers of the paddy fields. Impressive as it is – the cast of professionals and non-professionals show extraordinary commitment; the landscape, interiors and actors are finely photographed; and the tone is ably sustained – the film is somehow neither as moving nor as satisfying as it promises to be. Focused on a hard-pressed rice-growing family with its Russian-doll-pack of seven daughters, the film, based on a novel by Shannon Ahmad, follows their travails as the seasons turn and the wife takes over the burden of responsibilty after her husband succumbs to a deadly thorn. Rithy Panh elegantly evokes in ethnographic detail the centuries-old agrarian pattern of their lives, the Buddhist icons, the portentous owls. A mysterious dream of the Khmer Rouge entering the village and an end quote from Rilke suggest that narrative is a metaphor for the people's suffering as a whole under Pol Pot. This is not, however, fully developed. Heartbreaking depictions of pestilence, though, and some memorably expressive scenes with children. WH

Gentle Creature, A

see Femme Douce, Une

Gentle Gunman, The

(1952, GB, 86 min, b/w)
d Basil Dearden. *p* Michael Relph. *sc* Roger MacDougall. *ph* Gordon Dines. *ed* Peter Tanner. *ad* Jim Morahan. *m* John Greenwood. *cast* John Mills, Dirk Bogarde, Elizabeth Sellars, Robert Beatty, James Kenney, Joseph Tomelty, Barbara Mullen, Jack MacGowran.

●An Ealing production, this stiff, overplotted tale of IRA internal feuding, shot in spurious *noir* style, nevertheless betrays interesting attitudes. The fact that some emphasis is given to the IRA and its claims is defused by abandoning the political issue in favour of a generalised, wet humanism – Mills and Bogarde, as reconciled Irish brothers (!), slouching into the sunset – and by a typically English focus on Irish character. Beatty, the hard man, can say 'You English came into Ireland as if you stormed into a Cathedral and settled into the nave', and the sense of desecration is nevertheless lost because he is 'Irish', i.e. poetic, daft or sinister. If Ealing once mirrored English attitudes, then clearly film-making has progressed but the attitudes haven't. (Roger MacDowell adapted his own play.) CPea

Gentleman Jim

(1942, US, 104 min, b/w)
d Raoul Walsh. *p* Robert Buckner. *sc* Vincent Lawrence, Horace McCoy. *ph* Sid Hickox. *ed* Jack Killifer. *ad* Ted Smith. *m* Heinz Roemheld. *cast* Errol Flynn, Alexis Smith, Jack Carson, Alan Hale, Ward Bond, John Loder, Minor Watson, Arthur Shields.

●Walsh's reputation is as an action director, but he was equally good as a period illustrator (witness the lazily loving *The Strawberry Blonde*). Here he has the best of both worlds, matching a rich evocation of San Francisco in the 1880s (perhaps a bit heavy on the Irish family brawls) with a vivid account of the pre-Queensberry fight scene, and capping a rumbustious sequence of bouts with a superbly shot version of the gruelling heavyweight championship match between Gentleman Jim Corbett and John L Sullivan in 1892. Lavish, lustrous and none too accurate historically, it's Hollywood at its cavalier best, with a perfectly judged performance from Flynn, brash yet engaging, as the social-climbing Corbett. TM

Gentleman's Agreement

(1947, US, 118 min, b/w)
d Elia Kazan. *p* Darryl F Zanuck. *sc* Moss Hart. *ph* Arthur Miller. *ed* Harmon Jones. *ad* Lyle Wheeler, Mark Lee Kirk. *m* Alfred Newman. *cast* Gregory Peck, Dorothy McGuire, John Garfield, Celeste Holm, Anne Revere, June Havoc, Albert Dekker, Jane Wyatt, Dean Stockwell.

●Academy Award-winning but sentimental and muddled account of a journalist (Peck) who passes himself off as a Jew in order to research a series of articles on anti-Semitism, only to find the masquerade entailing a backlash of grief and pressure for his own family. Archetypal Hollywood social comment (from a novel by Laura Z Hobson) in that it wears its heart on its sleeve rather than offers any analysis of the problem; and the Fox studio's fondness for 'realism' looks remarkably dated in places. Good performances, however, particularly from Garfield and Holm. GA

Gentlemen Don't Eat Poets

see Grotesque, The

Gentlemen Prefer Blondes

(1953, US, 91 min)
d Howard Hawks. *p* Sol C Siegel. *sc* Charles Lederer. *ph* Harry J Wild. *ed* Hugh S Fowler. *ad* Lyle Wheeler, Joseph C Wright. *songs* Jule Styne, Leo Robin, Hoagy Carmichael, Harold Adamson. *cast* Jane Russell, Marilyn Monroe, Charles Coburn, Tommy Noonan, Elliot Reid, George Winslow.

●A classic musical/social satire, featuring tight script, Hawks' usual humanity of style, and a line-up of sardonic song'n'dance numbers ('Diamonds Are a Girl's Best Friend', etc). A cynical plotline (golddigging cabaret artistes on transatlantic liner crossing) is wonderfully belied by generous sentiment, and the Monroe/Russell sexual stereotypes are used ironically to generate a whole range of erotic gambits: innocence, brashness, temptation, seduction. Interesting, too, that the male parts remain mere foils to the sympathetic sparring relationship of the female leads. Smashing. CA

Gentle Sex, The

(1943, GB, 93 min, b/w)
d Leslie Howard. *p* Leslie Howard, Derrick de Marney. *sc* Moie Charles. *ph* Robert Krasker. *ed* Charles Saunders. *ad* Paul Sheriff. *m* John Greenwood. *cast* Rosamund John, Joan Greenwood, Lilli Palmer, Joan Gates, Jean Gillie, Joyce Howard, Barbara Waring, Leslie Howard.

●Howard's silly framework for this account of the initiation of seven women into the army is annoying and patronising; but beneath the sugary surface there is a frank acknowledgment of the changes wrought by the war. Under the inspired leadership of a wily, sweet-sucking Glaswegian (John), the group grasp their opportunities to become gunners and lorry-drivers with both hands, and unlike the women in the more widely lauded *Millions Like Us*, without the approval and support of men. The documentary realism necessary to fulfil the film's propagandist function is extended by Howard into a welcoming, if rather bemused celebration of the new equality between the sexes. A fascinating barometer of the changing moral climate of the '40s. RMy

Genuine

(1920, Ger, b/w, 33 min)
d Robert Wiene. *sc* Carl Mayer. *ph* Willy Hameister. *ad* César Klein. *cast* Fern Andra, Harald Paulsen, Ernst Gronau, John Gottoht, Hans von Twardowsky.

●Same director, same writer, same cameraman, but… Rushed out six months after *The Cabinet of Dr Caligari*, *Genuine* merely goes to prove how dependent the earlier film was on its cast and designers: painted cinema animated by the extraordinary acting skills of Veidt and Krauss. Here, with rotten actors mugging away in César Klein sets which look like recycled leftovers from a Christmas pantomime, *Caligari*-ism is reduced to grisly travesty. The Pygmalion plot concerns a painter whose creation comes alive, turns nasty after being sold in a slave market, and gloatingly drives her admirers to murder and suicide. Playing this supervamp in unfortunate costumes which at one point lend her a passing resemblance to the Tinman of Oz, Fern Andra leers and squirms like a demented Theda Bara. TM

Gen-X Cops (Tejing Xin Renlei)

(1999, HK, 113 min)
d Benny Chan. *p* Benny Chan, John Chong, Solon So. *sc* Benny Chan, Peter Tsi, Koan Hui, Lee Yee-Wah. *ph* Arthur Wong. *ed* Cheung Ka-Lai. *pd* Bruce Yu. *m* Nathan Wang. *cast* Nicholas Tse, Stephen Fung, Sam Lee, Grace Ip, Daniel Wu, Eric Tsang, Toru Nakamura, Francis Ng, Jackie Chan.

● Three delinquent police cadets are recruited to pose as underworld types to investigate the theft of rocket fuel which can be used as a powerful explosive – a theft seemingly connected with a spate of gangland killings. They uncover a feud between Japanese criminals and a (fulfilled) plot to blow up the HK Convention Centre. This relatively big budget action-comedy offers little more than a series of set pieces (gunfights, sky dives, car chases, etc), individually well enough staged but cumulatively boring. The biggest problem is the shapeless, witless script; minor pleasures include vivid supporting turns from Tsang, Ng and newcomer Wu. A US major has picked up international rights, presumably because of Jackie Chan's cameo in the final reel. TR

Gen-Y Cops (Tejing Xin Renlei 2)

(2000, HK, 113 min)
d Benny Chan. *p* Thomas Chung, John Chong, Solon So. *sc* Felix Chong, Chan Kiu-Ying. *ph* Anthony Pun. *ed* Cheung Ka-Fai. *pd* Bruce Yu. *m* Peter Kam. *cast* Edison Chen, Stephen Fung, Sam Lee, Maggie Q, Richard Sun, Rachel Ngan, Anthony Wong, Eric Kot.

● Interesting to see who bailed out from this mega-dull sequel, produced to order for the US video market – which will no doubt see a heavily recut version. The indestructible 'peace-keeping' robot RS1 is unveiled at an arms fair in the HK Convention Centre (evidently rebuilt since *Gen-X Cops*), but Kurt, the Chinese-American techno-geek who designed it and found himself sidelined, steals it for sale to a shadowy Arab buyer. Our anti-heroes, now fronted by fashion-plate Edison Chen, are still giving 'high jinks' a bad name as they mug, pratfall and wisecrack their way through endless CGI explosions and double-crosses to save the world. There's really nothing to enjoy except an athletic display of demented villainy by Richard Sun (son of matinée idol Qin Han) and cameos by Wong and Kot as defeated mainland Chinese scientists who'd rather sleep than deploy their low-tech robot. TR

Geordie (aka Wee Geordie)

(1955, GB, 99 min)
d Frank Launder. *p/sc* Frank Launder, Sidney Gilliat. *ph* Wilkie Cooper. *ed* Thelma Connell. *ad* Norman Arnold. *m* William Alwyn. *cast* Bill Travers, Alastair Sim, Norah Gorsen, Raymond Huntley, Miles Malleson, Duncan Macrae, Stanley Baxter.

● Worried he's going to lose out on the girl he's after, confirmed weakling Travers builds himself up and enters the Melbourne Olympics as a hammer thrower. An affectionate triumph-of-the-underdog fable from Launder and Gilliat, chock full of Scots clichés, with Sim stealing every scene as the local laird and lots of familiar faces right down the cast list. From a novel by David Walker. TJ

George and Mildred

(1980, GB, 93 min)
d Peter Frazer Jones. *p* Roy Skeggs. *sc* Dick Sharples. *ph* Frank Watts. *ed* Peter Weatherley. *ad* Carolyn Scott. *m* Les Reed. *cast* Yootha Joyce, Brian Murphy, Stratford Johns, Norman Eshley, Sheila Fearn, Kenneth Cope.

● Spun off from a spin-off of a TV sitcom that began in the '60s, this threadbare farce provides lamentable evidence of Wardour Street's profitless dependency on the British TV ratings chart. Murphy's runtish Roper, traditionally played as one of the gambling, grumbling unemployed, has been given a job (setting a Thatcherite example) as a traffic warden. Otherwise it's the same ageist, sexist class structure you know and loathe. Feeble humour even in its half-hour slot, and desperately unfunny at three times the length. MA

George Balanchine's The Nutcracker

see Nutcracker, The

Georg Elser

see Seven Minutes

George of the Jungle

(1997, US, 92 min)
d Sam Weisman. *p* David Hoberman, Jordan Kerner, Jon Avnet. *sc* Dana Olsen, Audrey Wells. *ph* Thomas Ackerman. *ed* Stuart H Pappé, Roger Bondelli. *pd* Stephen Marsh. *m* Marc Shaiman. *cast* Brendan Fraser, Leslie Mann, Thomas Haden Church, Richard Roundtree, Greg Crutwell, Abraham Benrubi, (voice) John Cleese.

● Based on the characters of Jay Ward's TV cartoon series, this live action feature pitches itself on the level of exotic, anything-goes pantomime, with Tarzan-like George, a talking ape, a pelican, a pet elephant, a pith-helmeted eco-villain (Church), and a willowy but plucky love interest (Mann). Fraser is a natural for the hero, brought up in Bukuvu National Park, Africa, by Ape, his snobbish bookworm butler – incompetently, though, since George can't swing on a vine without crashing his tackle. His mix of bare-faced cheek, infantilism and physical exuberance sets the tone, while the plot's absurdities are acknowledged with disarming candidness. The story is incidental – the villain wants to abduct the talking ape for financial gain – and thankfully the animatronics and computer effects aren't allowed to overwhelm the proceedings. WH

Georgette Meunier

(1989, WGer, 82 min)
d Tania Stöcklin, Cyrille Rey-Coquais. *p* Hans-Willy-Müller. *sc* Tania Stöclin, Cyrille Rey-Coquais. *ph* Ciro Cappellari, Anka Schmid. *ed* Tania Stocklin, Cyrille Rey-Coquais. *m* Mikolaus Utermohlein. *cast* Tiziana Jelmini, Diana Stöcklin, Dina Leipzig, Thomas Schunke, Manfred Hulverschiedt.

● This independent feature, indulgently described as 'black comedy', tells of Georgette's frustrated love affair with brother Emile and her career as a 'black widow' – seducing and poisoning the male citizens of a small German town circa 1900. The necessarily minimalist treatment and a paternal voice-over which prompts the action suggest an adult fairy tale of sorts, though the combination of Inexorable Destiny and inexplicable behaviour tends to obscure any quasi-feminist intent, the incest theme actually debasing the radical thrust of the *femme fatale*. Likewise, a potentially absorbing fantasy element (she kills with kisses) is thrown away. The writer-directors optimistically equate pretension with wit, and only Jelmini's alarmingly potent Georgette carries much conviction. A mainstream production might have demanded tighter logic, an exploitation movie could have pushed the subversive stuff, but this drab effort comes from no man's land. TCh

George Washington

(2000, US, 89 min)
d David Gordon Green. *p* David Gordon Green, Sacha Mueller, Lisa Muskat. *sc* David Gordon Green. *ph* Tim Orr. *ed* Steven Gonzales, Zene Baker. *pd* Richard Wright. *m* Michael Linnen, David Wingo. *cast* Candace Evanoiski, Donald Holden, Damien Jewan Lee, Curtis Cotton III.

● A little like *Gummo* re-imagined by Terrence Malick, Green's extraordinary debut feature is a film without a centre. Narrated by a young girl, it shows vignettes from life in a small Southern dirt town around 4 July, focusing mainly on the kids (most of whom are black) and a notably laidback railroad track repair crew. Nothing of consequence happens until one boy dies in an accident and the others decide to hide his body rather than report the death; after that, the group fragments and each kid starts to edge towards maturity. Lyrically shot in 'Scope by Tim Orr, the film absorbs elements of documentary and improvisation to produce a remarkably organic whole. TR

Georgia's Friends

see Four Friends

Georgy Girl

(1966, GB, 99 min, b/w)
d Silvio Narizzano. *p* Otto Plaschkes, Robert A Goldston. *sc* Margaret Forster, Peter Nichols. *ph* Ken Higgins. *ed* John Bloom. *ad* Tony Woollard. *m* Alexander Faris. *cast* Lynn Redgrave, Alan Bates, James Mason, Charlotte Rampling, Bill Owen, Clare Kelly, Rachel Kempson.

● Though tame by modern standards, this candid comedy of sexual manners in 'Swinging London' was considered bold for its day. Redgrave is a frumpy, unattractive dance teacher who is offered an escape from her loneliness by her ageing, married but amorous employer (Mason). Inevitably dated, yet often funny and sometimes surprisingly bleak. A nice cameo by Rampling, too, as Georgy's bitchy, sniping flatmate. NF

German Chainsaw Massacre, The (Das deutsche Kettensagenmassaker)

(1990, Ger, 63 min)
d Christoph Schlingensief. *p* Christian Fürst. *sc/ph* Christoph Schlingensief. *ed* Ariane Traub. *pd* Uli Hanisch. *m* Jacques Arr. *cast* Udo Kier, Karina Fallenstein, Susanne Bredehöft, Artur Albrecht, Volker Spengler, Alfred Edel.

● A bloody and demented blend of Brechtian political satire and *Texas Chainsaw Massacre*-style horror, this shrieking gore-fest is set during the first hours after German reunification. Fleeing from the East, hapless victims fall prey to a crazed family of human butchers, who introduce them to the pleasures of the Free Market by noisily hacking, bludgeoning and chainsawing them to death. Abrasive, relentless, cruelly funny and enjoyably deranged. NF

German Sisters, The (Die Bleierne Zeit)

(1981, WGer, 107 min)
d Margarethe von Trotta. *p* Eberhard Junkersdorf. *sc* Margarethe von Trotta. *ph* Franz Rath. *ed* Dagmar Hirtz. *ad* Georg von Kieseritzky, Barbara Kloth. *m* Nicolas Economou. *cast* Jutta Lampe, Barbara Sukowa, Rüdiger Vogler, Doris Schade, Verenice Rudolph, Luc Bondy.

● Inspired by the cases of Gudrun Ensslin – the Baader-Meinhof terrorist and Stammheim 'suicide' – and her journalist sister, von Trotta once again takes up questions of the roots and potential paths of women's resistance and revolt, creating a disturbing mosaic of personal and state histories around a sisterly relationship of intriguingly contradictory complexity. As in *The Lost Honour of Katharina Blum*, terrorism itself is an offscreen phenomenon; its ramifications at the personal level, and its unlabelled reactionary equivalents, marking the film's painful subject across at least a generation: from two schoolgirls watching film of the concentration camps to a young son almost burned alive in the '80s because of his now notorious parentage. A bold assertion of the continuity of history from the culture most willing to deny it, and fine, accessible political film-making. PT

Germany, Awake!

see Deutschland, Erwache!

Germany in Autumn (Deutschland im Herbst)

(1978, WGer, 134 min, b/w & col)
d Heinrich Böll, Alf Brustellin, Bernhard Sinkel, Hans Peter Cloos, Katja Rupé, Rainer Werner Fassbinder, Alexander Kluge, Beate Mainka-Jellinghaus, Maximiliane Mainka, Peter Schubert, Edgar Reitz, Volker Schlöndorff. *p* Theo Hinz, Herbert Kerz. *sc* Heinrich Böll, Peter Steinbach. *ph* Michael Ballhaus, Jurgen Jürges, Bodo Kessler, Dietrich

Lohmann, Colin Mounier, Jörg Schmidt-Reitwin. *ed* Heidi Genée, Mulle Gotz-Dickopp, Beate Mainka-Jellinghaus, Tanja Schmidbauer, Christine Warnck. *ad* Henning von Gierke, Winfried Henning. *m* Tchaikovsky, Haydn, Ennio Morricone. *cast* Hannelore Hoger, Katja Rupé, Hans Peter Cloos, Angela Winkler, Helmut Griem.

● A genuinely collaborative movie, aiming to deal with the state of the West German nation in the months between the Schleyer kidnapping and the Baader-Meinhof deaths in Stammheim Prison. The result centres on paranoia rather than on terrorism as such. Fassbinder brings the issues squarely back home, showing himself arguing with his mother and taking out his aggressions on his late boyfriend Armin. At its best, the film argues that it's impossible to have a 'coherent' left wing position on terrorism. TR

Germany, Pale Mother (Deutschland bleiche Mutter)

(1979, WGer, 150 min)
d/p/sc Helma Sanders-Brahms. *ph* Jürgen Jürges, Renato Fortunato. *ed* Elfi Tillack, Ute Periginelli, Nazrath Bey Jusia. *ad* Götz Heymann, Antje Petersen. *m* Jürgen Knieper. *cast* Eva Mattes, Ernst Jacobi, Elisabeth Stepanek, Angelika Thomas, Rainer Friedrichsen, Gisela Stein.

● This highly personal account of Sanders-Brahms' own childhood was made for her daughter. Broken into three parts, it simultaneously traces the history of Germany before, during and after World War II, and her own history. In the first part she's the as yet unborn child who comments ironically on her parents; during the war the angle shifts as we watch the mother gather strength and their relationship develop; after the war the husband/father returns, unwittingly bringing emotional destruction with him. The film is overloaded with visual symbolism and runs too long, but the concept and performances more than compensate for the flaws. HM

Germany, Year Zero (Germania, Anno Zero)

(1947, It/WGer, 74 min, b/w)
d Roberto Rossellini. *p* Alfredo Guarini. *sc* Roberto Rossellini, Carlo Lizzani, Max Kolpet. *ph* Robert Juillard. *ed* Eraldo Da Roma. *ad* Piero Filippone. *m* Renzo Rossellini. *cast* Edmund Moeschke, Werner Pittschau, Barbara Hintz, Franz Krüger, Erich Gühne, Alexandra Manys.

● A long opening tracking shot through Berlin's ruins under the Occupation in 1945 is both documentary and a hallucinatory voyage through a stone age city, the perfect illustration that realist film can also forge fantasy. It sparks against the story of a thirteen-year-old boy who works the black market, sells Hitler souvenirs for chewing-gum, and who will kill his sick father out of naïve mercy and regard for the whisperings of his old Nazi teacher. A horror movie that declines to tease. DMacp

Germinal

(1993, Fr/Bel/It, 158 min)
d/p Claude Berri. *sc* Claude Berri, Arlette Langmann. *ph* Yves Angelo. *ed* Hervé de Luze. *ad* Thanh At Hoang, Christian Marti. *m* Jean-Louis Roques. *cast* Gérard Depardieu, Judith Henry, Renaud, Miou-Miou, Jean Carmet, Jean-Roger Milo, Laurent Terzieff.

● This adaptation of Zola's novel looks superb, as befits the most expensive French film to date. From the opening with the coal mine, belching orange flame, looming out of the dark, to the strike and riot, all 160 million francs is on screen. In the novel the miners' unionisation and strike are matched by the frustrated love story of Etienne (folk singer Renaud, making an impressive debut) and Catherine (Henry), in the film, however, the miners are much to the fore – with the result that the pace slows. The film, from the director of *Manon des Sources*, is at its best exploring man's uneasy relationship with the earth; the coal dust these people extract from the ground is killing them as surely as it's keeping a roof over their heads. Depardieu, as Maheu, is solid if unspectacular; but Miou-Miou, as his long-suffering wife, is astonishing, her performance gaining strength as she loses her beloved family, one by one, to the pit. NKe

Geronimo: An American Legend

(1994, US, 115 min)
d Walter Hill. *p* Neil Canton, Walter Hill. *sc* John Milius, Larry Gross. *ph* Lloyd Ahern. *ed* Freeman Davies, Carmel Davies, Donn Aron. *pd* Joe Alves. *m* Ry Cooder. *cast* Jason Patric, Gene Hackman, Robert Duvall, Wes Studi, Matt Damon, Rodney A Grant, Kevin Tighe, Steve Reevis.

● This is the authentically bloody chronicle of the last Apache leader, as recorded in the memoirs of one of the cavalrymen who hunted him down. It's a film about the land and who owns it, the clash between incompatible cultures, and the telescoping of history with the apparently inexorable progress of 'civilisation'. Although Wes Studi (Geronimo) is only fourth billed in the title role, he has roughly equal screen time with the other three principals: Southern cavalry officer Gatewood (Patric), General Crook (Hackman) and chief scout Al Sieber (Duvall). This being a John Milius story, you'd expect to find some unspoken bond between enemies, and there is, but it's a surprise how uncompromisingly the film conveys the ruthlessness of both sides, the racism and hypocrisy of the white men, and the ferocity with which the Apache respond. Walter Hill proves unexpectedly reluctant to force the story, but he makes the red earth of the Moab desert burn with blood and shame. TCh

Gert and Daisy's Weekend

(1941, GB, 79 min, b/w)
d Maclean Rogers. *sc* Maclean Rogers, Kathleen Butler, HF Maltby. *ph* Stephen Dade. *ad* WJ Hemsley. *cast* Elsie Waters, Doris Waters, Iris Vandeleur, John Slater, Elizabeth Hunt, Wally Patch, Annie Esmond, Aubrey Mallalieu.

● Music hall's favourite Cockneys, Gert and Daisy (Elsie and Doris Waters) do their patriotic bit for British cinema in this ramshackle but lively wartime comedy when they help evacuate a gang of East End kids to a smart country house. Needless to say, neither the toffs nor their butlers and maids much care for the visitors, who are soon accused of stealing jewellery. Social historians will doubtless be fascinated by the ease with which the sisters turn the class system upside down. It's hard to believe that in real life, their brother was that nice Jack Warner, who used to play PC Dixon of Dock Green. GM

Gertrud

(1964, Den, 116 min, b/w)
d/sc Carl Theodor Dreyer. *ph* Henning Bendtsen. *ed* Edith Schlüssel. *ad* Kai Rasch. *m* Jorgen Jersild. *cast* Nina Pens Rode, Bendt Rothe, Ebbe Rode, Baard Owe, Axel Strobye, Anna Malberg.

● Dreyer's last film was adapted from a 1919 play by Hjalmar Söderberg, but it remains one of the most purely cinematic discourses of the 1960s. Its forty-ish protagonist rejects the compromise of her marriage, but suffers disappointment in her younger lover and retreats into a serene isolation. Dreyer directs his actors into performances that are understated to the point of stillness, and composes shots with a daring economy of decor and design; he also slows the overall pace to a contemplative minimum. At the same time, though, he explodes the film's syntax (consecutive shots that don't quite match; camera movements that are never quite resolved), so that the placid surface is undermined by a quarry of tiny fissures. Similarly, the spiritual serenity of the subject is built upon an aching sense of emotional pain – and the fact that it's only half-articulated makes it all the more shattering. TR

Gervaise

(1955, Fr, 116 min, b/w)
d René Clément. *sc* Jean Aurenche, Pierre Bost. *ph* Robert Juillard. *ed* Henri Rust. *ad* Paul Bertrand. *m* Georges Auric. *cast* Maria Schell, François Périer, Armand Mestral, Suzy Delair, Jany Holt, Jacques Harden.

● Always unpredictable, René Clément here turned to Zola's tale of alcoholism and the poor (*L'Assommoir*) to mount a terrific exercise in literalism. The movie's images are so carefully arranged as to sustain the illusion for whole stretches that its story of a club-footed laundress and her misfortunes was indeed shot on location in 1850s Paris. The film is a succession of set pieces designed to impress: the fight in the laundry between Gervaise and a rival, the bored wedding guests wandering round the Louvre, the crippling of Gervaise's roofer husband. And impress they do, though as usual with Clément it all seems a bit soulless. The last few moments – Gervaise's little daughter playing with a ribbon while the child's mother stuns herself on absinthe – are a reminder that in the Zola context, this counts as a prequel to Renoir's 1926 *Nana*. BBa

Geschichte der Dienerin, Die

see Handmaid's Tale, The

Geschichte der O

see Story of O, The

Geschichte des Prinzen Achmed, Die

see Adventures of Prince Achmed, The

Geschichtsunterricht

see History Lessons

Geschriebene Gesicht, Das

see Written Face, The

Getaway, The

(1972, US, 122 min)
d Sam Peckinpah. *p* David Foster, Mitchell Brower. *sc* Walter Hill. *ph* Lucien Ballard. *ed* Robert L Wolfe, Roger Spottiswoode *ad* Ted Haworth, Angelo Graham. *m* Quincy Jones. *cast* Steve McQueen, Ali MacGraw, Ben Johnson, Sally Struthers, Al Lettieri, Slim Pickens, Richard Bright, Dub Taylor, Bo Hopkins.

● An evident precursor to *The Driver* (Walter Hill scripted both, this one from Jim Thompson's novel). The major strength of *The Getaway* rests solidly on McQueen's central role, a cold tense core of pragmatic violence. Hounded by furies (two mobs, police, a hostile landscape), he responds with a lethal control, blasting his way through shootouts that teeter on madness to the loot, the girl, and Peckinpah's mythic land of Mexico. Survival, purification, and the attainment of grace are achieved only by an extreme commitment to the Peckinpah existential ideal of action – a man is what he does. Peckinpah's own control of the escalating frenzy is masterly; this is one of his coldest films, but a great thriller. CPea

Getaway, The

(1994, US, 115 min)
d Roger Donaldson. *p* David Foster, Lawrence Turman, John Alan Simon. *sc* Amy Jones, Walter Hill. *ph* Peter Menzies Jr. *ed* Conrad Buff. *pd* Joseph Nemec III. *m* Mark Isham. *cast* Alec Baldwin, Kim Basinger, Michael Madsen, James Woods, David Morse, Jennifer Tilly, Richard Farnsworth.

● An efficient if somewhat echoing remake of Sam Peckinpah's 1972 thriller. Basinger is loving wife Carol, who sleeps with crooked politico (Woods) to spring ungrateful husband Doc (Baldwin) from jail. A big heist turns bloody, and the couple head for the Mexican border with the Mob, the cops and double-crosser Madsen on their tail. Peckinpah's take on Jim Thompson's novel was scripted by young Walter Hill, and the remake is based on the same screenplay updated by Amy (*Indecent Proposal*) Jones. Director Donaldson keeps the atmosphere hot and sweaty, with salty dialogue ('The plan is: Shut Up'), exciting shoot-outs at regular intervals and plenty of suspense in between. It's a treat to see the double-barrelled menace of Woods and Madsen together at last. TCh

Get Back

(1991, GB, 89 min)
d Richard Lester. *p* Philip Knatchbull, Henry Thomas. *ph* Bob Paynter, Jordan Cronenweth. *ed* John Victor Smith. *songs* Paul McCartney, John Lennon. *with* Paul McCartney, Linda McCartney.

● This documentary chronicles, in sometimes dated intercut fashion, the spate of gigging from Paul McCartney that culminated in his 1990 Get Back world tour. Despite the fussiness of Lester's approach, which bungs in lots of '60s footage, wacky imagery, vegetarian propaganda and home movies, the best thing here is the music itself, from McCartney and a (mostly) very good band. On vintage Beatles rockers like 'Back in the

USSR', 'I Saw Her Standing There' and 'Can't Buy Me Love', McCartney's voice sounds as good as the editing room can make it. There are lots of shots of adoring fans, and Lester even tries to make them the stars by showing them 'off-duty': one in a nurse's uniform, another doing bodybuilding exercises. Generally, the style hits that level of coy futility throughout, split-screens and all, but at least there are some great songs to remember from Macca, shamelessly nostalgic in a way that most pop always has been. SGr

Get Carter

(1971, GB, 112 min)
d Mike Hodges. *p* Michael Klinger. *sc* Mike Hodges. *ph* Wolfgang Suschitzky. *ed* John Trumper. *pd* Assheton Gorton. *m* Roy Budd. *cast* Michael Caine, Britt Ekland, John Osborne, Ian Hendry, Bryan Mosley, Geraldine Moffatt, Dorothy White.

● Caine plays a London wide-boy who moves up to Newcastle to sort out a spot of bother, only to discover that his niece is up to her neck in a blue movie racket. It's slick and cynical, but interesting for the Newcastle locations and its study of a provincial crime syndicate. In fact it's one of the relatively few British films of the period, along with *Gumshoe*, to exploit its setting to advantage. CPe

Get Charlie Tully

see Ooh…You Are Awful

Get on the Bus

(1996. US, 122 min)
d Spike Lee. *p* Reuben Cannon, Bill Borden, Barry Rosenbush. *sc* Reggie Rock Bythewood. *ph* Elliot Davis. *ed* Leander T Sales. *pd* Ina Mayhew. *m* Terence Blanchard. *cast* Richard Belzer, DeAundre Bonds, Andre Braugher, Thomas Jefferson Byrd, Gabriel Casseus, Albert Hall, Harry Lennix, Isaiah Washington, Ossie Davis.

● Lee assembles a crew of African-Americans travelling from South Central LA to attend Louis Farrakhan's Million Man March in Washington, DC, not only to celebrate an historic event, but to depict a microcosm of black (male) America – and to highlight the experiences and attitudes that divide, define and unite men bent on achieving a sense of brotherhood. Despite evident good intentions and the sterling performances, this ambitious road movie, set over three days in October 1995, never gets very far. Ironically (given some of Lee's earlier efforts), that's partly down to the director's determination to create a sense of balance: as scripted by Reggie Rock Bythewood, the passengers are more ciphers than fully rounded characters, while the conflict-driven narrative, which embraces issues of colour, class, criminality, age, religion and sexual politics, is schematic. Whether Farrakhan himself is simply pro-black, or sexist, anti-white and anti-Semitic is never really confronted, but the problem is less one of ideology than drama: though Lee's deft expertise keeps things pacy and (mostly) plausible, the material can't avoid a certain predictability and, in the end, a preachy sentimentality. GA

Get Out Your Handkerchiefs

see Préparez vos Mouchoirs

Get Over It

(2001, US, 86 min)
d Tommy O'Haver. *p* Michael Burns, Marc Butan, Paul Feldsher. *sc* R Lee Fleming Jr. *ph* Maryse Alberti. *ed* Jeff Betancourt. *pd* Robin Standefer. *m* Steve Bartek. *cast* Kirsten Dunst, Ben Foster, Melissa Sagemiller, Sisqó, Shane West, Colin Hanks, Swoosie Kurtz, Ed Begley Jr, Zoë Saldana, Martin Short.

● This high school movie sees scriptwriter R Lee Fleming Jr play loose variations on *A Midsummer Night's Dream* – a rock-musical production of which features prominently and provides the climax – and headlines dimpled Dunst. Though she is on screen virtually throughout, her role calls for her to take an emotional backseat as helpmate to the potentially endearing sufferings of senior Foster (who can't get over being dumped by svelte but shallow Sagemiller). The tongue in cheek atmosphere is established early on: in a scene pitched somewhere between Gracie Fields propaganda and Farrelly Bros pastiche, cast members fall in step to perform Neil Sedaka's 'Love Will Keep Us Together'; cinematographer Maryse Alberti ensures the candy pop colours don't turn sickly; and thought-balloon graphics prick any pomposity in the characters' amusing fortune cookie philosophies. So far so likeable. So why does the film gently disappoint? Caricatured teachers are a teen movie staple, but Martin Short's elephantiasis-affected drama teacher is a lazy, irritating miscalculation; the music is too often crudely interpolated; and director O'Haver fails to supply any proper shape or development. WH

Get Real

(1998, GB/SAf, 110 min)
d Simon Shore. *p* Stephen Taylor. *sc* Patrick Wilde. *ph* Alain Almond. *ed* Barrie Vince. *pd* Bernd Lepel. *m* John Lunn. *cast* Ben Silverstone, Brad Gorton, Charlotte Brittain, Stacy A Hart, Kate McEnery, Patrick Nielsen, Tim Harris, James D White, Jacquetta May.

● In downtown Basingstoke, Steven is suffering the torment of so many 16-year-olds. The one person he wishes he could dance with at the school disco is taken already. Sigh. And sigh again, because Steven is gay, and that special someone is a very straight boy known to everyone in school. Shore's first feature plots a course through sixth form romance and intrigue, bringing Steven's problems to life for an audience which might not necessarily have shared *quite* the same experiences. The same theme could have served for a tract on the pain and isolation of growing up gay, yet while it never sidesteps the issues, the film (adapted by Patrick Wilde from his play *What's Wrong with Angry?*) has its eyes more on the John Hughes teen movies of Hollywood yesteryear, complete with bitchy dialogue and a bouncy pop soundtrack. Ben Silverstone as Steven adeptly combines the jaundiced perceptions of an habitual outsider with the reserve of someone who knows that he must never give too much of himself away, while Gorton, his 'friend', shows how sexual confusion bites hard when you're one of the good-at-everything types loved-yet-hated by all and sundry. The film is grounded in genuine emotions and its knowing humour serves it well. I laughed like a drain. TJ

Get Shorty

(1995, US, 105 min)
d Barry Sonnenfeld. *p* Danny DeVito, Michael Shamberg, Stacey Sher. *sc* Scott Frank. *ph* Mark Plummer. *ed* Jim Miller. *pd* Peter Larkin. *m* John Lurie. *cast* John Travolta, Gene Hackman, Rene Russo, Danny DeVito, Dennis Farian, Delroy Lindo, James Gandolfini, John Gries, David Paymer, Linda Hart, Barry Sonnenfeld.

● Miami loan shark Chili Palmer (Travolta) follows a bad debt from one coast to the other, but he feels right at home when he touches down in LA. Instead of putting the squeeze on schlock movie-maker Harry Zimm (Hackman), Chili pitches his own story concept, agrees to back-off Harry's most impatient investor, ruthless drugs kingpin Bo Catlett (Lindo), and casually breaks into showbiz. Retired scream queen Karen Flores (Russo) provides an intro to her ex, diminutive Hollywood superstar Martin Weir (DeVito), and soon the deal is taking shape: money, murder and mayhem in Lalaland. By sticking closely to Elmore Leonard's novel (often word for word), director Sonnenfeld and screenwriter Scott Frank have plugged straight into the king of crime's most underrated attribute: the comedy of manners. Leonard's flashy characters are always trying on personalities for size, feeling each other out with flip remarks and attitude – everybody's looking for a piece of the action, and the movie fair fizzes with memorable double-talk and backchat. As satire, it's pretty broad, and so throwaway it almost cancels itself out, but the film-makers never overplay their hand: it's a breezy, smoothly sophisticated affair, capitalising on Travolta's low-key charisma. Snappily scored and edited – everything clicks. TCh

Getting Any? (Minna Yatteruka)

(1994, Jap, 108 min)
d Takeshi Kitano. *p* Masayuki Mori, Yasushi Tsuge, Takio Yoshida. *sc* Takeshi Kitano. *ph* Katsumi Yanagishima. *ed* Takeshi Kitano. *ad* Norihiro Isoda. *m* Hidehiko Koike. *cast* Minoru Iikuza, Shouji Kabyashi, Testuya Yuuki, Dannkann, Yuuji Minakata, Renn Oosugi.

● Kitano may have recut this film since I saw it a few weeks ago [in October 1994], when it was half hilarious, half surprisingly leaden. It begins as an absurd comedy about a young dope bent on losing his virginity: because he believes a fast car or a first-class air ticket will make him irresistible, he gets up to a series of crazy antics in pursuit of sex. The repetitive gags about obsession and incompetence, not unlike those in a *Roadrunner* cartoon, are marvellous; then, when he gets a job acting in a samurai film, the humour drifts off into ever more tired parody (yakuza and monster movies follow). The export cut runs 76 minutes. GA

Getting Even With Dad

(1994, US, 109 min)
d Howard Deutch. *p* Katie Jacobs, Pierce Gardner. *sc* Tom S Parker, Jim Jennewein. *ph* Tim Suhrstedt. *ed* Richard Halsey. *pd* Virginia Randolph. *m* Miles Goodman. *cast* Macaulay Culkin, Ted Danson, Glenne Headly, Saul Rubinek, Gailard Sartain, Hector Elizondo.

● Widower Ray Gleason (Danson) is an ex-con who wants to go straight. Timmy (Culkin) is his estranged son who wants to have a father again. When the boy's aunt dumps him on Ray's doorstep, Timmy finds that dad is less interested in looking after him than in carrying out the final heist that will pay for his bakery business, so he videos the crime, hides the loot, and threatens to blow the whistle if father and son don't spend some time together. Hence, the way is paved for an ending visible from a distance of some miles. The script is formula and so is the direction, which leaves the acting. According to the credits, Danson had an acting coach, but he's a warm enough presence to be able to carry a film as slight as this without needing one; instead the coach should have worked with Culkin, who can't even eat a sandwich convincingly. AO

Getting It Right

(1989, US, 102 min)
d Randal Kleiser. *p* Jonathan D Krane, Randal Kleiser. *sc* Elizabeth Jane Howard. *ph* Clive Tickner. *ed* Chris Kelly. *pd* Caroline Amies. *m* Colin Towns. *cast* Jesse Birdsall, Helena Bonham Carter, Peter Cook, John Gielgud, Jane Horrocks, Lynn Redgrave, Shirley Anne Field, Pat Heywood, Bryan Pringle, Judy Parfitt.

● Poor Gavin (Birdsall), shy, sensitive, still living at home, and at 31 the oldest virgin in Christendom. But fear not: Gav is about to discover *gurls* in a big way, in all their stereotypical glory. There's Minerva (Bonham Carter), anorexic daughter of wealth-seeking Mr Buy-Rite; Joan (Redgrave), a flame-haired 40-year-old who has had material splendour heaped upon her but has 'never been loved'; and Jenny (Horrocks), heart-of-gold hairdresser's assistant. All have the hots for nice boy Gavin. Adapted by Elizabeth Jane Howard from her own novel, the film flits between light comedy and raging pathos, a male fantasy (despite the female author) drenched in a kind of Hampstead world-view. Cameos come and go: Cook adjusts his toupée, and Gielgud camps it up as Minerva's *arriviste* father. half-hearted attempts are made to evoke the style of '60s films like *Georgy Girl*, but it just never clicks. Birdsall is fine, but top marks to Pat Heywood as his mother, who fair steals the whole movie. MK

Getting of Wisdom, The

(1977, Aust, 101 min)
d Bruce Beresford. *p* Phillip Adams. *sc* Eleanor Witcombe. *ph* Donald McAlpine. *ed* William Anderson. *pd* John Stoddart. *cast* Susannah Fowle, Sheila Helpmann, Patricia Kennedy, John Waters, Barry Humphries, Kerry Armstrong.

● Drenched in lushly tasteful Victorian production values, this evocation of a warmly sentimental education, set in a Melbourne girls' boarding school, achieves little by way of justifying an adaptation of Ethel Richardson's autobiographical novel of 1910. A perky feminine independence may have proved controversial at the time of its writing, but here emerges as a mere cliché-ridden prelude to an unseen but inevitable brilliant career. Barry Humphries plays straight as a cleric, when a little of his invigorating vulgarity might have pepped the proceedings up considerably, while Beresford's display of versatility only points up his comparative strengths in the almost all-male worlds of *The Club* and *The Money Movers*. PT

Getting Straight

(1970, US, 125 min)
d/p Richard Rush. *sc* Robert Kaufman. *ph* Laszlo Kovacs. *ed* Maury Winetrobe. *ad* Sydney Z Litwack. *m* Ronald Stein. *cast* Elliott Gould, Candice Bergen, Robert F Lyons, Jeff Corey, Max Julien, Cecil Kellaway.
●Muddled (and now dated) campus revolt comedy, distinguished by Elliott Gould's marvellously grizzly performance as an ageing dropout who decides to drop back in again, and resolutely keeps his nose glued to his books in self-defence. Robert Kaufman's script casts a nicely caustic eye not only on the juvenility of the student demands, but also on the hopeless desiccation of academia. Instead of following up, he opts for the easy way out, offering a kitschy metaphor – make love not protest – in a ridiculous scene where Gould strips off to do just that amid the flying fists of a campus riot. Rush's mannered direction is no help, but there are some very funny scenes, not least an oral in which Gould is driven into a corner like a caged lion by an examiner determined to make him admit, through a reinterpretation of *The Great Gatsby*, that Scott Fitzgerald was a closet homosexual. TM

Getting to Know You

(1999, US, 96 min)
d. Lisanne Skyler. *p.* George La Voo, Laura Gabbert. *ph* Jim Denault. *ed* Julie Janata, Anthony Sherrin. *ad* Judy Asnes. *m* Michael Brook. *cast* Heather Matarazzo, Mark Blum, Bebe Neuwirth, Jacob Reynolds, Michael Weston, Bo Hopkins.
●Skyler's first feature is a quiet, oblique character study which gradually gains in intensity. Heather Matarazzo (the geeky outsider from *Welcome to the Dollhouse*) underplays beautifully as Judith, a shy 16-year-old waiting in a bus depot with her brother. Here, she meets an older boy called Jimmy (Weston) who spins her heart tugging, but far fetched yarns about the love lives and domestic problems of the other strangers waiting for buses. Judith listens fascinated. Every anecdote deals with broken families or dysfunctional relationships. Loosely based on a collection of Joyce Carol Oates stories. the material could have been very grim, but Skyler – a documentary maker by trade – treats her variously damaged characters with warmth and gentle humour. She's helped by low key but affecting performances from Bo Hopkins, as a small town cop haunted by a tragedy in his past, and the wonderful Bebe Neuwirth, as Judith's affectionate but highly strung mother. GM

Gettysburg

(1993, US, (Pt 1) 136 min, (Pt 2) 118 min)
d Ronald F Maxwell. *p* Robert Katz, Moctesuma Esparza. *sc* Ronald F Maxwell. *ph* Kees van Oostrum. *ed* Corky Ehlers. *pd* Cary White. *m* Randy Edelman. *cast* Tom Berenger, Martin Sheen, Stephen Lang, Jeff Daniels, Sam Elliott, C Thomas Howell, Brian Mallon, Ken Burns.
●This epic account (made for Turner Television) of the events of the American Civil War preceding, during and after the great battle of 1863 is, finally, a film about men with whiskers – the prodigious facial hair being a signifier of manly courage, moral resolve, undying honour and sensitivity to deathly resolve. It's a movie that parades authenticity, but never settles on its own point of view. Clearly, even now, film-makers are wary of stirring up or offending old allegiances, and here, regrettably, writer/director Maxwell wishes to have his cake and eat it. That said, as officers like Lee (Sheen), Longstreet (Berenger), Chamberlain (Daniels) and Buford (Elliott) struggle to cope with the heavy mantle of history, gazing off to the horizon or tearfully exhorting their men to sacrifice themselves for the greater good, Maxwell does make with the massed troops to spasmodically impressive effect (notably in the Little Round Top fiasco). Of interest chiefly to Civil War buffs and make-up artists. GA

Ghetto

(1996, Serbia, 72 min)
d Mladen Maticevic, Ivan Markov. *p* Veran Matic. *sc* Ivan Markov, Mladen Maticevic. *ph* Drasko Plavsic. *ed* Suzana Stevanovic. *pd* Goran Joksimovic. *m* Darkwood Dub. *cast* Goran Cavajda, Partibrejkers, DLM, Svarog, Direktori, Dead Ideas, Darkwood Dub, Plejboj, Supernaut.
●A drummer wanders though Belgrade in slo-mo, musing on how dreadful life in the city has become over the last few years, and visits rock bands, poets, alternative artists and other rebels and posers. If you know the city, its buildings and rock 'n' roll traditions, this all may mean something; others are likely to find it dull, cynical and pretentious. GA

Ghost

(1990, US, 127 min)
d Jerry Zucker. *p* Lisa Weinstein. *sc* Bruce Joel Rubin. *ph* Adam Greenberg. *ed* Walter Murch. *pd* Jane Musky. *m* Maurice Jarre. *cast* Patrick Swayze, Demi Moore, Tony Goldwyn, Whoopi Goldberg, Vincent Schiavelli, Rick Aviles.
●The premise is a staple of teen romance: separate hero and heroine so that there's plenty of yearning but no danger of any squelchy business. The difference here is that the young couple are allowed a brief but memorable moment of on-screen passion; and the thing that comes between them is death. Swayze, he of the acting ability of a corpse, is ideal as the murdered yuppie who learns how to use his ghostly powers to foil a dastardly plot; Moore, as the grieving girlfriend, displays the animation of a dishcloth. Luckily, Whoopi Goldberg is on hand to ham it up gloriously in abetting the lovers with her newly discovered psychic powers. But the real credit for turning a minor mystic romance into one of the most enjoyable movies of the year rests on an excellent script by Bruce Joel Rubin, and on the surprisingly sure direction of Jerry Zucker. He borrows a roving camera from Sam Raimi, a penchant for shooting into and through solid matter from David Lynch; and the dissolves between scenes cleverly echo Swayze's ability to walk through walls. DW

Ghost and Mrs Muir, The

(1947, US, 104 min, b/w)
d Joseph L Mankiewicz. *p* Fred Kohlmar. *sc* Philip Dunne. *ph* Charles Lang Jr. *ed* Dorothy Spencer. *ad* Richard Day, George Davis. *m* Bernard Herrmann. *cast* Gene Tierney, Rex Harrison, George Sanders, Edna Best, Vanessa Brown, Anna Lee, Robert Coote, Natalie Wood.
●Apprentice work, comparatively speaking, not scripted by Mankiewicz himself (although he contributed), but still astonishingly characteristic in its airy philosophical speculations about the imagination and its role as a refuge when the salty ghost of a sea captain (Harrison) befriends a beautiful widow (Tierney) and intervenes to save her from the cad she is thinking of marrying. Leaning too heavily towards light comedy, Mankiewicz doesn't get the balance quite right, so that the tale of a romance tenuously bridging two worlds isn't quite as moving as it should be when reality ultimately reasserts its claims. A hugely charming film, nevertheless, beautifully shot (by Charles Lang), superlby acted, and with a haunting score by Bernard Herrmann. TM

Ghost and the Darkness, The

(1996, US, 110 min)
d Stephen Hopkins. *p* Gale Anne Hurd, Paul Radin, A Kitman Ho. *sc* William Goldman. *ph* Vilmos Zsigmond. *ed* Robert Brown, Steve Mirkovich, Roger Bonelli. *pd* Stuart Wurtzel. *m* Jerry Goldsmith. *cast* Michael Douglas, Val Kilmer, Tom Wilkinson, Bernard Hill, John Kani, Om Puri, Emily Mortimer.
●The British Empire's steaming progress across East Africa is stalled by two lions that wreak such terror on the natives pressed into building a railway bridge that the project falls dangerously behind schedule. As the bodies mount, Irish engineer John Patterson (Kilmer) is joined by the famous game hunter Remington (Douglas) to tackle 'The Ghost' and 'The Darkness'. Teddy Roosevelt called Col Patterson's *The Man-Eaters of Tsavo* 'the most thrilling book of true stories ever written', and William Goldman's script begins with the boast: 'Even the most improbable parts of the story really happened.' Too bad director Hopkins (*Predator 2*) wouldn't know the truth if it bit him. He renders this mildly promising material so crassly, we might be watching a belated *Jaws* rip-off. All the elements are here: the prowling POV shots as the lions size up their next victim; the merciless capitalist who's the real villain of the piece (Wilkinson – 'I don't care about you; I don't care about 30 dead; I only care about my knighthood!'); and Douglas doing his Robert Shaw impression as the swaggering, whisky-swigging hunter. The film looks expensive and is, occasionally, tense. It's also risibly staged and edited, with incongruous cutaways to flora and fauna, and downright sheepish when it comes to explaining away colonialism. TCh

Ghost Breakers, The

(1940, US, 82 min, b/w)
d George Marshall. *p* Arthur Hornblow Jr. *sc* Walter de Leon. *ph* Charles Lang Jr. *ed* Ellsworth Hoagland. *ad* Hans Dreier, Robert Usher. *m* Ernst Toch. *cast* Bob Hope, Paulette Goddard, Richard Carlson, Paul Lukas, Willie Best, Anthony Quinn, Noble Johnson.
●One of Hope's finest comedies, a sequel from Paramount to the success of the previous year's *The Cat and the Canary*, this sees him accompanying the gorgeous Ms Goddard to the West Indies, where she has inherited a haunted Gothic castle. Meetings with ghosts, zombies, and all manner of spooky phenomena occur, allowing Hope ample space to demonstrate his customary capacity for cowardice and alarm. But although the general situation is much the same as in *The Cat and the Canary*, it works better here because the film provides thrills as well as laughs, thanks to Marshall's deft and delicate direction, Charles Lang's shadowy camerawork, and Hans Dreier's authentically Gothic art direction. GA

Ghost Brigade

see Killing Box, The

Ghostbusters

(1984, US, 105 min)
d/p Ivan Reitman. *sc* Dan Aykroyd, Harold Ramis. *ph* Laszlo Kovacs. *ed* Sheldon Kahn, David Blewitt. *pd* John F DeCuir. *m* Elmer Bernstein. *cast* Bill Murray, Dan Aykroyd, Sigourney Weaver, Harold Ramis, Rick Moranis, Annie Potts, William Atherton.
●*Ghostbusters* combines two of the most popular Hollywood products in recent years: *National Lampoon/Saturday Night Live*-style comedy and state-of-the-art special effects. But the story of a trio of incompetent 'experts' in the paranormal (Murray, Aykroyd and Ramis), who set up as ghostbusters after they are canned from their college sinecures, is less cynical a construction than it sounds. Reitman shows greater flair at controlling the anarchic comic rhythms of the *Lampoon/SNL* crowd than most of the directors who have attempted that hopeless task, and the effects are truly astonishing. *Close Encounters* meets *Animal House*, incidentally giving Murray's sleazily self-confident persona his best leading part to date. MB

Ghostbusters II

(1989, US, 108 min)
d/p Ivan Reitman. *sc* Harold Ramis, Dan Aykroyd. *ph* Michael Chapman. *ed* Sheldon Kahn, Donn Cambern. *pd* Bo Welch. *m* Randy Edelman. *ph* Franco Delli Colli. *m* Simon Boswell. *cast* Bill Murray, Dan Aykroyd, Sigourney Weaver, Harold Ramis, Rick Moranis, Ernie Hudson, Annie Potts, Peter MacNichol, Harris Yulin, David Margulies, Kurt Fuller, Janet Margolin, Wilhelm von Homburg.
●A river of gunk flows beneath the sidewalks of New York, growing ever bigger in response to people's nasty thoughts. The Ghostbusters confront the sticky philosophical issues with characteristic finesse, but overall this much-hyped sequel fails to recapture the energy of the original. Even the demonic stature of the chief villan (von Homburg), who wants to possess Weaver's baby, fails to inject consistent tension. The film is largely an excuse for a cast get-together, with the Ghostbusters, under judicial restraining order after the havoc wreaked in part one, suffering lives of semi-obscurity. Murray fronts a cable TV show, Aykroyd and Hudson are entertainers to the 'ungrateful yuppie larva' at children's parties, Ramis continues his research. Weaver is a single parent divorcee (and ex-lover of Murray), and her imperilled sprog brings the team back into action. This attempt to inject novelty into the plot by way of an endangered infant is little more than a convenience, while the rest is all too familiar. CM

Ghost Camera, The

(1933, GB, 64 min, b/w)
d Bernhard Vorhaus. *p* Julius Hagen. *sc* H Fowler Mear. *ph* Ernest Palmer. *ed* David Lean. *ad* James Carter. *cast* Henry Kendall, Ida Lupino, S Victor Stanley, George Merritt, Felix Aylmer, Fred Groves, John Mills, Davina Craig.

● A rough and ready little comic mystery, from a story by J Jefferson Farjeon, about a chemist who finds a camera in the backseat of his car, develops the film and smells a murder, with John Mills as the ultra innocent suspect of shifty detective Merritt. This 'quota quickie' was made by Vorhaus at Twickenham for Julius Hagen; and, aside from the David Lean editing credit, is chiefly of interest for the upper-class innocence and what now seems the utterly extraordinary accent and delivery of Henry Kendall, as the chemist. JPy

Ghost Catchers

(1944, US, 67 min, b/w)
d Edward F Cline. *p/sc* Edmund L Hartmann. *ph* Charles Van Enger. *ed* Arthur Hilton. *ad* John B Goodman, Richard H Riedel. *songs* Paul Francis Webster, Harry Revel, Edward Ward, others. *cast* Ole Olsen, Chic Johnson, Gloria Jean, Martha O'Driscoll, Leo Carrillo, Andy Devine, Lon Chaney Jr, Walter Catlett.

● Third of the four zany comedies with which Olsen and Johnson revived a flagging career during the '40s. Best remembered for *Hellzapoppin*, they were even better in *Crazy House*. This one, with the pair as nightclub entertainers exorcising a haunted house, is patchier, not least because it is saddled with far too much plot. Funny, though, with the same riot of non-sequiturs and vaudeville gags. TM

Ghost Chase

(1987, WGer, 89 min)
d Roland Emmerich. *sc* Roland Emmerich, Thomas Kubisch. *ph* Walter Lindenlaub. *ed* Brigitte Pia Fritsche. *pd* Ekkehard Schroeer, Sonja B Zimmer. *m* Hubert Bartholomae. *cast* Jason Lively, Jill Whitlow, Tim McDaniel, Paul Gleason, Chuck Mitchell, Leonard Lansink.

● With its silly script, lame acting, naff special effects, and laughable model work, this unfunny supernatural comedy looks like the sort of film its leading characters – a pair of teenage home movie-makers (Lively and McDaniel) – might have made themselves. Lively is hoping his grandfather's bequest will save their latest production and lure back his much put-upon leading lady, Whitlow. His inheritance, however, turns out to be a suitcase of junk, including an old clock. But piranha-loving studio boss Gleason is very interested in the suitcase, and hires a bumbling Kraut stereotype (Lansink) to steal it. The clock's chimes at midnight fail to turn McDaniel into Orson Welles, but they do help him to dream up some ideas for a new movie. Wisps of fog then bring to life an animatronic model of grandfather's old butler, and a predictable tale of stolen inheritance unfolds. The most inventive thing here is footage from *Night of the Living Dead* shown on a projector without the spools going round. NF

Ghost Dance

(1983, GB, 100 min, b/w & col)
d/p/sc Ken McMullen. *ph* Peter Harvey. *ed* Robert Hargreaves. *m* David Cunningtham, Michael Giles, Jamie Muir. *cast* Leonie Mellinger, Pascale Ogier, Robbie Coltrane, Jacques Derrida, Dominique Pinon, Stuart Brisley.

● A film to watch rather than to analyse or write about (though it stubbornly encourages both activities). Its pleasures – which are not consistent over 100 minutes – are intensely visual: a beachscape, blighted urban landscape, a city by night, evocatively photographed by Peter Harvey. Evocation is the film's key theme. A 'calling up' of images, myths and memories from a past which, according to philosopher Jacques Derrida (who is 'interviewed' in one sequence), was never present. Ghosts, then, but in the Freudian sense of 'internalised figures from the past' who collectively make their presence known to us. These myths, the film argues, seek to make historical sense out of historical chaos, and in the present electronic age they are omnipresent – in data banks, and even at the end of a telephone line. Quite how the thesis connects with the narrative – Ogier and Mellinger drifting around Paris and London and running into the bulky frame of Coltrane – remains a mythtery. MA

Ghost Dog: The Way of the Samurai

(1999, US, 116 min)
d Jim Jarmusch. *p* Richard Guay, Jim Jarmusch. *sc* Jim Jarmusch. *ph* Robby Müller. *ed* Jay Rabinowitz. *pd* Ted Berner. *m* RZA. *cast* Forest Whitaker, John Tormey, Cliff Gorman, Henry Silva, Isaach de Bankolé, Tricia Vessey.

● Jarmusch's engagingly offbeat variation on the hitman thriller finds Ghost Dog (Whitaker) under threat from the wiseguys who've been using his ultra efficient services after the boss's daughter witnesses one of his killings. On to this basic storyline, Jarmusch grafts an unlikely but coherent variety of moods, motifs, themes and gags: the Mob, though themselves memorably eccentric, simply can't cope with a black killer who communicates by carrier pigeon and lives by the ancient code of Japanese samurai. At once a tribute to traditional notions of honour, loyalty, friendship and professionalism, and a stylish, ironic pastiche inspired by the likes of Melville and Suzuki, it's very funny, insightful, and highly original, proving that Jarmusch has lost none of his wit, warmth or invention. Great camerawork (Robby Müller), score (RZA) and bird footage, too. GA

Ghost Goes West, The

(1936, GB, 90 min, b/w)
d René Clair. *p* Alexander Korda. *sc* Robert E Sherwood. *ph* Harold Rosson. *ed* William Hornbeck. *ad* Vincent Korda. *m* Mischa Spolianky. *cast* Robert Donat, Jean Parker, Eugene Pallette, Elsa Lanchester, Everley Gregg, Hay Petrie.

● Only the obsessively cosmopolitan Korda could have put together this British film, with its French director, its American writer (Robert Sherwood) and its story from *Punch* about a Scottish castle transported to Florida along with its ghost. The result of this geographical potpourri is so silly that it's almost disarming – especially with the gracefully romantic Donat wandering about with his honey voice, kilt and bagpipes. But total delight is kept at bay by the obviousness of the satire on US habits, the obviousness of the sets, and the comparative waste of Clair's talents. GB

Ghost in the Shell (Kokaku Kidotai)

(1995, Jap/GB, 83 min)
d Mamoru Oshii. *sc* Kazunori Ito. *ph* Hisao Shirai. *ed* Shuichi Kakesu. *ad* Hiromasa Ogura. *m* Kenji Kawai. *cast* voices: Richard George, Mimi Woods, William Frederick, Abe Lasser, Christopher Joyce, Mike Sorich.

● Set in 2029 and using inspired computer animation, Oshii's sci-fi *anime* conjures up a dazzling, futuristic cityscape that, sadly, is not matched by the human landscapes at the heart of the story. The *Blade Runner* theme of identity as a function of memory is raised but not explored. Cybercop Kusanagi has a synthetic personality, silicon breasts and an identity crisis. Ordered to track down the Puppetmaster, who can hack into human brains, she and her bland sidekick Bateau become embroiled in a conspiracy involving a secret government project, inter-departmental rivalries and a computer virus that's mutated into a being with a sense of its own destiny. All credit to Britain's Manga Entertainment for co-funding this ambitious project with the Japanese producers of *Akira*, but much more attention should have been paid to the script and disastrous dubbed dialogue. NF

Ghost of Frankenstein, The

(1942, US, 68 min, b/w)
d Erle C Kenton. *p* George Waggner. *sc* W Scott Darling. *ph* Milton Krasner, Woody Bredell. *ed* Ted J Kent. *ad* Jack Otterson. *m* Hans J Salter. *cast* Cedric Hardwicke, Lon Chaney Jr, Lionel Atwill, Bela Lugosi, Ralph Bellamy, Evelyn Ankers, Dwight Frye.

● No masterpiece but better than its reputation, this picks up where *Son of Frankenstein* left off, with Lugosi's Igor retrieving the monster (now played by Chaney, alas) from the sulphur pit. Relishable performances from Hardwicke and Atwill as scientists at cross-purposes, the former determined to endow the monster with a sane brain, the latter slyly playing along with Lugosi's mad plan to have his transplanted so that he can dominate the world in the monster's body. The pair make it great fun. TM

Ghost of St Michael's, The

(1941, GB, 82 min, b/w)
d Marcel Varnel. *p* Michael Balcon. *sc* Angus Macphail, John Dighton. *ph* Derick Williams. *ed* EB Jarvis. *ad* Wilfrid Shingleton. *m* Ernest Irving. *cast* Will Hay, Claude Hulbert, Charles Hawtrey, Derek Blomfield, Felix Aylmer, Raymond Huntley, John Laurie.

● Hay's first picture with Ealing stuck to a tried routine, with his seedy schoolmaster and boisterous pupils evacuated from the Blitz to a spooky castle on Skye where rebellious Hawtrey whisks up further mischief among his fellow students. Meanwhile, the rest of the plot (by Angus Macphail and John Dighton) works in a mystery bagpiper and the by now customary unmasking of a Nazi spy ring. TJ

Ghosts from the Past

see Ghosts of Mississippi

Ghost Ship, The

(1943, US, 69 min, b/w)
d Mark Robson. *p* Val Lewton. *sc* Donald Henderson Clarke. *ph* Nick Musuraca. *ed* John Lockert. *ad* Albert S D'Agostino, Walter Keller. *m* Roy Webb. *cast* Richard Dix, Russell Wade, Edith Barrett, Ben Bard, Edmund Glover, Skelton Knaggs, Lawrence Tierney, Sir Lancelot.

● This Val Lewton production may not scale the heights of *Cat People* or *I Walked with a Zombie*, but it has its impressive moments. A brooding tale of mysterious deaths on board a ship captained by the haunted, moody Dix, it's perhaps most notable for its scene of a sailor crushed to death by an enormous chain in the hold, and for its remarkable narration by a seemingly omniscient deaf-mute. The first, sea-girt half is best, darkly atmospheric and full of pulp poetry; when the story moves ashore, things come down to earth a little, but by then the spell is cast.

Ghosts of Kasane Swamp, The (Kaidan Kasane ga Fuchi)

(1957, Jap, 66 min, b/w)
d Nobuo Nakagawa. *p* Mitsugu Okura, Katsuji Tsuda. *sc* Kohan Kawauchi. *ph* Yoshimi Hirano. *ed* Toshio Goto. *ad* Akira Konami. *m* Chumei Watanabe. *cast* Katsuko Wakasugi, Takashi Wada, Noriko Kitazawa, Tetsuro Tanba.

● A bad-karma ghost story from future cult director Nakagawa, made for Shintoho (i.e., Japan's Republic Pictures) at a time when even a modest monochrome B-feature could boast decent performances and design. It's 1793. The foundling Shinkichi (Wada) works as a servant in a fabric shop. He's torn between the affections of Hisa (Kitazawa), the daughter of the house, and her music teacher Rui (Wakasugi), causing the usual complications. But none of them is aware that Shinkichi's samurai father killed Rui's debt collector father twenty years earlier. Karmic revenge begins when a shamisen plectrum hits Rui on the head, causing massive disfigurement. Pretty much everyone is dead by the end, something of a Nakagawa trademark. TR

Ghosts of Mars

(2001, US, 98 min)
d John Carpenter. *p* Sandy King. *sc* Larry Sulkis, John Carpenter. *ph* Gary B Kibbe. *ed* Paul C Warschilka. *pd* William Elliott. *m* John Carpenter. *cast* Ice Cube, Natasha Henstridge, Jason Statham, Pam Grier, Clea Duvall, Joanna Cassidy, Liam Waite, Wanda DeJesus, Duane Davis, Robert Carradine.

● Mars, 2176. Shapely cop Ballard (Henstridge) is quizzed by superiors after returning to base, apparently the sole survivor of a mission to retrieve dangerous criminal 'Desolation' Williams (Ice Cube) from a distant mining outpost. Flashbacks reveal Ballard's team arriving at the camp to discover a scene of slaughter, the colonists having been taken over by a mysterious ancient force and turned into cannibal zombie psychopaths. The movie is itself possessed by powerful older spirits: the spectres of Carpenter's back catalogue. Buffs will have a field day ticking off the self-homages, starting with the period setting – exactly 200 years after his breakthrough *Assault on Precinct 13*. It's easy to knock the hole-ridden plot, the *Blake's 7* effects, and the dated racket that is Carpenter's own synth-metal score. But to take it seriously would be to miss the point: the crazily complicated flashback structure and hilarious hardboiled dialogue are all the more amusing for being played dead-on straight. NY

Ghosts of Mississippi (aka Ghosts from the Past)

(1996, US, 130 min)
d Rob Reiner. *p* Rob Reiner, Fred Zollo, Nicholas Paleologos, Andrew Scheinman. *sc* Lewis Colick. *ph* John Seale. *ed* Robert Leighton. *pd* Lilly Kilvert. *m* Marc Shaiman. *cast* Alec Baldwin, Whoopi Goldberg, James Woods, Craig T Nelson, Susanna Thompson, Lucas Black, William H Macy.
●Thirty years after the event, Assistant DA Bobby DeLaughter (Baldwin) is out to secure a conviction for the murder of Medgar Evers, one-time chief civil rights worker in the frontline state of Mississippi. True, DeLaughter, in association with several hard-working colleagues and with the key involvement of Evers' widow Myrlie, tracked down new witnesses and a lost murder weapon to help bring a case against Byron De La Beckwith (Woods, Oscar nominated), originally acquitted after two hung juries. Certainly the DA, who'd been 11 at the time of the killing in 1963, had marital problems because of the pressure and unpopularity of the case, but no amount of emotional ballast in the film can make up for the tedium and repetition inevitable when a murder is shown and then dissected in two separate court hearings. Indeed, the only pluses are the ever-watchable Woods and Whoopi Goldberg's excellent, understated showing as Evers' widow. SGr

Ghosts...of the Civil Dead

(1988, Aust, 93 min)
d John Hillcoat. *p* Evan English. *sc* Gene Conkie, John Hillcoat, Evan English, Nick Cave, Hugo Race. *ph* Paul Goldman, Graham Wood. *ed* Stewart Young. *pd* Chris S Kennedy. *m* Nick Cave, Mick Harvey, Blixa Bargeld. *cast* Dave Field, Mike Bishop, Chris De Rose, Nick Cave, Freddo Dierck, Vincent Gil.
●Hillcoat makes a remarkable debut with this brutal depiction of prison life. The technology appears futuristic, but the New Generation prison under scrutiny is very much a contemporary phenomenon based on the production team's research. The film unfolds in flashback, detailing the violent incidents which necessitated a 'lock-down' at Central Industrial prison. Despite the protection offered to guards by hi-tech observation rooms, the inmates – after months of administrative provocation and manipulation – exact bloody revenge on what they perceive to be their oppressors. Hillcoat makes few concessions to commercial conventions, such as establishing a sympathetic protagonist. The result is unrelenting and harrowing as the focus rapidly shifts between all the aggrieved. Pornography, murder, rape, theft, and drugs are all dealt with in raw fashion, and although the cumulative effect is exceptionally disturbing, the film ultimately manages to elicit passionate concern over the future of our prison service. CM

Ghost Story

(1981, US, 110 min)
d John Irvin. *p* Burt Weissbourd. *sc* Lawrence D Cohen. *ph* Jack Cardiff. *ed* Tom Rolf. *ad* Norman Newberry. *m* Philippe Sarde. *cast* Fred Astaire, Melvyn Douglas, Douglas Fairbanks Jr, John Houseman, Craig Wasson, Patricia Neal, Alice Krige, Jacqueline Brookes.
●Disastrous distillation of Peter Straub's overrated but at least tolerably coherent novel. The action is now almost as arthritic as the performances of the quartet of golden oldies who sit around regaling each other with ghost stories while the demonic spirit of a girl they wronged in their youth rampages around wreaking vengeance. The horror, weakly and predictably managed by Irvin, is mainly confined to tiresomely repetitive shots of the rotting flesh that lurks beyond the demon's pretty face. TM

Ghost Story of Yotsuya (Tokaido Yotsuya Kaidan)

(1959, Jap, 76 min)
d Nobuo Nakagawa. *p* Mitsugu Okura, Hiroshi Onozawa. *sc* Masayoshi Onuki, Yoshihiro Ishikawa. *ph* Tadashi Nishimoto. *ed* Shin Nagata. *ad* Haruyasu Kurosawa. *m* Chumei Watanabe. *cast* Shigeru Amachi, Katsuko Wakasugi, Shutaro Emi, Noriko Kitazawa, Junko Ikeuchi, Jun Otomo.
●Now considered a classic, Nakagawa's adaptation of Nanboku Tsuruya's kabuki play went unhailed by critics at the time but was popular enough to prompt at least three remakes in short order (by Tai Kato in 1961, Shiro Toyoda in 1965 and Issei Mori in 1969). With the connivance of the servant Naosuke (Emi), destitute ronin Iemon (Amachi) marries O-Iwa (Wakasugi) after secretly murdering her disapproving father. Two years later they are living in poverty in Edo with a baby. Desperate for money, Iemon courts O-Ume (Ikeuchi) for her father's wealth and plots to kill O-Iwa after framing her as an adulterer. But O-Iwa is hideously disfigured by poison and kills herself and the baby – and then returns as a ghost to exact vengeance. Concisely plotted and fast-paced, the film somehow reconciles classical elegance with Nakagawa's patented shock effects. Both the remarkable use of sound and the colour expressionism influenced many other directors. Nakagawa's finest hour. TR

Ghost World

(2001, GB/US/Ger, 112 min)
d Terry Zwigoff. *p* Lianne Halfon, John Malkovich, Russell Smith, Janette Day. *sc* Daniel Clowes, Terry Zwigoff. *ph* Affonso Beato. *ed* Carole Kravetz-Aykanian, Michael R Miller. *pd* Edward T McAvoy. *m* David Kitay. *cast* Thora Birch, Scarlett Johansson, Steve Buscemi, Brad Renfro, Illeana Douglas, Bob Balaban, Stacey Travis, Charles C Stevenson Jr, Teri Garr.
●Enid (Birch) has an outré thing going on. She wears thriftshop cast-offs with pride. In her tortoiseshell specs and purple lip-gloss, she and best friend Rebecca (Johansson) like nothing better than to vent their wisecracking contempt for the conformity all around them. The way they see it, even going to college would be a sell-out. Instead they plan to take an apartment together, but they'll have to earn some money before they can afford to drop out. What makes the film special is how it relishes adolescent rebellion (it's based on Daniel Clowes' graphic novel). But doesn't stop there. It's clear that, for pretty Rebecca especially, this is 'just a phase' – and what's more, our heroines' knee-jerk cynicism, reverse snobbery and 'include me out' cool need to be subjected to the mundane complexities of human relationships. Enid picks up a middle-aged sad sack, Seymour (Buscemi), as a kind of hobby, until he becomes an emotional attachment that she needs more than he does. This sort-of love story could have been sticky, but in fact it's beautifully played. It isn't a perfect film, but it's never less than strikingly original. TCh

Ghoul, The

(1933, GB, 79 min, b/w)
d T Hayes Hunter. *p* Michael Balcon. *sc* Roland Pertwee, John Hastings Turner. *ph* Günther Krampf. *ed* Ian Dalrymple, Ralph Kemplen. *ad* Alfred Junge. *m* Louis Levy. *cast* Boris Karloff, Ernest Thesiger, Cedric Hardwicke, Dorothy Hyson, Anthony Bushell, Ralph Richardson, Kathleen Harrison.
●Slow-burning and extremely uneven chiller with Karloff as a professor who believes that a ring stolen from an Egyptian tomb will grant him immortality. However, when Karloff lays down to die, his servant steals the gem, and the professor comes back to life to wreak a terrible revenge. The build-up is too slow, and the later scenes degenerate into ill-judged humour and Old Dark House clichés. Keep an eye out for Richardson, making his screen debut as a phony vicar. NF

Ghoul, The

(1975, GB, 87 min)
d Freddie Francis. *p* Kevin Francis. *sc* John Elder [Anthony Hinds]. *ph* John Wilcox. *ed* Henry Richardson. *ad* Jack Shampan. *m* Harry Robinson. *cast* Peter Cushing, John Hurt, Alexandra Bastedo, Gwen Watford, Veronica Carlson, Don Henderson.
●We're back in the world of Hammer production values (now subtly calling themselves Tyburn), where no moorland scene is complete without a smoke-bomb billowing away just out of camera range, and well up to the usual mediocre level of British horror. Violin-playing ex-missionary Cushing arrives back from India with A Horrible Secret and a mystical servant (Watford). Bright young things crash their motor outside the front gate, and are whished away in by poor mad Tom (Hurt, sadly wasted). You should be able to fill in the other details. The familiar brisk script ('These marshes were used by the army as a training area, but they lost too many men') is by John Elder. AN

Ghoulies

(1984, US, 84 min)
d Luca Bercovici. *p* Jefery Levy. *sc* Luca Bercovici, Jefery Levy. *ph* Mac Ahlberg. *ed* Ted Nicolaou. *pd* Wayne Springfield. *m* Shirley Walker, Richard Band. *cast* Peter Liapis, Lisa Pelikan, Michael Des Barres, Jack Nance, Peter Risch, Tamara De Treaux.
●College kid inherits dead father's mansion and the parental obsession with black magic. Black arts movies tend to come cheap: a dark cellar, a few candles and a robe. Deep shadow is a blessing here too because the titular trolls are absurd puppets that merely wobble about and snarl a bit. The kid's proficiency in magical mumbling allows Dad to rise from the grave and unleash further low budget mayhem. As the house falls apart, the kid is helped by caretaker and kindly satanist Jack Nance, who duels with Dead Dad via lightning bolts from their eyes. Dad's lightning is pink, Jack's blue, so we can keep up with who's winning. The kid and pals escape and discover the greatest horror: the car's full of ghoulies and there will be a sequel. DO

Ghouls, The

see Flesh and the Fiends, The

Giant

(1956, US, 197 min)
d George Stevens. *p* George Stevens, Henry Ginsberg. *sc* Fred Guiol, Ivan Moffatt. *ph* William C Mellor. *ed* William Hornbeck. *pd* Boris Leven. *m* Dimitri Tiomkin. *cast* Elizabeth Taylor, Rock Hudson, James Dean, Mercedes McCambridge, Carroll Baker, Dennis Hopper, Chill Wills, Jane Withers, Sal Mineo, Rod Taylor.
●Stevens' sprawling epic of Texan life, taken from Edna Ferber's novel, strives so hard for Serious Statements that it ends up as a long yawn. Dealing with the two men who love Taylor – strait-laced cattle baron Hudson, and the less respectable rancher who strikes it rich with oil (Dean, a strange spectacle in himself as he turns grey) – the film attempts to conduct some sort of attack on rampant materialism, as well as offering an elegy for the times that have a-changed. But the pace is so plodding, and the general effect so stultifyingly unsubtle, that one is left impressed only by the fine landscape photography and Dean's surprisingly convincing portrayal of a middle-aged man. To see the overblown, soft-centred nature of the film, one need only compare it with Sirk's vitriolic account of Texan family life in *Written on the Wind*. GA

Giant of Marathon, The (La Battaglia di Maratona)

(1959, It/Fr, 87 min)
d Jacques Tourneur. *p* Bruno Vailati. *sc* Ennio De Concini, Augusto Frassinetti, Bruno Vailati. *ph* Mario Bava. *ed* Mario Serandrei. *ad* Marcello Del Prato, Massimo Tavazzi. *m* Roberto Nicolosi. *cast* Steve Reeves, Mylène Demongeot, Daniela Rocca, Daniele Varga, Sergio Fantoni, Alberto Lupo, Gianni Loti, Ivo Garrani, Philippe Hersent.
●Philippides (Reeves), victor of the 490 BC Olympics, is proclaimed leader of the Athenian Sacred Guard and in due course defeats Darius the Persian at the Battle of Marathon. A well-plotted (in a bare-bones sort of way) and quite sprightly tale of double dealing, photographed by Mario Bava (who a year later launched his career as a cult horror director), with Fantoni as the heartless woman-killer Theocritus, and Rocca as the matronly sacrificial love interest. Pretty ordinary (not to say ludicrous), but some inventive and brutal underwater sequences. JPy

Giant Spider Invasion, The

(1975, US, 76 min)
d Bill Rebane. *p* Bill Rebane, Richard L Huff. *sc* Richard L Huff, Robert Easton. *ph* Jack Willoughby. *ed* Barbara Pokras. *ad* Ito Rebane. *cast* Barbara Hale, Steve Brodie, Leslie Parrish, Alan Hale, Robert Easton, Kevin Brodie, Bill Williams.
●Something of a hotch-potch as Rebane jumbles comic strip with genuinely unsettling horror. Real spiders are used to reasonably good effect, whereas the one giant specimen, despite a spirited first appearance, is patently mechanical and sadly undemonstrative. Still, the film starts with gusto:

gamma rays crash into a Wisconsin farm, opening up a sort of grisly parallel universe, and scattering alien rocks that in addition to housing the spiders are lined with diamonds. Thereafter it becomes a tangle of technological mumbo-jumbo, an elderly courtship between Hale and Brodie, Old Testament fire and brimstone from a revivalist preacher, a painfully jolly sheriff, an asinine cub reporter, and a drunken wife who constantly berates her slobbish husband. Apart from the monumentally stilted script which provides many a chuckle, one of the highlights must be when Leslie Parrish (the drunken wife) sips a Bloody Mary which, unknown to her, contains a pulverised arachnid enemy. IB

G.I. Blues

(1960, US, 104 min)
d Norman Taurog. *p* Hal B Wallis. *sc* Edmund Beloin, Henry Garson. *ph* Loyal Griggs. *ed* Warren Low. *ad* Hal Pereira, Walter Tyler. *songs* Sid Tepper, Roy C Bennett, Bert Kaempfert, others. *cast* Elvis Presley, Juliet Prowse, Robert Ivers, Leticia Roman, James Douglas, Arch Johnson.

● First in a series of nine bland Presley vehicles directed by Taurog, and the film which engendered a career formula of tepid, routine comedy-musicals. Just out of the army himself, a subdued Elvis plays a guitar-strumming GI in West Germany, romances the forbidding Prowse, serenades unpardonably cute children, has the occasional fist fight, and sleepwalks to the set of his next film. AC

Gidget

(1959, US, 95 min)
d Paul Wendkos. *p* Lewis J Rachmil. *sc* Gabrielle Upton. *ph* Burnett Guffey. *ed* William A Lyon. *ad* Ross Bellah. *m* Morris W Stoloff. *cast* Sandra Dee, Cliff Robertson, James Darren, Arthur O'Connell, Joby Baker, Yvonne Craig, Doug McClure.

● Dee hangs out for the summer with clean-living college surfers on Malibu Beach. She falls for Darren, but he's in love with his surfboard. Sandra soon puts matters right by making the big chump jealous. This winsome comedy – a sort of *Baywatch* of its day – spawned several sequels and a TV series (with Sally Field) and made a mint for Columbia. GM

Gift, The

(1990, GB, 102 min)
d Marc Evans, Red Saunders. *p* Linda James. *sc* Anthony Horowitz. *ph* Jason Lehel. *ed* Rob Sylvester. *pd* Steve Hardie. *m* Michael Storey. *cast* Tat Whalley, Jodhi May, Emma-Louise Harrington, Cynthia Greville, Jeff Rawle, Jacqueline Tong.

● Loosely based on the TV series, this is a fairly gripping supernatural drama for older children. On a visit to his grandparents' Welsh cottage, 14-year-old Davy (Whalley) learns that he has inherited the family gift for clairvoyance. returning home with his young sister (Harrington), he is assailed by a stream of disturbing premonitions involving armed men in grotesque masks and Western-style coats – the very men with whom Davy's father has been overheard in clandestine converstation. Younger kids may get restive because of the lack of action with the situation only becoming clear towards the end. That said, there are a number of nail-biting moments, extremely inventive camera angles, and marvellously understated performances from Whalley, Jodhi May (as the only classmate to understand Davy's predicament), and Cynthia Greville as the kindly but somewhat sinister grandmother. Pity about the cotton-wool soundtrack. DA

Gift, The

(2000, US, 112 min)
d Sam Raimi. *p* James Jacks, Tom Rosenberg, Gary Lucchesi. *sc* Billy Bob Thornton, Tom Epperson. *ph* Jamie Anderson. *ed* Arthur Coburn, Bob Murawski. *pd* Neil Spisak. *m* Christopher Young. *cast* Cate Blanchett, Giovanni Ribisi, Keanu Reeves, Katie Holmes, Greg Kinnear, Hilary Swank, Michael Jeter, Kim Dickens, Gary Cole, Rosemary Harris.

● Annie Wilson (Blanchett) lives in a cabin out in the boondocks glumly reading other people's futures. Given that her regulars include nutsy mechanic Buddy (Ribisi) and perpetually black-eyed Valerie (Swank), tact is probably the most demanding aspect of her job. Still, when she bumps into school principal Wayne Collins (Kinnear) and his hot-to-trot fiancée Jessica (Holmes), she can't quite hide the apocalyptic visions which flood her senses. When Jessica disappears, it's Annie who holds the key to the crime. Blanchett gives it all she's got, but there's a fundamental flaw here: if your beleaguered heroine has second sight, how come everybody in the entire audience is streets ahead of her? This is one of those murder mysteries where the red herring is so scarlet only a Texan would convict, while the guilty party simpers soulfully trying to look unobtrusive. Director Raimi, meanwhile, treats the trashy material with sluggish solemnity and only wakes up in the dream sequences. TCh

Gifted City (Mesto Darovane)

(1965, Czech, 12 min, b/w)
d Vladimir Kressl.

● Short films don't come much more significant or disturbing than this measured reportage on the daily life and transports of Theresienstadt, the transit camp 'gifted' by Hitler to the Jews. Scenes of football games, concerts, relaxed dormitory shots and general community business are counterpointed with a calmly delivered listing of the reference codes for trains to the camps, the number of passengers and the numbers who survived – in one case just two out of thousands – making the film both a terrible reminder of the lives extinguished and a chilling memento of Nazi propaganda. Alongside readings of 'letters' sent home to relatives to reassure them about camp conditions, the 'normality' the Nazis faked as a show window to the world ironically reveals more about the culture they were hellbent on destroying than the often seen concentration camp atrocity footage ever could. GE

Gigantic (Absolute Giganten)

(1999, Ger, 81 min)
d Sebastian Schipper. *p* Stefan Arndt, Tom Tykwer. *sc* Sebastian Schipper. *ph* Frank Griebe. *ed* Andrew Bird. *pd* Andrea Kessler. *m* The Notwist, Sophia, Egoexpress. *cast* Frank Giering, Florian Lukas, Antoine Monot Jr, Julia Hummer, Jochen Nickel.

● 'Friendships are like dreams, big, great, absolutely gigantic; they won't let you go,' says Floyd, preparing for a rites-of-passage night on the town when he'll announce his departure from Hamburg and his two mates, Ricco 'the ultimate gigolo' and mechanic Walter. They traipse around each other's houses, have a miserable time in Horst's bar, cruise the city in Walter's beloved yellow Ford Granada, and pick up a waif-like girl, before an over-enthusiastic visit to a Turkish-run Elvis Stunt Show results in cross-town car chases and rumbles. With its T Rex and rap soundtrack, sub-Levinson chatter, early Wenders-style downbeat sweetness, and time-lapse neon nightscapes, this makes for unremarkable but engaging viewing. (It also has the best table-football game in the movies.) WH

Gigi

(1949, Fr, 100 min, b/w)
d Jacqueline Audry. *p* Claude Dolbert. *sc* Pierre Laroche. *ph* Gérard Perrin. *ed* Nathalie Petitroux. *ad* Raymond Druart. *m* Marcel Landowski. *cast* Danièle Delorme, Frank Villard, Gaby Morlay, Jean Tissier, Yvonne de Bray, Paul Demange.

● In between the Colette novella and the MGM musical came this quite intelligent elaboration, from which Alan Jay Lerner borrowed extensively. Fifteen-year-old Gilberte – Gigi – is being raised by her all-female family for the role of '*petite amie*', shortly to be assigned to an acceptable man of means, such as Gaston, the handsome sugar millionaire. Things, of course, work out differently. Unfortunately, Delorme adolescent spontaneity lacks … spontaneity. Well, she was 22 at the time. But de Bray is superb as the girl's grandmother. And the period detail – the horse-drawn bathing machines, the new Eiffel Tower restaurant, the skating fad – is quite evocative. BBa

Gigi

(1958, US, 116 min)
d Vincente Minnelli. *p* Arthur Freed. *sc* Alan Jay Lerner. *ph* Joseph Ruttenberg. *ed* Adrienne Fazan. *ad* William A Horning, Preston Ames. *m* Frederick Loewe. *cast* Leslie Caron, Maurice Chevalier, Louis Jourdan, Hermione Gingold, Jacques Bergerac, Eva Gabor, Isabel Jeans.

● Not a Broadway-based musical but a screen original, derived from Colette's short novel set in turn-of-the-century Paris, with famous if vapid songs by Lerner and Loewe ('I Remember It Well', 'Thank Heaven for Little Girls'). But the dominating creative contribution comes from Minnelli and Cecil Beaton (responsible for production design and costumes). The combination of these two visual elitists is really too much – it's like a meal consisting of cheesecake, and one quickly longs for something solid and vulgar to weigh things down. No doubt inspired by the finicky, claustrophobic sets and bric-à-brac, the cast tries (with unfortunate success) to be more French than the French, especially Chevalier. The exception is Gingold, who inhabits, as always, a world of her own. GB

G.I. Jane

(1997, US/GB, 125 min)
d Ridley Scott. *p* Ridley Scott, Roger Birnbaum, Demi Moore, Suzanne Todd. *sc* David N Twohy, Danielle Alexandra. *ph* Hugh Johnson. *ed* Pietro Scalia. *pd* Arthur Max. *m* Trevor Jones. *cast* Demi Moore, Viggo Mortensen, Anne Bancroft, Jason Beghe, Scott Wilson, Lucinda Jenney.

● This humourless variant on *Private Benjamin* puts Moore through her paces as an intelligence officer selected as the first woman to undergo combat training with the US Navy SEALs. Everyone expects her to fail. Mortensen – the sadistic/benevolent master chief – abuses his recruits, but Demi takes it like a man. She shaves her head – a moment covered with half a dozen cameras, as if it were the helicopter attack in *Apocalypse Now!* All the movie lacks is real combat, so the script cooks up an excuse for a raid on Libya, where the star can celebrate the ultimate emancipation: she can kill for her country. It's a toss up what's most depressing about all this. Moore's grim self-determinism is self-defeating. She's fit all right – but an exercise video might have been more entertaining. The hardline feminism is such a reductionist position, and the basic training genre affords so little room for manoeuvre, that the picture's an irrelevance before it's even begun. TCh

Gilda

(1946, US, 110 min, b/w)
d Charles Vidor. *p* Virginia Van Upp. *sc* Marion Parsonnet, Jo Eisinger. *ph* Rudolph Maté. *ed* Charles Nelson. *ad* Stephen Goosson, Van Nest Polglase. *m* Marlin Skiles. *cast* Rita Hayworth, Glenn Ford, George Macready, Joseph Calleia, Steve Geray, Gerald Mohr.

● Ford plays a drifting gambler who gets adopted by a German casino owner (Macready) in Buenos Aires, only to become embroiled in a misogynistic ménage-à-trois with the German and his wife (Hayworth). The script is laced with innuendoes and euphemisms; and Ford finds himself as a character whose sexual attributes are not only ambiguous, but bordering on the perverse as his misogyny gradually gains the upper hand. Never has the fear of the female been quite so intense; and the themes that took wing in this extraordinary piece of cinema finally came to roost in such sexual *noirs* as *Carnal Knowledge* and *Last Tango in Paris.* GSa

Giliap

(1975, Swe, 137 min)
d Roy Andersson. *p* Kalle Boman, Göran Lindgren. *sc* Roy Andersson. *ph* Jon Olsson. *ed* Roy Andersson, Kalle Boman. *ad* Anna Asp, Sören Brunes, Lotta Melanton. *m* Björn Isfält. *cast* Thommy Bergren, Mona Seilitz, Willie Andréason, Pernilla August, Lars-Levi Læstadius.

● A young-ish drifter takes a job waiting at an unprepossessing, old fashioned and strictly run hotel in small town Sweden, where he falls for a waitress and gets involved in the none too promising plans for a robbery dreamed up by another staff member. Andersson's commercially disastrous second feature is a real oddity. It starts as if it's a desert-dry deadpan comedy about hotel life, begins to take on allegorical/religious dimensions (purgatory, temptation, sin), and ends as a slightly overextended thriller-cum-romance. Though it is so low key that it's unsurprising it bombed, it's not without intelligence, wit or interest. GA

Gilsodom

(1985, SKor, 97 min)
d Im Kwon-taek. *p* Bak Jong-chan. *sc* Song Gilhaa. *ph* Jeong Il-seong. *ed* Bak Sun-duk. *pd* Kim Yu-jun. *m* Kim Jong-gil. *cast* Kim Ji-mi, Sin Song-il, Han Ji-il, Kim Ji-yong, Lee Sang-a, Kim Jong Sok.

● In the summer of 1983, South Korea's national obsession was a TV programme designed to reunite families separated in the Korean War thirty-three years earlier. Im Kwon-taek's movie takes the broadcasts as a documentary starting point, then spins off into a Fassbinderesque fiction about a dispersed family that comes back together, only to find that the pieces no longer fit. The issues are adult, and so is the treatment:no melodrama, no tub-thumping, but a piercing analysis of social and psychological blocks. TR

Gimme Shelter

(1970, US, 90 min)
d David Maysles, Albert Maysles, Charlotte Zwerin. *p* Ronald Schneider. *ph* David Maysles, Albert Maysles. *ed* Ellen Giffard, Joanne Burke, Robert Farren, Kent McKinney. *with* The Rolling Stones, Ike and Tina Turner, Jefferson Airplane.

● The Altamont movie, and something of a bummer: if you love the Stones, you're likely to be irritated by the fact that the camera stays on Mick Jagger for virtually every frame; if you're keen to understand why the notorious murder took place and what responsibility the musicians should admit to, you're left with a vacuous look of shock and confusion on the singer's face; and if you get off on violence accompanied by music played loud and raw, you'll love it. Still, it is a reminder that the '60s were not entirely about love, peace and limp liberalism. GA

Ginger & Fred (Ginger e Fred)

(1986, It/Fr/WGer, 127 min)
d Federico Fellini. *p* Alberto Grimaldi. *sc* Federico Fellini, Tonino Guerra, Tullio Pinelli. *ph* Tonino Delli Colli, Ennio Guarnieri. *ed* Nino Baragli, Ugo De Rossi, Ruggero Mastroianni. *ad* Dante Ferretti. *m* Nicola Piovani. *cast* Giulietta Masina, Marcello Mastroianni, Franco Fabrizi, Frederick von Ledenburg, Augusto Poderosi, Martin Maria Blau.

● The absence of Fellini's name before the title seems a just indication of a return to something warmer, quieter and more intimate than his grandiose freak shows. Confirming this is his reunion with his wife Masina after a gap of some 23 years, and with Mastroianni, so often his alter ego in the past. They play a couple of old hoofers, who used to tour the boards doing a respectful homage to Astaire and Rogers; they are being brought together after all these years by a TV show in Rome. A long first half, chronicling Ginger's return to the city, shows the place to be in the grip of much general urban decay, and allows Fellini his usual wallowing in all the quirky sideshows (a dead pig, lit up with fairy lights, dangles from the railway station roof). But once the couple finally get together, a warmth which Fellini has not displayed for years gradually seeps all over the screen. She is still trim, a courageous old fighter; he is seedy, but with an ironic detachment. Not even Fellini's deadly sarcasm about TV's horrible degradation of all human values can quite dim the magic that they restore with their little dance. As usual, Fellini doesn't have a lot to say; but it amounts to considerably more than his usual marginal doodlings, and it is irresistibly charming. CPea

Gingerbread Man, The

(1997, US, 114 min)
d Robert Altman. *p* Jeremy Tannenbaum. *sc* Al Hayes [Robert Altman]. *ph* Changwei Gu [Gu Changwei]. *ed* Geraldine Peroni. *pd* Stephen Altman. *m* Mark Isham. *cast* Kenneth Branagh, Embeth Davidtz, Robert Downey Jr, Daryl Hannah, Robert Duvall, Tom Berenger, Famke Janssen, Mae Whitman.

● Almost as soon as hotshot Savannah lawyer Rick Magruder (Branagh) picks up waitress Mallory Doss (Davidtz), you know he's being set up. If he's the shark here, she's the angler – that's the way these stories work. It's late and a hurricane's brewing, so Rick drives her home. She vents as she strips: her father is crazed, she explains, and threatening to kill her. She doesn't know where to turn, she says, turning to Rick, naked. He takes her and her case. Committed for psychiatric evaluation, her old man (Duvall) escapes with havoc in his heart. Altman and John Grisham make uneasy bedfellows, the one inspired by accident and chaos, the other a control freak, moralist and conservative. In this, Altman's wet and windy film of an unpublished Grisham story, the director keeps squeezing narrative strictures; it's an open and shut case with too much emotional baggage to fit. To a degree, the two authors cancel each other out – the movie probably won't satisfy fans of either. TCh

Ginger Snaps

(2000, Can, 104 min)
d John Fawcett. *p* Steven Hoban, Karen Lee Hall. *sc* Karen Walton. *ph* Thom Best. *ed* Brett Sullivan. *pd* Todd Cherniawsky. *m* Michael Shields. *cast* Emily Perkins, Katharine Isabelle, Kris Lemche, Jesse Moss, Danielle Hampton, Peter Keleghan, John Bourgeois, Mimi Rogers.

● Vampires, zombies and cat people may have their feminine side, but werewolves are almost always male. So when 16-year-old late-developer Ginger Fitzgerald starts experiencing heavy shit a couple of days after a hairy encounter with a savage dog, she automatically assumes it's related to menstruation. But her kid sister Brigitte realises the true nature of Ginger's lunar cycle, aghast as her former best friend in the whole world starts running wild with boys, staying out all night and leaving a trail of blood behind her. The film uncovers virgin territory in a genre we all thought had been flogged to death. It begins by establishing a bummed-out mood of suburban teen disaffection: Bailey Downs is a torpidly nondescript north American burg, hardly flattered by Fawcett's forceful low budget handiwork. Just as the Fitzgerald sisters get their kicks by photographing each other in staged suicide scenes, the movie gives off an exploitation movie buzz belied by its obvious intelligence. From Brigitte's 15-year-old perspective, lycanthropy is just a more extreme example of the gross hormonal hula hoops adolescence has in store; for Ginger, it's confusing – she feels she's grown a tail between her legs – but also liberating: 'I've got this ache, and I thought it was for sex, but it's to tear everything to fucking pieces.' With a trio of strong female performances (Isabelle is Ginger, Perkins her sister, Rogers her mom) and enough suspense to camouflage some dodgy special effects, this isn't just a good horror movie, it's a good movie. Period. TCh

Gion Festival Music (Gion Bayashi/aka A Geisha)

(1953, Jap, 87 min, b/w)
d Kenji Mizoguchi. *p* Masaichi Nagata. *sc* Yoshikata Yoda. *ph* Kazuo Miyagawa. *ed* Mitsuzo Miyata. *ad* Kazuyoshi Koike, Ichizo Kajitani. *cast* Michiyo Kogure, Ayaka Wakao, Seizaburo Kawazu, Kanji Koshiba, Eitaro Shindo, Ichiro Sugai, Haruo Tanaka.

● One of Mizoguchi's most affecting films, this concerns a geisha who takes a teenage novice under her wing and gives her gentle encouragement in rebelling against her fate at the hands of politicking, insensitive businessmen patrons. A hymn to women's mutual supportiveness, acutely aware that selling one's body is very different from selling one's emotions, and that sometimes it's just too late to change things for oneself. As elegantly made as ever, of course, and poignant in the extreme. GA

Giornata Particolare, Una

see Special Day, A

Giorno della prima di Close Up, Il (Day of the Premiere of Close Up)

(1995, It, 7 min)
d Nanni Moretti. *ph* Alessandro Pesci. *cast* Nanni Moretti.

● Pointed, poignant and marvellously droll Moretti short in which he worries about the opening, at his Nuovo Sacher cinema in Rome, of a Kiarostami masterpiece against stiff competition from the likes of *The Lion King*. One of the best and most honest movies ever made about the headaches of running an indie art cinema. GA

Giovanna d'Arco al Rogo (Jeanne au Bûcher/Joan at the Stake)

(1954, It/Fr, 70 min)
d Roberto Rossellini. *p* Giorgio Criscuolo, Franco Francese. *sc* Paul Claudel. *ph* Gabor Pogany. *ed* Jolanta Benvenuti, Robert Audenet. *ad* Carlo Maria Cristini. *m* Arthur Honegger. *cast* Ingrid Bergman, Tullio Carminati, Giancinto Prandelli, Augusto Romani, Agnese Dubbini.

● Anyone acquainted with the writings of the conservative Catholic mystic Paul Claudel will be best placed to fathom what his oratorio, scored by Honegger, is all about. The composer's references to medieval religious music and French folk song might possibly be apt, but this is still a tedious affair. The least of all the Joan of Arc pictures, it is perhaps best understood as a gift (of sorts) from a director to his wife/leading lady: prestigious, 'important' and finally rather private. Rossellini had already staged the oratorio in Milan and elsewhere, but evidently rethought it for the screen, at least to the extent of using glass shots and superimpositions; the colour is soft and soothing. BBa

Gips

(2000, Jap, 83 min)
d Akihiko Shiota. *p* Akio Saito, Hisanori Endo, Susumu Nakajima, Reiko Arakawa, Yuji Sadai, Hiroko Matsuda. *sc* Rena Horiuchi, Akihiko Shiota. *ph* Kazuhiro Suzuki. *ed* Takehiro Ishitani, Akihiko Shiota. *ad* Chie Matsumoto. *m* Gary Ashiya. *cast* Hinako Saeki, Machiko Ono, Kanji Tsuda, So Yamanaka, Hiromi Kuronuma.

● Ex-cinematographer Shiota specialises in disarmingly everyday stories of the desire to be dominated and humiliated, and this is his best yet. Tamaki (Saeki) discovered in high school that when she had to wear a gips cast after breaking her leg 'funny things' happened to her. Back then, a teacher killed himself over her. Now 22, she wears gips and walks on crutches for fun – and unfailingly attracts disposable 'slaves' to cater to her whims. Sometimes these 'slaves' meet sudden ends. The film centres on Tamaki's relationship with her first female 'slave' Kazuko (Ono), also 22, a transcription stenographer who lives in the same block and finds her life transformed the day she stops to help Tamaki. Funny, cruel, mildly suspenseful and (of course) deliciously perverse. TR

Girasoli, I

see Sunflower

Girl

(1998, US, 94 min)
d Jonathan Kahn. *p* Jeff Most, Chris Hanley, Brad Wyman. *sc* David Tolchinsky. *ph* Tami Reiker. *ed* Gillian Hutshing. *pd* Joanna Butler. *m* Michael Tavera. *cast* Dominique Swain, Sean Patrick Flanery, Tara Reid, Channon Roe, Summer Phoenix, Selma Blair, Portia Di Rossi.

● Ostensibly based on a novel by Blake Nelson, this is an unalloyed rip-off of the acclaimed US TV series *My So-Called Life*, in which straight-A student Claire Danes confided her romantic/hormonal confusions as she swapped her school books for boyfriends. This time it's Swain (Adrian Lyne's admirable Lolita) who falls head over heals for Portland, Oregon grunge rocker Todd Sparrow (Flanery), with plenty of smartsy asides to the audience but nothing new to say. TCh

Girl Can't Help It, The

(1956, US, 99 min)
d/p Frank Tashlin. *sc* Frank Tashlin, Herbert Baker. *ph* Leon Shamroy. *ed* James B Clark. *ad* Lyle Wheeler, Leland Fuller. *songs* Bobby Troup, Tony Iavello, Mel Leven, others. *cast* Jayne Mansfield, Tom Ewell, Edmond O'Brien, Julie London, Henry Jones, Little Richard, Fats Domino, Eddie Cochran, Gene Vincent.

● The quintessential '50s rock film, containing legendary appearances from Fats Domino, the Platters, Little Richard and Gene Vincent among its seventeen numbers, though the greatest musical moment is perhaps Eddie Cochran belting out '20 Flight Rock'. The story is a fairly biting satire on the PR worlds of rock and advertising, with Ewell as a press agent and Mansfield as a dumb blonde who rockets to stardom after imitating a prison siren on a rock record. This is the film in which Tashlin made Mansfield hold two milk bottles next to her boobs for a momentary visual gag; and he was capable of even crueller humour, as the sequel *Will Success Spoil Rock Hunter?* proved. DP

Girlfight

(1999, US, 110 min)
d Karyn Kusama. *p* Sarah Green, Martha Griffin, Maggie Renzi. *sc* Karyn Kusama. *ph* Patrick Cady. *ed* Plummy Tucker. *pd* Stephen Beatrice. *m* Theodore Shapiro. *cast* Michelle Rodriguez, Jaime Tirelli, Paul Calderon, Santiago Douglas, Ray Santiago, Elisa Bocanegra, Shannon Walker Williams, Victor Sierra.

● A volatile African American schoolgirl living in New York's projects decides to take up boxing, and inevitably faces incomprehension from her friends and opposition from her father, the kids already training at the gym, and, eventually, her boyfriend, who's reluctant to face her in the ring. At it's most basic, the story is pretty conventional. That said, however, Kusama's direction is imaginative, her attention to detail makes for credibility and clarity with regard to the dilemmas faced by her determined young heroine, and Rodriguez is quite astonishing in the lead role: tough, scary, stubborn, intelligent, and, when she finally lets down her defences, sweet, vulnerable and tender. GA

Girlfriend, The (La Amiga)

(1988, WGer/Arg, 108 min)
d Jeanine Meerapfel. *p* Jorge Estrada Mora, Kalus Volkenborn. *sc* Jeanine Meerapfel, Alcides Chiesa, Agnieszka Holland. *ph* Axel Block. *ed* Juliane Lorenz. *pd* Jorge Marchegiani, Rainer Schaper. *m* José Luis Castineira de Dios. *cast* Liv Ullmann, Cipe Lincovsky, Federico Luppi, Victor Laplace, Harry Baer, Lito Cruz.

●This fragmented history of a relationship between two women explores elasticity of friendship, loyalty and strength, and attempts to parallel the women's differing experiences of oppression. Raquel, a Jewish child refugee from Berlin, and Maria grow up in Buenos Aires in the '40s and '50s. Raquel (Lincovsky) realises her desire to become a well-known actress; Maria (Ullmann) marries a local boy and has three children. The two meet again in 1978, shortly after Maria's eldest has been abducted by 'security forces'. Anti-Semitic attacks scare Raquel into fleeing to Berlin, to return to an uneasy democracy of sorts when Argentina's military government falls. Maria has devoted herself to an uncompromising struggle to locate her missing son, one of many. Raquel has exorcised herself in Berlin (but it's a shady part of the narrative) and returns somehow more reflective; Maria has been transformed from passive onlooker to vociferous leader of 'The Mothers'. The story rattles on movingly and competently, but might have been more fulfilling had the themes been better balanced: the dialectic only hints at similarities between the opression faced in Europe in the thirties and Argentina in the seventies, at the anti-Semitism that surfaced during both traumatic periods. JGl

Girlfriends

(1978, US, 88 min)
d Claudia Weill. *p* Claudia Weill, Jan Saunders. *sc* Vicki Polon. *ph* Fred Murphy. *ed* Suzanne Pettit. *ad* Patrizia von Brandenstein. *m* Michael Small. *cast* Melanie Mayron, Anita Skinner, Eli Wallach, Christopher Guest, Amy Wright, Viveca Lindfors, Bob Balaban, Mike Kellin.

● The heroine of Weill's chronicle of a woman in New York today – not pretty, not gamine, not even *jolie laide* – is an apprentice 'art' photographer, an uneasy heterosexual in a world of obsessively potato-mashing males, who is bereft when her poetry-writing flatmate marries and moves out. The slightly spaced gay dance freak who replaces her gets chucked (nice touch) when she borrows our heroine's blouse. But not before she catalyses the film's sidelong appraisal of lesbianism – treated, unusually, as a fair option. The net effect is a warm (if not entirely cosy) liberal feminism. MM

Girlfriends, The

see Amiche, Le

Girl from Lorraine, A (La Provinciale)

(1980, Fr/Switz, 112 min)
d Claude Goretta. *p* Yves Peyrot, Raymond Pousaz. *sc* Claude Goretta, Jacques Kirsner, Rosine Rochette. *ph* Philippe Rousselot, Dominique Bringuier. *ed* Joële van Effenterre, Nelly Meunier. *ad* Jacques Bufnoir. *m* Arié Dzierlatka. *cast* Nathalie Baye, Angela Winkler, Bruno Ganz, Dominique Paturel, Roland Monod, Jean Obé, Henri Poirier.

●Single, stifled and 31, Baye's '*provinciale*' uproots for a Paris peopled largely with fellow exiles (Swiss pill salesman Ganz, struggling German actress Winkler) in search of work and...well, she's not quite sure what else. What she doesn't want, but all she finds, is a succession of relationships set in parentheses, circumscribed as much by economics as emotions. Ganz's promotion ends their affair; friend Winkler sells herself to keep kids and career together. Baye is an only slightly tougher cousin of Goretta's tragic 'lace-maker', but every bit as 'innocent', and her director really has nothing new to say in this insubstantially vague portrait of sensitivity and metropolitan moral recession. A romanticist's tut-tutting just doesn't cut deep enough: it's no more than a wistful sigh of a movie. PT

Girl from Maxim's, The

(1933, GB, 79 min, b/w)
d Alexander Korda. *p* Ludovico Toeplitz, Alexander Korda. *sc* Lajos Biro, Harry Graham, Henri Jeanson. *ph* Georges Périnal. *ed* Harold Young, R Bettinson. *ad* Vincent Korda. *m* Kurt Schroeder. *cast* Frances Day, Leslie Henson, George Grossmith, Stanley Holloway, Lady Tree, Evan Thomas, Eric Portman.

●Made before Korda hit the big time with *The Private Life of Henry VIII* and the lavish Denham epics, this adaptation of a Feydeau farce impresses despite the budgetary constraints. With brother Vincent's meticulous art direction and Périnal's photography, Korda convincingly creates the ambience of hypocritical decadence that epitomises the 'gay nineties'. Maxim's, presided over by Day's cunningly quixotic coquette, becomes a palace of boisterous female exhibitionism where men pay for their pleasure by exposing themselves as fatuous ninnies. The brilliant farce-playing from snorting old buffer Grossmith, splutteringly pompous Henson, and the gnarled and knotty Lady Tree, completes the ingredients for a bold, elegant, visually exciting film. RMy

Girl from Trieste, The (La Ragazza di Trieste)

(1983, It, 103 min)
d Pasquale Festa Campanile. *p* Achille Manzotti. *sc* Ottavio Jemma. *ph* Alfio Contini. *ed* Amedeo Salfa. *pd* Ezio Altieri. *m* Riz Ortolani. *cast* Ben Gazzara, Ornella Muti, Mimsy Farmer, Andrea Ferreol, Jean-Claude Brialy, William Berger.

●Muti is saved from a watery grave, artificially respirated, and then confronted on the beach by expatriate cartoonist Gazzara, who in no time is brazenly squinting down her bodice. When she confesses to doing such suicidal things for kicks, it's plain he should duck for cover, but as her eccentricity runs on down to barking lunacy, so he becomes more and more obsessive, the fool. By the time she has shaved her head bald, it's clear that it's going to end badly, and her desperate yearning for punishment is going to allow Campanile full rein in showing all its festering detail. Gazzara coasts through it, rumbling away in his best Hemingway manner; and Muti seems to be cornering the market in doe-eyed doxies with a serious Catholic problem; the rest is just a gaudy treadmill. CPea

Girl in a Boot (Einmal Ku'damm und Zurück)

(1983, WGer, 96 min)
d Herbert Ballmann. *sc* Jürgen Engert. *ph* Ingo Hamer. *ed* Hans Otto Krüger, Ruth Kusche. *ad* Hans-Jürgen Kiebach. *m* Jürgen Knieper. *cast* Ursela Monn, Christian Kohlund, Evelyn Meyka, Peter Schiff, Peter Seum, Bettina Martell, Brigitte Mira.

●The girl is Ulla, a spunky East Berlin fräulein, a little bored with her job at the Engineering Works and her long-standing boyfriend; given a lift one day by Thomas, a suave chef at the Swiss Embassy, she finds herself more than ready to indulge in a little nocturnal East-West relations. Thomas has taken to nipping across Checkpoint Charlie for pizzas at his favourite restaurant, so Ulla suggests he take her for a quick 'Ausflug' to the West, secreted in the boot of his Merc... But, oh yes, things go wrong. Shot with all the panache of a McDonalds advertisement with music to match, the movie adds up to little more than an unimaginative love story that reduces the traumas of life in the 'divided city' to casuistic cliché. Symptomatically, the only enlivening diversion is provided by two minor performances: Peter Schiff as Ulla's concerned Communist father, and Fassbinder regular Brigitte Mira as a toilet attendant. WH

Girl in Every Port, A

(1928, US, 5,500 ft, b/w)
d Howard Hawks. *p* William Fox. *sc* Seton I Miller, James K McGuinness, Howard Hawks, Sidney Lanfield. *ph* L William O'Connell, Rudolph J Berquist. *ed* Ralph Dixon. *ad* William Darling. *cast* Victor McLaglen, Robert Armstrong, Louise Brooks, Marcia Casajuana, Myrna Loy, William Demarest, Sally Rand.

●'That big ox means more to me than any woman!' says Armstrong's sailor (via an intertitle) in Hawks' engagingly naive fourth film, thus paving the way for decades of buddy love. A strange choice, you might think, when the ox is McLaglen and the woman is the almost divine Louise Brooks, glowing with beauty in a cloche hat and beguiling fringe. But the film's allegiances remain so much with the triangle's male sides – two sailors who stumble over each other befriending the same girls in the same ports – that the result is dramatically lopsided. Technically, however, it's perfectly adroit, swiftly paced, clearly detailed, with only a modicum of overacting from the lads when they're tanked up and spoiling for trouble ('Let's pick another fight and go fifty-fifty on the fun'). No Hawksperson should miss it. GB

Girl, Interrupted

(1999, US, 127 min)
d James Mangold. *p* Douglas Wick, Cathy Konrad. *sc* James Mangold, Lisa Loomer, Anna Hamilton Phelan. *ph* Jack Green. *ed* Kevin Tent. *pd* Richard Hoover. *m* Mychael Danna. *cast* Winona Ryder, Angelina Jolie, Clea Duvall, Brittany Murphy, Elisabeth Moss, Jared Leto, Jeffrey Tambor, Vanessa Redgrave, Whoopi Goldberg.

●An open wound of a girl, Susanna Kaysen (Ryder), puts up only minimal resistance when her parents bundle her off to a mental asylum. There she meets a pack of similarly troubled souls, led by rebel Lisa (Jolie). In this glossy adaptation of Kaysen's '60s memoir, it's the beauty of the two leads you first notice. Jolie has a flaming, slithery, childlike presence. During a group outing, Susanna is accosted by the wife of her former lover, unleashing Lisa's protective rage. As the humiliated woman backs away, the girls roar with delight and we feel like roaring with them. It's not just Susanna who's being seduced here, it's us. Does it matter that every time Jolie's off-screen the film wilts a little? Ryder should be perfect as the bright spark; her lines are sharp as a knife. There's a gap, however, between what we hear and what we see. Ryder's too wide-eyed and cutesy, and when we see her with nurse Valerie (Goldberg), we know it's only a matter of time before they start hugging. As Lisa's dark side turns pitch black, she hisses to Susanna: 'You need me to play the villain, 'cos it makes you the good guy' – a clever attempt by Lisa to wriggle free of her own guilt. As a summary of Ryder's schtick, though, it's bang on. CO'Su

Girl in the Picture, The

(1985, GB, 91 min)
d Cary Parker. *p* Patrick Higson. *sc* Cary Parker. *ph* Dick Pope. *ed* Burt Eels. *pd* Jemma Jackson. *m* Ron Geesin. *cast* John Gordon Sinclair, Irina Brook, David McKay, Gregor Fisher, Paul Young, Rikki Fulton.

●Sinclair plays a photographer's assistant who doesn't know when he's well off. Having decided to give his live-in girlfriend (Brook) the boot – some nice comic moments as he tries to pluck up the courage to tell her – he's soon mooning about wondering why he can never get a slice of the action; a feeling shared by his workmate Kenny (McKay), who is pining for a mystery 'girl in the picture' he has just developed. But of course there's always someone worse off, and into the shop to order some wedding photos comes Bill (Fisher), harbouring catastrophic doubts about his forthcoming marriage. The comic confusions and misunderstandings as these three incompetents try to help each other out look a little like pastiche Bill Forsyth. But it's still an engaging debut from writer/director Parker, a classy light comedy with a firmer hold on reality than most of its American teenage counterparts. CS

Girl in the Sneakers, The (Dokhtari Ba Kafsh-Hay-e Katani)

(1999, Iran, 110 min)
d/p Rassul Sadr Ameli. *sc* Peyman Qasemkhani, Fereydoun Farhudi. *ph* Dariush Ayyari. *ed* Mostafa Kherqe-Push. *pd* Ali Abedini. *m* Bahram Saeedi. *cast* Pegah Ahangarani, Majid Hajizade, Akram Mohammadi, Abdolreza Akbari, Mahmud Jafari.
●Not Iranian children this time, but an Iranian teenager. Opening as a realist family drama, the film develops into a freefloating portrait of a runaway girl's 24 hours in Tehran. Tadaei is strung out because, after walking and talking heart to heart with a boy her age, a policeman intervenes and returns her home. After medical and legal investigations, the family escorts her to school next day, whereupon she really walks. Structurally it's a little vague, but Tadaei's encounters with protective or preying strangers cut a swath through Tehrani society, and suggest what it takes to sap the spirit of a headstrong girl. NB

Girl Most Likely, The

(1957, US, 98 min)
d Mitchell Leisen. *p* Stanley Rubin. *sc* Devery Freeman. *ph* Robert Planck. *ed* Harry Marker, Dean Harrison. *ad* Albert S D'Agostino, George W Davis. *songs* Hugh Martin, Ralph Blane. *cast* Jane Powell, Cliff Robertson, Keith Andes, Tommy Noonan, Kaye Ballard, Una Merkel.
●Leisen's last theatrical feature – a musical remake of *Tom, Dick and Harry*, with Powell agonising prettily over which of three beaux (mechanic Robertson, wealthy Andes, real estate salesman Noonan) to wed – is admittedly far from his best, but not without interest. True, the cast don't have the necessary talent or fizz to do justice to either Gower Champion's choreography or the often splendidly gaudy art direction (shot in Technicolor, of course). But Leisen's handling of his hand-me-down material is civilised and vibrant, and while it's nowhere near as memorable as his *Lady in the Dark*, the film provides further evidence that he was one of Hollywood's most underrated directors. GA

Girl of Good Family, A (Liangjia funü)

(1985, China, 110 min)
d Huang Jianzhong. *p* Ma Qianli. *sc* Li Kuanding. *ph* Yun Wenyao. *ed* Huang Pu Keren. *pd* Shao Ruigang. *m* Sui Wanchun. *cast* Cong Shan, Zhang Weixin, Wang Jiayi, Liang Yan, Zhang Jian.
●Much influenced by *Yellow Earth* (whose director, Chen Kaige, worked as Huang Jianzhong's assistant on two previous movies), this tale of an arranged marriage between an 18-year-old girl and an infant boy confirms that Chinese cinema has acquired a new candour and readiness to broach 'difficult' material. The girl naturally get the hots for a strapping lad of her own age, pushing the film to a climax that comes straight from traditional melodrama. But most of it is freshly observed, understated, and lushly imagistic. TR

Girl on a Motorcycle (La Motocyclette/Naked Under Leather)

(1968, GB/Fr, 91 min)
d Jack Cardiff. *p* William Sassoon. *sc* Ronald Duncan. *ph* Jack Cardiff, René Guissart. *ed* Peter Musgrave. *ad* Russell Hagg, Jean d'Eaubonne. *m* Les Reed. *cast* Marianne Faithfull, Alain Delon, Roger Mutton, Marius Goring, Catherine Jourdan, Jean Leduc.
●Thrill as adulterous Faithfull zips off into the arms of former lover Delon for a bout of leather-clad, tank-straddling, high-octane how's-your-father, shot by director/cameraman Cardiff as if it were high art indeed. Proof that the Swinging '60s could be toweringly soporific. TJ

Girl on the Bridge, The (La Fille sur le Pont)

(1998, Fr, 92 min, b/w)
d Patrice Leconte. *p* Christian Fechner. *sc* Serge Frydman. *ph* Jean-Marie Dreujou. *ed* Joëlle Hache. *ad* Yvan Maussion. *cast* Daniel Auteuil, Vanessa Paradis, Claude Aufaure, Farouk Bermouga, Bertie Cortez, Nicola Donato.
●Vanessa Paradis brings out the fey side of older French male directors who should know better. Leconte has always been a sucker for a pretty curve, but he used to work around that with an idiosyncratic mix of flamboyant storytelling and a good nose for mischief making. What with its monochrome 'Scope photography and shake-a-limb camerawork, and the plot's magic-exotic conceits about knife throwing and telepathic love, here Leconte comes over all moonfaced romantic for a character who seems a wet rag even before she tries jumping in the Seine. Poor Adele, bad luck seems to follow her. Gabor (Auteil), who stops her jump, insists that her luck can change, and to prove it he throws knives at her, this being his stage act. They invest in some circus clothes, and ply their newfound luck around the Riviera. And because they're apparently psychic, they start wandering about talking to the ether like damn fools. Leconte too seems to be communing with himself, or some fantasy audience. The film has the precocious gloss of an advert, a similarly crass conception of human connection, and an utter lack of rhyme or reason. NB

Girl Rosemarie, The

see Mädchen Rosemarie, Das

Girls, The

see Bonnes Femmes, Les

Girls! Girls! Girls!

(1962, US, 106 min)
d Norman Taurog. *p* Hal B Wallis. *sc* Edward Anhalt, Allan Weiss. *ph* Loyal Griggs. *ed* Warren Low. *ad* Hal Pereira, Walter Tyler. *songs* Jerry Lieber, Mike Stoller, Sid Tepper, Otis Blackwell, others. *cast* Elvis Presley, Stella Stevens, Laurel Goodwin, Jeremy Slate, Guy Lee, Nestor Paiva.
●Elvis as a nightclub singer, pursued by girls but more concerned about his beloved fishing-boat. Co-scripted by Edward Anhalt, who won an Oscar for the 'Becket' screenplay two years later, this is not exactly a feast of wit and erudition; but it is one of Presley's better lightweight vehicles, thanks largely to the presence of Stella Stevens, one of the few leading ladies who gave him any competition. AC

Girl, She is 100%, A (Hyaku percent no Onna no Ko)

(1983, Jap, 11 min, b/w & col)
d Naoto Yamakawa. *p* Masayasu Kato. *sc/ph/ed/ad* Naoto Yamakawa. *cast* Yoshinari Kuwamoto, Shigeru Muroi, Kazunao Sakaguchi, Akifumi Yamaguchi.
●Yamakawa's second adaptation of a Haruki Murakami story (following *Attack on a Bakery*) is another brilliant rethink of Murakami's existential ambivalence in film terms, using stills, pixillation, minimal animation and voice-over to deconstruct a 'sentimental city romance'. A young man passes a young woman in a Harajuku backstreet; it occurs to him only later that she was the ideal woman he had always looked for. And so he imagines a scenario in which they meet, agree that they're all too perfectly matched and part, waiting to see if 'fate' will bring them back together. Sharp, witty and beyond fashion, this is a small, many faceted gem. TR

Girls He Left Behind, The

see Gang's All Here, The

Girl Shy

(1924, US, 88 min, b/w)
d Fred Newmeyer, Sam Taylor. *sc* Sam Taylor, Ted Wilde, Tim Whelan, Tommy Gray. *ph* Walter Lundin, Henry N Kohler. *ed* Allen McNeil. *ad* Liell K Vedder. *cast* Harold Lloyd, Jobyna Ralston, Richard Daniels, Carlton Griffin.
●Lloyd is a timid tailor's apprentice who after hours has been writing a fantasy book, 'The Secret of Making Love' (later retitled 'A Boob's Diary'), two episodes of which are exactly illustrated: 'My Vampire', in which Harold professes 'indifference', and 'My Flapper' in which he adopts the caveman approach. There are in addition three classic sequences: one in which Harold becomes glued to the girl he's wooing; another when he visits the LA publishers to whom he's submitted his book and is mobbed by the hysterical typing pool; and finally the climactic rescue chase, to prevent the marriage of the girl to a mustachioed bigamist, with its glorious string of knife-edge stunts. JPy

Girls in Uniform

see Mädchen in Uniform

Girl 6

(1996, US, 108 min)
d/p Spike Lee. *sc* Suzan-Lori Parks. *ph* Malik Sayeed. *ed* Sam Pollard. *pd* Ina Mayhew. *m* Prince. *cast* Theresa Randle, Isaiah Washington, Spike Lee, Jennifer Lewis, Quentin Tarantino, Debi Mazar, Naomi Campbell, Larry Pine, Madonna, John Turturro, Ron Silver.
●Lee's follow-up to *She's Gotta Have It* has been a long time coming, but this freewheeling comic celebration of an independent New York City gal fits the bill: it even starts with Judy (Randle) auditioning with a monologue from the earlier film. When the director (Tarantino) insists she strip, she quits, and her acting career appears to be over until she lands a job as a phone-sex operator. Although her friend Jimmy (Lee) is appalled, in many ways 'Girl 6' is a liberating, therapeutic role: sexually she's always in control, she's well paid, and there's no colour barrier. But is Judy hung-up on Girl 6? If this synopsis suggests a plot, Lee must have had other things on his mind. Instead, the film's eclectic, New Wave-ish pick-'n'mix of fantasy, parody and pastiche sets the stage for star cameos à go-go. Randle changes her look with every scene, throws in faultless impersonations of Dorothy Dandridge and Pam Grier, and almost holds it all together. After this role, she should never have to audition again. There's something refreshing about the film's reckless proximity to anarchy, the stylishly imaginative cinematography and lusciously exorbitant Prince soundtrack, even if it does ring hollow when Lee tries to get serious on us. TCh

Girls Just Want to Have Fun

(1985, US, 89 min)
d Alan Metter. *p* Chuck Russell. *sc* Amy Spies. *ph* Thomas Ackerman. *ed* David Rawlins, Lorenzo DeStefano. *pd* Jeffrey Staggs. *m* Thomas Newman. *cast* Sarah Jessica Parker, Lee Montgomery, Helen Hunt, Morgan Woodward, Jonathan Silverman, Ed Lauter, Holly Gagnier, Shannen Doherty.
●Sundry youth picture stand-bys one imagined were fossilised by the mid-'60s get an '80s spin in this piece of celluloid candy-floss, which has Parker outwitting the high school vicious circle to carry the day at a TV dance contest. All very mild indeed; and significantly less hard-hitting than the jaunty video for the Cyndi Lauper smash that gives the movie its title (this being a penny-pinching New World production, it's a soundalike version we actually get to hear). While Parker's lead is on the vapid side, Hunt's fizzing performance as her go-ahead best pal makes you wonder why the actress subsequently took so long to break through to the Hollywood front rank. TJ

Girls' Night

(1997, GB/US, 102 min)
d Nick Hurran. *p* Bill Boyes. *sc* Kay Mellor. *ph* David Odd. *ed* John Richards. *pd* Taff Batley. *m* Ed Shearmur. *cast* Brenda Blethyn, Julie Walters, Kris Kristofferson, George Costigan, James Gaddas, Philip Jackson, Sue Cleaver, Meera Syal.
●Jackie (Walters) and sister-in-law Dawn (Blethyn) are chalk 'n' cheese: Jackie, loud and flirty; Dawn, devoted to her family. They work in the same factory in a small northern town and live for bingo, but when Dawn hits the jackpot it's only to discover she has secondary cancer. The solution, Jackie decides, is a Las Vegas holiday. The women meet a grizzled, sexy cowboy (Kristofferson). Granada TV stumped up the money and it shows: the scenes in the factory are pure *Coronation Street*, circa 1975. But with the onset of Dawn's illness, the tone starts to wobble,

part *Shirley Valentine* cuteness, part *Bridges of Madison County* gloom. The best moments are those without dialogue (Dawn lying in hospital, the dimmed ward ghostly quiet, rain falling outside). Distinctly soapy, though. CO'Su

Girls to be Married, The (Chujia Nü)

(1990, China, 96 min)
d Wang Jin. *p* Zhao Qingqiang. *sc* He Mengfang. *ph* Zhao Xiaoshi. *ed* Yan Xiuying. *ad* He Qun. *m* Wang Shi. *cast* Shen Rong, Tao Huimin, Ju Xue.

● Five young girls, faced with the prospect of marriage (four of them arranged), make a suicide pact: it's to be hanging *en masse*, bedecked in festive red corduroy. As they wait, their family travails give them every reason to wish for a rapid getaway. From the shocking, perverse tableau at the beginning – a bride hangs herself during a wedding procession – the film draws links between love and death, underscoring the grim lot reserved for women in the rural community in which it is set. Admirers of *Ju Dou* will recognise some of the settings, and even some of the visual style; but in typical Hong Kong fashion, the more sober themes are tempered by splashes of spectacle and heart-tugging rhetoric (it's heavy on the soft-focus). Moving, beautiful, and not a little unsettling. JRo

Girls Town

(1996, US, 89 min)
d Jim McKay. *p* Lauren Zalaznick. *sc* Jim McKay, Denise Casano, Anna Grace, Lili Taylor. *ph* Russell Lee Fine. *ed* Kate Williams, Jim McKay, Alex Hall. *pd* David Doernberg. *m* Guru. *cast* Lili Taylor, Bruklin Harris, Anna Grace, Aunjanue Ellis, Ramya Pratt, Asia Minor.

● It's high school senior year for four gals from Hackensack, NJ, but this lot isn't going to the prom, and they don't give a toss either. Nikki (Ellis) has a place at college to look forward to, Angela (Harris) pours her innermost thoughts into her poetry, Emma (Grace) helps out at the women's shelter, while Patti (Taylor) has a kid to look after and car maintenance classes to go to, or she'll be kept behind yet another year. When they learn that one of them has been raped but not let on, it strengthens their bond, and sets them up for revenge. There's a terrific scene where the guy's car gets it: keys are scraped along paintwork, tyres ripped open, 'rapist' daubed on the bonnet; as the girls surprise themselves with the ferocity of their attack. A detailed, smartly observed chronicle about growing up, even if the girls' friendship crosses ethnic and class boundaries a little too easily, and the improv framework sometimes makes the plot a bit sticky. TJ

Girl with Brains in Her Feet, The

(1997, GB, 98 min)
d Roberto Bangura. *p* Don Boyd. *sc* Jo Hodges. *ph* Peter Butler. *ed* Adam Ross. *pd* Lynn Bird. *m* Rob Lane. *cast* Joanna Ward, Amanda Mealing, John Thompson, Jamie McIntosh, Joshua Henderson, Jodie Smith.

● This directorial debut may explore familiar territory (a girl's coming of age), but it opens up Jo Hodges' screenplay with a light touch, and elicits engaging performances from its principals, notably Joanna Ward as 13-year-old 'Jack'. Secret smoker, T-Rex fan and nascent track runner, this energetic Leicester schoolgirl shows a nifty ability to sidestep the challenges and irritations life throws up, be it domestic interference (her mum's a nag), scarcely veiled racism, the perils of adolescent sex – or the lack of training shoes. It's not in the league of *Kes*, on which it leans for inspiration, but it gives notice of sensitive new talent. WH

Girl with Green Eyes

(1963, GB, 91 min, b/w)
d Desmond Davis. *p* Oscar Lewenstein. *sc* Edna O'Brien. *ph* Manny Wyn. *ed* Brian Smedley-Aston. *ad* Edward Marshall. *m* John Addison. *cast* Rita Tushingham, Peter Finch, Lynn Redgrave, Marie Kean, Arthur O'Sullivan, Julian Glover, TP McKenna.

● Co Clare colleen Tushingham heads up to Dublin, where she shares digs with her best pal Redgrave, works in a grocer's, and falls for middle-aged writer Finch, whose wife and kids have long since left him. Unlike other British films of the time, cameraman Davis's assured debut, scripted by Edna O'Brien from her own novel, doesn't pile on the kitchen sink realism. It concentrates on the characters' fumbling emotional insecurities and the keenly observed background of emotional repression. Has worn well. TJ

Girl with the Red Hair, The (Het Meisje met het Rode Haar)

(1981, Neth, 114 min)
d Ben Verbong. *p* Chris Brouwer, Haig Balian. *sc* Ben Verbong, Pieter de Vos. *ph* Theo van de Sande. *ed* Ton de Graaff. *ad* Dorus van der Linden. *m* Nicola Piovani. *cast* Renée Soutendijk, Peter Tuinman, Ada Bouwman, Robert Delhez, Johan Leysen, Loes Luca.

● A remarkably assured first feature, charting the real-life resistance activities of the (for the Dutch) almost legendary World War II heroine Hannie Schaft. It paints a detailed, lucid portrait of a respectable woman abandoning her legal studies and overcoming qualms to become an efficient killer, hunted by the occupant Nazis and increasingly at odds with the acquiescent Dutch authorities. Avoiding 'aren't Nazis slimy' clichés, Verbong constructs a resonant context in which his courageous heroine discovers the personally tragic consequences of her militant choice. If the film is finally too restrained to achieve the emotional power of its acknowledged models (Melville's *L'Armée des Ombres*, Bertolucci's *The Conformist*), the precise, exquisite images – in desaturated sepia colours – and strong performances nevertheless convey both honesty and intelligence: it's engrossing, sensitive, and despite the period setting, totally relevant. GA

Giro City

(1982, GB, 102 min)
d Karl Francis. *p* Sophie Balhetchet, David Payne. *sc* Karl Francis. *ph* Curtis Clark. *ed* Neil Thomson. *ad* Jamie Leonard. *m* Alun Francis. *cast* Glenda Jackson, Jon Finch, Kenneth Colley, James Donnelly, Emrys James, Karen Archer.

● Exercising something of the fascination of a crossword puzzle, this angry parable about media censorship is cast as an investigative report about two investigative reports, often assuming thriller form as reporters lurk and cameras whirr, the stories are worried over and painstakingly reworked, until the exhilarating moment when the pieces finally fall into place. One story is about a Welsh farmer stubbornly resisting eviction, the other about the political situation in Ireland. Both prove to involve 'higher interests'; both end on the cutting-room floor; and the reporters are left to bite on the bullet: 'You never learn, do you? You have to compromise'. Guilty itself of a little (understandable) compromise in casting star names for what comes on like a documentary, the film nevertheless still bites, and is honest enough to query (without really exploring) the honesty of reporters who rage against, but accept, the status quo of compromise. TM

Giselle

(1981, Braz, 95 min)
d Victor Di Mello. *p* Carlo Mossy, Bernado Goldszal. *sc* Victor di Mello. *ph* Antonio Gonçalves. *ed* Giuseppe Baldacconi. *cast* Alba Valéria, Carlo Mossy, Maria Lucia Dahl, Nildo Parente, Ricardo Faria, Monique Lafond.

● Pretty Giselle returns from her studies in Europe to Brazil where, on the ranch that is home to her father and stepmother, she rolls head, shoulders and eyes in the orgasmic embrace of all and sundry to the accompaniment of an international MOR soundtrack. The distinguishing feature of this not unenjoyable softcore is the sheer variety of sexual permutation (homo and heterosexual two, three and foursomes, paedophilia), while elements of politics and violence which threaten to introduce a new dimension to the film are quickly manipulated to eliminate any hindrance to the family's lovemaking. All finally go their separate ways, with Giselle returning to Europe – for more of the same. FD

Gito, the Ungrateful (Gito, l'Ingrat)

(1992, Burundi/Switz/Fr, 90 min)
d Léonce Ngabo. *p* Jacques Sandoz. *sc* Léonce Ngabo, Patrick Herzig. *ph* Matthias Kaelin. *ed* Dominique Roy. *pd* Joseph Kpobly. *m* Pierre-Alain Hofmann. *cast* Joseph Kumbela, Marie Bunel, Aoua Sangare, Louis Kamatari.

● In outline, Ngabo's (and Burundi's) first feature sounds like an Eric Rohmer comedy of manners. Back home with a Parisian diploma in his pocket and expecting to walk into a civil service job, Gito finds himself both unemployed and caught between two women: his current French girlfriend Christine and his local old flame Flora. If it plays more like sit-com than Rohmer, then that reflects Ngabo's need to appeal to audiences at home *and* abroad and his well-developed sense of humour: the film runs rings round both male pride and the emerging African bourgeoisie. Minor, but highly watchable. TR

Giù la Testa (Duck, You Sucker/A Fistful of Dynamite/Once Upon a Time – the Revolution)

(1971, It, 150 min)
d Sergio Leone. *p* Fulvio Morsella. *sc* Luciano Vincenzoni, Sergio Donati, Sergio Leone. *ph* Giuseppe Ruzzolini. *ed* Nino Baragli. *ad* Andrea Crisanti. *m* Ennio Morricone. *cast* James Coburn, Rod Steiger, Romolo Valli, Maria Monti, Rik Battaglia, Franco Graziosi.

● Having already, in *Once Upon a Time in the West*, taken energetic liberties with the typical (John) Fordian Western, it's not surprising that Leone should have taken a sideswipe at another of the director's stereotypes, the revolutionary Irishman, in the second part of his trilogy of political fables. But the specific IRA background of Coburn's Sean is as ultimately unimportant as the specific Mexican setting: with characteristic flamboyance, Leone is more concerned to build a composite of the all-purpose, all-causes revolutionary 'John Doe' from Sean's informed commitment and the naïve brute force of Steiger's Juan. The most wry of the political spaghettis, and wholly wonderful. PT

Giulietta degli Spiriti

see Juliet of the Spirits

Give 'em Hell

see Ça va Barder…

Give My Regards to Broad Street

(1984, GB, 108 min)
d Peter Webb. *p* Andros Epaminondas. *sc* Paul McCartney. *ph* Ian McMillan. *ed* Peter Beston. *pd* Anthony Pratt. *m* Paul McCartney. *cast* Paul McCartney, Bryan Brown, Ringo Starr, Barbara Bach, Linda McCartney, Tracey Ullman, Ralph Richardson.

● Pop star Paul zooms around in his own Herbie car, records at the Beeb, attends board meetings, smiles kindly at aged autograph hunters, takes champers, and performs an awful lot of music. The documentary stuff is propped up by a plot about some missing master tapes (which has the distinction of being both uneventful and baffling), some embarrassingly old-fashioned visual set pieces, and cameo roles in which Ullman manages to be unfunny and Richardson looks understandably tired. Token attempt at street cred: if Paul doesn't get the tapes back, he'll be taken over by a sunglasses-wearing business shark. SGr

Give Us Tomorrow

(1978, GB, 94 min)
d/p/sc Donovan Winter. *ph* Austin Parkinson. *m* John Fox. *cast* Sylvia Syms, Derren Nesbitt, James Kerry, Donna Evans, Matthew Haslett, Alan Guy.

● Good old True Brit cinema does it again with this half-hearted headline exploitation, in a sub-TV thriller vein, that leaves you in no doubt that it was 'entirely shot on location in Orpington, Kent'. It's unlikely that it even disturbed the residents with its tale of a bank robbery gone wrong and a suburban siege in which heavyweight lumpen yob (Nesbitt) and dole-queue kid (Guy) hold 'respectable' bank manager's family hostage. If tempted to lay down money for this rubbish, you should get a few compensatory chuckles from a captor-captive slanging match on the economics of the class system, and from the instant love affair between virgin daughter and afore-mentioned kid; but you'll still want your cash back by the time the script's stabs at Social Comment are exhausted. PT

Gladiator

(1992, US, 102 min)
d Rowdy Herrington. *p* Steve Roth, Frank Price. *sc* Lyle Kessler, Robert Kamen. *ph* Tak Fujimoto. *ed* Peter Zinner. *pd* Gregg Fonseca. *m* Brad Fiedel. *cast* James Marshall, Cuba Gooding Jr, Brian Dennehy, Robert Loggia, Ossie Davis, John Heard, Jon Seda, Cara Buono, Lance Slaughter.
● Herrington follows up the state-of-the-art violence of *Road House* with a leaner, more controlled tale of back-street boxing in Chicago. Blackmailed by corrupt promoter Horn (Dennehy), white schoolboy boxer Tommy Riley (Marshall) is forced into a fight scene where cheating is normal. Horn bills Tommy as 'The Great White Hope', but Tommy's motivation – paying off his father's gambling debts – hardly sets him alongside 'hungry' white champions of the past. For his black opponents, on the other hand, their fists are their only passport out of the ghetto. It's this desperation, and the racial undercurrent of black versus white, that Horn is keen to exploit. Marshall makes a promising feature debut; and Herrington, pushing beyond the expected triumph-of-the-underdog clichés, underpins the crowd-pleasing Rocky-style fight action with some unobtrusive social comment and confident visual storytelling. NF

Gladiator (100)

(2000, US, 155 min)
d Ridley Scott. *p* Douglas Wick, David Franzoni, Branko Lustig. *sc* David Franzoni, John Logan, William Nicholson. *ph* John Mathieson. *ed* Pietro Scalia. *pd* Arthur Max. *m* Hans Zimmer, Lisa Gerrard. *cast* Russell Crowe, Joaquin Phoenix, Connie Nielsen, Oliver Reed, Richard Harris, Derek Jacobi, Djimon Hounsou, David Schofield, John Shrapnel, Tomas Arana, Ralf Moeller, Spencer Treat Clark, David Hemmings.
● The late second century: the Roman army is fighting Germania, but that's a small problem for general Maximus (Crowe), compared to his relations with the Imperial dynasty. Ailing Marcus Aurelius (Harris) would like his favourite soldier and confidant to take over and pass power to the Senate. His heir, however – the insecure Commodus (Phoenix) – feels miffed by the slight. Having ensured dad dies in his arms, the new Emperor exerts his murderous authority. But Maximus won't swear loyalty, and after a narrow escape, the enslaved ex-general, bent on vengeance, gets a chance to return to Rome as a gladiator. Scott's sword and sandal spectacular is a bloody good yarn, packed with epic pomp and pageantry, dastardly plots, massed action and forthright, fundamental emotions. That said, for all the efforts to suggest authenticity, it stays true to peplum tradition, not only in its age old clichés, but in saying as much about our era as that in which it's set. The implausibly efficient carnage of the opening battle evokes post-'Nam war movies; Maximus' improbably swift, deep bonding with an African slave lends a whiff of PC historicity; Commodus's vices arise from poor parental care. Still, the cast is strong (notably Nielsen as Commodus's vacillating sister, and the late Oliver Reed, unusually endearing as a gladiator owner), the pacing lively, and the sets, swordplay and Scud catapults impressive. GA

Glaneurs et la Glaneuse, Les

see Gleaners and I, The

Glass House, The

(2000, US, 106 min)
d Daniel Sackheim. *p* Neal H Moritz. *sc* Wesley Strick. *ph* Alar Kivilo. *ed* Howard E Smith. *pd* Jon Gary Steele. *m* Christopher Young. *cast* LeeLee Sobieski, Diane Lane, Stellan Skarsgård, Bruce Dern, Kathy Baker, Trevor Morgan, Chris Noth, Michael O'Keefe, Rita Wilson.
● Bolshy teen Ruby (Sobieski) and younger brother Rhett are orphaned when their parents career off the side of a cliff in a BMW. The kids are sent to live with their allotted guardians, former neighbours who moved to Malibu to live in a giant cinematic metaphor. Terry and Erin Glass live in a glass house, all chilly, unwelcoming angles and soulless hi-tech gadgets. Just for good measure there's a windowless concrete basement, perfect for stashing dark secrets in. No, the Glasses are not all they seem. Erin (Lane) is a doctor given to self-medication in her spare time, while Terry (Skarsgård) is a car dealer whose spiralling debts threaten to consume the unrealistic lifestyle he's created for himself. Could the Glasses be planning to embezzle the kids' sizeable inheritance in order to bankroll their monumental window cleaning bills? This ludicrous premise is artlessly realised, while the film's second half is littered with scenes added for no reason other than to plug another gaping plot-hole. WI

Glass Key, The

(1942, US, 85 min, b/w)
d Stuart Heisler. *sc* Jonathan Latimer. *ph* Theodor Sparkuhl. *ed* Archie Marshek. *ad* Hans Dreier, Haldane Douglas. *m* Victor Young. *cast* Brian Donlevy, Alan Ladd, Veronica Lake, Joseph Calleia, William Bendix, Bonita Granville, Richard Denning.
● Not quite so resonant an early example of *noir* as *The Maltese Falcon*, partly because the novel's ending has been clumsily softened, but still a remarkably successful Hammett adaptation. Best sequence by far is the marathon beating-up sustained by Ladd in a bout of grating sadomasochism as Bendix ('He's a tough baby, he likes this') coyly begs his 'little rubber ball' to bounce back for more. Shot and played with deceptive casualness, the sequence is central to the film, flaunting an erotic undertow that sows continuing doubts throughout. Playing with his usual deadpan as he weaves warily through a maze of political machinations and underworld snares in the service of his boss, Ladd remains equally frozen whether expressing his love for Lake or his loyalty to Donlevy. The result is a teasing sexual ambiguity, considerably enhanced (at least until the copout ending) by the fact that Hammett's hero – here callous enough to admit a willingness to let Lake hang if necessary in furtherance of his aims – has been toughened up by being reduced to a *noir* cipher for the film. TM

Glass Menagerie, The

(1987, US, 135 min)
d Paul Newman. *p* Burtt Harris. *sc* Tennessee Williams. *ph* Michael Ballhaus. *ed* David Ray. *pd* Tony Walton. *m* Henry Mancini. *cast* Joanne Woodward, John Malkovich, Karen Allen, James Naughton.
● Newman's movie of the Tennessee Williams play, about a family disintegrating in a gloomy, claustrophobic St Louis apartment during the depression, is uncompromising and at times unbearably poignant. The mother (Woodward) is a stifling combination of emotional blackmail and self-glorifying reverie; her crippled daughter Laura (Allen, a revelation here), is a timid, gentle creature, as fragile as the world of glass animals into which she retreats. When the long-awaited gentleman caller accidentally breaks both her favourite unicorn and her heart, she finally drifts away for good into her fantasies. Her brother Tom (Malkovich) is weak and aware of it, and his self-loathing testimony brackets the confined action. The acting is bruisingly true; the deep guilts of family are present throughout; everybody feels martyred. Newman trusts the words to conjure up the old crushed magnolia. BC

Glass Mountain, The

(1949, GB, 98 min, b/w)
d Henry Cass. *p* John Sutro, Joseph Janni, Fred Zelnik. *sc* Joseph Janni, John Hunter, Emery Bonnet, Henry Cass, John Cousins. *ph* Otello Martelli, William McLeod. *ed* Lister Laurence. *m* Nino Rota. *cast* Michael Denison, Dulcie Gray, Valentina Cortese, Tito Gobbi, Sebastian Shaw.
● Shot down over Italy in WWII, composer Denison is inspired by the glacial beauty of the Alps and his illicit desire for the young Cortese to write an opera based on the legend of the Glass Mountain. When he returns to Blighty, his wife Dulcie Gray waits stoically for his indifference to thaw. This solidly directed, lavishly mounted romantic tosh was a huge hit in its day. NF

Glass Shield, The

(1995, US, 108 min)
d Charles Burnett. *p* Tom Byrnes, Carolyn Schroeder. *sc* Charles Burnett. *ph* Elliot Davis. *ed* Curtiss Clayton. *pd* Penny Barrett. *m* Stephen Taylor. *cast* Michael Boatman, Lori Petty, Bernie Casey, Ice Cube, Michael Ironside, Elliott Gould, Richard Anderson, Don Harvey.
● Burnett's first film since the provocative *To Sleep with Anger* in 1990 is a Lumet-style *policier* inspired by an everyday tale of LAPD-sponsored murder, racism and corruption. Boatman is the first black cop to serve in Anderson's precinct. He's proud to pull on his uniform, and readily bends the truth to put away a bad guy, but he can't just stand by and watch when he realises his colleagues are framing an innocent man, and they'll kill to keep it quiet. It's a familiar story, but Burnett draws strong character work from the cast (Petty is outstanding as a rookie who latches on to Boatman as a fellow outsider). Ultimately, however, the movie feels sketchy, as if Burnett chopped the flesh off his screenplay and left us only the bare bones.

Glastonbury: The Movie

(1995, GB, 99 min)
d/p Robin Mahoney, Matthew Salkeld, William Beaton. Robin Mahoney, Matthew Salkeld, William Beaton. *ph* William Beaton, Mike Sarne, Matthew Salkeld, Robert Heath, Korak Ghosh, Colin Thompson, Paolo Proto, Robin Mahoney, Aubrey Fagon. *ed* Robin Mahoney, Matthew Salkeld, William Beaton. *with* The Verve, Lemonheads, Omar, Airto Moreira.
● A marvellously honest, beautifully shot documentary celebrating 25 years of rock 'n' rolling around in the mud somewhere in a field in Somerset. Filmed over several years, this widescreen Dolby digital excursion dispenses with voice-overs, interviews and scrolling subtitles and just lets the music – from crusty rockers The Verve, Evan Dando's Lemonheads, spaced-cadets Spiritualised, groove-meister Omar, percussion genius Airto Moreira, et al – do the talking. DA.

Gleaming the Cube

(1988, US, 105 min)
d Graeme Clifford. *p* Lawrence Turman, David Foster. *sc* Michael Tolkin. *ph* Reed Smoot. *ed* John Wright. *pd* John Muto. *m* Jay Ferguson. *cast* Christian Slater, Steven Bauer, Richard Herd, Le Tuan, Minh Luong, Art Chudabala, Ed Lauter, Charles Cyphers.
● 'Gleaming the cube' is the term applied for that moment when pirouetting skateboarders momentarily leave the ground to carve their way through the air. It's the type of thing rebel without a high school diploma Brian (Slater) loves to do, much to his parents' despair. But he's first to rally to their cause when tragedy strikes, getting his act together to take the law into his own hands. According to the hackneyed conventions of this so-so thriller, this involves ridding himself of tatty clothes and stubble. He delves into the Orange County underworld, which is racier than you might think. The Vietnamese community is up to no good, with corruption infiltrating a seemingly respectable medical supply business. Slater and Le Tuan (as a Vietnamese ex-colonel) put in decent performances, but the best moments come from the action sequences in which Brian and his buddies perform their sporty feats. But with the screenplay dabbling with too many issues and stereotypes, the characters are largely one-dimensional and the relationships unconvincing. CM

Gleaners and I, The (Les Glaneurs et la Glaneuse)

(2000, Fr, 77 min)
d/commentary Agnès Varda. *ph* Stéphane Krausz, Didier Rouget, Didier Doussin, Pascal Sautelet, Agnès Varda. *ed* Agnès Varda, Laurent Pineau. *m* Joanna Bruzdowicz.
● The French title of this delightful, encouraging documentary underlines how Agnès Varda identifies with her subjects – social marginals who 'glean' a living, from the earth (caravan dwellers) or from refuse (the teacher of Malian and Senegalese immigrants whom she befriends at a Paris street market). The veteran film-maker is newly inspired and energised by the freedom her DV camera brings. The film is marked by youthful freshness, and the integrity and sympathy of both the images and the commentary, as Varda hurtles us to Arras, Beaune or Paris in search of the new generation of foragers. Cheekily, she places a frocked lawyer in a crop field, so he can declaim on section 12.26.10 of the penal code enshrining the historic right to take harvest leftovers; persuades an art gallery to disinter a painting of *glaneurs* from its vaults; takes tips

from a young Michelin chef who gleans herbs for his restaurant; or marvels at the totem towers of a nonagenarian Russian '*poubelle*' artist. It's as if, in following the line of her inspiration, Varda has re-mapped France, her demography of 'marginalia' uniting a diverse community of individuals who're unearthed and celebrated with an intimacy and discretion that is essentially political. WH

Glengarry Glen Ross

(1992, US, 100 min)
d James Foley. *p* Jerry Tokofsky, Stanley Zupnik. *sc* David Mamet. *ph* Juan Ruiz-Anchia. *ed* Howard Smith. *pd* Jane Musky. *m* James Newton Howard. *cast* Al Pacino, Jack Lemmon, Alec Baldwin, Alan Arkin, Ed Harris, Kevin Spacey, Jonathan Pryce, Bruce Altman, Jude Ciccolella.

●David Mamet's play about the wheelings and dealings of real-estate salesmen gets dedicated playing from a splendid cast, but gains nothing by the transfer from stage to screen. Foley takes us outside the office a bit, but essentially it's a claustrophobic story of men under pressure revealing cracks in character. 'Always be closing,' is the motto of these high-pressure hustlers, but after a brutal pep talk from bossman Blake (Baldwin), many of the team are faced with personal closure if they don't perform at peak. In this competitive climate, one of them steals the 'leads' (names of prospective clients). Mamet's aphasic dialogue and profanities fit perfectly with the accents, and it's possible to imagine how hotshot Ricky Roma (Pacino) will end up like pitiful, pleading Levene (Lemmon). Both turn in superb performances, but it's an ensemble piece, and Harris, Arkin and Spacey are just as good. BC

Glenn Miller Story, The

(1954, US, 116 min)
d Anthony Mann. *p* Aaron Rosenberg. *sc* Valentine Davies, Oscar Brodney. *ph* William H Daniels. *ed* Russell Schoengarth. *ad* Bernard Herzbrun, Alexander Golitzen. *songs/numbers* Glenn Miller, Mitchell Parrish, Andy Razaf, Joe Garland, JE Winner, others. *cast* James Stewart, June Allyson, Harry Morgan, George Tobias, Frances Langford, Louis Armstrong, Gene Krupa, Charles Drake.

●This ends where Scorsese's *New York, New York* begins, at the height of the big band era in the '40s; and some striking similarities end with the remorseless good nature of the Glenn Miller movie. Allyson beams and twinkles as Miller's practical wife; Stewart, looking remarkably like Miller, is disarmingly eccentric. They make an exemplary American couple, finding the road to success lined with nice friends, swirling *Variety* headlines, and key moments like Glenn saying to wife (long-distance), 'My number's Pennsylvania 6-5000'. But it works beautifully, especially if you like the music. Musical direction is by Henry Mancini, who abandons his own particular 'sound' for a credible homage to Miller's. Watch for Louis Armstrong leading a jam session on 'Basin Street Blues' in a speakeasy in Harlem, and Frances Langford doing 'Chattanooga Choo-Choo' in a well-boned strapless. JS

Glenn O'Brien's New York Beat Movie

see Downtown 81

Glen or Glenda? (aka I Led Two Lives/ I Changed My Sex)

(1952, US, 61 min, b/w)
d Edward D Wood Jr. *p* George G Weiss. *sc* Edward D Wood Jr. *ph* William C Thompson. *ed* Bud Schelling. *ad* Jack Miles. *cast* Bela Lugosi, Lyle Talbot, Daniel Davis (ie. Edward D Wood Jr), Dolores Fuller, Tommy Haynes.

●This well-meaning disaster, rescued from the obscurity it surely craves, is without doubt a candidate for one of the worst films ever made. The main story – a documentary-style look at the problems of transvestites – is a masquerade of good intentions shot with all the panache of an Indian restaurant commercial. Glen (pseudonymously played by the director himself) eyes ladies' underwear in clothing stores, covets his fiancée's angora; and when dressed to kill s/he looks like a straggler from the Monty Python lumberjack song. Snicker, snicker. Presiding over proceedings – goodness knows why – is a senile Lugosi looking as though he had strayed in from another movie. His advice as an 'expert' takes the form of endless taunts…but see for yourself, it's a film that defies description. CPe

Glimmer Man, The

(1996, US, 92 min)
d John Gray. *p* Steven Seagal, Julius R Nasso. *sc* Kevin Brodbin. *ph* Rick Bota. *ed* Donn Cambern. *pd* William Sandell. *m* Trevor Rabin. *cast* Steven Seagal, Keenen Ivory Wayans, Bob Gunton, Brian Cox, Michelle Johnson, John M Jackson, Stephen Tobolowsky.

●Although this slick Seagal action pic won't convert die-hard detractors, aficionados will note that he's both gained weight and lightened up. Ever since playing the ship's cook in *Under Siege*, the slab-faced one has been leavening his straight man image with a pinch of humour. The magic ingredient here is Wayans who, as his fast-talking, street-wise partner, allows Seagal to introduce something new into the mix, self-mockery. While Seagal cleanses his mind with Tibetan prayer beads, Wayans worships Saint Jack – Daniels, that is. The mismatched buddies are hunting a California serial killer called 'The Family Man', who slaughters and crucifies entire Catholic families; but Seagal suspects the latest killing was the work of a pro. Anonymously scripted and directed, this at least suggests that if Seagal can ever learn to deliver a kiss-off line, he might get within shouting distance of being likeable. As his old Special Ops boss, an over-ripe Cox confirms his status as the Rod Steiger of the '90s. NF

Glissements Progressifs du Plaisir

(1974, Fr, 105 min)
d/sc Alain Robbe-Grillet. *ph* Yves Lafaye. *ed* Bob Wade. *m* Michel Fano. *cast* Olga Georges-Picot, Jean-Louis Trintignant, Anicée Alvina, Michel Lonsdale.

●Trintignant, in trenchcoat and trilby, investigates a bondage slaying, grilling the heroine in the victim's bedroom which somehow contrives to be also a monastery cell, with trussed-up nuns languishing compliantly in the adjacent sanctum sanctorum. This is Robbe-Grillet amusing himself by scrambling together images and situations out of the overlapping conventions of the murder mystery and the S/M fantasy, taking care never to join the dots to form a coherent narrative and indeed ensuring that no such joining-up can possibly be achieved. This being Robbe-Grillet, none of the characters is permitted anything so crass as everyday sexual congress, though the numerous erotic tableaux should stir even the jaded or disinclined, thanks to the presence of Olga Georges-Picot, playing (but of course!) both victim and defence counsel. Amid all the sleight of hand, the most impressive feat is Trintignant's performance which manages to be simultaneously poker-faced and extravagantly comic. BBa

Glitter

(2001, US/Can, 104 min)
d Vondie Curtis Hall. *p* Laurence Mark. *sc* Kate Lanier. *ph* Geoffrey Simpson. *ed* Jeff Freeman. *pd* Dan Bishop. *m* Terence Blanchard. *cast* Mariah Carey, Max Beesley, Da Brat, Tia Texada, Valarie Pettiford, Ann Magnuson, Terrence Howard, Dorian Harewood.

●Vocalist Billie Frank (US popstress Carey in her screen debut) is separated as a child from an addict mother with whom she sang in honky tonks. Years later, her high-octave talents are discovered on New York's early-'80s club scene by maverick DJ Dice (Beesley), who becomes Billie's manager and lover. Several tiffs and much schmaltz later, she's set to sell out Madison Square Garden – despite the (puzzling) fact that she's still able to roam Manhattan without being recognised. This fails to convince on several levels: Carey's assumed edginess; Beesley's faltering Brooklyn accent; turns from such celebs as rapper Da Brat and soul vocalist Eric Benet; the half-hearted '80s references and the haphazard retro effects. AHa

Glitterball, The

(1977, GB, 56 min)
d Harley Coklis. *p* Mark Forstater. *sc* Howard Thompson. *ph* Alan Hall. *ed* Thomas Schwalm, Nick Gaster. *ad* Robert Jones. *m* Harry Robinson. *cast* Ben Buckton, Keith Jayne, Ron Pember, Marjorie Yates, Barry Jackson, Andrew Jackson.

●Enterprising little feature from the Children's Film Foundation which told – but five years earlier– precisely the same story as Spielberg's *E.T.* The extraterrestrial (a metal sphere) is insufficiently characterised and the adults are a drag, but it's neat and pacy with (on a limited budget) some excellent special effects. TM

Glitter Dome, The

(1984, US, 94 min)
d Stuart Margolin. *p* Stuart Margolin, Justis Greene. *sc* Stanley Kallis. *ph* Michael Watkins, Fred Murphy. *ed* MS Martin. *pd* Douglas Higgins. *m* Stuart Margolin. *cast* James Garner, Margot Kidder, John Lithgow, John Marley, Stuart Margolin, Paul Koslo, Colleen Dewhurst.

●As a one-time member of the LAPD, Joseph Wambaugh presumably has the merit of authenticity in his very personal treatment of police procedure; all the more worrying, then, that he chooses to cast his scenarios in the form of black farce. Cases get solved more by accident and coincidence than by detection, the police chiefs are all rattled idiots, and the detectives are divided between the 'survivors' – hard-drinking wearies, given to carnal jags of mind-bending proportion – and the 'sensitives', who can't find the release of outrageous behaviour and tend to crack up. Margolin's direction of this Tinsel-town thriller about child porn and murder (designed for cable TV) is too diffuse to be faithful to the particularities of Wambaugh's vision. But Garner contributes a very watchable wrinkly 'tec with lines like 'In Hollywood, Halloween is redundant'; and as his partner, Lithgow acquits himself perfectly in the role of the 'sensitive' with nightmares of an especially nasty case of child abuse. CPea

Global Affair, A

(1963, US, 84 min, b/w)
d Jack Arnold. *p* Hall Bartlett. *sc* Arthur Marx, Bob Fisher, Charles Lederer. *ph* Joseph Ruttenberg. *ed* Bud Molin. *ad* George W Davis, Preston Ames. *m* Dominic Frontiere. *cast* Bob Hope, Lilo Pulver, Michèle Mercier, Elga Andersen, Yvonne De Carlo, Robert Sterling, John McGiver, Nehemiah Persoff, Mickey Shaughnessy.

●What did poor Jack Arnold do to deserve this? Bob Hope plays a bachelor United Nations official, saddled with a foundling baby and flatulent wisecracks, who spurs furious competition between the 117 member nations – hitherto uninterested in welcoming the orphan – by announcing that it will be awarded to the best and most deserving country. All patch up their differences to applaud his eventual decision to adopt the little charmer himself (surprise, surprise) after marrying Michèle Mercier. Nobody is likely to applaud anything else, except perhaps a brief flare from Lilo Pulver as a Russian gynaecologist. TM

Gloire de mon père, La (My Father's Glory)

(1990, Fr, 111 min)
d Yves Robert. *p* Alain Poiré. *sc* Lucette Andrei. *ph* Robert Alazraki. *ed* Pierre Gillette. *ad* Jacques Dugied. *m* Vladimir Cosma. *cast* Philippe Caubère, Nathalie Roussel, Didier Pain, Thérèse Liotard, Julien Ciamaca, Joris Molinas, Paul Crauchet, Victor Garrivier.

●The first part of Marcel Pagnol's four-volume autobiography represents an unclouded homage to a childhood of apparently unchanging sunshine. In comparison to *Jean de Florette* and its sequel, this is a film of small pleasures. Robert eschews the top rank of French actors in favour of those with a genuine Provençal background, a decision Pagnol would surely have admired. But other decisions seem less successful. The book's charm comes from the sly contrast between the grown-up Pagnol's narration and his young self's naivety. Robert does use a narrator, but much of the verbal humour is lost on audiences reliant on subtitling or struggling to decipher the vernacular. The child actors have charm in good measure, but charm cannot be built into a film: you have to let it arise. Although the landscape is as impressive as ever, the film always looks too pretty, and Robert can't resist the temptation to swamp key scenes with Vladimir Cosma's heavy Mantovani strings. JMo

Gloria

(1980, US, 121 min)
d John Cassavetes. *p* Sam Shaw. *sc* John Cassavetes. *ph* Fred Schuler. *ed* George C

Villasenor. *ad* René D'Auriac. *m* Bill Conti. *cast* Gena Rowlands, John Adames, Buck Henry, Julie Carmen, Lupe Guarnica, Basilio Franchina.
● A near stunner: half art movie, half chase thriller, with a breathless, commanding performance from Gena Rowlands as the ex-chorus girl of the title. Hard as nails and twice as brassy, she takes unwilling charge of a neighbour's doe-eyed kid after his family has been slaughtered by the Mafia; the mismatched pair find themselves on the run with a bookful of Mafia accounts. Cassavetes' movies are a kind of frenzied gulp, quivering with emotion, under-motivated, overlong, and this is no exception: sublime, but infuriating. CA

Gloria

(1998, US, 108 min)
d Sidney Lumet. *p* Gary Foster, Lee Rich. *sc* Steven Antin. *ph* David Watkin. *ed* Tom Swartwout. *pd* Mel Bourne. *m* Howard Shore. *cast* Sharon Stone, Jeremy Northam, Cathy Moriarty, Jean-Luke Figueroa, Mike Starr, Sarita Choudhury, Miriam Colon, Bobby Cannavale, George C Scott.
● This remake of John Cassavetes' 1980 odd-couple chase thriller is an unremarkable balls-up, nothwithstanding the creditable names involved – Sharon Stone taking Gena Rowlands' lead, Sidney Lumet directing. The press notes finger screenwriter Steven Antin for the fall, but in fact the blame lies fairly evenly. It was presumably Antin's decision to turn Cassavetes' preference for action over motivation on its head, filling out Gloria's relationship with the gangsters on her tail, having her newly paroled after doing time for her no-account mobster boyfriend (Northam) – all of which, ironically, means her link-up with the orphaned kid (Figueroa) is more tenuous than before – while the present-tense drama trots along without ever breaking into a sweat. On the upside, Stone isn't embarrassed by her predecessor's blistering example; it's a streetsmart turn with nothing to connect to. And George C Scott shows us what we're missing as the (now) rascally mob boss, sly bon mots dripping from his tongue as if he'd had decent lines written just for himself. NB

Glory

(1989, US, 133 min)
d Edward Zwick. *p* Freddie Fields. *sc* Kevin Jarre. *ph* Freddie Francis. *ed* Steven Rosenblum. *pd* Norman Garwood. *m* James Horner. *cast* Matthew Broderick, Denzel Washington, Cary Elwes, Morgan Freeman, Jihmi Kennedy, André Braugher, Raymond St Jacques, Cliff DeYoung.
● *Glory* heralds the bravery of the American Civil War's first black fighting unit. Most of the emphasis has gone into evoking a firm sense of period: screenwriter Kevin Jarre reveals less talent for full-blooded characterisation and dialogue. Led by white officers headed by Colonel Robert Gould Shaw (Broderick), the men set off from the North for confrontation, which culminates in the bloody storming of a Confederate fort. Among the soldiers (and giving the best performances) are a calm gravedigger (Freeman) and a belligerent runaway slave (Washington). Voice-over narration makes effective use of the real-life Shaw's correspondence, but in terms of authenticity the battle sequences are truly impressive. Marching across open fields amid cannon-shot, or plunging into hand-to-hand combat, the stark clarity of Freddie Francis' cinematography combined with Zwick's intimate style evokes immediacy and fear. CM

Glory Alley

(1952, US, 79 min, b/w)
d Raoul Walsh. *p* Nicholas Nayfack. *sc* Art Cohn. *ph* William H Daniels. *ed* Gene Ruggiero. *ad* Cedric Gibbons, Malcolm Brown. *m* Pete Rugolo, George Stoll. *cast* Ralph Meeker, Leslie Caron, Kurt Kasznar, Gilbert Roland, Louis Armstrong, John McIntire, Dan Seymour, Jack Teagarden.
● Set among the 'pugs and mugs' of Bourbon Street, New Orleans, this is long on atmosphere but short on credibility. Meeker plays (very well) a boxer who literally runs out on the bout that might have made him a contender. Hounded as a coward, especially by the blind father (Kasznar) of the girl he loves (Caron), he is too proud to explain that, as a child, he suffered a fractured skull at the hands of his drunken father; under the bright lights of the ring, the trauma recurred of schoolmates jeering at his shaven, stitched skull. After a bout with alcohol, he enlists, returning from the war a much-publicised hero. Only Kasznar refuses to relent, until an eye specialist (secretly summoned by Meeker) suggests an operation that might restore his sight. It doesn't, but ('there are various kinds of blindness') does effect a change of heart. Meeker, now a welcome son-in-law, goes on to become champ. Disgorged in clumsy chunks by Art Cohn's script, this farrago becomes much easier to take when leavened by Walsh's ebullient response to the low-life fellowship of the milieu. The jazz score, with Armstrong in good voice and Caron contributing some charmingly quaint honky tonk/ballet routines, is a bonus, too. TM

Glory Guys, The

(1965, US, 112 min)
d Arnold Laven. *p* Arnold Laven, Arthur Gardner, Jules Levy. *sc* Sam Peckinpah. *ph* James Wong Howe. *ed* Melvin Shapiro, Ernst R Rolf. *ad* Roberto Silva, Ted Haworth. *m* Riz Ortolani. *cast* Tom Tryon, Harve Presnell, Andrew Duggan, Senta Berger, James Caan, Michael Anderson Jr, Slim Pickens, Wayne Rogers.
● Screenwriter Sam Peckinpah might have made more of this fatalistic Western adventure, from the novel *The Dice of God* by Hoffman Birney, than journeyman Laven, but it's a diverting picture all the same. Tryon's the cavalry captain sent to join general Duggan's frontier regiment, only to find the latter obsessed with defeating the combined local Indian forces. If anything, the film should be called 'The Glory Guy' because it's Duggan's drive to personal fulfilment, even at the cost of his men's lives, which is the central strand of this examination of control-gone-mad. The result's hardly a masterpiece, but it builds to a nicely mounted battle that pushes the point home. TJ

Glory Stompers, The

(1967, US, 85 min)
d Anthony M Lanza. *p* John Lawrence. *sc* James Gordon White, John Lawrence. *ph* Mario Tosi. *ed* Len Miller. *m* Sidewalk Productions. *cast* Dennis Hopper, Jody McCrea, Chris Noel, Jock Mahoney, Saundra Gale, Jim Reader, Robert Tessier.
● AIP biker movie in which plastic Chris Noel ('I just want something more than being a Stomper's girl') gets herself kidnapped by a rival gang and sparks off a series of fantasies of varying violence among Dennis Hopper's boys. Hopper ogles Noel's reincarnation of high school days, while his younger brother (Reader) dreams of meaningful love (and gets run over by a primitive hulk for his pains). While its framework is that of a Western, the film sticks relentlessly to its B picture format, successfully exuding an atmospheric haze. There's the sad sight, though, of Jock Mahoney (erstwhile Tarzan and Range Rider, famous for vaultingon to his horse back in the '50s) so aged he can scarcely straddle his machine. CPe

'G' Men

(1935, US, 85 min, b/w)
d William Keighley. *p* Louis F Edelman. *sc* Seton I Miller. *ph* Sol Polito. *ed* Jack Killifer. *ad* John Hughes. *cast* James Cagney, Ann Dvorak, Margaret Lindsay, Robert Armstrong, Lloyd Nolan, Barton MacLane.
● The film that put Cagney on the right side of the law after pressure groups (and Hoover's FBI) had castigated Hollywood's glorification of the gangster hero. In fact, it's hard to distinguish Cagney's Brick Davis – a punk from the wrong side of the tracks who becomes a lawyer, turning federal agent to take on the mob who killed his buddy – from his earlier incarnations, since he's still violent, trigger-happy and motivated by personal impulses rather than a sense of legal justice. That said, however, it's a typical Warners thriller: fast, gutsy, as simplistic and powerful as a tabloid headline. GA

G:MT Greenwich Mean Time

(1998, GB, 117 min)
d John Strickland. *p* Taylor Hackford. *sc* Simon Mirren. *ph* Alan Almond. *ed* Patrick Moore. *pd* Luana Hanson. *m* Guy Sigsworth. *cast* Alec Newman, Melanie Gutteridge, Georgia MacKenzie, Steve John Shepherd, Chiwetel Ejiofor, Benjamin Waters.
● Sam (Shepherd), Charlie (Newman), Rix (Ejiofor) and Bean (Waters) have been friends since school. Because he has money and the mind of an operator, Sam manages Rix and Bean's jazz jungle group G:MT; aspiring photographer Charlie snaps some publicity shots and it looks like they're on their way. Then Charlie's paralysed in an accident, Bean storms off when Sam insists they need to bring in a vocalist, and next thing you know he's pushing drugs. Revolving around young Londoners making their way today, this clearly set out to tell it like it is, but unfortunately it's neither convincing nor compelling in terms of character or context. For the purposes of what little plot there is, we have to accept that Rix doesn't think about his erstwhile soulmate for months, and then gets all shirty when it turns out that, no, Sam never did phone Bean to let him know about that ccucial studio recording session. TCh

Gnome Named Gnorm, A (aka Upworld/Adventures of a Gnome Named Gnorm)

(1990, US, 88 min)
d Stan Winston. *p* Ted Field. *sc* Pen Densham, JohnWatson. *m* Richard Gibbs. *cast* Anthony Michael Hall, Jerry Orbach, Eli Danker, Claudia Christian, Mark Harelik, Robert Z'Dar.
● A particularly desperate addition to the cycle of buddy-cop pics, in which LAPD workhorse Hall (who's filled out somewhat from his geeky John Hughes days) finds himself teamed with one of the little people (a creature who's burrowed up from beneath the earth in search of a life-giving crystal) to track down some diamond thieves. Director Stan Winston made his name as the effects wizard behind *Aliens*. TJ

Go

(1999, US, 101 min)
d Doug Liman. *p* Paul Rosenberg, Mickey Liddell, Matt Freeman. *sc* John August. *ph* Doug Liman. *ed* Stephen Mirrione. *pd* Tom Wilkins. *m* BT. *cast* Sarah Polley, William Fichtner, Katie Holmes, Jay Mohr, Timothy Olyphant, Desmond Askew, Scott Wolf.
● Liman's second feature trades in the drop-dead cool of *Pulp Fiction*, and except for a couple of late cop-outs it's packed with gags, novelties and surprises. It's a balmy Christmas Eve: check-out girl Ronna (Polley) finishes a double shift, impetuously drops in on Todd (Olyphant), the not-so-friendly pusher of her British colleague Simon, and persuades him she's got a no-risk deal with Adam and Zack (Wolf and Mohr). She doesn't know, however, that they're really actors working a sting with a scarily intense cop (Fichtner). Meanwhile, Simon (Askew) is having a hell of a time in Vegas. Connections are sometimes forced (would Todd lend his credit card to Simon? Do Adam and Zack belong at a rave?), but Liman is always a jump ahead, switching tempo and point of view with sufficient alacrity to disguise how slight the stories are. Like his earlier *Swingers*, this isn't just confident, it's cocky. In the end, neither amounts to much, but they boast so many memorable bits of business that the sum of the parts easily exceeds the whole. TCh

Goalkeeper's Fear of the Penalty, The (Die Angst des Tormanns beim Elfmeter)

(1971, WGer/Aus, 101 min)
d/sc Wim Wenders. *ph* Robby Müller. *ed* Peter Przygodda. *ad* R Schneider Manss-Au, Burghard Schlicht. *m* Jürgen Knieper. *cast* Arthur Brauss, Kai Fischer, Erika Pluhar, Libgart Schwarz, Marie Bardischewski, Michael Toost.
● *The Goalkeeper's Fear of the Penalty* outdoes even Wenders' subsequent *Alice in the Cities* in its sense that everything shown is at once subjective and objective. German goalie Bloch (Brauss) walks out of a game in Vienna, hangs around, commits an arbitrary murder, and then takes a coach to the Austrian border to look up an old flame. It's the journey of a man who's getting too old for his job, living off his nerves, sustained by his taste for Americana, movies and rock (everything from Hitchcock to 'Wimaway'). Brauss' engagingly hangdog face anchors it all in recognisable human feelings, while avoiding the least hint of 'psychological' explanation. More

than in his later movies, Wenders' style here has a remarkably charged quality: every frame haunts you for goddam weeks. TR

Goat Horn, The (Koziyat Rog)

(1972, Bulg, 97 min, b/w)
d Metodi Andonov. *sc* Nilolai Haitov. *ph* Dimo Kolarov. *m* Simeon Pironkov. *cast* Katia Paskaleva, Anton Gortchev, Milene Penev, Kliment Dentchev.

● A straightforward 17th century tale of revenge which comes to the screen with the well-worn air of a film made at least a decade earlier. A Bulgarian farmer raises his daughter as a boy, training her to kill the men who raped and murdered her mother, a role against which she eventually revolts. The film fails because it refuses to explore the girl's growing awareness beyond the basic requirements of the plot, except once in a scene where she watches one of her mother's killers make love to a woman. In this instance her realisation of the inadequacies of her own concepts, founded as they are on revenge, is confidently handled. Elsewhere, as in her subsequent relationship with a young shepherd, cliché predominates. Altogether something of an anachronism. CPe

Go-Between, The

(1970, GB, 116 min)
d Joseph Losey. *p* John Heyman, Norman Priggen. *sc* Harold Pinter. *ph* Gerry Fisher. *ed* Reginald Beck. *ad* Carmen Dillon. *m* Michel Legrand. *cast* Julie Christie, Alan Bates, Dominic Guard, Margaret Leighton, Michael Redgrave, Michael Gough, Edward Fox.

● Losey's adaptation of LP Hartley's novel is one of his more impressive later works. Together with screenwriter Harold Pinter, he creates another of his depictions of the destructive side of the English class system, as a love affair between the daughter of an affluent country family and a local farmer is tragically thwarted by prejudice and convention. Seen through the eyes of a young boy who acts as the instrument for the couple's assignations, the affair becomes the nexus for all the repression and unspoken manipulations brewing under the polite facade of an apparently civilised society; battle becomes personal on the cricket field, and the chink of teacups hides vicious whispers and plotting. It occasionally becomes a bit too precious, especially with the inserts of the grown-up go-between visiting his past haunts, but it's strong on atmosphere (the Norfolk locations are beautifully shot by Gerry Fisher), performance and moral nuance. GA

GoBots: Battle of the Rocklords

(1986, US, 74 min)
d Ray Patterson, Don Lusk, Alan Zaslove. *p* Kay Wright. *sc* Jeff Segal. *ed* Larry Cowan. *cast* voices: Margot Kidder, Roddy McDowall, Michael Nouri, Telly Savalas.

● Whatever evil lurks in the dark corners of the galaxy, have no fear: the GoBots are there – a new line of toys from the Tonka corporation, now starring in their first feature-length animated advertisement by Hanna-Barbera. Leader One and the GoBots are faced with a dangerous mission. Cy-Kill, the renegade GoBot, has travelled through the dimensions of hyperspace to the planet Quartex to join forces with the evil Magmar (voice by Savalas). There, where inanimate rocks have the ability to transform themselves into living, breathing anthropomorphic forms, Magmar seeks to take the planet by force, and the GoBots aim to stop him. Save your pennies and watch the GoBots on TV instead. SGo

Godard on TV: 1960–2000 (Godard à la télé: 1960–2000)

(1999, Fr, 52 min)
d Michel Royer. *p* Christiane Graziani. *sc* Michel Royer. *ed* Antoine Moreau. *narrator* Jean Croc.

● A cheeky Godardian assembly of TV clips featuring everyone's favourite mad artist, from jeunesse to senility, you might say. The governing irony is that Jean-Luc, for all his latter-day conversion to video, attests to loathe television: 'With TV I feel I'm in occupied territory. My country is the imagination.' Or 'TV leaves you with the forgettable; cinema leaves you with memories.' Yet he doesn't hesitate to appear on the box, to pontificate on whatever with inscrutable sagacity. 'I love to talk with no meaning, I'm the champion of that,' he admits. And TV loves him for it. This jape is amusing and a little depressing, but it's worth it to see JLG walk on his hands, and occasional quips hit home: 'The films we see on TV aren't films, they're reproductions of films.' TCh

Goda Viljan, Den

see Best Intentions, The

Goddess, The

see Devi

Goddess, The

(1958, US, 105 min. b/w)
d John Cromwell. *p* Milton Perlman. *sc* Paddy Chayefsky. *ph* Arthur J Ornitz. *ed* Carl Lerner. *ad* Ted Haworth. *m* Virgil Thomson. *cast* Kim Stanley, Lloyd Bridges, Betty Lou Holland, Steven Hill, Patty Duke, Joan Copeland.

● Just as he later ridiculed the inanities of American TV in *Network*, writer Paddy Chayevsky took the Hollywood star system to task in this equally savage satire. He cribbed the story directly from Ava Gardner's life: a small town girl of the Depression marries her way out of her background, abandons her husband, changes her name and sleeps her way to stardom. Once at the top, she can't cope with her fame and becomes increasingy suicidal. Although brilliantly played in best Method style by Kim Stanley, this would-be screen goddess is more a caricature than a character. Given what happened to Monroe a few years later, the script seems both cruel and strangely prophetic. GM

Goddess, The (Shennü)

(1934, China, 78 min, b/w)
d Wu Yonggang. *cast* Ruan Lingyu, Li Keng, Zhang Zhizhi, Li Junpan.

● Written, directed and designed by the 27-year-old Wu Yonggang, this is the kind of film that demands a rewriting of the film history books. The Garbo-esque Ruan Lingyu plays a single mother driven into prostitution (the title is a euphemism) to pay for her young son's schooling. Her best efforts to maintain some personal dignity run aground on social hypocrisy and male misogyny, the latter personified by the brutal pimp who co-opts her services. Free of moralism and melodrama, expressively composed and lit and very naturalistically acted, this is a film of startling modernity. TR

Goddess of 1967, The

(2000, Aust, 118 min)
d Clara Law. *p* Peter Sainsbury, Eddie LC Fong. *sc* Clara Law Eddie LC Fong. *ph* Dion Beebe. *ed* Kate Williams. *pd* Nicholas McCallum. *m* Jen Anderson. *cast* Rose Byrne, Rikiya Kurokawa, Nicholas Hope, Elsie McCredie.

● The Goddess is the Citroën DS 19, as Francophiles will understand. The movie is an incongruity of stylish, bleached-out pop imagery, black comic road trip (Hong Kong hipster Kurokawa hitching a ride through the outback with blind girl Byrne), and a clumsy psychodrama which explains Byrne's mindset in long, choked flashbacks to a traumatic childhood. Rarely as much fun as it would like to be, this heads off in four directions at once and ends up in the middle of nowhere. TCh

Godfather, The

(1971, US, 175 min)
d Francis Ford Coppola. *p* Albert S Ruddy. *sc* Mario Puzo, Francis Ford Coppola. *ph* Gordon Willis. *ed* William H Reynolds, Peter Zinner. *pd* Dean Tavoularis. *m* Nino Rota. *cast* Marlon Brando, Al Pacino, James Caan, Richard Castellano, Robert Duvall, Sterling Hayden, John Marley, Richard Conte, Diane Keaton, John Cazale, Talia Shire.

● An everyday story of Mafia folk, incorporating a severed horse's head in the bed and a number of heartwarming family occasions, as well as pointers on how not to behave in your local trattoria (i.e. blasting the brains of your co-diners out all over their fettuccini). Mario Puzo's novel was brought to the screen in bravura style by Coppola, who was here trying out for the first time that piano/fortissimo style of crosscutting between religious ritual and bloody machine-gun massacre that was later to resurface in a watered-down version in *The Cotton Club*. See Brando with a mouthful of orange peel. Watch Pacino's cheek muscles twitch in incipiently psychotic fashion. Trace his rise from white sheep of the family to budding don and fully-fledged bad guy. Singalong to Nino Rota's irritatingly catchy theme tune. Its soap operatics should never have been presented separately from Part II. GA

Godfather Part II, The

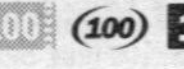

(1974, US, 200 min)
d/p Francis Ford Coppola. *sc* Francis Ford Coppola, Mario Puzo. *ph* Gordon Willis. *ed* Peter Zinner, Barry Malkin, Richard Marks. *pd* Dean Tavoularis. *m* Nino Rota, Carmine Coppola. *cast* Al Pacino, Robert Duvall, Diane Keaton, Robert De Niro, John Cazale, Talia Shire, Lee Strasberg, Michael V Gazzo.

● Coppola's superior sequel to his own very fine Mafia epic extends the original film's timeframe both backwards (to Vito Corleone's arrival and struggles to get by in New York at the start of the 20th century) and forwards (to his son Michael's ruthless protection of his own power as capo during a post-war period of expanded influence into Vegas, Cuba and elsewhere). The two strands alternate in Coppola's elliptical and elegantly orchestrated narrative, so that the seemingly inexorable progress from petty to corporate crime, from survival instinct to a steely obsession with power for power's sake, is charted with a terrifying lucidity. True, the film is so entranced by the dynastic dazzle that it neglects to show the Mob's baleful influence on America at large – the only people visibly harmed are either rival *mafiosi* or corrupt authority figures – but the performances, Gordon Willis' memorably gloomy camerawork, the stately pace and the sheer scale of the story's sweep render everything engrossing and so, well, plausible that our ideas of organised crime in America will forever be marked by this movie. GA

Godfather Part III, The

(1990, US, 162 min)
d/p Francis Ford Coppola. *sc* Mario Puzo, Francis Ford Coppola. *ph* Gordon Willis. *ed* Barry Malkin, Lisa Fruchtman, Walter Murch. *pd* Dean Tavoularis. *m* Nino Rota, Carmine Coppola. *cast* Al Pacino, Diane Keaton, Talia Shire, Andy Garcia, Eli Wallach, Joe Mantagna, George Hamilton, Bridget Fonda, Sofia Coppola, Raf Vallone, Donal Donnelly, Helmut Berger, John Savage.

● The chief impression is of déjà vu: extravagant ceremonies, parties, shady meetings behind closed doors. The implausible story doesn't help: Michael Corleone (Pacino), grey and bowed in 1979, misses his ex-wife (Keaton) and kids so much that he decides to abandon crime and make the family business legitimate. If it's nicely ironic that bastard nephew Vincent (Garcia), Michael's right-hand man, is almost psycopathically violent, this strand is weakened when Michael objects to daughter Mary's falling for Vincent. And the unwise insertion of elements from real life – the laundering of money through the Vatican – founders because so many details are skated over that the exact implications of Michael's brush with Old World power-brokers are often obscured. Plot apart – much of which concerns Michael's struggles to defend both his empire and his intergrity against Mafia peers – it often looks like Coppola is going through the motions. The acting is merely passable, several characters are given nothing to do, and Michael's paranoid self-pity lends the film an absurd morality: Coppola expects us to sympathise with the *semblance* of virtue. GA

God, Fatherland and Authority

see Deus, Patria e Autoridade

Godfather of Harlem, The

see Black Caesar

God's Alcatraz

(1993, GB, 36 min)
d Boris Stout. *p* Christian Martin. *ph* Stephen Gray. *ed* Soren Ebbe. *with* Dr Johnny Ray.

● Sketchy but intriguing documentary about one man's struggle to instil black pride into the impoverished 'village' of St Paul in East

Brooklyn. Radical Christian preacher Dr Johnny Ray has a mission, and self-acknowledged charisma. But as we follow him from sermons and men's consciousness-raising sessions to his Mississippi home, the precise import of his ideas (including voluntary segregation for the black community) are never fully examined – a pity, since his influence on his parishioners is evidently substantial. GA

Gods and Monsters

(1998, GB/US, 105 min, b/w and col)
d Bill Condon. *p* Paul Colichman, Gregg Fienberg, Mark R Harris. *sc* Bill Condon. *ph* Stephen M Katz. *ed* Virginia Katz. *pd* Richard Sherman. *m* Carter Burwell. *cast* Ian McKellen, Brendan Fraser, Lynn Redgrave, Lolita Davidovich, Kevin J O'Connor, David Dukes.

● Adapted from Christopher Bram's novel, this fictionalised biographical treatment-cum-tribute to James Whale – the ex-pat British director of *Frankenstein* and *Bride of Frankenstein*, who died mysteriously, face down in his California swimming pool in 1957, as if seeking refuge in one of his own horror film scenarios. Whiling away his early Hollywood retirement in incapacitated general lechery, lapsing into nostalgic reveries prompted by the visit of a young would-be biographer, McKellen's Whale latches on to Fraser's hunky but determinedly straight gardener, desperately seeking solace as his past glories and horrors begin crowding round. It's superficially reminiscent of *Love and Death on Long Island*, only less crusty, with McKellen giving a superb performance as the tormented old bugger; and the inserts from his past steadily and lucidly sound echoes of the *Frankenstein* themes and roles. 'Alone – bad! Friend – good!' – not a complicated film, but warm and clever. NB

God's Army (aka The Prophecy)

(1994, US, 96 min)
d Gregory Widen. *p* Joel Soisson. *sc* Gregory Widen. *ph* Bruce Douglas Johnson, Richard Clabaugh. *ed* Sonny Baskin. *pd* Clark Hunter. *m* David C Williams. *cast* Elias Koteas, Christopher Walken, Eric Stoltz, Virginia Madsen, Amanda Plummer, Viggo Mortensen.

● A novice priest-turned-cop (he lost his faith after a string of searing apocalyptic visions), Koteas finds himself caught between heaven and hell in a battle of the angels, as predicted in the 23rd chapter of Revelations (there's no 23rd chapter, Bible fans). For the God squad, we have Stoltz sucking face with a little girl to lodge the evil soul of a war criminal where fallen angel Gabriel (Walken) will not find it, he hopes. This weird metaphysical thriller comes on like a cross between *Wings of Desire* and an exploitation rip-off. Widen (who wrote *Highlander*) hasn't quite got the budget to stage Armageddon, but he would if he could. As it is, the movie never quite delivers on the Big Idea, but at least Walken comes through in spades: he's out of this world. Acting doesn't get more brazen than this. TCh

God's Country

(1985, US, 90 min)
d Louis Malle. *p* Vincent Malle. *sc/ph/narrator* Louis Malle. *ed* James Bruce.

● A truly lovely little film from the sadly underrated Malle. As ever, in this documentary about the inhabitants of the small farming town of Glencoe, Minnesota, the director reveals an extraordinary compassion for his subjects, viewed as well-meaning, dignified, but flawed. The gently comic tone of the beginning – happy, united families mowing the lawns, cow inseminators enjoying their literally shitty work, farmboys driving enormous tractors – gradually deepens to a darker hue as the legacies of Vietnam and Reagan are examined, and the tightly-knit community is shown as a breeding-ground of ignorance and intolerance (blacks are absent, gays invisible). Then, for the final 20 minutes, Malle shows us Glencoe six years on: dreams severely damaged, prosperity threatened, newlyweds become prematurely middle-aged. Malle never mocks, merely understands, in this extremely personal document of one European's love-hate for middle America. GA

Godsend, The

(1980, GB, 90 min)
d/p Gabrielle Beaumont. *sc* Olaf Pooley. *ph* Norman Warwick. *ed* Michael Ellis. *ad* Tony Curtis. *m* Aubrey Lewis. *cast* Malcolm Stoddard, Cyd Hayman, Angela Pleasence, Patrick Barr, Wilhelmina Green, Joanne Boorman.

● There's more than a hint of *The Omen* in this horror movie about a family that is slowly destroyed by a little girl they adopt after her mother has mysteriously vanished. Despite some moments of artfully sustained menace, and the fact that both little girls playing the cuckoo-child look superbly malevolent, the script by Olaf Pooley rapidly becomes stilted, and the narrative development makes little sense. DMcG

God's Favorite

(1999, US, 110 min)
d Roger Spottiswoode. *p* Nancy Hardin. *sc* Lawrence Wright. *ph* Pierre Mignot. *ed* Mark Conte. *pd* Owen Paterson. *cast* Bob Hoskins, Jeffrey DeMunn, Rosa Blasi, Luis Avalos, Denise Blasor, Richard Masur.

● Spottiswoode's biopic of Panamanian super thug Manuel Noriega sketches a corrupt, violent but not unsympathetic buffoon, beset by murderous Colombian drug gangs, bungling American diplomats, calculating Vatican officials, vengeful rebels – not to mention a nagging wife, ambitious girlfriend and a patronising Fidel Castro, plus worries about his bad complexion. Under such pressure, then, it's no wonder that he's driven to lop off the occasional rebel limb. The model could be *The Long Good Friday*, with Hoskins conducting another power struggle combining horror and black comedy. Noriega's regime fizzled out ignominiously and this account of it is obliged to follow suit. Otherwise it's an unexpectedly vigorous effort from the parallel universe of the telefeature. BBa

God's Little Acre

(1958, US, 110 min, b/w)
d Anthony Mann. *p* Sidney Harmon. *sc* Philip Yordan. *ph* Ernest Haller. *ed* Richard C Meyer. *pd* John S Poplin Jr. *m* Elmer Bernstein. *cast* Robert Ryan, Tina Louise, Aldo Ray, Buddy Hackett, Jack Lord, Fay Spain, Michael Landon.

● *God's Little Acre* completely bypasses its exotic origins in Erskine Caldwell's sensational novel. Instead, Mann and scriptwriter Philip Yordan transform their subject matter to create out of it a study of two 'over-reachers' struggling for control over the destiny of their family. Accordingly, the film is best seen in the light of the treatment of the family in *Man of the West* and *The Fall of the Roman Empire*. Ryan, the family's monomaniacal patriarch, has successfully harnessed the energy of his constantly squabbling flock for 15 years into an impossible search for his grandfather's mythic hidden gold. Similarly, Ray's son-in-law is driven by the dream of reinvigorating the homestead (and the valley) by turning the mill-power back on. While the film's resolution – peace and harmony – is impossible to take, the previous 100-odd minutes offer the most concise account of Mann's conception of the power and tensions that lie at the root of family life. PH

Gods Must Be Crazy, The

(1980, SAf, 109 min)
d/p/sc Jamie Uys. *ph* Buster Reynolds, Jamie Uys, Robert Lewis. *ed* Jamie Uys. *ad* Caroline Burls. *m* John Boshoff. *cast* N!Xau, Marius Weyers, Sandra Prinsloo, Nic de Jager, Louw Verwey, Michael Thys.

● Savour the profound imperialist symbolism of a Coke bottle dropping out of the sky like an apple of discord into a Botswana bush tribe of beatific innocents; delight in gags of such stunning originality as banana-skin pratfalls and speeded-up car chase scenes; gladden in positive, new images of the developing countries (bumbling black bureaucrats; evil but incompetent terrorists, of course routed mainly by the white 'stars'; and the simple, primitive tribe, with a plummy, patronising voice-over constantly reminding us how quaint and comical they are). Offensively racist and too gormless even for the kids at whom it is evidently aimed: Third World cinema of a quite...uncommon kind. SJo

Gods Must Be Crazy II, The

(1988, SAf, 98 min)
d Jamie Uys. *p* Boet Troskie. *sc* Jamie Uys. *ph* Buster Reynolds. *ed* Renee Englebrecht, Ivan Hall. *m* Charles Fox. *cast* N!Xau, Lena Farugia, Hans Strydom, Eiros.

● Mindless, immature, slapstick twaddle. Clearly aimed at under-fives, it follows the plight of several unconnected folk, all running about the vast Kalahari veldt like headless chickens: Bushman Xixo (N!Xau) has lost his two offspring on the back of a poacher's lorry; New York City lawyer Ann Taylor (Farugia), in Africa to front a conference, crashes on an airborne sightseeing trip and meets up with Tom Selleck-lookalike Dr Marshall (Strydom), who does his darndest to impress the city waif with his bushwhacking skills; and a couple of armed guerillas with nothing better to do than spend most of their time arresting each other. As with its predecessor, the Pathé-style 'gee, aren't these natives cute' narrative mingles speeded-up Keystone capers, a never-ending supply of mechanically-operated wildlife, and some of the naffest aerial SFX you're ever likely to see. DA

Gods of the Plague (Götter der Pest)

(1969, WGer, 91 min, b/w)
d Rainer Werner Fassbinder. *p* Rainer Werner Fassbinder, Michael Fengler. *sc* Rainer Werner Fassbinder. *ph* Dietrich Lohmann. *ed* Rainer Werner Fassbinder. *ad* Kurt Raab. *m* Peer Raben. *cast* Harry Baer, Hanna Schygulla, Margarethe von Trotta, Günther Kaufmann, Ingrid Caven, Carla Aulaulu.

● Remade (in more impressive form) as *The American Soldier* later the same year, Fassbinder's early gangster movie is slow, absurd, and quite mesmerising. Baer's the pretty criminal 'hero' who gradually sinks back into his underworld ways by hanging around with the wrong types: card-playing crooks and layabouts with trenchcoats and ever-present cigarettes, fickle molls hanging languorously on the sidelines. Any social comment is implicit rather than explicit, the world depicted is related more closely to classic American *noir* than any contemporary reality, and there is very little plot indeed. But it's a witty, stylish meditation on the genre, filtered through the decidedly dark and morbid sensibility of its director. GA

God Told Me To (aka Demon)

(1976, US, 95 min)
d/p/sc Larry Cohen. *ph* Paul Glickman. *ed* Arthur Mandelberg, William J Walters, Chris Lebenzon, Mike Corey. *m* Frank Cordell. *cast* Tony Lo Bianco, Sandy Dennis, Sylvia Sidney, Deborah Raffin, Sam Levene, Richard Lynch, Mike Kellin, Andy Kaufman.

● A delirious mix of sci-fi, pseudo-religious fantasy and horror detective thriller, with Lo Bianco as the perfect existential anti-hero – a New York cop and closet Catholic, guiltily trapped between wife and mistress. His investigations into a bizarre spate of mass murders lead right to the top: Jesus Christ, no less, is provoking innocent citizens to go on a murderous rampage. The wonderfully insane plot – involving spaceships, genetics and police corruption – builds to an ambiguous climax: a 'gay' confrontation which suggests an outrageous alternative to anal intercourse. *God Told Me To* overflows with such perverse and subversive notions that no amount of shoddy editing and substandard camerawork can conceal the film's unusual qualities. Digging deep into the psyche of American manhood, it lays bare the guilt-ridden oppressions of a soulless society. SW

Godzilla 1985

see Gojira 1984

Godzilla

(1998, US, 138 min)
d Roland Emmerich. *p* Dean Devlin. *sc* Dean Devlin, Roland Emmerich, Ted Elliott, Terry Rossio. *ph* Ueli Steiger. *ed* Peter Amundson, David J Siegel. *pd* Oliver Scholl. *m* David Arnold. *cast* Matthew Broderick, Jean Reno, Hank Azaria, Maria Pitillo, Michael Lerner, Harry Shearer.

● Toho's nuclear nightmare comes to America, like a very big chicken coming home to roost. This self-appointed box office behemoth from the makers of *Independence Day* is a plodding non-event. After a promising start, the movie falls apart almost as soon as Godzilla arrives in Manhattan – we'll buy a mutant lizard the size of a church, but it's a stretch to accept that the authorities keep losing track of the creature (then again, it does appear to change size according to the demands of the art director). Emmerich's sub-Spielbergian awe is constantly undercut by his own squeamishness – it's just not scary – and by the irritatingly drippy leads. You can't help praying for Broderick to get the chop, while Pitillo seems to think she's auditioning for a sitcom; only Reno comes out with head held high. Populist cataclysm requires a lighter touch than this. TCh

Godzilla vs the Bionic Monster (Gojira tai Mekagojira)

(1974, Jap, 80 min)
d Jun Fukuda. *p* Tomoyuki Tanaka. *sc* Jun Fukuda, Hiroyasu Yamaura. *ph* Yuzuru Aizawa. *ed* Michiko Ikeda. *ad* Kazuo Satsuya. *m* Masaru Sato. *cast* Masaki Daimon, Kazuya Aoyama, Akihiko Hirata, Hiroshi Koizumi.
●A patchy romp in which villainous spacemen (apes at heart) plan to devastate Earth using Mechagodzilla, a fearsome bionic ogre disguised to look like the real champ. After a breathless intro during which a royal geisha has visions of the impending disaster, a spooky cave is unearthed, pieces of 'space titanium' are found, and Mechagodzilla makes mincemeat of one of our hero's mates (a sort of inflated, leaping hedgehog), the film becomes bogged down in a clutter of subplots, characters and technicalities. Things begin to pick up in the final epic confrontation between the two Godzillas and war god Ghinrah, who is woken up from his million year kip to lend a hand. Death rays zigzag and mouths belch fire with cartoon gusto, through overall the special effects are disappointing. IB

Godzilla vs the Smog Monster (Gojira tai Hedora)

(1971, Jap, 85 min)
d Yoshimitsu Banno. *sc* Takeshi Kimura, Yoshimitsu Banno. *ph* Yuichi Manoda. *ed* Yoshitami Kuroiwa. *ad* Taiko Inoue. *m* Riichir Manabe. *cast* Akira Yamaguchi, Hiroyuki Kawase, Toshie Kimura, Toshio Shibaki, Keiko Mari.
●The tenth sequel to the original *Godzilla*. Your favourite Oriental monster's sparring partner here is a king-sized lump of sludge (supposedly evolved from the industrial waste of a coastal town) that poses under the name of Hedora (Hopper? tails? sexual?) and looks like a cross between an owl and a festering turd. While the special effects aren't exactly Harryhausen (in fact two Jap midgets in costumes stomping around shoe-boxes painted to look like factories), and it's certainly no great shakes as sci-fi, there are a few laughs and an unintentionally funny 'Save the Earth' theme tune. PM

Go Fish

(1994, US, 83 min, b/w)
d Rose Troche. *p/sc* Rose Troche, Guinevere Turner. *ph* Ann T Rossetti. *ed* Rose Troche. *m* Brendan Dolan, Jennifer Sharpe, Scott Aldrich. *cast* VS Brodie, Guinevere Turner, T Wendy McMillan, Migdalia Melendez, Anastasia Sharp.
●A lively romantic comedy set in Chicago which blows fresh air on the fusty conventions applied to the representation of lesbian and gay lives. Five women – aspirant writer Max, college lecturer Kia, reserved vet's assistant Ely, sharp-minded Daria, divorced nurse Evy – do the thing twenty- and thirty-somethings do. They hang out, cook, drink, talk and then talk some more. Here for a change are people who seem to come from somewhere. Troche makes sure that detail is minutely, tellingly observed, and quite naturally adds a moral political dimension. What's also welcome is that the characters' sexual identity is given – they're lesbians. If you can accept that, now we're talking. WH

Go for a Take

(1972, GB, 90 min)
d Harry Booth. *p* Roy Simpson. *sc* Alan Hackney. *ph* Mark McDonald. *ed* Archie Ludski. *ad* Lionel Couch. *m* Glen Mason. *cast* Reg Varney, Norman Rossington, Sue Lloyd, Dennis Price, Julie Ege, Patrick Newell, David Lodge.
●Varney and Rossington as two characters who find themselves pursued by a gang and seek refuge in a film studio, where Varney turns his hand to stunting and Rossington to hustling. They end up stealing a necklace and avoiding the gang in an extended chase sequence. A very weak comedy, equally uninspired whether hammering away at its twin themes of money and girls or putting Varney through yet another painful routine. DP

Go For Broke (Heng Shu Heng)

(2000, China, 87 min)
d Wang Guangli. *p* Tang Ying, Wang Guangli. *sc* Zhang Xian. *ph* Lu Yuqing. *ed* Li Tian, Chen Huifang. *cast* Zhang Baozhong, Zhou Yuhua, Zhong Lingjun, Gu Longxiang, Zhao Yongshen, Wang Jianxin, Zhang Jiangang, Xu Meijiang.
●Wang's first 'above-ground' film is one of the most engrossing docu-dramas ever made. Six Shanghainese (five men, one woman, all naturals) re-enact their real-life experiences of teaming up to run a private interior decorating company after losing jobs in state-owned factories. Their venture has its ups and downs (only a lottery win rescues it from bankruptcy), but it survives to face China's unpredictable economic future. Shooting handheld, using only first takes and jump cutting within scenes, Wang succeeds completely in capturing (a) the character of life in Shanghai, (b) the risks of being an entrepreneur in a near lawless country, and (c) the lure of shortcuts to wealth. He frames the story with brief fictional scenes showing a young couple who operate as con artists and score a lottery win, and ends with comments from the six non-actors about the experience of making the film. Amazing that he pulled this off so fluently, and amazing that the authorities let him get away with it. TR

Gohatto

see Taboo

Goin' Down the Road

(1970, Can, 88 min)
d/p Donald Shebib. *sc* William Fruet. *ph* Richard Leiterman. *ed* Don Shebib. *m* Bruce Cockburn. *cast* Doug McGrath, Paul Bradley, Jayne Eastwood, Cayle Chernin, Nicole Morin, Pierre La Roche.
●Joey and Pete are running from a poverty-stricken region of the Maritimes in a fated attempt to escape a sequence of drab inevitabilities. Of course Toronto can only offer the same sort of job; of course one of them's going to hit a girl on an unlucky night; of course he'll marry her and set up house on hire purchase; he's going to get laid off from work because that's the nature of the work; they're going to huddle in depressing rooms, and argue more and more as the money hits zero; they're going to try robbing a supermarket; something's going to go wrong. The whole inescapable spiral is charted without ever putting an emotional foot wrong. We've all had bad times, but there's usually been something to get us on to the next plateau: luck, background, education. These two have none of this, and Shebib's first feature awakens anger at a society that invites dreams it cannot fulfil, teaching us a bit more about what's wrong. JC

Going All the Way

(1997, US, 103 min)
d Mark Pellington. *p* Tom Gorai, Sigurjon Sighvatsson. *sc* Dan Wakefield. *ph* Bobby Bukowski. *ed* Leo Trombetta. *pd* Thérèse DePrez. *m* Tomandandy. *cast* Jeremy Davies, Ben Affleck, Amy Locane, Rose McGowan, Rachel Weisz, Jill Clayburgh, Lesley Ann Warren, Dan Wakefield.
●Adapted by Dan Wakefield from his 1970 novel, this is a spirited coming-of-age drama with a difference. For one thing, dealing with young men returning from war to the claustrophobic conformity of their families, it's concerned with the rift between different generations of adults, their ideas and aspirations. For another, while the story is set in 1954 among the Christian folk of Indianapolis, the film is as frankly libidinous and angst-ridden as any present-day equivalent. Confused, anxiously hormonal Sonny Burns (Davies) and self-confidant high school jock 'Gunner' Casselman (Affleck), whose experiences in the Far East have shown him the merits of thinking for himself, become friends – to the dismay of Sonny's apple-pie mom (Clayburgh) – and hang together through encounters with a succession of women. Part satire and part confessional memoir, the film is stronger on period flavour and Sonny's inner demons than on the humanity of some of the other characters. The leading men never quite show us the essence of their unlikely friendship. NB

Going in Style

(1979, US, 96 min)
d Martin Brest. *p* Tony Bill, Fred T Gallo. *sc* Martin Brest. *ph* Billy Williams. *ed* Robert Swink, C Timothy O'Meara. *pd* Stephen Hendrickson. *m* Michael Small. *cast* George Burns, Art Carney, Lee Strasberg, Charles Hallahan, Pamela Payton-Wright, Siobhan Keegan.
●The director of *Beverly Hills Cop* and *Scent of a Woman* made an auspicious start to a Hollywood career as a purveyor of neatly crafted commercial undertakings with this warm and entertaining story of old codgers Burns, Carney and Strasberg hitting back at the society that's abandoned them by successfully robbing a Manhattan bank. A trio of contrasting personalities, the veterans bring both a mischievous wit and a sense of subdued anger to a familiar comic plotline, and the film achieves a rare balance of laughter and compassion. TJ

Going My Way

(1944, US, 126 min, b/w)
d/p Leo McCarey. *sc* Frank Butler, Frank Cavett, Leo McCarey. *ph* Lionel Lindon. *ed* Leroy Stone. *ad* Hans Dreier, William Flannery. *songs* Johnny Burke, James Van Heusen, JR Shannon. *cast* Bing Crosby, Barry Fitzgerald, Rise Stevens, Gene Lockhart, Frank McHugh, Jean Heather, Stanley Clements.
●Godawful Oscar-winning schmaltz, with Crosby as a crooning, imbibing and golf-playing priest who saves the souls in his New York parish and wins over the man who holds the mortgage on the church as well. All this and Barry Fitzgerald doing his crotchety leprechaun act too. Go anywhere to avoid it. ATu

Going Off Big Time

(2000, GB, 87 min)
d Jim Doyle. *p* Ian Brady. *sc* Neil Fitzmaurice. *ph* Damian Bromley. *ed* Julian Day. *pd* David Butterworth. *m* Andy Roberts. *cast* Neil Fitzmaurice, Dominic Carter, Sarah Alexander, Nick Lamont, Gabbi Barr, Nick Moss, Vinnie Adams, Peter Kay, Bernard Hill.
●Scouse bloke Mark Clayton (Fitzmaurice) has kept out of trouble all his life, until he accidentally hits a cop and get four years in jail. Helped by old timer Hill, he learns survival skills (worthy of Alcatraz) and, once released, is soon heading a gang of ex-cons. Although scams and dodgy deals are lucrative and a laff, Mark begins to tire when he gets to know posh bird Natasha (Barr). Is he in too deep? The Liverpudlian production team have gone for a comic spin, and the film has its moments, such as Mark's first meeting with a crook who's 'more Stringfella than Goodfella – couldn't read or write but could spell Versace.' The acting, however, is variable, the mix of violence and capering uneasy, and the romance strictly routine. KW

Going Places

see Valseuses, Les

Going Steady (Yotz' im Kavua)

(1979, Isr, 88 min)
d Boaz Davidson. *p* Menahem Golan, Yoram Globus. *sc* Boaz Davidson, Eli Tavor. *ph* Adam Greenberg. *ed* Alain Jakubowicz, Arial Roshko. *ad* Eytan Levi. *cast* Yiftach Katzur, Yvonne Michaels, Zacki Noy, Rachel Steiner, Jonathan Segal, Daphna Armoni.
●Brought to you by the makers of the disastrous *Lemon Popsicle*, this is equally dire and unremittingly sexist. 'Never pass up a potential piece' is the philosophy of one of its puerile heroes, and the film indulges his every whim. It's supposed to be an Israeli version of *American Graffiti*, but all it manages is an obscene level of childishness, and the ruination of 22 classic '50s hits (from The Platters to Brenda Lee). HM

Goin' South

(1978, US, 108 min)
d Jack Nicholson. *p* Harry Gittes, Harold Schneider. *sc* John Herman Shaner, Al Ramrus, Alan Mandel. *ph* Nestor Almendros. *ed*

Richard Chew, John Fitzgerald Beck. *pd* Toby Carr Rafelson. *m* Van Dyke Parks, Perry Botkin Jr. *cast* Jack Nicholson, Mary Steenburgen, Christopher Lloyd, John Belushi, Veronica Cartwright, Richard Bradford, Danny De Vito.

●Nicholson's second film as director, a wonderfully beguiling Western in which he plays a sad sack outlaw (ex-cook to Quantrill's Raiders) snatched from the gallows by Steenburgen's prim spinster (taking advantage of a special ordinance occasioned by man shortage after the Civil War), who weds him and puts him to work mining for gold. Tender, bawdy and funny in its shaggy dog ramifications, their evolving relationship – she hankering for prosperous propriety in Philadelphia, he for lazy lustfulness in a Mexican cantina – is irresistible, and comes complete with a hilarious variation on the genre's inescapable shootout with the law. TM

Gojira 1984 (Godzilla 1985/Return of Godzilla)

(1985, Jap, 103 min/US re-edit 87 min)
d Kohji Hashimoto, RJ Kizer. *p* Tomoyuki Tanaka, Anthony Randel. *sc* Shuichi Nagahara, Lisa Tomei. *ph* Kazutami Hara, Takashi Yamamoto, Toshimitsu Ohneda. *ed* Yoshitami Kuroiwa, Michael Spence. *pd* Akira Sakuragi. *m* Reijiro Koroku. *cast* Raymond Burr, Keiju Kobayashi, Ken Tanaka, Yasuko Sawaguchi, Shin Takuma, Eitaro Ozawa.

●Godzilla ended his 1954 trip to Japan as a pile of ash, but the horny guy is back, redesigning the Tokyo skyline with extreme prejudice. Since the mid-'90s we've been able to compare the American re-edit (*Godzilla 1985*, incorporating added scenes featuring Raymond Burr) with the un-Burred original (*Return of Godzilla*). In these versions Godzilla is off-screen for almost an hour and both are dubbed, apparently by Australians. Not only does Godzilla have to be vanquished all over again but there's a cold war still on and, interestingly, in the Burr version, some nifty cutting reverses the Soviet navy's original reluctance to go nuclear. Not to be missed: the end titles love song, 'Take care now Godzilla, my old friend'. DO

Gojoe (Gojo Reisen Ki)

(2000, Jap, 137 min)
d Sogo Ishii. *p* Takenori Sento. *sc* Goro Nakajima, Sogo Ishii. *ph* Makoto Watanabe. *ed* Shuichi Kakesu. *pd* Shunya Isomi. *m* Hiroyuki Onogawa. *cast* Daisuke Ryu, Tadanobu Asano, Masatoshi Nagase, Jun Kunimura, Ittoku Kishibe.

●Ishii's epic rethink of the Genji-Heike clan wars of the 12th century is superbly cast and designed, full of visual magic and very different in tone from most Japanese *jidai-geki* – but not terrifically exciting. The oft-told clash between the warrior Benkei (Ryu, great), persuaded by the inscription on his chest that he is destined to defeat the forces of darkness, and the deposed Genji prince Shanao (Asano), conducting arcane rituals in secret with his *kagemusha* doubles, is seen here as an all-out spirit war. Decked out with ghosts and rumours of ghosts, cosmic portents (twin comets, a solar eclipse) and faster than light swordplay, it clearly hopes to reach the psychedelic heights of Ishii's *August in the Water*. It does succeed in blurring the line between the physical and the metaphysical, and in its repetitive way it's often very impressive. But it never quite takes off. (A recut 'international version' also exists.) TR

Go, Johnny, Go!

(1958, US, 75 min, b/w)
d Paul Landres. *p* Alan Freed, Hal Roach Jr. *sc* Gary Alexander, *ph* Ed Fitzgerald. *ed* Walter Hannemenn. *ed* McClure Capps. *m* Leon Klatzkin. *cast* Alan Freed, Jimmy Clanton, Sandy Stewart, Chuck Berry, Jo-Ann Campbell, Richie Valens, Eddie Cochran.

●As if the hilarious cynicism of *The Girl Can't Help It* had never happened, the almost-charming naïveté of Alan Freed's movies continued, ignoring racialism and presenting a painfully low-budget, cleaned-up version of rock'n'roll to calm parental fears. Hero Clanton (later to perpetrate 'Venus in Blue Jeans', but coming from the raunchy New Orleans school) grins his way stoically from rags to riches via a demo disc played on Freed's radio show. Everyone is so damned decent that the occasional sour comments from Freed and a studio bandleader sound like blasphemy. Laugh if you like, but as well as the crude fictionalising and dreadful miming, the film offers the only moving evidence of Ritchie Valens (even if Freed does rush out half-way through the song), a rare fragment of Eddie Cochran, the great Cadillacs camping through two Coasters-like numbers, and Chuck Berry struggling to be a nice guy in a 'major acting role'. JC

Gold

(1974, GB, 124 min)
d Peter Hunt. *p* Michael Klinger. *sc* Wilbur Smith, Stanley Price. *ph* Ousama Rawi. *ed* John Glen. *ad* Alex Vetchinsky, Syd Cain. *m* Elmer Bernstein. *cast* Roger Moore, Susannah York, Ray Milland, Bradford Dillman, John Gielgud, Tony Beckley, Simon Sabela.

●Moore fights a conspiracy to flood a gold mine and thus increase the world price of gold, allowing the villains to profit by prior investment. Apart from neat performances by Milland and Gielgud, the only point of note is that *Gold* was made in South Africa against union wishes. Predictably, black miners are depicted as a loyal army of cheery coons, a notion that concludes with a black overseer sacrificing his life to save Moore's. Ah, well, at least the film's idea of justice extends as far as having the villain (Dillman) run over by his own Rolls Royce. CPe

Gold Coast (aka Elmore Leonard's Gold Coast)

(US, 1997, 105 min)
d Peter Weller. *sc* Harley Peyton. *ph* Jacek Laskus. *cast* David Caruso, Marg Helgenberger, Jeff Kober, Barry Primus, Richard Bradford.

●Strange thing about Elmore Leonard adaptations, you can stick closely to the book, and it all comes right (*Get Shorty, Jackie Brown*), or you can stick closely to the book, and everything goes horribly wrong (as here). This has a plot set-up which takes some swallowing: Karen, a widowed Miami millionairess, appears to have it all – what she doesn't have is sex, because her husband decreed it in his will (the executor hires a heavy to enforce it, too). Ex-con/dolphin ringmaster Maguire (Caruso) comes into her life, and decides to help her out. Jeff Kober steals the show as Roland, the strong arm, but the leads are distinctly lacklustre, and Weller botches the behind-the-camera stuff – he seems to have discovered a new toy, 'shaki-cam'. TCh

Gold Diggers, The

(1983, GB, 89 min, b/w)
d Sally Potter. *sc* Lindsay Cooper, Rose English, Sally Potter. *ph* Babette Mangolte. *ed* Sally Potter. *ad* Rose English. *m* Lindsay Cooper. *cast* Julie Christie, Colette Laffont, Hilary Westlake, David Gale, Tom Osborn, Jacky Lansley.

●It's all happening in this feminist experiment: frantic chases, gold rushes, horseback escapes, ballroom dances. But this is no action movie, for its heart is in its mouth, and the value of each character and scene is measured in metaphors. Sadly, Potter's cyclical, stylised, surreal film about a quest for knowledge, power and much more, illustrates nothing better than the difficulties inherent in this kind of undertaking. Hers is a cryptic world of shadows and ciphers, with meanings that are too elusive (or didactic) to command attention or encourage interest; and it is ironic that the best made point is achieved off-camera (by the assembly of an all-women crew to make the film). FD

Gold Diggers of 1933

(1933, US, 96 min, b/w)
d Mervyn LeRoy. *sc* Erwin Gelsey, James Seymour. *ph* Sol Polito. *ed* George Amy. *ad* Anton F Grot. *songs* Al Dubin, Harry Warren. *cast* Warren William, Joan Blondell, Aline MacMahon, Ruby Keeler, Dick Powell, Ginger Rogers, Ned Sparks, Guy Kibbee.

●Second of the archetypal backstage musicals from Warners (it followed hard on the success of *42nd Street*) which established the idiosyncratic geometrics of Busby Berkeley. Some semblance of a plot (songwriter Powell turns against his wealthy parents in wishing to marry chorus girl Keeler), and much Depression wisecracking from Blondell, MacMahon and Rogers; but most notable is the vulgar, absurd and wonderfully surreal Berkeley choreography. Great numbers: Ginger Rogers adorned in dollars singing 'We're in the Money'; young lovers interrupted by rain while 'Pettin' in the Park'; and on a strangely bleak note, the files of unemployed ex-servicemen during 'Remember My Forgotten Man'. Delirious and delightful. GA

Gold Diggers of 1935

(1934, US, 95 min, b/w)
d Busby Berkeley. *p* Robert Lord. *sc* Manuel Seff, Peter Milne. *ph* George Barnes. *ed* George Amy. *ad* Anton F Grot. *songs* Harry Warren, Al Dubin. *cast* Dick Powell, Adolphe Menjou, Gloria Stuart, Alice Brady, Hugh Herbert, Gloria Farrell, Frank McHugh, Winifred Shaw.

●Not a patch on *Gold Diggers of 1933*, this is set in a hotel where Powell, a medical student doubling as hotel clerk, falls for the daughter (Stuart) of a stingy multi-millionairess (Brady). The annual charity show is naturally being put on, and the plot revolves around the efforts of a mad Russian director (Menjou) and assorted associates to take the millionairess for as much as they can. Since Berkeley (his first solo as director) seems to have no idea how to handle actors, the result is acres of atrocious mugging (Menjou being the worst offender) and a couple of Powell ballads. Survive the first 70 minutes, however, and there are two big production numbers. The first ('The Words Are in My Heart') is standard Berkeley fare, involving chorines and waltzing white pianos. But 'The Lullaby of Broadway' is one of his most inventive choreographies: a mini-chronicle of a day in the life of the Great White Way, ending with the night bringing on an exhilarating horde of tap dancers. TM

Gold Diggers of 1937

(1936, US, 100 min, b/w)
d Lloyd Bacon. *p* Hal B Wallis. *sc* Warren Duff. *ph* Arthur Edeson. *ed* Tommy Richards. *ad* Max Parker. *songs* Harry Warren, Al Dubin, EY Harburg, Harold Arlen. *cast* Dick Powell, Joan Blondell, Glenda Farrell, Victor Moore, Lee Dixon, Osgood Perkins.

●Dick Powell as a singing insurance salesman who interests ageing, hypochondriac producer Victor Moore in a million dollar policy, and puts on a show with the proceeds… Nuggets include two memorable Busby Berkeley set pieces. Fifty couples canoodling on fifty giant rocking-chairs in 'Let's Put Our Heads Together', and spunky Joan Blondell leading seventy chorus girls in a military-style tattoo called 'All's Fair in Love and War'. TCh

Golden Ball, The

see Ballon d'Or, Le

Golden Balls (Huevos de Oro)

(1993, Sp, 95 min)
d Bigas Luna. *p* Marivi de Villanueva. *sc* Cuca Canals, Bigas Luna. *ph* José Luis Alcaine. *ed* Carmen Frias. *ad* Antxón Gómez. *m* Nicola Piovani. *cast* Javier Bardem, Maria De Medeiros, Maribel Verdu, Elisa Touati, Raquel Bianca, Alessandro Gassmann.

●Bardem plays Benito Gonzalez, a hustler who dreams of building the biggest skyscraper in Benidorm. After plump, two-timing Rita (Touati) breaks his heart, he determines not to let any woman past his defences; model Claudia (Verdu) is strictly a trophy broad. He marries Marta (De Medeiros) for her money and juggles his sharp, intelligent wife and compliant mistress while doing dodgy deals and wailing along to Julio Iglesias on his home karaoke machine, showing off his Rollex and jingling his bollocks like so much small change. Director Luna mixes admiration for this full-blooded fool with a rueful warning about the dangers of machismo. Reinforcing the central image of a vaunting skyscraper – can he get it up? – are phallic symbols galore, with eggs and lobsters the key foodstuffs. SFe

Golden Bowl, The

(2000, GB, 137 min)
d James Ivory. *p* Ismail Merchant. *sc* Ruth Prawer Jhabvala. *pd* Tony Pierce-Roberts. *ed* John David Allen. *pd* Andrew Sanders. *m* Richard Robbins. *cast* Uma Thurman, Nick Nolte, Jeremy Northam, Kate Beckinsale, Anjelica Huston, James Fox.

●Arguably Merchant Ivory's best costumer, if only for a certain expertise with which Ruth Prawer Jhabvala has transformed Henry James' dense, allusive late novel into an easily manageable story. A crucial problem is Thurman, resplendently decorous but otherwise inadequate as the financially constrained Charlotte, still enamoured of fickle, pragmatic Italian aristo (Northam) who marries her best friend Maggie (Beckinsale), daughter of philanthropic, art-collecting American billionaire Adam Verver (Nolte) – whom Charlotte, desperate yet not quite resigned to her fate, weds. Inevitably, amid all the deception, love – sexual and familial – wreaks havoc, and the seemingly innocent New Worlders show the scheming Old Worlders a thing or two in matters of strategy. Mercifully, James' incisive ironies and insights just about survive the emphasis on discretion and visual opulence, but there's no denying the stolid clumsiness of direction and script (the metaphor of the beautiful but flawed objet d'art is hammered home relentlessly), nor the overall lack of passion. GA

Golden Boy

(1939, US, 99 min, b/w)
d Rouben Mamoulian. *p* William Perlberg. *sc* Daniel Taradash, Lewis Meltzer, Sarah Y Mason, Victor Heerman. *ph* Nick Musuraca, Karl Freund. *ed* Otto Meyer, Donald W Starling. *ad* Lionel Banks. *m* Victor Young. *cast* Barbara Stanwyck, William Holden, Adolphe Menjou, Lee J Cobb, Joseph Calleia, Sam Levene, Edward Brophy.

●If Clifford Odets' play seems impossibly shopworn today – boy from poverty row is tempted to abandon Art and his violin for the quick but brutalising rewards of the boxing-ring – at least this adaptation prunes away the worst, pseudo-poetical excesses of the original dialogue. Gone, too, is the character of the labour organiser, mouthpiece for Odets' flabby plea that the hero's choice is a matter for concern in terms of the ongoing struggle between Capital and Labour. What's left is melodrama, with the dilemma couched largely in moral and personal terms, and it stands up pretty well under Mamoulian's stylish direction, with its chiaroscuro lighting effects, savage final fight (shot with subjective camera), and gallery of excellent performances. Holden (in his film debut) is good in the title role; but the real treats are Menjou's mournfully cynical fight manager, Stanwyck's melting moll, and Calleia's wonderfully serio-comic, trigger-itchy gangster. TM

Golden Braid

(1990 Aust, 91 min)
d Paul Cox. *p* Paul Cox, Paul Ammitzboll, Samantha Naidu. *sc* Paul Cox, Barry Dickins. *ph* Nino Martinetti. *ed* Russell Hurley. *pd* Neil Angwin. *cast* Chris Haywood, Gosia Dobrowolska, Paul Chubb, Norman Kaye, Marion Heathfield, Monica Maughan.

●Inspired by Guy de Maupassant's short story 'La Chevelure', this is slighter than usual for Cox, but as witty as ever. Bernard (Haywood) is a fastidious clock-repairer with a history of collecting as many women as he does clocks. But his home is his true repository of pleasure, full of antiques and works of art, and chiming to the music of time. Into it he brings his newest conquest, the married Terese (Dobrowolska), but it's a perfect lock of golden hair, found secreted in a dresser, that unlocks his erotic passions and threatens to tip him into insanity. Though essentially a melancholy chamber piece, sustained by Haywood's quietly expressive performance, it is not without bursts of deliciously dark humour. Nino Martinetti's cinematography ensures a rich painterly surface, and the film is edited to produce a slow metronomic rhythm which lulls one rewardingly. WH

Golden Child, The

(1986, US, 94 min)
d Michael Ritchie. *p* Edward S Feldman, Robert D Wachs. *sc* Dennis Feldman. *ph* Donald Thorin. *ed* Richard A Harris. *pd* J Michael Riva. *m* Michel Colombier. *cast* Eddie Murphy, Charles Dance, Charlotte Lewis, Randall 'Tex' Cobb, James Hong, Shakti, JL Reate.

●Hot on the heels of *Big Trouble in Little China*, this similarly attempts to weld the thrills of oriental martial arts movies on to the Hollywood comic thriller, and similarly swan dives between the two stools to fall flat on its fanny. Murphy is a freelance LA social worker who specialises in finding lost children. Spotted by various wise oriental persons as The Chosen One, he embarks on his mission to retrieve The Golden Child, an appealing little waif who will convert the world to goodness, but has been captured for the forces of darkness by Dance. As in *Big Trouble*, there is much playing around with oriental mythic nonsense: underground caverns, magic daggers, even a trip to Tibet. But where the movie really misses a trick is its inability to reproduce the balletic splendours of martial arts. There is a comely Tibetan wench who can sink the odd villain, but her leaping wouldn't get her past an audition for the Peking Opera. Dance, sporting an orange goatee, is a splendid villain, looking like a Victorian actor-manager. The surprise is Murphy, who relies more on his undoubted charm than on the stream of wisecracks he usually delivers. CPea

Golden Coach, The (La Carrozza d'Oro/ Le Carrosse d'Or)

(1953, It/Fr, 100 min)
d Jean Renoir. *p* Francesco Alliata. *sc* Jean Renoir, Jack Kirkland, Renzo Avanzo, Giulio Macchi. *ph* Claude Renoir. *ed* Mario Serandrei, D Hawkins. *ad* Mario Chiari. *m* Antonio Vivaldi. *cast* Anna Magnani, Duncan Lamont, Odoardo Spadaro, Riccardo Rioli, Paul Campbell, Nada Fiorelli, Jean Debucourt.

●The first film in what came to be seen as a trilogy (completed by *French Cancan* and *Eléna et les Hommes*) celebrating Renoir's continuing love affair with the theatre. Magnani plays the lead actress in a troupe of commedia dell'arte players in 18th century Peru. The story (derived from Prosper Mérimée) revolves around her pursuit by three different lovers. Both story and characterisations are remarkably silly, in fact, but Renoir makes gold of the interaction between theatre and life, the distinction between them continually shifting with the plot. Exquisitely shot by Claude Renoir, this is one of the great colour films. RM

Golden Eighties

(1986, Fr/Bel/Switz, 96 min)
d Chantal Akerman. *p* Martine Marignac. *sc* Chantal Akerman, Leora Barish, Henry Bean, Pascal Bonitzer, Jean Gruault. *ph* Gilberto Azevedo, Luc Benhamou. *ed* Francine Sandberg. *ad* Serge Marzolff. *m* Marc Herouet. *cast* Delphine Seyrig, Myriam Boyer, Fanny Cottençon, Lio, Pascale Salkin, Charles Denner, Jean-François Balmer, John Berry.

●A zippy, brightly coloured musical – rather like Jacques Demy on speed – which is a far cry from Akerman's earlier slow, serious examinations of women and their place. The setting is the enclosed world of a shopping mall: on one side Lili's hair salon, busy with excitable young shampoo girls; on the other a clothes boutique run by Monsieur Schwartz and wife Jeanne (played with a nervous false smile by Seyrig). Their son Robert lusts after Madonna-lookalike Lili, who shamelessly shifts between him and a lovelorn gangster. One of her girls, Mado, is hopelessly in love with Robert. Then Jeanne's old American lover turns up… Akerman breathlessly switches from one group to another, merging bustling set pieces with wistful solos, until somehow the threads come together in a celebration of tears for fears and rampant amour. Dangerously flirting with kitsch – some sections do resemble a wacky French pop special – Akerman once again gets away with the impossible by virtue of her energy, insight and enveloping sensuality. DT

GoldenEye

(1995, GB/US, 130 min)
d Martin Campbell. *p* Michael Wilson, Barbara Broccoli. *sc* Jeffrey Caine, Bruce Feirstein. *ph* Philip Meheux. *ed* Terry Rawlings. *pd* Peter Lamont. *m* Eric Serra, Monty Norman. *cast* Pierce Brosnan, Sean Bean, Izabella Scorupco, Famke Janssen, Desmond Llewelyn, Joe Don Baker, Judi Dech, Robbie Coltrane, Tchéky Karyo, Alan Cumming, Minnie Driver, Samantha Bond.

●Six years after Timothy Dalton's last po-faced outing as 007, Brosnan takes over the role which Sean Connery once said was 'as difficult as Hamlet'. There's also a new Miss Moneypenny (Bond), a new M (Dench) and a new post-Communist world order. This Bond has been ruthlessly updated for '90s Russia: one scene takes place in a breaker's yard full of redundant Soviet statues. There's also an attempt to add depth to his character by introducing moral dilemmas – should he surrender, or let agent 006 (Bean) die? – and a hint of inner struggle. Thankfully, some things stay the same: Llewelyn makes his 15th appearance as Q, and there's another baddy who wants to inflict damage on the world, by stealing and controlling the 'GoldenEye' satellite activator, which disables everything electronic from outer space. Brosnan is most comfortable fighting, escaping or making the odd quip; in the more pensive scenes, particularly with impressive love interest Natalya (Scorupco), he seems lost. Director Campbell keeps matters bowling along and even manages to recapture something of the look of the earlier films. NKe

Golden Lady, The

(1979, GB/HK, 94 min)
d José Larraz. *p* Paul Cowan. *sc* Joshua Sinclair. *ph* David G Griffiths. *ed* David Campling. *ad* Norris Spencer. *m* Georges Garvarentz. *cast* Christina World, June Chadwick, Suzanne Danielle, Anika Pavel, Stephen Chase, Edward de Souza, Patrick Newell.

●Bizarrely unimaginative mix of ingredients from *Charlie's Angels* and the Bond series: cute women agents whose greatest victories are scored in the sack. The location is London, the plot too complicated to believe (KGB, CIA, Israelis and Arabs in one ridiculous espionage arena), the tone depressingly reminiscent of *The Bitch*. Forget it.

Golden Marie

see Casque d'Or

Golden Needles

(1974, US, 92 min)
d Robert Clouse. *p* Fred Weintraub, Paul Heller. *sc* S Lee Pogostin, Sylvia Schneble. *ph* Gil Hubbs. *ed* Michael Kahn. *m* Lalo Schifrin. *cast* Joe Don Baker, Elizabeth Ashley, Jim Kelly, Burgess Meredith, Ann Sothern, Roy Chiao, Frances Fong.

●Another of the Weintraub/Heller rip-offs of the Chinese cinema, and certainly the most dull, cynical and reactionary yet, lacking the slim saving graces of either *Enter the Dragon* or *Black Belt Jones*. Its plot ties itself in dreary knots around the attempts of a couple of hired freelancers (Ashley and Baker) to obtain possession of an ancient Chinese statue which indicates the seven forbidden acupuncture points. The martial arts are peripheral, and anyway no match for Western muscle. Clouse once again proves himself one of the least competent directors around. VG

Golden Rendezvous

(1977, US, 103 min)
d Ashley Lazarus. *p* André Pieterse. *sc* Stanley Price. *ph* Ken Higgins. *ed* Ralph Kemplen. *ad* Frank White. *m* Jeff Wayne. *cast* Richard Harris, Ann Turkel, David Janssen, Burgess Meredith, John Vernon, Gordon Jackson, Keith Baxter, Dorothy Malone, John Carradine.

●Dud ship-board drama based on one of Alistair MacLean's more preposterous yarns (a cargo ship catering to wealthy gamblers is taken over by terrorists as prelude to a dastardly caper). Attention is briefly held as mercenaries machine-gun the casino. Unfortunately they miss Burgess Meredith, wearing a silly hat, big Ann Turkel as the bitch with a heart of gold bullion, and dear old Dorothy Malone with her secret sorrow. JS

Golden Salamander

(1949, GB, 87 min, b/w)
d Ronald Neame. *p* Alexander Galperson. *sc* Lesley Storm, Victor Canning, Ronald Neame. *ph* Oswald Morris. *ed* Jack Harris. *ad* John Bryan. *m* William Alwyn. *cast* Trevor Howard, Anouk Aimée, Herbert Lom, Miles Malleson, Walter Rilla, Jacques Sernas.

●Lame thriller about an English art expert on the trail of some priceless antiques in North Africa (including the jewel-studded allegorical creature of the title), but crossing the path of a gang of gun-runners. At least there's Anouk to look at, along with some photogenic locations, and Howard gives a sturdier performance than the material warrants. TM

Golden Seal, The

(1983, US, 94 min)
d Frank Zuniga. *p* Samuel Goldwyn Jr. *sc* John Groves. *ph* Eric Saarinen. *ed* Robert Q Lovett. *pd* Douglas Higgins. *m* Dana Kaproff, John

Barry. *cast* Steve Railsback, Michael Beck, Penelope Milford, Torquil Campbell, Seth Sakai, Richard Narita.

●Set on one of the bleak Aleutian islands off the coast of Alaska, this is not in fact a Disney film but it has the formula down pat. Boy loves seal. Dad hunts seal. Boy hates dad. Dad sees light. Stir in some postcard scenery, plus some guff about the golden seal's magical ecological properties, and that's about it. TM

Golden Swallow (Jin Yanzi)

(1968, HK, 104 min)
d Chang Cheh. *p* Run Run Shaw. *sc* Chang Cheh. *ph* Pao Hsuie Lui. *ed* Chiang Shin Loong. *m* Wang Foo Ling. *cast* Wang Yu, Cheng Pei-Pei, Lo Lieh, Wu Ma, Gu Feng, Lin Chiao.

●Shaw Brothers produced this sequel to King Hu's *Come Drink with Me* to 'punish' Hu for ending his contract with them (and for cleaning up with his first Taiwanese film, *Dragon Gate Inn*). Cheng Pei-Pei returns as the righteous swordswoman Golden Swallow, lured out of hiding by news that her trademark pin has been found near the bodies of assorted dead villains. The man responsible is Silver Roc (Wang Yu at his most impassive), who has loved her since childhood and kills bad guys by the score to prove it. Trouble is, her friend Han (Lo Lieh) also secretly loves her – and so emotional complications underpin the plot's martial mayhem. Better written, shot and edited than Shaw movies of the '70s (Bao Xueli's 'Scope cinematography includes some daring hand-held work), this carries rhetorical excesses to sublime heights. High points include Roc, in spotless white, despatching an entire army singlehanded and the climax, in which Roc fights on with four daggers embedded in his chest. Yes, it was a seminal influence on John Woo, soon to be Chang's assistant. TR

Golden Voyage of Sinbad, The

(1973, GB, 105 min)
d Gordon Hessler. *p* Charles H Schneer, Ray Harryhausen. *sc* Brian Clemens. *ph* Ted Moore. *ed* Roy Watts. *pd* John Stoll. *m* Miklos Rozsa. *cast* John Philip Law, Caroline Munro, Tom Baker, Douglas Wilmer, Martin Shaw, Grégoire Aslan, Kurt Christian.

●Horror film director Hessler and special effects man Ray Harryhausen combine brilliantly to trace Sinbad's mystical voyage. The effects aren't simply fascinating for their own sake – they genuinely convey a sense of the magical and otherworldly. Younger kids sit through it happily enough but probably older kids and adults will enjoy it most. Regrettably, Brian Clemens' script remains resolutely earthbound. DP

Goldfinger

(1964, GB, 112 min)
d Guy Hamilton. *p* Harry Saltzman, Albert R Broccoli. *sc* Richard Maibaum, Paul Dehn. *ph* Ted Moore. *ed* Peter Hunt. *pd* Ken Adam. *m* John Barry, Leslie Bricusse, Anthony Newley. *cast* Sean Connery, Honor Blackman, Gert Froebe, Shirley Eaton, Harold Sakata, Bernard Lee.

●Vintage Bond from the moment our hero pops up out of the sea under a bobbing seagull attached to his frogman's suit which, having duly accomplished his explosive mission, he strips off to reveal an impeccable white dinner-jacket underneath. Ken Adam's sets, capped by the marvellous Fort Knox fantasy, are superb; and although Blackman's Pussy Galore is less than might be desired, there is suitably outsized villainy from Froebe and Sakata. Paul Dehn had a hand in the script, doubtless accounting for the unusually high incidence of wit in a script pleasantly laced with diabolic fantasy (from Eaton's demise by gold paint to Connery's near-emasculation by laser beam). TM

Goldfish (Huangjin Yu)

(1995, China, 70 min)
d Wu Di. *p* Zhou Wei. *sc* Wu Di, Ma Xiaoyong. *ph* Wu Wei. *ed* Niu Fang. *cast* Ma Xiaoyong, Zheng Tianwei, Yang Lu.

●This comic-edged first feature by Wu Di (cinematographer of *The Days* and *Postman*) has the same feel for street-level realities found in other Beijing indies, but a jauntier tone than most of them. Ma is the only guy his age in urban China who is scared to emigrate. One girlfriend has already left him over this issue; another gets him as far as the airport before he chickens out of flying to San Francisco. Trouble is, they've said their goodbyes to family and friends – and so they find themselves hiding in a rented farmhouse outside the city, pretending to be abroad. *Retour d'Afrique* had a similar premise, but this turns into a much sharper meditation on mental and other prisons when Ma starts breeding and selling goldfish, envying them their 'freedom'... TR

Gold Rush, The 100

(1925, US, 8,555 ft, b/w)
d/p/sc Charles Chaplin. *ph* Roland Totheroh, Jack Wilson. *ad* Charles D Hall. *cast* Charlie Chaplin, Mack Swain, Georgia Hale, Tom Murray, Henry Bergman, Betty Morrissey.

●The Little Tramp is here the Lone Prospector, poverty stricken, infatuated with Hale, and menaced by thugs and blizzards during the Klondike gold rush of 1898. Famous for various imaginative sequences – Charlie eating a Thanksgiving meal of an old boot and laces, Charlie imagined as a chicken by a starving and delirious Swain, a log-cabin teetering on the brink of an abyss – the film is nevertheless flawed by its mawkish sentimentality and by its star's endless winsome attempts to ingratiate himself into the sympathies of his audience. Mercifully, it lacks the pretentious moralising of his later work, and is far more professionally put together. But for all its relative dramatic coherence, it's still hard to see how it was ever taken as a masterpiece. GA

G'Olé!

(1982, GB, 101 min)
d Tom Clegg. *p* Drummond Challis, Michael Samuelson. *sc* Stan Hey. *ph* Harvey Harrison. *ed* Peter Boyle. *m* Rick Wakeman.

●Settling for redundantly regurgitating the spectacle of the final stages of the 1982 World Cup, this documentary compilation (narrated by Sean Connery, with commentary by Stan Hey) emerges as blandly unimaginative as its 'official film' status might imply. Where its 1966 precursor 'Goal' sustained itself on the potent novelty values of an England victory and flexible colour camerawork, this lags helplessly in the wake of high-quality blanket TV coverage, relying on a futile recreation of excitement over results and their immediate reverberations, while the penchant for low-angle close-ups on play ill serves a level of the game that's predominantly about finding and exploiting space. PT

Golem, The (Der Golem, Wie er in die Welt Kam)

(1920, Ger, 69 min, b/w)
d Paul Wegener, Carl Boese. *sc* Paul Wegener, Henrik Galeen. *ph* Karl Freund. *pd* Hans Poelzig. *cast* Paul Wegener, Albert Steinrueck, Ernst Deutsch, Lyda Salmonova, Hanns Sturm, Otto Gebühr.

●Spirited Ufa re-telling of the famous Jewish myth. When new anti-semitic laws are passed in 16th century Prague, an old rabbi, who's foreseen misfortune in the stars, brings the Golem to life. This ungainly hulking monster, made from clay with a pudding bowl haircut, terrorises the court into rescinding its laws against the Jews, but then goes on a wrecking spree of its own. Notable for its imaginative use of armies of extras and Karl Freund's expansive camerawork, Wegener's horror pic anticipates the many monster movies later made in Hollywood. The director was obsessed by the story of the Golem (he made two other films on the subject), quite an irony considering his later association with the Nazis. GM

Goliath and the Barbarians (Il Terrore dei Barbari)

(1959, It/US, 95 min)
d Carlo Campogalliani. *p* Emimmo Salvi. *sc* Carlo Campogalliani, Gino Mangini, Nino Stresa, Giuseppe Taffarel. *ph* Adalberto Albertini. *ed* Franco Fraticelli. *ad* Oscar D'Amico. *m* Carlo Innocenzi, Les Baxter. *cast* Steve Reeves, Chelo Alonso, Giulia Rubini, Livio Lorenzon, Andrea Checchi, Bruce Cabot.

●AD 568: The Longobards sack Verona, in the process killing the father of young Emiliano, aka Goliath (Reeves, aka Mr Universe). Goliath organises a guerilla band, counterattacks, and is taken prisoner. He falls in love with the daughter of his captor, a barbarian duke. Everything works out, thanks to Goliath returning the sacred crown of the Longobard king. After much bloodshed Emiliano marries the girl (Alonso). Kitsch fare from that fondly remembered, but in fact irredeemably tacky age of TotalScope Italian epics. JPy

Go Naked in the World

(1960, US, 103 min)
d Ranald MacDougall. *p* Aaron Rosenberg. *sc* Ranald MacDougall. *ph* Milton Krasner. *ed* John McSweeney Jr. *ad* George W Davis, Edward C Carfagno. *m* Adolph Deutsch. *cast* Gina Lollobrigida, Anthony Franciosa, Ernest Borgnine, Luana Patten, Will Kuluva, Philip Ober.

●Don't get excited, the title is only a lurid fly. Franciosa brings home his new girlfriend, La Lollo, but dad Borgnine and the Italian siren go way back already. The players do not seem to have their hearts in this lumpen melodrama. TJ

Gone in 60 Seconds

(1974, US, 103 min)
d/p/sc HB Halicki. *ph* John Vacek. *ed* Warner Leighton. *m* Philip Kachaturian, Ronald Halicki. *cast* HB Halicki, Marion Busia, Jerry Daugirda, James McIntyre, George Cole, Ronald Halicki.

●A rousing exercise in auto-snuff: how many cars can you demolish inside 103 minutes and still maintain interest in a plot? Almost half that time is taken up by another chase to end them all as 'Eleanor', the stolen Ford Mustang needed to complete a gigantic consignment (the title means how long it takes to steal a car, not to destroy it), creates a trail of havoc through LA and environs. 'Eleanor' is quite rightly credited at the start, since she has at least as much character as the human wrecking crew, who adopt a take-it-or-leave-it attitude about letting you know what's going on. If you take it, the wealth of sketched-in technical detail is fairly engrossing, and the energy of this Halicki production (he also wrote, directed, stars and supplied the vehicles) is arresting. It's a pity that it had to descend into such routine carnage. AN

Gone in Sixty Seconds

(2000, US, 118 min)
d Dominic Sena. *p* Jerry Bruckheimer, Mike Stenson. *sc* Scott Rosenberg. *ph* Paul Cameron. *ed* Tom Muldoon, Chris Lebenzon. *pd* Jeff Mann. *m* Trevor Rabin. *cast* Nicolas Cage, Angelina Jolie, Giovanni Ribisi, Delroy Lindo, Will Patton, Christopher Eccelston, Chi McBride, Robert Duvall, Scott Caan, Vinnie Jones, TJ Cross.

●Despite the flashy paint job and HipHop stereo soundtrack, Sena's reworking of HB Halicki's 1974 cult car-chase movie lacks grunt and growl beneath the hood. Where the original had too many car chases and not enough plot or characterisation, this has too much plot, too many characters and not enough metal crunching, tyre squealing action. The script is all chassis and no engine, while the messy direction lacks grip and acceleration. Forced out of retirement when his kid brother Kip (Ribisi) crosses some heavy duty criminals, legendary car thief 'Memphis' Raines (Cage) must reunite his old crew and steal 50 cars in one night, or kiss his sibling's ass goodbye. Hamstrung by the clunky script, the always watchable Cage is forced to overplay his modest hand, while Jolie has to content herself with a visually arresting cameo. Only charismatic ex-footballer Jones makes any impression – in part because his character, the mute and enigmatic Sphinx, is spared any embarrassing dialogue. In support, meanwhile, assorted seasoned actors stand around like spanners in search of the right-sized nut. NF

Gone To Earth

(1950, GB, 111 min)
d/p/sc Michael Powell, Emeric Pressburger. *ph* Christopher Challis. *ed* Reginald Mills. *pd* Hein Heckroth. *m* Brian Easdale. *cast* Jennifer Jones, David Farrar, Cyril Cusack, Esmond Knight, Sybil Thorndike, Edward Chapman, Hugh Griffith, George Cole, Beatrice Varley.

●A film much maligned in its time, not least by producer David O Selznick, who issued an American version retitled *The Wild Heart*, incorporating additional footage directed by Rouben Mamoulian and running only 82 minutes. Mary Webb's 1917 novel was the archetypal bodice-ripper – wicked squire, pious yokels, adultery and redemption – out of which Powell and Pressburger made a visually spellbinding romance. Christopher Challis' photography evokes Shropshire and the Welsh borders so that you can smell the earth. Menace, the bloodlust of the chase (of the fox or the outcast sinner), is omnipresent as trees bend and wild creatures panic before an unseen primal force. Cruelty besides beauty sweeps these pastoral vistas. Forget Jones' rustic English (Kentucky? Australian?) and the melodramatic clichés (boots trampling posies): the haunting, dreamlike consistency recalls that other fairy story of innocence and menace, *The Night of the Hunter*. MHoy

Gone With the Wind 100

(1939, US, 222 min)
d Victor Fleming. *p* David O Selznick. *sc* Sidney Howard. *ph* Ernest Haller, Ray Rennahan, Wilfrid M Cline. *ed* Hal C Kern, James E Newcom. *pd* William Cameron Menzies. *m* Max Steiner. *cast* Clark Gable, Vivien Leigh, Leslie Howard, Olivia de Havilland, Thomas Mitchell, Hattie McDaniel, Ona Munson, Ann Rutherford, Evelyn Keyes.
● What more can one say about this much-loved, much discussed blockbuster? It epitomises Hollywood at its most ambitious (not so much in terms of art, but of middlebrow, respectable entertainment served up on a polished platter); it's inevitably racist, alarmingly sexist (Scarlett's submissive smile after marital rape), nostalgically reactionary (wistful for a vanished, supposedly more elegant and honourable past), and often supremely entertaining. It never really confronts the political or historical context of the Civil War, relegating it to a backdrop for the emotional upheavals of Leigh's conversion from bitchy Southern belle to loving wife. It's also the perfect example of Hollywood as an essentially collaborative artistic production centre. Cukor, Sam Wood and Fleming directed from a script by numerous writers (including Scott Fitzgerald and Ben Hecht); William Cameron Menzies provided the art designs; there's a top-notch cast; and producer David O Selznick oversaw the whole project obsessively from start to finish. Yet, although anonymous, it's still remarkably coherent. GA

Gong Show Movie, The

(1980, US, 89 min)
d Chuck Barris. *p* Budd Granoff. *sc* Chuck Barris, Robert Downey. *ph* Richard C Glouner. *ed* James Mitchell, Sam Vitale, Jacqueline Cambas. *ad* Robert Kinoshita. *m* Milton DeLugg. *cast* Chuck Barris, Robin Altman, Brian O'Mullin, Mable King, Murray Langston, Jaye P Morgan, Jamie Farr.
● A hit on US TV in the latter part of the '70s, *The Gong Show* was a forum for the talentless – the dentist who played tunes on his drill, the man who blew his trumpet through his navel – who got laughed at by a celebrity panel, or, worse, suffered the ignominy of the gong which terminated their plucky efforts. Unfortunately, Barris, the show's creator/presenter, seemed to be succumbing to megalomania by the time this cringingly diabolical spin-off appeared, detailing his own crises of confidence and mounting personal problems as he tries to keep his beloved show on the road. TJ

Gonin

(1995, Jap, 109 min)
d Takashi Ishii. *p* Taketo Niitsu, Katsuhide Motoki. *sc* Takashi Ishii. *ph* Yasushi Sasakihara. *m* Goro Tasukawa. *cast* Koichi Sato, Masahiro Motoki, Jinpachi Nezu, Naoto Takenaka, Toshiyuki Nagashima, 'Beat' Takeshi Kitano.
● Five rank social outsiders (bankrupt businessman, unemployed salaryman, dismissed cop, pimp and male prostitute) team up to rob a huge amount of money from the outwardly respectable Ogoshi yakuza gang; an implacably gay hitman ('Beat' Takeshi in an eyepatch) is sent to hunt them down. Both the visuals and the all-star cast are knockout, but it's the mix of genre renewal, social allegory and dirty (mostly gay) sexuality which makes the film extraordinary. The climaxes are so exciting they should come with a health warning. TR

Gonin 2

(1996, Jap, 107 min)
d Takashi Ishii. *p* Kazuyoshi Okuyama. *sc* Takashi Ishii. *ph* Yasushi Sashikibara. *ed* Yoshiyuki Okuhara. *cast* Ken Ogata, Shinobu Otake, Kimiko Yo, Yui Natsukawa, Yumi Nishiyama, Mai Kitajima, Yumi Takigawa, Toshiyuki Nagashima.
● Not quite the equal of the first film, but it was a typically smart idea to make the five outsiders women this time. Each has a deftly sketched reason to hate society in general and men in particular. They are about to rob an ultra-chic jewellery story when the Ogoshi gang beats them to it, so they set about relieving the yakuza of their haul. The wild card in play is Toyama (Ogata), the owner of a metalworks, who has his own major grudge against the gang and is bent on violent revenge. For sheer graphic flair and visual attack, Ishii's film-making is head-and-shoulders above what passes for comics-influenced cinema in the West. TR

Gonza the Spearman (Yari no Gonza)

(1986, Jap, 126 min)
d Masahiro Shinoda. *p* Kiyoshi Iwashita, Mastake Wakita, Msayuki Motomichi. *sc* Taeko Tomioka. *ph* Kazuo Miyagawa. *ed* Sachiko Yamawaki. *pd* Kiyoshi Awazu. *m* Toru Takemitsu. *cast* Hiromi Go, Shima Iwashita, Shohei Hino, Misako Tanaka, Haruko Kato, Takashi Tsumura, Kaori Mizushima.
● Osai's husband, shogun leader of the clan of Izumo, is called away on business. In his absence, she asks his favoured retainer, Gonza, to marry her young daughter. But Gonza is caught up within the intra-clan power struggle, as others seek to usurp his prominent position. Beneath structured ritual, beneath the unstructured dichotomy of masculine and feminine culture, Shinoda uncovers the motivating passions which slowly simmer before boiling to the surface. Based on the 18th century play by Monzaemon Chikamatsu, the film's triumph comes with its final samurai confrontation, two dishonoured men left with no choice but to fulfil their prescribed roles. SGo

Goodbye, Boys (Do Svidanija, Maltsjiki)

(1966, USSR, 97 min)
d Mikhail Kalik. *sc* Boris Balter. *ph* Levan Paatashvili. *cast* Yevgeni Steblov, Mikhail Kononov, Nikolai Dostal, Natalia Bogoenova, Victoria Fedorova, Anna Rodjonova.
● Directed by a great lost name of '60s Soviet cinema, this was shelved and forbidden for export, emerging only 25 years later. It shouldn't be seen purely as a historical curio, though. Very much of its time, but still extremely fresh, it's an alternately lyrical and cynical evocation of youth in a Black Sea resort before World War II. Three adolescent boys enjoy their last summer together before being packed off reluctantly to military school. The use of newsreel footage – which was partly what got the film into trouble – is somewhat jarring, but otherwise it is light on polemic. The boys' quirks and follies are sympathetically observed, and the sense of place is flawless. JRo

Goodbye Charlie Bright

(2001, GB, 87 min)
d Nick Love. *p* Charles Steel, Lisa Bryer. *sc* Nick Love, Dominic Eames. *ph* Tony Imi. *ed* Patrick Moore. *pd* Eve Stewart. *m* Ivor Guest. *cast* Paul Nicholls, Roland Manookian, Phil Daniels, Jamie Foreman, Danny Dyer, Dani Behr, Richard Driscoll, David Thewlis, Sid Mitchell.
● This turns on the summer its young hero (Nicholls) realises his best mate Justin (Manookian) is a yob, a drawback and, worse, a danger to himself and anyone else within shouting distance. As their adolescent pranks edge towards something more serious, should Charlie stand by his friend, or step out for himself? It's scarcely a new story – *Mean Streets*, anyone? – but a true story none the less. Obviously, on some imaginative level, Charlie is director Nick Love. Refreshingly, Love skips grotty realism for a brighter, breezier style, popping chroma and whip pans, more *Do the Right Thing* than *Nil by Mouth*. The tone is larky and unpretentious, a little awkward as it shifts from the localised detail of a South London estate to wide-eyed wonder at the grown-up world beyond, but the film is more than carried by its strength of feeling for the lads back then, and the men they left behind. In fact, it's those who got away who come off worst: Charlie's dad (Thewlis) and his macho-riche uncle Hector (Driscoll). Vivid stuff, true to itself, and a promising debut. TCh

Goodbye, Columbus

(1969, US, 105 min)
d Larry Peerce. *p* Stanley R Jaffe. *sc* Arnold Schulman. *ph* Gerald Hirschfeld. *ed* Ralph Rosenblum. *ad* Manny Gerard. *m* Charles Fox. *cast* Richard Benjamin, Ali MacGraw, Jack Klugman, Nan Martin, Michael Meyers, Lori Shelle, Royce Wallace.
● A wonderfully beady-eyed adaptation of Philip Roth's novella satirising the Jewish nouveau riche and/or the American Dream, with Benjamin as the impoverished graduate courting a Radcliffe girl (MacGraw), and discovering what he's got into only when she invites him (to the exasperation of her socially ambitious mother) to stay as a house guest. Self-effacingly directed by Peerce, the film stakes everything on minute observation of detail: the ghastly gusto of mealtimes in the parvenu dining-room; the loose-limbed insolence in every movement made by the scion of the family; the worship of appearances rather than accomplishments in everything that is said or done. With Philip Roth's barbed dialogue retained intact, and faultlessly delivered by an admirable cast, the film is funnier than *The Graduate* (made a couple of years earlier) and much less pretentious. TM

Goodbye Emmanuelle

(1977, Fr, 98 min)
d François Leterrier. *p* Michel Choquet. *sc* Monique Lange, François Leterrier. *ph* Jean Badal. *ed* Marie-Josèphe Yoyotte. *ad* François de Lamothe. *m* Serge Gainsbourg. *cast* Sylvia Kristel, Umberto Orsini, Jean-Pierre Bouvier, Charlotte Alexandra, Jacques Doniol-Valcroze, Olga Georges-Picot, Alexandra Stewart.
● This awful episode in the *Emmanuelle* saga takes a curious moral turn. When one of her passing fancies calls her a whore, her only recourse is to fall in love with him. The double standard evident in previous adventures – where Kristel portrays a woman apparently choosing to practice sexual freedom, while in fact being savagely exploited – is dropped. Suddenly it's all jealousy, privacy and tears around bedtime. Much agony, low on ecstasy. JS

Goodbye Girl, The

(1977, US, 110 min)
d Herbert Ross. *p* Ray Stark. *sc* Neil Simon. *ph* David M Walsh. *ed* Margaret Booth. *pd* Albert Brenner. *m* David Grusin. *cast* Richard Dreyfuss, Marsha Mason, Quinn Cummings, Paul Benedict, Barbara Rhoades.
● Written by Neil Simon, it's no surprise that this is a classy piece of Broadway sitcom. Mason and Dreyfuss play with comic panache and vitality as the couple reluctantly obliged to cohabit, even if occasionally their physical energy adds to the impression that this is simply theatre on celluloid. Equally, interest flags after they get to bed, endorsing the line that 'It's amazing how flabby you get when you're happy'. But overall Simon's ego-splitting wisecracks make for many good laughs, even though, in contrast to Woody Allen's nervous New York humour, which has the discomforting ring of truth, Simon opts for a playwright's ring of confidence. JS

Goodbye Lover

(1998, US/Ger, 104 min)
d Roland Joffé. *p* Alexandra Milchan, Patrick McDarrah, Joel Roodman, Chris Daniel. *sc* Ron Peer, Joel Cohen, Alec Sokolow. *ph* Dante Spinotti. *ed* William Steinkamp. *pd* Stewart Starkin. *m* John Ottman. *cast* Patricia Arquette, Dermot Mulroney, Ellen DeGeneres, Mary-Louise Parker, Don Johnson, Ray McKinnon, André Gregory, Lisa Eichhorn, Max Perlich, Vincent Gallo.
● Patricia Arquette delivers another of her unlikely temptress turns as Sandra Dunmore, an over-sexed blonde with an insatiable appetite for, among other things, *The Sound of Music*. Observing something's amiss, her husband Jake (Mulroney) is hitting the bottle big time, but he'd never guess she was screwing his own brother Ben (Johnson). Ben in turn wants out, so tries it on with his improbably prim colleague Peggy Blaine (Parker); the scorned Sandra is somewhat put out. Or is she? Naturally the plot's not what it seems, twice over. Like its characters, the film operates in extreme bad faith, unloading a stream of narrative deceptions and obfuscations in an

attempt to maintain what semblance of suspense the hysterical melodrama, lumpen dialogue and farcical acting still allow. NB

Goodbye, Mr Chips

(1939, GB, 113 min, b/w)
d Sam Wood. *p* Victor Saville. *sc* RC Sherriff, Claudine West, Eric Maschwitz. *ph* Freddie Young. *ed* Charles Frend. *ad* Alfred Junge. *m* Richard Addinsell. *cast* Robert Donat, Greer Garson, Terry Kilburn, John Mills, Paul Henreid, Judith Furse, Lyn Harding, Milton Rosmer, Guy Middleton, Nigel Stock.

●With his cane, scarf, mortar-board and perpetual hangdog expression, Robert Donat seemed to embody Neville Chamberlain – 'I have a piece of paper and it's spelt incorrectly. One hundred lines, Master Hitler, or you'll be slippered'. Actually, the movie always was a museum piece, and– if you are in the right mood – a deeply affecting one. Donat's schoolmaster looks back upon his life – his surrogate fatherhood to scores of boys, his marriage to Mrs Miniver, who dies during childbirth – and Olde England passes before our very eyes. ATu

Goodbye, Mr Chips

(1968, GB, 147 min)
d Herbert Ross. *p* Arthur P Jacobs. *sc* Terence Rattigan. *ph* Oswald Morris. *ed* Ralph Kemplen. *pd* Ken Adam. *songs* Leslie Bricusse. *cast* Peter O'Toole, Petula Clark, Michael Redgrave, George Baker, Michael Bryant, Jack Hedley, Sian Phillips.

●Incredibly bloated remake, with Mrs Chips an ex-showgirl (allowing for some vacuous songs), a continental holiday (allowing for a travelogue wallow), and Herbert Ross (his first film as director), trying to match Wyler's choreographed camera movements on *Funny Girl* but failing to make them serve any meaningful purpose. The pity of it is that Peter O'Toole sketches an excellent performance amid the debris – angular and desiccated as a stick insect, but endowing the character with both an inside and an outside, so that his metamorphosis from passionless pedant into loveable eccentric is perfectly credible. Good support too, from Redgrave and Bryant in particular, but they're trapped like flies in the sticky confection. TM

Goodbye New York

(1984, Isr, 90 min)
d/p/sc Amos Kollek. *ph* Amnon Salomon. *ed* Alan Heim. *m* Michael Abene. *cast* Julie Hagerty, Amos Kollek, Shmuel Shiloh, Aviva Ger, David Topaz, Jennifer Babtist.

●Garrulous insurance saleswoman Hagerty, betrayed by her unfaithful hubby, sets out for Paris in seach of peace of mind, only to end up penniless and stranded in Israel. Kollek offers us a predictable plot and dismal propaganda about the values of kibbutz culture. A fatal flaw in the film is that both Hagerty and Kollek himself, playing an Israeli army reserve who becomes her chief suitor, are so unsympathetic. Another is that Hagerty's sub-Judy Holliday kook is simply not strong enough to carry such thin and clichéd material. GA

Goodbye, Norma Jean

(1975, US/Aust, 95 min)
d/p Larry Buchanan. *sc* Lynn Shubert, Larry Buchanan. *ph* Robert B Sherry. *ed* John S Curran, Larry Buchanan. *ad* John Carter. *m* Joe Beck. *cast* Misty Rowe, Terrence Locke, Patch Mackenzie, Preston Hanson, Marty Zagon.

●Managing the feat of holding its nose and leering at the same time, this 'biopic' mixes scurrility and a token feminism with rock-bottom production values. 'Not legend, nor the way she told it, this is how it was' promises the introduction, thereby allowing for a highly speculative hour-and-a-half about Marilyn Monroe's early career on the casting couch. Even the sustained loathing of men ('That's the last cock I'll ever have to suck' are the film's final words) is diluted by the presence of an unlikely father-figure producer who takes Marilyn's career in hand. Misty Rowe fails spectacularly as a reincarnation of Monroe.

Goodbye Pork Pie

(1980, NZ, 105 min)
d Geoff Murphy. *p* Nigel Hutchinson, Geoff Murphy. *sc* Geoff Murphy, Ian Mune. *ph* Alun Bollinger. *ed* Michael Horton. *ad* Kai Hawkins, Robert Outterside. *m* John Charles. *cast* Tony Barry, Kelly Johnson, Claire Oberman, Shirley Gruar, Jackie Lowitt, Don Selwyn.

●Using the well-established caper-chase road movie format, this follows two 'irrepressible' buddies on a 1,000 mile 'let's get smashed' odyssey in a stolen car, in pursuit of love and pursued by cops. But for all its admittedly speedy pace, the film pays mere lip service to the idea of characterisation and to 'earthy' humour with its lame, often objectionable jokes: 'irrepressible' means sexist antics such as betting on a girl's virginity, cursing 'stupid bloody bitches' ad nauseam, indulging in drink, dope and drearily juvenile zaniness. Only towards the end does the film pick up in its predictably darkening mood. But even then too many elements are plagiarised; *Sugarland Express*, especially, told a similar tale with far more thrills, wit and humanity. GA

Goodbye South, Goodbye (Nanguo Zai Jian, Nanguo)

(1996, Tai, 116 min)
d Hou Xiaoxian. *p* Katsuhiro Mizuno, Jieh-Wen King. *sc* Chu Tien-wen. *ph* Li Ping-Bin. *ed* Liao Ching-Song. *cast* Jack Kao, Hsu Kuei-ying, Lim Giong, Anne Shizuka Inoh, Hsi Hsiang.

●Though Hou has said that he wanted this to have a different rhythm from the slow, even static pace of his previous work, it remains immediately recognisable as a Hou movie, not only because of the very lengthy takes (here, admittedly, often of moving trains, cars, motorbikes, etc), but because of his determinedly oblique approach to narrative and the way it provides information. This time round, the 'story' of a group of small-time punks on the fringes of the underworld is designed to offer insights into the moral, political and economic climate of '90s Taiwan; it does, and the movie looks as marvellous as ever. But for all the expertise on view, one can't help feeling a sense of déjà vu. The film echoes much of Hou's own previous work, and the plot's central strand – an ambitious guy and his younger, more volatile buddy finally get their comeuppance in a car crash – is oddly reminiscent of *Mean Streets*. GA

Good Burger

(1997, US, 95 min)
d Brian Robbins. *p* Mike Tollin, Brian Robbins. *sc* Dan Schneider, Kevin Kopelow, Heath Seifert. *ph* Mac Ahlberg. *ed* Anita Brandt-Burgoyne. *pd* Steve Jordan. *m* Stewart Copeland. *cast* Kenan Thompson, Kel Mitchell, Abe Vigoda, Sinbad, Shar Jackson, Dan Schneider.

●This TV spinoff asks us to root for the trash food joint of the title, and specifically its hero, Ed (Mitchell), an exceptionally annoying imbecile. The staff of Good Burger are more adept at driving out would-be customers with execrable puns than serving their orders, so the bad boys across the road at Mondo Burger need no help in driving their small fry rivals out of business. Enter Dexter (Thompson), a more conventionally wayward adolescent than Ed, who needs to work through the school vacation to pay off the insurance on two sportscars he's wrecked. Dexter notes that Ed makes very nice homemade burger sauce, and suddenly Good Burger is back in business. Few people can be so big-hearted as to tolerate Ed's agonising brand of pedantic humour. NB

Good Companions, The

(1933, GB, 113 min, b/w)
d Victor Saville. *p* Michael Balcon. *sc* WP Lipscomb. *ph* Bernard Knowles. *ed* Frederick Y Smith. *ad* Alfred Junge. *songs* George Posford, Douglas Furber. *cast* Edmund Gwenn, Mary Glynne, John Gielgud, Jessie Matthews, Percy Parsons, AW Baskcomb, Max Miller.

●JB Priestley's fantasy, in which a demure spinster, an elderly mill-worker and an effete schoolteacher throw security to the winds to seek fortune and adventure with a broken-down band of travelling players, is so engaging that one easily forgives its sentimentality. Saville's direction is adequate rather than inspired, but he elicits marvellous performances from his disparate cast. Matthews' portrayal of a bubblingly neurotic soubrette is wonderful, and not surprisingly shot her to stardom. The film does feed on rather than explore the twee camaraderie of the provincial touring company, but an English backstage musical as witty and well-handled as this is something to be thankful for indeed. RMy

Good Companions, The

(1956, GB, 104 min)
d J Lee Thompson. *p* Hamilton G Inglis, J Lee Thompson. *sc* TJ Morrison. *ph* Gilbert Taylor. *ed* Gordon Pilkington. *ad* Robert Jones. *m* Laurie Johnson. *cast* Celia Johnson, Eric Portman, John Fraser, Janette Scott, Hugh Griffith, Joyce Grenfell, Rachel Roberts, Thora Hird, Mona Washbourne, Alec McCowen, John Le Mesurier, Anthony Newley.

●Priestley's novel is given a Technicolor and CinemaScope update making it far plusher than the tightly budgeted 1933 version. This time Johnson, Portman and Fraser are the spinster, the bluff Northerner and the teacher who bring new life to the Dinky Doos pierrot troupe, and put youngster Scott's name up in lights. It doesn't have quite the same charm as the earlier adaptation, but is solidly done all the same, with a regiment of familiar faces in the minor roles. TJ

Good Die Young, The

(1954, GB, 98 min)
d Lewis Gilbert. *sc* Vernon Harris, Lewis Gilbert. *ph* Jack Asher. *ed* Ralph Kemplen. *ad* Bernard Robinson. *m* Georges Auric. *cast* Laurence Harvey, Gloria Grahame, Richard Basehart, Joan Collins, John Ireland, Stanley Baker, Margaret Leighton, Robert Morley.

●Producer Clayton and director Gilbert (the most hard-working of all British post-war filmmakers) assembled a top Anglo-American cast for this predictable but not unentertaining thriller (from a novel by Richard Macauley). Psychotic playboy Harvey finds himself short of the readies so he persuades ex-GI Basehart, AWOL Air Force sergeant Ireland and no-hope boxer Baker to join him in holding up a mail van. This being a British picture from the '50s, you don't expect them to get away with it – but neither do you quite anticipate Joan Collins and Gloria Grahame popping up in such low-key supporting roles as they do here. GM

Good Earth, The

(1937, US, 138 min, b/w)
d Sidney Franklin. *p* Irving Thalberg. *sc* Talbot Jennings, Tess Slesinger, Claudine West. *ph* Karl Freund. ed Basil Wrangell. *ad* Cedric Gibbons. *m* Herbert Stothart. *cast* Paul Muni, Luise Rainer, Walter Connolly, Charley Grapewin, Jessie Ralph, Tilly Losch, Keye Luke.

●'Who wants to see a picture about Chinese farmers?' asked LB Mayer of his production chief Irving Thalberg. Thalberg had asked the same question about a Civil War picture called *Gone With the Wind*. The answer in both cases was millions, but in the case of *The Good Earth* the reasons are quite bewildering. A kind of 'Lychees of Wrath', it's a typically lumbering, cautious, overblown Thalberg project, saved by Rainer's genuinely moving, Oscar-winning portrayal of Chinese peasantry, and by an immensely spectacular storm of locusts. Thalberg died during the production, and Mayer accorded him a special tribute on the credits, the only time that the name of the last tycoon appeared on a film. (From the novel by Pearl Buck.) ATu

Good Father, The

(1986, GB, 90 min)
d Mike Newell. *p* Ann Scott. *sc* Christopher Hampton. *ph* Michael Coulter. *ed* Peter Hollywood. *pd* Adrian Smith. *m* Richard Hartley. *cast* Anthony Hopkins, Jim Broadbent, Harriet Walter, Frances Viner, Simon Callow, Miriam Margolyes, Joanne Whalley.

●Hopkins is a middle-aged, middle-class, middle-minded man, impaled on the post-feminist hook. Having once been a subscriber to the cause, he has since been thrown out of his home, and pays alimony for the privilege of having his child turned against him. The worm turns and he embarks on a none-too-fair legal battle, in order to 'jerk her lead'. The early stages of this battle of the sexes are by turns hilarious and squirm-making, but Christopher Hampton's script finally opts for an uneasy truce, perhaps a soft option after the initial viciousness. But it's a very brave foray across the minefield; its detonations will have you ducking for cover, whatever your sex or persuasion. CPea

GoodFellas (100)

(1990, US, 145 min)
d Martin Scorsese. *p* Irwin Winkler. *sc* Nicholas Pileggi, Martin Scorsese. *ph* Michael Ballhaus. *ed* Thelma Schoonmaker. *pd* Kristi Zea. *cast* Robert De Niro, Ray Liotta, Joe Pesci, Lorraine Bracco, Paul Sorvino, Frank Sivero, Gina Mastrogiacomo, Frank Vincent, Chuck Low.
● Scorsese's fast, violent, stylish mobster movie is a return to form, De Niro, and the Italian-American underworld. But in following, from '55 to the late '70s, the true-life descent into big-time crime of Henry Hill (Liotta), he and co-writer Nick Pileggi seem less concerned with telling a lucid, linear story than with providing sociological evidence of an ethically (ethnically?) marginalised society united by the desire to make a fast buck. Because Hill and the older 'good fellas' he first falls in with as an awestruck kid – De Niro, Pesci, Sorvino – exist almost totally on the surface, we watch shocked and beguiled but never come to care. The camera and cutting style is as forcefully persuasive as a gun in the gut, so that we are not enlightened but excited by the cocky camaraderie, bloody murder, and expansive sense of 'family' on view. Still, the movie excites the senses in a way few film-makers even dream of, and its epic sweep and brilliantly energetic film language rest on a cluster of effortlessly expert performances. GA

Good Fight, The

(1983, US, 98 min, b/w & col)
d/p Noel Buckner, Mary Dore, Sam Sills. *ph* Stephen Lighthill, Peter Rosen, Joe Vitagliano, Renner Wunderlich. *ed* Noel Buckner. *m* Wendy Blackstone, Bernardo Palombo. *with* Bill Bailey, Ed Balchowsky, Ruth Davidow, Evelyn Hutchins, Steve Nelson, Tom Page.
● Just about the most stirring documentary you'll ever see. Through newsclips, old photographs and interviews with survivors, it tells the story of the 3,200 men and women who fought with the American Lincoln Brigade during the Spanish Civil War: men like Bill Bailey, the longshoreman who laughs as he describes how, during an anti-Nazi demonstration in New York in 1935, he and a friend boarded a German ship and tore down its swastika; women like Evelyn Hutchins, who had to fight to persuade her colleagues into letting her serve as the only female ambulance driver. What seems to have motivated them was America's deliberate non-intervention. 'That was my brother out there', says one volunteer; 'You had to put up or shut up' says another; and they all describe 'an enormous feeling of wanting to come to grips' with what they saw as the tide of Fascism about to engulf Europe. What comes over most strongly is the resolute idealism of those who fought, and did so in a way that seems impossibly heroic in these unheroic times. They were young, 'just chickenshit kids', untrained, and with no idea of what they were letting themselves in for. Yet they went and suffered terrible casualties. Now, although in their seventies, their enthusiasm for the cause remains undimmed, and a bunch of them are seen marching proudly as Lincoln Brigade veterans in a huge demo against US involvement in El Salvador. They may have lost the battle, as one of them concludes, but the war against Fascism was won, and the good fight continues. CB

Good Green World, The

see Belle Verte, La

Good Guys and the Bad Guys, The

(1969, US, 90 min)
d Burt Kennedy. *p/sc* Ronald M Cohen, Dennis Shryack. *ph* Harry Stradling Jr. *ed* Howard Deane. *pd* Stan Jolley. *m* William Lava. *cast* Robert Mitchum, George Kennedy, David Carradine, Tina Louise, Douglas V Fowley, Martin Balsam, Lois Nettleton, John Davis Chandler, John Carradine, Marie Windsor.
● Burt Kennedy's characteristically affectionate Western comedy sees ageing sheriff Mitchum join forces with his old bandit enemy George Kennedy to outwit Carradine and his gang of younger, rather less honorable robbers, and in so doing, cock a snook at Balsam, the opportunist and self-inflated mayor who has demanded Mitchum's retirement. In noting the passing of the Old West, and upholding honour and age over expediency and youth, Kennedy comes closer to the Peckinpah of *Ride the High Country* than of *The Wild Bunch*; even so, the humour here is broad and cheery rather than elegiac and violent. The performances are delightful throughout, and Kennedy, quite rightly, gives them free rein. GA

Good Guys Wear Black

(1977, US, 95 min)
d Ted Post. *p* Allan F Bodoh. *sc* Bruce Cohn, Mark Medoff. *ph* Robert Steadman. *ed* William Moore, Millie Moore. *ad* BB Neel. *m* Craig Safan. *cast* Chuck Norris, Anne Archer, James Franciscus, Lloyd Haynes, Dana Andrews, Jim Backus.
● Whether taken as a cynical companion to prestigious Hollywood Vietnam movies, a twisting political conspiracy, or a starring vehicle for world karate champion Chuck Norris, this complicated action caper hovers between OK and mediocre. A mysterious spate of assassinations follow a top secret US raid into North Vietnam, with veteran Norris suspecting that they were set up by corrupt politicians as part of an expedient deal with the reds to end the war. Norris ties it all up and biffs sense into those too yellow to own up in a post-Watergate world where expediency is all, and honour is a dirty word. A successor to *Go Tell the Spartans* from the studiously unsentimental Post. DMacp

Good Housekeeping

(2000, US, 91 min)
d Frank Novak. *p* Mark Mathis, *sc* Frank Novak. *ph* Alex Vendler. *ed* Fritz Feick. *pd* Elizabeth Burhop. *cast* Bob Mills, Petra Westen, Zia, Tracey Adams, Scooter Stephan, Andrew Eichner, Al Schuermann.
● Coming on like an insane brew of Ishii's *Crazy Family* and Harmony Korine's freewheeling schizophrenic essays, this black satire on a North Hollywood white trash family who descend to near animal behaviour (in the period before the parents' divorce) pushes audience tolerance to the limit. Guntoting, *Puppetmaster*-obsessed Don (Mills) explodes when wife Donatella (Westen) takes a supportive lesbian lover; he divides the house down the middle and with his drinking cronies (including a militant men's rights activist and a so-called paralegal) prepares for battle to the end. Remarkable for its view of the cops (mere domestic go-betweens) and its all embracing cynicism, this bleak account of the sex war makes uncomfortable viewing, but it's fun seeing the actors rule the roost. May appeal to disillusioned youth. WH

Good Life, The (La Buena Vida)

(1997, Sp, 105 min)
d David Trueba. *p* Fernando Trueba, Ana Huete, Christina Huete. *sc* David Trueba. *ph* William Lubtchansky. *ed* Angel Hernandez. *pd* Christia Mampaso. *m* Antoine Duhamel. *cast* Fernando Ramallo, Lucía Jiménez, Luis Cuenca, Isabel Oetero, Joel Joan, Victoria Peña, Jordi Bosch.
● This uneven, but not uninteresting first feature starts alarmingly (in sub-*Toto the Hero* vein) with the 14-year-old protagonist, a would-be writer, recalling his life from pre-natal days – before picking up a little when he learns that his parents have died in a car crash, while he's planning to lose his cherry to a whore. Thereafter the film concerns the boy's efforts to overcome loneliness and guilt, to sort out his own problems and those of his relatives, and generally to get through growing up without too much pain. Weakest when most whimsical, the film is nevertheless sporadically perceptive about adolescent experience. Lively, amiable, and eminently forgettable. GA

Good Man in Africa, A

(1993, US, 94 min)
d Bruce Beresford. *p* Mark Tarlov, John Fiedler. *sc* William Boyd. *ph* Andrzej Bartkowiak. *ed* Jim Clark. *pd* Herbert Pinter. *m* John Du Prez. *cast* Colin Friels, Sean Connery, John Lithgow, Diana Rigg, Louis Gossett Jr, Joanne Whalley-Kilmer, Timothy Spall.
● Just as casting can be the making of a film, so it can be its ruination. A case in point is this adaptation of William Boyd's comic novel about the political, diplomatic and sexual machinations surrounding an impending election in the emerging oil-rich state of Kinjana. As frustrated mid-level British diplomat Morgan Leafy, a role tailor-made for Timothy Spall, we have the more bankably handsome Australian actor Colin Friels; as his boorish boss, High Commissioner Fanshawe, we have American John Lithgow, whose 'English' accent has improved not a jot since *Cliffhanger*; and as Professor Adekunle, wily would-be president of the corrupt African state, Louis Gossett Jr, who appears to be more basketball player than politician. Screenwriter Boyd has turned his laugh-out-loud novel into a groan-out-loud movie. NF

Good Marriage, A

see Beau Mariage, Le

Good Men, Good Women (Haonan, Haonü)

(1995, Jap/Tai, 108 min)
d Hou Hsiao-hsien. *p* Katsuhiro Mizuno. *sc* Zhu Tianwen. *ph* Chen Hwai-En. *ed* Liao Ching-Song. *pd* Huang Wen-ying, Lu Ming-ching, Ho Hsien-ko. *m* Chen Hwai-en. *cast* Annie Shizuka Inoh, Lim Giong, Jack Kao.
● Hou again looks at recent Taiwanese history. The story centres on an actress mourning her lover who's convinced she's receiving silent phone calls from the person who stole her diary. She begins to identify with the character she's playing in a movie about a couple involved in the Resistance during the '40s and '50s. With its narrative switching between past and present, 'reality' and the film-within-a-film, Hou's movie is complex and challenging, but never inaccessible. Blending the personal with the political to typically resonant effect, it's a multi-layered exploration of changing cultural ideals, haunted memories, and the joys and pains of love. With patience, it soon becomes clear this is some sort of masterpiece. GA

Good Morning

see Ohayo

Good Morning, Miss Dove

(1955, US, 107 min)
d Henry Koster. *p* Samuel G Engel. *sc* Eleanore Griffin. *ph* Leon Shamroy. *ed* William H Reynolds. *ad* Lyle Wheeler, Mark-Lee Kirk. *m* Leigh Harline. *cast* Jennifer Jones, Robert Stack, Kipp Hamilton, Robert Douglas, Peggy Knudsen, Chuck Connors, Jerry Paris.
● Sentimental but professionally assembled classroom chronicle follows much-loved spinster schoolma'm Jennifer Jones through generations of diverse pupils at a small town high school, before a spine tumour sends her to hospital where surgeon Stack, a former student, must undertake a risky operation to save her. Few sharp edges, but just the thing for a homespun Sunday afternoon wallow. TJ

Good Morning...and Goodbye (aka The Lust Seekers)

(1967, US, 78 min)
d/p Russ Meyer. *sc* John E Moran. *ph* Russ Meyer. *ed* Russ Meyer, Richard Brummer. *m* Igo Kantor. *cast* Alaina Capri, Stuart Lancaster, Pat Wright, Haji, Karen Ciral, Don Johnson, Tom Howland.
● Connoisseurs of camp who revere Russ Meyer's majestic *Beyond the Valley of the Dolls* will be disappointed by this low-budget earlier effort. Although loins quiver, studs flex their pectorals, and cantilevered breasts career across the screen, the film is distinctly skimpy and down-market. Despite the sonorous moralising in prologue and epilogue about 'humble sex, that three-letter word whose power cannot be demeaned by the foulness of four-letter words', such splendid silliness is not maintained throughout the story of Burt, impotent middle-aged businessman, and his randy, taunting wife Angel, for whose legs anytime is opening time. DJe

Good Morning Babylon (Good Morning Babilonia)

(1986, It/Fr/US, 113 min)
d Paolo Taviani, Vittorio Taviani. *p* Giuliani G De Negri. *sc* Paolo Taviani, Vittorio Taviani, Tonino Guerra. *ph* Giuseppe Lanci. *ed* Roberto Perpignani. *ad* Gianni Sbarra. *m* Nicola Piovani. *cast* Vincent Spano, Joaquim De Almeida, Greta Scacchi, Désirée Becker, Omero Antonutti, Charles Dance, Bérangère Bonvoisin.

●The Taviani brothers' first (mainly) English language film, set just before and during World War I, concerns two inseparable Tuscan brothers, stonemasons who – like their forefathers – restore Romanesque cathedrals. Suddenly finding themselves without work, they travel to America in search of the fortune that will allow them to return to revive their father's business; after endless setbacks, they finally win acclaim for their work on the Babylonian elephants for DW Griffith's *Intolerance*. As in their previous films, the Tavianis take an oblique and deeply personal look at history to create a fable of enormous resonance. Realism merges with the surreal, fact with fiction, and a *faux-naif* surface (not unlike that of the films from the period depicted) conceals a complex interweaving of familiar Taviani themes: the continuing strengths and shortcomings of tradition and patriarchy, the importance of imagination, memory and collective endeavour. Typically, sentimentality is held at bay by the cool, formalised direction. The performances throughout are splendid, the symbolism never intrusive, the entire achievement witty and elegant. GA

Good Morning, Boys! (aka Where There's a Will)

(1937, GB, 79 min, b/w)
d Marcel Varnel. *p* Edward Black. *sc* Val Guest, Leslie Arliss, Marriot Edgar. *ph* Arthur Crabtree. *ed* RE Dearing, Alfred Roome. *ad* Alex Vetchinsky. *m* Jack Beaver. *cast* Will Hay, Graham Moffatt, Lilli Palmer, Martita Hunt, Mark Daly, Charles Hawtrey.
●This brisk vehicle for Hay's idiosyncratic talents has him in the tailor-made role of a roguish schoolmaster, whose wayward teaching methods win him a trip to Paris with his French class. There's a stowaway in the party and they become involved in the theft of the Mona Lisa. Hay's persona is a much more cynical and devious than the gauche type George Formby played for director Varnel, which goes some way to explaining why this, his finest hour, hasn't dated too badly. TJ

Good Morning Vietnam

(1987, US, 108 min)
d Barry Levinson. *p* Mark Johnson, Larry Brezner. *sc* Mitch Markowitz. *ph* Peter Sova. *ed* Stu Linder. *pd* Roy Walker. *m* Alex North. *cast* Robin Williams, Forest Whitaker, Tung Thanh Tran, Chintara Sukapatana, Bruno Kirby, Robert Wuhl, JT Walsh, Noble Willingham.
●As US Armed Forces Radio DJ Adrian Cronauer, dumped in Saigon, in '65, Williams reveals how easy it is to hang a slim, bathetic idea on a virtuoso performance. Cronauer is your archetypal all-American anti-hero, an achingly funny, irreverent motormouth with a taste for hot soul and a subversive vision of the Vietnam conflict as a mad *Wizard of Oz* scenario which enrages the top brass as inevitably as it boosts the morale of the grunts. Williams' rendition of the broadcasting sequences is terrific, as speedily inventive as the comic's finest stand-up moments, even though Levinson has an irritating habit of cutting away to Cronauer's colleagues and audience cracking up, simply to show that the guy's funny. But the story itself is bunk. Besides the DJ's heroic set-to with petty-minded superiors, there's a crass romance with a shy young Vietnamese, and a friendship with her brother, which allows our fine liberal protagonist to play great white god to the gooks. Offering only hackneyed insights into the war, the film makes for stodgy drama. But Williams' manic monologues behind the mike are worth anybody's money. GA

Good Mother, The

(1988, US, 103 min)
d Leonard Nimoy. *p* Arnold Glimcher. *sc* Michael Bortman. *ph* David Watkin. *ed* Peter E Berger. *pd* Stan Jolley. *m* Elmer Bernstein. *cast* Diane Keaton, Liam Neeson, Jason Robards, Ralph Bellamy, Teresa Wright, James Naughton, Asia Vieira.
●Heartbreak time in this rigged tug-of-love drama. Divorced Anna (Keaton) brings up six-year-old daughter Molly (Vieira) on her own, and is making out nicely until she discovers the realm of the senses in the bed of sculptor Leo (Neeson). It's a shock when Molly reports to her father (Naughton) that Leo let her touch his penis, and he sues for custody. That was in fact all very innocent, but their taking the sleeping child into their bed during sex was questionable, and Anna's lawyer (Robards) advises her to throw Leo to the wolves if she wants to keep her kid. Is it possible to combine sexual ecstasy with motherhood, asks the blurb, but that's hardly made into a universal brain-teaser, nor into a comment on society's transition from permissive '60s to staid '80s, by this special case. Performances are good, though Keaton's snorting laughs and distracted manner are a bit of an obstacle course. Three hankie job. BC

Goodnight Vienna (aka Magic Night)

(1932, GB, 76 min, b/w)
d/p Herbert Wilcox. *sc* Holt Marvell, George Posford, Eric Maschwitz. *ph* Freddie Young. *ed* Ernest Aldridge. *pd* LP Williams. *songs* George Posford, Eric Maschwitz, Holt Marvell. *cast* Jack Buchanan, Anna Neagle, Clive Currie, Gina Malo, William Kendall, Joyce Bland.
●'Vienna in the summer of 1914 – gayest, handsomest city in Europe, famous alike for the lilt of its waltzes and the beauty of its women…Vienna, capital of love, where days are made for love and nights for kisses.' As the gushing introduction suggests, this romantic musical, adapted from a radio play, is sheer syrup from beginning to end. Buchanan plays a dashing Austrian cavalry officer (with his lopsided grin and braying diction, he looks and sounds as if he's just slipped out of a PG Wodehouse novel). Neagle, making her screen debut, is the Eliza Doolittle-like flower seller he falls in love with. War comes between them. He ends up a penniless shoe salesman, while she rises to become a great singer. The two are no longer on talking terms, but not even Neagle can resist Buchanan in full song. GM

Good Old Daze

see Péril Jeune, Le

Good People of Portugal, The (Bom Povo Português)

(1980, Port, 135 min, b/w)
d Rui Simoes. *narrator* José Mario Branco.
●An exemplary piece of agit-documentary which, in its own context, is as experimental and revolutionary as Vertov's *Man with a Movie Camera*. The events of Portugal's 'Carnation' Revolution and the subsequent eighteen months are complex, but this combination of heady lyricism and sharp political analysis transmits the popular energy that gave western Europe its most uplifting mass movement of recent years. Newsreel, satire, re-enactments and popular music come together dynamically in a film that is both about the people and for the people. MA

Good Son, The

(1993, US, 87 min)
d Joseph Ruben. *p* Mary Anne Page, Joseph Ruben. *sc* Ian McEwan. *ph* John Lindley. *ed* George Bowers. *m* Elmer Bernstein. *cast* Macaulay Culkin, Elijah Wood, David Morse, Wendy Crewson, Daniel Hugh Kelly, Jacqueline Brookes, Quinn Culkin.
●Now, here's a thing: two years after its US release, this bad seed thriller reaches Britain, by-passing cinemas despite healthy US box-office takings. The reason has nothing to do with the film's shortcomings and everything to do with the murder of the Liverpool toddler James Bulger by two small boys and the media uproar which followed. Based on an original screenplay by Ian McEwan (who disowned the film), the story concerns young Mark (Wood), who comes to stay with his aunt and uncle and gradually discovers that his cousin Henry (Macaulay Culkin) is psychotic. Despite a few crude philosophical stabs at the nature of evil, the film is basically a straight-ahead melodrama, driven home with force if not finesse by the director of *The Stepfather*. Kit Culkin apparently held Fox to ransom over *Home Alone 2* to extend his son's range with this role – in the event, young Mac is decisively upstaged by Wood, but the film's strongest selling point has to be a cliff-top finale in which the tyke's own mother has to choose whether he'll live or die. A summer camp classic. TCh

Good, the Bad and the Ugly, The (Il Buono, il Brutto, il Cattivo)

(1966, It, 180 min)
d Sergio Leone. *p* Alberto Grimaldi. *sc* Age, Scarpelli, Luciano Vincenzoni, Sergio Leone. *ph* Tonino Delli Colli. *ed* Nino Baragli, Eugenio Alabiso. *ad* Carlo Simi. *m* Ennio Morricone. *cast* Clint Eastwood, Eli Wallach, Lee Van Cleef, Aldo Giuffrè, Mario Brega, Luigi Pistilli.
●Hard to tell who's good, bad or ugly in this bitterly cynical portrait of America during the Civil War, with the three leads indulging in ruthless violence and self-help as they search for a buried fortune. Nevertheless, for all its shortcomings as a study in relative morality, Leone's final *Dollars* Western delights through its subversive, operatic parody of genre conventions, undercutting heroism by means of black comedy and over-the-top compositions, all deep focus and zooms. And Morricone's score is as powerful as always. It's enormous fun. GA

Good to Go

(1986, US, 90 min)
d Blaine Novak. *p* Doug Dilge, Sean Ferrer. *sc* Blaine Novak. *ph* Peter Sinclair. *ed* Gib Jaffe, Kimberly Logan, DC Stringer. *ad* Ron Downing. *cast* Art Garfunkel, Robert Doqui, Harris Yulin, Reginald Daughtry, Richard Brooks, Paula Davis.
●A vindictive cop (nastily well-played by Yulin) pursues a young black gang who've perpetrated rape and murder while low on Angel Dust and after they had been prevented from attending a Washington Go-Go gig. The music is culpable by association. Reporter/lush Garfunkel (limp) is duped into abetting the racist cop, until indignant blacks force Art's pink eyes open. The real star, of course, is the music of Trouble Funk, Chuck Brown & The Soul Searchers, and Redds & The Boys. Go-Go is Washington's form of superhard funk. It's heavy duty but clean and proud, and makes you dance like you always knew you could. GBr

Good Wife, The

see Umbrella Woman, The

Good Wife of Tokyo, The

(1992, GB, 52 min)
d/p Kim Longinotto, Claire Hunt. *ph* Kim Longinotto. *ed* John Mister. *m* Kazuo Hohki. *with* Kazuko Hokki.
●This thoroughly captivating, amusing documentary records singer Kazuko Hohki's visit to her home town of Tokyo where, in between performances with her group the Frank Chickens, she gets married and canvasses women's views on their changing role in Japanese society. The most fascinating revelations come from Hohki's wonderful mother who, as a priest in the religious group House of Development, preaches the benefits of laughter within a doctrine for positive living. Her Zen demonstration on the art of a long and happy marriage is a sequence to be cherished. CM

Good Will Hunting

(1997, US, 126 min)
d Gus Van Sant. *p* Lawrence Bender. *sc* Matt Damon, Ben Affleck. *ph* Jean-Yves Escoffier. *ed* Pietro Scalia. *pd* Melissa Stewart. *m* Danny Elfman. *cast* Robin Williams, Matt Damon, Ben Affleck, Stellan Skarsgård, Minnie Driver, Casey Affleck, Cole Hauser.
●*Good Will Hunting*'s sincerity comes capitalised, which is not to deny the film is honest and moving in its way. Damon (who co-scripted, with Ben Affleck) plays Will, a janitor at the Massachusetts Institute of Technology. He's a closet genius, a volatile orphan who'd rather hang out with his beer buddies than parlay his brains into the lucrative career that would seem to be his destiny. Appalled that such a talent should be lost to science, maths professor Lambeau (Skarsgård) takes the boy under his wing, arranges for him to get psychiatric help, and watches Will make monkeys of the shrinks. Sean (Williams) is the last resort: another South Boston guy who never really made it, maybe he can break through where his distinguished peers failed. There are tensions here. To an extent, the film challenges America's ingrained anti-intellectualism, yet its anti-elitist instincts lead it close to equating academia with a dubious effeminacy. In the end it

even falls back on that old cinematic panacea: get in touch with your inner Robin Williams. It's acted and directed with care, and Damon is outstanding, his scenes with Driver being especially sparky.TCh

Good Woman of Bangkok, The

(1991, Aust, 79 min)
d/p/sc/ph Dennis O'Rourke. *ed* Tim Litchfield. *with* Yaowalak Chonchanakun.

● The economics of prostitution out East haven't changed since Suzie Wong's day, and O'Rourke's documentary doesn't break new ground either, apart from his declaration of *mea culpa*. Aoi, from a village, becomes a bar girl to support her family. 'Good or bad, I don't think. I get money. OK'. Direct-to-camera interviews with Aoi and her mother are spuriously ennobled with opera, and there are plenty of shock cuts to the roaring life of the bar, bulging with lager louts demanding 'pussy shoot balloon'. BC

Goofy Movie, A

(1996, US, 77 min)
d Kevin Lima. *p* Dan Rounds. *sc* Jymm Magon, Chris Matheson, Brian Pimental. *ed* Gregory Perler, Catherine Rascon. *pd* Fred Warter. *m* Carter Burwell. *cast* voices: Bill Farmer, Jason Marsden, Jim Cummings, Kellie Martin, Rob Paulsen, Wallace Shawn.

● The first full-length movie starring Disney's toothy 63-year-old hound. For much of his career Goofy remained in the shadow of Mickey and Donald until the studio resurrected him for a series of 'Goof Troop' TV shorts, in which he played alongside his slightly more intelligent son Max. Here Max shows signs of adolescent rebellion. Realising he's gotta do something if he's to bridge the generation gap, Pa takes reluctant son on a mind-expanding fishing trip. Max would much rather be impressing his girl Roxanne with his Michael Jackson routine. Insipid songs and not much story. DA

Goonies, The

(1985, US, 114 min)
d Richard Donner. *p* Richard Donner, Harvey Bernhard. *sc* Chris Columbus. *ph* Nick McLean. *ed* Michael Kahn. *pd* J Michael Riva. *m* David Grusin. *cast* Sean Astin, Josh Brolin, Jeff Cohen, Corey Feldman, Kerri Green, Martha Plimpton, Ke Huy Quan.

● Dreamed up in a story by Steven Spielberg, the goonies are seven restless kids in a coastal town who, deserted by parents fighting a local real estate takeover bid, discover an old treasure map pointing to famed pirate One-Eyed Willie's galleon. Unfortunately, a family of incompetent thieves are also after the loot, and are not above shoving the hand of one of the little mites into a liquidiser to extort information. And while the pre-pubescents continually scream, their doting parents prove equally odious in a finale of astounding sentimentality. DT

Goopy Gyne Bagha Byne

see Adventures of Goopy and Bagha, The

Gordon's War

(1973, US, 90 min)
d Ossie Davis. *p* Robert Schaffel. *sc* Howard Friedlander, Ed Spielman. *ph* Victor J Kemper. *ed* Eric Albertson. *ad* Perry Watkins. *m* Andy Bodale, Al Elias. *cast* Paul Winfield, Carl Lee, David Downing, Tony King, Gilbert Lewis, Carl Gordon.

● Once director Davis settles down and leaves gimmickry well alone, this unfolds nicely enough. The idea is the old one of a group of professionals dedicated to wiping out crime and evil, this time in modern Harlem. Ex-Green Beret Winfield reassembles the old black platoon from 'Nam and declares war on the pusher after his wife is found dead from an overdose (cue for red-filtered flashbacks). Wartime expertise hits the concrete jungle, and from then on it's mindless action all the way, with the platoon having unlimited access to material – 'Hey, man, this infra-red is outta sight!' – to help wage their war. Raised out of the ordinary by an ingenious safe raid, an above-average car chase, and some nice location work.

Gorgeous Bird Like Me, A

see Belle Fille comme moi, Une

Gorgeous Hussy, The

(1936, US, 102 min, b/w)
d Clarence Brown. *p* Joseph L Mankiewicz. *sc* Ainsworth Morgan, Stephen Morehouse Avery. *ph* George Folsey. *ed* Blanche Sewell. *ad* Cedric Gibbons. *m* Herbert Stothart. *cast* Joan Crawford, Lionel Barrymore, Robert Taylor, Melvyn Douglas, Franchot Tone, James Stewart, Beulah Bondi.

● A lavishly appointed nineteenth century costumer in which Joan Crawford, as glamorous as she ever was, inveigles her way into a position of high influence in the White House of childhood friend Andrew Jackson (Barrymore, who steals the picture) – so much so that the President sacks his entire cabinet when rumours start to circulate. Crawford's role was based on the real Peggy Eaton, but it was Beulah Bondi, playing Jackson's bona fide wife, who came out of the film with an Oscar nomination. TJ

Gorgo

(1961, GB, 79 min)
d Eugène Lourié. *p* Wilfrid Eades. *sc* John Loring, Daniel Hyatt. *ph* Freddie Young. *ed* Eric Boyd-Perkins. *ad* Elliot Scott. *m* Angelo Francesco Lavagnino. *cast* Bill Travers, William Sylvester, Vincent Winter, Christopher Rhodes, Joseph O'Conor, Bruce Seton.

● An irresistibly tacky cross between *King Kong* and *The Beast from 20,000 Fathoms*. Midsize monster Gorgo is awoken from millennia of slumber and shipped off for exhibit in Battersea Funfair. This prompts its mammoth mummy to come and stomp a number of model-work London monuments in a display of maternal kinship. The final film, more's the pity, to be directed by Lourié, an art director who also perpetrated *The Beast from 20,000 Fathoms*, *The Colossus of New York* and *Behemoth the Sea Monster*. PT

Gorgon, The

(1964, GB, 83 min)
d Terence Fisher. *p* Anthony Nelson Keys. *sc* John Gilling. *ph* Michael Reed. *ed* James Needs. *pd* Bernard Robinson. *m* James Bernard. *cast* Peter Cushing, Richard Pasco, Barbara Shelley, Christopher Lee, Michael Goodliffe, Patrick Troughton, Prudence Hyman.

● One of the few Hammer films with a female monster, this very English slice of Grand Guignol is undermined by failings in the make-up department. The Gorgon, a harridan with a snake-encrusted wig, would be hard pressed to frighten the proverbial mouse, let alone turn anyone to stone. Barbara Shelley's the young woman who acts ghoulish whenever there's a full moon. (The actual monster was played by Prudence Hyman.) Given that so many thrillers are predicated on the idea of the murderous male gaze, it's a novelty to have the woman staring back. Fisher directs in his usual brisk style, as if he's making a public information documentary, not a baroque horror pic. The settings are disconcerting (we're in Vandorf, an imaginary country somewhere between Transylvania and suburban Surrey) and Christopher Lee's scientist always looks uncomfortable in his tweed suit. GM

Gorilla Bathes at Noon

(1993, Ger, 83 min)
d Dusan Makavejev. *p* Alfred Hürmer, Bojana Marijan, Joachim von Vietinghoff. *sc* Dusan Makavejev. *ph* Aleksandar Petokovic. *ed* Vuksan Lukovac. *pd* Veljdeko Despotovic. *m* Brynmor Llewelyn-Jones. *cast* Svetozar Cvetkovic, Anita Mancic, Alexandra Rohmig, Petar Bozovic, Andreas Lucius, Eva Ras.

● For Makavejev, it's as if nothing has changed in 20-odd years. This collage-comedy may be set in the no-man's-land at the heart of the unified Berlin, but the images, the ideas and the bathetic juxtapositions could all be out-takes from *Innocence Unprotected* or *W.R. – Mysteries of the Organism*. The protagonist is a Russian soldier left behind in Berlin when his platoon goes home, haunted by scenes from the 1949 Stalinist epic *The Fall of Berlin* and nonplussed by the demolition of a gigantic statue of Lenin. So: socialism dies, socialist illusions crumble, and we're back to the same old socialist punch-ups and social contradictions. Not riveting. TR

Gorillas in the Mist

(1988, US, 129 min)
d Michael Apted. *p* Arnold Glimcher, Terry Clegg. *sc* Anna Hamilton Phelan. *ph* John Seale. *ed* Stuart Baird. *pd* John Graysmark. *m* Maurice Jarre. *cast* Sigourney Weaver, Bryan Brown, Julie Harris, John Omirah Miluwi, Iain Cutherbertson, Constantin Alexandrov.

● Apted's biopic about the late Diane Fossey's mission to save the endangered mountain gorilla has, to some extent, been pre-empted by wildlife programmes on TV. This is not to denigrate Sigourney Weaver's committed performance, but to question the dramatic rigging around the humans. One of those spiky crusaders with tunnel vision, Fossey pitched herself on a wet, cold mountain in Rwanda, and set about her life's work. Her research cleared away a mass of misinformation about gorilla behaviour, and the scenes in which she gradually establishes a communication with the reclusive species are the real interest of the film. Her relationship with the photographer (Brown) who puts her cause on the map, initial hostility turning into love affair, feels like a box-office consideration; over the years, her battles with poachers and government officials distort her into a dangerous Messianic crank, but the transition here seems abrupt. Script problems apart, the film is too long, but the footage with the gorillas is always extraordinary. BC

Gorky Park

(1983, US, 128 min)
d Michael Apted. *p* Gene Kirkwood, Howard W Koch Jr. *sc* Dennis Potter. *ph* Ralf D Bode. *ed* Dennis Virkler. *pd* Paul Sylbert. *m* James Horner. *cast* William Hurt, Lee Marvin, Brian Dennehy, Ian Bannen, Joanna Pacula, Michael Elphick, Richard Griffiths, Rikki Fulton, Alexander Knox, Alexei Sayle.

● Neither Dennis Potter's screenplay nor the heavyweight cast can raise this adaptation of Martin Cruz Smith's best-selling spy novel above the ordinary. The discovery of three faceless bodies in Moscow's Gorky Park sets Soviet policeman Hurt's investigation in motion, but while subsequent interference by KGB man Dennehy hints at espionage, the involvement of fur-coated businessman Marvin suggests more mercenary motives. Hurt and Dennehy are excellent, as ever, but Marvin is badly miscast as a ruthless smoothie; and the film as a whole, while never less than involving, seldom generates any real suspense as it moves towards a curiously muffled showdown. NF

Gosford Park

(2001, GB/US, 137 min)
d Robert Altman. *p* Robert Altman, Bob Balaban, David Levy. *sc* Julian Fellowes. *ph* Andrew Dunn. *ed* Tim Squyres. *pd* Stephen Altman. *m* Patrick Doyle. *cast* Eileen Atkins, Bob Balaban, Alan Bates, Charles Dance, Stephen Fry, Michael Gambon, Richard E Grant, Tom Hollander, Derek Jacobi, Kelly Macdonald, Helen Mirren, Jeremy Northam, Clive Owen, Ryan Phillippe, Kristin Scott Thomas, Maggie Smith, Geraldine Somerville, Emily Watson, James Wilby.

● Altman's unexpected venture into Agatha Christie territory works a treat. The setting is an English country house, the year 1932, and the many and varied heirs to the McCordle family inheritance congregate for the weekend to bag pheasants, ruffle some feathers, and suck up to the old man (Gambon). Each has a maid or a valet in tow. Upstairs, everyone knows his or her place, and social proprieties are strictly observed. Downstairs, as above, so below, where the visiting servants are even known by their masters' names. Yet behind this orderly facade resentments fester, and when McCordle is found dead over his brandy, there's no shortage of suspects. We all know that Altman can throw a party, but it's a pleasant surprise how much respect he's accorded Julian Fellowes' witty, intricate screenplay, from an idea by Altman himself and actor/producer Balaban. The family relationships could be a bit clearer, but the danger that the audience might get swamped by the several dozen speaking parts is circumvented by a glittering, instantly recognisable cast, plus a couple of tour guides: first, Balaban's droll Hollywood producer, researching the mysteries of British etiquette for his next B-movie; then Kelly Macdonald's novice personal maid, getting pointers from her splendidly barbed mistress (Smith) and from a 'seen it all before' domestic (Watson). Altman has such fun satirising the affectations and casual cruelties of the class system, it's almost a shame when he finally gets down to plot machinations – whodunit is the least of it. TCh

Gospel According to St Matthew, The (Il Vangelo Secondo Matteo)

(1964, It/Fr, 142 min, b/w)
d Pier Paolo Pasolini. *p* Alfredo Bini. *sc* Pier Paolo Pasolini. *ph* Tonino Delli Colli. *ed* Nino Baragli. *ad* Luigi Scaccianoce. *m* JS Bach, Mozart, Prokofiev, Webern, Luis Enriquez Bacalov. *cast* Enrique Irazoqui, Margherita Caruso, Susanna Pasolini, Marcello Morante, Mario Socrate.

●Certainly Pasolini's most satisfying movie, devoid both of the frequent lapses into pretentiousness that mar (for example) *Theorem* and *Medea*, and the sloppy editing and awkward acting of movies like *The Decameron*. The director's Catholicism and Marxism serve him well here as the Messiah is presented as a determinedly political animal fuelled by anger at social injustice, while the miracles are allowed to remain unexplained (but also never presented in terms of flashy special effects). The film's beauty, in fact, derives from its simplicity, with the Italian landscape (and non-professional actors) turned into a convincing milieu for the all-too-familiar goings-on by marvellous monochrome camerawork. And Pasolini's use of music, from Bach to Billie Holiday, is astounding. GA

Gossip

(2000, US/Aust, 90 min)
d Davis Guggenheim. *p* Jeffrey Silver, Bobby Newmyer. *sc* Gregory Poirier, Theresa Rebeck. *ph* Andrzej Bartkowiak. *ed* Jay Cassidy. *pd* David Nichols. *m* Graeme Revell. *cast* James Marsden, Lena Headey, Norman Reedus, Kate Hudson, Marisa Coughlan, Sharon Lawrence, Eric Bogosian, Edward James Olmos, Joshua Jackson.

●Derrick (Marsden), Jones (Headey) and Travis (Reedus) are chic NY students shacked up together in loft luxury. By day they slouch through Bogosian's communications lectures; by night they flock to glam warehouse parties in the meat-packing district. Derrick spies chaste classmate Naomi (Hudson) the worse for drink and apparently in flagrante with her boyfriend. The pals decide to start a rumour and follow its progress. But what goes around, spins way out of control. The film's most fun while it's just wallowing in its good looks. There's nothing more spoilt than a student with money, and the crew duly go to town on the trio's lifestyle. Further the self-indulgent sets are initially complemented by a swagger in the actors' steps, and a verve about the editing. The ballyhoo the film makes about rumour mongering might be merely daffy, but once the story tries to crank itself into a *Shallow Grave*-style potboiler, it turns into unalloyed gibberish. NB

Go Tell the Spartans

(1977, US, 114 min)
d Ted Post. *p* Allan F Bodoh, Mitchell Cannold. *sc* Wendell Mayes. *ph* Harry Stradling Jr. *ed* Millie Moore. *ad* Jack Senter. *m* Dick Halligan. *cast* Burt Lancaster, Craig Wasson, Jonathan Goldsmith, Marc Singer, Evan Kim, Joe Unger, Dennis Howard.

●Moving from the home front – and tentative or oblique treatments of Vietnam – towards confrontation with the action, American cinema was gradually extricating itself from a position of silent complicity and stuttering out the sort of moralistic mush that permeates *Go Tell the Spartans*, one of the first 'platoon movies' of Vietnam. Post's film is fundamentally that old post-World War II standby, the anti-war-movie, a second generation offspring of the conscience-stricken cavalry movie. It's brought up to date to the extent that our human/wise/rebellious hero (Lancaster – count his speeches) can die with a final exclamation of 'Oh, shit!' – an apt summation of a film that parades characters and quotes expressly included to be dismissed with a self-satisfied cynical shrug. Message-mongering for morons. PT

Gothic

(1986, GB, 87 min)
d Ken Russell. *p* Penny Corke. *sc* Stephen Volk. *ph* Mike Southon. *ed* Michael Bradsell. *pd* Christopher Hobbs. *m* Thomas Dolby. *cast* Gabriel Byrne, Julian Sands, Natasha Richardson, Myriam Cyr, Timothy Spall, Alec Mango.

●June 16, 1816. The Villa Diodati on the shores of Lake Geneva. An illustrious gathering: Lord Byron and his biographer-physician Polidori play host to Shelley, his lover Mary Godwin, and her half-sister Claire. They're an unruly, incestuously entangled lot, as artistic types in Russell's films tend to be, given to imbibing laudanum, mauling each other, and tossing off gratuitous insults. Not surprisingly, matters get out of hand. As a storm gathers, the flamboyant fops and fantasists hold a séance, to test their propensity for wickedness by conjuring into life their innermost demons. With this fictionalised re-creation of the events leading to the writing of *Frankenstein*, Russell is in his element, revelling in the seething psychodramas, the fetid atmosphere of sexual abandon, the gloops of slime and decaying flesh. Unfortunately, Stephen Volk's script is so banal that the final eruption of absolute evil comes not as a nightmarish climax but as a nonsensical mish-mash of all we've seen before. Pretensions aside, it's an entertaining enough roller-coaster ride, but it's sad to see the darker, more fertile labyrinths of this particular literary funhouse ignored in favour of scatological silliness. GA

Goto, l'île d'amour (Goto, Island of Love)

(1968, Fr, 93 min, b/w & col)
d Walerian Borowczyk. *p* Louis Duchesne, René Thévenet. *sc* Walerian Borowczyk, Dominique Duvergé. *ph* Guy Durban. *ed* Charles Bretoneiche. *m* Handel. *cast* Pierre Brasseur, Ligia Branice, Ginette Leclerc, René Dary, Jean-Pierre Andréani, Guy Saint-Jean.

●Borowczyk's first live-action feature was simultaneously a brilliant debut and a seamless transition from his earlier animation-based work. The story is a simple fable of the destructive force of passion: on a mythical island, the beautiful wife (Branice) of the weak ruler Goto III (Brasseur) is shown to be unfaithful by his chief fly-catcher, Grozo (Saint-Jean). But Grozo's own infatuation for her leads to tragedy. Borowczyk's highly stylised direction, with consciously flattened images, and objects rendered as animate and as significant as human beings, is well complemented by the imperious Brasseur and the extraordinary beauty of Branice. The sudden flashes of colour in a very monochrome context, and the soaring use of a Handel organ concerto, further consolidate a true 'art' film, in the sense that everything is composed and designed to create a wholly imagined – yet tangible – world. DT

Gotti

(1997, US, 117 min)
d Robert Harmon. *p* David Coatsworth. *sc* Steve Shagan. *ph* Alar Kivilo. *ed* Zach Staneberg. *pd* Barbara Dunphy. *m* Mark Isham. *cast* Armand Assante, Anthony Quinn, William Forsythe.

●No-holds-barred four-letter words, strong acting from a name American-Italian cast and good writing from Steve Shagan add up to the life and crimes of the 'Teflon Don', John Gotti, who murdered his way to the top of the Gambino crime family of New York. There are some strange sanitisations: Gotti is known to have personally dismembered the neighbour who accidentally ran over his beloved son. Here the neighbour is simply shot by Gotti's close associate and betrayer Sam Gravano, who is now part of the witness protection program and presumably can't complain. A touch of cynical humour perhaps? Assante excels as Gotti, a man of undoubted complexity, while Quinn as his mentor Neil DeLaCroce absolutely peels away the years. Highly recommended. SGr

Goupi Mains Rouges (It Happened at the Inn)

(1943, Fr, 95 min, b/w)
d Jacques Becker. *sc* Pierre Véry. *ph* Pierre Montazel. *ed* Marguerite Renoir. *ad* Pierre Marquet. *m* Jean Alfaro. *cast* Fernand Ledoux, Georges Rollin, Blanchette Brunoy, Line Noro, Robert le Vigan, Maurice Schutz.

●The French peasantry sometimes affects that traditionally 'Welsh' habit of distinguishing each owner of a widely shared name by affixing some characteristic trait to it. Thus 'Goupi the Red-Handed', a poacher and the blackest sheep of a rural family in the throes of treasure-hunting. Black, not red, is in fact the dominant tonality of this bracingly mean-spirited melodrama, whose sombre, underlit visuals give the impression that the whole film was shot during a curfew. GAd

Goût des autres, Le

(2000, Fr, 113 min)
d Agnès Jaoui. *p* Charles Gassot, Christian Bérard. *sc* Agnès Jaoui, Jean-Pierre Bacri. *ph* Laurent Dailland. *ed* Hervé de Luze. *ad* François Emmanuelli. *cast* Anne Alvaro, Jean-Pierre Bacri, Alain Chabat, Agnès Jaoui, Gérard Lanvin, Christiane Millet, Wladimir Yordanoff.

●Castella (Bacri) is an industrialist, married, temporarily inconvenienced by the presence of a bodyguard while a sensitive business deal is ironed out. In his own world, he's king. A dutiful (groundbreaking) trip to the theatre is a revelation. It's not the play which moves him, but the lead actress, Clara (Alvaro). Neither young nor especially glamorous – she's stuck in subsidised theatre – Clara touches him so deeply, she opens up horizons he's never dreamed of: a new world of art, literature, philosophy and beauty, a world in which Castella simply doesn't fit. A critical and popular hit in France, *Le Goût des autres* (literally, 'Other People's Taste') is a culture clash comedy with the emphasis on 'culture'. Agnès Jaoui (making her directorial debut with a script co-written with longtime partner Bacri) aims for the droll slow burn, subtle ironies and wry observation. There's a lovely, funny-sad sequence in which the industrialist shaves off his moustache to impress his muse – only it takes ages before anyone notices. The film works as a one-sided love story, yet finds time to flesh out half a dozen peripheral characters, each in his or her own way as lovelorn and alone as the industrialist. TCh

Gouttes d'eau sur pierres brûlantes

see Water Drops on Burning Rocks

Governess, The

(1997, GB/Fr, 114 min)
d Sandra Goldbacher. *p* Sarah Curtis. *sc* Sandra Goldbacher. *ph* Ashley Rowe. *ed* Isabel Lorente. *pd* Sarah Greenwood. *m* Edward Shearmur. *cast* Minnie Driver, Tom Wilkinson, Harriet Walter, Florence Hoath, Bruce Myers, Jonathan Rhys Meyers.

●The 1840s. After the murder of her father, Rosina (Driver) sheds her Jewish identity and arrives on a Scottish island to work as a governess. Her charge's father, Charles (Wilkinson), is obsessed with the secrets of photography. Rosina is fascinated and soon the pair are entwined. Writer/director Goldbacher knows how to create atmosphere – the early London scenes have a musty, sensual sweetness straight out of *Daniel Deronda*. The edgy camera alerts us to potential fracture: even before the father's double life is exposed, we know something's amiss. When the action moves to Scotland, however, doubts begin to creep in – a voyage of female self-discovery set by the bleak sea? Surely *The Piano* and *Breaking the Waves* have been there, done that. Nevertheless, the script keeps you intrigued and the use of photography as a metaphor for emotional 'preservation' is delicately done. Driver is full of hoity-toity charisma. Luckily, however, Wilkinson's wonderfully quiet performance doesn't go to waste. CO'Su

Go West

(1925, US, 6,293 ft, b/w)
d Buster Keaton. *p* Joseph M Schenck. *sc* Raymond Cannon, Buster Keaton, Lex Neat. *ph* Elgin Lessley, Bert Haines. *cast* Buster Keaton, Howard Truesdale, Kathleen Myers, Ray Thompson, Brown Eyes.

●The only Keaton feature in which he discreetly tapped a vein of Chaplin pathos (his character is 'Friendless' and his leading lady a mournful cow), this is not one of his masterpieces, but is almost as enchanting in its quiet way. Some wonderful touches mark the progress of Buster's romance with the cow as he sits patiently waiting for her to milk herself after placing a pail in the appropriate position, ties antlers to her head so that she can defend herself against the herd, and – on realising that his liking is reciprocated – essays a gingerly pat while politely raising his hat. The spirited climax has Buster, dressed in a red Mephistopheles costume with demented cops clinging to his tail, trying to head off a stampeding herd as it rampages through town: a chase which never really escalates properly in the manner of *Cops* or *Seven Chances*, largely (as Keaton later explained) because of problems experienced in controlling the cattle. TM

Go West

(1940, US, 80 min, b/w)
d Edward Buzzell. *p* Jack Cummings. *sc* Irving Brecher. *ph* Leonard Smith. *ed* Blanche Sewell. *ad* Cedric Gibbons, Stan Rogers. *m* Bronislau Kaper. *cast* The Marx Brothers, John Carroll, Diana Lewis, Tully Marshall, Robert Barrat.
●Relatively late, and therefore far from great, Marxian mania, in which Groucho, Chico and Harpo find themselves victims both to a West they can barely hoodwink or subvert, and to a script which is only spasmodically funny. That said, it starts well enough, with Harpo and Chico gleefully outwitting Groucho's attempts to fleece them of ten dollars; and the final, frantic train chase climax – while falling dismally short of Keaton's The General – has its (admittedly slapsticky) moments. GA

Goya in Bordeaux (Goya en Burdeos)

(1999, Sp/It, 104 min)
d Carlos Saura. *p* Andrés Vicente Gómez. *sc* Carlos Saura. *ph* Vittorio Storaro. *ed* Julia Juaniz. *ad* Pierre Louis Thévenet. *m* Roque Baños. *cast* Francisco Rabal, José Coronado, Maribel Verdú, Eulalia Ramón, Dafné Fernández, Emilio Gutiérrez Caba, Joaquín Climent.
●Bordeaux, 1828: exiled from his native Spain, Francisco de Goya (Rabal), now aged 82, spends his final days in a house shared with his lover Leocadia (Ramón). He recounts the events of his life to their young daughter Rosarito (Fernández), cueing flashbacks to his time as court painter to King Charles IV, and his passionate affair with the intoxicating Duchess of Alba, who still haunts his thoughts. He describes the torment at going deaf at 46, and his anguish over the destruction of Spain during years of political turmoil, reflected in the tone of his later paintings. This is Saura's dream project and his dedication to it is evident in the detailed exposition. At once colourful, opulent and dark, it captures the delights and demons of genius. Singular, intriguing, mesmerising, there are rich rewards here for lovers of painting, history and spectacle. KW

Grace of My Heart

(1996, US, 115 min)
d Allison Anders. *p* Ruth Charny, Daniel Hassid. *sc* Allison Anders. *ph* Jean-Yves Escoffier. *ed* Thelma Schoonmaker. *pd* François Séguin. *m* Larry Klein. *cast* Illeana Douglas, Matt Dillon, John Turturro, Eric Stoltz, Bruce Davison, Patsy Kensit, Jennifer Lee Warren, Bridget Fonda.
●There's a lovely sequence about a third of the way into Anders' delightful movie which follows a song from conception – the street scene that inspires it – through the writing, to the recording session. This seamlessly edited passage swings like the snappy '60s girl pop it emulates. Like the film as a whole, it works as a musical in its own right, and as history and critique of the pop process. Anders charts the progress of Denise Waverly (the excellent Illeana Douglas), an aspiring singer signed up to write songs at the Brill Building by impresario Joel Millner (outrageously wigged-out Turturro). Denise is tough and smart, but often ill-served by a series of amorous and professional partners: beatnik radical Eric Stoltz, married DJ Bruce Davison, and finally surf sensation Matt Dillon, none of whom allows her to develop her own voice, though they all provide plenty of song material. Loosely inspired by the life of Carole King, this is a light, feminist take on 15 years of pop: hits and Ms, if you will. It begins with a bright, peppy tone, pastiching the nascent rock'n'roll scene with an affectionate smile and perfect pitch – the Larry Klein-produced soundtrack is spot on. But it's not all kitsch nostalgia: the period coincides with great social changes, particularly regarding the role of women, a recurrent Anders theme. Sharp cameos include Patsy Kensit's rival songwriter and Bridget Fonda's teen songbird with a secret love. TCh

Grace Quigley

(1984, US, 102 min)
d Anthony Harvey. *p* Menahem Golan, Yoram Globus. *sc* Martin Zweiback. *ph* Larry Pizer. *ed* Robert Reitano. *pd* Gary Weist. *m* John Addison. *cast* Katharine Hepburn, Nick Nolte, Kit Le Fever, Chip Zien, William Duell, Elizabeth Wilson, Walter Abel.
●Professional hit man Nolte lacks self-confidence. But when he fetches up against Hepburn, who hires him first to help ease her out of this life, and then to oblige all her old friends, he gains self-esteem from these philanthropic acts of euthanasia, and a mother figure to comfort him. Good black comedies about death are rare, and this certainly proves spry and knowing. But its tough line on sentimentality goes squashy at the three-quarter point, and there is evidence of re-editing to provide a soft-option ending. Originally screened as *The Ultimate Solution of Grace Quigley*, running 102 minutes, it was then re-edited, partly re-shot, and re-titled. CPea

Graduate, The

(1967, US, 108 min)
d Mike Nichols. *p* Lawrence Turman. *sc* Calder Willingham, Buck Henry. *ph* Robert Surtees. *ed* Sam O'Steen. *pd* Richard Sylbert. *songs* Paul Simon. *m* David Grusin. *cast* Anne Bancroft, Dustin Hoffman, Katharine Ross, William Daniels, Murray Hamilton, Elizabeth Wilson, Norman Fell, Buck Henry.
●Modish, calculated, but hugely popular film which, with the help of an irrelevant but diverting Simon and Garfunkel soundtrack, proved one of the biggest hits of the '60s. Hoffman, looking for the most part like a startled rabbit, got caught between the rapacious Mrs Robinson and her daughter, and suggested a vulnerability that was sufficiently novel to turn him into as big a movie star as all the he-men like McQueen and Newman. The film itself is very broken-backed, partly because Anne Bancroft's performance as the mother carries so much more weight than Katharine Ross' as the daughter, partly because Nichols couldn't decide whether he was making a social satire or a farce. As a comment on sex in the West Coast stockbroker belt, the film falls a long way short of Clint Eastwood's later *Breezy*, which makes much more of a lot less promising material. CPe

Grand Amour, Le

(1968, Fr, 86 min)
d Pierre Etaix. *p* Paul Claudon. *sc* Pierre Etaix, Jean-Claude Carrière. *ph* Christian Guillouet. *ed* Henri Lanoe. *pd* Daniel Louradour, Jean Gallaud. *m* Claude Stieremans. *cast* Pierre Etaix, Annie Fratellini, Nicole Calfan, Ketty France, Louis Mais, Alain Janey.
●The diminishing returns apparent in Etaix's films, derived from Tati but without the touch of genius (unmistakable even if you find Tati unfunny), came to a head with this tiresome whimsy which chose the unfortunate year of 1968 in which to satirise French bourgeois morality with a gentle affection that turns into approbation. About a respectable married man who escapes into fantasies about his nineteen-year-old secretary, only to return to the status quo a contentedly wiser man, it is witless, self-indulgent and cloyingly sentimental. TM

Grand Canyon

(1991, US, 134 min)
d Lawrence Kasdan. *p* Lawrence Kasdan, Charles Okun, Michael Grillo. *sc* Lawrence Kasdan, Meg Kasdan. *ph* Owen Roizman. *ed* Carol Littleton. *pd* Bo Welch. *m* James Newton Howard. *cast* Danny Glover, Kevin Kline, Steve Martin, Mary McDonnell, Mary-Louise Parker, Alfre Woodard, Jeremy Sisto, Tina Lifford, Patrick Malone.
●The things that can happen in LA! If you're an immigration lawyer, like Kline, you can break down in a poor black area and get saved from the homeboys by a black road-rescue driver (Glover). Or if you're the wife (McDonnell) of that lawyer, and he's had a fling with his secretary and your teenage son is turning to thoughts of love, you can go gooey-eyed over a baby you find abandoned in the bushes. Or if, like Glover, you've got a deaf daughter, and a poor but hard-workin' sister with a son who's tempted by the neighbourhood gangs, you can befriend the rich lawyer and wax philosophical about one of your country's loveliest natural landmarks. Or if you produce slasher movies, like Martin, and then get shot, you can reconsider your whole life and career. Then again, like Kasdan, you could make an ambitious, entertaining and seriously indulgent film about the modern malaise afflicting your home town. If this disaster-packed parable often smacks of melodramatic contrivance, it does at least benefit from solid performances and direction, and a leavening line in sardonic humour. GA

Grand Central Murder

(1942, US, 73 min, b/w)
d S Sylvan Simon. *p* BR Zeidman. *sc* Peter Ruric. *ph* George Folsey. *ed* Conrad A Nervig. *ad* Cedric Gibbons. *m* David Snell. *cast* Van Heflin, Sam Levene, Patricia Dane, Cecilia Parker, Virginia Grey, Tom Conway, Samuel S Hinds, Connie Gilchrist, Mark Daniels, Millard Mitchell.
●A traditional whodunit, scripted at a breathless pace by Peter Ruric from Sue MacVeigh's novel, with private eye Van Heflin solving the murder of a golddigging actress (Dane) under the nose of a biliously dim cop (Levene). After a couple of scenes edgily and excitingly staged amid the rolling stock at Grand Central Station, the suspects are assembled at police HQ. Fortunately, they're a lively bunch, and their stories keep the action jumping in unexpected directions by way of a series of intriguing flashbacks. The resolution stemming from a reconstruction of the murder is a little flat, but the rest makes for an enjoyable B movie: good performances, tolerably witty dialogue, excellent camerawork (George Folsey), and a pleasant leavening of both comedy and hard-boiled thriller. TM

Grand Chemin, Le

(1987, Fr, 107 min)
d Jean-Loup Hubert. *p* Pascal Hommais, Jean-François Lepetit. *sc* Jean-Loup Hubert. *ph* Claude Lecomte. *ed* Raymonde Guyot. *ad* Thierry Flamand. *m* Georges Granier. *cast* Anémone, Richard Bohringer, Antoine Hubert, Vanessa Guedj, Christine Pascal, Raoul Billerey.
●Hubert's story of a nine-year-old Parisian boy's billeting in a Breton village has the universal appeal of a beloved genre. Birth, death, sex, kids' games, and adult secrets are seen through the eyes of sensitive little Louis (Antoine Hubert). Dumped on Marcelle (Anemone) and Pelo (Bohringer) while his mother goes into hospital to have a baby, Louis finds himself in a desperately troubled and sometimes violent household. Pelo boozes, and has to be brought home in a wheelbarrow, because Marcelle has become unresponsive after the death of their child. Both clutch for the boy's love, and bicker over him. A little village tomboy (Guedj) teases and instructs him in the ways of grown-ups, but Louis has to go through his familial insecurity on his own. The squabbling couple won French Oscars and richly deserve them – Anemone for her sassy walk and prissy ways, Bohringer for his rough, bawdy tenderness. The sense of a childhood summer remembered is sensitively conveyed, the barley-sugar sweetness of days in the trees, the nocturnal alarms with the pillow over the ears. BC

Grande Bouffe, La

see Blow-Out

Grande Illusion, La 100

(1937, Fr, 117 min, b/w)
d Jean Renoir. *p* Frank Rollmer, Albert Pinkovitch. sc Jean Renoir, Charles Spaak. *ph* Christrian Matras. *ed* Marguerite Renoir, Marthe Huguet. *ad* Eugène Lourié. *m* Joseph Kosma. *cast* Jean Gabin, Pierre Fresnay, Erich von Stroheim, Marcel Dalio, Julien Carette, Gaston Modot, Jean Dasté, Dita Parlo, Jacques Becker.
●Renoir films have a way of talking about one thing while being about another. *La Grande Illusion* was the only one of his '30s movies to be received with unqualified admiration at the time, lauded as a warmly humane indictment of war, a pacifist statement as nobly moving as *All Quiet on the Western Front*. Practically nobody noted the irony with which this archetypal prison camp escape story also outlined a barbed social analysis, demonstrating how shared aristocratic backgrounds (and military professionalism) forge a bond of sympathy between the German commandant (von Stroheim) and the senior French officer (Fresnay); how the exigencies of a wartime situation impel Fresnay to sacrifice himself (and Stroheim to shoot him) so that two of his men may make good their escape; and how those two escapees (Gabin and Dalio), once their roles as hero-warriors are over, will return home reduced being working class and dirty Jew once more. *The Grand Illusion*, often cited

as an enigmatic title, is surely not that peace can ever be permanent, but that liberty, equality and fraternity is ever likely to become a social reality rather than a token ideal. TM

Grandes Manoeuvres, Les (Summer Manoeuvres)

(1955, Fr, 107 min)
d René Clair. *sc* René Clair, Jérôme Géronimi, Jean Marsan. *ph* Robert Lefebvre. *ed* Louise Hautecoeur, Denise Natot. *ad* Léon Barsacq. *m* Georges van Parys. *cast* Gérard Philipe, Michèle Morgan, Jean Desailly, Yves Robert, Brigitte Bardot, Magali Noel, Dany Carrel.

● A garrison town just before the First World War. Armand, rakish lieutenant in the Dragoons (Philipe), undertakes to seduce any woman – say, whoever wins tonight's raffle – by the time the regiment goes on summer manoeuvres. A decorous but unfoolable divorcée (Morgan) turns out to be the object of the wager and of course Armand falls genuinely in love: the rake's comeuppance. But Clair is the victim of his own nature just as much as the hapless Armand. His preferred 'voice' – the lightly ironical – and the distance he insists on maintaining between characters and audience ensure that the story seems only half-expressed, merely an agreeably rendered anecdote. Hard to resist imagining what Max Ophuls might have made of it. BBa

Grandeur et Décadence d'un Petit Commerce de Cinéma

see Rise and Fall of a Little Film Company

Grand Hotel

(1932, US, 115 min, b/w)
d Edmund Goulding. *p* Irving Thalberg. *sc* William A Drake. *ph* William H Daniels. *ed* Blanche Sewell. *ad* Cedric Gibbons. *cast* Greta Garbo, John Barrymore, Wallace Beery, Joan Crawford, Lionel Barrymore, Lewis Stone, Jean Hersholt.

● The 'Nashville' of its day, *Grand Hotel*'s reputation has outgrown its actual quality, and it is now interesting only as an example of the portmanteau style: an interwoven group of contrasting stories allowing a bunch of stars to do their most familiar turns. Cigarette cards here include lonely Garbo, mercurial John Barrymore, crusty Lionel, business-like Joan Crawford, bent Beery. Supervising and commenting on the operation are ageing Lewis Stone and twittering émigré Jean Hersholt. Throw in Cedric Gibbons as art director and cameraman William Daniels, and you have the perfect MGM vehicle – dead boring. Made a year later with a similar cast, *Dinner at Eight* is of more note in that it provides acidic insight into the star system that *Grand Hotel* represents. (From the play by William A Drake, itself an adaptation of a novel, *Menschen im Hotel*, by Vicki Baum.) AN

Grand Isle

(1991, US, 95 min)
d Mary Lambert. *p* Carolyn Pfeiffer. *sc* Hesper Anderson. *ph* Toyomichi Kurita. *ed* Tom Finan. *ad* Michelle Minch. *m* Elliot Goldenthal. *cast* Kelly McGillis, Adrian Pasdar, Glenne Headly, Julian Sands, Ellen Burstyn, Glenne Headly.

● A soporific adaptation of *The Awakening*, Kate Chopin's proto-feminist, turn-of-the-century novel about a Kentucky-born wife and mother of two (McGillis) whose summer season on Grand Isle with her husband's easy-going Creole friends frees her from inhibitions. Courted by the young Pasdar, she finds herself through swimming, unrequited love, painting and other unconventional behaviour. Produced by McGillis herself, this is primarily a celebration of her extraordinary beauty, with endless loving close-ups of her flattering costumes, veiled face and naked body. Thanks to *Siesta* director Lambert's inept direction, there's no erotic charge, and the liberating ideas that are so strong in the book are lost amid the frocks and period detail. NF

Grand Jeu, Le (Card of Fate)

(1934, Fr, 115 min, b/w)
d Jacques Feyder. *sc* Charles Spaak, Jacques Feyder. *ph* Harry Stradling, Maurice Forster. *ed* Jacques Brillouin. *ad* Lazare Meerson. *m* Hanns Eisler. *cast* Françoise Rosay, Pierre-Richard Willm, Marie Bell, Charles Vanel, Georges Pitoeff, Pierre Larquey.

● Once famed for its supposedly Pirandellian casting of Bell as a honky tonk temptress whose chiselled features remind hero Willm of the Parisian beauty (also played by Bell) he had joined the Foreign Legion precisely 'to forget'. *Le Grand Jeu* is short on directorial presence, but long on atmosphere: heat, sand, flies, cheap absinthe, and Rosay poring over greasy Tarot cards behind a rustling bead curtain. GAd

Grandma and Her Ghosts (Mo-fa A-Ma)

(1998, Tai/SKor, 90 min)
d Wang Shaudi. *p/sc* Huang Liming. *ph* Cho Bok-Dong. *ad* Mai Jan-Chieh. *m* Shih Jei-Yong.

● Wang and Huang's animated feature has things in common with their live-action films, especially the mix of 'dark' satire and 'light' fantasy, but this is a more purposive attempt to win back the Chinese audience lost to Hollywood. A small boy parked on his scary old grandma during a family crisis accidentally releases an evil spirit imprisoned in a jar in her back yard. It possesses grandma's cat Kulo and goes on a ghost-eating rampage before targeting grandma herself – she being a Taoist, adept at guiding hungry, roaming ghosts in the annual fortnight of freedom they enjoy before going for reincarnation. It gets the balance of frissons and laughs, cuteness and pathos just about right. (Park Jun-Nam was the animation director.) TR

Grandma's Boy

(1922, US, 65 min approx (silent version), b/w)
d Fred Newmeyer. *p* Hal Roach. *sc* Hal Roach, Sam Taylor, Jean Havez. *titles* HM Walker. *ph* Walter Lundin. *ed* Thomas J Crizer. *cast* Harold Lloyd, Mildred Davis, Anna Townsend, Charles A Stevenson, Dick Sutherland.

● This country comedy ('Ma wants some gasoline – she's scouring Pa's neck') contradicts the received wisdom about Lloyd being all gags and no character. The coward's redemption was a framework he often exploited, and it's remarkable how much conviction he puts into the scenes of humiliation, and how violent (and gag-free) is the climax, where Harold finally stands up to the bully. Parts of it *are* funny, though, notably the series of disasters when Harold goes courting, involving inappropriate dress, malevolent ornaments, importunate kittens and a pocketful of mothballs. Other delights include Mildred Davis, all dimples and ringlets, a stereotype from another age; and the rather poetic documentary going on in the background, as Harold makes his way across a patchwork of fields and building sites that was Hollywood 1922. BBa

Grand Meaulnes, Le

see Wanderer, The

Grand Prix

(1966, US, 175 min)
d John Frankenheimer. *p* Edward Lewis. *sc* Robert Alan Aurthur. *ph* Lionel Lindon. *ed* Fredric Steinkamp. *pd* Richard Sylbert. *m* Maurice Jarre. *cast* James Garner, Eva Marie Saint, Yves Montand, Brian Bedford, Toshiro Mifune, Jessica Walter, Antonio Sabato, Françoise Hardy, Jack Watson, Adolfo Celi, Claude Dauphin, Genevieve Page.

● Probably the best of the formula motor racing films, though that isn't saying much. Frankenheimer was a keen fan of the sport, and took great pains to convey the experience cinematically. There are no process shots; a 70mm camera was fixed to Garner's car, and the suspension jacked up on the other side to balance it. Long lenses were used for a slow-motion effect, and split screen boosts the racing footage. But in following an entire season, the movie was always too long, and the bits in-between are the usual soapy off-track drama. The Brian Bedford character, incidentally, was inspired by Stirling Moss. TCh

Grand Theft Auto

(1977, US, 89 min)
d Ron Howard. *p* Jon Davidson. *sc* Ranse Howard, Ron Howard. *ph* Gary Graver. *ed* Joe Dante. *ad* Keith Michael. *m* Peter Ivers. *cast* Ron Howard, Nancy Morgan, Marion Ross, Peter Isackson, Barry Cahill.

● Looking like something that Peckinpah might have made as a boy, this can best be described as an automotive snuff movie. Howard's debut as a director (he also scripts and stars), it leaves not a vehicle untotalled. There are some feeble attempts to make statements about young love, political ambition, money and the media, but wrecking cars is what it's all about. As stunts go, they don't go very far, but watching a Roller get wiped out in a demolition derby has its appeal. JCo

Grand Tour: Disaster in Time

see Timescape

Grandview U.S.A.

(1984, US, 97 min)
d Randal Kleiser. *p* William Blaylock, Peter W Rea. *sc* Ken Hixon. *ph* Reynaldo Villalobos. *ed* Robert Gordon. *pd* Jan Scott. *m* Thomas Newman. *cast* Jamie Lee Curtis, C Thomas Howell, Patrick Swayze, Jennifer Jason Leigh, Troy Donahue, Ramon Bieri, John Cusack, Joan Cusack.

● The assembled cast would've cost a great deal more ten years on. Howell does the rites-of-passage stuff, and Curtis looks after pa's demolition derby business while number one driver Swayze pines vigorously for her. It's pleasant enough, as a view of small-town Americana, but played very straight. No theatrical release in Britain. TJ

Grapes of Wrath, The

(1940, US, 129 min, b/w)
d John Ford. *p* Darryl F Zanuck. *sc* Nunnally Johnson. *ph* Gregg Toland. *ed* Robert Simpson. *ad* Richard Day, Mark-Lee Kirk. *m* Alfred Newman. *cast* Henry Fonda, Jane Darwell, John Carradine, Russell Simpson, Charley Grapewin, Dorris Bowden, John Qualen.

● This classic Ford film eclipses much of the action of John Steinbeck's well-known novel of the Oklahoma farmers' migration from the dustbowl to the California Eden during the Depression years. The Okies were unwelcome in California, of course; they threatened the jobs of the locals. The brutal police hassled and harassed them unmercifully. The migrants formed unions in self-defence and struck for decent fruit-picking wages. This inevitably multiplied the official violence. Ford's film, shot by Gregg Toland with magnificent, lyrical simplicity, captures the stark plainness of the migrants, stripped to a few possessions, left with innumerable relations and little hope. MH

Grass

(1925, US, 5,220 ft, b/w)
d Merian C Cooper, Ernest B Schoedsack. *p* Jesse L Lasky. *sc* Marguerite Harrison. *ph* Ernest Schoedsack. *ed* Terry Ramsaye, Richard P Carver.

● A fascinating, visually splendid film about the massive annual migration undertaken by Persia's Bakhtiari tribes in search of fresh pastures for their cattle. Due partly to some pretty awful intertitles ('Brrr. The water's cold!') as the nomads make their journey through fast-flowing rivers, across snowy glaciers and so forth, partly to the suspicion (encouraged by statements from the Persians themselves) that the odyssey was made more difficult at the insistence of the film-makers to render it more dramatic and picturesque, the film doesn't exactly fit the notion of a modern documentary. None the less, if viewed as a Herzog-like tribute to man's courage, determination, and ability to tame nature without destroying it, the film has an impressive scale and poetry. GA

Grass

(1999, US, 82 min, b/w & col)
d/p Ron Mann. *sc* Solomon Vesta. *ph* Robert Fresco. *ed* Robert Kennedy. *ad* Paul Mavrides. *m* Guido Luciani. *narrator* Woody Harrelson.

● Mann documents America's 'misguided and ineffective' prohibition of marijuana, and the billions of dollars of taxpayers' money expended thereon, with a plethora of movie extracts, press cuttings, songs and assorted graphics. He relates the ongoing ban to empire building by the Federal Bureau of Narcotics, to puritanism generally and to the weed's association with a shifting cast of the threatening and the undesirable (Mexicans pre-WWI, Red China in the '50s, the anti-war movement in the '60s/'70s). The tone is one of amused outrage, appropriate to such laws as the Tax Act of 1937, which stated that marijuana could be grown under licence, and that the issuing of such licences was prohibited; and to such law enforcers as the chain-smoking Culver City police chief c.1960, exhorting everyone to heed the perils of addiction. BBa

Grass Arena, The

(1991, GB, 90 min)
d Gillies MacKinnon. *p* Ruth Baumgarten. *sc* Frank Deasy. *ph* Rex Maidment. *ed* Michael Parker. *pd* Tony Burrough. *m* Philip Appleby. *cast* Mark Rylance, Lynsey Baxter, Pete Postlethwaite, Billy Boyle, Gerard Horan, Bunny May, Harry Landis.

● Having already impressed with *Conquest of the South Pole* and *Needles*, MacKinnon here offers a tough, intelligent version of John Healy's autobiography. Brutalised by his father during a sickly childhood, Healy later ditched a promising boxing career to indulge his obsession for booze among the dossers in London's parks. Repeated stints in prison didn't help, and only when a cell-mate taught him the game of chess did salvation seem a prospect. While MacKinnon makes great use of a highly mobile camera – though made for TV, this is real film-making – he and scriptwriter Frank Deasy respect the inherent drama of Healy's painful, often drily funny story, aided by an astonishing performance from Rylance as the shy, innocent and none-too-articulate Healy. GA

Grass Harp, The

(1995, US, 107 min)
d Charles Matthau. *p* Charles Matthau, Jerry Tokofsky, John Davis, James J Davis. *sc* Stirling Silliphant, Kirk Ellis. *ph* John A Alonzo. *ed* Sidney Levin, C Timothy O'Meara. *pd* Paul Sylbert. *m* Patrick Williams. *cast* Piper Laurie, Sissy Spacek, Walter Matthau, Edward Furlong, Nell Carter, Jack Lemmon, Mary Steenburgen, Sean Patrick Flannery, Joe Don Baker, Charles Durning, Roddy McDowall.

● The American South, a town full of eccentrics, the late '30s – and Furlong is the chap with the growing up to do when his mother dies and he's left in the company of his aunts (Spacek is the sensible one, Laurie the nature loving, touchy-feely sister she doesn't get on with). The plot (adapted from a Truman Capote novel by Stirling Silliphant and Kirk Ellis) rouses itself when Laurie's home-brew herbal dropsy cure attracts the attention of Lemmon's 'chemical engineer', a shyster with his eye on Spacek's fortune. His arrival causes such division in the household that Laurie retires to a tree house, a crisis requiring the intervention of kindly retired judge Matthau. Town barber McDowall, Durning's blustery reverend and Steenburgen's travelling evangelist also make their contributions to Furlong's life lessons, in a movie so old fashioned it makes *Fried Green Tomatoes* looks like a Gregg Araki picture. Old fashioned but not much cop, unfortunately, since director Charles Matthau (son of Walter) indulges his crusty old hams to the *n*th degree. Capote's prose glitters on the page, but this moves like treacle through its own wrong-headed sense of self-importance. TJ

Grass Is Always Greener, The (Uberall ist es besser, wo wir nicht sind)

(1989, WGer, 79 min, b/w)
d Michael Klier. *p* Daniel Zuta. *sc* Michael Klier, Gustav Barwicki. *ph* Sophie Maintigneux. *ed* Bettina Böhler. *ad* Jérôme Burckhardt-Latour. *cast* Miroslaw Baka, Marta Klubowicz, Michael Krause, Josef Zebrowski, Anna Pastewka, Anja Klein.

● Klier's dour black-and-white feature stars Baka (from Kieslowski's *Short Film About Killing*) as the gentle but alienated youth who tires of the futility of his eked-out existence in depressed Poland – changing money, fencing cheap stolen goods – and hotfoots it to Berlin while he prepares his emigration plans for the US. The film scores in its documentary-style comparative tour around the low dives and low-lives of the marginals and petty criminals found in the dead-end parts of Warsaw and West Berlin, but suffers overly from miserabilism, muted performances, and the lack of an overall organising perspective. WH

Grass Is Greener, The

(1960, US, 105 min)
d/p Stanley Donen. *sc* Hugh Williams, Margaret Williams. *ph* Christopher Challis. *ed* Jim Clark. *ad* Paul Sheriff. *songs* Noël Coward. *cast* Cary Grant, Deborah Kerr, Robert Mitchum, Jean Simmons, Moray Watson.

● Everyone in this movie – adapted from a flummery stage comedy by Hugh and Margaret Williams – stands around like mannequins in Bond Street stores. Dior and Hardy Amies are the real stars. On the plot front, Mitchum is an oil millionaire on holiday in England when he falls for Miss Kerr, a Countess who invites him for tea in her stately home. There follow some indiscretions in London and a duel with Mr Grant, as the cuckolded aristo. ATu

Grass Is Singing, The

(1981, Zam/Swe, 109 min)
d Michael Raeburn. *p* Mark Forstater. *sc* Michael Raeburn. *ph* Bille August. *ed* Thomas Schwalm. *pd* Disley Jones. *m* Lasse Dahlberg, Björn Isfält, Temba Tana. *cast* Karen Black, John Thaw, John Kani, Patrick Mynhardt, John Moulder-Brown, Margaret Heale.

● Two of Doris Lessing's recurring themes come together here: the descent into madness, and the debilitating effect of the environment (in this case, the oppressively permanent swelter of Southern Africa). In a courageously abandoned performance, Karen Black, overdressed and anxious about spinsterhood, leaves the relative social and physical comforts of the town for marriage with a none-too-successful bush farmer (Thaw). Installed in the ramshackle homestead, her automatic and unconsidered racism (it's only 1960) towards the African workers, and her pent-up loathing of the heat and the mean little farm, drive her towards complete breakdown and the film's violent, quasi-mystical resolution. A dramatically potent adaptation which, while seriously polemical, is also shot through with the hallucinatory and the poetic. JS

Gravesend

(1996, US, 85 min)
d/p/sc Salvatore Stabile. *ph* Joseph Dell'olio. *ed* Miranda Devin, Salvatore Stabile. *cast* Tony Tucci, Michael Parducci, Tom Malloy, Thomas Brandise, Sean Quinn, Carmel Altomare.

● Given that this first feature was written and directed by a 19-year-old, with a cast of unknowns and an initial budget of $5,000, it's hard not to be impressed by its raw, dark tale of four young, white Brooklyn friends who find themselves swept up in a spiralling nightmare after one of their number accidentally kills another's brother in one of his many moments of volatile, psychotically macho aggression. Cue the night-long search for a way, with help from Jojo the junkie, to dispose of the body… or, as it turns out, bodies. There's nothing especially new here, and the narrative is perhaps over-eventful, but Stabile clearly has talent; this is compulsively watchable, blessed by muscular performances, occasional incursions of grisly black humour, and a real sense of pace and place. GA

Graveyard of Dreams (Ochnebebis Sasaplao)

(1997, Georgia, 95 min, b/w)
d/p Georgi Khaindrava. *sc* Georgi Khaindrava, Irakli Solomonaschvili. *ph* Georgi Khaindrava, Michael Magalashvili. *ed* Georgi Khaindrava, Leila Muchigulaschvili. *pd* Zaza Tsitsischvili. *m* Naizi Diasamidze. *cast* Bacho Bachukaschvili, George Nakashidze, Avtandil Schitrladze, Tamaz Berejiani, Lascha Esebua, Surab Gorgadze.

● Every culture, it seems, needs to discover for itself that war is hell. Khaindrava's version of this *aperçu* is in every sense a front line bulletin: it's a b/w docu-drama about Georgia's attempts to subdue the rebellion in Abkhazia, made with real young soldiers and partly shot in the thick of battle. It starts from the eagerness of students and intellectuals to volunteer for the Georgian army and ends (with rather facile irony) with the deaths of many. Khaindrava, several times imprisoned for dissidence in USSR days, knows all about the conflict: he helped launch it when he was made Minister for Abkhazian Affairs – a post he soon quit. He should have watched *Hell Is for Heroes* before he took the job. TR

Graveyard Shift

(1990, US, 86 min)
d Ralph S Singleton. *p* William G Dunn Jr, Ralph S Singleton. *sc* John Espositio. *ph* Peter Stein. *ed* Jim Gross, Randy Jon Morgan. *pd* Gary Wissner. *m* Anthony Marinelli, Brian Banks. *cast* David Andrews, Kelly Wolf, Stephen Macht, Andrew Divoff, Vic Polizos, Brad Dourif, Robert Alan Beuth.

● Where *Misery* restored one's faith in Stephen King adaptations, this travesty buries his reputation alive. Bland hunk John Hall (Andrews) drifts into a small Maine town and lands a job at a dilapidated mill. Working the graveyard shift in a basement, he is on hand when a crew of disposable extras discover the subterranean lair of a giant rat-like monster. Introduced to up the love interest, spunky co-worker Jane (Wolf, making what she can of a poorly written role) sweats a lot and holds her own among the all-male crew. The most engaging character, Dourif's crazed Vietvet vermin exterminator, adds some much-needed humour and class before suffering a premature burial. Neither Singleton nor scriptwriter John Esposito has grasped the anti-capitalist undercurrents of King's story, relying instead on cheap shocks and dodgy creature effects. NF

Grayeagle

(1977, US, 104 min)
d/p/sc Charles B Pierce. *ph/ed* Jim Roberson. *ad* John Ball. *m* Jaime Mendoza-Nava. *cast* Ben Johnson, Iron Eyes Cody, Lana Wood, Jack Elam, Paul Fix, Alex Cord, Jacob Daniels.

● Right from the opening of this simple Cheyenne legend – an ageing chief intoning in his ancestors' graveyard – the mood evoked by the widescreen Montana landscape is fractured by nonsensical jumps. With 40 minutes removed, the film has been not so much cut as butchered for distribution here. What's left is a disjointed narrative, marvellous performances from Johnson and Elam (whose moments of quiet dignity are ludicrously curtailed), and a picture of Indian life that carries sufficient authenticity only to be undercut by some un-folkloric music and slow-motion. A mess, but one which carries intimations of something better: a would-be mood piece celebrating Indian cycles of death and rebirth. CPea

Gray Lady Down

(1977, US, 111 min)
d David Greene. *p* Walter Mirisch. *sc* James Whittaker, Howard Sackler. *ph* Stevan Larner. *ed* Robert Swink. *pd* William Tunke. *m* Jerry Fielding. *cast* Charlton Heston, David Carradine, Stacy Keach, Ned Beatty, Stephen McHattie, Ronny Cox, Rosemary Forsyth.

● A tedious disaster movie that amounts to no more than a straightforward salvage operation (the film is plastered with dedications to the US Navy). Heston, strong and silent commander of the jeopardised nuclear sub that sinks after a collision, is given lines which strain credulity even more than his hairpiece: 'Stow that crap, sailor, now!' Character makes little impression in this almost entirely pointless military exercise. David Carradine at least makes some impact as the strong, silent, nonconformist captain who mounts the rescue operation, but everyone else is more mechanical than the hardware. CPe

Grazie Zia (Thank You, Aunt)

(1968, It, 96 min, b/w)
d Salvatore Samperi. *p* Enzo Doria. *sc* Sergio Bazzini, Salvatore Samperi, Pier Luigi Murgia. *ph* Aldo Scavarda. *ed* Alessandro Giselli. *ad* Giorgio Mecchia. *m* Ennio Morricone. *cast* Lou Castel, Lisa Gastoni, Gabriele Ferzetti, Luisa De Santis.

● For his first feature, a black comedy modelled on Bellocchio's *Fists in the Pocket*, Samperi even borrowed Lou Castel to embody his anti-hero, the son of a business tycoon, who initially expresses his rebellion by pretending to be unable to walk, and snarling insults at all and sundry from his wheelchair. Sent to recuperate in the care of an aunt (Gastoni) – a doctor but also a beautiful woman – he snares her into a kind of sexual complicity, forcing her to humour him in a series of bizarre rites which rise in crescendo to his final invention, a game of euthanasia. Uneven, more black than comic, but capturing much the same sense of rapt perversity as Bellocchio's film: an undeniably striking debut. TM

Grease

(1978, US, 110 min)
d Randal Kleiser. *p* Robert Stigwood, Allan Carr. *sc* Bronte Woodard. *ph* Bill Butler. *ed*

John F Burnett. *pd* Philip M Jefferies. *songs* Jim Jacobs, Warren Casey. *cast* John Travolta, Olivia Newton-John, Stockard Channing, Jeff Conaway, Barry Pearl, Didi Conn, Eve Arden, Joan Blondell, Sid Caesar.

● The real progenitor of this musical celebrating the rock'n'roll '50s, had it not fudged some of the less adequate dance numbers by shooting above the knees, would be *West Side Story*. Otherwise, the film aspires to some of the pretensions of *Rebel Without a Cause*, from which it borrows liberally while saddled with the liabilities of its dumb stage musical script. Its flashy opportunism (nostalgia pitched squarely at an audience too young to even recall the era) quickly becomes very irritating. Allusions to french letters and high school pregnancies, and double entendres allowed by the hindsight of this more 'permissive' society, scarcely conceal the fact that *Grease* is even more simplistic (and finally reactionary) than the beach blanket movies of the era. Lots of colour, movement, surface glitter, only one decent song (the title track sung by Frankie Valli). RM

Grease 2

(1982, US, 114 min)
d Patricia Birch. *p* Robert Stigwood, Allan Carr. *sc* Ken Finkleman. *ph* Frank Stanley. *ed* John F Burnett. *pd* Gene Callahan. *m* Louis St Louis. *songs* Louis St Louis, Howard Greenfield, Michael Gibson, others. *cast* Maxwell Caulfield, Michelle Pfeiffer, Adrian Zmed, Lorna Luft, Didi Conn, Eve Arden, Sid Caesar, Tab Hunter.

● As gaudily tempting a soft-centre as ever graced a Woolworth counter. Liberally pick-ing'n'mixing assorted elements of American popular culture, Birch picks up the story of Rydell High a few years on from where Randal Kleiser left it. Travolta and Newton-John have moved on, Conn is back from beauty school, and straight skirts have replaced full ones; these changes apart, we're on familiar ground. Pink Lady Pfeiffer steals the heart of Caulfield, a straight A, strait-laced student from England who is excruciatingly dull (rating 8 on a chuckability scale of 10). However, he gets himself a pair of wheels and wins his girl. Such niceties as a plausible plot and three-dimensional characters are trampled under Weejun-shod foot, but sheer energy, a handful of good tunes (including a great theme song from the Four Tops), and some very funny one-liners save the day. FD

Greased Lightning

(1977, US, 96 min)
d Michael Schultz. *p* Hannah Weinstein. *sc* Kenneth Vose, Lawrence Dukore, Melvin Van Peebles, Leon Capetanos. *ph* George Bouillet. *ed* Robert Wyman, Randy Roberts. *ad* Jack Senter. *m* Fred Karlin. *cast* Richard Pryor, Beau Bridges, Pam Grier, Cleavon Little, Vincent Gardenia, Richie Havens.

● Anyone who enjoyed *Car Wash* should be warned that Schultz admits only to having done a wrap-up 'fireman's job' on this woeful biopic featuring a smiling Pryor as Wendell Scott, the first black US stock car driver. Although Melvin Van Peebles evidently directed most of it, a doubt still remains as to who should be held finally responsible for the finished cornball mish-mash, since Schultz's subsequent film (*Which Way Is Up?*) bears an ominous resemblance to the style and tone of this relentlessly indulgent comedy-romance. JPy

Great Armored Car Swindle, The

see Breaking Point, The

Great Balls of Fire!

(1989, US, 107 min)
d Jim McBride. *p* Adam Fields. *sc* Jack Baran, Jim McBride. *ph* Affonso Beato. *ed* Lisa Day, Pembroke J Herring, Bert Lovitt. *pd* David Nichols. *songs* Otis Blackwell, Jack Hammer, others. *cast* Dennis Quaid, Winona Ryder, John Doe, Joe Bob Briggs, Stephen Tobolowsky, Trey Wilson, Alec Baldwin, Steve Allen, Lisa Blount, Peter Cook.

● The trouble with this biopic is that it attempts to convey too many aspects of the Jerry Lee Lewis legend. His marriage (to his 13-year-old second cousin)and the ensuing scandal are the focus and deserve serious treatment, but instead the pace is disrupted by the kind of spontaneous musical routine that is more at home in a light-hearted romantic comedy. When the film switches to London, the playful approach is utterly out of keeping with the unfolding drama. And what is Peter Cook doing as a newspaper hack? Stranger yet is the miscasting of Quaid, whose attempts to affect Lewis' boundless energy and Southern naiveté are alternately amusing and perplexing. Taken in isolation. Quaid's keyboard scenes are splendidly carried by the strength of the music, but alas, such moments are short-lived. Other performances are better, notably from Alec Baldwin as Lewis' Bible-thumping, disapproving cousin, and Ryder as his winsome bride. CM

Great Day in Harlem, A

(1994, US, 60 min, b/w & col)
d/p Jean Bach. *sc* Jean Bach, Susan Peehl, Matthew Seig. *ph* Steve Petropoulos. *ed* Susan Peehl. *with* Art Kane, Dizzy Gillespie, Marian McPartland, Art Farmer, Milt Hinton, Sonny Rollins, Johnny Griffin. *narrator* Quincy Jones.

● Bach's documentary avoids all the clichés of jazz retrospection by concentrating on a single event on an August morning back in 1958. *Esquire* magazine's then art director, Robert Benton (yes, he of *Bonnie and Clyde* and *Nobody's Fool*), commissioned a photo from Art Kane containing as many jazz musicians as possible standing outside a brownstone in Harlem (57, plus one club-owner, in the event), and, unofficially, bassist Milt Hinton brought along his home-movie camera. There are so many stories here. The musicians had hardly seen each other in daylight before – 'They never knew there were two 11 o'clocks in one day,' said one. They were so pleased to talk to each other it was difficult to get them to stand still, and even then Dizzy Gillespie pulled a face which cracked up Roy Eldridge, and street urchins stole Count Basie's hat. Thelonious Monk was late. He'd been deciding on an outfit to eclipse the company. Johnny Griffin today remembered Monk with awe, and Sonny Rollins remembered Lester Young as someone briefly visiting from another planet. All the contemporary interviews are fascinating and touching, too: Blakey and Diz are gone now. The musical clips aren't over-familiar and are killingly good. A wonderful, warm little movie. BC

Great Day in the Morning

(1956, US, 92 min)
d Jacques Tourneur. *p* Edmund Grainger. *sc* Lesser Samuels. *ph* William Snyder. *ed* Harry Marker. *ad* Albert S D'Agostino, Jack Okey. *m* Leith Stevens. *cast* Robert Stack, Virginia Mayo, Ruth Roman, Alex Nicol, Raymond Burr, Leo Gordon.

● A fine Western, set on the eve of the Civil War, with Stack as a Southern gambler/gunslinger who agrees, for a price, to help ferry a shipment of gold desperately needed to buy guns for the Rebel cause. Adapted from a bestseller and set in the booming Colorado Territory, it starts with the advantage of a remarkably literate script by Lesser Samuels which beats a lucid path through the tangle of conflicting interests: not only between North and South, but between public need and private lust for gold, between the realities of love and the illusions of desire. Focal point of the various subsidiary battles between self-interest and selfless commitment is Stack's anti-hero, who is finally cornered not only into offering his services to the South free of charge, but to acknowledge that he loves Roman's shop-soiled saloon girl rather than Mayo's pristine lady. But he does so – the script never quite abandons its abrasive edge of cynicism – only when it is too late for his gold (otherwise all of it would fall into Northern hands) and for his girl (although he doesn't know it, he left her behind to be murdered). Tourneur stages it all impeccably, with outstanding performances from Stack and Roman. TM

Great Dictator, The

(1940, US, 128 min, b/w)
d/p/sc Charles Chaplin. *ph* Karl Struss, Rollie Totheroh. *ed* Willard Nico. *ad* J Russell Spencer. *m* Charles Chaplin. *cast* Charles Chaplin, Paulette Goddard, Jack Oakie, Reginald Gardiner, Maurice Moscovich, Billy Gilbert, Henry Daniell.

● Chaplin acts the roles of Hitler (alias Adenoid Hynkel) and a Jewish barber who returns as an amnesiac, decades after an accident in World War I, totally unaware of the rise of Nazism and the persecution of his people. The representation of Hitler is vaudeville goonery all the way, but minus the acid wit and inventive energy that Groucho Marx managed in his impersonation of authoritarianism gone berserk in *Duck Soup*. Mr Nobody is eventually carted away to a concentration camp, which leads to a reversal of roles when the barber escapes and is mistaken for Hynkel on the eve of the invasion of Austria. Cue for an impassioned speech about freedom and democracy calculated to jerk tears out of the surliest fascist, in a manner startlingly similar to Hitler's very own delivery. VG

Great Ecstasy of Woodcarver Steiner, The (Die Grosse Ekstase des Bildschnitzers Steiner)

(1975, WGer, 47 min)
d/p/sc Werner Herzog. *ph* Jörg Schmidt-Reitwein, Francisco Joan, Frederik Hettich, Alfred Chrosziel, Gideon Maron. *ed* Beate Mainka-Jellinghaus. *m* Popol Vuh. *with* Walter Steiner.

● A film about flying in the face of death. In Steiner's case, the flying is literal: he is a champion ski-jumper, in Herzog's view the best in the world because the most profoundly fearless. Convention would call this a 'documentary reportage', but convention would be wrong: the angle of approach is wholly unexpected, and Herzog's own participation as commentator/interviewer/hero-worshipper/myth-maker guarantees a really extraordinary level of engagement with the subject. Watch especially how he coaxes a truly revealing story about a pet raven out of a highly embarrassed Steiner in the closing moments. Herzog, a surrealist to the core, knows that the real world offers more fantastic phenomena than anything he can imagine. TR

Great Escape, The

(1962, US/WGer, 173 min)
d/p John Sturges. *sc* James Clavell, WR Burnett. *ph* Daniel L Fapp. *ed* Ferris Webster. *ad* Fernando Carrere. *m* Elmer Bernstein. *cast* Steve McQueen, James Garner, Richard Attenborough, James Donald, Charles Bronson, Donald Pleasence, James Coburn, Gordon Jackson, David McCallum.

● Uneven but entertaining World War II escape drama, which even when it first appeared seemed very old-fashioned. Based on Paul Brickhill's factual account of the efforts of Allied prisoners to break out of Stalag Luft North, it contains memorable sequences and a sea of well-known faces. McQueen comes off best as 'The Cooler King'; Bronson and Garner (perhaps surprisingly) give good support; Coburn is totally miscast as an Australian, yet turns in an amusing performance. Worth seeing the last half hour, if nothing else, for one of the best stunt sequences in years: McQueen's motor-cycle bid for freedom. CPe

Greatest, The

(1977, US/GB, 101 min)
d Tom Gries. *p* John Marshall. *sc* Ring Lardner Jr. *ph* Harry Stradling Jr. *ed* Byron 'Buzz' Brandt. *pd* Bob Smith. *m* Michael Masser. *cast* Muhammad Ali, Ernest Borgnine, Roger E Mosley, Lloyd Haynes, Malachi Throne, John Marley, Robert Duvall, David Huddleston, Ben Johnson, James Earl Jones.

● It's hard to define exactly where this highly selective biography, with Muhammad Ali playing himself, goes so wrong, but it's like one of his later fights: heavy in unrealised potential, poor value considering the stars involved, yet with Ali himself emerging unscathed at the end. The script – credited to Ring Lardner Jr – veers between some felicitous use of the young Clay's poetry which grows into the fluent speeches given to Ali himself, and hamfisted bridging passages that gloss over any details out of tune with the *Rocky* image (e.g. the death of his mentor Malcolm X, Zaire). Likewise the direction, which evokes some early nigger-baiting tensions, then as soon as Ali takes over the role and dodges the draft, settles for straight hero-worship. AN

Greatest Heroes, The (De Storste Helte/aka The Biggest Heroes)

(1996, Den, 90 min)
d Thomas Vinterberg. *p* Bo Ehrhardt, Birgitte Hald, Peter Aalbæk Jensen. *sc* Bo Hr. Hansen, Thomas Vinterberg. *ph* Anthony Dod Mantle.

ed Jesper W Nielsen, Valdis Oskarsdóttir. *m* Nikolaj Egelund. *cast* Thomas Bo Larsen, Ulrich Thomsen, Mia Maria Back, Bjarne Henriksen, Paprika Steen, Trine Dyrholm, Hella Joof.

● Vinterberg's first feature has its moments, but on the whole it's something of a mess. Much of the cast are familiar from *Festen*, notably Bo Larsen and Thomsen as delinquent buddies Karsten and Peter, a recidivist bank robber and a manic depressive pill-popper respectively; and the plot echoes both the latter film and Vinterberg's short *The Boy Who Walked Backwards* in its basis in family trauma and rebellion, following the pair and Karsten's newfound teenage daughter on a slapdash spree through Sweden in flight from the girl's abusive foster father and the authorities. Vinterberg's attempt at characterisation on the go doesn't come off: the action is too diffuse and the character background introduced too clumsily. The male lead performances are uncomfortably pitched somewhere between drama and farce, though the women are generally very assured. The shoot-out finale is particularly uninspired. NB

Greatest Show on Earth, The

(1952, US, 153 min)
d/p Cecil B DeMille. *sc* Fredric M Frank, Barré Lyndon, Theodore St John. *ph* George Barnes. *ed* Anne Bauchens. *ad* Hal Pereira, Walter Tyler. *m* Victor Young. *cast* James Stewart, Betty Hutton, Charlton Heston, Cornel Wilde, Dorothy Lamour, Gloria Grahame, Lawrence Tierney, Henry Wilcoxon.

● Characteristically elephantine Big Top epic from DeMille, thumped across with a winning brashness and garnering the veteran showman his first Best Picture Oscar. Heston crosses his Moses-to-be with Noah as he leads his 'children' and menagerie cross-country, while Stewart's killer-on-the-lam does a wonderfully affecting 'tears of a clown' number in the true, tacky circus tradition of sawdust, spectacle and sentiment. PT

Greatest Story Ever Told, The

(1965, US, 225 min)
d/p George Stevens. *sc* James Lee Barrett, George Stevens. *ph* William C Mellor, Loyal Griggs. *ed* Argyle Nelson, Frank O'Neill. *ad* Richard Day, William J Creber. *m* Alfred Newman. *cast* Max von Sydow, Carroll Baker, Pat Boone, Victor Buono, Richard Conte, Jose Ferrer, Van Heflin, Charlton Heston, Angela Lansbury, David McCallum, Roddy McDowall, Dorothy McGuire, Sal Mineo, Donald Pleasence, Sidney Poitier, Claude Rains, Telly Savalas, John Wayne, Shelley Winters, Ed Wynn.

● Interminable and intolerably reverential rendering of the Life of Christ, originally made in Ultra Panavision 70mm, and soon cut for general release to 225 minutes (with subsequent versions even further shorn, the most ruthless being 127 minutes). Max von Sydow's remarkable performance is consistently undermined by dozens of ill-chosen cameos, such as John Wayne's 'Truly, this man was the Son of Gaaard' Centurion, and Shelley Winters yelling 'I'm cured!' as the Woman of No Name. Sydow resists the temptation to engage the Devil (Pleasence) in a game of chess. ATu

Great Expectations

(1946, GB, 118 min, b/w)
d David Lean. *p* Ronald Neame. *sc* David Lean, Ronald Neame, Anthony Havelock-Allan, Cecil McGivern, Kay Walsh. *ph* Guy Green. *ed* Jack Harris. *pd* John Bryan. *m* Walter Goehr. *cast* John Mills, Valerie Hobson, Martita Hunt, Bernard Miles, Francis L Sullivan, Finlay Currie, Jean Simmons, Anthony Wager, Alec Guinness, Freda Jackson.

● Still Lean's best film, and probably – along with Cukor's *David Copperfield* – the best of all the cinema's many stabs at Dickens. It begins on a high note with young Pip's nervous scurry home along the bleak seashore as darkness falls, past lowering gibbets and blasted trees leading him straight into his hair-raising encounter with Magwitch the convict in the graveyard. A hard act to follow, but Lean tops it effortlessly with his eerie evocation of the Gothic yet strangely gentle fantasy world inhabited by poor, mad Miss Havisham, nesting her broken heart amid the cobwebby remains of her wedding finery. For once the transition from childhood (with Mills and Hobson taking over from Wager and Simmons) is managed with total credibility, and the fine performances keep on coming (Mills and Hobson have never been better; Hunt is fantastic; Currie, Guinness, Simmons and Sullivan all memorable). Visually flawless, perfectly paced, it's a small masterpiece. TM

Great Expectations

(1975, GB, 124 min)
d Joseph Hardy. *p* Robert Fryer. *sc* Sherman Yellen. *ph* Freddie Young. *ed* Bill Butler. *pd* Terence Marsh. *m* Maurice Jarre. *cast* Michael York, Sarah Miles, James Mason, Margaret Leighton, Robert Morley, Anthony Quayle, Joss Ackland, Rachel Roberts, Heather Sears, Andrew Ray.

● Many distinguished names who should have known better lend themselves to what looks like a TV musical version of Dickens' tale, minus the songs. This plodding, charmless adaptation is long on coincidences which become increasingly preposterous. Most notable, however, are the wigs: over a hundred, the press handout revealed. And you can spot every one of 'em. Poor old Joss Ackland's ruins an otherwise good performance (as Joe Gargery). And the same bowl of fruit rests on the sideboard…twenty years later. CPe

Great Expectations

(1997, US, 111 min)
d Alfonso Cuarón. *p* Art Linson. *sc* Mitch Glazer. *ph* Emmanuel Lubezki. *ed* Steven Weisberg. *pd* Tony Burrough. *m* Patrick Doyle. *cast* Ethan Hawke, Gwyneth Paltrow, Hank Azaria, Chris Cooper, Anne Bancroft, Robert De Niro, Josh Mostel, Kim Dickens.

● While remaining largely faithful to the narrative thrust of Dickens' novel, Cuarón's version is hugely different from the David Lean classic, displaying all the wit, vitality and unpretentious assurance the Mexican brought to his delightful *A Little Princess*. It kicks off with orphan Finn (Hawke) fatefully making the acquaintance of an escaped con (De Niro), crazy old Nora Dinsmoor (Bancroft), and her beautiful niece Estella (Paltrow) in '70s Florida; before fast-forwarding to '80s New York where, as a promising artist, Finn continues to pursue his childhood beloved, now engaged to rich, snobby Walter (Azaria). The transposition to modern America works very well. Since we're advised from the start that we're about to see the story not as it happened, but as it's remembered by the older, wiser Finn, both the magical, natural paradise of the Everglades and the success-oriented New York art world beautifully evoke the twin poles of hopeful innocence and harsh experience. Cuarón plays up this fabulous romance, never departing from Finn's obsessive view of the bewilderingly changeable Estella, and underlining the cruel ironies of a life transformed yet tainted by love. Stylish, sexy, involving, and great fun. GA

Great Garrick, The

(1937, US, 91 min, b/w)
d James Whale. *p* Mervyn Le Roy. *sc* Ernest Vajda. *ph* Ernest Haller. *ed* Warren Low. *ad* Anton F Grot. *m* Adolph Deutsch. *cast* Brian Aherne, Olivia de Havilland, Edward Everett Horton, Melville Cooper, Lionel Atwill, Luis Alberni, Etienne Girardot, Lana Turner, Marie Wilson, Albert Dekker.

● Not the 'ponderous biography' of Steven Scheuer's *Movies on TV*, but an unusual, comical divertissement in which the legendary 18th century English actor accepts an invitation to the Comédie Française in Paris, announcing that he'll teach them a thing or two about their craft. When they catch wind of his remark, the entire French company stages an elaborate hoax at a country inn in an attempt to humiliate their guest (who has a trick or two in hand). A swish, witty production with a droll performance from the underrated Aherne as David Garrick. TCh

Great Gatsby, The

(1949, US, 92 min, b/w)
d Elliott Nugent. *p* Richard Maibaum. *sc* Cyril Hume, Richard Maibaum. *ph* John F Seitz. *ed* Ellsworth Hoagland. *ad* Hans Dreier, Roland Anderson. *m* Robert Emmett Dolan. *cast* Alan Ladd, Betty Field, Macdonald Carey, Barry Sullivan, Ruth Hussey, Shelley Winters, Howard da Silva.

● The first sound adaptation of Scott Fitzgerald's classic. Although some of the detail of the novel has been changed (and Betty Field gives an unusually weak performance, miscast as Daisy Buchanan), this scores over Jack Clayton's lavish and longer 1974 version by the casting of Alan Ladd as Gatsby, so much more convincing as a man with a dark and mysterious past than one-dimensional glamour-puss Robert Redford. At the same time, the picture is less a '20s costume drama than a '40s *film noir*, shot in moody monochrome by the maestro John F Seitz. ATu

Great Gatsby, The

(1974, US, 146 min)
d Jack Clayton. *p* David Merrick. *sc* Francis Ford Coppola. *ph* Douglas Slocombe. *ed* Tom Priestley. *pd* John Box. *m* Nelson Riddle. *cast* Robert Redford, Mia Farrow, Bruce Dern, Karen Black, Scott Wilson, Sam Waterston, Lois Chiles, Howard da Silva.

● A literary adaptation that continually begs detrimental comparison with the novel, this relies too much on appearance, making little attempt to explore behind the beguiling '20s façade. Given little support, the characters are left scratching the surface, their feverishness expressed in an unfortunately literal manner, as though they're running high temperatures most of the time. Redford occasionally conveys Gatsby's private obsession and his unease, but too often he's merely decorative, certainly no enigmatic figure of gossip. Farrow's Daisy is disastrously lightweight, a cross between squeaky child and flapper hard to imagine as the object of anyone's infatuation. It's sadly logical that their love is celebrated as the ultimate Babycham experience. Although no catastrophe, uneven pacing and length make *The Great Gatsby* over-schematic and overt, at its best when dealing with the lesser characters, and safely middle-of-the-road.

Great Gilbert and Sullivan, The

see Story of Gilbert and Sullivan, The

Great Gundown, The

see 40 Graves for 40 Guns

Great Jewel Robber, The (aka After Nightfall)

(1949, US, 91 min, b/w)
d Peter Godfrey. *p* Bryan Foy. *sc* Borden Chase. *ph* Sid Hickox. *ed* Frank Magee. *ad* Stanley Fleischer. *m* William Lava. *cast* David Brian, Marjorie Reynolds, John Archer, Jacqueline de Wit, Claudia Barrett, Ned Glass.

● Blame Godfrey for everything that's missing here: mood, rhythm, conviction, point. But this crime yarn does have a quasi-auteur in writer Borden Chase (*Red River*, *Winchester '73*), whose penchant for hectic incident is evident. By the 30-minute mark TGJR has busted out of a Canadian jail, been double-crossed in Buffalo, plugged in New Rochelle and on the side romanced a nurse, a couple of shady ladies and the landlord's daughter. The idea of a movie narrated by an unmitigated rat is unusual for its time, but goes for nothing, thanks to the uninterested Godfrey and the uninteresting Brian, whose trademark sneer makes him seem torn between either throwing up or bursting into tears.BBa

Great K & A Train Robbery, The

(1926, US, 53 min, b/w)
d Lewis Seiler. *sc* John Stone. *ph* Dan Clark. *cast* Tom Mix, Dorothy Dwan, William Walling, Harry Grippe, Carl Miller, Edward Piel.

● Typically energetic escapist Western from one of the earliest stars to set the generic formula. Officially listed as an army deserter in 1902, Mix became national rodeo champion in 1909, and entered films with the Selig company a year later. With the accent on pace, stuntwork and a modicum of comic relief, his films achieved massive success, and a Fox contract followed from 1917 to 1928, until the coming of sound and the lure of the circus conspired to slow his prolific output. Here, as a railroad detective going undercover to foil a persistent gang, he crossed paths with versatile B director Seiler, a former Fox gagman who was still churning 'em out in 1958. PT

Great Lie, The

(1941, US, 107 min, b/w)
d Edmund Goulding. *sc* Lenore J Coffee. *ph* Tony Gaudio. *ed* Ralph Dawson. *ad* Carl Jules Weyl. *m* Max Steiner. *cast* Bette Davis, Mary Astor, George Brent, Lucile Watson, Hattie McDaniel, Grant Mitchell, Jerome Cowan.
●Sudsy melo as George Brent divorces concert pianist Astor, marries Davis, and then leaves a metaphorical Amazon jungle for the real one, where he apparently dies in a plane crash. Meanwhile, back in the big smoke, Astor discovers that she's pregnant and Davis wants to adopt the baby as a souvenir of her darling hubby. The leading ladies blast away at each other like pocket battleships, while Max Steiner and Tchaikovsky provide a sumptuous musical background. ATu

Great Manhunt, The

see State Secret

Great Man Votes, The

(1939, US, 72 min, b/w)
d Garson Kanin. *p* Cliff Reid. *sc* John Twist. *ph* Russell Metty. *ed* Jack B Hively. *ad* Van Nest Polglase. *m* Roy Webb. *cast* John Barrymore, Peter Holden, Virginia Weidler, Donald MacBride, William Demarest, Katharine Alexander.
●Virtually a B movie, but featuring a wittily outsize performance from Barrymore as a Harvard professor, turned nightwatchman and souse since his wife's death, who demands the right to educate his own children and finds himself arguing from a position of strength because of a quaint electoral anomaly. In Capra vein but rather too whimsical, the film is constantly dragged down by a pedestrian script which offers Barrymore no help at all (and indeed, often makes him appear to be guilty of cute overplaying). TM

Great McGinty, The

(1940, US, 81 min, b/w)
d Preston Sturges. *p* Paul Jones. *sc* Preston Sturges. *ph* William C Mellor. *ed* Hugh Bennett. *ad* Hans Dreier, Earl Hedrick. *m* Frederick Hollander. *cast* Brian Donlevy, Muriel Angelus, Akim Tamiroff, Allyn Joslyn, William Demarest, Louis Jean Heydt.
●Sturges' first film as writer/director, a wonderfully dry satire which takes the American political system apart through the tale of a bum (Donlevy) who rides on a tide of corruption to become state governor. A totally dishonest man, he gets his comeuppance only because – through the influence of his wife, a sweet prig whose liberal conscience comes in for some rude knocks – he is for one fatal moment tempted to be honest. Cast in flashback from the sleazy banana republic cantina where the disgraced Donlevy has found refuge as a barman – and tells his story to a bank cashier (Heydt) suicidally regretting a momentary temptation to embezzlement – the script is underpinned by some slyly subversive thoughts about the success ethic and living up to expectations. Although the Sturges stock company was not yet fully formed, a number of familiar faces keep popping up to give the whole thing a delightfully quirky vitality. TM

Great McGonagall, The

(1974, GB, 89 min)
d Joseph McGrath. *p* David Grant. *sc* Joe McGrath, Spike Milligan. *ph* John Mackey. *ed* Rusty Coppleman. *ad* George Djurkovic. *m* Derek Warne, John Shakespeare, Spike Milligan, Joe McGrath. *cast* Spike Milligan, Peter Sellers, Julia Foster, Julian Chagrin, John Bluthal, Valentine Dyall.
●Revue-type sketches inspired by the life of William McGonagall, the 19th century Scot and self-styled poet who wrote verse not unlike Milligan. Potentially amusing material comes to grief as the film fails to find an appropriate visual style for Milligan's predominantly verbal humour. The Goonery between Sellers (as Queen Victoria) and Milligan (as McGonagall) comes off, but elsewhere the humour is forced and the social/political comment embarrassingly exposed. With its musical hall setting, it looks like some tiresome theatrical junket brought out in the wake of the departing Lord Chamberlain, crammed full of previously vetoed references to the Royal Family.

Great Moment, The

(1944, US, 83 min, b/w)
d/sc Preston Sturges. *ph* Victor Milner. *ed* Stuart Gilmore. *ad* Hans Dreier, Ernst Fegté. *m* Victor Young. *cast* Joel McCrea, Betty Field, Harry Carey, William Demarest, Louis Jean Heydt, Franklin Pangborn, Grady Sutton, Jimmy Conlin.
●The odd Sturges film out, a more or less serious biopic of WTG Morton, the Boston dentist who accidentally discovered the use of ether as an anaesthetic in 1846, receiving neither fame nor fortune as a reward for this great service to humanity. But Sturges couldn't be solemn for long, and though telling a basically tragic story (like the hero of *The Great McGinty*, Morton ruined himself through one 'great moment' of charitable impulse), he injects some delightful doses of slapstick and verbal fancy, while using members of his stock company in very unexpected ways. Recut by the studio and generally considered to be a failure, it's nevertheless an oddly moving film that sticks obstinately and agreeably in the mind. TM

Great Mouse Detective, The (aka Basil the Great Mouse Detective)

(1986, US, 80 min)
d John Musker, Ron Clements, Dave Michener, Burny Mattinson. *p* Burny Mattinson. *sc* Pete Young, Burny Mattinson, Melvin Shaw, Steve Hulett, John Musker, Matthew O'Callaghan, Dave Michener, Vance Gerry, Ron Clements, Bruce M Morris. *ph* Ed Austin. *ed* Roy M Brewer Jr, James Melton. *ad* Guy Vasilovich. *m* Henry Mancini. *cast* voices: Vincent Price, Barrie Ingham, Basil Rathbone, Shani Wallis, Val Bettin, Susanne Pollatsched.
●Animated feature from Disney in which the one true rival to the old coke-fiend lives down in the basement of 221b Baker Street. Basil, like his alter ego, plays the violin; he also has his Moriarty, in the shape of the magnificent Professor Ratigan, a Napoleon of crime with the wardrobe and neurotic wit of a Nineties dandy, and the absolute conviction that his rat-like form is one of nature's mistakes. Donning his best mousestalker, Basil takes to the mean streets once more, in aid of an eight-year-old Scots mouse whose toymaker father has been abducted. As usual with *film noir*, however, it is the villain who steals the heart and one is rooting for in the breathtaking showdown high up in the cogs and ratchets of Big Ben. CPea

Great Muppet Caper, The

(1981, GB, 97 min)
d Jim Henson. *p* David Lazer, Frank Oz. *sc* Tom Patchett, Jay Tarses, Jerry Juhl, Jack Rose. *ph* Oswald Morris. *ed* Ralph Kemplen. *pd* Harry Lange. *m* Joe Raposo. *cast* Diana Rigg, Charles Grodin, John Cleese, Robert Morley, Peter Ustinov, Jack Warden, Joan Sanderson.
●Second big screen outing for TV's favourite inanimates, with Kermit, Fozzie and Gonzo as reporters intrepidly investigating the theft of jewels belonging to Rigg, an international couturière soon being besieged by Miss Piggy as an aspiring model. The songs are routine, but the inconsequential plot leaves plenty of time for engaging asides like the blandly silly dinner-table dialogue between a well-bred couple (Cleese and Sanderson) determined not to notice that their home has been invaded by little furry creatures. Or a charming moment when Kermit and friends tangle with a fold-up bed which shuts them away into the wall. Pause, then a contentedly muffled, 'Hey, this is nice!' TM

Greatness of the Small Man, The

(1999, Swe, 56 min)
d Kjell Andersson, Bo Harringer. *p* Kjell Andersson. *ph* Bo Harringer. *ed* Rasmus Ohlander. *m* Benny Andersson, Hans Ek.
●Not a standard 'making of' doc, this unassuming featurette on *Songs from the Second Floor*, co-directed by Roy Andersson's brother Kjell, spends time hanging out in a couple of Roy's inimitable sets – the disused hangar turned sweeping grey train station, and the gravel pit where a crowd of locals were assembled to witness the sacrifice of a nine-year-old – and observing the film's formation. Roy vouches a disdain for modern politics' illiberal technocratic bent, laughing gaily at anything that passes – and leaving his cameraman to knot his brow with artistic doubt. What registers is the human scale of the huge enterprise. NB

Great Northfield Minnesota Raid, The

(1971, US, 90 min)
d Philip Kaufman. *p* Jennings Lang. *sc* Philip Kaufman. *ph* Bruce Surtees. *ed* Douglas Stewart. *ad* Alexander Golitzen, George Webb. *m* David Grusin. *cast* Cliff Robertson, Robert Duvall, Luke Askew, RG Armstrong, Dana Elcar, Donald Moffa t, John Pearce, Matt Clark.
●This Western concerning the Younger and James brothers' gang covers familiar ground, borrowing freely from *Bonnie and Clyde*, *McCabe and Mrs Miller*, etc. Interesting for its demonstration of how exploitative capitalism leads simple-minded farmers' boys into outlawry, though somewhat marred by Duvall's manic interpretation of the role of Jesse James.

Great Rock'n'Roll Swindle, The

(1979, GB, 104 min)
d/sc Julien Temple. *ph* Adam Barker-Mill, Bill Patterson, Nic Knowland, John Metcalfe. *ed* Richard Bedford, Gordon Swire, Bernie Pokrzywa, Mike Maslin, Crispin Green, David Rea. *m* The Sex Pistols. *cast* Malcolm McLaren, Sid Vicious, Johnny Rotten, Steve Jones, Paul Cook, Ronnie Biggs, Irene Handl.
●A brilliant, infuriating final chapter in the Sex Pistols saga, exposing the corruption of a lethargic roll generation and the morbid tastes of the English. Smartly mixing early Pistols fragments with virtuoso set pieces (including Sid in 'My Way'), it adds up to the most innovative comic strip fantasy since Tashlin. DMacp

Great Santini, The

(1979, US, 115 min)
d Lewis John Carlino. *p* Charles A Pratt. *sc* Lewis John Carlino. *ph* Ralph Woolsey. *ed* Houseley Stevenson. *pd* Jack Poplin. *m* Elmer Bernstein. *cast* Robert Duvall, Blythe Danner, Michael O'Keefe, Stan Shaw, Lisa Jane Persky, Julie Anne Haddock.
●Duvall is Colonel 'Bull' Meechum – ace Marine fighter pilot, obsessive disciplinarian and family man who drives his wife and kids perilously close to the edge. His performance, and that of O'Keefe as his confused, loyal elder son, hold together the shoddy script by force of Method acting alone. But Carlino's direction doesn't help: he was responsible for the atrocious *Sailor Who Fell from Grace with the Sea*, and *The Great Santini* suffers from the same triteness, with its Deep South setting and a 'progressive' racial subplot that plunges deep into tear-jerk territory. See it for the acting; wallow in the sentiment. CA

Great Scout & Cathouse Thursday, The

(1976, US, 102 min)
d Don Taylor. *p* Jules Buck, David Korda. *sc* Richard Shapiro. *ph* Alex Phillips. *ed* Sheldon Kahn. *pd* Jack Martin Smith. *m* John Cameron. *cast* Lee Marvin, Oliver Reed, Robert Culp, Elizabeth Ashley, Strother Martin, Sylvia Miles, Kay Lenz.
●Marvin revives an old feud with a politically ambitious railroad man and teams up with Reed, who plays an improbable half-breed fired with an ambition to give all white women the clap. This dreary and eminently forgettable Western has Marvin's increasingly tedious hamming matched, and even topped, by Reed's hapless mugging; not a pretty sight. CPe

Great Sinner, The

(1949, US, 110 min, b/w)
d Robert Siodmak. *p* Gottfried Reinhardt. *sc* Ladislas Fodor, Christopher Isherwood. *ph* George Folsey. *ed* Harold F Kress. *ad* Cedric Gibbons, Hans Peters. *m* Bronislau Kaper. *cast* Gregory Peck, Ava Gardner, Melvyn Douglas, Walter Huston, Agnes Moorehead, Ethel Barrymore, Frank Morgan.
●The year is 1860, the great sin is gambling, and the sinner (Peck) is a young novelist, 'Fyodor', if you will. Isherwood had a hand in the script, which unceremoniously culls episodes and

characters from Dostoevsky's youth, *Crime and Punishment*, and *The Gambler*. Unfortunately, this prestigious MGM production is heavy-going and overdone. Moorehead plays a bleary pawnbroker; Barrymore, Morgan and Huston are roulette fiends; Gardner is the love interest. They're all out of luck. TCh

Great Smokey Roadblock, The

see Last of the Cowboys, The

Great Texas Dynamite Chase, The (aka Dynamite Women)

(1976, US, 90 min)
d Michael Pressman. *p* David Irving. *sc* David Kirkpatrick. *ph* Jamie Anderson. *ed* Millie Moore. *pd* Russell Smith. *m* Craig Safan. *cast* Claudia Jennings, Jocelyn Jones, Johnny Crawford, Chris Pennock, Tara Strohmeier, Miles Watkins.

●Traditionally raunchy New World fare, a gimmicky outlaw yarn that stands genre roles on their heads, with Jennings and Jones as dynamite-totin' best-buddy bankrobbers. It gleefully exhibits all the essential radicalism of the exploitation format, and brims with anarchic energy. PT

Great Train Robbery, The

see First Great Train Robbery, The

Great Waldo Pepper, The

(1975, US, 108 min)
d/p George Roy Hill. *sc* William Goldman. *ph* Robert Surtees. *ed* William H Reynolds. *ad* Henry Bumstead. *m* Henry Mancini. *cast* Robert Redford, Bo Svenson, Bo Brundin, Susan Sarandon, Geoffrey Lewis, Edward Herrmann, Margot Kidder.

●A surprising box-office flop next to its precursors, *Butch Cassidy and the Sundance Kid* and *The Sting*, this by and large refuses cute nostalgic manipulation (an easy option for a vivid yarn on the declining days and shrinking frontiers of aerial barnstorming) to place some coherent emphasis on a critique of the unquestioned 'heroic' hooks of the earlier films: adventurism, conmanship and male bonding. Redford's World War I flier has by 1926 tailored his sustaining lies about his daredevil rivalry with former German opponent Brundin (now extended into stuntsmanship) to the point where he almost believes them himself, and is certainly convincing enough to employ them with a dangerous seductiveness. His deeds and his deceptions (and his irresponsibility) are, however, rhymed with those of cinema itself, presented as the only scheme within which they really make any sense. An underrated attempt to scrutinise the immature American screen hero, which simultaneously works as a fine belated addition to Hollywood's recurrent romantic fascination with flying. PT

Great Wall, A

see Great Wall Is a Great Wall, The

Great Wall Is a Great Wall, The (aka A Great Wall)

(1985, US/China, 102 min)
d Peter Wang. *p* Shirley Sun. *sc* Peter Wang, Shirley Sun. *ph* Peter Stein, Robert Primes. *ed* Grahame Weinbren. *pd* Wing Lee, Feng Yuan, Ming Ming Cheung. *m* David Liang, Ge Ganru. *cast* Wang Xiao, Li Qinqin, Xiu Jian, Sharon Iwai, Shen Guanglan, Kelvin Han Yee, Peter Wang.

●The first American feature film shot in China amounts to rather more than an album of holiday snaps, thanks to the unfamiliarity of the resort and the universality of the situation. A Chinese-American computer executive (Peter Wang) takes his family to visit relatives in Peking. Both branches of the family are enormously curious about each other, so there is plenty of experimenting with language, lipstick, electric blankets, music and squat toilets. Ideological differences are kept at arm's length, and the concept of privacy which is debated would have been as incomprehensible in Imperial China as it is to the Red Chinese. There's no Chinese word for it. Comparative economics don't get much of a look in either, beyond the statistic that a bottle of Coke costs half a day's wages. West confronts East only at the ping-pong table, and the star of the film is Peking itself, still an elegant city of shady courtyards, tree-lined avenues and ancient pagodas, despite *Godzilla*-type redevelopers. BC

Great Waltz, The

(1938, US, 102 min, b/w)
d Julien Duvivier. *p* Bernard H Hyman. *sc* Samuel Hoffenstein, Walter Reisch. *ph* Joseph Ruttenberg. *ed* Tom Held. *ad* Cedric Gibbons. *m* Johann Strauss Jr, Dimitri Tiomkin. *cast* Luise Rainer, Fernand Gravey, Miliza Korjus, Hugh Herbert, Lionel Atwill, Minna Gombell, Sig Ruman.

●Sumptuous MGM kitsch, shot with great panache by Joseph Ruttenberg but treating Johann Strauss and his music to most of the clichés known to the biopic book (the snivelling romantic complications are very hard to take). Victor Fleming took over direction latterly from Duvivier, but the final sequence (Strauss' instant composition of 'The Blue Danube' and tearful farewell to his illicit love) was conceived and directed by Josef von Sternberg. TM

Great Waltz, The

(1972, US, 134 min)
d/p/sc Andrew L Stone. *ph* Davis Boulton. *ed* Ernest Walter. *ad* William Albert Havenmeyer. *m* Johann Strauss Sr, Johann Strauss Jr, Josef Strauss, Jacques Offenbach. *cast* Horst Buchholz, Mary Costa, Rossano Brazzi, Nigel Patrick, Yvonne Mitchell, James Faulkner.

●For perhaps half-an-hour, with every door opening to reveal couples whirling gaily in the Viennese waltz and Nigel Patrick cheerfully sending up the character of Johann Senior, this Strauss biopic is lively if exhausting. Then Senior dies, Junior gets amorous, and love's platitudes are given the freedom of the screen. There is even a moment when Strauss, struck by instant inspiration while dallying in the Vienna Woods, scribbles an immortal melody on his cuff. It makes the Duvivier film look like a masterpiece by comparison. TM

Great White Hype, The

(1996, US, 91 min)
d Reginald Hudlin. *p* Fred Berner, Joshua Donen. *sc* Ron Shelton, Tony Hendra. *ph* Ron Garcia. *ed* Earl Watson. *pd* Charles Rosen. *m* Marcus Miller. *cast* Samuel L Jackson, Peter Berg, Jeff Goldblum, Jon Lovitz, Damon Wayans, Corbin Bernsen, Cheech Marin, Salli Richardson.

●When it comes to heavyweight boxing: never bet on the white guy. But what if America got bored with blacks beating each other up? A flamboyant promoter, the Reverend Fred Sultan (Jackson), decides the sport needs a Great White Hope to bring back the big bucks. In the absence of any qualified contenders, he settles on retired amateur pugilist Terry Conklin (Berg), the peace-loving lead singer of Massive Head Wound, and the only man ever to floor the champ. Despite some promising credentials – notably a script by Ron Shelton (*Bull Durham*) and Tony Hendra (*Spinal Tap*) – this lackadaisical comedy stings like a butterfly and floats like a bee. Still, Jackson supplies an engaging gloss on Don King, and the script takes a refreshingly irreverent approach to media pieties ('Do you covet racism?' demands the politically correct Conklin of his bemused new manager). Indeed, the film's clued-in on most fronts. It doesn't insult the intelligence, lands a sucker punch or two, but fails to deliver a knock-out combination. A contender, then, but only a flyweight. TCh

Greed 100

(1923, US, 7,900 ft, b/w)
d Erich von Stroheim. *p* Louis Mayer. *sc* Erich von Stroheim. *ph* William Daniels, Ben Reynolds. *ed* Erich von Stroheim, Rex Ingram, June Mathis, Joseph W Farnham. *ad* Richard Day, Cedric Gibbons, Erich von Stroheim. *cast* Gibson Gowland, ZaSu Pitts, Jean Hersholt, Tempe Pigott, Frank Hayes, Dale Fuller.

●Originally planned to run around ten hours but hacked to just over two by Thalberg's MGM, von Stroheim's greatest film still survives as a true masterpiece of cinema. Even now its relentlessly cynical portrait of physical and moral squalor retains the ability to shock, while the Von's obsessive attention to realist detail – both in terms of the San Francisco and Death Valley locations, and the minutely observed characters – is never prosaic: as the two men and a woman fall out over filthy lucre (a surprise lottery win), their motivations are explored with a remarkably powerful visual poetry, and Frank Norris' novel is translated into the cinematic equivalent of, say, Zola at the peak of his powers. Never has a wedding been so bitterly depicted, never a moral denouement been delivered with such vicious irony. GA

Greek Tycoon, The

(1978, US, 106 min)
d J Lee Thompson. *p* Allen Klein, Ely Landau. *sc* Morton Fine. *ph* Anthony B Richmond. *ed* Alan Strachan, Derek Trigg. *pd* Michael Stringer. *m* Stanley Myers. *cast* Anthony Quinn, Jacqueline Bisset, Raf Vallone, Edward Albert, James Franciscus, Camilla Sparv, Charles Durning, Roland Culver.

●Set somewhere in a timeless Martini-land, *The Greek Tycoon* is an everyday love story of a shipping magnate and an assassinated president's widow – a sort of Harold Robbins out of *TitBits* tabloid biopic. Quinn's ageing Zorba is certainly no Citizen Kane, and Bisset's contribution rarely veers beyond the soulful pose, but it matters hardly a jot to a publicly rehearsed, pre-sold jet-set jamboree. Upmarket exploitation pics tend to make it (ie. profit) on the merest smell of money, sex and scandal, and this effort just reeks. Trashy it may be (though classily trashy, on a $6 million budget); vulgar it ain't – the Tomasis and the Cassidys are at bottom really ordinary, unhappy folks who just happen to have untold wealth and power. Your sympathy is earnestly solicited; it would be better spent on anyone tempted to sit through this glossy travesty. PT

Green Berets, The

(1968, US, 141 min)
d John Wayne, Ray Kellogg. *p* Michael Wayne. *sc* James Lee Barrett. *ph* Winton C Hoch. *ed* Otho Lovering. *pd* Walter M Simonds. *m* Miklós Rózsa. *cast* John Wayne, David Janssen, Jim Hutton, Aldo Ray, Raymond St Jacques, Jack Soo, Bruce Cabot, Patrick Wayne, Luke Askew.

●The Duke tells it like it was in Vietnam from a hawk's eye view, with the Vietcong spending their time setting fiendish booby-traps, while he and his gallant men defend the peace-loving, victimised peasantry. A war correspondent (Janssen) starts by expressing mild doubts about the situation, but grabs a rifle when he sees how it is. What offends about the film, even more than its flag-waving one-sidedness, is that it is such a ponderously silly, tear-jerking melodrama. Every cliché is given a whirl, even the Vietnamese orphan lurking about the camp as a cute mascot. At the end, when his favourite Yank is killed in action, Wayne leads the kid comfortingly off into the sunset (honest he does) saying 'You're what this is all about'. TM

Green Card

(1990, US, 107 min)
d/p/sc Peter Weir. *ph* Geoffrey Simpson. *ed* William Anderson. *ad* Wendy Stites *m* Hans Zimmer. *cast* Gérard Depardieu, Andie MacDowell, Bebe Neuwirth, Gregg Edelman, Robert Prosky, Jessie Keosian, Ethan Phillips, Mary Louise Wilson.

●French musician George Faure (Depardieu) needs a green card to work in America; New York horticulturist Brontë Parrish (MacDowell) is after an apartment with greenhouse available only to a married couple. So they undergo a marriage of convenience, which turns out to be anything but when the authorities decide to investigate. After months apart, flamboyant George and uptight Brontë must reunite in order to memorise a fictionalised life together… Rarely did New York look so exotic and entrancing; Weir's signature is evident in the driving beat of the opening musical sequence and in the lush splendours of Brontë's greenhouse. Weir's first romantic comedy boasts a central relationship which is tentative and hopeful, a mood beautifully realised by Depardieu (venturing into new territory with a major English-speaking role). Complemented by the refined MacDowell, his gracious, generous performance is never dominating, and their exchanges offer unexpected pleasures. In terms of the genre's conventions, Weir likens this film to 'a light meal'. It's one to savour. CM

Greenfingers

(2000, US/GB, 90 min)
d Joel Hershman. *p* Travis Swords, Daniel J Victor. *sc* Joel Hershman. *ph* John Daly. *ed* Justin Krish. *pd* Tim Hutchinson. *m* Guy Dagul. *cast* Clive Owen, Helen Mirren, David Kelly, Warren Clarke, Danny Dyer, Adam Fogerty, Paterson Joseph, Natasha Little, Peter Guinness.
● Based on the true story of a group of prisoners which won several prizes at the Hampton Court Palace Flower Show, this comedy is populated with English eccentrics and steeped in whimsy. Its theme – ordinary people achieving the extraordinary – is standard Ealing, and the gardening is treated with suitably affectionate reverence. This, unsurprisingly, is a fabricated vision of rural Britain rather than anything recognisably real: country folk drive vintage cars and live in crumbling mansions crammed with liftable heirlooms (spot the plot point?). Mirren's aristo celebrity gardener is from another age. Unfortunately, there's also a didactic tone, with the theme of redemption being hammered home at every opportunity, while the metaphor of convicted murderers finding peace in the act of creating new life (albeit in lupins rather than humans) is clumsy and self-satisfied. More positively, its sentimental tendencies are tempered by Owen, impressive in the central role of a prisoner institutionalised since the age of seventeen. WI

Green Fire

(1954, US, 100 min)
d Andrew Marton. *p* Armand Deutsch. *sc* Ivan Goff, Ben Roberts. *ph* Paul C Vogel. *ed* Harold F Kress. *ad* Cedric Gibbons, Malcolm Brown. *m* Miklós Rózsa. *cast* Grace Kelly, Stewart Granger, Paul Douglas, John Ericson, Murvyn Vye, José Torvay.
● Expansive but routine romantic adventure, with Kelly coming between expat emerald miners amid the local (Eastman) colour of South America. A profusion of natural disasters give Marton the chance to show his paces, usually better appreciated when confined to action sequences and second unit inserts on the films of others (as in the chariot races of *Ben Hur*). An early script from the writing team of Ivan Goff and Ben Roberts who, despite signing proficient stuff for directors like Walsh and Mann, will probably be best remembered for creating *Charley's Angels* over 20 years later. PT

Green Fish (Chorok Mulgoki)

(1997, SKor, 111 min)
d Lee Chang-Dong. *p* Yeo Kyun-Dong, Myung Kye-Nam. *sc* Lee Chang-Dong. *ph* Yoo Young-Kil. *ed* Kim Hyun. *pd* Joo Byung-Do. *m* Lee Dong-Jun. *cast* Han Suk-Kyu, Shim Hye-Jin, Moon Sung-Keun, Myung Kye-Nam, Song Kang-Ho.
● Screenwriter Lee's debut feature offers a wry, regretful chunk of recent social history in the guise of a gangster drama. Makdong (Han) comes home from military service to find his family fragmented and their village razed to make way for a vast new housing development. He drifts back to the outer suburbs of Seoul and into the employ of a seemingly sympathetic gang boss (Moon), whose much-put-upon mistress (Shim) seems in need of a friend. But Makdong is hopelessly out of his depth, not realising that he's barging into a sado-masochistic relationship and misunderstanding the politics of inter-gang rivalry. Lee's sense of his characters as unwitting victims of the moral/economic/architectural climate they live in is anchored in brilliantly judged imagery and in an acute sensitivity to ambiguities of mood and feeling. TR

Green for Danger

(1946, GB, 91 min, b/w)
d Sidney Gilliat. *p* Frank Launder, Sidney Gilliat. *sc* Sidney Gilliat, Claud Gurney. *ph* Wilkie Cooper. *ed* Thelma Myers. *pd* Peter Proud. *m* William Alwyn. *cast* Alastair Sim, Sally Gray, Rosamund John, Trevor Howard, Leo Genn, Megs Jenkins, Judy Campbell, Moore Marriott.
● Two murders in a cottage hospital leave the surgeon, the anaesthetist and three attendant nurses as major suspects. But this is no ordinary country house whodunit; Launder and Gilliat's long experience as scriptwriters enables them to undermine the conventions to macabrely humorous effect. Amid the unpredictable explosions of World War II 'doodlebugs', Sim's eccentrically fallible detective rakes over the dirty secrets of his guilt-ridden suspects and leads us carefully up the garden path. 'Not one of my most successful cases', he is driven to confess; but one of Launder and Gilliat's most likeable films. RMy

Greengage Summer, The (aka Loss of Innocence)

(1961, GB, 99 min)
d Lewis Gilbert. *p* Victor Saville. *sc* Howard Koch. *ph* Freddie Young. *ed* Peter Hunt. *ad* John Stoll. *m* Richard Addinsell. *cast* Kenneth More, Danielle Darrieux, Susannah York, Jane Asher, Maurice Denham.
● Before Gilbert descended to mush like *Friends* and *Paul and Michelle*, he made a number of interesting failures, of which this is probably one of the best. Susannah York, in one of her best performances, plays a young schoolgirl holidaying in France, where she falls in love with an Englishman, a mysterious older man (More). The main problem is that the plot degenerates into silly dramatics at the expense of character development, with More turning out to be – of all things – a jewel thief. (From the novel by Rumer Godden.) DP

Green, Green Grass of Home, The (Zai na Hepan Qing Cao Qing)

(1982, Tai, 89 min)
d Hou Xiaoxian. *p* Zhang Huakun. *sc* Hou Xiaoxian. *ph* Chen Kunhou. *ed* Liao Qingsong. *ad* Ji Kaiqin. *m* Zuo Hongyuan. *cast* Kenny Bee, Jiang Ling, Chen Meifeng, Gu Jun, Li Po, Mei Fang.
● Hou's third feature is as 'cute' and 'wholesome' as the worst government-sanctioned Taiwan movies of the 1970s, but it contains clear signs of the Hou to come in its long-take mise-en-scène and in its handling of child actors. Pop star Kenny Bee (allowed only one song) plays a temp teacher in a small town primary school in southern Taiwan. During his brief tenure he dumps a bossy, egocentric girlfriend from Taipei, falls in love with a sweet local girl, sorts out a delinquent in the making and launches an environmental movement to clean up the river and restock it with fish. Sitting through some of it takes nerves of steel, but there are shots and even some sequences capable of raising cinephile goosebumps. TR

Green Grow the Rushes (aka Brandy Ashore)

(1951, GB, 79 min, b/w)
d Derek Twist. *p* John Gossage. *sc* Howard Clewes, Derek Twist. *ph* Harry Waxman. *ed* Hazel Wilkinson. *ad* Fred Pusey. *m* Lambert Williamson. *cast* Richard Burton, Honor Blackman, Roger Livesey, Frederick Leister, Geoffrey Keen, Bryan Forbes.
● The film technicians' union ACTT (as it then was) set up its own production company to break the grip which the British majors then had on the industry and thus provide extra work for its members. Their first offering, from the novel by Howard Clewes, was this diluted combination of *Whisky Galore!* and *Passport to Pimlico* in which a bunch of Kent brandy smugglers call on ancient rights to prevent the men from the ministry shutting down their operations. The film had distribution problems at the time, and these days is chiefly of archival interest. TJ

Green Ice

(1981, GB, 116 min)
d Ernest Day. *p* Jack Wiener. *sc* Edward Anhalt, Ray Hassett, Anthony Simmons, Robert DeLaurentis. *ph* Gilbert Taylor. *ed* John Jympson. *pd* Roy Walker. *m* Bill Wyman. *cast* Ryan O'Neal, Anne Archer, Omar Sharif, Domingo Ambriz, John Larroquette, Philip Stone.
● Clodhopping attempt to make a jolly romantic comedy set against a background of torture, murder and rebel guerillas being fed to the hogs in the prisons of Colombia. O'Neal and Archer play a couple of Americans meeting cute in Mexico, then heading for Colombia, where she takes over from a sister shot while working for the rebel cause, and he (at first with itchy fingers for the loot) helps her replenish the rebel coffers through a daring heist of emeralds from a government stronghold right out of a James Bond movie (with Sharif a villain to match). Painfully miscalculated from the word go, it's a load of offensive old cobblers coated in picture postcard scenery. TM

Greenkeeping

(1992, Aust, 86 min)
d David Caesar. *p* Glenys Rowe. *sc* David Caesar. *ph* Simon Smith. *ed* Mark Perry. *pd* Kerith Homes. *m* David Bridie, John Phillips. *cast* Mark Little, Lisa Hensley, Max Cullen, Gia Carides, Syd Conabere, Rob Steele.
● A meandering, *very* low-key comedy in which Little, greenkeeper at the local bowls club, finds it hard to cope with a dope-dependent wife and her unpaid dealers, with a born-again moneylender brother, with racists and temptresses in the club, and with his own complete ignorance on matters horticultural. The script is often droll in its observation of the mind-numbing banalities of mate-culture, though there are times when it seems unfocused and all too ready to rest on sub-Jane Campion eccentricity. Slim, then, but finally rather likeable. GA

Green Light

(1936, US, 85 min, b/w)
d Frank Borzage. *p* Henry Blanke. *sc* Milton Krims. *ph* Byron Haskin. *ed* James Gibbons. *ad* Max Parker. *m* Max Steiner. *cast* Errol Flynn, Anita Louise, Margaret Lindsay, Cedric Hardwicke, Walter Abel, Henry O'Neill, Spring Byington.
● Adapted from a novel by Lloyd C Douglas, this is a typically heady brew of medico-religious claptrap. Flynn is a young surgeon, left to take the blame when a patient dies during an operation, who refuses to exculpate himself on realising that the senior colleague responsible (O'Neill) is an old man terrified of total ruin. It's love at first sight when Flynn meets the dead woman's daughter (Louise); but she blames him for her mother's death; so he departs for the wilds of Montana, places his life on the line as a human guinea pig, and comes up with a vaccine against the deadly spotted fever. The jello binding the characters together in a welter of forgiveness and redemption is a wise old crippled cleric (Hardwicke), who assures them that God's red light means man must pause to learn through suffering before getting the green light to go on into eternity. Given that the script comes on like a volubly po-faced sermon, Borzage directs with admirable cool, and gets excellent performances from the entire cast. TM

Green Man, The

(1956, GB, 80 min, b/w)
d Robert Day, [Basil Dearden]. *p/sc* Frank Launder, Sidney Gilliat. *ph* Gerald Gibbs. *ed* Bernard Gribble. *ad* Wilfrid Shingleton. *m* Cedric Thorpe Davie. *cast* Alastair Sim, George Cole, Terry-Thomas, Jill Adams, Raymond Huntley, Eileen Moore, Avril Angers, Dora Bryan, John Chandos, Colin Gordon, Peter Bull, Arthur Lowe.
● A splendid black comedy, adapted by Frank Launder and Sidney Gilliat from their own play *Meet a Body*. Sim is up to his old tricks as a timid watchmaker who is a professional assassin in his spare time. All the right people get bumped off (headmasters, businessmen, and other assorted dictators), and the movie is quite vulgar enough to be funny. It is fascinating to compare Sim's hilarious schizophrenia with Alec Guinness in *The Ladykillers*. Inside every Englishman there lurks a ruthless criminal, impatient to steal scenes. TCh

Green Mile, The

(1999, US, 189 min)
d Frank Darabont. *p* David Valdes, Frank Darabont. *sc* Frank Darabont. *ph* David Tattersall. *ed* Richard Francis-Bruce. *pd* Terence Marsh. *m* Thomas Newman. *cast* Tom Hanks, David Morse, Bonnie Hunt, James Cromwell, Michael Clarke Duncan, Michael Jeter, Graham Greene, Sam Rockwell, Gary Sinise.
● Now an inmate of an old folks' home, sometime Death Row guard Paul Edgecomb (Hanks) relates his Depression Era experiences on 'The Green Mile', the strip of lime linoleum that leads to the execution chamber. His memories centre on black inmate John Coffey (Duncan), a gentle giant convicted of murdering two white girls. Yet Coffey seems anything but violent: he's afraid of the dark

and later reveals a gift for spiritual healing. Where Darabont's earlier period prison drama *The Shawshank Redemption* (also based on a Stephen King original) was very much of a piece, this suffers from a surfeit of plot threads and characters, some more compelling than others: for example, the volatile relationship between Edgecomb and a fellow guard, whose sadistic behaviour must be tolerated because he's the state governor's nephew. By contrast, the sentimental scenes featuring a Cajun inmate and his pet mouse soon become tiresome. The supernatural elements carry an undeniable emotional charge, but the solution to the underlying murder mystery is disappointingly tidy and trite. The flawless production design ensures one can almost smell the burning flesh, but Thomas Newman's score turns up the 'triumph of the human spirit' meter to 11. NF

Green Pastures, The

(1936, US, 93 min, b/w)
d William Keighley, Marc Connelly. *p* Henry Blanke. *sc* Marc Connelly. *ph* Hal Mohr. *ed* George Amy. *ad* Allen Saalburg, Stanley Fleischer. *cast* Rex Ingram, Oscar Polk, Eddie Anderson, Frank Wilson, George Reed, Myrtle Anderson.

●There is nothing intrinsically offensive about this all-white use of all-black stereotypes to illustrate the artless simplicities of the gospel religion of Deep South slavery. Constructed as a series of Sunday School Bible stories linked by spirituals, it has enormous charm in its folklorish fancies (Heaven as a cushy cotton plantation, Babylon as a dingy backstreet dive), and a performance of great gentleness and good humour from Ingram ('Ain't no bed of roses bein' De Lawd') which is never tainted by the mawkish religiosity that creeps in towards the end. What is offensive is the way in which the depths of plangent suffering that inspired the spirituals are totally ignored. Instead we get white society's wish-fulfilment image of happy Uncle Toms who will be content with their due reward of a ten-cent cigar and a fish-fry in heaven. TM

Green Ray, The (Le Rayon Vert)

(1986, Fr, 99 min)
d Eric Rohmer. *p* Margaret Ménégoz. *sc* Eric Rohmer. *ph* Sophie Maintigneux. *ed* Maria-Luisa Garcia. *m* Jean-Louis Valero. *cast* Marie Rivière, Vincent Gauthier, Carita, Basile Gervaise, Béatrice Romand, Lisa Hérédia.

●It's July, and Delphine (Rivière), a young Parisian secretary, is suddenly at a loss regarding her holiday; a friend has just backed out of a trip to Greece, her other companions have boyfriends, and Delphine can't bear spending August in Paris. She also hopes to find a dream lover, but receives only the unwelcome attentions of pushy predators, until... There's a whiff of fairytale to this particular slice of realism à la Rohmer, but what's perhaps most remarkable is that the film was almost completely improvised; though not so as you'd know it. It's as flawlessly constructed, shot and performed as ever, with France's greatest living director effortlessly evoking the morose moods of holidaying alone among crowds, and revelling in the particulars of place, weather and time of day. Deceptively simple, the film oozes honesty and spontaneity; the word, quite bluntly, is masterpiece. GA

Green Room, The

see Chambre Verte, La

Greenwich Mean Time

see G:MT Greenwich Mean Time

Greenwich Village

(1944, US, 82 min)
d Walter Lang. *p* William Le Baron. *sc* Earl Baldwin, Walter Bullock. *ph* Leon Shamroy, Harry Jackson. *ed* Robert Simpson. *ad* James Basevi, Joseph C Wright. *songs* Leo Robin, Nacio Herb Brown. *cast* Carmen Miranda, Don Ameche, William Bendix, Vivian Blaine, Felix Bressart, Tony and Sally DeMarco, Adolph Green, Betty Comden, Judy Holliday, Alvin Hammer.

●The Village in the Roaring '20s and the new boy in town is dapper Don Ameche, a talented composer hoping to get his latest concerto performed at Carnegie Hall. What happens, though, is that he falls in with Carmen Miranda, exotic hostess at William Bendix's swingin' speakeasy, who persuades him to let her boss turn it into a Broadway revue – and just the vehicle for singing sensation Vivian Blaine, with whom young Ameche is already besotted. The fluff factor is high in this easygoing Fox frolic, but trainspotters will note the fleeting presence of cabaret artistes The Revuers, who included future star Billy Holliday and *Singin' in the Rain* writers Betty Comden and Adolph Green. TJ

Greetings

(1968, US, 88 min)
d Brian De Palma. *p* Charles Hirsch. *sc* Charles Hirsch, Brian De Palma. *ph* Robert Fiore. *ed* Brian De Palma. *songs* Children of Paradise. *cast* Jonathan Warden, Robert De Niro, Gerritt Graham, Megan McCormick, Ashley Oliver, Allen Garfield.

●De Palma's third feature freewheels and jump-cuts its three weirdo leads through a late '60s obstacle course of draft-dodging, sex and assassination politics, picking up more than its share of unforced laughs on the way. A quintessential Movie Brat apprentice piece. Godardian disruptions, documentary coups, peeping-tom Hitchcock incisions: the film school textbooks and movie house memories assimilated, evaluated, turned inside-out and spring-cleaned, with only the budget to keep it all streetbound. Silly *and* substantial.

Gregorio Cortez

see Ballad of Gregorio Cortez, The

Gregory's Girl

(1980, GB, 91 min)
d Bill Forsyth. *p* Davina Belling, Clive Parsons. *sc* Bill Forsyth. *ph* Michael Coulter. *ed* John Gow. *ad* Adrienne Atkinson. *m* Colin Tully. *cast* John Gordon Sinclair, Dee Hepburn, Jake D'Arcy, Claire Grogan, Robert Buchanan, William Greenlees, Allison Forster.

●Slight but highly entertaining comedy about a Scottish schoolgirl who becomes a wizard on the football team (arousing male resentment, naturally), and the lanky Gregory who fancies her from afar. Strong performances and a naturalistic script, which zooms in on adolescent delusions and embarrassments, keep things going at a leisurely pace. Quirky and utterly endearing, it nevertheless reveals the director's definite lack of interest in the visual textures of his films. GA

Gregory's Two Girls

(1999, GB/Ger, 116 min)
d Bill Forsyth. *p* Christopher Young. *sc* Bill Forsyth. *ph* John de Borman. *ed* John Gow. *pd* Andy Harris. *m* Michael Gibbs. *cast* John Gordon-Sinclair, Dougray Scott, Maria Doyle Kennedy, Kevin Anderson, Martin Schwab, Fiona Bell, Carly McKinnon, Hugh McCue.

●While this may be a belated sequel to *Gregory's Girl*, it's most certainly not a reprise. Gregory (Gordon Sinclair) is now a teacher at his old Cumbernauld comprehensive, unable to commit to the romantic demands of fellow teacher Bel (Doyle Kennedy) because he can't get guilty thoughts about Frances (McKinnon), one of his brightest students, out of his head. When the latter arranges an illicit rendezvous, his pulses are racing, but her boyfriend comes along and together they have secrets to reveal: in the nearby electronics factory they've discovered evidence of an export trade in torture technology to the Third World. There's still comic mileage in Gordon Sinclair's amiable fumbling Gregory: e.g. his hilarious confrontation with police and headmaster after his contact with McKinnon becomes known. She's another in the distinguished line of self-confident Forsythian young women, and so never allows the teacher/student subplot to become uncomfortable. Fascinatingly, attention is directed towards wider, broadly political issues, but Forsyth's assured craftsmanship ensures that they are deftly woven into the storytelling. Gordon Sinclair is a revelation, and although the film suffers from a lack of pace, its wealth of human insight and the premium it places on subtlety of expression make it a rare pleasure. TJ

Gremlins

(1984, US, 111 min)
d Joe Dante. *p* Michael Finnell. *sc* Chris Columbus. *ph* John Hora. *ed* Tina Hirsch. *pd* James H Spencer. *m* Jerry Goldsmith. *cast* Zach Galligan, Phoebe Cates, Hoyt Axton, Polly Holliday, Frances Lee McCain, Dick Miller, Keye Luke, Scott Brady.

●With a characteristic mix of narrative anarchy, cinephile allusion, cartoon-style slapstick and black-tinged comedy, Dante gleefully sinks his teeth into the kind of fluffy, sugary, sickly small town fantasy beloved of his pal and sometime producer Spielberg. It starts with a Christmas gift – a cute, cuddly little 'mogwai' – but the time of goodwill soon turns hellish when, splashed with water, the creature starts sprouting the titular monsters, whose sense of mischief extends to the murderous and beyond. As the all-American township falls prey to the little demons' destructive urges, Dante lets rip with fabulous special effects, hilariously sadistic set-pieces (most memorably the monsters wreaking havoc at a screening of Disney's *Snow White*) and in-jokes galore, all delivered at such a heady pace that the trashing of traditional American values and consumer goods even feels quite liberating. GA

Gremlins 2: The New Batch

(1990, US, 106 min)
d Joe Dante. *p* Michael Finnell. *sc* Charlie Haas. *ph* John Hora. *ed* Kent Beyda. *pd* James Spencer. *m* Jerry Goldsmith. *cast* Zach Galligan, Phoebe Cates, John Glover, Robert Prosky, Robert Picardo, Christopher Lee, Haviland Morris, Dick Miller, Jackie Joseph, Keye Luke, Kathleen Freeman, Paul Bartel, John Astin.

●A chaotic affair which eschews narrative coherence for rapid-fire sight gags and self-referential silliness. The risibly slender plot finds Billy (Galligan) and prissy girlfriend Kate (Cates) in the employ of the Clamp Organisation, into whose money-grubbing hands falls the newly-orphaned *mogwai* ('Gizmo' to his friends). Narrowly evading dissection by ever-so-slightly fiendish Dr Catheter (Lee), Gizmo is reunited with Billy, who hardly has time to say 'don't get them wet or feed them after midnight' before his moistened pet gives birth to a skyscraper full of late-night feasting beasties. Thereafter, film-inspired pandemonium reigns. Gizmo, his head full of Rambo, 'becomes war', gribblies wave dentists' drills about their ears and chatter 'Is it safe?', and the whole diminutive cast dons spangled dresses and top hats for a Busby Berkeley-style chorus of 'New York, New York'. There's almost enough in-joke ingenuity to justify the total absence of plot. MK

La Grenouille et la baleine

see Tadpole and the Whale

Grey Fox, The

(1982, Can, 91 min)
d Phillip Borsos. *p* Peter O'Brian. *sc* John Hunter. *ph* Frank Tidy. *ed* Ray Hall. *pd* Bill Brodie. *m* Michael Conway. *cast* Richard Farnsworth, Jackie Burroughs, Ken Pogue, Wayne Robson, Timothy Webber, Gary Reineke, David Petersen.

●Oldster stagecoach-robber Bill Miner (impeccably played by Farnsworth) emerges from the San Quentin rest home at the turn of the century, after a stay of some 30 years. Journeying through America into Canada, he discovers a country in transition: cars, cameras, rampaging Pinkerton men, etc. Still in love with the romance of the old West, Miner both disinters his career in crime and embarks on an oddball love affair, before committing himself to the inevitable one blag too many. The pacing is gentle, the style conditioned by documentary. Borsos infuses this story with wry observation, an appropriately elegiac feel, and a brooding sense of landscape. It's hard not to be charmed. RR

Grey Gardens

(1975, US, 95 min)
d David Maysles, Albert Maysles, Ellen Hovde, Muffie Meyer. *p/ph* David Maysles, Albert Maysles. *ed* Ellen Hovde, Muffie Meyer, Susan Froemke. *with* Edith Bouvier Beale, Edith B Beale Jr, Jerry Torre, Lois Wright.

●America's obsession with Jackie Kennedy-Onassis-who-next is overwhelming, and presumably the reason for the success there of this documentary about two of her family who live in isolated squalor on Long Island; a film that is voyeuristic in the extreme, extending no warmth to the bizarre mother and daughter as they battle out their lives together, but choosing instead to film them in the most offensive of ways. Like the shots of 'Little' Edith Bouvier Beale, a large 56-year-old, taken from below as she climbs upstairs in a miniskirt, rambling to herself; or 'Big' Edith, the demanding 79-year-old mother, with her towel falling off her withered, naked body. As Big Edie sings and Little Edie dances, both adoring the transient attentions of the film crew, you can only wonder what happened once the party was over. HM

Grey Owl

(1998, US/Can, 118 min)
d Richard Attenborough. *p* Jake Eberts, Richard Attenborough. *sc* William Nicholson. *ph* Roger Pratt. *ed* Lesley Walker. *pd* Anthony Pratt. *m* George Fenton. *cast* Pierce Brosnan, Annie Galipeau, Renée Asherson, Stephanie Cole, Nathaniel Arcand, Stewart Bick, Vlasta Vrana, Graham Greene.

●Grey Owl ('He Who Walks by Night' in Ojibwa, the tongue of the indigenous people of northern Canada) was an intrepid keeper of the native faith who spoke up for ecological providence and sustainability in the early '30s, simultaneously defending one tradition while establishing another, that of celebrity environmentalism. A trapper turned gamekeeper, he ploughed a lone furrow in the wilderness. Light came late to his life in the form of a part-Mohawk girl 20 years his junior, Anahareo, or Pony. Much of the film is about beavers. Pony rescues and nurtures an orphaned brood, and persuades her lover he has no business hunting them; instead he decides to describe to the world their charms. It's all perfectly literal: the furry critters are presented as self-evidently cute, the love story is entirely wholesome, and the moral all about clean living, in the broadest sense. Archie Grey Owl is played with quiet if unremarkable assurance by Brosnan, while Galipeau – who is part Algonquin – grows into the role of Pony after the rather irritating early stages of their courtship. Sedately middlebrow, sincere and minimally sanctimonious, it's one of the more likeable of Attenborough's 20th century biopics, and it staves off sentimentality at least until the conclusion. NB

Greystoke – The Legend of Tarzan Lord of the Apes

(1984, GB, 130 min)
d Hugh Hudson. *p* Hugh Hudson, Stanley S Canter. *sc* Robert Towne, Michael Austin. *ph* John Alcott. *ed* Anne V Coates. *pd* Stuart Craig. *m* John Scott. *cast* Christopher Lambert, Ralph Richardson, Ian Holm, James Fox, Andie MacDowell, Cheryl Campbell, John Wells, Nigel Davenport.

●What would it be like for a lost child of the British aristocracy to be reared by apes in the African jungle? Cue for some skilfully handled action and a vivid realisation of the ape community in which a man eventually becomes boss-cat. The film changes gear when our hero returns to Edwardian Britain and his ancestral home, Greystoke. Torn between two cultures, confused by his love for Jane, desolated by the loss of his grandfather (man) and his father (ape), he undergoes…culture schlock. It is here that *Greystoke* pops its valves, pushing a simple yarn to the point of philosophical overload. Rhetoric apart, the film offers some stirring entertainment, and a memorable ham sandwich from Richardson, allowed to steal the show as the grandfather in what proved to be his last film. RR

Gridlock'd

(1996, US/GB, 91 min)
d Vondie Curtis-Hall. *p* Damian Jones, Paul Webster, Eric Huggins. *sc* Vondi Curtis-Hall. *ph* Bill Pope. *ed* Chris Koefoed. *pd* Dan Bishop. *m* Stewart Copeland. *cast* Tim Roth, Tupac Shakur, Thandie Newton, Charles Fleischer, Howard Hessman, John Sayles, Vondie Curtis-Hall.

●When fellow musician Cookie (Newton) overdoses on New Year's Eve, Stretch and Spoon resolve to get into rehab asap. They reckon, however, without the federal welfare system, a bureaucratic spaghetti junction which isn't about to help anyone in a hurry, least of all a couple of itchy smack addicts with attitude. Trekking from office to office, queue to queue, the pair take another hit to help them through the day, only to get mixed up with a brutal gangster and a murder investigation. A hip take on heroin addicts kicking against the pricks (*Trainspotting in New York*, you might say), the film has a fairly uninteresting narrative motor in its thriller subplot, but hits on an edgy black comic tone for Stretch and Spoon's increasingly pained dealings with the unsympathetic representatives of authority. Roth (Stretch) and the late Tupac Shakur (Spoon) work up a delicious, deadpan rapport, in which Stretch is the wild card and Spoon the long-suffering straightman, and which climaxes with a hilariously sick scene in which the former repeatedly stabs his compliant pal in the chest, in a last desperate bid for medical attention. TCh

Grief

(1993, US, 87 min)
d Richard Glatzer. *p* Ruth Charny, Yoram Mandel. *sc* Richard Glatzer. *ph* David Dechant. *ed* Bill Williams, Robin Katz. *pd* Don Diers. *m* Tom Judson. *cast* Craig Chester, Jackie Beat, Illeana Douglas, Alexis Arquette, Carlton Wilborn, Lucy Gutteridge, Paul Bartel, Mary Woronov.

●'There are many ways to tell a story, realism is just the most dull.' That, at any rate, is the ethos of the writers of *The Love Judge*, a TV show set in a California divorce court. Here circus lesbians vie with schizophrenic opera divas and stripper nuns for truth, justice and alimony. The writers' lot seems mundane in comparison, though these maladjusted under-achievers are a colourful group: Mark (Chester) is still grieving for his lover who died a year ago of AIDS, but he's in with a chance for a production job and is besotted with Bill (Arquette). Jeremy (Wilborn) says Bill's a lost cause, and Leslie (Douglas) agrees with him; she prefers Ben, the photocopy repairman. Meanwhile, the boss, Jo (Beat), is incensed to find her new sofa despoiled with sperm stains every morning. While Glatzer's debut boasts a good number of campy, enjoyable scenes (notably 'extracts' from *The Love Judge* featuring the likes of Paul Bartel and Mary Woronov) and a standout performance from Jackie Beat, it's a surprisingly well structured, carefully nuanced affair (taking place over a working week, and, except in the extracts, never leaving the office). A genuinely moving comedy. TCh

Grieta, La

see Rift, The

Grievous Bodily Harm

(1988, Aust, 96 min)
d Mark Joffe. *p* Richard Brennan. *sc* Warwick Hind. *ph* Ellery Ryan. *ed* Marc Van Buren. *pd* Roger Ford. *m* Chris Neal. *cast* Colin Friels, John Waters, Bruno Lawrence, Shane Briant, Joy Bell, Chris Stalker.

●Flat Australian thriller which follows the uneasy partnership between crime journalist Friels and opportunistic cop Lawrence as they combine expertise to stop serial killer Waters from continuing a trail of mayhem. The film's habit of undercutting audience expectation is so over-used it becomes tiresome, so Joffe throws in the odd snippet of sexual perversity in a bid to restore interest. TJ

Grifters, The

(1990, US, 110 min)
d Stephen Frears. *p* Martin Scorsese, James Painten, Richard Harris. *sc* Donald E Westlake. *ph* Oliver Stapleton. *ed* Mick Audsley. *ad* Dennis Gassner. *m* Elmer Bernstein. *cast* Anjelica Huston, John Cusack, Annette Bening, Pat Hingle, Henry Jones, Michael Laskin, Eddie Jones, JT Walsh.

●The title refers to con artists like Roy Dillon (Cusack), who makes a living palming dollar bills in bars, or Myra (Bening), the feisty drifter who tries to steer him to the big time after a petty scam lands him in hospital. But the most ruthlessly survivalist is Roy's mother Lily (Huston), employed by the Mob to work a 'playback' scam at racetracks, and liable to be beaten up or have a cigar stubbed out on her hand just to teach her a lesson. Lily is perceived as a woman of great tragedy, still possessed of the maternal instincts she needs to try to save her long-neglected son, imbued with a toughness that helps her overcome constant terror and loneliness, and sufficiently tainted by life to both desire and finally destroy her offspring. Donald Westlake's excellent screenplay does some justice to the starkness of Jim Thompson's novel; and Frears' direction never fails to grab the attention, even given the weaknesses of Cusack and Bening as the existentialist young love interest. Anjelica Huston is quite astonishing; as Thompson is a kind of dime-store Dostoievsky, so Huston's Myra seems straight from the pages of Euripides and Sophocles. SGr

Grim Prairie Tales

(1990, US, 94 min)
d Wayne Coe. *p* Richard Hahn. *sc* Wayne Coe. *ph* Janusz Kaminski. *ed* Earl Ghaffari. *pd* Anthony Zierhut. *m* Steve Dancz. *cast* James Earl Jones, Brad Dourif, William Atherton, Lisa Eichhorn, Will Hare, Marc McClure, Michelle Joyner, Scott Paulin.

●This first feature by Coe (who designed the posters for *Back to the Future* and *Out of Africa*, among others) is a stand-out US independent. A prim New Englander (Dourif) finds his campsite invaded by a grizzled, smelly mountain man (Jones), who turns up with a fresh corpse slung over his saddle. Mutual mistrust spurs them to scare each other with horror stories through the night. The four tales are ingeniously varied (and intelligently keyed to the character of the teller and the situation around the camp-fire); but it's the writing of the framing story and the two lead performances that make the film so special. As the T-shirt has it, it sucks you in. TR

Grinch, The

see Dr Seuss' How the Grinch Stole Christmas

Grind

(1996, US, 96 min)
d Chris Kentis. *p* Laura Lau, Melissa Powell. *sc* Chris Kentis, Laura Lau. *ph* Stephen Kazmierski. *ed* Chris Kentis. *pd* Therese Deprez. *m* Brian Kelly. *cast* Adrienne Shelly, Billy Crudup, Paul Schulze, Frank Vincent, Saul Stein, Jenny Dundas.

●The filmic equivalent of a Springsteen song: Eddie (Crudup) returns to his industrial home town and moves in with his brother and his bored, brow-beaten wife, Janey. Eddie goes to work as a machinist, but switches to night shifts so he can work on his hotrod by day. It sounds grindingly predictable (and it doesn't disappoint), but this is a subtler, more emotionally honest film than most American indies are concerned to come up with. It doesn't look like much, but the cutting's sharp, and the three principals turn in carefully nuanced performances. It's easy to see why everyone's getting excited about Crudup – but don't write off Kentis either. In its own quiet, cumulative way this is an impressive, authoritative debut. TCh

Gringo in Mañanaland, A

(1995, US, 61 min, b/w & col)
d/p Dee Dee Halleck. *sc* Dee Dee Halleck, Nathalie Magnan, Che Che Martinez. *ed* Dee Dee Halleck, Nathalie Magnan, Che Che Martinez, Pennee Bender.

●This documentary constructs an argument about the representation of South America by its northern neighbours without recourse to commentary or interviews: the film is entirely made up of archive footage from Hollywood features, cartoons, ads and newsreels. At first it seems shapeless and neutral, but gradually the insidious political nature of the material becomes explicit, not least when the unmistakable Ronald Reagan turns up in a long-forgotton melodrama, *Tropic Zone*, and Charlton Heston takes to battling the armies of invading Red Ants in *The Naked Jungle*. TCh

Grip of Fear, The

see Experiment in Terror

Grip of the Strangler (aka The Haunted Strangler)

(1958, GB, 79 min, b/w)
d Robert Day. *p* John Croydon. *sc* Jan Read, John C Cooper. *ph* Lionel Banes. *ed* Peter Mayhew. *ad* John Elphick. *m* Buxton Orr. *cast* Boris Karloff, Elizabeth Allan, Jean Kent, Vera Day, Anthony Dawson, Tim Turner, Diane Aubrey.

●A Jekyll and Hyde tale set in London in the 1880s, with an immaculate performance from Karloff as a distinguished novelist and social reformer who investigates the case of 'The Haymarket Strangler' – suspecting that a sailor found guilty and executed was in fact innocent – and finds the trail leading in alarmingly compromising directions. Opening grimly with a public hanging (with callous crowd hungry for a spot of entertainment eagerly in attendance), and making evocative use of 'The Judas Hole' (a sleazy music hall whose scantily-clad girls become the target for murder), the whole film is powerfully underpinned by the repressive nature of Victorian society. Uncommonly gripping, wonderfully atmospheric, it has a real touch of the Val Lewtons. TM

Grisbi

see Touchez pas au Grisbi

Grissom Gang, The

(1971, US, 128 min)
d/p Robert Aldrich. *sc* Leon Griffiths. *ph* Joseph Biroc. *ed* Michael Luciano. *ad* James D Vance. *m* Gerald Fried. *cast* Kim Darby, Scott Wilson, Tony Musante, Robert Lansing, Connie Stevens, Irene Dailey.

● One of Aldrich's finest and most complex films, this adaptation of James Hadley Chase's notorious *No Orchids for Miss Blandish* is far more than just another contribution to the nostalgic rural gangster cycle initiated by *Bonnie and Clyde*. For one thing, the eponymous family, who kidnap '30s heiress Miss Blandish, are never glamorised but portrayed as a pathetic, ignorant bunch of grotesques; for another, as the petulant and spoilt heroine turns the sadistic and murderous Slim Grissom's love for her to her own cruelly humilating purposes, the film becomes an unsentimental exploration of perverse power-games played between two characters whose very different family backgrounds cannot conceal the latent vulnerability they both share. As such it is simultaneously witty and surprisingly touching, its disturbing emotional undercurrents lent depth by the assured playing of both Darby and Wilson. GA

Grizzly

(1976, US, 91 min)
d William Girdler. *p/sc* David Sheldon, Harvey Flaxman. *ph* William Asman. *ed* Bub Asman. *m* Robert O Ragland. *cast* Christopher George, Andrew Prine, Richard Jaeckel, Joan McCall, Joe Dorsey, Kermit Echols.

● 'No way!' twice in the first five lines of dialogue let you know what to expect from this attempt to ape *Jaws*, so to speak. The strictly B feature cast plays a team of Forest Rangers (including boozy maverick and fey conservationist, as in *Jaws*) chasing an alleged twenty-footer who eats girl campers. Alleged, because whenever the bear is seen from a normal angle, he is quite obviously of medium build; much of the other marauding is done from his own point of view (as in *King Kong*), which equally fails to convince. The heavy-breathing soundtrack accompanying these attacks is at least preferable to lines like 'While you've been sitting on your fat ass, I've made this forest part of me'. AN

Groove

(2000, US, 84 min)
d Greg Harrison. *p* Danielle Renfrew, Greg Harrison. *sc* Greg Harrison. *ph* Matthew Irving. *ed* Greg Harrison. *pd* Chris Ferreira. *cast* MacKenzie Firgens, Lola Glaudini, Denny Kirkwood, Hamish Linklater, Rachel True, Steve Van Wormer, Ari Gold, Chris Ferreira, Elizabeth Sun, Dimitri from the Lower Haight [Dimitri Ponce].

● Initially resembling a heist movie, this cash-in on the rave scene spirals around a warehouse party in San Francisco, its organisers and clubbers. Writer/director Harrison is knowledgeable and passionate about the scene, and the film is refreshingly unselfconscious about drugs and the intensity of relationships that mushroom on the dancefloor. It's beautifully shot too, the party sequences aglow with neon pinks and blues, jolting into unflattering starkness when one character discovers her fiancé's secret. And the wondrous soundtrack pumps garage, trance, breakbeats and tech-house through a cinema sound system. The insistence that raving constitutes a voyage of discovery, bonding uptight protagonist David (Linklater) and feisty New Yorker Leyla (Glaudini), is unpersuasive; but if this is often gauche, it's the most ardent film tribute yet to all-night escapism. AHa

Groove on a Stanley Knife

(1997, GB, 42 min)
d Tinge Krishnan, Beth Kotler. *cast* Alison Burrows, Samantha Hoyle.

● Two lasses hole up in a gross public lavatory, after a violent confrontation with three drug dealers. They gab about drugs and sex (one is a lesbian) until a dramatic revelation tears everything apart. At least one of the co-directors here has talent: there's a real intensity when the film pushes beyond its grimy realism. It's let down by some over-written dialogue and uneven acting, but on the whole it's an impressive calling card from Sheffield's Disruptive Element Films – let's hope MTV doesn't swallow them up. TCh

Groove Tube, The

(1974, US, 75 min)
d/p Ken Shapiro. *sc* Ken Shapiro, Lane Sarasohn. *ph* Bob Bailin. *ad* Carmen Bates. *cast* Ken Shapiro, Richard Belzer, Chevy Chase, Buzzy Linhart, Richmond Baier, Berkeley Harris.

● A series of one-dimensional parodies on aspects of American life that lampoons all the expected targets – corporations, TV, commercials, politics – but in a way that makes few dents. Jokes extend little beyond their not-so-original ideas: a news broadcast about Suk Muc Dik and Phuc Hu; some ads that make explicit the implicit sex of most advertising; a TV pundits' tea party; 'Fanny Hill' being read out on a tots' programme. The only permutations the film seems happy with are two sex sketches: one dealing with a heavy petting session in a cinema, the other a sporting commentary on the German performance in the International Sex Games. Throughout a fairly healthy vulgarity prevails over insight. CPe

Gross Anatomy (aka A Cut Above)

(1989, US, 109 min)
d Thom Eberhardt. *p* Howard Rosenman, Debra Hill. *sc* Ron Nyswaner, Mark Spragg. *ph* Steve Yaconelli. *ed* Bud Smith, Scott Smith. *pd* William F Matthews. *m* David Newman. *cast* Matthew Modine, Daphne Zuniga, Christine Lahti, Todd Field, John Scott Clough, Alice Carter, Zakes Mokae.

● The trials and tribulations of a first year med 'gross anatomy' class. Modine is a charismatic lead as Joe Slovak, the cocky young lad who bounces in with his basket-ball to find that not everyone views dissecting cadavers in the same carefree manner. The group's reaction to this maverick is sensitively – if not adventurously – scripted as they resist his influence and put him in his place. Mild and humorous, the film dodges the melodrama traps it sets for itself, making pleasant if forgettable viewing. RK

Grosse Fatigue

(1994, Fr, 92 min)
d Michel Blanc. *p* David Toscan du Plantier. *sc* Michel Blanc. *ph* Eduardo Serra. *ed* Marilyne Monthieux. *ad* Carlos Conti. *m* René-Marc Bini. *cast* Michel Blanc, Carole Bouquet, Philippe Noiret, Gilles Jacob, Charlotte Gainsbourg, Mathilda May, Josiane Balasko, Roman Polanski, Thierry Lhermitte.

● Actor Blanc's ambitious blend of doppelgänger fable and movie-movie comedy isn't, unfortunately, as funny as it'd like to be. It begins intriguingly, with Blanc up to mysteriously awful antics in Cannes and, later, Paris; then, as the puzzle moves towards its ingenious if excessively belated solution, matters get bogged down in in-jokes and bad timing. Noiret, especially, contributes an engaging cameo, but the film as a whole is much too clever for its own good. And really, Michel, gags about rape are a bit off. GA

Grosse Pointe Blank

(1997, US, 107 min)
d George Armitage. *p* Susan Arnold, Donna Roth, Roger Birnbaum. *sc* Tom Jankiewicz, DV DeVincentis, Steve Pink, John Cusack. *ph* Jamie Anderson. *ed* Brian Berdan. *pd* Stephen Altman. *m* Joe Strummer. *cast* John Cusack, Minnie Driver, Alan Arkin, Dan Aykroyd, Joan Cusack, Jeremy Piven, Hank Azaria, Barbara Harris.

● Contract killer Martin Blank (John Cusack) finds himself going home to Grosse Pointe, Detroit, for his high school reunion weekend. His shrink (Arkin) thinks it might help with his spiritual crisis. So does his secretary (Joan Cusack). And besides, there's a job in town. More to the point, maybe Debi (Driver) is ready to forgive him, ten years after he stood her up on prom night. Coming on the heels of *Swingers* and *Palookaville*, this hip black comedy is another droll study in the neuroses of the modern American male. As his name suggests, Blank is a void – his life has no meaning – but he thinks he's smart enough to get back on track, to buck those twin truisms: you can't go home again, and there are no second acts in American lives. Cusack is an engaging, lively actor with a keen sense of irony, and those qualities are much in evidence here. Director Armitage doesn't quite get the edge he brought to *Miami Blues*, but for what is essentially a one-joke movie, this has an awful lot going for it; not least the persuasive notion that psychiatrists all over America are being terrorised by angst-ridden hitmen intent on liberating their inner selves. TCh

Grotesque, The (aka Gentlemen Don't Eat Poets)

(1995, GB, 98 min)
d John-Paul Davidson. *p* Trudie Styler. *sc* Patrick McGrath, John-Paul Davidson. *ph* Andrew Dunn. *ed* Tariq Anwar. *pd* Jan Roelfs. *m* Anne Dudley. *cast* Alan Bates, Theresa Russell, Sting, Lena Headey, Steven Mackintosh, Jim Carter, Anna Massey, Trudie Styler, Maria Aitken, James Fleet, John Mills, Annette Badland.

● Having scripted this moribund adaptation of his own meticulously wrought, black comic novel, Patrick McGrath must take some blame, but Davidson's stultifying direction and listless performances from Sting and Bates deal the death blow. In the novel, McGrath evokes an atmosphere of Gothic gloom, moral decay and insidious malice; here his elegant weirdness and sly humour sink into a bog of boredom. The new obsequious butler Fledge (Sting) insinuates himself into the postwar household of Sir Hugo Coal (Bates), an eccentric aristo who hopes to stun the Royal Society with his crackpot theories of dinosaur genealogy. Seduced by Fledge's charm, Sir Hugo's wife Harriet (Russell) becomes embroiled in a subtle conspiracy that undermines her husband's authority, compromises her daughter Cleo's marriage plans, and culminates in the death of Cleo's would-be suitor Sidney Giblet (Mackintosh). Sting fails to capture the class hatred and sly ambition that inform Fledge's actions, and it's a crime to have wasted such character actors as Carter, Massey and Mills on such a dramatically dull, visually impaired treatment. NF

Groundhog Day

(1993, US, 101 min)
d Harold Ramis. *p* Trevor Albert, Harold Ramis. *sc* Danny Rubin, Harold Ramis. *ph* John Bailey. *ed* Pembroke J Herring. *pd* David Nichols. *m* George Fenton. *cast* Bill Murray, Andie MacDowell, Chris Elliott, Stephen Tobolowsky, Brian Doyle-Murray, Marita Geraghty.

● How would it feel to wake up to the same day *every* day? Would you crack up at the sheer tedium of it all? Cynically exploit others (*they* don't know they're trapped in a time warp) with what you learned about them the day before? Or use the situation to better yourself? That's the dilemma facing misanthropic TV weatherman Phil Connors (Murray) when he once more visits the small town of Punxsutawney, Pennsylvania – 'weather capital of the world' – to report on its annual Groundhog Day ceremony. What's so satisfying about Danny Rubin and Harold Ramis' script – besides the sheer plethora of gags – is the way it rigorously covers every last nuance of Connors' nightmarish predicament: he can drink himself legless without fear of the morning after, endlessly refine his chat-up lines, become an expert in 19th century French verse, but whatever he does he ends up back where he was on the dot of six. Ramis directs this surreal suburban fantasy with an admirably light touch, revelling in its absurd repetitions, surprising us with narrative ellipses, and allowing Murray ample space to indulge his special mix of sarcasm and smarm. But this is first and foremost a comedy of *ideas*, on which score it never falters. GA

Groundstar Conspiracy, The

(1972, US, 95 min)
d Lamont Johnson. *p* Trevor Wallace. *sc* Matthew Howard. *ph* Michael Reed. *ed* Edward Abroms. *ad* Cam Porteous. *m* Paul Hoffert. *cast* George Peppard, Michael Sarrazin, Christine Belford, Cliff Potts, James Olson, Tim Olson.
●Johnson fashions a neatly edgy film out of an investigation into sabotage at a space research plant, where the blank mind of an amnesiac (Sarrazin) lies at the centre of the mystery. With an excess of surveillance hardware on display, the film carefully sows the seeds of paranoia, and expresses grave doubts about the morality of security control as Peppard's security agent goes about his enquiry answerable to no one. Apart from one lapse into the field of human emotions, the script deals intelligently with the programmed responses of its automaton-like characters.

Group, The

(1966, US, 150 min)
d Sidney Lumet. *p/sc* Sidney Buchman. *ph* Boris Kaufman. *ed* Ralph Rosenblum. *pd* Gene Callahan. *m* Charles Gross. *cast* Candice Bergen, Joan Hackett, Elizabeth Hartman, Shirley Knight, Joanna Pettet, Mary-Robin Redd, Jessica Walter, Kathleen Widdoes, James Broderick, Larry Hagman, Richard Mulligan.
●Basically soap opera, but a beautifully crafted and brilliantly acted adaptation of Mary McCarthy's novel chronicling the fortunes of eight Vassar graduates, class of '33, up to the beginning of World War II. Sidney Buchman's script does a remarkable tailoring job on the book, pruning away all the fat and cutting the rest into hundreds of sharp little scenes which are pieced together as an attractively witty mosaic of the decade. Particularly clever is the way in which the girls, each one neatly and distinctively characterised, are seen to evolve personality-wise: looking, for instance, at the Dottie (Hackett) of the last scenes – proud wife of an Arizona oilman, growing slightly hatchet-faced and probably a pillar of the local ladies' league – and remembering her first, despairingly daring affair with a Greenwich Village painter, one thinks with astonishment that's exactly how she would turn out. Should the lengthy array of amorous hopes and disillusionments threaten boredom, there's always Boris Kaufman's wonderfully handsome camerawork to admire. TM

Grumpy Old Men

(1993, US, 103 min)
d Donald Petrie. *p* John Davis, Richard C Berman. *sc* Mark Stephen Johnson. *ph* Johnny Jensen. *ed* Bonnie Koehler. *pd* David Chapman. *m* Alan Silvestri. *cast* Jack Lemmon, Walter Matthau, Ann-Margret, Burgess Meredith, Daryl Hannah, Kevin Pollak, Ossie Davis, Buck Henry.
●The Odd Couple are reunited to curious effect, since Lemmon has long since moved convincingly into dramatic parts, while Matthau has stayed pretty much where he was. They play elderly, feuding neighbours in small-town Wabasha, Minnesota. They've been insulting each other about their fish catch for five decades, when on to the scene arrives wacko teacher Ariel (Ann-Margret) to intensify their rivalry. Who gets the newcomer is as predictable as the outcome of a subplot romance between their respective children (Hannah and Pollak). It's a dawdling affair – apart from the outtakes at the end, which are funnier than anything in the picture itself – memorable chiefly for the Hanna-Barbera appearance of Matthau in a trapper's cap uttering lines like, 'The guy's straight as a grizzly's dick.' Also on hand is Burgess Meredith as an L-Dopa grandpa – 'Didya mount her?' – and Buck Henry as the flinty repo man. Mediocre, regrettably. BC

Guadalcanal Diary

(1943, US, 93 min, b/w)
d Lewis Seiler. *p* Bryan Foy. *sc* Lamar Trotti, Jerry Cady. *ph* Charles G Clarke. *ed* Fred Allen. *ad* James Basevi, Leland Fuller. *m* David Buttolph. *cast* Preston Foster, Lloyd Nolan, William Bendix, Richard Conte, Anthony Quinn, Richard Jaeckel, Roy Roberts, Minor Watson, Lionel Stander.
●Twentieth Century-Fox lost no time in bringing the US Marines' successful Solomon Islands campaign to the screen (it was the first important victory of the Pacific war). Respected at the time for its authenticity, Seiler's film no longer seems particularly remarkable, featuring the usual cross-section of acceptable American types (with a heroic chaplain at their head) as they go about their business. The cast is better than most, and it is impressively staged, given that location filming actually took place in Camp Pendleton, California. (From the book by Richard Tregaskis.) TCh

Guantanamera

(1995, Cuba, 105 min)
d Tomás Gutiérrez Alea, Juan Carlos Tabio. *p* Gerardo Herrero. *sc* Eliseo Alberto de Diego Garcia Marroz, Tomás Gutiérrez Alea, Juan Carlos Tabio. *ph* Hans Burmann. *ed* Carmen Frias. *ad* Onelio Larralde. *m* José Nieto. *cast* Carlos Cruz, Mirtha Ibbara, Raúl Eguren, Jorge Perugorria, Raul Eguren, Pedro Fernandez.
●A familiar retread of the Cuban political satires of the '60s and '70s, this road movie deals with the aftermath of the now settling Cuban financial crisis of the early '90s. An ageing opera singer, 'Yoyita', the 'Guantanameran' of the song and title, who has been abroad to earn her fortune, returns to Cuba where she dies in the arms of her old flame. As a result, the intransigent bureaucrat husband of her unhappily married daughter, who has organised a crazy petrol-saving relay scheme for Havana burials, finds Yoyita is his first road test. There are jibes at shortages, the black market and sexual politics, but, as the daughter has a fling with a truck-driver, the film subsides into another celebration of the Cuban adage: 'Love is the Salt of Life'. WH

Guard, The (Karaul)

(1989, USSR, 96 min, b/w & col)
d Alexander Rogozhkin. *sc* Ivan Loschilin. *ph* Valeri Martynov. *ad* Tamara Denisova. *ad* Alexander Zogosin. *cast* Alexander Smirnov, Alexei Buldakov, Sergei Kupriyanov, Alexei Poluyan, Aleksej V Mozrun, Taras Denisenko.
●Less stunning than bludgeoning, Rogozhkin's grisly movie is like the old Living Theater play *The Brig*, but on wheels. It is set almost entirely on a prison train transporting jailbirds across the USSR. It focuses on a rookie guard, Chlustov, and the endlessly humiliating hazing he undergoes at the hands of his older colleagues; finally, the atmosphere of extreme violence and brutality causes him to crack. Prison metaphors aside, the movie is notable for pushing certain images of Russian masculinity as far as they will go; it strips men naked morally, spiritually and, ultimately, physically too. TR

Guardian, The

(1990, US, 93 min)
d William Friedkin. *p* Joe Wizan. *sc* Stephen Volk, Dan Greenburg, William Friedkin. *ph* John A Alonzo. *ed* Seth Flaum. *pd* Gregg Fonseca. *m* Jack Hues. *cast* Jenny Seagrove, Dwier Brown, Carey Lowell, Brad Hall, Miguel Ferrer, Natalia Nogulich.
●Deep in the lush canyons of upmarket LA, the tranquillity of an all-American family (Brown, Lowell and infant son) is threatened by the arrival of Camilla (Seagrove). Posing as a nanny sent by the Guardian Angel agency, she turns out to be a bloodthirsty, baby-sacrificing tree-worshipper. Based on Dan Greenburg's novel *The Nanny*, Friedkin's first foray into horror since *The Exorcist* contains many of the trademarks which characterised that epochal work: prying cameras track constantly through the shadowy corridors, sneaking up on occupants, while blinded scientists (police and doctors) impotently explain away supernatural disturbances. This time, though, Friedkin opts for up-front hokum, interspersed with impressively ridiculous special effects, including man-eating trees, flying nannies and coniferous chainsaw carnage. A severely flawed but not unamusing venture from a director who should know better. MK

Guardians of the Earth (Mankolangal)

(2000, Ind, 117 min)
d Subrahmanian Santakumar. *p* K Retnakumari. *sc* Viju Varma, Manikantan. *ph* Praveen Panicker. *ed* Ajith Kumar, Vijay Kumar. *m* Madhu Dev. *cast* Manikantan, Beena Antony, Viplavam Balan, Seema G Nair.
●Worthy but wooden and stilted melodrama set in a Kerala village dependent on pottery for survival. Much of the drama focuses on a womanising rebel and drunkard who treats his latest partner none too well and comes up against some local spivs. Of some interest, of course, for its depicition of a society somewhat different from our own, but in terms of drama, direction and performance (the forever simpering heroine is especially embarrassing), it's hard going. GA

Guarding Tess

(1994, US, 95 min)
d Hugh Wilson. *p* Ned Tanen, Nancy Graham Tanen. *sc* Hugh Wilson, Peter Torokvei. *ph* Brian Reynolds. *ed* Sidney Levin. *pd* Peter Larkin. *m* Michael Convertino. *cast* Shirley MacLaine, Nicolas Cage, Richard Griffiths, Austin Pendleton, Edward Albert, James Rebhorn.
●Doug Chesnic (Cage) has the worst assignment in the secret service: he's bodyguard to former First Lady Tess Carlisle (MacLaine). Doug wants to be where the action is; Tess wants to go golfing every three or four years (usually in the dead of winter), with perhaps an annual trip to the opera for variety. Worse, she treats her bodyguards like butlers; she expects breakfast in bed, and no guns in the house. Hugh Wilson, creator of the *Police Academy* series, was once responsible for some modestly engaging TV sitcoms – and that's essentially what this is. He gets some amiable, low-key play out of the slippery ground between protocol and authority, the battle of wills between the determined, by-the-book agent and stubborn, independent Tess, but it's going nowhere slow until an implausible kidnap plot is hatched much too late in the day. Cage is on best behaviour here, but he's not an especially sympathetic performer. MacLaine more than keeps her end up (picking an outfit for an official affair, she opts for 'elegant disdain, yet sincere concern'); and her tetchy hauteur just about keeps the movie alive. TCh

Guerre d'un Seul Homme, La

see One Man's War

Guerre des Boutons, La (The War of the Buttons)

(1962, Fr, 95 min, b/w)
d Yves Robert. *sc* Yves Robert, François Boyer. *ph* André Bac. *ed* Marie-Josèphe Yoyotte. *ad* Pierre Thévenet. *m* José Berghmans. *cast* André Treton, Michel Isella, Martin Lartigue, Jean Richard, Yvette Etiévant, Jacques Dufilho.
●The buttons in question belong to the trousers of two rival gangs of urchins and are snipped off, along with braces and shoelaces, in a crescendo of running battles. If that notion doesn't, as they say, grab you, then how about an atrociously mugging and coyly foul-mouthed little hero with a twinkle in his eye as big as the Ritz, who proposes to drive the enemy from their lair by farting them out? A huge commercial success, like all films with naked children. GAd

Guerre est finie, La (The War is Over)

(1966, Fr/Swe, 122 min, b/w)
d Alain Resnais. *sc* Jorge Semprun. *ph* Sacha Vierny. *ed* Eric Pluet. *ad* Jacques Saulnier. *m* Giovanni Fusco. *cast* Yves Montand, Ingrid Thulin, Genevieve Bujold, Dominique Rozan, Françoise Bertin, Michel Piccoli, Jean Bouise, Jean Dasté.
●Stylistically, *La Guerre est finie* is probably Resnais' most orthodox film, covering three days in the life of a Spanish exile in Paris involved in a plot to overthrow Franco. Working from a script by Jorge Semprun, Resnais explores his hero's doubts and insecurities through his relationships with two very different women: a mistress (Thulin) who represents potential stability, and a vivacious young student (Bujold) who offers him a new life. Perhaps it is the film's directness and obviously dated aspects (middle-age male angst faced with effervescent feminine adoration having become such a staple 'art movie' subject) that have made it seem a minor item in an often challenging director's career. DT

Guerre sans nom, La (The Undeclared War)

(1992, Fr, 240 min)
d Bertrand Tavernier. *p* Jean-Pierre Guerin. *sc* Bertrand Tavernier, Patrick Rotman. *ph* Alain Choquart. *ed* Luce Grunenwaldt, Laure Blancherie.

●The 1954–1962 Algerian War was undoubtedly one of the most bitter and destructive of modern conflicts. Nearly three million French combatants were involved, 25,000 lost their lives, and the French political establishment was shaken to its foundations. Officially, of course, there was no war, only 'a police action'. In the 30 years since, precious little has been written or filmed on the subject, and it was in a sense to break the taboo, to give voice to the repressed past, that producer Jean-Pierre Guérin and Tavernier undertook this documentary, hacked down from 50 hours of footage shot in Grenoble, the venue of one of the two largest anti-war riots in the '50s. They made the decision to focus exclusively on the testimonies of 28 veterans and a few of their wives; Tavernier uses a few of their own snapshots, a few shots of the Algerian desert, some footage of the site of the riots and of a veterans' rally; there is no stock footage, of carnage or otherwise. The film's remarkable power and universality lies in the human scale of these testimonies. The veterans – all of them conscripts, and of every shade of political conviction – are clearly talking about their experiences for the first time, and describe the events of 30-odd years ago with exceptional vividness and honesty. With anguished memory captured so tangibly, it is sometimes difficult to watch as so many of them break down in tears. The film, however, is shot with full allowance for their integrity. WH

Guerriere dal Seno Nuda, La

see Amazons, The

Guess Who's Coming To Dinner

(1967, US, 108 min)
d/p Stanley Kramer. *sc* William Rose. *ph* Sam Leavitt. *ed* Robert C Jones. *pd* Robert Clatworthy. *m* Frank De Vol. *cast* Spencer Tracy, Katharine Hepburn, Sidney Poitier, Katharine Houghton, Cecil Kellaway, Beah Richards, Roy E Glenn Sr.

●One can hardly complain about the performances when Tracy and Hepburn combine as the leads, but Kramer's well-meaning comedy-drama about racism – a liberal couple suffer a few doubts when their daughter brings home the black she intends to marry – is a leaden and stilted affair, wrecked by the cautious move of making the groom-to-be singularly good-looking, respectable (he's a doctor) and well-to-do. A wishy-washy, sanctimonious plea for tolerance, directed with Kramer's customary verbosity and stodginess. GA

Guest, The

see Caretaker, The

Guest House Paradiso

(1999, GB, 90 min)
d Adrian Edmondson. *p* Phil McIntyre. *sc* Adrian Edmondson, Rik Mayall. *ph* Alan Almond. *ed* Sean Barton. *pd* Tom Brown. *m* Colin Towns. *cast* Rik Mayall, Adrian Edmondson, Vincent Cassel, Hélène Mahieu, Bill Nighy, Simon Pegg, Fenella Fielding, Lisa Palfrey, Kate Ashfield.

●Edmondson's anarchic, loud, excessive comedy is so crude, so lewd, that it will probably try the patience of even TV's *Bottom* fans. A cheap take-off of *Fawlty Towers*, it's set in an island holiday pad run by dodgy voyeur and all-round fleecer Richie Twat (Mayall) and his thick buddy Eddie Elizabeth Ndingombaba (Edmondson). The food sucks; most rooms overlook a nuclear power station; and sex starved, foul mouthed Mr Twat just can't resist rummaging through his guests' underwear. The admittedly hilarious opening sight of Eddie speeding manically on his motorbike sets the tone: we're talking imbecilic bog humour, with stains; everything is pushed to the extreme. If your toes don't curl, that's because you've already left the cinema. DA

Gueule d'Amour

(1937, Fr, 102 min, b/w)
d Jean Grémillon. *p* Raoul Ploquin. *sc* Charles Spaak. *ph* Günther Rittau. *m* Lothar Brühne. *cast* Jean Gabin, Mireille Balin, René Lefèvre, Marguerite Deval, Jeanne Marken, Jean Aymé.

●When Gabin chances to return – older, sadder and in unbecoming civvies – to the shady bar where, as a legionnaire, he once held sway, a taxi-girl remarks incredulously (and callously) on his former reputation as the garrison's Don Juan. The intense poignancy of this 'privileged moment' is symptomatic of the way in which both actor and director have revitalised what is basically a trite, off-the-peg melodrama about a man destroyed by his passion for a woman. GAd

Gueule Ouverte, La

see Mouth Agape, The

Guide for the Married Man, A

(1967, US, 91 min)
d Gene Kelly. *p* Frank McCarthy. *sc* Frank Tarloff. *ph* Joseph MacDonald. *ed* Dorothy Spencer. *ad* Jack Martin Smith, William Glasgow. *m* John Williams. *cast* Walter Matthau, Robert Morse, Inger Stevens, Sue Ane Langdon, Claire Kelly, Elaine Devry, Lucille Ball, Jack Benny, Sid Caesar, Art Carney, Jeffrey Hunter, Jayne Mansfield, Carl Reiner, Phil Silvers, Terry-Thomas.

●Walter Matthau, who was passed over for the film version of *The Seven Year Itch* at the beginning of his Hollywood career after playing it on Broadway, comes down with the 12-year itch in this garbled bourgeois satire. Robert Morse is the adulterous neighbour who gives his friend the lowdown on the dos and don'ts of doing it, with star-studded illustrations featuring Lucille Ball, Phil Silvers, Jayne Mansfield and the like (among a host of guest cameos). These occasionally inventive situations score intermittently, but it's an unappealing effort on the whole. TCh

Guiltrip

(1995, Ire, 89 min)
d Gerard Stembridge. *p* Ed Guiney. *sc* Gerard Stembridge. *ph* Eugene O'Connor. *ed* Mary Finlay. *pd* David Wilson. *m* Brendan Power. *cast* Andrew Connolly, Jasmine Russell, Peter Hanly, Michelle Houlden, Frankie McCaffert, Pauline McLynn.

●Brutal, bleak, full of the bitterness of life, this isn't much fun. But it's an impressive, disturbing glimpse of fear and loathing in a provincial Irish town. Late at night, Tina (Russell) waits for her army corporal husband Liam (Connolly) to return from work. When he finally makes it, a long argument erupts. Each is suspicious of what the other's been up to. They never find out, but we do. Liam's a calculating skirt-chaser; Tina fancies the wares at a hi-fi shop and also an absurdly enthusiastic salesman (Hanly). Juggling flashbacks, writer/ director Stembridge masters a difficult structure: unfolding past and present, building up character, counterpoising word and deed, and finally suggesting a ruinously unbalanced relationship that obscures and distorts issues of blame and guilt. More than just a domestic drama, the film's an unflinching picture of communal discord and alienation amid the banalities of small-town life. It's also an indictment of the place of violence in society: the abuse of personal power and the hopelessness of keeping military-bred qualities confined to barracks. An auspicious debut. NB

Guilty as Sin

(1993, US, 107 min)
d Sidney Lumet. *p* Martin Ransohoff. *sc* Larry Cohen. *ph* Andrzej Bartkowiak. *ed* Evan Lottman. *pd* Philip Rosenberg. *m* Howard Shore. *cast* Rebecca De Mornay, Don Johnson, Stephen Lang, Jack Warden, Dana Ivey, Ron White.

●Though the title suggests a *Jagged Edge*-style thriller, Lumet has a taste for weightier courtroom dramas. Audiences expecting a legal thriller will get something deeper and darker, but if they stay long enough, they'll also get what they came for. Jennifer Haines (De Mornay), an ambitious lawyer with a killer instinct, meets her match in David Greenhill (Johnson), a 'ladies man' and alleged wife killer. Locked in a dangerous game with her seductive, manipulative client, yet bound by the rules of confidentiality, she slowly realises she was chosen for a reason: Greenhill knew he could push her buttons. Lumet and scriptwriter Larry Cohen emphasise the erotic tension and psychological cross-currents sparking between the couple. Regrettably, De Mornay resorts to quivering histrionics for Haines' slide from confident professional to hysterical victim, while the potentially fascinating battle, gives way to crass women-in-peril clichés, before finally tipping over the edge into melodrama. NF

Guilty by Suspicion

(1990, US, 105 min)
d Irwin Winkler. *p* Arnon Milchan. *sc* Irwin Winkler. *ph* Michael Ballhaus. *ed* Priscilla Nedd. *pd* Leslie Dilley. *m* James Newton Howard. *cast* Robert De Niro, Annette Bening, George Wendt, Patricia Wettig, Sam Wanamaker, Luke Edwards, Ben Piazza, Martin Scorsese, Barry Primus, Gailard Sartain, Stuart Margolin.

●Film director David Merrill (De Niro) refuses to name names to the House Un-American Activities Committee in 1951, despite the recommendations of studio boss Darryl F Zanuck (Piazza) that he resort to a slippery lawyer (Wanamaker). Everybody assumes he'll give in since his work means everything to him – it cost him his marriage – but will he? The only fringe benefit of blacklisting, since friends split for Europe, kill themselves or denounce each other, is the support of his ex-wife (Bening) and his developing relationship with his son. The resolute ban on heroics in Winkler's directorial debut spreads something of a monochrome mood. What happens to friendship, marriage and work when the blacklist descends is schematically displayed without mining much that's memorable. Still, it's an interesting film, convincingly played and mature in its conception. BC

Guinea Pig, The (aka The Outsider)

(1948, GB, 97 min, b/w)
d Roy Boulting. *p* John Boulting. *sc* Bernard Miles, Warren Chetham-Strode, Roy Boulting. *ph* Gilbert Taylor. *ed* Richard Best. *ad* John Howell. *m* John Wooldridge. *cast* Richard Attenborough, Cecil Trouncer, Robert Flemyng, Sheila Sim, Bernard Miles, Peter Reynolds, Timothy Bateson.

●Thanks to the first cinematic sounding of the word 'arse', a vaguely controversial examination of what would happen if you let working class yobs into the country's public schools. Attenborough is the tobacconist's son whose uncouth manners give him a hard time as he shocks the snobbish teachers and pupils of an old-established institution. Solid entertainment, even if barely convincing, distinctly soft on the political side (he eventually wins respect and friendship, of course, having been moulded to the public school image), and riddled with special pleading. GA

Gulag

(1984, US, 119 min)
d Roger Young. *p* Andrew Adelson. *sc* Dan Gordon. *ph* Kelvin Pike. *ed* John Jympson. *pd* Keith Wilson. *m* Elmer Bernstein. *cast* David Keith, Malcolm McDowell, David Suchet, Warren Clarke, John McEnery, Nancy Paul.

●A film thoroughly mediocre in every aspect – acting, writing, the very idea. An American journalist (Keith), victim of a KGB plot, is arrested while covering a sports tournament in Moscow. This honest and innocent hero is beaten and humiliated by various black-hearted flunkies of the Russian legal system before being carted off to a Siberian prison camp for ten years. There he eventually persuades a stiff-lipped Englishman (McDowell) – very democratic, this film, when it comes to handing out national stereotypes – to join him in an outrageous escape attempt across more than 1,000 miles of snowdriven Siberian wastes. At which point one roots for a pack of wolves to come and put an end to everyone's misery. A moving performance from Suchet (as a Jewish academic imprisoned for requesting an exit visa to Israel) simply points up what an insulting load of old cobblers the rest is. CS

Gulliver's Travels

(1976, GB, 81 min)
d Peter Hunt. *p* Raymond Leblanc, Derek Horne. *sc* Don Black. *ph* Alan Hume. *ed* Ron Pope, Robert Richardson. *pd* Michael Stringer. *m* Michel Legrand. *cast* Richard Harris, Catherine Schell, Norman Shelley, Meredith Edwards, Michael Bates, Denise Bryer.

●Singing Richard Harris is shipwrecked in pasteboard Lilliput, and junior patrons will find that the ensuing, distinctly un-Swiftian fun leaves almost everything to be desired. Immense trouble, so we're informed, went into the film's animation (though Harris, the only human being seen for most of the running time, gives the impression of having been uneasily shoe-horned into the frantic, scampering action). The enterprise as a whole, featuring a tubby king and a lacklustre court conspiracy, is bogged down in treacly sentiment. JPy

Gumball Rally, The

(1976, US, 106 min)
d/p Chuck Bail. *sc* Leon Capetanos. *ph* Richard Glouner. *ed* Gordon Scott, Stuart H Pappé, Maury Winetrobe. *ad* Walter M Simonds. *m* Dominic Frontière. *cast* Michael Sarrazin, Normann Burton, Raúl Julia, Gary Busey, Tim McIntire, Susan Flannery.
●The first, and some say best, of the cross-country car race cycle that spawned the likes of *The Cannonball Run*. As the customised cars burn rubber from New York to Long Beach, Florida, we are treated to the usual squealing tyres, clouds of dust and metal-crunching crashes. Pitched at cartoon level, with a bizarre collection of speed enthusiasts crudely taking care of the comedy, it relies almost exclusively on the exceptional stunt work, the plot only occasionally dropping into first gear for some boring and irrelevant dramatic stuff. NF

Gummo

(1997, US, 89 min)
d Harmony Korine. *p* Cary Woods. *sc* Harmony Korine. *ph* Jean-Yves Escoffier. *ed* Chris Tellefsen. *pd* Dave Doernberg. *m* Randy Poster. *cast* Jacob Sewell, Nick Sutton, Lara Tosh, Jacob Reynolds, Darby Dougherty, Chloe Sevigny, Carisa Glucksman, Max Perlich, Linda Manz.
●This impressionistic portrait of a half-imaginary Midwestern suburb confirms Harmony (*Kids*) Korine as a creative force to be reckoned with. Be warned, however, it is often an unpleasant experience. When the two teenage boys at its centre aren't killing stray cats, they're sniffing glue, paying for sex or messing with life support machines. But for all the immature fixation on depravity, Korine's refusal to condemn or condescend to his characters saves the film from freak show voyeurism. Twisting from *cinéma vérité* to improvisation to pre-scripted lines, often within the same scene, he's audaciously upfront about his stratagems (his command of rhythm and pace is also quite brilliant). Problematic, troubling, dangerous even, but breathtakingly original, and absolutely true to the times. The cutting edge doesn't get any sharper than this. TCh

Gumshoe

(1971, GB, 84 min)
d Stephen Frears. *p* Michael Medwin. *sc* Neville Smith. *ph* Chris Menges. *ed* Charles Rees. *pd* Michael Seymour. *m* Andrew Lloyd Webber. *cast* Albert Finney, Billie Whitelaw, Frank Finlay, Janice Rule, Fulton Mackay, Carolyn Seymour, George Silver.
●A beautifully observed and hilariously funny film about a bingo-caller in a Liverpool working-men's club (Finney) who dreams of writing (and starring in) *The Maltese Falcon* and recording 'Blue Suede Shoes', only to be plunged into a real murder mystery when he tries to bring his dream world to life. *Gumshoe*, unlike most pastiches, doesn't get bogged down in references beyond itself. The credit for this is due to Finney, who is careful to make it clear that Eddie is a self-conscious dreamer, and to Stephen Frears who, in his first feature, is similarly careful to anchor the film in the gritty world of petty Liverpool crime before animating Eddie's all-encompassing dreams. PH

Gun Crazy (aka Deadly Is the Female)

(1949, US, 87 min, b/w)
d Joseph H Lewis. *p* Maurice King, Frank King. *sc* MacKinlay Kantor, Millard Kaufman. *ph* Russell Harlan. *ed* Harry Gerstad. *pd* Gordon Wiles. *m* Victor Young. *cast* Peggy Cummins, John Dall, Berry Kroeger, Morris Carnovsky, Annabel Shaw, Harry Lewis, Nedrick Young.
●Basically a love-on-the-run saga, this concerns a misfit couple, drawn to each other by their mutual love for guns, who turn to robbing banks when married life gets tough. Much praised as an amoral, gripping study in the fraught relationship between sex, violence and money, it sees Lewis – one of the very finest B movie directors – firing on all cylinders, prompt ing his leads to a very real evocation of amour fou, and turning his budgetary limitations to advantage, notably in the lengthy uncut take (shot from inside a car) of a small-town heist, and in the finale, shot in a misty swamp to avoid the need for extras. Far more energetic than *Bonnie and Clyde* – the most famous of its many progeny – its intensity borders on the subversive and surreal. GA

Guncrazy

(1992, US, 93 min)
d Tamra Davis. *p* Diane Firestone, Zane W Levitt. *sc* Matthew Bright. *ph* Lisa Rinzler. *ed* Kevin Tent. *ad* Kevin Constant. *m* Ed Tomney. *cast* Drew Barrymore, James LeGros, Joe Dallesandro, Billy Drago, Michael Ironside, Rodney Harvey.
●Straight to video in Britain, but audience support in the US eventually won it a theatrical release. Inspired by *They Live by Night* and the original *Gun Crazy*, this is a love-on-the-run yarn, with the incendiary Barrymore immensely sympathetic as the promiscuous, sexually mistreated teen who goes on the lam with former prison penpal LeGross. They leave behind an unwitting trail of death and destruction, begun by her shooting of abusive guardian Dallesandro. Although it doesn't seek to excuse their wrongdoing, the film stands out for its convincing depiction of the up-against-it white-trash mentality and the overriding demands of youthful desire. TJ

Gunese Yolculuk

see Journey to the Sun

Gunfight, A

(1970, US, 89 min)
d Lamont Johnson. *p* A Ronald Lubin, Harold Jack Bloom. *sc* Harold Jack Bloom. *ph* David M Walsh. *ed* Bill Mosher. *ad* Tambi Larsen. *m* Laurence Rosenthal. *cast* Kirk Douglas, Johnny Cash, Jane Alexander, Raf Vallone, Karen Black, Keith Carradine.
●A self-conscious Western which conflates the showdown with showmanship, as ageing gunmen Douglas and Cash prepare to charge admission to townsfolk eager to view the eponymous event, to be held (in parodic homage to the 'corrida' finales of Leone's *Dollar* films) in the local bullring. Director Johnson's heavyweight tele-movie reputation was then still to be established; while writer Harold Jack Bloom, who here cheats badly with an inconclusive double ending, was also later to taste small-screen fame as a Jack Webb associate and creator of the series *The DA* and *Hec Ramsey*. PT

Gunfight at the O.K. Corral

(1957, US, 122 min)
d John Sturges. *p* Hal B Wallis. *sc* Leon M Uris. *ph* Charles Lang Jr. *ed* Warren Low. *ad* Hal Pereira, Walter Tyler. *m* Dimitri Tiomkin. *cast* Burt Lancaster, Kirk Douglas, Rhonda Fleming, Jo Van Fleet, John Ireland, Lee Van Cleef, Frank Faylen, Kenneth Tobey, DeForest Kelley, Earl Holliman.
●This peculiar film resembles Sturges' more famous *The Magnificent Seven*: not unlikeable, not uninteresting, but as many times as you see it, it gets neither better nor worse. Passion, certainly, is lacking, and being a 'town' Western, it's all very conventionally domestic. The Earp/Clanton family shootout is a Western legend, and was treated by Ford with romantic righteousness in *My Darling Clementine* a decade earlier. For Sturges, the shootout remains a kind of grudging necessity, and has no more relationship with any real historical truths than Ford's did. Curiously, Sturges returned to the Earp saga with *Hour of the Gun* (1967), which picked up where this one leaves off; but by then he was caught between a dying traditionalism and the growing audience need for the genre to criticise itself. CW

Gunfighter, The

(1950, US, 84 min, b/w)
d Henry King. *p* Nunnally Johnson. *sc* William Bowers, William Sellers. *ph* Arthur Miller. *ed* Barbara McLean. *ad* Lyle Wheeler, Richard Irvine. *m* Alfred Newman. *cast* Gregory Peck, Helen Westcott, Millard Mitchell, Jean Parker, Karl Malden, Skip Homeier, Richard Jaeckel, Mae Marsh.
●A superb Western, almost classical in its observance of the unities (clock-watching as obsessively as *High Noon*, it's an altogether tougher, bleaker film), and a ground-breaker in its day with its characterisation of Peck's notorious gunfighter Jimmy Ringo as a man just about over the hill, haunted by the dead weight of his reputation, the fear of loneliness, the certainty of dying at the hands of some fast-draw punk sneering 'He don't look so tough to me'. Riding into the small town where the wife and child he abandoned are living incognito, he insists on waiting in the saloon in the hope that she will agree to see him. The kids play hookey from school to gape open-mouthed; the bartender gleefully rubs his hands at the thought of the profits; indignant rustling from the good ladies of the town serve notice that an outlaw is unwelcome; and with assorted grudge-bearers already assembling, along with the aforesaid fast-draw punk, there is clearly no future for Johnny Ringo. Magnificently directed and shot (by Arthur Miller), flawlessly acted by Peck and a superb cast, governed by an almost Langian sense of fate, it's a film that has the true dimensions of tragedy. TM

Gun Fury

(1953, US, 83 min)
d Raoul Walsh. *p* Lewis J Rachmil. *sc* Irving Wallace, Roy Huggins. *ph* Lester H White. *ed* Jerome Thoms, James Sweeney. *ad* Ross Bellah. *m* Mischa Bakaleinikoff. *cast* Rock Hudson, Donna Reed, Phil Carey, Lee Marvin, Neville Brand, Leo Gordon.
●Straightforward Western from a generally straightforward film-maker. Hudson and new bride Reed are on their way West when she's kidnapped by bad 'un Carey and his gang (including youthful varmint Marvin), leaving her man no choice but to lay down his pacifist ideals and give chase. 'A man's gotta do,' in other words, though in this instance Rock's flamboyant performance rather overdoes it. TJ

Gunga Din

(1939, US, 114 min, b/w)
d/p George Stevens. *sc* Joel Sayre, Fred Guiol, Ben Hecht, Charles MacArthur. *ph* Joseph H August. *ed* Henry M Berman, John Lockert. *ad* Van Nest Polglase, Perry Ferguson. *m* Alfred Newman. *cast* Cary Grant, Victor McLaglen, Douglas Fairbanks Jr, Joan Fontaine, Sam Jaffe, Eduardo Ciannelli, Montagu Love.
●Of course one winces a little at the smug colonialist attitudes, and at the patronising 'You're a better man than I am, Gunga Din' which commemorates the humble native water-bearer's sacrifice after he dies blowing a bugle to save the Raj from falling into an ambush. All the same this is a pretty spiffing adventure yarn, with some classically staged fights, terrific performances, and not too much stiff upper lip as Kipling's soldiers three go about their rowdy, non-commissioned, and sometimes disreputable capers. What, one wonders, did William Faulkner contribute, uncredited, to the bulldozing Hecht/MacArthur script? TM

Gung Ho

(1986, US, 112 min)
d Ron Howard. *p* Tony Ganz, Deborah Blum. *sc* Lowell Ganz, Babaloo Mandel. *ph* Don Peterman. *ed* Daniel Hanley, Michael Hill. *pd* James Schoppe. *m* Thomas Newman. *cast* Michael Keaton, Gedde Watanabe, George Wendt, Mimi Rogers, John Turturro, Soh Yamamura.
●In a Pennsylvanian town, works foreman Keaton persuades a Japanese car company to reopen a local factory. But his problems have just begun, because as employee liaison officer, he has to smooth over the introduction of streamlined practices and zero-defect efficiency. Soon he is unable to contain the workers' resentment: a walkout threatens the future of the partnership. Keaton, with bizarre facial expressions and smart-aleck wisecracks, makes much of the comic situations, but Howard fails to keep the line moving. Further, the hero, though funny, is ultimately unsympathetic, securing through his cosy pacts nobody's position but his own, while the upbeat ending justifies strike-breaking. With comrades like this, who needs class enemies? NF

Gunhed

(1989, Jap, 100 min)
d Masato Harada. *p* Yoshishige Shimatani, Tetsuhisa Yamada. *sc* Masato Harada, James Bannon. *ph* Junichi Fujisawa. *ed* Fumio

Ogawa. *m* Tohiyuki Honda. *cast* Landy Leyes, Masahiro Takashima, Brenda Bakke, James B Thompson, Aya Enjyoji.
●It's the 21st century, and on the Pacific island 8J0, the super-computer Chiron 5 lies in the 400-storey Mother Tower, dormant since it defeated the World Union Government back in 2026. Arriving on 8J0, bounty hunter Brooklyn and Texas Ranger Nim team up after the Mother Tower's reactivated defence system has massacred their various comrades. With the help of two children who survived the robot war, they discover and repair the last 'Gunhed', an unmanned combat robot, and use it to save the world as they know it. Impenetrable tosh (at least in this English version). AO

Gunmen

(1993, US, 90 min)
d Deran Sarafian. *p* Laurence Mark, John Davis, John Flock. *sc* Stephen Sommers. *ph* Hiro Narita. *ed* Bonnie Koehler. *pd* Michael Seymour, Hector Romero. *m* John Debney. *cast* Kadeem Hardison, Christopher Lambert, Mario Van Peebles, Brenda Bakke, Sally Kirkland, Denis Leary, Patrick Stewart, Richard Sarafian.
●This buddy-buddy action movie begins promisingly with a South American drug baron Patrick Stewart attending his wife's funeral. 'Do you think I'm over-reacting?' he asks coolly, as the gravediggers shovel on the dirt, slowly muffling the poor woman's screams. He sends right-hand man Leary to find a cache of stolen loot, putting him on collision course with charming adventurer Lambert and US special agent Van Peebles, unlikely allies, each of whom knows half of the treasure's location. Sarafian is an unpretentious, easy-to-please director, with an eye for quirky character detail and a dab hand at the macho stuff. Leary makes a good fist of the heavy, but the movie's real subject is the elaborate bonding rituals of the hunks. TCh

Gunnar Hedes Saga

(1923, Swe, 70 min approx, b/w)
d/sc Mauritz Stiller. *ph* J Julius [Julius Jaenzon], Henrik Jaenzon. *ad* Axel Ebbensen. *cast* Einar Hanson, Mary Johnson, Pauline Brunius, Adolf Olchansky, Stina Berg, Hugo Björne, Thecla Ahlander, Gösta Hillberg.
●Reckless Gunnar adventures forth to make his fortune only to be concussed by stampeding reindeer. He returns home zombiefied but is finally restored to health and wealth by the love of a beautiful fiddle player from a travelling show. One way of approaching this odd but rewarding movie, from Selma Lagerlöf's novel, is to imagine a prologue in which a child announces 'Once upon a time…' The tale which follows, with its sinister/comforting mother and vigorous/passive hero, would play quite smoothly if the copious inter-titles were rendered in Daisy Ashford-ese. Freudians will find the film specially congenial, particularly the heroine's dream, in which Gunnar is carried into her bedroom on a sledge driven by an old woman and pulled by four enormous black bears. Hmm. BBa

Gunpoint

see At Gunpoint

Gun Runner, The

see Santiago

Guns Across the Veldt

see Spoor

Guns and the Fury, The

(1981, US, 99 min)
d/p Tony Zarindast. *sc* Donald Fredette, Tony Zarindast. *ph* Elly Zarindast. *ed* Michael Billingsley, Bill Cunningham. *pd* David Maleck. *m* Jack Wheaton. *cast* Peter Graves, Albert Salmi, Cameron Mitchell, Michael Ansara, Shaun Curry, Barry Stokes.
●An abysmal desert adventure which totally wastes the inherent promise of being set in Persia in 1908, amid early international conflict over Arab land and Gulf oil. What happens is that mercenary Yanks cluster manfully round a single drilling rig, getting furious as swarthy locals, gung-ho Bengal Lancers and dastardly Russians try to give them and each other some pragmatic lessons in gun-power ideology. The history's as risibly re-written as the dialogue; the only woman in sight is inevitably raped by marauding Cossacks; the local hero seems to have graduated from Oxford in guerilla tactics; and two charging horsemen fall dead for every shot fired. PT

Guns for San Sebastian (La Bataille de San Sebastian)

(1967, Fr/Mex/It, 111 min)
d Henri Verneuil. *p* Jacques Bar. *sc* James R Webb. *ph* Armand Thirard. *ed* Françoise Bonnot. *ad* Robert Clavel, Roberto Silva. *m* Ennio Morricone. *cast* Anthony Quinn, Anjanette Comer, Charles Bronson, Sam Jaffe, Silvia Pinal, Jaime Fernández, Ivan Desny, Fernand Gravey.
●Anthony Quinn plays a lusty rogue with a heart of gold (what else?) who allows himself to be mistaken for a priest, and goes on to inspire some craven villagers to defend themselves against assorted un-Christian marauders (including Bronson as a nasty half-breed who has taken up with the Indians). The setting is nominally 18th century Mexico. It's a one-man Seven Samurai by any other name, competently enough directed and with a Morricone score, but strictly routine stuff. TM

Guns in the Afternoon

see Ride the High Country

Guns of Darkness

(1962, GB, 102 min, b/w)
d Anthony Asquith. *p* Thomas Clyde. *sc* John Mortimer. *ph* Robert Krasker. *ed* Frederick Wilson. *ad* John Howell. *m* Benjamin Frankel. *cast* Leslie Caron, David Niven, James Robertson Justice, David Opatoshu, Derek Godfrey, Richard Pearson, Eleanor Summerfield, Ian Hunter.
●Set in South America, and at first glance a hangover from the Empire films of the '50s, with their familiar paraphernalia of rebellions, plantations and exotic locales. There is, in fact, rather more to it. The story, taken from a Francis Clifford novel, moves through similar territory to Graham Greene's 'entertainments'. Both writers deal with questions of conduct faced by the Englishman abroad, although Clifford's heroes show more practical application and less imagination in the face of moral crises, thereby skirting the spiritual malaise that besets Greene's characters. Here Niven's Britisher finds himself unwillingly dragged off the fence when his own and his wife's safety is threatened. John Mortimer manages an intelligent script. CPe

Guns of Navarone, The

(1961, GB, 157 min)
d J Lee Thompson. *p* Cecil F Ford. *sc* Carl Foreman. *ph* Oswald Morris. *ed* Alan Osbiston. *pd* Geoffrey Drake. *m* Dimitri Tiomkin. *cast* Gregory Peck, David Niven, Anthony Quinn, Stanley Baker, Anthony Quayle, James Darren, Irene Papas, James Robertson Justice, Richard Harris.
●Producer Carl Foreman specialised in downbeat movies questioning the nature of wartime heroism. But the on-going debates about the morality of warfare that are scattered through this Alistair MacLean adaptation only serve to drag out the action climaxes, in which our WWII heroes take out two big gun-posts on a Turkish cliff. Lots of studio rock-climbing, and everybody gets very wet. TR

Guru, The

(1968, US/Ind, 112 min)
d James Ivory. *p* Ismail Merchant. *sc* Ruth Prawer Jhabvala, James Ivory. *ph* Subrata Mitra. *ed* Prabhakar Supare. *ad* Bansi Chandragupta, Didi Contractor. *m* Ustad Vilayat H Khan. *cast* Utpal Dutt, Michael York, Rita Tushingham, Aparna Sen, Madhur Jaffrey, Barry Foster, Saeed Jaffrey, Ismail Merchant.
●Fox budget meets slender subject, and East uncomfortably meets West. With York as a '60s pop idol (he even sings) tripping to India for sitar lessons, and Tushingham on an unidentified spiritual quest, not even Utpal Dutt's splendid performance as their Western-susceptible guru can prevent Ivory's mockery from nose-diving into caricature, or his favourite theme – of incongruous cultural collisions – from being awkwardly reinforced by his own hybrid style. JD

Guru in Seven

(1997, GB, 107 min)
d/p/sc Shani Grewal. *ph* James Bishop. *ed* Shani Grewal. *m* Matthew Best, Neil Hourigan, Sean Maher, Sunny Sehegal. *cast* Saeed Jaffrey, Jacqueline Pearce, Nitin Chandra Ganatra, Lea Rochelle, Lynne Michelle, Elle Lewis, Amanda Pointer, Samantha Spiro.
●Sanjay (Ganatra), an immature charmer on the cusp of thirty, is struggling as an artist on the dole. Left by his black girlfriend because he refuses to marry, he accepts a bet from pub mates that he can sleep with seven women in a week and thus become 'the guru'. Will his smugness see him through? Or is he heading for a fall? This micro budget comedy will doubtless offend (or bore) many, not least members of the London Punjabi community who take some of Sanjay's sharpest jibes. With its cavalier, non-PC sexual mores (probably more representative than is usually allowed), this is not art cinema but it makes many '90s British-Asian movies seem distinctly old hat. Shot on the lam, Ganatra holds the film together with a mix of self-parody, flash Harry charm and little-boy-lost innocence. WH

Guy

(1996, GB/Ger, 94 min)
d Michael Lindsay-Hogg. *p* Renée Missel. *sc* Kirby Dick. *ph* Arturo Smith. *ed* Dody Jane Dorn. *pd* Kara Lindstrom. *m* Jeff Beal. *cast* Vincent D'Onofrio, Hope Davis, Kimber Riddle, Diane Salinger, Richard Portnow, Valente Rodriguez.
●This intriguing oddity attempts to blend the experimental with the mainstream. Shot with 'subjective camera', it begins with the unseen, anonymous film-maker (Davis) selecting Guy Dade (D'Onofrio) as the subject for her latest 'documentary'. Initially uncertain about her motives and understandably reluctant to let her invade his privacy, he eventually agrees to let her follow him around LA, shooting his dodgy car deals, dates with girlfriend Veronica (Riddle), and his endless vain attempts to get to know his chronicler/interrogator better. She, however, remains an aloof observer – or does she? This is an intelligent if rather unfocused examination of the way people may be both nervous about, and aroused by, the prospect of exposing themselves to the prying but sometimes liberating gaze of a voyeuristic camera. D'Onofrio is adept at suggesting Guy's increasingly evident, faintly desperate need to feel attractive or desired; though aware he's playing with fire, he's clearly turned on by – what? – the chance of fame, a woman's attention, self-revelation? Though entertaining and thought provoking, it's not a patch, say, on *Spinal Tap*, let alone *Close-Up*. GA

Guyana: Crime of the Century (Guyana: El Crimen del Siglo)

(1979, Mex/Sp/Pan)
d/p René Cardona Jr. *sc* Carlos Valdemar, René Cardona Jr. *ph* Leopoldo Villaseñor. *ed* Earl Watson. *m* Jimmie Haskell, Alfredo Diaz Ordaz. *cast* Stuart Whitman, Gene Barry, John Ireland, Joseph Cotten, Bradford Dillman, Jennifer Ashley, Yvonne De Carlo.
●Guyana, 1978: 912 members of James Jones' People's Temple cult commit mass suicide – an act of 'revolutionary death' – as their dream of a promised land shatters. Hounded by press, congressmen, and his own paranoid imagination, the Bible-thumping socialist visionary Jones (played by Whitman) emerges as no more than a cardboard cut-out in this penny-dreadful hash which is somehow both uninformative and tedious. The strictly token emphasis on lurid sex/torture, and its ageing rent-a-star cast, shows up producer/director Cardona's past reputation for factory-line quickies for South American markets. DMacp

Guys and Dolls

(1955, US, 150 min)
d Joseph L Mankiewicz. *p* Samuel Goldwyn. *sc* Joseph L Mankiewicz. *ph* Harry Stradling. *ed* Daniel Mandell. *pd* Oliver Smith. *songs* Frank Loesser. *cast* Marlon Brando, Jean Simmons, Frank Sinatra, Vivian Blaine, Stubby Kaye, Robert Keith.
●A musical fairly glittering with intelligence and invention. Too much talk, its critics said (not for the first time with Mankiewicz). But

quite apart from the fact that much of this talk is delectable Runyonese, some defence is necessary against the frenzied brilliance of Michael Kidd's choreography, which threatens to deluge the screen in energy and eccentricity right from the pyrotechnic opening number that establishes the teeming underworld of Times Square. Relaxed and caressing, the dialogue sequences serve as a kind of foreplay, enhancing not merely the exquisite eruptions of pleasure aroused by the musical numbers, but the genuine lyricism of the romance between gambler Sky Masterson and his Salvation Army doll. Inspired casting here, with Brando and Simmons – a Method counterbalance to the more traditional showbiz coupling of Sinatra and Blaine – lending an emotional depth rare in musicals. TM

Gycklarnas Afton (The Naked Night/Sawdust and Tinsel)

(1953, Swe, 96 min, b/w)
d Ingmar Bergman. *p* Rune Waldekranz. *sc* Ingmar Bergman. *ph* Sven Nykvist, Hilding Bladh. *ed* Carl-Olov Skeppstedt. *ad* Bibi Lindström. *m* Karl-Birger Blomdahl. *cast* Harriet Andersson, Ake Grönberg, Hasse Ekman, Anders Ek, Gudrun Brost, Annika Tretow, Gunnar Björnstrand.

●Acknowledging the influence of Dupont's *Variety* – one of the keystones of German expressionism, in which marriage was seen as a perilous high-wire act – Bergman here employs the circus as a metaphor for the humiliating hoops through which men and women are put by their sexual dreams and desires. Heavily masochistic in its anguished account of the futile attempts of an ageing circus owner (Grönberg) and his steely young mistress (Andersson) to escape the dreary limitations of their mutually destructive involvement, it isn't exactly prepossessing in theme. But visually it is a treat, with Bergman's richly baroque compositions and persistent use of deep focus brilliantly exploiting the circus and theatre settings. And the performances are first-rate. TM

Gymkata

(1985, US, 90 min)
d Robert Clouse. *p* Fred Weintraub. *sc* Charles Robert Carner. *ph* Godfrey Godar. *ed* Robert A Ferretti. *pd* Veljko Despotovic. *m* Alfi Kabiljo. *cast* Kurt Thomas, Tetchie Agbayani, Richard Norton, Edward Bell, Edward Bell, John Barrett.

●High-kicking balderdash featuring Thomas as a former US Olympic gymnast who enters an endurance test in the small Himalayan country of Gymkata just so he can biff his opponents and, if he wins, persuade the authorities to instal an American 'Star Wars' defence post on their soil. Mediocre action pulp. TJ

Gypsy

(1962, US, 149 min)
d/p Mervyn LeRoy. *sc* Leonard Spigelgass. *ph* Harry Stradling. *ed* Philip W Anderson. *ad* John Beckman. *songs* Jule Styne, Stephen Sondheim. *cast* Rosalind Russell, Natalie Wood, Karl Malden, Paul Wallace, Betty Bruce, Parley Baer, Ann Jilliann.

●Blowsy, miscast Technirama musical, with Rosalind Russell as the horrendous stage mother Mama Rose. Ethel Merman had a Broadway triumph with the role, but Russell is horrendous. As her unfortunate offspring, Ann Jillian isn't really there as June Havoc, and Wood doesn't have what it takes as stripper Gypsy Rose Lee. On the plus side: songs by Jule Styne and Stephen Sondheim. TCh

Gypsy

(1994, US, 142 min)
d Emile Ardolino. *p* Emile Ardolino, Cindy Gilmore. *sc* Arthur Laurents. *ph* Ralf D Bode. *ed* William H Reynolds. *pd* Jackson de Govia. *songs* Jule Styne, Stephen Sondheim. *cast* Bette Midler, Peter Riegert, Cynthia Gibb, Jennifer Beck, Ed Asner, Lacey Chabert, Elisabeth Moss, Keene Curtis.

●A second adaptation, this time for television, of the musical on the life of stripper Gypsy Rose Lee is a traditional genre piece in '40s mode. Midler's hellish showbiz mom steals the picture against not much opposition. JBa

Gypsy and the Gentleman, The

(1957, GB, 107min)
d Joseph Losey. *p* Maurice Cowan. *sc* Janet Greene. *ph* Jack Hildyard. *ed* Reginald Beck. *ad* Ralph Brinton. *m* Hans May. *cast* Melina Mercouri, Keith Michell, Patrick McGoohan, Lyndon Brook, June Laverick, Flora Robson, Mervyn Johns.

●In an uneven Regency-period melodrama, neither Mercouri as a flashy-eyed gypsy girl nor Michell as the arrogant minor aristocrat she pursues to raise her standing could be said to give subtle performances. Neither are they aided by by a story that echoes the worst aspects of the costume romp in its mechanical contrivance. But seen as a typical Losey film in which class and sexual passion lead to death and destruction, it's not without interest, particularly in view of the director's bold attempt to match prints by Rowlandson and avoid Technicolor prettiness. DT

Gypsy Moths, The

(1969, US, 106 min)
d John Frankenheimer. *p* Hal Landers, Bobby Roberts. *sc* William Hanley. ph Philip H Lathrop. *ed* Henry Berman. *ad* George W Davis, Cary Odell. *m* Elmer Bernstein. *cast* Burt Lancaster, Deborah Kerr, Gene Hackman, Scott Wilson, William Windom, Bonnie Bedelia, Sheree North.

●In many ways a flawed film – the attempt at mixing the action of a *Grand Prix* and the small town disillusionments of an *All Fall Down* doesn't entirely come off – *The Gypsy Moths* is none the less one of Frankenheimer's most satisfying works. Dealing with a trio of sky-divers who for a variety of reasons are growing ambivalent about their 'careers', and the inhabitants of a small town who feel both threatened and attracted to the parachutists, the film manages to catch equally well the quiet desperation of small town life and the growing disillusionment of incessant travellers in search of glamour. The performances by Lancaster, Kerr and Hackman are superb. PH

Gypsy Soul (Alma Gitana)

(1995, Sp, 92 min)
d Chus Gutiérrez. *p* Antonio Conesa, Juan Vicente Córdoba. *sc* Antonio Conesa, Juan Vicente Córdoba, Joaquin Jordà, Chus Gutiérrez. *ph* Arnaldo Catinari. *ad* Fernando Pardo. *pd* Angel Haro. *m* Adolfo Rivéro. *cast* Amara Carmona, Pedro Alonso, Peret, Loles León, Rafael Alvárez 'El Brujo', Julieta Serrano.

●Taking inspiration from *Romeo and Juliet*, and also probably *Strictly Ballroom*, this flamenco romance is a fairy tale set in Madrid. Handsome, womanising Antonio wants to become a flamenco star, but hasn't enough gypsy in his soul to pass muster – that's also the problem when he meets and falls for Lucia, a serious student whose patriarchal family don't want her hanging out with non-gypsies. Stylishly shot but with no new spin on macho mores. GA

h

Harry Potter and the Philosopher's Stone

Hackers

(1995, US, 105 min)
d Iain Softley. *p* Michael Peyser, Ralph Winter. *sc* Rafael Moreau. *ph* Andrzej Sekula. *ed* Chris Blunden, Martin Walsh. *pd* John Beard. *m* Simon Boswell. *cast* Fisher Stevens, Jonny Lee Miller, Angelina Jolie, Jesse Bradford, Matthew Lillard, Laurence Mason, Renoly Santiago.

● Blurring the line between heightened reality and hi-tech fantasy, this presents the virtual world that hackers imagine, rather than the one they inhabit. Busted seven years earlier for causing computer chaos on Wall Street, the legendary 'Zero Cool' (Miller) is now 18 and hooked up with a wacky, multi-ethnic gang of hackers and phone phreaks. While Zero and spiky femme 'Acid Burn' (Jolie) channel their sexual attraction into competing for the top hacker slot, 'Cereal Killer', 'Phantom Freak' and 'Crash Override' define their place in the rebel tribe by pulling harmless on-line stunts. But things get serious when the Secret Service cracks down and 'The Plague' (Stevens), hacker turned security expert, sets them up to take the fall for his internal scam, siphoning millions of dollars from the mega-corporation that employs him to keep them out. Directed with verve, and driven forward by a wrap-around electronic score, this brilliantly captures the energy and insolence of virtual teen rebellion. The sappy ending's hard to take, but the on-line showdown between The Plague, the Secret Service and the united worldwide community of hackers is nail-biting. NF

Hail! Hail! Rock'n'Roll

(1987, US, 121 min)
d Taylor Hackford. *p* Stephanie Bennett, Chuck Berry. *ph* Oliver Stapleton. *ed* Lisa Day. *with* Chuck Berry, Eric Clapton, Robert Cray, Johnnie Johnson, Etta James, Julian Lennon, Keith Richards, Linda Ronstadt, Jerry Lee Lewis, Bruce Springsteen.

● Early on in Hackford's well-researched documentary and concert film about the legendary Chuck Berry, we see Berry outside the Fox Theatre in St Louis, from which he was excluded as a boy because of his colour, and now to be the scene of his 60th birthday concert. Interviews with Berry's contemporaries – pianist and former partner Johnnie Johnson, wild man Little Richard and Bo Diddley – stress his originality, while family members fill in the personal background. Unusually, the emphasis is on the development of his unique guitar sound, with keen insights into his diverse influences. Berry's voice is shot, and several songs – 'School Days', 'Sweet Little Sixteen', 'Memphis' – fall hopelessly flat, but his guest stars do him proud: Richard's clanging riffs on 'Little Queenie', Clapton's bluesy licks on 'Wee Wee Hours', and R & B queen Etta James' gutsy, soulful singing on 'Rock'n'Roll Music'. The sound recording is excellent, and the fluid camerawork and sharp editing capture the live concert atmosphere. NF

Hail, Mary (Je Vous Salue, Marie)

(1984, Fr/Switz, 107 min)
d/sc Jean-Luc Godard. *ph* Jean-Bernard Menoud, Jacques Firmann. *m* Johann Sebastian Bach, Antonín Dvorak, John Coltrane. *cast* Myriem Roussel, Thierry Rode, Philippe Lacoste, Manon Andersen, Juliette Binoche, Malachi Jara Kohan.

● Wily Godard has located the Biblical story of the Virgin Birth among the present-day Swiss. Godard's Mary (beautifully incarnated by Roussel, his Karina-like discovery) has to cope with an unconvinced and irritable Joseph, eventually almost beaten into submission by an oafish Gabriel, who performs the Annunciation at a petrol station. While Joseph learns the hardest of ways that love is not all fleshly desire, a parallel story tells of a young girl called Eva receiving a painful lesson in male inconstancy. Composed like a brilliant mosaic, Godard's film gives fresh meaning to everyday images; makes us listen to Dvorak with renewed appreciation; and shows the female nude as though never filmed before. DT

Hail the Conquering Hero

(1944, US, 101 min, b/w)
d/sc Preston Sturges. *ph* John F Seitz. *ed* Stuart Gilmore. *ad* Hans Dreier, Haldane Douglas. *m* Sigmund Krumgold, Werner R Heymann. *cast* Eddie Bracken, Ella Raines, Raymond Walburn, William Demarest, Elizabeth Patterson, Jimmy Conlin, Franklin Pangborn, Vic Potel, Torben Meyer, Robert Warwick, Dewey Robinson.

● Wonderful satire on small-town jingoism, all the more remarkable in that it was made during World War II. Bracken is the scrawny Marine, son of a World War I hero, instantly invalided out because of hay fever. Terrified at this mortal blow to family pride, he hides out as a shipyard worker while pretending to be overseas, until forcibly escorted home by six sympathetic Marines who learn his story. But a quirk of the telephone wires has translated 'hay' into 'jungle' fever, and to his horror he finds a civic welcome awaiting him as a Pacific war hero, with worse to come when he is adopted by acclaim as candidate for mayor. The ending has been taxed with sentimentality, although it is in fact deeply ironic. Otherwise no Middle American sacred cow (from mom and apple pie to heroic fathers) is spared in this hilarious blend of satire, slapstick and comedy of manners, with marvellous dialogue full of dizzy non-sequiturs and an amazing gallery of grotesque characters. TM

Haine, La (Hate)

(1995, Fr, 98 min, b/w)
d Mathieu Kassovitz. *p* Christophe Rossignon. *sc* Mathieu Kassovitz. *ph* Pierre Aim. *ed* Mathieu Kassovitz, Scott Stevenson. *ad* Giuseppe Ponturo. *cast* Vincent Cassel, Hubert Koundé, Saïd Taghmaoui, Karim Belkhadra, Edouard Montoute, François Levantal.

● Twenty-four hours in the Paris projects: an Arab boy is critically wounded in hospital, gut-shot, and a police revolver has found its way into the hands of a young Jewish skinhead, Vinz (Cassel), who vows to even the score if his pal dies. Vinz hangs out with Hubert (Koundé) and Saïd (Taghmaoui). They razz each other about films, cartoons, nothing in particular, but always the gun hovers over them like a death sentence, the black-and-white focal point for all the hatred they meet with, and all they can give back. Kassovitz has made only one film before (the droll race-comedy *Métisse*), but *La Haine* puts him right at the front of the field: this is virtuoso, on-the-edge stuff, as exciting as anything we've seen from the States in ages, and more thoroughly engaged with the reality it describes. He combats the inertia and boredom of his frustrated antagonists with a thrusting, jiving camera style which harries and punctuates their rambling, often very funny dialogue. The politics of the piece are confrontational, to say the least, but there is a maturity and depth to the characterisation which goes beyond mere agitprop: society may be on the point of self-combustion, but this film betrays no appetite for the explosion. A vital, scalding piece of work. TCh

Hair

(1979, US, 121 min)
d Milos Forman. *p* Lester Persky, Michael Butler. *sc* Michael Weller. *ph* Miroslav Ondricek. *ed* Stan Warnow, Alan Heim. *pd* Stuart Wurtzel. *m* Galt MacDermot. *cast* John Savage, Treat Williams, Beverly D'Angelo, Annie Golden, Dorsey Wright, Don Dacus, Nicholas Ray, Twyla Tharp.

● Other than providing the full stop to his would-be '60s trilogy (previous episodes: *Taking Off* and *One Flew Over the Cuckoo's Nest*), it's difficult to determine what could have attracted Forman to a musical as hopelessly leaden as *Hair* and its uneasy amalgam of draft-card burning, cosmic consciousness, ill-judged comedy and dopey sentimentality. Sounding, and for the most part looking, like a National Lampoon parody of some ghastly Swinging Sixties compendium, it lacks even the vitality of the stage show (books/lyrics James Rado, Gerome Ragni), which was at least persuasively ingenuous. The problem with *Hair* is that it's neither old enough to have acquired the picturesque dignity of a period piece, nor young enough to have the slightest contemporary relevance. The result is a smug, banal fairytale-with-a-message, redeemed only by the intermittently imaginative staging of the songs. AC

Hairdresser's Husband, The (Le Mari de la coiffeuse)

(1990, Fr, 80 min)
d Patrice Leconte. *p* Thierry de Ganay. *sc* Claude Klotz, Patrice Leconte. *ph* Eduardo Serra. *ed* Joëlle Hache. *ad* Ivan Maussion. *m* Michael Nyman. *cast* Jean Rochefort, Anna Galiena, Roland Bertin, Maurice Chevit, Philippe Clévenot, Jacques Mathou, Tricky Holgado.

● Aged 12, Antoine has two passions: dancing to Arabic music, and having his hair cut by an ample Alsacienne who unwittingly introduces him to the world of sex. In middle age, Antoine (Rochefort) has lost none of his ardour: when he glimpses shy *coiffeuse* Mathilde (Galiena), he is so struck that he immediately proposes marriage. Amazingly she accepts, and he moves into her salon, where their blissful romance remains barely touched by the outside world... While Leconte's study in erotic obsession is, like *Monsieur Hire*, hardly sophisticated in its sexual politics, that's not to deny its eccentric charm. Lighter in tone than its predecessor, it benefits from a genuinely scatty performance by Rochefort, and from a fine line in off-the-wall humour. Less successful is the shift to a darker mood: this bitter-sweet comedy barely justifies its downbeat outcome. That said, Eduardo Serra's elegant photography and Michael Nyman's score perfectly complement the blend of wit and melancholia. GA

Hair Opera, The (Mohatsu Kageki)

(1992, Jap, 61 min)
d Yuri Obitani. *cast* Yuri Obitani, Yosefu Kosuzu, Tomoko Kamisaki.

● Obitani is a trainee opera singer and aspiring film-maker casting about for ways to entertain his audience when he learns of an exhibition by woman artist Yosefu Kosuzu; it comprises neatly mounted and dated specimens of pubic hair from all the men she has slept with. Obitani excitedly interviews her and then invites her to exchange film 'letters' with him. The film is mostly a compilation of those letters, chronicling a conceptual relationship which begins to break down when it emerges that what Obitani wants most is a place in Kosuzu's *next* exhibition. Already a classic of Japanese independent cinema, this is the most startling first-person film-making since David Holzman's famous *Diary*. The climactic shaving scene left me almost on the floor. TR

Hairspray

(1988, US, 92 min)
d John Waters. *p* Rachel Talalay. *sc* John Waters. *ph* David Insley. *ed* Janice Hampton. *ad* Vincent Peranio. *m* Kenny Vance. *cast* Divine, Debbie Harry, Sonny Bono, Ricki Lake, Colleen Fitzpatrick, Ruth Brown, Pia Zadora, Ric Ocasek, Mink Stole.

● Waters' most hygienically commercial film is a Retro schlock-fancier's delight. Remember backcombing and the beehive, pale-pink lipstick, acid yellows, that first kiss? Tracy Turnblad (Lake), fat teenie offspring of fatter Edna (Divine), dreams of winning the dance crown on *The Corny Collins Show* on TV, but falls foul of bitchy queen-of-the-hop Amber von Tussle (Fitzpatrick) and her grotesquely unscrupulous parents (Harry and Bono). Also on the strength are Ruth Brown as Motormouth Maybelle, Pia Zadora as a beatnik, and plenty of vigorous hoofing to the unlamented Madison. BC

Halbe Welt (Half World)

(1993, Aus, 83 min)
d Florian Flicker *p* Helmut Grasser. *sc* Florian Flicker, Michael Sturminger. *ph* Jerzy Palacz. *ed* Bernhard Weirather. *pd* Renate Martin, Andreas Donhauser. *m* Andreas Haller. *cast* Rainer Egger, Daniel Levy, Maria Schrader, Mercedes Echerer, Goran Rebic.

● This ultimately exasperating slice of Austrian sci-fi conjures up a metropolitan society where the sun's rays have become fatal and life continues at night or behind shades. Controlling all images of the sunlit world now off-limits is the all powerful Luna organisation, but a disparate band of rebels stands determined to free themselves from the dark and re-embrace the light. Unfortunately, this is only half the movie. There's the germ of an idea, excellent use of Vienna and Hamburg locations, and impressive high-contrast photography, yet the plotting and characterisation are dispiritingly minimal and one's interest soon flags. A missed opportunity. TJ

Half a Sixpence

(1967, GB/US, 146 min)
d George Sidney. *p* Charles H Schneer, George Sidney. *sc* Beverley Cross. *ph* Geoffrey Unsworth. *ed* William Lewthwaite, Frank Santillo. *pd* Ted Haworth. *m* David Heneker. *cast* Tommy Steele, Julia Foster, Cyril Ritchard, Penelope Horner, Elaine Taylor, Hilton Edwards, Pamela Brown, James Villiers, Alan Cuthbertson.
Tommy Steele originated the role of the draper's assistant who comes into money and moves up the social scale without automatically finding the happiness he desires in Beverley Cross's musical play adapted from HG Wells' novel *Kipps*. Made in the days when American studios were throwing money at anything British that could move under its own power, the film lays on the period charm rather exhaustingly, and the songs ('Flash! Bang! Wallop! What a Picture!' being the highlight) don't exactly sweep you along. The star smiles and smiles – and smiles. TJ

Half-Breed, The

(1952, US, 81 min)
d Stuart Gilmore. *p* Herman Schlom. *sc* Harold Shumate, Richard Wormser. *ph* William V Skall. *ed* Samuel E Beetley. *ad* Albert S D'Agostino, Ralph Berger. *m* Paul Sawtell. *cast* Robert Young, Janis Carter, Jack Buetel, Reed Hadley, Barton MacLane, Porter Hall, Connie Gilchrist.
● Well-meaning but rather dull Western, clearly derivative of the earlier *Broken Arrow* as it ladles out a message about how the Indians were only mean because some white men had been mean to them first. Buetel (Billy the Kid in *The Outlaw*) is ineffectual as the title character, trying to forge the bonds of friendship between whites and Indians in the face of gold-greedy shit-stirring from Hadley, although Young adds a touch of class as the good liberal gambler who saves the day. GA

Half Life

(1985, Aust, 84 min. b/w & col)
d/p/sc/ph Dennis O'Rourke. *ed* Tim Litchfield.
● After World War II, the Marshall Islands were entrusted by the United Nations to the care of Uncle Sam, who generously staged some 66 nuclear tests in this Pacific paradise. This documentary focuses on Operation Bravo, an explosion over 1,000 times bigger than Hiroshima, detonated in (the film claims) full knowledge that winds would carry radiation straight to two of the atolls. Navy officials stood by in specially insulated ships as kids played in the nuclear 'snow'; US propaganda films crowed over the 'stupendous blast' and the (quote) 'happy, amenable savages' providing 'valuable data' on the bomb's hideous long-term effects. Drawing on recently declassified US Defense Department footage, O'Rourke presents his case with textbook clarity and intelligence. The fallout from this blast from the past lingers on, and the breathtaking cynicism of the Americans in the whole affair should, at the very least, give pause to ponder the speed at which our own sceptred isle is turning into Airstrip One. SJo

Half Moon Street

(1986, US, 89 min)
d Bob Swaim. *p* Geoffrey Reeve. *sc* Bob Swaim, Edward Behr. *ph* Peter Hannan. *ed* Richard Marden. *pd* Tony Curtis. *m* Richard Harvey. *cast* Sigourney Weaver, Michael Caine, Patrick Kavanagh, Faith Kent, Ram John Holder, Keith Buckley, Annie Hanson.
● An American linguist and economist working in London, Dr Slaughter (Weaver) supplements her meagre income by prostitution. The relationship she strikes up with a regular client, troubleshooting diplomat Lord Bulbeck (Caine), not only follows the customary course of clandestine trysts and growing jealousy, but also entangles her in a web of violent political intrigue. Adapted from Paul Theroux's novel *Dr Slaughter*, Swaim's follow-up to *La Balance* is a dud. Without decent direction, Weaver's portrayal of a woman intent on exercising full control over her life, but unwittingly manipulated by all around her, seems merely embarrassed, while – with the exception of the dependable Caine – the supporting characterisations are woefully thin. London becomes a familiar topographical mish-mash, the narrative is ramshackle, and even the action set pieces – the most memorable aspect of the earlier film – are clumsily executed. GA

Half World

see Halbe Welt

Hallelujah, I'm a Bum (aka Hallelujah, I'm a Tramp/ Lazybones)

(1933, US, 82 min, b/w)
d/p Lewis Milestone. *sc* SN Behrman, Ben Hecht. *ph* Lucien Andriot. *ad* Richard Day. *songs* Richard Rodgers, Lorenz Hart. *cast* Al Jolson, Madge Evans, Harry Langdon, Frank Morgan, Chester Conklin, Bert Roach, Edgar Connor.
● An intriguing but curiously botched follow-up to the enchanting *Love Me Tonight*, again using a Rodgers & Hart score structured by rhyming recitative. Jolson, hardly the ideal R&H interpreter anyway, is horribly miscast as the leader of a band of Depression down-and-outs who haunt Central Park: he just hasn't the persona to play a Byronic hero of social protest who accepts a job because he falls in love, and drops out again when love fails him. The script, mixing cynicism with sentimentality in a manner typical of Ben Hecht (who co-authored with SN Behrman), also veers uncertainly between pursuing its Depression themes and elaborating its singularly turgid romantic complications (where the heroine, conveniently amnesiac, shuttles between two equally unlikely suitors). Some of the infelicities were probably due to production problems, since the film was started by Harry D'Abbadie D'Arrast, continued by Milestone (who brought in R&H), and completed (apparently at Jolson's insistence) by Chester Erskine. The songs make pleasant but not great listening. TM

Hallelujah the Hills

(1962, US, 86 min, b/w)
d Adolfas Mekas. *p* David C Stone. *sc* Adolfas Mekas. *ph* Ed Emshwiller. *ed* Adolfas Mekas. *m* Meyer Kupferman. *cast* Peter H Beard, Sheila Finn, Martin Greenbaum, Peggy Steffans, Jerome Raphael, Blanche Dee, Jerome Hill, Taylor Mead.
● A highpoint from the 'innocent' years of American underground cinema, and something of an enduring delight for real film buffs. Mekas' comedy starts from an enthusiastic parody of French 'new wave' concepts like using two actresses to play one character, and manages to go on to incorporate references (part satire, part homage) to what seems like every other branch of cinema extant. It ranges from samurai movies to Chaplinesque slapstick, and it hits the intended tone between love and scepticism far more often than you'd have thought possible. The main thing is that it's recklessly enthusiastic about itself and about cinema in general – and the enthusiasm is infectious. TR

Halliday Brand, The

(1956, US, 78 min, b/w)
d Joseph H Lewis. *p* Collier Young. *sc* George F Slavin, George W George. *ph* Ray Rennahan. *ed* Michael Luciano, Stuart O'Brien. *ad* David Garber. *m* Stanley Wilson. *cast* Joseph Cotten, Viveca Lindfors, Betsy Blair, Ward Bond, Bill Williams, Jay C Flippen, Christopher Dark, Jeanette Nolan, Peter Ortiz.
● If ever a movie justified the once-modish tag of 'psychological Western', it's this one. Lewis' film has been unforgiveably neglected, for it matches his unique visual intelligence to a remarkably explicit critique of patriarchal law. Ward Bond's tyrannical authority, exerted over both family and community (of which he is 'founding father' and sheriff) is classically grounded in an obsessive fear of otherness. His brutal defence of race purity (against the Indians whose fathers he 'tamed' and dispossessed) sparks off the conflict with his own son (Cotten) which gives the film its headlong impetus and its characteristic violence. The psychological – and political – resonances are specified in the clarity of Lewis' visual metaphors (the gun in the foreground; dead wood littering the frame), which gloriously transcend the minor irritants of miscasting and underbudgeting. Impressive. PT

Halloween

(1978, US, 91 min)
d John Carpenter. *p* Debra Hill. *sc* John Carpenter, Debra Hill. *ph* Dean Cundey. *ed* Tommy Lee Wallace, Charles Bornstein. *pd* Tommy Lee Wallace. *m* John Carpenter. *cast* Donald Pleasence, Jamie Lee Curtis, Nancy Loomis, PJ Soles, Charles Cyphers, Kyle Richards, Brian Andrews, John Michael Graham.
● A superb essay in Hitchcockian suspense, which puts all its sleazy *Friday the 13th* imitators to shame with its dazzling skills and mocking wit. Rarely have the remoter corners of the screen been used to such good effect as shifting volumes of darkness and light reveal the presence of a sinister something. We know, and Carpenter knows we know, that it's all a game as his psycho starts decimating teenagers observed in the sexual act; and he delights in being one step ahead of expectation, revealing nothing when there should be something, and something – as in the subtle reframing of the girl sobbing in the doorway after she finally manages to kill the killer, showing the corpse suddenly sitting up again behind her – long after there should be nothing. Perhaps not quite so resonant as *Psycho* to which it pays due homage, but it breathes the same air. TM

Halloween II

(1981, US, 92 min)
d Rick Rosenthal. *p* Debra Hill, John Carpenter. *sc* Debra Hill. *ph* Dean Cundey. *ed* Mark Goldblatt, Skip Schoolnik. *pd* J Michael Riva. *m* John Carpenter. *cast* Jamie Lee Curtis, Donald Pleasence, Charles Cyphers, Jeffrey Kramer, Lance Guest, Pamela Susan Shoop, Hunter Von Leer.
● The first *Halloween* had such an ancient maniac-on-the-loose theme that it was easy to miss just how original the film was in its use of the new gliding Steadicam to prolong audience identification with the villain. Rosenthal is no Carpenter, but he makes a fair job of emulating the latter's visual style in this sequel (co-scripted by Carpenter) which takes up where the earlier film left off. The action is now largely set in a terrorised local hospital, while the villain has so palpably become an agent of Absolute Evil that any associations with contemporary sexual violence are fortunately diminished. The result won't make any converts, but Jamie Lee Curtis is as good as ever. DP

Halloween III: Season of the Witch

(1983, US, 98 min)
d Tommy Lee Wallace. *p* Debra Hill, John Carpenter. *sc* Tommy Lee Wallace. *ph* Dean Cundey. *ed* Millie Moore. *pd* Peter Jamison. *m* John Carpenter, Alan Howarth. *cast* Tom Atkins, Stacey Nelkin, Dan O'Herlihy, Ralph Strait, Michael Currie, Jadeen Barbor, Bradley Schachter, Garn Stephens.
● The title is a bit of a cheat, since the indestructible psycho of the first two films plays no part here. With the possibilities of the character well and truly exhausted, *Season of the Witch* turns more profitably to a marvellously ingenious Nigel Kneale tale of a toymaker and his fiendish plan to restore Halloween to its witch cult origins (involving a TV commercial for toy masks that are in fact diabolical engines). Kneale had his name removed from the credits after tampering with his script had reduced O'Herlihy's toymaker – originally bathed in Celtic mists of myth and magic – to the conventional mad doctor. The end result is a bit of a mess but hugely enjoyable, and often (thanks to Dean Cundey's camerawork and John Carpenter's close supervision as producer) as striking visually as its predecessors. TM

Halloween 4: The Return of Michael Myers

(1988, US, 88 min)
d Dwight H Little. *p* Paul Freeman. *sc* Alan McElroy. *ph* Peter Lyons Collister. *ed* Curtiss Clayton. *ad* Roger S Crandall. *m* Alan Howarth. *cast* Donald Pleasence, Ellie Cornell, Danielle Harris, Michael Pataki, Beau Starr, Kathleen Kinmont, Sasha Jenson, George P Wilbur.
● Ten years after his incarceration in a maximum security prison, catatonic ex-knife-wielder Michael Myers (Wilbur) finds himself

transferred to a 'normal' hospital. In no time at all our boy snaps out of his decade-long coma, stiffs a few ambulance men, and trudges off to his old haunting ground of Haddonfield, intent upon introducing his cutesy-pop little niece (Harris) to the cutting edge of his eccentric behaviour. 'Evil... on two legs!' exclaims deranged, disfigured Dr Loomis (Pleasence), before steaming off in search of his favourite patient. Then it's the usual town-under-siege-by-indestructible-psycho nonsense: the Halloween celebrations are curtailed by Michael's festive antics; police officers are massacred (off-screen, naturally); kiddies are terrorised; promiscuous teenagers discover that if you make out behind your parents' backs the bogeyman will slice you up. *Halloween III* ditched Myers, realising that as an archetypal harbinger of doom he was a dead duck. It's a shame that the lure of the cash registers resurrected the beleagured bore. The shocks are infinitesimal, the script diabolical. MK

Halloween: The Curse of Michael Myers

(1995, US, 88 min)
d Joe Chappelle. *p* Paul Freeman. *sc* Daniel Farrands. *ph* Billy Dickson. *ed* Randy Bricker. *m* Alan Howarth. *cast* Donald Pleasence, Mitchell Ryan, Paul Rudd, Marianne Hagan, Mariah O'Brien. Leo Geter, George P Wilbur.

● You know you're in trouble when they stop numbering the sequels; this is the sixth, if anyone's counting. The unkillable chappie remains unkilled after offing a host of unknown faces on Halloween, only this time he's egged on by evil doctors and black magic. A series of competently engineered shock moments jollied along by a jazzed-up version of John Carpenter's original electronic score: slicker than crude oil and just as unattractive. AO

Halloween H20 – 20 Years Later

(1998, US, 87 min)
d Steve Miner. *p* Paul Freeman. *sc* Robert Zappia, Matt Greenberg. *ph* Daryn Okada. *ed* Patrick Lussier. *pd* John Willett. *m* John Ottman. *cast* Jamie Lee Curtis, Adam Arkin, Michelle Williams, Adam Hann-Byrd, Jodi Lyn O'Keefe, Janet Leigh, Josh Hartnett, Chris Durand.

● Curtis touches up her scream queen roots with a complex reworking of the Laurie Strode character she created for John Carpenter's groundbreaking original. Twenty years on, Laurie is the headmistress of a private school and the divorced, alcoholic and over-protective mother of a 17-year-old son. Still obsessed with the Halloween night when her homicidal brother Michael Myers came home, Laurie confronts the twentieth anniversary with paralysing fear and liberal doses of booze. Her son, meanwhile, skips a school camping trip in favour of an intimate party with his girlfriend and another couple; so when 'The Shape' reappears, right on cue, there's plenty of young flesh for him to slice up. Despite a tedious set-up and saggy middle section, things gather pace as the teen victims are dispatched in a variety of nasty ways. While Carpenter's film was all about economy and a skilful use of empty space, Miner's busy compositions have a cluttered feel that is echoed by superfluous orchestral music, which merely washes over the original's spare, atmospheric electronic score. NF

Halls of Montezuma

(1950, US, 112 min)
d Lewis Milestone. *p* Robert Bassler. *sc* Michael Blankfort. *ph* Winton C Hoch, Harry Jackson. *ed* William H Reynolds. *ad* Lyle Wheeler, Albert Hogsett. *m* Sol Kaplan. *cast* Richard Widmark, Walter [Jack] Palance, Reginald Gardiner, Robert Wagner, Skip Homeier, Richard Boone, Jack Webb, Karl Malden.

● Rough tough US Marines hunt down a Japanese rocket base in the Pacific Basin in this standard guts-or-glory WWII flagwaver. Capably put together by Milestone, who cut in real combat footage with the mock-up set-pieces shot in the US at Camp Pendleton, but it's hard to believe this is the same man who 21 years earlier made the landmark anti-war movie *All Quiet on the Western Front*. TJ

Hambone and Hillie (aka The Adventures of Hambone and Hillie)

(1983, US, 90 min)
d Roy Watts. *p* Gary Gillingham, Sandy Howard. *sc* Sandra Bailey, Michael S Murphey, Joel Soisson. *ph* Jon Kranhouse. *ed* RJ Kizer. *pd* Helena Reif. *m* Georges Garvarentz. *cast* Lillian Gish, Timothy Bottoms, Candy Clark, OJ Simpson, Robert Walker, Jack Carter, Alan Hale Jr, Anne Lockhart.

● Spunky li'l dog misplaces Lillian Gish at the airport. Not having the price of a transcontinental flight he's reduced to walking. Will he die or get lost, or will he take the scenic route and meet colourful characters before reaching California? Take a wild guess. There's the sheriff's pregnant wife who needs a hand – well, a paw – when a psychotic intruder shows up, there's a narrow escape from a vivisectionist and the retrospective delight of an OJ Simpson cameo. Having a supernatural sense of direction but no map, Hambone crosses Illinois and Monument Valley on the way to the Sunshine State. It would be a shame to reveal whether the pooch and Hillie are reunited. DO

Hamburger Hill

(1987, US, 110 min)
d John Irvin. *p* Marcia Nasatir, James Carabatsos. *sc* James Carabatsos. *ph* Peter MacDonald. *ed* Peter Tanner. *pd* Austen Spriggs. *m* Philip Glass. *cast* Dylan McDermott, Steven Weber, Tim Quill, Don Cheadle, Michael Patrick Boatman, Anthony Barrile, Michael Dolan, Don James.

● Highly conventional in form, this traces the brutally brief odyssey of a group of infantrymen from training to bodybags in Vietnam. Hamburger Hill, for which most of the attacking grunts die, proves as pointless as the objective in *Paths of Glory*, but Irvin and screenwriter James Carabatsos reserve their indignation for the unappreciative citizenry back home. It isn't quite the old ours-is-not-to-question-why encomium, however, since the troops are poor whites and uneducated blacks who bitch continually about protesting hippies, each other, and do-or-die largely unreconciled. Applied sociology is all over the dialogue, though the obscenity quota mercifully drops as battle begins. There are a couple of rocky moments, but the large cast of unknowns go through hell convincingly, and illustrate the randomness of mortality. BC

Hamlet

(1913, GB, 5,800 ft, b/w)
d Hay Plumb. *cast* Johnston Forbes-Robertson, Gertrude Elliott, Walter Ringham, Adeleine Bourne, JH Barnes, SA Cookson, Alex Scott-Gatty, JH Ryley.

● Forbes-Robertson was known by London's theatre critics as 'the supreme Hamlet of his time'. This film, made on location at a specially built castle on the Dorset coast under the auspices of producer Cecil Hepworth, attempts to preserve his stage performance, as in aspic. Featured alongside the actor-knight are his American wife Gertrude Elliott (Ophelia) and the rest of the cast from a famous Drury Lane production. It's fascinating to see Forbes-Robertson's mannered, gestural performance, but at 60, he was 35 years too old for the part. Shakespeare without sound: a typically quixotic endeavour from Britain's pioneer film-makers. GM

Hamlet

(1948, GB, 155 min, b/w)
d Laurence Olivier. *ph* Desmond Dickinson. *sc* Laurence Olivier, Alan Dent. *ed* Helga Cranston. *pd* Roger Furse. *m* William Walton. *cast* Laurence Olivier, Eileen Herlie, Basil Sydney, Jean Simmons, Felix Aylmer, Stanley Holloway, Terence Morgan, Peter Cushing, Esmond Knight, Anthony Quayle.

● Despite winning several Oscars, Olivier's (condensed) version of Shakespeare's masterpiece makes for frustrating viewing: for all its 'cinematic' ambitions (the camera prowling pointlessly along the gloomy corridors of Elsinore), it's basically a stagy showcase for the mannered performance of the director in the lead role (though he's ably supported by a number of British theatrical stalwarts). Not half as powerful as Kozintsev's marvellous Russian version. GA

Hamlet

(1964, USSR, 150 min, b/w)
d/sc Grigori Kozintsev. *ph* Jonas Gritsius. *ed* E Makhankova. *ad* E Ene, Georgi Kropachev. *m* Dimitri Shostakovich. *cast* Innokenti Smoktunovsky, Mikhail Nazvanov, Elza Radzin-Szolkonis, Yuri Tolubeyev, Anastasia Virtinskaya, V Erenberg, S Oleksenko.

● Featuring a positive hero (predictably, the 'Now might I do it pat' soliloquy of prevarication has been cut), the action unfolds between shots of lowering rocks and turbulent seas, with Hamlet pattering through a very tangible Elsinore of massive portcullises, stone walls, endless corridors and chunky oaken furniture. A little monolithic in theory, but it works magnificently because Kozintsev has thought his interpretation right through to the end with complete consistency, and gives the film a genuinely exciting epic sweep. What one remembers, though, is the superb marginal detail: the appearance of the Ghost on the battlements, vast black cloak billowing in the wind, like a Titan striding across the sea; the dying Polonius pulling down the arras to reveal row upon row of tailor's dummies in Gertrude's wardrobe; above all, the wonderfully moving conception of Ophelia as a frail blonde marionette, first seen jerked into motion by the tinkling music of a cembalo at her dancing lesson, and gradually becoming the helpless plaything of court politics. There's a genuine cinematic imagination at work here. TM

Hamlet

(1969, GB, 117 min)
d Tony Richardson. *p* Neil Hartley. *ph* Gerry Fisher. *ed* Charles Rees. *ad* Jocelyn Herbert. *m* Patrick Gowers. *cast* Nicol Williamson, Anthony Hopkins, Judy Parfitt, Mark Dignam, Marianne Faithfull, Michael Pennington, Gordon Jackson, Roger Livesey, Roger Lloyd Pack, Anjelica Huston.

● The perennial problem in filming Shakespeare is what to do with all those stagy settings and backdrops; or alternatively, what to do with all those words, which tend to sound impossibly literary when set off against natural surroundings. Filming entirely in the Round House, where he had previously staged the play, Richardson solves the dilemma by concentrating almost exclusively on faces. Flurries of dark stone, vague impressions of courtiers and rich hangings; but mostly faces lower obsessively from the screen, surrounded by mysterious pools of darkness in which figures stealthily appear and disappear. The reason may be economy, but the result is an extraordinarily naked emphasis on the words and their meaning. Nicol Williamson's Hamlet, not exactly mellifluous but intelligent, mocking and volcanically explosive, is neatly disciplined by this approach; and apart from some roughnesses in the casting (and some curious textual omissions), it's interesting, imaginative, and certainly Richardson's best film. TM

Hamlet

(1976, GB, 67 min)
d/p/sc Celestino Coronado. *ph* Robina Rose, Dick Perrin, Andy Humphries, R Anthony. *ed* Richard Melling. *ad* Celestino Coronado, Anthony Meyer. *m* Carlos Miranda. *cast* Anthony Meyer, David Meyer, Helen Mirren, Quentin Crisp, Barry Stanton, Vladek Sheybal, Valentine Moon.

● Made impossibly cheaply (shot and mixed on video, then transferred to film) this obviously took great effort and dedication. But was it worth it? As a compression of the play, it's initially inventive but all too soon predictable: the device of having twin brothers play Hamlet wears very thin indeed. As an interpretation, it is most notable for taking the misogyny of the 'get thee to a nunnery' scene and applying it liberally to the rest of the play: having Helen Mirren play both lead women helps Coronado to sustain this reading. The misogynist bias puts the film's overall gay-camp sensibility in a very questionable light, and preening performances from Crisp and Sheybal don't help. At worst, offensive; at best, joyless. TR

Hamlet

(1990, US, 135 min)
d Franco Zeffirelli. *p* Dyson Lovell. *sc* Christopher De Vore, Franco Zeffirelli. *ph*

David Watkin. *ed* Richard Marden. *ad* Michael Lamont. *m* Ennio Morricone. *cast* Mel Gibson, Glenn Close, Alan Bates, Paul Scofield, Ian Holm, Helena Bonham-Carter, Stephen Dillane, Nathaniel Parker, Pete Postlethwaite.

●There are very few actors who could carry the risks of another cinematic reworking of *Hamlet* in an age when many younger film fans think the name refers to a small cigar. Mel Gibson and Glenn Close are two such stars, and, though the name of Franco Zeffirelli is unlikely to mean much to anyone under the age of 30, it must have been the Italian director's cultish *Romeo and Juliet*, rather than his recent string of cinematic no-nos such as *Endless Love* and *The Champ*, that soothed the backers. It's a surprisingly successful venture, decked out in Anglo-Saxon styles and with a brooding, robust castle setting which oozes horse muck. Gibson never gets much beyond the antic disposition and sports some bizarre curls, but Close gambols lustily as Gertrude, Helena Bonham-Carter makes a splendidly under-age Ophelia and, in other supporting roles, both a boozy-looking Bates and a pompous-sounding Ian Holm add great worth to the parts of Claudius and Polonius. Zeffirelli's darting, aerial, I-spy perspective more often adds to, rather than repeats, the effect of the verse, and all the cuts (including the opening battlements sequence) are eminently justified in the cause of narrative thrust. SGr

Hamlet

(1996, US/GB, 242 min)
d Kenneth Branagh. *p* David Barron. *sc* Kenneth Branagh. *ph* Alex Thomson. *ed* Neil Farrell. *pd* Tim Harvey. *m* Patrick Doyle. *cast* Kenneth Branagh, Julie Christie, BillyCrystal, Gérard Depardieu, Charlton Heston, Richard Briers, Derek Jacobi, Jack Lemmon, Robin Williams, Rufus Sewell, Richard Attenborough, Brian Blessed, Michael Bryant, Judi Dench, Reece Dinsdale, Ken Dodd, John Gielgud, Rosemary Harris, Michael Maloney, John Mills, Timothy Spall, Kate Winslet.

●If Branagh's ambitious film needs any kind of compliment, it is that at around four hours it carries itself perfectly well. The star/director has assembled one of the finest casts ever seen on the big screen: so the Player King is played by Heston, who at least gets to speak, unlike Gielgud, Dench, John Mills and Ken Dodd in a succession of parts which underline the text through imagined interludes. Sometimes the casting is regrettable (Jack Lemmon looking ill-at-ease as a superannuated sentry); at others tongue-in-cheek (Attenborough as the English ambassador) or wasteful (Depardieu as a one-scene monosyllabic spy). The role-playing scores most in the world of work and politics, warfare and diplomacy, as imagined by Briers' superb Polonius and Jacobi's Claudius. Branagh's prince is admirable: popular, versatile, frank, kind, ruthless, athletic, straight-backed, with a little-boy-lost voice to go with the martial one. Tim Harvey's production design makes Elsinore a highlight, creating a snow-swept Ruritania of chessboard floors, mirrored corridors, freezing courtyards. Drawbacks: an intrusive score; spurious sex scenes between Kate Winslet's Ophelia and Branagh's pre-antic Hamlet; and a full-scale Norwegian invasion during the final duel. But all in all, as near to Branagh's masterwork as dammit, and far better fun than a jig, or even a tale of bawdry. SGr

Hamlet

(2000, US, 111 min)
d Michael Almereyda. *p* Andrew Fierberg, Amy Hobby. *sc* Michael Almereyda. *ph* John de Borman. *ed* Kristina Boden. *pd* Gideon Ponte. *m* Carter Burwell. *cast* Ethan Hawke, Kyle MacLachlan, Diane Venora, Sam Shepard, Bill Murray, Liev Schreiber, Julia Stiles, Karl Geary, Jeffrey Wright, Paul Bartel.

●This runs less than half the length of Branagh's would-be definitive full-text adaptation and updates events to contemporary New York. Following the unexpected demise of the CEO, MacLachlan's Claudius has taken over the reins at Denmark Corporation, and sealed the deal by marrying the old man's very willing widow (Venora). Hawke is her son, a slacker prince who hides his hurt behind designer shades, a Peruvian woolly hat and a digicam. The film buzzes with gadgets and gizmos. Shepard is the ghost in the machine – first spotted on security camera videos – whose baleful looks give focus to this thoroughly modern Hamlet's overwhelming sense of static. Writer/director Almereyda sets 'To be or not to be' in Blockbuster video, a none too subtle pointer that this in-action hero is mired in media saturation, as well as indecision and self-doubt. When he does make a move, he makes a movie, and shows it in the corporate screening room to stir Claudius's guilty conscience. This *Hamlet* fails to muster tragic grandeur, and it's not quite the dazzler Baz Luhrmann made of *Romeo & Juliet*, but Almereyda modernises and streamlines without trivialising, and amplifies poetic melodrama with regular ingenuity and energy. TCh

Hamlet Goes Business (Hamlet Liikemaailmassa)

(1987, Fin, 86 min, b/w)
d/p/sc Aki Kaurismäki. *ph* Timo Salminen. *ed* Paija Talvio. *ad* Pertti Hilkamo. *m* Dimitri Shostakovich. *cast* Pirkka-Pekka Petelius, Esko Salminen, Kati Outinen, Elina Salo, Esko Nikkari, Pentti Auer.

●Kaurismäki's idiosycratic reworking of Shakespeare is concerned with money rather than melancholia. Transposed to modern Finland, it begins with the poisoning of the head of a family firm, leaving shiftless son Hamlet with a controlling 51 per cent interest. Learning that unprofitable mills and factories are to be sold off to buy a world monopoly in rubber-duck manufacture, Hamlet vetoes the move and starts a boardroom battle. Kaurismäki keeps this wacky idea afloat with farcial plotting, deadpan humour and cryptic dialogue. The overall tone is pure B-movie, the exaggerated emotions and Timo Salminen's glistening *noir* photography recalling Warners' crime melodramas of the '40s. The characters are ciphers, too: reduced to pawns in the board games, they have no life outside their assigned roles. Viewed in isolation, this might have seemed merely promising; seen in combination with *Ariel* and *Leningrad Cowboys Go America*, it confirms Kaurismäki's unique and unpredictable talent. NF

Hammers Over the Anvil

(1992, Aust, 101 min)
d Ann Turner. *p* Richard Mason, Ben Gannon. *sc* Peter Hepworth, Ann Turner. *ph* James Bartle. *ed* Ken Sallows. *pd* Ross Major. *m* Not Drowning, Waving. *cast* Russell Crowe, Charlotte Rampling, Alexander Outhred, Frankie J Holden, Jake Frost.

●In a rural community in Australia at the turn of the century, handicapped teenager Outhred discovers the mysteries of the adult world when he becomes the unwitting go-between in the affair of lusty horse-trader Crowe and romantically inclined Englishwoman Rampling, wife of the local landowner. The result with its voice-over documenting the artistic growth of the teenager, its glimpses of half-understood sexuality, and its trail of conflict between father and son – isn't badly made, just familiar. Ann Turner's *Celia*, an arresting rites-of-passage story about the terrors of childhood, promised better than this literary saga. TJ

Hammett

(1982, US, 97 min)
d Wim Wenders. *p* Fred Roos. *sc* Ross Thomas, Dennis O'Flaherty. *ph* Philip H Lathrop. *ph* Joseph Biroc. *ed* Barry Malkin, Marc Laub, Robert Q Lovett, Randy Roberts. *pd* Dean Tavoularis, Eugene Lee. *m* John Barry. *cast* Frederic Forrest, Peter Boyle, Marilu Henner, Roy Kinnear, Lydia Lei, Elisha Cook, RG Armstrong, Richard Bradford, Sylvia Sidney, Samuel Fuller, Ross Thomas.

●Wenders' first American movie is no conventional biopic, but a stunningly achieved fiction about the art and mystique of creating fiction. By 1928, Dashiell Hammett is a retired Pinkerton agent, aridly glossing the exploits of his old sidekick Jimmy Ryan as raw material for his magazine stories. But when the real Ryan turns up in San Francisco to plunge Hammett into a Chinatown conundrum of underage hookers, gunsel punks, stag movies, blackmail and murder, he uncovers at first hand the characters and canvas for such subsequent triumphs as *The Maltese Falcon*, and discovers within himself the seeds of Sam Spade. Wenders' double-edged examination of what Spade later called 'the stuff that dreams are made of' is rich and audacious, as much a homage to bygone Hollywood as to Hammett and the 'roman noir' he pioneered: almost entirely studio-shot, bit-cast with iconic veterans, hauntingly scored. Forrest incarnates the writer as a rumpled but uncreased Bogart; Boyle is the archetypal Archer-type loser; the whole cast plays just one beat away from the genre staples their characters would become in print and the movies. One to savour. PT

Hamsin

(1982, Isr, 88 min)
d Daniel Wachsman. *p* Jacob Lifshin. *sc* Daniel Wachsman, Danny Verete, Jacob Lifshin. *ph* Benny Hoffman. *ed* Levi Zinni. *ad* Frank Gempel, Bashir Abu-Rabia. *cast* Shlomo Tarshish, Hemda Levy, Ruth Geler, Shawaf Yassin, Daou Selim.

●This shows that art can sometimes do what no amount of political commentary and reporting can accomplish: provide the understanding that comes from knowing people, rather than knowing about them. In a small farming village in Northern Israel in 1982, suspicions arise that the central government intends to expropriate the local Arab lands. The consequent bitterness and hostility destroy old Arab-Jewish friendships and loyalties. The film is particularly good at conveying the texture of Israel: the look and character of a country that combines Third World and Western ways. There are weaknesses – some clumsy exposition and a too obvious Lawrentian sexuality – but they do not seriously diminish the film's pleasures, nor its importance. MH

Hamster Factor and Other Tales of Twelve Monkeys, The

(1996, US, 90 min)
d/p/sc/ph/ed Keith Fulton, Louis Pepe. *m* John Benskin. *with* Terry Gilliam.

●A documentary on the making of *12 Monkeys*, giving insights into its director Terry Gilliam (perfectionist but pragmatic, ambitious but amiable), and taking us through virtually the entire production process, from receiving the script and working out the budget, through shooting, editing and other aspects of post-production, to the marketing, previews, promotion and final release of the movie. Entertaining and illuminating. GA

Hana-Bi

(1997, Jap, 103 min)
d Takeshi Kitano. *p* Masayuki Mori, Yasushi Tsuge, Takio Yoshida. *sc* Takeshi Kitano. *ph* Hideo Yamamoto. *ed* Takeshi Kitano. *ad* Norihiro Isoda. *m* Joe Hisaishi. *cast* 'Beat' Takeshi, Kayoko Kishimoto, Ren Osugi, Susumu Terajima, Tetsu Watanabe, Taro Itsumi, Makoto Ashikawa, Yuko Daike.

●Kitano's Venice prize-winner mixes tenderness, violence and droll humour. A recently retired cop drifts towards a one-off crime, to help out a suicidal colleague crippled in a disastrous stake-out, and to take his terminally ill wife on one last trip around Japan. It's exceptionally assured, imaginative and idiosyncratic: the violence is sudden, brutal and almost all in the editing; the working of Kitano's own delightful paintings into the story is astonishingly resonant; the *mise-en-scène* as sharp and inventive as in *Sonatine*; and it's all held together by Beat Takeshi's unprecedentedly taciturn, impassive, but expressive performance, which is crucial to the film's emotional punch. Fans of Melville, Keaton, Hawks and Peckinpah should be especially impressed, but anyone with a modicum of patience, an open mind and a little love in their heart will probably recognise it as a masterpiece. GA

Hand, The

(1981, US, 104 min)
d Oliver Stone. *p* Edward R Pressman. *sc* Oliver Stone. *ph* King Baggot. *ed* Richard Marks. *pd* J Michael Riva. *m* James Horner. *cast* Michael Caine, Andréa Marcovicci, Annie McEnroe, Bruce McGill, Viveca Lindfors, Rosemary Murphy, Oliver Stone.

●Anyone having seen *Salvador* or *Platoon* who thinks that Oliver Stone is the best thing since sliced bread would do well not only to remember his scripts for *Midnight Express* and *Year of the Dragon*, but to catch this grotesque, unimaginative fiasco – clearly ripped off from *The Beast with Five Fingers* – in which cartoonist Caine has his mitt severed in an accident, and sees it commit a series of murderously vengeful crimes against his enemies. Silly and nasty. GA

Handful of Dust, A

(1987, GB, 118 min)
d Charles Sturridge. *p* Derek Granger. *sc* Tim Sullivan, Derek Granger, Charles Sturridge. *ph* Peter Hannan. *ed* Peter Coulson. *pd* Eileen Diss. *m* George Fenton. *cast* James Wilby, Kristin Scott Thomas, Rupert Graves, Anjelica Huston, Judi Dench, Alec Guinness, Graham Crowden, Beatie Edney, Stephen Fry.

●Here we go again, with the inevitable follow-up to *Brideshead Revisited*: heritage, haircuts and hooray Henries. This time the country house is a Gothic pile called Hetton, where the 'madly feudal' Tony Last (Wilby) lives with wife Brenda (Thomas) and young son John Andrew. Brenda, out of boredom, has an affair with John Beaver (Graves), a common golddigger. As these are the '30s, she pays for her infidelity with the death of her son. Evelyn Waugh's novel is a savage, ironic indictment of worthless people, but you wouldn't know it from the film. Sturridge directs the proceedings with all the gob-smacked wonder of a stable-boy at the ball; everything is taken at face value. Only when Brenda thinks John Beaver has copped it, and is relieved to discover that it is John Andrew instead, do we register any moral disgust. Great performances, glorious scenery, a magnificent waste of time. MS

Handgun (aka Deep in the Heart)

(1982, US, 101 min)
d/p/sc Tony Garnett. *ph* Charles Stewart. *ed* William Shapter. *pd* Lilly Kilvert. *m* Mike Post. *cast* Karen Young, Clayton Day, Suzie Humphreys, Helena Humann, Ben Jones.

●Garnett's first American movie, set in Dallas, is a curious amalgam of 'concerned' docudrama and *Lipstick*-style exploitation. Kathleen (Young), a nice Irish Catholic girl from Boston, squares up to the cowboy charmer (Day) who dates her and then rapes her at gunpoint. Unfortunately for the film's sexual politics, Kathleen opts for rough justice the Charles Bronson way, arming herself with a new 'masculinised' image (cropped hair, combat gear), a handgun and sharpshooting skills, before luring the baddie out to a midnight face-off and dumping him symbolically outside the County Courthouse. Garnett is clearly as seduced as his heroine by Wild West frontier mythology and life in the Lone Star state. Misfiring as serious social commentary, this ends up, beneath its veneer of casual naturalism, as a pseudo-feminist vigilante movie that celebrates the attitudes it affects to deplore. SJo

Handgun

(1993, US, 90 min)
d Whitney Ransick. *p* Bob Gosse, Larry Meistritch. *sc* Whitney Ransick. *ph* Michael Spiller. *ed* Tom McCardle. *pd* Andras Kanegson. *m* Douglas J Cuomo. *cast* Treat Williams, Paul Schulze, Seymour Cassel, Toby Huss, Angel Caban, Frank Vincent, Anna Thompson.

●This engaging thriller, set in New York, starts with a bang, as villain Jack (Cassel), father of George (Williams), ends up the sole survivor of a mega-heist firefight. The cops descend on George, catch him in flagrante, and locate his handgun. He goes on the run and is finally forced to hole-up with his brother Mike, a sleazebag con-man with a Woody Allen-like verbal delivery. Indie writer/director Ransick's debut is another offbeat post-modern character study of thieves without honour. Hand-held, droll and well-observed: maybe some of the dialogue could have been tightened, and some of the scenes rehearsed one more time, but it's still a winner, and Treat's a treat. WH

Händler der vier Jahreszeiten

see Merchant of Four Seasons, The

Handmaid's Tale, The (Die Geschichte der Dienerin)

(1990, US/WGer, 108 min)
d Volker Schlöndorff. *p* Daniel Wilson. *sc* Harold Pinter. *ph* Igor luther. *ed* David Ray. *pd* Tom Walsh. *m* Ryuichi Sakamoto. *cast* Natasha Richardson, Faye Dunaway, Aidan Quinn, Elizabeth McGovern, Victoria Tennant, Robert Duvall, Blanche Baker, Traci Lind.

●Margaret Atwood's novel is a remarkable tour de force, a kind of feminist *1984* which gradually builds up detail so that the full horror of the world created creeps up like a killer in the night: a vision of an America so obsessed with physical, environmental and moral pollution that it returns to a mix of old Calvinism and newer Fascism. It should have transferred well to the screen, particularly as Schlöndorff is a veteran of literary adaptation. Of the fine cast, both Richardson (as the titular surrogate mother chosen to give birth on behalf of the state) and Duvall (as her unwelcome mate, an ageing military bigwig) are particularly fine. Sadly, the faults in the film lie in Harold Pinter's uncharacteristically bland script, and often woefully inadequate design and direction: the latter often missing opportunities in key scenes, the former full of rather tacky and silly uniforms, symbols, vehicles, and particularly crass watchtowers. SGr

Hands (Ladoni/aka Palms)

(1993, Rus, 129 min, b/w)
d/p/sc/ph/ed Artur Aristakisyan.

●Aristakisyan's debut, set among the beggar population of his native Kishinev, the capital of Moldavia, takes fundamental issue with the foundations of the post-Soviet madhouse, but would seem challenging in any context. First, its form is unlike any conventional cinematic genre or stratagem. Drafted as a cinematic epistle from the film-maker to his unborn son, it allies individual case studies of several beggars, the visible subjects of the film, with a philosophy of socio-economic degeneration and individual salvation expounded in voice-over through Aristakisyan's counsel to his boy, soon to be 'scooped out' of his mother's womb. Aristakisyan presents a moral and political argument that is complex, alien and enigmatic. Crucial (if undefined) terms here are 'the system' and 'the Spirit'; the former corrupts and suppresses while the latter must be embraced with a stoicism and asceticism akin to that by which the beggars live. Pitched somewhere between Christian dialectical materialism and metaphysical anarchism, Aristakisyan's treatise ranges in tone between mysticism, gnomic utterances and deep pessimism. It's not a funny movie, and too long, but the monochrome photography can be very beautiful and the beggars are filmed with a respect which is neither sentimental nor fatuous. NB

Hands Across the Table

(1935, US, 79 min, b/w)
d Mitchell Leisen. *p* E Lloyd Sheldon. *sc* Norman Krasna, Vincent Lawrence, Herbert Fields. *ph* Ted Tetzlaff. *ed* William Shea. *m* Frederick Hollander. *cast* Carole Lombard, Fred MacMurray, Ralph Bellamy, Astrid Allwyn, Ruth Donnelly, Marie Prevost, William Demarest.

●After telling a friendly paraplegic that she's after money, not love, hotel manicurist Lombard bumps into MacMurray's impecunious man-about-town hopscotching down the corridor, and her personal credo slowly crumbles. But not in the riotous way of some other Paramount comedies from the period: Leisen skilfully moves his players through some occasionally creaky set pieces (a meal full of hiccups, a simulated long-distance telephone call) to arrive, in the last half-hour, at thoughtful scenes of considerable tenderness whose erotic undertow prevails even when MacMurray is bared to the waist under a sun lamp. And Lombard, in the first part tailor-made for her, proves herself as the only Hollywood person ever to be a great beauty, a great comedienne and a great actress all at once. GB

Hands of Orlac, The (Orlacs Hände)

(1924, Aus, 92 min, b/w)
d Robert Wiene. *sc* Ludwig Nerz. *ph* Hans Androschin, Günther Krampf. *ad* Stefan Wessely, Hans Rovc, Karl Exner. *cast* Conrad Veidt, Alexandra Sorina, Carmen Cartellieri, Fritz Kortner, Paul Askonas, Fritz Strassny.

●Wiene spent the early '20s trying to repeat his surprise success with *The Cabinet of Dr Caligari*. This adaptation of Maurice Renard's celebrated novel finds him exploring another 'horrific' theme, but using his repertoire of Expressionist effects more coolly. His version of the story (about a concert pianist who loses his hands in a train crash, and has the hands of an executed murderer grafted on in their place) opts for a 'realistic' denouement rather than a 'fantastic' one, but it still manages to generate some potent shocks from its confrontation between the hero and villain. Its most enduring quality is Veidt's tormented performance as Orlac. TR

Hands of Orlac, The

see Mad Love

Hands of the Ripper

(1971, GB, 85 min)
d Peter Sasdy. *p* Aida Young. *sc* LW Davidson. *ph* Ken Talbot. *ed* Chris Barnes. *ad* Roy Stannard. *m* Christopher Gunning. *cast* Eric Porter, Angharad Rees, Jane Merrow, Keith Bell, Derek Godfrey, Dora Bryan, Marjorie Rhodes, Norman Bird, Margaret Rawlings.

●Late Hammer horror with a hefty dose of cod Freud, as Jack the Ripper's daughter grows up to become a sexually disturbed homicidal maniac after seeing daddy butcher mommy. Rees is particularly effective in the role, while Sasdy keeps the tension reasonably high; nevertheless, one can't help experiencing a certain sense of déjà vu, for all the narrative ingenuity. GA

Hands Over the City

see Mani sulla Città, Le

Hands Up! (Rece do Góry)

(1967/1981, Pol, 78 min, b/w & col)
d Jerzy Skolimowski. *sc* Jerzy Skolimowski, Andrzej Kostenko. *ph* Witold Sobocinski, Andrzej Kostenko. *ed* Jerzy Skolimowski. *ad* Jaroslav Switoniak ('67), Janusz Sosnowski ('81). *m* Krzysztof Komeda ('67), Krzysztof Penderecki, Józef Skrek ('81). *cast* Jerzy Skolimowski, Bogumil Kobiela, Joanna Szczerbic, Adam Hanuszkiewcz, Tadeusz Lomnicki; and ('81) Jane Asher, Alan Bates, David Essez, Bruno Ganz, Karol Kulik, Mike Sarne, Gerald Scarfe, Volker Schlöndorff, Feliks Topolski, Fred Zinnemann.

●Though doubts have been expressed as to the wisdom of re-editing the original footage to make space for a prologue shot in 1981 in London and Beirut, Skolimowski's film, more aptly titled than he realised, proves well worth waiting for since its suppression by the Polish authorities in 1967. Shot in sepia and grey, bursting with '60s energy and invention, funny yet vitriolic, it details in consistently vivid imagery a collective psychodrama staged by four disillusioned students in an abandoned cattle truck. Unforgettable. GAd

Handsworth Songs

(1986, GB, 61 min)
d John Akomfrah. *p* Lina Gopaul. *sc* Black Audio Collective. *ph* Sebastian Shah. *ed* Brand Thumin, Anna Liebschner. *m* Trevor Mathison. *with* Handsworth and Aston Welfare Association, Asian Youth Movement (Birmingham), Sachkhand Nanak Dham. *voice-overs* Pervais Khan, Meera Syal, Yvonne Weekes.

●An invigorating and thoughtful documentary from the London-based Black Audio Film Collective that examines elements of the Black experience in Britain from the perspective of the tragic events of 1985: the Handsworth riots, the death and funeral of Cynthia Jarrett, and the – seemingly – ever downward path of race relations, brought to a head by the deteriorating economic plight of Britain in the '80s. What is in evidence here is a fertile and imaginative cinematic intelligence which, in waging 'the war of naming the problem', musters a range of archive material, interviews, and filmed records of the disturbances in such a way as to provide an essay that is as full of subtle, rich and allusive argument as it is devoid of empty didacticism and stridency. WH

Hand That Rocks the Cradle, The

(1992, US, 110 min)
d Curtis Hanson. *p* David Madden. *sc* Amanda Silver. *ph* Robert Elswit. *ed* John F Link. *pd* Edward Pisoni. *m* Graeme Revell. *cast* Annabella Sciorra, Rebecca De Mornay, Matt McCoy, Ernie Hudson, Julianne Moore, Madeline Zima, John de Lancie.

● Claire (Sciorra), happily married and pregnant, is molested during a visit to her gynaecologist. The ensuing investigation results in the doctor's suicide, thus causing his pregnant wife (De Mornay) to miscarry. De Mornay finds solace in an elaborate revenge which involves posing as a nanny and gaining employment with Claire in order to wreak havoc. Screenwriter Amanda Silver gleefully exploits parental fears, and skilfully depicts the shifting loyalties, malevolence and escalating paranoia within Claire's household. But as the film progresses, malicious schemes and loony excesses are combined, with Hanson's self-conscious direction rendering one particularly sensational murder even more implausible. Subtler and more involving are sequences which show the splendidly unnerving De Mornay in coercive, threatening mode. CM

Hanged Man, The

(1964, US, 87 min)
d Don Siegel. *p* Raymond Wagner. *sc* Stanford Whitmore, Jack Laird. *ph* Bud Thackery. *ed* Richard Belding. *ad* John J Lloyd. *m* Stanley Wilson. *cast* Robert Culp, Edmond O'Brien, Vera Miles, Norman Fell, Brenda Scott, Gene Raymond, J Carrol Naish.

● Nowhere near as effective as Siegel's other telefilm (*The Killers*), this second version of Dorothy Hughes' *Ride the Pink Horse* comes over as a thriller with considerable directing flair and little substance. As Culp travels to New Orleans to take revenge on the man he believes responsible for the death of his friend, only to discover that he is the victim of manipulative deception, Siegel makes the most of his colourful locations (notably during the Mardi Gras festivities), but is let down by a hackneyed, incoherent script, which has Culp getting involved with a beautiful young girl of astonishing, implausible innocence. Of interest to Siegel completists only. GA

Hang 'em High

(1967, US, 114 min)
d Ted Post. *p* Leonard Freeman. *sc* Leonard Freeman, Mel Goldberg. *ph* Leonard South, Richard H Kline. *ed* Gene Fowler Jr. *ad* John Goodman. *m* Dominic Frontiere. *cast* Clint Eastwood, Inger Stevens, Ed Begley, Pat Hingle, Arlene Golonka, James MacArthur, Ben Johnson, Ruth White, Charles McGraw, LQ Jones, Alan Hale Jr, Dennis Hopper, Bruce Dern, Bert Freed, Bob Steele.

● More interesting as a way station in Eastwood's career than for anything intrinsic to its lawman/vigilante scenario, this was his first American Western after the spaghettis. Made by his own company, Malpaso, with an old 'Rawhide' director on board (Eastwood is said to have shot some of it himself), the film anticipates the obsession with the dichotomy between natural and legal justice. Saved by chance after being summarily strung up as a presumed rustler and left to die, Eastwood sets out to avenge himself on the nine men who constituted the lynch mob and left him with a scar on his neck. TCh

Hanging Garden, The

(1997, Can/GB, 91 min)
d Thom Fitzgerald. *p* Louise Garfield, Arnie Gelbart, Thom Fitzgerald. *sc* Thom Fitzgerald. *ph* Daniel Jobin. *ed* Susan Shanks. *pd* Taavo Soodor. *m* John Roby. *cast* Chris Leavins, Troy Veinotte, Kerry Fox, Sarah Polley, Seana McKenna, Peter MacNeill.

● Writer/director Fitzgerald's first feature starts conventionally as Sweet William (all the characters are named after plants) returns home to rural Nova Scotia after a long absence for his sister's wedding. Then matters turn spectacularly surreal: he encounters his former self, an unhappy grossly overweight teenager who hanged himself in despair over his homosexuality. A question mark hangs over which William is the 'true' one, and which the ghost, or the fantasy. Leavins and Fox head a strong cast in this unusual witty twist on the old dysfunctional family plot. SJo

Hanging Gardens

see Jardines Colgantes

Hanging Up

(2000, US, 95 min)
d Diane Keaton. *p* Laurence Mark, Nora Ephron. *sc* Delia Ephron, Nora Ephron. *ph* Howard Atherton. *ed* Julie Monroe. *pd* Waldemar Kalinowski. *m* David Hirschfelder. *cast* Meg Ryan, Diane Keaton, Lisa Kudrow, Walter Matthau, Adam Arkin, Cloris Leachman, Jesse James, Edie McClurg, Duke Moosekian, Ann Bortolotti.

● Nora Ephron helped pen this hideously synthetic film version of her sister Delia's novel, at least partly based on the last days of their screenwriter father Henry. Here Matthau plays the plucky old codger Lou, wheeled into hospital with the kind of terminal illness which has reduced his powers of speech to tart one-liners, leaving his three girls to spend all their time on the phone fretting over him and each other. Georgia (Keaton, who also directs) is the eldest, a power-suited dynamo who publishes her own successful style magazine; Eve (Ryan), the responsible middle one, is a permanently hassled party organiser; while Maddy (Kudrow) acts in one of the tackiest soaps on daytime TV. They laugh, they cry, they bond, and that's all there is to it. The painful demise of a parent is blithely Ephronised into easily digested gobbets of sticky sentiment, smart ass dialogue and fortune cookie insight. Amid autopilot performances from the ladies, Matthau deserves some credit for avoiding the mawkishness that might have made the proceedings even more unendurable. It does seem desperately trite however when his loss merely provides for a culminating image of sisterhood in a liberating food fight. TJ

Hangin' with the Homeboys

(1991, US, 89 min)
d Joseph B Vasquez. *p* Richard Brick. *sc* Joseph B Vasquez. *ph* Anghel Decca. *ed* Michael Schweitzer. *ad* Isabel Bau Madden. *m* Steven Ray. *cast* Doug E Doug, Mario Joyner, John Leguizamo, Nestor Serrano, Kimberly Russell, Mary B Ward, Reggie Montgomery.

● Four Bronx likely lads – two black, two Puerto Rican – start their Saturday night by being booted out of a salsa party, and end up, one battered car and several battered egos later, wiser guys. It's one of those films in which the lessons of a lifetime are learned in one night, but it all works to brisk comic effect. The guys are basically cutouts, each defined by his own tic, but they're done to a fault. There's Tom (Joyner), an aspiring actor, shiftless Willie (Doug), and shy, morose Johnny (Leguizamo). But the star turn is Nestor Serrano's obnoxious hustler, Vinnie. The film is a little too episodic, and being a buddy movie, never quite pulls the rug from under the boys' braggadocio. But Vasquez makes pointed play with some of the current movie clichés of race and sex politics, and the pace never lets up. A lot of fun, with a lot of heart, and pretty hip into the bargain. JRo

Hangmen Also Die!

(1943, US, 131 min, b/w)
d/p Fritz Lang. *sc* Fritz Lang, Bertolt Brecht, John Wexley. *ph* James Wong Howe. *ed* Gene Fowler Jr. *ad* William Darling. *m* Hanns Eisler. *cast* Brian Donlevy, Anna Lee, Walter Brennan, Gene Lockhart, Dennis O'Keefe, Alexander Granach, Margaret Wycherly.

● Marvellous anti-Nazi propaganda film structured as *noir* thriller, with Donlevy as the man who assassinates Heydrich in Prague in 1942, hiding out with the Resistance when the Gestapo implement a retributory reign of terror in the city. Brecht, who originally worked on the script with Lang, claimed that his ideas were betrayed by the final product; but Lang's insistence that for most of the film he did employ the writer's work seems borne out by many fine sequences, with the taut, typically Langian action often interrupted by speeches that comment both didactically and intelligently on the proceedings. The atmosphere is dark and oppressive, the Nazis are portrayed as ideological gangsters, and the themes of loyalty and betrayal, passive and active resistance, beautifully worked out. Superb performances throughout, while James Wong Howe's photography perfectly captures the spirit of the occupied city, where hiding places are few and far from safe. GA

Hangover Square

(1944, US, 78 min, b/w)
d John Brahm. *p* Robert Bassler. *sc* Barre Lyndon. *ph* Joseph La Shelle. *ed* Harry Reynolds. *ad* Lyle R Wheeler, Maurice Ransford. *m* Bernard Herrmann. *cast* Laird Cregar, Linda Darnell, George Sanders, Glenn Langan, Faye Marlowe, Alan Napier.

● Loosely based on Patrick Hamilton's novel, this is a slightly self-conscious attempt to repeat the success of *The Lodger*, immensely stylish in its evocation of Edwardian London but failing to reproduce quite the same sense of subtle psychological nightmare. Playing a composer driven to murderous blackouts by discordant sounds (a fine cue for Bernard Herrmann's score), Cregar – in his last film – again gives a superbly ambivalent performance; and Darnell is terrific as the scheming chanteuse who seduces him into prostituting his talent to supply her with popular songs. But with the script using histrionics to patch its holes, Brahm is sometimes forced to respond with Grand Guignol excesses like the climax, which provides flaming apotheosis in the concert hall for the composer and his finally-completed concerto; pitched on a far too hysterical and grandiose note, this finale never quite rhymes, as it should, with the superb earlier sequence in which Cregar, anonymous in the crowd of Guy Fawkes celebrants, casually consigns Darnell's body to a bonfire. TM

Hangup

(1973, US, 93 min)
d Henry Hathaway. *p* Martin Rackin. *sc* John B Sherry, Lee Lazich. *ph* Robert B Hauser. *ed* Chris Kaeselau. *ad* James Halsey. *m* Tony Camillo. *cast* William Elliott, Marki Bey, Cliff Potts, Michael Lerner, Wally Taylor, George Murdock, Midori.

● A curiously dated and unconvincing tone of moral outrage envelops this creaking tale of a black policeman (Elliott) who redeems and then falls in love with a young heroin addict (Bey), only to abandon her upon discovering that she lied about having worked as a hooker. Driven back to the toils, she dies and he is left with a 'hangup'. The septuagenarian Hathaway's creative powers were once to be reckoned with, intermittently, but this rudimentary, straggling revenge picture – his last – should have been left on the shelf. JPy

Hanky Panky

(1982, US, 107 min)
d Sidney Poitier. *p* Martin Ransohoff. *sc* Harry Rosenbaum, David Taylor. *ph* Arthur J Ornitz. *ed* Harry Keller. *pd* Ben Edwards. *m* Tom Scott. *cast* Gene Wilder, Gilda Radner, Kathleen Quinlan, Richard Widmark, Robert Prosky, Josef Sommer, Johnny Sekka.

● An unashamed attempt to repeat the success of *Stir Crazy*, again directed by Poitier and taking the high security leak of a weaponry system for its soft centre, this comedy-thriller lets Wilder do his hysterical hero act yet again as he gets unwittingly embroiled with double-crosses, moles and cabbies who are allergic to elephant shit. Unfortunately, *Hanky Panky* doesn't have Richard Pryor in a chicken suit. Instead, there's TV comedienne Radner, whose efforts to pull a performance out of a poorly drawn female romantic lead are valiant, to say the most. Shored up by the mildly funny situation jokes and a superbly evil performance from the papyrus-faced Widmark as a horrid henchman, this is slick fun at best and cringing nonsense at its worst. FL

Hanna's War

(1988, US, 148 min)
d Menahem Golan. *p* Menahem Golan, Yoram Globus. *sc* Menahem Golan. *ph* Elemér Ragalyi. *ed* Alain Jakubowicz. *pd* Kuli Sander. *m* Dov Seltzer. *cast* Ellen Burstyn, Maruschka Detmers, Anthony Andrews, Donald Pleasence, David Warner, Vincenzo Ricotta, Christopher Fairbank, Ingrid Pitt.

● 1944. When Hanna (Detmers) abandons the rough comforts of her kibbutz to help kilted Andrews chase the Nazis out of the Balkans, nothing goes as it should. They are astonished to discover cattle trucks full of Jews, and even more surprised to learn that the ferryman paid to smuggle them into Hungary is a German spy. Hanna consequently falls into the capable hands of torturer Pleasence, who persuades her to betray her mother, brave, moving Burstyn. But all's well that ends well. Mum is released, and Hanna finds the slick Hollywood martydom she seems to be after. Written, produced and directed by Golan, the film's supposed to be a serious piece, refuting the anti-Semitic slur that the Jews were a load of namby-pamby defeatists when, in fact, they fought the Nazis like everybody else. The bad script is based on a stale polemic, which produces an expensive and self-righteous piece of propaganda. Top-notch performances by Detmers and Pleasence do nothing to make it the slightest bit gripping. PHo

Hannah and Her Sisters

(1986, US, 107 min)
d Woody Allen. *p* Robert Greenhut. *sc* Woody Allen. *ph* Carlo Di Palma. *ed* Susan E Morse. *pd* Stuart Wurtzel. *cast* Woody Allen, Michael Caine, Mia Farrow, Carrie Fisher, Barbara Hershey, Lloyd Nolan, Maureen O'Sullivan, Daniel Stern, Max von Sydow, Dianne Wiest, Sam Waterston.

●Allen's previous three films (*Zelig, Broadway Danny Rose, The Purple Rose of Cairo*) were thin, clever sketches fleshed out with characteristic one-liners. Here he returns to the territory he knows best, Manhattan. Of the three sisters (this is very much Chekhov landscape), the youngest (Hershey) lives with a spiritual mentor (Von Sydow), an intellectual recluse who rails against the iniquities of modern culture. The middle one (Wiest) is a frantic urban neurotic, forever borrowing money to pursue her latest career whim. And the eldest (Farrow) is apparently the most stable, a successful actress and mother presiding over a warm family circle. All is not well, however; Farrow's husband (Caine) is pursuing an affair with the youngest sister; sibling rivalry is rife. Wandering in and out of this extended dissection of family love life is Allen himself, playing his familiar nebbish hypochondriac; when a medical crisis brings him uncomfortably close to death, he samples all the different religions, before turning to the Marx Brothers' films as evidence that life is to be enjoyed. It is an articulate, literate film, full of humanity and perception about its sometimes less-than-loveable characters, which nonetheless comes down on the side of the best things in life: the primacy of love and feeling, qualified hope, and the fragility of it all. It also returns to much of the humour from his 'early, funny' films; Allen seems finally to have found the ability to please not just everyone, but also himself. CPea

Hannibal

(2001, US, 131 min)
d Ridley Scott. *p* Dino De Laurentiis, Martha De Laurentiis, Ridley Scott. *sc* David Mamet, Steven Zaillian. *ph* John Mathieson. *ed* Pietro Scalia. *pd* Norris Spencer. *m* Hans Zimmer. *cast* Anthony Hopkins, Julianne Moore, Ray Liotta, Frankie R Faison, Giancarlo Giannini, Francesca Neri, Zeljko Ivanek, Gary Oldman.

●In case you haven't read the Thomas Harris bestseller on which Scott's film is based, this finds brilliant, sophisticated, cannibalistic serial killer Dr Lecter (Hopkins) lurking in comfy pseudonymity as a Florence curator. But he's on the FBI's Ten Most Wanted list, and horribly mutilated millionaire Mason Verger (Oldman), Lecter's sole surviving victim, has put a reward on his head. When Hannibal learns that his old acquaintance Clarice Starling (Moore) is being stitched up by her bosses at the Bureau, he's sufficiently sure of his secret life to write to her; but he hasn't bargained for cop Pazzi (Giannini), who has his doubts about the curator. The weight-watchers script sensibly dispenses with several characters to serve a brew that's enjoyably spicy but low on substance. So much story is squeezed into 131 minutes that little time's left for analysis or characterisation. Moore is impressive but saddled with the straight role, Hopkins ambles through, Giannini is engagingly morose, and Oldman manages to strike a fine balance between witty pastiche and wry pathos, aware that this grandiose Guignol is hokum. The bloated 'classical' score suits Harris's pretensions, while Scott wisely keeps things brisk and delivers the set pieces. Lip smacking fun, it's an improvement on the book, but it's never as rigorous, insightful or compelling as *Manhunter*. GA

Hannibal Brooks

(1968, GB, 102 min)
d/p Michael Winner. *sc* Dick Clement, Ian La Frenais. *ph* Bob Paynter. *ed* Peter Austen-Hunt, Lionel Selwyn. *pd* John Stoll. *m* Francis Lai. *cast* Oliver Reed, Michael J Pollard, Wolfgang Preiss, Helmut Lohner, Karin Baal, Peter Karsten, John Alderton, James Donald.

●British PoW Brooks (Reed) is assigned to look after an elephant named Lucy, to whom he grows devoted. En route with the elephant from Munich to a safer zoo in Innsbruck, Brooks accidentally kills the Nazi member of the escort (Karsten) and then sets off with Lucy over the mountains to Switzerland. Pollard is tiresomely flaky as one 'Packy', leader of a private army, and Oliver Reed is not much more than Oliver Reed. Pretty good, though, for a Michael Winner film. TJ

Hannie Caulder

(1971, GB, 85 min)
d Burt Kennedy. *p* Patrick Curtis. *sc* Burt Kennedy, David Haft. *ph* Ted Scaife. *ed* Jim Connock. *ad* José Alguero. *m* Ken Thorne. *cast* Raquel Welch, Robert Culp, Ernest Borgnine, Strother Martin, Jack Elam, Christopher Lee, Diana Dors.

●Gimmicky British-financed Western, terminally indecisive over whether to parody or indulge the then familiar motifs of the spaghetti style, featuring Welch as the poncho-clad avenger of her own gang-rape and her husband's murder by the gnarled triumvirate of Borgnine, Elam and Martin. An opportunistic hiatus in Kennedy's comedy-Western decline. PT

Hanover Street

(1979, GB, 108 min)
d Peter Hyams. *p* Paul N Lazarus III. *sc* Peter Hyams. *ph* David Watkin. *ed* James Mitchell. *pd* Philip Harrison. *m* John Barry. *cast* Harrison Ford, Lesley-Anne Down, Christopher Plummer, Alec McCowen, Richard Masur, Michael Sacks, Patsy Kensit, Max Wall.

●Gung-ho American World War II bomber pilot falls for an already married English rose during teatime rendezvous in war-torn Hanover Street. Presumably the fragile 'brief encounters' of war had some immediate poignancy for the audiences of that period; here, though, tricked out with all sorts of 'modern' intrusions (bed scenes, *Catch-22* aircrew) and saddled with dialogue of quite staggering banality, they merely straggle into the wayward irrelevancies of his creeping cowardice and her increasing guilt. The second half ignores the obvious irony of husband and lover circumstantially trapped on the same suicide mission, settling instead for heroics of the 'Tell her I died a brave man' variety. Anaemic and foolish. CPea

Hans Christian Andersen

(1952, US, 112 min)
d Charles Vidor. *p* Samuel Goldwyn. *sc* Moss Hart. *ph* Harry Stradling. *ed* Daniel Mandell. *ad* Richard Day. *m/lyrics* Frank Loesser. *cast* Danny Kaye, Farley Granger, Zizi Jeanmaire, Joey Walsh, Roland Petit, John Qualen.

●Determined that he was going to make a movie about the celebrated storyteller, producer Sam Goldwyn went through every conceivable permutation of directors (William Wyler!), stars (Gary Cooper!) and scripts (16 of 'em) before ending up with this garish epic of musical puerility. You'll remember the songs – from 'Wonderful, Wonderful Copenhagen' to 'The Ugly Duckling' – but does Kaye have to play it as though he has a mental age of ten? A sugary one. TJ

Hans Christian Andersen and The Long Shadow

see H.C. Andersen's The Long Shadow

Hanussen

(1988, Hun/WGer, 117 min)
d István Szabó. *p* Arthur Brauner. *sc* István Szabó, Péter Dobai. *ph* Lajos Koltai. *ed* Zsuzsa Csákány. *ad* József Romvári, László Makai, Gyula Tóth. *m* György Vukán. *cast* Klaus Maria Brandauer, Erland Josephson, Ildikó Bánsági, Walter Schmidinger, Károly Eperjes, Grazyna Szapolowska.

●The third collaboration, after Mephisto and Colonel Redl between Szabó, Brandauer and cinematographer Lajos Koltai. Klaus Schneider (Brandauer) is an Austrian sergeant whose clairvoyant gifts first attract moderate acclaim during his recuperation from fighting in WWI. In hospital he forms friendships with two people who will help him to shape his future: Jewish psychologist Bettelheim (Josephson) and Nowotny (Eperjes), an ambitious army acquaintance who decides to promote Schneider's talents. On tours of Vienna and Berlin under the stage name of Hanussen, Schneider's phenomenal predictions bring him into contact with the decadent post-war elite; and despite his apolitical stance, his prophecies of Hitler's rise to power inevitably implicate him with the Nazis, threatening his friendships and precarious sense of stability... Brandauer's dominating screen presence is perfectly suited to the role of the charismatic seducer, whose abilities to transfer his will and to control respondents serve as a not so subtle metaphor for the rise of Fascism. Szabó heightens the mysticism with a pervading sense of menace which, together with Koltai's exquisite visuals, captivates attention throughout. CM

Hap-Ki-Do (aka Heqidao)

(1972, HK, 97 min)
d Huang Feng. *p* Raymond Chow. *sc* Ho Jen. *ph* Li Yu Tong. *ed* Chang Yao Chu. *ad* Li Sheng. *m* Lay Shu Hua. *cast* Angela Mao, Carter Huang, Pai Ying, Ji Han Jae, Shih Chia-Yin, Whang In Sik.

●A well-mounted action pic with a female lead who practises the martial art of Hap-Ki-Do. There is an undoubted, if limited, kick to be had from seeing a woman in there giving as good as she gets instead of waiting under the cherry blossoms. Set in 1934 Korea, when the country was under the domination of those perennial baddies, the Japanese, the plot concerns the efforts of the Chinese to fight back against constant provocation. The biggest culprits are the denizens of the notorious Black Bear School, and inevitably it is left to Angela Mao to storm the place alone. VG

Happening, The

(1966, US, 101 min)
d Elliot Silverstein. *p* Jud Kinberg. *sc* Frank R Pierson, James D Buchanan, Ronald Austin. *ph* Philip H Lathrop. *ed* Philip Anderson. *pd* Richard Day. *m* Frank De Vol. *cast* Anthony Quinn, George Maharis, Michael Parks, Faye Dunaway, Robert Walker, Oscar Homolka, Martha Hyer, Milton Berle.

●Four Miami beach bums find they've kidnapped cleaned up gangster Quinn in this dated excuse for an anti-establishment comedy, which gave Dunaway her first role, as one of the abductors (a few months later she was to play Bonnie Parker), and The Supremes a chart-topping hit. Infuriated that his wife Martha Hyer, partner Berle, Mafia boss Homolka, and his mother won't pay up for his release, the gangster blows his top, takes over his own kidnapping, secures the ransom by a faked death and blackmail, and then, to the horror of the purblind hippies, who he's turned into his soldiers, burns the supposedly marked loot. Co-scripted by Frank R Pierson, with evocative camerawork by Philip Lathrop. TJ

Happiest Days of Your Life, The

(1950, GB, 91 min, b/w)
d/p Frank Launder. *sc* Frank Launder, John Dighton. *ph* Stan Pavey. *ed* Oswald Hafenrichter. *ad* Joseph Bato. *m* Mischa Spoliansky. *cast* Alastair Sim, Margaret Rutherford, Joyce Grenfell, Edward Rigby, Guy Middleton, Richard Wattis, George Cole.

●With hindsight, this uproarious farce, adapted from a play by John Dighton, heralds a retreat. Throughout the 1940s, Launder and Gilliat had been making ambitious, heartfelt films about ordinary people (*Millions Like Us, Waterloo Bridge*), but with the new decade, they began to rely more and more on stylised English humour and stock characters. Sim plays a headmaster who learns that thanks to Civil Service bungling, he's going to share his premises with a girls' school. Vintage moments include Rutherford, the tweedy, formidable headmistress, marching at the head of a column of girls, like Hannibal about to attack the Alps, and Joyce Grenfell's games mistress Miss Gossage ('just call me sausage') banging the school gong with the fervour of a bodybuilder auditioning for Rank. GM

Happiest Millionaire, The

(1967, US, 159 min)
d Norman Tokar. *sc* AJ Carothers. *ph* Edward Colman. *ed* Cotton Warburton. *ad* Carroll Clark, John B Mansbridge. *m* Jack Elliott. *cast* Fred MacMurray, Tommy Steele, Greer Garson, John Davidson, Lesley Ann Warren, Geraldine Page, Gladys Cooper, Hermione Baddeley.

● Antiseptic, over-long (there have been various cut-down versions) but not unpleasant Disney musical. MacMurray exudes characteristically quizzical charm as the eccentric Philadelphian millionaire with a penchant for fisticuffs and alligators, while Tommy Steele does a winsome Oirish act as the butler who takes care of problems that arise when his master's tomboy daughter (Warren) falls for a youth (Davidson) who initially doesn't quite come up to expectations. What with Greer Garson thrown in as MacMurray's gracious wife, it's all very bland and cosy. Best moment is when Gladys Cooper and Geraldine Page sing the respective praises of aristocratic and *nouveau riche* social graces in a nicely bitchy song called 'There Are Those'. TM

Happiness (Schaste)

(1934, USSR, 5,840 ft, b/w)
d/sc Alexander Medvedkin. *ph* Gleb Troianski. *ad* Alexander Utkin. *cast* Piotr Zinoviev, Elena Egorova, L Nenascheva, W Uspenski. G Mirgoryan. Lavrenyev.

● One of the last Soviet silent movies, rediscovered and restored by French cine-chameleon Chris Marker in 1971, *Happiness* proved an easily accessible counterpoint to the exotic obscurities of *The Wishing Tree*. For this rare and often hilarious example of socialist slapstick is likewise grounded in the seeming eccentricities of Russian folk culture; but on the less culturally specific dynamics of those hopes and dreams which forever sustain the exploited, and which may or may not flourish after the revolution. Medvedkin's infectiously happy oddity emerged surprisingly from a slough of social-realist orthodoxy, and prompted none other than Eisenstein to the admiring tribute: 'Today I saw how a Bolshevik laughs.' PT

Happiness

see Bonheur, Le

Happiness

(1998, US, 139 min)
d Todd Solondz. *p* Ted Hope, Christine Vachon. *sc* Todd Solondz. *ph* Maryse Alberti. *ed* Alan Oxman. *pd* Thérèse Deprez. *m* Robbie Kondor. *cast* Jane Adams, Dylan Baker, Lara Flynn Boyle, Philip Seymour Hoffman, Ben Gazzara, Louise Lasser, Jared Harris.

● Centred loosely on a New Jersey family of three grown-up sisters, their parents, partners and children, Solondz's brave and adventurous second feature takes misery, loneliness and cruelty as a given in contemporary life; everyone here is (justifiably or otherwise) unhappy with their lot – or should be, if they could only stop deluding themselves. Right from the painfully funny opening, it's a bible-black comedy of considerable assurance, but gradually the humour subsides to be replaced by a core of despairing human sympathy, most noticeably for the paedophile father whose heart-to-hearts with his teenage son come to form the emotional backbone of the movie. Very often, you're unsure whether you want to accompany Solondz on his journey into a modern purgatory, but you should take the trip; it's worth it, and something you'll never forget. GA

Happiness in Twenty Years (Le Bonheur dans 20 Ans)

(1971, Fr, 93 min, b/w)
d/sc Albert Knobler. *ed* Marc Pavaux. *narrator* (French version) Michel Bouquet, (English version) Orson Welles.

● Series of astonishing documentary sequences illustrating the Czech experience, from the arrival of the Russian liberating tanks after World War II to the 'confessions' of the show trials, from chunks of Stalinist newsreel to the first blossoming of what was to become the cinematic new wave in the café theatre satires of the '60s. Its argument is achieved visually: although it does inevitably relish the tatty absurdity of the whole iconography of the Stalinist period, the film also carefully charts its progress so that we actually see a visual expression of a political idea forming on the screen as crowds harden, literally, into massed ranks. VG

Happiness of the Katakuris, The (Katakuri-ke no Kofuku)

(2001, Jap, 113 min)
d Takashi Miike. *p* Tetsuo Sasho, Hirotsugu Yoshida. *sc* Kikumi Yamagishi. *ph* Hideo Yamamoto. *ed* Yasushi Shimamura. *ad* Tetsuo Harada. *m* Koji Makaino, Koji Endo. *cast* Kenji Sawada, Keiko Matsuzaka, Shinji Takeda, Naomi Nishida, Tetsuro Tamba, Naoto Takenaka, Kiyoshiro Imawano.

● One of the six or seven movies Miike made in 2001, this misfire is a musical remake of the Korean black comedy *The Quiet Family*, directed by Kim Ji-Woon. The Katakuri family decides to begin life afresh by opening a chalet hotel in the mountains. Family tensions are exacerbated by the non-arrival of guests. Then, when guests do show up, they keep dying on the premises; family head Masao (Sawada, the only pro singer in the starry cast) opts for hushing up the deaths to avoid giving the place a bad rep. Miike elaborates the storyline with claymation sequences, deliberately tacky songs, parodies of *The Sound of Music* and Brit aristocracy, and chorus-lines of rotting zombies – all of which sounds like a lot more fun than it is. TR

Happy Birthday, Wanda June

(1971, US, 105 min)
d Mark Robson. *p* Lester Goldsmith. *sc* Kurt Vonnegut. *ph* Fred Koenekamp. *ed* Dorothy Spencer. *ad* Boris Leven. *cast* Rod Steiger, Susannah York, George Grizzard, Don Murray, William Hickey.

● Kurt Vonnegut's adaptation of his own off-Broadway play about a big game hunter (Steiger) who returns from the jungle after being believed dead for eight years. He finds his dim wife (York) turned intellectual, and undecided whether to marry a pacifist doctor or a vacuum cleaner salesman. Though these ingredients may sound promising, add a precocious child and you have all the ingredients for the tedious satire of American attitudes that it is. Steiger's overacting and the film's obvious theatrical origins don't help either.

Happy Days (Stchastlivye Dni)

(1992, Rus, 80 min, b/w)
d Alexei Balabanov. *p* Alexei German. *sc* Alexei Balabanov. *ph* Sergei Astachow. *cast* Viktor Sukhorukov, Lika Nevolina.

● Balabanov's first feature could be described as a purgatorial allegory. As idiosyncratic as his later *Of Freaks and Men*, it takes its inspiration from Samuel Beckett. A character named Peter, Sergei or possibly Boris (Sukhorukov), his head wrapped in bandages since his release from hospital, roams the decaying flats and cemeteries bordering St Petersburg's Winter Palace square, in search of somewhere to stay. This is a world of Kafka-esque hostility and minatory mystery where only a blind man with a donkey and a fallen aristocratic woman offer the protagonist any amicable communicative signs. Could these be ironic reminders of the balms of religion, or the lost certainties of the old social order? The director employs b/w most expressively, whether in exquisite gliding crane shots, or in claustrophobically framed dark interiors, where the camera will often alight and pause, affectingly, on an object before moving on. Similarly, his mood effects are emphasised by canny use of non-naturalistic sound. An extraordinarily well-realised doom-lover's playground, the existential gloom makes way only for Svankmajer-like surrealism. WH

Happy End

(1999, SKor, 99 min)
d Jung Ji-Woo. *p* Lee Eun. *sc* Jung Ji-Woo. *ph* Kim Woo-Hyung. *ed* Kim Hyun. *ad* Kim Sang-Man. *m* Cho Young-Wook. *cast* Choi Min-Sik, Chun Do-Yeon, Ju Jin-Mo.

● First-time director Jung ventures into Chabrol territory with a sexual triangle drama which ends in murder and (literally) transferred guilt. The central couple are interestingly conceived: the man (Choi) has become a house-husband since losing his banking job and spends his time squatting in a used-book store when he isn't watching TV, doing domestic chores or minding the baby; the woman (Chun) runs a profitable language school and launches into a torrid affair with her first love from adolescence (Ju), evidently the only man she has ever really loved. Naturalistic playing and reasonably ingenious plotting carry the film quite a long way, but it never reaches the higher, allusive level it seems to be aiming for. Kim's superbly controlled camerawork couldn't be more different from his hand-held style on *Lies*. TR

Happy Ever After (aka Tonight's the Night)

(1954, GB, 84 min)
d/p Mario Zampi. *sc* Jack Davies, Michael Pertwee. *ph* Stan Pavey. *ed* Kathleen Connors. *ad* Ivan King. *m* Stanley Black. *cast* David Niven, Yvonne De Carlo, Barry Fitzgerald, George Cole, Robert Urquhart, Michael Shepley, AE Matthews, Liam Redmond.

● Passable comedy with Niven as the new squire of an Irish village, blissfully unaware that the devious locals are drawing lots to see who gets the chance to bump him off. It's actually not bad as these things go, because the money was spent on the cast, and they even went to Ireland to shoot it (in Technicolor). TJ

Happy Family, The (aka Mr Lord Says No)

(1952, GB, 86 min, b/w)
d Muriel Box. *p* William MacQuitty. *sc* Muriel Box, Sydney Box. *ph* Reginald Wyer. *ed* Jean Barker. *ad* Cedric Dawe. *m* Francis Chagrin. *cast* Stanley Holloway, Kathleen Harrison, Naunton Wayne, Dandy Nichols, George Cole, Miles Malleson, Margaret Barton.

● Another Ealing-style triumph for the 'little people' (adapted by Sydney and Muriel Box from a play by Michael Clayton Hutton): Holloway and family barricade themselves in their grocery store when the authorities inform them it has to be demolished to make way for an access road to the Festival of Britain site on London's South Bank. Nichols is fun as a spiritualist spinster, but otherwise there's not a great deal to celebrate. TJ

Happy Gilmore

(1996, US, 92 min)
d Dennis Dugan. *p* Robert Simonds. *sc* Tim Herlihy, Adam Sandler. *ph* Arthur Albert. *ed* Jeff Gourson. *pd* Perry Andelin Blake. *m* Mark Mothersbaugh. *cast* Adam Sandler, Christopher McDonald, Julie Bowen, Frances Bay, Carl Weathers, Alan Covert, Dennis Dugan.

● Happy Gilmore (Sandler) is a life-long ice hockey fanatic. Snags: his skating's wretched, and his temper short and explosive. In fact, his one talent's a thundering slap shot that's as liable to hit the spectators as the net. While the home of his beloved grandma is being repossessed by tax officials he discovers his power shooting lends itself to a 400-yard golf drive. So, hoping to rescue grandma from a diabolical nursing home, Happy goes on the Pro Golf Tour, hindered by his putting, his short fuse and the jealous attentions of smarmy favourite Shooter McGavin (McDonald). Given that the chief pleasure of Dugan's film is watching a maniac on golf greens, a liking for the sport is incidental to the enjoyment of this immensely silly film. And while it may be dumb, the film-makers refuse to force the fact as funny in itself, relying instead on well-drawn characters, goofy slapstick, cartoon violence and occasionally inspired dialogue. The result falls somewhere between early Steve Martin, the Marx Brothers and a Looney Tune. The only real let-down is the handling of the love interest; otherwise, this is superior disposable comedy. NB

Happy Hooker, The

(1975, US, 98 min)
d Nicholas Sgarro. *p* Fred Caruso. *sc* William Richert. *ph* Dick Kratina. *ed* Jerry Greenberg. *pd* Gene Callahan. *m* Don Elliott. *cast* Lynn Redgrave, Jean-Pierre Aumont,

Lovelady Powell, Nicholas Pryor, Elizabeth Wilson, Tom Poston, Conrad Janis, Richard Lynch.

●The only spark in this cheapskate version of Xaviera Hollander's much-touted life story is provided by Lynn Redgrave's believable and consistently interesting incarnation of Xaviera as a rather practical lady of no great imagination but a deal of energy. The script and direction are both doggedly routine. Anything like a sex scene is promptly elided out of existence, a promising line of social satire fails to develop, and the sorry light cast on the male characters, all roundly and condescendingly patronised by the women, is allowed to develop swiftly into overripe farce. A distinct aura of missed opportunity hangs about the proceedings, which make quite a good job of sidestepping the relevant issues. VG

Happy Man (Szczesliwy czlowiek)

(2000, Pol, 85 min)
d/sc Malgorzata Szumowska. *ph* Michal Englety, Marek Gajczak. *ed* Jacek Drosio. *pd* Marek Zawierucha. *m* Zygmunt Konieczny. *cast* Jadwiga Jankowska-Cieslak, Piotr Jankowski, Malgorzata Hajewska-Krzysztofik.

●This extremely promising first feature, extraordinarily assured given the writer/director's 27 years, builds up an elliptical, enigmatic but finally wholly lucid tale of a thirtyish slacker, a would-be writer who lives with his mother and decides to improve his ways when it appears she's dying. To make her happy, he determines to meet someone and marry, and settles on a single mother. Robust, imaginative imagery, long takes with little dialogue and marvellous performances serve to draw out the cruel ironies of the perceptive, unsentimental but poignant script. GA

Happy New Year

see Bonne Année, La

Happy Now?

(2001, GB, 97 min)
d Philippa Collie-Cousins. *p* Neris Thomas, Alison Owen. *sc* Belinda Bauer. *ph* Richard Greatrex. *ed* John Wilson. *pd* Eve Stewart. *m* Dario Marianelli. *cast* Ioan Gruffudd, Susan Lynch, Om Puri, Emmy Rossum, Paddy Considine, Richard Coyle. Jonathan Rhys Myers, Alison Steadman, Robert Pugh.

●This BBC Films production is a real oddball. Welsh coastal town Pen Y Wig (twinned with 3 Mile Island) is rocked by the killing of a local beauty queen Jenny. Joe (Coyle) and Marcus (Considine) fearfully cover up what started out as an accident, and the homeless Tin Man (Om Puri) is convicted of murder. Fourteen years later the Tin Man gets out of prison just as Marcus' electoral campaign is threatened by the unsettling appearance of Jenny's exact double, Nikki (Rossum). Oh, and there's a new sheriff in town, Gruffudd's handsome but disgraced cop Max. Jam-packed with good actors – Robert Pugh, Susan Lynch – and frankly overloaded with eccentricities like Max's fondness for TV's *Bonanza*, or the themed hotel presided over by a prone Alison Steadman in a giant metal lung, this never really hits a convincing, authoritative tone. Meanwhile the murder mystery is strictly potboiler. TCh

Happy Texas

(1999, US, 99 min)
d Mark Illsley. *p* Mark Illsley, Rick Montgomery, Ed Stone. *sc* Ed Stone, Mark Illsley, Phil Reeves. *ph* Bruce Douglas Johnson. *ed* Norman Buckley. *pd* Maurin Scarlata. *m* Peter Harris. *cast* Jeremy Northam, Steve Zahn, Ally Walker, Illeana Douglas, William H Macy, MC Gainey, Ron Perlman, Paul Dooley.

●Escaped cons Harry (Northam) and Wayne Wayne Wayne Jr (Zahn) hole up in Happy, Texas, after hijacking a camper van – and the locals are expecting them. That is, they're expecting a pair of homosexual beauty pageant directors to coach the town's pre-pubescent girls to the county finals. While the eminently ill-suited Wayne is stuck teaching the teenies to twirl, his much smoother partner sets about be-girlfriending the bank manager, Jo (Walker), and fending off the advances of the sheriff, Chappy Dent (Macy). The film is nothing if not easygoing, and it has its share of neat touches and good lines. Regrettably, most of them occur in the first five minutes. The rest is more slack than slick – which gives you ample time to consider the gaping holes in the plot. Zahn clucks dumb for all he's worth, but director Illsley is unaccountably more interested in Northam's bland, wistful encounters with lovelorn Texans. TCh

Happy Times (Xingfu Shiguang)

(2000, China, 98 min)
d Zhang Yimou. *p* Zhao Yu, Zhang Weiping. *sc* Guizi. *ph* Hou Yong. *ed* Zhai Ru. *pd* Cao Jiuping. *m* Sanbao. *cast* Zhao Benshan, Dong Jie, Li Xuejian, Dong Lifan, Niu Ben, Fu Biao.

●Another blow to Zhang's international reputation, this sentimental comedy drifts from low satire into high pathos without catching any recognisable aspects of present-day Beijing life. TV comic Zhao plays an unemployed chancer who tries to win the heart of a fat divorcee. By the time he discovers she has an equally fat fiancé, he has haplessly accepted responsibility for her blind stepdaughter Wu Ying (newcomer Dong Jie). His attempt to make money by converting an abandoned bus into a 'love hotel' founders on his prudishness (he insists on sitting with the customers) and ends when the authorities lift the bus to the scrapyard. Then, for no evident reason, he sets about creating a fake working environment for Wu Ying, mocking up a bath-house massage room is a disused factory and asking his friends to pose as customers; she twigs the deception, but gamely plays along – until the factory is demolished. Hou Yong's bright, gently stylised images are a plus, but the material remains hopelessly inconsequential and unresonant. TR

Happy Together

(1989, US, 96 min)
d Mel Damski. *p* Jere Henshaw. *sc* Craig J Nevius. *ph* Joe Pennella. *ed* O Nicholas Brown. *pd* Marcia Hinds. *m* Robert Folk. *cast* Patrick Dempsey, Helen Slater, Dan Schneider, Marius Weyers, Brad Pitt, Barbara Babcock.

●College comedy in which freshman Dempsey discovers that an admin error has given him Slater as a roommate, a situation that's bound to lead to embarrassment, amorous complications and a clunking resolution. If you're really interested a young Brad Pitt pops up as a fellow student. TJ

Happy Together (Chunguang Zhaxie)

(1997, HK, 97 min)
d/p/sc Wong Kar-Wai. *ph* Christoper Doyle. *ed* William Chang, Wong Ming-Lam. *pd* William Chang. *m* Danny Chung. *cast* Leslie Cheung, Tony Leung Chiu-Wai, Chang Chen.

●Under the Chinese title used for Antonioni's *Blow-Up* (it connotes the exposure of something indecent), Wong Kar-Wai and cameraman Chris Doyle have crafted their most lyrical film. The romance between two gay men from Hong Kong ends soon after they arrive in Argentina. Lai (Leung) gets a job as a doorman at a Buenos Aires tango bar and starts saving for his ticket home. Ho (Cheung) turns tricks for fun and profit, but comes running back to Lai for comfort when one of his clients leaves him bruised and bleeding. Lai befriends – and somehow draws emotional strength from – a Taiwanese kid on his way south to 'the end of the world'. The three main characters give Wong all he needs for a piercing meditation on the meaning of partings, reunions, and attempts to start over. From afar (Buenos Aires is Hong Kong's antipodes), he crystallises the anxieties and hopes of Hong Kong people on the eve of the return to China. TR

Happy We

see Tva Killar och en Tjej

Hardbodies

(1984, US, 87 min)
d Mark Griffiths. *p* Jeff Begun, Ken Dalton. *sc* Steve Greene, Eric Alter, Mark Giffiths. *ph* Tom Richmond. *ed* Andy Blumenthal. *pd* Gregg Fonscea. *m* Vic Caesar. *cast* Grant Cramer, Teal Roberts, Gary Wood, Michael Rapport, Sorrells Pickard.

●Soft porn from Columbia Pictures (let's name 'n shame 'em) without a single redeeming feature. Middle-aged cretins concoct a scheme for picking up girls by throwing parties and pretending to be talent scouts, with the Young Hero as front-man. The cretins are a hit with the party girls who can't wait to strip off. But they mess with Young Hero's steady, are duly humiliated and True Romance triumphs. Middle-aged cretins wanting to try this at home should put out a casting call for *Hardbodies 2* immediately. DO

Hard-Boiled (Lashou Shentan)

(1991, HK, 126 min)
d John Woo. *p* Linda Kuk, Terence Chang. *sc* Barry Wong. *ph* Wong Wing-Heng. *ed* John Woo, David Woo, Kai Kit Wai. ad James Leung, Joel Chong. *m* Michael Gibbs. *cast* Chow Yun-Fat, Tony Leung, Teresa Mo, Philip Chan, Anthony Wong.

●In essence, John Woo's characteristic take on movies like *Die Hard*: a supercharged thriller in which a renegade cop and an undercover man take on Triad gun-runners who store their munitions in a hospital morgue. Anyone who saw *The Killer* will have a fair idea what to expect, from the intense male bonding to the hyper-kinetic editing style. What's new here is a rich vein of anarchic humour (will they evacuate the maternity ward before the hospital blows up?) and a bluesy back-beat of philosophical musings on a cop's sad lot. No surprise that Woo (who cameos as a barman) has been courted by Hollywood. TR

Hard Contract

(1969, US, 106 min)
d S Lee Pogostin. *p* Marvin Schwartz. *sc* S Lee Pogostin. *ph* Jack Hildyard. *ed* Harry Gerstad. *ad* Ed Graves. *m* Alex North. *cast* James Coburn, Lee Remick, Lilli Palmer, Burgess Meredith, Patrick Magee, Sterling Hayden, Claude Dauphin, Helen Cherry, Karen Black.

●A sometimes intelligent examination of the mind of a professional killer (Coburn) sent to Europe to dispose of three men. Plans start to go awry when his emotional reserves (he deliberately seeks transactions with prostitutes) are plumbed by Remick. Unfortunately there are too many distractions for the film to really work: Coburn appears too inflexible, the pretty European locations look deliberately chosen for the American market, and too many well known faces (Magee, Palmer, Dauphin) are left with too little to do. CPe

Hardcore (aka The Hardcore Life)

(1978, US, 108 min)
d Paul Schrader. *p* Buzz Feitshans. *sc* Paul Schrader. *ph* Michael Chapman. *ed* Tom Rolf. *pd* Paul Sylbert. *m* Jack Nitzsche. *cast* George C Scott, Peter Boyle, Season Hubley, Dick Sargent, Leonard Gaines, David Nichols.

●Schrader tackled Middle American dilemmas with eloquence in the radical *Blue Collar*, and he had touched on incest and child sexuality in scripts like *Obsession* and *Taxi Driver*. *Hardcore* stakes out similar ground: the pre-teen daughter of Midwesterner Scott disappears from a Calvinist youth camp, then surfaces in a porn film. And Scott gets things off to a titanic start as we voyeuristically watch his agony when confronted with a porn movie of his own daughter. But credibility wavers when he impersonates a seedy producer with suspicious ease, then forms a sentimental detective partnership with a whore (Hubley). The action meanders around to a hackneyed end, and because *Hardcore* is softcore, it doesn't convincingly convey that climate of self-hatred which pervades the sexual ghetto. It's a reminder, though, that the culturally respected cinema demands far gorier, more inventive and more technically accomplished depictions of sexual violence than the flesh flicks. CR

Hard Day's Night, A

(1964, GB, 85 min, b/w)
d Richard Lester. *p* Walter Shenson. *sc* Alun Owen. *ph* Gilbert Taylor. *ed* John Jympson. *ad* Ray Simm. *m* John Lennon, Paul McCartney. *cast* The Beatles, Wilfrid Brambell, Norman Rossington, John Junkin, Victor Spinetti, Anna Quayle, Lionel Blair, Brian Epstein.

●A sanitised semi-documentary version of life on the road with John, Paul, George and Ringo, with a paper-thin storyline about difficulties with their manager and Paul's Grandpa (Brambell) serving as a linking device to connect scenes of the Fab Four in the studio, in concert, and in flight from frantic fans. Lester's gimmicky camera-trickery – jump-cuts, fast and slow motion, etc, etc – is so much icing on the cake, and has dated badly; but the mop-tops are likeably relaxed, with Lennon offering a few welcome moments of his dry, acerbic wit. GA

Hard Eight

(1996, US, 101 min)
d Paul Thomas Anderson. *p* Robert Jones, John Lyons. *sc* Paul Thomas Anderson. *ph* Robert Elswit. *ed* Barbara Tulliver. *ad* Michael Krantz. *m* Michael Penn, Jon Brion. *cast* Philip Baker Hall, John C Reilly, Samuel L Jackson, Gwyneth Paltrow, F William Parker.

●Sidney (Hall) – old, well-kept – approaches a roadside café. John (Reilly) – young, down-and-out – is slumped in front of the joint. Sidney offers John cigarettes and coffee, $50 and a ride to Vegas, and advice on playing the money at the crap tables. Reno, two years later, and the stakes have doubled. John's making a steady living gambling under Sidney's tutelage; he's also hooked up with Clementine (Paltrow), a cocktail waitress who turns tricks on the side. Outside Sidney's orbit is John's pal Jimmy (Jackson), a small-time hood with scant respect for Sidney – a catalyst for trouble. There's a timeless quality to this first feature (from the director of *Boogie Nights*): while owing particular debts to the low-life worlds of '40s B-movies and '70s neo-*noir*, it could have been made almost any time in the last 50 years. But it's in no way a pastiche. With a smart, savvy, but unshowy script and quietly confident direction, this is a subtle, understated reworking of *noir* conventions. Jackson and Paltrow both prove their talents as character actors; Reilly brings a credible, wide-eyed fecklessness to his part; and Baker Hall is a revelation. NB

Harder They Come, The

(1972, Jam, 110 min)
d/p Perry Henzell. *sc* Perry Henzell, Trevor D Rhone. *ph* Frank St Juste, David MacDonald, Peter Jessop. *ed* John Victor Smith, Reicland Anderson, Richard White. *ad* Sally Henzell. *m* Jimmy Cliff, Derek Harriot, Desmond Dekker, Maytals. *cast* Jimmy Cliff, Carl Bradshaw, Basil Keane, Janet Bartley, Winston Stona, Bobby Charlton.

●The age-old story of country boy, urban corruption, and a bad end. The guy is Jimmy Cliff, the city is Kingston, the bad business is the reggae industry, and the crime is killing a cop who's in on the 'ganja' trade. The film's tone is righteously angry, but it doesn't go for the easy targets: it views Cliff's image of himself as a hero as ironically as it denounces police violence and missionary-style religion. Along the way, it offers a richly textured picture of Jamaican shanty-town life, composed with a terrific eye for detail. The action is as gutsy as the well-integrated score, which makes the movie's Hollywood-style gloss a little anomalous, but the basic humour and toughness emerge unscathed. TR

Harder They Fall, The

(1956, US, 109 min, b/w)
d Mark Robson. *p/sc* Philip Yordan. *ph* Burnett Guffey. *ed* Jerome Thoms. *ad* William Flannery. *m* Hugo Friedhofer. *cast* Humphrey Bogart, Rod Steiger, Jan Sterling, Mike Lane, Max Baer, Edward Andrews, Carlos Montalban, Nehemiah Persoff.

●A boxing drama with Bogart (in his last role) typecast as the sports publicist who finally does the right thing and sets out to expose the syndicate, *The Harder They Fall* bears the hallmark of its producer/writer Philip Yordan all over it. Robson tries vainly to give the movie the look of a thriller with lots of shadows and bleak lighting, but Yordan consistently returns it to the field of melodrama by setting his drama in the home – as Bogart and his wife Sterling agonise over his job of exposing the fixed fights – rather than in the boxing ring. PH

Hard, Fast and Beautiful

(1951, US, 79 min, b/w)
d Ida Lupino. *p* Collier Young. *sc* Martha Wilkerson. *ph* Archie J Stout. *ed* George Shrader, William Ziegler. *ad* Albert S D'Agostino, Jack Okey. *m* Roy Webb. *cast* Claire Trevor, Sally Forrest, Carleton Young, Robert Clarke, Kenneth Patterson.

●An intriguing little melodrama from the underrated Lupino, with Trevor as an ambitious, domineering mother who pushes her daughter (Forrest) to become a tennis champion, only to accuse her of ingratitude when she falls for Clarke and tires of the tournament circuit. Rather like a *Mildred Pierce* of the sporting world but with sympathies reversed, it's a mite predictable in its plotting, but Trevor is typically excellent, and Lupino never sentimentalises the mother-daughter relationship. Nowhere near as rewarding as either *The Hitch-hiker* or *The Bigamist*, but a very watchable entertainment all the same from one of Hollywood's few women directors. GA

Hard Men

(1996, GB/Fr, 87 min)
d JK Amalou. *p* JK Amalou, Georges Benayoun. *sc* JK Amalou. *ph* Nick Sawyer. *ed* Victoria Boydell. *pd* Simon Elliott. *cast* Vincent Regan, Ross Boatman, Lee Ross, 'Mad' Frankie Fraser, Ken Campbell, Mirella D'Angelo.

●A bankrupt effort which begs to be seen as a British *Reservoir Dogs*. It's a callous, sentimental drama about an East End hitman who wants out, now he's a dad. The acting's uniformly terrible (imagine the cast of *Grange Hill* imitating Joe Pesci) and the dialogue's chiefly monotonous obscenity. Dire. TCh

Hard Rain

(1997, US/GB/Jap/Ger/Den, 97 min)
d Mikael Salomon. *p* Mark Gordon, Gary Levinsohn, Ian Bryce. *sc* Graham Yost. *ph* Peter Menzies Jr. *ed* Paul Hirsch. *pd* J Michael Riva. *m* Christopher Young. *cast* Morgan Freeman, Christian Slater, Randy Quaid, Minnie Driver, Edward Asner, Richard Dysart.

●After weeks of rain, the floods are rising around the town of Huntingburg, Indiana. Slater's armoured-car courier is out on his usual money collection run. It's bad enough being stuck in water with $3m in the back – what he doesn't need is a man like Freeman planning a robbery with his gang, nor a damsel in distress like Driver's art restorer, too stubborn to leave her beloved stained glass windows in the local church. Thankfully, good ol' sheriff Quaid is around, but maybe even he can't resist the temptation of an evacuated town there for the taking. Meanwhile, it's still bucketing. *Speed* screenwriter Graham Yost came up with this nifty spin on the high concept thriller, which puts everything under water several feet deep and rising. *Hard Rain* may not be the most inventive of thriller plots, essentially boiling down to an extended chase with all concerned after the moneybags, but it's extremely impressive as a physical production. TJ

Hard Road

(1989, GB, 90 min)
d Colin Finbow. *p* Brianne Perkins. *sc* Children's Film Unit. *ph* Alan Dunlop (supervisor). *ad* Petra Cox. *m* David Hewson. *cast* Francesca Camillo, Max Rennie, John Louis Mansi, Andrew Mulquin, David Savile, Amanda Murray, Peter Bayliss.

●The tenth feature from the Children's Film Unit centres on the adventures of two bored and disillusioned 13-year-olds: working class Kelly (Camillo), an incessant liar whose favourite pastime is winding up the Children's Help Line about her so-called abusing father; and quiet, withdrawn Max (Rennie), a poor rich kid with a fondness for faking suicides. Kelly persuades Max to take the driving seat (of a scarlet 1959 Ferrari he is due to inherit when he's 17) for an illegal spin round the countryside, where the joy of new-found freedom eventually has them settling Crusoe-style deep in the Sussex undergrowth. Although some children will find the pace a trifle slow at times, it's still easily the CFU's best work to date: technically proficient (especially bearing in mind that most of the production team are well under 16), and with shining performances from the children. DA

Hard Target

(1993, US, 97 min)
d John Woo. *p* Sean Daniel, Jim Jacks. *sc* Chuck Pfarrer. *ph* Russell Carpenter. *ed* Bob Murawski. *m* Graeme Revell. *cast* Jean-Claude Van Damme, Lance Henriksen, Yancy Butler, Arnold Vosloo, Wilford Brimley, Kasi Lemmons.

●Sporting hair extensions and a Cajun accent, Van Damme plays Chance Boudreaux, a drifter who comes to the aid of one Natasha Binder (Butler) as she searches for her transient father in New Orleans. He turns up dead, the luckless prey in a deadly bloodsport: a clandestine safari through the urban jungle in which the very rich hunt and kill derelicts. Matters improve considerably once the hunt is on – the movie's firepower would shame the devil. It's what Hollywood wanted Woo for: bigger, brighter explosions. That we can hope for more is evinced by the film's most memorable sequence: a wounded black man stumbles through a busy main street begging for help, ignored by everyone except his hunters. As the man becomes resigned to his fate, Woo homes in on his face in three arresting jump-cut freeze-frames. The scene doesn't just betray an alien viewpoint, it distils an undertow of social alienation more sharply than any American director would have dreamed of. TCh

Hard Times (aka The Streetfighter)

(1975, US, 97 min)
d Walter Hill. *p* Lawrence Gordon. *sc* Walter Hill, Bryan Gindorff, Bruce Henstell. *ph* Philip H Lathrop. *ed* Roger Spottiswoode. *ad* Trevor Williams. *m* Barry DeVorzon. *cast* Charles Bronson, James Coburn, Jill Ireland, Strother Martin, Maggie Blye, Michael McGuire, Robert Tessier, Frank McRae.

●Hill's debut as a director: a surprisingly arresting and tight film about illegal bare-knuckle fighting in Depression era New Orleans. Rather than open up the story with the type of pretentious moralising that bedevils the majority of American sporting and gambling films, this utilises Bronson's limited range to produce a laconic, unemotional, almost Oriental celebration of the mythic fighting hero. Strong supporting performances, good locations, and well-staged fights contribute to what is an impressive example of how to assemble this kind of material. CPe

Hard Times (Tempos Dificeis, Este Tempo)

(1988, Port/GB, 96 min, b/w)
d/p/sc Joao Botelho. *ph* Elso Roque. *ed* Joao Botelho. *ad* Jasmin Matos. *m* António Pinho Vargas. *cast* Luis Estrela, Julia Britton, Isabel de Castro, Ruy Furtado, Inêz de Medeiros.

●Botelho's third feature is a modern-day adaptation of Dickens' novel, set in a strangely timeless Lisbon. Constructed for the most part from static tableaux shot in stunning black-and-white, performed with a stylised detachment, and littered with intriguing, even startling narrative ellipses, it is serious but never solemn. Indeed, for all the personal tragedy on view, much of the film is very funny with Dickens' purple and eccentric text (often spoken in voice-over) complemented by and contrasted with Elso Roque's starkly poetic images. It's a tale of jealousy, robbery, and disillusionment; of stern, forbidding patriarchs, downtrodden wives and workers, and orphans making good, in a world both defined and confined by its unflinching commitment to facts as opposed to feelings. The film's manifest intelligence and profound sense of irony knocks spots off most British literary adaptations, while simultaneously constituting a love letter to cinema itself. GA

Hard to Handle

(1932, US, 75 min, b/w)
d Mervyn LeRoy. *p* Robert Lord. *sc* Wilson Mizner, Robert Lord. *ph* Barney McGill. *ed* William Holmes. *ad* Robert M Haas. *cast* James Cagney, Mary Brian, Ruth Donnelly, Allen Jenkins, Emma Dunn, Claire Dodd, Robert McWade.

●This breezy comedy is a real product of the Depression, with Cagney blustering away as the scheming promotions man ducking and diving his way from fronting marathon dance contests, to pushing new wonder diets and making

America grapefruit-conscious (an allusion perhaps to the star's notorious fruit-in-the-face scene from *Public Enemy*). He meets his match in determined mom Donnelly, who's set on marrying him off to daughter Brian, and if the whole thing doesn't make a heck of a lot of sense, at least it speeds along. TJ

Hard to Kill

(1990, US, 96 min)
d Bruce Malmuth. *p* Gary Adelson., Joel Simon, Bill Todman Jr. *sc* Steven McKay. *ph* Matthew F Leonetti. *ed* John F Link *pd* Robb Wilson King. *m* David Michael Frank. *cast* Steven Seagal, Kelly LeBrock, Bill Sadler, Frederick Coffin, Bonnie Burroughs.

●A routine cop thriller with plenty of bodies but no brains. Waking from a lengthy coma, LA cop Mason Storm (Seagal) swears revenge on the corrupt senator, crooked cops and vicious hoodlums who killed his wife and son and put him to sleep for seven years. With a little TLC from nurse Andy Stewart (LeBrock) and some help from a retired Internal Affairs officer, Storm regains gale force and blows away everyone in sight. he also recovers an incriminating videotape which will put the senator, now aspiring Vice President, behind bars for a long time. While Seagal is spraying bullets, breaking bones and throwing interchangeable bad guys through windows, this has a certain mindless appeal. But Malmuth's flaccid direction lacks the vicious muscularity and authentic edge of Seagal's previous feature, Nico; while the poorly integrated romantic subplot – not to mention the drippy, Chuck Norris-style flashback scenes involving the dead wife and son – lead to some awkward, choppy scene transitions. Why do these tough guys always insist on showing their sensitive side too? NF

Hardware

(1990, GB/US, 94 min)
d Richard Stanley. *p* Paul Trybits, Joanne Sellar. *sc* Richard Stanley, Mike Fallon. *ph* Chris Chivers. *ed* Derek Trigg. *pd* Joseph Bennett. *m* Simon Boswell. *cast* Dylan McDermott, Stacey Travis, John Lynch, William Hootkins, Iggy Pop, Carl McCoy, Mark Northover.

●In the barren wastelands of the future, a zone trooper stumbles upon the remains of an advanced killing machine, the Mark 13 cyborg. Purchased by rugged space trooper Mo (McDermott) as a gift for his sculptress girlfriend Jill (Travis), the dismembered fragments reconstruct themselves from household appliances, turning Jill's apartment into a combat zone as the reborn machinery goes on the rampage. Former pop-promo director Stanley's feature debut is an impressive assault on the senses, a shamelessly plagiaristic robotics nightmare laden with OTT apocalyptic symbolism and brash cinematic homages, from Argento's *Deep Red* to Cameron's *The Terminator*. Stanley's gaudy vision achieves a roller-coaster pace, swept along by an incessant industrial soundtrack, the perfect backdrop for Image Animation's deliciously fetishistic creation, all pumping pistons and sinewy flex. An energetic, low-budget Pandora's Box of delights, tailor-made for the disposable '90s. MK

Hard Way, The

(1991, US, 111 min)
d John Badham. *p* William Sackheim, Rob Cohen. *sc* Daniel Pyne, Lem Dobbs. *ph* Robert Primes, Don McAlpine. *ed* Frank Morriss, Tony Lombardo. *pd* Philip Harrison. *m* Arthur B Rubinstein. *cast* Michael J Fox, James Woods, Stephen Lang, Annabella Sciorra, Delroy Lindo, Luis Guzmán, Mary Mara, Christina Ricci, Penny Marshall.

●Action-man actor Nick Lang (Fox), tired of cartoon characters (his latest is 'Smoking Gunn II') wants to land the part of a gritty New York homicide detective, so his agent fixes up some real-life experience with John Moss (Woods). But this reluctant 'Yoda among cops' has no intention of babysitting, and continues his search for a dangerous killer, all the while dragging the movie star through his chaotic and dangerous life. This light, bright comedy counterbalances Hollywood convention with some very funny swipes at the film industry. A breathtaking opening chase sequence gives way to a gloriously playful, carping exchange between Lang and his agent (Marshall) as they review the current state of Hollywood, ranging from the success of *Henry V* ('It won awards for that little Scottish fellow') to the unstoppable career of Mel Gibson. Badham handles the numerous action sequences with confidence, but the real enjoyment comes from the interplay between the two leads, who revel in the opportunity to send up their images. The ever-amazing Woods recalls *Cop* during speeches about his life, and Fox's 'dickless Tracy' tries to debunk nice-guy McFly. CM

Harem

(1985, Fr, 114 min)
d Arthur Joffé. *p* Alain Sarde. Arthur Joffé, Tom Rayfiel. *ph* Pasqualino De Santis. *ed* Françoise Bonnot, Dominique Martin. *pd* Alexandre Trauner. *m* Philippe Sarde. *cast* Nastassja Kinski, Ben Kingsley, Dennis Goldson, Michel Robin, Zohra Segal, Juliette Simpson.

●It is hard not to be impressed by the single-mindedness of Joffé who, with only a few shorts to his credit, garnered $10 million, Kinski and Kingsley, and made his own movie. Kinski plays a single-minded New York demoiselle, working at full stretch on Wall Street and firmly not on the lookout for 9 weeks of passion. But mysterious gifts begin arriving, and before long she appears to be a prize catch for the white slave market, waking up one day in an isolated Arabian harem. Fortunately, though, her captor is an educated and lonely prince who has desired her from afar. What might have been an intriguing clash of cultures soon dissipates into a listless drama of will they/won't they, until the Tragic Irony of the finale falls completely flat. Fine credentials (attractive decor by Trauner, delicate photography by De Santis) but little inspiration. DT

Harem Suare (Le Dernier Harem)

(1999, Fr/It/Tur, 106 min)
d Ferzan Ozpetek. *p* Tilde Corsi, Régine Konckier, Jean-Luc Ormières, Gianni Romoli. *sc* Ferzan Ozpetek, Gianni Romoli. *ph* Pasquale Mari. *ed* Mauro Bonanni. *ad* Bruno Cesari, Mustafa Ziya Ulgenciler. *cast* Marie Gillain, Alex Descas, Lucia Bosé, Valeria Golino, Malick Bowens, Christophe Aquillon, Serra Yilmaz, Haluk Bilginer.

●Ozpetek's follow-up to *The Turkish Bath* is a murky historical drama slithering about the political and emotional convolutions of life in the Sultan's harem during the dying days of the Ottoman Empire, as recounted (get this) to Valeria Golino at a train station by an old woman who was there. It looks a million (at least, the costume budget does), but the human relations are too vague and diffused to hold the centre, and the sense of bygone traditions and practices is shallow, certainly compared to similar treatments in *The Silences of the Palace* and *Raise the Red Lantern*. NB

Harlan County, U.S.A.

(1976, US, 103 min, b/w & col)
d/p/sc Barbara Kopple. *ph* Hart Perry, Kevin Keating. *ed* Nancy Baker, Mary Lampson. *with* Nimrod Workman, EB Allen, Bessie Lou Cornett, Jim Thomas.

●With its plundering of Hollywood narrative conventions – notably an action pic crescendo climax, and establishment 'villains' who could have come straight from Central Casting – Kopple's documentary about a Kentucky miner's strike fails in ways typical of many American political films which strike a chord in the liberal conscience and go on to win Oscars. *Harlan County* inevitably gets very confused/confusing at times, but there's some extraordinary footage by the courageous crew, and to its credit the film eschews any BBC notions of 'impartiality' or 'balance'. The role of women in the strike (as pickets, debaters about tactics, morale-boosters and strengtheners of solidarity) begs comparison with *Salt of the Earth*. Required viewing, therefore, but there should have been more analysis and less emotive effect. RM

Harlem Nights

(1989, US, 116 min)
d Eddie Murphy. *p* Robert D Wachs, Mark Lipsky. *sc* Eddie Murphy. *ph* Woody Omens. *ed* George Bowers. *pd* Lawrence G Paull. *m* Herbie Hancock. *cast* Eddie Murphy, Richard Pryor, Redd Foxx, Michael Lerner, Danny Aiello, Della Reese.

●New York 1938, and the city's nocturnal revelries are centered upon Club Sugar Ray, where gambling, booze and hookers are available in equal quantities. Presided over by the paternal Sugar Ray (Pryor) and his hot-headed adopted son Quick (Murphy), the illegal venue's profitable future is threatened when rival clubster Bugsy Calhoune (Lerner) demands a slice of the action, aided and abetted by crooked cop Phil Cantone (Aiello). Resolving to head for pastures new, Ray and Quick plot to stitch up Calhoune and Cantone once and for all before exiting swiftly with the loot. Written, produced, directed by and starring Mr Murphy, *Harlem Nights* is a bloated period piece, brandishing big production values, one or two good performances (notably Pryor and Aiello), the occasional laugh, and a spectacularly duff sub-*Sting* storyline that doesn't so much climax as go prematurely limp. Murphy's screenplay abounds with the usual doses of misogynistic dialogue, interspersed with a few gags about people who stutter and multiple use of the word 'motherfucker', all of which are tiresome. the imposing Della Reese meanwhile camps it up as a ball-busting Madame, who says 'Kiss my entire ass' endlessly and beats Murphy up, which is a vicarious delight for all. MK

Harlequin

(1980, Aust, 93 min)
d Simon Wincer. *p* Antony I Ginnane. *sc* Everett De Roche. *ph* Gary Hansen. *ed* Adrian Carr. *pd* Bernard Hides. *m* Brian May. *cast* Robert Powell, David Hemmings, Carmen Duncan, Broderick Crawford, Gus Mercurio, Alan Cassell, Mark Spain.

●The multi-headed beast of international packaging got its fangs into the struggling Australian film industry and spat out this lump of drivelling horror. The potentially interesting notion of re-running the Rasputin legend in the context of a modern political campaign is sunk by a dumb script, a lot of telekinetic flummery, and a performance from Robert Powell which desperately lacks the sense of irony that might at least have transformed his studded leather and mascara into high camp instead of the simply ridiculous. With its English leads, its supporting cast dubbed into American, and its carefully non-specific locations, the whole miserable thing founders somewhere in mid-Pacific. CPea

Harley Davidson and the Marlboro Man

(1991, US, 98 min)
d Simon Wincer. *p* Jere Henshaw. *sc* Don Michael Paul. *ph* David Eggby. *ed* Corky Ehlers. *pd* Paul Peters. *m* Basil Poledouris. *cast* Mickey Rourke, Don Johnson, Chelsea Field, Daniel Baldwin, Giancarlo Esposito, Vanessa Williams, Tom Sizemore, Julius Harris.

●Set in sunny Burbank, this disastrous modern Western veers between camp pastiche and po-faced machismo as two tough but tenderhearted tearaways accidentally steal some drugs. Pursued by mobsters who want their merchandise back, Harley (Rourke) and Marly (Johnson) bike, smoke, flex biceps, jump off tall buildings, and indulge in various limp male-bonding rituals. They make a ludicrously vain double act, Johnson modelling sporty stetson and kinky boots, Rourke opting for a black-and-red leather jump-suit with his name emblazoned on the back. The baddies, meanwhile, are dressed to kill in fetching ankle-to-neck, wet-look overcoats. Utter rubbish, and badly dressed at that. MK

Harmonists, The

see Comedian Harmonists

Harold and Maude

(1971, US, 92 min)
d Hal Ashby. *p* Colin Higgins, Charles Mulvehill. *sc* Colin Higgins. *ph* John A Alonzo. *ed* William A Sawyer, Edward A Warschilka. *ad* Michael Haller. *m* Cat Stevens. *cast* Ruth Gordon, Bud Cort, Vivian Pickles, Cyril Cusack, Charles Tyner, Ellen Geers.

●Like Bob Rafelson, a director similarly obsessed with the trials and tribulations of the children of the rich, Ashby forever treads the thin line between whimsy and absurdity and 'tough' sentimentality and black comedy. *Harold and Maude* is the story of a rich teenager (Cort) obsessed with death – his favourite pastime is trying out different mock suicides – who is finally liberated by his (intimate) friendship with Ruth Gordon, an 80-year-old funeral freak. It is most successful when it keeps to the tone of an insane fairystory set up at the beginning of the movie. PH

Harper (aka The Moving Target)

(1966, US, 121 min)
d Jack Smight. *p* Jerry Gershwin, Elliott Kastner. *sc* William Goldman. *ph* Conrad Hall. *ed* Stefan Arnsten. *ad* Alfred Sweeney. *m* Johnny Mandel. *cast* Paul Newman, Lauren Bacall, Julie Harris, Arthur Hill, Janet Leigh, Pamela Tiffin, Shelley Winters, Robert Wagner, Robert Webber.

● Newman plays Ross MacDonald's private eye Lew Harper, a role he was to repeat for Stuart Rosenberg in 1975's *The Drowning Pool*. William Goldman, in his first solo script credit, plays knowing games with the Chandlerish conventions, while director Smight pumps up the pace and tags along with the allusive casting of Bacall. Enjoyable performances throughout. Just the same, a very minor *Big Sleep*. PT

Harrad Experiment, The

(1973, US, 97 min)
d Ted Post. *p* Dennis F Stevens. *sc* Michael Werner, Ted Cassedy. *ph* Richard H Kline. *ed* Bill Brame. *m* Artie Butler. *cast* James Whitmore, Tippi Hedren, Don Johnson, B Kirby Jr, Laurie Walters, Victoria Thompson, Robert Middleton.

● Or 'Gidget Meets Masters and Johnson'. Set in an American co-ed college where the pupils are taught self-discovery through sex and (discreet) nudity, the film merges teen romance and sexposé so beguilingly that it ends up as one of the most amusing Hollywood romps since *Beyond the Valley of the Dolls*. The sexual agonies and dilemmas are straight out of True Romances, and frequently crass; but occasionally they have a lurid authenticity, and Post, who employs long, voyeuristic takes, reveals more gusto here than one would ever have thought possible from his previous work. The film, with its incredibly awful theme song and old-fashioned conception of sexological research, well deserves the cult success it had in America. DP

Harriet the Spy

(1996, US, 101 min)
d Bronwen Hughes. *p* Marykay Powell. *sc* Douglas Petrie, Theresa Rebeck. *ph* Francis Kenny. *ed* Debra Chiate. *pd* Lester Cohen. *m* Jamshied Sharifi. *cast* Michelle Trachtenberg, Gregory Smith, Vanessa Lee Chester, Rosie O'Donnell, J Smith-Cameron, Robert Joy, Charlotte Sullivan, Eartha Kitt.

● Adapted from Louise Fitzhugh's 1964 novel about a determined 11-year-old, this primary-coloured piece is a sweet but flawed take on the inspirational children's film. Harriet (Trachtenberg) is indeed a spy – self-employed – roaming the neighbourhood, observing life in all its multi-cultural glory, and taking comprehensive readings in her private notebook. She wants to remember everything, because she's going to be a writer. Meet her world: best friends Janie (Lee Chester), a budding home chemist, and Sport (Smith), a house-kid tending to his starving-writer dad; the rest of her class, including prim Marion, class president; her well-to-do parents; and her guiding light, nanny Golly (O'Donnell). That's the set-up. Pity it takes most of an hour, without proposing where we might be going. Much of the Nickelodeon-assembled cast and crew share a background in commercials, and it shows: good-looking, insistently hip 'fun' – it's also quite boring. Then Marion steals Harriet's notebook, reads out her rather hurtful character assessments of all her friends; they take revenge; Harriet takes her revenge; everyone shuns her; her parents get worried and stop her note-taking; bad emotions take hold…and we have a story. Engaging dilemmas, solutions, experiences – great. And maybe it was worth the wait, but the wait wasn't needed. NB

Harry & Son

(1984, US, 117 min)
d Paul Newman. *p* Paul Newman, Ronald L Buck. *sc* Ronald L Buck, Paul Newman. *ph* Donald McAlpine. *ed* Dede Allen. *pd* Henry Bumstead. *m* Henry Mancini. *cast* Paul Newman, Robby Benson, Ellen Barkin, Wilford Brimley, Judith Ivey, Ossie Davis, Morgan Freeman, Joanne Woodward.

● Taken sequence by sequence, this is a well acted and elegantly photographed social drama, with Newman as a depressed widower who loses his job and quarrels with his kids. The plot is a little thin, but Big Acting Scene follows Big Acting Scene quite pleasantly for a while, until you begin to realise that Newman (who co-scripted as well as directed) has decided to compose his entire film out of them. It is nothing more than a constant succession of the kind of emotional peaks actors love to do on screen. Humbler scenes involving background or narrative, which may be immensely tedious to act but help the plot unfold, have in general been left out altogether. The result is a curiously indigestible phenomenon, like being forced to eat five courses of avocado by an overbearing dinner-party host. DP

Harry and the Butler (Harry og Kammertjeneren)

(1961, Den, 105 min)
d Bent Christensen. *p* Bent Christensen, Preben Philipsen. *sc* Bent Christensen, Leif Panduro. *ph* Kjeld Arnholtz. *ed* Kirsten Christensen, Lene Møller. *pd* Erik Aaes. *m* Niels Rothenborg. *cast* Osvald Helmuth, Ebbe Rode, Gunnar Lauring, Henning Moritzen, Lise Ringheim, Lily Broberg, Olaf Ussing, Palle Kirk.

● A gentle comedy offering the promise of easy social consensus. Harry (Helmuth) is a simple old-time shop porter offered a chance at self-realisation when he's bequeathed a sum by an unknown relative (via several levels of fiscal blood suckers). He decides to engage a butler to take good care of him for a time. This is a man of distinguished upper class service, but a generous nature which happily integrates with Harry's small but colourful world of drinking buddies and crackpot neighbourhood kids. Affable whimsy. NB

Harry and the Hendersons (aka Bigfoot and the Hendersons)

(1987, US, 111 min)
d William Dear. *p* Richard Vane, William Dear. *sc* William Dear, William E Martin, Ezra D Rappaport. *ph* Allen Daviau. *ed* Donn Cambern. *pd* James D Bissell. *m* Bruce Broughton. *cast* John Lithgow, Melinda Dillon, Margaret Langrick, Joshua Rudoy, Kevin Peter Hall, David Suchet, Lainie Kazan, Don Ameche, M Emmet Walsh.

● 'A William Dear Film'? Come off it, this has Steven Spielberg, whose Amblin company produced, written all over it. While the Hendersons are on a hunting holiday, their car collides with the legendary Bigfoot of the Pacific Northwest. Mistakenly believing the Yeti-like creature dead, they take him to their Seattle home, which he promptly demolishes before proving himself a genial giant of enormous compassion. Nevertheless, nosey neighbours and fame-hungry hunters smell something suspicious, and pretty soon the gun-crazy citizens of Seattle are on the trail of the hapless, hirsute 'Harry'. This cloying mixture of sitcom and fantasy is clearly designed to pluck the heart-strings, tickle the funnybone, and sow seeds of doubt about the moral worth of hunting. GA

Harry and Tonto

(1974, US, 115 min)
d/p Paul Mazursky. *sc* Paul Mazursky, Josh Greenfeld. *ph* Michael Butler. *ed* Richard Halsey. *ad* Ted Haworth. *m* Bill Conti. *cast* Art Carney, Ellen Burstyn, Chief Dan George, Geraldine Fitzgerald, Larry Hagman, Arthur Hunnicutt, Joshua Mostel, Melanie Mayron.

● Mazursky's odyssey traces elderly widower Harry's flight/trip across America with cat Tonto after the demolition of his NY apartment. It's *Candide* again, with Harry not so much an innocent as a sympathetic, who is mugged, seduced, welcomed, depended upon, rejected, ever so gently. Its charm has a calculated feel, though, its individualities an edge of whimsy, its poetry is rhyming couplets. Harry's freedom to mix it with the kids, squeezing out their oppressed parents, is hammered home. Still, Mazursky has escaped Fellini's shadow; when everyone's back from going to 'look for America', he might have something interesting to say. SG

Harry and Walter Go to New York

(1976, US, 111 min)
d Mark Rydell. *p* Don Devlin, Harry Gittes. *sc* John Byrum, Robert Kaufman. *ph* Laszlo Kovacs. *ed* Fredric Steinkamp, David Bretherton, Don Guidice. *pd* Harry Horner. *m* David Shire. *cast* James Caan, Elliott Gould, Michael Caine, Diane Keaton, Charles Durning, Lesley Ann Warren, Val Avery, Jack Gilford.

● A caper film set in the 1890s whose weightily established period atmosphere (carefully gaslit interiors, tones of muted brown and gold) creates a mausoleum-like environment in which all attempts at comedy die the death. The disastrous casting of Caan and Gould as a variety song-and-dance act – unsuccessful, as they demonstrate only too effectively – dooms the project further. There is some fleetingly acute re-creation of the mores of the upper crust of the criminal world, a climax of chaotic mayhem, and a neatly dotty performance from Lesley Ann Warren. The film provides its own epitaph when Caine's underworld star, asked why he keeps on cracking safes, remarks that 'every cell tingles with the possibility of failure'. Failure realised, and with precious little tingle. VG

Harry, He's Here to Help (Harry, un ami qui vous veut du bien/aka With a Friend Like Harry...)

(2000, Fr, 117 min)
d Dominik Moll. *p* Michel Saint-Jean. *sc* Dominik Moll, Gilles Marchand. *ph* Matthieu Poirot-Delpech. *ed* Yannick Kergoat. *pd* Michel Barthélémy. *m* David Sinclair Whitaker. *cast* Sergi Lopez, Laurent Lucas, Mathilde Seigner, Sophie Guillemin, Liliane Rovère, Dominique Rozan, Michel Fau, Victoire de Koster.

● This quirky comedy-thriller cum psychological study charts the encounter between a young couple facing a tough holiday in the Auvergne with their troublesome kids, and the likeable but clearly loopy Lopez – an old schoolmate of the husband, now wealthy, generous and determined to revive and encourage his long-forgotten (and hardly realistic) writing ambitions. At first, as Lopez and his girl (Guillemin, bovine as in *L'Ennui*) wheedle their way into Lucas and Seigner's lives, the tone is wittily offbeat (yet rooted in an impressively plausible portrait of everyday banality); as the demands of friendship become more complex, however, the film takes a turn into altogether darker territory. Lopez, excellent as ever, gets superb support all round, while director/co-writer Moll handles the shifts in tone with quiet assurance. GA

Harry In Your Pocket

(1973, US, 103 min)
d/p Bruce Geller. *sc* Ron Austin, James D Buchanan. *ph* Fred J Koenekamp. *ed* Arthur Hilton. *ad* William Bates. *m* Lalo Schifrin. *cast* James Coburn, Michael Sarrazin, Trish Van Devere, Walter Pidgeon, Michael C Gwynne, Tony Giorgio, Michael Stearns.

● Coburn as a jet-set pickpocket in a film that looks as if it should have been sold straight to the TV networks. Too much time is devoted to the least interesting aspect of the story, a rather silly love triangle involving Coburn. Sarrazin and Devere. Coburn's profession demands that he remain a cipher in the society in which he has chosen to operate, but this implication is never developed; and too little time is devoted to the art of the professional pickpocket at work, something else that would have made for a more interesting time. CPe

Harry Potter and the Philosopher's Stone (aka Harry Potter and the Sorcerer's Stone) (100)

(2001, US/GB, 152 min)
d Chris Columbus. *p* David Heyman. *sc* Steve Kloves. *ph* John Seale. *ed* Richard Francis-Bruce. *pd* Stuart Craig. *m* John Williams. *cast* Daniel Radcliffe, Rupert Grint, Emma Watson, John Cleese, Robbie Coltrane, Richard

Griffiths, Richard Harris, Ian Hart, John Hurt, Alan Rickman, Fiona Shaw, Maggie Smith, Julie Walters, Zoë Wanamaker, David Bradley, Tom Felton, Elizabeth Spriggs.
●Orphaned Harry (Radcliffe) is billeted in the suburbs with his cruel aunt and uncle until a blizzard of letters arrives from Hogwarts School offering a chance to study wizardry. He is yet to learn that he bears a famous name in that skill, and that the lightning-flash scar on his forehead was the result of a clash with the Most Evil One, Voldemort, in babyhood. Harry goes from deprivation to elevation in true fairytale style, school career benignly supervised by headmaster Dumbledore (Harris), the assistant head (Smith) and the kindly, hulking Keeper of Keys and Grounds, Hagrid (Coltrane), but threatened by sneering contemporary Draco Malfoy (Felton) and malevolent Professor Snape (Rickman). All the boarding school stuff is terrific, and the lessons quick and funny. Harry's pals are Ron Weasley (Grint) and Hermione Granger (Watson), both jumps ahead of the Children's Film Foundation. The game of Quidditch, the most eagerly awaited visualisation from JK Rowling's first book, is as fast as *Top Gun*, but then becomes incomprehensible. What a feast for children! Long, and engrossing. Kids will love it! Wizard! BC

Harry Potter and the Sorcerer's Stone

see Harry Potter and the Philosopher's Stone

Harry, un ami qui vous veut du bien

see Harry, He's Here to Help

Harvest, The

(1992, US, 97 min)
d David Marconi. *p* Morgan Mason, Jason Clark. *sc* David Marconi. *ph* Emmanuel Lubezki. *ed* Carlos Puente. *pd* J Rae Fox. *m* Dave Allen, Rick Boston. *cast* Miguel Ferrer, Leilani Sarelle, Harvey Fierstein, Henry Silva, Anthony Denison.
●One of those moody thrillers where down-on-his-luck gringo (Ferrer's blocked scriptwriter) heads down to Mexico and finds himself involved with a femme fatale, corrupt officialdom and various seedy ex-pats. Nothing very original, then, although there's a nice twist when Ferrer wakes to find himself short of one kidney. The hothouse atmosphere, boozy interludes and fishing-nets on the beach suggest that Marconi has seen the likes of *The Big Steal* and *Out of the Past* once too often. GA

Harvey

(1950, US, 104 min, b/w)
d Henry Koster. *p* John Beck. *sc* Oscar Brodney. *ph* William H Daniels. *ed* Ralph Dason. *ad* Bernard Herzbrun, Nathan Juran. *m* Frank Skinner. *cast* James Stewart, Josephine Hull, Cecil Kellaway, Peggy Dow, Jesse White, Charles Drake, Wallace Ford.
●Stewart in his batty but amiable persona as small-town boozer Elwood P Dowd, who imagines a close friendship with a 'pooka' (a mischievous familiar of Irish folklore), in this case a 6' 4" white rabbit called Harvey. His anxious sister (Hull) tries to get him certified, but the film suggests that the fantasy is quite harmless. Charming, lightweight stuff (from a play by Mary Chase), so long as you can take Stewart's ingenuousness, but it does wear thin. GA

Harvey Girls, The

(1946, US, 101 min)
d George Sidney. *p* Arthur Freed. *sc* Edmund Beloin, Nathaniel Curtis, Harry Crane, James O'Hanlon, Samson Raphaelson. *ph* George Folsey. *ed* Albert Akst. *ad* Cedric Gibbons, William Ferrari. *songs* Johnny Mercer, Harry Warren. *cast* Judy Garland, John Hodiak, Ray Bolger, Angela Lansbury, Virginia O'Brien, Preston Foster, Marjorie Main, Kenny Baker.
●A likeable but aimless musical which doesn't know what to make of its plot (designed to cash in on the pioneer spirit of *Oklahoma*) about the Harvey House restaurants which followed the railroad into the West, bringing demure waitresses into the domain of rowdy saloon girls. The highly inappropriate Harry Warren/Johnny Mercer songs are mostly romantic numbers or specialties for the deadpan O'Brien, with even the bustling 'On the Atchison, Topeka and the Santa Fe' failing to rouse any real echoes of the Western. It is symptomatic that the film's best and most legitimate number, with Angela Lansbury leading a saloon girl chorus of 'Oh, You Kid', is thrown away in favour of a dialogue exchange between Garland and Hodiak which could well have waited. TM

Harvey Middleman, Fireman

(1965, US, 76 min)
d Ernest Pintoff. *p* Robert L Lawrence. *sc* Ernest Pintoff. *ph* Karl Malkames. *ed* Hugh A Robertson Jr. *pd* Gene Callahan. *m* Ernest Pintoff. *cast* Gene Troobnick, Hermione Gingold, Patricia Harty, Arlene Golonka, Will Mackenzie, Charles Durning.
●In animator Pintoff's first live-action feature, Harvey is a fireman with a nice wife, nice children, nice house. He rescues a girl, falls in love with her, has attacks of conscience, and cools it; whereupon the girl stages another fire, falls into the arms of another fireman, and Harvey goes happily back to his domestic routine. At first this simple story is used as a peg for very effective humour derived from the contrast between the mundane, frightening 'normalness' of Harvey's daily routine, and the pride in it which he confides to camera in a series of monologues. But the film changes direction, and what started as sharp, subtle satire on a 'normal' American ends up as little more than standard domestic comedy, complete with pat happy ending. JC

Has Anybody Seen My Gal

(1952, US, 89 min)
d Douglas Sirk. *p* Ted Richmond. *sc* Joseph Hoffman. *ph* Clifford Stine. *ed* Russell Schoengarth. *ad* Bernhard Herzbrun, Hilyard Brown. *m* Joseph Gershenson. *cast* Charles Coburn, Piper Laurie, Rock Hudson, Gigi Perreau, Lynn Bari, Larry Gates, Skip Homeier.
●One of a projected series of films about small town America, this was Sirk's first in colour. Coburn plays an eccentric millionaire investigating the Blaisdell family, to whom he is thinking of leaving all his money. The $100,000 he gives them as a test goes to the parents' heads, but the children and their commonsensical values save the day. From this perspective the film is an admirable companion piece to *All That Heaven Allows*. In contrast to the devastating view of selfish children and mean-minded respectable citizens of that film, *Has Anybody Seen My Gal* is one of Sirk's gentler – and lesser – works, making charming use of its '20s setting and songs. James Dean made his brief debut in one of the drugstore scenes. PH

Hasards ou coïncidences

see Chance or Coincidence

Hasta Morir (Until Death)

(1994, Mex, 90 min)
d Fernando Sariñana. *sc* Marcela Fuentes Berain. *ph* Guillermo Granillo. *ed* Carlos Bolado. *m* Eduardo Gamboa. *cast* Demián Bichir, Juan Manuel Bernal, Dolores Beristain, Vanessa Bouche, Verónica Merchant.
●Well-directed, effective contemporary tragidrama of disenchanted Mexico City youth focusing on two friends since childhood. One is a cool criminal dude with a 'Pachucho' tattoo, a porkpie hat and a belief in knives (a noble weapon) rather than guns; the other a weak vessel with an dog who adopts an empty machismo when the pressure builds following a store robbery. Blending familar staples such as the Cain and Abel story, the doppelgänger and the conventions of the US ghetto movie, writer/director Sarinana nevertheless manages to turns a fresh eye on notions of couth and cool for today's barrio boys. Its enjoyable music track of acoustic guitar rock and Mexican-style funk sets the tone perfectly. No masterpiece, but it keeps you involved. WH

Hasty Heart, The

(1949, GB, 107 min, b/w)
d/p Vincent Sherman. *sc* Ranald MacDougall. *ph* Wilkie Cooper. *ed* EB Jarvis. *ad* Terence Verity. *m* Jack Beaver. *cast* Richard Todd, Patricia Neal, Ronald Reagan, Anthony Nicholls, Howard Marion Crawford, Ralph Michael, Orlando Martins, Alfie Bass.
●Leaden version of John Patrick's tearjerking play, set in a World War II army hospital in Burma, about a dour, chip-on-shoulder Scottish soldier who gradually discovers the meaning of friendship after learning that he has only weeks to live. Todd won some plaudits at the time for his stubborn performance, but subsequent appearances confirmed that the wooden look was habitual. TM

Hatari!

(1961, US, 157 min)
d/p Howard Hawks. *sc* Leigh Brackett. *ph* Russell Harlan. *ed* Stuart Gilmore. *ad* Hal Pereira, Carl Anderson. *m* Henry Mancini. *cast* John Wayne, Elsa Martinelli, Hardy Kruger, Red Buttons, Gérard Blain, Michèle Girardon, Bruce Cabot.
●Marked by the relaxed pace and tone of Hawks' later work, this could easily be seen as *Only Angels Have Wings* transferred from the Andes to the African bush. There's little plot but plenty of typically Hawksian situations as it follows the travails of a group of safari hunters (preservationists, not killers) working a game reserve. All the usual themes emerge as gently and naturally as bubbles from champagne: the need for professionalism and self-respect; the importance of the group and integration; attraction between men and women seen as conflict; and (echoing *Monkey Business* and *Bringing Up Baby*) asides on humans as animals. Light, sunny, and effortlessly switching between action and comedy, it also fascinates through its superb footage of the actual capture of the wildlife, in which the danger and the excitement of the chase are beautifully, precisely evoked. All in all, one of those rare films that genuinely constitutes a 'late masterpiece'. GA

Hatchet Man, The (aka The Honourable Mr Wong)

(1931, US, 74 min, b/w)
d William A Wellman. *sc* J Grubb Alexander. *ph* Sid Hickox. *ed* Owen Marks. *ad* Anton F Grot. *cast* Edward G Robinson, Loretta Young, Dudley Digges, Leslie Fenton, Tully Marshall, J Carrol Naish.
●Robinson is the hit man of the title, a Chinaman who has made it as an American businessman, and who is called back to his traditional responsibilities when a Tong War breaks out in San Francisco. To complicate matters, his task is to kill his best friend, and he must then look after the latter's daughter. It's a subject that would surely have excited Sam Fuller. As handled by Wellman, the idea of friendship and responsibility is called into question rather than that of cultural identity. An intriguing film (from a play by Achmed Abdullah and David Belasco). PH

Hate

see Haine, La

Hathi

(1998, Can/Ind, 97 min)
d Philippe Gautier. *p* Rock Demers. *sc* Prajna Chowta. *ph* Ivan Gekoff. *ed* Myriam Poirier. *m* Narasimhalu Vadavati. *cast* Jamedar Sabu Saab, Kawadi Makbul, Noorullah, Pyare Jan, Begum Jamila, Begum Kahurun, Nanny Ama, Shabanah Saab, Venkatesh.
●A film of few words and entrancing images, this tells of a villager who follows his father to become a mahout, working the declining population of Indian elephants. Things go awry when the Forestry Commission sells off his elephant to a private buyer (cue disingenuous mumblings about buyers cheating the government), but Gautier's film is less about story than mood (as measured and leisurely as an elephant's ambling) and message: the usual (quite justified) ecological truisms about skills and customs vanishing beneath the plough of progress. That said, it's a slightly dubious argument. While man and beast certainly work well together, one shouldn't forget the animals are forced to do so, by and purely for the benefit of humans. Still, the movie has a fairytale simplicity,the framing is superb, and the lead pachyderm deserves an Oscar (not to mention his freedom). GA

Hatter's Castle

(1941, GB, 102 min, b/w)
d Lance Comfort. *p* Isadore G Goldsmith. *sc* Paul Merzbach, Rudolf Bernauer, Rodney Ackland. *ph* Max Green. *ed* Douglas Robertson. *ad* James Carter. *m* Horace Shepherd. *cast* Robert Newton, Emlyn Williams, James Mason, Deborah Kerr, Beatrice Varley, Henry Oscar, Anthony Bateman.

●An entertaining slice of Victorian melodrama adapted from AJ Cronin's novel. Not quite Gothic, but edging that way through Newton's performance (one of his more controlled efforts) as the social-climbing Glasgow hatter who builds himself an opulent mansion, sets about keeping his family in line with a brutal relish that would have made Mr Barrett of Wimpole Street wince, and ends up in madness and conflagration. Damped down by flat direction, but the sets and camerawork are excellent. TM

Hatter's Ghosts, The

see Fantômes du Chapelier, Les

Hauch von Sonnenschein, Ein

see Sunshine

Haunted

(1983, US, 118 min)
d Michael Roemer. *p* Stanley D Plotnick. *sc* Michael Roemer. *ph* Franz Rath. *ed* Terry Lewis. *cast* Brooke Adams, Jon De Vries, Ari Meyers, Trish Van Devere, Mark Arnott, Scottie Bloch, Roseanna Cox.

●With Brooke Adams in fine form as the young woman fleeing an unhappy marriage and taking refuge with a family in a more drastic state of disintegration than her own, this out-and-out melodrama sees her confronting as heavy a mix of cruelty, confusion and incipient insanity as Barbara Stanwyck ever had to face in the '50s. Far darker than the likes of *Dallas* and *Dynasty* (since it avoids their drossy gloss and plasticky plotting), it impresses due to a careful script, superb naturalistic performances, and – perhaps most importantly – a profound and rare awareness that upset/unbalanced people sorely in need of help are very often a total pain in the ass. GA

Haunted

(1995, GB/US, 107 min)
d Lewis Gilbert. *p* Anthony Andrews, Lewis Gilbert. *sc* Lewis Gilbert, Timothy Prager, Bob Kellet. *ph* Tony Pierce-Roberts. *ed* John Jympson. *pd* John Fenner, Brian Ackland-Snow. *m* Debbie Wiseman. *cast* Aidan Quinn, Kate Beckinsale, Anthony Andrews, Alex Lowe, Anna Massey, Liz Smith, John Gielgud.

●Adapted from James Herbert's novel by veteran Lewis Gilbert, this old-fashioned ghost story benefits from craftsmanship, but lacks atmosphere and imagination. All is present and correct, from the Edwardian pile where things go bump in the night, to the ghostly figures by a moonlit lake. Quinn brings an emotional dimension to the professional sceptic David Ash whose rational beliefs are challenged by a confrontation with the spiritual world. Summoned to Edbrook House by dotty servant Miss Webb (Massey), David's drawn into the intrigues of its other three inhabitants, Christina and the brothers Robert (Andrews) and Simon (Lowe). Unsettled by the weird goings-on, David starts to lose his grip on reality. Massey's twitchy, unhinged old lady sets the tone for what will follow, while Beckinsale's sexy Christina fuses childlike recklessness with adult manipulation. Ironically, as the shocking revelations and sfx kick in with a vengeance, it's Quinn's disintegrating professor who holds things together, his outstanding performance a solid dramatic axis around which things spin wildly out of control. NF

Haunted and the Hunted, The

see Dementia 13

Haunted Honeymoon

(1986, US, 84 min)
d Gene Wilder. *p* Susan Ruskin. *sc* Gene Wilder, Terence Marsh. *ph* Fred Schuler. *ed* Chris Greenbury. *pd* Terence Marsh. *m* John Morris. *cast* Gene Wilder, Gilda Radner, Dom DeLuise, Jonathan Pryce, Paul L Smith, Peter Vaughan, Bryan Pringle.

●In the opening scene of this comedy chiller, a sinister spectre, seen only from his white spats down, kicks a loveable family dog. After which it's familiar formula: stick a group of loonies in a draughty mansion, kill one of them off, and kill the lights, with honeymoon couple Wilder and Radner – 1939 stars of radio's *Manhattan Mystery Theatre* – present because he's set to inherit if he can survive the night. Wilder, of course, is playing with genre here, and unlike Mel Brooks with *Young Frankenstein*, gets his fingers burnt. It's flat, unfunny, and full of slavish borrowings. SGo

Haunted Palace, The

(1963, US, 86 min)
d/p Roger Corman. *sc* Charles Beaumont. *ph* Floyd Crosby. *ed* Ronald Sinclair. *ad* Daniel Haller. *m* Ronald Stein. *cast* Vincent Price, Debra Paget, Lon Chaney, Frank Maxwell, Leo Gordon, Elisha Cook, John Dierkes.

●This supposed version of Poe's poem, beautifully scripted by Charles Beaumont with a good deal more than a dash of Lovecraft's *The Case of Charles Dexter Ward*, boasts a superb performance from Price as a New England warlock who is burned alive for his evil practices, though not before putting a curse on his tormentors. In due course he returns, taking over the body of his great-great-grandson to wreak a picturesque revenge, well-flavoured with ground fogs, creaking doors, cobwebs, electrical storms and mutant monsters. If there is a flaw, it is that Daniel Haller's art direction rings too few changes on the style he established in *House of Usher*; but Corman, with his prowling camera omnivorously probing the darker recesses of nightmare, paces his direction to perfection. TM

Haunted Strangler, The

see Grip of the Strangler

Haunted Summer

(1988, US, 106 min)
d Ivan Passer. *p* Martin Poll. *sc* Lewis John Carlino. *ph* Giuseppe Rotunno. *ed* Cesare D'Amico, Richard Fields. *pd* Stephen Grimes. *m* Christopher Young. *cast* Philip Anglim, Laura Dern, Alice Krige, Eric Stoltz, Alexander Winter.

●As in Ken Russell's *Gothic*, it is the summer of 1816. Shelley, his lover Mary Goodwin, and her half-sister Claire Clairmont, gather at the Hôtel d'Angleterre in Secheron, where who should turn up but Lord Byron. We can tell that Shelley (Stoltz) is an untrammelled spirit because he flashes his willy in a waterfall, and that Byron (Anglim) is a free-thinker because he smokes opium provided by his adoring catamite Dr Polidori (Winter). When they have nothing better to do, the queer quintet attempt to scare the hell out of each other in the dungeons of Chillon castle, but all that comes out is yawns. Quivering glances, sensitive silences, pretty photography, and Haydn harmonies do not in themselves make a film serious. Passer, who directed the excellent Cutter's Way, has turned coy here, opting for soft lighting, soft focus, and shots through sheets of gauze for the sedate sex scenes. MS

Haunting, The

(1963, GB, 112 min, b/w)
d/p Robert Wise. *sc* Nelson Gidding. *ph* Davis Boulton. *ed* Ernest Walter. *pd* Elliot Scott. *m* Humphrey Searle. *cast* Julie Harris, Claire Bloom, Richard Johnson, Russ Tamblyn, Fay Compton, Rosalie Crutchley, Lois Maxwell, Valentine Dyall.

●Often overwrought in its performances, this adaptation of Shirley Jackson's novel *The Haunting of Hill House* – a group of people gather in a large old house to determine whether or not a poltergeist is the source of rumours that it is haunted – still manages to produce its fair share of frissons. What makes the film so effective is not so much the slightly sinister characterisation of the generally neurotic group, but the fact that Wise makes the house itself the central character, a beautifully designed and highly atmospheric entity which, despite the often annoyingly angled camerawork, becomes genuinely frightening. At its best, the film is a pleasing reminder that Wise served his apprenticeship under Val Lewton at RKO. GA

Haunting, The

(1999, US, 113 min)
d Jan De Bont. *p* Susan Arnold, Donna Arkoff Roth, Colin Wilson. *sc* David Self. *ph* Karl Walter Lindenlaub. *ed* Michael Kahn. *pd* Eugenio Zanetti. *m* Jerry Goldsmith. *cast* Liam Neeson, Catherine Zeta-Jones, Owen Wilson, Lili Taylor, Bruce Dern, Marian Seldes, Virginia Madsen.

●While filming this bombastic supernatural thriller, director De Bont promised to eschew Robert Wise's 1963 version in favour of a faithful, if updated, adaptation of Shirley Jackson's source novel, *The Legend of Hill House*. De Bont also vowed to make sparing use of special effects. He reneged on both counts. Substituting dull computer generated spooks for atmosphere, scares and suspense, he has turned a frightening, unfathomable ghost story into a boring, solvable mystery. Like the human 'guinea pigs' drawn to Hill House by Dr David Marrow's alleged research into sleep disorders, we've been brought here under false pretences. The grotesque sets dwarf the actors, as the gliding camera pursues them down endless corridors, up staircases and into over-designed chambers. Thank heaven for Taylor, whose susceptible Nell occasionally succeeds in reducing things to a human scale. A timid soul who feels drawn to a Victorian house haunted by the unquiet souls of dead children – lured there 130 years before by childless textile tycoon Hugh Crain – Nell is the focus of the building's most extraordinary visual and aural manifestations. Sadly the ambiguity and complexity of Taylor's portrayal only shows up the insipidity of Neeson's bland psychologist, Zeta-Jones' bisexual vamp and Wilson's oddball sceptic. NF

Haunting of Julia, The

see Full Circle

Hauptdarsteller, Der

see Main Actor, The

Haut les Coeurs (Chin Up!/ aka Battle Cries)

(1999, Fr, 110 min)
d Sólveig Anspach. *p* Patrick Sobelman. *sc* Sólveig Anspach, Pierre-Erwan Guillaume. *ph* Isabelle Razavet. *ed* Anne Reigel. *pd* Catherine Keller. *m* Olivier Manoury, Martin Wheeler. *cast* Karin Viard, Laurent Lucas, Julien Cottereau, Claire Wauthion, Philippe Duclos, Charlotte Clamans.

●Forget the English titles. This first feature concerns a young woman expecting her first child, who learns that she also has breast cancer. The initial prognosis demands an abortion, but she wants her child and refuses to hear it. Specialist advice reveals a risky but worthwhile strategy, using chemotherapy to control the tumour long enough for her to give birth, then a mastectomy right after the delivery. Yes, this is a tough movie, but the central performance from Karin Viard – resolute, vulnerable, human – is one of the best you will see anywhere this year. Viard's battle for her baby and for herself reminds us that life is absolutely worth fighting for. Full stop. How many so-called 'feelgood' movies mean this much? TJ

Havana

(1990, US, 145 min)
d Sydney Pollack. *p* Sydney Pollack, Richard Roth. *sc* Judith Rascoe, David Rayfiel. *ph* Owen Roizman. *ed* Fredric Steinkamp, William Steinkamp. *pd* Terence Marsh. *m* Dave Grusin. *cast* Robert Redford, Lena Olin, Raul Julia, Alan Arkin, Tomas Milian, Daniel Davis, Richard Farnsworth, Mark Rydell.

●Cuba, 1958. Revolution is in the air, American gangsters and corrupt politicians enjoy a last taste of unrestrained capitalism. Slick gambler Jack Weil (Redford) prefers poker to politics, but then he meets glamorous Swedish revolutionary Bobby (Olin) and her rich husband (Julia). Suddenly he's making radical gestures, braving financial loss and life-threatening situations in a bid to save her from dictator Batista's men. Redford's seventh collaboration with Pollack has a romantic, dramatic sweep which glosses over some of the most intense scenes. Crisp, luminous images alternate with dusty filters to help create a sense of heightened reality. Sexual attraction leads to political awareness; the speed at which the central relationship develops provides an indication of social change, with Bobby betraying her class and Jack forced to acknowledge some difficult truths about himself. But the whole thing lacks conviction. CM

Havanna Mi Amor

(2000, Ger/Cuba, 80 min)
d Uli Gaulke. *p* Helge Albers, Roshanak Behesht Nedjad, Konstantin Kröning. *sc* Uli Gaulke. *ph* Axel Schneppat. *ed* Uli Gaulke.

●Charming documentary about Cuban romantics, making sly (dis-)connections between the sentimental stories on the popular local soaps and the touching but messy relationships of the people who watch them. The men are amorous but utterly dependent (even or especially on their ex-wives); the women make the best of it. It's fun, and you learn a lot about Cuba along the way. TCh

Having a Wild Weekend

see Catch Us If You Can

Having It All

(1982, US, 95 min)
d Edward Zwick. *p* John Thomas Lenox, Tristine Rainer. *sc* Elizabeth Gill, Ann Beckett. *ph* Michael D Margulies. *ed* Robert Florio. *pd* Steven P Sardanis. *m* Miles Goodman. *cast* Dyan Cannon, Barry Newman, Hart Bochner, Melanie Chartoff, Sylvia Sidney, Andra Millian.

●Glossy comedy featuring high fashion and the jet set life. Guilt-ridden Thera (Cannon), a rich, successful fashion designer, has a cool, sophisticated spouse in New York, and an artistic, passionate one in LA. Her personality changes too, one can tell by the changes in hairstyle from soignée to rampant curls. Bedroom doors are out of date, and it's more a question of popping in and out of airports, and even then you can get caught. Naturally the first husband finally wins out, and the comedy follows its predictable course unto its dreary end. Made for cable TV, it should have stayed there. JE

Hawaii

(1966, US, 186 min)
d George Roy Hill. *p* Walter Mirisch. *sc* Dalton Trumbo, Daniel Taradash. *ph* Russell Harlan. *ed* Stuart Gilmore. *pd* Cary Odell. *m* Elmer Bernstein. *cast* Max von Sydow, Julie Andrews, Richard Harris, Carroll O'Connor, Torin Thatcher, Gene Hackman, Jocelyn La Garde.

●A sprawling adaptation of James A Michener's doorstop novel about an 1820s Yale divinity student (Sydow) who becomes a missionary to the underdeveloped Hawaiian islands. The conflict between naïve dogma and naïve innocence is effectively established, but the spectacle is always broader than it is deep. Dashing sea captain Harris' desire for Sydow's friendly, outgoing wife (Andrews) provides the love interest, the storm scene a much-needed dose of riproaring spectacle. NF

Hawk, The

(1992, GB, 86 min)
d David Hayman. *p* Ann Wingate, Eileen Quinn. *sc* Peter Ransley. *ph* Andrew Dunn. *ed* Justin Krish. *m* Nick Bicât. *cast* Helen Mirren, George Costigan, Rosemary Leach, Owen Teale, Christopher Madin, Marie Hamer, Melanie Hill.

●Annie Marsh (Mirren) fears her husband (Costigan) may be the serial killer whom the media have dubbed 'The Hawk'. But is the father of her children – a roving service engineer – capable of bludgeoning women to death and gouging out their eyes? Hayman's low-key direction of Peter Ransley's script (from his own novel) and Andrew Dunn's moody urban photography work well in developing Mirren's escalating paranoia. But with so much of the detail taken directly from the Yorkshire Ripper case, it seems absurd and disorienting when, in a departure from both real and fictional sources, Annie finally finds the strength to turn the tables on her husband. GA

Hawks

(1988, GB, 110 min)
d Robert Ellis Miller. *p* Stephen Lanning, Keith Cavele. *sc* Roy Clarke. *ph* Douglas Milsome. *ed* Malcolm Cooke. *pd* Peter Howitt. *m* John Cameron, Barry Gibb. *cast* Timothy Dalton, Anthony Edwards, Janet McTeer, Camille Coduri, Jill Bennett, Robert Lang, Sheila Hancock, Geoffrey Palmer.

●It's a worthy idea: a dark comedy about two men, in their prime but terminally ill in hospital, who decide to live their last days to the full. So in surgeon's greens and hijacked ambulance, the handsome lawyer (Dalton) and American football player (Edwards) make for Amsterdam with the intention of bonking their balls off in a brothel. Waylaid, however, by a couple of Sharons (McTeer, Coduri), they discover that nice girls will do it for the dying with a glad heart and kinky négligée. Miller's attempts to set a life-affirming tone hit hysteria, although the script by Roy Clarke (*Last of the Summer Wine*) doesn't help, with its relentless innuendo and offensively stereotyped characters dragging the humour through black to blue. Ultimately, the over-zealous exploitation of anything that might make an unappealing subject more commercial kills the film. EP

Hawks and the Sparrows, The

see Uccellacci e Uccellini

Hawk the Slayer

(1980, GB, 94 min)
d Terry Marcel. *p* Harry Robertson. *sc* Terry Marcel, Harry Robertson. *ph* Paul Beeson. *ed* Eric Boyd-Perkins. *ad* Michael Pickwoad. *m* Harry Robertson. *cast* Jack Palance, John Terry, Bernard Bresslaw, Ray Charleson, Peter O'Farrell, Patricia Quinn, Annette Crosbie, Morgan Sheppard, Harry Andrews, Roy Kinnear, Patrick Magee.

●Somewhere in the mists of time (or dry ice to you and me), Hawk the Slayer (Terry) roamed a land of painted backdrops, cardboard castles, and gauze-infested forests, fighting Evil and bringing Peace. His team: a dwarf, an elf, a giant, and a witch who can turn a useful trick or two. His opponents: the rest of the world captained by big brother Palance, a dirty player if ever there was one. The object of the game: kill each other. The wonder of it is that the cast can deliver their lines without cracking up. It is all so unbelievably tacky that it almost works. FF

Häxan

see Witchcraft Through the Ages

Hazy Life (Donten Seikatsu)

(1999, Jap, 84 min)
d Nobuhiro Yamashita. *p* Kosuke Mukai, Nobuhiro Yamashita, Hayato Maeda, Ryuto Kondo, Akira Matsumoto. *sc* Kosuke Mukai, Nobuhiro Yamashita. *ph* Ryuto Kondo. *ed* Kosuke Mukai, Nobuhiro Yamashita, Hayato Maeda, Ryuto Kondo. *pd* Hayato Maeda. *m* Akainu. *cast* Hiroshi Yamamoto, Teppei Uda, Hiromichi Maeda, Ko Riran, Maki Imaeda.

●A slacker movie, Osaka indie style. Tsutomu (Uda) is hanging around waiting to play pachinko when he crosses paths with Kee (Yamamoto), who sports women's shoes and a Leningrad Cowboys hairdo. Next thing he's installed in Kee's cluttered room helping to dub copies of porno tapes made at home by a couple Kee knows. Tsutomu has the odd violent thought, especially when caught shoplifting, but spends as much time as possible asleep. Yamashita's rather wonderful film goes mainly for deadpan comedy, but doesn't flinch when things start to go wrong for the amiably degenerate characters. The fantasy ending, with everyone reconciled as one big happy family under the cherry blossoms, could have been sardonic. But Yamashita makes it as heartening as the end of *Kids Return*. TR

H.C. Andersen's The Long Shadow (H.C. Andersen og Den Skæve Skygge/aka Hans Christian Andersen and The Long Shadow)

(1998, Den, 78 min)
d Jannik Hastrup. *p* Marie Bro. *sc* Bent Haller, Jannik Hastrup. *pd* Ole Bidstrup. *m* Fuzzy. *cast* voices: Jesper Klein, Ghita Nørby, Jarl Kulle, Ditte Gråbøl, Claus Ryskjær, Ove Sprogøe, Bodil Udsen, Tammi Øst.

●A delightful reinterpretation of Andersen's life and work by the veteran Danish animator Jannik Hastrup, beginning with the great storyteller's fanciful, solitary boyhood and ending with his wistful, solitary death. Loneliness seems to be the long shadow here: the film posits Andersen's fervent imagination as being at least partly fired by his documented celibacy and unrequited passions, which forced him back on the companionship of a pet ugly duckling he calls Emma, his own wayward shadow, and the Devil himself. Shadow and Satan naturally find common cause, but in the last resort the power of Andersen's writings and fame grant him a bitter-sweet salvation. Hastrup mixes watercolours and inks, focusing on story, but occasionally letting loose with flights of freeflowing expressionism or apposite whimsy. NB

Head

(1968, US, 85 min)
d Bob Rafelson. *p/sc* Bob Rafelson, Jack Nicholson. *ph* Michael Hugo. *ed* Mike Pozen. *ad* Sydney Z Litwack. *m* Ken Thorne. *cast* The Monkees (Micky Dolenz, David Jones, Mike Nesmith, Peter Tork), Victor Mature, Annette Funicello, Timothy Carey, Logan Ramsey, Frank Zappa, Jack Nicholson.

●Rafelson's first feature, made when Monkee mania had all but died, *Head* proved too experimental for the diminishing weenybop audience which had lapped up the ingenious TV series. It flopped dismally in the US, and only achieved belated release here. Despite obviously dated aspects like clumsy psychedelic effects and some turgid slapstick sequences, the film is still remarkably vital and entertaining. Rafelson (who helped to create the group), together with Jack Nicholson (co-writer and co-producer), increased the TV show's picaresque tempo while also adding more adult, sardonic touches. The calculated manipulation behind the phenomenon is exposed at the start, when the Monkees metaphorically commit suicide. The typical zany humour is intercut with harsher political footage and satire on established genres of American cinema, exploding many a sacred cow into the bargain. IB

Head Above Water

(1996, US/GB, 92 min)
d Jim Wilson. *p* Jim Wilson, John M Jacobsen. *sc* Theresa Marie, Michael Blake. *ph* Richard Bowen. *ed* Michael R Miller. *pd* Jeffrey Beecroft. *m* Christopher Young. *cast* Harvey Keitel, Cameron Diaz, Craig Sheffer, Billy Zane, Shay Duffin.

●Alone in a remote holiday beach house in Maine, while her judge husband (Keitel) and local childhood friend (Sheffer) go sea-fishing, ex-party girl Diaz is visited by old flame Zane – whose dead body she finds next morning on the living room couch. Keitel's miscast as a pipe-chewing father figure, while Diaz, clad mostly in a one-piece yellow swimsuit, is left floundering in the shallows of a script which relies on ludicrous human behaviour and mechanical plot twists, the latter signposted by an over-emphatic score. (Remake of Nils Gaup's superior black comic thriller *Hodet Over Vannet*, 1993.) NF

Headhunter

(1988, SAf, 92 min)
d Francis Schaeffer. *p* Jay Davidson. *sc* Len Spinelli. *ph* Hans Kühle. *ed* Robert Simpson. *m* Julian Laxton. *cast* Kay Lenz, Wayne Crawford, John Fatooh, Steve Kanaly, June Chadwick, Sam Williams.

●A complete non-starter of a horror movie featuring a quite astonishing dearth of imagination: a pagan beast comes to Boston, kills off a lot of people, and then gets defeated in hand-to-hand combat with two cops. End of story. A subplot about one of the cops (Crawford) discovering that his wife is a lesbian comes and goes, leaving you wondering if somebody switched movies on you. Gratuitous tedium. MK

Head On (aka Fatal Attraction)

(1980, Can, 88 min)
d Michael Grant. *sc* James Sanderson, Paul Illidge. *ph* Anthony B Richmond. *ed* Gary

Oppenheimer. *pd* Antonin Dimitrov. *m* Peter Mann. *cast* Stephen Lack, Sally Kellerman, John Huston, Lawrence Dane, Michelle Keys, John Peter Linton.
●Stephen Lack, star of *Scanners*, and Sally Kellerman, her usual off-beam self, meet after a car crash and begin to act out their sexual fantasies. The process starts by taking inspiration from children's stories, but develops into something more dangerous. Much of this misfires, but there are sparks of interest. (Released in the US in 1985 – would you believe – as *Fatal Attraction*.) TJ

Head On

(1997, Aust, 104 min)
d Ana Kokkinos. *p* Jane Scott. *sc* Andrew Bovell, Ana Kokkinos, Mira Robertson. *ph* Jaems Grant. *ed* Jill Bilcock. *pd* Nikki Di Falso. *m* Ollie Olsen. *cast* Alex Dimitriades, Paul Capsis, Julian Garner, Elena Mandalis, Tony Nikolakopoulos, Damien Fotiou, Eugenia Fragos, Andrea Mandalis.
●The background is set up in the credit sequence: a montage of docking post-war immigrants to Australia, among whom are the family of Ari (Dimitriades), a second generation Greek rebel. This first feature, a big hit in Oz, follows 24 hours of Ari's life in Melbourne's underbelly: techno blasting in his ears, cocaine up his nose, risky fast sex, fights with his father. This is one confused gay man, who covers his feelings of insecurity and isolation with a bullish assertiveness that comes dangerously close to a desire for self-destruction. Director Kokkinos provides no easy solutions, preferring to keep more or less consistently to Ari's rollercoaster point of view, but the resulting aimlessness drifts towards punk-aesthetic nihilism. Things aren't helped by Dimitriades' sullen performance. Kokkinos sets up a few potentially progressive scenes, morally speaking, where Ari might acknowledge the difficulties faced by his sister or the courage of his trans-sexual friend Johnny (Capsis), but even here he registers no more emotion than any dumb bystander. WH

Head Over Heels (aka Chilly Scenes of Winter)

(1979, US, 98 min)
d Joan Micklin Silver. *p* Mark Metcalf, Amy Robinson, Griffin Dunne. *sc* Joan Micklin Silver. *ph* Bobby Byrne. *ed* Cynthia Scheider. *pd* Peter Jamison. *m* Ken Lauber. *cast* John Heard, Mary Beth Hurt, Peter Riegert, Kenneth McMillan, Gloria Grahame, Nora Heflin, Jerry Hardin, Griffin Dunne.
●Occasionally engaging romantic comedy (based on Ann Beattie's novel *Chilly Scenes of Winter*), with Heard as the Salt Lake City civil servant doing his damnedest to win back the woman with whom he had an affair the year before. The trouble is, she's not too sure about his idolisation of her, nor of whether she wants to leave her husband. Strong naturalistic performances and an unforced script keep the ogre of wackiness at bay, although – as in *Between the Lines* – Silver's attitude all too often becomes rather ingratiatingly indulgent towards the determinedly 'nice' characters, resulting in a soft, mushy centre. GA

Health

(1979, US, 102 min)
d/p Robert Altman. *sc* Frank Barhydt, Paul Dooley, Robert Altman. *ph* Edmond L Koons. *ed* Dennis M Hill, Tony Lombardo, Tom Benko. *ad* Robert Quinn. *m* Joseph Byrd. *cast* Lauren Bacall, Glenda Jackson, Carol Burnett, James Garner, Dick Cavett, Paul Dooley, Donald Moffat, Henry Gibson, Alfre Woodard.
●Never released theatrically in Britain, and widely considered as exemplifying the trap into which Altman's free-wheeling, loosely structured social comedies were sooner or later destined to fall, *Health* none the less has its admirers who claim that the movie's incidental jokes justify the thinness of the storyline. It's about a health foods convention in Florida, where leading lights from the yoghurt and museli industries are competing for the presidency of the national organisation. Jackson does her butch number, complete with cigar; Bacall plays an 83-year-old virgin (!); Garner contributes his engagingly wry *Rockford* persona; Burnett and Gibson are reliably wacky. But Altman's character-based, semi-improvised plotting, so successful in *Nashville*, misses its target more often than it scores. MA

Health Warning (Da Leitai)

(1983, HK, 83 min)
d Kirk Wong. *cast* Wong Lung-Wai, Ko Hung, Ray Lui, Venus Nguyen, Monica Lam, Alexandre Lee, Tsui Kam-Kong.
●Kirk Wong's most daring film: a deeply cynical take on the kung-fu genre crossed with dystopian sci-fi and an attitude towards sexual kinks straight out of an early Lou Reed song. Ray Lui (the nominal hero) is killed off early, allowing the chunky Wong Lung-Wai to move centre stage as the stolid but highly corruptible fighter who takes on transvestites, robotic dykes, newly synthesised hallucinogens and neo-Nazi megalomaniacs. This is what the French mean by *film maudit*. TR

Hear My Song

(1991, GB, 105 min)
d Peter Chelsom. *p* Alison Owen-Allen. *sc* Peter Chelsom, Adrian Dunbar. *ph* Sue Gibson. *ed* Martin Walsh. *pd* Caroline Hanania. *m* John Altman. *cast* Ned Beatty, Adrian Dunbar, Shirley Anne Field, Tara Fitzgerald, William Hootkins, Harold Berens, David McCallum, John Dair, Stephen Marcus.
●Loosely inspired by events in the life of Irish tenor Josef Locke, Chelsom's first feature is an 'old-fashioned' comedy whose shameless stabs at cockle-warming charm make for a sludge of ingratiating whimsy. Liverpool club owner Micky O'Neill (Dunbar, who co-wrote with Chelsom) is in a fix. His inability to say 'I love you' has provoked a walk-out by his girlfriend Nancy (Fitzgerald), and his ambitious plans to revive the club's fortunes by bringing back tax exile Locke (Beatty) go awry: the singer he has booked is an imposter (Hootkins) who takes advantage of Locke's old flame Cathleen (Field), who happens to be Nancy's mum. Micky's dreams can be fulfilled only if he tracks down the real Locke in Ireland and tempts him to Liverpool for one last concert. It's hard to fathom why this film was received so warmly. Despite Beatty's sterling performance, the overall tone is one of maudlin blarney. GA

Hear No Evil

(1993, US, 97 min)
d Robert Greenwald. *p* David Matalon. *sc* RM Badat, Kathleen Rowell. *ph* Steven Shaw. *ed* Eva Gardos. *pd* Bernt Capra. *m* Graeme Revell. *cast* Marlee Matlin, Martin Sheen, DB Sweeney, John C McGinley, Christina Carlisi, Greg Elam.
●Journalist McGinley finds a valuable ancient coin, stolen in a daring heist, and hides it in the bleeper of his deaf physical-trainer. When the journalist meets with an explosive 'accident', the physical-trainer, Matlin, doesn't know she's been left carrying the booty. But crooked psycho-cop Sheen does. Only reliable restaurateur Sweeney can save the day. A ludicrous variation on *Wait Until Dark* in which Matlin and Sweeney remain laudable deadpan, while Sheen goes swiftly into rent-a-mental overdrive. MK

Hearse, The

(1980, US, 95 min)
d George Bowers. *p* Mark Tenser. *sc* William Bleich. *ph* Mori Kawa. *ed* George Berndt. *ad* Keith Michl. *m* Webster Lewis. *cast* Trish Van Devere, Joseph Cotten, David Gautreaux, Donald Hotton, Med Flory, Donald Petrie.
●Still recovering from a mental collapse, Devere moves to an inherited house in a small town, an antique hearse keeps driving up at night, and, to add to her troubles, a diary suggests that she is related to a witch possessed by the devil. Standard guff.

Heart

(1997, UK, 85 min)
d Charles McDougall. *p* Nicola Shindler. *sc* Jimmy McGovern. *ph* Julian Court. *ed* Edward Mansell. *pd* Stuart Walker, Chris Roope. *m* Stephen Warbeck. *cast* Christopher Eccleston, Saskia Reeves, Kate Hardie, Rhys Ifans, Anna Chancellor, Bill Paterson, Matthew Rhys, Jack Deam, Kate Rutter, Nicholas Moss.
●A tawdry, laughable, blood-soaked melodrama. Businessman Eccleston is so stressed out by sexual jealousy that he has a heart attack, which, ironically, drives spouse Hardie, a TV producer, into the arms of maverick writer Ifans. Left in a wheelchair, Eccleston is given new hope by the possibility of a heart transplant, when a young man dies in a traffic accident and his mother, Reeves, gives permission for the organ donation. Big mistake. She becomes increasingly obsessed by Eccleston since he's now carrying her dead son's heart, and intent on protecting the same from the errant Hardie. One can sense major Jacobean mayhem coming a mile off. Screenwriter McGovern and the director obviously imagined that keeping every scene pared to the bone would build up a sense of foreboding, but the relentless cutting actually comes between the viewer and the staid characters. Worse is the treatment meted out to poor Hardie, if she's not naked or mouthing unspeakable dialogue, she's on the wrong end of a blunt instrument. Not since *Midnight Express* has a British film gloated over tender flesh and breaking bones with such prurient zeal. TJ

Heartaches

(1981, Can, 93 min)
d Donald Shebib. *p* Pieter Kroonenburg, David J Patterson, Jerry Raibourn. *sc* Terence Heffernan. *ph* Vic Sarin. *ed* Gerry Hambling, Peter Boita. *m* Simon Michael Martin. *cast* Margot Kidder, Annie Potts, Robert Carradine, Michael Zeiniker, Arnie Achtman, Winston Rekert, George Touliatos.
●Winsome (female) buddy movie which offers a roundly satisfying tragi-comic role to Kidder, but substantially less to its audience. The plot hinges on plain-looking Potts running away from her track-racer husband (Carradine) and shacking up with Kidder in downtown Toronto. One-time great hope of Canadian cinema, Shebib contents himself with schematic contrasts between the two women's approach to sex, and a sentimental excursion into an Italian immigrant community. Anyone homesick for Toronto might find compensations in the location photography; but if you ask more of a movie, this one is not answering. MA

Heart Beat

(1979, US, 108 min)
d John Byrum. *p* Alan Greisman, Michael Shamberg. *sc* John Byrum. *ph* Laszlo Kovacs. *pd* Jack Fisk. *m* Jack Nitzsche. *cast* Nick Nolte, Sissy Spacek, John Heard, Ray Sharkey, Anne Dusenberry, Margaret Fairchild, Tony Bill.
●A minor (low budget) gem, with Nolte ambling ruefully through twenty years of the American Dream as Neal Cassady, the superman-hero-hobo-lover of Jack Kerouac's *On the Road*. Based on the autobiography of Carolyn Cassady (who is played with calm brilliance by Spacek), the movie centres on her triangular life with two men, warily sidestepping the hype and narcissism of Beat mythology and the parallel temptation to indulge in an essay on Literary Genius. Instead, out of an episodic narrative emerges a quiet contemplation of the vast spaces and suburban dreams of the postwar period, a glowingly designed, occasionally tacky epic of America from the Bomb to the Pill. CA

Heart, Beating in the Dark (Yamiutsu Shinzo)

(1982, Jap, 75 min)
d Shunichi Nagasaki. *sc* Shunichi Nagasaki. *ph* Kiichi Muto. *cast* Shigeru Muroi, Takeshi Naito, Taro Suwa, Tesuji Onda.
●A boy and a girl in a room, seemingly on the run from something. Are they in love? They fuck compulsively, and their sex has a disturbing edge of sado-masochism. They enact 'flashbacks' to their pasts, but it's the girl who speaks the boy's aggressive, 'macho' lines and vice versa. What brought them there is finally revealed in a terrifying monologue. It often plays like a 'wrong side of the tracks' answer to Oshima's *In the Realm of the Senses*: a love story which is brutal, messy, hopeless and finally horrifying, but a love story none the less. (Shot on Super-8, transferred to video.) TR

Heartbreakers

(1984, US, 99 min)
d Bobby Roth. *p* Bob Weis, Bobby Roth. *sc* Bobby Roth. *ph* Michael Ballhaus. *ed* John

Carnochan. *m* Tangerine Dream. *cast* Peter Coyote, Nick Mancuso, Carole Laure, Max Gail, James Laurenson, Carol Wayne, Kathryn Harrold, Jerry Hardin.

●Blue is an angry young artist, facing up to the departure of his long-time girlfriend. His greatest buddy is Eli, a handsome, reluctant rich boy desperate to be in love. Written and directed with tremendous assurance, Roth's first commercial feature deals with the close friendships splintered by the competitive instincts of dissatisfied souls, and the secret jealousies and impulsive attractions that cause the greatest wounds. There are brilliant lead performances from Coyote and Mancuso; fine too are Laure, and Laurenson as a campy art dealer. Add a pulsating Tangerine Dream score and Michael Ballhaus' glowing photography, and the result is an emotional cocktail that is provocative, touching and witty as hell. DT

Heartbreakers

(2001, US, 124 min)
d David Mirkin. *p* John Davis, Irving Ong. *sc* Robert Dunn, Paul Guay, Stephen Mazur. *ph* Dean Semler. *ed* William Steinkamp. *pd* Lilly Kilvert. *m* John Debney; (theme) Danny Elfman. *cast* Sigourney Weaver, Jennifer Love Hewitt, Ray Liotta, Jason Lee, Jeffrey Jones, Gene Hackman, Anne Bancroft, Nora Dunn, Carrie Fisher.

●Mother and daughter, Max (Weaver) and Page (Hewitt) specialise in double-crossing wealthy, malleable men whom Max marries and then divorces, after 'catching' them being seduced by Page. The maternal/filial bond, however, has recently been weakened by competitiveness, Max determined to show she's not too old for the game, Page intent on proving herself as capable as mom. And while repellent billionaire William B Tensy (Hackman) is almost too much to handle, it's a previous victim, the inescapable Dean (Liotta), and a cute bartender, Jack (Lee), who cause the real problems. The film lacks funny jokes. But if you're interested in the blossoming of Love Hewitt, there'll be no refunds. Admittedly, she's playing a young woman who uses her sexuality overtly to seduce men, but such slavish attention to looks obscures the acting. Not offensively bad, but silly. KW

Heartbreakers, The (Die Heartbreakers)

(1983, WGer, 114 min)
d Peter F Bringmann. *p* Herbert Rimbach. *sc* Matthias Seelig. *ph* Helge Weindler. *ed* Annette Dorn. *ad* Toni Lüdi. *m* Charly Terstappen, Mark Eichenseher, Kurt Schmidt, Wolfgang Horn, Michael Dommers. *cast* Sascha Disselkamp, Mary Ketikidou, Uwe Enkelmann, Michael Klein, Mark Eichenseher, Hartmut Isselhorst.

●It's 1964, and bitten by the Beatle bug from Berlin to Bavaria, kids are buying guitars, forming groups with English names, and setting out to emulate the Fab Four. One such band is Die Heartbreakers: four pimply individuals, their pint-sized impresario and chanteuse excluded on the grounds that Mick Jagger would never have shared the stage with a girl. Bringmann tells their story with droll humour, drawing unforced performances from his cast of young unknowns, and playing the gigs and gags out against interesting locations. A likeable, unassuming movie whose very passable renditions of '60s classics will bring a glow of nostalgia to anyone who was there, and perhaps a flash of pleasurable surprise to those too young to remember. SJo

Heartbreak Island (Qunian Dongtian)

(1995, Tai, 122 min)
d Hsu Hsiao-Ming. *p* Grant Chang, Tommy Wang. *sc* Cheng Guo, John SC Chiang. *ph* Yang Wei-Han. *ed* Chen Bo-Wen. *pd* Chang Hong. *m* Chyi Ching. *cast* Vicky Wei, King Jieh-Wen, Chang Ching-Ju, Tsai Chen-Nan.

●An intelligent but rather studied film about idealism and its betrayal, set against the 'Formosa Incident' (a troubled pro-democracy rally of the '70s) and its aftermath. A woman is released from prison where she was locked up for a decade or so for terrorism; in seeking out friends and colleagues, and the lover who inspired her to become an activist, she comes painfully to realise that not only the world but people's feelings have changed. The movie, beautifully acted and visualised, is a blend of the personal and political, somewhat in the style of Hou Hsiao-hsien, but lacking the resonance and emotional punch that make Hou's films so compelling. GA

Heartbreak Kid, The

(1972, US, 106 min)
d Elaine May. *p* Edgar J Scherick. *sc* Neil Simon. *ph* Owen Roizman. *ed* John Carter. *ad* Richard Sylbert. *m* Garry Sherman. *cast* Charles Grodin, Cybill Shepherd, Jeannie Berlin, Eddie Albert, Audra Lindley, William Prince, Augusta Dabney, Mitchell Jason.

●Marital comedy with its characters distanced just enough to prevent the barbs coming too close to home. Lenny (Grodin) woos and weds Lila (Berlin), only to have his carefully nurtured prewedding romantic ideas bite the dust from the moment the ceremony is concluded. His inaccessible goddess becomes the all too accessible Lila, gorging herself on egg salad sandwiches, getting sunburned, and generally behaving like a normal human being. It's too much for Lenny, stuck as he is in a state of pre-wedding hots. He finds another object for his fantasies (Shepherd), and pursues her with a kind of crass desperation all the way to her midwest college, where she is, as expected, every football hero's dream date. Wittily directed by May, and neatly scripted by Neil Simon (from Bruce Jay Friedman's story *A Change of Plan*), though somewhere the film loses its thread and forgets how to draw things decently to a close. VG

Heartbreak Ridge

(1986, US, 130 min)
d/p Clint Eastwood. *sc* Jim Carabatsos. *ph* Jack N Green. *ed* Joel Cox. *pd* Edward C Carfagno. *m* Lennie Niehaus. *cast* Clint Eastwood, Marsha Mason, Everett McGill, Moses Gunn, Eileen Heckart, Bo Svenson, Boyd Gaines, Mario Van Peebles.

●After three tours in Vietnam, gunnery sergeant Tom Highway (Eastwood) approaches retirement, and is assigned to the Reconnaissance Platoon where he started. Alas, the US Marines are now run by penpushers, theorists and timeservers; so when Grenada looms, there is only Highway between his rookies and a row of bodybags. In format, this is no more than the classic mission movie: first they train, then they do it for real. But the film belongs to Eastwood. Now looking increasingly like an Easter Island statue, he has a voice pickled in bourbon, a tongue like razor wire, and a body so full of shrapnel that he can't walk through airport metal detectors. When he isn't putting his men through hell, he is sobering up in the brig or reading women's magazines to get a clue on how to speak to his ex-wife. CPea

Heartburn

(1986, US, 109 min)
d Mike Nichols. *p* Mike Nichols, Robert Greenhut. *sc* Nora Ephron. *ph* Nestor Almendros. *ed* Sam O'Steen. *pd* Tony Walton. *m* Carly Simon. cast Meryl Streep, Jack Nicholson, Jeff Daniels, Maureen Stapleton, Stockard Channing, Richard Masur, Milos Forman, Kevin Spacey, Mercedes Ruehl.

●This is taken from Nora Ephron's book about her marriage to Watergate champ Carl Bernstein. Streep and Nicholson play the two journalists (under different names), although you will be forgiven if this fact passes you by. For the substance of the film is the kind of *Guardian* Women's Page slop in which the getting and raising of babies is suddenly a unique experience, deemed to be of undying interest to all observers, and the greatest tragedy in a woman's life is the discovery of her husband's adultery. Real life in between is supplied by dinner party gossip and group therapy. A movie of colossal inconsequence. Heartburn? No, just a bad attack of wind. CPea

Heart Condition

(1990, US, 95 min)
d James D Parriott. *p* Steve Tisch. *sc* James D Parriott. *ph* Arthur Albert. *ed* David Finfer. *pd* John Muto. *m* Patrick Leonard. *cast* Bob Hoskins, Denzel Washington, Chloe Webb, Jeffrey Meek, Ray Baker, Roger E Mosley.

●This mismatched-buddy cop movie with a neat supernatural angle has Hoskins as an LA vice cop with a penchant for fast food, beer, smoking and using the 'N-word' when referring to his black brothers. So when he sees his old flame (Webb) being smuggled away from a crime scene by her new lover, a suave black lawyer (Washington), racist sparks fly. Hoskins' real problems start when he suffers a heart attack and, with Washington meanwhile dying, receives his black heart in a transplant. More problematically, Washington's ghost is along for the ride, complaining that he was murdered and coaxing Hoskins into smartening up his act. So Hoskins starts wearing flash clothes, driving a Merc, and asking awkward questions of a dead senator. Making effective use of its central conceit, this offbeat gem delivers the necessary plot twists and action, but never soft pedals on the racial angle. Chloe Webb contributes a finely balanced performance as a woman whose appreciation of both men's qualities finally finds expression in one composite male. NF

Heart in Winter, A

see Coeur en hiver, Un

Heart Is a Lonely Hunter, The

(1968, US, 123 min)
d Robert Ellis Miller. *p* Thomas C Ryan, Marc Merson. *sc* Thomas C Ryan. *ph* James Wong Howe. *ed* John F Burnett. *ad* LeRoy Deane. *m* Dave Grusin. *cast* Alan Arkin, Sondra Locke, Laurinda Barrett, Stacy Keach, Chuck McCann, Percy Rodriguez, Biff McGuire, Cicely Tyson.

●A deaf mute (Arkin), left alone when his only friend (similarly afflicted) is committed to an asylum, moves to a new town, waiting expectantly. This being the Deep South, assorted misfits soon gather round him: an alcoholic drifter (Keach), a gawkily unhappy teenage girl (Locke), a black doctor with an outsize chip on his shoulder (Rodriguez). All of them pour out their troubles in his silent, sympathetic presence, feeling that their lives are richer for the shared relationship. Yet suddenly, for reasons they know nothing about, the deaf mute commits suicide (he has learned of the death of his friend), and they are left to reflect bitterly on how much they took, how little they gave. The theme is sentimental, of course, but as directed by Miller in a series of oblique, self-contained scenes – with excellent performances all round and superb camerawork from James Wong Howe – the film has much the same haunting, poetic quality as the Carson McCullers novel (her first) on which it is based. TM

Heartland

(1979, US, 96 min)
d Richard Pearce. *p* Michael Hausman, Beth Ferris. *sc* Beth Ferris. *ph* Fred Murphy. *ed* Bill Yahraus. *pd* Patrizia von Brandenstein. *m* Charles Gross. *cast* Rip Torn, Conchata Ferrell, Barry Primus, Lilia Skala, Megan Folsom, Amy Wright.

●Directed by a former documentarist, and based on the letters and papers of real-life 'wilderness woman' Elinore Randall Stewart, this looks to be the kind of Western that Ken Loach might make. The Wyoming hills of 1910 may be past the earliest days of the frontier, but Rip Torn's taciturn Scots rancher hasn't changed his attitudes since his forebears disembarked the Mayflower. Ferrell is the housekeeper he first buys, then later weds, and she provides an admirable testimony to the central role that women must have played in building the new-found land. Rooted firmly in TV-style docu-drama, the film charts the appalling rigours of pioneer life (lost herds, lost children) with an oblique respect and an insistence on the gritty (see Torn up to his elbows in a cow's backside). Whether or not you go for it rather depends on whether you like your Westerns mythologised or demythologised: 'circle the wagons' versus the Wyoming hills with a washing-line stretched across them. CPea

Heartland Reggae

(1982, Can, 87 min)
d Jim Lewis. *p* John W Mitchell. *ph* John Swaby. *ed* Jim Lewis, Randal J Torno, John Mayes. *with* Bob Marley & The Wailers, The I-Threes, Peter Tosh, Jacob Miller Inner Circle Band, Junior Tucker, Althea & Donna.

●Using concert footage shot between 1977–78 (climaxing with the 'One Love Peace Concert' where Marley, elevated to prophet status, unites on stage the leaders of the two Jamaican political parties), this falls into exactly the same trap as its predecessors in reggae documentary. For whom was the film made? If Black, the rasta talk-over is unnecessary; if White, it is almost incomprehensible. Despite a scissors-and-sellotape approach to editing, and a sound quality never better than variable, the film does have its joyous moments: the gleeful Tosh as he anthemises the 'erb in 'Legalise It'; the sadly missed wobbling antics of Jacob Miller, whose enthusiasm is hard not to respond to and ultimately saves the film from being a ganja-fogged mess. FL

Heart Like a Wheel

(1983, US, 113 min)
d Jonathan Kaplan. *p* Charles Roven. *sc* Ken Friedman. *ph* Tak Fujimoto. *ed* O Nicholas Brown. *pd* James William Newport. *m* Laurence Rosenthal. *cast* Bonnie Bedelia, Beau Bridges, Leo Rossi, Hoyt Axton, Bill McKinney, Anthony Edwards, Dean Paul Martin, Dick Miller.

● This bold film yokes together two unlikely themes, the 'woman's picture' and drag racing, then stands slightly to the side of both and narrows its eyes. For while the roaring glamour of quarter-mile sprint cars would have tempted many action directors into dwelling at length on the spectacle, Kaplan's focus shifts slowly away from the flames and the noise and on to the problems facing the rise of a woman racer, Shirley Muldowney. Even then the movie is far from simple: of course there is unthinking prejudice from race officials and other drivers, but the real problem is Muldowney's struggles with her own affections and loyalties. Race fans won't be disappointed, but the real bonus comes from a perfect performance of tough understatement from Bonnie Bedelia as the three-time winner. The wheel may be a flash chrome slot-mag, but the heart is gold. CPea

Heart of Glass (Herz aus Glas)

(1976, WGer, 94 min)
d/p Werner Herzog. *sc* Werner Herzog, Herbert Achternbusch. *ph* Jörg Schmidt-Reitwein. *ed* Beata Mainka-Jellinghaus. *ad* Henning von Gierke, Cornelius Siegel. *m* Popol Vuh. *cast* Josef Bierbichler, Stefan Guttler, Clemens Scheitz, Volker Prechtel, Sepp Müller, Sonja Skiba, Brunhilde Klöckner.

● It's hard to imagine that anyone other than Herzog would have wanted to make a film like *Heart of Glass*. It returns to the formal and conceptual extremism of his work before *Kaspar Hauser*: almost the entire cast are performing under hypnosis throughout, and the plot unfolds in increasingly oblique fragments, making it Herzog's most stylised film to date. It's certainly extremely bizarre, but by no means unapproachable. The tale it tells is plainly allegorical: a glass factory declines into bankruptcy when its owner dies without divulging the formula for its special ruby glass, and the village that depended on the factory for employment goes down with it. But one doesn't have much chance to mull over the implications during the film itself: Herzog directs attention squarely at the performances (which are almost agonisingly intense) and at the imagery (which is very beautiful in a German Gothic way). Any film that dares to hover so close to sheer absurdity needs – and deserves – a sympathetic audience. TR

Heart of Light (Lysets Hjerte)

(1997, Greenland/Den, 90 min)
d Jacob Grønlykke. *p* Henrik Møller-Sorensen. *sc* Jacob Grønlykke, Hans Anthon Lynge. *ph* Dan Laustsen. *ed* Wadt Thomsen. *pd* Anders Engelbrecht. *m* Joachim Holbek. *cast* Rasmus Lyberth, Vivi Nielsen, Niels Platow, Kenneth Rasmussen, Laila Rasmussen, Anda Kristensen, Knud Petersen.

● An engaging if slightly ungainly venture into the recent history of Greenland and its indigenous inhabitants. After a stock silent newsreel prologue recalling the country's dilemma pre-subordination to Danish rule, the film begins in turbulent family-crisis mode with a drunken middle-aged father, Rasmus (Lyberth), alienating his two sons with his insistent nationalist traditions and old-time hunting bravado. This soon boils over, somewhat unconvincingly, but the ensuing numb self-exploration in the vast blank tundra – Rasmus finally picks up his sled for real and goes in search of his roots – makes singular unbound drama, combining historical and mystical elements to intriguing and moving effect. NB

Heart of Midnight

(1988, US, 105 min)
d Matthew Chapman. *p* Andrew Gaty. *sc* Matthew Chapman. *ph* Ray Rivas. *ed* Penelope Shaw. *pd* Gene Rudolf. *m* Yanni. *cast* Jennifer Jason Leigh, Peter Coyote, Brenda Vaccaro, Denise Dummont, Gale Mayron, Frank Stallone, Nick Love, Tico Wells, James Rebhorn, Steve Buscemi.

● Chapman's psychological thriller is an interesting failure, which so indulges the psycho viewpoint that it finally prevents his plot from working. Heroine Carol (Leigh) has a history of mental illness, and when she inherits a neglected downtown club, her raucous mum (marvellous Vaccaro) doubts the wisdom of letting her move in and renovate. Swiftly, so do we. Three degenerate builders turn into rapists one night, objects whizz about by telekinesis, taps drip blood, and upstairs is a maze of SM parlours, orgy dorms, and spyholes, besides which Carol has flashbacks, hallucinations, and an ankle in plaster. There is an explanation, but having gone through hell with camera angles and panting corridors, you may not buy it. The Powell of Peeping Tom, Polanski, and Lynch are in the mix, and there are disquieting and powerful sequences. BC

Heart of the Matter, The

(1953, GB, 105 min, b/w)
d George More O'Ferrall. *p/sc* Ian Dalrymple. *ph* Jack Hildyard. *ed* Sidney Stone. *ad* Joseph Bato. *m* Edric Connor. *cast* Trevor Howard, Elizabeth Allan, Denholm Elliott, Maria Schell, Gérard Oury, George Coulouris, Peter Finch, Earl Cameron, Michael Hordern, Cyril Raymond.

● Despite its betrayal of Graham Greene's concluding chapters, this is still an atmospheric adaptation; and as the tormented Scobie, Trevor Howard gives what is possibly his finest screen performance. The setting is Sierra Leone in 1942, and Scobie, a Catholic, is the deputy police commissioner whose sympathy for the Africans doesn't go down well with the ex-pats. But Scobie has more serious problems: no longer loving his wife yet consumed by his pity for her, he sends her back to Britain on holiday, having borrowed the money from a local trader. He then falls in love with Maria Schell, a survivor from a torpedoed liner, and when his wife returns, he is blackmailed. Sinking into the depths of despair and religious guilt, he dies fatefully by accident. In the novel he commits suicide, the gravest sin for Catholics, and the heart of the matter was God's capacity for forgiveness. Even so, the intensity of Howard's performance more than compensates, as does the supporting cast (including Finch as a priest, Oury as the blackmailer, and Hordern as Scobie's boss). ATu

Heart of the World, The

(2000, Can, 6 min)
d Guy Maddin. *p* Niv Fichman, Jody Shapiro. *sc/ph* Guy Maddin. *ed* Guy Maddin, deco dawson. *cast* Leslie Bais, Caelum Vatnsdal, Shaun Balbar, Hryhory Yulyanovitch Klymkyiev.

● Maddin's brilliant, delirious short is a spot-on pastiche/parody of a silent Soviet propaganda epic, full of phallic symbols, visionary heroes and splendidly emphatic montage. GA

Heart-Rending

see Love Hurts

Hearts and Minds

(1974, US, 110 min)
d Peter Davis. *p* Bert Schneider, Peter Davis. *ph* Richard Pearce. *ed* Lynzee Klingman, Susan Martin.

● An Oscar-winning documentary dissection of the post-Vietnam American conscience. Davis, a controversial documentarist whose previous work included the notorious *The Selling of the Pentagon* for CBS television, described it as 'more psychological than political'; which is precisely where it falls down, using pathos-eliciting footage (interviews with veterans, their parents, a Buddhist monk; footage of a bombed village) instead of the hard political analysis so obviously needed. The result is that, while this has the required emotional effect, the film's characters polarise all too easily into the heroes and villains of the anti-Commie, anti-gook propaganda movies extensively 'quoted'. Nevertheless, there is much interesting and exclusive interview material from American militarists and policymakers, and most notably a previous French president, to compensate for the overall mood of chest-beating remorse. RM

Hearts in Atlantis

(2001, US/Aust, 101 min)
d Scott Hicks. *p* Kerry Heysen. *sc* William Goldman. *ph* Piotr Sobocinski. *ed* Pip Karmel. *pd* Barbara C Ling. *m* Mychael Danna. *cast* Anthony Hopkins, Anton Yelchin, Hope Davis, Mika Boorem, David Morse, Alan Tudyk, Tom Bower, Celia Weston.

● Bobby Garfield (Morse), a middle-aged married man, returns to Smallsville, USA, for the funeral of a childhood friend. Wandering around his now dilapidated home, he recalls the events surrounding his 11th birthday, when his single mom (Davis) gave him an adult library ticket instead of the bicycle he yearned for. Things appear to take an upturn when Ted Brautigan (Hopkins), a psychic drifter, arrives as the Garfields' lodger. An enigmatic figure, he takes an avuncular interest in Bobby; he engages the boy to read aloud to him, and asks to be alerted to the arrival of the 'low men' who are pursuing him. Based on two Stephen King stories and set in the '50s, this turgid (but good-looking) 'loss of innocence' movie (first kiss, first fight) lopes towards a sinister denouement. But it lacks emotional depth – the characters are too thinly drawn – and frankly, as for tension, vague references to the CIA and anti-communist activity don't cut it. JFu

Hearts of Darkness: A Filmmaker's Apocalypse

(1991, US, 96 min)
d Fax Bahr, George Hickenlooper. *p* George Zaloom, Les Mayfield. *sc* Fax Bahr, George Hickenlooper. *ph* Larry Carney, Eleanor Coppola, Bill Neal, Doug Ryan, Les Blank, Shana Hagan, John Heller, Igor Meglic, Kevin O'Brien, Steve Wacks. *ed* Michael Hreer, Jay Miracle. *m* Todd Boekelheide.

● Even at the time *Apocalypse Now* was completed, back in 1979, Coppola likened its genesis to the Vietnam war itself: 'It was crazy…we had access to too much money and too much equipment, and little by little we went insane'. This documentary is entirely in agreement with that verdict. Assembled from later interviews and from some 60 hours of footage shot on location in the Philippines (much of it by Coppola's wife Eleanor), the documentary lists a catalogue of disasters: problems with weather and the Filipino government; massive over-expenditure; Martin Sheen's heart attack; actors spaced out on whatever drugs were available; and an elephantine Brando refusing to play a fat character. At once anecdotal and revealing, this excellent film both illuminates the catastrophes that beset one particular project, and shows, by way of comparison, exactly what American film has foregone since the '70s. GA

Hearts of Fire

(1987, US, 95 min)
d Richard Marquand. *p* Richard Marquand, Jennifer Miller, Jennifer Alward. *sc* Scott Richardson, Joes Eszterhas. *ph* Alan Hume. *ed* Sean Barton. *pd* Roger Murray-Leach. *m* John Barry. *cast* Fiona Flanagan, Bob Dylan, Rupert Everett, Suzanne Bertish, Julian Glover, Susannah Hoffmann, Larry Lamb, Ian Dury, Mark Rylance.

● A half-baked rock'n'roll fable. Star-struck teenager Flanagan quits her job and flies to England with retired rock star Dylan. Together, they are whisked off to a country house retreat by hot but jaded pop star Everett, and Flanagan launches herself into the recording of her debut album, while Everett recovers his song-writing ability. Nothing much happens, except that Flanagan is seduced by fame and Everett, while Dylan hovers enigmatically on the sidelines, offering jaundiced comments. Everett parades his affected proletarian accent once more, hilariously typecast as a talentless wanker. The only sympathetic character is the blind girl fan who wants to shoot him. Hampered by a meandering script, Marquand's last film has none of the functional slickness of *Jagged Edge*; the concert scenes in particular are hopelessly unexciting. NF

Hearts of the West (aka Hollywood Cowboy)

(1975, US, 103 min)
d Howard Zieff. *p* Tony Bill. *sc* Robert Thompson. *ph* Mario Tosi. *ed* Edward A Warschilka. *ad* Robert Luthardt. *m* Ken Lauber. *cast* Jeff Bridges, Blythe Danner, Andy Griffith, Donald Pleasence, Alan Arkin, Richard B Shull, Herbert Edelman.

●Few films in recent years have dealt with the Hollywood dream factory so wittily, sympathetically and incisively. In the early '30s, a hick from the sticks (Bridges) signs up with a bogus university to improve his talent at writing Zane Grey-style Western novels; stranded in LA, he takes a job as saddletramp extra for a film being made by the irascible Arkin. Rob Thompson's script gently nudges at the plagiarism, narcissism, corruption and rampant materialism infecting Tinseltown during its heyday, and allows sufficient space for the characters to grow, convince and command sympathy. A delicate balancing act is achieved as reality and fantasy are juxtaposed, and the performances are top-notch throughout (Bridges is particularly fine as the likeable innocent eager to make good). The jokes may not make you guffaw, but are carried out with a subtle, understated sense of timing and characterisation that will surely leave you with a quietly satisfied smile stretching from ear to ear. GA

Heartstrings (Xin Xiang)

(1992, China, 97 min)
d Sun Zhou. *sc* Miao Yue. *ph* Yao Li. ed Shi Haiying. *m* Zhao Jiping. *cast* Fei Yang, Wang Yumei, Zhu Xu, He Jielin.

●Jingjing, ten-year-old son of Peking Opera actors, is sent to stay with his grandfather in the Guangdong countryside while his parents get divorced. The boy hates Opera; the old man used to be an Opera star. Sun Zhou follows their progress from prickly estrangement to rapprochement with unblushing sentimentality, pausing only to dwell on the old man's emotional perplexity in romancing the local grass widow. Mushy stuff with rather too many ideas recycled from Hou Xiaoxian's *A Summer at Grandpa's*. TR

Heat (100)

(1971, US, 103 min)
d Paul Morrissey. *p* Andy Warhol. *sc* Paul Morrissey, John Hollowell. *ph* Paul Morrissey. *ed* Lana Jokel, Jed Johnson. *m* John Cale. *cast* Joe Dallesandro, Sylvia Miles, Andrea Feldman, Pat Ast, Ray Vestal, Lester Persky, Eric Emerson.

●A pool, a crummy hotel, a luxury mansion, and the ever-retreating charade of showbiz and stardom. Sylvia Miles plays an ageing actress with her hooks into Little Joe. Little Joe plays an out-of-work ex-child star in a TV Western series, buffeted languidly by circumstance. Andrea Feldman plays an unloved child/mother. *Sunset Boulevard* as it never was, often looking like a softcore foray into poolside sex. Some great lines, some campy sequences, much humour. VG

Heat

(1995, US, 171 min)
d Michael Mann. *p* Michael Mann, Art Linson. *sc* Michael Mann. *ph* Dante Spinotti. *ed* Dov Hoenig, Pasquale Buba, William Goldenberg, Tom Rolf. pd Neil Spisak. *m* Elliot Goldenthal. *cast* Robert De Niro, Al Pacino, Val Kilmer, Jon Voight, Amy Brenneman, Wes Studi, Dennis Haysbert, Tom Sizemore, Mykelti Wiliamson.

●Investigating a bold armed robbery which has left three security guards dead, LA cop Vincent Hanna (Pacino), whose devotion to work is threatening his third marriage, follows a trail that leads him to suspect a gang of thieves headed by Neil McCauley (De Niro). Trouble is, McCauley's cunning is at least equal to Hanna's, and that makes him a hard man to nail. Still, unknown to Hanna, McCauley's gang have their own troubles: one of their number is a volatile psychopath, while the businessman whose bonds they've stolen is not above some rough stuff himself. Such a synopsis barely scratches the surface of Mann's masterly crime epic. Painstakingly detailed, with enough characters, subplots and telling nuances to fill out half a dozen conventional thrillers, this is simply the best American crime movie – and indeed, one of the finest movies, period – in over a decade. The action scenes are better than anything produced by John Woo or Quentin Tarantino; the characterisation has a depth most American film-makers only dream of; the use of location, decor and music is inspired; Dante Spinotti's camerawork is superb; and the large, imaginatively chosen cast gives terrific support to the two leads, both back on glorious form. GA

Heat and Dust

(1982, GB, 130 min)
d James Ivory. *p* Ismail Merchant. *sc* Ruth Prawer Jhabvala. *ph* Walter Lassally. *ed* Humphrey Dixon. *pd* Wilfrid Shingleton. *m* Richard Robbins. *cast* Julie Christie, Greta Scacchi, Christopher Cazenove, Shashi Kapoor, Madhur Jaffrey, Charles McCaughan, Barry Foster, Nickolas Grace, Zakir Hussain.

●Adapted by Ruth Prawer Jhabvala from her own novel, *Heat and Dust* fuses several Merchant Ivory themes: the exoticism of India stirring English blood, the past hanging heavy over the present, dirty dealings flourishing behind a cloak of good manners. Anne (Christie) arrives in India to investigate the story of her great-aunt Olivia (Scacchi), cause of a considerable Raj scandal in the '20s. Ivory cuts back and forth between the newly-married Olivia's discovery of India, crashing colonial boredom relieved only by outings with the local Nawab (Kapoor); and Anne's as she follows obsessively in her great-aunt's footsteps. But whereas Olivia's spirited disregard for convention lands her in disgrace, the same path 60 years later leads Anne towards self-awareness and contentment. Directed with Ivory's customary charm, the film boasts fine performances (Christie and Scacchi in particular), and switches periods with effortless ease, striking up a fine network of ironies along the way. Passion, never one of Ivory's strong points, does get rather submerged beneath a welter of local colour; a delight none the less. JP

Heathers

(1988, US, 103 min)
d Michael Lehmann. *p* Denise DiNovi. *sc* Daniel Waters. *ph* Francis Kenny. *ed* Norman Hollyn. *pd* Jon Hutman. *m* David Newman. *cast* Winona Ryder, Christian Slater, Shannen Doherty, Lisanne Falk, Kim Walker, Penelope Milford, Glenn Shadix, Lance Fenton, Patrick Labyorteaux.

●A wicked black comedy about teenage suicide and pernicious peer-group pressure, this refreshing parody of high-school movies is venomously penned by Daniel Waters and sharply directed by Lehmann. The Heathers are three vacuous Westerburg High school beauties who specialise in 'being popular' and making life hell for socially inadequate dweebettes and pillowcases. Having sold out her former friends in these categories, Veronica (Ryder) becomes an honorary member of the select clique – but turns monocled mutineer. Aided by handsome rebellious newcomer JD (Slater), she devises a drastic plan to undermine the teen-queen tyranny, but underestimates JD's ruthlessness: the scheme backfirs dangerously. The compromised ending (forced on the film-makers by New World) is a serious let-down, but there is some exceptional ensemble acting, several stylish set pieces, and more imaginative slang than you could shake a cheerleader's ass at. More crucially, the film uses an intimate knowledge of teen-movie clichés to subvert their debased values from the *inside*. NF

Heatwave

(1981, Aust, 95 min)
d Phillip Noyce. *p* Hilary Linstead. *sc* Marc Rosenberg, Phillip Noyce. *ph* Vince Monton. *ed* John Scott. *pd* Ross Major. *m* Cameron Allan. *cast* Judy Davis, Richard Moir, Chris Haywood, Bill Hunter, John Gregg, Anna Jemison, John Meillon.

●Goon squads roughly evict demonstrating squatters: people in the way of 'progress', their homes on the site of a speculative prestige building project. No more than a scenario for worthy sentiments, it seems, until the focus rapidly narrows to the curious common-ground confrontation between an ambitious architect (Moir) and an impulsive local activist (Davis); and amid the heatwave that is Sydney's Christmas climate, the plot unexpectedly sours, thickens, and solidifies into a complex conspiracy thriller. A campaigning community journalist disappears, companies change hands, unions change sides, arson takes care of stubborn residents. Noyce puts the suspense screws on in time, and tight, and the odd allies' spiralling progress towards a nightmarish New Year's Eve shootout stylishly scars the unacceptable face of Lego-brick capitalism, with a memorably disturbing final image confirming this film as a genuine urban horror movie. PT

Heaven

(1986, US, 80 min, b/w & col)
d Diane Keaton. *p* Joe Kelly. *ph* Frederick Elmes, Joe Kelly. *ed* Paul Barnes. *ad* Barbara Ling. *m* Howard Shore. *with* John Paul Fiore, Albert Robles, Kenny Ostin, Victoria Sellers, Rev Hands, Dr Hymers, Don King, Mary Hall, Dorrie Keaton.

●Quirky first film from Diane Keaton which blows a great idea – various inhabitants of America talk about their ideas of death and the after-life – by tarting it up with horrendously pretentious studio sets, unnecessarily silly camera angles, and somewhat over-clever cutting. The use of old film and TV clips, while funny, palls after a while; but most damaging is Keaton's snidely condescending tone towards her manipulated subjects. A cooler, more conventionally objective approach would have produced a far more revealing, humane and witty documentary. GA

Heaven

(2001, Ger/US, 93 min)
d Tom Tykwer. *p* Anthony Minghella, Maria Köpf, William Horberg, Stefan Arndt, Frédérique Dumas. *sc* Krzysztof Kieslowski, Krzysztof Piesiewicz. *ph* Frank Griebe. *ed* Mathilde Bonnefoy. *ad* Uli Hanisch. *m* Arvo Pärt, Tom Tykwer. *cast* Cate Blanchett, Giovanni Ribisi, Remo Girone, Stefania Rocca, Alessandro Sperduti.

●Kieslowski died in 1996 while planning a *Heaven/Purgatory/Hell* trilogy with his long-term collaborator Piesiewicz; they'd done a 30-page outline for *Heaven*, now filmed in Italy by a gaggle of EU producers and a German director (for Miramax). Against all odds, it's faithful to the spirit of Kieslowski – and terrifically good. Philippa (Blanchett), an English teacher in Turin, is arrested for planting a bomb that killed four innocent bystanders. Her claim that she was targeting a drug czar is ignored by everyone except Filippo (Ribisi), a young cop who volunteers to translate for her, outwits his corrupt superiors – and ends up helping her to escape and kill the bad guy after all. Moral, social and political questions are bundled inextricably together in a fast on-the-run narrative that plays like a sun-drenched *film noir*. Blanchett isn't quite up to Philippa's wrenching inner conflicts, but Ribisi is brilliant as the boy who imagines piloting a helicopter straight up to heaven, a place he already knows in his heart. TR

Heaven & Earth

(1993, US, 140 min)
d Oliver Stone. *p* Oliver Stone, Arnon Milchan, Robert Kline, A Kitman Ho. *sc* Oliver Stone. *ph* Robert Richardson. *ed* David Brenner, Sally Menke. pd Victor Kempster. *m* Kitaro. *cast* Tommy Lee Jones, Joan Chen, Haing S Ngor, Hiep Thi Le, Debbie Reynolds.

●Admirable though it may be for Stone to have followed *Platoon* and *Born on the Fourth of July* with an account of the Vietnam War as experienced by a Vietnamese woman, good intentions don't necessarily make for good movies. This is awful. When a prologue set in 1953 introduces young Le Ly and her peaceful farming community just before the arrival of French troops, it's clear from an autobiographical voice-over, the gleeful peasant faces and the swelling music that we're not about to see an understated movie. And as Le Ly (Hiep Thi Le) proceeds on her physically dangerous and spiritually devastating odyssey, Stone scuppers what could have been an affecting story with visual, verbal and dramatic bombast. In going again for the big one, the director resorts to damp sentimentality, cod poeticism and facile preachiness – and it seems to last forever. GA

Heaven Can Wait

(1943, US, 112 min)
d/p Ernst Lubitsch. *sc* Samson Raphaelson. *ph* Edward Cronjager. *ed* Dorothy Spencer. *ad* James Basevi, Leland Fuller. *m* Alfred Newman. *cast* Don Ameche, Gene Tierney, Charles Coburn, Laird Cregar, Marjorie Main, Spring Byington, Allyn Joslyn, Eugene Pallette, Signe Hasso, Louis Calhern.
●Classic Lubitsch, disarmingly light in tone but in fact quite astute in its social and sexual satire. Ameche plays Henry Van Cleeve, a dandy who pitches up in Hell believing his past sex life in the naughty Nineties qualifies him admirably for eternal damnation; but as he recounts his story, he emerges as a kindly and sympathetic man. Tierney plays the faultless wife, and Lubitsch handles the whole delightful business with characteristic delicacy. The bonus is the brilliant Technicolor photography which shows off Basevi and Fuller's marvellous decor for Hell to memorable advantage. MA

Heaven Can Wait

(1978, US, 101 min)
d Warren Beatty, Buck Henry. *p* Warren Beatty. *sc* Elaine May, Warren Beatty. *ph* William A Fraker. *ed* Robert C Jones, Don Zimmerman. *pd* Paul Sylbert. *m* David Grusin. *cast* Warren Beatty, Julie Christie, James Mason, Jack Warden, Charles Grodin, Dyan Cannon, Buck Henry, Vincent Gardenia.
●Beatty's directing debut is a perverse remake of the 1941 *Here Comes Mr Jordan*, a whimsical tale of a dead boxer returning to earth in another chap's body through a celestial mix-up. What mordant wits like Elaine May (who co-scripted with Beatty) and Buck Henry saw in this is another heavenly mystery: the script provides only the thinnest of lunatic fringes to decorate the soggy comic material. Beatty ambles nicely enough through the hero's part (remodelled as a quarterback), and Charles Grodin turns up trumps playing another of his chinless, spineless wonders. But Christie's comedy gifts are as minuscule as ever, and the film drags its feet uncertainly from beginning to end. GB

Heaven Help Us (aka Catholic Boys)

(1984, US, 104 min)
d Michael Dinner. *p* Dan Wigutow, Mark Carliner. *sc* Charles Purpura. *ph* Miroslav Ondricek. *ed* Stephen A Rotter. *pd* Michael Molly. *m* James Horner. *cast* Donald Sutherland, John Heard, Andrew McCarthy, Mary Stuart Masterson, Kevin Dillon, Wallace Shawn, Kate Reid, Philip Bosco
●A sharply observed rites-of-passage comedy set in Brooklyn in 1965. At St Basil's Catholic School for Boys, the pupils find their growing pains made more painful by the ministrations of stern-faced Brethren, who lecture them on the Seventh Deadliest Sin just before a long-awaited junior prom, and patrol the dance floor ready to disentangle any clinches too close for chastity. Sutherland presides in a perm and a cassock over fellow-monks Heard and Shawn, the schoolboy cast give good-natured performances, and Dinner (his first film) brings sensitivity and freshness to a threadbare theme. SJo

Heaven Knows, Mr Allison

(1957, US, 105 min)
d John Huston. *p* Buddy Adler, Eugene Franks. *sc* John Lee Mahin, John Huston. *ph* Oswald Morris. *ed* Russell Lloyd. *ad* Stephen Grimes. *m* Georges Auric. *cast* Deborah Kerr, Robert Mitchum.
●On the one hand, Huston's typically wry contribution to Hollywood's long-established, censor-baiting fascination with nuns. On the other, a quirky and superior reworking of his own *The African Queen*. Deborah Kerr, back in the habit ten years after *Black Narcissus*, is stranded on a Jap-held Pacific island with Marine corporal Mitchum, whose wonderfully low-key portrait of melting machismo is everything Bogart's respectably Oscar-chasing irascibility wasn't. The favourite film of its veteran screenwriter, John Lee Mahin. PT

Heavenly Creatures

(1994, NZ, 98 min)
d Peter Jackson. *p* Jim Booth *sc* Frances Walsh, Peter Jackson. *ph* Alun Bollinger. *ed* Jamie Selkirk. *pd* Grant Major. *m* Peter Dasent. *cast* Melanie Lynskey, Kate Winslet, Sarah Peirse, Diana Kent, Clive Merrison, Simon O'Conner.
●Based on a real-life murder case that scandalised New Zealand in the '50s, Peter Jackson's movie marks a welcome change from the splatter of *Bad Taste* and *Braindead*. Rather than focus on the final act of violence, the film explores the overheated encounter between two teenagers: clever, cocky Juliet (Winslet), from a well-to-do English family, and pudgy, initially more introspective Pauline (Lynskey), a working-class girl. The pair's obsession with books, Mario Lanza, the fearsome Orson Welles and other 'saints' leads them to create their own 'Fourth World', a medieval fantasy involving royal romance and bloody intrigue; but when their parents decide that the friendship is 'wayward' and 'unhealthy', the girls' terror at the prospect of separation impels daydreams to invade reality, with deadly results. Jackson's film is distinguished by the intensity of the girls' secretive relationship. If the busy camera movements used to convey the heady exhilaration of their early encounters are irritating, the sense of claustrophobic immersion in private mysteries is palpable. Acted with conviction, and directed and written with febrile vibrancy. GA

Heavenly Pursuits

(1986, GB, 91 min)
d Charles Gormley. *p* Michael Relph. *sc* Charles Gormley. *ph* Michael Coulter. *ed* John Gow. *pd* Rita McGurn. *m* BA Robertson. *cast* Tom Conti, Helen Mirren, David Hayman, Brian Pettifer, Jennifer Black, Dave Anderson, Ewen Bremner.
●An engaging satire on the miracle business, set in a Catholic school in Glasgow whose status-seeking authorities are much taxed by the problem of canonisation for their patron, the Blessed Edith Semple, who died in 1917 with one authenticated miracle to her credit. She needs two more, the Vatican sternly decrees. Meanwhile a sceptical remedial teacher (Conti) is quietly performing miracles of his own with backward kids, and is as startled as anyone when a couple of bizarre circumstances intervening in his life seem to smack of the miraculous. Treated with tongue-in-cheek seriousness, the resulting confusion of cross-purposes as the media jump on the band wagon treads a delicate path through the morass of cynicism, gullibility and wishfulness. Quirkily funny and admirably acted, it works beautifully largely because Gormley (scripting as well as directing) refuses to undersell any of his characters: everybody has his reasons. TM

Heaven, Man, Earth

(1984, GB, 78 min)
d Laurens C Postma. *p* Laurence C Postma, Phillip Bartlett. *sc* Jonathan Frost. *ph* David Scott, Billy Wo. *ed* Hussein Younis. *m* David Hewson.
●The problem in making a film about the Triad gangs of Hong Kong is that there's very little you can actually show. This deeply dishonest movie used miles of irrelevant travelogue to cover the gap, and has clumsily staged sequences masquerading as 'documentary'. Even the alleged movie clips are actually scenes from TV. All this duplicity produces a very damp squib, despite the dogged sensation-seeking. TR

Heavens Above!

(1963, GB, 118 min, b/w)
d John Boulting. *p* Roy Boulting. *sc* Frank Harvey, John Boulting. *ph* Max Greene. *ed* Teddy Darvas. *ad* Albert Witherick. *m* Richard Rodney Bennett. *cast* Peter Sellers, Cecil Parker, Isabel Jeans, Eric Sykes, Bernard Miles, Brock Peters, Ian Carmichael, Irene Handl, Miriam Karlin, Joan Hickson.
●Playing a clergyman who applies his Christian charity literally, having been translated by error to a posh parish from his prison chaplaincy, Sellers works valiantly to wring a laugh or two out of this cringe-making satire on the church. Based on an idea by Malcolm Muggeridge, no less, the script is peopled exclusively by stereotypes, skitters uneasily into farce, and indulges a penchant for schoolboy sniggers that makes it a not-so-distant relative of the *Carry On* family. TM

Heaven's Burning

(1997, Aust, 99 min)
d Craig Lahiff. *p* Al Clarke, Helen Leake. *sc* Louis Nowra. *ph* Brian Breheny. *ed* John Scott. *pd* Vicki Niehaus. *m* Graeme Koehne. *cast* Russell Crowe, Youki Kudoh, Kenji Isomura, Ray Barrett, Robert Mammone, Petru Gheorghiu.
●It takes a while for this road movie thriller to take off, as the director labours through an opening section which lays out how Japanese honeymooner Midori (Kudoh) happens to find herself on the run (and loving it), chased by bank robbers and her 'disgraced' ex-husband, with only a hot-rodder (Crowe) as reluctant helpmate. In a film of blunt genre strokes, Kudoh's transition to kooky 'liberated' chick is as rudimentarily sketched as the reactions to her foreignness are awkwardly played out. Nevertheless, director Lahiff manages to balance the action and human interest, using transport truck metal and the horizontal swaths of the Australian landscape to emulate the sweep and gleam of the American prototype, and undercutting the machismo through the sympathetic playing of Kudoh and, especially, Crowe. WH

Heaven's Gate

(1980, US, 219 min)
d Michael Cimino. *p* Joann Carelli. *sc* Michael Cimino. *ph* Vilmos Zsigmond. *ed* Tom Rolf, William Reynolds, Lisa Fruchtman, Gerald Greenberg. *ad* Tambi Larsen. *m* David Mansfield. *cast* Kris Kristofferson, Christopher Walken, John Hurt, Sam Waterston, Brad Dourif, Isabelle Huppert, Joseph Cotten, Jeff Bridges, Geoffrey Lewis.
●For all the abuse heaped on it, this is – in its complete version, at least – a majestic and lovingly detailed Western which simultaneously celebrates and undermines the myth of the American frontier. The keynote is touched in the wonderfully choreographed opening evocation of a Harvard graduation in 1870: answering the Dean's ritual address urging graduates to spread culture through contact with the uncultivated, the class valedictorian (Hurt) mockingly replies that they see no need for change in a world 'on the whole well arranged'. Twenty years later, as Hurt and fellow-graduate Kristofferson become involved in the Johnson County Wars, their troubled consciences suggest that some change in the 'arrangements' might well have been in order. Watching uneasily as the rich cattle barons legally exterminate the poor immigrant farmers who have taken to illegal rustling to feed their starving families, they can only attempt to enforce the law that has become a mockery (Kristofferson) or lapse into soothing alcoholism (Hurt). Moral compromise on a national scale is in question here, a theme subtly echoed by the strange romantic triangle that lies at the heart of the film: a three-way struggle between the man who has everything (Kristofferson), the man who has nothing (Walken), and the girl (Huppert) who would settle for either provided no fraudulent compromise is asked of her. The ending, strange and dreamlike, blandly turns a blind eye to shut out the atrocities and casuistries we have witnessed, and on which the American dream was founded; not much wonder the American press went on a mass witch-hunt against the film's un-American activities. TM

Heaven-6-Box

(1995, Jap, 60 min)
d Hiroyuki Oki. *with* Yasuhisa Kiyooka, Gensho Takasaki, Yoshie Takasaki, Jun Osaki, Tei Osaki, Kenji Tsuzuki, Daijiro Hashimoto.
●Commissioned by the city of Kochi to mark the opening of its Museum of Modern Art, this experimental feature by Japan's foremost gay indie film-maker almost defies description. The film is divided into six 10-minute chapters (or 'boxes') which, says Oki, add up to an image of 'heaven'. They certainly do add up to a portrait of the city and its people, from the mayor posing outside the railway station to the undressed boys lying around Oki's own apartment, from a strange piece of performance art outside the new museum to the fish market and the youth orchestra playing on the seashore. Ineffably idiosyncratic and mildly sexy, it rewards repeated viewings. TR

Heaven's Prisoners

(1996, US, 131 min)
d Phil Joanou. *p* Albert S Ruddy, André E Morgan, Leslie Greif. *sc* Harley Peyton, Scott Frank. *ph* Harris Savides. *ed* William Steinkamp. *pd* John Stoddart. *m* George Fenton. cast Alec Baldwin, Kelly Lynch, Mary Stuart Masterson, Eric Roberts, Teri Hatcher, Vondie Curtis-Hall, Badja Djola.

●This unspeakably tedious adaptation of a book by James Lee Burke is hampered by the fact that the leading man looks and sounds like an LA tourist, rather than a bruised ex-New Orleans cop recovering from violence and alcoholism by running a bait farm. Taking on the role of Dave Robicheaux, Baldwin gets back into his old baddie routine when he rescues a child from a spectacular air wreck. The crash concerns villains involved in dope, women and illegal immigrants, and leads to the killing of Dave's wife, at which point Baldwin gives what is one of the most embarrassingly unconvincing examples of Hollywood emoting by refusing to believe that she's dead. Joanou has a strong affinity for the violent, the religiously symbolic and the musical – one of the best things about this film is a solid blues soundtrack. But he can also be a deeply boring storyteller, and at 131 minutes this piece is way over its natural timespan; by about two thirds in, you pray for the alligators to get you. SGr

Heaven Tonight

(1990, Aust, 93 min)
d Pino Amenta. *p* Frank Howson. *sc* Frank Howson, Alister Webb. *ph* David Connell. *ed* Philip Reid. *pd* Bernadette Wynack. *m* Andrew Rammage. *cast* John Waters, Kim Gyngell, Rebecca Gilling, Sean Cully, Guy Pearce.

●Although most films about the tribulations of rock stars are utterly awful, the occasional oddball which slips through the net keeps the 'pop film' genre alive and interesting. This tiny-budget Antipodean offering centres on an ageing has-been whose son's flourishing singing career provokes much domestic hassling and heartache. Taking a resolutely downbeat approach, and featuring some convincing footage in which the participants actually appear to be playing their instruments (a miracle!), this avoids all the naff 'let's-do-the-gig-here' clichés, for which praise is due indeed. Not as hard-hitting as *Slade in Flame*, perhaps, but nicely grim none the less. MK

Heavy

(1995, US, 103 min)
d James Mangold. p Richard Miller. *sc* James Mangold. *ph* Michael Barrow. *ed* Meg Reticker. pd Michael Shaw. *m* Thurston Moore. *cast* Pruitt Taylor Vince, Shelley Winters, Liv Tyler, Deborah Harry, Joe Grifasi, Evan Dando.

●The humming undertow of Thurston Moore's electronic score lends this American indie a brooding intensity right from the start. We're in small-town territory: a rundown diner, a new girl behind the counter, and growing romantic attachment from the owner's plump, retiring son. Disaster's rather obviously brewing; Tyler's fresh-faced Callie may be bringing new life to the place, but she's sparked resentment in fellow waitress Delores (Harry), while the occasional presence of her muso boyfriend Jeff (Dando) seems bound to cause the gentle, corpulent Victor (Vince) some ill-defined yet inevitable hurt. As proprietress Dolly (Winters) presides over failing business and a few loyal regulars, the future appears more uncertain than ever. Writer/director Mangold's careful, essentially serious approach puts the characters under the microscope and relies on the performers not to let him down. They don't. Newcomer Tyler is breezy and touching. Vince meanwhile is hugely sympathetic as the shy boy daring to reach out, capturing deep repression and tiny everyday acts of courage with meticulous command. A potent, if slightly precious first feature, that's distinctive enough to remain long in the mind. TJ

Heavy Metal

(1981, US, 90 min)
d Gerald Potterton. *p* Ivan Reitman. *sc* Dan Goldberg, Len Blum. *ed* Janice Brown. *pd* Michael Gross. *m* Elmer Bernstein. *cast* voices: Don Francks, Richard Romanus, John Candy, John Vernon.

●Among those listed in the credits are a handful of collaborators whose reputations should be rescued from the cosmic junkheap this deserves to rust on – notably writer Dan O'Bannon – but the collective animators of this dopey Disney parody (reportedly 1,000 artists working in five cities simultaneously) still have a lot to answer for. Fantasies that are gratuitously sexist and Fascist (macho whoring and warmongering), and whose roots reach all the way back to post-hippie paranoia, feed the tangled plot-lines of a movie that, given the orchestral overkill and surprisingly low profile of heavy metal music, should disappoint even the teenage wet-dreamers it's aimed at. MA

Heavy Petting

(1988, US, 80 min, b/w & col)
d/p Obie Benz. *sc* Suzanne Fenn, Lianne Halfron. *ph* Sandi Sissel. *ed* Judith Sobol. *with* David Byrne, Sandra Bernhard, Allen Ginsberg, William Burroughs, Ann Magnuson, Spalding Gray, Josh Mostel, Laurie Anderson, John Oates, Abbie Hoffman.

●A documentary whose subject matter (sexual initiation and education) tempted assorted celebrities and intellectuals to recount their earliest intimate encounters. Sandra Bernhard let a boy see her bottom in return for a fudgsicle, David Byrne wondered if he would use up all his sperm if he masturbated, Spalding Gray ponders whether the raccoon hats so popular during his adolescence were used to stimulate the wearer's genital area. By incorporating archival footage (educational, television, feature films), Benz and his researchers explore shifts in sexual codes of conduct in America from the '50s. They've unearthed some wonders, from *How to Say No* to *Physical Aspects of Puberty*; and as newshounds quiz teens about the evils of rock'n'roll, one presenter warns that moral depravity could leave the country vulnerable to Communist conquest. The 'witnesses' lend a structure of sorts; when it works, the material is funny and direct, even though the comparison of the two eras doesn't exactly prove revelatory. CM

Heavy Traffic

(1973, US, 75 min)
d Ralph Bakshi. *p* Steve Krantz. *sc* Ralph Bakshi. *ph* Ted C Bemiller, Gregg Heschong, John Vita, Ralph Bakshi. *ed* Donald W Ernst. *m* Ray Shanklin, Ed Bogas. *cast* voices: Joseph Kaufmann, Beverley Hope Atkinson, Franke de Kova, Terri Haven, Mary Dean Lauria, Jacqueline Mills, Lillian Adams.

●An animated follow-up to *Fritz the Cat* that must have been worked out on a computer. Take one pinball wizard, plus one godfather, plus one underground comic artist, plus black chickette power, plus anything else that grabbed the boppers ten years ago, and you should have what they all want to see. Despite the occasional stream of animated piss, stretched cock or flashed twat, or the 'innovation' of combined live and animated sequences, the movie falls apart at every seam, a humourless mess, a stale joke. The quality of the animation is cornflake packet standard, the script – one or two minor moments excepted – a disaster. JDuC

Hedda

(1975, GB, 102 min)
d Trevor Nunn. *p* Robert Enders. *sc* Trevor Nunn. *ph* Douglas Slocombe. *ed* Peter Tanner. *ad* Ted Tester. *m* Laurie Johnson. *cast* Glenda Jackson, Peter Eyre, Timothy West, Jennie Linden, Patrick Stewart, Constance Chapman.

●The abbreviated title of this Brut production (transposing Nunn's Royal Shakespeare Company staging of Ibsen's play) is the clue: leaving out the *Gabler* implies a Woman's Picture and the plastic surface of high-class soap opera. So it is for much of the time, with close-ups of Glenda Jackson reacting archly to the out-of-focus figures in the background. Luckily the supporting cast is outstanding; so that once the nods to opening out the play have been made, the film settles into its hypnotic story of manipulation and sexual tensions, with no fancy angles to obscure the power of Hedda's climactic burning of the Lovborg manuscript. AN

Hedd Wyn

(1992, GB, 110 min)
d Paul Turner. *p* Shan Davies. *sc* Allan Llwyd, Paul Turner. *ph* Ray Orton. *ed* Chris Lawrence. *ad* Jane Roberts, Martin Morley. *m* John Hardy. *cast* Huw Garmon, Sue Roderick, Catrin Fychan, Ceri Cunnington, Lilo Silyn, Grey Evans.

●Subtitled 'The Armageddon Poet', this Welsh-language feature is the story of WWI poet Ellis Evans, known under the pen name Hedd Wyn. Ellis – who failed on his first attempt to fulfil his ambition of winning the Chair at the National Eisteddfod – left school at 14 and three years later was conscripted (in place of his brother) into the Army. While serving in France, he used every spare moment to work on his poem 'Yr Arwr' (The Hero), which he finally completed and submitted by post. A month later, on the first day of the Battle of Passchendaele, he was mortally wounded, but his poem survived and he was awarded the prize he had always coveted. Little noted in England, *Hedd Wyn* received an Oscar nomination in 1994 for best foreign-language film. NF

He Died After the War

see Man Who Left His Will on Film

He Died with His Eyes Open (On ne Meurt que 2 Fois)

(1985, Fr, 106 min)
d Jacques Deray. *p* Norbert Saada. *sc* Jacques Deray, Michel Audiard. *ph* Jean Penzer. *ed* Henri Lanoë, Sylvie Pontoizeau. *ad* François De Lamothe. *m* Claude Bolling. *cast* Michel Serrault, Charlotte Rampling, Xavier Deluc, Elisabeth Depardieu, Jean Leuvrais, Jean-Paul Roussillon.

●An adaptation of Robin Cook's thriller (written under the pseudonym Derek Raymond). A washed-up concert pianist is found dead beside a railway track, leaving back at his apartment the biggest heap of clues anyone could wish for: a pile of tape recordings in which he rambles on about his obsessive love for one Barbara. When the lady in question turns up (Rampling), she immediately confesses to the bemused cop on the case (Serrault). In true *noir* style, however, this is only the beginning; there is now poor, ugly Serrault's long haul to establish proof, his fatal attraction to the femme fatale, his bizarre identification with the dead man, and of course his sad choice between feelings and duty. Rampling is fine as the sloe-eyed temptress with the murderous level gaze and a certain taste for incest; and Serrault is rapidly establishing himself as the French Walter Matthau, a marvellous melancholic with perfect timing. It's the sort of thriller at which the French excel; lovely stuff. CPea

Hedwig and the Angry Inch

(2001, US, 92 min)
d John Cameron Mitchell. *p* Christine Vachon, Katie Roumel, Pamela Koffler. *sc* John Cameron Mitchell. *ph* Frank G DeMarco. *ed* Andrew Marcus. *pd* Thérèse DePrez. *m/lyrics* Stephen Trask. *cast* John Cameron Mitchell, Andrea Martin, Michael Pitt, Alberta Watson, Stephen Trask, Rob Campbell, Theodore Liscinski, Michael Aronov, Miriam Shor.

●The Angry Inch is her band – a rare rock group named after a lesser member – and Hedwig a naturalised American icon in waiting, an 'internationally ignored song stylist' who used to be Hansel, a slip of an East German boy, before a botched backstreet sex op changed not quite everything. We catch the band in the act, touring suburban salad bars, obsessively tracking one Tommy Gnosis – Rock God, and defendant in Hedwig's forthcoming multi-million dollar plagiarism suit. The set is staged, you might say. Hedwig's performance (and you'd better believe she's never off) is a desperate plea for attention; it's autobiography as frock opera. At least she gives good barb. I love the idea that young Hansel's Berlin home was so cramped his Mütter made him play in the oven. But for a movie about a little prick, there's something monstrously self-aggrandising going on: Hedwig invokes the Berlin Wall as a metaphor for his/her sexual identity crisis, for example, and not the other way round; the relentless narcissism dominates every scene, every self-deprecating one-liner. It's easy to imagine that John Cameron Mitchell's full-on, wigged-in presence more than carried the live show off-Broadway and beyond; but despite the creator/actor/director's energetic efforts, the material never feels comfortable in its new form. TCh

He Got Game

(1998, US, 136 min)
d Spike Lee. *p* John Kilik, Spike Lee. *sc* Spike Lee. *ph* Malik Hassan Sayeed. *ed* Barry Alexander Brown. *pd* Wynn Thomas. *m* Aaron Copland. *cast* Denzel Washington, Ray Allen, Milla Jovovich, Rosario Dawson, Ned Beatty, Jim Brown, Lonette McKee, John Turturro.
●Father/son relationships have come to carry increasing weight in Spike Lee's films, and this one exhibits a sober moral force. A convict, Jake Shuttleworth (Washington), is unofficially paroled to Coney Island for a week. If he can persuade his son Jesus, the hottest basketball prospect in the country, to sign for the Governor's alma mater, Jake can get used to freedom. However, Jesus (NBA star Allen) has his own agenda, and the man who killed his mother comes at the end of a very long queue. The corrupt college scholarship system and the business of sport in general gets surprisingly ambivalent, vaguely satiric treatment – presented with these false profits and fast temptations, Lee puts his trust in Jesus. Flashbacks to Jake's tough-love training sessions are especially powerful, Washington exposing the aggression behind the determination, but cumbersome subplots involving Jovovich as a hooker and Dawson as Jesus' double-dealing girl don't help. Most scenes play too long, with a surplus of ideas, textures, tones and characters, and after 134 minutes it's clear Lee's problem with closure hasn't gone away. TCh

Heidi Fleiss – Hollywood Madam

(1995, GB, 106 min)
d Nick Broomfield. *p* Nick Broomfield, Kahane Corn. *ph* Paul Kloss. *ed* Susan Bloom. *m* David Bergeaud. *with* Heidi Fleiss, Ivan Nagy, Madam Alex, Cookie.
●Broomfield's characteristically feisty, intrusive documentary about the Tinseltown prostitute/madam is packed with biographical detail, eye-catchingly sleazy characters (but unfortunately no real stars), and lots of unanswered questions. Fleiss is clearly a pretty shrewd mover; Madam Alex, her mentor, now seems merely a sad eccentric; while Fleiss's on-off, love-hate relationship with film-maker, lover and alleged pimp Ivan Nagy, is a wonder to behold: exploitative in the extreme, but who's exploiting who? Fascinating, but then, however sharp or persuasive Broomfield's sleuthing methods, that's almost inevitable. GA

Heidi's Song

(1982, US, 94 min)
d Robert Taylor. *p* Joseph Barbera, William Hanna. *sc* Joseph Barbera, Jameson Brewer, Robert Taylor. *ph* Jerry Mills. *ed* Larry Cowan, Patrick Foley, Gregory V Watson Jr. *ad* Paul Julian. *m* Hoyt Curtin. cast voices: Lorne Greene, Sammy Davis Jr, Margery Gray, Michael Bell, Peter Cullen.
●The much loved, oft retold story of Heidi gets the Hanna-Barbera treatment: it remains the tale of a cute little blonde who refuses to see catastrophe (grandfather breaks his leg, Klara is still no better, and Heidi herself is almost devoured by rats) other than as an opportunity for a grating cheerfulness, spiced with a Disney-like catalogue of anthropomorphic mutts and vermin and a few tunes. But, interestingly, the film-makers seem to have taken the classic animation of Chuck Jones as their model (where they have not cannibalised their own TV series), introducing a saving strain of acerbity into an otherwise cloying cartoon. FD

Heimat (Homeland)

(1984, WGer, 924 min. b/w & col)
d/p Edgar Reitz. *sc* Edgar Reitz, Peter Steinbach. *ph* Gernot Roll. *ed* Heidi Handorf. *ad* Franz Bauer. *m* Nikos Mamangakis. *cast* Marita Breuer, Dieter Schaad, Michael Lesch, Eva Maria Bayerswaltes, Rüdiger Weigang.
●In this eleven-part film made for TV, Reitz portrays his country's difficult history from 1919 to the present day without recourse to soap operatics. Maria, born in 1900, is the still point around whom others move emotionally, economically, and politically, with the narrative developing through a superbly sustained accumulation of detail. Humane and comic, it's very finely acted, exact in period detail, and immaculately photographed in monochrome with occasional bursts of colour of an epiphanic resonance. A magnificent achievement that will reward every hour it demands of your time. DT

Heimspiel

see Home Game

Heiress, The

(1949, US, 115 min, b/w)
d/p William Wyler. *sc* Ruth Goetz, Augustus Goetz. *ph* Leo Tover. *ed* William Hornbeck. *pd* Harry Horner. *m* Aaron Copland. *cast* Olivia de Havilland, Ralph Richardson, Montgomery Clift, Miriam Hopkins, Vanessa Brown, Ray Collins, Mona Freeman.
●Wyler's version of Henry James' *Washington Square* (based on a play adaptation) is typically plush, painstaking and cold. James' heroine, whose young love is thwarted by a grasping fiancé and an equally selfish father, at least turned into a spinster with moral integrity, but Wyler's simply grows into a malevolent old witch. Olivia de Havilland is a millstone round many a film's neck, but she soon leaves off smiling sweetly in this one, clashing swords in deep focus with Richardson (magnificently imperious) and an oily Clift. And Aaron Copland contributes some suitably icy music. It's all highly professional and heartless. GB

Heist

(2001, US/Can, 109 min)
d David Mamet. *p* Art Linson, Elie Samaha, Andrew Stevens. *sc* David Mamet. *ph* Robert Elswit. *ed* Barbara Tulliver. *pd* David Wasco. *m* Theodore Shapiro. *cast* Gene Hackman, Danny DeVito, Delroy Lindo, Sam Rockwell, Rebecca Pidgeon, Ricky Jay, Patti LuPone.
●David Mamet has been talking this up as his homage to that perennial favourite, *film noir*. But as we should all know by now, you can't trust a word he says. In fact this movie belongs to a far more exclusive and readily identifiable sub-genre: the Mamet sting game. Hackman is a master cracksman persuaded by DeVito to go that job too far; Lindo and Jay are his expert team, and Mrs Mamet – Pidgeon – is totally miscast as the femme fatale who may or may not be Hackman's weakest link. Sure, you get the feeling Mamet could write this stuff before breakfast, and the only surprise on the home straight is how lazy it feels, but at least everyone's having fun – audience included – Mamet has finally learned how to direct action, and Hackman… 'He's so cool, when he goes to bed, sheep count him.' TCh

Heist, The

see $ [Dollars]

He Knows You're Alone

(1980, US, 94 min)
d Armand Mastroianni. *p* George Manasse. *sc* Scott Parker. *ph* Gerald Feil. *ed* George T Norris. *ad* Susan Kaufman. *m* Alexander Peskanov, Mark Peskanov. *cast* Don Scardino, Caitlin O'Heaney, Elizabeth Kemp, Tom Rolfing, Lewis Arlt, James Rebhorn, Tom Hanks.
●There's a psycho on the loose. Having once been traumatically jilted, Rolfing specialises in brutally despatching brides-to-be, and becomes obsessed with one in particular (O'Heaney). News reaches police chief Arlt, who snorts fire as his erstwhile bride-to-be was an early Rolfing victim. For a more curdled piece of chiller incompetence, this would be hard to beat. Newcomer Mastroianni directs with leaden predictability. A myopic eye for overblown and voyeuristic imagery, he moves from one murder to another, a synthesiser signpost helping to rob every spill of any surprise at all. The final twist is especially dumb and obvious. And characterisation means stereotype; Tupperware dialogue for passive women, racy dialogue for shower-room, protective men. It's almost distastefully bad. IB

Held for Questioning (Der Aufenthalt)

(1983, EGer, 102 min)
d Frank Beyer. *sc* Wolfgang Kohlhaase. *ph* Eberhard Geick. *ed* Rita Hiller. *ad* Alfred Hirschmeier. *m* Gunther Fischer. *cast* Sylvester Groth, Fred Düren, Klaus Piontek, Matthias Günther, Horst Hiemer.
●Beyer's film is a study of prison life and of personality. A young German soldier is imprisoned after the end of the war in 1945: is he wittingly or unwittingly a war criminal? Are the other inmates more dangerous than the guards? Never less than interesting, the film is flawed by a central inconsistency of approach: never quite a study of the minutiae and banality of the day-to-day existence of the prisoner, it also never fully explores the possibilities of a potentially Kafkaesque situation. SM

Helen, Queen of the Nautch Girls

(1973, Ind/GB, 31 min, b/w & col)
d Anthony Korner. *p* Ismail Merchant. *sc* James Ivory. *ph* Anwar Siraj, RM Rao. *ed* Andrew Page. *narrator* Anthony Korner. *with* Helen.
●A documentary on the Anglo-Indian Helen, best remembered by Western audiences, perhaps, as the Heroine in Gold dancing on the giant typewriter in Merchant Ivory's *Bombay Talkie*. The star of more than 500 Hindi films turns out to be straightforward, unaffected professional, modestly concerned that her film's have a consistent point of view and that, above all, her eyes hold the spectator's attention. Her ambition, when she finally retires? To open a modest boutique in Bombay's still to be completed Sheraton Hotel. JPy

Helicopter Spies, The

(1967, US, 93 min)
d Boris Sagal. *p* Anthony Spinner. *sc* Dean Hargrove. *ph* Fred Koenekamp. *ed* Joseph Dervin, John B Rogers. *ad* George W Davis, James W Sullivan. *m* Richard Shores, Jerry Goldsmith. *cast* Robert Vaughn, David McCallum, Carol Lynley, Bradford Dillman, Lola Albright, John Dehner, Leo G Carroll, John Carradine, Julie London.
●A *Man from UNCLE* film which sees Solo and Kuryakin on the trail of a notorious safecracker (Dillman) in Greece. Inevitably their quest leads to a plot to dominate the world, this time by a sect of white-haired mystics, and the team fight their way through several continents. It's all pretty static low-budget stuff, with only a few guest appearances to help things along: Carol Lynley, for example, as a mini-skirted all-American girl, bent on revenge. DP

Hell (Jigoku)

(1960, Jap, 101 min)
d Nobuo Nakagawa. *p* Mitsugu Okura. *sc* Ichiro Miyagawa, Nobuo Nakagawa. *ph* Mamoru Morita. *ed* Toshio Goto. *ad* Hiroyasu Kurosawa. *m* Chumei Watanabe. *cast* Shigeru Amachi, Yoichi Numata, Utako Mitsuya, Jun Otomo, Hiroshi Hayashi.
●Nakagawa's most ambitious film, a cult item in Japan, is wildly eccentric. Shot mostly on bare studio sets with a lighting style even more theatrical than the acting, it feels like a weird piece of fringe theatre in three acts. Act 1, in Tokyo, sets up the characters' moral failings. Shiro (Amachi) is a student engaged to his professor's daughter Yukiko (Mitsuya); under the influence of the demonic Tamura (Numata), he's involved in both a hit and run accident which kills a yakuza and a taxi crash which kills his fiancée. Act 2, in rural Tenjoen ('Paradise Garden'), adds assorted dissolute adults and has Shiro fall in love again, this time with Sachiko (Mitsuya again), who turns out to be his sister. Mass poisonings kill everyone. Act 3, in Hell, gives Shiro the chance to redeem himself by rescuing the soul of his and Yukiko's unborn daughter; everyone suffers lurid tortures. A Buddhist twist on the old US film *Dante's Inferno*, this actually anticipates the traits of Corman's contemporary Poe cycle: guilt-ridden characters, tacky visual effects, outré compositions in 'Scope. TR

Hell and High Water

(1954, US, 103 min)
d Samuel Fuller. *p* Raymond A Klune. *sc* Jesse L Lasky Jr, Samuel Fuller. J MacDonald. *ed* James B Clark. *ad* Lyle Wheeler, Leland Fuller. *m* Alfred Newman. cast Richard Widmark, Bella Darvi, Victor Francen, Cameron Mitchell, Gene Evans, David Wayne.
●Known for his uninhibited camera movements, Fuller was the obvious person for Fox to ask to make a CinemaScope movie in an

enclosed space in order to prove to doubting executives that the walls of the cinema would not appear to rotate during tracking shots or pans. The result was *Hell and High Water*, which is mostly set aboard a submarine, and tells the story of a group of patriots and mercenaries who stop the Chinese from dropping an atomic bomb from an 'American' plane at the time of the Korean war. A deeply pessimistic film, it questions the roots of loyalty and identity by examining the stated motives of its characters at every stage of the film. Widmark is at his ambiguous best. PH

Hellbound: Hellraiser II

(1988, GB, 93 min)
d Tony Randel. *p* Clive Barker. *sc* Peter Atkins. *ph* Robin Vidgeon. *ed* Richard Marden. *pd* Mike Buchanan. *m* Christopher Young. *cast* Claire Higgins, Ashley Laurence, Kenneth Cranham, Imogen Boorman, Sean Chapman, William Hope, Doug Bradley.

●A disappointing sequel to Clive Barker's innovatory 'body horror' pic, which – while making some effort to flesh out the Cenobite mythology – simply performs cosmetic surgery on the original. This time, it's a skinned Julia (Higgins) who writhes up from a blood-caked mattress, while depraved psychiatrist Dr Channard (Cranham) summons Pinhead and his pals with the help of Tiffany (Boorman), a dumb teenager with a penchant for solving puzzles. And when Kirsty (Laurence) receives a message in blood from her Hell-bound father, she plunges into a subterranean labyrinth to save him. Directed with staggering ineptitude, this never approaches the visceral intensity and flesh-crawling terror of the first film. The teenage heroines are too insipid to elicit either interest or sympathy, Julia's graduation from wicked stepmother to Evil Queen erasesa crucial element of moral ambiguity, and the labyrinth looks like a cross between an MC Escher painting and a '70s 'progressive rock' album cover. Only Channard's transformation into a Cenobite, and subsequent celebration of his perverse power, match the intellectual complexity and visual ferocity of *Hellraiser*. NF

Hellcat Mud Wrestlers

(1983, GB, 48 min)
d David Sullivan, John M East. *p* John M East. *ph* Alan Hall. *ed* Jim Connock. *with* Queen Kong, Shelley Selina Savage, Sadistic Sadie, Vickie Scott, Helen Hammer, Rosie Rock, Miss Death Wish.

●Grappling in the goo for the delectation of a bunch of drunks, Sadie, Kong and the rest try their best to be hellcats, but (good for them) their hearts aren't in it. Even the mud lacks conviction. It's generically a documentary, though it's hardly what John Grierson had in mind when he devised the term. The disquiet and loathing it induces correlate to the aims of a Buñuel or a Vigo. This is not to be confused with a recommendation. BBa

Hellcats of the Navy

(1957, US, 69 min, b/w)
d Nathan Juran. *p* Charles H Schneer. *sc* David Lang. *ph* Irving Lippman. *ed* Jerome Thoms. *ad* Rudi Feld. *m* Mischa Bakaleinikoff. *cast* Ronald Reagan, Nancy Davis, Arthur Franz, Robert Arthur, Henry Lauter, Selmer Jackson.

●Ron'n'Nancy's only screen appearance together is the chief reason why anyone still remembers this dull WWII actioner, from a book by CA Lockwood and Hans Christian Adamson. On a US Navy sub out to attack Japanese merchant shipping, Capt Reagan hits conflict with Chief Officer Franz over command decisions which may have been influenced by feelings for Miss Davis. (Actually scripted by the blacklisted Bernard Gordon.) TJ

Hell Drivers

(1957, GB, 108 min, b/w)
d C Raker Endfield [Cy Endfield]. *p* S Benjamin Fisz. *sc* John Kruse, C Raker Endfield. *ph* Geoffrey Unsworth. *ed* John D Guthridge. *ad* Ernest Archer. *m* Hubert Clifford. *cast* Stanley Baker, Herbert Lom, Peggy Cummins, Patrick McGoohan, William Hartnell, Wilfrid Lawson, Jill Ireland, Sidney James, Gordon Jackson, Sean Connery.

●Energetic and violent trucking thriller marked by the raw, angry edge of the best of blacklist victim Endfield's Hollywood work, and by his appreciation (shared, oddly enough, by fellow exile Joseph Losey) of the markedly out-of-the-mainstream talent of Stanley Baker. Playing an ex-con hired as one of a team of drivers forced to drive at dangerous speeds in rattletrap lorries over rugged roads to meet the daily quota of loads to be delivered (a touch of *The Wages of Fear* here), Baker further becomes involved in a deadly duel with a sadistic rival (McGoohan) on his way to smashing the haulage company's racket. Baker and Endfield eventually formed their own production company for *Zulu*. PT

Heller in Pink Tights

(1960, US, 100 min)
d George Cukor. *p* Carlo Ponti, Marcello Girosi. *sc* Dudley Nichols, Walter Bernstein. *ph* Harold Lipstein. *ed* Howard Smith. *ad* Hal Pereira, Eugene Allen. *m* Daniele Amfitheatrof. *cast* Sophia Loren, Anthony Quinn, Margaret O'Brien, Steve Forrest, Edmund Lowe, Eileen Heckart, Ramon Novarro.

●Cukor's one stab at the Western genre was a typically personal response to the conventions, playing much of the adventure for comedy, and centering the plot around a touring theatrical troupe. As in so many of his films, the relationship between life and theatre is explored as the company, performing to ramshackle communities in an untamed frontier, act out heroic tales of love, passion and honourable death, surrounded by an altogether less romantic reality in which people struggle simply to survive. As in *A Star Is Born* and *Les Girls*, Hoyningen-Huene's colour designs are magnificent, and under the expert eye of Cukor, even Loren and Quinn give superb performances. GA

Heller Wahn

see Friends and Husbands

Hellfire Club, The

(1960, GB, 93 min)
d/p Robert S Baker, Monty Berman. *sc* Leon Griffiths, Jimmy Sangster. *ph* Monty Berman. *ed* Frederick Wilson. *ad* Ray Sim. *m* Clifton Parker. *cast* Keith Michell, Peter Arne, Adrienne Corri, Kai Fischer, Peter Cushing, Bill Owen, Tutte Lemkow, Miles Malleson, Andrew Faulds.

●Baker and Berman produced, directed and shot this yarn, written by Leon Griffiths and Jimmy Sangster, and based, peripherally, on the dodgy doings of the 18th century club for sensation-seeking gentlemen. Jason, an orphaned acrobat in a travelling circus (Michell, suitably energetic), is heir to the Netherden estate, which has been usurped by his cousin Thomas, the Hellfire's decadent new president (Arne). To retrieve what's his, Jason becomes a Netherden groom, arouses Thomas's mistress (Corri) and ends in Newgate under sentence of death, until the Prime Minister intervenes to save him. Surprisingly light on debauchery and occasionally perhaps too jocular for its own good, this costume melodrama nevertheless occasionally skips out of the rut. TJ

Hellhounds of Alaska, The (Die Blutigen Geier von Alaska)

(1973, WGer, 90 min)
d Harald Reinl. *p* Gunther Storm. *sc* Kurt Nachmann. *ph* Heinz Holscher. *ed* Eva Zeyn. *ad* Zeljko Senecic. *m* Bruno Nicolai. *cast* Doug McClure, Harald Leipnitz, Angelika Ott, Roberto Blanco, Kristina Nel, Klaus Löwitsch.

●West German, or schnitzel Westerns, have never had the crossover appeal of the spaghettis, but there was quite a sub-genre there for a while. This is an obscure, moderate adventure, with McClure as a fur-trapper battling the elements and sundry villains to sled a sick boy cross country for medical treatment. TJ

Hell in Korea

see Hill in Korea, A

Hell in the Pacific

(1968, US, 103 min)
d John Boorman. *p* Reuben Bercovitch. *sc* Alexander Jacobs, Eric Bercovici. *ph* Conrad Hall. *ed* Thomas Stanford. *ad* Anthony DG Pratt, Masao Yamazaki. *m* Lalo Schifrin. *cast* Lee Marvin, Toshiro Mifune.

●Intriguing but finally dissatisfying movie in which Marvin and Mifune repeatedly get into macho standoffs as a US Marine pilot and a Japanese naval officer stranded together on a desert island during World War II. Boorman makes the most of a limited situation through strong performances and dramatically employed scope compositions, but it gradually descends into woolly allegory. Obviously on the principle that something was lacking, the British release prints were saddled with an ending in which a bomb from the skies literally blew everything apart. In Boorman's original, rather more acerbic ending, after the two men get happily drunk together, having just discovered civilisation (an abandoned military camp, with stocks of food, cigarettes and drink) they simply walk angrily off in opposite directions, their enmity rewakened by photographs of the war in an old magazine. GA

Hell Is a City

(1959, GB, 98 min, b/w)
d Val Guest. *p* Michael Carreras. *sc* Val Guest. *ph* Arthur Grant. *ed* James Needs, John Dunsford. *ad* Robert Jones. *m* Stanley Black. *cast* Stanley Baker, John Crawford, Donald Pleasence, Maxine Audley, Billie Whitelaw, Joseph Tomelty, George A Cooper.

●A persuasively sweaty crime thriller set in Manchester, written and directed by the once reliable Guest (from a novel by Maurice Proctor), this atypical Hammer production benefited from a strong cast and fine use of location photography (in 'Hammerscope'). Square-jawed Baker toughs it out as a harassed police inspector with a volubly frustrated wife (Audley) at home, and the arduous assignment on the streets of tracking down a jailbreaker (Crawford) wanted for murder. The atmosphere is persuasively seedy and downbeat, and there's a striking performance by Billie Whitelaw in a period when she seemed to specialise in 'fallen women'. DT

Hell Is for Heroes

(1962, US, 90 min, b/w)
d Don Siegel. *p* Henry Blanke. *sc* Robert Pirosh, Richard Carr. *ph* Harold Lipstein. *ed* Howard Smith. *ad* Howard Richmond. *m* Leonard Rosenman. cast Steve McQueen, Bobby Darin, Fess Parker, Nick Adams, Bob Newhart, Harry Guardino, James Coburn.

●A war film is a war film is a war film...except that Siegel, brought into the project at the last moment when Steve McQueen refused to work with the scheduled director, toughened the standard war-is-hell screenplay into an extraordinary study of psychopathology. He centres everything squarely on the McQueen character (one of his best performances, a human war machine), and emphasises the tensions within the American platoon rather than the conflict with the offscreen Germans. The ending, which stresses the enormous human cost of a small tactical gain, is remarkably powerful, precisely because it's the first time that Siegel allows his audience any perspective on what they've been seeing. TR

Hell Night

(1981, US, 102 min)
d Tom De Simone. *p* Irwin Yablans, Bruce Cohn Curtis. *sc* Randolph Feldman. *ph* Mac Ahlberg. *ed* Tony Di Marco. *ad* Steven G Legler. *m* Dan Wyman. *cast* Linda Blair, Vincent Van Patten, Peter Barton, Kevin Brophy, Jenny Neumann, Suki Goodwin.

●Producer Irwin Yablans spent the time between *Halloween* and *Halloween II* cooking up more of the same. This time the innocent lambs set up for slaughter are a quartet of students (sporting fancy dress for more picturesque effect) who are locked overnight into a haunted house as a fraternity initiation test. To nobody's surprise but their own, jokey efforts to stage manage some nocturnal frights turn into the real thing. Amazing, though, what a competent director, cameraman and cast can do to help out a soggy plot. Tolerably watchable by comparison with the average *Halloween* rip-off. TM

Hello Again

(1987, US, 96 min)
d/p Frank Perry. *sc* Susan Isaacs. *ph* Jan Weincke. *ed* Peter C Frank, Trudy Ship. *pd* Edward Pisoni. *m* William Goldstein. *cast* Shelley Long, Judith Ivey, Gabriel Byrne, Corbin Bernsen, Sela Ward, Austin Pendleton, Carrie Nye, Madeleine Potter.
●Lucy Chadman (Long) is the ideal suburban housewife, devoted to her medic hubby Jason (Bernsen) and son Danny, who wants to be a chef. Her sister is quite the opposite. In tune with the cosmos, zany Zelda (Ivey) has no problem bringing Lucy back from the dead when she chokes on a South Korean chicken ball. But in the meantime a year has elapsed, and Jason has married Lucy's horizontally-mobile friend Kim (Ward). Lucy doesn't like it. Enlisting the help of a doctor friend (Byrne), she fights off the attentions of the alerted media and sees off her rival in love. Merely the excuse for a parade of expensive clothes and opulent locations, with Shelley Long milking her role for any drop of pathos, this is good for a giggle at best. MS

Hello, Dolly!

(1969, US, 148 min)
d Gene Kelly. *p/sc* Ernest Lehman. *ph* Harry Stradling. *ed* William H Reynolds. *pd* John F De Cuir. *m/lyrics* Jerry Herman. *cast* Barbra Streisand, Walter Matthau, Michael Crawford, Marianne McAndrew, EJ Peaker, Tommy Tune, Louis Armstrong.
●Only Streisand's second movie, but already (as co-star Matthau grumbled) she was hogging the screen. The trouble is that there isn't much to hog in this elephant which gave *Star!* a helping hoof in burying the Hollywood musical. The Jerry Herman score is unmemorable, Michael Kidd's choreography is foreshortened to accommodate yards of additional dialogue by Ernest Lehman, and the rest is Streisand capably doing her thing in a series of plushily colossal sets. PT

Hell of a Day, A (Reines d'un jour)

(2001, Fr, 94 min)
d Marion Vernoux. *p* Alain Rozanès, Pascal Verroust. *sc* Marion Vernoux, Nathalie Kristy. *ph* Dominique Colin. *ed* Lise Beaulieu. *pd* Emmanuel Duplay. *m* Alexandre Desplat, (song) Catherine Ringer. *cast* Karine Viard, Hélène Fillières, Victor Lanoux, Jane Birkin, Sergi López, Clémentine Célarié, Gilbert Melki, Melvil Poupaud, Jonathan Zaccaï.
●This energetic Paris-based comedy begins in wild fashion with a furtive fling at a drunken wedding and then gets gradually more chaotic. There's attrition between the classes (Fillières, the pretty but bad-tempered assistant in a photo development shop has a grudge against the bourgeoisie), romantic conspiracy (we witness the comic but pathetic attempts of one self-conscious housewife to cheat on her husband), conflict between the sexes (Birkin takes gloating revenge on her patronising ex-husband), and there's plenty of knockabout farce, all orchestrated with considerable wit and charm. GM

Hello, Frisco, Hello

(1943, US, 98 min)
d H Bruce Humberstone. *p* Milton Sperling. *sc* Robert Ellis, Helen Logan, Richard Macauley. *ph* Charles G Clarke, Allen Davey. *ed* Barbara McLean. *ad* James Basevi, Boris Leven. *songs* Mack Gordon, Harry Warren, others. *cast* Alice Faye, John Payne, Jack Oakie, Lynn Bari, June Havoc, Laird Cregar, Ward Bond.
●Lush but formulaic Fox musical, set on the Barbary Coast during the Naughty Nineties and charting the constancy of Faye's broken heart as she quietly rises to fame as a singing star while Payne, brashly acquiring ideas above his station, gets into entrepreneurial messes and tags after a Nob Hill heiress. Notable mainly for the vivid Technicolor and Faye's rendition of the Oscar-winning song 'You'll Never Know' (although it's repeated once too often as she waits for Payne to get the message). GA

Hello, Hemingway

(1990, Cuba, 88 min)
d Fernando Pérez. *p* Ricardo Avila. *sc* Mayda Royero. *ph* Julio Valdés. *ed* Jorge Abello. *cast* Laura de la Uz, Raúl Paz, Herminia Sánchez, Caridad Hernández, Enrique Molina.
●'Why did they make birds so delicate and fine as those sea swallows when the ocean can be so cruel?', a bookseller quotes from Hemingway's The Old Man and the Sea; but his young friend Laurita (Laura de la Uz, terrific) dismisses the darker passages of the story. In '50s Cuba, she applies for a scholarship to an American university, thereby attempting the first steps away from her impoverished family. Pérez beautifully interweaves complex moods as his film ranges over personal and social upheaval. Laurita's decision to try to go to America unleashes increasingly hostile reactions from relatives and her politicised boyfriend, but this is balanced against tender exchanges with her grandmother. Initially, the film parallels Laurita's determination with that of Hemingway's Old Man; but more effectively, it dwells on the function of fantasy as both catalysing and comforting force. Fresh, lively and intelligent. CM

Hellraiser

(1987, GB, 93 min)
d Clive Barker. *p* Christopher Figg. *sc* Clive Barker. *ph* Robin Vidgeon. *ed* Richard Marden. *ad* Jocelyn James. *m* Christopher Young. *cast* Andrew Robinson, Clare Higgins, Ashley Laurence, Sean Chapman, Oliver Smith, Robert Hines.
●In the bare bedroom of a London suburban house, bored sensualist Frank Cotton solves the mystery of a Chinese puzzle-box and enters a world of exquisite cruelty presided over by the Cenobites, glamorous sadists with a penchant for ripped flesh, steaming viscera and flayed muscle. Later, restored to life by his brother Larry's blood, Frank rises half-formed from a pool of slime. When Larry's wife (and Frank's ex-lover) Julia agrees to provide the human meat he needs to put flesh on his bones, the three become involved in an infernal triangle…Barker's dazzling debut as a director creates such an atmosphere of dread that the astonishing visual set pieces simply detonate in a chain reaction of cumulative intensity. His use of the traditional 'teenage screamer' heroine (Larry's daughter) tends to undercut the unsettling moral ambiguities of the adult triangle, and the brooding menace of the Cenobites is far more terrifying than the climactic roller-coaster ride. These are small quibbles, however, in a debut of such exceptional promise. A serious, intelligent and disturbing horror film. NF

Hellraiser II

see Hellbound: Hellraiser II

Hellraiser III: Hell on Earth

(1990, US, 96 min)
d Anthony Hickox. *p* Lawrence Mortorff. *sc* Peter Atkins. *ph* Gerry Lively. *ed* Christopher Cibelli. *pd* Steve Hardie. *m* Randy Miller. *cast* Doug Bradley, Terry Farrell, Paula Marshall, Kevin Bernhardt, Ken Carpenter, Peter Boynton.
●With its bravura camerawork, fetishistic Cenobite designs, nerve-jangling soundtrack, and literate Peter Atkins script, Anthony Hickox's film is a worthy successor to Clive Barker's flesh-ripping original. Freed from the stone prison of the Pillar of Souls, Pinhead (Bradley) quickly dispatches decadent rock club owner JP Monroe (Bernhardt). Hearing of JP's gruesome death, TV reporter Joey Summerskill (Farrell) sniffs a scoop, but what she finds is something more nightmarish: Pinhead and his new purveyors of pain, Camerahead, CD and Barbie. Forget the disastrous *Hellbound: Hellraiser II*; this is adult horror to die for. NF

Hell's Angels

(1930, US, 135 min, b/w & col)
d/p Howard Hughes. *sc* Joseph Moncure March. *ph* Tony Gaudio, Harry Perry, E Burton Steene, Elmer Dyer, Harry Zech, Dewey Wrigley. *ed* Frank Lawrence, Douglas Biggs, Perry Hollingsworth. *ad* Julian Boone-Felming, Carroll Clark. *m* Hugo Riesenfeld. *cast* Ben Lyon, James Hall, Jean Harlow, John Darrow, Lucien Prival, Frank Clarke, Roy Wilson.
●The Hughes folly over which he laboured for nearly three years, going through a slew of directors (including Luther Reed, James Whale and Howard Hawks) at various stages in the hope of making the greatest and most impressively realistic flying movie ever. Saddled with an atrocious boy's own paper plot about a good brother and a bad brother, both in the Flying Corps and clashing over a girl, the end result is barely adequate. But it does feature a spectacularly elaborate World War I dogfight, and an equally fine Zeppelin sequence. And of course there's Harlow, unflatteringly lit and making a nonsense of the plot by playing her character as an unmistakable floozie, but undeniably making an impact. TM

Hell's Angels on Wheels

(1967, US, 95 min)
d Richard Rush. *p* Joe Solomon.*sc* R Wright Campbell. *ph* Laszlo Kovacs. *ed* William Martin. *m* Stu Phillips. *cast* Adam Roarke, Jack Nicholson, Sabrina Scharf, Jana Taylor, John Garwood.
●Rush's film came second after Corman's *Wild Angels* in the late '60s biker-movie cycle, and like the earlier film was banned by the British censor. It now looks a real weirdie: notorious Angel Sonny Barger is credited as 'adviser'; the Oakland Angels feature; B movie directors Jack Starrett and Bruno VeSota have cameo parts; and Jack Nicholson – as a gas pump attendant called Poet who falls in with the road rats by accident – already possesses, fully-fledged, the cynical charm that made him a star. But nothing prepares you for the simple brutality of the film and its off-the-cuff style (it was shot in two weeks). The camera (Laszlo Kovacs) thunders in and out of the pack on dusty roads; barroom fights boast bottles and chains; and Nicholson's nervousness looks real. The whole project, in fact, with its violence and love interest (Nicholson fighting for the leader's 'momma') is schizophrenic, cutting from psychedelia and group sex to private angst and night-time stompings. Rush said that he found the whole bike phenomenon 'distasteful', and it shows in the uneven treatment. But who can resist a bike movie whose pack-leader, asked for a motive, resorts to Milton: 'It is better to rule in Hell than to serve in Heaven.' Eat your heart out, Hunter Thompson. CA

Hellstrom Chronicle, The

(1971, US, 90 min)
d/p Walon Green. *sc* David Seltzer. *ph* Walon Green, Helmut Barth, Ken Middleham, Kobaiyashi, Gerald Thompson. *ed* John Soh. *m* Lalo Schifrin. *with* Lawrence Pressman.
●A curious mixture of entomological documentary and cheapjack horror movie, with Pressman impersonating a supposed visionary Swedish scientist called Nils Hellstrom, and intoning apocalyptic warnings about mankind's imminent come-uppance. The insects are taking over, is the message: scientifically possible and even probable, no doubt, but dramatised with laughable over-emphasis. The microphotography, on the other hand, is amazing, making the insects (everything from bees and termites to Black Widow spiders and driver ants) look like horrendous monsters, and containing quite enough chills in its own right. TM

Hell Up in Harlem

(1973, US, 96 min)
d/p/sc Larry Cohen. *ph* Fenton Hamilton. *ed* Franco Guerri, Peter Holmes. *pd* Larry Lurin. *m* Fonce Mizell, Freddie Perren. *cast* Fred Williamson, Julius W Harris, Gloria Hendry, Margaret Avery, D'Urville Martin.
●This sequel to *Black Caesar* sparks from a marked tension between blaxploitation conventions and Cohen's maintenance of an ironic distance from his 'hero', who survives an opening semi-reprise of the earlier film's ending (having Harlem Hospital commandeered at gunpoint) to rise/fall/resurrect himself as underworld overlord of New York. The jerkily episodic narrative loosens its tremendous pace about half-way in, even if Cohen keeps jostling the formula with inventive story loops and staccato bursts of action, but it's the overall evidence of a film shot literally 'on the run' that makes this such a delight. Action constantly erupts to general bewilderment and brilliant effect on unsanctioned New York streets, while tourist trap monuments to American democracy serve as hit-and-run locations for conspiracy or corruption, as if in a dry run for Cohen's *Private Files of J Edgar Hoover*. Black maids force-feeding soul food to Mafiosi, a colour-reverse lynching, and a ludicrous foot-plane-foot chase sequence constitute just a few of the sly energies emitted en route to a characteristically ambivalent ending. PT

Hellzapoppin'

(1941, US, 84 min, b/w)
d HC Potter. *sc* Nat Perrin, Warren Wilson. *ph* Woody Bredell. *ed* Milton Carruth. *ad* Jack Otterson. *m* Frank Skinner. *cast* Ole Olsen, Chic Johnson, Martha Raye, Mischa Auer, Hugh Herbert, Elisha Cook Jr, Jane Frazee, Robert Paige.

● A genuinely bizarre oddity, this madcap comedy is fascinating not only for its many very funny moments, but also for the way it includes, amid the material taken directly from the original stage revue, various purely cinematic gags which are surprisingly modern in tone and significance. The fact that Olsen and Johnson's revue-style material dispenses with plot, creating instead an almost Monty Pythonesque series of loosely, lunatically linked vignettes (many of them parodies of Hollywood clichés, such as Elisha Cook invariably getting filled with lead), allows them to ignore realism and play around with the medium itself: at one point the stars have problems with the careless projectionist screening the film out of rack, upside-down, etc. Although lacking the satirical edge of the Marx Brothers, *Hellzapoppin'* frequently outstrips the works of Groucho and Co in terms of speed, imagination and sheer craziness. GA

Help!

(1965, GB, 92 min)
d Richard Lester. *p* Walter Shenson. *sc* Marc Behm, Charles Wood. *ph* David Watkin. *ed* John Victor Smith. *ad* Ray Simm. *m* John Lennon, Paul McCartney. *cast* John Lennon, Paul McCartney, Ringo Starr, George Harrison, Leo McKern, Eleanor Bron, Victor Spinetti, Roy Kinnear, Patrick Cargill, Alfie Bass, Warren Mitchell.

● The second of Lester's two films with the Beatles is obviously a must on grounds of nostalgia, but it never really lives up to the engaging opening sequence in which the evil Maharajah throws darts at the Beatles performing on film. Many of the gags subsequently fall flat, and the final frenetic chase scarcely makes it as either slapstick or satire. *A Hard Day's Night* may be more primitive, but it also seems more spontaneous. DP

Help! I'm a Fish (Hjælp! Jeg er en fisk/Hilfe! Ich bin ein Fisch)

(2000, Den/Ger/Ire, 80 min)
d Michael Hegner, Stefan Fjeldmark. *p* Anders Mastrup, Eberhard Junkersdorf, Russell Boland. *sc* Stefan Fjeldmark, Karsten Kiilerich, John Stefan Olsen. *ed* Per Risager. *ad* Matthias Lechner. *m* Søren Hyldgaard. *cast* voices: Alan Rickman, Terry Jones, Aaron Poul, Jeff Pace; (Danish version) Nis Bank-Mikkelsen, Søren Sætter-Lassen, Mortern Kerrn Nielsen, Sebastian Jessen.

● Danish directors Hegner and Fjeldmark wanted 'to create an animated film based on an ordinary daily situation'; and this, believe it or not, is it. Thirteen-year-old Fly takes kid sister Stella and dweeby cousin Chuck on a fishing trip. Stranded by the tides, they stumble on an underground laboratory where dotty Professor Mac Krill has devised a potion to turn humans into fish (in anticipation of the polar ice caps melting and humans being forced to survive underwater). After Stella accidentally drinks some of the potion and turns into a starfish, the boys have to take it, too, to find her – but if she doesn't get the antidote within 48 hours, she'll remain a fish forever. This underwater adventure, complete with Busby Berkeley-style synchronised swimming sequences, is further complicated by the antidote falling into the fins of megalomaniac pilot fish Joe, enabling him to think and speak like a human. Capitalising on his newfound powers, he soon sets up a one-fish state, with himself as a kind of despotic Captain Nemo, supported by a 'dumb but dangerous' shark and bullyboy crabs. For a story about friendship and working together, the characters are cute, the animation pretty well executed, and Rickman is a fine choice to voice the menacing Joe. That said, the film lacks the technical precision of *Shrek* and the bold, well-rounded characterisation of the *Toy Story* films. More importantly, it lacks that extra dimension which would engage and entertain the adults in the audience as well as the kids. JFu

Helter Skelter

(1976, US, 92 min)
d/p Tom Gries. *sc* JP Miller. *ph* Jules Brenner. *ed* Gene Fowler, Bud S Isaacs, Byron 'Buzz' Brandt. *ad* Phil Barber. *m* Billy Goldenberg. *cast* George DiCenzo, Steve Railsback, Nancy Wolfe, Marilyn Burns, Christina Hart, Cathey Paine, Alan Oppenheimer.

● A dramatised documentary about the wave of brutal killings that swept LA back in 1969, and the investigations and trials that eventually led to the conviction of Charles Manson and several members of his 'family'. Based on the book of the same name by prosecuting DA Vincent Bugliosi, it's hardly surprising that the movie is factually reliable, although having been cut down to half its original length (it was first shown as a two-part telefilm), it inevitably omits many important details, such as the fact that one of the defence lawyers was killed by the 'family' during the trial. More disturbingly, it never really examines the generally confused and shifting moral climate in which the murders took place: the sympathy that Manson won from various far outposts of the counter-culture is totally ignored, while the lackadaisical and incompetent methods of the police investigations are barely mentioned. Still, it's thankfully low on gore, and (for an enormously complicated story) told with sufficient narrative simplicity to remain gripping, even though the premise that Manson and his right-hand woman Susan Atkins were mad is too often signalled by ludicrously widened staring eyes. GA

Hen in the Wind, A (Kaze no naka no mendori)

(1948, Jap, 84 min, b/w)
d Yasujiro Ozu. *sc* Ryosuke Saito, Yasujiro Ozu. *ph* Yuharu Atsuta. *ed* Yoshiyasu Hamamura. *ad* Tatsuo Hamada. *m* Sonji Ito. *cast* Shuji Sano, Kinuyo Tanaka, Chieko Murata, Chishu Ryu, Takeshi Sakamoto, Eiko Takamatsu.

● Ozu himself considered this a failure, but its tale of a soldier who returns home from the war to find his wife has resorted to prostitution in order to nurse their sick child shames many a lesser director's manifest successes despite its overtly melodramatic elements. The symmetrically structured narrative, concentrating first on the woman's plight, then on the husband's rejection of her and eventual reconciliation, and the outbreak of angry violence extraordinarily heightened against the placid domestic background, leave no doubt where Ozu's sympathies lie and of his concern for the erosion of the traditional family system. RM

Hennessy

(1975, GB, 104 min)
d Don Sharp. *p* Peter Snell. *sc* John Gay. *ph* Ernest Steward. *ed* Eric Boyd-Tompkins. *pd* Ray Simm. *m* John Scott. *cast* Rod Steiger, Lee Remick, Richard Johnson, Trevor Howard, Eric Porter, Peter Egan, Stanley Lebor, Ian Hogg, Patrick Stewart, Patsy Kensit.

● Only American International Pictures could come up with a rollicking cheapie based on the situation in Northern Ireland, utilising both the royal family and the cabinet as plausible extras. Steiger is better than he's been for ages as Hennessy, an embittered Belfast demolition worker who plans to blow up the Royal Opening of Parliament. The film deftly avoids the sectarian issue by making him a lone maverick, pursued by both Special Branch and the IRA (who are to all intents and purposes indistinguishable), and by moving so fast that the improbabilities simply don't have time to catch up. The casting (Porter, Remick and Howard especially), the locations and the use of newsreel at the climax are all spectacularly good, and Sharp's direction proves that he is more than a match for any of AIP's Hollywood hands. DP

Henri

(1993, GB, 60 min)
d Simon Shore. *p* Colin Tucker. *sc* John Forte. *ph* Eric Gillespie. *ed* Bill Wright. *pd* Leslie Wallace. *cast* Kara Bowman, John Hewitt, Joe McPartland, Cheryl O'Dwyer, Michael Gregory.

● A BBC 'Screenplay' from Northern Ireland which treats local events with a light comic touch, without losing sight of the serious underlying issues. John Forte's script uses the piano accordion as a symbol of the divided communities' mutual distrust, following rural Protestant schoolgirl Henri(etta) as she travels to Belfast to try her luck in a music competition – despite a repertoire limited to old Orange anthems. TJ

Henry & June

(1990, US, 136 min)
d Philip Kaufman. *p* Peter Kaufman. *sc* Philip Kaufman, Rose Kaufman. *ph* Philippe Rousselot. *ed* Vivien Hillgrove, William S Scharf, Dede Allen. *pd* Guy-Claude François. *m* Mark Adler. *cast* Fred Ward, Uma Thurman, Maria De Medeiros, Richard E Grant, Kevin Spacey, Jean-Philippe Ecoffey, Juan Luis Buñuel, Pierre Etaix.

● Kaufman's account of the triangular affair between Henry Miller (Ward), his wife June (Thurman) and Anais Nin (Medeiros) in '30s Paris is certainly good to look at, edited like a dream, and about an hour too long. Intelligently scripted, particularly good on the pain in relationships, it doesn't shed much light on the literary commerce between the writers. Bohemian society here sometimes resembles the setting for a Gene Kelly number, and the much-vaunted explicitness seems to have strayed in from a Zalman King production. Both Miller and Nin choose June as their Muse, draining away at her until she flees to preserve her sanity, but the actual disclosure that provokes the break – in bed with Nin, she learns that Nin and Miller have been a number – seems uncharacteristically illiberal. Neither Thurman nor Medeiros do much with their roles, but Ward has a fine old time screwing with his hat on and hammering at the Remington. BC

Henry Fool

(1997, US, 137 min)
d/p/sc Hal Hartley. *ph* Mike Spiller. *ed* Steve Hamilton. *pd* Steve Rosenzweig. *m* Hall Hartley. *cast* Thomas Jay Ryan, James Urbaniak, Parker Posey, Maria Porter, Kevin Corrigan, Veanne Cox.

● Looser, more expansive and certainly more scatological than Hartley's earlier work, this very funny, finally touching fable focuses on the way Henry Fool (Ryan) – a bawdy, rebellious, intellectually gifted drifter, and quite possibly a charlatan – transforms the lives of the inhabitants of a small town: notably, shy, put-upon Simon Grim (Urbaniak), who under Fool's auspices becomes both celebrated as a writer and demonised as a pornographer; his promiscuous sister (Posey) and depressive mother (Porter). For all its outrageous black humour, however, it remains a Hartley movie, with its wittily stylised dialogue, droll performances, crisp camerawork and its profoundly ironic musings on the nature of art and its status in society – musings which surely reflect on Hartley's own status as an ambitious but marginalised film-maker. GA

Henry: Portrait of a Serial Killer

(1986, US, 83 min)
d John McNaughton. *p* John McNaughton, Lisa Dedmond, Steven A Jones. *sc* Richard Fire, John McNaughton. *ph* Charlie Lieberman. *ed* Elena Maganini. *ad* Rick Paul. *m* Ronert McNaughton, Ken Hale, Steven A Jones. *cast* Michael Rooker, Tracy Arnold, Tom Towles.

● McNaughton's compelling study of a blithe sociopath makes the flesh crawl and the mind reel. Turning up at the Chicago apartment shared by old prison buddy Otis and his timid sister Becky, Henry (Rooker) slowly draws Otis into his dark, obsessive world of casual murder. The violence is at first oblique, with Henry's past murders presented as a series of grotesque tableaux accompanied by the (recorded?) sounds of the victims death struggles. Later, the violence becomes more graphic, but what makes it so disturbing, and sometimes almost unwatchable, is the cool matter-of-fact tone McNaughton sustains throughout. Whether presenting a halting conversation or bloody carnage, he observes events with the unblinking eye of a surveillance camera. It is this air of detachment that makes the blood run cold. Rooker achieves frightening intensity as an ice-killer for whom murder and taking a beer out of the fridge are much the same thing. The remote possibility of moral redemption seems to be held out by Henry's tentative relationship with Becky, but even that faint glimmer of hope is extinguished by a devastatingly downbeat ending. A film of ferocious, haunting power, and a highly impressive directing debut. NF

Henry VIII and His Six Wives

(1972, GB, 125 min)
d Waris Hussein. *p* Roy Baird. *sc* Ian Thorne. *ph* Peter Suschitzky. *ed* John Bloom. *pd* Roy Stannard. *m* David Munro. *cast* Keith Michell, Frances Cuka, Charlotte Rampling, Jane Asher, Jenny Bos, Lynne Frederick, Barbara Leigh-Hunt, Donald Pleasence, Michael Gough, Brian Blessed, Bernard Hepton.
●The BBC series *The Six Wives of Henry VIII* was a typically well-costumed and researched affair, if rather predictable in its desire to show that underneath the infamous king's bluff and headstrong exterior there lay a lonely and reasonable man. This big-screen spin-off retains that predictability, while losing a lot of historical detail in its compression of the nine-hour original. Most annoying, however, is Michell's mannered and determinedly larger-than-life performance. GA

Henry V

(1944, GB, 137 min)
d Laurence Olivier. *p* Laurence Olivier, Dallas Bower. *sc* Laurence Olivier, Alan Dent. *ph* Robert Krasker. *ed* Reginald Beck. *ad* Paul Sheriff. *m* William Walton. *cast* Laurence Olivier, Renée Asherson, Robert Newton, Leslie Banks, George Robey, Esmond Knight, Leo Genn, Felix Aylmer, Max Adrian.
●In Olivier's first attempt at direction there's a certain, limited delight in the possibilities of a new-found medium. The transitions from the stage-bound settings of the Globe to the ringing plains of Agincourt (as stirring as any sequence from *Triumph of the Will*) suggest a flexing of cinematic muscle that, sadly, he later allowed to atrophy by returning to acting his head off and simply recording it by camera. CPea

Henry V

(1989, GB, 137 min)
d Kenneth Branagh. *p* Bruce Sharman. *sc* Kenneth Branagh. *ph* Kenneth MacMillan. *ed* Mike Bradsell. *pd* Tim Harvey. *m* Patrick Doyle. *cast* Kenneth Branagh, Brian Blessed, Richard Briers, Robbie Coltrane, Judi Dench, Ian Holm, Derek Jacobi, Alec McCowen, Geraldine McEwan, Michael Maloney, Paul Scofield, John Sessions, Robert Stephens, Emma Thompson, Michael Williams.
●Branagh adapted and directed this opus as well as starring, and he's found jobs for all his pals. Look, there's John Sessions mugging frantically at the back! Scurvy knave Bardolph is a be-latexed Briers; Mistress Quickly is a dusty Judi Dench; plus there's the grim spectacle of Emma Thompson bounding around in a red wig, gabbling Franglais. Coltrane is Falstaff: great idea, but as the fat man doesn't appear in the play, he's wedged in by way of fumbling flashbacks. Most of the scenes, including exteriors, could have been filmed on the stage of the National, and devices like Jacobi's Chorus, in anachronistic black greatcoat and woolly scarf, serve to accentuate the theatricality of the enterprise, as does the fact that Hal appears to be attacking France with 25 men. The fog of war is convincingly portrayed, though other scenes have an unmistakable whiff of the BBC production: the clip-clop-whinny sound effects, the sudden downpours, the swirling dry ice. Quibbles apart, Branagh succeeds in his blunt, robust portrayl of the Soldier-King, hauling the film along in the wake of his own gung-ho performance. SFe

Her Alibi

(1989, US, 94 min)
d Bruce Beresford. *p* Keith Barish. *sc* Charlie Peters. *ph* Freddie Francis. *ed* Anne Goursaud. *pd* Henry Bumstead. *m* George Delerue. *cast* Tom Selleck, Paulina Porizkova, William Daniels, James Farentino, Hurd Hatfield, Ronald Guttman, Victor Argo, Patrick Wayne, Tess Harper.
●One of those predictable comedies about reclusive writers living vicariously through the adventures created in their work. Selleck is a mystery novelist, suffering from writer's block, who attends court one day in the hope that inspiration will strike, and encounters beautiful Romanian Nina (Porizkova). His powers of perception are such that he can tell straight away she's incapable of stabbing a man as charged, and it transpires that she's being coerced by nasty KGB agents. Suitably intrigued, he offers refuge at his palatial country hideout, in the knowledge that the unfolding adventures will offer him plenty of material. The plot is ludicrous, which in itself would be perfectly acceptable given sharper handling, but both script and direction devote so much time to romantic undercurrents that the central intrigue is further divested of credibility. CM

Herbie Goes Bananas

(1980, US, 93 min)
d Vincent McEveety. *p* Ron Miller. *sc* Don Tait. *ph* Frank Phillips. *ed* Gordon D Brenner. *ad* John B Mansbridge, Rodger Maus. *m* Frank De Vol. *cast* Cloris Leachman, Charles Martin Smith, John Vernon, Stephan W Burns, Elyssa Davalos, Harvey Korman, Richard Jaeckel.
●In the ten years since the Disney Organisation made *The Love Bug* and an off-white VW Beetle called Herbie shot to stardom, he's grown with the part and become more assertive, while his supporting actors become more and more like car components. This is Herbiefilm IV (last in the series), in which 26 versions of the star car got trashed; with that kind of turnover in stand-ins, it's not surprising that they haven't got around to changing the plot formula, only the scenery. This year's model chases around some of the less political clichés of Central America in pursuit of villains and pre-Colombian artefacts. If you can stomach the lovey bits, the film has a lot of good car stunts, some innuendo for the adults, and the ultimate accolade for the Chaplinesque Herbie – a chance to play opposite a cute Mexican orphan. RP

Herbie Goes to Monte Carlo

(1977, US, 105 min)
d Vincent McEveety. *p* Ron Miller. *sc* Arthur Alsberg, Don Nelson. *ph* Leonard J South *ed* Cotton Warburton. *ad* John D Mansbridge, Perry Ferguson. *m* Frank De Vol. *cast* Dean Jones, Don Knotts, Julie Sommars, Jacques Marin, Roy Kinnear, Bernard Fox.
●Herbie the thinking VW is all tuned up for the Paris to Monte Carlo road race, but falls for a pert little Lancia (who must be considerably underage), to the dismay of his handsome driver (Jones) and eye-rolling mechanic (Knotts). Successfully combining excitement, romance and simple comedy, this stock Disney (third in the series) follows an entirely predictable course with masterful precision. And there's sunny weather all the way. JS

Herbie Rides Again

(1974, US, 88 min)
d Robert Stevenson. *p/sc* Bill Walsh. *ph* Frank Phillips. *ed* Cotton Warburton. *ad* John B Mansbridge, Walter Tyler. *m* George Bruns. *cast* Helen Hayes, Ken Berry, Stefanie Powers, John McIntire, Keenan Wynn, Huntz Hall.
●Sequel to Disney's *The Love Bug*, about a Volkswagen with a mind of its own. Despite some insipid characterisation and one or two lapses, things move along at a fair pace and there's a surprising plot all about property speculation in San Francisco. Can Grandma Steinmetz save her home from the grasping magnate Alonzo Hawk? The comedy is on the whole inventive, occasionally aspiring to almost surrealist heights. CPe

Herbstonate

see Autumn Sonata

Hercules

(1997, US, 93 min)
d John Musker, Ron Clements. *p* Alice Dewey, John Musker, Ron Clements. *sc* Ron Clements, John Musker, Donald McEnery, Bob Shaw, Irene Mecchi. *ed* Tom Finan. *pd* Gerald Scarfe. *m* Alan Menken. *cast* voices: Tate Donovan, Danny DeVito, James Woods, Rip Torn, Samantha Eggar, Hal Holbrook.
●Ancient myth the Disney way, with all the incest, virgin-ravishing and animal cruelty merrily replaced by sound family values and a whole urnful of peppy 1990s pop references. It could easily seem crass, but it's hard to get all serious about a film that so revels in its own infectious humour, distributes gags to all ages, and displays great craft in art director Gerald Scarfe's angular integrated visual design. In short another benchmark achievement for the *Aladdin* team of Musker and Clements. As in *The Hunchback of Notre Dame*, the makers are clued-in enough to take a rise out of their conventional hero, and the grown-up Herc here is a likeable big lug, though not too smart – game enough to slay the Hydra, but not so savvy he can spot the machinations of honey-voiced siren Megara, who's secretly in league with Hades, the megalomaniac ruler of the Underworld. As voiced by Woods, this cigar-chomping super-bad guy remains the chief attraction for grown-ups, who'll also relish the gospelling divas of the none-too-Greek chorus, and the cheeky send-up of ancient Thebes' own merchandising industry. Littl'uns will go for DeVito's knockabout hero-training satyr. TJ

Hercules and the Captive Women

see Ercole alla conquista di Atlantide

Hercules Conquers Atlantis

see Ercole alla conquista di Atlantide

Hercules Returns

(1993, Aust, 80 min)
d David Parker. *p* Philip Jaroslow. *sc* Des Mangan. *ph* David Connell. *ed* Peter Carrodus. *pd* Jon Dowding. *m* Philip Judd. *cast* David Argue, Michael Carman, Mary Coustas, Bruce Spence, Brendon Suhr, Nick Polites.
●Brad (Argue) is booted out of the Kent Cinema Corporation, a heartless multiplex monolith, and fights back by reopening an old-fashioned picture palace with the help of projectionist Sprocket (Spence). But evil boss Sir Michael Kent tries to scupper them by ensuring that their trash-fest opener, *Hercules*, is supplied in the original Italian without subtitles. What to do? Why, dub it themselves of course, live from the projection box. Actually, this pretence doesn't hold up. But the merciless caricature of these baby-oil poseurs is pretty irresistible. SFe

Herd, The (Sürü)

(1978, Tur, 118 min)
d Zeki Ökten. *sc* Yilmaz Güney. *ph* Izzet Akay. *ed* Özdemir Aritan. *pd* Rauf Ozangil, Sabri Aslankara. *m* Zülfü Livaneli. *cast* Tarik Akan, Melike Demirag, Tuncel Kurtiz, Levent Inanir, Meral Niron, Erol Demiröz.
●Shot by Ökten under instruction from its writer Yilmaz Güney, at the time imprisoned for murdering a judge, this slice of social realism is never simplistic, always powerful as it follows the disintegration of a nomadic family of shepherds as they herd their sheep from the Anatolian pastures to the markets of modern Ankara. Problems abound: the traditional ways of the nomads – superstition, feuding, ignorance – are no better than the corrupt and exploitative officialdom of modern industrialised Turkey, although being poor and barely recognised as real human beings, the family are continually at the mercy of their more 'sophisticated' compatriots. Though never quite as telling or brilliant as the later *Yol*, it's a fine film that achieves its effect through its total sincerity and conviction. GA

Here Beneath the North Star

see Täällä Pohjantähden alla

Here Comes Mr Jordan

(1941, US, 94 min, b/w)
d Alexander Hall. *p* Everett Riskin. *sc* Sidney Buchman, Seton I Miller. *ph* Joseph Walker. *ed* Viola Lawrence. *ad* Lionel Banks. *m* Frederick Hollander. *cast* Robert Montgomery, Evelyn Keyes, Claude Rains, Rita Johnson, Edward Everett Horton, James Gleason.
●Mildly engaging fantasy, remade as *Heaven Can Wait* in 1978, with Montgomery as the boxer despatched to his eternal rest by clerical error and returned to earth with Rains as his avuncular guardian angel. Lovely supporting performances from Rains, Horton (the anxiously over-zealous heavenly messenger who made the mistake in the first place) and Gleason (a hopelessly bemused fight manager); but the comedy of errors as Montgomery casts around for a new body in which to pursue his championship ambitions is rather uncomfortably tinged with the fey archness which so often came over Hollywood when envisaging an afterlife. TM

Here Comes the Groom

(1951, US, 113 min, b/w)
d Frank Capra. *sc* Virginia Van Upp, Liam O'Brien, Myles Connolly. *ph* George Barnes. *ad* Hal Pereira, Earl Hedrick. *ed* Ellsworth Hoagland. *songs* Jay Livingston, Ray Evans. *cast* Bing Crosby, Jane Wyman, Franchot Tone, Alexis Smith, James Barton, Anna Maria Alberghetti.
●Typically whimsical Capra comedy (with lots of sentiment) in which Crosby adopts a couple of war orphans who will be exiled from the land of democracy unless he can win his fiancée Wyman back from an infatuation with a handsome millionaire (Tone). Tedious romantic shufflings slightly enlivened by some songs and a brief guest spot for Louis Armstrong (playing and singing 'Misto Christofo Columbo'). TM

Here Come the Waves

(1944, US, 99 min, b/w)
d/p Mark Sandrich. *sc* Allan Scott, Ken Englund, Zion Myers. *ph* Charles Lang Jr. *ed* Ellsworth Hoagland. *ad* Hans Dreier, Roland Anderson. *songs* Johnny Mercer, Harold Arlen. *cast* Bing Crosby, Betty Hutton, Sonny Tufts, Ann Doran, Catherine Craig, Gwen Crawford, Noel Neill.
●Fairly dull musical stacked full of patriotic propaganda as it pays tribute to the seafaring warriors – both men and women – of the US Navy. Bing croons and spoons as he joins up and falls in love with identical twin sisters (Hutton x 2). The variable score by Harold Arlen and Johnny Mercer includes 'That Old Black Magic' and 'Accentuate the Positive'. GA

Here We Go Round the Mulberry Bush

(1967, GB, 96 min)
d/p Clive Donner. *sc* Hunter Davies. *ph* Alex Thomson. *ed* Fergus McDonell. *ad* Brian Eatwell. *m* The Spencer Davis Group, Stevie Winwood, Traffic. *cast* Barry Evans, Judy Geeson, Angela Scoular, Sheila White, Adrienne Posta, Vanessa Howard, Diane Keen, Moyra Fraser, Denholm Elliott, Michael Bates, Maxine Audley.
●Swinging London days, so poor Hunter Davies' pleasant sub-Salinger novel, about the sexual tribulations of a grammar school sixth-former (he longs for something a bit more up-market than the snotty-nosed local bints), gets the full gloss treatment. Jamie McGregor (Evans) worked part-time for a small local Co-op, but here he's much more smartly located in a supermarket; the Stevenage council estate where he lives looks like King's Road-cum-Carnaby Street, fairly dripping with dolly birds; his dream fantasies are Dick Lester lookalikes, using speeded-up motion for good measure; and when he finally gets invited to a party, the scene looks as fashionably clichéd as the photographer's studio antics in Antonioni's *Blow-Up*. Donner's eagerness to pour 'swinging style' and pop songs over everything makes nonsense of the socially critical attitudes that filter weakly through from the script (by Hunter Davies himself). So charmless as to be almost unwatchable. TM

Heritage, The

(1993, Isr, 86 min)
d Amnon Rubinstein. *p* Marek Rozenbaum, Avi Toledano. *sc* Zvi Kerzner. *ph* Yoav Kosh. *ed* Tova Asher. *m* Avi Toledano. *cast* Avi Toledano, Yael Abekasis, Alon Aboutbul, Shlomo Bar-Shavit.
●An old-fashioned costume drama, which cuts between present-day Jerusalem and Toledo, Spain, at the time of the Inquisition and the suppression of the seders. Its parallel love stories – in the modern story an Israeli Jew befriends an air hostess on his trip to locate a house described on an ancient family document brought to him by a lawyer; in the past, a Gentile falls for the imprisoned Jewish woman he's assigned to spy on – function poorly as a means of bringing history 'alive'; and as a 'reconciliation' love story, the film leaves much to be desired, as do its awkward transitions and plot contrivances. It's strangely compulsive, none the less, in a sandal-saga kind of way. WH

Heritage...Africa

(1987, Ghana, 125 min)
d/p/sc Kwaw Ansah. *ph* Chris Tsui Hesse. *ed* Roger Hagon. *ad* Mike Amon Kwafo. *cast* Kofi Bucknor, Peter Whitbread, Ian Collier, Anima Misa, Tommy Ebow Ansah, Evans Oma Hunter.
●Set in 1955 in the violent run up to Ghanaian independence, this ambitious political drama follows the conversion of conscience of the first black District Commissioner, an anglicised Cambridge man so dedicated to his duties that he refuses to attend his mortally ill son. Ansah presents a diffuse political analysis – he is at pains to distinguish both between the 'enlightened self-interest' of the Governor (Whitbread) and the cruder reactionary methods of sneering civil servant Snyper (Collier), and the rivalries in the 'Association of Freedom' led by Kwame Nkrumah. Stilted acting and dramatic over-emphasis make it hard going, but the complex pains and ironies of colonialism come over only too strongly. WH

Her Last Affaire

(1935, GB, 67 min, b/w)
d Michael Powell. *p* Geoffrey Rowson. *sc* Ian Dalrymple. *ph* Leslie Rowson. *ed* Ian Dalrymple. *ad* J Elder Wills. *cast* Hugh Williams, Francis L Sullivan, Viola Keats, Sophie Stewart, Felix Aylmer, Googie Withers, John Laurie, Cecil Parker.
●A body lies crumpled on the floor. Enter maid, carrying breakfast tray. Scream! Crash! Ah, but not when the maid is Googie Withers. Without batting an eye, she steps across the corpse and trawls the room for clues, only then discharging her scream 'n' crash obligation. An adaptation of Walter Ellis's play *SOS*, this sample of Powell juvenilia turns on such issues as Sir Jervis's reputation, Lady Avril's weak heart, the secretary's secret. That the hero (Williams) is so dislikeable can be attributed to writing and casting, but Powell can be credited with encouraging what amounts to a comedic putsch by the supporting cast: John Laurie, a-quiver with Calvinist rectitude, Cecil Parker being, as ever, put upon. And of course the redoubtable Googie. BBa

Her Majesty, Love

(1931, US, 75 min, b/w)
d William Dieterle. *sc* Robert Lord, Arthur Caesar, Henry Blanke, Joseph Jackson. *ph* Robert Kurrle. *ed* Ralph Dawson. *ad* Jack Okey. *songs* Al Dubin, Walter Jurmann. *cast* Marilyn Miller, WC Fields, Ben Lyon, Leon Errol, Ford Sterling, Chester Conklin.
●Fields plays second fiddle to bright-eyed Marilyn Miller (a fellow Ziegfeld star) and the all-smiling, all-leaping Ben Lyon in his first sound feature, an adaptation of a German film with few belly laughs but much charm. He plays the unpresentable father of a barmaid engaged to a dashing young toff, and enjoys himself scandalising dinner guests with a few juggling routines perilously performed with food and kitchenware. Aside from such set pieces, he's still good value, for Fields is one of the few screen comics who could take on the part of a doting father and retain credibility. GB

Hero

see Accidental Hero

Hero

(1982, GB, 92 min)
d Barney Platts-Mills. *p* Andrew St John. *sc* Barney Platts-Mills. *ph* Adam Barker-Mill. *ed* Robert Hargreaves. *ad* Tom Paine. *m* Paul Steen. *cast* Derek McGuire, Caroline Kenneil, Alastair Kenneil, Stewart Grant, Harpo Hamilton.
●Brave venture for the fiercely independent Platts-Mills (who had been silent since making *Bronco Bullfrog* and *Private Road* over ten years previously): a Gaelic-speaking epic set in the fifth century, shot on some beautiful locations along the south-west coast of Scotland, and telling the tale of a young knight-errant who joins the band of 'heroes' led by Finn MacCool and sung by the bard Ossian. The non-professional cast, alas, are distressingly amateurish, and since the script seems half-strangled in what it is trying to say, the result looks not unlike a clumping village pageant. TM

Hero

(1986, GB, 86 min)
d Tony Maylam. *m* Rick Wakeman.
●For those who take on the task of making the official documentary of the FIFA World Cup, there is one crucial question: with an impossible number of games to cover, how do you make sure that the most important moments are committed to celluloid? This team thought they had all bases covered by concentrating on the progress of ten key players from various countries; and although, by and large, it's a fairly sensible way of approaching the problem, there is still too much left out for this film to be entirely satisfactory. The commentary, by an awestruck Michael Caine, is embarrassingly over the top, but the film's real weakness is that two of the tournament's most significant games – Russia's 6–0 drubbing of Hungary, and then their defeat by Belgium in the best game of the whole series – barely get a mention. As a celebration of the talent of Diego Maradona, it's spellbinding, but as a record of the 1986 World Cup, it stinks. DPe

Hero, The

see Bloomfield

Hero at Large

(1979, US, 98 min)
d Martin Davidson. *p* Stephen J Friedman. *sc* AJ Carothers. *ph* David M Walsh. *ed* Sidney Levin, David Garfield. *pd* Albert Brenner. *m* Patrick Williams. *cast* John Ritter, Anne Archer, Bert Convy, Kevin McCarthy, Harry Bellaver, Anita Dangler.
●Very obvious comedy with uncharismatic Ritter as an unemployed actor who gets a job running around in a costume to promote the Captain Avenger comic strip, then after bravely stopping a grocery store robbery decides he'd quite like to go into the superhero business himself. Archer's the wholly disinterested girl-next-door, Convy the scheming PR exec who sees a way of exploiting the Captain's derring-do to his own ends. TJ

Herod's Law (La Ley de Herodes)

(1999, Mex, 120 min)
d/p Luis Estrada. *sc* Luis Estrada, Jaime Sampietro, Fernando León, Vicente Leñero. *ph* Norman Christianson. *ed* Luis Estrada. *pd* Ana Solares, Salvador Parra. *m* Santiago Ojeda. *cast* Damián Alcázar, Pedro Armendáriz, Alex Cox, Leticia Huijara, Isela Vega, Salvador Sánchez, Guillermo Gil.
●Mexico, 1949. When a corrupt mayor is murdered by disgruntled villagers, Governor Lopez (Armendáriz), who's up for re-election, has him replaced by Vargas (Alcázar), an honest and loyal garbage supervisor. Attempts to improve the backwater are stifled when Vargas realises his predecessor stole the entire budget. Instead of money, Lopez hands Vargas a gun and explains Herod's Law: 'Screw them or they'll screw you.' Vargas gets the hang of it, with the help of greedy gringo Cox, and rapidly becomes a paranoid, misogynistic megalomaniac. This black comedy takes satirical swipes at connivance, corruption and the self-serving attitude of Mexican politicians in a country ruled by the same party for seven decades. In a spooky irony, the government tried to ban the film. They failed and lost the election. JFu

Heroes

(1977, US, 113 min)
d Jeremy Paul Kagan. *p* David Foster, Lawrence Turman. *sc* James Carabatsos. *ph* Frank Stanley. *ed* Patrick Kennedy. *pd* Charles Rosen. *m* Jack Nitzsche. *cast* Henry Winkler, Sally Field, Harrison Ford, Val Avery, Olivia Cole, Hector Elias, Verna Bloom.
●Henry 'The Fonz' Winkler's first starring feature purports to deal with the 'forgotten' subject of Vietnam veterans. But well-meaning references to a lost generation are quickly dropped in favour of routine odyssey as Winkler travels from NY to Eureka, California (yes, afraid so), teams up with Sally Field (casualty of a non-military engagement), and comes on like the only sane man in a crazy world (of course he's certified and on the run). 'The only one who is chasing you is you', she tells him, and he finally exorcises his ghosts of Vietnam with his gal by

his side. One brief interlude of interest features Harrison Ford as a speedy but kinda slow vet who'd make Clint Walker look smart. CPe

Heroes, The (Gli Eroi)

(1972, It/Fr/Sp, 110 min)
d Duccio Tessari. *p* Alfredo Bini. *sc* Luciano Vincenzoni, Sergio Donati. *ph* Carlo Carlini. *ed* Mario Morra. *ad* Walter Patriarca, Andrea Crisanti. *m* Riz Ortolani. *cast* Rod Steiger, Rosanna Schiaffino, Rod Taylor, Claude Brasseur, Terry-Thomas, Gianni Garko.
● Badly dubbed and inferior successor to *Kelly's Heroes* and other such wartime caper movies. A motley assortment of Germans and Allies call an uneasy truce and opt out of the desert conflict in pursuit of £2 million. Steiger does his German accent (which is beginning to pall a bit), Schiaffino shows a lot of leg, and everyone hams outrageously. A few happy coincidences and a lot of doublecrossing keeps a creaky plot going, and the photography helps some, but the relentless jokiness, plus the inevitable problems of co-production, ensure that it ends up being tedious.

Heroes in Love (Lian'ai Qi Yi)

(2001, HK, 91 min)
d Wing Shya; Nicholas Tse, Stephen Fung; GC Goo-Bi. *p* Gordon Chan, Jan Lamb. *sc* Chang Tze-Hin; Nicholas Tse, Stephen Fung; Patrick Kong; GC Goo-Bi. *ph* O Sing-Pui. *ed* William Chang, Chan Chi-Wai. *ad* Man Lim-Chung, Chau Sai-Hung. *cast* Tong Wing-Sze, Gloria Cheng, Wu Por, Charlene Choi, Lawrence Chou.
● How come old Wong Kar-Wai movies still exert so much influence on new HK directors? Of the contributors to this portmanteau feature, Wing Shya has the best excuse (he works as Wong's graphic designer), but his episode *Kidnap* lets an interesting premise peter out: an introverted dyke (Tong) locks up the lippy girl she's been stalking (Cheng), hoping to make her love her. *My Beloved* (by hip young actors Tse and Fung, the weakest episode) awkwardly crosscuts between a pizza delivery boy's handgun fantasies and TV reportage on his crimes. Best of the three is woman dee-jay GC's *Oh G!*, which updates *Chungking Express* into the tale of a romantic young woman (Choi) blind-dating a boy she met on the internet. But he (Chou) turns out to be an archetypal laddish geek. Co-producer Lamb adds a coda which recaps all three episodes and draws some conclusions about solitude and coupledom. Livelier than most HK features these days, but hardly a triumph. TR

Heroes of Telemark, The

(1965, GB, 131 min)
d Anthony Mann. *p* S Benjamin Fisz. *sc* Ivan Moffat, Ben Barzman. *ph* Robert Krasker. *ed* Bert Bates. *ad* Tony Masters. *m* Malcolm Arnold. *cast* Kirk Douglas, Richard Harris, Ulla Jacobsson, Michael Redgrave, David Weston, Anton Diffring, Eric Porter.
● Panavision vistas of Norwegian snowscapes dwarf the characters of Mann's spectacular World War II mission movie, in appropriate correlation to the atomic threat posed by the Nazi heavy water plant Douglas and his resistance allies must destroy. If the landscape no longer mirrors psychology as it did in Mann's classic Westerns, at least it still dominates the narrative with impressive ironic force. PT

Heroic Trio, The (Dongfang San Xia)

(1992, HK, 82 min)
d Johnny To. *p* Ching Siu-Tung. *sc* Sandy Shaw. *ph* Poon Hang-Sang, Tom Lau. *ed* Kam Wah Productions. *ad* Bruce Yu. *m* William Hu. *cast* Maggie Cheung, Michelle Yeoh, Anita Mui, Anthony Wong, Damian Lau, Paul Chin.
● The gimmick is all three are women. Superheroines of the near future battle ancestral evils in labyrinthine caverns beneath city streets. This is quintessential Hong Kong pulp fiction, conflating elements of sci-fi, horror, *noir*, thriller, the supernatural, action-adventure and instant pathos. The plot involves kidnapped boys, one of whom will be chosen as puppet monarch of some imaginary China, the rest turned into zombie cannibals. Good support from Anthony Wong as a meathead sentinel who eats his own severed fingers. TR

Herostratus

(1967, GB, 142 min)
d Don Levy. *p* Don Levy, James Quinn. *sc* Don Levy. *ph* J Keith Allams. *ed* Don Levy. *ad* Gerald Coral, James Meller. *m* Beethoven, Halim El Dabh, John Meyer, Verdi. *cast* Michael Gothard, Gabriella Licudi, Peter Stephens, Antony Paul, Mona Chin, Helen Mirren, Malcolm Muggeridge.
● This 'triumph' for the British avant-garde – an inverted Mephistopheles story in which a poet sells his suicide to an ad agency – now looks charmingly naive. It's Antonioni crossed with Lester's Beatles generation: polite, irreverent, inarticulate, with an irredeemably narrative construction (love story), and much proudly presented but embarrassed improvisation. While the film's choice of models (tragic grandiloquence versus minimalism, capitalism versus existential angst) remains confused, it's still clever and pretty. Leather fetish fantasy turns wittily into rubber glove ad, striptease is intercut with abattoir – and juxtaposition nearly reduces both to advertising slickness. Intriguing to see how even the avant-garde was mesmerised by the 'beautiful life' of the '60s. CA

Héros très discret, Un (A Self-Made Hero)

(1995, Fr, 106 min)
d Jacques Audiard. *p* Patrick Godeau. *sc* Alain Le Henry, Jacques Audiard. *ph* Jean-Marc Fabre. *ed* Juliette Welfling. *pd* Michel Vandestien. *m* Alexandre Desplat. *cast* Mathieu Kassovitz, Anouk Grinberg, Sandrine Kiberlain, Albert Dupontel, Nadia Barentin, Jean-Louis Trintignant.
● Audiard's marvellous follow-up to his impressive *Regarde les hommes tomber* is a deliciously inventive comedy about a shy, cowardly, none-too-bright nobody (Kassovitz, director of *La Haine*) who through a mixture of luck, determination and downright lies manages to pass himself off as a WWII Resistance hero. It may be seen as a sly satire on France's illusions about its own wartime record, but more importantly it's a dazzlingly written, consistently funny, and finally very moving tale about identity, fame, storytelling and the way heroic acts often occur on the most intimate plane. GA

Herr Arnes Pengar (Sir Arne's Treasure)

(1919, Swe, 105 min approx, b/w)
d Mauritz Stiller. *sc* Mauritz Stiller, Gustaf Molander. *ph* J Julius [Julius Jaenzon], Gustaf Boge. *ad* Harry Dahlström, Alexander Bakó. *cast* Mary Johnson, Richard Lund, Hjalmar Selander, Concordia Selander, Wanda Rothgardt, Eric Stocklassa, Bror Berger, Axel Nilsson, Gustaf Aronson, Stina Berg.
● Sweden, the 16th century. Three Scottish mercenaries on the run murder a parson and his household and make off with the family fortune. A foster daughter survives, and her subsequent dilemma – when she learns that the man she's fallen for was one of the killers – is the heart of the drama. The scenario partakes of the all-pervading religiosity of the setting, with dreams and premonitions, the reactions of animals, the behaviour of the weather all seen as the workings of a vengeful Old Testament God. Some bravura staging by Stiller, who had yet to find his Garbo; Mary Johnson didn't fit that bill, though she certainly was uncommonly pretty. BBa

Herz aus Glas

see Heart of Glass

He Said, She Said

(1991, US, 115 min)
d Ken Kwapis, Marisa Silver. *p* Frank Mancuso Jr. *sc* Brian Hohlfeld. *ph* Stephen H Burum. *ed* Sidney Levin. *pd* Michael Corenblith. *m* Miles Goodman. *cast* Kevin Bacon, Elizabeth Perkins, Sharon Stone, Nathan Lane, Anthony LaPaglia, Charlaine Woodard.
● A pair of yuppie Baltimore hacks use their romance as material for their rival newspaper columns. Later they become TV stars. The story's told from two perspectives, with Kwapis directing his and Silver hers. It may seem a novel conceit, but like the lifestyle journalism it celebrates, the film is grating, narcissistic and shallow. GM

He's a Woman, She's a Man (Jinzhi Yuye)

(1994, HK, 106 min)
d Peter Chan Ho-sun. *p* Eric Tsang Chi-Wai. *sc* Lee Chi, James Yuen. *ph* Chan Tseun-kit. *ed* Chan Ki-hop. *pd* Yee Chung-man. *m* Hui Yun, Tsiu Tsang-hei. *cast* Leslie Cheung, Anita Yuen, Carina Lau, Eric Tsang Chi-Wai, Lawrence Cheng.
● The United Film-makers Organisation (UFO) has made a splash in the tough Hong Kong market with a series of comedy-dramas about the problems facing yuppies. This one purports to deal with gender issues and has a smattering of gay supporting characters. A young woman (Yuen) tries to break into showbiz by posing as a male singer; a straight talent manager (Cheung) is disturbed to find himself fancying her, unaware of her actual gender. Almost unwatchably shallow and insincere, the film tries to give its affirmative hetero ending a gay-friendly spin. TR

Hester Street

(1974, US, 89 min, b/w)
d Joan Micklin Silver. *p* Raphael D Silver. *sc* Joan Micklin Silver. *ph* Kenneth Van Sickle. *ed* Katherine Wenning. *pd* Stuart Wurtzel. *m* William Bolcom. *cast* Steven Keats, Carol Kane, Mel Howard, Dorrie Kavanaugh, Doris Roberts.
● Tackling a potentially fascinating and neglected area – Jewish immigrants in end-of-last-century New York – this limits itself to an affectionate and predictable chronicle of the Americanisation of Jake and Gitl. Clarity of emotion at the expense of subtlety, larger than life performances (with the exception of Carol Kane, whose greenhorn wife ends up learning the fastest), confine the film to warmheartedness and gentle, ironic observation at the expense of any real insight. Only towards the end, as the couple split up and remarry, does the film satisfactorily come to terms with a society in a state of flux and its relation to the American Dream: the passing of old customs, self-improvement, ghetto mentality and matriarchy are all touched upon. But an unimaginative camera and misty monochromes do little beyond conveying some self-conscious period recreation. CPe

Hets (Frenzy/Torment)

(1944, Swe, 101 min, b/w)
d Alf Sjöberg. *p* Carl Anders Dymling. *sc* Ingmar Bergman. *ph* Martin Bodin. *ed* Oscar Rosander. *ad* Arne Akermark. *m* Hilding Rosenberg. *cast* Stig Järrel, Mai Zetterling, Alf Kjellin, Olof Winnerstrand, Stig Olin, Jan Molander, Gunnar Björnstrand.
● A vaguely rebellious teenager (Kjellin), bullied by his sadistic Latin master (Järrel), falls for a young prostitute (Zetterling) who tells him she is being persecuted by a sinister man; when the boy finds her dead, he also discovers the teacher hiding in the room... As scripted by Ingmar Bergman (it was his first filmed scenario), Sjöberg's film is a relentlessly cruel study in sadomasochistic relationships, structured as a bleak, sordid thriller. Full of superb expressionist shots which serve to highlight the intensity of the film's highly emotional subject matter, it also benefits from the excellent performances of Järrel and the young Mai Zetterling. Interestingly, Järrel was made up to resemble Himmler, prompting interpretations of the film as an allegory on Fascism; more crucially, however, its harsh pessimism anticipates the spiritually tormented universe of Bergman's own work. GA

He Walked By Night

(1949, US, 79 min, b/w)
d Alfred Werker. *p* Robert T Kane. *sc* John C Higgins, Crane Wilbur, Harry Essex. *ph* John Alton. *ed* Alfred DeGaetano. *ad* Edward Ilou, Armor Marlowe, Clarence Steensen. *m* Leonid Raab. *cast* Richard Basehart, Scott Brady, Roy Roberts, Whit Bissell, Jack Webb.
● Minor but taut thriller in the semi-documentary vein so popular in the second half of the '40s, about detectives tracking down thief-turned-cop killer Basehart (and making much play with the new Identikit methods). The fact that Anthony Mann had an uncredited hand in the direction may have something to do with the successful creation of a tense atmosphere, although most notable is the superb *noir* photography by John

Alton, who really comes into his own during the final chase through the LA sewers. Basehart is excellent as the strange, lone wolf electronics expert/killer, an enigmatic threat haunting the paranoid dreams of the witch-hunting era. GA

He Walks Like a Tiger

see King of Kung Fu

He Who Gets Slapped

(1924, US, 6,953 ft, b/w)
d Victor Sjöström. *sc* Victor Sjöström, Carey Wilson. *ph* Milton Moore. *ed* Hugh Wynn. *ad* Cedric Gibbons. *cast* Lon Chaney, Norma Shearer, John Gilbert, Tully Marshall, Marc MacDermott, Ford Sterling.

●Based on Leonid Andreyev's 1914 play, which prefigures Beckett and the Absurd in expressing the angst of pre-Revolutionary Russia, *He Who Gets Slapped* is about a scientist shattered to discover that his patron has appropriated not only his researches but his wife. Frozen into the fixation that he must become a clown in body as well as in spirit, he joins a circus. There, literally wearing his heart on his sleeve, he willingly suffers agonies of humiliation while the crowd roars. Chaney's performance is extraordinary, but the real amazement of the film is Sjöström's direction, incorporating incredibly subtle lighting effects (which are his, not the cameraman's), and perfectly blending its daring Expressionist devices with the horror movie ethos which takes over when the clown finally seeks revenge. This, undoubtedly, is the source Bergman drew on for *Sawdust and Tinsel*. TM

Hex

(1973, US, 93 min)
d Leo Garen. *p* Clark Paylow. *sc* Leo Garen, Steve Katz. *ph* Charles Rosher Jr. *ed* Robert Belcher, Antranig Mahakian. *ad* Gary Weist, Frank Sylos. *m* Charles Bernstein. *cast* Tina Herazo [Cristina Raines], Hilarie Thompson, Keith Carradine, Mike Combs, Scott Glenn, Gary Busey, Robert Walker, John Carradine.

●Largely a mess, but an engaging one. A horror film/Western/World War I biker movie, it exudes an improbable degree of charm precisely because of a freewheeling script that refuses to be tied to any one genre. Very obviously made in the shadow of Corman's *Gas-s-s-s*, it traces the consequences of the accidental meeting between two Lawrentian sisters – living alone on the Nebraskan farm left to them by their Indian father – and a gang of oddly innocent bikers in the early years of the century. While the expected thuggery and rape almost come about, mayhem of another kind is introduced when one of the sisters begins to conjure her dead father's familiars to do their worst, resulting in a string of psychedelic sequences. Although the girls' motivations remain consistently traditional (well, almost), on the whole the film exudes the feeling of being, almost subliminally, a nostalgic valediction to the counter-culture. VG

Hey Cousin!

see Salut Cousin!

Hi, Are You Alone? (Hola, estás sola?)

(1995, Sp, 90 min)
d Icíar Bollaín. *p* Fernando Colomo, Beatriz de la Gandara. *sc* Icíar Bollaín. Julio Medem. *ph* Teo Delgado. *ed* Angel Hernandez. *pd* Josune Lassa. *m* Bernardo Bonezzi. *cast* Silke, Candela Peña, Daniel Guzman, Alex Angulo, Elena Irureta, Arcadi Levin.

●Like her performance as the red-haired Maite in Ken Loach's *Land and Freedom*, actress-turned-writer/director Icíar Bollaín's first feature is simple, direct and infused with feeling. Part road movie and part domestic drama, it follows two 20-year-olds, moody Niña (Silke) and vivacious Trini (Peña), as they wander about Spain in search of money, love and a sense of belonging. Alternating between spells on the road and brief experiments with various forms of domesticity, the ill-matched pair share rooms, a boyfriend (the Russian-speaking 'Olaf') and, more problematically, Niña's estranged mother Mariló (Irureta). The uncontrived situations, flawed characters and unforced humour are revealing yet never judgmental. NF

Hibiscus Town (Furong Zhen)

(1986, China, 136 min)
d Xie Jin. *sc* Ah Cheng, Xie Jin. *ph* Lu Junfu. *ed* Zhou Dingwen. *ad* Jin Qifen. *m* Ge Yan. *cast* Liu Xiaoqing, Jiang Wen, Zheng Zaishi, Zhu Shibin, Xu Songzi.

●Cut for international distribution from the 165 minute, two-part original, this – like Xie Jin's *Two Stage Sisters* – is a potent blend of the political and personal. It begins in 1963, in the remote rural backwater of the title: through determination and hard work, beancurd-seller Hu Yuyin makes enough money to build a new house for herself and her timid husband. But Maoist plans are afoot to clean up the country, and Hu Yuyin is accused of self-enrichment at the expense of the state. Betrayal, denunciation and humiliation abound as her life steadily falls apart; with the advent of the 1966 'Cultural Revolution', intrigue and paranoia are epidemic. Xie's portrait of China's traumatic, turbulent history ranges from '63 to the post-'Gang of Four' years, his palette the changing fortunes of an entangled group of individuals. It's impressive both for the elegant precision with which the director fills his scope frame with small, significant details, and for the discreet understatement that controls his own special brand of epic melodrama. In some ways similar to the classic romances of Frank Borzage, *Hibiscus Town* is a moving account of survival in the face of widespread social and political madness, told with clarity, compassion and insight. GA

Hickey & Boggs

(1972, US, 111 min)
d Robert Culp. *p* Fouad Said. *sc* Walter Hill. *ph* Wilmer C Butler. *ed* David Berlatsky. *m* Ted Ashford. *cast* Bill Cosby, Robert Culp, Rosalind Cash, Carmen, Louis Moreno, Ron Henrique, Robert Mandan, Michael Moriarty, Vincent Gardenia, James Woods.

●The first film from a Walter Hill script turns out to be as interesting for the assurance of Culp's direction as for Hill's contribution. *Hickey & Boggs* pairs television's *I Spy* team of Cosby and Culp as two down-at-heel private eyes caught in the crossfire of a very messy attempt to fence a suitcase full of banknotes. The laconic and cynical pair inhabit a familiar '70s *noir* thriller world where if you blink you miss a crucial plot point, and Cosby's relationship with his estranged wife and kid more than once threatens to turn sentimental. But the film scores with set pieces like the complicated shootout in a baseball park (where neither of them manage to hit anything), and many moments of fine throwaway humour. Peckinpah or Siegel couldn't have done it any more crisply. RM

Hidden, The

(1988, US, 97 min)
d Jack Sholder. *p* Robert Shaye, Gerald T Olson, Michael Meltzer. *sc* Bob Hunt. *ph* Jacques Haitkin. *ed* Michael N Knue. *pd* CJ Strawn, Mick Strawn. *m* Michael Convertino. *cast* Kyle MacLachlan, Michael Nouri, Claudia Christian, Clarence Felder, Clu Gulager, Ed O'Ross, William Boyett.

●A fast-paced, blackly comic sci-fi thriller about a power-hungry alien organism which invades the bodies of law-abiding citizens and transforms them into deranged criminals with a penchant for fast cars, blasting rock music, and violent antisocial behaviour. When a respectable businessman robs a bank, guns down the security guards, and crashes into a road block, LA cop Nouri thinks it's all over. But at the hospital, the inciting organism slips into a neighbouring patient, who then continues the previous host's crime spree. Forced to team up with FBI cop MacLachlan, Nouri's frustration is exacerbated by his new partner's quirky behaviour and air of debauched stillness. Created by ace SFX man Kevin Yagher, the organism is a classic (mostly kept hidden); the developing relationship between the two cops is nicely handled; and there's a neat twist concerning the origins of MacLachlan's vendetta against the organism. Powered by a driving rock score, this is by turns sleek, reckless, and smoothly effective, like a Ferrari with a psycho killer at the wheel. NF

Hidden Agenda

(1990, GB, 108 min)
d Ken Loach. *p* Eric Fellner. *sc* Jim Allen. *ph* Clive Tickner. *ed* Jonathan Morris. *pd* Martin Johnson. *m* Stewart Copeland. *cast* Frances McDormand, Brian Cox, Brad Dourif, Mai Zetterling, Maurice Roëves, Bernard Bloch, Brian McCann, Michelle Fairley.

●Loach's film has the feel of a Costa-Gavras political thriller and a script by controversial Marxist Jim Allen. Despite its sometimes flailing conspiracy-theory narrative, and its upstaging by TV projects like *Stalker, Death on the Rock* and *Who Bombed Birmingham?*, this deserves to be seen simply because it takes the debate on Ireland further than most such docudramas, asking questions about the nature of the British presence and its effect on the mainland's justice system. The plot, based on both the Stalker and Colin Wallace affairs, concerns the murder of an American civil liberties campaigner by security forces, and the subsequent enquiry by Brian Cox's Stalker-style police officer which leads to the heart of the military and political establishment. Whatever one thinks of the political line on offer, there's plenty of evidence of Loach's undiminished power as a film-maker, and equally ample evidence that something is very rotten in the state of Northern Ireland. SGr

Hidden City

(1987, GB, 108, b/w & col)
d Stephen Poliakoff. *p* Irving Teitelbaum. *sc* Stephen Poliakoff. *ph* Witold Stok. *ed* Peter Coulson. *pd* Martin Johnson. *m* Michael Storey. *cast* Charles Dance, Cassie Stuart, Bill Paterson, Richard E Grant, Alex Norton, Tusse Silberg.

●Poliakoff's first film as writer/director, at least partly inspired by an article in Time Out on Secret London, in particular a building in Wandsworth which was used for the interrogation of prisoners during the war. The film bristles with deceptively mundane settings – tunnels, shafts, tearooms, workmen's huts – all throwing up secrets of the surveillance trade. Not merely the Le Carré kind either, but the sort which affects all of us in the end. The thriller plot in which Charles Dance and Cassie Stuart track down one of these secrets is chilling enough, but far less powerful than the superb use of real locations and the mazy, hazy recreation of a modern city of computers, chicanery and dark secrets. The sort of movie that ensures you never feel secure walking down the street again. SGr

Hidden Fortress, The (Kakushi Toride no San-Akunin)

(1958, Jap, 123 min, b/w)
d Akira Kurosawa. *p* Masumi Fujimoto. *sc* Ryuzo Kikushima, Hideo Oguni, Shinobu Hashimoto, Akira Kurosawa. *ph* Ichio Yamazaki. *ad* Yoshiro Muraki. *m* Masaru Sato. *cast* Toshiro Mifune, Misa Uehara, Takashi Shimura, Susumu Fujita, Eiko Miyoshi.

●The movie that confirmed Kurosawa's greatest strength, his innovative handling of genre. It's set amid the civil wars of 16th century Japan, and concerns samurai Mifune escorting a princess and two oafish peasants through enemy territory. Kurosawa's treatment is part traditional (the plotting, the concept, the use of Noh theatre music), part eclectic (there are reminiscences of John Ford Westerns), and part truly idiosyncratic (the Shakespearean contracts between clowns and heroes). It was clearly only a small step from this to the delights of *Yojimbo* and *Sanjuro*. TR

Hidden River

see Río Escondido (1947)

Hidden River

see Río Escondido (1999)

Hidden Room, The

see Obsession

Hidden Witnesses (Testigos Ocultos)

(2000, Arg/Sp, 96 min)
d/p Nestor Sanchez Solelo. *ph* Esteban Clausse. *cast* Carolina Touceda, Martin Loza, Fernando Aguilar, Esther Goris, Fernando Guillén Cuervo, Martin Coria, Roly Serrano, Alejandro Fiore.

●What starts as a small-scale tale of street folk – Maria Jose ('Majo') and violent addict boyfriend Federico blackmail rich men by secretly filming them with her – soon aims for more ambitious territory with its exploration of cult behaviour and psychology. But, a visually unremarkable telepic dressed up with social surface, the film is poorly equipped to deliver on such intentions. It's engaging enough in a familiar way, and, by default or association, it does have something to say about the pressure to find a niche, or simply survive, within a rabid free-market economy – it's probably most resonant in its clearsighted understanding of women's extra vulnerability within such a system, but it's too in thrall to North American filmic models to offer anything lasting. GE

Hide in Plain Sight

(1980, US, 98 min)
d James Caan. *p* Robert Christiansen, Rick Rosenberg. *sc* Spencer Eastman. *ph* Paul Lohmann. *ed* Fredric Steinkamp, William Steinkamp. *pd* Pato Guzman. *m* Leonard Rosenman. *cast* James Caan, Jill Eikenberry, Robert Viharo, Joe Grifasi, Barbra Rae, Kenneth McMillan, Danny Aiello.

●A promising subject for James Caan's directorial debut: the true story of a divorced Buffalo factory-worker who finds that his two children have disappeared because their stepfather has been given a new, secret identity by the government after testifying against underworld associates. But as a director, Caan's sense of mood and construction proves desperately uncertain, with the result that the film uneasily mixes suspense thriller elements in with its more realistic study of a blue collar worker up against civil authority; and his own mannered portrayal of the inarticulate, fiery hero with a heart of gold is frequently hard to take. DP

Hideous Kinky

(1998, GB/Fr, 99 min)
d Gillies MacKinnon. *p* Ann Scott. *sc* Billy MacKinnon. *ph* John de Borman. *ed* Pia Di Ciaula. *pd* Louise Marzaroli, Pierre Gompertz. *m* John Keane. *cast* Kate Winslet, Saïd Tagmaoui, Pierre Clémenti, Bella Riza, Carrie Mullan, Abigail Cruttenden, Ahmed Boulane, Sira Stampe.

●MacKinnon's film of Esther Freud's semi-autobiographical novel displays characteristic subtlety and intelligence. A penniless single mother (Winslet) and her two young daughters try to make a go of it in Morocco in the early '70s. The kids have no problems with mum's relationship with a local charmer, but they're less happy with her restless spirit of adventure and her desire to find herself in Sufism. Extremely clear eyed, the film's densely textured portrait of both Moroccan and middle-class hippy culture is unsentimental, evocative and convincing, and never takes sides with or against the mother. MacKinnon draws terrific performances from all involved (Winslet bravely refusing to court our sympathies), lets character, mood and meaning take precedence over story, and assembles a great music track as a bonus. Spot on. GA

Hider in the House

(1989, US, 108 min)
d Matthew Patrick. *p* Edward Teets, Michael Taylor. *sc* Lem Dobbs. *ph* Jeff Jur. *ed* Debra T Smith. *pd* Victoria Paul. *m* Christoper Young. *cast* Gary Busey, Mimi Rogers, Michael McKean, Kurt Christopher Kinder, Candy Hutson, Elizabeth Ruscio, Chuck Lafont.

●When Tom Sykes (Busey) is released from an institution some 20 years after murdering his sadistic parents, all he wants is a family and a home. Obsessively pragmatic, he installs himself into a newly refurbished house, building a secret room behind a false wall in the loft. By the time the Dryers take up residence, all the rooms are bugged and Sykes has his own entry. Adopting this 'perfect' family, he finds himself increasingly involved in family affairs: cowering like the kids when the parents argue, and then taking an overtly Oedipal role, manoeuvering the father (McKean) out of the picture and introducing himself to the mother (Rogers) as a friendly neighbour. Accept the unlikely premise (director Patrick puts economy over plot exposition), and you'll find a tense psychological suspense film which cannily explores family politics with sour wit and distinctly macabre conclusions. It's a very promising debut from Patrick, resisting the overt violence of the horror movie in favour of uneasy intimacy and intelligent characterisation. Rogers and McKean are first-rate, but Busey in particular has seldom been better employed, his hulking physique a reminder of the tragic monsters of movie yore, immensely threatening but intrinsically vunerable. TCh

Hi, Dharma! (Darmaya Nolja)

(2001, SKor, 95 min)
d Kwan Park [Park Chul-Kwan]. *p* Oh Seung-Hyun. *sc* Park Gyu-Tae. *ph* Park Hee-Joo. *ed* Kim Sang-Bum. *ad* Oh Sang-Man. *m* Park Jin-Seok. *cast* Park Shin-Yang, Chung Jin-Young, Park Sang-Myun, Lee Moon-Shik, Hong Kyung-In, Ryoo Seung-Soo.

●Five bloodied gangsters, needing to lie low after a disastrous clash with a rival gang, hide out in a remote temple in the mountains. The resident Buddhist monks greet them with horror and treat them with contempt, but the wise, elderly head monk lets them stay. By the time the gangsters' treacherous boss shows up, the two factions have learnt a grudging mutual respect. This culture-clash comedy (which echoes both *Performance* and Suo's *Fancy Dance* without really resembling either) trades in shameless stereotypes, but the gradual exposure of the underlying similarities between the monks and the hoods is witty and well managed. The casting also helps offset the general predictability of the plotting, and the first-time director's respect for the characters make the closing scenes surprisingly touching. TR

Hiding Out

(1987, US, 98 min)
d Bob Giraldi. *p* Jeff Rothberg. *sc* Joe Menosky, Jeff Rothberg. *ph* Daniel Pearl. *ed* Edward Warschilka. *pd* Dan Leigh. *m* Anne Dudley. *cast* Jon Cryer, Keith Coogan, Annabeth Gish, Gretchen Cryer, Oliver Cotton, Tim Quill, Anne Pitoniak.

●A twenty-something stockbroker (Jon Cryer), about to give evidence against a mobster, learns there's a contract out on his life. He flees town, dyes his hair, and enrolls in a suburban high school alongside his cousin. Predictable, slackly plotted nonsense, marginally redeemed by a genial young cast. GM

Hiding Place, The

(1974, US, 147 min)
d James F Collier. *p* Frank R Jacobson. *sc* Allan Sloane, Lawrence Holben. *ph* Michael Reed. *ed* Ann Chegwidden. *pd* John Blezard. *cast* Julie Harris, Eileen Heckart, Arthur O'Connell, Jeannette Clift, Robert Rietty, Nigel Hawthorne.

●At the centre of this story of Corrie and Betsie ten Boom, Dutch sisters who, with their family, helped smuggle countless Jews out of Holland during World War II and were incarcerated in a German concentration camp, lies a would-be celebration of Christian faith. The good intentions of all concerned notwithstanding, the film falls flat. Collier's ersatz heroic style is inadequate as suggesting either the torments of concentration camp life or the consolations of true faith; so much so that the real Corrie ten Boom appears personally in a prologue to testify how faith kept her and her sister alive. In short, the film – produced for Billy Graham's Evangelistic Association – lacks the commitment of its protagonist, preferring instead religious clichés and production values. PH

High and Dry

see Maggie, The

High and Low (Tengoku to Jigoku)

(1963, Jap, 143 min, b/w)
d Akira Kurosawa. *p* Tomoyuki Tanaka, Ryuzo Kikushima. *sc* Hideo Oguni, Ryuzo Kikushima, Eijiro Hisaito, Akira Kurosawa. *ph* Asakazu Nakai, Takao Saito. *ad* Yoshiro Muraki. m Masaru Sato.*cast* Toshiro Mifune, Kyoko Kagawa, Tatsuya Mihashi, Yutaka Sada, Tatsuya Nakadai, Takashi Shimura.

●Adapted, unexpectedly, from one of Ed McBain's 87th Precinct novels (*King's Ransom*), this emerges as part thriller and part morality play in the manner characteristic of Kurosawa. After bringing off a big financial coup, a tycoon finds that his son has been kidnapped. Prepared to ruin himself to pay the ransom, he realises that his chauffeur's son was abducted by mistake. The first half, set in a single room, echoes Hitchcock's *Rope* in exploring his moral dilemma while the action takes place off-screen. The second is disconcertingly different in that it focuses excitingly on the police procedures deployed in the hunt for the kidnapper. But the connections, though sometimes overly obvious in appealing to the liberal conscience, span fascinating Dostoevskian depths. TM

High Anxiety

(1977, US, 94 min)
d/p Mel Brooks. *sc* Mel Brooks, Ron Clark, Rudy DeLuca, Barry Levinson. *ph* Paul Lohmann. *ed* John C Howard. *pd* Peter Wooley. *m* John Morris. *cast* Mel Brooks, Madeline Kahn, Cloris Leachman, Harvey Korman, Ron Carey, Dick Van Patten, Rudy DeLuca, Barry Levinson.

●Generally juvenile and crass spoof of Hitchcock thrillers, filching themes and scenes from *Vertigo, Psycho, The Birds, Spellbound*, etc, in its story of a psychologist going to work at a very strange and sinister Institute for the Very Very Nervous. Most of the gags are either incredibly obvious or depressingly scatological, or both. But there are a couple of nice touches, one satirising Hitchcock's use of orchestral scores, and the other his relentlessly prowling, voyeuristic camera. GA

High Art

(1998, US, 102 min)
d Lisa Cholodenko. *p* Dolly Hall, Jeff Levy-Hinte, Susan A Stover. *sc* Lisa Cholodenko. *ph* Tami Reiker. *ed* Amy E Duddleston. *pd* Bernhard Blythe. *m* Shudder to Think. *cast* Ally Sheedy, Radha Mitchell, Tammy Grimes, Patricia Clarkson, Gabriel Mann, Ann Duong, Bill Sage.

●Cholodenko's debut is an ambitious, intelligent but ultimately frustrating account of a young woman (Mitchell) who gets a job on a trendy Manhattan photography mag and goes for a big break when she discovers, thanks to a leaky ceiling, that the woman who lives in the apartment above her is a famous but reclusive retired photographer (Sheedy). The girl's introduction to the smudger's druggy, bisexual, boho world leads to trouble with her boss, her boring boyfriend, and much overall intrigue. Decent performances mean that the movie's fine as far as it goes, but the tone uneasily straddles satire and straight drama, and there's rather less here than meets the eye. GA

High Boot Benny

(1993, Ire, 82 min)
d Joe Comerford. *p* David Kelly. *sc* Joe Comerford. *ph* Donal Gilligan. *pd* John Lucas. *m* Gaye Mcintyre. *cast* Frances Tomelty, Alan Devlin, Marc O'Shea, Fiona Nicholas.

●The occasional playfulness of *Reefer and the Model* (1987) is replaced here – another response by director Comerford to the political impasse in present-day Ireland – by a more sombre mood. This is a more straightforward allegorical tale than its predecessor, set around a 'neutral' school run by 'The Matron' (Tomelty) and Manley (Devlin), a maverick ex-priest, on the windswept border between North and South. Teenage delinquent Benny, who sports a mohican and steel-shinned boots, is a metaphorical and literal outsider, who wanders the rugged landscape that surrounds the former fort, looking after animals, and taking refuge (and physical comfort) at the school. When the school 'caretaker' is found dead, Benny is drawn into the conflict between the police, the British Army, the Loyalist paramilitaries, and the IRA. Into the arms of which group will he be drawn? This is a potent blend of didactic history lessons, flourishes of elegant dark beauty, brooding psycho-drama and cold-blooded analysis. Strong performances. WH

High Bright Sun, The (aka McGuire Go Home!)

(1965, GB, 114 min)
d Ralph Thomas. *p* Betty E Box. *sc* Ian Stuart Black. *ph* Ernest Steward. *ed* Alfred Roome. *ad* Syd Cain, Franco Fontana. *m* Angelo Francesco Lavagnino. *cast* Dirk Bogarde,

George Chakiris, Susan Strasberg, Denholm Elliott, Grégoire Aslan, Colin Campbell, Joseph Fuerst, Nigel Stock.

●A misguided Ralph Thomas/Betty Box production for the Rank Organisation which tries to create a romantic drama out of the British military presence in Cyprus in the late '50s. Bogarde's the British intelligence man whose efforts to stem Eoka guerilla activity are compromised when he falls for American-Cypriot gal Strasberg, an archeology student lodging at a villa where the chief guerilla (Aslan) is in hiding. Sadly the script by Ian Stuart Black (from his own novel) doesn't make it through the political minefield created by a very messy independence conflict. Chakiris lays it on as a fanatical student patriot. TJ

High Commissioner, The

see Nobody Runs Forever

High Encounters of the Ultimate Kind

see Cheech & Chong's Next Movie

Higher Animal, A

see Barking Dogs Never Bite

Higher Learning

(1995, US, 128 min)
d John Singleton. *p* John Singleton, Paul Hall. *sc* John Singleton. *ph* Peter Lyons Collister. *ed* Bruce Cannon. *pd* Keith Brian Burns. *m* Stanley Clarke. *cast* Ice Cube, Laurence Fishburne, Kristy Swanson, Jennifer Connelly, Michael Rapaport, Omar Epps, Jason Wiles, Tyra Banks.

●The setting is 'Columbus' University, where freshmen arrive believing that they're there in pursuit of higher learning, wilder parties or whatever – whereas what they're really after is some individual sense of sexual, racial or political identity: hard to achieve when they also want to belong, and when various teachers, cliques and loudmouths are out to influence them. Among the newcomers are Malik (Epps), a black athlete who soon has to work and run harder than expected, and finds himself caught between the conflicting attitudes to racial struggle of Fudge (Ice Cube) and Professor Phipps (Fishburne); Kristen (Swanson), a gullible WASP who after being date-raped falls under the spell of feminist Taryn (Connelly); and Remy (Rapaport), a gauche misfit whose loneliness renders him prey to the camaraderie of local neo-Nazis. A stylish, intelligent film-maker, Singleton interweaves the threads of his demographic tapestry with assurance, passion and a welcome awareness of the complexities of the college community's contradictory impulses towards integration and separatism. Minus points: some schematic stereotyping and a rather sniffy attituted towards lesbianism. GA

Highest Honor – A True Story, The

see Southern Cross

High Fidelity

(2000, US/GB, 114 min)
d Stephen Frears. *p* Tim Bevan, Rudd Simmons. *sc* DV De Vincentis, Steve Pink, John Cusack, Scott Rosenberg. *ph* Seamus McGarvey. *ed* Mick Audsley. *pd* David Chapman, Thérèse Deprez. *m* Howard Shore. *cast* John Cusack, Iben Hjejle, Todd Louiso, Jack Black, Lisa Bonet, Catherine Zeta-Jones, Joan Cusack, Tim Robbins, Lili Taylor, Natasha Gregson Wagner, Sara Gilbert.

●The movie of Nick Hornby's book has been transposed to Chicago, but with more fidelity than you might expect. Cusack, a wry and believably apathetic Rob, rakes over the ashes of dead relationships and casts a wary eye out for a midlife crisis he's too lethargic to put himself through. Director Frears' big idea is to have Rob break off from scenes to recount dry monologues on sex and vinyl. He does this so often you wonder why he doesn't write a book and have done with it. Then you remember: the book's written, this is the movie. That's not a putdown, really. I enjoyed the film – twice! I related! Taylor, Gilbert, Gregson Wagner: chicks so cool they endow the uncredited Zeta-Jones with honorary coolness. Black's a dynamo, a bullshitter in a vinyl store. Dylan, The Beta Band, The Chemical Brothers – the soundtrack's packed, but you wish they'd let you hear more of it; you wish that Hornby wrote women as funny as his blokes; and you wish it meant more than a one-night stand. TCh

High Heels

see Docteur Popaul

High Heels (Tacones lejanos)

(1991, Sp, 114 min)
d Pedro Almodóvar. *p* Augustín Almodóvar. *sc* Pedro Almodóvar. *ph* Alfredo Mayo. *ed* José Salcedo. *pd* Pierre-Louis Thévenet. *m* Ryuichi Sakamoto. *cast* Victoria Abril, Marisa Paredes, Miguel Bosé, Pedro Díez del Corral, Féodor Atkine, Ana Lizarán.

●Almodóvar ditches gender-bending, drug-abusing anarchy for a more sober meditation on the importance of family. Newsreader Rebecca (Abril) is obsessed by her glamorous pop singer mother (Paredes), who left her as a child. The reunion after 15 years is difficult, not least because Rebecca has married her mother's old boyfriend; and when he is murdered, suspicion alights on them both. The performances are superb, with a raw emotion that is uncomfortably voyeuristic to watch; and the central scene, around which the rest of the film was constructed, is an astonishing tragic-comic tour de force: Rebecca broadcasts the latest news on the murder of her own husband, then almost breaks down as she shows snapshots of ordinary household objects. It's sad and funny, but like the rest of the film, mostly sad. And therein lies the problem: the overwrought, almost physical love/hate relationship between the two women never quite rings true, and Almodóvar has crossed the thin comedic line that separated *Law of Desire* and *Matador* from cloying melodrama. You come out bruised, thoughtful, but unredeemed. DW

High Heels and Low Lifes

(2001, GB, 86 min)
d Mel Smith. *p* Uri Fruchtman, Barnaby Thompson. *sc* Kim Fuller. *ph* Steven Chivers. *ed* Christopher Blunden. *pd* Michael Pickwoad. *m* Charlie Mole. *cast* Minnie Driver, Mary McCormack, Kevin McNally, Mark Williams, Danny Dyer, Michael Gambon, Len Collin.

●In a bad mood with her boyfriend, a digital sound sculptor, for not paying her enough attention, nurse Shannon (Driver) spends the evening dancing at the disco and moaning with her pal Frances (McCormack), an actress tired of appearing in fringe theatre and voicing cartoons. Things brighten up when they're alone in a room with the boyfriend's scanner as it crackles to life. Scary, but they persevere with it, and are soon eavesdropping on a neighbourhood bank robbery. Opportunity knocks: they plan to fox the villains and pocket the cash. Scrapes ensue but a policy of non-violence ensures only minor injuries occur for which they can't apologise enough. So what do you get when you cross the director of *Mr Bean* with the writer of *Spice World*? A lecherous, reactionary Britcom that sneers at all things new and different while jumping on every bandwagon in town. Relying on lame self-referential questions to cover its tracks, it collapses into a directionless mess whose patronising brand of girlpower fails on every level to disguise its creators' hankering after the golden age of Miss World. SS

High Hopes

(1988, GB, 112 min)
d Mike Leigh. *p* Simon Channing-Williams, Victor Glynn. *sc* Mike Leigh. *ph* Roger Pratt. *ed* Jon Gregory. *pd* Diana Charnley. *m* Andrew Dickson. *cast* Philip Davis, Ruth Sheen, Edna Doré, Philip Jackson, Heather Tobias, Lesley Manville, David Bamber.

●Mike Leigh describes this film (his first for the big screen since his debut in 1971 with Bleak Moments) as his most optimistic work to date; and in the splendidly unfashionable figures of Cyril and Shirley (Davis and Sheen), two downmarket residents of old King's Cross, comes an enormous upsurge of warmth, despite Cyril's continuing confusion on the subject of procreation in a divided world. Less successful are the nastier creations of Leigh's blend of improvisation and script: the monstrous car salesman Martin and his consumerist spouse (Jackson and Tobias); two yuppie neighbours played by Bamber and Manville with a permanent sneer on their minds. But in the figure which draws all these strands together for a very amusing birthday party, Cyril's ageing and indomitable mum (Doré), he offers a superbly crafted and unsentimentalised study of age and survival. Very long, prone to the longueur, but finally triumphant in its sombre, raw meditation on how we live. SGr

Highlander

(1986, GB, 116 min)
d Russell Mulcahy. *p* Peter S Davis, William N Panzer. *sc* Gregory Widen, Peter Bellwood, Larry Ferguson. *ph* Gerry Fisher. *ed* Peter Honess. *pd* Allan Cameron. *m* Michael Kamen. *cast* Christopher Lambert, Roxanne Hart, Clancy Brown, Sean Connery, Beatie Edney, Alan North.

●Narrative coherence is not a quality which director Mulcahy brings to this mondial of machismo, about a bizarre (and shrinking) band of immortals engaged in mortal combat down the ages. Highlander hops to and fro, from the Scottish highlands in the middle ages to contemporary America, allowing Lambert to don a variety of kits to match the perpetually pained expression in his eyes, and Connery, as his mentor, to make tosh dialogue sound like it was written by Noël Coward. It has lots of energy, a frenzied pace, and a villain who sings Tom Waits while mowing down innocent pedestrians. It's a lot of utterly preposterous fun, even if it doesn't quite hang together. Scotch missed. RR

Highlander II – The Quickening

(1990, US, 100 min)
d Russell Mulcahy. *p* Peter S Davis, William Panzer. *sc* Peter Bellwood. *ph* Phil Meheux. *ed* Hubert C de la Bouillerie, Anthony Redman. *pd* Roger Hall. *m* Stewart Copeland. *cast* Christopher Lambert, Sean Connery, Virginia Madsen, Michael Ironside, Allan Rich, John C McGinley.

●The time travellers with a flair for decapitation and swordplay are back, though this time Mulcahy's slick visuals merely serve to emphasise how vacuous the concept has become. It's the 21st century, and the ozone layer has been replaced by a protective shield built by what rapidly becomes the world's most powerful, corrupt corporation. The shield's original creator is Connor MacLeod (Lambert), now an old man who has opted to end his days in peaceful oblivion on Earth. But back home on the planet Zeist, evil dictator Katana (Ironside) has other plans for him... The film-makers opt this time for plenty of comic-strip gore, with the irredeemably wicked Katana leering his way through a series of spine-shattering escapades. 'This is going to be fun,' he mutters before a particularly tedious sequence in which subway train passengers endure a bloody ride to hell. Leaden, laden with effects, short on imagination.

Highlander III – The Sorcerer

(1995, Can/Fr/GB, 98 min)
d Andy Morahan. *p* Claude Léger. *sc* Paul Ohl. *ph* Steven Chivers. *ed* Yves Langlois. *pd* Gilles Aird, Ben Morahan. *m* J Peter Robinson. *cast* Christopher Lambert, Mario Van Peebles, Deborah Unger, Mako, Raoul Trujillo, Jean-Pierre Pérusse.

●Evil magician Kane (Van Peebles), one of three immortals buried in a Japanese magician's cave for 400 years, returns to confront his nemesis, the Highlander (Lambert). Using brute strength and the power of illusion, he wrests the Prize from his adversary's grasp. Observing from the sidelines is research scientist Alex Johnson (Unger), whose archaeological dig first unearthed them. Lambert is as uncharismatic as ever, while Van Peebles is as frightening as a wrestler in mock angry mood, and just as ridiculous. The choicest moment is when Connor MacLeod's flashback romp in the hay with Sarah (Unger, again) is interrupted by a flunky who insists he's needed in Paris immediately, 'because the Revolution's started'. With dialogue and storylines like these, director Morahan is on a hiding to nothing. To his credit, however, he smoothly continues the series' tradition of flashy images, showy sfx, aerial landscape shots and driving rock tunes. Polished photography from Steven Chivers. NF

Highly Dangerous

(1950, GB, 88 min, b/w)
d Roy Baker. *p* Antony Darnborough. *sc* Eric Ambler. *ph* Reginald Wyer. *ed* Alfred Roome. *ad* Alex Vetchinsky. *m* Richard Addinsell. *cast* Margaret Lockwood, Dane Clark, Marius Goring, Naunton Wayne, Wilfrid Hyde-White, Michael Hordern, Anthony Newley.

●Eric Ambler must have enjoyed himself cooking up this daffy blend of espionage spoof and straightforward thriller. Lockwood's the rather prim entomologist who heads for the Balkans, is arrested as a spy, then escapes and teams up with crusading Yank journo Clark while under the influence of a truth serum that makes her believe she's the heroine in a radio serial. It doesn't really come off, but larky moments raise a smile – like casting Naunton Wayne as the Chief of the Imperial General Staff. TJ

High Noon

(1952, US, 85 min, b/w)
d Fred Zinnemann. *p* Stanley Kramer. *sc* Carl Foreman. *ph* Floyd Crosby. *ed* Elmo Williams. *pd* Rudolph Sternad. *m* Dimitri Tiomkin. *cast* Gary Cooper, Grace Kelly, Lloyd Bridges, Katy Jurado, Thomas Mitchell, Otto Kruger, Lon Chaney, Henry Morgan.

●A Western of stark, classical lineaments: Cooper, still mysteriously beautiful in ravaged middle-age, plays a small town marshal who lays life and wife on the line to confront a killer set free by liberal abolitionists from the North. Waiting for the murderer's arrival on the midday train, he enters a long and desolate night of the soul as the heat gathers, his fellow-citizens scatter, and it grows dark, dark, dark amid the blaze of noon. Writer Carl Foreman, who fetched up on the HUAC blacklist, leaves it open whether the marshal is making a gesture of sublime, arrogant futility – as his bride (Kelly), a Quaker opposed to violence, believes – or simply doing what a man must. *High Noon* won a fistful of Oscars, but in these days of pasteboard screen machismo, it's worth seeing simply as the anatomy of what it took to make a man before the myth turned sour. SJo

High Plains Drifter

(1972, US, 105 min)
d Clint Eastwood. *p* Robert Daley. *sc* Ernest Tidyman. *ph* Bruce Surtees. *ed* Ferris Webster. *ad* Henry Bumstead. *m* Dee Barton. *cast* Clint Eastwood, Verna Bloom, Mariana Hill, Mitchell Ryan, Jack Ging, Stefan Gierasch, Billy Curtis, Geoffrey Lewis.

●As gravestone inscriptions in the town of Lago (painted red and renamed Hell by the phantom drifter) make clear, this was supposed to be Eastwood's fond adieu to the worlds of Sergio Leone and Don Siegel; and indeed he cuts the operatic excess of the former with the punchy economy of the latter. Yet the way Ernest Tidyman's script is submitted to distortion and distension, and fitted with Bruce Surtees' almost surreal images (and several twists of the ghostly revenge plot itself), suggest nothing so much as Eastwood returning for reference to the popular Japanese cinema from which Leone himself first borrowed for the *Dollars* films. Whatever, there's a boldness, confident stylisation, and genuine weirdness to the movie that totally escaped other post-spaghetti American Westerns, with a real sense of exorcism running both through and beyond it. PT

High Risk

(1981, US/GB, 94 min)
d Stewart Raffill. *p* Joseph Raffill, Gerald Green. *sc* Stewart Raffill. *ph* Alex Phillips Jr. *ed* Tom Walls. *ad* Ron Foreman. *m* Mark Snow. *cast* James Brolin, Lindsay Wagner, Anthony Quinn, Cleavon Little, Bruce Davison, Chick Vennera, James Coburn, Ernest Borgnine.

●To the accompaniment of news bulletins dispensing gloom about inflation and unemployment, an out-of-work cameraman (Brolin) collects three similarly situated buddies for an improbable raid on the Colombian hacienda of dope-dealer Coburn. Veering between comic caper and homily on the danger of living out depression fantasies, *High Risk* has something of an identity problem. For all his bull-slaying bravado, the suavely sinister Coburn proves to be just a paper tiger, while Quinn and a band of corrupted revolutionaries provide little more than light relief. There are nicely observed moments – the trepidation with which these 'ordinary Americans' confront the necessity for violence, their righteous indignation at being taken for CIA agents ('Christ, we're on Welfare!') – but they do tend to get lost in a finale of dago-bashing heroics. RMy

High Road to China

(1983, US, 120 min)
d Brian G Hutton. *p* Fred Weintraub. *sc* Sandra Weintraub Roland, S Lee Pogostin. *ph* Ronnie Taylor. *ed* John Jympson. *pd* Roland Laing. *m* John Barry. *cast* Tom Selleck, Bess Armstrong, Jack Weston, Wilford Brimley, Robert Morley, Brian Blessed, Cassandra Gava.

●No better or worse than other film-making-by-numbers imitations of *Raiders of the Lost Ark*. Armstrong plays a headstrong '20s heiress searching for her father, an inventor; Selleck plays the grizzled alcoholic flying ace who owns the only available planes. There is absolutely no feeling for the period, and the actors make no attempt to rise above the script's feeble idea of verbal sparring. But the Yugoslav locations are scenic, the aerial stunts are efficient, and there's an explosion every time interest starts to flag. Assuming, of course, that the interest was there in the first place. TR

High School

(1968, US, 75 min, b/w)
d/p/sc Frederick Wiseman. *ph* Richard Leiterman. *ed* Frederick Wiseman.

●Wiseman's second film, one of the documentaries marked by a certain compulsive austerity – they reject the traditional crutches of commentary, background music, gloss colour or fancy camerawork – in which he explored aspects of American institutional life. In *High School*, as might be expected, the American Dream is watched in the making. It is in the oppression of the adult/child relations that the full squalor of the bourgeois ideal is squeezed out. JDuC

High School High

(1996, US, 85 min)
d Hart Bochner. *p* David Zuker, Robert LoCash, Gil Netter. *sc* David Zuker, Robert LoCash, Pat Proft. *ph* Vernon Layton. *ed* James R Symons. *pd* Dennis Washington. *m* Ira Newborn. *cast* Jon Lovitz, Tia Carrere, Mekhi Phifer, Guillermo Diaz, John Neville, Malinda Williams, Louise Fletcher.

●Gag-wise, this spoof from the Zucker Bros – actually just David plus major production help and lightweight scriptwriting assistance from Robert LoCash and Pat Proft – is an underachiever. Lovitz plays the naive teacher son of a WASP headmaster who escapes the paternal shadow by accepting a post in the internecine groves of Marion Barry High. His beliefs set him at odds with rival Latino/Afro gangs and headmistress Louise Fletcher, who wields a baseball bat, but soon gets him 'skin-slapping' with 'educational assistant' Victoria (Carrere). Strangely, the director plays too much of the movie straight, slow and slushily romantic. This grants us dangerous leisure time to notice the script's dependence on racism, sexism and homophobia, ensuring that the moments of unrestrained, non-PC excess (a hilarious travesty of Chinatown clichés, for instance) prove the most rewarding. WH

High Season

(1987, GB, 101 min)
d Clare Peploe. *p* Clare Downs. *sc* Mark Peploe, Clare Peploe. *ph* Chris Menges. *ed* Gabriella Cristiani. *pd* Andrew McAlpine. *m* Jason Osborn. *cast* Jacqueline Bisset, James Fox, Irene Papas, Sebastian Shaw, Kenneth Branagh, Lesley Manville, Robert Stephens.

●This messy moussaka of a film purports to identify the changes effected by tourism on a colour-brochure Greek village, but it is in fact symptomatic rather than diagnostic. A pack of foreigners, their cameras whirring, have descended upon an unspoilt location, made hoo-ha, ridiculed the natives, and gone home with their skin peeling but their preconceptions intact. Characteristically for such a Carry On, the feeble plot wanders all over the place and involves a Grecian urn, a statue of the unknown tourist and a Russian spy. Bisset is a photographer, and her estranged hubby (Fox) a sculptor. Their cultural pretensions are on a level with those of the script by Mark and Clare Peploe. MS

High Sierra

(1941, US, 100 min, b/w)
d Raoul Walsh. *p* Hal B Wallis. *sc* John Huston, WR Burnett. *ph* Tony Gaudio. *ed* Jack Killifer. *ad* Ted Smith. *m* Adolph Deutsch. *cast* Humphrey Bogart, Ida Lupino, Alan Curtis, Arthur Kennedy, Joan Leslie, Henry Hull, Henry Travers, Cornel Wilde, Barton MacLane.

●A momentous gangster movie which took the genre out of its urban surroundings into the bleak sierras, and in so doing marked its transition into *film noir*. It isn't just that Bogart's Mad Dog Earle is a man 'rushing towards death', infallibly doomed and knowing it, from the moment he is paroled and through the half-hearted hold-up to his last stand on the mountainside. He also in a sense wills his own destruction, his dark despair fuelled by the betrayal of an innocent, clubfooted country girl whose operation he pays for, and who casually abandons him as soon as she can 'have fun'. Terrific performances, terrific camerawork (Tony Gaudio), terrific dialogue (John Huston and WR Burnett from the latter's novel), with Walsh – who in fact reworked the material as *Colorado Territory* eight years later – giving it something of the memorable melancholy of a Peckinpah Western. TM

High Society

(1956, US, 107 min)
d Charles Walters. *p* Sol C Siegel. *sc* John Patrick. *ph* Paul C Vogel. *ed* Ralph E Winters. *ad* Cedric Gibbons, Hans Peters. *m* Cole Porter. *cast* Bing Crosby, Frank Sinatra, Grace Kelly, Celeste Holm, Louis Armstrong, Louis Calhern, John Lund.

●Musical remake of *The Philadelphia Story* which scores over the original only in its score. Crosby (especially) and Sinatra are miscast in the Cary Grant/James Stewart roles, and Grace Kelly only really catches the icy class of Tracy Lord, whereas Katharine Hepburn made her a complex comic creation. But despite many commentators' thumbs-down to one of Cole Porter's best late scores, the numbers are good, particularly the lesser-known ballads (like Bing's archetypal note-bending 'Samantha'). And there's not much gainsaying 'Well Did You Evah' (the only song not written for the movie, and it looks an intrusion) or 'Who Wants to Be a Millionaire?' (with the undervalued Celeste Holm). A slightly misbegotten musical, but with many pleasures and Louis Armstrong, growing into sweet avuncularity. SG

High Spirits

(1988, US, 96 min)
d Neil Jordan. *p* Stephen Woolley, David Saunders. *sc* Neil Jordan. *ph* Alex Thomson. *ed* Michael Bradsell. *pd* Anton Furst. *m* George Fenton. cast Peter O'Toole, Daryl Hannah, Steve Guttenberg, Beverly D'Angelo, Jennifer Tilly, Martin Ferrero, Liam Neeson, Ray McAnally.

●Written and directed by the man who gave you *Angel*, *Company of Wolves* and *Mona Lisa*, this dreadful movie carries on the love affair between Ireland and Hollywood with a vengeance, beginning as a tribute to '50s flea-bag theatre, continuing as a banal commercial for the joys of Celtic rural life, and ending as a cross between *Beetlejuice*, *Cymbeline* and *The Quiet Man*. O'Toole is the decrepit owner of decrepit Plunkett Castle, which he hopes to preserve from the hands of a rich American developer by renting it out to gullible, ghost-hunting rich Americans. Lo and behold, real ghosts emerge, time zones are crossed, silly buggers played, Hannah rattles her bones, and Guttenberg plays Guttenberg. The script seems a collection of loose ends and rewrites; the direction is deeply dispirited; and with the exception of O'Toole and a couple of engaging vignettes, it's a complete turkey. SGr

High Tide

(1987, Aus, 104 min)
d Gillian Armstrong. *p* Sandra Levy. *sc* Laura Jones. *ph* Russell Boyd. *ed* Nicholas Beauman. *pd* Sally Campbell. *m* Peter Best. *cast* Judy Davis, Jan Adele, Claudia Karvan, Colin Friels, John Clayton, Frankie J Holden.

●Lilli (Davis) is one of a trio of mophead backing singers for an Elvis lookalike. Bet (Adele) works in a fish factory, drives an ice-cream van in the summer, and sings at the local nightspot at weekends. Ally (Karvan), her granddaughter, wants to be as great a surfer as her late father. When Lilli gets the sack, she is stranded in the Australian backwater where Bet and Ally live in a caravan park. Ally is her abandoned daughter. Gillian Armstrong's terrific film centres on the after-shocks of this discovery. Without a trace of schlock or schmaltz, she depicts the viewpoints of these three women with great skill, aided in no small way by Laura Jones' admirable script. A distinctive sense of place, a generous sense of humour, and three remarkable performances comine to produce a movie with an undertow of astonishing emotional power. MS

High Time

(1960, US, 103 min)
d Blake Edwards. *p* Charles Brackett. *sc* Tom Waldman, Frank Waldman. *ph* Ellsworth J Fredricks. *ed* Robert Simpson. *ad* Duncan Cramer, Herman A Blumenthal. *m* Henry Mancini. *cast* Bing Crosby, Fabian, Tuesday Weld, Nicole Maurey, Richard Beymer, Patrick Adiarte, Yvonne Craig.

●Bing does a Rodney Dangerfield and goes back to school in this early Edwards offering, before *Breakfast at Tiffany's* made his name or the *Pink Panther* films lodged him in a creative rut. Had you been a bona fide teenager at the time, one suspects you'd probably have hated it, but from a '90s vantage point, it's an inoffensive caper, gamely played by the old groaner and prodded along by an easygoing Henry Mancini score and some Cahn/Van Heusen songs ('The Second Time Around' picking up an Oscar). TJ

Highway, The (Da Lu)

(1934, China, 111 min, b/w)
d Sun Yu. *p* Luo Mingyou. *sc* Sun Yu. *ph* Qiu Yiwei. *ed* Sun Yu. *ad* Liu Leisan. *m* Nie Er. *cast* Jin Yan, Li Lili, Chen Yanyan, Zhang Yi, Zheng Junli, Han Lan'gen, Liu Qiong.

●Shot as a late silent but released with music and effects, Sun's classic is pitched as a call for national defence against the Japanese, unnamed for censorship reasons. Six unemployed men leave the city to work as labourers on a new national highway. Sun starts out celebrating their camaraderie on and off the job and their flirtations with two young waitresses. The plot arrives when some of them are imprisoned and tortured by a local warlord in league with 'the enemy'. Sun was the only US-trained director in Shanghai, but his ideas are fresh and irreducibly Chinese. One scene, in which the estimable Li Lili refuses to avert her gaze from the sight of the men bathing naked, clearly derives from Borzage's *The River*. Otherwise, the main thing Sun picked up from Hollywood movies was his well developed sense of fun. TR

Highway Patrolman (El Patrullero)

(1991, US/Mex, 105 min)
d Alex Cox. *p/sc* Lorenzo O'Brien. *ph* Miguel Garzon. *ed* Carlos Puente. *pd* Cecilia Montiel. *m* Zander Schloss. *cast* Roberto Sosa, Bruno Bichir, Vanessa Bauche, Zaide Silvia Gutierrez, Pedro Armendariz Jr, Malena Doria.

●When he graduates from the National Highway Patrol Academy to the dusty desert roads around Durango, young Pedro (Sosa) is determined to serve with honour. He's even against bribes, though the woman he marries soon puts paid to that with her repeated demands for a more comfortable life. Gradually the poverty, crime, marital tension and growing self-hatred get to Pedro, and when he stumbles across a drugs operation, he must decide which path to take...back to his old lofty ideals, or on to ill-gained wealth, a new pragmatism, or death. Graced with an aura of authenticity, the movie succeeds as a low-key blend of cautionary tale and downbeat actioner, despite the sometimes glaring budgetary restraints. In short, not as ambitious, let alone as quirky, as most of Cox's earlier work, but it delivers. GA

Highways by Night

(1942, US, 62 min, b/w)
d Peter Godfrey. *sc* Lynn Root, Frank Fenton. *ph* Robert De Grasse. *ed* Harry Marker. *ad* Albert S D'Agostino. *m* Roy Webb. *cast* Richard Carlson, Jane Randolph, Jane Darwell, Barton MacLane, Ray Collins, Gordon Jones.

●Based on a story by Clarence Buddington Kelland but with one eye seemingly on Howard Hughes, this RKO B movie features Carlson as a millionaire whiz-kid content to enjoy a sheltered existence at home while contributing revolutionary designs to the family engineering plant. Since he is shortly to become a leader of men in the navy, his uncle (Collins) suggests he go and find out how those men live. Obediently visiting a sleazy nightclub, he witnesses a murder, is framed for the killing by a racketeer (MacLane), and finds shelter with a working girl (Randolph), whose brother (Jones) runs a one-man trucking firm the racketeer is trying to put out of business. Adding his brains to the brother's brawn, Carlson saves the day and wins the girl. It's all efficiently done, but not very interesting: *Sullivan's Travels* reworked by Capra, with the wit replaced by bromides about the sterling worth of ordinary folk, the benefits of manual labour, and the joys of ham sandwiches. TM

Highway Society

(1998, Ger/Fin, 92 min)
d Mika Kaurasmäki. *p* Mariette Rissenbeek. *sc* Paul Charles Bailly, Mika Kaurismäki, (German dialogue) Beate Langmaack. *ph* Timo Salminen. *ed* Inge Behrens. *pd* Michael Mölder, Markku Pättilä. *m* Steamhammer, Mauri Sumén. *cast* Kai Wiesinger, Marie Zielcke, Jochen Nickel, Michaela Rosen, Hannes Hellmann, Siegfried Terpoorten, Michael Schönborn.

●Rather more assured than Kaurismäki's *LA Without a Map*, this finds the director on familiar ground. It's a quirky, moody and likeable serio-comic road thriller, in which a mechanic, forced by former partners in crime to smuggle 'medical supplies' back from Finland to Germany, is lumbered with, and attracted to, the spoilt, eccentric daughter of a domineering rich woman determined to marry her off to a feckless aristo. It's an engaging tale of deceit and betrayal, executed with wry good humour and attractive camerawork. GA

Highway to Hell

see Running Hot

High Wind in Jamaica, A

(1965, GB, 103 min)
d Alexander Mackendrick. *p* John Croydon. *sc* Stanley Mann, Ronald Harwood, Denis Cannan. *ph* Douglas Slocombe. *ed* Derek York. *ad* John Howell, John Hoesli. *m* Larry Adler. *cast* Anthony Quinn, James Coburn, Dennis Price, Ben Carruthers, Lila Kedrova, Kenneth J Warren, Gert Fröbe, Nigel Davenport, Isabel Dean, Martin Amis.

●Mackendrick paved the way towards the risky triumph of *A High Wind in Jamaica* with an equally unsentimental scrutiny of the innocent savageries of childhood in the underrated *Sammy Going South*. But his adaptation of Richard Hughes' novel was still received uncomfortably on its release, for widescreen buccaneering adventures were hardly expected to incorporate emotional and psychological resonances of the sort only recently locked up in the art-house visions of *Lord of the Flies*. Yet the colourful gusto Mackendrick brings to his yarn of pirate-captured children adrift between primitivism and Victorianism is pure cinema and pure entertainment, with comedy and tragedy ironically balanced in the combination of childhood dreams and adult dread. PT

High Window, The

see Brasher Doubloon, The

Hilary and Jackie

(1998, GB, 122 min)
d Anand Tucker. *p* Andy Paterson, Nicolas Kent. *sc* Frank Cottrell Boyce. *ph* David Johnson. *ed* Martin Walsh. *pd* Alice Normington. *m* Barrington Pheloung. *cast* Emily Watson, Rachel Griffiths, James Frain, David Morrisey, Charles Dance, Celia Imrie, Rupert Penry Jones, Bill Paterson, Nyree Dawn Porter.

●This subjective double take transcends the limitations of the biopic to exult in the artistry of the great cellist Jacqueline du Pré, even as it poses profound troubling questions about communication, destiny and the artist's sense of her own identity. Taking its cue from the controversial memoir *A Genius in the Family*, by Jackie's siblings Hilary and Piers, the movie begins with the prodigy finding free expression in the cello, and rapidly overtaking her elder sister's musical development. This opening movement is played out in a florid, ostentatiously romantic style which is slowly undercut as the sisters – now played by Watson and Griffiths – go their separate ways. Jackie disappears into music's jet setting high society, while Hilary's self-confidence gets a boost from the courtship of the ebullient Kiffer Finzi (Morrisey). When they come together again, the trauma is a defining moment in their lives and the movie's emotional centrepiece. The film's most audacious inspiration is to track back from this shocking, very moving and apparently unforgivable act, to retrace events from Jackie's perspective, revealing her loneliness and her ambivalence towards her instrument and her calling. Watson's performance is virtuoso: passionate, sensitive, impressionable and sometimes grotesque; and she's well matched by the subtle Griffiths and vibrant Morrisey. TCh

Hilda Was a Goodlooker

(1986, GB, 59 min)
d/p/sc/ph/ed Anna Thew. cast Mary Thew, Hermine Demoriane, Jacky Davy, Kevin Allen, George Saxon.

●Broken fragments of narration accompany broken fragments of 'Hilda's' physique. A woman recalls the early aspects of her family's life, centering on her older sister's rejection and subsequent acceptance of her suitor (who, in a lighter moment, wins the girl over by banging his head against the wall). Thew's intention is unclear; we are able to get an idea of what Hilda's life might have been like, but to what end? The mystical images with their repetitious depictions of the parts of the whole, the passionate silhouettes, the fragments of thought and footwear, amount to little more than mystical images of parts of the whole, passionate silhouettes, and fragments of thought and footwear. SGo

Hill, The

(1965, GB, 123 min, b/w)
d Sidney Lumet. *p* Kenneth Hyman. *sc* Ray Rigby. *ph* Oswald Morris. *ed* Thelma Connell. *ad* Herbert Smith. *cast* Sean Connery, Harry Andrews, Ian Bannen, Alfred Lynch, Ossie Davis, Roy Kinnear, Jack Watson, Ian Hendry, Michael Redgrave.

●Sean Connery took a break from Bond to give a sterling performance in this awesomely intense drama set in a North African British army camp, where the favourite punishment for prisoners is to send them clambering up and down a man-made hill in the full heat of the day. A lot of screaming and barking issues from the British thesps, and every bead of sweat is visible in Oswald Morris' brilliant monochrome photography. Lumet's strengths (the moral universe as an all-male enclave) and weaknesses (set the volume high, then turn it up higher) are all here. Not for the faint-hearted. DT

Hillbrow Kids

(1999, Ger/SAf, 94 min)
d Michael Hammon, Jacqueline Görgen. *p* Mirjam Quinte. *ph* Michael Hammon. *ed* Michael Hammon, Yvonne Loquens. *m* Harald Bernhard, Matthias Kratzenstein. *with* Regina Ndlovu, the street children of Johannesburg.

●A documentary highlighting the legacy of apartheid. Once a vital city centre, Hillbrow has become a shambles of street markets and ignorant, homeless people. The tower blocks in this built-up area of Johannesburg are now boarded up, violent crime is rife, begging endemic. Silas, a goodlooking lad with a surprisingly mature head on his shoulders, should by rights be violently resentful of his lowly situation. Like most of his peers, his parents have disowned him, he has nowhere to live and he partakes in the odd bit of glue sniffing. Yet despite the squalor, the kid's optimistic, yearning for the day his ship comes in. It probably never will. Poignant, enlightening and heartbreaking. DA

Hill in Korea, A (aka Hell in Korea)

(1956, GB, 81 min, b/w)
d Julian Amyes. *p* Anthony Squire. *sc* Ian Dalrymple, Anthony Squire, Ronald Spencer. *ph* Freddie Francis. *ed* Peter Hunt. *ad* Cedric Dawe. *m* Malcolm Arnold. *cast* George Baker, Stanley Baker, Harry Andrews, Michael Medwin, Ronald Lewis, Stephen Boyd, Victor Maddern, Percy Herbert, Robert Shaw, Michael Caine.

● 'Old enough to fight, too young to vote' – the cry of National Service conscripts in Korea who resented being placed in the firing line of someone else's civil war. The conflict wasn't popular with British film-makers either – too many sensitive areas. This patrol movie, shot in Spain three years after the armistice, touches lightly on most of them, though it deflects the National Service issue by making the most hysterical malcontent (Lewis) equally indignant that a lad of his calibre is having to muck in with all these rough proles. Tension with army regulars and death from 'friendly fire' are also addressed. Otherwise, it all seems slightly pointless, though inventively shot by Freddie Francis (his first). BBa

Hill's Angels

see North Avenue Irregulars, The

Hills Have Eyes, The

(1977, US, 90 min)
d Wes Craven. *p* Peter Locke. *sc* Wes Craven. *ph* Peter Saarinen. *ed* Wes Craven. *ad* Robert A Burns. *m* Don Peake. *cast* John Steadman, Janus Blythe, Arthur King, Russ Grieve, Virginia Vincent, Susan Lanier, Dee Wallace, Robert Houston.

● A baby cries, granddaddy is crucified, cannibals with CB radios stalk a land where even the hills have eyes. Somewhere in the desert a clean WASP family of six are stranded; there are murmurs of atomic tests, and at the local gas station, an old man talks of a monster mutant son he abandoned in the wilds. To little avail: the Carters are besieged in their trailer and the nightmare begins. The baby is kidnapped (for supper), half the family die. From there, it's a question of the 'civilised' family acquiring the same cunning as their cannibal counterparts in a fight to the death. Parallel families, Lassie-style pet dogs who turn hunter-killers, savage Nature: exploitation themes are used to maximum effect, and despite occasional errors (the cannibal girl who protects the 'human' baby), the sense of pace never errs. A heady mix of ironic allegory and seat-edge tension. CA

Hi-Lo Country, The

(1998, GB/US, 114 min)
d Stephen Frears. *p* Barbara De Fina, Martin Scorsese, Eric Fellner, Tim Bevan. *sc* Walon Green. *ph* Oliver Stapleton. *ed* Masahiro Hirakubo. *pd* Patricia Norris. *m* Carter Burwell. *cast* Woody Harrelson, Billy Crudup, Patricia Arquette, Cole Hauser, Katy Jurado, Sam Elliott.

● Peckinpah toyed with adapting this 1961 novel by Max Evans: it echoes all those end-of-the-Old-West stories about taciturn men caught out by changing times. Two ex-GIs come home to the Midwest after WWII to find that old girlfriends have married other people and that cattle ranching has gone corporate. The big economic issues hang in the background, clouding the thoughts of 'Big Boy' Matson (Harrelson, wearyingly laddish) and his introverted friend Pete Calder (Crudup, excellent), but the story ultimately boils down to a display of emotional grandstanding, featuring adultery, jealousy, sibling rivalry and blood. Frears and Stapleton deliver an impeccably crafted film, but it's at best a polished retro item. Time and the Marlboro man have done for the kind of awe John Ford and others once conjured from expansive images of cattle drives across the big country. TR

Himalaya (Himalaya – L'Enfance d'un chef)

(1999, Fr/Switz/GB/Nepal, 109 min)
d Eric Valli. *p* Jacques Perrin, Christophe Barratier. *sc* Eric Valli, (adaptation/dialogue) Olivier Dazat. *ph* Eric Guichard, Jean-Paul Meurisse. *ed* (supervising) Marie-Josèphe Yoyotte. *ad* Jérôme Krowicki, Tenzin Norbu Lama. *m* Bruno Coulais. *cast* Thilen Lhondup, Gurgon Kyap, Lhakpa Tsamchoe, Karma Wangel, Karma Tensing Nyima, Labrang Tundup.

● Elemental, sweeping and often majestic, this is both an engaging drama and a labour of love in tribute to the Buddhist, semi-nomadic people of the Dolpo, a remote region deep in the interior of the NW Himalayas. At the film's heart is a stunning re-enactment of a strenuous, often perilous annual yak caravan through the mountains. As the harvest yields only three months' food, salt must be traded for extra grain. Around this the film-makers weave a story dramatising themes that typify the conflicts and traditions of a threatened culture. The non-professional cast are given roles to suit their abilities, but turn in uniformly winning performances. If there's a fault, it lies in the director's occasional difficulty in sustaining narrative and dramatic flow without sacrificing his concern to reproduce authentic ethnographic detail. WH

Himmel über Berlin, Der

see Wings of Desire

Hi, Mom!

(1969, US, 86 min, b/w & col)
d Brian De Palma. *p* Paul Hirsch. *sc* Brian De Palma. *ph* Robert Elfstrom. *ed* Paul Hirsch. *ad* Paul Bocour. *m* Eric Kaz. *cast* Robert De Niro, Jennifer Salt, Lara Parker, Gerrit Graham, Nelson Peltz, Allen Garfield, Charles Durning, Paul Bartel, Paul Hirsch.

● A blast from the past which recalls De Palma's beginnings as a really eclectic independent. Made for $95,000 after the unexpected success of his anarchic *Greetings*, this is the sequel to end all sequels. De Niro plays variations on a Vietnam vet returning to NY as, variously, a 'peep art' porno movie-maker, an urban guerilla, and an insurance salesman. At least that's the framing excuse for an increasingly lunatic series of set piece gags. 'Be Black Baby' is a skit on off-Broadway 'encounter theatre', in which a middle class white audience is terrorised by black actors in whiteface. Shot by De Palma in visceral *vérité*, it actually is terrifying. Structurally, the film never recovers – but then its main merit is a refusal to 'hang together'. Anarchic and very appealing. IC

Hindenburg, The

(1975, US, 125 min, b/w & col)
d/p Robert Wise. *sc* Nelson Gidding. *ph* Robert Surtees. *ed* Donn Cambern. *pd* Edward C Carfagno. *m* David Shire. *cast* George C Scott, Anne Bancroft, William Atherton, Roy Thinnes, Gig Young, Burgess Meredith, Charles Durning.

● The disaster movie whose big bang is based on the assumption that the Hindenburg airship, the pride of Nazi Germany, was in fact sabotaged when it burst into flames while landing at New York in 1937. The formula is much as one would expect – lots of switching from the dirigible to plot developments on land in the USA and Germany which are accompanied by day/time/place checks, all part of the big countdown to disaster. Special effects are reasonable, and the final holocaust is shot in black-and-white to enable the incorporation of newsreel footage. The cast, most of them under suspicion as potential saboteurs, are both more imaginatively selected and kept in better check than usual; but the picture of Nazi Germany scratches scarcely deeper than *Cabaret*.

Hindered (Behindert)

(1974, GB/WGer, 96 min)
d/p/sc/ph/ed Stephen Dwoskin. *m* Gavin Bryars. *cast* Stephen Dwoskin, Carola Regnier.

● Certainly one of Dwoskin's most immediately accessible movies, *Hindered* is also one of his most rigorous examinations of the 'look' of the spectator, of the camera, and of his actors. Made in cooperation with German TV, the film traces the ebbing and flowing relationship between Dwoskin – a polio victim who can only move, and then with great difficulty, with the use of crutches – and Carola Regnier. In contrast to most of Dwoskin's works, the content of *Hindered* is not overtly erotic. Nonetheless, like films such as *Dyn Amo* and *Girl*, it works by denying the spectator full satisfaction of the voyeuristic interests raised by the film's images. Dwoskin forces the spectator to take sides with the trapped actors – including Dwoskin himself, of course – whom his camera mercilessly probes. PH

Hindle Wakes

(1931, GB, 77 min, b/w)
d Victor Saville. *p* Michael Balcon. *sc* Victor Saville, Angus MacPhail. *ph* Max Greene. *ed* RE Dearing. *pd* Andrew Mazzei. *m* WL Trytel. *cast* Belle Chrystall, John Stuart, Sybil Thorndike, Norman McKinnel, Edmund Gwenn, Mary Clare, Muriel Angelus.

● This glitteringly effective celebration of the financial and sexual independence of Lancashire mill-girls, based on Stanley Houghton's celebrated play from 1912, must have aroused mixed feelings among working class audiences in the '30s, when unemployment was driving women into prostitution. While Sally Hardcastle of *Love on the Dole* sells her body and soul to the bookmaker, fierce, fiery Jenny Hawthorne (Chrystall) snubs her nose at marriage to the boss' son and gaily assures her parents that, 'I'm a Lancashire lass, and so long as there's weaving sheds in Lancashire I shall earn enough to keep me going'. Ironic that the economic basis of her independence had been eroded by the time the film appeared; but Jenny, storming out into the night in clogs and shawl, makes a splendidly indomitable icon of feminist independence. RMy

Hi, Nellie!

(1934, US, 75 min, b/w)
d Mervyn LeRoy. *sc* Abem Finkel, Sidney Sutherland. *ph* Sol Polito. *ed* Bill Holmes. *ad* Robert Haas. *m* Leo M Forbstein. *cast* Paul Muni, Glenda Farrell, Ned Sparks, Robert Barrat, Kathryn Sergava, Hobart Cavanaugh, Douglass Drumbrille, Donald Meek.

● Paul Muni, the Hollywood '30s favourite in heavyweight social-conscience roles, reteamed with his *I Am a Fugitive from a Chain Gang* director for a rare crack at a comedy in this Warners newspaper frolic, rather uncertainly pepped up with a gangster angle. Refusing to condemn an apparently embezzling banker, Brad (Muni) is demoted from managing editor of the *Times-Star* to the latest incumbent of the 'Nellie Nelson' agony column, a task he resents at first, before falling on a clue that might help clear his reputation. The title's a reference to the sardonic teasing he repeatedly receives from fellow journos. The studio had conveyed newspaper life with more veracity and punch three years earlier in *Five Star Final*. TJ

Hips of John Wayne, The (Le Bassin de J.W./aka The Pelvis of J.W.)

(1992, Port, 124 min)
d João César Monteiro. *p* José Mazeda, Daniel Toscan du Plantier, Frederic Sichler. *sc* João César Monteiro. *ph* Mario Barroso. *ed* Carla Bogalheiro. *pd* Nelson Fonseca, Jorge Spencer. *cast* João César Monteiro, Hugues Quester, Pierre Clémenti, Graziella Delerm, Manuel de Freitas, Joana Azevedo, Marie Makhando.

● Even by Monteiro's eccentric standards, this is a weirdo that taxes the patience. It starts with a lengthy rehearsal (in a warehouse) of a Biblical play by Strindberg, before moving on to a lunatic plot involving the actor's disreputable double and an odyssey to the Arctic inspired by the angle and sway of John Wayne's hips. Mad, then, with Monteiro's own typically seedy, cadaverous central performance only adding to the overall insanity. Still, the sheer, bold perversity of some scenes is transfixing. GA

Hired Hand, The

(1971, US, 90 min)
d Peter Fonda. *p* William L Hayward. *sc* Alan Sharp. *ph* Vilmos Zsigmond. *ed* Frank Mazzola. *ad* Lawrence G Paull. *m* Bruce Langhorne. *cast* Peter Fonda, Warren Oates, Verna Bloom, Robert Pratt, Severn Darden, Ted Markland, Ann Doran.

● Peter Fonda's follow-up to *Easy Rider* is a strange hybrid of a movie which starts off as a ghastly Western parody of Dennis Hopper's film, and then develops into something much more interesting: the last half is primarily concerned with the problems of a woman in a male-oriented Western culture, and Bloom captures the part magnificently, adding another dimension to the film by her performance. Oates, too, is as good as ever, and there are a few scenes between them of real subtlety and intelligence before the uninteresting mechanics of the plot reassert themselves. DP

Hireling, The

(1973, GB, 108 min)
d Alan Bridges. *p* Ben Arbeid. *sc* Wolf Mankowitz. *ph* Michael Reed. *ed* Peter Weatherley. *pd* Natasha Kroll. *m* Marc Wilkinson. *cast* Robert Shaw, Sarah Miles, Peter Egan, Elizabeth Sellars, Caroline Mortimer, Ian Hogg.

●Not uninteresting adaptation of LP Hartley's novel, consciously styled in echo of Losey's *The Go-Between*, with excellent performances from Miles as the upper class widow recuperating from a nervous breakdown, and Shaw as the chauffeur of the car she hires daily to escape her empty world of tinkling teacups and social chitchat.Talking to the chauffeur's back, reassured by the monosyllabic pragmatism of an ex-RSM who views life's problems in terms of black and white, she gradually realises the emptiness of her self-torment, becomes gay, flirtatious, ready to resume her place in society; he, meanwhile, is gradually caught in the toils of an inarticulate, almost mystic adoration. The social barrier is subtly evoked in terms which have nothing to do with *Lady Chatterley* snobbery and sexual challenge; the point Hartley makes is that because neither ever really sees the other as a human being, neither of them can consciously admit the other as a possible partner, and frustration is inevitable. At which point, alas, the film falls apart. Electing to sound a blast of contemporary social protest totally at odds with the '20s setting, it has the chauffeur going berserk and using his Rolls as a battering-ram to the accompaniment of ironical snatches of 'Rule Britannia' and 'God Save the Queen'. Crass is hardly the word for it. TM

Hiroshima, Mon Amour

(1959, Fr/Jap, 91 min, b/w)
d Alain Resnais. *sc* Marguerite Duras. *ph* Sacha Vierny, Michio Takahashi. *ed* Henri Colpi, Jasmine Chasney, Anne Sarraute. *ad* Esaka, Mayo, Maurice Petri. *m* Giovanni Fusco, Georges Delerue. *cast* Emmanuele Riva, Eiji Okada, Bernard Fresson, Stella Dassas, Pierre Barbaud.

●Hiroshima's mushroom cloud has probably inspired more glib statements and images than any other 20th century phenomenon. So it's particularly refreshing to find that it still has some meaning in Resnais' first feature, now almost thirty years old. Marguerite Duras' script – part *nouveau roman*, part Mills & Boon – centres on a Japanese man and a French woman coming together in Hiroshima, exploring each other and their past lives, both of which have been far from rosy. The woman was punished as a wartime collaborator after an affair with a German soldier; the man's whole life was shattered by the bomb. Duras and Riva revel masochistically in the woman's sad story (she had her head shaved in prison), but Resnais does his best to soft-pedal the novelettish touches, and presents a melancholy disquisition on the complex relationships between world calamities and personal histories, between the past, present and future. GB

His Affair

see This Is My Affair

His Girl Friday

(1939, US, 92 min, b/w)
d/p Howard Hawks. *sc* Charles Lederer. *ph* Joseph Walker. *ed* Gene Havlick. *ad* Lionel Banks. *m* Morris W Stoloff. *cast* Cary Grant, Rosalind Russell, Ralph Bellamy, Gene Lockhart, Porter Hall, Helen Mack, Roscoe Karns, John Qualen, Ernest Truex, Billy Gilbert.

●Perhaps the funniest, certainly the fastest talkie comedy ever made, this inspired adaptation of Hecht and MacArthur's *The Front Page* adds an extra dimension of exploitation by turning Hildy Johnson into Walter Burns' ex-wife. Grant's Burns performs astonishing feats of super-quick timing as he garrulously manipulates a gallows case – Qualen, a simpleton mercilessly jailed for killing a black policeman – to further his own ends: first, to win back his wife from staid insurance salesman Bellamy (wonderfully slow in gumboots and bovine smile); second, to win back his star reporter (Hildy again); and third, to beat the rival rags to the full story of the political corruption that casts a shadow over the judicial system demanding Qualen's death. But Grant is not alone in his masterly expertise: Charles Lederer's frantic script needs to be heard at least a dozen times for all the gags to be caught; Russell's Hildy more than equals Burns in cunning and speed; and Hawks transcends the piece's stage origins effortlessly, framing with brilliance, conducting numerous conversations simultaneously, and even allowing the film's political and emotional thrust to remain upfront alongside the laughs. Quite simply a masterpiece. GA

His Kind of Woman

(1951, US, 120 min, b/w)
d John Farrow. *p* Robert Sparks. *sc* Frank Fenton, Jack Leonard. *ph* Harry J Wild. *ed* Eda Warren, Frederick Knudtson. *pd* Joseph McMillan Johnson. *m* Leigh Harline. *cast* Robert Mitchum, Jane Russell, Vincent Price, Tim Holt, Charles McGraw, Marjorie Reynolds, Raymond Burr, Jim Backus.

●A supreme oddity from Howard Hughes' RKO, which starts off with a relatively straightforward *noir* thriller plot – gambler Mitchum is pressurised under threat of violence to help exiled hoodlum Burr return to the States – and about halfway through turns into surreal parody. Mitchum has said that much of it was made up as the production went along, and certainly scenes such as his ironing of dollar bills, and the frequent innuendo-laden backchat with Russell, have an air of spontaneity. Funniest, however, is Price as a mad and conceited actor, given to spouting cod Shakespeare even at the most dangerous of moments. The thing, not unlike a taut, sadistic thriller peppered with incursions from the Monty Python crew, hardly hangs together; but it is excellently performed and directed, and remains an unforgettable delight. GA

His Lordship

(1932, GB, 77 min, b/w)
d Michael Powell. *p* Jerry Jackson. *sc* Ralph Smart. *ph* Geoffrey Faithfull, Arthur Grant. *ed* A Seabourne. *ad* Frank Wells. *m/songs* Richard Addinsell, Walter Leigh, others. *cast* Jerry Verno, Janet Megrew, Ben Welden, Polly Ward, Muriel George, Peter Gawthorne.

●A dozen or so under-rehearsed chorines in suspenders shuffle through a bit of a number involving buckets and mops, and that's as near as this quota-quickie musical gets to Busby Berkeley. Long considered a 'lost' Powell and only lately rediscovered, it confirms the director's 'never say die' credo, here applied to a sluggish scenario which draws on such '30s indicators as a plumber who's really a lord, a publicity-mad film star and some comic Bolsheviks. (There can't be many English-language movies with a heroine named Leninia.) The songs are quite amusing in the cabaret style of the day, and the low key, fretful persona of Jerry Verno is not unattractive. BBa

His Other Woman

see Desk Set

Histoire d'Adèle H., L'

see Story of Adèle H., The

Histoire d'O

see Story of O, The

Histoire inventée, Une (An Imaginary Tale)

(1990, Can, 100 min)
d André Forcier. *p* Claudio Luca, Robin Spry. *sc* André Forcier, Jacques Marcotte. *ph* Georges Dufaux. *ed* François Gill. *ad* Réal Ouellette. *m* Serge Fiori. *cast* Jean Lapointe, Louise Marleau, Charlotte Laurier, Marc Messier, Jean-François Pichette, France Castel, Tony Nardi, Marc Gélinas.

●This bizarre farrago of Québecois humour raises a few laughs and just about makes sense, but rarely at the same time. It revolves around an arty production of *Othello*, staged by a manic director (Nardi) whose ex-mobster uncle has roped in the Palermo old folks club to attend every performance. Or around a boozy cop (Messier), first seen having a mild altercation with a rambunctious parrot; or a jazz trumpeter (Lapointe) whose on-the-skids trio is being rent asunder by sorrows romantic and religious; or a love goddess (Marleau) whose 40 ex-swains follow her around in a moonstruck cortège; or even her daughter (Laurier), agonising over a two-timing Othello. There's some of the flavour of an Alan Rudolph movie – the characters keep bouncing off each other in the same desultory way – but there's too much reliance on running gags that don't really run anywhere. The cast's great, though, and Forcier has a way of making bleak old Montreal look charmingly baroque. JRo

Histoires d'Amérique: Food, Family and Philosophy

see American Stories

Histoires Extraordinaires (Spirits of the Dead/ Tales of Mystery)

(1967, Fr/It, 121 min)
d Roger Vadim; Louis Malle; Federico Fellini. *sc* Roger Vadim, Pascal Cousin; Louis Malle, Daniel Boulanger; Federico Fellini, Bernadino Zapponi. *ph* Claude Renoir; Tonnino Delli Colli; Giuseppe Rotunno. *ed* Hélène Plemiannikov; Franco Arcalli, Suzanne Baron; Ruggero Mastroianni. *ad* Jean Forester, Carlo Leva; Ghislain Uhry; Piero Tosi. *m* Jean Prodromidès; Diego Masson; Nino Rota. *cast* Jane Fonda, Peter Fonda, Françoise Prévost; Alain Delon, Brigitte Bardot; Terence Stamp, Salvo Randone.

●A compendium of three Poe stories. Vadim's (*Metzengerstein*) carries with it an aura of perversity, due not so much to the fetishistic clothes and decor as to the casting of Jane Fonda and brother Peter as the lovers. With his death, she resorts to a totem black stallion as a substitute, and the film itself falls apart. Malle's piece (*William Wilson*), a not particularly riveting variation on the Doppelgänger theme, has Alain Delon 1 (looking slightly bewildered) being chased by Alain Delon 2 (looking even more bewildered). Bardot puts in an appearance, looking odd in a black wig. Meticulously done, but not much to do with Poe; only Fellini (*Toby Dammit*) really manages to make much of his source. Stamp comes to Rome as the actor chosen to play Christ in the first Catholic Western (a cross between Dreyer and Pasolini, with a touch of Ford). He plays a man at the end of his tether, and as his obsessions take over, so do Fellini's. In many ways the sequence foreshadows *Roma*. It's overdone and strained, but worthwhile for Stamp's curious performance. CPe

Historia Oficial, La

see Official Version, The

Historias del Kronen

see Stories of the Kronen

History Is Made at Night

(1937, US, 99 min, b/w)
d Frank Borzage. *p* Walter Wanger. *sc* Gene Towne, Graham Baker. *ph* David Abel. *ed* Margaret Clancy. *ad* Alexander Toluboff. *m* Alfred Newman. *cast* Charles Boyer, Jean Arthur, Leo Carrillo, Colin Clive, Ivan Lebedeff, George Meeker.

●A bizarre movie from Borzage, who invades the sophisticated territory of Lubitsch and Leisen – Paris hotels, cruise liners, impersonations, two-timing wives, jealous husbands – and turns it all into a romantic thriller, complete with an ending that recalls *A Night to Remember*. Jean Arthur's marriage to Colin Clive is on the rocks, and suave Boyer – a waiter who poses as a thief, later turning up as patron of a Manhattan restaurant – comes to her rescue. Emotions run high, implausibilities pile up, Borzage keeps the motor running, and the stars – especially the rather neglected Arthur, who is now a Carmelite recluse – are immensely watchable. ATu

History Lessons (Geschichtsunterricht)

(1972, It, 85 min)
d/p/sc Jean-Marie Straub, Danièle Huillet. *ph* Renato Berta, Emilio Bestetti. *ed* Jean-Marie Straub, Danièle Huillet. *cast* Gottfried Bold, Johann Unterpertinger, Henri Ludwigg, Carl Vaillant.

● *History Lessons* derives from sections of Brecht's incomplete novel *The Business Affairs of Mr Julius Caesar*. It comprises four interviews with contemporaries of Caesar's (every word on the soundtrack is Brecht's): a banker, a former soldier, a lawyer and a writer, all of whom place Caesar's exploits in direct political perspectives. Typically, though, the film-makers insist on doing more than merely re-examining historical fact. They inscribe the dissection of Rome's imperialist past within three detailed studies of Rome today, establishing links that work both ways. And they leave the city altogether for the scenes in which their actors quote Brecht's dialogue; these scenes make a radical (Brechtian) break with the 'rules' of narrative film grammar. Illusions of all kinds are, in fact, ruthlessly pared away, leaving a series of concrete facts and statements in the forms of sounds and images that the viewer is free to use to construct meanings. This is arguably political cinema at its most advanced and provocative. TR

History of a Man's Face, The (Otoko no Kao wa Rirekisho)

(1966, Jap, 89 min)
d Tai Kato. *p* Kinen Masumoto. *sc* Tai Kato, Seiji Hoshikawa. *ph* Tetsuo Takaha. *ed* Iwao Ishii. *ad* Chiyosuke Maiden. *cast* Noboru Ando, Ichizo Itami, Sanae Nakahara, Kanjuro Arashi, Bunta Sugawara.

● Startlingly unlike Kato's genre movies, this is a sprawling account of the rise of a ruthless Korean-Japanese gang in Osaka during the post-war depression of 1948. Much of it is presented through the eyes of Amamiya (Ando), a war hero now running the only medical clinic in the area targeted by the gang; the complicated flashback structure ushers in ancillary issues like the ambiguous identity of Koreans in Japan, attitudes to violence and sex shaped by experiences in the war, and so on. At heart it's all standard melodrama, but the fiction reflects social history rather accurately. The open ending forms a question mark as gutsy as anything in Sam Fuller's movies. TR

History of Mr Polly, The

(1949, GB, 95 min, b/w)
d Anthony Pélissier. *p* John Mills. *sc* Anthony Pélissier. *ph* Desmond Dickinson. *ed* John Seabourne. *ad* Duncan Sutherland. *m* William Alwyn. *cast* John Mills, Sally Ann Howes, Finlay Currie, Megs Jenkins, Diana Churchill, Dandy Nichols, Juliet Mills, Irene Handl.

● Timid draper Mills, tired of his dull life and nagging wife, torches his shop and takes to the open road, landing up at the Potwell Inn, where he battles with fearsome Currie before settling down with the pub's jolly plump landlady, Megs Jenkins. A pleasant, rosy-cheeked adaptation of HG Wells's rural fantasy novel. NF

History of Post-War Japan as Told by a Bar Hostess (Nippon Sengo Shi: Madamu Omboro no Seikatsu)

(1970, Jap, 105 min, b/w)
d/sc Shohei Imamura. *ph* Masao Toshibawa. *ed* Mutsuo Tanji, Moriaki Matsumoto. *m* Harumi Ibe. *with* Etsuko Akaza, Tami Akaza, Akemi Akaza, Masako Akaza, Chieko Akaza.

● The links between the two halves of the title are generally left to work themselves out in terms of American influence, which we see both in the newsreels of political events and, on its most basic level, in the hostess' bar. They are sufficiently tenuous for our interest to rest mainly with the hostess herself. Fortunately she's an amazing lady, talkative and humorous, possessor of enormous charm. Shot in an appropriately rough-edged style, partly to distance itself from its own claim that film is a manipulative medium. Imamura's film ironically has an ending like something out of Hollywood fantasy. Our hostess, rumoured to be about fifty by then, leaves for the States with her 23-year-old Marine husband in tow and her sights set on US citizenship.

History of the World Part I

(1981, US, 92 min)
d/p/sc Mel Brooks. *ph* Woody Omens, Paul Wilson. *ed* John C Howard, Danford B Greene. *pd* Harold Michelson, Stuart Craig. *m* John Morris. *cast* Mel Brooks, Dom DeLuise, Madeline Kahn, Harvey Korman, Cloris Leachman, Gregory Hines, Pamela Stephenson, Sid Caesar, Spike Milligan, John Hurt, Nigel Hawthorne.

● It's difficult to dislike Brooks' parody of the historical epic, as old-fashioned as it is anarchic: a series of comic sketches playing through scenes from Kubrick's *2001*, DeMille's *Ten Commandments*, Roman sandal epics, and Louis XIV's court immediately prior to the French Revolution. Brooks piles on the scatological humour thick and fast, including many of the world's worst jokes, and as usual there's a high number of misses for every gag that hits the target. Centrepiece is a lavish Busby Berkeley-style production number, 'The Inquisition', a bad taste attempt to recapture the kitsch glories of 'Springtime for Hitler' (in *The Producers*). And, like the Monty Python team, Brooks knows full well that one of his best jokes is production values at least as impressive as what he's lampooning. RM

His Wife's Diary (Dnevnik Yego Zheny)

(2000, Rus, 110 min)
d Alexei Uchitel. *p* Alexander Golutva, Alexei Uchitel. *sc* Dunya Smirnova. *ph* Yuri Klimenko. *ed* Elena Andreeva. *pd* Bera Zelinskaia, Nikola Samonov. *m* Leonid Desyatnikov. *cast* Andrei Smirnov, Galina Tyunina, Olga Budina, Eugeny Mironov, Elena Morozova, Dani Kogan, Tatiana Moskvina, Sergei Vinogradov.

● Purportedly a big deal in Russia because it discusses the ménage-à-trois of a revered poet, this historical reconstruction sports fine Chekhov-lite performances, superb set design and sublimely choreographed grand manners. It traces the years Nobel Laureate Ivan Bunin, of the white linen, spent mostly in exile, from 1928–45, in Paris or Provence. Cameraman Klimenko doesn't put a lens wrong and the performances are as strong as those of false memory syndrome, but the film consists of little more than endless domestic arrangements and rearrangements, flutters of the heart, and storms in breakfast table teacups which illuminate neither poet nor the condition of exile. In sum Bunin hated the Bolsheviks, followed his heart, broke others, travelled a lot. Must read the poetry. WH

Hit, The

(1984, GB, 98 min)
d Stephen Frears. *p* Jeremy Thomas. *sc* Peter Prince. *ph* Mike Molloy. *ed* Mick Audsley. *pd* Andrew Sanders. *m* Paco de Luca. *cast* John Hurt, Tim Roth, Laura del Sol, Terence Stamp, Bill Hunter, Fernando Rey, Jim Broadbent.

● After ten years meditating on his new life down in Spain, supergrass Willie Parker (Stamp) is rudely awakened by some visitors – two hit men come to take him back to Paris to settle a few scores. But Willie is a changed man, completely unfazed by the imminence of death, and it is the killers whose nerves are stretched on the long road back to 'the hit'. Frears returned here to the big screen thirteen years after *Gumshoe* and a retreat to the stunting effect of TV; the wide, sunlit plains of Spain seem to have broadened his horizons, allowed a flexing of cinematic muscle, and inspired him to something both exciting and lofty. Hurt is in good vicious form as the shaded hit man; Stamp once more wears a smile like a halo; and the prospect of approaching death is handled without too much metaphysical puffing and blowing. All in all, a very palpable hit. CPea

Hit!

(1973, US, 134 min)
d Sidney J Furie. *p* Harry Korshak. *sc* Alan R Trustman. David M Wolf. *ph* John A Alonzo. *ed* Argyle Nelson. *ad* Georges Petitot. *m* Lalo Schifrin. *cast* Billy Dee Williams, Richard Pryor, Paul Hampton, Gwen Welles, Warren Kemmerling, Janet Brandt, Todd Martin, Henri Cogan, Pierre Collet.

● Furie continued his association with Williams, Pryor and Hampton from *Lady Sings the Blues* into this over-stretched vendetta action movie, which also overdoes the improvised jive-talk comedy relief in its yarn about a renegade federal agent (Williams) forming his own ad hoc revenge squad to take out nine Marseilles heroin dealers after his daughter ODs. Furie's penchant for silly camera angles and meaninglessly arresting images is here muted, but not replaced by much of distinction. PT

Hitcher, The

(1986, US, 97 min)
d Robert Harmon. *p* David Bombyk, Kip Ohman. *sc* Eric Red. *ph* John Seale. *ed* Frank J Urioste. *pd* Dennis Gassner. *m* Mark Isham. *cast* Rutger Hauer, C Thomas Howell, Jennifer Jason Leigh, Jeffrey DeMunn, John Jackson, Billy Green Bush, Armin Shimerman, Henry Darrow.

● There's a killer on the road (everyone's favourite Dutch psycho, Hauer) with a Nietzschean gleam in his eye and an ugly knife in his pocket. When Howell picks him up at dawn on a deserted Texan highway, he immediately makes his intentions plain by scaring the boy witless. When the boy fights back, however, then the hitcher has found what he needs – a decent adversary – and the game begins. By an apparent near-magical ability to be in several places at once, Hauer embarks on his round of gory slaughters, while sucking Howell into appearing at the scene, only to be nabbed by the cops. If you can swallow the unlikely nature of the killer's powers (like dismembering an entire police station while the boy is asleep in a cell), then you are in for a good rough ride down a murky road. There's a little toying with the old *doppelgänger* idea of the hero and villain coming to resemble one another, and the ending is rather straightforward; but it's a highly competent sick-fright version of the evergreen chase formula. And you'll never eat french fries again without looking at them closely. CPea

Hitch-hiker, The

(1953, US, 71 min, b/w)
d Ida Lupino. *p* Collier Young. *sc* Collier Young, Ida Lupino, Robert Joseph. *ph* Nick Musuraca. *ed* Douglas Stewart. *ad* Albert S D'Agonstino. Walter E Keller. *m* Leith Stevens. *cast* Edmond O'Brien, Frank Lovejoy, William Talman, José Torvay, Sam Hayes, Jean Del Val, Natividad Vacio.

● Although made in the same year as Lupino's impressive weepie *The Bigamist*, this inhabits a totally different universe. Two men on a fishing trip pick up a mass-murdering hitcher (Talman), and are forced at gunpoint to drive him through Mexico until the fatal moment when he no longer needs them. Absolutely assured in her creation of the bleak, *noir* atmosphere – whether in the claustrophobic confines of the car, or lost in the arid expanses of the desert – Lupino never relaxes the tension for one moment. Yet her emotional sensitivity is also upfront: charting the changes in the menaced men's relationship as they bicker about how to deal with their captor, stressing that only through friendship can they survive. Taut, tough, and entirely without macho-glorification, it's a gem, with first-class performances from its three protagonists, deftly characterised without resort to cliché. GA

Hi, Tereska (Czesc, Tereska)

(2001, Pol, 91 min, b/w)
d Robert Glinski. *p* Filip Chodzewicz. *sc* Robert Glinski. *ph* Petro Aleksowski. *ed* Krzysztof Szpetmanski. *pd* Elwira Pluta. *cast* Alexandra Gietner, Karolina Sobczak, Zbigniew Zamachowski, Malgorzata Rozniatowska, Krzysztof Kiersznowski.

● Writer/director Glinski pulls no punches in his portrait of a teenager who longs to be a fashion designer. Shot in b/w to underscore the greyness of the communist-era apartment blocks where Tereska lives, it also highlights the drab existence of her fellow tenants. In such desperate surroundings it seems fated that gradually but surely the girl's dreams will be dashed, as she's drawn into the world of delinquency already inhabited by those around her. If Gietner's remarkable performance is uncomfortably natural, it might be explained by the fact that both she and screen friend Renata (Sobczak) were cast from a Polish reform school. JFu

Hitler – a Career (Hitler eine Karriere)

(1977, WGer, 157 min, b/w & col)
d Joachim C Fest, Christian Herrendoerfer. *p* Werner Rieb. *sc* Joachim C Fest. *ed* Fritz Schwaiger, Elisabeth Imholte, Karin Haban. *m* Hans Possegga. *narrator* (English version) Stephen Murray.

●The first big hit of the Hitler revival in West Germany: it came as a book-plus-film package, just like *Jaws*. The movie is a long compilation of documentary footage, tracing Hitler's political trajectory from its early setbacks in the '20s to its end, with just enough contexting material to support its simple linear-history argument; this English version is garnished with a grave, moralising commentary. There's a strong bias towards footage from the '20s and '30s, presumably because images of the blitzkrieg and the concentration camps would be less saleable to a modern German audience. British audiences, of course, haven't been protected from Hitler, and much of the material is familiar here from TV compilations and movies like *The Double-Headed Eagle* and *Swastika*. But whether one finds the material intrinsically interesting or not, there's no mistaking the nature of the packaging: this is 'history' conceived, edited and scored like fiction, self-sufficient and comfortably remote. TR

Hitler, a Film from Germany (Hitler, ein Film aus Deutschland)

(1977, WGer/GB/Fr, 429 min)
d/p/sc Hans-Jürgen Syberberg. *ph* Dietrich Lohmann. *ed* Jutta Brandstaedter. *pd* Hans Gailling. *m* Wagner, Mahler, Beethoven, Mozart, Haydn. *cast* Heinz Schubert, André Heller, Hellmuth Lange, Amelie Syberberg, Harry Baer, Peter Kern, Rainer von Artenfels, Peter Moland.
●The third and longest part of Syberberg's extraordinary trilogy on German culture, history and nationalism (the two earlier films were *Ludwig – Requiem for a Virgin King* and *Karl May*), best described as a high camp, heavy-duty analysis of both history and historical analysis itself. The chosen method is to single out, act out, alter, and finally comment on the lives of a handful of 'awkward' German historical figures, from Ludwig of Bavaria through fantasy author Karl May to Hitler, the 'madman'. Behind aesthetic complexity lies a simple purpose: to show up the sort of historical contradictions solved by Marxists with bare economic models, and by others with suspect reference to the 'greatness' or 'madness' of the figures involved. Visually lyrical, the style is eclectic to the point of hysteria; and the tone oscillates between the operatic (Wagner figures large) and the colloquial (Hitler in conversation with his projectionist) without ever quite coming unstuck. Humour mixes with mythology and analysis in the attempt to reunite art, history and ideology. It's a quite remarkable film, with a sense of metaphor equal to its intellectual courage. CA

Hitler Gang, The

(1944, US, 101 min, b/w)
d John Farrow. *p* Joseph Sistrom. *sc* Frances Goodrich, Albert Hackett. *ph* Ernest Laszlo. *ed* Eda Warren. *ad* Franz Bachelin. *ad* Hans Dreier. *m* David Buttolph. *cast* Robert Watson, Roman Bohnen, Martin Kosleck, Reinhold Schunzel, Fritz Kortner, Alexander Granach, Alexander Pope, Ludwig Donath.
●Although sometimes tempted to caricature and inclined to simplify by suggesting that Hitler was no more than an addle-pated psychotic, this stands head-and-shoulders above most of Hollywood's attempts to deal with the Nazi peril. Semi-documentary in approach, it traces the rise of the Nazi party from 1918 to 1934 with the aid of some brilliant impersonations of Hitler, Goebbels, Goering, Himmler, Hess, Ludendorff, Streicher, Strasser et al, mainly by refugee actors. Its set pieces, in particular the Munich putsch and the Night of the Long Knives, are staged with real flair. But the fascination of the film, as its title suggests and as Parker Tyler noted, is its view of Hitler as a gangster (and therefore likely to get his comeuppance from betrayal by his own generals), where gangsterism is defined as 'the interest of minorities hallucinated as the interest of majorities and prosecuted in an extra-legal or anti-legal way…so that the nation became a gang'. The lucidly intelligent script, surprisingly enough, is by Frances Goodrich and Albert Hackett, a partnership otherwise notable mainly for a clutch of distinguished musicals. TM

Hitler's Madman

(1943, US, 85 min, b/w)
d Douglas Sirk. *p* Seymour Nebenzal. *sc* Peretz Hirshbein, Melvin Levy, Doris Malloy. *ph* Jack Greenhalgh. *ed* Dan Milner. *ad* Fred Preble, Edward Willens. *m* Karl Hajos. *cast* John Carradine, Patricia Morison, Alan Curtis, Howard Freeman, Ralph Morgan, Edgar Kennedy, Jimmy Conlin, Ava Gardner.
●Sirk's first American film may, like Lang's *Hangmen Also Die!*, centre on the true story of the Nazi commander Heydrich, whose assassination by the Czechs brought about horrendous reprisals by the German forces, but it is less *noir*-thriller than a committed, moving tribute to the spirit of resistance among the occupied Czech people. Its low budget is all too evident in the back-lot sets and the none-too-inspiring cast (though Carradine is superb as the sadistic Heydrich, and Ava Gardner has a brief cameo as a peasant girl tormented by brutal Nazis), but the overall effect is surprisingly powerful; from the opening shots of a statue of St Sebastian pinned with arrows, the film's emphasis on physical suffering and martyrdom is kept well to the fore. GA

Hitler: the Last Ten Days

(1973, GB/It, 104 min)
d Ennio De Concini. *p* Wolfgang Reinhardt. *sc* Enni De Concini, Mari Pia Fusco, Wolfgang Reinhardt. *ph* Ennio Guarnieri. *ed* Kevin Connor. *ad* Roy Walker. *m* Mischa Spoliansky. *cast* Alec Guinness, Doris Kunstmann, Simon Ward, Adolfo Celi, Diane Cilento, Gabriele Ferzetti, Eric Porter, Joss Ackland, Sheila Gish, Timothy West.
●For all its specious moralising – the Simon Ward character is clearly intended to be the 'conscience of Germany', and Alistair Cooke's scene-setting narration is similarly intended as the 'voice of authority' – this account of life in the bunker quickly topples over into uneasy farce, with Alec Guinness' Hitler seeming more like a character from *Kind Hearts and Coronets* than the frightening political figure he was. Juxtaposing newsreel footage with dramatised reconstructions doesn't help either. PH

Hit List

(1989, US, 87 min)
d William Lustig. *p* Paul Hertzberg. *sc* John Goff, Peter Brosnan. *ph* James Lemmo. *ed* David Kern. *ad* Pamela Marcotte. *m* Garry Schyman. *cast* Jan-Michael Vincent, Lance Henriksen, Rip Torn, Leo Rossi, Jere Burns, Charles Napier.
●For people who like seeing heads being shut in doors, stuck inside ovens, or being cut to french fry size by a steel grid. Henriksen does a great job playing the psycho hitman working for Mafia boss Torn, but – all because of a floppy house number 9 – gets the wrong address for a hit, shoots the wrong man, gives the wrong wife a miscarriage, and even kidnaps the wrong child. Sadly for the Mob, the child belongs to civilian hero Vincent. Cue vengeance, thrills, gore, and even a touching finale. WSG

Hitmakers: The Teens Who Stole Pop Music

(2001, US, 90 min)
d/p/sc Morgan Neville. *ph* Craig Spirko. *ed* Shaun Peterson. *with* Carole King, Jerry Goffin, Barry Mann, Cynthia Weill, Jeff Barry, Ellie Greenwich, Burt Bacharach, Hal David, Jerry Leiber, Mike Stoller, Neil Sedaka, Shadow Morton. *narrator* John Turturro.
●For supposedly disposable music, pop of the last 50 years has drawn a parade of documentarists. Neville himself has been down Tin Pan Alley before with a film on songwriters Leiber and Stoller, and 1619 Broadway – the Brill Building – loomed large in Allison Anders' loose Carole King fictionalisation *Grace of My Heart*, with John Turturro in Phil Spector-esque wig. Perhaps by way of acknowledging the precedent, Turturro narrates this straightforward memento of the young '60s song factory workers – King and Goffin, Weill and Mann, Jeff Barry, Neil Sedaka – who knocked out, with remarkable fecundity, pop hits for the likes of The Shirelles, The Drifters, Bobby Vee and The Righteous Brothers. It swings into the story at a fair lick, zigzagging through the decade's cultural conditions, the shifting fortunes and the relationships at work, while present-day talking heads vouch for the ingenuousness of the songs' feelings. It's informative, comprehensive – and just a little too dry. NB

Hit Man

see Scousmoune, La

HMS Defiant (aka Damn the Defiant)

(1962, GB, 101 min)
d Lewis Gilbert. *p* John Brabourne. *sc* Nigel Kneale, Edmund H North. *ph* Christopher Challis. *ed* Peter Hunt. *ad* Arthur Lawson. *m* Clifton Parker. *cast* Alec Guinness, Dirk Bogarde, Anthony Quayle, Tom Bell, Nigel Stock, Murray Melvin, Victor Maddern, Maurice Denham, Bryan Pringle.
●This late 19th century seafaring saga has some impressive credentials: a strong cast, a script by Nigel Kneale and Edmund H North (the latter did the adaptation for Ray's *In a Lonely Place* and co-wrote *Patton*), beautiful CinemaScope photography by Christopher Challis, crisp editing by Peter Hunt (later to become a Bond stalwart), and superb design by Arthur Lawson. It was nothing special in 1962, but today seems rather cherishable, and to make it now would cost rather more than $40 million. As an evocation of class conflicts among the officers and bitter resentments among the press-ganged crew, the movie is tense and convincingly acted, with the traditional *Mutiny on the Bounty* roles reversed: Captain Guinness is the humanitarian, and First Lieutenant Bogarde is the unrepentant cat-lover. ATu

Ho! (aka Criminal Face)

(1968, Fr/It, 107 min)-
d Robert Enrico. *sc* Pierre Pélégri, Lucienne Hamon, Robert Enrico. *ph* Jean Boffety. *ed* Jacqueline Meppiel. *ad* Jacques Saulnier. *m* François de Roubaix. *cast* Jean-Paul Belmondo, Joanna Shimkus, Sydney Chaplin, Paul Crauchet, Stéphane Fey, Tony Taffin, Alain Mottet.
●Indulgent Belmondo fans only for this turgid, badly dubbed effort from the time when the star could churn out any old rubbish and still clean up at the French box office. In this one, he's a disgraced former racing driver reduced to chauffeuring for a bunch of thieves who simply call him 'Ho!' Meanwhile, his other interests in life are society girl Shimkus and (ahem) his collection of smart ties. TJ

Hobson's Choice

(1953, GB, 107 min, b/w)
d David Lean. *sc* David Lean, Norman Spencer, Wynyard Browne. *ph* Jack Hildyard. *ed* Peter Taylor. *ad* Wilfrid Shingleton. *m* Malcolm Arnold. *cast* Charles Laughton, Brenda de Banzie, John Mills, Daphne Anderson, Prunella Scales, Richard Wattis, John Laurie.
●Set in the 1890s, this adaptation of Harold Brighouse's working class comedy, a favourite rep company standby since it was first performed in 1916, sees Laughton's tyrannical Lancashire bootmaker brought to heel when his plain-speaking daughter (de Banzie) marries his downtrodden, simple-minded employee (Mills) and sets up a competitive business. It could so easily have been a load of old cobblers; but Lean's sharp direction and impeccable performances all round transform a slight comedy into a timeless delight. NF

Hochelaga

(2000, Can, 130 min)
d Michel Jetté. *p* Louise Sabourin, Michel Jetté. *sc* Michel Jetté. *ed* Michel Jetté, Louise Sabourin. *pd* Mylène Bilodeau, Sandrine Rousseau. *m* Gilles Grégoire. *cast* Dominic Darceuil, David Boutin, Ronald Houle, Jean-Nicolas Verreault, Michel Charette, Deano Clavet, Claudia Hurtubise.
●The eponymous district in Montreal's run-down eastern sector is the battleground for this biker movie with an almost anthropological heart. Strong on rituals and gang mores, it follows petty thief Marc as he descends into the hell that is street warfare between the Dark Souls and the Devil's Soldiers. Having to prove his loyalty and courage via several extreme transgressions, he finds himself caught in a conflict just beyond the border gates of conventional urban authority. Violent, authentic and pretty relentless, it more or less delivers on its intentions, which are definitely not for everyone. GE

Hocus Pocus

(1993, US, 95 min)
d Kenny Ortega. *p* David Kirschner, Steven Haft. *sc* Mick Garris, Neil Cuthbert. *ph* Hiro Narita. *ed* Peter E Berger. *pd* William Sandell. *m* John Debney. *cast* Bette Midler, Sarah Jessica Parker, Kathy Najimy, Omri Katz, Thora Birch, Amanda Shepherd.
● This comedy ghoulfest – about three hanged 17th century Salem witches revivified at Halloween 1993 – toes a wobbly line between genuinely scaring the tinies and diverting the seen-it-all teens. New-kid-in-town Katz believes witches and stuff to be all hocus pocus until heart-throb Shepherd takes him to her family's disused museum – the old witches' house – where he foolishly lights a black-flamed candle and brings back the blood-seeking daughters of darkness. The ugly trio – Midler, Najimy and Parker – perform a show-stopping version of 'I Put a Spell on You' at a Halloween party, but otherwise it's slim pickings. WH

Hoffa

(1992, US, 140 min)
d Danny DeVito. *p* Edward R Pressman, Danny DeVito, Caldecot Chubb. *sc* David Mamet. *ph* Stephen H Burum. *ed* Lynzee Klingman, Ronald Roose. *pd* Ida Random. *m* David Newman. *cast* Jack Nicholson, Danny DeVito, Armand Assante, JT Walsh, John C Reilly, Robert Prosky, Natalija Nogulich, Kevin Anderson, John P Ryan, Paul Guilfoyle.
● Written by David Mamet, and starring Nicholson as the legendary union boss who disappeared one summer's evening in 1975, DeVito's film disappoints, though there are always compensations. Nicholson's Hoffa and his all-purpose sidekick/co-conspirator Bobby Ciaro (De Vito) move all the way from hard-nosed pre-war trucking, through union organisation, struggle and arson, into the full-scale corruption and racketeering that were to lead Hoffa into the arms of attorney general Robert Kennedy (Anderson), to jail, and finally to an anonymous grave – courtesy, in all probability, of his erstwhile Mafia cohorts. DeVito's scale is grand, but the language is foul and the sets sometimes look tacky, while the score is unspeakable. Nicholson's performance dominates, but fails finally to hold the film together. Still, in the courtroom confrontations with Anderson's boyish Bobby, and in the flash-forward scenes with an aged DeVito, waiting for that last, late rendezvous in a freeway cafeteria, there is much to admire. Ambiguous, but probably not sufficiently so: yooze catch ma drift? SGr

Hog Wild

(1980, Can, 95 min)
d Les Rose. *p* Claude Héroux. *sc* Andrew Peter Marin. *ph* René Verzier. *ed* Dominique Boisvert. *pd* Carol Spier. *m* Paul Zaza. *cast* Patti D'Arbanville, Michael Biehn, Tony Rosato, Angelo Rizacos, Martin Doyle, Claude Phillipe.
● A mite pleasanter and funnier than the awful title suggests, this is a good-natured, dumb movie about a high school feud between Waspy wimps and leathered bike heavies. Quick to anger, easily moved to violence (of the custard pie sort), the bikers are led by Rosato, who has perfected an incomprehensible mumble (sounding like early Brando on a bad line) and is as menacing as anyone with doggy eyes and an owlish blink can be. Although the bikers are blessed with a Morricone-esque theme tune, the film lacks the sort of musical thread which might make it a viable teen movie (it's obvious that all the 'kids' should have graduated at least a decade earlier). JS

Höhenfeuer

see Alpine Fire

Hola, estás sola?

see Hi, Are You Alone?

Holcroft Covenant, The

(1985, GB, 112 min)
d John Frankenheimer. *p* Edie Landau, Ely Landau. *sc* George Axelrod, Edward Anhalt, John Hopkins. *ph* Gerry Fisher. *ed* Ralph Sheldon. *pd* Peter Mullins. *m* Stanislas. *cast* Michael Caine, Anthony Andrews, Victoria Tennant, Lilli Palmer, Mario Adorf, Michel Lonsdale, Bernard Hepton.
● From the blood soaked ashes that is Berlin 1945, rises a mighty plan hatched by the doomed *Übermensch*, involving some $4bn and a vault in Geneva. Caine, as the unwitting son of the ring-leader, is elected to administer the fund; a job which entails spending most of the movie jetting to international tourist locations so that he can be filled in on the next plot twist by an obliging minor character. From the blood soaked ashes of a dog's dinner like this it is yet possible to glean moments of derisive pleasure. And Caine, once again, strides through the rubble with the air of a man who has read the script but is still hoping for a miracle. CPea

Hold Back the Dawn

(1941, US, 115 min, b/w)
d Mitchell Leisen. *p* Arthur Hornblow Jr. *sc* Charles Brackett, Billy Wilder. *ph* Leo Tover. *ed* Doane Harrison. *ad* Hans Dreier, Robert Usher. *m* Victor Young. *cast* Charles Boyer, Olivia de Havilland, Paulette Goddard, Victor Francen, Walter Abel, Rosemary de Camp, Mitchell Leisen, Brian Donlevy, Veronica Lake.
● As scripted by Brackett and Wilder and directed by the underrated Leisen (who appears, as himself, in a brief cameo as the Hollywood director to whom Boyer tries to sell his story), this romantic weepie is both moving and effectively stylish. Boyer's vaguely sinister charm is well deployed as the stateless Latin gigolo who tricks a plain-jane schoolmarm (de Havilland) into marriage purely in order to gain entry to the US from Mexico, while the depiction of their faltering relationship is achieved with a welcome degree of dark, ironic wit. But it's Leisen's assured, polished handling of a potentially soapy story that lends surprising conviction to the whole affair; so fluent is the narrative that disbelief at de Havilland's naiveté is suspended throughout. GA

Hold Back the Night

(1999, GB/It, 104 min)
d Phil Davis. *p* Sally Hibbin. *sc* Steve Chambers. *ph* Cinders Forshaw. *ed* Adam Ross. *pd* Chris Roope. *m* Peter John Vettese. *cast* Christine Tremarco, Stuart Sinclair Blyth, Sheila Hancock, Richard Platt, Julie Ann Watson, Kenneth Colley, Tommy Tiernan.
● Three apparently ill-matched souls find a measure of understanding in this telegraphed drama. Charleen (Tremarco) is on the run from her home in the Midlands, where her dad has been abusing her handicapped sister; Declan (Sinclair Blyth) has left a conventional upbringing behind to find himself on the road as an eco-warrior. After a fracas with the police at his latest protest site, Declan and Charleen take refuge in a camper van by the roadside, and find themselves in the company of Vera (Hancock), who's on her way to the Ring of Brodgar in Orkney for a sentimental reunion of sorts before advancing illness gets the better of her. So the scene is set for a study in cross-generational misunderstanding and coming together. Young folk learn a little about life, old girl gets to realise they're not such a bad lot, and so forth. Thankfully, Hancock's performance is a wonder of restraint, which more or less keeps the film going while we wonder why the sexual abuse subplot feels so superficial, why Declan is relatively undeveloped, and what the film-makers thought they would gain by delivering exactly what we expect from beginning to end. TJ

Hold Me, Thrill Me, Kiss Me

(1992, US, 92 min)
d Joel Hershman. *p* Travis Swords. *sc* Joel Hershman. *ph* Kent Wakeford. *ed* Kathryn Himoff. *pd* Dominik Wymark. *m* Gerald Gouriet. *cast* Adrienne Shelly, Max Parrish, Sean Young, Diane Ladd, Andrea Naschak, Timothy Leary.
● It's probably inevitable that a thrusting young director on the make should come up with much the same 'outrageous' ideas as his predecessors of the last generation did, but it's kinda sad that Hershman's debut feature should turn out to be such a flabby rehash of *Pink Flamingos*. A burglar (Parrish) on the run from a shotgun marriage in which the gun went off hides out in a California trailer park peopled with would-be droll eccentrics, and finds true lurv with the virginal sister (Shelly) of a vicious go-go dancer. The casting is right – Young and Ladd parody their established screen images, Timothy Leary does a cameo – but the sense of going through the motions is overwhelming. This is more like an American *Carry On Columbus* than a brave new voice in alternative comedy. TR

Hold You Tight (Yue Kuai Le, Yue Duoluo)

(1998, HK, 93 min)
d Stanley Kwan. *p* Raymond Chow. *sc* Jimmy Ngai. *ph* Kwan Pun-Leong. *ed* Maurice Li. *pd* Bruce Yu. *m* Yu Yat-Yui, Keith Leung. *cast* Chingmy Yau, Sunny Chan, Ke Yulun, Eric Tsang, Sandra Ng, Tony Rayns.
● Kwan's '1997 movie' avoids politics and melodrama, focusing instead on characters who oscillate between Hong Kong and Taiwan, between marriage and divorce, between commitment and adultery. Chingmy Yau plays two Hong Kong career women (or is that one woman at two phases of her life?), one of them stuck in a not very fulfilling marriage with a computer obsessed husband, the other a divorcee who has emigrated to Taipei and opened a boutique. The story turns on the sudden death of the first woman in an air crash; her husband (Chan), more numbed than grief stricken, is helped through the aftermath by a gay friend (Tsang), only to be devastated afresh by discovering that he's long been an object of desire for a teenager confused about his sexuality (Ke). Sexually frank and emotionally intense, the film's stature is enhanced by strong performances and Kwan Poon-Leung's virtuoso cinematography. RG

Hole, The

see Trou, Le

Hole, The

see Onibaba

Hole, The

(2000, GB/Fr, 102 min)
d Nick Hamm. *p* Lisa Bryer, Jeremy Bolt, Pippa Cross. *sc* Ben Court, Caroline Ip. *ph* Denis Crossan. *ed* Niven Howie. *pd* Eve Stewart. *m* Clint Mansell. *cast* Thora Birch, Desmond Harrington, Daniel Brocklebank, Laurence Fox, Keira Knightley, Embeth Davidtz, Gemma Craven.
● When teenager Liz (Birch) staggers through the deserted corridors of an English boarding school to raise the alarm, the investigation is about to begin. She's the sole survivor of the four classmates who've been missing for two weeks, trapped inside a disused army bunker unbeknown to anyone. Under the sensitive promptings of a police psychologist (Davidtz), she's about to reveal the truth about what really happened in 'the hole', and why her classmates – cool dude Mike (Harrington), rugger bugger Geoff (Fox) and It-girl wannabe Frankie (Knightley) – didn't make it. Her story of an adolescent crush gone wrong points the finger at geeky resident fixer Martin (Brocklebank), yet under subsequent questioning his entirely different version of events is equally plausible. This British teen thriller, part-funded by the Film Council, comes on confidently. Clint Mansell's electro score creates a genuine sense of anticipation, while screenwriters Ben Court and Caroline Ip (working from Guy Burt's novel *After the Hole*) adeptly set up the central conundrum, which Birch's able performance subtly sustains. Is Liz sinned against or psycho? The trouble is, Nick Hamm's film, for all its intriguing ambiguity, does eventually have to make its mind up, at which point it swiftly starts to fall apart, blowing its hard-earned credibility with showy directorial button-pushing. TJ

Hole, The (Dong)

(1998, Tai/Fr, 95 min)
d Tsai Ming-Liang. *p* Peggy Chiao, Carole Scotta, Caroline Benjo. *sc* Yang Ping-Ying, Tsai Ming-Liang. *ph* Liao Peng-Jung. *ed* Hsaio Ju-Kuan. *pd* Lee Pao-Lin. *cast* Yang Kuei-Mei, Lee Kang-Sheng, Miao Tien, Tong Hsiang-Chu.
● The last week before the 21st century: a mysterious epidemic has resulted in mass evacuation from Taipei, with only a few residents refusing to leave their homes, two of whom – a man and the woman who lives in the flat below – become involved in a mysterious, unspoken relationship when the latter's ceiling collapses, due to the non-stop rain, and they suddenly become aware of one another. The premise is weird enough, but interrupting the metaphorical story with delightfully

amateurish song and dance sequences (by way of homage to '50s star Grace Chang, though they also reflect on the woman's fantasies) takes it still further into uncharted territory. Somehow, it all comes off: the characters are depicted with insight and wit, the mood is kept controlled, and the ending is genuinely moving. Idiosyncratic, of course, but immensely impressive. GA

Hole in the Head, A

(1959, US, 120 min)
d/p Frank Capra. *sc* Arnold Schulman. *ph* William H Daniels. *ed* William Hornbeck. *ad* Eddie Imazu. *m* Nelson Riddle. *cast* Frank Sinatra, Edward G Robinson, Eleanor Parker, Carolyn Jones, Thelma Ritter, Keenan Wynn.

●Capra's penultimate movie lacks the resonance of his '30s work, and is a fairly wilful attempt to make our hearts heave. Sinatra plays the widowed (with small son) owner of a peeling Miami Beach hotel which is about to be foreclosed by the banks. Robinson is his elder brother, and Parker is a lonely widow who might have the money to save the hotel, but Sinatra isn't that much of a heel. Frank sings 'High Hopes', and despite some good moments, one wishes the whole thing was a musical. ATu

Hole in the Sky (Sora no Ana)

(2001, Jap, 127 min)
d Kazuyoshi Kumakiri. *p* Hidetoshi Morimoto, Mayumi Amano, Kazuki Nakamura. *sc* Kazuyoshi Kumakiri. *ph* Kiyoaki Hashimoto. *ed* Kazuyoshi Kumakiri. *ad* Toru Nishimura. *m* Akira Matsumoto. *cast* Susumu Terajima, Yurioko Kikuchi, Bunmei Tobayama, Shunsuke Sawada, Shunsuke Gondo.

●From the splatter of *Kichiku* to a film about a middle-aged man in deep denial who begins to understand himself with the aid of a mystery girl. Ichio (Kitano regular Terajima, very good) cooks for passing truckers and travellers in his father's roadside diner (named 'Hole in the Sky') in remote Hokkaido; he's never forgiven dad for mum's departure when he was very young. The penniless Taeko (Kikuchi) is dumped on the premises by an absconding boyfriend; she sticks around as a helper, has a brief fling with Ichio, and helpfully points out that it's about time both men got over losing the woman in their lives – before sensibly moving on herself. There seems to be a really good movie buried in this meandering, repetitive mood piece with its vague but insistent symbolism, but Kumakiri can't quite find it. It might help if he moved beyond thinking of women as ciphers. TR

Holiday

(1938, US, 95 min, b/w)
d George Cukor. *p* Everett Riskin. *sc* Sidney Buchman. *ph* Franz Planer. *ed* Otto Meyer, Al Clark. *ad* Stephen Goosson. *m* Sidney Cutner. *cast* Cary Grant, Katharine Hepburn, Lew Ayres, Doris Nolan, Edward Everett Horton, Henry Kolker, Binnie Barnes, Henry Daniell.

●Marvellous 'sophisticated comedy' about a prototype dropout (Grant in one of his best performances) who takes a rich upper class family by storm: arriving engaged to the conventionally snobbish younger daughter (Nolan), stirring up latent doubts and resentments through his carefree disregard for material proprieties and properties, he ends up by showing the yearningly dissatisfied elder sister (Hepburn) the way to a declaration of independence. Despite some very funny barbed dialogue, mostly centering on two clashing couples among the engagement party guests (one liberal, the other proto-Fascist), the film is less a satire on the rich than an acknowledgment that privilege has its drawbacks; its key scene, accordingly, takes place in the nursery playroom, a place redolent of childhood hopes and dreams, which Hepburn and her unhappily alcoholic brother (Ayres) unconsciously use as a retreat from their unwelcome social obligations. Often underrated by comparison with *The Philadelphia Story* (both are based on plays by Philip Barry), but even better because its glitteringly polished surface is undermined by veins of real feeling, it is one of Cukor's best films. TM

Holiday Camp

(1947, GB, 97 min, b/w)
d Ken Annakin. *p* Sydney Box. *sc* Sydney Box, Muriel Box, Peter Rogers, Ted Willis, Mabel Constanduros, Denis Constanduros. *ph* Jack Cox. *ed* Alfred Roome. *ad* Richard Yarrow. *m* Bob Busby. *cast* Flora Robson, Dennis Price, Jack Warner, Kathleen Harrison, Hazel Court, Jimmy Hanley, Esmond Knight, Emrys Jones, Peter Hammond, Patricia Roc, Bill Owen, Charlie Chester.

●Surprisingly unpatronising in its portrayal of the working classes triumphing over organised leisure, Annakin's kaleidoscope of life in a Butlin's concentration camp reflects something of the populist feeling which swept the Labour Party to victory in 1945. Time has mellowed the documentary quality of the film, and location shooting and authentic detail now seem less important than the presence of the whole range of British acting talent, from Dame Flora Robson to Cheerful Charlie Chester, among the cast of thousands. Annakin is able to build up a microcosm of British society, with Price's killer airman embodying post-war anxiety, and acting as a sinister antidote to Warner and his Huggett family. The only thing missing is the presence of voluptuous Jean Kent, struck down by flu on the inhospitable East Coast location. RMy

Holiday in Mexico

(1946, US, 127 min)
d George Sidney. *p* Joe Pasternak. *sc* Isobel Lennart. *ph* Harry Stradling. *ed* Adrienne Fazan. *ad* Cedric Gibbons, Jack Martin Smith. *songs* Ralph Freed, Sammy Fain, Victor Herbert, others. *cast* Walter Pidgeon, Jane Powell, Jose Iturbi, Ilona Massey, Roddy McDowall.

●Absurdly over-extended musical confection in which Pidgeon as the US Ambassador to Mexico looks on in disdain as daughter Powell falls for local classical pianist Iturbi. That's the cue for a string of musical interludes bringing in everything from Xavier Cugat and his Latin combo doing the 'Walter Winchell Rumba', an arrangement of 'Three Blind Mice' by the then 17-year-old André Previn, and, to top it all, Schubert's 'Ave Maria'. MGM threw everything they had at this one, but it still just lies there and dies there. TJ

Holiday Inn

(1942, US, 100 min, b/w)
d/p Mark Sandrich. *sc* Claude Binyon. *ph* David Abel. *ed* Ellsworth Hoagland. *ad* Hans Dreier, Roland Anderson. *m* Irving Berlin. *cast* Fred Astaire, Bing Crosby, Marjorie Reynolds, Virginia Dale, Walter Abel, Louise Beavers.

●Despite opportunities for some fine dancing from Astaire at his most energetic, he's lumbered not only with Crosby, crooning 'White Christmas' for the first time, but also with Marjorie Reynolds, clearly no replacement for Ginger Rogers. But the Irving Berlin score, including 'Easter Parade' and 'Let's Say It with Firecrackers' (which gives Fred his best moment) makes up for the thin story about a love triangle at the eponymous vacation resort. GA

Hollow Man

(2000, US/Ger, 112 min)
d Paul Verhoeven. *p* Douglas Wick, Alan Marshall. *sc* Andrew W Marlowe. *ph* Jost Vacano. *ed* Mark Goldblatt. *pd* Allan Cameron. *m* Jerry Goldsmith. *cast* Elisabeth Shue, Kevin Bacon, Josh Brolin, Kim Dickens, Greg Grunberg, Joey Slotnick, Mary Randle, William Devane.

●Scientist grapples with particle modelling program; Isabelle the lab gorilla is restored to the realm of the visible; disregarding medical niceties, scientist volunteers own body to the cause of biological transparency. But has he cracked reversion, or will it crack him? This revamp of *The Invisible Man* begins entertainingly in cartoon medical sci-fi territory. The experiments proceed in a top secret underground lab masterminded by egomaniac Dr Caine (Bacon), under the loose auspices of the Pentagon. Verhoeven doesn't exploit the political angle, preferring to attend to the hammy sexual triangulation between Caine, his ex Linda McKay (Shue) who also happens to be his deputy, and her secret new lover (Brolin). Once invisible, Caine's licentiousness grows steadily nastier, while McKay, inexplicably, remains in two minds about her old flame's desirability. However, since the doctor's conscience was clearly only skin-deep, his degeneration offers little suspense and even less of a moral. Cue basement action/slasher movie effects (exploding lifts, innumerable false endings) which in themselves are impressive. NB

Hollow Reed

(1995, GB/Ger, 104 min)
d Angela Pope. *p* Elizabeth Karlson. *sc* Paula Milne. *ph* Remi Adefarasin. *ed* Sue Wyatt. *pd* Stuart Walker. *m* Anned Dudley. *cast* Sam Bould, Martin Donovan, Ian Hart, Joely Richardson, Jason Flemyng, Shaheen Khan, Roger Lloyd Pack, Annette Badland.

●Martyn (Donovan) is a gay doctor estranged from his wife Hannah (Richardson). Visited by their 9-year-old son Oliver, who lives with his mother, Martyn suspects that the blood on the boy's face is not the result of school bullying but something more sinister. Is Oliver being abused by Hannah's lover Frank (Flemyng)? Hannah, however, rejects the notion out of hand, impelling Martyn to sue for custody. Trouble is, Oliver's so frightened, and reluctant to upset his mum, that he won't speak out against Frank. Besides, there's also the fact that Martyn lives with Tom (Hart) – and a gay man, in the eyes of the law, is unlikely to be deemed a better parent than a heterosexual woman. Sensitive, intelligent and affecting, Pope's film derives much of its emotional punch from its cast: Donovan gives an especially fine, focused performance, Richardson scrapes together some sympathy for a character whose blinkered gullibility is frequently infuriating, and young Sam Bould is admirable as Oliver. GA

Hollow Triumph (aka The Scar)

(1948, US, 82 min, b/w)
d Steve Sekely. *p* Paul Henreid. *sc* Daniel Fuchs. *ph* John Alton. *ed* Fred Allen. *ad* Edward Ilou, Frank Durlauf. *m* Sol Kaplan. *cast* Joan Bennett, Paul Henreid, Eduard Franz, Leslie Brooks, John Qualen, Mabel Paige.

●Not half bad, despite a loopy plot about a conman/thief hiding from pursuit who kills a look-alike psychiatrist and assumes his identity (conveniently skilled in surgery through interrupted studies, he is even able to reproduce a facial scar). The tension is kept ticking nicely by a flaw in the impersonation (working by mirror, he scars the wrong cheek), even more so by the fact that he unexpectedly inherits dire troubles from the dead man's past. Good supporting performances, a satisfyingly bleak ending, and absolutely stunning lighting and LA location shooting from John Alton. TM

Hollywood Boulevard

(1976, US, 83 min)
d Joe Dante, Allan Arkush. *p* Jon Davison. *sc* Patrick Hobby. *ph* Jamie Anderson. *ed* Amy Jones, Allan Arkush, Joe Dante. *ad* Jack De Wolfe. *m* Andrew Stein. *cast* Candice Rialson, Mary Woronov, Rita George, Jeffrey Kramer, Dick Miller, Paul Bartel, Jonathan Kaplan.

●Prentice work from the carefree young persons who went on to give you *Piranha* and *Rock'n'Roll High School*. Reputedly cobbled together in ten days, most of which must have been spent collating the outtakes from *Death Race 2000*, this is probably the ultimate movie in-joke: a parody of Roger Corman's outfit (New World Pictures), made by the people who work for it. The plot includes several murders, an unscrupulous star (Woronov), a director (Bartel, of course) who can't decide whether to pay homage to Von Sternberg or Godzilla, and a great many clips from actual New World product. The relentless obviousness is ultimately rather wearying, but the finale manages to be suitably outrageous, and it's undoubtedly a treasure trove for Corman buffs. TR

Hollywood Cavalcade

(1939, US, 97 min)
d Irving Cummings. *p* Darryl F Zanuck. *sc* Ernest Pascal. *ph* Ernest Palmer, Allen Davey. *ed* Walter Thompson. *ad* Richard Day, Wiard Ihnen. *m* David Raksin, David Buttolph, Cyril Mockridge. *cast* Don Ameche, Alice Faye, J Edward Bromberg, Buster Keaton, Al Jolson, Mack Sennett, Chester Conklin, The Keystone Kops, Ben Turpin.

●Agent Ameche brings Faye to silent-era Hollywood in this loving re-creation of the movies' pioneer days. The first half is the best, with Mack Sennett on hand to supervise the slapstick and Buster Keaton to chuck a custard pie or two. Personal problems and unconvincing melodrama take over, but the sight of the genuine Rin-Tin-Tin Jr will send viewers off into the sunset well satisfied. TJ

Hollywood Cowboy

see Hearts of the West

Hollywood Ending

(2002, US, 114 min)
d Woody Allen. *p* Letty Aronson. *sc* Woody Allen. *ph* Wedigo von Schultzendorff. *ed* Alisa Lepselter. *pd* Santo Loquasto. *cast* Woody Allen, Téa Leoni, George Hamilton, Treat Williams, Mark Rydell, Isaac Mizrahi, Debra Messing, Tiffani Thiessen.

●Val Waxman (Allen) is so down on his movie-directing luck that when Hollywood offers the chance for a comeback, he's persuaded to take it, despite the fact that it means working for his ex (Leoni) and the studio head (Williams) who stole her away. Waxman's difficult anyway, but when something – jealousy, anger, or something else? – renders him psychosomatically blind, he has to try to behave himself while concealing his disability on set. Uncharacteristically broad, even coarse, in its comic tone, Allen's leaden movie-making satire also suffers from undue repetition, rampant illogicality (many gags operate as if Waxman were also deaf), lazy stereotyping (most notably of the young), poor pacing and excessively heavy-handed metaphor. Leoni and Williams do their best, but haven't a chance against the otherwise ubiquitous mugging and hand-me-down script. GA

Hollywood on Trial

(1976, US, 102 min, b/w & col)
d David Helpern Jr. *p* James Gutman, David Helpern Jr. *sc* Arnie Reisman. *ph* Barry Abrams. *ed* Frank Galvin. *with* Dalton Trumbo. Martin Ritt, Walter Bernstein, Zero Mostel, Edward Dmytryk, Howard DaSilva, Ring Lardner Jr, Gary Cooper, Otto Preminger, Ronald Reagan, Joseph McCarthy. *narrator* John Huston, Joseph Losey.

●It's hardly surprising that *Hollywood on Trial* ends up being interesting mostly for the footage of individual testimonies at the 1947 House Un-American Activities Committee hearings on Hollywood. Helpern's documentary begins with a short potted newsreel history of America from the early '30s until the end of World War II. From there it gradually zeroes in on the persecution of the group of (mainly) screenwriters who were to become known as the Hollywood Ten for their defiance of the burning question, 'Are you now, or have you ever been a member of the Communist Party?' The film sometimes succumbs to the simplistic in its attempts to adequately contextualise the HUAC hearings. And the interviews with the jailed and blacklisted thirty years on – Dalton Trumbo, Edward Dmytryk, Zero Mostel and many others – add little to our comprehension of the paranoia rampant in the McCarthy era. Worth seeing for the film of the hearings themselves, though. RM

Hollywood or Bust

(1956, US, 95 min)
d Frank Tashlin. *p* Hal B Wallis. *sc* Erna Lazarus. *ph* Daniel L Fapp. *ed* Howard Smith. *ad* Hal Pereira, Henry Bumstead. *songs* Sammy Fain, Paul Francis Webster. *cast* Dean Martin, Jerry Lewis, Pat Crowley, Maxie Rosenbloom, Ben Welden, Anita Ekberg.

●Last (and one of the best) of the Martin and Lewis comedies, in which Lewis is a mentally retarded movie freak enamoured with La Ekberg, and Martin a gambler on a losing streak. They team up and drive a Cadillac convertible, which they have both won as a prize, to Hollywood. For protection, Lewis takes along his Great Dane. A particular favourite of Truffaut, who pointed out that the title refers to financial insolvency as much as to Ekberg's chest, its gags have real momentum, and the parody of *War and Peace*, which Paramount were making at the time with Ekberg, is delightful. ATu

Hollywood Shuffle

(1987, US, 81 min)
d/p Robert Townsend. *sc* Robert Townsend, Kennen Ivory Wayans. *ph* Peter Deming. *ed* WO Garrett. *ad* Melba Katzman Farquhar. *m* Patrice Rushen, Udi Harpaz. cast Robert Townsend, Anne-Marie Johnson, Starletta Dupois, Helen Martin, Craigus R Johnson, Ludie Washington, Damon Wayans, Kennan Ivory Wayans, Rusty Cundieff.

●Bobby is a struggling black actor. The few roles offered by white movie writers and producers reek of artifice: punks, pimps, sassy soul brothers and Eddie Murphy clones. What's a man to do? Townsend's satire may be gentle, but more often than not it's spot on. As Bobby (Townsend) escapes the sad reality of racial stereotyping through daydreams that expose the absurdity of whites telling blacks how to be Black, we're treated to visions of a Black Acting School (learn how to play a yodelling butler Stepin Fetchit-style), a truly *noir* TV-*noir* (Sam Ace in *Death of a Breakdancer*), and best of all, a Bros' version of a Bazza Norman-type movie round-up. Despite the film's conspicuously minuscule budget and shaky narrative structure, it is funny. If you value enthusiasm and imagination more than glossy sophistication, you'll laugh. GA

Holocaust 2000 (aka The Chosen)

(1977, It/GB, 102 min)
d Alberto De Martino. *p* Edmondo Amati. *sc* Sergio Donati, Alberto De Martino, Michael Robson. *ph* Erico Menczer. *ed* Vincenzo Tomassi. *ad* Umberto Bertacca. *m* Ennio Morricone. *cast* Kirk Douglas, Simon Ward, Agostina Belli, Anthony Quayle, Virginia McKenna, Alexander Knox, Adolfo Celi.

●A straight rip-off from *The Omen*. This time it's an American industrialist, not an American ambassador, who sires the Antichrist, but in other respects the familiar rush-towards-apocalypse is all here, right down to the various decapitations. If only the film-makers had paid less attention to plot detail in *The Omen* and more to its acute construction and direction, they might have pulled it off; but *Holocaust 2000* bears most of the worst traces of international co-production, notably a sense of disunity between cast and direction, some poor dubbing, and lines of dialogue that sound just like subtitles ('Your mother used to blame you subconsciously for being the only one to survive'). Everyone's pulling hard, only it's all too obvious they're not pulling in the same direction. DP

Holy Innocents, The (Los Santos Inocentes)

(1984, Sp, 105 min)
d Mario Camus. *p* Pablo Núñez, Julián Mateos. *sc* Antonio Larreta, Manuel Matji, Mario Camus. *ph* Hans Burmann. *ed* José María Biurrun. *ad* Rafael Palmero. *m* Antón García Abril. *cast* Alfredo Landa, Terele Pávez, Francisco Rabal, Augustin González, Juan Diego.

●In the '60s, a young soldier on leave returns to the humble rural croft of his youth to visit his prematurely ageing parents, and recalls, in a series of flashbacks, the lives and quotidian grind of his family. This is Franco's Spain; and for the poorest workers on the estates, life is feudal and brutal. The scenes speak for themselves: the soldier's father crawling like a dog to sniff out fallen game, too proud of his prowess to notice his debasement; his simpleton uncle gently cradling the family's retarded child, only to infect her with lice; his ever-suffering mother, sadly and stoically accepting the loss of her child's chance of an education. If Camus places his sympathy firmly with these innocent victims rather than their morally impoverished employers, his mood is nevertheless one of restraint, shot through with moments of symbolism and dark spirituality. Save only finally, when the cruelty and claustrophobia are punctured by a moment of cold catharsis. A moving and mournful valediction to an unforgotten and unforgiven past. WH

Holy Man

(1998, US, 114 min)
d Stephen Herek. *p* Roger Birnbaum, Stephen Herek. *sc* Tom Schulman. *ph* Adrian Biddle. *ed* Trudy Ship. *pd* Andrew McAlpine. *m* Alan Silvestri. *cast* Eddie Murphy, Jeff Goldblum, Kelly Preston, Robert Loggia, Jon Cryer, Eric McCormack, Sam Kitchin.

●'G' (Murphy) is a pilgrim in sandals and kaftan with nowhere to go – until, that is, he's almost run over by Ricky Hayman (Goldblum), producer of TV's 'Good Buy Shopping Network,' and a man ripe for the chop unless he can reverse his channel's plummeting ratings. When G wanders on to the 'live' set and instructs viewers to stop buying, the phone lines go crazy, and stock begins flying off the shelf. Cue G's career in reverse-psychology marketing and a reprieve for Hayman, who begins to dream up new ways of exploiting naivety. This cynical yarn about the evils of consumerism has a roster of faults: the public's infatuation with the guru is complete nonsense; erratic editing ensures the plot shoots off all over the place; and some of the slapstick scenes are done to death. Nevertheless, Murphy's bemused manner works well against Goldblum's wisecracking asshole, and the kitsch on-air shopping sequences are often very funny. DA

Holy Matrimony

(1994, US, 93 min)
d Leonard Nimoy. *p* William Stuart, David Madden, Diane Nabatoff. *sc* David Weisberg, Douglas S Cook. *ph* Bobby Bukowski. *ed* Peter E Berger. pd Edward Pisoni. *m* Bruce Broughton. *cast* Patricia Arquette, Joseph Gordon-Levitt, Armin Mueller-Stahl, Tate Donovan, John Schuck, Lois Smith, Courtney B Vance.

●This comedy thriller has Arquette, the 'Marilyn Monroe' of her local Midwestern State Fair, hot-footing it with amour Donovan to a Hutterite colony on the Alberta plains, there to hide from the FBI following a cash robbery. Donovan is only cautiously welcomed back from the land of temptation by elder Mueller-Stahl; but when he's seen off in a car accident, Hutterite law demands that Arquette must marry his 12-year-old brother. The elders hope the law will provoke her swift egress. Instead, she accepts. Matching the culture clash of *Witness* with a rock'n'roll movie would be daunting for even the most inventive director. Leonard Nimoy plays it straight. Arquette is a vital, kooky presence, but here she looks merely embarrassed. WH

Holy Smoke

(1999, US, 115 min)
d Jane Campion. *p* Jan Chapman. *sc* Anna Campion, Jane Campion. *ph* Dion Beebe. *ed* Veronika Jenet. *pd* Janet Patterson. *m* Angelo Badalamenti. *cast* Kate Winslet, Harvey Keitel, Pam Grier, Julie Hamilton, Tim Robertson, Sophie Lee, Daniel Wylie, Paul Goddard, George Mangos, Kerry Walkers.

●Far from her suburban Sydney home, backpacker Ruth Barron (Winslet) is so touched by an Indian guru that even mum turning up with tales of dad's imminent demise can't lure her back. Ironically, mum's own asthmatic reaction to Delhi leads to Ruth escorting her to Oz, where awaits wizard 'cult exiter' PJ Waters (Keitel), hired by the family to rid Ruth of her plans to become one of her mentor's wives. His three-step process takes place in a cabin in the desert, a suitably scorched, remote arena for a blazing battle of wills that takes them beyond conventional power struggles into a heady realm of love, hate, doubt and desire. With its switches in tone, from searing psycho-drama to broad, exuberant comedy, its sometimes purposeful, sometimes meandering narrative and its bright hues, the film initially seems an efficient if uneven entertainment. As it progresses, however, with Ruth and PJ moving into ever murkier territory, it becomes easier to discern a thematic thread: how we're all conditioned, and how we must interrogate traditional assumptions to discover our real selves. It's brave, adventurous, refreshingly frank – qualities also marking the performances, particularly those of the leads. GA

Holy Terror

see Communion

Hombre

(1966, US, 111 min)
d Martin Ritt. *p* Martin Ritt, Irving Ravetch. *sc* Irving Ravetch, Harriet Frank Jr. *ph* James Wong Howe. *ed* Frank Bracht. *ad* Jack Martin Smith, Robert E Smith. *m* David Rose. *cast* Paul Newman, Fredric March, Richard Boone, Diane Cilento, Martin Balsam, Barbara Rush, Cameron Mitchell, Frank Silvera.

●Based on a novel by Elmore Leonard which works a neat variation on the *Stagecoach* theme, this has Newman first outcast by the passengers who think he is an Apache, then elected as their guardian angel when they are menaced by bandits. White, but brought up by Apaches to believe that civilisation is hell, Newman very sensibly – but to humanitarian protests from his flock –

starts coldly and calculatedly picking off the bandits one by one before they are ready for him. Developing its own liberal conscience, the film has Newman finally see the light – 'People must help each other' – so that he perishes (nobly rather than ironically) in making a doomed bid to rescue Rush, staked out by the bandits to die in the sun. Even so this is one of Ritt's best films, with fine performances all round, impressive Death Valley locations, and superlative camera-work from James Wong Howe. TM

Hombre del Rio Malo, El

see Bad Man's River

Hombre Mirando al Sudeste

(1986, Arg, 110 min)
d Eliseo Subiela. *cast* Lorenzo Quinteros, Hugh Soto, Ines Verengo.

●Faced with a patient who insists he's from another planet, a doctor reacts with incredulity, yet the better he gets to know his subject, the more inclined he is to believe him, even if this means challenging his most basic assumptions. A straight-faced Argentinian drama, which Hollywood would doubtless have played as farce. TJ

Hombres armados

see Men with Guns

Home Alone

(1990, US, 103 min)
d Chris Columbus. *p/sc* John Hughes. *ph* Julio Macat. *ed* Raja Gosnell. *pd* John Muto. *m* John Williams. *cast* Macaulay Culkin, Joe Pesci, Daniel Stern, John Heard, Roberts Blossom, Catherine O'Hara, John Candy, Kieran Culkin.

●After *Planes, Trains and Automobiles*, writer/producer John Hughes turns once more to the nightmare of travel, this time from a child's perspective. Set to spend Christmas in Paris with parents and assorted relatives, young Kevin (Culkin) wishes everyone would just disappear, a desire granted when he is accidentally left behind by his preoccupied parents (Heard and O'Hara). But the novelty starts to wear off when a couple of burglars (Stern and Pesci, excellent) target the house. Hughes confidently mixes elements of precocious self-awareness with childlike wonderment: the boy truly believes his dream has become manifest, so he gorges on junk food and television until the reality of the situation brings loneliness and fear. Broader in humour, however, with an inconsistency of mood not helped by abrupt editing and Columbus' sometimes self-conscious direction, *Home Alone* lacks the sustained tension of the earlier film. CM

Home Alone 2: Lost in New York

(1992, US, 120 min)
d Chris Columbus. *p/sc* John Hughes. *ph* Julio Mucat. *ed* Raja Gosnell. *pd* Sandy Veneziano. *m* John Williams. *cast* Macaulay Culkin, Joe Pesci, Daniel Stern, Catherine O'Hara, John Heard, Devin Ratray, Brenda Fricker, Eddie Bracken, Tim Curry.

●This routine sequel has a trio of nice cameos, but no surprises. Through mix-ups, Kevin (Culkin) gets detached from the family again, and while they fly on holiday to Florida, he fetches up alone in New York. Bad burglars Harry (Pesci) and Marv (Stern) turn up again to rob a toyshop of its Christmas takings, which owner Mr Duncan (Bracken) has earmarked for a children's hospital. Wandering about Central Park, Kevin encounters a sinister-seeming but actually lonely pigeon lady (Fricker), and advises her about love and life (much as he did the sinister-seeming but lonely snow-shoveller in the earlier film). His sojourn at the Plaza Hotel is fraught with suspicious staff (Curry), but his battle with the burglars – surely the point of these flicks – mistakes the pain threshold for hilarity. BC

Home Alone 3

(1997, US, 102 min)
d Raja Gosnell. *p* John Hughes, Hilton A Green. *sc* John Hughes, *ph* Julio Macat. *ed* Bruce Green, Malcolm Campbell, David Rennie. *pd* Henry Bumstead. *m* Nick Glennie-Smith. *cast* Alex D Linz, Olek Krupa, Rya Kihlstedt, Lenny Von Dohlen, David Thornton, Haviland Morris, Kevin Kilner.

●In place of Macaulay Culkin, comes mop-top newcomer Linz, and in place of Pesci and Stern, a quartet of similarly stupid espionage thieves. What remains the same is yet another chain of 'ouch that hurt' cartoon set-pieces. The first two films saw Kevin inadvertently left alone because of mistakes made by his preoccupied parents. Here writer/producer John Hughes has manufactured a situation whereby Alex, suffering from chicken pox, is intentionally left at home by his working parents. This low-IQ nonsense is becoming very tiresome. DA

Home and the World, The (Ghare-Baire)

(1984, Ind, 140 min)
d/sc Satyajit Ray. *ph* Soumendu Roy. *ed* Dulal Dutt. *ad* Ashoke Bose. *m* Satyajit Ray. *cast* Soumitra Chatterji, Victor Banerji, Swatilekha Chatterji, Gopa Aich, Jennifer Kapoor, Manoj Mitra.

●Based on a novel by Rabindranath Tagore and set in 1908 Bengal, this tells of a woman who, after being persuaded by her wealthy but liberal husband to break with the tradition of female seclusion, falls not only for his old friend but also for the latter's revolutionary ideals, intended to unite Bengalis against the British colonial policy of 'divide and rule' regarding Hindus and Moslems. Although it becomes clear where Ray's political sympathies lie, his customary sense of balance and generosity towards his characters prevents him from tipping the scales in facile fashion, while motivations and issues are presented with great clarity. One could accuse the film of being talky and static, but the formal elegance, sure sense of pace, and uniformly excellent performances guarantee a moving experience. GA

Home at Seven (aka Murder on Monday)

(1952, GB, 85 min, b/w)
d Ralph Richardson. *p* Maurice Cowan. *sc* Anatole de Grunwald. *ph* Jack Hildyard, Ted Scaife. *ed* Bert Bates. *ad* Fred Pusey, Vincent Korda. *m* Malcolm Arnold. *cast* Ralph Richardson, Margaret Leighton, Jack Hawkins, Meriel Forbes, Campbell Singer, Michael Shepley.

●Bank clerk Richardson returns home from work to quiet suburbia at his usual time, only to be told by his wife (Leighton) that he's been missing for 24 hours. Suffering from apparent amnesia, he gets another shock when evidence incriminates him in theft and murder committed during the time he can't account for. Richardson had starred on stage in RC Sherriff's source play. His air of concerned bewilderment is just right for this modest suspenser; and in his only time behind the camera, he makes a decent fist of maintaining tension, although the proscenium arch never seems far away. TJ

Home Before Midnight

(1978, GB, 111 min)
d/p Pete Walker. *sc* Murray Smith. *ph* Peter Jessop *ed* Alan Brett. *ad* Michael Pickwood. *m* Jigsaw. *cast* James Aubrey, Alison Elliot, Mark Burns, Juliet Harmer, Richard Todd, Debbie Linden, David Hamilton.

●A confused but salacious piece of exploitation which takes the tale of a London Lolita and places it in an unconvincing world of '70s rock'n'roll. Its only possible appeal is to the sexist who might be able to identify with David Hamilton's line about the girl at his side: 'I've got to handle this little hot shot here.' The script rarely rises above the asinine until the end, where it becomes truly offensive, making a case for believing that little girls who cry 'rape' are probably lying. HM

Homebodies

(1973, US, 96 min)
d Larry Yust. *p* Marshal Backlar. *sc* Larry Yust, Howard Kaminsky, Bennett Sims. *ph* Isidore Mankofsky. *ed* Peter Parasheles. *ad* John Retsek. *m* Bernardo Segall. *cast* Paula Trueman, Frances Fuller, William Hansen, Ruth McDevitt, Peter Brocco, Ian Wolfe, Douglas Fowley.

●Low budget black comedy about six senior citizens who, refusing to vacate their condemned brownstone haven for a gaunt, antiseptic block of flats, begin a murderous guerilla war against their opponents. The subsequent mayhem is depicted with much humour, nicely controlled tension, and – somehow – with dignity. Towards the end, the group's leader (76-year-old Paula Trueman, a saner version of Ruth Gordon) gets carried away into excess, and the film goes off the rails with her. But on balance it's remarkably convincing. GB

Homeboy

(1988, US, 116 min)
d Michael Seresin. *p* Alan Marshall, Elliott Kastner. *sc* Eddie Cook. *ph* Gale Tattersall. *ed* Ray Lovejoy. *pd* Brian Morris. *m* Eric Clapton, Michael Kamen. *cast* Mickey Rourke, Christopher Walken, Debra Feuer, Thomas Quinn, Kevin Conway, Antony Alda, Jon Polito, Reubén Blades.

●Rourke has usually played knock-nutty, but this time, as an ageing boxer from Arkansas, at least he has an alibi. Johnny Walker winds up at a run-down seaside resort, is befriended by small-time entertainer and petty thief Wesley (Walken), and falls for The Nice Girl (Feuer) who runs the carousel and pony rides. Resisting Wesley's plan to rob some orthodox Jews of diamonds, Johnny fights for the big purse, although he knows that with his cranium one blow can kill him (he needs the money to repair the carousel, see). Rourke is credited with the story, and it's a compendium of his screen characteristics – the inner tenderness postulate that can only be reached by cracking the kernel against the wall for reel upon reel, the preposterous walk, gobbing in two kinds (blood and saliva), lots of up-ended bottles, and very sparse dialogue. Sentimental and self-indulgent, with snot added. BC

Homecoming (Si Shui Liu Nian)

(1984, HK, 97 min)
d Yim Ho. *p* Jenny Choe. *sc* Kong Liang. *ph* Poon Hang-sang. *ed* Kin-Kin. *pd* Cheong Supping. *m* Kitaro. *cast* Siqin Gaowa, Josephine Koo, Xie Weixiong, Zhou Yun.

●After ten years in Hong Kong, a girl returns for a visit to her native village on the mainland. Cue for a familiar clash between nostalgia and necessity, busy fleshpots and rustic backwaters, the 'free' and the Communist worlds. But effortlessly confounding expectations, Yim Ho's film sidesteps all the pitfalls with grace, wit and even touches of quaint fantasy. A real charmer. TM

Homecoming, The

(1973, US/GB, 114 min)
d Peter Hall. *p* Ely Landau. *sc* Harold Pinter. *ph* David Watkin. *ed* Rex Pike. *pd* John Bury. *cast* Cyril Cusack, Ian Holm, Michael Jayston, Vivien Merchant, Terence Rigby, Paul Rogers.

●*The Homecoming* was first performed in 1965 after Pinter had taken a five-year pause over full-length stage work. Significantly, it concerns the return of academic son Teddy (Jayston) to his North London familial nest, a smouldering pyre of hatred and resentment presided over by Max (Rogers). This demonic Alf Garnett, when not spitting contempt for his poovy bachelor brother (Cusack), waxes hateful, rapturous and disgusted about his dead wife, best friend, and homebound sons, loquacious pimp Lenny (Holm) and dumbbell pugilist Joey (Rigby). In this battle of wills, Teddy's enigmatic wife (Merchant) finally triumphs, while hubby returns to his US campus unsure of his ability to operate 'on' situations rather than 'in' them. Hall has produced his best work for the cinema with this sensitive adaptation: a riveting, often hilarious piece (with outstanding performances from Holm, Cusack and Rogers) which makes one quite melancholy about Pinter's self-willed decline into a Bakerloo Line imitation of Samuel Beckett. SGr

Home for the Holidays

(1995, US, 103 min)
d Jodie Foster. *p* Peggy Rajski, Jodie Foster. *sc* WD Richter. *ph* Lajos Koltai. *ed* Lynzee Klingman. *pd* Andrew McAlpine. *m* Mark Isham. *cast* Holly Hunter, Anne Bancroft, Robert Downey Jr, Charles Durning, Dylan McDermott, Steve Guttenberg, Cynthia Stevenson, Claire Danes, Geraldine Chaplin, Austin Pendleton, David Strathairn.

●'Wait till you see your father's organ – he can't keep his hands off it!' No, not a line from some forgotten British farce, but Bancroft to Hunter in

Jodie Foster's family-relationships comedy that stoops to fart jokes and dotty maiden aunts before divesting itself of a none-too-pressing homily: 'We don't have to like each other – we're family.' Hunter is Claudia, who makes the pilgrimage home for Thanksgiving with a bad cold and a worse temper: her life's a mess. Her parents (Bancroft and Durning) bicker constantly, her brother (Downey) shows up with a mysterious male friend (McDermott), and her sister (Stevenson) can't contain her resentment towards all and sundry. It's shaping up to be a hell of a weekend. A modest film (in every sense) which pushes the gags too hard. TCh

Home from the Hill

(1959, US, 150 min)
d Vincente Minnelli. *p* Edmund Grainger. *sc* Harriet Frank Jr, Irving Ravetch. *ph* Milton Krasner. *ed* Harold F Kress. *ad* George W Davis, Preston Ames. *m* Bronislau Kaper. *cast* Robert Mitchum, Eleanor Parker, George Peppard, George Hamilton, Luana Patten, Everett Sloane, Constance Ford.
● In this small-town America melodrama, Mitchum plays the coolly licentious head of a Texan family, Parker his frigid wife. Both vie for the allegiance of their son (Hamilton), coming to terms with his patriarchal inheritance until he discovers the existence of an illegitimate half-brother (Peppard). Then all hell breaks loose as the sins of the father are visited on the son. Minnelli's intelligent use of scope, colour and all the technical resources Metro could offer would make it watchable enough. His ability to present the network of relationships between his quartet of characters so that all four are presented in a sympathetic light, and particularly his portrayal of the central oedipal psychodrama (Hamilton is excellent), make it explosive viewing. RM

Home Game (Heimspiel)

(1999, Ger, 101 min)
d Pepe Danquart. *p* Mirjam Quinte. *sc* Pepe Danquart. *ph* Michael Hammon. *ed* Mona Bräuer. *m* Walter W Cikan, Eddie Siblik. *with* Jörg Beslé, Liselotte Beutner, Mike Bullard, Ralf Czygan, Lorenz 'Lenz' Funk, Günther Gasch, Bernd Karrenbauer.
● This excellent, stylishly photographed doc introduces East Berlin's prize ice hockey team the Eisbären (the Polar Bears) and their fans, and takes off to explore how deeply divided Germany still is. Along the way we learn a good deal about the team's history (for years East Germany had a league consisting of just two teams, playing each other 18 times a season), about the effect of capitalism on sport, and about what the fans get out of it. TCh

Home in Indiana

(1944, US, 103 min)
d Henry Hathaway. *p* André Daven. *sc* Winston Miller. *ph* Edward Cronjager. *ed* Harmon Jones. *ad* James Basevi, Chester Gore. *m* Hugo Friedhofer. *cast* Walter Brennan, Jeanne Crain, June Haver, Charlotte Greenwood, Lon McCallister, Ward Bond.
● Homespun Americana to the max as orphan McCallister is packed off to uncle Walter's farm, teams with local lasses Crain and Haver, then finds his métier as a champion horse breeder. Brightly coloured and impossibly optimistic, it's a missive from another era, and not recommended to those of a curmudgeonly disposition. Later remade as the Pat Boone vehicle *April Love*. TJ

Home-Made Melodrama

(1982, GB, 51 min)
d Jacqui Duckworth. *cast* Lyndey Stanley, Joy Chamberlain, Cass Bream, Madelaine McNamara, Joy Watkins.
● This frankly autobiographical account of the director's painful experiences developing a lesbian ménage à trois remains caught in a cloistered domestic world that, despite a real concern to open up a wider perspective, masks the political dimension and external pressures enclosing intimate emotions. Its address is to a committed, if limited audience, which will doubtless disregard the mostly unimaginative visuals and 'home-made' technical quality dictated by lack of money, equipment and expertise. SJo

Home of Our Own, A

(1993, US, 104 min)
d Tony Bill. *p* Dale Pollock, Bill Borden. *sc* Patrick Duncan. *ph* Jean Lépine. *ed* Alex Hubert. *pd* James L Schoppe. *m* Michael Convertino. *cast* Kathy Bates, Edward Furlong, Clarissa Lassig, Sarah Schaub, Miles Feulner, Soon-Teck Oh.
● Frances Lacey (Bates) has no money, no husband, six kids and a broken-down '48 Plymouth. Undeterred, she settles on an abandoned farm shack in a middle-American pothole and convinces its owner, Mr Moon (Soon-Teck Oh), to let the Lacey clan set up house there in return for chores and odd jobs. With bits and pieces from the local scrap merchant, and a great deal of determination, the family begins to fix up the place. Hardship takes its toll, however, and the eldest son, Shayne (Furlong), becomes increasingly embittered towards his indomitable mom. It's hard to imagine much of an audience for this gritty, poignant movie. Tony Bill presents a vision of working-class American experience that is, perhaps, a shade sentimental, but still largely authentic and unpatronising. With notably tough and tender performances from Bates and Furlong, and good work from cinematographer Jean Lepine, this is a solid, small-scale film with its heart in the right place. TCh

Home of the Brave

(1986, US, 91 min)
d Laurie Anderson. *p* Paula Mazur. *sc* Laurie Anderson. *ph* John Lindley. *ed* Lisa Day. *pd* David Gropman. *cast* Paula Mazur, Laurie Anderson, William S Burroughs, Joy Askew, Adrian Belew, Richard Landry, Dollette McDonald.
● Written and directed by Anderson, this is far removed from the monochrome epics of her earlier shows, relying on colour imagery, dance, and fair helpings of Anderson's spooky humour. All the hits and album faves are here, although the adoption of the rock format contradicts the initial, idiosyncratic charm of her work. Fans should flock, while others are guaranteed 91 minutes of the strangest pop entertainment ever. If there is a flaw, it's in Anderson's work itself, which pretends to comment on weapon culture and information technology, when in fact all that Anderson is doing is playing around with signs. JG

Hometown (Furusato)

(1930, Jap, 86 min, b/w)
d Kenji Mizoguchi. *sc* Bin Kisaragi, Shuichi Hatamoto, Tadashi Kobayashi. *ph* Tatsuyuki Yokota, Yoshio Mineo. *m* Toyoaki Tanaka. *cast* Yoshie Fujiwara, Shizue Natsukawa, Fujiko Hamaguchi, Kunio Tamura, Heitaro Doi, Isumu Kosugu.
● Mizoguchi's first sound film (some of it's talkie, some with music and intertitles) may feature a fairly crude *Star Is Born*-style melodramatic story, broad humour and some distinctly unsubtle cutting, but it still impresses for its fluid camerawork and its sympathy for the woman whose singer husband, attracted by fame, fortune and a femme fatale, gradually grows more distant and uncaring. Very much of its time, but memorable for a dazzling party scene with jazzed-up Dvorak. (Original running time 107 minutes, but all extant copies 86 minutes.) GA

Homeward Bound: The Incredible Journey

(1993, US, 85 min)
d Duwayne Durham. *p* Franklin R Levy, Jeffrey Chernov. *sc* Caroline Thompson, Lida Wolverton. *ph* Reed Smoot. *ed* Jonathan P Shaw, Jay Cassidy, Michael Kelly, Brian Berdan. *pd* Roger Cain. *m* Bruce Broughton. *cast* Kim Greist, Don Adler, Ed Bernard; voices: Michael J Fox, Sally Field, Don Ameche, Don Adler.
● Disney's live-action hit *The Incredible Journey* (1963) saw two dogs and a cat trek across Canada on their way home. This is the remake. Verities are passed from age to youth; races and creeds bonded by adversity. The creatures are voiced – Fox is the tearaway pup, Ameche the venerable hound, Field the Himalayan cat. Totally uncorrupting. WH

Homework (La Tarea)

(1990, Mex, 85 min)
d Jaime Humberto Hermosillo. *p* Pablo Barbachano. Francisco Barbachano. *sc* Jaime Humberto Hermosillo. *ph* Toni Kuhn. *ad* Laura Santa Cruz. *m* Luis Arcaraz. *cast* María Rojo, José Alonso, Xanic Zepeda, Christopher.
● Virginia (Rojo) sets up a hidden video camera, discards jeans for figure-hugging dress, and awaits a knock on the door. Enter Marcelo (Alonso), an old paramour of the preening variety. Hermosillo's inventive and deceptive sex comedy comes on like a minimalist *sex, lies and videotape* revisited à la Mexicana, though the spin here is placing a woman in control of the camera. This is a less cool relative of the serious 'filming and fucking' movies from the likes of Soderbergh and Atom Egoyan, but here the meditations on power, pornography, voyeurism, the camera as weapon of control, fantasy and the like, have a more formal, old-fashioned feel. It's shot in ten-minute takes to fake real time, and being forced to view the proceedings from the static camera position is like participating in an experiment, with the viewer as object. Still, it's good to be implicated now and again. WH

Homicidal

(1961, US, 87 min, b/w)
d/p William Castle. *sc* Robb White. *ph* Burnett Guffey. *ed* Edwin Bryant. *ad* Cary Odell. *m* Hugo Friedhofer. *cast* Glenn Corbett, Patricia Breslin, Jean Arless, Eugenie Leontovich, Alan Bunce, Richard Rust.
● One from cult shock-meister William Castle, of *The Tingler* fame. Castle himself introduces this passably creepy tale about an Old Dark House, a murderous blonde, a paralysed old Swedish woman, and a mysterious young man. Not quite his loopiest film, it cribs brazenly from Psycho, to good effect. This time, the gimmick-fixated maestro didn't go as far as wiring up cinema seats or dangling creepy crawlies from the ceiling; instead, the faint-hearted were offered a 'fright break' in which to make their excuses and leave. JRo

Homicide

(1991, US, 102 min)
d David Mamet. *p* Michael Hausman, Edward R Pressman. *sc* David Mamet. *ph* Roger Deakins. *pd* Michael Merritt. *m* Alaric Jans. *cast* Joe Mantegna, William H Macy, Natalija Nogulich, Ving Rhames, Vincent Guastaferro, Rebecca Pidgeon, Lionel Mark Smith.
● Mamet's third film comes from a disturbing thriller, *Suspects*, by William Caunitz. Honest cop Bobby Gold (Mantegna) is taken off a hot case to babysit a Jewish family. An old pawnbroker has been murdered, and the family, fearing an anti-semitic conspiracy, believe that they're next. Gold starts out resenting the assignment, but gradually begins to accept their take on events. His long-suppressed Jewishness surfaces. The twist at the end is devastating, forcing you to view the film as a character study rather than a thriller, which places it in the *Detective Story* and *The Offence* bag. Unfortunately, the transitions are sometimes abrupt and unconvincing, despite Mantegna's intensity. We can see how bigotry drives him away from his adoptive police family toward his own people, but not how his new militancy escalates so steeply. Gripping, though. BC

Homme Amoureux, Un

see Man in Love, A

Homme au Chapeau de Soie, L' (The Man in the Silk Hat)

(1983, Fr, 97 min, b/w)
d/sc Maud Linder. *ed* Suzanne Baron, Pierre Gillett. *m* Jean-Marie Sénia. *with* Max Linder.
● Max Linder (1883–1925) was a pint-sized, dapper dynamo who bustled through his films wearing a permanent grin, partly benevolent, partly mischievous. By about 1910 he had fixed his persona – man about town, the silk topper his emblem, precise movement and fastidious timing his hallmark – and in a series of one-reelers (*Max the Bullfighter*, *Duellist*, *Skier*, etc) became internationally popular. Having overseen the revival of her father's later Hollywood movies Maud Linder now presents this biographical tribute, largely dealing with Max's pre-WWI work, via a profusion of extracts and actuality footage. She wraps things up swiftly and with discretion. With a year-old baby and on the eve of starting a new movie, Max and his wife cut their wrists and bled to death. 'No explanation came to light,' says Maud Linder tonelessly. BBa

Homme de Désir, L'

(1970, Fr, 100 min, b/w)
d/p/sc Dominique Delouche. *ph* Jean Bourgoin. *ed* Maryse Siclier. *ad* Georges Richar. *m* JS Bach. *cast* François Timmerman, Eric Laborey, Emmanuelle Riva, André Falcon.

●Delouche's film is reverentially shot in the style of Bresson: the pious, anguished hero inhabiting a world in which everyday objects are infused with mystical significance, and where natural sounds serve to emphasise the individual's essential isolation in a universe where man's only possible relationship is directly with God. Uneasily grafted on to this act of homage is the *ménage à trois* tale of a man's infatuation for a hitchhiking youth he has picked up, a relationship which develops with all due encouragement from his wife. The story is reminiscent of Chabrol's *Les Biches*, in fact, and is best enjoyed as a thriller. The contrast between the urbane, relaxed world of the man, and the underworld night existence of the youth, is handled with a remarkable sureness until the working-out of the respective fates of the two characters, when our sympathy is shifted from the corrupt impotence of the man to the unworthy pocket-picking boy unwillingly drawn into the man's cruel and ultimately masochistic pursuit.

Homme de Marrakech, L' (Our Man in Marrakesh/ That Man George)

(1965, Fr/It/Sp, 92 min)
d Jacques Deray. *sc* Henri Lanoë, José Giovanni, Jacques Deray. *ph* Henri Raichi. *ed* Paul Cayatte. *ad* Eduardo Torrede la Fuente. *m* Alain Goraguer. *cast* George Hamilton, Claudine Auger, Alberto De Mendoza, Daniel Ivernel, Tiberio Murgia.

●Dubbed '60s international hotchpotch with Hamilton and cohorts planning a gold bullion heist in the Moroccan desert. It's the sort of would-be-hip fluff that Belmondo had made popular in France and overseas (*L'Homme de Rio*, etc), but Hamilton's glazed presence doesn't do the business. TJ

Homme de ma vie, L' (The Man in My Life)

(1995, Fr/Can, 103 min)
d Jean-Charles Tacchella. *p* Gabriel Boustani. *sc* Jean-Charles Tacchella. *ph* Dominique Le Rigoleur. *ed* Marie-Aimée Debril. *pd* Serge Douy. *m* Raymond Alessandrini. *cast* Maria de Medeiros, Thierry Fortineau, Jean-Pierre Bacri, Anne Letourneau, Ginette Garcin, Ginette Mathieu.

●A very moderate comedy of manners, à la Woody Allen: Fortineau's impecunious bookseller Maurice affects an air of misanthropic mystery but needs de Medeiros' coquettish Aimée to put him at ease with the world. She, however, has determined to marry money, donning slinky red dress and cheesy grin to snare bastard restaurant-critic Malcolm (Bacri). The resolution is not unexpected, but along the way writer/director Tacchella toys with the audience to exasperating, if not terribly interesting effect. TJ

Homme de Rio, L' (That Man from Rio)

(1964, Fr/It, 120 min)
d Philippe de Broca. *p* Alexandre Mnouchkine, Georges Dancigers. *sc* Jean-Paul Rappeneau, Ariane Mnouchkine, Daniel Boulanger, Philippe de Broca. *ph* Edmond Séchan. *ed* Françoise Javet. *m* George Delerue. *cast* Jean-Paul Belmondo, Françoise Dorléac, Jean Servais, Simone Renant, Milton Ribeiro, Adolfo Celi.

●A delightfully preposterous thriller (the McGuffin is some stolen Amazonian treasure), wittier than any of the Bond spoofs that subsequently flooded the market and a good deal racier than *Raiders of the Lost Ark*. Handsomely shot on location in Brazil, with Belmondo as the cheerfully indestructible hero who cliffhangs, climbs buildings, imitates Tarzan, parachutes almost into the jaws of a crocodile, and does his best to cope with the enchantingly unpredictable Dorléac (late lamented sister of Catherine Deneuve). The dubbing in the transatlantic version isn't too disastrous. TM

Homme est Mort, Un

see Outside Man, The

Homme est une femme comme les autres, L'

see Man Is a Woman

Homme et une Femme, Un (A Man and a Woman)

(1966, Fr, 102 min)
d Claude Lelouch. *sc* Claude Lelouch, Pierre Uytterhoeven. *ph* Claude Lelouch. *ed* Claude Barrois, Claude Lelouch. *ad* Robert Luchaire. *m* Francis Lai. *cast* Anouk Aimée, Jean-Louis Trintignant, Pierre Barouh, Valérie Lagrange, Simone Paris, Paul le Person.

●The notoriously schmaltzy but still undeniably eye-catching film in which Aimée and Trintignant conduct an intense and often unhappy affair against an elegant, colourful background. Lelouch tricks it out with every elaborate cinematic effect he can beg, borrow or steal, ransacking both Welles and Godard for titillating devices which look good but never even begin to mesh with the subject matter (note in particular the 360 degree tracking shot at the end). In some ways the film's sheer zest and the talented cast might have won the day, were it not for Francis Lai's dreadfully corny and monotonous theme music. DP

Homme qui Aimait les Femmes, L'

see Man Who Loved Women, The

Homme qui Dort, Un (A Man in a Dream)

(1974, Fr/Tun, 90 min, b/w)
d Bernard Queysanne. *sc* Georges Perec. *p* Pierre Neurisse. *ph* Bernard Zitzermann. *ed* Andrée Davanture. *m* Groupe OIO. *cast* Jacques Spiesser; voice: Shelley Duvall.

●A hypnotic solo by its mute hero, a young man who decides to withdraw from the world and whose mental journal of his experience is confided to us by a girl's voice off-screen, *Un Homme qui Dort* is an astonishing tour de force. What distinguishes it from all those ventures in spiritual navel-gazing is that his decision to not-be is purely practical, and the parabola he traces from boredom to terror – as he gradually detaches himself to float free within an indefinable menace – is brilliantly conveyed by the other leading character in the film: the city of Paris. The influence of Franju is unmistakable, and wholly beneficial. TM

Hommes femmes Mode d'emploi

see Men, Women: User's Manual

Homme sur les Quais, Les

see Man by the Shore, The

Hondo

(1953, US, 84 min)
d John Farrow. *p* Robert Fellows. *sc* James Edward Grant. *ph* Robert Burks, Archie J Stout. *ed* Ralph Dawson. *ad* Alfred Ybarra. *m* Emil Newman, Hugo Friedhofer. *cast* John Wayne, Geraldine Page, Ward Bond, Michael Pate, James Arness, Rodolfo Acosta, Lee Aaker, Leo Gordon, Lassie.

●John Wayne's favourite John Wayne movie. Louis L'Amour's source novel is a variation on *Shane*, with Wayne as the eponymous stranger, a cavalry scout, whose manly ways recommend him to a homesteader (Page) and her boy, though here her husband's a ne'er-do-well the Duke kills in self-defence. The film extends liberal respect to the Indians, and even implicitly endorses a romance between a white woman and the half-breed Hondo. Page won an Oscar nomination for this, her first film role, but Wayne's guileless performance is even better: gently self-mocking, while still every inch the embodiment of the conviction that 'a man ought to do what he thinks is best'. Robert Burks' cinematography is a major plus (the film was originally released in 3-D, but there's precious little gimmickry). A rarity until restored by the John Wayne Society for re-release in 1995. TCh

Honest

(2000, GB/Fr, 110 min)
d David A Stewart. *p* Eileen Gregory, Michael Peyser. *sc* David A Stewart, Dick Clement, Ian La Frenais. *ph* David Johnson. *ed* David Martin. *pd* Michael Pickwoad. *m* David A Stewart. *cast* Nicole Appleton, Peter Facinelli, Natalie Appleton, Melanie Blatt, James Cosmo, Jonathan Cake, Rick Warden, Annette Badland, Sean Gilder, Corin Redgrave.

●Jewel heists, gender-bending and love in the Swinging '60s, with Nicole and Natalie Appleton and Melanie Blatt (three quarters of UK popsters All Saints), as Gerry, Mandy and Jo – East End sisters turned gangsters. As soon as you hear the Mockney accents, however, it's clear that absent member Shaznay was wise to avoid this particular affair. When a robbery flounders, Gerry encounters American journalist Daniel (Facinelli) – who provides further eye candy, while murmuring: 'It's a two pound cab ride from Carnaby Street to the East End, yet it's a different world.' Despite glimmers of effective comedy from hapless Jo and unhinged Mandy, who trades blow jobs for firearms, this is on the whole directionless, hackneyed and riddled with hysterical clichés, among them a sleazy fanzine editor and a traumatized father. AHa

Honest Courtesan, The

see Dangerous Beauty

Honey and Venom

(1990, GB, 41 min)
d Jun Mori. *cast* Georgia Byng, Tom Knight, Emma Croft.

●An intriguing but faintly over-aesthetic short feature, made in London by a young Japanese director. A woman painter, in a lifeless apartment that she must have designed herself, finds her privacy invaded by a drunken man from the noisy party upstairs. The incident seems trivial, but the reverberations are massive: the woman's house of cards begins to collapse. Mori films without comment or explanation, trusting his emphasis on details to tease out the unspoken implications. Hard to imagine the method working in a full-length feature, but he just about gets away with it at this length. TR

Honey, I Blew Up the Kid

(1992, US, 89 min)
d Randal Kleiser. *p* Dawn Steel, Edward S Feldman. *sc* Thom Eberhardt, Peter Elbling, Garry Goodrow. *ph* John Hora. *ed* Michael A Stevenson, Harry Hitner. *pd* Leslie Dilley. *m* Bruce Broughton. *cast* Rick Moranis, Marcia Strassman, Robert Oliveri, Lloyd Bridges, John Shea, Keri Russell, Ron Canada, Amy O'Neill.

●Kleiser's follow-up to *Honey, I Shrunk the Kids* is a disappointment. Much of the problem is that it's impossible to place a 112-foot high baby in peril, or excite the sort of concern that was generated by the miniaturised children. This big baby gurgles happily as he picks up cars with adults in them and toddles about grabbing neon signs in Las Vegas, threatened only – and briefly – by a man with a tranquilliser dart in a helicopter. The rest of the problem is lousy back-projection, with ill-matched scenes in which the proper-sized people seem to be responding several yards to the left and right of the stimulus. Very boring. BC

Honey, I Shrunk the Kids

(1989, US, 93 min)
d Joe Johnston. *p* Penny Finkelman Cox. *sc* Ed Naha, Tom Schulman. *ph* Hiro Narita. *ed* Michael A Stevenson. *pd* Gregg Fonseca. *m* James Horner *cast* Rick Moranis, Matt Frewer, Marcia Strassman, Kristine Sutherland, Thomas Brown, Jared Rushton, Amy O'Neill, Robert Oliveri.

●While batty inventor Szalinski (Moranis) boffins away in the attic, his kids Amy and Nick (O'Neill, Oliveri) are left to shift for themselves. Russ Thompson (Frewer), his sports-jock neighbour, looks on in scorn, but is comically insensitive to the needs of his own two sons (Brown, Rushton). The Thompson boys whack a baseball through the attic window, the as yet imperfect shrinking machine is activated, and the warring youngsters wind up tiny, swept into a bin-bag and dumped at the bottom of the garden. During their trek back, there are wonderful moments like a flight *on* the bumble bee, a fall into a giant flower, and the adoption of a discarded lego brick as a night shelter. Perhaps unavoidably, there are inconsistencies of scale, and though the c haracterisation is generally warm and believable, there's still the 'Your sister's all right – for a *gurl!*' syndrome. Sterling entertainment, though. SFe

Honeymoon (Luna de Miel)

(1959, Sp/GB, 109 min)
d Michael Powell. *p* Cesáreo Gonzalez, Michael Powell. *sc* Michael Powell, Luis Escobar. *ph* Georges Périnal. *ed* Peter Taylor, John Victor Smith. *ad* Ivor Beddoes. *m* Mikis Theodorakis, Manuel de Falla. *cast* Anthony Steel, Ludmilla Tcherina, Antonio, Leonide Massine, Rosita Segovia, Pepe Nieto.

●The last of Powell's ballet films, unfortunately not a patch on *The Red Shoes*, or even *The Tales of Hoffmann*. A slim story – prima ballerina Tcherina travelling on honeymoon with Steel in Spain, and being drawn into performing again by Antonio – is thankfully enlivened by a couple of beautifully shot ballet sequences (music by Theodorakis and de Falla) choreographed by Antonio and Massine. Many of Powell's customary themes are there, including that of the ambivalence of artistic creation, but delivered in fairly lifeless fashion compared to his best work. That said, Georges Périnal's Technicolor camerawork is as stunning as ever. GA

Honeymoon in Vegas

(1992, US, 105 min)
d Andrew Bergman. *p* Mike Lobell. *sc* Andrew Bergman. *ph* William A Fraker. *ed* Barry Malkin. *pd* William A Elliott. *m* David Newman. *cast* Nicolas Cage, Sarah Jessica Parker, James Caan, Pat Morita, Anne Bancroft, Peter Boyle, Seymour Cassel.

●A long awaited wedding between the maternally fixated Jack Singer (Cage) and his boisterous bride Betsy (Parker) seems finally on the cards when the couple take a break in Vegas. But the decks are stacked against Jack, who loses big in a poker game to arch knave Tommy Korman (Caan, sublimely slimy). In lieu of payment, Tommy demands a weekend with Betsy, who reminds him of his long-lost wife. Will Tommy steal Jack's ace from under his nose? Beautifully written and directed by Bergman, this paradoxically modern slice of nostalgia energetically revives the long mourned 'oddball' comedy. For once, Cage is pleasantly understated, playing the straight guy beset by nine shades of madness: lunatic mothers, deranged mobsters, singing Chieftains, and sky-diving Elvis impersonators by the dozen, they're all here in this joyous, uplifting romp. MK

Honeymoon Killers,The

(1969, US, 106 min, b/w)
d Leonard Kastle. *p* Warren Steibel. *sc* Leonard Kastle. *ph* Oliver Wood. *ed* Stan Warnow, Richard Brophy. *m* Gustav Mahler. *cast* Shirley Stoler, Tony Lo Bianco, Mary Jane Higby, Doris Roberts, Kip McArdle, Barbara Cason.

●This tells, bleakly, unsentimentally, in shady b/w tricked out with a scratchy Mahler soundtrack, the true tale of Martha Beck and Ray Fernandez: she a grotesquely overweight nursing sister from Mobile, Alabama; he a Latin gigolo living off aged spinsters and widows, tricking them of their money and, after a torrid team-up with Martha, bumping them off in a manner no way sanitised in Kastle's hands. The couple were electrocuted in 1951, but the film shows them not so much as monsters as a weird, passionate appendage to the love and marriage stakes glibly represented by the collection of down-home mommas, randy would-be wives and patriotic widows on whom the couple prey (with Martha posing as Ray's sister, though so overcome with jealousy that attempted suicide, murder, and eventually betrayal to the police ensue). An eerie, negected classic of its kind. (Martin Scorsese's first feature as director, until he got canned.) SGr

Honey Pot, The

(1966, US/It, 150 min)
d Joseph L Mankiewicz. *p* Charles K Feldman, Joseph L Mankiewicz. *sc* Joseph L Mankiewicz. *ph* Gianni Di Venzanzo. *ed* David Bretherton. *pd* John De Cuir. *m* John Addison. *cast* Rex Harrison, Susan Hayward, Cliff Robertson, Capucine, Edie Adams, Maggie Smith, Adolfo Celi, Herschel Bernardi.

●Adapted from a play out of a novel based on Ben Jonson's *Volpone*, Mankiewicz's screenplay finds a contemporary millionaire (Harrison in fine waspish form) inspired after a performance of Jonson's play to re-enact the same plot device on his three former mistresses (Hayward, Capucine and Adams) – posing as a dying man to test their reactions. The structure continually threatens to cave in under the weight of over-fussy dialogue and confusing plot twists, but the high-grade cast (with a pleasingly restrained Maggie Smith as the hypochondriac Hayward's nurse), and some sumptuous photography by Gianni Di Venanzo, make it highly watchable. If cinema and stage farce have to get in bed together, this is one of the more fruitful unions around. DT

Honeysuckle Rose

(1980, US, 119 min)
d Jerry Schatzberg. *p* Gene Taft. *sc* Carol Sobieski, William D Wittliff, John Binder. *ph* Robby Müller. *ed* Aram Avakian, Norman Gay, Marc Laub, Evan Lottman. *pd* Joel Schiller. *m* Willie Nelson. *cast* Willie Nelson, Dyan Cannon, Amy Irving, Slim Pickens, Joey Floyd, Diana Scarwid, Emmylou Harris.

●Schatzberg might be a very urban cowboy (*Panic in Needle Park*, *Puzzle of a Downfall Child*, *Sweet Revenge*, etc), but there's no evidence here of slick, Altman-style condescension to country 'n' western culture. Instead there's an unforced equation of the upfront emotional currency of C&W lyrics with a simple triangular plotline pared down from *Intermezzo* (singer Nelson and wife Cannon almost come apart over the lure of the road and one more infidelity). Nothing new under the sun – but the easy-going fringe benefits are well worth the ticket: Nelson's a natural, and the duets with Cannon are pure gold. PT

Honkers, The

(1971, US, 103 min)
d Steve Ihnat. *p* Arthur Gardner, Jules Levy. *sc* Steve Ihnat, Stephen Lodge. *ph* James Crabe. *ed* Tom Rolf. *m* Jimmie Haskell. *cast* James Coburn, Slim Pickens, Lois Nettleton, Anne Archer, Richard Anderson, Ted Eccles, Jim Davis.

●Ageing rodeo rider Lew Lathrop (Coburn) may not still be at his competitive best, but the cameraderie and womanising of the touring circuit continue to exert a strong pull when he makes a rare visit home to New Mexico to his estranged spouse Nettleton. Melancholy, slow, closely detailed post-Western drama which lets rip with the moralising at the close as Lew's partner Clete (Pickens) is trampled to death by a bucking bull. Coburn has a watchable charm, though *Junior Bonner* and *J.W. Coop* (both also from the early '70s) rode the same range with greater distinction. TJ

Honky Tonk Freeway

(1981, US, 107 min)
d John Schlesinger. *p* Don Boyd, Howard W Koch Jr. *sc* Edward Clinton. *ed* Jim Clark. *ad* Edwin O'Donovan. *m* George Martin, Elmer Bernstein. *cast* William Devane, Beau Bridges, Teri Garr, Beverly D'Angelo, Hume Cronyn, Jessica Tandy, Geraldine Page.

●Ealing in its heyday might have coaxed some mild satire out of the idea of a small town prepared to go to any lengths to ensure that it is not bypassed by a new freeway. Officials swallow bribes but fail to deliver, the townsfolk resort to terrorist tactics, hordes of grotesques converge on the town bringing the tourist money all the ghoulish greed is about. The material is there, but in Schlesinger's hands the whole thing is battered into a shapeless, witless mess as a barrage of slapstick gags, each more crudely conceived and badly timed than the last, leaves one numb with disbelief. Even Abbott and Costello were funnier. TM

Honkytonk Man

(1982, US, 123 min)
d/p Clint Eastwood. *sc* Clancy Carlile. *ph* Bruce Surtees. *ed* Ferris Webster, Michael Kelly, Joel Cox. *pd* Edward C Carfagno. *m* Steve Dorff. *cast* Clint Eastwood, Kyle Eastwood, John McIntire, Alexa Kenin, Verna Bloom, Matt Clark, Barry Corbin, Jerry Hardin.

●One of the most oddball and heroically unfashionable superstar vehicles ever contrived. Only Eastwood, with the rest of Hollywood obsessed with taking us up where we belong, could have the audacity to play a comparatively odious and untalented country singer dying of consumption during the Depression. Much of the film is concerned with his picaresque pilgrimage to a Nashville audition along with nephew (played by Eastwood's son) and grandpappy (the excellent McIntire), and it culminates in a last-chance recording session during which the singer nearly coughs himself to death. The whole thing veers wildly in quality, and no Eastwood-hater should go within a mile of it; but few lovers of American cinema could fail to be moved by a venture conceived so recklessly against the spirit of its times. DP

Honno

see Lost Sex

Honorary Consul, The (aka Beyond the Limit)

(1983, GB, 104 min)
d John MacKenzie. *p* Norma Heyman. *sc* Christopher Hampton. *ph* Philip Meheux. *ed* Stuart Baird. *pd* Allan Cameron. *m* Stanley Myers. *cast* Michael Caine, Richard Gere, Bob Hoskins, Elpidia Carrillo, Joaquim de Almeida, A Martinez, Geoffrey Palmer, Leonard Maguire, Zohra Segal.

●Deep in torpid, guerilla-riddled, brothel-centric South America (a currently popular destination for film-makers and a land Graham Greene's fiction has visited many times, always carrying two battered suitcases labelled 'Betrayal' and 'Errant Catholicism'), honorary British consul Charlie Fortnum (Caine) is mistakenly kidnapped. And no one really wants him back. MacKenzie directs with a literal flourish, brandishing Hoskins, charm-like, as an unlikely Argentinian policeman. But even a rabbit's foot as solid as Hoskins cannot ward off the evil charm of Gere reworking his unloving *American Gigolo* persona that is all wrong for Dr Eduardo Plarr, a character to whom machismo is totally alien. One wonders what Greene, whose thoughts on the cinema and charlatans are always worth hearing, would have to say. Yet even he could hardly find fault with Caine who, as the anti-heroic middle-aged lush (a character he first began to sketch in *Educating Rita*) gives the performance of his life. FD

Honor Thy Father

(1973, US, 92 min)
d Paul Wendkos. *p* Harold D Cohen. *sc* Lewis John Carlino. *ph* Arthur J Ornitz, Howard Schwartz. *ed* Richard Halsey. *ad* Rodger Maus. *m* George Duning. *cast* Joseph Bologna, Raf Vallone, Brenda Vaccaro, Richard S Castellano, Joe De Santis, Marc Lawrence.

●Based on Gay Talese's account of the '60s Mafia war between the Organisation and recalcitrant member Joe 'Bananas' Bonanno, Wendkos' film (actually made for TV) compares favourably with the more ambitious but superficial *The Godfather*. Against the familiar settings of anonymous rooms, city backlots, and streets at night, a feeling of futility erodes the Mafia assumptions of honour. An archetypal slob of a gunman giggles his way through old gangster movies, yet reads Sartre's *Being and Nothingness*. For all the shootings, the two most graphic deaths are natural: heart attack and cancer. Above all, there's the bewilderment of Bonanno's daughter-in-law (Vaccaro). Already a nervous wreck, her patience snaps when two more gangsters turn up expecting to eat. Apart from a weak ending and a plot that both needs and uses a narrator, an altogether intelligent film. CPe

Honourable Mr Wong, The

see Hatchet Man, The

Honour Among Thieves

see Touchez pas au Grisbi

Hoodlum Empire

(1952, US, 98 min, b/w)
d/p Joseph Kane. *sc* Bruce Manning, Bob Considine. *ph* Reggie Lanning. *ed* Richard Van Enger. *ad* Frank Arrigo. *m* Nathan Scott. *cast* Brian Donlevy, Claire Trevor, Luther Adler, John Russell, Forrest Tucker, Vera Ralston, Gene Lockhart, Grant Withers, Taylor Holmes.

●Designed to cash in on the televised Kefauver hearings, this was originally intended as a Frank Costello biopic. When George Raft refused to play his old buddy, the project metamorphosed into the story of Joe Gray (Russell), brought up in the rackets by his mobster uncle (Adler) until combat service in WWII teaches him the all-American values his army buddies are ready to die for. In feeble imitation of the vastly superior *The Enforcer*, a string of flashbacks from the Senate Committee hearings reveal how Gray tries to go straight in a rural community; how the Mob's expanding gambling activities encroach; and how he is deliberately inculpated so that, should threats fail and he decide to testify, his evidence will be compromised. Absurdly melodramatic when it isn't being pompous, sermonising or hopelessly simplistic about syndicate activities, the film is kept afloat solely by the fine cast (Adler, Russell and Trevor, in particular). TM

Hook

(1991, US, 144 min)
d Steven Spielberg. *p* Kathleen Kennedy, Frank Marshall, Gerald R Molen. *sc* Nick Castle, Malia Scotch Marmo. *ph* Dean Cundey. *ed* Michael Kahn. *pd* Norman Garwood. *m* John Williams. *cast* Dustin Hoffman, Robin Williams, Julia Roberts, Bob Hoskins, Maggie Smith, Caroline Goodall, Charlie Korsmo, Amber Scott, Laurel Cronin, Phil Collins.

●Spielberg's *Hook* looks like a theme park. The *Peter Pan* plot has been rejigged to suit Hollywood's dreary preoccupation with redemption; not that it matters much, since the story is largely becalmed so that we can wallow in the production values. The sets are variable but often unpleasant on the eye. To say that the best thing about the film is the miniaturised Roberts as Tinkerbell, wearing motorised Arthur Rackham wings, gives some idea how duff it is. The $60 million-plus enterprise first nosedives in the sprawling sequence where the Lost Boys train the paunchy grown-up Peter Pan (Williams) for combat against arch-enemy Hook (Hoffman), who has kidnapped his children. Hoffman's Old Etonian accent slips a bit; Hoskins as Hook's sidekick has nothing to do, and does it raucously. By the end, Peter has ditched his Wall Street cell phone and rediscovered the child in himself, so that's all right. BC

Hoop Dreams

(1994, US, 171 min)
d Steve James. *p/sc* Fred Marx, Steve James, Peter Gilbert. *ph* Peter Gilbert. *ed* Fred Marx, Steve James, Bill Haugse. *m* Tom Yore. *with* William Gates, Arthur Agee, Emma Gates, Ken Curtis, Sheila Agee, Arthur 'Bo' Agee.

●Steve James' essential inner-city epic chronicles the lives of two young blacks growing up in a Chicago housing project. At 14, basketball prodigies Arthur Agee and William Gates win scholarships to a suburban high school, St Joseph's. Then their fortunes diverge. William looks set to follow in the footsteps of St Joe's favourite son, all-star Isiah Thomas. Arthur doesn't make the cut. Skinny and immature, he finds himself back in the inner city when his parents fall behind on the fees. Over the next four years, however, the boys' lives are to intersect more than once, and in unexpected ways. A three-hour documentary about basketball is probably not most people's idea of a night out, but this one rewards the effort. James and his collaborators shot more than 250 hours of footage, and the cumulative emotional power is simply devastating. Sport is the only dream Arthur and William are allowed, their only ticket out of the ghetto, but they also have to carry the weight of their parents' aspirations – and if they make it, they will become role models for thousands of kids just like them. Unforgettable. TCh

Hooper

(1978, US, 99 min)
d Hal Needham. *p* Hank Moonjean. *sc* Thomas Rickman, Bill Kerby. *ph* Bobby Byrne. *ed* Donn Cambern. *ad* Hilyard Brown. *m* Bill Justis. *cast* Burt Reynolds, Jan-Michael Vincent, Sally Field, Brian Keith, John Marley, Robert Klein, James Best, Adam West.

●The rich vein of 'innocent' anarchy running through Burt Reynolds comedy showcases around this time is mined again to good effect as his *Smokey and the Bandit* persona transmutes seamlessly into the ace Hollywood stuntman of the title, and director Needham (an ex-stuntman himself) slips effortlessly into a lightweight satire of the movie biz and an almost Hawksian action-comedy of male-group professionalism. Formula stuff as Reynolds' over-the-hill stuntman faces the toll of his injuries, and battles against the multiple hazards of low budget, high risk production, irate girlfriend and challenge from younger rival. Plus, naturally, The Big Stunt. But it's all surmounted by the irrepressible and irresistible Reynolds ego, which accommodates both the hagiography of a Tammy Wynette soundtrack dirge and the self-mockery of a screening of stunt footage from *Deliverance* to a sleeping audience. PT

Hoosiers (aka Best Shot)

(1986, US, 115 min)
d David Anspaugh. *p* Carter De Haven, Angelo Pizzo. *sc* Angelo Pizzo. *ph* Fred Murphy. *ed* C Timothy O'Meara. *pd* David Nichols. *m* Jerry Goldsmith. *cast* Gene Hackman, Barbara Hershey, Dennis Hopper, Sheb Wooley, Fern Persons, Chelcie Ross.

●Back in 1951, a hick high school basketball team could achieve self-respect just by getting into the State Finals. Or so this cloyingly nostalgic sports movie would have us believe. Hackman plays the belligerent coach who, in knocking the underdogs into shape, is absolved of his past sins. Actually, the film starts promisingly, with his entry into the tight-knit rural community complicated by suspicion and by his prickly relationship with fellow-teacher Hershey. There's also a brilliant cameo by Hopper as the sometime player turned town drunk whom Hackman redeems by taking him on as his assistant. However, once Hackman's uncompromising integrity lures the team's recalcitrant star player out of self-imposed retirement and the team hits a winning streak, it's just a case of going through the hoops. NF

Hoots Mon!

(1939, GB, 77 min, b/w)
d Roy William Neill. *sc* Roy William Neill, Jack Henley, John Dighton. *ph* Basil Emmott. *ed* Leslie Norman. *ad* Norman Arnold. *cast* Max Miller, Florence Desmond, Hal Walters, Davina Craig, Garry Marsh, Gordon McLeod.

●Ramshackle vehicle for the Cheeky Chappie, who used to appear on stage through a trapdoor, 'up from the sewers, like the jokes you're going to get': his act is carefully deodorised here, though he still makes a pretence of keeping a wary eye on the wings in expectation of being hauled off-stage. The excuse for a plot has him get rather more than he bargained for when he accepts a challenge from a rival Scots comedienne (Desmond) to try his Cockney comedy on her native folk. Fast-moving, cheerful and a mite tiresome, it is enlivened by Desmond's impersonations of Miller himself, Syd Walker, Bette Davis and – best of all – a hideously simpering Elisabeth Bergner. TM

Hope and Glory

(1987, GB, 112 min)
d/p/sc John Boorman. *ph* Philippe Rousselot. *ed* Ian Crafford. *pd* Anthony Pratt. *m* Peter Martin. *cast* Sebastian Rice Edwards, Geraldine Muir, Sarah Miles, David Hayman, Sammi Davis, Derrick O'Connor, Ian Bannen.

●Boorman's autobiographical film about family life during the Blitz is subversively light on the blood, sweat, tears and sacrifice, and a joy throughout. Seen through the eyes of nine-year-old Bill Rohan (Rice Edwards), the war was a wonderland of superior fireworks displays every night, and adventure playgrounds of rubble and ruined houses. Dad joins up and Mum starts to see a lot of Dad's best friend Mac, while teenage sister Dawn runs wild with GIs. 'They know we're mad on jam' warns Mum, regarding a captured tin of German jam with deep suspicion; a barrage balloon breaks free of its moorings, bumps about the rooftops, and has to be shot down by a Home Guard firing squad. Tragedy is touched upon only in the episode of an orphan who refuses to leave her bombed home, and is offered a shrapnel collection by a sympathetic child. When the Rohan family are burned out, they take refuge with eccentric Granddad (Bannen, astonishingly good) at Shepperton on the river. The wind in the willows and the willow on the cricket ball – Boorman's long-lost England communicates its affectionate poetry. BC

Hope Floats

(1998, US, 114 min)
d Forest Whitaker. *p* Lynda Obst. *sc* Steven Rogers. *ph* Caleb Deschanel. *ed* Richard Chew. *pd* Larry Fulton. *m* Dave Grusin. *cast* Sandra Bullock, Harry Connick Jr, Gena Rowlands, Mae Whitman, Michael Paré, Rosanna Arquette.

●A small town Texas beauty queen, Birdee Pruitt (Bullock) returns to the nest after her husband announces he's in love with another – on a TV talk show. Her taxidermist mother (Gena Rowlands) is not immediately sympathetic, but that's all the excuse Birdee needs to take a bottle to bed for the foreseeable future, to the disgust of daughter Bernice (Whitman). We're squarely in *Terms of Endearment* territory here. With such staples as the eccentric, wilful mother, the smart-mouthed kid, and the 'aw shucks' cowboy suitor (Connick), the movie sets itself up as a gentle, humanist riposte to the theatre of shock therapy presided over by the likes of Jerry Springer and Ricki Lake. Director Whitaker repeatedly betrays the material, however, with schmaltzy slow motion and tear jerking ballads. A touching scene between Birdee and her dad (an Alzheimer's sufferer) is spoiled with a cop out when she manages to break through, and Connick's philosophical handyman turns out to be – but of course! – an architect on the side. TCh

Hopscotch

(1980, US, 107 min)
d Ronald Neame. *p* Edie Landau, Ely Landau. *sc* Bryan Forbes, Brian Garfield. *ph* Arthur Ibbetson. *ed* Carl Kress. *pd* William J Creber. *m* Ian Fraser. *cast* Walter Matthau, Glenda Jackson, Herbert Lom, Sam Waterston, Ned Beatty, George Baker, David Matthau, Ivor Roberts.

●Despite the equal star billing, this is not another comic two-hander following up *House Calls* in pitting the misanthropic slobbishness of Matthau against the elegant bitchery of Jackson. Really it's a solo vehicle for Matthau as a CIA operative who, disciplined by demotion to a desk job, takes his revenge through an elaborate practical joke: mysteriously disappearing, he starts mailing – with the order soon out that he has got to be stopped – chapter by chapter instalments of his memoirs (with the promise of revelations to come) to intelligence agencies in the world's capitals. Less weakly scripted and directed, less reliant on globetrotting locations and technological hardware, it could have become a worthy successor to *Charley Varrick*; as it is, Matthau just about carries it. But only just. RM

Hora Mágica, A

see Magic Hour, The

Horizon (Horizont)

(1971, Hun, 87 min, b/w)
d Pál Gábor. *p* András Nemeth. *sc* Gyula Marosi, Pál Gábor. *ph* János Zsombolyai. *ed* Zoltán Farkas. *ad* Lászlo Duba. *m* János Gonda. *cast* Péter Fried, Lujza Orosz, Szilvia Marossy, Zoltán Vadász, József Madaras.

●This study of the contemporary Hungarian generation gap is unfortunately reminiscent of the British social dramas of the early '60s (a sequence from Anderson's *If*... is included by way of indirect tribute), with the jazz and pop music used reinforcing the period feel: a dance-hall sequence looks like something from early Beatle days. A teenage boy, representative of many his age, rejects all that his parents have fought and been imprisoned for. He drops out of school, quits his job, dreams of nihilism, and ends up working in a factory, the despair of his elders. The film is best at gauging the fundamental confusion that lies behind the boy's facade of toughness (illustrated when he carefully copies an acquaintance's man of the world mannerisms, much to the scorn of his schoolfriends). Coming down on the side of youth, it does invest them with a mobility that contrasts pointedly with the often sedentary older generation. But it is in its assertion that the old has to make way for the new that *Horizon* flounders. Given his hero's lack of stance, Gábor is left making detailed observations and little else.

Horizons West

(1952, US, 81 min)
d Budd Boetticher. *p* Albert J Cohen. *sc* Louis Stevens. *ph* Charles P Boyle. *ed* Ted J Kent. *ad* Bernard Herzbrun, Robert Clatworthy. *m* Joseph Gershenson. *cast* Robert Ryan, Julie Adams, Rock Hudson, John McIntire, Raymond Burr, James Arness, Dennis Weaver.

●Still apprentice work, so don't expect anything quite so stylishly spare as the Boetticher-Randolph Scott cycle from this Western about two brothers returning to Texas after the Civil War, one to get rich quick by cattle rustling and terrorisation, the other to become his nemesis as town marshal. Burt Kennedy's superb scripting was probably the decisive factor in those later movies; here, despite impressive patches, the script by Louis Stevens too often settles for crude routine, while Hudson makes a slightly laborious meal of the good brother. But Ryan's performance as the gangster-tycoon reverberates in a manner that sometimes anticipates Boetticher's classic *The Rise and Fall of Legs Diamond*. TM

Horloger de St Paul, L' (The Clockmaker/The Watchmaker of Saint-Paul)

(1973, Fr, 105 min)
d Bertrand Tavernier. *p* Raymond Danon. *sc* Jean Aurenche, Pierre Bost, Bertrand Tavernier. *ph* Pierre-William Glenn. *ed* Armand Psenny. *ad* Jean Mandaroux. *m* Philippe Sarde. *cast* Philippe Noiret, Jean Rochefort, Jacques Denis, Yves Afonso, Sylvain Rougerie, Christine Pascal.
●For his film-making debut, ex-critic Tavernier took a novel by Simenon, made the lightly polemical choice to collaborate on the screenplay with veterans Aurenche and Bost (victims of Truffaut's early New Wave ire), set the result in Lyon, and emerged with a work of old-fashioned precision that the craftsman of the title would doubtless have been proud of. Noiret is superb as the eponymous 'horloger', realigning his self-willed solitude into credible relationships with his son, on the run with girlfriend after killing a swinish security guard, and the sympathetic police inspector (Rochefort) in charge of the case; while the physical and political ambience is rendered with a classically 'invisible' aura of authenticity. PT

Horror Chamber of Dr Faustus, The

see Yeux sans Visage, Les

Horror Express (Pánico en el Transiberiano)

(1972, Sp/GB, 90 min)
d Eugenio Martin. *p* Bernard Gordon. *sc* Arnaud D'Usseau, Julian Halevy. *ph* Alejandro Ulloa. *ed* Bob Dearberg. *ad* Ramiro Gomez Guadiana. *m* John Cavacas. *cast* Christopher Lee, Peter Cushing, Telly Savalas, Silvia Tortosa, Jorge Rigaud, Alberto de Mendoza, Julio Peña.
●An inferior reworking of *The Thing from Another World*, which still manages to keep interest alive despite some poor special effects, a flat jokiness and stereotype characters. The idea itself is intriguing enough: anthropologist Lee's ancient fossil found in China, believed to be the missing link, comes back to life on the Trans-Siberian railway, adding the knowledge of its victims to its own. From their first greeting of 'Well, well, look who's here!', Lee and his arch-rival Cushing, at their most urbane, ensure that it remains watchable, while the express train setting keeps it all moving at a better speed than it perhaps deserves. CPe

Horror Hospital

(1973, GB, 91 min)
d Antony Balch. *p* Richard Gordon. *sc* Antony Balch, Alan Watson. *ph* David McDonald. *ed* Robert Dearberg. *ad* David Bill. *m* De Wolfe. *cast* Michael Gough, Robin Askwith, Vanessa Shaw, Ellen Pollock, Skip Martin, Dennis Price, Kurt Christian.
●Anticipating the day of the video nasty, Balch – who had collaborated with William Burroughs on *Towers Open Fire* and *The Cut-Ups* – here twisted the conventional elements of the horror movie to a new level of grotesquerie. The plot concerns a mad Pavlovian doctor, whose body is a hulk of third-degree burnt tissue, boring holes in young persons' brains in an attempt to master their minds. The object is somehow to persuade beautiful ladies to fuck him, appearances notwithstanding; but despite turning into mindless zombies, they are still resistant to his charms. Hence much frustration vented by scything heads off with a Boadicea chariot of a Rolls-Royce, Cocteau-like biker henchmen given to beating people up, and mutant dwarves chopping skulls with hatchets or burning flesh with cigarettes. All of which takes place in a charming castle masquerading as a health farm. Cliché after cliché is ruthlessly hammed into a telling stomach-gripper: one for sophisticates of undergrowth horror of the Chas Addams variety. JDuC

Horror of Death

see Asphyx, The

Horror of Dracula

see Dracula

Horrors of the Black Museum

(1959, GB, 81 min)
d Arthur Crabtree. *p* Jack Greenwood. *sc* Aben Kandel, Herman Cohen. *ph* Desmond Dickinson. *ed* Geoffrey Muller. *ad* Wilfred Arnold. *m* Gerard Schurmann. *cast* Michael Gough, Graham Curnow, June Cunningham, Shirley Ann Field, Geoffrey Keen, Gerald Andersen, Beatrice Varley.
●The first of Anglo-Amalgamated's loose trilogy of Sadian horror movies – the others being *Circus of Horrors* and Michael Powell's infinitely superior *Peeping Tom* – anticipates Powell's interest in voyeurism with its opening scene of a woman's eyes being gouged out by a pair of viciously spiked binoculars. Thereafter, as Gough's novelist devises a series of horrible crimes in order to make his work more appealing to a sensation-hungry readership, the film continues as a tacky catalogue of gratuitously nasty tortures and murders. Indeed, it's as lascivious and leering in its approach as the great British public it purports to condemn. Lurid and innuendo-laden, it's an intriguing oddity. GA

Horse Feathers

(1932, US, 70 min, b/w)
d Norman Z McLeod. *sc* Bert Kalmar, Harry Ruby, SJ Perelman, Will B Johnstone. *ph* Ray June. *songs* Bert Kalmar, Harry Ruby. *cast* The Marx Brothers, Thelma Todd, David Landau, Robert Greig, Nat Pendleton, Reginald Barlow.
●The title means bunk or baloney, a fitting epithet for the Brothers' second screen original for Paramount, where the lads and their writers threw sanity to the winds with a wildly disorganised parody of academic life. Groucho is president of Huxley College, where no student appears to be under thirty-five. Chief subjects on the curriculum seem to be football, sex, the delivery of heinous puns (haddock/headache) and the refurbishing of old vaudeville routines (the biology lecture). The Brothers have never been so chaotic or so aggressively funny. GB

Horseman on the Roof, The

see Hussard sur le toit, Le

Horsemen, The

(1970, US, 109 min)
d John Frankenheimer. *p* Edward Lewis. *sc* Dalton Trumbo. *ph* Claude Renoir. *ed* Harold F Kress. *pd* Pierre-Louis Thévenet. *m* Georges Delerue. *cast* Omar Sharif, Jack Palance, Leigh Taylor-Young, David De, Peter Jeffrey, Mohammad Shamsi, George Murcell, Eric Pohlmann, Saeed Jaffrey.
●The story, adapted by Dalton Trumbo from Joseph Kessel's novel, is a good and suitably emblematic one about a champion Afghan horseman and the famous last-of-the-line stallion who undertake a perilous journey to regain the honour the man feels he has lost after his defeat in the ceremonial game of Buzkashi. On the journey he loses a leg, is confronted by his groom and an untouchable woman who want to kill him, meets a blind scribe who tells him the tale of his blindness, and a nomad who fights his scraggy one-horned sheep against a champion ram. Each encounter contains within it the seeds of his own predicament, from which a moral can be drawn. Sadly, the whole thing comes grindingly to grief on compromise (not least the absurdities of Hollywood stars speaking pidgin and rubbing shoulders with genuine Afghan extras). Some good things survive: the Afghan landscape, the horse-riders (including Sharif's double), and Palance (the only actor who seems to know what it's all about). VG

Horse's Mouth, The

(1958, GB, 95 min)
d Ronald Neame. *p* John Bryan. *sc* Alec Guinness. *ph* Arthur Ibbetson. *ed* Anne V Coates. *ad* Bill Andrews. *m* Ken Jones. *cast* Alec Guinness, Kay Walsh, Renee Houston, Mike Morgan, Robert Coote, Arthur MacRae, Michael Gough, Ernest Thesiger.
●Uneasy adaptation of Joyce Cary's marvellous novel (itself an integral part of a trilogy) about the anti-social nature of genius. Guinness builds a clever, painstakingly detailed character study as the scruffily disreputable Gulley Jimson, an ageing artist prepared to go to any lengths to ensure that he can go on setting down his vision in paint. But despite using John Bratby paintings to represent that vision, the film itself is more concerned with the artist's eccentricities than with his creativity. Flatly directed, loosely scripted, it emerges as little more than a lightweight slice of Ealing-style whimsy. TM

Horse Soldiers, The

(1959, US, 120 min)
d John Ford. *p/sc* John Lee Mahin, Martin Rackin. *ph* William H Clothier. *ed* Jack Murray. *ad* Frank Hotaling. *m* David Buttolph. *cast* John Wayne, William Holden, Constance Towers, Althea Gibson, Hoot Gibson, Anna Lee, Russell Simpson.
●Underrated Civil War Western, leisurely and sometimes simplistic, but mostly quintessential Ford as Wayne's pragmatic colonel and Holden's humanitarian doctor debate (and embody) aspects of war while leading a Union cavalry patrol deep behind Confederate lines, with their conflict extended by the presence of a fiery Southern belle (a lovely performance from Towers) taken along for the ride because she's overheard their plans and bursting to undermine their mission. There's a magnificent payoff in the sequence where children from the military academy cheerfully march off to the tune of fife and drum to mount a last-ditch defence of the Confederacy, flimsy toy soldiers so ripe for the slaughter that the baffled enemy simply turn tail and flee. TM

Horse Thief (Daoma Zei)

(1986, China, 88 min)
d Tian Zhuangzhuang. *sc* Zhang Rui. *ph* Hou Yong, Zhao Fei. *ed* Li Jingzhong. *ad* Huo Jianqi. *m* Qu Xiaosong. *cast* Tseshang Rigzin, Dan Jiji, Jayang Jamco, Gaoba, Daiba.
●This is Zhuangzhuang's dream project: a film about the real Tibet, from the hardship and cruelty of life on the plains to the splendour and mystery of Buddhist ceremonial, a film about life and death in the Buddhist scheme of things. The story is told in pictures, not words. Norbu is a horse thief, expelled from his clan, forced to become a nomad, pitching his tent wherever he can find casual work. He and his wife are devout Buddhists, regularly visiting the temples to turn the prayer-wheels, but their son falls sick and dies. Norbu reaches his lowest ebb when a tribe hires him to carry the death-totem in a ritual exorcism of a plague of anthrax. In desperation, he returns to his clan to beg to be taken back. Filmed on locations in Tibet, Gansu and Qinghai and acted by local people, it offers the most awesomely plausible account of Tibetan life and culture ever seen in the west. It's one of the few films whose images show you things you've never seen before. TR

Horse Whisperer, The

(1998, US, 169 min)
d Robert Redford. *p* Robert Redford, Patrick Markey. *sc* Eric Roth, Richard LaGravenese. *ph* Robert Richardson. *ed* Tom Rolf, Freeman Davies, Hank Corwin. *pd* Jon Hutman. *m* Thomas Newman. *cast* Robert Redford, Kristin Scott Thomas, Sam Neill, Dianne Wiest, Scarlett Johansson, Chris Cooper, Cherry Jones.
●Redford's Tom Booker is nothing less than the perfect man: stoical, wise, warm, at home in the world, ruggedly handsome and – most poignantly – ultimately elusive. This is horseshit. Redford is a thoughtful, attentive director, but where *The Bridges of Madison County* recognised that romance takes two, this movie, based on the novel by Nicholas Evans, is altogether more solipsistic – it's a film-maker's love letter to himself. Scott Thomas does her best with a severely compromised post-feminist role as a careerist wife and

mother, who drives across country to throw herself at the feet of horse trainer Booker. Her daughter (Johansson) is recovering from a riding accident which killed her friend and traumatised her horse. Tom tames the daughter first, then mother, and finally the quadruped – but patiently, over two and three-quarter painstakingly elongated hours of gorgeous scenery and weather to die for. Scott Thomas can only squint at her co-star, halo'd against yet another sunset: these are the aesthetics of the shampoo commercial, soft soap for adolescent girls of all ages. TCh

Hors la vie (Out of Life)

(1991, Fr/It/Bel, 97 min)
d Maroun Bagdadi. *p* Jacques Perrin, *sc* Maroun Bagdadi. *ph* Patrick Blossier. *ed* Luc Barnier. *pd* Dan Weil. *m* Nicola Piovani. *cast* Hippolyte Girardot, Rafic Ali Ahmad, Hussein Sbeity, Habib Hammoud, Magdi Machmouchi, Hassan Farhat.

● When Patrick Perrault (Girardot), a French photographer covering the war in Beirut, is taken hostage, his life turns into a waking nightmare. Kept blindfold in an airless, initially darkened room, prey to injury, illness and sheer terror, Perrault alternates between simply struggling to survive and trying to persuade the more communicative of his continually changing captors to help him escape. Lebanese director Bagdadi's gripping thriller is exemplary of its kind. Neither flinching from nor sensationalising the violence, humiliation and sordid circumstances of Perrault's ordeal (inspired by the real-life experiences of Roger Auque), the film comes across as frighteningly authentic. The captors are never just faceless villains, but rounded, often sympathetic characters evoking the variety of causes at work in the war. Bagdadi never takes sides or offers easy answers, and Girardot's powerhouse performance renders Perrault's fear remarkably palpable. GA

Hospital

(1970, US, 84 min, b/w)
d/p Frederick Wiseman. *ph* William Brayne. *ed* Frederick Wiseman, Susan Primm.

● Wiseman's fourth film, one of his celebrated vérité projects on American institutions: a series of despairing (or blackly comic) vignettes from the low priority end of the health/wealth equation, shot with comprehensive austerity at Metropolitan Hospital in New York City. As with most of Wiseman's films of this period, a marshalling of evidence that's angrily illustrative of symptoms of the 'system's' malaise, but mute with regard to analysis of their cause or their cure. PT

Hospital, The

(1971, US, 102 min)
d Arthur Hiller. *p* Howard Gottfried. *sc* Paddy Chayefsky. *ph* Victor J Kemper. *ed* Eric Albertson. *ad* Gene Rudolf. *m* Morris Surdin. *cast* George C Scott, Diana Rigg, Barnard Hughes, Nancy Marchand, Stephen Elliott, Donald Harron, Roberts Blossom.

● Paddy Chayefsky's black comedy about the head of a hospital facing disasters all round him while he undergoes a bout of personal depression. It starts off with some marvellously cruel moments, and Scott's performance towers over the proceedings throughout. But Hiller's direction is pretty shoddy, while the script eventually loses its way and begins to look increasingly hysterical, at the same time shamelessly trivialising Scott's crisis (sex cures all ills). GA

Hostile Hostages

see Ref, The

Hot Blood

(1956, US, 84 min)
d Nicholas Ray. *p* Howard Welsch, Harry Tatelman. *sc* Jesse L Lasky Jr. *ph* Ray June. *ed* Otto Ludwig. *ad* Robert Paterson. *m* Les Baxter. *cast* Jane Russell, Cornel Wilde, Luther Adler, Joseph Calleia, Jamie Russell, Nina Koshetz, Helen Westcott, Mikhail Rasumny.

● While admittedly far from being one of Ray's best films, his tale of the stormy courtship of Wilde and Russell – gypsies from rival tribes introduced to one another by their parents for an arranged marriage which obeys the laws not only of tradition but financial enterprise – is fascinating both for its *mise-en-scène* and as an example of the director's interest in ethnology. Indeed, the two elements combine to create a boldly flamboyant celebration of ritual, the gypsies' love of music, dance and colourful costumes allowing Ray to transform a potentially clichéd romantic sparring session into lurid, restless images often strangely reminiscent of the musical. An oddity, then, but one distinguished by Ray's characteristic refusal to patronise or glamorise his characters. GA

Hot Box, The

(1972, US, 89 min)
d Joe Viola. *p* Jonathan Demme. *sc* Joe Viola, Jonathan Demme. *ph* Felipe Sacdalan. *ed* Ben Barcelon. *ad* Ben Otico. *m* Resti Umali. *cast* Andrea Cagan, Margaret Markov, Rickey Richardson, Laurie Rose, Carmen Argenziano, Charles Dierkop.

● Though co-scripted and produced by Jonathan Demme, a film so hampered by basic lack of skill that an interesting storyline becomes buried under a whole load of destructive ambiguities. Four American Peace Corps nurses are kidnapped by the Revolutionary Army of a Latin American republic to teach medical aid. Having tasted ill-treatment by Government forces, they become sufficiently convinced of the rightness of the cause to fight a bloody battle on the revolutionaries' side. Their 'enlightenment', though, remains a perfunctory foible of the plot. VG

Hot Dog...The Movie

(1983, US, 98 min)
d Peter Markle. *p* Edward S Feldman. *sc* Mike Marvin. *ph* Paul G Ryan. *ed* Stephen Rivkin. *ad* Don DeFina. *m* Peter Bernstein. *cast* David Naughton, Patrick Houser, Tracy N Smith, John Patrick Reger, Frank Koppola, James Saito, Shannon Tweed.

● Target audience: boys of 15 who don't get out much. Predicting that we might soon weary of downhill action, this virtually plotless ski picture is decorated with hot tub frolics and a wet T-shirt contest. Rivalry is set up between the blonde, blue-eyed underdog hero and a party of unconvincing Germans, reinforcing the impression that skiing is an all-white, all-male activity. The lone black guy in the crowd is startlingly noticeable. Despite the timidity of the film's ambitions, the footage of ski skirmishing is artfully shot and assembled and occasionally (ski-borne ballet!) bizarre. Lingering shots of ski-wear brand names are unlikely to be accidental. DO

Hotel

(2001, GB/It, 109 min)
d Mike Figgis. *p* Annie Stewart, Mike Figgis, Etchie Stroh. *sc* Mike Figgis. *ph* Patrick Alexander-Stewart. *pd* Franco Fumagalli. *m* Mike Figgis, Anthony Marinelli. *cast* Saffron Burrows, Valeria Golino, Salma Hayek, Danny Huston, Rhys Ifans, Lucy Liu, John Malkovich, Chiara Mastroianni, Ornella Muti, Burt Reynolds, Julian Sands, David Schwimmer, Heathcote Williams, La Yerbabuena.

● A sort of 'Grand Guignol Hotel', if you'll settle for the likes of Hayek and Schwimmer as modern-day Garbos and Barrymores. Another Figgis DV experiment, this 'life meets art' movie-movie about a project to update John Webster's Jacobean drama *The Duchess of Malfi* flirts just occasionally with *Timecode*-style split-screens. But far from choreographing its action he lets the cast off the leash to chew up one another and the scenery. Hard to make much sense of the florid mix of murky hotelier intrigue (the setting is Venice and the Lido's once glamorous art deco Hungaria Palace Hotel), crude film-biz caricatures and eye-rolling improvisation, nor indeed of the baiting hypocrisy in Figgis' indulgence of exploitative nudity and supposedly Dogme-style 'bad lighting'. NB

Hôtel de la Plage, L'

(1977, Fr, 111 min)
d Michel Lang. *p* Marcel Dassault. *sc* Michel Lang. *ph* Daniel Gaudry. *ed* Hélène Plemiannikov. *ad* Enrique Sonois. *m* Mort Shuman. *cast* Daniel Ceccaldi, Myriam Boyer, Francis Lemaire, Guy Marchand, Jean-Paul Muel, Anne Parillaud, Michel Robin, Anna Gael.

● Michel Lang's dated (arrested?) preoccupation with the supposed comic dimensions of adolescent skirt-chasing –already displayed in *A Nous les Petites Anglaises!* – re-emerges intact in this omnibus version of every dire French holiday-romance movie you've ever seen. Ticking off the predictable, prudishly 'permissive' permutations of a dozen or so stereotyped holidaymakers lends the film about as much narrative tension as filling in last week's football coupon. Lang alternately indulges and exploits the intended objects of his satire, and for the genuine toughness of a generically related film like *The Lacemaker*, merely substitutes a cloying sentimentality. PT

Hotel de Love

(1996, Aust, 97 min)
d Craig Rosenberg. *p* Michael Lake, David Parker. *sc* Craig Rosenberg. *ph* Stephen Windon. *ed* Bill Murphy. *pd* Simon Dobbin. *m* Brett Rosenberg. *cast* Aden Young, Craig Rosenberg, Saffron Burrows, Simon Bossell, Pippa Grandison, Ray Barrett, Julia Blake.

● A gaudy, kitsch, neo-romantic Australian comedy, in which, by some oversight, there are no ABBA tunes, but 10CC serve almost as well. Twins Rick (Young) and Stephen (Bossell) both carry a ten-year torch for Melissa (Burrows), an old flame from their teens. Rick is cynical and assertive, Simon shy and romantic. Melissa re-enters their lives at the titular honeymoon hotel, arm in arm with her fiancé, the very week that the twins' bickering parents are to renew their wedding vows. With its dapper cocktail piano player, theme suites, and 'Niagara Smalls' water feature, the de Love is quite tacky enough to complement a handful of enjoyably broad performances, but writer/director Rosenberg doesn't allow the dressing to swamp the salad – yes, it's occasionally crass, but it's also sometimes laugh-out-loud funny. TCh

Hôtel du Nord

(1938, Fr, 90 min, b/w)
d Marcel Carné. *sc* Henri Jeanson, Jean Aurenche. *ph* Armand Thirard, Louis Née. *ed* Marthe Gottié. *ad* Alexandre Trauner. *m* Maurice Jaubert. *cast* Annabella, Arletty, Louis Jouvet, Jean-Pierre Aumont, André Brunot, Jane Marken, Paulette Dubost, Bernard Blier, François Périer.

● A very likeable film, but for once denied a Jacques Prévert script, Carné's 'poetic realism' seems a trifle thin and hesitant in this populist yarn about a sleazy Parisian hotel and its inhabitants. While the sad young lovers (Annabella, Aumont) defy their jobless future in a suicide pact, Arletty and Jouvet run cynically away with the film as a pair of hardbitten rogues. But the real star is Trauner, whose studio sets – the mournful canal bank, the little iron bridge, the shabby rooms – are as amazingly evocative as Maurice Jaubert's score. TM

Hôtel du Paradis

(1986, GB/Fr, 113 min)
d Jana Bokova. *p* Simon Perry. *sc* Jana Bokova. *ph* Gérard de Battista. *ed* Bill Shapter. *pd* Patrick Weibel. *m* Rodolfo Mederos. *cast* Fernando Rey, Fabrice Luchini, Bérangère Bonvoisin, Hugues Quester, Marika Rivera, Carola Regnier, Michael Medwin, Juliet Berto, Lou Castel.

● Joseph (Rey) is an ageing actor whose movie career has been dogged by a succession of villainous cameos in Bond movies. Spending a working vacation in Paris, he attempts in vain to stage Camus' *The Fall*, his path crossing with the hotel's other variously estranged residents: Frédérique (Bonvoisin), a photographer on the run from her ex-boyfriend; Arthur (Luchini), a would-be film-maker; and Maurice (Quester), a theatre owner in the grip of severly diminishing returns. Bokova's feature debut is a melancholy portrait of exile which threatens to fall into sentimentality. Yet her conviction that apparent non-events frequently embody the most important episodes of human communication, and her resolute refusal to compromise atmosphere by forcing the narrative forward, constantly elevates her work above such mundanity. Casting Rey was a stroke of genius; the almost painful parallel between his own career and that of the beleaguered Joseph is turned into caustic humour by his fatally grim, understated delivery. MK

Hotel New Hampshire, The

(1984, US, 108 min)
d Tony Richardson. *p* Neil Hartley. *sc* Tony Richardson. *ph* David Watkin. *ed* Robert K

Lambert. *pd* Jocelyn Herbert. *m* Jacques Offenbach. *cast* Rob Lowe, Jodie Foster, Beau Bridges, Nastassja Kinski, Paul McCrane, Lisa Banes, Jennie Dundas, Wallace Shawn, Wilford Brimley, Joely Richardson, Matthew Modine, Dorsey Wright, Seth Green.

●Richardson was obviously a brave man to adapt and direct this screen version of John Irving's ultra-whimsical 1981 novel, with serial hotelier Bridges eventually leading his family to Vienna in his quest for the perfect establishment. Along the way, daughter Foster gets gang raped, her sibling Lowe takes out his frustrated incestuous desire on the other female cast members, Kinski plays a lesbian in a bear suit, and there's a farting dog for good measure. If it worked on the page, however, it's glassy and bewildering on screen, somehow contriving torpor from a catalogue of sensationalism and eccentricity. Irving ties the novel together with oft-repeated pat homilies on the human condition ('Keep passing the open windows'), but writer/director Richardson's aim for stylistic continuity through relentlessly jolly Offenbach arrangements on the soundtrack is an ultimately self-defeating gesture further distancing the viewer from the on-screen shenanigans. TJ

Hotel Sahara

(1951, GB, 96 min, b/w)
d Ken Annakin. *p* George H Brown. *sc* Patrick Kirwan, George H Brown. *ph* Jack Hildyard. *ed* Alfred Roome. *ad* Ralph Brinton. *m* Benjamin Frankel. *cast* Yvonne De Carlo, Peter Ustinov, David Tomlinson, Roland Culver, Albert Lieven, Bill Owen, Ferdy Mayne, Sydney Tafler, Anton Diffring.

●Ustinov plays it very broad as the accommodating North African hotel owner, caught in WWII, who switches allegiances whenever a new army comes to town. There are fitful hints that satire may be intended, but the end result is basically jingoistic farce. One plus is a fine comic turn from Yvonne De Carlo (soon to be Mrs Munster) as Ustinov's fiancée.

Hotel Sorrento

(1994, Aust, 112 min)
d/p Richard Franklin. *sc* Richard Franklin, Peter Fitzpatrick. *ph* Geoff Burton. *ed* David Pulbrook. *pd* Tracy Watt. *m* Nerida Tyson-Chew. *cast* Caroline Goodall, Caroline Gillmer, Tara Morice, Ray Barrett, Joan Plowright, John Hargreaves.

●Meg Moynihan (Goodall), an Australian based in London, is the author of a feminist memoir nominated for the Booker Prize. The book's caused waves back in her small hometown. Here Meg's sister Hilary (Gillmer) has been joined by their youngest sibling Pippa (*Strictly Ballroom*'s Morice), who's flown in briefly from business in the US. By the time Meg's anxiety has sent her back to the family nest, a death has upped the stakes in sisterly recrimination. At which point, Marge Morrisey (Plowright), a literary local, turns the domestic turmoil into a debate on the changing face of Australian cultural identity. An earnest trawl through the personal and artistic legacy of Ocker patriarchy, based on a play by Hannie Rayson. TJ

Hotel Splendide

(1999, GB/Fr, 98 min)
d Terence Gross. *p* Ildikó Kemény. *sc* Terence Gross. *ph* Gyula Pados. *ed* Michael Ellis. *pd* Alison Dominitz. *m* Mark Tschanz. *cast* Toni Collette, Daniel Craig, Katrin Cartlidge, Stephen Tompkinson, Hugh O'Conor, Helen McCrory, Peter Vaughan, Len Hibberd.

●A one-off debut destined for the potential cult-movie drawer. The increasingly madcap plot gives only half a clue. Kath (Collette), one of life's intractable upsetters, returns to a crumbling, dysfunctional spa hotel on a remote island in hope of reuniting with old flame Ronald (Craig). The latter's one of the least bubo-encrusted of the Blanches – a family ruled with an invert's petty passion by Dezmond (Tompkinson) in accordance with their dead mother's grisly health regimen. Forces divide. Kath's 'liberated' cooking causes the guests to revolt on her behalf; and although Ronald's heart starts to thaw, Dezmond's hardens demonically, while sensitive Cora (Cartlidge) gets caught in the emotional crossfire. Watching this modest production is a strange, uneven experience, pulled along, as it is, by the divergent horses of satire, farce and psychological realism. But it's played with undisguised gusto and feeling. And though the images of the film's crumbling fabric (brown and green fungus, faeces-fired heating system and all) may have you heaving, writer/director Gross's surreal intelligence and sense of invention may well leave you moved and amused. A very English movie. WH

Hotel Terminus: The Life and Times of Klaus Barbie

(1987, US, 267 min)
d/p Marcel Ophuls. *ph* Michael Davis, Pierre Boffety, Ruben Aaronson, Wilhelm Rosing, Lionel Legros, Daniel Chabert, Paul Gonon. *ed* Albert Jurgenson, Catherine Zins. *voice* Jeanne Moreau.

●Ophuls' documentary about the Nazi war criminal, expelled from Bolivia and returned to France for trial, is a mass of interview and newsreel spliced and juxtaposed to produce a narrative *which* is also a moral and historical record *which* is also a set of questions *which* can be reduced here to two crunchers: who are you to judge? what would you have done? The film rarely flags, despite copious location shifts and languages and subtitles which run the gamut and the gauntlet. From wartime France to fascist Bolivia, from boyhood admirers to aggrieved business partners and victims of the Nazis' butchery turning almost as much upon each other as their persecutor, the film is as much about selective memory and the vagaries of moral responsibility as a story of one man who affected so many, and who managed to work for not only the SS but also the Allies, the Bolivian arms runners and the romantically conceived Bolivian navy, and return to Lyons at the age of 71 more sprightly and confident than most of the people whose lives he wrecked. Superb. SGr

Hot Enough for June

(1963, GB, 98 min)
d Ralph Thomas. *p* Betty E Box. *sc* Lukas Heller. *ph* Ernest Steward. *ed* Alfred Roome. *m* Angelo Francesco Lavagnino. *ad* Syd Cain. *cast* Dirk Bogarde, Sylva Koscina, Robert Morley, Leo McKern, Roger Delgado, John Le Mesurier, Richard Vernon, Derek Nimmo, Richard Pasco, Frank Finlay.

●A plodding spy spoof, with Czech-speaking writer Dirk Bogarde unwittingly hired by the British Secret Service for a mission in Prague. The early scenes are fun, as the late James Bond's effects are filed away, and as Robert Morley's spy chief shows his knowledge of geography. But the movie rapidly goes downhill until the ending, when the number one sightseeing spot in Britain for a Czech refugee turns out to be Aldermaston. ATu

Hot Money

(1986, Can, 80 min)
d Selig Usher. *p* Zale Magder. *sc* Phyllis Camesano, Joel Cohen, Neil Cohen, Carl de Santis. *ph* Stan Mestel. *ed* Adam Peden. *m* Rob McConnell. *cast* Orson Welles, Michael Murphy, Michelle Finney, Harry Ramer, Ken Pogue, Alfie Scopp.

●Presumably this Canadian offering kept Welles in cigar money for a couple of weeks, but it's sad to see him reduced to such dreck. (The film was started in 1979 by director George McCowan, but not completed until after his death.) Murphy's the ex-con, now working as a small-town deputy, who pulls off a $1m theft from a local widow, then worries that his boss, sheriff Welles, will lose his job because of it. (The producer apparently re-shot much of the original material – and the final director credit remains something of a mystery.) TJ

Hot One, The

see Corvette Summer

Hot Rock, The (aka How to Steal a Diamond in Four Uneasy Lessons)

(1972, US, 105 min)
d Peter Yates. *p* Hal Landers, Bobby Roberts. *sc* William Goldman. *ph* Edward R Brown. *ed* Frank P Keller, Fred W Berger. *pd* John Robert Lloyd. *m* Quincy Jones. *cast* Robert Redford, George Segal, Zero Mostel, Ron Leibman, Paul Sand, Moses Gunn, William Redfield.

●Donald E Westlake, who also writes under the name of Richard Stark, has quietly been providing material for some of the better American thrillers for some years. *Point Blank*, *The Split* and *The Outfit*, all with similar plots and themes, were adaptations from Stark novels. *Like Cops and Robbers*, *The Hot Rock* is by Westlake. Both of them touch on the themes of teamwork and capitalism, crime being just another form of free enterprise. Redford and Segal are both good, parodying their normal images, as the thieves who steal the Sahara Stone from the Brooklyn Museum and spend the rest of the film chasing after it. Like Cops and Robbers it's a lightweight film, but enjoyable nonetheless. CPea

Hot Roof, A (Gyaegotun Nalui Ohu)

(1996, SKor, 108 min)
d Lee Min-Yong. *p* Lee Soon-Yeoul. *sc* Lee Kyoung-Sik. *ph* Seo Jung-Min. *ed* Park Kog-Ji. *pd* Choo Yung-sam. *m* Lee Young Hoon. *cast* Sook Son, Ha You-Mi, Jung Sun-Kyoung, Lee Jean-Son.

●The subtitles are kind of dodgy and there's the odd lapse in the script, but Lee Min-Yong's debut feature is basically a gas. Already the most widely-sold Korean film ever made (but it doesn't have distribution in Britain), it's a daydream about a major skirmish in the sex-war: women, who come to the rescue of a battered wife and accidentally kill her husband, barricade themselves on the roof of their apartment block, resist arrest, and win national support. The women's struggle for solidarity (most tested when they find out that one of them is actually a drag queen) is wittily contrasted with the quasi-gay bonding of two burglars trapped in an apartment below by the police siege. Funny, raunchy and unashamedly pulpy, this knockout entertainment could only have come from a society and culture in the throes of rapid change. TR

Hot Shots!

(1991, US, 85 min)
d Jim Abrahams. *p* Bill Badalato. *sc* Jim Abrahams, Pat Proft. *ph* Bill Butler. *ed* Jane Kurson, Eric Sears. *pd* William A Elliott. *m* Sylvester Levay. *cast* Charlie Sheen, Cary Elwes, Valeria Golino, Lloyd Bridges, Kevin Dunn, Jon Cryer, William O'Leary, Kristy Swanson, Efrem Zimbalist Jr.

●Enlisted in a top secret bombing mission alongside the élite of the Navy's air corps, hot-headed flyboy Topper Harley (Sheen) must first convince the beautiful base psychiatrist (Golino) that his mental quirks won't endanger the operation. In the event, he earns her love, his comrades' respect, and a one-way ticket to Disneyland. This Kentucky Fried movie dogs *Top Gun* like canned laughter dogging a feeble joke. There's nothing as subtle as parody here. Instead, Abrahams and co-writer Pat Proft keep the narrative framework out of harm's way while taking pot shots at whatever takes their fancy, from *Nine ½ Weeks* to *Dances with Wolves*. These spoofs are funny up to a point, but Abrahams can't summon much conviction for the job; too often, a mere allusion does all the work, while wackier gags are stretched beyond breaking point. It might be funnier. TCh

Hot Shots! Part Deux

(1993, US, 89 min)
d Jim Abrahams. *p* Bill Badalato, Jim Abrahams. *sc* Jim Abrahams, Pat Proft. *ph* John R Leonetti. *ed* Malcolm Campbell. *pd* William A Elliott. *m* Basil Poledouris. *cast* Charlie Sheen, Lloyd Bridges, Richard Crenna, Valeria Golino, Brenda Bakke, Rowan Atkinson.

●*Part Deux* turns to the Rambo saga, reinventing Sheen's lunkhead 'Topper' Harley as a pseudo-Stallone, while drafting in the real Richard Crenna to reprise his sturdy colonel schtick. With President 'Tug' Benson (Bridges again) ensconced in the mother of all hostage crises – his country's finest captive in the Middle East – Charlie dons upper-body definition, bullet-belt and bandana to rescue 'the men who went in to get the men who went in to get the men'. Unlike its grim predecessor, there are at least two chuckles this time round, a slapstick routine at a Buddhist monastery and a witty *Apocalypse Now* gag. TJ

Hot Spot
see I Wake Up Screaming

Hot Spot, The
(1990, US, 130 min)
d Dennis Hopper. *p* Paul Lewis. *sc* Nona Tyson, Charles Williams. *ph* Ueli Steiger. *ed* Wende Phifer Mate. *pd* Cary White. *m* Jack Nitzsche. *cast* Don Johnson, Virginia Madsen, Jennifer Connelly, Charles Martin Smith, William Sadler, Jerry Hardin, Barry Corbin, Leon Rippy, Jack Nance.
● After an impressively laconic, enigmatic opening – Harry Madox (Johnson) drifts into a dusty Texan town and successfully makes a sale at a used-car lot owned by a complete stranger – Hopper's film sinks steadily into *film noir* cliché. Taken from Charles Williams' 1953 novel *Hell Hath No Fury*, it's a determinedly sleazy account of small-town corruption. When canny con-man Madox finds his affections torn between a troubled, virginal waif (Connelly) and his new employer's dangerously seductive wife (Madsen), you soon get the gist: he's headed for a fall. Robbery, adultery, blackmail and murder are on the agenda, but the pacing is so sluggish, the plotting so repetitive, and the characters so formulary that everything is imbued with an unilluminating inevitability. Ueli Steiger's camerawork conveys the overheated torpor of small-town Texas, and odd brief scenes bring a touch of fire; but for the most part the impression is of a talented man going rather lazily through the motions. GA

Hot Stuff
(1979, US, 91 min)
d Dom DeLuise. *p* Mort Engelberg. *sc* Michael Kane, Donald E Westlake. *ph* James Pergola. *ed* Neil Travis. *m* Patrick Williams. *cast* Dom DeLuise, Suzanne Pleshette, Jerry Reed, Ossie Davis, Luis Avalos, Marc Lawrence, Dick Davalos.
● The raucous comedy of *Hot Stuff* is even broader than its sizeable director/star. The plot, co-scripted by Donald Westlake, concerns four Miami cops who pose as fences in order to entrap a ridiculously bizarre gaggle of thieves (not as bizarre, though, as the perfect social mix back at the cop shop, which includes a black chief, a volatile Cuban, and Pleshette as the perfectly groomed policewoman who always has a fresh magnolia in her hair). But despite the right wing premise (the story is based on a real police entrapment operation) and tedious funny-chases, nice characterisations and witty dialogue make it almost winning. CR

Hot Times
(1974, US, 84 min)
d Jim McBride. *p* Lew Mishkin. *sc* Jim McBride. *ph* Affonso Beato. *ed* Jack Baran. *m* Victor Lesser. *cast* Henry Cory, Gail Lorber, Amy Farber, Steve Curry, Bob Lesser, Clarissa Ainley, Jack Baran.
● A kind of Jewish comic reply to *The Lords of Flatbush*, in which a number of misogynist, Portnoy-esque sex hang-ups are laid bare in a High School USA setting. However, if one peels away the phony zaniness lent by the bleeping out of 'offensive language' (defensive tampering by the producers) and the supposedly zappy voice-over narration, one is left with a film surprisingly true to McBride's underground origins, notable for some persuasively bizarre touches and a superlatively fluid visual style. Best scenes are those involving the shooting of a sex film in which a series of male performers struggle to come-or-not-to-come on cue, and a sequence involving a Times Square pick-up with a 'liberated' mother. Superb performances. VG

Hot War (Huan Yin Te Gong)
(1998, HK, 94 min)
d Jingle Ma. *p* Jackie Chan, Chu Siu-Chun, David Chan. *sc* Calvin Poon, Lo Chi-Leung, Ivy Chow. *ph* Chan Chi-Ying. *ed* Kwong Chi-Leung. *pd* Yee Chung-Man. *m* Peter Kam. *cast* Ekin Cheng, Jordan Chan, Kelly Chan, Terence Wan, Yeung Jang.
● Sterling Chinese scientists researching subliminal imagery in a CIA lab in Chicago are targeted by bleach-blond terrorist 'Alien' on behalf of a sinister mogul who plans to create economic chaos by inserting subliminals into television coverage of the Asian Games. With one wife murdered and one fiancée kidnapped, the two men submit to an experimental programme to turn them into hyper-skilled 'VR Fighters' and rush to Hong Kong and Kuala Lumpur for daring rescues, showdowns, etc. This expensive, derivative attempt at a virtual reality thriller with much dialogue in English is a misguided response to the decline of the HK film industry. The stars, charismatic elsewhere, might as well be CGI figures; cinematographer-turned-director Jingle Ma's only non-Hollywood idea is to give it a tragic/elegiac ending. Yawn. TR

Hot Winds (Garm Hava)
(1973, Ind, 136 min)
d MS Sathyu. *p* Abu Siwani, MS Sathyu. *sc* Kaifi Azmi, Shama Zaidi. *ph* Ishan Arya. *ed* S Chakraborty. *m* Ustad Bahadur Khan. *cast* Balraj Sahni, Vikas Anand, Rajendra Raghuvanshi, Raj Verma, Gita, Shama Zaidi.
● A highly ambitious first feature which examines the Indian situation just after the liberation, and the aftermath of the partition of the subcontinent. What is remarkable about the film is the degree to which it refuses to follow well-trodden 'epic' paths in its story of a Muslim family coming to terms with the political realities of an increasingly hostile Hindu Agra (where to remain is to be hounded as outcasts). Despite something of an undertow of conventional melodrama, particularly in the ill-fated romance and eventual suicide of the daughter of the house, Sathyu directs with grace and perceptiveness, and reveals a noteworthy political awareness. VG

Hound-Dog Man
(1959, US, 87 min)
d Don Siegel. *p* Jerry Wald. *sc* Fred Gipson, Winston Miller. *ph* Charles G Clarke. *ed* Louis Loeffler. *ad* Lyle Wheeler, Walter M Simonds. *m* Cyril J Mockridge. *songs* Ken Darby, Frankie Avalon, Mort Shuman, others. *cast* Fabian, Stuart Whitman, Carol Lynley, Arthur O'Connell, Betty Field, Royal Dano, Jane Darwell, Edgar Buchanan, Claude Akins.
● Fred Gipson's bucolic novel of Southern country folk was the main attraction for Siegel here (Peckinpah thought of filming it too), but he reckoned without producer Jerry Wald's insistence that Fabian get the lead as the young chap learning about life and love on a hunting jaunt with older, wiser Whitman. This meant eight songs from a star who admitted his own frailty in the vocal department, but Siegel integrates them into the action, has the rest of the cast join in on occasion, and swiftly moves on with the action. The music certainly doesn't detract from an amiable outdoor adventure with a pleasing line in deflating macho bullshit. And nothing whatsoever to do with Elvis. TJ

Hounded
see Johnny Allegro

Hound of the Baskervilles, The
(1939, US, 80 min, b/w)
d Sidney Lanfield. *p* Darryl F Zanuck. *sc* Ernest Pascal. *ph* J Peverell Marley. *ed* Robert Simpson. *ad* Richard Day, Hans Peters. *m* Cyril J Mockridge. *cast* Richard Greene, Basil Rathbone, Nigel Bruce, Lionel Atwill, Wendy Barrie, John Carradine, Morton Lowry.
● First in the Rathbone-Bruce Sherlock Holmes series, making disappointingly little of the baleful hound (Roy William Neill later provided much more imaginative direction). Highly enjoyable as a period thriller, nevertheless, with lovely support from Carradine and Atwill as a pair of richly sinister red herrings, and one scene enchantingly played by Bruce in which, unable to resist claiming to be Holmes in questioning a tramp, Watson has to pretend he knew all the time when the tramp reveals himself to be Holmes in disguise. This is the only film in the series to allude to Holmes' addiction, through his weary curtain-line aside: 'The needle, Watson!' TM

Hound of the Baskervilles, The
(1958, GB, 87 min)
d Terence Fisher. *p* Anthony Hinds. *sc* Peter Bryan. *ph* Jack Asher. *ed* Alfred Cox. *pd* Bernard Robinson. *m* James Bernard. *cast* Peter Cushing, Christopher Lee, André Morell, Marla Landi, David Oxley, Miles Malleson, Francis de Wolff, John Le Mesurier.
● The best Sherlock Holmes film ever made, and one of Hammer's finest movies. Fisher, at the peak of his career, used Conan Doyle's plot to establish a stylish dialectic between Holmes' nominally rational Victorian milieu and the dark, fabulous cruelty behind the Baskerville legend. This opposition is expressed within the first ten minutes, when he moves from the 'legend' with its strong connotations of the Hellfire Club (the nobleman tormenting a young girl with demonic satisfaction) to the rational eccentricities of Baker Street. Holmes is indeed the perfect Fisher hero, the Renaissance scholar with strong mystical undertones, and Cushing gives one of his very best performances, ably supported by Morell (who does not make the usual mistake of overplaying Watson). Lee is in equally good form as the Baskerville heir, and Jack Asher's muted Technicolor photography is superb. DP

Hound of the Baskervilles, The
(1977, GB, 85 min)
d Paul Morrissey. *p* John Goldstone. *sc* Peter Cook, Dudley Moore, Paul Morrissey. *ph* Dick Bush, John Wilcox. *ed* Richard Marden, Glenn Hyde. *pd* Roy Smith. *m* Dudley Moore. *cast* Peter Cook, Dudley Moore, Denholm Elliott, Joan Greenwood, Terry-Thomas, Max Wall, Irene Handl, Kenneth Williams, Hugh Griffith, Roy Kinnear, Prunella Scales, Spike Milligan.
● A 'homage' to the spirit of English film comedy that is truly one of the crummiest movies ever made. In case the idea of a Conan Doyle send-up doesn't itself have you in stitches, Morrissey and his stars/co-scripters Cook and Moore try to slay you with every other kind of joke their clapped-out minds can remember. There's even a pathetic lampoon of *The Exorcist*, a mere four years too late. Every single gag and every single comedy role is mistimed, misplayed or simply misconceived. It also looks worse than any film from a 'name' director in years: a first-year film student would be ashamed of the flat, stilted compositions and the dingy little sets. TR

Hounds of Notre Dame, The
(1980, Can, 95 min)
d Zale Dalen. *p* Fil Fraser. *sc* Ken Mitchell. *ph* Ron Orieux. *ed* Tony Lower. *ad* Richard Hudolin. *m* Maurice Marshall. *cast* Thomas Peacocke, Frances Hyland, Barry Morse, David Ferry, Lenore Zann, Lawrence Reece.
● Not, in fact, Quasimodo's pets, but the ice-hockey team of Notre Dame, a boys' school in the frozen Canadian outback, run by nuns and a priest, which dispenses the usual vile mixture of learning by rote, inedible food and patriotic speeches for World War II. Hero of the piece is the 'larger than life' headmaster/priest who runs the place like a Hitler Youth Camp and is duly loved by all the boys. Miss Jean Brodie on ice? CPea

Hounds of Zaroff, The
see Most Dangerous Game, The

Hour of Liberation – the Struggle in Oman, The (Saat el Tahrir Dakkat Barra Ya Isti'Mar)
(1974, Leb, 62 min, b/w & col)
d/sc Heiny Srour. *ph* Michel Humeau. *ed* Heiny Srour. *narrator* Youssef Salman Youssef.
● An urgent and fast-moving documentary/ propaganda film on the struggles of the People's Liberation Army in Oman, in the Persian Gulf. The resistance of the PLA in the early '60s is placed in the context of British/US economic and political interests, in which a sophisticated oil-extractive technology in the north has produced a deliberate political maintenance of poverty and underdevelopment elsewhere. Establishing their base in Dhofar, in the south, the PLA's task is both military and ideological. As they seek to gain ground, since 1970 they have started a school, trained a people's militia, helped stop inter-tribal feuding among the nomads by helping them to build secure water-holes and learn farming. It's technically compelling, using stills, slogans, songs, documentary material, aimed as much at the Arab-speaking world as at all national liberation movements. MV

Hour of the Gun

(1967, US, 101 min)
d/p John Sturges. *sc* Edward Anhalt. *ph* Lucien Ballard. *ed* Ferris Webster. *ad* Alfred C Ybarra. *m* Jerry Goldsmith. *cast* James Garner, Jason Robards, Robert Ryan, Steve Ihnat, Frank Converse, Albert Salmi, Jon Voight.
●Sturges' sequel to his own *Gunfight at the O.K. Corral*, written by Edward Anhalt and shot in Panavision by Lucien Ballard, is a notable addition to the run of Wyatt Earp movies chiefly for its unexpected bitterness of tone. Garner's lawman leaves the moral high ground to seek hot-blooded revenge for the murder of his brothers by henchmen working for Ryan's Ike Clanton. Classic opening gunfight and first-rate performances from Garner, and from Robards as the tubercular, laconically resigned Doc Holliday. A determinedly old-style Western, made two years before Peckinpah shook things up with *The Wild Bunch*. TJ

Hour of the Pig, The

(1993, GB/Fr, 117 min)
d Leslie Megahey. *p* David Thompson. *sc* Leslie Megahey. *ph* John Hooper. *ed* Isabelle Dedieu. *pd* Bruce Macadie. *m* Alexandre Desplat. *cast* Colin Firth, Donald Pleasence, Ian Holm, Nicol Williamson, Michael Gough, Harriet Walter, Elizabeth Spriggs.
●In darkest medieval France, legislation languishes beneath the pendulum sway of ecclesiastical caprice and peasant superstition. Against this backdrop, Renaissance man and Parisian lawyer Richard Courtois (Firth) makes his grand entrance, only to find that his first case in an isolated rural community is to defend a pig charged with the murder of a young boy. As the drama uncoils into folds of seigneurial corruption and forbidden sexuality, ethnic tension and church indifference, the slightly ramshackle narrative proves both educational and highly entertaining. Although revelling in the bawdy absurdities of lovingly textured authenticity, writer/director Megahey's film remains thoroughly modern in outlook, refreshingly irreverent in tone and remarkably accomplished in execution. TJ

Hour of the Star (A Hora da Estrela)

(1985, Braz, 95 min)
d Suzana Amaral. sc Suzana Amaral, Alfredo Oroz. *ph* Edgar Moura. *ed* Idê Lacreta. *ad* René Silbar. *m* Marcus Vinicius. *cast* Marcélia Cartaxo, José Dumont, Tamara Taxman, Umberto Magnani, Denoy De Oliveira, Fernanda Montenegro.
●Nineteen-year-old Macabéa works as a typist in Brasilia. With little money, less grace or beauty, and almost no education, she leads a wretched life: her roommates say she smells, her only pal calls her ugly, and her boyfriend Olimpico – no great shakes himself – tells her she's an idiot. Unusually, the director places this plain Jane nonentity centre-screen to present a beguilingly unsentimental portrait of ignorance, cultural poverty, and stunted emotions. Nothing much happens: the girl avoids being sacked, eats like a pig, rides the Metro, and takes aimless walks with her not exactly beloved Olimpico. But Amaral's precise and never condescending direction ensures that we follow this most unsympathetic of heroines to the end of the line, forestalling bathos by means of a stark, robust humour. Only Bresson's *Mouchette* suggests a precedent for this film's determination to reveal, rather than dignify, a life of utter banality; but what the comparison fails to evoke is Amaral's ability to uplift without Catholic contrivance. GA

Hour of the Wolf (Vargtimmen)

(1967, Swe, 89 min, b/w)
d/sc Ingmar Bergman. *ph* Sven Nykvist. *ed* Ulla Ryghe. *ad* Marik Vos-Lundh. *m* Lars Johan Werle. *cast* Max von Sydow, Liv Ullmann, Erland Josephson, Gertrud Fridh, Gudrun Brost, Ingrid Thulin.
●A brilliant Gothic fantasy about an artist who has disappeared, leaving only a diary; and through that diary we move into flashback to observe a classic case history of the Bergman hero haunted by darkness, demons and the creatures of his imagination until he is destroyed by them. The tentacular growth of this obsession is handled with typical virtuosity in a dazzling flow of surrealism, expressionism and full-blooded Gothic horror. First the hour of the wolf, the sleepless nights of watching and waiting, when the artist (von Sydow) describes – but we do not see – the horde of man-eating birdmen and insects who have invaded his sketch-book. Then the daylight encounters when a car crawling over the horizon, a girl picking her way through the rocks on a sun-bleached beach, look momentarily like weird, threatening insects. Finally, the full nightmare of the *soirée* at a château gradually transformed into Dracula's castle as its aristocratic inhabitants become werewolves and vampires, and the artist flees into a forest of blackened, clutching trees, pursued by monstrous birds of prey. In its exploration of the nature of creativity, haunted by the problem of whether the artist possesses or is possessed by his demons, *Hour of the Wolf* serves as a remarkable companion-piece to *Persona*. TM

Hours and Times, The

(1991, US, 60 min, b/w)
d/p/sc Christopher Münch. *ph* Christopher Münch, Juan Carlos Valls. *ed* Christopher Münch. *cast* David Angus, Ian Hart, Stephanie Pack, Robin McDonald, Sergio Moreno, Unity Grimwood.
●In the spring of 1963, John Lennon allowed Brian Epstein to take him away for four days in Barcelona. It was a chance for John to recharge his batteries. Also, Epstein was gay. Münch's film is a speculative fiction, based on these facts but with no pretence at Albert Goldman-style faction. Instead, he presents a lively, subtle conversation piece, an intimate dialogue between two very different men. Epstein is urbane, cosmopolitan and deeply insecure; Lennon working-class, intellectually curious and absolutely sure of himself. They discuss art, check out a Bergman film, discuss the ins-and-outs of buggery. Epstein is in love; Lennon pulls back from the brink. Both turn elsewhere to make half-hearted pick-ups. Whatever really happened, this poignant, fragmentary, assured and beautifully paced film rings true. Validation enough, surely? TCh

House

(1995, Can, 86 min)
d Laurie Lynd. *p* Karen Lee Hall. *sc* Laurie Lynd, Daniel MacIvor. *ph* David A Makin. *ed* Susan Maggi. *pd* Marian Wihak. *m* Jeff Bird. *cast* Daniel MacIvor, Patricia Collins, Stephen Ouimette, Ben Cardinal.
●Basically a one-man show, with MacIvor venting his spleen before an audience of small town curiosity-seekers. His Carver-esque, neurotic/psychotic autobiographical anecdotes touch on the lives of one or more of those in attendance. Sort of alternative group therapy. MacIvor is not happy: his mother's possessed by the devil, his father's the saddest man alive, his sister's in love with a dog, the one he loves does not love him, and he has no place to live. TCh

House

(1986, US, 93 min)
d Steve Miner. *p* Sean S Cunningham. *sc* Ethan Wiley. *ph* Mac Ahlberg. *ed* Michael N Knue. *pd* Gregg Fonseca. *m* Harry Manfredini. *cast* William Katt, George Wendt, Richard Moll, Kay Lenz, Mary Stavin, Michael Ensign.
●Struggling with his Vietnam novel, an author seeks solitude: where else but in a haunted house. Visions of his missing son and his war service intrude, along with a monster from the closet and flying garden tools. This could be played any number of ways: straight, paranoid fantasy, Abbott & Costello. The latter temporarily prevail: when the cops arrive just as he's hiding a body under the stairs our hero all but cries out 'Abbott!' and any seriousness is further undermined by having Norm from TV's *Cheers* living next door. In the last reel comes the revelation that most of the foregoing has been engineered by the crumbling but ambulatory corpse of a Vietnam buddy nursing a grudge. Fortunately the ghostly veteran packs non-ghostly, indeed live, hand grenades and it all ends, not before time, with a big bang. DO

House II: The Second Story

(1987, US, 88 min)
d Ethan Wiley. *p* Sean S Cunningham. *sc* Ethan Wiley. *ph* Mac Ahlberg. *ed* Marty Nicholson. *pd* Gregg Fonseca. *m* Harry Manfredini. *cast* Arye Gross, Jonathan Stark, Royal Dano, Bill Maher, John Ratzenberger, Lar Park Lincoln, Amy Yasbeck, Gregory Walcott.
●Jesse McLaughlin (Gross) inherits a house with a secret: his great-great grandpappy, a notorious outlaw from the Old West, was buried in the back garden with a valuable crystal skull imbued with magic powers. So Jesse digs him up. But once the skull is installed on its altar, it creates a series of magic portals by which various baddies travel through time to try to steal it. This sequel to *House* offers another blend of humour and horror, but the gags aren't particularly sweet, the chills aren't particularly spicy. On the whole an indigestible affair, which fortunately passes quickly through the system. SGo

House!

(1999, GB, 90 min)
d Julian Kemp. *p* Michael Kelk. *sc* Jason Sutton. *ph* Kjell Vassdal. *ed* Jonathan Rudd. *pd* Kit Line. *cast* Kelly Macdonald, Gwenllian Davies, Sue Hopkins, Eileen Edwards, Marlene Griffiths, Freddie Jones, Mossie Smith, Jason Hughes, Miriam Margolyes.
●This first feature is an unashamed stab at recapturing the magic of Ealing. And while the disarming innocence of '40s and '50s cinema is absent, the feelgood theme – the underdog triumphing against the odds – is reassuringly familiar. The film is set in a small town in S Wales, where the bingo hall is besieged on all sides. Not only are council inspectors threatening to demolish the building, but, less than a mile up the valley, the UK's biggest bingo arena is about to open. Employee Linda (Macdonald) is desperate: her job's on the line, debts are mounting, and porcine Aunt Beth (Margolyes) is threatening to sell her house. To make matters worse, she catches her boyfriend, bingo caller Gavin (Hughes), buried chin-first in the bosom of her friend Kay (Smith). Then Linda discovers she has an unexpected talent – the ability to predict numbers before they're called and rig the results. With the introduction of a supernatural element, the storytelling becomes too self-consciously whimsical. Nevertheless, there's charm to spare, and the spirited direction and likeable cast more than make up for the film's shortcomings, not least the mindlessly upbeat ending. WI

Houseboat

(1958, US, 110 min)
d Melville Shavelson. *p* Jack Rose. *sc* Melville Shavelson, Jack Rose. *ph* Ray June. *ed* Frank Bracht. *ad* Hal Pereira, John Goodman. *m* George Duning. *cast* Cary Grant, Sophia Loren, Martha Hyer, Harry Guardino, Eduardo Ciannelli, Murray Hamilton.
●Widower Grant takes his kids in tow and shacks up in a new floating domicile to find romance with maid Loren, who (surprise!) just happens to be a wealthy socialite doing a bit of slumming. Tame VistaVision family frolic. TJ

House by the Cemetery, The (Quella Villa accanto al Cimitero)

(1981, It, 86 min)
d Lucio Fulci. *p* Fabrizio De Angelis. *sc* Dardano Sacchetti, Giorgio Mariuzzo, Lucio Fulci. *ph* Sergio Salvati. *ed* Vincenzo Tomassi. *pd* Massimo Lentini. *m* Walter Rizzati. *cast* Katherine MacColl, Giovanni De Nari, Paolo Malco, Giovanni Frezza, Giovanni Frezza, Silvia Collatina, Dagmar Lassander.
●Cut-price spaghetti gore cooked up from the not exactly brand-new narrative premise of a nice middle class family moving to a house in New England with a sinister sitting tenant, the nefarious Dr Freudstein. Bits of *Amityville* and *The Shining*, plus every other imaginable mad-scientist, screaming-in-the-cellar, haunted-house horror cliché, shamelessly ripped off, cut and stuck together into (literally) a hack-work of almost awesome incoherence. Even Henry James, irreverently quoted in the closing epitaph, fails to confer any respectability upon the proceedings. Strictly for pulp cultists. SJo

House by the Lake, The

see Death Weekend

House by the River
(1949, US, 88 min, b/w)
d Fritz Lang. *p* Howard Welsch. *sc* Mel Dinelli. *ph* Edward Cronjager. *ed* Arthur Hilton. *ad* Boris Leven. *m* George Antheil. *cast* Louis Hayward, Jane Wyatt, Lee Bowman, Dorothy Patrick, Ann Shoemaker, Kathleen Freeman, Peter Brocco, Jody Gilbert.
●One of Fritz Lang's deathly constructs: a patently artificial period melodrama about an author (Hayward) who strangles his wife's maid and implicates his brother (Bowman) in the crime. It's a bleak, gloomy film, one in which the psychological undercurrents seem to be flooding over the banks, drowning any fleeting vestige of rationality in a perverse Teutonic romanticism. TCh

House Calls
(1978, US, 98 min)
d Howard Zieff. *p* Alex Winitsky, Arlene Sellers. *sc* Max Shulman, Julius J Epstein, Alan Mandel, Charles Shyer. *ph* David M Walsh. *ed* Edward A Warschilka. *pd* Henry Bumstead. *m* Henry Mancini. *cast* Walter Matthau, Glenda Jackson, Art Carney, Richard Benjamin, Candice Azzara, Dick O'Neill, Thayer David.
●Concocted by an unhealthy quartet of writers, this suggests a slightly wacky, liberated variant on Universal's comedies of eighteen years earlier, when Rock Hudson flashed his pearly teeth at Doris Day. Once again it's love between two pros: Matthau is a shambling, philandering doctor at a mediocre hospital, while Jackson leads one of those nebulous American business lives, making and selling cheesecake. He doesn't put a foot wrong, but the garrulous, charmless Jackson character comes over as the original pain in the neck. Background details of hospital life are handled much more astutely than the main plot. It's a big mystery how Zieff (of *Slither* and *Hearts of the West*) allowed it to go off at half-cock. GB

Householder, The
(1963, Ind, 101 min, b/w)
d James Ivory. *p* Ismail Merchant. *sc* Ruth Prawer Jhabvala. *ph* Subrata Mitra. *ed* Pran Mehra. *m* Ustad Ali Akbar Khan. *cast* Shashi Kapoor, Leela Naidu, Durga Khote, Achla Sachdev, Hariendernath Chattopadayaya.
●James Ivory's first feature was adapted by Ruth Jhabvala from her fourth novel and shot, on a shoestring, in Delhi, using a house belonging to a friend of the producer. A young teacher Prem (Kapoor) finds himself married to an exquisite but trying girl (the part-French Leela Naidu). He's not yet ready, however, to assume the responsibilities of a 'householder'. He feels, like many later Merchant Ivory protagonists – Olivia in *Heat and Dust*, Leonard Bast in *Howards End* – that there must be something more to life, something spiritual, something better and higher. Prem searches (comically), but in the end settles for domesticity. The predicaments of Olivia and Leonard were resolved with greater dramatic conviction, but there's much that's authentic and touching in this small, sharply observed drama about the necessity of a man turning a deaf ear to the sighs of his mother. Ivory showed an early version of the film to Satyajit Ray who offered to reshape it. The task took three days, and Ivory recalls the explosive force of the Master's repeated command, *Cut!* JPy

House in Nightmare Park, The
(1973, GB, 95 min)
d Peter Sykes. *p/sc* Clive Exton, Terry Nation. *ph* Ian Wilson. *ed* Bill Blunden. *ad* Maurice Carter. *m* Harry Robinson. *cast* Frankie Howerd, Ray Milland, Hugh Burden, Kenneth Griffith, John Bennett, Rosalie Crutchley, Ruth Dunning.
●Howerd plays a Victorian ham actor invited to an eerie stately home, supposedly to entertain. In reality it's a question of inheritance (he's the long-lost heir, and this is *The Cat and the Canary* all over again). Sykes directs in his best high romantic style (the opening is brilliant) and Howerd restrains himself sufficiently; but though some gags work, towards half time the strain begins to tell and it all falls apart.

Housekeeping
(1987, US, 116 min)
d Bill Forsyth. *p* Robert F Colesberry. *sc* Bill Forsyth. *ph* Michael Coulter. *ed* Michael Ellis. *pd* Adrienne Atkinson. *m* Michael Gibbs. *cast* Christine Lahti, Sara Walker, Andrea Burchill, Anne Pitoniak, Barbara Reese, Margot Pinvidic, Bill Smillie, Wayne Robson.
●Adolescent sisters Ruthie (Walker) and Lucille (Burchill) live by a threatening black lake; their mother lies at its bottom, and Aunt Sylvie (Lahti) flaunts death by rowing on it late at night. Sylvie rocks the boat in other ways too. Arriving out of the blue to care for her nieces, she has habits that challenge the small town's conventions and eventually come between the girls: she collects tins, sleeps on park benches, hoards newspapers, condones the girls' truancy, almost sets the house on fire while cooking. Gentle humour stems from such idiosyncrasies, but Sylvie is irresponsible, dangerously so. When Lucille's schoolgirl desire to be 'normal' forces her out of the house, we sense an ominous flipside to the kookie, childish adventures Sylvie dreams up to entertain Ruthie. Weather, period (the '50s) and place (Idaho) are so emphatically detailed they're oppressive; while Sylvie and the girls come to life with greater depth and wholeness than Forsyth's characters have hitherto enjoyed. Here the director's characteristic other-worldly charm is overshadowed by a dark intensity; with its backdrop of death, isolation and portent, the movie is sombre, very strange, but wonderful. EP

Housemaid, The (Hanyo)
(1960, SKor, 90 min)
d Kim Ki-Young. *cast* Lee Un-shim, Chu Jung-nyo, Kim Chin-kyu.
●An extraordinary film anywhere, not least in Korea, this heightened melodrama is often cited as the uneven maverick Kim Ki-Young's masterpiece. It's a deliberately overblown, if deadpan and Hitchcockian tale of a music teacher's demise through the twin agencies of his wife's greed (she wants a two-storey house) and his maidservant's supposed sexual predatoriness (she comes on like Kathleen Byron in *Black Narcissus*). Kim's is a bleak, Nietzschean view of human motivation, and the whole, with its jazz-score, location shooting, hot-house Sirkian drama and Clouseau-like horror suspense makes for a notably delirious experience. WH

House of America
(1996, GB/Neth, 96 min)
d Marc Evans. *p* Sheryl Crown. *sc* Edward Thomas. *ph* Pierre Aim. *ed* Michiel Reichwein. *pd* Mark Tildesley. *m* John Cale. *cast* Siân Phillips, Matthew Rhys, Steven Mackintosh, Lisa Palfrey, Richard Harrington, Pascal Laurent.
●In an isolated prairie-style house built from corrugated iron, the Lewis family – mad mam (Phillips), teenage dreamers Sid and Gwenny (Mackintosh and Palfrey), and their down-to-earth young brother Boyo (Rhys, sympathetic) – struggle to cope with the void left by their absent husband/father who 15 years before traded the green green grass of South Wales for the wide open spaces of America. More like an overwrought Sam Shepard psycho-drama than a downbeat study of doleful teenagers, this adapted play (by Edward Thomas) eschews miserabilism in favour of a poetic celebration of naive teen dreams about burning bright and dying young. With no local heroes to call their own, the Harley-riding Sid and Gwenny lose themselves in a drink and drug-fuelled fantasy of the American Dream derived from Kerouac's *On the Road*. The bleached photography and Welsh-dominated soundtrack adds notable texture to an ambitious debut. NF

House of Angels (Anglagård)
(1992, Swe, 119 min)
d Colin Nutley. *p* Lars Jönsson, Lars Dahlquist. *sc* Colin Nutley, Susanne Falck. *ph* Jens Fischer. *ed* Perry Schaffer. *ad* Ulla Herdin. *m* Björn Isfält. *cast* Helena Bergström, Rikard Wolff, Sven Wollter, Reine Brynolfsson, Ernst Gunter, Per Oscarsson.
●After a rural community's elderly patriarch snuffs it, anticipation runs high that his neighbour, wealthy farmer Axel (Wollter), will buy up his property, but his granddaughter Fanny (Bergström) turns up on a Harley Davidson with leather-clad companion Zac (Wolff) and decides to move into the house. The locals are suspicious that the pair will bring Big City ways to this sleepy corner of the country, and though harmony is eventually restored, Nutley by no means makes this a sure thing. The film's slow to start, but the measured pacing clearly delineates the two parties' separate agendas, as tension builds between them and the ostensibly decent villagers start haranguing the newcomers out of narrow-mindedness, anxiety and mistrust. While the portrayal of open-hearted oldster Gottfried (Gunter) sugars the pill, there's an unexpectedly trenchant analysis of simmering everyday prejudice: a movie that smiles at you with gritted teeth. TJ

House of Bamboo
(1955, US, 102 min)
d Samuel Fuller. *p* Buddy Adler. *sc* Harry Kleiner. *ph* Joseph MacDonald. *ed* James B Clark. *ad* Lyle Wheeler, Addison Hehr. *m* Leigh Harline. *cast* Robert Ryan, Robert Stack, Shirley Yamaguchi, Cameron Mitchell, Sessue Hayakawa, Brad Dexter.
●1954. American-led gang pulls raids in Tokyo, Yokohama. Ex-GI involvement suspected. Lone American infiltrates gang. Identity, motives unclear. *House of Bamboo* offers all Fuller's key themes and motifs in a characteristic thriller form: dual identities, divided loyalties, racial tensions, life (and cinema) as war. Part of it is Fuller the war correspondent, reporting from the front, leaving the viewer to fight out meanings alongside the characters. Part of it is Fuller the American tourist, shamelessly reducing Japan to stereotypes, twisting local colour to his own ends. Godard used to think it was Fuller's best movie. TR

House of Bernarda Alba, The (La Casa de Bernarda Alba)
(1987, Sp, 103 min)
d Mario Camus. *sc* Mario Camus, Antonio Larreta. *ph* Fernando Arribas. *ed* José M Biurrun. *ad* Rafael Palmero. *cast* Irene Gutiérrez Caba, Ana Belén, Florinda Chico, Enriqueta Carballeira, Vicky Peña, Aurora Pastor, Mercedes Lezcano.
●In this adaptation of Lorca's last play, the matriarchal edict proclaimed by Bernarda on her husband's death condemns her five unmarried daughters to an aeon in black behind the locked doors of an all-female household. The one male to get a look in is glimpsed in shadows, keeping minight trysts through barred windows; planned for the eldest daughter, he loves the youngest, stoking the flames of jealous rivalry until the whole pressurised can of blocked emotions blows apart. Camus' forte lies in his precise delineation of period detail and buttoned-up behaviour, and he makes palpable the savage destructiveness of Franco's dictatorship – here in its birth throes but rooted, as Lorca tried to show, in the restricted social and sexual codes of Spanish society. The performances play on one unrelenting note – fever-pitched misery – though the whole cast admirably sustains the intensity throughout. Camus rarely opens the drama out, but neither does he achieve the cathartic rush demanded by Lorca's denouement. The result is cold, and a little tiresome. WH

House of Cards (La Voce del Silenzio)
(1993, US/It, 109 min)
d Michael Lessac. *p* Dale Pollack, Lianne Halfon, Wolfgang Glattes. *sc* Michael Lessac. *ph* Victor Hammer. *ed* Walter Murch. *pd* Peter Larkin. *m* James Horner. *cast* Kathleen Turner, Tommy Lee Jones, Asha Menina, Park Overall, Shiloh Strong, Esther Rolle, Park Overall, Michael Horse, Anne Pitoniak.
●When the death of their archeologist father causes a family to return to the US after years on the site of a Mayan dig in Mexico, mom Turner grows concerned by daughter Menina's increasingly withdrawn behaviour. Jones is the kindly psychiatrist with whom she clashes when his diagnosis doesn't match her own theories. A mediocre family saga in which a striking turn from young Menina eclipses the two stars. TJ

House of Doom
see Black Cat, The

House of Dracula
(1945, US, 67 min, b/w)
d Erle C Kenton. *p* Paul Malvern. *sc* Edward T Lowe. *ph* George Robinson. *ed* Russell Schoengarth. *ad* John Goodman, Martin

Obzina. *m* Edgar Fairchild. *cast* Lon Chaney Jr, John Carradine, Martha O'Driscoll, Lionel Atwill, Glenn Strange, Onslow Stevens.
● A follow-up to Universal's *House of Frankenstein* monster omnibus, this time adding a girl hunchback to the usual fauna. Stevens plays a benevolent doctor who cures the Wolf Man, fails with Dracula, and while running amok himself with an inadvertently acquired bloodlust, gleefully revives the Frankenstein monster. It all ends in a grand holocaust borrowed from *The Ghost of Frankenstein*. Nicely shot by George Robinson, it's agreeably loony fun if you don't expect too much. TM

House of Evil

see House on Sorority Row, The

House of Exorcism, The (La Casa dell'Esorcismo)

(1975, It, 93 min)
d Mickey Lion. *p* Alfred Leone. *sc* Alberto Cittini, Alfred Leone, Mario Bava. *ph* Cecilio Paniagua. *ed* Carlo Reali. *ad* Nedo Azzini. *m* Carlo Savina. *cast* Telly Savalas, Elke Sommer, Sylva Koscina, Alida Valli, Robert Alda, Gabriele Tinti.
● A wildly incoherent *Exorcist* spin-off directed, in part at least, by the talented Mario Bava. The film alternates pointlessly between stops-out hocus pocus and some devilish comedy from a lollipop-sucking Telly Savalas. The pseudonymous director credit conceals the fact that this is Bava's *Lisa and the Devil* (1972), much hacked about and tricked out with clatteringly crude new footage involving Alda as an exorcising priest. RC

House of Fear, The

(1945, US, 69 min, b/w)
d/p Roy William Neill. *sc* Roy Chanslor. *ph* Virgil Miller. *ed* Saul A Goodkind. *ad* John Goodman, Eugène Lourié. *m* Paul Sawtell. *cast* Basil Rathbone, Nigel Bruce, Aubrey Mather, Paul Cavanagh, Dennis Hoey, Holmes Herbert, Gavin Muir.
● A cursed mansion named Drearcliff provides the setting for this passably atmospheric adaptation of Conan Doyle's *Adventure of the Five Orange Pips*, with Holmes and Watson joining the heavily insured old buffers of 'The Good Comrades' club for a weekend of cryptic warnings and mutilated corpses. Watson, for once, makes the elementary deduction. PT

House of Frankenstein

(1944, US, 74 min, b/w)
d Erle C Kenton. *p* Paul Malvern. *sc* Edward T Lowe. *ph* George Robinson. *ed* Philip Cahn. *ad* John B Goodman, Martin Obzina. *m* Hans Salter. *cast* Boris Karloff, Lon Chaney Jr, John Carradine, Glenn Strange, Lionel Atwill , George Zucco, J Carrol Naish.
● Universal's second horror stew, which tried to go one better than *Frankenstein Meets the Wolf Man* by featuring, in addition to those two luminaries, Dracula, a mad doctor, a psycho hunchback and a Chamber of Horrors. It's absurdly indigestible but surprisingly watchable, thanks to classy camerawork from George Robinson, with Carradine making – all too briefly – a superb Dracula. Mad doctor Karloff and the Frankenstein monster (Strange) meet their end in quicksands. TM

House of Fright

see Two Faces of Dr Jekyll, The

House of Games

(1987, US, 102 min)
d David Mamet. *p* Michael Hausman. *sc* David Mamet. *ph* Juan Ruiz-Anchia. *ed* Trudy Ship. *pd* Michael Merritt. *m* Alaric Jans. *cast* Lindsay Crouse, Joe Mantegna, Mike Nussbaum, Lilia Skala, JT Walsh, Steve Goldstein.
● In playwright David Mamet's directorial debut, best-selling psychiatrist Margaret Ford (Crouse) decides to confront the gambler who has driven one of her patients to the verge of suicide, and leaves her orderly, antiseptic life for a visit to the downtown lowlife House of Games. Mike (Mantegna) turns out to be swift and shifty, promising to cancel the patient's debts if Margaret sits in with him on a big money card game in the back room. Fascinated by the similarities between her trade and Mike's – both study human nature and trade on trust – Margaret hangs out with Mike and learns, to her cost, the intricacies of the sting. Mamet's glee in tracking the rackets and his ear for the great American aphasia – 'I'm from the United States of Kiss My Ass' – more than compensate for the sometimes flat direction, and the performances are splendid. BC

House of Madness (La Mansión de la Locura)

(1972, Mex, 88 min)
d Juan López Moctezuma. *p* J Guss Elster, J Borchowsky. *sc* Carlos Illescas, Juan López Moctezuma. *ph* Rafael Corkidi. *ed* Federico Landeros. *m* Nacho Méndez. *cast* Claudio Brook, Arthur Hansel, Ellen Sherman, Martin Lasalle, David Silva.
● A curiosity based on an obscure Poe story, *The System of Doctor Tarr and Professor Fether*, which is well worth a look. Definite echoes of Jodorowsky and Arrabal, but in general Moctezuma, who has a fetching visual style, steers clear of the obvious pitfalls of absurdist horror. His film is about a kind of 'kingdom' of madness which is established when the inmates of a vast and surreal insane asylum lock up their wardens and establish their own bizarre hierarchy of activities and ideas. Many of the images and sequences have a weird beauty, though the pace flags towards the end. DP

House of Mirth, The

(2000, GB, 140 min)
d Terence Davies. *p* Olivia Stewart. *sc* Terence Davies. *ph* Remi Adefarasin. *ed* Michael Parker. *pd* Don Taylor. *cast* Gillian Anderson, Eric Stoltz, Dan Ayrkroyd, Eleanor Bron, Laura Linney, Anthony LaPaglia, Jodhi May, Elizabeth McGovern.
● Terence Davies' adaptation of Edith Wharton's novel is a triumph which puts most recent screen versions of the classics to shame. It concerns a New York socialite beauty who ends in disgrace, despair, poverty and worse after she is wrongly rumoured to have had an affair with the philandering husband of one of her friends. Though period and place are sensitively evoked, Davies sidesteps superficial details to home in on both the cruel nuances of the wealthy set's polite social rituals and the resultant suffering. It's a marvellously elegant (but unflashy) film of faces in sombre close-up, an emotionally devastating study of injustice, enforced solitude, wasted opportunities and love never quite gratified. The casting is inspired, with Anderson, especially, repaying her director's faith with an immaculate, unsentimental but immensely moving performance, while Davies' writing, sense of pace, and customary honesty make for a film that profoundly affects both the heart and mind. GA

House of Mortal Sin

(1975, GB, 104 min)
d/p Pete Walker. *sc* David McGillivray. *ph* Peter Jessop. *ed* Matt McCarthy. *ad* Chris Burke. *m* Stanley Myers. *cast* Anthony Sharp, Susan Penhaligon, Stephanie Beacham, Norman Eshley, Sheila Keith, Hilda Barry.
● *House of Whipcord* and *Frightmare*, the first two films McGillivray scripted for Walker, suggested that the two of them might possibly invigorate low budget British exploitation. *Mortal Sin*, however, is a disappointment, although it has its moments. Crazed old Catholic priest terrorises young girl after her confession, while her sister is getting the curate, a young liberall, all hot under the collar. The script relies too much on mild sacrilege for its effects, instead of concentrating on more interesting aspects of religious repression. CPe

House of Pleasure

see Plaisir, Le

House of Rothschild, The

(1933, US, 88 min, b/w & col)
d Alfred Werker. *p* William Goetz, Raymond Griffith. *sc* Nunnally Johnson. *ph* Peverell Marley. *ed* Allen McNeil, Barbara McLean. *ad* Richard Day. *m* Alfred Newman. *cast* George Arliss, Boris Karloff, Loretta Young, Robert Young, C Aubrey Smith, Arthur Byron, Helen Westley, Reginald Owen, Alan Mowbray.
● A lavish Selznick biopic in which Arliss first plays Mayer, founder of the House of Rothschild, then his son Nathan, the financial wizard who made London his HQ. A lengthy prologue, set in Prussia in 1780, argues that money was the only way out of the ghetto for a Jew. Thereafter, infused with the spirit of the New Deal, Nunnally Johnson's script waxes lyrical over the great social good that Nathan achieved by putting his resources behind the fight to save Europe from Napoleon's empire-building (no comment is made on the fact that this also made him the richest man in Europe). Rather more interesting are details concerning the expansion of Mayer's humble money-changing business, and about the tricky insider deals which brought Nathan to a position of power. Commenting on the legacy of anti-semitism (with Karloff's sinister Prussian baron pointedly coming on like a Nazi), the film hedges its bets by casting non-Jews in the leading roles, and by bursting into Technicolor for a tendentious finale in which Nathan finally achieves social acceptance along with a knighthood from the Prince Regent. TM

House of Smiles (La Casa del sorriso)

(1990, It, 100 min)
d Marco Ferreri. *p* Giovanna Romagnoli, Augusto Caminito. *sc* Marco Ferreri, Liliana Betti, Antonio Marino. *ph* Franco Di Giacomo. *ed* Dominique B Martin. *pd* Livia Borgogoni. *cast* Ingrid Thulin, Dado Ruspoli, Vincenzo Cannavale, Maria Mercader, Elisabeth Kaza.
● Ferreri's film concerns old age (the old provocateur is in his sixties himself), and centres around the relationship between two 'inmates' of a home for the elderly: lively, eccentric Adelina (Thulin) and dapper charmer Andrea (Ruspoli). All Ferreri's films have elements of surreal black farce, and here the farce resides in the outrageous institutional repressiveness of the home and its staff. Ferreri turns everything on its head. Transgressors (and those unable any longer to perform basic functions for themselves) are threatened with dispatch to 'Africa', an outbuilding staffed by immigrant Maghrebi workers. It is there that the celebrant couple go for privacy and sex (in the Watermelon caravan belonging to their African friends). A film of sharp insight, filled with humanity and mischievous subversiveness. WH

House of Spirits, The

(1993, Ger/Den/Port, 138 min)
d Bille August. *p* Bernd Eichinger, Mark Rosenberg, Bille August. *sc* Bille August. *ph* Jörgen Persson. *ed* Janus Billeskov Jansen. *pd* Anna Asp. *m* Hans Zimmer. cast Jeremy Irons, Meryl Streep, Glenn Close, Winona Ryder, Antonio Banderas, Vanessa Redgrave, Armin Mueller-Stahl, Vincent Gallo.
● Isabel Allende's dynastic fable begins in the 1920s, when fate throws together the driven, macho Esteban Trueba (Irons) and the mysterious, magical Clara Del Valle (Streep). A self-made man, Esteban whisks Clara off to his sprawling estate, where they live in discord with his spinster sister Ferula (Close as a butch, black-eyed Catholic martyr). Time passes. The Truebas' felicitously named daughter Blanca grows up to be Winona Ryder: an independent-minded young woman who gets pregnant by peasant agitator Banderas. And so it goes on for two hours and five decades, until a dramatic political coup jerks these characters from the magical realist soap that is their life into a traumatic melodrama in which Blanca is brutally tortured by Esteban's bastard son. This final passage belatedly musters some conviction; elsewhere, director August plods through his own unwieldy, literal script without betraying any sensitivity to the material. Irons gives an excruciating performance – what Streep's genuinely warm, wonderful Clara sees in him you'd need ESP to fathom. TCh

House of Strangers

(1949, US, 101 min, b/w)
d Joseph L Mankiewicz. *p* Sol C Siegel. *sc* Philip Yordan. *ph* Milton Krasner. *ed* Harmon Jones. *ad* Lyle Wheeler, George W Davis. *m* Daniele Amfitheatrof. *cast* Edward G

Robinson, Richard Conte, Susan Hayward, Luther Adler, Paul Valentine, Efrem Zimbalist Jr, Debra Paget.
●The story of a patriarchal Italian-American banker and the internecine strife created by his attempts to dominate his four sons (remade as the Western *Broken Lance*). Much darker than most Mankiewicz movies, almost *noir* in fact, though cast in his favourite flashback form so that it becomes a sort of confessional memoir probing ambiguities of motive (and allowing Robinson to make a stunning first appearance, conjured in Conte's memory by a portrait, a Rossini aria, and the camera prowling endlessly up a grand stairway in the family mansion). Terrific performances (Conte, Robinson, Adler) and even better camerawork by Milton Krasner which uses lighting and composition to stake out the screen, the house and the family groupings into sharply defined areas of conflict. TM

House of the Long Shadows, The

(1982, GB, 101 min)
d Pete Walker. *p* Menahem Golan, Yoram Globus. *sc* Michael Armstrong. *ph* Norman Langley. *ed* Bob Dearberg. *ad* Michael Pickwoad. *m* Richard Harvey. *cast* Vincent Price, Christopher Lee, Peter Cushing, Desi Arnaz Jr, John Carradine, Sheila Keith, Richard Todd.
●A jumble of dark house clichés (loosely based on that old standby, *Seven Keys to Baldpate*) which stacks up the zzzzz for a good hour before even admitting it's a spoof. Thereafter, two gags for Price, the unavoidable sad ghoulishness of Carradine's mere presence, and a Christopher Lee so wooden that it's hard to tell if he's in a coffin or not. Only Cushing retains any dignity, even coming up with a fresh characterisation – a lisping, drunken rendition of the Upper Class Twit at 70 – that might turn Michael Palin green. The rest is vacuum: bus-ticket script, the usual faceless juvenile support, and bathchair direction. GD

House of Usher, The (aka The Fall of the House of Usher)

(1960, US, 80 min)
d/p Roger Corman. *sc* Richard Matheson. *ph* Floyd Crosby. *ed* Anthony Carras. *pd* Daniel Haller. *m* Les Baxter. *cast* Vincent Price, Myrna Fahey, Mark Damon, Harry Ellerbe.
●The first of Corman's eight-film Poe cycle, and one of his most faithful adaptations. Price is his usual impressive self as the almost certainly incestuously inclined Roderick Usher who, having buried his sister alive when she falls into a cataleptic trance, becomes the victim of her ghostly revenge; but it is Corman's overall direction that lends the film its intelligence and power. The sickly decadence and claustrophobia of the Usher household – which is both disturbed and temporarily cleansed by the fresh air that accompanies Damon's arrival as suitor to Madeline Usher – is admirably evoked by Floyd Crosby's 'Scope photography and Daniel Haller's art direction, the latter's sets dominated by a putrid, bloody crimson. But Richard Matheson's script is also exemplary: lucid, imaginatively detailed and subtle. GA

House of Wax

(1953, US, 88 min)
d André De Toth. *p* Bryan Foy. *sc* Crane Wilbur. *ph* Bert Glennon, J Peverell Marley. *ed* Rudi Fehr. *ad* Stanley Fleischer. *m* David Buttolph. *cast* Vincent Price, Phyllis Kirk, Frank Lovejoy, Carolyn Jones, Paul Cavanagh, Paul Picerni, Roy Roberts, Charles Bronson.
●One of the better 3-D epics (Warners' first, pioneering effort). Handsomely mounted and directed with great care, it nevertheless remains oddly lacklustre by comparison with the 1933 *Mystery of the Wax Museum*, despite being an often word-for-word remake. One reason is that where the original acquired an additional charge of bizarrerie by locating its Grand Guignol monster within a private enclave of bustling, contemporary New York, this remake is much more conventionally set in the fantasy world of gaslight, ground fogs and opera cloaks. Still, Price is fun (this was the film that typed him as a horror star), the fire in the waxworks is good for a gruesome thrill, and De Toth brings off one classic sequence with Kirk fleeing through the gaslit streets pursued by a shadowy figure in a billowing cloak. TM

House of Whipcord

(1974, GB, 101 min)
d/sc Pete Walker. *sc* David McGillivray. *ph* Peter Jessop. *ed* Matt McCarthy. *ad* Mike Pickwoad. *m* Stanley Myers. *cast* Barbara Markham, Patrick Barr, Ray Brooks, Ann Michelle, Penny Irving, Sheila Keith, David McGillivray, Pete Walker.
●An above average sexploitation/horror that has been put together with some polish and care from a fairly original script. The film is dedicated ironically to all those who wish to see the return of capital punishment in Britain, and it's about a senile old judge and his wife who are so appalled by current permissiveness that they set up a gruesome house of correction for young girls. The only trouble is that the film undercuts its potentially interesting Gothic theme by some leering emphases, and the final result is likely to be seen and appreciated only by the people who will take the dedication at its face value. DP

House of Yes, The

(1997, US, 85 min)
d Mark Waters. *p* Beau Flynn, Stefan Sichowitz. *sc* Mark Waters. *ph* Michael Spiller. *ed* Pamela Martin. *pd* Patrick Sherman. *m* Jeff Rona, Rolfe Kent. *cast* Parker Posey, Josh Hamilton, Tori Spelling, Freddie Prinze Jr, Genevieve Bujold, Rachael Leigh Cook.
●There's something quite lethal about Parker Posey in pearls, and for that inspiration director Mark Waters deserves our gratitude. The film plays like *Rocky Horror* rewritten by Strindberg and Oliver Stone: Hamilton brings his fiancée Spelling home to meet the family, arriving on a dark and stormy night to be greeted by the daintily bonkers Bujold (his mom), a deeply nervy Prinze (brother), and the glamorous Jackie-O, as Posey styles herself (his incestuous twin). Soon, Spelling is witness to a strange, erotic ritual of humiliation, role playing, sex and death – because blood doesn't just run in this family, it positively flows. Quite insane, very arch, and viciously funny (from a play by Wendy MacLeod). TCh

House on Carroll Street, The

(1987, US, 101 min)
d Peter Yates. *p* Robert Benton, Robert F Colesberry. *sc* Walter Bernstein. *ph* Michael Ballhaus. *ed* Ray Lovejoy. *pd* Stuart Wurtzel. *m* Georges Delerue. *cast* Kelly McGillis, Jeff Daniels, Mandy Patinkin, Jessica Tandy, Jonathan Hogan, Remak Ramsay, Ken Welsh, Christopher Rhode.
●Idealistic Emily (McGillis) comes up before a senate committee in 1951 and refuses to name names, loses her job on *Life* magazine, and is subjected to surveillance. By chance, she stumbles upon a plot to smuggle Nazis into the country, and FBI agent Cochran (Daniels) believes her story but is repeatedly warned off. Yates isn't Hitchcock, however, and the cruel cat-and-mouse structure of *Notorious* crumbles to allow for *The Janitor* to make another pass. Walter Bernstein's script unfortunately can't quite make up its mind to finger the American government for giving useful Nazi war criminals sanctuary in the early '50s, and hedges its bets. On the entertainment level, though, it's an efficient, good-looking movie, thanks to Michael Ballhaus' photography of period New York. The tension relies a bit too much on footfalls on gloomy stairwells, and the villain's silkinesss lacks menace. But there are plenty of nice touches: straight-arrow Cochran making love to Emily between surveillance duties at a stake-out; Tandy's imperious old lady with the binoculars. BC

House on Garibaldi Street, The

(1979, US, 101 min)
d Peter Collinson. *p* Mort Abrahams. *sc* Steve Shagan. *ph* Alejandro Ulloa. *ed* Gene Fowler Jr. *pd* Disley Jones, Fernando Gonzalez. *m* Charles Bernstein. *cast* Topol, Nick Mancuso, Janet Suzman, Martin Balsam, Leo McKern, Charles Gray, Derren Nesbitt, Alfred Burke.
●Topol as an Israeli secret agent kidnapping Nazi Eichmann from Buenos Aires? The mind boggles. In fact the problems of this humourless piece of faction (made for TV) are elementary: since the real raid (in the '60s) was a perfect success (ending in Eichmann's trial and execution in Israel), the possibilities for action and suspense are severely limited; the acting is often comic; the plot remains juvenile. What survives surprisingly well is a lack of pretension and a workmanlike sense of limitations which, at times – the nighttime kidnapping scene, for example – even generates a mood of gritty low-budget energy. CA

House on Haunted Hill

(1999, US, 93 min)
d William Malone. *p* Robert Zemeckis, Joel Silver, Gilbert Adler. *sc* Dick Beebe. *ph* Rick Bota. *ed* Anthony Adler. *pd* David F Klassen. *m* Don Davis. *cast* Geoffrey Rush, Famke Janssen, Taye Diggs, Ali Larter, Bridgette Wilson, Peter Gallagher, Chris Kattan, Max Perlich, Jeffrey Combs, Dick Beebe, Slavitza Jovan.
●This remake of William Castle's enjoyably creaky 1958 movie replaces Vincent Price's eccentric millionaire, who invites five hapless strangers to spend the night in an 'old dark house', with Rush's flamboyantly barking theme-park impresario, Steven Price. Thankfully, Rush's performance is more affectionate homage than slavish impersonation, and Malone's direction quickly wins us over with a blend of camp villainy, knockabout horror and twisted nastiness. Should any of the five strangers survive a night in the former Vannacutt Psychiatric Institute for the Criminally Insane, they will receive $1 million. And since the scares have been rigged by their playful host, we figure they might just make it. On the other hand, Mr Price and his beautiful wife Evelyn (Janssen) are so spitefully combative that they seem destined to kill each other before the night is out. But then the house itself takes a hand. The imaginative physical effects come into their own during the surreal dream sequences and hauntingly gruesome flashbacks to the madhouse's heyday, the latter featuring the old Re-Animator himself, Jeffrey Combs, as the sadistic Dr Vannacutt. NF

House on 92nd Street, The

(1945, US, 88 min, b/w)
d Henry Hathaway. *p* Louis De Rochemont. *sc* Barré Lyndon, Charles G Booth, John Monks Jr. *ph* Norbert Brodine. *ed* Harmon Jones. *ad* Lyle Wheeler, Lewis H Creber. *m* David Buttolph. *cast* William Eythe, Lloyd Nolan, Signe Hasso, Gene Lockhart, Leo G Carroll, Lydia St Clair, Harry Bellaver.
●Much touted at the time as the first of Louis (*The March of Time*) De Rochemont's documentary thrillers, made with the full cooperation of the FBI. It still works well enough, even though the breathless revelation of the hardware of counterespionage (hidden cameras, two-way mirrors, microfilm, etc) has become slightly old hat. More fascinating, given J Edgar Hoover's personal interest in the project – he even appears on screen to introduce it – is the way the Nazi spy ring, foiled before they can get away with the secrets of the atom bomb, could be read as dirty Commies. The low-key performances contribute effectively to the sense of actuality, despite clumsy mistakes like having Signe Hasso masquerade none too convincingly in drag as the mysterious spymaster. TM

House on Sorority Row, The (aka House of Evil)

(1982, US, 92 min)
d Mark Rosman. *p* Mark Rosman, John G Clark. *sc* Mark Rosman. *ph* Tim Suhrstedt. *ed* Jean-Marc Vasseur. *ad* Vincent Peranio. *m* Richard H Band. *cast* Kathryn McNeil, Eileen Davidson, Lois Kelso Hunt, Christopher Lawrence, Janis Zido, Robin Meloy, Harley Zokak, Jodi Draigie.
●Six out of seven sorority girls will hide a body rather than risk expulsion and the seventh is ready to stalk the stalker. They're so bright that they're down to four before they notice. But is the killer the house mother who they've left dead in the swimming pool, or is it the screwy baby she gave birth to 24 years earlier, pre-credits? Rosman's debut movie was a pretty fair showreel promising, falsely it seems, more and better to come. DO

House on Trubnaya, The (Dom na Trubnoi)

(1928, USSR, 5,765 ft, b/w)
d Boris Barnet. *sc* B Zoritch, Anatoly Marienhov, V Cherchenievitch, Nikolai

Erdman. *ph* E Alekseyev. *ad* Sergei Kozlovski. *cast* Vera Maretskaya, Vladimir Fogel, Anna Sudakevich, Yelena Tiapkina, Sergei Komarov.

●This is the greatest movie by Barnet, an ex-actor and boxer who made several of the freshest and most entertaining Soviet films of the 1920s. The plot hinges on a petit bourgeois hairdresser (hilariously caricatured by Fogel) who tries to hire a non-union housemaid; but the film's pleasures are less in the writing than in the try-anything-once attitude to film form, and the agile camerawork, which cranes up and down a crowded tenement and roams the streets of Moscow. It has much the same spontaneity that the early Godard films had, plus it's a whole lot funnier. A bona fide classic. TR

House Party

(1990, US, 104 min)
d Reginald Hudlin. *p* Warrington Hudlin. *sc* Reginald Hudlin. *ph* Peter Deming. *ed* Earl Watson. *pd* Bryan Jones. *m* Marcus Miller. *cast* Kid'n'Play (Christopher Reid, Christopher Martin), Robin Harris, Martin Lawrence, Tisha Campbell, AJ Johnson, Paul Anthony.

●Wanna party? Kid's grounded, but he's gotta itch to scratch, and tonite could be his night. Par-Tee! After *School Daze*, what else but school nights? The Hudlin brothers' rap comedy (Reggie wrote and directed, Warrington produced) doesn't aspire to Spike Lee's political attitude, but Spike set a precedent for the commercial black-youth pic, his influence evident here in bright day-glo colours, disparate characters, and righteous role models (no alcohol, no drugs, safe sex). Clearly this is no masterpiece, but as its US reception indicated, it is a product overdue in the market, and it compares well with its anaemic counterparts: it's loud, hip and vibrantly styled. Salt'n'Pepa labelmates Kid'n'Play take lead roles, and as someone says, 'they've got a cute thing happening'. Campbell and Johnson from *School Daze* impress again, Full Force and George Clinton crop up in cameos, and Marcus Miller contributes a funky score. TCh

Housesitter

(1992, US, 102 min)
d Frank Oz. *p* Brian Grazer. *sc* Mark Stein. *ph* John A Alonzo. *ed* John Jympson. *pd* Ida Random. *m* Miles Goodman. *cast* Steve Martin, Goldie Hawn, Dana Delany, Julie Harris, Donald Moffat, Peter MacNicol, Richard B Shull, Laurel Cronin, Christopher Durang.

●It's back to wacky mode for Hawn after her dismal adventures in *Deceived*. She plays waitress Gwen, whose modest means fail to support her grand ambitions. But that's before she meets stuffy architect Newton Davis (Martin): during their one-night stand, she learns of the custom-made dream house rejected by his long-term love (Delany). Gwen secretly traces his empty property to a New England town. She moves in, and proceeds to regale the locals with stories of her marriage to a dashing, professionally successful Newton. For a romantic comedy, there's little in the way of romance, but the film's strength lies in the escalating lies concocted by Gwen as she struggles to maintain a toehold on her new life. Although it doesn't add up to a whole, and screenwriter Mark Stein fudges the issue of Gwen's motivation, he does provide some very funny, cheerfully contrived scams. CM

House That Dripped Blood, The

(1970, GB, 102 min)
d Peter Duffell. *p* Max J Rosenberg, Milton Subotsky. *sc* Robert Bloch. *ph* Ray Parslow. *ed* Peter Tanner. *ad* Tony Curtis. *m* Michael Dress. *cast* Denholm Elliott, Peter Cushing, Christopher Lee, Jon Pertwee, Joanna Dunham, Joss Ackland, Chloë Franks, Nyree Dawn Porter, Ingrid Pitt, John Bennett.

●Third in the Amicus portmanteau horror series, incorporating four stories by Robert Bloch and marking Duffell's highly promising debut as a director. Three of the episodes are rough-and-ready but vigorous Grand Guignol fun, involving Elliott as a novelist confronted by the mad strangler created for his latest yarn; Cushing as a retired stockbroker whose head lands up in the hands of a waxworks Salome, image of his long-lost love; and Pertwee (it should have been Vincent Price) as a veteran star of horror movies who finds himself inexplicably in the grip of a vampiric urge. The fourth is something else again, a marvellous mood piece of chilling intensity about a lonely, angelic child (the remarkable Chloë Franks) who compensates rather nastily – with wax image and pins – for the neglect to which she has been condemned, not without cause, by her widowed father (Lee). TM

House with a View of the Sea, A (Una Casa con Vista al Mar)

(2000, Ven/Can/Sp, 93 min, b/w)
d Alberto Arvelo. *p* Pedro Mezquita Arcaya, Miguel Perelló, Christopher Zimmer. *sc* Alberto Arvelo Mendoza. *ph* Cezary Jaworski. *ed* José Ares. *m* Nascuy Linares, Loreena McKennitt. *cast* Gabriel Arcand, Imanol Arias, Leandro Arvelo, Alejo Felipe, Hector Manrique.

●Following his wife's death, Tomás Alonso, a campesino farmer, ponders whether God's justice is the same for all men. Struggling to raise his son, he's beset by poverty. Meanwhile, the fear of being unable to protect the boy from the bullying attention of the landowner's son brings tragedy to both their lives. This sometimes ponderous tale of love and death, violence and revenge is beautifully shot with a haunting, lushly minimalist score; moments of tenderness and humour, courtesy of a kindly travelling photographer, provide a little levity. JFu

Housing Problems

(1935, GB, 15 min, b/w)
d/p Arthur Elton, Edgar Anstey. *ph* John Taylor.

●The format is the same as any old item on any old *Newsnight*, and it's hard to regain mentally a state of affairs when such a film might have seemed groundbreaking. And although the social conditions described – bugs, squalor – seem like a call to arms, the fact is that the film was sponsored by a gas combine anxious to build blocks of flats which they could fill with their ovens and Ascots. The lasting interest lies in the unmediated (or so it appears) straight to camera monologues of the Stepney slum-dwellers themselves: a reminder of a time when kitchens were for toffs and everyone else just had a scullery. BBa

Howards End

(1991, GB, 142 min)
d James Ivory. *p* Ismail Merchant. *sc* Ruth Prawer Jhabvala. *ph* Tony Pierce-Roberts. *ed* Andrew Marcus. *pd* Luciana Arrighi. *m* Richard Robbins. *cast* Anthony Hopkins, Vanessa Redgrave, Helena Bonham Carter, Emma Thompson, James Wilby, Samuel West, Prunella Scales, Jemma Redgrave, Joseph Bennett, Simon Callow.

●Margaret, Helen and Tibby Schlegel are bright, beautiful and, compared with most Edwardians, open-minded. The Wilcoxes, with the sole exception of Mrs Wilcox, are not. When Helen (Bonham Carter) carries a torch for Paul Wilcox (Bennett), she gets her fingers burned, but Margaret (Thompson) strikes up a friendship with Mrs Wilcox (Vanessa Redgrave), who then goes and spoils it all by dying. Her last wish is for Margaret to have her house in the country, Howards End, but the wicked Wilcoxes destroy the will and deny Margaret her inheritance. Then, would you believe it, Mr Wilcox (Hopkins) falls for her... Thus the stage is set for a saga of marriage, idealism, despair, pregnancy, exile and manslaughter conducted to the sound of skeletons rattling in the closet. This is as close as EM Forster ever came to a revenger's tragedy, and the only way Ruth Prawer Jhabvala's overlong screenplay can incorporate all the incident is by having more black-outs than a convention of epileptics. The performances are impeccable, but honours go to Thompson, who manages to make Margaret's saintliness actually seem seductive. MS

Howard the Duck (aka Howard...a new breed of hero)

(1986, US, 111 min)
d Willard Huyck. *p* Gloria Katz. *sc* Willard Huyck, Gloria Katz. *ph* Richard H Kline. *ed* Michael Chandler, Sidney Wolinsky. *pd* Peter Jamison. *m* John Barry. *cast* Lea Thompson, Jeffrey Jones, Tim Robbins, Paul Guilfoyle, Liz Sagal, Dominique Davalos.

●Howard T Duck, of Marvel Comics, might well have a beef against Lucasfilm for transforming his magnetic comic strip personality into a zipperless polyester duck-suit (filled interchangeably by eight different actors, each apparently under four feet in height) in this aimless movie. As it begins, its hero is zapped out of his tranquil life in Duck World and mysteriously transported to Cleveland, Ohio, where he meets the lead singer (Thompson) of an all-girl punk band. Moved by the violent, anarchic lyrics which sink to depths of depravity only previously reached by the kids from *Fame*, Howard takes an interest in the girl. But the consummation of their love must wait, as the same forces which brought him to earth now threaten the planet iself. Eventually, some wonderful special effects mercifully take over as Jeffrey Jones is transformed into the evil 'Dark Overlord' and slugs it out with one of the duck-suited thespians. SGo

How Does It Feel

(1976, GB, 60 min)
d/p Mick Csaky. *sc* Mick Csaky, Adrian Munsey. *ph* John Bulmer, Mick Csaky, Charles Stewart. *ed* Philip Howe. *with* RD Laing, RL Gregory, Elkie Brooks, Joseph Beuys, Michael Tippett, David Hockney.

●This pretentious documentary, financed by the Arts Council, allegedly examines 'many ideas and activities developed to heighten our sensory awareness and feelings', but is in fact little more than an excuse for a stream of blather. Neuro-psychologist RL Gregory lectures on human sensory mechanisms while watching a movie of two people apparently making love; RD Laing pontificates ('We either want to live or we want to die, and while we're alive we surely want to live more abundantly...'), and later abstractedly watches the birth of his own son; David Hockney chatters engagingly about his art, and answers questions on the level of 'Can you see without your glasses?'; Annie Ross delivers a stentorian commentary, and Elkie Brooks interminably belts out Bob Dylan's 'Like a Rolling Stone'. Only Michael Tippett, passionately discussing the genesis of his Third Symphony, addresses himself to the subject with conviction. These matters were dealt with more energetically and with less solemnity in *WR – Mysteries of the Organism*. JPy

How Green Was My Valley

(1941, US, 118 min, b/w)
d John Ford. *p* Darryl F Zanuck. *sc* Philip Dunne. *ph* Arthur Miller. *ed* James B Clark. *ad* Richard Day, Nathan Juran. *m* Alfred Newman. *cast* Walter Pidgeon, Maureen O'Hara, Roddy McDowall, Donald Crisp, John Loder, Anna Lee, Barry Fitzgerald, Patric Knowles, Arthur Shields.

●The backlot mining village (impressive as it is) and the babel of accents hardly aid suspension of disbelief in this nostalgic recollection of a Welsh childhood, based on Richard Llewellyn's novel. An elegant and eloquent film, nevertheless, even if the characteristically laconic Fordian poetry seems more contrived here (not least in the uncharacteristic use of an offscreen narration). Its tale of the calamitous break-up of a traditional way of life – with immigration to America offering a despairing hope of salvation – looms larger in the mind if you think of it (as Ford obviously did) as dealing with Ireland rather than Wales. TM

How Harry Became a Tree

(2001, Ire/It/GB/Fr, 100 min)
d Goran Paskaljevic. *p* Riccardo Tozzi, Liam O'Neill, Clive Parsons, Antoine de Clermont-Tonnere. *sc* Goran Paskaljevic, Stephen Walsh, Christine Gentet. *ph* Milan Spasic. *ed* Petar Putnikovic. *pd* Lesley Oakley. *m* Stefano Arnaldi. *cast* Colm Meaney, Adrian Dunbar, Cillian Murphy, Kerry Condon.

●A multinational production, set in Ireland, written and directed by a Serb, based on an ancient Chinese folk tale – this has more edge than the usual blarney. 'A man is measured by his enemies,' avows Harry (Meaney in expansive mode): so he picks on George (Dunbar), the most successful and beloved man in the village. Caught up in this one-way feud is Harry's gormless son Gus (Murphy), who has his heart set on marrying George's latest girl, a catch so precious even Harry agrees to trade half a field of cabbages for her. The union only quickens Harry's descent into paranoia, with disastrous results for most of the characters. Hard not to read this earthy black comedy as an allegory for civil war. Certainly it's propelled by a strain of Balkan madness, a belief that extreme conviction is its own rationale. That fits Ireland in the 1920s well enough. Like poteen, it's unsubtle but potent. TCh

How I Won the War

(1967, GB, 110 min)
d/p Richard Lester. *sc* Charles Wood. *ph* David Watkin. *ed* John Victor Smith. *ad* Philip Harrison, John Stoll. *m* Ken Thorne. cast Michael Crawford, John Lennon, Roy Kinnear, Lee Montague, Jack MacGowran, Michael Hordern, Jack Hedley, Karl Michael Vogler, Ronald Lacey, Robert Hardy, Sheila Hancock, Dandy Nichols.
●Dated, maybe, but Lester's gruesomely black anti-war comedy still looks inventive, and manages occasionally to hit home with its blend of surreal lunacy and barbed satire. Concerning the futile mission of a troop of British soldiers in Egypt during World War II, sent behind enemy lines to set up a cricket pitch to impress a visiting VIP, Charles Wood's script, which attacks war movie conventions as much as war itself, is not always well served by Lester's determinedly zany direction; but the performances are well attuned to the single-minded mood of brash bitterness. GA

Howling, The

(1980, US, 90 min)
d Joe Dante. *p* Michael Finnell, Jack Conrad. *sc* John Sayles, Terence H Winkless. *ph* John Hora. *ed* Mark Goldblatt, Joe Dante. *ad* Robert A Burns. *m* Pino Donaggio. *cast* Dee Wallace, Patrick MacNee, Dennis Dugan, Christopher Stone, Belinda Balaski, John Carradine, Slim Pickens.
●Though it works well enough as a werewolf thriller (not, admittedly, a genre packed with masterpieces), Dante's film – which has TV reporter Wallace seeking therapy with bizarre consciousness-raising group 'The Colony' after a traumatic incident involving a serial killer – succeeds best as a witty, knowing commentary on the genre itself. References to lycanthropic lore, literature and cinema abound; gags are plentiful; and the whole thing casts a pleasingly sceptical glance at various social fashions and fads of the times. Hardly surprising, given Dante's irreverent sense of humour and the fact that the film was co-written by John Sayles. GA

How Old Is the River? (Fuyu no Kappa)

(1994, Jap, 114 min)
d Shiori Kazama. *sc* Shiori Kazama, Tomoko Ogawa. *ph* Akihiko Suzuki. *ed* Shiori Kazama. *cast* Akiko Ito, Cho Bang-Ho, Seiichi Tanabe, Rijin Wakuta, Makiko Kuno.
●Three half-brothers (their father was a serial husband) share an old-style house by a river outside Tokyo; but the house is on the market, and they have a week to vacate it. The youngest boy has a very secret crush on the eldest, and the other two are rivals for their female cousin; it doesn't take much to shatter their precarious emotional equilibrium. Making her first feature, Kazama sets out to pinpoint the exact moment when young adults surrender their adolescent sense of independence and begin to face a future in society. The film is sometimes so low-key that it threatens to float off down-river itself, but it sketches its characters with unassertive skill. TR

How Stella Got Her Groove Back

(1998, US, 124 min)
d Kevin Rodney Sullivan. *p* Deborah Schindler. *sc* Terry McMillan, Ron Bass. *ph* Jeffrey Jur. *ed* George Bowers. *pd* Chester Kaczenski. *m* Michel Colombier. *cast* Angela Bassett, Whoopi Goldberg, Regina King, Suzzanne Douglas, Taye Diggs, Michael J Pagan, Sicily, Carl Lumbly.
●Stella's got a spunky loving son, a big numbers job on the money markets (if it counts) and great-fitting pink running pants. But since she and her husband split, something's been missing. Still, a 40-year-old girl will dream, and when Stella appears to herself in a luscious vacation ad, Jamaica beckons – even if it takes her merrily dissolute friend Delilah (Goldberg) to force the issue. Lo, strapping Winston Shakespeare (Diggs) sees the shine in her, but as the fling turns serious, her cares return – he's half her age. *Shirley Valentine* meets *Harold and Maude*. The package holiday movie has its place and, as *Waiting to Exhale* suggested, Terry McMillan's cosmetic novels of the heart provide ideal material for this very literal type of cinematic escapism. Bassett is consistently watchable, but what with Stella's increasingly rambling relationship hesitancy, and Diggs' studious Jamaican accent adding 15 minutes to the running time, it's a long haul for such a flighty outing. NB

How Sweet Is Her Valley (Unterm Dirndl wird gejodelt)

(1974, WGer, 90 min)
d/p Alois Brummer. *sc* Peter Genzer. *ph* Hubertus Hagen. *ed* Jürgen Wolter. *m* Fred Turnow. *cast* Gisela Schwartz, Annemarie Wiese, Edgar Anliker, Margot Mahler, Bertram Edelmann.
●Unimaginably heavy-handed and ill-assembled German so-called sex comedy, populated by a brace of village idiots in lederhosen (one with a chicken in his shorts, the other fishing with a cowbell), several others who spend large amounts of time rubbing their privates in anticipation, and a couple of leading ladies got up to fulfil the more uninteresting fantasies of the pigtail, miniskirt and knicker brigade. VG

How Sweet It Is!

(1968, US, 98 min)
d Jerry Paris. *p/sc* Garry Marshall, Jerry Belson. *ph* Lucien Ballard. *ed* Bud Molin. *ad* Arthur Lonergan. *m* Patrick Williams. *cast* James Garner, Debbie Reynolds, Maurice Ronet, Paul Lynde, Terry-Thomas, Marcel Dalio, Penny Marshall.
●Garry Marshall and partner Jerry Belson wrote and produced this fairly ordinary comic travelogue, which follows concerned parents Garner and Reynolds to Europe so they can keep an eye on their son and his girlfriend on their continental vacation. Reynolds finds romance with dallying Ronet, best remembered for his searing portrayal of the suicidal playboy in Louis Malle's *Le Feu Follet*. Started life as a novel by Muriel Resnick titled *The Girl in the Turquoise Bikini*. TJ

How the Grinch Stole Christmas! (aka Dr Seuss's How the Grinch Stole Christmas!)

(1966, US, 26 min)
d Chuck Jones. *sc* Dr Seuss. *m* Albert Hague. *cast* voices: Thurl Ravenscroft, June Foray. *narrator* Boris Karloff.
●This 26-minute animated version of the children's story book is a seasonal classic on American TV, right up there with *It's a Wonderful Life*, variations on *A Christmas Carol*, and, I suppose, the Nativity. Chuck Jones keeps faith with the Dr Seuss visual style, and propels the slim storyline with dramatic panache (the Grinch takes his vengeance on the irritatingly cheerful Whos by stealing all their presents – but they celebrate anyway). It's less knowing than the Jim Carrey version, which sympathises more broadly with the mischievous monster. What's most striking about seeing this again is the shocking degree to which Tim Burton's *The Nightmare Before Xmas* obviously, uh, 'borrowed' from it. TCh

How the West Was Won

(1962, US, 155 min)
d Henry Hathaway, John Ford, George Marshall. *p* Bernard Smith. *sc* James R Webb. *ph* William Daniels, Milton Krasner, Charles Lang Jr, Joseph La Shelle. *ed* Harold F Kress. *ad* George W Davis, William Ferrari, Addison Hehr. *m* Alfred Newman. *cast* John Wayne, James Stewart, Henry Fonda, Gregory Peck, Carroll Baker, Debbie Reynolds, Richard Widmark, Walter Brennan, Raymond Massey, Agnes Moorehead, Karl Malden, Robert Preston, George Peppard, Eli Wallach. *narrator* Spencer Tracy.
●A vast, sprawling Western, shot in the short-lived three-strip Cinerama process, which chronicles the development of the American West through the adventures of one family over three generations. Hathaway's sequence, 'The Rivers, The Plains, The Outlaws', comes off best, while Ford's section on the Civil War looks as much a survey of his own career as of the war. The main problem remains the impossibility of subjecting a film that is fundamentally about landscape and history to the demands of such a coarse dramatic form. CPe

How to Be a Player

see Def Jam's How to Be a Player

How to Be a Woman and Not Die in the Attempt (Como ser mujer y no morir en el intento)

(1991, Sp, 89 min)
d Ana Belén. *sc* Carmen Rico-Godoy. *ph* Juan Amoros. *ed* Carmen Frias. *ad* Gerardo Vera. *m* Antonio Garcia De Diego, Pancho Varona, Mariano Diaz. *cast* Carmen Maura, Antonio Resines, Carmen Conesa, Tina Sainz, Juan Diego Botto, Paca Casares, Victor García, Juanjo Puigcorbé.
●This sweet film probably meant so much more in its native Spain, where director Belén is a film star and singer, and writer Carmen Rico-Godoy is a well-known novelist and journo. It's presumably autobiographical: the heroine (Maura) is also a journalist called Carmen, and the film has an episodic structure similar to a series of gently humorous newspaper columns. Carmen's husband (Resines) is a genial-slob record producer. It's up to Carmen to clean up, deal with the kids and the maid, and work. The point is hammered home quite relentlessly, but it's a mid-life crisis without the crisis. Maura is as watchable as ever, even when the material is as desultory as this. SFe

How to Be Very, Very Popular

(1955, US, 89 min)
d/p/sc Nunnally Johnson. *ph* Milton Krasner. *ed* Louis Loeffler. *ad* Lyle Wheeler, John F DeCuir. *m* Cyril J Mockridge. *cast* Betty Grable, Robert Cummings, Charles Coburn, Sheree North, Fred Clark.
●Originally, Marilyn Monroe was pencilled in to partner Forces pin-up Betty Grable in this frantic comedy about two chorus girls who hide out in a boys' college to escape a murderer. When Monroe turned down the role, Fox's platinum blonde in reserve, Sheree North, was brought in as replacement. Johnson tries too hard to be as zany as possible, but North's outrageous dance routines make this well worth a look. GM

How to Commit Marriage

(1969, US, 98 min)
d Norman Panama. *p* Bill Lawrence. *sc* Ben Starr, Michael Kanin. *ph* Charles Lang. *ed* Ronald Sinclair. *ad* Edward D Engoron. *m* Joseph L Lilley. cast Bob Hope, Jackie Gleason, Jane Wyman, Leslie Nielsen, Maureen Arthur, Joanna Cameron, Tim Matthieson, Tina Louise, Irwin Corey, Paul Stewart.
●One of the dire sitcoms in which Bob Hope latterly got bogged down. Hope and wife Wyman initiate divorce proceedings. Daughter (Cameron) learns this on the way to the altar, and decides to cohabit instead of marrying. Much ado, especially when she becomes pregnant, with Hope and Wyman adopting silly disguises and contriving to commit the young couple (and themselves, of course) to marriage. Hope also gets to masquerade as a hippy and an oriental guru, to play golf with a chimpanzee (he loses), and to see Jackie Gleason (as the prospective groom's cynical father) steal the few laughs on offer. TM

How to Destroy the Reputation of the Greatest Secret Agent (Le Magnifique)

(1973, Fr/It, 94 min)
d Philippe de Broca. *p* Alexandre Mnouchkine, Georges Danciger. *sc* Francis Verber. *ph* René Mathelin. *ed* Henri Lanoë. *ad* Francois de Lamothe. *m* Claude Bolling. *cast* Jean-Paul Belmondo, Jacqueline Bisset, Vittorio Caprioli, Monique Tarbès, Raymond Gérome.

●Nine years earlier, with *L'Homme de Rio*, de Broca and Belmondo came up with a delightful parody of James Bondery. They try again here, much less successfully, with Belmondo as a writer of pulp spy thrillers, pressured by deadline fever, who slips out of his seedy garret into the fantasy world of his novels. Imagining himself as his secret agent hero Bob Saint-Clair, he gets involved in the usual sub-Bond spy-jinks, and lures the girl across the courtyard, Christina/Tatiana (Bisset), between the covers. Routine shoot 'em up stuff is laced with casual sexism and marred by atrocious dubbing. GA

How to Get Ahead in Advertising

(1989, GB, 94 min)
d Bruce Robinson. *p* David Wimbury. *sc* Bruce Robinson. *ph* Peter Hannan. *ed* Alan Strachan. *pd* Michael Pickwoad. *m* David Dundas, Rick Wentworth. *cast* Richard E Grant, Rachel Ward, Richard Wilson, Jacqueline Tong, John Shrapnel, Susan Wooldridge, Mick Ford. Jacqueline Pearce, Roddy Maude-Roxby, Tony Slattery, Sean Bean.
●The very model of a successful '80s man, with a lifestyle to match, advertising executive Dennis Bagley (Grant) has a severe zit problem: he can't work up a pitch for a new pimple cream campaign. Things come to a head when he has a very real commercial break, realises that what's wrong with the world is advertising's fault, and proceeds to rid his home of anything that is contaminated with the deadly virus of the promoters. Pustules are forgotten, until a check in the mirror reveals a talking boil on his neck. As Bagley's disgust at his profession grows, so does the carbuncle, a wretched alter ego taking over his life. Grant, as the charmingly meglomaniac Bagley, turns in a high-energy, bravura performance. The opening half-hour is outrageously brilliant, but descends into a pot-boiler of repetitive, if animated, soapbox preaching about the manipulation of punters by the denziens of Madison Avenue and their international brotherhood. That said, writer/director Robinson's dark comedy is bursting with inspired scenes taking the pus out of this powerful industry, and is spot on. JGl

How to Make an American Quilt

(1995, US, 117 min)
d Jocelyn Moorhouse. *p* Sarah Pillsbury, Midge Sanford. *sc* Jane Anderson. *ph* Janusz Kaminski. *ed* Jill Bilock. *pd* Leslie Dilley. *m* Thomas Newman. *cast* Winona Ryder, Anne Bancroft, Dermot Mulroney, Ellen Burstyn, Kate Nelligan, Alfre Woodard, Kate Capshaw, Lois Smith, Jean Simmons, Rip Torn, Maya Angelou, Melinda Dillon, Gail Strickland.
●Struggling to finish a thesis on women's handiwork in tribal cultures and to come to terms with her imminent marriage, Berkeley student Finn Dodd (Ryder) returns to spend the summer with her grandmother (Burstyn) and great aunt (Bancroft). Their idyllic retreat is also the work place of the Grasse Quilting Bee, and as its members make her wedding quilt, Finn becomes privy to their tales of love and betrayal. Unlike the glib accounts of bonding in *Waiting to Exhale* and *Now and Then*, this adaptation of Whitney Otto's best-seller is a lyrical, intelligent attempt to create a specifically 'female' cinema. Moorhouse keeps the narrative, which spans 130 years, on a tight rein, never allowing it to wander aimlessly from one anecdote to the next. Admittedly, the metaphor (life's rich tapestry) is facile, but the direction, Janusz Kaminski's pastoral photography and Jane Anderson's finely tuned dialogue combine to produce a subtle, surprisingly witty film. Nevertheless, it's the remarkable performances which really enhance the mixture of nostalgia and world-weary realism: Ryder, as gamine as ever, delivers her most credible performance to date, while the luminous Simmons and imposing Angelou infuse the film with grace and understated charm. KM

How to Marry a Millionaire

(1953, US, 95 min)
d Jean Negulesco. *p/sc* Nunnally Johnson. *ph* Joseph MacDonald. *ed* Louis Loeffler. *ad* Lyle Wheeler, Leland Fuller. *m* Alfred Newman. *cast* Marilyn Monroe, Betty Grable, Lauren Bacall, William Powell, Rory Calhoun, David Wayne, Alex D'Arcy, Cameron Mitchell, Fred Clark.
●The first film to be shot in CinemaScope (although it was the second to be released) opens with a pre-credit sequence called *Street Scene*, which was designed to show off the new anamorphic and stereophonic system. Then follows this feeble little comedy, which hardly needed a wide screen and which just about gets by on star power. Filmed immediately after *Gentlemen Prefer Blondes*, it's basically the same story, with divorcee Bacall and her chums Monroe and Grable turning a New York apartment into a man-trap. It was made solely to boost Monroe's celebrity, and her short-sighted bimbo is the best thing in it. The men – including Calhoun's fur trapper, Powell's oil tycoon, and Wayne's tax evader – are a wan lot and meant to be. ATu

How to Steal a Diamond in Four Uneasy Lessons

see Hot Rock, The

How to Steal the World

(1968, US, 89 min)
d Sutton Roley. *p* Anthony Spinner. *sc* Norman Hudis. *ph* Robert B Hauser. *ed* Peter Tanner. *pd* Wilfrid Shingleton. *m* Richard Shores. *cast* Robert Vaughan, David McCallum, Barry Sullivan, Eleanor Parker, Leslie Nielsen, Daniel O'Herlihy, Leo G Carroll, Angela Bassett.
●Kitsch '60s thrills as the Men from UNCLE, Napoleon Solo and Illya Kuryakin, battle yet another evil genius, who's been kidnapping their fellow spies and plotting world domination from his hideaway high in the Himalayas. From the days when Leslie Nielsen was a serious actor. Well, sort of. TJ

How to Succeed in Business Without Really Trying

(1966, US, 121 min)
d/p/sc David Swift. *ph* Burnett Guffey. *ed* Ralph E Winters, Allan Jacobs. *ad* Robert Boyle. *m/lyrics* Frank Loesser. *cast* Robert Morse, Michele Lee, Rudy Vallee, Anthony Teague, Maureen Arthur, Sammy Smith, Murray Matheson.
●A blandly outrageous and occasionally sharp-toothed musical satirising big business, with a likeable score by Frank Loesser, which takes potshots at everything from coffee breaks to advertising campaigns. Morse, somehow contriving to be horrendous and endearing at one and the same time, repeats his stage role to brilliant effect as the all-American boy who employs scientific knowhow to rise like a meteor, licking asses and trampling heads every step of the way. Swift's direction is a little stiff and stagy, and there are dull patches; but with handsome camerawork from Burnett Guffey, witty Bob Fosse choreography, and the ineffable Vallee playing the compulsive-knitting, fussbudget boss, this was one of the livelist musicals of the '60s. TM

H.P. Lovecraft's Necronomicon

see Necronomicon

Huckleberry Finn (aka The Adventures of Huckleberry Finn)

(1939, US, 91 min, b/w)
d Richard Thorpe. *p* Joseph L Mankiewicz. *sc* Hugo Butler. *ph* John F Seitz. *ed* Frank E Hull. *ad* Cedric Gibbons. *m* Franz Waxman. *cast* Mickey Rooney, Walter Connolly, William Frawley, Rex Ingram, Minor Watson, Jo Ann Sayers, Elisabeth Risdon, Victor Kilian.
●Disappointingly routine follow up to *The Adventures of Tom Sawyer*, prosaically shot (in black-and-white) with none of the care lavished on the earlier film, despite extensive use of locations. With the characters stuck in cliché (Connolly and Frawley labouring for comic effect as the riverboat conmen, Ingram in the Uncle Tom bit as the runaway slave), the leisurely adventures – though entertaining enough, thanks largely to a subdued and admirable Rooney – seem to roll by as sluggishly as ol' man river. TM

Huckleberry Finn

(1974, US, 118 min)
d J Lee Thompson. *p* Arthur P Jacobs. *sc* Robert B Sherman, Richard M Sherman. *ph* Laszlo Kovacs. *ed* Michael F Anderson. *pd* Philip M Jefferies. *songs* Richard M Sherman, Robert B Sherman. *cast* Jeff East, Paul Winfield, Harvey Korman, David Wayne, Arthur O'Connell, Gary Merrill, Natalie Trundy, Lucille Benson.
●With the facsimile b/w minstrels crooning 'Huckle-berry, Huckle-berry, where you bin?' and Roberta Flack 'performing' (so the credits say) the title song, you get the tenor of this *Reader's Digest* musical adaptation. The lying and deception that run through Twain's original become incidental rather than thematic, and much of the sense of sheer adventure gets lost. Instead, Huck's adventures with runaway slave Jim remain amiable and episodic rather than memorable and integrated. Everyone 'performs' larger than life, singing their forgettable songs rather badly. Laszlo Kovacs' camerawork, consistently several notches above the rest of the production, remains its only distinctive feature. CPe

Hud

(1962, US, 111 min, b/w)
d Martin Ritt. *p* Martin Ritt, Irving Ravetch. *sc* Irving Ravetch, Harriet Frank Jr. *ph* James Wong Howe. *ed* Frank Bracht. *ad* Hal Pereira, Tambi Larsen. *m* Elmer Bernstein. *cast* Paul Newman, Melvyn Douglas, Patricia Neal, Brandon De Wilde, John Ashley, Whit Bissell, Crahan Denton, Val Avery.
●Along with *Hombre*, one of Ritt's best films, less abrasive than it thinks but still a remarkably clear-eyed account of growing up in Texas to mourn the old free-ranging ways of the frontier days. Its focus is the antagonism between a sternly moralising, patriarchal ranch-owner (Douglas) and his free-drinking, free-whoring 'no account' son (Newman); the conflict between them, ambivalently observed by the two other members of the household, both emotionally involved with Newman – the ranch housekeeper (Neal) and a hero-worshipping nephew (de Wilde) – boils to a head over a government order to slaughter the ranch's entire herd as a precaution against foot-and-mouth, with Newman urging outlaw defiance and Douglas siding with the law. The film sometimes seems to be busting its britches to attain the status of Greek tragedy in delineating the disintegration of a heritage, with dialogue haunted by images of death and decay. But pretensions are kept nicely damped down by the performances (all four principals are great) and by Wong Howe's magnificent camerawork. TM

Hudson Hawk

(1991, US, 100 min)
d Michael Lehmann. *p* Joel Silver. *sc* Steven E De Souza, Daniel Waters. *ph* Dante Spinotti. *ed* Chris Lebenzon, Michael Tronick. *pd* Jack DeGovia. *m* Michael Kamen, Robert Kraft. *cast* Bruce Willis, Danny Aiello, Andie MacDowell, James Coburn, Richard E Grant, Sandra Bernhard, David Caruso, Donald Burton, Frank Stallone.
●This quirkily amusing piece of vanity filmmaking is essentially a ludicrously expensive cult movie. Fresh from prison, reformed thief Hawk (Willis) is coerced by filthy rich megalomaniacs Darwin and Minerva Mayflower (Grant and Bernhard) into a plot to steal three Leonardo masterpieces that provide the key to an alchemical machine for turning lead into gold. Hovering in the backgroud are CIA man Coburn and beautiful Vatican spy MacDowell. Shades of TV's *Moonlighting* remain, with a cavalier disregard for plot logic and henchmen named after candy bars. Unfortunately, neither Lehmann's direction nor the in-jokey script achieve a consistent tone, veering from knockabout fun to vicious, throat-slashing gore. Willis smirks and smarms his way through some neatly staged set pieces, but funnier by far are MacDowell's drug-induced display of dolphin-speak and the deliciously demented antics of Grant and Bernhard. NF

Hudsucker Proxy, The

(1994, US, 111 min)
d Joel Coen. *p* Ethan Coen. *sc* Ethan Coen, Joel Coen, Sam Raimi. *ph* Roger Deakins. *ed* Thom Noble. *pd* Dennis Gassner. *m* Carter Burwell.

cast Tim Robbins, Paul Newman, Jennifer Jason Leigh, Charles Durning, Jim True, John Mahoney, William Cobbs, Steve Buscemi.
●New Year's Eve, 1958, Norville Barnes (Robbins) climbs on to a window-ledge of the Hudsucker Industries skyscraper in snowy Manhattan. We flash back a month: company chairman Waring Hudsucker (Durning) shocks board members by plunging 45 floors to the sidewalk below – at the moment young Norville, a hayseed business graduate from Indiana, first enters the building to take a post in the mail room. Norville didn't, however, expect immediate promotion to company boss, a move plotted by vice-chairman Sidney Mussburger (Newman); with an idiot pawn in charge, stock will plummet and Sid can take over. Or he could, if only hard-bitten hack Amy Archer (Leigh) hadn't smelt a rat and gone undercover as Norville's secretary. Directed by Joel Coen, produced by Ethan Coen, and scripted by both brothers (plus Sam Raimi), this is a notably well-executed, very funny and very well-acted movie: a quirky, sardonic take on '50s faddishness, fame, power, friendship, character and ethics. A minor work, but confirmation of the Coens' position among America's most ambitious, able and exciting film-makers. GA

Hu-Du-Men (aka Stage Door)

(1996, HK, 87 min)
d Shu Kei. *p* Raymond Chow. *sc* Raymond To. *ph* Bill Wong. *ed* Kwong Chi-leung. *pd* Bill Lui. *m* Otomo Yoshida. *cast* Josephine Siao, Anita Yuen, Daniel Chan, Chung King-fai, Lee Chi-hung.
●Tailored to fit the impossibly wonderful Josephine Siao, Shu Kei's comedy drama centres on a woman who makes her living playing men on stage and has trouble fulfilling the roles of wife and mother off stage. The film sensibly makes no attempt to disguise the story's own stage origins, but concentrates instead on weaving together the several strands of plot, the emotional complications and the rapid shifts from humour to pathos and back again. The slightly surprising appearance of a lesbian subplot confirms that sexual politics are somewhere on the agenda, but the stance is closer to farce than Freud. Charmingly old-fashioned. TR

Hue and Cry

(1947, GB, 82 min, b/w)
d Charles Crichton. *p* Michael Balcon. *sc* TEB Clarke. *ph* Douglas Slocombe. *ed* Charles Hasse. *ad* Norman G Arnold. *m* Georges Auric. *cast* Alastair Sim, Jack Warner, Harry Fowler, Valerie White, Douglas Barr, Jack Lambert, Harry Fowler, Frederick Piper, Vida Hope.
●Reminiscent of *Emil and the Detectives* as a gang of East End kids excitedly realise that their favourite blood-and-thunder comic is being used as a means of communication by crooks, and (since the police turn a deaf ear) set out in hot pursuit. One of Ealing's first postwar successes, it is given an enormous boost by locations around the bomb sites of London's East End and by Sim's sinister eccentricities as the author of the serial in question. Its charm, in these days of headlines about kids and video nasties, is of another world: capturing a blonde moll (White) and requiring information, the gang subject her to the most vicious tortures they can think of – tickling by feather (which doesn't work) and menace by white mouse (which does). TM

Huellas Borradas, Las

see Fading Memories

Huevos de Oro

see Golden Balls

Huggetts Abroad, The

(1949, GB, 87 min, b/w)
d Ken Annakin. *p* Betty Box. *sc* Gerard Bryant, Ted Willis, Mabel and Denis Constanduros. *ph* Reg Wyer. *ed* Gordon Hales. *ad* Norman Arnold. *m* Antony Hopkins. *cast* Jack Warner, Kathleen Harrison, Susan Shaw, Petula Clark, Jimmy Hanley, Dinah Sheridan.
●'It's like a little bit o' Bournemouth,' says Ma Huggett, unimpressed by her first glimpse of Algiers. Fed up with rain, rationing and drabness, the family have resolved to make a new start in South Africa. The idea of the Huggetts confronting apartheid is not unappealing, but as it happens, a Canadian crook and a nasty fellow Brit ensure they never leave French territory. East, West, home's best, conclude the admirable, exasperating tribe, and head back to Huggettland. These chronicles of the working class sector of the bourgeoisie are a goldmine for social historians, and still offer a degree of entertainment. A Huggett-ography: introduced in *Holiday Camp* (qv), then in their own little series comprising *Here Come the Huggetts*, *Vote For Huggett*, and this last one, *The Huggetts Abroad*. BBa

Hugo the Hippo

(1975, US, 90 min)
d William Feigenbaum. *p* Robert Halmi Sr. *sc* Thomas Baum. *pd* Graham Percy. *m* Robert Larimer. *cast* voices: Robert Morley, Paul Lynde, Ronny Cox, Percy Rodriguez.
●An animation feature with terrible songs from Burl Ives and Osmonds Marie and Jimmy. But at least there's an attempt at a liberal theme in its story about the friendship between a village boy (a black kid in Africa) and the sole survivor of a hippo slaughter, and how the local kids come to Hugo's aid against the mindless cruelty of the adults. VG

Huis Clos (No Exit/ Vicious Circle)

(1954, Fr, 96 min, b/w)
d Jacqueline Audry. *sc* Pierre Laroche. *ph* Robert Juillard. *ed* Marguerite Beaugé. *ad* Maurice Colasson. *m* Joseph Kosma. *cast* Arletty, Frank Villard, Gaby Sylvia, Yves Deniaud, Nicole Courcel, Danièle Delorme, Gianni Esposito.
●Down they go, another consignment of sinners, arriving in the lobby of Hell, where a very correct receptionist directs them to their quarters. A mother who murdered her child, a revolutionary who betrayed his comrades and a suicided lesbian, handpicked to drive each other up the wall, are designated room-mates for eternity. Their only distraction, a window on to the world of the living, is soon sealed as their old associates forget them. This adaptation can do little to mitigate the theatrical hokum of the Sartre source material, its pretensions pointed up by Philip Larkin when he rendered its most famous line – '*L'enfer, c'est les autres*' – as 'other people are hell'. Afterlife experts, though, may find this version interestingly of its time. BBa

8 Femmes

see 8 Women

Huitième Jour, Le

see Eighth Day, The

Hullabaloo over Georgie and Bonnie's Pictures

(1978, Ind/GB, 83 min)
d James Ivory. *p* Ismail Merchant. *sc* Ruth Prawer Jhabvala. *ph* Walter Lassally. *ed* Humphrey Dixon. *ad* Bansi Chandragupta. *m* Vic Flick. *cast* Peggy Ashcroft, Larry Pine, Saeed Jaffrey, Victor Banerjee, Aparna Sen, Jane Booker.
●Originally made for LWT's *The South Bank Show*, this is probably one of the most successful of all Merchant Ivory collaborations. Ruth Prawer Jhabvala's script sets two collectors (Ashcroft and Pine) and two adventurers (Jaffrey and Sen) after a group of Indian miniatures, hidden away in a glorious but crumbling palace. The owner, the Maharajah of Jodhpur (Banerjee), watches dispassionately as the four scrabble decorously but desperately after his family's fortune. As delicate and as beautiful as the miniatures at its centre, the film poses, in the most acceptable and accessible way, central questions about the function and value of art. JW

Human Beast, The

see Bête Humaine, La

Human Desire

(1954, US, 90 min, b/w)
d Fritz Lang. *p* Lewis J Rachmil. *sc* Alfred Hayes. *ph* Burnett Guffey. *ed* Aaron Stell. *ad* Robert Peterson. *m* Daniele Amfitheatrof. *cast* Glenn Ford, Gloria Grahame, Broderick Crawford, Edgar Buchanan, Kathleen Case, Grandon Rhodes, Dan Seymour.
●Lang's version of Zola's *La Bête Humaine* is, like all his best '50s work, as cold, hard and steely grey as the railway tracks which here mark out the action. Glenn Ford, the perfect embodiment of these qualities, returns from Korea, only to be pulled into the murderously destructive marriage between Grahame and Crawford (both superb). The bleak, dark marshalling yards are the perfect backdrop for the playing out of adulterous relationships where 'desire' signifies only fear, jealousy and hatred. SJ

Human Experiments

(1979, US, 86 min)
d/p Gregory Goodell. *sc* Richard Rothstein. *ph* Joao Fernandes. *ed* Barbara Pokras, Jon Gregory. *pd* Linda Spheeris. *m* Marc Bucci. *cast* Linda Haynes, Geoffrey Lewis, Ellen Travolta, Lurene Tuttle, Aldo Ray, Jackie Coogan, Mercedes Shirley.
●Solo country singer Linda Haynes runs foul of the law (Ray and Coogan cameos) and takes the rap for a mass killing that sees her committed to the state penitentiary, where a crazed regime zombifies its women inmates. Trailing well behind *Jackson County Jail*, but firing off a cruder mixture of backwoods misogyny and nightmarish incarceration, it's a severe case of Southern discomfort. MA

'Human' Factor, The

(1975, GB, 96 min)
d Edward Dmytryk. *p* Frank Avianca. *sc* Tom Hunter, Peter Powell. *ph* Ousama Rawi. *ed* Alan Strachan. *ad* Peter Mullins. *m* Ennio Morricone. *cast* George Kennedy, John Mills, Raf Vallone, Arthur Franz, Rita Tushingham, Haydée Politoff, Barry Sullivan.
●Despite some heavily loaded exploitation of middle class fears of irrational terrorist violence, this movie achieves a certain bulky conviction of its own. After the pointless slaughter of his family in Naples, the cerebral war-games of a NATO electronics expert (Kennedy) are undermined by baser instincts of revenge. Thrashing around like a stunned ox, Kennedy takes on the extremists single-handed, finally wiping them out after they take over a crowded supermarket. His disintegration into a brute force gives the film its momentum, and more or less everyone stands back in disbelief to let him get on with it. The computer hardware is diverting, and treated with greater respect than the terrorists, who are given no credibility whatsoever, ideological or otherwise. CPe

Human Factor, The

(1979, GB/US, 114 min)
d/p Otto Preminger. *sc* Tom Stoppard. *ph* Mike Molloy. *ed* Richard Trevor. *ad* Ken Ryan. *m* Richard Logan, Gary Logan. *cast* Nicol Williamson, Richard Attenborough, Joop Doderer, John Gielgud, Derek Jacobi, Robert Morley, Ann Todd, Richard Vernon, Iman.
●As directed by the erratic Preminger and scripted by Tom Stoppard, this is pretty faithful to Graham Greene's novel about loyalty and betrayal in the espionage world, at least in terms of plot. Dealing with a couple of British agents suspected of leaking information to the Russians, it comes across well enough in its portrait of loneliness and conscience, and – despite being worthy and almost totally bereft of any real action – the plot mechanics are unusually clear for a spy movie. But the whole thing badly lacks any sort of central thematic focus, and the strangely obsessive Englishness of Greene's world is altogether missing. Craftsmanlike rather than inspired, it's watchable thanks largely to its solid performances. GA

Humanité, L'

see Humanity

Humanity (L'Humanité)

(1999, Fr, 148 min)
d Bruno Dumont. *p* Jean Bréhat, Rachid Bouchareb. *sc* Bruno Dumont. *ph* Yves Cape. *ed* Guy Lecorne. *pd* Marc-Philippie Guerig. *m* Richard Cuvillier. *cast* Emmanuel Schotté, Séverine Caneele, Philippe Tullier, Ghislain Ghesquière, Ginette Allègre.
●Exhibiting all the faults and almost none of the virtues of Dumont's earlier, far superior *La Vie de Jésus*, this is again set in an unrelentingly glum Pas de Calais, where Schotté's police

lieutenant investigates the murder of a young girl whose mutilated body he's found in a field. The notion, that he's an ordinary, unremarkable man whose tendency to take the world's suffering – and sins – on his own shoulders makes him a latter-day saint, has a certain Bressonian appeal, but the clumsy performances (by local amateurs), the slow, faltering pace, and Dumont's seeming ignorance of the most basic police procedures (finger-printing, DNA, cross-examination, deduction) make for a turgid, pretentious and sometimes risibly implausible film. GA

Humanity and Paper Balloons (Ninjo Kamifusen)

(1937, Jap, 86 min, b/w)
d Sadao Yamanaka. *p* Masanobu Takemaya. *sc* Shintaro Mimura. *ph* Akira Mimura. *ad* Sentaro Iwata, Kazuo Kubo. *m* Tadashi Ota. *cast* Kanemon Nakamura, Chojuro Kawarazaki, Sukezo Suketakaya, Emitaro Ichikawa, Shizue Yamagishi.

● Yamanaka, a friend and contemporary of Ozu, was one of the giants of '30s Japanese cinema; this masterpiece marked the end of a six-year career directing period melodramas. (He was drafted on the day it premiered and died in battle in Manchuria the following year, aged 29.) It was his second collaboration with the (covertly leftist) theatre troupe Zenshin-za and represented a direct challenge to the militarist ethos rampant in other period movies of the time. Luckless ronin Matajuro (Kawarazaki) looks for work while his wife O-Taki (Yamagishi) makes paper balloons at home. His neighbour Shinza (Nakamura), a barber, kidnaps a young heiress and hides her in Matajuro's home; his attempt to extort a ransom from her father ends in grief. A deeply pessimistic view of poverty and crime in feudal society, it was drawn from a 19th century kabuki play, but Yamanaka thought and felt it in strongly cinematic terms. The performances are naturalistic and surprisingly 'modern'; the compositions have great depth of field, linking foreground and background action. And the pathos is distinctly hard-edged: the film stresses that the slum community comes alive only for funerals, and it opens and closes with offscreen suicides. TR

Human Monster, The

see Dark Eyes of London

Humanoid, The (L'Umanoide)

(1979, It, 100 min)
d George B Lewis [Aldo Lado]. *p* Giorgio Venturini. *sc* Adriano Bolzoni, Aldo Lado. *ph* Silvano Ippoliti. *ed* Mario Morra. *pd* Enzo Bulgarelli. *m* Ennio Morricone. *cast* Richard Kiel, Corinne Cléry, Leonard Mann, Barbara Bach, Arthur Kennedy, Ivan Rassimov, Massimo Serato.

● *Star Wars* may have been puerile, but at least it was fun, which is more than can be said for this space cowboys and Indians movie: a tedious compound of everything from *Frankenstein* (the irradiated mutant monster) to Zen Buddhism (the boy Dalai Lama floats in from Tibet on a glass ashtray), with Darth Vader baddies and a robodog thrown in for good measure. The sets resemble Brent Cross and the spaceships could have come out of a cornflakes packet. 'Nuff said? FF

Humanoids from the Deep (aka Monster)

(1980, US, 81 min)
d Barbara Peeters. *p* Martin B Cohen. *sc* Frederick James. *ph* Daniel Lacambre. *ed* Mark Goldblatt. *ad* Michael Erler. *m* James Horner. *cast* Doug McClure, Ann Turkel, Vic Morrow, Cindy Weintraub, Anthony Penya, Hoke Howell, Linda Shayne.

● Despite the sex of the director, a more blatant endorsement of exploitation cinema's current anti-women slant would be hard to find: the strain of humanoid ecological mutants featured here don't stick simply to killing everyone in sight, but carry the sexual premise of the Black Lagoon a stage further into a compulsion to rape. Peeters also lays on the gore pretty thick amid the usual visceral drive-in hooks and rip-offs from genre hits; and with the humour of an offering like *Piranha* entirely absent, this turns out a nasty piece of work all round. PT

Human Resources (Ressources Humaines)

(1999, Fr/GB, 103 min)
d Laurent Cantet. *p* Caroline Benjo, Carole Scotta. *sc* Laurent Cantet, Gilles Marchand. *ph* Matthieu Poirot Delpech, Claire Caroff. *ed* Robin Campillo, Stéphane Leger. *ad* Romain Denis, Caroline Bernard, Florent Maillot, Evariste Richer, Loic Lemoigne. *cast* Jalil Lespert, Jean-Claude Vallod, Chantal Barré, Véronique de Pandelaère, Michel Begnez, Lucien Longueville, Danielle Mélador.

● Business student Franck (Lespert) returns home as a management trainee in the same factory as his father, a tool operator. Like Bruno Dumont's *L'Humanité*, this rousing and moving drama grandly (and ironically) invokes our peculiar species in its title, even as it's marked by an understated directorial style that minimises visual flourish and favours non-professional actors. But where Dumont applies a mysterious and distanced gaze, Cantet, for all his formal restraint, fashions a film of communicative intimacy, offering a fresh, relevant and challenging view of work, class and family. If the choice of milieu, a concrete industrial satellite of Paris which we first see through Franck's eyes as he journeys home by train, recalls '60s political Godard, so does the film's evolving class-consciousness. But whatever Cantet's political stance, his methods are dramatic, not didactic. His realism is based on acute, telling observation. The film has its faults. Franck's discovery of secret management plans lacks credibility; the skullduggery of the bosses is overdone; and the father is a little too bovine. But these are quibbles. WH

Human Traffic

(1999, GB/Ire, 95 min)
d Justin Kerrigan. *p* Allan Niblo, Emer McCourt. *sc* Justin Kerrigan. *ph* David Bennett. *ed* Patrick Moore. *pd* David Buckingham. *m* Robert Mello, Matthew Herbert. *cast* John Simm, Lorraine Pilkington, Shaun Parkes, Danny Dyer, Nicola Reynolds, Dean Davies, Peter Albert, Jan Anderson, Jo Brand.

● Drawing on his experience of 'life in the bus lane', sticking dead end jobs for the promise of weekend clubbing, writer/director Kerrigan follows half a dozen Cardiff mates from the rush of Friday evening to the Sunday afternoon hangover. First up, there's Jip (Simm), party animal and bigtime romantic, temporarily handicapped by a case of Mr Floppy. Then there's vinyl pusher Coop (Parkes), his flirty girl Nina (Reynolds), her tough-talking pal Lulu (Pilkington) and wheeler dealer Moff (Dyer). There's not much you could call 'plot' here. Rather, the film proceeds through a kind of double-vision by which daily reality is warped, scratched and remixed in the fantasies of Jip and his friends. The film doesn't really come into its own until it hits the dance-floor. Put simply, the higher it gets, the funnier it is. The hyper, in-your-face style sometimes feels forced, and some gags fall crushingly flat, but I'd bet the chemical generation will embrace this movie, not only because it's wickedly good on the agony and the Ecstasy, but because Kerrigan's virtuosity is at the service of his honesty – you wouldn't be surprised to bump into any of these characters on a Friday night. The film emanates a bruvverly vibe that sends you out on a wave of euphoria. TCh

Hummingbird Tree, The

(1992, GB, 84 min)
d Noella Smith. *p* Gub Neal. *sc* Jonathan Falla. *ph* Remi Adefarasin. *ed* Mark Day. *pd* Tony Borough. *m* John Keane. *cast* Patrick Bergin, Susan Wooldridge, Clive Wood, Tom Beasley, Desha Penco, Sunil Y Ramjitsingh.

● A BBC 'Screen One' production, set in Trinidad at the time of the 1946 elections, when the vote was being extended to black Caribbeans and Indians and the call for independence was growing louder. A far from unpredictable take on the tensions wrought by racial, religious and class divisions, it focuses on a young white boy whose friendship with two local Hindustani kids is constantly being discouraged by his supposedly liberal parents. Performances, script and direction are adequate rather than inspired, though the flaws will probably be less apparent on the small screen. GA

Humoresque

(1946, US, 125 min, b/w)
d Jean Negulesco. *p* Jerry Wald. *sc* Clifford Odets, Zachary Gold. *ph* Ernest Haller. *ed* Rudi Fehr. *ad* Hugh Reticker. *m* Rimsky-Korsakov, Tchaikovsky, Gershwin, Wagner. *cast* Joan Crawford, John Garfield, Oscar Levant, J Carrol Naish, Craig Stevens, Tom D'Andrea, Paul Cavanagh, Robert Blake.

● Full-tilt Warner Brothers melodrama: slum kid Garfield rises to concert pitch as a classical violinist (dubbed by Isaac Stern) under the far from disinterested patronage of wealthy/lonely/bottle-happy/yearning socialite Crawford, and amid ludicrously intense shoulder-chip, tear-jerk sparrings, has to choose between his bow and her heartstrings. Levant plays resident cynic/voice of conscience from the piano stool; Clifford Odets, no less, contributes to the adaptation of Fannie Hurst's madcap tushery. PT

Hunchback of Notre Dame, The

(1923, US, 108 min, 2,593 ft, b/w)
d Wallace Worsley. *sc* Edward T Lowe, Perley Poore Sheehan. *ph* Robert S Newhard, Tony Kornman. *ad* EE Sheeley, Sidney Ullman, Stephen Goosson. *m* Hugo Riesenfeld. *cast* Lon Chaney, Patsy Ruth Miller, Ernest Torrence, Raymond Hatton, Norman Kerry, Tully Marshall, Brandon Hurst.

● Chaney's first big-budget film, and the one which made his reputation. Laden down with massive sets and milling extras, bowdlerised even by comparison with the Laughton version of 1939, it emerges more as a historical spectacle than as a horror movie – and a rather tedious one at that, thanks to Worsley's often painfully ponderous direction. Worth seeing mainly for Chaney's remarkable performance; even bowed and constricted by the heavy weights he used to help simulate Quasimodo's crippled gait, his body remains extraordinarily expressive. TM

Hunchback of Notre Dame, The

(1939, US, 116 min, b/w)
d William Dieterle. *p* Pandro S Berman. *sc* Sonya Levien. *ph* Joseph August. *ed* William Hamilton, Robert Wise. *ad* Van Nest Polglase. *m* Alfred Newman. *cast* Charles Laughton, Maureen O'Hara, Cedric Hardwicke, Thomas Mitchell, Edmond O'Brien, Harry Davenport, George Zucco.

● Although Laughton doesn't attempt the acrobatics that Lon Chaney performed in the silent version, his hunchback comes across as one of the cinema's most impressive 'grotesque' characterisations. Dieterle directs in a way that reminds you of his background as actor/director in the German expressionist cinema: the visuals here impressively recall earlier movies from *Metropolis* (the crowds) to *The Last Laugh* (tracking shots through the shadows). Richly entertaining. TR

Hunchback of Notre Dame, The (Notre Dame de Paris)

(1956, Fr/It, 107 min)
d Jean Delannoy. *p* Robert Hakim, Raymond Hakim. *sc* Jean Aurenche, Jacques Prévert. *ph* Michel Kelber. *ed* Henri Taverna. *ad* René Renoux. *m* Georges Auric. *cast* Anthony Quinn, Gina Lollobrigida, Jean Danet, Alain Cuny, Robert Hirsch, Jean Tissier.

● Embarrassingly awful, with Quinn labouring under a slapdash make-up and not rendering the crude dubbed dialogue (it's difficult to imagine that Jacques Prévert had a hand in the original script) any more palatable by indulging in some weird vocal mannerisms. A totally misbegotten venture. TM

Hunchback of Notre Dame, The

(1996, US, 91 min)
d Gary Trousdale, Kirk Wise. *p* Don Hahn. *sc* Tab Murphy, Irene Mecchi, Bob Tzudiker, Noni White, Jonathan Roberts. *ed* Ellen Keneshea. *ad* David Goetz. *songs* Alan Menken, Stephen Schwartz. *cast* voices: Tom Hulce, Demi Moore, Kevin Kline, Tony Jay.

● While Victor Hugo might not entirely recognise his novel, this Disney animated blockbuster more or less remakes the formidable 1939 Charles

Laughton version, marking another milestone for the studio with its dazzling technique and surprisingly mature content. As voiced by Hulce, Quasimodo is, despite the misshapen form that restricts him to the company of three bantering gargoyles in the cathedral bell tower, a fairly cuddly chap. But *Beauty and the Beast* directors Trousdale and Wise marshal their energies to different ends, lining up this King of Fools alongside the Parisian gypsies and beggars, united in the harsh treatment they receive from the chilling Judge Frollo – an index of society's attitude to the outsider which even the youngest minds should grasp. Elsewhere, while Kevin Kline injects a dash of irony into the conventionally heroic Phoebus, the modelling of free spirited Esmeralda on voice artist Demi Moore (vital statistics and all) confirms the underlying sexual tension – in a Disney cartoon! – of Frollo's confrontation with his own inner demons. Though Alan Menken's music misses the big tune that would cap Stephen Schwartz's nimble lyrics, it's the thematic sophistication that brings the movie to life, making older children and adults its best audience. Sure, the pacy slapstick is up to par, but the 'mobile' camera and extraordinary vistas really come into their own in the dramatic set-pieces, breakneck chases and the climactic assault on Notre Dame itself. TJ

Hundstage

see Dog Days

Hungarian Fairy Tale, A (Hol Volt, Hol nem Volt)

(1986, Hun, 97 min, b/w)
d Gyula Gazdag. *sc* Gyula Gazdag, Miklós Györffy. *ph* Elemér Ragályi. *ed* Júlia Sivó. *pd* József Romvari. *m* WA Mozart. *cast* Arpád Vermes, Mária Varga, Frantisek Husák, Eszter Czákányi, Szilvia Tóth.

●The fairytale in question is the legend of a giant bird that flies down to save Hungary, but Gazdag's film is less a reinvention of national myth than an attempt to get to the bottom of a typically communist paradox: the way that human impulses turn into inhuman pratices under the dead hand of bureaucracy. The bird turns up at the start in a TV cartoon; and reappears at the end to carry a little boy and his surrogate parents away from their troubles. In between, the film uses Mozart's *Magic Flute* to waft its way through the story of a young orphan searching for a father who was only ever a fictitious name on a birth certificate. Gazdag's approach has something in common with the 'magic realism' of Latin American novelists; he shoots in silvery black-and-white, and feels free to jump from social observation into areas of fantasy and absurdist humour. The result is undeniably distinctive, and the shifts in tone sometimes have a genuinely disconcerting punch; but basically, Gazdag is looking back nostalgically to earlier social fables like De Sica's *Miracle in Milan* than forward to the Hungary of the '90s. TR

Hunger, The

(1983, US, 99 min)
d Tony Scott. *p* Richard A Shepherd. *sc* James Costigan, Ivan Davis, Michael Thomas. *ph* Stephen Goldblatt, Tom Mangravite. *ed* Pamela Power. *pd* Brian Morris. *m* Michael Rubini. Denny Jaeger. *cast* Catherine Deneuve, David Bowie, Susan Sarandon, Cliff De Young, Beth Ehlers, Dan Hedaya, Suzanne Bertish, Bessie Love, Willem Dafoe.

●Deneuve is the ageless, possibly final survivor of an ancient immortal race dependent on humans for both sustenance and companionship. Her superior blood allows her lovers a triple lifetime until they ultimately succumb to instant decline. Not all of this is apparent in the film, where style rules at the expense of coherence. But that style is often glorious, from a bloody sun sinking over a gothic hi-tech Manhattan skyline to living quarters that are sumptuous. Neat touches of grim humour also: Deneuve and Bowie manhunt in a disco as Bauhaus sing 'Bela Lugosi's Dead'; and Bowie rots away in a hospital waiting room where the 20 minutes wait becomes a subjective century of ageing. Visual sensualities will have a feast, but you'll have to read Whitley Strieber's novel if you don't want to emerge with a badly scratched head. GD

Hungry Hill

(1946, GB, 109, b/w)
d Brian Desmond Hurst. *p* William Sistrom. *sc* Daphne du Maurier, Terence Young, Francis Crowdy. *ph* Desmond Dickinson. *ed* Alan Jaggs. *pd* Alex Vetchinsky. *m* John Greenwood. *cast* Margaret Lockwood, Cecil Parker, Michael Denison, Dermot Walsh, Dennis Price, Jean Simmons, Siobhan McKenna, Dan O'Herlihy.

●Lockwood isn't her usual Wicked Lady self in this overcooked piece of blarney about 19th century Irish copper-mining folk. She plays a high-spirited colleen who toys with the affections of two brothers, Denison and Price. The storyline, adapted by Daphne du Maurier (and Terence Young) from her own novel, ladles on fire, flood and disease in its grim moments, and throws in Irish jigs, horse riding and waltzing whenever a little levity is needed. There's the usual bad feeling between the villagers and the big businessman (Parker) who's taken over their land to open his mine. Lockwood is the one who suffers, losing her husband and ending up (somewhat improbably) as a sad old woman with a drug and gambling problem. The dialogue's often laughable, the attempts at Irish accents grate, but this is still enjoyable, full-blooded entertainment. GM

Hungry Wives

see Jack's Wife

Hunt, The

see Caza, La

Hunted (aka The Stranger in Between)

(1952, GB, 84 min, b/w)
d Charles Crichton. *p* Julian Wintle. *sc* Jack Whittingham. *ph* Eric Cross. *ed* Geoffrey Muller. *ad* Alex Vetchinsky. *m* Hubert Clifford. *cast* Dirk Bogarde, Jon Whiteley, Elizabeth Sellars, Kay Walsh, Frederick Piper, Julian Somers.

●A child stumbles on an edgy, well-dressed man in an abandoned warehouse. The man grabs the boy and drags him from the building, leaving the body of a murdered man lying in the rubble. From this taut beginning, the film (set in Glasgow and the surrounding country) develops into a study of the pair on the run and of the demons that pursue them. Bogarde, in one of his earlier starring roles, is persuasive as the jealous husband who has stepped outside the law, and his gradual redemption and growing fondness for young Robbie (Whitely) is believable and touching. Crichton's direction produces a tense, forbidding atmosphere with imagery occasionally echoing that of Laughton's *Night of the Hunter*. Melodramatic but compelling. TCo

Hunter, The

(1980, US, 117 min)
d Buzz Kulik. *p* Mort Engelberg. *sc* Ted Leighton, Peter Hyams. *ph* Fred J Koenekamp. *ed* Robert L Wolfe. *pd* Ron Hobbs. *m* Michel Legrand. *cast* Steve McQueen, Eli Wallach, Kathryn Harrold, LeVar Burton, Ben Johnson, Richard Venture, Tracey Walter.

●McQueen's last movie has him cast as a latter-day bounty hunter making a living bringing in bail absconders. Routinely scripted and directed, but McQueen gives a likeable enough performance as the anachronistic born-out-of- his-time man. Best running joke is his beaten-up auto which he seems unable to move without crunching metal. RM

Hunters, The

(1958, US, 108 min)
d/p Dick Powell. *sc* Wendell Mayes. *ph* Charles G Clarke. *ed* Stuart Gilmore. *ad* Lyle R Wheeler, Maurice Ransford. *m* Paul Sawtell. *cast* Robert Mitchum, Robert Wagner, Lee Phillips, Peter Egan, May Britt.

●Mitchum snoozes his way through this Korean War drama as an Air Force major so cool in the face of combat he's called 'the Iceman'. Not much flying, instead there's a soapy subplot involving the nerve-wracked Phillips and his two-timing spouse May Britt – more than enough going on though for those who'd happily watch the star recite the phone book. Filmed in 'Scope, from a novel by James Salter. TJ

Hunter's Blood

(1986, US, 102 min)
d Robert C Hughes. *p* Myrl A Schreibman. *sc* Emmett Alston. *ph* Tom DeNove. *ed* Barry Zetlin. *ad* Douglas Forsmith. *m* John D'Andrea. *cast* Sam Bottoms, Clu Gulager, Ken Swofford, Mayf Nutter, Joey Travolta, Kim Delaney, Lee DeBroux, Billy Drago, Mickey Jones, Billy Bob Thornton.

●A bunch of Real Men drive into the deep woods of Arkansas (apparently located in Ventura, California) to shoot something. There, to nobody's surprise but their own, they encounter poachers who are even Realer Men and who therefore shoot at everybody. The movie was optimistically promoted with the tag 'After *Deliverance* comes *Hunter's Blood*'. There's also a rerun of John Cazale's 'clumsy hunter' scene from *The Deer Hunter* and the night-camp ambush from *The Searchers*. Clu Gulager performs some *Last of the Mohicans*-style tracking and hand signals, but all that distinguishes hunter from poacher is neat hair and better dental work. Once the chase is on nothing much happens beyond miscellaneous running about and shooting. DO

Hunt for Red October, The

(1990, US, 135 min)
d John McTiernan. *p* Mace Neufeld. *sc* Larry Ferguson, Donald Stewart. *ph* Jan de Bont. *ed* Dennis Virkler, John Wright. *pd* Terence Marsh. *m* Basil Poledouris. *cast* Sean Connery, Alec Baldwin, Scott Glenn, Sam Neill, James Earl Jones, Joss Ackland, Richard Jordan, Peter Firth, Tim Curry, Stellan Skarsgård.

●The 'Red October' is a silent submarine. Virtually undetectable on sonar, it constitutes a deadly first strike weapon, more than enough to tip the nuclear balance in the Soviets' favour. No sooner has it left port on its maiden voyage than Captain Raimus (Connery, terrific) breaks from the official course and heads for the US. Will he start a war, or defect? Despite the Cold War implications (the action is set disingenuously before Gorbachev), there's enough nuclear frisson and multi-lateral cynicism here to evoke *Fail Safe*, if not *Dr Strangelove*. McTiernan guides us surely threough the convolutions of an admittedly over-complicated plot, and adeptly links hi-tech with character. At its best, with Soviets, Americans and Raimus all at cross-purposes, the movie is an engrossing and exciting battle of wits. But when it attemptsto suggest an interior life in the characters beyond the job at hand, the results are at best perfunctory, more often corny, despite the high-calibre cast. TCh

Hunting Scenes from Lower Bavaria (Jagdszenen aus Niederbayern)

(1968, W Ger, 90 min, b/w)
d/sc Peter Fleischmann. *ph* Alain Derobe. *ed* Barbara Mondy, Jane Seitz. *cast* Martin Sperr, Angela Winkler, Else Quecke, Michel Strixner, Maria Stradler, Hanna Schygulla.

●Between the seemingly idyllic opening and closing scenes depicting a rural community, first at church, then at the village festival, Fleischmann attacks that community's prejudices and ignorance without remorse. His very precisely observed portrait of Bavarian life begins with little more than a display of the villagers' constant ribbing, bawdy humour, continuous gossip, and more than a hint of their slow-wittedness. With the return of a young man, their idle malice and childish clowning, always on the edge of unpleasantness, receive some focus: quite without foundation, the lad is victimised as a homosexual. The crippling conformity of their ingrained conservatism leads the villagers to reject anything 'different': a young widow is ostracised, more for her crippled lover and idiot son than her morals; a teacher is frozen out because she's educated; the casual destruction of the young 'homosexual' is given no more thought than the cutting up of a pig. Not Germany in the '30s but the '70s; nevertheless the political parallels are clear. An impressive film. CPe

Hurlyburly

(1998, US, 123 min)
d Anthony Drazan. *p* Anthony Drazan, Richard N Gladstein, David S Hamburger. *sc* David Rabe. *ph* Changwei Gu. *ed* Dylan

Tichenor. *pd* Michael Haller. *m* David Baerwald, Steve Lindsey. *cast* Sean Penn, Kevin Spacey, Robin Wright Penn, Chazz Palminteri, Garry Shandling, Anna Paquin, Meg Ryan.
●What a cast and crew! What a disappointment! This cynical would-be dissection of the macho, self-oriented, coke-fuelled world of male film folk making up Hollywood's second rung is adapted by David Rabe from his own play. It shows Sundance prizewinner Drazan to be a formidable director of actors. Changwei Gu captures beautifully the cold, gleaming ambience of the Hollywood Hills apartments where ever-high Eddie (S Penn), 'flip' Mickey (Spacey), shallow Artie (Shandling) and near psychotic Phil (Palminteri) talk the talk like latter-day Rat Packers for whom the humour has soured into self-parody. Paquin's teenage drifter Donna, who uses her body as a meal ticket, and Ryan's rent-a-date Bonnie have the sad roles of the victims – providing evidence of the naked nature of the men's ugly misogyny – but their inadequately qualified passivity merely adds to the pervasive atmosphere of inhuman coldness. Unedifying. WH

Hurricane

(1979, US, 120 min)
d Jan Troell. *p* Dino De Laurentiis. *sc* Lorenzo Semple Jr. *ph* Sven Nykvist. *ed* Sam O'Steen. *pd* Danilo Donati. *m* Nino Rota. *cast* Jason Robards, Mia Farrow, Max von Sydow, Trevor Howard, Dayton Ka'ne, Timothy Bottoms, James Keach.
●This melodrama of murder and miscegenation was to have been directed by Polanski, who might perhaps have introduced some sexual curiosity. Troell's version is more polynesian pap than polymorphous perversity. American naval commander's virginal daughter (Farrow) is seduced by the pulsating beat of native loins in Pago Pago. The enviable loins belong to Dayton Ka'ne, a bronzed cross between Arnold Schwarzenegger and Robby Benson, but their love augurs badly – the entire cast overacts at the mention of it, and Mia's dad (Robards) can't decide whether he's Captain Queeg or Captain Ahab. As it becomes clear that lots of scenes didn't make it into the final cut, the hurricane does to the landscape what everyone else has done to the script. And even the effects don't cut it. SM

Hurricane, The

(1937, US, 102 min, b/w)
d John Ford. *p* Samuel Goldwyn. *sc* Dudley Nichols. *ph* Bert Glennon. *ed* Lloyd Nosler. *ad* Richard Day. *m* Alfred Newman. *cast* Dorothy Lamour, Jon Hall, Mary Astor, C Aubrey Smith, Raymond Massey, Thomas Mitchell, John Carradine, Jerome Cowan.
●A breezy South Seas melo, with Dorothy Lamour, having no need to apologise for slinking around in a sarong, canoodling with Hall and giving starchy Governor Raymond Massey the sweats. Ford knocks off the hour or so of filler efficiently enough before the special effects team (headed by James Basevi) take over for the biggest blow-job in Hollywood history. Infinitely more enjoyable than the 1979 remake. ATu

Hurricane, The

(1999, US, 145 min)
d Norman Jewison. *p* Armyan Bernstein, John Ketcham, Norman Jewison. *sc* Armyan Bernstein, Dan Gordon. *ph* Roger Deakins. *ed* Stephen Rivkin. *pd* Philip Rosenberg. *m* Christopher Young. *cast* Denzel Washington, John Hannah, Deborah Kara Unger, Liev Schreiber, Vicellous Reon Shannon, David Paymer, Dan Hedaya, Harris Yulin, Rod Steiger, Al Waxman.
●This facile and unpersuasive film is based on the true story of Afro-American middleweight boxer Rubin 'Hurricane' Carter, who served 20 years in prison for a murder he didn't commit. The problem stems, one suspects, from Jewison's debt to a simpler age, when the '60s Civil Rights movement was at its peak. But it's another century, and racial politics have moved on, leaving Jewison, a veteran of liberal conscience movies, with his embarrassing white-people-can't-dance jokes, a toe-curling script and leaden stereotypes. Not to mention pale imitations of boxing scenes from *Raging Bull*. Washington can't be faulted as the wronged fighter, while Shannon shows promise as the teenager who inspires Carter to fight for his release. But both soon become powerless observers of their own lives, dependant on the whim of heroic white knights and authority figures. GMu

Hurricane Streets

(1997, US, 89 min)
d Morgan J Freeman. *p* Galt Niederhoffer, Gill Holland, Morgan J Freeman. *sc* Morgan J Freeman. *ph* Enrique Chediak. *ed* Sabine Hoffman. *pd* Petra Barchi. *m* Theodore Shapiro. *cast* Brendon Sexton III, Shawn Elliott, José Zuñiga, David Roland Frank, Carlo Alban, Edie Falco, LM Kit Carson, Isidra Vega.
●This slice of wrong-side-of-the-tracks New York teenage life has a sympathetic heart, but lacks the passion and originality to convince. It centres on crew member Marcus (Sexton), a spotty, asthmatic, vulnerable 15-year-old being raised by his grandmother in the absence of his father, and with his mother in jail (for helping Mexicans hop the border). It's a story of breaking away, with Marcus making his first (sweetly outlined) romantic forays with pretty young Latino Melena (Vega), running in with her dad and being hauled up by the cops for thieving. Writer/director Freeman is initially at pains to restrain the usual hyperrealist clichés, patching out the boy's existence in desultory, almost inconsequential scenes of street life, hanging out in the 'club house', fencing stolen goods by the school gates. Here the movie seems most at ease, but as it gears up with gunplay episodes and an all too familiar heist, the uncertainties – inappropriateness, rather – of tone, and the shortcomings of the acting and directing become more evident. WH

Hurry Sundown

(1966, US, 146 min)
d/p Otto Preminger. *sc* Thomas C Ryan, Horton Foote. *ph* Milton Krasner, Loyal Griggs. *ed* Louis Loeffler, James D Wells. *pd* Gene Callahan. *m* Hugo Montenegro. cast Michael Caine, Jane Fonda, John Phillip Law, Robert Hooks, Diahann Carroll, Burgess Meredith, Faye Dunaway, George Kennedy, Rex Ingram.
●Set in Georgia in 1946 and dealing with the attempts of land-grabbers to dispossess a Negro smallholder, this is the sort of film in which the good guys are very, very good, the bad ones just plain horrid, and you recognise the hero because he gazes at his son, pauses for a count of three, and solemnly intones, 'A man's gotta do what his conscience says is right'. When Preminger makes a problem movie, he really piles on the agony: not just black-baiters and black-lovers, but a judge prejudiced to the point of imbecility, a conscienceful white minister serving his black brethren, a child traumatised after being tied up in his cot, and rampant sex all over the place. The Preminger flair which made *The Cardinal* so enjoyable, despite its hackneyed script, seems to have deserted him in this lumbering melodrama, put together with the sort of crudely opportunistic 'style' which alternates scenes of the rich folks parading in a stately mansion with shots of the poor sitting down to their humble fare while thumping mood music makes sure you get the point. TM

Husbands

(1970, US, 154 min)
d John Cassavetes. *p* Al Ruban. *sc* John Cassavetes. *ph* Victor J Kemper. *ed* Tom Cornwall, Jack Woods, Robert Heffernan. *ad* Rene D'Auric. *cast* Ben Gazzara, Peter Falk, John Cassavetes, Jenny Runacre, Jenny Lee Wright, Noelle Kao.
●One of the Cassavetes improvisations made before he began profitably subjecting the technique to genre limitations in *The Killing of a Chinese Bookie*, *Opening Night* and *Gloria*, this is a maddening mixture. Cliché is never too far away as three New York commuters, middle-aged, married and disturbed by the death of a friend, embark on a despairing odyssey (partly on a flying visit to London) of drink, sex and self-discovery. Yet for all the rambling repetitions and noisy generalisations, the film does add up to a devastatingly bleak view of the emptiness of suburban life. TM

Husbands and Wives

(1992, US, 108 min)
d Woody Allen. *p* Robert Greenhut. *sc* Woody Allen. *ph* Carlo Di Palma. *ed* Susan E Morse. *pd* Santo Loquasto. *cast* Woody Allen, Blythe Danner, Judy Davis, Mia Farrow, Juliette Lewis, Liam Neeson, Sydney Pollack, Lysette Anthony, Cristi Conaway, Ron Rifkin, Bruce Jay Friedman.
●When Sally (Davis) and Jack (Pollack) announce their amicable break-up, their friends Gabe and Judy (Allen and Farrow) start looking at their own marriage more critically. Do they keep secrets from each other? Why have they never had kids? Would Lit lecturer Gabe follow Jack's example and fall for a woman half his age – student Rain (Lewis), for example? Why is Judy so keen to get the highly-strung Sally together with her eligible colleague, the *very* romantic Michael (Neeson)? To put it another way, what is this thing called love? So vividly drawn are all the characters that one becomes wholly caught up in their tangled whirl of emotional/psychological confusion: though not consistently hilarious, the film is engrossing from start to finish. If the use of hand-held camera is occasionally overdone, Allen's decision to shoot and structure his study of mid-life crisis in the style of fly-on-the-wall documentary pays dividends. With excellent performances (Davis and Pollack in particular), it's his finest film since *Hannah and Her Sisters*. GA

Hush!

(2001, Jap, 135 min)
d Ryosuke Hashiguchi. *p* Tetsujiro Yamagami. *sc* Ryosuke Hashiguchi. *ph* Shogo Ueno. *ed* Ryosuke Hashiguchi. *pd* Fumio Ogawa. *m* Bobby McFerrin. *cast* Mazuya Takahashi, Seiichi Tanabe, Reiko Kataoka.
●Seriously disappointing third feature from the director of *A Touch of Fever* and *Like Grains of Sand*. Asako (Kataoka), a socially graceless dental assistant, decides that she fancies maternity and barges into the lives of a gay couple, wanting Katsuhiro (Tanabe) to provide sperm and be a father at arm's length. But he is already having trouble in his relationship with the still closeted Naoya (Takahashi), and matters are made worse by the fact that a flakey woman in Katsuhiro's office has a crush on him. All the tensions explode, soap opera-style, when Katsuhiro's family visits from Kyoto for a showdown. It wouldn't be a problem that the film gets bogged down in such dated 'gay issues' if the thirty-something characters were more engaging and the film didn't spend so much time showing how existentially lonely they all are. Add some decidedly awkward comedy relief and you have a misfire which is really no advance on Joji Matsuoka's rather similar *Twinkle*, made nearly ten years earlier. TR

Hush-a-Bye Baby

(1989, Ire, 72 min)
d Margo Harkin. *p* Tom Collins. *sc* Margo Harkin, Stephanie English. *ph* Breffni Byrne. *ed* Martin Duffy. *m* Sinead O'Connor. *cast* Emer McCourt, Michael Liebmann, Cathy Casey, Julie Marie Reynolds, Sinead O'Connor.
●A delightful film from the Derry film and Video Collective, about the lives of four working class convent school chums, one of whom (played by the excellent McCourt) forms a romantic affair – consolidated during an evening Irish class – with a boy who is later detained by the British Army. Something of an exemplar of low-budget, locality-based film-making, the film homesstraight in on the realities of its protagonists' lives, engaging such issues as adolescence, the British presence, isolation and abortion through finely observed and finely played details in their daily lives. Its vigour, clarity and compassion make the sad predicament of McCourt's heroine all the more moving. Sinead O'Connor has a cameo and provides an excellent music soundtrack. WH

Hush...Hush, Sweet Charlotte

(1964, US, 134 min, b/w)
d/p Robert Aldrich. *sc* Henry Farrell, Lukas Heller. *ph* Joseph Biroc. *ed* Michael Luciano. *ad* William Glasgow. *m* Frank De Vol. *cast* Bette Davis, Olivia de Havilland, Joseph Cotten, Agnes Moorehead, Cecil Kellaway, Victor Buono, Mary Astor, William Campbell, Wesley Addy, Bruce Dern, George Kennedy.
●Loony Grand Guignol, with Aldrich and Davis retreading the territory charted in *What Ever Happened to Baby Jane?* a couple of years earlier. This time round, Davis is the victim, a woman

suspected of murdering her fiancé and driven to the point of insanity by the dead man's repeated hauntings of her in her lonely Gothic mansion. Over the top, of course, and not a lot to it, but it's efficiently directed, beautifully shot (Joseph Biroc), and contains enough scary sequences amid the brooding, tense atmosphere. Splendid performances from Davis and Moorehead, too. GA

Hussard sur le toit, Le (The Horseman on the Roof)

(1995, Fr, 136 min)
d Jean-Paul Rappeneau. *p* René Cleitman. *sc* Jean-Paul Rappeneau, Nina Companeez, Jean-Claude Carrière. *ph* Thierry Arbogast. *ed* Noëlle Boisson. *ad* Ezio Frigerio. *m* Jean-Claude Petit. *cast* Oliver Martinez, Juliette Binoche, Claudio Amendola, Pierre Arditi, Isabelle Carré, François Cluzet, Jean Yanne, Gérard Depardieu.

●1832. Provence is gripped by cholera. Angelo (Martinez), a hussar, flees Austrian assassins determined to stamp out exiled Italian revolutionaries. Although he attempts to help victims with know-how garnered from a doctor, he's almost lynched as a suspected water-poisoner. To cap it all, he meets mysterious Pauline de Théus (Binoche), a woman so brave and loyal that she's prepared to travel the ravaged land alone in search of her husband. The entranced Angelo insists on delaying his return to Italy to accompany her on the quest. But is there hope? Rappeneau's follow-up to *Cyrano de Bergerac* is a sumptuous costumer adapted from another literary favourite (one of Jean Giono's 'Hussar' novels). He avoids the static pictorialism that afflicts most heritage movies by focusing on dynamic action and using a speedy, kinetic camera and cutting style. Sadly, however, this runs the risk of turning what is clearly intended to be a serious romance into a lusty romp. Binoche's customary gravitas lends the proceedings some emotional depth, while Martinez makes for a handsome, energetic hero. The Provençal villages and landscapes look good (as usual), but in the end there's not enough development, thematic or otherwise, to sustain interest. GA

Hussy

(1979, GB, 94 min)
d Matthew Chapman. *p* Jeremy Watt. *sc* Matthew Chapman. *ph* Keith Goddard. *ed* Bill Blunden. *pd* Hazel Peiser. *m* George Fenton. *cast* Helen Mirren, John Shea, Daniel Chasin, Murray Salem, Paul Angelis, Jenny Runacre, Patti Boulaye, Sandy Ratcliff.

●A love story requiring wads of tissue – if not for dabbing at the eyes, then for stuffing in the mouth to stifle frequent yawns – *Hussy* follows the path of true love as it never runs smooth for a whore with a heart of mould (Mirren) and the lighting man at the nightclub she operates. Set against the sex, drugs and chicken-in-the-basket ambience of London's niteries, their attempts to find happiness (like the scriptwriter's efforts to avoid clichés) get bogged down in a welter of increasingly banal plot devices. A violence-crazed ex-lover, a coke-crazed ex-friend, and a football-crazed 10-year-old son do all they can to mess things up, but like Mirren's virulent essays at acting, it's never quite enough. FL

Hustle

(1975, US, 118 min)
d/p Robert Aldrich. *sc* Steve Shagan. *ph* Joseph Biroc. *ed* Michael Luciano. *ad* Hilyard Brown. *m* Frank DeVol. *cast* Burt Reynolds, Catherine Deneuve, Ben Johnson, Paul Winfield, Eileen Brennan, Eddie Albert, Ernest Borgnine, Catherine Bach, Jack Carter.

●Remarkable contemporary *film noir* that cuts the dirt and corruption of Los Angeles with a strain of allusions to (and, in the case of Reynolds' cop, illusions of) European romance. A perverse network of lies, guilts and evasions encompasses even Reynolds' love for hooker Deneuve, despite his misguided sense that he can exorcise one world to gain access to another by pursuing a spiralling investigation into the death of a call-girl on behalf of her dangerously distraught father. The toughly ironic parallels Aldrich imposes on Steve Shagan's customarily bitter script draw out a sense that everyone is hustling masochistically for impossible dreams; most audaciously, if the love story is seen as central, Aldrich provides Reynolds and Deneuve with the ultimate tinsel role model of Lelouch's *A Man and a Woman*. PT

Hustler, The

(1961, US, 135 min, b/w)
d/p Robert Rossen. *sc* Robert Rossen, Sidney Carroll. *ph* Gene Shufton [Eugen Schüfftan]. *ed* Dede Allen. *pd* Harry Horner. *m* Kenyon Hopkins. *cast* Paul Newman, Jackie Gleason, George C Scott, Piper Laurie, Myron McCormick, Murray Hamilton, Michael Constantine, Jake La Motta, Vincent Gardenia.

●Newman is Fast Eddie, doing his best to convince the world that he can take on Minnesota Fats (Gleason) at pool and walk away with the world title. As always with Walter Tevis (the author of the original book), it takes defeat, and a longish dark night of the soul with Laurie, a drunken, lame waif of a woman, before he can summon the self-respect to return to battle. Rossen allows much space to the essentially concentrated, enclosed scenes of the film, and so it rests solidly on its performances. A wonderful hymn to the last true era when men of substance played pool with a vengeance. CPea

Hustler White

(1996, US, 80 min)
d Bruce LaBruce, Rick Castro. *p* Jürgen Brüning, Bruce LaBruce. *sc* Bruce LaBruce, Rick Castro. *ph* James Carman. *ed* Rider Siphron. *pd* Rick Castro, Bruce LaBruce. *cast* Tony Ward, Bruce LaBruce, Alex Austin, Kevin Kramer, Ron Athey, Glen Meadmore, Ivar Johnson, Rick Castro.

●Bruce LaBruce surfaces somewhere closer to the mainstream with this picaresque LA story. There are no women and, no drugs (and no AIDS-consciousness) in this sideways spin on the rituals of meeting cute. But there is LaBruce himself as visiting writer Jürgen Anger (no relation to Kenneth, as he says repeatedly), who falls for the beatific presence of fugitive hustler Ward, as the two negotiate Santa Monica Boulevard's parade of perversities. It's on the level of mid-'70s John Waters, delighting more in shock value than technical accomplishment (grungy 16mm). TJ

Hwa-om-kyong (Hwa-eom-gyung)

(1993, SKor, 110 min)
d Jang Sun-Woo. *p* Lee Tae-Won. *sc* Jang Sun-Woo. *ph* Yu Young-Gil. *ed* Kim Hyun. *m* Lee Chong-Ku. *cast* Oh Tae-Kyung, Lee Hye-Young, Kim Eun-Mi, Kim Hye-Sun, Chung Soo-Young.

●*Hwa-om-kyong* is the Korean name of the Avatamsaka Sutra, used by Ko Eun as the title for his novel about a young man's tortuous path to Buddhist enlightenment in the India of the Fifth Century BC. Jang proves that he's not only the bad-boy provocateur of Korea's 'new cinema' but a world-class talent by reinventing Ko's novel as a commentary on present day Korea. In Jang's version a boy orphan who never ages physically journeys through the country in search of the mother he never knew; he goes from city streets and polluted dumps to the remotest areas of the country, meeting a prostitute blinded by her pimp, a political prisoner, a professor of astronomy, a Goddess of Mercy. Less a Buddhist film than a way of seeing the chaos of the present from an unexpected perspective, this is a devastating achievement. TR

Hyenas (Hyènes/Ramatou)

(1992, Switz/Fr/Sen, 110 min)
d Djibril Diop Mambéty. *p* Pierre Alain Meier, Alain Rozanes. sc Djibril Diop Mambéty. *ph* Matthias Kalin. *ed* Loredana Cristelli. *m* Wasis Diop. *cast* Mansour Diouf, Ami Diakhate, Makhourédia Gueye, Issa Ramagelissa Samb, Faly Gueye, Djibril Diop Mambéty.

●Partly based on Friedrich Dürrenmatt's play *The Visit*, *Hyenas* could be read as a simple parable about political corruption, but it's far too strange to be reduced to that. Stylistically and visually, it's reminiscent of the García Márquez-inspired film *Erendira* – there's the same sense of heightened unreality and (dare one say it?) magic realism. Set in a small village which mysteriously blossoms into a metropolis (i.e. it's set nowhere), it's the story of a local notary shunted into the moral front line when the town is visited by one of its daughters made good – the now omnipotent *grande dame* Linguere. Director Mambéty displays a slightly cruel comic touch as he manipulates his cast of fools and avenging deities in what seems like Africa's equivalent of a Krazy Kat landscape. Not quite fascinating, but more than intriguing. JRo

Hyenas' Sun (Soleil des Hyènes)

(1977, Tun/Neth, 100 min)
d Rihda Behi. *p* Willum Thijssen. *sc* Rihda Behi. *ph* Theo van de Sande. *ed* Ton de Graaff. *ad* Jean-Robert Marquis. *m* Nicola Piovani. *cast* Larbi Doghmi, Mahmoud Morsi, Habachi, Ahmed Snoussi, Hélène Catzaras, El Omari.

●Tunisia turns up trumps with this rough but quite striking study in the awful consequences of capitalist madness and tourism in a small fishing village. The quick-witted jump on the bandwagon with the development's German financiers, the others tag behind as employees, deserting their boats to sell tinned sardines and hawk postcards to the overweight foreign funsters who crowd the beaches. Behi, making his first full-length feature, uses a strident visual style, with a little too much distorted camerawork for comfort; but the film's sense of commitment (and acidly ironic sense of humour) helps to steady the course. GB

Hypnotised and Hysterical (Hairstylist Wanted) (Filles Perdues, Cheveux Gras)

(2002, Fr, 96 mins)
d Claude Duty. *p* Bruno Levy. *sc* Claude Duty, Jean-Philippe Barrau, Pascale Faure. *ph* Bruno Romiguière. *ed* Agnès Mouchel. *ad* Jean-Pierre Clech. *m* Valmont. *cast* Amira Casar, Marina Fois, Olivia Bonamy, Charles Berling, Sergi Lopez, Léa Drucker.

●This belated first feature from short-film-maker Duty is a genuinely offbeat pop musical. Its allegiance to the Demy tradition is to be found not in the slightly uninspired sub-Madonna choreography and melodies (albeit with agreeably witty lyrics), but in the clever colour coding (lurid rather than pastel) and in the unusually downbeat story about three young women going through various crises. (One's an alky who lost her pussy, another a single 'unfit' mother, the last obsessed with vengeance on her faithless lover.) Then there's the animated and synchronised-swimming sequences, a finale tinged (tongue-in-cheek) with pantheistic mysticism, and an engagingly diverse array of minor characters (including a Masai warrior). Quite delightfully different. GA

Hypothesis of the Stolen Painting, The (L'Hypothèse du Tableau Volé)

(1978, Fr, 66 min, b/w)
d Raúl Ruiz. *p* Nedjma Ouichene. *sc* Raúl Ruiz, Pierre Klossowski. *ph* Sacha Vierny. *ed* Patrice Royer. *ad* Bruno Beauge. *m* Jorge Arriagada. *cast* Jean Rougeul, Gabriel Gascon, Chantal Paley, Jean Raynaud, Daniel Grimm.

●For anyone sceptical about the big claims made for Ruiz, this is the film to see. It's the equivalent of a vintage Ken Russell arts psycho-doc, commissioned by French TV as a study of the philosopher, novelist (and high-class pornographer) Pierre Klossowski. The result is more like a haunted-house occult whodunit in suspended animation. A bumbling collector of pictures takes us on a guided tour of his *Tonnerre* collection – not the canvases, but their weird compositions re-enacted as tableaux vivants in a mansion and its gardens. Between his far-fetched interpretations of these pictures (mythological subjects with relevance to the society of the day), an enigma takes shape that can only be explained through 'the hypothesis…etc'. A tale of mystery and imagination that gives new meaning to the phrase 'intellectual thriller'. This is the real thing. IC

Hysteric

(1999, Jap, 100 min)
d Takahisa Zeze. *p* Akira Toshikura, Yoshitaka Tanaka. *sc* Kishu Izuchi. *ph* Koichi Saito. *ed* Masaji Sakai. *ad* Nobumasa Oba. *m* Goro Yasukawa. *cast* Hijiri Kojima, Koji Chihara, Shingo Tsurumi, Jun Murakami, Susumu Terajima, Taro Suwa.

●The would-be Godard of Japan's porno underground makes another bid for the mainstream with this fictionalised reconstruction of a 1994 murder incident. Factory worker and night-school student Mami abandons her job and her nice, steady boyfriend Keiji to tag along with the violent and emotionally volatile Tomoaki on a crime spree. Hiding out in the absent Keiji's apartment, Tomoaki orders Mami to sexually lure the neighbour so that they can rob him – a plan which results in the man's death. Clearly shot in haste on a tight budget, the film soon becomes boring because (one easy voice-over aside) it fails to address the question which should have been its starting point: what keeps Mami in thrall to the psychotic Tomoaki? TR

i

If...

I Accuse!

(1957, GB/US, 99 min, b/w)
d José Ferrer. *p* Sam Zimbalist. *sc* Gore Vidal. *ph* Freddie Young. *ed* Frank Clarke. *ad* Elliott Scot. *m* William Alwyn. *cast* José Ferrer, Anton Walbrook, Emlyn Williams, Viveca Lindfors, Herbert Lom, Leo Genn, Donald Wolfit, David Farrar, Felix Aylmer, Harry Andrews, George Coulouris, Michael Horden, Laurence Naismith.

●MGM's version of Alfred Dreyfus' trial, imprisonment on Devil's Island, retrial, pardon and exoneration runs through the facts, and only once or twice touches on the ambiguities of the 'Dreyfus Affair' which made the infamous case, for France at the end of the 19th century, a compelling national tragedy. Ferrer, the star/director, plays Capt Dreyfus, of French military intelligence, with a contained dignity, highlighted by the histrionics of his outraged enemies (notably Lom and Wolfit). The film purrs along, helped by Freddie Young's b/w 'Scope photography and a competent all-star cast, and rises satisfyingly to its big moments, the public humiliation of Dreyfus and Emlyn Williams' impassioned rendition of Zola's noble call to arms (*'J'accuse'*). Scripted by Gore Vidal from a book by Nicholas Halasz, this is the sort of confident historical picture which from time to time Hollywood used to feel called upon to make, tackling big issues head on, while taking good care not to become mired in human and political paradoxes. JPy

I Am a Camera

(1955, GB, 99 min, b/w)
d Henry Cornelius. *sc* John Collier. *ph* Guy Green. *ed* Clive Donner. *ad* William Kellner. *m* Malcolm Arnold. *cast* Julie Harris, Laurence Harvey, Shelley Winters, Anton Diffring, Lea Seidl, Tutte Lemkow.

●Julie Harris is Sally Bowles in this version of Christopher Isherwood's '30s Berlin saga (via John Van Druten's stage adaptation), later filmed as the far superior *Cabaret*. You'd hardly expect an adult drama from the director of *Genevieve*, and sure enough the end result is sadly bowdlerised and lacking any sense of the divinely decadent. (The movie which inspired the famous critical quip: 'Me no Leica.') TJ

I Am a Dancer (Un Danseur: Rudolph Nureyev)

(1970, Fr, 93 min)
d Pierre Jourdain. *p* Evdoros Demitriou. *sc* Pierre Jourdain. *ph* Michel Kelber, Tony Imi. *ed* Catherine Henry, Timothy Gee. *ad* Sydney Beytex, Geoffrey Guy. *m* L Demitriou, K Stockhausen, F Liszt, P Tchaikovsky. *with* Rudolph Nureyev, Margot Fonteyn, Lynn Seymour, Deanne Bergsma, Carla Fracci, Sabine Sale.

●With a seemingly ideal subject to hand, one might have expected a film that would convey something of the excitement of disciplined movement, give some insight into the grinding commitment of a professional dancer's life. Instead, Jourdain has produced a badly lit, boringly photographed, *Vogue*-style portrait of a man with good cheek bones and a leap that regularly carries him out of the frame. Developing into a record of performances, it is useful to the archivist, but captures little of the Nureyev magic. Much the most impressive sequence is a rehearsal of Glen Tetley's 'Field Figures', watched by the choreographer and performed by Nureyev and Deanne Bergsma. Here the proximity of the camera is of real benefit, allowing exploration of this contemporary work in a way never possible over the gulf of an orchestra pit. But once again Jourdain neglects a valuable opportunity: instead of Tetley discussing his piece, which has baffled and intrigued many, we are simply offered Bryan Forbes' voice reading a narration written by John Percival. JMu

I Am a Fugitive from a Chain Gang

(1932, US, 90 min, b/w)
d Mervyn LeRoy. *p* Hal Wallis. *sc* Howard Green, Brown Holmes. *ph* Sol Polito. *ed* William Holmes. *ad* Jack Okey. *m* Leo F Forbstein. *cast* Paul Muni, Glenda Farrell, Helen Vinson, Preston Foster, Edward Ellis, Allen Jenkins, Edward Ellis, Sally Blane.

●Muni gives a brilliant performance as a regular guy wrongly convicted of murder and subjected to the hardships and beatings of a dehumanising chain gang regime. Later, Muni escapes and makes a successful career as a civil engineer, only to be dragged back to jail some years after when his real identity is discovered. Some of the social commentary now seems a little heavy-handed, but the film still packs a hefty punch. The details of chain gang life are tough and harrowing; the scene in which the governor cites Muni's outstanding contribution to society as evidence of the character-building benefits of the chain gang system defies belief; and the downbeat ending is a killer. NF

I Am Anna Magnani (Io Sono Anna Magnani)

(1979, Bel, 105 min, b/w & col)
d Chris Vermorcken. *p* Jacqueline Pierreux. *sc* Chris Vermorcken. *ph* Gianfranco Transunto, Rufus J Bohez. *ed* Eva Houdova. *m* Willy de Maesschalck. *with* Anna Magnani, Vittorio De Sica, Pier Paolo Pasolini, Roberto Rossellini, Luchino Visconti, Claude Autant-Lara, Marco Bellocchio, Susi Cecchi D'Amico, Federico Fellini, Marcello Mastroianni, Giulietta Masina, Franco Zeffirelli.

●This conventional scrapbook biography of legendary actress Anna Magnani features clips from her performances in vaudeville, neo-realist movies and Hollywood, alongside interviews with such directors as her former husband Rossellini, and De Sica and Visconti. Apart from trotting out showbiz paeans to her human warmth, dignified resistance to '50s sex-typing and so forth, it manages glimpses of a complex life scarcely touched upon before. DMacp

I Am an S+M Writer (Futai no Kisetsu)

(2000, Jap, 88 min)
d Ryuichi Hiroki. *p* Naoya Narita, Akira Fukunaga, Eiji Koide. *sc* Hitoshi Ishikawa. *ph* Kazuhiro Suzuki. *ed* Kikuchi. *m* Koji Endo, The Blue Hearts. *cast* Ren Osugi, Yoko Hoshi, Eri Yamazaki, Jun Murakami, William Brian Churchill.

●Hiroki's excellent film (adapted from a novel by SM connoisseur Oniroku Dan) starts out as sex farce but turns into a strange and quite provocative vision of what sexual empowerment might really mean. Kurosaki (Kitano movie regular Osugi) is a failed novelist who has turned to writing SM porn to earn a buck. Lacking expertise and inspiration, he has his assistant Kawada (Murakami) hire models to strike bondage poses and describe their feelings. But his wife (Hoshi) isn't that keen on finding nubile young things tied up in the living room. She responds by flirting with her athletic English teacher – and then by having a sexually adventurous affair with Kawada, which effectively ends the marriage. Kurosaki recalls these events in retrospect, but shows no sign of having gained real self-knowledge and never addresses one central question: can sex really be a dictation sport? TR

I Am a Sex Addict

(1993, GB/US, 98 min)
d Vikram Jean [Vikram Jayanti], John Powers. *p* Vikram Jayanti. *sc* Vikram Jayanti, John Powers. *ph* Maryse Alberti. *ed* Ila von Hasperg. *m* Charlie Skarbek. *with* Hubert Selby Jr.

●In America, it's said, 300,000 people are trying to break the habit of sex addiction. An off-shoot of the vogue sex-talk TV show, this documentary was deemed too explicit for the BBC. In fact, it's unsensational, but on occasion unapologetically voyeuristic. Most of the eight interviewees are sad and lonely – not so much dependent, perhaps, as just plain desperate. Hubert Selby Jr provides whimsical intellectual annotations. TCh

I Am Cuba (Ya – Cuba/Soy Cuba)

(1964, USSR/Cuba, 141 min, b/w)
d Mikhail Kalatozov. *sc* Yevgeni Yevtushenko, Enrique Pineda Barnet. *ph* Sergei Urussevsky. *ed* Evgeny Svidietelov. *m* Carlos Fariñas. *cast* Sergio Corrieri, Salvador Wood, Luz Maria Collazo, Jean Bouise.

●A Russo-Cuban tribute to the victorious revolution against the Battista regime, with Mother Cuba as the 'heroine' and the Cuban masses the 'hero'. Two poets were brought in to write the screenplay, while local peasants and students played themselves alongside professional colleagues. The result is a widescreen cine poem, loosely inspired by Eisenstein, that buries its Socialist Realist paean to communism beneath a ravishing, passionate, often Expressionist combination of sound and image from its eloquent 'travelogue' opening (seen from the sky), to its smiling, anthem chanting end. The four episodes are familiar, but totally altered by the intensity and inventiveness of the filming. This is heavily choreographed naturalism, accompanied by a powerful mix of Afro-Cuban music, natural sound and minimal, dubbed dialogue. Its highly lyrical locations, cityscapes, staged riots and brothel scenes are filmed in deep-focus b/w, using wide lenses, swooping cranes and long, elaborate travelling shots. WH

I Am Curious – Yellow (Jag är Nyfiken En Film i Gult)

(1967, Swe, 121 min, b/w)
d Vilgot Sjöman. *p* Göran Lindgren. *sc* Vilgot Sjöman. *ph* Peter Wester. *ed* Wic Kjellin. *m* Bengt Ernryd. *cast* Lena Nyman, Börje Ahlstedt, Peter Lindgren, Vilgot Sjöman, Holger Löwenadler; *with* Yevgeni Yevtushenko, Olof Palme, Martin Luther King.

●Its sexual frankness – very bold for '67 – and its satirical take on such liberal precepts as non-violence ensured that, in its time, the picture drew flak from all quarters. Mixing reportage and fiction, often conflating the two, Sjöman contrasts Lena's principles (her Dad's still in the doghouse over the Spanish Civil War) with her life-as-lived, specifically her affaire with a bourgeois rat. In a teasing subplot Sjöman accuses himself, not very vehemently, of similar inconsistencies. 'Describes the difficulties of a radical in a country with no serious problems,' sniped American commentator William O'Neill. The mix of frivolousness and moral reproach, though, seems altogether '60s, rather than particularly Swedish. BBa

I Am Frigid...Why? (Je Suis Frigide...Pourquoi?)

(1972, Fr, 92 min)
d/p/sc Max Pécas. *ph* Robert Le Febvre. *ed* Michel Pécas. *m* Derry Hall. *cast* Sandra Jullien, Marie-George Pascal, Jean-Luc Terrade, Anne Kerylen, Thierry Murzeau.

●If there's anything worse than a French underground movie, it's a French sex movie, especially those of Pécas: a less sensual director is hard to imagine, and he has a most calculated and unpleasant way of mixing instant trend into his banal little stories. Our heroine in this effort – last seen suffering from a contrary malady under the same director in *I Am a Nymphomaniac* – is frigid due to some sexual game-playing on the part of the son and daughter of her father's employer (she's just a gardener's daughter). One finishing school, accommodation agency, brothel and theatrical assistantship later, she's realised that her only hope lies with her first true love, he realises he always loved her too, and that's that. Hardly enlightening.

I Am My Own Woman (Ich bin meine eigene Frau)

(1992, Ger, 90 min)
d/p Rosa von Praunheim. *sc* Valentin Passoni, Rosa von Praunheim. *ph* Lorenz Haarmann. *with* Charlotte von Mahlsdorf. Jens Taschner, Ichgola Androgyn, Robert Dietl, Rainer Luhn.

●The best yet film from the generally dodgy Rosa von Praunheim: a German equivalent to *The Naked Civil Servant*, centred on the indomitable 'Charlotte von Mahlsdorf', who has braved familial rejection, social ostracism, Nazi persecution, East German Communist persecution, and latterly skinhead persecution with a frock and a smile. Skilfully scripted and paced, the film wisely allows Charlotte herself to shine; she even wanders into reconstructed scenes from her past to correct details. Magnus Hirschfeld should be alive to see it. TR

I Am Sam

(2001, US/Ger, 132 min)
d Jessie Nelson. *p* Jessie Nelson, Richard Solomon, Marshall Herskovitz, Edward Zwick. *sc* Kristine Johnson, Jessie Nelson. *ph* Elliot Davis. *ed* Richard Chew. *pd* Aaron Osborne. *m* John Powell. *cast* Sean Penn, Michelle Pfeiffer, Dianne Wiest, Dakota Fanning, Richard Schiff, Loretta Devine, Doug Hutchison, Laura Dern, Mary Steenburgen.

●Another contrived look at modern family matters from the director of *Corrina, Corrina*, this immediately set off alarm bells, if not for the sight of Penn finding fulfilment at work in the local Starbucks, then for the spectacle of him playing a man with a mental age of seven. Fathering a daughter by a homeless woman who immediately scarpers, Sam raises young Lucy solo until some years later the authorities decides to resettle Lucy with a family in which she won't have to play the grown-up. Looking for a legal advocate, Sam somehow makes his way to self-absorbed fancy attorney Rita Harrison (Pfeiffer). It's grand that Hollywood wants to tell stories of the handicapped, but the sentimental rhetoric it customarily chooses patronises everyone. This is no exception. NB

I Am the Law

(1938, US, 83 min, b/w)
d Alexander Hall. *p* Everett Riskin. *sc* Jo Swerling. *ph* Henry Freulich. *ed* Viola Lawrence. *ad* Stephen Goosson, Lionel Banks. *m* Morris Stoloff. *cast* Edward G Robinson, Otto Kruger, Barbara O'Neil, John Beal, Louis Jean Heydt, Marc Lawrence.

●It may not be terribly good, but this feisty vehicle for Edward G plays to the star's strengths. He's a never-say-die law professor who takes on the city's racketeers, and even carries on the good fight by himself after he's removed from the post, finally putting together the evidence that mayor's son Beal is actually the local crime kingpin. TJ

I Bought a Vampire Motorcycle

(1989, GB, 105 min)
d Dirk Campbell. *p/sc* Mycal Miller, John Wolskel. *ph* Tom Ingle. *ed* Mycal Miller. *ad* José Furtado. *m* Dean Friedman. *cast* Neil Morrissey, Amanda Noar, Michael Elphick, Anthony Daniels, Andrew Powell, George Rossi, Daniel Peacock, Burt Kwouk.

●Falling somewhere between *The Evil Dead* and *Carry On Screaming*, this refreshingly effective horror spoof throws caution to the wind and entrails to the floor when hirsute biker Noddy (Neil Morrissey) buys a Norton, which turns out to be a spawn of Hades. Garage-bound by day, at night the satanic cycle fuels up on the blood of Hell's Angels, traffic wardens and streetwalkers. When Noddy turns to a priest for assistance, he is met first with scepticism, then with steely resolve as the eccentric cleric (Daniels, neatly twitchy) tools up for an exorcism, God on his side and sacred Ninja weaponry in reserve. Filmed on a minute budget around Birmingham's back streets, Campbell's debut maintains a base level of quick-witted humour while ladling on grungy gore, courtesy of the Image Animation team. The uniformly respectable performances are rather overshadowed by Elphick's deadpan Inspector Cleaver (all sour-faced garlic-breathiness). Schoolboy toilet humour with teeth. MK

Ice

(1969, US, 132 min, b/w)
d Robert Kramer. *p* David C Stone. *sc* Robert Kramer. *ph* Robert Machover. *with* Robert Kramer, Tom Griffin.

●A film that has gained hugely with the passage of time. It may not 'explode in people's faces like a grenade' or 'open minds like a can-opener' as Kramer has stated he wished it to, but there's no doubt that it stands alone as a sympathetic, frequently brilliant ideological thriller. Dealing with urban insurrection and armed revolt by the youth of America, Kramer's film occupies intriguingly shifting territory between documentary and science fiction. The result is a unique testament to the political consciousness of a decade. Kramer constantly astonishes with his ability to draw performances and find images that fix this particular consciousness with unnerving precision. It is beautifully shot in black-and-white. VG

Ice Age

(2002, US, 81 min)
d Chris Wedge. *p* Lori Forte. *sc* Michael Berg, Michael J Wilson, Peter Ackerman. *ed* John Carnochan. *pd* Brian McEntee. *m* David Newman. *cast* voices: Ray Romano, John Leguizamo, Denis Leary, Goran Visnjic, Jack Black, Tara Strong.

●Fox's CGI feature fails to match the constant visual surprise and teeming invention provided by Disney-Pixar ever since *Toy Story*, and its uninflected anthropomorphism harks back to a lazier orthodoxy. That said, once you get used to the repetitive, cursorily sketched backgrounds and concentrate on the comic deeds of the central trio – a woolly mammoth, a sloth and a sabre-toothed tiger – there's enough classically derived Road Runner-type fun to keep most family audiences happy. But the characters betray their contrivance. The sloth, Sid, is a hapless orphan abandoned by the migrating herds of the opening sequences. He foists himself on reluctant lone mammoth Manfred with the same blithe insistence that Eddie Murphy's Donkey used to insinuate himself into the company of *Shrek*, and he cracks a similar brand of self-deprecating gag. Likewise, the screenplay has a magpie lack of discrimination. I liked the goggle-eyed squirrel, but who wouldn't identify with his Sisyphean efforts to secure that damned acorn? WH

Ice Castles

(1978, US, 109 min)
d Donald Wrye. *p* John Kemeny. *sc* Donald Wrye, Gary L Baim. *ph* Bill Butler. *ed* Michael Kahn, Maury Winetrobe, Melvin Shapiro. *pd* Joel Schiller. *m* Marvin Hamlisch. *cast* Robby Benson, Lynn-Holly Johnson, Colleen Dewhurst, Tom Skerritt, Jennifer Warren, David Huffman.

●The pirouetting free-skater heroine, blonde nymphette Lexie Winston (Johnson), leaves backwoods Iowa for the rigorous discipline of Olympic coaching. Escaping the claustrophobia of home (where her father sees her as a substitute for her dead mother), she attains a degree of independence comparable to that of her dilettante ice hockey-playing boyfriend Nick (Benson). Aided by worldly people (the coach, a TV sportscaster), she gains success and fame – at a price: the loss of her native innocence (competition is a cutthroat business), the estrangement of Nick, and finally the tragic loss of her eyesight through a fall. What this three-hanky weepie really says is 'Don't get ideas above your station', for Lexie can only come to terms with her handicap by re-accepting the dominance of her father and Nick, and rejecting her ambitions and herself. You'd have to be blind to miss the moral. FF

Ice Cold in Alex

(1958, GB, 132 min, b/w)
d J Lee Thompson. *p* WA Whittaker. *sc* TJ Morrison, Christopher Landon. *ph* Gilbert Taylor. *ed* Richard Best. *ad* Robert Jones. *m* Leighton Lucas. *cast* John Mills, Harry Andrews, Anthony Quayle, Sylvia Syms, Diane Clare, Richard Leech, Liam Redmond.

●It may not be a very good film, but as Raymond Durgnat demonstrates in *A Mirror for England*, it's an interesting account of 'Britain's sense of inferiority in the post war world'. After the fall of Tobruk in World War II, a battle-fatigued army captain (Mills), a sergeant-major (Andrews) and two nurses drive an ambulance back to Alexandria. On the way they pick up a Dutch South African officer (Quayle) who does everything brilliantly. He's pointedly tougher and more sensible than the suicidally, and manslaughterously, hysteric captain. He's pointedly stronger than the strong sergeant-major, and he's also, it seems, a brilliant diplomat (twice persuading ugly-looking panzers who've captured them to release them). Even when they've found out that he's a German spy, they reckon he's a decent chap as well, having saved their lives several times over. So they save his, by pretending he wasn't in Allied uniform when they caught him. The capability ranking is unmistakeable: Germans or colonial, top; loyal NCO, next; English officer last. PH

Iceland (aka Katina)

(1942, US, 79 min, b/w)
d H Bruce Humberstone. *p* William LeBaron. *sc* Robert Ellis, Helen Logan. *ph* Arthur Miller. *ed* James B Clark. *ad* Richard Day, Wiard Ihnen. *songs* Mack Gordon, Harry Warren. *cast* Sonja Henie, John Payne, Jack Oakie, Felix Bressart, Osa Massen, Joan Merrell, Fritz Feld.

●A sluggish comedy-romance with Payne as a marine stationed in Iceland and Henie working her tiresome pixie charm overtime as the local miss who determinedly snares him. Even the skating routines, loaded with fulsome tributes to the good old USA, are tough going. TM

Iceman Cometh, The (Jidong Qixia)

(1989, HK, 114 min)
d Clarence Fok Yiu-Leung. *sc* Stephen Shiu. *ph* Poon Hang-Sang. *ed* Poon Hung-Yiu. *cast* Yuen Biao, Maggie Cheung, Yuen Wah, Wong Jing, Yuan Kui.

●For reasons too complicated to explain, ancient antagonists Ah Ching (Yuen Biao, the good guy) and Fung San (Yuen Wah, the bad guy) are frozen alive in a glacier. The modern scientists who discover their entwined bodies take them as proof that homosexuality existed in imperial China, but no love is lost between them when they are defrosted and reanimated in present day Hong Kong. This is the cue for a barrage of serio-comic fight scenes, Buddhist mythology and special visual effects, much enhanced by Maggie Cheung's way with the stock character of a brassy hooker. TR

Ice Palace

(1960, US, 143 min)
d Vincent Sherman. *p* Henry Blanke. *sc* Harry Kleiner. *ph* Joseph Biroc. *ed* William Ziegler. *ad* Malcolm Bert. *m* Max Steiner. *cast* Richard Burton, Robert Ryan, Carolyn Jones, Martha Hyer, Jim Backus, Ray Danton, Shirley Knight.

●Edna Ferber's sprawling novels and populous plays were naturals for never-mind-the-quality-feel-the-width Hollywood (and occasionally produced such happy results as *Giant*, *Dinner at Eight* or the numerous versions of *Cimarron* and *Showboat*). This monster about the founding of Alaska, however, was well and truly betrayed, freezing into a series of icy confrontations between man of progress Burton and simple rival Ryan amid the Warners studio snow. Soap specialist Sherman had already logged the entry of Texas into the Union in 1951's *Lone Star*. PT

Ice Palace, The (Is-slottet)

(1988, Nor, 76 min)
d/sc Per Blom. *ph* Halvor Naess. *ed* Margit Nordqvist. *ad* Ingeborg Kvamme. *m* Geir Bohren, Bent Aserud. *cast* Line Storesund, Hilde Nyeggen Martinsen, Merete Moen, Sigrid Huun.

●In the depths of a deep-frozen Norwegian winter, two just-adolescent girls, Siss and Unn, sneak off to Unn's attic bedroom and undress for each other. Although nothing concrete happens, the following day Unn is so overwhelmed by guilt that she runs off to a nearby frozen waterfall, and wandering through caves of ice, finally lays down and dies. The rest of the film focuses on Siss' almost wordless grieving, unable to tell the town elders why her friend disappeared, becoming progressively numbed herself by her inability to understand what has happened. With little dialogue and minimal action, Blom uses the landscape of winter to express strong longing and stronger repression. A cross between *Picnic at Hanging Rock* and the poetic melancholia of an Ibsen play, *The Ice Palace* is a bitter-sweet dream of snow and shadow, beautiful to watch. RS

Ice Station Zebra

(1968, US, 152 min)
d John Sturges. *p* Martin Ransohoff, John Calley. *sc* Douglas Heyes. *ph* Daniel L Fapp. *ed* Ferris Webster. *ad* George W Davis, Addison Hehr. *m* Michel Legrand. *cast* Rock Hudson, Ernest Borgnine, Patrick McGoohan, Jim Brown, Tony Bill, Alj Kjellin, Gerald S O'Loughlin, Lloyd Nolan.

●A passable yarn about a race for a Russian satellite that comes down near the North Pole, blighted by some heavy-handed irony. Borgnine hams outrageously, Hudson manages better than you'd expect, and McGoohan turns in a good performance. It's not saying much, but Sturges has been responsible for two of the more successful Alistair MacLean adventures, this and *The Satan Bug*. CPe

Ice Storm, The

(1997, US, 113 min)
d Ang Lee. *p* Ted Hope, James Schamus, Ang Lee. *sc* James Schamus. *ph* Frederick Elmes. *ed* Tim Squyres. *pd* Mark Friedberg. *m* Mychael Danna. *cast* Kevin Kline, Sigourney Weaver, Joan Allen, Jamey Sheridan, Christina Ricci, Elijah Wood.

●With its meticulous script by James Schamus, strong performances and elegant direction, this tragi-comic look at the lives of a couple of comfortably-off small town Connecticut families in the winter of 1973 is a gem of witty, perceptive observation. Unbeknown to Allen his wife, Kline is carrying on with neighbour Weaver, an affair discovered when he comes across his teenage daughter Ricci playing her own sexually explorative games with Weaver's sons. Cue marital discord, adolescent disenchantment and family crises in a thoroughly enjoyable blend of comedy and melodrama which is spot-on both in its evocative re-creation of the fads, habits and attitudes of the early '70s, and in its sense of an America at a particular point in its socio-political history. GA

Ichabod and Mr Toad (aka The Adventures of Ichabod and Mr Toad)

(1949, US, 68 min)
d Jack Kinney, Clyde Geronimi, James Algar. *p* (supervisor) Ben Sharpsteen. *sc* Erdman Penner, Winston Hibler, Joe Rinaldi, Ted Sears, Homer Brightman, Harry Reeves. *songs* Don Raye, Gene De Paul. *cast* voices: Basil Rathbone, Eric Blore, Pat O'Malley (*The Wind in the Willows*); Bing Crosby (*The Legend of Sleepy Hollow*).

● Misleading title: Disney hasn't contrived the insertion of Ratty, Mole and company into Washington Irving's grisly tale of Sleepy Hollow. These are two separate featurettes, released in harness. *The Wind in the Willows* adaptation has a gag-a-shot scenario, breakneck pace and plays like an extended Donald Duck short. Great fun, provided you disregard the spirit of the original as comprehensively as Disney did. More uneven is the story of bumptious schoolmaster Ichabod Crane and his nemesis the Headless Horseman. It's a trite, chocolate box picture of colonial days – until the Horseman shows up for one of those nightmare sequences with which Uncle Walt so relished terrifying his kiddie audience. BBa

I Changed My Sex

see Glen or Glenda?

Ichi the Killer (Koroshiya Ichi)

(2001, Jap/SKor/HK, 126 min)
d Takashi Miike. *p* Dai Miyazaki, Akiko Funatsu, Toshiki Kimura, Elliot Tong, Cho Yuchul. *sc* Sakichi Sato. *ph* Hideo Yamamoto. *ed* Yasuji Shimamura. *ad* Takashi Sasaki. *m* Karera Musication. *cast* Tadanobu Asano, Nao Omori, Shinya Tsukamoto, Sabu, Alien Sun, Susumu Terajima.

● 'All events and characters in the film are entirely sick, any resemblance to persons living or dead is a sad coincidence.' As disclaimers go, that's on the nail: Miike's adaptation of Hideo Yamamoto's notorious *manga* is alarmingly faithful. Which means that these two hours of extreme violence, sadism and masochism are calculated to challenge every censor in the world: no part of the male or female body is left unsliced, and no bodily fluid is left unsplattered. The yakuza Kakihara (Asano, flinching from *nothing*) mobilises his gang to track down the legendary killer Ichi, suspected murderer of their boss; Kakihara is also searching for a sadist who can torture him with the same love he used to get from the dead man. No one suspects that Ichi (Omori, son of *butoh* legend Akaji Maro) is a helpless cry-baby who becomes the ultimate killer in a superhero costume only when under hypnosis from the vengeful Jijii (Tsukamoto), whose secret agenda is to stir up a gang-war. Funny, absurd, nightmarishly visceral and – of course – deeply serious. TR

Ich war Neunzehn

see I Was Nineteen

Icicle Thief (Ladri di Saponette)

(1989, It, 98 min, b/w & col)
d Maurizio Nichetti. *p* Ernesto Di Sarro. *sc* Maurizio Nichetti, Mauro Monti. *ph* Maria Battistoni. *ed* Rita Rossi, Anna Missoni. *pd* Ada Legori. *m* Manuel De Sica, Franco Godi. *cast* Maurizio Nichetti, Caterina Sylos Labini, Heidi Komarek, Federico Rizzo, Renato Scarpa.

● The director of a monochrome *hommage* to *Bicycle Thieves* is invited on to a TV programme to discuss his film before a screening. But during the transmission, his movie is interrupted by colour commercials, the characters slip from one world into another, and eventually the director himself intervenes to sort out the mess. Nichetti's wacky satire on the big screen/small screen war is technically very effective, but his own manic performance as the mustachioed director is a major irritant. Some good in-jokes (like a housewife complaining about boring introductions to films on TV) help to pass the time. DT

I Confess

(1953, US, 95 min)
d Alfred Hitchcock. *sc* George Tabori, William Archibald. *ph* Robert Burks. *ed* Rudi Fehr. *ad* Ted Haworth. *m* Dimitri Tiomkin. *cast* Montgomery Clift, Anne Baxter, Karl Malden, Brian Aherne, OE Hasse, Roger Dann, Dolly Haas.

● One of Hitchcock's most overtly 'serious' and portentous murder plots, about a Catholic priest who faces the death penalty because of his refusal to break the secrecy of the confessional. Its theological theme and exploration of personal guilt once made it a cardinal point in the pro-Hitchcock arguments of the French critics, notably Chabrol and Rohmer. But now that most critics accept Hitchcock as more than just entertainment, the more strained and serious movies look a lot less formidable than the so-called roller-coaster rides like *Psycho*. Clift (as the priest) and Malden (as the cop) make this worth watching, but it's heavy going at times and the more literary aspects of the script, adapted from Paul Anthelme's play (written in 1902), are uncinematic to say the least. DP

I Could Go On Singing

(1963, GB, 100 min)
d Ronald Neame. *p* Lawrence Turman. *sc* Mayo Simon. *ph* Arthur Ibbetson. *ed* John Shirley. *ad* Wilfrid Shingleton. *m* Mort Lindsey. *cast* Judy Garland, Dirk Bogarde, Jack Klugman, Aline MacMahon, Gregory Phillips, Pauline Jameson, Jeremy Burnham.

● Well-built people have been known to keel over under the intense glare of Garland's emotions in this old-fashioned tug-of-love melodrama (her last film). And the narrative provides very little shelter, as she plays a famous singer topping the bill at the London Palladium, struggling to wrest her illegitimate son away from his surgeon father (Bogarde). Naturally, this is required viewing for Garland devotees, but with Neame's glacial, humourless manner of directing it's hardly the film if you just want fun. GB

I Could Read the Sky

(1999, Ire/GB/Fr, 86 min)
d Nichola Bruce. *p* Janine Marmot. *sc* Nichola Bruce. *ph* Seamus McGarvey, Owen McPolin. *ed* Catherine Creed. *pd* Jane Bruce. *m* Iarla O'Lionáird. *cast* Dermot Healy, Stephen Rea, Brendan Coyle, Maria Doyle Kennedy, Roy Larkin, Lisa O'Reilly, Sezso.

● Timothy O'Grady and Steve Pyke's photonovel *I Could Read the Sky* juxtaposed words and images, landscape and interiority, memory and loss to evoke the Irish emigrant experience. This adaptation imposes sound and movement on the mix: the burr of Irish writer Healy's voice; an eclectic soundtrack that ebbs and flows around the images; gauzy layers and transitions of film textures and fragments. The narrator is an old Irish exile in a Kentish Town bedsit, lying back and listening as the memories come crowding in. In no particular order, he revisits his childhood in the West of Ireland, his family diaspora, friends and pub society, romance, marriage and widowerhood. Hard toil is the one constant, be it in potato fields, abattoirs, construction sites and on the streets, sweeping and busking. At last he faces the moment of retirement, wracked but unbroken, clear-minded but still yearning. As testimony, the film is unimpeachable; as art cinema, it's not always technically equal to its ambitions; but in its modesty there's a fluid, fleeting grace. NB

i.d.

(1994, GB/Ger, 107 min)
d Philip Davis. *p* Sally Hibbin. *sc* Vincent O'Connell. *ph* Thomas Mauch. *ed* Inge Behrens. *m* Will Gregory. *cast* Reece Dinsdale, Warren Clarke, Claire Skinner, Richard Graham, Perry Fenwick, Philip Glenister, Saskia Reeves, Sean Pertwee, Charles De'Ath, Philip Davis.

● An impressive first feature following a group of undercover policemen who attach themselves to the louts who follow a fictional second-division London football club. John (Dinsdale) is your average ambitious cop, early twenties, eye on promotion, a charmer with a nice wife at home, but still with some mileage in the pulling and rucking stakes. The film takes him through the stages of brutalisation, from learning how to drink, smoke and fight dirty, through the addiction of fandom, to eventual disintegration as he loses family, dignity and much more in a descent into the kind of violence he's been sent to prevent. The film has weaknesses: sometimes the low budget shows, and there are irritating lapses (the fans' scarves are all brand new and the same design), while the script's notes on aggression are far more convincing than its attempt to tackle racism – almost a politically correct afterthought. But Dinsdale's riveting, and the supports, notably Clarke's tattoo-encrusted, skinhead pub landlord and Skinner's housewife, more than make up the numbers. Intriguing stuff, and as English as a cold bacon butty. SGr

Ideal Husband, An

(1947, GB, 96 min)
d/p Alexander Korda. *sc* Lajos Biro. *ph* Georges Périnal. *ed* Oswald Haffenrichter. *ad* Vincent Korda *m* Arthur Benjamin. *cast* Paulette Goddard, Michael Wilding, Diana Wynyard, Hugh Williams, C Aubrey Smith, Glynis Johns, Constance Collier, Michael Medwin.

● Producer/director Korda had fellow Hungarian Lajos Biro adapt Wilde's play for this rather turgid screen version, which has imported American star Goddard as a reasonable Mrs Cheveley, the Victorian adventuress whose blackmail attempt on politico Williams is stymied by nobleman Wilding's decisive counter-attack. Lots of technical gloss on display, including costumes by Cecil Beaton and Georges Périnal's elegant camerawork, but the film is so reverent towards its source material it's almost embalmed. TJ

Ideal Husband, An

(1998, GB/US, 98 min)
d Oliver Parker. *p* Barnaby Thompson, Uri Fruchtman, Bruce Davey. *sc* Oliver Parker. *ph* David Johnson. *ed* Guy Bensley. *pd* Michael Howells. *m* Charlie Mole. *cast* Cate Blanchett, Minnie Driver, Rupert Everett, Julianne Moore, Jeremy Northam, John Wood, Lindsay Duncan, Peter Vaughn, Jeroen Krabbé, Nickolas Grace, Simon Russell Beale.

● Sir Robert Chiltern (Northam) has a devoted wife, an impeccable character, and expectation of a Cabinet post. Then he's introduced to the unconventional Mrs Cheveley (Moore) and his world is upended. She has evidence that he made his fortune in a stock market scam, and threatens exposure unless he reports favourably to the House on an expensive canal project in which she has invested heavily. While Chiltern struggles with his conscience, his wife Gertrude (Blanchett) and his urbane best friend Lord Goring (Everett) conspire against Cheveley, whose true character they know full well. Wilde's play still feels all too relevant in its witty dissection of public and private morality,but this adaptation doesn't really capitalise on its strengths. For a start, writer/director Parker has 'opened out' the material with such breathless zeal the effect is quite suffocating. He seems to want us to empathise with Sir Robert and the insufferably virtuous Gertrude, in effect nullifying Wilde's satire and landing poor Northam and Blanchett with thankless roles. The comedy works better, and the film brightens up considerably whenever the insouciant Everett and flighty Driver (as Mabel Chiltern) get down to the serious business of small talk. In fact, for those of a patient disposition, the last act is very enjoyable. The bright, crisp design, Wilde's arch eloquence and a classy company help to camouflage the shortcomings. TCh

Identification of a Woman (Identificazione di una Donna)

(1982, It/Fr, 131 min)
d Michelangelo Antonioni. *p* Giorgio Nocella, Antonio Macri. *sc* Michelangelo Antonioni, Gérard Brach. *ph* Carlo Di Palma. *ed* Michelangelo Antonioni. *ad* Andrea Crisanti. *m* John Foxx. *cast* Tomas Milian, Daniela Silverio, Christine Boisson, Sandra Monteleoni, Giampaolo Saccarola, Marcel Bozzuffi.

● Very much the film of an elder statesman arrogantly conscious of being the most 'modern' director of his generation. It is a contemporary love story – based upon a film-maker's chance encounters with two women – designed to bury the controversies of his courageous video manifesto (*The Oberwald Mystery*) and to regain access to Hollywood. Visually this is perhaps Antonioni's most beautiful film to date, effortlessly fleshing out familiar themes around the difficulties of establishing relationships in our times. But there is much more. Most notably, a refreshing irony prevents the hardened art house pundit from wallowing in nostalgia and the metaphysics of 'portentous messages'. Emphasis is very much on the 'investigation' suggested by the title rather than possible meanings to be derived from it. Everything in the film comes in twos: two women from different social and sexual backgrounds, two films about to be made, two extraordinary key sequences – the first enshrouded in thick fog, the other in the desolation of the Venetian lagoon. In the end the central character chooses not to make his film about the 'ideal woman' but to lose himself in a space oddity with skull-like spacecrafts journeying towards the sun. Probably not a sign of Spielbergian things to come from Antonioni – more a subdued admission from the 'apostle of incommunicability' that the best place for alienation these days is in megabuck fantasies. DR

I Died a Thousand Times

(1955, US, 109 min)
d Stuart Heisler. *p* Willis Goldbeck. *sc* WR Burnett. *ph* Ted McCord. *ed* Clarence Kolster. *ad* Edward Carrere. *m* David Buttolph. *cast* Jack Palance, Shelley Winters, Lori Nelson, Lee Marvin, Gonzales Gonzales, Lon Chaney, Earl Holliman.

● While not a patch upon Walsh's version of WR Burnett's *High Sierra*, of which this is a remake, there are still entertaining moments in this tale of a con out to pull one last bank job before retiring. It's often too talky and lethargically paced, but Heisler has an enthusiastic eye for spectacle (notably in the climax up in the mountains), while Palance and Winters, though no real replacement for Bogart and Ida Lupino, demonstrate their own rough charm. GA

Idiot, The (Hakuchi)

(1951, Jap, 165 min, b/w)
d Akira Kurosawa. *p* Takashi Koide. *sc* Eijiro Hisaita, Akira Kurosawa. *ph* Toshio Ubukata. *ed* Yoshi Sugihara. *ad* So Matsuyama. *m* Fumio Hayasaka. *cast* Masayuki Mori, Toshiro Mifune, Setsuko Hara, Takashi Shimura, Yoshiko Kuga, Chieko Higashiyama.

● Kurosawa's adaptation from his favourite novelist Dostoevsky has an undeserved reputation as a failure. True, it has a plot which is at first extremely difficult to follow if you don't know the novel, but its literal faithfulness (transferred from St Petersburg to modern Hokkaido) hardly deserves rebuke. The acting has an eerie, trance-like quality; and the perpetually snowbound sets and locations, warmed by scarcely adequate fires and bulky clothing, together with a continually turbulent music soundtrack, make up the perfect expressionist metaphor for the emotional lives of Dostoievsky's characters. Tom Milne has noted similarities to Dreyer's *Gertrud*; like that film, it repays the initial effort required to get into it. RM

Idiots, The (Idioterne)

(1998, Den, 117 min)
d Lars von Trier. *p* Vibeke Windelov. *sc/ph* Lars von Trier. *ed* Molly Malene Stensgaard. *pd* Lene Nielsen. *cast* Bodil Jørgensen, Jens Albinus, Louise Hassing, Troels Lyby, Nikolaj Lie Kaas.

● Often looking rather like a filmed acting workshop, von Trier's first movie made according to the back-to-basics 'Dogma 95' manifesto centres on the emotional and social dynamics of a group of people who, for various reasons, go around pretending to be mentally and/or physically handicapped. What little plot there is charts the tensions that lead some of them to consider leaving the cult, but the film's real interest lies in its exploration of different kinds of 'performance', and in its often very funny satirical look at the way 'normal' society treats 'abnormal' people. Emotionally and intellectually, the movie never quite delivers on its promise, and the frequent views of the boom, the shadow of the camera crew and so forth are irritating distractions (manifesto or not, this is *not* 'pure' cinema), but it is consistently intriguing, involving, and finally quite unlike anything else. GA

Idiot's Delight

(1939, US, 105 min, b/w)
d Clarence Brown. *p* Hunt Stromberg. *sc* Robert E Sherwood. *ph* William H Daniels. *ed* Robert J Kern. *ad* Cedric Gibbons. *m* Herbert Stothart. *cast* Clark Gable, Norma Shearer, Edward Arnold, Charles Coburn, Joseph Schildkraut, Burgess Meredith, Virginia Grey.

● Crass adaptation of Robert Sherwood's pacifist play, which not only reduces Sherwood's political arguments to a few whimpers about futility (they weren't any too hot in the first place), but adds a prologue revealing how the broken-down hoofer (Gable) and the mysterious Russian mistress of an armaments king (Shearer) had met and fallen in love when she too was just an all-American showbiz hopeful. What we are then faced with is simply the cloyingly predictable romance when they meet again – she now shorn of all dramatic mystery and all too obviously ripe for comeuppance because she put ambition before love. To make matters worse, the fateful romance takes place in a hotel somewhere in Europe with war hammering ominously at the doors: a hollow Ship of Fools peopled by the usual token selection of rats about to desert (armaments king, German scientist, fervent Communist, etc). Although Clarence Brown works hard to cast his usual elegant spell, the film remains as dead as a doornail, with the exception of one scene in which Gable does a delightfully shoddy top hat and white tie Astaire routine, raising morale in the audience if not the hotel guests. TM

Idle on Parade

(1959, US, 92 min, b/w)
d John Gilling. *p* Harold Huth. *sc* John Antrobus. *ph* Ted Moore. *ed* Bert Rule. *ad* Ray Sim. *m* Bill Shepherd. *cast* Anthony Newley, William Bendix, Anne Aubrey, Lionel Jeffries, David Lodge, Sidney James.

● An interesting curiosity, this is a kind of folksy British parody of Elvis Presley's controversial drafting into the US Army: Newley plays a prototype rock singer who is called up, with all the ensuing complications. In retrospect it all seems very quaint, but it was the film that launched Newley (up to that point a straight actor) on a singing career; and the rock songs that Newley sings ('Idle Rock-a-boogie', 'I've Waited So Long', etc) were great hits in their time. DP

I Don't Kiss

see J'embrasse pas

I Don't Want to Be Born (aka The Devil Within Her)

(1975, GB, 94 min)
d Peter Sasdy. *p* Norma Corney. *sc* Stanley Price. *ph* Ken Talbot. *ed* Keith Palmer. *ad* Roy Stannard. *m* Ron Grainer. *cast* Joan Collins, Eileen Atkins, Donald Pleasence, Ralph Bates, Caroline Munro, Hilary Mason.

● Sasdy, once thought by many to be the great black hope for British horror films, here turned in – aptly enough – an abortion. Comparing unfavourably with *It's Alive* (made the previous year), it is both derivative and disastrous in every respect: a poor idea (Joan Collins gives birth to a big baby possessed by a devil whose medium is a dwarf she once spurned), an abominable screenplay by Stanley Price ('I keep getting these awful premonitions'), ludicrous acting (poor Eileen Atkins as an Italian nun), and worst of all, Sasdy's direction. The market for this film must have been planned as the Continent or the States, because almost every foot of film not concerned with the baby is travelogue at its most banal – extraneous shots of Westminster and Oxford Street, plugs for Fortnum & Mason and Holiday Inns. Completing this sorry tale of rip-off is borrowing from *The Exorcist*, Hilary Mason from *Don't Look Now*, and any number of details from Amicus, Hammer and Swinging London horrors. Give it a wide berth. AN

I Dream of My Friends (Onirevome tous Filous Mou)

(1993, Greece, 114 min)
d/sc Nikos Panayotopoulos. *ph* Giorgos Frentzos. *ed* Giorgos Triantafyllou. *ad* Dionysus Fotopoulos, Maria Kaltsa. *cast* Lefteris Voyiatzis, Minas Hatzisavvas, Akilas Karazissis, Yannis Karatzoyiannis, Stathis Livathinis, Alekos Koliopoulos.

● This low key, episodic mood piece, from a book by Dimitris Nollas, spans the years from 1965 to '90 in a quartet of remembered moments. West Germany 1965: Kyriakos and a friend attempt to sell encyclopedias on US bases, but end up scamming on a Bible deal. This opener sets the mood – as in early Wim Wenders, the world is a muted, empty place; a zone of transit, of occasional communion with strangers and creeping Americanisation. Whether hitching in Yugoslavia in 1973, waiting for a plane in the blackout of a terminal hall, or facing a friend's sudden death in the marble toilets of a plush wedding reception, Kyriakos is a displaced observer. Best to view the vignettes as self-contained works: there is little sense of any character development, and that is perhaps the writer/director's point. GE

I Escaped from Devil's Island

(1973, US, 89 min)
d William Witney. *p* Roger Corman, Gene Corman. *sc* Richard L Adams. *ph* Rosalio Solano. *ed* Tom Walls, Barbara Pokras. *ad* Roberto Silva. *m* Les Baxter. *cast* Jim Brown, Christopher George, Richard Rust, Rick Eli, James Luisi, Bob Harris, Paul Richards, Robert Phillips.

● Despite an air of unrelieved cruddiness, relentless machismo, bad acting and over-insistent animal imagery of a dog-eats-dog nature, this Corman-produced epic, unlike *Papillon*, at least adopts the right approach. As the title suggests, the film is very much on the level of those old 'True Adventure' stories. Jim Brown has no apparent motive for escaping, but then prison life is painted in sufficiently graphic terms for that not to matter. Favouritism and brutality are rife, prisoners are prepared to rat on each other, and the film admits (albeit crudely) an aura of homosexuality and political agitation that was never properly allowed to infiltrate *Papillon*. Life after the escape looks like a rejected draft of the other film, and includes an encounter with lepers, a tumble with a native girl, and an equally perfunctory ending. Not exactly recommended, unless you misspent your youth reading stories like 'How I Wrestled with a Python and Won'. CA

If...

(1968, GB, 111 min, b/w & col)
d Lindsay Anderson. *p* Michael Medwin, Lindsay Anderson. *sc* David Sherwin. *ph* Miroslav Ondricek. *ed* David Gladwell. *pd* Jocelyn Herbert. *m* Marc Wilkinson. *cast* Malcolm McDowell, David Wood, Richard Warwick, Robert Swann, Christine Noonan, Hugh Thomas, Peter Jeffrey, Arthur Lowe, Mona Washbourne, Charles Sturridge.

● A modern classic in which Anderson minutely captures both the particular ethos of a public school and the general flavour of any structured community, thus achieving a clear allegorical force without sacrificing a whit of his exploration of an essentially British institution. The impeccable logic of the conclusion is in no way diminished by having been lifted from Vigo's *Zéro de Conduite*, made thirty-five years earlier. *If...* was also a timely film – shooting began two months before the events of May 1968 in Paris. Along with *The White Bus*, it put Anderson into a pretty high league; the major disappointment of *O Lucky Man!*, followed by the disastrous *Britannia Hospital*, took him back out of it again. SG

If All the Guys in the World...

see Si tous les gars du monde...

If I Had a Million

(1932, US, 88 min, b/w)
d Ernst Lubitsch, Norman Taurog, Stephen Roberts, Norman Z McLeod, James Cruze, William A Seiter, H Bruce Humberstone. *p* Louis D Lighton. *sc* Claude Binyon, Malcolm Stuart Boylan, Sidney Buchman, Isabel Dawn, Oliver HP Garrett, Grover Jones, Lawton Mackall, William Slavens McNutt, Whitney Bolton, John Bright, Lester Cole, Boyce DeGaw, Harvey Gates, Ernst Lubitsch, Joseph L Mankiewicz, Robert Sparks, Walter DeLeon, Seton I Miller, Tiffany Thayer. *cast* Gary Cooper, George Raft, WC Fields, Charles Laughton, Jack Oakie, Charlie Ruggles, Mary Boland, Wynne Gibson, Gene Raymond, May Robson.

● The title tells all in this episodic entertainment (variations on the theme of what happens to assorted characters each left a million dollars by a wealthy eccentric), written by eighteen pairs of hands and directed by seven, from cool geniuses like Lubitsch to jolly hacks like Humberstone. The famous Lubitsch episode in which Charles Laughton's mild-mannered clerk gives his boss the raspberry now warrants nothing stronger than a wet smile, but the WC Fields episode is still fun (he goes on a joyride in various old cars, bashing them vengefully against every passing road-hog). The non-comic sequences, however, are all very painful; this is one of those curate's eggs with far more curate than egg. GB

If Only (Lluvia en los zapatos)

(1998, Sp/Fr/Can/GB/Luxembourg, 95 min)
d Maria Ripoll. *p* Juan Gordon. *sc* Rafa Russo. *ph* Javier Salmones. *ed* Nacho Ruiz-Capillas. *pd* Grant Hicks. *m* Luis Mendo, Bernardo Fuster, Angel Illarramendi. *cast* Lena Headey, Douglas Henshall, Penelope Cruz, Gustavo Salmeron, Mark Strong, Elizabeth McGovern.

● Victor Bukowski (Henshall) is a struggling an actor. Sylvia (Headey) broke up with him after he confessed to an affair, and now she's decided to marry someone he despises. Nothing for it but to slump over a drink and pour it all out to barmaid Diane (McGovern), who might just be a mysterious catalyst for change. Unlikely as it sounds, a magic umbrella and the intervention of some Spanish bin men are about to give Victor an unexpected second chance. What if he went back in time and didn't own up to his infidelities? This patchy comedy with a twist begins to creak when it strains for Quixotic fantasy, lays on the Notting Hill local colour with a trowel, and awkwardly introduces Cruz as belated, unpersuasive love interest. Most winning, however, is the mid-section where Henshall gets to retrace his own footsteps, and a piercing eye is cast over the tensions between trust and temptation. Henshall may not be everyone's idea of a romantic leading man, but he's hassled, human, bitterly funny, and he matures before our very eyes. And Headey is perfectly cast as the beautiful but vacant Sylvia. TJ

I.F. Stone's Weekly

(1973, US, 62 min, b/w)
d Jerry Bruck Jr. *with* IF Stone. *narrator* Tom Wicker.

● A fascinating portrait of the maverick Washington journalist who, blacklisted during the McCarthy era, started his own paper (running it for some seventeen years) and became a master political gadfly. Stone himself is a delight: witty, irreverent, forever puncturing the lies he claims it is in the nature of all politicians to tell. Brilliantly edited throughout, the real triumph of the film is the way it intercuts Stone's comments with newsreel footage to demonstrate how much of a point he has. TM

If These Walls Could Talk

(1996, US, 94 min)
d Nancy Savoca, Cher. *sc* Nancy Savoca, Susan Nanus, Marlene King. *ph* Ellen Kuras, Bobby Bukowski, John Stainer. *ed* Elena Magnani, Peter Honess. *pd* Hilda Stark Manos. *m* Cliff Eidelman. *cast* Demi Moore, Shirley Knight; Sissy Spacek, Xander Berkeley; Cher, Anne Heche.

● A triptych of half-hour films, set in the same house, in 1952, 1974 and 1996, with new occupants reflecting rather obviously the changing times. (Cher makes her directing debut in the third film.) The theme is abortion and the sometimes life-threatening responsibility faced by pregnant women: nurse Demi Moore widowed in the war and pregnant after a fling; harassed housewife/mature student Spacek; and student Anne Heche, who has no home and little income. The films suffer from dramatic compression (there's enough social context to service a soap opera series) and a didactic liberal tone, but they're fleshed out with strong performances and a keen sense of the women's dilemmas. Cher casts herself as a clinic doctor (in bulletproof vest) who literally takes her life in her hands in the fight against hysterical pro-life Christians. WH

If You Feel Like Singing

see Summer Stock

I Hate Your Guts

see Intruder, The

I Hired a Contract Killer

(1990, Fin/Swe, 79 min)
d/p/sc Aki Kaurismäki. *ph* Timo Salminen. *ed* Aki Kaurismäki. *pd* John Ebden. *cast* Jean-Pierre Léaud, Margi Clarke, Kenneth Colley, Trevor Bowen, Nicky Tesco, Charles Cork, Serge Reggiani, Peter Graves.

● This droll thriller displays the same melancholy vision as Kaurismäki's brilliant *Ariel*. After 15 years as a London waterworks clerk, French émigré Henri (Léaud) is made redundant. Lonely and friendless, he hires a hit-man to put him out of his misery; but after meeting flower-seller Margaret (Clarke) in a pub, he tries to cancel the contract. Shot in English on barely recognisable London locations, the film's oblique camera angles, moody colours and short, sharp scenes create a stylised world which still has the feel of everyday life. Kaurismäki's plots and dialogue often give the impression of having been improvised at the last moment, but his framing and narrative concision are extremely rigorous. He also allows lots of space for some sympathetic performances, in particular the laconic Léaud, Colley as the hangdog assassin, Tesco and Cork as a pair of small-time villains. Meanwhile, Timo Salminen's atmospheric images once again catch the seedy ambience of a B movie world where talk is cheap but love is precious. In short, it plays like an Ealing comedy on downers. NF

I Huvet på en Gammal Gubbe

see Out of an Old Man's Head

Iki Kadin

see Two Women

Ikinai

(1998, Jap, 101 min)
d Hiroshi Shimizu. *p* Masayuki Mori. *sc* Dankan. *ph* Katsumi Yanagishima. *ed* Yoshinori Ota. *pd* Norihiro Isoda. *m* Maya. *cast* Dankan, Nanano Okouchi, Toshinori Omi, Ippei Soda, Youichi Nukumizu, Great Gidayu.

● This fascinating first feature from Takeshi Kitano's regular first assistant shares certain traits with the master's movies: stylish camerawork, deadpan black comedy, and a concern with the value of life and how best to live it. Nine men – all in debt – embark on a private coach tour which will end in a fatal crash, thus ensuring insurance payouts to creditors and dependants. Unfortunately, just before the bus starts off, they are joined by a young woman determined to make use of her now deranged uncle's ticket. The droll humour gradually yields to a darker, more contemplative and affecting mood, without sacrificing any of the film's quirky originality. An engrossing debut. GA

Ikíngut

(2000, Ice/Nor/Den, 87 min)
d Gisli Snaer Erlingsson. *p* Hrönn Kristinsdóttir. *sc* Jón Steinar Ragnarsson. *ph* Sigurdur Sverrir Pálsson. *ed* Sigvaldi J Kárason, Skule Eriksen. *pd* Jón Steinar Ragnarsson. *m* Vilhjálmur Gudjónsson. *cast* Hjalti Rúnar Jónsson, Hans Tittus Nakinge, Pálmi Gestsson, Magnus Ragnarsson, Freydis Kristófersdóttir, Finnur Gudmundsson.

● Like Hal Hartley's unreleased *No Such Thing*, this is an allegorical Icelandic monster movie backed by Fridrik Thór Fridriksson – only this one's for kids. Set a couple of centuries ago, it's about the superstition and fear that overtake a remote village when a furry monster is spotted roaming the nearby wastes – but then, when the 11-year-old parson's son gets to meet the mysterious creature, it turns out to be a kid from Greenland. Cue a pleasant if predictable fable about friendship, prejudice and tolerance. GA

Ikiru (Living/To Live)

(1952, Jap, 143 min, b/w)
d Akira Kurosawa. *p* Shojiro Motoki. *sc* Shinobu Hashimoto, Hideo Oguni, Akira Kurosawa. *ph* Asaichi Nakai. *ed* Akira Kurosawa. *ad* So Matsuyama. *m* Fumio Hayasaka. *cast* Takashi Shimura, Nobuo Kaneko, Kyoko Seki, Miki Odagiri, Makoto Kobori, Kumeko Urabe, Kamatari Fujiwara.

● Easy to patronise as a classic of humanism; a celebration of the intrinsic nobility of human nature as a humble civil servant, following a drunken bout of panic, aimless wandering, and odd encounters on learning that he is dying of cancer, finally discovers a meaning to his empty life by patiently pushing through a project to turn a city dump into a children's playground. An intensely moving film all the same, elegiac and sometimes quirkishly funny in the manner of Kurosawa's elective model, John Ford. Shimura is superb in the central role, and not the least of Kurosawa's achievements is his triumphant avoidance of happy ending uplift; in the crucial (and beautiful) shot of the old man sitting huddled alone in the park on a child's swing, as the snow falls and he croons happily to himself as he waits for death, the sense of desolation remains complete. TM

I Know I'll See Your Face Again (Verboden te zuchten)

(2000, Bel, 98 min, b/w)
d Alex Stockman. *p* Kaat Camerlynck. *sc* Alex Stockman. *ph* Michel Baudour. *ed* Erik Lamens. *pd* Hubert Pouille. *m* Daan Stuyven. *cast* Stefan Perceval, Stefanie Bodien, Senne Rouffaer, Jacqueline Bir, Marie Bulté, Josse De Pauw.

● Another intriguingly strange Belgian film. Here's a droll, leisurely, rather enigmatic b/w comedy-drama in which a twenty-something coming out of a broken romance decides to leave Brussels for brighter climes. But instead, for no clear reason, he checks into a little hotel, whence he starts wandering the city and having odd encounters with various characters – including, of course, a girl. Faintly surreal in its use of non sequiturs, dramatic ellipses and subtly offbeat gags; regrettably, the film is so modest that it never quite lives up to the promise of its first half. GA

I Know What You Did Last Summer

(1997, US, 101 min)
d Jim Gillespie. *p* Neal Moritz, Erik Feig, Stokely Chaffin. *sc* Kevin Williamson. *ph* Denis Crossan. *ed* Steve Mirkovich. *pd* Gary Wissner. *m* John Debney. *cast* Jennifer Love Hewitt, Sarah Michelle Gellar, Ryan Phillippe, Freddie Prinze Jr, Johnny Galecki, Bridgette Wilson, Anne Heche.

● This crude slasher movie from *Scream* scriptwriter Kevin Williamson fails to spice up the old recipe and is far too sparing with the basic ingredient – the gruesome slaughter of nauseating American teenagers by a terrifying killer. Here a hook-handed fisherman (a sort of transmogrified Cap'n Birds Eye) terrorises four teenagers involved in a hushed-up hit-and-run accident. There are shoals of red herrings, lots of dumb 'Behind you!'-type scares, and not a scrap of imagination. Heche adds a dash of class as a weird country hick haunted by her brother's suicide, but otherwise the bland teenage cast simply go through the motions. NF

I Know Where I'm Going!

(1945, GB, 92 min, b/w)
d/p/sc Michael Powell, Emeric Pressburger. *ph* Erwin Hillier. *ed* John Seabourne. *pd* Alfred Junge. *m* Allan Gray. *cast* Wendy Hiller, Roger Livesey, Finlay Currie, Pamela Brown, John Laurie, Norman Shelley, Nancy Price, Catherine Lacey, George Carney, Petula Clark.

● Alongside *A Canterbury Tale*, Powell's most eloquent tribute to the mysteries of the British landscape. Hiller is the headstrong young girl who travels to Scotland to marry a wealthy but elderly man, only to be confused and distracted by the presence of dashing young laird Livesey. Full of well-integrated symbols (islands, hawks, a whirlpool) and lyrically shot in monochrome by Erwin Hillier, it's all quite beautiful, combining romance, comedy, suspense and a sense of the supernatural to winning effect. GA

Ile au trésor, L' (Treasure Island)

(1991, Fr/US, 115 min)
d Raúl Ruiz. *p* Paolo Branco. *sc* Raúl Ruiz. *ph* Acácio de Almeida. *ed* Rodolfo Wedeles. *ad* Maria-José. Branco.*m* Georges Arriagada. *cast* Melvil Poupaud, Martin Landau, Vic Tayback, Lou Castel, Jeffrey Kime, Anna Karina, Jean-François Stévenin, Charles Schmidt, Jean-Pierre Léaud, Pedro Armendariz Jr.

●Not so much an adaptation as an extended riff on a Robert Louis Stevenson standard. It begins with young Jim Hawkins – who's really called Jonathan, played in excruciating dubbed American by the angelic Poupaud in the English language version – watching his favourite TV serial, and then making the rest up from life when a power failure cuts him off in mid-episode. The hotel where he lives with his ill-matched parents (Castel and Karina) is visited by a motley crew of salt-encrusted sea-wrecks, and by Léaud as Jim's mentor in narrative, or as his alter ego. Midway, the film turns into something like a traditional seafaring yarn, and takes a decided downturn from the wildly artificed first half. But through the morass of entangled story, false clues, and literary references to Borges, Melville and quite possibly Thomas Pynchon, it weaves a dense web of allusions that carry it away from straight narrative into a strange terrain that's part dream, part psychoanalysis, part film theory, and several parts piss-take. Delayed for five years by litigation, cut down from the original four-hour conception, it's extraordinary, if patchy. JRo

I Led Two Lives

see Glen or Glenda?

I Like It Like That

(1994, US, 106 min)
d Darnell Martin. *p* Ann Carli, Jane Jangler. *sc* Darnell Martin. *ph* Alexander Gruszynski. *ed* Peter C Frank. *pd* Scott Chambliss. *m* Sergio George. *cast* Lauren Vélez, Jon Seda, Griffin Dunne, Rita Moreno, Tomas Melly, Desiree Casado, Jesse Borrego.

●Chino (Seda), a monstrous husband, is outraged to discover that his wife Lisette (Vélez) wants to work in order to pay for a new stereo. When their Puerto Rican neighbourhood in the South Bronx is hit by a blackout, he goes looting to procure the hi-fi himself, but is caught and jailed – leaving Lisette to raise their three children alone. Helped by her transsexual brother Alexis (who lends her his false breasts), she heads uptown to try to make it as a model. A series of chance encounters gets her a job in a record company working for Stephen Price (Dunne), who falls in lust with her, and drives her home in his red Lamborghini, much to the displeasure of Chino's mother (Moreno). An impressive fast-paced first feature. Director Darnell Martin emerges as an unusually perceptive chronicler of fragile sexual relationships and complex family ties, and draws strong performances from an inspired cast. A singular, hard-edged romantic comedy. ACh

I Like You, I Like You Very Much (Anata-ga suki desu, dai suki des')

(1994, Jap, 58 min)
d/sc/ph/ed Hiroyuki Oki. *cast* Kazunori Shibuya, Hisanori Kitakaze, Kazufumi Nishimoto, Hiroyuki Oki, Yoji Tanaka.

●Made by the most high-profile of Japan's avant-garde film-makers, this is in the same free-wheeling style as Hiroyuki's Oki personal short films: hand-held camerawork, refocusing, reframing and adjustment to the camera aperture. These informal methods are used to tell the committedly everyday story of a relationship between two boys which threatens to break apart when one impulsively cruises a straight guy on the street. Shot in the port city of Kochi, the film offers a panorama of small-town gay lives from quasi-monogamous partnerships to night-groping in the park. Highly credible as an account of a glitch in a relationship, it strikes me as one of the most candid films ever made about the vagaries of male desire, albeit with a deliciously romantic ending. TR

I Lived With You

(1933, GB, 98 min, b/w)
d Maurice Elvey. *p* Julius Hagen. *sc* Ivor Novello, George A Cooper, H Fowler Mear. *ph* Sydney Blythe, Ernest Palmer. *ed* Jack Harris. *ad* James Carter. *m* William Trytel. *cast* Ivor Novello, Ursula Jeans, Ida Lupino, Eliot Makeham, Minnie Rayner, Jack Hawkins.

●Another exotic stranger moves in on another stable, complacent household, with seismic results. Novello's penniless Russian prince lodging with a working class London family emerges as part-Boudu, part-Shane, liberating the elder daughter, but inadvertently steering Dad towards crime, while Mum quietly hits the bottle. It's smooth entertainment, with the crowd-pleasing elements of Novello's play fine-tuned during its West End run. And as usual with the campy, languid Ivor, you can hardly miss a sly playfulness, e.g. making royalty a code for gayness – 'Why do they hate me for what I cannot help?' The cast includes slimline Jack Hawkins as a cockney loudmouth and chubby Ida Lupino as a teenage temptress. BBa

I Live in Fear (Ikimono no Kiroku)

(1955, Jap, 113 min, b/w)
d Akira Kurosawa. *p* Shojiro Motoki. *sc* Shinobu Hashimoto, Hideo Oguni, Akira Kurosawa. *ph* Asakazu Nakai. *ed* Akira Kurosawa. *ad* Yoshiro Muraki. *m* Fumio Hayasaka. *cast* Toshiro Mifune, Eiko Miyoshi, Takashi Shimura, Yutaka Sada, Minoru Chiaki, Haruko Togo, Kamatari Fujiwara.

●Made between *Seven Samurai* and *Throne of Blood*, this contemporary social problem movie is Kurosawa's least commercially successful work. Mifune is the ageing, patriarchal head of a Tokyo family who, terrified at the prospect of a nuclear war, decides to sell up the family business and emigrate to a farm in Brazil. With Mifune uncomfortable playing a character twice his real age, and the character himself rendered incoherent by a script which seems uncertain whether it's him or society which is insane, a volunteer court official (Shimura) – required to adjudicate in the ensuing family squabble – a little awkwardly assumes the role of moral centre. It's a problematic film, wearing its uncertainties on its sleeve; but whether shooting in long takes or cutting the footage from multiple camera shooting, Kurosawa remains the cinema's supremely humanist emotional manipulator. See it and worry. RM

I Live in Grosvenor Square (aka A Yank in London)

(1945, GB, 114 min, b/w)
d/p Herbert Wilcox. *sc* Maurice Cowan, Nicholas Phipps, William D Bayles, Capt Arvid O Dahl. *ph* Otto Heller. *ed* Vera Campbell. *pd* William T Andrews. *m* Anthony Collins. *cast* Anna Neagle, Rex Harrison, Dean Jagger, Robert Morley, Jane Darwell, Irene Vanbrugh.

●Wilcox's demonstration of Anglo-American inter-dependence has become as quaint a wartime artifact as a Mickey Mouse gas mask. Toff Morley gives up his ancestral home to house GIs; heroic officer Harrison steps aside with exquisite grace when he realises fiancée Neagle prefers USAAF sergeant Jagger. In response to such abasement Jagger sacrifices his life to prevent his bomber crashing on the film's emblematic English village (where Tory Harrison has just been defeated in a by-election). Hard to imagine how this mournful account of the 'special relationship' could have had much appeal on either side of the Atlantic, but it's helped by Harrison's languid charm, Jagger's studied amiability and Neagle's loose-limbed jitterbugging at the USO. BBa

I'll Be Seeing You

(1944, US, 85 min, b/w)
d William Dieterle. *p* Dore Schary. *sc* Marion Parsonnet. *ph* Tony Gaudio. *ed* William H Ziegler. *ad* Mark-Lee Kirk. *m* Daniele Amfitheatrof. *cast* Ginger Rogers, Joseph Cotten, Shirley Temple, Spring Byington, Tom Tully, Chill Wills, John Derek.

●Interestingly cast mainstream melodrama with Rogers a late replacement for Joan Fontaine as the woman shell-shocked soldier Cotten falls in love with before her 17-year-old daughter (Shirley Temple in her first adult role) blurts out a well-kept secret that threatens to destroy their romance. The contrivance is handled with a good deal of dignity by the ever-refined Dieterle, but producer Selznick wasn't satisfied with Temple's key monologue and hired in George Cukor to reshoot the crucial scene. Spot the joins? TJ

Ill Fares the Land

(1982, GB, 102 min)
d Bill Bryden. *p* Robert Love. *sc* Bill Bryden. *ph* John Coquillon. *ed* Lesley Walker. *pd* Ken Bridgeman. *m* John Tams. *cast* Fulton Mackay, James Grant, David Hayman, Robert Stephens, Morag Hood, JG Devlin.

●From Michael Powell to Bills Forsyth and Douglas, Scotland endures as the resonant repository for British cinematic mythology. An impressive addition to that tradition, this is a moving, factually-based investigation of the last gasps of life on remote St Kilda. Besieged by hunger, inbreeding, and a remarkable lack of contact with the outside world, the five families remaining in 1929 finally wrench themselves from their wild, beautiful island in a semi-voluntary act of evacuation to the mainland. The film both celebrates the close-knit community's daily life and examines why, in its reluctance to adapt, it could not but disappear. Neither pastoral idyll nor a 'we had it tough' catalogue of survival strategies, it's more a laconic account of the strengths and strictures of family and ritual – the Sabbath, funerals, a wedding, work and coming-of-age. Here, indeed, lie the connections with Bryden's script for Walter Hill's *The Long Riders*, and with his stylistic idol John Ford. GA

Illicit Interlude

see Sommarlek

Ill Met by Moonlight (aka Night Ambush)

(1957, GB, 104 min, b/w)
d/p/sc Michael Powell, Emeric Pressburger. *ph* Christopher Challis. *ed* Arthur Stevens. *ad* Alex Vetchinsky. *m* Mikis Theodorakis. *cast* Dirk Bogarde, Marius Goring, David Oxley, Cyril Cusack, Laurence Payne, Wolfe Morris, Michael Gough, Christopher Lee.

●It's sad that Powell and his long-standing collaborator Emeric Pressburger were forced into the grind of British war movies so soon after they had managed to transcend the limitations of most local cinema in movies like *The Red Shoes* and *A Matter of Life and Death*. Like their *The Battle of the River Plate*, this is superior of its kind, but that isn't enough to lift it into the areas that Powell and Pressburger mastered a few years earlier. It's based on an actual incident in World War II: British officer Bogarde is working with partisans in occupied Crete, and decides to kidnap the German commander-in-chief to boost the war effort. General Kreipe (Goring) is duly hijacked and trekked across country by night into custody on a British vessel. The scrupulous reconstruction is all pluck, stiff upper lips and mutual respect for one's foe. It's distinguished by Powell's sense of landscape (as in *49th Parallel*), and by a vigorous Theodorakis score. TR

Illumination (Iluminacja)

(1972, Pol, 91 min)
d Krzysztof Zanussi. *p* Andrzej Kotaczynski, M Kesy. *sc* Krzysztof Zanussi. *ph* Edward Klosinski. *ed* Urszula Sliwinska. *ad* Stefan Maciag. *m* Wojciech Kilar. *cast* Stanislaw Latallo, Monika Denisiewicz-Olbrzychska, Malgorzata Pritulak, Edward Zebrowski, Jan Skotnicki.

●Zanussi's film follows its questing hero, a physics student, through his twenties. A meditation on the human condition, its title is taken from medieval philosophy. The hero's development is episodic and familiar: student days, first sexual encounter, the death of a friend, a marriage that falters and recovers, economic security – a development marked by the gradual abandoning of his search for absolutes. With maturity comes a limiting of horizons and the beginning of decline. The film's depth and individual perception stem from its background of physics, mathematics and medicine, which transforms it into an objective look at the human species. The rapid editing and self-conscious technique is sometimes irritating, but more often proves sufficiently provocative to hold attention. CPe

Illusions

(1984, US, 34 min)
d Julie Dash. *cast* Lonette McKee, Ned Bellamy, Rosanne Katon.

●In which McKee repeats her black-seen-as-a-white role from *The Cotton Club*, this time as a '40s Hollywood producer's assistant determined to fight the way the movies rewrite history (particularly war propaganda) without reference to blacks. Some nice lines, performances and music, although the narrative could be much tighter, and – as in so many low-budget independents – the quality of the sound recording is abysmal. In general, what tends to be described as 'worthy'. GA

Illustrated Man, The

(1968, US, 103 min)
d Jack Smight. *p* Howard B Kreitsek, Ted Mann. *sc* Howard B Kreitsek. *ph* Philip H Lathrop. *ed* Archie Marshek. *ad* Joel Schiller. *m* Jerry Goldsmith. *cast* Rod Steiger, Claire Bloom, Robert Drivas, Don Dubbins, Jason Evers, Tim Weldon.

●A much maligned film, loosely derived from Ray Bradbury's collection of short stories and spinning out a fascinating triangle relationship which ranges disconcertingly through past, present and future, and in which the three participants never meet on the same time plane. A young hitchhiker (Drivas) encounters a stranger on the road (Steiger) whose skin is covered with fantastic tattoos which foretell the future. They were done, he says, by a witch-woman (Bloom) who disappeared 'back into the future', leaving him to roam the earth like the Wandering Jew in quest of vengeance against the woman who made him an outcast. Fascinated, already falling in love, the young man begins to conjure an image of the witch; and through the Illustrated Man's tattoos, sees three stories from the distant future in which he, the witch and the Illustrated Man play the leading roles, all hingeing obliquely on the betrayal of love, with sometimes one character, sometimes another, becoming the victim. Time suddenly ceases to exist, and the characters are caught in a reenactment of the story of the Garden of Eden (or of Cain and Abel) over a campfire where the Illustrated Man and the young hitchhiker fight a mental/physical battle over their enigmatic, absent Eve. Hesitantly directed by Smight, the script is nevertheless genuinely imaginative, and both settings and performances are admirable. TM

Illustrious Corpses (Cadaveri Eccellenti)

(1975, It/Fr, 120 min)
d Francesco Rosi. *p* Alberto Grimaldi. *sc* Francesco Rosi, Tonino Guerra, Lino Jannuzzi. *ph* Pasqualino De Santis. *ed* Ruggero Mastroianni. *ad* Andrea Crisanti. *m* Piero Piccioni. *cast* Lino Ventura, Alain Cuny, Paolo Bonacelli, Marcel Bozzuffi, Tina Aumont, Max von Sydow, Fernando Rey, Charles Vanel, Renato Salvatori.

●While not as immediately tough as Rosi's political case histories, *Illustrious Corpses* burns on a slow fuse. A lone policeman (Ventura) investigates the murders of prominent legal figures. But as he stumbles on a conspiracy of national dimensions, the mystery thriller expands into an exploration of the mysteries of political power. The machinations of both Right and Left are set against the constant fact of human mortality (as referred to in the film's title). And a sense of the past is ever present: huge public monuments sit in judgment on the grey men who move through their corridors of power. What impresses most are scenes displaying Rosi's bravura: an obsessive judge shot in his tomb-like mansion; a party calculatedly shocking in its lavishness; Ventura alone in his flat when the horror of his discovery hits him. The photography serves perfectly the growing sense of unease, and Ventura is as quietly excellent as ever. CPe

I Love a Man in Uniform

(1993, Can, 97 min)
d David Wellington. *p* Paul Brown. *sc* David Wellington. *ph* David Franco. *ed* Susan Shipton. *pd* John Dondertman. *m* Ron Sures and The Tragically Hip. *cast* Tom McCamus, Brigitte Bako, Kevin Tighe, David Hemblen, Alex Karzis, Graham McPherson.

●Henry Adler realises his acting ambitions when he lands the part of a tough-guy sergeant in a TV cop show. Sporting the full black-leather regalia, he acquires a sense of self-importance he can't wait to test out by walking the streets and passing himself off as a real police officer. At first, Wellington's debut plays Henry's misadventures as dark comedy; but when shooting begins of the authentically cheesy *Crimewave* and Henry's off-screen relationship with his co-star fails to develop satisfactorily, the writer/director's wider scheme falls into place. McCamus's compelling lead performance delineates the increasingly violent results when one anguished individual starts blurring the distinctions; and the film as a whole is provocative and disturbing in the way it leaves viewers to decide how much their sympathies are implicated in the power trip from alienation to psychosis. TJ

I Love Melvin

(1952, US, 76 min)
d Don Weis. *p* George Wells. *sc* George Wells, Ruth Brooks Flippen. *ph* Harold Rosson. *ed* Adrienne Fazan. *ad* Cedric Gibbons, Jack Martin Smith, Eddie Imazu. *songs* Mack Gordon Josef Myrow. *cast* Donald O'Connor, Debbie Reynolds, Una Merkel, Allyn Joslyn, Jim Backus, Richard Anderson.

●Really attractive little musical, with O'Connor as a magazine photographer's gofer pretending to make a cover girl of a chorine (Reynolds) in order to impress her, then heading for disaster as he tries to make good his empty promises. The family scenes have a touch of *Meet Me in St Louis*, and the numbers choreographed by Robert Alton – including a football ballet (with Reynolds as the football) and a roller-skating dance for O'Connor – are bright and breezily inventive. TM

I Love Trouble

(1994, US, 123 min)
d Charles Shyer. *p* Nancy Meyers. *sc* Nancy Meyers, Charles Shyer. *ph* John Lindley. *ed* Paul Hirsch, Walter Murch, Adam Bernardi. *pd* Dean Tavoularis. *m* David Newman. *cast* Julia Roberts, Nick Nolte, James Rebhorn, Robert Loggia, Saul Rubinek, Olympia Dukakis, Marsha Mason.

●Ace columnist Peter Brackett (Nolte), a Pulitzer hack, is scooped out of complacency by cub reporter Sabrina Peterson (Roberts). They clash on the story of a train wreck, and spur each other on until they've got to the bottom of a not very interesting corporate conspiracy – and each other. Charles Shyer and producer Nancy Meyers usually purvey old-fashioned comedies with a topical twist, but this is just old fashioned: a '90s star vehicle transposed from the '30s. You can't replicate charm, however, and the Shmeyers' movie isn't witty or glamorous; it's smug and glossy, sparkling as tap water, and – when it finally decides it's a suspense picture – tense as an arthritic earthworm. TCh

I Love You Again

(1940, US, 99 min, b/w)
d WS Van Dyke. *p* Lawrence Weingarten. *sc* Charles Lederer, George Oppenheimer, Harry Kurnitz. *ph* Oliver T Marsh. *ed* Gene Ruggiero. *ad* Cedric Gibbons. *m* Franz Waxman. *cast* William Powell, Myrna Loy, Frank McHugh, Edmund Lowe, Nella Walker, Donald Douglas, Pierre Watkin.

●Powell, Loy and 'one-shot Woody' Van Dyke (the latter didn't dawdle) put *The Thin Man* series on hold to film this equally zestful screwball comedy. The gambit's a corker: when he's clocked with an oar, fusty small-town businessman Powell suddenly remembers he's a con-man, not the model citizen he's been playing for eight years. He forgets everything else about his life while he's an amnesiac and falls in love anew with his beautiful but bored wife. Loy, however, wants a divorce. The pace flags after the first reel, but cracking dialogue and the stars' perfect rapport ensure plenty of giddy fun. GM

I Love You, Alice B. Toklas!

(1968, US, 93 min)
d Hy Averback. *p* Charles H Maguire. *sc* Paul Mazursky, Larry Tucker. *ph* Philip Lathrop. *ed* Robert C Jones. *pd* Pato Guzman. *m* Elmer Bernstein. *cast* Peter Sellers, Jo Van Fleet, Joyce Van Patten, Leigh Taylor-Young, David Arkin, Herbert Edelman, Grady Sutton.

●Dispiritingly trendy comedy, co-scripted by Paul Mazursky, in which Sellers briefly sketches a brilliant performance as a middle-aged lawyer tormented by asthma, by a mistress intent on being a wife, and by a car with parking problems. When everyone begins romping around under the influence of marijuana cookies, Sellers becomes a long-haired dropout, and one can only cringe in embarrassment. TM

I Love You, I Don't (Je t'aime, moi non plus)

(1975, Fr, 88 min)
d Serge Gainsbourg. *p* Jacques-Eric Strauss. *sc* Serge Gainsbourg. *ph* Willy Kurant. *ed* Kénout Peltier, Elizabeth Servouze, Sylvie Quester. *ad* Constantin Mejinsky, Théo Meurisse. *m* Serge Gainsbourg, Jean-Pierre Sabar. *cast* Jane Birkin, Joe Dallesandro, Hugues Quester, René Kolldehoff, Gérard Depardieu, Michel Blanc.

●'Some days I just feel I could flush myself down the bowl,' bemoans Dallesandro, summing up the excremental flavour of this riotously bleak and brutalised love story. Writer/director Gainsbourg employs a ludicrously grotesque approach – monosyllabic script, overblown symbolism, high-pitched performances, refuse-tip landscape, and small town aggressive boredom. A romance for our times. IB

I Love You, I'll Kill You (Ich liebe Dich, Ich töte Dich)

(1971, WGer, 94 min)
d/p/sc Uwe Brandner. *ph* André Dubreuil. *ed* Heide Genée. *m* Uwe Brandner, Heine Hotter, Kid Olauf. *cast* Rolf Becker, Hannes Fuchs, Helmut Brasch, Stefan Moses.

●A young, vaguely effete schoolteacher takes a post in a remote village community, which turns out to be an 'ideal' society: the all-but unemployed macho cops administer downers to keep public deviations in check, but anything from whips to sheep-fucking goes in private. Teach meets his butch 'opposite', the hunter of wolves; the two recognise their hidden kinship, and become lovers. But the experience leads our hero off the rails. He starts poaching (the game is reserved for the 'masters' who descend on the village by helicopter once a year), and so his lover has to track him down…Brandner presents all this in short, seemingly oblique fragments (his own metaphor is a kaleidoscope), a method that takes a while to adjust to: it really takes a second viewing to realise how funny the film is, for example. Brandner seems to have aimed at a *L'Age d'or* for the valium generation, but the result is very close indeed to a rural version of *Performance* (right down to a similarly unsatisfactory ending). TR

I Love, You Love (Ja Milujem, Ty Milujes)

(1980, Czech, 96 min)
d Dusan Hanak. *p* Karol Bakos. *sc* Dusan Hanak. *ph* Jozef Ort-Snep, Alojz Hanusek. *ed* Alfred Bencic. *pd* Milos Kalina. *m* Miroslav Korinek. *cast* Roman Klosowski, Milan Jelic, Iva Janzurova, Vaclav Baka, Marie Motlova, Milada Jezkova.

●Humour doesn't travel too well in this gentle Slovakian comedy about two railway mailmen: Vinco, a successful, devil may care womaniser, and Pista, lovelorn and a disaster with the ladies – the archetypal comic 'nobody', in fact. Of some interest for its focus on provincial Slovakian life (all bee keeping, boozing, and eccentricity, apparently), but otherwise predictable and rather sentimental. (Not released until 1989, in which year Hanak took the prize for best director at the Berlin Film Festival.) GA

I Love You to Death

(1990, US, 97 min)
d Lawrence Kasdan. *p* Jeffrey Lurie, Ron Moler. *sc* John Kostmayer. *ph* Owen Roizman. *ed* Anne V Coates. *pd* Lilly Kilvert. *m* James Horner. *cast* Kevin Kline, Tracey Ullman, Joan Plowright, River Phoenix, William Hurt, Keanu Reeves, James Gammon, Jack Kehler, Miriam Margolyes.

●Based on a real-life story – jealous wife Fran Toto made or contracted for five attempts on her unfaithful husband's life, landed in prison, and was eventually reconciled with her forgiving spouse – this sketchy comedy sinks beneath the weight of predictability. While Joey (Kline) spins pizzas and compliments female customers, his wife Rosalie (Ullman) puts his flirtation down to Italian blood. When she learns that the dalliances involve sex, however, her murderous rage knows no bounds. But assorted ploys to end his life are all futile; not even bullets fired at point blank range can kill him. A starry cast assists Ullman in her plans – Hurt, Plowright and Phoenix all have a go at Joey – but their presence is just one more symptom of the film's extraordinary lack of restraint. In straining towards humour, John Kostmayer's script falls back on crude exaggeration, and the result is woefully unfunny. CM

Images

(1972, Ire, 101 min)
d Robert Altman. *p* Tommy Thompson. *sc* Robert Altman. *ph* Vilmos Zsigmond. *ed* Graeme Clifford. *pd* Leon Ericksen. *m* John Williams. *cast* Susannah York, René Auberjonois, Marcel Bozzuffi, Hugh Millais, Cathryn Harrison, John Morley.

●Underrated film about a lonely woman cracking up and suffering disturbing hallucinations about sex and death. Unlike most of Altman's movies, which parody and reinvent genres, *Images* stands rather in a loose trilogy with *That Cold Day in the Park* and *3 Women*, in its investigation of madness and its concentration upon a female character. The fragmented style of the film, in which York's mental life is portrayed as substantially as her 'real' life, might have become pretentious; but the director controls things beautifully, proffering credible biographical reasons for her inner disturbances, and borrowing shock effects from the thriller genre to underline the terrifying nature of her predicament. It's brilliantly shot by Vilmos Zsigmond (wtihout a hint of psychedelic trickery in sight), superbly acted, and lent extra menace by the sounds and music of, respectively, Stomu Yamashta and John Williams. GA

Imaginary Crimes

(1994, US, 105 min)
d Anthony Drazan. *p* James G Robinson. *sc* Kristine Johnson, Davia Nelson. *ph* John J Campbell. *ed* Elizabeth Kling. *pd* Joseph T Garrity. *m* Stephen Endelman. cast Harvey Keitel, Fairuza Balk, Kelly Lynch, Vincent D'Onofrio, Diane Baker, Chris Penn, Seymour Cassel, Annette O'Toole.
●Keitel is good but not stretched as Ray, a small man with big dreams, doomed both as a barely legit businessman and as a husband and father. His eldest daughter (Balk, good) is a bright high school kid and budding author, who uses the emotions he provokes as raw material for her stories about one girl's experience growing up in '60s Colorado. It's a rites-of-passage story in which the daughter's loss of innocence is compared and contrasted with the father's almost childlike destructiveness and delusion; his crimes, real or imaginary, provide the pain which she will use to shape her success. Drazan's careful direction certainly suits the heartfelt script (from a book by Sheila Ballantyne), but more than lashings of honest emotion is required. AO

Imaginary Tale, An

see Histoire inventée, Une

Imagine (aka Imagine: John Lennon)

(1988, US, 106 min, b/w & col)
d Andrew Solt. *p* David L Wolper, Andrew Solt. *sc* Sam Egan, Andrew Solt. *ph* Nestor Almendros. *ed* Bert Lovitt. *with* Cynthia Lennon, Julian Lennon, Yoko Ono, Sean Lennon.
●When a poor boy who can do nothing else but play in a rock and roll band dies, we the public get treated to more golden tributes than all the barbiturates he ever took. This documentary uses acres of footage shot on Lennon's orders, and documents the one time in the '70s when he was not continually nodding out. The 1971 recording session in the Lennon's country mansion which produced 'Imagine' is the core; the whole of the narration is taken from Lennon interviews, tracing his life in his own words. The result is a mythological media history that paints the man to be more than a saint: he is a *human* saint. He made mistakes, and he admits to them. No one, not even his ex-wife, has a bad word to say about him. It's a lesson in how to use celluloid to create your own personal version of reality. But then, when did Lennon ever truly deal with reality? MPe

Imago – Meret Oppenheim

(1989, Switz, 90 min)
d Pamela Robertson-Pierce, Anselm Spoerri. *narrator* Glenda Jackson.
●Her fur-lined tea cup is one of the most famous surrealist objects ever made, but its creator, Oppenheim, is practically unknown. Ironically, the success of the sculpture eclipsed other achievements, and contributed to a depression that sent her back to Switzerland. Her self-doubt lifted in 1954, when she began the extraordinary paintings and sculptures shown at the ICA in 1989. This film was begun in collaboration with the artist, but sadly she died before shooting got under way. Glenda Jackson reads letters and diaries with a dull matter-of-factness to an irritating soundtrack. The edifice creaks, and Oppenheim is made to seem ordinary. The woman who said 'Imagination is the landscape in which the artist goes for a walk' deserves more imaginitive treatment. SK

I'm All Right, Jack

(1959, GB, 105 min, b/w)
d John Boulting. *p* Roy Boulting. *sc* Frank Harvey, John Boulting, Alan Hackney. *ph* Max Greene. *ed* Anthony Harvey. *ad* Bill Andrews. *m* Ken Hare. *cast* Ian Carmichael, Peter Sellers, Irene Handl, Richard Attenborough, Terry-Thomas, Dennis Price, Liz Fraser, Margaret Rutherford, Miles Malleson, John Le Mesurier.
●The best of the Boultings' warm, vulgar, affectionate satires. The travails of silly-ass hero Carmichael are only mildly amusing, but the film blazes into life with the arrival of Sellers' Stalinist Don Quixote, tilting with alarming predictability at the windmills constructed by his class enemies. The Red Robbos of this world may be an unfairly easy target, but Sellers' caricature is affectionate, not malicious. Accusations of union-bashing are misplaced. The workers may all be dumb clods who sleep with their vests on, but there's a grudging appreciation of their truculent cynicism, and Attenborough's horrid little entrepreneur discovers that in making them the dupes of his capitalist crookery he brings about his own downfall. RMy

I Married a Communist (aka The Woman on Pier 13)

(1949, US, 73 min, b/w)
d Robert Stevenson. *p* Jack J Gross. *sc* Charles Grayson, Robert Hardy Andrews. *ph* Nick Musuraca. *ed* Roland Gross. *ad* Albert S D'Agostino, Walter Keller. *m* Leigh Harline. *cast* Laraine Day, Robert Ryan, John Agar, Thomas Gomez, Janis Carter, Richard Rober, William Talman, Paul Guilfoyle.
●This was the notorious project with which eager beaver Howard Hughes did his bit for Uncle Sam during the witch hunt days, assigning it to a string of RKO directors (turn it down, and you labelled yourself pinko or worse). Day is the lady who marries Ryan after a whirlwind courtship, knowing only that he is a top executive with a San Francisco shipping company who used to be a stevedore. The Commies, though, know that he was briefly a Party member during the Depression, and begin blackmailing him (Carter just wanting revenge because he ditched her along with the Party, but Gomez intent on forcing him to help foment labour disputes at the shipyard). Ryan plays ball until the game gets rough and corpses start piling up, when he does the right thing (conveniently dying in the process, after explaining that he only joined because he was a disgruntled kid out of a job: 'I thought I'd quit, but you can't quit. They won't let you'). The sterling cast can make no headway against cartoon characters, a fatuous script that defies belief, and an enveloping sense of hysteria. Nick Musuraca's *noir*-ish camerawork, mercifully, is stunning. TM

I Married a Monster from Outer Space

(1958, US, 78 min, b/w)
d/p Gene Fowler Jr. *sc* Louis Vittes. *ph* Haskell Boggs. *ed* George Tomasini. *ad* Hal Pereira, Henry Bumstead. *cast* Tom Tryon, Gloria Talbott, Peter Baldwin, Robert Ivers, Ty Hungerford [Ty Hardin], Ken Lynch, John Eldridge, Alan Dexter.
●Though trailing in the wake of *Invasion of the Body Snatchers* and saddled with a singularly schlocky title, this is a remarkably effective cheapie about an alien takeover, which even manages an undertow of sexual angst as the tentacular creature inhabiting Tryon, inadvertently giving itself away to Talbott on the sentimental occasion of their wedding anniversary, struggles to come to terms with a mysterious humanisation of its instincts. Good performances, strikingly moody camerawork, a genuinely exciting climax (with a particularly nice touch in that the posse of bona fide humans which finally routs the aliens is recruited from expectant fathers at the maternity ward of the local hospital). TM

I Married a Nazi

see Man I Married, The

I Married a Witch

(1942, US, 76 min, b/w)
d René Clair. *sc* Robert Pirosh, Marc Connelly. *ph* Ted Tetzlaff. *ed* Eda Warren. *ad* Hans Dreier, Ernst Fegté. *m* Roy Webb. *cast* Veronica Lake, Fredric March, Cecil Kellaway, Robert Benchley, Susan Hayward, Elizabeth Patterson, Robert Warwick.
●Heresy here: Clair's '30s musical comedies have always been acclaimed as enormously original, innovative classics, far superior to his American films. But where those French films now seem dated and Chaplinesque in their twee sentimentality and naïve desire to make a serious point, the American films remain delightful: unpretentious, pacy and genuinely witty. *I Married a Witch* sees Clair at his peak, with an ambitious, puritanical politician (March) being plagued by the mischievous Lake, a witch reincarnated and bent on revenge after being burned at the stake by his ancestors. Lake is delightfully effective as the malicious woman, whose ideas of punishment are often beautifully absurd, and March provides an excellent foil. GA

I Married a Woman

(1956, US, 84 min, b/w & col)
d Hal Kanter. *p* William Bloom. *sc* Goodman Ace. *ph* Lucien Ballard. *ed* Otto Ludwig. *ad* Albert S D'Agostino, Walter Keller. *m* Cyril J Mockridge. *cast* George Gobel, Diana Dors, Adolphe Menjou, Jessie Royce Landis, Nita Talbot, Angie Dickinson, John Wayne.
●One of two disastrous movies British siren Dors made in Hollywood for RKO, this has her opposite timid US TV comic Gobel as a neglected wife of an ad-man who sets out to make her husband jealous. Dors later sued the studio, charging that they'd made her 'an object of disgrace, ill-will and ridicule,' which gives some idea of the movie's quality. TJ

I'm Expecting

see Jag Är Med Barn

I'm Going Home (Vou Para Casa/ Je Rentre à la Maison)

(2001, Port/Fr, 90 min)
d Manoel de Oliveira. *p* Paulo Branco. *sc* Manoel de Oliveira. *ph* Sabine Lancelin. *ed* Valérie Loiseleux. *pd* Yves Fournier. *cast* Michel Piccoli, Antoine Chappey, Leonor Baldaque, Leonor Silveira, Ricardo Trepa, Jean-Michel Arnold, Adrien de Van, Sylvie Testud, Isabel Ruth, Catherine Deneuve, John Malkovich.
●Thanks to the dependably marvellous Piccoli, this heartfelt but slim, slightly predictable and sometimes silly study of an actor in his twilight years manages to hold the attention throughout, despite longueurs as we see him on stage and in rehearsal (for, obviously, *The King Is Dead* and *The Tempest* and, very implausibly, as Buck Mulligan – *to be sûr!* – in a Malkovich movie of *Ulysses*). The film has its moments – the sudden news that he's lost almost his entire family in an accident, some gentle comedy with café tables, Piccoli's expression as make-up is applied – but without the actor's charm, warmth, expertise and sheer presence, the pickings would be slim. GA

I'm Gonna Git You Sucka

(1988, US, 89 min)
d Keenen Ivory Wayans. *p* Peter McCarthy, Carl Craig. *sc* Keenen Ivory Wayans. *ph* Tom Richmond. *ed* Michael R Miller. *m* David Michael Frank. *cast* Keenen Ivory Wayans, Bernie Casey, Antonio Fargas, Steve James, Isaac Hayes, Jim Brown, Ja'Net DuBois, Dawnn Lewis, John Vernon, Clu Gulager, Kadeem Hardison, Damon Wayans.
●In this spoof of the mean-ass blaxploitation actioners of the '70s, a crisis has struck New York's black neighbourhoods: the brothers are 'OG'-ing (overdosing on gold medallions, etc) in their thousands. Into the fray comes army sergeant Jack Spade (Wayans); returning from years of brave desk and latrine duty to find his younger rother has fallen victim, he decides to hunt down evil Mr Big (Vernon). Wayans tosses out black stereotypes in arresting profusion, adopting the *Airplane!* approach: broad rather than subtle visual gags and parodic encounters. The greatest pleasure comes from seeing '70s veterans send themselves up: an overweight Hayes 'tooling up' with enough weaponry to bomb Libya; Fargas' Flyguy, winner of the 'Pimp of the Year' competition, in ludicrous flamboyant threads. The music ranges from Hayes through Curtis Mayfield to rap. The film was co-scripted

by Robert Townsend, which may account for a faint smell of complacent yuppie bad faith in the air, but that is blown away by the enthusiasm and innocence of the playing. WH

Imitation Game, The

(1980, GB, 95 min)
d/p Richard Eyre. sc Ian McEwan. *ph* Peter Bartlett. *ed* David Martin. *pd* Geoff Powell. *cast* Harriet Walter, Lorna Charles, Bernard Gallagher, Gillian Martell, Simon Chandler, Brenda Blethyn, Patricia Routledge.

●Ian McEwan's brilliant script, perfectly realised on film by Eyre, was the TV drama of 1980. During WWII, an ATS wireless operator (Walter) casually penetrates, and is eventually destroyed by, the circles of secrecy surrounding the code-breaking operation Ultra. Power, patriarchy, and the moral basis of war are threaded together in a drama concerned with history yet charged with contemporary resonance. JW

Imitation of Life

(1934, US, 109 min, b/w)
d John M Stahl. *p* Carl Laemmle Jr. *sc* William Hurlblut. *ph* Merrit B Gerstad. *ed* Philip Cahn, Maurice Wright. *ad* Charles D Hall. *m* Heinz Roemheld. *cast* Claudette Colbert, Warren William, Louise Beavers, Rochelle Hudson, Fredi Washington, Ned Sparks, Alan Hale, Henry Armetta, Franklin Pangborn.

●More character study than polemic, wonderfully warm and witty in its observation of two women (one black, one white) who not only crash the race barriers in their friendship but successfully go it alone in a man's world, Stahl's version of Fannie Hurst's novel makes fascinating comparison with Sirk's remake. Where Sirk pushes the final melodramatics into social confrontation, Stahl withdraws in discretion, almost reducing them to naturalistic credibility. But one shot, of a staircase mathematically dividing the house into upstairs and downstairs as the guests arrive for a party which white Colbert hostesses and black Beavers serves from the kitchen, acknowledges Stahl's awareness of the hypocrisy that underlies the script's apparently 'liberal' treatment of blacks. TM

Imitation of Life

(1958, US, 124 min)
d Douglas Sirk. *p* Ross Hunter. *sc* Eleanore Griffin, Allan Scott. *ph* Russell Metty. *ed* Milton Carruth. *ad* Alexander Golitzen, Richard H Riedel. *m* Frank Skinner. *cast* Lana Turner, John Gavin, Sandra Dee, Juanita Moore, Susan Kohner, Daniel O'Herlihy, Robert Alda, Troy Donahue, Mahalia Jackson.

●There is a marvellous moment towards the end of Sirk's film which encapsulates the cruel cynicism that permeates his best work. As successful actress Turner, leaning over her dying black maid and long-term friend, lifts her head in tears, we see in the background a photograph of the dead woman's half-caste daughter, smiling. The romantic sentimentality of the moment is totally undercut by the knowledge that the girl, who has rejected her mother out of a desire to pass for white, has found a tragic release with her kindly parent's death. Sirk's last movie in Hollywood is a coldly brilliant weepie, a rags-to-riches tale of two intertwined families, in which the materialist optimism is continually counterpointed by an emphasis upon racist tension and the degeneration of family bonds. Despite the happy ending, what one remembers from the film is the steadily increasing hopelessness, given its most glorious visual expression in the scene of the maid's extravagant funeral, the only time in the film when her subordinate status and unhappy distance from her daughter are abolished. Forget those who decry the '50s Hollywood melodrama; it is through the conventions of that hyper-emotional genre that Sirk is able to make such a devastatingly embittered and pessimistic movie. GA

Im Juli

see In July

I'm Jumping Over Puddles Again (Uz zase Skácu pres Kaluze)

(1970, Czech, 92 min)
d Karel Kachyna. *sc* Ota Hofman, Karel Kachyna. *ph* Josef Illik. *ed* Miroslav Hájek. *ad* Oldrich Okac, Ester Krumbachová. *m* Zdenek Liska. *cast* Vladimir Dlouhy, Karel Hlusicka, Zdena Hadrbolcová, Vladimir Smeral, Darja Hajska.

●About a young boy's passion for horses, his paralysis from polio, and subsequent triumph over his handicap by learning to ride. Village life of the period (just before World War I) is well evoked, and the boy's relationship to his wastrel father, anxious mother, and the somewhat scornful village kids is treated with some feeling. It's a whimsical, rather drowsy film, overlaid with an unfortunate technical tricksiness and an insistent music score. Unexpectedly, it improves enormously with the boy's illness and his feverish hallucinations in hospital. Later, treated with a nicely quirky sense of humour, neither his crippled state nor his determination to overcome it are trivialised. Altogether a bit of an oddity, pleasant and irritating in equal proportions as it avoids the obvious pitfalls and then falls flat where least expected.

Im Lauf der Zeit

see Kings of the Road

Immaculate Conception

(1991, GB, 120 min)
d/p/sc Jamil Dehlavi. *ph* Nic Knowland. *ed* Chris Barnes. *pd* Mike Porter. *m* Richard Harvey. *cast* James Wilby, Melissa Leo, Shabana Azmi, Zia Mohyeddin, James Cossins, Ronny Jhutti, Tim Choate.

●Eccentric at first sight, this ends up delivering pretty much what you'd expect from a 'Film on Four' movie: thoughtful scripting, solid acting, questions of cultural and sexual identity. Wilby and Leo play a well-heeled white couple in Karachi – she's Jewish-American with free-spirit mystic tendencies, he's a no-nonsense Brit conservationist. Unable to conceive, they have recourse to a holy shrine attended by a bevy of eunuchs in full drag. After a three-day fertility work-out, their dream seems likely to come true; but there, of course, the trouble begins. This is plentiful premise to be getting on with, but writer-director Dehlavi chooses to stitch in more subplot than his two hours can reasonably accommodate: Wilby's relationship with journalist Samira (Azmi) and her dying uncle; Cossins as a camp old colonial who steps out of line with Islam; and Leo's pushy diplomat brother (Choate), who turns up to nudge matters into the international incident bracket. Dehlavi goes out of his way to skirt the risk of sensationalism, but his diffuse, overcautious approach dilutes matters to the point of tedium. JRo

Immoral Tales (Contes Immoraux)

(1974, Fr, 103 min)
d Walerian Borowczyk. *p* Anatole Dauman. *sc* Walerian Borowczyk. *ph* Bernard Daillencourt, Guy Durban, Michel Zolat, Noël Véry. *ed/ad* Walerian Borowczyk. *m* Maurice Le Roux. *cast* Lise Danvers, Fabrice Luchini, Charlotte Alexandra, Paloma Picasso, Pascale Christophe, Florence Bellamy, Jacopo Berinizi, Lorenzo Berinizi.

●Made between *Blanche* and *Story of Sin*, *Immoral Tales* takes Borowczyk's celebrated eye for erotic representation about as far as it can go. The result, which is Borowczyk's slightest and most commercial offering to date, has provoked wildly differing responses: great pagan art or ultimate softcore? In one sense it hardly matters: although cool and stylised in approach, the film displays the most sustained erotic content yet seen publicly in this country. Four episodes – three stories of women from history, plus a contemporary Surrealist text – explore manifestations of feminine eroticism in relation to various taboos: a cosmic initiation, a religious ecstasy, incest and a bloodlust. There is nothing to censor as such, because everything is controlled through atmosphere and suggestion. Objects, even decor, are invested with an erotic tactile quality. The story of Countess Bathory, for example, who bathed in the blood of murdered girls, is predominantly a visual catalogue of liquids on flesh. CPe

Immortal Beloved

(1994, GB/US, 120 min)
d Bernard Rose. *p* Bruce Davey. *sc* Bernard Rose. *ph* Peter Suschitzky. *ed* Dan Rae. *pd* Jiri Hlupy. *m* Ludwig van Beethoven. *cast* Gary Oldman, Jeroen Krabbé, Johanna Ter Steege, Valeria Golino, Isabella Rossellini, Marco Hofschneider, Miriam Margolyes, Alexandra Pigg, Barry Humphries.

●This passionately committed Beethoven biopic proves there's life in the old music yet. Held together by Oldman's harrumphing portrayal of the bad-tempered genius, it structures itself around the enduring enigma of the great man's last will (his entire estate went to an unidentified 'Immortal Beloved'), offering a potted personal history, a judicious selection of greatest hits, and an awe-struck contemplation of the creative process. Regrettably, the film-makers' defining question – is the Immortal Beloved youthful heart-throb Golino, world-weary countess Rossellini, or even his brother's wife, Ter Steege? – makes for only limited dramatic interest; and Oldman's performance consists chiefly of a wig, a scowl and a tantrum. The film's strength is writer/director Rose's determination to let the music carry as much of the emotional weight as possible. He builds exhilarating set-pieces from the Violin Concerto and the *Eroica* and proves a persuasive evangelist for the classical repertoire. The film may plod and pulse in equal measure, but the ecstatic visualisation of the climactic *Ode to Joy* is a triumph. TJ

Immortal Sergeant, The

(1943, US, 90 min, b/w)
d John M Stahl. *p/sc* Lamar Trotti. *ph* Arthur Miller, Clyde De Vinna. *ed* James B Clark. *ad* Richard Day, Maurice Ransford. *m* David Buttolph. *cast* Henry Fonda, Thomas Mitchell, Maureen O'Hara, Allyn Joslyn, Reginald Gardiner, Melville Cooper, Bramwell Fletcher, Morton Lowry, Peter Lawford.

●Standard WWII issue lost-in-the-desert exercise set during the North African campaign, with Fonda as the diffident Canadian corporal who has to shape up and assume command of a depleted British Eighth Army patrol on the death of Thomas Mitchell's stalwart veteran sergeant. Flashbacks fill us in on Fonda's background. He's pleasant but gauche, a would-be writer and a timorous lover who still considers himself 'a civilian with a couple of chevrons on my sleeve'. Rations are low, the Eyeties are everywhere, and an impressive sandstorm is brewing. Fortunately, at moments of crisis Fonda is prompted by the voice of experience (that is to say, the voice of Thomas Mitchell), and he returns a hero with a valuable lesson under his belt: 'If I want anything worthwhile in this life, I have to fight for it. That's not a bad thing for a man to learn, is it…or a nation? To fight!' TCh

Immortal Story, The (Histoire Immortelle)

(1968, Fr, 60 min)
d Orson Welles. *p* Micheline Rozan. *sc* Orson Welles. *ph* Willy Kurant. *ed* Yolande Maurette, Marcelle Pluet, Françoise Garnault. *ad* André Piltant. *m* Erik Satie. *cast* Orson Welles, Jeanne Moreau, Norman Eshley, Roger Coggio.

●Though shot for television on a low budget, this is a sumptuous experience, a fairytale-like story, taken from Isak Dinesen, of a wealthy Macao merchant (Welles) who hires a young sailor to sleep with his wife (actually also hired, since he is unmarried) to make an old legend come true. Basically, it's about the conflict between the cold-blooded realism of the merchant and a romanticism he refuses to accept; and inevitably, the myth turns upon him. Welles is his usual megalomaniacal self, and the use of deep focus, deep shadow and colour is superb. The material itself is fascinating, and Erik Satie's music is perfectly chosen. RM

Immortelle, L'

(1962, Fr/It/Tur, 100 min, b/w)
d Alain Robbe-Grillet. *p* Samy Halfon, Michel Fano. *sc* Alain Robbe-Grillet. *ph* Maurice Barry. *ed* Robert Wade. *ad* Konnell Melissos. *m* Georges Delerue, Tashin Kavalcioglu. *cast* Françoise Brion, Jacques Doniol-Valcroze, Guido Celano, Catherine Carayon, Catherine Blisson.

●The first feature directed by *nouveau roman* writer and film-maker Robbe-Grillet (who had scripted Resnais' *Last Year in Marienbad*), this is a characteristically fragmented mystery-romance set in Istanbul. The arty narrative is occasionally irritating, and one could easily argue that the images of the elusive femme fatale in underwear and bondage are misogynist; but there is no denying the film's extraordinary creation of that strange, unsettling atmosphere one encounters in a foreign and labyrinthine city. GA

I'm No Angel

(1933, US, 87 min, b/w)
d Wesley Ruggles. *p* William Le Baron. *sc* Mae West, Lowell Brentano, Harlan Thompson. *ph* Leo Tover. *ed* Otho Lovering. *ad* Hans Dreier, Bernard Herzbrun. *m* Harvey Brooks. *cast* Mae West, Cary Grant, Edward Arnold, Gertrude Michael, Kent Taylor, Gregory Ratoff.

●Single-handed, Mae saved Paramount from bankruptcy and provoked the birth of the League of Decency. *I'm No Angel* contains an extraordinary scene in which she's tended by a bevy of black maids ('Hey, Beulah! Peel me a grape'). Sexism coupled with racism. You can't beat it. Grant, Mae's protégé, once said 'I learned everything from her. Well, almost everything.' The films are pretty awful, but no one ever notices. Mae still lays them in the aisles. SG

I, Mobster (aka The Mobster)

(1957, US, 80 min, b/w)
d Roger Corman. *p* Edward L Alperson, Roger Corman, Gene Corman. *sc* Steve Fisher. *ph* Floyd Crosby. *ed* William B Murphy. *ad* Daniel Haller. *m* Gerald Fried, Edward L Alperson Jr. *cast* Steve Cochran, Lita Milan, Robert Strauss, Celia Lovsky, Lili St Cyr, John Brinkley, Grant Withers.

●Corman's second gangster movie, contemporary in setting and made on a bigger budget than he was accustomed to after Fox picked up on the success of *Machine Gun Kelly*. Characteristically taut and vivid in chronicling Cochran's rise from bookie's runner to crime czar and candidate for the attentions of Murder Inc, it basically repeats the gangster movie's age-old story. What lifts it right out of the rut, aside from the excellent performances and Floyd Crosby's beautifully crisp camerawork, is the perfectly judged ambivalence that attends Cochran's ruthless drive for the top. A slum kid ready and willing to kill to avoid remaining on the receiving end of life's kicks, he nevertheless retains a streak of puritan conscience; and having seen himself disowned by his adoring mother, seen the innocent girl who loves him deliberately sacrifice her integrity in order to be with him, seen the shallowness of the loyalties he has chosen to live by, he finally comes to understand the inevitability of his own death. In its modest way, a fascinating film. TM

I, Monster

(1971, GB, 75 min)
d Stephen Weeks. *p* Max J Rosenberg, Milton Subotsky. *sc* Milton Subotsky. *ph* Moray Grant. *ed* Peter Tanner. *ad* Tony Curtis. *m* Carl Davis. *cast* Christopher Lee, Peter Cushing, Mike Raven, Richard Hurndall, George Merritt, Kenneth J Warren, Susan Jameson.

●Directed with a remarkably mature visual sense by Weeks at the age of twenty-two (his first feature), this Amicus adaptation of Stevenson's *Dr Jekyll and Mr Hyde* – with Lee giving a low-key performance in the lead – suffers from its prosaic fidelity to its source, as well as from a rather forced 'moral' parallel between Victorian and contemporary drug cultures. Clearly made on a shoestring, it was apparently started in an abortive 3-D process that eventually had to be abandoned. PT

Impasse

(1968, US, 99 min)
d Richard Benedict. *p* Hal Klein. *sc* John C Higgins. *ph* Mars B Rasca. *ed* John F Schreyer. *m* Philip Springer. *cast* Burt Reynolds, Anne Francis, Lyle Bettger, Rodolfo Acosta, Jeff Corey, Miko Mayama.

●The sort of film that now probably sorely embarrasses Burt Reynolds, a tedious action-man adventure that has him searching for a cache of gold in the Philippines, stashed away by five soldiers (using a complicated system of safeguards) during World War II. Screenwriter John C Higgins was once under contract to MGM's B unit, bringing him assignments like Zinnemann's *Kid Glove Killer* and Anthony Mann's *Border Incident*; but by this time he'd gone through *Untamed Youth* towards the ultimate dross of *Daughters of Satan*, also made on the cheap in the Philippines. PT

Imperfect Love (L'Amore imperfetto)

(2001, It, 92 min)
d Giovanni Davide Maderna. *p* Andrea Occhipinti, Umberto Massa. *sc* Giovanni Davide Maderna. *ph* Yves Cape. *ed* Paola Freddi. *pd* Massimo Santomarco. *m* Bernardo Bonezzi. *cast* Enrico Lo Verso, Marta Belaustegui, Federico Scribani, Francesco Carnelutti.

●Judging by his two films (the first was *Questo è il giardino?*), Maderna is that rare item, a devout Catholic film-maker. Here Belaustegui plays Angela virtually as a latter-day saint who undergoes a time of trial when the doctors tell her that her baby cannot live more than a few days. She goes through with the birth, and finds herself at the centre of a media storm (it's an hour into the film before the details of the baby's condition emerge). Lo Verso is her depressed husband, who may or may not be responsible for the rape of a trainee at the supermarket where he works. Downplaying emotionalism, this is a serious film, not to say dour, sermonising and visually pedestrian – an agnostic's point of view, admittedly. TCh

Importance of Being Earnest, The

(1952, GB, 92 min)
d Anthony Asquith. *p* Teddy Baird. *ph* Desmond Dickinson. *ed* John D Guthridge. *ad* Carmen Dillon. *m* Benjamin Frankel. *cast* Michael Redgrave, Joan Greenwood, Edith Evans, Dorothy Tutin, Michael Denison, Margaret Rutherford, Miles Malleson.

●It is typical of Asquith – Grand Master of the Filmed English Classic – that he never attempts any cinematic wit to complement the verbal ping-pong of Wilde's play: his cameras do little more than reverently record a great patriotic theatrical event. But the settings are the epitome of Victorian plushness, the colour is Technicolor at its fruitiest, and most of the playing is disarming, particularly Edith Evans and her handbag. GB

Impostors

(1979, WGer/US, 110 min)
d/p/sc Mark Rappaport. *ph* Fred Murphy. *ed* Mark Rappaport, Meri Weingarten. *pd* Robert Edmonds. *cast* Peter Evans, Ellen McElduff, Charles Ludlam, Michael Burg, Lina Todd, Randy Danson.

●Five chameleon New York characters (twin magicians/assassins, two enigmatic women, a rich wimp), their passions masked by aggressive cool, wend their absurdly entertaining way through Rappaport's customary comic-opera catalogue of melodramatic disparities: a series of tableau visuals bursting with allusive emotional movement, sense of skeletal slapstick, a superabundance of inconsequential plot trails. There's enough for anyone half-familiar with out-of-the-rut New York independent film-making to latch onto; and in terms of the wide audience Rappaport deserves, reservations about this film based on higher enthusiasm for the earlier, underexposed *Local Color* and *The Scenic Route* begin to seem pretty irrelevant. PT

Impostors, The

(1998, US, 101 min)
d Stanley Tucci. *p* Beth Alexander, Stanley Tucci. *sc* Stanley Tucci. *ph* Ken Kelsch. *ed* Suzy Elmiger. *pd* Andrew Jackness. *m* Gary DeMichele. *cast* Stanley Tucci, Oliver Platt, Teagle F Bougere, Elizabeth Bracco, Steve Buscemi, Billy Connolly, Hope Davis, Alfred Molina, Isabella Rossellini, Campbell Scott, Tony Shalhoub, Lili Taylor, Woody Allen.

●After the charming delights of Tucci's *Big Night*, this knockabout '30s farce comes as a severe disappointment. Its intentions are made clear from the opening credits sequence: with its style and intertitles recalling silent movies, hapless pair Arthur (Tucci) and Maurice (Platt) vie to play the 'death scene' for one of their cons. Two poverty-stricken thesps, they stow away as stewards on the 'Continental' liner to escape a charge of assault on a boozy, talentless English theatrical knight (Molina), only for the great man to appear, cops in tow. This is distictly old-fashioned fare, with Keystone-age capers and dastardly disguises, pitched at the edge of self-parody, ham with egg on the face. In scenes that blend the worst of Agatha Christie with the ignoblest of Brian Rix, cameos come a-plenty, each more embarrassing than its predecessor. Plots hatch, robberies occur, deceit descends, lies are plied – our spirits flag. WH

Impromptu

(1989, GB, 107 min)
d James Lapine. *p* Stuart Oken, Daniel A Sherkow. *sc* Sarah Kernochan. *ph* Bruno de Keyser. *ed* Michael Ellis. *ad* Gérard Daoudal. *m* Chopin, Liszt, Beethoven. *cast* Judy Davis, Hugh Grant, Mandy Patinkin, Bernadette Peters, Julian Sands, Ralph Brown, Anton Rodgers, Emma Thompson, Anna Massey.

●Directed by Sondheim collaborator Lapine, this tells the romantic story of Bohemian cross-dressing novelist George Sand's protracted pursuit of Chopin through salon and château, variously foiled and abetted by Liszt (Sands) and mistress (Peters), Alfred de Musset (Patinkin) and Delacroix (Brown). Driven by a quest for perfect love, Sand (Davis), though knee-deep in an operetta of rejected lovers, hears Chopin pelting at the piano through a door and is a goner. Given that the sick stick of a Pole is played by Hugh Grant, her passion seems inexplicable, and the only scene that convinces has the novellist lying aswoon under the piano as the soundtrack pours it on. The acting comes in different sizes: in contrast to the naturalism of Davis – heiress to the Jeanne Moreau Estate – stands the high camp of Emma Thompson as the Art-struck Duchess, and the swashbuckling of Patinkin. A longish haul. BC

Improper Conduct (Mauvaise Conduite)

(1983, Fr, 114 min)
d Nestor Almendros, Orlando Jimenez Leal. *p* Margaret Ménégoz, Barbet Schroeder, Michel Thoulouze. *ph* Dominique Merlin. *ed* Michel Pion, Alain Tortevoix. *with* Lorenzo Monreal, Jorge Lago, Julio Medina, César Bermudez, José Mario, Rafael De Palet, Guillermo Cabrera Infante, Fidel Castro, Susan Sontag. *narrator* Michel Dumoulin.

●A quietly terrifying documentary on the (mis)treatment of gays in Cuba which opened up a hornet's nest of controversy and political schizophrenia. While Fidel smiles for the cameras, thousands of homosexuals are being rounded up, sent to concentration camps, imprisoned in medieval castles and tortured. The system of family and neighbour denunciation (for as little as a flowery shirt or long hair) echoes Nazi Germany; the work camp banner of 'Work Will Make You Men' echoes Belsen's '*Arbeit macht Frei*'. While the likes of Sartre and Sontag recant their support on camera, others still insist on the wider goal of a socialist state. Bullshit. One innocent person oppressed is one too many. JG

Improperly Dressed (Herkulesfürdöi emlék)

(1976, Hun, 85 min)
d Pál Sándor. *sc* Zsuzsa Toth. *ph* Elemér Ragalyi. *ed* Andrásné Karmentö. *pd* László Makai. *m* Zdenkó Tamassy. *cast* Endre Holman, Margit Dayka, Irma Patkós, Carla Romanelli, Dezsö Garas.

●An oddly elliptical, mournfully elegiac tale of a young Communist, hounded for political reasons, who seeks haven in a remote sanatorium where, disguised as a woman among women, he becomes increasingly seized by the inertia of his time out of war. The year is 1919, the oppressors are White Russians, and the sanatorium stands nicely as a symbol for what is wrong with Hungary, then as now. The trouble is that Sándor seems uncertain what to make of the parable, and the bizarre situation, left pretty much to its own devices, simply fritters itself away in a haze of half-hinted sexual ambiguities and dreamy atmospherics (the camerawork is exquisite). TM

Impudent Girl, An (L'Effrontée)

(1985, Fr, 97 min)
d Claude Miller. *p* Marie-Laure Reyre. *sc* Claude Miller, Luc Béraud, Bernard Stora, Annie Miller. *ph* Dominique Chapuis. *ed* Albert Jurgenson. *ad* Jean-Pierre Kohut-Svelko. *m* Alain Jomy. *cast* Charlotte Gainsbourg, Bernadette Lafont, Jean-Claude Brialy, Raoul Billerey, Clothilde Baudon, Jean-Philippe Ecoffey, Julie Glenn, Simon de la Brosse.

●The wayward Miller has always pursued his own fancy; from the adolescent problems of *The Best Way to Walk*, through the detections of *This Sweet Sickness* and *The Inquisitor*, up to the scatty *Mortelle Randonnée*, there has been no obvious thread running through his work. *An Impudent Girl*, however – an uncredited adaptation of Carson McCullers' *The Member of the Wedding* – returns to what was his surest ground in his first film: the pangs of adolescence. Sweet Charlotte (Gainsbourg) is a 13-year-old problem looking for somewhere to happen. She is the despair of her widowed father, drives her brother mad, knows she wants something better, but doesn't know what it is. Until Clara (Baudon) walks into her life. Clara too is 13, but she is also a successful concert pianist, wears pretty white dresses, lives in a lakeside mansion, and is generally just too good to be true. All Charlotte's mad hopes and fears, her desires and heel-stamping jealousies, come pouring out with the appearance of this young catalyst; but the experience is therapeutic, and the outcome one of adult optimism. The film exhibits all of Miller's strengths, in particular his canny way with actors; but best of all is its emotional truth. Adolescence is never comfortable; to face its memories honestly is part of being adult. CPea

Impulse

(1984, US, 99 min)
d Graham Baker. *p* Tim Zinnemann. *sc* Bart Davis, Don Carlos Dunaway. *ph* Thomas Del Ruth. *ed* David Holden. *ad* Jack T Collins. *m* Paul Chihara. *cast* Tim Matheson, Meg Tilly, Hume Cronyn, John Karlen, Bill Paxton, Amy Stryker.

●Smalltown USA. After a minor earth tremor, a farmer's wife tries to blow her brains out in the middle of an irrationally abusive phone call to her daughter. Armed with her doctor boyfriend, the girl returns home to see what drove momma mad, and finds people acting totally on impulse: elderly folk rob banks, barroom brawlers break their own fingers, and mischievous brats attempt to roast her alive. All too reminiscent, most notably of *Invasion of the Body Snatchers*, the film wastes its predictable but promising premise and quickly degenerates into virtual absurdity. With the exception of its heroine (Tilly), the entire cast is transformed into an almost comic collection of screaming harridans and snarling gunmen, while the 'hints' at what lies behind the epidemic of aggression are delivered with sledgehammer subtlety. Aiming for a realistic ecological allegory, Baker simply stumbles from cliché to cliché. GA

Impulse

(1990, US, 108 min)
d Sondra Locke. *p* Albert S Ruddy, André Morgan. *sc* John De Marco, Leigh Chapman. *ph* Dean Semler. *ed* John W Wheeler. *ad* William A Elliott. *m* Michel Colombier. *cast* Theresa Russell, Jeff Fahey, George Dzundza, Alan Rosenburg, Nicholas Mele, Eli Danker, Charles McCaughan, Lynne Thigpen.

●Theresa Russell (excellent) plays an undercover cop on the edge, burned out and unable to sustain her relationship with men. Under assessment by the police shrink after shooting a criminal, she is still moonlighting as a decoy hooker, a role that feeds her desire to lose control. Assistant DA Fahey, meanwhile, is looking for a second witness to secure a watertight case against a drug kingpin. Russell is recruited to make a fake drugs buy designed to force a low-life dealer into testifying, but her cover is blown and things get very complicated. Although a subsequent plot twist, linking Russell's dangerous impulsiveness to a loose thread of Fahey's complex case, is a shade too convenient, Sondra Locke directs with great assurance. The action is tough, the low-life atmosphere authentic, and the relationship between Russell and Fahey charged with tremulous eroticism. Stylish, exciting, and emotionally satisfying. NF

Im Zeichen des Kreuzes

see Due To an Act of God

Inadmissible Evidence

(1968, GB, 96 min, b/w)
d Anthony Page. *p* Ronald Kinnoch. *sc* John Osborne. *ph* Ken Hodges, Tony Imi. *ed* Derek York. *ad* Seamus Flannery. *m* Dudley Moore. *cast* Nicol Williamson, Eleanor Fazan, Jill Bennett, Peter Sallis, David Valla, Eileen Atkins, Ingrid Brett, Gillian Hills, Lindsay Anderson.

●Misfiring adaptation of John Osborne's play about a middle-aged solicitor oppressed by his sense of failure and his feeling that the whole world is conspiring to exclude him, with Williamson repeating his brilliant stage performance to lesser effect. The main problem is the intrusive camera/editing style which reduces the original lengthy diatribes to tetchy little snippets, simultaneously cutting Osborne's magnificently theatrical anti-hero down to size: instead of being effectively inside a man's mind, we are now left outside, wondering why we should be expected to sympathise with such an unprepossessing, self-centred bore. TM

In All Innocence (En plein coeur)

(1998, Fr, 101 min)
d Pierre Jolivet. *p* Alain Goldman. *sc* Roselyn Bosch. *ph* Pascal Ridao. *ed* Yves Deschamps. *ad* Thierry Flamand. *m* Serge Perathoner, Jannick Top. *cast* Gérard Lanvin, Virginie Ledoyen, Carole Bouquet, Guillaume Canet, Aurélie Vérillon, Jean-Pierre Lorit, Denis Podalydès, Anne Le Ny, Nadia Barentin.

●After crashing a posh Parisian soirée in search of food and wallets, wide-girl Cécile (Ledoyen) and her friend Samira pull a shoplifting stunt which goes awry; Samira is deported, Cécile arraigned. Making the most of her meagre resources, Cécile shoplifts a skirt suit and cold-calls on the law offices of the man whose wallet she stole, demanding help. Initially merely tickled by her chutzpah, Michel (Lanvin) quickly finds his fancy stoked. He takes both case and defendant. He's less enamoured of Vincent (Canet), a former boyfriend Cécile won't shake; but then his wife Viviane (Bouquet) isn't exactly keen on Cécile. A confidently appointed French thriller with a sense of class, Jolivet's adaptation of Georges Simenon's *En cas de malheur* offers an intelligent narrative dynamic spanning social and generational divisions, and cogent characterisations by an eminently watchable cast. A pity, then, that the basic dramatic situation's so hidebound. If Michel's dormant class-consciousness promises a variation on the usual midlife-affair material, it's never really pushed beyond the obvious. And while the subsequent passion play is often quite compelling, it gradually sinks into crude revenge drama. NB

In a Lonely Place

(1950, US, 93 min, b/w)
d Nicholas Ray. *p* Robert Lord. *sc* Andrew Solt. *ph* Burnett Guffey. *ed* Viola Lawrence. *ad* Robert Peterson. *m* George Antheil. *cast* Humphrey Bogart, Gloria Grahame, Frank Lovejoy, Robert Warwick, Jeff Donnell, Martha Stewart, Carl Benton Reid.

●The place is Hollywood, lonely for scriptwriter Dixon Steele (Bogart), who is suspected of murdering a young woman, until girl-next-door Laurel Gray (Grahame) supplies him with a false alibi. But is he the killer? Under pressure of police interrogation, their tentative relationship threatens to crack – and Dix's sudden, violent temper becomes increasingly evident. Ray's classic thriller remains as fresh and resonant as the day it was released. Nothing is as it seems: the *noir* atmosphere of deathly paranoia frames one of the screen's most adult and touching love affairs; Bogart's tough-guy insolence is probed to expose a vulnerable, almost psychotic insecurity; while Grahame abandons femme fatale conventions to reveal a character of enormous, subtle complexity. As ever, Ray composes with symbolic precision, confounds audience expectations, and deploys the heightened lyricism of melodrama to produce an achingly poetic meditation on pain, distrust and loss of faith, not to mention an admirably unglamorous portrait of Tinseltown. Never were despair and solitude so romantically alluring. GA

In & Out

(1997, US, 91 min)
d Frank Oz. *p* Scott Rudin. *sc* Paul Rudnick. *ph* Robert S Hahn. *ed* Daniel Hanley, John Jympson. *pd* Ken Adam. *m* Marc Shaiman. *cast* Kevin Kline, Joan Cusack, Matt Dillon, Debbie Reynolds, Wilford Brimley, Bob Newhart, Tom Selleck, Dan Hedaya.

●Howard Brackett (Kline), an English teacher in a Midwestern town, gets the shock of his life when a protégé turned movie star (Dillon) unthinkingly 'outs' him before the whole world during the Oscar ceremony. Howard isn't even out to himself – in fact he's supposed to be marrying Emily (Cusack) at the weekend. So what if he's a virgin who loves to dance and adores Barbra Streisand movies? A mainstream comedy with a twist, this is surprisingly waspish about gay manners and sexual hypocrisy, especially as practised by Brackett himself. As long as the script by Paul Rudnick (inspired by Tom Hanks' announcement when he won an Academy Award for *Philadelphia*) is taking itself flippantly, the movie works well enough. Oz wants it both ways, though, and can't resist hammering home the message with a prolonged *Spartacus*-style climax quite as ludicrous as the Oscar winning film-within-the-film. TCh

In a Savage Land

(1999, Aust, 116 min)
d Bill Bennett. *p/sc* Bill Bennett, Jennifer Bennett [Jennifer Cluff]. *ph* Dann Ruhlmann. *ed* Henry Dangar. *pd* Nicholas McCallum. *m* David Bridie. *cast* Martin Donovan, Maya Stange, Rufus Sewell, John Howard, Max Cullen, Andrew S Gilbert, Marshall Napier.

●This is a drama with massive travelogue potential. On the Trobriand Islands north of Australia, an anthropologist couple (Donovan and Stange) embark on a year-long study of the 'natives' as war is declared in 1939. Sewell is the more pragmatic American pearl trader who stays to comfort Strange when her husband dies of dysentery. Bennett has a dour way with social observation and romantic storytelling – though the script involves some interesting conflicts – and the ending is unsatisfactory. WH

Inauguration of the Pleasure Dome, The

see Anger Magick Lantern Cycle, The

In a Wild Moment

see Moment d'Egarement, Un

In a Year with 13 Moons (In einem Jahr mit 13 Monden)

(1978, WGer, 129 min)
d/p/sc/ph/ed/pd Rainer Werner Fassbinder. *m* Peer Raben. *cast* Volker Spengler, Ingrid Caven, Gottfried John, Elisabeth Trissenaar, Eva Mattes, Günther Kaufmann.

●Elvira (Spengler) was Erwin until s/he went to Casablanca for a discreet operation. She now lives in Frankfurt, abandoned by her lover, befriended by a hooker who's not much better off than herself, and ripped to shreds by cruelties and social inequalities. *In a Year with 13 Moons* is not only Fassbinder's last word on victimised innocence, it's also a subjective response to the suicide of his own lover Armin Meier, and a sincere admission that life is messier than his earlier films acknowledged. A movie riven with contradictions and fuelled by vehemence and passion. TR

In Bed with Madonna

see Truth or Dare

Inbetweeners

(2000, GB, 86 min)
d/p/sc Danny Paul Fisher. *ph* Matthew Woolf. *ed* Danny Paul Fisher. *cast* Johnny Ball, Philippa Forrester, Anthea Turner, Sarah Vandebergh.

●No 'student' cliché is left unexamined in this gauche Britcom styling itself 'the first film about the British University experience'. Shot cheaply on DV, the result is not unlike a video training manual. When you first arrive at university, we learn, it's de rigueur to break the ice by asking all new acquaintances the same three questions (about their A levels, origins and course). No one's here to work; the library and dance hall are your pick-up joints; some girls and boys will hook up in a trice, others will instantly get off on the wrong foot; everyone will drink and talk shit all night. NB

In Caliente

(1935, US, 85 min, b/w)
d Lloyd Bacon. *sc* Jerry Wald, Julius Epstein. *ph* Sol Polito, George Barnes. *ed* James

Gibbons. *songs* Mort Dixon, Allie Wrubel, Al Dubin, Harry Warren. *cast* Dolores Del Rio, Pat O'Brien, Glenda Farrell, Edward Everett Horton, Leo Carrillo, Judy Canova, Phil Regan, Winifred Shaw.
● Magazine editor O'Brien gives Mexican firebrand Del Rio a bad review for her dance extravaganza, but when best pal Horton whisks him south of the border to evade ruthless gold-digger Farrell, there are no prizes for guessing who's back in her home town of Agua Caliente to meet and greet him. Sadly slack Warners extravaganza, but it does warm up a bit for the Busby Berkeley numbers, including the ultra-kitsch 'Muchacha'. TJ

In Cane for Life (A Vida em Cana)

(2000, Braz, 69 min)
d/p Jorge Wolney Atalla.
● Picking up a crop of festival awards, this committed exploration of the lives of São Paulo state's sugar cane cutters fuses the hard realities of their labour with received images of Brazil and its attendant mythologies. Spirited endurance and the ability to find brief joys despite hardship are bracketed by the awareness that encroaching mechanisation might threaten even these small victories. GE

In Celebration

(1974, GB/Can, 131 min)
d Lindsay Anderson. *p* Ely A Landau. *sc* David Storey. *ph* Dick Bush. *ed* Russell Lloyd. *ad* Alan Withy. *m* Christopher Gunning. *cast* Alan Bates, James Bolam, Brian Cox, Constance Chapman, Gabrielle Daye, Bill Owen.
● Stage to screen transfer of the David Storey play directed at the Royal Court by Lindsay Anderson in 1969, with the cast remaining the same. Not strictly autobiographical, but rooted in the playwright's Nottinghamshire mining background, *In Celebration* is set in the family home on the night three grown-up sons return somewhat reluctantly to celebrate their parents' 40th wedding anniversary. Anderson has said, 'The stage gives the audience a broader aspect of a scene than film, and therefore the rehearsals were perhaps more valid for me than for the actors.' The play was re-rehearsed for three weeks before shooting, and location scenes were filmed in the colliery town, but it still emerges as an awkward compromise between the two forms, though Bates is splendid as Andrew, the failed painter. MA

Incense for the Damned

(1970, GB, 87 min)
d Michael Burrowes [Robert Hartford-Davis]. *p* Graham Harris. *sc* Julian More. *ph* Desmond Dickinson. *pd* George Provis. *m* Bobby Richards. *cast* Patrick MacNee, Peter Cushing, Alex Davion, Johnny Sekka, Madeline Hinde, Patrick Mower, Imogen Hassall, Edward Woodward.
● An adaptation of Simon Raven's novel *Doctors Wear Scarlet* which bears a fictional director credit: Hartford-Davis took his name off the picture after unexplained difficulties, and it must be the first time in screen history that a film-maker has disowned the only remotely good thing he's done. The film bears some marks of its production difficulties, but in general it sticks closely to Raven's novel, in which the act of vampirism becomes for the hero (Mower) a therapeutic acting-out of the stifling, parasitic mental processes of Oxford that surround him. Probably the theme really needs a Polanski or a Franju to do it justice, but here it is at least put together neatly and coherently, with some elegant location camerawork from Desmond Dickinson. DP

In Cold Blood

(1967, US, 134 min, b/w)
d/sc Richard Brooks. *ph* Conrad Hall. *ed* Peter Zinner. *ad* Robert Boyle. *m* Quincy Jones. *cast* Robert Blake, Scott Wilson, John Forsythe, Paul Stewart, Gerald S O'Loughlin, Jeff Corey, Charles McGraw.
● A low-key adaptation of Truman Capote's 'novel of fact' about the murder of a whole family by two disturbed petty criminals, *In Cold Blood* forever shies away from trying to understand the killers (played by Blake and Wilson). Accordingly, in contrast to Capote, whose obsessive documentation of the pair's every act betrays his fear than he (and his readers) could well do something similar, Brooks explains and sympathises away their act as being unique to them. PH

Incognito

(1997, US, 107 min)
d John Badham. *p* James G Robinson. *sc* Jordan Katz. *ph* Denis Crossan. *ed* Frank Morriss. *pd* Jamie Leonard. *m* John Ottman. *cast* Jason Patric, Irène Jacob, Thomas Lockyer, Ian Richardson, Rod Steiger, Dudley Sutton, Ian Holm.
● Three art dealers employ a tormented forger (Patric) to paint a 'lost' Rembrandt. Director Badham opts to play it straight, as if this will somehow render the whole exercise less preposterous. Choice moments include Patric daubing furiously in an Amsterdam garret, his sweaty torso decoratively splashed with paint, and the jaw-dropping revelation that a gauche Parisian art student (Jacob) is in fact the world authority on the Dutch master. A plot to frame the forger for murdering one of the dealers culminates with a ludicrous scene at the Old Bailey in which Donovan attempts to prove his innocence by reproducing 'live' his fake masterpiece. NF

In Country

(1989, US, 115 min)
d Norman Jewison. *p* Norman Jewison, Richard Roth. *sc* Frank R Pierson, Cynthia Cidre. *ph* Russell Boyd. *ed* Antony Gibbs, Lou Lombardo. *pd* Jackson DeGovia. *m* James Horner. *cast* Bruce Willis, Emily Lloyd, Joan Alley, Kevin Anderson, Richard Hamilton, Judith Ivey, Peggy Rea, John Terry.
● Jewison's post-Vietnam movie concentrates on bereavement, with the consequence that it's decent but dull. Kentucky teenager Samantha (Lloyd) never knew her father who died in the war, but discovers his letters and photos. 'Gee, you missed *ET* and the Bruce Springsteen concerts', she says. Her role throughout is to reconcile the community with its unacknowledged tragedy, whether coddling her withdrawn Viet vet Uncle Emmett (Willis) or encouraging an impotent mechanic. Her generation not only knows naught of Country Joe & the Fish, but double-naught about GIs collecting VC ears and burning hooches, an ignorance which recalls post-war Germany. The emotional climax arrives at the Vietnam memorial tablets in Washington, with the family finally achieving closeness as they find their lad's nme among the thousands. The mass grave, little more than a hole in the ground as a relative says, is a good visual equivalent for America's attitude towards the shameful defeat. Vietnam had a closed casket funeral. BC

Incredible Hulk, The

(1978, US, 104 min)
d Kenneth Johnson, Sigmund Neufeld Jr. *p* Kenneth Johnson. *sc* Kenneth Johnson, Thomas E Szollosi, Richard Christian Matheson. *ph* Howard Schwartz, John McPherson. *ed* Jack W Schoengarth, Alan Marks, Edward W Williams, Lawrence J Vallario. *ad* Charles R Davis, Frank Grieco Jr. *m* Joseph Harnell. *cast* Bill Bixby, Susan Sullivan, Jack Colvin, Lou Ferrigno, Susan Batson.
● This fills you in on what's happened to American TV veteran Bixby since the days when he hosted *My Favourite Martian*. In a nutshell: his marriage (soft-focus flashback) ended when he couldn't pry a two-ton heap of flaming metal off his wife after an accident, and the trauma sent him on a 'scientific' crusade for the secret of superhuman strength. He checks out the possibilities: adrenalin? dextrose? no, you guessed it, another cinematic dose of radiation. Unfortunately, someone has been souping up the radiation equipment as well as the 'magnification' tools. So Bixby by accident becomes The Hulk, re-enacts a monster-and-little-girl scene reminiscent of James Whale's *Frankenstein*, and spends aeons of airtime saving a 747 jet. The moral is: two TV shows (which is what this is) do not one coherent movie make. CR

Incredible Journey, The

(1963, US, 80 min)
d Fletcher Markle. *sc* James Algar. *ph* Kenneth Peach, Jack Couffer, Lloyd Beebe. *ed* Norman Palmer. *ad* Carroll Clark, John B Mansbridge. *m* Oliver Wallace. *cast* Emile Genest, John Drainie, Tommy Tweed, Sandra Scott, Syme Jago, Marilyn Finlayson, Ronald Cohoon.
● Triumphantly painful Disney adventure; guaranteed to sear the memory, in spite of the 'Derek the Lonely Dingo'-style narration that has always stood for 'nature' in Walt's wonderful world. Across the changing seasons, three anthropomorphised pets find, incredibly, their way home through 250 miles of Canadian tundra to make some back-handed point about the nuclear family.

Incredible Melting Man, The

(1977, US, 86 min)
d William Sachs. *p* Samuel W Gelfman. *sc* William Sachs. *ph* Willy Curtis. *ed* James Beshears. *ad* Michael Levesque. *m* Arlon Ober. *cast* Alex Rebar, Burr DeBenning, Myron Healey, Michael Alldredge, Ann Sweeney, Jonathan Demme.
● What to do with the incredible melting man except have him melt some more? The film-makers never really resolve this sticky problem once their burned-up astronaut busts out of hospital and, at a snail's pace, starts eating the local population. This Z-grade effort, lacking any low-budget energy, takes its cue from the central character: it's tacky and bumbling and sinks into its own morass long before its subject finally dribbles apart, slurp, glub. CPe

Incredible Sarah, The

(1976, US, 106 min)
d Richard Fleischer. *p* Helen M Strauss. *sc* Ruth Wolff. *ph* Christopher Challis. *ed* John Jympson. *pd* Elliot Scot. *m* Elmer Bernstein. *cast* Glenda Jackson, Daniel Massey, Yvonne Mitchell, Douglas Wilmer, David Langton, Simon Williams, John Castle, Edward Judd.
● An obvious chore for Fleischer (as well as for the audience), this is a pretty traditional attempt at the biopic which threads together scenes-from-the-life of Sarah Bernhardt, from tyro rejection to triumph via social ostracism. The script makes an attempt or two to link Bernhardt's tendency to turn her daily life into constant theatricals with the magnetism of her on-stage appearances, but they remain very token. This *Reader's Digest* film carries the bland signature of its sponsors writ large over every set-up. Glenda Jackson emotes effectively enough through a series of cameo pieces from the classics, but is floored by the bits in between. VG

Incredible Shrinking Man, The

(1957, US, 81 min, b/w)
d Jack Arnold. *p* Albert Zugsmith. *sc* Richard Matheson. *ph* Ellis Carter. *ed* Al Joseph. *ad* Alexander Golitzen, Robert Clatworthy. *m* Joseph Gershenson. *cast* Grant Williams, Randy Stuart, April Kent, Paul Langton, Raymond Bailey, William Schallert, Billy Curtis.
● Not merely the best of Arnold's classic sci-fi movies of the '50s, but one of the finest films ever made in that genre. It's a simple enough story: after being contaminated by what may or may not be nuclear waste, Williams finds himself slowly but steadily shedding the pounds and inches until he reaches truly minuscule proportions. But it is what Richard Matheson's script (adapted from his own novel) does with this basic material that makes the film so gripping and intelligent. At first, Williams is merely worried about his mysterious illness, but soon, towered over by his wife, he begins to feel humiliated, expressing his shame and impotence through cruel anger. And then his entire relationship with the universe changes, with cats, spiders and drops of water representing lethal threats in the surreal and endless landscape that is, in fact, his house's cellar. And finally, to the strains of Joseph Gershenson's impressive score, we arrive at the film's philosophical core: a moving, strangely pantheist assertion of what it really means to be alive. A pulp masterpiece. GA

Incredible Shrinking Woman, The

(1981, US, 88 min)
d Joel Schumacher. *p* Hank Moonjean. *sc* Jane Wagner. *ph* Bruce Logan. *ed* Jeff Gourson, Anthony Redman. *pd* Raymond A Brandt. *m* Suzanne Ciani. *cast* Lily Tomlin, Charles Grodin, Ned Beatty, Henry Gibson, Elizabeth Wilson, Mark Blankfield.

●One more high-promise comedy down the drainpipe: *The Incredible Shrinking Woman* still sounds better on paper after you've seen it. The theme should be watertight in the *Nine to Five*, would-be progressive mould: Woman suffering (literal) diminution under the weight of patriarchal, consumerist culture; while the advance prospect of seeing Lily Tomlin biting ankles is tasty enough to quell doubts about the wisdom of tampering with Richard Matheson's original sci-fi premise. But good intentions and one's own goodwill are soon diminished as script and direction conspire to render a sitcom satire that's indistinguishable from its target. A cloying cuteness soon pervades as Tomlin, shrinking after being sprayed with a new perfume marketed by her advertising executive husband, becomes a media celebrity; and the conclusion – curse becomes cure – is recuperative in more ways than one. PT

Incredible Times...

see Epoque formidable..., Une

Incredibly Strange Creatures Who Stopped Living and Became Mixed-Up Zombies, The (aka Teenage Psycho Meets Bloody Mary)

(1964, US, 82 min)
d/p Ray Dennis Steckler. *sc* Gene Pollock, Robert Silliphant. *ph* Joseph V Mascelli. *ed* Don Schneider. *ad* Mike Harrington. *m* Libby Quinn. *cast* Cash Flagg [Ray Dennis Steckler], Brett O'Hara, Carolyn Brandt, Atlas King, Sharon Walsh.

●Steckler's imagination seems to have stalled after thinking up the title(s), neither of which is especially valid. A few cheap masks don't transform lurching extras into creatures strange or zomboid; and the teenager isn't a psycho until he runs into 'Mary' who in any case is called Estrella. The carnival setting could have been tackier, weirder, more sinister if, instead of stopping at cribs from *House of Wax* and *I Was a Teenage Frankenstein*, the makers had indulged in a bit of imaginative theft from *Nightmare Alley*. DO

Incredibly True Adventure of Two Girls in Love, The

(1995, US, 94 min)
d Maria Maggenti. *p* Dolly Hall. *sc* Maria Maggenti. *ph* Tami Reiker, Melissa Painter. *ed* Susan Graef. *pd* Ginger Tougas. *m* Terry Dame. *cast* Laurel Hollomon, Nicole Parker, Dale Dickey, Stephanie Berry, Maggie Moore, Kate Stafford, Sabrina Artel.

●Punky 17-year-old Randy Dean (Hollomon) is having a desultory affair with a married woman, lives with her aunt in a 'regular lesbo household', and daydreams to the strains of Zeppelin and Hendrix. Evie Roy (Parker) is a glamorous, well-to-do African-American who lives with her mum, prefers Mozart and Walt Whitman, and is getting tired of her insensitive, immature boyfriend. Though they're both in their senior year at the same high school they don't meet until Evie's car starts giving her trouble and she calls in at the garage where Randy works. Still, it's an encounter that will change their lives. This feature debut offers a perky look at the trials of first love as experienced by two very different girls from two very different backgrounds. If there's nothing hugely original about the story, there's a lot of charm here, thanks largely to the easy naturalism of the performances. This is such a conventional telling of a modern-day fairy story that its (vaguely) subversive content should offend virtually no one. There's tenderness, humour, lyricism and a heartfelt plea for universal tolerance; and if the farcical finale seems obvious and contrived, it's hard to resist a movie so gentle that its most shocking transgression is the unwitting wasting of a bottle of Château Latour. GA

In Crowd, The

(2000, US, 104 min)
d Mary Lambert. *p* James G Robinson. *sc* Mark Gibson, Philip Halprin. *ph* Tom Priestley Jr. *ed* Pasquale Buba. *pd* John D Kretschmer. *m* Jeff Rona. *cast* Susan Ward, Lori Heuring, Matthew Settle, Nathan Bexton, Ethan Erickson, Laurie Fortier, Kim Murphy, Tess Harper.

●Anarchists ponder how to contain crime in a free society without recourse to the authority of law and suggest that public opinion and social stigma might do the trick – but with the qualm that majority opinion can exert its own tyranny. Few would expect this dilemma to be expressed in the post-teen pulp currently favoured by Hollywood, but with their hermetic social universe, marginalised authority figures and rapt attention to the dynamics of the peer group, such films provide an oddly expedient test model. There are two salient moments in this tacky 'beautiful set' thriller concerning mistrust and treachery among a South Carolina beachside country club clique, which together demonstrate the twin sides of the anarchist dilemma. Assigned probationary work at the club, Adrien (Heuring), an ex-delinquent, is falsely arrested for a grisly crime of passion. She makes a walk of shame past the massed ranks of her putative new pals, and the film's avid attention to the silent stares speaks louder and more sincerely than anything else in this befuddled romp. Later, of course, justice prevails and in a mirroring scene, the crowd's censure is redirected at the true villain of the piece, whose look of exposed terror suggests punishment is already in effect. Elsewhere, there's little noteworthy. NB

Incubus

(1981, Can, 92 min)
d John Hough. *p* Marc Boyman, John M Eckert. *sc* George Franklin. *ph* Bert Dunk. *ed* George Appleby. *pd* Ted Watkins. *m* Stanley Myers. *cast* John Cassavetes, Kerrie Keane, Helen Hughes, Erin Flannery, Duncan McIntosh, John Ireland.

●A demon-rape flick of unusually high technical ineptitude, even for this egregious genre, which features Canada doubling as California and Cassavetes as the doctor trying to solve the problem of just what is doing all those shower-curtain murders and inflicting such massive internal injuries on the female victims. We are indebted to *The Monthly Film Bulletin* for their scholarly note pointing out that the movie chickens out of the central image of Ray Russell's novel – the huge size of the incubus' phallus – and it's a castration that reaches out into the whole film. Cassavetes' presence inevitably raises echoes from *Rosemary's Baby*, but his baleful looks are miscast on the side of the angels. The only decent hope is that this nonsense made him enough money for one of his own independent films. CPea

In Custody (Hifazaat)

(1993, GB/Ind, 126 min)
d Ismail Merchant. *p* Wahid Chowan. *sc* Anita Desai, Shahrukh Husain. *ph* Larry Pizer. *ed* Roberto Silvi. *pd* Suresh Sawant. *m* Zakir Hussain, Ustad Sultan Khan. *cast* Shashi Kapoor, Om Puri, Shabana Azmi, Sushma Seth, Neena Gupta, Tinnu Anand, Prayag Raj.

●As the long-time producer of the Merchant Ivory partnership, Ismail Merchant should have understood the problems of adapting literary texts to the cinema. All credit to him, then, for having the sang froid to choose for his first feature as director, Anita Desai's spare, uneventful novel about a once-revered elderly Urdu poet. The film follows the efforts of a pedantic college tutor, Deven (Puri), to record his hero, the poet Nur (Kapoor), reciting his own work. On a visit to the city of Bhopal, Deven finds Nur living in seclusion, drinking and over-eating, or bickering with his two wives, tired of casting pearls before swine. Deven is no master of technology: the tape-recorder is a mystery to him, and much low comedy is extracted from his incompetence; and the arch, awkward quality of these scenes typify the film. Shashi Kapoor as the embittered, decayed poet is, regrettably, made to carry more weight than any man can bear – to symbolise a whole tradition: the neglect of the Urdu language and the oral tradition with its attendant philosophies of authority and respect. WH

Indecent Obsession, An

(1985, Aust, 106 min)
d Lex Marinos. *p* Ian Bradley. *sc* Denise Morgan. *ph* Ernest Clark. *ed* Philip Howe. *pd* Michael Ralph. *m* Dave Skinner. *cast* Wendy Hughes, Gary Sweet, Richard Moir, Jonathan Hyde, Bruno Lawrence, Mark Little, Tony Sheldon, Bill Hunter.

●A hospital drama with a difference: it's World War II, the Far East, and the Japs have just surrendered. The inmates of Ward X, a wing for psychiatric and problem patients, have their routines shattered by the arrival of a new, mysterious patient. Lust, homophobia, violent death, cowardice and an exotic location should make for the sort of soap you can get your teeth into; but apart from a few reasonable impressions of mild insanity, the performances are never good enough to make you believe what's happening on screen. The confrontations fizzle out, the flashbacks are incredibly heavy-handed, and the sexual intrigue is...well, limp. Colleen McCullough's source novel provides a decent enough formula, but the film-makers manage to reduce it to housewives' afternoon TV-slot tedium. DPe

Indecent Proposal

(1993, US, 117 min)
d Adrian Lyne. *p* Sherry Lansing. *sc* Amy Holden Jones. *ph* Howard Atherton. *ed* Joe Hutshing. *pd* Mel Bourne. *m* John Barry. *cast* Robert Redford, Demi Moore, Woody Harrelson, Oliver Platt, Seymour Cassel, Billy Connolly, Herbie Hancock.

●Great hook, crap movie. Here's the zinger: Redford offers a seven-figure sum for a night of hormonal judo with Moore, but she loves some other schmuck. This is so high-concept it practically needs breathing apparatus, but Lyne's flash-trash panache reduces it to mere hi-gloss. To call the characters cardboard would ennoble them. David (Harrelson) and Diana (Moore) are happily married, successful architect and real estate salesperson respectively, until the recession all but wipes them out. They head for Las Vegas, hoping to win an instant fortune, but ill luck polishes them off, and only the million dollar proposition from Redford's enigmatic magnate stands between the couple and financial ignominy. Can their relationship survive this sternest of all tests? The eventual triumph of love over money is so moving, you'd need a heart of stone not to laugh. At last, a movie for people who cry at pop videos. TJ

Inde Fantôme, L'

see Phantom India

Independence Day

(1996, US, 145 min)
d Roland Emmerich. *p* Dean Devlin. *sc* Dean Devlin, Roland Emmerich. *ph* Walter Lindenlaub. *ed* David Brenner. *pd* Oliver Scholl, Patrick Tatopoulos. *m* David Arnold. *cast* Bill Pullman, Will Smith, Jeff Goldblum, Robert Loggia, Margaret Colin, Mary McDonnell, Vivica A Fox, Judd Hirsch, James Rebhorn, Harvey Fierstein, Harry Connick Jr.

●Act I is an Anarchists' Ball. Massive metal spaceships loom over the cities of the world. The destruction of the White House is just for starters. Annihilation of the human race is on the agenda. US President Pullman, a wimp ex-fighter jock, listens to communications expert Goldblum (only in a Rupert Murdoch film could a TV exec save the world!). Act II, the survivors regroup at a secret military base in New Mexico to organise Act III, the fightback. Emmerich's globe-buster is an index of American populist fantasy. Forget subtext. This scrappy, spectacular, juvenile remake of *War of the Worlds* and 101 other sci-fi movies can be taken at face value. It's not about *Them*, it's about *US*: At least this America is strongly pluralist; it's black (Smith as the heroic top gun); it's Jewish (Goldblum and Hirsch as comic relief); it's even a little bit feminine – though Fierstein, Margaret Colin, et al, are really just emotional punctuation marks. The politics cut both ways, balancing pro- and anti-government impulses with Pullman as a vaguely Clinton-esque figure in the middle, pacifist by inclination, warrior by experience. Everything feels anti-climactic after the fireworks, but the moral is clear: it's the end of the world as we know it. And we feel fine. TCh

Indiana Jones and the Last Crusade

(1989, US, 127 min)
d Steven Spielberg. *p* Robert Watts. *sc* Jeffrey Boam. *ph* Douglas Slocombe. *ed* Michael Kahn. *pd* Elliot Scott. *m* John Williams. *cast* Harrison Ford, Sean Connery, Denholm Elliot, Alison Doody, John Rhys-Davies, Julian Glover, River Phoenix, Michael Byrne, Robert Eddison, Alexei Sayle.

●A film which smacks of *Raiders of the Lost Ark* in both mood and effects, even down to a tank chase which drags Jones' well-worn heels along the desert floor. Saving us from a sense of complete déjà vu is the introduction of Connery, Medievalist professor and Indiana's father. His screen image provides the perfect fatherly foil to the larger-than-life hero. Pursuing a life-long obsession with the Holy Grail brings the prof into the grip of dastardly Nazis, who of course are after the same thing. It's Indiana Jones to the rescue of his father, the Grail, nay democracy itself. Wisely dispersing with attempts to recapture the central romance of *Raiders*, the emotional core is served this time by the sparring relationship between Indiana and his dad. Jeffrey Boam's script dabbles with themes of neglect and reconciliation, but there's nothing ponderous about the duo's near death scrapes and light-hearted tussels over the same blonde Fräulein. CM

Indiana Jones and the Temple of Doom

(1984, US, 118 min)
d Steven Spielberg. *p* Robert Watts. *sc* Willard Huyck, Gloria Katz. *ph* Douglas Slocombe. *ed* Michael Kahn. *pd* Elliot Scott. *m* John Williams. *cast* Harrison Ford, Kate Capshaw, Ke Huy Quan, Amrish Puri, Roshan Seth, David Yip, Philip Stone, Dan Aykroyd.

●Conceived as a prequel to *Raiders of the Lost Ark*, this kids off in old Shanghai and quickly hotfoots it to the Himalayas in pursuit of another magical talisman. While the set pieces are as spectacular as ever (a neat Busby Berkeley pastiche of 'Anything Goes' as an opener, a corker of an underground helter-skelter ride), the intervening filler shows signs of desperation. Part of the trouble is that anything clearly does go, including the slender hold on credibility that *Raiders* managed to maintain. Gone is Karen Allen's tough, no nonsense heroine, and instead we have the off-putting sight of Capshaw wittering on about her broken nails. Foreigners are generally perceived as an exotic bunch who are essentially savages at heart. The thrills are there all right, and delivered by the hand of a master, but the frantic flash-bang-wallop sounds altogether more hollow than last time around. JP

Indian Fighter, The

(1955, US, 85 min)
d André De Toth. *p* William Schorr. *sc* Frank Davis, Ben Hecht. *ph* Wilfred M Cline. *ed* Richard Cahoon. *ad* Wiard Ihnen. *m* Franz Waxman. *cast* Kirk Douglas, Elsa Martinelli, Walter Matthau, Walter Abel, Diana Douglas, Lon Chaney Jr, Elisha Cook Jr, Alan Hale Jr.

●A brisk and very polished Western, lacking the intensity of De Toth's later *Day of the Outlaw*, but notable for its sumptuous 'Scope photography and for its interest in the Sioux Indians and their closeness to nature. Douglas is typically robust as the scout hoping to make a peace treaty with the Sioux as he escorts a wagon train through their territory, while Martinelli, as the Indian girl he falls for, achieved some notoriety with a fairly explicit bathing sequence. The storyline is hardly original, but the solid cast and De Toth's effortless, elegant direction lend it a certain flair. GA

Indian in the Cupboard, The

(1995, US, 96 min)
d Frank Oz. *p* Kathleen Kennedy, Frank Marshall, Jane Startz. *sc* Melissa Mathison. *ph* Russell Carpenter. *ed* Ian Crafford. *pd* Leslie McDonald. *m* Randy Edelman. *cast* Hal Scardino, Litefoot, Lindsay Crouse, Richard Jenkins, David Keith, Steve Coogan, Sakina Jaffrey.

●A delightful adaptation of Lynne Reid Banks' children's classic: Omri (Scardino), whose parents (Crouse and Jenkins) are sufficiently well off to afford kids' bedrooms large enough to be film sets, receives an old lock-up cupboard for his ninth birthday, and does swapsy for a plastic model of an 'Indian' with his pal Patrick. After a night in the cupboard, the model becomes Little Bear, an 18th century Onondaga-Iroquois brave (Litefoot). Once Little Bear realises Omri is no 'Great Spirit', they swiftly make friends and explain each other's worlds, until, that is, sole confidant Patrick 'brings to life' a 19th century cowboy (Keith), and their game becomes a matter of life and death. The film's conceit ('you should not do magic you do not understand') is prompted by the heart attack from fear of an old Native American chief, which is typical of the neatly (and lightly) concealed moral thrust of Melissa Mathison's screenplay, which teaches respect for people, knowledge and technology. Fine enlarged production design and effects, and appealing acting from the little and the large. WH

Indian Runner, The

(1991, US, 126 min)
d Sean Penn. *p* Don Phillips. *sc* Sean Penn. *ph* Anthony B Richmond. *ed* Jay Cassidy. *pd* Michael Haller. *m* Jack Nitzsche. *cast* David Morse, Viggo Mortensen, Valeria Golino, Patricia Arquette, Charles Bronson, Sandy Dennis, Dennis Hopper, Jordan Rhodes.

●Plattsmouth, Nebraska, 1968. Tattooed tearaway Frank Roberts (Mortensen) returns from Vietnam to be uncomfortably reunited with his brother Joe (Morse), a law-abiding family man. 'Some of the boys are coming back confused,' muses Bronson, excellently cast against type as the helpless father who needs constant reminding that 'Frank *left* confused'. As Joe strives in vain to rekindle the bond which once joined him to his brother, Frank descends into alcohol-addled oblivion. Inspired by Bruce Springsteen's 'Highway Patrolman', Penn's first project as writer/director is a film out of time, drenched in an overbearing '60s world-view which veers between the dated and the dopey. As a brother, Joe is heartbroken; as casual onlookers, we soon tire both of Frank's drunken philosophising and of Penn's reverence for his suffering. Potentially potent and not without naive charm, but ultimately a masturbatory ejaculation of all too personal juices. MK

Indians Are Still Far Away, The (Les Indiens Sont Encore Loin)

(1977, Switz/Fr, 95 min)
d/sc Patricia Moraz. *ph* Renato Berta. *ed* Thierry Deroclès. *ad* Jacques Magnien, Rolf Knutti. *cast* Isabelle Huppert, Christine Pascal, Mathieu Carrière, Nicole Garcia, Anton Diffring.

●One of the problems facing Swiss cinema is finding interesting and engaging ways of discussing the country's provincialism. The problem is emphasised in this film about the last week in the life of a schoolgirl because it opts for accumulating banalities. Isabelle Huppert, of *The Lacemaker*, registers another flawless recording of passive teenage despair. CPe

Indian Story, An

(1981, Ind, 59 min, b/w)
d Tapan K Bose. *p* Suharini Mulay. *ph* Salim Shaikh. *ed* Prakash Kothare. *narrator* Naseeruddin Shah.

●In 1980, thirty-three people were blinded by police in the Bhagalpur district of India's eastern state of Bihar. The police claimed they were criminals and that the measures were necessary to curb the soaring crime rate in that area. In fact most of them had no criminal record, had not been convicted, or even charged with any specific crime, but were picked almost at random from the streets and villages around Bhagalpur and subjected to this quite horrendous justice. The Bihar government and its henchmen managed to cover up the whole thing so well that the only man punished was the police officer who leaked the affair. This documentary recounts the story with a simple, chilling clarity. It also makes the necessary connection between the Bhagalpur blindings and the repressive machinery inherited from the British and still maintained. MBo

Indian Summer

see Alive and Kicking

Indian Summer (Indiánské Léto)

(1994, Czech Rep, 65 min)
d Sasa Gedeon. *p* Petr Oukropec, Pavel Strnad. *sc* Sasa Gedeon. *ph* Milos Kabyl. *ed* Petr Turyna. *pd* Ondrej Nekvasil. *cast* Tatiana Vilhelmová, Klára Issová, Olga Karaskova, Robert Stepánek, Jirí Ployhar.

●Petty rivalries, spitefulness and a very tentative symbiosis are the subjects of this first feature, a low key study – adapted from a story by F Scott Fitzgerald – of two mismatched cousins spending a summer together in their granny's country home. One, Marie (Vilhelmová), is an average girl of the world, callow and unimpressed with her choice of admirers; the other, Klára (Issová), seems like an alien next to her, gauche, rigid and clueless about the conventions of teen dating. Writer/director Gedeon's deliberate, understated style is already much in evidence, and though not as lyrical as *Return of the Idiot*, nor finally as affecting, the film offers similarly discreet performances, a fastidious eye, and gently deprecating humour. Not to mention its intriguingly odd, and oddly effective, choice of imagery – apples, bobs, and Indian scalping. NB

Indian Tomb, The

see Tiger of Eschnapur, The

India Song

(1974, Fr, 120 min)
d Marguerite Duras. *p* Stéphane Tchalgadjieff. *sc* Marguerite Duras. *ph* Bruno Nuytten. *ed* Solange Leprince. *m* Carlos d'Alessio. *cast* Delphine Seyrig, Michel Lonsdale, Mathieu Carrière, Claude Mann, Vernon Dobtcheff, Didier Flamand, Marguerite Duras, Benoît Jacquot.

●Duras' main protagonist is Anne-Marie Stretter (Seyrig), a bored consular wife in '30s India, and the film details the languorous desperation that drives her to suicide. But the formal approach to this subject is like nothing before in film history: the 'drama' is entirely aural (a play of off-screen voices blending with Carlos d'Alessio's utterly compulsive score), and the elegant visuals counterpoint it by creating an atmosphere of sumptuous enervation. Many will find it fascinating, not least because its sense of stifled anguish emerges without the least hint of aggression in the style. TR

Indiscreet

(1958, GB, 99 min)
d/p Stanley Donen. *sc* Norman Krasna. *ph* Freddie Young. *ed* Jack Harris. *ad* Don Ashton. *m* Richard Rodney Bennett, Ken Jones. *cast* Cary Grant, Ingrid Bergman, Phyllis Calvert, Cecil Parker, David Kossoff, Megs Jenkins.

●Despite the casting, far from a re-run of *Notorious*. In fact the Norman Krasna script for this romantic comedy fluff (about diplomat Grant's insistence that he's already married in the face of actress Bergman's attentions) originated in a play of his that flopped on Broadway some five years previously, *Kind Sir*. Here the New York setting gave way to Mayfair, and Donen piled on the civilised charm. PT

Indiscretion of an American Wife

see Terminal Station

Indochine

(1991, Fr, 154 min)
d Régis Wargnier. *p* Eric Heumann. *sc* Erik Orsenna, Louis Gardel, Catherine Cohen, Régis Wargnier. *ph* François Cantonné. *ed* Geneviève Winding. *pd* Jacques Bufnoir. *m* Patrick Doyle. *cast* Catherine Deneuve, Vincent Perez, Linh Dan Pham, Jean Yanne, Dominique Blanc, Henri Marteau, Carlo Brandt.

●Before Vietnam, there was Indochina; before the Americans, the French. The languorous first half of Wargnier's epic historical romance is pretty much as you'd expect: plantation-owner Deneuve in impeccably starched jodhpurs, coolies in their place, civilisation transplanted to a hothouse. She begins a passionate affair with a young naval officer (Perez), but he falls in love with her adopted Vietnamese daughter (Linh Dan Pham). When he is sent to a remote outpost on the Gulf of Tonkin, the girl takes after him. And Wargnier follows. Midway through, having involved us so deeply in colonial enterprise, he abruptly cuts our cultural ties and plunges into sweeping revolutionary myth: the lovers go on the run, the girl discovers her people, their struggle, what her role must be. If Bertolucci tried his hand at a mini-series, it would probably look something like this. The allegorical intimations may not be entirely credible, given the piece's lush romanticism; it's rather enervatingly composed; and the pacing could certainly be tighter. But such grand old-fashioned melodrama is almost as exotic as the stunning Vietnamese landscape; it's easy to be seduced by it. TCh

In Dreams

(1998, US, 100 min)
d Neil Jordan. *p* Stephen Woolley. *sc* Bruce Robinson, Neil Jordan. *ph* Darius Khondji. *ed*

Tony Lawson. *pd* Nigel Phelps. *m* Elliot Goldenthal. *cast* Annette Bening, Katie Sagona, Aidan Quinn, Robert Downey Jr, Stephen Rea, Paul Guilfoyle, Prudence Wright Holmes, Krystal Benn, Pamela Payton-Wright.
●Immediately signalling its blend of supernatural horror and intense psychological drama, Jordan's film opens with a visually arresting, breathtaking sequence. Police divers searching for the victims of a child killer glide gracefully through the clear flood waters covering a New England town, the rooms of its abandoned buildings still intact below the surface. Above, clairvoyant children's book illustrator Claire Cooper plunges into her unconscious, delving for clues about where the killer might strike next. Sadly, this is merely the haunting overture to an essentially prosaic variation on the 'abused child grows into serial killer' plot. While Downey hams it up something rotten as bad apple Vivian, Bening's portrayal of Claire has a diamond clarity that deserve a better setting. If her illustrations for a book of Grimms' fairy tales provided a conduit for the killer to enter her mind, by descending into madness she can confront him on his home ground: in order to destroy him, she must become him. Yet for all Jordan's imaginative use of skewed nightmare logic, this is a b/w photocopy of a serial killer plot that has merely been coloured in with super-saturated dream sequences and over-elaborate art house imagery. NF

I Never Promised You a Rose Garden

(1977, US, 96 min)
d Anthony Page. *p* Daniel H Blatt, Michael Hausman, Terence F Deane. *sc* Gavin Lambert, Lewis John Carlino. *ph* Bruce Logan. *ed* Garth Craven. *pd* Toby Carr Rafelson. *m* Paul Chihara. *cast* Bibi Andersson, Kathleen Quinlan, Sylvia Sidney, Ben Piazza, Lorraine Gary, Darlene Craviotto, Reni Santoni, Susan Tyrrell, Signe Hasso, Diane Varsi.
●This Roger Corman production, faithful in detail to Hannah Green's book (generally regarded as one of the best lay descriptions of schizophrenia), has 16-year-old Deborah Blake (Quinlan) struggling with her fantasy-world-turned-remorseless-possessor and gradually being rehabilitated with the help of her hospital doctor. Unlike the book, though, the film fairly hurtles along, missing any real analysis of mental disturbance while going all out for Emotion. The inevitably beautiful victim suffers heavily sexual demons; the tragi-comic antics of her fellow inmates are exploited to the full; and the end is imbued with the peachy tints of a full-blown rose. But it's enjoyable and the performances are excellent, in particular Bibi Andersson's doctor and Kathleen Quinlan's staggering portrayal of Deborah. Nutsploitation of a superior kind. HM

I Never Sang for My Father

(1969, US, 92 min)
d/p Gilbert Cates. *sc* Robert Anderson. *ph* Morris Hartzbrand, George Stoetzel. *ed* Angelo Ross. *ad* Hank Aldrich. *m* Al Gorgoni, Barry Mann. *cast* Melvyn Douglas, Gene Hackman, Dorothy Stickney, Estelle Parsons, Elizabeth Hubbard, Lovelady Powell, Daniel Keyes.
●*Summer Wishes, Winter Dreams*, and indeed *The Affair*, showed how fine a director of actors Cates is, and this earlier movie provides even more convincing evidence. Based on Robert (*Tea and Sympathy*) Anderson's play, *I Never Sang for My Father* is a close and fraught piece about that curious, inarticulated love that turns blood relationships tacky and sour. Hackman makes something remarkable of the wrestling with himself as well as with his father – Melvyn Douglas in full flight – and Cates keeps the saccharine, if not always the over-emphasis, at bay. If you're not too laid back to stomach a film about emotions, this is more than just a worthy affair. SG

Inevitable, The (Parinati)

(1988, Ind, 125 min)
d/ph/ed Prakash Jha. *m* Raghunath Seth. *cast* Basant Josalkar, Surekha Sikri, Sudhir Kulkarni, Sharda De Soares, BD Singh.
●Set in an indeterminate period, this flawlessly tells a folk tale that has all the elemental power of myth. A humble but respected potter, his wife, and young boy are encouraged by the local chief to leave town to manage a remote desert well and inn for travellers. Slowly, ineluctably, the seductive power of potential riches causes their downfall. First they allow their beloved son to be taken away to be trained as a Seth (merchant). Later, they abuse their reputation of service to prey on their trusting guests. Jha, primarily a documentary film-maker, here serving as his own cinematographer, never puts a foot wrong. he suffuses the screen with colour (gold, ochre, yellows), mines extraordinary performances from his players, and uses faces and spaces to perfection, controlling and sustaining a mood of tragic intensity. WH

In Expectation

see Rainclouds Over Wushan

In Fading Light

(1989, GB, 107 min)
d Murray Martin, Amber Films. *sc* Tom Hadaway. *ad* Judith Tomlinson. *m* Alasdair Robertson, Ray Stubbs. *cast* Joe Caffrey, Mo Harold, Dave Hill, Brian Hogg, Sammy Johnson, Joanna Ripley, Amber Styles.
●The admirable Amber Films collective comes up trumps again, after *Seacoal*, with another Loach-ian account of the disillusioned and dispossessed up North. A teenage girl (Ripley) visits her estranged father (Hill) in North Shields, and in joining him aboard his fishing boat, comes up against male chauvinism, female jealousy, and the despair of running a traditional small business in the face of Thatcherite corporate investment. If it's sometimes hard to follow the authentic dialect, there is no denying the conviction of the naturalistic performances or the intelligence of the script, while a suspenseful gale sequence effortlessly belies the lowly budget. GA

Infernal Street

see Return of the Dragon

Infernal Trio, The (Le Trio Infernal)

(1974, Fr/It/WGer, 100 min)
d Francis Girod. *p* Raymond Danon, Jacques Dorfmann. *sc* Francis Girod, Jacques Rouffio. *ph* Andréas Winding. *ed* Claude Barrois. *ad* Jean-Jacques Caziot. *m* Ennio Morricone. *cast* Michel Piccoli, Romy Schneider, Mascha Gomska, Andréa Ferréol, Monica Fiorentini, Philippe Brizard.
●An elegant and outrageous black opera, handled with a panache that deliberately flouts notions of good taste. Piccoli enjoys himself hugely as the civic eminent (a distinguished lawyer newly invested with the Legion of Honour) who swindles and murders unscrupulously with the help of his lovers, two sisters (Schneider and Gomska). The result is a finely balanced fairytale (complete with 'happy' ending), full of a subversive mockery of pathetic respectabilities, unkind but not callous. Avoid the English-dubbed version, which coarsens the film to such an extent that it's scarcely recognisable: the exuberant excesses of Piccoli's performance are made to look merely hammy. CPe

Inferno

(1953, US, 83 min)
d Roy Baker. *p* William Bloom. *sc* Francis Cockrell. *ph* Lucien Ballard. *ed* Robert Simpson. *ad* Lyle Wheeler, Lewis H Creber. *m* Paul Sawtell. *cast* Robert Ryan, Rhonda Fleming, William Lundigan, Henry Hull, Carl Betz, Larry Keating.
●A tight and involving essay in suspense which works on the ingenious idea of leaving the audience alone in the desert with an unsympathetic and selfish character (all the more so considering that he's a millionaire), left to die with a broken leg by his wife and her lover. Baker then forces us to change our attitude of contempt to one of sympathy and admiration for his sheer will to survive. The suspense is well handled, especially a descent into a canyon with just one rope and a fall of hundreds of feet. The excellent Ryan plays the millionaire, Fleming his wife. *Inferno* was one of the best and last movies to be made in 3-D during the boom in the early '50s. Certainly its use of space emphasised the dramatic possibilities of 3-D and reveals, as more than one person has observed, that the device had largely been squandered in other films made at the time. CPe

Inferno

(1980, It, 107 min)
d Dario Argento. *p* Claudio Argento. *sc* Dario Argento. *ph* Romano Albani. *ed* Franco Fraticelli. *ad* Giuseppe Bassan. *m* Keith Emerson. *cast* Leigh McCloskey, Irene Miracle, Eleonora Giorgi, Daria Nicolodi, Sacha Pitoeff, Alida Valli, Feodor Chaliapin, Veronica Lazar.
●Argento's career has largely centred on a series of outlandish thrillers, notable for their bizarre set pieces, elaborate editing and camerawork. These bravura displays of technique remained at odds with his banal handling of actors and narrative, but his best known film, *Suspiria*, seemed to indicate that Argento had begun to devise a style of commercial film-making which was moving away from the limitations of conventional narrative (or certainly treating it in the most perfunctory fashion), and thrilling the audience only through sound, image and movement. Sadly, *Inferno* – murder and the occult in a New York apartment house – is a much more conventional and unexciting piece of work. Argento's own over-the-top score has been replaced by religioso thunderings from the keyboards of Keith Emerson, and the meandering narrative confusions are amplified by weak performances. Even the set pieces fail to set the screen alight, and the film's remaining virtue is a series of remarkable individual shots illuminated like masterworks of comic book art. SM

Informer, The

(1935, US, 91 min, b/w)
d John Ford. *sc* Dudley Nichols. *ph* Joseph August. *ed* George Hively. *ad* Van Nest Polglase. *m* Max Steiner. *cast* Victor McLaglen, Heather Angel, Preston Foster, Margot Grahame, Wallace Ford, Una O'Connor, JM Kerrigan, Donald Meek.
●What do critics dream about? John Ford got the best reviews of his career for this heavy-handed, humourless and patronising art film ('Many consider it the greatest talking picture ever made in America,' wrote Theodore Huff a few years later), roundly, and rightly, debunked by Lindsay Anderson for having the 'painstaking explicitness of a silent film grimly determined to tell its story without the aid of titles'. Liquored up by Ford, McLaglen won an Oscar for his lumbering portrait of a brainless, boozy Dubliner, Gypo Nolan, who betrays his buddy to the Black and Tans for a kingly £20, then suffers sweatily under the torments of conscience. There were further awards for the director, Dudley Nichols' script, and Max Steiner's score – all equally over-emphatic. Today, only Joe August's foggy expressionist camerawork still captures the imagination, but even this becomes enervatingly portentous before long. TCh

Ingaló

(1992, Ice, 100 min)
d Asdís Thoroddsen. *p* Martin Schlüter, Albert Kitzler. *sc* Asdís Thoroddsen. *ph* Tahvo Hirvonen. *ed* Valdís Oskarsdottir. *m* Christoph Oertel. *cast* Sólveig Arnarsdóttir, Haraldur Hallgrimsson, Ingvar Sigurdsson, Thorlákur Thorleifsson.
●Bearing an uncanny resemblance to Amber Films' *In Fading Light*, this centres on a 'difficult' (i.e. feisty and aggressive) 18-year-old, who leaves her family home on the northern coast of Iceland to join her brother on board a trawler: much gutting ensues. A low-key fable that leavens its raw emotional authenticity with an unexpectedly sly wit, it's deftly acted, crisply shot, and eventually about issues of sexual chauvinism, economics, and labour intrigue. If it never gets as sharply political as Amber's movie, it's a fine effort all the same. GA

In Georgia (In Georgien)

(1987, EGer, 107 min)
d Jürgen Böttcher. *p* Frank Löprich, Kerstin Lindenberg, Dia Kurdgelia. *sc* Jürgen Böttcher. *ph* Thomas Plenert. *ed* Gudrun Plenert.
●There's a sense of wonder to Böttcher's graceful film about the republic of Georgia on the Black Sea. With a minimal crew, he travels along the coastline, visiting the main cities and holiday resorts and the most isolated mountain villages, touching on the region's history, culture and simplicity of life. Breath-taking panoramic views of misty blue-grey mountains, and long, long takes that allow for uncoaxed responses from the peasant subjects, create an impression of a mystical lost land. EP

In Harm's Way

(1965, US, 167 min, b/w)
d/p Otto Preminger. *sc* Wendell Mayes. *ph* Loyal Griggs. *ed* George Tomasini, Hugh S Fowler. *pd* Lyle Wheeler. *m* Jerry Goldsmith. *cast* John Wayne, Kirk Douglas, Patricia Neal, Tom Tryon, Paula Prentiss, Brandon de Wilde, Burgess Meredith, Henry Fonda, Dana Andrews, Franchot Tone, Slim Pickens.

● Preminger, having already revealed a taste for excessive length in films like *Advise and Consent*, *Exodus* and *The Cardinal*, here stretches out a relatively conventional WWII drama to the point of tedium. Wayne is the discredited admiral whose reactions to the Japanese attack on Pearl Harbor finally convince both the Navy's top brass and his alienated, contemptuous son of his worth; subplots include his romance with nurse Neal, and his executive officer Douglas's trajectory towards self-destruction after he learns of his faithless wife's death. It goes on and on, the slowness exacerbated by Preminger's customary long takes and by the endless parade of star cameos. So what's it all add up to? War may be hell, but courage and honour will triumph in the end. GA

Inheritance, The

see Uncle Silas

Inheritance, The (L'Eredità Ferramonti)

(1976, It, 103 min)
d Mauro Bolognini. *p* Gianni Hecht Lucari. *sc* Ugo Pirro, Sergio Bazzini. *ph* Ennio Guarnieri. *ed* Nino Baragli. *ad* Luigi Scaccianoce. *m* Ennio Morricone. *cast* Anthony Quinn, Fabio Testi, Dominique Sanda, Luigi Proietti, Adriana Asti, Paolo Bonacelli, Rossella Rusconi.

● The insipid Sanda seduces her way into the affections and bed of self-made millionaire Quinn, to get her hands on his closely guarded lucre. Passionless characterisations abound, and the periodic spasms of carnality offer little relief as we are swanned around the meticulously realised Rome of the 1880s. Punters dishing out good money in the hopes of seeing a sexually explicit version of TV's *Dynasty* may well be disappointed. WH

Inheritors, The (Die Siebtelbauern)

(1997, Aus/Ger, 95 min)
d Stefan Ruzowitzky. *p* Danny Krausz, Kurt Stocker. *sc* Stefan Ruzowitzky. *ph* Peter von Haller. *ed* Britta Nahler. *ad* Isi Wimmer. *m* Erik Satie. *cast* Sophie Rois, Simon Schwarz, Lars Rudolph, Tilo Prückner, Ulrich Wildgruber, Julia Geschnitzer.

● This darkening parable of pre-WWII farm life is a variation on the German 'Heimat' film – a genre of idealised, romantic depictions of rural communities that developed in an increasingly sentimental direction in the inter-war years. Writer/director Ruzowitzky has a revisionist agenda. Seven peasants are bequeathed an alpine smallholding following the mysterious demise of the elderly landowner. Having inherited their earth, can these unprotected 'communards' survive the twin threats of internal divisions and the external opposition from the outraged burghers of a nearby town? This cold-eyed movie combines keen observation with political/historical critique – but one at the expense of the other. The peasants are a motley bunch: a libidinous charmer, an authoritarian foreman, an icy spinster, a naive halfwit. And it is in intimately detailing their stratified daily lives in all their variety that allows Ruzowitzky to lighten the preponderantly portentous mood. WH

Inherit the Wind

(1960, US, 128 min, b/w)
d/p Stanley Kramer. *sc* Ned Young, Harold Jacob Smith. *ph* Ernest Laszlo. *ed* Frederick Knudtson. *ad* Rudolph Sternad. *m* Ernest Gold. *cast* Spencer Tracy, Fredric March, Gene Kelly, Florence Eldridge, Dick York, Donna Anderson, Harry Morgan, Noah Berry Jr.

● Courtroom drama meets pious liberalism in this stolid adaptation of the Jerome Lawrence-Robert E Lee play about the Tennessee 'Monkey Trial' of 1925 (when a young schoolmaster – played by York – was indicted for illegally teaching Darwinian theory). Tolerably gripping in its old-fashioned way, thanks chiefly to old pro performances from Tracy and March as the rival lawyers and ideologists, but rather let down by Kelly's inadequacy as the cynical journalist who is comfortably denounced as the real villain of the piece. TM

Inhibitions

(1976, It, 120 min)
d Paul Price [Paolo Poeti]. *p* Giulio Scanni. *sc* Adriano Belli. *ph* Giancarlo Ferrando. *ed* Luigia Magrini. *pd* Carlo Gentili. *m* Guido De Angelis, Maurizio De Angelis. *cast* Claudine Beccarie, Ivan Rassimov, Ilona Staller, Cesare Barro, Adolfo Caruso, Patrizia Gori.

● Veteran porn star Claudine Beccarie shows her years in this lavish sex film, set in North Africa (and heavily cut for British distribution). The more than usually fatuous plot revolves around the inhibited proprietress of a stud ranch who spends her time indulging in casual affairs and snubbing an impecunious upper-class Englishman. In the last reel she succumbs to his sincerity, and the proceedings conclude with a bout of passionate, long-delayed grappling. Some dreadful bits of half-baked philosophising crop up from time to time. JPy

Inhumaine, L'

(1924, Fr, 6,120 ft, b/w)
d Marcel L'Herbier. *sc* Marcel L'Herbier, Pierre Mac Orlan. *ph* Georges Specht. *ad* Fernand Léger, Albert Cavalcanti, Claude Autant-Lara, Robert Mallet-Stevens. *m* Darius Milhaud, Jean-Christophe Desnoux. *cast* Georgette Leblanc, Jaque Catelain, Philippe Hériat, Marcelle Pradot, Fred Kellerman, Bonambellas, Jean Börlin.

● Part-financed by American singer Georgette Leblanc, who also stars, this was designed as a sort of showcase for contemporary French arts. So, decorating a tolerably camp story about a heartless woman (Leblanc) who is poisoned by one disappointed lover (Hériat) and scientifically resuscitated into new humanity by another (Catelain), it boasts extravagant Cubist settings (by Fernand Léger, Robert Mallet-Stevens, Claude Autant-Lara and Alberto Cavalcanti), features costumes by Paul Poiret, incorporates a Jean Borlin ballet, makes coy reference to radio and TV, and was originally accompanied by a Darius Milhaud score. The result, resolutely chic, brought instant sneers about aesthetic dilettantism which L'Herbier was subsequently never quite able to shake off. But despite the wretched acting and daft script (by Pierre Mac Orlan), the last third of the film, in which L'Herbier's attempt to apply a different mood and rhythm to each setting begins to pay dividends, is often remarkable in the way it manipulates space as an autonomous element in the drama. TM

In Ismail's Custody

(1994, GB, 48 min)
d Derrick Santini. *with* Anthony Hopkins, Simon Callow, Ruth Prawer Jhabvala, Vanessa Redgrave, Andrew Sarris, Shashi Kapoor.

● This documentary, by Merchant Ivory stillsman Derrick Santini, courses through the life of Ismail Merchant, from childhood in Bombay, the son of a Muslim textile merchant, to his heights in 1994 as producer of *The Remains of the Day*. Bombay is the Indian Hollywood, but it was on a trip to New York for university studies that Merchant first saw the work of De Sica and Satyajit Ray and realised the type of film he wished to make. Santini has rounded up the usual suspects: Anthony Hopkins, Emma Thompson, Vanessa Redgrave, Simon Callow ('He's a maverick,' echoing the rest), collaborator/writer Ruth Jhabvala, et al. Shashi Kapoor has been a friend since the first MI film, *The Householder* in 1963, so his comments on working on *In Custody*, Merchant's feature debut – 'He's the most fascist director in the world!' – could be humorous. Critic Andrew Sarris and ex-Disney supremo Jeffrey Katzenberg's testimony shows the Yanks have been wowed too. After 30 years of struggle, the world seems to be his oyster – or perhaps his chicken *tikka*. WH

In July (Im Juli)

(2000, Ger, 99 min)
d Fatih Akin. *p* Stephan Schubert, Ralph Schwingel. *sc* Fatih Akin. *ph* Pierre Aïm. *ed* Andrew Bird. *ad* Jürgen Schnell. *m* Ulrich Kodjo Wendt. *cast* Moritz Bleibtreu, Christiane Paul, Mehmet Kurtulus, Idil Üner, Jochen Nickel, Branka Katic, Birol Ünel, Sandra Borgmann, Fatih Akin.

● Basically an understated, shaggy-dog romantic comedy, and an inconsequential one at that, the film is played with near effortless assurance. Daniel (Bleibtreu) is a bespectacled Hamburg student teacher. A market vendor (Paul) sells him a lucky sun ring, which he soon matches with the image on the dress of a lovely Turkish tourist (Üner) he meets for the night. It's the holidays, so he decides to return the visit. En route to Turkey he picks up the same, now hitch-hiking street vendor; is picked up by a nutty Serbian woman trucker (Katic) and a Turkish driver (Kurtulus) with a body in his trunk; loses two cars, his wallet and passport, and gets the wrong side of several nations' border guards. The cast are extremely confident, and there's a winning soundtrack, fine photography and never a longueur. NB

In-Laws, The

(1979, US, 103 min)
d Arthur Hiller. *p* William Sackheim, Arthur Hiller. *sc* Andrew Bergman. *ph* David M Walsh. *ed* Robert E Swink. *pd* Pato Guzman. *m* John Morris. *cast* Peter Falk, Alan Arkin, Richard Libertini, Nancy Dussault, Penny Peyser, Arlene Golonka, Michel Lembeck, Paul Smith.

● Much Arkin and Falkin about enlivens this MOR buddy-comedy, which has a bewildered dentist and a loony CIA man hauling stolen Treasury engravings through a Central American banana-joke republic just before their kids' wedding. Too silly to be particularly offensive or even particularly funny – it's simply outstandingly ordinary stuff.

In Like Flint

(1967, US, 115 min)
d Gordon Douglas. *p* Saul David. *sc* Hal Fimberg. *ph* William H Daniels. *ed* Hugh S Fowler. *ad* Jack Martin Smith, Dale Hennesy. *m* Jerry Goldsmith. *cast* James Coburn, Lee J Cobb, Jean Hale, Andrew Duggan, Anna Lee, Hanna Landy, Totty Ames, Steve Ihnat.

● Dire sequel to the already desperately flashy *Our Man Flint*, with its nudging innuendo stuck at the level of its punning title. Coburn's super-Bond saves the world from women. Ray Danton took over when TV unwisely revived the spoof formula in the '70s. PT

In Love (aka Strangers in Love)

(1983, US, 90 min)
d/p Chuck Vincent. *sc* Rick Marx, Chuck Vincent. *ph* Larry Revene. *ed* James MacReading. *pd* Larry Revene. *m* Ian Shaw. *cast* Kelly Nichols, Jerry Butler, Jack Wrangler, Tish Ambrose, Joanna Storm, Samantha Fox, Michael Knight.

● The John Ford legend about tearing pages out of the script to get back on schedule may have inspired director Vincent, but he only seems to get the pages out of order, doggedly pursuing his labyrinthine plot down blind alleys, stopping on the way for a number of discreetly shot couplings, as his leads endure years of separation and a passionate reuniting. Great romantics like Griffith and Chaplin never had the advantage of hot-tubs, but Vincent's blend of slush and flesh must presumably be considered part of the tradition. DO

In Love and War

(1958, US, 111 min)
d Philip Dunne. *p* Jerry Wald. *sc* Edward Anhalt. *ph* Leo Tover. *ed* William Reynolds. *ad* Lyle R Wheeler, George W Davis. *m* Hugo Friedhofer. *cast* Robert Wagner, Jeffrey Hunter, Bradford Dillman, Dana Wynter, Hope Lange, Sheree North, France Nuyen, Mort Sahl, Veronica Cartwright.

● A best-selling source novel, *The Big War* by Anton Myrer, provides the canvas for a selection of Fox's contract artistes to impress in at least one big scene each. Characters include a rich rebel (Dillman), a poor rebel (Wagner) and a tough but tender family man (Hunter). There's a dash of miscegenation, a moralising streak (promiscuous Wynter dies horribly) and some well-designed and choreographed combat scenes, the blood and madness mostly left out. There's no pop star on parade, but briefly fashionable comedian Mort

Sahl is featured. As to which of these young lions will stop a bullet: the status of fatherhood, adding poignancy as it provides consolation, is mostly decisive in formula stuff like this. BBa

In Love and War

(1996, US, 115 min)
d Richard Attenborough. *p* Dimitri Villard, Richard Attenborough. *sc* Allan Scott, Clancy Sigal, Anna Hamilton Phelan. *ph* Roger Pratt. *ed* Lesley Walker. *pd* Stuart Craig. *m* George Fenton. *cast* Sandra Bullock, Chris O'Donnell, Mackenzie Astin, Emilio Bonucci, Ingrid Lacey, Margot Steinberg, Tara Hugo.

●Singularly uninspiring three-handed dramatisation (of a book by Henry S Villard and James Nagel) of the passionate but ill-fated affair of Ernest Hemingway (O'Donnell) and nurse Agnes von Kurowsky (Bullock). This was during the author's formative spell as a volunteer orderly on the Austro-Italian front in 1918. Bullock simply doesn't have a period face, and looks hopelessly lost. Love, war and grand passion ain't her thing, though you can forgive her for looking unconvinced in the clinches with eternal jock O'Donnell, who gives the same faintly irritating performance he always does. Attenborough conjures up hordes of extras for the battle scenes and stunning Venetian locations for the subplot involving wealthy Italian suitor Bonucci, yet the film's vision of the horrors of war proves so blandly approximate it never quite fixes the central relationship in sharp focus. Bereft of startling thematic insight or leavening gallows humour, such old-fashioned selfless heroism and breast-heaving romance doesn't really play any more. The kind of movie the director might have made 30 years ago, and after the very moving *Shadowlands*, a considerable let-down. TJ

In My Father's House (In Het Huis van Mijn Vader)

(1997, Neth, 67 min)
d Fatima Jebli Ouazzani. *ph* Maarten Kramer.

●This elegantly shot, brave and impassioned documentary deals with the director's own family experiences. She tells her own story, how she stayed single and childless since leaving home, refusing arranged marriages. She also interviews her grandmother – 'a deflowered in yesterday's couscous' – and other family members, including her father, who repudiated her mother when she died young to take another 17-year-old wife. Alongside these personal episodes, to show continuity, the director adds film of a young Dutch Muslim woman embarking on an arranged marriage in Morocco and presents interviews with gynaecologists charged with providing evidence of a woman's virginity before a marriage is allowed (one tells of how stinging nettles are used the night before to provide the bloodied sheets required by tradition). WH

In Name Only

(1939, US, 102 min, b/w)
d John Cromwell. *p* George Haight. *sc* Richard Sherman. *ph* J Roy Hunt. *ed* William Hamilton. *ad* Van Nest Polglase. *m* Roy Webb. *cast* Carole Lombard, Cary Grant, Kay Francis, Charles Coburn, Helen Vinson, Jonathan Hale, Anne Baxter, Peggy Ann Garner.

●Cary Grant has it all: money, a beautiful wife (Francis) – then he goes and falls in love with artist Carole Lombard, and the Mrs won't give him a divorce. It has all the trappings of a wonderful screwball comedy: in fact it's a mushy tearjerker, handled with a certain amount of style by John Cromwell.

Inner Circle, The (Il Proiezionista)

(1991, It, 137 min)
d Andrei Konchalovsky. *p* Claudio Bonivento. *sc* Andrei Konchalovsky, Anatoly Usov. *ph* Ennio Guarnieri. *ed* Henry Richardson. *pd* Ezio Frigerio. *m* Eduard Artemyev. *cast* Tom Hulce, Lolita Davidovich, Bob Hoskins, Aleksandr Zbruev, Feodor Chaliapin Jr, Bess Meyer, Maria Baranova.

●*Glasnost* and *perestroika* have a bit to answer for with this true-ish story. Allowed back into Russia to film, Konchalovsky was given access to secret police chief Beria's bullet-proof train compartment and the dreaded KGB building. And that, plus Hoskins' amused performance as Beria, is the upside. Ivan (Hulce), believing that he's under arrest, is whisked off to work the projector for movie-fan Stalin (Zbruev), and is soon boasting to his wife Anastasia (Davidovich) about his importance. She doesn't share his worship of Stalin, and is obsessed with the fate of an orphaned Jewish girl (Baranova). None of this is convincing, and errors of judgment reach surreal proportions (passing cattle urinating into the couple's basement flat, an enormous gilt bust of Stalin bulging out the wardrobe). While serving on a train, Anastasia is 'requisitioned' by Beria, though Ivan registers only the honour of it all – until she returns pregnant. Grinning Hulce is unbelievably gormless throughout. BC

Innerspace

(1987, US, 120 min)
d Joe Dante. *p* Michael Finnell. *sc* Jeffrey Boam, Chip Proser. *ph* Andrew Laszlo. *ed* Kent Beyda. *pd* James H Spencer. *m* Jerry Goldsmith. *cast* Dennis Quaid, Martin Short, Meg Ryan, Kevin McCarthy, Fiona Lewis, Vernon Wells, Henry Gibson, Dick Miller, Chuck Jones.

●After an accident, scientifically miniaturised marine Quaid finds himself floating, complete with miniaturised submersible, around the body of neurotic wimp Short. The pair's attempts to return him to normal size are hampered by evil saboteurs keen in killing Short in order to get hold of the magical miniaturising whatsit. Where Dante transcended the formulaic ingredients of *Gremlins* and *Explorers* by means of dark, droll wit, here for the most part he indulges in frenetic slapstick, broad parody, and juvenile mugging. And while the anatomical special effects are imaginative enough, the manic rather than magical tone fails to achieve the sense of awe that made *Fantastic Voyage* – clearly this film's inspiration – so fascinating. GA

Innocence Unprotected (Nevinost Bez Zastite)

(1968, Yugo, 78 min, b/w & col)
d/sc Dusan Makavejev. *ph* Branko Perak, Stevan Miskovic. *ed* Ivanka Vukasovic. *m* Vojislav Dostic. *with* Dragoljub Aleksic, Ana Milosavljevic, Vera Jovanovic, Bratoljub Gligorijevic.

●Makavejev's third film, an entrancing collage using excerpts from the first Serbian talkie, a hilariously naïve melodrama made in occupied Belgrade in 1942 with film stock stolen from the Germans. Bad as the film was, it was apparently a huge success, mainly because audiences delighted in flouting German movies to wallow in its pouting heroine's adventures as she is saved from a wicked stepmother and a leering lecher by a strong man with the heart of a lion (played by a real life Charles Atlas-cum-Houdini type). Innocence, though, is preserved in more ways than one, for Makavejev reassembled the surviving members of cast and crew, older, greyer and sadder. The strong man demonstrates that he can still manage some of his milder tricks (and defends himself against a charge of wartime collaboration); the stepmother wistfully recalls that she once won a competition for the most beautiful legs in Belgrade (and does a song-and-dance to prove it); and as they exchange memories of the old days, Makavejev cuts in newsreel shots of the Occupation so that one begins to see the hoary old melodrama with the eyes of 1942. The film, the people, their youth and their dreams, hover before us as miraculously preserved as flies in amber. TM

Innocent, The (L'Innocente)

(1976, It/Fr, 128 min)
d Luchino Visconti. *p* Giovanni Bertolucci. *sc* Suso Cecchi D'Amico, Enrico Medioli, Luchino Visconti. *ph* Pasqualino De Santis. *ed* Ruggero Mastroianni. *ad* Mario Garbuglia. *m* Franco Mannino. *cast* Giancarlo Giannini, Laura Antonelli, Jennifer O'Neill, Rina Morelli, Massimo Girotti, Didier Haudepin, Marie Dubois.

●After several misguided projects, Visconti's last film returns to the territory he knew best, and forms a worthy finale to a distinguished career. The plot is understated melodrama: a turn-of-the-century gentleman of leisure indulges all his own extra-marital whims, but is mortified when his wife has an affair; his whole philosophy crumbles as he desperately tries to preserve his self-respect. It's based (faithfully) on a novel by Gabriele D'Annunzio, and Visconti's treatment is much more novelistic than melodramatic: the style is uninflected, and the stately camerawork directs attention to the period manners and environments and the notably convincing characterisations. The film resolves itself into an almost painfully sincere meditation on masculine self-delusion. It has a great performance from Laura Antonelli as the wife, and excellent ones from Giannini and Jennifer O'Neill as husband and lover. TR

Innocent, The

(1984, GB, 96 min)
d John MacKenzie. *p* Jacky Stoller. *sc* Ray Jenkins. *ph* Roger Deakins. *ed* Tony Woollard. *pd* Andrew Mollo. *m* Francis Monkman. *cast* Andrew Hawley, Kika Markham, Kate Foster, Liam Neeson, Patrick Daley, Paul Askew, Lorraine Peters, Tom Bell, Miranda Richardson.

●Set in a cotton-mill town in the depths of the '30s depression, this professes to offer a truthful picture of life and love on the dole, but too often settles for quaint nostalgia. A young epileptic roams the Yorkshire dales (spectacularly shot) in search of the rare, wonderful kingfisher when the adult world becomes too bewildering and tough. The film has all the makings of a Sunday afternoon tearjerker, only MacKenzie is too honest to pull too heavily on the heartstrings. He is rewarded by merely revealing the thinness of the characterisation and the meagreness of the script. JE

Innocent, The (...und der Himmel steht still)

(1993, GB/Ger, 119 min)
d John Schlesinger. *p* Norma Heyman, Chris Sievernich, Wieland Schultz-Keil. *sc* Ian McEwan. *ph* Dietrich Lohmann. *ed* Richard Marden. *pd* Luciana Arrighi. *m* Gerald Gouriet. *cast* Anthony Hopkins, Isabella Rossellini, Campbell Scott, Hart Bochner, Ronald Nitschke, James Grant, Jeremy Sinden.

●Berlin, 1955. A gauche young electronics expert, Leonard Marnham (Scott), arrives in a city drawn and quartered by the Cold War. Already dazed to be enlisted by British Intelligence, he's even more at sea when he finds himself working on a top-secret American project under the command of one Bob Glass (Hopkins), and completely out of his depth when he's seduced by the strange, lovely German Maria (Rossellini). Before they're through, the three will be party to a secret as terrible as any covert international operation. The film didn't have an easy route to the screen. The production lost both director (Mike Newell) and leading lady (Lena Olin) before Schlesinger stepped into the breach. Surprising, then, to discover just how much this absorbing, intelligent picture (from a novel by Ian McEwan) has going for it: a strong sense of time and place, interesting characters, an intriguing scenario. Not that the film works. The pace is altogether too genteel, and, crucially, the casting doesn't stick. TCh

Innocent Blood

(1992, US, 113 min)
d John Landis. *p* Lee Rich, Leslie Belzberg. *sc* Michael Wolk. *ph* Mac Ahlberg. *ed* Dale Beldin. *pd* Richard Sawyer. *m* Ira Newborn. *cast* Robert Loggia, Anne Parillaud, Anthony LaPaglia, David Proval, Don Rickles, Rocco Sisto, Chazz Palminteri.

●If you've been waiting since 1981 for Landis to reprise the clever blend of horror and humour of *An American Werewolf in London*, this black-comic vampire movie will answer some of your prayers. Parillaud plays Maria, a modern-day vampire with glinting eyes and selective eating habits: she only feeds on bad guys, which puts ambitious Mafia boss Sal Macelli (Loggia) on the menu. Also staking out Macelli is undercover cop Joe Gennaro (LaPaglia) who, despite discovering Maria's secret, teams up with her to prevent Sal turning Pittsburgh into an open-air restaurant for Mafia blood brothers. Going easy on the tomato sauce and fx trimmings, Landis and Parillaud instead emphasise the loneliness of Maria's nocturnal existence. Drawing a parallel with Gennaro's undercover isolation and hinting at a cautious affinity in a bravura sex scene, Landis brilliantly captures a carnal craving laced with blood lust and dangerous eroticism; but, regrettably, all too often the tone lurches from stylish suspense to smart-ass in-jokiness and silly slapstick. NF

Innocent Man, An

(1989, US, 113 min)
d Peter Yates. *p* Ted Field, Robert W Court. *sc* Larry Brothers. *ph* William A Fraker. *ed* Stephen A Rotter, William S Scharf. *pd* Stuart Wurtzel. *m* Howard Shore. cast Tom Selleck, F Murray Abraham, Laila Robins, David Rasche, Richard Young, Peter Van Norden, Bruce A Young.
●When wealthy aircraft engineer Jimmie Rainwood (Selleck) is first shot, then framed by a pair of carelessly corrupt drug (taking) cops, his cosily ordered world is thrown into chaos. Considering himself a 'model citizen' (with only an old marijuana conviction to blot his copybook), Rainwood soon discovers that while the law may be an ass, his own ass is in serious danger. Sentenced to prison, where warring gangs of blacks and whites beat , rape and humiliate each other, the naive idealist is taken under the wing of veteran inmate Virgil Cane (Abraham). Rainwood learns that to survive in this hell-hole he must stand up and fight – knowledge he carries with him on his eventual parole. With the exception of Abraham's world-weary performance, and a couple of nicely nasty cameos from David Rasche and Richard Young as the crooked cops, this is a disposable affair. Yates' ham-fisted direction cranks the film up into melodramatic hyperbole, but Selleck is the real villan, portraying his transformation from wide-eyed innocent to hardened man of the world by changing from clean-shaven mop top to stubbly slicked-back, with reflecting shades to boot. Laughable. MK

Innocent Moves

see Searching for Bobby Fischer

Innocents, The

(1961, GB, 99 min, b/w)
d/p Jack Clayton. *sc* William Archibald, Truman Capote. *ph* Freddie Francis. *ed* Jim Clark. *ad* Wilfrid Shingleton. *m* Georges Auric. *cast* Deborah Kerr, Martin Stephens, Pamela Franklin, Megs Jenkins, Michael Redgrave, Peter Wyngarde, Clytie Jessop, Isla Cameron.
●Extremely impressive chiller based on Henry James' *The Turn of the Screw*, with Kerr perfectly cast as the prim, repressed Victorian governess who begins to worry that her young wards may be possessed by the evil spirits of dead servants. No shock tactics here, just the careful creation of sinister atmosphere through decor, Freddie Francis' haunting camerawork, and evocative acting. Kerr, especially, is excellent: rarely was her air of struggling to veil growing hysteria under a civilised facade so appropriately deployed. GA

Innocents in Paris

(1953, GB, 102 min, b/w)
d/p Gordon Parry. *sc* Anatole De Grunwald. *ph* Gordon Lang. *ed* Geoffrey Foot. *pd* Georges Wakhévitch. *m* Joseph Kosma. *cast* Alastair Sim, Ronald Shiner, Margaret Rutherford, Claire Bloom, Laurence Harvey, Jimmy Edwards, Richard Wattis, Louis de Funès, Christopher Lee, Kenneth Williams.
●It's national stereotyping well to the fore when assorted Brits launch themselves at Gay Paree for the weekend in this dim spot of '50s portmanteau flummery. Treasury man Sim winds up downing a few with the intransigent Russian delegate; Jimmy Edwards zeroes in on an English pub; and Harvey displays his complete lack of any comic timing as a waiter on the make. It makes TV's *'Allo, 'Allo* look relatively sophisticated, but the likes of Sim and Rutherford perk it up while they're on. TJ

Innocent Sleep, The

(1995, GB, 99 min)
d Scott Michell. *p* Scott Mitchell, Matthew Vaughn. *sc* Ray Villis. *ph* Alan Dunlop. *ed* Derek Trigg. *pd* Eve Mavrakis. *m* Mark Ayres. *cast* Rupert Graves, Annabella Sciorra, Michael Gambon, Graham Crowden, Franco Nero, John Hannah.
●Down and out in London, Alan (Graves) witnesses the assassination of a businessman, left hanging under Tower Bridge. At the local police station, he's horrified to recognise Insp Stephens (Gambon) from the crime. While Stephens sets about tying up this unexpected loose end, Alan begs reporter Billie Hayman (Sciorra) to check out his story. From the very first sequence, Michell's directorial debut belies its no-budget origins to take us on a journey from the fetid humanity of Cardboard City to the cold, hidden bastions of power. Some of the supporting turns are uneven (Crowden holds nothing back as an alcoholic tramp with useful connections), and Ray Villis's underwritten script runs out of ingenuity on the final lap, but Michell keeps the pacing tight and enlists some lively work from Sciorra and Graves (much more interesting now he's out of those linen suits). It's a classical, rather old-fashioned film, with a symphonic score by Mark Ayres and impressive 'Scope cinematography by Alan Dunlop. TCh

Innocent Sorcerers (Niewinni Czarodzieje)

(1960, Pol, 86 min, b/w)
d Andrzej Wajda. *p* Stanislaw Adler. *sc* Jerzy Andrzejewski, Jerzy Skolimowski. *ph* Krzysztof Winiewicz. *ed* Wieslawa Otocka, Aurelia Rut. *ad* Leszek Wajda. *m* Krzysztof T Komeda. *cast* Tadeusz Lomnicki, Krystyna Stypulkowska, Zbigniew Cybulski, Wanda Koczewska, Teresa Szmigielowna, Roman Polanski, Krzysztof Komeda, Jerzy Skolimowski.
●After his war trilogy, Wajda made this 'new wave' style film about contemporary youth from a script by Skolimowski. The subject is the ritual game-playing of the post-war generation, focusing on a dissolute young man (Lomnicki) who finds himself alone one night with a spikily garrulous young woman (Stypulkowska). They play out a kind of psychological striptease that ends with nothing actually happening, since neither will expose any raw feeling to the other. Wajda himself was unhappy with the result, feeling no particular sympathy for such an 'ineffective' hero. If the film still has value, it lies in the compelling lead performances and the vivid portrait of a newly restless milieu – among them (in a small role), one Roman Polanski, clearly eager to leave this Communist *huis clos*. DT

Innocents with Dirty Hands (Les Innocents aux Mains Sales)

(1975, Fr/WGer/It, 125 min)
d Claude Chabrol. *p* André Génoves. *sc* Claude Chabrol. *ph* Jean Rabier. *ed* Jacques Gaillard. *ad* Guy Littaye. *m* Pierre Jansen. *cast* Romy Schneider, Rod Steiger, Paolo Giusti, Jean Rochefort, François Maistre, Pierre Santini, Hans Christian Blech, Dominique Zardi, Henri Attal.
●A superbly stylish and baroque crime thriller which marks a return for Chabrol to the bravura incorporation of pulp conventions that distinguished some of his earlier work. But here the convoluted plot draws us inexorably through a minefield of kaleidoscopically changing relationships at the kind of measured pace that allows the film to accumulate all sorts of tragic resonances. There are innumerable bold strokes as Chabrol treads from irony to irony, ambiguity to ambiguity. Romy Schneider is fascinating as the icy wife plotting to rid herself of her boorish husband (doubts about Steiger fade as the film progresses), and the minor characters – including a characteristically histrionic lawyer and two policemen given to discussing the case over meals of various dimensions – are drawn with absolute precision. VG

Inn of the Frightened People

see Revenge

Inn of the Sixth Happiness, The

(1958, GB, 159 min)
d/p Mark Robson. *sc* Isobel Lennart. *ph* FA Young. *ed* Ernest Walter. *ad* John Box, Geoffrey Drake. *m* Malcolm Arnold. *cast* Ingrid Bergman, Curt Jurgens, Robert Donat, Noel Hood, Athene Seyler, Richard Wattis, Ronald Squire.
●The renowned story of Gladys Aylward (played by Bergman), an ex-housemaid who became a missionary in China in the 1930s. Sketchily scripted and shamelessly glamorised (Aylward bitterly resented being depicted as having had an affair with a Chinese army officer, played by Jurgens), the film is nevertheless a proficiently mounted blend of spectacle and human interest; and the famous climax (Aylward leading the orphaned children over the mountains) is a throat-tightener. The last film of Robert Donat, who looked very ill in his part as the Mandarin. DMcG

In Nome della Legge (In the Name of the Law)

(1949, It, 103 min, b/w)
d Pietro Germi. *p* Luigi Rovere. *sc* Giuseppe Mangione, Mario Monicelli, Federico Fellini, Tullio Pinelli, Aldo Bizzarri, Pietro Germi. *ph* Leonida Barboni. *ed* Rolando Benedetti. *ad* Guido Morici. *m* Carlo Rustichelli. *cast* Massimo Girotti, Charles Vanel, Saro Urzi, Jone Salinas, Camillo Mastrocinque.
●A new magistrate arrives in a baking, crumbling Sicilian village over which Il Barone and his henchmen hold sway. Battling against corruption and inertia, he eventually achieves ... well, nothing much. A murderer is arrested, but at the end Il Barone is still in situ, and despite Rustichelli's thunderous musical salutes, the magistrate still looks to have an impossible mountain to climb. The Mafia charge about the countryside on horseback, a law unto themselves but, it says here, a force for good if appealed to in the right terms. The sense is of Germi and Co desperately wanting to appear positive and optimistic about Sicily's social order, but conceding implicitly that such a response is hardly justified. The movie's climax was featured in *Cinema Paradiso*, where the villagers award it a rousing cheer. BBa

In Old Chicago

(1938, US, 111 min, b/w)
d Henry King. *p* Darryl F Zanuck. *sc* Sonya Levien, Lamar Trotti. *ph* J Peverell Marley. *ed* Barbara McLean. *ad* William Darling, Rudolph Sternad. *m* Louis Silvers. *cast* Tyrone Power, Alice Faye, Don Ameche, Alice Brady, Andy Devine, Brian Donlevy, Phyllis Brooks, Tom Brown.
●MGM famously mounted the West Coast's most notorious earthquake in 1936's *San Francisco*, so rival studio Fox came up with their own equally spectacular disaster flick in this impressive re-creation of the 1871 Great Fire of Chicago. With a star-filled cast and a fitful sense of drama, it's pretty much the same old recipe as the equivalent cycle of megabudget '70s exploiters, but the climactic conflagration – shot on the backlot under such dangerous conditions that no women were allowed on set and stuntmen in dresses took all the female parts – is certainly worth the wait.

In Praise of Love

see Eloge de l'amour

In Praise of Older Women

(1977, Can, 110 min)
d George Kaczender. *p* Robert Lantos, Claude Héroux. *sc* Paul Gottlieb. *ph* Miklos Lente. *ed* George Kaczender, Peter Wintonick. *ad* Wolf Kroeger. *m* Tibor Polgar. *cast* Tom Berenger, Karen Black, Susan Strasberg, Helen Shaver, Marilyn Lightstone, Alexandra Stewart, Marianne McIsaac, Alberta Watson.
●Despite its title, this tediously faithful adaptation of Stephen Vizinczey's book proves to be no more than the picaresque adventures of a highly self-satisfied Hungarian Romeo. Glibly reflecting on the nature of Women, Love, etc., hero and film skate arm-in-arm across an utterly conventional series of sexual encounters: from adolescent seduced by his neighbour (whatever is Karen Black doing here?), via cabaret artiste and 'revolutionary', to the women he meets as a philosophy lecturer in Canada. The film hits a high when one of his pupils has the temerity to declare her sexual preferences. But as that immediately writes her out of the picture, we are back to the soft-focus, softcore actions of a limp prick; a guy who can rise no further than his own dire simile: love is like a supermarket – you can come out with goods you just didn't need. HM

Inquisitor, The

see Garde à Vue

Ins and the Outs, The

see Uns et les Autres, Les

Insatiable

(1980, US, 80 min)
d/p Godfrey Daniels. *sc* Daniel Short. *ph* JR Baggs, Anthony Welsh. *ed* Joe Diamond. *ad* Skip Davis. *m* Don G Sciarrotta, Dennis C Nicklos. *cast* Marilyn Chambers, John C Holmes, Serena, Jesie St James, John Leslie, Mike Ranger, David Morris.
●Stash the old raincoat if you venture out to sample this vehicle for American porno star Chambers which, to judge from the marketing, is being offered in Britain as middle class 'acceptable' skinflick. The original *Insatiable* that set Manhattan dinner parties a-chatter was longer by thirteen minutes, as was stud star Holmes by several inches. The censor has snipped all the hardcore but passed the macho brutality of the foreplay and orgasmic cutaways, leaving a handful of reels that could be projected in any order to the same numbing effect. MA

In Search of Famine (Aakaler Sandhane)

(1981, Ind, 125 min)
d Mrinal Sen. *p* Dhiresh Chakraborty. *sc* Mrinal Sen. *ph* KK Mahajan. *ed* Gangadhar Naskar. *ad* Suresh Chandra. *m* Salil Chowdhury. *cast* Dhritiman Chatterjee, Smita Patil, Sreela Majumdar, Gita Sen, Dipankar Dey.
● A polemical feature from India's leading political film-maker, whose strident radicalism constrasts starkly with the liberal humanism of fellow-Bengali Satyajit Ray. In 1980, a film unit arrives in a Bengali village to film a story about the terrible famine of 1943. However, their failure to understand or communicate with the villagers threatens the viability of the project. The film-makers' intention is to recreate the dire poverty of a disabled peasant's household, yet they seem oblivious to the fact that the lot of the villagers has improved very little in the intervening years. Using this film-within-a-film device, Sen calls into question the insensitive assumptions of the privileged film-makers – an afternoon's shopping for the crew, for example, cleans out the village's vegetable market. NF

Insect Woman, The (Chung Nyo)

(1972, SKor, 110 min)
d Kim Ki-Young. *cast* Namgung Won, Yun Yo-jong, Chon Kye-hyon.
● A delirious, overheated melodrama in which a young woman, forced to support her unappreciative family, slides into a life of prostitution, exploitation and sexual violence, with deadly results. Shot in expressionist style, complete with weird camera effects, this is a movie about madness, inflamed passions, impotence, sadism and, unfortunately, 'Ma Cherie Amour'. GA

Inserts

(1975, GB, 117 min)
d John Byrum. *p* Davina Belling, Clive Parsons. *sc* John Byrum. *ph* Denys Coop. *ed* Michael Bradsell. *ad* John Clark. *cast* Richard Dreyfuss, Jessica Harper, Veronica Cartwright, Bob Hoskins, Stephen Davies.
● Very few sex films are actually about sexuality. While this makes a few moves in that direction, it takes an unconscionably long time about it. Set in '30s Hollywood, the stagebound action takes place on a single set where a faded director (Dreyfuss) has been reduced by the talkies to grinding out a porno silent, complete with gay stud and junked-up ex-DeMille actress. Stale repartee and Golden Age gags proliferate; nor does the action pick up with the arrival of other characters and the porno queen's overdose. But when the film finally reaches its erotic confrontation between Dreyfuss and his backer's girlfriend (beautifully played by Jessica Harper), it does momentarily move into a different league. The censor has spared the scissors here, but someone should have used them on the first hour. DP

Inside Daisy Clover

(1965, US, 128 min)
d Robert Mulligan. *p* Alan J Pakula. *sc* Gavin Lambert. *ph* Charles Lang Jr. *ed* Aaron Stell. *ad* Robert Clatworthy. *m* André Previn. *cast* Natalie Wood, Christopher Plummer, Robert Redford, Ruth Gordon, Katharine Bard, Roddy McDowall.
● This story of the rise and fall of a '30s musical starlette left audiences rather cold on its release, and it's not hard to see why. Gavin Lambert's screenplay (from his own novel) lives in the land of the ambiguous and fey, which is probably why the film now seems subtle and attractive. Wood's performance is no Meryl Streep number (and arguably the better for it), while Redford as her possibly gay husband is extraordinarily handsome, which all adds to the air of innocence. The songs by André and Dory Previn are nothing to get excited about, though. DT

Inside Job

see Alpha Caper, The

Inside Moves

(1980, US, 113 min)
d Richard Donner. *p* Mark M Tanz, RW Goodwin. *sc* Valerie Curtin, Barry Levinson. *ph* Laszlo Kovacs. *ed* Frank Morriss. *pd* Charles Rosen. *m* John Barry. *cast* John Savage, David Morse, Diana Scarwid, Amy Wright, Tony Burton, Bert Remsen, Harold Russell.
●Savage, crippled as a result of a suicide attempt, is reborn in a seedy LA bar where most of the regulars are disabled. As if this weren't difficult enough material in itself, the plot is also determinedly optimistic, mingling its neo-realist surface with dreams of basketball stardom which eventually come true. Sheer eccentricity and ambitiousness place *Inside Moves* above the Kramer class, but ultimately the film only reconfirms that good liberal intentions rarely produce good Hollywood movies.

Inside Out

(1975, GB/WGer, 97 min)
d Peter Duffell. *p* Judd Bernard. *sc* Judd Bernard, Stephen Schneck. *ph* John Coquillon. *ed* Thom Noble. *ad* Peter Lamont. *m* Konrad Elfers. *cast* Telly Savalas, Robert Culp, James Mason, Aldo Ray, Günter Meisner, Adrian Hoven, Charles Korvin.
● After Duffell's impressive *England Made Me*, this vehicle for Telly Savalas' continuing overexposure comes as a disappointment. Based around the springing from gaol of a top Nazi general who can tell a band of ageing misfits about a cache of gold, what emerges is a rather forlorn middle-aged men's fantasy. After some awkward exposition and flashbacks over 30 years, the film settles into a knowing heist caper whose script desperately papers over the implausibilities with wisecracks. One moment of high farce in which the general is confronted with an apparently resurrected Führer in his bunker suggests that events might be taking a belated turn for the better. Sadly, this is not the case. CPe

Insider, The

(1999, US, 158 min)
d Michael Mann. *p* Michael Mann, Pieter Jan Brugge. *sc* Eric Roth, Michael Mann. *ph* Dante Spinotti. *ed* William Goldenberg, Paul Rubell, David Rosenbloom. *pd* Brian Morris. *m* Pieter Bourke, Lisa Gerrard. *cast* Al Pacino, Russell Crowe, Christopher Plummer, Diane Venora, Philip Baker Hall, Lindsay Crouse, Debi Mazar, Stephen Tobolowsky, Colm Feore, Bruce McGill, Gina Gershon, Michael Gambon, Rip Torn, Lynne Thigpen, Pete Hamill, Michael Moore.
● This is the real life tale of two guys battling corporate corruption and compromise: Jeffrey Wigand (Crowe), a research scientist for the tobacco giant Brown & Williamson, which threatens litigation if he breaks a confidentiality agreement about the harmful properties of nicotine; and Lowell Bergman (Pacino), producer for CBS's *60 Minutes*, who encourages Wigand to speak out on TV. A potent aspect of the story is that while it works as a suspenseful *film noir*, it never shortchanges us on the details and issues or oversimplifies the pair's heroism. Moreover, the movie reveals Michael Mann's unparalleled ability to fashion taut suspense from unpromising material. Through careful pacing, music, moody lighting, nervy camera movement and imaginative compositions that subtly play on claustrophobia and agoraphobia, he makes even the most mundane situation suggestive of menace and paranoia, and creates a genuine sense of scale, so that intimate insights into private lives and emotions are balanced by an almost epic sense of historical and political import. Splendid. GA

Insignificance

(1985, GB, 109 min)
d Nicolas Roeg. *p* Jeremy Thomas. *sc* Terry Johnson. *ph* Peter Hannan. *ed* Tony Lawson. *pd* David Brockhurst. *m* Stanley Myers. *cast* Michael Emil, Theresa Russell, Tony Curtis, Gary Busey, Will Sampson.
●1954. As Monroe, Einstein, DiMaggio and McCarthy, Roeg assembles an excellent cast of non-stars, confines them in anonymous hotel rooms, and lets them rip on all his favourite topics: life, love, fame, hate, jealousy, atomic firestorm and the whole damn thing. As usual with Roeg, the firmament is streaming with large ideas and awkward emotions, which grow larger and larger in significance, and most of which come together in a delightful scene when Marilyn (Russell) explains relativity to Einstein (Emil) with the aid of clockwork trains and balloons. Curtis is Senator McCarthy, still witch-hunting phantoms of his mind; Busey is the washed-up ballplayer, aching for Marilyn's return. It may be a chamber piece, but its circumference is vast. CPea

Insomnia

(1997, Nor, 96 min)
d Erik Skjoldbjærg. *p* Petter J Borgli, Tomas Backström, Tom Remlov. *sc* Nikolaj Frobenius. *ph* Erling Thurmann-Andersen. *ed* Håkon Øverås. *pd* Eli Bø. *m* Geir Jenssen. *cast* Stellan Skarsgård, Sverre Anker Ousdal, Bjørn Floberg, Gisken Armand, Maria Bonnevie, Maria Mathiesen.
● Two city cops arrive to help the locals investigate a murder. Jonas (Skarsgård) and partner Erik (Ousdal) are unimpressed by the wastes of northern Norway – land of the midnight sun – and the killer has covered his tracks all too well: the only clue is the victim's school satchel. Jonas uses the bag to lure his man back to the crime scene. As the fog rolls in off the Arctic Ocean, the trap is sprung. In the confusion, Jonas shoots his partner dead, but ducks the blame. Can he solve one murder, salve his conscience, and save himself? The first feature by Erik Skjoldbjærg (a graduate of our National Film and TV School) may be lacking in the plot department, but it wrings some ingenious twists from the formula. The light in this '*film blanc*' assumes a toxic quality, insistent and piercing as the truth – at least in Jonas's exhausted eyes. A superbly controlled actor, Skarsgård shows us an incisive mind shutting out humanity to fall into perilous complicity with his prey. A taut and distinctive example of genre film-making. TCh

Inspecteur Lavardin

(1986, Fr, 100 min)
d Claude Chabrol. *p* Marin Karmitz. *sc* Claude Chabrol, Dominique Roulet. *ph* Jean Rabier. *ed* Monique Fardoulis, Angela Braga-Mermet. *ad* Françoise Benoît-Fresco. *m* Matthieu Chabrol. *cast* Jean Poiret, Jean-Claude Brialy, Bernadette Lafont, Jean-Luc Bideau, Jacques Dacqmine, Hermine Clair.
● Shortly after investigating the banning as blasphemous of a play entitled 'Our Father Which Farts in Heaven', a high-minded paterfamilias is found dead on the beach, PIG scrawled insultingly on his naked backside. With the widow offering a regal display of indifference, a teenage stepdaughter skulking furtively in drug-pushing circles, and a gay uncle gloating madly over his collection of glass eyes, this is Chabrol at odds with the bourgeoisie again. But there is a difference as Poiret's police inspector arrives for his second murder investigation following *Cop au Vin*, this time trailing memories of his former love for the widow, a fallen angel who has innocently sinned in her emotional affairs. Discovering what amounts to a paradise lost, Lavardin elects to play God in order to rout the otherwise unassailable forces of evil. Strangely tender, bizarrely funny, with gorgeous performances from Lafont (the widow) and Brialy (the uncle), this is Chabrol back to the mood of eccentric metaphysical mystery he mined in the marvellous *Ten Days' Wonder*. TM

Inspector Calls, An

(1954, GB, 79 min, b/w)
d Guy Hamilton. *p* AD Peters. *sc* Desmond Davis. *ph* Ted Scaife. *ed* Alan Osbiston. *ad* Joseph Bato. *m* Francis Chagrin. *cast* Alastair Sim, Jane Wenham, Arthur Young, Olga Lindo, Brian Worth, Bryan Forbes, George Cole.

●JB Priestley's play comes to the screen (adapted by Desmond Davis) with a minimum of cinematic imagination. Alastair Sim is still highly watchable, however, as the Yorkshire policeman who materialises in the midst of a comfortably off Edwardian family to reveal how each one of its complacent members bears some responsibility in the suicide of a pregnant pauper. The play survives, just. TJ

Inspector Clouseau

(1968, US, 96 min)
d Bud Yorkin. *p* Lewis J Rachmil. *sc* Tom Waldman, Frank Waldman. *ph* Arthur Ibbetson. *ed* John Victor Smith. *pd* Michael Stringer. *m* Ken Thorne. *cast* Alan Arkin, Delia Boccardo, Frank Finlay, Patrick Cargill, Beryl Reid, Barry Foster, Michael Ripper, Tutte Lemkow.

●The bumbling French policeman – immortalised by Peter Sellers, but only impersonated here by Alan Arkin – is called to Swinging London to help the Yard track down a gang using the proceeds of the Great Train Robbery to siphon funds from every bank on Swiss soil. Sorely contrived.

Inspector Gadget

(1999, US, 78 min)
d David Kellogg. *p* Jordan Kerner, Roger Birnbaum, Andy Heyward. *sc* Kerry Ehrin, Zak Penn. *ph* Adam Greenberg. *ed* Thom Noble, Alan Cody. *pd* Michael White, Leslie Dilley. *m* John Debney. *cast* Matthew Broderick, Rupert Everett, Joely Fisher, Michelle Trachtenberg, Andy Dick, Cheri Oteri, Michael G Hagerty, Dabney Coleman, DL Hughley, René Auberjonois.

●Disney's live-action rendition of the animated TV series starts encouragingly enough, in cartoon style – replete with jerky camera movements – in which geeky security guard John Brown (Broderick) apprehends a baddie. The arrest goes awry, however, and John finds himself strung up in a hospital bed – the perfect candidate, thinks Government scientist Dr Brenda Bradford (Fisher), on whom to try out a wacky new experiment. Unaware of her intentions, the helpless John has every conceivable crime-fighting gizmo grafted to his body; days later, sporting a Bogart-like grin, he stumbles out of hospital as the Government's new one-man police force, a veritable Swiss Army Knife on legs. It's roughly at this point (about 10 minutes in) that the film goes horribly pear shaped. The plot jackknifes as soon as Everett enters the fray as the obligatory English baddie, with a grand scheme to build a rogue clone of the inspector. DA

Instinct

(1999, US, 124 min)
d John Turteltaub. *p* Michael Taylor, Barbara Boyle. *sc* Gerald DiPego. *ph* Pilippe Rousselot. *ed* Richard Francis-Bruce. *pd* Garreth Stover. *m* Danny Elfman. *cast* Anthony Hopkins, Cuba Gooding Jr., Donald Sutherland, Maura Tierney, George Dzundza, John Ashton, John Aylward, Thomas Q Morris.

●In the world's eyes, renowned primatologist Ethan Powell (Hopkins) has gone mad: when park rangers tried to drag him away from a group of gorillas, he murdered two of them. Now he has a chance to be 'reassessed', and ambitious psychotherapist Theo Calder (Gooding) wants the case. Powell, though, has a few surprises in store. This is not a breezy ride. Set mostly in a high security detention centre, it has one of those soundtracks that beat you around the head. Similarly, the interaction between the men is like a series of body blows. The effect is not macho; this is a film about controlling the desire to 'penetrate'. Theo – his high, soft voice so at odds with Powell's growl – is that rare thing, a virginal male whose sexuality is allowed to remain undefined. And Gooding makes you believe in the contradiction. Hopkins' contribution is equally intense, even Lear-like in its muddle of wisdom, spite and foolishness. But you can't watch him without thinking of *Silence of the Lambs*. Worse, in the film's second half, the script's often acute observations about prisons and systems of control are overwhelmed by ocean-sized dollops of melodrama. CO'Su

Institute Benjamenta

(1995, GB, 105 min, b/w)
d Brothers Quay. *p* Keith Griffiths, Janine Marmot. *sc* Alan Passes, Brothers Quay. *ph* Nic Knowland. *ed* Larry Sider. *pd* Jennifer Kernke. *m* Lech Jankowski. *cast* Mark Rylance, Gottfried John, Alice Krige, Daniel Smith, Joseph Alessi, Jonathan Stone.

●Sometime this century, somewhere in Europe: Jakob von Gunten (Rylance) enrols at the Institute Benjamenta, a run-down edifice headed by an eccentric tyrant (John) and dedicated to the training of suitably unambitious, humble servants. Though Jakob readily submits to the repetitive regime of incredibly banal lessons in servility, he begins to wonder whether he might be sufficiently princely to rescue his melancholy tutor, Benjamenta's sister Lisa (Krige), from the suffocating half-life she leads inside the school's sinister, shadowy walls. Inspired by the writings of Swiss novelist Robert Walser, the first feature from the Brothers Quay is as outlandishly beautiful, bizarre, mysterious and inventive as one might expect; more surprising, perhaps, given their history as animators specialising in puppetry and rather abstract metaphor, is the firm grasp of narrative and the intense performances elicited from a strong international cast. Overall, the film can be seen as a (finally subversive) variation on traditional fairytale motifs, as an allegory on our progress through – as an alternative title would have it – 'This Dream People Call Human Life', or as a loving tribute to cinema's fantastic capacity for poetry. Genuinely unsettling. GA

Instrument: Ten Years with the Band Fugazi

(1998, US, 115 min, col & b/w)
d/p Jem Cohen, Fugazi. *ph* Jem Cohen. *ed* Jem Cohen, Fugazi, David Frankel. *with* Ian MacKaye, Guy Picciotto, Joe Lally, Brendan Canty

●This feature length 'measurement' (the title plays with the idea of musicians taking measure of their world) of the US alt-rock band Fugazi ('a messed-up situation') collates material of the band at work and play, on the road and on public access TV, with portraits of and interviews with their fans and other concertgoers. Its core, however, is built around promo- and film-maker Jem Cohen's own accumulation of film and video footage spanning a decade. The documentary emphasises what makes the band special both onstage (its angular, distended, semi-improvised brand of agit-rock and freeform performance) and off (a dedication to affordable popular access, commercial independence and political activism), but not, significantly, on record – and the songs themselves not being immediately endearing to the uninitiated, the incorporation of 20-odd numbers over two hours can certainly wear. NB

Intelligence Men, The

(1965, GB, 104 min)
d Robert Asher. *p* Hugh Stewart. *sc* SC Green, RM Hills. *ph* Jack Asher. *ed* Gerry Hambling. *ad* Carmen Dillon. *m* Philip Green. *cast* Eric Morecambe, Ernie Wise, William Franklyn, April Olrich, Gloria Paul, Richard Vernon, Warren Mitchell, Tutte Lemkow, Peter Bull.

●In the late '50s and early '60s, producer Hugh Stewart had success with Norman Wisdom. He hoped to do even better with Eric and Ernie, whose genius was already evident to millions of British TV viewers. Unfortunately, the pair made only three films, and none had the improvisatory wit or cheek of their best TV work. This is their debut, a feeble spy spoof, culminating in the attempted assassination of a Russian ballerina (Olrich) during a performance of *Swan Lake* at Covent Garden. A long way short of a classic, but it does have its sunshine moments. GM

Interiors

(1978, US, 91 min)
d Woody Allen. *p* Charles H Joffe, Jack Rollins. *sc* Woody Allen. *ph* Gordon Willis. *ed* Ralph Rosenblum. *pd* Mel Bourne. cast Kristin Griffith, Mary Beth Hurt, Richard Jordan, Diane Keaton, EG Marshall, Geraldine Page, Maureen Stapleton, Sam Waterston.

●*Interiors* must rank as one of the most spectacular changes of direction for an American artist since Clint Eastwood made *Breezy*. Working as director and writer only, Allen put together a beautifully acted, lyrically written exploration of an intelligent middle class American family whose three grown-up daughters are thunderstruck when their father trades in his elegant depressive wife for a lively, but jarringly vulgar, divorcee. The film has moments of humour, but they are integrated into a totally serious structure which isolates the family's countervailing tensions with a scalpel-like penetration. Only in a single character, the failed husband of one of the daughters, does the tone falter towards soap. Otherwise the approach is rock steady and, if the film's surface invites superficial comparisons with Bergman, its real roots lie in the very finest American art. DP

Interlude

(1957, US, 90 min)
d Douglas Sirk. *p* Ross Hunter. *sc* Daniel Fuchs, Franklin Coen. *ph* William H Daniels. *ed* Russell.Schoengarth. *ad* Alexander Golitzen, Robert E Smith. *m* Frank Skinner. *cast* June Allyson, Rossano Brazzi, Marianne Koch, Françoise Rosay, Keith Andes, Jane Wyatt.

●A minor but entirely delightful film, based on a James M Cain story previously filmed in 1939 by John M Stahl as *When Tomorrow Comes*: American-girl-in-Europe falls in love with famous classical conductor (Brazzi, oozing charm from every pore). Redolent with guidebook sentiment, and resolutely egalitarian, Sirk's film (as always) subverts the crude dictates of his studio model. The lover comes to rely increasingly on the heroine's 'naïve' strength, and Sirk uses a 'dark secret' subplot (Brazzi's dramatically insane wife) to weave fairytale darkness into a landscape of wide, clear colour. The woman's desire, and her (transient) happiness are allowed to transcend the usually tyrannical alternative: torrid passion or marital affection. CA

Interlude

(1968, GB, 113 min)
d Kevin Billington. *p* David Deutsch. *sc* Lee Langley, Hugh Leonard. *ph* Gerry Fisher. *ed* Bert Bates. *pd* Tony Woollard. *m* Georges Delerue. *cast* Oskar Werner, Barbara Ferris, Virginia Maskell, Donald Sutherland, Nora Swinburne, Alan Webb, Bernard Kay, John Cleese, Derek Jacobi.

●A remake of Sirk's 1958 film about a young girl who falls in love with a married musician seemed a bizarre choice for Billington's first film. Updated to contemporary London and featuring an *Evening Standard* journalist as the heroine, it is an often successful attempt to relate the clichéd story to people working and living against a precisely drawn (albeit trendy) background. Billington mercifully avoids the excesses of 'Swinging London', and his observant delineation of the discrepancy between the characters' would-be sophistication and their actual stock responses is, on the whole, well supported by the performances. CPe

Intermezzo (aka Escape to Happiness)

(1939, US, 69 min, b/w)
d Gregory Ratoff. *p* David O Selznick. *sc* George O'Neil. *ph* Gregg Toland. *ed* Hal C Kern, Francis D Lyon. *ad* Lyle R Wheeler. *cast* Leslie Howard, Ingrid Bergman, Edna Best, Cecil Kellaway, John Halliday.

●The ultimate in coffee table weepies, with Howard's unhappily married violinist and Bergman's sympathetic piano teacher making sweet music together during a Riviera idyll, ended when paternal longings drag him reluctantly home and the child has a convenient accident to effect marital reconciliation. Making her radiant Hollywood debut in a part she had played in Sweden, Bergman almost makes you believe the tosh, but Howard (dubbed on violin by Jascha Heifetz) comes on like a smarmy elocution teacher, enunciating atrocious dialogue full of arch emptinesses. TM

Internal Affairs

(1990, US, 115 min)
d Mike Figgis. *p* Frank Mancuso Jr. *sc* Henry Bean. *ph* John A Alonzo. *ed* Robert Estrin. *pd* Waldemar Kalinowski. *m* Mike Figgis, Anthony Marinelli, Brian Banks. *cast* Richard Gere, Andy Garcia, Nancy Travis, Laurie Metcalf, Richard Bradford, William Baldwin, Michael Beach, Faye Grant, Katherine Borowitz, John Kapelos, Annabella Sciorra.

●Gere (a brilliant return to form) plays an experienced LA street cop who clashes with the tight-assed pen-pushers from Internal Affairs ('the cops of the cops'). But what do these bureaucrats (Garcia and Metcalf) know? Well, for a start, they know that Gere's ex-wives own a fortune in real estate, and that his partner's wife drives a Merc and wears a Rolex. At this point, the morality begins to shift and slide, leaving no clear identification figure. A key element in Gere's modus operandi is his ability to identify and exploit the weaknesses of others, something he uses to advantage against Garcia, with taunts about his wife's alleged infidelity. But as the Internal Affairs officers home in on Gere's strung-out partner (Baldwin), they show much the same killer instinct. Also, impressively, the film highlights both the working-class contempt Gere feels for college-boy Garcia, and the fact that Garcia's lesbian partner seems driven by resentment of Gere's macho persona. How much of this was in Henry Bean's excellent script is impossible to tell, but Figgis (in his first American feature) handles the explosive action and the psychological undercurrents with equal assurance. Dark, dangerous and disturbing. NF

International House

(1933, US, 73 min, b/w)
d A Edward Sutherland. *sc* Francis Martin, Walter DeLeon, Lou Heifetz, Neil Brant. *ph* Ernest Haller. *songs* Ralph Rainger, Leo Robin. *cast* WC Fields, George Burns, Gracie Allen, Peggy Hopkins Joyce, Stuart Erwin, Franklin Pangborn, Bela Lugosi, Rudy Vallee, Sterling Holloway, Cab Calloway and His Band.

● A bizarre, juicy comedy in which dozens of eccentric characters are quarantined in a Shanghai hotel where a crazy local doctor has devised a 'radioscope' – a television set. Over the airwaves we get turns by Rudy Vallee, Baby Rose Marie, and Cab Calloway singing about 'that funny reefer man'. Meanwhile, Burns and Allen perform their shtick, and the incomparable WC Fields cocks a snook at Prohibition by his ostentatious consumption of beer – in flight too! TCh

International Velvet

(1978, GB, 132 min)
d/p/sc Bryan Forbes. *ph* Tony Imi, Edward R Brown. *ed* Timothy Gee. *pd* Keith Wilson. *m* Francis Lai. *cast* Tatum O'Neal, Christopher Plummer, Anthony Hopkins, Nanette Newman, Peter Barkworth, Dinsdale Landen.

● A pretty equestrian fairytale, in which an orphaned American teenager (O'Neal) sets her sights on a Gold Medal for Great Britain in the 3-day event at some future South African Olympic Games. This gelatinous story, devised by producer/director Forbes, is so unashamedly sentimental, so resolutely devoid of authentic emotion or motivation, that one can only marvel at its lavish audacity. Do families still go to such tosh? Forbes presumably banked the film's appeal on middle-aged parents recalling Elizabeth Taylor winning the Grand National in *National Velvet* and hauling their children off to see this, its woeful – and very belated – sequel. JPy

Internecine Project, The

(1974, GB, 89 min)
d Ken Hughes. *p* Barry Levinson, Andrew Donally. *sc* Barry Levinson, Jonathan Lynn. *ph* Geoffrey Unsworth. *ed* John Shirley. *pd* Geoffrey Drake. *m* Roy Budd. *cast* James Coburn, Lee Grant, Harry Andrews, Ian Hendry, Michael Jayston, Keenan Wynn, David Swift, Julian Glover.

● An American professor of economics (Coburn) gets offered a top level advisory job in Washington, on condition that he eliminates four people in London who operate his European industrial espionage network. Once under way, *The Internecine Project* turns into a straightforward, very enjoyable if somewhat implausible murder story. Rather than despatch his victims himself, Coburn sets them to kill each other by orchestrating their motives and their moves. Despite the plot turning around a succession of calls from conveniently empty public phone boxes (all in working order), and the presence of a stereotype female journalist acting as Coburn's conscience, the film gains in weight thanks to its topical implications. All in all, a neat and unpretentious thriller that offers more food for thought than most such unashamedly commercial movies. CPe

Interno Berlinele

see Berlin Affair, The

Interno di un Convento, L'

see Behind Convent Walls

Interrogation (Przesluchanie)

(1982, Pol, 116 min)
d/sc Ryszard Bugajski. *ph* Jacek Petrycki. *ed* Katarzyna Maciejko, Jacek Palubinsky. *ad* Janusz Sosnowski, Edward Papierski, Magdalena Dipont, Jan Szwagrsyk. *cast* Krystyna Janda, Adama Ferencego, Agnieszka Holland, Janusz Gajos, Anna Romantowska.

● Bugajski's horrifying film was originally banned under martial law. When cabaret artiste Tonia (Janda) is imprisoned without explanation, she assumes there has been a bureaucratic slip-up. Gradually, however, it becomes clear she is there for a reason: betrayal. Days become months. The monotonous deprivation of the prison cell is varied only by the persuasion, intimidation and torture of interrogation, but Tonia will not break. If, in a sense, this is a period film twice over – made in '82, set in '51 – its impact is as current as it ever was, and its allegorical implications have proved prophetic: the trajectory is very much freedom through fortitude and perseverance. Drained of colour, largely without music, resolutely intimate, it makes for a harrowing couple of hours, but the shifting power-plays between Tonia and her inquisitors are subtly conveyed, while the nuances distinguishing subjective and objective guilt inevitably suggest Kafka and Orwell. TCh

Intersection

(1994, US, 98 min)
d Mark Rydell. *p* Bud Yorkin, Mark Rydell. *sc* David Rayfiel, Marshall Brickman. *ph* Vilmos Zsigmond. *ed* Mark Warner. *pd* Harold Michelson. *m* James Newton Howard. *cast* Richard Gere, Sharon Stone, Lolita Davidovich, Martin Landau, David Selby, Jenny Morrison.

● A reworking of Claude Sautet's *Les Choses de la Vie* (1970), this meticulously directed, flawlessly written, romantic melodrama unfolds in flashback – in the time it takes for a fatal car accident to happen. Successful architect Vincent Eastman (Gere) is experiencing a mid-life crisis: his 16-year marriage to the equally talented Sally (Stone) is empty, held together only by inertia and a mutual responsibility to their daughter Megan (Morrison). Vincent's affair with sensual, spontaneous Olivia (Davidovich) at first seems the perfect way out, yet he continues to hanker for the familiar pleasures his loveless marriage continues to offer. As he vacillates, the failure to choose between wife and mistress causes pain and confusion all round. Less neurotic and sexually charged than usual, Gere digs deep to find the source of his character's chronic indecisiveness. The casting of the vampish Stone as a socially proper, sexually repressed woman is a bold stroke, and Davidovich makes much of her role as the emotionally demanding 'other woman'. NF

Interview With the Vampire

(1994, US, 122 min)
d Neil Jordan. *p* Stephen Woolley, David Geffen. *sc* Anna Rice. *ph* Philippe Rousselot. *ed* Mick Audsley, Joke van Wijk. *pd* Dante Ferretti. *m* Elliot Goldenthal. *cast* Tom Cruise, Brad Pitt, Antonio Banderas, Stephen Rea, Christian Slater, Kirsten Dunst, Domiziana Giordano, Thandie Newton, Roger Lloyd Pack.

● Contemporary San Francisco – Louis de Pointe du Lac (Pitt) tells a journalist (Slater) the strange details of his life: how two centuries earlier he was attacked by the degenerate vampire Lestat (Cruise); how he rejected his mentor's advice by feeding on rats and poodles; how the pair 'adopted' a young orphan, Claudia (Dunst), whose thirst for blood outstripped even Lestat's; how their individual inclinations and ethical codes gave rise to lethal tensions between the various members of this bizarre, undead 'family'; and so on. For all its ambitions and visual flair, Jordan's adaptation of Anne Rice's novel is a disappointment. It's not only not scary, it's also dull and conventional. True, the emphasis on Dante Ferretti's lavish production design makes for some heavy dollops of 'atmosphere'; true, too, that the acting is adequate. The major problem lies with Rice's own script which is dramatically repetitive and philosophically banal. Profoundly unremarkable. GA

Intervista

(1987, It, 105 min)
d Federico Fellini. *p* Ibrahim Moussa. *sc* Federico Fellini, Gianfranco Angelucci. *ph* Tonino Delli Colli. *ed* Nino Baragli. *pd* Danilo Donati. *m* Nicola Piovani. *cast* Federico Fellini, Marcello Mastroianni, Anita Ekberg, Sergio Rubini, Maurizio Mein, Lara Vendel.

● The wait is over! Here is yet another episode from Fellini's relentlessly colourful past: a free-form reminiscence of his first arrival in the Cinecittà studios, prompted by questions from a Japanese TV crew. The searching period reconstruction includes some dark notes (peasants sing Fascist anthems in the fields), but this is mostly a starry eyed celebration of the time when Movies were still Magic, complete with a bitter-sweet pastiche Nino Rota score. As expected, Mastroianni pops up, and Fellini sweeps everyone off to Anita Ekberg's villa, where a clip from *La Dolce Vita* is screened and quiet tears are shed for the Good Old Days. Groundbreaking stuff. TR

In That Land (V toi Stranje)

(1997, Rus, 85 min)
d Lidia Bobrova. *cast* Dmitri Clopov, Vladimir Borchaninov, Anna Ovsiannikova, Alexander Stakheev, Svetlana Gaytan.

● The spectre of allegory haunts every frame of this handsome and intriguing movie, but clear-cut meanings remain elusive. The mayor of a snowbound rural community in the north faces two severe problems: traditional farming skills are dying out because of the exodus of young people to the cities, and too many of the remaining residents are drinking themselves to death on moonshine liquor. Director Lidia Bobrova spreads her dramatic focus evenly between several households, building up a viable microcosm of Russian society in the late 1990s; there are elements of dark, absurdist humour, but in general she's less inclined than her contemporary Muratova to stress regressive and stupid tendencies. Her ending, appropriately enough, leaves us on a knife edge: will the ex-con brought into the village as a mail-order husband turn out to be the community's saviour or its nemesis? TR

In the Bedroom

(2001, US, 130 min)
d Todd Field. *p* Graham Leader, Ross Katz, Todd Field. *sc* Rob Festinger, Todd Field. *ph* Antonio Calvache. *ed* Frank Reynolds. *pd* Shannon Hart. *m* Thomas Newman. *cast* Sissy Spacek, Tom Wilkinson, Nick Stahl, William Mapother, William Wise, Celia Weston, Marisa Tomei, Karen Allen.

● A supremely confident, controlled US indie, this debut from actor Field isn't the sex romp its title might suggest, but a well-tempered study of communion and claustrophobia, trespass and transgression. In the first place it's an immaculate family portrait of a middle-aged New England couple (Spacek and Wilkinson) on the brink of losing their grown son (Stahl) to college, hoping his fling with an older single-mum (Tomei) won't outlast the summer. The film conveys these relationships, their intimacies and tensions, with enveloping ease and lucidity, before taking first one and then another abrupt turn into unpredictable terrain. All this is acted with immense delicacy and authority so that when peace erupts, the emotional violence is visceral. At the film's core is a portrait of grief and the healing process, evoked with remarkable containment by Spacek and Wilkinson, she burrowing deep into repressed reproachfulness, he correspondingly lost in a daze of uncertainty. And if the final stage alone nudges up against genre bounds, it none the less raises some pertinent questions. Meanings here are fluid, but ultimately it's a film about the implacable face of bourgeois composure: the surface is ruffled, something stirs in the deep, but finally tranquillity reasserts itself. NB

In the Belly of the Dragon (Dans le Ventre du Dragon)

(1989, Can, 102 min)
d Yves Simoneau. *p* Michel Gauthier. *sc* Yves Simoneau, Pierre Revelin, Marcel Beaulieu. *ph* Alain Dostie. *ed* André Corriveau. *ad* Norman Sarrazin. *m* Richard Grégoire. *cast* Rémy Girard, Michel Coté, David La Haye, Pierre Curzi.

● Simoneau's commendable shot at a sci-fi fantasy with teeth is better than most contemporary Canadian movies, but that isn't saying much. A butch young man drops out of his dead-end job (delivering shop brochures to strife-torn tenements) and sells his body to a mysterious research institute, whose crazed woman diretcor is bent on maximising brain power without regard for the physical cost to her subjects. The movie wants to be a cross between *Brazil* and *Subway*, but it's crippled by unimaginitive designs and weak scripting; it comes closest to working in its elements of black comedy, which peter out around the half-way mark. TR

In the Best Interests of the Children

(1977, US, 51 min)
d Elizabeth Stevens, Cathy Zheutlin, Frances Reid. *with* Betty Knickerbocker, Lorraine Norman, Pat Norman, Bernice Augenbraun, Camille Le Grand.

● A documentary which argues the right of lesbian mothers to custody of their children. Constructed in a series of interviews with several mothers and their staggeringly articulate children, the film eschews any real analysis of the situation, but works instead on an emotive level to convince that lesbians are really OK people. Thus, unfortunately, the visual correlative to the spoken statement is given in the clichéd form of these particular women at their housewifely best (the film's homely, non-alienating stance was designed for TV). HM

In the Bleak Midwinter (aka A Midwinter's Tale)

(1995, GB, 98 min, b/w)
d Kenneth Branagh. *p* David Barron. *sc* Keneth Branagh. *ph* Roger Lanser. *ed* Neil Farrell. *pd* Tim Harvey*m* Jimmy Yuill. *cast* Richard Briers, Hetta Charnley, Joan Collins, Nicholas Farrell, Michael Maloney, Julia Sawalha, Celia Imrie, Jennifer Saunders, John Sessions.

● After the monstrous hubris of *Mary Shelley's Frankenstein*, Branagh was wise to get back to basics with this unpretentious backstage comedy, and to cede the limelight to a stand-in. That said, Maloney's actor-director Joe Harper is irresistibly Branagh-esque. A passionate apostle of Shakespeare, Joe's determined to mount his own production of *Hamlet*, even if it means the last of his meagre savings and a mere week's rehearsal in a rundown country church. With the help of his agent (Collins), he rounds up a group of unlikely thespians desperate enough to work for nothing over Christmas (Briers, Farrell, Sawalha). Shot quickly and cheaply, this is Branagh's most modest film, and his most successful. This is not to say there aren't irritations: too many of the jokes have seen better days, and the sit-com characterisations can't support the director's increasingly sentimental designs on them. Still, Branagh knows his way round an ensemble, his screenplay combines heartfelt commitment to the theatre with a healthy degree of self-mockery, and the film is crisply photographed in b/w. A palpable hit. TCh

In the Company of Men

(1997, US, 93 min)
d Neil LaBute. *p* Mark Archer, Stephen Pevner. *sc* Neil LaBute. *ph* Tom Hettinger. *ed* Joel Plotch. *pd* Julia Henkel. *m* Ken Williams, Karel Roessingn. *cast* Aaron Eckhart, Matt Malloy, Stacy Edwards, Emily Cline, Jason Dixie.

● Playwright Neil LaBute's film-directing debut is an impressively witty yet unsettling study of male insecurity, misogyny and rivalry. Away on a six-week business trip in a strange town, grouchy, resentful thirty-something execs Eckhart and Malloy decide to take revenge for their recently broken relationships by choosing a vulnerable, lonely woman for both of them (unbeknown to her) to date and dump. The scheme is put into action with deaf typist Edwards (a remarkable performance), but the best laid plans… Poised precariously but skilfully between realism and allegory, black comedy and straight drama, the movie makes the very most of its few locations by opting for a strangely timeless feel, and by focusing attention squarely on the three central performances and LaBute's clever, insightful script. Cruel, cool and pleasingly provocative. GA

In the Deep Woods

(1992, US, 94 min)
d Charles Correll. *p* Joe Fields, Ron Gilbert. *sc* Robert Nathan, Robert Rosenblum. *ph* James Glennon. *ed* Mark W Rosenbaum. *pd* Jonathan Carlson. *m* Sylvester LeVay. *cast* Anthony Perkins, Rosanna Arquette, Will Patton, DW Moffett.

● Perkins' last film isn't one you'd care to remember him by. He looks haggard and tired as a private investigator on the trail of the 'Deep Woods' killer, who's already murdered one of Arquette's best pals and looks like he's made her his next target. A make-weight filler, from a novel by Nicholas Conde, for completists only. Straight to video in Britain. TJ

In Thee I Trust (Na Tebya Upovayu)

(1993, Rus, 86 min)
d Elena Tsiplakova. *p* Alexander Mikhailov. *sc* Nadejda Pokornaya. *ph* Ilia Diomin. *ed* Natalia Volchek. *ad* Vladimir Murzin, Alexander Kholodtsev. *m* Valery Miagkih. *cast* Evgeniya Dobrovolskaya, Natasha Sokoreva, Irina Rozanova, Vladimir Ilyin, Dimitri Pevtsov..

● Alla, a lonely, disfigured woman, takes a priest's advice and volunteers at the local orphanage. It's a grim institution, the staff hardened by corruption and contempt for their charges, the facilities barely adequate. But Alla feels for the children and they respond to her warmth. The authority figures are perhaps too harsh, and the kids too cute, but this is a hard-hitting, moving film about the lost souls of the 'New Russia'. TCh

In the Forest

(1978, GB, 80 min, b/w)
d/p/sc Phil Mulloy. *ph* Ian Dobbie. *ed* Phil Mulloy. *ad* Anne Marie Schöne, Tina Carr, Sue Barnes. *m* Carys Hughes. *cast* Barrie Houghton, Anthony O'Donnell, Ellen Sheean, Joby Blanchard, Nick Burton, Larry Dann.

● An English *Travelling Players?* Three peasant types trek across a forest…and through a polemically structured account of 400 years of British history. Not the 'standard' history of monarchs, battles, disasters and dates (although all of those are there), but an 'alternative' history of political and cultural fragments. What emerges is a militant analysis of the origins of the modern British working class, fashioned by Mulloy with exceptional acuity and a brilliant gift for synthesis. TR

In the French Style

(1962, US/Fr, 105 min)
d Robert Parrish. *p* Robert Parrish, Irwin Shaw. *sc* Irwin Shaw. *ph* Michel Kelber. *ed* Renée Lichtig. *ad* Rino Mondellini. *m* Joseph Kosma. *cast* Jean Seberg, Stanley Baker, Philippe Forquet, Jack Hedley, Addison Powell, James Leo Herlihy, Claudine Auger, Moustache.

● An ambitious but ultimately flawed attempt to capture the feelings of an American art student in Paris (Seberg) and her passionate but brief love affairs (with Stanley Baker, among others). For Parisophiles, there's some really nice location photography (by Michel Kelber), but Irwin Shaw's scripts from two of his own short stories doesn't succeed in avoiding the obvious sentimental pitfalls. DP

In the Good Old Summertime

(1949, US, 102 min)
d Robert Z Leonard. *p* Joe Pasternak. *sc* Albert Hackett, Frances Goodrich, Ivan Tors. *ph* Harry Stradling. *ed* Adrienne Fazan. *ad* Randall Duell. *songs* George Evans, Fred Fisher, others. *cast* Judy Garland, Van Johnson, SZ Sakall, Spring Byington, Buster Keaton, Clinton Sundberg, Liza Minnelli.

● A musical remake of Lubitsch's *The Shop Around the Corner*, with the period moved back to 1906, the setting shifted to a Chicago music store, and Garland at her most captivating as the shop assistant waging a war of attrition with her bossy superior (Johnson), unaware that he is the lonelyhearts pen pal with whom she has already fallen in love. The fragile charm is rather let down by an indifferent score, although Garland makes the most of her numbers and the rest of the cast give sterling support. Liza Minnelli made her bow as the child at the end. TM

In the Heat of the Night

(1967, US, 109 min)
d Norman Jewison. *p* Walter Mirisch. *sc* Stirling Silliphant. *ph* Haskell Wexler. *ed* Hal Ashby. *ad* Paul Groesse. *m* Quincy Jones. *cast* Sidney Poitier, Rod Steiger, Warren Oates, Quentin Dean, James Patterson, Lee Grant, Scott Wilson, Matt Clark.

● Jewison's multi-Oscared murder melodrama of racial tension – set in a small Mississippi cotton town where Steiger's bigoted sheriff finds himself forced into collaboration with Poitier's arrogant black homicide expert from Philadelphia – oozes sufficient Southern sweat and features enough admirably crumpled character faces to make up for its over-strident liberal rhetoric. It certainly ranks as superior in every respect to the two Virgil Tibbs vehicles (*They Call Me MISTER Tibbs!* and *The Organisation*) with which Poitier subsequently exploited his homicide cop role. Stirling Silliphant's adaptation of the John Ball novel was still deemed controversial enough, in 1967, to require the recreation of a Mississippi small town in the less sensitive environs of Illinois. PT

In the Heat of the Sun (Yang-guang Canlan de Rizi)

(1994, China, 134 min)
d Jiang Wen. *p* Ki Po, Hsu An-chin, Gou Youliang. *sc* Jiang Wen. *ph* Gu Changwei. *ed* Zhou Ying. *cast* Xia Yu, Ning Jing, Geng Le, Shang Nan, Tao Hong, Siqin Gaowa.

● Actor Jiang Wen's first feature is a archetypal rites-of-passage film about a group of boys entering puberty one hot summer in Beijing: fooling around, showing off and bonding, spying on girls, clashing with other gangs, dealing with pesky erections. Two things distinguish it. One is Jiang's own wry voice-over, admitting that these are romanticised and sometimes wished-for episodes from his own childhood. The other is the mid-1970s setting, the dog days of the Cultural Revolution, after all the Maoist frenzy, which it shows as no movie has ever done before. TR

In the King of Prussia

(1982, US, 90 min)
d/p/sc Emile de Antonio. *ph* Judy Irola. *ed* Mark Pines. *with* 'The Plowshares Eight', Martin Sheen, John Randolph Jones, Richard Sisk, George Tynan, John Connelly.

● Reconstructing the trial that followed a 1980 direct action against a General Electric nuclear weapons facility (the title refers to the name of the plant), this has the 'Plowshares Eight' (Daniel and Philip Berrigan, et al) as their eloquent selves, and Martin Sheen in excellent greasy form as the judge. With all the structural advantages of a courtroom drama, it's a wonderful vehicle for the radical Christian anti-nuclear message, and as agitprop it's far superior to even well-done preaching-to-the-converted documentaries such as *Dark Circle*. An intense, low-key production, which itself shows up the flashy decontextualising of *Atomic Cafe*, it ranges from Nagasaki survivors, through neighbours of a plutonium plant, to the fiasco of Diablo, the nuclear plant described as 'the most analysed building in the world', which at the last minute turned out to have been built back to front. JCo

In the Line of Fire

(1993, US, 129 min)
d Wolfgang Petersen. *p* Jeff Apple. *sc* Jeff Maguire. *ph* John Bailey. *ed* Anne V Coates. *pd* Lilly Kilvert. *m* Ennio Morricone. *cast* Clint Eastwood, John Malkovich, Rene Russo, Dylan McDermott, Gary Cole, Fred Dalton Thomas, John Mahoney.

● An enjoyably slick if not unfamiliar thriller (by Jeff Maguire) in which the fiendishly brilliant psycho-killer repeatedly taunts the cop to man-to-man confrontation. As Secret Service agent Horrigan, Eastwood is as outspokenly independent as ever: at odds with superiors, caught in a teasing, argumentative romance with colleague Lilly Raines (Russo), and determined to do his job. This time, however, he's haunted by the past (30 years ago he failed to stop the bullet that killed Kennedy) and when he learns that a would-be assassin (Malkovich) has plans for the current Presidential elections, professional duty provides the opportunity for personal redemption or personal failure. Directing each set-piece for all he's worth, Petersen highlights the plot with vivid details and invests several of the action sequences with moral/psychological dimensions. He's helped no end by Malkovich, and by his lead, whose fine, easy performance extends even to tears. GA

In the Mood for Love (100) (Huayang Nianhua)

(2000, HK/Fr, 97 min)
d Wong Kar-Wai. *p* Wong Kar-Wai, Chan Ye-Cheng, Jackie Pang. *sc* Wong Kar-Wai. *ph* Tor Hor Feng, Lee Ping Bing. *ed/pd* Chan Suk-Ping. *m* Michael Galasso. *cast* Maggie Cheung, Tony Leung [Leung Chiu-Wai], Rebecca Pan, Lai Chin, Siu Ping-Lam, Chin Tsi-Ang.
● Wong's paean to the agony'n ecstasy of buttoned-up emotions is a kind-of sequel to *Days of Being Wild*, shaped and scored as a *valse triste*. In Hong Kong, 1962, Mr Chow (Leung) and Mrs Chan (Cheung) are neighbours who discover that their spouses are having an affair. He finds excuses to spend time with her, apparently intending to jilt her. Then they fall in love, but (aside from one reckless moment in a hotel) repress their feelings. He runs away to work as a journalist in Singapore; in 1966, covering De Gaulle's state visit to Cambodia, he's in Angkor Wat trying to unburden himself of the secret which overwhelms his life… Every charged frame of the film pulses with the central contradiction between repression and emotional abandon; the formalism and sensuality are inextricable. Career-best performances from both leads, Leung having a Cannes 'Best Actor' prize to show for his. TR

In the Mouth of Madness

(1994, US, 95 min)
d John Carpenter. *p* Sandy King. *sc* Michael De Luca. *ph* Gary B Kibbe. *ed* Edward A Warschilka. *pd* Jeff Steven Ginn. *m* John Carpenter. *cast* Sam Neill, Julie Carmen, Jürgen Prochnow, Charlton Heston, Frances Bay, Wilhelm von Homburg.
● In this lightweight but entertaining horror movie, seasoned genre director Carpenter realises the Lovecraftian weirdness hinted at in the eerie atmospherics of *The Fog* and the monstrous excesses of *The Thing*: in short, the idea of an order of beings that exists in a parallel dimension, expelled from this world but waiting patiently to cross back and take control again. There are shades of both HP Lovecraft and Stephen King in the central character, Sutter Cane (Prochnow), a popular horror writer whose works allegedly influence his more susceptible readers, transforming them into homicidal harbingers of global chaos. When Cane vanishes just before his new book is due for delivery, his publishers panic and hire sceptical insurance investigator John Trent (Neill) to track him down. Trent suspects an elaborate publicity stunt; but having entered the writer's hometown of Hobb's End, he too experiences a blurring of the line between reality and fiction. The script by New Line's head of production, Michael (*Freddy's Dead*) de Luca, does not allow Carpenter free range, nevertheless he manages some neat flourishes of his own, handling the narrative twists and unsettling sfx sequences with customary skill. NF

In the Name of the Father (Nel Nome del Padre)

(1971, It, 107 min)
d Marco Bellocchio. *p* Franco Cristaldi. *sc* Marco Bellochio. *ph* Franco Di Giacomo. *ed* Franco Arcalli. *ad* Amedeo Fago. *m* Nicola Piovani. *cast* Yves Beneyton, Renato Scarpa, Lou Castel, Piero Vida, Aldo Sassi, Laura Betti, Marco Romizi.
● As title and opening make clear, a film about the tyrannies of paternalism: with a great deal of surrealist wit and much venom, Bellocchio lays into the absurdities of authority and its institutions. And by setting his film in a seedy boarding school for rich delinquents, run by Jesuits along military lines, Bellocchio creates a rich target indeed: what monsters are spawned! The result is sheer anarchic fantasy, alternately feverish and despondent, but always superbly realised. On a tougher, allegorical register, it's about the failure of a revolution, about the Italian church's capacity to survive, and about replacing one oppression with another. What lifts the film into that special area inhabited by Buñuel is Bellocchio's capacity for healthy blasphemy and its translation into startling images. Rich, bizarre and original. CPe

In the Name of the Father

(1993, Ire/GB/US, 132 min)
d/p Jim Sheridan. *sc* Terry George, Jim Sheridan. *ph* Peter Biziou. *ed* Gerry Hambling. *pd* Caroline Amies. *m* Trevor Jones. *cast* Daniel Day-Lewis, Pete Postlethwaite, Emma Thompson, Corin Redgrave, John Lynch, Beatie Edney, Britta Smith.
● Sheridan's movie seeks to engage and enrage. It's not, however, a film with an ideological axe to sharpen, but one which unfolds, with a sense of passionate conviction, a story of injustice – that of the four people wrongly convicted of the IRA's Guildford pub bombings in October 1974. Tracing back to Belfast in the early '70s to uncover the roots of the tragedy, the narrative goes on to chronicle the British judicial system's wilful imprisonment of the Guildford Four – Gerry Conlon (Day-Lewis), fellow tearaway Paul Hill (Lynch), and their London acquaintances Carole Richardson and Paddy Armstrong – plus their alleged accomplices, Conlon's father (Postlethwaite) and relatives in the Maguire family. It then follows events leading to the highly publicised release of the Four in 1989. Sheridan and co-writer Terry George make some minor factual alterations in order to underscore the emotional pain of the long fight for legal reappraisal. TJ

In the Name of the Law

see In Nome della Legge

In the Name of the People

(1984, US, 75 min)
d Frank Christopher. *p* Alex W Drehsler, Frank Christopher, *sc* Alex W Drehssler. *ph* John Chapman. *ed* Frank Christopher. *narrator* Martin Sheen.
● A clandestine documentary by American filmmakers following eighteen months in the lives (and deaths) of guerrillas and peasants in the liberated areas of El Salvador. The subdued narration by Martin Sheen details the problems of daily life, food, weapons, recruitment, training, education, health and military actions. JCo

In the Navel of the Sea (Sa Pusod Ng Dagat)

(1998, Phil, 114 min)
d Marilou Diaz-Abaya. *cast* Jomari Yllana, Elizabeth Oropesa.
● Abaya builds up a convincing portrait of day to day life on a poor Philippine island, using local non-actors, an observational style and a simple, laidback narrative. There's a stunning moment when one villager is crucified to mark Easter, nails and all, though none of the villagers seems particularly impressed. Ethnographic interest aside, however, there's not an awful lot going on here. To his embarrassment, Pepito grows up to become a male midwife ('Sometimes when I look at a woman's face all I can see is a uterus!'), but his romantic longings touch on wider concerns about the future of this way of life. A bit too soft to hold the attention. TCh

In the Realm of the Senses

see Ai No Corrida

In the Rye (Co Chytnes v Zite)

(1998, Czech Rep, 100 min)
d Roman Vávra. *p* Alexej Guha, Cestmir Kopecky, Richard Nemec Jr. *sc* Jaroslav Pozzi, Martin Rysav, Roman Vávra. *ph* David Ployhar ('The Awn'), Antonín Chundela ('The Haystack'), Miro Gábor ('The Path'). *pd* Petr Kunc. *cast* Ladislav Frej Jr ('The Awn'); Andrea Elsnerova, Klára Issová, Daniel Oliva, Václav Jakoubek ('The Haystack'); Iva Janzurová ('The Path').
● The seasons change, and a field of rye hosts three ages of folk making their own delicate romantic rites of passage. In 'The Awn' (originally an award-winning student short), a young friendly couple wander through the fertile field discussing crop circles and wheat that chafes; in 'The Haystack', a young village lad and his three mates find a pregnant girl in their hideout and learn of grown-up love and responsibility; in 'The Path', an ageing new bride and groom meet their first test of faith when their wedding train sticks in the mud en route to their honeymoon destination. Naturalistic, tender and unassuming, it's a pastoral beauty. NB

In the Shadow of the Sun

(1972/80, GB, 51 min)
d/p/ph/ed Derek Jarman. *m* Throbbing Gristle. *with* Christopher Hobbs, Gerald Incandela, Andrew Logan, Kevin Whitney, Luciano Martinez, Lucy Su.
● A collection of Jarman's 1972–74 home footage of friends superimposed around and over 1980 footage of a 'car trip to Avebury'. The 'effects' were all architected at the Super-8 stage, before the arty-fact achieved its final 16mm form. It features recurrent themes: a figure at a typewriter who may/may not be composing/dreaming the experience; slow cavortings by would-be mythopoeic figures (i.e. naked folk); flames; dunes; a woman swinging her skirt; a couple dancing; lots of robed and masked movers; knockoff plaster heads after the Grecian; and a depiction of angst that could easily be mistaken for an Anadin commercial. Mitigating against that sort of mistake is the soundtrack music by Throbbing Gristle (i.e. much electronic doodling with swells of 'meaningful' sound as a persistent shuffler of Tarot cards discovers an antique key and waves it at the viewer). Influences are legion here: Tai Chi movement, Murnau's *Nosferatu*, the wonders of the colour Xerox machine, Windscale-style protective clothing, Alan Alan's Holborn magic shop, and thermography. But, alas, zilch emerges from them; indeed, Jarman's genuine imagination as a designer seems totally in abeyance. Over fifty minutes, it's just not possible to keep your mind from wandering out to make a baloney sandwich. CR

In the Soup

(1992, US, 95 min, b/w)
d Alexandre Rockwell. *p* Jim Stark, Hank Blumenthal. *sc* Alexandre Rockwell, Tim Kissel. *ph* Phil Parmet. *ed* Dana Congdon. *pd* Mark Friedberg. *m* Mader. *cast* Seymour Cassel, Steve Buscemi, Jennifer Beals, Will Patton, Stanley Tucci, Jim Jarmusch, Carol Kane, Elizabeth Bracco.
● New Yorker Adolpho Rollo (Buscemi) is your classic head-movie auteur. In his mind he's creating deathless classics of the screen. Back in the real world, he can't pay the rent on the downtown grothole he calls home. He knows he must be getting really desperate when he puts a script 'Unconditional Surrender' – 500 pages of angst-drenched gobbledygook – up for sale and attracts the attentions of one 'Joe' (Cassel), a warm-hearted minor gangland figure. Director Rockwell's affectionate screenplay pits innocence against experience, artist against philistine, but unexpectedly weighs sympathies towards Cassel's force-of-nature mob mentor, who's soon giving his po-faced protégé a life-lesson masterclass in generosity of spirit, wooing the girl-next-door (Beals), and seat-of-the-pants petty crime. Rockwell's wonderfully unassuming movie throws a big hug around youthful ambition, b/w filmstock, and the glowing screen charisma of Cassel. An unheralded gem. TJ

In the Spirit

(1990, US, 94 min)
d Sandra Seacat. *p* Julian Schlossberg, Beverly Irby. *sc* Jeannie Berlin, Laurie Jones. *ph* Dick Quinlan. *ed* Brad Fuller. *ad* Michael C Smith. *m* Patrick Williams. *cast* Jeannie Berlin, Olympia Dukakis, Peter Falk, Elaine May, Marlo Thomas, Melanie Griffith, Michael Emil, Christopher Durang.
● At a time when alternative, holistic medicine is rampaging its ugly way through every town in the world, this satirical swipe at all things new-age comes as a welcome antidote. When a prostitute is killed, a chalk-and-cheese pair of women (one worldly, one fey) set about tracking down her killer, using the notorious 'netherworlds' as their unreliable guide. Deftly scripted by Jeannie Berlin, *In the Spirit* is packed with acerbic gibes which deflate the air-headed arrogance of such leading new-agers as Shirley MacLaine. Berlin and Dukakis are fab in the lead roles, Peter Falk is rip-roaring in a sadly brief cameo, and Melanie Griffith is hardly on screen at all. MK

In the White City (Dans la Ville Blanche)

(1983, Port/Switz, 108 min)
d Alain Tanner. *p* Paulo Branco, Alain Tanner, Antonio Vaz da Silva. *sc* Alain Tanner. *ph* Acácio de Almeida. *ed* Laurent Uhler. *ad* Maria José Branco. *m* Jean-Luc Barbier. *cast* Bruno Ganz, Teresa Madruga, Julia Vonderlinn, José Carvalho, Victor Costa.

●Ganz, that great loner of modernist cinema, here plays a Swiss seaman who jumps ship in Lisbon, gets involved with a barmaid, and sends reels of home movies back to his wife. Adrift in the exotic *White City*, he is robbed and then stabbed, loses the barmaid after a passionate fling, and finally hitting rock bottom he raises the fare home. The home movies, accompanied by Jean-Luc Barbier's beautiful, hard-edged jazz score, terrifyingly reflect the disintegration of a man in flight from himself. But this is no idling tract on alienation, more an intrigue built around silences, blankness, deceptions of space and time. A teasingly simple film that compels and stimulates. JCo

In the Winter Dark

(1998, Aust, 92 min)
d James Bogle. *p* Rosemary Blight. *sc* James Bogle, Peter Rasmussen. *ph* Martin McGrath. *ed* Suresh Ayyar. *pd* Nicholas McCallum. *m* Peter Cobbin. *cast* Brenda Blethyn, Ray Barrett, Richard Roxburgh, Miranda Otto.

●Spectres of the past and present haunt this chilly, enigmatic vision of isolated life in the Australian outback. Farming couple Horace and Ida (Barrett and Blethyn) live out their barren years in an uneasy, unspoken truce over a lost young daughter, their only distant company now a neighbouring grizzled retiree and a newly single mother-to-be. The bloody visitations of an unknown predatory animal bring the four together spatially – and send them flying apart. The bleak, pregnant ambience is handled effectively, but there's a mute hysteria at the heart of the marriage, which is hardly clarified by a confusion of flashbacks. It's hard to follow a narrator who's gone barking mad. (From a novel by Tim Winton.) NB

In This Our Life

(1942, US, 97 min, b/w)
d John Huston. *sc* Howard Koch. *ph* Ernest Haller. *ed* William Holmes. *ad* Robert M Haas. *m* Max Steiner. *cast* Bette Davis, Olivia de Havilland, George Brent, Dennis Morgan, Charles Coburn, Frank Craven, Billie Burke, Hattie McDaniel, Lee Patrick.

●Bette Davis steals her sister's husband and ruins her life in this out-of-control family melodrama. 'No one is as good as Bette when she's bad,' claimed the publicity, and she's bad in this all right. John Huston (whose second film this was) wrote that 'there is a demon within Bette which threatens to break out and eat everybody, beginning with their ears. I let the demon go'. In the roadhouse sequence, the sharp-eyed will spot most of the cast from Huston's first picture, *The Maltese Falcon*, including Bogart, Astor, Greenstreet, Lorre, and the director's father, Walter. TCh

Intimacy (Intimité)

(2000, Fr/GB, 120 min)
d Patrice Chéreau. *p* Charles Gassot. *sc* Anne-Louise Trividic, Patrice Chéreau. *ph* Eric Gautier. François Gédigier. *ad* Hayden Griffin. *m* Eric Neveux. *cast* Mark Rylance, Kerry Fox, Timothy Spall, Alastair Galbraith, Philippe Calvario, Marianne Faithfull, Susannah Harker, Frazer Ayres.

●This English-language European art movie (from stories by Hanif Kureishi) examines the anonymous, almost wordless, sexual relationship that married, working-class Claire (Fox) and embittered head barman and divorced father Jay (Rylance) embark on in his seedy flat in New Cross, London. The media's concentration on the explicit sex angle in this troubling, uneven but stimulating and cinematically intriguing film has been excessive, as the treatment is resolutely serious and meaningful. The film is about inevitable human incompleteness, living with contradictions, the irreconcilable conflicting hungers of the body and the heart. Fox and Rylance's performances, their lack of ingratiation and their plain, professional courage are the most remarkable things about the film – cameraman Eric Gautier's exciting, jagged, rich-toned rendering of London notwithstanding. At their best in the little theatre of the bedsit room, trouble only starts outside, where they, and the film, lose direction. The behaviour of other Londoners seems all wrong, if entirely plausible. This process of de-familiarisation is fascinating: it's invigorating to be made to feel, for an hour or so, an alien in your own city. WH

Intimate Affair, An

see Liaison Pornographique, Une

Intimate Confessions of a Chinese Courtesan (Ai Nu)

(1972, HK, 91 min)
d Chu Yuan. *p* Runme Shaw. *sc* Chieu Kang-chien. *ph* Wu Cho-hua. *ed* Chiang Hsing-lung, Li Yen-hai. *ad* Chen Ching-sheng. *cast* Lily Ho, Yueh Hua, Betty [Ting Pei], Tung Lin, Wan Chung-shan.

●A good looking production, but a rather embarrassed cross between archetypal kung-fu and the sex film. Set in medieval China, the plot involves the Lesbian head of an exclusive brothel who hires a gang of louts to kidnap likely young girls, who are then broken in and sold off to a series of more or less geriatric local officials with inflated ideas of their own desirability. Our heroine, a young teacher, even undergoes multiple rape, almost entirely in reaction shots and freeze frames; in fact almost everything is filmed in reaction shots, whose over-familiarity just makes this comic strip fable that much more ridiculous. Women with any kind of consciousness, however, will be interested in the superbly acted 'false' ending in which the two women are reconciled – hastily followed, of course, by the hugely predictable 'real' climax.

Intimate Games

(1976, GB, 90 min)
d Tudor Gates. *p* Guido Coen. *sc* Tudor Gates. *ph* Frank Watts. *ed* Pat Foster. *ad* Tony Curtis. *m* Roger Webb. *cast* Peter Blake, Suzy Mandell, Anna Bergman, George Baker, Ian Hendry, Joyce Blair, Hugh Lloyd, Mary Millington.

●A tediously unfunny sex comedy masquerading (for censorship reasons?) as a spuriously moral exposure movie. 'Abnormal phantasies', we learn late in the proceedings, cause Professor Gottlieb (Baker) to pounce on one of his female psychology students, after which he is carted off to hospital frothing at the mouth. Earlier, Gottlieb's students have been despatched for the summer vac to write up each other's sexual phantasies. Theory, however, inevitably gives way to softcore practice: slow-motion, dimly-lit, featherweight Lesbian groping; some singularly unerotic tumbling in the back seat of a Rolls; frequent old-fashioned naturist shots of pleasant, well-scrubbed girls in the buff; a notable absence of genitalia. Ian Hendry, Hugh Lloyd and Joyce Blair make brief, decidedly uncomfortable appearances; Anna, Ingmar Bergman's daughter, strips off with good humour. JPy

Intimate Reflections

(1975, GB, 86 min)
d/p Don Boyd. *sc* Richard Meyrick, Don Boyd. *ph* Keith Goddard. *ed* Clive Muller. *cast* Anton Rodgers, Lillias Walker, Sally Anne Newton, Jonathan David, Peter Vaughan, Derek Bond.

●Surely the worst film of the year. It would, of course, be wrong to expect a conventional moviegoing experience from something as specifically non-narrative as this concoction of nuance and gesture; but no amount of special pleading, bonhomie towards experiment, or explanation of motive can hide the fact that the result is like a synthesis of every bad detail of every bad undergraduate film you've ever seen. That Anton Rodgers keeps audience interest going during the film's second half is a tribute to a standard of professionalism eschewed elsewhere. AN

Intimate Relations

(1995, GB/Can, 99 min)
d Philip Goodhew. *p* Angela Hart, Lisa Hope, Jon Slan. *sc* Philip Goodhew. *ph* Andrés Garreton. *ed* Pia DiCiaula. *pd* Caroline Greville-Morris. *m* Lawrence Shragge. *cast* Julie Walters, Rupert Graves, Matthew Walker, Laura Sadler, Holly Aird, Les Dennis.

●An English market town, 1954. Harold (Graves) takes a room in the Beasley household. All seems dandy, but then Mrs Beasley (Julie Walters – 'Call me Mum') slips into the sheets with him, and won't take no for an answer. The man of the house remains oblivious, but the 13-year-old daughter begins to get ideas of her own, and Harold finds himself in a pickle. Like *The Young Poisoner's Handbook*, this first feature maliciously satirises the sexual hypocrisy of the time. Walters, needless to add, takes full advantage of the material. TCh

Intimate Stranger, The (aka Finger of Guilt)

(1956, GB, 94 min, b/w)
d Joseph Walton [Joseph Losey]. *p* Alec C Snowden. *sc* Peter Howard [Howard Koch]. *ph* Gerald Gibbs. *ed* Geoffrey Muller. *ad* Wilfred Arnold. *m* Trevor Duncan. *cast* Richard Basehart, Mary Murphy, Constance Cummings, Roger Livesey, Mervyn Johns, Faith Brook.

●Pseudonymously directed by Losey, who had been driven from Hollywood by the McCarthyite purge of the studios, *Intimate Stranger* is a wonderfully slow thriller with a baroque climax in a film studio. Richard Basehart is the studio executive pursued by blackmailing letters from a mysterious girl claiming to be his mistress, his problems complicated by the fact that his wife is the boss' daughter, while the star of his current film is a still-amorous ex-lover. As usual with Losey, both predator and victim take an almost pathological pleasure from their game of mutual destruction. PH

Intimate with a Stranger

(1994, GB, 94 min)
d Mel Roberts. *p* Roderick Mangin-Turner. *sc* Mel Roberts, Roderick Mangin-Turner. *ph* Nick Tebbett. *ed* Brian Smedley-Aston. *pd* Graeme Story. *m* Ledsam and Pugh. *cast* Roderick Mangin-Turner, Daphne Nayer, Amy Tolsky, Lorelei King, Janis Lee, Darcey Ferrer.

●Los Angeles. After the break-up of his relationship with fellow academic Michelle (Nayer), ex-philosophy professor Jack Hawkins (producer/co-writer Mangin-Turner) walls off his emotions and becomes a gigolo. However, while Hawkins is meant to be an intellectual masquerading as a gigolo, Mangin-Turner looks more like a gigolo masquerading as an intellectual. 'You can be intimate with a stranger, but a stranger to intimacy.' The development and visualisation of this notion leave much to be desired. It doesn't help that the first in a series of women who drift into the jaded gigolo's life is Summer (Lee), a beautiful schoolgirl wanting to lose her virginity to an older man who won't brag about it. Nor that his other clients (frustrated housewife, unfulfilled career-woman) are chiefly 'types' – each with her own monologue (sometimes straight to camera) explaining why she's after sex and solace in unequal measure. Tediously talky. NF

Intimité

see Intimacy

Intolerance 100

(1916, US, 12,598 ft, b/w)
d/p/sc DW Griffith. *ph* Billy Bitzer. *ed* James Smith, Rose Smith. *ad* R Wllis Wales, Frank Wortman. *m* Joseph Carl Breil. *cast* Lillian Gish, Mae Marsh, Robert Harron, Constance Talmadge, Miriam Cooper, Alfred Paget, Elmo Lincoln, Walter Long, Bessie Love, Seena Owen.

●Griffith's immensely influential silent film intercuts four parallel tales from history (spanning Babylon, Christ's Judaea, Reformation Europe, and turn-of-the-century America) to embroider a moral tapestry on personal, social and political repression through the ages. The thematic approach no longer works (if it ever did); the title cards are stiffly Victorian and sometimes laughably pedantic; but the visual poetry is overwhelming, especially in the massed crowd scenes. And the unbridled eroticism of the Babylon harem scenes demonstrate just what Hollywood lost when it later bowed to the censorship of the Hays Code. CA

In Too Deep

(1999, US, 97 min)
d Michael Rymer. *p* Paul Aaron, Michael Henry Brown. *sc* Michael Henry Brown, Paul Aaron. *ph* Ellery Ryan. *ed* Dany Cooper. *pd* Dan Leigh. *m* Christopher Young. *cast* Omar Epps, LL Cool J, Nia Long, Stanley Tucci, Hill Harper, Jake Weber, Richard Brooks, David Patrick Kelly, Pam Grier.

●How far can an undercover cop go before he risks not coming back out again? That was the question posed in Bill Duke's *Deep Cover*, where officer Laurence Fishburne inveigled his way into an LA narcotics ring. Here, Cincinnati detective Epps is set the same challenge: to walk the walk and talk the talk with sufficient credibility to get close to the local drugs kingpin. If the 1992 movie's still in your memory, the new version will seem undercharacterised, but for those coming fresh to *In Too Deep* the core situation still plays, even if there's not much else on offer, solid performances not withstanding, though. Epps may not have had a lot of room to work with, but behind the eyes is a moral quandary and rising anxiety. Such is the case whether he's playing the role, or it's playing him. His fear is palpable, too, being focused on LL Cool J's major supplier. If Aussie director Rymer finds it hard not to revel in the latter's macho grandstanding, well, once the action moves outside the gangland milieu there isn't much else to shoot. TJ

Into the Arms of Strangers: Stories of the Kindertransport

(2000, US, 117 min, b/w & col)
d Mark Jonathan Harris. *p* Deborah Oppenheimer. *ph* Don Lenzer. *ed* Kate Amend. *m* Lee Holdridge. *with* Steve Harvey, DL Hughley, Cedric the Entertainer. *narrator* Judi Dench.

●During 1938/9, the *Kindertransport* initiative placed more than 10,000 Jewish children in British foster homes, rescuing them from the Nazis, but separating them from parents in Germany, Austria and Czechoslovakia. Twelve former *Kinder* tell their stories, intercut with rare archive footage. The impact lies in the details (clothes carefully embroidered and packed; a preserved identity tag; spelling mistakes in letters home; kippers for breakfast; news of parents 'deported to Auschwitz'; preparations for rare, uneasy reunions) and the straightforward chronological presentation, unhampered by intrusive stylistic devices or the minimal narration spoken by Judi Dench. These are not random testimonies from randomly selected subjects – they shed particular light on different perspectives of the evacuation. As the emotional confusion that is the lifelong legacy of these exceptional childhoods is gradually revealed their stories converge, around loss, thankfulness, resentment towards parents for sending (or not sending) them away, guilt, limbo – and later, subtle shifts in understanding, the pleasure of grandchildren, and the profound realisation of what it means to have survived. SS

Into the Night

(1985, US, 115 min)
d John Landis. *p* George Folsey Jr, Ron Koslow. *sc* Ron Koslow. *ph* Bob Paynter. *ed* Malcolm Campbell. *pd* John J Lloyd. *m* Ira Newborn. *cast* Jeff Goldblum, Michele Pfeiffer, Richard Farnsworth, Irene Papas, Dan Aykroyd, David Cronenberg, John Landis, Waldo Salt, Daniel Petrie, Jack Arnold, Paul Mazursky, Jonathan Lynn, Paul Bartel, Don Siegel, David Bowie.

●Goldblum abandons a safe suburban existence in favour of nocturnal prowlings through Los Angeles, and encounters a mysterious blonde on the run. The plot is minimal, but the film scores partly because of a high sense of fun, and partly because of the way Landis uses his LA locations. As the characters race from the yachts of Marina Del Rey via Rodeo Drive to the Marion Davies mansion in Beverly Hills, he adds a visual running commentary of old film and TV ads, to milk our movie fantasies for all they're worth, and to convey a sense of Los Angeles as a truly mythical city. The casting of innumerable major filmmakers in small roles seems an unnecessary bit of elbow-jogging, but David Bowie makes an excellent contribution as an English hit man, and the two leading players are excellent: Pfeiffer in particular takes the sort of glamorous yet preposterous part that generally defeats even the best actress and somehow contrives to make it credible every inch of the way. DP

Into the West

(1992, Ire, 102 min)
d Mike Newell. *p* Jonathan Cavendish, Tim Palmer. *sc* Jim Sheridan. *ph* Tom Sigel. *ed* Peter Boyle. *pd* Jamie Leonard. *m* Patrick Doyle. *cast* Gabriel Byrne, Ellen Barkin, Ciarán Fitzgerald, Ruaidhri Conroy, David Kelly, Johnny Murphy, Brendan Gleeson.

●Screenwriter Jim Sheridan follows *My Left Foot* and *The Field* with a soppy tale of life among the Travellers. In his Dublin tower block, a broken man since the death of his wife, one time Traveller king Papa Riley (Byrne) is swayed from his determination to give his sons (Conroy and Fitzgerald) a conventional home when Grandpa Ward (Kelly) returns from his travels, bringing fanciful tales and a white horse which is lodged in the cramped flat. The authorities take a predictably dim view of this, but in confiscating the horse, provide both father and sons with a new lease of life. But the film lapses into tired whimsy when the boys masquerade as lawless cowboys. It's hard to share their vision of the west of Ireland as America's Western frontier, and impossible to perceive any danger from the uniformed incompetents in pursuit. CM

Intruder, The (aka The Stranger/ I Hate Your Guts)

(1961, US, 80 min, b/w)
d/p Roger Corman. *sc* Charles Beaumont. *ph* Taylor Byars. *ed* Ronald Sinclair. *m* Herman Stein. *cast* William Shatner, Frank Maxwell, Beverley Lunsford, Robert Emhardt, Jeanne Cooper, Leo Gordon, Charles Barnes, Charles Beaumont.

●Raw-edged and startling, scripted by Charles Beaumont from his own novel based on real-life rabble-rouser John Kasper, Corman's film about Southern desegregation was shot on location in Missouri in a mere three weeks, with threats and obstruction from white locals mirroring the fictional action. Adam Cramer (Shatner, mesmerising) represents an organisation which seeks to stop the process of educational desegregation and thus frustrate plans of the 'Communist front headed by Jews' to 'mongrelise' society. Cramer is an insidious outsider whose impassioned speeches rouse the populace; the result is heightened Klu Klux Klan activity, attacks on black families and a liberal white newspaper editor, a near-hanging. Complex characterisation is sacrificed in the interests of representing the broad socio-political issues. Emotions intensify in accord with searing summer temperatures; visuals emphasise the economic disparities, memorably in shots of the black ghetto and of Cramer in his pristine white suit. Chilling, and especially at the moment Cramer delivers his battle-cry, 'This is just the beginning', painfully prophetic. CM

Intruder in the Dust

(1949, US, 86 min, b/w)
d/p Clarence Brown. *sc* Ben Maddow. *ph* Robert Surtees. *ed* Robert J Kern. *ad* Cedric Gibbons, Randall Duell. *m* Adolph Deutsch. *cast* Claude Jarman Jr, David Brian, Juano Hernandez, Elizabeth Patterson, Porter Hall, Will Geer.

●By far the best of the race prejudice cycle of the '40s, a subtle adaptation (by Ben Maddow) of William Faulkner's novel which goes out of its way to avoid the usual special pleading in dealing with Lucas Beauchamp (Hernandez), the elderly black facing a lynch mob when accused of shooting a white man in the back. Lucas is clearly innocent but also 'stubborn and insufferable', so scornful of whitey and his patronage that he refuses to stoop to defending himself; an arrogant sonofabitch so hard to like that when two lone citizens come forward in his defence (an old woman and a young boy), they do so against their wills, purely so that they can go on sleeping easy. An amazingly laid back conception for the period, echoed by Brown's calmly dispassionate direction and by the unobtrusively persuasive ambience (most of the film was shot in Faulkner's home town of Oxford, Mississippi). TM

Inutile Envoyer Photo

(1977, Fr, 95 min)
d Alain Dhouailly. *cast* Paul Le Person, Hélène Dieudonné, Danièle Ajoret, Bernard Lajarrige, Rémy Carpentier, Jenny Cleve.

●Gentle, almost soporific rural drama about the travails of a 55-year-old bachelor farmer when faced by the imminent prospect of two unsought partnerships. While the dairy demands that he modernise his milking equipment and a neighbour offers to pool resources, his feisty old mother starts placing lonelyheart ads for him in the photo-romance magazines that she reads interminably with her two cronies. A French TV production that's a little too impressed by its own observation of quirky custom and character, and ends up as naively 'charming' as its unlikely hero. PT

Invaders from Mars

(1953, US, 78 min)
d William Cameron Menzies. *p* Edward L Alperson. *sc* Richard Blake. *ph* John F Seitz. *ed* Arthur Roberts. *pd* William Cameron Menzies. *m* Raoul Kraushaar. *cast* Helena Carter, Arthur Franz, Jimmy Hunt, Leif Erickson, Hillary Brooke, Morris Ankrum.

●A sci-fi cheapie about another invasion of the body snatchers, which has some chillingly effective moments but doesn't really live up to its reputation, despite the unusual ploy of being told largely from the point of view of a small boy (Hunt) who is the first to spot the invaders and whose parents are the first to go under. Interesting, though, for the extremeness of its Cold War aura of military preparedness, which even throws in actuality shots of tanks and troops massing as the earthlings prepare to fight back against the green tentacular midget things that live in glass globes. Its backyard setting, a nostalgic slice of small town Americana which is the territory to be defended, inspired the opening sequence of Scorsese's *Alice Doesn't Live Here Any More*. TM

Invaders from Mars

(1986, US, 99 min)
d Tobe Hooper. *p* Menahem Golan, Yoram Globus. *sc* Dan O'Bannon, Don Jakoby. *ph* Daniel Pearl. *ed* Alain Jakubowicz. *pd* Leslie Dilley. *m* Christopher Young. *cast* Karen Black, Hunter Carson, Timothy Bottoms, Laraine Newman, James Karen, Bud Cort, Louise Fletcher.

●An updated version of the '50s paranoia classic in which a young boy wakes up in the middle of the night to see a spaceship landing over the hill behind his house. The rest of the film consists of his efforts to make the adults around him believe his story, and his increasing despair as more and more people are taken over by the Martians. The effects are magnificent (the tripod drones and the supreme Martian intelligence are horrific), but whereas the original worked by building up an increasingly black mood, this version relies almost entirely on the special effects; and such limited brooding tension as it has is gratuitously undermined by a string of sequences played purely for laughs. Black is good as the near-hysterical school nurse who becomes the boy's only ally, and forms a lovely double act with her real son (Carson), who is commendable as the poor lad. The lame twist in the original's ending has been retained. Fun, but very silly. DPe

Invasion

(1966, GB, 82 min, b/w)
d Alan Bridges. *p* Jack Greenwood. *sc* Roger Marshall. *ph* James Wilson. *ed* Derek Holding. *ad* Scott MacGregor. *m* Bernard Ebbinghouse. *cast* Edward Judd, Valerie Gearon, Yoko Tani, Tsai Chin, Lyndon Brook, Eric Young, Barrie Ingham, Glyn Houston, Anthony Sharp.

●Strikingly imaginative little sci-fi thriller in which two Oriental women, actually aliens but peaceful in intent, throw a force field round a hospital while attempting to retrieve a colleague, a criminal who escaped from their charge and has been knocked down by a car. Little happens as the telephones go dead and panic mounts in the hospital along with the temperature, but the sense of threat from the unknown becomes almost tangible as Bridges weaves his Losey-influenced camera through shadowy landscapes, or lets it linger broodingly on innocent objects until they begin to acquire an air of alien malevolence. TM

Invasion of the Body Snatchers

(1955, US, 80 min, b/w)
d Don Siegel. *p* Walter Wanger. *sc* Daniel Mainwaring. *ph* Ellsworth J Fredricks. *ed* Robert S Eisen. *pd* Ted Haworth. *m* Carmen Dragon. *cast* Kevin McCarthy, Dana Wynter, Larry Gates, Carolyn Jones, King Donovan, Virginia Christine, Tom Fadden, Sam Peckinpah.

●There's something strange going on in Santa Mira. Children don't recognise their parents. Husbands have become estranged from their wives. Mass hysteria? Mass alienation more likely. Dr Kevin McCarthy discovers the secret: pod people are colonising the earth, taking human form but dispensing with the soul. Shot in just 19 days, Siegel's economical adaptation of a Jack

Finney story (script by Daniel Mainwaring of *Out of the Past* fame) is one of the most resonant sci-fi movies, and one of the simplest. It has been interpreted as an allegory against McCarthyism, though it could equally stand as anti-Communist. (In his book *A Siegel Film*, the director has nothing to say on the matter.) It's still a chilling picture, gaining over Phil Kaufman's smart remake by virtue of its intimate small town setting, and it has one of the greatest endings ever filmed. Too bad the studio insisted on adding a lame book-end framing device and voice-over narration to diffuse it. TCh

Invasion of the Body Snatchers

(1978, US, 115 min)
d Philip Kaufman. *p* Robert H Solo. *sc* WD Richter. *ph* Michael Chapman. *ed* Douglas Stewart. *pd* Charles Rosen. *m* Denny Zeitlin. *cast* Donald Sutherland, Brooke Adams, Leonard Nimoy, Veronica Cartwright, Jeff Goldblum, Art Hindle, Lelia Goldoni, Kevin McCarthy, Don Siegel, Tom Luddy, Robert Duvall.

●Though it lacks the awesome allegorical ambiguousness of the 1956 classic of sci-fi/political paranoia (here paid homage in cameo appearances by Kevin McCarthy and Don Siegel), Kaufman and screenwriter WD Richter's update and San Francisco transposition of Jack Finney's novel is a far from redundant remake. The extraterrestrial pod people now erupt into a world where seemingly everyone is already 'into' changing their lives or lifestyles, and into a cinematic landscape already criss-crossed by an endless series of conspiracies, while the movie has as much fun toying with modern thought systems (psychology, ecology) as with elaborate variations on its predecessor. Kaufman here turns in his most Movie Brattish film, but soft-pedals on both his special effects and knowing in-jokiness in a way that puts De Palma to shame; even extra bit appearances by Robert Duvall (Kaufman's Jesse James in *The Great Northfield Minnesota Raid*) and Hollywood archivist Tom Luddy are given a nicely take-it-or-leave-it dimension. PT

Invasion of the Body Stealers

see Body Stealers, The

Invasion of the Flying Saucers

see Earth vs the Flying Saucers

Invasion of the Saucermen (aka Invasion of the Hell Creatures)

(1957, US, 67 min, b/w)
d Edward L Cahn. *p* James H Nicholson, Robert J Gurney Jr. *sc* Robert J Gurney Jr, Al Martin. *ph* Frederick E West. *ed* Charles Gross Jr. *ad* Don Ament. *m* Ronald Stein. *cast* Steve Terrell, Gloria Castillo, Frank Gorshin, Raymond Hatton, Ed Nelson.

●Low-budget '50s sci-fi which doesn't quite descend to the level of Ed Wood-style ineptitude, but isn't too far above it either. 'Little green men' pop in on Middle America, the town drunk gets zapped, teenagers show their pluck, the military get called in. All the usual genre elements are here, though Cahn hasn't the money or the imagination to do more than the barest minimum with them. TJ

Invasion U.S.A.

(1985, US, 107 min)
d Joseph Zito. *p* Menahem Golan, Yorma Globus. *sc* James Bruner, Chuck Norris. *ph* Joao Fernandes. *ed* Daniel Lowenthal, Scott Vickrey. *pd* Ladislav Wilheim. *m* Jay Chattaway. *cast* Chuck Norris, Richard Lynch, Melissa Prophet, Alexander Zale, Alex Colon, Eddie Jones, Billy Drago.

●We can all sleep easy with Chuck 'Neanderthal' Norris to protect the free world single-handed from the commie guerrilla force that attempts *Invasion U.S.A.* A machine-pistol hanging at each hip, Norris blasts his way through an invasion force that blows up innocent family homes as the occupants prepare for Christmas. Terrorists disguised as Miami cops, they massacre crowds of Hispanics, place bombs in hypermarkets, and generally sow the seeds for the street warfare that will undermine the fabric of democracy. Norris, who doesn't so much act as point his beard at the camera, weaves his way through so many explosions that the money saved on the cast was obviously blown on pyrotechnics. Leaden, xenophobic, and utterly stupid, it's far more offensive than *Rambo* and far less well executed. DPe

Inventing the Abbotts

(1997, US, 107 min)
d Pat O'Connor. *p* Ron Howard, Brian Grazer, Janet Meyers. *sc* Ken Hixon. *ph* Kenneth MacMillan. *ed* Ray Lovejoy. *pd* Gary Frutkoff. *m* Michael Kamen. *cast* Joaquin Phoenix, Billy Crudup, Will Patton, Kathy Baker. Jennifer Connolly, Michael Sutton, Liv Tyler, Alessandro Nivola.

●Haley, Illinois, 1957: Phoenix and Crudup are the blue-collar Holt brothers who dare to glance at the glittering Abbott daughters – smart, gawky Tyler, typecast 'bad girl' Connelly – whose father has expressly forbidden such contact. This rankles with the boys, especially since rumours persist that the Abbott paterfamilias (Patton) had an affair with their teacher mother, just after their father died, and is also purported to have snaffled the dead man's design for a suspension file drawer. The central notion of the gentry callously exploiting the labour of those less fortunate brings an element of class tension to the film which, as the title suggests, shows how the Abbotts' carefully groomed public image is in fact their strongest suit in perpetuating their social status. While we see behind the facade, the film eschews real bitterness in favour of the hesitant romance between Tyler and Phoenix, and a hope that future generations can break the cycle of deception and resentment. O'Connor's follow-up to *Circle of Friends* looks the part and is adeptly played, but isn't quite distinctive enough to be much more than a pleasant non-event. TJ

Investigation of Murder, An

see Laughing Policeman, The

Invincible

(2001, Ger/Ire/GB/US, 133 min)
d Werner Herzog. *p* Gary Bart, Werner Herzog, Christine Ruppert. *sc* Werner Herzog. *ph* Peter Zeitlinger. *ed* Joe Bini. *pd* Ulrich Bergfelder. *m* Hans Zimmer, Klaus Badelt. *cast* Tim Roth, Jouko Ahola, Anna Gourari, Max Raabe, Jacob Wein, Gustav Peter Wöhler, Udo Kier, Herbert Golder, Gary Bart, Renate Krössner.

●Herzog's first narrative feature in a decade is an embarrassment. Backed by FilmFour and consequently presented in what sounds like dubbed English, his Weimar-era fable aims for simplicity and innocence but comes off as simpleminded and naive. The promising material concerns Zishe (Ahola), a blacksmith in a Polish schtetl whose colossal strength catches the eye of a showbiz agent with car trouble. Persuaded to pursue his destiny in Berlin, Zishe is put on stage in Hanussen's Theatre of the Occult club as 'Siegfried the Gladiator', the strongest man in the world. The club is a favourite haunt of the Nazis, who flock to hear the seer Hanussen (Roth), so when the lovesick Zishe declares himself a Jew, chaos erupts. Unfortunately, the confusion extends to the film itself. The sluggish pace, broken-backed storytelling and unspeakable dialogue leave the non-professional actors spooning like fish out of water. Even more surprising is the film's visual poverty. Its most memorable image – a plague of red crabs – is recycled from the director's documentary *Little Dieter Needs to Fly*. TCh

Invincible Barbarian, The (Gunan el Guerriero)

(1982, It, 90 min)
d Frank Shannon [Franco Prosperi]. *p* Pino Buricchi. *sc* Piero Regnoli. *ph* Pasquale Fanetti. *ed* Alessandro Lucidi. *ad* Francesco Cuppini. *m* Roberto Pregadio. *cast* Peter McCoy [Pietro Torrisi], Sabrina Siani, Malisa Longo, David Jenkins, Emilio Messina.

●In a dark barbaric age gone by, savage tyrant destroys village and massacres inhabitants. Surviving child grows up into incredibly strong/manly/muscular hunk who eventually murders tyrant and avenges dead family. Sounds familiar? No, it's not *Conan the Barbarian* but *Gunan the Warrior*, an Italian rip-off which has neither the style nor the special effects of the real McCoy. But the bills for designer loincloths, eye make-up and tomato ketchup must have been astronomic. MG

Invincible Pole Fighters, The

see 8-Diagram Pole Fighter, The

Invisible Adversaries (Unsichtbare Gegner)

(1978, Aus, 109 min)
d/p Valie Export. *sc* Peter Weibel. *ph* Eric Timmermann, Wolfgang Simon. *ed* Juno Sylva Englander, Valie Export, Herbert Baumgartner. *cast* Susanne Widl, Peter Weibel, Dr Josef Plavee, Monika Helfer-Friedrich, Helke Sander.

●Dancing a forlorn quickstep along the interface between dreams and waking, Austrian Anna surfaces to that sinister sound of white noise on the radio informing her that aliens, or at least *Invisible Adversaries*, have invaded human beings. Noticeably blasé about this looming revelation, she seems to regard it as yet more evidence of the way that modern life disfigures its artists, men dump on women, the police hit you on the head, and Kreisky's Austria represses everyone. It's possible that this state of mind is brought on by her boyfriend urinating on her head in the mornings, but whatever the reason, she does seem fairly unhappy, morosely photographing faces and leaving the baby in the fridge. It's either a feverish deconstruction of the bourgeois modes of representation, or more likely what you'd expect to find on *Time Out*'s back page under 'The Way It Was, Dec 1972'. Not unlike *W.R. – Mysteries of the Organism*; it will probably age as badly. CPea

Invisible Circus, The

(2000, US, 93 min)
d Adam Brooks. *p* Julia Chasman, Nick Wechsler. *sc* Adam Brooks. *ph* Harry Braham. *ed* Elizabeth Kling. *pd* Robin Standefer. *m* Nick Laird-Clowes. *cast* Cameron Diaz, Jordana Brewster, Christopher Eccleston, Blythe Danner, Camilla Belle, Patrick Bergin, Isabelle Pasco, Moritz Bleibtreu.

●The past is another country, or sometimes a rhubarb of several: in this sentimental relic, Holland, France, Germany and Portugal. Home is, or was, San Francisco for two sisters, but they end up in turn at opposite ends of the '70s in these old world haunts where they sow and reap the decade's upheavals like a before and after tagteam. First forward was Faith (Diaz), who fell from mischief to mayhem, and finally on to the coastal rocks of Cabo Espichel, leaving a hole in the heart of sister Phoebe (Brewster). This is where the film begins, with Phoebe contemplating her inner limbo in listless prose: 'I am sure there was a time when everything was perfect.' So she ventures to follow in Faith's footsteps. In Paris, she looks up Faith's old boyfriend Wolf (Ecclestone), and they revisit radical Berlin through his memories, and floral Portugal for real, waxing reminiscent. 'You guys were reinventing the world every single day,' she assures him. 'I thought I'd put it behind me, but the truth is I never let go,' he assents. A pork barrel of clichés, the film has a remarkably narrow, centripetal vision: it makes the political personal and it prunes away the personalities of two of its three main characters – blank satellites orbiting a black hole. NB

Invisible Man, The

(1933, US, 71 min, b/w)
d James Whale. *p* Carl Laemmle Jr. *sc* RC Sherriff. *ph* Arthur Edeson. *ed* Ted J Kent. *ad* Charles D Hall. *cast* Claude Rains, Gloria Stuart, Una O'Connor, William Harrigan, EE Clive, Dudley Digges, Dwight Frye, Walter Brennan, John Carradine.

●Engrossing adaptation of HG Wells' tale of a scientist made invisible by his experiments with the drug monocaine. The megalomania that ensues upon Rains' ability to go about unseen is played for suspense, pathos and tongue-in-cheek humour (he can't go out in the rain, because it would make him look like a ridiculous bubble). The real strengths of the movie are John P Fulton's remarkable special effects (Rains removing his bandages to reveal nothing, footsteps appearing as if by magic in the snow), lending much-needed conviction to the blatant fantasy; and the fact that we never see the scientist without his bandages until the very end of the film. No wonder Karloff, disdainful of a role in which he would for the most part only be heard, turned down the part; but Rains, with his clear, sensitively inflected voice, was lucky: it made him a star. GA

Invisible Man Returns, The

(1940, US, 81 min, b/w)
d Joe May. p Ken Goldsmith*sc* Lester Cole, Curt Siodmak. *ph* Milton Krasner. *ed* Frank Gross. *ad* Jack Otterson. *m* Charles Previn. *cast* Vincent Price, Cedric Hardwicke, John Sutton, Nan Grey, Alan Napier, Cecil Kellaway.
●Not as stylishly bizarre as Whale's original, but a very enjoyable sequel, with Price as a man wrongly convicted of murder who goes invisible with the help of the original invisible man's brother (Sutton). Riding out the madness that is one of the drug's unfortunate side effects, he proves his innocence by unmasking the real killer. The whodunit element is less gripping than the original's study in soaring megalomania, but Price's urbanely mellifluous voice makes him an admirable successor to Claude Rains, and John P Fulton's special effects are well up to par. TM

Invisible Ray, The

(1936, US, 81 min, b/w)
d Lambert Hillyer. *p* Edmund Grainger. *sc* John Colton. *ph* George Robinson, John P Fulton. *ed* Bernard Burton. *ad* Albert S D'Agostino. *m* Franz Waxman. *cast* Boris Karloff, Bela Lugosi, Frances Drake, Frank Lawton, Walter Kingsford, Beulah Bondi, Violet Kemble Cooper.
●Last and least of Universal's three co-starring vehicles for Karloff and Lugosi in the '30s, with the latter overshadowed by Karloff in the first of his many mad scientist roles. After a superb opening in the Carpathian laboratory where Karloff learns the secret of 'capturing light rays from the past', it gets a bit rickety in the African scenes, where a meteorite provides his ray with the necessary 'Radium X' and where a demonstration goes disastrously wrong. But it's briskly staged with some fine camerawork, and Karloff – turned into a radioactive killer and melting down a symbolic statue after each death on his vengeance trail against his wife and the colleagues he feels have betrayed him – is great. TM

Invisible Stripes

(1939, US, 82 min, b/w)
d Lloyd Bacon. *sc* Warren Duff. *ph* Ernest Haller. *ed* James Gibbon. *ad* Max Parker. *m* Heinz Roemheld. *cast* George Raft, Jane Bryan, William Holden, Humphrey Bogart, Flora Robson, Paul Kelly, Lee Patrick, Henry O'Neill, Marc Lawrence, Leo Gorcey.
●A thoroughly predictable tale of the tribulations of an ex-con. Released from jail simultaneously, bad boy Bogart goes back to the rackets, good guy Raft to a careworn mother (Robson), a hopeful younger brother (Holden), a fiancée who snottily ditches him (Patrick), and an ill-paid job from which he is summarily fired as untrustworthy. Unable to make a decent living because of his 'invisible stripes', in despair because he can see his brother edging towards crime in his turn, he emulates Sydney Carton's 'far, far better thing' to team up with Bogart in a series of robberies. The gesture costs him his life, but does stake Holden to a garage and enable him to marry his sweetheart (Bryan). The terminally dreary Raft does little to brighten the soggily soapy proceedings. TM

Invitation, The (L'Invitation)

(1973, Switz/Fr, 100 min)
d Claude Goretta. *p* Yves Peyrot. *sc* Michel Viala, Claude Goretta. *ph* Jean Zeller. *ed* Joële van Effenterre. *ad* Yanko Hodjis. m Patrick Moraz. *cast* Michel Robin, Jean-Luc Bideau, Jean Champion, Pierre Collet, Corinne Coderey, Rosine Rochette, François Simon.
●Truly delightful comedy from Goretta, later better known for *The Lacemaker*. A very simple plot – quiet office clerk inherits a marvellous country house when his beloved mother dies, and invites his 'friends' from work over for a summer garden party. But what distinguishes the film is its acute observation, and the way it gently scrapes away the stereotypes – office lecher, buffoon, nymphet, henpecked husband, etc – to reveal more complex figures all locked in private worlds of hope, loneliness, and despair. The film has aptly been compared to the work of Renoir, not only for its narrative similarity to *La Règle du Jeu*, but also because Goretta's tender yet unsentimental generosity towards his characters is akin to the French master's dictum that 'everybody has his reasons'. GA

Invitation to Bed (Les Confidences Erotiques d'un Lit Trop Accueillant)

(1973, Fr, 90 min)
d Michel Lemoine. *p* Louis Duchesne. *sc* Michel Lemoine. *ph* Philippe Théaudière. *ed* Bob Wade. *m* Guy Bonnet. cast Olga Georges-Picot, Janine Reynaud, Michel Le Royer, Anne Libert, Marie-Gabrielle Pascal, Nathalie Zieger, Emile Mathis.
●The erotic adventures of a large white fluffy bed, which could almost be a fugitive from a Claes Oldenburg art exhibit. Various characters lie on it and find that their passions increase tenfold. The fadeout joke is when the hero and heroine make love in a square one. GB

Invocation Maya Deren

(1987, GB, 53 min)
d Jo Ann Kaplan. *with* Hella Hammid, Sasha Hammid, Amos Vogel, Marcia Vogel, Stan Brakhage, Jonas Mekas.
●Maya Deren is one of the most important figures in the history of American experimental cinema. Her '40s films established her as a flamboyant, original film poet whose work not only inspired other avant-garde movie-makers but gave rise to America's Creative Film Foundation and the progressive distribution company Cinema 16. This informative documentary may use a familiar format – clips (including unfinished work), talking heads (Jonas Mekas, Stan Brakhage, et al), footage of Deren herself – but its tone, at once celebratory and objectively distanced, is beguiling. The film paints a portrait of a fascinating woman: extrovert, strong-willed, eccentric, deeply competitive, and immensely energetic. Recommended to anyone interested in dance, alternative cinema, forceful women, and ecstatic imagery. GA

In weiter Ferne, so nah!

see Faraway, So Close

In Which We Serve

(1942, GB, 116 min, b/w)
d David Lean, Noël Coward. *p/sc* Noël Coward. *ph* Ronald Neame. *ed* Thelma Myers. *ad* David Rawnsley. *m* Noël Coward. *cast* Noël Coward, John Mills, Bernard Miles, Celia Johnson, Joyce Carey, Kay Walsh, Michael Wilding, James Donald, Daniel Massey, Kathleen Harrison, Richard Attenborough.
●The story of a destroyer, its crew, and their flashback memories of the folks back home from a raft after being dive-bombed during the Battle of Crete. Staged with what passed at the time for honest understatement, it now looks impossibly patronising, the epitome of stiff upper lip as Coward's captain graciously condescends to his forelock- touching crew like an indulgent auntie. Interesting chiefly as a reminder of the structures of snobbery and privilege in the services which were largely responsible for Labour's postwar election victory. TM

In With the New

see Sylvester Countdown

Io ballo da sola

see Stealing Beauty

Iodo

(1977, SKor, 110 min)
d Kim Ki-Young. *cast* Lee Hwa-si, Kim Jong-choi, Choi Yun-sok.
●More sex and death from iconoclast Kim Ki-Young in this bizarre and beautifully shot 'Scope drama. It takes the form of an investigation by a resort promoter and a newspaper editor of the strange death of an Iodo islander turned ecology reporter, who disappears overboard on a trip back to the island. Unfolding in flashback, it relates in mock mythological terms the fate of the island, populated almost entirely by Amazon-like female deep sea divers and their shamans. Atmospheric, ghostly and oneiric, it's a Freudian mind-boggler, filled with male sexual anxiety, culminating in one of the most shocking copulatory denouements in the movies. WH

I Ought to Be in Pictures

(1982, US, 108 min)
d Herbert Ross. *p* Herbert Ross, Neil Simon. *sc* Neil Simon. *ph* David M Walsh. *ed* Sidney Levin. *pd* Albert Brenner. *m* Marvin Hamlisch. *cast* Walter Matthau, Ann-Margret, Dinah Manoff, Lance Guest, Lewis Smith, Martin Ferrero.
●One of those cases of long-lost family rashly turning up unexpectedly and causing radical (also unlikely) changes in peoples' personalities. This time it's the daughter, the unbearably cute and outspoken Libby (Manoff), who sets off for Hollywood to seek fame and her father (Matthau), last seen when she was in diapers. Matthau is a grumpy, scared bachelor who has given up on work and relationships, and who, until transformed by his daughter, is driving his sensible girlfriend (Ann-Margret) into the arms of another man. Far too few jokes to soak up Neil Simon's soggy material. JE

Ipcress File, The

(1965, GB, 109 min)
d Sidney J Furie. *p* Harry Saltzman. *sc* Bill Canaway, James Doran. *ph* Otto Heller. *ed* Peter Hunt. *pd* Ken Adam. *m* John Barry. *cast* Michael Caine, Nigel Green, Guy Doleman, Sue Lloyd, Gordon Jackson, Aubrey Richards, Frank Gatliff.
●First and best of Caine's three appearances as Len Deighton's Harry Palmer, despite Furie's penchant for flashy images. There's a suitably complex plot involving a missing scientist, an enigmatic piece of recording tape, electronic brainwashing, and top-level treachery; but the best sequences linger in the mind long after the narrative details have been forgotten. Palmer's perky Cockney personality may be irritating at times, but it's worth putting up with it for scenes like the encounter in the reading-room, the unsuccessful raid on a mysterious warehouse, or the psychedelic torture-chamber. DP

IP5

(1992, Fr, 119 min)
d/p Jean-Jacques Beineix. *sc* Jean-Jacques Beineix, Jacques Forgeas. *ph* Jean-François Robin. *ed* Joëlle Hache. *ad* Dan Weil. *m* Gabriel Yared. *cast* Yves Montand, Olivier Martinez, Sekkou Sall, Géraldine Pailhas, Colette Renard, Sotigui Kouyate.
●Beineix's film ('5' because it's his fifth, 'IP' for *Isle aux Pachydermes*) is another idiosyncratic slice of hard-edged romantic whimsy, which sees a pair of Paris delinquents – a graffiti artist and his very young black pal – head south in search of escape and/or love. Down in Toulouse, they come across Montand's asylum-escapee shaman, a man who talks to the trees and walks on water, but carries a gun. It looks great – urban reds, moon blues and forest greens – and is replete with the usual chic irony and cinematic pyrotechnics. Well acted, too, especially by the two juve leads, Martinez and Sall. It was Montand's last film, and he is visibly – and movingly – dying. A likeable film, but whether it adds up to much is up to you. WH

I.Q.

(1994, US, 96 min)
d Fred Schepisi. *p* Carol Baum, Fred Schepisi. *sc* Andy Breckman, Michael Leeson. *ph* Ian Baker. *ed* Jill Bilcock. *pd* Stuart Wurtzel. *m* Jerry Goldsmith. *cast* Tim Robbins, Meg Ryan, Walter Matthau, Lou Jacobi, Gene Saks, Joseph Maher, Stephen Fry, Tony Shalhoub, Charles Durning.
●To judge from the movies, Albert Einstein was a goofy comedian who dabbled in algebraic abstractions on the side. Matthau plays fairy godmother to his brainy niece Catherine (Ryan) and besotted local mechanic Ed (Robbins). Unable to see beyond the size of a man's Mensa score, Catherine is engaged to a stuffy English psychologist (Fry); she only becomes interested in Ed when uncle Albert and his cronies conspire to recognise his (entirely imaginary) scientific genius. Unfortunately, the media become interested too, and soon President Eisenhower is on the phone. A sappy, old-fashioned romantic comedy in pastel hues, which might have been given some backbone by a Billy Wilder or a Howard Hawks. Robbins is amiable enough as a Gary Cooper type, and Meg Ryan does her own sweet thing, but the equation is overbalanced by Matthau's matey old man. TCh

Ireland: Behind the Wire

(1974, GB, 110 min)
d Berwick Street Film Collective.

●A bleak alternative to the bland footage of Northern Ireland that we normally get to see. The makers of this documentary offer not so much an analysis of the political situation as a record of the psychological toll. The mesh of sectarianism and nationalism is scarcely touched upon. Rather, the film argues in terms of the legacies of British capitalism and colonialism, and states that a minority is being persecuted just as relentlessly as anywhere else in the world. Through interviews with men who have been tortured, images of barricades and destruction, the sight of a decidedly non-passive army in action, and the strain registered on faces young and old, one can begin to understand what it is like to live in perpetual fear in a country that has become a breeding ground for violence. The film, in revealing the economic discrepancies between England and Northern Ireland, and showing up much of the complacency that dominates our thinking, makes a little more comprehensible the desperate measures taken by extremists.

I Remember Mama

(1948, US, 134 min, b/w)
d George Stevens. *p* Harriet Parsons. *sc* DeWitt Bodeen. *ph* Nick Musuraca. *ed* Robert Swink. *ad* Albert S D'Agostino, Carroll Clark. *m* Roy Webb. *cast* Irene Dunne, Barbara Bel Geddes, Oskar Homolka, Philip Dorn, Cedric Hardwicke, Rudy Vallee, Edgar Bergen, Ellen Corby, Florence Bates.

●A rosily nostalgic valentine to family life in San Francisco circa 1910, rather in the manner of *Meet Me in St Louis*, though cast (without the music) in the form of memories set down by a budding authoress looking back in gratitude and affection. The homespun philosophy with which these Norwegian immigrants face up to life's hard knocks makes it more sentimental than Minnelli's film. A charmer, nevertheless, directed and acted with real delicacy, not least by Hardwicke as the lodger, a broken-down old actor who pays his way with readings from the classics. Beautifully adapted by DeWitt Bodeen from the John Van Druten play (itself based on Kathryn Forbes' book *Mama's Bank Account*). TM

Irezumi – Spirit of Tattoo (Sekka Tomurai Zashi)

(1981, Jap, 108 min)
d Yoichi Takabayashi. *p* Yasuyoshi Tokuma, Masumi Kanamura. *sc* Chiho Katsura. *ph* Hideo Fuji. *ad* Seiten Shimoishizaki. *m* Masaru Sato. *cast* Tomisaburo Wakayama, Masayo Utsunomiya, Yusuke Takita, Masaki Kyomoto, Taiji Tonoyama.

●Once more into the mystique of Japanese sex. This one is about a grizzled old master tattooist who will only work on his subjects while they are in the act of screwing. Both the tattooing and the sex are tastefully sanitised: no blood, no unsightly scabs, no erotic complications. There's lashings of picturesque old Japan, and it all turns into jolly melodrama for the finale, with suicides, murders and revelations of hidden identities. RG

Irgendwo in Berlin...

see Somewhere in Berlin...

Iris

(2001, GB/US, 91 min)
d Richard Eyre. *p* Robert Fox, Scott Rudin. *sc* Richard Eyre, Charles Wood. *ph* Roger Pratt. *ed* Martin Walsh. *pd* Gemma Jackson. *m* James Horner. *cast* Judi Dench, Jim Broadbent, Kate Winslet, Hugh Bonneville, Penelope Wilton, Juliet Aubrey, Eleanor Bron, Angela Morant, Joan Bakewell, Samuel West, Timothy West.

●Eyre's film of John Bayley's bestselling memoirs has the virtues one imagines Iris Murdoch would have hoped for: it's an intelligent, literate film with a sure sense of its world and honest, moving performances. If it's also underwhelming, perhaps these virtues can become vices: it's overly literal, solipsistic and even a little academic. For the benefit of those dozing at the back, Murdoch was a very fine British novelist and philosopher. Educated at Oxford in the 1950s, she fashioned herself as a free spirit – yet oddly, when the stammering John Bayley paid court, she chose him to be her husband, and they lived together until her death in 1999. Eyre's film switches between the couple's courtship and the painful last years when Murdoch suffered from Alzheimer's disease, often eliding four decades in a single, eloquent pan. The twin casts are perfectly matched: Dench and Winslet as the flinty, hay-haired Iris; and Broadbent and Bonneville as John, almost a caricature of the absent-minded don, the cuckold happy with his nest. She sees decency in him, an intellect to parry, and an unworldliness which obviously suited her purposes. Eyre is interested in how dependency shifts between them, in what keeps a couple together even in the face of Alzheimer's – and in watching a brilliant mind regress. Yet, perhaps inevitably, the film becomes less interesting as it goes on. TCh

Irma la Douce

(1963, US, 147 min)
d/p Billy Wilder. *sc* Billy Wilder, IAL Diamond. *ph* Joseph LaShelle. *ed* Daniel Mandell. *ad* Alexandre Trauner. *m* André Previn. *cast* Jack Lemmon, Shirley MacLaine, Lou Jacobi, Bruce Yarnell, Herschel Bernardi, Hope Holiday, Joan Shawlee, James Caan.

●Wilder's two-and-a-half-hour comedy set in the prostitute milieu of Paris (Hollywood-built, courtesy of Alexandre Trauner's designs) looks more than anything like a gaudy musical (which it once was) without the songs (which Wilder removed). It's a chance for Lemmon to go through his paces in various guises – zealous boulevard cop, pimp, and moonlighting worker in Les Halles food-market impersonating an English lord by day. Even for Lemmon, there's too much self-pity in the part of a naïve ex-gendarme who falls heavily for a tart, but Shirley MacLaine redresses the balance as the whore with a heart of gold. Wilder's soft-centred cynicism provides frequent enough laughs without too many longueurs. As in *The Seven Year Itch* and despite the French setting, they come mainly from the hypocritical vulgarity of contemporary American sexual morality. RM

Irma Vep

(1996, Fr, 98 min)
d Olivier Assayas. *p* Georges Benayoun. *sc* Olivier Assayas. *ph* Eric Gautier. *ed* Luc Barnier, Tina Baz, Marie Lecoeur. *ad* François-Renaud Labarthe. *cast* Maggie Cheung, Jean-Pierre Léaud, Nathalie Richard, Alex Descas,Bulle Ogier, Lou Castel, Jacques Fieschi.

●Named after the slinky heroine of Feuillade's *Les Vampires* (which neurotic, idealistic director Léaud is here planning to remake), Assayas' partly improvised film charts the experiences of Hong Kong actress Cheung (playing herself) when she turns up in Paris to take the lead in Léaud's doomed movie. Crew members come on to her; journalists lecture her on the future of cinema, Léaud cracks up and is replaced by the gloriously seedy Castel, and Cheung starts having strange dreams. A delightfully nonchalant movie, complete with some nice satirical barbs aimed at contemporary French film culture, and fine performances throughout. GA

Iron & Silk

(1991, US, 92 min)
d/p Shirley Sun. *sc* Mark Salzman, Shirley Sun. *ph* James Hayman. *ed* Geraldine Peroni, James Y Kwei. *ad* Calvin Tsao. m Michael Gibbs. *with* Mark Salzman, Pan Qingfu, Jeanette Lin Tsui, Vivian Wu, Sun Xudong, Zheng Guo.

●Actor/writer Salzman's autobiography provides the source material for this winning semi-documentary outsider's take on contemporary Chinese society. A youthful fan of kung-fu movies, Salzman travels to China, works as an English teacher and falls for student Vivian Wu, while also training with (real-life) martial arts guru Pan Qingfu. Although the film doesn't probe that deeply into the political arena, cultural differences certainly emerge as the enthusiastic protagonist embraces a way of life far removed from his Western upbringing. TJ

Iron Curtain, The (aka Behind the Iron Curtain)

(1948, US, 87 min, b/w)
d William A Wellman. *p* Sol C Siegel. *sc* Milton Krims. *ph* Charles G Clarke. *ed* Louis Loeffler. *ad* Lyle R Wheeler, Mark-Lee Kirk. *m* Shostakovich, Prokofiev, Khachaturian, Miaskovsky. *cast* Dana Andrews, Gene Tierney, June Havoc, Leslie Barrie, Edna Best, Berry Kroeger, Noel Cravat.

●By the late '40s, anti-communist fervour in Hollywood and throughout the US had reached fever pitch. This brisk, documentary-style thriller, based on the experiences of a code clerk in the Russian embassy in Washington, captures the mood of the times. Andrews is the turncoat who wants asylum in the West so his son can grow up in 'freedom'. Given that he's prepared to share all the latest dope about Soviet espionage techniques, it is not surprising his old colleagues are so keen to assassinate him. GM

Iron Eagle

(1985, US, 119 min)
d Sidney J Furie. *p* Ron Samuels, Joe Wizan. *sc* Kevin Elders, Sidney J Furie. *ph* Adam Greenberg. *ed* George Grenville. *pd* Robb Wilson-King. *m* Basil Poledouris. *cast* Louis Gossett Jr, Jason Gedrick, David Suchet, Tim Thomerson, Larry B Scott, Caroline Lagerfelt.

●A film which captures the misunderstood rationale behind the Reagan administration's foreign policy, and translates it into dramatic form. Doug Masters (Gedrick), high school graduate, is fighting mad: his dad is being held prisoner in an 'Islamic Fundamentalist State'. In a country where negotiation has become an eleven-letter word no one can pronounce, Doug is left with one option; if he's going to save his old man, he's going to have to blast him out. So he and a retired colonel (Gossett) abscond with two US Airforce fighters and splatter the 'little goochies' across the face of the desert. It is regrettable that the highest of production values have been invested in this, the cheapest of stories. SGo

Iron Eagle II

(1988, Can, 100 min)
d Sidney J Furie. *p* Jacob Kotzky, Sharon Harel, John Kemeny. *sc* Kevin Elders, Sidney J Furie. *ph* Alain Dostie. *ed* Rit Wallis. *ad* Robb Wilson-King. *m* Amin Bhatia. *cast* Louis Gossett Jr, Mark Humphrey, Stuart Margolin, Alan Scarfe, Sharon H Brandon, Maury Chaykin.

●A cheapskate sequel to a *Top Gun* rip-off, with veteran flyer Colonel 'Chappy' Sinclair (Gossett) heading a top-secret combined US/Soviet mission against a common Arab enemy. The villain this time is Iran, apparently only two weeks away from nuclear capability. Circumventing attempts by hawkish top brass on both sides to sabotage the mission (and thereby Soviet-American military cooperation) by assigning a bunch of rebel, misfit flyers, Chappy and his Soviet counterpart get together, disobey orders, and launch an unofficial attack on the Iranian missile base. While the conciliatory attitude towards the Soviet Union is a welcome development, the drippy romance between macho US pilot Humphrey and glamorous Soviet fly-girl Brandon is entirely dispensable. Long on clichéd characters, ludicrous dialogue, and flying sequences accompanied by nondescript rock music, but short on credibility. NF

Iron Giant, The

(1999, US, 87 min)
d Brad Bird. *p* Allison Abbate, Des McAnuff. *sc* Tim McCanlies. *ph* Mark Dinicola. *ed* Darren T Holmes. *pd* Mark Whiting. *m* Michael Kamen. *cast* voices: Jennifer Aniston, Harry Connick Jr, Vin Diesel, James Gammon, Cloris Leachman, M Emmet Walsh.

●As entertaining as it's intelligent, this delightful 'Scope animation from Warner Bros is adapted from Ted Hughes' anti-Cold War children's book. In a small town in Maine in 1957 (year of the Sputnik launch), young adventurer Hogarth, son of single mother and waitress Annie, is obsessed with things extra-terrestrial. Due in part to his school's nuclear-protection TV sessions, he's especially concerned about the Red Invader. He's the only one to take seriously a fisherman's frantic reports of the landing of a metal giant, and his search is rewarded by the sighting of a metal crunching, electricity-immune 50-footer in the forest. A friendship grows – the 'brain-damaged', perhaps war-oriented machine is educated by the boy like a 'wild child' – as government agents close in. Thank heaven, Hogarth's beatnik pal Dean runs the scrapyard and can provide, simultaneously, food and shelter – but for how long? This moral film effectively dramatises the war between imaginative, responsible solutions on the one hand, and gung ho, nuke 'em rule of force on the other, without losing sight of youngster friendly action-movie requirements. WH

Iron Horse, The

(1924, US, 11,335 ft, b/w)
d John Ford. *sc* Charles Kenyon. *ph* Gene Schneiderman, Burnett Guffey. *m* Erno Rapee. *cast* George O'Brien, Madge Bellamy, Charles Edward Bull, William Walling, Fred Kohler, Cyril Chadwick, Delbert Mann.

● *The* epic silent Western, made as Fox's response to *The Covered Wagon* and effortlessly surpassing it. A paean to Lincoln and the notion of Manifest Destiny, it recounts the building of the first transcontinental railroad. Gangs start from both coasts, rebuffing Indian attacks, thwarting greedy landowners, initiating a sweeping trail drive and moving whole towns along the line. After battles against the rigours of blizzard and desert, the final spike is driven home as the hero avenges his father's murder and wins back his childhood sweetheart. Visual glories (and stirring piano accompaniment) sweep aside objections to the tedious passages, the psychological ineptitude, and the racist portrayal of Indians, Irish and 'coolies'. As in *Stagecoach*, each scene and each character looks fresh struck at the mint of myth, while every frame asserts that this is the making of America and of the American cinema. JW

Iron Ladies (Satree Lek)

(1999, Thai, 105 min)
d/p Yongyoot Thongkongtoon. *sc* Visuttichai Boonyakarnjana, Jira Maligool, Yongyoot Thongkongtoon. *ph* Jira Maligool. *ed* Sunit Assavinikul. *pd* Naruecha Vijitvanit. *m* Saranat Kitpraamote. *cast* Jesdaporn Pholdee, Sashaparp Virakamin, Awkkachai Buranaphanit, Gokgorn Benjathikul, Chaichan Nimpoolsward.

● A global hit, Yongyoot's debut feature is improbably based on fact: in 1996, a team of *khatuey* (ladyboys) really did win a Thai national volleyball championship – as men. But this ain't no docu-drama: it offers a deathlessly entertaining mix of riotous comedy, right-on anti-homophobe stings and sporting triumph kicks. The Lampang volleyball team hits the rocks when its macho 'star' leads a mass walkout in protest against the appointment of a lesbian coach. Starting with drag queens Mon and Jung, coach Bee sets about rebuilding the team and ends up with a rainbow coalition of gays and transvestites, with one token transsexual and one token straight. Of course their path to the top is strewn with personal traumas, professional tensions and broken fingernails, but most viewers take the low humour and elements of sit-com in their stride. And many emerge from the cinema dancing with joy. TR

Iron Maiden, The

(1962, GB, 98 min)
d Gerald Thomas. *p* Peter Rogers. *sc* Vivian A Cox, Leslie Bricusse. *ph* Alan Hume. *ed* Archie Ludski. *ad* Carmen Dillon. *m* Eric Rogers. *cast* Michael Craig, Anne Helm, Jeff Donnell, Alan Hale Jr, Noel Purcell, Cecil Parker, Roland Culver, Joan Sims.

● A sad film, a kind of traction engine version of *Genevieve*, with Michael Craig as the man of the future (he's an aircraft designer) getting into trouble because of his love of the past, and finally solving his problems through the realisation that 'Britain is the place of continuity...' etc. Thematically the film makes (reactionary) sense, but cinematically it's a disaster. Scenes at Henley, Ascot and Woburn are supplemented by the Duke of Bedford in person. PH

Iron Mask, The

(1929, US, 104 min, b/w)
d Allan Dwan. *sc* Lotta Woods. *ph* Henry Sharp, Warren Lynch. *ed* William Nolan. *ad* Laurence Irving, Carl Oscar Borg, William Cameron Menzies. *m* (new score 1999) Carl Davis. *cast* Douglas Fairbanks, Leon Bary, Tiny Sandford, Gino Corrado, Marguerite De La Motte, Belle Bennett, Dorothy Revier, Nigel de Brulier, Ulrich Haupt, William Bakewell, Rolfe Sedan, Gordon Thorpe.

● An effortlessly high-spirited, beautifully bedecked romp through Dumas, with Fairbanks revisiting his favourite role as D'Artagnan. It's also a fond farewell to Fairbanks' own screen youth and the gaiety he'd shared with audiences over a decade, with the plot following the valiant musketeers through a 20-year separation, reunification and a final leap into heaven and a greater adventure beyond. Aside from a shaky five minutes at the start of the second half, it's perfectly pitched, paced and performed. (The print under review was restored by Photoplay Productions, London, in association with MoMA, New York.) NB

Iron Maze

(1991, US/Jap, 102 min)
d Hiroaki Yoshida. *p* Ilona Herzberg, Hidenori Ueki. *sc* Tim Metcalfe. *ph* Morio Saequsa. *ed* Bonnie Koehler. *pd* Tony Corbett, Toro Ueno. *m* Stanley Myers. *cast* Jeff Fahey, Bridget Fonda, Hiroaki Murakami, JT Walsh, Gabriel Damon, John Randolph, Peter Allas, Carmen Filpi.

● Based on the same short story as Kurosawa's *Rashomon*, this shifts the action to a Pennsylvania 'Rust Belt' town where the son (Murakami) of a billionaire Japanese businessman plans to replace the old steel mill with an amusement park. When he is found at the mill with a potentially fatal head injury, an embittered ex-steelworker (Fahey) confesses that he acted in self-defence, a story backed up by the injured man's American wife (Fonda). The local police chief (Walsh) is suspicious, and his investigation reveals a complex maze of personal and cultural conflicts. *Rashomon* addressed the subjective nature of perception, but Yoshida's debut feature reduces this idea to a mere plot device, designed to sustain suspense. The attempt to deal with the huge subject of US/Japanese economic and cultural relations is similarly fudged by focusing on the triangular relationship between Murakami, Fahey and Fonda. By the time you reach the centre of this iron maze, you may wish you'd opted for the rollercoaster instead. NF

Iron Triangle, The

(1988, US, 91 min)
d Eric Weston. *p* Angela D Shapiro, Tony Scotti. *sc* Eric Weston, John Bushelman, Lawrence Hilbrand. *ph* Irv Goodnoff. *ed* Roy Watts. *pd* Errol Kelly. *m* Michael Lloyd, John D'Andrea, Nick Strimple.*cast* Beau Bridges, Haing S Ngor, Liem Whatley, Johnny Hallyday, Jim Ishida, Ping Wu, Jack Ong, Sophie Trang.

● Billed as the first Vietman film to show both sides of the conflict, this tries to have its cake and eat it. Based on the diary of a young, idealistic Vietcong soldier (here called Ho, played by Whatley), it is narrated by the equally sympathetic US officer who finds it, Captain Keen (Bridges). It therefore dispels the myth of the 'faceless enemy', while retaining a convienient Western identification figure. To be fair, as the opposing forces vie for tactical advantage in the heavily militarised 'Iron Triangle', this strategy does yield some intriguing moments. In the American camp, Keen clashes with his ruthless South Vietnamese and French colleagues over their relentless propagandising and routine use of torture. Likewise, Ho's professional soldiering is compromised by the ideological point-scoring of Communist party official Khoi (Ishida). Naturally, when Keen is later captured by Ho and his men, a professional respect develops between the two. Sadly, the sporadic battle scenes are too messy to be fully effective, so one's over-riding feeling is that writer/director Weston has his heart in the right place, but his liberal politics and cinematic technique all over the place. NF

Ironweed

(1987, US, 143 min)
d Hector Babenco. *p* Keith Barish, Marcia Nasatir. *sc* William Kennedy. *ph* Lauro Escorel. *ed* Anne Goursaud. *pd* Jeannine C Oppewall. *m* John Morris. *cast* Jack Nicholson, Meryl Streep, Carroll Baker, Michael O'Keefe, Diane Venora, Fred Gwynne, Margaret Whitton, Tom Waits, Jake Dengel.

● At last, a real part for Nicholson to sink his teeth into. As Francis Phelan, one-time family man and baseball contender reduced by guilt to Depression-era drifter, the star drives for the marrow, for the spiritual dimension beyond the stubble and staggers that eluded Rourke in *Barfly*. Decades ago, Phelan fatally dropped his baby son; during a trolley strike he threw a rock at a scab, accidentally killing him; a boxcar brawl over shoes resulted in another death: ghosts rise up to rebuke him. 'I don't hold grudges for more than five years,' he tells the apparitions, companionably. 'See ya'. His horizons have shrunk to somewhere to sleep for the night, the price of a bottle, and a new pair of shoelaces, but like the Beckett characters who can't go on, he goes on. Weaker derelicts attach themselves to him – Rudy, cheerfully dying of cancer (Waits, terrific), and Helen, a pathetic, muttering bag-lady down from gentility (Streep, resembling Worzel Gummidge). Down here on the wintry streets of Albany, the characteristic Babenco concern for flotsam gets a sombre and lengthy workout, but it's Nicholson's film. BC

Irreconcilable Differences

(1984, US, 113 min)
d Charles Shyer. *p* Arlene Sellers, Alex Winitsky. *sc* Nancy Myers, Charles Shyer. *ph* William A Fraker. *ed* John F Burnett. *pd* Ida Random. *m* Paul de Senneville, Olivier Toussaint. *cast* Ryan O'Neal, Shelley Long, Drew Barrymore, Sam Wanamaker, Allen Garfield, Sharon Stone.

● This is essentially about the excesses of the Hollywood lifestyle, the egomania it generates, and how success and failure can change 'normal' people into monsters overnight. O'Neal and Long both turn in sensitive and gently comic performances as a couple consumed by it all, and Drew Barrymore is superb as the neglected daughter caught in the middle. It ruthlessly parodies film industry types, and the superficial Beverly Hills set, by way of one-liners, some truly touching moments, and a great cast. Lovely. DPe

Isabelle Eberhardt

(1991, Fr/Aust, 115 min)
d Ian Pringle. *p* Jean Petit, Daniel Scharf. *sc* Stephen Sewell. *ph* Manuel Téran. *ed* Ken Sallows. *pd* Bryce Perrin, Geoffroy Larcher. *m* Paul Schütze. *cast* Mathilda May, Tchéky Karyo, Peter O'Toole, Richard Moie, Arthur Dignam, Françoise Brion.

● Eberhardt is remembered mainly for her diaries, eventually translated into English by Paul Bowles. This deals with her travails in Algeria and Morocco between 1899 and her death in 1904: her marriage to a consumptive Legionnaire, her belligerent journalism, her clashes with the forces of colonialism, whether brutish (Moie) or benign (O'Toole). Primarily it's a vehicle for May, the nude space vampire in *Lifeforce*, here a beguiling cross-dresser when not swathed in a burnous, and looking every inch a star. But this stilted Saharan slog does her no favours. O'Toole, who must know a thing or two about deserts by now, coasts in an undemanding role. BBa

Isadora

(1968, GB, 138 min)
d Karel Reisz. *p* Robert Hakim, Raymond Hakim. *sc* Melvyn Bragg, Clive Exton. *ph* Larry Pizer. *ed* Tom Priestley. *pd* Jocelyn Herbert. *m* Maurice Jarre. *cast* Vanessa Redgrave, James Fox, Jason Robards, Ivan Tchenko, John Fraser, Bessie Love, Cynthia Harris.

● Many hands dabbled in the script – Clive Exton, Melvyn Bragg, Margaret Drabble – which is perhaps why this lavish biopic is rather impersonal, lacking a consistent viewpoint. Isadora Duncan, like Lawrence of Arabia, is an enigma; and whereas David Lean and Robert Bolt found only an enigma and sought to perpetuate it, Reisz seeks to unravel and explain this bizarre, scandalising appendage to the '20s. In some ways it's like a Ken Russell movie at 33 rpm, discovering the ageing Isadora dictating her memoirs and flashing back to her affairs in Berlin (Fox) and France, where she marries Mr Singer (Robards) of sewing-machine fame, then her second marriage to a Russian poet, her rejection and disillusion, and her final ride in a red Bugatti with scarf flying. The source of the scandal, her uninhibited sexuality and her Classical Greek dancing at the height of the Jazz Age, gives the film a semblance of unity, something to hang on to, and a visual beauty. And there is also Vanessa Redgrave, giving a quite superb performance in which the mannerisms are Isadora's, not hers. ATu

I Saw What You Did

(1965, US, 82 min, b/w)
d/p William Castle. *sc* Wiliam P McGivern. *ph* Joseph Biroc. *ed* Edwin Bryant. *ad* Alexander Golitzen, William M Simonds. *m* Van Alexander. *cast* Joan Crawford, John Ireland, Andi Garrett, Sarah Lane, Sharyl Locke, Leif Erickson, Patricia Breslin.

●Typical Castle suspense shocker with a nice premise about a couple of silly teenage girls (Garrett, Lane) who while away the tedium of babysitting by making hoax phone calls ('I saw what you did! I know who you are!'), but unfortunately chance on a psycho (Ireland) who has just done away with his wife. A few chilling moments, but it all depends on your susceptibility. In spite of her star billing, Crawford – given to appearing in this type of film in the later stages of her career – has a supporting role, and makes a violent exit as an overwrought mistress jealously trying to blackmail the psycho into marrying her. DP

I See a Dark Stranger (aka The Adventuress)

(1946, GB, 112 min, b/w)
d Frank Launder. *p* Frank Launder, Sidney Gilliat. *sc* Frank Launder, Sidney Gilliat, Wolfgang Wilhelm. *ph* Wilkie Cooper. *ed* Thelma Myers. *pd* David Rawnsley *m* William Alwyn. *cast* Deborah Kerr, Trevor Howard, Raymond Huntley, Liam Redmond, Michael Howard, Norman Shelley, Brefni O'Rorke.
●A briskly entertaining (if ideologically cosy) espionage thriller set during World War II, with Kerr as an Irish colleen brought up on her father's tales of his exploits against the wicked English. Setting out to join the IRA but sidetracked into innocently spying for the Nazis in Dublin, she is run ragged all over the place – including the Isle of Man – before suffering a change of heart when she falls for a British officer (Howard). Rather too whimsical, but littered with engagingly Hitchcockian conceits like the disposal of a corpse by taking it for a stroll in a wheelchair. TM

I Shall Return

see American Guerilla in the Philippines

I Shot Andy Warhol

(1996, US/GB, 100 min)
d Mary Harron. *p* Tom Kalin, Christine Vachon. *sc* Daniel Minahan, Mary Harron. *ph* Ellen Kuras. *ed* Keith L Reamer. *pd* Thérèse DePrez. *m* John Cale. *cast* Lili Taylor, Jared Harris, Martha Plimpton, Stephen Dorff, Lothaire Bluteau, Danny Morgenstern, Michael Imperioli. Myriam Cyr.
●Engrossing, informative and beautifully performed account of the psychological turmoil and various other pressures that led Valerie Solanas, founder and sole member of SCUM (the Society for Cutting Up Men), to gun down Andy Warhol. Despite a long, rather too self-conscious party scene, complete with Velvets, various superstars and conversations on couches, the re-creation of the Factory and its population is mostly spot-on: Taylor's paranoid but spikily intelligent Solanas is a triumph, as is Dorff's Candy Darling. And if Harris is perhaps a little too enervated as Andy, the film's sharp take on sexual politics, the allure of fame and the artistic pretensions of a vanished era lends it substance a-plenty. There's a score by John Cale, too. GA

I Shot Jesse James

(1948, US, 81 min, b/w)
d Samuel Fuller. *p* Clark K Hittleman. *sc* Samuel Fuller. *ph* Ernest Miller. *ed* Paul Landres. *ad* Frank Hotaling. *m* Albert Glasser. *cast* Preston Foster, Barbara Britton, John Ireland, Reed Hadley, J Edward Bromberg, Victor Kilian, Tom Tyler, Byron Foulger.
●Fuller's first film is a virtual illustration of his dictum that the cinema is like a battleground: 'Love, hate, action, violence, death…in one word, Emotion.' Having to choose between loyalty to the past and a love for Jesse James (Hadley), or a desire for a future and the love of a woman, Fuller's outlaw hero Bob Ford (Ireland) makes the wrong choice. He shoots James, only to discover that his whole life has become defined by this deed: doomed to re-enact the murder on stage, and condemned to notoriety in 'The Ballad of Jesse James'. His vision of the future fades into jealousy, economic hardship and, as Phil Hardy has pointed out, 'misplaced love'. As such, more a psychological drama (emphasised by the use of close-up) than a Western, and a highly original film. CPe

Ishtar

(1987, US, 107 min)
d Elaine May. *p* Warren Beatty. *sc* Elaine May. *ph* Vittorio Storaro. *ed* Stephen A Rotter, William H Reynolds, Richard Cirincione. *pd* Paul Sylbert. *m* John Strauss. *cast* Warren Beatty, Dustin Hoffman, Isabelle Adjani, Charles Grodin, Jack Weston, Tess Harper, Carol Kane, David Margulies.
●So bad it could almost have been deliberate. The faults are many, but the casting of Hoffman and Beatty as a talentless and tacky cabaret duo is fatal: perverse logic makes Hoffman the smooth-talking womaniser and Beatty the bozo. The complex plot takes far too long to establish that they are to Simon and Garfunkel what McGonagall is to Burns before they are whisked off on a tour of the mythical Sahara republic of Ishtar, where they are lured into spying for opposing sides of a planned revolution, each tailing the other while trying to impress the same beautiful freedom fighter (Adjani). Of course the pair make worse spies than they do songwriters, and soon they're trekking into the desert with only a blind camel and CIA snipers for company. May's script is unfunny, and anything approximating a joke is wrung dry; but accept that you're watching one of the worst films ever made and you may find it hilarious. EP

Island, The (Hadaka no Shima)

(1961, Jap, 92 min, b/w)
d Kaneto Shindo. *p* Kaneto Shindo, Eisaku Matsura. *sc* Kaneto Shindo. *ph* Kiyoshi Kuroda. *ed* Toshio Enoki. *m* Hikaru Hayashi. *cast* Nobuko Otowa, Taiji Tonoyama, Shinji Tanaka, Masanori Horimoto.
●The film that brought Shindo to international attention is a meditatively-paced study of life on the far side of privation: a small family group struggle for survival on a barren island off the west coast of Japan. The 'poetry' is highly contrived, but the feeling is probably authentic. TR

Island, The

(1980, US, 114 min)
d Michael Ritchie. *p* David Brown, Richard D Zanuck. *sc* Peter Benchley. *ph* Henri Decae. *ed* Richard A Harris. *pd* Dale Hennesy. *m* Ennio Morricone. *cast* Michael Caine, David Warner, Angela Punch McGregor, Frank Middlemass, Don Henderson, Dudley Sutton, Colin Jeavons.
●Peter Benchley's script from his own novel is a mad concoction in which Michael Caine and son stumble on a Caribbean island inhabited by bloodthirsty pirates, inbred over 300 years and now sterile, who survive by plundering consumer goodies from luxury yachts. Caine is designated as stud to the only female capable of child-bearing, the son is happily absorbed into the patriarchal dream world, and a thoroughly Oedipal conflict begins between the pair which looks like ending in patricide. The plot's inversion of *Lord of the Flies* (adults without children running amok on an island paradise), the inanely prattling buccaneers straight out of Disneyland, and the anti-materialist glee of their attack against the rich – smashing videos and taunting sunbathers – all add up to one of the most ludicrous yet entertaining mis-hits since *The Other Side of Midnight*. DP

Island at the Top of the World, The

(1973, US, 94 min)
d Robert Stevenson. *p* Winston Hibler. *sc* John Whedon. *ph* Frank Phillips. *ed* Robert Stafford. *pd* Peter Ellenshaw. *m* Maurice Jarre. *cast* Donald Sinden, David Hartman, Jacques Marin, Mako, David Gwillim, Agneta Eckemyr.
●Despite the promise of its Jules Verne-ish title, a thoroughly pedestrian effort that doesn't even merit comparison with such earlier Disney adventures as *20000 Leagues Under the Sea.* Unimaginative plot, interminable dialogue in 'Old Norse', some pointless love interest, and a particularly repulsive poodle. DP

Island in the Sun

(1957, US, 123 min)
d Robert Rossen. *p* Darryl F Zanuck. *sc* Alfred Hayes. *ph* Freddie Young. *ed* Reginald Beck. *ad* William C Andrews. *m* Malcolm Arnold. *cast* James Mason, Harry Belafonte, Joan Fontaine, Dorothy Dandridge, Joan Collins, Stephen Boyd, Michael Rennie, Diana Wynyard.
●Eager yet compromised tilt at a mid-'50s race relations movie, which hasn't quite got the courage of its convictions. Diluted from a novel by Alec Waugh, it's set on a fictional West Indian island, Santa Marta, where wealthy would-be politico Mason stirs up matters by opposing union leader Belafonte in the local election, and the challenger's sister Collins frets at the effect it might have on her impending engagement to Governor's son Boyd. Self-important and rather phoney. TJ

Island of Dr Moreau, The

(1977, US, 104 min)
d Don Taylor. *p* John Temple-Smith, Skip Steloff. *sc* John Herman Shaner, Al Ramrus. *ph* Gerry Fisher. *ed* Marion Rothman. *pd* Philip M Jefferies. *m* Laurence Rosenthal. *cast* Burt Lancaster, Michael York, Nigel Davenport, Barbara Carrera, Richard Basehart, Nick Cravat.
●HG Wells' novel (about a mad doctor who rules an island by grafting men and animals together on his operating table) is ideal material for screen horror because it's filled with subversive political undertones. The 1933 version with Charles Laughton (*Island of Lost Souls*) made the most of these, but here director Don Taylor seems determined to iron out all the interesting emphases in favour of a visual and narrative style that reduces everything to the level of schoolboy adventure. The island becomes an antiseptic paradise, and Moreau (Lancaster) is no longer a white-suited colonial sadist but the standard misguided scientist. Only Michael York's metamorphosis into a beast has any impact, and the film predictably fails to follow through even on that. DP

Island of Dr Moreau, The

(1996, US, 96 min)
d John Frankenheimer. *p* Edward R Pressman. *sc* Richard Stanley, Ron Hutchinson. *ph* William A Fraker. *ed* Paul Rubell. *pd* Graham Walker. *m* Gary Chang. *cast* Marlon Brando, Val Kilmer, David Thewlis, Fairuza Balk, Ron Perlman, Marco Hofschneider, Temuera Morrison.
●Third adaptation of HG Wells' sci-fi novel, begun by Richard Stanley (*Hardware*) and completed by John Frankenheimer. Like one of Moreau's creatures, it is a sorry patchwork, its jumbled good and bad parts in constant conflict. Yet despite the ludicrous antics of Brando's Moreau, and the lazy, narcissistic Kilmer as his ex-neuro-surgeon sidekick Montgomery, flashes of inspiration remain, not least in Brando's idiosyncratic but chilling delivery of the key speech that begins, 'I have seen the Devil in my microscope, and I have chained him.' One feels sorriest for Thewlis and Balk, who as morally repulsed castaway Douglas and Moreau's beautiful, feline daughter Aissa, vainly try to counter the indulgent excesses of their co-stars. Smeared with sunblock and sporting a range of absurd headgear, Brando is too whimsical to convince as either the gene-splicing genius or the benevolent dictator, dispensing justice with the aid of pain-inducing implants that he activates whenever his half-human subjects threaten to revert to their animalistic ways. In a more coherent context, Stan Winston's varied creature designs might have had more impact; here they barely serve to distinguish one mutant creation from another. NF

Island of Lost Souls

(1932, US, 72 min, b/w)
d Erle C Kenton. *sc* Waldemar Young, Philip Wylie. *ph* Karl Struss. *cast* Charles Laughton, Richard Arlen, Leila Hyams, Kathleen Burke, Bela Lugosi, Stanley Fields.
●Not a great success at the time, probably because its horror is more intellectual than graphic, this adaptation of HG Wells' *The Island of Dr Moreau* (repudiated by the novelist, and originally banned in Britain) is nevertheless a remarkably powerful film. Laughton is magnificently repellent as the fiendish doctor whose evolutionary experiments, involving painful vivisectional graftings, have resulted in a pitiful island community of hideous man-beasts. Satanically bearded, the epitome of imperialist arrogance in his immaculate white ducks, the whip-toting Moreau rules his 'natives' through rituals of fear and pain; and in a subplot that suffuses the film with a perverse erotic sadism, he indulges his intellectual curiosity by plotting to mate a human (Arlen) with the beautiful girl he has created from a panther (Burke), but who is already reverting to her animal state. In the delirious final sequence, superbly staged and shot by Karl Struss as the 'natives' rebel and drag the screaming Laughton away to his own 'House of Pain', the film's subversive spirit surfaces with a real vengeance. TM

Island of Mutations (L'Isola degli Uomini Pesce)

(1979, It, 100 min)
d Sergio Martino. *p* Luciano Martino. *sc* Sergio Donati, Cesare Frugoni, Sergio Martino. *ph* Giancarlo Ferrando. *ed* Eugenio Alabiso. *pd* Massimo Antonello Geleng. *m* Luciano Michelini. *cast* Barbara Bach, Claudio Cassinelli, Richard Johnson, Joseph Cotten, Beryl Cunningham.

●Irresistibly giggly hokum that gives an uncredited airing to *The Island of Dr Moreau*, boasts a whole school of amphibious 'Black Lagoon'-styled creatures, and works up a reasonable head of cheap thrills in a finale uniting an erupting volcano, voodoo, the treasure of Atlantis, the mad biologist's secret, and a good old graveyard fist-fight. Some rather dry verbal humour, stylish camerawork, and performances above par for the Saturday afternoon genre easily offset the variable SFX, and overall it makes welcome second feature material. PT

Island of the Burning Heat

see Night of the Big Heat

Island of the Damned

see ¿Quién Puede Matar a un Niño?

Island Rescue

see Appointment with Venus

Islands in the Stream

(1976, US, 105 min)
d Franklin J Schaffner. *p* Peter Bart, Max Palevsky. *sc* Denne B Petitclerc. *ph* Fred J Koenekamp. *ed* Robert Swink. *pd* William J Creber. *m* Jerry Goldsmith. *cast* George C Scott, David Hemmings, Gilbert Roland, Susan Tyrrell, Richard Evans, Claire Bloom, Julius Harris, Hart Bochner.

●The strongest thing about this ponderous movie is the redoubtable George C Scott. Basing the character on Hemingway himself as much as upon the Hemingway hero of this late novel, Scott contrives mostly to play Scott; and what makes his performance so interesting is the tension between conscientious craftsmanship and an intelligence too keen to take seriously the whole charade of acting. Set in the Caribbean in 1940, this film about father and sons uncomfortably mixes reflection and action: ageing artist comes to terms with life (during sons' school holidays) and death (heroic self-sacrifice). Scott performs the Hemingway clichés with vigorous conviction, whether trying to catch the big fish, idealising the memory of his first wife, or displaying gruff affection for the obligatory rummy friend. Mostly it's heavy going, though, especially Schaffner's direction, which languishes in the tropical sun as it did with *Papillon*. CPe

Island Tales, The (You Shi Tiaowu)

(1999, HK/Jap, 100 min)
d Stanley Kwan. *p* Shinya Kawai, Naoko Tsukeda. *sc* Jimmy Ngai. *ph* Kwan Pun-Leung. *ed* Maurice Li, Jimmy Ngai. *pd* William Chang. *m* Yu Yat-Yiu. *cast* Takao Osawa, Shu Qi, Michele Reis, Julian Cheung, Kaori Momoi, Elaine Jin, Gordon Liu.

●Kwan's seriously misjudged movie recycles the old plot about strangers thrown together by a quarantine scare; during a day and night of enforced isolation on an island they learn some fairly rudimentary lessons about inspiration, motivation, careerism and death. Audience sympathy for the often tiresome characters is assumed rather than earned; a scrambled time-frame, scrappy editing and a women's magazine approach to characterisation don't help. Michele Reis comes off worst as a bossy American-Chinese dyke with a would-be waspish line in put-downs. More idiosyncratic, Shu Qi and Japanese star Momoi fare better. Ex-kung fu star Gordon Liu puts in a surprising appearance as a gay hotel proprietor. TR

Isle, The (Seom)

(2000, SKor, 89 min)
d Kim Ki-Duk. *p* Seok Dong-Jun, Lee Eun. *sc* Kim Ki-Duk. *ph* Hwang Seo-Sik. *ed* Kyung Min-Ho. *pd* Kim Ki-Duk. *m* Cocore, Super String, Huckleberry Finn, Double M Brothers, Dream & Delusion. *cast* Seo Jeong, Kim Yu-Seok, Cho Jae-Hyun, Park Seong-Hee, Jang Hang-Seon.

●Women! Can't live with 'em, can't live without 'em! Notorious for causing viewers to scream, vomit and pass out at its Venice premiere, Kim's fourth feature is a juvenile allegory of man's love/hate relationship with woman. The mute Hee-Jin (Seo) operates a number of fishing rafts on a remote lake, supplying provisions, fishing aids and sometimes sexual services to the men who rent them. The suicidal Hyun-Sik (Kim), evidently on the run, rents a raft. She seduces him, he beats her, she takes revenge, he swallows fish hooks, she saves his life, he kicks her crotch, etc etc. At least it's all framed in striking images, but the ideas are banal, the shock tactics are desperate (fish hooks in the vagina) and the cruelty to animals is indefensible. In sum, obnoxious. TR

Isle of Love, The

(1922, US, 5 reels, b/w)
d/sc Fred J Balshofer. *ph* Tony Gaudio. *cast* Rudolph Valentino, Julian Eltinge, Virginia Rappe, Alma Francis, Lydia Knott.

●A drag artist, Valentino in his days before stardom, and the actress who was to die in the Arbuckle scandal: a list perhaps dreamed up in desperation for a story about the wilder shores of early Hollywood? In fact, these three came together for a 1920 film, *An Adventuress* (written by Charles Taylor, Tom J Geraghty). In 1922, after Virginia Rappe had died and Valentino had become a star, director Fred Balshofer recut his footage and boosted Valentino's part with out-takes. The outcome is pretty loopy: Eltinge in drag, a palace revolution, saucy bathing belles, and huge plugs for US intervention in foreign affairs. Most of the film's interest comes from its blatant efforts to cash in: a silent conversation between Rappe and Valentino takes on dimensions that Balshofer could never have dreamed of in 1920. CPe

Isle of the Dead

(1945, US, 71 min, b/w)
d Mark Robson. *p* Val Lewton. *sc* Ardel Wray. *ph* Jack MacKenzie. *ed* Lyle Boyer. *ad* Albert S D'Agostino, Walter Keller. *m* Leigh Harline. *cast* Boris Karloff, Ellen Drew, Marc Cramer, Katherine Emery, Helene Thimig, Alan Napier.

●Set on a Greek island threatened by the plague at the end of the Balkan war of 1912, this moody but slightly muddled RKO horror movie involves the premature burial of the British consul's wife (Emery), who rises as a new Britannia, a silent, emblematic figure killing with a trident and saving Greek womanhood (Drew) from the Greek general (Karloff) to enable her to fall into the arms of an American. Producer Val Lewton occasionally manages to evoke the wondrous effects achieved by Jacques Tourneur (who made Lewton's name as a producer) in *I Walked with a Zombie*. The film comes magnificently alive with the burial sequence, and with the zombie-like, white-robed woman roaming through shadowy galleries and shuttered rooms. PW

Isn't She Great

(1999, US/Ger/GB/Jap, 95 min)
d Andrew Bergman. *p* Mike Lobell. *sc* Paul Rudnick. *ph* Karl Walter Lindenlaub. *ed* Barry Malkin. *pd* Stuart Wurtzel. *m* Burt Bacharach. *cast* Bette Midler, Nathan Lane, David Hyde Pierce, Stockard Channing, John Cleese, John Larroquette, Amanda Peet.

●What a screech that went up in heaven the day Jacqueline Susann heard that, in the movie version of her life, she was to be played by Bette Midler. Susann, best known for her sleazy novel *Valley of the Dolls*, always thought of herself as crashingly beautiful. Confronting the issue head on, the film is all about the gap between how we'd like to be seen and how others see us. But, based on an article 'Wasn't She Great' by Michael Korda, Paul Rudnick's script keeps staggering like a drunk towards sentimentality (an autistic son, breast cancer and a supportive husband get slobbered over at embarrassing length), only to sober up suddenly. Things work best when Jackie and pal Flo (Channing) get together. It's a reminder not only that Midler and Channing can act, but that vanity and a taste for Venus flytrap clothing don't necessarily blunt your powers of observation. Extolling the profundity of the superficial, there are lines here Wilde would appreciate. Visually, the costumes do all the time travel work, with director Bergman shooting in that '70s-lite haze which Midler drags into her films. CO'Su

I Stand Alone (Seul contre tous)

(1998, Fr, 92 min)
d/p/sc Gaspar Noé. *ph* Dominique Colin. *ed* Lucille Hadzihalilovic, Gaspar Noé. *cast* Philippe Nahon, Blandine Lenoir, Frankye Pain, Martine Audrain, Zaven, Jean-François Rauger, Guillaume Nicloux.

●Nahon gives a stunningly courageous performance as the racist, misanthropic, unemployed horsemeat butcher, who dumps his pregnant fiancée, gets a gun and trawls the gutter. His purpose in life is basic survival and the possibility of springing his mentally retarded daughter from care. Noé's first feature bombards the audience with a vile voice-over and jarring gunshot zooms, forcing us to face the bristling hatred of one of society's ultimate outsiders. By so doing he tests his audience's moral convictions, but it's a gruelling battle. A film of alarming intensity. TJ

I Start Counting

(1969, GB, 105 min)
d/p David Greene. *sc* Richard Harris. *ph* Alex Thomson. *ed* Keith Palmer. *pd* Brian Eatwell. *m* Basil Kirchin. *cast* Jenny Agutter, Bryan Marshall, Clare Sutcliffe, Simon Ward, Gregory Phillips, Lana Morris, Madge Ryan, Fay Compton.

●Misfired psychological thriller revolving around Agutter's schoolgirl fantasies about her older foster brother and a series of local murders, and evoking unproductive associations with such precursors as *The Fallen Idol*. A disappointment to admirers of *The Shuttered Room* and *The Strange Affair*, with which Greene appeared to be establishing himself in the feature market, and a prompt to his resumption of prolific TV work (previously in Britain, Canada and the States, subsequently with such heavyweights as *Rich Man, Poor Man* and *Roots*) from which he has sporadically emerged for such impersonal chores as *Godspell* or *Gray Lady Down*. PT

Is There Sex After Marriage?

(1973, US, 87 min)
d/p/sc Richard Robinson. *ph/ed* David Worth. *cast* John Dunn, Lori Brown, Keith Benedict, Candy Samples, Tony Grillo.

●This little sex epic tells of a housewife and her husband getting outside rejuvenations (such titillations as a porno movie or two prostitutes in lesbian embrace) to overcome their awful inhibitions. The acting is reasonably natural and the number of couplings reasonably plentiful; everything happens with pace and economy, and a lady named Candy Samples boasts a fine pair of breasts. What more can you possibly want? GB

I Still Know What You Did Last Summer

(1998, US/Ger, 100 min)
d Danny Cannon. *p* Neal H Moritz, Erik Feig, Stokely Chaffin, William S Beasley. *sc* Trey Callaway. *ph* Vernon Layton. *ed* Peck Prior. *pd* Douglas Kraner. *m* John Frizzell. *cast* Jennifer Love Hewitt, Freddie Prinze Jr, Brandy, Mekhi Phifer, Muse Watson, Bill Cobbs, Matthew Settle, Jeffrey Combs, Jennifer Esposito.

●Irredeemably dire follow-up to *I Know What You Did Last Summer*. What do you do if, a year on, you're still traumatised by the wholesale slaughter of your friends by a hook-handed Cap'n Bird's Eye lookalike? Go on an all-expenses-paid vacation, courtesy of a local radio competition, to an off-season Bahamas hotel, together with your sassy college roommate Karla (Brandy), her horny boyfriend Tyrell (Phifer) and a love-struck classmate you hardly know. But dead, demented fisherman Ben Willis shows up on cue, his oilskin and sou'wester proving mighty handy for stalking hapless teens through tropical storms. NF

I Take This Woman

(1939, US, 97 min, b/w)
d WS Van Dyke. *p* Bernard Hyman. *sc* James Kevin McGuinness. *ph* Harold Rosson. *ed* George Boemler. *ad* Cedric Gibbons, Paul Groesse. *m* Bronislau Kaper. *cast* Spencer Tracy, Hedy Lamarr, Verree Teasdale, Kent Taylor, Laraine Day, Mona Barrie, Jack Carson, Marjorie Main.

●Tracy as a dedicated doctor who dissuades Lamarr from committing suicide, marries her, and then an old flame of his shows up, making Lamarr go off the rails again. Much more interesting than the soapy histrionics is the film's production history: the supporting cast was changed in mid-stream, and director Josef von Sternberg was replaced by Frank Borzage, who was finally replaced by Van Dyke. Known in Hollywood as 'I Re-take This Woman', it was really a project of Louis B Mayer's, which would have been junked had it not been for the mogul's insistence that Hedy Lamarr would become a star in it. ATu

Italianamerican

(1974, US, 49 min)
d Martin Scorsese. *p* Paul Rubin, Elaine Attias. *ph* Alec Hirschfeld. *ed* Bert Lovitt. *with* Catherine Scorsese, Charles Scorsese, Martin Scorsese.

●Scorsese used to wrap up each feature by hustling through a fast documentary on its tail, a practice that unfortunately he seems to have discontinued. Made just after *Mean Streets*, *Italianamerican* proves just as instructive about life in Little Italy as Johnny Boy's saga. It's simply Catherine and Charles Scorsese sitting reminiscing on a plastic sofa; but their son Marty demonstrates an early maturity by allowing them a lot of living-space and little interference, from which a likeable and affectionate portrait emerges. Charles is a regular, unpretentious guy; Catherine an engaging, garrulous mama, from whom Scorsese obviously inherited his furious logorrhea. She also makes meatballs, whose recipe is included on the credits. CPea

Italian for Beginners (Italiensk for Begyndere)

(2000, Den, 112 min)
d Lone Scherfig. *p* Ib Tardini. *sc* Lone Scherfig. *ph* Jørgen Johansson. *ed* Gerd Tjur. *cast* Anders W Berthelsen, Ann Eleonora Jørgensen, Anette Støvelbæk, Peter Gantzler, Lars Kaalund, Sara Indrio Jensen, Elsebeth Steentoft.

●There's some mileage yet in the Dogme franchise. Shot on some of the same locations as *Dancer in the Dark*, this immensely likeable movie about six unhappy loners eking out an existence in a dead end town starts in bleak fashion, but once the losers start attending evening classes in Italian, the mood begins to lighten. By the final reel, the film has turned into something approaching a conventional romantic comedy. Scherfig (the first woman to direct a Dogme movie) dènies that she was trying to serve up a fairytale ending. 'I just hope people who see the film can see the possibility of turning a not so good fate into a slightly better one,' she says. GM

Italian Job, The

(1969, GB, 100 min)
d Peter Collinson. *p* Michael Deeley. *sc* Troy Kennedy Martin. *ph* Douglas Slocombe. *ed* John Trumper. *pd* Disley Jones. *m* Quincy Jones. *cast* Michael Caine, Noël Coward, Benny Hill, Raf Vallone, Tony Beckley, Rossano Brazzi, Maggie Blye, Irene Handl, John Le Mesurier, Fred Emney, Robert Powell.

●The planning and execution of a Turin bullion heist take, for once, a back seat to the stunt-riddled getaway (subsequently pastiched, after numerous TV screenings of the film, by at least one car commercial). As a modest fun movie, it works, much helped by deep casting contrasts and a nice sense of absurd proportions from scriptwriter (and *Z Cars* originator) Troy Kennedy Martin. PT

It All Starts Today (Ça commence aujourd'hui)

(1999, Fr, 118 min)
d Bertrand Tavernier. *p* Alain Sarde, Frédéric Bourboulon. *sc* Dominique Sampiero, Tiffany Tavernier, Bertrand Tavernier. *ph* Alain Choquart. *ed* Sophie Brunet. *ad* Thierry François. *m* Louis Sclavis. *cast* Philippe Torreton, Maria Pitarresi, Nadia Kaci, Véronique Ataly, Nathalie Bécue, Emmanuelle Bercot, Françoise Bette, Christine Citti, Christina Crevillen.

●A war movie that happens to take place in a nursery school in northern France, this is wrenching, unpatronising social conscience cinema. Daniel (Torreton) is the embattled headteacher, fighting to do the best by his kids in a former mining community – a job that's tantamount to social work. Daniel's convictions are fiercely and unapologetically socialist, and Tavernier plunges us into the life of the school without pause. Using the documentary-style Steadicam technique of his policier *L.627*, Tavernier conveys the stimulation, the inspiration, and the frustration of teaching, as well as the limitless demands it makes on the teacher's compassion. Torreton is intense and dynamic, persuading us of Daniel's anger at a post-socialist political agenda and a quieter, poetic sensibility. It's Ken Loach territory, and like Loach, not beyond melodrama – Daniel's crisis of faith is linked to the fate of an alcoholic mother and an abused child – but also like Loach, too salutary to be fobbed off with condescension. Some critics have found the ending over-optimistic, but after the many troubled parental relationships in Tavernier's films, from *The Watchmaker of Saint-Paul*, through *'Round Midnight* to *These Foolish Things*, this precious affirmation is surely merited. TCh

It Always Rains on Sunday

(1947, GB, 92 min, b/w)
d Robert Hamer. *p* Michael Balcon. *sc* Angus Macphail, Robert Hamer, Henry Cornelius. *ph* Douglas Slocombe. *ed* Michael Truman. *ad* Duncan Sutherland. *m* Georges Auric. *cast* Googie Withers, John McCallum, Jack Warner, Edward Chapman, Susan Shaw, Patricia Plunkett, Alfie Bass, Jimmy Hanley, John Slater, Sydney Tafler.

●A resolutely downbeat – remarkably so for Ealing Studios – account of a day in the life of Bethnal Green when an escaped convict (McCallum) seeks shelter at the home of a former girlfriend (Withers), now respectably married but bored and waspishly discontented. No attempt is made to elicit easy sympathy for either of the protagonists as they pursue their selfish ends, and the sense of drab squalor, with pursuit ending in the railway yards, is a minor key echo of the poetic realism (also carefully studio-built) of prewar Carné and Renoir. Only slightly compromised by a certain pawkiness in some of the minor Cockney characterisations. TM

Italy: Year One (Anno Uno)

(1974, It, 123 min)
d Roberto Rossellini. *sc* Roberto Rossellini, Marcella Mariani, Luciano Scaffa. *ph* Mario Montuori.*ed* Jolanda Benvenuti. *ad* Giuseppe Mangano. *m* Mario Nascimbene. *cast* Luigi Vannucchi, Dominique Darel, Valeria Sabel, Rota Forzano, Ennio Balbo, Rita Calderoni, Omero Antonutti.

●Rossellini's return to the cinema after twelve years working for television: a sympathetic, idealised – and almost universally reviled – portrait of Italy's postwar statesman Alcide De Gasperi (played by Vannucchi), the Christian Democrat leader who successfully kept the Communists out of the government, it is indeed hard to swallow. Its flaw is obvious: from 1945's chaos through anti-Communist coalitions, the historical realities are too close to bear De Gasperi's saint-like depiction. Its major saving irony is that it shows the conditions for historical choices in a much more illuminating light than its reactionary ticket would allow. So, although by no means the best, it's the most provocative of Rossellini's historical biographies, looking suspiciously like a triumph for the devil's advocate. DMacp

It Came from Beneath the Sea

(1955, US, 78 min, b/w)
d Robert Gordon. *p* Charles H Schneer. *sc* George Worthing Yates, Hal Smith. *ph* Henry Freulich. *ed* Jerome Thoms. *ad* Paul Palmentola. *m* Mischa Bakaleinikoff. *cast* Kenneth Tobey, Faith Domergue, Donald Curtis, Ian Keith, Harry Lauter.

●Good to see supporting stalwart Tobey get a lead for once, even if it is in this minor entry in the '50s cycle of radiation-paranoia sci-fi pics (effects by Ray Harryhausen). Our man is a sailor whose submarine is almost sunk by an unidentifed object in the Pacific. Before long San Francisco itself is threatened by the mystery marauder, an octopus mutated to giant dimensions by nuclear tests. (The budget allowed for a creature with only six tentacles.) TJ

It Came from Hollywood

(1982, US, 80 min, b/w & col)
d Malcolm Leo, Andrew Solt. *p* Susan Strausberg, Jeff Stein. *sc* Dana Olsen. *ed* Bert Lovitt. *cast* Dan Aykroyd, John Candy, Cheech Marin, Tommy Chong, Gilda Radner.

●A sloppy compilation of the lowlights of schlock. Z-movie monsters and specious effects are wheeled on for a few easy laughs, with unfunny introductions by the likes of Dan (*My Stepmother Is an Alien*) Aykroyd. Most of the clips didn't come from Hollywood at all; they came from Britain, Japan and garages in the Midwest. Some of them do, but anyone who laughs at scenes from classics like *War of the Worlds* and *The Incredible Shrinking Man* is off my Christmas card list for good. TCh

It Came from Outer Space

(1953, US, 81 min, b/w)
d Jack Arnold. *p* William Alland. *sc* Harry Essex. *ph* Clifford Stine. *ed* Paul Weatherwax. *ad* Bernard Herzbrun, Robert Boyle. *m* Joseph Gershenson. *cast* Richard Carlson, Barbara Rush, Charles Drake, Russell Johnson, Joseph Sawyer, Kathleen Hughes.

●An early attempt at the theme of an encounter with benign but awe-inspiring aliens. The script (nominally from Ray Bradbury's story *The Meteor*) rattles through all the formulary clichés: an amateur astronomer who 'understands', a belligerent sheriff, a woman used as a pawn. But seen in its original 3-D, it's clear that Arnold's direction gives it more than a passing lift. He isn't much good with his second-rate cast, but his compositions in depth are consistently interesting, and his sparing use of special effects keeps the level of visual interest high. The 3-D process leaves the image somewhat murky, but you can discern sparks of authentic pulp poetry throughout. TR

It Conquered the World

(1956, US, 71 min, b/w)
d/p Roger Corman. *sc* Lou Rusoff. *ph* Frederick E West. *ed* Charles Gross. *m* Ronald Stein. *cast* Peter Graves, Beverly Garland, Lee Van Cleef, Sally Fraser, Charles B Griffith, Russ Bender, Dick Miller.

●*It Conquered the World* makes *Dr Who* look like *2001*. A large, triangular Venusian arrives in a California sandpit and starts belching out little bats to vampirise the locals, much to the consternation of the military. You have to see a movie like this to realise that film-makers who feel they have nothing to lose are rarer than you'd think. TR

It Could Happen to You

(1994, US, 101 min)
d Andrew Bergman. *p* Mike Lobell. *sc* Jane Anderson. *ph* Caleb Deschanel. *ed* Barry Malkin. *pd* Bill Groom. *m* Carter Burwell. *cast* Nicolas Cage, Bridget Fonda, Rosie Perez, Wendell Pierce, Isaac Hayes, Victor Rojas, Seymour Cassel, Stanley Tucci.

●'Cop Tips Waitress $2 Million': that was the headline in the New York press when Charlie Lang showed up at a coffee shop on his beat and presented Yvonne Biasi with the winnings he'd promised to split with her if his number came up in the lottery. This fairy tale is narrated by a tabloid journalist 'Angel' (Hayes) and comes complete with a wicked witch, Charlie's wife Muriel, who wants all the money for herself. Perez has a field day as Muriel, injecting a welcome note of good old-fashioned greed into what is otherwise a relentlessly edifying story. As Charlie, Cage is on best behaviour, while the wan Fonda is white-bread-with-crusts-off as the waitress worth her heart of gold. TCh

It Couldn't Happen Here

(1987, GB, 86 min)
d/p Jack Bond. *sc* Jack Bond, James Dillon. *ph* Simon Archer. *ed* Rodney Holland. *ad* James Dillon. *cast* Neil Tennant, Chris Lowe, Joss Ackland, Dominique Barnes, Neil Dickson, Carmen Du Sautoy, Gareth Hunt, Barbara Windsor.

●At a tawdry English seaside resort, mummy's boy Tennant, winsome and sad-eyed in full evening dress, surveys the scene: a ranting blind priest (Ackland) stumbles across shingle trailed by a troop of schoolboys; nuns in suspenders and kinky boots gambol in the shallows; at a funfair drug addicts, gorging fat ladies and perverts whizz past on the big wheel; and Tennant sings that everything he's ever done is a sin. Meanwhile Tennant's pop group sidekick Lowe breaks free of a garish boarding-house where Barbara Windsor is serving mountainous breakfasts. Director Bond's attempt at a narrative stringing together of the Pet Shop Boys' pop themes is witless, aimless and pretentious. If this sickbag of kitsch communicates anything it's the anguish of a young aesthete on discovering that flying ducks still adorn the walls of his mother's house. EP

It Happened at the Inn

see Goupi-Mains-Rouges

It Happened Here

(1963, GB, 99 min, b/w)
d/p/sc Kevin Brownlow, Andrew Mollo. *ph* Peter Suschitzky. *ed* Kevin Brownlow. *ad* Andrew Mollo. *m* Jack Beaver. *cast* Pauline Murray, Sebastian Shaw, Fiona Leland, Honor Fehrson, Percy Binns, Frank Bennett.

●With an immense reputation as a doggedly meticulous historical fantasy, Brownlow/Mollo's low-budget film of a Nazi invasion of Britain now seems more than ever like a Borges newsreel: though the event never happened, a film of it perhaps exists from which only these scraps of footage survive. A genuinely eccentric curio which names but cannot express its fears or desires.

It Happened in Brooklyn

(1946, US, 103 min, b/w)
d Richard Whorf. *p* Jack Cummings. *sc* Isobel Lennart. *ph* Robert Planck. *ed* Blanche Sewell. *ad* Cedric Gibbons, Leonid Vasian. *songs* Jule Styne, Sammy Cahn. *cast* Frank Sinatra, Kathryn Grayson, Jimmy Durante, Peter Lawford, Gloria Grahame.

●Sinatra was still in the bobby-soxer phase when he made this fluffy musical about a returning GI who moves in with Brooklyn janitor Durante, falls for teacher Grayson, and sets his sights on a career in showbiz. 'Time After Time' (not the Cyndi Lauper hit) stands out among the tunes, though Frank and the Schnozz kick up a storm on 'The Song's Gotta Have Heart'. TJ

It Happened One Night

(1934, US, 105 min, b/w)
d Frank Capra. *sc* Robert Riskin. *ph* Joseph Walker. *ed* Gene Havlick. *ad* Stephen Goosson. *m* Louis Silvers. *cast* Claudette Colbert, Clark Gable, Walter Connolly, Roscoe Karns, Jameson Thomas, Alan Hale, Arthur Hoyt, Ward Bond.

●The film which lifted Columbia Studios into the big league by winning five Academy Awards and putting Capra's future output among the biggest box-office successes of the '30s. Gable plays a ruthless reporter who adopts a fugitive heiress making her way across America by bus. She (Colbert) is spoiled and snobbish, he is poor but honest, and his attempts to convert her to homespun pleasures hit the right emotional chord in Depression-weary audiences. Opinions divide about whether the film's comedy and sententious notions about the miserable rich and happy poor have dated, but some of the set pieces definitely haven't aged. Capra's sense of humour is a little like that of Preston Sturges, though less caustic; and the film shows its stars at their best, Colbert as one of Hollywood's fresher comediennes, Gable as dumb-but-loveable hunk. RM

It Happened One Summer

see State Fair

It Happened Tomorrow

(1944, US, 84 min, b/w)
d René Clair. *p* Arnold Pressburger. *sc* Dudley Nichols, René Clair. *ph* Archie J Stout. *ed* Fred Pressburger. *ad* Erno Metzner. *m* Robert Stolz. *cast* Dick Powell, Linda Darnell, Jack Oakie, Edgar Kennedy, Edward Brophy, John Philliber.

●An engaging fantasy about a cub reporter (1890 period) granted a peek at tomorrow's news by a ghostly old man who presents him with newspapers a day ahead of schedule. The resulting scoops bring him star status and a load of troubles, culminating on the third day with headlines accouncing his own death: a rendezvous which he tries frantically – though with unexpected results – to avoid. Not always as inventive as it might have been, but an elegantly beguiling movie. TM

I, the Executioner (Minagoroshi no Reika)

(1968, Jap, 90 min, b/w)
d Tai Kato. *p* Kunio Sawamura. *sc* Haruhiko Mimura. *ph* Keiji Maruyama. *ed* Shizu Osawa. *ad* Kyohei Morita. *cast* Makoto Sato, Chieko Baisho, Sanae Nakahara, Kin Sugai, Yoshiko Sawa, Oh Ran-Fan.

●Up there with Oshima's *Violence at Noon* and Imamura's *Vengeance Is Mine* as one of Japan's most disturbing anatomies of a serial killer, Kato's shattering film eschews suspense (it confronts male violence against women head-on from its very first shot) in favour of mystery. What links the murders of five women with the suicide of a 16-year-old delivery boy? Plodding cops (one with a bad case of piles) investigate, and solarised flashbacks eventually provide a denouement, but the near metaphysical ending ensures that the mystery somehow lingers. Kato anchors it in location-shot observation of Tokyo's quotidian realities, which makes the unorthodox approach to questions of sexual politics all the more bracing. TR

I, the Jury

(1981, US, 111 min)
d Richard T Heffron. *p* Robert H Solo. *sc* Larry Cohen. *ph* Andrew Laszlo. *ed* Garth Craven. *pd* Robert Gundlach. *m* Bill Conti. *cast* Armand Assante, Barbara Carrera, Laurene Landon, Alan King, Geoffrey Lewis, Paul Sorvino, Judson Scott.

●Apart from Aldrich's extraordinary *Kiss Me Deadly*, the blood-and-guts thrillers of Mickey Spillane have not translated well to cinema. This adaptation delivers more sex and violence than ever before, and Assante plays Mike Hammer in a shambling Italian style, pleasingly reminiscent of De Niro in *Mean Streets*. But (possibly because Larry Cohen was replaced as director after a week) the film soon becomes repetitious, lacking the overall atmosphere of paranoia that makes Spillane's fictions bearable, and dwelling in a nauseating way (even by the standards of its source material) on sadistic sexual violence. The updated plot concerns sex clinics, post-Watergate cover-ups, and such a multitude of bad guys that even Hammer is only able to despatch about eighty of them. But the modern references just get in the way: as with Ian Fleming, an authentic Spillane adaptation would have to be set in the hysterical atmosphere of the Cold War. DP

I, the Worst of All (Yo, la peor de todas)

(1990, Arg, 105 min)
d María Luisa Bemberg. *p* Lita Stantic. *sc* María Luisa Bemberg, Antonio Larreta. *ph* Felix Monti. *ed* Juan Carlos Macias. *pd* Voytek. *m* Luis María Serra. *cast* Assumpta Serna, Dominique Sanda, Héctor Alterio, Lautaro Murúa, Alberto Segado, Franklin Caicedo, Graciela Araujo.

●Bemberg's dramatisation of the life of Sister Juana Inés de la Cruz, the 17th century Mexican writer, moves from an austere series of tableaux to a charged atmosphere of repression and calculating ambition. Flashbacks reveal Sister Juana's fatherless, impoverished and intellectually precocious childhood, and there's a suggestion that her decision to enter the convent was a tactical manoeuvre enabling her to pursue her studies and writing. When the archbishop later conspires to stop her work, she becomes embroiled in a counterplot to undermine his authority, with disastrous results. Serna's intense performance in the lead role is never allowed to dominate a plot built around internecine conflict, shifting loyalties, betrayals and individual acts of courage. The drama is progressively unsettling, particularly as the spiritual malaise becomes manifest in the horrific ravages of the plague. CM

I Think I Do

(1997, US, 94 min)
d Brian Sloan. *p* Lane Janger. *sc* Brian Sloan. *ph* Milton Kam. *ed* François Keraudren. *pd* Debbie Devilla. *cast* Alexis Arquette, Christian Maelen, Lauren Vélez, Tuc Watkins, Marianne Hagan, Maddie Corman.

●*The Big Chill* warmed over. A group of friends reunite for a wedding: Bob (Arquette) humiliated himself at college when he made a pass at best friend Brendan (Maelen), who went on to sleep with Sarah (Hagan); now Bob's got a boyfriend of his own, soap star Scott Sterling (Watkins), and it's Brendan who wants Bob; someone better tell Sarah... The chief problem with this would-be screwball comedy is Bob. A man supposedly witty, charming and adorable, he is, in fact, an obnoxious, petulant bore who deserves to be beaten about the head. With a sinking heart you realise this ain't gonna happen. Meanwhile, poor undesirable Sarah, the uptight, square, voracious bitch who we're supposed to hate, makes great sense. Indeed, the only character for whom we feel what we're supposed to feel is the ageing, superficial hunk Sterling. Watkins is a natural comedian and delivers his lines with a mix of vanity and sweetness. He's a clue, perhaps, to what might have been. CO'Su

It Hurts Only When I Laugh

see Only When I Laugh

It Lives Again

(1978, US, 91 min)
d/p/sc Larry Cohen. *ph* Fenton Hamilton. *ed* Curt Burch, Louis Friedman, Carol Oblath. *m* Bernard Herrmann. *cast* Frederic Forrest, Kathleen Lloyd, John P Ryan, John Marley, Andrew Duggan, Eddie Constantine, James Dixon.

●Cohen gives his sequel to *It's Alive* a human angle by placing his monster – a large baby of ferocious tendencies – well inside a normal family context and examining the strain this puts on relationships (Kathleen Lloyd is particularly touching as the wife). But on the whole this is a good film in theory rather than practice. The script is written in the Albert Memorial style – ungainly in structure, weighed down with extraneous detail. And Cohen remains a director of parts, capable of imaginatively conceived shocks once the monster babies being kept under observation get on the rampage (crawling about under bedclothes, putting feet into birthday cakes), but less capable of providing a cumulative effect. GB

It's a Gift

(1934, US, 73 min, b/w)
d Norman McLeod. *p* William LeBaron. *sc* Jack Cunningham. *ph* Henry Sharp. *ad* Hans Dreier, John B Goodman. *cast* WC Fields, Kathleen Howard, Jean Roverol, Julian Madison, Tom Bupp, Baby Le Roy, Morgan Wallace, Charles Sellon.

●It's a masterpiece, and Fields' definitive study in the horrors of small town family life. Every person and thing around causes sublime winces of irritation, from the town's horrid disabled citizen Mr Muckle, and a passing insurance salesman looking for 'Karl LaFong', to a squeaking hammock and a rolling coconut. And Fields himself is so curmudgeonly that he almost snatches food from his son's mouth. There's little sentiment (or plot) to provide any relief, either; the film's string of set pieces (three of them taken from the 1925 Ziegfeld Follies) maintains a relentless pace and tone, making this easily the most devastating comedy of the '30s. GB

It's Alive

(1973, US, 91 min)
d/p/sc Larry Cohen. *ph* Fenton Hamilton. *ed* Peter Honess. *m* Bernard Herrmann. *cast* John P Ryan, Sharon Farrell, Andrew Duggan, Guy Stockwell, James Dixon, Michael Ansara, Robert Emhardt.

●Although it doesn't finally have the courage of its convictions and raises more questions than its standard horror/sci fi format can cope with, there's still a lot that comes off here. The premise is blackly humorous: every monster has a Mom who loves it. A banal Los Angeles family discover that they have brought a homicidal vampire baby into the world when Junior, straight out of the womb, goes on a murder spree and pits his wits against a mobilised police force. Despite such potentially sidesplitting material, the film often manages to instil a genuinely chilling atmosphere, with its initially kitsch family growing into human beings as they plummet into a world unhinged and apart at the seams. John Ryan's performance as the husband is particularly astute, and Bernard Herrmann's score milks the suspense for all it's worth. CPe

It's All Happening

(1963, GB, 101 min)
d Don Sharp. *p* Norman Williams. *sc* Leigh Vance. *ph* Ken Hodges. *ed* John Jympson. *ad* Scott MacGregor. *m* Philip Green. *cast* Tommy Steele, Angela Douglas, Michael Medwin, Bernard Bresslaw, Walter Hudd, Jean Harvey, Richard Goolden.

●Cheesy British pop musical of the early '60s has Tommy (fresh and chipper) doing his bit for 'charidee' as a hard-working talent scout for a recording company, who puts on a benefit concert to save the orphanage where he was brought up. It's nostalgia parade time as the gig goes ahead with the likes of Shane Fenton and the Fentones, Russ Conway, and The Clyde Valley Stompers. TJ

It's All True

(1993, Fr/US, 85 min)
d Richard Wilson, Myron Meisel, Bill Krohn. *p* Régine Conckier, Jean-Luc Ormieres. *sc* Bill Krohn, Myron Meisel, Richard Wilson. *ph* Gary Graver. *ed* Ed Marx. *m* Jorge Arriagada. *narrator* Miguel Ferrer

●Some years back, footage of Orson Welles' 'lost' multi-part film – started in South America in 1942 but never completed (the fiasco basically ruined his career) – surfaced in a short documentary. What little there was (some Rio carnival footage, scenes from the fishing story 'Four Men on a Raft') looked stunning. In this documentary, happily, there's much more to show, including a half-hour sequence, with interviews detailing the film's bedevilled history, and an apparently pretty complete restoration of 'Four Men'. GA

It's a Long Way to the Sea (Hkhagoroloi Bohu Door)

(1995, Ind, 106 min)
d Jahnu Barua. *p* Sailadhar Barua, Jahnu Barua. *sc* Jahnu Barua. *ph* P Rajan. *ed* Hue-en Barua. *ad* Phatik Barua. *m* Satya Barua. *cast* Bishnu Kharghoria, Arun Nath, Kashmiri Saikia Barua, Sushanta Barua.

●A village boatman Puwai (Kharghoria) and his grandson (KS Barua) attempt to stay in touch with relatives in the city and to cope with a new bridge across the river that has provided the family with employment for generations. Beneath the surface of this modest Assamese tale, with its familiar metaphorical Indian river, is a moral lesson on the human cost of 'development'. Bar one slight lurch in the middle, the film unfolds with delightful openness and simplicity. NB

It's Always Fair Weather

(1955, US, 102 min)
d Gene Kelly, Stanley Donen. *p* Arthur Freed. *sc* Betty Comden, Adolph Green. *ph* Robert Bronner. *ed* Adrienne Fazan. *ad* Cedric Gibbons, Arthur Lonergan. *m* André Previn. *cast* Gene Kelly, Dan Dailey, Cyd Charisse, Dolores Gray, Michael Kidd, David Burns, Jay C Flippen.

●Donen and Kelly's last musical together, and an exhilarating – if rather odd – follow-up to the marvellous *On the Town*. Dealing with three soldier buddies who reunite ten years after the war, only to discover that they now have nothing in common, it features some great dance numbers (Kelly on roller-skates, the trio dancing with dust-bin-lids for shoes, Charisse and a chorus of plug-uglies in the gym), and a strangely cynical sense of humour about their incompatibility and about television. GA

It's a Mad, Mad, Mad, Mad World

(1963, US, 192 min)
d/p Stanley Kramer. *sc* William Rose, Tania Rose. *ph* Ernest Laszlo. *ed* Frederick Knudtson *ad* Rudolph Sternad. *m* Ernest Gold. *cast* Spencer Tracy, Milton Berle, Sid Caesar, Ethel Merman, Mickey Rooney, Buddy Hackett, Dick Shawn, Phil Silvers, Terry-Thomas, Jonathan Winters, Edie Adams, Peter Falk, Eddie 'Rochester' Anderson, William Demarest.

●Originally filmed in Ultra Panavision for showing in Cinerama (subsequent prints were cut to 154 minutes), Kramer's 'comedy to end all comedy' stretches its material to snapping point but offers happy hours of star-spotting (everyone has a cameo, from Buster Keaton, Jimmy Durante and Jim Backus to Jack Benny, Jerry Lewis and the Three Stooges). There are several great sequences, most of which involve Terry-Thomas, whose image of America as a bosom- and money-fixated society is spot on. It's an epic allegory about greed, centering on a frantic treasure hunt for buried bank loot. ATu

It's a 2' 6" Above the Ground World (aka The Love Ban)

(1972, GB, 93 min)
d Ralph Thomas. *p* Betty E Box. [*sc* Kevin Laffan.] *ph* Tony Imi. *ed* Roy Watts. *ad* Anthony Pratt. *m* Stanley Myers. *cast* Hywel Bennett, Nanette Newman, Russell Lewis, Simon Henderson, Sally-Ann Ferber, Milo O'Shea, Georgina Hale, John Cleese.

●Heartwarming (?) comedy about a well-off Catholic family with six kids where the wife exiles husband to the spare bedroom until he feels brave enough to buy himself some contraceptives. It compromises itself right, left and centre in an effort not to offend, and ends up not saying anything at all, but throwing out on the way a couple of nasty lines in doublethink. The wife, for instance, decides to go on the pill – which is OK for her as she's C of E – without telling her husband; and having been celibate for ten months, they both start having sex fantasies. As a comedy it relies on played-down double entendres and the lady driver joke.

It's a Wonderful Life 100 (100)

(1946, US, 129 min, b/w)
d/p Frank Capra. *sc* Frances Goodrich, Albert Hackett, Frank Capra. *ph* Joseph Walker, Joseph Biroc. *ed* William Hornbeck. *ad* Jack Okey. *m* Dimitri Tiomkin. *cast* James Stewart, Donna Reed, Lionel Barrymore, Henry Travers, Beulah Bondi, Gloria Grahame, Thomas Mitchell, HB Warner, Ward Bond.

●An extraordinary, unabashed testament to the homely small-town moral values and glossy studio production values that shaped Capra's films so successfully in the late '30s and rapidly disappeared thereafter. It's a film designed to grab your cockles and warm them till they smoulder, particularly at the end, with its Christmas card setting, its whimsical angel sent down to save the despairing do-gooder (Stewart) from doing evil by committing suicide. Capra has total command of his cast and technical resources, and a touching determination to believe that it is indeed a wonderful life. GB

It's a Wonderful World

(1956, GB, 89 min)
d Val Guest. *p* George Minter. *sc* Val Guest. *ph* Wilkie Cooper. *ed* John Pomeroy. *ad* Evelyn Webb. *cast* Terence Morgan, George Cole, Kathleen Harrison, Mylène Demongeot, James Hayter, Richard Wattis, Ted Heath and His Music.

●Groan-worthy British musical comedy from the days before rock'n'roll. Cole (at his spivviest) and Morgan are a couple of hard-pressed songwriters, about to be chucked out of their digs by landlady Harrison, when they get their big break – fellow lodger Demongeot, a young mademoiselle in England for her studies, manages to sell one of their tunes to the Ted Heath orchestra. The ensuing complications are unsurprising, but there are enough familiar faces in the cast to make you feel at home, and a pleasing diversion when our chaps pass off a backwards recording as their new progressive jazz opus 'City of Lost Souls'. TJ

It's Great to Be Young

(1956, GB, 93 min)
d Cyril Frankel. *p* Victor Skutezky. *sc* Ted Willis. *ph* Gilbert Taylor. *ed* Max Benedict. *ad* Robert Jones. *m* Ray Martin, Lester Powell, John Addison. *cast* John Mills, Cecil Parker, Mona Washbourne, Dorothy Bromiley, Jeremy Spenser, Brian Smith, Eleanor Summerfield.

●Tempting to see this as a typically British forerunner of Hollywood's cute campus radical movies, with a bunch of musically-minded grammar school kids rebelling against the dismissal of their piano-playing teacher. Actually, it is just a botched imitation of those Garland/ Rooney putting-on-a-show musicals, tediously tame and producing one absurdity to treasure in the sight of John Mills (the teacher in question) jiving over a hot jazz piano in a pub. The music is dubbed by Humphrey Lyttleton's Band (among others less reputable). TM

It Should Happen to You

(1953, US, 86 min, b/w)
d George Cukor. *p* Fred Kohlmar. *sc* Garson Kanin. *ph* Charles Lang Jr. *ed* Charles Nelson. *ad* John Meehan. *m* Frederick Hollander. *cast* Judy Holliday, Peter Lawford, Jack Lemmon, Connie Gilchrist, Michael O'Shea, Vaughn Taylor, Walter Klavun, Whit Bissell.

●One of Judy Holliday's delicious dumb blonde performances as the nobody despairing of being somebody who makes it by splashing her savings on splashing her name across a billboard in Manhattan. Garson Kanin's script doesn't really bite hard enough in its satire of TV and its eager promotion of the nonentity celebrity, nor – after a wonderful opening – does the comedy have anywhere much to go. Bright moments and irresistible performances, though, with Lemmon (in his debut) making a superb foil for Holliday as the solemn documentary film-maker who observes, loves and is baffled by her. TM

It Shouldn't Happen to a Vet

(1976, GB, 93 min)
d Eric Till. *p* Margaret Matheson. *sc* Alan Plater. *ph* Arthur Ibbetson. *ed* Thom Noble. *pd* Geoffrey Drake. *m* Laurie Johnson. *cast* John Alderton, Colin Blakely, Lisa Harrow, Bill Maynard, Richard Pearson, Paul Shelley, John Barrett, Liz Smith, Richard Griffiths.

●A sequel to the fresh-faced, scrubbed and earnest *All Creatures Great and Small*, based on James Herriot's bestselling tales of the life of a Yorkshire vet in the '30s. What Richard Gordon's *Doctor* books were to the '50s, Herriot's vet books are to the '70s. Certainly both have won their way into the hearts of the middle classes, presumably because both are so reassuring about the order of things (an impending world war is kept discreetly in the background of this instalment). And in both, our medical hero mixes self-deprecation with an ability to pull it off when it really counts. Alderton plays the part originated by Simon Ward with a greater natural ability; but otherwise the film offers the same round of people chasing animals and vice versa, farmyard gags, and nostalgia for a vanished rural lifestyle. CPe

It's Love I'm After

(1937, US, 90 min, b/w)
d Archie Mayo. *p* Harry Joe Brown. *sc* Casey Robinson. *ph* James Van Trees. *ed* Owen Marks. *ad* Carl Jules Weyl. *m* Heinz Roemheld. *cast* Bette Davis, Leslie Howard, Olivia de Havilland, Patric Knowles, Eric Blore, Bonita Granville, George Barbier, Spring Byington, Veda Ann Borg.

●Howard and Davis, as feuding thespians too busy to have got around to getting married yet, have more fun with this romantic comedy than its overwritten script by Casey Robinson deserves. When matinée idol Howard has to cope with the consequences of a young de Havilland's backstage advances, the plot degenerates into a rather uninspired Comedy of Errors set in a well-to-do WASPish family's country house. For connoisseurs of bad acting, however, there's an execrable but funny performance from Blore (as a manservant, naturally), with whom Howard has most of the fun. RM

It's Magic

see Romance on the High Seas

It's My Life

see Vivre sa Vie

It's My Party

(1996, US, 110 min)
d Randal Kleiser. *p* Joel Thurm, Randal Kleiser. *sc* Randal Kleiser. *ph* Bernd Heinl. *ed* Ila von Hasperg. *pd* Clark Hunter. *m* Basil Poledouris. *cast* Eric Roberts, Gregory Harrison, Lee Grant, Marlee Matlin, Bronson Pinchot, Margaret Cho, Olivia Newton-John, Roddy McDowall, Bruce Davison, George Segal, Sally Kellerman, Nina Foch.

●Nick (Roberts) is a Los Angeles architect, HIV-positive and now, says his doctor, suffering progressive brain lesions, giving him perhaps another ten days of consciousness. Time to implement Plan B: one final shindig with family and friends, at the end of which Nick will take an overdose, dignity intact. But he won't, or can't, invite Brandon (Harrison), his ex-lover with whom he parted acrimoniously after testing positive. Most of the film consists of Nick's two-day party, at which the ensemble cast mill around, joke and squabble, and gradually slide into a ruminative disconsolateness. Brandon too turns up, is first shunned, and finally makes his peace with Nick. Despite the occasional longueur, all this is quietly engaging. Still, for a weepie, let alone one about AIDS, it's peculiarly upbeat. The real traumas stay in flashbacks, to the death of other infected friends, or in photos arranged in testament on Nick's wall; even moments of frisson, as when Nick's estranged father appears unexpectedly, are kept to the edges of frame. NB

It's Only Money

(1962, US, 84 min, b/w)
d Frank Tashlin. *p* Paul Jones. *sc* John Fenton Murray. *ph* W Wallace Kelley. *ed* Arthur P Schmidt. *ad* Hal Pereira, Tambi Larsen. *m* Walter Scharf. *cast* Jerry Lewis, Zachary Scott, Joan O'Brien, Mae Questel, Jesse White, Jack Weston.

● TV-radio repairman Lewis turns shamus in the search for the inheritor of a millionaire's fortune, and finds he's the missing heir. It's a very funny losing battle against the gadgets and machines, as Lewis turns high energy against cannibal electronic lawn-mowers, TV sets, and living stereo. Up-tempo, satirical, and despite a lame plot, it's a collection of excellent gags. DMacp

It Started in Naples

(1960, US, 100 min)
d Melville Shavelson. *p* Jack Rose. *sc* Melville Shavelson, Jack Rose, Suso Cecchi D'Amico. *ph* Robert Surtees. *ed* Frank Bracht. *ad* Hal Pereira, Roland Anderson. *m* Alessandro Cicognini, Carlo Savina. *cast* Clark Gable, Sophia Loren, Vittorio De Sica, Marietto, Paolo Carlini, Claudio Ermelli, Giovanni Filidoro.

● One-joke romantic comedy in which Gable (stiff with American honesty and hygiene) and Loren (voluble with Italian guile and grubbiness) squabble over the future of an orphan child fast turning into a delinquent amid the *dolce far niente* temptations of a travelogue Italy. Originally intended as a vehicle for Gracie Fields (it happens on Capri), it is kept afloat chiefly by Loren's engaging ebullience. TM

It Started with Eve

(1941, US, 90 min, b/w)
d Henry Koster. *p* Joe Pasternak. *sc* Norman Krasna, Leo Townsend. *ph* Rudolph Maté. *ed* Bernard W Burton. *ad* Jack Otterson. *m* Hans J Salter. *cast* Charles Laughton, Deanna Durbin, Robert Cummings, Guy Kibbee, Margaret Tallichet, Walter Catlett.

● Far better than most Durbin vehicles, enlivened no end by the presence of Laughton as the cantankerous old millionaire who insists on meeting his grandson's fiancée before he dies. The girl can't be reached and so Durbin, a hatcheck girl, is enlisted to deceive the old man, with predictable complications. Cheerful and charming, although one could well do without the chirpy songs warbled by Durbin. GA

It's the Old Army Game

(1926, US, 77 min, b/w)
d Edward Sutherland. *sc* Tom J Geraghty, J Clarkson Miller. *ph* Alvin Wyckoff. *cast* WC Fields, Louise Brooks, Blanche Ring, William Gaxton, Mary Foy.

● In her book *Lulu in Hollywood*, Louise Brooks recalls this as a chaotic, drunken shoot ('Nobody in Ocala seemed to have heard of Prohibition'), and dismisses her own role as 'the love interest'. She's right: it's a hit-and-miss affair, and her appearance is peripheral. Centre stage is Fields, playing the small town drugstore proprietor Prettywillie. He has ghastly relatives (including an obnoxious infant), never gets an uninterrupted nap, gets dragged into a seemingly crooked real estate deal, and makes a disastrous visit to New York. In short, Fields gets to recreate many of his stage routines, and in a much 'purer' form than in most of his later movies. Remade as *It's a Gift*. TR

It's the Rage

see All the Rage

It's Trad, Dad!

(1962, GB, 73 min, b/w)
d/p Dick Lester. *sc* Milton Subotsky. *ph* Gilbert Taylor. *ed* Bill Lenny. *ad* Maurice Carter. *m* Ken Thorne. *cast* Helen Shapiro, Craig Douglas, Felix Felton, Timothy Bateson, Frank Thornton, Bruce Lacey, Chubby Checker, Temperance Seven, Kenny Ball, Chris Barber, Gene Vincent.

● Having cut his teeth on Telegoon shows like *Idiots Weekly* and *A Show Called Fred*, expatriate American Lester proceeded to take the staid British film industry by storm with this firework display of cinematic trickery. Boldly throwing realism out of the window, he uses a wafer-thin plot about a Toy Town mayor determined to stamp out creeping jazzism as a device to explore the '60s music scene (25 numbers in 73 mintes), and to celebrate the coming 'Youth Revolution'. Some of the acts stand up better than others – Gene Vincent singing 'Space Ship to Mars', Gary (US) Bonds, the witty, modish Temperance Seven – but even the more boring trad jazz is filmed with such energy and inventiveness that it entertains. RMy

It Takes Two

(1988, US, 79 min)
d David Beaird. *p* Robert Lawrence. *sc* Richard Christian Matheson, Thomas Szollosi. *ph* Peter Deming. *ed* David Garfield. *pd* Richard Hoover. *m* Carter Burwell. *cast* George Newbern, Leslie Hope, Kimberly Foster, Barry Corbin, Anthony Geary.

● While his new bride is stalling in neutral at the altar, a soon-to-be-ex-bachelor spends his last hours of freedom test driving the car of his dreams with a rather attractive saleswoman for company. Breezy Texas-set caper with a few good jokes. One of the better movies of hit-and-miss director Beaird, best known in Britain for writing the over-heated stage melodrama *0900 Oneanta*, and the squiffy celluloid Southern galumphry *Scorchers*. TJ

It Takes Two

(1995, US, 100 min)
d Andy Tennant. *p* James Orr, Jim Cruickshank. *sc* Deborah Dean Davis. *ph* Kenneth Zunder. *ed* Roger Bondelli. *pd* Edward Pisoni. *m* Sherman Foote, Ray Foote. *cast* Kirstie Alley, Steve Guttenberg, Mary-Kate Olsen, Ashley Olsen, Jane Sibbett, Philip Bosco.

● Brooklyn: spinster and orphanage worker Diane (Alley) wants to adopt her favourite charge, spunky nine-year-old Amanda (Mary-Kate Olsen). Trouble is, she's still looking for Mr Right, and the adoption authorities would rather she'd already found him. Upstate New York: widower Roger (Guttenberg), millionaire and part-time parent, would like to find a new mum for his daughter, pristine nine-year-old Alyssa (Ashley Olsen). Trouble is, he's just got engaged to gold-digging Clarice Kensington (Sibbett), and Alyssa would rather she took her claws out of him. Funnily enough, Amanda and Alyssa are identical strangers. Two comedy genres – mistaken identity and true romance – are married in forgettable fashion. And, alas, the Olsen girls are not immediately heart-warming. NB

It Was an Accident

(2000, GB, 100 min)
d Metin Hüseyin. *p* Paul Goodman. *sc* Ol Parker. *ph* Guy Dufaux. *ed* Annie Kocur. *pd* Joseph Bennett. *m* Courtney Pine. *cast* Chiwetel Ejiofor, Max Beesley, James Bolam, Nicola Stapleton, Neil Dudgeon, Hugh Quarshie, Thandie Newton, Sidh Solanki.

● After four years in jail, Nicky's determined to start fresh. A get-rich scheme isn't strictly legit, but stealing from one-armed bandits hardly counts, does it? Yet he can't move in Walthamstow without running into aggro. While cashing a benefit cheque, he reluctantly foils an armed raid and becomes a 'have a go hero' – to the irritation of local Mr Big, Mickey Cousins (Beesley). Mickey's rival (Solanki) wants him on side and doesn't take kindly to being told 'no'. Retaining the distinctive linguistic linguini of Jeremy Cameron's novel, but only the bones of his plot, the film-makers have fashioned a droll, larger than life, if occasionally scrappy comedy about how shit happens when good blokes do as little as possible. Nicky means well – a copper's daughter (Newton) sees to that – but he tries to please everyone, and never really stands up for himself. Ejiofor makes Nicky agreeably personable. Licensed to play it wide, some of the other actors stray into laddish shenanigans, but for all the hijinks, this has a firm moral underpinning. Snappy Courtney Pine score, rich verbals and an unpretentious desire to entertain. TCh

Ivanhoe

(1952, GB, 107 min)
d Richard Thorpe. *p* Pandro S Berman. *sc* Noel Langley. *ph* Freddie Young. *ed* Frank Clarke. *ad* Alfred Junge, Roger Furse. *m* Miklós Rózsa. *cast* Robert Taylor, Elizabeth Taylor, Joan Fontaine, George Sanders, Finlay Currie, Guy Rolfe, Robert Douglas, Emlyn Williams.

● One of the vintage MGM costume epics from the early '50s when Thorpe was making countless medieval movies 'over at Metro' (this usually meant on location in England). *Ivanhoe* is one of the best, with Robert Taylor in the title role, Elizabeth Taylor as Rebecca, and Fontaine as Rowena. The dialogue and script are fatuously Americanised from Scott's original, but these chivalric Hollywood sagas still have a strange poetic quality about them, perhaps partly because of the way they unscrupulously and inaccurately ransacked literature and history for ideas and images. DP

Ivan Mosjoukine, or The Carnival Child (Ivan Mosjoukin ili Ditya Karnavala)

(1999, Rus, 65 min, col & b/w)
d Galina Dolmatovskaya. *p* Ludmila Boudiar. *sc* Galina Dolmatovskaya. *ph* Pavel Sukhov, Vladimir Lozovsky. *ed* Nelli Zhdanova. *m* Taras Buyevsky.

● This fascinating documentary opens a window on the life and milieu of the great Russian-born silent actor Ivan Mosjoukine. A cross between John Barrymore, Valentino and Chaplin, he dominated Russian movies. Moving to Paris to work with L'Herbier when the Bolsheviks took power, his star soared on, before his rejection of the role of Napoleon for Gance, a fizzled relationship with Laemmle in Hollywood, and the long slow decline. The commentary offers no deep analysis, but the footage and ample documentation speak for themselves. Renoir, having watched Mosjoukine in *Blazing Fire*, decided cinema was to be his passion. WH

Ivan's Childhood (Ivanovo Detstvo)

(1962, USSR, 95 min, b/w)
d Andrei Tarkovsky. *sc* Vladimir Bogomolov, Mikhail Papava. *ph* Vadim Iusov. *ed* L Feyginovoy. *ad* V Chernyaev. *m* Vyacheslav Ovchinnikov. *cast* Kolya Burlyaev, Irina Tarkovskaya, Valentine Zubkov, Yevgeny Zharikov, Dimitri Milyutenko, S Krylov, Nikolai Grinko, Andrei Konchalovsky.

● Tarkovsky's first feature is in many ways an orthodox Russian film of its period. Ivan is a teenage Soviet spy on the German front in World War II who undertakes dangerous missions behind enemy lines, until the inevitable mission from which there is no return. Many of Tarkovsky's later images and themes are already present and correct: Ivan silently wading through still water, eerily immanent forestscapes, the poetry of forbidden zones, and life-and-death struggles played out in slow motion. But the glittering black-and-white camerawork has a florid, bravura quality that Tarkovsky later rejected, as if determined to invest this more or less familiar material with touches of 'visionary' beauty. The irony is that the generic storyline provides a much stronger foundation for his visual ambitions than do the religiose and feebly philosophical abstractions that ostensibly underpin the films from *Solaris* onwards. Tha aura of holiness around Ivan registers neither as religious bombast nor as patriotic myth-making, but rather as an awed respect for childhood mysteries. This is Tarkovsky before his peasant sentimentality and sense of self-importance got the better of him, and it still looks hugely impressive. TR

ivansxtc.

(2000, GB/US, 92 min)
d Bernard Rose. *p* Lisa Enos. *sc* Bernard Rose, Lisa Enos. *ph* Bernard Rose, Ron Forsythe. *ed*

Bernard Rose. *m* Elmo Weber. *cast* Danny Huston, Peter Weller, Lisa Enos, Joanne Duckman, Angela Featherstone, Caroline Feeney, Valeria Golino, Adam Kreutzman, Heidi Jo Markel, James Merendino.

● The trivial and misleading text message of the title masks what is at heart a serious attempt – inspired by Tolstoy's *Ivan Ilyich* – to confront mortality at a time of spiritual vacancy in the penthouse of decadent culture. We're straight into the court intrigues of the Hollywood fast lane for this initially familiar tale of A list agent Ivan, celebrating the poaching of Weller's homophobe, misogynist actor Don West at the same time as receiving a diagnosis of lung cancer. That he loses the battle is no surprise, as the film opens with his demise. But his belated redemption is genuinely powerful, unfolding as it does within a striking, digitally shot LA of burnished, terminal light, its streets as empty as the souls of its brokers. GE

Ivan the Terrible (Ivan Grozny)

(1944/1946, USSR, 100 min (Pt I)/88 min (Pt II), b/w & col)
d/p Sergei Eisenstein. *ph* Eduard Tissé, Andrei Moskvin. *ed* Sergei Eisenstein. *ad* Isaac Shpinel. *m* Sergei Prokofiev. *cast* Nikolai Cherkasov, Serafima Birman, Ludmila Tselikovskaya, Mikhail Nazvanov, Pavel Kadochnikov, Mikhail Zharov, Mikhail Kuznetsov, Vsevolod I Pudovkin.

● Probably the most enjoyable of all Eisenstein's films, his last work, a projected trilogy of which only two parts were completed. The historical subject – Tsar Ivan's struggle to consolidate the Russian empire, freeing it from Eastern domination and (in Part II) the self-serving interests of the Boyars – is sufficiently removed from the crucial problem (for Eisenstein) of reconciling film theory and political practice for it to work as comic melodrama. Often criticised for its lack of historical truth, the film still holds up as a camp essay in authoritarian paranoia. Cherkassov's contorted performance as Ivan, absurdly stylised though it is, beautifully expresses the conscience of the state torn between absolutism and factionalism, while managing a miraculous integration with a superbly operatic visual style. RM

I've Gotta Horse

(1965, GB, 92 min)
d Kenneth Hume. *p* Larry Parnes, Kenneth Hume. *sc* Ronald Wolfe, Ronald Chesney. *ph* Ernest Steward. *ed* Ernest Hosler. *ad* Scott McGregor. *songs* David Heneker, John Taylor. *cast* Billy Fury, Amanda Barrie, Michael Medwin, Bill Fraser, Leslie Dwyer, The Gamblers, The Bachelors.

● At the start of his career, Billy Fury's love of animals proved a constant source of embarrassment to his management, who were trying to mould him into a surly rock'n'roller. By 1965, Fury had broadened into a lukewarm entertainer, and this effort, which desperately plugged his affection for his four-legged friends, was a misguided attempt to (a) widen his appeal to mums, and (b) to regain some of the fans that he and other solo artists had lost since the advent of groupmania in 1963. The film slipped by unnoticed. CPe

I've Heard the Mermaids Singing

(1987, Can, 83 min)
d Patricia Rozema. *p* Patricia Rozema, Alexandre Raffé. *sc* Patricia Rozema. *ph* Douglas Koch. *ed* Patricia Rozema. *ad* Valanne Ridgeway. *m* Mark Korven. *cast* Sheila McCarthy, Paule Baillargeon, Ann-Marie MacDonald, John Evans, Brenda Kamino, Richard Monette.

● When Polly, a gauche, 'organisationally impaired' temp who indulges in absurdly ethereal daydreams and photography, gets a job at a trendy gallery, she develops a crush on her sophisticated, seemingly imperturbable boss, Gabrielle, and unwittingly becomes involved in an art fraud. Unlike her protagonist, Rozema never puts a foot wrong. Polly is granted her own subtle dignity, Gabrielle and her lesbian lover transcend conventional villainy, and an allegorical subtext warning against blind faith in false gods is handled so lightly as to be virtually invisible. For all its social satire, however, this is Polly's film. She is, perhaps, the most memorable, genuinely likeable screen creation in years, and Rozema's debut – touching, hilarious, as fresh as a summer breeze – does her ample justice. GA

Ivory Hunter

see Where No Vultures Fly

Ivy

(1947, US, 99 min, b/w)
d Sam Wood. *p* William Cameron Menzies. *sc* Charles Bennett. *ph* Russell Metty. *ed* Ralph Dawson. *pd* William Cameron Menzies. *m* Danielel Amfitheatrof. *cast* Joan Fontaine, Patric Knowles, Herbert Marshall, Richard Ney, Cedric Hardwicke, Henry Stephenson.

● Russell Metty's gorgeous low-key camerawork sets the tone for this Edwardian chiller with a wonderfully moody opening sequence at a fortune-teller's where Fontaine learns that her destiny is to become a murderess. Demurely grasping ambition aiding, she is soon on her way to black widowhood by poisoning her husband, framing her lover, and setting her sights on the next victim. Based on a novel by Mrs Belloc Lowndes (of *The Lodger*) and given an exquisite period gloss by William Cameron Menzies' designs, it's a little bland but a real pleasure on the eye. TM

I Wake Up Screaming (aka Hot Spot)

(1942, US, 82 min, b/w)
d H Bruce Humberstone. *p* Milton Sperling. *sc* Dwight Taylor. *ph* Edward Cronjager. *ed* Robert Simpson. *ad* Richard Day, Nathan Juran. *m* Cyril J Mockridge. *cast* Victor Mature, Betty Grable, Laird Cregar, Carole Landis, Elisha Cook Jr, Alan Mowbray, Allyn Joslyn, William Gargan.

● A fine thriller in which the familiar situation of the man wrongly accused of his girl's murder is given a number of brilliant twists. Visually, adhering to the Fox style, the film is basically naturalistic, but its mood becomes increasingly murky as the hero plumbs the depths of nightmare, culminating in his discovery that the obese, soft-spoken detective relentlessly hounding him (the marvellously sinister Cregar) knows he didn't kill her but, himself hopelessly infatuated with the dead girl, blames him for her death and means to exact a perverse vengeance. Intimations of *noir* proliferate in the fact that the dead girl's sister is irresistibly attracted to the presumed killer, in the sleazy little dream world inhabited by the real killer, and in a scene of nightmarish ambivalence where the hero wakes to find the detective brooding lovingly over him as he sleeps. It's a pity that the script, developing cold feet, prevents the film from developing its full *noir* potential by toning down Steve Fisher's source novel in several respects. Most notably, Fisher's detective (intriguingly, a pen portrait of Cornell Woolrich), was presented as a man dying of TB ('He looked sick. He looked like a corpse. His clothes didn't fit him'); this sickness, creeping like a cancer through the story, made more sense of his obsessive vendetta against a man healthy enough not only to live but to win love. TM

I Walked with a Zombie

(1943, US, 69 min, b/w)
d Jacques Tourneur. *p* Val Lewton. *sc* Curt Siodmak, Ardel Wray. *ph* J Roy Hunt. *ed* Mark Robson. *ad* Albert S D'Agostino, Walter Keller. *m* Roy Webb. *cast* Frances Dee, Tom Conway, James Ellison, Edith Barrett, Christine Gordon, Sir Lancelot, Darby Jones.

● The most elegant of Val Lewton's low budget horrors for RKO, an imaginative updating of *Jane Eyre* which anticipates Jean Rhys' *Wide Sargasso Sea* by transposing the action to the Caribbean, with Rochester's first wife not mad but the victim of a voodoo spell. The script, weaving a delicately intricate web of local superstition around a litany of oblique references to the relativity of good and evil, does wonders in creating an ambiguously unsettling atmosphere. But it is Tourneur's caressingly evocative direction, superbly backed by Roy Hunt's chiaroscuro images, that makes sheer magic of the film's brooding journey into fear by way of voodoo drums, gleaming moonlight, somnambulistic ladies in fluttering white, and dark, silent, undead sentries. TM

I Wanna Hold Your Hand

(1978, US, 104 min)
d Robert Zemeckis. *p* Tamara Asseyev, Alex Rose. *sc* Robert Zemeckis, Bob Gale. *ph* Donald M Morgan. *ed* Frank Morriss. *ad* Peter Jamison. *songs* The Beatles. *cast* Nancy Allen, Bobby Di Cicco, Marc McClure, Susan Kendall Newman, Theresa Saldana, Wendie Jo Sperber, Eddie Deezen, Will Jordan.

● Spielberg-exec-produced debut for Zemeckis: the zany adventures of four teeny fans from New Jersey determined to crash the Ed Sullivan Show the night the Beatles appeared in 1964 (you never actually see the Fab Four, of course). A personal recollection of the more arcane details of Beatlemania is almost essential, plus familiarity with youth movies like *American Graffiti* and characters like The Fonz. The comedy is far too diverse, ranging from pastiche through farce (old elevator and corridor gags) to plain good humour. In the best scenes, Zemeckis suggests how the Beatles' blend of irreverence, romance and innocence encouraged a kind of youthful rebellion that was almost completely sanctioned. Loved the music. JS

I Wanted to See Angels (Ja Chtela Uwidetj Angelow)

(1992, Rus, 85 min)
d Sergei Bodrov. *p* Carolin Cavallero. *sc* Sergei Bodrov, Carolin Cavallero. *ph* Alosha Radionov. *ed* Olga Grinspan. *ad* Valeri Kostrin. *m* Mongol Shundan. *cast* Alexi Baranov, Natasha Ginko, Lia Ahedjanov, Alex Jarkov.

● Bodrov (director of *Freedom Is Paradise*) divides his time between Moscow and California, which may explain why this vision of Moscow's chaotic sub-culture has a perspective and elegance lacking in other similar Russian movies about juvenile tearaways. Twenty-year-old Bob rides 1000 km to Moscow on his vintage motorbike to collect a bad debt for his boss; the city chews up and spits out this naive country boy, whose head is full of *Easy Rider* dreams. Less *film noir* than elegy for lost chances, the movie gets inside young Russian heads with an acuity that's almost psychedelic. Sexy, bruising and quite haunting. TR

I Want to Go Home (Je veux rentrer à la maison)

(1989, Fr, 110 min)
d Alain Resnais. *p* Marin Karmitz. *sc* Jules Feiffer. *ph* Charlie Van Damme. *ed* Albert Jurgenson. *ad* Jacques Saulnier. *m* John Kander. *cast* Adolph Green, Gérard Depardieu, Linda Lavin, Micheline Presle, Laura Benson, Geraldine Chaplin.

● To make a movie inspired by comic strip art has been a long term ambition for Renais; sadly, fulfilment of the dream seems too have come to late. Scripted by Jules Feiffer, this is a predictable tale of a boorishly xenophobic American cartoonist (in Paris for an exhibition of his work) and his estranged daughter (an unforgiving Francophile academic), who belatedly make friends thanks to unwitting intermediary Depardieu, a Sorbonne genius with a characteristically French love of pulp art. If it's meant to be funny, moving *or* an essay on the gulf between American and European mores, it fails; worse, however, the central characters are all so downright egocentric and unpleasant that they virtually drive you screaming from the cinema. GA

I Want to Live!

(1958, US, 120 min. b/w)
d Robert Wise. *p* Walter Wanger. *sc* Nelson Gidding, Don Mankiewicz. *ph* Lionel Lindon. *ed* William Hornbeck. *ad* Edward Haworth. *m* John Mandel. *cast* Susan Hayward, Simon Oakland, Virginia Vincent, Theodore Bikel, Wesley Lau, John Marley, Dabbs Greer, Gavin MacLeod.

● One of the great anti-capital punishment movies, this is based on the life and death of Barbara Graham. At one time or another, Graham was convicted of prostitution, perjury, forgery, and finally murder. Basing their screenplay on contemporary newspaper files and her own letters, Nelson Gidding and Don Mankiewicz make no bones about Graham's anti-social tendencies, but conclude that she was probably innocent of the last charge. Wise paces the film so that the last half-hour, taking us into the gas chamber, is incredibly powerful, and Hayward won an Oscar for her unforgettable performance. The jazz score is by Johnny Mandel. TCh

I Want What I Want

(1971, GB, 105 min)
d John Dexter. *p* Raymond Stross. *sc* Gillian Freeman. *ph* Gerry Turpin. *ed* Peter Thornton. *ad* Bill Andrews. *m* Johnny Harris. *cast* Anne Heywood, Harry Andrews, Jill Bennett, Paul Rogers, Michael Coles, Sheila Reid, Virginia Stride, Rachel Gurney.

●Anne Heywood as the transsexual son of a Major (Rtd, currently working as a supermarket manager) who decides to fully become a woman (one year later he/she has a 'completely successful' operation). Dexter's *The Virgin Soldiers*, his only previous film, had its points; but this absurd non-exploration has none, aside from one image of sexual frustration powerful only because the rest of the film is so misconceived, misbegotten and coy.

I Want You

(1951, US, 101 min, b/w)
d Mark Robson. *p* Samuel Goldwyn. *sc* Irwin Shaw. *ph* Harry Stradling. *ed* Daniel Mandell. *ad* Richard Day. *m* Leigh Harline. *cast* Dana Andrews, Dorothy McGuire, Farley Granger, Peggy Dow, Robert Keith, Mildred Dunnock, Ray Collins, Jim Backus.

●Having achieved tremendous success five years earlier with *The Best Years of Our Lives*, producer Samuel Goldwyn had high hopes for this slightly less distinguished domestic drama, written by Irwin Shaw, exploring the effects of the Korean war on a small-town family construction business. Suggested by the recent experiences of the mogul's own son, future movie-maker Sam Jr, it's a well intentioned, low-key effort, and though it never quite escapes the feeling that all concerned are walking on eggshells, a valuable record of the times still emerges. TJ

I Want You

(1998, GB, 87 min)
d Michael Winterbottom. *p* Andrew Eaton. *sc* Eoin McNamee. *ph* Slawomir Idziak. *ed* Trevor Waite. *pd* Mark Tildesley. *m* Adrian Johnston. *cast* Rachel Weisz, Alessandro Nivola, Labina Mitevska, Luka Petrusic, Graham Crowden, Ben Daniels.

●This seems to be aiming at obsessive *noir* romance – though these things play better in San Francisco or New York than in pointedly fictional English seaside resorts. Martin (Nivola) returns home after serving nine years for murder. Violating the conditions of his parole, he begins to stalk his old girlfriend Helen (Weisz), unaware that she's under the surveillance of a mute refugee, Honda (Petrusic), who lives on the beach with his older sister, Smokey (Mitevska). For light relief, Martin pays a local prostitute to strip to Elvis Costello's 'I Want You'. The script is too thinly plotted to support the levels of enigma, alienation and abstraction piled on top. TCh

I Was a Fireman

see Fires Were Started

I Was a Male War Bride (aka You Can't Sleep Here)

(1949, US, 105 min)
d Howard Hawks. *p* Sol C Siegel. *sc* Charles Lederer, Leonard Spigelgass, Hagar Wilde. *ph* Norbert Brodine, Osmond Borradaile. *ed* James B Clark. *ad* Lyle Wheeler, Albert Hogsett. *m* Cyril J Mockridge. *cast* Cary Grant, Ann Sheridan, Marion Marshall, Randy Stuart, William Neff, Kenneth Tobey.

●Neatly reversing the usual comic model, where marriage only ever signals 'The End', this is a classic demonstration of Hawks' unsentimental optimism, and a comedy on frustration and sex-roles that is romantic, subversive and extremely funny, all at the same time. Grant is the priggish, bemused French army officer who hates, loves, and marries smart American army lieutenant Sheridan…then discovers that to follow his bride back to the USA and consummate their interrupted wedding night, he must fill in a million forms, wander disconsolately from barrack to barrack in search of a bed, and, final humiliation, dress up in drag to beat the bureaucracy. CA

I Was a Teenage Werewolf

(1957, US, 74 min, b/w)
d Gene Fowler Jr. *p* Herman Cohen. *sc* Ralph Thornton. *ph* Joseph La Shelle. *ed* George Gittens. *ad* Leslie Thomas. *m* Paul Dunlap, Jerry Blaine. *cast* Michael Landon, Yvonne Lime, Whit Bissell, Tony Marshall, Dawn Richard, Barney Phillips, Ken Miller, Vladimir Sokoloff, Guy Williams.

●All-time zero-budget schlock classic capitalising on the late '50s trend for teen problem pictures, and starring Michael Landon, later Little Joe in *Bonanza* and Dad in *Little House on the Prairie*. As a juvenile delinquent, he's sent to an unscrupulous psychiatrist (Bissell) in the hope he'll get the help he needs to reform; instead, said shrink's experiments turn the hapless youth into a werewolf whenever the school bell sounds. CR

I Was Born, But... (Umarete wa Mita Keredo)

(1932, Jap, 91 min, b/w)
d Yasujiro Ozu. *sc* Akira Fushimi, Geibei Ibushiya. *ph/ed* Hideo Mohara. *ad* Takashi Kono. *cast* Tatsuo Saito, Mitsuko Yoshikawa, Hideo Sugawara, Tokkan Kozo [Tomio Aoki], Takeshi Sakamoto, Teruyo Hayami, Seiichi Kato, Chishu Ryu.

●This is the original version of the story about rebellious kids who feel betrayed by their father that Ozu remade as *Ohayo* thirty-seven years later. *I Was Born, But…* doesn't have the later film's oscillations between comedy and a tragic sense of defeat; rather, it begins as a particularly riotous comedy, and then abruptly switches to a darker tone when the boys lose their respect for their father. It's silent (Ozu resisted talkies until 1935), but its visual style is so dynamic that you hardly notice; both the gags and the emotional disappointments are anchored in a sure sense of characterisation that remains wholly fresh, and the pace of the whole film is worthy of Buster Keaton at his best. TR

I Was Fifteen (Den Sommeren jeg fylte 15)

(1974, Nor, 98 min)
d Knut Andersen. *p* Svein Toreg. *sc* Knut Faldbakken, Knut Andersen. *ph* Knut Gløersen. *ed* Bente Kaas. *m* Eyvind Solås. *cast* Steffen Rothschild, Anne-Lise Tangstad, Kaare Kroppan, Grethe Ryen, Carina Rude, Arne Lendl.

●This Norwegian entry in the adolescent-initiation stakes tastefully refrains from an explicit depiction of its hero's first faltering attempts at sexual congress, and instead diverts us at inordinate length with phallic symbols and boyish customs (boasting, blowing up condoms, chaste kissing in the rain). The plot concerns a youngster sent to his uncle's farm for the summer; the uncle is extremely randy, and his homely wife makes up for his neglect of her by overfeeding their nephew. Going for a swim, uncle discovers the body of an orphaned girl made pregnant by him (her pasty make-up washes off before our very eyes). Set sometime in the past, judging from the magazines the boy ogles, this sombre film aims, rather uncertainly, at highlighting the hypocrisy of adulthood and the winsomeness of youth. JPy

I Was Happy Here

(1965, GB, 91 min, b/w)
d Desmond Davis. *p* Roy Millichip. *sc* Edna O'Brien, Desmond Davis. *ph* Manny Wynn. *ed* Brian Smedley-Aston. *ad* Tony Woollard. *m* John Addison. *cast* Sarah Miles, Cyril Cusack, Julian Glover, Sean Caffrey, Marie Kean, Eve Belton, Cardew Robinson.

●A horribly pretentious and sentimental film which still manages to retain a degree of emotional power, with moments of real intensity and conviction. It's about an Irish girl (Miles) who returns to her home in Ireland after an unhappy marriage, and is pursued there by her bullying husband (Glover). The film is certainly much better than Davis' earlier Irish story *The Girl with Green Eyes* (also adapted from Edna O'Brien), but it's dogged by the awful tricks of overemphasis which he seems to have learned from his patron Tony Richardson. DP

I Was, I Am, I Shall Be (Ich war, ich bin, ich werde sein)

(1974, EGer, 71 min, b/w)
d/sc Walter Heynowski, Gerhard Scheumann. *ph* Peter Hellmich, Horst Dowth, Winifried Goldner. *ed* Traute Wischnewski, Robert Michel, Wolfgang von Polentz. *m* Sergio Ortega, Aparco Instrument Group, Mathias Remmert.

●Some months after the Chilean coup of September 1973, an East German camera crew managed to obtain permission to visit one of the Pinochet regime's prison camps, a former disused saltpetre mine in the arid desert of northern Chile. But they were able to film only under close surveillance, and the chief interest of *I Was, I Am, I Shall Be* is the material with which this footage is intercut. Shot mainly before the coup, it places Chatabuco in a historical context, both as mine and as prison camp. The factual testimony of former mineworkers, including a witness of the 1925 massacre at Marusia, makes a striking contrast with the blandly explanatory Pinochet. One shot provides a continual refrain: a prisoner holds up the handle of a miner's spade with the words, 'It was found here and I think it speaks for itself. It can be interpreted in many ways' – a statement whose multiple ambiguities become increasingly clear as the film progresses. AS

I Was Monty's Double

(1958, GB, 100 min, b/w)
d John Guillermin. *p* Maxwell Seton. *sc* Bryan Forbes. *ph* Basil Emmott. *ed* Max Benedict. *pd* Wilfrid Shingleton. *m* John Addison. *cast* John Mills, Cecil Parker, ME Clifton James, Marius Goring, Michael Hordern, Leslie Phillips, Patrick Allen, Bryan Forbes, Victor Maddern, John Le Mesurier.

●Released in America under the marvellous title of *Heaven, Hell and Hoboken*, *I Was Monty's Double* is a low-budget tour de force. Based on real events – an actor (James, who really was used as a double for General Montgomery during the Allied invasion of Europe in World War II) is hired to impersonate Monty and so confuse the Germans by popping up in odd places – the film neatly uses the elevation of a nobody to honoured hero to question the notions of heroism that so many British war movies unquestioningly supported. Highly enjoyable. PH

I Was Nineteen (Ich war Neunzehn)

(1967, EGer, 119 min, b/w)
d Konrad Wolf. *sc* Konrad Wolf, Wolfgang Kohlhaase. *ph* Werner Bergmann. *ed* Evelyn Carow. *ad* Alfred Hirschmeier. *cast* Jaecki Schwarz, Vasili Livanov, Alexey Eyboshenko, Johannes Wieke.

●Germany, April–May 1945: officials cling to their authority as the Nazi fantasy collapses around them; a girl numbly mounts guard over her suicided parents; bands of recalcitrant SS shoot up everything that moves. The film consists of such vignettes, all precisely dated and evidently transcribed from the director's own recollections. Like his alter ego in the film, the teenage Wolf served with the advancing Red Army. The technique – meticulously authentic settings, pseudo-spontaneous handheld camerawork – generates a tremendous sense of reality. But the inevitable sanitised portrayal of Russian soldiery – noble fellows all – undermines it considerably. BBa

I Was on Mars

(1991, Ger/US/Switz, 87 min)
d Dani Levy. *p* Ted Hope, James Schamus. *sc* Dani Levy, Maria Schrader. *ph* Carl-F Koschnick. *ed* Susann Lahaye. *pd* Dan Ouellette. *m* Niki Reiser. *cast* Maria Schrader, Dani Levy, Mario Giacalone, Antonia Rey.

●It's taken a few years for them to gestate, but Jarmusch's *Stranger Than Paradise* has fathered a brood of low-budget Euro-movies about the trials and tribulations of foreigners newly arrived in New York. This is one of them: a relentlessly in-your-face tragi-comedy about a young woman from Warsaw who speaks no English and loses the few greenbacks she has to the first guy she meets, a loud-suited spiv. Levi himself plays the conman as a sleazeball who takes the bit-players in *GoodFellas* as role models; co-writer Maria Schrader plays the Polish girl as dogged perseverance personified. Sometimes raucous, sometimes forlorn, but very rarely convincing. TR

I Went Down

(1997, Ire/GB/Sp, 107 min)
d Paddy Breathnach. *p* Robert Walpole. *sc* Conor McPherson. *ph* Cian De Buitléar. *ed*

Emer Reynolds. *pd* Zoë MacLeod. *m* Dario Marianelli. *cast* Brendan Gleeson, Peter McDonald, Peter Caffrey, Tony Doyle, Antoine Byrne, David Wilmot, Michael McElhatton, Joe Gallagher.

●Lovely, slow-burning shaggy-dog Irish crime movie built around the uneasy partnership of two small-time Dublin chancers. Thrown together for an errand, the lads are to retrieve a fugitive associate of the local crime boss, and return him to face the music. Git (McDonald) is the quiet type, only doing it to help get a mate out of trouble; Bunny (Gleeson) is a bruiser with ginger sideburns and rockabilly shoes, who likes to think he's on top of the situation when, patently, he isn't. Playwright Conor McPherson's mixes broad humour and dialogue (in the Roddy Doyle vein) into a neat thriller plot. He's well served by an as-yet relatively unknown cast, who never allow the skew-whiff turns of phrase to sound self-conscious, and by the director's guiding sense of equilibrium. It's all beguilingly entertaining as we move through a landscape of rural petrol stations, stand-offs on the peat bog, and deepening intrigue; deceptively rich, too, as it reflects on how its reluctant protagonists stand up to the demands of modern masculinity when they're estranged from their womenfolk, and to consider the whys and wherefores of loyalty and integrity when greed and violent persuasion have blurred the lines of moral probity. TJ

I Will...I Will...For Now

(1975, US, 108 min)
d Norman Panama. *p* George Barry. *sc* Norman Panama, Albert E Lewin. *ph* John A Alonzo. *ed* Robert Lawrence. *pd* Fernando Carrere. *m* John Cameron. *cast* Elliott Gould, Diane Keaton, Paul Sorvino, Victoria Principal, Warren Berlinger, Candy Clark, Robert Alda.

●*Harry and Walter Go to New York* demonstrated that the talents of Diane Keaton, that beautifully composed comedienne who neatly partnered the cack-handed and physically inconsequential Woody Allen, were not equally suited to those of the exuberant and brawny Elliott Gould. The main problem with this leaden marital farce climaxing in a Californian sex clinic, however, is not so much that the Keaton/Gould partnership again fails to spark, but that Norman Panama's lamentable script, based on a Hollywood approach to sex and marriage decades out of date, is executed with all the lack of subtlety and brightly lit jollity of a Doris Day heartwarmer. Though hardly surprising in view of Panama's creaky comedy antecedents, it is still wincingly embarrassing to see accomplished performers cavorting in such rubbish. JPy

I Will Survive (Sobreviviré)

(1999, Sp, 102 min)
d Alfonso Albacete, David Menkes. *p* Francisco Ramos. *sc* Alfonso Albacete, David Menkes, Lucia Etxebarría. *ph* Gonzalo Fernández-Berridi. *ed* Miguel Angel Santamaria. *m* Paco Ortega. *cast* Emma Suárez, Juan Diego Botto, Mirta Ibarra, Rosana Pastor, Manuel Manquiña, Alex Brendemühl, Javier Martín, Adriá Collado.

●Emma Suárez, familiar to Julio Medem fans from *Vacas, The Red Squirrel* and *Tierra*, plays Marga, a young woman with a knack for being in the wrong place at the wrong time – most tragically when the father of her unborn baby dies in a car accident. At least she has her friends – most of them gay men, as it happens. Pitched somewhere between wistful romantic comedy and melodrama, this has something in common with Nicholas Hytner's 'Dad to be Gay' movie *The Object of My Affection*. Unfortunately, as in that case, potentially absorbing material is neutered by a domesticated, sitcom sense of cinema. Suárez is a honey, though. TCh

I Won't Go Back Home (No quiero volver a casa)

(2000, Arg, 74 min, b/w)
d Albertina Carri. *p* Hernán Musaluppi. *sc* Albertina Carri, Paula Carri. *ph* Paula Grandio. *ed* Rosario Suarez. *pd* Valeria Ambrosio, Monica Van Asperen. *m* Edgardo Rudnitzki. *cast* Martín Churba, Gabriela Toscano, Manuel Callau, Analia Couceyro, Fabiana Falcón, Ricardo Merkin, Manuel Vicente, Márgara Alonso.

●Shot in moody b/w, this bemusing, tedious little number begins with a murder, then goes back to trace the movements of the assassin, revealing a disintegrating family background in his restless past. The film brings out nothing definite by way of characterisation or narrative tension, lumbering from one lifeless encounter to another, as its 70-odd minutes pass with glacial slowness. One scene where the protagonist rolls marbles at length around a glass-topped table will have you screaming for him to get on with it. TJ

I...You...He...She

see Je tu il elle

j

Jubilee

Jabberwocky

(1977, GB, 101 min)
d Terry Gilliam. *p* Sandy Lieberson. *sc* Charles Alverson, Terry Gilliam. *ph* Terry Bedford. *ed* Michael Bradsell. *pd* Roy Smith. *m* De Wolfe. *cast* Michael Palin, Max Wall, Deborah Fallender, John Le Mesurier, Annette Badland, Warren Mitchell, Harry H Corbett, Rodney Bewes, Bernard Bresslaw, Terry Jones, Brian Glover.
●Honestly, the things people do to make you laugh in this Python-esque medieval epic. They hire a cast of British notables, ranging from Max Wall to Christopher Logue. They seek out some of Britain's nicest ancient monuments. They create a monster with enough horrible features to stock two series of *Dr Who*. They pile on the atmosphere with mist, candles, crowds, dust and blood. They construct a complicated plot and then only give you glimpses of it, as in the foreign films. Oh yes, they write gags too: some are good (jousting knights with daft things like bananas and fish on their helmets), some are bad, and some ugly. Max Wall's fruity enunciation boosts almost all his lines, and Michael Palin makes a pleasingly gormless hero. But nice bits here and there don't amount to a good movie: like the portmanteau words in Lewis Carroll's poem, there's just far too much packed together for anything to make proper sense. GB

Jabula – A Band in Exile

(1981, GB, 41 min)
d Jan Bernard Bussemaker.
●No great shakes as a movie, but a sympathetic profile of this black South African group, exiled to the 100 Club in London and discussing the problem of maintaining indigenous roots in music designed to help fight apartheid through popular appeal. The mainstay is a rousing performance of their number 'Wake Up!', intercut with stills of Sharpeville. TM

J'Accuse

(1918, Fr, 130 min approx, b/w)
d/sc Abel Gance. *ph* L-H Burel, Marc Bujard, Maurice Forster. *ed* Andrée Danis, Abel Gance. *cast* Séverin-Mars, Romuald Joubé, Marise Dauvray, Angèle Guys, Maxime Desjardins.
●The film begins with a close-up of Gance himself staring into the camera: *j'accuse!* But who is he accusing of what? This WWI melodrama is bursting with ideas and energy but void of such concepts as consistency, subtlety, credibility. Taking his characters from 19th century romance (the poet, the brute, the dying mother, the illegitimate tot), applying lashings of symbolism (from nature and religion), Gance compounds the artifice – unwisely – with some frontline actualité. The climax is the shellshocked hero's vision of the war dead returning to judge their families, who are found sadly unworthy of the sacrifice. So after all, it's ungrateful stay-at-homes and unfaithful wives Gance is accusing. He would have more to say two decades later. BBa

J'Accuse

(1937, Fr, 119 min, b/w)
d Abel Gance. *sc* Abel Gance, Steve Passeur. *ph* Roger Hubert. *ed* Madeleine Cretolle. *ad* Henri Mahé. *m* Henry Verdun. *cast* Victor Francen, Line Noro, André Nox, Jean Max, Marcel Delaitre.
●In the first third, Gance reprises his 1918 film of the same title, in the second third he carries the story forward, and the final third is something else again. Exploring the old Verdun battlefield in a thunderstorm, trench veteran Francen undergoes some unspecified transforming experience. Later, with world conflict about to break out again, he invokes the spirits of the war dead who, in an echo of the earlier picture, rise up and parade about reproachfully. A 'Universal Council' is convened, the war is called off, the dead return to their graves. Historically, these passages are an invaluable complement to Munich '38. As cinema, their unself-conscious absurdity and vulgarity (genuine disfigured veterans alongside extras in ghoul make-up) mark them as pure Gance. BBa

Jack

(1996, US, 113 min)
d Francis Ford Coppola. *p* Ricardo Mestres, Fredric S Fuchs, Francis Ford Coppola. *sc* Gary Nadeau, James DeMonaco. *ph* John Toll. *ed* Barry Malkin. *pd* Dean Tavoularis. *m* Michael Kamen. *cast* Robin Williams, Diane Lane, Brian Kerwin, Jennifer Lopez, Bill Cosby, Fran Drescher, Michael McKean.
●The Francis Ford Coppola signature, usually reserved for personal projects, doesn't appear to square with what looks like another excuse for Robin Williams to do his infantile routine. The plot conceit has Williams as a lad, Jack, whose over-active metabolism masks a 10-year-old in the hairy body of a 40-year-old man; but in taking the time to explore this scenario in genuine human terms, Coppola delivers an ungainly but undeniably arresting hybrid. While the film's too mature for the kids' audience, its juvenile slapstick trappings – collapsed chairs and the like – may blind grown-ups to the deeply felt emotions at its core. Jack's dispatched to school for the first time, and the way he wins over his alarmed classmates proves refreshingly clear-sighted: he can buy porn mags, light his farts, and dominate the basketball court. It's good to see a movie in touch with such realities – though Bill Cosby's sticky turn as Jack's kindly tutor should have been cut at script stage. Where things switch up a gear, however, is in the confrontation with the adult world, for an ill-fated attempt at wooing teacher introduces Jack to a confusing arena of failed relationships and sexual hang-ups, while a simple 'What I want to be when I grow up' assignment impresses on him the sobering burden of time: when his chums are twenty-something, he'll be approaching his century. The star, kept under firm control, grates less than usual, though you wouldn't come to 'a Robin Williams movie' for what you get here: a divided soul, and just possibly Coppola's most honest movie in years. TJ

Jackal, The

(1997, US, 124 min)
d Michael Caton-Jones. *p* Jim Jacks, Sean Daniel, Michael Caton-Jones, Kevin Jarre. *sc* Chuck Pfarrer. *ph* Walter Lindenlaub. *ed* Jim Clark. *pd* Michael White. *m* Carter Burwell. *cast* Bruce Willis, Richard Gere, Sidney Poitier, Diane Venora, Mathilda May, JK Simmons, Tess Harper, Leslie Phillips.
●The Cold War's over, but Russia's gangsters don't like FBI interference on their patch. Angered by the death of his brother, one of the Russians decides to punish the Bureau by hiring a top assassin, the Jackal (Willis), to eliminate a high profile target in full view of the American public. Working with Russian intelligence officer Koslova (Venora), the FBI's Deputy Director (Poitier) reckons the only way to stop the killer is to enlist imprisoned IRA terrorist Mulqueen (Gere) – who has his own reasons for hating the Jackal. So begins a race against time as the assassin, an anonymous master of disguise, moves in on his as-yet unidentified prey. Structurally, of course, this film echoes *The Day of the Jackal*, but where Fred Zinnemann opted for a meticulous, even dull study in procedural methods, Caton-Jones goes for pacy, well-staged action, colourful characters, and determinedly contemporary atmosphere. If it's sometimes hard to accept Gere's accent and tough guy stuff, Willis plays the lone, heartless killer with menace, flair and evident glee. Excellent performances, too, from Poitier and Venora. GA

Jackal of Nahueltoro, The (El Chacal de Nahueltoro)

(1969, Chile, 88 min, b/w)
d/sc Miguel Littin. *ph* Héctor Rios. *ed* Pedro Chaskel. *m* Sergio Ortega. *cast* Nelson Villagra, Shenda Román, Luis Melo, Ruben Sotoconil, Armando Fenoglio, Marcelo Romo.
●Chile's first feature, like other Third World films, was made specifically for its own people and intended as a critique of the social conditions in that country. Littin chose the true story of an illiterate peasant who had murdered a widow and her five children when drunk, to dramatise his belief that the crime was as much the responsibility of the state as it was the individual's. The killing is reconstructed as a blind emotional reflex against the accumulated despair of a life of abject, uncomprehended poverty. Sentenced to death amid enormous publicity, the 'jackal' is taught to read and write, to make guitars, to be a 'useful' citizen. The society which is responsible for his original illiteracy and poverty gives him his first 'sense of life' with one hand and a firing-squad with the other. The film leaves you enraged not only at the futility of capital punishment, but also at the whole repressive system whose essential inhumanity is never more clearly indicated than in the final, furtive murder of their scapegoat, a shallow exorcism of their own guilt. JDuC

Jack & Sarah

(1995, GB, 110 min)
d Tim Sullivan. *p* Pippa Cross, Simon Channing-Williams, Janette Day. *sc* Tim Sullivan. *ph* Jean-Yves Escoffier. *ed* Lesley Walker. *pd* Christopher J Bradshaw. *m* Simon Boswell. *cast* Richard E Grant, Samantha Mathis, Judi Dench, Eileen Atkins, Ian McKellen, Cherie Lunghi, Imogen Stubbs, Kate Hardie, David Swift.
●As English as it gets, this romantic comedy about a one-parent family is not without a modest charm. Jack (Grant) loses his wife in childbirth but commits to raising baby Sarah himself. The upside is the sympathetic reaction of young women, and the downside the busybody visits of his mother (Dench) and his wife's mother (Atkins). All is solved when he hires a nanny (Mathis), except that her proximity around the house brings a new cargo of woe. The tale avoids most of the fumbling man-and-baby stuff, but tries to beat the formula elsewhere in overly bizarre fashion. Who would believe a posh alcoholic tramp (McKellen), discovered outside sleeping in a builder's skip, pressed into service as a butler? Yes, the film is thesped to the hilt in the minor roles. Grant is very good at conveying his love for his baby and his impatience with family interference, and possibly only stretched when it comes to being enamoured of the American nanny, an intensely dislikeable bill of goods. Passable. BC

Jack Be Nimble

(1992, NZ, 95 min)
d Garth Maxwell. *p* Jonathan Dowling, Kelly Rogers. *sc* Garth Maxwell. *ph* Donald Duncan. *ed* John Gilbert. *pd* Grant Major. *m* Chris Neal. *cast* Alexis Arquette, Sarah Smuts-Kennedy, Bruno Lawrence, Tony Barry, Elizabeth Hawthorne, Brenda Simmons.
●A heady witches' brew of fairy-tale grimness, melodramatic excess and dark supernatural horror, Maxwell's first feature induces disequilibrium and unease. After their father's affairs precipitate their mother's flight into insanity, Jack (Arquette) and Dora (Smuts-Kennedy) endure a painful childhood separation with very different adoptive families. Jack's sadistic 'father' whips him with barbed wire while his hatchet-faced 'mother' and ghoulish 'sisters' look on. By contrast, Dora's parents are kind, if stiflingly respectable, although at school she is ridiculed and bullied. A long-dreamed-of reunion in their teens, after Jack's escape and Dora's discovery of hidden psychic powers, cannot match the damaged Jack's idealised memories; consumed by desperate, frustrated rage, he lashes out at those closest to him. Meanwhile, his vengeful sisters are on his trail. As the disturbed creator of a steam-driven, hypnosis-inducing light-machine, Alexis Arquette proves that his sisters Rosanna and Patricia have no monopoly on the family talent for flakiness, while Sarah Smuts-Kennedy brings a luminous inner strength to the outwardly frail Dora. NF

Jack Frost

(1998, US, 102 min)
d Troy Miller. *p* Mark Canton, Irving Azoff. *sc* Mark Steven Johnson, Steve Bloom, Jonathan Roberts, Jeff Cesario. *ph* Laszlo Kovacs. *ed* Lawrence Jordan. *pd* Mayne Berke. *m* Trevor Rabin. *cast* Michael Keaton, Kelly Preston, Joseph Cross, Mark Addy, Andy Lawrence, Eli Marienthal.
●Jack Frost (Keaton) pursues his dream of becoming a musician while neglecting wife Gabby (Preston) and son Charlie (Cross). Ironically, however, when he abandons a career-making gig in favour of a family Christmas he piles his car into a snowdrift and dies. A year later, he's reincarnated as a snowman, and has the chance to be the attentive father he should have been first time around. Here things go soft, since Jack's 'born-again father' routine chiefly involves helping Charlie to snow board circles around the school bully, or teaching him an ice hockey shot that dispels the boy's lethargy and gets him back on the school team. The snowman's a bland shuffling blob (from Jim Henson's Creature Shop) with two expressions, an all-purpose smile and a vague look of resignation. NF

Jackie Brown

(1997, US, 154 min)
d Quentin Tarantino. *p* Lawrence Bender. *sc* Quentin Tarantino. *ph* Guillermo Navarro. *ed* Sally Menke. *pd* David Wasco. *cast* Pam Grier, Samuel L Jackson, Robert Forster, Bridget Fonda, Michael Keaton, Robert De Niro, Michael Bowen, Lisa Gay Hamilton, Chris Tucker.

● A pretty faithful adaptation of Elmore Leonard's *Rum Punch*, Tarantino's finest, most mature movie to date centres on airline steward Jackie (Grier), picked up by the Feds at LAX with cash and drugs destined for gun trader Ordell (Jackson). Reluctant to do time and aware that Ordell tends to murder anyone he suspects might turn informer, she decides to play cops and criminals – not only Ordell, but his former cellmate Louis (De Niro) and pothead girlfriend Melanie (Fonda) – against each other, confiding only in Max (Forster), the world-weary bail bondsman Ordell hired to get her out of jail in the first place. What's immediately rewarding is that Tarantino forgoes flash patter, stand-offs and stylistic flourishes in favour of a closer focus on character (women included), relationships, motives and mood. Also crucial to our actually coming to care about these people is the terrific acting (Grier and Forster make you wonder where they've been all these years). But perhaps most surprising and welcome is that this is a subtle poignant account of middle-aged people trying to come to terms with failing faculties, fading looks, diminishing options and a need to make their lives count somehow. GA

Jacknife

(1988, US, 103 min)
d David Jones. *p* Robert Schaffel, Carol Baum. *sc* Stephen Metcalfe. *ph* Brian West. *ed* John Bloom. *pd* Edward Pisoni. *cast* Robert De Niro, Ed Harris, Kathy Baker, Charles Dutton, Elizabeth Franz, Tom Isbell, Loudon Wainwright III.

● As Megs, a clearly unstable Vietvet whose sudden reappearence in the life of his now nearly alcoholic former buddy Dave (Harris) is part theraputic, part traumatic, De Niro is touching, funny and entirely convicing. The moment he arrives out of the blue at the Conneticut home Dave shares with his schoolmarm sister Martha (Baker), we immediately believe in Megs' inarticulacy, slobbishness and sensitivity. Dave's welcome is less than warm; Martha shifts from horror through hesitant acceptance to friendship. Unsurprisingly, as Megs' hidden strengths rise to the surface, he and Martha fall for each other; equally unsurprisingly, Dave – afraid of being alone – opposes their relationship. The stage origins (Stephen Metcalfe's play *Strange Snow*) of this gently humorous, lyrical study in loneliness and the lasting legacy of 'Nam are all too evident; but Jones focuses attention on his three actors, all of whom serve him well. The obligatory 'Nam flashbacks are clumsy, the resolution a little pat; but De Niro, compelling from start to finish, carries the film. GA

Jackpot

(2001, US, 92 min)
d Michael Polish. *p/sc* Mark Polish, Michael Polish. *ph* M David Mullen. *ed* Shawna Callahan. *pd* Michele Montague. *m* Stuart Matthewman. *cast* Jon Gries, Garrett Morris, Daryl Hannah, Anthony Edwards, Crystal Bernard, Peggy Lipton, Adam Baldwin, Patrick Bauchau, Mac Davis, Rosie O'Grady.

● A change of direction from *Twin Falls Idaho*, the Polish Brothers' second feature is a likeably low key road movie following American dreamer Sunny (Gries) as he drives his old pink Cadillac and partner Les (Morris) on the endless 'Disco Cowboy' trail to the town of Jackpot. This downbeat set-up is familiar, but like a good blues or country melody, you don't mind hearing it again. There are some tricks (shots through the opening of a car cassette), offputting silences and leftfield digressions, but the basics – the singing, the clubs, the roadstops – are all present and correct. Like an easy-over version of *Midnight Cowboy*, it's obvious the relationship of Sunny and his wife (Hannah) can't compete with the all-male comforts of artist and road manager. WH

Jackson County Jail

(1976, US, 84 min)
d Michael Miller. *p* Jeff Begun. *sc* Donald Stewart. *ph* Bruce Logan. *ed* Caroline Ferriol. *ad* Michael McCloskey. *m* Loren Newkirk. *cast* Yvette Mimieux, Tommy Lee Jones, Robert Carradine, Frederic Cook, Severn Darden, Howard Hesseman, John Lawlor, Betty Thomas, Mary Woronov, Hal Needham.

● As the best of the current batch of rape pictures, *Jackson County Jail* – perhaps not surprisingly – exploits its heroine the least. With her job and domestic life in shreds, a middle class career woman leaves the security of LA to drive across the States. On the road she is subjected to by now familiar humiliations, culminating with life on the run after a jail rape. What lifts the film beyond the offensive indignities of its lesser relations is an insistence on the violence and discrimination in American society, and the assured and straightforward progression through the country's underbelly. In addition, unlike *Death Weekend*, it is unequivocally sympathetic towards its heroine. Right from the deceptive opening, Miller's direction knows what it's about, and the continual emphasis on the woman's plight and her silent bewilderment lends the film dimensions of reflection and compassion probably not in the original script. The assurance of Yvette Mimieux's performance is a real surprise. CPe

Jack's Wife (aka Hungry Wives/Season of the Witch)

(1972, US, 89 min)
d George A Romero. *p* Nancy M Romero. *sc/ph/ed* George A Romero. *m* Steve Gorn. *cast* Jan White, Ray Laine, Anne Muffly, Joedda McClain, Bill Thunhurst, Neil Fisher, Esther Lapidus.

● Following his hugely successful debut with *Night of the Living Dead*, Romero flopped with a romantic comedy (*There's Always Vanilla*) as well as this curious hybrid, before returning to successful formula with *The Crazies*. Although there's an occult tinge to its story of a woman who turns to witchcraft for relief from her troubles and ends up shooting her husband in the belief that he is the prowler of her nightmares, it's a strange, experimental film, with an unmistakable (but amateurish) aura of Bergman in its fragmented study of a woman caught up in frustrations very much of the '60s. The drug references and abstract devices date it badly, but it's intriguing to see Romero torn between genre and art. On the evidence of this film (at least in the 89 minute version generally available), he eventually made the right choice. DP

Jack the Bear

(1992, US, 98 min)
d Marshall Herskovitz. *p* Bruce Gilbert. *sc* Steve Zaillian. *ph* Fred Murphy. *ed* Steven Rosenblum. *pd* Lily Kilvert. *m* James Horner. *cast* Danny DeVito, Robert J Steinmiller, Miko Hughes, Gary Sinise, Julia Louis-Dreyfuss, Bert Remsen, Reese Witherspoon.

● Oklahoma, c. 1972. The house that 12-year-old Jack lives in looks like it was abandoned by the Addams family. Mom's dead, Dad (DeVito), the host of a midnight schlock-horror show, teases the neighbours' kids with his realistic monster impressions. He's got a drink problem and he's close to a breakdown. There's little bro' Dylan, but at three years old, he's more of a responsibility than an ally. The loony next door, forever polishing his car, is rumoured to be a Nazi. This weird – if never quite wonderful – entertainment is a rites-of-passage drama in horror-movie clothing. DeVito gives a blue-collar truth to a hard role, and it's rare to find a Hollywood film which tackles such troubling subjects, however uneasily. WH

Jack the Giant Killer

(1961, US, 94 min)
d Nathan Juran. *p* Edward Small. *sc* Orville Hampton, Nathan Juran. *ph* David S Horsley. *ed* Grant Whytock. *ad* Fernando Carrere, Frank McCoy. *m* Paul Sawtell, Bert Shefter. *cast* Kerwin Mathews, Judi Meredith, Torin Thatcher, Walter Burke, Roger Mobley, Barry Kelley, Don Beddoe, Anna Lee.

● Amiable children's fantasy, looking uncannily like one of the Schneer-Harryhausen series. Hardly surprising, perhaps, since Edward Small turned down the chance to produce *The Seventh Voyage of Sinbad*, then set out to duplicate it when it turned out to be a huge success. Unable to persuade Harryhausen to cooperate along with Juran, Mathews and Thatcher, Small had 'Harryhausen' special effects created by Project Unlimited. Far more persuasive than the jerky demonic creatures (including a griffin and an octopedic sea monster) is Torin Thatcher's sinister, Lugosi-like performance as the wicked Master of Demons. TM

Jacky

(2000, Neth, 77 min)
d Hu Fow-Pyng, Brad Ljatifi. *p* Jeroen Beker, Frans van Gestel. *sc* Hu Fow-Pyng, Brad Ljatifi. *ph* Benito Strangio. *ed* Hu Fow-Pyng, Brad Ljatifi, Casper Koetsveld. *ad* Martine de Schipper. *cast* Hu Fow-Pyng, Eveline Wu, Gary Guo, Zhou Xuanwei, Toh Jian-Pau.

● A little too oblique for its own good, this modest indie feature from two first-time directors (of Chinese and Yugoslav descent respectively) usefully counters the feel good tone of most Asian-American movies about the immigrant experience. Hu himself plays the title character, an unassertive 25-year-old stuck in boring Eindhoven who trundles refreshment trolleys up and down Dutch trains. Ordered to marry by his tough-old-bird mother, Jacky finds himself sharing an Amsterdam apartment with a mail-order bride from China (Wu). But he also passively accepts the friendship of an opera queen (Guo) – until his mother intervenes. Composed of short and often wordless scenes, the film seems to have more subtext than text. TR.

Jacob's Ladder

(1990, US, 113 min)
d Adrian Lyne. *p* Alan Marshall. *sc* Bruce Joel Rubin. *ph* Jeffrey L Kimball. *ed* Tom Rolf. *pd* Brian Morris. *m* Maurice Jarre. *cast* Tim Robbins, Elizabeth Peña, Danny Aiello, Matt Craven, Pruitt Taylor Vince, Jason Alexander, Patricia Kalember, Ving Rhames, Macaulay Culkin.

● Lyne's chilling film bombed in the States, probably because of its origins in the murkier side of the now done-to-death Vietnam War. But, messy and maddening though some of it is, *Jacob's Ladder* is also a truly scary film which is never simply a war or horror vehicle. Jacob Singer (Robbins) is a man whose life totters continually between past, present and future, between reality and terrifying illusion brought on by his experiences in Vietnam, where his unit was dosed with a vicious derivative of LSD to improve its killing power. Where the problem arises is that this scenario is only one alternative in the life of a man variously shown as divorced, studying and cohabiting, married and prosperous with children, or dead on a Vietnam field-hospital table. But Lyne's giddying, unsettling direction conjures up moments of horrifying hallucinogenic power from the bad-trip hell of his protagonist. SGr

Jacqueline Susann's Once Is Not Enough

(1974, US, 122 min)
d Guy Green. *p* Howard W Koch. *sc* Julius J Epstein. *ph* John A Alonzo. *ed* Rita Roland. *pd* John F DeCuir. *m* Henry Mancini. *cast* Kirk Douglas, Alexis Smith, David Janssen, George Hamilton, Melina Mercouri, Gary Conway, Brenda Vaccaro, Deborah Raffin.

● A film that has Kirk Douglas exclaim 'You just cut my balls off in front of my daughter,' that feels moved to rattle such skeletons in the cupboard as impotence and artificial insemination, that has its central character called January because (in the words of her father) 'she was born on New Year's Day and I swore I'd give her the world,' and that bothers to incorporate into the plot a minor-league astronaut with an 'aw shucks' attitude to his job. *Once Is Not Enough* brings Jacqueline Susann's's characteristically unshadowed world of wealth and deodorised amorality to the screen with all the ringing confidence of a sanitary towel commercial. Green's direction is highly professional, and the overall slickness is fascinatingly allowed to lie like the very thinnest of veneers over absolutely nothing. VG

Jacquot de Nantes

(1991, Fr, 118 min, b/w & col)
d Agnès Varda. *p* Agnès Varda, Danielle Vaugon, Perrine Bauduin. *sc* Agnès Varda. *ph* Patrick Blossier, Agnès Godard, Georges Strouvé. *ed* Marie-Jo Audiard. *ad* Robert Nardone, Olivier Radot. *m* Joanna Bruzdowicz. *cast* Philippe Maron, Edouard Joubeaud, Laurent Monnier, Brigitte de Villepoix, Daniel Dublet, Marie-Sidonie Benoist.

● Varda's tribute to her husband Jacques Demy, who died in 1990, takes the form of a fictional reconstruction of the boy Jacquot's childhood, deriving its sense of authenticity not only from being shot in the real locations where Demy grew up, but from the fact that he himself collaborated with Varda, sifting through his memories. Home footage of Demy – together with clips from his films – casts an uncomfortably melancholic gaze on the proceedings. Extremely evocative, and vivaciously played by a cast of unknowns, this is a curious hybrid: part essay, part nostalgic reconstruction, at times sitting a little too cosily with the French vogue for faultlessly authentic reminiscence. Varda's valedictory may not bring you any closer to Demy the director, but it's an engrossing, moving tribute. JRo

Jade

(1995, US, 95 min)
d William Friedkin. *p* Robert Evans, Gary Adelson, Craig Baumgarten. *sc* Joe Eszterhas. *ph* Andrzej Bartkowiak. *ed* Augie Hess. *pd* Alex Tavoularis. *m* James Horner. *cast* David Caruso, Linda Fiorentino, Richard Crenna, Chazz Palminteri, Michael Biehn, Donna Murphy.
● This is Friedkin back to the hackery of *The Guardian*. Indeed, from the prowling camera tour of the baroque oriental San Francisco mansion of a millionaire playboy, to the creepy choral music and jarring soundtrack, this ugly murder thriller pushes close to horror movie territory. It's motored by the same engine common to many of that genre: male fear of the female libido. Predictability, risibility and degeneracy vie in Joe Eszterhas's script: assistant DA Corelli (Caruso), regarding the millionaire's flailed corpse, remarks, 'This is rage!', while a colleague, noting it's election year, laments, 'The media is going to turn this into an X-rated gang bang!' The libido in question belongs to unlikely psychologist of workplace violence Trina Gavin (Fiorentino): married to amoral lawyer Matt (Palminteri), and one-time lover of the still ardent Corelli, she was the last person to see the millionaire alive and is thus prime supect. The role strips Fiorentino of charisma and grace. Caruso, too, has little to do and does it poorly. Thrown in are a few hackneyed Friedkin 'show-stoppers': an extended car chase, and a variation on the car-with-cut-brake-cables number. Camerman Andrzej Bartkowiak does little more than provide a sheeny gloss on standard ritzy SF locations. Bad. WH

Jade Love (Yu Qing sao)

(1984, Tai, 104 min)
d Chang Yi. *p* Li Hsing. *sc* Chang Yi. *ph* Lin Tzu-jung. *ed* Lin Shan-liang. *pd* Tsou Chih-liang. *m* Chang Hung-yi. *cast* Yang Hui-shan, Juang Sheng-t'ien, Ling Ting-feng.
● An affecting and well-acted period melodrama, based on a Chinese short story but suspiciously similar to *The Go-Between*, right down to a climactic glimpse of coitus. It's about a spoiled young brat who becomes the unwitting messenger between his adored nanny and her mysteriously reclusive 'brother'. The atmosphere is rather cloyingly literary, doubtless because the youngish director (rallying from two recent flops) was determined to prove his 'cultural' mettle. Still, accomplished in its backward-looking way. TR

Jadviga's Pillow (Jadviga Párnája)

(1999, Hun, 127 min)
d Krisztina Deák. *p* György Marosi. *sc* Krisztina Deák, Pál Závada. *ph* Gábor Balog. *ed* Zsuzsa Csákány. *m* György Selmeczi. *cast* Ildikó Tóth, Viktor Bodó, Roman Luknár, Mari Csomós, Eszter Ónodi, Béla Fesztbaum.
● Ondris (Bodó) and his Slovakian friends drunkenly celebrate his prospective marriage. Jadviga the bride (Tóth) is clothed, with deliberate care, in traditional Hungarian finery. A sense of palpable anticipation builds. Jadviga's a woman with secrets. It isn't long before the differences between the strong, passionate wife and her doting, but weak and impetuous husband lead to a rift. Disaster beckons. The tale, from a novel by Pál Závada, is set against a backdrop of violence and secession in the period before and during WWI. The fractured relationship of the antagonists, their friends and family is reflected in that of war-torn Hungary, riven by power struggles between monarchists, communists and Slovakian nationalists. JFu

Jag Är Med Barn (Father-to-Be/I'm Expecting)

(1979, Swe, 107 min)
d Lasse Hallström. *p* Ole Hellbom. *sc* Brasse Brannstom, Lasse Hallstrom, Ole Hellbom. *ph* Roland Lundin. *ed* Lasse Hallstrom. *pd* Bengt Peters. *m* Bengt Palmers. *cast* Magnus Härenstam, Anki Lidén, Micha Gabay, Ulf Brunnberg, Lis Nilheim.
● Moderately diverting social comedy, from the director who went on to make *My Life as a Dog*, in which carefree Härenstam dreams of a career as a famous novelist but is brought right back down to earth by girlfriend Lidén's announcement of a new arrival. TJ

Jagdszenen aus Niederbayern

see Hunting Scenes from Lower Bavaria

Jagged Edge

(1985, US, 109 min)
d Richard Marquand. *p* Martin Ransohoff. *sc* Joe Eszterhas. *ph* Matthew F Leonetti. *ed* Sean Barton, Conrad Buff. *pd* Gene Callahan. *m* John Barry. *cast* Jeff Bridges, Glenn Close, Maria Mayenzet, Peter Coyote, Lance Henriksen, Sarah Cunningham, Robert Loggia.
● This shows that a contemporary whodunit can still rivet sophisticated modern audiences without retreating into horror or camp. Marquand and screenwriter Joe Eszterhas achieve this coup by ringing brilliant changes on ancient material: Close plays a woman defence lawyer who becomes involved with client Bridges, fighting to prove he's innocent of murdering his wife. The trial scenes are scripted and played with electrifying skill, as every turn and twist is amplified through Close's emotions. But it is much more than a courtroom picture. These days it is almost unheard of for a movie to keep you guessing until the last frame, but this one does, partly because Marquand plays it so beautifully straight. DP

Jaguar

(1979, Phil, 110 min)
d Lino Brocka. *sc* José Lacaba, Ricardo Lee. *ph* Conrado Balthazar. *ed* René Tala. *m* Max Jocson. *cast* Phillip Salvador, Amy Austria, Menggie Cobarrubias, Anita Linda, Johnny Delgado, Tonio Gutierrez.
● Originally banned for export by the Marcos government, and only released after pressure from the Cannes Film Festival, where it was the first Filipino film to be shown in competition. Just as *Manila: In the Claws of Darkness* plundered melodrama, *Jaguar* plunders the American gangster movie (plus possibly blaxploitation pix such as *Shaft*) to express Brocka's rage about poverty and repression. Jaguar is slang for bodyguard, and the hero guards a smart apartment block, supports his family, and stays out of trouble. But when he intervenes in a fight, saving the life of a wealthy playboy and landowner, he gets hired as the man's personal guard and falls for his girlfriend. Gradually, in spite of himself, he is dragged down into crime, becoming a murderer and finally going berserk in jail. Despite budgetary limitations and some wooden acting, the passion of the picture comes across powerfully, as does its portrait of a society in which violence and resentment are endemic. ATu

Jaguar Lives

(1979, US, 90 min)
d Ernest Pintoff. *p* Derek Gibson. *sc* Yabo Yablonsky. *ph* John Cabrera. *ed* Angelo Ross. *pd* Ron Talsky. *m* Robert O Ragland. *cast* Joe Lewis, Christopher Lee, Donald Pleasence, Barbara Bach, Capucine, Joseph Wiseman, Woody Strode, John Huston.
● Time-warp film-making from ex-cartoonist and once-touted director Pintoff: a no-interest, multi-location 'action movie' that takes its cues from early James Bond and cheapo kung-fu thrillers. The listless, tedious hokum of the old secret-agent-busts-international-crime-ring plot would have looked tacky (and its martial arts catchpenny) at the turn of the last decade; today it looks hopelessly anachronistic in even the baldest commercial terms. Dead from the neck up; dead from the wallet down. PT

Jailhouse Rock

(1957, US, 97 min, b/w)
d Richard Thorpe. *p* Pandro S Berman. *sc* Guy Trosper. *ph* Robert Bronner. *ed* Ralph E Winters. *ad* William A Horning, Randall Duell. *songs* Jerry Lieber, Mike Stoller. *cast* Elvis Presley, Judy Tyler, Mickey Shaughnessy, Vaughn Taylor, Dean Jones, Jennifer Holden, Anne Neyland.
● Wrestling with the problem of what to do with a rock'n'roll star, MGM hit on the addled brainwave of using Richard Thorpe, who had made *The Student Prince* for them three years earlier and had a background in costume musicals and adventures. The story, about a rock star with a prison background, was tougher than some of the other Presley pictures, but the musical numbers especially were shot in the MGM tradition, which was totally wrong for rock. DP

Jaime

(1999, Port/Luxembourg, 111 min)
d António-Pedro Vasconcelos. *p* Jani Thiltges. *sc* Carlos Saboga. *ph* Edgar Moura. *ed* Frédéric Fichefet. *pd* Veronique Sacrez. *m* Alain Jomy. *cast* Saúl Fonseca, Fernanda Serrano, Joaquim Leitão, Sandro Silva, Vitor Norte, Guilherme Leme, Nicolau Breyner, Rogerio Samora, Zita Duarte.
● Well acted, well-intentioned but faintly predictable slice of social realism about kids forced by poverty, broken families, etc, into illegal and highly exploitative under-age labour. Set in an emphatically seedy Porto, the film blends social comment and melodrama pretty effectively, although it seldom transcends stereotyping, and lacks the bizarre lugubrious poetry of the best Portuguese cinema. GA

Ja, Ja, Mein General! But Which Way to the Front?

see Which Way to the Front?

Jake Speed

(1986, US, 105 min)
d Andrew Lane. *p* Andrew Lane, Wayne Crawford, William Fay. *sc* Wayne Crawford, Andrew Lane. *ph* Bryan Loftus. *ed* Fred Stafford. *pd* Norman Baron. *m* Mark Snow. *cast* Wayne Crawford, Dennis Christopher, Karen Kopins, John Hurt, Leon Ames, Roy London, Barry Primus, Monte Markham.
● The remarkable thing is that here is a movie that wants to be bad and still fails. There's nothing wrong with its fecund premise: a fictional comic-strip hero let loose on the screen to lampoon and parody himself through every thrills-and-spills adventure caper that has graced our cash-tills in recent years. But Crawford plays Speed with his foot in his mouth rather than tongue-in-cheek, and instead of glorying in the experiences of the pulp novel dialogue, dissipates all the comic potential by his evident bewilderment. The feckless and dupable Kopins is the sex interest, romanced down the Zambesi in the quest to rescue her abducted sister from an evil gang of white slave traders, led by almost cynically OTT gay nasty Hurt. In danger of making the targeted teen audience kick the cinema habit altogether. WH

Jakob the Liar

(1999, US, 120 min)
d Peter Kassovitz. *p* Marsha Garces Williams, Steven Haft. *sc* Peter Kassovitz, Didier Decoin. *ph* Elemér Ragályi. *ed* Claire Simpson. *pd* Luciana Arrighi. *m* Edward Shearmur. *cast* Robin Williams, Alan Arkin, Bob Balaban, Hannah Taylor Gordon, Michael Jeter, Armin Mueller-Stahl, Liev Schreiber, Nina Siemaszko, Mathieu Kassovitz.
● After Roberto Benigni in the camps, Robin Williams in the ghetto (this was actually shot before *Life Is Beautiful*). Radios and newspapers are banned in the Jewish quarter of an unnamed, Nazi-held Polish city, which places a real premium on reports Jakob (Williams) overhears from a German army broadcast when coincidence finds him inside their barracks. No one believes that he was able to talk his way out again, so Jakob must surely have an illicit radio himself. Realising the morale boosting effect of his revelations, he starts spinning out a few more creative untruths. Broadly, the central conceit is similar to *Life Is Beautiful*, that when the world becomes too awful you simply invent your own. Benigni's dubious airbrushing is largely avoided, but Kassovitz's film is still a contrived affair, since the misunderstanding which sets the plot rolling is tiresomely stretched out in order to draw something positive from harrowing historical fact.

Moreover, face set in that characteristically sincere grimace, Williams gets to bond with an orphaned girl and provide knockabout fun with a faked Churchill radio address. TJ

Jalsaghar (The Music Room)

(1958, Ind, 100 min, b/w)
d/p/sc Satyajit Ray. *ph* Subrata Mitra. *ed* Dulal Dutta. *ad* Banshi Chandra Gupta. *m* Ustad Vilayat Khan. *cast* Chabi Biswas, Ganga Pada Basu, Pinaki Sen Gupta, Kali Sarkar, Padma Devi, Tulsi Lahari.

● Ray's fourth film, a wonderfully evocative anecdote about an elderly aristocrat, slowly dying amid the crumbling splendours of the past, who decides to defy the egalitarian age that is encroaching. For all the rough edges, there is something of Welles here as the ageing aristocrat sits alone in his Xanadu, like Mr Clay in *The Immortal Story*, dreaming amid the remnants of past magnificence while the bulldozers of modern civilisation hum outside the walls. Something, too, of Chekhov's tender irony as he rebels in a gesture of glorious folly, bankrupting himself to hire the best classical musicians around, dust off the vast chandelier, and bring his ancestral music room to glittering life once more for just one last regal extravaganza. Slow, rapt and hypnotic, it is – given some appreciation of Indian music – a remarkable experience. TM

Jam (Guojiang)

(1998, Tai/Jap, 102 min)
d Chen Yi-wen. *p* Yu Wei-yen. *sc* Chen Yi-wen. *ph* Li Yi-shu, Zhu Pei-ji, Zhou Yi-wen. *ed* Chen Bo-wen. *pd* Yu Wei-yen. *m* Ed Yen. *cast* Cai Xing-hong, June Cai, Vina Xu, Gao Ming-jun.

● Edward Yang protégé Chen Yi-wen makes a super-confident directorial debut with this snappy exercise in overlapping narrative. Four chronologically shuffled chapters introduce us to the main players: a film producer who is having an affair with the studio boss and an aspiring director; a thoughtful gangster (the dullest strand); and two kids, Kai and Jiajia, whose ill-advised car jacking prank collides social barriers. It's funny, clever stuff, but never excessively or incestuously cinephilic – the youngsters' ambiguous unconsummated relationship gives the film its heart. TCh

Jamaica Inn

(1939, GB, 108, b/w)
d Alfred Hitchcock. *p* Erich Pommer. *sc* Sidney Gilliat, Joan Harrison. *ph* Harry Stradling. *ed* Robert Hamer. *ad* Tom Morahan. *m* Eric Fenby. *cast* Charles Laughton, Maureen O'Hara, Leslie Banks, Robert Newton, Emlyn Williams, Wylie Watson.

● Acting as co-producer as well as star, Laughton ruled the roost even more than usual in this murky melodrama of 18th century Cornish wrecking, smuggling and thuggery, parading about in the top hat, boots and leering eyebrows of the local JP, and giving poor Maureen O'Hara the fright of her life. Hitchcock, who slipped in this Daphne du Maurier adaptation before leaving for America, clearly found it impossible to secure a strong grip on either Laughton or the material. And while the star himself effortlessly commands attention, the film around him too often collapses in a welter of rhubarbing locals, piffling model work, and the most cardboard sets Elstree could offer. The result is weird, but not wonderful. GB

J.A. Martin, Photographer (J.A. Martin Photographe)

(1976, Can, 101 min)
d Jean Beaudin. *p* Jean-Marc Garand. *sc* Jean Beaudin, Marcel Sabourin. *ph* Pierre Mignot. *ed* Jean Beaudin, Hélène Girard. *ad* Vianney Gauthier. *m* Maurice Blackburn. *cast* Marcel Sabourin, Monique Mercure, Marthe Thierry, Catherine Tremblay, Mariette Duval, Denis Hamel.

● Leaden venture into the world of the period 'art' movie, not so much meditative as cataleptic. Primarily about Rose-Aimée and her decision to abandon her household temporarily to accompany her photographer husband on one of his annual tours (in 19th century Quebec), the title seems misplaced; indeed, this sort of erratic emphasis dogs the whole farrago. The structure works by too simple a process of accretion – a succession of 'telling' vignettes at each halt, as the couple photographically encounter capitalism, death, marriage, love, sex, even a miscarriage (he impassively reaches for his shovel). Their final rekindling of passion is only barely justified by the previous pedestrian episodes. And it's all heavily sunk with the usual up-market trappings: ochre tints, half-lit interiors, blank inter-scene pauses, long-held reaction shots; as if Bergman had got hold of *The Archers*. CPea

James and the Giant Peach

(1996, US, 79 min)
d Henry Selick. *p* Denise DiNovi, Tim Burton. *sc* Karey Kirkpatrick, Jonathan Roberts, Steven L Bloom. *ph* Pete Kozachik, Hiro Narita. *ed* Stan Webb. *pd* Harley Jessup. *m* Randy Newman. *cast* Paul Terry, Steven Culp, Pete Postlethwaite; voices: Simon Callow, Richard Dreyfuss, Joanna Lumley, Miriam Margolyes, Susan Sarandon.

● Made by the director of *The Nightmare Before Christmas*, this has an enchanting, at times ghoulish, appeal. An adaptation of Roald Dahl's classic story, Selick's film may not have made any spectacular technical advance on his previous work (the animated central section is sandwiched by stylised live-action sequences), but, despite a lightness of plot, it most beautifully captures the book's free-floating, fantastic sense of adventure and wonder. Forced into a life of drudgery by his evil aunts Sponge and Spiker (Margolyes and Lumley), orphan James dreams of escape to New York. An old man (Postlethwaite) appears and gives the boy a jigging handful of fluorescent, magical crocodile tongues. A dead peach tree bears a gigantic fruit, and diving Alice-like into its core, James enters a world of strange invertebrates. As his wishes take flight, so does the peach, putting to sea and soaring up in the air, hauled majestically by a flock of tethered seagulls. The songs and music have the inimitable signature of Randy Newman. WH

James Baldwin: The Price of the Ticket

(1989, US, 87 min)
d Karen Thorsen. *p* Karen Thorsen, William Miles. *sc* Karen Thorsen, Douglas K Dempsey. *ph* Don Lenzer. *with* James Baldwin, Maya Angelou, Amiri Baraka [Leroi Jones], David Baldwin, William Styron, Bobby Short, David Leeming, Lucien Happersberger.

● Born in Harlem in 1924, a preacher's son, Baldwin was himself a boy preacher. In some ways the vocation stuck through his life. Thorsen's non-narrated documentary mixes footage covering his speeches, interviews, lectures; extracts from TV plays; testimony from friends, family, pupils, colleagues; and Maya Angelou reading from his letters and books. A powerful portrait emerges of a fighter, idealist, teacher and liberal-baiter; a man whose anger grew in the face of ignorant interviewers. His long search for self and his education into the politics of race, equality and revolution fascinate: from his flight in '48 from a suffocating America to hyperventilation in Paris; his support of Algerians ('Paris's niggers'); writing *Go Tell It on the Mountain* in a Swiss village (where, the visual antithesis of all he surveyed, he was a friend to every child); coming out with the publication of *Giovanni's Room*; further flight to Turkey; Eldridge Cleaver's vicious attack on him as a traitor to macho Black politics; and the deaths of King, Malcolm X, JFK. Deeply moving, educational and engaging though the film is, the man's lovers are conspicuously absent. Which of these talking heads were they? *Were* they white? Did that matter to him? At 87 minutes, this is tantalising proof that less is not always more. TC

James Brothers, The

see True Story of Jesse James, The

James Dean Story, The

(1957, US, 82 min, b/w)
d/p George W George, Robert Altman. *sc* Stewart Stern. *ed* Robert Altman, George W George. *pd* Louis Clyde Stoumen. *m* Leith Stevens. *with* Marcus Winslow, Ortense Winslow, Markie Winslow, Mr and Mrs Dean [James Dean's grandparents], Adeline Hall. *narrator* Martin Gabel.

● Something of a curiosity, this documentary about the life and character of the cultish star who had died a couple of years before is short on analysis, long on (sometimes insufferably pretentious) poetic symbolism, and extremely fine for its sharp black-and-white photography, especially effective in the bleak wastelands where Dean grew up. A few nice rare clips are included (notably a stunning outtake from *East of Eden*), but otherwise this is probably of interest only to Dean fanatics or Altman collectors. GA

James Dean – the First American Teenager

(1975, GB, 80 min)
d Ray Connolly. *p* David Puttnam, Sandy Lieberson. *sc* Ray Connolly. *ph* Mike Molloy, Robert Gersicoff. *ed* Peter Hollywood. *m* Elton John, David Bowie. *narrator* Stacy Keach. with Carroll Baker, Natalie Wood, Sal Mineo, Dennis Hopper, Nicholas Ray, Sammy Davis Jr, Leonard Rosenman, Leslie Caron, Vampira.

● Connolly's catch-all compilation follows the trail blazed by Joe Boyd's Hendrix movie: lotsa clips of the Star in action (including obscure TV footage and a 'rare' screen test), lotsa glossy interviews with those who loved or hated him, as much rock music as possible, and fragments of memorabilia like a hilariously stilted road safety commercial. The most lucidly evasive contribution comes from Dean's long time 'mentor' Leonard Rosenman; the most affably stoned from Dennis Hopper. But Connolly makes his reliance on the original movies a real problem: when someone mentions Dean getting into a car, for instance, we're shown a clip from *Giant* of him doing just that…and so the film constantly reinforces the Hollywood 'image' it purports to question. And the dismal coyness about Dean's sex life means the movie scarcely makes it even as gossip. TR

James Gang, The

(1997, GB/Can, 95 min)
d Mike Barker. *p* Andrew Eaton. *sc* Stuart Hepburn. *ph* Ben Seresin. *ed* Guy Bensley. *pd* Alice Normington. *m* Bernard Butler. *cast* John Hannah, Helen McCrory, Jason Flemyng, Toni Collette, Darren Brownlie, David Brownlie, Lauren McMurray, Tim Woodward.

● With its stylish cinematography, eye catching direction and groovy pop soundtrack, this is a British first feature (Scottish characters, Welsh locations) that desperately wants to be hip. Helen McCrory, who gave her all in Karl Francis' *Streetlife*, is similarly committed here, as the mum trying to hold her family together by launching an impromptu crime spree – though errant husband Hannah and trailing policewoman Collette don't really have the grit required. What's more, Stuart Hepburn's script never begins to carry the weight that would justify the involvement of McCrory's children in the various robberies, or lend conviction to the characterisation. TJ

Jamón, Jamón

(1992, Sp, 94 min)
d Bigas Luna. *p* Andrés Vicente Gómez. *sc* Cuca Canals, Bigas Luna. *ph* José Luis Alcaine. *ed* Pablo Del Amo. *ad* Chu Uroz, Noemi Campano. *m* Nicola Piovani. *cast* Penélope Cruz, Anna Galiena, Javier Bardem, Stefania Sandrelli, Juan Diego, Jodi Molla.

● This is 'Carry On' as scripted by Lorca, a hysterically sombre sex farce pointing up the connections between sex and food. The title is an obscure sexual compliment: machinist Silvia (Cruz) enslaves wealthy stripling José with her ham-flavoured nipples. But as one might expect from a man so fixated, José is in thrall to his mother Conchita, who doesn't want him married to the daughter of the town whore. Conchita enrols a chunky would-be *torero*, Raúl, to distract the nymphet. Before long he's up under Silvia's miniskirt, and it's bound to end in tears. One just wants to slap Silvia, a woman who habitually traipses around wailing in wet, clingy, baby-doll dresses. But there are compensations in Sandrelli's monstrous Conchita and Bardem's hilarious Raúl. The sex scenes are so bizarre as to be parodic and it all looks terribly ugly. But wonderful vignettes of rural life, and a terrific performance from Pablito the piglet. Ham indeed. SFe

Jam Session: The Official Bootleg of Kikujiro

(1999, Jap, 93 min)
d Makoto Shinozaki. *p* Takio Yoshida, Masayuki Mori. *ph* Kawazu Taro. *ed* Kikawa Manabu. *m* Joe Hisaishi. *with* 'Beat' Takeshi Kitano, Hou Xiaoxian.

● When Office Kitano commissioned Shinozaki to record Kitano's work on *Kikujiro* from the start of shooting to the screening of the 'A' copy, they knew he wouldn't do a standard 'Making of'. Since Kitano shot the film more or less in sequence and improvised a lot, Shinozaki is able to turn his documentary into an authentic 'bootleg': an anthology of out-takes, mistakes and deleted scenes which adds up to a 'parallel' version of the film itself. It's also a very candid portrait of Kitano in his self-deprecatory prime – especially when nearly lost for words during a social chat with Hou Xiaoxian. One caveat: Kitano himself sings the song under the end credits. TR

Jan Dara

(2001, Thai, 120 min)
d Nonzee Nimibutr. *p* Nonzee Nimibutr, Duangkamol Limcharoen, Jojo Hui, Yuet Chun. *sc* Nonzee Nimibutr, Sirapak Paoboonkerd. *ph* Nattawut Kitikun. *ed* Sunit Asvinkul. *pd* Arkadech Kaewkotr, Rach-Chanon Khayanngan. *m* Pakawat Waiwitaya, Chartchai Pongprapapan. *cast* Vipavee Charoenpura, Christy Chung, Suwinit Panjamawat, Santisuk Promsiri, Eakarat Sarsukh, Pataravarin Timkul.

●Thailand's most famous and successful director Nonzee Nimibutr's third feature is a gorgeous film based on *The Story of Jan Dara*, a controversial erotic novel of the 1960s. It begins in Bangkok in the 1930s and scrutinises Thai social history through the life of the protagonist. Born into a wealthy and corrupt family, Jan is rejected by his father because his mother died during his birth. He searches for nurturing female companionship throughout his life and uses sex as revenge and consolation, each encounter characterised by a palpable lack of love. The film is shot in hues of white, cream and sepia, with splashes of crimson to suggest family skeletons of lesbianism, incest, adultery and betrayal. Ultimately, resistance is futile: Jan's frustration turns him into a version of the man he most abhors. EG

Jane

(1963, US, 51 min, b/w)
d DA Pennebaker, Richard Leacock, Hope Ryden, Gregory Shuker, Abbott Mills. *with* Jane Fonda, Bradford Dillman, Lee Strasberg, Madeleine Sherwood, Walter Kerr.

●One of the early Drew/Leacock efforts, a *cinéma-vérité* portrait of Jane Fonda which tracks her through rehearsals for her Broadway debut in 1960 (a comedy called *The Fun Couple*). Since Vadim and *Barbarella* were still to come, this is Jane the eager *ingénue*, with political protest not rating even a whisper. The tensions of rehearsal and opening night are well caught, but the rest of the story (Sardi's after the show, unkind reviews, ephemeral heartbreak) is no different from the average showbiz epic. TM

Jane and the Lost City

(1987, GB, 92 min)
d Terry Marcel. *p* Harry Robertson. *sc* Mervyn Haisman. *ph* Paul Beeson. *ed* Alan Jones. *pd* Michael Pickwoad. *m* Harry Roberston. *cast* Sam Jones, Maud Adams, Jasper Carrott, Kirsten Hughes, Graham Stark, Robin Bailey, Ian Roberts, Elsa O'Toole.

●This would-be romp based around the saucy exploits of the oft-déshabillée, cami-knickered heroine (Hughes) of the *Daily Mirror*'s wartime 'Jane' strip cartoon is bad beyond the promptings of idle curiosity. Churchill stabs at a map of Africa and dispatches clipped-upper-lip Colonel (Bailey) and secretary Jane in search of much-needed diamonds to save the Empire at its darkest hour. A haphazard journey later, they team up with life-saving Yank Jungle Jack Buck (Jones), and trek through the veldt two comic capers ahead of evil Nazis Lola Pagoda (Adams) and hysterical Herr Heinrich (Carrott, a deep mistake), before reaching the cardboard Lost City presided over by Sheba the Leopard Queen, late of Roedean. Notwithstanding the spasmodic salacious shots of Jane's principal silk-clad joints, the film translates the innocent eroticism and tongue-in-cheek adventurism of the strip into a pile of puerile, enervative folie. WH

Jane Austen in Manhattan

(1980, GB/US, 111 min)
d James Ivory. *p* Ismail Merchant. *sc* Ruth Prawer Jhabvala. *ph* Ernest Vincze, Larry Pizer. *ed* David McKenna. *ad* Jeremiah Rusconi. *m* Richard Robbins. *cast* Anne Baxter, Robert Powell, Michael Wager, Sean Young, Tim Choate, Nancy New, John Guerrasio, Katrina Hodiak, Kurt Johnson, Charles McCaughan.

●A study in cultural cross-pollination from the Merchant-Ivory-Jhabvala team. Prompted by the recent discovery of a piece of Jane Austen juvenilia – a schoolgirl fantasy playlet about abduction at the hands of a rake – the film again finds them exploring the ways in which the past becomes appropriated and re-processed in the present. Two small New York theatre companies, with widely differing ideas about how the unearthed play ought to be staged (period operetta versus avant-gardist 'performance' event), vie with each other for the patronage of a wealthy cultural foundation which has acquired the rights to the manuscript. The contending claims of tradition, experiment and capital are given narrative thrust, but no real focus or amplification, by the developing feud between the two rival directors: an ageing Anne Baxter and her protégé-turned-Svengali, Robert Powell. Personal differences are allowed to oust artistic differences so comprehensively that the film simply loses its way, disappointingly playing itself out as a series of flashy real-life variations on Austen's original abduction theme. Really, it's all just a little too clever for its own good. MPo

Jane Eyre

(1943, US, 96 min, b/w)
d Robert Stevenson. *p* David O Selznick. *sc* Aldous Huxley, Robert Stevenson, John Houseman. *ph* George Barnes. *ed* Walter Thompson. *pd* William L Pereira. *m* Bernard Herrmann. *cast* Orson Welles, Joan Fontaine, Margaret O'Brien, Peggy Ann Garner, John Sutton, Sara Allgood, Henry Daniell, Agnes Moorehead, Hillary Brooke, Elizabeth Taylor.

●Charlotte Bronte reduced to straight Gothic romance, but surprisingly effective right from the opening shot of a wavering candle being carried down a long, dark corridor. The early sequences of Jane's schooling are probably the most stylistically consistent and vividly realised (Daniell's chillingly pious sadism as the headmaster, Moorehead sourly petting a piggish little fat boy, young Elizabeth Taylor dying from cruel negligence). After Welles makes his thunderous appearance out of the mist, thrown from his startled horse but still able to swirl a cape with fine braggadocio, the film becomes more erratic, but always looks as though Orson had at least one eye behind the camera. And the cracks (notably the discrepancies in acting styles between pallid Jane and full-blooded Rochester) are neatly papered over by a fine Bernard Herrmann score. TM

Jane Eyre

(1970, GB, 110 min)
d Delbert Mann. *p* Frederick H Brogger. *sc* Jack Pulman. *ph* Paul Beeson. *ed* Peter Boita. *ad* Alex Vetchinsky. *m* John Williams. *cast* George C Scott, Susannah York, Ian Bannen, Jack Hawkins, Nyree Dawn Porter, Rachel Kempson, Kenneth Griffith, Peter Copley, Michele Dotrice.

●A typical hybrid of 'tasteful' adaptation, shot and (briefly) released in Britain before finding its US TV home. For all the Yorkshire location work and pedantic respect for Charlotte Brontë, it's not a patch on the gloriously artificial 1943 movie; and for all Scott's actorly huff and puff as Rochester, he can't disturb memories of Orson Welles. PT

Jane Eyre

(1995, GB/It/Fr/US, 113 min)
d Franco Zeffirelli. *p* Dyson Lovell. *sc* Hugh Whitemore, Franco Zeffirelli. *ph* David Watkin. *ed* Richard Marden. *pd* Roger Hall. *m* Alessio Vlad, Claudio Capponi. *cast* Charlotte Gainsbourg, William Hurt, Joan Plowright, Anna Paquin, Geraldine Chaplin, Billie Whitelaw, Maria Schneider, Fiona Shaw, Elle Macpherson, John Wood, Amanda Root, Samuel West.

●A faithful adaptation, by Hugh Whitemore and director Franco Zeffirelli, aimed squarely at the middle ground. Its cinematic effects are generally banal – the elegant, slow dissolves that befit a prestige classic, hollow footsteps and an eerie laugh echoing through the Tower – but such restraint is welcome given what Zeffirelli is capable of. Mostly, he seems satisfied to let the actors get on with it, tacitly acknowledging that Charlotte Gainsbourg's Jane is his strongest asset. It's unusual to see a lead actress photographed so harshly. She is sallow with shadows under her eyes, yet has a defiant tilt of the chin and embodies a guilelessness which makes her deeply sympathetic. (She's also a credible match for Anna Paquin's forlorn young Jane.) Gainsbourg's so sparing with her smile, that each one cuts to the quick. William Hurt makes a strong fist of a less intimidating Rochester: he's brusque and morose, but altogether more accessible than the brooding romantics portrayed by Welles and Scott in earlier versions. In a way, that's the problem with this adaptation. It's too tame to stir the blood. We understand Jane's pain but not her passion. For all its melodramatic hyperbole, the 1943 version caught Charlotte Bronte's tenor more honestly than this. Very capable support, though, from Fiona Shaw (Mrs Reed), Amanda Root (Miss Temple), Joan Plowright (Mrs Fairfax), and Billie Whitelaw (Grace Poole). TCh

Jang Sun-Woo Variations, The (Jang Sun-Woo Pyeonjuguk)

(2001, SKor, 119 min)
d Tony Rayns. *p* Park Ki-Yong, Park Jin-Sung. *sc* Tony Rayns. *ph* Kim Woo-Hyung. *ed* Kim Sun-Min. *m* Dal Palan. *with* Jang Sun-Woo, Moon Sung-Kun, Park Joong-Hoon, Byun Young-Joo, Wonkyong.

●Rayns – long-term TO contributor and an acknowledged expert on Asian cinema – gets to grips with the iconoclastic Jang, interviewed (characteristically?) as he is massaged and relaxes in a bathhouse. The division of the movie into chapters allows for a lucid, informative and often witty look at Jang's preoccupations, film-making style, career, his place in Korean society and his extraordinary haircut. An exemplary introduction to an important and very idiosyncratic film-maker. GA

Janice

(1973, US, 84 min)
d/p Joseph Strick. *sc* Judith Rascoe. *ph* Don Lenzer. *ed* Sylvia Sarner. *m* Stanley Myers. *cast* Robert Drivas, Regina Baff, Barry Bostwick, David Bauer, Beatrice Colen, Laura Esterman, Barton Heyman, Joe Pantoliano.

●Strick's rather belated foray into the world of the road movie and through the dregs of the American dream. Two truck drivers (Drivas, Bostwick), leading a life sufficiently precarious to keep them on the fringes of petty crime, pick up Janice (Baff), a prostitute who alternately helps them and helps to destroy them. Strick looks to expose the myth of the road movie through his characters, whose main form of communication lies in outbursts of destructive violence. But with his over-riding concern to make the film look good – the vergeside shots at hubcap height, the rain swirling up from the wheels of overtaking lorries – he ends up merely glamorising the myth that he's purporting to strip bare. CPe

Janice Beard 45 WPM

(1999, GB, 81 min)
d Clare Kilner. *p* Judy Counihan. *sc* Clare Kilner, Ben Hopkins. *ph* Richard Greatrex, Peter Thwaites. *ed* Mary Finlay. *pd* Sophie Becher. *m* Paul Carr. *cast* Rhys Ifans, Patsy Kensit, David O'Hara, Eileen Walsh, Sandra Voe, Frances Gray, Zita Sattar, Amelia Curtis, Mossie Smith, Maynard Eziashi.

●Janice's dad died right there in the delivery room when she was being born, leaving mum a traumatised agoraphobic ever since. Through childhood, she made a point of telling very tall tales, hoping to cajole her mother out of their Glasgow flat. Now, however, the time is ripe for Janice Beard (Walsh) to spread her own wings. She plans to make enough money in London to buy expensive treatment for the old girl. Starting on the bottom rung of a motor company, she has the unwritten rules of typing pool etiquette to learn, like not getting on the wrong side of the Essex gal supervisor (Kensit). Still, she may have found a kindred spirit in Sean (Ifans), a happy go lucky junior. Kilner's first film charms because it makes the best of its own modest parameters. Though the audience is ahead of the plotting throughout, it matters less than the quality time we spend with the likeable characters caught up in the creaking farce. Walsh's screen debut is a gem, while the ubiquitous Ifans gives of his best and Kensit brings surprising heart to her secretarial role. TJ

Janis

(1974, Can, 97 min)
d/sc Howard Alk, Seaton Findlay. *ph* Michael Wadleigh, Don Lenzer, Richard Pearce, Chuck Levey, Al Wertheimer, Richard Chew, Ted Churchill, Jim Desmond, Nicholas Proferes, Albert Maysles, DA Pennebaker, Richard

Leacock, WP Hassenstein, Peter Biziou, Bob Fiore, Clarke Mackey, Paul Goldsmith. *ed* Howard Alk, Seaton Findlay. *with* Janis Joplin.
●On film, as on stage, Janis Joplin is like a child in complete isolation: holding dialogues with herself that never end, moving gently over her own pain like someone trying to compose an instant autobiography. It's a tribute to the makers of this documentary that you do come out feeling that there will never be anyone else like her. The film contains no mention of her death, only the merest suggestion in a wistful tracking shot around her empty car, but from the amount of energy that we see released it doesn't seem surprising. Her own words, plus a montage of early pictures, go quite a way towards explaining how the quiet suburban kid from Port Arthur who was never asked to the High School prom could have developed into one of the greatest American rock singers. Alk and Findlay simply allow the story to be told in its own terms, especially by the performances: all of the good ones are here, from the legendary Monterey 'Ball and Chain' to 'Try'. DP

Janitor, The

see Eyewitness

January Man, The

(1989, US, 97 min)
d Pat O'Connor. *p* Norman Jewison, Ezra Swerdlow. *sc* John Patrick Shanley. *ph* Jerzy Zielinski. *ed* Lou Lombardo. *pd* Philip Rosenberg. *m* Marvin Hamlisch. *cast* Kevin Kline, Susan Sarandon, Mary Elizabeth Mastrantonio, Harvey Keitel, Danny Aiello, Rod Steiger, Alan Rickman, Faye Grant.
●In New York, eleven murders have taken place in as many months, and the serial killer is about to strike again. So bellicose mayor Steiger reluctantly reinstates maverick sleuth Nick Starkey (Kline), and despite the reservations of the police commissioner (Keitel), who also happens to be Nick's estranged brother, Nick is put on the case. In idiosyncratic fashion, Nick miraculously identifies the apartment that is the killer's next port of call…at which point plot and dramatic tension plummet. Black humour becomes knockabout comedy. Sarandon, as Keitel's wife and sometime lover of his brother, and Mastrantonio as the mayor's daughter who falls for Nick, give good enigmatic performances, but are mislaid in the ensuing tumult. John Patrick Shanley's screenplay, touching on themes of betrayal and corruption, honesty and trust, promises and teases but suffers from coitus interruptus. JGl

Japan

see Japón

Japón (Japan)

(2002, Mex/Sp, 129 min)
d/p/sc Carlos Reygadas. *ph* Diego Martínez Vignatti. *ed* Carlos Serrano Azcona, Daniel Melguizo, David Torres. *ad* Alejandro Reygadas. *m* Arvo Pärt, Dimitri Shostakovich, JS Bach. *cast* Alejandro Ferretis, Magdalena Flores, Yolanda Villa, Martín Serrano, Rolando Hernández, Bernabé Pérez, Carlos Reygadas Barquín, Fernando Benítez.
●Perhaps too self-conscious a stab at a 'great' movie, Reygadas' debut is nevertheless an impressive, engrossing account of a man – a little lame, probably in his sixties, possibly an artist – who travels to a remote valley with thoughts of suicide. Renting a room in an elderly woman's house high above a village, he slowly rediscovers, through a tangle of unexpected emotions, the will to live. Little is explicit in this slow, measured, parable-like film; we're left to deduce motivation from a telling use of music (memorably the final movement from Shostakovich's 15th and Pärt's *Cantus*), landscape (shot in Super16 'Scope), and the performances of an almost wholly non-pro cast of local peasants. Mesmerising – even after one drunken actor hilariously shatters suspension of disbelief with a whinge about the crew. GA

Jardin del Eden, El (The Garden of Eden)

(1994, Mex, 104 min)
d Maria Novaro. *p* Jorge Sanchez. *sc* Maria Novaro, Beatriz Novaro. *ph* Eric Alan Edwards. *ed* Sigfrido Barjau. *cast* Renée Coleman, Bruno Bichir, Gabriela Roer, Ana Ofelia Murguia, Rosario Sagrav, Joseph Culp.
●From the 'feminist' director of the delightful *Danzón*, this is set in Tijuana and concerns the relationship between three disparate women, all in their way border-dwellers – Jane, an American going south, Liz her Spanish-American friend (who can't speak Spanish and is sister of blocked writer Frank who can), and Mexican Serena, a widow struggling to bring up her children alone. It's a discursive, rambling narrative, which may offer a good few insights into the difficulties of both racial identity and the building of alternate means of communication and support between women, but its message or meaning is a little obscure. Likeable and good-hearted none the less. WH

Jardines Colgantes (Hanging Gardens)

(1993, Sp, 116 min)
d/sc Pablo Llorca. *ph* Gerardo Gormezano. *ed* Pablo Llorca. *pd* Monica Burnuy. *m* Saimon Simonet. *cast* Féodor Atkine, Iciar Bollaín, Luis Flete, Rafael Diaz.
●Joining the long line of cinema's shy, bespectacled voyeurs is Flete's repressed tailor, obsessed by his dream of clothing absolutely without decoration. In search of a perfect piece of leather, he falls into the hands of a ruthless warehouse owner (Atkine), who purloins his precious tailor's knife and compels him to make a dashing suit to win the heart of an unwilling local girl (Bollaín). Sexual and professional jealousy entwine to make this a slow-burning tale of desire and perversity, studded with erotic symbols (roses, blood, tattoos, knives, tight corsetry). Atkine is stunning as the vain, garrulous, frightening mobster. SFe

Jason and the Argonauts

(1963, GB, 103 min)
d Don Chaffey. *p* Charles H Schneer. *sc* Raymond Bowers, Jan Read, Beverley Cross. *ph* Wilkie Cooper. *ed* Maurice Rootes. *pd* Geoffrey Drake. *m* Bernard Herrmann. *cast* Todd Armstrong, Nancy Kovack, Gary Raymond, Laurence Naismith, Niall MacGinnis, Michael Gwynn, Douglas Wilmer, Honor Blackman, Patrick Troughton, Nigel Green.
●Jolly juvenile adventure in which Jason (the rather stolid Armstrong) is aided – or hindered – by assorted whimsical gods on Olympus as he quests for the Golden Fleece, and the film itself is given an enormous boost by Ray Harryhausen's special effects. The bronze Titan is an arthritic disappointment, but most of the other inventions are pleasingly imaginative, not least the army of waspishly pugnacious, sword-wielding skeletons which pop out of the ground when the Hydra's teeth are sown. Great fun, as these things go, with a Bernard Herrmann score to boot. TM

Jason's Lyric

(1994, US, 119 min)
d Doug McHenry. *p* Doug McHenry, George Jackson. *sc* Bobby Smith Jr. *ph* Francis Kenny. *ed* Andrew Mondshein. *pd* Simon Dobbin. *m* Afrika. *cast* Allen Payne, Jada Pinkett, Forest Whitaker, Bokeem Woodbine, Suzanne Douglas, Anthony 'Treach' Criss, Lisa Carson.
●This begins in lyrical Deep South mood with Jason (Payne) sitting on a Greyhound bus and recalling his traumatic Houston childhood, when his estranged Viet-vet father Maddog (Whitaker) would go on binges brutally proclaiming his love for Jason's mom (Douglas); the gunshot that put an end to his attacks resulted in Jason's younger brother Josh (Woodbine) turning to a life of drugs and imprisonment. Years later, Jason's still trying to keep the volatile Josh in check, but when he takes up with gang leader Alonzo, elder brother of Lyric (Pinkett), whose romantic sensitivity has allowed Jason's nightmares to turn into dreams of a better life, it's clear that Jason will have to choose between his family and his lover. Bobby Smith Jr's script is an all-black blend of themes from *Romeo and Juliet* and the Cain and Abel story – a risky conceit, but one that in general works surprisingly well, thanks to muscular performances, and an atmospheric portrayal of life in and around the Houston suburbs that rarely descends into stereotype. The movie's a touch too long, and its romantic interludes are sometimes too highly coloured, but McHenry's control of the nicely unsentimental tone is pretty assured, while there's a bonus in the soundtrack which mixes bluesy electric guitar and soul standards. GA

Jassy

(1947, GB, 102 min)
d Bernard Knowles. *p* Sydney Box. *sc* Dorothy Christie, Campbell Christie, Geoffrey Kerr. *ph* Jack Asher, Geoffrey Unsworth. *ed* Charles Knott. *ad* George Provis. *m* Henry Geehl. *cast* Margaret Lockwood, Patricia Roc, Dennis Price, Basil Sydney, Dermot Walsh, Nora Swinburne, Cathleen Nesbitt.
●Splendid tosh from Gainsborough, home of the postwar British movie melodrama, with Lockwood as a 19th century gypsy girl who has the gift of second sight and is saved from the forfeit for witchcraft (a ducking in the village pond) by Dermot Walsh, rightful owner of the local manor house. Later involved in tortuous romantic complications culminating in an accusation of murder, she nevertheless contrives to find true love and see justice done all round. Stock 'period' characters in full-blooded performances; not to everyone's taste, but a testament to the vigour of Gainsborough's style in a period of otherwise dour British cinema. MA

Jaws (100)

(1975, US, 125 min)
d Steven Spielberg. *p* Richard D Zanuck, David Brown. *sc* Peter Benchley, Carl Gottlieb. *ph* Bill Butler. *ed* Verna Fields. *pd* Joseph Alves Jr. *m* John Williams. *cast* Roy Scheider, Robert Shaw, Richard Dreyfuss, Lorraine Gary, Murray Hamilton, Carl Gottlieb, Jeffrey Kramer, Susan Backlinie.
●A reminder that, once upon a time, Spielberg used to make films for adults rather than infants and critical regressives. Maybe it is just a monster movie reminiscent of all those '50s sci-fi films, but it's at least endowed with intelligent characterisation, a lack of sentimentality (in contrast to, say, *E.T.*), and it really is frightening. And, added to the Ahab/Moby Dick echoes in the grizzled sailor Shaw's obsession with the Great White Shark, there are moments of true darkness, expressed most eloquently in the John Milius-scripted speech about the wreck of the 'Indianapolis'. GA

Jaws 2

(1978, US, 116 min)
d Jeannot Szwarc. *p* Richard D Zanuck, David Brown. *sc* Carl Gottlieb, Howard Sackler. *ph* Michael Butler. *ed* Neil Travis, Steve Potter, Arthur Schmidt. *pd* Joe Alves. *m* John Williams. *cast* Roy Scheider, Lorraine Gary, Murray Hamilton, Joseph Mascolo, Jeffrey Kramer, Collin Wilcox, Ann Dusenberry.
●'Children of Jaws' might have been a better title for this teen version of the big fish story. The switch in emphasis – away from an adult world in which expert and monster play out their duel, to one where healthy, wealthy but dumb kids are merely terrorised prawns – can't disguise the sense of *déjà vu*. The townsfolk of Amity appear to be suffering from amnesia as far as sharks are concerned; the mayor is still corrupt and money-hungry; the disappearance of tourists is shrugged off; and as usual, nobody believes Scheider. Suspension of disbelief might have been possible had this been a ripping good yarn; but the kids are just plain silly, and it's a toss-up to decide which is more unconvincing, the shark or Scheider. FF

Jaws 3-D

(1983, US, 99 min)
d Joe Alves. *p* Rupert Hitzig. *sc* Carl Gottlieb, Richard Matheson. *ph* James A Contner. *ed* Randy Roberts, Corky Ehlers. *pd* Woods MacKintosh. *m* Alan Parker. *cast* Dennis Quaid, Bess Armstrong, Simon MacCorkindale, Louis Gossett Jr, John Putch, Lea Thompson, PH Moriarty, Dan Blasko.
●Just when you thought it was safe (yet again) to go back into the cinema, a new *Jaws* hits the screen, this time in 3-D (you need some form of gimmick to sell a film with little or no storyline). A new 'Undersea Kingdom', fashioned out of a lagoon at Sea World, Florida, is about to be opened to the public. Everything goes according to plan until…dum-da-dum…enter Great White through a damaged sea gate, and the usual havoc begins. Quaid is the constructor of this giant aquarium, Armstrong the girl obsessed with dolphins and other sea creatures; of course neither of them realises anything is afoot until people start disappearing and end up as bits and pieces floating out towards the cinema audience. Put in a baking tray, gas mark 7, and enjoy a turkey. DA

Jaws – The Revenge

(1987, US, 100 min)
d/p Joseph Sargent. *sc* Michael De Guzman. *ph* John McPherson. *ed* Michael Brown. *pd* John J Lloyd. *m* Michael Small. *cast* Lorraine Gary, Lance Guest, Mario Van Peebles, Karen Young, Michael Caine, Judith Barsi, Lynn Whitfield, Mitchell Anderson, Melvin Van Peebles.
●That naughty shark spoils everyone's holiday by eating a policeman (son of Scheider from *Jaws* and *Jaws 2*) on Christmas Eve. Thereafter the movie focuses on the mother and remaining son, who happens to be a marine biologist (and to have a wife and daughter), as both become obsessed by what appears to be a vendetta against the family. While it's mostly just a matter of waiting till feeding time (and some keen anticipation as to when the jaws will silence forever a particularly irritating Cute Child), there is a hint that somebody was trying to foist some Symbolism onto the shark: as mother and son suffer an attack of the Oedipals, the creature keeps popping up grinning. Sadly, this attempt at a bit of Art (which could have had hilarious consequences) is ditched, and the film concludes with a few people getting chewed before a messy happy ending amid chunks of exploding shark. RS

Jaya Ganga (Jaya, Fille du Gange)

(1996, Ind/Fr/US, 85 min)
d/sc Vijay Singh. *ph* Piyush Shah. *ed* Renu Saluja. *m* Vanraj Bhatia. *cast* Asil Raïs, Smriti Mishra.
●Nishant (Raïs), a young Indian writer based in Paris, is tracing the Ganges from its Himalayan source to the sea. He's haunted by memories of Jaya, a woman (or possibly a river goddess) he met in France; nevertheless he soon falls for Zehra (Mishra), a sensuous, uncommonly poetic dancing girl who performs in a brothel. Nishant uses his Western buying power to take Zehra away from all that. Can happiness be theirs, or will the past catch up with them? Adapted from his own semi-autobiographical novel, the first feature by Vijay Singh may have made waves in Paris, but here it's hard to endorse, or even to divine the thinking behind the praise offered by that otherwise discerning cinephile city. From the opening, with Nishant wandering the hills in meditative mood, turgid metaphor and empty pictorialism hold sway. GA

Jay and Silent Bob Strike Back

(2001, US, 104 min)
d Kevin Smith. *p* Scott Mosier. *sc* Kevin Smith. *ph* Jamie Anderson. *ed* Kevin Smith, Scott Mosier. *pd* Robert 'Ratface' Holtzman. *m* James L Venable. *cast* Jason Mewes, Kevin Smith, Ben Affleck, Matt Damon, Shannen Doherty, Carrie Fisher, Mark Hamill, Chris Rock.
●When Jay (Mewes) and Silent Bob (Smith) discover that the 'Bluntman & Chronic' comic strip which they've unwittingly inspired is to be made into a movie – without their permission – they're not best pleased. Worse, they're being badmouthed on movie websites. There's nothing for it but to head out Hollywood way to sabotage the production. Wickedly silly tangents and dream sequences ensue. Smith's quick, cartoon-like direction complements the absurd premise and through straight to camera asides, he makes his film feel like a big joke we're all in on, while his savvy pop observations are as smart as ever. Packed with knowing movie references and pulling together strands from Smith's past work, this absurd and surreal road movie, peppered with frat boy humour, is the perfect curtain call for these much-loved, wise but oh so stupid slackers. AL

Jazz in Exile

(1982, US, 59 min)
d/p Chuck France. *ph* Chuck France, Bruce Maim. *ed* Chuck France. *with* Dexter Gordon Quartet, Johnny Griffin Quartet, Art Ensemble of Chicago, Woody Shaw Quintet, Art Farmer, Phil Woods Quartet.
●In an earlier, shorter release (1978) this was a drag; extensive re-editing produced a delight. Too little music and too much talk – about jazzers escaping to enthusiastic Europe from a cool reception in the States (after all, the music's black) – has been rebalanced by the greatly increased concert footage. The music is mainly Hard Bop (tenorists Dexter Gordon and Johnny Griffin trading gutsy phrases, Phil Woods' sliding, striding alto, virtuoso bassist Richard Davis punching out an agile blues with Ben Sidran), but covers enough ground to include archive footage of Billie Holiday and Lester Young, and the modern histrionics of the Art Ensemble of Chicago. More could have been heard from the women (Carla Bley and Betty Carter), and sometimes the solos are cut too short. By and large, though, the film certainly delivers the goods. GA

Jazz on a Summer's Day

(1959, US, 86 min)
d/p Bert Stern. *sc* Arnold Pearl, Albert D'Anniable. *ph* Bert Stern, Courtney Hafela, Ray Phealan, Mike Cuesta, Jack Schatz, Pierre Streit. *ed* Aram A Avakian. *with* Louis Armstrong, Big Maybelle, Chuck Berry, Dinah Washington, Gerry Mulligan, Thelonious Monk, Anita O'Day, Mahalia Jackson, Sonny Stitt, Jack Teagarden.
●This documentary record of the 1958 Newport Jazz Festival is often hailed as one of the first and most influential live concert films, paving the way for later classics like *Monterey Pop* and *Woodstock*. A dazzling array of jazz and rock'n'roll giants are captured on celluloid, including Chuck Berry duck-walking his way through 'Sweet Little Sixteen'. Unquestionable highlight, however, is the extraordinary Mahalia Jackson, whose soulful renditions of 'Didn't It Rain', 'Shout All Over' and 'The Lord's Prayer' send a shiver down the spine. NF

Jazz Singer, The

(1980, US, 116 min)
d Richard Fleischer. *p* Jerry Leider. *sc* Herbert Baker. *ph* Isidore Mankofsky. *ed* Maury Winetrobe. *pd* Harry Horner. *m* Leonard Rosenman. *cast* Neil Diamond, Laurence Olivier, Lucie Arnaz, Catlin Adams, Franklyn Ajaye, Paul Nicholas, Sully Boyar, Mike Kellin, James Booth.
●Neil Diamond, as the New York synagogue cantor's son who trades his yarmulke for the glitter of the LA music biz, makes the most cautious soft-rock superstar movie debut you'll ever get to see. The recording and music publishing businesses are just made for clean-living folk, and guarantee almost immediate recognition and success to anyone of Diamond's obvious talent – or so the film would have you believe. But although nothing is presented to put his family-audience persona at risk, the character comes across as curiously unthinking and irresponsible. The performance is okay…but then Diamond never attempts anything so difficult as chewing gum and walking at the same time. RM

Jazzwomen

(2001, It/US, 79 min)
d/p/ph Gabriella Morandi. *ed* Federica Lang. *with* Abbey Lincoln, Annie Ross, Dakota Station, Teri Thornton, Barbara Carroll, Etta Jones, Mintzy Berry, Vivian Lord, Nancy Miller Elliott, Jackie Cain, Awilda Rivera.
●This documentary is a hymn of praise to women in jazz music and, like most hymns, it's worthy, depressing and slightly dull. The setting is a modern day, neon-lit, late night Manhattan that resembles a trendy lager commercial, filmed in juddering Steadicam and undergoing irritating drop frame/field removed treatment. Such gimmickry only interferes with director Morandi's frank, simple interviews with female musicians. Abbey Lincoln, Annie Ross and Jackie Cain are among the bigger names, but there are many moving testaments delivered to camera from hugely talented young hopefuls who – at best – can dream of a modest clubland career. But the interviewees might just as well be male jazz musicians – only in the last few minutes does the film touch on the uniquely female nature of their problems. JL

Jealousy (Celos)

(1999, Sp, 106 min)
d Vicente Aranda. *p* Fernando Bovaira. *sc* Vicente Aranda, Alvaro del Amo. *ph* José Luis Alcaine. *ed* Teresa Font. *pd* Josep Rosell. *m* José Nieto. *cast* Aitana Sánchez-Gijón, Daniel Gimenéz Cacho, Maria Botto, Luis Tosar, Alicia Sánchez, José Luis Oliva.
●Another preposterous tale of obsessional love from the director of *Lovers* finds Aranda still peddling his mix of TV movie visuals, faux-liberationist misogyny and tired storylines. Lorry driver Antonio is due to wed the gorgeous Carmen, but all that goes awry when he finds a photo of her in the company of an old flame. Cue seriously pathological behaviour from a character whose problems are rumoured to originate with southern inbreeding, and you have the makings of a plot with nada in the empathy stakes. 'What's he looking for?' asks one trucker. 'His own downfall,' the other replies (it's that kind of diner). A showdown in the rain is lifted from the previous film; and along the way the crudest of expositions is matched only by the vulgar portrayal of women as sex-obsessed primitivists equated with the fecund orange crops of the region. GE

Jealousy, Italian Style

see Dramma della Gelosia

Jean de Florette

(1986, Fr/It, 121 min)
d Claude Berri. *sc* Claude Berri, Gérard Brach. *ph* Bruno Nuytten. *ed* Arlette Langmann, Hervé de Luze, Noëlle Boisson. *pd* Bernard Vézat. *m* Jean-Claude Petit. *cast* Yves Montand, Gérard Depardieu, Daniel Auteuil, Elisabeth Depardieu, Ernestine Mazurowna, Marcel Champel, Armand Meffre, André Dupon.
●In the mid-'20s, hunchback tax collector Jean Cadoret (Depardieu) inherits a Provence farm, moving there with wife and daughter to fulfil his naive city-dweller's dreams of an idyllic pastoral life. The map shows a valuable spring on his land, but the cunning Soubeyrans – Montand and son Auteuil – have stopped it up, and plan to wait for him to go broke so that they can buy up his property for a song. Depardieu, though, has some scientific knowledge up his suit sleeve, and at first his crops thrive…Berri and scriptwriter Gérard Brach brilliantly capture the rhythm of the countryside, where the pace of life is dictated by inexorable seasonal changes and the often cruel vagaries of the weather. An object lesson in literary adaptation, the film eschews mere illustration to favour an elliptical narrative which embodies, through the subtlest nuances of dialogue and the most delicate shadings of light and colour, the atmosphere and meaning of Marcel Pagnol's source novel, *L'Eau des collines*. But it is Depardieu who supplies the heart and soul of the film with a performance of towering strength and heart-breaking pathos. *Manon des Sources*, the second part of the diptych, followed in the same year. NF

Jeanne au Bûcher

see Giovanna d'Arco al Rogo

Jeanne d'Arc

see Joan of Arc

Jeanne Dielman, 23 Quai du Commerce, 1080 Bruxelles

(1975, Bel/Fr, 225 min)
d Chantal Anne Akerman. *p* Evelyne Paul, Corinne Jenart. *sc* Chantal Anne Akerman. *ph* Babette Mangolte. *ed* Patricia Canino. *ad* Philippe Graff. *cast* Delphine Seyrig, Jan Decorte, Henri Storck, Jacques Doniol-Valcroze, Yves Bical.
●Chantal Akerman's feature is one of the few 'feminist' movies that's as interesting aesthetically as politically. It covers three days in the life of a bourgeois widow who supports herself and her somewhat moronic son by taking in a 'gentleman caller' each afternoon. Much of the film simply chronicles her ritualised routine, but does it in an ultra-minimal, precise style that emphasises the artifice of the whole thing…and gradually the artifice (coupled with the fact that Delphine Seyrig plays the woman) shifts the plot into melodrama, so that the film becomes a bourgeois tragedy. TR

Jeanne et le Garçon Formidable

(1997, Fr, 105 min)
d Olivier Ducastel, Jacques Martineau. *p* Cyriac Auriol, Pauline Duhault. *sc* Olivier Ducastel, Jacques Martineau. *ph* Matthieu Poirot-Delpech. *ed* Sabine Mamou. *pd* Louis Soubrier. *m* Philippe Miller. *cast* Virginie Ledoyen, Mathieu Demy, Jacques Bonaffé, Valérie Bonneton, Frédéric Gorny, Laurent Arcaro, Michel Raskine, Damien Dodane, Denis Podalydes.
●This ambitious contemporary musical quite literally makes a big production number out of AIDS. The virus looms large in the life of Jeanne

(Ledoyen, gamine to a fault), who thinks she has found the perfect guy until he starts getting dizzy spells and ends up in the hospital. He's played by Mathieu Demy, son of Jacques, who of course made the definitive Gallic musical in *The Umbrellas of Cherbourg*. No Michel Legrand score here, however, just bustling sub-Eurovision tunelessness which leaves the heart resolutely untouched. The jaunty choreography and vivid colours make a piquant contrast with the serious subject matter, but we never really believe in the characters enough for it to count. An enterprising idea, disappointing in execution. TJ

Jeanne la Pucelle (Joan of Arc)

(1994, Fr, (*Les Batailles*) 117 min/ (*Les Prisons*) 121 min)
d Jacques Rivette. *p* Martine Marignac. *sc* Christine Laurent, Pascal Bonitzer. *ph* William Lubtchansky. *ed* Nicole Lubtchansky. *pd* Manu de Chauvigny. *m* Jordi Savall. *cast* Sandrine Bonnaire, André Marcon, Jean-Louis Richard, Marcel Bozonnet, Patrick Le Mauff, Didier Sauvegrain, Jean-Pierre Lorit, Tatiana Moukhine, Jean-Luc Petit, Edith Scob.

●This two-part version of the great story has the space to take matters beyond the theological debate, and the agnostic, ascetic sensibility and to explore the socio-political currents which shaped an enduring popular legend. Jacques Rivette's sedulous, distanced approach is a matter of cumulative impact. The period reconstruction is undemonstrative, the screenplay (by Christine Laurent and Pascal Bonitzer) allows events to gain weight over time, and judicious bursts of Jordi Savall's soundtrack convey moments of release. All this demands a film-maker of immense confidence, but it might be arid were it not for the physical presence and spiritual ambiguity of Bonnaire's performance. Unlike Dreyer's Falconetti, she's no fiery angel, but a strong, courageous, essentially human individual. Rivette refuses to underline the truth or otherwise of her holy visions; instead, he's more interested in showing the power of an idea in moulding events, and the disposability of that idea when its usefulness in Realpolitik is at an end. He's with his heroine in showing the shock created by her explosion of gender demarcation, and in detailing the institutionalised repression of thought by a monolithic church. All this may sound the dourest of history lessons, but Rivette's mastery of the long form makes for a compelling experience; involving, thought-provoking and, as Jeanne mounts the stake, profoundly moving. TJ

Jeder für sich und Gott gegen alle (The Enigma of Kaspar Hauser/Every Man for Himself and God Against All/The Mystery of Kaspar Hauser)

(1974, WGer, 110 min)
d/p/sc Werner Herzog. *ph* Jörg Schmidt-Reitwein, Klaus Wyborny. *ed* Beata Mainka-Jellinghaus. *ad* Henning von Gierke. *m* Pachebel, Albinoni, Orlando Di Lasso, WA Mozart. *cast* Bruno S, Walter Ladengast, Brigitte Mira, Willy Semmelrogge, Gloria Dör, Volker Prechtel, Enno Patlas.

●A film that shares with *Aguirre, Wrath of God* a fascination with historical manuscripts, an uneasy laughter at human aspiration, and an awe of landscape. 19th century Germany: Kaspar arrives like a time traveller, found standing in a sleepy town square, his origins shrouded in mystery. After learning to talk, he tells of being kept in a cellar and never having seen a human being. The learned confront this enigma with the power of their logic, dissection and annotation, but Kaspar shows up the limitations of such rationalism. He departs as mysteriously as he arrived, stabbed by an unknown assailant, leaving behind a deathbed vision that he knows to be only the beginning of a story, and an enlarged liver and overdeveloped brain for doctors to ponder over. Not the same dizzy folly as *Aguirre*, but Herzog's similarly long perspective conjures as powerful a picture of man's aimless tracks through an impassive landscape. Stunning. CPea

Jeepers Creepers

(2001, Ger/US, 91 min)
d Victor Salva. *p* Barry Opper, Tom Luse. *sc* Victor Salva. *ph* Don E Fauntleroy. *ed* Ed Marx. *pd* Steven Legler. *m* Bennett Salvay. *cast* Gina Philips, Justin Long, Jonathan Breck, Patricia Belcher, Brandon Smith, Eileen Brennan.

●The opening blends *Duel* and *Texas Chain Saw Massacre*, as college kids Darius (Long) and sister Trish (Philips) drive home by the backroads and are menaced by an aggressively driven old truck. Barely surviving the ordeal, they stumble across something nasty in the cellar of a deserted church. It's part of the film's appeal that we discover the truth at the same rate as Trish and Darius. As tension builds with bracing economy and ingenuity, a seemingly standard teen-shocker gradually shifts into darker *Twilight Zone* territory. A stunning climax lifts things to another level, throwing a new, blackly comic light on the whole enterprise. The film nimbly incorporates urban myth and post-*Scream* post-modernism with sufficient nastiness to sate the gorehound. NY

Jefferson in Paris

(1995, US, 140 min)
d James Ivory. *p* Ismail Merchant. *sc* Ruth Prawer Jhabvala. *ph* Pierre Lhomme. *ed* Andrew Marcus, Isabelle Lorente. *pd* Guy-Claude François. *m* Richard Robbins. *cast* Nick Nolte, Greta Scacchi, Thandie Newton, Gwyneth Paltrow, Simon Callow, Seth Gilliam, Michael Lonsdale, Nancy Marchand, James Earl Jones, Jean-Pierre Aumont, Lambert Wilson.

●In 1785, some ten years after he drafted the Declaration of Independence, Thomas Jefferson became America's first ambassador to the court of Louis XVI. There he observed the decadence which was to ignite the French Revolution, and there, according to this film, he twice fell in love, with the married Anglo-Italian artist Maria Cosway, and then with the half sister of his late wife, the household slave Sally Hemings. As usual with Merchant Ivory, dramatic tension, such as it is, centres on the conflict between love and convention, or, as Jefferson famously expressed it, the head and the heart. A man of reason and principle, Jefferson nevertheless embodied the contradictions of his time: he wrote that all men are created equal, yet remained a slave owner until his death; a widower who swore to remain true to his wife, he wooed Cosway (Scacchi), and had children by Hemings (Thandie Newton – very fly). Nick Nolte brings a starchy grace to Jefferson, but it's as if, regrettably, he's acting in a corset. For all the prettily embroidered rhetoric, Ruth Jhabvala's screenplay is too reticent to skewer hypocrisy, and Ivory's direction too inert to stir the passions. TCh

Jeffrey

(1995, US, 94 min)
d Christopher Ashley. *p* Mark Balsam, Mitchell Maxwell, Victoria Maxwell. *sc* Paul Rudnik. *ph* Jeffrey Tufano. *ed* Cara Silverman. *m* Stephen Endelman. *cast* Steven Weber, Patrick Stewart, Michael T Weiss, Sigourney Weaver, Bryan Batt, Nathan Lane, Olympia Dukakis.

●Exasperated by the stresses and contradictions of AIDS-era gay sexuality, Jeffrey (Weber), a New York waiter-cum-actor, decides celibacy is the only way forward. Next thing, of course, he meets Weiss' charming gym trainer, and is hesitating over whether he might just be The One, when a much anticipated date brings the announcement that the object of his desire is HIV-positive. Paul Rudnick's loose but often hilarious screenplay (from his play) adopts a scattershot approach to just about every aspect of the contemporary gay experience: the painful loss of friends and lovers is here, and there's a big showing for New York's Gay Pride march, though it's the sparkling comic set-pieces that leave the strongest impression. There's also a showy cameo for Weaver as the hucksterish self-help guru of Sexual Compulsives Anonymous, and a stand-out routine in gay priest Lane's proclamation that sex and the great Broadway musicals prove the existence of God. On the debit side, not everything adds up, with stage director Ashley ill at ease at the helm, and Stewart rather uncertain as the queeny father figure coping with a crisis of his own. TJ

J'embrasse pas (I Don't Kiss)

(1991, Fr, 116 min)
d André Téchiné. *p* Maurice Bernart, Jacques Eric Strauss, Jean Labadie. *sc* André Téchiné, Jacques Nolot, Michel Grisolia. *ph* Thierry Arbogast. *ed* Claudine Merlin, Edith Vassard. *ad* Vincent Mateu-Ferrer. *m* Philippe Sarde. *cast* Philippe Noiret, Emmanuelle Béart, Manuel Blanc, Hélène Vincent, Ivan Desny, Christophe Bernard, Roschdy Zem.

●He doesn't kiss; nor, according to the subtitles laying down conditions to prospective male clients, does this Paris rent boy (Blanc) 'suck off or take it up the bum'. The innocent country boy has come a long way since arriving with high hopes of making it in the big city. His only contact (with equally vulnerable middle-aged widow Vincent) provides a bed to sleep in, but under impossible conditions. Film producer Noiret offers 'no sex' overtures of friendship, which he only later realises are more predatory than they seemed. Auditions end in humiliation and flight from his tentative ambition to become an actor. Only tart-with-a-troubled-heart Béart seems honest in this world without pity. Despite odd moments of truth and affecting scenes, Téchiné's episodic film is a downhill racer: what at first seems art house austerity reveals itself to be mere posturing. WH

Jennifer

(1953, US, 73 min, b/w)
d Joel Newton. *p* Berman Swartz. *sc* uncredited. *ph* James Wong Howe. *ed* Everett Douglas. *ad* uncredited. *m* Ernest Gold. *cast* Ida Lupino, Howard Duff, Robert Nicholls, Mary Shipp, Ned Glass, Kitty McHugh, Russ Conway, Lorna Thayer.

●Lupino takes a job as caretaker of an isolated mansion, from which her predecessor has mysteriously disappeared. Outside, the hot California sun; inside, cool, empty corridors, the ominous basement boiler room. This is gothic romance crossed with early-'50s *noir*, worth a look for the sake of the great Wong Howe. Grey-listed and taking what work he could get, he tackles even this B-picture for Monogram with unfailing artistry, creating images that are strong without being showy, atmospheric yet perfectly naturalistic. From a story by Virginia Myers. BBa

Jennifer 8

(1992, US, 127 min)
d Bruce Robinson. *p* Gary Lucchesi, David Wimbury. *sc* Bruce Robinson. *ph* Conrad Hall. *pd* Richard Macdonald. *m* Christopher Young. *cast* Andy Garcia, Uma Thurman, Lance Henriksen, Kathy Baker, John Malkovich, Kevin Conway.

●Focusing on the dubious obsession of Garcia, a burnt-out Los Angeles cop, with an alleged serial killer – whose latest victim he dubs 'Jennifer 8' – English writer/director Bruce Robinson's first Hollywood feature fails to reconcile the conflicting demands of psychological character study and generic suspense thriller. Garcia's transfer to the small town of Eureka, California, ruffles a few feathers, especially when he starts exhuming corpses and digging into long-dead cases. The key witness, Thurman, is a young blind woman whose growing affection for Garcia and fragments of knowledge about the killer put her at risk. Garcia too is stumbling in the dark, so much so that FBI 'observer' Malkovich points the finger at *him*. The opening scene on a rain-drenched rubbish tip hints at great things, but despite strong writing and an exceptional cast, the plotting is suspect and the murderer's identity is obvious from very early on. NF

Jenseits der Stille

see Beyond Silence

Jenseits der Wolken

see Beyond the Clouds

Jeopardy

(1952, US, 69 min, b/w)
d John Sturges. *p* Sol Baer Fielding. *sc* Mel Dinelli. *ph* Victor Milner. *ed* Newell P Kimlin. *ad* Cedric Gibbons, William Ferrari. *m* Dimitri Tiomkin. *cast* Barbara Stanwyck, Barry Sullivan, Ralph Meeker, Lee Aaker.

●Solid performances and slick direction give this thriller a certain edge, but the situation is contrived, the tension spurious. On holiday in Mexico, Sullivan is trapped by timber from a collapsing pier on a remote beach. With the tide rising, his wife (Stanwyck) drives off to seek help, leaving their young son (Aaker) to tend to his dad. She runs into an escaped killer (Meeker), who cynically appropriates the car to make good his own escape; but surprised by the way Stanwyck continues to fight him, he returns to the beach after she reminds him that he can use her husband's clothes and papers, and promises to go with him herself (as decoy for police roadblocks, or whatever he wants) provided her husband is freed. It's an MGM film, so you know that family and the love of a good woman will weigh heavily in the end. TM

Jeremiah Johnson

(1972, US, 108 min)
d Sydney Pollack. *p* Joe Wizan. *sc* John Milius, Edward Anhalt. *ph* Duke Callaghan. *ed* Thomas Stanford. *ad* Ted Haworth. *m* John Rubinstein. *cast* Robert Redford, Will Geer, Stefan Gierasch, Allyn Ann McLerie, Delle Bolton, Charles Tyner, Josh Albee, Matt Clark.
●A flawed but immensely appealing film adapted in part from Vardis Fisher's *Mountain Man*, a superb historical novel which explores the myth and the reality of the tough trappers who roamed the unconquered West in the 1850s. Shot on location in fantastically beautiful, desolate snowscapes in Utah, the first part of the film is terrific: tenderfoot Redford's first, baffled steps in the battle for survival; the weird encounter with a corpse frozen upright in the snow which provides him with his first real gun; the old man of the mountains who takes time out from hunting grizzlies to teach him how to fish, trap beaver, tell one Indian from another, and stay alive. After this things switch from documentary to picaresque adventure, and John Milius' script begins to stumble uncertainly. But it does come back on course towards the end as the Indians, half-worshipping and half-contemptuous, begin their hunt for the strange white man who has broken their taboos and disappeared into the snows – the legend of the West in the making. TM

Jeremy

(1973, US, 90 min)
d Arthur Barron. *p* George Pappas. *sc* Arthur Barron. *ph* Paul Goldsmith. *ed* Zina Voynow. *ad* Peter Bocour. *m* Lee Holdridge. *cast* Robby Benson, Glynnis O'Connor, Len Bari, Leonardo Cimino, Ned Wilson, Chris Bohn.
●A good example of the sucker punch. Make a nicely photographed New York boy-meets-girl story, done with the same glossy colour supplement superficiality that the boy condemns in his parents, and you too can win best first film prize at Cannes. Have Jeremy, an aspiring cellist of 16, meet aspiring ballet dancer just as shy and sensitive. Make them fall in love as they sing the theme song to each other on the soundtrack. Then one day, when it's raining and they're bored with their game of chess, get Jeremy to take off his glasses and fuck her ever so tastefully. Sew it all up by having tragedy strike three weeks and four days later. Vaguely liberal parents and moist-palmed adolescents may succumb, but most will probably emerge feeling somewhat redundant. CPe

Je Rentre à la Maison

see I'm Going Home

Jericho Mile, The

(1979, US, 97 min)
d Michael Mann. *p* Tim Zinnemann. *sc* Patrick J Nolan, Michael Mann. *ph* Rexford Metz. *ed* Arthur Schmidt. *ad* Stephen Berger. *m* Jimmie Haskell. *cast* Peter Strauss, Richard Lawson, Roger E Mosley, Brian Dennehy, Geoffrey Lewis, Billy Green Bush, Ed Lauter, Beverly Todd, William Prince.
●Made for TV, this is part gritty prison movie, part equally gritty fairytale (sympathetic killer obsessively runs to Olympic standard). It's generally upbeat without being remotely wimpish or excessively naive: the walls don't simply fall, and the optimism has to seep through a quasi-documentary context of racism and violence. It's really well acted by pros and inmates, crafted to manipulative perfection; and it beats *Rocky* every which way. See it, be suckered, be entertained. PT

Jerk, The

(1979, US, 94 min)
d Carl Reiner. *p* David V Picker, William E McEuen. *sc* Carl Reiner, Steve Martin, Carl Gottlieb, Michael Elias. *ph* Victor J Kemper. *ed* Bud Molin. *pd* Jack T Collis. *m* Jack Elliott. *cast* Steve Martin, Bernadette Peters, Catlin Adams, Mabel King, Richard Ward, Dick Anthony Williams, Bill Macy, M Emmet Walsh, Carl Gottlieb.
●America's rediscovery of lame-brain comedy brought this starring debut for Steve Martin. Behind the stoned humour, it's basically a Depression romance about a sucker in the big city, boosted and updated by some pleasingly irreverent twists like his black plantation home (a foundling, he reluctantly has to accept the awful truth that he's white). The trouble with retard comedy is that it rapidly degenerates into banana-skin jokes; but at its best, *The Jerk* manages to move its central character away from the merely moronic to a truly hysterical Pollyannaism, as when he becomes ecstatic at seeing his name in the phone-book, or jumps for joy at the sight of his new home (a men's toilet: 'Like it? I love it!'). The comedy runs out of steam when the jerk makes good, but laugh for laugh it's probably a better investment than *10*. DP

Jerry Maguire

(1996, US, 139 min)
d Cameron Crowe. *p* James L Brooks, Laurence Mark, Richard Sakai, Cameron Crowe. *sc* Cameron Crowe. *ph* Janusz Kaminski. *ed* Joe Hutshing. *pd* Stephen Lineweaver. *m* Nancy Wilson. *cast* Tom Cruise, Cuba Gooding Jr, Renee Zellweger, Kelly Preston, Jerry O'Connell, Jay Mohr, Regina King, Bonnie Hunt, Beau Bridges.
●When sports agent Jerry Maguire (Cruise) writes an uncharacteristically idealistic manifesto suggesting his company should opt for fewer clients and a more caring approach, he's applauded by his colleagues who, as soon as he's fired, desert him – along with all but one of his clients, mouthy footballer Rod Tidwell (Gooding). But then Jerry also has support from single mum Dorothy Boyd (Zellweger), who happens to have fallen for him. Will the prospect of failure allow him to open up to his emotions, instead of just half-hearted affairs, as before? Lauded as a witty moral fable with a revelatory performance from its star, this romantic comedy is in fact meretricious, manipulative and reactionary. Cruise is still limited to three modes of expression: anxious, determined and smugly smiling. Since Maguire never really breaks with the money-oriented definition of success favoured by the agency that fired him, his 'failure' and diatribes against cynicism are meaningless. As for his 'redemption' through the love of a good woman: she's a doting doormat who even apologises for his mistakes, and he's so peremptory about getting what he wants that the film comes over as unthinkingly sexist. Sterling performances, nevertheless, from Zellweger and Gooding. GA

Jersey Girl

(1992, US, 95 min)
d David Burton Morris. *p* Amanda DiGiulio. *sc* Gina Wendkos. *ph* Ron Fortunato. *ed* Norman Hollyn. *pd* Lester Cohen. *m* Misha Segal. *cast* Jami Gertz, Dylan McDermott, Molly Price, Aida Turturro, Star Jasper, Sheryl Lee, Joseph Bologna.
●New Jersey schoolteacher Toby (Gertz) wants to trade loyal friends and the local diner for ritzy dates on Fifth Avenue. At the Mercedes showroom parking lot, she collides her battered VW into the new Mercedes belonging to Prince Charming, aka Sal (McDermott), whose vast wealth conceals his blue-collar background. His involvement with snobbish Tara (Lee) comes to an abrupt end when she makes one too many allusions to having helped him from the gutter; but can he and Toby overcome class differences and her declared ambition to look like a 'city girl'? This shamelessly contrived romance, which makes a half-hearted attempt to denigrate materialism and '80s aspirations, lurches from one predictable exchange to the next. Mind-numbing. CM

Jerusalem File, The

(1971, US/Isr, 96 min)
d John Flynn. *p* R Ben Efraim. *sc* Troy Kennedy Martin. *ph* Raoul Coutard. *ed* Norman Wanstall. *ad* Peter Williams. *m* John Scott. *cast* Bruce Davison, Nicol Williamson, Daria Halprin, Donald Pleasence, Ian Hendry, Koya Yair Rubin, Zeev Revah.
●A slice of ill-disguised (and painfully dull) Zionist propaganda masquerading as a thriller about an idealistic American archaeology student (Davison) caught in the Arab-Israeli crossfire. Set in Jerusalem after the Six Day War, it purports to be on the side of peace and love, but in fact depicts all the violence as coming from various unspecified Arab groups, while the benevolent Israelis try to stop them fighting each other.

Jesse James

(1939, US, 105 min)
d Henry King. *p* Darryl F Zanuck. *sc* Nunnally Johnson. *ph* George Barnes, W Howard Greene. *ed* Barbara McLean. *ad* William Darling, George S Dudley. *m* Louis Silvers. *cast* Tyrone Power, Henry Fonda, Nancy Kelly, Randolph Scott, Henry Hull, Brian Donlevy, John Carradine, Jane Darwell, Donald Meek.
●An influential, sympathetic biography of the West's most famous outlaw, 'One of the doggonedest, dad-blamedest buckaroos that ever rode across the United States of America' (not a description that immediately brings to mind Tyrone Power). Shot in new, improved Technicolor by George Barnes, the film looks well, and King directs with uncharacteristic spurts of vitality whenever Jesse gets busy, though Nunnally Johnson injects too many moral disclaimers into his script: it's all the railroad's fault. TCh

Jester, The (O Bobo)

(1987, Port, 127 min)
d José Alvaro Morais. *sc* José Alvaro Morais, Rafael Godhino. *ph* Mario de Carvalho. *ed* José Nascimento. *pd* Jasmim. *m* Carlos Azevdo, Carlos Zingaro, Pedro Caldeira Cabral. *cast* Fernando Heitor, Paula Guedes, Luis Lucas, Luísa Marques, Victor Santos Ramos, Glicinia Quartin.
●This takes patience (a degree in Portuguese studies wouldn't go amiss, either), but ultimately rewards it by pulling a dozen apparently separate threads together into a vivid picture of Lisbon's young intelligentsia in 1978, when the idealism roused by the Portuguese revolution finally died. Most of the central characters are involved in putting on a play (adapted from Alexandre Herculano's novel *The Jester*), and the film gets astonishing mileage from the old device of counterpointing their on-stage and off-stage lives. The off-stage issues include gun-running, a sexually ambivalent triangle, and a murder; the on-stage scenes are designed sumptuously enough to recall the heyday of Michael Powell. TR

Je suis né d'une cigogne (Children of the Stork)

(1999, Fr, 80 min)
d/sc Tony Gatlif. *ph* Claude Garnier, Eric Guichard. *ed* Monique Dartonne. *pd* Brigitte Brassart. *m* Tony Gatlif. *cast* Romain Duris, Rona Hartner, Ouassini Embarek, Christine Pignet, Marc Nouyrigat, Muse Dalbray, Suzanne Flon, Daniel Laloux.
●Far more fanciful and pretentious than Gatlif's gypsy films, this metaphorical road movie reunites *Gadjo Dilo*'s Duris and Hartner as a rebellious young couple on the run from a life of tedious conformism. Stealing a car, they meet up with an Arab kid and a wounded stork whom they take for an illegal Algerian immigrant and decide to reunite with his family in Germany. The camera trickery and wacky, noisome 'comedy' soon grate, the attempts to emulate early Godard are mainly offbeam, and the overriding thesis about borders and alienation is woolly and unilluminating. GA

Jesus Christ Superstar

(1973, US, 107 min)
d Norman Jewison. *p* Norman Jewison, Robert Stigwood. *sc* Melvyn Bragg, Norman Jewison. *ph* Douglas Slocombe. *ed* Antony Gibbs. *pd* Richard MacDonald. *songs* Tim Rice, Andrew Lloyd Weber. *cast* Ted Neeley, Carl Anderson, Yvonne Elliman, Barry Dennen, Bob Bingham, Larry T Marshall, Joshua Mostel.
●It's possible that Tim Rice and Andrew Lloyd Webber originally intended their de-theologisation of Christ quite seriously, in which case they were probably nonplussed by the way the stage show generated a pop version of 'religious' awe, like an updated Miracle Play. But the whole thing was out of their hands by the time it came to the movie, and so here the contradictions are writ very large indeed. Jewison ranges a ten stone weakling Christ (Neeley) against a powerhouse black Judas (Anderson), resurrects the latter rather than the former (in a Sly Stone jumpsuit, yet), and still manages to send audiences into transports of spiritual exaltation; the final credits roll in hushed silence. Despite the 'impressive' desert locations and an array of tanks (to represent the ills of modern militarism), it's still staged like a student revue. Most notable moments are

the garden of Gethsemane scene, where Jewison cuts in leering Pharisees and crucifixion details from Flemish masters to supremely kitschy effect, and the scene of Christ being flogged, shot in sadistic slow motion. TR

Jesus of Montreal (Jésus de Montréal)

(1989, Can/Fr, 119 min)
d Denys Arcand. *p* Roger Frappier, Pierre Gendron. *sc* Denys Arcand. *ph* Guy Dufaux. *ed* Isabelle Dedieu. *ad* François Séguin. *m* Yves Laferriere, François Dompierre, Jean-Marie Benoit. *cast* Lothaire Bluteau, Catherine Wilkening, Johanne-Marie Tremblay, Rémy Girard, Robert Lepage, Gilles Pelletier, Yves Jacques, Denys Arcand.

● Unknown actor Daniel (Bluteau) is asked by the Church to revive and revitalise a version of the Passion Play. Although the result is a critical and commercial success, his employers take exception to his radical account of Christ's life – was the Messiah the bastard son of a Roman soldier? – and Daniel's reluctance to compromise sees him heading towards modern martyrdom. Thematically or tonally, few recent films have been as rich as Arcand's delicious satire on contemporary mores. If it is fundementally a witty, free-wheeling variation on the Gospel of St Mark, it is never constrained by allegorical schematism, and manages to make deft, original swipes at a plethora of modern 'evils': media hype, advertising, hospital bureaucracy, and of course the hypocrisy of the religious establishment. But what really makes the film so enjoyable is its capacity to surprise, not least in the way that a wide variety of potentially academic issues are introduced into a classy, clever, thoroughly entertaining format. Even if you're normally scared off by things theological, this visually elegant, uncluttered movie is serious fun. GA

Jesus' Son

(1999, US, 105 min)
d Alison Maclean. *p* Lydia Dean Pilcher, Elizabeth Cuthrell, David Urrutia. *sc* Elizabeth Cuthrell, David Urrutia, Oren Moverman. *ph* Adam Kimmel. *ed* Stuart Levy. *pd* David Doernberg. *cast* Billy Crudup, Samantha Morton, Holly Hunter, Dennis Hopper, Denis Leary, Will Paton, Jack Black, Greg Germann.

● Its been a long time since *Crush*, but New Zealander Maclean's first US film is a frisky adaptation of a collection of short stories by Denis Johnson, recounting the misadventures of the drug-addled Fuck Head (FH for short) in the Midwest in the early '70s. The freewheeling tone (Maclean modifies her style between episodes) somewhat resembles *Drugstore Cowboy*. A sequence involving a knife and an eyeball is the funniest thing I've seen all year. The redemptive thrust of the second half is obviously a bit harder to swallow, but see the film for Billy Crudup's wonderful central performance, which holds everything together and justifies all the buzz which has gathered around him. TCh

Je t'aime, Je t'aime

(1967, Fr, 94 min)
d Alain Resnais. *p* Mag Bodard. *sc* Jacques Sternberg. *ph* Jean Boffety. *ed* Albert Jurgenson, Colette Leloup. *ad* Jacques Dugied. m Krzysztof Penderecki. *cast* Claude Rich, Olga Georges-Picot, Anouk Ferjac, Annie Fargue, Bernard Fresson, Yvette Etievant.

● One of Resnais' most underrated explorations of the tone of time and memory. Claude Ridder (Rich), a failed suicide, is visited by two men who invite his cooperation in an experiment (already tried with a mouse) to project him into the past to see if he can recapture a moment of his life (since he has no wish to live, and therefore has no future, he is the perfect subject). Indifferently he agrees, is whisked through a suburban no man's land to a laboratory, and – accompanied by the mouse as an experienced travelling companion – sets off on his weird, fairytale trip through time, only to become hopelessly lost. As the scientists frantically try to trace their missing guinea-pig, fragments of his past surface momentarily, recurringly. Beautiful, tranquil, but increasingly menacing clues to a love affair with a girl he may or may not have killed. The fragments remain teasingly undertain, just out of Ridder's grasp, but his feelings lead him inexorably back to the key moment of suicide; and in the present, Ridder's body – the body of a man projected into his death – is found in the laboratory grounds. On one level a witty sci-fi adventure, on another a poetic apprehension of man's helpless entrapment by time, the film is perfectly summed up by the extraordinary last shot of the mouse, still caged by the glass dome in which it has travelled, standing with its paws spread out against the glass in mute appeal. TM

Je t'aime, moi non plus

see I Love You, I Don't

Jetée, La 100 (The Jetty/The Pier)

(1962, Fr, 29 min, b/w)
d/sc Chris Marker. *ph* Jean Chiabaud. *ed* Jean Ravel. *m* Trevor Duncan. *cast* Hélène Chatelain, Davos Hanich, Jacques Ledoux, William Klein, Ligia Branice, Etienne Becker.

● This classic 'photo-roman' about the power of memory – 'the story of a man marked by an image of his childhood' – begins at Orly airport a few years before WWIII. That image is of a woman's face at the end of the pier; and in the post-apocalyptic world the man now inhabits as a prisoner, he is given the chance to discover its true significance as a guinea-pig in a time travel experiment. Marker uses monochrome images recognisably from the past, such as the ruins of Europe after WWII, and with a few small props and effects, subtly suggests a future environment. The soundtrack's texture is similarly sparse, and the fluid montage leads the viewer into the sensation of watching moving images. Until, that is, an extraordinary epiphany when an image genuinely does move: the man's sleeping lover opens her eyes. DT

Jet Pilot

(1957, US, 112 min)
d Josef von Sternberg. *p/sc* Jules Furthman. *ph* Winton C Hoch. *ed* Michael R McAdam, Harry Marker, William H Moore. *ad* Albert S D'Agostino, Feild Gray. *m* Bronislau Kaper. *cast* John Wayne, Janet Leigh, Jay C Flippen, Richard Rober, Paul Fix, Roland Winters, Hans Conried.

Turgid and risible Cold War drama enlivened only by the superb aerial footage so beloved of its producer Howard Hughes, who re-shot, re-cut and generally tinkered with the film so obsessively that it was finally released some seven years after shooting began. Clearly uninspired by the material, Von Sternberg focused all his attention on Leigh, an improbably beautiful Soviet pilot who lands in Alaska to seek political asylum and falls in love with Major Wayne. But, it transpires, she's an agent sent to turn a high-ranking officer into an informer, and he returns with her to Russia. Needless to say, she soon realises that Moscow doesn't measure up to Palm Springs, but not before some pretty daft stuff involving sexual innuendo, patriotic sentiments, and very obvious double-cross. For Von Sternberg completists only. GA

Jetsons: The Movie

(1990, US, 81 min)
d William Hanna, Joseph Barbera. *sc* Dennis Marks. *ph* Daniel Bunn. *ed* Pat Foley, Terry W Moore, Larry C Cowan; Gregory V Watson Jr, Gilbert Iverson, Tim Iverson, Karen Doulac. *pd* Al Gumer, Judith Holmes Clarke, Ric Estrada. *m* John Debney. *cast* voices: George O'Hanlon, Penny Singleton, Mel Blanc, Tiffany.

● Hanna/Barbera's futuristic follow-up to *The Flintstones* was launched on TV in 1962 and cancelled after a single season. Syndication has kept it alive for three decades, long enough for Hanna/Barbera to believe that there would be a market for a comeback in the shape of an animated feature film. Big mistake. Top-notch computer graphics, star voices and a gaggle of gadgets cannot disguise the fact that this family of the future is stuck firmly in 1962. Dad struggles for promotion while Mom remains sickeningly supportive, Sis digs shopping and dreamy rock stars, Sonny plays basketball with his robot friend, and the future is a technological Utopia where every man's need is catered for at the push of a button – Dad's job being 'digital index operator' at Spacely Space Sprockets. Not such a bad idea, but who needs it? DW

Jet Storm

(1959, GB, 99 min, b/w)
d Cy Endfield. *p* Steven Pallos. *sc* Cy Endfield, Sigmund Miller. *ph* Jack Hildyard. *ed* Oswald Hafenrichter. *ad* Scott MacGregor. *m* Thomas Rajna. *cast* Richard Attenborough, Stanley Baker, Hermione Baddeley, Bernard Braden, Diane Cilento, Paul Eddington, Megs Jenkins, David Kossoff, Virginia Maskell, George Rose, Harry Secombe, Elizabeth Sellars, Sybil Thorndike, Marty Wilde, Mai Zetterling.

● A British prototype for the *Airport* disaster movies of the '60s and '70s, with Shepperton's version of an all-star cast among the 40 passengers and crew of a first class transatlantic flight. Attenborough is the disaster in question, a specialist in unstable compounds who is more than a little unstable himself after his daughter's death in a hit-and-run incident. It transpires that the guilty party (Rose) is also on the flight, and twitchy Dickie has a bomb stowed away. 'You think you have a plane-load of people? It's a travelling zoo!' he explains to Captain Stanley Baker – with some justification. Like its later supersonic counterparts, Endfield's film is naive and contrived, but not without interest as the alarmed passengers soon divide into groups: reactionary (advocating torture) and liberal (patience and persuasion). TCh

Jetty, The

see Jetée, La

Je tu il elle (I...You...He...She)

(1974, Bel, 85 min, b/w)
d/p/sc Chantal Anne Akerman. *ph* Bénédicte Delsalle, Charlotte Slovak, Renelde Dupon. *ed* Luc Freche. *cast* Chantal Anne Akerman, Niels Arestrup, Claire Wauthion.

● The force of Akerman's disquieting and mesmeric first feature has been lost amid critical praise (for its modish sexual preoccupations) or blame (for its arrogant omission of plot). Look again. Sexually frank, coolly passionate, it's a spiritual odyssey on a low budget as we follow 'Je' (played by Akerman herself) writing a love letter ('Tu'), in a masturbatory affair with a lorry driver playing Marlon Brando ('Il'), and an unresolved encounter with her female lover ('Elle'). Minimal in style, maximum in impact, it achieves a feeling of quiet desperation most reminiscent of Fassbinder's early features; and similarly it's a daring prototype for more remarkable later work. DMacp

Jeu de l'oie, Le (Snakes and Ladders)

(1980, Fr, 32 min)
d Raúl Ruiz. *cast* Pascal Bonitzer

● A concise essay on maps and orientation, made in the context of a cartography exhibition at the Pompidou Centre, this is a slightly flimsy fantasy that covers some of the same ground as Greenaway's *A Walk Through H*, but with less conviction. A man finds himself embroiled in the board game '*Le Jeu de l'oie*', first across Paris, then on a cosmic level. Some of Rivette's fictions, like *Le Pont du Nord*, have covered similar ground more convincingly; but the footnotes from Borges, et al, are informative, at least. JRo

Jeune Fille Assassinée, La

see Charlotte

Jeune Werther, Le (Young Werther)

(1992, Fr, 94 min)
d Jacques Doillon. *p* Hervé Duhamel. *sc* Jacques Doillon. *ph* Christophe Pollock. *ed* Nicole Lubtchansky. *m* Philippe Sarde. *cast* Ismaël Jolé-Ménébhi, Thomas Brémond, Simon Clavière, Faye Anastasia, Pierre Mézerette, Miren Capello.

● Like the hero of Goethe's *The Sorrows of Young Werther*, on which this is based, adolescent Guillaume – much discussed but never seen – commits suicide over a love affair. Despite his death, the pangs of unrequited love that brought it about continue among his friends. Indeed, Ismaël (Jolé-Ménébhi) and Théo (Brémond), having found Miren (Capello), the object of Guillaume's love, make a move on her themselves, breaking up with girlfriends and straining their own friendship. But just as Guillaume's friends never really knew him (or, for that matter, themselves), so we never really get to understand them. AO

Jeux Interdits (Forbidden Games/The Secret Game)

(1952, Fr, 90 min, b/w)
d René Clément. *p* Paul Joly. *sc* Jean Aurenche, Pierre Bost, François Boyer. *ph* Robert Juillard. *ed* Robert Dwyre. *ad* Paul Bertrand. *m* Narciso Yepes. *cast* Brigitte Fossey, Georges Poujouly, Lucien Hubert, Suzanne Courtal, Jacques Marin, Laurence Badie.

●Clément's notorious eclecticism can surely never have been so marked within a single film as in this all-purpose allegory, anti-war tract and *noir*-ish morality. Waifish children create their own secret animal cemetery and honour it with the monuments of the human dead, while World War II holocaust and petty family feuds form a perverse backdrop to their 'innocence' – or, perhaps, a mirror to the 'perversion' of their forbidden games. Unfortunately, such a potentially fascinating patchwork is glossed over with an irritating layer of heartstring humanism, and now looks 'touching' rather than challenging. PT

Jeux sont Faits, Les

(1947, Fr, 91 min, b/w)
d Jean Delannoy. *sc* Jean-Paul Sartre. *ph* Christian Matras. *ed* Henri Taverna. *ad* Serge Pimenoff. *m* Georges Auric. *cast* Marcel Pagliero, Micheline Presle, Marguerite Moréno, Charles Dullin, Jacques Erwin, Marcel Mouloudji, Howard Vernon.

●Sartre wrote this rare survivor from those Left wing movies which loomed large in Europe after 1945. English liberal critics missed their class issues and saw only poetic fatalism. Stalinist hacks punished them for lacking positive heroes and singing tomorrows. Then English Marxists fell for Cahiers' twee formalism and whored after Hollywood culture. This forgotten gem cries out for rehabilitation. In this *Heaven Can Wait* fantasy, a de luxe lady (Presle) falls in love with the workers' militia leader just before they die. The afterworld (a Tati-like bureaucracy) gives them a second chance. The Communist street-fighting man is played by Pagliero, a Gabin-Montand hybrid who also directed bleak proletarian melodramas. The plot bitterly laments the lost opportunity for a 1945 French Revolution. Though it's sapped by Delannoy's stiffish direction, it's kitted out with 'cubist Heaven' decor and a L'Herbier-type aesthetic. Compulsive for connoisseurs. RD

Je veux rentrer à la maison

see I Want to Go Home

Je Vous Salue, Marie

see Hail, Mary

Jew-Boy Levi (Viehjud Levi)

(1998, Ger, 97 min)
d Didi Danquart. *p* Martin Hagemann. *sc* Didi Danquart, Martina Döcker. *ph* Johan Feindt. *ed* Katja Dringenberg. *pd* Susanne Hopf. *m* Cornelius Schwehr. *cast* Bruno Cathomas, Caroline Ebner, Martina Gedeck, Ulrich Noethen, Eva Mattes, Gerhard Olschewski, Bernd Michael Lade, Günther Knecht, Alexander May, Stefan Merki.

●Slight, clichéd and often overly theatrical, this account of the rise of anti-Semitism, as suffered by a cattledealer in love with an Aryan girl wooed by one of her own kind, in a Black Forest farming community in 1935 never offers insights of originality or interest. Every development is signposted, and the only surprise is that Eva Mattes, once a sexy Fassbinder siren, can now so convincingly play a lumpenly bovine hausfrau. (From a play by Thomas Strittmatter.) GA

Jewel of the Nile, The

(1985, US, 106 min)
d Lewis Teague. *p* Michael Douglas. *sc* Mark Rosenthal, Lawrence Konner. *ph* Jan De Bont. *ed* Michael Ellis, Peter Boita. *pd* Richard Dawking, Terence Knight. *m* Jack Nitzsche. *cast* Michael Douglas, Kathleen Turner, Danny DeVito, Spiros Focas, Avner Eisenberg, Paul David Magid, Howard Jay Patterson.

●The end of *Romancing the Stone* found the likeable team of Turner and Douglas sailing off down a Manhattan avenue in their schooner. By *Jewel*, they are comfortably afloat in the south of France, and agreeing to go their separate ways after she is approached by a handsome sheik to write up his story and thus promote his accession to leader of some unspecified Middle Eastern kingdom. When the schooner gets blown out of the water, it's then a ripping chase, in and out of prisons, up and down the desert in an effort to locate the famous 'Jewel' which alone will restore the rightful leader to his people. The film is still as crazy and hectic as its predecessor, without ever quite coming up to the bench mark set by the original. More distressing is that, like *Indiana Jones and the Temple of Doom*, it falls into a kind of unthinking racism, in which all Arabs are seen as dishcloth-wearing fanatics, all screaming 'Aieee' and bent on murdering An infidel for Allah. CPea

Jezebel

(1938, US, 106 min, b/w)
d William Wyler. *p* Henry Blanke. *sc* Clements Ripley, Abem Finkel, John Huston. *ph* Ernest Haller. *ed* Warren Low. *ad* Robert M Haas. *m* Max Steiner. *cast* Bette Davis, Henry Fonda, George Brent, Margaret Lindsay, Donald Crisp, Fay Bainter, Spring Byington, Richard Cromwell.

●New Orleans, 1852, the Lympus Ball. Enter Julie Marston (Davis) dressed in scarlet. Deep shock from the maidens in white and the matrons in grey. She starts to waltz and couples shrink from the contaminating touch of her red gown. This justly famous scene from *Jezebel* (filmed, incidentally, in black-and-white) telescopes many of the film's themes. Julie is socially and sexually transgressive. Indeed her defiance of conventions threatens the very Social Order, and she is soon associated with the fever and fires that devastate the town. Preston Dillard (Fonda), engaged to Julie but already insecure in his masculinity, cannot cope with her dangerous sexuality and finds refuge with a safe woman from the North. But when Preston returns to the South, he meets Julie again and gets the fever… JCl

Jezebels, The

see Switchblade Sisters

JFK

(1991, US, 189 min, b/w & col)
d Oliver Stone. *p* A Kitman Ho, Oliver Stone. *sc* Oliver Stone, Zachary Sklar. *ph* Robert Richardson. *ed* Joe Hutshing, Pietro Scalia. *pd* Victor Kempster. *m* John Williams. *cast* Kevin Costner, Gary Oldman, Sissy Spacek, Tommy Lee Jones, Laurie Metcalf, Michael Rooker, Jay O Sanders, Sally Kirkland, Ed Asner, Jack Lemmon, Vincent D'Onofrio, Brian Doyle-Murray, Joe Pesci, Walter Matthau, Tomas Milian, John Candy, Kevin Bacon, Donald Sutherland.

●Stone goes for the gut, but the complexity of theories surrounding the Kennedy assassination might have benefited from a cooler assessment. Understandably, he is hostile to the lone assassin findings; here, Oswald (Oldman) is merely the 'patsy' of a nebulous conspiracy cover-up involving just about *everyone;* sadly, their exact roles in the '*coup d'état*' are never properly clarified. The investigation conducted between '66 and '69 by DA Jim Garrison (whitewashed as Costner) allows Stone to proffer a dazzling array of facts, hypotheses and flashbacks, intercutting archive footage, reconstructions, and more conventional dramatic material. While his logic is often murky, the data overload is forceful, if not wholly persuasive. Though the huge cast performs strongly, characterisation is minimal, and the overall structure uninspiring. Often the film seems a garbled rant, but mostly it's more complex and less flashy than Stone's other work; the urgent editing packs a powerful punch, and if the conclusions are vague and ready to see conspiracy everywhere, one can't deny the force of Stone's call for more open debate. GA

Jigsaw

(1980, GB, 67 min, b/w & col)
d/ph/ed Robina Rose.

●An impressive film, this sharply conceived yet sympathetic look at a group of autistic children uses formal experiment (elements of documentary, avant-garde and narrative cinema) to reflect the alienated world of its subjects. Images and sounds build up to the obsessive isolation of the film's climax: a representation of 'tunnel vision' which turns the metaphor outside in and takes you with it. HM

Jimi Hendrix

(1973, US, 102 min)
d Joe Boyd, John Head, Gary Weis. *p* Joe Boyd. *ph* Gary Weis. *ed* Peter Colbeck. *with* Jimi Hendrix, Pete Townshend, Eric Clapton, Al Hendrix, Major Charles Washington, Little Richard, Mick Jagger, Lou Reed, Germaine Greer.

●Thanks mainly to the technical dexterity of producer/director Joe Boyd, this succeeds in communicating a real sense of Hendrix via his music and his friends. There are amusing and enlightening appearances from Noel Redding, Clapton, Townshend, Jagger, Little Richard, and even Lou Reed. But more importantly, the music is for once really well chosen: amazing and formerly unseen things from Monterey, Isle of Wight, Woodstock, Fillmore East, and even the Marquee Club. DP

Jimi Plays Berkeley

(1971, US, 45 min)
d/p/sc Peter Pilafian. *ph* Eric Saarinen, Joan Churchill, Peter Smokler, Johann Rush. *ed* Baird Bryant. *with* The Jimi Hendrix Experience.

●A record of the historic Berkeley concert on Memorial Day, 1970. For Hendrix admirers only; others are unlikely to be converted. Pilafian intercuts the concert with shots of rioting students to little effect. People flash their peace signs and say things like 'It's my country, right or wrong'. Hendrix just plays; best are 'Purple Haze' and 'Voodoo Chile'. And what did you do in the youth revolution, Daddy?

Jimmy Hollywood

(1994, US, 109 min)
d Barry Levinson. *p* Mark Johnson, Barry Levinson. *sc* Barry Levinson. *ph* Peter Sova. *ed* Jay Rabinowitz. *pd* Linda DeScenna. *m* Robbie Robertson. *cast* Joe Pesci, Christian Slater, Victoria Abril, Jason Beghe, John Cothran Jr, Rob Weiss, Chad McQueen.

●It's a sign of the times that Barry Levinson's slick, gimmicky *Disclosure* got a major theatrical release in Britain, while the same director's quirky, fascinating *Jimmy Hollywood* snuck out straight to video virtually unnoticed. Ironically (as the title implies), Hollywood is at the heart of the picture. Pesci plays an out-of-work actor, Jimmy Alto, so frustrated by his stillborn career that he turns vigilante instead. Not that he's a *Falling Down*, mad-as-hell kind of guy; he's more an accidental hero – and his media friendly alter ego, guerilla crime-fighter Jericho, turns out to be the role of a lifetime. The pacing might be tighter, but much of the movie is a delight. With shades of *Bugsy* and *Rain Man*, as well as the verbal riffs and gender tensions which distinguished *Diner* and *Tin Men*, it's a key film in Levinson's oeuvre. TCh

Jimmy Neutron Boy Genius

(2001, US, 83 min)
d John A Davis. *p* Steve Oedekerk, John A Davis, Albie Hecht. *sc* John A Davis, David N Weiss, J David Stern, Steve Oedekerk. *ed* Jon Michael Price, Gregory Perler. *pd* Fred Cline. *m* John Debney. *cast* voices: Megan Cavanagh, Mark DeCarlo, Debi Derryberry, Jeff Garcia, Bob Goen, Mary Hart, Carolyn Lawrence.

●Visually, the rendering of this sci-fi animation from the Nickelodeon stable is hardly Pixar-perfect, but it's not far off. Jimmy Neutron is Retroville's brightest young spark, an expert problem solver and prolific inventor. When his usually easy-going parents insist that, like his mates, he must miss the opening of a new amusement park, the kids sneak out anyway. On returning home, they find their parents have been abducted by aliens. Initially, the kids think it's a dream come true and riotously indulge, *Home Alone*-style, in all things previously prohibited. Soon, though, they realise they miss their folks, so Jimmy fashions a miraculous fleet of spaceships from the town's hardware and together they hit the intergalactic road with a view to kicking some alien butt. Youngsters will no doubt be charmed by the cute caricatures with their big round faces, whacky hairstyles and chirpy voices. Parents, too, should find a modicum of time-passing amusement in some of the jocular dialogue and the garish '50s milieu. DA

Jimmy Reardon

see Night in the Life of Jimmy Reardon, A

Jimmy the Kid

(1982, US, 85 min)
d Gary Nelson. *p* Ronald A Jacobs. *sc* Sam Bobrick. *ph* Dennis Dalzell. *ed* Richard C Meyer. *ad* Bill Ross. *m* John Cameron. *cast* Gary Coleman, Paul LeMat, Walter Olkewicz, Dee Wallace, Ruth Gordon, Don Adams, Cleavon Little.

●Gary Coleman was a child star who waged a personal battle against a growth-repressing illness and the parents who spirited away the fortune he made from the hit TV series *Diff'rent Strokes*. In this indifferent comedy, however, he mugs gracelessly as the listless son of showbiz folk. LeMat is the kindly kidnapper who teaches him that life (cue retching) is worth living after all. Tell it to Donald Westlake, who must have wept when he saw what they did to one of his novels. TJ

Jingle All the Way

(1996, US, 89 min)
d Brian Levant. *p* Chris Columbus, Mark A Radcliffe, Michael Barnathan. *sc* Randy Kornfield. *ph* Victor J Kemper. *ed* Kent Beyda, Wilton Henderson, Adam Weiss. *pd* Leslie McDonald. *m* David Newman. *cast* Arnold Schwarzenegger, Sinbad, Phil Hartman, Rita Wilson, Robert Conrad, Martin Mull, Jake Lloyd, James Belushi.

●Arnie's the dad running round town trying to buy his son an action man toy for Christmas, but they're all sold out. And that's about it. This valiantly hypocritical, uninflected movie keeps its most cynical role for the 'good father' Ted (Hartman), a character pilloried for having the prescience to buy his son's 'Turbo Man' early. WH

Jin-Roh (Jinro/aka The Wolf Brigade)

(1998, Jap, 98 min)
d Hiroyuki Okura. *p* Tsutomu Sugita, Hidekazu Terakawa. *sc* Mamoru Oshii. *ph* Hisao Shirai. *ed* Shuichi Kakesu. pd Hiromasu Ogura. *m* Hajime Mizoguchi. *cast* voices: Yoshikatsu Fujiki, Kazuki Fusé, Sumi Mutuo.

●Despite an incomprehensibly complex backstory, this is the most interesting animation feature from Japan since *Memories*. Fusé, a military policeman battling subversives in the late 1950s is covertly a member of an elite force known as the Wolf Brigade; he is sent for retraining and put under surveillance after failing to shoot a girl suicide bomber. The dead girl's sister (or is she?) encounters him and subverts his macho, hyper-obedient mind-set by introducing him to the Little Red Riding Hood story. But the more he gets drawn into the story, the more he identifies with the wolf. Fine work from all the designers, animators and voice actors, but the key talent is writer Mamoru Oshii, himself a leading animation director. His concept here plays like a re-reading of Angela Carter on lupine myth – from the wolf's point of view. (Tetsuya Nishio and Toshiyuki Inoue were the key animation supervisors.) TR

Jinxed!

(1982, US, 103 min)
d Don Siegel. *p* Herb Jaffe. *sc* Bert Blessing. *ph* Vilmos Zsigmond. *ed* Douglas Stewart. *pd* Ted Haworth. *m* Bruce Roberts, Miles Goodman. *cast* Bette Midler, Ken Wahl, Rip Torn, Val Avery, Jack Elam, Benson Fong, Don Siegel.

●Siegel's last film, and, by all accounts, an unhappy experience. Midler conspires with blackjack dealer Wahl to kill her partner Rip Torn, which would leave her free to continue their romance and him free from the uncomfortable winning streak Torn had been enjoying at his tables. An obvious lack of rapport between Midler and Wahl doesn't help Frank D Gilroy's much rewritten script (credited to 'Bert Blessing'). TJ

Jit

(1990, Zim, 92 min)
d Michael Raeburn. *p* Rory Kilalea. *sc* Michael Raeburn. *ph* João (Funcho) Costa. *ed* Justin Krish. *pd* Lindie Pankiv. *m* Oliver Mtukudzi. *cast* Dominic Makuvachuma, Sibongile Nene, Farai Sevenzo, Winnie Ndemera, Oliver Mtukudzi.

●If *The Harder They Come* was a tough-nosed bus ride around Kingston, Jamaica, Raeburn's romp is a comedic scooter tour of Harare, Zimbabwe, to the lively jump of Jit music. Both are ready-made tales of poor country boys in the big bad city. The main character here, UK, is an orthodontic wonder, whose only collateral (besides his teeth) is a combination of optimism and charm. He takes to following around Sofi (Nene), the local stunner, who thinks he must be kidding, and who, to add injury to insult, has a gangster boyfriend who agrees. Undeterred, UK approaches Sofi's dad for her hand, and the venal old sod suggests a wedding price of a radiogramophone and $500 to see what happens. What happens is that the boy chases around Harare like Pee-Wee Herman on speed to earn the money, dogged at every step by the twin forces of his village 'Jukwa' (a wizened old village 'spirit' with magic powers and an alcohol problem), and the gangster's stitched-faced cronies. It's Zimbabwe's first feature, a bit of a tourist trip, with lots of musical entertainment thrown in. WH

Jitterbugs

(1943, US, 74 min, b/w)
d Malcolm St Clair. *p* Sol M Wurtzel. *sc* W Scott Darling. *ph* Lucien Andriot. *ed* Norman Colbert. *ad* James Basevi, Chester Gore. *m* Emile Newman. *cast* Stan Laurel, Oliver Hardy, Vivian Blaine, Bob Bailey, Lee Patrick, Douglas Fowley, Noel Madison.

●By far the best of the later L & H features, with the pair playing a two-man jazz band who fall foul of a gang of conmen in attempting to help singer Vivian Blaine recover the money they have swindled. Although one or two close-ups show Laurel looking distinctly ravaged, his illness never hampers the film, which is elegant, inventive, and beautifully paced by Mal St Clair. Even the musical numbers are attractive, thanks to Vivian Blaine and the jitterbug sequence near the beginning which sees L & H handling all the instruments in the band (including trumpet in the Harry James manner). One gem of a sequence has Laurel in hilarious drag as auntie, while Hardy, masquerading as a gallant Southern colonel, exchanges wonderful sweet nothings with Lee Patrick. TM

Jo

(1971, Fr, 85 min)
d Jean Girault. *p* Léo L Fuchs. *sc* Claude Magnier. *ph* Henri Decae. *ed* Armand Psenny. *ad* Sydney Bettex. *m* Raymond Lefevre. *cast* Louis de Funès, Claude Gensac, Christiane Muller, Bernard Blier, Carlo Nell, Jacques Marin, Ferdy Mayne.

●Alec Coppel's play *The Gazebo* transposed to studio-bound France. About a writer who pretends he's writing a murder story but is in fact attempting to carry out the perfect crime, it is often predictable and sometimes repetitive. Some surprising gems, nevertheless: Bernard Blier as the Hitchcockian inspector, for instance; and de Funès, operating in that difficult area where everything is forced into the determinedly lightweight, is a unique farceur.

Joan at the Stake

see Giovanna d'Arco al Rogo

Joan of Arc

see Jeanne la Pucelle

Joan of Arc (Jeanne d'Arc)

(1999, Fr, 158 min)
d Luc Besson. *p* Patrice Ledoux. *sc* Andrew Birkin, Luc Besson. *ph* Thierry Arbogast. *ed* Sylvie Landra. *pd* Hugues Tissandier. *m* Eric Serra. *cast* Milla Jovovich, John Malkovich, Faye Dunaway, Dustin Hoffman, Pascal Greggory, Vincent Cassel, Tchéky Karyo, Richard Ridings, Desmond Harrington, Timothy West, Timothy Bateson, Richard Leaf.

●This take on the angelic upstart again proves that Besson is incapable of melting substance into style. His Joan (Jovovich) is a preposterous creature, a peasant with a cut-glass accent. Cassel, as a grizzled military leader, performs like a man with his mind on other matters, while Malkovich, as the spoilt Dauphin, simply mugs. That said, a few things – like Joan's blood-bolted visions – do work. She's haunted by a wretchedly pious young man (Leaf), a frail beauty except for his grotesque joke shop eyes. Hoffman is also surprisingly bearable as Joan's hooded, whispery-voiced 'conscience'. His scepticism may strip away the film's potential for mystery, but at least he presents some sort of stick against which to measure Joan. Trying to upgrade this sword 'n' sorcery epic, Besson has reduced myth to delusional fantasy. The story only rings true when Joan is exposed as mad and friendless – as soon as we're asked to believe she's politically dangerous, the whole edifice collapses. CO'Su

Joan of Arc of Mongolia (Johanna d'Arc of Mongolia)

(1989, WGer, 165 min)
d/p/sc/ph Ulrike Ottinger. *ed* Dörre Völz. *ad* Ulrike Ottinger. *m* Wilhelm Dieter Siebert. *cast* Delphine Seyrig, Irm Hermann, Jean Marais, Christoph Eichhorn, Gillian Scalici, Inés Sastre, Xu Re Huor, Peter Kern.

●Thanks to subsidy from German TV, Ottinger has carved out a niche for herself as the foremost lesbian adventurist film-maker in Europe. This particular farrago imagines four disparate women meeting on the Trans-Siberian Express (where their repartee falls pitifully short of the Noël Coward tone it aspires to), and then finding themselves hijacked by a nomadic Mongolian princess and dragged through a tour of 'exotic' Mongolian culture that changes their lives. The assumptions about western and eastern cultures on which this rests are every bit as repulsive as they sound, and don't stand up to a moment's thought; but the really nauseating thing about the movie is its phony reverence for Mongolian traditions, seen as a matriarchal web of ethnic ceremonies and unfathomable secrets. Shameless. TR

Joan Sees Stars

(1993, US, 60 min, b/w & col)
d Joan Braderman, Dana Master. *p/sc* Joan Braderman. *ph* Gene Gort. *ed* Joan Braderman, Dana Master. *cast* Joan Braderman, Elizabeth Taylor, Vivien Leigh, Ava Gardner.

●This essay by the 'media-holic' video artist Joan Braderman is in two parts. The first ('Starsick') finds Joan – via Master's video technology – in bed with Liz Taylor (*BUtterfield 8*) discoursing on friendship and shared movie passion with the stage director Leland Moss (who died of AIDS), her own illness (ulcerated colitis), and her autobiographical feminist deconstruction of the nature of the TV/video image. She mugs to the camera, breathes fire, and places herself in various physically, aesthetically and ideologically compromised positions. Thoughtful, affecting, amusing and highly consumable. Part Two ('MGM: Movie Goddess Machine') is another persuasive melange of stills, clips and images marrying *Frankenstein* with *Gentlemen Prefer Blondes*; the Vivien Leigh of *GWTW* with that of *Streetcar*; and Ava Gardner (in *On the Beach*) with Joan herself, ending with a justification of S&M ('a parody of romance') and tattooing ('our refusal written in pain, blood and skin'). A witty slap in the face to all meanie manipulators, not least 'figure fascists' and 'aerobic storm troopers'. Light-hearted and strangely moving. WH

Job, The

see Posto, Il

Jobman

(1990, SAf, 97 min)
d Darrell James Roodt. *p* Christopher Coy. *sc* Darrell James Roodt, Greg Latter. *ph* Paul Witte. *ed* Shelly Wells. *ad* Dave Barkham. *m* Joel Goldsmith. *cast* Kevin Smith, Tertius Meintjies, Lynn Gaines, Marcel van Heerden, Goliath Davids, Josephine Liedeman.

●Smith, the deaf and dumb son of a rural black preacher, refuses to accept the menial labour on offer in the small farming community where he's grown up. He tries to earn a living in the city, but this ends in assault, and his return home sparks off a cycle of vengeful violence. What Roodt's film lacks in subtlety, it makes up for in dirty authenticity. A hard-hitting independent venture (the director went on to make *Sarafina!*), completed and released against the odds in apartheid South Africa. TJ

Joe Albany...A Jazz Life

(1980, US, 57 min)
d/p Carole Langer. *ph* Jonathan Smith. *ed* Michael Schenkein. *with* The Joe Albany Trio, Phil Schapp.

●Carole Langer's documentary is a delight every time jazz pianist Joe Albany sits down to play, amply justifying his reference to Charlie Parker as the one influence he acknowledges in his style. The interview material, focusing almost exclusively on the Albany 'mystery', is less satisfying. After making an almost legendary name with Bird and others in the '40s, Albany became a drug addict and dropped out of sight for decades. The story of his long climb back from degradation, happily ending in renewed fame, is obviously crucially important to Albany himself, but is an almost too familiar tale. More about Parker and the 52nd Street past would have added just the right touch of cream in the coffee. TM

Joe Gould's Secret

(2000, US, 108 min)
d Stanley Tucci. *p* Chuck Weinstock, Beth Alexander, Stanley Tucci. *sc* Howard Rodman. *ph* Maryse Alberti. *ed* Suzy Elmiger. *pd* Andrew Jackness. *m* Evan Lurie. *cast* Stanley Tucci, Ian Holm, Hope Davis, Susan Sarandon, Patricia Clarkson, Steve Martin.

●Joseph Mitchell encountered Joe Gould, an eccentric, erudite tramp, drunk and rogue, in the 1940s, and later wrote about him in two beguiling, time-separated investigative essays for the *New Yorker*. The pieces asked whether the bum's claim to have composed, in the form of a massive unpublished oral history, one of the most profoundly important books of all time held up to inspection. The tale had colourful characters, decent themes – fame and neglect; loyalty, faith and betrayal; creativity and destructivenes – and the ring of truth. Tucci's well-meaning but staid simplification is clumsily sentimental, with a horribly indulged 'larger than life' turn from Holm as the boho derelict, who, incidentally, is one of the most fragrantly clean tramps ever to grace a cinema screen. After *The Impostors*, this calls into question the promise shown by Tucci (or was it Campbell Scott after all?) with *Big Night*. GA

Joe Hill (aka The Ballad of Joe Hill)

(1971, Swe, 115 min)
d/p/sc Bo Widerberg. *ph* Peter Davidsson, Jörgen Persson. *ed* Bo Widerberg. *ad* Ulf Axen. *m* Stefan Grossman. *cast* Thommy Berggren, Anja Schmidt, Evert Anderson, Cathy Smith, Franco Molinari, Kelvin Malave, Sven Sjolander.

●Berggren plays Joe Hillstrom, a Swedish immigrant to the US in 1902, who attempts to organise the poor through speeches and songs, and is eventually executed for murder on circumstantial evidence. Like *Adalen '31*, it's distractingly pretty to look at for a factually inspired film about the man who became a labour songwriter and organiser with the IWW. But when Widerberg is accused of diluting his message by making his films too sentimental and beautiful to look at, he argues that this attracts a wider audience than would go to a more rigorous political film, and that preaching to the converted is a waste of time…

Joe Kidd

(1972, US, 87 min)
d John Sturges. *p* Sidney Beckerman. *sc* Elmore Leonard. *ph* Bruce Surtees. *ed* Ferris Webster. *ad* Alexander Golitzen, Henry Bumstead. *m* Lalo Schifrin. *cast* Clint Eastwood, Robert Duvall, John Saxon, Don Stroud, Stella Garcia, James Wainwright, Paul Koslo, Gregory Walcott.

●Photographed by the admirable Bruce Surtees, but a curiously strangled Western which can't make up its mind whether it wants to wring straight action out of the range war between poor Mexicans and a tycoon rancher (Duvall), or to explore the moral standing of the disreputable character (Eastwood) who takes law and order into his hands. Not unlikeable, but its irresolution is typified by the inappropriately rumbustious scene in which Eastwood drives a train through a saloon. TM

Joe Louis – For All Time

(1984, US, 90 min, b/w & col)
d Peter Tatum. *p* Jack Healy, Jim Jacobs, William Cayton, Peter Tatum. *sc* Budd Schulberg. *ph* Isidore Mankofsky. *ed* Anthony Zaccaro. *m* Bill Zampion. *narrator* Brock Peters.

●Why does boxing so consistently make for good movies? Maybe it's because the subject provides action and lurid out-of-ring lives galore, maybe because boxers always seem to be such sad figures, reliant on powerful punches for their brief period of glory and then often doomed to years of neglect and poverty. Even with as popular and long-reigning a pugilist as Louis, this element of despair is present, and along with the marvellous archive footage on view, gives this documentary its compulsive and touching quality. The only complaints, in fact, lie surprisingly with the commentary written by Budd Schulberg; not only does it never question the values of physical violence as sport, but it frequently degenerates into absurdly purple bombast. GA

Joe Macbeth

(1955, GB, 90 min, b/w)
d Ken Hughes. *p* MJ Frankovich. *sc* Philip Yordan. *ph* Basil Emmott. *ed* Peter Rolfe Johnson. *ad* Alan Harris. *m* Trevor Duncan. *cast* Paul Douglas, Ruth Roman, Bonar Colleano, Grégoire Aslan, Sidney James, Nicholas Stuart, Robert Arden, Harry Green, Minerva Pious.

●A somewhat misbegotten attempt to transpose *Macbeth* as a gangster movie, though by no means the total disaster as which it was generally written off. The main problem, aside from the British studio stab at a New York '30s ambience, is the pedantically literal adaptation by Philip Yordan, which seems to be constantly inviting recognition for its daring by drawing needless attention to its source (even the names are uncomfortably echoed, Banquo becoming Banky, for instance). Some of the transpositions work (the three witches as an old flower-seller outside a nightclub), others emphatically do not (Banquo's ghost materialising unconvincingly at a country-house dinner). If the end result is disappointingly hollow, it is often directed with style: the gangland execution in a deserted nightclub at the beginning; the murder of 'Duncan' (Aslan) as he takes an early morning dip in a lake; the eerie self-haunting of Macbeth (Douglas, really rather good), left deserted in his castle by the defection of the two murderer-hoods and the madness of his wife. A distinct curate's egg oddity. TM

Joe Versus the Volcano

(1990, US, 102 min)
d John Patrick Shanley. *p* Teri Schwartz. *sc* John Patrick Shanley. *ph* Stephen Goldblatt. *ed* Richard Halsey. *pd* Bo Welch. *m* Georges Delerue. *cast* Tom Hanks, Meg Ryan, Lloyd Bridges, Robert Stack, Abe Vigoda, Dan Hedaya, Barry McGovern, Amanda Plummer, Ossie Davis.

●Shanley's full-blown romantic fantasy, shot almost entirely on stylised sets, is a dreamlike allegory about heroism and personal fulfilment. Curiously, in a film so dependent on narrative and visual artifice, it is Hanks' multi-faceted performance as a clerk-turned-adventurer that binds the disparate elements together. After learning that he has a 'brain cloud' and only six months to live, Joe realises he has been too scared to live properly, and accepts a challenge from magnate Graynamore (Bridges): the inhabitants of a Polynesian island need a hero who will jump into a volcano to appease their gods; in return, Joe will get to live like a king and die like a man, while Graynamore gets the rights to valuable mineral deposits. Passing from the depressing grey-blue of Joe's office through LA's neon brashness to the abstract colours of the later scenes, this engaging fable builds from a slow bubble to an outright eruption of comedy, romance and tear-jerking sentiment. If you go with the flow of Joe's Capraesque journey of self-discovery, you may be swept along. NF

Johan

(1921, Swe, 85 min approx, b/w)
d Mauritz Stiller. *sc* Mauritz Stiller, Arthur Nordeen. *ph* Henrik Jaenzon, Gustaf Boge. *ad* Axel Ebbensen. *cast* Jenny Hasselquist, Urho Somersalmi, Mathias Taube, Hildegard Harring, Lilly Berg.

●Marit weds farmer Johan, a dull old stick with a poisonous mother living across the river. Along comes a fat-arsed lumberjack who easily seduces Marit away, taking her on a perilous journey over the rapids, with Johan in hot pursuit. It ends with the seducer taking a beating and a penitent Marit returning to the farm – happy ending for Johan, his 'property' restored, but most modern audiences will feel frustrated at Marit's inability to kiss off both these jerks and head for the bright lights. (In *Juha*, the Kaurismäki remake, she suffers even more grievously.) Stiller deadpans the morality of the tale, more intent on having his camera commune with the rugged Scandinavian landscape. The inter-titles are unusual, being in the form of a trad-sounding ballad with a mocking refrain. From a novel by Juhani Aho. BBa

Johanna d'Arc of Mongolia

see Joan of Arc of Mongolia

John and Mary

(1969, US, 92 min)
d Peter Yates. *p* Ben Kadish. *sc* John Mortimer. *ph* Gayne Rescher. *ed* Frank P Keller. *pd* John Robert Lloyd. *m* Quincy Jones. *cast* Dustin Hoffman, Mia Farrow, Michael Tolan, Sunny Griffin, Stanley Beck, Tyne Daly, Olympia Dukakis, Cleavon Little.

●Part two of Peter Yates' step-by-step demonstration of his abilities to Hollywood: first the cars (in *Bullitt*), here the characters (in the archetypal late '60s morning-after-the-night-before movie). Hoffman and Farrow awake to each other in a New York bed and interminably worry, via chat, fantasy, flashback and some trendy cultural reference, whether they should do it again. PT

John Carpenter's Escape from L.A.

(1996, US, 102 min)
d John Carpenter. *p* Debra Hill, Kurt Russell. *sc* John Carpenter, Debra Hill, Kurt Russell. *ph* Gary B Kibbe. *ed* Edward A Warschilka. *pd* Lawrence G Paull. *m* Shirley Walker, John Carpenter. *cast* Kurt Russell, Stacy Keach, Steve Buscemi, Peter Fonda, Cliff Robertson, George Corraface, AJ Langer, Pam Grier, Valeria Golino, Paul Bartel, Robert Carradine.

●When *Escape from New York* was released in 1981, its innovative computer graphics, satirical dystopian vision and tongue-in-cheek humour had a freshness that disguised its ramshackle narrative. Equally enjoyable was Russell's cynical anti-hero Snake Plissken, with his eye-patch and tight-lipped, Eastwood-style one-liners. After 15 years of computer-generated effects, apocalyptic sci-fi and Arnie movies with flippant kiss-off lines, the sequel feels hackneyed and pointless. In the original, Snake was sprung from prison in order to rescue the US President from Manhattan, a lawless maximum-security island populated exclusively by hardened criminals. An explosive device injected into his neck enforced safe and timely delivery. This time, the Snake's injected with a fatal virus, despatched to the earthquake-created prison island of LA, and charged with terminating the President's daughter, Utopia (Langer), a Patti Hearst-style runaway who's stolen the government's 'doomsday device' and shacked up on the island with South American drug dealer turned revolutionary Cuervo Jones (Corraface). Once ashore, he crosses the urban wasteland to Jones' fortified lair, encountering tough transsexual Hershe (Grier), weaselly tour-guide 'Map to the Stars' Eddie (Buscemi), and spaced-out surfer Pipeline (Fonda). NF

John Carpenter's Vampires

see Vampires

John Grisham's The Rainmaker

see Rainmaker, The

John Heartfield: Photomonteur

(1977, WGer, 60 min)
d Helmut Herbst.

●A documentary which looks at Heartfield primarily as a political activist working in a specific historical context. It demonstrates this relationship by the use of documentary material, such as archive footage of inter-war Germany, in juxtaposition with Heartfield's works. (These are here frequently shown, as they are rarely reproduced, in their original format as magazine or book covers.) Far from manifesting an obsequious reverence for the works, the film takes the bold step, thoroughly justified by its results, of re-using the elements of Heartfield's montages for short snippets of photo-animation. It also documents artistic influences on Heartfield's work – Berlin Dada, which was in general more immediately political in nature than its Zurich counterpart, and George Grosz in particular – and includes a detailed demonstration of how the photomontages were produced and printed. AS

John Huston War Stories

(1998, GB, 90 min, b/w & col)
d/p Midge Mackenzie. *ph* Richard Leacock. *ed* Neil Thomson. *with* John Huston.

●A fascinating interview with Huston conducted by Mackenzie and Leacock in the early '80s, together with extracts from his wartime documentaries, *The Battle of San Pietro* (1944) and *Let There Be Light*. (1946). Both Huston's films were originally banned, the former through fear that its frank reportage of the horrifying US casualty rate in the invasion of Italy might discourage new recruits (the ban was lifted only after General Marshall approved it, promoting Huston to Major); the latter for its unblinking focus on combat neuroses in a psychiatric hospital. BC

Johnny Allegro (aka Hounded)

(1949, US, 81 min, b/w)
d Ted Tetzlaff. *p* Irving Starr. *sc* Karen DeWolfe, Guy Endore. *ph* Joseph Biroc. *ed* Jerome Thoms. *ad* Perry Smith. *m* George Duning. *cast* George Raft, George Macready, Nina Foch, Will Geer, Gloria Henry, Ivan Triesault.
●Passable thriller with Raft as a reformed criminal persuaded (mainly by the appearance of Foch as a mysterious siren) to hunt down a traitorous counterfeit gang on behalf of the Treasury Department. Things take a lift as the action shifts to an island off the Florida coast, the script begins to filch from *The Hounds of Zaroff*, and Macready's suavely decadent villain proceeds to hunt Raft with bow-and-arrow (he doesn't get him, sad to say). TM

Johnny Angel

(1945, US, 79 min, b/w)
d Edwin L Marin. *p* William A Pereira. *sc* Steve Fisher. *ph* Harry J Wild. *ed* Les Millbrook. *ad* Albert S D'Agostino, Jack Okey. *m* Leigh Harline. *cast* George Raft, Claire Trevor, Signe Hasso, Lowell Gilmore, Hoagy Carmichael, Marvin Miller, Margaret Wycherly.
●A ghost ship emerges out of the fog: bullet-holes, overturned chairs and broken photographs point to a perturbed past. The world of *Johnny Angel* is very *noir* indeed. Raft plays Captain Johnny Angel, who's out to avenge the murder of his father, but gets only bland sympathy from the babyish Gusty, his father's boss. Trevor, as Gusty's scheming wife, is playing a shady game of her own, while French girl Paulette (Hasso) is hunted by an unknown killer and trusts no one. They all inhabit a closed world, where even pastoral idylls reek of claustrophobia and obsession. The men struggle against the towering shadows of their fathers, the women are dangerously enigmatic, and the docks of New Orleans glisten under the diffuse light of a single street-lamp. Even Hoagy Carmichael sounds eerie singing 'Memphis in June'. There are no black diamonds, but *Johnny Angel* glitters like one. RB

Johnny Aquarius (Jancio Wodnik)

(1993, Pol, 100 min)
d/sc Jan Jakub Kolski. *ph* Piotr Lenar. *ed* Ewa Pakulska. *m* Zygmunt Konieczny. *cast* Franciszek Pieczka, Grazyna Blecka-Kolska, Boguslaw Linda, Katarzyna Aleksandrowicz.
●Kolski's idiosyncratic blend of pantheistic mysticism and bucolic comedy is here applied to an obscure fable about a peasant blessed with mysterious healing powers who abandons his pregnant wife to tour the countryside. The fame attendant upon his miracles and the machinations of a charlatan Christ impersonator turn his head – but a curse put on his family by a crazed vagrant brings him, eventually, to his senses. Certainly Kolski's images are often startlingly eccentric, as are the shifts between 'reality', fantasy and symbolism, but quite what it all means, beyond its warning against the temptations of the flesh, remains a mystery. GA

Johnny Dangerously

(1984, US, 90 min)
d Amy Heckerling. *p* Michael Hertzberg. *sc* Norman Steinberg, Bernie Kukoff, Harry Colomby, Jeff Harris. *ph* David M Walsh. *ed* Pembroke J Herring. *pd* Joseph R Jennings. *m* John Morris. *cast* Michael Keaton, Jo Piscopo, Marilu Henner, Maureen Stapleton, Peter Boyle, Griffin Dunne, Glynnis O'Connor, Dom DeLuise, Danny DeVito, Ray Walston, Carl Gottlieb.
●Parody of '30s gangster movies in which Michael Keaton's meteoric rise to cleanest-cut hood in town (after turning to crime at the age of 12) is matched only by his incorruptible brother's rise to fame as a crime-busting DA, complete with inevitable courtroom confrontation between the two. Some delightfully unexpected visual gags and off-the-wall one-liners, along with the good-looking period settings and a wealth of minor characters, give the film its strength. It becomes a little predictable in the middle, but the pace picks up in time for the classic final shootout. Despite lapses, infectiously good-humoured. GO

Johnny Eager

(1941, US, 107 min, b/w)
d Mervyn LeRoy. *p* John W Considine Jr. *sc* John Lee Mahin, James Edward Grant. *ph* Harold Rosson. *ed* Albert Akst. *ad* Cedric Gibbons. *m* Bonislau Kaper. *cast* Robert Taylor, Lana Turner, Edward Arnold, Van Heflin, Robert Sterling, Patricia Dane, Glenda Farrell, Henry O'Neill, Barry Nelson, Charles Dingle, Paul Stewart.
●The John Lee Mahin/James Edward Grant script for this gangster movie proposes an intriguingly sleazy scenario about a cold-blooded hoodlum (Taylor), his homosexual whipping-boy (Heflin), and the masochistic society girl (Turner) who can't wait to sample his wares ('I think he'd beat a woman if she made him angry'). Given the full-gloss-and-redemption MGM treatment, it emerges as the sudsiest of soaps. Taylor seduces Turner for his own nefarious purposes, conning her into thinking she killed a man; having discovered *l'amour fou*, she starts going round the guilt-ridden bend; and after much prodding from the drunkenly philosophising Heflin, Taylor does the far, far better thing. LeRoy handles the grand operatics with a certain style and excellent camerawork from Harold Rosson; but nothing can salvage a film which suggests that its hero went to the bad because he never owned a dog as a boy. TM

Johnny Frenchman

(1945, GB, 112 min, b/w)
d Charles Frend. *p* Michael Balcon. *sc* TEB Clarke. *ph* Roy Kellino. *ed* Michael Truman. *ad* Duncan Sutherland. *m* Clifton Parker. *cast* Françoise Rosay, Tom Walls, Patricia Roc, Paul Dupuis, Ralph Michael, Paul Dupuis, Frederick Piper, Arthur Hambling, James Knight, Alfie Bass.
●Hands-across-the-water propaganda for the Allied effort at the end of the war, as a Cornish fishing village is eventually led, by means of true love, to abandon its hatred of a rival Breton community and realise that the French are people too. Pretty dim drama (and comedy), though it is psychologically acute in revealing Patricia Roc's romantic preference for a visiting Frenchman over the local lad who woos her by shoving pilchards down her back. GA

Johnny Got His Gun

(1971, US, 111 min, b/w & col)
d Dalton Trumbo. *p* Bruce Campbell. *sc* Dalton Trumbo. *ph* Jules Brenner. *ed* Millie Moore. *pd* Harold Michelson. *m* Jerry Fielding. *cast* Timothy Bottoms, Jason Robards, Marsha Hunt, Diane Varsi, Donald Sutherland, Kathy Fields, Charles McGraw.
●Trumbo lays on every emotional effect and then some to get across his tale of a World War I casualty left limbless, faceless, deaf, dumb and blind, confined to a semi-existence in a hospital back room, who learns to communicate with the world through a painful morse code tapped out with his head on the pillow, and whose final request – that people be allowed to see him or that he be allowed to die – is refused. Trumbo adapted his own novel, incredibly based on fact, some thirty years after he wrote it, and he tells the seemingly unfilmable story through a sustained interior monologue and a series of flashbacks to Johnny's childhood, his failure of a shoe-salesman father, his job in the local bakery, his first-and-last night with his girl before leaving for the front, and through a series of fantasy sequences (the most effective involving Donald Sutherland as Christ). The film is often sentimental, sometimes brilliant as well as horrifying, and it is intriguing to speculate on what Buñuel, whom Trumbo originally wanted to direct, would have made of it. VG

Johnny Guitar

(1954, US, 110 min)
d Nicholas Ray. *p* Herbert J Yates. *sc* Philip Yordan. *ph* Harry Stradling. *ed* Richard L Van Enger. *ad* James W Sullivan. *m* Victor Young. *cast* Joan Crawford, Sterling Hayden, Mercedes McCambridge, Scott Brady, Ward Bond, John Carradine, Ernest Borgnine, Ben Cooper, Royal Dano.
●Emma (McCambridge) has the hots for The Dancing Kid (Brady). The Kid is wild about Vienna (Crawford). But Vienna can't drive Johnny Guitar (Hayden) out of her head. Ray's film is not a romantic comedy, but a Western. Or is it? Taking a story about two gutsy, gun-totin' matriarchs squabbling over the men they love and the ownership of a gambling saloon, Ray plays havoc with Western conventions, revelling in sexual role-reversals, turning funeral gatherings into lynch mobs, and dwelling on a hero who finds inner peace through giving up pacifism and taking up his pistols. Love and hate, prostitution and frustration, domination and humiliation are woven into a hypnotic Freudian web of shifting relationships, illuminated by the director's precise, symbolic use of colour, and strung together with an unerring sense of pace. The whole thing is weird, hysterical, and quite unlike anything else in the history of the cowboy film: where else can one find a long-expected shootout between two fast and easy killers averted by a woman's insistence that they help her prepare breakfast? Crawford and McCambridge are fallen angel and spinster harpy, while Hayden is admirably ambivalent as the quiet saddletramp with a psychopathic temper. Truffaut called the film 'the Beauty and the Beast of the Western', a description which perfectly sums up Ray's magical, dreamlike emotionalism. GA

Johnny Handsome

(1989, US, 94 min)
d Walter Hill. *p* Charles Roven. *sc* Ken Friedman. *ph* Matthew F Leonetti. *ed* Freeman Davies, Carmel Davies, Donn Aron. *pd* Gene Rudolf. *m* Ry Cooder. *cast* Mickey Rourke, Ellen Barkin, Elizabeth McGovern, Morgan Freeman, Forest Whitaker, Lance Henriksen, Scott Wilson.
●Part criminological essay, part revenge thriller, this adaptation of John Godey's novel *The Three Worlds of Johnny Handsome* casts Mickey Rourke as freakish villain John. Shunned even by the criminal fraternity, he's left carrying the can for a brutal robbery by ruthless associates (Barkin and Henriksen) who also kill his only friend (Wilson). At this stage the mood becomes uncertain; a surgeon (Whitaker) links recidivism with physical deformity, and decides to perform plastic surgery. But will good looks prevent Johnny's return to crime? Jaded cop (Freeman) doesn't think so; Johnny's new girlfriend (McGovern) hopes they will. The look of the film, at least, is fixed; the New Orleans backdrop assumes sinister, *noirish* hues, and the action sequences are crisp and agressive. Barkin and Henriksen perform with relish, Whitaker and Freeman are pleasantly understated. Rourke tries harder than ever to minimise, nay obscure, his good looks, a process which merely serves to emphasise them. 'You guys did a good job' utters Johnny as he emerges from bandages with the face of a heart-throb. Hollywood can bear only so much gloom. CM

Johnny Mnemonic

(1995, US, 96 min)
d Robert Longo. *p* Don Carmody. *sc* William Gibson. *ph* François Protat. *ed* Ronald Sanders. *pd* Nilo Rodis Jamero. *m* Brad Fiedel. *cast* Keanu Reeves, Dina Meyer, Ice T, Takeshi Kitano, Denis Akiyama, Dolph Lundgren, Barbara Sukowa, Udo Kier.
●He-man Johnny (Reeves, playing mannequin) has two chips, one on his shoulder, the other in his brain, the latest in data-storage enhancers. For this mnemonic courier inhabits the cyberpunk future. The banal dystopia, virtually realised here, is a weird mix of the familar and unfamilar: architecturally, decayed hi-tech; politically, gangster-like international neo-capitalism – an interspace between *Blade Runner* and '70s James Bond. The plot: Johnny is forced to double-load his memory to transport one last mega-program. Short of space, he's already sacrificed recall of his childhood (despite painful disjointed flashes), and now has quickly to download before his head explodes. Realising the info's importance, he joins forces with punkette Jane (Meyer) to elude Pharmakon agents and the yakuza through the streets of 'Free' New Jersey. Directing his first feature, artist Longo seems dazzled, like a rabbit, by sheer visual overload. Lundgren's arch-villain, half Visigoth, half demented Jesus freak, fits perfectly, but Takeshi's yakuza is sadly wasted. Might suit very undemanding teenagers. WH

Johnny O'Clock

(1946, US, 95 min, b/w)
d Robert Rossen. *p* Edward G Nealis. *sc* Robert Rossen. *ph* Burnett Guffey. *ed* Warren Low. *ad* Stephen Goosson, Cary Odell. *m* George Duning. *cast* Dick Powell, Evelyn Keyes, Lee J Cobb, Ellen Drew, Nina Foch, Thomas Gomez, John Kellogg, Jim Bannon, Mabel Paige, Phil Brown, Jeff Chandler.

●Despite good performances and fine camerawork from Burnett Guffey, Rossen's first film as director is a disappointingly flat thriller. His script weaves a nicely complex web around Powell's Johnny O'Clock, co-owner of a gambling club who, interested only in money and women and turning a blind eye to the dubious activities of his partner (Gomez), ends up wanted for two murders and up to his ears in treachery. The trouble lies in the pacing: as director, Rossen seems so uncertain of himself that he often fails to give his actors sufficient time or space to imprint their presence on screen (true throughout, but in particular of the two murder victims: Bannon as the corrupt cop who tries to muscle in on the partnership, and Foch as the girlfriend he cruelly discards). Since they remain totally unmemorable (through no fault of the actors concerned), the subsequent action tends to become little more than a sequence of events mechanically strung together. TM

Johnny 100 Pesos (Johnny Cien Pesos)

(1993, Chile, 90 min)
d/p Gustavo Graef-Marino. *sc* Gerardo Caceras. Gustavo Graeff-Marino. *ph* Jose Luis Arredondo. *ed* Danielle Fillios. *pd* Juan Carlos Castillo. *m* Andres Pollak. *cast* Armando Araiza, Patricia Rivera, Willy Semler, Luis Gnecco, Armando Silvestre.

●A heist on a high-rise black market bank goes wrong, presenting government and police officials with a tricky prime-time hostage situation. While the gang sweat it out, the media go into a feeding frenzy, particularly regarding schoolboy crook Johnny (Araiza). Inspired by a 1990 Santiago news event, this *Dog Day* thriller is cynical and relatively slick, but not especially compelling or original (it perhaps seemed more daring back in Chile). TCh

Johnny Suede

(1991, US/Switz/Fr, 97 min)
d Tom DiCillo. *p* Yoram Mandel, Ruth Waldburger. *sc* Tom DiCillo. *ph* Joe DeSalvo. *ed* Geraldine Peroni. *pd* Patricia Woodbridge. *m* Jim Farmer. *cast* Brad Pitt, Nick Cave, Alison Moir, Catherine Keener, Calvin Levels, Peter McRobbie, Samuel L Jackson.

●Right from the start, it's clear that the young eponymous hero (Pitt) is madly in love with suede shoes, Ricky Nelson's songs, his plans to become a rock'n'roll idol, the romantic notion of finding a dream girl, and – most of all – himself. So when, after a flattering fling with alarmingly changeable damsel in distress Darlette (Moir), Johnny meets the more down-to-earth Yvonne (Keener), you know he'll finally have to choose between his immature fantasies and the love of a good woman. On to this slim, slightly moralistic fable, DiCillo grafts an appealing veneer of droll slow-burn humour, wacky caricature, and pseudo-hip posing. Much of what is said and done is deliberately and delightfully absurd. But the movie is saved from becoming too knowingly flip not only by DiCillo's sure sense of pace and mood, but by the performances; especially Keener, who displays a fine mix of strength, savvy and vulnerability. GA

John Q

(2002, US, 116 min)
d Nick Cassavetes. *p* Mark Burg, Oren Koules. *sc* James Kearns. *ph* Rogier Stoffers. *ed* Dede Allen. *pd* Stefania Cella. *m* Aaron Zigman. *cast* Denzel Washington, Robert Duvall, James Woods, Anne Heche, Eddie Griffin, Kimberly Elise, Shawn Hatosy, Ray Liotta, David Thornton, Ethan Suplee.

●Washington rubbed off his customary sheen of integrity in *Training Day*, and picked up an Oscar. In this misbegotten blend of populist rabble-rouser and medical tearjerker, he plays blue collar hero John Quincy Archibald. True, John Q – a desperate industrial worker on shortened hours who takes over a hospital ER at gunpoint to secure his sick kid a heart transplant – is the best thing in the film, a beacon of acting sincerity in a sea of thespian bemusement. However, enveloping a significant political issue like healthcare provision in the US in such a psychologically crude, *Dog Day Afternoon*-style siege drama gives the film an unsavoury exploitative dimension. It also leaves Washington with a credibility problem, not helped by director Nick Cassavetes' standard over-emphasis, guilelessness and poor timing. WH

Johns

(1995, US, 96 min)
d Scott Silver. *p* Beau Flynn, Stefan Simchowitz. *sc* Scott Silver. *ph* Tom Richmond. *ed* Dorian Harris. *pd* Amy Beth Silver. *m* Charles Brown, Danny Caron. *cast* David Arquette, Lukas Haas, Wilson Cruz, John C McGinley, Keith David, Elliott Gould, Arliss Howard.

●John (Arquette) wakes up homeless, shoeless and consequently resourceless in Hollywood (he'd stashed his savings in his sneakers). It's Christmas Eve, and he's set his heart on one night of luxury at the Plaza. A back-seat encounter with a cruising movie exec soon puts him back on his feet. With his sensitive friend Donner (Haas) to help out, perhaps he can still hustle up $300 in time? Former documentarist Silver's feature debut captures the acrid tang of downtown LA's sun-swept strips and telescopes some half-dozen tricks of the trade into vivid, colourful vignettes. The stories are all true, apparently, right down to the saga of the stolen shoes and an invisible bogeyman figure who haunts the street hustlers' worst nightmares, though the 24-hour time-frame is a substantial dramatic contrivance, and undercuts the on-going despair, boredom and frustration which must be central to these lives. The movie is funnier than you'd expect, and extremely well played, particularly the touching rapport between Arquette, a meridian cowboy working overtime, and Haas, the softer new kid on the block. The excellent score is by the septuagenarian bluesman Charles Brown. TCh

Joint Security Area/JSA (Gongdong Gyungbi Guyeok JSA)

(2000, SKor, 110 min)
d Park Chan-Wook. *p* Lee Eun, Shim Jae-Myung. *sc* Kim Hyun-Seok, Lee Moo-Young, Jung Seong-San, Park Chan-Wook. *ph* Kim Seong-Bok. *ed* Kim Sang-Beom. *pd* Kim Sang-Man. *m* Cho Young-Wook. *cast* Song Kang-Ho, Lee Byung-Heon, Lee Young-Ae, Kim Tae-Woo, Shin Ha-Kyun.

●An incident in the JSA (the demilitarised zone between North and South Korea) leaves two N Korean border guards dead and one S Korean wounded. The Swiss-Korean woman officer (Lee Young-Ae) heading the neutral enquiry into the skirmish gets nowhere until she stumbles upon a history of secret fraternisation between some of the border guards on both sides. It's decently directed and acted; easy to see why it did better than *Shiri* in Korea, although it fudges the political questions by casting the ultra-charismatic Song Kang-Ho as the main commie soldier. But the message that all Koreans could get along fine if it wasn't for those pesky ideologies and uniforms doesn't mean a thing outside Korea, and the film is too entranced by all the male bonding to begin to function as an effective mystery. TR

Joko, Invoca Dio...e Muori

see Vengeance

Joli mai, Le

(1962, Fr, 180 min, b/w)
d/commentary Chris Marker. *p* Catherine Winter. *sc* Cathérine Varlin. *ph* Pierre Lhomme. *ed* Eva Zora. *m* Michel Legrand. *narrator* Yves Montand (French version), Simone Signoret (English version).

●A marvellous, highly influential *cinéma-vérité* examination of a specific time and place: Paris in May 1962, going through its first spring of peace since 1939 (the signing of the Evian agreement in March 1962 having finally put an end to the long-running Algerian troubles). The basic method is simple: Marker and his colleagues (unseen) elicit comments on work, money, happiness, etc, from a cross-section of Parisians. But these personal thoughts are firmly and evocatively placed within a wider socio-political context, as the film proceeds to show footage of police charges, rioters, strikers, and so forth. What distinguishes the film most, however, is its wit, both verbal and visual, so that it is simultaneously illuminating and funny. (The film was cut under Marker's supervision from the original 180 minutes to 123 minutes.) GA

Jolly Bad Fellow, A

(1963, GB, 96 min, b/w)
d Don Chaffey. *p* Michael Balcon, Donald Taylor. *sc* Robert Hamer, Donald Taylor. *ph* Gerald Gibbs. *ed* Peter Tanner. *ad* George Provis. *m* John Barry. *cast* Leo McKern, Janet Munro, Maxine Audley, Duncan MacRae, Dennis Price, Miles Malleson, Leonard Rossiter, Alan Wheatley.

●Blackish comedy about a science academic (McKern) doing away with his enemies and rivals by a new, traceless poison. It never reaches the *Kind Hearts and Coronets* level at which it was evidently pitched (it was developed by that film's director, Robert Hamer, before his death in 1963, and co-produced by Michael Balcon), but nevertheless still manages a grinning gusto. PT

Jolly Boys' Last Stand, The

(1999, GB, 88 min)
d Christopher Payne. *p* Craig Woodrow, Richard Conway. *sc* Christopher Payne. *ph* Will Jacob, Robin Cox. *ed* Tullio Brunt. *m* Jeremy Panufnik. *cast* Andy Serkis, Milo Twomey, Sacha Baron Cohen, Rebecca Craig, Jo Martin.

●Budgeted on pocket money, this DV movie features a bunch of writer/director Payne's mates, who fortunately include actor Andy Serkis (*Mojo*) and an almost unrecognisable Sacha Baron Cohen (aka Ali G). Like *The Blair Witch Project*, it purports to be found documentary footage, though in this case it's nothing more sinister than a home video tribute to Spider (Serkis), filmed by his mate Des (Twomey) as a wedding present. It looks like a lark, but then the video reveals a malevolent undercurrent. Spider is Hon. El Presidente of the 'Jolly Boys': a bunch of beer-swilling pranksters who've known each other forever – and Des in particular is miffed that Spider's abdicating his irresponsibilities. Fake documentary demands nothing less than nothing but the truth, and when you sense the artifice (an unconvincing line, an awkward performance), it all goes flat. But you needn't make too many allowances. This has promise, bags of laughs, and a sincerity that sneaks up and smacks you with a dead fish. TCh

Jolson Story, The

(1946, US, 128 min)
d Alfred E Green. *p* Sidney Skolsky. *sc* Stephen Longstreet. *ph* Joseph Walker. *ed* William A Lyon. *ad* Stephen Goosson. Walter Holscher. *songs* George Gershwin, Ira Gershwin, Al Dubin, Harry Warren, Al Jolson, others. *cast* Larry Parks, Evelyn Keyes, William Demarest, Ludwig Donath, Bill Goodwin, Scotty Beckett.

●Probably the most famous Hollywood showbiz biography, in which the black-faced Al (Parks) bellows his way from burlesque to Broadway and beyond, falls in love with musical comedy star 'Julie Benson' (read Ruby Keeler), but falls more in love with his audience's applause. Jolson himself sings on the soundtrack ('Avalon', 'Toot, Toot, Tootsie' and many more), Larry Parks impersonates him with studied sincerity, and the musical numbers are attractively staged by Joseph H Lewis (whose more usual territories were Westerns and *films noirs*). More of the same followed, with contrived plot and without Lewis, in *Jolson Sings Again* (1949). GB

Jonah Who Will Be 25 in the Year 2000 (Jonas qui aura 25 ans en l'an 2000)

(1976, Switz/Fr, 115 min)
d Alain Tanner. *p* Yves Gasser, Yves Peyrot. *sc* John Berger, Alain Tanner. *ph* Renato Berta. *ed* Brigitte Sousselier, Marc Blavet. *ad* Yanko Hodjisi, Olivier Bierer. *m* Jean-Marie Sénia. *cast* Jean-Luc Bideau, Rufus, Miou-Miou, Jacques Denis, Dominique Labourier, Roger Jendly, Myriam Mézières, Myriam Boyer, Raymond Bussières, Jonas.

●Through circumstance, coincidence and necessity, eight characters find themselves drawn together. In various ways they're all irrevocably marked by the spirit of May '68, individually representative of the diverse political utopianism operating in the annus mirabilis of which Mailer wrote, 'One had the thought that the gods were back in human affairs'. Tanner gives us a Trotskyist journalist, an anarchic shopgirl who steals food, a transcendental mysticist, an educationalist; and labourer Mathieu Vernier (Rufus), who accommodates his friends' philosophies but realises that their enduringly optimistic visions can only be achieved through class struggle. Mathilde (Boyer), his wife, is pregnant with the Jonah of the title. Tanner again collaborated with John Berger, and the script is didactic and compact, though *Jonah* has a lighter and more humorous touch than *The Middle of the World*. It's a heady experience following their agile ruminations on time, language and perception, deftly superimposed on a film that pleases visually and formally. JS

Jonathan Livingston Seagull

(1973, US, 120 min)
d/p Hall Bartlett. *sc* Richard Bach, Hall Bartlett. *ph* Jack Couffer. *ed* Frank P Keller. *pd* Boris Leven. *m* Neil Diamond, Lee Holdridge. *cast* voices: James Franciscus, Juliet Mills, Hal Holbrook, Philip Ahn, David Ladd, Dorothy Maguire, Richard Crenna.

● Richard Bach's best-selling parable for freshmen becomes on screen a very spelled-out allegory, complete with flat voice-overs and pretentious Neil Diamond soundtrack. The film's renegade seagull hero enacts the theme of spiritual development and human achievement, moving through an obsession with speed (maybe seagulls can't fly faster than 62 mph, but wouldn't it be great if they could) towards a more fashionable Oriental philosophy (perfect speed is being there), and final apotheosis as a Messiah figure. Ignore all that (admittedly difficult) and you have a finely photographed essay on birds which uses its coastal locations to good effect.

Jory (Un Niño Llamado Muerte)

(1972, US/Mex, 97 min)
d Jorge Fons. *p* Howard G Minsky. *sc* Gerald Herman, Robert Irving. *ph* Jorge Stahl. *ed* Fred Chulack, Sergio Ortega. *pd* Earl Hedrick. *m* Al DeLory. *cast* John Marley, BJ Thomas, Robby Benson, Brad Dexter, Claudio Brook, Patricia Aspillaga,Todd Martin, Linda Purl.

● A simple and fairly strong tale about a 15-year-old kid (Benson) who turns revenge killer after watching his father murdered. But it's submerged beneath an impenetrably fruity script littered with clichés on Life with a capital L and a man finding 'a place with his name on it'. 'So what's so special about Texas?' 'It's the meanin' that's different, not the dirt'. Unremarkable direction, routine performances, and a pair of uninteresting juvenile leads finish the thing off. VG

Joseph Andrews

(1976, GB, 104 min)
d Tony Richardson. *p* Neil Hartley. *sc* Allan Scott, Chris Bryant. *ph* David Watkin. *ed* Thom Noble. *pd* Michael Annals. *m* John Addison. *cast* Ann-Margret, Peter Firth, Michael Hordern, Beryl Reid, Jim Dale, Natalie Ogle, Peter Bull, John Gielgud, Hugh Griffith, Timothy West, Wendy Craig, James Villiers, Peggy Ashcroft.

● Attempting to repeat the commercial success of *Tom Jones*, this adaptation of Fielding's first novel is little more than a middlebrow's *Carry On*. Richardson allows his photographer and designers to make pretty pictures à la *Barry Lyndon*, while himself showing little interest in Fielding's essentially moralistic themes – innocence beset by rapacious experience, physically with Joseph and Fanny, mentally with Parson Adams. Indeed he violates the novel's guts and narrative coherence, at the same time reducing it to little more than a headlong tumble of bits of knockabout bedroom farce loosely hung together. Saddest of all is the usually brilliant Michael Hordern's performance as Adams. The one potentially interesting scene, a Ken Russell pastiche – a Black Mass with Fanny as victim – merely hints at a real depravity which might have been allowed to threaten. RM

Joseph Conrad's The Secret Agent

see Secret Agent, The

Joseph Cornell: Worlds in a Box

(1992, GB, 52 min)
d Mark Stokes.

● Arguably one of modern art's best kept secrets, Joseph Cornell spent his life quietly creating in New York's suburbia. His best work has a curious *Alice in Wonderland* quality to it: glass-fronted boxes in which he stored 20th century detritus, from marbles and stamps to fluff. The film reveals how Cornell wanted to create a universe for his brother, who was confined to the house with cerebral palsy. Cornell later re-edited old films to entertain his brother, and these jittery, anti-narrative works bridge the gap between Dadaism and Pop Art. It's no surprise that John Lennon and Andy Warhol were among his fans. What is more surprising is prize ham Tony Curtis' in-depth knowledge of Cornell's art. The jury might still be out on whether Cornell is a Great Artist, but this reveals a man whose view of modern times is never less than fascinating. BD

Josephine (Die Ortliebschen Frauen)

(1979, WGer, 106 min)
d Luc Bondy. *p* Renée Gundelach. *ph* Ricardo Aronovich. *cast* Edith Heerdegen, Libgart Schwarz, Elisabeth Stepanek, Klaus Pohl.

● After a slow and confused opening, this stylised study of claustrophobic, incestuously possessive familial repression makes compulsive viewing. Josephine assumes her late father's mantle of domestic tyranny, binding mother, sister and crippled brother to an increasingly rigid notion of respectability that shades towards sadism as outside relationships are severed and minor cruelties escalate. A fine, blackly bizarre first film from theatre director Bondy; based on the appropriately-titled novel *The Grave of the Living* by Franz Nabl, it's both co-scripted and hauntingly acted (as Josephine) by Libgart Schwarz, the wife of Peter Handke. PT

Joseph Kilián (Postava k Podpírání)

(1963, Czech, 40 min, b/w)
d/sc Pavel Jurácek, Jan Schmidt. *ph* Jan Curík. *ed* Zdenék Stehlik. *ad* Oldrich Bosák. *m* Wiliam Bukovy. *cast* Karel Vasicek, Consuela Morávková, Pavel Bártl, Zbynek Jirmar.

● A bizarre, consciously Kafkaesque allegory in which a young man wanders the streets of Prague fruitlessly searching for a man called Joseph Kilián, of whom no one seems to have heard. Passing a state cat-shop, he impulsively hires a cat for the day, only to find, nightmarishly, that the shop is no longer there when he tries to return the cat as required. Wittily poking fun at the personality cult (a huge portrait of Stalin looms over a roomful of frayed agit-prop posters and Cold War slogans), Jurácek and Schmidt scarcely put a foot wrong in evoking the incomprehensible mazes – simultaneously absurd and terrifying – of totalitarian bureaucracy. TM

Josh and S.A.M.

(1993, US, 98 min)
d Billy Weber. *p* Martin Brest. *sc* Frank Deese. *ph* Don Burgess. *ed* Chris Lebenzon. *pd* Marcia Hinds-Johnson. *m* Thomas Newman. *cast* Jacob Tierney, Noah Fleiss, Martha Plimpton, Stephen Tobolowsky, Joan Allen, Chris Penn.

● Driven to despair by his dysfunctional extended family, angst-ridden Josh Whitney (Tierney) strings his younger sibling Sam a fanciful line – Sam is not a real kid, but a Strategically Altered Mutant, sold by his parents for government warfare. Perversely, Sam embraces the lie, which miraculously explains his feelings of isolation, aggression, obsession with death, and his detachment from mom and dad. When Josh and Sam make a run for the open road, freaky coincidences conspire to prop up the delusion. Ultra-jowly newcomer Fleiss (Sam) ably portrays a child's sullen confusion when faced with the tawdry grottiness of the real world. Yet even with him, and some bitter one-liners in its favour, the overall picture is as confused and disjointed as Sam's own tortured outlook. MK

Josie and the Pussycats

(2001, US, 98 min)
d Deborah Kaplan, Harry Elfont. *p* Marc Platt, Tracey E Edmonds, Chuck Grimes, Tony DeRosa-Grund. *sc* Deborah Kaplan, Harry Elfont. *ph* Matthew Libatique. *ed* Peter Teschner. *pd* Jasna Stefanovich. *m* John Frizzell. *cast* Rachael Leigh Cook, Tara Reid, Rosario Dawson, Alan Cumming, Gabriel Mann, Paulo Costanzo, Missi Pyle, Parker Posey.

● 'I'm a trend pimp!' exclaims a character in this double-think pop-rock comedy extravaganza, 'inspired' by the old Archies cartoon and directed with juvenile exuberance by writers Kaplan and Elfont. The character is offered by way of instructive contrast to the trio of grungy Riverdale heroines, high school friends Josie (Cook), Melody (Reid) and Valerie (Dawson), whose self-determined if overly wacky cultural and personal identity is threatened after their garage band is signed up by big-shot manager Wyatt (Cumming). Watch the classic dramatic parabola: make-overs, promos and instantaneous chart-topping success under their manipulative Mega Records boss (Posey); self-absorption, interband rivalry, fallouts and failure; and finally, hard-won reconciliation. Aaaaah, what a classic! And what an important, laudable message it could provide, too, for its target ten- to 20-year-old female market, if it weren't complete bollocks. WH

Jour de Fête

(1948, Fr, 85 min, b/w & col)
d Jacques Tati. *p* Fred Orain. *sc* Jacques Tati, Henri Marquet, René Wheeler. *ph* Jacques Mercanton. *ed* Marcel Moreau. *ad* René Moulaert. *m* Jean Yatove. *cast* Jacques Tati, Guy Decomble, Paul Frankeur, Santa Relli, Maine Vallee, Roger Rafal.

● Like Keaton before him, Tati devised gags of such sheer intricacy as to prove on occasion just too beautiful to be laughed at (it's no accident that the truly funniest talkies – Fields, the Marx Brothers – were hardly directed at all). In this, his first feature, reissued in its original 'splash colour' version (never shown at the time), an almost plotless tale of a village postman's endeavours to streamline his service *à l'américaine* is enhanced by a radiographic vision of rural minutiae which one might call hyper-realist, were it not for that term's sleek urban connotations. As for Tati the performer, he makes cycling along a tranquil country lane as spellbinding as if it were taking place on a high wire. GAd

Journal d'un Curé de Campagne

see Diary of a Country Priest

Journal d'une Femme de Chambre, Le

see Diary of a Chambermaid, The

Journal de Lady M, Le (The Diary of Lady M)

(1993, Switz/Bel/Sp/Fr, 112 min)
d Alain Tanner. *p* Alain Tanner, Jacques de Clercq, Dimitri de Clercq, Gerardo Herrero, Marta Estaban, Christophe Rossignon, *sc* Myriam Mézières. *ph* Denis Jutzeler. *ed* Monica Goux. *ad* Jordi Canora, Alain Chennaux. *m* Arié Dzierlatka. *cast* Myriam Mézières, Juanjo Puigcorbé, Félicité Wouassi, Antoine Basler.

● It's a stormy Parisian night. Tempestuous Spanish painter Diego (Puigcorbé) shelters in a club doorway and is strangely attracted by the music within. Soon he's transfixed before girl pop-group Lady M, ogling the lead singer (Mézières) undulating in a silk slip. Their ensuing tangled affair is written up in Lady M's diary, with much pen-sucking and curling up on sofas. This project clearly meant something to Mézières and Tanner, but, like their first collaboration, *A Flame in My Heart*, it turns out to be little more than ill-written (but graphic) soft porn. When Diego's wife Nuria (Wouassi) joins the couple in bed, M pleads, 'Save me from becoming a dead tree.' Worth seeing, if at all, for the sex, but mostly just plain silly. SFe

Journée dans la Vie d'Andrei Arsenevitch, Une

see One Day in the Life of Andrei Arsenevitch

Journey for Margaret

(1942, US, 81 min, b/w)
d WS Van Dyke. *p* BP Fineman. *sc* David Hertz, William Ludwig. *ph* Ray June. *m* Franz Waxman. *cast* Robert Young, Laraine Day, Margaret O'Brien, Fay Bainter, Nigel Bruce, William Severn, Signe Hasso.

● MGM's weepy follow-up to the hugely successful hands-across-the sea Anglophilia of *Mrs Miniver*, this time featuring a nice, average American couple who adopt two orphaned (and disturbed, oh yes indeed) children during the Battle of Britain. Awesomely glutinous, but the fascinating thing about Margaret O'Brien is that, even at the age of five and in only her second film, she was already an accomplished actress rather than a cute personality. TM

Journey Into Autumn

see Kvinnodröm

Journey Into Fear

(1942, US, 69 min, b/w)
d Norman Foster. *p* Orson Welles. *sc* Joseph Cotten, Orson Welles. *ph* Karl Struss. *ed* Mark Robson. *ad* Albert S D'Agostino, Mark-Lee Kirk. *m* Roy Webb. *cast* Joseph Cotten, Dolores Del Rio, Orson Welles, Everett Sloane, Agnes Moorehead, Ruth Warrick, Jack Moss.

●'Designed' rather than directed by Welles, though you wouldn't care to bet on it as things get under way with the camera craning up to a sleazy window in Istanbul and peering in – as a tinny gramophone with a stuck needle maddeningly grinds out the same phrase – for its first glimpse of the slug-like babyfaced killer played (brilliantly) by Jack Moss. Thereafter, with Cotten on the run from Gestapo agents and Welles having fun in the first of his monster roles as the Turkish chief of secret police (he directed all his own scenes), the tone veers through nightmare chases, bizarre encounters, and deflating jokes. Eminently watchable, but it does tail away. TM

Journey of a Young Composer (Akhalgazrda Kompozitoris Mogzauroba)

(1985, USSR, 105 min)
d Georgi Shengelaya. *sc* Georgi Shengeleya, Erlom Achwlediani. *ph* Levan Paatashvili. *ed* Sofi Machaidze. *pd* Boris Tskhakaya. *cast* Giya Peradze, Levan Abashidze, Zurab Kipshidze, Rusudan Kvlividze.

●The year is 1907 and tensions are running high in the Eastern Georgian countryside, with the Tsar's cossacks seeking to crush any further insurrection. Nikusha, the young composer, drifts innocently into the area to record the music of the local peasants. Accompanied by the boisterous Leko, who's convinced that he's connected with the underground, he makes his appointed rounds on the nobility, who go about their business like extras in a George Romero feature. Leko, swaggering and spitting, leering and swearing, stomping his feet and chewing with his mouth open (all before dinner is served), quickly inspires the wrath of his grey hosts…Shengelaya meticulously records the events of the pair's mysterious adventure, but sadly neglects the spectator. A lot is happening but there's very little to see, apart from Leko's (Peradze's) embarrassing performance. SGo

Journey of Hope (Reise der Hoffnung)

(1990, Switz, 110 min)
d Xavier Koller. *p* Alfi Sinniger, Peter Fueter. *sc* Xavier Koller, Feride Çiçekoglu. *ph* Elemér Ragalyi. *ed* Galip Iyitanir. *ad* Luigi Pelizzo, Kathrin Brunner. *cast* Necmettin Cobanoglu, Nur Srer, Emin Sivas, Erdinç Akbas, Yaman Okay, Dietmar Schönherr.

●In this moving, resolutely unglamorous drama, based on a real-life incident, a Turkish couple decide to escape their hand-to-mouth existence by upping sticks to Switzerland. Selling their possessions, they travel illegally with one of their sons, eventually getting caught up with unscrupulous smugglers who promise transport over the Swiss border. The ultimate test comes when they attempt to cross a stretch of the Alps on foot. Compelling as the unfolding horrors are, the real strength of the film rests in its strong central characterisations. Koller resists sentimentalising relationships, building up the tension slowly so that by the time their nightmare deepens the couple have built up an unspoken bond. Less satisfactory are some of the colourless depictions of the Swiss, which merely serve to throw into relief the plight of the refugees. CM

Journey of Natty Gann, The

(1985, US, 101 min)
d Jeremy Kagan. *p* Mike Lobell. *sc* Jeanne Rosenberg. *ph* Dick Bush. *ed* David Holden, Steven Rosenblum. *pd* Paul Sylbert. *m* James Horner. *cast* Meredith Salenger, John Cusack, Ray Wise, Lainie Kazan, Scatman Crothers, Barry Miller, Verna Bloom.

●Set at the time of the Depression, this suggests something like a return to form after a series of Disney disappointments. Natty's one-parent family unit is upset when daddy is forced to leave to look for work in a lumber camp in the north; subjected to the whim of a sadistic guardian landlady, she sets off to find him. On the way she has a string of adventures, runs into the obligatory wild dog whom she befriends, and you can guess the rest. Beautifully shot and well acted (Meredith Salenger in a fine performance as Natty), there's a real sense of period, even if the film does occasionally become over-sentimental. DPe

Journey's End

(1930, US/GB, 120 min, b/w)
d James Whale. *p* George Pearson. *sc* Joseph Moncure March, V Gareth Gundrey. *ph* Benjamin Kline. *ed* Claude Berkeley. *ad* Hervey Libbert. *cast* Colin Clive, Ian MacLaren, David Manners, Billy Bevan, Anthony Bushell, Robert Adair.

●Whale's first film, marred by some strangulated performances, is fascinating primarily as a record of his stage production of RC Sherriff's enormously successful play. The passionate sincerity of Sherriff's lament for the death of idealism in the mud of World War I still comes across with intermittent power, but is undercut by textual tampering. Though the structure of the play is respected, with opening-out limited to a prologue and brief punctuating scenes in no man's land, the speeches have all been pruned. As a result, the curiously plangent rhythms of the text (which still make it a masterpiece on stage today) are lost, with the meticulously built-up tension – in which you can almost hear the playing fields of Eton in the background as youthful veterans of the trenches mask their fear so as to live up to the hero worship of even younger schoolfellows – frittered away much of the time into an exchange of banalities. TM

Journey to Beijing (Bei Zheng)

(1998, HK/US, 112 min)
d Evans Chan. *p* Willy Tsao. *ph* Wong Ping Hung. *ed* Evans Chan. *m* Milos Raickovich.

●Ostensibly a documentary about a four-month charity walk from Hong Kong to Beijing, which was timed to reach its destination on the eve of Hong Kong's reversion to Chinese sovereignty, Chan's film is in fact a wide ranging 'essay' on the narrowing – or is it? – gap between Hong Kong and the 'mother country'. Part of the film does focus on the walkers, examining their motives and their reactions to the experience, and on the people they meet on the road, but there are frequent sidetracks: for instance, a sequence examining the progress of the gay rights movement in Hong Kong and questioning its future prospects. Facing up to the inevitable sense of anti-climax which followed the hand over, Chan cuts to the heart of Hong Kong's conflicting feelings about its own way forward, and clears away all the evasions and half-truths of the full-on media coverage of the hand over itself. TR

Journey Together

(1945, GB, 95 min, b/w)
d/p John Boulting. *sc* Terence Rattigan. *ph* Harry Waxman. *pd* John Howell. *m* Gordon Jacob. *cast* Richard Attenborough, Jack Watling, David Tomlinson, Edward G Robinson, Bessie Love, John Justin, George Cole, Ronald Squire, Sebastian Shaw.

●Produced by the RAF Film Unit with much the same brief as Powell and Pressburger's *A Matter of Life and Death*, Boulting's first feature opted for semi-documentary rather than fantasy. Terence Rattigan's script follows three aspiring pilots (Attenborough, Watling, Tomlinson) through training in Britain, America and Canada, thereby paying tribute to Allied cooperation without fuss or fanfare, while national idiosyncrasies are amusingly acknowledged in a scene where an American instructor (Robinson) and his wife (Love) entertain two of the trainees to dinner. The focus is on the scope and stresses of the training programme, with only one of the trio (Watling) making the grade. The script comes perilously close to convention in detailing Attenborough's tribulations (he's the working-class lad), but comes back on course with a detailed, superbly handled account of the preparations made by a crippled bomber's crew before it is ditched in the sea. With most of the cast serving in the RAF at the time, the keynote is authenticity, and the film remains surprisingly effective. TM

Journey to Italy

see Viaggio in Italia

Journey to the Beginning of the World (Viagem ao pricipio do mundo/Voyage au début du monde)

(1997, Port/Fr, 95 min)
d Manoel de Oliveira. *p* Paulo Branco. *sc* Manoel de Oliveira. *ph* Renata Berta. *ed* Valérie Loiseleux. *ad* Maria José Branco. *m* Emmanuel Nunes. *cast* Marcello Mastroianni, Jean-Yves Gautier, Leonor Silveira, Diogo Dória, Isabel,de Castro, Isabel Ruth, Manoel de Oliveira.

●Manoel de Oliveira was born in 1908 and made his first movie in 1929. It's no surprise then that this 1997 production feels like an old man's film. Manoel, a Portuguese director (Mastroianni), revisits childhood haunts on a pilgrimage with his actors and collaborators, Afonso (Gautier), Judite (Silveira) and Duarte (Dória). Oliveira keeps it simple. Conversations are interspersed with shots from the moving car. They stop by a river and look across to the Jesuit college Manoel attended. He reminisces and flirts with Judite – then they drive on. The first half is rambling and pretentious – unless you share Oliveira's obvious fondness for Manoel. Then a strange thing happens. With scant warning, attention shifts to Afonso – in fact, it transpires that this pilgrimage is for his benefit, a visit to his dead father's sister in a remote peasant village. They've never met before, and Afonso's aunt is hostile and suspicious. The scene in which he breaks through is a sustained tour de force. Oliveira's insistence on stasis and change, *saudades* – nostalgia, history, atavism – these themes find an emotional hold in the face of actress Isabel de Castro. TCh

Journey to the Centre of the Earth

(1959, US, 132 min)
d Henry Levin. *p* Charles Brackett. *sc* Charles Brackett, Walter Reisch. *ph* Leo Tover. *ed* Stuart Gilmore, Jack W Holmes. *ad* Lyle Wheeler, Franz Bachelin, Herman A Blumenthal. *m* Bernard Herrmann. *cast* James Mason, Pat Boone, Arlene Dahl, Diane Baker, Thayer David, Alan Napier, Peter Ronson.

●Pat Boone gives this colourful, exciting story its few nauseating moments (as when he sings 'My Heart's in the Highlands'). Otherwise it's one of the very best Hollywood adventure movies, with lots of monsters, underground oceans, sinister villains, and touches which would have delighted Jules Verne himself. James Mason as usual carries his part superbly, and there are plenty of good supporting actors like Napier and Ronson. Some of the special effects are intriguing, and believe it or not there's also quite a bit of effective sexual symbolism in typical Hollywood style, which greatly enhances the syrupy romantic subplot. Watch for the ending in which the girl is blown up on a giant funnel, with close-ups of her on her back smiling orgastically. DP

Journey to the Sun (Günese Yolculuk/Reise zur Sonne)

(1999, Tur/Neth/Ger, 105 min)
d Yesim Ustaoglu. *p* Behrooz Hashemian. *sc* Yesim Ustaoglu. *ph* Jacek Petrycki. *ed* Nicolas Gaster. *pd* Natali Yeres. *cast* Nazmi Oirix, Newroz Baz, Mizgin Kapazan, Ara Güler, Lucia Marano.

●Ex-architect Yesim Ustaoglu was inspired to make this film after reading newspaper articles about Kurdish villages laid waste in southeastern Turkey. Given the level of censorship she faced, this lyrical, deceptively simple tale about love, loss, and identity (brilliantly shot by Kieslowski's old cameraman Jacek Petrycki) is all the more courageous. The story starts with two outsiders, Mehmet and Berzan, meeting in Istanbul, where both are eking out an existence in the face of police oppression. When Berzan is killed, Mehmet embarks on an epic journey across country to return his body to his home village. Ustaoglu is never didactic. Instead, she shows the bafflement and yearning of the young friends as they struggle to make sense of their predicament. GM

Journey to the Western Xia, The (Xi Xia Lu Tiaotiao)

(1997, China, 99 min)
d Lu Wei. *p* Zhang Peimin. *sc* Lu Wei. *ph* Chi Xiaoning. *ed* Liu Xiaoqing. *ad* Huang Xinming. *m* Chang Yuhong. *cast* Ni Dahong, Badema, Wang Ning, Gong Qujia.

●The directorial debut of Lu Wei, who scripted *Farewell My Concubine*, is another historical drama, this time set in the 11th century. A group of warlike 'tax-collectors' from the Tangut tribe in the province of Xixia forcibly take ten boys from a defenceless Chinese village as their tithe; when one of the infants disappears, the leader abducts a pregnant woman to avert the Emperor's wrath. But the cost of duty is high. Making splendid use of the north western landscapes (though the camerawork is raw and gutsy rather than abstract and picturesque), this is a vigorous if slightly predictable tale of barbarism modified by respect, sympathy and suffering. GA

Journey to Wisdom (Desaadanam)

(1996, Ind, 114 min)
d/p Jayaraj. *sc* Madampu Kunjukuttan. *ph* Radhakrishnan. *ed* B Lenin, VT Vijayan, *ad* Nadhan Kannur. *m* Mohan Sithara. *cast* Vijaya Raghavan, Kumar, VK Sreeraman, Unnikrishnan Nambutiri, Chitrabhanu Nambutiri, Mini Nair, Soumya.

●When Pachu's chosen to become the new leader of the ashram, his grandfather's overjoyed. This is an inordinate honour for the family. Pachu's parents, however, are horrified. Dearly loving their only child, they cannot stand the thought of him being taken. Producer/director Jayaraj (from Kottayam in Kerala) explores the nature of family and duty with a keen and tender eye, probing the consequences of tradition and status without resorting to polemic: the family's elevated position in the village dissolves the intimacy of friendship, bringing an uncomfortable isolation, yet to reverse the decision would bring shame and dishonour to all. FM

Jour se lève, Le (Daybreak)

(1939, Fr, 87 min, b/w)
d Marcel Carné. *p* Brachet. *sc* Jacques Viot, Jacques Prévert. *ph* Curt Courant, Philippe Agostini, André Bac. *ed* René Le Hénaff. *pd* Alexandre Trauner. *m* Maurice Jaubert. *cast* Jean Gabin, Arletty, Jules Berry, Jacqueline Laurent, Bernard Blier, René Génin, Mady Berry.

●Possibly the best of the Carné-Prévert films, certainly their collaboration at its most classically pure, with Gabin a dead man from the outset as his honest foundry worker, hounded into jealousy and murder by a cynical seducer, holes up with a gun in an attic surrounded by police, remembering in flashback how it all started while he waits for the end. Fritz Lang might have given ineluctable fate a sharper edge (less poetry, more doom), but he couldn't have bettered the performances from Gabin, Berry, Arletty, and (as the subject of Gabin's romantic agony) Laurent. Remade in Hollywood as *The Long Night* in 1947. TM

Jours Tranquilles à Clichy

see Quiet Days in Clichy

Joy

(1983, Fr/Can, 95 min)
d Serge Bergon. *p* Benjamin Simon. *sc* Marie-Françoise Hans, Christian Charrière, Serge Bergon, Robert Geoffrion. *ph* René Verzier. *ed* Michel Lewin. *pd* Csaba Kertesz, Eric Moulard. *m* Alain Wisniak. *cast* Claudia Udy, Gérard Antoine Huart, Agnès Torrent, Elisabeth Mortensen, Jeffrey Kime, Claire Nadeau.

●The movie that launched the film career of model Claudia Udy, a career that lasted until the film opened. Seeing her parents fornicating left Joy prone to sexual anxiety, made worse by her father-like lover introducing her to the softcore orgy circuit. Joy abandons him for a new lover whose orgies are Fujicolor tantric group sex encounters, and thus healthier. Four scriptwriters and a novelist are credited, plus a bunch of translators whose further gloss is dubbed by graduates of the What's Up Tiger Lily academy. DO

Joyless Street, The (Die freudlose Gasse)

(1925, Ger, 95 min, 7,121 ft, b/w)
d GW Pabst. *p* Hirschel Sofar. *sc* Willy Haas. *ph* Guido Seeber, Curt Oertel, Robert Lach. *ed* GW Pabst. *ad* Hans Sohnle, Otto Erdmann. *cast* Greta Garbo, Asta Nielsen, Valeska Gert, Einar Hanson, Jaro Fürth, Werner Krauss, Tamara Tolstoi, Henry Stuart.

●Pabst's record of the process of destitution in the middle classes of Vienna in the '20s (from the novel by Hugo Bettauer) was banned in Britain when first released. As such, it later came as a major revelation, both when compared with Pabst's later work and in the context of the development of a film narrative able to accommodate a large number of characters. Its squalid realism is given conviction by a sureness of technique and a sensuousness of imagery, continually creating contrasts between the misery of the have-nots and the uncaring gaiety of the champagne-swilling affluent, the threadbare and the luxurious. (Original length: 12,264 ft.) RM

Joy Luck Club, The

(1993, US, 139 min)
d Wayne Wang. *p* Wayne Wang, Amy Tan, Ronald Bass, Patrick Markey. *sc* Amy Tan, Ronald Bass. *ph* Amir Mokri. *ed* Maysie Hoy. pd Donald Graham Burt. *m* Rachel Portman. *cast* Kieu Chinh, Tsai Chin, Ming-Na Wen, Tamlyn Tomita, Rosalind Chao, France Nuyen, Victor Wong.

●An intimate chronicle of the lives of three generations of Chinese-American women, this sophisticated weepy contains enough 'life events' for a season of soap operas, but it is to director Wang's credit that he never allows the tides of emotion to erode the essential truthfulness of the film's characterisations and insights. The Joy Luck Club is a mah-jong club at which four well-to-do immigrant Shanghai women swap recipes, memories and support. At one gathering – when, on the eve of a trip to China, American-born June (Ming-Na Wen) takes the place of her recently deceased mother Suyuan – the film flashes back to the critical moments in the relationships between the four pairs of mothers and daughters. Barring a lull towards the end, the film successfully sustains momentum through sensitive mise-en-scène, the all-round excellence of performance and design, its rhythmic emotional flow, and the sour-sweet blend of humour and tears. WH

Joy of Living

(1938, US, 90 min, b/w)
d Tay Garnett. *p* Felix Young. *sc* Gene Towne, Graham Baker, Allan Scott. *ph* Joseph Walker. *ed* Jack B Hively. *ad* Van Nest Polglase. *songs* Jerome Kern, Dorothy Fields. *cast* Irene Dunne, Douglas Fairbanks Jr, Alice Brady, Guy Kibbee, Eric Blore, Lucille Ball, Franklin Pangborn, Billy Gilbert, Jean Dixon.

●Musical screwball comedy from RKO which had its title changed from *Joy of Loving* (naughty, naughty, said the Production Code). Dunne plays a musical comedy star driven to the brink of exhaustion by the demands of the greedy, money-grubbing family she supports; Fairbanks is the carefree hero who helps her to opt out of the rat race by showing her the joys of loving (ie. eating in romantically cosy neighbourhood restaurants and running about barefoot in the rain). Dunne sings several Jerome Kern numbers, all very stiffly staged; and the dropout message characteristic of the period hedges its bets all the way (Fairbanks may be against money-grubbing, but with an island paradise and a small cargo business of his own he's all right). Faintly tiresome and full of flat stretches, but the excellent supporting cast helps. TM

Joy Parade, The

see Life Begins in College

Joy Ride (aka Roadkill)

(2001, US, 97 min)
d John Dahl. *p* JJ Abrams, Chris Moore. *sc* Clay Tarver, JJ Abrams. *ph* Jeffrey Jur. *ed* Eric L Beason, Scott Chestnut, Todd E Miller. Glen Scantlebury. *pd* Rob Pearson. *m* Marco Beltrami. *cast* Steve Zahn, Paul Walker, LeeLee Sobieski, Jessica Bowman, Stuart Stone, Basil Wallace, Brian Leckner, Mary Wickliffe, McKenzie Satterthwaite, Matthew Kimbrough.

●Dahl's surprisingly effective mad trucker thriller, his most enjoyable offering since *The Last Seduction*, is a mesh of quotations from classics like *Duel* and *The Hitcher*. Lewis (Walker) is a college freshman whose plans to drive across the US with almost girlfriend Venna (Sobieski) are scuppered when he has to bail out his troublemaking brother Fuller (Zahn), who then invites himself along for the ride. At Fuller's suggestion, the duo buy an old CB radio and amuse themselves en route to Venna's by playing a prank on a trucker, 'Rusty Nail' (Kimbrough), inviting him in a faux-female voice to meet them at a roadside motel. In the film's finest moment, Mr Nail makes the extent of his anger at being duped crunchingly clear to the unwitting resident of their rendez-vous room, while the boys cower next door and the camera fixes blankly on a kitsch painting gracing the thin partition wall. Such Hitchcockian panache is, however, in short supply. Never mind *Roadkill* – 'Overkill' would make a more fitting title, as Rusty wreaks his revenge, and set piece is piled on implausible set piece. JO'C

Joyriders

(1988, GB, 96 min)
d Aisling Walsh. *p* Emma Hayter. *sc* Andy Smith. *ph* Gabriel Beristain. *ed* Thomas Schwalm. *pd* Leigh Malone. *m* Hal Lindes, Tony Britten. *cast* Patricia Kerrigan, Andrew Connolly, Billie Whitelaw, David Kelly, John Kavanagh.

●Walsh's directorial debut is the story of downtrodden Dubliner Mary Flynn (Kerrigan), who breaks away from her domineering husband and leaves her kids at the railway left luggage to go in search of something more. Something more turns out to be leather-jacketed Perky Rice (Connolly), an incorrigible car thief and desperate romantic who whisks her off on a joyride through the rolling Irish countryside. Along the way, Mary meets an ageing country and western star (Whitelaw), who orgainses tea-dances in a dilapidated seaside resort, and a weathered hill farmer (Kelly), whose observations bring some humour to an otherwise straight-laced film. Andy Smith's screenplay occasionally touches poignantly on the insurmountable breach between the characters' wishful flights of fancy and the reality of their cramped lives, but in the end the film suffers from a narrowness of vision: lighting, camerawork, and direction all seem bound by the constraints of the small plot, so that neither the passion nor the tragedy of the runaways is ever given full rein. EP

Juarez

(1939, US, 132 min, b/w)
d William Dieterle. *sc* John Huston, Wolfgang Reinhardt, Aeneas MacKenzie. *ph* Tony Gaudio. *ed* Warren Low. *ad* Anton Grot. *m* Erich Wolfgang Korngold. *cast* Paul Muni, Bette Davis, Brian Aherne, Claude Rains, John Garfield, Gale Sondergaard, Donald Crisp, Gilbert Roland, Louis Calhern, Joseph Calleia.

●Only Bette Davis and Gale Sondergaard have any fire in this otherwise plodding Warner Bros costume drama about the French attempt to colonise Mexico in the 1860s, the romance between the puppet dictator (Aherne) and the Empress Carlota (Davis), and the exploits of Juarez himself (Muni), the proponent of Mexican independence. The script, by John Huston and historical researchers, was rewritten by Muni's brother-in-law. Huston commented: 'His changes did the picture irreparable damage. In Mr Muni's estimation, his contributions to the dramatic arts were for the enrichment of the world. It was heavy going around Muni'. ATu

Jubilee

(1978, GB, 104 min)
d Derek Jarman. *p* Howard Malin, James Whaley. *ph* Peter Middleton. *ed* Nick Barnard. *m* Brian Eno. *cast* Jenny Runacre, Little Nell, Toyah Willcox, Jordan, Hermine Demoriane, Ian Charleson, Orlando.

●It's almost an understatement to say that *Jubilee* has a lot going for it. Jarman has conceived the ingenious idea of transporting Queen Elizabeth I through time to witness the future disintegration of her kingdom as marauding girl punks roam a junky and violent urban landscape. Its patchily humorous evocation of this landscape lays the film open to criticism: several sequences stoop to juvenile theatrics, and the determined sexual inversion (whereby most women become freakish 'characters', and men loose-limbed sex objects) comes to look disconcertingly like a misogynist binge. But in conception the film remains highly original, and it does deliver enough of the goods to sail effortlessly away with the title of Britain's first official punk movie: 'Rule Britannia', as mimed by Jordan, should have 'em pogoing in the aisles. DP

Judas Was a Woman

see Bête Humaine, La

Jude

(1996, GB, 122 min)
d Michael Winterbottom. *p* Andrew Eaton. *sc* Hossein Amini. *ph* Eduardo Serra. *ed* Trevor Waite. *pd* Joseph Bennett. *m* Adrian Johnston. *cast* Christopher Eccleston, Kate Winslet, Liam Cunningham, Rachel Griffiths, June Whitfield, James Nesbitt, Vernon Dobtcheff, Freda Dowie, Dexter Fletcher.

●This determinedly non-heritage adaptation of Thomas Hardy's *Jude the Obscure* is an often impressive but oddly frustrating movie. Mostly, it's faithful to the story of the lowly but academically ambitious Wessex stonemason (Eccleston) who, after a disastrous marriage to Arabella (Griffiths), daughter of a pig farmer, heads off to the university town of Christminster, where he falls for his strong-willed, comparatively worldly-wise cousin Sue (Winslet). Somehow, however, the film never delivers the punch deserved by one of the 19th century's most movingly cruel English novels. Part of the trouble is that, in trying to cram Hardy's narrative into a mere two hours, Hossein Amini's brisk screenplay rarely does more than skate over the key dramatic moments. The leads, too, lack the chemistry to render the tragic outcome of Jude and Sue's socially unacceptable *amour fou* as devastating as it should be; Eccleston is too relentlessly 'intense' for Jude to seem a truly attractive prospect, while Winslet's Sue is such a thoroughly modern miss that she finally fails to convince. Eduardo Serra's 'Scope camerawork is eye-catching, and the film is never stilted, but it's hard to see how its emphasis on being 'modern' make the content really relevant to today. Ambitious, sensitive, but ultimately uninvolving. GA

Judex

(1963, Fr, 95 min, b/w)
d Georges Franju. *sc* Jacques Champreux, Francis Lacassin. *ph* Marcel Fradetal. *ed* Gilbert Natot. *ad* Robert Giordani. *m* Maurice Jarre. *cast* Channing Pollack, Edith Scob, Francine Bergé, Jacques Jouanneau, Sylva Koscina, Michel Vitold.

●Franju's superbly elegant and enjoyable tribute to the adventure fanatasies of Louis Feuillade sees the eponymous righter-of-wrongs (Pollack) abduct a wicked banker in order to prevent villainess Diana (Bergé, glorious in black cat suit) laying her hands on a fortune the banker's daughter (Scob) is due to inherit. Cue for a magical clash between good and evil, with the director revelling in poetic symbolism (the opening masked ball finds our hero, with forbidding bird mask, creating a dove out of thin air), black-and-white photography that thrills with its evocation of a lost, more innocent era, and surreal set pieces. GA

Judge Dredd

(1995, US, 95 min)
d Danny Cannon. *p* Charles M Lippincott, Beau EL Marks. *sc* William Wisher, Steven E de Souza. *ph* Adrian Biddle. *ed* Alex Mackie, Harry Keramidas. *pd* Nigel Phelps. *m* Alan Silvestri. *cast* Sylvester Stallone, Armand Assante, Max von Sydow, Diane Lane, Rob Scheider, Jürgen Prochnow, Joanna Miles, Joan Chen, Balthazar Getty, Maurice Roëves, Ewen Bremner.

●Stallone certainly has the square jaw-line and iconic presence to play Judge Dredd, a helmeted, emotionless future-cop who dispenses summary justice on the riot-torn streets of Mega City One. When Dredd is falsely convicted of murder and, like his honest mentor Judge Fargo (von Sydow), driven out into the lifeless deserts of the Cursed Earth, the resulting vacuum is filled by corrupt Judge Griffin (Prochnow), who springs Dredd's cloned criminal brother Rico (Assante) from prison and foments social chaos. Dredd, however, is not so easily vanquished and returns to settle old family scores. Indicative of worries that Dredd's heartless, neo-fascistic persona would result in too dark a tone, the uneven script throws in femme cop Hershey (Lane) and irritating side-kick Fergie (Schneider) to add human feeling and comic relief. Despite some fuzzy flying sequences, the precocious technical mastery displayed by 27-year-old Brit director Cannon is extraordinary; but as with his flawed debut, *The Young Americans*, a question mark still hangs over his handling of actors and narrative fluidity. As a result, this slam-bang Stallone vehicle never quite delivers what its confident, fizzing visuals seem to promise. NF

Judgement in Stone, A

see Cérémonie, La

Judgement in Stone, A

(1986, Can, 100 min)
d Ousama Rawi. *p* Harve Sherman. *sc* Elaine Waisglass. *ph* David Herrington. *ed* Stan Cole. *ad* Reuben Freed. *m* Patrick Coleman, Robert Murphy. *cast* Rita Tushingham, Ross Petty, Shelley Peterson, Jonathan Crombie, Jessica Steen, Jackie Burroughs.

●Lord! The things that happen when you're dyslexic! Eunice (Tushingham) is thus afflicted, and according to a prologue, her inability to read causes all sorts of traumas at school. Worse, it makes her grow up into a mousy, embittered spinster, bullied by her unshaven father and given to wearing silly wigs. Dad, in fact, gets on her nerves so much (what with his ludicrous attempts at a cockney accent) that she kills him and then, still concealing her disability, contrives to find a job in middle America as housekeeper with a kind and wealthy family. But what happens when she has to provide a shopping list? Yep, you guessed it: Eunice goes off her rocker, and pretty soon all hell is let loose. It's hard to tell whether this inept adaptation of Ruth Rendell's novel is meant as a straightforward psychological thriller or as a peculiarly camp black comedy. The awful acting – not merely Tushingham, all wide-eyed bathos and twitchy hysteria, but the entire cast – and the leaden direction suggest the former. GA

Judge Priest

(1934, US, 80 min, b/w)
d John Ford. *p* Sol Wurtzel. *sc* Dudley Nichols, Lamar Trotti. *ph* George Schneiderman. *ad* William Darling. *m* Samuel Kaylin. *cast* Will Rogers, Henry B Walthall, Tom Brown, Anita Louise, Stepin Fetchit, Rochelle Hudson, Hattie McDaniel.

●A loose amalgam of Irwin S Cobb stories which Ford later reshaped, personalised and perfected as *The Sun Shines Bright*. This was the second of three Ford films to star Rogers, the cracker-barrel humorist perfectly cast here as the lazy gadfly who stings a small-town Southern community, still divided by prejudice and the lingering legacy of Civil War conflicts, into shamed awareness of its intolerances. A warmly funny, richly atmospheric slice of Americana, it ran some front office interference (removal of a scene involving the attempted lynching of Stepin Fetchit was one reason for the remake), and shows Ford sometimes fumbling for the touch of poetry that later came so easily (the scene in which Rogers talks to his dead wife was more fully achieved in *Young Mr Lincoln* and *She Wore a Yellow Ribbon*). But it's still terrific. TM

Judgment at Nuremberg

(1961, US, 190 min, b/w)
d/p Stanley Kramer. *sc* Abby Mann. *ph* Ernest Laszlo. *ed* Frederick Knudtson. *ad* Rudolph Sternad. *m* Ernest Gold. *cast* Spencer Tracy, Burt Lancaster, Richard Widmark, Marlene Dietrich, Judy Garland, Maximilian Schell, Montgomery Clift, William Shatner, Edward Binns.

●With his reputation for tackling only Big Issues, the Holocaust had to be on Kramer's list of cinematic 'lest we should forget' achievements. That said, this assembly of star turns in the court – including token 'Germans' Dietrich and Schell, the latter collecting an Oscar for his efforts as the defence attorney – are often very impressive. Tracy puts in an effortlessly brilliant performance as the superjudge, and Clift as a confused Nazi victim is painfully convincing in his emotional disintegration. There are no surprises in the direction, and Abby Mann's screenplay plays the expected tunes, but there's enough conviction on display to reward a patient spectator. DT

Judgment in Berlin

(1988, US, 96 min)
d Leo Penn. *p* Joshua Sinclair, Ingrid Windisch. *sc* Joshua Sinclair, Leo Penn. *ph* Gabor Pogany. *ed* Teddy Darvas. *ad* Jan Schlubach, Peter Alteneder. *m* Peter Goldfoot. *cast* Martin Sheen, Sam Wanamaker, Max Gail, Jürgen Heinrich, Heinz Hoenig, Carl Lumbly, Max Volkert Martens, Sean Penn, Christine Rose, Marie-Louise Sinclair, Joshua Sinclair, Jutta Speidel, Harris Yulin.

●'No one has ever been tried in the West for escaping from the East' announces Sheen early in this docudrama based upon the trial of two East German citizens who in 1978 hijacked a plane to defect to the 'free West' – or did they? Tried under American jurisdiction, their case rose to notoriety when presiding judge Herbert J Stern refused to yield to political pressure, and granted Helmut Thiele and Sigrid Radke the right to trial by jury. Penn's adaptation of Stern's book is an uncertain affair, an intriuging courtroom drama marred by heavy-handed pathos and symbolic flag-waving. Sheen hams it up as Stern, delivering Lincoln-esque speeches about freedom while gazing meaningfully at newsreels of refugees. 'I'm just trying to understand these people', he tells his German-hating Jewish wife (Rose), who soon tires of the whole performance. Hoenig and Speidel are admirable as the errant Easterners, but the real surprise is Sean Penn, whose portrayal of a recently liberated, hesitant student is exemplary. MK

Judith

(1965, US/Isr, 109 min)
d Daniel Mann. *p* Kurt Unger. *sc* John Michael Hayes. *ph* John Wilcox, Nicolas Roeg. *ed* Peter Taylor. *pd* Wilfrid Shingleton. *m* Sol Kaplan. *cast* Sophia Loren, Peter Finch, Jack Hawkins, Hans Verner, Zaharira Charifai, Joseph Gross, André Morell.

●Sophia Loren, Jewish survivor of a concentration camp arriving as an illegal immigrant in Palestine on the eve of Israeli independence in 1947, steps out of the packing-case in which she has been nailed up for a taxing sea voyage looking as fresh as a film star. Yes, it's that sort of movie, and it gets worse as she searches for the Nazi husband who denounced her, a wanted war criminal now training Arabs for the coming struggle. Terminally dreary as well as totally unbelievable. TM

Ju Dou

(1990, Jap/China, 94 min)
d Zhang Yimou, Yang Fengliang. *p* Shigeru Mori, Hiroyuki Kato, Zhao Hangao. *sc* Liu Heng. *ph* Gu Changwei, Yang Lun. *ed* Du Yuan. *ad* Cao Jiuping, Xia Rujin. *m* Zhao Jiping. *cast* Li Wei, Gong Li, Li Baotian, Zheng Jian, Zhang Yi.

●A magnificent melodrama, even more visually sumptuous and emotionally draining than the same director's earlier *Red Sorghum*, even though its cruel tale of adultery and revenge constitutes, to some extent, a blatant reworking of themes. This time, it's set in and around a dyeing workshop in a remote town in the 1920s, where the young wife of the ancient, impotent and sadistic dyer decides to make the old man's adopted nephew her lover and protector. Even when she finds herself with child, their affair remains a secret; but after the dyer is left partly paralysed by an accident, they brazenly flaunt their love, so that the vengeful cuckold's only hope is to turn the child against its parents. Hardly surprising, perhaps, that the Chinese authorities virtually dissociated themselves from this Japanese-financed, less-than-rosy picture of a country given over to unfettered sexual desire and murderous hatred. But it's this vision – expressed through superbly forthright performances, and in images whose stunning colours are sure to stick in the mind – that lends Zhang's movie the stark, searing power of Greek tragedy. Its dark wit and fiery pace ensure that even the occasional overheated moments carry conviction. GA

Judy Berlin

(1998, US, 94 min, b/w)
d Eric Mendelsohn. *p* Rocco Caruso. *sc* Eric Mendelsohn. *ph* Jeffrey Seckendorf. *ed* Eric Mendelsohn. *pd* Charlie Kulsziski. *m* Michael Nicholas. *cast* Barbara Barrie, Bob Dishy, Edie Falco, Carlin Glynn, Aaron Harnick, Bette Henritze, Madeline Kahn, Julie Kavner, Anne Meara.

●Ever feel that life's passing you by? Perhaps the torpor afflicting David (Harnick), a 30-year-old failed film-maker who returns home to Long Island, is infectious, because his parents (Kahn and Dishy) seem to be suffering from related conditions. 'I feel like I'm still 14,' his mom reflects. 'I just don't know what I'm doing,' his father repeats, on the verge of acknowledging his amorous feelings for a fellow teacher, Sue Berlin (Barrie). Babylon is that kind of a town where nothing much changes, David reminds himself. Then he bumps into an old face from school, Judy (Falco), and of course they reminisce. But Judy still has plans for the future. The film's grainy b/w visuals take on a luminous, poetic quality in the second half, when an eclipse plunges the town into darkness. That's the most obvious 'artistic' moment, and perhaps the most heavy-handed. The film's virtues are quiet and self-effacing – the director's sensitivity to body language and personal space, his respect for each of his characters. Marry the finely tuned, mature sensibility with a droll comic touch and you have the makings of a film-maker of rare distinction. TCh

Juge Fayard dit le Sheriff, Le

see Sheriff, Le

Juggernaut

(1974, GB, 110 min)
d Richard Lester. *p/sc* Richard Alan Simmons. *ph* Gerry Fisher. *ed* Antony Gibbs. *pd* Terence Marsh. *m* Ken Thorne. *cast* Richard Harris, Omar Sharif, David Hemmings, Anthony Hopkins, Ian Holm, Shirley Knight, Roy Kinnear, Roshan Seth, Cyril Cusack, Freddie Jones.

●*Juggernaut* has been stuck with a 'disaster movie' tag when in fact it bears little relation to the Hollywood crop of calamities. The potential catastrophe here is seven steel drums of amatol timed to go off and destroy 1,200 passengers unless a ransom is delivered to the mysterious Juggernaut. But Lester's movie is no glossy catalogue of modern living with a holocaust thrown in for the climax. On the contrary, it is a penetrating and sardonic commentary on a fading and troubled Britain, neatly characterised by the lumberingly chaotic ocean liner, 'The Britannic', in which everything is falling apart: newly fitted stabilisers rock the boat, the general facilities are shabby and run down, bombs keep exploding to the dismay of the stoical passengers. Anyone who's ever had to endure that peculiar form of torture, the luxury ocean liner, will find an exact description here with not a jot of misery omitted. The pace of the thriller aspect is unflagging, and the characters are unerringly drawn, from the perfect casting of Sharif as the seedy, demoralised captain, to Harris as the bomb expert (the film's research in this direction is painstaking). Without a doubt, one of the best movies of 1974. DP

Juha

(1999, Finland, 78 min, b/w)
d Aki Kaurismäki. *p* Aki Kaurismäki, Ilkka Mertsola. *sc* Aki Kaurismäki. *ph* Timo Salminen. *ed* Aki Kaurismäki. *pd* Markku Lumme. *m* Anssi Tikanmäki. *cast* Sakari Kuosmanen, Kati Outinen, André Wilms, Esko Nikkari.

●Based on a much-filmed Finnish novel from 1911: a farmer's wife is seduced into running away from her stolid, older husband Juha by a city slicker, who enslaves her in a brothel. This plot is an ideal vehicle for Kaurismäki's riotous miserabilism – dour characters in dire situations – but for once the glum Finn goes beyond one-note comedy. He shoots it as a neo-silent movie and turns it into a sophisticated reflection on the evolution of silent cinema, from its heavily intertitled, melodramatic beginnings to the rarely equalled visual expressiveness of its maturity. (The soundtrack similarly evolves from a musical base, gradually adding sound effects and then a fragment of sync-sound as a woman sings.) The result curiously resembles parts of *Twin Peaks*, but it plays as an oblique indictment of the mediocrity of most modern cinema. TR

Juice

(1992, US, 91 min)
d Ernest R Dickerson. *p* David Heyman, Neal H Moritz, Peter Frankfurt. *sc* Gerard Brown, Ernest R Dickerson. *ph* Larry Banks. *ed* Sam Pollard, Brunilda Torres. *pd* Lester Cohen. *m* Hank Shocklee, Keith Shocklee, Carl Ryder, Gary G Wiz. *cast* Omar Epps, Khalil Kain, Jermaine Hopkins, Tupac Shakur, Cindy Herron, Vincent Laresca.

●This Harlem-set rap thriller examines the implosive relationship between four African-American high school 'crew' members. Q (Epps) is an aspiring scratch'n'mix DJ, holding down a relationship with an older divorcee; Raheem (Kain) has an estranged wife and child; Steel (Hopkins) is the kid, a gentle butt to their jokes; and Bishop (Shakur) is the loaded gun with no safety catch. Their average day – the light-hearted first half of the movie – is spent ditching school in favour of playing the video-game arcades, having close encounters with rival gangs, and taking in some shoplifting of records. But an attempted hold-up instigated by Bishop goes badly wrong, and comedy turns to tragedy as fear and mutual suspicion conspire to blow the four apart. What distinguishes Dickerson's 'ghetto' movie is less the anti-violence message than the sense it gives of *inhabiting* the lives of these Harlem kids. Stylishly shot, it works well as a thriller; the result is energetic and entertaining, without the feeling of difficult truths being forgotten. WH

Jules and Jim (Jules et Jim)

(1961, Fr, 105 min, b/w)
d François Truffaut. *sc* François Truffaut, Jean Gruault. *ph* Raoul Coutard. *ed* Claudine Bouché. *m* Georges Delerue. *cast* Jeanne Moreau, Oskar Werner, Henri Serre, Marie Dubois, Vanna Urbino, Sabine Haudepin, Boris Bassiak.

●Truffaut's film about a dilettantish ménage-à-trois focusing around the First World War, with Moreau as the fatalistic heroine at its centre, has dated a little and the influence of Renoir is more obvious now that we are some distance from the New Wave. The lightning changes of mood from pathos to whimsy and back again still make it watchable, though. Remade by Paul Mazursky as *Willie and Phil* in 1980. RM

Jules Verne's Rocket to the Moon (aka Those Fantastic Flying Fools)

(1967, GB, 101 min)
d Don Sharp. *p* Harry Alan Towers. *sc* Dave Freeman. *ph* Reginald Wyer. *ed* Ann Chegwidden. *ad* Frank White. *m* Patrick John Scott. *cast* Burl Ives, Troy Donahue, Gert Fröbe, Terry-Thomas, Hermione Gingold, Daliah Lavi, Lionel Jeffries, Dennis Price, Joan Sterndale-Bennett.

●Like the rocket in question, this soppy farce has great difficulty in getting off the ground. Jules Verne had little to do with the proceedings, which involve a large star cast getting repeatedly blown up. Reminiscent of *First Men in the Moon* (even to the extent of Lionel Jeffries playing the irascible inventor in both films), but there's no comparison entertainment-wise. DP

Julia

(1977, US, 117 min)
d Fred Zinnemann. *p* Richard Roth. *sc* Alvin Sargent. *ph* Douglas Slocombe. *ed* Walter Murch, Marcel Durham. *pd* Gene Callahan, Willy Holt, Carmern Dillon. *m* Georges Delerue. *cast* Jane Fonda, Vanessa Redgrave, Jason Robards, Maximilian Schell, Hal Holbrook, Rosemary Murphy, Meryl Streep, Dora Doll.

●Lillian Hellman's tight autobiographical story about memory and friendship gets the full Zinnemann gloss-wash. Julia, disaffected Anglo-American aristocrat, strides into womanhood wearing golf shoes and that brave Redgrave grin. Swept up in the anti-Fascist movement, she persuades Hellman (Fonda) to smuggle money to Berlin. One-legged and a liability to any underground movement, Julia is murdered. Hellman returns to Dashiell Hammett (Robards) for grizzled comfort. Suckers for frontier drama, trains, NY literary society and the '30s will enjoy. Zinnemann blows it most of all in the Fonda-Redgrave relationship, and no credibility is given to Hellman's ferocious talent and dominant personality. Reverential to the end, a suggestion of homosexuality is laughingly tossed off in one glittering scene. No one bothers to mention that lesbianism is central to 'The Children's Hour', the play Hellman is trying to write while, as per synopsis, 'her memory returned again and again' to Julia. JS

Julia Has Two Lovers

(1990, US, 86 min)
d/p Bashar Shbib. *sc* Daphna Kastner, Bashar Shbib. *ph* Stephen Reizes. *ed* Bashar Shbib, Dan Foegelle. *m* Emilio Kauderer. *cast* Daphna Kastner, David Duchovny, David Charles, Tim Ray, Clare Bancroft, Martin Donovan, Anita Olanick.

●Alone in her Californian beach apartment, Julia (Kastner) receives a call from a stranger (Duchovny). It's a wrong number, but that doesn't stop them from embarking on a revealing, lengthy conversation conducted while he shaves, she tidies. Julia only puts the receiver aside when her live-in boyfriend (Charles) arrives for lunch and demands sex. Once he's gone, the conversation is resumed, and the two agree to meet the next day. This low-budget comedy makes the most of limited means, but its resourcefulness goes beyond cautious budgeting. Long-distance intimacy exposes the characters' sense of displacement, while poking fun at life in LA. The pace picks up once there's direct interaction between the strangers, leading to the inevitable conflict between long-term security and short-term excitement. Kastner and Duchovny offer engaging performances, and although the film could do with tightening, it's good-natured and uplifting. CM

Julian Po

(1997, US, 83 min)
d Alan Wade. *p* Jon Glascoe, Joseph Pierson. *sc* Alan Wade. *ph* Bernd Heinl. *ed* Jeffrey Wolf. *pd* Stephen McCabe. *m* Patrick Williams. *cast* Christian Slater, Robin Tunney, Bruce Rohne, Roy Cooper, Frankie Faison, Zeljko Ivanek, Allison Janney, Cherry Jones, Michael Parks, Harve Presnell, Anne Pitoniak, LaTanya Richardson.

●Slater is the stranger (one 'Julian Po') who walks into a sleepy small town, and soon admits that he is there to commit suicide. This revelation makes him the man of the moment: women throw themselves at his feet, storekeepers and bakers shower him with freebies, and a sweepstake takes bets on naming the fateful day. But, of course, Mr Po starts to enjoy his celebrity, and confrontation looms in a film which looks like a novella padded out for the big screen (it's based on *La Mort de Monsieur Golouja* by Branimir Scepanovic). Slater brings little to the material, apart from one of the more regrettable moustaches in recent celluloid history. TJ

Julien Donkey-Boy

(1999, US, 94 min)
d Harmony Korine. *p* Cary Woods, Scott Macaulay, Robin O'Hara. *sc* Harmony Korine. *ph* Anthony Dod Mantle. *ed* Valdis Oskarsdottir. *cast* Ewen Bremner, Chloë Sevigny, Werner Herzog, Evan Neumann, Joyce Korine, Chrissy Kobylak, Alvin Law, Brian Fisk.

●Harmony Korine's eagerly awaited follow-up to the controversial *Gummo* has, on the whole, had a much warmer reception from the critics. It's less gratuitously shocking, 'more mature', I suppose, and then it carries with it the excitement of being the first American Dogma film (Korine used dozens of lightweight DV cameras to shoot it). It's with some reluctance then that I confess to a little disappointment. A jazzy free-associative cine poem about a dysfunctional family, headed by stern disciplinarian Werner Herzog, it's never less than fascinating, sometimes bizarrely funny, occasionally moving (Bremner is stunning as the schizophrenic Julien), but too much of it feels like improvisation in a vacuum. The vérité-like scenes out in the real world (mixing it up with a gospel congregation, or an armless magician, for example) have an edge the domestic scenes mostly miss. And then, I can't think of a director less in need of purgation than enfant terrible Korine. He's still the most exciting talent in American cinema, but this is two steps forwards, two steps back. TCh

Juliet of the Spirits (Giulietta degli Spiriti)

(1965, It/Fr, 145 min)
d Federico Fellini. *p* Angelo Rizzoli. *sc* Federico Fellini, Tullio Pinelli, Brunello Rondi, Enio Flaiano. *ph* Gianni Di Venanzo. *ed* Ruggero Mastroianni. *ad* Piero Gherardi. *m* Nino Rota. *cast* Giulietta Masina, Mario Pisu, Sandra Milo, Valentina Cortese, Caterina Boratto, Sylva Koscina, Lou Gilbert, Valeska Gert.

●What *8½* did for its bourgeois film-director hero, *Juliet of the Spirits* does for his female opposite number, a repressed, paranoid, bourgeois housewife (played, of course, by Fellini's wife). That's to say it's a gaudy, hyperbolic pageant, in which a 'reality' composed of séances, film-star neighbours, tyrannous relatives, and a large helping of Catholic guilt is gradually invaded by 'flashbacks' and 'fantasies'. The overall charm just about carries the glibness of the psychological payoff, and the way that different veins of imagery interlock gives the film a cogency that later Fellini has woefully lacked. TR

Julius Caesar

(1953, US, 120 min, b/w)
d Joseph L Mankiewicz. *p* John Houseman. *sc* Joseph L Mankiewicz. *ph* Joseph Ruttenberg. *ed* John Dunning. *ad* Cedric Gibbons, Edward C Carfagno. *m* Miklós Rozsa. *cast* Marlon Brando, James Mason, Louis Calhern, John Gielgud, Edmond O'Brien, Deborah Kerr, Greer Garson, George Macready.

● Although it lacks the excitement of *Macbeth* or *Othello* as imagined by Welles, a remarkably successful stab at Shakespeare. Mankiewicz, as one might expect, respects the words and films without tricks, letting the camera concentrate on performance and on preserving the rhythms of the text. Discreetly pruned, this emerges boldly and lucidly as (in producer John Houseman's words) 'a political thriller', with the motley cast pulling together surprisingly well. At least three outstanding performances (Gielgud, Calhern, Brando), the only disappointments being Mason's muffled Brutus and the two ladies on standby. TM

July 14th

see Quatorze Juillet

July Rhapsody (Nanren Sishi)

(2001, HK, 103 min)
d Ann Hui. *p* Alex Wong, Derek Yee, Ann Hui. *sc* Ivy Ho. *ph* Kwan Pun-Leung. *ed* Kwong Chi-Leung. *ad* Man Lim-Chung. *m* Tommy Leung. *cast* Jacky Cheung, Anita Mui, Karena Lam, Shaun Tam, Tou Chung-Hwa, Eric Kot.

● The Chinese title suggests a companion-piece to Hui's *Summer Snow*: in Chinese that was called 'A Woman at Forty' and this is 'A Man at Forty'. What the two films have in common is a keen sense of middle-aged bewilderment and exasperation, not the usual substance of HK movies these days. Lam Yiu-Kwok (Cheung) is a secondary-school teacher facing two emotional crises. His wife Man-Ching (Mui, remarkable) needs time away from him to come to terms with the impending death of her first boyfriend, who fathered her first child. At the same time, in school, he faces a barrage of flirtation from precocious pupil Choi-Nam (newcomer Lam, clearly a star in the making), who claims to be in love with him and knows very well that she could get him into serious trouble. Restrained, grown-up drama, not especially exciting, but engagingly written, acted and directed. TR

Jumanji

(1995, US, 104 min)
d Joe Johnston. *p* Scott Kroopf, William Teiter. *sc* Jonathan Hensleigh, Greg Taylor, Jim Strain. *ph* Thomas Ackerman. *ed* Robert Dalva. *pd* James D Bissell. *m* James Horner. *cast* Robin Williams, Bonnie Hunt, Kirsten Dunst, Bradley Pierce, Bebe Neuwirth, Jonathan Hyde.

● Young Alan Parrish lives in a postcard '60s American town. One day, he and his only friend Sarah find a Victorian jungle-based board-game, 'Jumanji'. That night, as they play, the jungle comes to life. Her throw of the dice brings bats swooping through the lounge; his takes him into the game, whence he can return only if an opponent throws a seven. Unfortunately, a terrified Sarah runs off into the night, leaving Alan trapped in 'Jumanji'. Cut to the depressed '90s. Two young orphans move into the now decrepit Parrish house and find the game in the attic. They start to play, bringing into being a marauding lion, monkeys and an older Alan (Williams), presumed murdered for over 20 years. To reverse the effects of the game, Parrish knows they must play to the end. Subsequent throws produce a psychotic Victorian hunter (Hyde, excellent), earthquakes, floods and, best of all, a herd of rhinos, zebras and elephants stampeding through the town. This is an sfx movie par excellence. Although leading actors Williams and Hunt (as the older Sarah) give competent performances, script, direction and story are all subservient to Industrial Light and Magic's extraordinary computer-generated animals and effects. Hollow, but very spectacular. NKe

Jumbo

see Billy Rose's Jumbo

Jumping for Joy

(1955, GB, 88 min, b/w)
d John Paddy Carstairs. *p* Raymond Stross. *sc* Jack Davies, Henry E Blyth. *ph* Jack Cox. *ed* John D Guthridge. *ad* Michael Stringer. *m* Larry Adler. *cast* Frankie Howerd, Stanley Holloway, AE Matthews, Tony Wright, Alfie Bass, Joan Hickson, Lionel Jeffries, Richard Wattis.

● Lame, optimistically titled Britcom with young Howerd as the dog-track gopher who's sacked on suspicion of involvement in a doping scandal, but gets his own back on his old bosses by nursing a sick greyhound back to peak condition and winning the big race. Holloway's the con artist in support. TJ

Jumpin' Jack Flash

(1986, US, 105 min)
d Penny Marshall. *p* Lawrence Gordon, Joel Silver. *sc* David H Franzoni, JW Melville, Patricia Irving, Christopher N Thompson. *ph* Matthew F Leonetti. *ed* Mark Goldblatt. *pd* Robert Boyle. *m* Thomas Newman. *cast* Whoopi Goldberg, Stephen Collins, John Wood, Carol Kane, Annie Potts, Peter Michael Goetz, Roscoe Lee Browne, Jeroen Krabbé, Jonathan Pryce, Tracey Ullman.

● Funky computer operator Terry Doolittle (Goldberg) is suffering the usual terminal boredom when someone code-named Jumping Jack Flash appears on her VDU screen. The mystery man is a British agent trapped in Eastern Europe, so Terry is soon rushing around town reading contact names off the bottom of frying pans, meeting strange Dutchmen on moonlit dockside piers, gatecrashing swanky diplomatic dinners dressed as Diana Ross, and getting her slinky outfit, not to mention her nerves, well and truly shredded. Striking an effective balance between suspenseful intrigue and wacky humour, director Marshall handles both the spy-jinks and Goldberg's eccentric antics with confident panache. There are occasions when Goldberg does rather too much, arresting the action by lapsing into stand-up comic routines; fortunately, the plot soon regains its brisk momentum. NF

Jump into the Void (Salto al Vacio)

(1995, Sp, 86 min)
d Daniel Calparsoro. *p* Enrique Fernandez Ayuso. *sc* Daniel Calparsoro. *ph* Kika De La Rica. *ed* Pite Pinas. *ad* Jon Escuder. *cast* Najwa Nimry, Robert Chalu, Alfredo Villa, Tom Gabella, Karra Elejalde, Saturnino Garcia.

● Raw, radical, post-*Reservoir Dogs* thriller from the Basque new wave. A portrait of the hopelessness of youth – with violent trimmings – the film centres on the character of Alex, a muttering, lovelorn punkess with the word 'Void' inscribed on her pate. This is her day: 'Shitty hopheads, shitty work, spiderman shorts, the old woman's coffeepot, Esteban's thumb, the stiff, those two bastards…who the fuck loves me?' The salty, confrontational dialogue, jumpcuts, handheld camerawork and grotesque black comic elements all signal 26-year-old writer/director Calparsoro as a significant talent, while Nimry is outstanding in the lead role. TCh

Jump the Gun

(1996, UK/SAf, 124 min)
d Les Blair. *p* Indra de Lanerolle. *sc* Les Blair. *ph* Seamus McGarvey. *ed* Norrie Ottey. *pd* David Barkham. *m* Joe Nina. *cast* Baby Cele, Lionel Newton, Michele Burgers, Thulani Nyembe, Rapulana Seiphemo.

● Johannesburg, a town where a violent crime occurs every 17 seconds. This is the first film to take the lid off the new South Africa, to create a scenario around living, breathing individuals coming to terms with life in these post-Mandela times. There's poor white Clint, who thinks that the country's getting 'very black' and gun-ownership will solve his problems; there's Minnie, a white prostitute who drinks and has lost her kid; Gugu, who's black and wants to sing in a band, and will sleep with whoever it takes. There's Thabo, who studied and got out of Soweto, and Zoo, who stayed but has changed from township activist to car-hijacking gang leader – even if he is confined to a wheelchair. How these people, who've been brought up apart, get together, is a mix of sex, music and common decency. Great performances, notably from Newton's Clint and Michele Burgers' Minnie, make this a film, written and directed by one-time Mike Leigh collaborator Les Blair, that's genuinely original and genuinely magnificent. SGr

Jump Tomorrow

(2001, GB/US, 96 min)
d Joel Hopkins. *p* Nicola Usborne. *sc* Joel Hopkins. *ph* Patrick Cady. *ed* Susan Littenberg. *pd* John Paino. *m* John Kimbrough. *cast* Tunde Adebimpe, Hippolyte Girardot, Natalia Verbeke, Patricia Mauceri, Isiah Whitlock Jr, Kaili Vernoff.

● This takes its cue from classic Hollywood screwball farce, shoots it with Jim Jarmusch deadpan timing and a Tati-esque delight in the oddities of people and places, then binds everything together with a faith in romantic affirmation so straightforward it seems like some cutting edge discovery. The road movie plot cranks up at the airport when shy New York office worker George (Adebimpe, destined for stardom) arrives on the wrong day to meet his arranged bride from Nigeria, is smitten with Latin flirt Alicia (Verbeke), and provides a diffident shoulder for Frenchman Gérard (Girardot) to cry on after a rebuffed marriage proposal. Destinies will tangle en route to Niagara Falls, where George's nuptials await, and if it's not hard to anticipate a feelgood resolution, the shaggy dog progress upstate never allows the outcome to become a contrived certainty. TJ

Junge Törless, Der

see Young Törless

Jungfrauenmaschine, Die

see Virgin Machine

Jungfrukällan

see Virgin Spring, The

Jungle Book, The

(1967, US, 78 min)
d Wolfgang Reitherman. *sc* Larry Clemmons, Ralph Wright, Ken Anderson, Vance Gerry. *ed* Tom Acosta, Norman Carlisle. *m* George Bruns. *cast* voices: Phil Harris, Sebastian Cabot, Louis Prima, George Sanders, Sterling Holloway.

● 'I thought you were entertaining someone up there in your coils,' Shere Khan the Tiger purrs malevolently (with the unmistakable voice of George Sanders) as Kaa the Snake endeavours to squeeze Mowgli the Man Cub in his horrible clutches. This animated Disney feature based on Kipling, the last to be supervised by Big D himself, is chock-a-block with such shapely lines (with Baloo the dim-witted bear, voiced by Phil Harris, getting the best). It's also got great knockabout visual gags, mercifully little cutey-poo sentiment, and reasonable songs, including 'The Bare Necessities'. The animation has only the bare necessities, too, and the storyline is weak, but it doesn't seem to matter much. GB

Jungle Book, The (aka Rudyard Kipling's The Jungle Book)

(1994, US, 111 min)
d Stephen Sommers. *p* Edward S Feldman, Raju Patel. *sc* Stephen Sommers, Ronald Yanover, Mark D Geldman. *ph* Juan Ruiz-Anchia. *ed* Bob Ducsay. *pd* Allan Cameron. *m* Basil Poledouris. *cast* Jason Scott Lee, Cary Elwes, Lena Headey, Sam Neill, John Cleese, Jason Flemying.

● In this live-action adventure, Mowgli (Scott Lee) is five before he's jungle-bred. The animals act like animals, sort of, which means that Mowgli wrestles with Baloo the bear, tumbles with wolves, but doesn't discuss philosophy with 'em. He swims in sun-shafted rivers like Johnny Weissmuller and runs like the wind. Re-entering society in proud manhood, this beautiful, innocent wild child stuns Kitty Brydon (Headey), daughter of the local divisional officer (Neill, stiff but decent), much to the consternation of a pack of snivelling subalterns led by bad-egg Elwes. Sensing that romance and animal magic won't sew up the audience, director Sommers hots up the pace with abductions and a treasure hunt in the Lost City; this seems like a loss of nerve. But Scott Lee is an unexpectedly appealing hero, partly because he's never indulged, and his dialogue is kept to a minimum. WH

Jungle Burger (La Honte de la Jungle)

(1975, Fr/Bel, 85 min)
d Picha [Jean-Paul Walravens], Boris Szulzinger. *p* Boris Szulzinger. *sc* Picha, Pierre Bartier; (US dubbed version) Michael O'Donoghue, Anne Beatts. *ph* Raymond Burlet. *ed* Claude Cohen. *cast* voices: Georges Aminel, Bernard Dhéran, Claude Bertrand, Pierre Trabaud, Roger Carel; (US dubbed version) Johnny Weissmuller Jr, John Belushi, Bob Perry, Bill Murray.

●A softcore pornish cartoon Tarzan, Englished in this version to conform to the *Animal House* spirit of pre-anal comedy: the eternally adolescent class clown with the Harvard diploma stapled to his fly. There are glimpses of riotously idiosyncratic wit; but the viewer is soon left to drown in a wave of crassness while each animated participant grabs the nearest sex object and heads for the closest pile of leaves. CR

Jungle Fever

(1991, US, 132 min)
d/p/sc Spike Lee. *ph* Ernest Dickerson. *ed* Sam Pollard. *pd* Wynn Thomas. *m* Stevie Wonder, Terence Blanchard. *cast* Wesley Snipes, Annabella Sciorra, Spike Lee, Ossie Davis, Ruby Dee, Samuel L Jackson, Lonette McKee, John Turturro, Frank Vincent, Anthony Quinn, Tyra Ferrell, Tim Robbins, Brad Dourif.

●When happily married black architect Flipper Purify (Snipes) begins an affair with his Italian-American secretary Angie (Sciorra), all hell breaks loose: his wife (McKee) throws him out, Angie leaves home after being beaten by her father, and families, friends and neighbours chip in with horrified reactions… Lee's 'joint' looks good, features a chorus of garrulous characters (most of them heavily into racial hatred), makes stirring use of music (by Stevie Wonder and others), and never allows the forgiving women a fair share of the deal. But instead of *showing* how prejudice seeps into the private intimacies of daily life, the film turns its attention to the other characters, including Flipper's junkie brother Gator (Jackson), who fuels a subplot evoking the destructive effects of crack on black society. Sadly, this aspect, which allows Lee his most unsettling and impressive scene, seems loosely tacked on to the main thrust of the film. GA

Jungle Sex

see Black Bunch, The

Jungle Story

(1996, SKor, 87 min)
d Kim Hong-Joon. *p* Kim In-Soo. *sc* Kim Hong-Joon, Kang Heon, Lee Jeong-Wook. *ph* Byun Hee-Sung. *ed* Park Gok-Ji. *m* Shin Hae-Chul. *cast* Yoon Do-Hyun, Kim Chang-Wan, Cho Yong-Won, Kim Min-Soo.

●In this film about the struggle to establish and promote a rock band in rock-hostile South Korea, the music stands for a spirit of non-conformity and rebellion – concepts which mean something in the country's fast-changing but still overwhelmingly feudal-Confucian society. The story elements are very familiar: endless rehearsals, dodgy contracts, 'musical differences', a bullying manager whose faith in the band never dies. But the details ring true, and there's no hint of MTV excess in the performances or visuals. Kim's taste in music seems more '70s than '90s, but he directs with real elegance and makes very smart use of vignettes like the glimpses of the girl at the pharmacy counter who measures out her life in Neil Young songs. TR

Jungle 2 Jungle

(1997, US, 105 min)
d John Pasquin. *p* Brian Reilly. *sc* Bruce A Evans, Raynold Gideon. *ph* Tony Pierce-Roberts. *ed* Michael A Stevenson. *pd* Stuart Wurtzel. *m* Michael Convertino. *cast* Tim Allen, Sam Huntington, JoBeth Williams, Lolita Davidovich, Martin Short, LeeLee Sobieski, Joan Copeland, David Ogden Stiers.

●Allen's a top New York commodities trader dragged to the depths of the Amazon to get estranged medic spouse JoBeth Williams' signature on their divorce papers. There's a 13-year-old surprise waiting for him, however: a son (Huntingdon) he never knew about, called Mimi-Siku and raised entirely by the local Indians. Naturally, the filial bonding routine comes as something of a shock, but before long, junior and pet spider wind up back in the US, where jungle-trained blowpipe skills may just come in handy for sorting out dad's financial contretemps with a gang of dodgy Russian mafiosi. Allen is nothing if not personable, and though the material here is awfully predictable, he never makes the mistake of overplaying it into submission. No, that's left to business partner Short, who rolls his eyeballs and wrings his hands as the pair's trading balance turns life threatening. Typically for Disney, the villains aren't made of very stern stuff, nor indeed is fey spear-carrying Mimi-Siku. TJ

Jung (War) – in the Land of the Mujaheddin (Jung (Giang) – nella Terra dei Mujaheddin)

(2000, It, 114 min)
d Fabrizio Lazzaretti. *p* Lorenzo Torraca, Fabrizio Lazzaretti, Alberto Vendemmiati. *ph* Fabrizio Lazzaretti. *ed* Giuseppe Petitto. *m* Mario Crispi. *with* Ettore Mo.

●Superb and unsettling documentary which follows in the footsteps of journalist and one-time special envoy Ettore Mo in the war-torn Mujaheddin districts of northern Afghanistan, a region that has been at war continuously for 25 years, first against the Russians, now against the Taliban. There are fascinating interviews with the ousted President, and notably, with an Italian doctor and a British nurse who are trying to set up hospital facilities. Most powerful is the footage of ordinary soldiers and citizens – seemingly few left unwounded, few far from poverty, all possessing a strange nobility under fire. The West comes out badly. WH

Junior

(1994, US, 110 min)
d/sc Ivan Reitman. *sc* Kevin Wade, Christian Conrad. *ph* Adam Greenberg. *ed* Sheldon Kahn. *pd* Stephen Lineweaver. *m* James Newton Howard. *cast* Arnold Schwarzenegger, Danny DeVito, Emma Thompson, Frank Langella, Pamela Reed, Judy Collins.

●Nothing is inconceivable: big Arnie's having a baby – and he's the mother. In the past, movie scientists with the hubris to play God over nature have met with thundering Gothic retribution; no such fate befalls Dr Hesse (Schwarzenegger) after experimenting on himself with a new wonder drug. Arnie has dabbled with the comic implications of genetic science before in *Twins*. This too is a one-joke movie, but at least it's a good joke. Once more director Reitman pulls the strings, slackly at first, but with ever-increasing assurance, and DeVito is back on board as Hesse's collaborator Dr Arbogast. Just as Cary Grant was once the apotheosis of masculinity and therefore ripe for humiliation, so there is something inherently, essentially funny about a feminised Arnie. He's more than matched by the hilariously dizzy Thompson as the unwitting 'father'. They must be the unlikeliest couple of 1994, but, I swear, they're great together. Call it…chemistry. TCh

Junior Bonner

(1972, US, 103 min)
d Sam Peckinpah. *p* Joe Wizan. *sc* Jeb Rosebrook. *ph* Lucien Ballard. *ed* Robert Wolf. *ad* Ted Haworth. *m* Jerry Fielding. *cast* Steve McQueen, Robert Preston, Ida Lupino, Joe Don Baker, Barbara Leigh, Mary Murphy, Ben Johnson, Bill McKinney, Don Barry, Dub Taylor.

●Peckinpah coasting enjoyably between *Straw Dogs* and *The Getaway* with an elegiac reworking of Nick Ray's *The Lusty Men*, an alternately wistful and raucous family Western about the shrinking frontiers of the rodeo circuit and the anachronism of honour (a suited middle-class horseman rides by with *The Wild Bunch* embroidered on his saddle-blanket). Some of the symbolism's a bit heavy-handed (wild bulls: bulldozers), but the performances are finely affecting, and Peckinpah captures the contradictory flavours of the new west with a multi-camera set-up at the real Prescott, Arizona rodeo and judicious use of split screen. PT

Junk Mail (Budbringeren/ Postbudet der vidste for meget)

(1997, Nor/Den, 81 min)
d Pål Sletaune. *p* Dag Nordahl, Peter Boe. *sc* Pål Sletaune, Jonny Halberg. *ph* Kjell Vassdal. *ed* Pål Gengenbach. *ad* Karl Juliusson. *m* Joachim Holbek. *cast* Robert Skjærstad, Andrine Sæther, Per Egil Aske, Eli Anne Linnestad, Trond Høvik, Henriette Steenstrup, Trond Fausa Aurvåg.

●This droll Norwegian first feature shows that Aki Kaurismäki doesn't have the monopoly on deadpan Nordic humour and oddball working class characters. Lugubrious, love-struck postman Roy (Skjærstad) falls for pretty, partially deaf dry cleaning assistant Line (Sæther), whose lowlife boyfriend recently embroiled her in a mugging that left a security guard in a coma. Too shy to declare his love, Roy eavesdrops on Line's unhappy life, becoming involved in a bizarre sequence of events that unfolds like a cheap B-movie plot tinged with Nordic melancholy. The downbeat, fatalistic storyline relies a bit too heavily on ironic coincidences, but the observations are always generous and the humour never forced. NF

Jupiter's Darling

(1954, US, 96 min)
d George Sidney. *p* George Wells. *sc* Dorothy Kingsley. *ph* Paul C Vogel, Charles Rosher. *ed* Ralph E Winters. *ad* Cedric Gibbons, Urie McCleary. *songs* Burton Lane, Harold Adamson. *cast* Esther Williams, Howard Keel, Marge and Gower Champion, George Sanders, Norma Varden, William Demarest, Richard Haydn.

●Elephantine musical (literally, given that the Champions do one number with performing pachyderms), set in 218 BC and featuring Hannibal's march on Rome alongside a lavish underwater ballet for Esther Williams. Disarmingly dotty rather than good, although the Champions have one beautifully choreographed slave market routine. TM

Jurassic Park

(1993, US, 127 min)
d Steven Spielberg. *p* Kathleen Kennedy, Gerald R Molen. *sc* Michael Crichton, David Koepp. *ph* Dean Cundey. *ed* Michael Kahn. *pd* Rick Carter. *m* John Williams. *cast* Sam Neill, Laura Dern, Richard Attenborough, Jeff Goldblum, Bob Peck.

●*Jaws* with claws. Now, however, with state-of-the-art computer-generated effects, the creatures are so good you hardly care what the rest of the film is like. Unfortunately, Spielberg seems to share the disinterest. The premise is solid – scientist clones dinosaurs from blood found in insects trapped in amber, invites distinguished guest and children to his living theme park, and watches helplessly as the behemoths run amok – but the plot is full of inconsistencies and shipwrecks from Michael Crichton's novel. The performances are merely passable (save the kids and Dern), and Goldblum is ludicrous as the chaos theorist. His cod mottos are all that's left of the ethical debate, and the only discernible theme is pure Spielberg: palaeontologist Neill starts off hating children but learns to love them. But why quibble? Spielberg is still supreme as an action director, and when the T Rex makes beefburger of the jeep, or the vicious 'Raptors stalk their human prey, the film inspires wonder and awe. DW

Jurassic Park: The Lost World

see Lost World: Jurassic Park, The

Jurassic Park III

(2001, US, 92 min)
d Joe Johnston. *p* Kathleen Kennedy, Larry Franco. *sc* Peter Buchman, Alexander Payne, Jim Taylor. *ph* Shelly Johnson. *ed* Robert Dalva. *pd* Ed Verreaux. *m* (original themes) John Williams; (new) Don Davis. *cast* Sam Neill, William H Macy, Teá Leoni, Alessandro Nivola, Trevor Morgan, Michael Jeter, John Diehl, Bruce A Young, Laura Dern.

●For the third instalment of his blockbuster creature-feature franchise, Steven Spielberg has passed the reins to Johnston, who works to a copycat script. Jeff Goldblum is out, Sam Neill back; the kid this time is Trevor Morgan, son of mega-rich Macy and Leoni; and Dern is demoted to final reel cavalry. Morgan gets lost parascending over the dinosaur-infested Isla Sorna, and Neill and young colleague Nivola are conned into a search and rescue mission. True, the film offers little new, but it's still stirring family entertainment, even if Spielberg's elegance of construction and his preservation of the element of wonder are replaced by vamped-up sound effects and violent large-scale action sequences. The shift from wonder to spectacle is epitomised by the now depleted crew drifting downstream in an old tug, gazing at grazing dinosaur herds, and passing on by. Johnston feels little interest here, nor a need for Michael Crichton-style lectures – he's more a bloody meat man. However, the film's souped-up animatronics give it the fun feel of a '50s B-movie; the child's grace and self-sufficiency are interesting, too, as Johnston knows how to dignify his kids. WH

Juror, The

(1996, US, 118 min)
d Brian Gibson. *p* Irwin Winkler, Rob Cowan. *sc* Ted Tally. *ph* Jamie Anderson. *ed* Robert Reitano. *pd* Jan Roelfs. *m* James Newton Howard. *cast* Demi Moore, Alec Baldwin, Anne Heche, Joseph Gordon-Levitt, James Gandolfini, Lindsay Crouse, Tony Lo Bianco, Matt Craven, Michael Constantine.

●Sculptress and single mom Annie (Moore) is thrilled to be selected for jury duty on a big Mafia trial, and even happier when an attractive art dealer (Baldwin) picks up on her work and asks her out. He's too good to be true, she tells her best friend (Heche) – and so it transpires, when he whispers these sweet nothings on the first date: if Annie doesn't swing the jury to an acquittal, then she's art history. This pappy, semi-enjoyable legal thriller (from a book by George Dawes Green) raises a number of questions, the most intriguing of which must be: is this woman the most exciting screen actress in America? No, no – not Ms Moore, though she's hit on what must be her perfect movie vocation, making sculptures you can't see (they come boxed). She's very up in the early scenes, very down thereafter, and perfectly watchable throughout, but it's still a stretch watching her persuade 11 angry jurors that black is white and 'the big spaghetti-o' should walk. No, Anne Heche is the one to look for. In just a handful of perfunctory scenes, this mercurial newcomer blows the stars off the screen and the film rings momentarily true. For the rest, screenwriter Ted Tally appears to be aiming for a low-brow companion piece to his *Before and After*, Baldwin contributes a silky, Zen hood ('If I can keep you scared, I can save you'), but director Gibson shows real bad faith by resorting to a laughably primitive climax in Guatemala, of all places. TCh

Just a Gigolo (Schöner Gigolo – Armer Gigolo)

(1978, WGer, 105 min)
d David Hemmings. *p* Rolf Thiele. *sc* Ennio De Concini, Joshua Sinclair. *ph* Charly Steinberger. *ed* Alfred Srp. *pd* Peter Rothe. *m* Günther Fischer. *cast* David Bowie, Sydne Rome, Kim Novak, David Hemmings, Maria Schell, Curd Jürgens, Marlene Dietrich.

●Hemmings recut his film (reputedly the most expensive ever made in Germany to date), restoring some footage originally deleted by the producer, who radically reduced its 147 minute running time after preliminary screenings. These alterations may well have helped, but no amount of tinkering could turn it into the comedy-drama that it was clearly intended to be. Its main problem is its tone: its story of a young Prussian (Bowie) returning to a turbulent Berlin after World War I, and finding himself torn between a team of homosexual Nazis and a flotilla of wealthy widows, never finds its level, but swings wildly between coarse knockabout farce and aspirations to tragic dignity. Bowie's vacant performance reflects these uncertainties precisely, and the cluster of star names around him are reduced to delivering awkward party pieces. TR

Just a Little Whistle (Jen si Tak Trochu Písknout)

(1980, Czech, 79 min)
d Karel Smyczek. *sc* Radek John, Ivo Pelant. *ph* Viktor Ruzucka. *ad* Jirí Hlupy. *m* Zdenek John. *cast* Michal Suchánek, Dan Sedivák, Pavel Kohout, Libuse Heczková, Renata Pokorná.

●Back to schooldays with a couple of kids from differing backgrounds forming an unholy alliance and beginning to wonder what girls are all about. Parental neglect and/or misunderstanding, a drift towards delinquency, a final betrayal. Sounds familiar? Too right, it might almost be a remake of Truffaut's *Les Quatre Cents Coups*. Competently done, with excellent performances from the two boys, but desperately predictable. TM

Just Another Girl on the I.R.T.

(1992, US, 97 min)
d Leslie Harris. *p* Erwin Wilson, Leslie Harris. *sc* Leslie Harris. *ph* Richard Connors. *ed* Jack Haigis. *pd* Mike Green. *cast* Ariyan Johnson, Kevin Thigpen, Ebony Jerido, Chequita Jackson, Jerard Washington.

●Chantal (Johnson) lives in the Brooklyn projects. She's an A student, but her street sassiness leads to her downfall, alienating teachers and attracting Tyrone (Thigpen), a jeep-driving fly guy, who smooth talks Chantal into unprotected sex. Soon she's facing abortion or teenage motherhood. Being generous to Harris's debut would earn PC credibility, since this is the first film written and directed by an African-American woman to gain British distribution. One could dwell on Johnson's in-your-face performance, or how refreshing it is to see a black New York drama played out by home*girls*. But, facing facts, the climax is unpersuasive and the happy end a cop-out. CO'S

Just Another Night (aka Mystery Date)

(1991, US, 99 min)
d Jonathan Wacks. Cathleen Summers. *sc* Parker Bennett, Terry Runte. *ph* Oliver Wood. *cast* Ethan Hawke, Teri Polo, Fisher Stevens, Brian McNamara, BD Wong, Tony Rosato, Don Davis.

●Darker humour than you might anticipate raises this erratic teen comedy out of the usual rut. Hawke thinks he's got it made when brother McNamara sets him up with siren next door Teri Polo, but he's about to become an unwitting pawn in his brother's dodgy business dealings as a corpse turns up in the back of the car. Straight to video in Britain. TJ

Just Ask for Diamond

(1988, GB, 94 min)
d Stephen Bayly. *p* Linda James. *sc* Anthony Horowitz. *ph* Billy Williams. *ed* Scott Thomas. *pd* Peter Murton. *m* Trevor Jones. *cast* Susannah York, Colin Dale, Dursley McLinden, Peter Eyre, Nickolas Grace, Patricia Hodge, Saeed Jaffrey, Roy Kinnear, Bill Paterson, Jimmy Nail.

●This junior private eye spoof on *The Maltese Falcon*, scripted by Anthony Horowitz from his novel *The Falcon's Malteser*, soon degenerates into superficial pastiche and becomes increasingly tiresome. Handed a box of Maltesers by a South American dwarf, teenage shamus Tim Diamond (McLinden) is soon out of his depth and forced to rely on his younger, smarter brother Nick (Dale). The Fat Man demands an audience, Inspector Snape (Paterson) and his sadistic assistant (Nail) apply the pressure, and comically inept heavies Gott and Himmell (Eyre and Grace) fall over each other to get their hands on the chocs. Sadly, only York as the drink-sodden romantic Laura Bacardi, and Patricia Hodge as the enigmatic Baroness, leave a lasting impression. NF

Just Before Nightfall (Juste avant la Nuit)

(1971, Fr/It, 107 min)
d Claude Chabrol. *p* André Génoves. *sc* Claude Chabrol. *ph* Jean Rabier. *ed* Jacques Gaillard. *ad* Guy Littaye. *m* Pierre Jansen. *cast* Stéphane Audran, Michel Bouquet, François Périer, Anna Douking, Dominique Zardi, Henri Attal, Jean Carmet, Marina Ninchi.

●Chabrol's tortuous, entertaining study of murder and the expiation of guilt in a small suburban town, a low-key thriller about a husband who murders his mistress (his best friend's wife), tries to confess and accept punishment, but finds a bland bourgeois unwillingness to recognise guilt from his own wife and friends. Organised in Chabrol's lurid, witty and elegant manner, this was his last productive mining of the themes of *La Femme Infidèle* before they were transmuted through repetition into the farcical intrigues of *Les Noces Rouges*. Direction, acting and script are all meticulous, and the use of subplot (the meek accountant who robs the hero's safe) is especially fine. DP

Just Between Friends

(1986, US, 120 min)
d Allan Burns. *p* Edward Teets, Allan Burns. *sc* Allan Burns. *ph* Jordan Cronenweth. *ed* Anne Goursaud. *pd* Sydney Z Litwack. *m* Patrick Williams. *cast* Mary Tyler Moore, Ted Danson, Christine Lahti, Sam Waterston, Salome Jens, Jane Greer.

●In this pseudo-sophisticated weepie, the ongoing relationships are those between two buddy seismologists, and between a loving wife and her lonely female newscaster friend who is having an affair with one of the quake-quacks, who just happens to be married to the aforesaid wife (a fit but wizened MTM). As is usual in such cases, the wife is the only person not to know what is going on, but after the adulterer's death in an auto smash while attending an anti-nuclear rally in Washington, she does find out. And the adulteress is pregnant…Even given the sensitive performances and fitfully humorous script, the end product is exactly what might be expected to eradicate stains from white-collar conscience: soap. But for those who can pause-button the mind, it works. MS

Just Cause

(1995, US, 102 min)
d Arne Glimcher. *p* Lee Rich, Arne Glimcher, Steve Perry. *sc* Jeb Stuart, Peter Stone. *ph* Lajos Koltai. *ed* William Anderson. *pd* Patrizia von Brandenstein. *m* James Newton Howard. *cast* Sean Connery, Laurence Fishburne, Kate Capshaw, Blair Underwood, Ed Harris, Ruby Dee, Ned Beatty, Daniel J Travanti, Hope Lange, Kevin McCarthy, George Plimpton.

●There's a Hollywood dictum about not going on the floor until you've fixed the script, but it's obviously news to the makers of this picture. The novel by John Katzenbach, from which it's taken, may have been an overweight airport buy, but it did have two startling plot twists, both fumbled by the script. For some reason, Armstrong (Connery) has had a career change from investigating journalist to Harvard law professor, and this effectively destroys the humiliation of his Pulitzer backing up on him when he realises his newspaper campaign has released the wrong man from Death Row. Another no-good reason issues him with a wife (Capshaw), and to give her something to do, the script babbles about a past entanglement with the killer. Briefly, Armstrong is persuaded to take the case of black convict Bobby Earl (Underwood), railroaded for raping and killing a little girl. He was beaten into a confession by police chief Tanny Brown (Fishburne), and at the retrial is set free, after which the killings begin again. Harris as a mad serial killer is lit from under; Connery and Fishburne are adversarial along *Heat of the Night* lines, but director Glimcher makes little of the small-town Deep South locations. Pity. BC

Juste avant la Nuit

see Just Before Nightfall

Just Heroes

(1993, HK, 93 min)
d John Woo. *cast* David Chiang, Danny Lee, Chow Sing Chi.

●Bizarrely moralistic gangster picture in which Woo orchestrates the gunplay with customary virtuosity, but also argues that violence is wrong and 'nobody wins' in gangland feuds. As usual, the family's foregrounded. *The Godfather*-like plot charts the bloody happenings after the boss of a crime syndicate is murdered and his relatives fight to take over the reins. As in the best mobster movies, it's never quite clear who's betraying who. The director includes some self-reflexive comedy in the shape of a youngster who wants to emulate the heroes of *A Better Tomorrow* (Woo, 1986), but learns that shoot-outs in 'real life' are tough, unglamorous work. Such corny moralistic humour can't help but undermine an otherwise impressive hardboiled thriller. GM

Justine

(1969, US, 116 min)
d George Cukor. *p* Pandro S Berman. *sc* Lawrence B Marcus. *ph* Leon Shamroy. *ed* Rita Roland. *ad* Jack Martin Smith, William Creber. *m* Jerry Goldsmith. *cast* Anouk Aimée,

Michael York, Dirk Bogarde, Anna Karina, John Vernon, Philippe Noiret, George Baker, Robert Forster, Jack Albertson, Marcel Dalio, Michael Dunn, Barry Morse.
●A foredoomed attempt to compress Lawrence Durrell's *Alexandria Quartet* for Hollywood consumption, begun by Joseph Strick on location and continued by Cukor in studio sets, with the former's Tunisian exteriors cut in (irrespective of disruptive colour-matching) or back-projected from time to time to make the whole thing look doubly phony. Exuding the disastrous smell of compromise in every shot, it emerges as a farrago of sex (romantic, incestuous, homosexual, nymphomaniac) and high-flown political intrigues concerning Coptic Christians and gun-running in Palestine. Only Bogarde, as the tormented Pursewarden, manages to rise above the inanities and deliver his lines as though they meant something. TM

Justine

(1976, GB, 90 min, b/w)
d Stewart Mackinnon. *p* Stewart Mackinnon, Nigel Perkins. *sc* Stewart Mackinnon, Clive Myer, Nigel Perkins. *ph* Clive Myer. *ed* Stewart Mackinnon, Clive Myer, Nigel Perkins. *m* Johnny Hawksworth. *cast* Alison Hughes, Robin Phillimore, Patrick Good, Peter Marples, Patrisha Despond, Ken Campbell.
●Who nowadays reads de Sade? His precise, logical catalogues of moral and sexual behaviour belong to a vanished time with a vanished language. If de Sade lives, it's through his present-day interpreters: de Beauvoir, Barthes, Pasolini. And the Film Work Group, whose *Justine* is an isolated and very honourable attempt to bring an important strain in contemporary European thinking into British consciousness. The film comprises a series of non-dramatic tableaux, representing incidents from the first third of the book: although the period trappings are all there, there's no attempt to 'involve' the audience by creating a 'plausible' historical reality. Instead, the visual tableaux and long speeches set out to present de Sade's book in a form that modern viewers can broach and try to come to terms with. No one could pretend that it's a complete success, but its challenge is real. RG

Justine de Sade

see Violation of Justine, The

Just Like a Woman

(1992, GB, 106 min)
d Christopher Monger. *p* Nick Evans. *sc* Nick Evans. *ph* Alan Hume. *ed* Nicolas Gaster. *pd* John Box. *m* Michael Storey. *cast* Julie Walters, Adrian Pasdar, Paul Freeman, Susan Wooldridge, Gordon Kennedy, Ian Redford.
●Monica (Walters) has her life turned a-tizz by the arrival of dashing city-slicker lodger Gerald (Pasdar), whose hunky eligibility only seems enhanced by fastidiously plucked eyebrows. For Gerald is happier as Geraldine; and Monica, too, soon discovers she prefers it that way. Tailored to the transatlantic *Shirley Valentine* market, the film soft-pedals shamelessly. Any sense of challenge is defused by the accent on the naughty-but-normal, and by a time-wasting 'Wall Street' subplot that allows Freeman to breeze through as a boardroom nasty, while Pasdar rides to the rescue in an embarrassing reprise of Dustin Hoffman's *Tootsie* turn. Pasdar's performance, and his suits, are straight out of a Burton's window. Walters busks it on her dependable big bright smile. And Monger stitches it all together into a slickly pedestrian TV *(sic)* movie. JRo

Just Like Weather (Meiguo Xin)

(1986, HK, 98 min, b/w)
d Allen Fong. *p* Cheung Chi-sing. *sc* Ng Ching-chau. *ph* George Chang, Michael Chin. *ed* Lee Yuk-wai. *pd* Wong Kwai-ping. *m* Law Wing-fei. *cast* Christine Lee, Lee Chi-keung, Allen Fong, Cheng Chi-hung, Yung Man-ching.
●An object lesson in finding hidden depths in everyday material. A young Hong Kong couple are on the verge of separating, although a trip to New York might save their marriage. Fong himself interviews them about their problems, then spins them off into fictional episodes (an abortion, an arrest, an interlude with a randy vet whose chat-up line is the mating habits of dogs), and finally whisks them off to the States, where they get stuck in a New Mexican snowdrift. Underlying it all are very candid worries about the future of Hong Kong after 1997. TR

Just the Ticket

(1998, US, 115 min)
d Richard Wenk. *p* Gary Lucchesi, Andy Garcia. *sc* Richard Wenk. *ph* Ellen Kuras. *ed* Christopher Cibelli. *pd* Franckie Diago. *m* Rick Marotta. *cast* Andy Garcia, Andie MacDowell, Richard Bradford, Elizabeth Ashley, Fred Asparagus, André Blake, Patrick Breen, Ronald Guttman. Abe Vigoda, Irene Worth,
●Garcia is allowed free rein as NY 'scalper' (tout) Gary Starke, a bumptious, philanthropic charmer in slanted pork-pie hat and Ratso Rizzo sneakers (and mannerisms). He might come on like cock of the walk with his gang of associates and hangers-on in Tony's Bar, but he feels impelled to get a social security card – and a life – by reuniting with old flame and aspiring chef Linda (MacDowell, muted). The plot turns on his efforts to raise funds for a restaurant lease, borrowing over his head to buy black market tickets for the Pope's upcoming Yankee Stadium visit. The *Diner*-esque banter is enjoyable, thanks to a rich list of character actors (notably Bradford as the protagonist's pal, lonely ex-boxing coach Benny, whose tearful flurry of hurt, anger and confusion at a diatribe from Gary provides the film's best scene). Garcia himself, in a screen-hogging role, is a little stretched: his De Niro-style set pieces – selling a TV to an unwilling customer, helping Linda cook for a snobby English tight arse – jar against his subsequent low life lethargy. WH

Just the Way You Are

(1984, US, 94 min)
d Edouard Molinaro. *p* Leo L Fuchs. *sc* Allan Burns. *ph* Claude Lecomte. *ed* Claudio Ventura, Georges Klotz. *ad* François de Lamotte. *m* Vladimir Cosma. *cast* Kristy McNichol, Michael Ontkean, Kaki Hunter, André Dussollier, Catherine Salviat, Robert Carradine.
●Childhood polio has left musician Kristy McNichol feeling as if life hasn't treated her right, so she heads for a ski resort in the French Alps, puts her leg in a cast, and waits to see what people – particularly men – make of her now. This comedy-drama-romance, from the director of *La Cage aux Folles*, never quite hangs together and threatens to get rather spongy, but McNichol's appealing performance holds the interest throughout. TJ

Just Us

(1986, Aust, 95 min)
d Gordon Glen. *cast* Scott Burgess, Catherine McClements, Merfyn Owen, Gina Riley, Jay Mannering, Kim Gyngell, Marie Redshaw.
●Another of those 'How I became good friends with a convict and discovered he wasn't such a bad type after all' sagas, this time based on a book by crusading Australian journalist Gabrielle Carey (played somewhat sanctimoniously by McClements). Burgess is the prisoner. Earnest, numbing fare with none of the bite of *In Cold Blood*. GM

Just Visiting (Les Visiteurs en Amérique)

(2001, Fr/US, 88 min)
d Jean-Marie Gaubert [Jean-Marie Poiré]. *p* Patrice Ledoux, Ricardo Mestres. *sc* Christian Clavier, Jean-Marie Poiré, John Hughes. *ph* Ueli Steiger. *ed* Michael A Stevenson. *pd* Doug Kraner. *m* John Powell. *cast* Jean Réno, Christina Applegate, Christian Clavier, Matthew Ross, Tara Reid, Bridgette Wilson-Sampras, John Aylward, George Plimpton, Malcolm McDowell.
●The poor record of Hollywood remakes of French comedy smashes is scarcely enhanced by writer/director Gaubert's transposition of his time-travel farce *Les Visiteurs* from Languedoc to Chicago. The original stars Réno and Clavier more or less reprise their Quixotic duo as haughty medieval knight and craven manservant who land in the present, courtesy of a wizard's potion. As you'd expect, the digs at changed manners, class attitudes and status have been coarsened to reflect urban American realities rather than provincial French mores, but it hardly matters in this intentionally puerile romp. WH

Juvenile Court

(1973, US, 135 min, b/w)
d/p/sc Frederick Wiseman. *ph* William Brayne. *ed* Frederick Wiseman.
●A distillation of over sixty hours of footage taken during a month in Memphis. The material that is kept is obviously that which most clearly reveals the layers of assumption and prejudice that form the basis of the entire court process, but also that which contains the most tension, irony, pathos and drama of one kind or another. All Wiseman's work has this sort of ambiguity, of apparent objectivity and latent distortion. Despite this, his films are more intelligent documentaries than you'd ever expect from the likes of the Beeb, demonstrating how much a film-maker actually robs his audience when he wants to seduce more than inform. Generally Wiseman informs. JDuC

Juvenile Liaison

(1975, GB, 97 min)
d/p/sc/ph/ed Nicholas Broomfield, Joan Churchill.
●A devastating exposé of the now notorious police scheme to cope with potential young (from 7 years old) offenders. The film is a deliberately modest effort (it follows the work of one Lancashire juvenile liaison division over a seven-week period, is shot in available light, and made without TV-style window-dressing), yet it is hard to think of another British film that has so succinctly revealed the day-to-day mechanics whereby class and paternalistic authority are sustained. The collusion of the educational establishments is perhaps the hardest thing of all to take. VG

Juvenile Liaison 2

(1990, GB, 85 min)
d Nicholas Broomfield, Joan Churchill. *p* Rita Ord. *sc/narrator* Nicholas Broomfield. *ph* Joan Churchill. *ed* Richard Vick, Aaron Weissblatt.
●Documentary film-maker Broomfield has a knack of catching life in the raw, and it's not always a pretty sight. Hence, Juvenile Liaison was banned fifteen years ago for undermining the image of the friendly bobby. Blackburn is the setting and some pre-teen kids are the subjects. Seven-year-old Glen, accused of stealing a cowboy suit, quakes with fear before a bullying, burly sergeant, and one little girl is given the third degree over a missing apple. The 'seen and not heard' axiom is brought disturbingly to life. This updated version includes footage shot in Blackburn in 1989 in which the original 'juveniles' are traced to discover what scars their 'liaisons' with authority may have left. Depressingly, the grown-up kids have inherited the same misguided attitudes towards children. Bristling with characteristic Broomfield tension, the film's interest goes beyond its content. Compare the anguish of the original footage with the latent irony of the additional scenes. Broomfield has picked up a black sense of humour along the way. EP

J.W. Coop

(1971, US, 112 min)
d/p Cliff Robertson. *sc* Cliff Robertson, Gary Cartwright, Bud Shrake. *ph* Frank Stanley. *ed* Alex Beaton. *m* Don Randi, Louie Shelton. *cast* Cliff Robertson, Geraldine Page, Cristina Ferrare, RG Armstrong, RL Armstrong, John Crawford, Wade Crosby.
●Cliff Robertson's debut as director emerges as very flawed but sufficiently interesting to deserve escape from total neglect. The film's benefits are pretty much on the fringe, all the more so because it treads ground already covered by *Junior Bonner*. It's a pity, then, that the film gets hung up on its own narrative development, with Coop's efforts to win the rodeo championship (too lazy to work, too scared to steal) and his relationship (embarrassing) with a hippie girl, because Robertson's at his best with the peripheries. This comes over strongest in the first half-hour, with Coop trying to pick up the threads after ten years in prison, only to find that there aren't any. Above all he makes you understand what it's like to have been away for that long through observing his own reactions: talking to a man about his brother who has made it big; watching a couple of women going bowling; sitting drinking; realising that everything's different but that nothing much has changed. The decaying small towns have a feel that Bogdanovich, for all his painstaking efforts, never realised in *The Last Picture Show*. CPe

k

Kiss Me Kate

Kabhi Khushi Kabhie Gham...

(2001, Ind, 210 min)
d Karan Johar. *p* Yash Johar. *sc* Sheena Parikh, Karan Johar. *ph* Kiran Deohans. *ed* Sanjay Sankla. *ad* Sharmishta Roy. *lyrics* Sameer. *cast* Amitabh Bachchan, Jaya Bachchan, Shah Rukh Khan, Kajol, Hrithik Roshan, Kareena Kapoor, Alok Nath, Rani Mukherjee.

● 'It's all about loving your parents,' runs the opening declaration from writer/director Karan Johar, also behind the Bollywood blockbuster *Kuch Kuch Hota Hai*. Johar's second picture takes standard musical ingredients, and with the help of a stellar cast (including longtime luminaries Amitabh and Jaya Bachchan), creates something tremendously vibrant. Rahul Raichand (the charmingly jocular Khan) is the adopted heir to a Delhi business empire, ardently loyal to his family, until he falls for a girl without his father's approval. His brother Rohan (Roshan), having matured from pudgy youth into high school hunk, endeavours to reunite the clan with the help of flirtatious Pooja (Kapoor). This is a film with celebration in its heart: the musical routines are triumphantly lavish, boasting pounding *dhol* percussion and gorgeously fluid choreography, whether the characters are rejoicing in Diwali, weddings, birthdays or cricket scores. Unfortunately, the song lyrics aren't translated from Hindi. AHa

Kabloonak

(1994, Fr/Can, 105 min)
d Claude Massot. *p* Pierre Gendron. *sc* Claude Massot, Sébastien Régnier. *ph* Jacques Loiseleux. *ed* François Protat. *pd* Valodin Aronine, Jean-Paul Gunet, Jean-Pierre Nossereau. *cast* Charles Dance, Adamie Quasiak Inukpuk, Georges Claisse, Matthew Saviakjuk-Jaw, Natar Ungalaq, Tony Vogel.

● Robert Flaherty – the 'father' of the documentary, who died in 1951 – sits in a New York bar in 1922 like he's just been treasure hunting in the Sierra Madre. The well-received premiere of *Nanook of the North* has just prompted Paramount Pictures to offer him money for another movie. Flashback to 1919: in Port Harrison, Hudson Bay, on a snow-stiffened whaler, Flaherty embarks on his three-month trip to film the Eskimo way of life, under circumstances that would have daunted even Scott of the Antarctic. Dance makes Flaherty a fine taciturn hero, and Jacques Loiseleux's (presumably brave) cinematography makes the film a visual feast. Director Massot skirts the contentious issue of exactly what kind of documentary Flaherty was making (faked igloos, stage-managed sexual manners, etc) by concentrating on the man at work – and fascinating work it is. WH

Kadosh

(1999, Isr/Fr, 110 min)
d Amos Gitai. *p* Laurent Truchot. *sc* Amos Gitai, Eliette Abecassis, Jacky Cukier. *ph* Renato Berta. *ed* Monica Coleman, Kobi Netanel. *ad* Miguel Markin. *m* Philippe Eidel. *cast* Yaël Abecassis, Meital Barda, Yoram Hattab, Uri Ran Klauzner, Yussef Abu Warda, Sami Hori.

● Gitai's slow, simple and (presumably) controversial study of the suffering inflicted on women according to the laws of strict Hassidic Judaism makes for depressing but wholly compelling viewing. It focuses on the experiences of two sisters: one is married without kids, with a husband of ten years who is being advised by the local rabbi to dump her in favour a young woman who might bear a male heir; the other is forced into an unwelcome arranged marriage, even though she already loves another. The film never explicitly takes sides, but merely observes, in long, immaculately acted scenes, how women's happiness is of no consquence whatsoever in such an unthinkingly traditional patriarchal religion. Notwithstanding the quiet, contemplative tone, it will probably arouse anger in virtually every viewer. GA

Kafka

(1991, US/Fr, 98 min. b/w & col)
d Steven Soderbergh. *p* Stuart Cornfeld, Harry Benn. *sc* Lem Dobbs. *ph* Walt Lloyd. *ed* Steven Soderbergh. *pd* Gavin Bocquet. *m* Cliff Martinez. *cast* Jeremy Irons, Theresa Russell, Joel Grey, Ian Holm, Jeroen Krabbé, Armin Mueller-Stahl, Alec Guinness.

● Post-WWI Prague. After the disappearance of a colleague, Kafka (Irons), an aspiring writer and toiling clerk, is torn between a diffident policeman (Mueller-Stahl) and an angry revolutionary (Russell). Slowly but inexorably he's drawn into the deadly political machinations of the times, and an experiment in social engineering more nightmarish than even his own imaginings. At night, leprous, lobotomised creatures skulk in the shadows, while anarchists conspire and the authorities despatch body-snatchers from the castle high above the cobbled gas-lit city streets. Shot in inky b/w Soderbergh's follow-up to *sex, lies and videotape* took a hammering from the US critics. It is, however, an intriguing, idiosyncratic and often highly entertaining movie – a biopic which conflates elements of the author's life and writings into a fiction much bigger than life. It takes a sluggish half hour to take shape, and even then the absurdist comedy seems misjudged, but it's more playful than pretentious, and it works as a genuinely eye-catching mystery thriller. TCh

Kagemusha

(1980, Jap, 181 min)
d Akira Kurosawa. *sc* Akira Kurosawa, Masato Ide. *ph* Takao Saito, Masaharu Ueda. *ad* Yoshiro Muraki. *m* Shinichiro Ikebe. *cast* Tatsuya Nakadai, Tsutomu Yamazaki, Kenichi Hagiwara, Daisuke Ryu, Masayuki Yui, Toshihiko Shimizu.

● Though acclaimed as a magnificent return to form, Kurosawa's first Japanese film since Dodes'ka-den' is something of a disappointment. The basic story, clearly Shakespearean in inspiration, is fine enough: a disreputable thief is spared execution due to his physical resemblance to the lord of a warring clan, in order that the enemy might not learn of the lord's death in battle. Ample scope, then, for the depiction of deceitful intrigues in court, not to mention the occasionally touching attempts of the double to acquire the noble demeanour of the clan chief. But for all Kurosawa's splendidly colourful recreation of 16th century Japan, and though Nakadai's performance is impressive enough, it's all ultimately rather empty and tedious; it could easily have been cut by almost an hour, while the grating Morricone-like score only serves to underline the fact that the director fails to achieve the emotional force of his finest work. GA

Kagero-za

(1981, Jap, 139 min)
d Seijun Suzuki. *p* Genjiro Arata. *sc* Yozo Tanaka. *ph* Kazue Nagatsuka. *ed* Akira Suzuki. *ad* Norihatsu Iketani. *m* Kaname Kawauchi. *cast* Yusaku Matsuda, Michiyo Ogusu, Katsuo Nakamura, Eriko Kusuda, Mariko Kaga.

● The title translates literally as 'Heat-haze Theatre', which is a fair enough description of these two hours of hallucinatory goings-on, in which four increasingly abstracted men and women wander through a series of riddles about their identities, marital status, motives, and indeed their very existence. Veteran director Suzuki was idolised by Japanese students for his outré gangster movies during the '60s. TR

Kalamazoo

(1994, US, 29 min)
d Claudia Silver. *cast* Adrienne Shelley, Wally Shawn.

● Struggling actress Shelley may believe her WASP lover broke with her due to her mom's anti-semitism, but Jewishness hardly impinges on this sentimental comedy about a girl's long-term obsession with her ex. True, there are nice scenes with shrink Wally Shawn, but this is just as much a film about love and life on the fringes of the New York art scene as it is about cultural identity. Slight, light, sturdily performed, and not without charm. GA

Kaleidoscope

(1966, GB, 103 min)
d Jack Smight. *p* Elliott Kastner. *sc* Robert Carrington, Jane-Howard Carrington. *ph* Christopher Challis. *ed* John Jympson. *ad* Maurice Carter. *m* Stanley Myers. *cast* Warren Beatty, Susannah York, Clive Revill, Eric Porter, Murray Melvin, George Sewell, John Junkin, Yootha Joyce, Jane Birkin.

● Its tricksy flashiness conjured by its title, this Swinging London caper features Beatty as a playboy gambler (who's contrived to mark the printing plates at a playing-card factory) being manipulated into collaring a dope smuggler for the Yard. Down the credit list, Jane Birkin features as an 'exquisite thing': just about par for the course from Hollywood-on-Thames. PT

Kalifornia

(1993, US, 118 min)
d Dominic Sena. *p* Steve Golin, Sigurjon Sighvatsson, Aristide McGarry. *sc* Tim Metcalfe. *ph* Bojan Bazelli. *ed* Martin Hunter. *pd* Michael White. *m* Carter Burwell. *cast* Brad Pitt, Juliette Lewis, David Duchovny, Michelle Forbes, Sierra Pecheur, Gregory Mars Martin.

● Erotic photographer Carrie (Forbes) and her lover Brian (Duchovny), a writer researching serial murders, are not so complacent about their lives that they don't feel the need to quit their Pittsburgh pad, head for California and start afresh. But their self-conscious liberalism is shaken when they meet the couple they've agreed to car-share with: Early (Pitt) and Adele (Lewis), poor white trash with few pretensions, minimal manners and even less in the way off intellectual ability. Worse, Early is a psychopath, and even Brian's initial voyeuristic fascination turns to fear and revulsion when the blood starts flowing. Many of the images from this road-thriller look as if they're from a pop promo. More damagingly, Lewis's implausibly gullible Adele suggests that as an actress, she's limited to a handful of coy mannerisms. The plot is schematic, too, loaded with stark polarities, blunt ironies and repetition. That said, however, the film is oddly watchable. Yes, this is opportunistic, shallow and over-extended – but somewhere behind all the faddishness, there's a taut, pleasingly nasty B-thriller trying to get out. GA

Kama Sutra: A Tale of Love

(1996, Ind/GB/Jap/Ger, 114 min)
d Mira Nair. *p* Mira Nair, Lydia Dean Pilcher.*sc* Helena Kriel, Mira Nair. *ph* Declan Quinn. *ed* Kristina Boden. *pd* Mark Friedberg. *m* Mychael Danna. *cast* Naveen Andrews, Sarita Choudhury, Ramon Tikaram, Rekha, Indira Varma.

● In 16th century India, two virgins – Princess Tara (Choudhury) and servant girl Maya (Varma) – play at being friends. They're destined to grow apart, but sex, as taught by the Kama Sutra, soon has them inextricably entwined. Tara and Maya appear equally spoilt and pouty; meanwhile, the objects of their affection, lecherous Raj Singh (Andrews) and brooding sculptor Jai (Tikaram), defy belief. Raj is the sort of man who flares his nostrils when aroused, while Jai is prone to such insights as, 'My work has a power even I can't explain.' The film is visually delicious (peacock colours nestling in a dusty postcard haze), but that it comes from Mira Nair, director of the heart-pummelling *Salaam Bombay!*, is dispiriting. If there's an underlying message, it's conservative. Even before her lessons in the art of love, Maya is instinctively more sensuous than Tara – low class babes, you see, have natural rhythm. And what's behind the deluge of sex tips? Be imaginative in bed, girls, or the man in your life will stray. Ye gods! It's like being stuck in a lift with Jane Seymour: slave-girl chic turned nauseatingly fragrant. CO'Su

Kameradschaft

(1931, Ger/Fr, 93 min, b/w)
d GW Pabst. *p* Seymour Nebenzal. *sc* Ladislaus Vajda, Karl Otten, Peter Martin Lampel, Fritz Eckardt. *ph* Fritz Arno Wagner, Robert Baberske. *ed* Hans Oser. *ad* Ernö Metzner. *cast* Fritz Kampers, Alexander Granach, Ernst Busch, Gustav Püttjer, Daniel Mendaille, Georges Charlia, Pierre Louis, Hélèna Manson.

● The absolute high-point of German socialist film-making of its period. Pabst imagines a coal-mine on the French-German border, where the aftermath of World War I is still being played out: French prosperity and chauvinism hard up against German inflation and unemployment. There's a disaster in the French wing of the mine...and the German miners go to the rescue. Both the visual style and the 'message' of solidarity owe a lot to Soviet Socialist Realism, but Pabst was a more sophisticated social critic than any of the Russian film-makers. Only a bruised and cynical Berlin pessimist could produce a film as moving, sincere and committed as this. TR

Kamikaze

(1986, Fr, 89 min)
d Didier Grousset. *p* Luc Besson. *sc* Luc Besson, Didier Grousset. *ph* Jean-François Robin. *ed* Olivier Mauffroy. *pd* Dan Weil. *m* Eric Serra. *cast* Richard Bohringer, Michel Galabru, Dominique Lavanant, Riton Leibman, Kim Massée, Harry Cleven, Romane Bohringer.

● When brilliant but batty boffin Galabru is fired from his lab job, he retreats into a private world. Incensed by the banal idiocy of the TV he endlessly watches, he invents a gizmo which can kill the presenters, who both fascinate and repel him. The death ray is so ingenious that no one can fathom how the murderer operates, and investigating detective Bohringer comes into bitter conflict with the Ministry of Communications. As co-scripted and produced by Luc Besson (who passed it to his former assistant to direct), *Kamikaze* is an ambitious if somewhat slim satire on a society enthralled by the bland output of the box; not only Galabru's savagely demented performance, but the sharp, sumptuous, and very mobile widescreen photography, constitute a contemptuous attack on a medium which anybody in their right mind will already know is inferior to cinema. Not exactly substantial, but stylish fun. GA

Kamikaze Hearts

(1986, US, 77 min)
d Juliet Bashore. *p* Heinz Legler, Sharon Hennessey, Bob Rivkin. *sc* Juliet Bashore, Tigr Mennett, John Knoop. *ph* David Golia. *ed* John Knoop. *ad* Hans Fuss, Miriam Tinguely. *m* Paul M Young, Walt Fowler. *cast* Sharon Mitchell, Tigr Mennett, Jon Martin, Sparky Vasque, Jerry Abrahms, Robert McKenna, Jennifer Blowdryer.

● Bashore's gritty, grimy film about the porn industry and the status of women within it continually throws the audience up against problems of interpretation: sometimes the camera is a coolly discriminating, independent viewpoint, sometimes a goggling, peeping eye. The peg the film hangs on is the relationship between lithe, gorgeous porn star Sharon Mitchell and doggedly devoted Tigr, her lover and director; the viewer's sympathy switches nervously back and forth between the two women. Mitch is a shameless camera-hog, rabbiting on about joy and fulfilment through porn; Tigr is superficially less flaky, but collapses dramatically in the harrowing last scene. There are moments of humour, and the glimpses of the porn movie set enthral; but the film belongs to the frighteningly blank Mitch, who has clearly been turned inside out and torn in the process. A tough cookie who's also a figure of supreme availability, she embodies the contradictions explored in the film. SFe

Kamikaze Taxi

(1995, Jap, 169 min)
d Masato Harada. *p* Narihiko Yoshida. *sc* Masato Harada. *ph* Yoshitaka Sakamoto. *ed* Hirohide Abe. *pd* Hiroshi Maruyama. *m* Masahiro Kawasaki. *cast* Koji Yakusho, Kazuya Takahashi, Reiko Kataoka, Kenichi Yajima, Mickey Curtis.

● One of the discoveries of the 1995 London Film Festival (and let's face it, a 169-minute first film from a Japanese director is unlikely to get a proper theatrical release in Britain). This is a young, angry, combative movie about those endemically racist, sexist, and corrupt institutions, the yakuza and the government. Disillusioned by the brutal murder of his girlfriend, Tatsuo (Yakusho) turns against the mob to rip off a wealthy minister, but the heist goes wrong, and Tatsuo finds himself on the run – his days numbered – with only a Peruvian-Japanese taxi-driver and a young hooker to help him. A freewheeling original. TCh

Kanal

(1956, Pol, 95 min, b/w)
d Andrzej Wajda. *p* Stanislaw Adler. *sc* Jerzy Stefan Stawinski. *ph* Jerzy Lipman. *ed* Halina Nawrocka. *ad* Roman Mann. *m* Jan Krenz. *cast* Wienczyslaw Glinski, Tadeusz Janczar, Teresa Izewska, Emil Karewicz, Vladek Sheybal, Stanislaw Mikulski.

● The setting for the second film in Wajda's trilogy about WWII (coming between *A Generation* and *Ashes and Diamonds*) is the sewers of Warsaw, through which a group of partisans attempt to make their escape from the Nazis during the 1944 Uprising. This was the film that made Wajda's name in the West, and it certainly has a unique intensity and gloom, with most of the characters enduring appalling fates: two lovers reach an exit to find it sealed off with a grill, another man surfaces right into German hands. Nevertheless, scenes such as the musician playing Chopin amid the ruins have a peculiar poetry that speaks of an experience that demands to be reinvented. DT

Kanchenjungha

(1962, Ind, 102 min)
d/sc Satyajit Ray. *ph* Subrata Mitra. *ed* Dulal Dutta. *ad* Bansi Chandragupta. *m* Satyajit Ray. *cast* Chhabi Biswas, Pahari Sanyal, Anil Chatterjee, Karuna Banerjee, Alaknanda Ray, Subrata Sen.

● Set in the beautiful hill station of Darjeeling – a point suspended in time between modern India and the past – Ray's first colour film would have delighted Henry James with its sense of the past and concern for the future. While on holiday with his downtrodden family, whose lives he has unconsciously ruined by benevolently but firmly bending them to his will, an ageing industrial tycoon finds his values shattered by a chance meeting with a young man who refuses to be ruled. As the characters converse on the circling terraces of Observatory Hill in a strictly formalised pattern of walks whose musical structure is underlined by recurring images (the paths crossed and recrossed in different circumstances; a little girl eternally circling on her pony), the themes begin to harmonise contrapuntally and subtly shape all these lives into new configurations. And over it all broods Kanchenjungha, a majestic, inscrutable éminence rose… TM

Kandahar (Safar é Ghandehar)

(2001, Iran/Fr, 85 min)
d/p/sc Mohsen Makhmalbaf. *ph* Ebraham Ghafouri. *ed* Mohsen Makhmalbaf. *m* Mohamad Reza Darvishi. *cast* Niloufar Pazira, Hassan Tantaï, Sadou Teymouri, Hayatalah Hakimi.

● Now living in Canadian exile, Afghan journalist Nafas returns to her country's border with Iran after receiving a letter from her younger sister, who warns that she intends to commit suicide during an imminent eclipse of the sun. Nafas tries to reach the girl in Kandahar, but en route repeatedly encounters obstacles: the fear, wariness and dishonesty of those she asks to escort her, poverty and illness, the threat of landmines, the Taliban oppression of women. Makhmalbaf's film is characteristically jam-packed with metaphors and striking visual epiphanies – artificial legs being parachuted into the desert are even used twice! – and certainly packs some sort of visceral punch as it depicts the harsh realities of life in Afghanistan. But there are also enough clumsy or obvious moments, uncertainties of tone and brazenly rhetorical flourishes to seed doubts about just how heartfelt it all is. Moreover, by attacking the Taliban regime so fiercely, is Makhmalbaf serving as an apologist for, say, the treatment of women in Iran, or implicitly criticising certain aspects of his own country as well? As so often with his work, it's hard to know for sure. GA

Kanehsatake (Oka) – 270 Years of Resistance

(1990, Can, 120 min)
d Alanis Obomsawin.

● In this passionate, affecting documentary, Alanis Obomsawin – a member of the Abenaki tribe – describes the 11-week battle fought by the Mohawks of Montreal during 1990 to stop one of their sacred burial grounds being developed into a golf course. It was a war of wills with no winners. The Mohawk 'warriors' (in army dress and with movie names like 'Psycho' and 'Freddy Krueger') and women (with real names and with their children) set up barricades, blocked off the nearby Messier bridge, and made a peace camp. They were prepared to die. Facing them were the regional police – the 'SQ' – and the Canadian Army, who weren't. An army corporal *was* killed, however, which rocketed the confrontation from local to national news. This fascinating, condemnatory document, including a historical section and interviews with politicians, captures much of the Mohawk (and native Indian) identity and struggle. It also makes clear why Canada is in the process of breaking up. WH

Kangaroo

(1952, US, 84 min)
d Lewis Milestone. *p* Robert Bassler. *sc* Harry Kleiner. *ph* Charles G Clarke. *ed* Nick De Maggio. *ad* Lyle Wheeler, Mark-Lee Kirk. *m* Sol Kaplan. *cast* Maureen O'Hara, Peter Lawford, Richard Boone, Finlay Currie, Chips Rafferty, Charles Tingwell.

● A highly unlikely Australian Western, substituting Aborigines for Indians. Lawford and Boone plot to outwit a wealthy ranch-owner (Currie), but Lawford screws things up by falling in love with his daughter (O'Hara). Routine in all departments, it's one long yawn. DP

Kangaroo

(1986, Aust, 110 min)
d Tim Burstall. *p* Ross Dimsey. *sc* Evan Jones. *ph* Dan Burstall. *ed* Edward McQueen-Mason. *pd* Tracy Watt. *m* Nathan Waks. *cast* Colin Friels, Judy Davis, John Walton, Julie Nihill, Hugh Keays-Byrne, Peter Hehir.

● Novelist Richard Somers (Friels) and his wife (Davis) abandon the emotional and cerebral sterility of Europe in the early '20s for a new life in Australia. The couple are quickly befriended by their neighbours in Sydney; and at first captivated by the Australian couple's openness and hospitality, Somers soon comes to suspect something lurking beneath the sugary surface. This adaptation of DH Lawrence's autobiographical novel (which he called his 'thought-adventure') faithfully re-examines the issue of authority as it exists on the personal and political level. Somers finds a fresh surface in his new world, but remains contemptuous of the colonial; caught between the conflicting attractions of the all-embracing love of 'Kangaroo' (leader of a paramilitary movement) and the fraternity of the trade unionists, he must simultaneously resolve the ambiguity of his relationship with his wife. Burstall's characters are well defined, his exotic settings beautifully photographed (in contrast with the grim depiction of England), yet the film as a whole seems encumbered with a forced vitality. The literary origins almost inevitably serve to constrict the action rather than offer a point of departure. SGo

Kansas

(1988, US, 113 min)
d David Stevens. *p* George Litto. *sc* Spencer Eastman. *ph* David Eggby. *ed* Robert Barrere. *pd* Mathew Jacobs. *m* Pino Donaggio. *cast* Matt Dillon, Andrew McCarthy, Leslie Hope, Alan Toy, Andy Romano, Brent Jennings, Kyra Sedgwick.

● An uneven blend of crime thriller and rural romance, this aims for an adult complexity but misses the target by a mile. En route from LA to New York, directionless middle class kid McCarthy meets the slightly older Dillon, an insistently friendly drifter returning to his Kansas home town, and unwittingly gets caught up in an armed bank robbery. Forced to split up as they make a run for it, Dillon draws the heat and McCarthy hides the dough under a bridge. While McCarthy finds refuge on a ranch, and falls for the wealthy owner's daughter, Dillon goes on a crime spree, makes the wanted list, and subsequently turns up to demand his share of the loot…Though more morally ambivalent than the Depression era scripts it echoes, Stevens' film never follows through. McCarthy's character is distinctly unsympathetic – disloyal, opportunist, and shallow – but as Dillon becomes increasingly unhinged, the blame is clearly shifted in his direction. Like the eponymous state, this has corn for as far as the eye can see. NF

Kansas City

(1996, US, 115 min)
d/p Robert Altman. *sc* Robert Altman, Frank Barhydt. *ph* Oliver Stapleton. *ed* Geraldine Peroni. *pd* Stephen Altman. *cast* Jennifer Jason Leigh, Dermot Mulroney, MirandaRichardson, Harry Belafonte, Steve Buscemi, Brooke Smith, Michael Murphy, JeffFeringa, Ajia Mingnon Johnson, Albert J Burnes, AC Smith.

● It's 1934, and Kansas City – the wide-open capital of jazz, gambling and crime run by 'Boss' Tom Pendergast – is hotting up, not only for the local elections, but for a 'cutting contest' between top tenors Lester Young and Coleman Hawkins. But the only thing that concerns 'Blondie' O'Hara (Leigh), apart from wanting to be like her idol Jean Harlow, is how to get back her beloved Johnny (Mulroney), a petty thief held by gang-boss and night-club owner Seldom Seen (Belafonte) after a heist gone wrong. In kidnapping laudanum-addict Carolyn Stilton (Richardson), the wife of a bigwig adviser to Roosevelt, O'Hara hopes to force an exchange. Notwithstanding a slim central narrative thread (the shifts in the relationship between O'Hara and Stilton) and a mannered performance from Leigh, Altman's film mostly succeeds as a rich tapestry of characters, subplots, themes and events. Though the structure may seem loose (the film repeatedly abandons the plotline proper for scenes of the blowing jazzers at the Hey-Hey Club), it's actually subtle and tight, with a strange, adventurous arrangement of flashbacks, and unexpected links gradually and cleverly revealed between seemingly unconnected characters. Of the many fine performances, Belafonte, Richardson and the ever dependable Brooke Smith (as Blondie's sister) are probably the stand-outs, while the music (from the likes of Joshua Redman, Craig Handy, James Carter, David Murray, Geri Allen and Ron Carter) is simply a blast. GA

Kansas City Bomber

(1972, US, 99 min)
d Jerrold Freedman. *p* Martin Elfand. *sc* Thomas Rickman, Calvin Clements. *ph* Fred J Koenekamp. *ed* David Berlatsky. *ad* Joseph R Jennings. *m* Don Ellis. *cast* Raquel Welch, Kevin McCarthy, Helena Kallianiotes, Norman Alden, Jeanne Cooper, Cornelia Sharpe, Jodie Foster.

●Raquel Welch is a mother-of-two neglecting her kids to get a piece of the action on the roller-derby circuit, and soon agonising over fame versus family. The derby sequences are shot with an unbelievably heavy hand – could anyone really make them this dull? The script is unspeakable. Forget it.

Kaos

(1984, It, 187 min)
d Paolo Taviani, Vittorio Taviani. *p* Giuliani G De Negri. *sc* Paolo Taviani, Vittorio Taviani. *ph* Giuseppe Lanci. *ed* Roberto Perpignani. *ad* Francesco Bronzi. *m* Nicola Piovani. *cast* Margarita Lozano, Biagio Barone, Enrica Maria Modugno, Ciccio Ingrassia, Franco Franchi, Claudio Bigagli, Omero Antonutti, Regina Bianchi.

●A bandit plays bowls with the head of an old woman's husband, a peasant turns werewolf, a hunchback gets trapped in an outsized olive jar, a tyrant denies tenants the right to bury their dead, and Pirandello shares his sorrows with his mother's ghosts. The common link between the stories, adapted from Pirandello, is the vast, empty Sicilian landscape harbouring a richness of dramatic tales at once emotional and elemental. This is a film of fierce sunlight, bleached rocks, dark interiors, silent stares, and dialogue as rough and sparse as the land. In the years since the Tavianis' *Padre Padrone*, naturalism has given ground to a more grotesque vision of the past, allowing black comedy to creep into the always subtle socio-historical subject matter. Exhilarating. MA

Kapo

(1960, It/Fr, 115 min, b/w)
d Gillo Pontecorvo. *sc* Franco Solinas, Gillo Pontecorvo. *ph* Goffredo Bellisario, Aleksandar Sekulovic. *ed* Roberto Cinquini. *ad* Piero Gherardi. *m* Carlo Rustichelli. *cast* Susan Strasberg, Laurent Terzieff, Emmanuelle Riva, Didi Perego, Gianni Garko.

●Susan Strasberg is the Parisian Jewish teenager who's orphaned by the Nazis and, in order to save herself, becomes in time the heartless 'Kapo' of a Polish concentration camp. The Red Army advances and an escape is effected during which the Kapo (who has by this time fallen in love with Russian inmate Terzieff) redeems herself through self-sacrifice. Pontecorvo, a former commander in the wartime Italian resistance, who co-scripted this luridly realistic film with Franco Solinas, strives to say something about the nature of survival in the pit of degradation, but becomes mired in an overloaded plot peopled with stereotypes and filled out with signposted moral questions. Five years later, having made his mistakes here, the director executed his flawless, harrowing masterpiece, *The Battle of Algiers*. JPy

Karakter (Character)

(1997, Neth, 120 min)
d Mike van Diem. *p* Laurens Geels. sc Mike van Diem, Laurens Geels, Ruud van Megen. *ph* Rogier Stoffers. *ed* Jessica de Koning. *pd* Jelier & Schaaf *m* Het Paleis van Boem. *cast* Jan Decleir, Fedja van Huêt, Betty Schuurman, Victor Löw, Tamar van den Dop, Hans Kesting.

●Adapted from a classic novel by Ferdinand Bordewijk, this sombre, handsome costume pic set in turn of the century Rotterdam is distinguished by Jan Decleir's superb character turn as the villainous bailiff, Dreverhaven, who thinks nothing of evicting the poor, the elderly and the infirm from their homes. He's a forbidding figure with a touch of the Old Testament prophet. He seems determined to destroy his illegitimate son, a self-taught lawyer who likewise hates him. At times, the naturalistic detail is cluttering and leaves the film looking like a museum piece, but as oedipal drama, this is dark and often strangely powerful. (Winner of the 1998 foreign language Oscar.) GM

Karate Kid, The

(1984, US, 127 min)
d John G Avildsen. *p* Jerry Weintrab. *sc* Robert Mark Kamen. *ph* James Crabe. *ed* Bud Smith, Walt Mulconery, John G Avildsen. *pd* William J Cassidy. *m* Bill Conti. *cast* Ralph Macchio, Noriyuki 'Pat' Morita,Elisabeth Shue, Martin Kove, Randee Heller, William Zabka.

●A surprise summer hit in the States, this is another film-making-by-numbers exercise in teenage wish-fulfilment. A Jewish divorcée moves to California from New Jersey, and her son, a male Carrie called Daniel, has terrible trouble fitting in with West Coast ways. His first incipient romance runs foul of the girl's ex, a blond thug who trains at the local karate dojo run by a deranged Vietnam veteran. Fortunately his E.T. comes along in the form of an elderly Okinawan karate master, who not only becomes his special, secret friend but also handily teaches him persistence, inner strength, moral values and karate – which lead him into an apotheosis worthy of *Rocky*. This is actually director Avildsen's first hit since *Rocky*, and it has the same mixture of calculation and apparent naïveté. It borrows its formula from both East and West with good humour, and is completely free of intelligence, discrimination and originality. No wonder it was a hit. TR

Karate Kid: Part II, The

(1986, US, 113 min)
d John G Avildsen. *p* Jerry Weintrab. *sc* Robert Mark Kamen. *ph* James Crabe. *ed* David Garfield, Jane Kurson, John G Avildsen. *pd* William J Cassidy. *m* Bill Conti. *cast* Ralph Macchio, Noriyuki 'Pat' Morita, Nobu McCarthy, Danny Kamekona, Yuji Okumoto, Tamlyn Tomita, Charlie Tanimoto.

●This sequel retains the strengths of its predecessor, the gawky charm of Ralph Macchio (is he really 24?) as the cute boy-next-door turned hero, and Noriyuki 'Pat' Morita as his ever-smart, ever-wisecracking oriental mentor Miyagi. This time the action switches to Okinawa as Miyagi (with boy-next-door tagging along) returns to straighten out his dying father's estate, but also has to face up to a matter of honour that he had left unfinished. The plotline is classic Western morality-play stuff, with the goodies and baddies clearly delineated, but the set pieces are well constructed, and the whole thing is beautifully staged and shot. DPe

Karate Kid Part III, The

(1989, US, 112 min)
d John G Avildsen. *p* Jerry Weintrab. *sc* Robert Mark Kamen. *ph* Steve Yaconelli. *ed* John Carter, John G Avildsen. *pd* William Matthews. *m* Bill Conti. *cast* Ralph Macchio, Noriyuki 'Pat' Morita, Robyn Lively, Thomas Ian Griffith, Martin L Kove, Sean Kanan, Jonathan Avildsen.

●Via a quick flashback, we review the Kid's triumph in the championships and his mentor Mr Miyagi's triumph over rival trainer Kreese in a car-park bust-up. Now, a year later, the title's up for grabs, but Daniel (Macchio) doesn't want to defend it – it's not important any more. Kreese wants to force him to fight Mike Barnes (Kanan), who has been trained to fight dirty; and a delightful villain, ruthless millionaire Silver (a stunning debut from Griffith) vows to help him humiliate the Kid and discredit the Master and the Way. Daniel accepts the challenge, but Mr Miyagi won't train him, and suddenly he's in deep trouble. After suffering endless abuse, Daniel wins with just a few well placed whacks: those expecting standard wish-fulfilment fantasy will be disappointed that (in tune with the philosophy, of course) he didn't give the punk a pasting. SFe

Karate Killers, The

(1967, US, 92 min)
d Barry Shear. *p* Boris Ingster. *sc* Norman Hudis. *ph* Fred J Koenekamp. *ed* William B Gulick, Ray Williford. *ad* George W Davis, James W Sullivan. *m* Gerald Fried. *cast* Robert Vaughn, David McCallum, Curd Jürgens, Joan Crawford, Herbert Lom, Telly Savalas, Terry-Thomas, Kim Darby, Diane McBain, Jill Ireland, Leo G Carroll.

●A damp *Man from UNCLE* squib, directed with pace, and hopefully throwing in a string of star cameos plus some slapstick knockabout, but still refusing to ignite. It's the one in which the redoubtable duo of Solo and Kuryakin chase clues to a secret process (extracting gold from sea-water) entrusted to the dead inventor's four daughters. TM

Karate King – On the Waterfront

see Kung Fu – Girl Fighter

Karl May

(1974, WGer, 180 min)
d/p/sc Hans-Jürgen Syberberg. *ph* Dietrich Lohmann. *ed* Hans-Jürgen Syberberg. m Mahler, Chopin, Liszt. *cast* Helmut Käutner, Kristina Söderbaum, Käthe Gold, Attila Hörbiger, Willy Trenk-Trebitsch, Heinz Moog, Lil Dagover.

●The second film in Syberberg's trilogy forming, with *Ludwig – Requiem for a Virgin King* and *Hitler, a Film from Germany*, a unique analysis of the dominant forces in German history and culture. Like a German Rider Haggard, May was an 'imperialist' novelist with a strong romantic idealism (best remembered for his American 'noble savage' character, Winnetou), and part of Syberberg's aim is to celebrate the fragile beauty of his fantasies. But the film is structured as a kind of biography, and the long central scene of a courtroom battle marks the collapse of May's dreams as he gets more and more deeply embroiled in the realities of Prussian jurisprudence. The matter-of-fact historical framework acquires an added resonance from the fact that all the main parts are played by prominent figures from the Nazi cinema of the '30s. The mesh of fact, fiction, realism and expressionism is complex and fascinating. And the film's 'plastic' qualities are at least as sumptuous as those in *Ludwig*. TR

Kaseki

(1974, Jap, 209 min)
d Masaki Kobayashi. *p* Mayasuki Sato, Ginichi Kishimoto, Yutaka Kamioka. *sc* Shun Inagaki, Takeshi Toshida. *ph* Kozo Okazaki. *ed* Keiichi Uraoka. *m* Toru Takemitsu. *cast* Shin Saburi, Keiko Kishi, Hisashi Igawa, Kei Yamamoto, Orié Sato, Komaki Kurihara.

●The film reveals its entire plot in its opening moments: Itsuki, widower and successful businessman, will learn in Europe that he has cancer, and reappraise his dealings with family, colleagues and friends. Dropping the element of narrative 'surprise' works as a bold distancing device, the last thing you'd expect from the director of *Kwaidan* and *Rebellion;* it enables him to view Itsuki with a kind of engaged dispassion, and to make clear-eyed points about Japanese social conventions and ethics without troubling to keep a melodrama on the boil. Despite stretches that betray its origin in a TV serial (of twice the length), the result is exceptionally innovative for a Japanese film-maker of the older generation. The web of documentary, fiction and fantasy coalesces into a commitment to change that's emotionally tough, and never for a second sentimental. TR

Kashima Paradise

(1973, Fr, 110 min, b/w)
d Yann Le Masson, Benie Deswarte. *sc* Benie Deswarte. *ph* Yann Le Masson. *ed* Isabelle Ratheray, Sarah Taouss. *m* Hiroshi Hara.

●A documentary, with commentary by Chris Marker (spoken by John Atherton in the English version), which focuses on Kashima Paradise, an industrial complex some sixty miles from Tokyo. It examines the effect of total change in Japan, and the transition in one part-village from an almost medieval way of life to advanced industrial practice all within the space of a year. Japan is probably the country most susceptible to this type of rapid change at the moment, but it's something that's happening to us all.

Kaspar Hauser (Verbrechen am Seelenleben eines Menschens)

(1993, Ger, 139 min)
d Peter Sehr. *p* Andreas Meyer. *sc* Peter Sehr. *ph* Gernot Roll. *ed* Heidi Handorf, Susanne Hartmann. *ad* O Jochen Schmidt, Karel Vacek. *m* Nikos Mamangakis. *cast* André Eisermann, Udo Samel, Jeremy Clyde, Katharina Thalbach, Cécile Paoli, Hansa Czypionka, Hermann Beyer, Dieter Mann.

●Karlsruhe, 1812. Shortly after his birth, Kaspar, son of Crown Prince Karl of Baden, is exchanged with an ailing baby by Karl's philandering brother Ludwig, who has ambitions for the throne. The child is deposited with a nurse, but when Ludwig becomes Grand Duke and manifests hostility to Bavaria, with which Baden is in dispute, the boy is sold to a Bavarian minister, who has him hidden away for 12 years in a cellar. In 1828, Kaspar (Eisermann) is released in Nuremberg, unable to talk, walk or fend for himself; he's taken under the wing of kindly Prof Daumer (Samel), whose efforts to educate and protect the youth fail to take account of the fact that his charge is political dynamite. Whereas Herzog's *The Enigma of Kaspar Hauser* (1974) was a sorrowing, darkly comic meditation on the pitfalls of 'civilisation' and the way education destroys man's essential innocence, Sehr's Kaspar is simply a disposable pawn in Machiavellian power games between and within German states. So complex are these strategies, and so difficult is it to keep up with the narrative, that it's hard to care very much about Kaspar. A polished drama, but not much more than a rather arcane, even academic conspiracy hypothesis. GA

Kate & Leopold

(2001, US, 118 min)
d James Mangold. *p* Cathy Konrad. *sc* James Mangold, Steven Rogers. *ph* Stuart Dryburgh. *ed* David Brenner. *pd* Mark Friedberg. *m* Rolfe Kent. *cast* Meg Ryan, Hugh Jackman, Liev Schreiber, Breckin Meyer, Natasha Lyonne, Bradley Whitford, Paxton Whitehead, Spalding Gray, Philip Bosco.

●New York ad exec Kate (Ryan) is lovelorn; her last boyfriend, Stuart (Schreiber), was more interested in time travel than commitment. He inadvertently introduces her, however, to yummy Leopold (Jackman), a 19th century duke. She assumes Leo's delusional, but realises his brand of old world charm will work well on TV. It does, and together they impress her ruthless boss, who hints she may be promoted. But, disgusted by the hollow values of corporate life, Leopold begs her to return with him to the 1800s. This film wants to have its cake and gorge on it. Jackman's the product being promoted here. Bored with Mel Gibson? Missing Hugh Grant? Come on in. Ironically, what jeopardises the transaction is Ryan. Normally a by-word for formular fun, here she simply cannot make us believe Leopold is the answer to Kate's problems, always seeming on the verge of tears even when she's grinning. Or maybe director Mangold is stuck in *Girl, Interrupted* mode. CO'Su

Katia Ismaïlova (Podmoskovnye vechera)

(1994, Rus/Fr, 95 min)
d Valerii Todorovsky. *p* Igor Tolstunov, Marc Ruscart. *sc* Alla Krinitsyna, François Guérif, Cécile Vargaftig. *ph* Sergei Kozlov. *ed* Alla Strelnikova, Hélène Gargarin, Konstantin Charmadov. *pd* Aleksandr Osipov. *m* Leonid Desiatnikov. *cast* Vladimir Mashkov, Ingeborga Dapkounaite, Aleksandr Feklistov, Alisa Freindlikh, Natalia Shchukina.

●Adapted from Leskov's 1864 novella, this is a blend of idyll and murderous *film noir*. Set in present-day Russia, it centres on Katia (Dapkounaite), a mousy housewife reluctantly typing up the the latest novel by her famous mother-in-law Irina. During a visit to the family's country house, Katia's husband Mitia abandons the women to go on a business trip, leaving his wife prey to Sergei (Mashkov), a carpenter who's been restoring the house for Irina. The affair is discovered by the tyrannical author, who insists it cease. Katia, however, has other ideas. Traditionally an icon of unbridled passion, Katia is here a muted, impassive heroine. While her later actions betoken a deep-felt desire to transform her life, her resentment against mother-in-law and husband and her longing for Sergei is barely voiced – less a consequence of Dapkounaite's sturdy performance than of the script, which vacillates between subtle allusion, unembroidered simplicity and enigmatic ellipsis. The director appears to be saying that the heated emotions of the literary classics no longer suit the modern world (or cinema) – despite plot twists that echo moments from such steamy adulterous suspensers as *The Postman Always Rings Twice* and even *Blood Simple*. Very different from most Russian movies released in Britain, this is elegant, intelligent and intriguing, even if the cool tone and languorous pace forestall deeper involvement. GA

Katinka (Ved Vejen)

(1988, Den/Swe, 96 min)
d Max von Sydow. *p* Bo Christensen. *sc* Klaus Rifbjerg. *ph* Sven Nykvist. *ed* Janus Billeskov Jansen. *ad* Peter Høimark. *m* Georg Riedel. *cast* Tammi Øst, Ole Ernst, Kurt Ravn, Erik Paaske, Tine Miehe-Renard, Ghita Nørby.

●Von Sydow's directorial debut, an adaptation of a Herman Bang story, is as unfashionably reserved in its portrait of a woman stifled by a loveless marriage as Dreyer's *Gertrud*. Nothing happens in this triangle between Katinka (Ost), her insensitive station-master husband (Ernst), and the romantic newcomer (Ravn), but the depths of feeling are subtly pastelled in. Sven Nykvist's camera of feeling conjures up an idyllic turn-of-the-century small town atmosphere for the heroine to dream her life away in. Pressed flowers. BC

Katok i Skrypka (Roller and Violin/The Steamroller and the Violin)

(1961, USSR, 46 min)
d Andrei Tarkovsky. *sc* Andrei Konchalovsky, Andrei Tarkovsky. *ph* Vadim Yusov. *ed* L Buruzovoi. *pd* S Agoyan. *m* Vyacheslav Ovchinnikov. *cast* Igor Fomchenko, V Zamansky, N Arkhangelskaya, Marina Adzhubei.

●Tarkovsky's graduation project at the VGIK film school in Moscow offers a key to all the later 'mature' work: it's his clearest statement of frustrated longing for a perfect union with an idealised father-figure. Six-year-old Sasha (Fomchenko) lives with his domineering, unsympathetic mother (Adzhuberi), and studies the violin under an even more domineering and even less sympathetic female music teacher. His idealised father-figure is Sergei (Zamansky), a butch-but-sensitive roadmender, who saves him from being bullied, gives him bread, milk and lessons in self-confidence and respect, and promises to take him to the movies – to see *Chapayev*, the venerable romantic portrait of a Communist hero. The 'romance' between man and boy receives the benediction of a prototypical Tarkovskian rainstorm, incidentally yielding a charming cine-poem about drops of water and puddles. Some ten years later, Tarkovsky reworked all of this much more elaborately in *Solaris*. TR

Katzelmacher

(1969, WGer, 88 min, b/w)
d/sc Rainer Werner Fassbinder. *ph* Dietrich Lohmann. *ed* Franz Walsch [Rainer Werner Fassbinder]. *pd* Rainer Werner Fassbinder. *m* Peer Raben. *cast* Hanna Schygulla, Lilith Ungerer, Elga Sorbas, Doris Mattes, Rainer Werner Fassbinder, Rudolf Waldemar Brem, Harry Baer, Peter Moland, Irm Hermann.

●Fear and loathing in the mean streets of suburban Munich, where all behaviour obeys the basest and most basic of drives, and fleeting allegiances form and re-form in almost mathematically abstract permutations until disrupted by the advent of an immigrant Greek worker (played by Fassbinder himself; the title is a Bavarian slang term for a gastarbeiter, implying tomcatting sexual proclivities) who becomes the target for xenophobic violence. Fassbinder's sub-Godardian gangster film début, *Love is Colder than Death*, was dismissed as derivative and dilettanté-ish; this second feature, based on his own *anti-teater* play, won immediate acclaim. It still seems remarkable, mainly for Fassbinder's distinctive, highly stylised dialogue and minimalist *mise-en-scène* that transfigures a cinema of poverty into bleakly triumphant rites of despair. SJo

Kawashima Yoshiko (Chuandao Fangzi/aka The Last Princess of Manchuria)

(1990, HK, 111 min)
d Eddie Fong. *p* Anthony Chow, Eric Tsang. *sc* Li Pak Wah. cast Anita Mui, Andy Lau, Patrick Tse, Derek Yee.

●Writer/director Fong denies that he set out to parody *The Last Emperor*, but his excellent film certainly kicks the shit out of Bertolucci. It gives Anita Mui her best role since *Rouge* as the eponymous bisexual spy who sailed through some 25 years of Sino-Japanese tension and war alternately claiming Chinese and Japanese nationality and (according to Fong) covertly intervening in the politics of both sides. The film mocks all the received pieties about modern Chinese history (even the Nanking Massacre is presented in kitsch terms), subordinating them to the high-camp melodrama of Yoshiko's torrid love affairs. Variant endings exist: the one most often seen has Yoshiko executed by firing squad in 1948, but the best one shows her with her pet monkey on her shoulder in present day Tokyo, ageless and immortal. TR

Kazablan

(1973, Isr, 114 min)
d/p Menahem Golan. *sc* Menahem Golan, Haim Hefer. *ph* David Gurfinkel. *ed* Dov Hoenig. *ad* Shlomo Zafrir. *m* Dov Seltzer. *cast* Yehoram Gaon, Arie Elias, Efrat Lavie, Yehudah Efroni, Joseph Graber.

●An Israeli musical directed by the dreaded Menahem Golan that manages to come off as an uncomfortable cross between *Jesus Christ Superstar, Fiddler on the Roof* and *West Side Story*. Probably the most interesting aspect of the film is the acknowledgment it makes of divisions in Israeli society, notably that between the 'white' or European Jews and the 'black' or non-European Jews. The analysis is somewhat blunted by making the outcast gang-leader a forgotten war hero (although it does make a valid point in a sense). The songs sound familiar. The dance routines are dismally repetitive. VG

Kaza-hana

(2000, Jap, 116 min)
d Shinji Somai. *p* Masa-aki Wakasugi. *sc* Raimi Mori. *ph* Hiroshi Machida. *ed* Yoshiyuki Okuhara. *pd* Tomio Ogawa. *m* Otomo Yoshihide. *cast* Kyoko Koizumi, Tadanobu Asano, Shingo Tsurumi, Yoshiko Kagawa, Choei Takahashi.

●Another turgid exercise in up-market soap from Somai, who enjoys an inexplicably high critical reputation in Japan. This one gives Kyoko 'Kyon-Kyon' Koizumi (20 years earlier Japan's top 'idol') her first adult role as a burnt-out hooker and bar hostess who heads home to Hokkaido to see her daughter, raised by her mother and stepfather. Her accidental companion on the trip is an alcoholic civil servant (Asano making yet another bad career choice), who has just been suspended from work for shoplifting while on a drunken binge. Both are clearly heading for early graves, but Somai piles on the agony with interminable driving sequences, tortured flashbacks and soap-style scenes of heartbreak. The ironic title refers to dancing snowflakes, held to be harbingers of spring. TR

Kedma

(2002, Isr, 100 min)
d/p Amos Gitai. *sc* Amos Gitai, Marie-José Sanselme. *ph* Yorgos Arvanitis. *ed* Kobi Netanel. *pd* Eitan Levi. *m* David Darling, Manfred Eicher. *cast* Andrei Kashkar, Helena Yaralova, Yussef Abu Warda, Moni Moshonov, Juliano Merr, Menachem Lang, Sandy Bar, Tomer Ruso.

●Set in May 1948, this deals with the first hours in Palestine of a platoon of Holocaust survivors fighting to estabish the Zionist state of Israel. Coming, however, after the triumphs of Gitai's *Kadosh* and *Kippur*, it proves disappointingly uneven. There are fine scenes, of course, blessed with the director's trademark long takes (here shot with typical elegance by Angelopoulos regular Yorgos Arvanitis), but too often the precise details of the narrative remain unclear, while the over-explicit final mad rant (following a very fine scene in which the protagonist is an Arab) merely undermines much of what has gone before. And, incidentally, the characterisation of the British troops ('you guys!') is way off. GA

Keep, The

(1983, US, 96 min)
d Michael Mann. *p* Gene Kirkwood, Howard W Koch Jr. *sc* Michael Mann. *ph* Alex Thomson. *ed* Dov Hoenig, Pamela Power. *pd* John Box. *m* Tangerine Dream. *cast* Scott Glenn, Alberta Watson, Jürgen Prochnow, Robert Prosky, Gabriel Byrne, Ian McKellen, Morgan Sheppard.
●There is a secret buried deep within the walls of the keep, an ancient mystic shrine in the Carpathian Alps of Romania. It is an Evil so long contained that it has since been forgotten. It is an Evil more vile than the World War II German troops who have unwittingly released it, having violated the mausoleum. But there is a Man, a Man who has risen from a forgotten age who can stop the growing demon. First he must sleep with the beautiful Eva Cuza (evil demons take time to reach maturation), which he proceeds to do with infinitely more finesse than the final confrontation with the awakened Evil. Mann's film was first buried in video distribution after it flopped in the US (by that time Mann was already involved in the highly successful television series *Miami Vice*). Resurrected for cinema screening, it proves to be eerie, chilling, at times engaging. But Mann's attempt to superimpose an analysis of the emotional attraction of Fascism simply doesn't work within the Heavy Metal magazine cartoon format. SGo

Keep Cool (You Hua Hao Hao Shuo)

(1997, China, 95 min)
d Zhang Yimou. *p* Wang Qipeng. *sc* Shu Ping. *ph* Lu Yue. *ed* Du Yuan. *ad* Cao Jiuping. *m* Zang Tianshuo. *cast* Jiang Wen, Li Baotian, Qu Ying, Ge You, Zhang Yimou.
●Cut off from foreign financing by China's new Film Regulations, Zhang did the smart thing by making this low budget quickie primarily for domestic release. It's his first contemporary urban movie, his first comedy and his first without Gong Li. The great Jiang Wen plays a bookseller who won't accept that his hip young girlfriend has left him for someone richer. The first half details his attempts to confront her (he can't remember which of a thousand identical apartments she lives in); the second his wait with murderous intent in a restaurant, refusing to be pacified by a stranger whose new laptop he has broken. With ultra-mobile handheld camerawork and no pre-blocking of the scenes, Zhang achieves a spontaneity new in his work. But it's Jiang's performance which makes the film astonishing and funny. TR

Keeper, The

(1995, US, 90 min)
d Joe Brewster. *p* Jordi Torrent, Joe Brewster. *sc* Joe Brewster. *ph* Igor Sunara. *ed* Tom McArdle. *pd* Flavia Galuppo. *m* John Petersen. *cast* Giancarlo Esposito, Isaach de Bankolé, Regina Taylor, Ron Brice, OL Duke, Alvaleta Guess, Samuel E Wright, Arthur French.
●Esposito's a warder at a detention centre. A liberal studying law, he treats the prisoners with respect; his colleagues regard them as scum. When he helps bail out a Haitian baker (de Bankolé) accused of rape, whom he believes innocent, he forgets that the man will have difficulties finding a job or somewhere to live. When the man turns up on his doorstep, the warder persuades his wife (Taylor) to let him stay in their house, with alarming consequences. Fine cast, authentic early scenes, but melodrama eventually swamps the proceedings. GA

Keeper of the Flame

(1942, US, 100 min, b/w)
d George Cukor. *p* Victor Saville. *sc* Donald Ogden Stewart. *ph* William Daniels. *ed* James E Newcom. *ad* Cedric Gibbons, Lyle Wheeler. *m* Bronislau Kaper. *cast* Spencer Tracy, Katharine Hepburn, Richard Whorf, Margaret Wycherly, Forrest Tucker, Howard da Silva.
●Bizarre political melodrama which has its eye firmly glued on *Citizen Kane* as Tracy's reporter arrives at another Xanadu, gleans another mess of information for his biography of a Great American Citizen who has died in mysterious circumstances, and learns – having fallen for the widow (Hepburn) whose reticence he misinterprets – that his hero had feet of Fascist clay. It works well if rather stiffly for a while, with excellent performances (Wycherly and da Silva are outstanding), but blows up into absurd histrionics and naive propaganda. TM

Keepers, The

see Tête contre les Murs, La

Keeping the Faith

(2000, US, 129 min)
d Edward Norton. *p* Hawk Koch, Edward Norton, Stuart Blumberg. *sc* Stuart Blumberg. *ph* Anastas Michos. *ed* Malcolm Campbell. *pd* Wynn Thomas. *m* Elmer Bernstein. *cast* Ben Stiller, Edward Norton, Jenna Elfman, Anne Bancroft, Eli Wallach, Ron Rifkin, Milos Forman, Holland Taylor, Lisa Edelstein.
●Norton's directorial debut feature (discounting his re-cut of *American History X*) is a romantic triangle dating movie as confected, and nearly as wholesome, as a '50s Universal bedroom farce, but lacking the confidence and zest. The script sandwiches svelte exec Anna (Elfman) between two former girlhood chums, Jake (Stiller) and Brian (Norton), after her return to Manhattan from a contrived 10 years in California. In the interim, Jake's become a rabbi, and Brian a priest. Can Jake tell Rabbi Lewis (Wallach) he's to marry a shiksa? Can celibate Brian declare his heart and break Jake's? Norton sets this up with intriguing effect, playing the listener as Stiller carries off all the funny lines, but drops the ball halfway, losing the humour among a string of confessionals. Elfman (the star of TV's *Dharma and Greg*) has the hardest task, to humanise, sweeten and give credibility to a character who's a paragon of wealth and beauty. All credit to her, she manages it pretty well, though her poise can sometimes seem like disengagement. WH

Keep It Quiet

see Pas de Scandale

Keep It Up, Jack!

(1973, GB, 87 min)
d Derek Ford. *p* Michael L Green. *sc* Derek Ford, Alan Selwyn. *ph* Geoffrey Glover. *ed* Patrick Foster. *ad* Bernard Sarron. *m* Terry Warr. *cast* Mark Jones, Sue Longhurst, Maggi Burton, Paul Whitsun-Jones, Frank Thornton, Queenie Watts.
●Screamingly unfunny farce in which a tenth-rate seaside quick-change artist inherits a brothel, and finds himself for some unfathomable reason acting first the part of the recently expired madam, and then that of her clients. Hence the title gag, such as it is. If you miss it the first time round, there's a chorus of voices off and even a theme song to remind you. What with performers who enunciate like rejects from a RADA elocution course, a script that must have taken all of a weekend to elaborate, a handful of arbitrary flesh shots, and a relentlessly one-note sense of humour (off-key, of course), it is hardly hyperbolic to see *Keep It Up, Jack!* as defining a whole new low in British comedy. VG

Keep the Aspidistra Flying (aka A Merry War)

(1997, GB, 101 min)
d Robert Bierman. *p* Peter Shaw. *sc* Alan Plater. *ph* Giles Nuttgens. *ed* Bill Wright. *pd* Sarah Greenwood. *m* Mike Batt. *cast* Richard E Grant, Helena Bonham Carter, Julian Wadham, Jim Carter, Harriet Walter, Lesley Vicerage, Liz Smith, Barbara Leigh Hunt, Bill Wallis.
●This adaptation of Orwell's '30s satire on the advertising game is a dull, timid movie, all romantic flurry, tarted-up design and chocolate box London location photography. Grant seems to fit the bill, looks and character-wise, as Gordon Comstock, the frustrated copywriter at New Albion Publicity who jacks it all in for the life of a bohemian writer in the Lambeth slums. There's a period angularity about his face and body, and his mannerisms suggest the requisite vanity and naivety. And Bonham Carter, the smart side of prim in three-quarter-length velvet coats and idiosyncratic millinery, is controlled exasperation itself as the designer who would be his bride. But Bierman, working from an uninspired script by Alan Plater, finds no way to engage with, or make relevant, the satire, and concentrates instead on routine romantic comedy. The project thus emasculated, all that remains is archaic dalliance, coy sex, tea shop chatter and laughable class caricature. Worse, the language remains flat, and – unintentionally or not – it's a reactionary reading. WH

Keiner Liebt Mich (Nobody Loves Me)

(1995, Ger, 104 min)
d Doris Dörrie. *p* Gerd Huber, Renate Seefeldt. *sc* Doris Dörrie. *ph* Helge Weindler. *ed* Inez Regnier. *pd* Claus Kottmann. *m* Niki Reiser. *cast* Maria Schrader, Pierre Sanoussi-Bliss, Michael von Au, Elisabeth Trissenaar, Peggy Parnass, Ingo Naujoks.
●Yet another German 'comedy' that lives down to the stereotype, this centres on 29-year-old, death-obsessed Fanny Fink (Schrader), who despairs of ever meeting a man; encouraged by a gay African 'psychic' who lives in the same tenement block, she tries to get it on with her new landlord, but things go awry. Dörrie's predictable plotline, derived from the unappealing premise that her heroine's happiness depends on the company of men, relies excessively on supposedly weird and wonderful characters. Actually, it's hard to care about them, especially as it's also hard to believe Schrader – intelligent, pretty, vivacious – would be in this predicament anyway. GA

Këita! The Voice of the Griot (Këita! L'Héritage du Griot)

(1994, Fr/Burkina Faso, 94 min)
d/sc Dani Kouyaté. *ph* Robert Millie. *ed* Zoë Dourouchoux. *ad* Catherine Franck. *m* Sotigui Kouyaté. *cast* Sotigui Kouyaté, Hamed Dicko, Abdoulaye Komboudri,Seydou Boro.
●This charming and extremely direct first feature tells the story of a 13-year-old boy's introduction to the tales and myths of his 'forgotten ancestors', when a village griot (folk teacher), 'on a mission', sets up his hammock in the garden of the boy's middle-class city home. The simplicity with which the director films both the problems that this precipitates – the boy skips school, partly because the Western view of history seems far less relevant and engrossing than the old man's story – and the flashbacks to the magical past, pays strong dividends. Acted with appealing grace and dignity, the film is finely shot by Robert Millie and has a gentle unobtrusive score by Sotigui Kouyaté. WH

Kelly's Heroes

(1970, US/Yugo, 145 min)
d Brian G Hutton. *p* Gabriel Katzka, Sidney Beckerman. *sc* Troy Kennedy Martin. *ph* Gabriel Figueroa. *ed* John Jympson. *ad* Jonathan Barry. *m* Lalo Schifrin. *cast* Clint Eastwood, Telly Savalas, Donald Sutherland, Don Rickles, Carroll O'Connor, Stuart Margolin, Harry Dean Stanton.
●A truly silly formula World War II adventure film – lots of familiar faces, lots of explosions, and the odd 'meaningful' remark – in which Eastwood's disreputable platoon (and assorted buddies) take a time out of war to rob a bank in occupied France containing 14,000 bars of German gold. Interesting only in so far as it reveals Eastwood's nonchalant attitude to the blockbuster. Unlike Sutherland, who tries desperately to act his way out of Troy Kennedy Martin's laboured script, Eastwood just strolls through the film, along the way creating its few cinematic moments. PH

Kennel Murder Case, The

(1933, US, 73 min, b/w)
d Michael Curtiz. *sc* Robert N Lee, Peter Milne. *ph* William Reese. *ed* Harold McLernon. *ad* Jack Okey. *m* Leo Forbstein. *cast* William Powell, Mary Astor, Eugene Pallette, Ralph Morgan, Helen Vinson, Jack LaRue, Robert Barrat.
●Probably the best of all the Philo Vance mysteries (from the series by SS van Dine), with Powell as the super-suave private eye investigating a suicide that turns out to be murder. The plot is fairly preposterous, but Powell brings just

enough credibility to the task to make the film at once ingenious and entertaining. In all there were a dozen Philo Vance novels, and many more films featuring the character (*The Kennel Murder Case* was remade only seven years later as Calling Philo Vance), but this one is vintage. MA

Kenoma

(1998, Braz, 110 min)
d Eliane Caffé. *p* Alain Fresnot. *sc* Eliane Caffé, Luiz Alberto de Abreu. *ph* Hugo Kovensky. *ed* Idê Lacreta. *pd* Clovis Bueno. *m* Grupo Uakti. *cast* José Dumont, Enrique Diaz, Jonas Bloch, Mariana Lima, Matheus Nachtergaele, Eliana Carneiro.

●On the evidence of this parable on the contradictory nature of human aspiration, there's as rich a tradition of obsessive, idiosyncratic behaviour in Brazil as in Borges' Argentina. A handsome young drifter (Diaz, moody) turns up in the flaky frontier town of Kenoma ('the end of the world,' somebody at the bar volunteers). Enticed by the presence of an attractive daughter (Lima, thoughtful/dutiful), he helps madcap inventor Lineu (Dumont, eyeball-popping) with the Heath Robinson-style Perpetual Motion Machine he's been manufacturing in the barn of the local landowner these last 20 years. Director Caffé's first feature (co-written with poet Luiz Alberto de Abreu) is delicately scored and often looks beautiful, but its tragic arc seems more predictable than predestined, likewise the performances often tip over from the passionate to the mannered. WH

Kentuckian, The

(1955, US, 104 min)
d Burt Lancaster. *p* Harold Hecht. *sc* AB Guthrie Jr. *ph* Ernest Laszlo. *ed* William B Murphy. *ad* Ted Haworth. *m* Bernard Herrmann. *cast* Burt Lancaster, Dianne Foster, Diana Lynn, Ronald MacDonald, Walter Matthau, John Carradine, John McIntire, Una Merkel.

●Lancaster's only film as a director is a slow-moving, lack-lustre Western in which he plays a Kentucky frontiersman who, travelling to Texas with his young son to make a new start, becomes involved with two women and a family feud. Matthau makes an impressively villainous debut (though the scene in which he bullwhips the unarmed Lancaster tends to be censor-trimmed), and Carradine is good value as a garrulous doctor; but in general the direction tends to get bogged down in not very interesting characters and relationships while neglecting to deliver the action. TM

Kentucky

(1938, US, 96 min)
d David Butler. *p* Gene Markey. *sc* Lamar Trotti, John Tainto Foote. *ph* Ernest Palmer, Ray Rennahan. *ed* Irene Morra. *ad* Bernard Herzbrun. *m* Louis Silvers. *cast* Loretta Young, Richard Greene, Karen Morley, Moroni Olsen, Walter Brennan, Douglass Dumbrille.

●*Romeo and Juliet* meets the Kentucky Derby in this cheesy tale of hoss breedin' folk. Sweet-hearts Greene and Young come from families who've been feuding since the Civil War, but he runs off, assumes a false identity and prepares his beloved's mount for victory in the big race. It's not exactly unpredictable, but Ernest Palmer and Ray Rennahan's colour camerawork displays the possibilities of the then experimental Technicolor process a year before the milestones of *Gone With the Wind* and *The Wizard of Oz*. TJ

Kentucky Fried Movie, The

(1977, US, 90 min)
d John Landis. *p* Robert K Weiss. *sc* David Zucker, Jim Abrahams, Jerry Zucker. *ph* Stephen M Katz. *ed* George Folsey Jr. *ad* Rick Harvel. *m* Igo Kantor. *cast* David Zucker, George Lazenby, Donald Sutherland, Henry Gibson, Jerry Zucker, Evan Kim, Master Bong Soo Han, Bill Bixby, Tony Dow, Boni Enten.

●A simple case of the media munchies: a post Groove Tube variety pack offering some twenty different send-ups of American movies, TV and commercials. Sticking quite happily to the level of parody, it's full of energy, good nature, and the gross-out humour of fairly obvious targets (the tits and bums of a sexploitation trailer; the festering stiff of a TV charity appeal for the dead). The central sketch is an excellent spoof of *Enter the Dragon*. Great fun for an undemanding night out. HM

Kermesse Héroique, La (Carnival in Flanders)

(1935, Fr, 115 min, b/w)
d Jacques Feyder. *sc* Charles Spaak, Jacques Feyder. *ph* Harry Stradling, Louis Page, André Thomas. *ed* Jacques Brillouin. *ad* Lazare Meerson, Alexandre Trauner, Georges Wakhévitch. *m* Louis Beydts. *cast* Françoise Rosay, Louis Jouvet, Jean Murat, Alerme, Micheline Cheirel, Lyne Clévers, Alfred Adam.

●A minor gem of pre-war French cinema, about a small bourgeois town invaded by Spanish soldiers in early 17th-century Flanders. Feyder declared his intention of bringing to life Flemish painting, an end he achieves nearly perfectly through a combination of masterly use of studio sets and costumes and Harry Stradling's gorgeous photography. Faced by the cowardly reaction of their burgher husbands, the women of the town decide to save themselves by preparing a lavish welcoming feast for the bloodthirsty Spaniards. The film is distinctly ambiguous about which appetites are being satisfied and how, and about the politics of occupation – is it advocating collaboration or subversion? For this reason, Feyder found it wise to exile himself from Nazi-occupied France a few years later. Either way, though, it remains a distinctly amiable sex comedy. RM

Kerouac

(1984, US, 72 min)
d/p John Antonelli. *sc* John Tytell, Frank Cervarich. *cast* Jack Coulter, David Andrews, Jonah Pearson, Allen Ginsberg, Lawrence Ferlinghetti, Gregory Corso, Neal Cassady.

●This feature length documentary, narrated by Peter Coyote, reminds us that Kerouac wasn't just a handsome beatnik drifter who hung out with Burroughs and Ginsberg, and travelled across America striking moody poses. He was also a formidably talented writer. (One pundit, his biographer Ann Charters, rates him alongside Hemingway, Wolfe and Whitman.) The story is dispiriting – five unpublished novels before *On the Road* catapulted him on to the chat show circuit, then decline to a premature, drunken death at age 49. Antonelli has assembled a gallery of old rogues (Corso, Burroughs, Ferlinghetti) to reminisce about their pal Jack. He's also dug up archive footage of Neal Cassady, 'the flaming comet from the west' who inspired much of Kerouac's best work. Almost inevitably, the dramatic reconstructions of the writer's life seem dreary by comparison. GM

Kes

(1969, GB, 113 min)
d Kenneth Loach. *p* Tony Garnett. *sc* Barry Hines, Kenneth Loach, Tony Garnett. *ph* Chris Menges. *ed* Roy Watts. *ad* Bill McCrow. *m* John Cameron. *cast* David Bradley, Lynne Perrie, Freddie Fletcher, Colin Welland, Brian Glover, Bob Bowes, Robert Naylor.

●Barry Hines' novel, about a young schoolboy in Barnsley who attempts to escape the tedium and meaninglessness of his uninviting working-class future by caring for and training a kestrel that he finds, is never allowed to fall into undue sentimentality by Loach's low-key direction (his first feature). Rather than a tale of a boy and his pet, the film is a lucid and moving examination of the narrow options open to people without money, family stability and support, or education. Terrific performances, illuminated by Chris Menges' naturalistic but often evocative photography. GA

Kevin & Perry Go Large

(2000, GB/US, 83 min)
d Ed Bye. *p* Peter Bennett-Jones, Jolyon Symonds, Harry Enfield. *sc* Harry Enfield, David Cummings. *ph* Alan Almond. *ed* Mark Wybourn. *pd* Tom Brown. *cast* Harry Enfield, Kathy Burke, Rhys Ifans, Laura Fraser, James Fleet, Louisa Rix, Tabitha Wady, Paul Whitehouse, Natasha Little, Ken Cranham, Patsy Byrne.

●The modest dimensions of a TV sketch no longer able to contain their raging hormones, Kevin and Perry graduate to the kind of exposure any self-respecting, self-obsessed teenage boy would regard as his birthright: a big screen outing chocka with drugs, women and music. Ibiza it is, then, for the petulant Kevin Patterson (Enfield), his monosyllabic chum Perry (Burke) and, er, Kevin's mum and dad. Inevitably, mishap after mishap befall the pair's attempts to stage their own Balearic summer of love; a chance meeting with top DJ 'Eyeball' Paul (Ifans) reveals the seedier side of the Mediterranean idyll, and the chums are left chasing the sole two women on the island. As proven from Morecambe and Wise to *Saturday Night Live*, what works in a three minute skit often falls flat in a 90 minute feature. So it goes with Enfield's admittedly memorable creations. How much slack you're prepared to cut this sub-Farrelly Brothers gross out comedy probably depends on your fondness for the televised original. MHi

Key, The

(1958, GB, 134 min, b/w)
d Carol Reed. *p/sc* Carl Foreman. *ph* Oswald Morris. *ed* Bert Bates. *pd* Wilfrid Shingleton. *m* Malcolm Arnold. *cast* Sophia Loren, Trevor Howard, William Holden, Kieron Moore, Oscar Homolka, Carl Möhner. Bernard Lee, Beatrix Lehmann, Noel Purcell, Bryan Forbes, Irene Handl.

●Extraordinary, unwieldy World War II naval epic which fails to deliver as much as it promises, but promises so much as to be worth while none the less. Swiss waif Loren shelters and succours a succession of war-weary tugboat captains who are never quite sure whether she's a goddess or a whore, an island of love in the cold, cruel sea or a siren leading them on to their doom. Loren is excellent, and the film plays interestingly with the idea of a woman's mystery being the product of male prejudice and fear. But the dictates of the international box-office – lots of naval manoeuvres and a turgidly wooden American hero – result in a fascinatingly enigmatic melodrama being buried within a stolidly conventional war film. RMy

Keyhole, The (Noeglehullet)

(1974, Den, 88 min)
d Gerhard Poulsen [Paul Gerber]. *p* Gunnar Kryger. *sc* Gerhard Poulsen. *ph* Dirk Brüel. *ed* Lizzi Weischenfeldt, Knud Hauge. *cast* Marie Ekorre, Torben Larsen, Bent Warburg, Max Horn, Pia Larsen, Lene Andersen.

●A businessman in the opening minutes has the wonderful idea of making the first porno film to be completely realistic and believable – a notion which raised a few sniggers in the mackintoshed rows of the cinema where this epic was being screened. Nothing else in the movie, however, seemed to raise anything, although the leading couple (an aspiring movie-maker and the businessman's daughter) display a little more vivacity than one expects. According to Variety, Marie Ekorre previously appeared in the centre pages of *Penthouse*. She must have been relieved to get away from the staples. GB

Key Largo

(1948, US, 101 min, b/w)
d John Huston. *p* Jerry Wald. *sc* Richard Brooks, John Huston. *ph* Karl Freund. *ed* Rudi Fehr. *ad* Leo K Kuter. *m* Max Steiner. *cast* Humphrey Bogart, Edward G Robinson, Lauren Bacall, Lionel Barrymore, Claire Trevor, Thomas Gomez, Dan Seymour, Monte Blue.

●Reworking of a Maxwell Anderson play about a gangster under threat of deportation who holes up with his henchmen in a semi-derelict hotel on an island off Florida, holding the occupants at gunpoint and remaining blind to the menace posed by a coming hurricane. The debt to *The Petrified Forest* is obvious, but instead of wallowing in world-weary pseudo-philosophy, *Key Largo* has altogether sharper things to say about post-war disillusionment, corruption in politics, and the fact that the old freebooting ways of the gangster were about to change into something more sinisterly complex. Huston skilfully breaks up the action (basically one set and one continuous scene), working subtle variations on his groupings with the aid of superb deep-focus camera-work by Karl Freund. And although the characters are basically stereotypes, they are lent the gift of life by a superlative cast: Robinson as the truculent Little Caesar, Bogart as an embittered ex-Army officer, Bacall as the innocent who loves him, and above all Trevor as the gangster's disillusioned, drink-sodden moll. TM

Keys to Tulsa

(1996, US, 114 min)
d Leslie Greif. *p* Leslie Greif, Harley Peyton. *sc* Harley Peyton. *ph* Robert Fraisse. *ed* Eric L Beason, Louis F Cioffi, Michael R Miller. *pd*

Derek R Hill. *m* Stephen Endelman. *cast* Eric Stoltz, Cameron Diaz, Randy Graff, Mary Tyler Moore, James Coburn, Deborah Kara Unger, Michael Rooker, Peter Strauss, James Spader, Joanna Going.

● Tulsa, Oklahoma, a seedy sweat-joint propped up on a little oil – Jim Thompson would know his way around here. Stoltz is a reporter, not fundamentally bad, just weak and in with the wrong crowd, who gets ever busier wallowing in trouble. His ex (Unger), a sometime femme fatale, has started batting eyelids at him again. Her brother and Stoltz's old buddy (Rooker) likes to run around drunk waving guns in the air. Her lowrent husband (Spader) looks like an Elvis impersonator in black and wants Stoltz in on a plan to blackmail the local oilman's son for the murder of a black prostitute. Meanwhile his mum (Moore) is repossessing her offspring's home. Spader and Unger make their mark, but the film's initial possibilities all close down long before the finish. Harley Peyton's screenplay (from a novel by Brian Fair Berkey) is weak on plot and motivation, and the finale – side-lining characters at its own convenience (signs of a last minute change?) – comes as a considerable anti-climax. NB

Khartoum

(1966, GB, 128 min)
d Basil Dearden. *p* Julian Blaustein. *sc* Robert Ardrey. *ph* Ted Scaife. *ed* Fergus McDonell. *ad* John Howell. *m* Frank Cordell. *cast* Charlton Heston, Laurence Olivier, Richard Johnson, Ralph Richardson, Alexander Knox, Johnny Sekka, Nigel Green, Michael Hordern, Zia Mohyeddin, Hugh Williams.

● A massive all-star cast and a huge budget help to make the more vacuous moments of this epic comparatively painless. It is scripted with a ponderous attention to detail by the notorious pseudo-zoologist Robert Ardrey (author of *The Territorial Imperative*), but it has some very heavyweight performances, with Heston as General Gordon and Olivier as his bloodthirsty opponent the Mahdi (the face-to-face confrontation between the two is entirely fictitious). There's also Richardson as Gladstone, Nigel Green as General Wolseley, and Michael Hordern as Lord Granville, so despite inadequacies in both direction and screenwriting, anyone interested in the period will probably find quite a lot to enjoy. DP

Khroustaliov, ma voiture!

see Khrustalyov, My Car!

Khrustalyov, My Car! (Khrustalyov, mashinu!/ Khroustaliov, ma voiture!)

(1998, Fr/Rus, 137 min, b/w)
d Alexei Gherman. *p* Aleksandr Golutva, Armen Medvedev, Guy Séligmann. *sc* Alexei Gherman, Svetlana Karmalita, Pekka Lehto. *ph* Vladimir Ilyin. *ed* Irina Gorokhovskaya. *pd* Mikhail Gerasimov, Georgi Kropachyov, Vladimir Svetozarov. *m* Andrei Petrov. *cast* Yuri Tsurilo, Nina Ruslanova, Misha Dementyev, Jüri Jarvet.

● Being the line given to Beria, Stalin's soon to be doomed henchman, near the end of this crazy carnival of a movie. Gherman's first film since his 1982 masterpiece, *My Friend Ivan Lapshin*, similarly takes the form of a b/w reconstruction of times past – here the worlds surrounding drunken brain specialist General Glinsky, who's in charge of a Moscow hospital and master of a large domestic arena. Both circuses reflect the anarchic, anti-Semitic last days of Stalin's paranoid rule. Gherman's style refracts the everyday horror in a series of Fellini-esque, people-filled scenes, traced out with an extremely mobile camera, that is as likely to peek into a moving taxi window as glide around the demented faces of a brutal anal rape scene. The effect is relentless and overpowering, yet the film is often poetic in its blend of pathos, freneticism, surrealism and matter of factness. WH

Kichiku (Kichiku Dai Enkai)

(1997, Jap, 112 min)
d Kazuyoshi Kumakiri. *p* Kazuyoshi Kumakiri, Tomohiro Zaizen. *sc* Kazuyoshi Kumakiri. *ph* Kiyoaki Hashimoto. *ed* Kazuyoshi Kumakiri. *ad* Satoko Yasui. *m* Akainu. *cast* Sumiko Mikami, Shunsuke Sawada, Shigeru Bokuda, Toshiyuki Sugihara, Kentaro Ogiso.

● Made for around $20,000 as a graduation project at Osaka Art College, Kumakiri's 16mm feature shows the remnants of a left wing activist group holed up in an abandoned country house around 1970. Its leader has been arrested and imprisoned. When word comes that he has killed himself in jail, his girlfriend Masami (Mikami) goes berserk. Convinced that the group harbours a traitor, she goes on a killing spree, spreading psychosis all around. Much splatter ensues. As a comment on the student radicalism of the past, this is childish and risible. As a homemade rerun of *The Evil Dead* with inner demons replacing ancient Sumerians, it's not that bad. TR

Kickboxer

(1989, US, 103 min)
d Mark DiSalle, David Worth. *p* Mark DiSalle. *sc* Glenn Bruce. *ph* Jon Kranhouse. *ed* Wayne Wahrman. *pd* Shay Austin. *m* Paul Hertzog. *cast* Jean-Claude Van Damme, Dennis Alexio, Dennis Chan, Tong Po, Haskell Anderson, Rochelle Ashana, Steve Lee.

● Kickboxing is what it says it is: fisticuffs with feet. *Kickboxer* is an upfront title, too – don't see it for psychological complexity, social comment, acting, plot or humour; go, if you nust, just for kicks. There is a story. Two brothers: Eric (Alexio), all-American asshole, is KB champion stateside; Kurt (Van Damme) is the sensitive type – mother made him take ballet lessons before he learned karate! Big brother goes on an ego-trip to Bangkok 'to kick ass', gets pulped, and ends up paralysed to boot. Given the choice of caring for his bro' or beating the shit out of his opponent, Kurt goes into training with an oriental guru and emerges 'a man'. Further motivated by the knifing of his dog, raping of his girl, and kidnapping of Eric, Kurt is not about to turn the other cheek when he finally gets into the ring. In some movies these events might suggest a dehumanising process; here they are a route to mythification. It's the facistic tale of the making of a man, the 'white warrior', virgin avenger Van Damme. At least he ain't Chuck Norris. TCh

Kicked in the Head

(1997, US, 87 min)
d Matthew Harrison. *p* Barbara DeFina. *sc* Matthew Harrison, Kevin Corrigan. *ph* John Thomas, Howard Krupa. *ed* Michael Berenbaum. *pd* Kevin Thompson. *m* Stephen Endelman. *cast* Kevin Corrigan, Linda Fiorentino, Michael Rappaport, James Woods, Burt Young, Lili Taylor.

● A self-consciously 'cool' US indie comedy-drama from the director of the similarly derivative *Rhythm Thief*, in which Corrigan (who co-wrote it) – horribly indulged, self-indulgent and unsympathetic in his 'cute' confusion and adolescent desires – pursues his dopey spiritual quest for truth while dealing with a petty criminal uncle (Woods), manic entrepreneur buddy (Rappaport), devoted admirer (Taylor) and the object of his desire, an improbably yielding world-weary air hostess (Fiorentino). Too determinedly offbeat, and much too perniciously flip – gunfights are funny, men's immature sexual fantasies are to be indulged by mature women – for its own good. GA

Kick the Moon (Shilla ui Dalbam)

(2001, SKor, 119 min)
d Kim Sang-Jin. *p* Kang Woo-Suk, Gwon Byung-Gyun, Kim Mi-Hee. *sc* Park Jung-Woo. *ph* Jung Kwang-Suk. *ed* Ko Im-Pyo. *ad* Cho Sung-Won. *m* Sohn Moo-Hyun. *cast* Lee Sung-Jae, Cha Seung-Won, Kim Hae-Soo, Lee Jong-Soo, Lee Won-Jong.

● No less punch-drunk than Kim's previous *Attack the Gas Station!*, but noticeably broader in its anatomy of Korea's social contradictions, this comedy-drama centres on a romantic triangle: a tough-love schoolteacher whose inner bully is barely latent and a suave gangland enforcer with straight-but-not-too-narrow principles vying for the affections of a big sister/noodle-shop proprietor who could give the world lessons in pragmatism. Ten years ago, on a school trip to the historic town of Gyeongju, an epic rumble took place, led by alpha-male Choi Gi-Dong; the one kid who chickened out was nerdy Park Young-Joon. Cut to the present: Park (Lee Sung-Jae) is now a smooth Seoul gangster back in town to sort out a thuggish local crimelord, while Choi (Cha) is the local school's high-minded sports teacher. This distant descendant of *Angels with Dirty Faces* is a live-action cartoon that acts out a social conundrum and gives the moral compass a good spin. Ineffably hip. TR

Kid

(1990, US, 91 min)
d John Mark Robinson. *p* Robert L Levy, Peter Abrams, Natan Zahavi. *sc* Leslie Bohem. *ph* Robert Yeoman. *ed* Natan Zahavi. *pd* Sharon Seymour. *m* Tim Truman. *cast* C Thomas Howell, Sarah Trigger, Brian Austin Green, R Lee Ermey, Dale Dye, Michael Bowen, Damon Bowen.

● A fairly obvious attempt to refashion *High Plains Drifter* for youthful audiences, and for about two minutes it looks like it might be fun. It isn't. A mysterious stranger rides into town on a Greyhound. When a couple of local thugs give him strife, Kid leaves them begging for mercy. He checks into an empty motel. Then people start to die strange, perverse deaths. Kid? Uh-huh. Any film that devises a murder from a tennis ball and a can of bug spray may claim some ingenuity, but *Kid* just isn't trashy enough for its own good. Instead of nihilistic exploitation, we get half-cocked teen romance and a tiresomely sentimental vigilante. Howell is no substitute for Clint Eastwood, and love interest Trigger gives an unspeakably awful performance. Such relief as there is comes from R Lee Ermey as Sheriff Luke Clanton, who extends the nice range in invective he first shared with us in *Full Metal Jacket*. 'Seems to me' he cautions 'you stuck your dick in the wrong hole, Slick'. Quite. TCh

Kid, The

(1921, US, 5,300 ft, b/w)
d/p/sc Charles Chaplin. *ph* Roland Totheroh. *cast* Charles Chaplin, Edna Purviance, Jackie Coogan, Carl Miller, Tom Wilson, Henry Bergman, Lita Grey.

● 'A picture with a smile and perhaps a tear' says the opening title of Chaplin's first feature. There's no perhaps about it, what with Charlie struggling to nurture a cast-off illegitimate child in the face of unfeeling cops, doctors and orphanage workers. As always, Chaplin's opulent Victorian sentimentality is made palatable both by the amazing grace of his pantomimic skills and the balancing presence of harsh reality: the drama and the intertwining gags are played out amongst garbage, flophouses, a slum world depicted with Stroheim-like detail. As for the smiles, they're guaranteed too, although the gags don't coalesce into great sequences the way they do in later features. GB

Kid, The

see Disney's The Kid

Kid Blue

(1973, US, 100 min)
d James Frawley. *p* Marvin Schwartz. *sc* Edwin Shrake. *ph* Billy Williams. *ed* Stefan Arnsten. *pd* Joel Schiller. *m* Tim McIntire, John Rubinstein. *cast* Dennis Hopper, Warren Oates, Peter Boyle, Ben Johnson, Lee Purcell, Janice Rule, Ralph Waite, Clifton James.

● A magical Western, this companion piece to the marvellously eccentric *Steelyard Blues* features Dennis Hopper as a one-time minor desperado, turned would-be solid citizen and failing manfully. Calmly orchestrated by Frawley, who transforms even the smallest of parts into a rounded character and allows his story-line to develop out of those characters, *Kid Blue* never strains for meaning; even the web of references to the Greece of mythology is never too pointed. Oates, Boyle, Ben Johnson and Janice Rule offer solid support. PH

Kid Brother, The

(1927, US, 82 min, b/w)
d Ted Wilde, JA Howe. *sc* John Grey, Lex Neal, Howard Green. *ph* Walter Lundin. *ed* Allen McNeil. *ad* Liell K Vedder. *cast* Harold Lloyd, Jobyna Ralston, Walter James, Leo Willis, Olin Francis, Frank Lanning.

● Sources claim that half this film was directed by Lewis Milestone, but it's a Harold Lloyd movie through and through, and perhaps only slightly less of an achievement than *Safety Last*. Lloyd's penultimate silent movie, made for Paramount, *The Kid Brother* is not an urban story (which was his trademark) but a rural one, which brings it quite close to the world of Keaton. Lloyd, like

Keaton in *The Navigator*, is the living proof that every family tree must have its sap. Despised by his father and two strapping brothers, he proves he is a man after a girl catches his bespectacled eyes. The plot, of course, is just an excuse for a string of pratfalls, chases and derring-do, while the climax aboard an abandoned ship is a tour de force, and sometimes painfully violent. ATu

Kid for Two Farthings, A

(1955, GB, 96 min)
d/p Carol Reed. *sc* Wolf Mankowitz. *ph* Ted Scaife. *ed* Bert Bates. *ad* Wilfrid Shingleton. *m* Benjamin Frankel. *cast* Jonathan Ashmore, Celia Johnson, Diana Dors, David Kossoff, Sidney Tafler, Sidney James, Alfie Bass, Brenda de Banzie, Joe Robinson, Primo Carnera, Lou Jacobi, Sidney James, Irene Handl.
●Before he plunged headlong into 'international' film-making (never to be seen again), Carol Reed took this fanciful Wolf Mankowitz screenplay and tried to re-imagine Petticoat Lane in the poetic realist vein of Marcel Carné and Jacques Prévert. A young boy (Ashmore) mistakes a one-horned goat for a miraculous unicorn, and eagerly anticipates good fortune for his friends about the neighbourhood. A whimsical film, it may have seemed horribly patronising in the '50s; but from today's perspective, an intriguing, even adventurous attempt to resurrect a national cinema that had clearly lost its legs. TCh

Kid from Spain, The

(1932, US, 98 min, b/w)
d Leo McCarey. *sc* William Anthony McGuire, Bert Kalmar, Harry Ruby. *ph* Gregg Toland. *ed* Stuart Heisler. *ad* Richard Day. *songs* Bert Kalmar, Harry Ruby. *cast* Eddie Cantor, Lyda Roberti, Robert Young, Ruth Hall, John Miljan, Noah Beery, J Carrol Naish, Stanley Fields.
●Eddie Cantor's talent is for those of an antique taste, but this extravagant Goldwyn production has a few other things going for it, most notably a couple of blatant routines choreographed for the Goldwyn Girls by Busby Berkeley (the chorus line is said to include Lucille Ball, Jane Wyman, Betty Grable and Paulette Goddard, but you'll need sharp eyes to spot them). The plot has Cantor and his college buddy Young innocently caught up in a bank robbery and hiding out in Mexico, where Cantor is mistaken for a famous matador. No prizes for guessing where he ends up. TCh

Kid Galahad

(1937, US, 102 min, b/w)
d Michael Curtiz. *sc* Seton I Miller. *ph* Tony Gaudio. *ed* George Amy. *ad* Carl Jules Weyl. *m* Heinz Roemheld, Max Steiner. *cast* Edward G Robinson, Bette Davis, Humphrey Bogart, Wayne Morris, Jane Bryan, Harry Carey, Ben Welden, Veda Ann Borg.
●A none too subtle exposition of the now well-worn theme of corruption in the boxing-ring, with Robinson as the go-getting manager who finds himself a contender in the shape of a bellhop (Morris) who summarily knocks out the reigning heavyweight champion for insulting Robinson's mistress (Davis). It all boils up to a shoot-out between Robinson and racketeer Bogart when the former – having vengefully fixed a fight under the impression that Davis is cheating on him with Morris – suffers a change of heart. Actually, in one of those woozy subplots so beloved of Hollywood in the '30s, Davis has fallen for Morris all right, but he's making sheep's eyes at the innocent kid sister (Bryan) Robinson keeps in the background. Sleek direction and excellent performances keep it enjoyable. Remade in a circus setting (as *The Wagons Roll at Night*, 1941) and again as a dim Elvis Presley vehicle in 1962. TM

Kid Galahad

(1962, US, 96 min)
d Phil Karlson. *p* David Weisbart. *sc* William Fay. *ph* Burnett Guffey. *ad* Cary Odell. *m* Jeff Alexander. *songs* Fred Wise, Hal David, others. *cast* Elvis Presley, Gig Young, Lola Albright, Joan Blackman, Charles Bronson, Ned Glass, Michael Dante, Robert Emhardt.
●A musical remake of the 1937 Warner Bros boxing drama that starred Robinson, Bette Davis and Bogart. Gig Young is OK as the trainer, but the flabby Presley, recently demobbed from the army, looks as if he couldn't survive a round with Donald Duck. His songs aren't exactly knockouts either. ATu

Kid Glove Killer

(1942, US, 72 min, b/w)
d Fred Zinnemann. *p* Jack Chertok. *sc* Allen Rivkin, John C Higgins. *ph* Paul C Vogel. *ed* Ralph E Winters. *ad* Cedric Gibbons, Randall Duell. *m* David Snell. *cast* Van Heflin, Marsha Hunt, Lee Bowman, Samuel S Hinds, Cliff Clark, Eddie Quillan, John Litel, Robert Blake, Ava Gardner.
●Fred Zinnemann's feature debut, a neat, unpretentious and really rather enjoyable whodunit about the hunt for the killer of the town's crusading mayor. Obviously developed out of the MGM *Crime Does Not Pay* featurettes on which Zinnemann served his apprenticeship, it places the accent squarely – but not entirely seriously – on laboratory detection methods: among the gimmicks gleefully demonstrated by Heflin, as the dedicated forensic scientist, is a mini-dustette designed to collect evidence from human scalps. Likeably fresh performances, too, from Heflin, Hunt as his wisecracking assistant who despairs of his ever realising that she's a woman, and Bowman as the blandly suave killer. Ava Gardner has a tiny role as a waitress. TM

Kidnapped

(1971, GB, 107 min)
d Delbert Mann. *p* Frederick H Brogger. *sc* Jack Pulman. *ph* Paul Beeson. *ed* Peter Boita. *pd* Alex Vetchinsky. *m* Roy Budd. *cast* Michael Caine, Lawrence Douglas, Trevor Howard, Donald Pleasence, Jack Hawkins, Vivien Heilbron, Freddie Jones, Gordon Jackson, Peter Jeffrey.
●Umpteenth adaptation of Stevenson's adventure, set in the last days of the Jacobite rebellion, and you'd have thought they might have gotten it right by now. Instead, sluggish pacing and a meandering plot, that also takes in elements from *Catriona*, kill off interest early on. Caine's Alan Breck is somewhat softened in Jack Pulman's adaptation, and the ending of the tale revised so that Breck surrenders to the English for the murder of Mungo Campbell. The cast are decent, but not much more. Filmed in Panavision and angled at children. TJ

Kidnappers, The (aka The Little Kidnappers)

(1953, GB, 95 min, b/w)
d Philip Leacock. *p* Sergei Nolbandov, Leslie Parkyn. *sc* Neil Paterson. *ph* Eric Cross. *ed* John Trumper. *ad* Edward Carrick. *m* Bruce Montgomery. *cast* Duncan Macrae, Jean Anderson, Adrienne Corri, Theodore Bikel, Jon Whiteley, Vincent Winter.
●1904: two Scottish orphans are sent to live with their sternly Calvinist grandfather in Nova Scotia. Starved of affection, forbidden a pet dog, they appropriate a neighbour's baby and after gravely debating whether to name it Rover, they look after it most tenderly. After a flurry of melodrama, it all ends well. This children's classic (Neil Paterson adapting his own novella) is rather too self-consciously heart-warming, and it's hard to read the setting as Nova Scotia when the look is so Pinewood-esque. But cutting through all the artifice, fat-faced, five-year-old Vincent Winter seems pricelessly, artlessly unaffected. BBa

Kidnapping of the President, The

(1979, Can, 113 min)
d George Mendeluk. *p* John Ryan, George Mendeluk. *sc* Richard Murphy. *ph* Mike Molloy. *ed* Michael McLaverty. *ad* Douglas Higgins. *m* Paul Zaza. *cast* William Shatner, Hal Holbrook, Van Johnson, Ava Gardner, Miguel Fernandes, Cindy Girling, Elizabeth Shepherd.
●Oh yeah. Verily. For it is he of Starship Enterprise (Shatner). He cometh and walketh with the American Prez in the valley of the shadow of death (a pedestrian mall in Toronto). He faceth up to the Cubans and Weathermen and psychos and he saith unto them: 'Fuck off. For we shall fear nothing. Especially not you creeps and Commies'. And they reply: 'Look upon us. We are Moloch and Satan. We come creeping forth as vermin on our bellies , the legacy of Chile and El Salvador and American imperialism. We take your Prez and hold him in our chariot (a booby-trapped armoured car), using implements of destruction from *Hawaii Five-O, Mission Impossible* and other halls of TV fame.' But Captain Kirk turns upon the Commies and Cubans and Weathermen, and his voice is as thunder, saying: 'Lo. I did once (in the '70s, in fact) what you do now, and I did it well. But I look upon you and ask, is it good? It is not good'. And there is a great flashing of lightning (TNT), a beating of brows and rattling of bones, and the Prez walks on, free, down the American Way with his wife on his right hand and Kirk on his left. For although we walk through the valley of crap… CA

Kids

(1995, US, 91 min)
d Larry Clark. *p* Cary Woods. *sc* Harmony Korine. *ph* Eric Edwards. *ed* Christopher Tellefsen. *pd* Kevin Thompson. *m* Lou Barlow, John Davis. *cast* Leo Fitzpatrick, Justin Pierce, Chloe Sevigny, Yakira Peguero.
●If Clark's raw, controversial, documentary-style account of 24 hours in the lives of a group of New York early-teens is to be believed, we'd better watch and worry. Few of the kids seem bothered about *anything* except meaningless sex, whatever drugs or booze is available, and the odd bit of mindless violence. True, Clark and his writer Harmony Korine try to adopt some sort of cautionary standpoint (one girl is diagnosed as HIV-positive after just one sexual experience; drugs are not exactly glamorised), but the tone is relentlessly sordid, the view of these pubescent hedonists so hermetic, that the film-makers' 'honesty' seems exploitative and sensational. The film may not say anything new, but the way it says it does, in the end, make it some sort of landmark. Depressing. GA

Kids Are Alright, The

(1978, US, 101 min, b/w & col)
d Jeff Stein. *p* Bill Curbishley, Anthony Klinger. *sc* Jeff Stein. *ph* Peter Nevard, Norman Warwick, Anthony B Richmond. *ed* Ed Rothkowitz. *with* The Who, Tom Smothers, Jimmy O'Neil, Russell Harty, Melvyn Bragg, Ringo Starr, Steve Martin.
●That rare animal, a rock documentary which entertains and informs in equal quantities, *The Kids Are Alright* is a movie that comes over as a celebration of rock'n'roll itself as much as of one of its more masterful exponents. Covering The Who's 'turbulent' history from the days of sweaty Shepherd's Bush cellars to the super-technicalities required for the recording of 'Who Are You' (mercifully stopping before Moon's death), the film captures some of the most powerful rock music of the last two decades. Patching together snippets of hilarious interviews (witness the anarchic terror Moon wreaks on a panic-stricken Russell Harty) with footage of live gigs (culminating in a laser-streaked finale), plus a few fantasy sequences, the film will fascinate the under-twenties and delight the over-thirties. FL

Kids in the Hall: Brain Candy

(1996, US, 89 min)
d Kelly Makin. *p* Lorne Michaels. *sc* Norm Hiscock, Bruce McCulloch, Kevin McDonald, Mark McKinney, Scott Thompson. *ph* David A Makin. *ed* Christopher Cooper. *pd* Gregory P Keen. *m* Craig Northey. *cast* David Foley, Bruce McCulloch, Kevin McDonald, Mark McKinney, Scott Thompson, Kathryn Greenwood, Janeane Garofalo.
●'Kids in the Hall', a quintet of Canadian TV comedians, hit the cinema screen with a splat. This cautionary satire is intended to showcase (in multiple roles) the protean talents of these lame gagsters. The story – forgive the word – concerns the effects of Gleemonex, a Prozac-like happiness drug sweeping the country. It's a conspiracy, of course, by Mr Big Business (McKinney), and resistance is led by an initially gullible scientist (McDonald). Irrelevant, but well done, are the special effects (a psychedelic shot of a pill's journey to the stomach) and the production design. WH

Kids of Survival: The Art and Life of Tim Rollins & K.O.S.

(1996, US, 87 min)
d/p/ph Daniel Geller, Dayna Goldfine. *ed* Elizabeth Finlayson, Eve Goldberg, Dayna Goldfine, Daniel Geller. *m* Todd Boekelheide. *with* Tim Rollins.
●Fly-on-the-wall documentary about artist Tim Rollins and his disciplined but productive after-school classes in modern art for the troubled, often troublesome kids of the impoverished South Bronx. The proof of the pudding is in the fact that

KOS paintings – usually inspired by literary texts – show in New York's Museum of Modern Art: no bad achievement when the kids start off as truants, Nintendo addicts or worse. But the film itself, while worthy, is conservative in the extreme. GA

Kids Return

(1996, Jap, 107 min)
d Takeshi Kitano. *p* Masayuki Mori, Yasushi Tsuge, Takio Yoshida. *sc* Takeshi Kitano. *ph* Katsumi Yanagishima. *ed* Takeshi Kitano, Yoshinori Ota. *ad* Norihiro Isoda. *m* Joe Hisaishi. *cast* Masanobu Ando, Ken Kaneko, Leo Morimoto, Hatsuo Yamaya, Mitsuko Oka, Ryo Ishibashi, Susumu Terajima.
●Masaru and Shinji are problem kids who enter society without apparent talents or prospects; their setbacks and failures as, respectively, a yakuza and a pro boxer are contrasted with the career paths of others from their school, two of whom struggle to make the grade as stand-up comics. Although it's set in the present, the indefinable retro flavour tips you the wink that these are memories and reflections from 'Beat' Takeshi's own adolescence – which doubtless explains the way the film extends such warmth to its characters without indulging or excusing their flaws. Unlike previous Takeshi protagonists, these kids don't have the easy option of 'dying well'; their quests for a viable way to survive are, however, seen with all the director's usual visual and rhythmic flair. TR

Kika

(1993, Sp, 114 min)
d/sc Pedro Almodóvar. *ph* Alfredo Mayo. *ed* José Salcedo. *pd* Javier Fernandez, Alain Bainée. *cast* Verónica Forqué, Peter Coyote, Victoria Abril, Alex Casanovas, Bibi Andersen, Rossy de Palma, Santiago Lajusticia.
●You may already know that a) this is supposed to be Almodóvar's flop; and b) you must wax all indignant over That Rape Scene. The sang froid displayed by Kika (Forqué, brilliant) during her ordeal is, if anything, the director's cock-eyed tribute to the power of women, as is the reason for the attack: a crazed ex-porn actor and escaped criminal Pablo (Lajusticia) breaks into Kika's house, finds her asleep, but can't resist sniffing her fanny. Yes, it's grotesque, but also touching, daring and very funny. Male viewers seem to resent having to recognise themselves in dim-witted Pablo. The film also fields Coyote, clinging on to youth by what appears to be false teeth and a pageboy wig. Kika's narcoleptic lover Ramón is played by cute Casanovas, and Abril's stylish Andrea Scarface presents a true-crime show which gives the film its funniest moments. When the fuss has died down, most people will agree that this is a return to form after the slightly disappointing *High Heels*, and is full of magic Almodóvar moments. SFe

Kikuchi

(1990, Jap, 68 min)
d Kenchi Iwamoto. *p* Suichi Ohi. *sc* Kenchi Iwamoto. *ph* Hideo Fukuda. *ed* Keiichi Okada. *cast* Jiro Yoshimura, Yasuhiro Oka, Misa Fukuma, Papa Akiyama, Mama Akiyama.
●Saddled with a slavish, boring laundry job and no social life whatsoever, Kikuchi rarely leaves his bare apartment except to follow home and spy on a supermarket check-out girl. But there's no one he can tell about his secret passion, least of all his gawping, work-shy colleague. Even a stray kitten can't alleviate Kikuchi's frustration; clearly, something's got to give... This first film by a former *manga* illustrator, a terse and enigmatic blend of black comedy and psychodrama, has been compared to both *Eraserhead* and Chantal Akerman's *Jeanne Dielman;* another point of reference might be the slow, deceptively banal domestic dramas of Ozu, with whom Iwamoto shares a penchant for a mostly static camera, simple compositions, and an eye for the absurd details of everyday life. Only that old problem – how to show tedium without being tedious – occasionally undermines an otherwise impressive debut. GA

Kikujiro (Kikujiro no Natsu)

(1998, Jap, 121 min)
d Takeshi Kitano. *p* Masayuki Mori, Takio Yoshida. *sc* Takeshi Kitano. *ph* Katsumi Yanagishima. *ed* Takeshi Kitano. *ad* Norihiro Isoda. *m* Joe Hisaishi. *cast* Yusuke Sekiguchi, 'Beat' Takeshi, Kayoko Kishimoto, Akaji Maro, Great Gidayu.
●Kitano's violence-free 'road movie' (inspired by *The Wizard of Oz*, he says) is his most idiosyncratic film yet. He plays Kikujiro, a gone-to-seed yakuza who reluctantly looks after a small boy during summer vacation. On impulse they set off across country (initially in a stolen taxi) in search of the kid's absent mother. Strange things happen on the road, including odd dreams and encounters with punks, bikers, and a paedophile; Takeshi's ex-partner 'Beat' Kiyoshi pops up as a man at a bus stop. But there's no moral turning point; it's not a rite-of-passage story. The episodes are more like chapters from a child's picture book: memories-to-be in the making. Shot and cut in the distinctive Kitano style, the film has great spontaneity. The comedy elements bring the author's two personae, writer/director Takeshi Kitano and TV comedian 'Beat' Takeshi, closer together than ever before. TR

Killer

(1994, US, 98 min)
d Mark Malone. *p* Robert Vince, William Vince. *sc* Gordon Melbourne. *ph* Tobias Schliessler. *ed* Robin Russell. *pd* Lynne Stopkewich. *m* Graeme Coleman. *cast* Anthony LaPaglia, Mimi Rogers, Matt Craven, Peter Boyle, Monika Schnarre, Joseph Maher.
●A professional hit-man agrees to carry out a rush job on a woman for his usual fee – plus therapy sessions. When he meets the victim, however, she's only too willing to cooperate, and of course he falls in love. Malone's directorial debut (after script credits for *Dead of Winter* and *Signs of Life*) gets a certain amount of mileage out of this little *noir* conceit, but conceit is all we get: the movie's all talk and no action. It's let down by the leads, LaPaglia and Rogers (both shown up by Peter Boyle's genial mob boss), who fail to generate any kind of spark. TCh

Killer, The (Da Sha Shou)

(1971, HK, 93 min)
d Chu Yuan. *p* Run Run Shaw. *sc* Kuo Chia. *ph* Wu Chu-hua. *ed* Chaing Hsing-loong. *ad* Chen Ching-sheng. *m* Chou Fu-liang, Chen Ying Shu. *cast* Chin Han, Wang Ping, Tsung Hua, Ching Miao, Yang Chih Ching.
●Another kung-fu assembly line gore product according to the brothers Shaw. The film exists for its fight routines, and these go to heady extremes in taking our hero out of the realm of human fallibility (dozens fall at one blow) and inching him towards complete invincibility. The plot involves heroin smuggling, romantic meetings after many years under assumed names, and so on; but the scene in which 'The Killer' confronts the head of the Black Dragon gang – a remarkable picture of sword-wielding malevolence – is a rare spark in a movie that remains routine despite its exoticism. VG

Killer, The (Diexue Shuang Xiong)

(1989, HK, 111 min)
d John Woo [Wu Yusen]. *p* Tsui Hark. *sc* John Woo. *ph* Wong Wing-Hang, Peter Pau. *ed* Fan Kung-Wing. *pd* Luk Man-Wah. *m* Lowell Lo. *cast* Chow Yun-Fat, Danny Lee, Sally Yeh, Chu Kong, Paul Chu, Kenneth Tsang, Lam Chung.
●The most dementedly elegiac thriller you've ever seen, distilling a lifetime's enthusiasm for American and French *film noir*, with little Chinese about it apart from the soundtrack and the looks of the three beautiful leads. It started out as a homage to Martin Scorsese and Jean-Pierre Melville, but the limitless arsenal of guns and rocket-launchers appears somehow to have got in the way. Exquisitely-tailored contract killer Jeff (Chow Yun-Fat, Hong Kong's finest actor) accidentally damages the sight of nightclub singer Jennie while blasting a dozen gangsters to kingdom come. He befriends the near-blind girl, and decides to take One Last Job to finance the cornea graft she needs. Meanwhile he is stalked by a misfit cop (Lee), who eventually falls in love with him and winds up fighting alongside him. There are half-a-dozen mega-massacres along the way, plus extraordinary spasms of sentimentality, romance and soul-searching. The tone is hysterical from start to finish, but Woo's lush visual stylings and taste for baroque detail give the whole thing an improbably serene air of abstraction. TR

Killer, The (Tueur à Gages)

(1998, Kazakhstan/Fr, 80 min)
d Darejan Omirbaev. *p* Joël Farges, Elise Jalladeau, Gaziz Shaldybaev. *sc* Darejan Omirbaev. *ph* Boris Troshev. *ed* R Beliakova. *pd* Alim Sabitov. *cast* Talgat Assetov, Roksana Abouova.
●The former Soviet Republic of Kazakhstan isn't richly represented in world film archives, so at the very least this drama affords a glimpse of unfamiliar territory. But this austere, miserabilist film won't do much for the local tourist industry. Clearly meant as a state of the nation address, it finds an impoverished society undergoing moral breakdown. Traffic breakdown, too. Chauffeur Marat, distracted by his newborn child, drives into the Mercedes in front of him and tumbles into a cycle of debt. This is an in-action movie: various beatings, thefts and deaths all take place off camera. Instead we get lots of static shots of doors – mostly closed. Patient viewers will find it builds up a grim moral momentum. TCh

Killer!

see Que la Bête Meure

Killer: A Journal of Murder

(1995, US, 92 min, b/w & col)
d Tim Metcalfe. *p* Janet Yang, Mark Levinson. *sc* Tim Metcalfe. *ph* Ken Kelsch. *ed* Richard Gentner. *pd* Sherman Williams. *m* Graeme Revell. *cast* James Woods, Robert Sean Leonard, Ellen Green, Cara Buono, Robert John Burke, Richard Riehle, Harold Gould, Lili Taylor.
●1929: Two newcomers enter Leavenworth prison, Kansas. Henry Lesser, an idealistic guard, and Carl Panzram, a hard-bitten con who spits out a confession to 21 unsolved murders. The pair form a bond. Henry smuggles in paper and pen so America's first serial killer can write his memoirs – a journal so shocking it wasn't published for more than 40 years. Writer/director Metcalfe switches to b/w for the journal, but that approximates the harshness of the material, not any moral distinction. Indeed, Metcalfe holds to a liberal perspective which Panzram, for one, may not have agreed with. Woods is typecast as Panzram, but he's terrifyingly alive in the part – even double-chained and ringed by a dozen guards, he's a palpable threat. A very nasty piece of work, he none the less insists that he is a piece of work: the sum of his exposure to the indifference and sadism of others. Leonard is just an on-looker as Lesser, but he, like the film, never flinches from the disturbing truths Panzram represents. This tough, gritty movie is shot by Abel Ferrara's regular cameraman Ken Kelsch, produced by Oliver Stone and dedicated to Sam Peckinpah – so you know where it's coming from. TCh

Killer Butterfly (Salin Nabireul Cchotneun Yeoja)

(1978, SKor, 110 min)
d Kim Ki-Young. *cast* Kim Jung-chi, Kim Man, Kim Cha-ok.
●Not unlike one of Corman's Poe films updated to '70s Seoul (with a little *Ugetsu Monogatari* thrown in), this tells of a feckless, morose student torn between life and death, Eros and Thanatos, when he meets a variety of strange and supernatural beings. Some of the special effects look a little elementary, but the whole thing is extremely enjoyable, and the scene where the hero has sex with a ghost next to an automatic toaster has to be seen to be believed. GA

Killer Elite, The

(1975, US, 120 min)
d Sam Peckinpah. *p* Martin Baum, Arthur Lewis. *sc* Marc Norman, Stirling Silliphant. *ph* Philip H Lathrop. *ed* Tony De Zarraga, Monte Hellman. *pd* Ted Haworth. *m* Jerry Fielding. *cast* James Caan, Robert Duvall, Arthur Hill, Gig Young, Mako, Bo Hopkins, Burt Young, Helmut Dantine.
●After a brilliantly cryptic opening, *The Killer Elite* settles into Peckinpah's most apparently straightforward action film since *The Getaway.* Built around the internal politics of a San Francisco company which sidelines in dirty work that even the CIA won't touch, it concentrates on the painful recovery of an agent (Caan), wounded in knee and elbow in a double-cross, and his search for revenge. During Caan's lengthy recuperation, Peckinpah contemplates the old themes

of betrayal, trust and humiliation. And through the action of the second half, Caan (like other Peckinpah heroes) comes to some sort of understanding. The set pieces (a Chinatown shoot-out, a dockland siege, the superb ships' graveyard climax) are excellent, as are so many secondary scenes. There are echoes here of *Point Blank*, and behind the deceits and manipulations both are essentially simple films. Unmistakable Peckinpah – not a masterpiece, but enough to be going on with. CPe

Killer Fish (Agguato sul Fondo)

(1978, Braz/It/US, 101 min)
d Anthony M Dawson [Antonio Margheriti]. *p* Alex Ponti. *sc* Kenneth Ross. *ph* Alberto Spagnoli. *ed* Roberto Sterbini. *ad* Francesco Bronzi. *m* Guido De Angelis, Maurizio De Angelis. *cast* Lee Majors, Karen Black, Margaux Hemingway, Marisa Berenson, James Franciscus, Roy Brocksmith, Gary Collins.
●One of the first of Carlo Ponti's exile productions, and the sort of international film-making-by-numbers tailor-made for distribution by Lew Grade, this manages to conspicuously waste more than twice the budget of New World's *Piranha* without approaching anything like the imagination, relevance or sense of fun of its sharp-toothed, small-fry predecessor. The piranha here guard an underwater stash of stolen jewels, and take regular nibbles from the double-crossing crooks. Majors out-machos everyone else, while Hemingway arrives halfway through for – what else? – some location modelling work. PT

Killer Inside Me, The

(1975, US, 99 min)
d Burt Kennedy. *p* Michael W Leighton. *sc* Edward Mann, Robert Chamblee. *ph* William A Fraker. *ed* Danford B Greene, Aaron Stell. *m* Tim McIntire, John Rubinstein. *cast* Stacy Keach, Susan Tyrrell, Tisha Sterling, Keenan Wynn, Don Stroud, Charles McGraw, John Dehner, John Carradine, Royal Dano, Julie Adams.
●Not even the offices of the excellent Burt Kennedy can save this hopelessly stodgy and psychologising story about a self-consciously good cop (Keach) who finds a traumatic childhood experience catching up on him. Kennedy none the less does ensure that the film is crammed with enough pleasing incidental detail to make it watchable. Don Stroud lopes through the part of a naive and ape-ish slob with evident enjoyment; now perhaps if he and Keach had swapped roles… The pity of it is that the script by Edward Mann and Robert Chamblee wrecks a very good novel by Jim Thompson. VG

Killer Is Loose, The

(1955, US, 73 min, b/w)
d Budd Boetticher. *p* Robert L Jacks. *sc* Harold Medford. *ph* Lucien Ballard. *ed* George Gittens. *ad* Leslie Thomas. *m* Lionel Newman. *cast* Joseph Cotten, Rhonda Fleming, Wendell Corey, John Larch, Michael Pate, Virginia Christine.
●A low budget quickie which bustles through its itinerary (bank heist, jail break, manhunt, about one sudden death per reel) with efficiency and despatch, if not much credibility. The manhunt is for soft-spoken psycho Corey, who's prowling a rainswept LA, fixated on killing cop's wife Fleming. The latter character is the film's big liability (no fault of the actress), forever nagging husband Cotten to forget all this police stuff and come away with her to the beach. BBa

Killer Is on the Phone, The (Assassino...è al Telefono)

(1972, It, 102 min)
d Alberto De Martino. *p* Vittorio Bartattolo, Aldo Scavarda. *sc* Alberto De Martino, Vincenzo Mannino, Adriano Bolzoni, Renato Izzo. *ph* Aristide Massaccesi. *ed* Otello Colangeli. *ad* Antonio Visone. *m* Stelvio Cipriani. *cast* Anne Heywood, Telly Savalas, Rossella Falk, Giorgio Piazza, Osvaldo Ruggeri, Willeke Van Ammelrooy, Roger van Hool.
●Crippled thriller along is-she-insane-or-are-they-trying-to-make-her-believe-it lines, shot in Ostend and featuring Savalas, in his pre-lollipop days, and Heywood, who has the knack of picking hopeless projects. De Martino rapidly forfeits interest or suspense by loading every action with equal suggestiveness.

Killer Klowns from Outer Space

(1988, US, 88 min)
d Stephen Chiodo. *p/sc* Edward Chiodo, Stephen Chiodo. *ph* Alfred Taylor. *ed* Chris Roth. *m* John Massari. *cast* Grant Cramer, Suzanne Snyder, John Allen Nelson, Royal Dano, John Vernon.
●You'll never guess what this one is about. Funnily enough, it's about this huge circus tent that mysteriously appears up in the woods by a small American town, and then there's all these totally weird clowns who go around doing, like, gross things to people with projectile candy floss. Seems the clowns are on a mission from (surprise) outer space to collect human bodies for food. However, they are foiled by the young hero, who discovers that you can kill 'em if you knock off their big red noses. Utterly ridiculous, the dialogue exquisitely dumb, the acting soooooooo bad, it's one for cheap laughs. DA

Killer Nun (Suor omicidio)

(1978, It, 90 min)
d Giulio Berruti. *p* Enzo Gallo. *sc* Giulio Berriti, Alberto Tarallo. *ph* Tonino Maccoppi. *ed* Mario Giacco. *pd* Franco Vanorio. *m* Alessandro Alessandroni. *cast* Anita Ekberg, Alida Valli, Massimo Serato, Lou Castel, Joe Dallesandro, Laura Nucci.
●A dated blend of softcore sleaze, routine bloodletting and explicable coyness, this stars an over-the-hill Ekberg as a nun who has given up *la dolce vita* for a life behind convent hospital walls. A secret junkie whose past sexual traumas and drug-induced hallucinations transform her from a caring angel into an avenging one, Ekberg loses her patience and starts killing patients. Given this excessive scenario, why the quaint evasions? Lesbianism is hinted at but not shown, scenes of Ekberg shooting up are filmed with her back to the camera. Isolated scenes spill over into camp humour, as when the hysterical Ekberg repeatedly stamps on an old lady's dentures. A censored version, running 81 minutes, removed two 'nasties' (the needle in the eye/scalpel to the skull sequences). NF

Killer of Killers

see Mechanic, The

Killer of Sheep

(1977, US, 84 min, b/w)
d/p/sc/ph/ed Charles Burnett. cast Henry Gayle Sanders, Kaycee Moore, Charles Bracy, Angela Burnett, Eugene Cherry, Jack Drummond.
●A gritty, grainy slice of everyday lumpen American black struggle, marking the difficulty of maintaining slow-buck integrity – the title refers to a family breadwinner's slaughterhouse job. Shot with a telling near-documentary technique on a poverty-row budget, but lifted right out of any cinematic ghetto by the best compilation sound-track you'll hear for many a year, ranging through an unfamiliar black catalogue from Paul Robeson to electric blues. PT

Killer on a Horse

see Welcome to Hard Times

Killers, The

(US, 1946, 105 min, b/w)
d Robert Siodmak. *p* Mark Hellinger. *sc* Anthony Veiller. *ph* Woody Bredell. *ed* Arthur Hilton. *ad* Jack Otterson, Martin Obzina. *m* Miklós Rózsa. *cast* Edmond O'Brien, Ava Gardner, Burt Lancaster, Albert Dekker, Sam Levene, Vince Barnett, Charles McGraw, William Conrad, Virginia Christine.
●If anyone still doesn't know what's signified by the critical term *film noir*, then *The Killers* provides an exhaustive definition. The quality isn't in the rather average script (elaborated from Hemingway's short story) but in the overall sensibility – the casting, the use of shadows, the compositions alternating between paranoid long shots and hysterical close-ups. After the brilliant opening murder scene, what follows is a series of flashbacks as Edmond O'Brien's insurance investigator looks into the circumstances of Lancaster's death. Ava Gardner is an admirably tacky femme fatale, and her fickleness/faithfulness provides the not very surprising denouement. Worth attention as a '40s thriller, but more than that as a prime example of post-war pessimism and fatalism. TR

Killers, The

(1964, US, 95 min)
d/p Don Siegel. *sc* Gene L Coon. *ph* Richard L Rawlings Sr. *ed* Richard Belding. *ad* Frank Arrigo, George Chan. *m* John Williams. *cast* Lee Marvin, Angie Dickinson, John Cassavetes, Clu Gulager, Ronald Reagan, Claude Akins, Norman Fell, Virginia Christine, Seymour Cassel.
●Not exactly a remake of Siodmak's film, but a very similar adaptation of Hemingway's short story, except that the old *noir* ambience has given way to broad daylight, with the two killers now characterised as corporate executives rather than as emblematic figures from the shadows. Like its predecessor, Siegel's version is at its best while setting up the chillingly ruthless detail of the opening execution (here unnervingly set in an asylum for the blind), less satisfying when it starts providing an answer to the mysterious passivity of the victim (Cassavetes). A familiar tale of robbery and betrayal unfolds, not enhanced by the glossy colour but given a terrific boost by the fact that the two killers stick around (since they now conduct the investigation themselves in the interests of better business efficiency) and are superbly characterised by Marvin and Gulager. Originally made for TV, the film was tactfully switched to cinema release following the JFK assassination. TM

Killer's Kiss

(1955, US, 67 min, b/w)
d Stanley Kubrick. *p* Stanley Kubrick, Morris Bousel. *sc/ph/ed* Stanley Kubrick. *m* Gerald Fried. *cast* Frank Silvera, Jamie Smith, Irene Kane, Jerry Jarret, Julius Adelman.
●Written, edited, shot, produced and directed by Kubrick for a mere $75,000, his second feature is a moody but rather over-arty B thriller whose prime pleasures lie in the high contrast b/w camerawork (Kubrick had been a top photographer for *Look*). The story is nothing original – a down-at-heel boxer (Smith) falls for a night-club dancer (Kane) after saving her from being raped by her boss (Silvera), who consequently determines to put an end to their romance – but Kubrick makes the most of flashback and dream sequences, and a surreal climactic fight in a warehouse full of mannequins. The dialogue was post-synched, making for a certain stiltedness in the performances, but at least the brief running-time ensures that the film's more pretentious moments tend to flash past, rather than linger as in Kubrick's later work. (Incidentally, the film – and a fictionalised account of its making – became the subject of *Strangers Kiss* in 1983). GA

Killers of Kilimanjaro

(1959, GB, 91 min)
d Richard Thorpe. *p* John R Sloan. *sc* John Gilling, Earl Felton. *ph* Ted Moore. *ed* Geoffrey Foot. *ad* Ray Sim. *m* William Alwyn. *cast* Robert Taylor, Anne Aubrey, Anthony Newley, Gregoire Aslan, John Dimech, Orlando Martins, Donald Pleasence.
●Among the rash of Anglo-American oddities from circa 1960 (*Suddenly Last Summer*, *A Terrible Beauty*) this encomium for the British empire at its moment of maximum disintegration is in a class by itself. Victorian railway builder Taylor adventures off into the bush kitted out with lovable native urchin (Dimech), pretty white woman in distress (Aubrey), plus comic relief (Newley). A compendium of provocation (regarding Africans, wildlife, feminism, everything) the picture is both incident packed and deadly slow: a Thorpe speciality. Evelyn Waugh crossed paths with the production in Kenya, an encounter he described in *A Tourist in Africa*. BBa

Killer Tongue (La lengua asesina)

(1996, Sp/GB, 99 min)
d Alberto Sciamma. *p* Christopher Figg, Andrés Vicente Gómez. *sc* Albert Sciamma. *ph* Denis Crossan. *ed* Jeremy Gibbs. *pd* José Luis Del Barco, Cath Pater Lancucki. *m* Fangoria. *cast* Melinda Clarke, Jason Durr, Mapi Galán, Mabel Karr, Robert Englund, Doug Bradley.
●This calculatedly outrageous mix of jokey horror, road movie clichés and transvestite camp leaves a nasty taste in the mouth, but not in the way intended. Writer/director Sciamma's shambolic first feature is simply a catchy title in search of cult status. The presence of horror icons

Englund (*A Nightmare on Elm Street*), Bradley (*Hellraiser*) and Clarke (*Return of the Living Dead III*) might lead you to think he's got it licked, but while Clarke looks fetching in latex bodysuit, the one-gag scenario about her talking tonsil tickler soon wears thin. To impose a spurious logic on the wayward plot, Candy (Clarke) acquires her *lengua asesina* after flakes from a crashed meteorite land in her soup. Having eaten from the same bowl, her poodles inexplicably metamorphose into a pair of screeching drag queens. Most incovenient, since she's on the run from a bank job she's pulled with boyfriend Johnny (Durr), who himself has just escaped from a prison run by a sadistic guard (Englund). NF

Killing, The

(1956, US, 84 min, b/w)
d Stanley Kubrick. *p* James B Harris. *sc* Stanley Kubrick, Jim Thompson. *ph* Lucien Ballard. *ed* Betty Steinberg. *ad* Ruth Sobotka. *m* Gerald Fried. *cast* Sterling Hayden, Coleen Gray, Vince Edwards, Jay C Flippen, Marie Windsor, Elisha Cook Jr, Ted de Corsia, Timothy Carey.

●Characteristically Kubrick in both its mechanistic coldness and its vision of human endeavour undone by greed and deceit, this *noir*-ish heist movie is nevertheless far more satisfying than most of his later work, due both to a lack of bombastic pretensions and to the style fitting the subject matter. Hayden is his usual admirable self as the ex-con who gathers together a gallery of small-timers to rob a race-track; for once it's not the robbery itself that goes wrong, but the aftermath. What is remarkable about the movie, besides the excellent performances of an archetypal *noir* cast and Lucien Ballard's steely photography, is the time structure, employing a complex series of flashbacks both to introduce and explain characters and to create a synchronous view of simultaneous events. Kubrick's essentially heartless, beady-eyed observation of human foibles lacks the dimension of the genre's classics, but the likes of Windsor, Carey and Cook more than compensate. (From the novel *Clean Break* by Lional White.) GA

Killing Box, The (aka Ghost Brigade)

(1993, US, 86 min)
d George Hickenlooper. *p* Basil Krevoy, Steve Stabler, Fred Kuchnert. *sc* Matt Greenberg. *ph* Kent Wakeford. *ed* Monte Hellman. *pd* Mick Strawn. *m* Cory Lerios. *cast* Corbin Bernsen, Adrian Pasdar, Dylan McDermott, Ray Wise, Cynda Williams, Martin Sheen, Alexis Arquette.

●An arty zombie movie, this atmospheric American Civil War tale is described by director George (*Hearts of Darkness*) Hickenlooper as 'Conrad with a twist of Bram Stoker'. Confederate soldiers thought killed in an earlier skirmish are now suspected of a gruesome massacre. Forced into an alliance with Union captain Pasdar, captive Confederate colonel Bernsen finds Union soldiers crucified upside down on X-shaped crosses. Is an army of the undead abroad in this war-torn land? Involving, with dark undertones. NF

Killing Dad

(1989, GB, 93 min)
d Michael Austin. *p* Iain Smith. *sc* Michael Austin. *ph* Gabriel Beristain. *ed* Edward Marnier, Derek Trigg. *pd* Adrienne Atkinson. *m* Chas Jankel, David Storrs. *cast* Denholm Elliot, Julie Walters, Richard E Grant, Anna Massey, Laura Del Sol, Ann Way, Tom Radcliffe.

●A brief tour through the stock-room of British film comedy: seaside town out of season; molly-coddled son; overbearing neurotic mother; hopeless ventriloquist with drinking problem; faded femme fatale with drinking problem. Writer/director Austin's caricatures go through the motions of an Oedipal murder plot in perfunctory fashion; he seems to aspire to the satirical bite of Mike Leigh, but never achieves the accuracy, let alone the truth. Grant, struggling against being upstaged by a 1964 Beatles wig, employs his usual nose-wrinkling, eye popping mannerisms, but is unable to master the nasal tones of Harlow New Town. Elliott, object of Grant's murder mission, is wonderfully seedy. Walters brings much-needed warmth to her gin-sodden vamp: convincing, funny and sad. But Austin generally prefers to observe his characters as if they were insects under a stone: comedy needs a little more compassion. Southend looks suitably authentic and shabby, but the film is not located in real time at all, only somewhere between *Brighton Rock* and *The Punch and Judy Man*. JMo

Killing Fields, The

(1984, GB, 142 min)
d Roland Joffé. *p* David Puttnam. *sc* Bruce Robinson. *ph* Chris Menges. *ed* Jim Clark. *pd* Roy Walker. *m* Mike Oldfield. *cast* Sam Waterston, Haing S Ngor, John Malkovich, Julian Sands, Craig T Nelson, Spalding Gray, Bill Paterson, Athol Fugard, Patrick Malahide.

●Though it gradually turns into a somewhat sentimental buddy movie, with NY journo Sydney Schanberg (Waterston) longing for news of Dith Pran (Ngor), the Cambodian aide he left behind to suffer the horrors of the Khmer Rouge after the fall of Pnomh Penh in 1975, this is still very much a superior look at one country's troubles in the wake of American involvement in South East Asia. The first hour, sprawling, chaotic and violently messy, is very good indeed, conveying both the complexity and the essential absurdity of war, while the photography by Chris Menges is stunningly convincing in detailing the scale of the carnage. The use of Lennon's 'Imagine' at the end is a severe error of judgment, but the film's overall thrust – angry, intelligent, compassionate – makes this producer Puttnam's finest movie to date. GA

Killing Floor, The

(1985, US, 117 min, b/w & col)
d Bill Duke. *p* George Manasse. *sc* Leslie Lee, Ron Milner. *ph* Bill Birch. *ed* John Carter. *pd* Maher Ahmad. *m* Elizabeth Swados. *cast* Damien Leake, Alfre Woodard, Clarence Felder, Moses Gunn, Jason Green, Jamarr Johnson.

●Black migration from the Deep South at the time of World War I, as seen through the eyes of Frank Custer (Leake), a sharecropper who comes to the 'Promised Land' of Chicago, to sweep animal remains from the floor of the slaughterhouse. Finding himself caught up in an emerging trade union movement, he attempts to convince his fellow black workers that the struggle for decent working conditions must transcend traditional racial antagonisms. Director Duke's work is like a large wooden spoon filled with gristle, blood, black and trade union history; it's kind of hard to swallow all at once. Still, it does portray an often neglected aspect of American history, while offering a less than loving glimpse at what really goes into the all-American cheeseburger. SGo

Killing Me Softly

(2001, US/GB, 100 min)
d Chen Kaige. *p* Lynda Myles, Joe Medjuck, Michael Chinich. *sc* Kara Lindstrom. *ph* Michael Coulter. *ed* Jon Gregory. *pd* Gemma Jackson. *m* Patrick Doyle. *cast* Heather Graham, Joseph Fiennes, Natascha McElhone, Ulrich Thomsen, Ian Hart, Jason Hughes, Kika Markham, Alan Rickman.

●A debased update of those *films noirs* in which an unsuspecting girl starts to wonder if she's carelessly married a murderous sadist. Alice (Graham, miscast as a raving beauty) enjoys a vigorous fuck with Adam Tallis (Fiennes) just minutes after making eye-contact at the traffic lights; she's an American in London, he's a mountaineer who lives at permanently high altitude, even in Islington. When they marry, Adam's honeymoon treat is an uphill hike followed by sex enhanced with strangulation games in a country cottage. Bliss for the literally breathless Alice – until the anonymous notes start arriving, warning her that she's married a heel. Inane and shopworn material with a truly cheesy final twist, this is made excruciating by direction that takes it all deadly seriously. The fact that Chen chose this for his first non-Chinese film suggests that (a) he *really* wanted to direct a sex scene or two, and (b) he can't tell a Mandarin duck from a turkey. (From the novel by Nicci French.) TR

Killing of a Chinese Bookie, The 100

(1976, US, 109 min)
d John Cassavetes. *p* Al Ruban. *sc* John Cassavetes. *ph* Frederick Elmes, Michael Ferris, Mitchell Breit. *ed* Tom Cornwell. *pd* Sam Shaw, Phedon Papamichael. *m* Bo Harwood. *cast* Ben Gazzara, Timothy Carey, Seymour Cassel, Azizi Johari, Virginia Carrington, Meade Roberts, Alice Friedland, Soto Joe Hugh.

●Cassavetes doesn't believe in gangsters, as soon becomes clear in this waywardly plotted account of how a bunch of them try to distract Gazzara from his loyalty to his barely solvent but chichi LA strip joint, the Crazy Horse West. Or rather Cassavetes doesn't believe in the kind of demands they make on a film, enforcing clichés of action and behaviour in return for a few cheap thrills. On the other hand, there's something about the ethnicity of the Mob – family closeness and family tyranny – which appeals to him, which is largely what his films are about, and which says something about the way he works with actors. The result is that his two gangster films – this one and the later *Gloria* – easily rate as his best work criss-crossed as they are by all sorts of contradictory impulses, with the hero/heroine being reluctantly propelled through the plot, trying to stay far enough ahead of the game to prevent his/her own act/movie being closed down. It's rather like a shaggy dog story operating inside a chase movie. *Chinese Bookie* is the more insouciant, involuted and unfathomable of the two; the curdled charm of Gazzara's lopsided grin has never been more to the point. (After its initial release, Cassavetes re-edited the film, adding sequences previously deleted but reducing the overall running time from 133 minutes.) MA

Killing of Angel Street, The

(1981, Aust, 101 min)
d Donald Crombie. *p* Anthony Buckley. *sc* Evan Jones, Michael Craig, Cecil Holmes. *ph* Peter James. *ed* Tim Wellburn. *ad* Lindsay Hewson. *m* Brian May. *cast* Elizabeth Alexander, John Hargreaves, Alexander Archdale, Reg Lye, David Downer.

●Factually based political thriller in which a girl exposes the involvement of both government and organised crime after her father dies in mysterious circumstances while fighting attempts to 'persuade' the inhabitants of a row of terraced houses to make way for high-rise development. Not bad, though very lightweight and lumbered with a silly romance. Phillip Noyce's *Heatwave*, made the same year, did much better by the same facts. TM

Killing of Sister George, The

(1968, US, 138 min)
d/p Robert Aldrich. *sc* Lukas Heller. *ph* Joseph Biroc, Brian West. *ed* Michael Luciano. *ad* William Glasgow. *m* Gerald Fried. *cast* Beryl Reid, Susannah York, Coral Browne, Ronald Fraser, Patricia Medina, Hugh Paddick, Cyril Delevanti.

●Although one can't deny the entertainment value of Aldrich's adaptation of Frank Marcus's play about an ageing lesbian actress whose life falls apart as she loses first her job in a TV soap series and then her young lover, it could never be described as either realistic or sensitive. Rather, with its grotesque stereotyping and tour de force bitchiness and hysteria, it's like yet another instalment in the *What Ever Happened to Baby Jane?* saga. Cynical, objectionable, and fun, distinguished by Beryl Reid's marvellously energetic performance. GA

Killing Zoe

(1994, US, 96 min)
d Roger Avary. *p* Samuel Hadida. *sc* Roger Avary. *ph* Tom Richmond. *ed* Kathryn Himoff. *pd* David Wasco. *m* Tomandandy. *cast* Eric Stoltz, Julie Delpy, Jean-Hugues Anglade, Gary Kemp, Tai Thai, Bruce Ramsay, Kario Salem.

●Zed (Stoltz) arrives in Paris to participate in a bank robbery at the invitation of an old friend, Eric (Anglade). A professional safecracker, he's swept up in a maelstrom of sex and drugs which turns to blood and guts when the robbery goes wrong. Avary's crooks make his pal Quentin Tarantino's reservoir dogs look like Cary Grant – this is a grotesquely sleazy, brutal, bloody crime flick. Not a particularly interesting one, though. Utterly unedifying. TCh

Kill Me Again

(1989, US, 96 min)
d John R Dahl. *p* David W Warfield, Sigurjon Sighvatsson, Steve Golin. *sc* John R Dahl, David W Warfield. *ph* Jacques Steyn. *ed* Frank Jiminez, Jonathan Shaw, Eric Beason. *pd*

Michelle Minch. *m* William Olvis. *cast* Val Kilmer, Joanne Whalley-Kilmer, Michael Madsen, Jonathan Gries, Pat Mulligan, Nick Dimitri.

●Desperate to evade her psychotic partner-in-crime Vince (Madsen, memorably nasty if over-Methody) after stealing money from the Mob, treacherous femme fatale Fay (Whalley-Kilmer) asks down-at-heel private investigator Jack Andrews (Val Kilmer) to help her fake her own death. Somewhat inevitably, Jack takes the job, loses his heart, and finds that he is wanted by cops, Mob *and* Vince. Derived from assorted Hitchcocks and *noir* classics, the tortuous storyline of writer-director Dahl's determinedly sordid thriller has its moments, but the whole thing is fatally scuppered by the Kilmer pairing. Joanne is trying far too hard and looks like it, while Val, whose pudgy baby-face makes nonsense of his world-weary, tough-guy posturing, alternates between two expressions: troubled (unsmiling) and beguiled (faintly smiling). Setting its study of betrayal and deceit in and around the gambling towns of the Nevada desert, the film sporadically achieves a truly seedy atmosphere, but there are too many symbols, too many loose ends, and too many vaguely sensationalist scenes. GA

Kill-Off, The

(1989, US, 97 min)
d Maggie Greenwald. *p* Lydia Dean Pilcher. *sc* Maggie Greenwald. *ph* Declan Quinn. *ed* James Kwei. *pd* Pamela Woodbridge. *m* Evan Lurie. *cast* Loretta Gross, Andrew Lee Barrett, Jackson Sims, Steve Monroe, Cathy Haase, William Russell, Jorjan Fox, Sean O'Sullivan, Ellen Kelly, Ralph Graff.

●For her second feature, an adaptation of Jim Thompson's novel, Greenwald *almost* gets it perfect. As she charts the sordid lives of various no-hopers struggling to make it in a seedy, wintry East Coast resort, she revels in the laconic dialogue, vicious motivations and downbeat mood beloved by Thompson fans. What these losers, each involved in activities like drug abuse, adultery, incest and so on, have in common is their hatred for Luane Devore, an elderly, bed-ridden gossip whose malicious mouth is itself a reason for killing. But which of her victims, finally, will murder her? Loretta Gross, memorably nasty as the twisted invalid, is backed up by equally efficient unknowns, while Declan Quinn's camerawork creates a vivid atmosphere of claustrophobic despair. As a thriller, however, the movie is short of real suspense: comparison with *Blood Simple* highlights Greenwald's slow pace, while *Le Corbeau*, Clouzot's misanthropic masterpiece of 1943, provides far more psychological complexity, moral rigour and nail-biting tension in its corrosive examination of paranoid corruption. GA

Killpoint

(1984, US, 89 min)
d Frank Harris. *p* Frank Harris, Diane Stevenett. *sc/ph/ed* Frank Harris. *ad* Larry Westover. *m* Herman Jeffreys, Daryl Stevenett. *cast* Leo Fong, Cameron Mitchell, Richard Roundtree, Stack Pierce, Hope Holiday, Diana Leigh.

●When a State arsenal is raided and machine-guns get into the hands of local gangs, the result is a lot of dead people. Before you can say soy sauce, a peaceful Chinese restaurant is awash in a sea of blood; but *Killpoint* caters for most tastes, ranging from simple strangulation and sexual abuse, knives and razor blades, plenty of martial arts, right through to grenades and real 'heavy metal' automatics. Dispensing with sissy things like stockings and disguises, the roaming robber gangs work on the simplistic principle of leaving no witnesses behind in colourful encounters with splashes of red everywhere. The dialogue is a bit stilted, but then most people don't last long enough to say much and the goodies win in the end anyway. Oh well, pass the ketchup. HR

Kim

(1950, US, 112 min)
d Victor Saville. *p* Leon Gordon. *sc* Leon Gordon, Helen Deutsch, Richard Schayer. *ph* William V Skall. *ed* George Boemler. *ad* Cedric Gibbons, Hans Peters. *m* André Previn. *cast* Errol Flynn, Dean Stockwell, Paul Lukas, Robert Douglas, Thomas Gomez, Cecil Kellaway, Reginald Owen.

●Colourful location work scarcely makes up for the frequent turgid passages in this Hollywood version of Rudyard Kipling's novel. Stockwell essays the British-born, Indian-bred orphan who carves out a niche for himself as a spy for the Empire. Lukas is the Lama who teaches him a thing or two, Flynn the red-bearded spy who takes over his education. Politically indecorous, too. TCh

Kin

(1999, GB, 90 min)
d Elaine Proctor. *p* Margaret Matheson. *sc* Elaine Proctor. *ph* Amelia Vincent. *ed* Nicolas Gaster. *pd* Mark Wilby. *m* Justin Adams. *cast* Miranda Otto, Isaiah Washington, Chris Chameleon.

●Shot widescreen in Namibia, writer/director Elaine (*Friends*) Proctor's well directed and good looking romance blends themes of incest and a love of nature with racial, ethnic, sexual and historical concerns to diverting, often charged, but finally conventional effect. Otto's Anna is an interesting mix of naivety and passion as the game reserve worker passionate about her elephants. Her relationship with black American lawyer Stone (Washington) brings the wrath of Marius, her pastor brother. Her internal conflicts about racial matters are mirrored by Stone's sense of identity, torn as he is between an idealistic commitment to defend a local Himba tribesman – and thereby stay with Anna – and his desire to return to America and potential riches. WH

Kindergarten Cop

(1990, US, 111 min)
d Ivan Reitman. *p* Ivan Reitman, Brian Grazer. *sc* Murray Salem, Herschel Weingrod, Timothy Harris. *ph* Michael Chapman. *ed* Sheldon Kahn, Wendy Greene Bricmont. *pd* Bruno Rubes. *m* Randy Edelman. *cast* Arnold Schwarzenegger, Penelope Ann Miller, Pamela Reed, Linda Hunt, Richard Tyson, Carroll Baker.

●The trouble with comedy-thrillers is that while they are sometimes funny, they rarely thrill. If Reitman's film gets closer than most to covering the bases, there remain huge gaps in plausibility and a romantic subplot any ten-year-old could tell you is just plain icky. That the film works at all is down to Big Arnie. Far more successfully than in *Twins*, Reitman cannily exploits and debunks the Schwarzenegger screen persona. The exposition is particularly to the point, establishing him as the meanest cop on the block, a hard man who persuades a reluctant witness to testify by threatening to hang out with her forever. Weighed down by a female partner (the delightfully cheeky Reed) and an unlikely undercover assignment as a kindergarten teacher, Macho Man looks set to become New Man. Faced with the kids from hell, Arnie has never been so helpless or so funny. All too soon, though, the cop is back in charge; the nagging feeling that his high discipline and relentless Phys Ed is creating a class of *Überkinder* rather blunts the bite of the humour. TCh

Kinderspiel

see Child's Play

Kind Hearts and Coronets 100 (100)

(1949, GB, 106 min, b/w)
d Robert Hamer. *p* Michael Balcon. *sc* Robert Hamer, John Dighton. *ph* Douglas Slocombe. *ed* Peter Tanner. *ad* William Kellner. *m* WA Mozart. *cast* Dennis Price, Alec Guinness, Joan Greenwood, Valerie Hobson, Audrey Fildes, Miles Malleson, Clive Morton, Hugh Griffith.

●The gentle English art of murder in Ealing's blackest comedy, with Price in perfect form as the ignoble Louis, killing off a complete family tree (played by Guinness throughout) in order to take the cherished d'Ascoyne family title. Disarmingly cool and callous in its literary sophistication, admirably low key in its discreet caricatures of the haute bourgeoisie, impeccable in its period detail (Edwardian), it's a brilliantly cynical film without a hint of middle-class guilt or bitterness. GA

Kind of Hush, A

(1997, GB, 95 min)
d Brian Stirner. *p* Roger Randall-Cutler. *sc* Brian Stirner. *ph* Jacek Petrycki. *ed* David Martin. *pd* Mark Stevenson. *m* Arvo Pärt. *cast* Harley Smith, Marcella Plunkett, Ben Roberts, Paul Williams, Nathan Constance, Mike Fibbens, Roy Hudd.

●At first this raw, low budget, 'realistic' look at a group of King's Cross rent boys (out for revenge on the adults who abused them) seems stylistically clumsy and rather too keen on suggesting its characters' irrepressible energy. As the film proceeds, however, the performances and camerawork become more assured, a few quieter, more reflexive scenes provide some emotional depth and the overall conviction of the piece more or less compensates for the often awkward scripting. GA

Kind of Loving, A

(1962, GB, 112 min, b/w)
d John Schlesinger. *p* Joseph Janni. *sc* Willis Hall, Keith Waterhouse. *ph* Denys Coop. *ed* Roger Cherrill. *ad* Ray Simm. *m* Ron Grainer. *cast* Alan Bates, June Ritchie, Thora Hird, Bert Palmer, Gwen Nelson, Malcolm Patton, James Bolam, Leonard Rossiter.

●Schlesinger's first feature, an adaptation of Stan Barstow's novel directed with a quiet sympathy he subsequently lost (except for *Sunday, Bloody Sunday*) in pursuing flashy stylistics. The plot has seen sterling service (man trapped into marriage by an unplanned pregnancy), the setting is the then fashionable one of North Country factory and lower-middle-class aspirations, and the dialogue has the sort of terse, tape-recorder saltiness that scriptwriters Willis Hall and Keith Waterhouse used to churn out by the mile. Yet with all faults (which include a clumsily episodic structure), it remains keenly observant in detail and rather moving in its very unpretentiousness. TM

Kindred, The

(1986, US, 92 min)
d Jeffrey Obrow, Stephen Carpenter. *p* Jeffrey Obrow. *sc* Stephen Carpenter, Jeffrey Obrow, John Penney, Earl Ghaffari, Jospeh Stephano. *ph* Stephen Carpenter. *ed* John Penney, Earl Ghaffari. *pd* Chris Hopkins. *m* David Newman. *cast* David Allen Brooks, Rod Steiger, Amanda Pays, Talia Balsam, Kim Hunter, Timothy Gibbs, Peter Frechette.

●Geneticist John Hollins (Brooks) is shocked when his dying scientist mother refers to Anthony, a brother he never knew he had. With a crew of fresh-faced research assistants, he sets out to dismantle his old ma's cranky experiments, and discovers the mysterious Anthony in a cavernous slime-pit below stairs, the monstrous result of a hybridisation experiment. The thing shows scant regard for sibling attachments, and attempts to eat Hollins and anyone else it can lay talons on. It should be put down, but one man wants to keep the creature alive for his own devious ends. He is Dr Lloyd (Steiger in a wig resembling a pressed sparrow and looking as mean as the Ghostbusters' Stay-Puft marshmallow man). Lloyd fails and is eaten, shortly before Anthony is exploded into McNuggets of gristle and mucus. An adequate idea for a horror flick, ruined by bad pacing and a woolly plot. Not even mealy-mouthed Amanda Pays sprouting gills and fins can redeem this one. EP

King & Country

(1964, GB, 86 min, b/w)
d Joseph Losey. *p* Norman Priggen, Joseph Losey. *sc* Evan Jones. *ph* Denys Coop. *ed* Reginald Mills. *pd* Richard MacDonald. *m* Larry Adler. *cast* Dirk Bogarde, Tom Courtenay, Leo McKern, Barry Foster, James Villiers, Peter Copley, Jeremy Spenser.

●After three years at the front in World War I, a young soldier simply walks away from the guns; he is court-martialled, found wanting, and shot. For Losey, 'a story about hypocrisy, a story about people who are brought up to a certain way of life, who are given the means to extend their knowledge and to extend their understanding, but are not given the opportunity to use their minds in connection with it, and who finally have to face the fact that they have to be rebels in society…or else they have to accept hypocrisy.' This recasting of *The Servant* as a war film, with Courtenay playing the working-class deserter whose helplessness traps the liberal middle-class officer (Bogarde) assigned to defend him at his court-martial, fails precisely because the sexual element in the relationship, so explicit in *The Servant*, is so repressed.

Moreover, the intense questioning tone of John Wilson's source play (*Hamp*) is replaced with what are little more than academic debates about morality. PH

King and Four Queens, The

(1956, US, 84 min)
d Raoul Walsh. *p* David Hempstead. *sc* Margaret Fitts, Richard Alan Simmons. *ph* Lucien Ballard. *ed* David Bretherton. *ad* Wiard Ihnen. *m* Alex North. *cast* Clark Gable, Eleanor Parker, Jean Willes, Jo Van Fleet, Barbara Nichols, Sara Shane, Jay C Flippen.

● World-weary con artist Gable sets out to convince a quartet of widows that he was a member of their men's gang and thus throroughly deserving of a share in the lucrative stash they've buried, but he doesn't count on wily matriarch Van Fleet taking hold of the situation in the way she does. Gable's Hollywood nickname ('The King') is reflected in the title of this pared-down Western which is striking mainly for undercutting its leading man's macho authority.

King and I, The

(1956, US, 133 min)
d Walter Lang. *p* Charles Brackett. *sc* Ernest Lehman. *ph* Leon Shamroy. *ed* Robert Simpson. *ad* Lyle Wheeler, John F DeCuir. *cast* Deborah Kerr, Yul Brynner, Rita Moreno, Martin Benson, Terry Saunders, Carlos Rivas, Alan Mowbray.

● Over-long but visually spectacular musical version, by Rodgers and Hammerstein, of *Anna and the King of Siam*, with Kerr (dubbed for singing by Marni Nixon) as the prim widowed teacher gradually falling for Brynner's autocratic monarch. Poor songs ('Hello Young Lovers', 'Getting to Know You'), fair choreography, poor script, nice photography. GA

King and I, The

(1999, US, 89 min)
d Richard Rich. *p* James G Robinson, Arthur Rankin, Peter Bakalian. *sc* Peter Bakalian, David Seidler, Jacqueline Feather. *ed* James E Koford, Paul Murphy, Joseph Campana. *m* Richard Rodgers. *lyrics* Oscar Hammerstein II. *cast* voices: Miranda Richardson, Martin Vidnovic, Ian Richardson, Darrell Hammond, Allen D Hong, David Burnham.

● Rodgers and Hammerstein's songs are the mainstay of this animated update of the classic 1956 Hollywood musical. Little else surprises. It opens at sea in a thunderstorm as determined English schoolteacher, Anna Leonowens, and her young son battle through waves en route to a teaching post in Siam. The country's opinionated King wants his children educated in a Western fashion, but insists his new arrival toes the line and respects local mores. The story now includes a scheming Prime Minister and his toothsome assistant, whose combined attempts to overthrow the King are thwarted at every turn. The animation may be merely functional but it's explosively colourful. The voice-overs, though, are mostly perfunctory, and you'll have to search hard for a less funny comic sidekick. DA

King and Mister Bird, The (Le Roi et l'Oiseau)

(1980, Fr, 82 min)
d/p Paul Grimault. *sc* Jacques Prévert, Paul Grimault. *ph* Gérard Soirant. *m* Wojciech Kilar. *cast* voices: Pascal Mazzotti, Raymond Bussières, Agnès Viala, Renaud Marx, Hubert Deschaps. Roger Blin.

● The result of a long collaboration (and tortured production history) between animator Grimault and the respected screenwriter Jacques Prévert, this animated cartoon tells of the downfall of the king and kingdom of Tachycardia. Drawing upon ideas and images as different as Fritz Lang's *Metropolis* and the writings of Hans Christian Andersen, the film is distinguished by stylish graphics and an elegant visual and verbal humour that is guaranteed to appeal to all tastes and ages. The characterisations are a delight, and if the pace is occasionally as stately as the Tachycardian royal title (King Charles V-and-III-makes-VIII-and-VIII-makes-XVI), it merely allows more time to gape at the architecture of Tachycardia, a cool collage of Venetian canals, Bavarian castles, and New York tower blocks that is vast, monolithic, and truly vertiginous. FD

King Blank

(1982, US, 72 min, b/w)
d/p Michael Oblowitz. *sc* Michael Oblowitz, Rosemary Hochschild. *ph* Michael Oblowitz. *ed* Susanne Rostock. *cast* Rosemary Hochschild, Ron Vawter, Will Patton, Fred Neuman, Nancy Reilly, Peyton Smith, Cookie Mueller.

● A film that perfectly captures the true spirit of Christmas. Somewhere in the vicinity of Kennedy airport, two lost souls, trapped in a web of obscenity and loathing, play out their terminal lives. All that divides the couple is the little problem of sexual difference, which of course drives the male into psychosis and leads inevitably to a destructive climax. Oblowitz charts their drift through a twilight zone of motel rooms, highways and bars in beautiful black-and-white, but pays equal attention to the sound-track, a dense collage of voices adrift from bodies, music and demented radio stations – an ice-pick for the viewer's ear. It's very funny and deeply moving, and Oblowitz's association with New York's 'New Wave' thankfully counts for nothing. Think instead of Glen or Glenda, Throbbing Gristle and Eraserhead. What the latter did for one-parent families, *King Blank* does for nice heterosexual couples. SJ

King Boxer (Tianxia Diyi Quan/aka Five Fingers of Death)

(1972, HK, 105 min)
d Zheng Changhe. *p* Run Run Shaw. *sc* Chiang Yang. *ph* Wang Yung Lung. *ed* Chang Hsing Lung, Fan Kung Yung. *ad* Chen Chi Jui. *m* Wu Ta Chiang. *cast* Lo Lieh, Wang Ping, Wang Ching-Feng.

● Made by Shaw Brothers in direct response to Golden Harvest's huge success with Bruce Lee, this took the formula for the studio's swordplay genre and adapted it (minimally) for the needs of the new kung-fu. The righteous, virginal Chi-Hao (Lo Lieh, more often cast as a villain) wins a regional martial arts tournament, thereby avenging his two treacherously murdered teachers. Obstacles in his path to victory include black-hearted Chinese, evil Japanese and the ambush which leaves him with broken hands. Director Zheng (who is Korean) delivers by-the-numbers action melodrama, never rising above the studio's house-style, and falls back on tacky colour and sound effects to render the hero's winning 'iron palm' technique. But the *joli laid* Lo is kind of cute, and it's nice to see action choreography (by Lau Kar-Wing) that relies on trampolines rather than wires to enhance the fighters' skills. TR

King Creole

(1958, US, 116 min, b/w)
d Michael Curtiz. *p* Hal B Wallis. *sc* Herbert Baker, Michael V Gazzo. *ph* Russell Harlan. *ed* Warren Low. *ad* Joseph McMillan Johnson. *songs* Jerry Lieber, Mike Stoller, Claude DeMetrius, others. *cast* Elvis Presley, Carolyn Jones, Dolores Hart, Dean Jagger, Walter Matthau, Liliane Montevecchi, Vic Morrow, Paul Stewart.

● Curtiz's intelligent, austere, film *noir*-ish direction provides the perfect antidote to the occasional excesses of a script based on a Harold Robbins novel (*A Stone for Danny Fisher*), and an ideal complement to Presley's performance as a street hustler who forges himself a magnetic rebel image through his music. The sequence in which he sings 'If you're looking for trouble' in a bus-boy's uniform in response to gangster Walter Matthau's dare is prime stuff. VG

King David

(1985, US, 114 min)
d Bruce Beresford. *p* Martin Elfand. *sc* Andrew Birkin, James Costigan. *ph* Donald McAlpine. *ed* William Anderson. *pd* Ken Adam. *m* Carl Davis. *cast* Richard Gere, Edward Woodward, Alice Krige, Denis Quilley, Niall Buggy, Cherie Lunghi, Hurd Hatfield, Jack Klaff, John Castle, Tim Woodward, Gina Bellman.

● The fairly gentle, civilised tone of Beresford's movies marks him as an unlikely choice to render the tall tales of bathos and lyricism and Jehovah-sanctioned savagery that make up the Old Testament account of the exploits of David. On the plus side, the morality hasn't been sanitised for the 20th century, and there are all sorts of rich and strange elements in the visuals. But it seems a fundamental error to approach such a gory fantasia as though it were sober, four-square history. BBa

Kingdom, The (Riget)

(1994, Den, 279 min)
d Lars von Trier, Morton Arnfred. *p* Ole Relm. *sc* Lars von Trier, Tómas Gislason. *ph* Eric Kress. *ed* Jacob Thuesen, Molly Malene Stensgaard. *ad* Jette Lehmann. *m* Joachim Holbek. *cast* Ernst-Hugo Järegård, Kirsten Rolffes, Ghita Nørby, Søren Pilmark, Holger Juul Hansen, Annevig Schelde Ebbe.

● This mordant blend of hospital soap, occult schlocker and social satire makes David Lynch seem prim. Set in a Copenhagen hospital, it's a farce which puts a dead man's grip on the clichés of TV soap opera. The fun comes partly from the deadpan performances – from Järegård's consultant, a universally loathed Dane-hating Swede, to Rolffes' Mrs Drusse, a career patient determined to exorcise from the building the unquiet spirit of a murdered girl. No opportunity for going over the top is missed, no ethical interdict is left untransgressed, no sensibility untrammelled. As a social indictment, it's structured in tiers, from the top-floor, which houses the administrators' Masonic lodge, to the building's bowels, in which work the dishwashers, savants with Down's syndrome who function as an eerie Greek chorus. Shot in breathless *vérité*-style, and marked by von Trier's customary jaundiced tone, it's a compulsive, bizzarely plausible witches' brew of interweaving storylines, conspiracy theories and paranoiac visions, held together by manic conviction right up to its Grand Guignol finale. WH

Kingdom II, The (Riget II)

(1997, Den, 289 min)
d Lars von Trier, Morton Arnfred. *p* Vibeke Windeløv, Svend Abrahamsen. *sc* Lars von Trier, Niels Vørsel. *ph* Eric Kress. *ed* Molly Malene Stensgaard, Pernille Bech Christensen. *ad* Jette Lehmann, Lars Christian Lindholm. *m* Joachim Holbek. *cast* Ernst-Hugo Järegård, Kirsten Rolffes, Ghita Nørby, Søren Pilmark, Holger Juul Hansen.

● It's back to our favourite Copenhagen hospital for another four episodes (with more to come!) of von Trier's surreal soap about medical corruption and monstrous apparitions. No recaps are supplied (some homework is necessary for the uninitiated) while further layers of plot build up with less tension and more extravagant fantasy. Little of this should be revealed in advance – be warned, however, that the emerging baby sporting Udo Kier's head was no bad dream, but a living creature who refuses to stop growing. DT

Kingdom of the Spiders

(1977, US, 95 min)
d John 'Bud' Cardos. *p* Igo Kantor, Jeffrey M Sneller. *sc* Richard Robinson, Alan Caillou. *ph* John Morrill. *ed* Steven Zaillian, Igo Kantor. *m* Igo Kantor. *cast* William Shatner, Tiffany Bolling, Woody Strode, Lieux Dressler, David McLean, Natasha Ryan, Hoke Howell.

● The scene is Arizona, here and now. A calf mysteriously falls ill and dies, baffling local vet and Marlboro' man Shatner. Tissue samples are sent to the big-town university, and the 'liberated' Bolling (insect expert) appears, diagnosing a huge overdose of spider venom. Together they discover a spider hill, a kind of grand convention for all arachnids everywhere. Nature is up-ended. Tarantulas, usually cannibals, have become community conscious. Man's insecticides have destroyed their natural food and so they are turning to…guess what? Wooden performances, ham-fisted direction, an achingly bad script, plus a grisly Country and Western sound-track amount to a must to avoid even for the diehard kitsch fan. IB

King Elephant

see African Elephant, The

King in New York, A

(1957, GB, 105 min, b/w)
d/p/sc Charles Chaplin. *ph* Georges Périnal. *ed* John Seabourne. *ad* Allan Harris. *m* Charles Chaplin. *cast* Charles Chaplin, Dawn Addams, Oliver Johnston, Maxine Audley, Harry Green, Michael Chaplin, Sidney James, Jerry Desmonde, George Woodbridge.

● The Old Man's penultimate movie is very odd indeed – set in America but made in England with a cast of old lags like George Woodbridge (which never helps any film) and filled with Chaplin's loathing for the country which turned against him in the late '40s, forcing him into exile. The film reverses the real-life situation: Chaplin plays the deposed king of Estrovia who flees to the States, where he is tormented by McCarthyish investigations and more innocuous '50s phenomena (rock'n'roll, widescreen movies, TV advertising). In *Limelight*, Chaplin's acute egocentricity paid dividends, but here he seems unable to use his personal feelings for comedy: the bulk of the gags are incredibly crude. One watches the proceedings with constant interest and constant embarrassment. GB

King Is Alive, The

(2000, Den, 109 min)
d Kristian Levring. *p* Patricia Kruijer, Vibeke Windeløv. *sc* Kristian Levring, Anders Thomas Jensen. *ph* Jens Schlosser. *ed* Nicholas Wayman Harris. *cast* Miles Anderson, Romane Bohringer, David Bradley, David Calder, Bruce Davison, Jennifer Jason Leigh, Janet McTeer, Lia Williams.

● Levring's Dogme film takes a familiar situation – a bunch of strangers (in this case, coach passengers) is stranded in the middle of nowhere (here, the African desert) with scant chance of rescue before at least some of their number succumb to hostile nature and/or in-fighting – and adds resonance by having them stave off boredom and fear by putting on a play: *King Lear*. Nothing enormously original, then, as fevers and tensions rise and hopes sink – Levring wisely doesn't push the Lear parallels too far – but it's all very watchable, thanks to excellent performances all round, Jens Schlosser's camerawork (equally good on close-up faces and parched landscapes) and taut pacing. GA

King Kong

(1933, US, 100 min, b/w)
d Merian C Cooper, Ernest B Schoedsack. *sc* James Ashmore Creelman, Ruth Rose. *ph* Eddie Linde, Vernon L Walker, JO Taylor. *ed* Ted Cheesman. *ad* Carroll Clark, Al Herman. *m* Max Steiner. *cast* Fay Wray, Bruce Cabot, Robert Armstrong, Noble Johnson, Frank Reicher, Sam Hardy, James Flavin.

● If this glorious pile of horror-fantasy hokum has lost none of its power to move, excite and sadden, it is in no small measure due to the remarkable technical achievements of Willis O'Brien's animation work, and the superbly matched score of Max Steiner. The masterstroke was, of course, to delay the great ape's entrance by a shipboard sequence of such humorous banality and risible dialogue that Kong can emerge unchallenged as the most fully realised character in the film. Thankfully Wray is not required to act, merely to scream; but what a perfect victim she makes. The throbbing heart of the film lies in the creation of the semi-human simian himself, an immortal tribute to the Hollywood dream factory's ability to fashion a symbol that can express all the contradictory erotic, ecstatic, destructive, pathetic and cathartic buried impulses of 'civilised' man. WH

King Kong

(1976, US, 135 min)
d John Guillermin. *p* Dino De Laurentiis. *sc* Lorenzo Semple Jr. *ph* Richard H Kline. *ed* Ralph E Winters. *pd* Mario Chiari, Dale Hennesy. *m* John Barry. *cast* Jeff Bridges, Charles Grodin, Jessica Lange, John Randolph, René Auberjonois, Julius Harris, Ed Lauter, John Agar.

● The results of this technological bonanza are pretty mixed. With the ape's human characteristics exaggerated, the new Kong lacks his predecessor's noble, yet truly alien ferocity. Seemingly too human, his relationship with the nauseating Jessica Lange is pushed to mawkish and degrading lengths. But Lorenzo Semple's script tries hard to build on its more interesting components. He is unreservedly on the side of Kong and the anthropologist (Bridges), against the oil/sexploitation company who are out to exhibit the ape (and Lange) as commercial objects. And the film's spirited climax is worthy of its ancestry, while a highly ambiguous ending allows the plot to reassert its old political strength and redeem the more grotesque and sexist moments of this resurrection. DP

King Lear

(1970, GB/Den, 137 min, b/w)
d Peter Brook. *p* Michael Birkett. *ph* Henning Kristiansen. *ed* Kasper Schyberg. *pd* Georges Wakhévitch. *cast* Paul Scofield, Irene Worth, Alan Webb, Tom Fleming, Susan Engel, Annelise Gabold, Jack MacGowran, Cyril Cusack, Patrick Magee, Jack MacGowran, Robert Langdon Lloyd, Ian Hogg.

● Made on location in what looks like a perilously cold Denmark, Brook's only Shakespeare on celluloid found a similarly frosty reception, especially as it came out just after Kozintsev's grandly conceived Russian version. Brook's filming is graceless – looming close-ups, perverse camera moves – but there are some remarkable performances (developed from his much praised stage production a few years before with Scofield). The conception is consistent with the influential views of Jan Kott, who saw Lear as a precursor to Beckett's plays about human blindness and nothingness (a line reinforced by the casting of MacGowran as the Fool, and Magee as the Duke of Cornwall). A bleak interpretation, in every sense. DT

King Lear (Korol Lir)

(1970, USSR, 139 min, b/w)
d/sc Grigori Kozintsev. *ph* Jonas Gritsius. *ad* Yevgeni Yenei, Vsevelod Ulitko. *m* Dimitri Shostakovich. *cast* Yuri Yarvet, Elsa Radzinya, Galina Volchek, Valentina Shendrikova, Karl Sebris, Regimantis Adomaitis, Oleg Dal.

● Kozintsev's lusty adaptation succeeds in finding memorable equivalents for Shakespeare's verbal imagery, although the narrative is necessarily somewhat truncated. He makes Lear and his daughters act like a conceivable family, and brings the people into the affairs of the nobility more than usual, but the women fare badly. YevgeniYarvet (whose energetic though foolish king is far from the doddering dope Lear is usually made out to be) and Oleg Dal (the Fool) are incredible. Music by Shostakovich; subtitles by Shakespeare. VG

King Lear

(1987, US, 90 min)
d Jean-Luc Godard. *p* Menahem Golan, Yoram Globus. *sc* Jean-Luc Godard. *ph* Sophie Maintigneux. *ed* Jean-Luc Godard. *cast* Burgess Meredith, Peter Sellars, Molly Ringwald, Jean-Luc Godard, Woody Allen, Norman Mailer, Kate Miller, Léos Carax.

● Godard's dullest and least accomplished for some time. Expectedly, only the odd line of Shakespeare's text survives, mouthed by bratpacker Molly Ringwald. People wander in and out; connections are tenuous in the extreme. Mailer gets a scene or two, suggests a Mafia reading of the play, and exits. Enter Burgess Meredith to pick up the cue as an ex-hoodlum, Don Learo, bewailing to his sullen daughter Ringwald, at a lakeside restaurant, the fate of the crime barons of old at the hands of the big corporations. Godard plays a shambling 'professor', his telephone-cable dreadlocks suggesting he may be the Fool. The fragmentation of image, narrative, sound and music are familiar, but here employed to no effect. Intercut are stills of dead, great directors. Intertitles like 'C-Lear-ings' and 'No-thing' testify to Godard's continuing fidelity to the ideas of modern French existentialism. Another of his essays on the impossiblity of making movies in our time, this has all the dreariness of a pathologist's dictated notes. WH

King of Alcatraz

(1938, US, 56 min, b/w)
d Robert Florey. *p* William C Thomas. *sc* Irving Reis. *ph* Harry Fischbeck. *ed* Eda Warren. *ad* Hans Dreier, Earl Hedrick. *m* Boris Morros. *cast* Lloyd Nolan, Robert Preston, Gail Patrick, J Carrol Naish, Harry Carey, Anthony Quinn, Dennis Morgan.

● A terrific B movie from Paramount's resident backlot maestro, Robert Florey. Naish makes an unclean break from the prison island, landing up (initially in drag, accompanied by hijacking henchmen) on a tramp steamer whose wireless is manned by operators Nolan and Preston, buddies currently under disciplinary downgrading because of their perpetual brawling rivalry. They get to show their mettle to pretty Gail Patrick. The script has no time for subtleties, but the movie is extremely well put together, and it moves at a tremendous lick. TCh

King of Burlesque

(1936, US, 83 min, b/w)
d Sidney Lanfield. *p* Kenneth MacGowran. *sc* James Seymour, Gene Markey, Harry Tugend. *ph* Peverell Marley. *ed* Ralph Dietrich. *ad* Hans Peters. *songs* Jimmy McHugh, Ted Koeller. *cast* Warner Baxter, Jack Oakie, Mona Barrie, Alice Faye, Dixie Dunbar, Fats Waller.

● Backstage musical with Baxter as a burlesque producer from the wrong side of town who tries to make it big on Broadway. Mona Barrie is the leech-like socialite who marries him, then bleeds him dry of all his cash. Alice Faye is on hand to soothe him back to success in the final reel. The song and dance is chipper enough, but the storyline needs more beef. Fats Waller makes a rare (but brief) appearance. GM

King of Comedy, The

(1982, US, 109 min)
d Martin Scorsese. *p* Arnon Milchan. *sc* Paul D Zimmerman. *ph* Fred Schuler. *ed* Thelma Schoonmaker. *pd* Boris Leven. *m* Robbie Robertson. *cast* Robert De Niro, Jerry Lewis, Diahnne Abbott, Sandra Bernhard, Ed Herlihy, Lou Brown, Catherine Scorsese, Martin Scorsese.

● Scorsese and De Niro have been pushing each other so far for so long that audience polarisation now automatically accompanies the risk of their major-league collaboration. *The King of Comedy* guarantees a split even at the level of expectations: it's definitively not a comedy, despite being hilarious; it pays acute homage to Jerry Lewis, while requiring of the man no hint of slapstick infantilism; its uniquely repellent prize nerd is De Niro himself. The excruciating tone is set by an early freeze-frame of fingernails frantically scraping glass. Flinch here, and you're out, because Scorsese never does while detailing fantasist Rupert Pupkin's squirmily obsessive desperation to crash TV's real-time as a stand-up comic on the Carson-modelled Jerry Langford Show. Buttonholing its star (Lewis), then rebounding from brush-offs to hatch a ludicrous kidnap plot, De Niro's Pupkin isn't merely socially inadequate; he's a whole dimension short – happily rehearsing with cardboard cut-outs, choosing the flatness of videoscreen space for his schmucky jester's tilt at being 'king for a night'. Whereas the film itself is all unexpected dimensions and unsettling excesses, with the ambiguous fulfilment of Pupkin's dream frighteningly echoing the news-headline coda of *Taxi Driver*. Creepiest movie of the year in every sense, and one of the best. PT

King of Hearts (Le Roi de Coeur)

(1966, Fr/It, 110 min)
d/p Philippe de Broca. *sc* Daniel Boulanger. *ph* Pierre Lhomme. *ed* Françoise Javet. *ad* François de Lamothe. *m* Georges Delerue. *cast* Alan Bates, Geneviève Bujold, Jean-Claude Brialy, Françoise Christophe, Julien Guiomar, Pierre Brasseur, Michel Serrault, Micheline Presle, Adolfo Celi.

● One of the sleepers of all time in that, tried out in a small Boston cinema years after it flopped in the UK and in America, it became a kind of *Mousetrap* in student cinemas across the States. On a World War I mission, Bates discovers a town of lunatics which is due to be blown up at midnight. The fairy-tale atmosphere and carnival energy are nicely placed, but the whole excessively whimsical thing would have worked so much better if de Broca had toughened up the overall (wartime) context instead of letting everything slide towards farce. PT

King of Jazz, The

(1930, US, 105 min)
d John Murray Anderson. *p* Carl Laemmle. *sc* Frederick T Lowe Jr, Harry Raskin. *ph* Hal Mohr, Jerome Ash, Ray Rennahan. *ed* Robert Carlisle. *ad* Herman Rosse. *songs* Buddy de Sylva, Robert Katscher, Jack Yellen, others. *cast* Paul Whiteman and His Orchestra, John Boles, Bing Crosby and the Rhythm Boys, Slim Summerville, Laura LaPlante.

● Jazz? Whiteman may not have been the hottest swinger in town, but this is still hugely enjoyable, partly because of the marvellous two-strip Technicolor, partly because it dispenses with story altogether to focus on a lavishly designed musical revue. Catch Joe Venuti on fiddle, and Whiteman and his boys pounding out Gershwin's 'Rhapsody in Blue'. GA

King of Kings

(1961, US, 168 min)
d Nicholas Ray. *p* Samuel Bronston. *sc* Philip Yordan. *ph* Franz Planer, Milton Krasner, Manuel Berenguer. *ed* Harold F Kress. *ad* Georges Wakhévitch. *m* Miklós Rózsa. *cast* Jeffrey Hunter, Robert Ryan, Siobhan McKenna, Frank Thring, Hurd Hatfield, Rip Torn, Harry Guardino, Viveca Lindfors, Rita Gam.
●Despite being churlishly described at the time as 'I Was a Teenage Jesus' (in reference to the youth rebellion of *Rebel Without a Cause*), this is one of the most interesting screen versions of the Gospels. As so often in the work of script-writer Philip Yordan, the central conflict is seen in terms of political struggle and betrayal; detailing the Jews' rebellion against the oppressive power of Rome, it elevates Barabbas in particular to the status of an almost proto-Zionist nationalist leader, and the dynamics of the narrative are presented as the consequence of wide-ranging historical movements rather than the whims of charismatic individuals. As a result, some of the performances appear to lack depth, but one can't deny the effectiveness of Miklós Rózsa's fine score, and of Ray's simple but elegant visuals which achieve a stirring dramatic power untainted by pompous bombast. Despite producer Samuel Bronston's meddlesome editing, in fact, it's an intelligent, imaginative movie devoid of conventional Hollywood pieties. GA

King of Kung Fu (Shi Xiong Chu Ma/aka He Walks Like a Tiger)

(1973, HK, 93 min)
d Jiang Yixiong. *p* Pai Chin. *sc* Jiang Yixiong. *ph* Chen Chao-Yung. *ed* Lee Yen Hai. *ad* Lu Chien-Ming. cast Alex Lung, Christine Hui, Yukio Someno, Steve Yu, Yu Lung.
●This is a straight-up Chinese actioner with no trimmings, a few decidedly graceful moments (an acrobatic group performing in slow motion), and a virtue that several of the independent productions seem to share, that of incorporating a genuine street feeling, however fleetingly, into the proceedings. Out of the same stable as *Headcrusher*, the film is marred by the usual rambly story-line, some sentimentality, and exec producer Jimmy L Pascual's continuing love affair with the police (the 'man with no name' turns out to be an investigating officer). The fights are spirited. VG

King of Marvin Gardens, The

(1972, US, 104 min)
d/p Bob Rafelson. *sc* Jacob Brackman. *ph* Laszlo Kovacs. *ed* John F Link II. *ad* Toby Carr Rafelson. *cast* Jack Nicholson, Bruce Dern, Ellen Burstyn, Julia Anne Robinson, Scatman Crothers, Charles Lavine, John Ryan, Sully Boyar.
●An irresistible movie, not least for its haunting vision of Atlantic City as Xanadu, a stately pleasure dome of genteelly decaying palaces, rundown funfairs, and empty boardwalks presided over by white elephants abandoned to their brooding fate. It's like some unimaginable country of the mind, and so in a sense it is as two brothers embark on a sort of game (Atlantic City provided the original place names for the Monopoly board) in which they exchange their lives, their loves and their dreams. One has retreated, like Prospero, from the pain outside into the island of his mind; the other pursues an endless mirage of get-rich-quick schemes which will let him escape to an island paradise. Their fusion is a stunningly complex evocation of childish complicity and Pinterish obsessions, inevitably leading to tragedy as the obsessions founder on reality. One of the most underrated films of the decade. TM

King of Masks (Bian Lian)

(1995, HK, 101 min)
d/p Wu Tianming. *sc* Wei Minglun. *ph* Mu Dayuan. *ed* Hui Yulan. *pd* Wu Xujing. *m* Zhao Jiping. *cast* Chu Yuk, Chao Yim Yin, Zhao Zhi Gang, Zhang Riu Yang.
●The first film in ten years from the one-time godfather of China's 'fifth generation' directors is an eloquent and deeply felt protest against greed and inhumanity; any relevance to the state of Chinese society in the 1990s is, of course, purely coincidental. The story centres on an elderly street entertainer in the rural Sichuan of the 1930s (his act involves switching masks with uncanny speed) who realises that he risks dying without an heir to inherit the secrets of his art. He decides to adopt a son, but the boy he buys from a penniless man turns out to be a tomboy who brings him little but grief. The film's allegorical implications are almost as plain as its attacks on sexual inequalities and political misrule, but Wu lets nothing get in the way of very expressive images and a very emotive plot. TR

King of New York

(1989, US, 103 min)
d Abel Ferrara. *p* Mary Kane. *sc* Nicholas St John. *ph* Bojan Bazelli. *ed* Anthony Redman. *pd* Alex Tavoularis. *m* Joe Delia. *cast* Christopher Walken, David Caruso, Larry Fishburne, Victor Argo, Wesley Snipes, Janet Julian, Joey Chin, Giancarlo Esposito, Steve Buscemi.
●Quite easily the most violent, foul-mouthed and truly nasty of current gangster movies. It might be charitable to say that Ferrara, who made the reasonably decent *Cat Chaser*, is doing a *Scarface* by pointing up the designer nature of modern urban crime, its brutality and ethnic mixture, and its attempts to infiltrate the mainstream. Certainly, in the person of Walken, spare, elegant, slightly spaced and lording it over a black/hispanic gang, the film has an impressively charismatic central character: the kind of powerbroker who does favours for the poor and makes love on subway trains, but still manages the right burst of psychosis when dealing with racist rivals, Chinese nasties, or treacherous black brothers. Sadly, his performance is wasted on a film which, despite splendid location work, lurches sloppily and messily from kill to kill, orgy to orgy, coke to crack, cliché to cliché. SGr

King of Paris, The

see Roi de Paris, Le

King of the Children (Haizi Wang)

(1987, China, 106 min)
d Chen Kaige. *p* Wu Tianming. *sc* Chen Kaige, Wan Zhi. *ph* Gu Changwei *ed* Liu Miaomiao. *ad* Chen Shaohua. *m* Qu Xiaosong. *cast* Xie Yuan, Yang Xuewen, Chen Shaohua, Zhang Caimei, Xu Guoqing, Gu Changwei.
●An unschooled young man, one of the countless victims of Mao's Cultural Revolution, is labouring in the countryside when he is suddenly assigned to teach in a near-by village school. Gradually, he finds the confidence to ditch the Maoist textbook and encourage the barely literate kids to write about their own lives and feelings. At the same time, through a series of dream-like meetings with a young cowherd, he begins to sense the possibilities of a life beyond the parameters of traditional education. There are echoes here of a film like *Padre Padrone*, but Chen's film is completely free of flabby humanist sentimentality. It takes its tonality from the harsh beauty of the Yunnan landscape of soaring forests and misty valleys: a territory of the mind where hard-edged realism blurs easily into hallucination. By Chinese standards, this is film-making brave to the point of being visionary. By any standards, this follow-up to *Yellow Earth* and *The Big Parade* is also something like a masterpiece. TR

King of the Damned

(1935, GB, 76 min, b/w)
d Walter Forde. *p* Michael Balcon. *sc* Charles Bennett, Sidney Gilliat. *ph* Bernard Knowles. *ed* Cyril Randell. *ad* OF Werndorff. *cast* Conrad Veidt, Helen Vinson, Noah Beery, Cecil Ramage, Edmund Willard, Raymond Lovell, Percy Parsons.
●Basically just another of those penal colony movies, set in a Caribbean Devil's Island, with the convicts rebelling against a sadistic regime. Not uninteresting, though, in the Popular Front slant to its script whereby Veidt, having led a successful revolt against the cruelly oppressive (but temporary) governor, plays desperately for time before the news gets out because his main objective is to prove that the island can be run profitably and peacefully by the convicts themselves. Though too good to be true as a character (as is his bluff sidekick, played by Beery), Veidt gives his usual admirable performance; the camera-work (Bernard Knowles) is remarkably atmospheric; and Forde's direction is more than capable. TM

King of the Gypsies

(1978, US, 112 min)
d Frank Pierson. *p* Federico De Laurentiis. *sc* Frank Pierson. *ph* Sven Nykvist, Ed Lachman. *ed* Paul Hirsch. *pd* Gene Callahan. *m* David Grisman. *cast* Sterling Hayden, Shelley Winters, Susan Sarandon, Judd Hirsch, Eric Roberts, Brooke Shields, Annette O'Toole, Annie Potts, Michael V Gazzo.
●This starts in the rematch-for-retards category – reuniting Sarandon and Shields as the selfish mother/saleable daughter team from *Pretty Baby* – then tries to filter *The Godfather* through *Fiddler on the Roof*. Result: a gypsy vernacular of incredible brayings, bleatings, and raspings painfully laced with the Bronx (where much of the action occurs), and numerous crowd scenes resembling some *Night of the Living Loviches*. Sarandon outcrasses everyone else (matched only by the scene by scene disintegration of Shelley Winters). The Gypsy King's young successor (Roberts) – his decline predestined by the current recession of interest in fortune-telling – tries to make it all mean something: 'This is just temporary…and it's all trashy.' If only he were right; really it's endless and doggedly in earnest. CR

King of the Hill

(1993, US, 103 min)
d Steven Soderbergh. *p* Barbara Maltby, Albert Berger, Ron Yerxa. *sc* Steven Soderbergh. *ph* Elliot Davis. *ed* Steven Soderbergh. *pd* Gary Frutkoff. *m* Cliff Martinez. *cast* Jesse Bradford, Jeroen Krabbé, Lisa Eichhorn, Karen Allen, Spalding Gray, Elizabeth McGovern, Adrien Brody.
●St Louis, 1933. The Great Depression. Twelve-year-old Aaron (Bradford) has the richest imagination in the class and the poorest parents. They board in a dilapidated hotel in the wrong part of town. Mother (Eichhorn) goes into hospital, suffering from what looks like general malaise. Father (Krabbé) sends away Aaron's younger brother to live with his aunt, and when a job finally comes his way, he has no choice but to go on the road as a travelling salesman. That leaves Aaron to fend for himself, with some help from his steetwise pal Lester (Brody), and the kindly concern of the odd sympathetic adult. If Soderbergh could be said to be playing safe here, who could blame him after the ambitious but neglected *Kafka*? True the coming-of-age scenario holds few surprises, but this beautifully played film's sensitivity speaks volumes; Soderbergh lets his camera do the talking. What seems initially a nostalgic hue eventually becomes a harder, tougher tone. The result is both heartening and astringent. TCh

King of the Roaring 20's – The Story of Arnold Rothstein (aka The Big Bankroll)

(1961, US, 106 min, b/w)
d Joseph M Newman. *p* Samuel Bischoff, David Diamond. *sc* Jo Swerling. *ph* Carl Guthrie. *ed* George White. *ad* David Milton. *m* Franz Waxman. *cast* David Janssen, Dianne Foster, Jack Carson, Dan O'Herlihy, Mickey Rooney, Keenan Wynn, Joseph Schildkraut, Mickey Shaughnessy, William Demarest, Regis Toomey, Diana Dors.
●Cavalier about its facts, this biopic of the infamous, short, chubby gambling kingpin Arnold Rothstein (played by tall smoothie Janssen) contrives to suggest that all went wrong for this middle-class whizz-kid because his child-hood peccadillos were dogged by a bent cop (O'Herlihy) eternally on the take. His achievement of fame, fortune and true love (Foster) comes crashing around his ears when his schemes lead to the gangland murder of his longtime buddy and partner (Rooney). Rothstein has to hold himself morally responsible; but the real culprit, we are assured, is racketeer Big Tim O'Brien (Carson), working hand-in-glove with O'Herlihy (among others) to gain control of the gambling scene by manipulating Rothstein. Terminally dreary in its convolutions, the script eventually disappears up the backside of its plodding plot, while only Jack Carson manages to invest his character with any conviction. TM

King of the Wind

(1989, US, 102 min)
d Peter Duffell. *p* Michael Guest, Paul Sarony, Peter S Davis, William Panzer. *sc* Phil Frey. *ph*

Brian Morgan. *ed* Lyndon Matthews. *pd* Ken Sharp. *m* John Scott. *cast* Frank Finlay, Jenny Agutter, Nigel Hawthorne, Navin Chowdry, Ralph Bates, Barry Foster, Anthony Quayle, Ian Richardson, Norman Rodway, Peter Vaughan, Richard Harris, Glenda Jackson, Melvyn Hayes.
●HTV's adaptation of Marguerite Henry's children's adventure story boasts the sort of cast usually reserved for Agatha Christie (a couple of lines apiece for Harris and Jackson; others guilty of accepting insupportable roles). The leads, however, go to young Navin Chowdry (from *Madame Sousatzka*) as a mute Arab orphan, and the feisty colt he grooms for the Bey of Tunis. Presented as a gift to King Louis XV of France, the pair's fortunes swing from aristocratic patronage to plebeian servitude, and back again, and back again, taking in at least six owners and locations as diverse as the French court and Newgate jail. This viewer would have been happy to trade the surfeit of plot for a touch of subtlety. But horses for courses: children will probably respond to these equestrian escapades, Chowdry makes a natural hero, and Duffell's economic direction at least ensures that the going is firm. TCh

Kingpin

(1996, US, 114 min)
d Peter Farrelly, Bobby Farrelly. *p* Brad Krevoy, Steve Stabler, Bradley Thomas. *sc* Barry Fanaro, Mort Nathan. *ph* Mark Irwin. *ed* Chris Greenbury. *pd* Sidney Jackson Bartholomew Jr. *m* Freedy Johnston. *cast* Woody Harrelson, Randy Quaid, Vanessa Angel, Bill Murray, Chris Elliott, William Jordan, Lin Shaye.
●Harrelson's Roy Munson, the 1979 Odor Eaters Ten-Pin Bowling Champion, has been 17 years on the skids, paying off the bubo-encrusted landlady of his verminous flophouse with vomit-inducing bouts of sex. If he's lucky. Only with the arrival of fright-wigged con artist Ernie McCracken (Murray, gleefully camp) do things look up, McCracken teaching him to make money hustling ten-pin, until he's abandoned to a bunch of rednecks who twig to him and slash off his bowling hand. Undaunted, he happens upon Quaid's Ishmael Boorg, an ingenuous Amish and fellow bowling natural, and they take off for the National Championships in Reno, pausing only to pick up mini-skirted 'personal companion' Claudia (Angel). There's something arresting in the sheer commitment the Farrelly brothers bring to the naff gags, pratfalls and ritual humiliations these three go through. More beguiling still is their warts-and-all depiction of low life, so upfront it ends up quite affectionate; equally, the keen observations quash charges of cynicism. Dumbfounding. WH

King, Queen, Knave (Herzbube)

(1972, WGer/US, 92 min)
d Jerzy Skolimowski. *p* Lutz Hengst. *sc* David Shaw, David Seltzer. *ph* Christopher Steinberger. *ed* Melvin Shapiro. *ad* Rolf Zehetbauer. *m* Stanley Myers. *cast* Gina Lollobrigida, David Niven, John Moulder-Brown, Mario Adorf, Carl Fox-Duering, Barbara Valentin, Sonia Hofmann.
●Probably the most unjustly underrated of all Skolimowski's films, a surreal black comedy – based on Nabokov's novel retailing a triangle situation, with puckish overtones of obsession and perversion, between a wealthy businessman, his luscious wife, and an orphaned boy – that pushes some of the satirical extravagances of Frank Tashlin and Jerry Lewis to their most logical and deathly conclusions. Hilarious, misanthropic and disturbing, the movie amply fulfils Tom Milne's description of it as 'the most Nabokovian film the cinema has thrown up to date'. Despite reservations about its hybrid nature as an English version of a West German production, it certainly warrants a look. JR

King Ralph

(1991, US, 97 min)
d David S Ward. *p* Jack Brodsky. *sc* David S Ward. *ph* Kenneth MacMillan. *ed* John Jympson. *pd* Simon Holland. *m* James Newton Howard. *cast* John Goodman, Peter O'Toole, John Hurt, Camille Coduri, Richard Griffiths, Leslie Phillips, Joely Richardson, Julian Glover, Judy Parfitt.
●When the entire English royal family is killed in a freak accident, a team of scholars sets about finding an heir to the throne. Meet Ralph Jones (Goodman), Las Vegas entertainer and all-round loser. The reluctant monarch makes his way to face the horrors of etiquette, corgis and entourage, and before long Buckingham Palace comes to resemble a fun-fair. Meanwhile, dastardly Lord Graves (Hurt, wonderfully hammy) plots his fall from grace. This lame hybrid of travelogue and (attempted) satire introduces the unwary American to English cuisine, cricket and newspapers, and any notions that the film is irreverent are trashed by a concluding homage to the monarchy. The ever-watchable Goodman is given no opportunity to exercise his intelligence here, while Hurt and O'Toole (impeccable as the King's private secretary) go through the paces. Laughable – without the laughs. CM

King Rat

(1965, US, 134 min, b/w)
d Bryan Forbes. *p* James Woolf. *sc* Bryan Forbes. *ph* Burnett Guffey. *ed* Walter Thompson. *ad* Robert Smith. *m* John Barry. *cast* George Segal, Tom Courtenay, James Fox, Denholm Elliott, Todd Armstrong, Patrick O'Neal, James Donald, John Mills, Alan Webb, Leonard Rossiter.
●Interesting but flawed adaptation of James Clavell's novel about a Japanese POW camp in Singapore towards the end of World War II. Taking a leaf out of Billy Wilder's *Stalag 17*, it similarly sets out to demonstrate that survival was the name of the game (with Segal taking the William Holden role as the cynical collaborator/fixer-upper), but goes a stage further to delete all notions of heroism. The trouble is that the script gets lost between too many options, setting up a number of character conflicts but taking them nowhere much. Effective performances and camera-work (Burnett Guffey), but Forbes directs with his usual lapses into overstatement. TM

Kings and Desperate Men

(1981, Can, 118 min)
d/p Alexis Kanner. *sc* Edmund Ward, Alexis Kanner. *ph/ed* Alexis Kanner. *ad* Will McGow. *m* Michel Robidoux, Pierre Brault. *cast* Patrick McGoohan, Alexis Kanner, Andréa Marcovicci, Margaret Trudeau, Jean-Pierre Brown, Robin Spry.
●A generally inept psychological thriller, loosely taking off from the last episode of *The Prisoner* with its conflict between McGoohan and Kanner. The former's a radio phone-in host, the latter some sort of leftie who holds McGoohan hostage and demands the retrial of a recent court case over the airwaves. Pretty over the top, not to mention ill-conceived in its woolly thinking about terrorism. GA

Kings Go Forth

(1958, US, 109 min, b/w)
d Delmer Daves. *p* Frank Ross. *sc* Merle Miller. *ph* Daniel L Fapp. *ed* William B Murphy. *ad* Fernando Carrere. *m* Elmer Bernstein. *cast* Frank Sinatra, Tony Curtis, Natalie Wood, Karl Swenson, Leora Dana.
●Well-crafted but unconvincing mixture of war movie and melodramatic problem picture, with Sinatra and Curtis as GIs in France in 1944, falling out over Wood, an expatriate American girl who is beautiful but proves to be not entirely white. Daves, as so often, does a careful salvage job on a soapy script, but the best sequence is a brief jazz interlude with Curtis (giving the best performance in the film) grabbing a trumpet in a dive and (ghosted by Pete Candoli) sitting in with Red Norvo and group. GA

Kings of the Road (Im Lauf der Zeit)

(1976, WGer, 176 min, b/w)
d/p/sc Wim Wenders. *ph* Robby Müller. *ed* Peter Przygodda. *ad* Heidi Lüdi, Bernd Hirskorn. *m* Axel Linstädt. *cast* Rüdiger Vogler, Hanns Zischler, Lisa Kreuzer, Rudolf Schündler, Marquard Böhm.
●...or, King of the Road Movies. Wenders' epic, during which little happens, is one of the great films about men (with each other, without women), about travelling, about cinema (one of the central characters is a projection engineer visiting rundown cinemas), and about the effect of America in 'colonising' the European subconscious. The plot, such as it is, about two men meeting up, moving around Germany, and then splitting up again, is a loose framework for an investigation in various subjects that is marked by its emotional honesty, stunning visual organisation, lack of contrivance, and use of music. Marvellous. GA

Kings of the Sun

(1963, US, 107 min)
d J Lee Thompson. *p* Lewis J Rachmil. *sc* Elliott Arnold, James R Webb. *ph* Joseph MacDonald. *ed* William H Reynolds. *ad* Alfred Ybarra. *m* Elmer Bernstein. *cast* Yul Brynner, George Chakiris, Shirley Anne Field, Richard Basehart, Brad Dexter, Barry Morse, Armando Silvestre, Leo Gordon.
●An ambitious, if ludicrous, pre-Western, marking the struggles between exiled Mayan tribesmen (led by Chakiris as Prince Balam) and the native Indians (Brynner as Chief Black Eagle) in what eventually became Texas, achieving peaceful coexistence after the Mayans abandon their rites of human sacrifice. On the heels of this portentous exotica, co-writer James R Webb picked up the same year's Oscar for what might be construed as the continuing story, *How the West Was Won*. PT

King Solomon's Mines

(1937, GB, 80 min, b/w)
d Robert Stevenson. *sc* Michael Hogan, Roland Pertwee. *ph* Glen MacWilliams. *ed* Michael S Gordon. *ad* Alfred Junge. *m* Mischa Spoliansky. *cast* Paul Robeson, Cedric Hardwicke, John Loder, Roland Young, Anna Lee, Sydney Fairbrother, Robert Adams.
●Not quite Rider Haggard's ripping adventure, given that Robeson's Umbopo is required to sing (singularly soggy stuff, too, with full orchestral accompaniment) and a soppily conventional love interest has been injected. But there are two fine performances (Hardwicke as Allan Quartermain, Young as Captain Good), Stevenson keeps things moving quite briskly to the volcanic climax, and it's a damn sight better than the 1985 remake (or the 1950 Stewart Granger version for that matter). TM

King Solomon's Mines

(1985, US, 100 min)
d J Lee Thompson. *p* Menahem Golan, Yoram Globus. *sc* Gene Quintano, James R Silke. *ph* Alex Phillips. *ed* John Shirley. *pd* Luciano Spadoni. *m* Jerry Goldsmith. *cast* Richard Chamberlain, Sharon Stone, Herbert Lom, Bernard Archard, John Rhys-Davies, Ken Gampu.
●Haggard's magnificently cynical Allan Quartermain gives way to Richard Chamberlain's bland incompetent, a man with the sex appeal of a sheep and the comic timing of a manatee. Sharon Stone is trapped in the role of a silly woman who needs rescuing, much like the heroine of the *Indiana Jones and the Temple of Doom* farrago, a film which this clearly imitates. The friendly Umbopo turns out, for reasons a shade obscure, to be Twala, the book's bad number. And the feral relentlessness of tribal bloodshed is nowhere to be seen; instead there are comic Huns with pointy helmets and bad manners. It's stone cold dead on the slab. CPea

King Solomon's Treasure

(1978, Can, 88 min)
d Alvin Rakoff. *p* Alvin Rakoff, Susan A Lewis. *sc* Colin Turner, Allan Prior. *ph* Paul van der Linden. *ed* Stan Cole. *ad* Vianney Gauthier, James Wetherup. *m* Lew Leham. *cast* David McCallum, John Colicos, Patrick MacNee, Britt Ekland, Yvon Dufour, Ken Gampu, Wilfrid Hyde-White.
●Credited as based on Rider Haggard's *Allan Quartermain*, but suspicions of 'poetic licence', creeping in with the appearance of the first prehistoric monster, are confirmed as full-blown travesty by the time our three bluff Victorian hearties, setting out for Solomon's legendary city, start using a pseudopod as a beast of burden. Cheapness aside (polystyrene pillars will bounce), it's the multitude of nationalities that becomes confusing (Viking vessel crewed by Romans, Queen Britt as Cleopatra, an ancient Greek and Madame de Pompadour in the space of an afternoon). But it's hard to dislike the blimpish trio, who miraculously survive rebellious priests, erupting volcanoes and tumbling cities to return to the old country with nothing but a tale to tell their grandchildren. FF

Kings Row

(1940, US, 127 min, b/w)
d Sam Wood. *sc* Casey Robinson. *ph* James Wong Howe. *ed* Ralph Dawson. *pd* William Cameron Menzies. *m* Erich Wolfgang Korngold. *cast* Ann Sheridan, Robert Cummings, Ronald Reagan, Betty Field,

Claude Rains, Charles Coburn, Judith Anderson, Maria Ouspenskaya, Nancy Coleman.
●Question: connect President Reagan with the following quotation, 'A good town to live in. A good place to raise your children.' No, not one of Ron's election promises; it's the roadside sign that gets this glorious, maggot's-eye view of mid-town America under way, the film that made Reagan a star. Twenty years later he was back to second billing, but was busying himself as President of the Screen Actors Guild, leading and winning a strike for residual payments for non-theatrical releases. Twenty years later still, and the SAG won another deal on residuals while our Ron bid for a bigger presidency. Strange to think he'd probably protest about a contemporary *Kings Row* as un-American, and that he drew up anti-union legislation. The movie, though, is one of the great melodramas (from the same Wood/Menzies stable that made *Gone With the Wind*), as compulsive and perverse as any election, a veritable Mount Rushmore of emotional and physical cripples, including a surgeon with a penchant for unnecessary amputations, a girl who 'made friends on one side of the tracks and made love on the other', and best of all, a legless Reagan wondering 'Where's the rest of me?' PK

King Steps Out, The

(1936, US, 85 min, b/w)
d Josef von Sternberg. *sc* Sidney Buchman. *ph* Ernst Marischka. *ph* Lucien Ballard. *ed* Viola Lawrence. *ad* Stephen Goosson. *m* Fritz Kreisler. *cast* Grace Moore, Franchot Tone, Walter Connolly, Raymond Walburn, Elizabeth Risdon, Frieda Inescort, Herman Bing, Victor Jory.
●Exchanging Paramount and Dietrich for Columbia and Miss Grace Moore (as she is rather crassly credited), Sternberg's heart was all too obviously not in this adaptation of a Fritz Kreisler operetta. Moore, overdoing the skittish charm, plays Princess Elizabeth of Bavaria, who ends up in the arms of the Emperor Franz Josef (Tone) after intervening to save her sister (Inescort) – who loves a young officer (Jory) – from becoming his prearranged bride. Sternberg makes heavy weather of the comic opera conventions; he lumbers his star with several unflattering close-ups (notably when she sings: unusually, the songs were shot 'live'); and he gets his act together (his interest obviously captured by the bustling movement and quaint sideshow attractions of a rustic fair) only during a lengthy sequence in which the Emperor steps out incognito with the princess he believes to be a humble dressmaker. The rest is tasteless puff pastry for operetta buffs only. TM

King Ubu (Král Ubu)

(1996, Czech Republic, 84 min)
d FA Brabec. *p* Pavel Borovan. *sc* Milos Macourek. *ph* FA Brabec. *ed* Boris Machytka. *pd* Jindrich Goëtz. *m* Petr Kurka. *cast* Marian Labuda, Lucie Bilá, Karel Roden, Boleslav Polívka, Chantal Poullain.
●A 'bawdy black farce', this downgrading of the Scottish Play, from former Czech cameraman FA Brabec, does to Shakespeare's tragedy what Macbeth did to Duncan. Having made his military mark with army manoeuvres signalled by burps and farts, cretinous general Ubu and his lieutenant M'Nure knock off King Wenceslas at the behest of the Medusa-locked Mrs Ubu. Once enthroned, Ubu molests maidens, impose prohibitive taxes (on death, rheumatism and pickles), tours the land by motorbike, with trailing gallows rig, and declares war on Russia. It's cheerfully scattershot nonsense, but Milos Macourek's script from Alfred Jarry's play is witless, and there's a loud desperation about Brabec's direction. NB

Kini & Adams

(1997, Zim/GB, 93 min)
d Idrissa Ouedraogo. *p* Cedomir Kolar, Frédérique Dumas, Sophie Salbot. *sc* Idrissa Ouedraogo, Olivier Lorelle, Santiago Amigorena. *ph* Jean-Paul Meurisse. *ed* Monica Coleman. *pd* Heather Cameron. *m* Wally Badarou. *cast* Vusi Kunene, David Mohloki, Nthati Moshesh, Chigwendere Netsayi, John Kani, Claudia Cardinale.
●Kunene and Mohloki fall out over women, work and the car they see as a passport to wealth in an Africa defined by poverty, prostitution and the corruption of traditional values. Ouedraogo uses the 'Scope frame to vivid visual effect, holds the whole ramshackle affair together through the sheer good nature of the performances, and shows us a modern, semi-industrialised Africa all too often ignored by that continent's cinema – but the fairy tale simplicity and contrived tragic climax sit uneasily together and make for a certain superficiality. GA

Kippur

(2000, Isr/Fr, 123 min)
d Amos Gitai. *p* Michel Propper, Amos Gitai, Laurent Truchot. *sc* Amos Gitai, Marie-José Sanselme. *ph* Renato Berta. *ed* Monica Coleman, Kobi Netanel. *ad* Miguel Markin. *m* Jan Garbarek. *cast* Liron Levo, Tomer Ruso, Uri Ran Klauzner, Yoram Hattab, Guy Amir, Juliano Merr, Ran Kauchinsky.
●Gitai's autobiographically inspired account of the harrowing experiences of a first-aid team in the aftermath of Syria and Egypt's surprise attack on Israel in October 1973 typically features long, sinuous takes to chart the way in which patriotic enthusiasm is steadily eroded and replaced by fatigue and disillusionment. There's not a lot in terms of story, but the sheer,visceral physicality of the mise-en-scène makes the movie engrossing throughout – save the over-extended opening and closing love-making scenes,which taxed even this writer's love for a piece by Jan Garbarek, used several times in the movie as musical accompaniment to some stunning images; and an unexpected attack on the team's helicopter is quite frightening in its immediacy. Impressive. GA

Kira's Reason – A Love Story (Ein Kærlighedshistorie)

(2001, Den, 92 min)
d Ole Christian Madsen. *p* Bo Ehrhardt, Morten Kaufman. *sc* Ole Christian Madsen, Mogens Rukov. *ph* Jørgen Johansson. *ed* Søren B Ebbe. *m* Øyvind Ougaard, César Bertil. *cast* Stine Stengade, Lars Mikkelsen, Sven Wollter, Peacheslatrice Petersen, Camilla Bendix, Lotte Bergstrøm.
●Bourgeois revelations violently surface as Kira (Stengade, carrying the picture) returns home, still troubled, after a period in hospital. A model of intimate distance, she tries to deliver as housewife, lover and mother but it all becomes too much once again. The difficulties of relationships and the sometimes intolerable facade of social situations are given the rough and ready stylistic support they require. It's the familiar Scandinavian pressure cooker – well executed Dogme-style, but not particularly appealing. GE

Kisapmata

(1981, Phil, 97 min)
d Mike de Leon. *p* Rolando Atienza. *sc* Doy del Mundo, Raquel Villavicencio, Mike de Leon. *ph* Rody Lacap. *ed* Jess Navarro. *pd* Cesar Hernando. *m* Lorrie Ilustre. *cast* Vic Silayan, Charito Solis, Charo Santos, Jay Ilagan, Ruben Rustia.
●De Leon's film amply confirms the power of the work currently being done in the Filipino cinema. Based on a real- life murder scandal dating from 1961, its carefully handled story of incestuous obsession, bolstered by strong performances, builds to a climax which would be melodramatic in less skilful hands. But on the way it also paints a frightening portrait of terrible family tensions, edge-of-insanity patriarchy, and Catholic repression which makes its wider social implications abundantly and devastatingly clear. SM

Kismet

(1955, US, 113 min)
d Vincente Minnelli. *p* Arthur Freed. *sc* Charles Lederer, Luther Davis. *ph* Joseph Ruttenberg. *ed* Adrienne Fazan. *ad* Cedric Gibbons, Preston Ames. *m* Alexander Borodin. *cast* Howard Keel, Ann Blyth, Dolores Gray, Monty Woolley, Sebastian Cabot, Vic Damone, Jay C Flippen, Mike Mazurki, Jack Elam.
●Magicians and caliphs, poets and lovers, all involved in Arabian Nights-style romantic intrigues: the ideal material, one would have thought, for a full-blown exotic musical. But despite the ripe melodies borrowed from Borodin and the expensively luscious sets, it never really takes off, thanks partly to a less than top-notch cast, partly to Minnelli's often indifferent direction. Minnelli himself has commented: 'Arthur (Freed) had already asked me to direct the picture, but I didn't relate to it, and declined. Now I was being asked again (by Dore Schary), and the implication was that I wouldn't get the Van Gogh picture (*Lust for Life*) if I didn't direct *Kismet*. I capitulated…' GA

Kiss, The

(1929, US, 5,760 ft, b/w)
d Jacques Feyder. *sc* Hans Kräly, Jacques Feyder. *ph* William H Daniels. *ed* Ben Lewis. *ad* Cedric Gibbons. *m* William Axt. *cast* Greta Garbo, Conrad Nagel, Anders Randolf, Holmes Herbert, Lew Ayres.
●Both MGM's and Garbo's last silent, this is one of the actress' most memorable films, simply because it combines characteristic studio gloss (art direction by Cedric Gibbons, luminous close-ups by William Daniels) with a genuine feeling for her mixture of erotic glamour and doomy passion. As a woman tried for the murder of a husband who refuses her a divorce, she is perfectly cast, while Ayres makes a fine show as the youngster whose kiss seals her fate. And Feyder's direction contrives to transcend the novelettish nature of the material by means of its elegance, ambiguity, and sheer commitment to the melodramatic emotions. GA

Kiss, The

(1988, US, 101 min)
d Pen Densham. *p* Pen Densham, John Watson. *sc* Stephen Volk, Tom Ropelewski. *ph* François Protat. *ed* Stan Cole, *pd* Roy Forge Smith. *m* J Peter Robinson. *cast* Joanna Pacula, Meredith Salenger, Pamela Collyer, Peter Dvorsky, Mimi Kuzyk, Nicholas Kilbertus, Sabrina Boudot.
●Densham's daft and derivative 'possession' pic (his debut) starts in the Belgian Congo, with a sickly child miraculously revived when her aunt kisses her passionately, passing on an invigorating power before herself expiring. Some years later in America, soon after child-woman Salenger's religious confirmation, her mysterious aunt (Pacula) materialises at a family funeral. With the help of a blood-dripping African talisman and a bright-eyed black cat, Pacula seduces Salenger's father and incites much psychic chaos. The film soon degenerates into screeching incoherence, and – crucially – fails to explore the erotic undercurrents hinted at by Salenger's burgeoning sexuality and her aunt's corrupting desire. Salenger's tearful teen is too pathetic to elicit either sympathy or interest, Pacula hams it up as the demonic aunt, and Mimi Kuzyk provides the only shred of credible humanity as a sympathetic neighbour. Chris (*The Fly*) Walas' special effects are often more eye-catching than the inane plot deserves. NF

Kiss Before Dying, A

(1955, US, 89 min)
d Gerd Oswald. *p* Robert L Jacks. *sc* Lawrence Roman. *ph* Lucien Ballard. *ed* George Gittens. *ad* Addison Hehr. *m* Lionel Newman. *cast* Robert Wagner, Jeffrey Hunter, Joanne Woodward, Mary Astor, Virginia Leith, George Macready.
●An early Ira Levin thriller, predating *Rosemary's Baby*, *The Stepford Wives* and *Deathtrap*, superbly adapted as an icily acute nightmare (and as a riposte to the academicism of *A Place in the Sun*) by the great Oswald, giving a criminally myopic Hollywood its first glimpse of a unique visual talent, idiosyncratically developed from that of his father, German silent director Richard Oswald. Wagner is perfect as the college kid psycho coolly removing the pregnant Woodward from his life, and both he and Hunter were picked up from here by Nick Ray to play his James Brothers the following year. PT

Kiss Before Dying, A

(1991, US, 93 min)
d James Dearden. *p* Robert Lawrence. *sc* James Dearden. *ph* Mike Southon. *ed* Michael Bradsell. *pd* Jim Clay. *m* Howard Shore. *cast* Matt Dillon, Sean Young, Max von Sydow, Jim Fyfe, Ben Browder, Diane Ladd, James Russo, Martha Gehman.
●Writer/director Dearden's version of Ira Levin's novel is routine stuff, neither thrilling nor revealing as a portrait of a psychopath. Jonathan Corliss (Dillon) comes from the wrong side of the tracks and dreams of being tycoon Thor Carlsson (von Sydow). Getting that status means marrying into the family, but the first daughter (Young) gets inconveniently pregnant, so he courts and marries the second (also Young). But the fly in the ointment is her obsession with investigating her sister's

death. There's an untidiness about the film that suggests something else was intended. Why those fierce opening shots of the copper furnace if we are to be denied Levin's final Götterdämmerung? Dillon does his best; Young doesn't seem equipped to do a lot with a woman who discovers she's nurtured a viper at her bosom; Ladd brings pathos to the role of the killer's mother. BC

Kissed

(1996, Can, 78 min)
d Lynne Stopkewich. *p* Dean English, Lynne Stopkewich. *sc* Angus Fraser, Lynne Stopekewich. *ph* Greg Middleton. *ed* John Pozer, Peter Roeck, Lynne Stopkewich. *pd* Eric McNab. *m* Don MacDonald. *cast* Molly Parker, Peter Outerbridge, Jay Brazeau, Natasha Morley, Jessie Winter Mudie, Joe Maffei.

●This independent first feature, from story by Barbara Gowdy about a young mortician's deviant sexuality, is an edgy, challenging mix of style and content. A cross between a young Annette Bening and Isabelle Adjani, Molly Parker gives a formidable and engaging performance as an 'ordinary' woman, simultaneously chaste and sexual (she's turned on by corpses), who bravely sets out to chart her own adventurous course. The tone is, surprisingly, romantic – almost ecstatic. There are shocks (the embalming lesson is not for the faint-hearted), but overall director/co-writer Stopkewich's calm, non-judgmental approach pays rich dividends: the film is convincing, tender, and more than a little subversive. WH

Kissin' Cousins

(1963, US, 96 min)
d Gene Nelson. *p* Sam Katzman. *sc* Gerald Drayson Adams, Gene Nelson. *ph* Ellis Carter. *ed* Ben Lewis. *ad* George W Davis, Eddie Imazu. *songs* Fred Wise, Doc Pomus, Mort Shuman, others. *cast* Elvis Presley, Arthur O'Connell, Glenda Farrell, Jack Albertson, Pamela Austin, Yvonne Craig, Donald Woods.

●A seventeen-day quickie, produced by Sam Katzman as a lesson to Col. Tom Parker in how to make money, with Presley back in khaki as an air-force officer trying to move hillbillies – including himself as his blond-wigged cousin – in favour of missile bases. So thin that it barely exists. AC

Kissing a Fool

(1998, US, 94 min)
d Doug Ellin. *p* Tag Mendillo, Andrew Form, Rick Lashbrook. *sc* James Frey, Doug Ellin. *ph* Thomas Del Ruth. *ed* David Finfer. *pd* Charles Breen. *m* Joseph Vitarelli. *cast* David Schwimmer, Jason Lee, Mili Avital, Bonnie Hunt, Vanessa Angel, Kari Wuhrer.

●Romantic casualty and first time novelist Jay (Lee) sets up his best friend, ladies' man and TV sportscaster Max (Schwimmer), with his editor Sam (Avital). He won't date her himself, since she knows everything about him from his confessional memoirs ('Here's to You, Bitch Slut'). Sam hates sports, Max hates books, and with sickly sweet rapidity they announce their engagement. Whereupon Max's primitive anxieties surface, and to Jay's horror he asks his friend to put Sam's fidelity to the test. A women's movie for men (it takes up the implications of the two boys' neuroses, while Sam remains the luckless object of their affection), this could have used a shot of the raucous mischief Lee sported as Banky in *Chasing Amy*. But there's a sense of rising damp as Jay's dilemma rambles on and he falls sick at any sign of trouble. The framing device – Jay's publisher (Hunt) unfolding the narrative at the wedding, as if omniscient matchmaker – is also a distraction. NB

Kiss Me Deadly

(1955, US, 105 min, b/w)
d/p Robert Aldrich. *sc* AI Bezzerides. *ph* Ernest Laszlo. *ed* Michael Luciano. *ad* William Glasgow. *m* Frank Devol. *cast* Ralph Meeker, Albert Dekker, Maxine Cooper, Paul Stewart, Gaby Rodgers, Cloris Leachman, Jack Lambert, Wesley Addy, Nick Dennis, Marian Carr, Jack Elam.

●A key film from the '50s, a savage critique of Cold War paranoia bounded by two haunting sound effects: at the beginning, the desperate, panting sobs of the girl hitching a lift from Mike Hammer on the dark highway, and her despairing plea to 'Remember me' as she disappears to her death; and at the end, the strange, groaning sigh that escapes as the Pandora's box containing the Great Whatsit is finally opened to unleash an incandescent nuclear blast. Aldrich's distaste for the unprincipled brutality of Mickey Spillane's hero is evident throughout the film; but nevertheless given a sort of dumb-ox honesty by Ralph Meeker, the character acquires new resonance as an example of mankind's mulish habit of meddling with the unknown regardless of consequences. Brilliantly characterised down to the smallest roles, directed with baroque ferocity, superbly shot by Ernest Laszlo in *film noir* terms, it's a masterpiece of sorts. TM

Kiss Me Goodbye

(1982, US, 101 min)
d/p Robert Mulligan. *sc* Charlie Peters. *ph* Don Peterman. *ed* Sheldon Kahn. *pd* Philip M Jefferies. *m* Ralph Burns. *cast* Sally Field, James Caan, Jeff Bridges, Paul Dooley, Claire Trevor, Mildred Natwick, Dorothy Fielding, William Prince.

●Light fantastical comedy in which Sally Field moves into her old home and bumps into the ghost of her dead husband just as she's about to marry a new one. A ménage à trois with one party invisible naturally upsets her fiancé, who wonders what he is letting himself in for. *Blithe Spirit* without Madame Arcati. Noël Coward did it more entertainingly and less sentimentally years ago (though in fact it derives from the Brazilian *Doña Flor and Her Two Husbands* of 1976). JE

Kiss Me, Guido

(1997, US/GB, 89 min)
d Tony Vitale. *p* Ira Deutchman, Christine Vachon. *sc* Tony Vitale. *ph* Claudia Raschke. *ed* Alexander Hall. *pd* Jeffrey Rathaus. *cast* Nick Scotti, Anthony Barrile, Anthony DeSandro, Molly Price, Craig Chester, David Deblinger, Christopher Lawford, Tony Vitale.

●Having found his fiancée in bed with his brother, Frankie wants out of the Bronx. He answers an ad for a roommate placed by actor Warren (Barrile), not realising that G stands for gay, not guy. Scotti's Frankie – naive and ambitious – is sweet beyond belief, and the pizza parlour where he works is portrayed as a hubbub of insular passions, where a working class man's shyness is taken for self-sufficiency. It's the gay world which, ironically, rings false. Barrile has befuddled chipmunk looks, but lacks comic timing, while Chester, as the queeny best friend, also shows a heavy hand. A first feature which goes from bad to dire as writer/director Vitale tries to hurry things on to a feel-good climax. CO'Su

Kiss Me Kate

(1953, US, 109 min)
d George Sidney. *p* Jack Cummings. *sc* Dorothy Kingsley. *ph* Charles Rosher. *ed* Ralph E Winters. *ad* Cedric Gibbons, Urie McCleary. *songs* Cole Porter. *cast* Kathryn Grayson, Howard Keel, Ann Miller, Keenan Wynn, James Whitmore, Tommy Rall, Bob Fosse, Bobby Van, Ron Randell.

●Cole Porter's amazing score wasn't the only standout when this tricksy backstage/onstage parallel version of *The Taming of the Shrew* first appeared. Contemporary fashion caused Sidney the headache of shooting in both 3-D and 'flat' formats, and he accentuated the planes of artifice by employing a succession of frames within frames (doors, windows, proscenia) and, for the stage scenes, shooting head-on from something like the third row of the 'audience'. The Chinese box play-within-a-play construction is worked out to a tee, and even extends to Randell playing a character called Cole Porter, scoring a Broadway musical. Brilliantly choreographed by Hermes Pan, Ann Miller's dance numbers (variously partnered by Rall, Fosse and Van) are the champagne that go with the film. PT

Kiss Me Kate: 3-D

(1953, US, 109 min)
d George Sidney. *p* Jack Cummings. *sc* Dorothy Kingsley. *ph* Charles Rosher. *ed* Ralph E Winters. *ad* Cedric Gibbons, Urie McCleary. *songs* Cole Porter. *cast* Kathryn Grayson, Howard Keel, Ann Miller, Keenan Wynn, James Whitmore, Tommy Rall, Bob Fosse, Bobby Van, Ron Randell.

●Brush up your antiquated novelties, courtesy of this BFI revival. We open on the full three-dimensional munificence of the leading man's living room: with Cole Porter (actually Randell) looking on, silver-tongued impresario Fred Graham (Keel) tries to court his combative ex-wife Lilli Vanessi (Grayson) into starring opposite him in a musical version of *The Taming of the Shrew*. The effect is spoilt just a little when Lilli's eager-beaver rival Lois Lane (Miller) arrives to hoof it around the couch to the tune of 'Too Darn Hot'. And so the show goes on. This *42nd Street*-style, backstage stuff is tantamount to social realism so far as musicals are concerned. Certainly the film never attempts the cinematic fancifulness of, say, Minnelli or Donen, and Sidney's tricksiest 3-D application is to have his players throw objects at the camera. With querulous lovers, waspish dialogue and erudite hoodlums for comic relief, it's really a screwball musical, rooted in the 'comedies of remarriage' of a decade earlier. Think *The Awful Truth*, *The Palm Beach Story* and especially *His Girl Friday*; and as a musical resetting, rather than a travesty, this is to *Shrew* almost what *High Society* is to *The Philadelphia Story*. That said, all the sophistication here is in the original play and score, though the final number, 'From This Moment On', choreographed by a young Bob Fosse, is admittedly quite something. NB

Kiss Me, Stupid

(1964, US, 124 min, b/w)
d/p Billy Wilder. *sc* IAL Diamond, Billy Wilder. *ph* Joseph LaShelle. *ed* Daniel Mandell. *pd* Alexander Trauner. *m* André Previn. *songs* George Gershwin, Ira Gershwin. *cast* Dean Martin, Kim Novak, Ray Walston, Felicia Farr, Cliff Osmond, Barbara Pepper, Doro Morande, Henry Gibson, Mel Blanc.

●Drawing heavily on Martin's offscreen persona, this sees him as an arrogant, sex-crazed crooner stranded in a remote Californian town and feigning interest in the songs of amateur composer Walston in return for the sexual favours of the latter's wife (Farr). Anticipating this, the desperately ambitious but possessively jealous Walston has in fact substituted a local tart-with-a-heart (Novak) for his wife; but his wife, meanwhile... Wilder's vulgar satire on greed, lust and sexual game-playing was decried as tasteless upon release; the effect is less outrageous now, but the epithet stands, particularly in the light of feminist awareness. Characteristically cynical, clever and brash, it's helped out enormously by the performances of Martin, Farr and (particularly) Novak as Polly the Pistol, but for all its ambitions it isn't really all that funny. GA

Kiss of Death

(1947, US, 98 min, b/w)
d Henry Hathaway. *p* Fred Kohlmar. *sc* Ben Hecht, Charles Lederer. *ph* Norbert Brodine. *ed* J Watson Webb. *ad* Lyle R Wheeler, Leland Fuller. *m* David Buttolph. *cast* Victor Mature, Brian Donlevy, Richard Widmark, Coleen Gray, Karl Malden, Taylor Holmes, Mildred Dunnock, Millard Mitchell.

●Late '40s Fox saw several attempts to conceal the split in the gangster film between *noir* expressionism and 'procedural' authenticity, but few as bizarre as this. Mature is the stool-pigeon torn apart by two kinds of family loyalty: the Mob and the Missus. Widmark debuts as a psycho hood with an unforgettable chuckle and a nice line in helping wheelchair-ridden old ladies down stairs. Of its period, of course, but extraordinarily modern too: nighttime New York peopled only by daylight's misfits (à la *The Warriors*); and when Mature's wife kills herself, a neighbour happily takes her place. PK

Kiss of Death

(1994, US, 101 min)
d Barbet Schroeder. *p* Barbet Schroeder, Susan Hoffman. *sc* Richard Price. *ph* Luciano Tovoli. *ed* Lee Percy. *pd* Mel Bourne. *m* Trevor Jones. *cast* David Caruso, Samuel L Jackson, Nicolas Cage, Helen Hunt, Kathryn Erbe, Stanley Tucci, Michael Rapaport, Ving Rhames.

●Ex-con Jimmy Kilmartin's a decent guy who'd rather babysit than hijack cars. Lured back for One Last Job – a favour to no-account cousin Ronnie – Jimmy takes a bullet and the fall. Worse, his wife, Bev, dies in an accident after a one-night stand with Ronnie. Jimmy plays the DA off against a psychotic mobster, Little Junior, to execute his revenge from behind bars, which puts him in double jeopardy on his release. Schroeder's honourable, rather onerous remake of Hathaway's gripping *film noir* is too restrained for its own good

– it barely musters a climax – but it's a solid, atmospheric thriller all the same, with smart dialogue by Richard Price and a strong line-up of downbeat actors: Tucci as a DA of questionable integrity, Rhames as a scary drug-dealer, and Jackson as a cop with a weeping eye. Caruso's okay in the lead, but you can feel the weight of the movie (or is it destiny?) on his shoulders; in any case, he, along with the rest, is effectively steamrollered by Cage. 'I have an acronym for myself,' boasts Little Junior: 'Bad: Balls. Attitude. Direction'. I can't vouch for the direction, but he's definitely big on balls and attitude – no one's quite as bad as Nic when he's in this kind of mood: whether bench-pressing bargirls, confiding that he can't stand metal in his mouth, or taking another jolt of oxygen from his inhaler, this is larger-than-life villainy worthy of Elmore Leonard or Carl Hiaasen. TCh

Kiss of Evil

see Kiss of the Vampire

Kiss of the Dragon (Le Baiser mortel du dragon)

(2001, Fr/US, 98 min)
d Chris Nahon. *p* Luc Besson, Jet Li, Steven Chasman, Happy Walters. *sc* Luc Besson, Robert Mark Kamen. *ph* Thierry Arbogast. *ed* Marco Cave. *pd* Jacques Bufnoir. *m* Craig Armstrong. *cast* Jet Li, Bridget Fonda, Tchéky Karyo, Ric Young, Burt Kwouk, Laurence Ashley, Cyril Raffaelli, Didier Azoulay, John Forgeham.

●A sorry martial arts movie in which, once again, an Oriental supercop (Li) is sent on loan to tackle crime in the West. Here the streets he's cleaning up are those of a very normal and unthreatening Paris. Set up by Karyo's spectacularly bent cop, Li races against time to clear his name, rescue a junkie prostitute (Fonda) and kick most of Paris into tiny pieces. The fight scenes are sliced up by flashy quick cuts that reduce Li's awesome athleticism to little more than the backdrop to an MTV video. WI

Kiss of the Spider Woman (Beijo da a Mulher Aranha)

(1985, Braz/US, 121 min, b/w & col)
d Hector Babenco. *p* David Weisman. *sc* Leonard Schrader. *ph* Rodolfo Sanchez. *ed* Mauro Alice. *ad* Clovis Bueno. *m* John Neschling. *cast* William Hurt, Raúl Julia, Sonia Braga, José Lewgoy, Milton Gonçalves, Miriam Pires, Nuno Leal Maia.

●Flamboyant queen Molina (Hurt) and aggressive straight revolutionary Valentin (Julia) share a prison cell in an unnamed Latin American dictatorship. Molina, to Valentin's decreasing disgust, escapes the cell walls by recounting the camp French Resistance film of the title. The performances of Hurt and Julia win votes by the minute, Babenco directs their growing relationship with subtlety and depth, and the structure – mixing flashback, arch movie fantasy and powerful cell sequences – knocks the shit out of the gimmicks in Schrader's dubious *Mishima*. A film of fine balance and tone, not least in the dramatic turnaround ending. JG

Kiss of the Vampire (aka Kiss of Evil)

(1962, GB, 87 min)
d Don Sharp. *p* James Needs, Anthony Hinds. *sc* Anthony Hinds. *ph* Alan Hume. *ed* James Needs. *pd* Bernard Robinson. *m* James Bernard. *cast* Clifford Evans, Noel Willman, Edward de Souza, Jennifer Daniel, Barry Warren, Isobel Black.

●A beautifully photographed film in which an English honeymoon couple are lured towards a fate worse than death by a Bavarian disciple (Willman) of the late Count Dracula. The main trouble is that some of the acting, especially from de Souza and Daniel as the young couple, is terribly stiff (against which must be set Isobel Black, playing a very fetching vampire). The use of scenery is particularly superb, giving it an almost Dreyerian quality. Ironically, the film's release was delayed until 1964 because the distributors thought that the bat-infestation climax (one of the best scenes) flew dangerously close to *The Birds*, even though it was made quite some time before Hitchcock's film. DP

Kiss or Kill

(1997, Aust, 96 min)
d Bill Bennett. *p* Bill Bennett, Jennifer Cluff. *sc* Bill Bennett. *ph* Malcolm McCulloch. *ed* Henry Dangar. *pd* Andrew Plumer. *cast* Frances O'Connor, Matt Day, Chris Haywood, Barry Otto, Andrew S Gilbert, Barry Langrishe, Max Cullen.

●There's one richly absurdist scene here between two cops in a diner. There's an iota of interest in that writer/director Bennett has edited the film entirely in jump cuts (very aggravating). There's a choice quotation from Dylan Thomas to get the ball rolling ('We watch the show of shadows kiss or kill, / Flavoured of celluloid, give love the lie'). And then there's yet another ho-hum story of young lovers on the run from the law, this time through the Australian outback. TCh

Kiss the Girls

(1997, US, 115 min)
d Gary Fleder. *p* David Brown, Joe Wizan. *sc* David Klass. *ph* Aaron E Schneider. *ed* William Steinkamp, Harvey Rosenstock. *pd* Nelson Coates. *m* Mark Isham. *cast* Morgan Freeman, Ashley Judd, Cary Elwes, Tony Goldwyn, Jay O Sanders, Alex MacArthur, Bill Nunn, Brian Cox, Jeremy Piven.

●Detective Alex Cross (Freeman) reassures a woman that she was justified in killing her abusive husband. Then we learn that the next victim of camp serial killer Casanova – Dr Kate McTiernan (Judd) – is no gimmicky 'new' woman. Neither saintly, nor 'GI Jane' macho, her best scenes occur in the killer's hideout, where he's collecting an array of female talent. Kate's desire to connect with these other women is palpable, and, thanks to Judd, notably moving. Nor does Kate's boldness become diluted once she joins forces with Cross. On the subject of race, the film is less impressive – its intentions are good, but it never digs deep. Why, for instance, are Freeman and Judd not allowed to develop their relationship (as they do in the James Patterson novel)? Nevertheless, a surprising, atmospheric treat. CO'Su

Kiss Them for Me

(1957, US, 105 min)
d Stanley Donen. *p* Jerry Wald. *sc* Julius Epstein. *ph* Milton Krasner. *ed* Robert Simpson. *ad* Lyle R Wheeler, Maurice Ransford. *m* Lionel Newman. *cast* Cary Grant, Jayne Mansfield, Suzy Parker, Ray Walston, Larry Blyden, Leif Erickson, Harry Carey Jr.

●Jayne Mansfield in *Kiss Them For Me*? Well, tee-hee. But such ribaldry is misplaced: this is a WWII movie, based on Frederic Wakeman's novel *Shore Leave*, about three combat veterans who wangle a few days in San Francisco, where the skyvers, profiteers and complacent home front types finally send them hastening back in disgust to their buddies on the battle line. This balancing of the cynical and the romantic was really a job for Billy Wilder, just as the part of the embittered, livewire hero cried out for Kirk Douglas. Casting mishaps among the women too, with Mansfield as unable to calm down as Parker is to liven up. Still, worth seeing for its mixture of provocation and Fox gloss, plus other anomalies, like Mansfield in a Rosie the Riveter outfit. BBa

Kiss Tomorrow Goodbye

(1950, US, 102 min, b/w)
d Gordon Douglas. *p* William J Cagney. *sc* Harry Brown. *ph* J Peverell Marley. *ed* Truman K Wood, Walter Hannemann. *ad* Wiard Ihnen. *m* Carmen Dragon. *cast* James Cagney, Barbara Payton, Luther Adler, Ward Bond, Barton MacLane, Steve Brodie, Helena Carter, Neville Brand.

●Excellent gangster thriller based on Horace McCoy's novel about an escaped con first ruthlessly betraying his partner, and then planning an ambitious robbery. Strong performances from a great cast and Douglas' taut, classical direction place it among the best of the post-war gangster movies, but it is of course Cagney who is most memorable: strutting, snarling, and lashing out in almost psychopathic anger at all around him, his immense energy conveys the spirit of callous violence far more effectively than the explicit acts perpetrated in later movies. GA

Kitami (Kurutta Butokai/ aka Lunatic Theatre)

(1993, Jap, 60 min)
d Hisayasu Sato. *p* Syuji Kataoka. *sc* Shiro Yumeno. *ph* Fumio Sato. *ed* Seiji Sakai. *m* So Hayakawa. *cast* Takeshi Ito, Simone Kumai, Yo Suzuki, Kiyomi Ito, Koyama Hageki.

●Notorious for clearing cinemas at festival screenings, Sato's gay s/m weird-out is a direct to video title in Britain. Ryuzaki gets involved with Yukihiro Kitami without realising that his lover is a big-time sadist; he ends the relationship by slashing off Kitami's left arm with (what else?) a samurai sword. One year later, while scouring Tokyo for a multi-system video player to watch his Pasolini tapes, he's invited back to the 'secret theatre' where he first met Kitami. Simultaneously earnest and blackly comic, Sato's film seems less interested in either sadism or masochism as such than in the even more specialised tradition of louche psycho-drama. TR

Kitchen

(1965, US, 70 min, b/w)
d Andy Warhol, Ronald Tavel. *sc* Ronald Tavel. *cast* Edie Sedgwick, Roger Trudeau, Albert René Ricard.

●Drawn from a Ronald Tavel script that is frequently visible in shot, this has Edie Sedgwick and several half-undressed studs enacting a primitive psycho-drama in a single set. Best seen as a documentary on non-actors struggling to cope with a script which they haven't learned. TR

Kitchen (Wo ai Chufang)

(1997, HK/Jap, 124 min)
d Yim Ho. *p* Yim Ho, Akira Morishige. *sc* Yim Ho. *ph* Poon Hang-Sang. *ed* Poon Hung-Yiu. *ad* James Leung, Jason Mok. *m* Otomo Yoshihide, Uchihashi Kazuhisa. *cast* Jordan Chan, Yasuko Tomita, Law Kar-Ying, Karen Mok, Lau Siu-Ming.

●Banana Yoshimoto's fey novella about a psychologically damaged girl falling in with a nice young man and his transsexual father-turned-mother was first filmed – wretchedly – by Yoshimitsu Morita in 1989. Yim Ho sensibly rethinks the book, transposing the setting to Hong Kong and focusing on the boy rather than the girl. He also opts to shoot much of it in underlit close-ups, paving the way for a real visual coup in the final scene. But he can't do anything about the fundamental lack of energy in the characters and story; elegant languor inexorably slides towards torpor. Jordan Chan is excellent as the terminally tongue-tied 'hero', but has to cope with one of the worst haircuts in screen history. TR

Kitchen, The

(1961, GB, 74 min, b/w)
d James Hill. *p/sc* Sidney Cole. *ph* Reginald Wyer. *ed* Gerry Hambling. *ad* William Kellner. *m* David Lee. *cast* Carl Mohner, Mary Yeomans, Eric Pohlmann, Tom Bell, Martin Boddey, Sean Lynch, James Bolam.

●In the steamy atmosphere of a large and in-salubrious West End kitchen, chefs fight, philosophise and finally go berserk, while waitresses pout, dance and have miscarriages. An unlikely vehicle for the ACTT (the cine technicians' union) to choose for their incursion into commercial film-making, but the fact that it was the first play from socialist bright boy Arnold Wesker makes it explicable. Good intentions are perilously flimsy foundations for constructing worthwhile films; Wesker and director Hill (more at home with Elsa the lioness and Worzel Gummidge) fall into the trap of making clichéd pontification on the meaning of life, work, capitalism, the world. A strange mix of utopian whimsicality and rather unlikely melodrama. RMy

Kitchen Toto, The

(1987, GB, 95 min)
d Harry Hook. *p* Ann Skinner. *sc* Harry Hook. *ph* Roger Deakins. *ed* Tom Priestley. *pd* Jamie Leonard. *m* John Keane. *cast* Edwin Mahinda, Bob Peck, Phyllis Logan, Nicholas Charles, Ronald Pirie, Robert Urquhart, Kirsten Hughes, Edward Judd.

●Kenya, 1950. Mwangi (Mahinda) takes the job of kitchen toto or scullion in the household of police chief John Graham (Peck) after the murder of his pacifist clergyman father by Mau Mau revolutionaries. Events in the build-up to the slaughter that was to follow are presented only as they touch Mwangi, who fast becomes an embarrassment to both sides. Soon the boy is forced to take a rebel oath, swearing to take the head of a white man if required to do so, but he is already growing fond of Graham and his supremely cloying son (Pirie). The outcome of this division of loyalties is depressing, inevitable and unremarkable. All the performances are effective, particularly Peck and Mahinda – who carries the weight of the whole conflict upon his shoulders. Hook's low-key approach packs a surprisingly hard punch. He is clearly a talent to watch. RS

Kitty

(1945, US, 104 min, b/w)
d Mitchell Leisen. *sc* Darrell Ware, Karl Tunberg. *ph* Daniel L Fapp. *ed* Alma Macrorie. *ad* Hans Dreier, Walt Tyler. *m* Victor Young. *cast* Paulette Goddard, Ray Milland, Patric Knowles, Reginald Owen, Cecil Kellaway, Constance Collier, Sara Allgood, Eric Blore.
●One of the elegant Leisen's very best, with a lovely performance from Goddard as the 18th century London slum wench who gatecrashes society after being painted as a lady by Gainsborough. The tartly witty script (from a novel by Rosamund Marshall) owes something to *Pygmalion* as the grubby waif is taken up by Milland's raffish young man-about-town and taught the secrets of speech and deportment by his aunt. But tone and mood come closer to Renoir's *Diary of a Chambermaid*, blending sharp cynicism with shafts of tenderness as Milland seeks to capitalise on his creation, she sacrifices herself to save him from debtor's prison, and a couple of profitable marriages intervene before romance has its way. Stunningly shot by Daniel Fapp, scrupulously authentic in period detail (gorgeous sets and costumes), it's wholly delightful. TM

Klansman, The

(1974, US, 112 min)
d Terence Young. *p* William Alexander. *sc* Millard Kaufman, Samuel Fuller. *ph* Lloyd Ahern, Aldo Tonti. *ed* Gene Milford. *pd* John S Poplin. *m* Stax Organization. *cast* Lee Marvin, Richard Burton, Cameron Mitchell, OJ Simpson, Lola Falana, David Huddleston, Luciana Paluzzi, Linda Evans.
●Small town Alabama in the late '60s: rape, murder and rampant racism tear apart a sordid little community under the watchful, apathetic eyes of sheriff Marvin. Young directs with an alarming lack of subtlety, concentrating purely on (voyeuristically portrayed) action and rarely investigating the gradations in morality that inform the various characters. A pity, because the script by Sam Fuller and Millard Kaufman suggests the potential for something far better, a study in universal corruption pitched somewhere between Arthur Penn's *The Chase* and the inbred psychoses of Jim Thompson's novels. GA

Klassenverhältnisse

see Class Relations

Kleine Godard, Der

see Little Godard, A

Kleine Teune

see Little Tony

Kleine Vampir, Die

see Little Vampire, The

Klondike Annie

(1936, US, 77 min, b/w)
d Raoul Walsh. *p* William LeBaron. *sc* Mae West, Marion Morgan, George B Dowell. *ph* George Clemens. *ed* Stuart Heisler. *ad* Hans Dreier, Bernard Herzbrun. *m* Sam Coslow. *cast* Mae West, Victor McLaglen, Philip Reed, Harold Huber, Esther Howard, Soo Young, Lucile Gleason.
●Action man Raoul Walsh must have been chafing at the bit as Mae West let the suggestive drawl of her dialogue dictate the film's measured pace. 'She Made the Frozen North Red Hot' said the posters, but the film could do with being a bit hotter: considering the story – Mae in the Klondike, adopting the identity of a Salvation Army missionary – the humour is tame indeed. But by 1936 censorship problems were beginning to knock the stuffing out of our heroine, though she still had her eyebrows to flutter and her blue-beat songs to sing ('I'm an Occidental Woman in an Oriental Mood for Love'). And watered down or not, Mae still remains – in the words she uses to describe her co-star McLaglen – 'no oil painting but…a fascinating monster'. GB

Klute

(1971, US, 114 min)
d/p Alan J Pakula. *sc* Andy K Lewis, Dave Lewis. *ph* Gordon Willis. *ed* Carl Lerner. *ad* George Jenkins. *m* Michael Small. *cast* Jane Fonda, Donald Sutherland, Charles Cioffi, Roy Scheider, Dorothy Tristan, Rita Gam, Anthony Holland, Richard B Shull, Shirley Stoller.
●Fonda's Oscar-winning performance as New York call-girl Bree Daniels is the real focus of Pakula's thriller, rather than Sutherland's Klute, the private eye whose increasingly obsessional 'protection' she reluctantly receives when menaced by a former client. Though it's obviously valid to follow the line that *Klute*, with its abstracted updates of private eye and urban *noir* conventions, initiated Pakula's string of paranoid thrillers (*The Parallax View*, *All the President's Men*), it's just as fruitful to see it as belonging to a trio of features (with *Comes a Horseman* and *Rollover*), each starring Fonda, that hinge on the contradictions of autonomy and emotional commitment facing would-be independent women. The threats of dependency and destruction here become Sutherland's investigator and Cioffi's telephone breather, and Pakula's open ambivalence about Bree's eventual 'fate' will be repeated in Fonda's dealings with Caan's war-hero/Western stranger and Kristofferson's Wall Street cowboy. For once, a genuinely psychological thriller. PT

Knack...and how to get it, The

(1965, GB, 84 min, b/w)
d Richard Lester. *p* Oscar Lewenstein. *sc* Charles Wood. *ph* David Watkin. *ed* Antony Gibbs. *ad* Assheton Gorton. *m* John Barry. *cast* Rita Tushingham, Ray Brooks, Michael Crawford, Donal Donnelly, John Bluthal, Wensley Pithey, Dandy Nichols, Charles Wood, Charlotte Rampling.
●Patchily funny but generally dated and embarrassing Swinging Sixties tale of Crawford's meek and mild schoolteacher learning 'the knack' of picking up women from lecherous lodger Brooks, and trying out his technique on new-girl-in-town Tushingham. A misogynistic basis for comedy, not redeemed by the moralistic and predictable ending, and all shot in Lester's characteristically 'zany' style, with people running around all over the place for no apparent reason. Some of the tricks work; most don't; and Crawford, as always, is a pain. GA

Knave of Hearts (aka Lovers, Happy Lovers!/ Monsieur Ripois)

(1954, GB, 103 min, b/w)
d René Clément. *p* Paul Graetz. *sc* Hugh Mills, René Clément. *ph* Oswald Morris. *ed* Vera Campbell. *ad* Ralph Brinton. *m* Roman Vlad. *cast* Gérard Philipe, Valerie Hobson, Joan Greenwood, Margaret Johnston, Natasha Parry, Germaine Montero, Diana Decker, Eric Pohlmann.
●Clément's first film in English proved once again that a foreign eye can often find more in a familiar setting. Philipe, in an engagingly sweet performance, plays the fickle French lover of a succession of London ladies, wooing them by playing the role they prefer to see him in. This French insight into the dreams of English womankind caused a contemporary furore, as did the use of a hidden camera on London locations to show aspects of the city rarely glimpsed in British cinema. Today it still looks remarkably authentic, with a particularly touching performance from Joan Greenwood in an unusually timid role. DT

Knickers Ahoy (Frau Wirtins tolle Töchterlein)

(1973, WGer/It, 90 min)
d/p François Legrand [Franz Antel]. *sc* Kurt Nachmann. *ph* Siegfried Hold. *ad* Ferry Windberger. *m* Stelvio Cipriani. *cast* Terry Torday, Femi Benussi, Gabriele Tinti, Paul Löwinger, Marika Mindzenthy.
●Period romp in which five convent girls try in turn to prove they are the daughter of Europe's greatest courtesan and heir to her fortune. Classical bawdy tales pad out a thin plot, and a number of crowd scenes sugggest a fair-sized budget. The film requires little comment beyond the mystery of its English title (not a pair to be seen), and a passing reference to the camera's lingering obsession with buttocks to the virtual exclusion of everything else.

Knife in the Head (Messer im Kopf)

(1978, WGer, 113 min)
d Reinhard Hauff. *p* Eberhard Junkersdorf. *sc* Peter Schneider. *ph* Frank Brühne. *ed* Peter Przygodda. *ad* Heidi Lüdi. *m* Irm Schmidt. *cast* Bruno Ganz, Angela Winkler, Hans Christian Blech, Hans Hönig, Hans Brenner, Udo Samel.
●From a mix of classic American paranoia and German police gangsterism, Hauff weaves a disturbing and suspenseful yarn. Surviving a police bullet, scientist Berthold Hoffmann (Ganz) awakes in hospital as a stranger in his own land: without memory or speech, branded a terrorist by the police and a martyr by leftists – neither of which is 'Hoffmann' – his future depends upon retracing the events of an alien past. Shot in cold and clinical fashion, the film's drive depends upon an atmosphere so angst-laden the characters struggle for breath. Doubly disquieting – for the society it depicts, but even more for the film's own dispassion: a calculated gamble in trying to come to cool, dramatic terms with an impossibly over-dramatic reality. DMacp

Knife in the Water (Noz w Wodzie)

(1962, Pol, 94 min, b/w)
d Roman Polanski. *p* Stanislaw Zylewicz. *sc* Roman Polanski, Jerzy Skolimowski, Jakub Goldberg. *ph* Jerzy Lipman. *ed* Halina Prugar. *m* Krzysztof Komeda. *cast* Leon Niemczyk, Jolanta Umecka, Zygmunt Malanowicz.
●Polanski's first feature, a model of economic, imaginative film-making which, in many ways, he has hardly improved upon since. The story is simplicity itself: a couple destined for a yachting weekend pick up a hitch-hiker, and during the apparently relaxing period of sport and rest, allegiances shift, frustrations bubble up to the surface, and dangerous emotional games are played. Like much of Polanski's later work, it deals with humiliation, sexuality, aggression and absurdity; but what makes the film so satisfying is the tenderness and straightforward nature of his approach. With just three actors, a boat, and a huge expanse of water, he and script-writer Jerzy Skolimowski milk the situation for all it's worth, rarely descending into dramatic contrivance, but managing to heap up the tension and ambiguities. GA

Knight Moves

(1992, US/Ger, 116 min)
d Carl Schenkel. *p* Ziad El Khoury, Jean-Luc Defait. *sc* Brad Mirman. *ph* Dietrich Lohmann. *ed* Norbert Herzner. *pd* Graeme Murray. *cast* Christopher Lambert, Diane Lane, Tom Skerritt, Daniel Baldwin, Ferdinand Mayne, Katherine Isobel, Charles Bailey-Gates.
●Set during a chess championship at which widowed Grand Master Lambert is making a comeback, this irritating and over-complicated thriller features a clever opening gambit, a series of predictable moves, and a disappointing end game. A classic case of all plot and no substance, it embroils Lambert in a serial killer's sick and dangerous game of nerves: taunted by cryptic phone calls and clues written on the wall in the female victims' blood, he teams up with the police to trap the killer. But Lambert's casual sexual involvement with the first victim means the cops still regard him as the prime suspect. The film's chief difficulty is in persuading us not only that its handsome star (playing opposite his real-life wife) could be the killer, but that the chess player could have both opportunity and motive. In a vain effort to disguise this inherent implausibility, Schenkel piles on the baroque camerawork, over-designed sets and flashy editing; but the denouement erases all the interesting and subversive possibilities at a stroke. NF

Knightriders

(1981, US, 145 min)
d George A Romero. *p* Richard P Rubinstein. *sc* George A Romero. *ph* Michael Gornick. *ed* George A Romero, Pasquale Buba. *pd* Cletus Anderson. *m* Donald Rubinstein. *cast* Ed Harris, Gary Lahti, Tom Savini, Amy Ingersoll, Patricia Tallman, Christine Forrest, Warner Shook.

●When first shown in Britain at the London Film Festival, *Knightriders* was met with bewilderment, largely because it was such an anomaly within the Romero canon. In the light of his later aberrations, it looks more to the point now. The tale of a latter-day motorbiking King Arthur and his noble knights, who stage medieval jousts, it's a genuinely idiosyncratic exercise in anachronism, as well as scoring a few telling points about the nature of role-playing in modern America. Romero's regular effects man Tom Savini (later a director in his own right) features in the cast, as does scribbler Stephen King – surely the most macabre sight in the movie – in a boozy cameo. JRo

Knight's Tale, A

(2001, US, 132 min)
d Brian Helgeland. *p* Brian Helgeland, Tim Van Rellim, Todd Black. *sc* Brian Helgeland. *ph* Richard Greatrex. *ed* Kevin Stitt. *pd* Tony Burrough. *m* Carter Burwell. *cast* Heath Ledger, Mark Addy, Rufus Sewell, Paul Bettany, Shannyn Sossamon, Alan Tudyk, Laura Fraser, Christopher Cazenove, Bérénice Bejo, James Purefoy.

●The right to compete at jousting in the 14th century comes only by noble birth, but William (Ledger), a thatcher's son determined to realise a childhood dream of knighthood, reinvents himself as Ulric von Liechtenstein of Gelderland. He's soon travelling with a crowd of supporters and winning tournaments across Europe, to the chagrin of his rival Count Adhemar (Sewell). And though he displays little interest in the beautiful Lady Jocelyn – a regular spectator at tournaments and desperately coveted by Adhemar – she soon wins him over, so that he's fighting for her too. Whipping along at speed, with elaborate camera movements and rousing speeches, this knows how to engage a crowd. It's corny, of course, but a guilty pleasure: romantic, diverting, with mildly amusing modern gags. A medieval dance morphs into something funkier, a scrabbling crowd reaches for a flying helmet as if it were a Wimbledon ball, a shield momentarily displays a Nike sign, and crowds chant in French bars before a Paris tournament. But the film is also let down by soppy childhood flashbacks and a mostly gruesome rock soundtrack. KW

Knight Without Armour

(1937, GB, 109 min, b/w)
d Jacques Feyder. *p* Alexander Korda. *sc* Arthur Wimperis. *ph* Harry Stradling. *ed* Francis D Lyon. *ad* Lazare Meerson. *m* Miklós Rózsa. *cast* Marlene Dietrich, Robert Donat, Irene Vanbrugh, Herbert Lomas, Austin Trevor, John Clements, Hay Petrie, Miles Malleson.

●Reality never held much sway at Korda's Denham studios, least of all during the making of this lavishly preposterous melodrama of Russian life before and after the 1917 Revolution. Dietrich is the cool, fur-swathed Countess Vladinoff, who strips down for two titillating baths during her protracted rush to freedom organised by much-bearded Donat, who pretends to be a Russian Commissar but is actually AJ Fothergill, British secret agent. Feyder's typically stylish direction raises the film way above its subject matter, almost at times towards art. GB

K-9

(1988, US, 102 min)
d Rod Daniel. *p* Lawrence Gordon, Charles Gordon. *sc* Steven Siegel, Scott Myers. *ph* Dean Semler. *ed* Lois Freeman-Fox. *pd* George Costello. *m* Miles Goodman. *cast* James Belushi, Mel Harris, Kevin Tighe, Ed O'Neill, James Handy, Daniel Davis.

●Tom Dooley (Belushi) is an unorthodox but dedicated narcotics officer, possessed of a motormouth, a battered car and an unpartnerable personality. Following a lead, he persuades a colleague to let him have a sniffer-dog so that he can investigate a suspected illegal shipment of drugs by bad guy Lyman (Tighe). The only dog available (special agent K-9, geddit?) is Jerry Lee, a good snifer but a touch unhinged after previous scrapes with malevolent hoods. From here on in it's the odd-couple scenario, with lots of jokes about disobedience, and graduation from enforced stand-off to grudging respect and finally mutual love between man and dog. Daniel directs with a light touch, clearly aimed low enough for juvenile audiences; but Belushi ain't the comic genius of all time, and it's a lot of footage to account for with a silent mutt for a foil. WH

Knock Off

(1998, US/HK, 91 min)
d Tsui Hark. *p* Nansun Shi. *sc* Steven E De Souza. *ph* Arthur Wong. *ed* Mak Chi-Sin. *pd* James Leung, Bill Lui. *m* Ron Mael, Russell Mael. *cast* Jean-Claude Van Damme, Rob Schneider, Lela Rochon, Michael Fitzgerald Wong, Paul Sorvino, Carmen Lee, Glen Chin, Jeff Joseph Wolfe.

●A mediocre yarn, set against the backdrop of the handover of Hong Kong to China. Marcus Ray (Van Damme), an archetype of the successful Westerner in the Far East, is a sales rep for a jeans company who discovers the Russians are orchestrating a plot to introduce button-sized silver 'microbombs' to the terrorist market. Ray, his boss Karen Leigh (Rochon), and his partner Tommy (Schneider), who doubles as a CIA man, are soon embroiled in trying to put a stop to this mischief – a job which involves the destruction of large chunks of HK real estate. For hardcore Van Damme and Sparks fans only. HK

Knock on Any Door

(1949, US, 100 min, b/w)
d Nicholas Ray. *p* Robert Lord. *sc* Daniel Taradash, John Monks Jr. *ph* Burnett Guffey. *ed* Viola Lawrence. *ad* Robert Peterson. *m* George Antheil. *songs* Sylvia Fine. *cast* Humphrey Bogart, John Derek, George Macready, Allene Roberts, Mickey Knox, Jimmy Conlin, Susan Perry, Dewey Martin.

●Nick Romano must be the ideal name for a flawed Ray hero-victim. As embodied to vulnerable, narcissistic perfection by John Derek (long before he took up with Bo), he's the centre of a fascinating, slightly askew mix of social document and romantic agony. The basic material may be determinist melodrama – slum boy with deck stacked against him winds up on Death Row despite the efforts of a liberal lawyer (Bogart, whose Santana company made the film). But it's hard hitting in its own right, tautly crafted, and repeatedly stabbed through with Ray's impulsive generosity and anguish towards his characters. TP

Knock on Wood

(1953, US, 103 min)
d/p/sc Norman Panama, Melvin Frank. *ph* Daniel L Fapp. *ed* Alma Macrorie. *ad* Hal Pereira, Henry Bumstead. *m* Sylvia Fine. *cast* Danny Kaye, Mai Zetterling, Torin Thatcher, David Burns, Leon Askin, Abner Biberman, Steve Geray.

●Danny Kaye's a ventriloquist with an outspoken dummy. Shrink Zetterling lays on the therapy, but a major plot device gets in her way when secret agents deposit a microfilm inside the dummy, whisking the movie into chase thriller mode, and giving the star a chance to dance with a troupe of Cossacks (choreography by Michael Kidd) and burst into balladry at an Irish convention. Funny, but a bit too much. TJ

Knots

(1975, GB, 62 min)
d David I Munro. *p* Simon Perry. *sc* David I Munro. *ph* Mike Berwick. *ed* Norman Wanstall. *ad* Peter Price. *m* Martin Duncan. *cast* Edward Petherbridge, Caroline Blakiston, Tenniel Evans, Robin Ellis, Robert Eddison, RD Laing.

●For anyone less than sold on the RD Laing cult, Munro's skilled direction of uncinematic material makes this film of the play based on his book *Knots* something less of an ordeal than might be expected. It centres on a series of classic double-bind situations which are personified by individual members of the Actors Company, and revealed by way of dialogue that consists entirely of a series of riddle-like verbal 'knots': 'You can't bear that I'm not interested in you being interested in me', or 'I'm afraid of the self that's afraid of the self that's afraid of the self'. It's not particularly earth-shattering, quite slight overall and a little didactic, in fact, but at least it's tackled with reasonable good humour and no psychological hair-tearing. VG

Knowledge of Healing, The (Das Wissen vom Heilen)

(1996, Switz, 93 min)
d Franz Reichle. *p* Marcel Hoehn, Paul Riniker. *sc* Franz Reichle. *ph* Pio Corradi. *ed* Myriam Flury, Franz Reichle. *with* HH Tenzin Gyatso (XIV Dalai Lama), Tenzin Choedrak, Chimit-Dorzhi Dugarov, Karl Lutz, Alfred Hässig.

●Could centuries-old Tibetan medical manuscripts hold the secret key to cures which still leave Western doctors baffled? That's just one of the tantalising notions in this feature length documentary exploring the subject of Tibetan medicine. Dr Tenzin Choedrak, personal physician to the Dalai Lama, unfurls ancient manuscripts and introduces the theories, which view the body as a series of elements, energy centres and channels. There's much fascinating material here, but writer/director Reichle seems unsure how best to use it. Information overload is the problem, since we barely have time to get a handle on the basics of the Tibetan approach before sundry Western eggheads blind us with science. TJ

Koks i Kulissen

see Ladies on the Rocks

Kolya (Kolja)

(1996, Czech Republic/GB/Fr, 105 min)
d Jan Sverák. *p* Eric Abraham, Jan Sverák. *sc* Zdenek Sverák. *ph* Vladimír Smutny. *ed* Alois Fisárek. *ad* Milos J Kohout. *m* Ondrej Soukup. *cast* Zdenek Sverák, Andrej Chalimon, Libuse Safránková, Ondrej Vetchy, Stella Zázvorková.

●Prague, 1988. Since being chucked out of the Czech Philharmonic, cellist Frantisek Louka (Sverák) has been reduced to playing at funerals. With the bills mounting, the middle-aged loner agrees to a marry a Russian woman in return for enough cash to pay his debts and buy a Trabant. The bogus bride, armed with her new Czech papers, exits to join a lover in West Germany, thus threatening to land Louka in trouble with the authorities, and lumbering him with her five-year-old son Kolya (Chalimon). With each film, Czech director Jan Sverák moves ever closer to the mainstream: the oddball sci-fi parody *Accumulator 1* and the dark social insights of the road movie *The Ride* are here replaced by sentimental comedy-drama. The script (by the director's father and lead actor) is contrived, obvious and shallow, and benefits not a jot from being set during the decline of communism. That said, however, it is a polished affair, and thanks to Sverák Sr's subtle, quietly charismatic performance as the cynic softened by responsibility, it's not entirely without charm. GA

Komitas

(1988, WGer, 96 min, b/w & col)
d Don Askarian. *cast* Samuel Ovasapian, Onig Saadetian, Margarita Woskanjan, Yegishe Mangikian.

●Askarian's film attempts to find a cinematic correlative for the suffering and madness of Soghomon Soghomonian ('Komitas'), a great Armenian musician who spent his last 20 years in mental institutions, traumatised by the 1915 genocide of two million of his people. Presented in a series of eight or so sections, it has the mind-opening intensity of Tarkovsky's spiritual odysseys, the visual beauty of Paradjanov's celebrations of ethnic cultures, and an almost surreal, miraculous poetry that is Askarian's own. The images have the visionary logic of the maddened imagination: faded paintings on a ruined church wall crumble in the rain to reveal jugs foaming with colour; jam-jars are smashed, their contents left to bleed down; strange music echoes from rain drumming on a graveyard of musical instruments; a woman breast-feeds a lamb; Komitas lies on a bed of flames. The pace is leisurely, and the camera moves gently or not at all; time – too much, perhaps – is given to meditate on what is shown. At one point, Komitas says art is worthless, that only nature and light matter. This film affirms that they all matter. WH

Konfrontation – Assassination in Davos (Konfrontation)

(1974, Switz, 114 min, b/w)
d Rolf Lyssy. *p* Rolf Lissy, HR Willner. *sc* Rolf Lyssy, George Janett. *ph* Fritz Maeder. *ed* George Janett. *ad* Edith Peier. *m* Arthur Paul Huber. *cast* Peter Bollag, Gert Haucke, Marianne Kehlau, Hilde Ziegler, Wolfram Berger, Max Knapp.

●Based on the factual case of a young Jewish student who fled Germany and shot the leader of the Swiss Nazi party in 1936, *Konfrontation* remains unfortunately limited by its scrupulous efforts to be faithful to actual events. The quality of the film well matches the frequent insertions of newsreel footage. But beyond that, its technical limitations make the deliberate stylisation of events appear increasingly awkward. As an essay on the gradual rise and acceptance of persecution (by the oppressed in particular), it remains conscientious but unmoving, mainly because the protagonist's dilemmas (the act of political assassination grows out of personal crises rather than moral or intellectual convictions) are never satisfactorily explained. And on the question of Swiss neutrality, the film becomes increasingly hampered, ending with an interminable trial in which the film's themes are hammered out. CPe

Konga

(1960, GB, 90 min)
d John Lemont. *p* Herman Cohen. *sc* Aben Kandel, Herman Cohen. *ph* Desmond Dickinson. *ed* Jack Slade. *ad* Wilfred Armold. *m* Gerard Schürmann. *cast* Michael Gough, Margo Johns, Jess Conrad, Claire Gordon, George Pastell, Austin Trevor, Jack Watson, Leonard Sachs, Steven Berkoff.

● Inept, silly, and ludicrously enjoyable monster movie, with Gough as the mad boffin who injects a chimp with a growth serum, only to see it turn into an uncredited actor in a gorilla suit. Thereafter the ape grabs a Michael Gough doll and heads for Big Ben. Deeply political. GA

Korczak

(1990, Pol/Ger/Fr/GB, 118 min, b/w)
d Andrzej Wajda. *p* Regina Ziegler, Janusz Morgenstern, Daniel Toscin du Plantier. *sc* Agnieszka Holland. *ph* Robby Müller. *ed* Ewa Sma. *pd* Allan Starski. *m* Wojciech Kilar. *cast* Wojtek Pszoniak, Ewa Dalkowska, Piotr Kozlowski, Marzena Trybala, Wojciech Klata.

● The life and death of Janusz Korczak, the Polish-Jewish doctor who defied the Nazis and tended the children in the Warsaw ghetto, was first filmed (rather well, if memory serves) by Rudolph Cartier for the BBC in 1962. Wajda's version covers the same ground, and adds nothing to the sum of human knowledge of the Holocaust; since he himself has been accused of anti-Semitism in the past, it looks suspiciously like a director's heart-on-sleeve riposte to his critics. Agnieszka Holland's script starts from the German occupation of Warsaw in 1939 and the brutal herding of the city's Jews into the makeshift ghetto; it concludes with the inevitable journey to Treblinka in 1942. Korczak (more than adequately played by Pszoniak) is seen as a pugnacious academic, tough on adults – Zionist elders as well as Nazis – but soft on kids. Everything from Robby Müller's monochrome photography to Wojciech Kilar's score is a model of 'taste' and sensitivity, and all concerned work overtime to avoid sentimentality. The problem is that the film's very existence is itself a sentimental gesture. After *Shoah*, earnest humanist tracts are no longer enough. TR

Korea

(1995, Ire, 87 min)
d Cathal Black. *p* Darryl Collins. *sc* Joe O'Byrne, Cathal Black, John D'Alton. *ph* Nic Morris. *ed* Emer Reynolds. *pd* Ned McLoughlin. *m* Stephen McKeon. *cast* Donal Donnelly, Andrew Scott, Fiona Molony, Vass Anderson, Eileen Ward.

● Ireland, 1952, and the coming of the electricity to a remote village threatens the traditional way of life forever, forcing a fisherman and his college-age son to reappraise their stagnant relationship. The death of a local lad in the Korean War, fighting for the Americans, is the metaphor for the onslaught of the outside world in this well-acted but rather stodgy rerun of familiar themes. The camerawork captures the grey dankness of the lakeside landscape, but we've been here before and insight is not forthcoming. TJ

Kotch

(1971, US, 114 min)
d Jack Lemmon. *p* Richard Carter. *sc* John Paxton. *ph* Richard H Kline. *ed* Ralph E Winters. *ad* Jack Poplin. *m* Marvin Hamlisch. *cast* Walter Matthau, Deborah Winters, Felicia Farr, Charles Aidman, Ellen Geer, Arlene Stuart, Darrell Larson.

● Sentimental generational comedy, with Matthau mugging through as an irascible senior citizen, resisting all attempts made by his family to uproot him, and generally sprinkling Grey Power with sparks of a second childhood. A bit of an easy option for Jack Lemmon's debut as a director, and a strange project to involve former blacklist victim John Paxton (*Crossfire, Murder, My Sweet*) as screenwriter. PT

Koyaanisqatsi

(1983, US, 86 min)
d/p Godfrey Reggio. *sc* Godfrey Reggio, Michael Hoenig, Alton Walpole. *ph* Ron Fricke. *ed* Alton Walpole, Ron Fricke. *m* Philip Glass.

● A wildly charitable viewer might describe this as an ecological documentary. Less than 90 minutes transport us from the primordial cuteness of the American South-West (a Good Thing) to the squalor of a Manhattan rush hour (a Bad Thing); and in case you still don't get the message, there's plenty of time-lapse photography to make people look like machines, and an apocalyptic score by Philip Glass to tell you off for daring to find visual pleasure in New York's skyline. At once maudlin and doggedly sarcastic, the film gives you the uncomfortable sensation of being condescended to by an idiot; it is, transparently, a product of the advanced technology it purports to despise. The title, by the way, is pilfered from the Hopi tongue and means 'vacuous hippy'. KJ

K-PAX

(2001, US/Ger, 121 min)
d Iain Softley. *p* Lawrence Gordon, Lloyd Levin, Robert F Colesberry. *sc* Charles Leavitt. *ph* John Mathieson. *ed* Craig McKay. *pd* John Beard. *m* Edward Shearmur. *cast* Kevin Spacey, Jeff Bridges, Alfre Woodard, Mary McCormack, Peter Gerety, Saul Williams, David Patrick Kelly, Celia Weston, Ajay Naidu.

● Dr Mark Powell (Bridges) is reluctant to dismiss mild-mannered 'Prot' (Spacey) – who claims to be a visitor from the planet K-PAX – as the incurable loony diagnosed by his colleagues at the Psychiatric Institute of Manhattan. For one thing, Prot is logical, and his knowledge of the cosmos rivals top boffins; for another, he has an uncanny ability to calm and help the institute's other inmates. But could he really be an alien? And if not, who is he? Softley and his stars invest this mystery with more respect than it deserves. Since Charles Leavitt's adaptation of Gene Brewer's book can never decide whether Prot's a starman, madman or Messiah, the film steadily turns into a murky mélange of banal explanation, far-fetched wish fulfilment and moralistic metaphor. The Oliver Sacks-lite psychiatric seasoning simply sours the brew. GA

Krakatoa – East of Java

(1968, US, 132 min)
d Bernard Kowalski. *p* William R Forman. *sc* Clifford Newton Gould, Bernard Gordon. *ph* Manuel Berenguer. *ed* Maurice Rootes, Warren Low, Walter Hannemann. *pd* Eugène Lourié. *m* Frank De Vol. *cast* Maximilian Schell, Diane Baker, Brian Keith, Barbara Werle, John Leyton, Rossano Brazzi, Sal Mineo, Marc Lawrence, Niall MacGinnis.

● Originally made in Cinerama, this takes as its starting point the world's most spectacular recorded natural disaster; and then, just to make things a little more interesting, adds a mutiny, sunken hidden treasure, a new type of diving bell, balloonists galore, an orphan boy, a fire, and even a little bit of strip-tease. In short, for disaster movie addicts only; and as reviewers everywhere gleefully pointed out, Krakatoa is west of Java. PH

Kramer vs Kramer

(1979, US, 105 min)
d Robert Benton. *p* Stanley R Jaffe. *sc* Robert Benton. *ph* Nestor Almendros. *ed* Jerry Greenberg. *pd* Paul Sylbert. *cast* Dustin Hoffman, Meryl Streep, Jane Alexander, Justin Henry, Howard Duff, George Coe, JoBeth Williams.

● A high class modern weepie. While Hoffman and Streep come to terms with divorce and battle over who gets the brat, Benton forsakes the eccentric and original delights of his earlier films (*Bad Company*, *The Late Show*) and turns in a very solid and professional domestic melodrama, helped no end by some very fine naturalistic performances. As sensitive and as unremarkable as your average Truffaut film, and as ambivalent in its sexual politics. GA

Krapp's Last Tape

(2000, Ire/GB, 58 min)
d Atom Egoyan. *p* Michael Colgan, Alan Moloney. *sc* Samuel Beckett. *ph* Peter Mettler, Paul Sarossy. *ed* Atom Egoyan. *pd* Clodagh Conroy. *cast* John Hurt.

● While John Hurt had already honed his magisterial interpretation on stage in London, the involvement of Egoyan is surprisingly appropriate, since a play about an old man remorsefully responding to a taped recording of his younger self obviously chimes with one of the film-maker's longstanding themes, the interaction between technology, memory and self-perception. Within a realist one-room setting, Hurt's performance strikes a compellingly intimate note, as Egoyan's camera underlines a telling sense of drifting time through attentive long takes. The uninterrupted 20-minute closing shot proves utterly hypnotic and deeply moving, a humbling display of a great actor's craft. TJ

Krays, The

(1990, GB, 119 min)
d Peter Medak. *p* Dominic Anciano, Ray Burdis. *sc* Philip Ridley. *ph* Alex Thomson. *ed* Martin Walsh. *pd* Michael Pickwood. *m* Michael Kamen. *cast* Billie Whitelaw, Tom Bell, Gary Kemp, Martin Kemp, Susan Fleetwood, Charlotte Cornwell, Kate Hardie, Avis Bunnage, Gary Love, Steven Berkoff, Jimmy Jewel, Barbara Ferris, Victor Spinetti, John McEnery, Murray Melvin.

● Medak's biopic skirts *Sweeney*-style fair-cop-guv clichés for bolder terrain, in which the macabre beginnings of the identical angels – all chirpy cockney, poor-but-spotless nostalgia – are placed as much within womb, hearth and home as in the streets, clubs and fairground booths through which Ron and Reg came to criminal prominence between Elvis and early Beatles. If Philip Ridley's script charts most of the signposts – school, army, protection, murder – it seems keen to establish the female connection, be it through Reggie's tormented, finally destroyed wife (Hardie, magnificent), or the endless, loyal patience of the kray brood, presided over by mother (Whitelaw) and consumptive but awesome Aunt Rose (Fleetwood). Most surprising is the impressive showing of Gary and Martin Kemp (of Spandau Ballet) as the twins, despite fears that the 'youth cult' dimension might be too strong a factor in the concept; most riveting, a series of cameos including Bell (ultra-seedy as victim Jack McVitie), Berkoff (OTT as victim George Cornell), Jimmy Jewel as the tall-tale-telling grandad every young thug should have. Little about the Krays' position as social climbing roughnecks, and not in the *Badlands* league, but a lot better than one dared hope. SGr

Kremlin Letter, The

(1969, US, 121 min)
d John Huston. *p* Carter De Haven Jr, Sam Wiesenthal. *sc* John Huston, Gladys Hill. *ph* Ted Scaife. *ed* Russell Lloyd. *pd* Ted Haworth. *m* Robert Drasnin. *cast* Richard Boone, Bibi Andersson, Max von Sydow, Patrick O'Neal, Orson Welles, Ronald Radd, Nigel Green, Dean Jagger, Lila Kedrova, Barbara Parkins, George Sanders, John Huston.

● Starting out as an all-star espionage saga with a state secret as the supposed Grail, this quickly reveals itself as a serpentine tale of treachery and double-dealing. What makes the film so powerful is that where before such films have generally titillated us with their stories of violence and sex in defence of one's country, Huston structures his film around such expectations, so forcing us to take account of his spies' actions. The resulting film is possibly the clearest statement of Huston's vision of a cruel and senseless world in operation. CPe

Kreutzer Sonata, The (Kreitzerova Sonata)

(1987, USSR, 135 min)
d Mikhail Schweitzer, Sofia Milkina. *sc* Mikhail Schweitzer. *ph* Mikhail Agranovich. *ed* Lyudmila Feiginova. *pd* Igor Lemeshev, Vladimir Fabrikov. *m* Sofia Gubaidulina.

cast Oleg Yankovsky, Aleksandr Trofimov, Irina Seleznyova, Dmitri Pokrovsky, Alla Demidova, Lidia Fedoseyeva-Shukshina.
●This version of the Tolstoy novel is cinematically conventional, but grips like a drowner in the writing and acting. Pozdnyshev (Yankovsky), who murdered his wife, pours out an agonised confession to a fellow-traveller on a train. His chastening tale of a relationship which stifled both parties, twisted into jealousy, and ended in violence, is explored in flashback. She (Seleznyova) first caught his eye in a drawing room entertainment by the sheer physical joy of her response to music. Life with him soon snuffed that out; and years later, he sees it again on her face as she plays the Beethoven piece with a philandering violin virtuoso. Only when she is dying does he realise what he has destroyed, and feel for another's life. Neither Albee nor Bergman dug any deeper into the pain of the loveless marriage, and Tolstoy, of course, rises to more universal levels. Yankovsky's performance is a tour de force; it invades the emotions and forces you to understand. BC

Krieger und die Kaiserin, Der

see Princess + the Warrior, The

Kristina Talking Pictures

(1976, US, 90 min, b/w & col)
d/sc Yvonne Rainer. *ph* Roger Dean, Babette Mangolte. *ed* Yvonne Rainer. *cast* Bert Barr, Kate Parker, Frances Barth, Lil Picardi, James Barth, Yvonne Rainer.
●Rainer's third feature is arguably the closest she has yet come to the Godard wing of 'art cinema'. Like her other movies, it's a shifting collage of narrations (some visual, mostly verbal), loosely anchored in the central relationship between Kristina and her lover Raoul. Except that Kristina, generally sketched as a middle-class NYC artist concerned about the environment, about relationships and such-like, is played by several different women…and given a personal history (archive flashbacks) as a former lion tamer in Europe who came to America to work as a choreographer. Dunno if this is 'political art', but it's certainly lively, unpredictable, and in several senses challenging. Also, it prominently features a photo of James Cagney. WW

Krug and Company

see Last House on the Left, The

Krull

(1983, GB, 121 min)
d Peter Yates. *p* Ron Silverman. *sc* Stanford Sherman. *ph* Peter Suschitzky. *ed* Ray Lovejoy. *pd* Stephen Grimes. *m* James Horner. *cast* Ken Marshall, Lysette Anthony, Freddie Jones, Francesca Annis, Alun Armstrong, David Battley, Bernard Bresslaw, Liam Neeson, Robbie Coltrane.
●The main interest here lies in the fantasy world created, a cross between *Mad Max 2* and *Excalibur* in which pugnacious Celtic chieftains, on the point of making peace by marriage, are overcome by the Slayers, a warrior band ruled over by the mercurial Beast, a protean monster who makes Jabba the Hutt look like the boy next door. The story, with many romantic overtones of *The Thief of Bagdad*, is concerned with the quest of Prince Colwyn for his abducted betrothed: meeting dangers, encountering perils and helpers (including a Cyclops-style Bresslaw and several talented RSC-National Theatre stalwarts in disguise), and aided by a magical weapon, the Glaive (a jewel-encrusted starfish with prongs). Strong on stunts and special effects but often rambling and ponderously lurching into comedy, it's not the greatest of Christmas treats, but does have enough cherishable moments between the wordy longueurs; and in Lysette Anthony's Princess Lyssa, a heroine for whom many a young Turk would walk through fire and ice. SGr

Krush Groove (aka Rap Attack)

(1985, US, 97 min)
d Michael Schultz. *p* Michael Schultz, Doug McHenry. *sc* Ralph Farquar *ph* Ernest Dickerson. *ed* Jerry Bixman, Conrad M Gonzalez. *cast* Blair Underwood, Joseph Simmons, Sheila E, Fat Boys, Daryll McDaniels, Kurtis Blow.
●One would have thought a movie based on rap, the hip (not to say hop) sound of the mid-'80s, and featuring some of its hottest protagonists, would be sure to inspire an original story-line. But this is a Grade A stop-me-if-you've-heard-this-one-before plot. Young bloods form label, have hit, need cash to press yet more records. Enter loan shark, enter Big Deal record co, enter romance (Sheila E), entertainment. A subplot features the Three Stooges, aka the Fat Boys, attempting to make good in glamorous pop despite a noticeable lack of physical allurements. Clearly these doings are merely a device to break up the songs performed (Kurtis Blow and Sheila E are the best acts). Stick with the soundtrack. EBr

Krzysztof Kieslowski: I'm So So

(1995, Pol, 56 min)
d Krzysztof Wierzbicki.
●As a documentary maker himself, Kieslowski was renowned for his fascination with people: the patient, sympathetic way in which he would elicit their opinions. Here, the tables are turned. He is the subject. Wierzbicki, an old friend and collaborator, quizzes him about his childhood, career and aspirations. Early on, various experts (a doctor, a priest and a clairvoyant among them) are invited to analyse Kieslowski's personality. They're all off the mark. So, perhaps, is Wierzbicki. But that's the point – Kieslowski, like the characters in his films, defies easy categorisation. Still, this documentary, made a few months before his untimely death, offers a warm, humorous profile of one of the recent cinema's greatest storytellers. GM

KT

(2001, Jap/SKor, 138 min)
d Junji Sakamoto. *p* Lee Bong-Ou, Yukiko Shii. *sc* Haruhiko Arai. *ph* Norimichi Kasamatsu. *ed* Toshihide Fukano. *ad* Mitsuo Harada. *m* Toyomasu Hotei. *cast* Koichi Sato, Yoshio Harada, Kim Gap-Soo, Choi Il-Hwa, Akira Emoto, Go Riju.
●A speculative reconstruction of a never fully explained incident from 1973: the five-day disappearance in Japan of Kim Dae-Jung (then a politician opposed to South Korea's military dictatorship, later president of South Korea and a Nobel Peace Prize laureate). Kim (codenamed 'KT') was on a secret fund-raising visit to Tokyo when he was snatched from a hotel room; the film says the kidnappers were Korean CIA men abetted by Japan's army-in-all-but-name, the Jieitai, both working with the tacit approval of the United States. A director transformed since his success with *Face*, Sakamoto forgets about most of the conventions of thrillers and docu-dramas and approaches this as an analysis of the failure of post-war politics in Japan *and* South Korea. The film's moral compass points are provided by Tomita (Sato), a Mishima-worshipping fascist from the Jieitai, and Kamikawa (Harada), a cynical journalist: two tattered anti-heroes guaranteed to enrage viewers who come to the film from entrenched left- or right-wing positions. A smart piece of work. TR

K2

(1991, US, 111 min)
d Franc Roddam. *p* Jonathan Taplin, Marilyn Weiner, Tim Van Rellim. *sc* Patrick Meyers, Scott Roberts. *ph* Gabriel Beristain. *ed* Sean Barton. *pd* Andrew Sanders. *m* Chaz Jankel. *cast* Michael Biehn, Matt Craven, Raymond J Barry, Hiroshi Fujioka, Luca Bercovici, Patricia Charbonneau, Julia Nickson-Soul.
●This abyssal action adventure details the efforts of two American buddies to scale the world's second highest peak. Roddam's intentions are made clear early on: climbing as metaphor – take risks! you've only got one shot in life! go for the dream! The film opens with drunken jock-lawyer Taylor (Biehn) in post-party garb scaling the outside walls of his erstwhile climbing chum's apartment building. Will his scientist mate Harold (Craven) – he's the married, sensitive type – team up for the big one? Much philosophical debating later, Who's-a-Wimp Harry is *in*. The rest is snowbound, rope-and-piton daredevil drivel. On trip one (Alaska) two dorks die. Trip two involves much palaver with porters, challenges from old rivals, and beyond-the-cliché dialogue. Cinematographer Gabriel Beristain does wonders filming the mountain landscapes of Pakistan and British Columbia. WH

Kuch Kuch Hota Hai

(1998, Ind, 185 min)
d Karan Johar. *p* Yash Johar. *sc* Karan Johar. *ad* Sharmashita Roy. *m* Jatin-Lalit. *cast* Shah Rukh Khan, Kajol, Rani Muckerjee, Salman Khan, Sana Saeed, Anupam Kher, Farida Jalal, Archana Puran Singh, Aruna Irani.
●A runaway success on its limited British release, Johar's lavish debut feature has been made up in an English subtitled print. The story's pure corn: a spunky young lass grows up reading one new letter left for her by her dead mummy each birthday; the eighth and last reveals the story of the girl she was named after, cueing with infectious confidence an extended flashback to her daddy's romantic school daze. After the interval it's time to go find the lost lady, who's about to go compromise everything. The second, grown-up love triangle drags on far too long, but for well over two hours the film is hectically entertaining, its performances, camerawork, storytelling and extensive musical numbers all energetically colourful. NB

Kuffs

(1991, US, 102 min)
d Bruce A Evans. *p* Raynold Gideon. *sc* Bruce A Evans, Raynold Gideon. *ph* Thomas Del Ruth. *ed* Stephen Semel. *pd* Victoria Paul, Armin Ganz. *m* Harold Faltermeyer. *cast* Christian Slater, Milla Jovovich, Tony Goldwyn, Bruce Boxleitner, Troy Evans, George De La Pena, Leon Rippy.
●'I'm only going to stick around until I clean up the neighbourhood,' announces reformed rebel George Kuffs (Slater). He lives on the mean streets of San Francisco where, we learn, it's customary for police districts to be sold off to private enterprise. After witnessing the death of his cop brother (Boxleitner), Kuffs inherits the family patch and sets about finding the killer. It's hard to believe that the writing team behind the beautifully understated *Stand by Me* concocted this hotch-potch, which mixes buddy-cop-thriller with rites-of-passage drama with slapstick farce. Amid the explosions and pratfalls, Evans (making his directorial debut) and Raynold Gideon throw in direct-to-camera monologues in which our hero comments on the action: this is as useful as Elmer Fudd analysing a Bugs Bunny escapade, but less funny. Granted, both characters and situations are deliberately exaggerated; but the romantic subplot, which sees Kuffs baulking at commitment (to Jovovich) also fails to ring true. CM

Kuhle Wampe

(1931, Ger, 73 min, b/w)
d Slatan Dudow. *p* George Hoellering, Robert Scharfenberg. *sc* Bertolt Brecht, Ernst Ottwald. *ph* Günther Krampfe. *ad* Robert Scharfenberg, Carl P Haacker. *m* Hanns Eisler. *cast* Hertha Thiele, Ernst Busch, Martha Wolter, Lili Schönborn, Adolf Fischer, Max Sablotzki, Gerhard Bienert, Anna Müller-Linke.
●Brecht scripted and participated in the making of this film, an unsentimental view of life in Kuhle Wampe, a camp for the dispossessed. Brecht saw its docile inhabitants (who struggled to maintain their dignity through an obsessive tidiness and attention to the forms of 'respectable' life) as wasting the opportunity for class solidarity and revolution. The heroine rejects this stifling of her spirit, to find moral renewal and purpose with a left wing youth movement. Brecht employs his usual mixture of didacticism (the film bears the alternative title, *To Whom Does the World Belong?*) and an almost lyrical naturalism that encourages the viewer to put across his own socio-economic analyses. What is curiously absent, however, is any treatment of the rise of the Nazis. Hitler came to power only nine months after the premiere of *Kuhle Wampe* in May 1932, and wasted little time in banning this charming and subversive film. MH

Kundun

(1997, US, 134 min)
d Martin Scorsese. *p* Barbara DeFina. *sc* Melissa Mathison. *ph* Roger Deakins. *ed* Thelma Schoonmaker. *pd* Dante Ferretti. *m* Philip Glass. *cast* Tenzin Thuthob Tsarong, Gyurme Tethong, Tulku Jamyang Kunga Tenzin, Tencho Gyalpo, Tsewang Migyur Khangsar.

●Scorsese's early life of the 14th Dalai Lama is the simplest and strangest movie he has yet made. An act of self-imposed exile, it's a Hollywood film only in the production credits and language. There's minimal contextualising. The scenario (by Melissa Mathison) sticks to the Dalai Lama's point of view: his discovery by Buddhist monks searching for the reincarnation of the 13th Dalai Lama among the farming communities of northern Tibet in 1935; his upbringing and tutelage in Lhasa; through the Communist Chinese invasion of 1950, to his own exile to India nine years later. The biographical detail is honest and illuminating, be it the rodents given free range of the Potala palace, the boy's fascination with mechanics, or his wonder at the opulent religious ceremonies. The film isn't remotely slow, yet Scorsese rejects the tenets of Western melodrama and dispenses with the history in so swiftly that it's easy to get lost in the sombre raptures of red, gold and blue. Urged on by Philip Glass's throbbing, blaring score, the director conjures a phenomenal, trance-like climax, owing more to dreams, second sight and the mind's eye than conventional dramatic rhetoric. TCh

Kung Fu Fighting (Tang Shou Taiquandao/aka Crush)

(1972, HK, 86 min)
d Tu Guangqi. *p* Tsui Pao Chu. *sc* I Kuang. *ph* Wang Chien Han. *ed* Liang Yung-Tsan. *ad* Tang Kuo-Shih. *m* Wu Ta-Chiang. *cast* Jason Pai Piau, Chen Hung Lieh, Ingrid Hu, Kung Pei Shi, Lu Chun.

●It is ironic that the first martial arts film to have been specially shorn (down to 60 minutes) for children's consumption should show every sign, even in its drastically curtailed state, of having been among the best Chinese films released here. Shooting on location in Korea, the director (a stalwart of the sword film in the '60s) balances off the weighty proportions of Korean architecture with its snow-covered courtyards and poses his figures in space to quietly dramatic effect. His use of colour and the wide screen is brilliantly controlled, and for once it looks as if the dialogue on restraint and oppression, tradition and revolt, imperialism and national identity, had found a worthy environment in a film full of incidental thematic riches. The relationship of the two children and the character played by Ingrid Wu (superb) is profoundly enigmatic and seemingly totally original; it would be interesting to see how this related to the coarser, more conventional elements. VG

Kung-Fu Gangbusters (Nanzi Han/aka Smugglers)

(1973, HK, 98 min, b/w)
d John Sun [Sun Jiawen]. *p* Yang Man-Wu. *sc* I Kuang. *ph* Fan Chieh. *ed* Liang Yung-Tsan. *ad* Tang Kuo-Shih. *m* Wu Ta-Chiang. *cast* Jason Pai Piau, Tommy Lu Chun, Thompson Kao Kang, Ingrid Hu, Liang Tien.

●This comprises sundry inadequate visual accompaniments to selections from *West Side Story* and *Shaft*, and finally reveals itself as a hymn to the valour of the Hong Kong police in their drug-gang busting efforts. To be avoided. TR

Kung Fu Girl, The (Tiewa/aka None But the Brave)

(1973, HK, 89 min)
d Lo Wei. *p* Raymond Chow. *sc* Lo Wei. *ph* Chen Ching-Chu. *ed* Chang Yao-Chung. *cast* Cheng Pei Pei, Ou Wei, James Tien, Jo Shishido, Lo Wei.

●This traces the activities of a group of revolutionaries in the period during which General Yuan Shih-kai was attempting to subvert the new republic and have himself made emperor, a move which entailed signing away North China to Japanese control. Lo Wei turns in an atmospheric film, possibly – in some of its imagery, and in its use of a 'family' as the cell which infiltrates Japanese High Command and the upper echelons of Peking government – revealing influences from Communist China. Cheng Pei Pei (from *Golden Swallow*) builds a character of muted but intense single-mindedness, wit and intelligence. Lo Wei obviously delights in his own role as a particularly unpleasant turncoat commissioner, and (directorically) cannot resist adding his familiar humorous brush-strokes. Nevertheless, the more delicate mood of encroaching horror and staunch resistance dominates the film. VG

Kung Fu – Girl Fighter (Can Nü Kongshoudao/aka Karate King – On the Waterfront)

(1970, Tai, 88 min)
d Hou Jing. *p* Hou Un-Chian. *ph* Lai Chung-Yin. *ed* Chang Hong-Ming. *ad* Chow Tsu-Lian. *m* Wang Mo-San. *cast* Tang Paoyun, Chang Yu, Chen Hong Rie, Tien Yie, Hou Jing.

●A slightly haphazard film that nevertheless frequently achieves an intense visual grace as it weaves its discursive plot around the theme of China's need for national regeneration and rebirth, specifically through a wandering hero figure. It even foreshadows Bruce Lee's charismatic smashing of a 'No Dogs or Chinese Allowed' sign. Its uncertain period recreation is less important than its general description of a shady and manipulated world, laden with political innuendoes which are probably more intelligible to Chinese than Western eyes. It is no doubt a clue of sorts that the film was produced by a brother of Chiang Kai Shek's personal bodyguard, and hence makes (somewhat odd) use of Taiwan's military establishments, but then again it's hardly a rabid political tract. There's a superbly sensual bath-house murder scene, sadly and with ridiculous prurience cut by the censor. VG

Kung-fu Soccer

see Shaolin Soccer

Kung Fu Street Fighter (Gekitotsu! Satsujinken)

(1974, Jap, 88 min)
d Shigehiro Ozawa. *p* Norimichi Matsudaira. *sc* Koji Takada, Motohiro Torii. *ph* Kenji Horikoshi. *ed* Kozo Horiike. *ad* Takatoshi Suzuki. *m* Toshiaki Tsushima. *cast* Shinichi Chiba, Goichi Yamada, Yutaka Nakajima, Tony Cetera, Tatsuro Endo.

●Japan had its Bruce Lee craze like everywhere else, and this offers a taste of the ultra-violent unarmed combat movies the Japanese started making after Lee's death in 1973. Chiba stars as Terry Tsuguri, the meanest bastard who ever gouged eyes, in an incomprehensible kidnap plot which rises to a wonderfully hysterical climax with samurai-style swordplay aboard an oil-tanker. If you can take the film's formulary nature, its rampant misogyny, and the peculiarly Japanese notion of tortured personal honour that Chiba's 'hero' represents, it's quite impressive. TR

Kung Fu – The Headcrusher (Ying Han/aka Tough Guy)

(1972, HK, 90 min)
d Jiang Hong. *p* Jimmy L Pasqual. *sc* Kwok Teng Hung. *ph* Hua San. *ed* Kwok Teng Hung. *m* Chow Fu Liang. *cast* Chen Xing, Linda Ling, Henry Yue Young, Charly Chiang, Sin Lan.

●Routine stuff, taking its title from a particularly lethal grip its hero is able to administer to the skulls of those who cross his path. The unspoiled rural locations (Taiwan?) lend freshness, but otherwise this fable of a cop who goes undercover to trace a gang of smugglers lacks the spark that would have lent its perfunctorily well staged fight scenes the touch of bravura achieved only once (the climactic fight, with the hero momentarily foiled by the iron skullcap his opponent wears, but the villain nevertheless ending up hammered waist deep into the mud). Otherwise there's some fairly meretricious sex (the 'boss' suffers from ejaculatio praecox) and a fair range of physique shots. VG

Kuragejima – Legends from a Southern Island

see Profound Desire of the Gods: Tales from a Southern Island, The

Kuroneko (Yabu no Naka no Kuroneko)

(1968, Jap, 99 min, b/w)
d/sc Kaneto Shindo. *ph* Kiyomi Kuroda. *ed* Hisao Enoki. *ad* Takashi Marumo. *m* Hikaru Hayashi. *cast* Kichiemon Nakamura, Nobuko Otowa, Kiwako Taichi, Kei Sato, Hideo Kanze.

●Shindo hit big with a movie called *Onibaba*, about an elderly woman and her daughter-in-law preying on lost samurai, and so it wasn't surprising that he cobbled together this variation on the earlier film. This time the two women are cat spirits (cue aerial somersaults), and the overall ambience is a great deal artier (cue eccentric 'scope compositions). Passable as a horror fantasy, but it hasn't an entrail of the gut impact of *Onibaba*. TR

Kurosawa

(2001, GB, 115 min)
d Adam Low. *p* Sonoko Aoyagi Bowers. *sc* Adam Low. *ph* Dewald Aukema. *ed* David Kitson. *m* Fratelli Brothers.

●Produced by BBC TV's *Arena*, this critical biography of the Japanese master film-maker, who died in 1998, reuses 10-year-old British interview footage from a previous *Arena* programme, extensive archive footage, interviews with Kurosawa's old colleagues, critics (Tadao Sato and Donald Richie) and celebrity American admirers (Clint Eastwood, James Coburn), and filmed visits to his places of work. Writer/director Low makes much of Kurosawa's background – the family was samurai class, his mother from Osaka merchants; his brother, a silent film narrator, committed suicide at 27 – and his experience of the catastrophic 1923 Tokyo earthquake. He made some 38 films, his status ever on the rise, until the box-office disaster of *Dodes'ka-den* in 1970, when he himself made a suicide attempt. A thorough introduction to a great humanist. WH

Kurt & Courtney

(1997, GB, 95 min)
d/p Nick Broomfield. *ph* Joan Churchill, Alex Vendler. *ed* Mark Atkins, Harley Escudier. *with* Nick Broomfield, Mari Earle, Tracy Marander, Alice Wheeler, Hank Harrison, Rozz Rezabek, Larry Flynt, Courtney Love.

●Who killed Kurt Cobain? That's the mystery at the root of this funny, angry, provocative film. Nick Broomfield visits the scene of the crime, sleuths around the rock star's old stomping grounds in Seattle and Portland, questioning ex-girlfriends, family and hangers-on. At the heart of it all is the femme fatale, the vamp, the 'ambitious psycho queen', Courtney Love. Broomfield is intuitive, opportunistic and upfront. 'I didn't have an angle or a theory, I was just trying to find my way through it,' he claims. He casts himself as the hero, and does achieve a moment of bluff courage, berating the American Civil Liberties Union for their star-struck hypocrisy in Love's presence. TCh

Kvinnodröm (Dreams/Journey Into Autumn)

(1955, Swe, 86 min, b/w)
d/sc Ingmar Bergman. *ph* Hilding Bladh. *ed* Carl-Olov Skeppstedt. *ad* Gittan Gustafsson. *cast* Eva Dahlbeck, Harriet Andersson, Gunnar Björnstrand, Ulf Palme, Inga Landgré, Naima Wifstrand.

●Bergman's movies in the '50s tend to lack any real perspective on their obsessive themes; each film looks like a more or less strained effort to find a 'dramatic' solution to the 'problem' of the ideas it contains. *Journey Into Autumn* tries for irony, but still ends up looking more forced than measured as fashion editor Eva Dahlbeck and model Harriet Andersson dream of reconciliation with former lovers, only to face disillusionment. TR

Kvinnorna på taket

see Women on the Roof, The

Kwaidan

(1964, Jap, 164 min)
d Masaki Kobayashi. *sc* Yoko Mizuki. *ph* Yoshio Miyajima. *ad* Shigemasa Toda. *m* Toru Takemitsu. *cast* Rentaro Mikuni, Michiyo Aratama, Misako Watanabe, Ganemon Nakamura, Takashi Shimura, Keiko Kishi, Tatsuya Nakadai.

●Kobayashi's first independent production (after years of working under contract to a major studio) drew extensively on his own training as a student of Japanese painting and fine arts. It is a compendium of four ghost stories adapted from Lafcadio Hearn, so determinedly aesthetic in their design and style that horror frissons hardly get a look in. Very beautiful, though. One episode was removed when the film was released in Britain, reducing the running time to 125 minutes. TR

The Lord of the Rings: The Fellowship of the Ring

La Baule-les pins (C'est la vie)

(1990, Fr, 96 min)
d Diane Kurys. *p* Alexandre Arcady. *sc* Diane Kurys, Alain Le Henry. *ph* Giuseppe Lanci. *ed* Raymonde Guyot. *ad* Tony Egry. *m* Philippe Sarde. *cast* Nathalie Baye, Richard Berry, Zabou, Jean-Pierre Bacri, Vincent Lindon, Valéria Bruni-Tedeschi, Didier Benureau, Julie Bataille, Candice Lefranc, Alexis Derlon.
●Another autobiographical slice of life from Diane Kurys, a bitter-sweet recollection of summer at the seaside in 1958. Packed off with their nanny, Frédérique (13) and Sophie (6) are happy enough playing on the beach, but it's clear that all is not right between their parents. Léna (Baye) joins them only when summer is beginning to pall, and she is alone. For the most part, Kurys concentrates on the childish hi-jinks of the sisters and their cousins, but she subtly incorporates other perspectives too, exploring the ramifications of the parents' divorce through countless quietly affecting details. This is delightfully evocative film-making, bringing an unerringly authentic touch to the most intangible circumstances – childhood, memory, love gone sour – maintaining an even, unblinking vision that allows for a great deal of humour as well as heartache, and extracting performances from children and adults alike that ring absolutely true. A less heroic, harsher tale than the liberating *Coup de foudre*, but in many ways better judged. TCh

Laberinto de pasiones

see Labyrinth of Passions

Labyrinth

(1986, GB, 101 min)
d Jim Henson. *p* Eric Rattray. *sc* Terry Jones. *ph* Alex Thomson. *ed* John Grover. *pd* Elliot Scott. *m* Trevor Jones. *cast* David Bowie, Jennifer Connelly, Toby Froud, Shelley Thompson, Christopher Malcolm, Natalie Finland.
●Terry Jones scripted this fairy tale fantasy in which pubescent Connelly must negotiate the myriad dangers of a mazy goblin city and cross the Bog of Eternal Stench to reclaim her baby brother from the talons of Goblin King Bowie. If the narrative's an enthusiastic assemblage of elements from the likes of Maurice Sendak and Frank L Baum, Henson's Creature Shop were on hand to provide the necessary, and rather impressive supporting cast of assorted gnomes and pixies. Still, although the film's initial energy and engaging finale are rather muffled by a mid-section that spends too much time idling in neutral, you can at least wonder at David Bowie's saddest ever haircut (no mean achievement) and bask in the pleasurable sight of an ill-tempered gnome scornfully squishing sweet little fairy creatures underfoot. TJ

Labyrinth

(1991, Ger/Czech, 90 min)
d Jaromil Jires. *p* Karel Dirka. *sc* Jaromil Jires, Hans-Jorg Weyhmüller, Alex Koenigsmark. *ph* Ivan Vojnar. *ed* Alois Fisarek. *pd* Jiri Barta. *m* Lubos Fiser. *cast* Maximilian Schell, Christopher Chaplin, Milos Kopecky, Vida Neuwirth, Jiri Krejcik, Dita Bochnickova, Martin Huba.
●This unclassifiable oddity is *not* a movie about Franz Kafka, how his Jewish-Czech heritage (pogroms, the ghetto, the Golem) worked on his imagination, or how the bureaucracy of irrational persecution which he postulated surfaced monstrously in the real world after his death. Instead, it's about a director (Schell) who aspires to make a movie which explores all those things, but who is unable to find a suitable cinematic form, and finally abandons the project. Thus, it's a scrapbook of random observations, a series of tentative drafts, a movie about its own inadequacies, a 90-min admission of failure. Ruefully aware of Kafka's dim view of the cinema's potential, the film-makers' inability to treat the material properly has a mortifying appropriateness. BBa

Labyrinth of Dreams (Yume no Ginga)

(1996, Jap, 90 min, b/w)
d Sogo Ishii. *p* Atsuyuki Shimoda, Kenichi Kamata. *sc* Sogo Ishii. *ph* Norimichi Kasamatsu. *ed* Kan Suzuki. *pd* Toshihiro Isomi. *m* Hiroyuki Onodera. *cast* Tadanobu Asano, Rena Komine, Kotomi Kyono, Kiriko Mano, Tomoko Kurotani.
●Ishii's thriller, as oneiric in its way as *Angel Dust* and *August in the Water* were, updates a story by novelist maudit Kyusaku Yumeno to the monochrome 1950s. The virginal Tomiko (Komine) is a bus conductor in a small country town who grows convinced that the handsome new driver of her bus (Asano) is the man who loved and murdered her friend in another town. She steels herself to work with him, testing him at every opportunity. And then she falls in love. A Freudian fable of the night, filled with moons, rain, dark tunnels and imminent collisions. As Tomiko matures from repressed adolescence into womanhood the key question is less whether the man's a murderer, but whether it's possible for a man to murder with sincerity. TR

Labyrinth of Passion (Laberinto de pasiones)

(1982, Sp, 99 min)
d/sc Pedro Almodóvar. *ph* Angel Luis Fernandez. *ed* José Salcedo. *pd* Pedro Almodóvar. *cast* Cecilia Roth, Imanol Arias, Helga Liné, Marta Fernández-Muro, Angel Alcazar, Antonio Banderas, Agustín Almodóvar, Cristina S Pascual, Fabio McNamara.
●This is a home movie for the *Movida* set, a glamorous clash of frocks and jocks (and jocks *in* frocks) in a Madrid peopled by drug-takers, pop stars, wannabes, terrorists and sex maniacs. Briefly, rock singer Sexi (Roth) is the neurotic nympho daughter of a creepy gynaecologist who's treating the wife of a Shah-like potentate, whose son, bisexual Riza (Arias) also becomes a rock singer, and is torn between the charms of Sexi and an Arab terrorist (Banderas) with a keen sense of smell. Meanwhile, Sexi's biggest fan, a laundry maid, is raped continually by a father who snorts aphrodisiac. When her heroine comes into the dry-cleaners, the two join forces to outwit their parents, beat their beauty problems, and fulfil their dreams. A sense of humour is the string that will guide you through this tacky labyrinth, which includes an appearance by legendary mini-skirted pop duo Almodóvar and McNamara performing a rap song about fabulous drugs. Drag till you gag. SFe

LaCapaGira

(1999, It, 75 min)
d Alessandro Piva. *p* Valerio Bariletti, Umberto Massa, Alessandro Piva. *sc* Andrea Piva. *ph* Gianenrico Bianchi. *ed* Alessandro Piva, Thomas Woschitz. *m* Ivan Iusco, Nicola Cipriani, Russolo. *cast* Dino Abbrescia, Mino Barbarese, Mimmo Mancini, Dante Marmone, Paolo Sassanelli, Teodosio Barresi, Nicola Pignataro.
●A portrait of the various classes of criminal of the Italian heel town of Bari, this bears traces of sub-Jarmusch comedy, as two petty drug mules hang out waiting, not for Godot, but a crack delivery from the Balkans. Meanwhile the owners of an illegal video poker den feel the heat from the cops; and the local kingpin tries to enforce discipline. The director is as interested in faces, manners and slang as he is in plot mechanics – maybe the atmosphere he creates of casual violence, automatic criminality and survivalist humour is his point. His amoral stance allows for some droll downbeat portraiture, but as character studies, they lack the bite and power that Pasolini in his early frescos brought to the mid-20th century Roman cousins of these southern types. WH

Lac aux Dames

(1934, Fr, 94 min, b/w)
d Marc Allégret. *sc* Jean-Georges Auriol, Colette. *ph* Jules Kruger. *ed* Denise Batcheff. *ad* Lazare Meerson. *m* Georges Auric. *cast* Jean-Pierre Aumont, Simone Simon, Rosine Deréan, Illa Meery, Michel Simon, Odette Joyeux, Vladimir Sokoloff.
●Novelist Vicki Baum was the author of *Grand Hotel* and of this variant, set in a lakeside spa in the Tyrol. Aumont is a swimming instructor whose charms enthral, to varying degrees, a gold-digger on the run (Meery), an heiress (Deréan) and a saucy teenager from across the lake (Simon). Colette's dialogue, some moody photography and Allégret's showcasing of his youthful cast are the main attractions. It's easy to see why Hollywood snapped up Simone Simon, though not why the equally vivacious Meery was declined, unless her nude scenes scared them off. BBa

Lacemaker, The

see Dentellière, La

Lacho Drom

(1993, Fr, 103 min)
d Tony Gatlif. *p* Michèle Ray-Gavras. *sc* Tony Gatlif. *ph* Eric Guichard. *ed* Claude Garnier.
●Gatlif's *Les Princes* was an impressive addition to that small but fascinating genre, the gypsy film; since he was Romany himself, authenticity came easily. This film, whose title means 'safe journey', is another invaluable contribution, an impassioned, semi-allegorical odyssey traced, using one group of Roms after another, from India – by way of Egypt, Istanbul, Romania, Hungary, Slovakia and the annual pilgrimage to Saintes Maries de la Mer in the Camargue – to Spain. A document of customs, craftsmanship, costumes, faces and, most especially, song and dance, it's a musical celebration of the gypsies' sense of community and ability to survive in the face of upheaval, prejudice and persecution. Technically, the film, shot in numerous locations in 'Scope and stereo, is a triumph, transcending the staged nature of many sequences by means of colour and movement. Crucial to the film's success, however, is the music, not only as an expression of the gypsies' feelings about distance, love, exile, history and hope, but glorious in its own right. Only the cavalier way with bird song on the soundtrack and the sentimental use of a non-Romany mother and child in the Hungarian episode ring false. Otherwise, it's a joy. GA

Lacombe Lucien

(1974, Fr/It/WGer, 137 min)
d Louis Malle. *sc* Louis Malle, Patrick Modiano. *ph* Tonino Delli Colli. *ed* Suzanne Baron. *ad* Ghislain Uhry. *cast* Pierre Blaise, Aurore Clément, Holger Löwenadler, Thérèse Giehse, Stéphane Bouy, Jean Rougerie, Jacques Rispal.
●Out of school into a job, Lucien Lacombe shoots rabbits in his spare time. Then almost imperceptibly a particular historical perspective is slipped in behind him. World War II France is under German occupation, and Lucien finds himself acting out his adolescent emotions, gun in hand, within the eerie schema of Fascism. Malle's film has two strengths: one is Lucien, Malle's answer to the question, who becomes a Fascist? The second is the precision and total lack of histrionics with which the mechanics of compromise are mapped. It has one major weakness; having drawn Lucien from the fringe of the action to the centre of the screen, Malle seems unable to bridge the gap between himself and the character. He attempts to compensate with weighty (and unnecessary) symbolism, and fades out making pretty pictures around his protagonist. Perhaps Malle's seductive style, carried over intact from *Dearest Love,* cannot go any further. VG

LA Confidential

(1997, US, 138 min)
d Curtis Hanson. *p* Arnon Milchan, Curtis Hanson, Michael Nathanson. *sc* Brian Helgeland, Curtis Hanson. *ph* Dante Spinotti. *ed* Peter Honess. *pd* Jeannine C Oppewall. *m* Jerry Goldsmith. *cast* Kevin Spacey, Russell Crowe, Guy Pearce, James Cromwell, Kim Basinger, Danny DeVito, David Straithairn, Ron Rifkin.
●Dime store detective stories have inspired more great movies than Dostoevsky ever will, but local-boy-made-bad James Ellroy always seemed too tough a proposition for Hollywood to take on. Hanson's adaptation of Ellroy's most complex novel is a towering achievement, probably the finest mystery thriller since *Chinatown*. Set in the '50s, this punchy cocktail of gangland violence, police brutality, racism and sex-scandal cover-ups feels torn from today's headlines. It operates on the principles of an exposé, highlighting the parallax between image and reality. As Danny DeVito's muck-raising, 'Hush Hush' magazine hack guides us on a gleeful trawl through the seedier, sleazier aspects of this, the last of the frontier towns, we meet three very different lawmen: Spacey's cynical showboat Jack Vincennes; Ed Exley (Pearce), a straight-arrow cop headed for the top; and Crowe's Bud White, the strong arm of the law, brawn to Exley's brains. Contrasting not only their approaches to procedure, justice and

respect, but also their vividly etched, distinctly volatile psycho-pathologies, Hanson inexorably draws these three cases to one conclusion: when the trio do take a stand, it's inspired less by idealism than self-disgust. As the emotional nexus, a Veronica Lake lookalike trapped in a web of male desires, Basinger is arguably the pick of a perfect cast. Subtle, shocking, compelling and immensely assured. TCh

Ladder of Swords

(1988, GB, 98 min)
d Norman Hull. *p* Jennifer Howarth. *sc* Neil Clarke. *ph* Thaddeus O'Sullivan. *ed* Scott Thomas. *pd* Caroline Hanania. *m* Stanley Myers. *cast* Martin Shaw, Eleanor David, Juliet Stevenson, Bob Peck, Simon Molloy, Pearce Quigley.

●A desolate moor is the setting for murder, but despite the hackneyed backdrop, Neil Clarke's script for the most part creates genuinely suspenseful drama. Much of the film's credibility stems from strong performances. Shaw plays Don Demarco, an escaped convict who evades the law with his travelling circus act. In his caravan on the edge of the moor, awaiting his next engagement, he loses a disgruntled, thieving wife (David) and gains a caring lover (Stevenson). Meanwhile, obsessive Detective Inspector Atherton (Peck) takes an instant dislike to Demarco, accusing him of one offence after another, from a local robbery to murdering his wife. It's just a matter of time before the past catches up. Amid the elements of kitchen-sink realism, Atherton's character unbalances the film: as he tracks his quarry with the refinement of a rabid dog, it's hard to imagine him lasting two minutes in a real police station. This has less to do with Peck's fine performance than with misguided efforts to inject belly laughs amid more subtle humour. CM

Ladies and Gentlemen, the Rolling Stones

(1973, US, 90 min)
d Rollin Binzer. *p* Rollin Binzer, Marshall Chess, Bob Freeze, Steve Gebhardt. *ph* Jay Cassidy, Bob Freeze, Steve Gebhardt. *ed* Laura Lesser. *with* The Rolling Stones.

●Documentary record of an average Stones concert (1972 repertoire), filmed by cameramen with a Jagger fixation. With Mick in close-up eighty percent of the time, and no visual sense of the band as a working unit, the movie relies on the gimmick of Dolby quad sound to make its impact. It's not enough. TR

Ladies in Retirement

(1941, US, 92 min, b/w)
d Charles Vidor. *p* Lester Cowan. *sc* Garrett Fort, Reginald Denham. *ph* George Barnes. *ed* Al Clark. *ad* Lionel Banks. *m* Ernest Toch. *cast* Ida Lupino, Louis Hayward, Evelyn Keyes, Elsa Lanchester, Edith Barrett, Isobel Elsom, Emma Dunn.

●In this stage-bound yet surprisingly involving Gothic melodrama, Lupino plays a housekeeper who murders her ex-actress employer (Elsom) in order to prevent her two mentally disturbed sisters (Lanchester and Barrett) from being sent to an asylum. The blend of eccentricity and (genteel) Grand Guignol works well, though the events portrayed are nothing like as shocking as they must have seemed at the time of the film's original release. Remade in 1968 as *The Mad Room*. NF

Ladies' Man, The

(1961, US, 106 min)
d/p Jerry Lewis. *sc* Jerry Lewis, Bill Richmond. *ph* W Wallace Kelley. *ed* Stanley Johnson. *ad* Hal Pereira, Ross Bellah. *m* Walter Scharf. *cast* Jerry Lewis, Helen Traubel, Kathleen Freeman, Hope Holiday, Pat Stanley, Jack Kruschen, Doodles Weaver, George Raft.

●Jerry Lewis' second film as director is one of his greatest, with its star almost overwhelmed by his one major set, the split-level interior of a Hollywood boarding hotel for aspiring actresses, where one Herbert Heebert, practising misogynist, has been taken on in all innocence as a houseboy. Lewis' camera performs some virtuoso movement around the rooms (Jean-Luc Godard and Julien Temple were to borrow this device), and the ultra-loose plotline allows for some hilarious sequences, and even a touch of surrealism in one entirely white interior. Highlights include Lewis breaking up a television show and dancing a tango with George Raft. DT

Ladies Man, The

(2000, US, 84 min)
d Reginald Hudlin. *p* Lorne Michaels. *sc* Tim Meadows, Dennis McNicholas, Andrew Steele. *ph* Johnny E Jensen. *ed* Earl Watson. *pd* Franco de Cotiis. *m* Marcus Miller. *cast* Tim Meadows, Karyn Parsons, Billy Dee Williams, Tiffani Thiessen, Lee Evans, Will Ferrell, Sofia Milos, Jill Talley, John Witherspoon, Ken Campbell, Tamla Jones, Julianne Moore, Eugene Levy.

●Leon Phelps (Meadows) hosts a late night radio talk show on sex. What with his minimal IQ, speech impediment and a free-associative style that makes Howard Stern sound like Frasier Crane, you might question his qualifications for the job – but as he says, 'I have done it to a lot of lay-dees!' His success with the fair sex is no mystery. It's not so much that his funky mid-'70s wardrobe makes them laugh (though that afro is probably part of it); rather, they love his confidence – and his enormous wang. Sophisticates may want to look elsewhere, but hell, we've seen worse and lived to smile about it. Meadows is a nine-year veteran of TV's *Saturday Night Live*, and this spin-off sticks close to the formula: take a tried-and-tested character (usually a socially incongruous innocent) and place him in barely linked, sketch-like scenes. Leon loses his job and is hunted by a group of cuckolded husbands (including Lee Evans), but you could probably move five minutes from the beginning to the end without anyone noticing. Is it funny? After I swallowed my disbelief and gave my critical faculties a break, yeah, I was tickled every 40 minutes or so. Is it sexist? Like Woody Allen said, 'It is if you're doing it right.' TCh

Ladies of the Chorus

(1948, US, 60 min, b/w)
d Phil Karlson. *sc* Harry Sauber, Joseph Carole. *ph* Frank Redman. *ed* Richard Fantl. *ad* Robert Peterson. *songs* Allan Roberts, Lester Lee, Buck Ram *cast* Adele Jergens, Rand Brooks, Marilyn Monroe, Nana Bryant.

●Marilyn's first sizeable role came in this Columbia programme-filler, shortly before the studio scrapped her contract after only six months. Here she steps out of the chorus and into the limelight when the star walks out on a burlesque show. Mama Jergens warns her, however, to be wary of involvement with wealthy socialite Brooks. It's formula stuff, but if you've seen all the other Monroe pictures you might want to catch this one. TJ

Ladies on the Rocks (Koks i Kulissen)

(1984, Den, 110 min)
d Christian Braad Thomsen. *sc* Christian Braad Thomsen, Helle Ryslinge, Annemarie Helger. *ph* Dirk Brüel. *ed* Grete Møldrup. *m* Helle Ryslinge. *cast* Helle Ryslinge, Annemarie Helger, Flemming Quist-Møller, Hans Henrik Clemmensen, Gyda Hansen.

●The original title translates as *Chaos Behind the Scenes*, a neat summary of the lives and art of Micha and Laura, heroines of Thomsen's anti-romantic film and stars of their own comic cabaret. Abandoning loved ones, the women take to touring Denmark's damp autumnal provinces with their increasingly truculent show. The act is a success, but Micha and Laura's pleasure in their new life is spoiled by the failure of the old one, and by a suspicion that the ideals of both are largely fantasy. Although the message is unclear, it is delivered with an ingenuous vitality. And a curious optimism emerges from the film's waxy gloom: a triumph of large spirit over small aspirations, of bravura performance over pallid script. FD

Ladri di Biciclette

see Bicycle Thieves

Ladri di Saponette

see Icicle Thief

Ladro di bambini, Il

see Stolen Children, The

Lady & the Duke, The (L'Anglaise et le duc/Die Lady und der Herzog)

(2001, Fr/Ger, 129 min)
d Eric Rohmer. *p* Françoise Etchegaray. *sc* Eric Rohmer. *ph* Diane Baratier. *ed* Mary Stephen. *set decorator* Antoine Fontaine. *cast* Jean-Claude Dreyfus, Lucy Russell, Alain Libolt, Charlotte Very, Rosette, Léonard Cobiant, François Marthouret, Caroline Morin, Marie Rivière.

●Rohmer's third historical feature and literary adaptation is taken from the memoirs of Grace Elliott (Russell, even more impressive than she was in Chris Nolan's *Following*), a wealthy, well-connected Brit trapped in Paris at the time of the Revolution. Though an intimate of an influential Republican, the Duc d'Orléans (Dreyfus), she nevertheless falls under suspicion after reluctantly helping the governor of the Tuileries to evade the guillotine. Partly a suspense drama, partly a very relevant study in how political ideals may be tainted by fanaticism, partly a typically astute moral disquisition, this magisterial film finds the octogenarian auteur embracing the new opportunities afforded by digital – it resembles a contemporary painting come exquisitely to life. A splendid and remarkable achievement. GA

Lady and the Tramp

(1955, US, 75 min)
d Hamilton Luske, Clyde Geronimi, Wilfred Jackson. *sc* Erdman Penner, Joe Rinaldi, Ralph Wright, Don Da Gradi. *ed* Don Halliday. *m* Oliver Wallace. *songs* Sonny Burke, Peggy Lee. *cast* voices: Peggy Lee, Barbara Luddy, Larry Roberts, Stan Freberg, George Givot, Alan Reed.

●In 1956, when *Woof Back in Anger* was challenging perceptions on the London stage, a few critics remarked that it had all been done the year before in a Disney cartoon musical with songs by Peggy Lee. Like Osborne's play, *Lady and the Tramp* probes one of the great social fusses of the '50s: canine hypergamy – marriage or liaison above one's social caste or class – and was inspired by the tale of Walt's family spaniel. All tame stuff today; the humans are disgusting, Tramp is streetwise but sanitary, and the Lady is a wet. Happily the cameo lowlife, an excellent manic beaver, the famously villainous Siamese, and classic songs rescue the film from dumb animal sentiment. Best of these is the almost raunchy 'He's a Tramp', in which Peggy Lee shows that part of being a bitch is knowing when not to be too much of a lady. RP

Ladybird Ladybird

(1994, GB, 101 min)
d Ken Loach. *p* Sally Hibbin. *sc* Rona Munro. *ph* Barry Ackroyd. *ed* Jonathan Morris. *pd* Martin Johnson. *m* George Fenton. *cast* Crissy Rock, Vladimir Vega, Sandie Lavelle, Mauricio Venegas, Ray Winstone, Clare Perkins.

●Matters start promisingly: in a pub, Maggie (Rock) belts out a ballad and transfixes Jorge (Vega), a Paraguayan exile settled in London. He's gentle and supportive, just as well, given her foul-mouthed temper and troubled life. A mother of four living in a refuge, she's persistently hounded as an unfit parent by social workers who threaten to remove her children, because of her tendency to involve herself with violent, drunken louts. Truth to tell, she's a walking disaster area, though Jorge's love and understanding finally break through her defences, encouraging her to move in with him and start their own family. But modern Britain's an unjust place: can their fragile happiness last? Ken Loach sledgehammers his points. As social critique, the film provokes pity and anger, not thought: understandable, since it's never quite clear exactly what Loach is attacking. The methods of the social services? The bureaucracy of Tory Britain? Life itself? GA

Lady by Choice

(1934, US, 71 min, b/w)
d David Burton. *sc* Jo Swerling, Dwight Taylor. *ph* Ted Tetzlaff. *ed* Viola Lawrence. *cast* Carole Lombard, May Robson, Roger Pryor, Walter Connolly, Arthur Hohl, Raymond Walburn.

●A sequel to Capra's Damon Runyon adaptation of the previous year, *Lady for a Day*, this helping of Hollywood hogwash has a second-hand feel.

Lombard reprises her role as a fan-dancer, this time ripe for reform when she 'adopts' curmudgeonly old bag lady Robson in a Mother's Day publicity stunt. Mildly agreeable, but it would be very easy to overstate its modest quality. TJ

Lady Caroline Lamb

(1972, GB/It, 123 min)
d Robert Bolt. *p* Fernando Ghia. *sc* Robert Bolt. *ph* Oswald Morris. *ed* Norman Savage. *ad* Carmen Dillon. *m* Richard Rodney Bennett. *cast* Sarah Miles, Jon Finch, Richard Chamberlain, John Mills, Margaret Leighton, Pamela Brown, Ralph Richardson, Laurence Olivier, Peter Bull, Sonia Dresdel.
● Bolt's debut as a director from his own script about the darling of English society who rocked the boat with her scandalous behaviour – ha, ha. She bolts through the woods in boy's clothing, marries a conscientious liberal politician (Finch), and outrages the British way of life by not being discreet (as Mother was) in who she chooses to fuck, where, when, and how often, as well as by turning up at a fancy- dress ball near-naked and blacked up as Byron's slave. Plus the film has a theme: reason versus passion. It's the end of the Age of Reason, and she is all passion while most of those around her still bow to reason. But it is impossible to take seriously on a historical or an ideas level – the 2D characters refuse to be plugged in to anything beyond the studio sets around them. On the other hand, the film won't deliver Hollywood-type glamour either. Bright spot: Richard Chamberlain as Byron gets the white-clad early 19th century ladies' knickers twisted very effectively in eye-liner and lip-colour.

Lady Chatterley's Lover

(1981, GB/Fr, 104 min)
d Just Jaeckin. *p* Christopher Pearce, André Djaoui, Marc Behm. *sc* Christopher Wicking, Just Jaeckin. *ph* Robert Fraisse. *ed* Eunice Mountjoy. *pd* Anton Furst. *m* Stanley Myers, Richard Harvey. *cast* Sylvia Kristel, Nicholas Clay, Shane Briant, Ann Mitchell, Elizabeth Spriggs, Bessie Love.
● A ghastly movie. For all his funny ideas, DH Lawrence could string a sentence together. Take away the words, leave the story and the sex, and you have something very trite indeed. Jaeckin's prissy-pretty approach in concept, direction and photography is simply the pornography of mediocrity; Lawrence needs the runaway Ken Russell touch. Kristel gives a boring performance, even allowing for the English dubbing, and she plays it with the expression of a pall-bearer – her contribution to the film's good taste pretensions. She may think she's sloughed off the *Emmanuelle* image. Wrong. This stupid movie conclusively proves that there's nothing to choose between an airplane lay and a gamekeeper's hut. JS

Lady Eve, The 100

(1941, US, 97 min, b/w)
d/sc Preston Sturges. *ph* Victor Milner. *ed* Stuart Gilmore. *ad* Hans Dreier, Ernst Fegté. *cast* Barbara Stanwyck, Henry Fonda, Charles Coburn, Eugene Pallette, William Demarest, Eric Blore, Melville Cooper.
● A beguilingly ribald sex comedy, spattered with characteristic Sturges slapstick (Fonda can hardly move without courting disaster) and speech patterns ('Let us be crooked, but never common,' urges Coburn's conman). Fonda and Stanwyck are superbly paired as the prissy professor and the brassy card-sharp who meet on a liner for a ferociously funny battle of the sexes in which she proves triumphantly that Eve and the serpent still have the drop on poor old Adam. The glittering screwball comedy of love's labours that ensues – denounced as a brazen gold-digger and cast off, Stanwyck vengefully seeks revenge by reconquering Fonda's heart while masquerading (inimitably) as a flower of English society – is not just funny but surprisingly moving, given the tender romantic warmth of the early shipboard scenes in which, with Stanwyck's veneer slowly melted by Fonda's vulnerability, the pair first fall irrevocably in love. Very nearly perfection, and quintessential Sturges. TM

Lady for a Day

(1933, US, 95 min, b/w)
d/p Frank Capra. *sc* Robert Riskin, *ph* Joseph Walker. *ed* Gene Havlick. *ad* Stephen Goosson. *m* Mischa Bakaleinikoff. *cast* Warren William, May Robson, Guy Kibbee, Glenda Farrell, Jean Parker, Walter Connolly, Ned Sparks, Nat Pendleton.
● The story (derived from Damon Runyon) is pure sentiment. A lady known as Apple Annie (Robson) is reduced to selling apples on the sidewalk for a living. She keeps the awful truth from her daughter by writing fanciful letters about high society on purloined headed notepaper... until her daughter (Parker) decides to come to New York with her fiancé, a Spanish count. What will the poor gin-soaked old body do? As it's a Capra fable, everyone from fellow street bums to the mayor is eventually galvanised in her cause. You can tell just how rich the comedy is by the fact that not even a plot like that can sink it. Robert Riskin's razor-sharp dialogue is matched by Capra's super-subtle visuals, and backed by an array of suitably Runyonesque characters. In fact it is just about worth swallowing your cynicism (and scruples) for Ned Sparks' definitive stone-faced Broadway sharpie alone. Remade by Capra himself as *Pocketful of Miracles* in 1961.

Lady from Louisiana

(1941, US, 82 min, b/w)
d Bernard Vorhaus. *sc* Vera Caspary, Michael Hogan, Guy Endore. *ph* Jack Marta. *ed* Edward Mann. *ad* John Victor MacKay. *m* Cy Feuer. *cast* John Wayne, Ona Munson, Ray Middleton, Henry Stephenson, Dorothy Dandridge, Helen Westley, Jack Pennick.
● Wayne plays an idealistic young lawyer whose plans to clean up a rootin'-tootin' frontier town are in jeopardy as soon as he falls for alluring Southern belle Munson, whose father runs the local organised crime racket. Plodding second feature (co-scripted by Guy Endore) from German-born director Vorhaus who graduated (if that's the word) from British quota quickies to programmers like this at Republic Pictures. After *Stagecoach*, the Duke deserved better. TJ

Lady from Shanghai, The

(1947, US, 87 min, b/w)
d/p/sc Orson Welles. *ph* Charles Lawton Jr. *ed* Viola Lawrence. *ad* Stephen Goosson, Sturges Carne. *m* Heinz Roemheld. *cast* Orson Welles, Rita Hayworth, Everett Sloane, Glenn Anders, Ted de Corsia, Erskine Sanford, Gus Schilling.
● Don't attempt to follow the plot – studio boss Harry Cohn offered a reward to anyone who could explain it to him, and many critics have foundered on it – because Welles simply doesn't care enough to make the narrative seamless. Indeed, the principal pleasure of *The Lady from Shanghai* is its tongue-in-cheek approach to story-telling. Welles is an Irish sailor who accompanies a beautiful woman (Hayworth, then Mrs Welles) and her husband on a sea cruise, and becomes a pawn in a game of murder. One intriguing reading of the movie is that it's a commentary on Welles' marriage to Hayworth – the impossibility of the 'boy genius' maintaining a relationship with a mature woman – and the scene in the hall of mirrors, where the temptress' face is endlessly reflected back at him, stands as a brilliant expressionist metaphor for sexual unease and its accompanying loss of identity. Complex, courageous, and utterly compelling. MA

Lady from the Shanghai Cinema, The (A Dama do cine Shanghai)

(1988, Braz, 117 min)
d Guilherme De Almeida Prado. *p* Assunção Hernandes. *ph* Cláudio Portioli, José Roberto Eliezer. *ed* Jair Garcia Duarte. *pd* Hector Gomez. *m* Hermelino Neder. *cast* Maite Proença, Antonio Fagundes, José Lewgoy, Jorge Doria, José Mayer, Miguel Falabella.
● Prado pays tribute to *film noir* in general, and to *The Lady from Shanghai* in particular; but given that Welles' mirror-play classic was itself a genre deconstruction, it's little wonder that Prado's film ends up being more labyrinthine than its play on fantasy and reality, death and desire, can quite accommodate. On a chance visit to a fleapit, seedy estate agent Lucas (Fagundes) enjoys a steamy near-encounter with femme fatale Suzana (Proença); the next day, he finds himself selling a flat to her sinister husband. A slave to his hormones, and intrigued by this rapidly developing B-pic scenario, he is plunged into the customary abyss of mistaken identity, secret societies, drug runners and dead sailors. The film impresses with its hothouse look – all neon, sweat and ceiling fans – but its narrative obfuscation, spiked with Godardian distancing, is too complex to hold the attention. JRo

Lady Godiva Rides Again

(1951, GB, 90 min, b/w)
d Frank Launder. *sc* Frank Launder, Val Valentine. *ph* Wilkie Cooper. *ed* Thelma Connell. *ad* Joseph Bato. *m* William Alwyn. *cast* Pauline Stroud, Dennis Price, John McCallum, Stanley Holloway, George Cole, Diana Dors, Alistair Sim, Kay Kendall, Sidney James, Dora Bryan, Trevor Howard, Joan Collins.
● Would-be comic satire in which Pauline Stroud, winner of a local Lady Godiva contest, goes on to top a national beauty contest, the prelude to celluloid charm school training and an eventual descent into the burlesque arena. Disappointingly mundane, and done with enough discretion to claim a 'U' certificate from the censor. TJ

Lady Hamilton

see That Hamilton Woman

Ladyhawke

(1985, US, 121 min)
d Richard Donner. *p* Richard Donner, Lauren Schuler. *sc* Edward Khmara, Michael Thomas, Tom Mankiewicz. *ph* Vittorio Storaro. *ed* Stuart Baird. *pd* Wolf Kroeger. *m* Andrew Powell. *cast* Matthew Broderick, Rutger Hauer, Michelle Pfeiffer, Leo McKern, John Wood, Ken Hutchison, Alfred Molina.
● Broderick plays a Dark Ages version of the Artful Dodger, befriending the traumatised but bold Etienne of Navarre (camp Hauer), who is eternally separated from his true love Isabeau (decorative Pfeiffer) by a horrible, nasty spell that only outrageous bravery and special effects can undo. All rather facile sword-and-sorcery stuff, of course, but at times very funny (special mention to McKern as a bumbling priest) and always beautifully photographed in the Italian Dolomites. DPe

Lady Ice

(1973, US, 92 min)
d Tom Gries. *p* Harrison Starr. *sc* Alan R Trustman, Harold Clemins. *ph* Lucien Ballard. *ed* Robert Swink, William Sands. *pd* Joel Schiller. *m* Perry Botkin Jr. *cast* Donald Sutherland, Jennifer O'Neill, Robert Duvall, Patrick Magee, Jon Cypher, Eric Braeden, Buffy Dee.
● A diamond caper movie that promises well but wastes its opportunities and ends up modish and vacuous. Sutherland plays an insurance agent tracking down Jennifer O'Neill's poor little rich girl. He clearly enjoys himself, giving the complete antithesis of his silent detective in *Klute*, but she is hardly a worthy opponent. The film falls to pieces half-way through when the emphasis shifts away from the plot (which becomes too boring to follow anyway) and onto the two main characters, who spend the rest of the film in mutual admiration, eyeing each other and making half-hearted passes. CPe

Lady in Cement

(1968, US, 93 min)
d Gordon Douglas. *p* Aaron Rosenberg. *sc* Marvin H Albert, Jack Guss. *ph* Joseph Biroc. *ed* Robert Simpson. *ad* LeRoy Deane. *m* Hugo Montenegro. *cast* Frank Sinatra, Raquel Welch, Richard Conte, Martin Gabel, Dan Blocker, Lainie Kazan, Steve Peck.
● Plodding sequel to *Tony Rome*, with Sinatra's indomitable private eye fighting his way through an unexciting collection of freaks, perverts and villains. Carbon-copy stuff, with the Florida setting and characterisation of Tony Rome recalling John D Macdonald's Travis McGee, Dan Blocker playing a variation on Chandler's Moose Malloy, and a leering attitude to sex and violence not improved by bouts of gay-baiting. A good cast and loose-limbed direction from Douglas help things out. TM

Lady in Red, The

(1979, US, 93 min)
d Lewis Teague. *p* Julie Corman. *sc* John Sayles. *ph* Daniel Lacambre. *ed* Larry Bock, Ron Medico, Lewis Teague. *pd* Jac McAnelly.

m James Horner. *cast* Pamela Sue Martin, Robert Conrad, Louise Fletcher, Robert Hogan, Laurie Heineman, Glenn Withrow, Christopher Lloyd, Dick Miller.
●Writer John Sayles, playing fast and loose with the known facts, inverts the gender of the Dillinger myth and backtracks with outrageous relish over the history of his scarlet companion, punching out scene after great scene of Corman New World depression sleaze. Through farm girl, sweat-shop organiser, taxi-dancer, whorehouse, slammer, Dillinger's avenging angel outguns them all in one long hard slide down the wild side. Director Teague revels in the regular motifs of guns, money, fast cars and bizarre death, grafts on a layer of social comment lately absent in exploiters, and still slams through it all with an anarchic humour sometimes worthy of Sam Fuller. Very much the thinking person's crunch movie – chomp a cigar and see Dillinger go down again. CPea

Lady in the Car with Glasses and a Gun, The (La Dame dans l'auto avec des lunettes et un fusil)

(1970, Fr, 105 min)
d Anatole Litvak. *p* Raymond Danon, Anatole Litvak. *sc* Richard Harris, Eleanor Perry. *ph* Claude Renoir. *ed* Peter Thornton. *ad* Willy Holt. *m* Michel Legrand. *cast* Samantha Eggar, Oliver Reed, John McEnery, Stéphane Audran, Billie Dixon, Bernard Fresson, Marcel Bozzuffi, Jacques Fabbri.
●Eggar, an English secretary with an international advertising agency in Paris, is asked by her boss (Reed, so sinisterly smooth that you know he's up to no good) to work overnight at his house. Next day, she agrees to see him off at the airport with his family, then drive his car back to the house. But finding herself heading in the wrong direction, she impulsively drives on – towards the Riviera and nightmarish happenings which include encounters with various strangers who apparently recognise her, assault in the rest-room at a service station, an interlude with an enigmatic hitchhiker (McEnery), and the discovery of a body in the boot of the car. Echoes of *Psycho* proliferate (including a visit to an old dark house), but the tortuous mystifications and ponderings (shakily shored up by the revelation that she sometimes suffers bouts of amnesia) wear out their welcome long before the final gush of explanations. The presence of Stéphane Audran, as Reed's glacially neurotic wife, makes one wonder wistfully what Chabrol might have made of it all. TM

Lady in the Dark

(1943, US, 100 min)
d Mitchell Leisen. *p* Richard Blumenthal. *sc* Frances Goodrich, Albert Hackett. *ph* Ray Rennahan. *ed* Alma Macrorie. *ad* Hans Dreier, Raoul Pène DuBois.. *songs* Kurt Weill, Ira Gershwin*cast* Ginger Rogers, Ray Milland, Warner Baxter, Jon Hall, Barry Sullivan, Mischa Auer, Gail Russell.
●A gorgeously garish adaptation of the Moss Hart musical, with songs by Kurt Weill and Ira Gershwin, in which a high-powered fashion magazine editor (Rogers) turns to psychoanalysis to resolve her inability to choose between three loves: a middle-aged backer (Baxter), an attractive but independent-minded employee (Milland), and a hunky movie star (Hall). It doesn't bear too close examination, since Hollywood got cold feet about the lady's Electra complex, leaving only hints of her competition with mommy for daddy's love, and completing the bowdlerisation by removing the haunting key song 'My Ship'. What's left is a cardboard charade, but one given a dynamic charge by Leisen's witty visual styling. The three dream sequences, in particular, are superb, with the first two coolly designed, respectively in shades of blue and gold, the third – the circus sequence in which Jenny finds herself on trial for emotional delinquency – bursting into full colour. TM

Lady in the Lake

(1946, US, 103 min, b/w)
d Robert Montgomery. *p* George Haight. *sc* Steve Fisher. *ph* Paul C Vogel. *ed* Gene Ruggiero. *ad* Cedric Gibbons, Preston Ames. *m* David Snell. *cast* Robert Montgomery, Audrey Totter, Lloyd Nolan, Leon Ames, Tom Tully, Jayne Meadows, Dick Simmons, Lila Leeds.
●Suffering by comparison with *The Big Sleep* (made a year earlier), this celebrated Chandler adaptation is stubbornly loopy: shot entirely with subjective camera, it lets the audience see the world through Marlowe's eyes. Hired to track down someone's hated wife, you stumble on a dead body, and as Audrey Totter offers you her lips, darkness fills the screen: you have closed your eyes. Even novelty items like mysterious puffs of smoke from invisible cigarettes cannot disguise the high irritation factor in what Chandler himself described as 'a cheap Hollywood trick'. It really needed the magnificent panache of an Orson Welles, who had planned a '40s version of *Heart of Darkness* – about another Marlowe – in the same subjective style. DMacp

Lady in White

(1988, US, 113 min)
d Frank LaLoggia. *p* Andrew G La Marca, Frank LaLoggia. *sc* Frank LaLoggia. *ph* Russell Carpenter. *ed* Steve Mann. *pd* Richard K Hummel. *m* Frank LaLoggia. *cast* Lukas Haas, Len Cariou, Alex Rocco, Katherine Helmond, Jason Presson, Renata Vanni, Sydney Lassick, Jack Holland.
●A winning, if uneven, blend of affectionate nostalgia and supernatural scariness, set in an idealised small town community in 1962. Haas gives a luminous performance as a young boy whose innocence is tainted when he finds himself caught between a serial child murderer, the ghost of one of the killer's victims, and the unquiet spirit of the dead girl's mother. Seen through the boy's eyes, the events have a haunting quality that is reinforced by the juxtaposition of ethereal apparitions with the more tangible terror of the child killer. An undercurrent of social reality makes itself felt, particularly when the townspeople turn on the school's black janitor, exposing an undercurrent of incipient racism. But LaLoggia is also guilty here and there of questionable excess: the cosy Italian-American family scenes tend to slip into sentimentality, while the special effects overkill of the fairytale ending threatens to drown out the more restrained character development. NF

Lady Jane

(1985, GB, 142 min)
d Trevor Nunn. *p* Peter Snell. *sc* David Edgar. *ph* Douglas Slocombe. *ed* Anne V Coates. *pd* Allan Cameron. *m* Stephen Oliver. *cast* Helena Bonham Carter, Gary Elwes, John Wood, Michael Hordern, Jill Bennett, Jane Lapotaire, Sara Kestelman, Patrick Stewart, Joss Ackland, Richard Johnson.
●A fervent supporter of the Reformation, Lady Jane Grey (Bonham Carter) was brought up at a time when England was riven with religious dissension, and to prevent the Catholic Mary ascending to the throne, was compelled to marry Guilford Dudley (Elwes), son of the Duke of Northumberland. This seemingly ill-matched marriage was unexpectedly a success, but her brief period of happiness was destroyed when, on Edward VI's death, she was forced unwillingly on to the throne for nine days and died on the scaffold a few months later. A political pawn, indeed. With a script by David Edgar and a cast including all the stalwarts of the RSC, it was not too much to expect that more would be made of her life than just another costume drama. But despite its radical gloss, this over-long, lifeless epic of doomed true love falls into all the predictable traps: excessive pageantry, Monty Python-like peasants, dialogue that drips with sentiment, and even the sight of young lovers running through rural England. JE

Lady Killer

(1933, US, 76 min, b/w)
d Roy Del Ruth. *p* Henry Blanke. *sc* Ben Markson, Lillie Hayward. *ph* Tony Gaudio. *ed* George Amy. *ad* Robert Haas. *cast* James Cagney, Mae Clarke, Leslie Fenton, Douglass Dumbrille, Margaret Lindsay, Henry O'Neill, Willard Robertson, George Chandler.
●Cagney in comedy: a talent often forgotten when one thinks of this most energetically violent of actors. Here the story is tailor-made for his persona. He plays a hood who, for reasons of hiding out and making big money, goes to Hollywood; he serves his time in small parts (very funny, this), but by using the shrewdness and dishonesty he exploited in his life of crime (and writing enormous quantities of fan mail to himself), he graduates to star; whereupon his past threatens to catch up with him. The whole film is witty and fast, hurtled along by Cagney's stylish delivery, and offers a few sharply satirical swipes at Hollywood en route. GA

Ladykillers, The

(1955, GB, 97 min)
d Alexander Mackendrick. *p* Michael Balcon. *sc* William Rose. *ph* Otto Heller. *ed* Jack Harris. *ad* Jim Morahan. *m* Tristram Cary. *cast* Alec Guinness, Cecil Parker, Herbert Lom, Peter Sellers, Danny Green, Katie Johnson, Jack Warner, Frankie Howerd.
●Mackendrick and Ealing's resident American writer William Rose had already collaborated on *The Maggie* when they came together again for this, the last, most enduring and best known of all the studio's comedies, in which the sheer blackness of the central concept is barely disguised by the accomplished farce which surrounds it. Little Katie Johnson, the innocent hostess to a gang who find it easier to silence each other than her, proves resistant to science (Guinness' fanged 'Professor'), strategy (Parker's 'Major') and all shades of brute force and ignorance as she unwittingly foils a criminal getaway that never reaches beyond St Pancras. A finely wrought image of terminal stasis, national, political (Charles Barr suggests the gang as the first post-war Labour government), and/or creative (the house as Ealing, Johnson as Balcon??). Whatever, Mackendrick immediately upped for America and the equally dark ironies of *Sweet Smell of Success*. PT

Lady L

(1965, Fr/It, 124 min)
d Peter Ustinov. *p* Carlo Ponti. *sc* Peter Ustinov. *ph* Henri Alékan. *ed* Roger Dwyre. *ad* Jean d'Eaubonne, Auguste Capelier. *m* Jean Françaix. *cast* Sophia Loren, Paul Newman, David Niven, Claude Dauphin, Philippe Noiret, Michel Piccoli, Marcel Dalio, Cecil Parker, Peter Ustinov, Jacques Dufilho, Sacha Pitoeff.
●A glossy and very silly period costume piece (from a novel by Romain Gary) about the life of a laundress (Loren) who dallies with international anarchists (including Newman) before marrying an English lord (Niven). Despite the impressive cast and Ustinov's attempts to emulate Max Ophüls, it looks sadly like a case of MGM having locked funds in Europe and wanting to burn them quickly. Not content with writing, directing and playing a fuddy-duddy Bavarian prince, Ustinov also dubs Philippe Noiret's voice. ATu

Lady of Burlesque (aka Striptease Lady)

(1943, US, 91 min, b/w)
d William Wellman. *p* Hunt Stromberg. *sc* James Gunn. *ph* Robert De Grasse. *ed* James E Newcom. *pd* Joseph B Platt. *m* Arthur Lange. *cast* Barbara Stanwyck, Michael O'Shea, J Edward Bromberg, Charles Dingle, Frank Conroy, Gloria Dickson, Marion Martin, Pinky Lee, Iris Adrian.
●Stanwyck, as 'Dixie Daisy, the Darling of Burlesque', gets the show off to a good start with her spirited rendition of a Sammy Kahn/Harry Akst number, 'Take it off the E-String, play it on the G-String'. A strangler is loose among the showgirls in this comedy-thriller adapted from Gypsy Rose Lee's *The G-String Murders* (actually ghosted by Craig Rice). Although a stream of hard-boiled wisecracks keeps things amusing, the plot gets tied up in the usual dreary whodunit business of providing motives for all and sundry, and it's difficult to care very much about the jealousies, lecheries and treacheries between cardboard characters. On the other hand, one has to admire the technical skill with which Wellman choreographs the action non-stop all over the theatre, unobtrusively dovetailing it with a number of fascinatingly authentic-looking samples of old-time burlesque shtick. TM

Lady of Deceit

see Born to Kill

Lady of the Boulevards

see Nana

Lady on a Train

(1945, US, 94 min, b/w)
d Charles David. *p* Felix Jackson. *sc* Edmund Beloin, Robert O'Brien. *ph* Woody Bredell. *ed* Ted J Kent. *ad* John Goodman, Robert Clatworthy. *m* Miklós Rozsa. *cast* Deanna Durbin, Ralph Bellamy, Edward Everett Horton, George Coulouris, Allen Jenkins, David Bruce, Dan Duryea, Patricia Morison.
●Durbin plays a girl who witnesses a murder from the window of a train pulling into New York, is believed by no one, and so turns to detection herself, becoming entangled with the victim's sinisterly bizarre family (which includes the killer). With a strong supporting cast, it's surprisingly entertaining. The plot, derived from a story by Leslie Charteris previously filmed in Britain as *A Window in London*, doesn't delve into the dark chaos beloved of *noir* thrillers in the '40s so much as play it slightly tongue-in-cheek. Light, cheery and shading into darker areas for the climax, it's fun. GA

Lady Sings the Blues

(1972, US, 144 min)
d Sidney J Furie. *p* Jay Weston, James S White. *sc* Terence McCloy, Chris Clark, Suzanne De Passe. *ph* John A Alonzo. *ed* Argyle Nelson. *pd* Carl Anderson. *m* Michel Legrand. *cast* Diana Ross, Billy Dee Williams, Richard Pryor, James Callahan, Paul Hampton, Sid Melton, Virginia Capers, Scatman Crothers, Ned Glass.
●A staple biopic of Billie Holiday with all the time-hallowed mundanity of the genre (its preoccupation with her heroin addiction, for instance, or the sequence that 'explains' the song 'Strange Fruit'). What it tells you most about is those kitschy concepts of 'stardom' and the like on a soap-opera/ backstage drama level. Diana Ross, managing to avoid doing a Supremes-type number and keeping the songs this side of pastiche, comes out with a straightforward performance that only modulates to pure DR in an outrageous last shot that reduces Billie Holiday's death to the transience of a newspaper cutting, while holding on Diana Ross doing the pinnacle of success bit.

Lady Takes a Chance, A

(1943, US, 86 min, b/w)
d William A Seiter. *p* Frank Ross. *sc* Robert Ardrey. *ph* Frank Redman. *ed* Theron Warth. *ad* Albert S D'Agostino, Alfred Herman. *m* Roy Webb. *cast* John Wayne, Jean Arthur, Charles Winninger, Phil Silvers, Mary Field, Don Costello.
●Naive Easterner Jean Arthur takes Phil Silvers' bus trip, '14 Breathless Days in the West', but gets more than she bargained for when cowpoke Wayne shows her round some. Easygoing comic Western with the stars looking relaxed. TJ

Lady und der Herzog, Die

see Lady & the Duke, The

Lady Vampire, The (Onna Kyuke Tsuki)

(1959, Jap, 78 min, b/w)
d Nobuo Nakagawa. *p* Mitsugu Okura, Katsuji Tsuda. *sc* Shin Nakazawa, Katsuyoshi Nakatsu. *ph* Yoshimi Hirano. *ed* Toshio Goto. *ad* Haruyasu Kurosawa. *m* Hisashi Inoue. *cast* Shigeru Amachi, Keinosuke Wada, Yoko Mihara, Junko Ikeuchi, Torahiko Nakamura, Baku Mizuhara.
●Unlike giant monsters and invading aliens, vampires evidently seemed too 'foreign' for Japanese B-movies in the '50s. Nakagawa's attempt to create a Japanese vampire (from a story by Sotoo Tachibana) works overtime to accommodate this 'foreignness'. It opens in a Tokyo suburb so westernised it even has numbered streets, sets plot developments in a western-style hotel and art gallery, has a crime reporter (Wada) for a hero, and winds up explaining that the vampirism stems obliquely from Shiro of Amakusa, a 17th century Christian. The lady vampire is actually a helpless victim (Mihara) who returns to her family unaged 20 years after disappearing; the villain is Takenaka (Amachi), who lives in a subterranean castle with an entourage of freaks, uses little gold crosses to turn cuties into statues and develops uncontrollable urges when exposed to the full moon. Fun enough. TR

Lady Vanishes, The

(1938, GB, 96 min, b/w)
d Alfred Hitchcock. *p* Edward Black. *sc* Sidney Gilliat, Frank Launder. *ph* Jack Cox. *ed* RE Dearing. *ad* Alex Vetchinsky. *m* Cecil Milner. *cast* Margaret Lockwood, Michael Redgrave, Paul Lukas, Cecil Parker, Dame May Whitty, Linden Travers, Naunton Wayne, Basil Radford, Mary Clare, Googie Withers.
●Critical orthodoxy has it that Hitchcock's move to Hollywood in 1940 was some kind of breakthrough in his career; that his American movies are his 'mature' work, making the earlier English ones look trivial and provincial. It's true that the qualities of his work changed in America, but a look at an early movie like this knocks the rest of the orthodox view sideways. It still looks as fresh and funny as it must have done in 1938: what does the strangling of a Tyrolean street singer have to do with the tweedy English lady in the over-crowded hotel, and why (later) does everyone on a train deny ever having seen the lady in question? There's a sheer pleasure in watching the way the plot turns so smoothly round these questions, and it's compounded by Launder & Gilliat's consistently witty dialogue and the all-round excellence of the cast. TR

Lady Vanishes, The

(1979, GB, 97 min)
d Anthony Page. *p* Tom Sachs. *sc* George Axelrod. *ph* Douglas Slocombe. *ed* Russell Lloyd. *pd* Wilfrid Shingleton. *m* Richard Hartley. *cast* Elliott Gould, Cybill Shepherd, Angela Lansbury, Herbert Lom, Ian Carmichael, Arthur Lowe, Gerald Harper, Jenny Runacre.
●Comparisons are odious, but this remake of Hitchcock's thriller continually begs them by trampling heavily over its predecessor. The original anticipated, with some poignancy, a Europe at war. This version uses hindsight entirely to disadvantage. In fact, its picture of 1939 Europe reflects nothing more than current market demands. Thus the plot – madcap American heiress enlists support of *Life* magazine photographer when cosy English nanny disappears on train in Nazi Germany – serves merely as the packaging for American stars, British support, and German villains still swaggering from the glorious victories of *Cabaret* and *The Sound of Music*. Cybill Shepherd and Elliott Gould cover their lack of chemistry with a lot of noise. The film-makers have trouble with their suspense – did she imagine it? who cares? – and it's left to Arthur Lowe and Ian Carmichael, as the cricket lovin' Blimps, to provide solid middle-order batting. CPe

Lady Without Camellias, The

see Signora senza camelie, La

Lady Without Passport, A

(1950, US, 74 min, b/w)
d Joseph H Lewis. *p* Samuel Marx. *sc* Howard Dimsdale. *ph* Paul C Vogel. *ed* Frederick Y Smith. *ad* Cedric Gibbons, Edward C Carfagno. *m* David Raksin. *cast* Hedy Lamarr, John Hodiak, James Craig, George Macready, Steve Geray, Bruce Cowling, Nedrick Young.
●Stylishly directed by the low-budget wizard who brought you *Gun Crazy* and *The Big Combo*, this is a *Casablanca*-type tale of European immigrants trying to get into America, and being forced to stop off in corrupt, seedy Havana en route. Lamarr is the gorgeous woman with a past who will do anything to reach the land of promise, Hodiak the immigration official who bends the rules when he falls for her. A tight little script and economically etched characters provide a strong foundation, but it is Lewis' evocative visuals that really turn this into a poverty row gem. GA

Lady With the Little Dog, The (Dama s Sobachkoi)

(1959, USSR, 90 min, b/w)
d/sc Josif Heifits. *ph* Andrei Moskvin, D Meschiev. *ed* S Dereviansky. *ad* B Manevitch, I Kaplan. *m* N Silmonian. *cast* Iya Savvina, Alexei Batalov, Ala Chostakova, N Alisova.
●Much to the surprise of the Mosfilm commissars, art movie buffs throughout the world took this low-key Chekhov adaptation to their hearts. An impossible love affair begins on a Black Sea holiday, and continues in snatched and furtive meetings, encounters at the theatre, and so on. Heifits' palpable nostalgia for turn-of-the-century manners and styles invests the melancholy tale with astonishing undercurrents of emotion. Until Mikhalkov made his *Unfinished Piece for Mechanical Piano*, this was by far the best Chekhov movie in Soviet cinema. TR

Lair of the White Worm, The

(1988, GB, 93 min)
d/p/sc Ken Russell. *ph* Dick Bush. *ed* Peter Davies. *ad* Anne Tilby. *m* Stanislas Syrewicz. *cast* Amanda Donohoe, Hugh Grant, Catherine Oxenberg, Peter Capaldi, Sammi Davis, Stratford Johns, Christopher Gable.
●This Russell rigmarole, nominally based on the Bram Stoker novel, seems to have been made up as it went along, possibly inspired by props left over from his last. The function of much of the writing (Russell again) is to throw rickety pontoon bridges between the yawning set pieces, and you can hear it ticking. Everywhere lies the evidence of carelessness. Davis and Capaldi cower in terror, babbling about a car without its headlights on. The standard crucified Christ and raping Romans round out a nightmare. High Priestess Lady Sylvia Marsh (Donohue) paralyses a boy scout with a bite to the willy, after leading him on in leather stockings and suspenders over snakes-and-ladders, then fits a giant dildo for an assault upon the virgin Eve (Oxenberg). Archaeologist Angus Flint (Capaldi) produces a mongoose from his sporran, and later a grenade, to combat the ancient evil of the white worm. Tiresome. BC

Lait de la tendresse humaine, Le

see Milk of Human Kindness, The

Lakeboat

(2001, US, 98 min)
d Joe Mantegna. *p* Eric R Epperson. *sc* David Mamet. *ph* Paul Sarossy. *ed* Christopher Cibelli. *pd* Thomas Carnegie. *m* Bob Mamet. *cast* Charles Durning, Peter Falk, Robert Forster, JJ Johnson, Denis Leary, Tony Mamet, Jack Wallace, George Wendt.
●Grad student Dale (Tony Mamet, persuasive in a largely passive role) takes a summer job as a night cook on a freighter working the Great Lakes. It's a man's world (script by David Mamet, wordy and theatrical) and Dale's initiation, a tongue-lashing from the captain (Durning) for not knowing his evacuation number, is harsh. Before long, however, the men start to open up to him, particularly Joe (Forster), who confides in the youngster about his lost dream to become a ballet dancer) and his emotional state (a suicide attempt). Forster's performance hints at a world of pain beyond the boredom and bonding of the month-long voyages. NRo

Lake Consequence

(1992, US, 90 min)
d Rafael Eisenman. *p* Avram Butch Kaplan. *sc* Zalman King, Melanie Finn, Henry Cobbold. *ph* Harris Savides. *ed* James Gavin Bedford, Curtis Edge. *pd* Dominic Watkins. *m* George S Clinton. *cast* Billy Zane, Joan Severance, May Karasun, Whip Hubley, Courtland Mead.
●Wealthy housewife Irene (Severance) is seeing her husband and son off on a camping trip when she spies hard-torsoed Billy (Zane), a shaven-headed, eye-kohled tree-feller. They talk by nightlight, he pulls out his blues guitar. Next day, she's fingering the objects in his caravan when it jerks into motion, and she's whipped away on a trip of sensual personal discovery. This is producer/ writer Zalman King's movie for the uncertain '90s: gone is the techno-bright SM cinematic vocabulary of his previous *Nine ½ Weeks*. It positively drips with responsibility and eco-soundness. Director Rafael Eisenman shows his pop-promo background in a recurrent use of shock-editing, and subliminal sound and image. Despite such effects, the film has its pleasures: soporific sex scenes; Zane manfully failing to portray New Man; the amusing clichés in George Clinton's jazzy score; and the bejewelled dialogue. WH

Lake Placid

(1999, US, 82 min)
d Steve Miner. *p* David E Kelley, Michael Pressman. *sc* David E Kelley. *ph* Daryn Okada. *ed* Marshall Harvey, Paul Hirsch. *pd* John Willett. *m* John Ottman. *cast* Bill Pullman, Oliver Platt, Bridget Fonda, Brendan Gleeson, Betty White, David Lewis, Tim Dixon, Natassia Malthe, Mariska Hargitay, Meredith Salenger.

● This is a bouillabaisse of aquatic exploitation pics. Indeed, so similar is the opening scene to *Jaws*, you'll wonder whether it's homage, spoof or rip off. Stylistically, it's all three. Scriptwise, it's almost up there with the likes of *Piranha*, *Alligator* and *Tremors*. Something strange lurks beneath the surface of a Maine lake – how else could a law enforcer have been bitten in half, with only his big toe left as evidence? The culprit, it transpires, is a giant Asian croc. Before long a group of interested parties – Pullman's fussy game warden; sheriff Gleeson; wealthy slouch Platt; Fonda's nature-hating paleontologist – are on the case, falling over each other's feet and exchanging wonderfully cutting and often deadpan dialogue. Platt and Gleeson get most of the best lines, along with local dear Mrs Delores Bickerman (White), whose obscenities recall the Zucker brothers at their peak. If you don't find *something* to laugh about here, you've clearly stumbled into the wrong movie. As for the effects, they veer from the genuinely impressive – ever seen a crocodile eat a bear? – to the jerky and poorly rendered, as in the overblown finale. DA

Lalka

see Doll, The

Lamb

(1985, GB, 110 min)
d Colin Gregg. *p* Neil Zeiger. *sc* Bernard MacLaverty. *ph* Mike Garfath. *ed* Peter Delfgou. *pd* Austen Spriggs. *m* Van Morrison. *cast* Liam Neeson, Harry Towb, Hugh O'Conor, Frances Tomelty, Ian Bannen, Denis Carey, Eileen Kennally.

● Lamb (Neeson), a Catholic priest teaching at a grim remand home for boys on the Irish coast, focuses his charity upon a young ten-year-old (O'Conor) who is subject to fits. When left a small legacy, he takes flight with the boy to London. Alas, as the money slowly runs out, the little good they had between them is threatened by a sordid and uncaring city. Taken from the novel by Bernard MacLaverty, the film very movingly achieves many of those things which are often so difficult in cinema. A portrait of goodness, religion at work, and a multi-faceted view of human character. CPea

Lambada

(1990, US, 104 min)
d Joel Silberg. *p* Peter Shepherd. *sc* Sheldon Renan, Joel Siberg. *ph* Roberto D'Ettore Piazzoli. *ed* Andy Horvitch. *pd* Bill Cornfield. *m* Greg DeBelles. *cast* J Eddie Peck, Melora Hardin, Shabba Doo, Ricky Paull Goldin, Basil Hoffman.

● A hideous mutation which combines cartoon heroism with dance-floor sex, Brazilian rhythms with Midwest (rather than West Coast) platitudes, and makes *Saturday Night Fever* look like class movie-making. Peck plays Kevin Laird, a 32-year-old maths teacher at the local high, whose biggest selling point is his 'nice buns' rather than his skill with a set-square, and who leaves the classroom to don leather and prowl the dance-floors of the East LA community from which he sprung (gee, he was adopted as a boy). This Clark Kent of the Dirty Dance movement uses his gift for pump-and-grind to convince the deprived that maths can be groovy and career options more extensive than club bouncer or drug pusher. It ends not with a knife-fight but a school quiz, and of course Kevin doesn't lay a hand on posh Sandy (Hardin), who's nuts about him. It has an abysmal script, acting which makes Madame Tussaud's look like a roller disco, and some more than passable music and dancing from over 200 local beauties. SGr

Lancelot du Lac (Lancelot of the Lake)

(1974, Fr/It, 84 min)
d Robert Bresson. *p* Jean Yanne, Alfredo Bini. *sc* Robert Bresson. *ph* Pasqualino De Santis. *ed* Germaine Lamy. *ad* Pierre Charbonnier. *m* Philippe Sarde. *cast* Luc Simon, Laura Duke Condominas, Humbert Balsan, Vladimir Antolek-Oresek, Patrick Bernard.

● Malory, Tennyson, Richard Thorpe and Richard Harris wouldn't recognise Bresson's Knights of the Round Table. They clank around the Camelot area making more noise with their armour than a one-man band, confused about their purpose and even about people's identities; at the end they lie dead in a gloomy forest piled up on a scrap-heap. This is the Arthurian legend stripped bare, spotlighting the characters' cruelty, pride, and the aching need for human affection. Bresson's shooting style has always been bare, and he manipulates his small inventory of images and sounds with masterful ease. The tournament provides a virtuoso example: the cameras mostly stick with the horses' feet or the jousters' weapons, and refuse to show us the whole spectacle; the tension which builds up as a result ought to make Michael Winner throw in his cards. It's stunningly beautiful, mesmerising, exhausting, uplifting, amazing – all the things you could possibly expect from a masterpiece. GB

Lancer Spy

(1937, US, 88 min, b/w)
d Gregory Ratoff. *sc* Philip Dunne. *ph* Barney McGill. *ed* Louis Loeffler. *ad* Albert Hogsett. *m* Arthur Lange *cast* George Sanders, Dolores Del Rio, Peter Lorre, Joseph Schildkraut, Virginia Field, Sig Ruman, Fritz Feld.

● Sanders displaying his Prussian mannerisms for the first time in a dual role as a British naval lieutenant is required to impersonate a captured German baron for purposes of World War I espionage. You've seen it all before, what with Lorre and Ruman leading the nasty Huns, while Del Rio is mightily torn between love and duty as the siren assigned to trap Sanders. The title? That's a bit of a mystery. TM

Land and Freedom

(1995, GB/Sp/Ger, 110 min)
d Ken Loach. *p* Rebecca O'Brien. *sc* Jim Allen. *ph* Barry Ackroyd. *ed* Jonathan Morris. *pd* Martin Johnson. *m* George Fenton. *cast* Ian Hart, Rosana Pastor, Iciar Bollain, Tom Gilroy, Eoin McCarthy, Frédéric Pierrot.

● Loach's film charts the experiences of an unemployed young Liverpudlian (Ian Hart) when he goes to join the Republicans in the Spanish Civil War, and for the first half-hour or so it seems that Jim Allen's script is going to be a sentimental celebration of fraternal unity among the good guys. Then, mercifully, things get more complex, as Hart's confusion and divided loyalties mirror the in-fighting that plagued the Left and led to Franco's victory. The film has its shortcomings – notably the didactic discussions on, for example, the ideology of collectivism – but Loach handles what is for him an unprecedentedly large canvas with aplomb. The action scenes in particular have a raw, plausible immediacy. Nor is this just a movie which simply fills us in on fascinating historical details; thanks to muscular performances (especially from Hart), it also packs an emotional punch. GA

Land and Sons (Land og Synir)

(1980, Ice, 93 min)
d Agúst Gudmundsson. *p* Jon Hermannsson. *sc* Agúst Gudmundsson. *ph* Sigurdur Sverrir Palsson. *m* Gunnar Reynir Sveinsson. *cast* Sigurdur Sigurjónsson, Jón Sigurbjörnsson, Gudny Ragnarsdóttir, Jónas Tryggvasson.

● The title tells it all – generations of hill farmers struggling to force an existence from the unyielding land, and getting ripped off by the co-operative movement set up to help them. Relationships made with sheepdogs last longer than those with women. Yet for all the bleakness (rainswept landscapes) and the occasional awkwardness in performance and editing, this is an honourable first feature on the familiar theme of country boy drifting to big city. It may not do for Iceland what *The Harder They Come* did for Jamaica, but it recommends itself for its unusual setting and modest ambitions. MA

Land Before Time, The

(1988, US, 69 min)
d Don Bluth. *p* Don Bluth, Gary Goldman, John Pomeroy. *sc* Stu Krieger. *ph* Jim Mann. *ed* Dan Molina, John K Carr. *pd* Don Bluth. *m* James Horner. *cast* voices: Gabriel Damon, Helen Shaver, Bill Erwin, Candice Huston, Pat Hingle.

● After *An American Tale*, Bluth surely had the clout to make a more adventurous animated feature than this, with its anthropomorphic espousal of American nuclear family values and its static, unimaginatively rendered backgrounds. You'd have thought, too, that a film about dinosaurs could have been mildly educational: giving the species' proper names for instance, rather than just 'Three-horns' or 'Longnecks', or – since the plot concerns a group of youngsters learning to travel together to find the Great Valley, where they'll all be saved from extinction – bringing in at least one of the theories about why the food chain became broken. Still, it has its moments: an earthquake scene is genuinely scary, the tension between the two would-be leaders should strike a chord with any kid who's ever wanted to be accepte by a gang, and some of the voices are well, if irritatingly done. DW

Land Girls, The

(1997, GB/Fr, 111 min)
d David Leland. *p* Simon Relph. *sc* David Leland, Keith Dewhurst. *ph* Henry Braham. *ed* Nick Moore. *pd* Caroline Amies. *m* Brian Lock. *cast* Catherine McCormack, Rachel Weisz, Anna Friel, Steven Mackintosh, Tom Georgeson, Maureen O'Brien, Lucy Akhurst.

● This adaptation of Angela Huth's WWII novel follows the fortunes of – take three girls! – fun-loving Lancashire lass Prue (Friel), innocent Cambridge graduate Ag (Weisz), and responsible but romantic officer's fiancée Stella (McCormack), sent to work by the Land Army on a Dorset farm. Old man Lawrence's surliness is softened by his wife, but son Joe (Mackintosh), keen to be a pilot, presents a different problem. Though he's already engaged, Prue sets her cap at him. There are frequent hints of a bigger picture, but the focus is so firmly on individual experience that the significant details get lost in the overall lyricism. The schematic plot seems at first set to focus on the changes undergone by the three women, but by the end has almost forgottent about two of them (including, unfortunately, Prue, whose vitality far outshines that of her plummy colleagues). GA

Landlord, The

(1970, US, 110 min)
d Hal Ashby. *p* Norman Jewison. *sc* Bill Gunn. *ph* Gordon Willis. *ed* William A Sawyer, Edward A Warschilka. *pd* Robert Boyle. *m* Al Kooper. *cast* Beau Bridges, Pearl Bailey, Diana Sands, Louis Gossett, Douglas Grant, Melvin Stewart, Lee Grant, Susan Anspach.

● Ashby's first film as director – produced by Norman Jewison, whose regular editor Ashby had been – this was coolly received when first released. Presumably its anarchic satire on the mores and assumptions of the American Way of Life, which range from Sidney Poitier movies to events like the spinal meningitis summer ball, were thought to be in bad taste. Like *Leo the Last*, the film deals with the problems of a man of property once he enters into human, rather than economic, relationships with his tenants. But whereas Boorman's film is a carefully constructed whole, from its colour scheme to its casting of Marcello Mastroianni in the lead, Ashby's film (like the later and much more successful *The Last Detail*) operates through the freewheeling juxtaposition of characters in unlikely situations. Worth a look. PH

Land of Silence and Darkness (Land des Schweigens und der Dunkelheit)

(1971, WGer, 85 min)
d/p Werner Herzog. *ph* Jörg Schmidt-Reitwein. *ed* Beate Mainka-Jellinghaus. *m* JS Bach, A Vivaldi. *with* Fini Straubinger, Miss Juliet, Mr Mittermeier, Else Fährer, Ursula Riedneier, Joseph Riedneier. *narrator* Rolf Illig

● A stunning documentary about 56-year-old Fini, blind and deaf since her late teens. After 30 years of being confined to her bed by her mother, she fought to overcome her immense isolation by helping others similarly afflicted. While some of these tragically incommunicable individuals make for painful viewing, Herzog also demonstrates the humour and joys of a day at the zoo, or of a first plane flight, where touch and togetherness in suffering offer the sole but undeniable reason for living. The courage on view is astounding, and Herzog's treatment is never voyeuristic or sentimental, but sensuous and overwhelmingly moving. GA

Land of the Monsters

see Maciste Contro i Mostri

Land of the Pharaohs

(1955, US, 103 min)
d/p Howard Hawks. *sc* William Faulkner, Harry Kurnitz, Harold Jack Bloom. *ph* Lee Garmes, Russell Harlan. *ed* Rudi Fehr, V Sagovsky. *ad* Alexandre Trauner. *m* Dimitri Tiomkin. *cast* Jack Hawkins, Joan Collins, Dewey Martin, James Robertson Justice, Alexis Minotis, Sydney Chaplin.

● Hawks was always better with small groups of characters, but this Egyptian epic, concerning intrigue at the Pharaoh's court during the building of a massive pyramid, is far from uninteresting. Although the script (by Faulkner, among others) gets stranded with the usual slightly wooden dialogue considered necessary for ancient times, the story moves along at a stately but never sluggish pace, and is scattered with lovely moments, most notably the grim finale when Collins gets her ironic come-uppance. With sets by Trauner and camerawork by Lee Garmes, it looks great; certainly, alongside those of Nick Ray, one of the best epics. GA

Landru

(1962, Fr/It, 119 min)
d Claude Chabrol. *p* Georges de Beauregard, Carlo Ponti. *sc* Françoise Sagan. *ph* Jean Rabier. *ed* Jacques Gaillard. *ad* Jacques Saulnier. *m* Pierre Jansen. *cast* Charles Denner, Michèle Morgan, Danielle Darrieux, Hildegarde Neff, Juliette Mayniel, Stéphane Audran, Catherine Rouvel, Raymond Queneau, Jean-Pierre Melville.

● Enigmatic, slyly amused, fastidious, swinging from bleak introspection to boisterous knockabout, such is the style of Landru, the character and the film both. Its first half is a series of repetitions: WW1 newsreels to confirm the period, Landru selecting a victim, winning her confidence; then a freeze-frame on a trusting face, followed by a smoking chimney and the English neighbours complaining about nasty smells. The remainder – arrest, trial, execution – is slightly anti-climactic, but carried along by Denner, his mincing movements, booming bass voice and his mesmerising strangeness making for a plausible mass murderer. It's violence-free, though not without visual shocks: bilious purple upholstery intruding into a world of pale pastel, a victim-to-be ominously aligned with a row of brimming coal scuttles. BBa

Landscape After Battle (Krajobraz po Bitwie)

(1970, Pol, 111 min)
d Andrzej Wajda. *sc* Andrzej Wajda, Andrzej Brzozowski. *ph* Zygmunt Samosiuk. *ed* Halina Prugar. *ad* Jerzy Szeski. *m* Zygmunt Konieczny. *cast* Daniel Olbrychski, Stanislawa Celinska, Aleksander Bardini, Zygmunt Malanowicz, Tadeusz Janczar.

● Wajda's strange, turbulent, bracing film sees him returning to his old stomping ground of World War II, but the style is far more expressionist and fragmentary, the political analysis more complex, than in his famous trilogy. The landscape in question is a former concentration camp which, after the liberation, houses Polish 'displaced persons', including the disillusioned poet Tadeusz – presumably named after the author of the film's source material, Tadeusz Borowski, who committed suicide after surviving Auschwitz. Wajda's Tadeusz (played with precision by Olbrychski) seems to have a happier time of it: his belief in humanity is rekindled by an affair with a Jewish girl escaping from Poland. But there's still no easy sentimentality here, no easy solution to the problems of national and human identity. Wajda uses his darting camera to extract endless cruel ironies from the grim setting, and even presents the final credits in an odd, unsettling manner – they're daubed up on the side of railway wagons. GB

Landscape in the Mist (Topio stin Omichli)

(1988, Greece/Fr/It, 124 min)
d/p Theo Angelopoulos. *sc* Theo Angelopoulos, Tonino Guerra, Thanasis Valtinos. *ph* Yorgos Arvanitis. *ed* Yannis Tsitsopoulos. *ad* Mikes Karapiperis. *m* Eleni Karaindrou. *cast* Michalis Zeke, Tania Palaiologou, Stratos Tzortzoglou, Nadia Mourouzi.

● A small boy and his pubescent sister leave home in search of their missing father (said to be in Germany), and cross paths with various characters perhaps intended to evoke a nation in crisis; an uncle unwilling to take charge of the infant vagrants, a brute trucker, a luckless troupe of itinerant actors whose explorations of Greek history are no longer in demand. The one person to offer help is the troupe's roadie Orestes, whose own solitude, enhanced by imminent army service, prompts him to play father to the resolute waifs. A sombre, even disturbing road movie, this is no glossy Greek travelogue; endless train journeys and walks along wintry roads lead througha succession of dingy waiting-rooms, grey towns, muddy laybys, and mountains scarred by industry. But the children's slow, dreamlike odyssey also gives rise to surreal, startling epiphanies: wedding celebrants in the snow, a massive Godlike hand rising from the sea to soar over a city. If the overall tone is bleak in its portayal of betrayals, loneliness and disillusionment, Angelopoulos' assured control of mood, Giorgos Arvanitis' superb camerawork, and the kids' glowing performances provide ample pleasures. GA

Land That Time Forgot, The

(1974, GB, 91 min)
d Kevin Connor. *p* John Dark. *sc* James Cawthorne, Michael Moorcock. *ph* Alan Hume. *ed* John Ireland. *pd* Maurice Carter. *m* Douglas Gamley. *cast* Doug McClure, John McEnery, Susan Penhaligon, Keith Barron, Anthony Ainley, Godfrey James.

● The combination of a script co-written by Michael Moorcock, the largest budget Amicus has ever utilised, and director Connor (who made such a promising debut with *From Beyond the Grave*) should have added up to a lot more than this occasionally amusing Boy's Own Paper adventure. It starts off promisingly with some stylised and ridiculous heroics involving a German sub, but once the island has been occupied and a few excellent monsters vanquished, the plot settles down to some very ordinary machinations. In fact, by the time the ape-men arrive we might as well be back in one of Hammer's sub-anthropological sagas. It's better than Disney's similar attempt at family fantasy, *Island at the Top of the World*, but that's hardly a recommendation. DP

Langer Gang

see Passages

Language of Love (Kärlekens Språk)

(1969, Swe, 107 min)
d Torgny Wickman. *p* Inge Ivarson. *sc* Inge Hegeler, Sten Hegeler. *ph* Max Wilén. *ed* Carl-Olov Skeppstedt. *m* Mats Olsson. *with* Inge Hegeler, Sten Hegeler, Maj-Brith Bergström-Walan, Sture Cullhed.

● Living-room-type discussion of sex, interspersed with mimed or actual illustrative sequences. Genital close-ups, at one stage including five penises in a row – sight for sore eyes. Should be shown in schools rather than to the raincoat trade. VG

Lan Yu

(2001, HK, 86 min)
d Stanley Kwan. *p* Zhang Yongning, James Tsim. *sc* Jimmy Ngai. *ph* Yang Tao. *ed/ad* William Chang. *m* Zhang Yadong. *cast* Hu Jun, Liu Ye, Su Jin, Li Huatong, Zhang Yongning, Luo Fang, Li Shuang, Zhang Fan.

● Beijing, 1988. Successful commodities trader Handong (Hu) takes his one-night stand with architecture student Lan Yu (Liu) very lightly, but it was a life-changing experience for the boy. One major obstacle after another gets in the way of the two of them becoming a couple: Handong's compulsive promiscuity, Handong's impulsive (and short-lived) marriage, Lan Yu's involvement in the Tiananmen Square demos of 1989. They end up together anyway, only to find that fate isn't always kind to true lovers. Kwan's adaptation of an anonymous novel published only on the Internet (it galvanised the vast underground gay community in 1996 and established a new kind of samizdat publishing in China) is courageously simple and frank. The film eliminates most of the novel's near-porno sex scenes and tones down the melodrama, producing a matter of fact and emotionally truthful account of a relationship marked by its time and place. Superbly acted, too. TR

La Passione

(1996, GB, 106 min)
d John B Hobbs. *p/sc* Chris Rea. *ph* Roger Bonnici. *ed* Paul Endacott. *pd* Garry Freeman. *m* Chris Rea. *cast* Sean Gallagher, Thomas Orange, Paul Shane, Jan Ravens, Carmen Silvera, Shirley Bassey.

● Aside from creating bland AOR rock, Chris Rea also has a passion for motor racing and cars, especially those bearing the Ferrari marque. So much so that he's committed his childhood memories to celluloid with this semi-autobiographical 'musical fantasy'. It begins well enough with a sepia-toned Rea (played by Orange and later Gallagher) showing early signs of his Grand Prix obsession, but then the whole structure goes awry as we try to make sense of the jumps back and forth through stages of the singer's youth, the weird dream sequences, the absurdity of Shirley Bassey's cabaret turn, and the fact that his music is mostly out of kilter with the surreal imagery. The Ferraris look good, though. DA

Lara Croft: Tomb Raider

(2001, US/Ger/GB/Jap, 101 min)
d Simon West. *p* Lawrence Gordon, Lloyd Levin, Colin Wilson. *sc* Patrick Massett, John Zinman. *ph* Peter Menzies Jr. *ed* Dallas S Puett, Glen Scantlebury. *pd* Kirk M Petruccelli. *m* Graeme Revell. *cast* Angelina Jolie, Jon Voight, Noah Taylor, Iain Glen, Daniel Craig, Christopher Barrie, Julian Rhind-Tutt, Richard Johnson, Leslie Phillips, Richenda Carey.

● This was not, director West insisted, a visualisation of the computer game that made the aristocratic adventurer into a virtual icon; it was a 21st century action movie based on the character of Lara, with a powerful heroine and a strong emotional undertow. So while Lara's globe-trotting adventure pits her against villain Manfred Powell (Glen) and a secret cult known as the Illuminati, her search for 'the clock of ages' is underpinned by an emotional quest – the mystery surrounding the death of her father, Lord Croft (Voight). Regrettably, precious little of this has reached the screen, and what has survived has been sliced into tiny, meaningless slivers by the staccato editing. Even so, Angelina Jolie is amazing as Lara Croft, launching herself into the action with reckless abandon and pushing beyond the sexist silliness of her projectile-breasted character into something credible and human. But not even her burning charisma can disguise the airlessness of a jerky, fragmented tale that jumps from one exotic location to the next without any explanation or flow. NF

Larger Than Life

(1996, US, 93 min)
d Howard Franklin. *p* Richard B Lewis, John Watson, Pen Densham. *sc* Roy Blount Jr. *ph* Elliot Davis. *ed* Sidney Levin. *pd* Marcia Hinds. *m* Miles Goodman. *cast* Bill Murray, Janeane Garofalo, Matthew McConaughey, Keith David, Pat Hingle, Jeremy Piven, Lois Smith, Anita Gillette, Harve Presnell, Linda Fiorentino.

● Mr Cynical Chops, Murray, certainly meets his match in this buddy pic with a difference. His Jack Corcoran, motivational guru on the conference circuit, puts his success down to losing his dad at an early age, so he's in for a shock when he discovers the old man has only just passed away, bequeathing his son a circus clown's red nose and Vera, a performing elephant. Countless comic opportunities present themselves as Murray and his new pal make their way across country to settle her future: will it be with kindly researcher Garofalo, who'll return the beast to the wild, or seductive trainer Linda Fiorentino, who'll put her in a Vegas show but pay big bucks up front? Well, you don't need second sight to figure that one out. We know the elephant will knock lots of things over, tricks will be performed at significant plot points, and Bill will turn into a big softie along the way. If there's not much room for manoeuvre, Murray in curmudgeon mode is as watchable as ever. We learn, of course, to be kind to animals, though whether this sits easily with the well-trained antics of the co-star is another matter. Disgracing itself only with McConaughey's over-extended bit as a psychotic trucker, the film delivers more or less comfortably on what you'd expect, then sits down for a rest. TJ

Larks on a String (Skrivanci na niti)

(1969, Czech, 90 min)
d Jiri Menzel. *p* Karel Kochman. *sc* Bohumil Hrabal, Jiri Menzel. *ph* Jaromir Sofr. *ed* Jirina Lukesova. *ad* Oldrich Bosak. *m* Jiri Sust. *cast* Rudolf Hrusinsky, Václav Neckar, Vladimir Brodsky, Leos Sucharipa, Jitka Zelenohorska, Nada Urbankova.

●This satire was completed in 1969 and promptly banned by the authorities put in place in Czechoslovakia after the Soviet invasion of 1968. If it's easy to see why the apparatchiks weren't exactly chuffed with it, Menzel's still not the most hard-hitting of film-makers: here, as sundry bourgeois types are relocated to a '50s Stalinist factory workplace for 're-education', the focus is as much on their romantic misadventures with the women in the adjoining camp as it is on dissecting the harsh injustice of the system. For those who savour whimsy. TJ

Laserblast

(1978, US, 80 min)
d Michael Rae. *p* Charles Band. *sc* Franne Schacht, Frank Ray Perilli. *ph* Terry Bowen. *ed* Jodie Copelan. *ad* Pat McFadden. *m* Joel Goldsmith, Richard Band. *cast* Kim Milford, Cheryl Smith, Gianni Russo, Ron Masak, Roddy McDowall, Keenan Wynn, Dennis Burkley.

●A Jekyll/Hyde quickie rip-off, *Laserblast* is the epitome of what Frank Zappa once hymned as 'cheapness'. Shot in the director's front room, space creatures courtesy of Kelloggs, and a laser-gun that must have cost several dollars, it has all the sincerity of a plastic dashboard Jesus. The power that the alien laser confers on weedy Billy does allow him some vengeful destruction, but this is stingily confined to police cars and he duly pays the dreadful price – terminal alienship ('Billy, why can't you be more ordinary?'). Brain-addling. CPea

Lásky Jedné Plavovlásky (A Blonde in Love/Loves of a Blonde)

(1965, Czech, 82 min, b/w)
d Milos Forman. *sc* Milos Forman, Jaroslav Papousek, Ivan Passer. *ph* Miroslav Ondricek. *ad* Karel Cerny. *m* Evcen Hilin. *cast* Hana Brejchová, Vladimír Pucholt, Vladimír Mensík, Antonin Blazejovsky, Milada Jezkova, Josef Sebánek, Jana Novakova.

●Forman's second film is a small gem. The story is almost classical in its simplicity: a pretty little blonde meets a young pianist at a dance hall, and they spend a happy night of love together. But she takes the affair altogether more seriously than he does, and when she pays an unannounced call on his parents, everybody is appalled. He feels he is being trapped, she feels betrayed, and the parents see both sides in turn, until in the end nobody knows what to think because nobody seems to be playing according to any known rules. Much of Forman's humour comes from the fact that his characters peer out at the world like timid nocturnal animals, always prepared to defend themselves against attack, but constantly having the ground cut from under their feet by the discovery that people are never quite what they seem at first glance. Using mostly non-professional actors, letting them improvise, then refining, shaping and perfecting, he achieves something indescribably exact, touching and funny. TM

Lassie Come Home

(1943, US, 89 min)
d Fred M Wilcox. *p* Samuel Marx. *sc* Hugo Butler. *ph* Leonard Smith. *ed* Ben Lewis. *ad* Cedric Gibbons. *m* Daniele Amfitheatrof. *cast* Roddy McDowall, Donald Crisp, Dame May Whitty, Edmund Gwenn, Nigel Bruce, Elsa Lanchester, Elizabeth Taylor, Ben Webster.

●The daddy of dog movies has down-on-his-luck Yorkshireman Crisp reluctantly selling his son McDowall's prize collie to local aristo Bruce, but after a couple of canine escape attempts the good duke moves himself, dog and granddaughter Taylor to Scotland for some peace of mind. No sooner have they arrived, however, than Lassie's off on the arduous road to her young master. Nobody made this heart-warming fluff better than MGM. (From the novel by Eric Knight.) TJ

Lassiter

(1983, US, 100 min)
d Roger Young. *p* Albert S Ruddy. *sc* David Taylor. *ph* Gilbert Taylor. *ed* Benjamin A Weissman, Richard Hiscott. *pd* Peter Mullins. *m* Ken Thorne. *cast* Tom Selleck, Jane Seymour, Lauren Hutton, Bob Hoskins, Joe Regalbuto, Ed Lauter, Warren Clarke.

●Somewhere in the Hollywood hills there's a computer loaded with a software programme called BuildaStar. A hack punched in the script requirements for this intended star vehicle for Selleck: an action yarn pitting an American loner against evil Nazis, bent coppers, a sultry girlfriend; sardonic sex with a lashing of perversity and gratuitous nudity; dare-devil stunts and chases for excitement; pseudo-moral dilemmas for the more intellectually inclined; period London settings (1939) for a hint of authenticity. The computer duly scanned the files in its memory, notably the ones labelled *James Bond, The Sting, Steve McQueen's Motor-Bike Scenes* and *Cary Grant/Negligée Number from Bringing Up Baby*, and cobbled them all together into an Adult Entertainment. HH

Last Action Hero, The

(1993, US, 131 min)
d John McTiernan. *p* Steve Roth, John McTiernan. *sc* Shane Black, David Arnott. *ph* Dean Semler. *ed* John Wright. *pd* Eugenio Zanetti. *m* Michael Kamen. *cast* Arnold Schwarzenegger, F Murray Abraham, Art Carney, Charles Dance, Frank McRae, Mercedes Ruehl, Austin O'Brien, Anthony Quinn, Ian McKellen, Joan Plowright, Tina Turner, Michael V Gazzo.

●'No one likes a smart-ass,' Jack Slater (Schwarzenegger) advised young Danny (O'Brien), the kid who keeps insisting that Jack's fictional. He has a point. Here's the set-up: an elderly projectionist allows 11-year-old Danny to sneak into the midnight preview of the new Schwarzenegger action movie, *Jack Slater IV*. A magic ticket (!) transports him into the flick, where he helps his hero tackle the evil Benedict (Dance), until the killer in turn breaks through the screen to wreak havoc in 'reality'. It's a promising scenario but McTiernan pitches ham-fistedly at a post-modern attention span and shoots with the subtlety of a rampaging rhino. This is film-making of the 'more-is-more' school: heavy metal action, but no character, no suspense. It may be the first action art movie but this po-mo parody is so self-reflexive it scarcely requires an audience. TCh

Last American Hero, The

(1973, US, 95 min)
d Lamont Johnson. *p* William Roberts, John Cutts. *sc* Wiliam Roberts. *ph* George Silano. *ed* Robbe Roberts. *ad* Lawrence G Paull. *m* Charles Fox. *cast* Jeff Bridges, Valerie Perrine, Geraldine Fitzgerald, Ned Beatty, Gary Busey, Art Lund, Ed Lauter.

●With an absolutely top-notch cast headed by the excellent Bridges, this loose adaptation of a series of articles by Tom Wolfe could hardly fail. Telling of young Carolina hill-billy Junior Jackson (based on Junior Johnson), it traces his rise from moonshine-runner to stock-car and demolition-derby champ, and then on to fame as a big-time racer. But this is no mere celebration of fame, since it lightly but firmly sketches in the many compromises and losses met on the road to success. Johnson directs with a keen eye for the subculture of the car tracks and the whisky brewers, so that the film emerges as a winning, intelligent portrait of an aspect of America all too rarely seen in the movies. Like a *Thunder Road* filtered through the perceptions of the '70s, it's an invigorating and touching movie. GA

Last American Virgin, The

(1982, US, 92 min)
d Boaz Davidson. *p* Menahem Golan, Yoram Globus. *sc* Boaz Davidson. *ph* Adam Greenberg. *ed* Bruria Davidson. *ad* Jim Dultz. *cast* Lawrence Monoson, Diane Franklin, Steve Antin, Joe Rubbo, Louisa Moritz, Brian Peck, Kimmy Robertson, Tessa Richarde.

●Accompanied by a mediocre music score (Commodores, Cars, Blondie, etc), three moronic youths are herded through puberty and the dreary rites of passage all too familiar from endless similar films (comparing pricks, humping hookers, necking in the back of borrowed cars, spying on girls in the shower). The viewpoint is predictably phallic: fear/contempt of the female festers like a squeezed pimple; an abortion is shown more lasciviously than any sex. *Puberty Blues* and *Porky's* look positively progressive beside such sickening junk. Boaz Davidson should stick to sucking Popsicles. SJo

Last Battle, The (Le Dernier Combat)

(1983, Fr, 92 min, b/w)
d/p Luc Besson. *sc* Luc Besson, Pierre Jolivet. *ph* Carlo Varini. *ed* Sophie Schmit. *ad* Christian Grosrichard, Thierry Flamand, Patrick Leberre. *m* Eric Serra. *cast* Pierre Jolivet, Jean Bouise, Fritz Wepper, Jean Reno, Maurice Lamy, Pierre Carrive.

●That Besson previously assisted on a couple of features by the anarcho-eccentric Claude Faraldo is significant: the grim, wordless, post-holocaust humour of *The Last Battle* bears more than a passing resemblance to the latter's devastating *Themroc*. Unlike most *Mad Max* spin-offs, this is much more than a transplanted Western, with a hero who's as often required to be tender as he is ferocious. The result is a neat, wry, pocket-size adventure with several magic moments such as a rain-storm of fresh fish, and a touching scene where two of the most human characters manage to exchange a fragment or two of speech with the aid of a gas inhaler. The monochrome photography enhances a bare-bones atmosphere, and the small cast is splendid. A welcome addition to the post-holocaust barbarism boom. GD

Last Boy Scout, The

(1991, US, 105 min)
d Tony Scott. *p* Joel Silver, Michael Levy. *sc* Shane Black. *ph* Ward Russell. *ed* Stuart Baird, Mark Goldblatt, Mark Helfrich. *pd* Brian Morris. *m* Michael Kamen. *cast* Bruce Willis, Damon Wayans, Chelsea Field, Noble Willingham, Taylor Negron, Danielle Harris, Halle Berry, Bruce McGill, Joe Santos.

●Every element is present and correct in this violent, smart-mouthed, buddy-buddy action comedy, with just enough of an ironic inflection to ensure that familiarity breeds content. Willis plays a washed-up LA private eye whose partner is killed after passing on a case. With his marriage on the rocks and his daughter under threat, he reluctantly teams up with sartorially smooth ex-football player Jimmy Dix (Wayans) to crack the case. Naturally, the initial murder is just the tip of an iceberg, which engulfs major league football, prime-time sports coverage, and the gambling interests of a ruthless businessman (Willingham). Limited though his range is, Willis was born to play this type of role; the bonus here is that his flip smarm is matched by Wayans' suave charm. Despite the testosterone-charged violence and jaw-dropping sexism, the tone is one of self-conscious excess – a strategy which constantly undercuts the film's celebration of male bonding conventions. NF

Last Broadcast, The

(1998, US, 86 min)
d/p/sc Stefan Avalos, Lance Weiler. *ph* Lance Weiler. *ed* Stefan Avalos. *m* AD Roso, Stefan Avalos. *cast* David Beard, James Seward, Stefan Avalos, Lance Weiler, Rein Clabbers, Michele Pulaski, Tom Brunt, Mark Rublee, AD Roso, Dale Worstall.

●The Pine Barrens, New Jersey, 1995: a young, amateurish TV crew set up a live web/cable simulcast on the legendary Jersey Devil, keeping a video diary as they go deeper into the woods. After the gruesome deaths of two of the party and the disappearance of another, the fourth (psychic, psycho or sad nerdy fake?) was convicted of murder. But documentarist Leigh (Beard) reckons injustice may have been done, and explores further – and it's his investigative film we have here. It's not, of course, as anyone who's seen *The Blair Witch Project* will know. Weiler and Avalos' film is also fake documentary, and its publicity implies that since it was (allegedly) made months before *BWP*, it may have influenced it (though Sanchez and Myrick would have had to move sharpish). It may even be better. Baloney. While there are striking parallels, this film's more complex ambitions – it's less a horror chiller, and more a thriller-mockumentary with modernist pretensions – are its fatal flaw. The decision to indict the media as a source of injustice, even evil, means that the laboured narrative goes wildly awry towards the end; and the use of the investigative documentary format renders some lines so portentous, they're unintentionally funny, while also wrecking any potential for tension. GA

Last Castle, The

(2001, US, 131 min)
d Rod Lurie. *p* Robert Lawrence. *sc* David Scarpa. *ph* Shelly Johnson. *ed* Michael Jablow, Kevin Stitt. *pd* Kirk M Petruccelli. *m* Jerry Goldsmith. *cast* Robert Redford, James Gandolfini, Mark Ruffalo, Clifton Collins Jr, Delroy Lindo, Steve Burton, Paul Calderon, Samuel Ball, Robin Wright Penn.

● A prison movie with military trappings, this feels like something Hollywood might have made with Burt Lancaster or Gregory Peck during the Cold War. Director Lurie evidently believes in heroes, and he's found his perfect actor in Redford. He stars as Gen Eugene Irwin, who is court-martialled and thrown in military prison – to the awe of Col Winter (Gandolfini), the tinpot in charge. 'They should be naming a base after him, not sending him here,' he marvels. Irwin has served in 'Nam, the Gulf and Bosnia. He's 'a great man' who's 'done so much for the country' that his fellow prisoners genuflect. He just wants to do his time and keep his nose clean, but he's appalled by Winter's petty tyrannies, his callous disregard for human life, and the two are soon locked in an escalating battle for control of the inmates. Like most prison movies, this is broadly anti-authoritarian. But Lurie is so devoted to Irwin's 'enlightened' authority, he has ended up making a deeply conservative film, not to mention a ludicrous one, which at one particular low point involves an impromptu prisonyard rendition of 'The Halls of Montezuma'. TCh

Last Challenge, The (aka The Pistolero of Red River)

(1967, US, 96 min)
d/p Richard Thorpe. *sc* John B Sherry, Robert Emmett Ginna. *ph* Ellsworth J Fredricks. *ed* Richard W Farrell. *ad* George W Davis, Urie McCleary. *m* Richard Shores. *cast* Glenn Ford, Angie Dickinson, Chad Everett, Gary Merrill, Jack Elam, Delphi Lawrence, Royal Dano.

● The veteran Thorpe's last film, a Western gallantly attempting to ring the changes on an old situation, with Ford as the gunfighter turned marshal and yearning to settle down, Everett as the feisty youngster out to challenge him, and Dickinson as the saloon gal who doesn't want him dead. Watchable, thanks to solid performances, but pretty turgid. TM

Last Chance Hotel

see Emmène-moi

Last Chants for a Slow Dance

(1977, US, 88 min)
d/p Jon Jost. *sc* Jon Jost, Peter Trias. *ph/ed* John Jost. cast Tom Blair, Steve Vooheis, Jessica St John, Wayne Crouse, Mary Vollmer, John Jackson.

● The subject of Jost's excellent movie is the content of the most dirge-like Country and Western lyrics, and what that kind of indulgence leads to. His tale of a dole-queue loser, estranged from wife and kids, living an anachronistic male stud cowboy life and slowly drifting into crime, was apparently suggested by the life of Gary Gilmore. It's particularly scathing about the American macho psyche, but in a novel fashion; the music (all written and performed by Jost himself) comments on the action in a manner that's anything but the fashionably cosy way country is used in films these days. Jost shoots in long takes, relying on imaginative use of natural lighting à la early Godard. RM

Last Command, The

(1928, US, 95 min, b/w)
d Josef von Sternberg. *p* Joseph Bachman. *sc* John Goodrich, (titles) Herman J Mankiewicz. *ph* Bert Glennon. ed William Shea.*ad* Hans Dreier. *cast* Emil Jannings, Evelyn Brent, William Powell, Nicholas Soussanin, Michael Visaroff, Jack Raymond.

● *The Last Command* starts from a brilliant script idea: a Czarist general, defeated in the Russian revolution, finds himself down and out in Hollywood, working for peanuts as a bit-player in movies; he is spotted and hired by his former adversary, a Mayakovskian stage director turned Hollywood film-maker; and both men loved the same woman ten years earlier. (Goodrich's script was apparently from an original story by Sternberg, based on an incident told by Ernst Lubitsch to Lajos Biro…) Half the movie is an acid vision of the gap between success and the breadline in contemporary Hollywood, and the other half is a long flashback to revolutionary Russia, with the general seducing the woman Communist, imprisoning his rival, falling from power, and discovering abject humiliation. In other words, this is the first Sternberg masterpiece, the first of his glitteringly stylised rhapsodies of commitment and betrayal, expertly poised between satire and 'absurd' melodrama. The cast are fully equal to it; Jannings, in particular, turns the characteristic role of the general into an indelible portrait of arrogance, fervour and dementia. Even more incredible, the sheer sophistication of Sternberg's visuals makes nearly all current releases look old-fashioned. TR

Last Command, The

(1955, US, 106 min)
d Frank Lloyd. *sc* Warren Duff. *ph* Jack Marta. *ed* Tony Martinelli. *ad* Frank Arrigo. *m* Max Steiner. *cast* Sterling Hayden, Anna Maria Alberghetti, Richard Carlson, Arthur Hunnicutt, Ernest Borgnine, J Carrol Naish, Virginia Grey, Ben Cooper, John Russell, Slim Pickens.

● In the '20s and '30s, directors came no bigger than Frank Lloyd: he helmed *Cavalcade* and *Mutiny on the Bounty* and won a couple of Oscars. Hardly remembered now, his career ended with this reconstruction of the siege of the Alamo. As with the John Wayne epic of 1960, it's a travesty of history, and focuses on Jim Bowie (Hayden) rather more than Davy Crockett (Hunnicutt). The message is the same as in Wayne's film – better Tex than Mex – though the production values are considerably less impressive. This is a Republic Studios Western, so don't look for thousands of extras. But Lloyd's old professionalism produces some good battle footage. ATu

Last Crop, The

(1990, GB/Aust, 58 min)
d Sue Clayton. *p* Billy McKinnon. *sc* Richard Burridge, Mick O'Hanlon. *ph* Geoff Burton. *ed* Nicholas Beauman. *pd* Peta Lawson. *m* Felicity Foxx. *cast* Kerry Walker, Noah Taylor.

● Ann Sweeney has a peculiar perspective on how the other half live: as charwoman to a number of Sydney apartments owned by wealthy business folk who spend months abroad, she not only cleans the trappings of financial success, but makes good use of them, letting friends take over the luxury flats in the owners' absence for romantic weekends, wedding receptions, or simply a break from routine. But not everything is rosy for Ann, burdened as she is with a delinquent son, a daughter given to bursts of moody ingratitude, and a surly father in an old peoples' home who refuses to make everyone's life easier by selling the family's derelict farm. Deceptively slight, this adaptation of Elizabeth Jolley's short story charms partly for its bitter-sweet sense of humour, partly for its beautifully convincing performances (especially Kerry Walker as the pragmatic Ann). Also impressive are the way Clayton subtly injects trenchant social and economic observations into her oblique narrative, and the crisp, clear lines of Geoff Burton's camerawork. GA

Last Dance

(1995, US, 103 min)
d Bruce Beresford. *p* Steven Haft. *sc* Ron Koslow. *ph* Peter James. *ed* John Bloom. *ad* Monroe Kelly. *m* Mark Isham. *cast* Sharon Stone, Rob Morrow, Randy Quaid, Peter Gallagher, Jack Thompson, Skeet Ulrich.

● A painfully earnest, painfully inadequate anti-capital punishment movie, this asks us to take pity on Stone as a butch redneck hardcase whose death-row time is all used up. And we do pity her, but for the wrong reason: because Stone gives a rigorous, unglamorous and admirably low-key performance. There's a tendency to overpraise sex symbols when they take off the make-up in roles like this, as if ugliness somehow has more integrity than beauty – it doesn't – but Stone's work here is centred and hard, as layered as anything she's done, and all the more impressive for the lack of help she gets from the script. Compelling as Stone is, the film chooses to make Morrow's lawyer the dramatic focal point – and that's its undoing, because the character never rings true. A rich kid whose brother (Gallagher) gets him on the Governor's staff as a favour, Morrow is told to assess Stone's appeal for clemency before her politically expedient execution is carried out. For reasons which remain sketchy, he throws himself into the job and soon sets about re-opening the case. This legal beagle stuff is thin and risibly melodramatic. The film isn't a travesty, but it feels uncomfortably close to one. TCh

Last Date (De Laatste Sessie)

(1992, Neth, 92 min, b/w & col)
d Hans Hylkema. *p* Marian Browwer. *sc* Hans Hylkema, Thierry Bruneau. *ph* Deen van der Zaken. *ed* Ot Louw. *m* Eric Dolphy. *with* Eric Dolphy, Misha Mengelberg, Buddy Collette, Han Bennink, Ted Curson, Jaki Byard.

● Hylkema's portrait of the late jazz multi-instrumentalist Eric Dolphy certainly talks to the right people. As well as the expected survivors of Dolphy's European and Mingus periods – said Mingus: 'Eric, I'm gonna miss ya, asshole' – we go all the way back to Roy Porter, Buddy Collette and his bride-to-be in LA, and neighbours who heard the teenage prodigy practising his eight hours a day. No wonder he told pianist Mischa Mengelberg he was lazy. Dedicated, clean-living Dolphy had diabetes – Gunther Schuller puts it down to diet deficiency, since the jazzman survived on white beans and water when broke – but when he was admitted to a Berlin hospital in 1964, the authorities, assuming he'd overdosed, left him to die. Lots of old footage of Dolphy in action, mainly on bass clarinet . BC

Last Day of Summer

(1983, GB, 55 min)
d Derek Banham. *p* Nigel Stafford-Clark. *sc* Ian McEwan. *ph* Nic Knowland. *ed* Richard Trevor. *ad* Anton Furst. *m* Rachel Portman. cast Annette Badland, Graham McGrath, James Gaddas, Christina Jones, Saskia Reeves.

● Adapted by Ian McEwan from one of his own stories, this is a film of moods, overheard indistinct voices, slowed hypnotic time, and particularly a troubling sense of false security and impending tragedy. In a pot-addled Thames-side commune, Tom, a 12-year-old orphan (McGrath), is befriended by Jenny, a cheerful, overweight ex-teacher (Badland, excellent), who derives a passive contentment from attending to his conventional needs (Tom likes to go to school in uniform). Their affecting idyll is played out chiefly in Tom's rowing boat on the deceptively passive river at the end of a very filmic English summer. JPy

Last Day of Winter, The (Zuihou Yige Dongri)

(1986, China, 92 min)
d Wu Ziniu. *p* Huang Weide. *sc* Qiao Xuezhu. *ph* Yang Weidong. *pd* Na Shufeng. *m* Wang Xilin. *cast* Li Ling, Tao Zheru, Hong Yuzhou, Zhang Xiaomin, Yu Meng.

● This is the first movie to show the Chinese Gulag, a huge labour camp in the remote north-west, and so it's no surprise that its director is one of China's ground-breaking 'fifth generation' film-makers. The stylised flashbacks to the inmates' crimes teeter on the brink of melodramatic excess, but the framing scenes in the prison are as coolly controlled and visually striking as anything in New Chinese Cinema. The movie is also startlingly candid in matters of detail, like the scene in which a woman inmate breaks down over her brother's gift – of a suitcaseful of sanitary towels. TR

Last Days, The

(1998, US, 87 min, b/w & col)
d Jim Moll. *p* June Beallor, Ken Lipper. *ph* Harris Done. *ed* James Moll. *m* Hans Zimmer. *with* Irene Zisblatt, Renée Firestone, Alice Lok Cahana, Bill Basch, Congressman Tom Lantos, Dr Randolph Braham, Hans Munch.

●In this first Spielberg/Shoah Foundation feature documentary, the testimony of its five US-domiciled witnesses traces the history of the Final Solution as it affected Hungarian Jews in the last stages of the war. According to historian Randolph Braham, Hitler and the Nazis cared more about accelerating the extermination of Jews – at whatever cost in manpower, trains or fuel – than winning the war. Moll and his collaborators have laboured hard to be true both in describing the horrors of the survivors' experiences and in providing a positive educative message about the indomitability of the human spirit/soul. Ironically, the very slickness of the film and the attention grabbing 'sensitivity' of Hans Zimmer's score at times become intrusive. Essential viewing, none the less. WH

Last Days of Chez Nous, The

(1990, Aust, 97 min)
d Gillian Armstrong. *p* Jan Chapman. *sc* Helen Garner. *ph* Geoffrey Simpson. *ed* Nicholas Beauman. *pd* Janet Patterson. *m* Paul Grabowsky. *cast* Lisa Harrow, Bruno Ganz, Kerry Fox, Miranda Otto, Kiri Paramore, Bill Hunter, Lex Marinos, Mickey Camilleri.

●Everyday routine and a long-standing relationship with her French husband (Ganz) threatens to make Beth (Harrow) cynical and complacent, and to blind her to the possibility of change. But the arrival of her lovelorn sister Vicki (Fox) causes the family to implode, with three generations forced to re-evaluate their relationships. Armstrong skilfully and gently teases out the subtexts underlying each interaction, exposing individual selfishness which insulates and provides protection against domestic insecurity. Harrow heads the strong cast with a performance of considerable power and restraint. CM

Last Days of Disco, The

(1998, US, 114 min)
d/p/sc Whit Stillman. *ph* John Thomas. *ed* Andrew Hafitz, Jan Pires. *pd* Ginger Tougas. *m* Mark Suozzo. *cast* Chloë Sevigny, Kate Beckinsale, Chris Eigeman, Mackenzie Astin, Matt Keeslar, Robert Sean Leonard, Jennifer Beals, Matthew Ross.

●Manhattan, the early '80s. Recent graduates from an upper crust college, Alice (Sevigny) and Charlotte (Beckinsale) – flatmates and friends of a sort – pass their days working as trainee publishing editors, and most of their nights discussing social niceties at a fashionable disco where assistant manager Des (Eigeman) courts the boss's disfavour by admitting the wrong kind of clientele. The girls hang out at the disco with a preppy bunch of Harvard admen and lawyers; rumour, rivalry and falling-out is rife and relationships are frequently at risk. The third comedy of manners in Stillman's loose trilogy about the 'doomed bourgeois in love' again highlights the writer/director's expertise with naturalistically articulate dialogue whose idioms, ironies and absurdities provide vivid insights into the delusions, desires and often ludicrous tribal rituals of the young, privileged and, mostly, pretty ineffectual. Like *Metropolitan* and *Barcelona*, it's a brittle, sporadically brilliant film, very funny but rooted in social, political, historical and emotional realities. Beckinsale, especially, is a revelation, making Charlotte smug, spiteful, sexy and, underneath, rather sad, all with a spot-on accent. GA

Last Days of Man on Earth, The

see Final Programme, The

Last Days of Pompeii, The

(1935, US, 96 min, b/w)
d Ernest B Schoedsack. *p* Merian C Cooper. *sc* Ruth Rose, Boris Ingster. *ph* J Roy Hunt. *ed* Archie Marshek. *ad* Van Nest Polglase. *m* Roy Webb. *cast* Preston Foster, Basil Rathbone, Alan Hale, Dorothy Wilson, John Wood, Louis Calhern, Ward Bond.

●Mt Vesuvius blows its top in fine fashion somewhere near the end of this sword-and-sandal spectacular, but all the molten lava the special effects team can cook up isn't enough to atone for a cool, dreary script. Marcus, an honest blacksmith (Foster), is driven by misfortune to become an amoral gladiator. He repents just in time to save Pompeii's Christians from being frazzled. The acting honours, such as they are, go to Basil Rathbone, as a memorably dapper Pontius Pilate.

Last Detail, The

(1973, US, 104 min)
d Hal Ashby. *p* Gerald Ayres. *sc* Robert Towne. *ph* Michael Chapman. *ed* Robert C Jones. *pd* Michael Haller. *m* Johnny Mandel. *cast* Jack Nicholson, Otis Young, Randy Quaid, Clifton James, Carol Kane, Michael Moriarty, Luana Anders, Nancy Allen.

●Despite Robert Towne's often sharp script – about two veteran sailors detailed to escort a young and naïve rating to prison, and showing him a sordidly 'good time' en route – and despite strong performances all round, one can't help feeling that the criticism of modern America hits out at all too easy targets in a vague and muffled manner. Also that the overlay of bleak cynicism barely conceals a troubled – and, dare one say, sometimes misogynist – sentimentality about what it means to be men together. (From the novel by Darryl Ponicsan.) GA

Last Dinosaur, The

(1977, US, 100 min)
d Alex Grasshoff, Tom Kotani. *p* Arthur Rankin Jr, Jules Bass. *sc* William Overgard. *ph* Shosi Ueda. *ed* Tatsuji Nakashizu, Minoru Kozono. *ad* Zazuhiko Fujiwara. *m* Maury Laws. *cast* Richard Boone, Joan Van Ark, Steven Keats, Luther Rackley, Masumi Sekiya, William Ross.

●Difficult to know which is the more ludicrous in this shoddy monster pic: the Joke Shop tyrannosaurus galumphing through the polar icecap landscape, or Richard Boone's completely erratic portrayal of Masten Thrust (yessir, that's his name) – the richest, most bored man in the world, who gathers together a little band of stereotypes (Nobel prizewinning scientist, spunky woman photographer) to track the last of the breed. With his unkempt hair, dark glasses, and habit of closing his eyes between words, Boone shows all the signs of enjoying a massive hangover; but when you have to talk about a 'forty foot monster with a brain the size of a dried pea', this is probably a distinct advantage. Japan provided the special effects and the extras who play hairy prehistoric savages; someone should complain. GB

Last Dragon, The

(1985, US, 109 min)
d Michael Schultz. *p* Rupert Hitzig. *sc* Louis Venosta. *ph* James A Contner. *ed* Christopher Holmes. *pd* Peter Larkin. *m* Misha Segal. *cast* Taimak, Vanity, Chris Murney, Julius J Carry III, Faith Prince, Leo O'Brien, Mike Starr, Jim Moody.

●The Motown company were responsible for this utterly wigged-out kung-fu disco extravaganza, which manages to throw together chopsocky thrills, a passing video-jock to show off the label's latest recording sensations, and the dreariest kid-takes-on-mobsters plot you could imagine. The juxtaposition of head-spinning break dancing and mild martial arts (in which the fighters glow to show their level of mental attainment and nobody gets badly hurt) provides lots of whirling limbs, but the working into the storyline of a crook who wants to take over the nightclub to provide valuable exposure for his aspirant rock-goddess girlfriend seems lame indeed. Aka *Berry Gordy's The Last Dragon* and a sure sign that somewhere along the way the man from Hitsville USA lost it badly. Talk about 'Ball of Confusion'. TJ

Last Embrace

(1979, US, 101 min)
d Jonathan Demme. *p* Michael Taylor, Dan Wigutow. *sc* David Shaber. *ph* Tak Fujimoto. *ed* Barry Malkin. *pd* Charles Rosen. *m* Miklós Rozsa. *cast* Roy Scheider, Janet Margolin, John Glover, Sam Levene, Charles Napier, Christopher Walken, Jacqueline Brookes, Mandy Patinkin.

●A delicious excursion into the world of Hitchcockian suspense. A taut, complex conspiracy thriller, it sees Scheider – a former 'agent' for an assassination firm – threatened by mental breakdown (guilt over his wife's death), by his former employers who find him dangerously superfluous, and by an obscure Hebraic society bent on revenge for some unknown reason. Scheider is admirably haunted as the justifiably paranoid gunman (who gets involved with a strange, duplicitous femme fatale), the whole thing is beautifully shot by Tak Fujimoto, and Miklós Rosza's stunning score augments Demme's careful control of atmosphere and set pieces. But what finally impresses is the way that the various references to Hitchcock and other classic thrillers are never used as an end in themselves; rather, they simply add resonance and depth to a film that works perfectly well in its own right. GA

Last Emperor, The

(1987, China/It, 163 min)
d Bernardo Bertolucci. *p* Jeremy Thomas. *sc* Mark Peploe, Bernardo Bertolucci. *ph* Vittorio Storaro. *ed* Gabriella Cristiani. *pd* Ferdinando Scarfiotti. *m* Ryuichi Sakamoto, David Byrne, Cong Su. *cast* John Lone, Joan Chen, Peter O'Toole, Ying Ruocheng, Victor Wong, Dennis Dun, Ryuichi Sakamoto, Lisa Lu, Chen Kaige, Zhang Jungxiang.

●The odyssey of Emperor Pu Yi, from ruler of half the world's population to humble gardener in the People's Republic of China, is a saga of tidal historical turbulence with a small, often supine centre. Nations treated Pu Yi as a blank screen upon which they projected their ambitions, but Bertolucci's epic strives not to follow suit. The vast, gorgeous tapestry of visual delights is built around the question of one man's capacity for personal redemption, which – up to a point – transforms the puppet into protagonist. Pu Yi ascended the Dragon Throne at three but was forced to abdicate at six when China became a republic, and from then until his expulsion from the Forbidden City, his puissance was an empty charade, his palace a prison. This section of the film is sumptuously rich and strange, from the bewildering maze of the Forbidden City itself (with its 9,999 rooms) to the daily rituals surrounding the little Living God. Thousands of courtiers indulge his every whim, but can never allow him to venture outside; to some extent his Scottish tutor (O'Toole) replaces the forfeited warmth of his mother and wet nurse, later supplemented by an Empress (Chen). Given this outlandish upbringing, it is impossible to judge his subsequent showing as playboy in exile and dupe of the Japanese – neither section memorable. The film covers over half-a-century in flashbacks, contrasting at the start the rainbow glories with the grey reality of Communist confession, and gradually monitors its spectrum as Pu Yi rejoins the human race. John Lone is superb as the sad mediocrity; and if spectacle finally triumphs over sympathy, it is not without a decent struggle. BC

Last Exit to Brooklyn (Letzte Ausfahrt Brooklyn)

(1989, WGer, 98 min)
d Ulrich Edel. *p* Bernd Eichinger. *sc* Desmond Nakano. *ph* Stefan Czapsky, Bob Hanna. *ed* Peter Przygodda. *pd* David Chapman. *m* Mark Knopfler. *cast* Stephen Lang, Jennifer Jason Leigh, Burt Young, Peter Dobson, Jerry Orbach, Alexis Arquette, Zette, Frank Military, Ricki Lake, John Costelloe.

●A violent, harrowing, but oddly tender adaptation of Hubert Selby Jr's novel about life in a working class Brooklyn neighbourhood in the '50s. In this harsh, poverty-stricken enviroment, human feeling is sacrificed to expediency as prostitute Tralala (Leigh), union leader Harry Black (Lang), and assorted workers, hustlers, wives, pimps and homosexuals struggle to survive. While a strike at a loca factory explodes into violent confrontation, Harry uses embezzled union funds to explore the homosexual desire provoked in him by transvestite Georgette (Arquette). Tralala, meanwhile, frightened by an offer of love she cannot comprehend, plunges into a rampage of self destruction. From the fragments of an experimental novel, Edel has forged a remarkably coherent whole, cross-cutting from one story to another while retaining a precise delineation of character, picking out slender, golden threads of compassion and love from a bleak tapestry of pain. Not a comfortable film, but humane and savagely beautiful. NF

Last Feelings (L'Ultimo Sapore dell'Aria)

(1978, It, 105 min)
d Ruggero Deodato. *p/sc* Roberto Gandus, Tito Carpi. *ph* Claudio Cirillo. *ed* Daniele Alabiso. *pd* Carmelo Patrono. *m* Ubaldo Continiello. *cast* Maurizio Rossi, Vittoria Galeazzi, Carlo Lupo, Angela Goodwin, Fiorenzo Fiorentini, Jacques Sernas.
●Slim, dark, good-looking teenage boy, misunderstood but eager to please, speaks dubbed English, seeks substitute family, wants sincere girl-friend and wishes to become swimming champion. Only months to live, however. Is this why my eyes swim as much as I do and why I am wetter than any swimming-pool you care to think of? Write soonest with s.a.e. CPe

Last Flight, The

(1931, US, 77 min, b/w)
d William Dieterle. *sc* John Monk Saunders. *ph* Sid Hickox. *ed* Alexander Hall. *ad* Jack Okey. *cast* Richard Barthelmess, Helen Chandler, John Mack Brown, David Manners, Elliott Nugent, Walter Byron, Luis Alberni.
●A study of the Lost Generation more quintessentially Fitzgerald than anything Scott Fitzgerald ever wrote: a doomed, innocently mad-cap frolic over which hangs the aura of despair. Adapted by John Monk Saunders from his own novel *Single Lady*, it chronicles the dark night of the soul of four young aviators, invalided out as 'spent bullets' at the end of World War I and lingering on in Paris to drown their shattered nerves in dry Martinis and zany banter with a dreamily dotty rich girl in whom they instantly recognise a kindred spirit when they see her in a bar solemnly guarding someone's false teeth in her champagne glass. Nothing happens, and 'nothing matters' echoes as an ominous motif through the brilliantly racy conversations, until suddenly, within the space of a few minutes running time, three of the four have died or disappeared, and a curtain seems to fall on an era as the fourth is left to mourn the comradeship that alone survived the war. With superb dialogue that paints hell in wisecracks and an extraordinary performance by Helen Chandler as the girl, it's a small masterpiece. TM

Last Flight of Noah's Ark, The

(1980, US, 98 min)
d Charles Jarrott. *p* Ron Miller. *sc* Steven Carabatsos, Sandy Glass, George Arthur Bloom. *ph* Charles F Wheeler. *ed* Gordon D Brenner. *pd* Preston Ames. *m* Maurice Jarre. *cast* Elliott Gould, Genevieve Bujold, Ricky Schroder, Tammy Lauren, Vincent Gardenia, John Fujioka, Yuki Shimoda.
●There must be a computer in the Disney studios programmed to produce live-action shooting scripts at the drop of various switches (probably labelled 'Children', 'Animals', 'Moral Homilies' and 'Some Current Cinema Fashions'). It's certainly been in use here. A plane full of two orphans, sundry animals, an evangelist (wonderful Bujold) and a hard-nosed pilot (boring Gould) crash-lands in the Pacific, with ensuing struggle back to civilisation. There's the tousle-haired faucet Schroder crying over his small zoo; an encounter with a shark; and umpteen sermons on tolerance and togetherness, with all the cast – including two Jap soldiers still fighting World War II – learning to live together in a wonderful warm glow. GB

Last Gangster, The

(1937, US, 81 min, b/w)
d Edward Ludwig. *p* JJ Cohn. *sc* John Lee Mahin. *ph* William Daniels. *ed* Ben Lewis. *ad* Cedric Gibbons, Daniel Cathcart. *m* Edward Ward. *cast* Edward G Robinson, James Stewart, Rose Stradner, Lionel Stander, John Carradine.
●A typically edgy Robinson, continually threatening to turn things nastier at the drop of a snarl, returns from a 10-year stretch in stir during which he's become obsessed by the time he's missed with his small son. This is bad news for ex-wife Stradner, who's since married newspaperman Stewart and watched the bond grow between the boy and his stepdad. Stewart looks much younger than his 29 years, and he's not much of a match for the headliner, but this is still an absorbing exercise in contrasting styles. (From a story by William A Wellman and Robert Carson.) TJ

Last Good Time, The

(1994, US, 90 min)
d Bob Balaban. *p* Max Kishiyama, Mark Irwin, Dean Silvers. *sc* John Mclaughlin. *ph* Claudia Raschke. *ed* Hughes Winborne. *pd* Wing Lee. *m* Jonathan Tunick. *cast* Armin Mueller-Stahl, Lionel Stander, Maureen Stapleton, Olivia D'Abo, Adrian Pasdar, Zohra Lampert, Kevin Corrigan, Molly Powell.
●Very different from the ghoulish Americana of his debut, the horror-satire *Parents*, character actor Balaban's second feature is a compassionate and assured portrait of old age. Isolated in his Brooklyn apartment, Mueller-Stahl's immigrant German violinist broods on his past, haunted by sexual images of his late wife. An unlikely friendship with D'Abo's youthful stray, however, is to prove that he hasn't loosened his grip on life entirely, while the fortitude of cigar-chomping pal Stander in the face of terminal odds gives him renewed courage to continue. Adapted by Balaban and John McLaughlin from the novel by Richard Bausch, the result's a honed, if conventional testament to human resilience, delivered with unsentimental grit by the reliably excellent Mueller-Stahl, and toppped by an affecting performance from the veteran Stander – his last, and a worthy closer. TJ

Last Grave at Dimbaza

(1974, GB, 54 min)
d Nana Mahomo.
●A documentary shot by a British team who wanted to remain anonymous for fear of reprisals (not just against them, but the people who helped them). Most of the white South Africans they encountered were persuaded that they were simply making home movies. Consequently, and illegally, they went where camera teams had never penetrated: into the heart of the Bantustan (the tiny waste area designated for black development), the various ghettos, even into the vast houses of the white farmers. The film continually juxtaposes the two communities of South Africa to ghastly effect, and the cold statistics of its commentary are unbearable. Everyone knows that conditions in South Africa are bad. This film presents proof that they are genocidal. DP

Last Hard Men, The

(1976, US, 103 min)
d Andrew V McLaglen. *p* Russell Thacher, Walter Seltzer. *sc* Guerdon Trueblood. *ph* Duke Callaghan. *ed* Fred Chulack. *ad* Edward C Carfagno. *m* Jerry Goldsmith. *cast* Charlton Heston, James Coburn, Barbara Hershey, Christopher Mitchum, Jorge Rivero, Michael Parks, Thalmus Rasulala.
●Appalling tough-guy actioner, based on a novel called *Gun Down* by Brian (*Death Wish*) Garfield, in which Coburn and a gang of cons escape and plan revenge on sheriff Heston, whose daughter (Hershey) they kidnap and threaten to rape. The occasional elegiac tone lamenting the passing of the West seems entirely out of place. Only Michael Parks, still aping James Dean at nearly 40, provides some welcome distraction. GA

Last Hole, The (Das letzte Loch)

(1981, WGer, 92 min)
d/sc Herbert Achternbusch. *ph* Jörg Schmidt-Reitwein. *ed* Micki Joanni. *cast* Herbert Achternbusch, Gabi Geist, Annamirl Bierbichler, Franz Baumgartner, Wolfgang Ebert, Helga Loder, Alois Hitzenbichler.
●Even the fact that Achternbusch scripted the most wilfully bizarre Herzog feature – *Heart of Glass*, in which the entire cast performed under hypnosis – doesn't prepare one for the strangeness of his own films. Where Herzog has sought increasing comfort in grandiose visions and international travel, Achternbusch is less romantic and more defiantly Bavarian. However, his central character (played by himself) reminds one more of Spike Milligan than of any German: a fly-catcher and private detective, who loves only waitresses called Susan and drinks to forget the figure of six million that haunts him. As with Milligan, any attempt at synopsis is foolhardy. Suffice it to say that Achternbusch's self-elected task is to point up the absurd complacency of post-war Germany by reconnecting the raw nerves that the Germans have tried so hard to forget, and what pulls it all together is a desperate manic seriousness. One hesitates to call this unsettling film a comedy, as its laughter is the stuff of nightmare. What right has anyone to laugh after too many are dead? But, says Achternbusch, what else can one do? CPe

Last Holiday

(1950, GB, 88 min, b/w)
d Henry Cass. *p* Stephen Mitchell, AD Peters, JB Priestley. *sc* JB Priestley. *ph* Ray Elton. *ed* Monica Kimick. *ad* Duncan Sutherland. *m* Francis Chagrin. *cast* Alec Guinness, Kay Walsh, Beatrice Campbell, Bernard Lee, Wilfrid Hyde-White, Muriel George, Helen Cherry, Grégoire Aslan, Ernest Thesiger, Sidney James.
●A bitter-sweet little film written by JB Priestley. Informed that he has no more than a few weeks to live, a hard-working nonentity (Guinness) collects his savings, checks into a posh hotel, and resolves to go out like a gentleman. Here his life changes beyond all recognition: he finds love and happiness, and has an equally beneficent effect on those around him. It's a charming notion, Utopia on the never-never; and while the final twist is a bit tricky, the picture is surprisingly moving, delicately handled and full of lovely vignettes. Unlikely as it may seem, this was the inspiration for Aki Kaurismäki's *I Hired a Contract Killer*. TCh

Last House on the Left, The (aka Krug and Company/ Sex Crime of the Century)

(1972, US, 91 min)
d Wes Craven. *p* Sean S Cunningham. *sc* Wes Craven. *ph* Victor Hurwitz. *ed* Wes Craven. *m* David Alexander Hess. *cast* David Hess, Lucy Grantheim, Sandra Cassel, Marc Sheffier, Jeramie Rain, Fred Lincoln.
●Craven's first horror movie is pretty strong meat, though it never quite lives down to its infamous reputation. Two teenage girls (Grantheim and Cassel), on their way to a rock concert, are abducted, tortured and raped by a pair of psycopathic killers, Krug and Weasel, their dyke accomplice Sadie, and Krug's heroin-addicted son Junior. Then, in a twist borrowed from Ingmar Bergman's *The Virgin Spring*, the criminals ask for help when their car breaks down at a nearby house, where Cassel's parents (surprise, surprise) discover the truth and wreak brutal revenge. Rape, disembowelment and death by chainsaw are now standard horror fare, but Craven's cold, flat style of filming emphasises the fact that the violence dehumanises not only the victims but the aggressors. Craven fans will also note an early use of the domestic booby traps and dream sequences which were to be central to the later *Nightmare on Elm Street*. NF

Last Hunt, The

(1955, US, 98 min)
d Richard Brooks. *p* Dore Schary. *sc* Richard Brooks. *ph* Russell Harlan. *ed* Ben Lewis.*ad* Cedric Gibbons, Merrill Pye. *m* Daniele Amfitheatrof. *cast* Robert Taylor, Stewart Granger, Debra Paget, Lloyd Nolan, Russ Tamblyn, Constance Ford.
●This bleak and impressive Western pitches ruthless, Indian-hating buffalo hunter Taylor ('One less buffalo means one less Indian') against the more sympathetic Granger, who later falls for Indian squaw Paget. The extended massacre scene is chillingly effective, and the film not only condemns the senseless slaughter of bison, but also raises questions about the Western myths of heroism and the pioneering spirit. Russell Harlan's admirably low-key cinematography complements writer/director Brooks' down-beat tone. NF

Last Hurrah, The

(1958, US, 121 min, b/w)
d/p John Ford. *sc* Frank S Nugent. *ph* Charles Lawton Jr. *ed* Jack Murray. *ad* Robert Peterson. *cast* Spencer Tracy, Jeffrey Hunter, Dianne Foster, Basil Rathbone, Pat O'Brien, Donald Crisp, James Gleason, John Carradine, Edward Brophy, Ricardo Cortez, Jane Darwell.
●Often shrugged off as a Ford failure, but it improves with acquaintance. Sentimental, certainly, and featuring a perilously protracted death-bed scene, but with Ford superbly at ease on his Irish-American home ground in an elegiac account of the last, doomed campaign of a New England political boss (based by way of

Edwin O'Connor's novel on Boston's Mayor Curley), defeated by time and new-fangled media image-making. Sidestep-ping the corruption inseparable from this sort of old-style politicking, Ford prints the legend with a warm, rueful (almost testamentary) sense of recollection. Outstanding camera-work by Charles Lawton, and a rich gallery of performances in which Hollywood veterans and Ford's stock company are well to the fore. TM

Last Hurrah for Chivalry (Haoxia)

(1979, HK, 97 min)
d John Woo. *cast* Wei Bai, Liu Songren, Liu Jiang, Wei Zhuohua, Feng Ke'an.

● Dishonour among outlaws, John Woo style – except that this time the conflicts are fought out with fists, blades and spears, not guns. Woo claims it started out as a zen movie about internalised conflicts, but it plays like a regular martial arts melodrama; only the tone is darker and more cynical than usual. Kao recruits skilled fighters to exact vengeance on his old foe Pai, but is himself far from the paragon of wounded virtue he seems. The emphasis on betrayal and treachery is pretty relentless, although there's the odd visual gag and 'magic' feat to lighten the tone. Homosexual overtones are rife. TR

Last Images of the Shipwreck (Ultimas Imágenes del naufragio)

(1989, Arg/Sp, 129 min)
d Eliseo Subiela. *p* Hugo Lauria. *sc* Eliseo Subiela. *ph* Alberto Basail. *ed* Marcela Saenz. *pd* Abel Facello. *m* Pedro Aznar. *cast* Lorenzo Quinteros, Noemi Frenkel, Hugo Soto, Pablo Brichta, Sara Benítez, Andres Tiengo.

● Ensnared in the web of the alluring Estelita (Frenkel), who repeatedly uses a suicidal charade to drum up custom for 'the oldest profession', 40-year-old insurance salesman-cum-author Robert (Quinteros) is introduced to a bizarre family whose lunatic personalities he believes will provide the inspiration for his long-dreamed-of novel: from brother José, a gun-toting psychotic thief with a grudge against God, to brother Claudio, a withdrawn obsessive who methodically removes from his lexicon words for which he no longer has use, Estelita's family is a fictional goldmine. But as the family's initial hostility towards Robert turns to acceptance, he finds his characters demanding answers to their misery, insisting that he rewrite their lives and fill the space left by their long-departed philandering father. Building on a meticulous script, Subiela crafts a finely-honed vision of society in retreat, simultaneously evoking the despair of abandonment and the joyous sparkle of salvation through error. Anchored throughout by resiliently credible performances, this is a unique blend of satirical madness and spine-tingling fantasy. MK

Last Italian Tango, The (Ultimo Tango a Zagarol)

(1973, It, 98 min)
d Nando Cicero. *p* Mario Mariani. *sc* Mario Onorati. *ph* Luciano Trasatti. *ed* Sandro Peticca. *ad* Alberto Boccianti. *m* Ubaldo Continiello. *cast* Franco Franchi, Martine Beswick, Gina Rovere, Nicola Arigliano, Franca Valeri.

● Supposedly comic adaptation of Bertolucci's *Last Tango in Paris* which has its buffoonish hero beset by dominant females. It's terribly unfunny (the butter joke is pushed for all it's worth, and predictably it ends up being spread on bread), all the worse for sticking closely to the original (whole scenes are lifted) and trying to look like Bertolucci. The dubbing is bad as well. Bertolucci's film appears a comic masterpiece by comparison.

Last Journey, The

(1935, GB, 64 min, b/w)
d Bernard Vorhaus. *p* Julius Hagen. *sc* H Fowler Mear, John Soutar. *ph* Percival Strong, Billy Luff. *ed* Jack Harris, Lister Laurance. *ad* James Carter. *cast* Hugh Williams, Godfrey Tearle, Judy Gunn, Eve Grey, Nelson Keys, Frank Pettingell.

● The runaway train came down the track, and the passengers on board…Vorhaus' nippiest movie demonstrates many prime cinematic virtues from an era when British film was largely theatrical. His largest cast of actors have their roles characterised with incredible economic precision. The split-second editing is superb. And as Wenders was later to discover, the emotion comes from the motion. As usual, however, it is the loco, in this case a Great Western steamer, that steals the show. CPea

Last Laugh, The (Der letzte Mann)

(1924, Ger, 7,595 ft, b/w)
d FW Murnau. *p* Erich Pommer. *sc* Carl Mayer. *ph* Karl Freund. *pd* Robert Herlth, Walter Röhrig. [*m* Giuseppe Becce. *cast* Emil Jannings, Maly Delschaft, Max Hiller, Emilie Kurz, Hans Unterkircher, Olaf Storm.

● A tragic tale of status and its loss, made explicit in the archetypal German symbol of uniform, the reverse of Zuckmayer's classic play *The Captain of Köpenick*. Jannings, pre-eminent in the field of gigantic pathos, gives his all as the ageing hotel doorman humiliatingly stripped of his peaked cap and epaulettes and demoted to basement lavatory attendant. Murnau makes a film of mythic resonance from almost nothing – the door motif is particularly striking – and sends up rotten the happy resolution that the studio, UFA, insisted be grafted on. SG

Last Lieutenant, The (Secondløitnanten)

(1993, Nor, 100 min)
d Hans Petter Moland. *p* Harald Ohrvik. *sc* Axel Hellstenius. *ph* Harald Paalgard. *ed* Einar Egeland. *pd* Karl Juliusson. *m* Randall Meyers. *cast* Espen Skjønberg, Lars Andreas Larsen, Gard B Eidsvold, Bjørn Sundquist, Morten Faldaas.

● Decent, classy, rather old-fashioned drama about the confusion, divided loyalties and unadulterated fear which beset Norway in 1940 following the unexpected Nazi invasion. It centres on a retired naval lieutenant who, much to his younger colleagues' surprise, enlists in the army and then, when the government surrenders, sets up a resistance force. Nothing hugely original here, but Skjønberg's lead performance is impressive, the film avoids sentimentality, and the account of conflicting notions of collaboration and nationalism is deftly handled. GA

Last Man Standing

(1996, US, 101 min)
d/p/sc Walter Hill. *ph* Lloyd Ahern. *ed* Freeman Davies. *pd* Gary Wissner. *m* Ry Cooder. *cast* Bruce Willis, Christopher Walken, Alexandra Powers, Bruce Dern, David Patrick Kelly, William Sanderson, Karina Lombard, Ned Eisenberg, Michael Imperioli.

● Hill's remake of Kurosawa's samurai classic *Yojimbo* places the story in the Prohibition era, with Italian and Irish bootleggers clashing over Mexican liquor supplies in Jericho, Texas. 'John Smith' (Willis) takes one look at the dead horse in the middle of Main Street and gets the full measure of this godforsaken ghost town. Before long both factions are vying for his services as hired gun, and Smith cynically plays one off against the other until, steeped in blood and sickened by what he's seen, he sets about wiping out every last man. The plot will be familiar not only from *Yojimbo* but from Leone's *A Fistful of Dollars*. Hill's Tex-Mex version suggests he hasn't got the Western out of his system yet, and this highly stylised film looks like an uncomfortable exercise in cross-breeding, as if a handful of mobsters had wandered on to the wrong studio backlot. Hill goes all out for spiritual fable, with Smith bringing down the walls of Jericho, shooting for his own bloody Calvary. The conceit might have played better in a Western. As a thriller, the film tries to camouflage its lack of suspense with profligate and repetitive gunplay and a deafening barrage of noise (Ry Cooder's score is a plus, however). There's too much voice-over, and not enough for arch-nemesis Walken to do. but at least Willis has the hard-boiled hero down. An honourable failure. TCh

Last Married Couple in America, The

(1979, US, 102 min)
d Gilbert Cates. *p* Edward S Feldman, John Herman Shaner. *sc* John Herman Shaner. *ph* Ralph Woolsey. *ed* Peter E Berger. *pd* Gene Callahan. *m* Charles Fox. *cast* George Segal, Natalie Wood, Richard Benjamin, Arlene Golonka, Allan Arbus, Valerie Harper, Bob Dishy, Dom DeLuise.

● 'I've heard of the sexual revolution, but I've never had it sit down so close to me,' says comfortably married Natalie Wood, shuddering at the memory of Valerie Harper casually mentioning that she'd had her most private part tightened. But fear not for Natalie: the sexual revolution gets no closer, and America's last married couple (Wood and Segal) survive all threats and end up happily munching hamburgers with their kids. But it's a hollow victory. Throughout, the film's support for old-fashioned morality is as thinly felt as its sour ridicule of the new permissiveness. Wood's comic style always was of the galumphing kind, but even Segal loses his potency with this material. Luckily some of their friends and neighbours show more life (Richard Benjamin's manic depressive in particular), but the only word to describe the film is horrible. GB

Last Melodrama, The (Le Dernier Mélodrame)

(1977, Fr, 80 min)
d Georges Franju. *p* Céline Baruch. *sc* Bernard Dimey, Georges Franju. *ph* Marcel Fradetal. *ed* Fernand Mannella. *ad* Michel Blaise. *m* Albert Lévy. *cast* Michel Vitold, Raymond Bussières, Edith Scob, Juliette Mills, Luis Masson, Georges Koulouris [George Colours].

● Nostalgic, ironic, with flashes of what-might-have-been, this film (made for TV from a story by Pierre Brasseur) by master of melodrama Georges Franju is really a prolonged disappointment. Dealing with a touring theatre group in a provincial French town, it's a lament for the passing of an era of entertainment, and the human emotions it evoked. DMacp

Last Metro, The (Le Dernier Métro)

(1980, Fr, 131 min)
d François Truffaut. *sc* François Truffaut, Suzanne Schiffman. *ph* Nestor Almendros. *ed* Martine Barraque-Curie, Marie-Aimée Debril, Jean-François Giré. *ad* Jean-Pierre Kohut-Svelko. *m* Georges Delerue. *cast* Catherine Deneuve, Gérard Depardieu, Jean Poiret, Heinz Bennent, Andréa Ferréol, Paulette Dubost, Jean-Louis Richard, Richard Bohringer.

● Once the Prince Charming of the French cinema, Truffaut latterly carried his talent for crowd-pleasing to the brink of turning into an Ugly Sister. Watching this smugly hermetic tale of the artistic pangs suffered by a French theatre company under the German Occupation in World War II, you would never guess that films like *The Sorrow and the Pity* and *Lacombe Lucien* had irretrievably lifted the lid off those years. Playing for cute nostalgia, Truffaut lets the realities go to hell. TM

Last Moments (Venditore di Palloncini)

(1974, It, 106 min)
d Mario Gariazzo. *sc* Luisa Montagnana, Massimo Franciosa. *ph* Claudio Racca. *ed* Amedeo Giomini. *ad* Francesco Cuppini. *m* Stelvio Cipriani. *cast* Renato Cestié, James Whitmore, Marina Malfatti, Lee J Cobb, Maurizio Arena, Adolfo Celi, Cyril Cusack.

● Revolting tear-jerker about a child who dies (lingeringly but sweetly) of neglect after mum runs off and dad goes on an extended bat. A companion in awfulness to the same team's *The Last Snows of Spring*, it doesn't miss a manipulative trick, even ripping off the earlier film's bitter-sweet climax: there it was a last-ditch trip to the fairground, here it's the last-wish gratification of a trip to a circus. TM

Last Movie, The

(1971, US, 108 min)
d Dennis Hopper. *p* Paul Lewis. *sc* Stewart Stern. *ph* Laszlo Kovacs. *ed* David Berlatsky, Antranig Mahakian. *ad* Leon Ericksen. *m* Kris Kristofferson, John Buck Wilkin, Cabuca Granda, Severn Darden. *cast* Dennis Hopper, Stella Garcia, Julie Adams, Tomas Milian, Don Gordon, Roy Engel, Donna Baccala, Samuel Fuller, Kris Kristofferson, Sylvia Miles, Peter Fonda, Dean Stockwell.

●Dennis Hopper's second film as director: dazzling, chaotic, indulgent. Movie stunt-man Kansas (Hopper), filming a Western in the Andes and staying on with a mini-skirted Peruvian prostitute after gruff father-figure Fuller and his crew return to Hollywood, is inextricably drawn into the peasants' own film-making ritual with wickerwork cameras but real violence (and himself as sacrificial victim). Caught within his own movie myths – prospecting for gold with only *The Treasure of the Sierra Madre* for guidance – Hopper's Romantic hero obstinately refuses to come to terms with the harsh exoticism of South American peasant culture. The film, too, never quite sure how the last movie should end, persistently sabotages its own resolution. But as it disintegrates, it shoots out enough ideas to fill a dozen movies. RMy

Last Night

(1998, Can, 93 min)
d Don McKellar. *p* Niv Fichman, Daniel Iron. *sc* Don McKellar. *ph* Douglas Koch. *ed* Reginald Harkema. *pd* John Dondertman. *m* Alexine Louie, Alex Pauk. *cast* Don McKellar, Sandra Oh, Callum Keith Rennie, David Cronenberg, Sarah Polley, Genevieve Bujold, Tracy Wright.
●This directorial debut is an apocalyptic movie with a difference: the last six hours before the world's end are played out on an intimate scale, as various inhabitants of Toronto – some connected, some not – prepare for their final moments: holding family dinners, living out sexual fantasies, trying to get home to a loved one, finishing off a piece of work, while the world (sort of) carries on around them. It's a witty, perceptive movie, exceptionally well structured by writer/director McKellar, with a keen feeling for detail, a nice line in the unexpected and a strong sense of the wider context. Absorbing, insightful and suspenseful from start to finish. GA

Last Night at the Alamo

(1984, US, 80 min, b/w)
d Eagle Pennell. *p* Kim Henkel, Eagle Pennell. *sc* Kim Henkel. *ph* Brian Huberman, Eric A Edwards. *ed* Eagle Pennell, Kim Henkel. *ad* Fletcher Mackey. *m* John Sarget, Paul Cox. *cast* Sonny Carl Davis, Louis Perryman, Steven Mattilla, Tina-Bess Hubbard, Amanda Lamar, Peggy Pinnell.
●The Alamo is a seedy, smoke-filled bar in contemporary Houston, populated by proud, foul-mouthed Texans hell-bent on defending their favourite haunt against demolition. All hopes focus on rough, tough Cowboy (Davis), a braggart hero concealing his balding pate beneath a ten-gallon hat and his fear of impotence beneath boasts of high connections in the state capital. Pennell's razor-sharp black comedy overcomes its low budget and limited locations by means of marvellous monochrome camerawork and a vivid, ironic script by Kim Henkel (who co-wrote the similarly dark and delirious *Texas Chain Saw Massacre*) to produce a caustic commentary on filmic myths and male foibles ('A man's gotta do...'). Yet the colourful collection of no-hope good ole boys are never reduced to mere cardboard to be satirised; through excellent performances, our emotions are enlisted for these beautiful losers, boozing and brawling their way towards a final violent conflict that would touch the heart of John Ford himself. GA

Last of England, The

(1987, GB, 87 min, b/w & col)
d Derek Jarman. *p* James Mackay, Don Boyd. *ph* Derek Jarman, Christopher Hughes, Cerith Wyn Evans. *ed* Peter Cartwright, Angus Cook, John Maybury, Sally Yeadon. *pd* Christopher Hobbs. *m* Simon Fisher Turner. *cast* Spring, Gerrard McArthur, John Phillips, Gay Gaynor, Matthew Hawkins, Tilda Swinton, Spencer Leigh, Nigel Terry.
●'What proof do you need the world's curling up like an autumn leaf?' Jarman's most uncompromisingly personal film is of many parts. Shots of the man himself are accompanied by the mournful voice of Nigel Terry. Clips from home movies are spliced with endless scenes of inner-city decay and rent-boys throwing bricks. Pop video techniques are substituted for dialogue and linear progression. References to the Falklands War, drugs, the Bomb and the Royal Wedding are supposed to indicate the state of Britain today. Jarman, however, is not engaged with his subject but playing with it, a suspicion strengthened by continual allusions to his other work. The recurring images of desolate beauty are poetical not polemical, mesmerising not shocking – style has subverted substance. This is art of the state. Still, no one else could have made it. MS

Last of His Tribe, The

(1992, US, 90 min)
d Harry Hook. *p* John Levoff, Robert Lovenheim. *sc* Stephen Harrigan. *ph* Martin Fuhrer. *ed* Bill Yahraus. *pd* Michael Baugh. *m* John E Keane. *cast* Jon Voight, Graham Greene, David Ogden Stiers, Jack Blessing, Anne Archer, Daniel Benzali.
●Hook's third feature (actually made for cable) has the same fine intentions as *The Kitchen Toto* and *Lord of the Flies*, and the same lack of narrative drive and originality. It stars Greene (from *Dances with Wolves*) as the 'Wild Indian', 'a free-ranging man of nature', the last of his tribe of Californian Native Americans, found robbing a slaughterhouse for sustenance in 1911. Voight is the San Franciscan museum anthropologist who takes him in, studies, and employs him. 'That man's soul is in your hands, Alfred,' he is told , a message he finally takes to heart, much in the way, presumably, Hook hopes the viewer may do. Unfortunately, the movie is so filled with clichés, so devoid of character development and insight, that it's hard to see anybody sustaining interest long enough to hang in for the film's sincere but bathetic denouement. Never have scenes suggestive of genocide been encased in such a vacuum. WH

Last of Sheila, The

(1973, US, 123 min)
d/p Herbert Ross. *sc* Stephen Sondheim, Anthony Perkins. *ph* Gerry Turpin. *ed* Edward A Warschilka. *pd* Ken Adam. *m* Billy Goldenberg. *cast* Richard Benjamin, Dyan Cannon, James Coburn, Joan Hackett, James Mason, Ian McShane, Raquel Welch, Yvonne Romaine.
●The most interesting thing about this game-playing thriller seemed to be that it was scripted by real-life puzzle-freaks Anthony Perkins and Stephen Sondheim. The presence of an all-star cast promised...well, something. The film itself turned out to be heavily plotted hokum in which a group of six unlikely Hollywood luminaries, each with a guilty secret to hide, are brought together on a yacht anchored off a smart Mediterranean coast so that the film's Machiavellian villain (Coburn) – whose wife was killed in a hit-and-run accident after a party at which they were all present – can wreak impossible havoc on their psyches. Campy stuff, not as much fun as it should be.

Last of the Blue Devils, The

(1979, US, 91 min)
d Bruce Ricker. *p* John Kelly, Bruce Ricker, Edward Beyer. *sc* John Arnoldy, Bruce Ricker. *ph* Arnie Johnson, Eric Menn. *ed* Thomasin Henkel. *with* Count Basie, Joe Turner, Jay McShann, Jesse Price, Eddie Durham, Jo Jones, Baby Lovett, Speedy Huggins.
●Ricker's delightful documentary centres on a reunion in their old Musician's Hall of many of the great Kansas City blues and jazzmen as they joke and jam away a joyous time of reminiscence and musical celebration. Ricker skilfully interlaces the proceedings with archive footage of Basie, McShann, Charlie Parker, Dizzy Gillespie, Billie Holiday, Coleman Hawkins and many others, in eloquent illustration of the extraordinary influence these Kansas City men were to bring to bear. Simply one of the best musical documentaries ever made. GA

Last of the Cowboys, The (aka The Great Smokey Roadblock)

(1976, US, 106 min)
d John Leone. *p* Allan F Bodah, Susan Sarandon. *sc* John Leone. *ph* Ed Brown Sr. *ed* Corky Ehlers. *m* Craig Safan.*cast* Henry Fonda, Eileen Brennan, John Byner, Robert Englund, Susan Sarandon, Melanie Mayron, Austin Pendleton, Dub Taylor.
●A road movie starring, not the inevitable Peter Fonda, but Henry as a terminally ailing truck driver who steals his vehicle back after it is repossessed, picks up six evicted prostitutes during his cross-country career, and becomes a folk hero to the media and cheering public. Sounds kinda familiar? Beware movies that undergo successive title changes (it also became known as *Elegant John and His Ladies*) and get cut to boot. TM

Last of the Dogmen

(1995, US, 117 min)
d Tab Murphy. *p* Joel B Michaels. *sc* Tab Murphy. *ph* Walter Lindenlaub. *ed* Richard Halsey. *pd* Trevor Williams. *m* David Arnold. *cast* Tom Berenger, Barbara Hershey, Kurtwood Smith, Steve Reevis, Andrew Miller, Gregory Scott Cummins, Mark Boone Jr, Helen Calahasen.
●Kevin Costner has a lot to answer for. Take this contemporary Western, for instance, where tracker Berenger and anthropologist Hershey run across a Cheyenne tribe which has managed to survive in the mountains of Montana for a century or so without anyone noticing. The portrayal of the Native Americans seems so keen to avoid any negative stereotyping that the Cheyenne are reduced to benign, mystical, eco-friendly ciphers whose all-round good-eggness undercuts any tension in the narrative set-up. The inference is that they've lasted so long by killing anyone who came near, yet the reality is more fluffy, turning an arresting B-picture action premise into touchy-feely inanity. Berenger is a watchable lug, but he's saddled with a routine assignment as the boozy bounty hunter given one last chance to redeem himself in the eyes of sheriff Smith by locating a trio of escaped convicts in the Rockies. For 20 minutes we get *The African Queen*, but first-time director Murphy's screenplay works up to a slump when the Cheyennes' cover is blown. Great landscapes, though. TJ

Last of the Finest, The (aka Blue Heat)

(1990, US, 106 min)
d John MacKenzie. *p* John A Davis. *sc* Jere Cunningham, George Armitage, Thomas Lee Wright. *ph* Juan Ruiz-Anchia. *ed* Graham Walker. *pd* Lawrence G Paull. *m* Jack Nitzsche, Michael Hoenig. *cast* Brian Dennehy, Joe Pantoliano, Jeff Fahey, Bill Paxton, Michael C Gwynne, Henry Stolow, Deborra-Lee Furness, Lisa Jane Persky, Guy Boyd.
●Like MacKenzie's *The Fourth Protocol* (though achieving greater narrative coherence), this densely plotted cop thriller seems to be straining for a significance that constantly eludes its grasp. So while Dennehy gives yet another faultless performance as a veteran LA cop disillusioned by compromise and corruption, the potentially explosive political undercurrents fail to ignite. Suspended after an abortive raid, Dennehy and his undercover narcotics team pursue their own freelance investigations. Acting on a pimp's tip-offs, they uncover a conspiracy involving fellow cops, drug enforcement agents and wealthy businessmen, which proves to be a front for supplying arms to right-wing rebels in Latin America. Dennehy's relationship with his team (Pantoliano, Fahey and Paxton) and their various blue-collar backgrounds are deftly handled, the unobtrusive camerawork leaving space for the actors to interact convincingly. But the filming of the action scenes is also slightly distanced, leading to some distinctly unexciting set pieces. NF

Last of the High Kings, The

(1995, Ire/GB/Den, 104 min)
d David Keating. *p* Tim Palmer. *sc* David Keating, Gabriel Byrne. *ph* Bernd Heinl. *ed* Ray Lovejoy [Humphrey Dixon]. *pd* Frank Conway. *m* Michael Convertino. *cast* Gabriel Byrne, Catherine O'Hara, Jared Leto, Christina Ricci, Colm Meaney, Stephen Rea, Lorraine Pilkington.
●Coming-of-age movie, produced and co-written by Gabriel Byrne, as fresh as a newly pulled pint of the dark stuff. Dublin, 1977: Thin Lizzy bestride the charts in black leather kecks, but for Frankie (Leto in a career-launching turn) exam results loom, girls seem unobtainable, and his mum's insistence that he's descended from the High Kings of Ireland doesn't really help. A familiar mix, but the fashions are suitably terrifying, the cynicism about 'Oirish' bullshit is refreshing, and there's a neat cameo from Stephen Rea as the taxi driver who's 'had 'em all' in his cab. TJ

Last of the Mohicans, The

(1992, US, 122 min)
d Michael Mann. *p* Michael Mann, Hunt Lowry. *sc* Michael Mann, Christopher Crowe. *ph* Dante Spinotti. *ed* Dov Hoenig, Arthur Schmidt. *pd* Wolf Kroeger. *m* Trevor Jones, Randy Edelman. *cast* Daniel Day Lewis, Madeleine Stowe, Russell Means, Eric Schweig, Jodhi May, Steven Waddington, Wes Studi, Maurice Roëves, Patrice Chereau.
●Set in the mountainous frontier wilderness of the colony of New York in 1757, this charts the role played by Hawkeye (Day Lewis) in the complex war waged between the English and the French and their respective allies among both settlers and Indians. Adopted as a child by the Mohican Chingachgook (Means) after his white settler parents were killed, Hawkeye belongs to neither one culture nor the other. Similarly, he is both warrior and peacemaker; and it is this dichotomy which simultaneously alienates him from the English military and wins him the love of the colonel's daughter (Stowe). While few would deny the impressive spectacle Mann provides in some truly magnificent battle scenes, criticisms have been levelled at the way the film changes from a historically accurate account of the war into a full-blown love story. Indeed, it is best seen as an epic romantic adventure of a sort seldom executed with much intelligence these days. As such, Mann's characteristic mix of rousing, profoundly physical action, lyrical interludes, and strikingly stylish imagery, serves to create superior mainstream entertainment. (From the novel by James Fenimore Cooper.) GA

Last of the Red Hot Lovers

(1972, US, 98 min)
d Gene Saks. *p* Howard W Koch. *sc* Neil Simon. *ph* Victor J Kemper. *ed* Maury Winetrobe. *ad* Ben Edwards. *m* Neal Hefti. *cast* Alan Arkin, Sally Kellerman, Paula Prentiss, Renee Taylor, Bella Bruck.
●From a Neil Simon play about a conventionally married 40-year-old proprietor of a fish restaurant who finds himself wanting to have an affair. He borrows his old mum's apartment and lures various ladies there, all of whom – wait for it – turn out to have 'impossible' hang-ups, and none of whom he actually screws. A few laughs are wrung out of the situation, and Sally Kellerman provides more as a raunchy lady on a fish diet, but it's all 'heart', of course. Pretty dire.

Last Orders

(2001, GB/Ger, 110 min)
d Fred Schepisi. *p* Fred Schepisi, Elisabeth Robinson. *sc* Fred Schepisi. *ph* Brian Tufano. *ed* Kate Williams. *pd* Tim Harvey. *m* Paul Grabowsky. *cast* Michael Caine, Tom Courtenay, David Hemmings, Bob Hoskins, Helen Mirren, Ray Winstone, JJ Feild, Cameron Fitch, Nolan Hemmings, Anatol Yusef, Kelly Reilly, Stephen McCole.
●Schepisi's adaptation of Graham Swift's Booker-winning tale of three old Bermondsey chums' drive to Margate to bury the ashes of their old mucker and drinking partner, Jack Dodds, is richly entertainment. Sober, even elegiac in tone, and elegantly shot in 'Scope, the film attempts to flesh out in full these Londoners' lives by the accretion of detail, history and context. To that end, it uses – problematically – continual flashback to show significant scenes from the lives of the principals, their wives and their families, from their youthful hop-picking escapades in the '30s, through the war, to the present (the late '80s). At the film's heart is an attempt to suggest the extraordinary nature of ordinary people, and if it fails to achieve profundity, it still makes for one of the most rewarding and authentic depictions of/tributes to the Cockney way of life in recent years. Caine (butcher Jack), deflecting his almost iconic status, modulates vitality with obduracy and pathos; Winstone (Jack's gabby car-salesman son, who chauffeurs) is his usual easeful self; while Courtenay (fair undertaker Vic) and Hemmings (volatile ex-boxer Len) make a highly enjoyable pair of opposites. The revelations are, however, Hoskins (gambler and divorcee Ray) and Helen Mirren (Jack's wife, whom Ray has always loved), whose scenes together have a quiet depth that overshadows all else. WH

L.A. Story

(1991, US, 95 min)
d Mick Jackson. *p* Daniel Melnick, Michael Rachmil. *sc* Steve Martin. *ph* Andrew Dunn. *ed* Richard A Harris. *pd* Lawrence Miller. *m* Peter Melnick. *cast* Steve Martin, Victoria Tennant, Richard E Grant, Marilu Henner, Sarah Jessica Parker, Susan Forristal, Kevin Pollak, Rick Moranis.
●Nothing's going right for wacky TV weatherman Harris K Telemacher (Martin): out of a job, madly in love, he pines for dippy English journalist Sara (Tennant). But she's contemplating a reconciliation with her ex-husband (Grant), prompting Telemacher to embark on a hopeless affair with bimbette SanDeE* (Parker, wonderful). Steve Martin's script, a delightfully scatty account of life in the city of angels, exposes romance lurking beyond the snobbish restaurants and routine muggings; while British director Jackson conjures a lush vision that makes Los Angeles appear positively exotic. Rising above mundane reality, Telemacher is further confused during mystical communication with the electronic freeway information sign; and after a tour of the mock period architecture, there's a strange encounter with Rick Moranis's mock-Cockney gravedigger. Ultimately, the transforming powers of love infuse the whole with a sense of wonder. CM

Last Picture Show, The

(1971, US, 118 min, b/w)
d Peter Bogdanovich. *p* Stephen J Friedman. *sc* Larry McMurtry, Peter Bogdanovich. *ph* Robert Surtees. *ed* Donn Cambern. *pd* Polly Platt. cast Timothy Bottoms, Jeff Bridges, Cybill Shepherd, Ben Johnson, Cloris Leachman, Ellen Burstyn, Eileen Brennan, Clu Gulager, Sam Bottoms, Randy Quaid.
●Bogdanovich may have proved a wayward disappointment, but along with *Targets* this is a reminder that somewhere inside him the man has talent. Adapted from Larry McMurtry's novel, it tells of the problems of adolescence in a small roadside town in 1950s Texas. Sexual intrigue, the disillusionment of growing up, and gentle humour are common enough in many similar films. But where Bogdanovich scores is in his accurate depiction of period and place, so detailed as to be almost tangible, and in the unbridled sympathy he extends to his characters. The closing of the local cinema signifies the end of both personal and historical eras, but characteristically its function is never that of forced symbolism. In fact, the nostalgia for a simpler, quieter age is equally conveyed by the style of the film, which recalls nothing so much as the emotionally draining dramas of John Ford. Superb performances all round add to the charm of this fine, if now unfashionable film. GA

Last Plane Out

(1983, US, 92 min)
d David Nelson. *p* Jack Cox. *sc* Ernest Tidyman. *ph* Jacques Haitkin. *cast* Jan-Michael Vincent, Julie Carmen, Mary Crosby, David Huffman, William Windom, Lloyd Battista.
●Produced by Dallas newspaperman Jack Cox in a bid to shoulder his way into that elite corps of journalists whose names have outlasted the Big Story that made them – in Cox's case, Nicaragua. We first see him (Vincent) on assignment in 1978, the palmy days before the storm when his friendship with General Somoza eases his way in a difficult country. Months later he returns to the same country now frenziedly at war with itself, to discover that the same friendship makes him a target for Sandinista guerillas. Although purportedly based on Cox's story, what we get is largely the usual mundane journalistic fantasy of fast living and slow sex in foreign climes while the realities of the situation go hang. Somoza is shown as an avuncular nice guy pining for a plebiscite; the Sandinistas as bloodthirsty curs. Heady days for Cox, perhaps, but for us the tension hardly mounts. FD

Last Princess of Manchuria, The

see Kawashima Yoshiko

Last Resort

(2000, GB, 77 min)
d Pawel Pawlikowski. *p* Ruth Caleb. *sc* Pawel Pawlikowski, (co-writer) Rowan Joffe. *ph* Ryszard Lenczewski. *ed* David Charap. *pd* Tom Bowyer. *m* Max de Wardener, Rowan Oliver. *cast* Dina Korzun, Paddy Considine, Artiom Strelnikov, Lindsey Honey, Perry Benson, Dave Bean, Adrian Scarborough.
●Tanya (Korzun) and son Artiom (Strelnikov) arrive at Stansted airport from Moscow but don't get past immigration. Her fiancé never shows. She claims political asylum. The pair are dumped in Stonehaven (aka Margate) in midwinter, where they are expected to subsist on vouchers until their case can be considered. But the desolation of this grey open prison (Britain is made to look like the old Eastern Bloc) is not allowed to overshadow a tentative, tender courtship between Tanya and a sympathetic local bingo caller Alfie (Considine). Compassion, it seems, tempers the Polish-born director's fiery conviction. TCh

Last Rites

(1988, US, 103 min)
d Donald P Bellisario. *p* Donald P Bellisario, Patrick McCormick. *sc* Donald P Bellisario. *ph* David Watkin. *ed* Pembroke J Herring. *m* Bruce Broughton. *cast* Tom Berenger, Daphne Zuniga, Chick Vennera, Anne Twomey, Paul Dooley, Dane Clark.
●As a priest and the son of a mob boss, Berenger is caught between 'family' codes of honour and a higher authority when he shelters a young woman (Zuniga) whose name is on a Mafia hit list. Needless to say, the pair fall in love in this contrived plod of a thriller. An MGM picture sent straight to video on both sides of the Atlantic. TJ

Last Run, The

(1971, US, 99 min)
d Richard Fleischer. *p* Carter De Haven Jr. *sc* Alan Sharp. *ph* Sven Nykvist. *ed* Russell Lloyd. *ad* Roy Walker, José Maria Tapiador. *m* Jerry Goldsmith. *cast* George C Scott, Tony Musante, Trish Van Devere, Colleen Dewhurst, Aldo Sambrell.
●Scott as an ageing Chicago gangster, once an ace wheelman for the syndicate who, with wife run off and child dead, comes out of morose retirement (in Portugal) to do one last job and prove to himself, etc etc. Huston and Boorman both opted out of directing, not surprisingly given the sententiously overstated script, which is always laboriously explaining things you've already guessed for yourself. But the action sequences are fine, so is Scott, and Sven Nykvist's camera-work is great. TM

Last Seduction, The

(1993, US, 110 min)
d John Dahl. *p* Jonathan Shestack. *sc* Steve Barancik. *ph* Jeffrey Jur. *ed* Eric L Beason. *pd* Linda Pearl. *m* Joseph Vitarelli. *cast* Linda Fiorentino, Peter Berg, Bill Pullman, JT Walsh, Bill Nunn, Herb Mitchell.
●When Wendy (Fiorentino) arrives out of the blue in a small, cow-country town near Buffalo, New York, the locals – notably Mike (Berg) – don't know what's hit them. She's smart, sexy, refuses to use the customary verbal niceties, and can twist the male population round her little finger. More importantly, unknown to Mike, who soon falls in love with her, she's not Wendy but Bridget, in hiding from husband Clay (Pullman), ever since she ran out on him, taking the entire proceeds of a drug deal he'd almost died perpetrating. And that's just the start of this tortuous, well-acted, witty, crisply photographed and immensely enjoyable thriller. GA

Last September, The

(1999, Fr/Ire/GB, 103 min)
d Deborah Warner. *p* Yvonne Thunder. *sc* John Banville. *ph* Slawomir Idziak. *ed* Kate Evans. *pd* Caroline Amies. *m* Zbigniew Preisner. *cast* Maggie Smith, Michael Gambon, Jane Birkin, Fiona Shaw, Lambert Wilson, David Tennant, Richard Roxburgh, Keeley Hawes, Tom Hickey, Gary Lydon.
●Neil Jordan, one of the exec producers, suggested that Elizabeth Bowen's novel about the twilight of the Ascendancy in Ireland would be ideal for the first film of Deborah Warner, esteemed theatre and opera director. In the event, she has surrounded herself with the very best, developing the screenplay with John Banville, and drawing on cinematography and music from two of Kieslowski's former collaborators. Casting, too, for this story of the Anglo-Irish aristocracy in the autumn of 1920 is exemplary: Smith as the imperious lady of the manor, Gambon as the husband who's not quite as vague as he seems, Shaw the 'bohemian' vamp of a houseguest who sees through all of them. The centre of attention, however, is newcomer Hawes as Smith's young

charge, whose yearning for excitement sees her torn between a British army officer and a notorious Republican terrorist. The film delivers quality performances and creates a suitably persuasive country house setting in which events unfold, but surprises are few on this well trodden ground, and the insights are hardly devastating. Though Warner does some eccentric things with the camera, she mainly concentrates on giving the actors their due. Against such competition, Hawes' trembling between passion and reticence looks accomplished indeed. TJ

Last Snows of Spring, The (L'Ultima Neve di Primavera)

(1973, It, 91 min)
d Raimondo del Balzo. *p* Enzo Doria. *sc* Antonio Troisio, Raimondo del Balzo. *ph* Roberto D'Ettorre Piazzoli. *ed* Angelo Curi. *pd* Gisella Longo. *m* Franco Micalizzi. *cast* Bekim Fehmiu, Agostina Belli, Renato Cestié, Nino Segurini, Margherita Horowitz.

● A 10-year-old boy starts to die of neglect when his widowed father spends too much time forsaking his parental duties in favour of playboy activities and a jet-set life-style. With the onset of leukaemia remorse comes by the bucketful, ending with a particularly grisly final trip to the fairground. Never have the artifacts of high living seemed so unattractive, or a film looked so much like somebody's holiday snaps. More of the same was provided by *Last Moments* the following year.

Last Starfighter, The

(1984, US, 101 min)
d Nick Castle. *p* Gary Adelson, Edward O Denault. *sc* Jonathan Betuel. *ph* King Baggot. *ed* C Timothy O'Meara. *pd* Ron Cobb. *m* Craig Safan. *cast* Lance Guest, Dan O'Herlihy, Catherine Mary Stewart, Barbara Bosson, Norman Snow, Robert Preston.

● Turning to his favourite video game for solace after everything's gone wrong, Alex Rogan (Guest) finds that the game is a sophisticated recruitment aid for the galactic equivalent of the RAF. By beating the high score, he gets whisked off to shoot the baddies out of the cosmos and save our sector of the universe. All pretty preposterous stuff, but it doesn't take itself seriously for one moment, and even aspires to a gentle parody of the genre. The special effects are mind-expanding: computer-generated animation that is so good it's barely distinguishable from the conventional kind. Great fun, with some truly comical moments; a must for pulp-heads and video-junkies. DPe

Last Summer

(1969, US, 97 min)
d Frank Perry. *p* Alfred Crown, Sidney Beckerman. *sc* Eleanor Perry. *ph* Gerald Hirschfeld. *ed* Marion Kraft. *ad* Peter Dohanos. *m* John Simon. *cast* Richard Thomas, Barbara Hershey, Bruce Davison, Cathy Burns, Ralph Waite, Ernesto Gonzalez, Conrad Bain.

● One of those winsome, nostalgic beach movies (this one has a wounded seagull). Four gawky teenagers spend the summer on Long Island, learning the usual, bittersweet rites-of-passage lessons about life, love and loyalty. Director Perry was renowned for the way he probed human relationships. He's helped here by an insightful script adapted by his wife Eleanor Perry from a novel by Evan Hunter. The acting is also a cut above the average: Cathy Burns, who's since disappeared without trace, was Oscar-nominated for her depiction of a troubled adolescent. GM

Last Summer in the Hamptons

(1995, US, 108 min)
d Henry Jaglom. *p* Judith Wolinsky. *sc* Henry Jaglom, Victoria Foyt. *ph* Hanania Baer. *ed* Henry Jaglom. *ad* Bruce Postman, Jeff Monte. *cast* Victoria Foyt, Viveca Lindfors, Jon Robin Baitz, Savannah Smith Bouchér, Roscoe Lee Browne, André Gregory, Melissa Leo, Roddy McDowall, Martha Plimpton.

● Marginally less irritating than most of Jaglom's work, this nevertheless concerns a gallery of characters you'd probably hate to spend more than a couple of minutes with, let alone a whole weekend in the country: namely, three generations of a pretentious, bitchy theatrical dynasty dominated by matriarch Lindfors, playing host to various friends, including Foyt, a successful but none too respected Hollywood actress hoping to make it as a serious actress. As they mingle, fuck, discuss art and sex, and shift allegiances, Jaglom offers a few insights into family tensions and the relationship between theatre and life, but the attempts at comedy are mostly embarrassing, and the whole thing is typically indulgent. GA

Last Sunset, The

(1961, US, 112 min)
d Robert Aldrich. *p* Eugene Frenke, Edward Lewis. *sc* Dalton Trumbo. *ph* Ernest Laszlo. *ed* Edward Mann, Michael Luciano. *ad* Alexander Golitzen, Alfred Sweeney. *m* Ernest Gold. *cast* Kirk Douglas, Rock Hudson, Dorothy Malone, Carol Lynley, Joseph Cotten, Regis Toomey, Neville Brand, Jack Elam, Rad Fulton.

● Aldrich's film is in some senses an attempt to transpose to the Western genre the elements of Sirkian melodrama – same studio, similar casting, and a plot about sexual neurosis. Kirk Douglas is an unstable gunfighter who has murdered Sheriff Hudson's brother-in-law and wants to revive his own love for his ex-wife (Malone). At the same time, Douglas' daughter (Lynley) falls in love with her estranged father, and Malone falls in love with Hudson. Those tensions are resolved during a cattle drive from Mexico to Texas. The movie is more lyrical than Aldrich's usual macho posturings, and Dalton Trumbo's script is abrim with classical allusions. ATu

Last Supper, The (La Ultima Cena)

(1976, Cuba, 113 min)
d Tomás Gutiérrez Alea. *p* Santiago Llapur, Camilo Vives. *sc* Tomás González, María Eugenia Haya, Tomás Gutiérrez Alea. *ph* Mario García Joya. *ed* Nelson Rodriguez. *ad* Carlos Arditti. *m* Leo Brouwer. *cast* Nelson Villagra, Silvano Rey, Luis Alberto García, José Antonio Rodriguez, Samuel Claxton, Mario Balmaseda.

● A brilliant Godardian parable, reflecting the contemporary Cuban situation through a tale of a slave revolt on a sugar plantation in late 18th century Havana (historically, the moment when the old slave-based industry was under pressure from the new mechanised European techniques of sugar refining, and when the heady scent of freedom was sniffed in the air). The action takes place over the days of Easter, culminating when a rich, fanatically religious landowner reconstructs the Last Supper with twelve slaves. But when the slaves' response theatens his economic interests, the pious Christian suppresses the uprising. This complex indictment of religious hypocrisy and cultural colonisation reflects the same subtlety as Alea's earlier *Memories of Underdevelopment*. LM

Last Supper, The

(1995, Can, 96 min)
d Cynthia Roberts. *p* Greg Klymkiw. *sc* Hillar Liitoja, Greg Klymkiw, Cynthia Roberts. *ph* Harald Bachmann. *ed* Cynthia Roberts, Su Rynard. *ad* Wendy White, Hillar Liitoja. *m* Nicholas Sterling. *cast* Ken McDougall, Jack Nicholsen, Daniel MacIvor.

● An unflinching portrait of a man's final hours. The camera never leaves the room where Chris, withered by AIDS, wishes his life to be terminated after a last supper with his partner (Nicholsen). It's a tribute to Roberts and McDougall (who died four days after filming) that the film's power derives less from the latter's physical condition than from his persisting dignity. In body, Chris looks and sounds barely human; in spirit, he transcends his affliction, particularly in two set-pieces: a dance he performs, with white death-mask and carnations, to 'Dido's Lament' (a riveting sequence that puts the comparable scene in *Philadelphia* in the shade), and the candle-lit song during which he passes away. A simple but devastating study of the human condition in extremis: grit your teeth and go see. NB

Last Supper, The

(1995, US, 91 min)
d Stacy Title. *p* Matt Cooper, Larry Weinberg. *sc* Dan Rosen. *ph* Paul Cameron, Teresa Medina. *ed* Luis Colina. *pd* Linda Burton. *m* Mark Mothersbaugh. *cast* Cameron Diaz, Ron Eldard, Annabeth Gish, Jonathan Penner, Courtney B Vance, Jason Alexander, Nora Dunn, Charles Durning, Bill Paxton, Ron Perlman.

● A mordant black comedy with a sharp political edge: If you could go back to 1919 and meet Hitler, would you kill him? This ethical conundrum preoccupies a group of liberal grad students after an unexpected dinner guest turns violent and ends up fertilising the tomato plants. Why shouldn't humanists be more pro-active, they reason, inviting a string of rightwing reactionaries to a hearty last meal. It falls apart, but the cool cast and caustic script will leave most right-thinking people well satisfied. TCh

Last Tango in Paris

(1972, It/Fr, 129 min)
d Bernardo Bertolucci. *p* Alberto Grimaldi. *sc* Bernardo Bertolucci, Franco Arcalli. *p* Vittorio Storaro. *ed* Franco Arcalli. *pd* Ferdinando Scarfiotti, Maria Paola Maino. *m* Gato Barbieri. *cast* Marlon Brando, Maria Schneider, Maria Michi, Cathérine Allégret, Marie-Hélène Breillat, Catherine Breillat, Jean-Pierre Léaud, Darling Legitimus, Catherine Sola, Mauro Marchetti.

● 'Even if a husband spends two hundred fuckin' years, he's never going to comprehend his wife's true nature,' says Brando, and in reaction to her death he establishes an anonymous, masturbatory relationship with Schneider in an empty Paris apartment. The resentment of his observation suggests that the film is less about coming together than about more private, chauvinist obsessions: partly about Bertolucci's overriding desire to love every image to death and indulge his doubts about the role of director in movie-making (through the whole Léaud subplot). But mostly the film is Brando's, his comeback after too many bad movies. The monumental narcissism is still there, coupled with the inability to take himself seriously – no one else could play a death scene concentrating on removing the gum from his mouth. Against him, Schneider hasn't a chance, which says a lot about the imbalances of the film; Bertolucci doesn't seem too interested in her either. CPe

Last Temptation of Christ, The

(1988, US/Can, 163 min)
d Martin Scorsese. *p* Barbara DeFina. *sc* Paul Schrader. *ph* Michael Ballhaus. *ed* Thelma Schoonmaker. *pd* John Beard. *m* Peter Gabriel. *cast* Willem Dafoe, Harvey Keitel, Paul Greco, Steven Shill, Verna Bloom, Barbara Hershey, Roberts Blossom, Barry Miller, Irvin Kershner, André Gregory, Harry Dean Stanton, David Bowie.

● Neither blasphemous nor offensive, this faithful adaptation of Nikos Kazantzakis' book sees Christ torn between divine destiny and an all too human awareness of pain and sexuality, departing most dramatically from the gospels in the last 40 minutes, a clearly fantastic sequence in which Jesus is led from the cross by an angel who offers him a normal life as husband and father. The performances – especially Keitel (Judas) and Bowie (Pontius Pilate) – are excellent; the recreation of biblical times is effective and plausible; and the percussive ethnic score for the most part admirably complements the superb photography. The dialogue, however, is often astonishingly banal and the miracles mundane. More seriously, Scorsese fails to illuminate the soul of Christ – essentially what the film is all about. Nevertheless, it remains a sincere, typically ambitious and imaginative work from America's most provocatively intelligent film-maker. GA

Last Time I Committed Suicide, The

(1996, US, 93 min, b/w & col)
d Stephen Kay. *p* Edward Bates, Louise Rosner. *sc* Stephen Kay. *ph* Bobby Bukowski. *ed* Dorian Harris. *pd* Amy Ancona. *m* Tyler Bates. *cast* Keanu Reeves, Thomas Jane, Claire Forlani, Gretchen Mol, Adrien Brody.

● The credits of this likeable, but lightweight feature, describe it as 'based on a letter from Neal Cassady' and boasts Carolyn Cassady as consultant: indeed, it comes across as a bebop-influenced, free-form mood piece, spun off this source, delineating the life of the guy who was later to prove beat 'genius' Jack Kerouac's major inspiration. The time is 1946, a period of hard readjustment, and fresh out of Leavenworth, hipster Cassady (Jane) is dreaming of kids and picket fences with suicidal girlfriend Joan (Forlani), but spending what spare time is left over from the graveyard shift at the tyre company shooting pool with dissolute Harry (Reeves). It's a film of bits and pieces, with the evidently talented first-time director going for atmospheric flourishes, cutting in slo-mo sequences and jagged hand-held shots, seemingly modelled on jeans ads, alongside back lighting and superimpositions. As a portrait of a 'cool dude', it's a mite self-conscious – and sidesteps Cassady's bisexuality – but it exudes energy and sympathy, and the performances are winning. WH

Last Time I Saw Paris, The

(1954, US, 116 min)
d Richard Brooks. *p* Jack Cummings. *sc* Julius J Epstein, Philip G Epstein, Richard Brooks. *ph* Joseph Ruttenberg. *ed* John Dunning. *ad* Cedric Gibbons, Randall Duell. *m* Conrad Salinger. *cast* Elizabeth Taylor, Van Johnson, Donna Reed, Walter Pidgeon, Eva Gabor, Kurt Kasznar, Roger Moore.

●Despite a very corny script from Julius and Philip Epstein which borrows clichés from Casablanca and countless 'American in Paris' yarns, this remains an enjoyable (if heavy-handed) melodrama. Van Johnson wants to be the next Hemingway, but while he's a prodigious drinker, he doesn't show much ability as a writer. Taylor, looking unbelievably glamorous, is his long-suffering wife. Pidgeon steals the show as her father, a penniless chancer who still manages to live the good life. (Began life as a Scott Fitzgerald story.) GM

Last Train from Gun Hill

(1959, US, 98 min)
d John Sturges. *p* Hal B Wallis. *sc* James Poe. *ph* Charles Lang Jr. *ed* Warren Low. *ad* Hal Pereira, Walter Tyler. *m* Dimitri Tiomkin. *cast* Kirk Douglas, Anthony Quinn, Carolyn Jones, Earl Holliman, Brad Dexter, Ziva Rodann, Brian Hutton.

●Douglas as the sheriff determined to take in the rapist who killed his wife, Quinn as the old friend who happens to be the delinquent's father and is equally determined to stop him. An enjoyable Western, remarkably similar but much inferior to *3.10 to Yuma*, made a couple of years earlier. Vigorous performances, superb camerawork from Charles Lang and muscular direction are let down by a conventional script which creates characters without any real depth or resonance. TM

Last Train from Madrid, The

(1937, US, 78 min, b/w)
d James Hogan. *p* George M Arthur. *sc* Louis Stevens, Robert Wyler. *ph* Harry Fischbeck. *ed* everett Douglass. *m* Boris Morros. *cast* Dorothy Lamour, Lew Ayres, Gilbert Roland, Karen Morley, Lionel Atwill, Helen Mack, Robert Cummings, Anthony Quinn, Olympe Bradna, Evelyn Brent, Lee Bowman.

●The Spanish Civil War is pressganged as a backdrop for this atrocious farrago of love, duty and tearful self-sacrifice in which assorted characters jockey for the limited number of permits which will enable them (or loved ones) to take the last train out of war-torn Madrid. Roland and Quinn are army officers, now on opposite sides, who once swore an oath of comradeship; Lamour is the woman they both love; Ayres is an American journalist who falls for the daughter of a political activist executed as he arrived to interview him; Cummings is a callow soldier in love with a fallen woman, his innocence letting her hope for redemption. And so it goes, in a torrent of tawdry clichés, made no more palatable by inserted newsreel shots of the bombardment of Madrid. Roland, Quinn and Atwill give as sterling performances as their dialogue will permit; Lamour and Cummings challenge, respectively, for most zomboid and most embarrassing performance of the year. TM

Last Tycoon, The

(1976, US, 124 min)
d Elia Kazan. *p* Sam Siegel. *sc* Harold Pinter. *ph* Victor J Kemper. *ed* Richard Marks. *pd* Gene Callahan. *ad* Jack T Collis. *m* Maurice Jarre. *cast* Robert De Niro, Tony Curtis, Robert Mitchum, Jeanne Moreau, Jack Nicholson, Donald Pleasence, Ingrid Boulting, Ray Milland, Dana Andrews, Theresa Russell, John Carradine, Seymour Cassel, Anjelica Huston.

●Another episode in Hollywood's belated love affair with Scott Fitzgerald, this takes his unfinished novel about the movie colony in the '30s and goes for quality at the risk of squeezing the life out of the picture. It's often pretty ponderous despite a Pinter script, especially the protracted central relationship between quizzically intense, hot-shot producer De Niro and a wispy unknown (Boulting). But De Niro proves again how well he can carry a part, and is particularly good in scenes dealing with the day-to-day business of movie-making. For once a starry cast pulls its weight; when all else fails they at least remain interesting, mainly because Kazan's direction favours the actors at the expense of anything else. Although uneven, the result is still a lot better than Hollywood's last look at itself (*Day of the Locust*) and its last slice of Fitzgerald (*The Great Gatsby*). CPe

Last Unicorn, The

(1982, US, 93 min)
d/p Arthur Rankin Jr, Jules Bass. *sc* Peter S Beagle. *ph* Hiroyasu Omoto. *ed* Tomoko Kida. *pd* Arthur Rankin Jr. *m* Jimmy Webb. *cast* voices: Alan Arkin, Jeff Bridges, Mia Farrow, Tammy Grimes, Angela Lansbury, Christopher Lee, Keenan Wynn.

●Rather groovy little fable, based on Peter Beagle's fantasy about a unicorn's search for company (there are no singles bars in fairy-tales), that overcomes the Disney influence with some acid characterisation of the baddies (in particular Mommy Fortuna, a warty witch, and the mythical Harpy, whom legend or the animators have seen fit to give three tits). Some horrific moments, too (the mark of the best fairytales), and some sublimely witty lines, as when a bungling magician, caught in the branches of a tree that he has brought to amorous life, cries, 'Oh my God, I'm engaged to a Douglas Fir!' FD

Last Valley, The

(1970, GB, 129 min)
d /p/sc James Clavell. *ph* John Wilcox. *ed* John Bloom. *ad* Peter Mullins. *m* John Barry. *cast* Michael Caine, Omar Sharif, Florinda Bolkan, Nigel Davenport, Per Oscarsson, Arthur O'Connell, Madeline Hinde, Ian Hogg, Vladek Sheybal, Jack Shepherd.

●Turgid epic set in the 23rd year of the Thirty Years War (that's 1641, to save you looking it up) in which Cockney Caine leads his troops into a fertile valley which, just for once, they decide not to pillage. Reason? Caine has met refugee philosopher Omar Sharif and they've reached a mutual understanding. Clear-as-mud plotting and Tower of Babel accents don't help the allegory to make its point. A solid snore. MA

Last Voyage, The

(1959, US, 91 min)
d Andrew L Stone. *p* Andrew L Stone, Virgina Stone. *sc* Andrew L Stone. *ph* Hal Mohr. *ed* Virginia Stone. *cast* Robert Stack, Dorothy Malone, George Sanders, Edmond O'Brien, Woody Strode, Jack Kruschen.

●Disaster for the passengers and crew of a luxury liner when an exploding boiler blows a hole in her side and it's all boats away. A certain realism is ensured by using the Ile de France on her way to the scrap-yard. But with Dorothy Malone trapped in her cabin and gurgling just above the waterline through the frenzied rescue operations, what price anything but absurdity along with the tension? TM

Last Wagon, The

(1956, US, 99 min)
d Delmer Daves. *p* William Hawks. *sc* James Edward Grant, Delmer Daves, Gwen Bagni Gielgud. *ph* Wilfred M Cline. *ed* Hugh S Fowler. *ad* Lyle Wheeler, Lewis H Creber. *m* Lionel Newman. *cast* Richard Widmark, Felicia Farr, Susan Kohner, Tommy Rettig, James Drury, Timothy Carey, Nick Adams.

●Like *Broken Arrow*, a liberal Western, but contriving some complexity around the Widmark character: the son of a white missionary brought up by Comanches, he exacts revenge on the four brothers who raped and killed his Indian wife and children, falls in with the more or less racist members of a wagon train, and is left with the survivors on his hands after an Indian attack. Stylishly directed, superbly shot on location, and with a first-rate performance from Widmark, it retains a certain fascinating ambiguity: its hero, displaying an inflexible sense of purpose and charismatic qualities of leadership, could equally well be defined as an embryo Fascist. TM

Last Waltz, The

(1978, US, 117 min)
d Martin Scorsese. *p* Robbie Robertson. *ph* Michael Chapman, Laszlo Kovacs, Vilmos Zsigmond, David Myers, Bobby Byrne, Michael Watkins, Hiro Narita. *ed* Yeu-Bun Yee, Jan Roblee. *pd* Boris Leven. *cast* The Band, Bob Dylan, Joni Mitchell, Neil Diamond, Emmylou Harris, Neil Young, Van Morrison, Muddy Waters, Dr John, Ronnie Hawkins.

●An embellished record of The Band's farewell concert, mostly shot at San Francisco's Winterland in 1976, on a set borrowed from a local opera company. Largely wonderful music, a stage crowded with guests from Dr John to Muddy Waters, and consummately stylish film-making. Scorsese intersperses it with fragments of interview, shot around pool tables and in bars, treating Robbie Robertson and the others for all the world like refugees from one of his own movies. TR

Last Warrior, The

see Flap

Last Wave, The

(1977, Aust, 106 min)
d Peter Weir. *p* Hal McElroy, Jim McElroy, Jim McElory. *sc* Peter Weir, Tony Morphett, Petru Popescu. *ph* Russell Boyd, Ron Taylor, George Greenough, Klaus Jaritz. *ed* Max Lemon. *pd* Goran Warff. *m* Charles Wain. *cast* Richard Chamberlain, Olivia Hamnett, David Gulpilil, Frederick Parslow, Vivean Gray.

●Weir up to his usual tricks with 'civilised' man coming up against an alien, apparently less rational, society. In this case it's Chamberlain's white liberal lawyer who, in defending a group of Aborigines accused of murder, stumbles across a world of ritual mysteries and prophecies of apocalyptic proportions. From the opening scene, in which an inexplicable and ferocious hailstorm hits Sydney, Weir creates an impressively unsettling atmosphere; sad, then, that all the stuff about primeval voodoo is both simplistic and patronising. Even sadder, however, is the final, climactic image, in which the threat to civilisation as we know it is presented in the form of a puddle shot through a fish-eye lens. GA

Last Winter, The (Hakhoref Ha'Acharon)

(1983, Isr, 89 min)
d Riki Shelach Nissimoff. *p* Ya'akov Kotzky. *sc* John Herzfeld. *ph* Amnon Solomon. *ed* Kavin Connor. *ad* Ofer Lalush. m Nahum Heyman. *cast* Yona Elian, Kathleen Quinlan, Stephen Macht, Zippora Peled, Michael Schneider.

●Tel Aviv, autumn, 1973. During a hiatus in the Yom Kippur war, two soldiers' wives (Quinlan and Elian) anxiously awaiting news from the front are thrown together when each identifies the same man as her husband in a blurred film of PoWs. Tracing their relationship from initial hostility to mutual support, *Last Winter*, filmed in English, is rather blander than its subject matter might lead you to expect. The director, himself a war veteran, carefully skirts controversy, keeping political events strictly as background colour to the human interest angle; and after teasingly suggesting an erotic attraction between the women, has Quinlan seal their bond by 'loaning' the widowed Elian her husband for a night. Still, it's tasteful, workmanlike, and a reminder that the Israeli cinema can produce something else besides Popsicles. SJo

Last Woman, The (L'Ultima Donna)

(1976, It/Fr, 109 min)
d Marco Ferreri. *p* Edmondo Amati. *sc* Marco Ferreri, Rafael Azcona, Dante Matelli. *ph* Luciano Tovoli. *ed* Enzo Meniconi. *ad* Michel de Broin. *m* Philippe Sarde. *cast* Gérard Depardieu, Ornella Muti, David Biggani, Michel Piccoli, Renato Salvatori, Giuliana Calandra, Zouzou, Nathalie Baye.

●If Paul Morrissey's *Flesh* had examined any of the many questions it raised instead of simply parading them like fashions, it might well have turned into something like Ferreri's movie. Here the boyish male sex object is Depardieu, but both he and the women in his life are painfully conscious that man cannot live by his cock alone; his wife (Zouzou) has turned feminist and left him; his girlfriend (Muti) is frigid, somewhat neurotic, and very unsure of herself; and Depardieu, whose ideal is a life of eating, fucking and sleeping, is finally driven to self-mutilation in his inability to live up to his own patriarchal image of himself. It's as fraught and desperate as it sounds, and as laboriously worked out as you'd expect from the director of *La Grande Bouffe*; as there, though, the freshness of the performances just about makes the pessimism tolerable. TR

Last Woman on Earth, The

(1958, US, 71 min)
d/p Roger Corman. *sc* Robert Towne. *ph* Jacques R Marquette. *ed* Anthony Carras. *m* Ronald Stein. *cast* Anthony Carbone, Betsy Jones-Moreland, Edward Wain [Robert Towne].

● Anybody impressed with Robert Towne's scripts for movies like *Chinatown* and *The Last Detail* will be interested to catch up with *The Last Woman on Earth*, his first script for Corman. Ineffably pretentious, the movie sends its three unsympathetic characters skin-diving while the nuclear holocaust breaks; they emerge from the waves to fight out a momentous ménage à trois in a deserted Puerto Rico. Most striking features are the ultra-ripe dialogue and the jaundiced view of pre-nuclear society. TR

Last Year in Marienbad

see Année Dernière à Marienbad, L'

Last Yellow, The

(1999, GB/Ger, 94 min)
d Julian Farino. *p* Jolyon Symonds. *sc* Paul Tucker. David Odd. *ed* Pia Di Ciaula. *pd* John Paul Kelly. *m* Adrian Johnston. *cast* Mark Addy, Charlie Creed-Miles, Samantha Morton, Kenneth Cranham, Alan Atherall, Glen Cunningham, James Hooton, Emil Marwa.

● The Leicester film industry rolls on! After *The Girl with Brains in Her Feet* comes director Farino's gentle comedy thriller. Mother's boy and self-professed ex-SAS man Frank (Addy) is employed by new chum Kenny (Creed-Miles), simpleton brother of wheelchair-bound Keith (Hooton), to kill the Cockney nasty responsible for the latter's condition. This is a game of two legs: the first, at home, 40 minutes of nicely played if routine observational comedy, trading on the delights of nondescript Leicester council estates, cheap B&Bs and working men's clubs; the away leg sees the pair coaching down to Polanski territory as their intended hit in South London proves more complex than envisaged. The film is an audacious, if not always credible attempt to break away from the clichés of macho Tarantino-like thrillers in favour of gentler, more ironic characterisations, but despite strong performances, it never entirely frees itself from TV associations. In adapting his stage play, Paul Tucker has exposed its holes – the proud provincial bias, affectionate in the first half, feels parochial in the second. The absence of sentimentality is impressive, however, and the film is full of unexpected charms. WH

Las Vegas Story, The

(1952, US, 88 min, b/w)
d Robert Stevenson. *p* Robert Sparks. *sc* Earl Felton, Harry Essex. *ph* Harry J Wild. *ed* George Shrader. *ad* Albert S D'Agostino. Feild Gray. *songs* Hoagy Carmichael, Harold Adamson. *cast* Jane Russell, Victor Mature, Vincent Price, Hoagy Carmichael, Brad Dexter, Jay C Flippen.

● A minor RKO gem showing all the preferences of its then owner Howard Hughes (aeroplanes, brunettes, breasts and disenchanted heroes). Jane Russell, with amused detachment, plays a singer returning to Las Vegas with wealthy but despicable husband Price in tow, and picking up with her erstwhile lover, hunky Mature. Initially the script relies on innuendo-laden repartee and a couple of wonderful numbers from Hoagy Carmichael. But then a man is murdered, the pace changes, and the film charges into a superb action climax with a helicopter swooping through deserted hangars and Mature making a fifty-foot leap (to save Jane, of course). It all finishes with a perfunctory nod toward family values (by marrying off an irrelevant young couple), but the film wears its intentions on its sleeve with the final shot: Hoagy looks first at the seductive Russell, then winks at us as he sings, 'My resistance is low…' HM

Late August, Early September (Fin août, début septembre)

(1999, Fr, 111 min)
d Olivier Assayas. *p* Georges Benayoun, Philippe Carcassonne. *sc* Olivier Assayas. *ph* Denis Lenoir. *ed* Luc Barnier. *pd* François-Renaud Labarthe. *cast* Mathieu Amalric, Virginie Ledoyen, Jeanne Balibar, François Cluzet, Jeanne Balibar, Alex Descas, Arsinée Khanjian, Nathalie Richard, Mia Hansen-Løve.

● From the Ozu-like title, referring to a timespan of a little over a year, one might divine that writer/director Assayas is interested in mood, character and maturity. In the wake of their break-up, Gabriel and Jenny (Amalric and Balibar) attempt to sell their flat; Gabriel moves on to the sexy Anne (Ledoyen), while Jenny seems to want him back. Their mutual friendship with the writer Adrien (Cluzet) affords contrasting perspectives on their progress, especially when Adrien falls ill, forcing his younger companions to deal with their dependency on him. Assayas has a recognisable vision of a world – late twenty-somethings running around, stumbling into careers they're unsure of, falling into relationships they're not committed to – but he lets the story happen offscreen. Chapter headings and fade-outs bookend brief, elliptical snatches of apparently mundane activities, posting oblique updates on matters of life and death. It's a bit like a Woody Allen film without the kvetching or the wisecracks, but younger and more vital. TCh

Late for Dinner

(1991, US, 93 min)
d WD Richter. *p* Dan Lupovitz, WD Richter. *sc* Mark Andrus. *ph* Peter Sova. *ed* Richard Chew, Robert Leighton. *pd* Lilly Kilvert. *m* David Mansfield. *cast* Brian Wimmer, Peter Berg, Marcia Gay Harden, Colleen Flynn, Kyle Secor, Michael Beach, Peter Gallagher, Bo Brundin.

● A dusty gas-guzzler slithers along a desert road. Frank (Berg) can't drive – he's not quite right in the head – but at least he doesn't have a bullet in his chest like his brother Willie (Wimmer). In the limbo of LA's sub-suburbs, these two hapless fugitives come to rest in the laboratory of one Doc Chilblains (Brundin), experimenter in cryonics. It is 1962. The next morning, it is 1991. Nonplussed, Frank maintains they must be late for dinner. The rest of the world supposes these defrosting hicks are simply out to lunch. This starts in quirky fashion, shifts into an amiable retread of *Back to the Future*, then trundles to a standstill on the home straight. Willie and Frank return to Santa Fe, an ageing wife (Harden) and grown-up child (Flynn), and suddenly it's terms of endearment time, a laborious restoration of family, hearth and home. Even if you can stomach this sentimental retardation, the film still manages to outstay its welcome. TCh

Late Marriage (Hatouna Mehuheret/Mariage tardiff)

(2001, Isr/Fr, 100 min)
d Dover Kosashvili. *p* Marek Rozenbaum, Edgard Tenembaum. *sc* Dover Kosashvili. *ph* Dani Schneor. *ed* Yael Perlov. *pd* Avi Fahima. *m* Joseph Bardanashvili. *cast* Lior Louie Ashkenazi, Ronit Elkabetz, Moni Moshonov, Lili Kosashvili, Aya Steinovits Laor, Rozina Cambos, Simon Chen.

● Zaza (Ashkenazi) is 31, unwed, and in most respects a pretty typical modern Israeli. But everyone else in his family is a stickler for Georgian tradition, and his parents are forever trying to hitch him up to some nice young Jewish virgin. They introduce him to some beauties, too, but still Zaza's uninterested. Is it possible none of the girls appeals, or is he too shy? Or might he be keeping a secret from his doting folks? Most immediately impressive is the remarkably assured negotiation of some audacious shifts in tone the film starts as a deliciously deadpan comedy of embarrassed manners, suddenly turns uncommonly erotic for the second act, then takes an even more unexpected twist for an emotionally forceful, morally sophisticated finale. Superbly acted all round, expertly paced and surprisingly graphic in places, this witty, provocative film transcends its specific cultural context to mount a universally relevant exploration of different kinds of love and responsibility. GA

Late Night Shopping

(2000, GB/Ger, 91 min)
d Saul Metzstein. *p* Angus Lamont. *sc* Jack Lothian. *ph* Brian Tufano. *ed* Justine Wright. *pd* Mike Gunn. *m* Alex Heffes. *cast* Luke de Woolfson, James Lance, Kate Ashfield, Enzo Cilenti, Heike Makatsch, Shauna MacDonald, Sienna Guillory.

● An easygoing first feature about a group of twenty-somethings 'trapped in a twilight world of permanent night work'. The director began his career as a runner on *Shallow Grave*, but the protagonists here are nothing like the characters in that film. Despite their unsocial hours, they're a curiously wholesome, good-looking bunch who while away their spare time drinking endless cups of coffee and cooking up romantic conspiracies. The inspiration was clearly *Diner*. The dialogue here doesn't come near Barry Levinson's heights and the film suffers from being set in nowhere-land (like where are we?), but it's an ingeniously shot and easy film to warm to. GM

Late Night Talks with Mother (Nocní Hovory s Matkou)

(2001, Czech Rep, 69 min, b/w & col)
d Jan Nemec. *p* Iva Ruszeláková, Jan Nemec. *sc/ph* Jan Nemec. *ed* Iva Ruszeláková. *m* Jan Nemec. *cast* Karel Roden, Zuzana Stivínová, Jan Nemec, Marta Kubisová, Václav Havel, Vera Jirousová, Ester Krumbachová.

● In his experimental, largely autobiographical digital diary-cum-essay, veteran director/musician Nemec rakes over memories and ideas as he wanders around Prague trying to explain himself to his dead mother. There is some interesting stuff here, including doctored footage Nemec shot during the Russian invasion, but his fish-eye lens-style images (he shot with a specially made camera), the squiggly music (his too), and the overall solemnity soon become irritating. GA

Late Show, The

(1977, US, 93 min)
d Robert Benton. *p* Robert Altman. *sc* Robert Benton. *ph* Charles Rosher Jr. *ed* Lou Lombardo, Peter Appleton. *pd* J Allen Highfill. *m* Ken Wannberg. *cast* Art Carney, Lily Tomlin, Bill Macy, Ruth Nelson, Howard Duff, Joanna Cassidy, Eugene Roche, John Considine.

● *The Late Show* pretty much divides its time between paying tribute to the private-eye films of the '30s and '40s, and undercutting its nostalgia with a sourer modern note. Carney plays an old, ulcerous 'eye' who gets involved in a complex plot set in modern Los Angeles. Nothing much has changed. The characters are fundamentally the same, and the story matters less than the people. Here, the central relationship develops between the laconic Carney and Tomlin's scatty, neurotic fast-talker. Benton's direction never entirely overcomes the character-acting styles of his stars (particularly Tomlin who, like many gifted impersonators, condescends towards her character). However, Benton's script hits a note of defensive humour that's just right in relation to the theme of urban loneliness. Some great lines and terrific wisecracks keep doubts at bay. All in all, maybe best seen…at a late show. CPe

Late Spring (Banshun)

(1949, Jap, 108 min, b/w)
d Yasujiro Ozu. *sc* Kogo Noda, Yasujiro Ozu. *ph* Yuharu Atsuta. *ed* Yoshiyasu Hamamura. *ad* Tatsuo Hamada. *m* Senji Ito. *cast* Chishu Ryu, Setsuko Hara, Yumeji Tsukioka, Haruko Sugimura, Hohi Aoki, Jun Usami, Kuniko Miyake.

● A widowed professor (Ryu) and his grown-up daughter (Hara) share a life of domestic tranquillity in a Tokyo suburb, but when he is made to realise that this girl should now be married, Ryu gently overrules her reluctance and arranges a suitable match – a Gary Cooper lookalike! Some rate this simple, affecting film even above *Tokyo Story*. Certainly it contains passages of great beauty and humanity, and there can be no faulting the heartbreaking performances of Ryu and Hara in roles very similar to the ones they play in the later picture. It was a favourite of the director's too (Ozu lived with his own mother throughout his life) – but it must be said that while the emotions are universal, the social customs which engender them seem more 'foreign' here than in most of the oeuvre. Hara's disgust at the thought that a widower should remarry, for example. Nevertheless, this is a remarkable, piercing film, and central to an understanding of Ozu's work. He tackled much the same story in colour in 1962's *An Autumn Afternoon*, his last film. TCh

Latin Boys Go to Hell

(1997, US/Ger/Sp/Jap, 70 min)
d Ela Troyano. *p* Jürgen Brüning. *sc* André Salas, Ela Troyano. *ph* James Carman. *ed* Brian Kates. *pd* Uzi Parnes. *m* John Zorn. *cast* Irwin Ossa, John Bryant Davila, Alexis Artiles, Mike Ruiz, Jennifer Lee Simard, Guinevere Turner.

● Imagine the matador sequence from *Pink Narcissus* mixed with all the elements of a particularly cheesy Spanish soap and you're halfway to picturing this send-up of Latin passions. A gay Mexican boy from Brooklyn falls for his straight cousin – and a hunky male model has his penis chopped off by his jealous lover and stuffed down his throat. The acting is wooden, the plot a mess, and the limits of the budget show. But the whole thing's so deliriously over the top, it hardly matters. PBur

Latino

(1985, US, 108 min)
d Haskell Wexler. *p* Benjamin Berg. *sc* Haskell Wexler. *ph* Tom Sigel. *ed* Robert Dalva. *ad* Fernando Castro. *m* Diane Louie. *cast* Robert Beltran, Annette Cardona, Tony Plana, Ricardo Lopez, Luis Torrentes, Juan Carlos Ortiz.

● After the impressive but inevitably compromised *Under Fire*, it's good to see a movie that deals with conflict in Central America with a real sense of commitment. Wexler's brazenly partisan film may lack the artistic sophistication of its mainstream counterparts, but it gains in power by focusing not on the familiar 'neutral' journalist/photographer figure, but on an invading American soldier, a Green Beret lieutenant (Beltran) drafted to Honduras to train a platoon of 'Contras' for secret raids on Nicaragua. There he becomes embroiled not only in the infliction of death, torture and US propaganda upon the Sandinistas, but in the contradictions of his position. First, he's a Latin American himself; second, he falls for a woman working in Honduras who hails from the village that is his prime target. Wexler's methods involve passion rather than 'balance': black-and-white moralising may occasionally be the result, but there's no denying the emotional punch dealt by the assured combination of taut narrative and intelligently researched context. GA

Laughing Policeman, The (aka An Investigation of Murder)

(1973, US, 112 min)
d/p Stuart Rosenberg. *sc* Thomas Rickman. *ph* David Walsh. *ed* Robert Wyman. *m* Charles Fox. *cast* Walter Matthau, Bruce Dern, Lou Gossett, Albert Paulsen, Anthony Zerbe, Val Avery, Clifton James.

● As police clinically and methodically follow up a multiple killing on a San Francisco bus, this adaptation of the Sjöwall/Wahlöö novel looks as if it's setting the record straight on recent cop films. But in its desire to make no concessions to *Dirty Harry* and its ilk, it destroys any potential interest with almost wilful perversity. Matthau's disgruntled cop, alienated from family and superiors, emerges as a tedious protagonist, relating to nothing, continually bored and boring. The plot hops around in an unengaging manner, while the excursions into the underworld (pimps, dopers, transvestites, Angels, etc) are patchily directed. Ironically, by the end, complete with car chase and split-second shooting, the film has become indistinguishable from all those movies it's trying so hard to disown. CPe

Laughter

(1930, US, 80 min, b/w)
d Harry D'Abbadie D'Arrast. *p* Monta Bell. *sc* Donald Ogden Stewart. *ph* George Folsey. *ed* Helene Turner. *cast* Nancy Carroll, Fredric March, Frank Morgan, Glenn Anders, Leonard Carey, Diane Ellis.

● Brilliant Donald Ogden Stewart script (his first, aside from one silent credit) about an ex-Follies girl who has snared her ageing millionaire, finds society stifling, and happily plays with the fire of old flames from her Bohemian days. Wittily acute in its insight into Bright Young Thing nihilism, the film anticipates Cukor's marvellous *Holiday* (also scripted by Stewart) in steering a precarious path between screwball comedy and darker abysses. If D'Arrast isn't quite Cukor, he is at least Lubitsch without the nudges. TM

Laughterhouse (aka Singleton's Pluck)

(1984, GB, 93 min)
d Richard Eyre. *p* Ann Scott. *sc* Brian Glover. *ph* Clive Tickner. *ed* David Martin. *ad* Jamie Leonard. *m* Dominic Muldowney. *cast* Ian Holm, Penelope Wilton, Bill Owen, Richard Hope, Stephen Moore, Rosemary Martin.

● When one of farmer Holm's pluckers loses a joint off his finger in the plucking machine and the TGWU block the transport of his Christmas geese to market, he determines to take them on foot from Norfolk to Smithfield. The anti-union stance is soon conveniently dropped as the trek turns into a protest against factory farming, with another bunch of media shits (cf *The Ploughman's Lunch*) tagging along for the story. Presumably intended as a tribute to the continuing virtues of British pluck, the result is rather more off-putting than stirring. The main problem is that Eyre, as in the past, seems unable to invest his characters with a modicum of sympathy. That the film should have been 'inspired' by Howard Hawks' *Red River* is a point best glossed over. Comparisons are indeed odious. JP

Laughter in Paradise

(1951, GB, 93 min, b/w)
d/p Mario Zampi. *sc* Michael Pertwee, Jack Davies. *ph* William McLeod. *ed* Giulio Zampi. *ad* Ivan King. *m* Stanley Black. *cast* Alastair Sim, Fay Compton, Beatrice Campbell, George Cole, Hugh Griffith, Joyce Grenfell, AE Matthews, John Laurie, Audrey Hepburn.

● After kicking the bucket Griffith has the last laugh on his grasping relatives, each of whom stands to inherit £150,000 if, and only if, they perform the unlikely tasks designated by the deceased. Mild-mannered Sim, for instance, mercilessly hen-pecked by the priceless Grenfell, has to get himself thrown in jail. This is one of the brighter moments in a movie that's saddled with too much plot and then has to grind a way through it. Fitfully felicitous though, with a glimpse of young Audrey Hepburn. TJ

Laughter in the Dark

(1969, GB/Fr, 104 min)
d Tony Richardson. *p* Neil Hartley. *sc* Edward Bond. *ph* Dick Bush. *ed* Charles Rees. *ad* Julia Trevelyan Oman. *m* Raymond Leppard. *cast* Nicol Williamson, Anna Karina, Jean-Claude Drouot, Peter Bowles, Siân Phillips, Sebastian Breaks.

● Despite being transplanted from the sado-masochistic gloom of the German '30s to the Swinging London of the '60s, this adaptation of Nabokov's teasingly perverse variation on the eternal triangle is not as bad as one might expect. It's shot as a series of brief, impressionistic scenes with Monteverdi tinkling tranquilly on the soundtrack: a style which works well at the beginning as the ageing art critic (Williamson, excellent) meets his cinema usherette (Karina) and finds her worming herself into his obsessions; and it serves at the end, when the critic, blinded after a lover's quarrel and believing himself alone with the repentant girl in a lonely villa, gradually realises that there is a third presence in the house, playing mocking games with him. In between times, though, the film sags horribly into all sorts of destructively non-Nabokovian vulgarities: a swinging party shot in swinging style, a surfeit of semi-nude couples cavorting on beds, etc. TM

Laura

(1944, US, 88 min, b/w)
d/p Otto Preminger. *sc* Jay Dratler, Samuel Hoffenstein, Betty Reinhardt, Ring Lardner Jr. *ph* Joseph La Shelle. *ed* Louis Loeffler. *ad* Lyle Wheeler, Leland Fuller. *m* David Raskin. *cast* Gene Tierney, Dana Andrews, Clifton Webb, Vincent Price, Judith Anderson, Dorothy Adams, James Flavin.

● Not just another *noir* classic of '44, Laura almost succeeds in pulling the screen apart at the seams, if only to stitch it together again in a visibly frantic finale. The narrator's a critic, the cop a would-be necrophiliac, and the femme fatale a faceless corpse…or are they? Less investigative thriller than an investigation of that genre's conventions – voyeurism (looking at, and for, Laura), a search for solutions (not just whodunit but whodunwhat), and the race against time (clues and clocks, fantasies and flashbacks) – the plot is deliberately perfunctory, the people deliciously perverse, and the *mise-en-scène* radical. (From the novel by Vera Caspary.) PK

Laura (Laura, les Ombres de l'Eté)

(1979, Fr, 100 min)
d David Hamilton. *p* Serge Laski, Malcolm James Thomson. *sc* Joseph Morhaim, André Szöts. *ph* Bernhard Daillencourt. *ed* Joële van Effenterre. *ad* Eric Simon. *m* Patrick Juvet. *cast* Dawn Dunlap, James Mitchell, Maud Adams, Maureen Kerwin, Pierre Londiche, Louise Vincent.

● Even cut for British release, *Laura* runs for 90 minutes. Mere moments into this soft focus, soft-core story of a talented sculptor and a young girl whose love overcomes her mother's objections, his blindness, and the law relating to sex with minors, you will grasp the importance of this piece of information: only paedophiles are likely to stay to the end. Priapic men and pubescent girls wrestling with Art, Love and each other in the exotic south of France may sound very merry; but wet people in an arid landscape don't add up to much more than muck, no matter how tastefully photographed. FD

Lautrec

(1998, Fr/Sp, 127 min)
d Roger Planchon. *p* Margaret Ménégoz. *sc* Roger Planchon. *ph* Gérard Simon. *ed* Isabelle Devinck. *ad* Jacques Rouxel. *m* Jean-Pierre Fouquey. *cast* Régis Royer, Elsa Zylberstein, Anémone, Claude Rich, Jean-Marie Bigard, Philippe Clay, Roger Planchon.

● Noticing only the melodramatic possibilities of Lautrec's life and taking no hint from the steady, unsentimental gaze of the paintings, Planchon's movie embraces the values of the average Hollywood telefeature. Everyone is madly Belle Epoque, rushing from the CanCan to the centre-fold-strewn brothel to another picnic on the banks of the Marne. Nothing remotely unexpected happens. As HTL, Royer is hopelessly miscast, to put it kindly. It's symptomatic that the Leg Situation is resolved by photographing him almost entirely from the waist up. BBa

Lava

(2001, GB, 99 min)
d Joe Tucker. *p* Michael Riley, Gregor Truter. *sc* Joe Tucker. *ph* Ian Liggett, Roger Eaton. *ed* St John O'Rorke. *pd* Philip Robinson. *m* Simon Fisher-Turner. *cast* Joe Tucker, James Holmes, Nicola Stapleton, Grahame Fox, Mark Leadbetter, Tameka Empson, Leslie Grantham, Tom Bell, Johann Myers.

● A simpleton whose brother has been brain-damaged in a beating teams up with a fantasist who claims to have served in the SAS to knock off the brute who did the beating. When they get to the guy's flat, they find his girlfriend home alone, so they tie her up and wait. That, in a nutshell is the plot of *Lava*, written, directed and starring Joe Tucker. It was also the plot of *The Last Yellow*, Julian Farino's 1999 black comedy, written by Paul Tucker – Joe's brother – based on his stage play. Any resemblance is presumably genetic. Okay, there are differences. Most obviously, *Lava* is set during the Notting Hill Carnival, making for bags of local colour, Yardie action and a kilo of cocaine. When you get right down to it, though, the drama basically takes place in a flat, and plays out as a mordant farce of mistaken identities, bloody pratfalls and unreliable firearms. Unfortunately, it peddles a leering, lewd and crude misanthropy for cheap frills and laffs. Tucker shuffles deference, bravado and bullets to fitfully amusing effect as the boastful Smiggy. As director, he aims for gross post-Tarantino highs, and misses. One positive point: Simon Fisher-Turner deserves singling out for his innovative and accomplished 'music and noise'. TCh

Lavender Hill Mob, The

(1951, GB, 78 min, b/w)
d Charles Crichton. *p* Michael Balcon. *sc* TEB Clarke. *ph* Douglas Slocombe. *ed* Seth Holt. *ad* William Kellner. *m* Georges Auric. *cast* Alec Guinness, Stanley Holloway, Sidney James, Alfie Bass, Marjorie Fielding, John Gregson, Clive Morton, Robert Shaw, Audrey Hepburn.
●Probably not the finest Ealing comedy (although it does include an astute parody of the car chase in Ealing's own *The Blue Lamp*), but still one of the few enduringly funny movies in British cinema. Seemingly mousy bank teller (Guinness) teams up with seedy entrepreneur (Holloway) and two Cockney spivs (Bass and James) to steal gold bullion and turn it into Eiffel Tower paperweights. It won a script Oscar for TEB Clarke, who divides his satirical jibes between the police, the press and the City. Come in late and you'll miss a glimpse, in the opening scene in Rio, of a young Audrey Hepburn. TR

Law and Disorder

(1958, GB, 76 min, b/w)
d Charles Crichton. *p* Paul Soskin, George Pitcher. *sc* TEB Clarke, Patrick Campbell, Vivienne Knight. *ph* Ted Scaife. *ed* Oswald Hafenrichter. *ad* Alan Harris. *m* Humphrey Searle. *cast* Michael Redgrave, Robert Morley, Elizabeth Sellars, Ronald Squire, George Coulouris, Joan Hickson, Lionel Jeffries, Brenda Bruce, John Le Mesurier, Irene Handl.
●Sub-Ealing caper from the regular team of Crichton and writer TEB Clarke (with help from Patrick Campbell): clergyman Redgrave is actually a crook who passes off his frequent spells inside as missionary trips to Africa, but when his innocent son gets a job assisting judge Morley, the swindler's underworld cronies snap into action to prevent the truth being revealed. Mild fun sustained by the usual slew of British character types. Based on the novel *Smugglers' Circuit* by Denys Roberts. TJ

Law and Disorder

(1974, US, 102 min)
d Ivan Passer. *p* William Richert. *sc* Ivan Passer, William Richert, Kenneth Harris Fishman. *ph* Arthur J Ornitz. *ed* Anthony Protenza. *ad* Gene Rudolf. *m* Andy Badale. *cast* Carroll O'Connor, Ernest Borgnine, Karen Black, Anne Wedgeworth, Anita Dangler, Leslie Ackerman, Rita Gam.
●Passer's first American film is an engaging and remarkably successful, if lightweight, merger of the Czech comedy of social observation with the American police vigilante genre. It's framed against the background of a disintegrating New York residential district, whose inhabitants join the Auxiliary Police unit in an attempt to preserve a veneer of civilisation. There's a deliciously broad parody performance from Karen Black (a Monroe send-up) as a hairdresser given to slanging her customers, and Passer reveals a natural delight in perceiving the comedy inherent in all forms of pomp and ceremony. The emotional judgment is more problematic, especially in the final escalation towards tragedy; but despite its unevenness the film is refreshingly entertaining, and the blue-collar ambience is stunningly well used. VG

Law and Jake Wade, The

(1958, US, 86 min)
d John Sturges. *p* William Hawks. *sc* William Bowers. *ph* Robert Surtees. *ed* Ferris Webster. *ad* William A Horning, Daniel B Cathcart. *cast* Robert Taylor, Richard Widmark, Patricia Owens, Robert Middleton, Henry Silva.
●A highly watchable Western – probably Sturges' best – stunningly shot by Robert Surtees, and with an excellent script by William Bowers (*The Gunfighter, Support Your Local Sheriff*) which breathes new life into the old yarn about the outlaw-turned-sheriff (Taylor) trying to resist the blandishments of a former colleague he rescues from hanging (Widmark), who then relentlessly tries all he knows to coax/force his old buddy into helping him locate the whereabouts of the buried proceeds of a bank robbery they pulled. Widmark (especially) and Taylor are both excellent, and the climactic Indian attack (with shoot-out) in a ghost town is superbly staged. TM

Law and Order

(1969, US, 81 min, b/w)
d/p/sc Frederick Wiseman. *ph* William Brayne. *ed* Frederick Wiseman.
●One of the best of Wiseman's documentaries, an impressionistic account of the daily police routine in a predominantly black neighbourhood of Kansas City, Missouri. Although violence abounds, with a black prostitute almost strangled by a vice-squad cop, the film avoids grinding axes about police brutality. Instead, sitting back and coolly observing the situation from multiple perspectives, it suggests that any sickness in the forces of law and order is a symptom of disease in the society that breeds them. TM

LA Without a Map

(1998, GB/Fr/Fin/Luxembourg, 107 min)
d Mika Kaurismäki. *p* Julie Baines, Sarah Daniel, Pierre Assouline. *ph* Michel Amathieu. *ed* Ewa J Lind. *pd* Caroline Hanania. *m* Sebastien Cortella. *cast* David Tennant, Vinessa Shaw, Vincent Gallo, Julie Delpy, Cameron Bancroft, Joe Dallesandro, Anouk Aimée, Saskia Reeves, Leningrad Cowbows, Amanda Plummer, Jerzy Skolimowski, Don Ranvaud.
●A brief encounter, after a funeral, with vivacious Californian Barbara (Shaw) induces Bradford undertaker and obituary scribe Richard (Tennant) to quit his job and steady girlfriend for Los Angeles – and, perhaps, a dream screenwriting career. Barbara, however, is a bit iffy about his unexpected arrival at the restaurant where she waitresses. While she likes her limey admirer, she's anxious his presence might spoil her relationship with director Patterson (Bancroft), whose proprietorial desire for her could be a passport to an acting career. Pretty soon, Richard's jealousy is almost as strong as the nagging fear that he'll never really fit in in Tinseltown. Mika Kaurismäki's film, which he adapted with Richard Rayner from the latter's book, is a light, lively culture clash/meeting cute caper that never quite fulfils its promise. The pacing's perky enough for there always to be something to distract from the fact that, both as social satire and sentimental odyssey, the film's seldom as sharp as it might be. The problem, regrettably, lies with the choice of lead: Tennant is too weak to convince as someone who'd act so impulsively, let alone to engage our sympathies. Meanwhile, the affectionate and usually appropriate movie references are entertaining, but too liberally scattered. GA

Lawless, The (aka The Dividing Line)

(1949, US, 83 min, b/w)
d Joseph Losey. *p* William H Pine, William C Thomas. *sc* Geoffrey Homes. *ph* J Roy Hunt. *ed* Howard Smith. *ad* Lewis H Creber. *m* Mahlon Merrick. *cast* MacDonald Carey, Gail Russell, Lalo Rios, John Sands, Lee Patrick, John Hoyt, Argentina Brunetti, Martha Hyer.
●Losey's second feature, a lynching drama set in a small Southern Californian town beset by racial tensions: local newspaper reporter (Carey), after conquering self-interest under pressure from the girl he loves (Russell), crusades on behalf of a Mexican youth (Rios) falsely accused of having raped a 'white' girl. So far, so conventional, but what gives it an edge of brilliance is Losey's eye for the smalltown locations: the shabby dance hall in the Mexican quarter, the sleepy high street, the one-horse newspaper office, the cosy front porches and the churchgoers, all swept away in sudden primitive starkness as the fugitive is relentlessly hunted over a fantastic wasteland of rocks and rubble. The film also fairly reeks of fear, doubtless a testament to the HUAC witch-hunts, but beautifully woven into Daniel Mainwaring's script in a complex pattern (not just the racial divide, suspicion of the outsider or of anyone challenging the status quo, but the sexual anxieties that drive the 'white' youths to macho bravado in invading the Mexican dance-hall, the fear of losing his job that makes the reporter try to turn a blind eye, and so on). TM

Lawless Heart, The

(2001, GB/US, 100 min)
d Neil Hunter, Tom Hunsinger. *p* Martin Pope. *sc* Neil Hunter, Tom Hunsinger. *ph* Sean Bobbit. *ed* Scott Thomas. *pd* Lynne Whiteread. *m* Adrian Johnston. *cast* Bill Nighy, Douglas Henshall, Tom Hollander, Clémentine Célarié, Ellie Haddington, Sukie Smith, Josephine Butler, Stuart Laing.
●This witty, warm and imaginative British movie uses an ingenious triple-perspective story structure to chart the effects of a man's death on his brother-in-law, his lover and his long lost friend. Set in and around the small towns, farmland and estuaries of the Essex coast, the film is as perceptive and precise about the society it depicts as it is about indvidual emotions. That said, it never feels parochial; think Rohmer or Altman or, at a pinch, Winterbottom's *Wonderland*. GA

Lawless Street, A

(1955, US, 78 min)
d Joseph H Lewis. *p* Harry Joe Brown. *sc* Kenneth Gamet. *ph* Ray Rennahan. *ed* Gene Havlick. *ad* George Brooks. *m* Paul Sawtell. *cast* Randolph Scott, Angela Lansbury, Warner Anderson, Jean Parker, Wallace Ford, John Emery, Ruth Donnelly, Michael Pate.
●The first, and better, of the two colour Westerns Lewis made with Scott, this may lack the bizarre originality of *7th Cavalry* but certainly makes up for it in solid craftsmanship and vivid characterisation. Scott is the marshall, about to retire, who'd like to rid the town of its rowdy, gun-totin' villains before throwing in the towel; the job is complicated, however, by his involvement with faithless music-hall chanteuse Lansbury, whose fickle ways weaken his resolve. Strikingly shot, tersely plotted, it's no masterwork, but once again reveals Lewis as a superior director of low-budget material. GA

Lawman

(1970, US, 99 min)
d/p Michael Winner. *sc* Gerald Wilson. *ph* Bob Paynter. *ed* Frederick Wilson. *pd* Stan Jolley. *m* Jerry Fielding. *cast* Burt Lancaster, Robert Ryan, Lee J Cobb, Sheree North, Joseph Wiseman, Robert Duvall, Albert Salmi, John McGiver, Richard Jordan.
●Typically ham-fisted Western from *Death Wish* Winner. Stoic lawman Lancaster arrives in the town of Sabbath on the trail of seven killers (carousing cowboys who accidentally caused the death of an old man); their protective boss, Cobb, and the town's lily-livered sheriff (Ryan) don't plan on giving him much help; neither do the townspeople. Would-be thoughtful Western which ultimately resorts to killing and ketchup to make up for its lack of style and originality. A remake of *Man with the Gun* (1955). NF

Lawn Dogs

(1997, GB, 101 min)
d John Duigan. *p* Duncan Kenworthy. *sc* Naomi Wallace. *ph* Elliot Davis. *ed* Humphrey Dixon. *pd* John Myhre. *m* Trevor Jones. *cast* Sam Rockwell, Christopher McDonald, Kathleen Quinlan, Bruce McGill, Mischa Barton.
●Rural Kentucky. Ten-year-old Devon (Mischa Barton, hypnotic) strikes up a dangerous friendship with Trent (Rockwell), a trailer-trash lawnmower man. Their bond is established early on: Trent stripping in a traffic jam to dive off a bridge into the river; Devon stripping off her nightdress to howl naked at the moon. He's literally an outsider, exiled before dusk from the suburban fortress whose lawns he keeps from growing wild; she's a metaphorical outsider, a sickly child who dreams of Baba Yaga and the fleeing girl who drops a comb and causes an impenetrable wood to spring up behind her. While innocent, Devon's proto-sexual adoration of Trent makes their relationship as uncomfortable for the viewer as for her hypocritically straight parents. When they're dancing on the roof of Trent's truck and mooning at the security guard, they're carefree kids; when they start to compare scars, it's childhood's end. Australian director John Duigan's best films have dealt with the passage from childhood to adolescence, and here, in his first US film (from British producer Duncan *Four Weddings* Kenworthy), he maintains an atmosphere where dream is a short step from nightmare. Quirkily haunting. DW

Lawnmower Man, The

(1992, GB/US, 108 min)
d Brett Leonard. *p* Gimel Everett. *sc* Brett Leonard, Gimel Everett. *ph* Russell Carpenter. *ed* Allan Baumgarten. *pd* Alex McDowell. *m* Jurgen Brauninger. *cast* Jeff Fahey, Pierce Brosnan, Jenny Wright, Mark Bringleson, Geoffrey Lewis, Jeremy Slate, Dean Norris, Colleen Coffey.
●The first feature film to explore the possibilities opened up by Virtual Reality is derived in part from a Stephen King story, merged with an

existing project. Using mentally retarded gardener Jobe (Fahey) as a guinea pig, mad scientist Dr Angelo (Brosnan) exposes him to Virtual Reality teaching technology and powerful drugs which accelerate his learning ability, transforming him into a calculating genius. But tampering by a mercenary Cybertech executive produces unforeseen and dangerous side effects. Despite the hackneyed sub-Frankenstein plot, the dazzling computer-generated special effects almost carry the film. The irony is that almost nothing that matters actually depends upon, or takes place within, Virtual Reality. Until the final showdown between Jobe and his creator, what we see is merely the way Jobe's exposure to Virtual Reality affects his behaviour in the real world. Only when he and the lubricious Marnie (Wright) suit up to enjoy 'cybersex' are the storyline and computer effects fused, like their fluid bodies, together. NF

Lawnmower Man 2: Beyond Cyberspace

(1995, US, 92 min)
d Farhad Mann. *p* Edward Simons, Keith Fox. *sc* Farhad Mann. *ph* Ward Russell. *ed* Peter Berger, Joel Goodman. *pd* Ernest Roth. *m* Robert Folk. *cast* Matt Frewer, Patrick Bergin, Austin O'Brien, Ely Pouget, Camille Cooper, Patrick le Brecque, Crystal Celeste Grant, Kevin Conway.

●Having jettisoned all but one of the original cast, this cynical sequel retreads familiar ground, provoking both disorientation and déjà vu. Simpleton gardener Jobe, last seen merging with the US phone system, has returned in physical form (instead of a virtual Jeff Fahey, we now have limbless *Max Headroom* star Frewer, who presumably came as a package with that show's director Farhad Mann). O'Brien's young, minor character Peter has been retained, however, as an identification figure for viewers who may buy the spin-off computer games. Nursed to health by Dr Cori Platt (Pouget), Jobe is then exploited by her evil boss Walker (Conway), who wants him to complete work on a powerful computer chip he's stolen from virtual reality genius Dr Benjamin Trace (Bergin). Walker plans to seize control of the Internet, but Jobe has grander ideas – to merge with, and become lord of, the virtual domain. But first he must crack the 'Egypt' code, incorporated into the chip by Trace to prevent such megalomaniac schemes. As before, almost nothing of significance takes place in cyberspace, the effects look disconcertingly artificial, and all trace of Stephen King's source story has been lost. NF

Law of Desire, The (La Ley del Deseo)

(1987, Sp, 100 min)
d Pedro Almodóvar. *p* Ester García. *sc* Pedro Almodóvar. *ph* Angel Luis Fernández. *ed* José Salcedo. *pd* Javier Fernández. *cast* Eusebio Poncela, Carmen Maura, Antonio Banderas, Miguel Molina, Manuela Velasco, Bibi Andersen, Fernando Guillén.

●Seventh feature by a Spanish writer/director hitherto unknown in this country: a lush, overblown, steamy, tragi-comedy murder thriller set in Madrid, there's something to offend and delight everyone. It opens intercutting between the filming, dubbing and première of one of fictional director/writer Pablo Quintero's homo-erotic movies. Pablo leaves the first-night party without his quasi-lover, Juan, who's straight and loves him dearly, but…desire's off his menu. Pablo sends Juan to the country to put distance between them, and a handsome stranger, Antonio, obsessed by the director, makes his move to fill the gap. Actress Tina, the director's sex-changed brother (the stupendous Carmen Maura), now a lesbian, has her own problems to deal with, plus her lover's precocious daughter. Pablo, Tina and Antonio take up their themes in a passionate fugue which accelerates fast. Wit, sex, drugs and topsy-turvy clichés abound; Almodóvar's sensuous style carries all before him. A life-affirming joy. TC

Law of Enclosures, The

(2000, Can, 111 min)
d John Greyson. *p* Damon D'Oliveira, John Greyson, Phyllis Laing. *sc* John Greyson, Dale Peck. *ph* Kim Derko. *ed* Michael Munn. *pd* Réjean Labrie. *m* Don Pyle, Andrew Zealley. *cast* Sarah Polley, Brendan Fletcher, Diane Ladd, Sean McCann, Kristen Thomson, Rob Stefaniuk, Shirley Douglas, Victor Cowie.

●Taken from a novel by writer/provocateur Dale Peck, this charts the 40-year decline of a marriage, from its inception at a moment of personal crisis (to the backdrop of constant Gulf War televisual bombardment) to a point, after decades of petty routine, habit and argument, at which the submerged love might just surface one last time. Typically Canadian in its fascination with a left-field view of the everyday, and with the impact of the media on psychology, the film shares something with Egoyan's *Exotica* in its use of time frames. Performances are on the whole convincing, but some slippages in character motivation affect audience empathy with figures who have to a great degree bought their problems upon themselves. Nevertheless, it's an intriguing if flawed adaptation. GE

Lawrence of Arabia 100 (100)

(1962, GB, 222 min)
d David Lean. *p* Sam Spiegel. *sc* Robert Bolt. *ph* Freddie Young. *ed* Anne V Coates. *pd* John Box. *m* Maurice Jarre. *cast* Peter O'Toole, Alec Guinness, Anthony Quinn, Jack Hawkins, Omar Sharif, Jose Ferrer, Anthony Quayle, Claude Rains, Arthur Kennedy, Donald Wolfit.

●Presented virtually as a desert mirage, this epic biopic of TE Lawrence constructs little more than an obfuscatory romantic glow around its enigmatic hero and his personal and political contradictions: Lean had obviously learned the 'value' of thematic fuzziness from the success of *Bridge on the River Kwai*, and duly garnered further Oscar successes here. Somewhere between Robert Bolt's literariness and Freddie Young's shimmering cinematography, there should be direction: all there is is a pose of statuesque seriousness. PT

Laws of Gravity

(1992, US, 98 min)
d Nick Gomez. *p* Bob Gosse, Larry Meistrich. *sc* Nick Gomez. *ph* Jean de Segonzac. *ed* Tom McArdle. *pd* Monica Bretherton. *m* Douglas Cuomo. *cast* Peter Greene, Edie Falco, Adam Trese, Arbella Field, Paul Schulze, Saul Stein.

●We're back among the low-life on the mean streets of Brooklyn. Jimmy (Greene) and Jon (Trese) are two hustlers, the first under pressure from a loan-shark, the second so volatile he'll punch out anyone who annoys him, including girlfriend Celia (Field). Though hope springs eternal for the no-hoper men, Jimmy's wife (Falco) is tiring of it all, and when the guys get involved with gun-dealer Frankie (Schulze), tensions come to a head. Writer/director Gomez's first feature is nothing if not authentic. The performances are raw and itchy, the camerawork (by Jean de Segonzac) and cutting determinedly *vérité*, the script a frazzled blend of inconsequential character-chatter and aggressive outbursts. But if it's hard to fault the overall execution – the performances, especially, are solid – there's a problem that the film is so *familiar*. The pairing recalls early Scorsese, the gritty visual and verbal style Cassavetes. Efficient, but derivative. GA

Lawyer, The

(1968, US, 120 min)
d Sidney J Furie. *p* Brad Dexter. *sc* Sidney J Furie, Harold Buchman. *ph* Ralph Woolsey. *ed* Argyle Nelson Jr. *ad* Pato Guzman. *m* Malcoln Dodds. *cast* Barry Newman, Harold Gould, Diana Muldaur, Robert Colbert, Kathleen Crowley, Warren Kemmerling, EJ Andre.

●Remember *Petrocelli*, the mid-'70s TV series about a hip and groovy American lawyer? Well, it all started here in the movie version of the Dr Sam Sheppard murder case, where a hot shot attorney battles his way through legal technicalities and a difficult client to defend a doctor accused of killing his wife. Newman takes centre stage as the small town defence counsel grabbing his chance for national attention, though the proceedings go through some familiar moves. Watchable rather than scintillating. TJ

Laxdale Hall (aka Scotch on the Rocks)

(1952, GB, 77 min, b/w)
d John Eldridge. *sc* John Eldridge, Alfred Shaughnessy. *ph* Arthur Grant. *ed* Bernard Gribble. *ad* Ray Simm. *m* Frank Spencer. *cast* Ronald Squire, Kathleen Ryan, Raymond Huntley, Sebastian Shaw, Fulton MacKay, Prunella Scales.

●Amiable but uninvolving Ealing-esque comedy, adapted from Eric Linklater's novel, follows the clash between Hebridean car owners who refuse to cough up their road tax until the government actually builds a road on their island and the MPs who arrive to look into the matter. (Co-produced by John Grierson for Group 3.) TJ

Lazybones

see Hallelujah I'm a Bum

Lazybones

(1934, GB, 66 min, b/w)
d Michael Powell. *p* Julius Hagen. *sc* Gerard Fairlie. *ph* Ernest Palmer. *ed* Ralph Kemplen. *ad* James Carter. *cast* Ian Hunter, Claire Luce, Bernard Nedell, Michael Shepley, Sara Allgood, Bobbie Comber.

●Adapted from a play by Ernest Denny, this is a slow starter, with Hunter as an indolent baronet being urged by his impecunious family to marry an American heiress (Luce). He loves her, but scruples won't let him propose until he learns that she has lost all her money, whereupon he whisks her off to the registry office before his family can object. Complications arise, since she is led to believe he thought she was only pretending to have lost her money as a test; and her crooked cousin (Nedell) turns up to involve her in his theft of oil-related diplomatic papers from Hunter's brother-in-law (Shepley). Hereabouts, earlier moments of puckish humour escalate as Hunter rouses himself from his lethargy to resolve all problems; and graduate into dotty fantasy as he proves his ability to provide for a wife by turning his stately home into a 'Work Centre for the Wealthy Weary', where the idle rich can pay to enjoy honest toil as butlers, gardeners, etc. Modest but intelligently directed, the result is very engaging. TM

Leadbelly

(1976, US, 127 min)
d Gordon Parks. *p* Marc Merson. *sc* Ernest Kinoy. *ph* Bruce Surtees. *ed* Harry Howard. *pd* Robert Boyle. *m* Fred Karlin. *cast* Roger E Mosley, James E Brodhead, John McDonald, Earnest L Hudson, Dana Manno, Art Evans, Paul Benjamin.

●The casting of Roger Mosley, with his boyish good looks, forewarns of the total blandness of yet another tragic-black-musician biopic. While pretending to stress the realism of this version of the life of Huddie Ledbetter, Parks can't disguise the fact that the details of the black folk-hero's life have been laundered for the widest possible audience. Totally inexcusable, and downright offensive to the legacy of the man's music, is the re-recording of some of Leadbelly's best-known songs (emasculated vocals, string and woodwinds even). Best moments are some early scenes involving encounters with musicians from whom he learns humility: the anonymous old-timer who introduces him to the 12-string guitar, and his early travels with Blind Lemon Jefferson (well played by Art Evans). RM

Leading Man, The

(1996, GB, 100 min)
d John Duigan. *p* Bertil Ohlsson, Paul Raphael. *sc* Virginia Duigan. *ph* Jean-François Robin. *ed* Humphrey Dixon. *pd* Caroline Hanania. m Edward Shearmur. *cast* Lambert Wilson, Jon Bon Jovi, Thandie Newton, Anna Galiena, Barry Humphries, Patricia Hodge, Diana Quick, Harriet Walter, David Warner, Nicole Kidman.

●With Duigan directing a script by his sister Virginia, there's a whiff of indulgence about this backstage drama. A new play, 'The Hit Man,' is in rehearsal in London. Its author, Felix Webb (Wilson), is conducting a clandestine affair with ingénue Hilary (Newton), and he'd leave middle-aged wife Elena (Galiena) like a shot, if he thought she could handle it. Enter American movie star Robin Grange (Bon Jovi). He's the play's lead, but slyly offers to double as the wife's lover. Thisis watchable, but old hat. Duigan makes only token stabs at satirising the luvvies, despite the copious egos on hand and muted support from such troupers as Warner, Humphries, Hodge and Quick. TCh

Leaf on a Pillow (Daun Di Atas Bantal)

(1998, Indon, 83 min)
d Garin Nugroho. *p* Christine Hakim. *sc* Armantono, Garin Nugroho. *ph* Nur Hidayat. *ed* Sentot Sahid. *ad* Roedjito, Ong Heri Wahyu, Tonny Trimarsanto. *m* Djaduk Ferianto. *cast* Kancil, Sugeng, Heru, Christine Hakim.
●Producer Hakim is the only professional actor involved in Nugroho's quietly devastating account of the lives and deaths of street kids in Yogyakarta. She plays a market vendor of batik who sensibly refuses to be a surrogate mother to the homeless boys who subsist in the area – but anyway does her best to watch out for them. The film centres on the ways that three of the boys meet bad ends, but the plotting avoids melodrama and the staging avoids the clichés of docudrama; simply as a realist sketch of the ways these literally hopeless kids bond, compete, masturbate, sniff glue and reach for premature adulthood, the film is a landmark in East Asian cinema. Thanks to the overthrow of Suharto, it was the first of Nugroho's four features to get a general release in Indonesia – and was a huge success. TR

League of Gentlemen, The

(1960, GB, 113 min, b/w)
d Basil Dearden. *p* Michael Relph. *sc* Bryan Forbes. *ph* Arthur Ibbetson. *ed* John D Guthridge. *ad* Peter Proud. *m* Philip Green. *cast* Jack Hawkins, Richard Attenborough, Roger Livesey, Nigel Patrick, Bryan Forbes, Kieron Moore, Terence Alexander, Norman Bird, Robert Coote, Melissa Stribling, Nanette Newman, Gerald Harper.
●A terrific caper movie, adapted by Bryan Forbes from a novel by John Boland. Hawkins is at his gruff best as an embittered ex-army colonel who assembles a seven-man team of similarly disgruntled former military men to execute a million pound bank robbery. Plotting and direction are as rigorously organised as the operation itself, making this a crisply enjoyable picture with typically excellent character playing from a lovable set of old lags. TJ

League of Their Own, A

(1992, US, 128 min)
d Penny Marshall. *p* Robert Greenhut, Elliot Abbott. *sc* Lowell Ganz, Babaloo Mandel. *ph* Miroslav Ondricek. *ed* George Bowers. *pd* Bill Groom. *m* Hans Zimmer. *cast* Tom Hanks, Geena Davis, Lori Petty, Madonna, David Strathairn, Jon Lovitz, Garry Marshall, Rosie O'Donnell, Megan Cavanagh, Tracy Reiner.
●This fictionalised account of the All American Girls' Professional Baseball League (formed in 1943, with male players lost to the war) captures heartbreaks, home runs, and little vigour. Things start promisingly as a scout (Lovitz) scours the country recruiting players, including farm-girls Dottie and Kit (Davis and Petty), dance-hall hostess 'All the Way' Mae (Madonna) and bouncer Doris (O'Donnell). As they train, rivalries emerge, focusing too heavily on Kit's jealousy over sister Dottie's physical and social advantages. Marshall piles on the sentiment, notably in framing sequences which see the film unfold in flashback and culminate in a tearful reunion; even worse, scriptwriters Lowell Ganz and Babaloo Mandel neglect the ensemble, emphasising a sense of historical occasion over character development. As the cynical manager/coach who learns to love his team, Hanks has more to wrestle with, but Madonna makes do with a spot of dancing. CM

Leap into the Void (Salto nel Vuoto)

(1980, It/Fr, 120 min)
d Marco Bellocchio. *sc* Marco Bellocchio, Piero Natoli, Vincenzo Cerami. *ph* Giuseppe Lanci. *ed* Roberto Perpignani. *ad* Amedeo Fago, Andrea Crisanti. *m* Nicola Piovani. *cast* Michel Piccoli, Anouk Aimée, Michele Placido, Gisella Burinato, Antonio Piovanelli, Anna Orso.
●Bellocchio's quirky subversion of bourgeois family values revives all the strengths of two earlier works (*Fists in the Pocket* and *In the Name of the Father*) with its tale of a middle-aged, incestuously puritanical judge (Piccoli) gradually destroyed by the hesitant love affair between his sister (Aimée) and a young anarchist actor. The treatment is perhaps less cruel, but Bellocchio continues the stylisation and claustrophobia of his earlier images – and with them the debt to the wise, angry, anti-patriarchal cinema of Jean Vigo. CA

Leap of Faith

(1992, US, 108 min)
d Richard Pearce. *p* Michael Manheim, David V Picker. *sc* Janus Cercone. *ph* Matthew F Leonetti. *ed* Don Zimmerman, Mark Warner, John F Burnett. *pd* Patrizia von Brandenstein. *m* Cliff Eidelman. *cast* Steve Martin, Debra Winger, Lolita Davidovich, Liam Neeson, Lukas Haas, Meat Loaf, Philip Seymour Hoffman.
●Obviously seeking a role where he can seriously emote and turn in the goofy stuff as well, Martin has backed a loser in this confused spin on *Elmer Gantry*. His Jonas Nightengale is a cynical charlatan, whose travelling gospel revue mixes showbiz pizzazz and cracker-barrel sentiment to con gullible townsfolk out of their cash. Rustwater, Kansas, is the next Bible Belt burg on the hit-list, but Mr Ultra-cynical has to rethink his heartless cool when perky waitress Davidovich engages his romantic attentions, and her kid brother (Haas) starts to believe the showman-preacher can actually make him walk again. Pearce's uncertain entertainment builds a conscience-impaired comic creation from Martin's sham shaman, then asks us to give credence to his part in a sudden crop of bona fide 'miracles' – a dumb plot development as shamelessly manipulative as his earlier slick hick schtick. This is just nonsense, and the star, whose would-be spiritual patter looks like an over-extended sketch anyway, can't save it. TJ

Lease of Life

(1954, GB, 94 min)
d Charles Frend. *p* Michael Balcon. *sc* Eric Ambler. *ph* Douglas Slocombe. *ed* Peter Tanner. *ad* Jim Morahan. *m* Alan Rawsthorne. *cast* Robert Donat, Kay Walsh, Denholm Elliott, Adrienne Corri, Vida Hope, Richard Wattis.
●A Yorkshire parson (Donat) is given a year to live by his doctor, but conceals the news from his family in this tepid saga of conscience, written by Eric Ambler for Ealing. His remaining concern is to provide for daughter Corri, but the money for her musical scholarship will be harder to find when a contentious sermon loses him the opportunity of a better-paid post. Sincerity is never in doubt, but the drama's so low-key as to be almost non-existent. TJ

Leatherface: The Texas Chainsaw Massacre III

(1989, US, 81 min)
d Jeff Burr. *p* Robert Engelman. *sc* David Schow. *ph* James L Carter. *ed* Brent A Schoenfeld. *m* Jim Manzie, Pat Regan. *cast* RA Mihailoff, Kate Hodge, Ken Foree, Viggo Mortensen, William Butler, Joe Unger.
●Banned from general release by the BBFC on the grounds that it is excessively violent – and you'd have a hard time arguing the point. Blending the gritty, documentary quality of Tobe Hooper's original with the whacked-out psycho-comedy of Part II, Burr's darkly self-referential nightmare concerns a young couple's journey into the broiling Texan hinterlands, where Leatherface and his monstrously inbred companions await. Pursued by a jeepster from hell, covered in tanned and tortured human flesh, the 'normal' pair soon find themselves on the menu at a dinner engagement with the cannibal family: Leatherface, his two moronic brothers, feisty grandmother and corpulent grandfather, and the newest addition, a 12-year-old blond moppet who can't wait to get busy with the sledgehammer. While the on-screen gore is actually no more overt than in many mainstream horrors, what gives this its edge is the extent to which it revels in the atrocities depicted. A relentlessly sadistic and worryingly amusing movie, which will entertain and offend in equal measure. MK

Leave Her to Heaven

(1945, US, 119 min)
d John M Stahl. *p* William A Bacher. *sc* Jo Swerling. *ph* Leon Shamroy. *ed* James B Clark. *ad* Lyle Wheeler, Maurice Ransford. *m* Alfred Newman. *cast* Gene Tierney, Cornel Wilde, Jeanne Crain, Vincent Price, Mary Philips, Ray Collins, Gene Lockhart, Darryl Hickman.
●Wonderful all-stops-out melodrama (from a novel by Ben Ames Williams) drawing luridly on gimcrack psychology to tell the tale of a father-fixated girl (Tierney) who picks a husband because of his resemblance to Daddy, and is then gripped by a mounting paroxysm of jealousy which inclines her to dispose violently of anyone else laying claim to his affection. The potential for absurdity is enormous, not least in an unforgettable scene where Tierney roams the mountain-top on horseback at dawn (the colour, incidentally, is Fox-bright but exquisitely toned), scattering her father's ashes to the winds. But Stahl is totally in control, his precise pacing and compositions lending a persuasive dimension of *amour fou*, while Leon Shamroy's camerawork makes each image a purring pleasure on the eye. TM

Leaving (Bounce – Ko Gals)

(1997, Jap, 109 min)
d Masato Harada. *cast* Hitomi Sato, Yasue Sato, Yukiko Okamoto, Jun Murakami.
●The 'high gals' are Shibuya schoolgirls who finance their abortions, drug intake and desire for brand name fashions by hanging out – or having sex with – middle aged businessmen. Into town comes comparative innocent Lisa, about to fly off to New York the next day. After an appearance in a very softcore video goes wrong, she becomes embroiled with two high gals, not to mention a yakuza angry at the way the girls are deflecting business from his own professionals. Despite winning performances and a lively (if self-conscious) visual style, there's an air of hip posturing about this predictable, sporadically amusing urban fable. And even the bright surface can't prevent the narrative from congealing into sentimentality. GA

Leaving Las Vegas

(1995, US, 112 min)
d Mike Figgis. *p* Lila Cazes, Annie Stewart. *sc* Mike Figgis. *ph* Declan Quinn. *ed* John Smith. *pd* Waldemar Kalinowski. *m* Mike Figgis. *cast* Nicolas Cage, Elisabeth Shue, Julian Sands, Richard Lewis, Steven Weber, Valeria Golino, Ed Lauter, Mike Figgis, Danny Huston, Bob Rafelson.
●Alcoholic scriptwriter Ben (Cage) is blowing his options. Our first glimpse sees his beyond-niceties collaring of an agent friend in a smart restaurant to demand drink money, a symptomatic preamble to what's staring him in the face: a 'sadly, we have to let you go' dismissal from his studio job. Figgis sets the crap game running here: the pay-off finances a one-way ticket to oblivion or, to give hell its name, Las Vegas, city of permanent after-hours. Cash the cheque, burn the past, take the freeway – we're in the booze movie, that most fascinatingly flawed form of the modern urban tragedy. This modestly budget masterpiece pools the Vegas streets with reflected neon and watches Ben drown. Shue is good as the young hooker he falls for, but Cage is extraordinary, producing an Oscar-winning performance of edgy, utterly convincing suicidal auto-destruct. In fact, Figgis makes of him something of an existential saint, a man for whom terminal self-knowledge leads to a kind of grace. If the film lacks the depth and structural sophistication of, say, *The Lost Weekend* (it was shot fast, with Declan Quinn's saturated Super-16 photography blown up, which may explain its kinetic buzz), it certainly has the courage of its convictions. WH

Leaving Lenin (Gadael Lenin)

(1993, GB, 90 min)
d Endaf Emlyn. *p* Pauline Williams. *sc* Endaf Emlyn, Siôn Eiri. *ph* Ray Orton. *ed* Chris Lawrence. *ad* Vera Zelinskaya. *m* John ER Hardy. *cast* Sharon Morgan, Wyn Bowen Harries, Ifan Huw Dafydd, Steffan Trevor, Catrin Mai.
●A funny and arresting portrait of a group of Welsh sixth-formers accidentally left to fend for themselves in a St Petersburg where the dissolution of the old certainties has landed the local youth in pretty much the same position. Detached from their teachers by the uncoupling of a train, these strangers in a strange land are suddenly charged with defining their emotional independence amid the emergent bohemia of a city in transition. Shooting on the hoof in the new Russia, Emlyn's camera displays an equal sense of discovery, negotiating leafy backwaters where the errant staff face ideological and marital upsets of their own. Although the film assays a grandiose overview of the relationship between

artistic and personal freedoms, it works best as a witty but compassionate study of familiar types under pressure. Performed with assurance all the way, this is one to applaud. TJ

Leaving Normal

(1991, US, 110 min)
d Edward Zwick. *p* Lindsay Doran. *sc* Ed Solomon. *ph* Ralf D Bode. *ed* Victor Du Bois. *ad* Patricia Norris. *m* WD Snuffy Walden. *cast* Christine Lahti, Meg Tilly, Lenny Von Dohlen, Maury Chaykin, James Gammon, Patrika Darbo, Eve Gordon.

● *Thelma & Louise* without the turbo charge, this never seems certain where it's going. When Darly & Marianne set out on their voyage of self-discovery, their lives are a mess. Lahti's Darly is a brassy barmaid, as capable of putting her drunken customers down ('It takes more than two fingers to make me come') as of fireman's-lifting them outside. She seems to know where she's going, especially in comparison to Tilly's little-girl-lost Marianne. But on the road from Normal (Wyoming) to Alaska, it becomes clear that both are dominated by unresolved pain and unsuccessful relationships. The script, from *Bill and Ted* writer Edward Solomon, is full of detours where we meet enjoyably surreal supporting players who seem to have wandered in from a Lynch or a Waters movie. Solomon also supplies sharp lines, mostly to Lahti, who delivers them with great style. But there is a spurious mystical element, and this shunts the film off track in the direction of sentimentality, despite its quirky charm and photogenic locations. CO'S

Leaving No Trace

see Que no quede huella

Lebanon...Why? (Liban...Pourquoi?)

(1978, Leb/GB, 97 min)
d/p FN Georges Chamchoum. *ph* Vassilis Christomoglou. *ed* Marwan Akkawi, Bassem Abdallah. *m* Hussein Nazek.

● Lebanon... Why? is a pertinent and necessary question, given British TV's repeated simplification of the conflict into 'leftist Moslems versus rightist Christians'. The 'why' of Chamchoum's film, however, is unfortunately little more than an index of incomprehension, not a stimulus to analysis: this irritating documentary ends with the question rather than proceeding from it. Under the production circumstances, no one could reasonably expect a structured, fully coherent, text-book presentation, but that hardly excuses the editing strategy of fragmenting every interview, cutting fast between talking heads, the repeated use of redundant footage of gesturing fighters and scarred landscapes overlaid with a melodramatic score, or the tricksy effects of emotive freeze-frames. Indeed, most information has to be gleaned from the (added) English intertitles. PT

Leben ist eine Baustelle, Das

see Life Is All You Get

Lebenszeichen

see Signs of Life

Lebewohl Fremde

see Farewell, Stranger

Le Cop (Les Ripoux)

(1984, Fr, 107 min)
d/sc Claude Zidi. *ph* Jean-Jacques Tarbes. *ed* Nicole Saunier. *ad* Françoise De Leu. *m* Francis Lai. *cast* Philippe Noiret, Thierry Lhermitte, Régine, Grace De Capitani, Claude Brosset, Albert Simono, Julien Guiomar, Henri Attal.

● Corrupt Parisian cop René initiates naive police-academy graduate François (Lhermitte) into the advantageous corruption of the sleazy Goutte d'Or quarter in Paris, where shirts, meals, drink, whores and drugs are there for the taking – provided one turns a blind eye to certain criminal activities. Noiret is in his element as the slobbish René, Lhermitte's metamorphosis is nicely handled, and director Zidi's attention to the back-street milieu helps to sustain a believable air of comic amorality. NF

Le Cop 2 (Ripoux contre ripoux)

(1989, Fr, 108 min)
d Claude Zidi. *p* Pierre Gauchet. *sc* Simon Michael, Claude Zidi. *ph* Jean-Jacques Tarbes. *ed* Nicole Saunier. *ad* Françoise De Leu. *m* Francis Lai. *cast* Philippe Noiret, Thierry Lhermitte, Guy Marchand, Line Renaud, Grace De Capitani, Michel Aumont, Jean-Pierre Castaldi, Jean-Claude Brialy.

● A few droll set pieces, but on the whole this disappointing sequel is wretchedly put together. Lhermitte, as painfully couth as before, wants to go straight. To prove that Paris is universally crooked, his seasoned cop partner Noiret picks up a citizen at random, and within half-an-hour, a respectable banker (Brialy) has confessed to a long-forgotten misdemeanour. Regrettably, Zidi betrays this anarchic element for a contrived corruption and conspiracy scenario. For a black comedy, the film is unconscionably sentimental about prostitutes, horses and the countryside. Worst of all, it is maudlin towards its heroes. Noiret, a sharp fixer in the first film, looks ready to be put out to pasture, while Lhermitte proves unpersonable when asked to go beyond his straight man act. TCh

Lectrice, La

(1988, Fr, 98 min)
d Michel Deville. *p* Rosalinde Deville. *sc* Rosalinde Deville, Michel Deville. *ph* Dominique Le Rigoleur. *ed* Raymonde Guyot. *pd* Thierry Leproust. *cast* Miou-Miou, Régis Royer, Christian Ruché, Marianne Denicourt, Charlotte Farran, Maria Casarès, Pierre Dux, Patrick Chesnais.

● *La lectrice*, wonderfully played by Miou-Miou, is Constance, a girl who likes reading to her boyfriend in bed. One night she begins a novel by Raymond Jean called *La Lectrice*, whose leading character, Marie also likes reading... The camera follows Constance /Marie between the covers as she has social intercourse with four people who are disabled in some way: a boy in a wheelchair, a little girl whose mother is too busy to look after her, a bedridden war widow, an impotent company director. The texts chosen are appropriate (*L'Amant, Alice, War and Peace, Les Fleurs du Mal*). It becomes clear that each client is after attention of a different kind, but as soon as Marie plays along, a minor disaster ensues; only when she has to read the mucky Marquis to a geriatric judge does she begin to have doubts. This elegantly erotic and erudite games-playing has something for everyone: voyeurs will delight in the nudity, poseurs will prefer the many and various striking of attitudes, and penseurs will ponder on the way language is both a lexical and a sexual minefield. Set, too, against the beautiful wintry background of Arles as it contrasts with the colour-coded cast and the soundtrack of Beethoven sonatas. MS

Leda

see A Double Tour

Left Handed Gun, The

(1958, US, 102 min, b/w)
d Arthur Penn. *p* Fred Coe. *sc* Leslie Stevens. *ph* J Peverell Marley. *ed* Folmar Blangsted. *ad* Arthur Loel. *m* Alexander Courage. *cast* Paul Newman, John Dehner, Hurd Hatfield, Lita Milan, James Congdon, Colin Keith-Johnston, James Best, John Dierkes.

● Newman as Billy the mixed-up Kid, an ebullient young illiterate who takes to slinging a gun when his substitute father is killed, only to face another, sterner father figure. Endlessly fascinated by his own image, blindly following a death-wish to its logical conclusion, this Billy is very much of the rebel- without-a-cause breed, a hero unable to match up to his legend. Violent, stylised, occasionally top-heavy with symbolism (although the religious parallel is convincingly carried by Hatfield's marvellous performance as Billy's Judas disciple), *The Left Handed Gun* is a remarkable attempt to communicate an understanding (ours of Billy, his of himself) viscerally, felt through movement and gesture. Penn's first film, it is in many ways a key stage in the development of the Western. TM

Left-Handed Woman, The (Die linkshändige Frau)

(1977, WGer, 113 min)
d Peter Handke. *p* Wim Wenders. *sc* Peter Handke. *ph* Robby Müller. *ed* Peter Przygodda. *cast* Edith Clever, Bruno Ganz, Angela Winkler, Markus Mühleisen, Bernhard Minetti, Bernhard Wicki, Rüdiger Vogler, Michel Lonsdale, Gérard Depardieu.

● A train shatters the stillness of a Paris suburb, leaves a puddle on the station platform quivering with some unsolicited, mysterious, moving energy. This Romantic metaphor is at the very centre of Handke's grave, laconic film, produced by Wim Wenders, which begins where *The American Friend* left off: in the ringing void of Roissy airport. Here, the Woman (Edith Clever, superb in the role) meets her husband (Ganz) and, for no apparent reason, rejects him in favour of a solitary voyage through her own private void. In her house, with her child, the film records a double flight of escape and exploration, her rediscovery of the world, her relocation of body, home and landscape. This emotional labour makes its own economy: silence, an edge of solemnity, an overwhelming painterly grace. Self-effacement is made the paradoxical means of self-discovery, and the film becomes a hymn to a woman's liberating private growth, a moving, deceptively fragile contemplation of a world almost beyond words. CA

Left Hand of God, The

(1955, US, 87 min)
d Edward Dmytryk. *p* Buddy Adler. *sc* Alfred Hayes. *ph* Franz Planer. *ed* Dorothy Spencer. *ad* Lyle Wheeler, Maurice Ransford. *m* Victor Young. *cast* Humphrey Bogart, Gene Tierney, Lee J Cobb, Agnes Moorehead, EG Marshall, Benson Fong.

● Big, worthy production from Fox that looks like an all-out assault on the Oscars. Set in China in 1947, Bogart's an American ex-pilot on the run (posing as a Catholic priest) from Lee J Cobb's ruthless warlord. TJ

Left Luggage

(1997, Neth/Bel, 100 min)
d Jeroen Krabbé. *p* Ate De Jong, Hans Pos, Dave Schram. *sc* Edwin de Vries. *ph* Walther Vanden Ende. *ed* Edgar Burcksen. *ad* Hemmo Sportel. *m* Henny Vrienten. *cast* Isabella Rossellini, Maximilian Schell, Laura Fraser, Jeroen Krabbé, Marianne Sagebrecht, David Bradley, Adam Monty, Chaim Topol, Miriam Margolyes.

● Holland, 1972. To pay the rent, a young Jewish student protester (Fraser, effervescent) reluctantly takes a job as nanny with a Hassidic family and falls in love with their hitherto silent five-year-old son (Monty). She stays on for the boy's sake despite battling with the paterfamilias Mr Kalman (Krabbé) and the apartment's sneering janitor. As director, Krabbé refrains from giving the ever-darkening tale a portentous air. Furthermore, he shows a sure hand with the actors: coaching Rossellini to reveal a quietly humane, unglamorous stoicism as Mrs Kalman; keeping the freshness in Fraser's performance; and teasing fine cameos from Topol, as the girl's wise, reassuring friend Apfelschnitt. The trouble lies with the script (from Carl Friedman's novel *The Shovel and the Loom*), which propels the story like a fizzling three-stage rocket. It begins jauntily as a study of a young woman's search for self, before occupying itself with the relationship between the nanny and the sealed-off boy, and finally mutates into an examination of the divided wings within Jewry, using tragic events as a reminder of the shared history of suffering. WH

Left, Right and Centre

(1959, GB, 95 min, b/w)
d Sidney Gilliat. *p* Frank Launder, Sidney Gilliat. *sc* Sidney Gilliat, Val Valentine. *ph* Gerald Gibbs. *ed* Geoffrey Foot, Gerry Hambling. *ad* John Box. *m* Humphrey Searle. *cast* Ian Carmichael, Patricia Bredin, Alastair Sim, Eric Barker, Richard Wattis, Gordon Harker, Moyra Fraser, Irene Handl.

● More a mild sitcom than a political satire, since ideological breezes are conspicuously absent from the storm which brews when the Tory by-election candidate (peer's nephew and TV panellist) falls in love with his Labour rival (fishmonger's daughter and LSE student). Best moments come from Sim as a peer busily commercialising his stately home and counting the shekels. TM

Legacy

(1975, US, 90 min)
d/p Karen Arthur. *sc* Joan Hotchkis. *ph* John Bailey. *ed* Carol Littleton. *ad* Dixie Lee. *m* Roger Kellaway. *cast* Joan Hotchkis, George

McDaniel, Sean Allen, Dixie Lee, Richard Bradford III, Sarah Hotchkis.
●Superficially, there are resemblances to the Hollywood soap opera about the bored, anxiety-ridden wife, left alone to brood in her automated and luxurious household. However, with its edge of pain moving towards madness and suicide, and its sexual accuracy and eroticism, the film emerges as something fresher and truer. Despite being totally unsympathetic, the heroine increasingly engages our feelings with her intense frustration and rage. A small, claustrophobic work, and though the director tries to turn her heroine's anger into a metaphor for the death of an old America, its power derives from the raw image of a solitary woman, trapped and crying, 'I hate!' LQ

Legacy, The

(1978, GB, 102 min)
d Richard Marquand. *p* David Foster. *sc* Jimmy Sangster, Patrick Tilley, Paul Wheeler. *ph* Dick Bush, Alan Hume. *ed* Anne V Coates. *pd* Disley Jones. *m* Michael J Lewis. *cast* Katharine Ross, Sam Elliott, John Standing, Ian Hogg, Margaret Tyzack, Charles Gray, Lee Montague, Hildegard Neil, Roger Daltrey.
●A typically loony English-country-house horror from the pen of Jimmy Sangster, which dumps its statutory American leads (Katharine Ross and Sam Elliott) into a hardly-stirred plot-pot of diabolic conspiracy – and slowly congeals. In other words, the legacy in question is really the British industry's continuing forlorn attempt to crack the international market with a 'nowhere' story of an England where everything stops for tea, a Rolls prowls the leafy lanes, devoted rustic retainers do little but dispose of untidy corpses, and the dark family secret resides upstairs. And the true curse is that an actor of the calibre of Ian Hogg is limited to scowling from beneath a chauffeur's cap, and Charles Gray and Lee Montague have to affect hilarious Euro-accents, while the very presence of the Hollywood 'names' (plus a dreadful Roger Daltrey cameo) turns a hackneyed script into a 'package' with 'potential'. Horror, indeed. PT

Legal Eagles

(1986, US, 116 min)
d/p Ivan Reitman. *sc* Jim Cash, Jack Epps Jr. *ph* Laszlo Kovacs, Bill Butler. *ed* Sheldon Kahn, Pembroke J Herring, William Gordean. *pd* John F DeCuir. *m* Elmer Bernstein. *cast* Robert Redford, Debra Winger, Daryl Hannah, Brian Dennehy, Terence Stamp, Steven Hill, John McMartin, Roscoe Lee Browne, Christine Baranski.
●Never trust a film with a character named 'Chelsea'. Here, the silly moniker belongs to Daryl Hannah, a New York boho accused of murder and saved by two crusading attorneys in the shape of Redford and Winger. The plot meanders through trial scenes, further killings, a ludicrous performance-art display by the shapely Hannah, and various tussles – sexual and otherwise – between La Winger and la Redford. It all concludes with a big fire and an even bigger courtroom drama. Everything seems to revolve around an art fraud, though that's never quite clear since this plot falls into the category kindly known as 'baggy'. RR

Legally Blonde

(2001, US, 97 min)
d Robert Luketic. *p* Marc Platt, Ric Kidney. *sc* Karen McCullah Lutz, Kirtsen Smith. *ph* Anthony B Richmond. *ed* Anita Brandt Burgoyne, Garth Craven. *pd* Melissa Stewart. *m* Rolfe Kent. *cast* Reese Witherspoon, Luke Wilson, Selma Blair, Matthew Davis, Victor Garber, Jennifer Coolidge, Holland Taylor, Ali Larter, Jessica Cauffiel, Raquel Welch.
●Californian sorority queen Elle Woods (Witherspoon) dreams of the day she'll marry her ambitious boyfriend Warner. Unfortunately, he won't play ball. Just off to Harvard Law School, he dumps her, saying: 'If I'm going to be President, I need a Jacqueline Kennedy, not a Marilyn Monroe.' Undeterred, Elle enrols alongside him and sets out to prove she can be both. The film likewise attempts to give two for one. Boasting conscience, cleavage and bags of money, Elle is Cher from *Clueless* by way of Erin Brockovich. She pulls off the double act with aplomb; the film as a whole, however, is less assured. The writers do best when the jokes revolve around school; the acid-tongued law professors are well observed, so too the competitive, politicised students. But sophistication deserts them when they stray into the real world, whether the beauty parlour or the courts themselves. Elle's ultimate girl-power test is to defend a fitness queen on a murder charge, and here her 'spontaneous' wisdom begins to sound as post-feminist as TV's *Are You Being Served?* CO'Su

Legend

(1985, US, 94 min)
d Ridley Scott. *p* Arnon Milchan. *sc* William Hjortsberg. *ph* Alex Thomson. *ed* Terry Rawlings, Pam Power. *pd* Assheton Gorton. *m* Tangerine Dream (US version)/Jerry Goldsmith (European version). *cast* Tom Cruise, Mia Sara, Tim Curry, David Bennent, Alice Playten, Billy Barty, Cork Hubbert, Peter O'Farrell, Kiran Shah.
●If *Blade Runner* was his *Metropolis*, Scott's next was his *Die Nibelungen*: a Teutonic myth in which the Lord of Darkness castrates a unicorn and thereby transforms a pastoral Eden into an arctic wasteland. Fortunately, sprightly Jack (Cruise) is on hand to set things to rights. Beautifully shot and designed, but in a cloyingly self-conscious manner, the film lacks the narrative drive that propels Peter Jackson's *Lord of the Rings*. There are a handful of impressive sequences though – and Tim Curry is a magnificent horned Beelzebub (though Cruise's original gnashers are as scary in their own way). A director's cut has emerged on Region 1 DVD. TCh

Legend from Southern Island

see Profound Desire of the Gods: Tales from a Southern Island, The

Legend of Bagger Vance, The

(2000, US, 126 min)
d Robert Redford. *p* Robert Redford, Michael Nozik, Jake Eberts. *sc* Jeremy Leven. *ph* Michael Ballhaus. *ed* Hank Corwin. *pd* Stuart Craig. *m* Rachel Portman. *cast* Will Smith, Matt Damon, Charlize Theron, Bruce McGill, Joel Gretsch, J Michael Moncrief, Peter Gerety, Harve Presnell, Jack Lemmon.
●In 1984, Robert Redford starred in Barry Levinson's film of Bernard Malamud's Arthurian baseball saga *The Natural*. It was, against all odds, very decent, but it must've turned his head: as director, he'd later wax mystical over fly fishing (*A River Runs Through It*), equestrian skills (*The Horse Whisperer*), and now golf, with God as a caddy. The one imaginable motive (besides lucre) for perpetrating such mush must be that Hollywood types feel the need to justify/dignify time spent schmoozing on artificial oases of sprinklered sward that despoil and damage the environment. The script, allegedly from 'a novel' by Steven Pressfield, concerns Rannulph Junuh (Damon) who, since returning from the Great War, has lost his 'authentic swing', not to mention his drive and his desire for Savannah heiress Adele (Theron). Seeing daddy's luxury links menaced by the Depression, she plans to save them by staging a match between Bobby Jones, Walter Hagen and the local hero. But can Junuh overcome his fear, self-pity, pride and poor concentration? As if by destiny, out of the darkness comes canny caddy Bagger Vance (Smith) to teach him how to read greens, to hear tides and the turning of the eart' – to know himself and clinch the contest. Uncle Tom cobblers and all, this risible bloated excuse for a parable of spiritual redemption insults racial egalitarians, the religious, any golfer remotely realistic about the game, and those with brains not addled by what passes for the good life in LaLaland. Fore! GA

Legend of Billie Jean, The

(1985, US, 95 min)
d Matthew Robbins. *p* Rob Cohen.*sc* Mark Rosenthal. Lawrence Konner.*ph* Jeffrey Kimball. *ed* Cynthia Scheider.*pd* Ted Haworth. *m* Craig Safan. *cast* Helen Slater, Keith Gordon, Christian Slater, Richard Bradford, Peter Coyote, Martha Gehman,Dean Stockwell.
●When brainless jocks vandalise young Binx's scooter, he and his sister Billie Jean (Helen 'Supergirl' Slater) seek compensation from the father of the chief 'fucker'; but he (Bradford) is some mean bastard, and when he starts molesting BJ, Binx accidentally shoots him in the shoulder. Bro, Sis and a coupla chums take to the road, pursued by a paternal cop (Coyote), condemned by the media, and worshipped as upholders of justice by what seems to be the entire weeny and teeny population of Texas. Robbins co-wrote Spielberg's *Sugarland Express*, to which this bears more than a passing resemblance plotwise. But there similarities end. The sentimental elevation of BJ to legendary status ('She's everywhere') is ludicrously implausible, the characterisation cardboard and cute, the humour puerile, and the squandering of the considerable talents of Coyote and Bradford criminal. Four-letter words and gags about periods fail to disguise the adolescent wish-fulfilment quality of script and direction. GA

Legend of Bruce Lee (Xi Siwang Youxi/aka The New Game of Death)

(1975, Tai, 96 min)
d Lin Bing. *p* Chang Jung-Hua. *sc* LinBing. *ph* Tony Shang. *m* Appad Bondy.*cast* Lee Roy Lung, Lung Fei, Kus Lai, San Dus, Ronald Brown.
●Despite an opening sequence which suggests that what follows may back up the title (a collage of stills and articles, cutting to a suitably heroic training session featuring Lee Roy Lung, the film's 'lookalike' find), this sidetracks into an undistinguished contemporary kung-fu action film whose protagonist is apparently – in an odd confusion of reality and fiction – supposed to be the real-life Bruce Lee. Failing as a homage, and not aspiring to the exposé scurrility of *A Dragon's Story*, it misses out on every count. Lee Roy Lung masters only the least relevant of the star's mannerisms, and is a very boring fighter, a point underscored by the feeble-looking opponents he confronts. Heavily cut, the film is further burdened with an all-purpose soul score. VG

Legend of Frenchie King, The (Les Pétroleuses)

(1971, Fr/It/Sp/GB, 96 min)
d Christian-Jaque. *p* Raymond Eger, Francis Cosne. *sc* Guy Casaril, Daniel Boulanger. *ph* Henri Persin. *ed* Henri Taverna. *ad* José-Luis Galicia. *m* Christian Gaubert. *cast* Brigitte Bardot, Claudia Cardinale, Michael J Pollard, Micheline Presle, Georges Beller, Emma Cohen, Henry Czarniak.
●This lame attempt to repeat the success of Malle's *Viva Maria* sees Bardot and Cardinale as gunfighters in the West, feuding and scratching each other's eyes out over the title-deeds to a ranch soaked in oil, with the baby-faced Pollard mugging away as the harassed sheriff. Set in a French settlement, with the characters making wiz ze ooh-la-la accents in the dubbed version. Dreadfully unfunny. GA

Legend of Hell House, The

(1973, GB, 94 min)
d John Hough. *p* Albert Fennell, Norman T Herman. *sc* Richard Matheson. *ph* Alan Hume. *ed* Geoffrey Foot. *ad* Robert Jones. *m* Brian Hodgson, Delia Derbyshire. *cast* Pamela Franklin, Roddy McDowall, Clive Revill, Gayle Hunnicutt, Roland Culver, Peter Bowles, Michael Gough.
●Richard Matheson's disappointing adaptation of his own rather disappointing novel, a haunted-house tale in which a dying multi-millionaire (Culver) offers a physicist (Revill) £100,000 to investigate a mansion in which several psychic investigators have been killed, and to provide an answer to the perennial question about survival after death. Trivialising the theme, saddled with some terrible dialogue, needlessly tricked out with a lot of countdown-style dates, it founders into innocuous routine. Pamela Franklin, however, gives a convincing performance as the 'mental medium'. DP

Legend of Lylah Clare, The

(1968, US, 127 min)
d/p Robert Aldrich. *sc* Hugo Butler, Jean Rouverol. *ph* Joseph Biroc. *ed* Michael Luciano. *ad* George W Davis, William Glasgow. *m* Frank DeVol. *cast* Kim Novak, Peter Finch, Ernest Borgnine, Milton Seltzer, Valentina Cortese, Rossella Falk, Coral Browne, Gabriele Tinti, Michael Murphy.
●Hollywood picking its scabs is always a riveting sight, and never more enjoyably so than in Aldrich's supremely vulgar movie, which feeds

gluttonously off movie myth and experience to create a vigorously animated Hollywood Babylon where dead stars talk and everyone's laundry is filthy. Kim Novak stars as the moulded reincarnation of Lylah Clare, whose stellar career ended in mysterious death on the night of her wedding to director Lewis Zarkan (Finch), now attempting a semi-confessional biopic on the subject, which naturally involves an outrageous gallery of grotesques and innocents in its revelatory course from concept to screen. Necrophilia, cancer, cripples, French critics, lesbianism, ignorant producers, nepotism, abortion, 'film-artists', Italian studs and TV are the tasty elements Aldrich ghoulishly (and a little masochistically) juggles into a film-fan's delight, a side-splitting charade of satire, sarcasm and sheer perverse affection. PT

Legend of 1900, The (La Leggenda del pianista sull'oceano)

(1998/1999, It, 125 min)
d/sc Giuseppe Tornatore. *ph* Lajos Koltai. *ed* Massimo Quaglia. *pd* Francesco Frigeri. *m* Ennio Morricone. *cast* Tim Roth, Pruitt Taylor Vince, Mélanie Thierry, Bill Nunn, Peter Vaughan, Niall O'Brien, Gabriele Lavia, Alberto Vásquez, Clarence Williams III.

●Man walks into a musical instrument shop, dumps his tooter on the counter and asks for a good price; proprietor tells him to sod off and puts on a record. Man says: hmm, that reminds me, let me tell you a story... There was a transatlantic steamer, *The Virginian*, which ferried immigrants to the US. On it, a furnace man found an abandoned baby in a crate, named him Danny Boon TD Lemon 1900, and raised him on many white lies, before being killed by a loose chain hoist. One day, 1900 (Roth) sat down at the ship's grand piano and discovered his preternatural gift for playing jazz. He beat Jelly Roll Morton in a jazz duel. There was a girl he fancied, but she got off the ship. He once considered disembarking himself, but in the end rejected 'the infinite keyboard that is the city – God's piano.' 'This is an incredible story – incredible,' says the shop proprietor, before threatening to have the narrator (Vince) arrested. The ancient trumpeter takes his story to a demolition crew setting about *The Virginian*, but still the ship goes 'Boom!' (boom!). NB

Legend of Teddy Edwards, The

(2001, Den/US, 85 min)
d/p Don McGlynn. *ph* Steve Wacks, Stefan V Jensen, Randy Drummond, Chris Mosio, Elvis Restainu. *ed* Christian Moltke-Leth, Don McGlynn. *m* Teddy Edwards. *with* Teddy Edwards, Ernie Andrews, Dan Morgenstern.

●Documentary on the undersung but quietly influential Mississippi-born LA tenorist Teddy Edwards. Despite recording perhaps the first tenor bebop solo in 1942, and his close friendships with Charlie Parker, Fats Navarro, Clifford Brown and Benny Goodman, Edwards never received the acclaim he deserved. McGlynn's sluggish, murky film clearly lacks Ken Burns' aesthetic touch, and it desperately misses an authorial voice-over. But there are some revealing moments: it opens up the oft-ignored LA scene, while Edwards openly says that heroin improved his playing by releasing his subconscious and removing his inhibitions. And, aged 77, his playing is still as garrulous and soulful as ever, as are his anecdotes. JL

Legend of the Holy Drinker, The (La Leggenda del Santo Bevitore)

(1988, It, 128 min)
d Ermanno Olmi. *p* Roberto Cicutto, Vincenzo De Leo. *sc* Tullio Kezich, Ermanno Olmi. *ph* Dante Spinotti. *ed* Ermanno Olmi. *pd* Gianni Quaranta. *cast* Rutger Hauer, Anthony Quayle, Sandrine Dumas, Dominique Pinon, Sophie Segalen, Jean-Maurice Chanet.

●A tramp, exiled in Paris and haunted by a criminal past, sees no way out of his predicament until, almost miraculously, he is offered 200 francs by a wealthy stranger whose only request is that, when he can afford it, he return the money to a chapel dedicated to St. Thérèse. A man of honour but weak will, the derelict takes the chance to rejoin a world to which he had become a stranger, finding work, keeping company with women, dining out and sleeping in beds; such luxuries, however, distract him from his obligation... Olmi's adaptation of Joseph Roth's novella is faithful and charming, filmed with a simplicity that mirrors the original's economy. As the alcoholic, though a tad too clean, Rutger Hauer effortlessly suggests the character's blend of pride, dignity and vunerability, while Olmi eschews prosaic realism in his evocation of Paris, seen as an oddly timeless, universal city; the lyricism matches the almost magical coincidences of the plot. Indeed the film has the resonance and innocence of a parable, its religious elements widely subordinated to a story that is told with a minimum of fuss and explanatory dialogue. Quite why the film is so affecting is hard to hard to pin down: maybe it's because Olmi is so sure of his gentle, generous touch that he feels no need for overstatement. GA

Legend of the Lone Ranger, The

(1981, US, 98 min)
d William A Fraker. *p* Walter Coblenz. *sc* Ivan Goff, Ben Roberts, Michael Kane, William Roberts. *ph* Laszlo Kovacs. *ed* Thomas Stanford. *pd* Albert Brenner. *m* John Barry. *cast* Klinton Spilsbury, Michael Horse, Christopher Lloyd, Matt Clark, Juanin Clay, John Bennett Perry, Jason Robards, Richard Farnsworth.

●The mystery is how Fraker, a gifted cameraman who made a superb directing debut in Westerns with *Monte Walsh*, could produce such a clinker as this. Purporting to be a biography of John Reid, alias the Lone Ranger, it starts with an interminable account (in gooey soft focus) of how 11-year-old John saved young Tonto from a fate worse than death, found his own parents butchered by outlaws, and took to the tepee to swear a blood pact with his Indian buddy. His adult campaign to right all wrongs is, if anything, even more flabbily inept, saddled with flavourless performances and an off-screen narrator who elucidates an already painfully limpid plot like nanny explaining to a retarded child. TM

Legend of the Lost

(1957, US, 109 min)
d/p Henry Hathaway. *sc* Robert Presnell Jr, Ben Hecht. *ph* Jack Cardiff. *ed* Bert Bates. *ad* Alfred Ybarra. *m* Angelo Francesco Lavagnino. *cast* John Wayne, Sophia Loren, Rossano Brazzi, Kurt Kasznar.

●A lost-city desert yarn of near-classic lunacy, flecked with notions of (Christian) faith and (cinematic) illusion, as religious nut Brazzi, pragmatic guide Wayne, and wavering sinner Loren investigate mirages both Saharan and psychological. As writer Ben Hecht has Wayne put it, 'A couple of men and a dame are a strain on any civilisation.' PT

Legend of the Mountain (Shan Zhong Chuanqi)

(1978, HK, 180 min)
d King Hu. *cast* Hsu Feng, Sylvia Chang, Shih Chun, Tung Lin, Tien Feng.

●As long as the same director's *Touch of Zen*, but with only a quarter of the substance, this classical ghost story wanders interminably until it reaches its hugely predictable conclusion. Along the way there are some ropey performances, some ropier effects, and a lot of fabulous scenery. There are also moments of genuine delicacy and beauty, but few will have the perseverance to wade through all the self-conscious artfulness to get to them. RG

Legend of the 7 Golden Vampires, The

(1974, GB/HK, 89 min)
d Roy Ward Baker. *p* Don Houghton, Vee King Shaw. *sc* Don Houghton. *ph* John Wilcox, Roy Ford. *ed* Chris Barnes. *ad* Johnson Tsau. *m* James Bernard. *cast* Peter Cushing, David Chiang, Julie Ege, Robin Stewart, Shih Szu, John Forbes-Robertson, Robert Hanna, Liu Chia Yung.

●Hammer and Shaw Brothers combine to provide a fusion of kung-fu and vampirism in which Cushing's Van Helsen tracks Dracula to China, perceiving his hand behind the terrorising of a village by the malevolent undead. With early scenes that suggest a true marriage of forms as a Chinese pilgrim makes his way through Transylvanian forests to worship at Dracula's tomb, and later ones where the undead astonishingly hobble and dance their way across the screen, it is a shame that the film should muff some of the simplest set-ups, and rely for effect on some rather mechanically intercut vampire attacks. VG

Legend of the Suram Fortress, The (Legenda Suramskoi Kreposti)

(1984, USSR, 87 min)
d Sergo Paradjanov, Dodo Abashidze. *p* X Gogiladze, M Simxaev. *sc* Vazha Ghigashvili. *ph* Sergo Sixarulidze. *ed* K'ora Ts'ereteli. *ad* Aleksandre Dzhanshiev. *m* Dzhansugh K'axidze. *cast* Venerik'o Andzhaparidze, Dodo Abashidze, Sopik'o Ch'iaureli, Duduxana Ts'erodze, Tamar Tsitsishvili.

●A visually striking but rather inscrutable depiction of a Georgian myth, Paradjanov's film concerns a young boy who saves the constantly crumbling Suram Fortress by allowing himself to be covered with earth and eggs and walled up alive. The undeniable visual pleasures offered by the imaginative images and rich colours are unfortunately undercut by the stylised presentation – much of the action takes place amid the ruins of the fortress as it survives today – a confusing plot and some esoteric cultural references. NF

Legend of the Werewolf

(1974, GB, 90 min)
d Freddie Francis. *p* Kevin Francis. *sc* Anthony Hinds. *ph* John Wilcox. *ed* Henry Richardson. *ad* Jack Shampan. *m* Harry Robinson. *cast* Peter Cushing, Ron Moody, Hugh Griffith, Roy Castle, David Rintoul, Stefan Gryff, Lynn Dalby, Renee Houston.

●This carries all the earmarks of a disaster-ridden project. Lurching from a hopeless opening sequence – in which a *Look at Life* voice-over 'explains' the werewolf in decidedly bland terms – into a disastrously unfocused section featuring Hugh Griffith as a travelling showman, it finally settles down to being an only faintly more coherent tale of werewolf murders, set in a grade-school version of *fin de siècle* Paris. The script is particularly preposterous, and even Cushing looks disconcerted by the shambles around him. VG

Legend of Zu, The (Shushan Zhuan)

(2001, HK/China, 104 min)
d Tsui Hark. *p* Tsui Hark, To Wan, Wellson Chin. *sc* Tsui Hark, Li Man-Choi. *ph* Poon Hang-Sang, Herman Yau, William Yim. *ed* Marco Mak. *ad* Cyrus Hoh. *m* Ricky Ho. *cast* Ekin Cheng, Cecilia Cheung, Louis Koo, Patrick Tam, Kelly Lin, Wu Jing, Sammo Hung, Zhang Ziyi.

●Not so much a sequel to the 1983 *Zu*, more a way of life: Tsui's later films are so concerned with *process* that they hardly stand up as dramatic structures at all, and this barrage of digital effects (more than 1,500 shots involving CGI, they say) plays more like an extended showreel for a digital studio than a movie as such. This time around, no human character gets a look in; everyone on screen is a sword god, an enigmatic goddess (aside from a tiny cameo by Zhang Ziyi, virtually all the women are played by Cecilia Cheung) or a cosmic villain. China's sacred peaks are under attack from the dreaded Insomnia, whose Blood Cloud threatens total annihilation. King Sky (Cheng) is the sole survivor when the Kunlun School is wiped out (he was waiting 200 years for his beloved woman teacher to be reincarnated at the time); he flies around urging the other schools to set aside their differences and rally for the defence. Matters aren't helped when his chief ally (Koo) goes over to the Dark Side. TR

Legends of Rita, The (Die Stille nach dem Schuss)

(1999, Ger, 101 min)
d Volker Schlöndorff. *p* Arthur Hofer, Emmo Lempert. *sc* Wolfgang Kohlhasse, Volker Schlöndorff. *ph* Andreas Höfer. *ed* Peter Przygodda. *pd* Susanne Hopf. *cast* Bibiana

Beglau, Martin Wuttke, Nadja Uhl, Harald Schrott, Alexander Beyer, Jenny Schily, Mario Irrek, Franca Kastein.
●Those disappointed by Schlöndorff's stolid output in the '90s will welcome this look back at the '70s and the era of 'idealist' terrorism. A group robs banks in the name of the international victims of capitalism. Flash forward to the aftermath, when the remnants of the group go into hiding in E Germany, the state sponsoring of their activities, which they discover is less than a socialist utopia. Adjusting to life as a worker and ever nervous of recognition, 'Rita' (Beglau, excellent) is forced to analyse her past activities and loyalties, as she forms new relationships which test her principles and her freedom of action. A mature work directed with thoughtful sobriety. WH

Legends of the Fall

(1994, US, 133 min)
d Edward Zwick. *p* Edward Zwick, Bill Wittliff, Marshall Herskovitz. sc Susan Shilliday, Bill Wittliff. *ph* John Toll. *ed* Steven Rosenblum. *pd* Lilly Kilvert. *m* James Horner. *cast* Brad Pitt, Anthony Hopkins, Julia Ormond, Aidan Quinn, Henry Thomas, Karina Lombard, Tantoo Cardinal, Gordon Tootoosis, Paul Desmond.
●Zwick turns Jim Harrison's lean, macho novella into a purple, three-hankie Western: Mills and Daniel Boone. Set in the years around WWI, it's the story of the Ludlows: three brothers brought up in the wilds of Montana under the stern eye of their father, the Colonel (Hopkins). Alfred (Quinn), the eldest, is respectful and ambitious, as dutiful as his brother Tristan (Pitt) is rugged and untamed, but when Samuel (Thomas), the youngest, returns home from college with a beautiful wife, Susannah (Ormond), it's not long before discord blossoms. For all that it's blatantly ludicrous tosh, *Legends* performed very respectably at the American box office, and it's not hard to see why: the entire film plays like a commercial for Brad Pitt. You can imagine half the audience wondering, 'Where can I get one of those?' Every young male star should have a role like this: cowboy, soldier, adventurer, bootlegger, vigilante. He wrestles bears, scalps Jerries, sails the seven seas and nobly renounces the woman he loves (his brother's wife). Small wonder that Hopkins resorts to scene-stealing: picture Charles Laughton as Popeye out West. TCh

Leggenda del pianista sull'oceano, La

see Legend of 1900, The

Leggenda del Santo Bevitore, La

see Legend of the Holy Drinker, The

Leila

(1997, Iran, 129 min)
d Dariush Mehrjui. *p* Dariush Mehrjui, Faramarz Farazmand.*sc* Dariush Mehrjui, Mahnaz Ansarian. *ph* Mahmoud Kalari. *ed* Mostafa Kherqepush. *ad* Zhila Mehrjui, Fariar Javaherian. *m* Keivan Jahanshahi. *cast* Leila Hatami, Ali Mosaffa, Jamileh Sheikhi, Mohammad Reza Sharifi-Nia, Turan Mehrzad, Amir Pievar, Shaqayeq Farahani.
●This sensitively directed, slowly paced, spare, painful and finally very moving drama describes a marriage torn apart by the prejudices and self-tormenting ordinances forced on a childless young couple under Islam. The director uses the simplest of narrative strategies: he takes a well-to-do middle class couple, happy and contented, for whom the compulsion to have children is a sole product of traditional and parental pressure (the telephone in this film is the primary symbol of threatening interference), and watches their gradual sundering. After the endless hormone and AI treatments, endoscopy, herbal remedy and the rest, the wife, Leila, is convinced by her mother-in-law that she must persuade her husband to take a second wife. A little over-extended, but intelligent, well-acted and compassionately clear-eyed throughout. WH

Leila and the Wolves

(1984, GB/Leb, 93 min)
d/sc Heiny Srour. *ph* Curtis Clark, Charlet Recors. *ed* Eva Houdova. *ad* Ahmed Maala, Nooman El Joud. *cast* Nabila Zeitouni, Rafiq Ali Ahmed, Raja Nehme, Emilia Fowad, Ferial Abillamah.
●A docu-drama about the fight against victimisation of Arab women. An unlikely interlocutor garbed in a sheer white dress, Leila time-travels through the eight decades of this century, stopping here (at a time of revolution when women larded wedding invitations with news of hidden arms) and there (when young girls at the barricades are goaded into fatal action by chauvinist remarks). Visually, Heiny Srour's film is a treat, combining tinted newsreel footage with memorable images and clearly loving shots of a strife-torn nation; the acts of courage she reveals, and the example she sets to other film-makers to engage their own history, are exalting. FD

Lektionen in Finsternis

see Lessons in Darkness

Le Mans

(1971, US, 108 min)
d Lee H Katzin. *p* Jack N Reddish. *sc* Harry Kleiner. *ph* Robert B Hauser, René Guissart Jr. *ed* Don Ernst, John Woodcock, Ghislaine des Jonquères. *pd* Phil Abramson. *m* Michel Legrand. *cast* Steve McQueen, Siegfried Rauch, Elga Andersen, Ronald Leigh-Hunt, Fred Haltiner.
●Despite a valiant attempt at editing some excitement into the repetitive spectacle of circuiting Porsches and Ferraris, this self-congratulatory advert for Steve McQueen's driving prowess really feels like it's taking the obligatory 24 hours to unwind. PT

Lemon Popsicle (Eskimo Limon)

(1977, Isr, 100 min)
d Boaz Davidson. *p* Menahem Golam, Yoram Globus. *sc* Boaz Davidson, Eli Tabor. *ph* Adam Greenberg. *ed* Alain Jakbowicz. *ad* Ariel Roshko, Alfred Gershoni. *cast* Yiftach Katzur, Anat Atzmon, Jonathan Segal, Zacki Noy, Deborah Kaydar.
●A brazen and none-too-kosher attempt to transplant *American Graffiti* to 1958 Tel Aviv, where (despite the Hebrew signs in the ice-cream parlour) the juke-boxes pound out the California sound. Parading its tastelessness like a strong suit, the movie graphically follows a trio of sexually obsessed teenage boys through their first experiences of love, sex and rejection, and the classroom sweetheart through her first abortion. Were it not for their (and the camera's) fixation on private parts, the characters might be seen as taking their emotional range from the ever-present hit parade – with which the movie shares a blind indifference to the social and political climate. Lots of milk and honey, but there has to be more to the promised land than this. JD

Lemon Sisters, The

(1990, US, 93 min)
d Joyce Chopra. *p* Diane Keaton, Joe Kelley. *sc* Jeremy Pikser. *ph* Bobby Byrne. *ed* Joseph Weintraub, Michael R Miller. *pd* Patrizia von Brandenstein. *m* Dick Hyman. *cast* Diane Keaton, Carol Kane, Kathryn Grody, Joe Kelly, Elliott Gould, Ruben Blades, Aidan Quinn, Estelle Parsons, Matthew Modine.
●'Three lemons are just lemons. Three lemons together are a jackpot.' Atlantic City, 1959 – cue ragtime music, the seaside, boardwalks, childhood friendship. Sound familiar? This is a cheery version of the ultimate girly weepie, *Beaches*. Lifelong pals Grody, Keaton and Kane have ambitions to own a nightclub where they can perform their quirky singing act. But money isn't the only obstacle: friendship has its pressures too. A pleasing cast (including Aidan Quinn as a sleazy PR man) struggles manfully with a banal script, but there's very little here that you haven't seen before, including the mushy ending. YS

Lengua asesina, La

see Killer Tongue

Lengua de las Mariposas, La

see Butterfly's Tongue

Leningrad Cowboys Go America

(1989, Fin/Swe, 79 min)
d Aki Kaurismäki. *p* Klas Oloffson, Katinka Farago. *sc* Aki Kaurismäki. *ph* Timo Salminen. *ed* Raija Talvio. *cast* Matti Pellonpää, Nicky Tesco, Kari Väänänen, Jim Jarmusch, Sakke Järvenpää, Heikki Keskinen, Pimme Korhonen, Sakari Kuosmanen, Puka Oinonen, Silu Seppälä, Mauri Sumén, Mato Valtonen, Pekka Virtanen.
●Unable to make it big in frozen Finland, the Leningrad Cowboys, a talent-free pop group with a bizarre image and an idiosyncratic sound, head for America, where – a local promoter assures them – people will 'swallow any kind of shit'. En route to a wedding reception gig in Mexico, they drive their newly acquired Cadillac from one seedy venue to the next, taking in what Kaurismäki calls 'the steamy bars and honest folk and backyards of the Hamburger Nation'. Even without his cameo appearance as a used-car dealer, Jim Jarmusch's influence would be obvious from the tracking shots of dingy downtown areas, the stylised dialogue, and cryptic inter-titles. But Kaurismäki makes this engaging, comic road movie his own with a distinctive visual style, great running gags (the band carry with them a coffin containing their frozen bass guitarist), some memorably dreadful tunes, and his generosity towards the characters and the ordinary people they meet. Looked at superficially, it's a one-joke movie, but as with Jarmusch, the textured images and oblique nuances take priority over the wacky premise and slender storyline. NF

Lenny

(1974, US, 111 min, b/w)
d Bob Fosse. *p* Marvin Worth. *sc* Julian Barry. *ph* Bruce Surtees. *ed* Alan Heim. *pd* Joel Schiller. *cast* Dustin Hoffman, Valerie Perrine, Jan Miner, Stanley Beck, Gary Morton, Rashel Novikoff.
●Julian Barry's adaptation of his own stage play has all the worst faults of the Hollywood biopic: Lenny Bruce's complex life and personality are manhandled into the fable of an eager Jewish kid working second-rate clubs, who courts his future wife with flowers, rises to fame by being 'true to his art', and finds life at the top fraught with drugs, marital problems and notoriety. The monochrome photography and pseudo-documentary interpolations can't disguise the basic Harold Robbins material, and the good performances (Hoffman and Perrine) stand little chance against Fosse's withering direction: the subject matter needs far defter psychological handling than it gets. There are two powerful nightclub scenes carried by Hoffman, but otherwise Bruce emerges quite unfairly as little more than a tiresome, self-obsessed trouper. DP

Lenny Bruce Performance Film, The

(1967, US, 68 min, b/w)
d John Magnuson. *with* Lenny Bruce.
●As a historical document, this is a priceless piece of celluloid; as a slice of cinema, it's a little hard-going. The visual record of his penultimate performance at the Basin Street West Club in San Francisco (at that time, August '65, just about the only city where Bruce was still kosher), it's the result of a collaboration between the 'comedian' and an educational film-maker, John Magnuson. The Bruce trademark of a whiplash wit packaged in scatological and scaldingly accurate language is in abundant evidence, even if delivered in a diction akin to Joe Strummer on speed with his jaws super-glued together. Yet for a film about a funny man, there's a disquieting air of desperation. Lit only by a single spot which gives the film a dark and grainy feel, the car-coated figure is pinned against a dungeon-like backdrop as he reads obsessively from the transcripts of his New York obscenity trial. It makes you grimace with its truth, if not howl with its hilarity. An exhausting but still astonishing experience. FL

Lenny Bruce Without Tears

(1972, US, 85 min, b/w)
d/p/sc Fred Baker. *ed* Edward Deitch. *with* Lenny Bruce, Steve Allen, Malcolm Muggeridge, Kenneth Tynan, Jean Shepard, Mort Sahl, Nat Hentoff. *narrator* Fred Baker.
●Lenny Bruce would have hated this film. He would have called it sloppy, both in execution and in feeling. Although it contains some brilliant and excruciatingly funny routines from various stages in Bruce's career (and some interesting

interviews), it is linked together by a moralistic continuity, hammered home by Fred Baker's heavy-voiced, humourless narration, concerned to point out how Bruce was driven to his death by a society fighting back against the vision of itself that he revealed. The moral may be true, in part; but it is too simple. Still, careless and sentimentalised as it is, the film is well worth seeing for every frame of Bruce (except the truly obscene final shots). MH

Lenny Live and Unleashed

(1989, GB, 97 min)
d Andy Harries. *p* Andy Harries, Martyn Auty. *sc* Lenny Henry, Kim Fuller. *ph* Peter Sinclair. *ed* Gerry Hambling. *pd* Christopher Hobbs. *with* Lenny Henry, Robbie Coltrane, Jeff Beck, Clinton Derricks Carroll, Cleveland Watkins, Fred Dread Band.

●It takes a truck-load of ego and one hell of a track record to take on 90 minutes of one-person stand-up comedy on the big screen. Richard Pryor, Eddie Murphy and Steve Martin can do it, and here Lenny Henry fulfils his aspirations to be fourth on the list with relative ease. In the Hackney Empire, Lenny keeps the live audience on their toes with a script devised by himself and his long-standing writing partner Kim Fuller. Tried and tested favourites Delbert Wilkins, Deakus and Theophilus P Wildebeeste are all pulled out of the trunk, as well as a less exposed character, blues singer Hound Dog Smith. Henry has successfully overridden the criticisms of black stereotyping (simply by ignoring the issue), but there's never been any debate over his skills as an impersonator; and here he excels as he miraculously transforms himself into mirror images of Pryor, Murphy and Martin. IA

Léolo

(1992, Can, 107 min)
d Jean-Claude Lauzon. *p* Lyse Lafontaine, Aimée Danis. *sc* Jean-Claude Lauzon. *ph* Guy Dufaux. *ed* Michel Arcand. *ad* François Séguin. *m* Richard Gregoire. *cast* Maxime Collin, Ginette Reno, Julien Guiomar, Pierre Bourgault, Giuditta del Vecchio, Denys Arcand.

●Léo is no ordinary child. Convinced that his mother was impregnated by an Italian tomato, the French-Canadian boy insists on being called Léolo; disturbed by the lunatic behaviour of his father, sisters and brother, he finds refuge in his imagination and sexual fantasy. Director-writer Lauzon pulls off a bold fusion of the mystical and the macabre. Bleak humour combines with images of startling richness; heightened by Richard Grégoire's evocative score, hallucinatory passages conjure a very real sense of childhood isolation. Dark, disturbing and utterly compelling, this is coming-of-age as the stuff of nightmare. CM

Leon (aka (100) The Professional)

(1994, Fr, 110 min)
d/p/sc Luc Besson. *ph* Thierry Arbogast. *ed* Sylvie Landra. *pd* Dan Weil. *m* Eric Serra. *cast* Jean Reno, Gary Oldman, Natalie Portman, Danny Aiello, Peter Appel, Michael Badalucco, Ellen Greene.

●Besson's first American movie begins promisingly with a stylish action sequence, but goes off the rails. Hitman Leon (Reno) lives in isolation in his starkly appointed New York apartment, but when a neighbouring family is massacred by corrupt cop Stansfield (Oldman) and his thugs, he becomes reluctant protector of 12-year-old Mathilda (Portman), who asks him to instruct her in the art of killing. Initial wariness between the two turns to something warmer, mutually affecting and sentimental. If this sounds familiar that's because it's so reminiscent of (but nowhere near as good as) *Gloria*. Leaving aside the question of paedophilia, the film is devoid of subtlety. Reno brings a likeably naive, quiet panache to his role; Portman is overbearingly cute and sassy; and Oldman is hammy. Besson fails to make much of New York's visual potential, and lazily asks that Leon's expertise be taken on trust. The shallowness was to be expected; the slackness is surprising. GA

Leone Have Sept Cabecas, Der

see Lion Has Seven Heads, The

Leon Morin, Priest (Léon Morin, Prêtre)

(1961, Fr/It, 128 min, b/w)
d Jean-Pierre Melville. *p* Carlo Ponti, Georges de Beauregard. *sc* Jean-Pierre Melville. *ph* Henri Decaë. *ed* Jacqueline Meppiel, Nadine Marquand, Marie-Josephe Yoyotte, Denise de Casabianca, Agnès Guillemot. *ad* Daniel Guéret, Donald Cardwell. *m* Martial Solal, Albert Raisner. *cast* Jean-Paul Belmondo, Emmanuelle Riva, Irène Tunc, Nicole Mirel, Howard Vernon, Marielle Gozzi, Patricia Gozzi, Volker Schlöndorff.

●Melville's extraordinary excursion into Bressonian territory, set in a provincial town during the World War II German Occupation of France. With perfect formal control and an extreme emotional intensity, he forges links between the disparate themes of the Occupation, profane love, and spiritual quest. Superb performances from Belmondo as the priest with radical ideas and an eye for the women; and from Emmanuelle Riva as the young girl who, like her town, surrenders to an alien force – she is quite literally invaded by God. In exactly the same fashion as his priest, Melville uses the barest of material assets, but maximum emotional and metaphysical toughness, to inveigle the most sceptical of observers into acknowledging the operation of divine grace. With the Liberation comes a concomitant slackening of intensity; then detachment, loss, and the conclusion that even God has a sense of irony. Miraculous cinema, even for heretics. CPea

Leon the Pig Farmer

(1992, GB, 104 min)
d/p Vadim Jean, Gary Sinyor. *sc* Gary Sinyor, Michael Normand. *ph* Gordon Hickie. *ed* Ewa J Lind. *pd* Simon Hicks. *m* John Murphy, David Hughes. *cast* Mark Frankel, Janet Suzman, Brian Glover, Connie Booth, David De Keyser, Maryam D'Abo, Gina Bellman, Annette Crosbie, Bernard Bresslaw.

●A polished low-budget effort, this derives its laughs from the confusion that blights a Jewish boy (Frankel) who discovers that he's the product of early experiments in artificial insemination; his biological father is not North London net-curtain king Sidney Geller (De Keyser), but one Brian Chadwick (Glover), a far from kosher pig farmer in the Yorkshire Dales. The guilt of it all! Sharply shot, cut and performed, this slight but very smart comedy proffers plenty of wittily absurd lines, a wealth of offbeat visual gags, and more than its fair share of invention. Curiously, however, it seems (for want of a better term) ideologically incoherent, or at least unreadable. Is it for or against the cosy repressions of Jewish family life? Endorsing or guying stereotypes? Are we meant to agree that personal and racial identity are defined primarily by the donor of sperm? Or that the hybridisation of farm animal species is somehow analogous to procreation between humans of different creeds? Still, it's pacy enough for its generous, mostly unsentimental humour to override more serious doubts. GA

Leopard, The (Il Gattopardo)

(1963, It, 205 min)
d Luchino Visconti. Goffredo Lombardi. *sc* Suso Cecchi D'Amico, Pasquale Festa Campanile, Enrico Medioli, Massimo Franciosa, Luchino Visconti. *ph* Giuseppe Rotunno. *ed* Mario Serandrei. *ad* Mario Garbuglia. *m* Nino Rota. *cast* Burt Lancaster, Alain Delon, Claudia Cardinale, Paolo Stoppa, Rina Morelli, Serge Reggiani, Romolo Valli, Leslie French, Ivo Garrani, Mario Girotti, Pierre Clémenti.

●Prince Salina has always been the biggest cat on the block. Guys call him The Leopard. He growls, they shift ass. Now some biscuit-brain named Garibaldi wants to run the whole show from City Hall. Did 20th Century-Fox think this was the movie Visconti sold them back in 1963, the way they hacked, dubbed and reprocessed? At last, 20 years later, we have the original version in a restored Technicolor print, revealing this as one of the finest 'Scope movies ever made, and Visconti's most personal meditation on history: muscular in its script, which deals with the declining fortunes of a Sicilian aristocratic clan under the Risorgimento, vigorous in performance, and sensuous in direction, changing moods through subtle shifts of lighting to give a palpable sense of the place and the hour. Lancaster, in the first of his great patrician roles, is superb; the rest of the players, right down to the hundreds of extras in the justly celebrated ball scene, are flawlessly cast, each of them living a moment of history for which Visconti, Marxist aristocrat himself, privately sorrowed. MA

Leopard in the Snow

(1977, GB/Can, 94 min)
d Gerry O'Hara. *p* John Quested, Chris Harrop. *sc* Anne Mather, Jill Hyem. *ph* Michael Reed. *ed* Eddy Joseph. *ad* Anthony Pratt. *m* Kenneth Jones. *cast* Susan Penhaligon, Keir Dullea, Jeremy Kemp, Billie Whitelaw, Kenneth More, Yvonne Manners.

●From the moment Susan Penhaligon is rescued from a dangerous blizzard in the Cumberland fells by a limping and morose racing driver (Dullea) out for a walk with his pet leopard, addicts of the Mills & Boon publishing formula will know they're on safe ground. There is the usual deft substitution of anger for sex ('You're so twisted,' cries Susan, in tears), and the careful manipulation of a colourless fiancé figure. It's fortunate that the film takes itself so seriously, since the poker-faced approach helps to define and dilute the blatant sexism. Alternatively funny or disarmingly old-fashioned. DP

Leopard Man, The

(1943, US, 66 min, b/w)
d Jacques Tourneur. *p* Val Lewton. *sc* Ardel Wray. *ph* Robert De Grasse. *ed* Mark Robson. *ad* Albert S D'Agostino, Walter Keller. *m* Roy Webb. *cast* Dennis O'Keefe, Margo, Jean Brooks, Isabel Jewell, James Bell, Margaret Landry, Abner Biberman, Ben Bard.

●Last of the three films with which Jacques Tourneur got producer Val Lewton's series of low-budget horrors at RKO off to a marvellous start, based on Cornell Woolrich's novel *Black Alibi*. Is it the leopard from a travelling zoo which has escaped after a publicity stunt, or something more sinister wreaking havoc in the Mexican border town? This slim question is transformed by Tourneur's fluent and expressive use of shadows into a stylistic tour de force. A film for lovers of pools of darkness. PH

Leo the Last

(1969, GB, 104 min)
d John Boorman. *p* Irwin Winkler, Robert Chartoff. *sc* William Stair, John Boorman. *ph* Peter Suschitzky. *ed* Tom Priestley. *pd* Tony Woollard. *m* Fred Myrow. *cast* Marcello Mastroianni, Billie Whitelaw, Calvin Lockhart, Glenna Forster-Jones, Graham Crowden, Gwen Ffrangcon-Davies, David De Keyser, Vladek Sheybal.

●Boorman's brief return to Britain, after *Point Blank* and *Hell in the Pacific* and before *Deliverance*, produced this calculatedly bizarre art movie that won him the best director award at Cannes and met with zero commercial success. A surreal vision of Notting Hill culture clash, between Mastroianni's reclusive, convalescent aristocrat and his variously deprived neighbours, it takes place in some impossible overground extension of Turner's basement from *Performance*, and yet assumes the visual and intellectual contours of a down-to-earth, contemporary *Zardoz*, by turns insightful and infuriating as it intervenes in 'social problem' areas armed only with precarious fantasy. PT

Lepke

(1974, US, 110 min)
d/p Menahem Golan. *sc* Wesley Lau, Tamar Simon Hoffs. *ph* Andrew Davis. *ed* Dov Hoenig, Aaron Stell. *pd* Jackson De Govia. *m* Ken Wannberg. *cast* Tony Curtis, Anjanette Comer, Michael Callan, Warren Berlinger, Gianni Russo, Vic Tayback, Milton Berle.

●Weighty and uninspired attempt to do a Jewish *Godfather* that makes nothing at all of its promising material: the rise of the Syndicate and Murder Inc, and the subtle change of tack (to a corporate business ethic and image) under pressure from the clean-up campaigns of the late '30s and early '40s. VG

Les Girls

(1957, US, 114 min)
d George Cukor. *p* Sol C Siegel. *sc* John Patrick. *ph* Robert Surtees. *ed* Ferris Webster. *ad* William A Horning, Gene Allen. *songs* Cole

Porter. *cast* Gene Kelly, Kay Kendall, Mitzi Gaynor, Taina Elg, Jacques Bergerac, Leslie Phillips, Henry Daniell, Patrick MacNee.
●A delight to match that other Cukor musical, *A Star Is Born*. With a fine score by Cole Porter, and Kelly performing some marvellous dances, it works as a highly entertaining piece of entertainment. But there is, as in the earlier film, an interesting dramatic idea: here, it's a *Rashomon*-style look at the romantic accomplishments of philanderer Kelly, seen in flashback through the eyes of three women. Great photography, too, from Robert Surtees. GA

Les Misérables

(1935, US, 109 min, b/w)
d Richard Boleslawski. *p* Darryl F Zanuck. *sc* WP Liscomb. *ph* Gregg Toland. *ed* Barbara McLean. *ad* Richard Day. *m* Alfred Newman. *cast* Fredric March, Charles Laughton, Cedric Hardwicke, Rochelle Hudson, Jessie Ralph, Frances Drake, John Beal, Florence Eldridge.
●Fredric March may take the central role of Valjean, but it is Laughton's stunning performance as the sadistic Javert that really sticks in the mind. As the ruthless nemesis who hounds Valjean, from his youthful days as a galley-slave convicted for stealing bread through to respectable, wealthy middle-age, Laughton convinces with a panoply of controlled sneers, leers and ingratiating gulps, while providing the character – devoted to the law rather than to justice – with touching, credible undertones of shame and frustration. Despite occasional incursions of Hol lywoodian sentimentality, the film is still perhaps the best screen version of Victor Hugo's harrowing epic of social conscience, strong on period atmosphere and endowed with fine performances. GA

Les Miserables

(1952, US, 105, b/w)
d Lewis Milestone. *p* Fred Kohlmar. *sc* Richard Murphy. *ph* Joseph LaShelle. *ed* Hugh Fowler. *ad* Lyle Wheeler, J Russell Spencer. *m* Alex North. *cast* Michael Rennie, Robert Newton, Debra Paget, Sylvia Sidney, Edmund Gwenn, James Robertson Justice, Cameron Mitchell, Elsa Lanchester, Florence Bates.
●Rennie's Valjean is a stormy Biblical prophet (in the chiselled cinematic manner), while Robert Newton's Javert is a puffed-up turkeycock always, it seems, about to burst his buttons. Neither the escaped convict nor the 'imprisoned' policeman holds back. In the end, however, the honours go to Newton. He knows when to lay aside the bluster and movingly touch in the details which make his character pitiable. This lavish and very carefully mounted version of Hugo's novel was scripted by Richard Murphy for Fox; it's well acted by a roster of star secondary players, all of whom rise to the dignity of the proceedings, and was shot in rich, chiaroscuro b/w by Joseph LaShelle. Notable finale in the Paris sewers; but, regrettably, somewhat lacking in passionate conviction. JPy

Les Misérables

(1998, US, 134 min)
d Bille August. *p* Sarah Radclyffe, James Gorman. *sc* Rafael Yglesias. *ph* Jörgen Persson. *ed* Janus Billeskov-Jansen. *pd* Anna Asp. *m* Basil Poledouris. *cast* Liam Neeson, Geoffrey Rush, Uma Thurman, Claire Danes, Hans Matheson, Peter Vaughn, Kathleen Byron.
●This is the sort of bland, star-packed, international production you'd expect from a film-maker who plods through the bestseller lists with more perspiration than inspiration (Isabelle Allende, Peter Høeg and now Victor Hugo). We get lots of muttering extras, impressive set pieces (shot in Prague) and a cast who look like they've just stuck on their whiskers and applied a light dusting of soot for that authentic peasant effect. The central thrust about the nature of justice holds the attention, and Rush's compelling presence as the obsessive Javert gives a slight edge to the prevailing earnestness, but it's still a stodgy, old-fashioned movie that's very difficult to get excited about. TJ

Les Patterson Saves the World

(1987, Aust, 94 min)
d George Miller. *p* Sue Milliken. *sc* Barry Humphries, Diane Millstead. *ph* David Connell. *ed* Tim Wellburn. *pd* Graham Walker. *m* Tim Finn. *cast* Barry Humphries, Pamela Stephenson, Thaao Penghlis, Andrew Clarke, Henri Szeps, Hugh Keays-Byrne.
●Sir Leslie Patterson, KBE – Australia's putrescent Cultural Attaché, the man who made the meat pie a fashion accessory – is one of the great comic creations of the last decade. Better, though, to chew one's foot off than spend more than ten minutes in the bugger's company, especially by way of this grotesquely charmless film, entirely devoid of mirth, wit or style. The plot is a shotgun wedding of the *Carry On Follow That Camel* with those ropey James Coburn spy comedies from the '60s: bad enough, but worse when the deadly virus threatening the world is a dead ringer for AIDS. Worse yet, the director is not George (*Mad Max*) Miller but a namesake who should be occluding dental cavities in Moonee Ponds. DAt

Lessons in Darkness (Lektionen in Finsternis)

(1992, Fr/Ger, 52 min)
d Werner Herzog. *p* Werner Herzog, Paul Berriff. *ph* Paul Berriff.
●After the Gulf War, Herzog and cameraman/co-producer Paul Berriff travelled to Kuwait. What they found in the sand, besides bones, craters, rusting military debris and the shattered shells of buildings, was a blazing inferno. The bleak landscape on view was even more dramatic than the wreckage Herzog had shot in the Sahara for *Fata Morgana* (1971); small wonder, then, that as an accompaniment to the images, instead of the (ironic) creation myth he used for the earlier film, he concocted a 'narrative' to point up the apocalyptic aspects of Saddam Hussein's conflagration. The result, in 13 'chapters', is an evocation of hell on earth. Massive towers of flame and billowing black smoke transform the desert into a surreal, expressionist nightmare-world; Kuwaitis turn shocked, saddened eyes to the camera, without recrimination; fire fighters appear to be involved in bizarre, primeval rituals as they go silently about their seemingly ineffectual work. Herzog's own hushed, awestruck voice intones the poetic narration, while the likes of Wagner, Mahler, Verdi and Pärt are enlisted to furnish an epic, elegaic musical backdrop. GA

Lethal Weapon

(1987, US, 109 min)
d Richard Donner. *p* Richard Donner, Joel Silver. *sc* Shane Black. *ph* Stephen Goldblatt. *ed* Stuart Baird. *pd* J Michael Riva. *m* Michael Kamen, Eric Clapton. *cast* Mel Gibson, Danny Glover, Gary Busey, Mitchell Ryan, Tom Atkins, Darlene Love, Traci Wolfe.
●In this classy all-action thriller, Mel Gibson oozes charm the way his victims ooze blood. As a Vietvet-turned-cop, his only talent is for killing: since his wife's death in a road accident, he's known to his LAPD colleagues as a man with a death wish. After a Kim Basinger lookalike walks off the top of a multi-storey block, investigating detective Glover – a family man, just turned 50 and keen to see 51 – is given the dubious pleasure of having Gibson as his new partner. However, he soon comes to appreciate the virtues of having this 'lethal weapon' at his side when the two unlikely buddies are faced with a murderous gang of ex-CIA trained killers running a massive drugs syndicate. Stylish and brutally violent, the film escapes the usual clichés of the ex-soldier fighting a war back home by virtue of Gibson's blue-eyed smile. CB

Lethal Weapon 2

(1989, US, 114 min)
d Richard Donner. *p* Richard Donner, Joel Silver. *sc* Jeffrey Boam. *ph* Stephen Goldblatt. *ed* Stauart Baird. *pd* J Michael Riva. *m* Michael Kamen, Eric Clapton, David Sanborn. *cast* Mel Gibson, Danny Glover, Joe Pesci, Joss Ackland, Derrick O'Connor, Patsy Kensit, Darlene Love, Traci Wolfe, Steve Kahan.
●This wastes no time in assuring fans that Martin Riggs still loves getting involved in crazy things. A high-speed chase, explosive crash and helicopter rescue all slot neatly into the opening ten minutes. The villains are South African diplomats who run a lucrative drugs syndicate, and it's up to Riggs (Gibson) and his long-suffering partner Murtaugh (Glover) to throw away the rule books and bring justice to bear. Various trademarks of the original are repeated, notably the violence and the grudging affection between the mis-matched partners. Indeed, in this sequel their friendship has been enhanced, with Riggs virtually a member of Murtaugh's family. Joe Pesci makes a welcome appearance, albeit in a silly role as a bumbling accountant who has laundered narcotics money. By concentrating on the often frustrating, funny relationship between the three men, the film gains in humour but loses some of the momentum and panache which distinguished the original. CM

Lethal Weapon 3

(1992, US, 118 min)
d Richard Donner. *p* Richard Donner, Joel Silver. *sc* Jeffrey Boam, Robert Mark Kamen. *ph* Jan De Bont. *ed* Robert Brown, Battle Davis. *pd* James Spencer. *m* Michael Kamen, Eric Clapton, David Sanborn. *cast* Mel Gibson, Danny Glover, Joe Pesci, Rene Russo, Stuart Wilson, Steve Kahan, Darlene Love, Traci Wolfe, Gregory Millar, Damon Hines.
●This excels in the fast-paced action sequences more than in the sometimes over-developed buddy-gag exchanges between Gibson's manic cop Riggs and Glover's dependable Murtaugh. An example comes early on: Murtaugh, a perilous week away from retirement, and Riggs, carefree as ever, bypass the bomb squad and contrive to blow up an entire skyscraper office block, a spectacular destructive orgasm which isn't aided by rather crass dialogue. Following on from this is a set-to on an ice-hockey rink, a hair-raising chase between two speeding security vehicles, and some typically vicious violence. Though Gibson gets a martial arts girlfriend (Russo), Murtaugh has asked the crazed Leo Getz (Pesci) to sell his house, and the plot occasionally touches on the stuff of the LA riots, what this sequel delivers is still the kind of high-speed roller-coaster action that producer Joel Silver's films often do so well. SGr

Lethal Weapon 4

(1998, US, 128 min)
d Richard Donner. *p* Joel Silver, Richard Donner. *sc* Channing Gibson. *ph* Andrzej Bartkowiak. *ed* Frank J Urioste, Dallas Puett. *pd* J Michael Riva. *m* Michael Kamen, Eric Clapton, David Sanborn. *cast* Mel Gibson, Danny Glover, Joe Pesci, Rene Russo, Chris Rock, Jet Li, Steve Kahan.
●Back in '87, Gibson and Glover's mismatched, bickering buddies, Richard Donner's loose-wristed direction and Shane Black's slick dialogue coined a harder edged style of action comedy. But Hollywood action movies have moved on since then, becoming more flippant, knowing and cynical. So how did it all turn out so well? In a word, familiarity...both in the sense of 'breeds content', and in the sense of familial relationships: here is a new sub-genre, the action-sitcom, in which the heroes' complicated emotional lives are as important as the gunplay, car chases and explosions. Glover's daughter is pregnant, but won't say who the father is; glamorous detective Russo, Mel's love interest from 3, is also pregnant, and she, like the audience, is waiting to see if the haunted Mel will finally bury the memories of his dead wife by asking her to marry him. On the action front, it's business as usual, but with creakier limbs. 'We're getting too old for this shit,' gasps Glover, as he and Mad Mel drag their ageing bodies around LA in pursuit of a Triad smuggling gang that's selling Chinese immigrants into slavery. The climactic streetfighting clash between Mel and coldly charismatic martial arts star Jet Li is a bone-crunching classic. NF

Let Him Have It

(1991, GB, 115 min)
d Peter Medak. *p* Luc Roeg, Robert Warr. *sc* Neal Purvis, Robert Wade. *ph* Oliver Stapleton. *ed* Ray Lovejoy. *pd* Michael Pickwoad. *m* Michael Kamen. *cast* Chris Eccleston, Paul Reynolds, Tom Courtenay, Tom Bell, Eileen Atkins, Clare Holman, Mark McGann, Michael Gough, Ronald Fraser, James Villiers, Clive Revill, Michael Elphick, Murray Melvin.
●Nearly 40 years after his execution, the case of Derek Bentley – backward, epileptic, and hanged for a shooting committed by someone else – looks unlikely to be shut away in the drawer of history. Medak's first film since *The Krays* shares a concern for post-war London low-life, justice, and – on the downside – a preoccupation with early

yoof-culture and a too gangsterish treatment of sordid crimes. On November 2, 1952, Bentley and his under-age mentor in criminality, Chris Craig, were caught on the roof of a Croydon warehouse by police, one of whom was fatally shot by 16-year-old Craig after Bentley had uttered the ambiguous words, 'Let him have it, Chris.' Medak's film is an angry story told with great force by very fine actors: notably, Courtenay as Bentley's decently impotent dad, Atkins as his tortured mother, Reynolds as the yobbish Craig, and Eccleston's doomed Derek, rising manfully to a climax that will leave only the heartless without need of a hanky. SGr

Let It Be

(1970, GB, 81 min)
d Michael Lindsay-Hogg. *p* Neil Aspinall. *ph* Tony Richmond. *ed* Tony Lenny. *with* The Beatles, Yoko Ono.

● A *cinéma-vérité* documentary of the Beatles at work. The sycophancy of the direction notwithstanding, this survives as a fascinating record of both the Beatles' collapse and their unending power over their audience (us). After an hour in which one watches the Fab Four bickering and disintegrating before our eyes, almost magically they reform and take us back to happier times with their impromptu concert on the Apple rooftop. PH

Let It Come Down: The Life of Paul Bowles

(1998, Can, 73 min)
d Jennifer Baichwal. *p/ph* Nick de Pencier. *ed* David Wharmsby. *m* Paul Bowles. *with* Paul Bowles, Ned Rorem, David Herbert, Allen Ginsberg, William S Burroughs

● Paul Bowles was an accomplished American composer who left for Paris, turned his hand to prose and never looked back, not least when he became fascinated by the freedom of North Africa and spent much of his life in Tangier. Director Baichwal built up a friendship with the author of *The Sheltering Sky* over a number of visits to his home in Morocco, securing the long interview with the 87-year-old which makes up the core of this intimate but never over-adulatory portrait. In person Bowles appears as incisive and laconic as his writing style, recalling the difficulties of marriage to ill-fated spouse Jane, and offering a final assessment on Bertolucci's film of his most famous novel. American composer Ned Rorem comments on Bowles' musical achievement, the Hon David Herbert dishes the dirt on wild Tangier nights gone by, and the most fascinating footage reunites Bowles, Ginsberg and Burroughs in a New York hotel room. It was the last time these three giants of the counter-culture ever saw each other. TJ

Let It Ride

(1989, US, 86 min)
d Joe Pytka. *p* David Giler, Ned Dowd, Randy Ostrow. *sc* Nancy Dowd. *ph* Curtis J Wehr. *ed* Dede Allen, Jim Miller. *pd* Wolf Kroeger. *m* Giorgio Moroder. *cast* Richard Dreyfuss, Teri Garr, David Johansen, Jennifer Tilly, Allen Garfield, Mary Woronov, Robbie Coltrane.

● Although a straight-to-video special in Britain, this quirky farce has its moments and the often underrated Dreyfuss makes the most of them. The plot is ripped off from an old *Bilko* episode: a compulsive gambler has the luckiest day of his life at the track – suddenly he can't lose – but he's soon to find that hitting the jackpot doesn't necessarily make him any happier. One to ponder when you shell out your weekly lottery stake. Adapted by Nancy Dowd, under the name Ernest Morton, from the novel *Good Vibes* by Jay Cronley. TJ

Let It Snow (aka Snow Days)

(1999, US, 89 min)
d Adam Marcus. *p/sc* Kip Marcus. *ph* Ben Weinstein. *ed* Joe Klotz. *pd* Melissa Schrock. *m* Sean McCourt. *cast* Kipp Marcus, Alice Dylan, Bernadette Peters, Henry Simmons, Miriam Shor, Judith Malina, Sandra Prosper.

● Five-year-old James is left in the care of his 'grammy' (Malina) while Dad goes to find himself and Mom (Peters) searches for her chakras. Grammy's advice to little James is 'stay away from love', believing the family to be cursed – 'the men always leave and the women go crazy'. Grown-up James (Marcus) meets and shares special 'snow days' off school with girl next door Sarah (Dylan), but, believing he's cursed, he doesn't let her know his true feelings. Years after they've gone their separate ways, they meet up again, but by now she's met another man. Desperate to prevent her marriage to the wrong man, James attends hilarious open-mic therapy sessions and above all prays for another snow day. Something of a departure for the director of *Jason Goes to Hell*, the last of the 'Friday the 13th' series, this is unashamedly romantic and entertaining by turns. JFu

Let's Do It Again

(1975, US, 113 min)
d Sidney Poitier. *p* Melville Tucker. *sc* Richard Wesley. *ph* Donald M Morgan. *ed* Pembroke J Herring. *pd* Alfred Sweeney. *m* Curtis Mayfield. *cast* Sidney Poitier, Bill Cosby, Calvin Lockhart, John Amos, Denise Nicholas, Lee Chamberlain, Jimmy Walker, Ossie Davis, Billy Eckstine.

● A follow-up to *Uptown Saturday Night*, with the acidic touches reduced to broad, Disney-like comedy. Poitier and Cosby raise money, for an organisation that bears a closer resemblance to the Elks than the Black Muslims, by good-humouredly fixing and betting on a couple of boxing matches. Blaxploitation 'family entertainment' with a few genuinely funny moments. PH

Let's Get Laid!

(1977, GB, 96 min)
d James Kenelm Clarke. *p* Brian Smedley-Aston. *sc* Michael Robson. *ph* Philip Meheux. *ed* Jim Connock. *ad* Ken Bridgeman. *m* James Kenelm Clarke. *cast* Fiona Richmond, Robin Askwith, Anthony Steel, Graham Stark, Linda Hayden, Roland Curram, Tony Haygarth.

● If there's anything even vaguely surprising about this would-be comedy-thriller set in post-war London, it's how unbelievably old-fashioned it is, as if the geriatric former patrons of the Windmill were being offered one last, far from great prick-tease this side of the Reaper.The equine Ms Richmond displays the acting abilities of a chair and two of the most suspiciously buoyant sachets of flesh this side of Sainsbury's. Not unlike a George Formby movie with tits. GD

Let's Get Lost

(1988, US, 120 min, b/w)
d/p Bruce Weber. *sc* Susan Stribling. *ph* Jeff Preiss. *ed* Angelo Corrao. *with* Chet Baker, Carol Baker, Vera Baker, Paul Baker, Dean Baker, Missy Baker, Dick Bock, William Claxton, Jack Sheldon, Cherry Vanilla.

● Weber's documentary on jazz-trumpeter Chet Baker collects an impressive number of witnesses to his con-man charm and unreliability. None of his ex-wives finds much good to say about him – he was bad, he was trouble, and he was beautiful – and his children scarcely knew him. Even his Oklahoman mother takes the Fifth. Every body wanted to save Chet, but Chet just wanted to get lost, and he evaporated from all responsibilities when his habit took over. Just about the only constant love affair over the years was with the camera, from image-making West Coast photographer William Claxton in the '50s to Weber himself. The contemporary Chet in interview takes evasive action in a zonked Bertie Woosterish sort of way, and sings folorn ballads in an exhausted voice. Pity there isn't any footage of Chet's trumpet heyday, but there are rare extracts from terrible movies like *Hell's Horizon* and *Love at First Sight*. BC.

Let's Hope It's a Girl (Speriamo che sia Femmina)

(1985, It/Fr, 119 min)
d Mario Monicelli. *p* Giovanni Di Clemente. *sc* Leo Benvenuti, Piero De Bernardi, Suso Cecchi D'Amico, Tullio Pinelli, Mario Monicelli. *ph* Camillo Bazzoni. *ed* Ruggero Mastroianni. *pd* Enrico Fiorentini. *m* Nicola Piovani. *cast* Liv Ullmann, Catherine Deneuve, Giuliana De Sio, Philippe Noiret, Giuliano Gemma, Bernard Blier, Stefania Sandrelli.

● Men are the butt of the jokes in this gently humorous homage to sisterhood. Count Leonardo (Noiret) returns to his ex-wife Elena (Ullmann) at their run-down country estate with a hare-brained scheme to turn the stables into a spa. The plan is pipped by the Count's death, for which senile Uncle Gugo (Blier, timing his comic bumbling impeccably) is largely responsible. Their home threatened by bankruptcy, the female members of the household look to men for security. But the men create more problems than they resolve, and soon the women are scampering back to the domestic bliss of the farmhouse, where the mentally defused Gugo is the only tolerable male presence. It's a raggedy plot which tries to cover too much ground; but Monicelli's touch sets a heartening tone, and the dialogue, though slight, carries some delightfully barbed perceptions. EP

Let's Make Love

(1960, US, 118 min)
d George Cukor. *p* Jerry Wald. *sc* Norman Krasna. *ph* Daniel L Fapp. *ed* David Bretherton. *ad* Lyle R Wheeler, Gene Allen. *m* Lionel Newman. *songs* Cole Porter, Sammy Cahn, James Van Heusen. *cast* Yves Montand, Marilyn Monroe, Tony Randall, Wilfrid Hyde-White, Frankie Vaughan, David Burns.

● A rambling romance in a backstage musical setting, with Montand as a stuffy millionaire determined to take legal action against a little revue in which he is lampooned – until he meets Monroe. She, starring in the show and believing him to be an out-of-work actor, gets him a job impersonating himself; and he, trying to make good, hires the best (Bing Crosby, Gene Kelly and Milton Berle in cameos) to give him a showbiz polish. The teaming of Monroe and Montand works like a charm (the love affair was real, and you feel it), and Cukor contrives to lend the whole thing a witty sense of enchantment that isn't really there. Not so much a good film as a delightful experience, with one moment of true magic: Marilyn making her stage entrance down a fireman's pole and purring her way into Cole Porter's 'My Heart Belongs to Daddy'. TM

Let's Spend the Night Together (aka Time Is on Our Side)

(1982, US, 91 min)
d Hal Ashby. *p* Ronald L Schwary. *ph* Caleb Deschanel, Gerald Feil. *ed* Lisa Day. *with* The Rolling Stones.

● An account of three gigs, filmed during the Stones' 1981 American tour, that rarely strays beyond the confines of the vast stages. There's no attempt to penetrate the carefully constructed cliché images of 20 years – the monkishly-tonsured backroom boy Watts, the phlegmatic Wyman, and Jagger's posturing posterior are all present and correct. Although one may mourn the lost opportunity to say something about the Stones other than that they are twenty years older than they were twenty years ago (cue 'Time Is on My Side'), a Stones concert is still worthwhile entertainment. The sound is of high quality, the music is as you'd expect, and some of the helicopter shots are a wheeze; but the relevance of those newsreel clips of burning Buddhists and headless soldiers is dubious – this is not Woodstock, even though Ashby obviously wishes it was. FL

Letter, The

(1940, US, 95 min, b/w)
d William Wyler. *p* Hal B Wallis. *sc* Howard Koch. *ph* Tony Gaudio. *ed* George Amy, Warren Low. *ad* Carl Jules Weyl. *m* Max Steiner. *cast* Bette Davis, Herbert Marshall, James Stephenson, Frieda Inescort, Gale Sondergaard, Sen Yung, Cecil Kellaway,Bruce Lester.

● A superbly crafted melodrama, even if it never manages to top the moody montage with which it opens – moon scudding behind clouds, rubber dripping from a tree, coolies dozing in the compound, a startled cockatoo – as a shot rings out, a man staggers out onto the verandah, and Davis follows to empty her gun grimly into his body. The contrivance evident in Maugham's play during the investigation and trial that follow is kept firmly at bay by Wyler's technical expertise and terrific performances (not just Davis, but Stephenson as her conscience-ridden lawyer), although Maugham's cynical thesis about the hypocrisies of colonial justice is rather undercut by the addition of a pusillanimous finale in which Davis gets her comeuppance at private hands. A pity, too, that Tony Gaudio's camerawork, almost worthy of Sternberg in its evocation of sultry Singapore nights and cool gin slings, is not matched by natural sounds (on the soundtrack Max Steiner's score does a lot of busy underlining). TM

Letter, The (La Lettre/A Carta)

(1999, Fr/Port/Sp, 107 min)
d Manoel de Oliveira. *p* Paulo Branco. *sc* Manoel de Oliveira, (French dialogue) Jacques Parsi. *ph* Emmanuel Machuel. *ed* Valérie Loiseleux. *pd* Ana Vaz da Silva. *m* Pedro Abrunhosa, Franz Schubert. *cast* Chiara Mastroianni, Pedro Abrunhosa, Antoine Chappey, Leonor Silveira, Françoise Fabian, Maria João Pires, Anny Romand, Luis Miguel Cintra.

●This distinctly odd version of the classic novel *The Princess of Clèves*, from Portuguese director Manoel de Oliveira (b. 1908), falls between a rather studied literalism and a woebegone updating. The chaste wife (Mastroianni) is here wooed by real-life rock singer Pedro Abrunhosa, who to non-Portuguese may well seem an utter prat. Some reckon the film is intentionally funny, but this writer's in the larger camp that considers it misconceived and out of touch. (See also *La Fidélité*.) GA

Letter for an Angel (Surat Untuk Bidadari)

(1994, Indon, 118 min)
d Garin Nugroho. *p* A Alatas Fahmi. Robert S Sumendap, Benny V Aboebakar, Amoroso Katamsi. *sc* Garin Nugroho. *ph* Winaldha E Melalatoa. *ed* Arturo G Pradjawisastra. *m* Tony Prabowo. *cast* Nurul Arifin, Adi Kurdi, Windy, Viva Westi.

●Nugroho is the one director in Indonesian cinema who is challenging taboos and opening up new ground, and so it's a pity that his movies lack formal rigour and lapse so easily into vacuous pictorialism. Nine-year-old Lewa, motherless since infancy, but deeply attracted to his horse, writes regular letters to an angel about his problems; these include a local feud between villages, the deaths of his father and a family friend, and a suspicion that a poster of Madonna might represent his missing mother. Nugroho focuses on a tribal community caught between tradition and strong influences from outside, but loses grip when he drifts off into dime-store surrealist interludes, indulges in cheap-shot satire and gets fixated on colourful/bloody ethnic rituals. TR

Letter from an Unknown Woman 100

(1948, US, 90 min, b/w)
d Max Ophüls. *p* John Houseman. *sc* Howard Koch. *ph* Franz Planer. *ed* Ted J Kent. *ad* Alexander Golitzen. *m* Daniele Amfitheatrof. *cast* Joan Fontaine, Louis Jourdan, Mady Christians, Marcel Journet, Art Smith, Carol Yorke, John Good.

●Of all the cinema's fables of doomed love, none is more piercing than this. Fontaine nurses an undeclared childhood crush on her next-door neighbour, a concert pianist (Jourdan); much later, he adds her to his long list of conquests, makes her pregnant – and forgets all about her. Ophüls' endlessly elaborate camera movements, forever circling the characters or co-opting them into larger designs, expose the impasse with hallucinatory clarity: we see how these people see each other and why they are hopelessly, inextricably stuck. TR

Letters from a Dead Man (Pisma Myortvovo Chelovyeka)

(1986, USSR, 87 min)
d Konstantin Lopushansky. *sc* Konstantin Lopushansky, Vyacheslav Ribakov. *ph* Nikolai Pokoptsev. *ed* T Pulinoi. *ad* Elena Amshinskaya, Viktor Ivanov. *m* Alexander Zhurbin. *cast* Rolan Bikov, I Riklin, V Mikhailov, A Sabinin, N Gryakalova.

●This parable of the last days of civilisation as we know it takes place mostly underground, as the survivors of what seems to have been an accidental missile exchange wait for each other to die. The letters of the title are interior monologues by an elderly scientist (Bikov), addressed to the son he knows must have perished amid the briefly glimpsed devastation on the surface. What is most remarkable to find in a Soviet film, apart from the resolutely unpartisan pessimism, is a clear religious thread. The band of silent children who represent the hope of the future are initially in the care of a priest, before the dying scientist takes upon himself their salvation. Old hands will detect shades of Tarkovsky in this; in fact, Lopushansky was assistant on *Stalker*. It may not be a masterpiece – it's often static and rhetorical – but it is a humane and timely film, and few will resist the sheer emotion of its ending. IC

Letters from My Windmill

see Lettres de Mon Moulin, Les

Letters from the East

(1995, GB/Ger/Fin/Swe, 107 min)
d Andrew Grieve. *p* Ene Vanaveski. *sc* Andrew Grieve. *ph* Ian McMillan. *ed* Derek Bain. *pd* Bernd Lepel. *m* John Keane. *cast* Ewa Fröling, Mark Womack, Ingeborga Dapkunaite, Märta Laurent, Rein Oja, Mikk Mikiver.

●Writer/director Grieve's story of self-discovery and self-determination in occupied Estonia is a worthy take on recent Estonian history, personal and national. With a timespan book-ending 45 years of Soviet occupation, the story cuts between the 1944 exodus of thousands of refugees before the advancing Red Army, and the strengthening of the national independence movement in 1989. In the latter year, London-based cellist Anna (Fröling) discovers among her late father's effects photographs and correspondence from Estonia which stoke her curiosity about the real fate of her mother, supposedly a casualty of the family's flight from the country when Anna was eight. Had her father been hiding something? Against advice, she returns to her birthplace; followed by local film-maker Rein (Womack), she slowly, awkwardly, begins to uncover her heritage against a background of emerging nationhood. With a capable pan-European cast, Grieve's keen eye for a view, Ian McMillan's equally arresting photography, and Dvorak on the soundtrack, this has its virtues; dramatically, however, the film falls down. Anna's investigation typically involves a succession of fruitless and repetitive interviews with obscure locals; and the flashback structure is hackneyed and confusing, never fully convincing us that these are Anna's memories rather than just the film's. NB

Letters to an Unknown Lover (Les Louves)

(1985, GB/Fr, 101 min)
d Peter Duffell. *p* Ian Warren, Jaques Mader, Serge Bany. *sc* Hugh Whitemore. *ph* Claude Robin. *ed* Teddy Darvas. *pd* Michel Janiaud. *m* Raymond Alessandrini. *cast* Cherie Lunghi, Yves Beneyton, Mathilda May, Ralph Bates, Cadine Constant, Gabriel Gobin, Andrea Ferréol.

●Based on a story by Boileau and Narcejac (*Les Diaboliques*, *Vertigo*), and it shows. In occupied France, an escaped PoW pretends to be his dead friend in order to take refuge with two beautiful sisters. But things, inevitably, are not what they seem. Duffell contributes strong atmosphere, disturbing nuances, and wins some fine performances (particularly from Andrea Ferréol), but the thriller aspect (not too far from *The Beguiled*) could do with tauter direction. Interesting, nevertheless. GA

Letters to Katja

(1994, GB/Fin, 57 min)
d Amber Production Team.

●Finnish-born photographer Sirkka-Liisa Konttinen (a member of the estimable Amber film collective) returns after two decades in Britain to visit her family in Helsinki and at their country holiday home. Structured as a letter to her daughter (who soon gets bored of the stunning, empty landscapes her mother adores), the film is an impressionistic meditation on exile, nostalgia, nature, nationality and family. Occasionally a little too poetic, but its overall intelligence transcends purely personal concerns. GA

Letter to Brezhnev

(1985, US, 95 min)
d Chris Bernard. *p* Janet Goddard. *sc* Frank Clarke. *ph* Bruce McGowan. *ed* Lesley Walker. *ad* Lez Brotherston, Nick Englefield, Jonathan Swain. *m* Alan Gill. *cast* Alfred Molina, Peter Firth, Margi Clarke, Alexandra Pigg, Tracy Lea, Ken Campbell.

●Two girls bus it optimistically into Liverpool one night. One works as a chicken stuffer, the other is unemployed. The former rediscovers the joys of shameless rumpy-pumpy, while the other finds romance in the shape of a Russian sailor. He legs it back to Omsk, leaving matters to be fixed by 'a letter to Brezhnev'. Writer Frank Clarke and director Chris Bernard have made an escapist fantasy of cartoon-like simplicity (the love affair is, at times, ridiculously overblown) but rooted it in realistic observation which is gritty, energetic, and wonderfully funny. Exuberantly performed, the result is seductive – something like Bill Forsyth, except tougher, and taking due mileage from the fact that Liverpool is England's only mythological city. RR

Letter to Jane

(1972, Fr, 52 min, b/w & col)
d/p/voices Jean-Luc Godard, Jean-Pierre Gorin.

●This is a detailed, perceptive analysis of a news-photo which shows Jane Fonda in Vietnam, looking concerned in conversation with some Vietnamese. Godard/Gorin argue very soundly that this emphasis on the concern of the West, through an image of a film star, rather than on the Vietnamese themselves and what they have to say, is only another form of the colonialism which dominates the Third World. The use of film to analyse the ideologies of still images is very effective; but by turning what should be an investigation of the photo into 'a letter to Jane' telling her off for constructing her image, Godard/ Gorin fail to engage with the way meanings are constructed in news images (and other media). JWi

Letter to Three Wives, A

(1949, US, 103 min, b/w)
d Joseph L Mankiewicz. *p* Sol C Siegel. *sc* Joseph L Mankiewicz. *ph* Arthur Miller. *ed* J Watson Webb Jr. *ad* Lyle Wheeler, J Russell Spencer. *m* Alfred Newman. *cast* Kirk Douglas, Ann Sothern, Linda Darnell, Paul Douglas, Jeanne Crain, Jeffrey Lynn, Thelma Ritter, Florence Bates.

●Traditional wisdom has Mankiewicz as more writer than director, but consider the marvellously cinematic opening of *A Letter to Three Wives*: shots of a prosperous town and its stately avenues of rich men's houses, all placidly awaiting the start of the country club season, as the venomously honeyed voice of an unseen female narrator (beautifully done by Celeste Holm) begins spinning a web of speculation and suspicion round three married women, shortly to be completed by their receipt of a poisonous letter indicating that the narrator has run away with one of the husbands. With the three wives trapped for the day supervising a children's picnic, flashbacks start exploring their marital worries, perceptively probing sensitive areas of social and cultural unease. Glitteringly funny at one end of the scale (Kirk Douglas and Ann Sothern), dumbly touching at the other (Paul Douglas and Linda Darnell), it's absolutely irresistible. TM

Letter Without Words, A

(1997, US, 62 min, col & b/w)
d/p/sc Lisa Lewenz. *ph* (contemporary) Lisa Lewenz; (historical) Ella Lewenz. *ed* Ruth Schell, Lisa Lewenz, Anand Kamalaker, Penelope Falk. *m* Bob Telson, Lewis Spratlan, Lisa Lewenz, Paul Bartholomew.

●This documentary about the European Jewish experience before and during the Holocaust, as understood by descendants of the survivors, uses photography as a keyhole to remembrance. The director finds an archive of her grandmother's 8mm home movies. It contains extraordinary footage shot from the point of view of a privileged Berliner (Albert Einstein was a friend). Then the swastikas start to appear, and the family's Jewishness becomes an issue for the first time. TCh

Let the Good Times Roll

(1973, US, 99 min)
d Sid Levin, Robert Abel. *p* Gerald I Isenberg. *sc* Sid Levin, Robert Abel. *ph* Robert Thomas, David Myers, Erik Daarstad, Richard Pearce, Stevan Larner, Paul Lohmann, Mike Livesey, Peter Powell, Juliana Wang, Peter Echo, James Wilson. *ed* Sid Levin, Hyman Kaufman, Bud

Friedgen, Yeu-Bun Yee. *with* Chuck Berry, Little Richard, Fats Domino, Chubby Checker, Bo Diddley, The Shirelles, The Five Satins, Bill Haley and the Comets.
●Shot in three days at three of Richard Nader's *Rock Revival* productions in the States, this is not the exploitative quickie you might expect but the first attempt to put rock'n'roll culture in some sort of perspective. Using split-screen, the performances at the revival concerts are set against clips of the same artists in the '50s, and against a collage of related fragments: town officials railing against beat music, Nixon appealing to the nation, the Lone Ranger ordering silver bullets, Khrushchev banging the table at the UN. Chuck Berry starts and ends the film (in duet with Bo Diddley: worth the ticket price), the Five Satins revive memories of the Moonglows and the Penguins, the Shirelles show a leg, and even the relatively talent-free interloper from the '60s, Chubby Checker, carries it off acceptably. Minor quibbles aside, the film succeeds totally. JC

Let the People Sing

(1942, GB, 109 min, b/w)
d/p John Baxter. *sc* John Baxter, Barbara K Emary, Geoffrey Orme. *ph* Jimmy Wilson. *ed* Jack Harris. *ad* Holmes Paul. *m* Kennedy Russell. *cast* Alastair Sim, Fred Emney, Edward Rigby, Patricia Roc, Oliver Wakefield, Annie Esmond.
●John Baxter was the British director probably least patronising and most sympathetic to the working classes and their culture during the '30s and '40s, and even if his films now often seem naïve and simplistic, it's good at least to see an honest and humorous attempt to deal with life outside Mayfair. Less scathing than *Love on the Dole* (his best known film), this adaptation of a JB Priestley novel is a spritely, vaguely Capra-esque comedy about a couple of men on the run from the law, turning up in a town where the music hall is threatened with takeover, both by museum-loving dullards and by commerce. The pair join together with the locals to fight the move, while Fred Emney steals the show as a government arbitrator susceptible to the charms of alcohol. GA

Lettre, La

see Letter, The

Lettres de Mon Moulin, Les (Letters from My Windmill)

(1954, Fr, 160 min, b/w)
d/p/sc Marcel Pagnol. *ph* WillyFactorovitch. *ed* Monique Lacombe.*ad* Robert Giordani, Jacques Mandaroux.*m* Henri Tomasi. *cast* Roger Crouzet, Henri Crémieux, Fernand Sardou, Henri Vilbert, Rellys, Edouard Delmont.
●Alphonse Daudet leaves Paris for Provence, where he moves into a windmill and sets about recycling the local scene for his short stories. There follow adaptations of three of these. Two are whimsical tales about lovable priests, the other tells how Daudet helped out an obstreperous miller. A lot of this is so rambling it hardly seems to have been directed at all, but occasionally the affection and humanity of Pagnol's early work shines through.The version released on video omits the prologue but adds *Le Curé de Cucugnan*, another Daudet adaptation which Pagnol directed for TV in 1967. The original was released in the US (shorn to 132 min) with subtitles by Preston Sturges. BBa

Letzte Loch, Das

see Last Hole, The

Letzte Mann, Der

see Last Laugh, The

Leviathan

(1989, US/It, 98 min)
d George Pan Cosmatos. *p* Luigi De Laurentiis, Aurelio De Laurentiis. *sc* David Peoples, Jeb Stuart. *ph* Alex Thomson. *ed* Roberto Silvi, John F Burnett. *pd* Ron Cobb. *m* Jerry Goldsmith. *cast* Peter Weller, Richard Crenna, Amanda Pays, Daniel Stern, Ernie Hudson, Michael Carmine, Meg Foster, Lisa Eilbacher, Hector Elizondo.
●Dear Hollywood: I have this astounding movie idea, so hold on to your hairpieces and picture this: an isolated group of professionals, totally cut off from the world, their deadline fast approaching, happen across and Ancient Enigma…but before they know what's going down, they are cut down to size, violently, one by one. Yeah, I know it sounds kinda like *Alien* and *The Thing*, but that's the beauty of it, and you haven't heard the clincher. See, it ain't set in space or the Arctic, but in a Studio Preview Theatre! We get the usual motley crew of critics: the ambitious looker who really wants to pen a blockbuster (Amanda Pays could do it); the cynical old hack who is beginning to slip (a role for Richard Crenna, this); the egotist who panics as soon as the blood begins to flow; the standard no-hopers, strictly sfx fodder (we could throw in Ernie Hudson or Daniel Stern); and of course the hero, a lean, silent type who susses the Corporate Conspiracy, destroys the monster, and escapes to tell the world (how about Peter Weller?). Alternatively, you could transpose the situation to a sub-aquatic mining project, call it something imposing like *Leviathan*, and watch all those *DeepStar Six* and *Abyss* punters stay home again. TCh

Level Five

(1996, Fr, 106 min)
d/sc/ph/ed Chris Marker. *m* Michel Krasna. *cast* Catherine Belkhodja, Kenji Tokitsu, Nagisa Oshima, Junishi Ushiyama.
●Level one is reserved for Communists, Catholics, anarchists and the rest. Level two is for those with with a modicum of wit and self-awareness. That's as high as we get – except perhaps in death. Like Marker's masterpiece, *Sunless*, this is an essay film drawing on documentary and fiction techniques (crucially, aspects of correspondence); it uses the future as a conduit to the past – sci-fi as memory – a theme that takes us, naturally, to Japan. The central authorial conceit here is not without problems: Belkhodja interfacing with computer and remote-controlled camera, trying to complete a game which reconstructs the battle of Okinawa, 1945. It's easy to get lost in cyberspace. Marker goes from odd socks to military annihilation in the blink of an eye; he can be too quick to make connections, too indulgent of the muse (a toy parrot comes to mind). Yet the history of Okinawa is fascinating: 150,000 died, one third of the island's population, many by mass suicide (we meet a man who killed his entire family, rather than let them fall to the Yankee demons). Here are the foundations for Hiroshima. If ever there was a film-maker who might come up with a Theory of Everything, it's Marker. TCh

Lewis & Clark & George

(1996, US, 84 min)
d Rod McCall. *p* Dan Gunther, J Todd Harris. *sc* Rod McCall. *ph* Michael Mayers. *ed* Ed Marx. *pd* John Huke. *m* Ben Vaughn. *cast* Dan Gunther, Salvator Xuereb, Rose McGowan, James Brolin, Paul Bartel.
●This quirky black comedy by writer/director McCall musters more pizzazz than most contemporary crime capers. Lewis (Xuereb) and Clark (Gunther) are escaped convicts criss-crossing the West with a tricky treasure map. Lewis is an illiterate Monty Clift-lookalike with a penchant for mindless violence, Clark a white collar criminal, a useful navigator but an unreliable ally – especially after he bumps into George (Rose McGowan), a mute femme fatale with a poisonous snake in her valise. This is the kind of lark the Jonathans Demme or Kaplan might have dashed off for the drive-in market in the '70s. It both satirises and typifies Texan trailer park culture – there's a funny throwaway bit when Lewis massacres a busload of New York tourists who've come to gawp at the cowboys, and a novel scene involving the consumption of frozen beer. Cult credentials are further enhanced by the reunion of the darkly handsome Xuereb and the voluptuous McGowan from Gregg Araki's little-seen youth classic *The Doom Generation*. This is nothing like as cutting-edge, but it's fun while it lasts. Propelled by a hip, surprisingly eclectic soundtrack by Ben Vaughn, and directed with a dab hand, it isn't a second too long. TCh

Ley de Herodes, La

see Herod's Law

Ley Lines (Nihon Kuro Shakai – Ley Lines)

(1999, Jap, 105 min)
d Takashi Miike. *p* Toshiki Kimura. *sc* Ichiro Ryu. *ph* Naosuke Imaizumi. *ed* Taiji Shimamura. *ad* Akira Ishige. *m* Koji Endo. *cast* Kazuki Kitamura, Li Dan, Michisuke Kashiwaya, Tomoro Taguchi, Ren Osugi, Sho Aikawa, Naoto Takenaka.
●The final part of Miike's *Triad Society* trilogy offers a more street-level perspective on the tensions between Chinese and Japanese criminals than *Shinjuku Triad Society* or *Rainy Dog*. Three immigrant kids abandon their small town homes in rural Japan for the bright lights of Tokyo, where they suffer all the humiliations and setbacks of their kind and eventually come up against a psychotic Mr Big (guest star Takenaka at his most pervy). Miike characteristically minimises the sociological aspects and turns the film instead into a paean to romantic folly; the elegiac ending is up there with *Pierrot le fou*. The implication is that Japan itself is now the triad society, forcing those it denies 'membership' into desperate acts of love and crime. TR

Liaison Pornographique, Une (An Intimate Affair)

(1999, Fr/Bel/Luxembourg/Switz, 82 min)
d Frédéric Fonteyne. *p* Patrick Quinet. *sc* Philippe Blasband. *ph* Virginie Saint Martin. *ed* Chantal Hymans. *ad* Véronique Sacrez, Marc-Philippe Guerig. *m* Jeannot Sanavia, André Dziezuk, Marc Mergen. *cast* Nathalie Baye, Sergi López, Jacques Viala, Paul Pavel, Sylvie van den Elsen, Pierre Geranio, Hervé Sogne, Christophe Sermet.
●Presented in that already dated pseudo-documentary style, wherein interviews give rise to unreliable flashbacks, this teasing adult movie purports to dissect a relationship between two apparently respectable, middle-aged Parisians who share a very peculiar fetish. He (López) responds to a lonely hearts ad that she (Baye) placed in the paper, or was it on the Internet? Their stories differ. Both well satisfied by the anonymous tryst, they resolve to meet weekly, and repair to a modest hotel room. What started as a purely physical attraction imperceptibly shifts into an emotional and spiritual realm. But the persistent documentary-maker probes – what about the sex? An elegantly droll romance, this feels rather like a belated riposte to *Last Tango in Paris*. The mise-en-scène is beautifully modulated, a pitch-perfect exercise in imbuing emotional resonance through composition, cutting and camera movement, while Baye and the soulful López instil their roles with a tender sense of possibility cherished and resigned. TCh

Liaisons Dangereuses 1960, Les

(1959, Fr, 108 min, b/w)
d Roger Vadim. *sc* Roger Vadim, Claude Brulé. *ph* Marcel Grignon. *ed* Victoria Mercanton. *ad* Robert Guisgand. *m* Jack Murray, Thelonious Monk. *cast* Jeanne Moreau, Gérard Philipe, Annette Vadim, Jean-Louis Trintignant, Jeanne Valérie, Boris Vian, Gillian Hills, Roger Vadim.
●Anyone familiar with the Frears (*Dangerous Liaisons*) and Forman (*Valmont*) versions will immediately see the problem about updating this story. The innocence and lack of guile which the preyed-upon characters must embody is not convincingly available in a contemporary setting and neither, therefore, is the cruelty which exploits those qualities; and Annette Vadim's flight into madness would surely have lacked conviction even in 1782, when de Laclos was writing. Though this is the weakest of the three adaptations, it does have in Moreau and Philipe the choicest of scheming monsters. The Thelonious Monk score natters on, without discernible relevance; and Vadim himself appears at the start to put us right about men and women, deploying with exquisite negligence his cigarette holder, the overcoat draped around his shoulders. What did all those gorgeous women see in this noodle? BBa

Liam

(2000, GB/Ger/It, 91 min)
d Stephen Frears. *p* Colin McKeown, Martin Tempia, Ulrich Felsberg. *sc* Jimmy McGovern. *ph* Andrew Dunn. *ed* Kristina Hetherington. *pd* Stephen Fineren. *m* John Murphy. *cast* Ian Hart, Claire Hackett, Anne Reid, Anthony Borrows, Megan Burns, David Hart, Russell Dixon, Julia Deakin.
●Liverpool in the 1930s. Seven-year-old Liam (Borrows) lives in a working class Irish Catholic neighbourhood, with an older brother and sister,

devout mam (Hackett) and hard working dad (Ian Hart). But the Depression is beginning to kick, and work on the docks becomes scarce. The once proud breadwinner becomes embittered as he's forced to beg for a day's work. He blames his bosses first, then the Church, and finally he falls in with the Black Shirts and blames the Jews. Meanwhile Liam's suffering spiritual torment in religious instruction as he prepares to take his First Communion. McGovern's tub-thumping and angry humour is potent enough, and the film forces a kind of grim compassion for its painfully misdirected anti-hero. Hart doggedly refuses to soften this man, and that in itself commands respect. But the movie (made for BBC TV) goes straight where you'd expect, and the running gag involving Borrows' saucer-eyed urchin soon wears thin. (From the book *The Back Crack Boy* by Joseph McKeown.) TCh

Lianna

(1982, US, 112 min)
d John Sayles. *p* Jeffrey Nelson, Maggie Renzi. *sc* John Sayles. *ph* Austin de Besche. *ed* John Sales. *ad* Jeanne McDonnell. *m* Mason Daring. *cast* Linda Griffiths, Jane Hallaren, Jon DeVries, Jo Henderson, Jessica Wight MacDonald, Jesse Solomon, John Sayles.

●Sayles is spokesman for his generation, the babies of the post-war boom who made love and fought their wars within themselves. Their growing pains came late: Lianna (Griffiths) is thirty, married and the mother of two, when she falls in love with Ruth (Hallaren), her night-school teacher. Sayles sympathetically maps the hurricane-like effects of this on Lianna's life – thrown out by her philandering husband, cold-shouldered by her straight friends, stormy scenes with her lover – his sparkling dialogue illuminating every aspect of Lianna's sexuality with a zeal that is almost proselytising. The love scenes are infused with a tender erotic glow that deepens the shadows around the titillation of *Personal Best*, and the comedy in Lianna's post-coital glee as she cruises other women and announces herself as gay to people in launderettes is irresistible. A gem, rough-hewn by Sayles and polished to perfection in peerless performances. FD

Liar (aka Deceiver)

(1997, US, 102 min)
d Jonas Pate, Josh Pate. *p* Peter Glatzer. *sc* Jonas Pate, Josh Pate. *ph* Bill Butler. *ed* Dan Lebental. *pd* John Kretschmer. *m* Harry Gregson-Williams. *cast* Tim Roth, Chris Penn, Michael Rooker, Renee Zellweger, Ellen Burstyn, Rosanna Arquette.

●Deceit, infidelity and murder. Sex, drugs and guns. Obsession, schizophrenia and psychosis. Roth, Penn and Rooker. Yup, another hard-boiled US indie offering. There's a murdered woman (Zellweger), so rich bad boy Roth sits across a polygraph machine from detective Rooker and junior trainee Penn, and tells his story. Then he tells it again. Then he tells another one. Cue flashbacks while we puzzle out what's going on: Roth's character seems to be playing power games with his interrogators, confidence tricks with the lie detector and generally misbehaving, but like everyone else he has his problems, not the least of which is that he's an alcoholic epileptic. There's fun to be had watching the three leads each turning the screw; the knotty flashback structure is handled with some lucidity; and the film often looks striking. Finally, though, the screenplay by twin writer/directors Jonas and Josh Pate fails to unearth any fresh insights into the nature of memory and duplicity. NB

Liar Liar

(1997, US, 87 min)
d Tom Shadyac. *p* Brian Grazer. *sc* Paul Guay, Stephen Mazur. *ph* Russell Boyd.*ed* Don Zimmerman. *pd* Linda DeScenna.*m* John Debney. *cast* Jim Carrey, Maura Tierney, Justin Cooper, Cary Elwes, Anne Haney, Jennifer Tilly, Amanda Donohoe, Swoosie Kurtz.

●The father of five-year-old Max has missed one too many special occasions through alleged overwork, so when he's not there to see his son blow out the candles, a birthday wish lays down the gauntlet – daddy has to stop telling lies for one day. Since dad's in the legal profession, this obviously complicates matters, but, this being a Jim Carrey vehicle, it also provides the springboard for the usual panoply of elastic twitchery and broad knockabout. The first third of the movie pitches Carrey's aspiring attorney into professional anxieties over a career-making case, the second unleashes a 24-hour truth spell, and the rest is spent on a fairly predictable resolution. Pretty rudimentary, but it keeps Carrey's occasional over-exuberance in check and delivers likeable, effective, but decidedly mainstream comedy. TJ

Libel

(1959, GB, 100 min, b/w)
d Anthony Asquith. *p* Anatole de Grunwald. *sc* Anatole de Grunwald, Karl Tunberg. *ph* Robert Krasker. *ed* Frank Clarke. *ad* Paul Sheriff. *m* Benjamin Frankel. *cast* Dirk Bogarde, Olivia de Havilland, Paul Massie, Robert Morley, Wilfrid Hyde White, Richard Wattis, Millicent Martin, Kenneth Griffith, Richard Dimbleby.

●A genteel British courtroom drama, adapted from Edward Wooll's 1934 play. Aristo Bogarde's convenient amnesia prevents him from recalling anything of his life before his flight from a German PoW camp, whereupon Canadian airman Massie reveals to the press that the real baronet died during the escape and, ergo, Bogarde is an imposter. Even spouse de Havilland has her doubts in this fustian and rather creaky piece of plot-heavy fluff. TJ

Libera

(1992, It, 85 min)
d/sc Pappi Corsicato. *ph* Roberto Meddi, Raffaele Mertes. *ed* Fabio Nunziata. *ad* Pappi Corsicato. *cast* Iaia Forte, Ninni Bruschetta, Cristina Donadio.

●First time director Pappi Corsicato has been called Naples' answer to Pedro Almodóvar, a description which might be more accurate if the Italian learned to temper his stylistic exuberance with a sense of overriding purpose. Three stories each swivel round an individual woman's misfortune at the hands of male caprice – two faithless husbands and a dope-addict son – but only the last comes up with a storyline outrageous enough to match the primary colour scheme and off-kilter wit. Here, a plucky news-vendor turns her partner's womanising to profit by taping his activities and selling the results. TJ

Libera Me

(1993, Fr, 107 min)
d Alain Cavalier. *p* René Fauvél. *sc* Alain Cavalier, Bernard Crombey, Andrée Fresco. *ph* Patrick Blossier. *ed* Marie-Pomme Carteret. *pd* Claire Seguin. *cast* Annick Concha, Pierre Concha, Thierry Labelle, Christophe Turrier.

●An elegant, original and just occasionally irritating oddity, this film – from the director of *Thérèse* – consists entirely of wordless, enigmatic tableaux (many of them close-ups of faces, hands and objects). These slowly coalesce into an elliptical narrative about the spirit of resistance in an authoritarian state given over to imprisonment and torture. It looks, as one might expect, marvellous (though one can't help thinking that it rather aestheticises cruelty), and in the end it's Bressonian, in its focus on essentials, rather than gimmicky. Unlike Bresson's best, however, it remains rather soulless. GA

Liberation of L.B. Jones, The

(1969, US, 102 min)
d William Wyler. *p* Ronald Lubin. *sc* Stirling Silliphant, Jesse Hill Ford. *ph* Robert Surtees. *ed* Robert Swink, Carl Cress. *pd* Kenneth A Reid. *m* Elmer Bernstein. *cast* Lee J Cobb, Anthony Zerbe, Roscoe Lee Browne, Lola Falana, Lee Majors, Barbara Hershey, Yaphet Kotto, Arch Johnson, Chill Wills.

●A surprisingly tough-minded adaptation of Jesse Hill Ford's novel of Southern racism, with co-scriptwriter Stirling Silliphant eschewing the easy options of his earlier *In the Heat of the Night* for a grim demonstration of the inadequacies of liberal compromise over the institutional conflicts of class and colour. Wyler's final film, set in Tennessee, finds its catalyst in the divorce action brought by middle class black undertaker Browne, in which a white cop (Zerbe) is named as co-respondent. PT

Libero Burro

(1999, It, 108 min)
d Sergio Castellitto. *p* Massimo Ferrero. *sc* Piero Bodrato, Sergio Castellitto, Margaret Mazzantini, Giulia Mibelli. *ph* Gianfilippo Corticelli, Noelie Ungaro. *ed* Mauro Bonanni. *pd* Sonia Peng. *m* Angélique Nachon, Jean-Claude Nachon. *cast* Sergio Castellitto, Margaret Mazzantini, Michel Piccoli, Chiara Mastroianni, Bruno Armando, Paolo Porto.

●In this diverting light crime comedy, Sergio Castellitto, sometime theatre director and ebullient star of Tornatore's *The Starmaker*, plays a Southern Italian ex-reform school boy, Burro, who crosses an old rival – now a violent big cheese – over a property redevelopment in Turin. His rival puts Burro's partner on ice; Burro, with new partner Catherine (Mazzantini), kidnaps the cheese's neglected son. Basically it's a nicely judged, well acted, romantic riff on family, love and ambition centred on Castellitto's larger than life persona. Piccoli is Burro's chef pal with a dubbed accent suitable for the capo of capos. WH

Libertad, La (Freedom)

(2001, Arg, 73 min)
d Lisandro Alonso. *p* Hugo Alonso. *sc* Lisandro Alonso. *ph* Cobi Migliora. *ed* Lisandro Alonso, Martin Mainoli. *m* Juan Montecchia. *cast* Mizael Savavedr, Humberto Estrada, Rafael Estrada, Omar Didino, Javier Didino.

●So low-key as to come across as a kind of real-time sociological documentary, this uses long, slow, uneventful takes to chart a day in the life of a woodcutter who spends most of his time working alone in the Argentinian countryside. So we see him select and chop down trees, empty his bowels, listen to the radio, drive the staves to a buyer, drive back, and finally kill, roast and eat an armadillo(!). Certainly, there's an integrity to the film, and it's fascinating to watch someone so at home with nature, so isolated from people; but whether there's any deeper purpose to Alonso's austere methods than just showing how its subject lives is unclear. GA

Libertarias

(1995, Sp/Bel, 131 min)
d Vicente Aranda. *p* Andrés Vicente Gómez, Manfredi Traxler, Thasi Vanhuysse. *sc* Vicente Aranda, José Luis Guarner, Antonio Rabinad. *ph* Jose Luis Alcaine. *ed* Teresa Font. *pd* Joseph Rosell. *m* José Nieto. *cast* Ana Belén, Victoria Abril, Adriana Gil, Loles Leon, Laura Maña, Miguel Bosé.

●Aranda's big number on the Spanish Civil War deserves praise for its feminist perspective on the course of the 1936–7 revolution, when women's liberation was a logical, if hardly well-recognised, constituent of the libertarian ideals that the Spanish working class rose up to assert. Seen through the eyes of Maria (Gil), an initially fragile nun driven into a female militia by the revolution in Barcelona, it also takes a thoroughly circumscribed stance on the role of religion in this history. The film crams and elides both events and characters, and, after a brave start, loses its direction and our involvement – particularly problematic is a sudden final outburst of brutal violence. NB

Libertin, Le

(2000, Fr, 102 min)
d Gabriel Aghion. *p* Gaspard de Chavagnac. *sc* Gabriel Aghion, Eric-Emmanuel Schmitt. *ph* Jean-Marie Dreujou. *ed* Luc Barnier. *pd* Dan Weil. *m* Bruno Coulais. *cast* Vincent Perez, Fanny Ardant, Josiane Balasko, Michel Serrault, Arielle Dombasle, Christian Charmetant, Françoise Lépine, François Lalande.

●There's little doubt that the life and experiences of Denis Diderot – writer and co-ordinator of the mid-18th century *Encyclopédie*, a milestone publication which offered a rallying point for Enlightenment ideas – would make a fascinating movie. Not this one, regrettably. With so much juicy potential to play with, we're offered an all-star romp, with the occasional thudding epigram jostling for attention among the double entendres, shagging jokes and gratuitous nudity. A baronial country chateau provides the location for the sundry fun and frolics, with the chapel crypt hiding the illicit presses of the *Encyclopédie*, which both the hosts and Diderot himself (Perez) are keen to keep from the prying eyes of the local police and Serrault's visiting Cardinal. While the lady of the house (Balasko) distracts the prelate's attention with a series of deeply unfunny ruses, Diderot struggles over his latest entry on

'*Moralité*', thanks in no small part to the allure of fellow house guest Mme Therbouche (Ardant) and the strain it puts on his already faithless marriage. And so it plods wearily on with the sort of single-track 'fnarr-fnarr' puerility you hoped had gone out of fashion with the 'Carry On' series. TJ

Liberty Heights

(1999, US, 127 min)
d Barry Levinson. *p* Barry Levinson, Paula Weinstein. *sc* Barry Levinson. *ph* Chris Doyle. *ed* Stu Linder. *pd* Vincent Peranio. *m* Andrea Morricone. *cast* Adrien Brody, Bebe Neuwirth, Joe Mantegna, Ben Foster, Rebekah Johnson, Orlando Jones, David Krumholtz.

●'Where is the jawbone of an ass?' ponders young Ben Kurtzman (Foster). 'You mean there's an animal called an ass?!' We are in Baltimore, 1954. Writer/director Levinson set *Diner* here, *Tin Men* and *Avalon*, a series distinguished by a choice strain of comic exasperation at girls, cars and smorgasbord and an underlying sadness at the on-rush of modernity which you might call pop-Proustian. It's a rich, personal tapestry he's weaving, film by film. This droll and sometimes delectable film is, however, exactly how it seems: like the edges of an expansive, but rather flat and loose threaded tapestry. Ben reaches puberty and comes to the alarming realisation that the world is not universally Jewish; meanwhile brother Van (Brody) sets his cap at a Gentile Cinderella several leagues out of his class. Their pop (Mantegna) is being put out of the burlesque business by the arrival of TV, and gets mixed up in the numbers racket. About an hour in, the movie stirs itself to muster some sort of drama, but then it all dies away again before anything too drastic happens. Lovingly recreated with some delicious comic scenes, this is a warm, soft, picture going nowhere. TCh

Libido

(1973, Aus, 92 min, b/w)
d John B Murray, Tim Burstall, David Baker. *sc* Craig McGregor, Hal Porter, David Williamson. *ph* Eric Lomas, Robin Copping, Bruce McNaughton. *ed* Ted Lewis, David Bilcock Jr, Edward McQueen-Mason. *m* Tim Healy, Billy Green; Peter Best, Bruce Smeaton. *cast* Elke Neidhart, Byron Williams; John Williams, Jill Forster; Jack Thompson, Max Gillies.

●Three episodes dealing, more or less, with the theme of infidelity. *The Husband*, directed by Murray, is a depressingly flat and unimaginatively shot venture into trendy married life. *The Child* is a studiously evocative period piece, based on a story by Hal Porter that ends up a direct crib of *The Go-Between*, with no point beyond proving that Tim Burstall can direct with a trace less vulgarity than he showed in *Stork* or *Alvin Purple*. *The Family Man*, written by David Williamson, is the best of the three, managing to at least begin to explore inter-personal tensions and latent sexual aggressions. The women picked up by the appalling male duo (cruising while the wife of one is in hospital giving birth) are drawn in a strongly idiosyncratic way; finally, though, the piece falls clumsily between TV drama, fringe theatre, and Cassavetes-style *cinéma vérité*. A fourth story, written by Thomas Keneally and directed by Fred Schepisi, has been excised. VG

Licence to Kill

(1989, US, 133 min)
d John Glen. *p* Albert R Broccoli, Michael G Wilson. *sc* Michael G Wilson, Richard Maibaum. *ph* Alec Mills. *ed* John Grover, Carlos Puente. *pd* Peter Lamont. *m* Michael Kamen. *cast* Timothy Dalton, Carey Lowell, Robert Davi, Talisa Soto, Anthony Zerbe, Frank McRae, Everett McGill, Benico Del Toro, David Hedison.

●Not as witty as *The Living Daylights*, but it doesn't let the audience down in the arena of effects, gadgetry, and locations. It even makes muddled concessions towards a feisty Bond girl (Lowell) – one who must prove her sincerity by splitting skulls and fingernails with equal abandon. The plot kicks off with Bond and ex-CIA friend Felix Leiter capturing billionaire drug lord Sanchez (Davi), then deftly parachuting into Leiter's wedding. But Sanchez escapes to exact bloody revenge on Leiter and his bride, leaving Bond with a personal vendetta and a revoked licence to kill. The settings range from the Florida Keys (shark attacks, spectacular aerial rescues, scuba diving) to the fictitious Isthmus City in Latin America. It's all very pacy, with the overly straightforward plotting dimmed but not obscured by the hi-tech effects. CM

Licence to Live (Ningen Gokaku)

(1998, Jap, 109 min)
d Kiyoshi Kurosawa. *p* Tsutomu Tsuchikawa, Satoshi Kanno. *sc* Kiyoshi Kurosawa. *ph* Junichiro Hayashi. *ed* Masahiro Onaga. *pd* Tomoyuki Maruo. *m* Gary Ashiya. *cast* Koji Yakusho, Hidetoshi Nishijima, Shun Sugata, Lily, Sho Aikawa, Ren Osugi.

●Yutaka (Nishijima), aged 24, awakes from a ten-year coma and struggles to come to terms with everything from the collapse of the USSR to his own missed puberty and the fact that his family has fallen apart. Fish farmer Fujimori (Yakusho), an iconoclastic and eccentric family friend, takes him in and watches him try to reunite his parents and sister – and then supports him when he concludes there's more to life than family ties. Sundance alumnus Kurosawa previously looked more like an ambitious genre technician than the commentator on existential dilemmas he proves to be here. To his great credit, he frames the whole thing as black comedy and delivers the wryest of surprise endings. TR

License to Drive

(1988, US, 88 min)
d Greg Beeman. *p* Andrew Licht, Jeffrey A Mueller. *sc* Neil Tolkin. *ph* Bruce Surtees. *ed* Wendy Green Bricmont. *pd* Lawrence G Paull. *m* Jay Ferguson. *cast* Corey Haim, Corey Feldman, Carol Kane, Richard Masur, Heather Graham, Michael Manasseri, Harvey Miller, Nina Siemaszko.

●Young Corey Haim suffers the ultimate humiliation: he fails his driving test. He's not about to let legal niceties spoil his hot date with Mercedes (Graham), however, so he lies to his parents and borrows grandfather's classic car. Everything you've ever hated about American teenagers, their music, money, fashion sense, their values, and most of all their pin-ups, in one auto-destructive movie. TCh

Lie, The (Mensonge)

(1992, Fr, 89 min)
d François Margolin. *p* Alain Sarde. *sc* Denis Saada, François Margolin. *ph* Caroline Champetier. *ed* Martine Giordano. *pd* Julie Sfez. *cast* Nathalie Baye, Didier Sandre, Hélène Lapiower, Marc Citti, Dominique Besnéhard.

●Emma (Baye) discovers that she's both pregnant and HIV-positive – then that she was infected by her husband Charles (Sandre), a secret bisexual. Relationships with family and friends become strained as her life begins to disintegrate. Despite worthy intentions, Margolin, on his first time out as director and co-writer, sketches only a bare outline of the issues raised. AO

Liebe der Jeanne Ney, Die

see Love of Jeanne Ney, The

Liebe in Deutschland, Eine

see Love in Germany, A

Liebe ist kälter als der Tod

see Love Is Colder Than Death

Liebelei

(1932, Ger, 85 min, b/w)
d Max Ophüls. *p* Fred Lissa. *sc* Hans Wilhelm, Kurt Alexander. *ph* Franz Planer. *ed* Friedel Buchott. *ad* Gabriel Pellon. *m* Theo Mackeben. *cast* Wolfgang Liebeneiner, Magda Schneider, Luise Ullrich, Willy Eichberger, Paul Hörbiger, Gustaf Gründgens.

●'What is eternity?' a young girl asks her soldier lover. What indeed? As in Ophüls' *Lola Montès*, *La Ronde* and *Madame de...* this early German melodrama – which treats the passionate, whirlwind love affair between a young lieutenant and a shy sensitive fräulein – acknowledges both the liberating joy of love and its sad transience. For humans are never entirely free of their past, and young Fritz has a skeleton in his closet that makes a mockery of the pair's vows of undying love. Most similar to *Madame de...*, the film may be a little slow and ragged at times, but its final emotional power is undeniably immense. EA

Liebestraum

(1991, US, 113 min)
d Mike Figgis. *p* Eric Fellner. *sc* Mike Figgis. *ph* Juan Ruiz Anchia. *ed* Martin Hunter. *pd* Waldemar Kalinowski. *m* Mike Figgis. *cast* Kevin Anderson, Pamela Gidley, Bill Pullman, Kim Novak, Graham Beckel, Zach Grenier, Thomas Kopache, Catherine Hicks, Taina Elg.

●Figgis's temple-throbbing suspenser is a convoluted tale of lust and jealousy, moodier and more elegiac than his earlier *Internal Affairs*. Nick Kaminsky (Anderson), an architectural journalist, is summoned to the death-bed of the mother he never knew (Novak). Mooching around the unfamiliar town, he meets old friend Paul (Pullman), a property developer about to demolish a unique cast-iron department store, boarded up since a gruesome '50s murder. He becomes obsessed with the fate of the building, which Paul is sworn to destroy, and with Paul's wife Jane (Gidley), a photographer who records the ruin's final hours. And amid all the dust and debris, is a shadowy, malevolent figure who seems bent on harm towards all three. Kaminsky's adventures in the eerie small town have a Lynchian flavour: there's a paunchy, psychotic police chief, a curious doubling of whorehouse and nun scenes, and the final plot gyrations defy analysis. But the performances are great, especially Gidley's innocent and moving femme fatale. SFe

Lied für Beko, Ein

see Song for Beko, A

Liens de Sang

see Blood Relatives

Lies

(1983, US, 102 min)
d Ken Wheat, Jim Wheat. *p* Ken Wheat, Jim Wheat, Shelley Hermann. *sc* Ken Wheat, Jim Wheat. *ph* Robert Ebinger. *ed* Michael Ornstein. *pd* Christopher Henry. *m* Marc Donahue. *cast* Ann Dusenberry, Bruce Davison, Gail Strickland, Clu Gulager, Terence Knox, Bert Remsen, Dick Miller.

●Surfacing contemporaneously with *Blood Simple* and with a comparably sophisticated approach to genre manipulation, this variation on the *My Name Is Julia Ross* scenario briefly allowed the Wheats and the Coens to be mentioned in the same breath. Dusenberry makes a lively heroine-in-distress, sucked into an impersonation scheme that leaves her facing death or a fate worse-than. 'Promising' remains the best description, thus begging the question: Whither the Wheats? BBa

Lies (Kojitmal)

(1999, SKor, 122 min)
d Jang Sun-Woo. *p* Charles Shin. *sc* Jang Sun-Woo. *ph* Kim Woo-Hyung. *ed* Park Gok-Ji. *ad* Kim Myeong-Kyeong. *m* Dal Palan. *cast* Lee Sang-Hyun, Kim Tae-Yeon.

●Based on a novel banned as 'pornographic', Jang's follow-up to *Timeless, Bottomless Bad Movie* is a devastating account of amour fou. A married sculptor (his wife is abroad) blind-dates a high school girl and quickly takes her virginity. They launch into an affair in which the girl submits more or less willingly to a series of whippings and beatings. The man sees these as no more than strenuous foreplay, but when the roles are reversed, the girl proves to be made of sterner stuff – not least when touches of coprophilia and murder enter the frame. And when it's all over, the ending contrasts the intensity of the affair with the 'lies' on which conventional relationships rest. Made with two absolutely fearless first-time actors, this amazing film recaptures something of the shock *L'Age d'or* provoked in 1930. TR

Lies My Father Told Me

(1975, Can, 102 min)
d Ján Kádar. *p* Anthony Bedrich, Harry Gulkin. *sc* Ted Allan. *ph* Paul van der Linden. *ed* Edward Beyer, Richard Marks. *pd* François Barbeau. *m* Sol Kaplan. *cast* Yossi Yadin, Len Birman, Marilyn Lightstone, Jeffrey Lynas, Ted Allan, Barbara Chilcott.

●A distinctly warm-hearted tale of a Jewish childhood in Montreal in the 1920s. Grandfather, a rag-and-bone man, adheres to the old ways, frowning upon the brash commercial instincts of his son-in-law, and winning the favour of his grandson with his whimsical ways. Some attempt is made to sketch in ghetto life and to draw out a child's emotional reading of an adult world. But too often the film merely begs the audience's indulgence, asking it to register no more than its clucking approval or disapproval.

Lies to Live by (Babylon) (Babylon: la paura e la migliore amica dell'uomo)

(1994, It, 100 min, b/w)
d Guido Chiesa. *p* Carlo Degli Esposti, Agnese Fontana. *sc* Guido Chiesa, Antonio Leotti. *ph* Gherardo Gossi. *ed* Anna Napoli. *m* Giuseppe Napoli, Marlene Kunz. *cast* Paolo Lorimer, Valeria Milillo, Sophie Bernhard, Bill Sage, Andrea Prodan.

●An ambitious effort to evoke the Euro-Angst movies of the '70s this starts with images in blown-up 8mm of the wringing of hands and razor-blades being run across chests, before launching into a story about a disconnected foursome in post-industrial Turin. Francesco (Lorimer) is an ex-hard-left, ex-musician, factory worker married dysfunctionally to university worker Carla (Milillo). She's recently had a fling in the States with the mysterious house detective Charles (Sage, from Hartley's *Simple Men*), who's visiting Turin, staying at the house of her best friend Gabriella. Francesco falls into a murderous mood. With its mix of political-era Godard, '90s avant-garde anomie and Euro rock, Chiesa's film sets up a series of teasing conundrums about modern urban alienation, doppelgängers, and the like, but manages to leave them all unresolved. Photography by Gherardo Gossi gives the film an interesting surface (mainly composed of abandoned factory interiors and waste lands), but in the end the relentless lack of humour or seeming point make it a disappointing show. WH

Lieu du Crime, Le

see Scene of the Crime, The

Life

(1999, US, 109 min)
d Ted Demme. *p* Brian Grazer, Eddie Murphy. *sc* Robert Ramsey, Matthew Stone. *ph* Geoffrey Simpson. *ed* Jeffrey Wolf. *pd* Dan Bishop. *m* Wyclef Jean. *cast* Eddie Murphy, Martin Lawrence, Obba Babatundé, Ned Beatty, Bernie Mac, Miguel A Nuñez Jr, Clarence Williams III, Bokeem Woodbine, R Lee Ermey.

●Starting as a 1930s gangster caper, this quickly turns into a broad prison comedy about two chalk 'n' cheese black men – motor-mouthed conman Ray (Murphy) and grouchy, would-be bank clerk Claude (Lawrence) – flung together by cruel chance and Southern racism. Stuck with one another for life, they enjoy a 60-year vacation on a Mississippi prison farm as the result of a trumped up murder charge, their habitual 'odd couple' antagonism disguising a grudging respect that deepens with time. Demme soft pedals the harshness of the prison regime, with gruelling work leavened with ribaldry, baseball, barbecues and conjugal visits. But the tone slowly darkens, as the years of false imprisonment, failed escapes and frustrated dreams take their toll. At its most ambitious, this echoes *The Shawshank Redemption*. Rick Baker's ageing make-up effects are striking, but would not have worked without the leads' subtly effective changes in posture, movement and speech. The feelgood ending is signposted, but the restrained performances still convey a powerful sense of dignity in the face of hardship and injustice. NF

Life, The

see Dérobade, La

Life and Death of Colonel Blimp, The

100

(1943, GB, 163 min)
d/p/sc Michael Powell, Emeric Pressburger. *ph* Georges Périnal. *ed* John Seabourne. *pd* Alfred Junge. *m* Allan Gray. *cast* Roger Livesey, Anton Walbrook, Deborah Kerr, John Laurie, Roland Culver, James McKechnie, Ursula Jeans, David Hutcheson.

●At a time when 'Blimpishness' in the high command was under suspicion as detrimental to the war effort, Powell and Pressburger gave us their own Blimp based on David Low's cartoon character – Major General Clive Wynne-Candy, VC – and back-track over his life, drawing us into sympathy with the prime virtues of honour and chivalry which have transformed him from dashing young spark of the Nineties into crusty old buffer of World War II. Roger Livesey gives us not just a great performance, but a man's whole life: losing his only love (Deborah Kerr) to the German officer (Walbrook) with whom he fought a duel in pre-WWI Berlin, then becoming the latter's lifelong friend and protector. Like much of Powell and Pressburger's work, it is a salute to all that is paradoxical about the English; no one else has so well captured their romanticism banked down beneath emotional reticence and honour. And it is marked by an enormous generosity of spirit: in the history of the British cinema there is nothing to touch it. CPea

Life and Extraordinary Adventures of Private Ivan Chonkin, The (Zycie i Niezwykile Przygodv Szeregowca Iwana Czonkina)

(1994, GB/Fr/It/Czech Republic/Rus, 111 min)
d Jiri Menzel. *p* Eric Abraham. *sc* Zdenek Sverák, Vladimir Voinovich. *ph* JaromírSofr. *ed* Jiri Brozek, Elisabeth Guido.*pd* Milan Bycek. *m* Jiri Sust. *cast* Gennadiy Nazarov, Zoya Buryak, Zinovij Gert, Vladimir Ilyin, Valeriy Dubrovin, Alexei Zharkov, Yuriy Dubrovin.

●Menzel takes his sly mastery of the 'cinema of Occupation' to Russia for an adaptation of Vladimir Voinovich's (ex-samizdat) mega-hit novel of WWII. In the circumstances, the result is something of a miracle. The director, who has the average Czech's limited Russian vocabulary, marshals his actors very ably. He'd need to since for most of the movie they run around like chickens. His drill sergeant has Chonkin in mind when, quoting Stalin, he lectures, 'The enemy always seeks out the weakest in the chain.' When, however, the hapless, libidinous private (Nazarov) is dumped on the village of Dead End (renamed Red End), the Collective is seen in its eccentric, individualistic disarray as all weak links. Only young, fat-buttocked postmistress Nyura (Buryak), whom Menzel likes to film from the rear, to show it's a broad comedy, no doubt, proves welcoming, in and out of doors. There are some tougher swipes (the frenzy at the shop when invasion is announced, the pornographic interrogation of an old Jewish man by the NKVD), but mostly it's hayseed farce. Well shot, however, and finely acted. WH

Life and Nothing But (La Vie et rien d'autre)

(1989, Fr, 134 min)
d Bertrand Tavernier. *p* René Cleitman. *sc* Jean Cosmos, Bertrand Tavernier. *ph* Bruno de Keyzer. *ed* Armand Psenny. *pd* Guy-Claude François. *m* Oswald d'Andrea. *cast* Philippe Noiret, Sabine Azéma, Pascale Vignal, Maurice Barrier, François Perrot, Jean-Pol Dubois, Daniel Russo, Michel Duchaussoy.

●In 1920 in Northern France, haute Parisienne Irène (Azéma) and local teacher Alice (Vignal) search, respectively, for the husband and fiancé they have lost in the war. They find themselves thrown on the mercy of the head of the Missing in Action office, Major Dellaplane (Noiret), whose unending efforts to identify the countless dead, shell-shocked and missing are continually being diverted by a military establishment bent on glorifying French courage with a funeral ceremony for the Unknown Soldier. The film focuses on the way these three interact, but in so doing, broaches bureaucratic hypocrisy and corruption, postwar poverty and racism, social inequality and the deceptions of romantic involvement. But it's Tavernier's careful orchestration of his medium that most expressively colours the motifs of solitude, grief and loss. Subtle, fluid camera movements explore grey fields and stark, impeccably designed sets to supply a palpable sense of time and place; unsentimental yet dignified performances (with Noiret outstanding in his hundredth film role) underline the discreet humanism of Tavernier's approach. GA

Life and Times of Allen Ginsberg, The

(1986, US, 82 min, b/w & col)
d/p Jerry Aronson. *ph* Jean de Segonzac, Roger Carter, Richard Lerner. *ed* Nathaniel Dorsky, Jerry Aronson. *m* Tom Capek. *with* Allen Ginsberg, William Burroughs, Hannah Litsky, Eugene Brooks Ginsberg, Ken Kesey, Timothy Leary, Joan Baez.

●Burroughs, Kerouac, Cassidy, Orlovsky, Huncke – there's amusement to be derived from the respectable Ginsberg family remembering their nice Jewish boy and wondering how he fell in with the wrong crowd. His Russian mother's terror of being trapped led to insanity, and drove him to a conspicuous emancipation. Protest, poetry, drugs: the best quote – 'walking on water wasn't built in a day' – came from Catholic Kerouac on the effects of LSD. Fascinating cultural history. BC

Life and Times of Judge Roy Bean, The

(1972, US, 124 min)
d John Huston. *p* John Foreman. *sc* John Milius. *ph* Richard Moore. *ed* Hugh S Fowler. *ad* Tambi Larsen. *m* Maurice Jarre. *cast* Paul Newman, Jacqueline Bisset, Ava Gardner, Tab Hunter, John Huston, Stacy Keach, Roddy McDowall, Anthony Perkins, Victoria Principal, Anthony Zerbe, Ned Beatty.

●A beguiling Western, even if the John Milius script got semi-strangled along the way. Hawkish mythmaker extraordinary, Milius saw Judge Bean – outlaw turned self-appointed law-giver – as an embodiment of the ambivalent virtues of the old West: evil but necessary, a robber baron achieving tragic grandeur as 'a man who comes in and builds something and then is discarded by what he built'. As such, he should have had the same outsize dimensions as the Teddy Roosevelt of *The Wind and the Lion*, but emerges somewhat diminished in Newman's portrayal of a winsome charmer straight out of *Butch Cassidy* (complete with lyrical interludes and a stickily dreadful song). Playing both ends against the middle, Huston turns it into a rumbustious, episodic lark stuffed with eccentric cameos, but still manages to invest it with his own quizzical attitude to all myths and mythmakers, so that it can be read as an allegory about the capitalistic corruptions of Nixon's America. On the whole, an underrated film. TM

Life and Times of Rosie the Riveter, The

(1980, US, 65 min, b/w & col)
d/p/sc Connie Field. *ph* Cathy Zheutlin, Bonnie Friedman, Robert Handley, Emiko Omori. *ed* Lucy Massie Phenix, Connie Field. *with* Lola Weixel, Margaret Wright, Lyn Childs, Gladys Belcher, Wanita Allen.

●'Do the job HE left behind' the wartime posters urged American women. Connie Field's documentary explores and exposes the sexual hierarchy of labour operated during (and after) World War II as women quit their homes for the factories while the menfolk did their bit for 'Democracy'. Despite guarantees of continued work for women, the end of the war saw men resume their traditional position in the economy, and women encouraged 'Back to the stove and the marital bed'. Combining propaganda film and newsreel footage – often to hilarious effect – Field contrasts it with recollections from some of the women today in interviews that reveal the extent of sexual and racial discrimination they encountered. Consummately skilful in articulating vital political issues through a strong sense of humour. MA

Life at a Gallop (Cwal)

(1995, Pol, 104 min)
d/sc Krzysztof Zanussi. *ph* Jaroslaw Zamojda. *ed* Marek Denys. *m* Wojciech Kilar. *cast* Maja Komorowska, Bartosz Obuchowicz, Andrzej Szejnach, Karolina Wajda.

●A young boy arrives in the city to live with his aunt and continue his education. Aunt Idalia (Komorowska) is a determined non-conformist with a passion for riding, not exactly a recreation encouraged in Eastern bloc Europe. She and her renegade old friends seek relief from their drab lives by going for exhilarating gallops in the country. Nothing, not even tanks or stone throwing villagers, puts them off. Zanussi's autobiographical drama unfolds in the Poland of the early 1950s. Although it portrays a grim, bureaucratic society in which even schoolboys denounce each other and every sign of bourgeois individualism is frowned upon, it's also surprisingly witty and uplifting. Magnificently shot, and with an outrageously inventive ending, it belies its director's reputation as a film-maker who privileges ideas over emotions. GM

Life at the Top

(1965, GB, 117 min, b/w)
d Ted Kotcheff. *p* James Woolf. *sc* Mordecai Richler. *ph* Oswald Morris. *ed* Derek York. *ad* Edward Marshall. *m* Richard Addinsell. *cast* Laurence Harvey, Jean Simmons, Honor Blackman, Michael Craig, Donald Wolfit, Margaret Johnston, Allan Cuthbertson, Robert Morley, Nigel Davenport, Denis Quilley.
●John Braine's resistible anti-hero Joe Lampton (Harvey) returns in this lacklustre sequel to *Room at the Top* for another double-edged demonstration of 'making it', this time in the glossier muck 'n' brass world of the swinging south. A slightly curious outsiders' view of British capital culture comes from resident Canadians Kotcheff and writer Mordecai Richler, but it's no great leap from here to the subsequent routine teleseries, *Man at the Top*. PH

Life Begins in College (aka The Joy Parade)

(1937, US, 94 min, b/w)
d William A Seiter. *p* Harold Wilson.*sc* Karl Tunberg, Don Ettlinger. *ph* Robert Planck. *ed* Louis Loeffler. *ad* Hans Peters. *songs* Lew Pollack, Sidney Mitchell. *cast* Ritz Brothers, Joan Davis, Tony Martin, Gloria Stuart, Fred Stone, Nat Pendleton, Lon Chaney Jr.
●Cast for the first time without the bolster of their regular support star Alice Faye, the Ritz Brothers provide their usual second-rank comic fizz as the proprietors of Klassy Kampus Klothes, a firm of college-based tailors eager to help the local football team climb the inter-varsity league tables. It's a typically insubstantial caper with complicated plotting to the fore and the dullest juvenile leads imaginable. TJ

Lifeboat

(1944, US, 96 min, b/w)
d Alfred Hitchcock. *p* Kenneth MacGowan. *sc* Jo Swerling. *ph* Glen MacWilliams. *ed* Dorothy Spencer. *ad* James Basevi, Maurice Ransford. *m* Hugo Friedhofer. *cast* Tallulah Bankhead, Walter Slezak, John Hodiak, William Bendix, Hume Cronyn, Henry Hull, Canada Lee, Mary Anderson, Heather Angel.
●The setting is confined to a lifeboat in the Atlantic occupied by survivors from a torpedoed passenger-carrying freighter and the commander of the U-Boat responsible (Slezak). The idea was to contrast the singleminded Nazi against democracy's comparatively feeble representatives, but the script, started by Steinbeck and finished by Hitchcock, appears too calculated. It's worth seeing, though, for Hitchcock's handling of actors in a confined setting, which incidentally introduces an elusive sense of size, a perspective that is heightened by much of the film being shot in close or semi-close-up. Half the time you'd swear the lifeboat is enormous. CPe

Lifeforce

(1985, GB, 101 min)
d Tobe Hooper. *p* Menahem Golan, Yoram Globus. *sc* Dan O'Bannon, Don Jakoby. *ph* Alan Hume. *ed* John Grover. *pd* John Graysmark. *m* Henry Mancini. *cast* Steve Railsback, Peter Firth, Frank Finlay, Mathilda May, Patrick Stewart, Michael Gothard, Nicholas Ball.
●Wows-a-routie! If you've never seen this mind-reeling schlocko sci-fi spectacular then hang on to your brains. Adapted by Dan O'Bannon from the Colin Wilson novel *The Space Vampires*, it starts with something strange happening to a trio of astronauts investigating the path of Halley's Comet, and proceeds with nude extra-terrestrial May turning half of London into sex-crazed zombies. Gasp as Chancery Lane tube goes up in smoke and St Paul's cathedral communicates with another galaxy! Wonder as Messrs Firth and Finlay get through reams of daft expository dialogue without cracking up! Utter nonsense, but great fun. TJ

Lifeguard

(1976, US, 96 min)
d Daniel Petrie. *p* Ron Silverman. *sc* Ron Koslow. *ph* Ralph Woolsey. *ed* Argyle Nelson Jr. *m* Dale Menten. *cast* Sam Elliott, Anne Archer, Stephen Young, Parker Stevenson, Kathleen Quinlan, Steve Burns.
●Given direction that tends toward the same stolid beefiness as Sam Elliott's over-the-hill-at-thirty lifeguard, this still manages to perform an interesting autopsy on the psyche of the American male. The sub- (and not so sub-) text is homosexual. Heterosexual relationships, infinitely demanding and fraught with chauvinism, pale by comparison with the romantic glow of the male/male encounters; and it's every bit as haunted by the spectral fear of ageing as *Death in Venice*. A film that can narrow choices down to making a million as a car salesman, or drifting with alternate complacency and anxiety into middle-age as a superannuated beach bum, has something going for it in the way of cumulative obsessiveness. VG

Life in Shadows (Vida en Sombras)

(1948, Sp)
d Lorenzo Llobet Gracia. *cast* Fernando Fernán Gómez, Maria Dolores Pradera, Isabel de Pomes, Alfonso Estela.
●Born in a fairground tent during a screening of films by the Lumière brothers, Carlos spends his childhood watching Chaplin, falls in love with his bride-to-be during Thalberg's *Romeo and Juliet*, abandons his job as critic and documentary-maker when she's killed while he's out filming political riots, and finally finds his faith again after seeing Hitchcock's *Rebecca*. This semi-autobiographical film, produced on a small budget as part of Spain's 'amateur cinema' movement (yet looking totally professional in execution), deals with a man whose entire life is shaped by and dedicated to the movies…for better and for worse. As it examines the twisted relationship between life and art, it includes enough references to movies to make the likes of Godard, Wenders and De Palma seem relatively uninterested in the history of their chosen medium. But this is no clever academic work: in evoking its hero's obsession for both film and his wife, it predates (appropriately) the Hitchcock of, say, *Vertigo*, and achieves its emotional power through a fine performance from Fernán Gómez, later to become one of Spain's most impressive actors. GA

Life Is a Bed of Roses

see Vie est un Roman, La

Life Is a Dream

see Mémoire des apparences

Life Is All You Get (Das Leben ist eine Baustelle)

(1997, Ger, 118 min)
d Wolfgang Becker. *p* Stefan Arndt. *sc* Wolfgang Becker, Tom Tykwer. *ph* Martin Kukula. *ed* Patricia Rommel. *pd* Mathias Schwerbrock. *m* Jürgen Kniepe.cast Jürgen Vogel, Christiane Paul, Ricky Tomlinson, Christina Papamichou, Rebecca Hessing, Armin Rohde.
●Director and co-writer Wolfgang Becker weaves a loose, wry and finally tender tale around Jan (Vogel) and his meandering negotiation of the various people in his life: enigmatic lovers, grown-up drop-outs, washed-up lonely parents, irresponsible (incomprehensible) siblings, drifting immigrants, and men with bad haircuts (for this is Germany). A neater film would have given the script another couple of drafts, but the ill-defined narrative is part of the tentative fly-by-night charm. Being about the quixotic, unpredictable paths to reconstructing a social family, it sees opening up to someone as, in the end, an affirmative act of faith and optimism. NB

Life Is a Long Quiet River (La Vie est un long fleuve tranquille)

(1988, Fr, 91 min)
d Etienne Chatiliez. *p* Charles Gassot. *sc* Florence Quentin, Etienne Chatiliez. *ph* Pascale Lebègue. *ed* Chantal Delattre. *pd* Geoffroy Larcher. *m* Gérard Kawczynski. *cast* Benoît Magimel, Valerie Lalande, Tara Romer, Jérôme Floch, André Wilms, Daniel Gélin, Catherine Hiegel, Christine Pignet, Maurice Mons.
●Meet the Quesnoys, smugly conscious of their wealth, righteousness and impeccable taste. Meet, too, the Groseilles, a scurvy brood of slobs and small-time criminals living at the other end of town. Their paths cross when their mutual obstetrician's nurse (and spurned lover) spitefully reveals that she once deliberately swapped the cradles of two new-born babies. Horrified by their son's life to date, the Quesnoys decide to bring Momo (Magimel) into their sheltered fold; the Groseilles agree, for a fee, but don't give a shit about retrieving their Bernadette (Lalande). Momo's habits, however, are deeply ingrained; Bernadette's curiosity about her real parents is aroused; and all hell breaks loose at the Quesnoy mansion. Chatiliez' engaging, anarchic satire on the charmless discretion of the bougeoisie revels in the downfall of the Quesnoys, charting a descent into alcoholism, drugs and easy sex with a wicked logic reminiscent of Bertrand Blier. Nor are the Groseilles glamorised: repression, racism, hypocrisy and greed are rampant. More rigour might have helped, but there is enough beadiness in Chatiliez' first feature to suggest that he may be a talent to watch. GA

Life Is Beautiful (La Vita è Bella)

(1997, It, 116 min)
d Roberto Benigni. *p* Elda Ferri, Gianluigi Braschi. *sc* Vincenzo Cerami, Roberto Benigni. *ph* Tonino Delli Colli. *ed* Simona Paggi. *pd* Danilo Donati. *m* Nicola Piovani. *cast* Roberto Benigni, Nicoletta Braschi, Giorgio Cantarini, Marisa Paredes, Horst Buchholz.
●Audacious but misguided, this determinedly Chaplinesque comic fable starts well enough with the innocent, childlike Guido (Benigni) arriving in a Tuscan town in 1939 to visit his uncle, and courting, in typically eccentric fashion, local teacher Dora (Braschi), whom he manages to seduce away from her Fascist fiancé. So far, so amusing – but then, when the film flashes forward to the couple and their son being sent to a concentration camp, with Guido imaginatively turning events around them into a bizarre child's game in order to protect the boy from the ugly realities of the Holocaust, the whole thing turns sickly, not to say disingenuous (how come the villains are now German rather than Italian?). Well-meaning humanistic 'charm' and a 'poetic' approach to horror (including fuzzy shots of mountains of corpses) are inadequate to the task, and soon bogs down in manipulative and maudlin sentimentality. GA

Life Is Cheap...But Toilet Paper Is Expensive

(1989, US, 88 min)
d Wayne Wang. *p* Winnie Fredriksz. *sc* Spencer Nakasako. *ph* Amir M Mokri. *ed* Chris Sanderson, Sandy Nervig, Rupert Miles, Ma Po Shan, Alasdair Whitelaw, Kevin A Canamar. *ad* Colette Koo. *m* Mark Adler. *cast* Chan Kim Wan, Spencer Nakasako, Victor Wong, Cheng Kwan Min, Cora Miao, Lam Chung, Allen Fong.
●As different from *Dim Sum* as one could possibly imagine, Wang's bizarre look at contemporary Hong Kong is one of the most foul-mouthed, scatological, gorily shocking and relentlessly energetic movies in years. Strung very loosely around an almost non-existent thriller plot, it continually provokes its audience into a reaction, whether it be horror, bewilderment, admiration, or simply hilarity. It is often very, very funny, and its vision of a city on the brink (of change, of an ocean, of complete social and moral breakdown) is wholly plausible. But be warned: this is not easy viewing, and whether it's a seven-minute hand-held camera chase that virtually turns into a kinetic abstract painting, ducks being killed with no pretence at humaneness, or a guy taking a shit while talking to camera, there is no question but that you'll be, shall we say, affected. GA

Life Is Sweet

(1990, GB, 103 min)
d Mike Leigh. *p* Simon Channing-Williams. *sc* Mike Leigh. *ph* Dick Pope. *ed* Jon Gregory. *pd* Alison Chitty. *m* Rachel Portman. *cast* Alison Steadman, Jim Broadbent, Claire Skinner, Jane Horrocks, Stephen Rea, Timothy Spall, David Thewlis, Moya Brady.

●A splendid follow-up to *High Hopes*, in which Leigh's improvisational method achieves symmetry in the form of two very different chefs and twin daughters who are very different from their indomitably normal parents. Andy (Broadbent), is a good-natured cook with an ambition to run his own business from a disgusting mobile snack-bar flogged to him by a drunken mate (Rea); Aubrey (Spall) is a clueless fatty with a desire to be supercool, mastermind of a disastrous venture to bring gourmet cooking to Enfield. Offering such hideous fare as liver in lager and duck in chocolate sauce, Aubrey ropes in Andy's innuendo-prone wife Wendy (Steadman) as a replacement waitress. While the restaurant opening provides narrative focus, Leigh divides his interest between this and the plight of Andy and Wendy's teenage daughters, one (Skinner) a tomboy plumber, the other (Horrocks) an antisocial anorexic whose only enthusiasms are bulimic binges and casual sex with the aid of a jar of peanut butter. Despite two performances of insufficient conviction (Spall and Horrocks), the film is magnificent, mixing enormous fun with sad, serious subjects: the enterprise rip-off, adolescent despair, parents' lost dreams for their children, role-playing, the gutsy optimism of decent, ordinary humanity (represented by Broadbent and Steadman in two stunningly unflashy performances). SGr

Life Is to Whistle (La Vida es silbar)

(1998, Cuba, 110 min)
d Fernando Pérez. *sc* Eduardo del Llano, Humberto Jiménez, Fernando Pérez. *ph* Paúl Pérez Ureta. *ed* Julia Yip. *pd* Raúl Oliva. *m* Edesio Alejandro. *cast* Luis Alberto García, Coralia Veloz, Claudia Rojas, Bebe Pérez, Isabel Santos, Rolando Brito, Joan Manuel Reyes, Monica Guffanti.
●This philosophical, gently magical movie tells of the lives of three Cubans – a nurse to the elderly Julia, 'bum' Elpidio and ballet dancer Mariana – all in the throes of emotional change. It's narrated by 20-year-old Bebe (whom we see in various places: in flashback as a child at the same orphanage as the three principals; burbling words from inside an aquarium). Like a benign Greek god, he oversees the struggles of the others, using a taxi driver to ferry them about Havana in order to accelerate their fates. It's an affirmative movie in a 'seize the day' mould, which sighs at, rather than attacks, Cuba's unfinished revolution. WH

Life Less Ordinary, A

(1997, GB, 102 min)
d Danny Boyle. *p* Andrew Macdonald. *sc* John Hodge. *ph* Brian Tufano. *ed* Mashiro Hirakubo. *pd* Kave Quinn. *m* David Arnold. *cast* Ewan McGregor, Cameron Diaz, Holly Hunter, Delroy Lindo, Ian Holm, Dan Hedaya, Ian McNeice, Stanley Tucci, Tony Shalhoub, Maury Chakin.
●Not a complete write-off, the first US venture by the *Trainspotting* team is still a misfire. A screwball comedy, set in Utah, with a contemporary twist, it aims for a liberating sense of anything goes, but falters on a fantasy element that doesn't play. McGregor is Robert, a whimsical Scot, stuck in a menial job in an American corporation. Sacked, dumped and evicted in the same day, he abducts the boss's daughter Celine (Diaz), who soon takes the kidnapping in hand just to spite her dad. Meanwhile, the private detectives gunning to get her back, Hunter and Lindo, are in fact angels on a mission to ensure the couple fall for each other. Love through jeopardy is their game plan. McGregor is charming, a hopeless soft touch, easily outclassed in the brains department by the mercurial Diaz (a real livewire who jump starts the movie more than once). They make an attractive couple, doing very nicely, thanks, without the Almighty's contrived interventions – gratuitously violent scrapes which lurch the film into forced, mostly unfunny black comedy and even animation. The Coens meet Frank Capra – a mismatch made in heaven. TCh

Life of a Peking Policeman, The

see This Whole Life of Mine

Life of Chikuzan, The (Chikuzan Hitori Tabi)

(1977, Jap, 122 min)
d Kaneto Shindo. *p* Susumu Takashima, Sadaki Sato, Setsuo Noto, Manabu Akashi. *sc* Kaneto Shindo. *ph* Kiyomi Kuroda. *ed* Mitsuo Kondo. *ad* Kazumasa Otani. *m* Hikaru Hayashi. *cast* Chikuzan Takahashi, Ryuzo Hayashi, Nobuko Otowa, Dai Kanai, Yoshie Shimamura, Mitsuko Baisho.
●Chikuzan Takahashi, in his late sixties at the time of filming, is a blind musician who has spent most of his life on the roads of Northern Japan, earning his living as a *tsugaru shamisen* player. Latterly he acquired a devoted following among Japanese students, which is why Shindo made *The Life of Chikuzan*. The movie opens with Chikuzan himself in concert, then moves into a drama-documentary reconstruction of his early years, from his impoverished parents' desperate attempts to find a livelihood for him to his successful second marriage. Shindo keeps the travelogue elements to a decent minimum, and doesn't shy away from the harshness of Chikuzan's stoicism or lapse into sentimentality. He also chooses incidents with an eye to more than his subject's biography alone. The music, of course, is sublime. TR

Life of Emile Zola, The

(1937, US, 116 min, b/w)
d William Dieterle. *sc* Norman Reilly Raine, Heinz Herald, Geza Herczeg. *ph* Tony Gaudio. *ed* Warren Low. *ad* Anton Grot. *m* Max Steiner. *cast* Paul Muni, Joseph Schildkraut, Gale Sondergaard, Gloria Holden, Donald Crisp, Louis Calhern, Robert Barrat, Erin O'Brien Moore.
●Plodding briefly, inaccurately and somewhat risibly through Zola's early career, this solemn biopic improves no end when it gets to its main course: an account of the Dreyfus affair and how the now prosperously ageing Zola rediscovered his youthful ideals in an impassioned fight for justice. Carefully mounted, well directed and acted, but basically the sort of well-meaning pap out of which Oscars are made. TM

Life of Jesus, The

see Vie de Jésus, La

Life of Oharu, The (Saikaku Ichidai Onna)

(1952, Jap, 148 min, b/w)
d Kenji Mizoguchi. *p* Hideo Koi. *sc* Yoda Yoshikata, Kenji Mizoguchi. *ph* Yoshimo Kono, Yoshimi Hirano. *ed* Toshio Goto. *ad* Hiroshi Mizutani. *m* Ichiro Saito. *cast* Kinuyo Tanaka, Tsuki Matsura, Ichiro Sugai, Toshiro Mifune, Tashiaki Konoe, Masao Shinizu.
●This chronicle of the decline of a woman, from service in the imperial court of 17th-century Japan through exile, concubinage and numerous stages of prostitution, should further enhance Mizoguchi's reputation as the cinema's greatest ever director of women, and one of the most meticulous craftsmen of the period film. To place too much emphasis on the period setting is misleading, however; for despite the historical distance from feudal Japan, the social evils exposed have an unmistakable contemporary relevance. Feminists should unequivocally applaud the narrative simplicity and the clarity with which the second-class status of women is implicitly questioned almost everywhere in the film. It's also an extremely elegant movie whichever way you look at it: tiny details of movement by the actors, beautiful compositions and photography throughout, single fluid takes often serving to state a whole scene. RM

Life of Stuff, The

(1997, GB, 90 min)
d Simon Donald. *p* Lynda Myles. *sc* Simon Donald. *ph* Brian Tufano. *ed* Justin Krish. *pd* Zoë MacLeod. *m* John Lunn. *cast* Ewen Bremner, Liam Cunningham, Jason Flemyng, Ciaran Hinds, Gina McKee, Stuart McQuarrie
●Willie Dobie (Flemyng) is a man with ambition, imagination and lots of drugs. He also has a warehouse where he's preparing a party to celebrate the fact that, by means of a flaming van, he's just got shot of rival-in-crime Alec Sneddon. Where, too, variously crazed individuals are on hand: a pair of party girls; unloved eczematic Leonard (McQuarrie) and volatile janitor Arbogast (Hinds); and, meeting decidedly uncute down in the dank basement, nauseously hungover Janice (McKee) and skinny Fraser (Bremner), the last shivering in his smalls since he returned from what he believed was just some insurance scam involving a burnt-out van. Donald's dark, surreal, Scottish low-life farce may have delivered a sickening punch on stage, but on screen, as directed heavy-handedly by himself, the relentlessly OTT scuzziness, violence and hysteria is merely oppressive. True, the dry, black humour's still there in the dialogue, and most of the cast manage some semblance of recognisably human behaviour. But the ironic (?) use of inappropriately lush music, the cluttered, sometimes near-incoherent narrative, and the contrived metaphysics and humanism simply don't convince on the screen. GA

Life on a String (Bian Zou Bian Chang)

(1991, China/GB/Ger, 108 min)
d Chen Kaige. *p* Don Ranvaud. *sc* Chen Kaige. *ph* Gu Changwei. *ed* Pei Xiaonan. *ad* Shao Ruigang. *m* Qu Xiaosong. *cast* Liu Zhongyuan, Huang Lei, Xu Qing, Zhang Zhengyuan, Ma Ling, Zhang Jinzhan, Zhong Ling, Yao Erga.
●If it's hard occasionally to divine the precise meanings of Chen Kaige's lush, mystical fable, its poetic beauty and overall clarity of purpose are impossible to deny. An old, blind master musician wanders from desert village to desert village, accompanied by his headstrong, likewise afflicted pupil and amanuensis. As a child, the master was promised by his own mentor that when he had finally broken the thousandth string on his *sanxian*, he might open up the instrument and find a prescription to restore his sight. But his teenage apprentice, sceptical of his master's ascetic beliefs, is resolved to lead his own life, and takes up with a village girl against the wishes of both the old man and her family. Chronicling the widening of the gulf between man and boy, Chen explores the conflicts between age and youth, spirituality and physicality, discipline and disobedience, and – most movingly – the persistence and absence of faith and hope. Rarely have landscapes been photographed so sumptuously; rarely, too, has music in a film been used to such spine-tingling effect. GA

Life on Earth (La Vie sur Terre)

(1998, Fr, 61 min)
d Abderrahmane Sissako. *p* Pierre Chevalier, Caroline Benjo, Carole Scotta, Barbara Letellier, Simon Arnal. *sc* Abderrahmane Sissako. *ph* Jacques Besse. *ed* Nadia Ben Rachid. *m* Salif Keita, Anouar Brahem, Balafons et Tamours d'Afrique.*cast* Abderrahmane Sissako, Nana Baby, Mohamed Sissako, Bourama Coulibaly, Keita Bina Gaoussou, Mahamadou Drame.
●A rejoinder to the West's millennial hysteria, this beautiful feature debut follows writer/director Sissako from France to his father's Malian hometown, where the locals observe the developed world's excitement over the changing of the digits, relayed over the radio, with a casual interest while life goes on otherwise as normal. The film is quietly contemplative, overlaying scenes of apparently relaxed rural habitude with Sissako's occasional voice-over musing on the fate and fears of post-colonial Africa. Dramatic it ain't, the postmaster's mixed fortunes with the town's telephone being the nearest thing to a narrative motif. Among others the film quotes the Martinique writer Aimé Césaire, while simultaneously celebrating the gentle rhythms and colours of the present, typified by Anouar Brahem's delightful music. NB

Life Size (Tamaño Natural)

(1973, Sp/Fr/It, 100 min)
d Luis García Berlanga. *p* Alfredo Matas, Christian Ferry. *sc* Rafael Azcona, Luis García Berlanga, Jean-Claude Carrière. *ph* Alain Derobe. *ed* Françoise Bonnot. *pd* Alexandre Trauner. *m* Maurice Jarre. *cast* Michel Piccoli, Valentine Tessier, Rada Rassimov, Claudia Bianchi, Queta Claver, Manolo Alexandre.
●Piccoli, as a chic dentist, forsakes his 'liberated' but arid marriage for a new love. His job slides as he devotes himself entirely to her; they marry, but soon their bliss becomes contaminated and

he tries to kill her. What makes *Life Size* a suitably bizarre project for Piccoli in his running battle with the bourgeoisie is that the object of his affections is a lifelike doll, complete with mucous membranes. Best are the ways in which the film tackles the problems of fantasy in an apparently permissive society, and how the doll takes on a symbolic importance beyond Piccoli's conceptions. Slightly less successful: the running gag of women as living dolls (apart from one extraordinary sequence where Piccoli's wife behaves like one in order to attract him back), and the intimations of social apocalypse at the end. CPe

Lifespan

(1975, US/Neth, 85 min)
d/p Alexander Whitelaw. *sc* Alexander Whitelaw, Judith Roscoe, Alva Ruben. *ph* Eddy van der Enden. *ph* Guust Verschuuren, Jann Dopp. Hetty Konig. *ad* Dick Schillemans. *m* Terry Riley. *cast* Hiram Keller, Tina Aumont, Klaus Kinski, Fons Rademakers, Eric Schneider, Frans Mulders.

●Though visibly a low-budget Euro-thriller, *Lifespan* is none the less lent weight by its ingenious narrative and thematic audacity. In evoking and combining Faustian mythology, the modern pharmaceutical trade, Nazi medical experimentation, and Kinski's demonic search for eternal life, it perversely brings to the 'mad scientist' movie tradition a serious view of research ethics. Its horror resides in the fact of natural death, its questers after immortality working at the point where liberal science and fascist idealism collide in attempts to improve humanity by prolonging life. Its humour is equally unexpected: even what looks like a catchpenny bondage scene has Aumont tied in the knot symbolising DNA. Get past Hiram Keller's woodenness, and this is a bold and intelligent fun-movie. PT

Life Stinks

(1991, US, 95 min)
d/p Mel Brooks. *sc* Mel Brooks, Rudy De Luca, Steve Haberman. *ph* Steven Poster. *ed* David Rawlins. *pd* Peter Larkin. *m* John Morris. *cast* Mel Brooks, Lesley Ann Warren, Jeffrey Tambor, Stuart Pankin, Howard Morris, Rudy De Luca, Teddy Wilson, Billy Barty, Carmine Caridi.

●Having spent many fallow years producing sub-standard slapstick, Brooks here returns to the message-in-the-madness formula which once made him great; and if the result is extremely uneven, it's a huge leap forward from the inanities of *Spaceballs*. Selfish billionaire Goddard Bolt (Brooks) bets rival Vance Crasswell (Tambor, superbly slimy) that he can survive a sojourn communing with the city's homeless. Temporarily stripped of his wealth and taking to the streets, Bolt is swiftly swamped by the manic milieu of urban deprivation. Brooks plays out the inevitable schmaltzy conclusions with predictably tepid results: Bolt finds true friendship and love in the midst of misery, and finally turns the tables on the money-grabbing developers. More rewardingly, the grim, black humour of yore sporadically breaks through the glossy sheen, providing moments of vintage vitriol. MK

Life Story of Baal, The

(1978, GB, 58 min)
d Edward Bennett. *sc* Edward Bennett, Ben Brewster. *ph* Clive Tickner, Jeremy Brigden. *ed* Brand Thumim. *ad* Phoebe De Gaye, Miranda Melville, Tim Wheeler. *m* Jeremy Barlow. *cast* Neil Johnston, Patti Love, Jeff Rawle, Nick Edmett, Dinah Stabb, Roger Booth, Timothy Spall, Jim Broadbent. *narrator* Caroline Heller.

●Brecht never produced a fully revised version of this, his first play, and so the text can be considered fair game for further work. Bennett hasn't simply filmed it, but has risen to the challenge of producing a reading of it. Brecht at one level retains sympathy for Baal; Bennett never does. He reformulates the play as a powerful critique of the notion of the artist as a kind of social outlaw, and resolves the sexual, moral and political issues into urgent, provocative questions. TR

Life Upside-Down

see Vie à l'Envers, La

Life with Father

(1947, US, 118 min)
d Michael Curtiz. *p* Robert Buckner. *sc* Donald Ogden Stewart. *ph* Peverell Marley, William V Skall. *ed* George Amy. *ad* Robert M Haas. *m* Max Steiner. *cast* William Powell, Irene Dunne, Jimmy Lydon, Elizabeth Taylor, Edmund Gwenn, ZaSu Pitts, Martin Milner, Emma Dunn, Moroni Olsen, Elizabeth Risdon.

●Clarence Day Jr's tribute to his stern philosophising dad was turned into a play (by Howard Lindsay and Russel Crouse) that ran for more than 3,000 performances on Broadway, a record in its day, so it's no surprise Donald Ogden Stewart's film adaptation should prove such a satisfying entertainment. Powell dominates an episodic collection of domestic vignettes, with Dunne as the long-suffering wife, young Lydon the future author, and teenage Elizabeth Taylor the intermittent romance angle. Rudimentary comic strategies – the old boy's manful resistance to his belated baptism can only last so long – come up shining thanks to Powell's neatly judged inscription of the reluctant softie behind just so much self-important bluster and a theory on everything. Curtiz knocks it together without so much as breaking sweat. TJ

Lift, The (De Lift)

(1983, Neth, 99 min)
d Dick Maas. p Mattthijs Van Heijningen. sc Dick Maas. ph Marc Felperlaan. ed Hans Van Dongen. ad Harry Ammerlaan. m Dick Maas. cast Huub Stapel, Willeke Van Ammelrooy, Josine Van Dalsum, Piet Römer, Gerard Thoolen, Hans Veerman.

●This confirms all the creeping fears of those of us who stare glassily at the ceilings of lifts. In a Dutch high-rise building, one of the elevators suddenly gets a mind of its own, and since it is not one of those nice, charitably disposed Otis jobs with open grille-work, it decides to take revenge on all the sweaty claustrophobes who have been making its life such an up-and-down misery. The body count is low to middling for this kind of thing, although the methods of disposal are ingenious enough to compensate. Unfortunately, the movie is shafted by confusions of script and execution, neither of which match up to the original good idea. *The Shining* still holds the field among the all-too-rare horror films which explore the notion of an inanimate world exerting its revenge. CPea

Lift to the Scaffold

see Ascenseur pour l'Echafaud

Light, The

see Brightness

Light Ahead, The (Fishke der Krummer)

(1939, US, 120 min, b/w)
d/p Edgar G Ulmer. *sc* Chaver Pahver. *ph* J Burgi Contner, Edward Hyland. *ed* Jack Kemp. *cast* Isidore Cashier, Helen Beverly, David Opatoshu, Yudel Dubinsky, Rosetta Bialis, Tillie Rabinowitz.

●An inside job: made in Yiddish for the American immigrant Jewish population, this celebrates the trials and joys of being one of the 'chosen' people, chosen to suffer, too, it often seemed. Set in a Chagall-like Russian shetl near Odessa, where to be a Jew was synonymous with being impoverished, the film combines a sentimental love story – between a lame young man and a beautiful blind orphan – with a conflict between the working Jews and the village leaders over the spending of community funds. The two stories are brought together through the character of Reb Mendele, an avuncular bookseller who spreads hope and wisdom but privately laments in passionate tones the fate of his people. Ulmer's film touches the wellsprings of both Jewish sentimentality and hard-headed realism, exposing superstition as it praises true faith and courageous action. MH

Light at the Edge of the World, The

(1971, US/Sp/Liechtenstein, 99 min)
d Kevin Billington. *p* Kirk Douglas. *sc* Tom Rowe. *ph* Henri Decaë. *ed* Bert Bates. *ad* Enrique Alarcón. *m* Piero Piccioni. *cast* Kirk Douglas, Yul Brynner, Samantha Eggar, Jean-Claude Drouot, Fernando Rey, Renato Salvatori.

●1865, an island off Cape Horn: Lighthouse keeper Douglas battles murderous old seadog Brynner for the affections of shipwrecked maiden Eggar in this less than beacon-bright international co-production, based on a novel by Jules Verne. Over-enthusiastic performances.TJ

Lighthorsemen, The

(1987, Aust, 131 min)
d Simon Wincer. *p* Ian Jones, Simon Wincer. *sc* Ian Jones. *ph* Dean Semler. *ed* Adrian Carr, Peter Burgess. *pd* Bernard Hides. *m* Mario Millo. cast Peter Phelps, Tony Bonner, Gary Sweet, John Walton, Tim McKenzie, Jon Blake, Sigrid Thornton, Anthony Andrews.

●An account of a hard-fought WWI victory for the Australian mounted infantry in Palestine, with details of place and strategy clearly delineated, captions popping up everywhere, and much pointing at maps by moustachioed generals. The British were at a stalemate when the Lighthorse were summoned in 1917 to help plan an attack on the Turco-German army at the desert town of Beersheba, site of an 'unlimited' water supply. A British military intelligence officer (Andrews, a smart Alec with sneering nostrils) sets up a decoy which enables the Lighthorse to take the town by charging the enemy artillery cannons; he also forms the link between the facts and the fictional element. The plot straddles *Boy's Own* action as represented by four veterans of Gallipoli who are roped in to assist Andrews with his undercover activities, and *Women's Own* love interest as a fresh-faced recruit (Phelps) discovers he's unable to kill, joins the medical corps, and falls for a nurse (Thornton). It's good to look at: plumed hats, prancing thoroughbreds, and Aussie brute force shot against the clean desert light. Should appeal to people who like to play soldiers. EP

Light in the Piazza

(1961, US, 101 min)
d Guy Green. *p* Arthur Freed. *sc* Julius J Epstein. *ph* Otto Heller. *ed* Frank Clarke. *ad* Frank White. *m* Mario Nascimbene. *cast* Olivia de Havilland, Yvette Mimieux, George Hamilton, Rossano Brazzi, Isabel Dean, Barry Sullivan.

●Elizabeth Spencer's baroque, almost Jamesian novel of New World corruption versus Old World integrity is brought to the screen in the form of a 'grand tour' of North Italy. In the course of this, Olivia de Havilland tries to marry off her mentally retarded daughter (Mimieux) to a wealthy Italian (Hamilton). Sadly, it quickly falls prey to that most awesome of cinema's horrors – Rossano Brazzi – as attraction develops between de Havilland and the boy's father. A terrible film. PH

Lightning Jack

(1994, Aust, 114 min)
d Simon Wincer. *p* Greg Coote, Simon Wincer. *sc* Paul Hogan. *ph* David Eggby. *ed* O Nicholas Brown. *pd* Bernard Hides. *m* Bruce Rowland. *cast* Paul Hogan, Cuba Gooding Jr, Beverly D'Angelo, Kamala Dawson, Pat Hingle, Frank McRae, Roger Daltry, Richard Riehle, LQ Jones.

●This film, written by Paul Hogan, is essentially a straight Western with comic touches. Lightning Jack Kane (Hogan) is the self-styled sharpest shooter in the West. Unfortunately, the authorities don't share Jack's high opinion of himself, and consistently refuse to up the price on his head. Only when Jack teams up with mute novice desperado Ben Doyle (Gooding) do things start going his way. Now, can he get the girl (D'Angelo) as well? The central conceit, of two outlaws obsessed by their 'reviews' in the press, is a nice one, and the interplay between them is at times mildly amusing. NKe

Lightning Over Water (aka Nick's Movie)

(1980, WGer/Swe, 91 min)
d Nicholas Ray, Wim Wenders. *p* Chris Sievernich, Pierre Cottrell. *sc* Nicholas Ray, Wim Wenders. *ed* Peter Przygodda. *m* Ronee Blakley. *with* Nicholas Ray, Wim Wenders, Susan Ray, Tim Ray, Gerry Bamman, Ronee Blakley.

●Fittingly made on very dangerous ground as a celebratory last testament to an idea(l) of cinema that died along with Nicholas Ray. Developed haphazardly over the last two months of Ray's life, as a roughly improvised collaboration between the maverick Hollywood veteran and his *German Friend* Wim Wenders, it documents rawly but honestly the paradoxes of lives devoted to conjuring the sort of privileged moments the title alludes to. Ray, degenerating physically day by day, sustained by an irrepressible imaginative vitality; daily striving to reinvent cinema as Godard long ago predicted he would. Wenders, at an interim impasse on the protracted production of *Hammett*, constantly doubting his own methods and motives, unsettled by his own gestures of tribute. Two exiles trying to help each other find their ways back home, like Robert Mitchum in *The Lusty Men*. You needn't be steeped in film lore to appreciate the extraordinary emotions on which all this is strung. Even with its painful contradictions and discomfitures, it's that current rarity: one for the heart. PT

Lightning Swords of Death (Kozure Ohkam – Ko Wo Kashi Ude Kashi Tsukamatsuru)

(1972, Jap, 83 min)
d Kenji Misumi. *sc* Kasuo Koike. *ph* Shishi Makiura. *ad* Akira Nato. *m* Hideakira Sakurai. *cast* Tomisaburo Wakayama, Akhiro Tomikawa, Goh Kato, Yuko Hama, Fumio Watanabe.

●Originally a popular Japanese comic strip, the *Lone Wolf* character in this film is the star of a whole series of hugely successful features. The lugubrious and podgy hero travels around, pushing his young son along in a wooden pram, journeying through a Japan where the samurai tradition has become debased to little more than a licence to rape and kill. It's the hero's job, of course, to define the true code in a series of episodic adventures that end in displays of amazing swordplay. Meanwhile, the kid just looks on. Best is the climax in which the Lone Wolf is confronted by the Warlord's army, about 200 strong. What to do? Start with a fusillade of rockets from the front of the pram (yes, the kid's still sitting in it), followed by dynamite hand grenades, the remaining 50-odd dispatched with spears (hidden in the pram's handles) and of course sword. Tired, wounded and as glum as at the beginning of the film, our hero staggers off, still pushing the pram. One can almost forgive the appalling dubbing. CPe

Light of Day

(1987, US, 107 min)
d Paul Schrader. *p* Rob Cohen, Keith Barish. *sc* Paul Schrader. *ph* John Bailey. *ed* Jacqueline Cambas, Jill Savitt. *pd* Jeannine Claudia Oppewall. *m* Thomas Newman. *cast* Michael J Fox, Gena Rowlands, Joan Jett, Michael McKean, Thomas G Waites, Cherry Jones, Jason Miller.

●Joe Rasnick (Fox) works in a factory. In the evenings he plays in a group called The Barbusters which also features his sister Patti (Jett), a rock'n'roll rebel and mother of an illegitimate son. Their mother (Rowlands) has found the Lord and lost the ability to communicate with her daughter. When Joe is laid off, the group take to the road, but Patti's light fingers in a supermarket lead to a further schism, this time with her brother. More trauma when their mother succumbs to The Big C. What at first seems just another dreary blue-collar melodrama turns out to be something infinitely superior. Schrader's strong sense of place exploits the wintry wastelands of Cleveland, Ohio, and the familiar hallmarks of alienation and resistance to repression – in this case to religion, rammed home with a vicious plot twist – compensate for the superabundance of rancid rock, presumably included to titillate the teenies. The cast make the most of an intelligent script, with Rowlands and (especially) Jett providing most of the emotional punch. They create a powerful feeling of real lives being lived and lost. MS

Light of My Eyes (Luce dei miei occhi)

(2001, It, 114 min)
d Giuseppe Piccioni. *p* Lionello Cerri. *sc* Giuseppe Piccioni, Umberto Contarello, Linda Ferri. *ph* Arnaldo Catinari. *ed* Esmeralda Calabria. *pd* Giancarlo Basili. *m* Ludovico Einaudi. *cast* Luigi Lo Cascio, Sandra Ceccarelli, Silvio Orlando, Barbara Valente, Toni Bertorelli, Paolo Pierobon, Mauro Marino.

●This is handsomely shot, and nicely played by Lo Cascio as the love-lorn chauffeur Antonio, and especially by Ceccarelli as the long-suffering single mother who becomes the reluctant object of his adoration and kindness. A voice-over in which the driver imagines himself a 'space traveller' takes the material away from *Mona Lisa* thriller territory towards something more imaginative. But unfortunately director Piccioni and his two co-writers opt for an egregiously sentimental ending. TCh

Lightship, The

(1985, US, 88 min)
d Jerzy Skolimowski. *p* Moritz Borman, Bill Benenson. *sc* William Mai, David Taylor.*ph* Charly Steinberger. *ed* Barrie Vince,Scott Hancock. *ad* Holger Gross. *m* Stanley Myers. *cast* Robert Duvall, Klaus MariaBrandauer, Tom Bower, Robert Costanzo, Badja Djola, William Forsythe, Arliss Howard, Michael Lyndon.

●Taken from Siegfried Lenz's dour allegorical novella about what you might do if Hitler arrived on your ship, Skolimowski's adaptation mercifully junks the more overt political dimension, and concentrates successfully on the suspense element, with sufficient metaphysical undercurrent for those who want it. Brandauer is the pacifist captain of a rusting lightship, anchored off the coast of Norfolk, Virginia in the '50s. When they rescue a drifting boat, the trio that come aboard prove to be a set of psychos, on the run to a rendezvous with their pickup boat. Their leader, a menacing dandy played by Duvall at his most wilfully extravagant, threatens to set the ship adrift, and backs it up with the cool logic that the devil always presents. Brandauer, however, continues in a kind of dumb, passive resistance. Fortunately, Skolimowski keeps the schematic struggle between good and evil sufficiently well submerged beneath an atmosphere of menace and increasing hostility, as the crew bicker and fall apart under ill-fated attempts at heroism, and Duvall enacts his increasingly bizarre Übermensch tactics. If it puts you in mind of *Key Largo*, that is no bad thing. CPea

Light Sleeper

(1991, US, 103 min)
d Paul Schrader. *p* Linda Reisman. *sc* Paul Schrader. *ph* Ed Lachman. *ed* Kristina Boden. *pd* Richard Hornung. *m* Michael Been. *cast* Willem Dafoe, Susan Sarandon, Dana Delany, David Clennon, Mary Beth Hurt, Victor Garber, Jane Adams, Paul Jabara.

●A further instalment in Schrader's on-going study of confused loners, this stylish *film noir* offers yet another take on the possibility of redemption from sin and guilt in the modern world. At 40, John LeTour (Dafoe), an up-market dealer who delivers drugs to chic clubs and apartments, has hit a crisis. His boss (Sarandon) is contemplating trading in her cocaine business for herbal cosmetics; his psychic advisor (Hurt) reckons he's due for a change; and the recently reencountered love of his life (Delany) fears that he's never quite kicked his own suicidal habit. LeTour needs a push before he can break with the past; but the requisite jolt comes in the shape of a murder. Schrader certainly has his finger on the pulse of the times, and the universally strong performances do ample justice to his sensitive ear for dialogue. But the story meanders, and it echoes *Taxi Driver* and *American Gigolo* so closely that Schrader is working less than fresh variations on over-familiar themes. For all the film's conspicuously adult intelligence, it elicits a disappointing sense of déjà vu. GA

Lights of Variety

see Luci del Varietà

Light Years Away

(1981, Fr/Switz, 107 min)
d Alain Tanner. *p* Pierre Héros. *sc* Alain Tanner. *ph* Jean-François Robin. *ed* Brigitte Sousselier. *ad* John Lucas. *m* Arié Dzierlatka. *cast* Trevor Howard, Mick Ford, Odile Schmitt, Louis Samier, Joe Pilkington, John Murphy, Mannix Flynn, Bernice Stegers.

●An abandoned petrol pump in a desolate and beautiful Irish landscape is a curiously encouraging image for the future. The year is 2000, and the central character is an intelligent, tousled vagabond called Jonas (Ford) – the product of those good-hearted socialists who nurtured him in Tanner's earlier *Jonas qui aura 25 ans en l'an 2000*. Forsaking the city, Jonas is drawn to the remote Pallas Garage and its querulous, occasionally uproarious owner Yoshka (Howard). Here, Jonas endures a pointless, arduous apprenticeship (manning the dry pump, polishing the junkheap) before he is initiated into Yoshka's wondrous secret. The themes are large – the wilderness, Icarus, the earth. The film is mysterious without being mystifying or unduly solemn. Clear as mud, in fact, with the compelling logic of a dream. The real puzzle (though it's not a complaint) is why a politically discursive film-maker like Tanner – here working in English – has taken up this mystic and ritualistic fable. JS

Ligne de Démarcation, La

(1966, Fr, 120 min, b/w)
d Claude Chabrol. *p* Georges de Beauregard. *sc* le colonel Rémy. *ph* Jean Rabier. *ed* Jacques Gaillard. *ad* Guy Littaye. *m* Pierre Jansen. *cast* Maurice Ronet, Jean Seberg, Daniel Gélin, Stéphane Audran, Jacques Perrin, Jean Yanne, Jean-Louis Maury, Paul Gégauff, Claude Berri.

●If you believe his autobiography, Chabrol shot this picture in an alcoholic stupor, partly due to physical discomfort (on location in the mid-winter Jura countryside), but mainly because he felt no affinity with the material, a wartime resistance drama with daring escapes, heroic self-sacrifice and little moral complexity. And yet it seems a well-controlled, perfectly respectable piece, directed for its surface values and not undermined by any knowing winks at the audience (except perhaps in the scenes with leather-coated Gestapo agents Maury and Gégauff). It's a rural counterpart of *L'Armée des Ombres*, and although that comparison is by no means annihilating, it does point up the low intensity of Chabrol's involvement. BBa

Like a Bride (Novia que te Vea)

(1992, Mex, 115 min)
d Guita Schyfter. *p* Tita Lombardo. *sc* Hugo Hiriart. *ph* Toni Kuhn. *ed* Carlos Bolado. *cast* Angélica Aragon, Claudette Maille, Maya Mishalska, Ernesto Laguardia.

●Having trained with the BBC in London, Schyfter returned to Mexico to make this decently crafted, undeniably sincere and slightly underwhelming portrait of the country's Jewish community. Moving through the decades, the story charts the friendship of an aspiring painter, Oshinica, from a strict Sephardic family of Turkish origin, and her more liberal-thinking pal Riffke, the daughter of refugees from the Holocaust. Spanning the currents of feminism, Zionism and socialism, the two women seek to break free from the roles assigned to them by society. The end result is more arresting as social history than drama, but the careful performances and unusual content make it worthwhile for those with an interest in the subject matter. TJ

Like a Rolling Stone (Bo no Kanashimi)

(1994, Jap, 118 min)
d Tatsumi Kumashiro. *p* Hidehiro Ito, Yasuhide Kidota, Kinya Yagi, Misa Okatsu. *sc* Tatsumi Kumashiro, Hideohiro Ito. *ph* Junichiro Hayashi. *cast* Eiji Okuda, Eiko Nagashima, Reiko Takashima, Haku Ryu.

●Kumashiro's brilliant last film (based on a hard-boiled novel by Kenzo Kitakata) subverts the yakuza genre by creating a new type of anti-hero. Tanaka (Okuda, previously more associated with worthy social dramas) is a cool, high-ranking yakuza despised by his snobbish boss. Bored by his work, increasingly adrift from his own mental moorings, he debauches the girl from the local florist's shop just to give himself something to do and stitches his own stab wounds just to see what it feels like. The tension between this deeply alienated man and his job yields a film of compulsive, cumulative power, much of it shot in long, real-time takes. TR

Like Father

(2000, GB, 90 min)
d/p/sc/ph/ed Amber Production Team: Richard Grassick, Ellin Hare, Sirkka-Lissa Konttinen, Murray Martin, Pat McCarthy,

Lorna Powell, Peter Roberts. *ad* Irena Pietruszka. *m* Joe Adler. *cast* Joe Armstrong, Ned Kelly, Jonathan Dent, Anna Gascoigne, Derek Walmsley, Willie Ross, Brian Hogg, Ashley Gutsell.
●The Amber collective paints a typically droll, touching and perceptive portrait of three generations of men – a music teacher whose increasing absence from home and taste for booze is putting pressure on his marriage; his confused young son; and his ex-miner father, facing eviction from the land where he has his allotment and racing pigeons. In the process, Amber maps out the socio-political contours of life in the modern North East. The film deals deftly with civic corruption, the sex war, class conflict, the generation gap, idealism, compromise, recrimination and regret – not bad for a low budget film. But Amber's distinctive blend of documentary-style 'realism' and melodrama (literally 'drama with music', here as in Sirk) has always worked miracles, and *Like Father* is infinitely more honest, adult and affecting than the vast majority of current Hollywood movies. GA

Like Father, Like Son

(1987, US, 100 min)
d Rod Daniel. *p* Brian Grazer, David Valdes. *sc* Lorne Cameron, Steven L Bloom. *ph* Jack N Green. *ed* Lois Freeman-Fox. *pd* Dennis Gassner. *m* Miles Goodman. *cast* Dudley Moore, Kirk Cameron, Margaret Colin, Catherine Hicks, Patrick O'Neal, Sean Astin, Cami Cooper.
●A dud movie wrapping Moore's 'kid in a man's body' routine around a convenient age-swap plot. Dad (Moore) is a successful surgeon committed to good medicine for all; son Chris (Cameron) is a raunchy teenage tearaway. Dad wants Chris to follow in his footsteps and do good for others; Chris just wants to get laid. Enter a desert potion that enables 'transference of souls'. Dad drinks it, looks into son's eyes, the souls transfer, and – surprise, surprise – Dad's in Chris's body, and Chris in Dad's. This enables Dudley to play Arthur all over again with his dad's Gold Amex card. Meanwhile Chris turns up at the hospital to take patients' temperatures and shock the starchy surgeon fraternity with snazzy one-liners. The scam would have had a longer lifespan had Moore played true to the character of 16-year-old Chris instead of turning up as some generic 13-year-old. As it turns out, Cameron gets most of the laughs. EP

Like Grains of Sand (Nagisa no Sindbad)

(1995, Jap, 129 min)
d Ryosuke Hashiguchi. *p* Yoshishige Shimatani, Kazuo Hayashi, Kiyomi Kanazawa, Yuuka Nakazawa. *sc* Ryosuke Hashiguchi. *ph* Shogo Ueno. *ed* Miho Yoneda. *m* Kazuya Takahashi. *cast* Yoshinori Okada, Kota Kusano, Ayumi Hamazaki, Koji Yamaguchi, Kumi Takada, Shizuka Isami.
●A searing drama of love, compassion and sexual identity, this is the *War and Peace* of high school romances. Shy, sensitive Ito (Okada) yearns for the love of his best friend, but though the straight Yoshida (Kusano) stands by Ito when their classmates realise he's gay, Yoshida cannot – will not – embrace him. It's an audacious, brave film, with strongly developed themes and characters (exceptionally well played by the teenage cast), but the director's narrative grasp is less impressive, and in the end, the search for a big, uncompromising statement shows signs of strain.

Like It Is

(1997, GB, 92 min)
d Paul Oremland. *cast* Dani Behr, Roger Daltrey, Ian Rose, Steve Bell.
●This so-so first feature gets away with casting Behr as a disco diva and Daltrey as an amoral record company boss. Amazingly, it's not camp. Rather, it's a surprisingly touching love story between a Blackpool virgin (Bell) and an up-and-coming producer (Rose) who shows him the ropes in the old smoke. Polished to the point of blandness, but sincere nevertheless. TCh

Likely Lads, The

(1976, GB, 90 min)
d Michael Tuchner. *p* Aida Young. *sc* Dick Clement, Ian La Frenais. *ph* Tony Imi. *ed* Ralph Sheldon. *ad* Robert Jones. *m* Mike Hugg. *cast* Rodney Bewes, James Bolam, Brigit Forsyth, Mary Tamm, Sheila Fern, Zena Walker, Alun Armstrong.
●Full credit to writers Dick Clement and Ian La Frenais for trying to open out *The Likely Lads* into a feature-length story, with no need of the TV series as a constant reminder. It works a lot of the time, with a solid background of the lads' sentimental attachment to old Newcastle, and the realities of high-rise flats and married life as they increasingly look their age. And of course the characters and gags (Terry: 'I'd offer you a beer, Bob, but I've only got six cans') are terrific. Brigit Forsyth's Thelma is a genuine monster. Unfortunately, Michael Tuchner's direction is so flat that after about an hour the film does begin to seem like an extended TV special. AN

Like Water for Chocolate (Como Agua para Chocolate)

(1991, Mex, 114 min)
d/p Alfonso Arau. *sc* Laura Esquivel. *ph* Emmanuel Lubezki, Steve Bernstein. *ed* Carlos Bolado, Francisco Chiu. *ad* Marco Antonio Arteaga. Mauricio De Aguinaco, Denise Pizzini. *m* Leo Brower. *cast* Marco Leonardi, Lumi Cavazos, Regina Torne, Mario Ivan Martinez, Ada Carrasco, Yareli Arizmendi, Claudette Maille.
●Set during the Mexican revolution, this is a women's movie in that it shows the secret face of political events. Of three sisters, Gertrudis (Maille) becomes a general in the revolutionary army; Rosaura (Arizmendi) is married and has children; and the youngest, sweet-faced Tita (Cavazos), who was cheated of the chance to wed, experiences life through the disciplines of the kitchen. It might sound a bit like *Babette's Feast*, except that the rows, rapes, gunfire, ghosts and sex are a million miles from 19th century Denmark. Tita is doomed by tradition to spend her life looking after her ramrod mother (Torne), while her true love (Leonardi) perversely weds Rosaura. Director Arau doesn't linger over laborious cooking and sensual ingredients, perhaps because he has much to cover: 40 years, three generations, love wasted and renewed. Recipes are milestones as the women eat, fantasise and crave. It's overlong, but that reflects the nature of Mexican cooking: like water for chocolate, which must be brought to the boil three times, the characters continually bubble and boil over. SFe

Li'l Abner

(1959, US, 114 min)
d Melvin Frank. *p* Norman Panama. *sc* Norman Panama, Melvin Frank. *ph* Daniel L Fapp. *ed* Arthur P Schmidt. *ad* Hal Pereira, J McMillan Johnson. *cast* Peter Palmer, Leslie Parrish, Stubby Kaye, Howard St John, Stella Stevens, Julie Newmar, Robert Strauss.
●Having written the book for the Broadway musical based on Al Capp's comic strip featuring the hillbilly world of Dogpatch USA, Panama and Frank did it little service here with a flaccid script, even more flaccid direction, and choreography merely 'based' on Michael Kidd's original. The script, with the inhabitants shaggy-doggily resisting a plan to turn Dogpatch into an atomic testing site, could do with a nuclear blast to liven it up; but the casting is excellent, and the marvellous Johnny Mercer/Gene de Paul songs survive intact. TM

Lilac Domino, The

(1937, GB, 85 min, b/w)
d Fred Zelnik. *p* Isadore G Goldsmith. *sc* Basil Mason, Neil Gow. *ph* Bryan Langley, Roy Clark. *ed* Lynn Harrison. *ad* OF Werndorff. *m* Hans May, Charles Cuvillier. *cast* June Knight, Michael Bartlett, Athene Seyler, Richard Dolman, SZ Sakall, Fred Emney, Joan Hickson.
●Hungarian fun and games perpetrated on an unsuspecting populace by Max Schach, the endearing little Viennese expatriate who charmed £2m out of the City to make the most exhilaratingly awful extravaganzas in the history of cinema. This one involves a dashing cavalryman hero, a school-girl heiress heroine – afflicted with a neurotic need to sing and dance even when they're on the telephone – stuffed donkeys, mad waiters, and myriads of satin-pyjama-clad starlets. Music-hall comedian Emney adds a bit of class as an impeccably English Hungarian millionaire, while the gypsy dances and masked balls on the Denham studio backlot have the surreally exciting quality of truly bad cinema. RMy

Lili

(1952, US, 81 min)
d Charles Walters. *p* Edwin H Knopf. *sc* Helen Deutsch. *ph* Robert Planck. *ed* Ferris Webster. *ad* Cedric Gibbons, Paul Groesse. *songs* Helen Deutsch, Bronislau Kaper. *cast* Leslie Caron, Mel Ferrer, Kurt Kasznar, Jean-Pierre Aumont, Zsa Zsa Gabor, Amanda Blake.
●Perhaps too deliberately charming for its own good, but this adaptation of a Paul Gallico novel about a 16-year-old waif who falls unhappily in love with a carnival magician (Aumont), thus adding to the bitterness of the crippled puppeteer (Ferrer) who loves her from afar, is actually rather delightful, thanks to Caron's touching performance and Walters' delicately stylish direction. Caron's scenes with the puppets (through whom Ferrer talks to her, and whom she accepts as her living friends and confidants) are in fact brushed with a touch of genuine fairy-tale magic. Not really a musical (though it has one hit song, 'Hi Lili, Hi Lo'), it ends with an ambitious ballet which is attractive but seems oddly out of key with the rest of the film. GA

Li Lianying, the Imperial Eunuch (Da Taijian Li Lianying)

(1991, HK/China, 105 min)
d Tian Zhuangzhuang. *p* Tam Wing-Chuen, Cheng Zhigu. *sc* Jiang Wen, Tian Zhuangzhuang. *ph* Zhao Fei. *ed* Qian Lengleng. *pd* Yang Yuhe, Qao Qing. *m* Mo Fan. *cast* Jiang Wen, Liu Xiaoqing, Zhu Yu, Tian Xiaojun, Xu Fan, Lin Wei.
●Tian admits that this chamber epic was not a 'personal' project; for a film which began shooting only a few months after the Tiananmen Square massacre, it certainly feels more like a flight into history than even an oblique response to the moment. Spanning the last five decades of the Qing Dynasty, it centres on the oddly affectionate relationship between Empress Dowager Cixi (Liu) and her chief eunuch (Jiang); the stars were a real life couple at the time. The often filmed historical facts are rehearsed efficiently enough: the folly of deflecting naval funds to the building of the Summer Palace, puppet emperor Guangxu's ill fated bid for autonomy as a reformist and so on. But the film is vindicated by its prime mover Jiang Wen's colossal performance as Li; no other actor has ever gone deeper into the implications of castration and living as a neutered animal. TR

Lilies (Les Feluettes, ou La Répétition d'un drama romantique)

(1996, Can, 92 min)
d John Greyson. *p* Anna Stratton, Robin Cass, Arnie Gelbart. *sc* Michel-Marc Bouchard, (English version) Linda Gaboriau. *ph* Daniel Jobin. *ed* André Corriveau. *pd* Sandra Kybartas. *m* Mychael Danna. *cast* Brent Carver, Marcel Sabourin, Aubert Pallascio, Jason Cadieux, Matthew Ferguson, Danny Gilmore.
●Quebec, 1952: a bishop's visit to a prisoner seeking confession becomes an unexpected encounter with the past. The prisoner, a boyhood friend, near the end of a life sentence, has mounted an elaborate performance by his fellow inmates, his purpose to prick the prelate's guilty conscience and pierce the passions of their hidden teenage years. It's easy to see how the theatrical artifice eliding past and present might have impressed in Michel-Marc Bouchard's stage original, but on screen, for all the florid intercutting, it remains in the shadow of Robert Lepage. Still, strong performances from an all-male cast (in drag where necessary), and Mychael Danna's chóral score for the Hilliard Ensemble decorate the gay melodrama with an aura of keening nostalgic melancholy. TJ

Lili Marleen

(1980, WGer, 120 min)
d Rainer Werner Fassbinder. *p* Luggi Waldleitner. *sc* Manfred Purzer, Joshua Sinclair, Rainer Werner Fassbinder. *ph* Xaver Schwarzenberger. *ed* Rainer Werner Fassbinder, Juliane Lorenz. *pd* Rolf Zehetbauer. *m* Peer Raben. *cast* Hanna Schygulla, Giancarlo Giannini, Mel Ferrer,

Karl Heinz von Hassel, Erik Schumann, Hark Bohm, Rainer Werner Fassbinder.
●Fassbinder's determinedly 'tasteless' brew of sentiment and swastikas annexes the original two-way forces' favourite to a totally apocryphal cloak-and-dagger romance, camped up into a one-song musical comedy. Its basic joke is that Schygulla, required to sing 'Lili Marlene' umpteen times, can't sing; but when a variation on that has her Jewish lover (Giannini) tortured with the song by his German gaolers, one's incredulous guffaws just keep rolling. Elaborate proof that the devil really does have all the best tunes. PT

Lilith

(1964, US, 114 min, b/w)
d/p Robert Rossen. *sc* Robert Rossen, Robert Alan Aurthur. *ph* Eugen Schuftan. *ed* Aram Avakian. *ad* Richard Sylbert. *m* Kenyon Hopkins. *cast* Warren Beatty, Jean Seberg, Peter Fonda, Kim Hunter, Anne Meacham, James Patterson, Jessica Walter, Gene Hackman, René Auberjonois, Olympia Dukakis.
●Rossen's sadly underrated last film (from a novel by JR Salamanca), an ambitious reworking of legend through the emotional involvement of a trainee therapist (Beatty) with a schizophrenic girl (Seberg). Stylistically, the framework of Lilith is established by the ironic contrasts of the two walks that Vincent (Beatty) completes: the first, a purposeful one towards the asylum, and the last, a desperate zig-zag through the various corridors and stairways of the asylum itself, out into the gardens, and finally winding up where the first one began, with an exhausted and curiously childish plea for help. The irony is extended even to the cry for help, since the same social worker (Hunter) had, in the first instance, politely enquired if she could help him. It is within this framework that Rossen develops the shifting relationship between Vincent and Lilith, beginning as patient and guide, and ending as beguiler and beguiled. CL

Lillian Russell

(1940, US, 127 min, b/w)
d Irving Cummings. *p* Gene Markey. *sc* William Anthony McGuire. *ph* Leon Shamroy. *ed* Walter Thompson. *ad* Richard Day, Joseph C Wright. *songs* Gus Kahn, Bronislau Kaper, Mack Gordon, Alfred Newman and others. *cast* Alice Faye, Don Ameche, Henry Fonda, Edward Arnold, Warren William, Leo Carrillo, Nigel Bruce, Claud Allister, Lynn Bari.
●Sumptuous but turgid biopic of The American Beauty – star of burlesque and light opera from the 1880s – with Fonda and Ameche as her two husbands (she had four, but who's counting?). It comes alive only when Alice Faye sings such standards as 'After the Ball' and 'The Band Plays On'. Nigel Bruce and Claude Allister appear in cameos as Gilbert and Sullivan. TM

Lily Tomlin

(1986, US/GB, 90 min)
d/p Nicholas Broomfield, Joan Churchill. *with* Lily Tomlin, Jane Wagner, Peggy Feury.
●Not a great documentary – one learns little about Tomlin herself – but it is of interest for the way we are allowed to see how she develops her one-woman show over a period of almost two years: lines are changed, characters developed, and timing refined during 'works-in-progress' shows. But the main reason to catch this is for Tomlin's superbly funny performances, sharply satirising contemporary American stereotypes, and proving herself an actress of countless faces and voices. GA

Limbo

(1999, US, 127 min)
d John Sayles. *p* Maggie Renzi. *sc* John Sayles. *ph* Haskell Wexler. *ed* John Sayles. *pd* Gemma Jackson. *m* Mason Daring. *cast* Mary Elizabeth Mastrantonio, David Strathairn, Vanessa Martinez, Kris Kristofferson, Casey Siemaszko, Kathryn Grody, Rita Taggart.
●Audacious and ambitious even for Sayles, this starts, *City of Hope*-style, by tracing the connections between various inhabitants of an Alaskan coastal town on the verge of becoming a tourist trap. Gradually, country singer Mastrantonio and ex-fisherman Strathairn begin to put their painful pasts behind them as they embark on a relationship (though her damaged, resentful daughter Martinez is far from sure she wants to see yet another man in mom's life) – but then the seriously unexpected happens, forcing all three to question their priorities and to take risks. Stunningly acted and superbly shot (by Haskell Wexler), it is written, with Sayles' customary ear for vivid phrasing and telling details, as a meditation on man's desire to divorce himself not only from Nature but from his own true nature, imbuing the film with the intensity and rigour of an allegorical fable. And the ending truly makes you think about what you've just seen. GA

Limelight

(1952, US, 140 min, b/w)
d/p/sc Charles Chaplin. *ph* Karl Struss. *ed* Joseph Engel. *ad* Eugène Lourié. *m* Charles Chaplin. *cast* Charles Chaplin, Claire Bloom, Sydney Chaplin Jr, Nigel Bruce, Buster Keaton, Norman Lloyd, André Eglevsky, Melissa Hayden.
●Chaplin's final film before his exile in Europe is far and away his most personal: he recreates the London of his boyhood (a world of abject poverty, alcoholism, seedy tenement dwellings, pubs and music halls), and contemplates with supreme narcissism the onset of old age and the decline of his comic instinct. It's also Chaplin's least funny film: tears outweigh titters by several kilos (and the person who gets most laughs isn't Chaplin but Keaton, appearing briefly as his partner in a violin-and-piano routine), and there is much moralising about life's meaning and the artistic urge better suited to *Reader's Digest* or the back of a matchbox ('Life is splendid...it must be enjoyed...it is all we have'). It's over-long, shapeless, overblown, and...a masterpiece. Few cinema artists have delved into their own lives and emotions with such ruthlessness and with such moving results. GB

Limey, The

(1999, US, 91 min)
d Steven Soderbergh. *p* John Hardy, Scott Kramer. *sc* Lem Dobbs. *ph* Ed Lachman. *ed* Sarah Flack. *pd* Gary Frutkoff. *m* Cliff Martinez. *cast* Terence Stamp, Peter Fonda, Luis Guzman, Lesley Ann Warren, Barry Newman, Nicky Katt, Joe Dallesandro.
●Funny, touching, and as effortlessly assured, in its own relatively low budget way, as *Out of Sight*, this consistently imaginative, comic crime movie milks the fish-out-of-water theme for all it is worth, and then some. Stamp is superb as the ageing Cockney ex-con whose investigations into his daughter's death in LA lead him to surprise the locals not only with his (wonderfully OTT) rhyming slang, but with his hard-man resilience and ingenuity; moreover, he's given sterling support by Fonda (who as a rock impresario out of his depth in murky water inspires some lovely in-jokes about '60s counter-culture), Newman and Guzman (not, for once, typecast). Lem Dobbs' script is witty; Ed Lachman's images and Cliff Martinez' music are perfectly in keeping with the light, relaxed mood; and Soderbergh's customary playfulness with the narrative deftly underlines Stamp's obsession. A joy. GA

Limit Up

(1989, US, 88 min)
d Richard Martini. *p* Jonathan D Krane. *sc* Richard Martini, Luana Anders. *ph* Peter Lyons Collister. *ed* Sonny Baskin. *pd* R Clifford Searcy. *m* John Tesh. *cast* Nancy Allen, Dean Stockwell, Brad Hall, Danitra Vance, Ray Charles, Rance Howard, Sandra Brogan, Luana Anders, Sally Kellerman.
●Do you have to lose your soul in order to become a success on the stock exchange? Well, yes – or maybe, in the last analysis, no – writer/ director Martini can't quite make up his mind. This feeble comedy plays it both ways, lambasting the get-rich-quick mentality while showing that beneath even the meanest, dirtiest trader's chest beats a heart of gold. Runner Casey Falls (Allen) wants to become a trader, but her career path is blocked by her womanising boss (Stockwell). So she strikes a Faustian deal with a wacky, hip woman (Vance) who claims to be the devil's assistant. Casey will get the promotion, the mansion, the car, but she has to put up with endless pranks and supernatural displays from the mischievous demon. And there's the small matter of her soul. Characterisation is two-dimensional, and the intrigues fall flat. Ray Charles crops up intermittemtly; Sally Kellerman puts in an appearence; and it's disappointing to find Stockwell and Allen's roles so underdeveloped. CM

Lina Braake

(1974, WGer, 85 min)
d/p/sc Bernhard Sinkel. *ph* Alf Brustellin, Detlev Niedballa. *ed* Heidi Genée, Traudl Egger. *pd* Nicos Perakis. *m* Joe Haider. *cast* Lina Carstens, Fritz Rasp, Herbert Bötticher, Erica Schramm, Benno Hoffmann, Ellen Mahlke.
●An 'audience' movie that knows exactly what it wants. It deceptively begs respectability with its display of social concern – old people, immigrant workers – similar to Fassbinder's *Fear Eats the Soul*. More blatantly, the film offers a package: an art house, old folks' version of *The Sting*. Lina Braake, evicted from her home by the bank, is left to rot in an old people's home. Teaming up with an aristocratic old man, she swindles the bank and buys a house in Sardinia for a foreign worker family. The performances should crack even the surliest spectator; but the film's judgments and comparisons become increasingly dubious as the film moves towards its upbeat ending (like the juxtaposition of the bleak old people's home with the family celebration in Sardinia, all earthy peasant vitality and room for everyone from eldest to youngest). Does writer/director Sinkel really care for his characters? CPe

Lincoln County Incident

(1980, NZ, 48 min)
d Tony Brittenden. *cast* Shane Simms, Cornella Schaap, David Wright, Stephen Meyer, Grant McPhie, Pablo Rickard.
●An extremely polished comedy Western made by the students and staff of Lincoln High School in Christchurch. The pint-sized hero is Samson Peabody-Jones (Simms), whose stature stands in comic contrast to the greatness of his name and the enormity of his courage, which is severely tested by ghostly apparitions, unshaven villains, and a bar-tending floozie. The discovery of a dead prospector's map sends Jones – resplendent in green velvet knickerbockers – on his way through the contusion colours (yellow rocks, green ranges, blue skies) of 1881 New Mexico, accompanied by a chicken and a narration whose authentic American accent lets the cast concentrate on getting the action on the screen rather than the kiwi out of the voice. Full of charm, the film has the audacity to decorate its Wildish West with a telephone, a Coca-Cola can, and an anarchic ending; and the aplomb to get away with it. FD

Line, The

(1980, US, 95 min)
d Robert J Siegel. *p* Virginia Largent, Robert J Siegel. *sc* Reginald Shelborne, Patricia Maxwell. *ph* Sol Negrin, Al Lhota. *ed* Virginia Largent, Dennis Golub, Reginald Shelborne. *ad* Robert Wrightman. *m* Rod McBrien. *cast* Russ Thacker, Lewis J Stadlen, Brad Sullivan, Kathleen Tolan, Jacqueline Brookes, David Doyle, Andrew Duncan.
●Based on the true story of a Vietnam deserter who, after several suicide attempts in the army stockade, provokes a guard into killing him. As he crosses one line, fellow prisoners cross another, literally and metaphorically, by stepping out of parade in protest, and get life sentences for mutiny. Despite some powerful performances (Sullivan is outstanding as the senior stockade NCO), the film is top-heavy with a script whose painful honesty isn't always balanced: the strong story is over-compressed, notably in the media/civilian demonstration shit-storm that comes awkwardly out of nowhere into the closed world of the stockade. Well done up to a point and uncompromisingly relentless, but it makes you realise how good Costa-Gavras is at this kind of thing. JCo

Linea del cielo, La

see Skyline

Lines from the Heart (I Rollerna Tre)

(1996, Swe, 75 min)
d/p/sc Christina Olofson. *ph* Lisa Hagstrand. *ed* Christina Olofson, Stefan Sundlof. *m* Johan Zachrisson. *with* Bibi Andersson, Harriet Andersson, Gunnel Lindblom.

●The Swedish actresses Harriet Andersson, Gunnel Lindblom and Bibi Andersson spend a few days in the Provençal home of the late Mai Zetterling, the actress and director for whom they worked together in *The Girls* three decades before. The three discuss Zetterling, their lives and careers, Ingmar Bergman, the effects of ageing, maternity, etc, intercut are clips from Zetterling's movie. A 'fly on the wall' documentary – but the three celebrated actresses often look cramped by the camera and the need to 'perform' naturally. GA

Lineup, The

(1958, US, 86 min, b/w)
d Don Siegel. *p* Frank Cooper. *sc* Stirling Silliphant. *ph* Hal Mohr. *ed* Al Clark. *ad* Ross Bellah. *m* Mischa Bakaleinikoff. *cast* Eli Wallach, Robert Keith, Warner Anderson, Emile Meyer, Richard Jaeckel, Mary LaRoche, William Leslie.

●Psycho-killers Julian and Dancer (Keith and Wallach) are hired to recover a heroin haul. Among their professional touches is noting down their victim's last words ('Why be greedy?'). But they can be unprofessional too – like wanting to know more about The Man who hired them. From this premise of hitmen rising above their station, Siegel was later to remake *The Killers*. But this b/w B version, with its passionless psychos stalking San Francisco, is the more brutal, sadistic and threatening. DMacp

Linguini Incident, The

(1991, US, 98 min)
d Richard Shepard. *p* Arnold Orgolini. *sc* Tamara Brott, Richard Shepard. *ph* Robert Yeoman. *ed* Sonya Polonsky. *m* Thomas Newman. *cast* Rosanna Arquette, David Bowie, Eszter Balint, André Gregory, Buck Henry, Viveca Lindfors, Lewis Arquette, Marlee Matlin, Wallace Shawn, Kelly Lynch.

●In an ultra-fashionable restaurant, Monte (Bowie) and Lucy (Arquette) are the silver-suited bar staff. Naturally they must fall in love after first disliking each other; less evident is why the bored, cynical restaurateurs should be making million-dollar bets with Monte about whether Lucy can escape from a locked mailbag in a tank of water. Presumably someone, somewhere, must have thought they could get some jokes out of the situation. They were wrong. Bowie drifts through, elegant, unconcerned and vaguely supercilious, leaching the energy from the narrative. Arquette emotes gamely as the waitress who dreams of following in Houdini's footsteps, but even she looks bored, and the sexual chemistry between the two wouldn't singe a gnat's wing. There's some amusement from the Tweedledum/Tweedledee antics of Gregory and Henry as the restaurateurs, but it's slim pickings. DW

Link

(1985, GB, 116 min)
d/p Richard Franklin. *sc* Everett De Roche. *ph* Mike Molloy. *ed* Andrew London. *pd* Norman Garwood. *m* Jerry Goldsmith. *cast* Elisabeth Shue, Terence Stamp, Steven Pinner, Richard Garnett, David O'Hara, Kevin Lloyd.

●Link is a morning-suited monkey who acts as valet for Terence Stamp, the mad professor who lives in a strange, dark mansion high on the cliffs in the middle of nowhere. Also around the house are Voodoo, and Imp, a chimp which apparently has the strength of eight men and the mind of a one-year-old. Franklin was responsible for *Psycho II*, so it's not long before, in best Hitchcock tradition, the master goes missing and the young American student assistant (Shue) is left to fight for her life against the unstoppable furry ones. Incidental pleasure comes from Link himself, a sly charmer with big paws and a penchant for cigars, who seems to have strayed in from *The Jungle Book*; but it's a slight affair which comes down to nothing more than frights in the cellars and who will survive? Too much monkey business. CPea

Linkshändige Frau, Die

see Left-Handed Woman, The

Lion, The

(1962, GB, 96 min)
d Jack Cardiff. *p* Samuel G Engel. *sc* Irene Kamp, Louis Kamp. *ph* Ted Scaife. *ed* Russell Lloyd. *ad* Alan Withy. *m* Malcolm Arnold. *cast* William Holden, Trevor Howard, Capucine, Pamela Franklin, Makara Kwaiha Ramadhani, Paul Oduor.

●A girl's best friend is her lion in this cross-eyed savannah drama. Her game warden stepfather (Howard) has to swallow his pride when his wife (Capucine) invites her ex-husband (Holden) to come over from America to 'civilise' this wild child (Franklin). A depressing, patronising conclusion sees the original family returning to domesticity and the States. Ironically, in real life Holden liked Kenya so much that he decided to live there. TCh

Lion Has Seven Heads, The (Der Leone Have Sept Cabecas)

(1970, It/Fr, 103 min)
d Glauber Rocha. *p* Claude Antoine, Gianni Barcelloni. *sc* Glauber Rocha, Gianni Amico. *ph* Guido Cosulich. *ed* Glauber Rocher, Eduardo Escorel. *cast* Rada Rassimov, Giulio Brogi, Gabriele Tinti, Jean-Pierre Léaud, Aldo Bixio, Bayak, Reinhard Kolldehoff.

●Rocha's film intends to demonstrate the contradictions of imperialism in Africa and to reveal the dynamics of the revolutionary process, of struggle against it. It is filmed theatre, self-consciously and confessedly Brechtian in its method. Seventy rather stilted, second-hand tableaux dramatise relations between a stereotypic blonde goddess (imperialism), a grotesquely posturing Léaud as Catholicism, the CIA, a black bourgeois reformist politician, and their opposition, a classic Ché figure, an African militant, and 'the people'. Very didactic and banally filmed, it tends toward a condescending populism, a rip-off analysis that doesn't seem to stem from a strong engagement with the subject, despite the clarity/accuracy of the general argument. The signs have no life. JDuC

Lion in Winter, The

(1968, GB, 134 min)
d Anthony Harvey. *p* Martin H Poll. *sc* James Goldman. *ph* Douglas Slocombe. *ed* John Bloom. *ad* Peter Murton, Gilbert Margerie. *m* John Barry. *cast* Peter O'Toole, Katharine Hepburn, Jane Merrow, John Castle, Anthony Hopkins, Nigel Terry, Timothy Dalton, Nigel Stock.

●Domestic squabbles concerning the succession at the court of Henry II in 1183. O'Toole's Henry is a grizzled, decaying old man, a continuation of the same part in *Becket*. Hepburn won her third Oscar for her role as his wife, Eleanor of Aquitaine. Harvey's direction is intelligent enough, though the reduction of power struggles to fits of personal pique – where the fate of nations hangs in the balance – becomes a little irritating. Enjoyable for its two lead performances, however. RM

Lion Is in the Streets, A

(1953, US, 88 min)
d Raoul Walsh. *p* William Cagney. *sc* Luther Davis. *ph* Harry Stradling. *ed* George Amy. *pd* Wiard Ihnen. *m* Franz Waxman. *cast* James Cagney, Barbara Hale, Anne Francis, Warner Anderson, John McIntire, Jeanne Cagney, Lon Chaney Jr, Frank McHugh.

●The title alludes to one assassinated overreacher, Julius Caesar; this oddball Cagney family production concerns another, Huey Long – or, as the script has it, Hank Martin. A somewhat compromised treatment of the life and political crimes of 'The Kingfish' (director Walsh advised abandonment rather than capitulation to Long family threats of legal action), this covers much the same ground as Robert Rossen's earlier feature, *All the King's Men*, and Robert Collins' later telemovie, *The Life and Assassination of the Kingfish*. In decidedly more idiosyncratic style, however, with Cagney's aggressive energy suggesting the particular populist allure of the Southern shyster-cum-demagogue. PT

Lion King, The

(1994, US, 88 min)
d Roger Allers, Ron Minkoff. *p* Don Hahn. *sc* Irene Mecchi, Jonathan Roberts. *ed* Tom Finan, John Carnochan, Ivan Bilancio. *pd* Chris Sanders. *m* Hans Zimmer. *songs* Tim Rice, Elton John. *cast voices:* Rowan Atkinson, Matthew Broderick, Whoopi Goldberg, Jeremy Irons, James Earl Jones, Cheech Marin.

●Following the inspired *Aladdin* and the emotionally involving *Beauty and the Beast*, Disney caps a hat trick of box-office hits with this breathtaking picture. The story hews to Joseph Campbell's maxim: first act, cosy; second act, despair; third act, redemption and transfiguration. As before, the camera treats the animated material like a feature film with humans – dollies, zooms, deploying the movements you'd expect in a James Cameron movie. How's the little lion king in waiting? Not too yucky. He has to learn the responsibilities of kingship, his father (Jones) explains, but Uncle Scar (Irons) tempts him off course. Villains and irresponsibles always have more fun. The hyenas have sharp one-liners to fledge their jive-ass flight (leader Whoopi Goldberg). The layabout beasts that Simba, Lion King Jr, hangs with in the wasted years are very funny. Pumbaa the farting warthog and Timon the meerkat still offer a viable hippie alternative. Songs variable. Animation staggering. A winner. BC

Lion of the Desert

(1980, US, 163 min)
d/p Moustapha Akkad. *sc* HAL Craig. *ph* Jack Hildyard. *ed* John Shirley. *pd* Mario Garbuglia, Syd Cain. *m* Maurice Jarre. *cast* Anthony Quinn, Oliver Reed, Irene Papas, Raf Vallone, Rod Steiger, John Gielgud, Andrew Keir, Gastone Moschin.

●Oliver Reed, the megalomaniac vanguard of Mussolini's Roman Empire, mumbles his way across Libya in 1929, decimating and concentrating and finally hanging Bedouin leader Quinn. At which, with smug hindsight, we do not blanch, knowing that everyone gets their just deserts (pronounce this either way) eventually. History furnishes an eventful plot, the film-makers supply the stereotyped characters, and the heavens (apparently) an ethereal chorus, resulting in a not unenjoyable ripping yarn. FD

Lion's Den, The (La Boca del Lobo)

(1988, Peru/Sp, 116 min)
d Francisco J Lombardi. *p* Gerardo Herrero, Francisco J Lombadi. *sc* Augusto Cabada, Giovanna Pollarolo. Gerardo Herrero. *ph* José Luis Lopez Linares. *ed* Juan Ignacio San Mateo. *ad* Marta Méndez. *m* Bernardo Bonezzi. *cast* Gustavo Bueno, Toña Vega, José Tejada, Gilberto Torres, Bertha Pagaza.

●Lombardi's anti-war film is set high in the remote mountains of Peru, where the communists are in revolt against the government. A small platoon of soldiers establish a post in an Indian village. Their indecisive officer is ambushed and butchered, but none of the citizenry will admit to any knowledge of the guerillas. Career soldier Luna (Vega) is initially reassured by the arrival of tough Lieutenant Roca (Bueno), but increasingly alienated by the behaviour of his friend Gallardo (Tejada), who treats the Indians as sub-human. The enemy never surfaces, though the decimation of the army post continues, and it is this sense of impotence that finally sparks off a massacre of the villagers. *Platoon*, *The Deer Hunter*, and in particular, Philip Caputo's *Rumours of War*, tap into similar psychological terrain, though continents removed. A bit more heat under the pressure cooker and a bit more characterisation would have been welcome, but the film works steadily towards its final impact. BC

Lions Love

(1969, US, 110 min)
d/p/sc Agnès Varda. *ph* Stevan Larner. *ed* Robert Dalva. *ad* Jack Wright III. *m* Joseph Byrd. *cast* Viva, Gerome Ragni, James Rado, Shirley Clarke, Carlos Clarens, Agnès Varda, Eddie Constantine, Peter Bogdanovich, Billie Dixon, Richard Bright.

●A film bedevilled by its intellectualism. It attempts to analyse the media-Unwelt of fringe Hollywood in June '68, the material being: avant-garde theatre (Michael McLure's *The Beard*), experimental art film (Shirley Clarke), the hip-hype pop musical (Rado and Ragni of *Hair*), underground superstardom (Viva), and the TV news. Varda's presentation is a peculiarly confused mix of ancient Godard, cliché'd surrealism, '50s pop, and a half-arsed imitation of Warholian stylistics, with some rancid cream – an unconvincing triangular love trip à la *Le*

Bonheur – thrown in for good measure. Set off against the love triangle garbage is a neat doom package of assassination (Robert Kennedy), attempted murder (Andy Warhol) and attempted suicide (Shirley Clarke). A nakedly bad film, a melange of incompatibles that induces embarrassment or irritation, but hardly humour or interest. JDuC

Lipstick

(1976, US, 90 min)
d Lamont Johnson. *p* Freddie Fields. *sc* David Rayfiel. *ph* Bill Butler. *ed* Marion Rothman. *pd* Robert Luthardt. *m* Michel Polnareff. *cast* Margaux Hemingway, Chris Sarandon, Anne Bancroft, Perry King, Robin Gammell, John Bennett Perry, Mariel Hemingway.

● The provocative invitations of a top model (Margaux Hemingway) on lipstick advertising hoardings are taken up by a meek music teacher (Sarandon), who responds to her lack of interest by attacking and raping her. The subsequent court proceedings make much of the model's professional life as provocation: a theme reminiscent of Clint Eastwood's (superior) *Play Misty for Me*, which points to one way the subject could have been handled. In failing to reveal the model's persona as the materialisation (maintained at some cost to herself) of collective male fantasy, the script underlines its teleplay blandness. The final vision of Hemingway's flaming red-clad avenger, emerging from her sterile cocoon to line up her violator in her gun sights, seems like a gesture in search of a movie. VG

Liquid Dreams

(1991, US, 98 min)
d Mark Manos. *p* Zane W Levitt, Diane Firestone. *sc* Mark Manos, Zack Davis. *ph* Sven Kirstein. *ed* Ed Tomney. *pd* Pam Moffat.*cast* Candice Daly, Richard Steinmetz, Barry Dennen, Juan Fernandez, Tracey Walter, Frankie Thorn, Paul Bartel, Mink Stole, John Doe.

● In this sleekly designed, sub-Cronenbergian sci-fi pic, Candice Daly's investigations into her sister's death from an alleged drugs overdose draw her into the twilight world of Neurovid, a kinky satellite TV channel inspired by *Videodrome*. Aided by a sympathetic cop (Steinmetz), Daly tries to discover the secret of the ultimate thrill, known as The Ritual. The sex is mildly perverse, the tone coldly cerebral, with a fine debut from the striking Daly, and strong support from Barry Dennen as The Major, Neurovid's icy supremo. NF

Liquid Sky

(1982, US, 112 min)
d/p Slava Tsukerman. *sc* Slava Tsukerman, Anne Carlisle, Nina V Kerova. *ph* Yuri Neyman. *ed* Sharyn L Ross, Slava Tsukerman. *pd* Marina Levikova. *m* Slava Tsukerman, Brenda I Hutchinson, Clive Smith. *cast* Anne Carlisle, Paula E Sheppard, Bob Brady, Susan Doukas, Elaine C Grove, Otto von Wernherr.

● Film-maker Tsukerman's personal comment on, er, the State of Western Man, magnified through a thoroughly unpleasant bunch of New York junkies, poseurs and twits. Claiming to subvert a host of Hollywood verities, Tsukerman unleashes a parasitic alien being on the New York smack'n'sex demi-monde. Junkies and sex fiends start dropping like flies, and not even the Bruno Ganz-alike scientist can stop the voracious bug. Tsukerman stops short of his original intention of offing the whole cast, allowing for an extraordinary fairy-tale ascension at the end, but his aim of highlighting social malaise gets happily mislaid in a bizarre, often hilarious melee of weird drugs, weird sex and off-the-wall camp SF. *Close Encounters* for acid casualties. JG

Lisa and the Devil

see House of Exorcism, The

Lisa Theory, The

(1993, US, 80 min)
d/p/sc Steven Okazaki. *ph* D Matthew Smith. *ed* Steven Okazaki. *pd* Julie Slinger, Zand Gee. *m* Jim Matison. *cast* Devon Morf, Honey O Yates, Avel Sosa II, Jim Matison, Mark Gorney, Bucky Sinister.

● A layabouts' movie – for layabouts even being a slacker takes too much energy – about half a dozen young dozos who share a cooperative flat. The 'theory' states that anyone named Jennifer needs a good leaving alone: a theory that seemingly applies to Lisa (Yates) who befriends Devon (Morf) then leaves him – rendering him catatonic for the rest of the movie. This is TV's *The Young Ones* as directed by Andy Warhol, with writer/director Okazaki anatomising their relationship in flashback. These naff punk rockers, pseudo-existentialists, and non-macho deadbrains don't impress Lisa, that's for sure. If it's hard to understand quite how false naive the director's stance is supposed to be, there's throw away intelligence here to spare, good observation, and a nice line in self-deprecating humour. Let's hope it's not autobiographical. WH

Lisboa (Lisbon)

(1999, Sp, 100 min)
d Antonio Hernández. *p* Federico Bermúdez de Castro, Enrique González Macho, Marcelo Itzkoff, Ramón Pilaces, Eduardo Pérez Climent. *sc* Enrique Brasó, Antonio Hernández. *ph* Aitor Mantxola. *ed* Santiago Ricci. *ad* Gabriel Carrascal. *m* Víctor Reyes. *cast* Carmen Maura, Sergi López, Federico Luppi, Antonio Birabent, Laia Marull, Miguel Palenzuela, Saturnino García.

● A supremely stylish, witty and enjoyable road-movie cum thriller in the Hitchcockian mould (spot the discreet allusion to *North by Northwest*). Portuguese travelling salesman López reluctantly gives a lift to the mysterious, maybe mad Maura in the middle of the Spanish desert; pretty soon he's trying to decide whether to walk away from her on-going battle with the dysfunctional family that's in hot pursuit, or to lend the clearly distressed woman his support. As the tone turns steadily darker, and a frighteningly unpleasant Luppi appears on the scene as Maura's tyrannical husband, Hernández packs in more than enough twists to sustain interest in his perfectly paced narrative, while the 'Scope camerawork and orchestral score lend the proceedings a real whiff of epic drama. GA

Lisbon Story

(1995, Fr/Port, 105 min)
d Wim Wenders. *p* Paulo Branco, Joao Canijo, Ulrich Felsberg. *sc* Wim Wenders. *ph* Lisa Rinzler. *ed* Peter Przygodda, Anne Schnee. *m* Madredeus, Jürgen Knieper. *cast* Rüdiger Vogler, Patrick Bauchau, Vasco Sequeira, Teresa Salgueiro, Manoel de Oliveira, Madredeus.

● Summoned to Lisbon by director Bauchau, who's having problems with the silent movie he's shooting there, soundman Vogler arrives late, to discover that his friend has gone missing. He determines, nevertheless, to record a soundtrack for the unfinished film and, in so doing, comes to love Lisbon (and fado/pop singer Salgueiro), falling in with various kids and crooks in the meantime. All this is both pretty (Lisbon, after all, is very photogenic) and pretty lame; Wenders has never been comfortable with the kind of gentle comedy he essays here. But it's when Vogler finally catches up with Bauchau that the movie really goes off the rails, tottering into a tedious, redundant hypothesis about the lost innocence of the cinematic edge. Wenders has escorted us around this territory before, and far more entertainingly than here. GA

Listen to Me

(1989, US, 110 min)
d Douglas Day Stewart. *p* Mary Kay Powell. *sc* Douglas Day Stewart. *ph* Fred J Koenekamp. *ed* Anne V Coates. *pd* Gregory Pickrell. *m* David Foster. *cast* Kirk Cameron, Jami Gertz, Roy Scheider, Amanda Peterson, Tim Quill, George Wyner, Anthony Zerbe, Christopher Atkins.

● Welcome to Kenmont College, CA, and the prestigious debating team run by Professor Scheider. Among its luminaries, two scholarship students: poor country boy Tucker (Cameron) who used to make his shoes out of tyres, and bookish beauty Monica (Gertz) who doesn't date. Blonde cripple Donna (Peterson) is determined to 'dance again', but rebuffs invitations from surfer Bruce (Atkins). Topping them all is hunky Garson 'Dostoevsky' McKellar (Quill), whose writing ambitions are thwarted by a politician dad (Zerbe). Their aim to debate 'Is Abortion Immoral?' before the Supreme Court isn't helped by writer-director Stewart's supply of brainless platitudes. By the final half-hour, desperate plotting, uninspired casting and clichéd dialogue leave one student dead, another with a split lip, and Scheider lost for words. CM

Listen Up: The Lives of Quincy Jones

(1990, US, 115 min)
d Ellen Weissbrod. *p* Courtney Sale Ross. *ph* Stephen Kazmierski. ed Milton Moses Ginsberg, Pierre Kahn, Andrew Morreale, Laure Sullivan, Paul Zehrer. *m* Quincy Jones. *with* Quincy Jones, Clarence Avant, George Benson, Richard Brooks, Ray Charles, Miles Davis, Ella Fitzgerald, Frank Sinatra, Lionel hampton, Michael Jackson.

● Quincy Jones has been at or near the centre of black music since the '40s, as player, composer, arranger and producer: hence 'Lives'. He has also had rather a hard time. Unfortunately, this film biography, though laudatory, looks like one more cross to bear. To give Weissbrod her due, she has collected some astonishing material: home movies, newsreels, low-grade video, interviews (Ray Charles, Miles, Dizzy, Sinatra, Lionel Hampton, Ella Fitzgerald, Michael Jackson and many more), and masses of still photographs, handwritten scores and printed material. But the way she has assembled the film is deplorable. Weissbrod edits with crass brutality, presumably following a half-baked analogy with musical styles and techniques. Interviewees, seldom allowed whole phrases, let alone intelligible ideas, are made to speak simultaneously. No one is captioned until the end, an utterly elitist device. More damagingly, music barely gets a look in (plenty of sounds, but no completed musical statements). A little humility (R.E.S.P.E.C.T., even) in the presence of great artistry might have been in order. JMo

List of Adrian Messenger, The

(1963, US, 97 min, b/w)
d John Huston. *p* Edward Lewis. *sc* Anthony Veiller. *ph* Joseph MacDonald. *ed* Terry Morse, Hugh Fowler. *ad* Stephen Grimes, George Webb. *m* Jerry Goldsmith. *cast* George C Scott, Kirk Douglas, Jacques Roux, Dana Wynter, Clive Brook, Herbert Marshall, Bernard Archard, Gladys Cooper, Marcel Dalio, John Huston.

● Saddled with an incredibly creaky whodunit plot, this thriller should really have been set in Victorian times to accommodate its villain with a passion for disguises, its Holmesian detective in a bowler hat, its murder in a fog-bound Limehouse that is pure Griffith. As it is, archly playing the country-house game complete with drawing-room teas, fox-hunting guests, and port passed to the left, Huston never seems entirely sure whether he means to parody or play straight. Though not without longueurs, the result is surprisingly rich in fun, not least the insolent assurance with which Huston can give away the murderer's identity, knowing he has four guest stars (Mitchum, Lancaster, Curtis and Sinatra) also prancing around in disguise to act as mystificatory red herrings. (From the novel by Philip MacDonald.) TM

Lisztomania

(1975, GB, 104 min)
d Ken Russell. *p* Roy Baird, David Puttnam. *sc* Ken Russell. *ph* Peter Suschitzky. *ed* Stuart Baird. *ad* Philip Harrison. *m/songs* Rick Wakeman. *lyrics* Jonathan Benson, Roger Daltrey, Ken Russell. *cast* Roger Daltrey, Sara Kestelman, Paul Nicholas, Fiona Lewis, Veronica Quilligan, Nell Campbell, John Justin, Ringo Starr, Murray Melvin, Andrew Faulds, Oliver Reed.

● Since *Tommy* was Ken Russell's first real commercial hit, it's not surprising that *Lisztomania* should be a blatant attempt to repeat the formula. But without Pete Townshend behind him, Russell has to fall back on his own notion of a 'rock opera'...which means casting the hapless Daltrey as yet another Messiah and Ringo (ho ho) as the Pope, and hiring Rick Wakeman to play garbled rearrangements of Liszt and Wagner. The result is not only catastrophically wide of the mark as a 'sense experience', but misogynistic, addled and gracelessly witless. The most pitiable aspect is that Russell is here patronising his collaborators as much as he's always patronised his audience. TR

Litany for Survival: The Life and Work of Audre Lorde, A

(1995, US, 90 min)
d Michelle Parkerson, Ada Gay Griffin. *with* Audre Lorde.

● 'It is the work of the poet within us to bridge contradictions.' Audre Lorde – black, lesbian, feminist warrior – knew plenty about that. Though determined to survive as who she was, it wasn't an easy option: she suffered a backstreet abortion, married a white man and had two children along the way. Griffin and Parkerson interviewed the poet extensively in the eight years before her death by cancer in 1992: Lorde tells her story eloquently, too involved in the evolutionary struggle to waste time on regrets and bitterness, too involved in life to fear death. At the forefront of liberation movements in America, Lorde did not shrink from the political at home. In a revealing interview her son talks about having to define his own version of what manhood meant – one that wouldn't repulse his mother. An inspirational figure who believed her poetry was a means rather than an end – 'The power you feel is a power you own' – Lorde is well remembered here. FM

Little Angel (Engelchen)

(1996, Ger, 93 min)
d Helke Misselwitz. *ed* Thomas Wilkening. *sc* Helke Misselwitz. *ph* Thomas Plenert. *ed* Gudrun Steinbrueck. *pd* Lothar Holler. *cast* Susanne Lothar, Cezary Pazura, Sophie Rois, Herbert Fritsch, Kathrin Angerer.

● Something of a caged bird, Ramona (Lothar) works in a lipstick factory and lives alone near the Ostkreuz station in East Berlin. One day a stranger, Andrzej (Pazura), grabs and kisses her. He's a Pole working the black market, avoiding the police. Ramona sees him again, then some more. She becomes pregnant, and happy – then she loses the baby. Something of a downer, this quiet, sombre film has its heart in the right place, but never finds the devices to engage its audience. Given that the protagonist is (apparently) psychologically unbalanced, the realist method (writer/director Helke Misselwitz has a documentary background) of slowly recording her ups and downs isn't enough to help us get inside her head. A sense of helpless Central European melancholia percolates through, but as drama it's all too grey and worthy. NB

Little Big League

(1994, US, 119 min)
d Andrew Scheinman. *p* Mike Lobell. *sc* Gregory K Pincus, Adam Scheinman. *ph* Donald E Thorin. *ed* Michael Jablow. *pd* Jeffrey Howard. *m* Stanley Clarke. *cast* Jason Robards, Ashley Crow, Luke Edwards, Timothy Busfield, John Ashton, Dennis Farina, Ken Griffey Jr, Sandy Alomar Jr, Carlos Baerga, Lou Piniella.

● Twelve-year-old Billy Heywood (Edwards) has a problem: what to do when super-rich Grandpa (Robards) leaves him an entire major league baseball team of his own. When faced with the impending school vacation and the prospect of handling the day-to-day running of the Minnesota Twins, his response is to rekindle among the primadonna players a sheer love of the sport, resurrect their hopes of making the play-offs, and hope that Mom (Crow) doesn't get too upset over the odd cussword emanating from his lips due to big game tension. Making his directorial debut after producing such improving fare as *The Princess Bride* and *Stand by Me*, Scheinman is so keen to pile on the moral precepts, that the proceedings never really take on an imaginative life of their own. The film does, however, avoid tub-thumping triumphalism and manages better than most Hollywood sports movies to integrate its roster of real-life players within the contrivances of the storyline. TJ

Little Big Man

(1970, US, 147 min)
d Arthur Penn. *p* Stuart Millar. *sc* Calder Willingham. *ph* Harry Stradling Jr. *ed* Dede Allen. *pd* Dean Tavoularis. *m* John Hammond. *cast* Dustin Hoffman, Faye Dunaway, Martin Balsam, Richard Mulligan, Chief Dan George, Jeff Corey, Amy Eccles, Kelly Jean Peters, Alan Howard.

● Penn's adaptation of Thomas Berger's novel is an epic post-Western that sets out to demythologise its subject-matter through the eyes of Jack Crabb (Hoffman), either a 121-year-old hero who's seen it all or a phenomenal liar. Ambiguity, both towards fact and character, is the keynote, as Hoffman's protagonist is orphaned, adopted by Indians, returned to the whites as a conman, and finally acclaimed as the sole white survivor of Custer's downfall at Little Big Horn. It's a shaggy, picaresque tale, laden with off-beat but pertinent observations as Crabb exchanges cultures and bears witness to the white man's genocidal treatment of 'the human beings'. Parallels with Vietnam naturally abound, but finally it's a wryly ironic rewriting of American history that makes up for its occasionally facile debunking of heroic targets by means of vivid direction and effortless performances. Funny, humane, and a work of brave intelligence. GA

Little Buddha

(1993, Fr/GB, 140 min)
d Bernardo Bertolucci. *p* Jeremy Thomas. *sc* Rudy Wurlitzer, Mark Peploe. *ph* Vittorio Storaro. *ed* Pietro Scalia. *pd* James Acheson. *m* Ryuichi Sakamoto. *cast* Keanu Reeves, Ying Ruocheng, Alex Wiesendanger, Chris Isaak, Bridget Fonda, Raju Lal.

● Nine-year-old Jesse (Wiesendanger), son of Seattle teacher Fonda and architect Isaak is identified as a possible reincarnation of a Tibetan Buddhist lama. On a visit to their apartment, dying lama Norbu (the sympathetic Ying Ruocheng) gives Jesse a picture-book of the life of Siddhartha/Buddha and suggests a visit to his monastery. Facing bankruptcy, Jesse's father accepts, and on the subcontinent Jesse witnesses Siddhartha's cosmic battle to banish evil, the multi-form Lord Mara, and finds he is just one of three candidates from whom Norbu must choose. Bertolucci's epic is a disappointment. With its once-upon-a-time structure, it has the feeling of a beautiful but very expensive kids' movie, intercut with a '50s 'Scope sandal-saga. Reeves makes a pretty, exotic, bare-breasted icon as the damask-cloaked prince turned rasta-style ascetic. On a deeper level, the film seems not to be specifically about Buddha, but about resistance and acceptance, weirdly resolving itself into an confusing essay on the deification of children. WH

Little Caesar

(1930, US, 80 min, b/w)
d Mervyn LeRoy. *p* Darryl F Zanuck. *sc* Francis Edwards Faragoh. *ph* Tony Gaudio. *ed* Ray Curtiss. *ad* Anton F Grot. *cast* Edward G Robinson, Douglas Fairbanks Jr, Glenda Farrell, Stanley Fields, Sidney Blackmer, Ralph Ince, William Collier Jr.

● Though it looks somewhat dated now, there's no denying the seminal importance of this classic adaptation of WR Burnett's novel. Robinson – vain, cruel, jealous and vicious – is superb as the ruthlessly ambitious mobster Rico Bandello, determined to gain sole control of the city's criminal empire, anxious that his dancing-gigolo sidekick Massara (Fairbanks) should not leave him for a woman, and ending in bland astonishment that death should have overtaken him ('Mother of God, is this the end of Rico?'), despite the cautionary opening title assuring one and all that those who live by the sword, etc. Like many early talkies, the film often in fact errs on the slow side, at least in terms of dialogue; but the parallels with Capone, Tony Gaudio's photography, and LeRoy's totally unrepentant tone ensure that it remains fascinating. GA

Little Cheung (Xilu Xiang)

(1999, HK/Jap, 115 min)
d Fruit Chan. *p* Doris Yang, Makoto Ueda. *sc* Fruit Chan. *ph* Lam Wah-Chuen. *ed* Tin Sam-Fat. *ad* Chris Wong. *m* Lam Wah-Chuen, Chu Hing-Cheung. *cast* Yiu Yuet-Ming, Mak Wai-Fan, Mak Yuet-Man, Gary Lai.

● There are three Cheungs in Chan's complex and inventive film: the dying Cantonese opera star Tang Wing-Cheung (to whom the film is dedicated), the original Kid Cheung (child star Bruce Lee in a '50s movie) and the film's nine-year-old protagonist, who helps out in his family's restaurant in the working class district of Mongkok, surrounded by hookers, gangsters, coffin makers and illegal immigrants from China. Framed as an investigation into the community's economic structures and dynamics, the film (set in 1996, on the eve of the handover) uses a non-pro cast and a free form plot to assert what's specific and distinctive about HK's culture – albeit defined across Chan's now-familiar scatological obsessions. With a Kieslowskian flourish the protagonists of *Made in Hong Kong* and *The Longest Summer* turn up in the closing moments, making this the third part of an informal 'handover trilogy'. TR

Little City

(1998, US, 87 min)
d Roberto Benabib. *p* Jeffrey L Davidson, Beau Flynn, Stefan Simchowitz, Ron Wechsler. *sc* Roberto Benabib. *ph* Randall Love. *ed* Norman Buckley, Sloane Klevin. *pd* Don De Fina. *m* Mader. *cast* Jon Bon Jovi, Penelope Ann Miller, Josh Charles, Annabella Sciorra, JoBeth Williams, Joanna Going, Peter Gardiner.

● This easy-going, believable and nicely played relationship comedy explores the process of commitment in familiar, but perfectly watchable ways. Adam (Charles) and Kevin (Bon Jovi) are good friends, but the latter's affair with the former's partner Nina (Sciorra) is just the beginning in a series of bed and heart exchanges as new arrivals, some lesbian confusions and a challenging pregnancy add spice to the brew. Bon Jovi forgoes hair for heart, Charles is well-judged and all the women – it is, after all, a great cast – deliver on mature and serious, yet lightly handled roles. Package this differently (it went straight to tape in the UK) and you could pitch it to the 'low key US indie' appreciation crowd. GE

Little Darling (Petite chérie)

(2000, Fr, 106 min)
d Anne Villacèque. *p* Jean Bréhat, Rachid Bouchareb. *sc* Anne Villacèque, Elisabeth Barrière-Marquet. *ph* Pierre Milon. *ed* Anne Riegel. *pd* Laurent Deroo. *cast* Corinne Debonnière, Jonathan Zaccaï, Laurence Février, Patrick Préjean, Pierre Louis-Calixte, Sarah Haxaire, Philippe Ambrosini.

● Is this a black, miserabilist comedy or a serious drama? As with *L'Humanité*, produced by the same team, it's sometimes hard to tell. My guess is that writer/director Villacèque is trying to do a Mike Leigh, but in slightly more serious mode, as she charts the courtship of the plain, virginal and naive thirty-something of the title (that's how she's addressed, at any rate, by her over-protective and likewise worldly-unwise suburban parents) by a seedy, insecure and utterly unreliable chancer. Inexplicably all three look up to him, welcoming him as a romantic, canny hero. It's a rather patronising, even ugly film, not without some visual virtues and brave performances, but it leaves a sour taste in the mouth. GA

Little Darlings

(1980, US, 94 min)
d Ronald F Maxwell. *p* Stephen J Friedman. *sc* Kimi Peck, Dalene Young. *ph* Beda Batka. *ed* Pembroke J Herring. *pd* William M Hiney. *m* Charles Fox. *cast* Tatum O'Neal, Kristy McNichol, Armand Assante, Matt Dillon, Krista Errickson, Alexa Kenin, Maggie Blye.

● Setting out as a rough edged youthsploiter (factions at summer camp take bets on whether Tatum O'Neal or Kristy McNichol will lose her virginity first), it soon becomes apparent that the real message is that 'growing up' is not to be achieved by the simple act of defloration. *Little Darlings* proceeds to hammer the point home, till you emerge from its setting of woods, handy boathouses and the boys' camp across the lake, head ringing with the maxim, 'At 15, sex is bad, friendship good, and clean fun the answer.' If you can get over the moralising, there's a treat from Kristy McNichol as the rough talking, Marlboro-smoking kid who can deliver a kick to the cobblers to rival Paul Newman, while Matt Dillon as her 'gentle giant' initiator and the soundtrack (Blondie, Bonnie Raitt) also provide welcome relief. FF

Little Dorrit

(1987, GB. 176 min [Part I]/181 min [Part II])
d Christine Edzard. *p* John Brabourne, Richard Goodwin. *sc* Christine Edzard. *ph* Bruno de Keyser. *ed* Olivier Stockman, Fraser MacLean. *pd* Sands Film. *m* Giuseppe Verdi. *cast* Derek Jacobi, Alec Guinness, Eleanor Bron, Michael Elphick, Joan Greenwood, Sarah Pickering, Miriam Margolyes, Max Wall, Cyril Cusack, Patricia Hayes, Roshan Seth, Bill Fraser.

● 'Make money, sir. Be as rich as you honestly can,sir.' *Little Dorrit* is about lucre – filthy and otherwise – so Christine Edzard's masterful two part adaptation of Dickens' novel has a peculiar relevance for today. Part I (*Nobody's Fault*) tells the tale of fortunes lost and found, of secrets buried and unearthed, from the viewpoint of Arthur Clennam (Jacobi), who in his attempts to help the Dorrits abandons wealth and is brought to The Marshalsea, a debtors' prison. Part II (*Little Dorrit's Story*) relates the same story through the eyes of Little Dorrit herself (Pickering), the dutiful daughter of the 'Father of The Marshalsea' (Guinness), who forms a deep love for the oblivious Clennam. In the first part the powerful momentum of the narrative is broken by abrupt shifts back in time, but in the second the events ingeniously begin to overlap. Besides the excitement of the story, the chief delight of this epic production lies in the superb performances, which manage to convey Dickens' penchant for the grotesque while suggesting the inner life that many critics deny exists in the novel. Impressive camerawork and Verdi's music help make the six hours roll by far too quickly. MS

Little Drummer Girl, The

(1984, US, 130 min)
d George Roy Hill. *p* Robert L Crawford. *sc* Loring Mandel. *ph* Wolfgang Teu. *ed* William H Reynolds. *pd* Henry Bumstead. *m* David Grusin. *cast* Diane Keaton, Yorgo Voyagis, Klaus Kinski, Sami Frey, Michael Cristofer, David Suchet, Anna Massey, Thorley Walters.

●Keaton stars as Charlie, a right-on actress recruited by Israeli intelligence to help winkle out a top Palestinian terrorist. The film's misfortune is that it capturesm all too faithfully the tortuous, pretentious and rather unimaginative approach of John Le Carré's more recent work. Kinski is allowed a few show-stealing scenes as the officer who masterminds the seduction, both mental and physical, of the reluctant Charlie, but Keaton is altogether too much the star to portray effectively a woman who is supposed to be without qualities, a blank sheet who allows herself to be written all over by a bunch of strangers. This process of character is the most interesting idea. As for the rest of the film, there's just too little action, too much talk. RR

Little Foxes, The

(1941, US, 116 min, b/w)
d William Wyler. *p* Sam Goldwyn.*sc* Lillian Hellman, Arthur Kober, Dorothy Parker, Alan Campbell. *ph* Gregg Toland.*ed* Daniel Mandell. *ad* Stephen Goosson.*m* Meredith Willson. *cast* Bette Davis, Herbert Marshall, Teresa Wright, Patricia Collinge, Dan Duryea, Charles Dingle, Richard Carlson, Carl Benton Reid.

●Lillian Hellman's play about the malevolence of human greed, as displayed in the internecine machinations of a wealthy Southern family, now creaks audibly. But you are unlikely ever to see a better version than this, caressed by Gregg Toland's deep focus camerawork, embalmed by Wyler's direction and Goldwyn's sumptuous production values, galvanised by some superlative performances. The sulphurous Davis, her face a livid mask as she dispenses icy venom behind feline purrs, outdoes herself to provide the proceedings with a regally vicious centre; even so, she is in constant danger of being upstaged by Duryea, Dingle and Collinge. TM

Little Girl...Big Tease

see Snatched

Little Girl Who Sold the Sun, The (La Petite Vendeuse de Soleil)

(1999, Sen/Switz/Fr, 45 min)
d Djibril Diop-Mambéty. *p* Silvia Voser.*sc* Djibril Diop-Mambéty. *ph* Jacques Besse.*ed* Sarah Taouss Matton. *m* Wasis Diop.*cast* Lissa Baléra, Taïrou M'Baye, Oumou Samb, Moussa Baldé, Dieynaba Laam,Martin N'Gom.

●The last film of the Senegalese director Diop-Mambéty, fable-like in its simplicity, tells of a partly crippled young beggar, Sili, who after being knocked down by some unruly kids selling papers on the streets of Dakar, decides to take them on at their own game. Inevitably she meets with cruel competition and prejudice, but the kindness of a few strangers, coupled with her own courage, honesty and determination, eases her burden. The film's measured rhythms, vivid camerawork and confidence of tone make for enthralling viewing. GA

Little Godard, A (Der kleine Godard)

(1978, WGer, 81 min)
d Hellmuth Costard. *cast* Hellmuth Costard, Jean-Luc Godard, Rainer Werner Fassbinder, Andrea Ferréol, Hark Bohm.

●Costard here contrasts two approaches to film-making practice. In the red corner, Costard himself and Jean-Luc Godard, the former struggling to set up a Super-8 Co-op, the latter running rings around cultural officials in Hamburg Council. In the blue corner, Fassbinder shooting *Despair* on a huge tax-shelter budget, and Hark Bohm shooting his supremely idiotic movie about kiddie rebellion, *Moritz, lieber Moritz*. What emerges most strongly is a sense of the political and aesthetic chaos that Costard has made of his life. How do you take a movie whose director stages a scene showing himself leaping out of bed to answer a doorbell in order to display his own erection? TR

Little Hut, The

(1956, US/GB, 90 min)
d Mark Robson. *p* F Hugh Herbert, Mark Robson. *sc* F Hugh Herbert. *ph* Freddie Young. *ed* Ernest Walter. *ad* Elliot Scott. *m* Robert Farnon. *cast* Stewart Granger, David Niven, Ava Gardner, Walter Chiari, Finlay Currie, Jean Cadell, Jack Lambert.

●A neglected wife (Gardner), her husband (Granger) and an admirer (Niven) are shipwrecked on a desert island. André Roussin's stage farce ran for two years in Paris, and almost three in London (in an adaptation by Nancy Mitford), but this screen version is unbelievably bad; all talk, no action, and utterly superficial. These three layabouts wouldn't survive five minutes on a traffic island. TCh

Little Ida (Liten Ida)

(1981, Nor/Swe, 79 min)
d Laila Mikkelsen. *p* Kirsten Bryhni, Merete Lindstad. *sc* Marit Paulsen. *ph* Hans Welin, Kjell Vassdal. *ed* Peter Falck. *ad* Anders Barréus. *m* Eyvind Solås. *cast* Sunniva Lindekleiv, Howard Halvorsen, Lise Fjeldstad, Arne Lindtner Naess, Ellen Westerfjell.

●A return to the theme of childhood innocence spoiled by the rigours of war which has recently seen distinguished service in *Spirit of the Beehive* and *Muddy River*. Here the setting is Northern Norway, 1944–5, and the child seven-year-old Ida, cruelly ostracised for her mother's liaison with a German soldier. Mikkelsen mostly stays the right side of the line between sensitivity and sentimentality, delicacy and dullness, supported by Sunniva Lindekleiv's winning performance as a mercifully un-cute child, and by some stunning cinematography, all in muted tones of grey and brown which suddenly explode, in the final victory procession, into a proud flurry of red Norwegian flags. In its own unassuming way, a small gem of miniaturist observation. SJo

Little Kidnappers, The

see Kidnappers, The

Little Lord Fauntleroy

(1980, GB, 103 min)
d Jack Gold. *p* Norman Rosemont. *sc* Blanche Hanalis. *ph* Arthur Ibbetson. *ed* Keith Palmer. *pd* Herbert Westbrook. *m* Allyn Ferguson. *cast* Ricky Schroder, Alec Guinness, Eric Porter, Colin Blakely, Connie Booth, Rachel Kempson, Patsy Rowlands.

●Basically unacceptable advertisement for the concepts of philanthropy practised by an oppressive aristocracy in capitalist Victorian England. Presented with such intractable material, director Gold conspires with a cast of British character actors (immaculate) against the unacceptable face of American child acting (Schroder, wondrous). Zzzz. CPe

Little Malcolm and His Struggle Against the Eunuchs

(1974, GB, 110 min)
d Stuart Cooper. *p* Gavrik Losey. *sc* Derek Woodward. *ph* John Alcott. *ed* Ray Lovejoy. *ad* Edward Marshall. *m* Stanley Myers. *cast* John Hurt, John McEnery, Raymond Platt, David Warner, Rosalind Ayres.

●This film would probably be produced by C4 or Handmade now. Back then it was financed by the Beatles' crumbling Apple empire, with George Harrison as fledgling executive producer. It won an award in Berlin, died in the West End, and vanished. In fact, David Halliwell's stage satire on Fascism, in the form of an art student's revolt against authority, translated fairly well to the screen, and the themes of paranoia and impotence are handled with enough kick for it to have deserved more success. There are particularly strong performances from the men (admittedly rather old for students), but it is Ayres as the only woman who steals the show. CPe

Little Man Tate

(1991, US, 99 min)
d Jodie Foster. *p* Scott Rudin, Peggy Rajski.*sc* Scott Frank. *ph* Mike Southon. *ed* Lynzee Klingman. *pd* Jon Hutman. *m* Mark Isham.*cast* Jodie Foster, Dianne Wiest, Adam Hann-Byrd, Harry Connick Jr, David Pierce, Debi Mazar, PJ Ochlan, Celia Weston, George Plimpton, Josh Mostel.

●Fred Tate (Hann-Byrd) is a gifted child: by age seven, he can play the piano backwards, paint like a master, and solve complex maths problems. But at school he's bored in lessons, and left doodling Da Vinci-style while other pupils frolic in the playground. Single parent mother Dede (Foster) comes into conflict with child psychologist Jane Grierson (Wiest), who takes the boy under her wing: tough-talking Dede is ready with the hugs, while Jane serves up macrobiotics and disciplinary lectures. Foster's directorial debut is a worthy attempt to explore a little understood subject, but the film is bogged down by an approach to Wiest and Foster's characters which polarises intellect and emotion. Hann-Byrd has more to grapple with, and perfectly conveys Fred's jumbled motives and acute sensitivity. Tackling a difficult project, Foster draws good performances from her cast, but could have done with a better script. CM

Little Man, What Now?

(1934, US, 98 min, b/w)
d Frank Borzage. *sc* William Anthony McGuire. *ph* Norbert Brodine. *ed* Milton Carruth. *ad* Charles D Hall. *m* Arthur Kay. *cast* Margaret Sullavan, Douglas Montgomery, Alan Hale, Muriel Kirkland, Alan Mowbray, Mae Marsh, Catherine Doucet.

●One of Frank Borzage's remarkable romantic weepies, dealing – like *A Farewell to Arms*, *Three Comrades* and *The Mortal Storm* – with the transcendent power of love to survive in times of horrific spiritual and economic poverty. Here the couple – Sullavan, at her most radiant, and Montgomery – manage to stay together whatever the '20s depression in post-war Germany can throw at them. Beautiful, committed, and deeply moving, it's the sort of film that it would be virtually impossible to make today without falling into banality. (From the novel by Hans Fallada.) GA

Little Matchgirl, The

see Petite Marchande d'allumettes, La

Little Mermaid, The

(1989, US, 83 min)
d John Musker, Ron Clements. *p* Howard Ashman, John Musker. *sc* John Musker,Ron Clements. *ph* John Cunningham.*ed* Mark Hester. *ad* Michael A Peraza Jr, Donald A Towns. *m* Alan Menken. *cast*voices: René Auberjonois, Christopher Daniel Barnes, Jodi Benson, Pat Carroll, Buddy Hackett, Kenneth Mars.

●Hans Christian Andersen is given the update in Disney's animated fairytale, the action punctuated by calypso and sweeping ballads as 16-year-old rebellious mermaid Ariel follows her one true, human love, handsome Prince Eric. When the affair is thwarted by her domineering father Triton, sea-witch Ursula offers to turn Ariel into a human for three days; but if she fails to secure a royal kiss in that time, she becomes Ursula's property. This return to traditional Disney territory is geared to captivate children while allowing them to maintain their street cred, largely by combining extravagant animated technique with ranging musical styles. The underwater scenes are spectacular: shimmering, illusory images set behind bold, primary sea life. Why, given this kind of creative care, do the film-makers resort to racial stereotyping for Ariel's crustacean servant? CM

Little Miracles (Pequeños Milagros)

(1997, Arg, 102 min)
d Eliseo Subiela. *p* Omar Romay, Eliseo Subiela. *sc* Eliseo Subiela. *ph* Daniel Rodriguez Maseda. *ed* Marcela Saenz. *pd* Margarita Jusid. *m* Osvaldo Montes. *cast* Julieta Ortega, Antonio Birabent, Monica Galán, Paco Rabal, Ana Maria Picchio, Héctor Alterio.
●Young check-out girl Rosalia (Ortega), who spends her spare time reading to the blind, sits dreaming at a Buenos Aires supermarket till, distressing shoppers with her ethereal talk and smiling to herself at her compassionate telekinetic skills, realising she may indeed be a 'good fairy' with extraordinary powers – isn't that how maturity feels? Elsewhere in the city, a young scientist (Birabent) employed in a government astronomical survey searching for extra-terrestrial intelligence, daily checks his internet for closed circuit shots of a bus-shelter, where he has regularly spotted Rosalia waiting for her bus. This is a sweet but daft 'magical' romance which cross-cuts between – and thus connects – these two romantics, side-stepping sentimentality by way of sure, graceful performances. Héctor Alterio as the girl's 'frightened' father is superb, as ever. WH

Little Miss Marker

(1980, US, 102 min)
d Walter Bernstein. *p* Jennings Lang. *sc* Walter Bernstein. *ph* Philip H Lathrop. *ed* Eve Newman. *pd* Edward C Carfagno. *m* Henry Mancini. *cast* Walter Matthau, Julie Andrews, Tony Curtis, Sara Stimson, Bob Newhart, Lee Grant, Brian Dennehy, Kenneth McMillan.
●A calculated line-up: Matthau as a tight-fisted bookie, Julie Andrews as an English Rose, Tony Curtis as a camp hoodlum, and the doe-eyed Sara Stimson as Damon Runyon's Little Miss Marker. The setting is some hack's idea of '30s Depression New York, depressing all right in its complete lack of conviction, and the story is as contrived as the set: a father hands his daughter over as surety for a $10 racing debt, and proceeds to disappear into the river. Matthau, landed with the child and regretting the lost money, is gradually softened up by Childish Charms – though any audience, one suspects, would be left stone cold by this cynical attempt to engage their emotions. A film which aspires to a heart of gold, but is clearly alloy all the way. JCl

Little Mother

see Don't Cry for Me Little Mother

Little Murders

(1971, US, 110 min)
d Alan Arkin. *p* Jack Brodsky. *sc* Jules Feiffer. *ph* Gordon Willis. *ed* Howard Kuperman. *pd* Gene Rudolph. *m* Fred Kaz. *cast* Elliott Gould, Marcia Rodd, Vincent Gardenia, Elizabeth Wilson, Jon Korkes, John Randolph, Donald Sutherland, Lou Jacobi, Alan Arkin, Doris Roberts.
●A wryly funny parable, scripted by Jules Feiffer from his own play, about a photographer living in a metropolis where murder, rape and arson are so commonplace that nobody notices any more. Happily spending his days shooting shit in all shapes and sizes ('*Harper's Bazaar* wants me to do its Spring issue'), he naturally gets beaten up from time to time (but the muggers, he says, soon get tired and go away). Into his life comes a happy, beautiful girl who insists that everyone should wake up with a smile in the mornings; and just as he begins to discover what it is to have feelings, a sniper's bullet intervenes. Some of the fun poked at the nervous disintegration of Establishment authority (judge, cop, clergyman) is done in blatantly extraneous revue-type sketches. But the performances are perfection, and at the end you are left with a haunting image of the Feiffer world, where little daily murders done to man's soul have made feeling not merely dangerous but impossible. TM

Little Nellie Kelly

(1940, US, 100 min, b/w)
d Norman Taurog. *p* Arthur Freed. *sc* Jack McGowan. *ph* Ray June. *ed* Frederick Y Smith. *ad* Cedric Gibbons, Henry McAfee. *songs* George M Cohan, Roger Edens, Nacio Herb Brown, Arthur Freed. *cast* Judy Garland, George Murphy, Charles Winninger, Douglas MacPhail, Arthur Shields, Forrester Harvey.
●Sentimental tosh based on an old George M Cohan musical, about a young girl striving to placate her bilious old grandfather (Winninger, obviously meant to be charmingly-cutely Irish but emerging as truly obnoxious) when he objects to her marriage to a sworn enemy. Lots of irritating Irish blarney, with only Garland's clear tones leavening the brew in a number of songs (naturally including 'It's a Great Day for the Irish'). GA

Little Nemo Adventures in Slumberland

(1992, US/Jap, 87 min)
d (animation) Masami Hata, William Hurtz; (voices) David Swift. *p* Yutaka Fujioka. *sc* Chris Columbus, Richard Outten. *pd* Jean Moebius Giraud. *m* Thomas Chase, Steve Rucker. *songs* Richard M Sherman, Robert B Sherman. *cast* voices: Gabriel Damon, Mickey Rooney, René Auberjonois, Danny Mann, Laura Mooney, Michael Gough.
●Nemo looks too cute and the period sense is missing, along with the comically stilted conversation. But the flavour of Winsor McCay's original strip cartoon (dating from 1905) still lingers, thanks to the likes of Ray Bradbury (concept), Robert Towne and Disney veteran Ollie Johnston ('consultants'). Nemo's dreamworld encompasses Slumberland, all candy stores and bandstands; and Nightmareland, where monsters prowl amid bizarre wreckage. Fantasies of triumph give way to ones of shame, with much flying and falling through the air. The Shermans' songs, alas, are straight out of a musical Nightmareland, and Nemo's first dream – being pursued by a homicidal locomotive – sets the tone. Visually remarkable, but with a gallon of Sherman syrup poured over it. BBa

Little Night Music, A

(1977, Aus/WGer, 125 min)
d Harold Prince. *p* Elliott Kastner. *sc* Hugh Wheeler. *ph* Arthur Ibbetson. *ed* John Jympson. *ad* Herta Pischinger. *m/lyrics* Stephen Sondheim. *cast* Elizabeth Taylor, Diana Rigg, Len Cariou, Lesley-Anne Down, Hermione Gingold, Laurence Guittard, Christopher Guard, Chloe Franks.
●Stephen Sondheim's adaptation of Ingmar Bergman's *Smiles of a Summer Night* is an elaborate musical homage-cum-variation. It still centres on a yearn-of-the-century country house party, at which virginities are lost, adulteries are floated, and True Love wins through. Sondheim muffles the Freud but constructs some wonderful contrapuntal duets and trios, with characters in different places singing on top of each other. Harold Prince's film version is devoid of filmic ideas, but does give Elizabeth Taylor her least ridiculous part in a decade, and generally has decent performances. However, it also cuts the original score in a way that reduces the emotional credibility, and crassly highlights the weakest (because most conventional) song, 'Send in the Clowns'. Not offensive, just silly. TR

Little Nikita (aka Sleepers)

(1988, US, 98 min)
d Richard Benjamin. *p* Harry Gittes. *sc* John Hill, Bo Goldman. *ph* Laszlo Kovacs. *ed* Jacqueline Cambas. *ad* Gene Callahan. *m* Marvin Hamlisch. *cast* Sidney Poitier, River Phoenix, Richard Jenkins, Caroline Kava, Richard Bradford, Richard Lynch, Loretta Devine, Lucy Deakins.
●Despite a screenplay by the esteemed Bo Goldman (*One Flew Over the Cuckoo's Nest*, *Scent of a Woman*), this lacklustre espionage thriller is bogged down with the sort of clichés you'd expect from the height of the Cold War. It's none too credible either, with River Phoenix as a typical American teen who discovers that his parents are in fact dormant Soviet spies. Phoenix and Poitier (as the FBI man who sets him straight) invest the material with more emotional authenticity than you'd think possible, but it's an uphill struggle. TJ

Little Odessa

(1994, US, 98 min)
d James Gray. *p* Paul Webster. *sc* James Gray. *ph* Tom Richmond. *ed* Dorian Harris. *pd* Kevin Thompson. *cast* Tim Roth, Edward Furlong, Moira Kelly, Vanessa Redgrave, Maximilian Schell, Paul Guilfoyle.
●Josh (Roth) can't enter the Russian Jewish area of Brighton Beach, New York, where he grew up, so he makes his hits elsewhere. A contract on a jeweller, nevertheless, forces him back. There he fences with his kid brother, who loves him; his father, who certainly doesn't; his ailing mother, whom he loves beyond words; and a girl… The film has a thesis: hitmen must have psychopathy on their CVs; but even bad guys have souls. It's Roth's tough job to illustrate this, which, in his finest performance to date, he does magnificently. James Gray, aged 25, directs this dark, spare piece – his first feature – as to the manor born. WH

Little People

(1982, US, 88 min)
d/p Jan Krawitz, Thomas Ott. *ph* Thomas Ott. *ed* Jan Krawitz, Thomas Ott. *m* Randy Arneson. *with* Len Sawisch, Karla Eastburg, Mark Trombino, Beth Loyless, Billy Barty.
●Although the term 'dwarf' is now acceptable in the US when referring to people of short stature, in this country it still conjures up images of circus freaks and Snow White, and remains part of the vocabulary of prejudice. It is this prejudice that this piquant documentary undermines by introducing us through interviews to people of short stature. FD

Little Prince, The

(1974, US, 89 min)
d/p Stanley Donen. *sc* Alan Jay Lerner. *ph* Christopher Challis. *ed* Peter Boita, John Gutheridge. *pd* John Barry. *songs* Frederick Loewe, Alan Jay Lerner. *cast* Richard Kiley, Steven Warner, Bob Fosse, Gene Wilder, Joss Ackland, Clive Revill, Victor Spinetti, Graham Crowden, Donna McKechnie.
●A sad disaster for Donen with what was surely a misconceived project from the beginning. At each scene change, *The Little Prince* intrusively fractures the delicate mood of Saint-Exupéry's allegorical fable about a crashed pilot's encounter with a being from another planet. The book linked its simple line drawings to its text in a way that avoided both cuteness and sentimentality; the film frequently amazes with its grossness, notably in the planet sequence, where a nuance-less distorting lens technique is heavily overworked. Frederick Loewe's music is unmemorable (with Richard Kiley belting through the desert bawling out particularly un-singable lyrics) and the sentimentality often outrageously glutinous. Only Bob Fosse's Snake comes off in a regulation classic dance routine. VG

Little Princess, A

(1995, US, 97 min)
d Alfonso Cuarón. *p* Mark Johnson. *sc* Richard LaGravenese, Elizabeth Chandler. *ph* Emmanuel Lubezki. *ed* Steven Weisberg. *pd* Bo Welch. *m* Patrick Doyle. *cast* Eleanor Bron, Liam Cunningham, Liesel Matthews, Rusty Schwimmer, Arthur Malet, Vanessa Lee Chester, Errol Sitahal.
●An exemplary version of Frances Hodgson Burnett's novel has been updated to WWI. When her father, an army captain and a widower, is posted to France from India, young Sara (Matthews, excellent) is lodged in the New York boarding school of Miss Minchin (Bron). No sooner has her classmates' resentment at her wealth abated (Sara keeps them spellbound with accounts of the Hindu myths) than news arrives of father's death in the trenches. The ogreish Miss Minchin casts off her hypocrite's cloak and dispatches Sara to the school's Gothic attic, her only solace being secret meetings with the black servant Becky. Director Cuarón transforms these elements of Victorian melodramatic contrivance with skill and sensitivity into a humanist rites-of-passage story. He's audacious, too: the Bollywood pastels of the myth sequences; an exciting, Lean-like rooftop escape; a magical snow-shake which is a moment of sheer cinematic elan. And when Sara offers her passionate, outraged response – 'Every little girl is a little princess!' – to Miss Minchin's scorn, she turns the declaration into a defiant defence of dignity and dreams. WH

Little Rascals, The

(1994, US, 83 min)
d Penelope Spheeris. *p* Michael King, Bill Oakes. *sc* Paul Guay, Stephen Mazur, Penelope Spheeris. *ph* Richard Bowen. *ed* Ross Albert.

pd Larry Fulton. *m* William Ross. *cast* Travis Tedford, Bug Hall, Brittany Ashton Holmes, Kevin Jamal Woods,Zachary Mabry, Whoopi Goldberg, Mel Brooks, Daryl Hannah.
●This feature version of the old Hal Roach 'Our Gang' comedy series plays so young we could be watching another species. None of the cast is over three feet tall, and what they lack in acting ability they make up in freckles. Smarmed-down hair with spikes, sideways caps, bowlers and bow-ties give an old-fashioned look to the diminutive members of the He-Man Woman-Haters Club, and speeded-up sequences and venerable visual gags give the token nod to the original series. There's plot: Alfalfa (Hall) falls for a cutesy girl and incurs the ire of club president Spanky (Tedford), who pronounces the death sentence; and their rocket-shaped little car is threatened with its first defeat in the Go-Kart Derby. Director Spheeris (*Wayne's World*) seems to have taken her obsession with youth culture beyond the limit, including a scene of dancing teenies in pink leotards that would make John Waters blush. Many reaction shots feature Petey the dog covering his heart-branded eye with his paws. WH

Little Romance, A

(1979, US, 108 min)
d George Roy Hill. *p* Yves Rousset-Rouard, Robert L Crawford. *sc* Allan Burns. *ph* Pierre-William Glenn. *ed* William H Reynolds. *pd* Henry Bumstead. *m* Georges Delerue. *cast* Laurence Olivier, Diane Lane, Thelonious Bernard, Arthur Hill, Sally Kellerman, Broderick Crawford, David Dukes,Anna Massey.
●Hard to dismiss completely a film in which Broderick Crawford turns up as 'Brod', but with Olivier overdoing it dreadfully as the crinkly old ne'er-do-well who persuades misfit American teen Lane and French youth Bernard to run off to Venice and consolidate their love by the Bridge of Sighs, it's not one that'll win over hardened cynics either. Georges Delerue's delightful score won an Oscar. Adapted from a novel by Patrick Cauvin. TJ

Little Shop of Horrors, The

(1960, US, 70 min, b/w)
d/p Roger Corman. *sc* Charles B Griffith. *ph* Arch R Dalzell. *ed* Marshall Neilan Jr. *ad* Daniel Haller. *m* Fred Katz. *cast* Jonathan Haze, Jackie Joseph, Mel Welles, Dick Miller, Myrtle Vail, Leola Wendorff, Jack Nicholson.
●Made by Corman – with Daniel Haller credited as art director, though you have to see it to appreciate that joke – on a sheer nothing budget in one dust corner of a studio, complete with re-used cardboard and paste sets, this is worth seeing if only for Jack Nicholson's definitive role as a masochistically-inclined dental patient named Wilbur Force. A suitably Freudian story about a demanding plant that just keeps on growing, it's dressed up with *Dragnet* takeoffs as well. Its spoofy comedy keeps you tittering, sniggering and occasionally laughing out loud right to the last ridiculous frame. PG

Little Shop of Horrors

(1986, US, 94 min)
d Frank Oz. *p* David Geffen. *sc* Howard Ashman. *ph* Bob Paynter. *ed* John Jympson. *pd* Roy Walker. *m* Miles Goodman. *songs* Alan Menken, Howard Ashman. *cast* Rick Moranis, Ellen Greene, Vincent Gardenia, Steve Martin, Tichina Arnold, Tisha Campbell, Michelle Weeks, James Belushi, John Candy, Christopher Guest, Bill Murray, Miriam Margolyes.
●In the basement of Mushnik's Skid Row florist's, weedy shop-boy Seymour pines for bubbly-blonde shop-girl Audrey. But the basement is also home to a strange and unusual plant, a growing, bloodthirsty demon determined to devour mankind. It's hard to pinpoint just what makes this surreal saga such a delight. There's the music, a wonderful doowop score from the off-Broadway hit based on Corman's 1960 cult classic. There's the antics of Second City veteran comedians (Murray, Candy, Belushi). There's Steve Martin as 'The Dentist', Audrey's biker-boyfriend, a happy-go-lucky sadist who nearly steals the show. And finally there's the plant, a 50-ft jiving, root-stomping, vegetable from whose 49-ft lips comes the voice of Levi Stubbs of the Four Tops. Though Frank Oz will be damned for changing the play's original ending – let them eat carrots – this wild and witty musical is great fun. SGo

Little Sister (Zusje)

(1995, Neth, 91 min)
d Robert Jan Westdijk. *p* Robert Jan Westdijk, Clea de Koning. *sc* Robert Jan Westdijk, Jos Driessen. *ph* Bert Pot. *ed* Herman P Koerts. *pd* Anouk Danoiseaux. *cast* Kim van Kooten, Hugo Metsers III, Roeland Fernhout, Ganna Veenhuysen.
●Low budget pseudo-documentary about a film-maker's return to Amsterdam and the troubled relationship he shared with his little sister, now a fashion design student. Using a subjective camera – shots of the floor when the film-maker gets drunk, etc – it self-consciously explores themes of voyeurism and real-time film-making, but without much insight. As intimations of an incestuous relationship between the two become more explicit, so do the film's faults. Everything's signposted, from the name of the hotel to which he's forced to go, to the sub-Freudian resolution. A discomforting exercise in self-therapy, about a film-maker's exercise in self-therapy. WH

Little Soldier, The

see Petit Soldat, Le

Littlest Horse Thieves, The

see Escape from the Dark

Littlest Rebel, The

(1935, US, 70 min, b/w)
d David Butler. *p* Darryl F Zanuck. *sc* Edwin Burke. *ph* John Seitz. *ed* Irene Morra. *ad* William Darling. *m* Cyril J Mockridge. *cast* Shirley Temple, John Boles, Jack Holt, Karen Morley, Bill 'Bojangles' Robinson, Willie Best, Guinn Williams.
●A sentimental and none too enlightened Civil War picture, painting our Shirl as the heroine of the hour. She lives with her ma, her 'Uncle Billy' (Robinson), and her other happy slaves while pop (Boles) is fighting for the Confederacy. He returns when ma starts ailing, but Shirl persuades the nice Yankee colonel (Holt) to let him escape. Mr Lincoln is not impressed and executions seem in order, but a tug on his beard from the littlest rebel and all is back to rights. The problem with this picture is that it's still charming, despite all of the above. The tap routines with Robinson are the highlights, and go at least some way towards absolving the inherently patronising attitudes. TCh

Little Theatre of Jean Renoir, The

see Petit Théâtre de Jean Renoir, Le

Little Tony (Kleine Teune)

(1998, Neth, 100 min)
d Alex van Warmerdam. *p* Ton Schippers, Alex van Warmerdam. *sc* Alex van Warmerdam. *ph* Marc Felerlaan. *pd* Rikke Jelier, Alfred Schaaf. *m* Alex van Warmerdam. *cast* Alex Van Warmerdam, Annet Malherbe, Ariane Schluter, Sebastiaan te Wierik.
●This Dutch comedy drama suffers from its lugubrious, deadpan storytelling style. However bizarre their circumstances, none of the protagonists betrays a flicker of emotion. Van Warmerdam stars as an illiterate farmer, Malherbe is his scheming, formidable wife and Ariane Schluter is the pretty town woman enlisted to teach him to read. As in Kaurismäki films, the characters deal with lust, misfortune and domestic upheaval in phlegmatic fashion. As a study of a ménage à trois in which power is shifting all the time, it is often witty and acute, but Van Warmerdam's low key approach becomes increasingly wearisome – if the characters don't care about what is happening to them, why should we? GM

Little Toys (Xiao Wanyi)

(1933, China, 108 min, b/w)
d Sun Yu. *p* Luo Mingyou, Lu Hanzhang. *sc* Sun Yu. ph Zhou Ke. *ad* Fang Peilin. *cast* Ruan Lingyu, Li Lili, Yuan Congmei, Luo Peng, Liu Jiqun, Han Lan'gen.
●The most sophisticated of Sun's silent melodramas for the United Photoplay (Lianhua) company is the one least influenced by von Sternberg's Dietrich films. Mrs Ye (Ruan, extraordinary as ever) is a village wife pretty enough to catch the eye of passing city slickers. When her fisherman husband dies in a clash between regional warlords, she decamps with her daughter Zhu'er (Li) and neighbours to Shanghai, where she tries to re-establish their cottage industry making handcrafted toys. But times are tough. Modern mechanical toys are being imported in bulk, and most buyers aren't patriotic enough to think of buying local products as a priority. And then, in 1932, the Japanese shell Shanghai. Zhu'er is one of the many casualties, and Mrs Ye is last seen hysterically trying to warn middle-class shoppers on the Nanking Road of further impending disasters. The film's urgent topicality speaks volumes about the situation in Shanghai at the time, but it's Ruan's performance that raises it to greatness. TR

Little Vampire, The (Die kleine Vampir)

(2000, Ger/Neth/GB/US, 95 min)
d Uli Edel. *p* Richard Claus. *sc* Karey Kirkpatrick, Larry Wilson. *ph* Bernd Heinl. *ed* Peter R Adam. *pd* Joseph Nemec III. *m* Nigel Clarke, Michael Csányi-Wills. *cast* Jonathan Lipnicki, Richard E Grant, Jim Carter, Alice Krige, Pamela Gidley, Tommy Hinkley, Anna Popplewell, Dean Cook, Rollo Weeks, John Wood.
●Bespectacled nine-year-old Californian Tony Thompson (Lipnicki) has recently moved with his parents to a remote corner of Scotland, yet already he's plagued by nightmares about vampires and dark mythological occurrences. To his horror, a bat flies through his window and transforms itself into a vampire of similar age. Tony discovers, however, that not all vampires are nasty; like any mortal, they too have problems. The trouble is, Rudolph's problem is more pressing than most: his family (headed by Grant and Krige) is stuck in purgatory and desperate for the lad's help. This Burton-esque fantasy-cum-comedy thriller has plenty of bite, with just the right level of lightweight horror to give little ones a shock or two without inducing nightmares. Much of the film's success is down to the costume design, the novel SFX and the mildly foreboding atmosphere of the mist enshrouded Scottish countryside. DA

Little Vera (Malenkaya Vera)

(1988, USSR, 134 min)
d Vasili Pichul. *sc* Mariya Khmelik. *ph* Yefim Reznikov. *ed* Lena Zabolotskaya, Yelena Semyonovykh, Sofya Yaroslavskaya. *ad* Vladimir Pasternak. *m* Vladimir Matetski. *cast* Natalya Negoda, Ludmila Zaitseva, Andrei Sokolov, Yuri Nazarov, Alexander Alexeyev-Negreba, Alexandra Tabakova.
●The film that shocked the Soviets with its depiction of your average Russian family as a squalid, sottish, violent bunch of amoral no-hopers. Filtered through Western eyes, the sex scenes seem mild, the foul language blunted by subtitles, and the rebellious stance tame. But the film's message is still subtly affecting. The circumscribed sadness of life in a dull industrial town; the inability of the generations to understand each other; the hard eyed look at love as an explosive and divisive, not redemptive force; these themes are mercilessly delineated. There's also a welcome anarchic humour at work: when stolid Sergei bemoans Vera's lack of purpose, she writhes on top of him purring: 'You and I share the same goal. *Communism*'. You can feel the shock waves from here. The film's chief revelation is Negoda's searing performance as Vera, a feisty, mean-minded hellcat who injects chaos into every life that touches hers. The booze fuelled tale is wildly melodramatic, but the performances, pitilessly shot in gritty, realistic settings, are excellent. SFe

Little Voice

(1998, GB, 97 min)
d Mark Herman. *p* Ellizabeth Karlsen. *sc* Mark Herman, Jim Cartwright. *ph* Andy Collins. *ed* Michael Ellis. *pd* Don Taylor. *m* John Altman. *cast* Jane Horrocks, Michael Caine, Ewan McGregor, Jim Broadbent, Brenda Blethyn.
●A waif comes out of her shell only when she sings in the style of her late Dad's beloved Garland, Monroe, Bassey, et al. Her domineering Mum and a small-time agent try to turn her into a star. That's about it for plot, which hangs on two questions: is timid 'Little Voice' (Horrocks)

up to showcasing her talents in public, and if so, will this destroy her or set her free? Based on Jim Cartwright's play *The Rise and Fall of Little Voice*, Herman's film is a polished, populist effort whose virtues and flaws are soon apparent. The former include a river of verbal and visual gags, Broadbent and McGregor's supporting turns as a nightclub boss and LV's innocent soulmate, and, best of all, Caine's complex tour de force as the sleazy impresario desperate for a last shot at the big time. On the downside, Blethyn's monstrous mum is an OTT caricature of working class vulgarity, Horrocks is irritatingly gormless until she transforms into a sock it to 'em diva, and Herman derives as little mileage from most of the underwritten minor characters as he does from the tatty glamour of the Scarborough setting. A lively if finally rather cruel comic fantasy. GA

Little Women

(1933, US, 115 min, b/w)
d George Cukor. *sc* Sarah Y Mason, Victor Heerman. *ph* Henry Gerrard. *ed* Jack Kitchin. *ad* Van Nest Polglase. *m* Max Steiner. *cast* Katharine Hepburn, Joan Bennett, Paul Lukas, Frances Dee, Jean Parker, Edna May Oliver, Douglass Montgomery, Henry Stephenson, Spring Byington.
●Surely the definitive version of Louisa May Alcott's novel, sweet, funny, perfectly cast, and exquisitely evocative in its New England period reconstruction. Cukor rightly emphasises the seasons, starting with a winter of discontent as, with father serving in the Civil War, the four March girls face the prospect of growing up in reduced circumstances. But as the seasons change, so do joys return, and the film offers an endlessly pleasurable series of vignettes: the breaching of the ogre's castle next door (to find it inhabited by a very kind old man and a very personable young one); the disastrous performance of Jo's play; the business of Beth's piano, and the fluttering alarms of her bout with scarlet fever; the first stirrings of romantic interests. The cement that holds all this together is Hepburn's miraculous performance as the tomboy Jo, angrily resisting the approach of womanhood ('Why can't we stay as we are?'). Cukor mines a rich vein of sentiment, never over-stepping the mark into slush, but it is Hepburn's Jo, making a subversive *choice* of what she wants her life to be, who ensures that the cosiness isn't everything. TM

Little Women

(1994, US, 118 min)
d Gillian Armstrong. *p* Denise DiNovi. *sc* Robin Swicord. *ph* Geoffrey Simpson. *ed* Nicholas Beauman. *pd* Jan Roelfs. *m* Thomas Newman. *cast* Winona Ryder, Gabriel Byrne, Trini Alvarado, Susan Sarandon, Samantha Mathis, Kirsten Dunst, Claire Danes, Mary Wickes, Eric Stoltz, John Neville, Christian Bale.
●Hard times in New England during the Civil War, again. Winona Ryder's Jo is full of puppyish enthusiasm, brimming with enthusiasm and the thrill of anticipated passion, with Byrne's Professor Bhaer; Trini Alvarado is gentle Meg; newcomer Claire Danes is fragile Beth; and Kirsten Dunst's precocious Amy is suitably adorable. Presiding over Louisa May Alcott's family is Susan Sarandon's long-suffering Mrs March, going some way to cut through the sweetness. Gillian Armstrong resists the urge to revel in period detail, offering a somewhat clouded vision of the family, paying attention, for example, to their Transcendental beliefs. Be prepared, however, for a large beaker of the milk of human kindness. SFra

Live a Life

(1982, GB, 78 min)
d Maxim Ford. *p* Sally Hibbin. *ph* Bruce McGowan, Maxim Ford, Chris Plevin. *ed* Lynda Fowke, JR Davies. *with* The Beat, Black Slate, Tom Robinson, Barry Ford, OK Jive, Martin Besserman, Alexei Sayle.
●A documentary that takes the Rainbow concerts at the end of the Jobs Express march as its springboard. The musical interludes lighten an otherwise relentless parade of disaffected youth whose hopes of getting a job are as low as the interest shown in them by the Tory Government. Videoed off the TV screen, the rhetoric of such government bods as Tebbit is set against that of the country's young as they outline their grievances. Perhaps their over-familiar points of argument would be more incisive and less repetitive with a bit of judicious editing; and perhaps if the makers had tried to provide a concrete answer to their problems, this film would be more than the worthy but – alas – boring piece of work it is. FL

Live and Let Die

(1973, GB, 121 min)
d Guy Hamilton. *p* Harry Saltzman, Albert R Broccoli. *sc* Tom Mankiewicz. *ph* Ted Moore. *ed* Bert Bates, Raymond Poulton, John Shirley. *ad* Syd Cain. *m* George Martin. *cast* Roger Moore, Yaphet Kotto, Jane Seymour, Clifton James, Julius W Harris, Geoffrey Holder, David Hedison, Gloria Hendry, Bernard Lee, Lois Maxwell.
●Destructive tomfoolery on a typically grand scale, with Moore – trying on 007's white jacket for the first time – matched against a battery of colourful villains (blacks are the baddies this time) and voodoo chiles. Two hours long and anti-climactic, but Bond fans won't be disappointed. VG

Live Flesh (Carne Trémula/ En chair et en os)

(1997, Sp/Fr, 101 min)
d Pedro Almodóvar. *p* Augustín Almodóvar. *sc* Pedro Almodóvar, Ray Loriga, Jorge Guerricaechevarria. *ph* Affonso Beato. *ed* José Salcedo. *ad* Antxon Gomez. *m* Alberto Iglesias. *cast* Francesca Neri, Javier Bardem, José Sancho, Angela Molina, Liberto Rabal, Penelope Cruz, Pilar Bardem.
●This free but sensitive adaptation of Ruth Rendell's thriller is Almodóvar's most impressive film to date – darker, straighter and far more controlled than his camp extravaganzas. A story of obsession, hatred, jealousy and revenge, it concerns a young man sent to prison for his accidental involvement in a police raid that went disastrously wrong. He comes out – and he wants the crippled cop who helped to put him away. The performances are spot on, the control of pace, mood and narrative is assured, the visuals are crisp, stylish and imaginative, and the whole film has, for Almodóvar, an unprecedented weight and substance. GA

Live for Life

see Vivre pour Vivre

Live in Peace

(1997, China, 97 min)
d Hu Binliu. *cast* Pan Yu, Bai Xueyun.
●Despite a promising fragmented start, which suggests a wide ranging look at familial and generational tensions in contemporary China, this soon settles into a heartwarming tale of a curmudgeonly crone, who makes unreasonable demands of her work-exhausted son and his wife, but is finally won over by the country girl the couple hires as her maid and companion. Very pedestrian. GA

Lives of Performers

(1972, US, 90 min, b/w)
d/sc Yvonne Rainer. *ph* Babette Mangolte. *ed* Yvonne Rainer. *with* John Erdman, Valda Setterfield, Shirley Soffer, Fernando Torm, James Barth, Tannis Huill, Epp Kotkas, Sarah Soffer, Yvonne Rainer.
●Yvonne Rainer's characteristically witty and episodic first feature draws together the different strands of her own work (as dancer, choreographer, director) in a multi-faceted reflection of and on the elements of role playing within role playing. Three dancers, whose emotional triangle provides the film's narrative centre, are observed – from one another's points of view, in rehearsal and performance, public and private, expressing their own feelings and other people's – with Babette Mangolte's tightly choreographed camerawork visually equating Rainer's zig-zagging approach to a central theme. JD

Living

see Ikiru

Living Blood (Sangue vivo)

(2000, It, 95 min)
d Edoardo Winspeare. *p* Maurizio Tini. *sc* Giorgia Cecere, Edoardo Winspeare. *ph* Paolo Carnera. *ed* Luca Benedetti. *pd* Sabrina Balestra. *m* Gruppo Zoè. *cast* Pino Zimba, Lamberto Probo, Claudio Giangreco, Alessandro Valenti, Ivan Verardo, Luicia Chiuri, Addolorata Turco.
●A pedestrian story about two grown brothers in a village in Puglia, southern Italy. One has financial troubles and gets in hock to the local Mafia boss; the other is addicted to drugs. The treatment is also straightforward and naturalistic. But writer/director Winspeare has a trick up his sleeve. Zimba and Probo are real-life musicians (they play the local folk music, *La Pizzica*), and at about the one hour mark, the movie stops while Pino and his band play an open air concert. And they're tremendous. The passion and excitement of the music flesh out the rest of the still predictable story, to the point where the ending is even quite moving. TCh

Living Daylights, The

(1987, GB, 131 min)
d John Glen. *p* Albert R Broccoli, Michael Wilson. *sc* Richard Maibaum, Michael Wilson. *ph* Alex Mills. *ed* John Grover, Peter Davies. *pd* Peter Lamont. *m* John Barry. *cast* Timothy Dalton, Maryam d'Abo, Jeroen Krabbé, Joe Don Baker, John Rhys-Davies, Art Malik, Desmond Llewelyn, Robert Brown.
●Confused plot and digressive globe trotting notwithstanding, the best Bond in years. A radical rethink on 007 accommodates the new man; Dalton brings a positive emotional commitment to tight spots and courtship, and emerges as a Buchanite romantic hero. The pre-credits sequence on the Rock of Gibraltar grips like wet rope; the murderous milkman's raid on HQ is a chiller; the final shoot-out with Joe Don Baker's arms dealer amid toy soldiers and model battlefields is a fruitful metaphor. Lethal gizmos and digital countdowns are kept to the minimum, which leaves more room for the acting. On the debit side, in place of the usually globally ambitious mastermind, the writers have given us a couple of seedy dealers who keep moving the goalposts: arms, drugs, diamonds. That and unmemorable events in Afghanistan apart, enjoy. BC

Living Dead, The (Unheimliche Geschichten)

(1932, Ger, 89 min, b/w)
d Richard Oswald. *p* Gabriel Pascal. *sc* Heinz Goldberg, Eugen Szatmari. *ph* Heinrich Gärtner. *ed* Max Brenner. *m* Rolf Marbot, Bert Reisfeld. *cast* Paul Wegener, Eugen Klöpfer, Harald Paulsen, Roma Bahn, Mary Parker, Paul Henckels, Viktor de Kowa.
●Paul (*Golem*) Wegener's first talkie is a glorious horror comic that plays like *Great Moments of Expressionist Fantasy*. Poe and RL Stevenson are so much grist to its pulp-fiction mill: it knocks off a creditable *Black Cat* in the first ten minutes, and then races through a waxwork chamber of horrors and an insane asylum to put *Charenton* in the shade, before climaxing breathlessly in *The Suicide Club*. Villainous Wegener storms through mass murder, incitement to murder, alchemy, sedation, a guillotining, and even a den of sci-fi gadgetry on the way; the amusingly stolid hero never knows what hit him. Incredibly, the film has virtually no reputation. TR

Living Dead at the Manchester Morgue, The (Fin de Semana para los Muertos)

(1974, Sp/It, 93 min)
d Jorge Grau. *p* Edmondo Amati. *sc* Alessandro Continenza, Marcello Coscia. *ph* Francisco Sempere. *ed* Vincenzo Tomassi. *pd* Carlo Leva. *m* Giuliano Sorgini. *cast* Ray Lovelock, Christine Galbo, Arthur Kennedy, Aldo Massasso, Giorgio Trestini, Roberto Posse, José Ruiz Lifante.
●Although made in the Lake District with a mainly dubbed cast, Arthur Kennedy as a very American English policeman, and a plot indebted to *Night of the Living Dead*, this works against all the odds. Through intelligent handling of locations, England becomes a very bleak place indeed, full of sinister quietness. Hero and heroine, thrown together by chance, find themselves pursued by both police and an army of cannibalistic living dead through this increasingly nightmarish landscape. It's a film of unrelieved blackness, from the seedy photographer who

snaps his junkie wife cowering in the bath to homicidal babies, from mongol child at a petrol station to Kennedy's brutal sergeant. It's all the more absurdly fatalistic for refusing to draw political, moral or social conclusions. VG

Living Doll

(1989, GB, 92 min)
d Peter Litten, George Dugdale. *p* Dick Randall. *sc* George Digdale, Mark Ezra. *cast* Gary Martin, Katie Orgill, Mark Jax, Freddie Earlle, Eartha Kitt.

●Shy adolescent Martin can't find nobody to love, least of all the attractive young woman (Orgill) who runs the flower concession at the hospital where he works. Until, that is, her nubile body turns up on the mortuary slab, whereupon Martin steals it and takes it home to his seedy bed-sit. Then, while Orgill's body decomposes on the sofa, he tries to woo her with gooey talk and silky underwear. Nosey landlady Eartha Kitt, meanwhile, keeps threatening to discover her lodger's rotten secret. There's the seed of an idea here, but this necrophiliac romance never germinates, let alone flowers. Sensitively handled, as in Dominique Deruddere's *Crazy Love*, it might have smelled quite sweet; instead, it gives off the sickening whiff of unimaginative exploitation. NF

Living End, The

(1992, US, 84 min)
d Gregg Araki. *p* Marcus Hu, Jon Gerrans. *sc/ph/ed* Gregg Araki. *m* Cole Coonce. *cast* Craig Gilmore, Mike Dytri, Darcy Marta, Mary Woronov, Johanna Went, Paul Bartel.

●Araki used to make fumbling anti-dramas about the flotsam of Los Angeles: depressed, ambivalent, uncommitted. This is really different. It's a queer 'couple-on-the-lam' movie, crammed with genre memories but closer to a bent *Pierrot le Fou* than to anything out of Hollywood. Two body-positive guys, a raunchy hustler and a passive movie critic, fall violently in love and flee a caricatured LA together after the hustler carelessly shoots a cop. Their aimless, fuck-the-world rampage through the void of Middle America has the same weight and impact as a good Act-Up slogan or a solid punk thrash. Groovy. TR

Living in Oblivion

(1995, US, 90 min, b/w & col)
d Tom DiCillo. *p* Michael Griffiths, Marcus Viscidi. *sc* Tom DiCillo. *ph* Frank Prinzi. *ed* Camilla Toniolo. *pd* Thérèse DePrez. *m* Jim Farmer. *cast* Steve Buscemi, Catherine Keener, James LeGros, Dermot Mulroney, Danielle Von Zerneck, Rica Martens, Michael Griffiths.

●DiCillo's second feature gets great mileage out of the simple, familiar premise of an idealistic film-maker struggling to complete his movie. The director is Nick (Buscemi), an arty tyro believed by some to be 'tight with Tarantino' and by himself to be in love with leading lady Nicole (Keener). Nick's main headache, however, is leading man Chad Palomino (LeGros), a petulant hunk whose vanity outweighs his doubtful commitment, and whose philandering inflames rivalries between various women on set, notably Nicole and producer Wanda, whose lover Wolf was never too fond of Chad in the first place. And then, as further irritants, there are the errant booms and malfunctioning smoke-machines, the eye-patches and goatees, the senile mothers, psycho-analysing drivers and hypersensitive extras – a total nightmare. The ingenious narrative, told from differing perspectives and incorporating tales within tales and teasing elisions between 'film' and 'reality', is actually informative about the nuts and bolts of shooting a movie, and not only as a catalogue of technical disasters – through the shamefully under-rated Keener, we get a real insight into screen acting and the way fatigue, memory, stress and surroundings can take their toll. Hers, however, is merely the finest of a whole host of spot-on performances. A treat. GA

Living It Up (La Bella Vita)

(1993, It, 97 min)
d Paolo Virzi. *p* Paolo Vandini. *sc* Francesco Bruni, Paolo Virzi. *ph* Paolo Carnera. *ed* Sergio Montanari. *ad* Attilio Caselli. *m* Claudio Cimpanelli. *cast* Claudio Bigagli, Sabrina Ferilli, Massimo Ghini, Giorgio Algranti, Emanuele Barresi, Paola Tiziana Cruciani.

●Lightly likeable study of a marriage in decline, set against a backdrop of widespread unemployment and a shift from socialism to free market get-up-and-go. Bigagli's steelworker gets laid off, suffers poor health, and sees his hitherto faithful wife (the somewhat stunning Ferilli) have an affair with a smarmy local TV celeb. What's interesting is that she's viewed at least as sympathetically as the film's nominal hero; indeed, it's unfathomable why such a lively, intelligent, resourceful woman would be attracted to a lazy, depressive, self-pitying ugly mug like Bigagli in the first place. A minor but promising first feature. GA

Living on the Edge

(1987, GB, 86 min)
d Michael Grigsby. *p* John Furse. *sc* John Furse, Michael Grigsby. *ph* Ivan Strasburg. *ed* Julian Ware. *with* Frank, Mary, Alison and Stacey Rolfe, Tess, Joanne, Helen and TJ Casey, Dave, Deneice and Alan Smith.

●A documentary examining the lives and attitudes of working class Britons: a Devon farming family forced through bankruptcy to abandon their land after 40 years; a jobless family imprisoned on a Birkenhead housing estate; members of a South Wales mining community, bemoaning their reputation during the strike as 'the enemy within'; young Glaswegians travelling to London in search of work. Keenly analytical and wide ranging, Grigsby's film presents an impressionistic mosaic of the sundry intertwined forces that have wrecked the lives of these intelligent, articulate people. Political history, increasingly rampant consumerism, popular songs, archive radio and film material, all serve to illuminate the feeling that a massive portion of the population has been sold down the line. Poetic, perceptive and often profoundly moving as it monitors the sine wave from the Depression of the '30s to that of the present, the film's illustration that 'in the '30s people had principles; now they've got mortgages and cars' would be totally depressing, were it not for the sheer resilience of these people about whom the government barely cares. GA

Living Out Loud

(1998, US, 100 min)
d Richard LaGravenese. *p* Danny DeVito, Michael Shamberg, Stacey Sher. *sc* Richard LaGravenese. *ph* John Bailey. *ed* Jon Gregory, Lynzee Klingman. *pd* Nelson Coates. *m* George Fenton. *cast* Holly Hunter, Danny DeVito, Queen Latifah, Martin Donovan, Elias Koteas, Richard Schiff.

●Judith (Hunter) is divorced and lonely. For all the intense conversations going on in her head, when she talks to Pat (DeVito), the elevator man in her NY apartment building, it's the first meaningful human contact she's had in weeks. Pat is no one's idea of a dreamboat, but he may just be Judith's best hope. The film namechecks *Looking for Mr Goodbar* and plays like a contemporary revision of that once notorious story. Gone, mercifully, is the bloody retribution; instead, there's a very open, hard-won sense of female liberation enacted both in outrageous fantasy sequences and, more subtly, in the central, not-quite-romantic relationship. Scriptwriter LaGravenese proves a whimsical, sympathetic director (in his first feature), but his playfulness sometimes leads him astray. Inspired by Chekhov's stories *The Kiss* and *Misery*, the movie's too cute to be more than remotely plausible. Still, it's honestly felt and pitched with some charm by the leads, Martin Donovan and the redoubtable Queen Latifah. TCh

Lizards, The (I Basilischi)

(1963, It, 85 min, b/w)
d/sc Lina Wertmüller. *ph* Gianni Di Venanzo. *ed* Ruggero Mastroianni. *m* Ennio Morricone. *cast* Toni Petruzzi, Stefano Satta Flores, Sergio Farrannino, Luigi Barbieri, Flora Carabella, Mimmina Quirico.

●*The Lizards* is that perennial Italian favourite, the portrait of small town loafers constantly hatching half-hearted plans but hopelessly trapped in their own lethargy. Wertmüller's first feature, it's not fundamentally very different from Fellini's *I Vitelloni* of a decade earlier, with Morricone's score a definite plus. Later, in the mid-'70s, Wertmüller became a dubious art-house smash hit in America with films like *Love and Anarchy*, *Swept Away* and *Seven Beauties*. TR

Loaded

(1994, GB/NZ, 104 min)
d Anna Campion. *p* David Hazlett, Caroline Hewitt, Bridget Ikin, John Maynard. *sc* Anna Campion. *ph* Alan Almond. *ed* John Gilbert. *pd* Alistair Kay. *m* Simon Fisher Turner. *cast* Oliver Milburn, Dearbhla Molloy, Danny Cunningham, Catherine McCormick, Thandie Newton, Nick Patrick, Biddy Hodson.

●In this feature debut by Jane Campion's sister Anna, a party of English school leavers travels to a remote country house to shoot a low budget horror movie. But during filming, and especially during a videotaped collective acid trip, tensions surface threatening to tear the group apart. The writer/director's sympathy for her characters is, regrettably, not matched by her understanding of them. Emotional revelations that should explode in the tranquil silence of the forest are curiously muffled. NF

Local Hero

(1983, GB, 111 min)
d Bill Forsyth. *p* David Puttnam. *sc* Bill Forsyth. *ph* Chris Menges. *ed* Michael Bradsell. *pd* Roger Murray-Leach. *m* Mark Knopfler. *cast* Burt Lancaster, Peter Riegert, Denis Lawson, Peter Capaldi, Fulton Mackay, Jenny Seagrove, Jennifer Black, Christopher Rozycki, Rikki Fulton, John Gordon Sinclair.

●For all the ballyhoo about *Chariots of Fire*, Forsyth's is the more significant film because it rediscovers a genre that was once among the British cinema's proudest achievements. *Local Hero*, which concerns the frustrations of a Texas oilman's attempts to buy up an idyllic Scottish village, ranks as a lyrical anti-urban comedy in the great tradition of films like *I Know Where I'm Going* and *Whisky Galore!*; and its essential triumph is to prove that comedy can still contain a gentle, almost mystical, aspect without necessarily being old-fashioned. The film achieves this best in its superb sense of location and the haunting contrast between Texas and Scotland. Forsyth cannot quite tease out of his characters the kind of strange sublety that Powell and Pressburger delivered, but it is enough that he and producer David Puttnam succeed in making you realise just how badly this kind of film has been missed. DP

Locataire, Le

see Tenant, The

Loch Ness

(1994, GB, 101 min)
d John Henderson. *p* Tim Bevan. *sc* John Fusco. *ph* Clive Tickner. *ed* Jon Gregory. *pd* Sophie Becher. *m* Trevor Jones. *cast* Ted Danson, Joely Richardson, Ian Holm, Harris Yulin, James Frain, Keith Allen, Nick Brimble, Kirsty Graham, Harry Jones, Julian Curry, John Savident.

●Expect wall to wall effects, and you'll be disappointed. Here's a jaunty family fable where the power of legend and imagination, and the affection for people and place vanquish all-comers. Rarer than a sighting of Nessie is, of course, a sparkling movie performance from Danson, but that's what we get, self-deprecating and sympathetic as the has-been LA zoologist sent to disprove the existence of the mythic beastie once and for all. The witty script sticks to the formula in confronting him with Richardson's no-nonsense lochside innkeeper (to supply the romance) and her lively daughter (Graham, agreeably unprecocious). No, it's not original, but with terrific support from wax-jacketed water bailiff Holm, bright eyed expedition helper Frain, some perfectly judged shock moments from John Henderson (directing his first features after the children's TV series *The Borrowers*), and a lush, classy, folk-tinged score from Trevor Jones, it's a compact winner that hits the bull's eye in almost every department. TJ

Locked Room, The

see Beck

Locket, The

(1946, US, 86 min, b/w)
d John Brahm. *p* Bert Granet. *sc* Sheridan Gibney. *ph* Nicholas Musuraca. *ed* JR Whittredge. *ad* Abert S D'Agostino, Alfred Herman. *m* Roy Webb. *cast* Laraine Day, Brian

Aherne, Robert Mitchum, Gene Raymond, Ricardo Cortez, Sharyn Moffet, Henry Stephenson, Katherine Emery.
● One of the many émigrés to Hollywood who gave a distinctively Germanic twist to established genres, Brahm hit a winning streak of baroque melodramas in the mid-'40s which are all visually remarkable and emotionally supercharged. Virtually all action in *The Locket* is contained in the ever-receding flashbacks that present an imminent bride and 'hopelessly twisted personality' almost exclusively through the eyes of her past lovers. A psychodrama, definitely, complete with analyst, but strangely ambivalent about its own insights, right up to the mesmerising finale of the bride meeting her traumatic Calvary on her way up the aisle. NA

Lock, Stock and Two Smoking Barrels

(1998, GB, 106 min)
d Guy Ritchie. *p* Matthew Vaughn.*sc* Guy Ritchie. *ph* Tim Maurice-Jones.*ed* Niven Howie. *pd* Iain Andrews, Eve Mavarakis. *m* John A Hughes, John Murphy. *cast* Jason Flemyng, Dexter Fletcher, Nick Moran, Jason Statham, Steven Mackintosh, Vinnie Jones, PH Moriarty.
● Four East End lads (Moran, Flemyng, Statham and Fletcher) are desperate to get sumfin' for nuffin'. Their fate hinges on a card game with mobster Hatchet Harry (Moriarty), but he's a wise old bird and by the end of the evening they're half a million in debt. The four hatch a new plan to intercept a shipment of drugs. And that's where a few others – like debt collector Big Chris (soccer player Jones) and the public school druggies – come in. Whatever else, writer/director Ritchie knows how to wield a camera; and his feature debut comes alive every time the soundtrack rears its beautiful head. He also knows how to pick faces. But is Jones more than just an ugly face? On the A–Z of emotions, he barely makes it to B. So why is he here? The gangster genre has always dabbled in cross-fertilisation, but here it seems a particularly lazy move. Ritchie's not interested in exploring the economics behind the 'Cockney rebel' facade, nor the real sadism (and masochism) crawling alongside. Expect plenty of laughs and some edge-of-your-seat sweats, but not a whole lot else. Attempting to marry *Oliver Twist* with *Trainspotting*, this ends up more like a bloody episode of TV's *Minder*. CO'Su

Lock Up

(1989, US, 109 min)
d John Flynn. *p* Lawrence Gordon, Charles Gordon. *sc* Richard Smith, Jeb Stuart, Henry Rosenbaum. *ph* Donald E Thorin. *ed* Michael N Knue, Donald Brochu, Barry B Leirer, Robert A Ferretti. *pd* Bill Kenney. *m* Bill Conti. *cast* Sylvester Stallone, Donald Sutherland, John Amos, Sonny Landham, Tom Sizemore, Frank McRae, Darlanne Fluegel, Larry Romano.
● Although reviled for his macho roles, Stallone is a shrewd star who knows his limitations; the problem is that he tends to give his audience exactly what they expect, and no more. In this tough prison drama, he plays Frank Leone, a model prisoner with only six months to serve. Suddenly transferred to a maximum security hell-hole presided over by sadistic warden Drumgoole (Sutherland) – whose custody he previously escaped – he is pushed to the edge by a systematic campaign of harrasment and beatings. Leone at first resists, but finally cracks when a psycho about to be released says he's been hired by Drumgoole to rape and kill Leone's girlfriend (Fluegel). Always at his best when smouldering before the burn, Stallone makes the most of a tailor-made role, with useful support from a gallery of multi-ethnic archetypes. Effectively cast against type, Sutherland sports a fearsome haircut and spits out hackneyed hate with more conviction than it deserves. A competent action picture, directed with considerable kinetic power. NF

Lock Up Your Daughters!

(1969, GB, 103 min)
d Peter Coe. *p* David Deutsch. *sc* Keith Waterhouse, Willis Hall. *ph* Peter Suschitzky. *ed* Frank Clarke. *pd* Tony Woollard. *m* Ron Grainer. *cast* Christopher Plummer, Susannah York, Glynis Johns, Ian Bannen, Tom Bell, Elaine Taylor, Jim Dale, Kathleen Harrison, Roy Kinnear, Georgia Brown, Patricia Routledge.
● An amalgam of Fielding's *Rape Upon Rape* and Vanbrugh's *The Relapse*, based on the stage musical version, translated to the screen without the Laurie Johnson/Lionel Bart score. It's terrible. Life in lusty 18th century London, rife with innuendo and much elbow-digging humour. Certainly one of the worst films of the year. CPe

Loco de Amor

see Two Much

Lodger, The

(1926, GB, 96 min (5760 ft), b/w)
d Alfred Hitchcock. *p* Michael Balcon, Carlyle Blackwell. *sc* Eliot Stannard, (titles) Ivor Montagu. *ph* Baron Ventimiglia. *ed* Ivor Montagu. *ad* C Wilfred Arnold, Bertram Evans. *cast* Ivor Novello, Miss June, Marie Ault, Athur Chesney, Malcolm Keen.
● 'In truth you might almost say that *The Lodger* was my first picture.' Indeed, what makes the film (from a novel by Mrs Belloc Lowndes) so fascinating is the way it dissolves into pre-echoes of Hitchcock's later work. His concern with the uncertain line between guilt and innocence, his confident dismissal of the minutiae of the plot, the disturbing intrusions of fetishistic sexuality, are as apparent here as they are in *Psycho*. The tone is lighter (despite the Ripper-esque story) and the tone more superficial, but the film has its own vigorous identity, and there are moments – Novello coming out of the fog to make the lights dim and the cuckoo clock go berserk – which are memorably effective. RMy

Lodger, The

(1944, US, 80 min, b/w)
d John Brahm. *p* Robert Bassler. *sc* Barré Lyndon. *ph* Lucien Ballard. *ed* J Watson Webb Jr. *ad* James Basevi, John Ewing. *m* Hugo Friedhofer. *cast* Merle Oberon, George Sanders, Laird Cregar, Cedric Hardwicke, Sara Allgood, Doris Lloyd, Aubrey Mather, Queenie Leonard.
● One of the great evocations of that strange lost city of Hollywood imagination, the fogbound London of *Jack the Ripper*. It might almost be a continuation of *Pandora's Box* as a blind man haltingly taps his way through Whitechapel past posters announcing a reward for the Ripper's capture, a hulking figure prowls in the obscurity, a woman's screams are accompanied by animal panting while the camera stares blindly into a dark hole in the wall. Huge, feline, softly obscene as he builds his sonorous facade of biblical quotations and secretly rinses his bloody hands in the waters of the Thames, Laird Cregar gives a remarkable portrayal of perverted sexuality, at once horrific and oddly moving. Stunningly shot by Lucien Ballard, this is one of those rare films – like *Casablanca* – in which everything pulls together to create a weirdly compulsive atmosphere. TM

Lodz Ghetto

(1988, US, 103 min, b/w & col)
d Kathryn Taverna, Alan Adelson. *p/sc* Alan Adelson. *ph* Josef Piwkowski, Eugene Squires. *ed* Kathryn Taverna. *m* Wendy Blackstone.
● Six months after Hitler's troops marched into Lodz to the welcoming salutes of German Poles, all the city's Jews were rounded up and either locked up in the slums or shot. After the 'de-Jewing' of Prague, another large contingent of Jews was sent to the Lodz ghetto as slave labour, swelling the population fighting for survival there to 200,000. This chilling photo documentary reconstructs the horrors of the imprisoned, from starvation to separation as many were carted off to concentration camps towards the end of the war, using rare colour and other archive footage and heart-wrenching stills. The commentary is taken from diaries and monographs of the ghetto people, from scrupulously traced documents of the period. Only 800 survived in the ghetto until liberation. JGl

Logan's Run

(1976, US, 118 min)
d Michael Anderson. *p* Saul David. *sc* David Zelag Goodman. *ph* Ernest Laszlo. *ed* Robert Wyman. *ad* Dale Hennesy. *m* Jerry Goldsmith. *cast* Michael York, Richard Jordan, Jenny Agutter, Roscoe Lee Browne, Farrah Fawcett-Majors, Michael Anderson Jr, Peter Ustinov.
● Logan (York) is a security guard in a computer-controlled bubble civilisation whose hedonistic inhabitants are compelled to die at 30. His job is to hunt the fugitives, but one day outside the bubble he discovers 'new' emotions with Jenny Agutter. The lavish production has some good effects sequences, but its plot is as corny as the dreadful lurex drape costumes and Jerry Goldsmith's slushy score. Fundamentally, this is just further proof of Hollywood's untiring ability to reduce all science fiction to its most feeble stereotypes. DP

Lohngelder für Pittsville

see Catamount Killing, The

Loin

see Far Away

Loin des Barbares (Far from the Barbarians)

(1993, Fr, 95 min)
d Liria Bégéja. *p* Michèle Ray-Gavras. *sc* Liria Bégéja, Olivier Douyère, Philippe Barassat. *ph* Patrick Blossier. *ed* Luc Barnier. *pd* Pierre Decraen, Pierre Daroo. *m* Piro Cako. *cast* Dominique Blanc, Timo Flloko, Sulejman Pitarka, Piro Mani, Ronald Guttman.
● An impressive thriller-style investigation into the realities of exile for Paris's Albanian community. Zana (Blanc), a painter, spirited out of Albania as a baby, receives a call from a compatriot refugee at the airport saying he has news of the father she assumed was dead. She helps the man escape and embarks on an eye-opening tour through a little-seen side of Paris – the refugee camps, hotels and places of political asylum. Shot in a dark, frenetic style, the movie doesn't pull its punches, and nor does it offer any simplistic insights. Fine performances. WH

Loin du Viêt-nam

see Far From Vietnam

Lola

(1960, Fr/It, 91 min, b/w)
d Jacques Demy. *p* Carlo Ponti, Georges de Beauregard. *sc* Jacques Demy. *ph* Raoul Coutard. *ed* Anne-Marie Cotret. *ad* Bernard Evein. *m* Michel Legrand. *cast* Anouk Aimée, Marc Michel, Jacques Harden, Elina Labourdette, Margo Lion, Alan Scott, Corinne Marchand.
● Simultaneously a tribute to Max Ophüls (to whom it is dedicated), Nantes (its setting), American musicals, and the joyous but always glorious romantic roundelay centred on the alluring and enigmatic presence of Aimée's eponymous cabaret-dancer, forced to choose between a trio of lovers. Its breezy tone, narrative coincidences, circling camera, and overall *brio* suggest a certain superficiality, but at its heart lies a wistful awareness that happiness in love is both transient and largely dependent on chance. Very beautifully shot, in widescreen and luminous black-and-white, it is also formally astonishing, with all the minor characters serving as variations on the central couple. GA

Lola

(1981, WGer, 115 min)
d Rainer Werner Fassbinder. *p* Horst Wendlandt. *sc* Peter Märthesheimer, Pea Fröhlich, Rainer Werner Fassbinder. *ph* Xaver Schwarzenberger. *ed* Juliane Lorenz, Franz Walsch [Rainer Werner Fassbinder]. *ad* Helmut Gassner. *m* Peer Raben. cast Barbara Sukowa, Armin Mueller-Stahl, Mario Adorf, Mathias Fuchs, Helga Feddersen, Karin Baal, Ivan Desny, Hark Böhm.
● A wonderfully upfront narrative rendered in garish primary colours, this discursive update of *The Blue Angel* poses Lola (Sukowa) and the blue-eyed trembling-pillar-of-rectitude building commissioner who helplessly falls for her (Mueller-Stahl) as barometers of the moral bankruptcy at the heart of Germany's post-war 'economic miracle'. Lola (owned, like most of the city, by Mario Adorf's bluffly sleazy building profiteer) threads sinuously through the civic corruption of reconstruction, accruing sufficient manipulative credit to buy a slice of the status quo, seductively scuttling several shades of idealism with the oldest of come-on currencies. Business as usual. The prostitution metaphors come undiluted from

early Godard, the poster-art visuals from the magnificent melodramas of Sirk and Minnelli; the provocations are all Fassbinder's own. PT

Lola Montès (aka Lola Montez)

(1955, Fr/WGer, 140 min)
d Max Ophüls. *p* Ralph Baum, Albert Caraco. *sc* Max Ophüls, Jacques Natanson, Annette Wademant. *ph* Christian Matras. *ed* Madeleine Gug. *ad* Jean d'Eaubonne, Jacques Guth. *m* Georges Auric. *cast* Martine Carol, Peter Ustinov, Anton Walbrook, Ivan Desny, Will Quadflieg, Oskar Werner, Lise Delamare, Paulette Dubost.

● A biography of the celebrated 19th century adventuress, but not a biography in the conventional sense: the lady's life is chronicled in a highly selective series of flashbacks, framed by scenes in a New Orleans circus where she allows herself to be put on show to a vulgar and impressionable public. The space between her memories and her circus appearance is the distance between romantic dreams and tawdry reality, or between love and the knowledge that love dies. Ophüls conjures that space into life – indeed, makes it the very subject of his film – by means of the most sumptuous stylistic effects imaginable: compositions unmatched in their fluidity, moving-camerawork that blurs the line between motion and emotion. If ever a director 'wrote' with his camera, it was Ophüls, and this still looks like his most sublime work. TR [Note: Shot in three separate language versions – French, German and English – this was premiered at around 140 minutes, but subsequently much recut. The English version – *The Sins of Lola Montes* in the US, *The Fall of Lola Montes* in GB – ran 90 minutes, but is seldom seen now. Prints of the French and German versions currently in circulation are approximately 112 minutes. – Ed]

Lola + Bilidikid

(1998, Ger, 95 min)
d Kutlug Ataman. *p* Martin Hagemann. *sc* Kutlug Ataman. *ph* Chris Squires. *ed* Ewa J Lind. *pd* John Di Minico. *m* Arpad Bondy. *cast* Baki Davrak, Gandi Mukli, Erdal Yildiz, Michael Gerber, Murat Yilmaz, Inge Keller, Hakan Tandogan, Cihangir Gümüsturkmen.

● Murat, 17, comes from what might be called, in the context of Berlin's Turkish-immigrant transvestite subculture, a traditional family. Short on a father (dead) and one brother (a runaway), the family's broken and tormented by Murat's remaining sibling Osman, a fearful bully who's also evidently stupid going by his attempts to force a prostitute on his brother. Murat (Davrak) prefers the action in the town's underground cabaret and drag bars, where a diva called Lola (Mukli) catches his interest. He draws closer to this fringe world, with its muckers and misfits – and discovers that Lola is his missing brother. This second feature from Turkish writer/director Ataman is a wracked, high pitched drama driven only so far by its sincerity, conviction and feel for the emotional jeopardy of life in the margins. At a generous stretch you could discern the spirit of Fassbinder in its involvement with Berlin's ghettocracy; dramatically, though, the film's overwrought and alienating. NB

Lola Rennt

see Run Lola Run

Lolita

(1961, GB, 153 min, b/w)
d Stanley Kubrick. *p* James B Harris. *sc* Vladimir Nabokov. *ph* Oswald Morris. *ed* Anthony Harvey. *ad* William Andrews. *m* Nelson Riddle. *cast* James Mason, Sue Lyon, Shelley Winters, Peter Sellers, Diana Decker, Jerry Stovin, Gary Cockrell, Marianne Stone.

● Less genuinely ecstatic in its portrait of paedophiliac obsession than Nabokov's novel – Kubrick is too cold and distanced a director ever to portray happiness, it seems – but nevertheless far more satisfying than his later works (one hesitates to call them mere movies). Mason is highly impressive as Humbert Humbert – all repressed passion and furrowed brow – and Winters contributes just the right amount of vulgarity as Lo's mother. Kubrick manages to handle the moral and psychological nuances with surprising lucidity, but the decision to indulge Peter Sellers' gift for mimickry in the role of Quilty tends to scupper the movie's tone. Fascinating, nevertheless. GA

Lolita

(1997, Fr/US, 137 min)
d Adrian Lyne. *p* Mario Kassar, Joel B Michaels. *sc* Stephen Schiff. *ph* Howard Atherton. *ed* Julie Monroe, David Brenner. *pd* Jon Hutman. *m* Ennio Morricone. *cast* Jeremy Irons, Melanie Griffith, Frank Langella, Dominique Swain, Suzanne Shepherd, Erin J Dean, Ronald Pickup.

● This deploys body doubles, mostly avoids anything more explicit than a kiss, and is unlikely to foment paedophile activity, especially as it goes out of its way to stress the wretched consequences of Humbert Humbert's poisoned/poisonous infatuation with teenage nymphet Lo. One might, perhaps, concede that it's so concerned to make us understand Humbert at the same time as recognising his guilt that we learn little of Lolita's feelings, but the same is essentially true of Nabokov's novel. Moreover, the acting is spot on: Swain is excellent as Lo; Irons suitably impassioned, befuddled and tormented as Humbert; Griffith well cast as Charlotte Haze; and Langella's Quilty infinitely preferable to Peter Sellers' grandstanding in the Kubrick version. If the film has a problem, it's that its moral circumspection renders it a touch dull. Here, what humour there is consists largely of clumsy slapstick; any irony is generally heavy-handed; and the few moments of more florid mise-en-scène still evoke the fast-and-flashy aesthetic of an ads director. Nevertheless, the movie is neither sensationalist nor unintelligent, and some may even find the performances finally achieve a genuine poignancy. GA

e'Lollipop

(1975, SAf, 93 min)
d Ashley Lazarus. *p* André Pieterse. *sc* Ashley Lazarus. *ph* Arthur J Ornitz. *ed* Lionel Selwyn. *ad* Wendy Malan, Phil Rosenberg, Anita Friedberg. *m* Lee Holdridge. *cast* José Ferrer, Karen Valentine, Bess Finney, Muntu Ben Louis Ndebele, Norman Knox, Simon Sabela, Ken Gampu, Alice Webb.

● An all-stops-out tale of the undying friendship of two boys – one white, the other coloured – raised by a Catholic mission in a small South African village. The main message of the film is a liberal one about the need for tolerance and harmonious coexistence. More difficult to understand is the unquestioning attitude towards the American presence in South America. When the chips are down, it's US know-how and technology that saves the day. CPe

Lolly-Madonna XXX (aka The Lolly-Madonna War)

(1973, US, 105 min)
d Richard C Sarafian. *p* Rodney Carr-Smith. *sc* Rodney Carr-Smith, Sue Grafton. *ph* Philip H Lathrop. *ed* Tom Rolf. *ad* Herman A Blumenthal. *m* Fred Myrow. *cast* Rod Steiger, Robert Ryan, Scott Wilson, Jeff Bridges, Season Hubley, Katherine Squire, Ed Lauter, Randy Quaid, Gary Busey.

● This moves in on Peckinpah/Boorman territory, and comes adrift through lack of the singleness of purpose which those directors' obsessive preoccupations might have given it. It starts as a kind of thriller, with a gang of backwoodsmen capturing a girl at a lonely bus stop, then moves on to take in inter-family feuding (the Feathers headed by Steiger versus the Gutshalls led by Ryan), rape, mental deficiency, illicit moonshining, revenge killings, and some flashbacks to the death of the wife of one of the kidnappers. Sarafian can bring off the odd key scene in a fresh and convincing way, but seems unable to establish the drive the film needs to take it past its complicated plot and on to a satisfactory climax. Basically, rather over-decorated backwoods mayhem, memorable for the sequence where Ed Lauter fantasises himself as a Country & Western star and goes out to die like Elvis waving to his cheering fans. VG

Lolo

(1991, Mex, 88 min)
d Francisco Athié. *p* Gustavo Montiel. *sc* Francisco Athié. *ph* Jorge Medina. *ed* Tlacatéotl Mata. *m* Juan Cristobal. *cast* Lucha Villa, Roberto Sosa, Damián Alcazar, Alonso Echanove, Esperanza Mozo.

● A Mexican slum melodrama and a very pale shadow of Buñuel's *Los Olvidados*, Lolo (short for Dolores) loses his job when he's hospitalised after a mugging; the shock screws up his sense of personal mortality, and when he causes the accidental death of an old woman his only instinct is to grab his girlfriend and run. Unpersuasive in all departments. TR

London

(1994, GB, 85 min)
d Patrick Keiller. *p* Keith Griffiths. *sc/ph* Patrick Keiller. *ed* Larry Sider. *narrator* Paul Scofield.

● This lies in that fertile territory between fiction and documentary. Everything you see is actually there, but as Scofield's anonymous Narrator takes us through his 'journal' of 1992, what we hear goes way beyond the mere facts to embrace meditative reflection, political satire, erudite literary anecdote, mythification and offbeat humour. The 'story' is structured round three journeys undertaken by the Narrator and his friend/ex-lover Robinson (also unseen) to research the source of English Romanticism. But as the pair attempt to get a grip on the city's history, contemporary events distract them from their planned route and their focus on the past. Both a fascinating study of a culture in decline, and a scathing commentary on the effects of more than a decade of Conservatism, the film touches on figures as diverse as Baudelaire, John Major and the Chippendales. One of the most original British features in a long time. GA

London Belongs To Me (aka Dulcimer Street)

(1948, GB, 112 min, b/w)
d Sidney Gilliat. *p* Frank Launder, Sidney Gilliat. *sc* Sidney Gilliat, JB Williams. *ph* Wilkie Cooper. *ed* Thelma Myers. *ad* Roy Oxley. *m* Benjamin Frankel. *cast* Alastair Sim, Stephen Murray, Richard Attenborough, Fay Compton, Wylie Watson, Susan Shaw, Joyce Carey, Hugh Griffith, Gladys Henson.

● A shabby London lodging-house has the usual assortment of oddballs, including Alastair Sim – that staple of eccentricity – as a phony medium. Most particularly, there is garage-hand Attenborough, who lives with his mum (Henson). For a while, the picture looks like out-takes from *This Happy Breed*, but it swerves into thrillerdom, and then into something else again when Attenborough steals a car and his former girlfriend is killed in a hit-and-run accident. Attenborough is sentenced to hang for murder, and his fellow-lodgers march to Whitehall demanding a reprieve. Gilliat handles the thematic lurching very ably, even if it does look like a filmed play, and Attenborough's performance uses the left-over menace and panic of *Brighton Rock*. (From a novel by Norman Collins.) ATu

London Connection, The (aka The Omega Connection)

(1979, GB, 84 min)
d Robert Clouse. *p* Jan Williams. *sc* Gail Morgan Hickman, David E Boston. *ph* Godfrey Godar. *ed* Peter Boita, Mike Campbell. *ad* Jack Shampan. *m* John Cameron. *cast* Jeffrey Byron, Larry Cedar, Roy Kinnear, Lee Montague, Mona Washbourne, Nigel Davenport, David Kossoff, Frank Windsor, Kathleen Harrison.

● When Walt was alive, Disney films were great: fifteen-Kleenex tearjerkers, lots of monkey business with Hayley Mills, and the promise of Annette Funicello if only you'd Stay in School. But since their presiding genius copped it, the studio's films have developed increasingly terminal 'cute plots': flying beds, cars that think faster than they run, brontosauri that get shunted around town by stuntmen in drag. This one features the clean-cut Hardy boy and a fellow American he visits in London; together they help a defected East European scientist save his 'unique energy formula' from the clutches of a dubious syndicate. Back home, our jock hero works for his 'uncle' (Uncle Sam – geddit?), and things are made pretty easy by his array of sub-Bond defence devices. There is one impressive stunt, but the plot is such a bland-out you may be asleep when it happens. CR

London Kills Me

(1991, GB, 107 min)
d Hanif Kureishi. *p* Tim Bevan. *sc* Hanif Kureishi. *ph* Ed Lachman. *ed* Jon Gregory. *pd* Stuart Walker. *m* Mark Springer, Sarah

Sarhandi. *cast* Justin Chadwick, Steven Mackintosh, Emer McCourt, Roshan Seth, Fiona Shaw, Brad Dourif, Tony Haygarth, Stevan Rimkus, Eleanor David, Alun Armstrong, Naveen Andrews, Garry Cooper, Gordon Warnecke.
● Twenty, unemployed and tired of being in debt, Notting Hill drugs dealer Clint (Chadwick) decides to go straight. Trouble is, friend and posse boss Muffdiver (Mackintosh) is reluctant to let him go. Worse, Clint not only rivals Muff for the affections of junkie Sylvie (McCourt), but he lacks the shoes he needs to become a waiter at a local diner. Ready to beg, steal or borrow from anyone, Clint embarks on a quest for footwear. Kureishi's directing debut means well, but wayward plotting, charmless performances and flat direction ensure that tedium sets in early. Evidently intended as an authentic look at Notting Hill life, it rarely rings true; and Kureishi buries the flaws beneath sporadic bursts of running about to music (hoary clichés for showing the wild, irresponsible joys of youth). It's hard, finally, to know exactly what it's all about, or even whether it's meant as a comedy. GA

London Rock and Roll Show, The

(1973, GB, 84 min)
d/p Peter Clifton. *ph* Peter Whitehead, Mike Whittaker, Bruce Dowse, Martin Rolfe, Peter Jessop, Tony Coggans, Steffan Sargent. *ed* Thomas Schwalm. *with* Mick Jagger, Chuck Berry, Little Richard, Bill Haley and The Comets, Jerry Lee Lewis, Bo Diddley, Lord Sutch.
● A spotty record of the 1973 Wembley concert, this is finally worth it for the performances. The twitchy style is of the zoom-in-and-cut-away variety, and secondary content offers sparse interviews with performers and too much crowd 'atmosphere'. There could have been more talk, because the interviews provide some lighter moments: Bill Haley theorises on fraternity, while Jerry Lee Lewis and Little Richard squabble for the title of king; Little Richard supports his claim with an impromptu, quivering solo of 'I Believe' as proof of his range. Darkness brings some relief from the overall restlessness as cameras concentrate more on performers and less on crowds. Chuck Berry's triumphant climactic set is shot in a thankfully straightforward manner. CPe

Lone Hand, The

(1953, US, 80 min)
d George Sherman. *p* Howard Christie. *sc* Joseph Hoffman *ph* Maury Gertsman. *ed* Paul Weatherwax. *ad* Alexander Golitzen, Eric Orbom. *m* Joseph Gershenson. *cast* Joel McCrea, Barbara Hale, Jimmy Hunt, Charles Drake, Alex Nicol, James Arness.
● This modest Universal Western (from a story by Irving Ravetch) only really becomes interesting if regarded as a companion piece to Cameron Menzies' *Invaders from Mars*, made the same year. Here, too, the rather dazed-looking Jimmy Hunt sees his slice of idealised Americana (ranch, faithful dog, strong Pa, pretty step-Ma) turn sinister, even nightmarish, this time when he finds out that Pa (McCrea) is a member of the outlaw gang that's terrorising the county. Sherman is hardly the director to make the most of such a situation, and indeed the film chickens out at the end – Pa's an undercover Pinkerton. But as a little-known contribution to the '50s cinema of unease, it repays investigation. BBa

Loneliness of the Long Distance Runner, The

(1962, GB, 104 min, b/w)
d/p Tony Richardson. *sc* Alan Sillitoe. *ph* Walter Lassally. *ed* Anthony Gibbs. *ad* Ralph Brinton, Edward Marshall. *m* John Addison. *cast* Tom Courtenay, James Bolam, Avis Bunnage, Michael Redgrave, Alec McCowen, James Fox, Joe Robinson, Topsy Jane, Julia Foster, John Thaw, Frank Finlay.
● Alan Sillitoe's fiction fuelled the excellent *Saturday Night and Sunday Morning*, but this one started life as a short story and grew flabbier for the screen. Courtenay's Borstal boy is crabbed and corroded by class hatred, and his only moment of satisfaction comes when he throws a cross-country race against a local public school to spite the upper class Governor (Redgrave). Chariots of Bile. Even in this softened-up version, *Time* found the hero 'prolier-than-thou'. Most of the period hallmarks of the British New Wave are paraded here. The disaffected hero treats us to Hoggartian interior monologues and climbs the nearest hill so that we can see the hopeless urban sprawl – Nottingham, in this case – laid out like his future. He gets the obligatory lyrical day off, a bracing trip to Skegness. Courting couples snog beside the barbed wire, and there's no shortage of editing between lads being flogged and choirs singing 'Jerusalem'. The general thrust is that Britain provides no sustenance for the working class soul, and consumerism spearheaded by telly comes in for some stick. It all seems a long time ago. BC

Lonely Are the Brave

(1962, US, 107 min, b/w)
d David Miller. *p* Edward Lewis. *sc* Dalton Trumbo. *ph* Phil Lathrop. *ed* Leon Barsha. *ad* Alexander Golitzen, Robert E Smith. m Jerry Goldsmith. *cast* Kirk Douglas, Gena Rowlands, Walter Matthau, Michael Kane, Carroll O'Connor, George Kennedy, William Schallert.
● A striking modern Western, with Douglas' ex-con cowboy pitting his horse and wits against technocrat sheriff Matthau and the world of 'progress', in an attempt to hold on to his dream of freedom and the pioneering spirit. The message of Dalton Trumbo's script (adapted from Edward Abbey's novel *Brave Cowboy*) is often a little too heavily underlined, with Douglas' martyrdom buttressed by some rather obvious symbols, but Miller directs with an eloquent feeling for landscape, making excellent use of Philip Lathrop's monochrome photography as the cowboy is pursued by helicopters into the mountains. Beautifully acted by a superb cast, it's a gripping, elegiac movie, imbued with a very real nostalgia for a vanished world. GA

Lonelyhearts

(1958, US, 101 min, b/w)
d Vincent J Donehue. *p/sc* Dore Schary. *ph* John Alton. *ed* Aaron Stell, John Faure. *ad* Serge Krizman. *m* Conrad Salinger. *cast* Montgomery Clift, Robert Ryan, Myrna Loy, Maureen Stapleton, Dolores Hart, Jackie Coogan.
● This adaptation of Nathanael West's novel *Miss Lonelyhearts* proves an ideal vehicle for a vintage Clift display of raw-nerved sensitivity. Scarred by the childhood catastrophe of his mother's murder and his father's imprisonment, his job as a newspaper agony aunt piles on a daily dose of human misery; and he has also to endure the goadings of Ryan, his *Sun*-hearted editor, 'Slop for the slobs!' The confrontations between compassionate Clift and embittered Ryan are the heart of the film, leavened by a little drama when Clift gets too close to one of his correspondents. It's gripping if a little repetitive; Clift is fascinating to watch as usual, though physically he would have suited the part better ten years earlier. Donehue was a TV director, and the production has the cramped look (that newsroom set!) of a live episode of *Playhouse 90*. BBa

Lonely Hearts

(1981, Aust, 95 min)
d Paul Cox. *p* John B Murray. *sc* Paul Cox, John Clarke. *ph* Yuri Sokol. *ed* Tim Lewis. *ad* Neil Angwin. *m* Norman Kaye. *cast* Wendy Hughes, Norman Kaye, Jon Finlayson, Julia Blake, Jonathan Hardy.
● As crankily bizarre in its own way as the later *Man of Flowers*, this is a sort of neo-realist comedy with a touch that Buster Keaton would have admired, not least the opening funeral sequence in which hearse and solitary mourner's car, befuddled by traffic lights, engage in a startled *pas de deux* of overtaking before settling down again in dignified procession. Pushing 50, alone for the first time with his mother now dead, Peter the piano-tuner (Kaye) is free at last to find out if there's life in the old dog yet. Splashing out on a new toupee, amusing himself by pretending to be blind as he goes about his work, he acquires a girl (Hughes) through a lonely-hearts agency, hesitantly suspecting that she may be rather too young but not that over-protective parents have induced in her a pathological fear of sex. Tenderly and wittily, Cox nurses their relationship along through assorted ups and downs, in particular their involvement in a production of Strindberg's *The Father* (a wickedly accurate satire of amateur dramatics). Beautifully observed and beautifully acted, it's a small gem. TM

Lonely Hearts Club (Jimo Fangxin Julebu)

(1995, Tai, 110 min)
d Yee Chih-Yen. *p* Hsu Li-Kong. *sc* Yee Chih-Yen. *ph* Yang Wei-Han. *ed* Chen Sheng-Chang, Chen Hsiao-Tong. *ad* Timmy Yeh. *m* Huang Su-Chin. *cast* Pai Yueh-O, Yang Kuei-Mei, Denys Hsieh, Gao Chien-Guo.
● The former critic Yee Chi-Yen's debut feature traces an intricately linked network of romantic dreams, delusions and desires across half a dozen well-drawn and superbly acted characters. At its core, a middle-aged office accountant (played against type by the woman who is Taiwan's answer to Oprah), endlessly frustrated by her daughter, husband and mother-in-law, starts imagining that she could have an affair with the new office boy. He, of course, is gay, and has more than enough problems of his own. Yee reveals the complexities of the characters bit by bit, and maintains a sense of humour even when things start to go badly wrong for them. TR

Lonely in America

(1990, US, 96 min)
d Barry Alexander Brown. *p* Tirlok Malik, Phil Katzman. *sc* Satyajit Joy Palit, Barry Alexander Brown, Nicholas Spencer. *ph* Phil Katzman. *ed* Tula Goenka. *ad* Eduardo Capilla. *m* Gregory Arnold. *cast* Ranjit Chowdhry, Adelaide Miller, Tirlok Malik, Robert Kessler, David Toney, Melissa Christopher.
● Indian immigrant Arun (Chowdhry) arrives in New York with little to his name besides a turquoise suit, computer literacy and boundless optimism. 'I feel I own the place already!' he declares. He dumps the largesse – a job on Max's newsstand, an apartment and extended-familial support – offered by his uncle, in favour of embracing the American dream (and white girlfriend) in his own inimitable fashion. The script based on a story by producer Tirlok Malik contains some comic gems, but what insights it offers into the experience of New York's Asian community are largely travestied by Brown's inexperienced, clumsy direction and his over-forced atmosphere of naive triumphalism. This low-budget romantic comedy oscillates like a metronome between likeable and naff. WH

Lonely Lady, The

(1982, US, 92 min)
d Peter Sasdy. *p* Robert R Weston. *sc* John Kershaw, Shawn Randall. *ph* Brian West. *ed* Keith Palmer. *pd* Enzo Bulgarelli. *m* Charles Calello. *cast* Pia Zadora, Lloyd Bochner, Bibi Besch, Joseph Cali, Anthony Holland, Jared Martin, Ray Liotta.
● Hollywood on Hollywood again: Harold Robbins' sleazy little yarn features Pia Zadora as a wide-eyed ingénue in a slashed dress, fresh out of high-school creative-writing courses, and learning about Beverly Hills on the wrong side of a very nasty rape with a garden hose. In no time at all she is scrabbling her way to a screenwriting Oscar through the land where every Mercedes convertible has a toupee. It's hardly her talent with a pen that knocks them horizontal, but apart from a curious tendency to shower all the time with her dress on, such rogueries threw this spectator into a deep state of lacquered composure. CPea

Lonely Passion of Judith Hearne, The

(1987, GB, 116 min)
d Jack Clayton. *p* Peter Nelson, Richard Johnson. *sc* Peter Nelson. *ph* Peter Hannan. *ed* Terry Rawlings. *pd* Michael Pickwoad. *m* Georges Delerue. *cast* Maggie Smith, Bob Hoskins, Wendy Hiller, Marie Kean, Ian McNeice, Alan Devlin, Rudi Davies, Prunella Scales, Sheila Reid.
● Brian Moore's novel makes for a depressing experience in Clayton's hands. Everything seems congealed in a time warp, and if the forlorn, shabby-genteel dreams of a Dublin boarding-house conjure up the feeling of '40s Rattigan, the treatment could be a late '50s *Room at the Bottom*. Judith Hearne's lonely passion is for being loved, and failing that, the hard stuff. Neither of her amulets – a photo of her late aunt and a picture of The Lord – can save her from the bottle, and she regularly loses her piano students and her lodgings. It's a hermetic story in which hope springs eternal despite the treadmill

of character, and Maggie Smith calibrates her suffering to a nicety, rising to ferocious anguish before an uncommunicative altar shrine. The landlady's brother, James Madden (Hoskins), returned from the States and full of bull, appears to be a romantic contender, but is only interested in her putative savings. The landlady's lecherous son (McNeice) is grotesque beyond the call of duty. A downer. BC

Lonely Wife, The

see Charulata

Lonely Woman, The

see Viaggio in Italia

Loners (Samotari)

(2000, Czech Rep, 104 min)
d/p David Ondrícek. *sc* Petr Zelenka. *ph* Richard Rericha. *ed* Michael Lánsky. *pd* Radek Hanák. *m* Jan P Muchow. *cast* Jitka Schneiderová, Labina Mitevska, Dana Sedláková, Ivan Trojan, Sasa Rasilov, Jirí Machácek.

●If you caught Petr Zelenka's Buñuel-like *Buttoners* and enjoyed it (who didn't?), you're in for a treat with this likewise wry, faintly surreal black comedy – Zelenka wrote it while making *Buttoners* – interweaving the exploits of seven not-so-bright young things looking for love and a sense of purpose in modern Prague. It's a story of loneliness, obsession, betrayal, misunderstanding and confusion; it's also about chance, coincidence, destiny, responsibility, radio DJs, medical science, parents, car crashes, dope, and a Japanese take on Western life, all of which suggests this might be seen as 'Buttoners 2'. Well, it's similarly quirky, stylish and often very funny, yet at the same time fresh enough to feel quite original. GA

Lonesome Cowboys

(1968, US, 110 min)
d/p/sc Andy Warhol. cast Viva, Taylor Mead, Tom Hompertz, Louis Waldon, Joe Dallesandro, Eric Emerson, Julian Burroughs, Francis Francine.

●Fans of Warhol's work, with its complete disregard for logic, characterisation and chronology, will revel in this 'Western'. It encapsulates the essence of '60s decadence, with all of the cast (and probably the crew) high on acid and passing the joints around, but it does raise several interesting questions about the early pioneering days. The naturalness of sex between men who were living together, riding together and dying together on the lonesome trail is a concept not even hinted at in conventional Westerns, let alone explored. The film is by turns hilarious, camp, aggravating and bizarre; no awards for the acting, however, which varies between the incompetent and the amateur. MG

Lone Star

(1995, US, 135 min)
d John Sayles. *p* Paul Miller, Maggie Renzi. *sc* John Sayles. *ph* Stuart Dryburgh. *ed* John Sayles. *pd* Dan Bishop. *m* Mason Daring. *cast* Chris Cooper, Matthew McConaughey, Elizabeth Peña, Joe Morton, Kris Kristofferson, Stephen Mendillo, Clifton James, Miriam Colon, Frances McDormand.

●A skeleton's discovered in the desert just outside the Tex-Mex bordertown of Frontera, and sheriff Sam Deeds (Cooper) soon concludes that the dead man – 'bribes 'n' bullets' lawman Charlie Wade (Kristofferson), reputedly run out of town 40 years ago by Sam's late, legendary father Buddy (McConaughey) – was murdered. But who killed him, and why? It may, of course, be connected with the racial tensions that have always divided Frontera's population. After all, his own teenage romance with Pilar Cruz (Peña), now a teacher with a troubled son of her own, was frowned on by their parents; and even now the blacks are still marginalised: if they're not unemployed, most are stuck out at the army base headed by Delmore Payne (Morton), a by-the-book colonel whose faith in rugged individualism has alienated him from both his father and his son. Writer/director Sayles' witty, vividly demotic dialogue knocks even Tarantino for six, the characterisations are uniformly colourful and credible, the soundtrack and the widescreen camerawork exemplary, and the sense of a living, working, interrelating community is superbly realised. All this – and one of the most quietly subversive endings in American cinema. GA

Lone Wolf McQuade

(1983, US, 107 min)
d Steve Carver. *p* Yoram Ben-Ami, Steve Carver. *sc* BJ Nelson. *ph* Roger Shearman, Michael Sibley, Jerry G Callaway. *ed* Anthony Redman. *pd* Norman Baron. *m* Francesco De Masi. *cast* Chuck Norris, David Carradine, Barbara Carrera, Leon Isaac Kennedy, Robert Beltran, LQ Jones, RG Armstrong.

●As senseless violence goes, this is very senseless and very violent. Norris is a Texas Ranger, Carradine an oily Senator smuggling weapons to 'Central American terrorists', but the storyline has more non sequiturs than bodies, which is saying something. JCo

Long Ago, Tomorrow

see Raging Moon, The

Long and the Short and the Tall, The

(1960, GB, 105 min, b/w)
d Leslie Norman. *p* Michael Balcon. *sc* Wolf Mankowitz, Frederic Gotfurt, TJ Morrison. *ph* Erwin Hillier. *ed* Gordon Stone. *ed* Terence Verity, Jim Morahan. *m* Stanley Black. *cast* Laurence Harvey, Richard Todd, David McCallum, Richard Harris, Ronald Fraser, John Meillon, Kenji Takaki.

●Willis Hall's play, about a British patrol in Burma intent on killing an innocent Japanese prisoner in hysterical retribution for atrocities committed against British soldiers, was a hit at the Royal Court Theatre as directed by Lindsay Anderson, with Peter O'Toole in the key role of the doubter. Michael Balcon, when he produced the film, replaced Anderson with Leslie Norman, an Ealing veteran, and junked O'Toole in favour of Laurence Harvey. The result was suitably meretricious. PH

Long Arm, The (aka The Third Key)

(1956, GB, 96 min, b/w)
d Charles Frend. *p* Michael Balcon. *sc* Janet Green, Robert Barr. *ph* Gordon Dines. *ed* Gordon Stone. *ad* Edward Carrick. *m* Gerard Schurmann. *cast* Jack Hawkins, Richard Leech, John Stratton, Dorothy Alison, Geoffrey Keen, Ursula Howells, Sydney Tafler.

●The last Ealing film actually made at the famous studios before the move to Borehamwood, this paean to the middle-class copper's lot (with Scotland Yard 'tec Hawkins harassed at home and at work) was, like *The Blue Lamp* of six years before, highly influential on British TV cop shows of the '60s. As if to stress the genre's development, a close viewing reveals Stratford Johns as a mere constable in those days. PT

Long Day Closes, The

(1992, GB, 85 min)
d Terence Davies. *p* Olivia Stewart. *sc* Terence Davies. *ph* Michael Coulter. *ed* William Diver. *pd* Christopher Hobbs. *m* Robert Lockhart. *cast* Marjorie Yates, Leigh McCormack, Anthony Watson, Nicholas Lamont, Ayse Owens, Tina Malone, Jimmy Wilde.

●Like *Distant Voices, Still Lives*, Davies' final autobiographical film rings wholly true, due to the richness and the *rightness* of the allusions he makes through sets, costumes, dialogue, music, radio and cinema itself. Such is Davies' artistry that he shapes his material (an impressionistic series of brief, plotless scenes recalled from 1955–6, when he was about to leave junior school) into a poignant vision of a paradise lost. While economic constraints, school bullies, religious terror and barely-felt sexual longing are present, the accent is on the warmth 11-year-old 'Bud' receives from his family and neighbours. Indeed, it's primarily about the small, innocent but very real joys of being alive, recreated with great skill and never smothered by sentimentality. The stately camera movements; the tableaux-like compositions; the evocative use of music and movie dialogue; the dreamy dissolves and lighting – all make this a movie which takes place in its young protagonist's mind. Beautifully poetic, never contrived or precious, the film dazzles with its stylistic confidence, emotional honesty, terrific wit and all-round audacity. GA

Long Day's Dying, The

(1968, GB, 95 min)
d Peter Collinson. *p* Harry Fine. *sc* Charles Wood. *ph* Brian Probyn. *ed* John Trumper. *pd* Disley Jones. *cast* David Hemmings, Tom Bell, Tony Beckley, Alan Dobie.

●A clumsy adaptation of Alan White's fine novel about four lost soldiers – three British paratroopers and a German who becomes their prisoner – wandering around a World War II battlefield in Europe which becomes a private hell. The novel's rather interesting argument, that a highly trained soldier can revel in his skill as a killer and yet remain a pacifist, gets lost in hysterical overstatement, much camera trickery, insistent soft-focus photography, and a script by Charles Wood which is unwisely cast as a poetic stream-of-consciousness monologue. Excellent performances, though, especially from Tom Bell. TM

Long Day's Journey Into Night

(1962, US, 174 min, b/w)
d Sidney Lumet. *p* George Justin. *ph* Boris Kaufman. *ed* Ralph Rosenblum. *pd* Richard Sylbert. *m* André Previn. *cast* Katharine Hepburn, Ralph Richardson, Jason Robards, Dean Stockwell, Jeanne Barr.

●A straightforward transposition which captures much of the claustrophobic cannibalism of Eugene O'Neill's autobiographical play about a family tearing itself to pieces in a chain of quarrels, with love and hatred describing vicious circles around the self-centred parsimony of the actor father, the nervy drug-addiction of the mother, the incipient alcoholism of the elder son, and the tubercular condition of the younger one. Described by him as 'a play of old sorrow, written in tears and blood', it imposes itself by sheer weight of emotion. Terrific performance from Robards as the drunk, good ones from Hepburn (despite miscasting), Richardson (his mannerisms for once in character) and Stockwell (though a bit lightweight to represent O'Neill the future writer). TM

Longest Day, The

(1962, US, 180 min, b/w)
d Ken Annakin, Andrew Marton, Bernhard Wicki. *p* Darryl F Zanuck. *sc* Cornelius Ryan. *ph* Jean Bourgoin, Walter Wottitz. *ed* Samuel E Beetley. *ad* Ted Haworth, Léon Barsacq, Vincent Korda. *m* Maurice Jarre.*cast* John Wayne, Robert Mitchum, Henry Fonda, Robert Ryan, Mel Ferrer, Robert Wagner, Eddie Albert, Edmond O'Brien, Richard Burton, Kenneth More, Peter Lawford, Richard Todd, Leo Genn, Bourvil, Jean-Louis Barrault, Arletty, Curd Jürgens, Hans Christian Blech, Peter Van Eyck.

●Three main directors (plus Darryl Zanuck and Gerd Oswald filling in), five writers (including Romain Gary and James Jones), a block-buster source novel by Cornelius Ryan, and one of the biggest all-star casts of all time (many of them with damn all to do) make this one of the last true war epics. High on noise, spectacle and heroism as the Allies invade Normandy, generally strong on performances and humour, but still over-long and laden with the usual national stereotypes. GA

Longest Summer, The (Qunian Yanhua Tebie Duo)

(1998, HK, 128 min)
d Fruit Chan. *p* Andy Lau, Daniel Yu. *sc* Fruit Chan. *ph* Lam Wah-Chuen. *ed* Tin Sam-Fat. *pd* Yeung Sau-Sing. *m* Lam Wah-Chuen, Kenneth Bi. *cast* Tony Ho, Sam Lee, Jo Kuk, Chan Sang, Pang Yick-Wai, Lai Chi-Ho.

●Chan's recklessly original film centres on Chinese soldiers from the HK Military Service Corps (two played by real ex-members) who are left penniless and jobless when the Brits disband the force three months before Hong Kong is handed back to China. Ga-Yin (dancer Tony Ho making a terrific acting debut) gets work as a driver for a triad gang because his brother Ga-Suen (Lee, from *Made in Hong Kong*) is a member; then he and several unemployed mates decide to rob a bank. Everything goes wrong, but they end up with the money anyway – and with both cops and robbers on their trail. Shot to look like docu-drama and integrating vivid documentary footage of the handover, the whole film has a street authenticity rare in Hong Kong movies. The only bum notes are some misogynistic asides about delinquent schoolgirls. Otherwise, impressive and gripping. TR

Longest Yard, The (aka The Mean Machine)

(1974, US, 122 min)
d Robert Aldrich. *p* Albert S Ruddy. *sc* Tracy Keenan Wynn. *ph* Joseph Biroc. *ed* Michael Luciano. *pd* James S Vance. *m* Frank De Vol. *cast* Burt Reynolds, Eddie Albert, Ed Lauter, Michael Conrad, Jim Hampton, Harry Caesar, Bernadette Peters, Mike Henry, Richard Kiel.

● A fiercely anti-authoritarian parable mixing broad, black comedy and fast action, this portrays the conflict between prison inmate Reynolds and head warden Albert when a football game is organised between prisoners and guards; the inmates see it as their chance to take revenge for all the brutality they've suffered, while the guards are pressurised by Albert into playing dirty and humiliating their opponents. The themes are dignity and compromise, freedom and betrayal; if it all gets bogged down occasionally in its macho-violence trip, it's nevertheless very exciting, very witty, and elevated above its action-movie status by Aldrich's deliberate references to Nixon in Albert's characterisation of the warden. GA

Long Goodbye, The

(1973, US, 111 min)
d Robert Altman. *p* Jerry Bick. *sc* Leigh Brackett. *ph* Vilmos Zsigmond. *ed* Lou Lombardo. *m* John T Williams. *cast* Elliott Gould, Nina Van Pallandt, Sterling Hayden, Mark Rydell, Henry Gibson, David Arkin, Jim Bouton, Warren Berlinger.

●Despite cries of outrage from hard-line Chandler purists, this is, along with Hawks' *The Big Sleep*, easily the most intelligent of all screen adaptations of the writer's work. Altman in fact stays pretty close to the novel's basic narrative (though there are a couple of crucial changes), but where he comes up with something totally original is in his ironic updating of the story and characters: Gould's Marlowe is a laid-back, shambling slob who, despite his incessant claim that everything is 'OK with me,' actually harbours the same honourable ideals as Chandler's Marlowe; but those values, Altman implies, just don't fit in with the neurotic, uncaring, ephemeral lifestyle led by the 'Me Generation' of modern LA. As Marlowe attempts to protect a friend suspected of battering his wife to death, and gets up to his neck in blackmail, suicide, betrayal and murder, Altman constructs not only a comment on the changes in values in America over the last three decades, but a critique of *film noir* mythology: references, both ironic and affectionate, to Chandler (cats and alcoholism) and to earlier private-eye thrillers abound. Shot in gloriously steely colours by Vilmos Zsigmond with a continually moving camera, wondrously scripted by Leigh Brackett (who worked on *The Big Sleep*), and superbly acted all round, it's one of the finest movies of the '70s. GA

Long Good Friday, The

(1979, GB, 114 min)
d John MacKenzie. *p* Barry Hanson. *sc* Barrie Keeffe. *ph* Philip Meheux. *ed* Mike Taylor. *ad* Vic Symonds. *m* Francis Monkman. *cast* Bob Hoskins, Helen Mirren, Dave King, Bryan Marshall, Derek Thompson, Eddie Constantine, Brian Hall, Stephen Davis, Pierce Brosnan.

●Overrated thriller, often ludicrously compared to the only superficially similar *Performance*. About an East End gangland leader, with plans to develop the Docklands with the help of organised crime from overseas, who sees his empire threatened with extinction after a number of disasters are inflicted on him by mysterious rivals, it certainly manages to create a more convincing and contemporarily relevant London underworld than is usually seen in movies; and there's no denying the charismatic quality of Hoskins' slightly mannerised and stereotypical characterisation of yer typical Cockney 'ood. But the gangsters' connections with Mafia, IRA, big business and so on, are paraded like the latest fashions rather than examined, and the admittedly well-constructed set pieces are all too often diminished in effect by the uninspired camera-work. GA

Long Gray Line, The

(1955, US, 137 min)
d John Ford. *p* Robert Arthur. *sc* Edward Hope. *ph* Charles Lawton Jr. *ed* William A Lyon. *ad* Robert Peterson. *m* George Duning. *cast* Tyrone Power, Maureen O'Hara, Ward Bond, Donald Crisp, Robert Francis, Betsy Palmer, Phil Carey, Harry Carey Jr, Peter Graves.

● A beautifully crafted film, every image composed with graceful simplicity, but all that emerges is a lame 'Goodbye Mr Chips of West Point'. As a clumsy young man fresh off the boat from Ireland, hired by West Point Military Academy as a waiter, Marty Maher (Power) enlists to escape the mounting bill for breakages set against his wages, and becomes an instructor despite his ineptitude. Fifty years later, he is still there, a living monument to West Point, revered (he and his wife O'Hara having lost their only child at birth) as a beloved surrogate father to generations of cadets. The placid endorsement of military tradition (a straw dummy doubt about raising boys up to be cannon-fodder is easily disposed of) would be easier to take were it not for the rampant Irishry (jigs and pseudo-poetic blarney at every opportunity) that makes the sentimentality flow in buckets. Good performances, nevertheless. TM

Long Holidays of 1936, The (Las Largas Vacaciones del 36)

(1976, Sp, 107 min)
d Jaime Camino. *p* José Fradé. *sc* Manuel Guitiérrez Aragón, Jaime Camino. *ph* Fernando Arribas. *ed* Teresa Alcocer. *pd* José María Espada. *m* Xavier Montsalvatge. *cast* Amalia Gadé, Ismael Merlor, Angela Molina, Vincente Parra, Francisco Rabal, José Sacristán, Charo Soriano, Concha Velasco.

●Breaking with the defensive, allegorical style imposed by Franco's regime, Jaime Camino burst into the brightening days of the post-Franco era with this oblique but compelling study of the Spanish Civil War. Set in a middle-class resort outside Barcelona during 1936–39, his film charts the social, sexual and personal transformations which those momentous yet tragic revolutionary events brought in their wake. Through the alert and radicalised children and the impotent, squabbling adults, trapped on permanent 'vacation' by the Fascist uprising of 1936, we are made to understand in microcosm the wider political canvas. Using up till now 'forbidden data', trivial events are drawn large in humorous and tragic detail as the Civil War pervades everything. CG

Long, Hot Summer, The

(1958, US, 117 min)
d Martin Ritt. *p* Jerry Wald. *sc* Irving Ravetch, Harriet Frank Jr. *ph* Joseph LaShelle. *ed* Louis Loeffler. *ad* Lyle Wheeler, Maurice Ransford. *m* Alex North. *cast* Paul Newman, Joanne Woodward, Orson Welles, Anthony Franciosa, Lee Remick, Angela Lansbury, Richard Anderson.

● A steamy, Freudian tale of family intrigue set in the deep South, based on a compilation of stories by William Faulkner. Welles is the tyrannical Varner, whose rejected weakling son (an excessively neurotic performance from Franciosa) seeks consolation in bed with his sexy wife (Remick). A suspected 'barn burner' and definite trouble-maker, Ben Quick (Newman) arrives in town, and is welcomed by Varner as a suitable heir to his empire. The sparks fly between Quick and Varner's schoolmistress daughter (Newman and Woodward together for the first time), but under her cold exterior beats a passionate heart, and predictably they are in each other's arms by the final shot. The ending is an unconvincing cop out, but it can't spoil the film's compulsive dramatic tension (or a marvellous comic cameo from Angela Lansbury as Welles' long-suffering mistress). JE

Long Kiss Goodnight, The

(1996, US, 120 min)
d Renny Harlin. *p* Renny Harlin, Stephanie Austin, Shane Black, *sc* Shane Black. *ph* Guillermo Navarro. *ed* William Goldenberg. *pd* Howard Cummings. *m* Alan Silvestri. *cast* Geena Davis, Samuel L Jackson, Patrick Malahide, Craig Bierko, Brian Cox, David Morse, GD Spradlin, Tom Amandes.

●Samantha Caine's an amnesiac suburban wife. Her violent past surfaces, however, when rogue US intelligence agents recognise her as sometime assassin Charly Baltimore, missing for years and believed dead. By amazing coincidence, just as her ex-colleagues decide to protect their current dirty-tricks scam by terminating her, Sam/Charly starts having flashbacks to her former self. She's also nudged along by fragments of evidence uncovered by low-rent private eye and reluctant sidekick Mitch Henessey (Jackson). So when the bad guys' sadistic henchman (Bierko) kidnaps her 8-year-old daughter, Sam hacks off her long dark hair and emerges with a dyed blonde bob, a really bad attitude and a weapons training that's second to none. The film's unconventional only in the sense that, as visualised by Harlin, the $4m script by Shane Black dispenses entirely with traditional storytelling techniques. Instead, this violent escapist fantasy detonates a string of atomised action sequences so knowingly ironic that they aspire to the condition of post-modern pastiche. The only saving graces are Davis's stripped-down, mean-as-a-wildcat portrayal of the Uzi-toting Charly, and Jackson's engagingly ineffectual turn. Like Charly's alter ego, however, you may have trouble remembering what happened once it's all over. NF

Long Live the Lady! (Lunga Vita alla Signora!)

(1987, It, 106 min)
d Ermanno Olmi. *p* Giuseppe Cereda. *sc* Ermanno Olmi. *ph* Ermanno Olmi, Maurizio Zaccaro. *ed* Ermanno Olmi. *cast* Marco Esposito, Simona Brandalise, Stefania Busarello, Simone Dalla Rosa, Lorenzo Paolini, Lorenzo Paolini, Tarcisio Tosi.

● A slight but charming comedy set in a remote chateau, to which come six catering-school teenagers to wait at a banquet. Seen largely through the watchful eyes of shy, solemn Libenzio (Esposito), the absurdly militaristic preparations, the meal, and the post-prandial relaxation away from the silent stare of the stern, cadaverous hostess, become as magically tantalising and dreamily sinister as the transition from childhood to adulthood. The often unpredictable, faintly surreal satire is distinguished by Olmi's subtle eye for detail; while the exact significance of relationships and events is left intriguingly ambiguous, a wealth of emotion is conveyed not by the remarkably sparse dialogue but by faces, glances and gestures momentarily caught by the camera's serene and tender gaze. GA

Long Memory, The

(1953, GB, 96 min, b/w)
d Robert Hamer. *p* Hugh Stewart. *sc* Robert Hamer, Frank Harvey. *ph* Harry Waxman. *ed* Gordon Hales. *ad* Alex Vetchinsky. *m* William Alwyn. *cast* John Mills, John McCallum, Elizabeth Sellars, Eva Berg, Geoffrey Keen, Michael Martin-Harvey, Thora Hird.

●One of the marker posts of Hamer's decline after *Kind Hearts and Coronets*, this revenge thriller (from a novel by Howard Clewes) has John Mills, trying hard to summon up some grit, as a vengeful convict who's just spent 12 years inside for a crime he didn't commit. Hamer makes the most of the marshes and mud flats of the Thames Estuary, but the over-familiar plotting never springs to life. TJ

Long Night, The

(1947, US, 97 min, b/w)
d Anatole Litvak. *p* Anatole Litvak, Robert Hakim, Raymond Hakim. *sc* John Wexley. *ph* Sol Polito. *ed* Robert Swink. *ad* Eugène Lourié. *m* Dimitri Tiomkin. *cast* Henry Fonda, Barbara Bel Geddes, Vincent Price, Ann Dvorak, June Duprez, Queenie Smith, Elisha Cook Jr, Howard Freeman.

●Hollywood's cannibalisation (sometimes shot for shot) of Carné's *Le Jour se lève*. Bowdlerised and tricked out with a silly happy ending, but a better film than critics allowed at the time with Carné's film under threat of definitive suppression to make way for it. Excellent performances (with Price at his smarmiest, and Fonda only a shade self-pitying where Jean Gabin gave the role sheer, mutinous power), but above all a wonderful *noir* sheen from Sol Polito's camerawork. TM

Long Night's Journey into Day

(1999, US, 95 min)
d Frances Reid, Deborah Hoffmann. *p* Frances Reid, Johnny Symons. *ph* Frances Reid, Ezra

Jwili. *ed* Deborah Hoffmann, Kim Roberts. *m* Lebo M. *with* Mary Burton, Pumla Gobodo-Madikizela, Jann Turner, Desmond Tutu, Tony Weaver, Glenda Wildschut.
● Four stories brought before S Africa's Truth and Reconciliation Commission, the forum established in the wake of apartheid to negotiate a compromise between the needs of punitive and restorative justice. They concern the black killers of US student Amy Biehl; the police officers who abducted and murdered the Cradock Four; the ANC fighters who bombed a Saturday night bar in Durban; and the undercover agents who assassinated the Gugulu Seven 'terrorists'. The testimonies of perpetrators and relatives of the dead – both to the commission and to camera – bear witness to the social and emotional fissures wrought by apartheid, but it's the evidence of the healing process at work, with all its painful, grievous and unpredictable effects, which provides the real fascination of the film. NB

Long Ride, The

(1983, US/Hun, 93 min)
d Pál Gábor. *p* Robert Halmi Sr. *sc* William W Lewis. *ph* Elemér Ragalyi. *ed* Eva Karmentö, Norman Gay. *ad* József Romvari. *m* Charles Gross. *cast* John Savage, Kelly Reno, Ildikó Bánsági, László Mensáros, Ferenc Bács, Dzsoko Rosszics, László Horvath.
● A US pilot bales out over Hungary during World War II, and the Resistance helps him to flee to freedom across the Yugoslavian border. There being no cars, and with the Germans watching the trains, our hero (Savage) escapes on horseback, and *The Long Ride* becomes an excuse for lavish tracking and helicopter shots over the great Hortobagy plain. Not a hugely expensive picture, but co-production with Hollywood bought Gábor chopper shots and an indifferent American star. It also saddled him with a compromised script – just to keep the ideology straight, the pilot first considers fleeing East to join the advancing Red Army – and a sentimental ending whereby the plucky peasant lad who helps the hero to flee dies on reaching the border. MA

Long Riders, The

(1980, US, 99 min)
d Walter Hill. *p* Tim Zinnemann. *sc* Bill Bryden, Steven Philip Smith, Stacy Keach Sr, James Keach. *ph* Ric Waite. *ed* David Holden, Freeman Davies. *pd* Jack T Collis. *m* Ry Cooder. *cast* David, Keith and Robert Carradine, James and Stacy Keach, Dennis and Randy Quaid, Nicholas and Christopher Guest, Harry Carey Jr, Pamela Reed, James Remar.
● Hill's film holds its head high in a distinguished company of movies about the Jesse James/Cole Younger gang, refusing to bother too much about historical facts or psychological motivation, instead serving up a potted commentary on the conventions of the genre itself. Concentrating on familiar rituals – the funeral, the hoe-down, the robbery (a stunning tour de force in slow motion) – Hill pays tribute to such directors as Ford, Hawks and Ray, emphasises the mythic aspects of the Western, and focuses on the subjects of kinship and the land (probably suggested by Scotsman Bill Bryden's screenplay). This last theme is emphasised by Hill's coup of casting real-life brothers as the members of the gang. A beautiful, laconic and unsentimental film. GA

Long Ships, The

(1963, GB/Yug, 124 min)
d Jack Cardiff. *p* Irving Allen. *sc* Berkely Mather, Beverley Cross. *ph* Christopher Challis. *ed* Geoffrey Foot. *ad* John Hoesli. *m* Dusan Radic. *cast* Richard Widmark, Sidney Poitier, Rosanna Schiaffino, Russ Tamblyn, Oscar Homolka, Beba Loncar, Colin Blakely, Gordon Jackson, Lionel Jeffries.
● Awful international Technirama hodge-podge, adapted from a novel by Frank G Bengtsson, in which the Vikings wrestle with the Moors to lay hands on the legendary Golden Bell of St James (rather an anti-climax when it finally appears). Chief North African Poitier seems to be taking matters seriously, while Scandinavian rival Widmark clearly does not. Homolka overplays the role of Krok, a Viking shipbuilder, quite enjoyably. TJ

Long Shot

(1978, GB, 85 min)
d/p Maurice Hatton. *sc* Eoin McCann and the cast. *ph* Michael Davis (Edinburgh), Michael Dodds, Ivan Strasburg, Maurice Hatton (London), Teo Davis (Hollywood). *ed* Howard Sharp. *m* Terry Dougherty. *cast* Charles Gormley, Neville Smith, Ann Zelda, David Stone, Suzanne Danielle, Wim Wenders, Stephen Frears, Bill Forsyth, Jim Haines, Alan Bennett, John Boorman, Susannah York.
● An incestuous, half-hoax docu-farce, largely set against the background of the Edinburgh Festival, on the travails of setting up a British feature film. Scots producer Gormley hustles to package Neville Smith's commercial-sounding script about Aberdeen oilmen (called Gulf and Western), fighting to retain some semblance of meaning for the words 'independent' and 'British' in the face of temptations to grab an American director, Euro-market stars, and even the remotest whiff of Québecois finance. If you can imagine a picaresque comedy being forged from the repeated lament for a native cinema, this is it – and its hard-knocks humour probably succeeds in carrying it beyond an in-joke. PT

Longtime Companion

(1990, US, 99 min)
d Norman René. *p* Stan Wlodkowski. *sc* Craig Lucas. *ph* Tony Jannelli. *ed* Katherine Wenning. *pd* Andrew Jackness. *m* Gregg DeBelles. *cast* Stephen Caffrey, Patrick Cassidy, Brian Cousins, Bruce Davison, John Dossett, Mark Lamos, Dermot Mulroney, Mary-Louise Parker, Michael Schoeffling, Campbell Scott.
● Like much of the AIDS-related art now coming out of New York, this anodyne, apolitical movie about the impact of the virus on a group of well-heeled, white New Yorkers seems curiously remote from British experience. *Longtime Companion* (the euphemism for 'lover' in the obit columns of NY papers) opens on a Fire Island beach in the halcyon summer of 1981, just as news breaks of rare cancers in the gay community, and then leapfrogs through the following decade, taking one day from each year as a spot-sample of the HIV epidemic's grisly progress. Headed by Davison, Lamos and Caffrey, a stalwart cast of theatre actors attacks the bitty, anecdotal script with fair gusto and considerable conviction, building up an affecting picture of the collapse of a network of friends and lovers. But director René and scriptwriter Lucas spend all their energy avoiding sentimentality and pushing 'positive attitudes', when what the movie desperately needs is some larger perspective on the issues and the characters. The film is decent, no less but no more. TR

Long Time Dead

(2001, GB, 94 min)
d Marcus Adams. *p* James Gay-Rees. *sc* Eitan Arrusi, Daniel Bronzite, Chris Baker, Andy Day. *ph* Nic Morris. *ed* Lucia Zucchetti. *pd* Alison Riva. *m* Don Davis. *cast* Joe Absolom, Lara Belmont, Melanie Gutteridge, Lukas Haas, James Hillier, Alec Newman, Tom Bell, Michael Feast.
● Chilling out at a rave club, six students (including heart-throb Absolom from TV soap *EastEnders*) seek their kicks with a ouija board. The fun turns sour when the message 'all die' is spelled out, and soon the pals are being eliminated (off screen) by an unstoppable demonic djinn. There are a couple of jolts along the way, but the clunky dialogue undermines any real chills and a lame FX-heavy climax makes no sense at all. NY

Long Voyage Home, The

(1940, US, 105 min, b/w)
d John Ford. *sc* Dudley Nichols. *ph* Gregg Toland. *ed* Sherman Todd. *ad* James Basevi. *m* Richard Hageman. *cast* John Wayne, Thomas Mitchell, Ian Hunter, Ward Bond, Barry Fitzgerald, John Qualen, Arthur Shields, Mildred Natwick, Wilfrid Lawson.
● Adapted from four one-act plays by O'Neill, Ford's tribute to the plight of plucky seamen aboard a British freighter as WWII begins features his usual mixture of romanticised camaraderie and courage, boisterous braggadocio and brawling, and banal homespun philosophy. Beginning with an erotic skirmish with exotic island maidens, and ending with the death of Mitchell, shanghaied while drunkenly rescuing Wayne (oddly cast as an innocent Swedish farmlad) from the clutches of another crew, the film is chiefly noted for Gregg Toland's remarkable high-contrast camerawork which even manages to alleviate Ford's most maudlin excesses. None the less, a strong cast of risibly mixed accents copes gamely. GA

Long Way Home

(2002, US, 88 min)
d Peter Sollett. *p* Peter Sollett, Alain de la Mata, Robin O'Hara, Scott Macaulay. *sc* Peter Sollett. *ph* Tim Orr. *ed* Myron Kerstein. *pd* Judy Becker. *m* Roy Nathanson, Brad Jones. *cast* Victor Rasuk, Judy Marte, Melonie Diaz, Altagracia Guzman, Silvestre Rasuk, Krystal Rodriguez, Kevin Rivera.
● New York's Lower East Side: Like so many other Latino teens, Victor feels the need to impress the girls with smooth talk – conquest is everything. But then he falls for a local beauty, and his heartbreaker reputation won't wash any more. Meanwhile, his grandmother is blaming him for corrupting his younger brother and sister. A small, slightly too sweet, but otherwise wholly charming low key comedy about dating rituals, coming of age and familial responsibility, this succeeds thanks to winning performances from all concerned, an unpretentious, direct approach to narrative, and an air of authenticity that even informs the many fine one-liners. Delightful, and refreshingly free from cynicism and sensationalism. GA

Long Weekend

(1977, Aust, 97 min)
d/p Colin Eggleston. *sc* Everett de Roche. *ph* Vincent Monton. *ed* Brian Kavanagh. *pd* Larry Eastwood. *m* Michael Carlos. *cast* John Hargreaves, Briony Behets, Mike McEwen, Michael Aitkens, Roy Day, Sue Kiss von Soly.
● The message here is: mess with the primeval forces of Nature, and Nature will get you in the end. It seems that if you wife-swap, have abortions, or run over a kangaroo, you are going to have a lousy weekend. You won't be able to find the beach; ants will mess up your picnic; the chicken will go off pong, the spear-gun will go off ping; and God knows how the lager will stay cold. These and many other 'mysterious' events are so heavily laden with symbolism that any possibility of suspense or credibility is sunk even before Nature can start to get really raw. *Walkabout* and *The Last Wave* did it much better. DSi

Look Back in Anger

(1959, GB, 101 min, b/w)
d Tony Richardson. *p* Gordon LT Scott. *sc* Nigel Kneale. *ph* Oswald Morris. *ed* Richard Best. *ad* Peter Glazier. *m* John Addison. *cast* Richard Burton, Mary Ure, Claire Bloom, Edith Evans, Gary Raymond, Glen Byam Shaw, Phyllis Neilson-Terry, Donald Pleasence, George Devine.
● Archetypal squalid British realism in an effectively scripted and well acted version of John Osborne's now dated play about the miseries induced by angry young graduate Jimmy Porter, railing against society and taking out his frustrations on his long-suffering wife (Ure). Burton is too old for the part, and Richardson's turgidly literal approach is none too involving. GA

Looker

(1981, US, 94 min)
d Michael Crichton. *p* Howard Jeffrey. *sc* Michael Crichton. *ph* Paul Lohmann. *ed* Carl Kress. *pd* Dean Edward Mitzner. *m* Barry DeVorzon. *cast* Albert Finney, James Coburn, Susan Dey, Leigh Taylor-Young, Dorian Harewood, Tim Rossovich, Darryl Hickman.
● This tediously convoluted sci-fi thriller combines elements from *Westworld* and *Coma*, with Coburn as a tycoon experimenting with subliminally hypnotic TV commercials featuring replicated holograph models (the original girls, 'perfected' by Finney's plastic surgeon, are subsequently murdered for no apparent reason). Mostly pretty silly and uncertain whether to be tongue-in-cheek, it has one or two good scenes and some intriguing hardware, including the Looker (Light Ocular Oriented Kinetic Energetic Responsers) disorientation gun. TM

Looking for Angel (Tenshi no Rakuen)

(1999, Jap, 61 min)
d Akihiro Suzuki. *p* Toshiko Takashi. *sc* Akihiro Suzuki, Toshiko Takashi, Jun

Kurosawa. *ph* Jun Kurosawa. *ed* Akihiro Suzuki. *m* Kujun, Hiroyuki Oki, Koichi Fujishima. *cast* Koichi Imaizumi, Akira Suehiro, Hotaru Hazuki, Akira Kuroiwa, Hiroyuki Oki, Akihiro Suzuki.
● Producer/distributor Suzuki's directorial debut recaptures the waywardness of some New York underground movies of the '60s with its mix of sexual uncertainties, memories, regrets and all too fleeting friendships, not to mention its informal, jazz-riff visual style. Shinpei (Suehiro) is a country boy alone in Tokyo – maybe gay, maybe not – invited to a party by a girl he hasn't seen in a while. It turns out to be a wake for Takachi (Imaizumi), a gay guy who 'acted' in straight porn, now apparently murdered by a casual pick-up. During the night Shinpei pieces together Takachi's story: his friendship with a beautiful rent boy, his move to Kochi (where 'the boys are like angels'), his return to Tokyo – and his heart-breaking plea for gentleness on what turned out to be the last night of his life. Suzuki calls it 'anti-heterosexist', which seems about right. TR

Looking for Langston

(1988, GB, 45 min, b/w)
d Isaac Julien. *p* Nadine Marsh-Edwards. *sc* Isaac Julien. *ph* Nina Kellgren. *ed* Robert Hargreaves. *cast* Ben Ellison, Matthew Baidoo, John Wilson, Akim Magaji, Dencil Williams, Guy Burgess.
● A poetic visual fantasy of the lives of black gay men in '20s Harlem, shot in beautiful monochrome and packed with startling images of dream and desire. Scenes alternate between a dark, smoky club where men in formals dance and cruise, windswept beaches, secluded bedrooms, and scary alleyways where the same men make love, while the poetry of Langston Hughes and contemporary black gay writer Essex Hemphill meditates on the aesthetics of sexual desire. It may sound painfully arty, but the images are fresh and exciting enough to sweep away any such reservations. RS

Looking for Mr Goodbar

(1977, US, 136 min)
d Richard Brooks. *p* Freddie Fields. *sc* Richard Brooks. *ph* William A Fraker. *ed* George Grenville. *ad* Edward C Carfagno. *m* Artie Kane. *cast* Diane Keaton, Tuesday Weld, William Atherton, Richard Kiley, Richard Gere, Alain Feinstein, Tom Berenger, Julius Harris, LeVar Burton, Brian Dennehy.
● Judith Rossner's calculated bestseller, about a contemporary woman's sexuality and her 'descent' into the world of New York singles bars, gets what it deserves in this old-fashioned adaptation. Behind the apparent sexual frankness lurks the familiar spectre of moral puritanism, while Brooks' script disastrously employs two standard Hollywood bulwarks as major reference points: cod Freud and American Gothic. Theresa (Keaton) hangs out in bars cruising for men, fuelled with the certain knowledge that, starting with her father, all men are pricks. Her dislocated sexuality is clumsily related back to her family: with cartoon loud-mouth Irish bigot cop for a father, Tuesday Weld as an air-hostess sister, memories of a crippled childhood and suspicions of hereditary illness, it could hardly be otherwise. As a result, Theresa is merely acted upon, an American *Emmanuelle* whose dreary promiscuity is driven on guilt. Only Diane Keaton's performance counters the overall heavy-handedness. CPe

Looking for Richard

(1996, US, 112 min)
d Al Pacino. *p* Michael Hadge, Al Pacino. *ph* Robert Leacock. *ed* Pasquale Buba, William A Anderson, Ned Bastille. *ad* Kevin Ritter. *m* Howard Shore. *with* Al Pacino, Kevin Spacey, Winona Ryder, Alec Baldwin, Harris Yulin, Aidan Quinn, John Gielgud, Vanessa Redgrave, Kenneth Branagh, Kevin Kline, Peter Brook, James Earl Jones, Rosemary Harris, Estelle Parsons.
● Pacino's first film as writer/director is a marvellously intelligent, witty and imaginative exploration of the problems faced by anyone wishing to act in Shakespeare or translate the plays to film. The movie's part documentary, part adaptation of *Richard III*: Pacino scours the streets of New York for vox-pop comments on the playwright; elicits opinions from academics, critics and celebrated thesps on questions of performance, the text and the history behind it; holds readings and rehearsals; and provides dramatic renditions of key scenes. Besides offering an enthralling abridged account of the play, Pacino's film is a hugely informative and entertaining attempt to measure Shakespeare's accessibility and value to the modern world. Whether visiting Stratford, arguing with co-writer Frederic Kimball or producer Michael Hadge, allowing a derelict to wax lyrical about Shakespeare's poetry, or staging a sparsely populated but impressively cinematic version of the climactic battle on Bosworth Field, Pacino seduces us with his enthusiasm, energy and passion. GA

Looking Glass War, The

(1969, GB, 107 min)
d Frank R Pierson. *p* John Box. *sc* Frank R Pierson. *ph* Austin Dempster. *ed* Willy Kemplen. *ad* Terence Marsh. *m* Wally Stott. *cast* Christopher Jones, Pia Degermark, Ralph Richardson, Anthony Hopkins, Paul Rogers, Susan George, Ray McAnally, Robert Urquhart, Maxine Audley, Anna Massey.
● Typically convoluted Cold War espionage antics from Le Carré. Fine and quirky while the young Polish defector (Jones) selected as a pawn in the espionage game is guided through his training process by a series of bored eccentrics, with delicious performances from Rogers and Richardson (one nursing a permanent cough, the other a mad glint in his eye) as the Blimpish security chiefs hankering for the good old days when they weren't just a Civil Service backwater, and dreaming of the grand come-back they are busily setting in motion. But with the mission itself comes a swift descent into banal action, totally tedious as the sense of authenticity is dissipated in a welter of incredibly silly dialogue spoken by incredibly silly characters. TM

Look Me in the Eye

(1994, GB, 80 min)
d Nick Ward. *p* Simon Relph. *sc* Nick Ward. *ph* Seamus McGarvey. *ed* Jane Headland. *pd* Teresa McCann. *m* Nick Russell-Pavier. *cast* Caroline Catz, Seamus Gubbins, Barnaby Stone, Mat Patresi, Kelly Hunter, Alan Cooke, John Sandford.
● A woman allows herself to be picked up by a mysterious photographer. She strips slowly for his camera, but he walks out when she tries to consummate the relationship. A schoolteacher, recently married, Ruth is both exhibitionist and voyeur, a fantasist driven to act out her desires. Returning to the photographer's studio, she spies on him making love to a prostitute and, when they've gone, recreates the scene by seducing an estate agent. Alone, she tears the place apart. Ward's second film mines female sexual psychology in the guise of enigmatic melodrama. The result is intriguing, but not entirely convincing. Despite a bold central performance from Catz (who doubles as the prostitute), it's hard to see what triggers the teacher's increasingly reckless behaviour, while Stone's photographer remains a cipher, perhaps a figment of Ruth's over-heated imagination. Ward is good on the seedy hotels and sex shops around King's Cross. There's almost a surfeit of texture – you can practically sniff the wall-paper, taste the chemical skin of Seamus McGarvey's cinematography. Ultimately, though, the film proves too tricky for its own good. A heady, enigmatic brew all the same. TCh

Looks and Smiles

(1981, GB, 104 min, b/w)
d Kenneth Loach. *p* Irving Teitelbaum. *sc* Barry Hines. *ph* Chris Menges. *ed* Steve Singleton. *ad* Martin Johnson. *m* Marc Wilkinson, Richard and the Taxmen. *cast* Graham Green, Carolyn Nicholson, Tony Pitts, Roy Haywood, Phil Askham, pam Darrell, Tracey Goodlad.
● Sheffield, 1980: the evening paper warns of yet more redundancies in the steel industry, and the choice before school leavers Alan and Mick is either the forces or the dole. Alan (Pitts) enlists and is posted to Belfast, where he develops a taste for duffing up Catholics. Mick (Green) stays at home, tinkers with his bike, scours the sits vac, and takes up with shop-girl Karen (Nicholson) amid rising despair. Familiar Loach territory, and presented in characteristically spartan documentary style. Excellent performances from the three principals (all amateurs), resolutely unfussy black-and-white photography by Chris Menges, and a complete absence of self-consciousness on either side of the camera add up to a quietly devastating portrayal of human waste. JP

Look Who's Talking

(1989, US, 96 min)
d Amy Heckerling. *p* Jonathan D Krane. *sc* Amy Heckerling. *ph* Thomas Del Ruth. *ed* Debra Chiate. *ad* Reuben Freed, Graeme Murray. *m* David Kitay. *cast* John Travolta, Kirstie Alley, Olympia Dukakis, George Segal, Abe Vigoda, Louis Heckerling.
● From the opening shots of wriggling white tadpoles swimming through a neon womb, Amy Heckerling tackles motherhood humorously and head on, alternating between mucky-diaper realism and bright fantasy. Baby Mikey comes complete with snappy personality and the streetwise voice of Bruce Willis. Slapdash mum Mollie (Alley, a convincingly falliable parent) falls out with the already married father (Segal) just before the birth, and is tended instead by a taxi-driver who ferries her to hospital. Baby instantly likes the look of feckless cabbie James (Travolta), but Mollie is resistant to true love, especially when *her* mum (the admirable Dukakis) is striving to fix her up with someone more respectable. It's what-is-a-good-father time. Of course, we know it's the guy that's poor but *fun*. Heckerling directs this dippy but delightful film with a light, zany touch and a reasonably low yuck-factor (dribbles notwithstanding). Particularly cute is the way Travolta sends up his most famous role in a parodic disco dance routine. SFe

Look Who's Talking Now

(1993, US, 95 min)
d Tom Ropelewski. *p* Jonathan D Krane. *sc* Tom Ropelewski, Leslie Dixon. *ph* Oliver Stapleton. *ed* Michael A Stevenson, Harry Hitner. *pd* Michael Bolton. *m* William Ross. *cast* John Travolta, Kirstie Alley, Olympia Dukakis, Lysette Anthony, David Gallagher, Tabitha Lupien, George Segal.
● Travolta and Alley return as doting parents James and Mollie Ubriacco, their two kids now firmly ensconced in infanthood and the household recently extended by the arrival of mongrel Rocks – whose innermost thoughts are voiced by gruff Danny DeVito. The plot arrives in the shape of Lysette Anthony's power businesswoman Samantha, perky pilot James's new boss and keen to do more than fly with him. The action cranks itself up into a dilemma: Will 'work' prevent dad from spending the Yuletide period with the family? Comic interest is sustained by the entrance of prissy poodle Daphne (voice-over: Diane Keaton), but the preponderance of nudging innuendo was enough to earn the film a '12' certificate, thus excluding the audience of younger children who might otherwise have enjoyed the movie. TJ

Look Who's Talking Too

(1990, US, 80 min)
d Amy Heckerling. *p* Jonathan D Krane. *sc* Amy Heckerling, Neal Israel. *ph* Thomas Del Ruth. *ed* Debra Chiate. *pd* Reuben Freed. *m* David Kitay. *cast* John Travolta, Kirstie Alley, Olympia Dukakis, Elias Koteas, Twink Kaplan.
● Mikey, the tot with the Bruce Willis voice-over, is about to acquire a sister (thoughts by Roseanne Barr). 'Don't you just hate it when you get your head caught in your placenta?' muses the yet-to-be-born sprog. That's about as good as the gags get in this uninspired sequel to 1989's blockbuster. The story picks up with accountant Mollie (Alley) and cabbie James (Travolta) semi-settled in domestic bliss. But after the birth of their daughter, problems start to escalate: will James ever realise his dream to become an airline pilot and thus earn a decent salary? Will Mikey make it through toilet training? And when will Mollie stop giving money to her no-good, gun-crazy brother (Koteas)? This is formulaic stuff as the once-happy couple bicker incessantly, with a fire and rainstorm thrown in to lend a sense of danger when complacency threatens to become overwhelming. Crucially, this forgettable sequel lacks its predecessor's lively pace and comic tension. CM

Loophole

(1980, GB, 105 min)
d John Quested. *p* Julian Holloway, David Korda. *sc* Jonathan Hales. *ph* Michael Reed. *ed* Ralph Sheldon. *pd* Syd Cain. *m* Lalo Schifrin.

cast Albert Finney, Martin Sheen, Susannah York, Colin Blakely, Jonathan Pryce, Robert Morley, Alfred Lynch, Christopher Guard.
● This pedestrian bank heist 'thriller', with its resolutely old-fashioned air bolstered by the token presence of an American star (Sheen) and the crushing earnestness with which everyone else approaches their hackneyed roles as if they were fresh-minted, was released to critical and box-office responses of consensual indifference. London's sewers (though which the bank is approached, and which are of course menaced by a rainstorm flood) don't have quite the cinematic resonance of LA's storm drains, and only tend to throw the mind even further back and off course to numerous POW tunnel movies. PT

Loose Cannons

(1990, US, 93 min)
d Bob Clark. *p* Aaron Spelling, Alan Greisman. *sc* Richard Matheson, Richard Christian Matheson, Bob Clark. *ph* Reginald H Morris. *ed* Stan Cole. *ad* Harry Pottle. *m* Paul Zaza. *cast* Dan Aykroyd, Gene Hackman, Dom DeLuise, Ronny Cox, Nancy Travis, Robert Prosky, Paul Koslo, Dick O'Neill, Jan Triska, David Alan Grier.
● A reeking stinker of a comedy: Aykroyd and Hackman are Washington, DC, cops searching for a Nazi sex film in which a West German politician is caught with his pants down. Mossad agents, pornographers and rabbis all cross their path, without eliciting a laugh between them. From the director of *Porky's* I and II, but this one didn't hit pay dirt. GM

Loose Connections

(1983, GB, 96 min)
d Richard Eyre. *p* Simon Perry. *sc* Maggie Brooks. *ph* Clive Tickner. *ed* David Martin. *ad* Jamie Leonard. *m* Dominic Muldowney. *cast* Lindsay Duncan, Stephen Rea, Carole Harrison, Frances Low, Jan Niklas, Gary Olsen, Robbie Coltrane, Andy De La Tour.
● A welcome attempt to revive and update – steering clear of crass stereotypes – the bitter-sweet romance of classics like *I Was a Male War Bride* and the Tracy-Hepburn vehicles. Having built her own car, dogmatic feminist Sally drives off to Munich, accompanied by mild chauvinist Harry, who fits none of her requirements that her co-driver be vegetarian, gay and German-speaking. As their odyssey turns into a series of disasters, their differences (in class, education and attitudes to sex) flare up and then fizzle out under the benevolent influence of Glenfiddich. Maggie Brooks' script, from her own novel, may be a mite too schematic, and in the first half creates a Sally too cold and condescending to win much sympathy, but Duncan and Rea are both impressive. Best of all, however, is the portrayal of the English abroad: Bedford boozers in Rhineland bierkellers, Liverpool loonies celebrating after a soccer victory, and fleeting bonhomie between strangers stranded in strange lands are all wittily and subtly observed. GA

Loot

(1970, GB, 101 min)
d Silvio Narizzano. *p* Arthur Lewis. *sc* Ray Galton, Alan Simpson. *ph* Austin Dempster. *ed* Martin Charles. *ad* Anthony Pratt. *songs* Keith Mansfield, Richard Willing-Denton. *cast* Richard Attenborough, Lee Remick, Hywel Bennett, Milo O'Shea, Roy Holder, Dick Emery, Joe Lynch, Harold Innocent.
● A sad example of the process of literary castration. By the time Galton and Simpson's script (which adds 'comic' scenes like a police bulldozer destroying a garden of gnomes and removes the more outrageous lines from Joe Orton's play) has passed through Narizzano's hands, all that is left is a caricature of the original. In place of the absurdity and emotional intensity, a collection of British character actors and a couple of stars go through their paces while the director milks Orton's story of misplaced affection and an elusive corpse for all it's worth. PH

Lord Camber's Ladies

(1932, GB, 80 min, b/w)
d Benn W Levy. *p* Alfred Hitchcock. *sc* Edwin Greenwood, Gilbert Wakefield, Benn W Levy. *ph* James Wilson. *ad* David Rawnsley. *cast* Gerald du Maurier, Gertrude Lawrence, Benita Hume, Nigel Bruce, Clare Greet, A Bromley Davenport.
● Swerving in and out of an assortment of subgenres (showbiz comedy, terminal illness weepie, hospital whodunit), wildly inconsistent in tone, this quite entertaining appendage to Hitchcock's filmography shows absolutely no sign of any masterly guiding hand. An adaptation of HA Vachell's 1915 play, it's most notable for its casting. Randy rotter Lord Camber is played by Nigel Bruce, usually the bumbling comic relief. Performing one number only, Gertrude Lawrence combines pleasingly off-hand insolence with the purest ham. Most interesting is du Maurier (Daphne's dad). Though aging and visually nondescript, he instantly takes control of everything going on around him. His movements are extraordinary, a testament to decades of West End and Broadway domination. BBa

Lord Jim

(1964, GB, 154 min)
d/p/sc Richard Brooks. *ph* Freddie Young. *ed* Alan Osbiston. *pd* Geoffrey Drake. *m* Bronislau Kaper. *cast* Peter O'Toole, Paul Lukas, Daliah Lavi, Eli Wallach, Curd Jürgens, James Mason, Akim Tamiroff, Jack Hawkins, Ichizo Itami, Jack MacGowran, Christian Marquand.
● Brooks' adaptation of Conrad's novel is immeasurably better than its reputation, and a scene towards the end – on a raft in the middle of a fog-bound river as O'Toole's Jim and Mason's Gentleman Brown discuss the age of the world and the price of evil – is an extraordinary attempt to convey Conradian metaphysics. 'Attempt', because Brooks is not entirely successful, with a major structural flaw (as in the novel itself) when the story ends two-thirds of the way through and has to start up again. Nevertheless, the film's pleasures far outweigh its inadequacies: Freddie Young's photography does for the Asian jungles what he did for the desert in *Lawrence of Arabia*, and the same might be said in praise of O'Toole's all-aquiver, neurotic performance. ATu

Lord Love a Duck

(1965, US, 105 min, b/w)
d/p George Axelrod. *sc* Larry H Johnson, George Axelrod. *ph* Daniel L Fapp. *ed* William A Lyon. *ad* Malcolm Brown. *m* Neal Hefti. *cast* Roddy McDowall, Tuesday Weld, Lola Albright, Martin West, Ruth Gordon, Max Showalter, Harvey Korman, Martin Gabel.
● Axelrod's patchy but often brilliant first attempt at direction: a kooky fantasy, very funny in its satire of contemporary teen morals and mores. McDowall plays a high school student of enormous IQ and fabulous powers, which he exercises in order to grant a pretty co-ed (Weld) her every heart's desire, starting with the thirteen cashmere sweaters she requires to join an exclusive sorority, and ending with a husband whom he obligingly murders to leave her free to realise her true dream of movie stardom. Whereupon, realising he did it all for love, he ends up in the booby-hatch, happily dictating his memoirs. Taking in some delicious side-swipes at the 'Beach Blanket' cycle, Axelrod reveals much the same penchant (and talent) for cartoon-style sight gags as Tashlin, and coaxes a marvellous trio of variations on the American female from Tuesday Weld, Lola Albright and Ruth Gordon. Daniel Fapp's stunningly cool, clear monochrome camerawork is also a distinct plus. TM

Lord of Illusions

(1995, US, 122 min)
d Clive Barker. *p* JoAnne Sellar, Clive Barker. *sc* Clive Barker. *ph* Ron Schmidt. *ed* Alan Baumgarten. *ad* Stephen Hardie. *m* Simon Boswell. *cast* Scott Bakula, Kevin J O'Connor, Famke Janssen, Vincent Schiavelli, Daniel Von Bargen, Barry Del Sherman, Sheila Tousey.
● Barker's full-blooded adaptation of his story *The Last Illusion* arrives in Britain on video as a 'director's cut', with an extra 12 minutes, but since it's not letter-boxed, half the film's missing anyway. Hired by the enigmatic Dorothea (Janssen) to look out for her illusionist husband, Philip Swann (O'Connor), private eye Harry D'Amour (Bakula) enters a world where magic and illusion imperceptibly mingle. At the heart of the mystery is another of Barker's Faustian pacts: having learned his craft from religious cult leader Nix (Von Bargen), Swann recanted and sent Nix into temporary limbo. Now another Nix acolyte, the effete Butterfield (Sherman), has engineered his vengeful mentor's resurrection. Barker feels that the extra scenes flesh out the characters and explain their motivations, but much of this expository detail could be inferred from the studio's shorter cut. More fascinating are the imaginatively perverse images, the parallels between magic and cinematic illusion, and a gay subtext that presents the central struggle as a sexual/professional ménage à trois involving Nix, his heir apparent, Swann, and the aspiring Butterfield. NF

Lord of the Dance

(1985, Fr/Switz/WGer, 113 min)
d Richard Kohn.
● An excellent documentary, filmed at the Thubten Choling Monastery, high on the remote northern slopes of Everest, where in a form unchanged for over 400 years, the followers of the Tibetan Buddhist 'Diamond Path' have performed their spectacular and beautiful religious dance festival known as 'Mani-Rimdu': a three-week ceremony of empowerment, ritual and celebration wherein the initiates assume the form of 'Lord of the Dance' and annually banish the destructive spiritual forces of the universe. WH

Lord of the Flies

(1963, GB, 91 min, b/w)
d Peter Brook. *p* Lewis Allen. *sc* Peter Brook. *ph* Tom Hollyman, Gerald Fiel. *ed* Peter Brook, Gerald Feil, Jean-Claude Lubtchansky. *m* Raymond Leppard. *cast* James Aubrey, Tom Chapin, Hugh Edwards, Roger Elwin, Tom Gaman.
● An underrated adaptation of William Golding's 1954 novel about a gang of English schoolboys stranded on a desert island after a nuclear holocaust. At first their unscheduled outward bound adventure is a great wheeze. But then things degenerate into tribal warfare based on class differences – the public school chaps are the hunters, and the oicks are virtual slaves. Golding's novel took Darwin's theories of natural selection to their ultimate conclusion, and while the apocalyptic parable is hardly the subtlest ever devised, the imagistic prose made it a devastating one. Brook knows he can't have his 10- to 12-year-olds mouthing philosophical and poetic paragraphs, so he shoots it like a documentary, overcoming the starvation budget, the location problems, and the sometimes awkward performances. However, the principals are excellent: Aubrey's Ralph, who just about keeps his dignity while all around are losing theirs, Chapin's beastly Jack, and Edwards' tragic Piggy, who loses his glasses and then his life. ATu

Lord of the Flies

(1990, US, 90 min)
d Harry Hook. *p* Ross Milloy. *sc* Sara Schiff. *ph* Martin Fuhrer. *ed* Tom Priestley, Harry Hook. *pd* Jamie Leonard. *m* Philippe Sarde. *cast* Balthazar Getty, Chris Furrh, Danuel Pipoly, Andrew Taft, Edward Taft, Gary Rule.
● In this second version of William Golding's novel, a group of cadets from an American military school are stranded on a desert island, along with the wounded pilot, after their plane crashes. Eventually the camp divides; Ralph (Getty) and Piggy (Pipoly) represent the values imposed by adults and civilisation; while they struggle to maintain a signal fire, Jack (Furrh) and his band of hunters, giving way to more primitive impulses, run rampage and turn murderous. The film, simplistically assuming the book's central metaphor to be imperialism – hence the military slant – retains the bare bones of Gollding's narrative, but that's all. There's little attempt to hint at the deeper issues, while the revelatory moment when the impaled pig's head looms in the clearing to reveal man's inner darkness, is merely flat. Executive producer Lewis Allen also produced Peter Brook's superior 1963 version; he took on the project after learning that TV producers planned a remake with an 'upbeat ending'. This is better than that, but not nearly good enough. CM

Lord of the Rings, The

(1978, US, 133 min)
d Ralph Bakshi. *p* Saul Zaentz. *sc* Chris Conkling, Peter S Beagle. *ph* Timoth Galfas. *ed* Donald W Ernest. *m* Leonard Rosenman. *cast* voices: Christopher Guard, William Squire, Michael Scholes, John Hurt, Simon Chandler, Dominic Guard, Norman Bird.

●Disney first held the rights to Tolkien's epic in the late '50s, so it's surprising that we had to wait so long, particularly since Kubrick and Boorman both tried unsuccessfully to set up productions. Mercifully, the book has escaped the typical Disney demolition; Bakshi's version, using animation and live-action tracings, is uniformly excellent, sticking closely to the original text and visually echoing many of Tolkien's own drawings. Use of British voices, together with the sensitive Leonard Rosenman sound-track, augments the impression of authenticity; and Bakshi wisely chose to leave Vol. 3 for a later date, which allows him to avoid simplification to the point of superficiality. NFe

Lord of the Rings: The Fellowship of the Ring, The (100)

(2001, US/NZ, 178 min)
d Peter Jackson. *p* Barry M Osborne, Peter Jackson, Fran Walsh, Tim Sanders. *sc* Fran Walsh, Philippa Boyens, Peter Jackson. *ph* Andrew Lesnie. *ed* John Gilbert. *pd* Grant Major. *m* Howard Shore. *cast* Elijah Wood, Ian McKellen, Liv Tyler, Viggo Mortensen, Sean Astin, Cate Blanchett, John Rhys-Davies, Billy Boyd, Dominic Monaghan, Orlando Bloom, Christopher Lee, Hugo Weaving, Sean Bean, Ian Holm, Andy Serkis.

●Unlike so many big budget productions, the first movie instalment of JRR Tolkien's Middle Earth trilogy doesn't condescend to a teenage audience, but creates a sophisticated universe which abides by its own laws: a primordial world older than history and legend, back in the realm of myth. Here young hobbit Frodo Baggins (Wood) comes into possession of the ring of power – a talisman of evil so potent it corrupts everyone who touches it. Under the guidance of the wizard Gandalf (McKellen), Frodo escapes the clutches of the fearsome ring wraiths along with his faithful friend Sam (Astin), and heads for the kingdom of the elves, where they hope to thwart the encroaching forces of doom. Mostly, the film makes light work of Tolkien's richly Celtic imagination. You don't so much admire its virtuoso camerawork as lose yourself in the grandeur of the Gothic design, the bucolic Shire and mountain ranges riddled with mines and fire pits. Granted, there's a sermonising element which invites parody, but it never wants for menace (parents should probably steer young children clear). In unveiling the Holy Grail for action-fantasy aficionados, director and co-writer Peter Jackson has begun a series to rival *Star Wars* in the pantheon. TCh

Lords of Discipline, The

(1982, US, 103 min)
d Franc Roddam. *p* Herb Jaffe, Gabriel Katzka. *sc* Thomas Pope, Lloyd Fonvielle. *ph* Brian Tufano. *ed* Michael Ellis. *pd* John Graysmark. *m* Howard Blake. *cast* David Keith, Robert Prosky, GD Spradlin, Barbara Babcock, Michael Biehn, Rick Rossovich, John Lavachielli, Bill Paxton.

●Another in that most unlikely of 1980s genres: the US military college saga, this time a liberal conspiracy thriller, pitting its hero against the racist secret society which controls the college. If the blend doesn't quite work, it is no fault of Roddam, who gives the film the pace, energy and excitement he instilled into the action sequences of *Quadrophenia*. In the first half, Roddam admirably conveys the notion of an enclosed world with its own insane rules and rituals; but as the conspiracy format becomes more obvious, the sheer confinement of the setting and period begins to work heavily against the film, closing down its narrative options precisely at the point when, in this kind of thriller, you want them to open up. DP

Lords of Flatbush, The

(1974, US, 84 min)
d Stephen F Verona, Martin Davidson. *p* Stephen F Verona. *sc* Stephen F Verona, Gayle Glecker, Martin Davidson. *ph* Joseph Mangine, Edward Lachman. *ed* Stan Siegel, Muffie Meyer. *ad* Glenda Miller. *m* Joe Brooks. *cast* Perry King, Sylvester Stallone, Henry Winkler, Paul Mace, Susan Blakely, Maria Smith, Renée Paris, Paul Jabara, Ray Sharkey, Armand Assante.

●A small masterpiece that places the mood and general ethos of the '50s with absolute precision and total affection. The Lords are a teenage high school leather gang in Brooklyn – or as they winningly call themselves, 'a social and athletic club'. The film observes their relationships and muffed sexual encounters over some months in 1958, the year one of their number gets married. Verona and Davidson direct superbly – the film's silences are every bit as telling as the perfectly judged dialogue – and it is shot and edited with a welcome degree of wit. Above all, the characters are all real, rather than academic or sentimental recreations. VG

Lorenzo's Oil

(1992, US, 135 min)
d George Miller. *p* Doug Miller, George Mitchell. *sc* George Miller, Nick Enright. *ph* John Seale. *ed* Richard Francis-Bruce, Marcus D'Arcy, Lee Smith. *pd* Kristi Zea. *cast* Nick Nolte, Susan Sarandon, Peter Ustinov, Kathleen Wilhoite, Gerry Bamman, Margo Martindale, James Rebhorn, Ann Hearn, Maduka Steady.

●Miller's 'true story' medical drama is based on the case of the Odones, an economist and his linguist wife, whose five-year-old son Lorenzo was diagnosed as having ALD, a degenerative, quickly fatal, and little understood brain disease. The couple (Nolte and Sarandon) refuse to accept the inevitable, abandon work to care for their son at home, and set about learning biochemistry to find a cure, in so doing taking on the medical profession and the received wisdom of the charity organisations. The film comes over as a tour de force version of the disease-of-the-week TV movie: half scientific detective story, half domestic drama, replete with scenes of suffering. Throughout, Miller points up every least thing: religious symbolism, snow-dusted Christmas windows for pathos, spinning news headlines, and swirling, diving camera movements. Finally, it begins to seem a little dishonest and self-conscious, as if Miller were trying to make an AIDS movie with hope and a positive ending. The night of San Lorenzo, after all, is the night when wishes come true. WH

Loser

(1991, US, 83 min)
d Erik Burke. *p* Steve Deshle. *sc* Erik Burke. *ph* John Shepphird. *ed* Erik Burke. *pd* Ruth Amman. *m* Joey Harrow, Matthew Fritz. *cast* Brendan Kelly, John Salemmo, Bernice De Leo, Nadine Miral.

●This punchy, low-rent New York comedy turns the yuppie nightmare genre on its head by taking a lunkheaded blue-collar no-hoper and dropping him into the heat of Manhattan glitzery. Hank (the amiably lumbering Kelly) is at the bottom of the heap – out of work, out of money, out of love – with only his klutz of a wide-boy buddy for comfort. Then his number comes up in the lottery, and everyone wants to know him. You know from the start that there has to be a sting in store, but while you wait it's a very enjoyable ride. Crammed with larger-than-life stereotypes – hopheads, hustlers and ludicrous hipsters – it treads a narrow line between cracker barrel humanism and gleeful misanthropy, but mainly it exudes delight at its own cheap and cheerful sense of fun. JRo

Loser

(2000, US, 95 min)
d Amy Heckerling. *p* Amy Heckerling, Twink Caplan. *sc* Amy Heckerling. *ph* Rob Hahn. *ed* Debra Chiate. *pd* Steven Jordan. *m* David Kitay. *cast* Jason Biggs, Mena Suvari, Zak Orth, Tom Sadoski, Jimmi Simpson, Greg Kinnear, Dan Aykroyd, Twink Caplan, Colleen Camp.

●That this so neatly expounds the changeless themes of US teen romance is a reflection of its creator's credentials: Heckerling graduated with the 1982 classic *Fast Times at Ridgemont High* and pulled teen cinema back to form in the mid-'90s with *Clueless*. Paul (Biggs) moves to NY from Hicksville, carrying comforting adages from Pa (Aykroyd). He at once stands out as a socially awkward scholarship student, dissed by his camp rich-kid roommates. Meanwhile, sparky Dora (Suvari) struggles with college fees and conducts a clandestine affair with tutor Kinnear. These opposites find refuge in one another. The film is less explicitly bawdy than others of its ilk, and its sentimentalism is cut with wit. There are references to youth dramas such as *My So-Called Life*, angsty rockers Everclear make a noisy cameo, and Paul admits his Sarah McLachlan T-shirt is seriously uncool. *American Beauty* starlet Suvari even sneaks into Sam Mendes' Broadway production of *Cabaret*. Heckerling has described *Losers* as 'the anti-*Clueless*', but it's also an entertaining fantasy. And on screen, being the outsider is always a plus. AHa

Loser Takes All

(1956, GB, 88 min)
d Ken Annakin. *p* John Stafford. *sc* Graham Greene. *ph* Georges Périnal. *ed* Jean Barker. *ad* John Howell. *m* Alessandro Cicognini. *cast* Rossano Brazzi, Glynis Johns, Tony Britton, Robert Morley, Albert Lieven, Felix Aylmer, AE Matthews, Joyce Carey, Geoffrey Keen.

●Graham Greene adapted his own least interesting novella for the screen, but later admitted that the result was 'a disaster'. The film is stymied by the miscasting of Rossano Brazzi as the middle-aged accountant who loses his fiancée Johns when he breaks the bank at Monte Carlo (understandably, Greene wanted Alec Guinness for the part). Filmed in 'Scope for no apparent reason; remade almost as indifferently in 1990 as *Strike It Rich*. TCh

Losin' It

(1983, US, 100 min)
d Curtis Hanson. *p* Bryan Gindoff, Hannah Hempstead. *sc* Bill L Norton. *ph* Gilbert Taylor. *ed* Richard Halsey. *pd* Robb Wilson-King. *m* Ken Wannberg. *cast* Tom Cruise, Jackie Earle Haley, John Stockwell, John P Navin Jr, Shelley Long, Henry Darrow, Hector Elias.

●Sundry clean-cut teens head South of the Border to get laid. End of story really, since this is well short of hardcore country. Write your own movie including the following: there's a semi-experienced stud, a boasting faker, a nerd and a sincere sensitive one, plus a woman tagging along for a Tijuana divorce. The movie you think up will probably be more entertaining than this amiable, but entirely predictable trifle. Formerly of interest to Cruise-completists only, now with an extended life thanks to Hanson's ascension to the directorial A-list. DO

Los Olvidados

see Olvidados, Los

Loss of Innocence

see Greengage Summer, The

Loss of Sexual Innocence, The

(1998, US/GB, 106 min)
d Mike Figgis. *p* Mike Figgis, Annie Stewart. *sc* Mike Figgis. *ph* Benoît Delhomme. *ed* Matthew Wood. *pd* (Newcastle) Jessica Worrall, Mark Long, (Italy) Giorgio Desideri. *m* Mike Figgis. *cast* Julian Sands, Saffron Burrows, Stefano Dionisi, Kelly MacDonald, Gina McKee, Jonathan Rhys-Meyers, Bernard Hill, Rossy De Palma, Red Mullet [Mike Figgis].

●Figgis's long nurtured compendium of linked autobiographical stories sees him break for experimental ground. Framed by an inversion of the tale of Adam and Eve set in his childhood home of East Africa, it depicts episodes in the life of Nic (blue-remembered '50s Carlisle streets; Rhys-Meyers having his first sexual experiences in '60s Newcastle; in the present, Sands making documentaries in Tunisia) to weave a tapestry of memories, insights and reflections. It's a fascinating, brave, teeming inventory, notebook and memoir which, despite occasional melancholy episodes, mostly invokes the spirit of Godard in its restless, risk-taking energy. In many ways it reads as a child's lament, something echoed by the emotive use of solo piano and, in the childhood/adolescent sequences, by the saturated colour effects. Style is driven by content. The endgame of Nic's marriage is shot entirely from outside the wintry window of the farmhouse home; and his meeting with enigmatic twin females (Burrows) is imbued with Kieslowskian mystery. WH

Lost and Found

(1979, GB, 105 min)
d/p Melvin Frank. *sc* Melvin Frank, Jack Rose. *ph* Douglas Slocombe. *ed* Bill Butler. *pd* Trevor Williams. *m* John Cameron. *cast* George Segal,

Glenda Jackson, Maureen Stapleton, Hollis McLaren, John Cunningham, Paul Sorvino, John Candy, Martin Short.
●A belated and redundant re-teaming of *Touch of Class* pair Segal and Jackson has them sparring interminably through married life, to increasingly wearying effect. She gets soft-focus close-ups; both get witless lines. If life is indeed the 'crock of shit' that well-read taxi-driver Sorvino helpfully explains it to be, this movie's the perfect mirror.

Lost Angels (aka The Road Home)

(1989, US, 116 min)
d Hugh Hudson. *p* Howard Rosenman, Thomas Baer. *sc* Michael Weller.*ph* Juan Ruiz-Anchia. *ed* David Gladwell.*pd* Assheton Gorton. *m* Philippe Sarde.*cast* Donald Sutherland, Adam Horovitz,Amy Locane, Don Bloomfield, Celia Weston, Graham Beckel, Patricia Richardson, Kevin Tighe, Nina Siemaszko.
●In Hudson's characteristically flashy foray into the cinema of delinquency, Horovitz (of the Beastie Boys) plays an LA brat repeatedly driven to commit antisocial acts of violence by his middle class folks: mom and stepdad are assholes, the brother he idolises is already well on the road to ruin, and dad naturally is an ex-cop. No wonder the boy's a nihilist. Girls, for once, offer scant succour, since Locane, met at a corrective centre, is not only into drugs but suffers from hammily mobile facial grimaces. Salvation is at hand, however, in the hapless form of Dr Sutherland, the traditionally troubled good guy, a shrink forever at odds with the money-obsessed psychotherapy establishment. For all Hudson's determination to tell it like it is (inmates eat own shit – shock!), and his evident love of bombastic flourishes (craning camera, lotsa loud music, weirdo slo-mo), the film serves up only trite melodrama and hackneyed moral homilies. GA

Lost Boys, The

(1987, US, 97 min)
d Joel Schumacher. *p* Harvey Bernhard. *sc* Janice Fischer, James Jeremias. Jeffrey Boam. *ph* Michael Chapman. *ed* Robert Brown. *pd* Bo Welch. *m* Thomas Newman. *cast* Jason Patric, Corey Haim, Dianne Wiest, Barnard Hughes, Edward Herrmann, Kiefer Sutherland, Jami Gertz, Corey Feldman.
●This pathetic attempt at comic horror (deriving from an initial project to rework *Peter Pan* in vampiric terms) not only plays fast and loose with vampire mythology but also fails to deliver either frights or laughs. Soon after moving to the coastal town of Santa Clara with his mother (Wiest) and elder brother Michael (Patric), young MTV addict Sam (Haim) is warned against vampires by the two Goonies who run the local comic shop. Lured to a wild cave party, Michael gets his first taste of blood (out of a bottle?). Forewarned is forearmed, however, and when Michael starts wearing shades, sleeping all day and flying around, Sam and the comic kids reach for the holy water, garlic and wooden stakes. Directed with a cavalier disregard for intelligibility, this has to be one of the most anaemic vampire flicks ever made. NF

Lost Continent, The

(1968, GB, 98 min)
d/p Michael Carreras. *sc* Michael Nash. *ph* Paul Beeson. *ed* Chris Barnes. *ad* Arthur Lawson. *m* Gerard Schurmann. *cast* Eric Porter, Hildegard Knef, Suzanna Leigh, Nigel Stock, Tony Beckley, Nigel Stock, Neil McCallum, Benito Carruthers, Jimmy Hanley, Dana Gillespie, Victor Maddern.
●Outrageously plotted (after Dennis Wheatley's novel *Uncharted Seas*), garishly shot and played poker straight, this Hammer masterwork mutates the Gothic into the surreal as Porter's potentially explosive ship drifts into the uncharted nightmare world of the Sargasso, where the seaweed bites and the natives live in a time warp. Sad that after Carreras took over control of Hammer from his father, his sole directorial credit should have been on *Shatter* (following Monte Hellman's sacking). PT

Lost Highway

(1996, US, 134 min)
d David Lynch. *p* Deepak Nayar, Tom Sternberg, Mary Sweeney. *sc* David Lynch, Barry Gifford. *ph* Peter Deming. *ed* Mary Sweeney. *pd* Patricia Norris. *m* Angelo Badalamenti. *cast* Bill Pullman, Patricia Arquette, Balthazar Getty, Gary Busey, Robert Blake, Natasha Gregson Wagner, Richard Pryor, Gary Busey, Robert Loggia.
●Jazz saxophonist Fred (Pullman) is haunted by anxiety about the fidelity of his wife Renee (Arquette) and the mysterious arrival of video recordings shot inside their house. Fred sees himself, on one tape, next to his wife's battered body, and is arrested for murder. Overnight, Fred vanishes, to be replaced by garage mechanic Pete (Getty), who hasn't a clue how he ended up in jail. To make matters more mystifying, Pete presently becomes involved with Alice (Arquette again), mistress of his gangster pal Mr Eddy (Loggia), leading him into a nightmarish intrigue which only gradually begins to connect, obscurely, with Fred. The plotting, with its inexplicably metamorphosed protagonist and its various doubles, makes one suspect Lynch may be having us on. It's ironic, then, that narrative is the most intriguing thing about the film, leading us either to dismiss it as pretentious rubbish or to try to make sense of it on a metaphorical level. Fortunately, Lynch's mastery of mood through sound, space, decor and lighting means that we're more or less engrossed throughout, even though some of the sillier moments – not to mention the uncharacteristically clumsy use of music – try one's patience. GA

Lost Honour of Katharina Blum, The (Die verlorene Ehre der Katharina Blum)

(1975, WGer, 106 min)
d Volker Schlöndorff, Margarethe von Trotta. *p* Eberhard Junkersdorff. *sc* Volker Schlöndorff, Margarethe von Trotta. *ph* Jost Vacano, Peter Arnold. *ed* Peter Przygoda, Heidi Handorf, Ursula Götz. *m* Hans Werner Henze. *cast* Angela Winkler, Mario Adorf, Dieter Laser, Heinz Bennent, Hannelore Hoger, Harald Kuhlmann, Karl-Heinz Vosgerau, Jürgen Prochnow.
●A disturbingly powerful version of Heinrich Böll's novel about the irresponsibility of the gutter press and their ability to destroy lives. Winkler is excellent as the shy, apolitical young woman who sleeps with a man she meets at a party, unaware that he's a terrorist; next morning, after he's gone, armed police burst in, arrest her, and the nightmare begins. A smear campaign is started against her character, her privacy is repeatedly violated, and the links between single-minded, right-wing police and news-hungry press are made clear. It's a frightening account of how external, arbitrary forces can ruin lives, which simultaneously portrays the heroine as a courageous, dignified upholder of her freedom. Sometimes surreal, always intelligent and menacing, it's far superior to Schlöndorff's later *The Tin Drum*. GA

Lost Horizon

(1937, US, 117 min, b/w)
d/p Frank Capra. *sc* Robert Riskin. *ph* Joseph Walker. *ed* Gene Havlick, Gene Milford. *ad* Stephen Goosson. *m* Dimitri Tiomkin. *cast* Ronald Colman, Jane Wyatt, John Howard, Edward Everett Horton, Margo, Sam Jaffe, HB Warner, Thomas Mitchell, Isabel Jewell.
●Classic fantasy epic based on James Hilton's novel, with a number of air-passengers hijacked after leaving war-torn China, and ending up in Tibet's Shangri-La, where peace, good health and longevity are the rule. Colman is torn between staying and returning to normal 'civilisation', and the result is a full-blown weepie, complete with kitschy sets, admirable if incredibly naïve sentiments, and fine acting from Colman. Not at all the sort of film one could make in these considerably more jaundiced times, as was evident with the appearance of the atrocious remake in 1973. GA

Lost Horizon

(1972, US, 143 min)
d Charles Jarrott. p Ross Hunter. sc Larry Kramer. ph Robert Surtees. ed Maury Winetrobe. ad Preston Ames. m Burt Bacharach. cast Peter Finch, Liv Ullmann, Sally Kellerman, George Kennedy, Michael York, Olivia Hussey, Bobby Van, James Shigeta, Charles Boyer, John Gielgud.
●A disastrous remake of James Hilton's novel that replaces the old-fashioned hokum and wish-fulfilment of the Capra version with a melodramatic confrontation of the 'real' (the plane and its passengers are refugees from an unnamed Asian war) with the worst of recent cultural mythology (Shangri-La is little more than Disneyland with beads, and is overseen by a very Maharishi-like Charles Boyer). PH

Lost in America

(1985, US, 91 min)
d Albert Brooks. *p* Marty Katz. *sc* Albert Brooks, Monica Johnson. *ph* Eric Saarinen. *ed* David Finfer. *pd* Richard Sawyer. *m* Arthur B Rubinstein. *cast* Albert Brooks, Julie Hagerty, Michael Green, Tom Tarpey, Raynold Gideon, Maggie Roswell, Hans Wagner, Gary Marshall.
●Brooks and Hagerty are a well-off professional couple with fond memories of *Easy Rider* and a 'nest egg' they've put by should they ever decide to abandon their life of comfy capitalism for the freedom of the open road. Unexpectedly and by accident, they suddenly find themselves out of work, selling up, and going to live in a mobile home. The nest egg will keep the wolves from the door – until, that is, they decide to bid farewell to everything they abhor with one last visit to Vegas, and find themselves penniless in Nevada. A deft satire on self-delusion, complacency and compromised ideals, played to perfection by the two leads; only the slightly too soft ending strikes a false note. GA

Lost in Siberia (Zateryani v Sibiriy)

(1991, USSR/GB, 108 min)
d Alexander Mitta. *p* Anthony Andrews, Gagik Gasparyan, Alexander Moody. *sc* Alexander Mitta, Valery Fried, Yuri Korotkov (Russian version), James Brabazon (English version). *ph* Vladimir Shevtsik. *ad* Valery Yurkevitch, Vatali Klimenkov. *ed* Anthony Sloman, Nadezhda Veselovskaya. *m* Leonid Desyatnikov. *cast* Anthony Andrews, Yelena Mayorova, Vladimir Ilyin, Ira Mikhalyova, Yevgeni Mironov, Alexei Zharkov, Hark Bohm, Nicolas Chagrin, Elena Secota.
●This co-production describes the horrors of Stalin's camps and Arctic gulags in the '40s from the perspective of a British archaeologist falsely arrested for spying. Andrei Miller, a Brit of Russian grandparentage, is pulled off his dig and cattle-trucked to Siberia, where an escape attempt adds 25 years to his sentence. Living down in life's base camp, his identity stripped to bare bone, he finds only love and friendship can save the spirit. This is basically a journey-through-hell movie, with scenes of Doré-like torment, dehumanising injustice, hunger, privation and terror. Most harrowing is the depiction of violence among prisoners. Here the film's style veers closer at times to the visceral expressionism of Alan Parker's *Midnight Express* than, say, to that of Caspar Wrede's *One Day in the Life of Ivan Denisovich*; what holds it back is the acrid whiff of authenticity. Despite the excesses, it's an impressive effort, with a strong, committed performance from Andrews as Miller. WH

Lost in Space

(1998, US, 130 min)
d Stephen Hopkins. *p* Mark W Koch, Stephen Hopkins, Akiva Goldsman, Carla Fry. *sc* Akiva Goldsman. *ph* Peter Levy. *ed* Roy Lovejoy. *pd* Norman Garwood. *m* Bruce Broughton. *cast* Gary Oldman, William Hurt, Matt LeBlanc, Mimi Rogers, Heather Graham, Lacey Chabert, Jared Harris, Edward Fox.
●It's an axiom of modern SFX-dominated blockbusters – and this spin-off from the '60s TV series (itself a reworking of *Swiss Family Robinson*) boasts 750 such effects – that story and characterisation limp along in the rear. And despite the hard work of Hurt (as Prof Robinson who is rocketed with his family on a ten-year journey to Alpha Prime for a colonisation recce), deadpanning LeBlanc (his cocky top-gun captain Don West), and villainous Oldman (mad stowaway saboteur Dr Zachary Smith), this proves the rule. The response of a family under duress (while avoiding a collision with the sun, they get lost in deep space and time the other side of the 'Hyper Space Gate') is addressed in only token fashion. Most effort has gone into the impressive *Star Wars*-style opening dogfight and the edge-of-your-seat closing sequences, leaving a drawn out mid-section on the ship, with only a standard mutant insect invasion to pass the time. WH

Lost in the Stars

(1974, US, 114 min)
d Daniel Mann. *p* Ely Landau. *sc* Alfred Hayes. *ph* Robert Hauser. *ed* Walt Hannemann. *ad* Jack Martin Smith. *m* Kurt Weill. *cast* Brock Peters, Melba Moore, Raymond St Jacques, Clifton Davis, Paula Kelly.

● One of the weakest of the American Film Theatre's 'stage records', this adaptation of Alan Paton's *Cry, the Beloved Country* was the last musical scored by Kurt Weill. Opened up by screenwriter Alfred Hayes to little effect, and ploddingly directed by Daniel Mann, Paton's story of a black clergyman (Peters), who discovers the horrors of repression and racism when he travels to Johannesburg in search of his son, is transformed into a series of well-intentioned clichés. Weill's music is marvellous. PH

Lost in Transit

see Tombes du Ciel

Lost in Yonkers (aka Neil Simon's Lost in Yonkers)

(1993, US, 114 min)
d Martha Coolidge. *p* Ray Stark. *sc* Neil Simon. *ph* Johnny E Jensen. *ed* Steven Cohen. *pd* David Chapman. *m* Elmer Bernstein. *cast* Richard Dreyfuss, Mercedes Ruehl, Irene Worth, Brad Stoll, Mike Damus, David Strathairn, Robert Guy Miranda, Jack Laufer.

● Movies of Neil Simon plays never seem to be *directed by* anyone – and this film is a case in point. Two little brothers (Stoll and Damus) are dumped on Grandma by their father, a recent widower, and find themselves unwelcome. Grandma (Worth) runs her candy store and her family on an inhumanly tight rein. Her inability to show love has turned her son, the boys' Uncle Louie (Dreyfuss), into a feckless crook on the run, and daughter Bella (Ruehl) into a near retard, forever thwarted in her dreams of marriage and children. This sounds like a Jewish take on *The Glass Menagerie*, though Simon leaves one feeling faintly furtive about the odd manipulated tear. Irene Worth is outstanding as the matriarch, rising to the soundless scream that reveals the cost of her regime upon herself. Dreyfuss is in finger-popping mode, but Ruehl seems to have strayed in from the Broadway stage. BC

Lost Killers

(2000, Ger, 100 min)
d Dito Tsintsadze. *p* Peter Rommel. *sc* Dito Tsintsadze. *ph* Benedict Neuenfels. *ed* Stephan Krumbiegel. *pd* Thilo Mengler. *m* Dito Tsintsadze, Mirian, Udo Schö, Adrian Sherwood, Skip McDonald. *cast* Nicole Seelig, Misel Maticevic, Lasha Bakradze, Elie James Blezes, Franca Kastein Ferreira Alves, Franz Koller, Michael Holz.

● Mannheim, Germany, is the setting for another portrait of immigrants struggling against the odds. Familiar fare, you might think, or at least it would be if writer/director Tsintsadze hadn't taken a leaf out of Kusturica's book and brought a strong vein of anarchic comedy to their tribulations. A Vietnamese prostitute, who went into a coma after sex, is out for vengeance against the crocodile who ate her mother; a Haitian refugee is prepared to sell one of his kidneys if this will take him to Australia; and a Croatian-Georgian double act have set themselves up as hired assassins, but are having problems pulling the trigger. The plotting is episodic, and although the proceedings are too self-consciously absurd to generate much credibility, the raucous acting is cumulatively ingratiating. TJ

Lost Lover, The (L'Amante Perduto)

(1999, It/GB, 97 min)
d Roberto Faenza. *p* Elda Ferri. *sc* Sandro Petraglia, Roberto Faenza. *ph* José Luis Alcaine. *ed* Massimo Fiocchi. *pd* Giovanni Natalucci. *m* Paolo Buonvino. *cast* Ciaran Hinds, Juliet Aubrey, Stuart Bunce, Clara Bryant, Erick Vazquez, Cyrus Elias, Edoardo Moscone, Phyllida Law.

● In this controlled slice of heartfelt liberal whimsy, based on AB Yehoshua's *The Lover*, Adam (Hinds), a Tel Aviv garage-owner, allows his teacher wife Asya (Aubrey) to be seduced by Gabriel (Bunce), a caricatured 'stranger', in the hope that it might assuage her long-held guilt over their deaf son's accidental death. When the stranger disappears, his wife's spirit hits bottom, and Adam is forced on a lengthy quest to find Gabriel (and therefore Asya). Faenza dovetails a more interesting subplot about the tentative relationship growing between Adam's more practical daughter Dafi (Bryant, first rate) and one of her father's young Palestinian employees, the sensitive but torn Naim (the equally excellent Vazquez). WH

Lost Moment, The

(1947, US, 89 min, b/w)
d Martin Gabel. *p* Walter Wanger. *sc* Leonardo Bercovici. *ph* Hal Mohr. *ed* Milton Carruth. *ad* Alexander Golitzen. *m* Daniele Amfitheatrof. *cast* Robert Cummings, Susan Hayward, Agnes Moorehead, Joan Lorring, Eduardo Ciannelli, John Archer, Frank Puglia.

● A remarkably effective adaptation of Henry James' *The Aspern Papers*, closer to the shivery ambience of *The Innocents* than to the oh-so-discreet charm of *Daisy Miller* or *The Europeans*. An opportunist publisher (Cummings) lodges incognito in the Venetian house of a long-dead poet's lover, hoping to find the literary treasure trove of letters hidden there, and gradually comes under the spells of the past incarnate – the 105-year-old former loved one (Moorehead) and her schizophrenic niece (Hayward). The ghostly web of shifting identities and sexual tensions is superbly spun, making one regret that Martin Gabel subsequently confined himself to an acting career. PT

Lost One, The

see Verlorene, Der

Lost Paradise, The (Het Verloren Paradijs)

(1978, Bel, 94 min)
d Harry Kümel. *p* Jacqueline Pierreux. *sc* Harry Kümel, Kees Sengers. *ph* Ken Hodges. *ed* Susan Rossberg. *ad* Philippe Graff. *m* Roger Mores. *cast* Willeke van Ammelrooy, Hugo van den Berghe, Bert André, Gella Allaert, Stephen Windross.

● This may have little of the fantastic frenzy that dominated *Malpertuis* or *Daughters of Darkness*, but it's just as peculiar. A Flemish village is threatened by a motorway, whose siting provokes full-scale battle between the nature-loving burgomaster, the boorish but aspiring seed merchant, two *dummkopf* surveyors, and a crowd of stammering, vacillating, bewildered villagers. Then in strides Willeke van Ammelrooy, stately lady with a past, red hair, red mac and red fingernails, who adds a dose of arty sex to the buffoonery and broad satire. If Kümel hadn't such a heavy hand with everything the mix might have been quite explosive. But it remains one for curio-hunters: there can't be that many ecological-political-sex-comedy-dramas around. GB

Lost Patrol, The

(1934, US, 74 min, b/w)
d John Ford. *sc* Dudley Nichols, Garrett Fort. *ph* Harold Wenstrom. *ed* Paul Weatherwax. *ad* Van Nest Polglase, Sidney Ullman. *m* Max Steiner. *cast* Victor McLaglen, Boris Karloff, Wallace Ford, Reginald Denny, Alan Hale, JM Kerrigan, Billy Bevan, Alan Hale.

● At first glance, a fairly commonplace war-in-the-desert picture (with Yuma standing in for Mesopotamia), about a British patrol stranded during World War I falling prey to Arab snipers. Three main things distinguish it: Ford's adroit avoidance of 'Foreign Legion' clichés in the characterisation and plotting; Max Steiner's excellent score, which won an Oscar; and Karloff's extraordinary 'expressionist' performance as a soldier convinced that doom is at hand. The latter, in particular, represents an aspect of Ford's work that is often forgotten: a bold use of visual and dramatic stylisation, often associated with religious themes and characters. (From a novel by Philip MacDonald.) TR

Lost Sex (Honno)

(1966, Jap, 103 min, b/w)
d/sc Kaneto Shindo. *ph* Kiyomi Kuroda. *m* Hikaru Hayashi. *cast* Hideo Kanze, Nobuko Otowa, Eijiro Tono, Yoshinobu Ogawa, Kaori Shima.

● Given Shindo's predilection for either pretentious symbolism or heady sex 'n' violence, you might well fear the worst for this study of a middle-aged man who lost his virility at Hiroshima, regained it, lost it again after Bikini, and is patiently coaxed back to vim and vigour by his obliging widowed housekeeper. Surprisingly, it turns into an engaging character study, coloured by a wry wit more characteristic of Ichikawa. Few other directors could have brought the correct serio-comic touch to a scene in which the housekeeper, seeking to stimulate her master, stage manages an 'ancient custom' in which three masked males besiege her house by night, miaowing like rampant toms. Adding greatly to the pleasure are some marvellously melancholy (and beautifully photographed) snowy mountain locations. TM

Lost Son, The

(1998, GB/Fr, 102 min)
d Chris Menges. *p* Finola Dwyer. *sc* Eric Leclere, Margaret Leclere, Mark Mills. *ph* Barry Ackroyd. *ed* Pamela Power, Luc Barnier. *pd* John Beard. *m* Goran Bregovic. *cast* Daniel Auteuil, Nastassja Kinski, Katrin Cartlidge, Ciaran Hinds, Marianne Denicourt, Bruce Greenwood, Billie Whitelaw.

● A hardboiled genre film with queasy subject matter. Paris cop Xavier Lombard (Auteuil) has turned his back on the past and is now a private eye living in a crumbling Soho flat. Bumping into an old friend, Carlos (Hinds), Lombard agrees to track down his errant brother-in-law, Spitz, for a hefty fee, but when he turns up a videotape of child abuse at the missing man's flat, he decides to keep his cards close to his chest. There's something about Carlos's wife Deborah (Kinski) which he can't bring himself to trust. The locale and personalities notwithstanding, this is firmly in the classic gumshoe tradition, down to Lombard's friendship with loyal callgirl Nathalie (Denicourt). Auteuil gives a nuanced account of the down-at-heel operator, his stubborn integrity in the Marlowe mould. Director Menges has made two sensitive films about children (*A World Apart* and *Second Best*), and his treatment of the paedophilia theme here is discreet, but without soft-pedalling the rage and disgust it arouses. TCh

Lost Souls

(2000, US, 98 min)
d Janusz Kaminski. *p* Nina R Sadowsky, Meg Ryan. *sc* Pierce Gardner. *ph* Mauro Fiore. *ed* Anne Goursaud, Andrew Mondshein. *pd* Garreth Stover. *m* Jan AP Kaczmarek. *cast* Winona Ryder, Ben Chaplin, Philip Baker Hall, Elias Koteas, Sarah Wynter, John Beasley, Victor Slezak, John Diehl, Brad Greenquist, John Hurt.

● Catholic schoolteacher Maya Larkin (Ryder) – herself the victim of an earlier Satanic possession – assists at the unsuccessful exorcism of a crazed murderer, which renders her mentor and saviour Father Lareaux (Hurt) catatonic. Cryptic numerical codes in the psychopath's journals suggest the Devil is planning to take human form by possessing bestselling 'true crime' author Peter Kelson (Chaplin). Kelson, of course, is a resolute sceptic who believes there is no such thing as pure Evil. And why should he? Although orphaned as a child, he is supported by his wealthy uncle, Father James (Hall), and has a gorgeous girlfriend who doesn't seem to mind him running around with Ryder's shrewish, straggly-haired harbinger of doom. Director Kaminski's use of eerie shadows and desaturated colours helps envelop us in a world of ominous foreboding. He also borrows from the best, notably *Rosemary's Baby*. But unlike that other modern Polanski acolyte, M Night Shyamalan, Kaminski lacks the emotional insight and clarity that might infuse these supernatural happenings with a credible human dimension. So even as Jan Kaczmarek's textured musical score adds depth to some scary hallucinatory images, the tedious storytelling sucks the life and soul out of the characters far more effectively than Satan ever manages. NF

Lost Squadron, The

(1932, US, 79 min, b/w)
d George Archainbaud. *sc* Wallace Smith, Horace Jackson, Herman J Mankiewicz, Robert S Presnell. *ph* Leo Tover, Edward Cronjager. *ed* William Hamilton. *ad* Max Rée. *m* Max

Steiner. *cast* Richard Dix, Mary Astor, Erich von Stroheim, Joel McCrea, Dorothy Jordan, Robert Armstrong, Hugh Herbert, Ralph Ince.
●With a cynically acidic script by Herman J Mankiewicz, among others, this early talkie is one of the most enjoyably scabrous examples of Hollywood on Hollywood. Veteran airmen from World War I, desperate for work, get jobs as stuntmen on a movie (cue for some fine aerial photography), but they don't reckon with their director, an egotistical and obsessive (not to mention homicidally jealous) tyrant who'll stop at nothing in his desire to make a great film. Von Stroheim was perfect for the part: not only does he have a whale of a time strutting around in jodhpurs, snapping his whip and snarling through the megaphone, the role is also wonderfully reminiscent of his own reputed past as a sadistically cruel and inspired film-maker. GA

Lost Weekend, The

(1945, US, 99 min, b/w)
d Billy Wilder. *p* Charles Brackett. *sc* Charles Brackett, Billy Wilder. *ph* John F Seitz. *ed* Doane Harrison. *ad* Hans Dreier, Earl Hedrick. *m* Miklós Rózsa. *cast* Ray Milland, Jane Wyman, Philip Terry, Howard da Silva, Doris Dowling, Frank Faylen.
●A scarifyingly grim and grimy account of an alcoholic writer's lost weekend, stolen from time intended to be spent on taking a cure and gradually turning into a descent into hell. What makes the film so gripping is the brilliance with which Wilder uses John F Seitz's camerawork to range from an unvarnished portrait of New York brutally stripped of all glamour (Milland's frantic trudge along Third Avenue on Yom Kippur in search of an open pawnshop is a neo-realist *morceau d'anthologie*) to an almost Wellesian evocation of the alcoholic's inner world (not merely the justly famous DTs hallucination of a mouse attacked by bats, but the systematic use of images dominated by huge foreground objects). Characteristically dispassionate in his observation, Wilder elicits sympathy for his hero only by stressing the cruelly unthinking indifference to his sickness: the male nurse in the alcoholic ward gleefully chanting, 'Good morning, Mary Sunshine!', or the pianist in the bar leading onlookers in a derisive chant of 'somebody stole my purse' (to the tune of 'Somebody Stole My Gal') after he is humiliatingly caught trying to acquire some money. A pity that the production code demanded a glibly unconvincing ending in which love finds a way. TM

Lost World, The

(1925/(restored version) 2001, US, 63 min/ (restored version) 101 min, b/w)
d Harry Hoyt. *p* Earl Hudson. *sc* Marion Fairfax. *ph* Arthur Edeson. *ed* George McGuire, (chief editor restored version) Mathieu Dubosq. *ad* Marcel Delgado. *cast* Wallace Beery, Lewis Stone, Lloyd Hughes, Bessie Love, Arthur Hoyt, Frank Finch Smiles, Jules Cowes, Bull Montana, Alma Kennett, Arthur Conan Doyle.
●The idea that a film of Arthur Conan Doyle's *The Lost World* was itself lost seems so apt, you'd almost suspect it was mislaid on purpose – but wait, it was. A pioneering exercise in stop-motion animation effects in its day (1925) courtesy of 'research and technical director' Willis O'Brien, it was withdrawn just four years later, deemed obsolete by the arrival of the talkies. All known prints and export negatives were destroyed in favour of a sound remake. That of course became *King Kong*, and you can see how not only O'Brien but the latter's dramatic team learnt from the first film's successes and failures. Collated from some eight known sources, including a 35mm print rediscovered in the Czech film archives, this best-possible restored and remastered version shows the drama skewed towards the adventurers' exploratory rumpus in the jungle, with the more startling spectacle of a brontosaurus loose in London almost tacked on as an epilogue (the Blue Posts on Berwick Street really gets it). Lloyd Hughes makes a rather earnest strong jaw of a lead, and the sex (human/human) is almost a shaggy-dog story; worse (unless this edit does him a disservice), dramatic director Harry Hoyt flunks the suspense, introducing and cutting to his show-stopping monsters almost at random so that tension is muffled and the danger obscured. That said, the film retains a certain naive wonderment, the story (Eurocentric as it may be) still holds up, and Wallace Beery is an inimitably hirsute Professor Challenger. NB

Lost World, The

(1960, US, 98 min)
d/p Irwin Allen. *sc* Irwin Allen, Charles Bennett. *ph* Winton C Hoch. *ed* Hugh S Fowler. *ad* Duncan Cramer, Walter M Simonds. *m* Bert Shefter, Paul Sawtell. *cast* Michael Rennie, Jill St John, Claude Rains, David Hedison, Richard Haydn, Fernando Lamas, Richard Haydn.
●Dreary version of Conan Doyle's yarn about an expedition to a prehistoric enclave in the South American jungle (the silent version of 1925 was at least fun). The characters are insufferable, the dialogue abominable, and Willis O'Brien's special effects are hamstrung by Allen's decision to use real reptiles disguised as monsters. TM

Lost World: Jurassic Park, The

(1997, US, 129 min)
d Steven Spielberg. *p* Gerald R Molen, Colin Wilson. *sc* David Koepp. *ph* Janusz Kaminski. *ed* Michael Kahn. *pd* Rick Carter. *m* John Williams. *cast* Jeff Goldblum, Julianne Moore, Pete Postlethwaite, Arliss Howard, Vince Vaughn, Richard Attenborough, Peter Stormare.
●Despite the tighter script, this sequel suffers by provoking a sense of déjà vu: crucially, our wonder at the dinosaurs – the first film's trump card – is severely diminished second time around, while the suspense set-pieces are simply more of the same. Story and characterisation, such as they are, are contrived; it now turns out there's a second secret island populated by the beasts, which Goldblum reluctantly visits with a 'good' research expedition, while Postlethwaite leads a 'bad' team of hunters hired to transport them to a San Diego theme park. There's much hiding from T Rexes on the rampage after the baddies have messed with their young; indeed, there's much stuff about parenting, too, with Goldblum now lumbered with an (inexplicably black) daughter – presumably an identification figure for younger viewers, who may find some of the nastier attacks (men torn in two, faces bitten by initially sweet-seeming mini-monsters) hard to take. And the eco message is pap, an excuse for a climactic scene of a T Rex terrorising the LA suburbs (when, oddly, the model work is most conspicuous and unreal). In short, what you'd expect, and no more. GA

Lost World of Sinbad, The (Daitozoku)

(1963, Jap, 97 min)
d Senkichi Taniguchi. *p* Tomoyuki Tanaka, Kenichiro Tsunoda. *sc* Takeshi Kimura, Shinichi Sekizawa. *ph* Takao Saito. *ed* Yoshitami Kuroiwa. *ad* Takeo Kita. *m* Masaru Sato. *cast* Toshiro Mifune, Makoto Satoh, Jun Funato, Ichiro Arishima, Mie Hama, Takashi Shimura.
●So little of the Japanese popular cinema reaches Britain that it's been hard to judge whether the movies are as fanatically Americanised as most of the other Japanese mass media. Here is Exhibit A for the Prosecution: a Western-style swashbuckling fantasy which the dubbers have been able to turn into a Sinbad story without missing a beat. Although it's by no means rank, it remains the kind of film that gives a 'formula' a bad name. All the ingredients are there, including decent, if limited, special effects, but the emphases are curiously misjudged: there's too much plot, Mifune's presence goes for nothing, the comedy is hopelessly non-integrated, and the Gothicisms are too perfunctory. But the saddest thing is the bland rejection of the entire Oriental fantasy tradition. TR

Louise

see Chère Louise

Louisiana Story

(1948, US, 77 min, b/w)
d/p Robert J Flaherty. *sc* Frances Flaherty, Robert J Flaherty. *ph* Richard Leacock. *ed* Helen van Dongen. *m* Virgil Thomson. *with* Joseph Boudreaux, Lionel LeBlanc, E Bienvenu, Frank Hardy, CT Guedry.
●Flaherty's last work, like his first, *Nanook of the North*, was the product of one of those fluke occasions when a sponsor (in this case, the Standard Oil Company) offers money with no strings attached. With no disciplining 'purpose', Flaherty's totally intuitive method was tested to its limits – and his editor Helen van Dongen has recorded the extraordinary convolutions of plot and readings that his material underwent en route to its ravishing conclusion. As an account of oil exploration, Flaherty's narrative may seem slightly naive; but his vision of a child's myth-world, and the oilmen's intrusion and acceptance into it, is perhaps his greatest achievement. DC

Louis Prima: The Wildest

(1999, US, 82 min, col & b/w)
d Don McGlynn. *p* Joe Lauro. *ph* Steve Wacks, Randy Drummond, Alex Vlacos. *ed* Christian Moltke-Leth, Don McGlynn.
●Like too many US showbiz docs, this is marred by excessive indulgence of the sticky sentiments of the subject's erstwhile collaborators: Prima was 'a genius'; 'of the top five entertainers of the century, he's the top!'; 'he really was a real person'. No: what this entertaining film eventually shows is that he was a real swinger. The real person eludes his collaborators, just as he seems to have eluded his closest friends and his five wives. In the '50s Prima rated alongside Sinatra. Today he's best remembered for his songs on *The Jungle Book*. TV archive material catches him in his heyday and it's a wonderful sight: looking less like a ladykiller than a portly Frankie Howerd, he lets loose call and response rhythm 'n' blues to a shuffle beat, with honkin' sax, raucous vocals and manic clowning; and all the while his wife Keeley Smith stands about looking bored. TCh

Loulou

(1980, Fr, 105 min)
d Maurice Pialat. *p* Klaus Hellwig, Yves Gasser. *sc* Arlette Langmann, Maurice Pialat. *ph* Pierre-William Glenn, Jacques Loiseleux. *ed* Yann Dedet, Sophie Coussein. *ad* Max Berto, Jean-Pierre Sarrazin, Alain Alitbol. *m* Philippe Sarde. *cast* Isabelle Huppert, Gérard Depardieu, Guy Marchand, Humbert Balsan, Bernard Tronczyk, Christian Boucher, Frédérique Cerbonnet. .
●Pialat's film boasts France's two currently most important film stars: Depardieu as the slobbish drifter Loulou, and Huppert as the bright, rather aimless Nelly, who abandons her lover-boss and bourgeois friends for better sex and a simpler life (drink and TV, inarticulate tenderness and lost opportunities). With its combination of story-telling and social observation, *Loulou* sketches a portrait of France in the '70s (blue collar, big-bellied, chauvinist); and in its pessimism about social and sexual revolution, the film mocks the prosperity wrought by Giscard. At the end, as Nelly and Loulou stumble, drunk, out of the bar and into the Parisian suburbs, this really is 'darkness on the edge of town'. CA

Love (Szerelem)

(1971, Hun, 92 min, b/w)
d Károly Makk. *sc* Tibor Déry. *ph* János Tóth. *ed* György Sivó. *ad* József Romvári. *m* András Mihályi. *cast* Lili Darvas, Mari Töröcsik, Iván Darvas.
●Two women from different worlds whose lives have become rituals around an absent man: Makk catches the nuances of their relationship. One is the man's bedridden mother, who believes her imprisoned son is hitting the big time in America. The other is his wife, carefully sustaining the illusion in the old lady. The film is set in 1953, and shades of the consequences of the cult of the personality hang in Makk's references to the extravagant exploits of the son in the States. Finely shot by János Tóth, the film exhibits a concern for the quality of people's lives that stays this side of the nostalgic, and seems a characteristic of current Hungarian cinema. It may sound grim, it isn't in the least.

Love Affair (aka An Affair to Remember)

(1994, US, 108 min)
d Glenn Gordon Caron. *p* Warren Beatty, Glenn Gordon Caron. *sc* Warren Beatty, Robert Towne; (1939 original) Delmer Daves, Donald Ogden Stewart. *ph* Conrad L Hall. *ed* Robert C Jones. *pd* Ferdinando Scarfiotti. *m* Ennio Morricone. *cast* Warren Beatty, Annette Bening, Pierce Brosnan, Katharine Hepburn, Garry Shandling, Chloe Webb, Kate Capshaw, Paul Mazursky, Brenda Vaccaro, Harold Ramis.

●This remake of Leo McCarey's *An Affair to Remember* (1957), the vacuous weepie to which *Sleepless in Seattle* tipped its cap, went straight to video in Britain after a dismal outing in the US. As 'written' by Warren Beatty and Robert Towne – the updating aside, it's a virtual carbon copy of McCarey's film – the tale of a hesitant romance between Beatty's playboy sports celeb and Bening's music teacher looks little more than a vanity project. Impossibly exotic and glossy, its emotional dynamics make no sense today, so that all we're left with is a trite celebration of Warren and Annette as lovers made for each other. Only one scene works: when Beatty confronts Bening over why she failed to meet him as planned at the Empire State Building, his playing of humiliation, bruised vanity, confusion and uneasy bluffing sets the screen alight for a minute or two. But that's it. Even Hepburn is wasted. GA

Love Among the Ruins

(1975, US, 102 min)
d George Cukor. *p* Allan Davis. *sc* James Costigan. *ph* Douglas Slocombe. *ed* John F Burnett. *ad* Carmen Dillon. *m* John Barry. *cast* Katharine Hepburn, Laurence Olivier, Colin Blakely, Richard Pearson, Joan Sims, Leigh Lawson, Robert Harris.

●Cukor's last really impressive film was, ironically, made for television, and as such is stylistically rather less ambitious than his finest work. That said, his strengths were always his way with actors and his interest in the nuances of the battle between the sexes, and this remains a minor gem on both counts. Hepburn is the Edwardian dowager being sued for breach of promise by a much younger man (Lawson); Olivier is the eminent barrister whose course of defence – born of outrage at her inability to remember their brief affair years previously – is to portray her (falsely) as a senile old duffer incapable of passion. A gently sentimental comedy that never patronises the aged, the film charms with its subtle insights, quiet generosity, and sympathy for the plight of women in a repressive, male-dominated society. In short, it's a Cukor film through and through. GA

Love and Action in Chicago

(1999, US, 91 min)
d Dwayne Johnson-Cochran. *p* David Basulto, Leszek Burzynski, Danny Gold, Dwayne Johnson-Cochran, Richard Mann, BJ Rack. *sc* Dwayne Johnson-Cochran. *ph* Phil Parmet. *ed* J Kathleen Gibson, Carol Oblath. *pd* Cydney M Harris. *m* Russ Landau. *cast* Courtney B Vance, Regina King, Jason Alexander, Kathleen Turner, Edward Asner, Robert Breuler, Michael Gilio.

●The pitch here would be a black *Grosse Pointe Blank*. Vance is 'an eliminator', a hit-man who wipes out bad guys for the government. He wants out – but he has nothing in his life except his work. Turner is 'Middle Man', his controller, who doesn't want him to quit, and who fixes him up on a blind date with King. The tone is jokey, but it's supposed to work as a thriller, which it doesn't. Writer/director Johnson-Cochran fails to impress in either capacity; you wonder what attracted the quality cast to this uninspired material. TCh

Love and a .45

(1995, US, 101 min)
d CM Talkington. *p* Darin Scott. *sc* CM Talkington. *ph* Tim Richmond. *ed* Bob Ducsay. *pd* Deborah Pastor. *m* Tom Verlaine. *cast* Gil Bellows, Renee Zellweger, Peter Fonda, Rory Cochrane, Jeffrey Combs, Jace Alexander, Michael Bowen.

●Bellows pulls a hold-up with an empty pistol before toddling home to TV and girlfriend Zellweger, but soon a botched heist forces them to abandon their mobile-home for the open road, pursued by various cops and robbers. Pleny of excessive, derivative violence, but anyone desperate for a fix of style and sassiness will be disappointed. Fonda has a daft cameo as a trippy hippy who speaks through a device on his neck. AO

Love & Basketball

(2000, US, 125 min)
d Gina Prince-Bythewood. *p* Spike Lee, Sam Kitt. *sc* Gina Prince-Bythewood. *ph* Reynaldo Villalobos. *ed* Terilyn Shropshire. *pd* Jeff Howard. *m* Terence Blanchard. *cast* Omar Epps, Sanaa Lathan, Alfre Woodard, Dennis Haysbert, Debbi Morgan, Harry J Lennix, Kyla Pratt, Glenndon Chatman, Christine Dunford.

●This first feature is a tale of 'four quarters', each marking a milestone in the lives of two kids from a leafy LA suburb. Basketball-crazy neighbours Monica (Lathan) and Quincy (Epps) are rivals-cum-true loves chasing NBA ambitions. All is not equal: he plays to crowds and fends off groupies; she makes do with a poster of Magic Johnson and a mom who doesn't show up to games. Affluent hoop dreams? It's still different for girls. Writer/director Gina Prince-Bythewood turns what might have been an undemanding sporty-spice romance into a delicately executed, asskicking reminder of the obstacles faced by young women with zero interest in cheerleading. Her film takes its love of sport (and sexual politics) seriously, yet maintains broad appeal – not least because of the sympathy extended to its characters. It offers an unusual perspective on female alienation and the desire for emotional attachment, while intelligent questions about gender are never far from the surface. Stylishly shot and bursting with visual and sexual energy, this is confident black women's film-making and an eloquent tribute to the girl with the permanently grazed knees – and about time too. SS

Love and Bullets

(1978, US, 103 min)
d Stuart Rosenberg. *p* Pancho Kohner. *sc* Wendell Mayes. *ph* Fred J Koenekamp, (Europe) Anthony B Richmond. *ed* Michael F Anderson. *pd* John F DeCuir. *m* Lalo Schifrin. *cast* Charles Bronson, Jill Ireland, Rod Steiger, Henry Silva, Strother Martin, Bradford Dillman, Michael V Gazzo, Paul Koslo.

●Bronson sheds his enigmatic rough-tough persona, dons suit, and coifs hair to join Jill Ireland (impersonating Tammy Wynette) and Rod Steiger (taking off Brando) in this routine tale of witness wanted by FBI and mobsters alike. Characterisation becomes caricature, dialogue is diabolic, and with the whole of Switzerland to frolic in, the ability of both hunter and hunted to arrive in the same place at the same time transcends the realms of coincidence and enters those of ESP. *Love and Bullets*, my eye; embarrassment and tedium is more like it. FF

Love and Death

(1975, US, 85 min)
d Woody Allen. *p* Charles H Joffe. *sc* Woody Allen. *ph* Ghislain Cloquet. *ed* Ralph Rosenblum, Ron Kalish. *ad* Willy Holt. *m* Prokofiev. *cast* Woody Allen, Diane Keaton, Olga Georges-Picot, Harold Gould, Jessica Harper, Alfred Lutter, James Tolkan.

●On the same inspired wavelength as the Mel Brooks *2000 Year Old Man* routines, Stephen Leacock's parodies of the Russian novel, and any number of insane SJ Perelman dialogues. It's another episode in Allen's Jewish-neurotic romance with Diane Keaton, this time with Napoleon's invasion of Russia interfering. This allows a string of terrific visual gags using battles, Death the Grim Reaper, swords, grand opera, village idiots, snow, Napoleon and Olga Georges-Picot: 'Are you in the mood?' 'I've been in the mood since the late 1700s'. Less stylised than *Sleeper*, it's somehow not as satisfying to watch: in the cod-Russian manner, there are a lot of dark interior conversations between the lovers which tend to indulgence. But the running metaphor of Wheat is excepted honourably from this criticism, and as less than half-a-dozen lines are bum, *Love and Death* is an almost total treat. AN

Love and Death on Long Island

(1996, GB/Can, 93 min)
d Richard Kwietniowski. *p* Steve Clark-Hall, Christopher Zimmer. *sc* Richard Kwietniowski. *ph* Oliver Curtis. *ed* Susan Shipton. *pd* David McHenry. *m* Insects. *cast* John Hurt, Jason Priestley, Fiona Loewi, Sheila Hancock, Maury Chaykin, Gawn Grainger.

●Kwietniowski's feature debut, a marvellous adaptation of Gilbert Adair's novel, tells the hilariously unlikely tale of the obsession harboured by reclusive old fart London novelist Giles De'ath (Hurt) for hunky but not very talented American teen pin-up Ronnie Bostock (Priestley) after seeing him in an appalling movie. Unquestioningly hetero until his wife died, and barely cognisant of the modern technological world, let alone Long Island (where he fetches up in an attempt to meet his unwitting beloved), De'ath is simultaneously embarrassed, confused, tormented and rejuvenated by his infatuation. A genuinely literate, affectionate fish-out-of-water comedy, which never overplays its *Death in Venice* references, the film benefits hugely from Hurt's superb performance and from Kwietniowski's lovely parodies of straight-to-video fare. GA

Love and Duty (Lian'ai yu Yiwu)

(1931, China, 152 min, b/w)
d Richard Poh [Bu Wancang]. *cast* Ruan Lingyu, Raymond King [Jin Yan], Chen Yanyan, Li Ying.

●Believed lost until a near-pristine tinted print was discovered in Uruguay (!) in 1994, this epic-length melodrama is something of a revelation: a sophisticated account of love as the force most likely to upset a 'well ordered' society. The legendary Ruan Lingyu (21 at the time) plays a woman from adolescence to old age and doubles as the character's teenage daughter in the climactic scenes. Nai-Fan marries on the orders of her stern, traditional father and gives her rich, boring husband two children; but she runs away to be with the struggling writer she really loves, only to face a life of disappointment, hardship and poverty. Recent (1997) screenings confirm the film's lasting power to move audiences – and to make them laugh, thanks to the witty sketch of a shy courtship and the dream-sequence parody of a Douglas Fairbanks movie. TR

Love and Human Remains

(1993, Can, 100 min)
d Denys Arcand. *p* Roger Frappier. *sc* Brad Fraser. *ph* Paul Sarossy. *ed* Alain Baril. *pd* François Seguin. *m* John McCarthy. *cast* Thomas Gibson, Ruth Marshall, Cameron Bancroft, Mia Kirshner, Joanne Vannicola, Rick Roberts.

●Brad Fraser's *Unidentified Human Remains and the True Nature of Love* was praised as a play, but here, adapted for the screen, it seems much ado about very little. It's full of big issues, but what's said about them is less substantial, provocative or witty than in Arcand's previous attempt to monitor the contemporary pulse, *Jesus of Montreal*. The film centres on two flat-sharing friends: actor/writer David (Gibson), a manipulative bisexual cynic, and book-reviewer Candy (Marshall), whose quest for romance leaves her torn between a barman and a woman met at the gym. Add a dominatrix, a teenage busboy with a crush on David, a transvestite and others, and you have a fashionable cross-section of young Montreal – but which, if any, is the serial killer terrorising the city? Unfortunately, it's a half-hearted mystery. The characters are so unsympathetic, and the tone so determinedly cool, that the movie ends up as cautious and emotionally tepid as the behaviour it depicts. Not bad, but certainly not very likeable or illuminating. GA

Love and Music

see Stamping Ground

Love and Other Catastrophes

(1996, Aust, 79 min)
d Emma-Kate Croghan. *p* Stavros Efthymiou. *sc* Yael Bergman, Emma-Kate Croghan, Helen Bandis. *ph* Justin Brickle. *ed* Ken Sallows. *ad* Lisa Collins. *m* Doron Kipen. *cast* Frances O'Connor, Alice Garner, Radha Mitchell, Matt Day, Matthew Dyktynski, Suzi Dougherty.

●Made on a shoestring by a bunch of film school graduates (director and co-writer Croghan was 23 at the time), this sweet, brisk campus comedy has a refreshingly current feel. For once, you believe the actors are the age they're playing. The romantic musical chairs are routine, but Croghan has a light touch, and a shrewd eye for the rules of attraction. It's too unassuming to be brattily obnoxious. Film buffs will doubtless enjoy the frequent in-jokes (and come out numbering their three favourite films, and why). TCh

Love & Sex

(2000, US, 82 min)
d Valerie Breiman. *p* Timothy Scott Bogart, Martin J Barab, Brad Wyman. *sc* Valerie Breiman. *ph* Adam Kane. *ed* Martin

Apelbaum. *pd* Sara Sprawls. *cast* Famke Janssen, Jon Favreau, Noah Emmerich, Cheri Oteri, Ann Magnuson, Josh Hopkins, Robert Knepper, Vincent Ventresca.
● As a feature writer for 'Monique' magazine, Kate (Janssen) is stuck with a piece about what makes relationships last – a subject she fears she knows next to nothing about. Mulling over failed trysts with the likes of Eric (Emmerich), married with children, and actor Joey (Hopkins), Kate knows in her heart that she and Adam (Favreau) were the real thing. This rom-com gets a long way on the smart pairing of the sharp-featured Janssen and the big-boned Favreau. When they're together, the movie has the natural playfulness and relaxed quality associated with good relationships. You can tell that they enjoy each other. Favreau in particular has a comic delivery which makes his material seem wittier than it has any right to be. But when you get down to it, it's still pretty thin and over-familiar: the guy freaked out by his lover's sexual experience; the video rental fights (*Nosferastu* or *Ninja Babes?*); the tit for tat revenge dating. From Woody Allen to Nora Ephron, we've been through this cycle before. TCh

Love at First Bite

(1979, US, 96 min)
d Stan Dragoti. *p* Joel Freeman. *sc* Robert Kaufman. *ph* Edward Rosson. *ed* Mort Fallick, Allan Jacobs. *pd* Serge Krizman. *m* Charles Bernstein. *cast* George Hamilton, Susan Saint James, Richard Benjamin, Dick Shawn, Arte Johnson, Sherman Hemsley, Michael Pataki.
● A camp and knowing spoof along the lines of Rowan and Martin's *Laugh-In*, in which Count Dracula (Hamilton), dispossessed by the People's Commissar in his native Transylvania, moves to New York to have a bite out of the Big Apple and Susan Saint James. Atrociously directed and full of groan-making jokes, but the cast are having such a good time that it's difficult not to respond in a similar way. See it when you feel at your silliest.

Love at Large

(1990, US, 97 min)
d Alan Rudolph. *p* David Blocker. *sc* Alan Rudolph. *ph* Elliot Davis. *ed* Lisa Churgin. *pd* Steven Legler. *m* Mark Isham. *cast* Tom Berenger, Elizabeth Perkins, Anne Archer, Kate Capshaw, Annette O'Toole, Ted Levine, Ann Magnuson, Kevin J O'Connor, Ruby Dee, Barry Miller, Neil Young.
● Rudolph regularly pitches his movies somewhere between reality and unreality, which makes his work very uneven: either charming or frustratingly whimsical. Sadly, this foray into *film noir* territory, despite delightful moments, is mostly dispiritingly inconsequential. When Harry Dobbs (Berenger) – a PI about to break with his jealous girlfriend (Magnuson) – is asked by mysterious Miss Dolan (Archer) to keep tabs on a guy named Rick, the down-at-heel dick finds himself trailing a bigamist to a ranch, while being trailed in turn by a novice shamus, Stella (Perkins), hired by his jealous lover. Harry and Stella eventually join forces to right marital wrongs; but what they – and everyone else – really seek is love, a fleeting, indefinable emotion that Rudolph appears to be making his life's study. Because he can't decide whether his romantic comedy is also a thriller, it lacks suspense and memorable gags. If Berenger and Archer are unconvincing, the rest of the women – notably Perkins – hint at depths unexplored by the script. But hints are not enough, and unless the film's elusive, brittle mood traps you in the first few minutes, you may well find it much ado about nothing. GA

Love Ban, The

see It's a 2'6" Above the Ground World

Love Bewitched, A (El Amor Brujo)

(1986, Sp, 98 min)
d Carlos Saura. *p* Emiliano Piedra. *sc* Carlos Saura, Antonio Gades. *ph* Teo Escamilla. *ed* Pedro Del Rey. *ad* Gerardo Vera. *m* Manuel De Falla. *cast* Antonio Gades, Cristina Hoyos, Laura Del Sol, Juan Antonio Jimenéz, Emma Penella, La Polaca, Gomez de Jerez.
● The third collaboration between Saura and choreographer Gades, once again teeming with hot gypsy passions. But this one suffers from high-styled pretensions, and is short-circuited by non-musical scenes that have all the subtlety of old-fashioned, flaring-nostrils melodrama. The story is a supernatural love triangle about a woman possessed by the soul of her dead husband and pursued by the man who murdered him. The camera-work is straightforward and strong, the dance sizzling and authentic; but as with most series, *Flamenco III* isn't quite as satisfying as its predecessors. AR

Love Bug, The

(1968, US, 107 min)
d Robert Stevenson. *p* Bill Walsh. *sc* Bill Walsh, Don Da Gradi. *ph* Edward Colman. *ed* Cotton Warburton. *ad* Carroll Clark, John B Mansbridge. *m* George Bruns. *cast* David Tomlinson, Dean Jones, Michele Lee, Buddy Hackett, Joe Flynn, Benson Fong, Joe E Ross, Pedro Gonzalez-Gonzalez.
● The first instalment in the long-lived Disney series, based on Gordon Burford's story *Car–Boy–Girl*, reveals how Jones, an unsuccessful San Francisco racing driver, discovers that his Beetle has rather more personality than he expected. 'Herbie' and his plucky stunt drivers steal the show in this agreeable family entertainment. TJ

Love, Cheat & Steal

(1993, US, 96 min)
d William Curra. *p* Brad Krevoy, Steve Stabler. *sc* William Curran. *ph* Kent Wakeford. *ed* Carole Kravetz. pd Jane Ann Stewart.*cast* John Lithgow, Eric Roberts, Mädchen Amick, Richard Edson, Donald Moffat, Daniel O'Herlihy.
● Not exactly bad, but in no way notable. When Roberts reads that old flame Amick – whose evidence put him away in the Ravensville State Prison, Nevada, seven years ago – has married wealthy banker Lithgow, he breaks out of stir together with cellmate Edson and heads straight for the newly-weds' California love nest, where he passes himself off as her brother. Not that he wants to kill her, understand: rather, he's set on robbing Lithgow's bank (with her reluctant help, naturally). Meanwhile honest John has other problems since he's uncovered a money-laundering scam perpetrated by bank officials in cahoots with Colombian drug barons. Lithgow does a decent turn, of course, but Edson seems to have picked up Roberts' taste for ham, and Amick is as shallow as those other youngsters who emerged from *Twin Peaks*. GA

Love Child

see Child Under a Leaf

Love Child, The

(1987, GB, 100 min)
d Robert Smith. *p* Angela Topping.*sc* Gordon Hann. *ph* Thaddeus O'Sullivan.*ed* John Davies. *pd* Caroline Hanania. *m* Colin Gibson, Kenny Craddock. *cast* Sheila Hancock, Peter Capaldi, Percy Herbert, Lesley Sharp, Alexei Sayle, Arthur Hewlett, Stephen Frost, Steven O'Donnell.
● If Bill Forsyth teamed up with the Comic Strip, the result might be something like this: a determinedly whimsical, slightly-too-surreal look at working-class life on a Lambeth housing estate. Neither quite funny enough for comedy nor realistic enough for satire, but some strong cameos, warmth and wry wit make it enjoyable. Capaldi is a wide-eyed, gangling delight as an orphaned love child of the '60s (his father played with cult rock group the Pink Frogs) who fails to develop the 'bijou little killer streakette' required by his accounting-firm boss, and instead discovers magic 'shrooms and free love with an artist from the local squat. Meanwhile, in an amusing reversal, his dope-smoking gran (Hancock) plans to leave him for a place of her own. Though these two, by sheer force of personality, flesh out their stereotypes, the over-casting of alternative TV comedians (particularly Frost and O'Donnell as bully-boy policemen) was a mistake. DW

Lovecraft (aka Cast a Deadly Spell)

(1991, US, 92 min)
d Martin Campbell. *p* Gale Anne Hurd.*sc* Joseph Dougherty. Alexander Gruszynski. *ed* Dan Rae. *pd* Jon Bunker. *m* Curt Sobel.*cast* Fred Ward, David Warner, Julianne Moore, Clancy Brown, Alexandra Powers, Charles Hallahan.
● An engagingly left-field brew of gumshoes and ghouls, originally made for cable. The premise is that in Los Angeles in 1948, everyone is using magic – except, that is, for Marlowesque private eye H Philip Lovecraft (Ward). The plot, in this slapdash homage to Cthulhu, Yog-Sothoth and all the other unspellable regulars of horror writer HP Lovecraft's demonology, is the thinnest of McGuffins: the sinister Amos Hackshaw (Warner in prime eye-rolling mode) wants Lovecraft to get back his copy of the notorious grimoire, The Necronomicon, and to watch over the virtues of his virginal daughter. Distractions are added by the mandatory femme fatale, a nefarious club-owner and his sorcerous stooge, and a malevolent beastie. The narrative founders precariously between *film noir* verisimilitude and total cloud nine daffiness, with lurid but ultimately tame special effects, and a disappointing apocalyptic showdown. But there's much jaw-dropping flipness to be savoured on the way. JRo

Love Crazy

(1941, US, 99 min, b/w)
d Jack Conway. *p* Pandro S Berman. *sc* William Ludwig, Charles Lederer, David Hertz. *ph* Ray June. *ed* Ben Lewis. *ad* Cedric Gibbons, Paul Groesse. *m* David Snell. *cast* William Powell, Myrna Loy, Gail Patrick, Jack Carson, Florence Bates, Sidney Blackmer, Sig Ruman, Vladimir Sokoloff, Elisha Cook Jr, Donald MacBride.
● One of Conway's better movies, thanks to perfect casting and a brightly inventive script. Powell and Loy, both in cracking form, are blissfully celebrating their fourth anniversary when he gets stuck in a lift with an old flame (Patrick). Complications ensue, mother-in-law (Bates) gleefully smells a rat, and Loy sues for divorce. Powell obtains a postponement on the grounds of insanity (which he demonstrates at every opportunity). Loy retaliates by having him committed; he escapes disguised as his sister; and... well, it all comes out in the wash. This is screwball territory, so questions of implausibility or tastelessness don't really come into it; besides, it really is very funny, with every member of the cast contributing. Highlights include Powell's wonderfully refined drag act, and his efforts to explain, for the benefit of a lunacy commission, what a runaway cockatoo and playing boats with top hats in the swimming-pool had to do with his falling naked out of a tree onto a patio full of party guests. TM

Loved

(1996, US, 103 min)
d Erin Dignam. *p* Philippe Caland, Sean Penn. *sc* Erin Dignam. *ph* Reynaldo Villalobos. *ed* Gillian Hutshing, David Rogow. *pd* Barry Robison. *m* David Baerwald. *cast* William Hurt, Robin Wright Penn, Amy Madigan, Lucina Jenny, Joanna Cassidy, Sean Penn.
● Writer/director Dignam's film is part earnest TV movie and part that elusive beast, the American Art Film. Hurt's a DA trying to convince Robin Wright Penn to testify against her abusive ex-husband. Trouble is, she still loves him. More ambitious than it sounds, this elliptical, superbly acted film aims for spiritual intangibles. The tone is set by Sean Penn's haunting cameo as a man tormented by the fences we put up around us. TCh

Loved One, The

(1965, US, 119 min, b/w)
d Tony Richardson. *p* John Calley. *sc* Terry Southern, Christopher Isherwood. *ph* Haskell Wexler. *ed* Antony Gibbs, Hal Ashby, Brian Smedley-Aston. *pd* Rouben Ter-Arutunian. *m* John Addison. *cast* Robert Morse, Anjanette Comer, Jonathan Winters, Rod Steiger, Dana Andrews, Milton Berle, James Coburn, Ayllene Gibbons, John Gielgud, Tab Hunter, Margaret Leighton, Liberace, Roddy McDowall, Robert Morley, Lionel Stander.
● Evelyn Waugh's satirical novel about the British in Hollywood and Californian funeral practices was long a Buñuel project, but it finally fell to Richardson and a potentially riotous cast. Morse, unfortunately, as the British poet who ends up in the pet cemetery business, is no match for the expert wackiness on display, in particular Ayllene Gibbons as Steiger's bedridden (and food-bound) mother, and Liberace as a casket salesman. Sadly, the script, by Terry Southern out of Christopher Isherwood, just tries too hard to pack too much in, and the frenetic pacing becomes tiresome very quickly. DT

Love, etc.

(1996, Fr, 104 min)
d Marion Vernoux. *p* Patrick Godeau. *sc* Marion Vernoux, Dodine Herry. *ph* Eric Gautier. *ed* Jennifer Augé. *pd* François Emmanuelli. *m* Alexandre Desplat. *cast* Charlotte Gainsbourg, Yvan Attal, Charles Berling, Thibault de Montalembert, Elodie Navarre, Marie Adam, Charlotte Maury, Yvan Martin.

● A Georges Delerue-like Gallic version of Julian Barnes' novel *Talking It Over*, about a ménage à trois, this second feature from Vernoux (director Jacques Audiard's partner) is a self conscious attempt, complete with its 'Scope visuals and 180-degree circling camera, to refract modernity through a period lens – with one eye on the '60s New Wave, and the other on the more contemplative '70s. Gainsbourg, in fashionably mismatched outfits, plays strong-headed Marie, who marries orthodox Benoît (Attal) but becomes more and more intrigued by his 'crazier' lecturer pal of 20 years, Pierre (Berling). Attal and Berling give strong performances, notably in a passionate, confrontational head to head, but despite the evident intention to examine 'a man's world', it's Gainsbourg's lively gamine who provides the most compelling portrait. The film's retro chic aesthetic admits a certain waywardness and the odd longueur (the early pacing is variable, to say the least), but it grows considerably in interest and confidence as it progresses. WH

Love Eternal

see Eternel Retour, L'

Love Field

(1991, US, 104 min)
d Jonathan Kaplan. *p* Midge Sanford, Sarah Pillsbury. *sc* Don Roos. *ph* Ralf D Bode. *ed* Jane Kurson. *pd* Mark Freeborn. *m* Jerry Goldsmith. *cast* Michelle Pfeiffer, Dennis Haysbert, Stephanie McFadden, Brian Kerwin, Louise Latham, Peggy Rea.

● Lurene (Pfeiffer), a Dallas housewife infatuated with Jackie Kennedy, puts her marriage at risk when she takes the Greyhound to Washington to see the President's funeral. On the bus, she makes friends with a black fellow passenger (Haysbert) and the daughter he may or may not be abducting. This affecting romantic comedy probes the gradations of racial prejudice still prevalent in the South despite JFK's best efforts. Kaplan has a light touch throughout (the assassination itself is evocatively understated) and Pfeiffer gives a marvellously touching, funny and credible performance. Unaccountably denied a theatrical release in Britain, this is a most impressive and enjoyable work. GA

Love Goddesses, The

(1965, US, 87 min, b/w & col)
d/sc Saul J Turell, Graeme Ferguson. *ed* Nat Greene, Howard Kuperman. *m* Percy Faith. *narrator* Carl King.

● A fascinating but maddeningly snippety compilation of clips purporting to trace the changing face of the vamp and Hollywood's treatment of sex. The thesis is negligible, and not helped by the evident non-cooperation of some studios (notably MGM), so that Garbo is represented only by an early Swedish short, and Hedy Lamarr by the nude bathing scene from *Ecstasy*. But after its splendid opening coup (Dietrich emerging from the gorilla skin in *Blonde Venus*), it does offer pleasing glimpses, from Louise Glaum to Monroe, Taylor, et al. Pity the print quality is variable and the silent footage printed at the wrong speed. TM

Love Happy

(1949, US, 85 min, b/w)
d David Miller. *p* Lester Cowan, Mary Pickford. *sc* Frank Tashlin, Mac Benoff. *ph* William C Mellor. *ed* Basil Wrangell, Al Joseph. *ad* Gabriel Scognamillo. *m/songs* Ann Ronell. *cast* The Marx Brothers, Ilona Massey, Vera-Ellen, Marion Hutton, Raymond Burr, Eric Blore, Marilyn Monroe.

● A depressing final bow for the Marx Brothers. Groucho (who wrote the original story) has about ten minutes of screen time, one or two of them in the company of Marilyn Monroe, and there is a decent rooftop chase amongst advertising hoardings for Harpo. But it's a dead duck as a comedy, and the brothers look ill, old and jaded. ATu

Love, Honour and Obey

(1999, GB, 98 min)
d/p/sc Dominic Anciano, Ray Burdis. *ph* John Ward. *ed* Rachel Meyrick. *pd* Nick Burnell. *cast* Sadie Frost, Ray Winstone, Jonny Lee Miller, Jude Law, Sean Pertwee, Kathy Burke, Denise Van Outen, Rhys Ifans, Dominic Anciano, Ray Burdis, John Beckett.

● Music lovers who liked Winstone's 'Hound Dog' in *Fanny & Elvis* may enjoy his fuller rendition of 'The Harder They Come' in this tough nut caper comedy, written, produced and directed by Anciano and Burdis (who also show up, quite amusingly, as a couple of bouncers, named – surprisingly – Dom and Burdis). Observing the familiarity, bordering on self-parody, with which Winstone plays North London gangster and karaoke king Ray Creed, cinemagoers may be less impressed. The film proposes aggravation between north and south, the latter run by Sean (Pertwee), who in Matthew (Ifans) has a henchman as trigger happy and incompetent as any of Ray's unlikely crew. Matthew's rivalry with the upcoming Jonny (Miller), a chum of Ray's dapper consigliere Jude (Law), leads to full scale turf war. Dispiriting. WH

Love Hurts

(1990, US, 115 min)
d/p Bud Yorkin. *sc* Ron Nyswaner. *ph* Adam Greenberg. *ed* John C Horger. *pd* Armin Ganz. *m* Frank DeCaro. *cast* Jeff Daniels, Cynthia Sikes, Judith Ivey, John Mahoney, Cloris Leachman, Amy Wright, Mary Griffin.

● Paul Weaver (Daniels) gets his divorce papers on the eve of his sister's wedding, and rather than seek oblivion in another one-night stand, he decides to attend the ceremony. Guess who else is there? But Weaver's attempts at impressing his wife (Sikes) and two children are distracted by the presence of scatty Susan (Ivey), who has marriage problems of her own. By and large, Ron Nyswaner's script (written nearly a decade earlier) refuses the easy sympathies which affect too many such films; as Weaver confronts an unforgiving wife and daughter, his situation becomes progressively irredeemable. When it works, this relatively unpredictable approach is very effective – as when Weaver and his wife make a desperate attempt at reconciliation – but other sequences are too indulgent and unfocused. CM

Love Hurts (Hartverscheurend/ Heart-Rending)

(1993, Neth, 85 min)
d Mijke de Jong. *p* René Scholten. *sc* Jan Eilander, Mijke de Jong. *ph* Joost van Starrenburg. *ed* Menno Boerema. *ad* Jolein Laarman. *cast* Marieke Heebink, Mark Rietman, Andre-Arend Van Noord, Mientje Kleijer, Tanar Catalpinar, Roef Ragas.

● Well-meaning, not unintelligent, but rather tiresome look at the volatile relationship of two ill-matched lovers: a fully paid-up member of 'alternative Amsterdam' (she sings, helps out Kurdish refugees, worries about her HIV-positive friend, gets smashed, and laughs and screams a lot), and a comparatively strait-laced lawyer. Intended, surely, as a realistic study of the fragility of love in a divided, crumbling world, the film not only takes a few unnecessary turns into melodrama, but is relentlessly PC as its heroine, even more than her sullen lover, soon becomes an acute pain in the arse. GA

Love in a Fallen City (Qingcheng zhi Lian)

(1984, HK, 97 min)
d Ann Hui. *p* Lawrence Wong. *sc* Ann Hui. *ph* Anthony Hope. *ad* Tony Au. *m* Lam Man-yee. *cast* Cora Miao, Chow Yun-Fat, Keung Chung Ping, Chiu Kao.

● Using the masks and hieratic gestures of Peking Opera as a governing metaphor, Ann Hui describes the social and familial plight of a young divorcée in wartime China. The film centres on her nervous romance with a self-assured, westernised playboy in the Hong Kong of 1941, as the city falls to the Japanese. The loving reconstruction of the period tends to run away with itself, and there are some cloying romantic clichés. An interesting, ambitious failure. TR

Love in a Women's Prison (Diario Segreto da un Carcere Femminile)

(1972, It, 100 min)
d Rino Di Silvestro. *p* Giuliano Anellucci. *sc* Rino Di Silvestro, A Sangermano. *ph* Fausto Rossi. *ed* Angelo Curi. *ad* Piervittorio Marchi. *m* Franco Bixio. *cast* Anita Strindberg, Eva Czemerys, Olga Bisera, Jenny Tamburi, Paolo Senatore, Roger Browne, Valeria Fabrizi, Massimo Serato.

● Unimaginative and ludicrously inept offering, consisting of flatly directed examples of a variety of turn-ons (lesbians, fighting femmes, mild bondage and spanking), and a schoolboy plot involving drug smuggling, the Mafia, and intergang rivalry. Dull and unerotic, and the hit-and-miss dubbing doesn't help. CGi

Love in Germany, A (Eine Liebe in Deutschland)

(1983, WGer/Fr, 107 min)
d Andrzej Wajda. *p* Artur Brauner. *sc* Boleslaw Michalek, Agnieszka Holland, Andrzej Wajda. *ph* Igor Luther. *ed* Halina Prugar. *ad* Allan Starski, Götz Heymann, Jürgen Henze. *m* Michel Legrand. *cast* Hanna Schygulla, Marie-Christine Barrault, Armin Mueller-Stahl, Elisabeth Trissenaar, Daniel Olbrychski, Piotr Lysak, Bernhard Wicki.

● Of the many films on the nature of Nazism, very few scrutinise its manifestation in the daily lives of ordinary people. Adapted from Rolf Hochhuth's novel, this may be framed as a particular historical enquiry into the events surrounding an illicit love affair between a small-town shopkeeper (Schygulla) and a Polish PoW (Lysak), but their predicament is so movingly embodied that it lifts the film out of semi-autobiographical dredging and into the realm of tragedy. Their love is destroyed by the local petit bourgeoisie, so infected with political disease that the village is rotten with gossip, greed, suspicion. Alongside Schygulla's aching gravity, Mueller-Stahl weighs in a tremendous performance as the perplexed and irritable Gestapo chief. CPea

Love in Las Vegas

see Viva Las Vegas

Love in Limbo

(1992, Aust. 102 min)
d/p David Elfick. *sc* John Cundill. *ph* Stephen Windon. *ed* Stuart Armstrong. *m* Peter Kaldor. *cast* Aden Young, Craig Adams, Rhondda Findleton, Martin Sacks, Russell Crowe, Samatha Murray.

● Perth, 1957: a bespectacled adolescent (Young) is expelled from school for marketing his highly detailed drawings of naked women among his innocent classmates, whereupon he's parcelled off into a job in his uncle's clothing firm, and real life begins. Taken under the wing of the office rake (Adams), the lad is introduced to drink, women, cigarettes, etc, but his reactions are complicated when his widowed mum and his mentor begin to take an interest in each other. Assembling the story in a mosaic of kitsch furnishings and day-glo colours, Elfick finds both humour and pathos in the material, piecing events together with a rollercoaster rhythm. Most enjoyable. TJ

Love in the Afternoon

(1956, US, 120 min, b/w)
d/p Billy Wilder. *sc* Billy Wilder, IAL Diamond. *ph* William C Mellor. *ed* Léonide Azar. *ad* Alexandre Trauner. *m* Franz Waxman. *cast* Gary Cooper, Audrey Hepburn, Maurice Chevalier, John McGiver, Van Doude, Paul Bonifas, Lise Bourdin.

● An over-long and only spasmodically amusing romantic comedy, clearly made as a tribute to Lubitsch. Set in Paris, it concerns the predictably blooming love between wealthy American playboy Cooper and Hepburn, the innocent but determined daughter of Chevalier's private detective, whose cuckold client (John McGiver) intends to take revenge on Cooper with a pistol. The script – Wilder's first with IAL Diamond – has its moments, but by and large it's conspicuously lacking in insight or originality, while Hepburn's fresh-faced infatuation for her all too visibly ageing guide to the adult, sensual world comes across as faintly implausible. GA

Love in the Afternoon (L'Amour, l'Après-midi)

(1972, Fr, 97 min)
d Eric Rohmer. *p* Pierre Cottrell. *sc* Eric Rohmer. *ph* Nestor Almendros. *ed* Cécile Decugis. *ad* Nicole Rachline. *m* Arié Dzierlatka. *cast* Bernard Verley, Zouzou, Françoise Verley, Daniel Ceccaldi, Malvina Penne, Babette Ferrier, Frédérique Hender, Claude-Jean Philippe, Marie-Christine Barrault, Béatrice Romand.
●The last of Rohmer's *Six Moral Tales* sees its hero married – in contrast to the protagonists of the earlier films, who were merely contemplating marriage – and resisting the temptation of an affair, almost out of perversity. Equally, the film is a homage to the late afternoon – seen by Rohmer as a sunny parallel to 3am and the dark night of the soul – the time Bernard Verley eccentrically chooses as his regular lunch time. A formal, elegant examination of someone puzzled by marital fidelity, *Love in the Afternoon* is a wonderfully cool and lucid exposition of the twists and turns of its hero's thoughts. PH

Love in the Mirror (Amor nello specchio)

(1999, It, 110 min)
d Salvatore Maira. *p* Mariella Li Sacchi, Gian Marco Feletti. *sc* Salvatore Maira. *ph* Maurizio Calvesi. *ed* Alfredo Muschietti. *pd* Antonello Geleng, Marina Pinzuti. *m* Nicola Piovani. *cast* Anna Galiena, Peter Stormare, Simona Cavallari, Antonello Aglioti, Francesco Feletti, Jacques Sernas.
●This slick, glossy Italian costume drama is heavily laced with exposed (female) flesh, sex, sinister intrigues and somewhat facile philosophical musings on life's relationship with art, namely the theatre of a *commedia dell'arte* troupe led by the appallingly dubbed Stormare. Galiena's his leading lady and wife, jealous and vengeful over his attraction to ambitious and scheming new thesp Cavallari. Meanwhile, besides trying to keep the marital peace, he's putting on an innovative production which he hopes will win him the patronage to perform at Versailles. Po-faced and pretentious, heavy on female hair (pubic and permed), and really memorable only for some ingenious scenes involving weird stagecraft. GA

Love in the Strangest Way (Elles n'oublient pas)

(1994, Fr, 107 min)
d Christopher Frank. *p* Michelle de Broca. *sc* Christopher Frank. *ph* Bertrand Chatry. *ed* Catherine Dubeau. *m* Jean-Maria Sénia. *cast* Thierry Lhermitte, Maruschka Detmers, Nadia Fares, Johann Martel, Vincent Planchais, Patrick Timsit, Umberto Orsini.
●Light leading-man Lhermitte gets the chance to open up his emotional range as Julien, a hard-nosed operator for a debt collection agency. He comes a cropper when tangling with seductive Angela (Detmers) whose blatant come-on is conveniently timed to coincide with the wife and kids' annual holiday. One seedy fling later, we find Julien beating a retreat, but, after spouse Anne's return, Angela continues to seek his help in waiving her boyfriend's overdue loan, and soon turns up again as the family's new childminder. So far, so perfunctory; but where writer/ director Frank really hits the rocks is in trying to raise the passion level when murder enters the fray. TJ

Love Is a Ball (aka All This and Money Too)

(1963, US, 112 min)
d David Swift. *p* Martin H Poll. *sc* David Swift, Tom Waldman, Frank Waldman. *ph* Edmond Séchan. *ed* Tom McAdoo, Catherine Kelber. *ad* Jean d'Eaubonne. *m* Michel Legrand. *cast* Charles Boyer, Glenn Ford, Hope Lange, Ricardo Montalban, Telly Savalas, Ruth McDevitt, Ulla Jacobsson.
●A syrupy Michel Legrand score, European locations and much Hollywood Franglais mark this disposable filler (from Lindsay Hardy's novel *The Grand Duke and Mr Pimm*) as society matchmaker Boyer hopes to fix up penniless duke Montalban with Lange's American heiress, who of course falls for Ford's dashing racing driver. Neither film title quite hits the mark. TJ

Love Is a Many-Splendored Thing

(1955, US, 102 min)
d Henry King. *p* Buddy Adler. *sc* John Patrick. *ph* Leon Shamroy. *ed* William H Reynolds. *ad* Lyle Wheeler, George W Davis. *m* Alfred Newman. *cast* Jennifer Jones, William Holden, Isobel Elsom, Torin Thatcher, Murray Matheson, Jorja Curtright, Virginia Gregg.
●East meets West for some lush tripe based on a novel by Han Suyin, who had company in disliking it. Set in a full deck of CinemaScope Hong Kong postcards as an American journalist and a Eurasian doctor lady wallow in an ill-fated romance conducted in pidgin poetry ('Sadness is so ungrateful'). With that title and an Oscar-winning theme song, what did you expect? TM

Love Is Colder than Death (Liebe ist kälter als der Tod)

(1969, WGer, 88 min, b/w)
d/p/sc Rainer Werner Fassbinder. *ph* Dietrich Lohmann. *ed* Franz Walsch [Rainer Werner Fassbinder]. *ad* Ulli Lommel, Rainer Werner Fassbinder. *m* Peer Raben, Holger Münzer. *cast* Ulli Lommel, Hanna Schygulla, Rainer Werner Fassbinder, Hans Hirschmüller, Katrin Schaake, Ingrid Caven, Irm Hermann, Kurt Raab.
●A restless and sombre foray into the b/w world of the Hollywood gangster film as interpreted by B-movie mavericks such as Sam Fuller, and ex-*Cahiers* iconoclasts such as Godard, here stripped bare by Fassbinder to reveal the cold underlying mechanism of love, death, loneliness, friendship, hate, betrayal and manipulation. Shot on a pfennig budget, this – his first feature – is both an assured 'revolutionary' critique of genre, and at the same time a constantly searching experiment in style and treatment. The plot? For what it is worth, the worn-leather-jacket-and-boots, chain-smoking ex-con and pimp (Fassbinder) refuses the brutal 'persuasions' of the Syndicate, befriends a felt hat and raincoat (Lommel), only to be betrayed by a jealous prostitute lover (Schygulla) in an attempted bank robbery. In this bleak world of bare sets, static camera shots, and stylised acting, was awkwardly born one of the greatest 'lives in film' the cinema has seen. WH

Love Is Like a Violin

(1977, GB, 54 min)
d Jana Bokova. *p* Michael Radford. *ph* Charles Stewart. *ed* Jana Bokova, Robert Wynne-Simmons.
●Jana Bokova's observational portraits (her NFS films *Jokey* and *Militia Battlefield*; her TV films on Don McCullin and *Marevna and Marika*) have been highly achieved and entertaining examples of *cinéma-vérité* that engage with character through 'performance'; a film about a community theatre group would seem a natural progression. Yet the film emerges as an intriguing bundle of contradictions. In attempting to document how the Common Stock theatre company creates a performance for, and with material gathered from, pensioners in Hammersmith, Bokova appears torn between an analysis of a process and a series of contrasted group portraits of actors and OAPs. PT

Love Is My Profession

see En Cas de Malheur

Love Is Not Enough

(2001, GB, 89 min)
d/p/sc Mark Norfolk. *ph* Martin Scanlan. *ed* Suryaprath, Mark Norfoik. *m* Diesel Bug. *cast* Mark Vidoll, Stewart Wickham, Sharon Duncan-Brewster, David Case.
●Here's something different. I guess you could call it a faux first-person documentary (Beta SP). It begins with images of Che, Ali and writer/director Norfolk. Chutzpah or what? (Later he cites King, X and Sid James as his role models.) Commissioned by Welsh band Diesel Bug to record them live, Norfolk takes the measly budget and tries to finish off the feature he started five long years ago. Trouble is, his leading lady is now pregnant, his actor won't talk to him, and it doesn't take long for the crew to lose patience. Even Diesel Bug get suspicious. 'It's like a student film – only less organised,' they complain. They're right. You could call it an avant garde deconstruction of independent film practice and process – or you could call it a piss-take. It's a shambles, but engagingly so. I laughed lots. TCh

Love Is the Devil – Study for a Portrait of Francis Bacon (Ai no Akuma)

(1998, GB/Fr/Jap, 91 min)
d John Maybury. *p* Chiara Menage. *sc* John Maybury, James Cohen, Don Jordan. *ph* John Mathieson. *ed* Daniel Goddard. *pd* Alan MacDonald. *m* Ryuichi Sakamoto. *cast* Derek Jacobi, Daniel Craig, Tilda Swinton, Anne Lambton, Annabel Brooks.
●Maybury's film about Francis Bacon (Jacobi) focuses on the slow but inexorable downward spiral of his seven-year relationship with his lover, model and muse George Dyer (Craig), a smalltime villain whom the painter first met burgling his house. It's the tale of a charged but uncomfortable encounter, not only between two very different personalities, but between two different (but both very English) worlds: the arty, boozy Soho set and, ironically rather less amoral and more sympathetic, the East End criminal fraternity. At its heart is a raw, painful, even cruel love affair based on dominance, submission, snobbery and sadism, which is brought vividly to life by images often (but never excessively) reminiscent of Bacon's paintings. The performances are terrific, with Jacobi particularly astonishing as Bacon. GA

love jones

(1997, US, 109 min)
d Theodore Witcher. *p* Nick Wechsler, Jeremiah Samuels. *sc* Theodore Wechsler. *ph* Ernest Holzman. *ed* Maysie Hoy. *pd* Roger Fortune. *m* Darryl Jones. *cast* Larenz Tate, Nia Long, Isaiah Washington, Lisa Nicole Carson, Khalil Kain, Leonard Roberts.
●Disappointed in love, twenty-something Nina Mosley (Nia Long) plays it cool when publicly courted by Darius Lovehall (Tate) at Chicago nightspot The Sanctuary. With further effort, subterfuge, wit, charm and a spot of dancing, Darius and Nina finally come together. The pair duly make a splendid hash of things. By the way, she's a promising photographer; he's a promising writer – so much in common. A shame to split up, no? Both, probably, have much to learn about themselves and love: Sorry, please try again later. They do. A very (self-consciously) adult love story of temperate disposition, sage demeanour and protracted passage. Kudos to first-time writer/director Witcher for his level-headed attempt to tackle well trodden subject matter with a modern black twist. Unfortunately, a relationship has to be pretty special if the couple are going to pair up thrice over. The script seems to lose interest in its latter stages and Witcher never evinces a depth of insight such that you sit up and take notice. NB

Love/Juice

(2000, Jap, 78 min)
d Kaze Shindo. *p* Kazutoshi Wadakura, Tsuyoshi Sugino, Chikako Nakabayashi. *sc* Kaze Shindo. *ph* Koji Kanaya. *ed* Yukio Watanabe. *m* Kenichiro Isoda. *cast* Mika Okuno, Chika Fujimura, Toshiya Nagasawa, Hidetoshi Nishijima.
●Chinatsu and Kyoko share an apartment in Tokyo and work as hostesses in a bunny-type bar to pay the bills. The girlish Kyoko gets a crush on the guy in a nearby tropical fish store, but he hardly notices. The lesbian Chinatsu enjoys hanging out and sharing things with her roommate (brushing teeth, doing dope, etc), but doesn't think of her as a sexual partner until a girlfriend dumps her. Suddenly it's make or break time: will they become lovers or never see each other again? Shindo (the 23-year-old granddaughter of veteran director Kaneto Shindo) subtly teases out the sexual and psychological undercurrents – including a very Japanese suggestion of cannibalism – from scenes which never stray far from quotidian realities. Excellent performances and smart, thoughtful direction make this debut a striking account of female friendship at the turn of the century. TR

Loveless, The

(1981, US, 84 min)
d Kathryn Bigelow, Monty Montgomery. *p* Grafton Nunes, A Kitman Ho. *sc* Kathryn Bigelow, Monty Montgomery. *ph* Doyle Smith. *ed* Nancy Kanter. *pd* Lilly Kilvert. *m* Robert Gordon. *cast* Willem Dafoe, Robert Gordon, Marin Kanter, J Don Ferguson, Tina L'Hotsky, Lawrence Matarese.
●'Man, I was what you call ragged … I knew I was gonna hell in a breadbasket' intones the hero in the great opening moments of *The Loveless*, and as he zips up and bikes out, it's clear that this is one of the most original American independents in years: a bike movie which celebrates the '50s through '80s eyes. Where earlier bike films like *The Wild One* were forced to concentrate on plot, *The Loveless* deliberately slips its story into the background in order to linger over all the latent erotic material of the period that other films could only hint at in their posters. Zips and sunglasses and leather form the basis of a cool and stylish dream of sexual self-destruction, matched by a Robert Gordon score which exaggerates the sexual aspects of '50s music. At times the perversely slow beat of each scene can irritate, but that's a reasonable price for the film's super-saturated atmosphere. DP

Love Lessons (Laererinden/ Lust och fägring Stor)

(1995, Swe/Den, 130 min)
d Bo Widerberg. *p* Per Holst. *sc* Bo Widerberg. *ph* Morten Bruus. *ed* Bo Widerberg. *ad* Palle Arestrup. *cast* Johan Widerberg, Marika Lagercrantz, Tomas von Brömssen, Karin Huldt, Björn Kjellman, Nina Gunke, Kenneth Milldoff, Frida Lindholm.
●Sweden, 1943: six months in the life of 15-year-old Stig (Bo's son Johan Widerberg), who's come to the attention of his wispily carnal teacher Viola (Lagercrantz). She's dissatisfied with her salesman husband Frank (von Brömssen), and an affair duly begins. At first, Stig thinks Frank's the enemy; as it turns out, however, Viola's the one to watch. All starts well enough. Shot with mouth-watering crispness, the early scenes between Viola and Stig are tinglingly erotic and oddly authentic. Von Brömssen, too, is wonderful as a man so full of tears and alcohol he's all but leaking. But what next? Writer/director Widerberg's baffled. In the baggiest of second halves, he plies us with bland new characters and increasingly wordy monologues, labouring at humour like a tired man with a shovel. He even has a go at war, reducing real-life horrors to winsome marginalia. Stig himself is too good to be interesting, while Viola proves far too bad. And so, as dappled light plays on yet another of her silky suspender-belts and a crashing concerto swells for the umpteenth time, you find yourself stiff with indifference. CO'Su

Love Letter

(1995, Jap, 117 min)
d Shunji Iwai. *p* Suji Abe. *sc* Shunji Iwai. *ph* Noboru Shinoda. *ed* Shunji Iwai. *pd* Terumi Hosoya. *m* Remedios. *cast* Miho Nakayama, Etsushi Toyokawa, Bunjaku Han, Katsuyuki Shinohara, Miki Sakai.
●Japan's Fuji Television produced this glossy exercise in adolescent longing, and it looks it. A vehicle for pop idol Miho Nakayama to sigh and offer melancholy looks aplenty, it gives her a double role as Hiroko, the prim, grief-stricken young woman who sends a letter to her dead boyfriend's old address, and Itsuki, the rather feistier type who (happening to share a name with the chap in question) gets this unexpected missive, and whose initially tentative response is to send both girls on a voyage of discovery. TJ

Love Letter, The

(1999, US, 87 min)
d Peter Ho-Sun Chan. *p* Sarah Pillsbury, Midge Sanford, Kate Capshaw. *sc* Maria Maggenti. *ph* Tami Reiker. *ed* Jacqueline Cambas. *pd* Andrew Jackness. *m* Luis Bacalov. *cast* Kate Capshaw, Blythe Danner, Ellen DeGeneres, Geraldine McEwan, Julianne Nicholson, Tom Everett Scott, Tom Selleck, Gloria Stewart.
●We open with postcard-style snapshots of a sleepy New England fishing town, still cloaked in morning mist. The denizens of Loblolly-by-the-Sea – look, this won't get anywhere if you just sneer… It wants acquaintanceship, a sense of intimacy, a feel for the gentle rhythms of the place. Close in on the gritted face of Helen MacFarquhar (Capshaw) on her morning run; out again on other local folk going about their rounds. Helen keeps the town bookshop, where congregate a close circle of friends and employees. Going through a pile of papers after work, Helen finds a love letter. Oh, her beating heart! But who could it be from? Suddenly phrases from the letter are on everyone's lips; a violin rhapsody swells. At this point an asteroid hits the sleepy town of Loblolly-by-the-Sea and wipes out all its inhabitants. And the voice of God (me) booms out, and says: 'Peter Ho-Sun Chan, give us a break. Who's going to swallow romantic lines about peeling potatoes? What kind of a name is Miss Scattergoods? Quit with this gentle *real life* stroll – you're not Ozu – and show us someone interesting.' Well! A drastic turn of events, but this really wasn't getting anywhere. And maybe the final act's a tad unfair – but that's life, too. NB

Love Letters

(1945, US, 101 min, b/w)
d William Dieterle. *p* Hal B Wallis. *sc* Ayn Rand. *ph* Lee Garmes. *ed* Anne Bauchens. *ad* Hans Dreier, Roland Anderson. *m* Victor Young. *cast* Jennifer Jones, Joseph Cotten, Ann Richards, Cecil Kellaway, Gladys Cooper, Anita Louise, Reginald Denny.
●A florid romantic melodrama about an amnesiac cured – and cleared of her husband's murder – by the love of a soldier (Cotten) who had earlier dreamed up the letters supposedly written by his buddy (whom she then married). Never mind the dottily contrived plot and the tiresomely fey Jones; the superlative camerawork (Lee Garmes) and Dieterle's brooding direction make it a really rather ravishing experience. TM

Love Letters

(1983, US, 89 min)
d Amy Jones. *p* Roger Corman. *sc* Amy Jones. *ph* Alec Hirschfeld. *ed* Gwendolyn Greene. *ad* Jeannine C Oppewall. *m* Ralph Jones. *cast* Jamie Lee Curtis, James Keach, Amy Madigan, Bud Cort, Bonnie Bartlett, Matt Clark, Sally Kirkland.
●Put together in the corner of the Corman factory reserved for 'art', this proves once more that Corman can beat Hollywood mainstream in any genre. After the death of her mother, Jamie Lee Curtis discovers a cache of love letters which point to an affair of the heart indulged by her mother after she was born. They trigger the need, and soon she is knee-deep in a similar heartbreaker with a professional photographer (Keach), who is married but not about to leave. Just another triangle, perhaps, but this one is distinguished on several fronts. The passion is strong; the strength is hers; the obsession is not comfortable; and the treatment is uncompromising in its head-on stare at the sweet sickness. The last film to have sufficiently encompassed the derangement of love unto death was Truffaut's *The Woman Next Door*, and this film is very much more in the European tradition of *Last Tango in Paris* than in the Hollywood one of soft-focus romance. CPea

Love Letters from Teralba Road, The

(1977, Aust, 50 min)
d Stephen Wallace. *p* Richard Brennan. *sc* Stephen Wallace. *ph* Tom Cowan. *ed* Henry Dangar. *pd* Joanna Collard. *m* Ralph Schneider. *cast* Bryan Brown, Kris McQuade, Gia Carides, Joy Hruby, Kevin Leslie, Ashe Venn, Don Chapman.
●A working-class marriage is on the rocks: the partners separate, move in with their respective families, and then tentatively try to make amends. The strength of this modest movie, financed by the Sydney Filmmakers Co-operative, largely derives from what writer/director Stephen Wallace has chosen to leave unstated, and the way in which what seems at first an intolerable bind – especially from the point of view of the wife, authoritatively played by Kris McQuade – is finally revealed to be something much more complex and less pessimistic. JPy

Love Lottery, The

(1953, GB, 89 min)
d Charles Crichton. *p* Monja Danischewsky. *sc* Harry Kurnitz. *ph* Douglas Slocombe. *ed* Seth Holt. *pd* Tom Morahan. *m* Benjamin Frankel. *cast* David Niven, Peggy Cummins, Anne Vernon, Herbert Lom, Gordon Jackson, Felix Aylmer, Theodore Bikel, Sebastian Cabot, Hattie Jacques, Humphrey Bogart.
●Worn down by the pressures of Hollywood stardom and the attentions of his female fans, Niven, a British movie star, flees Hollywood for the sanctuary of Italy, only to allow Lom, the head of a gambling syndicate, to put him up as the prize in a so-called 'Love Lottery'. Thereafter, Vernon buys up hundreds of tickets to boost her chances, while London typist Cummins hopes the real thing will measure up to her daydreams. Humphrey Bogart – in his only film for Ealing Studios! – pops up unbilled in the final reel of this misfiring satire. TJ

Lovely Rita

(2001, Aus/Ger, 79 min)
d Jessica Hausner. *p* Antonin Svoboda, Philippe Bober, Heinz Stussak. *sc* Jessica Hausner. *ph* Martin Gschlacht. *ed* Karin Hartusch. *ad* Katharina Wöppermann. *cast* Barbara Osika, Christoph Bauer, Peter Fiala, Wolfgang Kostal, Karina Brandlmayer.
●Hausner's first feature focuses on a gauche teenage schoolgirl. The younger daughter to lower middle class parents who're slightly more disciplinarian than usual, she's misunderstood by her teachers and largely ignored by her schoolmates. Though she's still able to enjoy childhood japes with a fragile boy a few years younger than herself, she's also sufficiently curious about the adult world to start falling for a bus driver who barely notices her deliberately applied make-up. Try as she might (which isn't always very hard), she can't stay out of trouble, so she decides to take control. Opinions differ as to the effectiveness of the film's final ten minutes, required to give the narrative more obvious shape and raison d'être, perhaps, but it's also a touch redundant given the absolute authenticity of Hausner's witty, insightful depiction of adolescent growing pains, small town life and the way good intentions may dramatically backfire. Osika is perfect as Rita, half-child, half-woman, but then Hausner's cool, compassionate, naturalistic script, reminiscent of early Fassbinder, gives her plenty to play with. GA

Lovely to Look at

see Thin Ice

Lovely Way to Die, A (aka A Lovely Way to Go)

(1968, US, 103 min)
d David Lowell Rich. *p* Richard Lewis. *sc* AJ Russell. *ph* Morris Hartzbrand. *ed* Sidney Katz. *ad* Willard Levitas. *m* Kenyon Hopkins. *cast* Kirk Douglas, Sylva Koscina, Eli Wallach, Kenneth Haigh, Sharon Farrell, Gordon Peters, Philip Bosco.
●Douglas as a tough New York cop who turns in his badge after being ticked off for roughing up a crook or two in the cause of justice. He is promptly hired as a private eye by a lawyer friend (Wallach) who has a pretty client (Koscina) accused of murdering her wealthy husband and in need of protection. The attraction is very mutual, and soon Douglas is busy warding off assorted thuggish intruders with one hand, while romancing the lady with the other. A lumbering mixture of screwball romantic comedy and tortuously-plotted thriller, trying desperately to be 'with it' (lots of swinging New Wave stylistics), it relies on a relentlessly jolly score to keep things going and avoid flying off in all directions at once. TM

Lovely Way to Go, A

see Lovely Way to Die, A

Love Machine, The

(1971, US, 110 min)
d Jack Haley Jr. *p* MJ Frankovich. *sc* Samuel A Taylor. *ph* Charles Lang Jr. *ed* David Blewett. *pd* Lyle Wheeler. *m* Artie Butler. *cast* John Phillip Law, Dyan Cannon, Robert Ryan, Jackie Cooper, David Hemmings, Jodi Wexler, Shecky Greene.
●The love machine isn't a sex aid (unless you like your sex sleek, ruthless and sadistic), it's television, and its embodiment the glacier-profiled person of newscaster Robin Stone (Law). We're taken, courtesy of Jacqueline Susann's novel, on a

picaresque trip of the American television industry, in hot pursuit of Robin's rise to fame and power over the bodies of various ladies, including the network chief's wife (who gives him a final boost to the top in exchange for a key to his apartment) and a top model who commits suicide when he rejects her love. The world is the glossy ideal of Western consumer society (silk, models, fashion, even a camp photographer), and the film works on the crudest level possible. Pernicious crap. MV

Love Maker, The

see Calle Mayor

Love Match

see Partie de Plaisir, Une

Love Me

(1999, Fr, 107 min)
d Laetitia Masson. *p* Nicolas Daguet, Christine Gozlan, Alain Sarde. *sc* Laetitia Masson. *ph* Antoine Héberle. *ed* Aïlo Auguste-Judith. *m* John Cale. *cast* Sandrine Kiberlain, Johnny Hallyday, Jean-François Stévenin, Aurore Clément, Julie Depardieu, Anh Duong, Salomé Stévenin, Julian Sands.

●Reality and fantasy are confusingly intertwined in this striking but self-indulgent drama about a young schizophrenic. Gabrielle (Kiberlain), unemployed and eking out an existence in a small seaside town, has a huge crush on Lennox (Hallyday), a fading rock star who specialises in Elvis songs. We follow her to the US, where she takes a job as a waitress, tries to insinuate herself into Lennox's life, and hangs out in smoky bars. The whole American jaunt seems to be a figment of her imagination. To confuse matters further, we're presented with another character (Salomé Stévenin) who's supposed to be Gabrielle as a teenager. Masson has undoubted visual flair, but her attempts at combining *film noir*, melodrama and social realism in one unwieldy package are disorienting. She claims she wanted to induce a kind of vertigo in viewers – she risks baffling them instead. GM

Love Me or Leave Me

(1955, US, 122 min)
d Charles Vidor. *p* Joe Pasternak. *sc* Daniel Fuchs, Isobel Lennart. *ph* Arthur E Arling. *ed* Ralph E Winters. *ad* Cedric Gibbons, Urie McCleary. *songs* Nicholas Brodzsky, Sammy Cahn; Chilton Price. *cast* Doris Day, James Cagney, Cameron Mitchell, Robert Keith, Tom Tully, Harry Bellaver, Veda Ann Borg.

●The story of torch singer Ruth Etting and her involvement with racketeer Gimp Snyder, who used his muscle to launch her career, was rewarded with marriage, and ran into trouble when she hit the big time and outgrew his adoring but bullying machinations. Cagney, hovering constantly on the verge of *White Heat* mania, plays well off Doris Day's girl-next-door persona, lending a genuinely explosive edge to their relationship as, finding his demands increasingly inhibiting both personally and professionally, she begins to yearn for the less complicated devotion of her piano-player (Mitchell). Not quite as tough as it thinks it is – the script contrives to skirt the notion of any pre-marital sex deal – the film nevertheless has more substance than most musical biopics. And the stream of standards sung by Day, often used with dramatic point – 'You Made Me Love You', 'Mean to Me', 'Shaking the Blues Away', 'Ten Cents a Dance' – are a treat. TM

Love Me Tender

(1956, US, 89 min, b/w)
d Robert D Webb. *p* David Weisbart. *sc* Robert Buckner. *ph* Leo Tover. *ed* Hugh S Fowler. *ad* Lyle R Wheeler, Maurice Ransford. *m* Lionel Newman. *cast* Richard Egan, Debra Paget, Elvis Presley, Robert Middleton, William Campbell, Neville Brand, Mildred Dunnock, Bruce Bennett.

●Presley's debut film. It's basically a standard Western, about three Confederate brothers who steal a Union payroll and take it back to the family farm when the war is over. This is where Elvis comes in and the Western opts out – he's the younger, fourth brother, who has married the older brother's girl. A feud ensues, Presley gets filled with lead (but not before his pelvis and voice-box have had a workout), and finally reappears as a ghost, reprising the title number over his own grave. From debut to necropolis all in the space of a single movie. ATu

Love Me Tonight

(1932, US, 96 min, b/w)
d/p Rouben Mamoulian. *sc* Samuel Hoffenstein, Waldemar Young, George Marion Jr. *ph* Victor Milner. *ad* Hans Dreier. *songs* Richard Rodgers, Lorenz Hart. *cast* Maurice Chevalier, Jeanette MacDonald, Charles Ruggles, Charles Butterworth, Myrna Loy, C Aubrey Smith, Robert Greig, Elizabeth Patterson.

●A superb musical, outstripping the possible influences of René Clair and Lubitsch, to whose work this has been compared. A tale of the gradual dawn of romance between 'the best tailor in Paris' (Chevalier) and a haughty princess (MacDonald), the film is a stylish masterwork of technical innovations, and a delirious result of Mamoulian's desire to incorporate movement, dancing, acting, music, singing, décor and lighting into a cogent cinematic whole. The songs develop the action and characters, the dialogue is witty and rhythmic, and the entire film, with its fine score by Rodgers and Hart, is a charming, tongue-in-cheek fantasy that never descends into syrupy whimsy. GA

Love, Mother (Csók, Anyu)

(1987, Hun, 105 min)
d János Rózsa. *sc* Miklos Vámos. *ph* Elemér Ragályi. *ed* Zsuzsa Csáhány. *pd* József Romvári. *m* János Bródy. *cast* Dorottya Udvaros, Róbert Koltai, Kati Lajtai, Simon G Gévai, Sándor Gáspár.

●The Kalmars, a remarkably affluent Budapest family, are united only by brief communications on a kitchen blackboard. Secret affairs and even more secret depressions are observed through an ingenious telescopic device by their young son, a mute witness to this domestic parade of follies. Rózsa's film is a virtuoso piece of tiresome whimsy, which collapses when the general air of circumspection turns to serious moralising. DT

Love of Jeanne Ney, The (Die Liebe der Jeanne Ney)

(1927, Ger, 8,671 ft, b/w)
d GW Pabst. *sc* Ladislao Vajda, Rudolph Leonhardt, Ilya Ehrenburg. *ph* Fritz Arno Wagner, Walter Robert Lach. *ed* GW Pabst. *ad* Otto Hunte, Victor Trivas. *cast* Edith Jeanne, Brigitte Helm, Fritz Rasp, Hertha von Walther, Uno Henning, Vladimir Sokoloff, Sig Arno.

●Pabst's adaptation of a novel by Ilya Ehrenburg is in many ways a trial run for his masterpiece *Pandora's Box*, made the following year. Its German heroine flees from the Crimea after her Bolshevik lover has assassinated her diplomat father; the main part of the film finds her in Paris, struggling to maintain her integrity amid sundry corruptions and betrayals. The characters are not drawn with the depth of the later film, and the sheer density of plot tends to dominate everything else. The extraordinary richness of Pabst's visual articulation, however, turns this into an advantage: the narrative courses along vigorously, taking both Pabst's social insights and his aesthetic effects in its stride without wavering. TR

Love on the Dole

(1941, GB, 100 min, b/w)
d/p John Baxter. *sc* Walter Greenwood, Barbara K Emary, Rollo Gamble. *ph* Jimmy Wilson. *ed* Michael C Chorlton. *ad* R Holmes Paul. *m* Richard Addinsell. *cast* Deborah Kerr, Clifford Evans, Joyce Howard, Frank Cellier, Mary Merrall, George Carney.

●Despite the relevance of its theme, Walter Greenwood's sentimental tragedy remains very much a '30s period piece. The Salford slums look as irredeemably picturesque as the surrounding Pennine countryside, and 'Honest' Sam Grundy in his big car and check suit looks more like a teddy bear than a repulsive villain. Kerr is hardly the archetypical Lancashire mill-girl, but her mixture of coolness and fragility works surprisingly well in the scenes with the grumbling, bullying father she 'disgraces' and the fawningly lecherous bookie she pawns her body to. The real bite, though, comes from the gaggle of black-coated gossips – Mrs Dorbell, Mrs Nattle, Mrs Jike and Mrs Bull – who, Greek-chorus-like, pronounce judgment over their hap'orth of gin. RMy

Love on the Ground

see Amour par terre, L'

Love on the Run

(1936, US, 80 min, b/w)
d WS Van Dyke II. *p* Joseph L Mankiewicz. *sc* John Lee Mahin, Manuel Seff, Gladys Hurlbut. *ph* Oliver T Marsh. *ed* Frank Sullivan. *ad* Cedric Gibbons, Harry McAfee, Edwin B Willis. *m* Franz Waxman. *cast* Clark Gable, Joan Crawford, Franchot Tone, Reginald Owen, Mona Barrie, Ivan Lebedeff, William Demarest.

●Ducking out on the brink of her marriage to a European prince, American heiress Crawford enlists Gable's help in making her getaway, not knowing he's a journalist assigned to cover the nuptials but more interested in tracking down shady flying ace Owen. Busy, inconsequential romantic comedy with too much exposition for the stars to make much of it. TJ

Love on the Run (L'Amour en Fuite)

(1978, Fr, 95 min)
d François Truffaut. *p* Marcel Berbert, Roland Thénot. *sc* François Truffaut, Marie-France Pisier, Jean Aurel, Suzanne Schiffman, *ph* Nestor Almendros. *ed* Martine Barraque-Curie, Jean Gargonne, Corinne Lapassade. *ad* Jean-Pierre Kohut-Svelko, Pierre Compertz, Jean-Louis Povéda. *m* Georges Delerue. *cast* Jean-Pierre Léaud, Marie-France Pisier, Claude Jade, Dani, Dorothée, Rosy Varte, Daniel Mesguich, Julien Bertheau.

●Fifth and final instalment in the saga of Truffaut's narcissistic hero, Antoine Doinel, who hardly seems to have matured at all in this piece of whimsy. Encounter follows encounter in (ho hum) picaresque fashion, while Antoine remains bewildered at the vicissitudes of both women and life. There are welcome moments of irony and some sharply handled scenes, but they don't succeed in lifting the film above the most self-indulgent level of sentimentality. HM

Lover, The (L'Amant)

(1992, Fr/GB, 115 min)
d Jean-Jacques Annaud. *p* Claude Berri, Timothy Burrill. *sc* Gérard Brach, Jean-Jacques Annaud. *ph* Robert Fraisse. *ed* Noëlle Boisson, Diane Logan. *pd* Thanh At Hoang. *m* Gabriel Yared. *cast* Jane March, Tony Leung, Frédérique Meininger, Arnaud Giovaninetti, Melvil Poupaud, Lisa Faulkner, Xiem Mang.

●Late '20s Indo-China. A 15-year-old schoolgirl leans wistfully on the rail of a ferryboat crossing the Mekong. Observing her is an elegant, rich Chinese. With exquisite Parisian manners he offers her a lift to her lowly Saigon boarding-house. Thus meet the Young Girl (March) and the Chinaman (Leung) referred to in Marguerite Duras's assumedly autobiographical '80s novel (controversially, Annaud opted for a Gérard Brach script rather than Duras' own). For all the footage of glistening flesh – most of the film takes place in a darkened room where the two explore the realm of the senses – this is basically a melancholic piece about the remembrance of times, places and passions lost (with voice-over narration by Jeanne Moreau). The Young Girl, altogether too complex for the inexperienced March to do more than simply embody, was then in the process of taking her life into her own hands. She will become a writer, and has developed the strength to avoid both the predatoriness of her mother and the romantic dependence of her lover. But at a price. This sombre quality dignifies an otherwise shoddily directed movie. WH

Loverboy

(1989, US, 99 min)
d Joan Micklin Silver. *p* Gary Foster, Willie Hunt. *sc* Robin Schiff, Tom Ropelewski, Leslie Dixon. *ph* John Hora. *ed* Rick Shaine. *pd* Dan Leigh. *m* Michel Colombier. *cast* Patrick Dempsey, Kate Jackson, Kirstie Alley, Carrie Fisher, Robert Ginty, Nancy Valen, Charles Hunter Walsh, Barbara Carrera, Vic Tayback.

●Continuing in his niche as put-upon teen stud, Dempsey plays hopeless student Randy (who else?). Dumped by his disillusioned girlfriend (Valen), he's also in imminent danger of having college funds cut off by angry Dad (Ginty). A summer job delivering pizzas introduces him to rich, sophisticated Barbara Carrera, and before long he's on call to her friends, all wealthy, frustrated wives who pay handsomely for his services (wild sex, cosy chats, dancing sessions). By some strange logic, the accumulated sums are supposed to get Randy back to college, and thus back into the arms of his girl. But that's if deceived husbands remain ignorant. This is very silly stuff, but mildly engaging none the less. Silver adeptly juggles the set pieces, orchestrating a frantic, slapstick climax; and the likeable Dempsey is supported by a dependable cast, including Kirstie Alley as a vengeful doctor and Carrie Fisher as a body-builder's cynical wife. CM

Lovers (Amantes)

(1991, Sp, 103 min)
d Vicente Aranda. *p* Pedro Costa. *sc* Carlos Perez Merinero, Alvaro del Amo, Vicente Aranda. *ph* José Luis Alcaine. *ed* Teresa Font. *ad* Josep Rosell. *m* José Nieto. *cast* Victoria Abril, Jorge Sanz, Maribel Verdú, Enrique Cerro, Mabel Escaño, José Cerro.

●Madrid in the '50s. Young soldier Paco (Sanz) is courting his major's maid Trini (Verdú), the only tension between them being her determination to preserve her virginity until they are married. When Paco is discharged from the army and takes a room in the home of beautiful young widow Luisa (Abril), he is delighted at the happy 'resolution' to his ferocious sexual frustration: he has a passionate affair with Luisa, while Trini remains pure. But he had not bargained on the mad jealousy which both women develop, and is soon faced with an impossible choice. Aranda focuses tightly on his three principals, effectively conveying the dreadful, consuming power of passion. But he fails to imbue this true story with enough depth for the grand tragedy to which he aspires. We are never given any reason to care about these lovers, and Franco's Spain serves merely as a richly photographed backdrop. CO'S

Lovers, The

see Amants, Les

Lovers!, The

(1972, GB, 89 min)
d Herbert Wise. *p* Maurice Foster. *sc* Jack Rosenthal. *ph* Bob Huke. *ed* Bernard Gribble. *pd* Peter Mullins. *m* Carl Davis. *cast* Richard Beckinsale, Paula Wilcox, Susan Littler, Nikolas Simmonds, Anthony Naylor, Rosalind Ayres.

●Spin-off from a TV comedy series, but better than average because someone has bothered to think of it as a film, not just prolonged television. The boy and girl of the title, surrounded by the myth of the permissive society, find the reality of living at home with the parents in middle-class Manchester somewhat different. The film gains from being set in specific locations, so the characters acquire a degree of reality that the lot in *Coronation Street* will never have. It also creates the right degree of gaucheness in the protagonists without ever becoming condescending. Not recommended, really, just put together and acted with a surprising degree of conscientiousness. CPe

Lovers – Dogme 5

(1999, Fr, 95 min)
d Jean-Marc Barr. *p/sc* Pascal Arnold, Jean-Marc Barr. *ph* Jean-Marc Barr. *cast* Elodie Bouchez, Sergei Trifunovic, Geneviève Page, Thibault de Montalembert, Dragan Nicolic, Jean-Christophe Bouvet, Philippe Duquesne, Irina Decermic.

●Finally, the wheels fall off the Dogme 95 bandwagon. Although he acted for von Trier in *Europa* and *Breaking the Waves*, Barr is the first director from outside the founding group of Danish collaborators to be awarded their Dogme seal of authenticity. Here the no-frills proscription is only too evident in the final product, where the hand-held digital camerawork seems so murky it almost looks like amateur holiday footage. Not that the storyline is anything radical either, a case of the love-that-cannot-be when Parisian bookshop assistant Bouchez meets Serbian artist and illegal immigrant Trifunovic. As in *The Dream Life of Angels,* she is radiance personified, yet powerless in the face of a story which reveals the fine line between classic romance and banal cliché. Barr whirls the camera feverishly. Terribly wearing. TJ

Lovers, Happy Lovers!

see Knave of Hearts

Lovers in Woomuk-Baemi (Woomuk-Baemi ui Sarang)

(1989, SKor, 110 min)
d Jang Sun-Woo. *p* Byung-Gi Suh. *sc* Jang-Sun-Woo, Im Jong-Jai. *cast* Park Joong-Hoon, Yu Hae-Ri, Choi Myong-Gil, Lee Dae-Kun, Choi Ju-Bong, Shin Chung-Sik.

●The nearest Jang has ever come to straight social realism, this describes a stormy sexual triangle in the outer city suburb of the title. A male supervisor in a small sewing factory consoles one of the workers, a woman battered by her impotent husband, and they find themselves having an affair. Trouble is, he already has a steady partner, a former bargirl who won't give him up without a fight. Jang doesn't take sides (each of the characters has his/her reasons) but relishes the spontaneity of the emotions and the impossibility of concealing the scandal from the rest of the community. There's no symbolism, but the film's verve prefigures the imminent renaissance in Korean cinema. TR

Lovers of the Arctic Circle, The (Los Amantes del Círculo Polar/Les Amants du Cercle Polaire)

(1999, Sp/Fr, 108 min)
d Julio Medem. *p* Fernando Bovaira, Enrique López Lavigne. *sc* Julio Medem. *ph* Gonzalo F Berridi. *ed* Iván Aledo. *pd* Satur Idarreta, Karmele Soler, Estíbaliz Markiegi, Itziar Arrieta. *m* Alberto Iglesias. *cast* NajwaNimri, Fele Martínez, Nancho Novo, Maru Valdivielso, Peru Medem, Sara Valiente,Victor Hugo Oliveira.

●Otto is just eight years old when he falls in love with Ana. The first time she lays eyes on him, she sees her dead father looking back at her. And Otto's father, Alvaro, he too falls in love, with Ana's mother Olga. They make a family with a faultline running through its heart. Teasing, allusive and elusive, this is also Medem's most deeply felt movie to date. He can't resist games, patterns and stratagems; his latest is a kaleidoscope of circles revolving within circles, as his young lovers settle into an uneasy and intense emotional orbit. He alternates points of view, relating events from Otto's perspective, then from Ana's. It's an inspired ploy, accomplished with a magical sleight of hand: both these youngsters live – and love – inside their heads; their relationship is almost telepathic, a secret from their parents and, virtually, themselves. As they get older and look back, there's also much play on something Ana likes to call 'Fate', but which we're free to read as coincidence: recurring motifs interlace the fleeting years. Witty, thrilling, ineffably and tragically romantic, with a distinguished, delicate score by Alberto Iglesias, and sharp, shrewd performances, this is fabulous film-making; a love story which burns like ice. TCh

Lovers of Verona, The

see Amants de Vérone, Les

Love's a Bitch

see Amores perros

Lovesick

(1983, US, 96 min)
d Marshall Brickman. *p* Charles Okun. *sc* Marshall Brickman. *ph* Gerry Fisher. *ed* Nina Feinberg. *pd* Philip Rosenberg. *m* Philippe Sarde. *cast* Dudley Moore, Elizabeth McGovern, Alec Guinness, John Huston, Wallace Shawn, Gene Saks, Alan King, Ron Silver, Christine Baranski.

●Moore's a Manhattan psychiatrist who falls for one of his patients (McGovern). This comedy-romance, with the emphasis firmly (and often unbearably) on the latter, smacks more than a little of Woody Allen: no surprise when you consider that Brickman collaborated on *Sleeper, Annie Hall* and *Manhattan.* Unfortunately, the Allen trademarks are only superficially exploited; where Woody might have gloried in uncovering and lampooning the psychiatrist's guilt, Brickman avoids any real conflicts, and has the ghost of Sigmund Freud make frequent appearances as a mixed guardian angel/agent provocateur. Guinness fleshes out the role somewhat stiffly, and the result is nothing to compare with the similar function served by Gielgud in *Arthur.* What's left is a love story slightly less moving than an 'Interflora' ad. GD

Lovesick on Nana Street (Hole ahava be'shikun gimel)

(1995, Isr, 94 min)
d Savi Gabizon. *p* Anat Asoulin, Savi Gabizon. *sc* Savi Gabizon. *ph* Yoav Kosh. *ed* Tali Halter-Shenkar. *ad* Emanuel Amrami. *m* Ehud Banai. *cast* Moshe Ivgi, Hana Azulai-Hasfari, Avigail Arieli, Menashe Noy, Tuvia Gelber, Shmil Ben-Ari.

●Chauvinist braggart Victor (Ivgi) has a reputation around his Israeli estate as the local lewd boy, so it's nothing unusual when he propositions a good-looking stranger in town, Michaella (Hasfari), inviting her to a supposed orgy with two Norwegian girls. She's not interested, but the days pass and Victor won't move on, dreaming up an affair and so losing his grip that he is incarcerated in the local asylum, alongside a host of similarly lovelorn fellows. This is one odd number: certainly captivating in its vision of unrequited love en masse, the town a cuckoo's nest of personal breakdown and pandemia. It's also highly problematic, given the director's evident yet obscure identification with Victor's plight: in particular, it's hard to unravel the congruence or otherwise of the character's sexist erotomania with his sudden fit of helpless amour fou. Intriguing, none the less. NB

Love's Labour's Lost

(1999, GB/Fr/US, 94 min)
d Kenneth Branagh. *p* David Barron,Kenneth Branagh. *sc* Kenneth Branagh.*ph* Alex Thomson. *ed* Neil Farrelll, Dan Farrell. *pd* Tim Harvey. *m* Patrick Doyle.*cast* Kenneth Branagh, Nathan Lane,Adrian Lester, Matthew Lillard, Natascha McElhone, Alessandro Nivola, Alicia Silverstone, Timothy Spall, Richard Briers, Geraldine McEwan.

●Branagh's all singing, all dancing version of Shakespeare's least funny comedy cuts nearly three quarters of the text, sets the action in a Hollywood Europe of the golden age (1939–45), and incorporates musical numbers by Gershwin, Berlin and Cole Porter. Few would maintain that this represents the desecration of a great play. The King of Navarre (Nivola) and his entourage (Branagh, Lillard and Lester) forswearing female companionship for three years of serious study and contemplation. Naturally, these idealists are found wanting as soon as a French princess (Silverstone) and her ladies come a-courting. As Branagh has recognised, it's a classic template for screwball comedy. But as he's also recognised, the laborious word play has a suffocatingly arcane ring to it – hence the need for wholesale cutting and rejigging. The result is an oddity, an ersatz but curiously literal musical comedy, an act of double homage to antique artifice. It has a pleasant romantic feel, Technicolor-coded design, and a cast who are ready and willing, if not always able. 'Drowsy with harmony,' at least the songs really are sublime – you can't take that away from 'em. TCh

Loves of a Blonde

see Lásky Jedné Plavovlásky

Loves of Liszt, The (Szerelmi Almok – Liszt)

(1970, Hun/USSR, 185 min)
d Márton Keleti. *sc* Imre Keszi, D Delj. *ph* István Hildebrand. *ed* Mihály Morell. *ad* Alexei Rudiakov, Lászlo Duba. *m* Ferenc Farkas; Liszt, Chopin, Beethoven, Glinka. *cast* Imre Sinkovits, Ariadne Shengelaya, Klara Lutchko, Igor Dmitriev, Sándor Pécsi, Irina Gubanova, Larissa Trembovelskaya, Támas Major.

●A film with all the grace of a dinosaur and the liveliness of a dodo. For two and a half hours (mercifully, 32 minutes were cut for British release) we're treated to a childishly reverential biography that outdoes even Hollywood biopics in its horde of clichés and name-dropping. The settings, both interior and exterior, are attractive in their holiday-brochure way, yet they are never treated with any imagination (the director's main trick is to make the camera pirouette round the piano during Liszt's recitals, which only makes it seem as though he's performing on ice). And while the dollops of music are finely performed (mostly by György Cziffra and Sviatoslav Richter), the selection signally fails to support the script's claim that Liszt is a key figure in the development of modern music. GB

Love Song
see Affair, The

Love Story
(1944, GB, 108 min, b/w)
d Leslie Arliss. *p* Harold Huth. *sc* Leslie Arliss, Doreen Montgomery. *ph* Bernard Knowles. *ed* Charles Knott. *ad* John Bryan. *m* Hubert Bath. *cast* Margaret Lockwood, Stewart Granger, Patricia Roc, Tom Walls, Moira Lister, Reginald Purdell, AE Matthews.
●If you thought the Erich Segal *Love Story* was a bit much, then try this one for size. Lockwood is a pianist dying of heart trouble, Granger a mining engineer going blind. Down in Cornwall where English movie passions bloom, she's composing a swan-song ('The Cornish Rhapsody') while he dickers over an operation that may restore his sight (but thereby hangs much soul-searching and self-sacrifice). Fulsome, indeed. TM

Love Story
(1970, US, 100 min)
d Arthur Hiller. *p* Howard G Minsky. *sc* Erich Segal. *ph* Dick Kratina. *ed* Robert C Jones. *ad* Robert Gundlach. *m* Francis Lai.*cast* Ali MacGraw, Ryan O'Neal, John Marley, Ray Milland, Russell Nype, Katherine Balfour, Tommy Lee Jones.
●The bland mating of love and leukaemia which brought a box-office bonanza. 'What can you say about the girl you loved, and she died?' muses O'Neal before looking back to his days of clichéd happiness with Ali MacGraw. 'Very little of any interest,' replies Arthur Hiller, as he leads us through a turgid, trauma-ridden tale of Harvard students falling in lerv, making it financially, and then separating, thankfully, for ever. Dated before it was made. GA

Love Stories (Historie Milosne)
(1997, Pol, 84 min)
d Jerzy Stuhr. *p* Juliusz Machulski, Jacek Moczydlowski, Jacek Bromski. *sc* Jerzy Stuhr. *ph* Pawel Edelman. *ed* Elzbieta Kurkowska. *pd* Allan Starski. *m* Adam Nowak. *cast* Jerzy Stuhr, Dominika Ostalowska, Katarzyna Figura, Irina Alfiorowa, Karolina Ostrozna, Jerzy Nowak.
●Written, directed by and starring Jerzy Stuhr in four different roles, this morose comic fable interweaves the stories of four inhabitants of Krakow – a lecturer, an army officer, a priest and a drug smuggler – to mount a subtle exploration of the diverse roles played by love in contemporary life. It's a movie about fear, guilt, cowardice, responsibility, trust and betrayal, but despite occasional forays into allegorical fantasy, it mercifully never sermonises or descends into maudlin sentiment. Ingenious, insightful and finally rather touching. (Dedicated to Krzysztof Kieslowski, for whom Stuhr regularly acted.) GA

Love Streams
(1984, US, 141 min)
d John Cassavetes. *p* Menahem Golan, Yoram Globus. *sc* John Cassavetes, Ted Allan. *ph* Al Ruban. *ed* George C Villasenor. *ad* Phedon Papamichael. *m* Bo Harwood. *cast* Gena Rowlands, John Cassavetes, Diahnne Abbott, Seymour Cassel, Margaret Abbott, Jakob Shaw, Al Ruban.
●As so often in Cassavetes' work, there's little plot: desperate attempts at a sexual life from a boozy, middle-aged writer staving off loneliness; a divorced woman's struggles to hang on to her husband, daughter and sanity. Halfway through, when the woman takes refuge in the writer's chaotic household, the nature of their relationship (they're brother and sister) gradually unfolds. Very little else happens; but sparks fly throughout as the characters, guided firmly by the director's customary emphasis on spontaneous, naturalistic performance, search for closeness, warmth and self-definition. It's a long and wayward path, but humour, aching sadness, and sensitivity to the inner lives of people deemed eccentric, mingle to produce a rich, impressionistic tapestry. The oblique treatment occasionally leads to infuriating obscurity, but the movie's sense of 'real life', dynamic performances, and admirable lack of moralising make it compulsive. (From a play by Ted Allan.) GA

Love Test, The
(1934, GB, 63 min, b/w)
d Michael Powell. *p* John Findaly. *sc* Selwyn Jepson. *ph* Arthur Crabtree. *cast* Judy Gunn, Louis Hayward, David Hutcheson, Googie Withers, Morris Harvey, Bernard Miles, Eve Turner.
●A romantic comedy set in a chemistry lab up against a deadline to produce a formula for fireproof celluloid. Hoping to be made department head, Thompson (Hutcheson) stirs up chauvinist resentments when the appointment goes provisionally to Mary (Gunn), a serious young woman with no time for men; and he ensures that John (Hayward), already interested in Mary, is elected in a plot to distract her from her work. With the pair soon head-over-heels in love, Thompson throws another spanner in by telling Mary that John is actually making a play for her job, meanwhile ensuring that work comes to a standstill. Only John, though repulsed by the angry Mary, goes on working selflessly to find the formula… Scripts like this were the bread-and-butter of British movies, the difference being that Powell's stylishness, invention and impeccable direction of actors turn this one into a real charmer. Hayward and Gunn are touchingly sincere as the lovers, and Googie Withers (among several fine supporting performances) contributes a gem of a cameo as a pertly predatory secretary. TM

Love Unto Waste (Dixia Qing)
(1986, HK, 97 min)
d Stanley Kwan. *p* Dickson Poon. *sc* Lai Kit, Chiu Tai An-ping. *ph* Johnny Koo. *ed* Chow Cheung-kan. *pd* William Chang. *m* Violet Lam. *cast* Tony Leung, Chow Yun-Fat, Irene Wan, Elaine Jin, Ts'ai Ch'in.
●Here, at last, are images of Hong Kong life that readers of *The Face* and *i-D* would recognise. Four smart young things spend their time dressing, bonking, and getting smashed – until one of them is brutally, arbitrarily murdered in a burglary. The survivors come under the scrutiny of an eccentric cop, and their underlying fears and regrets slowly but surely emerge. Thanks to ace performances, the effect is surprisingly fresh and moving. TR

Love! Valour! Compassion!
(1997, US, 114 min)
d Joe Mantello. *p* Doug Chapin, Barry Krost. *sc* Terrence McNally. *ph* Alik Sakharov. *ed* Colleen Sharp. *pd* François Séguin. *m* Harold Wheeler. *cast* Jason Alexander, Stephen Spinella, Stephen Bogardus, Randy Becker, John Benjamin Hickey, Justin Kirk, John Glover.
●Forget the title. Adapted by Terrence McNally from his own play, this is the stinging tale of eight gay friends and their trysts and tangles over three holiday weekends. Technically, rookie director Mantello is desperate to play straight. And, at times, the savoured tastefulness of the setting (a New York country house), not to mention the clothes, makes you want to rush out and hug something ugly. *Seinfeld*'s Alexander shines as Buzz, a stage show fan as flamboyant as Liza Minnelli and twice as depressed. This is a man who's played phoney so long he doesn't feel real even to himself. Glover is also marvellous as John, the cynical Brit. He looks perfect, and even when he goes through the standard cathartic revelation, he manages to remain stiff with mistrust. Strangely, Glover's atrocious in a second part, as John's twin James. Certainly it's an uneven ride, with many of the emotional climaxes drifting into bathos. What saves the film is that its theme – that most sexual relationships don't last a lifetime – is a bomb which explodes with absolute quiet. When the kiss-off finally comes, it leaves the neck hairs standing. CO'Su

Love Will Tear Us Apart (Tian Shang Renjian)
(1999, HK, 113 min)
d Yu Lik-Wai. *p* Stanley Kwan, Tony Leung. *sc* Yu Lik-Wai. *ph* Lai Yiu-Fai. *ed* Chow Keung. *pd* Elbut Poon. *cast* Tony Leung [Leung Ka-Fai], Wong Ning, Lü Liping, Rolf Chow.
●Ace cinematographer Yu (*Xiao Wu, Ordinary Heroes*) has come up with the kind of debut feature that vindicates shoestring indie film-making. He focuses on the new underclass of recent immigrants to Hong Kong from Mainland China – the 'hicks' stuck in the sex industry or crappy menial jobs – but looks beyond sociology. Ah Ying (Wong, a recent graduate from drama college in Beijing) gives up karaoke bar work in China to try her luck in Hong Kong. Trapped in prostitution and shoplifting, she heads for a crack-up. Her path crosses those of porn tape vendor Ah Jian (Leung, from *L'Amant*, also the co-producer), exdancer and fantasist Ah Yan (Lü, from *The Blue Kite*) and elevator repairman Ah Chun (first-timer Chow). Yu's real subject is the masochistic resignation that keeps these people locked in their personal hells; he approaches it with unexpected wit and good humour. TR

Love With the Proper Stranger
(1963, US, 102 min, b/w)
d Robert Mulligan. *p* Alan J Pakula. *sc* Arnold Schulman. *ph* Milton Krasner. *ed* Aaron Stell. *ad* Hal Pereira, Roland Anderson. *m* Elmer Bernstein. *cast* Natalie Wood, Steve McQueen, Edie Adams, Herschel Bernardi, Tom Bosley, Harvey Lembeck, Nick Alexander, Penny Santoni.
●Charmingly bitter-sweet tale of the carefree jazz musician and the romantic shop-girl he gets pregnant, leading her to a back-street abortionist as a preferable alternative to facing her strict Italo-American family. Familiar in theme, but given a delightfully fresh flavour by Mulligan's atmospherically low-key direction, excellent performances from Wood and McQueen, and vivid location shooting in New York's Little Italy (the musician's union hall at the beginning, the amusement park, the sad and shabby street of the abortionist). Edie Adams is outstanding as the quizzically cynical stripper with whom McQueen is shacked up, but who is given a characteristically raw deal by a script working its way toward the obligatory happy ending. TM

Loving
(1970, US, 89 min)
d Irvin Kershner. *p/sc* Don Devlin. *ph* Gordon Willis. *ed* Robert Lawrence. *pd* Walter Scott Herndon. *m* Bernardo Segall. *cast* George Segal, Eva Marie Saint, Sterling Hayden, Keenan Wynn, Nancie Phillips, Janis Young, David Doyle, Sherry Lansing, Roland Winters, Roy Scheider.
●Brilliantly observed comedy, somehow at once screwball, satirical and sensitive, taking a refreshingly cynical angle on the clichés of Misunderstood Artist vs The Rest. Segal is the commercial illustrator turned egotistically Angry, scattering contracts, colleagues, wife and mistress in the wake of his empty 'bohemian' anarchy; a less easily indulged figure than Sean Connery's rebel poet in Kershner's earlier *A Fine Madness*, ending up as nakedly absurd as the institutions he takes such glee in attacking. A timely reminder of Kershner's true (major) worth, subsequently dimmed by a series of faceless 'projects' like *Return of a Man Called Horse* and *The Empire Strikes Back.* (Based on a novel by JM Ryan.) PT

Loving Couples
(1980, US, 98 min)
d Jack Smight. *p* Renée Valente. *sc* Martin Donovan. *ph* Philip Lathrop. *ed* Greyfox, Frank J Urioste. *ad* Jan Scott. *m* Fred Karlin. *cast* Shirley MacLaine, James Coburn, Susan Sarandon, Stephen Collins, Sally Kellerman, Nan Martin, Shelly Batt, Pat Corley.
●Flat champagne has nothing on this drearily predictable sitcom about a marriage crisis, solved when each partner seeks temporary refuge with a younger mate. Handsome young stud Collins, in other words, whisks MacLaine into a rejuvenating bout of disco dancing. Meanwhile Coburn, faced with the self-doubts of Sarandon's insecure young career girl, relearns the male prerogative of bolstering the feminine ego. Described as an irreverent romantic comedy about morality in the '80s, the film in fact subscribes to conventions as old as the hills and twice as rocky, burying any hints of feminist awareness beneath the routines of macho courtship. Faced with direction paced at a lethargic crawl and dialogue of inconceivable banality, the cast respond with performances of glazed charm. TM

Lovin' Molly
(1973, US, 98 min)
d Sidney Lumet. *p/sc* Stephen J Friedman. *ph* Edward R Brown. *ed* Joanne Burke. *ad* Robert Drumheller, Paul Hefferan. *m* Fred Hellerman.

cast Blythe Danner, Anthony Perkins, Beau Bridges, Edward Binns, Susan Sarandon, Conrad Fowkes.
●A slow and rambling replay of threads from *The Last Picture Show*, similarly based on a Larry McMurtry novel (*Leaving Cheyenne*) and seen through the same misty eyes. The film attempts to trace the relationship of its three protagonists over some forty years, overcome with a deepening sense of loss as youthful rural idyll turns sour with age and material success. Perkins is the withdrawn Gid; Bridges the placid brother; and Blythe Danner the woman intermittently shared by the brothers but refusing to marry either of them. It is her character the film has most difficulty with, battling to cope with her conscious quest for independence but sliding back into earth-mother cliché. While Lumet elicits very watchable performances, he doesn't really manage to imbue the film's sentimental fabric with enough insight to sustain its weighty format. VG

Loving the Dead

(1991, GB, 52 min)
d/sc Mira Hamermesh. *ph* Jacek Mierolawski. *ed* Terry Twigg. *m* Rosalie Coopman.
●Mira Hamermesh's film about her return to Poland to search for her mother's grave yields a wider picture of the Holocaust. Poland was the killing floor for most European Jews under the Nazis, and few, understandably, have moved back since the war. The culture is kept marginally alive through the efforts of various custodians; one craftsman makes clay models of traditional stetl figures, a group stages reenactments of village life, and Auschwitz has its ghastly museum. Those who escaped return to pore over the ghetto photos. Most Poles, however, seem indifferent. BC

Loving Walter

see Walter

Low Down, The

(2000, GB, 96 min)
d Jamie Thraves. *p* John Stewart, Sally Llewellyn. *sc* Jamie Thraves. *ph* Igor Jadue-Lillo. *ed* Lucia Zucchetti. *pd* Lucy Reeves. *m* Nick Currie, Fred Thomas. *cast* Aidan Gillen, Kate Ashfield, Dean Lennox Kelly, Tobias Menzies, Rupert Proctor, Samantha Power, Dena Smiles.
●Frank (Gillen) is dimly aware he'll have to grow out of this life. He's stuck in a slummy flatshare in Dalston, N London, passing girlfriends, dull contract work, and pals who take the piss. An appointment with Ashfield's easy-going estate agent Ruby offers him the chance to mark his card in more ways than one, but will he take it? Maintaining the promise of his short films, Thraves' unassuming feature debut offers an incisive, impressionistic inscription of twentysomething London experience: moving on, settling somewhere and making the mistakes you'll live with. As before, the writer/director's focus is on the everyday minutiae of friendship, betrayal and romantic diffidence – Frank's problem is his hesitancy, inarticulacy and indecision – here presented in a freewheeling style that's light as a postcard. The cast, too, are apropos. Gillen is bashful and brooding, Ashfield infectiously optimistic, and Menzies, Kelly and Proctor engagingly gabby and/or unsettled as Frank's friends and flatmates. Fresh, funny, new wavey and wistful, it's quite a delight. NB

Low Down Dirty Shame, A

(1994, US, 108 min)
d Keenan Ivory Wayans. *p* Joe Roth, Roger Birnbaum. *sc* Keenan Ivory Wayans. *ph* Matthew F Leonetti. *ad* Robb Wilson King. *m* Marcus Miller. *ed* John F Link. *cast* Keenan Ivory Wayans, Charles S Dutton, Jada Pinkett, Andrew Divoff, Salli Richardson, Corwin Hawkins, Gary Cervantes.
●Having profitably ransacked the '70s blaxploitation genre for the jaunty send-up *I'm Gonna Git You Sucka*, writer/director/star Wayans comes up with a few clichés of his own in this contemporary action-comedy. Turned out of the LAPD, Andre Shame is a struggling PI whose street wisdom and rough charm win him no new cases – until DEA agent Rothmiller (genre stalwart Dutton) offers him a lucrative covert job, tracking down $20m in drug money from narcotics baron Mendoza (Divoff, courtesy of Scumbags Inc). So far, so hackneyed, but when Shame's perky assistant Peaches (Pinkett) starts overdoing the enthusiastic incompetence in a vain bid to up the humour quotient, and the gumshoe's old flame Angela (Richardson) turns up on Mendoza's arm to add a dash of romantic rivalry, the plot starts running on tramlines. TJ

Lower Depths, The

see Bas-Fonds, Les

Lower Depths, The (Donzoko)

(1957, Jap, 137 min, b/w)
d Akira Kurosawa. *sc* Akira Kurosawa, Hideo Oguni. *ph* Ichio Yamazaki. *ed* Akira Kurosawa. *ad* Yoshiro Muraki. *m* Masaru Sato. *cast* Toshiro Mifune, Isuzu Yamada, Ganjiro Nakamura, Kyoko Kagawa, Bokuzen Hidari.
●It's difficult to get too worked up these days over Gorky's classic proletarian drama (one of the showpieces of Stanislavsky realism) about the human flotsam washed up in a Moscow dosshouse and living on illusions: very much of its period in its sturdy affirmation of life amid deprivation and degradation, it has dated as awkwardly as most social documents. But Kurosawa's very faithful transplant to the Tokyo slums, prerehearsed and shot with three cameras in long takes, makes astonishingly skilful use of space within the constricted main set (there are in fact only two), and is fascinating simply as a tour de force. Marvellous performances, too, mining a rich vein of ironic humour amid all the misery. TM

Loyal 47 Ronin of the Genroku Era, The (Genroku Chushingura)

(1941, Jap, 219 min, b/w)
d Kenji Mizoguchi. *p* Nobutaro Shirai. *sc* Kenichiro Hara, Yoshikata Yoda. *ph* Kohei Sugiyama. *ed* Takata Kuji. *ad* Hiroshi Mizutani, Kaneto Shindo. *cast* Utaemon Ichikawa, Isamu Kosugi, Mieko Takamine, Yoshisaburo Arashi, Manpo Misamu, Chojuro Kawarazaki.
●Made during the work-up to war, Mizoguchi's retelling of the traditional tale of the four dozen loyal feudal samurai who, in 1700, avenged the clan lord Asano's death (he committed *seppuku* after impetuously attacking a lord who had insulted him) is concerned with the place and meaning of the Bushido warrior code, which was in decline after 70 years of peace. An immense popular success, the film was approved by the propaganda authority and at near four hours may strain viewers not unduly interested in military ethics. Lovers of Mizoguchi, however, will marvel at the technical accomplishment, the elegance of compositional line and camera movement, and note the relegation of battle to reported speech and the concentration on human drama, notably the role of the chief vassal Oishi and the end sequence concerning the plight of a samurai's betrothed. WH

L-Shaped Room, The

(1962, GB, 142 min, b/w)
d Bryan Forbes. *p* James Woolf, Richard Attenborough. *sc* Bryan Forbes. *ph* Douglas Slocombe. *ed* Anthony Harvey. *ad* Ray Simm. *m* John Barry. *cast* Leslie Caron, Tom Bell, Brock Peters, Cicely Courtneidge, Bernard Lee, Avis Bunnage, Patricia Phoenix, Emlyn Williams, Brock Peters, Anthony Booth, Nanette Newman.
●A queasy sample of the 'new British realism' of the early '60s, based on a novel by Lynne Reid Banks, with Caron as a pregnant French girl who holes up in a Notting Hill bedsit. The house, of course, is peopled by a surefire stockpot of picturesque characters, from seedy doctor and gay black to lesbian actress and chatty tart, not forgetting the tyro writer (Bell) who falls for Caron and draws literary inspiration from their story. Good performances, but it's all a bit like a pofaced trial run for TV's *Rising Damp*. TM

L.627

(1992, Fr, 146 min)
d Bertrand Tavernier. *p* Frédéric Bourboulon, Alain Sarde. *sc* Michel Alexandre. *ph* Alain Choquart. *ed* Ariane Boeglin. *pd* Guy-Claude François. *m* Philippe Sarde. *cast* Didier Besace, Charlotte Kady, Philippe Torréton, Nils Tavernier, Jean-Paul Comart, Jean-Roger Milo, Lara Guirao, Cécile Garcia-Fogel, Claude Brosset.
●Parisian drugs-squad detective Lulu (Besace) has an obsessive mission, born of a hatred for the way drugs waste lives, as in the case of his junkie-prostitute friend Cécile (Guirao). But the department is underfunded; he's saddled with several colleagues who are incompetent, naive or racist; and his various relationships, with his superiors, his wife (Garcia-Fogel), addicts and informants, merely serve to muddy his idealistic code. Tavernier's documentary-style *policier* is admirable, intriguing, and finally something of a disappointment. On the credit side, it never pulls its punches, it's unsentimental in its depiction of both law enforcers and breakers, it acknowledges that both the system and racial inequality exacerbate the drugs problem, and its raw, rambling narrative makes for an impressively authentic alternative to the slick, heroic clichés produced by the Hollywood mainstream. But the film – engrossing enough in any ten-minute excerpt – lacks dramatic drive, frequently slipping into tedious procedural detail. GA

Lucas

(1986, US, 100 min)
d David Seltzer. *p* David Nicksay. *sc* David Seltzer. *ph* Reynaldo Villalobos. *ed* Priscilla Nedd. *ad* James Murakami. *m* Dave Grusin. *cast* Corey Haim, Kerri Green, Charlie Sheen, Courtney Thorne-Smith, Winona Ryder, Thomas E Hodges, Ciro Poppiti.
●Refreshing teen movie that takes the side of the dweebs. Lucas (Haim) is an awkward 13-year-old, more Adrian Mole than Luke Perry. He befriends and falls in love with an 'older' woman – 16-year-old Kerri. But she betrays him for the school football hero, attractively played by Charlie Sheen. More subdued and much more honest that any of John Hughes' egregious forays into adolescence, the film's only drawback is an artificially upbeat ending.

Luce dei miei occhi

see Light of My Eyes

Lucia

(1969, Cuba, 161 min, b/w)
d Humberto Solas. *sc* Humberto Solas, Julio Garcia Espinosa, Nelson Rodriguez. *ph* Jorge Herrera. *ed* Nelson Rodriguez. *ad* Pedro Garcia Espinosa, Roberto Miqueli. *m* Leo Brouwer, Joseito Fernández. *cast* Raquel Revuelta, Eslinda Nuñez, Adela Legra, Eduardo Moure, Ramón Brito, Adolfo Llaurado.
●Easily the finest film to come out of Cuba in the '60s, Solas' powerful triptych depicts three stages in his country's – and his countrywomen's – struggle for liberation. Using a different idiom and visual style for each era (high-contrast melodrama for the 1890s, nostalgic irony for the 1930s, carnival slapstick for the 1960s), he manages, without any political simplifications, to bring the historical process palpably, and humanly, to life. The film was way ahead of its time in linking sexual and political oppression: interest stays focused on the three heroines, but part of that interest lies in the extent to which they take their political colour from the men they love. Free from dogmatic orthodoxy, the film also observes how contradictions and imperialist emotions survive even the best-programmed revolutions. In an upbeat ending, the struggle is seen to continue. JD

Lucia

(1998, GB, 102 min)
d Don Boyd. *p* Stephanie Mills, Alison Kerr. *sc* Don Boyd. *ph* Dewald Aukema. *ed* Adam Ross. *m* (contemporary) Kiran Shiva Akal. *cast* Amanda Boyd, Mark Holland, Richard Coxon, Ann Taylor, John Daszak, Andrew Greenan, John Osborn.
●Part of the fun of Donizetti's opera *Lucia di Lammermoor* (from the novel by Sir Walter Scott) is watching grandiose Italian emotions unfold in a Scottish setting. A promising idea then to shoot his version in a fetching ancestral pile just outside Edinburgh, yet this is not quite a straight opera movie, since writer/director Boyd has picked on the chestnut of life imitating art to mould music with drama. Amanda Boyd plays Kate, a budding singer, whose brother

Hamish (Holland) wants to marry her off to an alcoholic American to save the family's crumbling home. But she loves hunky tenor Sam (Coxon). The production of *Lucia* they stage to celebrate the nuptials goes horribly wrong when fictional identities take over. Recording the arias on location has been unkind to the voices, while the lame scripting of the dramatic interpolations gets performances to match. The interjections from Kiran Akal's banal hybrid electronic score add precisely nothing. TJ

Lucía y el sexo

see Sex and Lucía

Luci del Varietà (Lights of Variety/Variety Lights)

(1950, It, 94 min, b/w)
d/p Alberto Lattuada, Federico Fellini. *sc* Federic Fellini, Alberto Lattuada, Tullio Pinelli. *ph* Otello Martelli. *ad* Aldo Buzzi. *m* Felice Lattuada. *cast* Carla Del Poggio, Peppino De Filippo, Giulietta Masina, John Kitzmiller, Folco Lulli, Franca Valeri, Carlo Romano, Silvio Bagolini.

●Despite the shared directorial credit, there's no doubt into whose filmography this cherishable oddity fits; and more than just the parade of eccentric dreamers and melancholy misfits identifies it. In the margin of its brash and tolerably sentimental story of the punctured pretensions of a troupe of second-rate travelling music-hall players, is examined a tension between 'artist' and 'showman' that not only anticipates the subsequent polarity of critical attitudes to Fellini, but also chimes perfectly with the elements of reflexive stock-taking in *Casanova*. PT

Lucie Aubrac

(1997, Fr, 116 min)
d Claude Berri. *p* Patrick Bordier. *sc* Claude Berri. *ph* Vincenzo Marano. *ed* Hervé de Luze. *pd* Olivier Radot. *m* Philippe Sarde. *cast* Carole Bouquet, Daniel Auteuil, Patrice Chéreau, Eric Boucher, Jean-Roger Milo, Heino Ferch, Jean Martin, Pascal Greggory.

●Based on the true story of two Resistance heroes, Berri's typically meticulous WWII drama concerns the efforts of Lucie Aubrac to liberate her husband Raymond from Gestapo incarceration. While Bouquet and Auteuil are dependably solid, they never really achieve the chemistry that might have made this into a more moving love story; the real problem, however, lies in the leaden pacing, and Berri's superficial, somewhat repetitive screenplay, which offers no particularly revealing insights, let alone dramatic excitement. Not exactly bad, the film is rather dull, and serves mainly as a reminder of how grippingly Melville's *L'Armée des Ombres* treated similar material. GA

Lucifer Rising

see Anger Magick Lantern Cycle, The

Luck of Ginger Coffey, The

(1964, Can/US, 99 min, b/w)
d Irvin Kershner. *p* Leon Roth. *sc* Brian Moore. *ph* Manny Wynn. *ed* Antony Gibbs. *pd* Harry Horner. *m* Bernardo Segall. *cast* Robert Shaw, Mary Ure, Liam Redmond, Tom Harvey, Libby McClintock, Leo Leyden.

●A quiet, compellingly probing adaptation of Brian Moore's novel about a man's painful growth into self-realisation. Shaw is excellent as the eponymous hero, a blarneying Irish immigrant who comes to the land of opportunity (Canada) convinced that he is the man it has been waiting for. Told of a vacancy as sub-editor on a newspaper, he immediately sees himself as becoming the editor within weeks; offered a good job as assistant to the owner of a diaper-cleaning service, he turns it down as beneath his dignity; and it is only after successive disappointments, when his despairing wife (Ure, equally good) has left him to take a job in order to support their teenage daughter, that Ginger begins to take realistic stock. Kershner's even, penetrating direction makes marvellous use of the Montreal locations, perfectly capturing the weird beauty of the city's mixture of gleaming skyscrapers and tall, old-fashioned houses festooned with iron staircases, all draped under a layer of snow and ice. TM

Luck, Trust & Ketchup: Robert Altman in Carver Country

(1994, US, 90 min)
d/p Mike Kaplan, John Dorr. *ph* John Dorr. *ed* Michael Masucci. *with* Robert Altman, Tess Gallagher, Anne Archer, Bruce Davison, Robert Downey Jr, Peter Gallagher, Buck Henry, Jennifer Jason Leigh, Jack Lemmon, Huey Lewis, Lyle Lovett, Andie MacDowell, Frances McDormand, Matthew Modine, Julianne Moore, Christopher Penn, Tim Robbins, Annie Ross, Lori Singer, Madeleine Stowe, Lili Taylor, Lily Tomlin, Tom Waits, Fred Ward.

●Kaplan has been an associate of Robert Altman since the mid-'70s, so you'd hardly expect his documentary on the making of *Short Cuts* to be in any way critical. That said, it avoids the sort of hagiographic gush that mars most on-set promos, while one evident advantage of his friendship with Altman was that he had unprecedented access to cast, crew and director alike. True, long-term admirers of the great man won't learn very much they didn't already know, but more recent converts should find this movie-on-the-movie intelligent and illuminating. Kaplan's prime achievement is his film's clarity; it's structured chronologically, charting the production from inception to wrap party, and interviewing each member of the large cast in sequence while they were on set. GA

Lucky Break

(1994, Aust, 94 min)
d Ben Lewin. *p* Bob Weis. *sc* Ben Lewin. *ph* Vince Monton. *ed* Peter Carrodus. *pd* Peta Lawson. *m* Paul Grabowsky. *cast* Anthony LaPaglia, Gia Carrides, Sio Bantuke, Jacek Koman, Rebecca Gibney, Robyn Nevin, Marshall Napier.

●Bizarre semi-black comedy charting the on-off relationship between Carrides (a polio victim whose erotic fantasies fuel her novels) and shady jeweller LaPaglia, who's torn between his wealthy fiancée and the woman whose leg he believes is only temporarily broken. The film, which occasionally gets rather too broad to work as properly romantic comedy, is frank about the difficulties of physical impairment, and even seems to celebrate it here and there.

Lucky Break

(2001, GB/Ger/US, 108 min)
d Peter Cattaneo. *p* Barnaby Thompson, Peter Cattaneo. *sc* Ronan Bennett. *ph* Alwin Küchler. *ed* David Gamble. *pd* Max Gottlieb. *m* Anne Dudley. *cast* James Nesbitt, Olivia Williams, Timothy Spall, Bill Nighy, Lennie James, Ron Cook, Frank Harper, Christopher Plummer, Celia Imrie.

●Director Cattaneo's follow-up to *The Full Monty* is set in a remote prison where the inmates are preparing a show as a smoke screen for an escape: a good excuse for another blokey bonding session, less so for the bland heterosexual romance at the film's heart. It's a tale of love across the divide, with cocky upstart Jimmy (Nesbitt) rightly accusing support officer Annabel (Williams) of talking crap before falling for her in rehearsals. What is surprising is how little dramatic tension surrounds even the escape; the film aims for low key, but limps, each character either following a predictable trajectory or remaining in total stasis. The clichés are strictly televisual: pompous governor, camp fraudster, clueless bleeding-heart drama teacher – it's assumed we know and like these people from the TV prison sitcom *Porridge*. There's a general laziness and complacency in the air, and the gags are guilty as charged. SS

Lucky Jim

(1957, GB, 95 min, b/w)
d John Boulting. *p* Roy Boulting. *sc* Patrick Campbell. *ph* Max Greene. *ed* Max Benedict. *ad* Elliot Scott. *m* John Addison. *cast* Ian Carmichael, Terry-Thomas, Hugh Griffith, Sharon Acker, Maureen Connell, Jean Anderson, Clive Morton, Kenneth Griffith.

●Kingsley Amis' novel about redbrick university life turned into likeable but harmless knockabout farce by the Boulting Brothers. The situation of accident-prone, caustic-minded young lecturer Jim Dixon having problems with his girlfriend and his professor – he was promptly annexed as an example of 'Angry Young Man' protest – here lacks all sense of satire, not surprisingly given the casting of the wet Carmichael in the central role. Cosy, undemanding, and quite forgettable. GA

Lucky Lady

(1975, US, 118 min)
d Stanley Donen. *p* Michael Gruskoff. *sc* Willard Huyck, Gloria Katz. *ph* Geoffrey Unsworth. *ed* Peter Boita. *pd* John Barry. *m* Ralph Burns. *cast* Gene Hackman, Liza Minnelli, Burt Reynolds, Geoffrey Lewis, John Hillerman, Robby Benson, Michael Hordern.

●The only vaguely remarkable thing about *Lucky Lady* is that it presents an overtly troilist relationship to its family audience with so little fuss: Hackman, Reynolds and Minnelli share a bed in '30s America, and make their living by running booze across the Mexican border. Unfortunately, the film's originality stops there, which is surprising since it was scripted by the talented Huyck/Katz partnership (*American Graffiti*, *The Second Coming*). Donen's determined 'lightness' is typified by the ghastly, insistent score which punctuates almost every action with a corny tune. The story is virtually non-existent, the period detail coyly derivative, and much of the comedy would be shamed even by the most meagre Anna Neagle vehicle of the '40s. DP

Lucky Luciano

(1973, It/Fr, 115 min)
d Francesco Rosi. *p* Franco Cristaldi. *sc* Francesco Rosi, Lino Jannuzzi, Tonino Guerra. *ph* Pasqualino De Santis. *ed* Ruggero Mastroianni. *ad* Andrea Crisanti. *m* Piero Piccioni. *cast* Gian Maria Volonté, Rod Steiger, Edmond O'Brien, Charles Siragusa, Vincent Gardenia, Charles Cioffi, Silverio Blasi, Jacques Monod.

●Rosi's characteristic dossier on power and corruption tracks the enigmatic figure of repatriated Mafioso gangster Luciano through the web of political/criminal complicity that set the course of Italy's post-war 'recovery'. While specific judgment on Luciano himself is open-endedly reserved, the evidence adduced from a variety of sources (mosaic-style, with Siragusa, for instance, playing himself as a US Narcotics Bureau investigator) is damningly clear on the way the Americans established the Mafia as a 'friendly' buffer against communist influence, only to later have the worm turn vengefully with a flood of drugs back to the States. *Film noir* meets the conspiracy thriller in a flurry of masterful set pieces, operatic intensity segues into documentary-like observation of the complex machinery of manipulable power, and Rosi provides a context for the *Godfather* films which threatens to outdo their own cinematic forcefulness. PT

Lucky Luke

(1971, Fr/Bel, 76 min)
d René Goscinny. *sc* René Goscinny, Morris, Pierre Tchernia. *ph* François Léonard. *ed* R Chanceux. *m* Claude Bolling. *cast* voices: (French version) Marcel Bozuffi, Jean Berger, Pierre Trabaud, Jacques Balutin, Jacques Jouanneau; (English version) Rich Little.

●Animated adventures of the popular European comic-strip cowboy, rendered in cheap and listless graphics, but augmented on the English version's soundtrack by Rich Little's verbal imitations of a host of Hollywood Western stars. PT

Lucky Mascot

see Brass Monkey, The

Lucky People Center International

(1999, Swe/Den/Nor, 81 min)
d Johan Söderberg, Erik Pauser. *p* Lars Jönsson. *sc* Johan Söderberg, Erik Pauser. *ph* Jan Röed. *ed* Johan Söderberg, Erik Pauser. *m* Lucky People Center.

●The Lucky People Center is a Swedish collective of dance musicians and multi-media artists, here concerned with complementary concepts of sensual and spiritual fulfilment offered by cultures or individuals from around the world. Thus we meet a voodoo priestess; a man inspired to mimic gibbon song; a yoga virtuoso; an angry forest tribe; a Japanese banker-cum-avant garde headbanger; a benevolent community rapper; a troupe of Maori activists; erotic adventurer Annie Sprinkle; and, in occasional counterpoint, less happy glimpses of the physically or spiritually misguided – Chinese soldiers, Heaven's Gate cultists, Bill Clinton. Advocations of song and dance, positive thinking, and wild living mingle with critiques of Western urban gridlock and credit cards; none of which is radically illuminating, but the cumulative effect is a palatable representation of alternative life styles. The film's most obvious formal antecedents are *Koyaanisqatsi* and *Baraka* where the collision of landscapes produced a pat, self-contradictory polemic. But here the slightly slipshod technique never enables the director/editors to editorialise – instead it's their subjects who are given voice. NB

Lucky Star

(1929, US, 90 min, b/w)
d Frank Borzage. *p* William Fox. *sc* Sonya Levien, Tristram Tupper, (dialogue) John Hunter Booth. *ph* Chester A Lyons, William Cooper Smith. *ed/titles* HH Caldwell, Katherine Hilliker. *ad* Harry Oliver. [*m* Stuart Hancock.] *cast* Charles Farrell, Janet Gaynor, Guinn 'Big Boy' Williams, Paul Fix, Hedwiga Reicher, Gloria Grey, Hector Sarno.

● With a prizewinning new score from Stuart Hancock, Borzage's long-lost wisp of a romance was made, like *Blackmail*, in both sound and silent versions (a silent print was rediscovered in the Netherlands Film Museum). It offers two fairytales for the price of one: while Gaynor's poor overburdened farm girl is given a Cinderella-like make-over by her seemingly platonic admirer Farrell, he in turn is abjuring his feelings for her, as the Beast did for Beauty, having come home a cripple from the Great War. His ultimate transformation, if taken literally, is hard to swallow these days; it's also far from clear what the villain of the piece thinks he's up to. Still, Borzage's romantic conception of love – as hard-won, shared innocence buffeting the world's ignorance and exploitation – is assuredly expressed, and the glancing realism of the war and family scenes gives it a firm grounding. NB

Lucky Texan, The

(1933, US, 53 min, b/w)
d Robert N Bradbury. *p* Paul Malvern. *sc* Robert N Bradbury. *ph* Archie J Stout. *ed* Carl Pierson. *cast* John Wayne, Barbara Sheldon, Lloyd Whitlock, George Hayes, Yakima Canutt, Ed Parker, Gordon Demaine, Earl Dwire.

● Jerry Mason (Wayne) goes prospecting with Jake, his father's old pardner (Hayes), but is duped by a couple of assayers. Charley's aunt saves the day when Jerry is had up for murdering Jake. One of Lone Star's more lively Westerns, with a gold-seeking dog, a somnolent sheriff (Canutt), an above-average final chase (automobile, horse, train), and Wayne somewhat flummoxed by the details of lady's underwear. Pretty primitive, none the less. JPy

Ludwig

(1972, It/Fr/WGer, 255 min)
d Luchino Visconti. *p* Ugo Santalucia. *sc* Luchino Visconti, Enrico Medioli, Suso Cecchi D'Amico. *ph* Armando Nannuzzi. *ed* Ruggero Mastroianni. *ad* Mario Chiari, Mario Scisci. *m* Offenbach, Schumann, Richard Wagner.*cast* Helmut Berger, Romy Schneider, Trevor Howard, Silvana Mangano, Helmut Griem, Nora Ricci, Gert Fröbe, John Moulder Brown.

● Interested only in Ludwig of Bavaria as a neurotic individual, Visconti centres everything on the king's fears, sublimations and fantasies. He therefore produces a loving, uncritical portrait of a mad homosexual recluse, whose passions are opera, fairy-tale castles, and exquisite young men. Nothing is more sumptuous than Helmut Berger's performance in the lead, the brooding mad scenes, the deliberately contrived hysterical outbursts, and it takes only a flicker of scepticism to find the whole charade risible. But suspension of disbelief has its own rewards: Visconti's connoisseurship of historical detail and manners is as acute as ever, and his commitment to his subject is total. The film was originally released in cut versions ranging between 186 and 137 minutes; this uncut one, obviously more coherent, simply doubles the interest/boredom rate. TR

Ludwig – Requiem for a Virgin King (Ludwig – Requiem für einen jungfräulichen König)

(1972, WGer, 139 min)
d Hans Jürgen Syberberg. *p* Hans Jürgen Syberberg, Christoph Holch. *sc* Hans Jürgen Syberberg. *ph* Dietrich Lohmann. *ed* Peter Przyggoda. *ad* Chr Dank, J Hoffmann, H Döll, A Quaglio, G Dehn, H Breling, M Schultze, F Seitz, F Knab, J Lange. *m* Richard Wagner. *cast* Harry Baer, Balthasar Thomas, Peter Kern, Peter Moland, Günther Kaufmann, Oskar von Schab, Ingrid Caven, Peter Przyggoda.

● The first part of Syberberg's remarkable trilogy (followed by *Karl May* and *Hitler, a Film from Germany*), this takes the legend of Ludwig II of Bavaria (Wagner's patron, virgin homosexual, mad visionary, builder of impossible castles, aesthetic recluse) and filters it through the subsequent chaos of German history: the rise of Bismarck and the Prussians at the turn of the century, and the rise of Hitler in the '30s. It's constructed as a series of 28 tableaux, which makes it more like a pageant than a conventional drama: it's full of deliberate disjunctions and contradictions (both Wagnerian stage designs and modern video footage are used as back-projections, for instance), and it feels free to use elements of kitsch (a Nazi rhumba) alongside moments of 'high art' (Isolde's *Liebestod*) without apparent distinction. The slow pace and ultra-mannered staging compel either fascination or outright rejection. Those fascinated are rewarded with constant surprises and delights, because it's one of the most beautiful and defiantly original movies of the '70s. TR

Ludwig's Cook (Theodor Hierneis oder wie man ein ehemaliger Hofkoch wird)

(1973, WGer, 84 min)
d/p Hans Jürgen Syberberg. *sc* Hans Jürgen Syberberg, Walter Sedlmayr. *ph* Hermann Reichmann. *cast* Walter Sedlmayr.

● Made by Syberberg immediately after *Ludwig – Requiem for a Virgin King*, *Ludwig's Cook* sets out to deal with some of the historical 'truths' about the fairytale monarch that the earlier film ignored. But Syberberg's approach is typically sly and oblique: Walter Sedlmayr (best known here as the grocer in *Fear Eats the Soul*) starts by taking us on a guided tour of Ludwig's castle, but soon slips into the role of Theodor Hierneis, who became Ludwig's head cook in 1882. And so everything that we learn about Ludwig comes from the (literal or metaphorical) perspective of his kitchens. The approach is a wonderfully subversive corrective to the orthodox histories, and at the same time a starting-point for a fascinating reflection on fact and fiction as opposite sides of the same coin. In its unmomentous way, a major film. TR

Lukewarm Water Under the Red Bridge (Akai Hashi Noshitano Nurui Mizu)

(2001, Jap. 119 min)
p Shohei Imamura. *sc* Shohei Imamura, Motofumi Tomikawa, Daisuke Tengan. *ph* Shigeru Komatsubara. *ed* Hajime Okayasu. *pd* Hisao Inagaki. *m* Shinichiro Ikebe. *cast* Koji Yakusho, Miho Shimizu, Mitsuko Baisho, Mansaku Fuwa, Kazuo Kitramura, Isao Natsuyagi.

● With a number of moments and themes reminiscent of *The Eel*, but with none of that film's tonal assurance, this bizarre, allegorical comedy-drama sees jobless Yakusho leave the streets of Tokyo in search of a golden Buddha which a now dead tramp and philosopher told him lies hidden in a house in a remote coastal town; there he meets and is revitalised by a strange kleptomaniac who vents water by the gallon every time she attains sexual pleasure – which, with him, is often – until jealousy kicks in. Rambling, discursive, uneven, fantastical, sometimes just plain silly, the film has a number of decent gags which, sadly, soon get overused; and quite what it's all about – other than a celebration of women's primeval powers in the age of technology – is up for grabs. GA

Lullaby of Broadway

(1950, US, 92 min)
d David Butler. *p* William Jacobs. *sc* Earl Baldwin. *ph* Wilfred M Cline. *ed* Irene Morra. *ad* Douglas Bacon. *songs* Al Dubin, Harry Warren, Cole Porter, George Gershwin, Buddy De Sylva and others. *cast* Doris Day, Gene Nelson, SZ Sakall, Billy de Wolfe, Gladys George, Florence Bates.

● Amiable backstage Warners musical with Doris Day as an up-and-coming British comedienne and singer who goes to New York in the mistaken belief that mum is a huge star on the stage there. Thanks to sweetie-pie millionaire 'Cuddles' Sakall, the truth is hidden long enough for her to launch her own crack at Broadway. A handful of Gershwin and Porter tunes include 'Please Don't Talk About Me When I'm Gone', but the stuff in between is just so much fluff. TJ

Lulu Belle

(1948, US, 87 min, b/w)
d Leslie Fenton. *sc* Everett Freeman. *ph* Ernest Laszlo. *ed* James Smith. *ad* Duncan Kramer. *m* Henry Russell. *cast* Dorothy Lamour, George Montgomery, Otto Kruger, Albert Dekker, Glenda Farrell, Greg McClure.

● Lamour vamps in a none too persuasive attempt to extend her range, playing an ambitious chanteuse who's also something of a femme fatale. Yes, we know, Dottie dallied with Bob Hope's affections when she only ever had eyes for Bing, but this is ridiculous. Where's Rita Hayworth when you need her? From a play by Charles MacArthur and Edward Sheldon. GM

Lulu the Tool

see Classe Operaia Va in Paradiso, La

Lumière

(1966, Fr, 61 min, b/w)
d Marc Allégret. *p* Pierre Braunberger. *sc* Marc Allégret. *ed* Mireille Mauberna. *m* Henri Sauguet. *narrator* Claude Dauphin.

● This was the longest in a Lumière quartet assembled by Allégret in collaboration with Marie Epstein and the Cinémathèque Française. It comprises material filmed by Louis, Auguste and their staff in Europe and N America between 1894 and 1900. There are street scenes, royal processions, travelling shots taken from train, gondola and the Eiffel Tower lift, vignettes of Warholian banality ('Card Players', 'Demolishing a Wall') and two versions of the 'watered gardener', that first tentative foray into narrative. Full marks to the informative commentary, with its wry awareness of the images' acquired poetic resonance. Print quality is excellent, doing full justice to that remarkable depth of focus. BBa

Lumière et Compagnie

(1995, Fr, 92 min, b/w & col)
d (Lumière et Compagnie) Sarah Moon; (the segments) Patrice Leconte, Gabriel Axel, Claude Miller, Jacques Rivette, Michael Haneke, Fernando Trueba, Merzak Allouache, Raymond Depardon, Wim Wenders, Jaco Van Dormael, Nadine Trintignant, Régis Wargnier, Hugh Hudson, Zhang Yimou, Liv Ullmann, Vicente Aranda, Lucian Pintilié, John Boorman, Claude Lelouch, Abbas Kiarostami, Lasse Hallström, Costa-Gavras, Kiju Yoshida, Idrissa Ouedraogo, Gastone Kabore, Youssef Chahine, Helma Sanders, Francis Girod, Cédric Klapisch, Alain Corneau, Ismail Merchant-James Ivory, Jerry Schatzberg, Spike Lee, Andrei Konchalovsky, Peter Greenaway, Bigas Luna, Arthur Penn, David Lynch, Theo Angelopoulos. *p* Fabienne Servan Schreiber. *ph* Philippe Poulet, Didier Ferry. *ed* Roger Ikhlef, Timothy Miller. *m* Jean-Jacques Lemêtre. *with/cast* the film-makers, François Mitterrand, Sven Nykvist, Bruno Ganz, Otto Sander, Lena Olin.

● A Lumière centenary production (cf *Les Enfants de Lumière*). Forty film-makers were invited, or challenged, to make a Lumière movie: one shot, 52 seconds long, no direct sound, using an original 1895 camera. The result is a series of tableaux – elaborate, banal, enigmatic – in which the favourite gambit has been to include the past and the present in the same shot (Boorman, Yimou, Merchant Ivory). Several look like fragments that have shaken loose from one of their director's features (Wenders, Rivette), while the most distinctive (Greenaway, Lynch) blithely ignore the ground rules. Even 40 of these film-lets don't add up to a feature, so each director is quizzed on such topics as 'Is cinema mortal?' and even *'Pourquoi filmez-vous?'* And yes, in principle there's a 1995 'train arriving at La Ciotat station' – that's Leconte, opening the proceedings. Except the train doesn't stop there now. BBa

Lumière Noire (Black Night)

(1994, Fr, 107 min)
d/p Med Hondo. *sc* Med Hondo, Didier Daeninckx. *ph* Ricardo Aronovich. *ed* Christine Lack. *cast* Patrick Poivey, Inês de Medeiros, Roland Bertin, Pascal Legitimus, Charlie Bauer, Gilles Sagal, Gérard Hernandez.

●Med Hondo made an international breakthrough in 1968 with his Burkina Faso-based warrior-queen epic *Sarraounia*. Here he brings an outsider's eye to a Parisian thriller: Poivey's an airport technician caught up in a terrorist attack who has to fight police bureaucracy to clear his name when he's suspected of involvement in the violence.

Lumumba

(2000, Fr/Bel/Ger/Haiti, 110 min)
d Raoul Peck. *p* Jacques Bidou. *sc* Pascal Bonitzer, Raoul Peck. *ph* Bernard Lutic. *ed* Jacques Comets. *pd* Denis Renault. *m* Jean-Claude Petit. *cast* Eriq Ebouaney, Alex Descas, Théophile Moussa Sowie, Maka Kotto, Dieudonné Kabongo, Pascal N'Zonzi, André Debaar.

●This is a first rate fictionalised story of the last year or so of Patrice Lumumba, the first post-colonial prime minister of the Democratic Republic of the Congo. It may assume a little prior knowledge of Central/West African political affairs, but it makes its point about his abandonment and lonely sacrifice clear enough. At its core is an extremely dignified performance by Eriq Ebouaney as the beer salesman turned leader of his people. WH

Luna, La

(1979, It, 142 min)
d Bernardo Bertolucci. *p* Giovanni Bertolucci. *sc* Giuseppe Bertolucci, Clare Peploe, Bernardo Bertolucci. *ph* Vittorio Storaro, Ed Lachman. *ed* Garbriella Cristiani. *ad* Gianni Silvestri, Maria Paola Maino. *cast* Jill Clayburgh, Matthew Barry, Laura Betti, Veronica Lazar, Renato Salvatori, Fred Gwynne, Alida Valli, Tomas Milian, Franco Citti, Roberto Benigni.

●An Oedipal parable, in which Matthew Barry's young junkie falls in love with his opera-singer mother (Clayburgh). Ravishing to look at, but the movie's real curiosity is the way it fails to reverse Bertolucci's usual preoccupations: it emerges that the boy's real problem is the lack of a father and need for a family – an emphasis that Bertolucci himself vehemently denies. CA

Luna e l'Altra

(1996, It, 100 min)
d Maurizio Nichetti. *p* Ernesto Di Sarro. *sc* Maurizio Nichetti, Stefano Albé, Nello Correale, Laura Rischetto. *ph* Luca Bigazzi. *ed* Rita Rossi. *pd* Maria pia Angelini. *m* Carlo Siliotto. *cast* Iaia Forte, Aurelio Fierro, Luigi Burruano, Ivano Marescotti, Maurizio Nichetti, Eraldo Turra.

●Nichetti's characteristically broad, sentimental comedy concerns a well-meaning but strait-laced teacher living with her disenchanted father in mid-'50s Milan. A magic lantern which she confiscates from some kids from a travelling circus liberates the teacher's free-spirited shadow. The shadow takes a room in the local bordello and generally scandalises the town (still partly inhabited by fascist sympathisers), causing much embarrassment to the woman's more stolid self. It's winsome and ingratiating, and not helped by all the obligatory circus and brass-band stuff, or by the director's own performance as the school janitor in love with the heroine. Technically clever, though. GA

Luna en el Espejo, La

see Moon in the Mirror, The

Luna Papa

(1999, Aus/Jap, 106 min)
d Bakhtiar Khudojnazarov. *p* Heinz Stussak, Karl Baumgartner, Kenzo Horikoshi. *sc* Irakli Kwirikadze. *ph* Martin Gschlacht, Rotislav Pirumov, Dusan Joksimovic, Rali Ralchev. *ed* Kirk von Heflin. *ad* Negmat Dzhuraev. *m* Daler Nasarov. *cast* Chulpan Khamatova, Moritz Bleibtreu, Merab Ninidze, Ato Mukhamedshanov.

●Six years on from *On Equal Terms*, Khudojnazarov tries to do it again with a romantic fable about a movie-struck 17-year-old girl left pregnant by an encounter one moonlit night with a faceless stranger who claims to be friends with Tom Cruise. While her father and brother scour the land for the seducer, Mamlakat herself (Khamatova) befriends a young doctor (Bleibtreu) who agrees to be a father to her child – and just might be the real one. Semi-detached from his Tajik roots, the director seems to be aiming for some nebulous ground between Bertolucci's *La Luna* and a Central Asian folktale. Even before the not-very-special effects take over at the climax, the visual poetry of his previous films has been eclipsed by the clichés of roistering 'magic realism' in the Kusturica manner. TR

Lunatic, The

(1990, US, 94 min)
d Lol Creme. *p* Paul Heller, John Pringle. *sc* Anthony C Winkler. *ph* Richard Greatrex. *ed* Michael Connell. *m* Wally Badarou. *cast* Julie T Wallace, Paul Campbell, Carl Bradshaw, Reggie Carter, Winston Stona, Linda Gambrill.

●This mind-boggling, often boring comedy/drama sex romp presents a disarmingly naive view of Jamaican life. It's centred on gentle lunatic Aloysius (Campbell) and the ménage à trois he sets up with blonde German tourist Inga (Wallace) and mad, machete-wielding goat-butcher Service Johnson (Bradshaw). They take to sex, then to crime, thence retribution. You could read the movie as a kind of upbeat reggae satire-cum-parody. It dances through all the major social and cultural themes: poverty, education, magic and animism, racism, class, religion, sexual politics, and finally cricket! The music score is by Wally Badarou, and the soundtrack sports such as Black Uhuru and Toots and the Maytals. The *patois* is easier to understand than in *The Harder They Come*, and Jamaica looks stunning in a touristy kind of way. A movie that asks to be laughed at. WH

Lunatic Theatre

see Kitami

Lunch Hour

(1962, GB, 63 min, b/w)
d James Hill. *p* John Mortimer, Harold Orton. *sc* John Mortimer. *ph* Wolfgang Suschitzky. *ed* Ted Hooker. *ad* Jack Stevens. *m* James Hill, Ian Orton. *cast* Shirley Ann Field, Robert Stephens, Kay Walsh, Hazel Hughes, Nigel Davenport, Peter Ashmore.

●Further evidence that, indeed, sexual intercourse didn't begin until 1963, as Field and Stephens, frustrated office colleagues, vainly seek somewhere to bonk. In fact the whole piece is redolent of the early '60s (post-Austerity, pre-Swinging), from its Theatre of the Absurd affectations to the way it manages to be simultaneously liberating and oppressive. It's also quite amateurish, going unreleased at the time and only latterly, some 40 years on, finding a niche as late night TV fodder for cine-socio-nostalgists. BBa

Lunch on the Grass

see Déjeuner sur l'Herbe, Le

Lune dans le Caniveau, La

see Moon in the Gutter, The

Lune et le téton, La

see Tit and the Moon, The

Lunes de fiel

see Bitter Moon

Lunga Vita alla Signora!

see Long Live the Lady!

Lured (aka Personal Column)

(1947, US, 102 min, b/w)
d Douglas Sirk. *p* James Nasser. *sc* Leo Rosten. *ph* William H Daniels. *ed* John M Foley. *pd* Nicolai Remisoff. *m* Michel Michelet. *cast* George Sanders, Lucille Ball, Charles Coburn, Boris Karloff, Cedric Hardwicke, Joseph Calleia, Alan Mowbray, George Zucco, Robert Coote.

●A remake of Siodmak's *Pièges*, transposed to London, with Lucille Ball as the taxi-dancer recruited by the police to help trap a serial killer preying on girls by way of lonely hearts ads. The ambience is strangely indeterminate (contemporary London wavers between Edwardian Gothic and transatlantic chic), and the script – mostly a slavish copy of the original, with all its faults – is not helped by a fatuous 'inspiration' (doubtless intended to add a bit of French decadence) whereby the killer is said to be inspired by Baudelaire's poetry. The lighter scenes work well enough, with Ball's heroine turned into a chorus-line Nancy Drew, and the ambivalently debonair Sanders (a vast improvement on Chevalier) more plausible as both romantic interest and chief suspect. But the darker corners are sadly neglected. Siodmak's superb depiction of the killer's slow, hapless self-betrayal goes for very little here; and the wonderfully sinister, yet touching sequence involving von Stroheim's mad couturier (now played by Karloff) is truncated into crude stereotype. TM

Lure of the Jungle, The

see Paw

Lush Life

(1993, US, 104 min)
d Michael Elias. *p* Thom Colwell. *sc* Michael Elias. *ph* Nancy Schrieber. *ed* Bill Yahraus. *m* Lennie Niehaus. *cast* Jeff Goldblum, Forest Whitaker, Kathy Baker, Tracey Needham, Lois Chiles, Zack Norman, Don Cheadle.

●A middlebrow take on the life of two jobbing jazzers in contemporary New York. Goldblum (stretching for louche) is a married-but-improvising sax player, Whitaker (far more credible) is his trumpet-blowing buddy. It meanders along quite happily, until 'untimely death' intervenes, somewhat unpersuasively. TCh

Lust and Desire (Le Désir et la Volupté)

(1973, Fr, 84 min)
d Julien Saint-Clair. *sc* Christian Daniel Watton, Julien Saint-Clair. *ph* Claude Beausoleil. *ed* Pauline Fraisse. *cast* Claire Gregory, Denyse Roland, Alan Scott, Vania Vilers, Catherine Lafont, Billy Kearns, Francis Lax.

●A hot title masking cool exploitation, this is an identikit example of the French sex cinema, down to the last chic ensemble and piano arpeggio. Flagging eroticism, with the married antagonists suffering sexual estrangement, is given a typically contrived boost by the introduction of a night-club stripper. The only point in the film's favour is that it does pay a mite more attention than usual to the sexual needs of its female characters, even allowing that lesbianism and bisexuality may offer liberating potential rather than being just another variation. VG

Lust for Life

(1956, US, 122 min)
d Vincente Minnelli. *p* John Houseman. *sc* Norman Corwin. *ph* Freddie Young, Russell Harlan. *ed* Adrienne Fazan. *ad* Cedric Gibbons, Hans Peters, Preston Ames. *m* Miklós Rózsa. cast Kirk Douglas, Anthony Quinn, James Donald, Pamela Brown, Everett Sloane, Niall MacGinnis, Jill Bennett, Henry Daniell.

●In contrast to the normal Hollywood biopic of 'The Great Artist', in which Art forever takes second place to the Man, Minnelli here offers an account of the developing intensity of Van Gogh's art. Throughout *Lust for Life*, Van Gogh, brilliantly portrayed by Kirk Douglas as a man forever on a knife-edge, struggles to explain himself to his family and to Anthony Quinn's Gauguin. However, Minnelli, with the colours he chooses – which follow those of the paintings – and with his dramatic counterpointing of events in Van Gogh's life with his canvases, undermines all explanations. Minnelli neither explains Van Gogh's art in terms of his life or vice versa, but celebrates both. (From Irving Stone's novel.) PH

Lustful Amazon, The (Maciste contre la Reine des Amazones)

(1973, Fr, 65 min)
d Clifford Brown [Jesús Franco]. *p* Robert de Nesle. *sc* Jesús Franco. *ph* Gérard Brissaud. *ed* Gérard Kikoine. *m* Robert Viger. *cast* Val Davis, Alice Arno, Robert Woods, Montie Prolis, Lina Romay, Chantal Broquet.

● Unrelievedly unimaginative offshoot from the Italian strong-man series, with a distinctly European garden standing in for the Amazonian jungle as Maciste sets off in quest of lost treasure, only to be pressed into service as a stud by the Amazon queen. Bored robot actresses walk through their non-roles in an understandable daze; and to cap it all, far from being staunchly independent, the Amazons are depicted as woeful figments of a chauvinistic male ego. VG

Lust in the Dust

(1985, US, 84 min)
d Paul Bartel. *p* Allan Glaser, Tab Hunter. *sc* Philip John Taylor. *ph* Paul Lohmann. *ed* Alan Toomayan. *pd* Walter Pickette. *m* Peter Matz. *cast* Tab Hunter, Divine, Lainie Kazan, Geoffrey Lewis, Henry Silva, Cesar Romero, Gina Gallego, Woody Strode.

● Laughs are hard to come by in Bartel's campy take on the Spaghetti Western, though it may provoke a few guilty sniggers. If that cast-list doesn't tell you all you need to know, be aware that the plot involves Divine's tattooed buttocks, a piano player named Red Dick and Tab Hunter's Clint Eastwood imitation. BBa

Lust Seekers, The

see Good Morning…and Goodbye

Lusty Men, The

(1952, US, 113 min, b/w)
d Nicholas Ray. *p* Jerry Wald. *sc* Horace McCoy, David Dortort. *ph* Lee Garmes. *ed* Ralph Dawson. *ad* Albert S D'Agostino, Al Herman. *m* Roy Webb. *cast* Susan Hayward, Robert Mitchum, Arthur Kennedy, Arthur Hunnicutt, Frank Faylen, Glenn Strange, Lane Chandler.

● Nick Ray understood character and psychological pressures better than almost any of his contemporaries, and *The Lusty Men* was one of his happiest breaks: sympathetic producers, a great cameraman (Lee Garmes, who shot Sternberg's Dietrich movies), and one of Robert Mitchum's finest performances. The story isn't much (the security of family life versus the rootlessness and danger of working as a rodeo rider), but the situation is rich in emotional resonances which Ray conjures into life convincingly. TR

Luther

(1973, US/GB/Can, 112 min)
d Guy Green. *p* Ely Landau. *sc* Edward Anhalt. *ph* Freddie Young. *ed* Malcolm Cooke. *pd* Peter Mullins. *m* John Addison. *cast* Stacy Keach, Patrick Magee, Hugh Griffith, Robert Stephens, Alan Badel, Julian Glover, Judi Dench, Leonard Rossiter, Maurice Denham.

● At school history classes, Luther emerged as one of the more interesting figures of history because of his constipation, the type of detail that posterity often overlooks. But even Fifth Formers should be disappointed with this version of John Osborne's scatological account of Luther, the bowel movements of history, and the rupture with the Catholic Church. Although Stacy Keach occasionally conveys Luther's intensely felt, near physical relationship with Mother Church, the proceedings are mounted in a totally undynamic manner. This leaves Osborne's dialogue in the lurch, either sounding stupidly matey ('Here's the man who did in four of the sacraments') or downright silly ('Look at Erasmus. He never really gets into serious trouble'). What remains is a few tormented ramblings and a sweating, tonsured cast.

Luv

(1967, US, 96 min)
d Clive Donner. *p* Martin Manulis. *sc* Elliott Baker. *ph* Ernest Laszlo. *ed* Harold F Kress. *pd* Albert Brenner. *m* Gerry Mulligan. *cast* Jack Lemmon, Peter Falk, Elaine May, Nina Wayne, Eddie Mayehoff, Paul Hartman, Severn Darden.

● A dire kooky farce (based on a play by Murray Schisgal) about contemporary sexual lunacy. The characters behave like berserk idiots, jumping in and out of love like so many rabbits, getting rid of unwanted partners by pushing them off the Brooklyn Bridge, and generally falling about in incoherent ecstasy. One sits bemused as joke after joke misfires, and the hapless actors are left mugging in a vacuum of chic settings. Some sense of comedy timing in the direction might have helped; and the cast could have been introduced to the atrociously post-synchronised dialogue which trails disconsolately behind them. TM

Luzhin Defence, The

(2000, GB/Fr/It/Hun/US, 108 min)
d Marleen Gorris. *p* Caroline Wood, Stephen Evans, Louis Becker, Philippe Guez. *sc* Peter Berry. *ph* Bernard Lutic. *ed* Michaël Reichwein. *pd* Tony Burrough. *m* Alexandre Desplat. *cast* John Turturro, Emily Watson, Geraldine James, Stuart Wilson, Christopher Thompson, Fabio Sartor, Peter Blythe, Orla Brady, Mark Tandy, Kelly Hunter.

● Alexander Luzhin (Turturro) is a chess grandmaster. The game has been his only world since childhood, and he's entirely lacking in social skills. His unconventional behaviour raises eyebrows at the Italian lakeside resort where he's taking part in the 1929 world chess tournament, but also draws the attention of Natalia (Watson), a Russian woman holidaying with her overbearing mother Vera (James), who's anxious for her daughter to marry well. As the attraction between Natalia and Luzhin grows, so too does Vera's dismay at the liaison. Luzhin, meanwhile, grapples with the demands and conflicts of his dedication to the game, and his love for Natalia. This does not quite live up to Nabokov's novella. But it's a valiant attempt to capture the spirit of the original, and the overall result is engaging, gently humorous and ultimately quite moving, with Turturro emanating a beguiling purity and exuberance. KW

Lydia

(1941, US, 104 min, b/w)
d Julien Duvivier. *p* Alexander Korda. *sc* Ben Hecht, Samuel Hoffenstein. *ph* Lee Garmes. *ed* William Hornbeck. *ad* Vincent Korda. *m* Miklós Rózsa. *cast* Merle Oberon, Edna May Oliver, Alan Marshal, Joseph Cotten, Hans Yaray, Sara Allgood.

● This seductive Hollywood remake of Duvivier's earlier *Carnet de Bal* can't quite compete with the swoony romantic pessimism that engulfed the '30s French cinema, but as an ersatz exercise in old-school charm it has its moments. Oberon is at the centre of another episodic structure as a New England grande dame reflecting over the string of varied lovers life turned up for her. TJ

m

Monsoon Wedding

M

(1931, Ger, 118 min, b/w)
d Fritz Lang. *p* Seymour Nebenzal. *sc* Fritz Lang, Thea von Harbou. *ph* Fritz Arno Wagner. *ad* Emil Hasler, Karl Vollbrecht. *cast* Peter Lorre, Otto Wernicke, Ellen Widmann, Inge Landgut, Gustav Gründgens, Theodor Loos.

●Lang's first sound film was based on the real-life manhunt for the Düsseldorf child-murderer (an extraordinary performance by Peter Lorre). A radical, analytical film that entertains many of Lang's fascinations: innovative use of sound; the detail of police procedure; the parallels drawn between organised police behaviour and the underworld... a construction which carries Lang's own view of the arbitrariness of the Law. A subversive film, or more simply a movie brimming over with the ferment of Lang's imagination at its height? You choose. RM

M

(1951, US, 88 min, b/w)
d Joseph Losey. *p* Seymour Nebenzal. *sc* Norman Reilly Raine, Leo Katcher, Waldo Salt. *ph* Ernest Laszlo. *ed* Edward Mann. *ad* Martin Obzina. *m* Michel Michelet. *cast* David Wayne, Howard da Silva, Luther Adler, Martin Gabel, Steve Brodie, Raymond Burr, Glenn Anders, Karen Morley, Norman Lloyd.

●Losey's remake of Lang's most famous film was inevitably subjected to invidious comparisons when it was first released. The main problem, as Losey admitted ('I couldn't believe myself in the idea of the whole underworld ganging up against the killer') is the weak ending. Where Lang achieved a double knockout with Lorre's great speech in which he turns the accusation against his accusers – effecting a complete turnabout in sympathies, not just because we understand that he is helpless to combat his sickness, but because he has turned into a victim of persecution – Losey manages only a sucker punch because the setting is no longer Nazi Germany. This said, the first half of the film is excellent, with the Los Angeles locations wonderfully used as a strange and terrifying concrete jungle, and a remarkable performance from David Wayne that bears comparison with Lorre. TM

Maborosi (Maboroshi no Hikari/ The Beckoning Light)

(1995, Jap, 109 min)
d Hirokazu Koreeda. *p* Naoe Gozu. *sc* Yoshihisa Ogita. *ph* Masao Nakabori. *ed* Tomoyo Oshima. *ad* Kyoko Heya. *m* Chen Ming-Chang. *cast* Makikio Esumi, Takashi Naito, Tadanobu Asano, Goki Kashiyama, Naomi Watanabe, Midori Kiuchi.

●Documentarist Koreeda's quietly devastating first fiction feature is about a young woman deeply troubled by the fear that she brings death to her nearest and dearest. Having lost her grandmother (to old age) and her first husband (to an inexplicable suicide), she lives happily in a fishing village with her second husband, but something inside remains frozen. Made under the benign influence of Hou Xiaoxian, the tale is told in contemplative wide-angle shots; the absence of any spurious, unearned intimacy with the characters makes the climactic scenes profoundly moving. TR

Mac

(1992, US, 118 min)
d John Turturro. *p* Nancy Tenebaum, Brenda Goodman. *sc* John Turturro, Brandon Cole. *ph* Ron Fortunato. *ed* Michael Berenbaum. *pd* Robin Standefer. *m* Richard Termini, Vin Tese. *cast* John Turturro, Katherine Borowitz, Michael Badalucco. Carl Capotorto, Ellen Barkin, John Amos, Olek Krupa.

●Queens, New York, 1953. Mac (Turturro) and his younger brothers Vito (Badalucco) and Bruno (Capotorto) work together in the building trade. Mac's obsessive perfectionism brings him into constant conflict with foreman Polowski (Krupa), who is only interested in cutting corners. Eventually Mac persuades his brothers that they should go into business for themselves, but the intensity of work inevitably takes its toll. Turturro's directorial debut is – appropriately – a labour of love. It's an ambivalent portrait of a Willy Loman figure, a man whose pride in his craft verges on egomania. There are strong performances throughout. The psychodrama which emerges towards the end infringes Cassavetes territory, but without the essential rigour. This, however, is a serious, likeable effort, not always successful, perhaps, but shot through with insight and conviction. TCh

Macabre

(1957, US, 73 min, b/w)
d/p William Castle. *sc* Robb White. *ph* Carl Guthrie. *ed* John F Schreyer. *ad* Jack T Collis, Robert Kinoshita. *m* Les Baxter. *cast* William Prince, Jim Backus, Christine White, Jacqueline Scott, Philip Tonge, Ellen Corby, Susan Morrow.

●The cheapo horror king's first venture in the genre. Not as good as *The Tingler*, though it gets a good start by being set predominantly in a foggy cemetery, where a frantic search is going on for a child supposedly buried alive in one of the graves. But then rather laborious flashbacks start explaining the whys and wherefores of the mystery with small town 'revelations' in the Peyton Place manner. TM

Macadam Tribu

(1996, Fr/Zaire, 87 min)
d José Laplaine. *p* Raphael Vion. *sc* José Laplaine. *ph* Lionel Cousin. *ed* Clare Pinheiro. *pd* Fallo Baba Keita. *m* Papa Wemba. *cast* Lydia Ewandé, Hassane Kouyaté, Sidy Camara, Habibou Dembélé, Djibril Kouyaté, Djémba Diawara.

●Centred on two brothers – one a womanising wastrel, the other an upcoming boxer – and their anxieties about their mother, heavily into the booze since her husband abandoned her, this funny, racy, pacy and poignant debut feature (from a Zairean-born writer/director now based in Europe) is full of vitality, in terms of both performances and cinematic style. It's an unpretentious but dazzling, deceptively loose-structured portrait of a community (the setting is non-specific 'urban Africa') obsessed with sex, money and social standing. It treats adultery, neighbourly rivalries and political posturing with an admirably light touch while offering serious food for thought on such issues as unemployment and the erosion of local communities. GA

Mac and Me

(1988, US, 99 min)
d Stewart Raffill. *p* RJ Lewis. *sc* Steve Feke, Stewart Raffill. *ph* Nick McLean. *ed* Tom Walls. *pd* W Stewart Campbell. *m* Alan Silvestri. *cast* Christine Ebersole, Jonathan Ward, Tina Caspary, Lauren Stanley, Jade Calegory, Vinnie Torrente, Martin West.

●First the good news: Jade Calegory, who plays the boy-hero in this cuddly alien yarn, was born with spina bifida, and the film is neither sentimental nor exploitative in dealing with its wheelchair-confined star. Unfortunately, there's little else to commend. Unless you missed *E.T.*, you know the story: an alien, separated from its family and hunted by nameless agents, hides in suburban California, befriends a boy, and is saved by the neighbourhood kids. Directed by Raffill with no hint of wit, personality or invention, the film soon degenerates into a litany of product placements: every frame is littered with Coke cans, and the invitation to interpret 'Mac' as 'Mysterious Alien Creature' is unlikely to fool anyone even before the song-and-dance number that pops up in a well-known junk-food chain. Mind-blowingly, the last item on the shopping list of hard sells is America itself: the alien no longer wants to go home, he's found a better life in LA. Give the kids a break; take them to something else. TCh

Macao

(1952, US, 81 min, b/w)
d Josef von Sternberg. *p* Alex Gottlieb. *sc* Bernard C Schoenfeld, Stanley Rubin. *ph* Harry J Wild. *ed* Samuel E Beetley, Robert Golden. *ad* Albert S D'Agostino, Ralph Berger. *m* Anthony Collins. *cast* Robert Mitchum, Jane Russell, William Bendix, Gloria Grahame, Thomas Gomez, Brad Dexter, Philip Ahn, Vladimir Sokoloff.

●Not an entirely happy production – Sternberg, according to Mitchum, shot and cut it in such a way that characters kept walking into themselves, with the result that Nicholas Ray was called in to reshoot (uncredited) many of the action scenes – but still a delightful bit of RKO exotica. The thin story, set in the port of the title, sees Mitchum's drifter joining up with Russell's sultry singer and helping the local cops catch a criminal bigwig. But what is so enjoyable, apart from Harry Wild's shimmering camerawork, is the tongue-in-cheek tone of the script and performances, best evidenced in the sparkling banter and innuendo between Mitchum and Russell. GA

Macaroni (Maccheroni)

(1985, It, 106 min)
d Ettore Scola. *p* Luigi De Laurentiis, Franco Committieri. *sc* Ruggero Maccari, Scarpelli, Ettore Scola. *ph* Claudio Ragona. *ed* Carla Simonelli. *pd* Luciano Ricceri. *m* Armando Trovaioli. *cast* Jack Lemmon, Marcello Mastroianni, Daria Nicolodi, Isa Danieli, Maria Luisa Santella, Patrizia Sacchi, Bruno Esposito.

●Forty years after World War II, an American executive (Lemmon) returns to Naples on business, only to be confronted by an amiable eccentric (Mastroianni) who over the years has been writing to his own sister, pretending to be Lemmon, in order to console her for being wooed and abandoned by Lemmon as a GI. A loopy enough premise for a crazy farce, but Scola avoids the obvious and turns in a touching comedy about friendship and the importance of imagination. While Lemmon is as effectively professional as ever as the surly grouch regenerated by the Neapolitan way of life, it is Mastroianni who steals the show. Perfectly attuned to the film's easygoing examination of the gulf between reality and fantasy, hopes and disillusionment, Mastroianni manages to make convincing a man stricken with a singularly fertile form of insanity and blessed with a heart as huge and warm as Vesuvius. Gently ironic, remarkably relaxed, he is Lancaster-like in his effortless ability to demonstrate pathos, humour and dignity. GA

MacArthur – The Rebel General

(1977, US, 130 min)
d Joseph Sargent. *p* Frank McCarthy. *sc* Hal Barwood, Matthew Robbins. *ph* Mario Tosi. *ed* George Jay Nicholson. *pd* John J Lloyd. *m* Jerry Goldsmith. *cast* Gregory Peck, Ivan Bonar, Ward Costello, Nicolas Coster, Marj Dusay, Ed Flanders, Art Fleming, Dan O'Herlihy, GD Spradlin.

●Typical Hollywood biopic (released in the US simply as *MacArthur*) which, despite proclamations of objectivity, tilts in the direction of hagiography. Inadvertently, the movie mirrors MacArthur in its own hubris: epic ambitions way beyond all budgetary control. The script is sprinkled with walking-on-the-water jokes in a half-hearted attempt to have its MacArthur and demystify him as well, but these merely enhance the image of the Perfect American General ('40s vintage) – a commodity which, as can be seen here, should never be exported. SM

Macbeth

(1948, US, 87 min, b/w)
d/p/sc Orson Welles. *ph* John L Russell. *ed* Louis Lindsay. *ad* Fred A Ritter. *m* Jacques Ibert. *cast* Orson Welles, Jeanette Nolan, Dan O'Herlihy, Roddy McDowall, Edgar Barrier, Alan Napier, Erskine Sanford, John Dierkes, Gus Schilling.

●Not entirely successful, hardly surprisingly in that it was shot in 23 days on a cheap Western backlot at Republic Studios. Also, Ms Nolan's Lady Macbeth is something of a disaster. That said, though, the film – unlike so many adaptations of the Bard – is pure cinema: moodily magnificent photography by John L Russell reinforces the sense of a nightmarish world before time, where primitive emotions hold sway with absolute, compelling simplicity. Adventurous film-making that takes risks, and full of imaginative flourishes. GA

Macbeth

(1971, GB, 140 min)
d Roman Polanski. *p* Andrew Braunsberg. *sc* Roman Polanski, Kenneth Tynan. *ph* Gilbert Taylor. *ed* Alastair McIntyre. *pd* Wilfrid Shingleton. *m* Third Ear Band. *cast* Jon Finch, Francesca Annis, Martin Shaw, Nicholas Selby, John Stride, Stephan Chase, Sydney Bromley.

●The opening shot of a yellow, withering moonscape stretching away to infinity – revealed to be a desolate sea-shore on which the three witches proceed to the ritual burial of a noose, a severed arm and a dagger – effortlessly establishes the cold, barbarous climate of Shakespeare's play. Polanski's imagery, evoking a characteristically cruel, irrational and blood-boltered world, is often magnificently strange and hieratic: the death of the Thane of Cawdor, for instance, hanged by way of a massive iron collar and chain from a high tower in a courtyard ringed by cloaked soldiers; or the almost pagan ritual of Macbeth's coronation, starting with his bare feet stepping into the huge footprints embedded in the sacred stone. The relative weakness is that Polanski's evident desire to elicit understated, naturalistic performances from his cast also underplays the poetry of the play, which as a result never quite spirals into dark, uncontrollable nightmare as the Welles version (for all its faults) does. TM

McCabe and Mrs Miller

(1971, US, 121 min)
d Robert Altman. *p* David Foster, Mitchell Brower. *sc* Robert Altman, Brian McKay. *ph* Vilmos Zsigmond. *ed* Lou Lombardo. *pd* Leon Ericksen. *songs* Leonard Cohen. *cast* Warren Beatty, Julie Christie, Rene Auberjonois, Hugh Millais, Shelley Duvall, Michael Murphy, John Schuck, William Devane, Keith Carradine.

●One of the best of Altman's early movies, using classic themes – the ill-fated love of gambler and whore, the gunman who dies by the gun, the contest between little man and big business – to produce a non-heroic Western. McCabe (Beatty) hasn't the grand dimensions of a Ford, Fuller or Leone hero; he is an amiable braggart, a bungling lover, a third-rate entrepreneur with chronic indigestion and a penchant for bad jokes. Mrs Miller (Christie) is a whorehouse madame who prefers her opium pipe to McCabe's amorous overtures. Their relationship is to a large extent a mournful background to Altman's central concern of chronicling the harsh conditions of life in a rawly developing mining town in the Northwest. His vision of the role of the individual represents another removal from genre tradition. Confronted with the primitive character of social organisation and the brutality of nature, Altman's Westerner is insignificant, isolated and vulnerable; his survival is chancy, a question of luck rather than skill. JdeG

Macchina Ammazzacattivi, La

see Machine That Kills Bad People, The

McGuire Go Home!

see High Bright Sun, The

Machine Gun Kelly

(1958, US, 80 min, b/w)
d/p Roger Corman. *sc* R Wright Campbell. *ph* Floyd Crosby. *ed* Ronald Sinclair. *ad* Daniel Haller. *m* Gerald Fried. *cast* Charles Bronson, Susan Cabot, Morey Amsterdam, Jack Lambert, Wally Campo, Barboura Morris, Connie Gilchrist.

●Corman's first gangster movie is one of the most ambitious and rewarding of his '50s quickies: not because it transcends any of its inherent limitations, but rather because it indulges them recklessly. Apparently modelling itself on Siegel's *Baby Face Nelson*, it sees Kelly (Bronson) as a child-like thug with a pathological fear of death, helplessly dominated by his moll Flo (Cabot, Corman's favourite femme fatale until Barbara Steele came along). The post-Freudian motifs aren't imposed on the dime-novel material; they grow with a hysteria all of their own from the sleazy settings and one-note performances. The movie reveals Corman as a director entirely in touch with his audience, and Floyd Crosby as one of the most prodigiously resourceful cameramen in Hollywood history. TR

Machine That Kills Bad People, The (La Macchina Ammazzacattivi)

(1948, It, 83 min, b/w)
d Roberto Rossellini. *p* Luigi Rovere, Roberto Rossellini, Salvo D'Angelo. *sc* Sergio Amidei, Roberto Rossellini, Franco Brusati, Liana Ferri, Giancarlo Vigorelli. *ph* Tino Santoni. *ed* Jolanda Benvenuti, Luigi Rovere. *ad* Virgilio Marchi. *m* Renzo Rossellini. *cast* Gennaro Pisano, Giovanni Amato, Marilyn Buferd, Bill Tubbs, Helen Tubbs, Pietro Carloni.

●Minor but mildly pleasing Rossellini, set in a small town in Southern Italy thrown into a tizzy by the machinations of a mysterious old man. Saint or devil, he endows a camera with the power not merely to kill people, but to ferret out sources of wealth. Cue for a flurry of treachery and greed, all casually swept under the carpet in a final pirouette. The neo-realist techniques don't always mix too comfortably with the fantasy, making it an Ealing comedy with an edifying bent. TM

Maciste all'Inferno (Maciste in Hell/ The Witch's Curse)

(1962, It, 90 min)
d Robert Hampton [Riccardo Freda]. *p* Ermanno Donati, Luigi Carpentieri. *sc* Oreste Biancoli, Piero Pierotti, Ennio De Concini. *ph* Riccardo Pallottini. *ed* Ornella Micheli. *pd* Luciano Spadoni. *m* Carlo Franci. *cast* Kirk Morris, Hélène Chanel, Vera Silenti, Andrea Bosic, Angelo Zanoli.

●Sporting only his trademark loincloth, Italian superhero Maciste shows up in the Scottish village of Loch Lake in the 17th century, where the winsome Martha is about to be burned as a witch. Hang about, says Big M, I'll nip down to Hades and sort this out. Pushing aside an evil-looking tree he descends into the Netherworld – a pile of cardboard rocks in some dusty corner of Cinecittà – in search of the real witch who's framed Martha. En route, he faces such perils of hell as serpents, a giant, an evil vulture and, curiously, stampeding cattle. Such unembarrassed loopiness should be amusing, but Freda's poker-faced manner plus the dullest of casts ensure that tedium sets in early: confirmation that the early-'60s muscleman cycle produced only small pleasures at best. BBa

Maciste Contro i Mostri (Colossus of the Stone Age/Fire Monsters Against the Son of Hercules/Land of the Monsters)

(1962, It, 82 min)
d Guido Malatesta. *p* Giorgio Marzelli, Alfio Quattrini. *sc* Arpad De Riso. *ph* Giuseppe La Torre. *ed* Enzo Alfonsi. *ad* Umberto Cerasano. *m* Gian Stellari, Guido Robuschi. *cast* Reg Lewis, Margaret Lee, Luciano Marin, Myra Kent, Andrea Aureli, Fulvia Gasser, Bergit Bergen, Rocco Spataro.

●Dreadful muscle-man epic featuring some prehistoric monsters which look as though they were created by Harryhausen's third junior assistant stand-in. The human battle scenes are atrociously choreographed (you can almost imagine The Anvil Chorus over the penultimate one), and Malatesta shows no signs of being able to direct his way out of a paper bag, let alone Reg Lewis act his way out of one. The dubbing is above-par stupid. PM

Maciste in Hell

see Maciste all'Inferno

Mackenna's Gold

(1968, US, 136 min)
d J Lee Thompson. *p* Carl Foreman, Dimitri Tiomkin. *sc* Carl Foreman. *ph* Joseph MacDonald. *ed* Bill Lenny. *pd* Geoffrey Drake. *m* Quincy Jones. *cast* Gregory Peck, Omar Sharif, Telly Savalas, Camilla Sparv, Keenan Wynn, Julie Newmar, Ted Cassidy, Eduardo Ciannelli, Eli Wallach, Edward G Robinson, Raymond Massey, Burgess Meredith, Anthony Quayle, Lee J Cobb.

●Matinee adventure material (from a novek bt Will Henry) blown up to deliciously absurd proportions, as the gold-lust clichés tumble from Carl Foreman's typewriter to be treated by the assembled stellar multitudes as if they were fresh-minted bullion. Peck's sheriff has The Map, everyone else wants it. Everyone double-crosses everyone else. And in the Lost Canyon of Gold there's…(wait for it)…an ironic Conclusion. Treasure of the Sierra Madness. PT

McKenzie Break, The

(1970, GB, 106 min)
d Lamont Johnson. *p* Arthur Gardner, Jules Levy. *sc* William Norton. *ph* Michael Reed. *ed* Tom Rolf. *pd* Frank White. *m* Riz Ortolani. *cast* Brian Keith, Helmut Griem, Ian Hendry, Jack Watson, Patrick O'Connell, Horst Janson, Alexander Allerson.

●Rare reversal of the PoW camp formula, with Germans the potential escapees from a Scottish internment. Keith and Hendry do ideological battle with fanatical Nazi Griem, who is willing to sacrifice half his less politicised men to cover his planned breakout. Elaborated with unusual care for authenticity, it's tautly handled by Johnson (better known for abrasive telemovies), and adapted from Sidney Shelley's novel by William Norton (father of *Convoy* adaptor and *More American Graffiti* director BWL Norton). PT

Mackintosh Man, The

(1973, GB, 99 min)
d John Huston. *p* John Foreman. *sc* Walter Hill. *ph* Oswald Morris. *ed* Russell Lloyd. *pd* Terence Marsh. *m* Maurice Jarre. *cast* Paul Newman, Dominique Sanda, James Mason, Harry Andrews, Ian Bannen, Michael Hordern, Nigel Patrick, Peter Vaughan, Roland Culver, Jenny Runacre, Leo Genn.

●Reasonably entertaining old-fashioned thriller, with British intelligence hiring a freelance agent (Newman) to expose Communist infiltration in high places. A quick stretch inside to gain credibility with the opposition, then a well-handled break-out leads Newman to a remote and mysterious house in Ireland. A spot of bother, another nicely handled escape across the moors; a resumé of the plot for Dominique Sanda, who can't work it out; then everyone's off to Malta for the climax. If you can accept Newman as a totally unconvincing Australian (thankfully only for about 20 minutes), an appalling array of accents (mainly Irish), and Dominique Sanda as an unlikely member of the British Secret Service, then it whiles away the time pleasantly enough. (From a novel by Desmond Bagley.) CPe

Macomber Affair, The

(1946, US, 90 min, b/w)
d Zoltan Korda. *p* Benedict Bogeaus, Casey Robinson. *sc* Casey Robinson, Seymour Bennett, Frank Arnold. *ph* Karl Struss, John Wilcox, Freddie Francis, Osmond Borradaile. *ed* George Feld, Jack Wheeler. *ad* Erno Metzner. *m* Miklós Rózsa. *cast* Gregory Peck, Joan Bennett, Robert Preston, Reginald Denny, Carl Harbord, Jean Gillie.

●Archetypal Hemingway tale of the rich dilettante on safari (Preston) – tormented by his own cowardice, taunted by his wife (Bennett), and finally rendered superfluous as she turns to their white hunter guide (Peck). Surprisingly persuasive (considering the stars stayed in Hollywood while three second unit cameramen shot the backgrounds), thanks to an admirably terse script and excellent performances. But it gradually begins to fall apart in the last third as courage is put to the test among the big game. TM

Macon County Line

(1973, US, 89 min)
d Richard Compton. *p* Max Baer. *sc* Max Baer, Richard Compton. *ph* Daniel Lacambre. *ed* Tina Hirsch. *ad* Roger Pancake. *m* Stu Phillips. *cast* Alan Vint, Cheryl Waters, Geoffrey Lewis, Joan Blackman, Jesse Vint, Max Baer, Stan Gilman, Tim Scott.

●Alan Vint and his brother Jesse form an agreeable duo, playing roistering brothers on a spree in Macon County, Georgia, in the '50s. They pick up a girl, fool around some, and run up against a redneck cop (Baer), who warns them on their way, then mistakenly goes on the rampage after them when he finds his wife raped and murdered. As the film moves from rompish comedy into something altogether darker, its moral tone becomes more overbearing, and the blood-spattered ending (the script is based on fact, but fails to prepare its ground adequately) seems to come from a different movie altogether. CPe

McQ

(1974, US, 111 min)
d John Sturges. *p* Jules Levy, Arthur Gardner, Lawrence Roman. *sc* Lawrence Roman. *ph* Harry Stradling Jr. *ed* William Ziegler. *pd* Walter M Simonds. *m* Elmer Bernstein. *cast* John Wayne, Eddie Albert, Diana Muldaur, Colleen Dewhurst, Clu Gulager, David Huddleston, Julie Adams, Al Lettieri.

●Perhaps the first commercial film to show the indirect influence of Watergate. It's also the best of the current spate of cop movies, despite the presence of an overage and cumbersome Wayne. He plays a Seattle lieutenant who goes on the rampage when his best friend gets killed, only to discover that it's the force itself that is corrupt, even to the point where they can double-cross the local crime syndicate in a dope deal. Wayne comes over not so much the lone crusader as an anachronism in a world of institutionalised crime. Rather than solve the plot, Wayne merely reveals that everything he has stood for is corrupt. The accusing finger even rests on him for a while; a pity, then, that he's too thick-skinned to let it register. CPe

Macunaima

(1969, Braz, 108 min)
d/p/sc Joaquim Pedro de Andrade. *ph* Guido Cosulich, Affonso Beato. *ed* Eduardo Escorel. *ad* Anisio Medeiros. *m* Mário de Andrade, Silvio Caldas, Geraldo Nunes, Antônio Maria, Heitor Villa-Lobos, Sady Cabral, Jards Macalé. *cast* Grande Otélo, Paulo José, Dina Sfat, Milton Gonçalves, Rodolfo Arena, Jardel Filho, Joana Fomm.

●De Andrade's film has a plot of fairytale simplicity. Macunaima, born black and middle-aged in the Brazilian jungle, turns into a young white on his way to the city. There, he and his stooge-like brothers, wide-eyed but their native shrewdness still intact, are buffeted around by the Marx Brothers-type logic that dominates the plot, while the film takes constant delight in visual incongruities. Macunaima takes up with a girl revolutionary, but she is killed by her own time bomb; the villain is the local industrial magnate, the Cannibal Giant, who feeds his guests to man-eating fish. The film, the introduction tells us, is about consumerism as cannibalism, about a Brazilian devoured by Brazil. It's a bizarre and often very funny comedy that applies its central thesis with unerring accuracy.

McVicar

(1980, GB, 112 min)
d Tom Clegg. *p* Roy Baird, Bill Curbishley, Roger Daltrey. *sc* John McVicar, Tom Clegg. *ph* Vernon Layton. *ed* Peter Boyle. *pd* Brian Ackland-Snow. *m* Jeff Wayne. *cast* Roger Daltrey, Adam Faith, Cheryl Campbell, Billy Murray, Georgina Hale, Ian Hendry, Steven Berkoff, Tony Haygarth.

●Despite the excellent teamwork of Daltrey and Faith, a cracking cast, and inspiring raw material, this musical version of *Scum*-meets-*Out* somehow buries these advantages deep inside a saucy action thriller format. Having read the headlines, bought the book, etc, few surprises are left: why no mention of the real life characters (Charlie Richardson, Ian Brady) of the prison inmates? Though it's good to see someone Escape from Durham rather than Alcatraz, the dependable British fascination with villains is played out once too often for anyone to care, and leaves McVicar's unique insights into crime more or less untouched. If you want to see Daltrey prove himself a straight actor, see it; otherwise read the book. DMacp

Madadayo (Not Yet)

(1993, Jap, 134 min)
d Akira Kurosawa. *p* Hisao Kurosawa. *sc* Akira Kurosawa. *ph* Takao Saito, Masaharu Ueda. *ed* Akira Kurosawa. *ad* Yoshiro Muraki. *m* Shinichiro Ikebe. *cast* Tatsuo Matsumura, Kyoko Kagawa, Hisashi Igawa, George Tokoro, Masayuki Yui, Akira Terao.

●Kurosawa's thirtieth film is, regrettably, as trite and embarrassing as its immediate predecessors, *Dreams* and *Rhapsody in August*. About Hyakken Uchida, a teacher who retires, in 1943, to concentrate on his writing career, and abandons his reclusive ways, once a year only, to welcome his adoring former students to his birthday celebrations, it's a maudlin, fulsomely nostalgic affair. The turgid narrative consists almost entirely of static, predictable, repetitive scenes in which the grown students, after reminiscing with the prof about the good old days, are overcome by tearful emotion and told by their mentor to shape up. 'Humanism' at its mushiest. GA

Mad Adventures of 'Rabbi' Jacob, The (Les Aventures de Rabbi Jacob)

(1973, Fr/It, 100 min)
d Gérard Oury. *p* Bertrand Javal. *sc* Gérard Oury, Danielle Thompson, Roberto De Leonidas. ph Henri Decaë. *ed* Albert Jurgenson. *ad* Théo Meurisse. *m* Vladimir Cosma. *cast* Louis de Funès, Suzy Delair, Marcel Dalio, Claude Giraud, Claude Piéplu, Renzo Montagnani, Miou-Miou.

●As the name implies, one big Jewish (not to mention Moslem and Catholic) joke in which Rabbi Jacob (de Funès) becomes inadvertently entangled with inefficient Arab terrorists and various other neurotic characters. The script is so banal and full of the most appalling jokes (to an Arab: 'You bet on the wrong *camel*'), that the film's success (if any) depends on reactions to de Funès' brand of humour (a mixture of slapstick and idiotic facial expressions). It might appeal to kids who like to see their protagonists wallowing in vats of green chewing-gum. GSa

Madagascar Skin

(1995, GB, 93 min)
d Chris Newby. *p* Julie Baines. *sc* Chris Newby. *ph* Oliver Curtis, *ed* Chris Newby, Annabel Ware. *pd* Paul Cross. *cast* John Hannah, Bernard Hill, Mark Anthony, Mark Petit, Danny Earl.

●This playful second feature is a world away from the medieval meditations of *Anchoress*. A virtual two-hander, it's a disarming love stories featuring a very odd couple: Hannah's young gay man, a fugitive from the club scene where the Madagascar-shaped birthmark on his face makes him feel ill at ease; and Hill's slightly shady Harry, a thumping heterosexual whose sheltered coastal hideaway may indicate that he too is running away from a past he'd rather not have to deal with. There's plenty of quirky humour, much that's the unexpected, and a gleeful eye for the absurd, as the film quizzically picks its way towards the triumph of their affections. TJ

Madame Bovary

(1934, Fr, 100 min, b/w)
d/sc Jean Renoir. *ph* Jean Bachelet. *ed* Marguerite Renoir. ad Georges Wakhévich, Robert Gys.*m* Milhaud. *cast* Valentine Tessier, Pierre Renoir, Daniel Lecourtois, Max Dearly, Fernand Fabre, Robert Le Vigan.

●Butchered by its original distributor (who cut it by an hour), surviving in a merely adequate print, this is nevertheless superb early Renoir. Valentine Tessier, mannered and theatrical – though not inappropriately so – is something of an acquired taste as Flaubert's unfortunate provincial lady, dreaming of romance while trapped in marriage to a bovine village doctor (magnificently played by Pierre Renoir), but the direction is masterly. Making systematic (and stunning) use of deep focus, Renoir captures perfectly the eternally irreconcilable beauty and boredom of the provinces, rooting Emma squarely in lovely Norman landscapes which her pathetic yearnings for a fantasy world turn into a bleak desert. TM

Madame Bovary

(1991, Fr, 129 min)
d Claude Chabrol. *p* Marin Karmitz. *sc* Claude Chabrol. *ph* Jean Rabier. *ed* Monique Fardoulis. *pd* Michèle Abbé. *m* Matthieu Chabrol. *cast* Isabelle Huppert, Jean-François Balmer, Christophe Malavoy, Jean Yanne, Lucas Belvaux.

●Chabrol's long-delayed adaptation of Flaubert's novel is as suffocating as its heroine's predicament. Emma, the ambitious farmer's daughter taken for a wife by arch-mediocrity Dr Bovary (Jean-François Balmer in a perfectly controlled performance), has been the subject of see-sawing literary interpretations since the 1860s. Chabrol sticking to the letter of the text avoided the temptation to cast her in a modernised feminist role and stressed instead her stifling limitation of choices in provincial 19th century France. Isabelle Huppert, often a blood-drained, internalised actress, outdoes herself here, playing Emma in a distracted, half-comatose state, resuscitated briefly by the odd gowned ball or the lifeline to passion proffered by heart-breaker Rodolphe (Malavoy). The birth of a child fails to bring light into her eyes. A classical art movie saturated with Chabrol's dark romantic pessimism. WH

Madame Butterfly

(1995, Fr/Jap/Ger/GB, 134 min)
d Frédéric Mitterrand. *p* Daniel Toscan du Plantier, Pierre-Olivier Bardet. *sc* Frédéric Mitterrand. *ph* Philippe Welt. *ed* Luc Barnier. *ad* Michel Glotz, Daniel Zalay, Michèle Abbe-Vannier, Taïb Jellouli. *cast* Ying Huang, Richard Troxell, Ning Liang, Richard Cowan, Jing Ma Fan.

●A few snippets of archive footage from turn-of-the-century Japan provide the most arresting moments in this rarely more than adequate film of the Puccini warhorse (routine accompaniment from the Orchestre de Paris under James Conlon). What we get is a realist, meat-and-two-veg rendition in picture postcard 'Japanese' settings rigged up for the occasion on the coast of Tunisia, where the chief location is the heroine's unhappy home. Mitterrand's camera moves in and out from behind the paper screens with a certain nimbleness, but you'd be forgiven if you wanted a bit more cinematic flair from a movie billed as 'A Martin Scorsese Presentation'. TJ

Madame Claude

(1976, Fr, 111 min)
d Just Jaeckin. *p* Claire Duval. *sc* André G Brunelin, Just Jaeckin. *ph* Robert Fraisse. *ed* Marie-Sophie Dubus. *ad* Maurice Sergent. *m* Serge Gainsbourg. *cast* Françoise Fabian, Murray Head, Dayle Haddon, Klaus Kinski, Robert Webber, Marc Michel, Maurice Ronet.

●Jaeckin, the man to blame for initiating the deadly rash of Emmanuelliana, has a knack for making movies in which sex appears about as much fun as a trip to the launderette. Perhaps realising this, he has bolstered the regulation softcore sighs with a purportedly 'political' thriller plot. Unfortunately the latter is equally inane, and one can only surmise that Jaeckin has a knack for making movies about as interesting...etc. Klaus Kinski looks like he'd give anything to be on a raft up the Amazon. PT

Madame Curie

(1943, US, 124 min, b/w)
d Mervyn LeRoy. *p* Sidney Franklin. *sc* Paul Osborn, Paul Rameau. *ph* Joseph Ruttenberg. *ed* Harold F Kress. *ad* Cedric Gibbons, Paul Groesse. *m* Herbert Stothart. *cast* Greer Garson, Walter Pidgeon, Henry Travers, Albert Bassernan, Robert Walker, C Aubrey Smith, Dame May Whitty, Reginald Owen. *narrator* James Hilton.

●Medical history MGM-style as the on-screen husband and wife who battled through the Blitz in the Oscar-winning *Mrs Miniver* roll up their sleeves in the lab and get on with the dogged business of discovering radium. Actually, the pop science angle is done rather well, but Garson's evident sanctity brings an air of portentousness to the film that it could clearly do without. If you want the basics on where X-ray technology came from, you could do worse. From the book by Eve Curie. TJ

Madame de... (The Earrings of Madame de...)

(1953, Fr/It, 102 min, b/w)
d Max Ophüls. *p* Ralph Baum. *sc* Max Ophüls, Marcel Achard, Annette Wademant. *ph* Christian Matras. *ed* Boris Lewin. *pd* Jean d'Eaubonne. *m* Oscar Straus, Georges Van Parys. *cast* Danielle Darrieux, Charles Boyer, Vittorio De Sica, Jean Debucourt, Lia de Léa, Mireille Perrey, Jean Galland.

●Ophüls' penultimate film, indulging a characteristically tender irony in its adaptation of Louise de Vilmorin's novel, is – even by his standards – exceptionally elegant in its rendering of its fin de siècle Paris milieu of ballrooms, the opera, and dashing young military officers paying their attentions to the unnamed heroine (Darrieux) of the title. The story concerns this beautiful woman's adulterous affair with an Italian diplomat (De Sica), with a pair of earrings playing an implausible and extraordinary role in their relationship. What is particularly brilliant about the film is the way Ophüls constantly draws attention to this improbable plot device, to allow a distanced and unmoralistic meditation on actions and their consequences. Also fine is the sumptuous decor, photographed in superb monochrome, and there is a particularly good performance from Boyer as the discreet 'wronged' husband. RM

Madame Rosa (La Vie devant Soi)

(1977, Fr, 120 min)
d Moshe Mizrahi. *p* Raymond Danon, Roland Girard, Jean Bolvary. *sc* Moshe Mizrahi. *ph* Nestor Almendros. *ed* Sophie Coussein. *ad* Bernard Evein. *m* Philippe Sarde. *cast* Simone Signoret, Claude Dauphin, Samy Ben Youb, Gabriel Jabbour, Michal Bat Adam, Costa-Gavras.
●Badly adapted from a rather good novel by Emile Ajar, this is art cinema at its artless, exploitative worst. An essentially simple tale – of a prostitute's child, Momo, brought up with a bevy of similar kids by professional foster-mother/aged ex-prostitute Madame Rosa – is used to screw the audience for every ounce of its social conscience, with Signoret evidently (and mistakenly) convinced that she's in a 'political' film. Far from reflecting the realities of streetwalking in Pigalle, or of childhood in the ghetto of Belleville, the film trades instead on Rosa's memories of Auschwitz (to which she refers with objectionable facility) and the boy's Algerian background to fabricate a pretentious allegory on Israeli/Arab conflict. Eventually, thank God, Rosa dies and doe-eyed Momo is 'rescued' – in a crowning example of nauseating, complacent sentimentality – by a chic young couple. CA

Madame Satã

(2002, Braz, 105 min)
d Karim Aïnouz. *p* Marc Beauchamps, Donald K Ranvaud, Vincent Maraval, Juliette Renaud. *sc* Karim Aïnouz. *ph* Walter Carvalho. *ed* Isabela Monteiro de Castro. *pd* Marcos Pedroso. *m* Marcos Suzano, Sacha Amback. *cast* Lázaro Ramos, Marcélia Cartaxo, Flavio Bauraqui, Felippe Marques, Emiliano Queiroz, Renata Sorrah.
●João Francisco dos Santos was a cook, nanny, transvestite, con-artist, kickboxer and adoptive father to the kids of his various low-life friends in the Rio slums; he also attained some success as a cabaret drag-queen. Writer/director Aïnouz flashes back from his incarceration for murder to focus on his faltering rise to some kind of stardom. It's a small film, effectively exploring a Genet-like netherworld of gay criminality, while taking the time to let us get to know 'Satã', so that his charm and perverse but distinctive sense of honour finally win us over too. Walter Carvalho's burnished camerawork oozes atmosphere, but in the end it's surely Lázaro Ramos' dazzling lead turn that carries the day. GA

Madame Sin

(1972, GB, 90 min)
d David Greene. *p* Julian Wintle, Lou Morheim. *sc* Barry Oringer, David Greene. *ph* Anthony B Richmond. *ed* Peter Tanner. *pd* Brian Eatwell. *m* Michael Gibbs. *cast* Bette Davis, Robert Wagner, Denholm Elliott, Gordon Jackson, Dudley Sutton, Catherine Schell.
●Lips a venomous scarlet slash, hair in Gorgonic braids, eyes popping ad lib, Bette Davis is a criminal arch-fiend plotting to hijack a Polaris sub ('Just one'). Lots of exotic sets and outlandish secret weapons, just a pity it's all rather old hat Bond stuff. Still, with Denholm Elliott giving sterling support as her sycophantic aide, Davis has a ball with some genuinely monstrous lines. 'Poor quality photography,' she rasps apologetically while showing Robert Wagner some footage of his fiancée being tortured to death, 'but we can't always choose the best camera positions.' TM

Madame Sousatzka

(1988, GB, 122 min)
d John Schlesinger. *p* Robin Dalton. *sc* Ruth Prawer Jhabvala, John Schlesinger. *ph* Nat Crosby. *ed* Peter Honess. *pd* Luciana Arrighi. *m* Gerald Gouriet. *cast* Shirley MacLaine, Peggy Ashcroft, Twiggy, Shabana Azmi, Leigh Lawson, Geoffrey Bayldon, Lee Montague, Navin Chowdhry.
●Schubert, Chopin, Beethoven, Schumann – the music moves the emotions, though nothing else does in this pedestrian version of Bernice Rubens' novel. Let's hear it again for the faded rooming-house full of types: the ageing osteopath queen (Bayldon), the ageing no-hope pop singer pushover in the attic (Twiggy), the aged, distracted, aristocratic owner in the basement (Ashcroft). And, in cloak and comic walk, severe but mush underneath, the ageing, imperious piano teacher of the title (MacLaine). Into this overworked literary armature arrives 14-year-old Manek (Chowdhry), a talented Indian lad with a domineering mother in back, for lessons. Madame soon has him in her grip, reining him in from concert exposure – though he is obviously mustard – before heading him off from the inevitable rite-of-passage in the attic. Probably conceived as more dislikeably monomaniacal than MacLaine plays her, this teacher has to get used to the painful fact that her chicks will fly the coop. Who could blame them? Fusty stuff. BC

Madame X

(1977, WGer, 141 min)
d Ulrike Ottinger. *p* Tabea Blumenschein. *sc/ph* Ulrike Ottinger. *cast* Tabea Blumenschein, Roswitha Jantz, Irena von Lichtenstein, Yvonne Rainer.
●A militant film, albeit one of a highly unorthodox kind. Ulrike Ottinger's lesbian feminist pirate adventure deliberately flouts every rule of orthodox film syntax, and is so uneventful and repetitive that many may well find it impossible to take. The evident aim is a destruction of traditional spectacle, and a construction of a new way of presenting women on film. The pirate plot is a high-camp pretext (and not in any sense a vehicle) for 'heroic' new images of women. The most obviously impressive scenes are those involving Yvonne Rainer as an artist disillusioned with the artocracy around her, who takes off for the high seas on roller skates, pausing only to declaim her disillusionment (as recorded in her notebooks) to a passing TV interviewer. TR

Mad Bomber, The

(1972, US, 95 min)
d/p/sc/ph Bert I Gordon. *ed* Gene Ruggiero. *m* Michel Mention. cast Vince Edwards, Chuck Connors, Neville Brand, Christina Hart, Faith Quabius, Ilona Wilson, Ted Gehring.
●Detective Vince Edwards hunts Los Angeles for dynamiter Chuck Connors (a nicely quirky characterisation), who is writing to the papers to explain that his bombs are punishments meted out to society. The victims include a high school, a hospital, a Women's Lib group…and aid comes from the unlikely quarter of a pathetic rapist (Brand, another fine performance). Shoddily assembled, but brightly conceived and very well acted, it has a genuine B movie vitality. (From a story by Marc Behm.) VG

Mädchen in Uniform (Girls in Uniform/Maidens in Uniform)

(1931, Ger, 98 min, b/w)
d Leontine Sagan. *sc* Christa Winsloe, FD Andam. *ph* Reimar Kuntze, Fritz Weihmayr. *ad* Fritz Maurischat. *m* Hansom Milde-Meissner. *cast* Dorothea Wieck, Hertha Thiele, Ellen Schwanneke, Emilia Unda, Hedwig Schlichter.
●A key early German talkie: a powerful melodrama about life in a Prussian boarding school for the daughters of the bourgeoisie – a bastion of the ideology of 'strength through suffering'. The plot mechanics are predictable – unhappy pupil with crush on housemistress is driven to attempt suicide – but the atmosphere and sensitivity to teenage fears are not: stage actress Leontine Sagan brings an exceptionally warm touch to her depiction of female friendships, and her denunciation of the Prussian orthodoxy is more a matter of subtle imagery than shrill accusations. Whether it adds up to a precursor of militant lesbianism is another question… TR

Mädchen Rosemarie, Das (The Girl Rosemarie)

(1958, WGer, 100 min, b/w)
d Rolf Thiele. *sc* Eric Kuby, Rolf Thiele, Joe Herbst, Rolf Ulrich. *ph* Klaus von Rautenfeld. *ed* Lisbeth Neumann. *ad* Wolf Englert, Ernst Richter. *m* Norbert Schultze. *cast* Nadja Tiller, Peter Van Eyck, Carl Raddatz, Gert Fröbe, Mario Adorf, Horst Frank, Karin Baal.
●The murder of Rosemarie Nitribitt, callgirl, on which Rolf Thiele based this film was one of those events which stir popular imagination for a long time because they seem to sum up an era. The mixture of provincial pettiness, ruthless money-making, and post-war shabbiness which propelled Rosemarie, her poodles and her white Mercedes to something more poignant than notoriety proved lethal in the end. Thiele's sharply directed film provides a more direct account of the grotty side of the economic miracle than Fassbinder, who was to portray it as belonging to such a remote and giddy past. RB

Mad City

(1997, US, 115 min)
d Costa-Gavras. *p* Arnold Kopelson, Anne Kopelson. *sc* Tom Matthews. *ph* Patrick Blossier. *ed* Françoise Bonnot. *pd* Catherine Hardwicke. *m* Thomas Newman. *cast* Dustin Hoffman, John Travolta, Alan Alda, Mia Kirshner, Ted Levine, Robert Prosky, Blythe Danner, William Atherton.
●Talented, ambitious but down on his luck, TV news reporter Max Brackett (Hoffman) resents working for the station in Madeline, CA, and having to cover, say, the funding of the local natural history museum. As luck would have it, while he's in the museum, none-too-bright security guard Sam Baily (Travolta) turns up to argue over his recent sacking with his former boss (Danner); shooting another employee in panic, he half-reluctantly creates a siege situation, complete with schoolkids at risk. Faced with an exclusive inside story, Brackett decides to try to prolong – indeed, to stage manage – the crisis. But can he revive his career without endangering his fellow hostages? Costa-Gavras' film is far from original but serves as a taut, tidy thriller with an engagingly cynical take on the opportunism of the media. It benefits from a decent cast (including Alda in a typically slimy turn as the network anchorman determined to profit from Brackett's scoop), while Travolta gives one of his finest performances in perhaps his most dramatically demanding role to date. GA

Mad Cows

(1999, GB, 91 min)
d Sara Sugarman. *p* Frank Mannion, Aaron Simpson. *sc* Sasha Hails, Sara Sugarman. *ph* Pierre Aïm. *ed* John Jympson. *pd* Joseph Nemec III. *m* Mark Thomas. *cast* Anna Friel, Joanna Lumley, Anna Massey, Phyllida Law, Greg Wise, John Standing, Nicholas Woodeson, Judy Cornwell, Prunella Scales, Geoffrey Robertson QC, Mohamed Al-Fayed, Jodie Kidd, Sophie Dahl, Kathy Lette.
●An adaptation of a novel by Kathy Lette: Maddy (Friel) is a spunky young Australian determined to make caddish English toff Alex (Wise) acknowledge her and their baby son Jack. Unfortunately, the evil British class system is against her and she soon finds herself in prison, where a batty psycho-therapist (Massey) tricks her into signing adoption papers. And when her only ally, posh totty Gillian (Lumley), agrees to look after Jack, even she turns traitor. Friel is a vital if spindly presence, and Lumley is riveting, exposing desperation beneath the immaculate whore's facade. Gillian doesn't invite easy pity, but shocks us into realising how futile self-awareness is in keeping loneliness at bay. As a result, her transformation into a baby-loving housewife makes a perverse, tender kind of sense. So what's the problem? Lette's one-liners, when spoken, reduce her characters to Tourette victims; they ejaculate punchlines even when no one's around, destroying any sense of naturalism. Newcomer Sugarman directs with her finger on the FF button, but to no avail. All her attempts to hurry time merely make you aware of how much is being wasted. CO'Su

Mad Doctor of Market Street, The

(1942, US, 60 min, b/w)
d Joseph H Lewis. *p* Paul Malvern. *sc* Al Martin. ph Jerry Ash. *ed* Ralph Dixon. *ad* Jack Otterson, Ralph M DeLacey. *m* Hans J Salter. *cast* Lionel Atwill, Una Merkel, Claire Dodd, Nat Pendleton, Anne Nagel, Noble Johnson.
●Lewis at his low budget looniest, and barely the worse for that. The material is preposterously absurd. It begins with mad boffin Atwill chased out of a recognisably modern American city for his sinister experiments, shifts to a swish ocean liner for a quick dash of social comedy (Merkel) and disaster movie, then ends up on a ludicrously unexotic desert island where the few shipwreck survivors are menaced by Atwill's desire to take up his old work again. *Everything* is cheap, tacky and infantile, but you can't help but admire the way Lewis balances his evident, slyly humorous disdain for the script and production values with a surprisingly professional pretence at some sort of commitment. Zomboid fun. GA

Mad Dog and Glory

(1992, US, 97 min)
d John McNaughton. *p* Barbara DeFina, Martin Scorsese. *sc* Richard Price. *ph* Robby Müller. *ed* Craig McKay, Elena Maganini. *pd* David Chapman. *m* Elmer Bernstein. *cast* Robert De Niro, Bill Murray, Uma Thurman, Kathy Baker, David Caruso, Mike Starr.
●This intriguing but not wholly successful blend of thriller, comedy and romance is essentially a buddy movie. It's concerned more with the friendship between Chicago forensic detective Wayne 'Mad Dog' Dobie (De Niro) and loan-shark Frank Milo (Murray), than the feelings between De Niro and Glory (Thurman), a salesgirl sent by the gangster as a gift after the cop saves his life. Just as Glory is merely a prize to be won, so Richard Price's script and McNaughton's direction relegate her to the function of a catalyst. Sexual politics aside (the film also avoids acknowledging its gay dimensions), it nevertheless exerts a quirky charm. Back on form, De Niro seems committed to the part of the sensitive loner, while Murray all but succeeds in mixing smooth and sinister, heartfelt and hot-tempered. But the film's real strength lies in incidentals: marginal characters; Dobie's love of photography and Louis Prima records; the drugs-murder which gets the whole thing started. Here, Price's street savvy and McNaughton's taut pacing bind the disparate elements impressively. GA

Mad Dog Morgan (aka Mad Dog)

(1976, Aust, 110 min)
d Philippe Mora. *p* Jeremy Thomas. *sc* Philippe Mora. *ph* Mike Molloy. *ed* John Scott. *ad* Bob Hilditch. *m* Patrick Flynn. *cast* Dennis Hopper, Jack Thompson, David Gulpilil, Frank Thring, Michael Pate, Wallas Eaton, Bill Hunter, John Hargreaves.
●An excellent early example of the Australian revival, this is a pacy, violent bushranger saga; basically a Western in all but locale, with the same sort of critical kinship to its US models as *Backroads*. Hopper's hirsute Irish outlaw (a first-rate performance) is the victim of social barbarities inflicted at the behest of bald, bullish policeman Thring, and David Gulpilil again represents the unknowable forgotten option like some 'good Injun'. PT

Mad Dogs and Englishmen

(1971, US, 118 min)
d Pierre Adidge. *p/sc* Pierre Adidge, Harry Marks, Robert Abel. *ph* David Myers. *ed* Sidney Levin. *with* Joe Cocker, Leon Russell, Rita Coolidge, Claudia Linnear.
●Leon Russell organised the caravan tour of the States in the spring of 1970 which featured Joe Cocker, the Greaseband and about forty others, and which this film documents. A team of 16mm cameramen followed them around, concentrating on simple, multi-camera coverage of concert numbers, and filling in the touring gaps with ungimmicky shots of the troupe in buses, hotels and streets. The sound recording for the first few numbers leaves something to be desired; but considering the pleasantly chaotic formation of the 'family' onstage, this is perhaps understandable, and is made up for in the unpretentious appearance of the movie as a whole. So it comes down to whether you like the music of the Cocker/ Russell team. If you do, you won't be disappointed. JC

Mad Dogs and Englishmen

(1994, GB, 97 min)
d Henry Cole. *p* Peter Watson-Wood, Nigel Thomas. *sc* Tim Sewell. *ph* John Peters. *ed* Lionel Selwyn, Simon Hilton. *pd* Tony Stringer. *m* Barrie Guard. *cast* Elizabeth Hurley, C Thomas Howell, Joss Ackland, Jeremy Brett, Claire Bloom, Frederick Treves, Patrick Lichfield.
●Rich bitch Antonia Dyer's heroin habit has led her into a dangerous world where crime and punishment easily become confused. The audience, too: Ackland's Insp Stringer of the the Yard, a bent copper struggling with incestuous desires and imminent retirement, seems more like a decent actor who's wandered into the wrong thriller. Bike messenger Mike is so infatuated with Antonia he'll pick up smack at 3 am on her whim, but Howell is so inexpressive his behaviour might as well be motivated by suicidal impulses. Antonia fits Hurley like 'that dress', but despite her plummy, punky credentials, she can do little to humanise a Sloane who spends most of her time lolling in silk lingerie, burning tin foil. The handling is clumsy, the moralising dire, and gestures towards genre movie-making are laughable. TCh

Mad Dog Time (aka Trigger Happy)

(1996, US, 93 min)
d Larry Bishop. *p* Judith James. *sc* Larry Bishop. *ph* Frank Byers. *ed* Norman Hollyn. *pd* Dina Lipton. *m* Earl Rose. *cast* Ellen Barkin, Gabriel Byrne, Richard Dreyfuss, Jeff Goldblum, Diane Lane, Larry Bishop, Gregory Hines, Kyle MacLachlan, Burt Reynolds, Michael J Pollard, Angie Everhart, Paul Anka, Rob Reiner, Richard Pryor, Joey Bishop.
●Writer/director Bishop, son of the old Rat Pack member Joey Bishop, looks set on founding his own pack with this spoof of gang warfare. Whereas Sinatra's pack made sneery, slick movies together, Bishop can organise his material and he shares his jokes. Gang boss Vic (Dreyfuss) is released from mental hospital, but finds his turf threatened with ambitious weeds like mortician MacLachlan, who longs to see everyone professionally, and his own once-faithful caretaker, Byrne. The new blood presents him with a commemorative straitjacket at his welcome home party, so the chances of détente are slim. Vic is also preoccupied with settling scores with his former hitman Nicky (Goldblum), who took up with his mistress once the boss was banged up. There's byzantine plotting, trade-offs and double-bluffs aplenty, plus an amusing ritual in which rival hitmen duel to the death from facing executive desks. The leads play up enthusiastically with the brass ring shared by Goldblum and Barkin's shifty moll Rita. There's a conveyor belt of faded or fuddled walk-ons from the likes of Pollard, Pryor, Reynolds and Anka, while the soundtrack is vintage cuff-shooting crooner. Fair fun. BC

Made

(1972, GB, 104 min)
d John MacKenzie. *p* Joseph Janni. *sc* Howard Barker. *ph* Ernest Day. *ed* David Campling. *ad* Philip Harrison. *m* John Cameron. *cast* Carol White, Roy Harper, John Castle, Margery Mason, Doremy Vernon, Sam Dastor, Michael Cashman, Brian Croucher.
●Rather dated already, MacKenzie's film swerves uneasily between social realism and melodramatic clichés as it follows a girl's attempts to find a way out from her miserable life looking after her illegitimate child and an invalid mother. Salvation is offered by a do-gooding priest and a boring old folksinger (Harper playing himself, quite well actually). It has its moments of acute perception, but much of the time is content with a typically British glamorisation of seedy lives. Ken Loach, one feels, would have handled it far better. GA

Made

(2001, US, 94 min)
d Jon Favreau. *p* Vince Vaughn, Jon Favreau. *sc* Jon Favreau. *ph* Christopher Doyle. *ed* Curtiss Clayton. *pd* Anne Stuhler. *m* John O'Brien, Lyle Workman. *cast* Jon Favreau, Vince Vaughn, Sean Combs, Famke Janssen, Faizon Love, David O'Hara, Vincent Pastore, Peter Falk, Joe Goossen, Makenzie Vega, Reanna Rossi.
●The arrested adolescents from *Swingers* tangle with the Mob in this belated follow-up to the 1996 indie hit written by Jon Favreau. This time he and Vaughn play hapless Angeleno ex-boxers, Bobby and Ricky, who get a chance to atone for their misdemeanours as delivery boys for old-style crime figure Max (Falk). All they have to do is fly to New York on expenses, hook up with major player Ruiz (Combs), and do the deal. Sounds simple, but fast-talking Ricky has a gift for saying the wrong thing at the wrong time, every time. No wonder Bobby's a worried man. Favreau's first directorial effort risks feeling repetitive until you realise it's playing a set of variations on a theme as bigmouth Ricky puts his foot in it and his ever-loyal buddy tries to smoothe things over. Though the scenario echoes *Mean Streets*, it's actually a comedy of manners in crime-flick garb. If the film's too ready to go with the flow of Chris Doyle's handheld camera-work, and sometimes seems ad hoc, its spot-on attention to the faux pas of the moment certainly raises a smile. If it's never quite a knockout, Vaughn's cannily judged display of virtuoso assholery is something to see. TJ

Made for Each Other

(1971, US, 107 min)
d Robert B Bean. *p* Roy Townshend. *sc* Renée Taylor, Joseph Bologna. *ph* William Storz. *ed* Sonny Mele. *ad* Robert Ramsey. *m* Trade Martin. *cast* Renée Taylor, Joseph Bologna, Paul Sorvino, Olympia Dukakis, Helen Verbit, Louis Zorich.
●Jewish girl from the Bronx meets an Italian boy from Brooklyn at an emergency encounter group on Christmas Eve. From there develops an erratic relationship that continually erupts into near-sadistic confrontations: the girl wants to be loved but not possessed, the guy wants to possess but not love (explicitly anyway). Much of the film is taken up by the couple's violent exchanges, which at times come over as childishness; but the chauvinistic attitudes and the film's unresolved tensions make it just about worth a look (although you have to sit through a lot of ego-shit before getting your head into the overall trip). JPi

Made in America

(1993, US, 110 min)
d Richard Benjamin. *p* Arnon Milchan, Michael Douglas, Rick Bieber. *sc* Holly Goldberg Sloan. *ph* Ralf Bode. *ed* Jacqueline Cambas. *pd* Evelyn Sakash. *m* Mark Isham. *cast* Whoopi Goldberg, Ted Danson, Will Smith, Nia Long, Frances Bergen, Phyllis Avery, Jennifer Tilly.
●Director Benjamin makes amiable but bland comedies, and here's another. The pitch is ebony (Goldberg) meets ivory (Danson) as bio-chemical parents of, well, a light-brown daughter (Long) when they belatedly discover she was the fruit of a sperm bank mix-up. Whoopi's a successful, politicised, single working-mother; Danson's a lovable, reconstructable cowpoke. After the first half sets up intriguing racial/political/biological conundrums, the second simply lets them go hang. Energetically directed with a fair smattering of funny lines. WH

Made in Heaven

(1987, US, 102 min)
d Alan Rudolph. *p* Raynold Gideon, Bruce Evans, David Blocker. *sc* Bruce Evans, Raynold Gideon. *ph* Jan Kiesser. *ed* Tom Walls. *pd* Paul Peters. *m* Mark Isham. *cast* Timothy Hutton, Kelly McGillis, Maureen Stapleton, Ann Wedgeworth, James Gammon, Debra Winger, Ellen Barkin, Don Murray, Timothy Daly, Amanda Plummer.
●Back in the '50s, Mike (Hutton) dies saving a family from a car accident. In heaven he falls in love with Annie (McGillis), a new soul waiting to be born, and he's forced to gamble on 30 more years on earth in order to search out his lost love. Will they meet again? Unlikely; he's reincarnated as under-achieving would-be musician Elmo, she as wealthy, talented Ally, spliced to an ambitious film-maker. Offbeat and very imaginative, Rudolph's movie displays the same absolute control of atmosphere – both celestial and worldly – that made his earlier work so tantalising. The narrative drifts a little as Elmo and Ally make their separate ways through the '60s, and the ending taxes credibility. But the film looks a treat, the performances are convincing and charismatic, and the result, as they say, is a real charmer. GA

Made in Hong Kong (Xiang-gang Zhizao)

(1997, HK, 107 min)
d Fruit Chan. *p* Andy Lau, Doris Yang. *sc* Fruit Chan. *ph* O Sing-Pui, Lam Wah-Chuen. *ed* Tin Sam-Fat. *ad* Ma Ka-Kwan. *m* Lam Wah Chuen. *cast* Sam Lee, Neiky Yim, Wenbers Li, Amy Tan.
●Bad things start happening to Moon, a kid from a housing estate, when he comes into possession of two bloodstained letters left behind by a schoolgirl suicide: his mother walks out, he starts having pesky wet dreams, his mentally handicapped best friend gets into trouble – and he falls for a girl who turns out to be seriously ill. The irresistibly named Fruit Chan, a long-serving assistant director in the film industry, got this indie feature made on a wing and a prayer: vari-

ous industry figures (notably Andy Lau) helped out, hardly anyone got paid and the non-pro cast was recruited on the street. Much of it is fresh, truthfully observed and touching in its honesty, but the climactic escalation into triad melodrama and the several false endings suggest that old industry habits die hard. None the less, a striking achievement. TR

Madeleine

(1949, GB, 114 min, b/w)
d David Lean. *p* Stanley Haynes. *sc* Nicholas Phipps, Stanley Haynes. *ph* Guy Green. *ed* Geoffrey Foot. *ad* John Bryan. *m* William Alwyn. *cast* Ann Todd, Leslie Banks, Elizabeth Sellars, Norman Wooland, Ivan Desny, Ivor Barnard, Andre Morell, Edward Chapman.

● One of three films Lean made virtually as star vehicles for his wife Ann Todd. Here she manages to extend the range of her semi-hysterical screen personality into a flimsily forceful character who pits her amoral deviousness against the rigid hypocrisy of Victorian Glasgow. Lean strongly emphasises her vulnerability: her French lover (Desny) is a preening bully, her father (Banks) a fire-eating patriarch, and her passage to the courtroom (accused of poisoning the lover) is marked by the furious rantings of a male mob. Where the film is remarkable, though, is in never allowing her to become simply a victim. She dares to expose and enjoy her sensuality, and cunningly exploits the prim reticence expected of a Victorian miss to avoid submission to marriage, deflecting the hostile gaze of outraged society with a proudly enigmatic vanity. RMy

Madeline

(1998, US/Ger, 89 min)
d Daisy von Scherler Mayer. *p* Saul Cooper, Pancho Kohner, Allyn Stewart. *sc* Mark Levin, Jennifer Flackett. *ph* Pierre Aïm. *ed* Jeffrey Wolf. *pd* Hugo Luczyc-Wyhowski. *m* Michel Legrand. *cast* Frances McDormand, Nigel Hawthorne, Hatty Jones, Ben Daniels, Arturo Venegas, Stéphane Audran, Katia Caballero, Chantal Neuwirth, Kristian de la Osa.

● Once you've seen Ludwig Bemelmans' idiosyncratic drawing of the twelve little girls in two straight lines dissolve into little actors, you've seen it all. We're at a school for young ladies in Paris in the '50s. Hatty Jones as the fearless heroine is likeable, while McDormand is, as ever, absolutely in her role. Her Miss Clavel presents physical comedy instead of the rather neurotic tilt of the original; her panics are very watchable as she tries to keep tabs on her brood. Hawthorne could have phoned in his Lord Covington, who decides to sell the school, so little does he have to do. The various ambassadors who arrive as potential buyers are put off by pranks, none memorable. Another plot, presumably born of desperation, involves the kidnapping of the Spanish ambassador's son, who registers a faintly leering presence astride a motor scooter. BC

Mademoiselle

(1966, GB/Fr, 103 min, b/w)
d Tony Richardson. *p* Oscar Lewenstein. *sc* Jean Genet. *ph* David Watkin. *ed* Antony Gibbs. *ad* Jacques Saulnier. *cast* Jeanne Moreau, Ettore Manni, Keith Skinner, Umberto Orsini, Jane Berretta, Mony Reh, Rosine Luguet.

● After *Tom Jones*, Tony Richardson launched into a series of extremely ambitious films (*The Loved One*, *The Sailor from Gibraltar* and *Mademoiselle*) which were all lambasted by the critics for their pretentiousness. This one boasts a script by Jean Genet which was partially rewritten by no less than four writers (David Rudkin, Michel Cournot, Oscar Lewenstein, and Richardson himself), and the results were understandably mixed, though not nearly as awful as *The Sailor from Gibraltar*, which deserves its reputation as the most meaningless movie of the '60s. Here, Jeanne Moreau plays a strung-up French schoolteacher who is driven by her lust for a woodcutter to commit a series of atrocities, but the whole thing suffers from Richardson's terrible addiction to artistic overstatement (not to mention the difficulty of making an intimate drama with an international cast speaking several languages). DP

Mademoiselle Docteur (aka Salonique, nid d'espions)

(1936, Fr, 96 min, b/w)
d GW Pabst. *sc* Georges Neveux, Madame I Cube, Jacques Natanson. *ph* Eugen Schüfftan. *ed* Marc Sorkin, Louise Haudecoeur. *ad* Serge Pimenoff. *m* Arthur Honegger. *cast* Dita Parlo, Pierre Fresnay, Louis Jouvet, Pierre Blanchar, Viviane Romance, Charles Dullin, Jean-Louis Barrault, Gaston Modot.

● A lunatic with a craving for melons accidentally strays into a den of spies. The ensuing encounter is hilarious, prototype Pinter. But it has nothing to do with the rest of the movie (WWI, glamorous German spy, handsome French officer, background of minarets, sweaty cabarets, danger under every fez), and you can appreciate the dismay of '30s cinephiles, finding that the great socialist-humanist Pabst had turned to such 'meaningless' melodrama. In any case, Pabst – glum, unromantic – was clearly miscast as director, and the result is a hodgepodge, redeemed by odd flashes of brilliance, like the melon scene. Parlo, fine as the bedraggled bride in *L'Atalante*, lacks the requisite Dietrich blend of insolence and melancholy, while the movie's finale is so perfunctory as to suggest production problems. BBa

Mad Genius, The

(1931, US, 81 min, b/w)
d Michael Curtiz. *sc* J Grubb Alexander, Harvey Thew. *ph* Barney McGill. *ed* Ralph Dawson. *ad* Anton Grot. *cast* John Barrymore, Marian Marsh, Donald Cook, Carmel Myers, Charles Butterworth, Mae Madison, Luis Alberni, Boris Karloff.

● Barrymore enjoys himself immensely in this ripe horror effort as a demented and crippled Svengali figure who takes over the running of a ballet company. Alberni is way, way over the top as the drugged dancing master, and Boris Karloff pops up as the sadistic dad. The finale, which involves a brutal murder in the middle of a ballet performance, is well worth the wait. TJ

Madhouse

(1974, GB, 92 min)
d Jim Clark. *p* Max J Rosenberg, Milton Subotsky. *sc* Greg Morrison. *ph* Ray Parslow. *ed* Clive Smith. *ad* Tony Curtis. *m* Douglas Gamley. *cast* Vincent Price, Peter Cushing, Robert Quarry, Adrienne Corri, Natasha Pyne, Linda Hayden, Catherine Willmer.

● Basically an actor's revenge plot in the wake of *Theatre of Blood*, but reasonably witty in its use of inter-penetrating fantasies born of the Dream Factory. The film has its faults, not least a tendency to allow things to go over the top; but the interweaving of the character of Paul Toombes, fictional veteran star of the *Doctor Death* series who is no longer able to tell fantasy and reality apart (he is glimpsed roaming Sunset Boulevard in his Doctor Death costume), with the real-life career of Vincent Price (who plays the part), is quite inspired and lends the film some sharp moments. Sequences from *The Fall of the House of Usher*, *The Raven* and other Price movies add a deeper piquancy to the mixture. A number of small parts are nicely filled, and in-jokes include the total dispensability of the TV series director: his death goes all but unnoticed. VG

Madhouse

(1990, US, 90 min)
d Tom Ropelewski. *p* Leslie Dixon, *sc* Tom Ropelewski. *ph* Denis Lewiston. *ed* Michael Jablow. *pd* Dan Leigh. *m* David Newman. *cast* John Larroquette, Kirstie Alley, Alison LaPlaca, John Diehl, Jessica Lundy, Bradley Gregg, Dennis Miller, Robert Ginty.

● Mark (Larroquette) and Jessie (Alley) are an LA couple on the threshold of their dreams. The money they earn – he as a finance manager, she as a TV journalist – just about enables them to mortgage their futures away on a cramped starter-home a mile from Venice Beach. Both eye their very own bedroom with delicious expectation, but – this being a comedy – coitus is forever interrupted. First, cousin Fred (Diehl), a newly-redundant sewage treatment operative, arrives with his wife (Lundy), who is pregnant, neurotic, and owner of a murderable cat; they take over the bedroom. Then Jessie's sister (La Placa), a rich bitch who has left her oil-sheik husband, gets the spare room. Having the neighbour (Ginty) about the place when his house burns down ain't so bad, but his kids have seriously bad attitudes. Then there's the elephant… A standard extremist farce, lazily written and fumblingly directed. WH

Madigan

(1967, US, 101 min)
d Don Siegel. *p* Frank P Rosenberg. *sc* Henri Simoun, Abraham Polonsky. *ph* Russell Metty. *ed* Milton Shifman. *ad* Alexander Golitzen, George Webb. *m* Don Costa. *cast* Richard Widmark, Henry Fonda, Inger Stevens, Harry Guardino, James Whitmore, Susan Clark, Michael Dunn, Steve Ihnat, Don Stroud, Sheree North.

● A film that marks a crossroads in Siegel's career. The methods of the two strongarm cops (Widmark and Guardino), given seventy-two hours to find a killer, invite comparisons with those of the two professional gunmen in Siegel's earlier *The Killers*. But the film also looks forward to *Coogan's Bluff* and *Dirty Harry* as the first to exploit the ambivalent enforcer/protector role of the police in society, with Fonda as the martinet police commissioner enforcing strict public morality while practising marital infidelity at home.

Mad Little Island

see Rockets Galore

Mad Love (aka The Hands of Orlac)

(1935, US, 70 min, b/w)
d Karl Freund. *p* John W Considine Jr. *sc* PJ Wolfson, John L Balderston, Guy Endore. *ph* Chester Lyons, Gregg Toland. *ed* Hugh Wynn. *ad* Cedric Gibbons, William A Horning, Edwin B Willis. *m* Dimitri Tiomkin. *cast* Peter Lorre, Frances Drake, Colin Clive, Isabel Jewell, Ted Healy, Sara Haden, Edward Brophy, Henry Kolker, Keye Luke.

● A classic slab of Grand Guignol, with Lorre in great form – bald, bulging-eyed and blessed with a magnificent leer – as the insane surgeon who lusts after the gorgeous Ms Drake, and in order to win her, operates on her concert pianist husband (Clive) after his hands are mutilated in an accident, deliberately grafting on the hands of a guillotined, knife-throwing murderer. The usual Gothic motifs, in fact – dismemberment, murder, madness, and the threat of rape – all played out in semi-serious fashion with some delirious set pieces, atmospherically shot by Gregg Toland and performed (with the exception of the wooden Clive) with gleeful abandon. Great fun. GA

Mad Love

(1995, US, 96 min)
d Antonia Bird. *p* David Manson. *sc* Paula Milne. *ph* Fred Tammes. *ed* Jeff Freeman. *pd* David Brisbin. *m* Andy Roberts. *cast* Drew Barrymore, Chris O'Donnell, Joan Allen, Matthew Lillard, June Ciccolella, Kevin Dunn, Liev Schreiber.

● When Matt (O'Donnell) gets a load of Casey (Barrymore), he has no idea what he's looking at. She's wild and impetuous and just a little crazy. A lot crazy, her father says, forbidding the relationship and putting her in psychiatric care when things get heavy. The young lovers hit the road, and the radio is their compass ('If the next song's country, we go north, if it's rock, we go south'), guiding them from watery Seattle to dusty New Mexico (rock'n'roll all the way). Things get heavier. Written by Paula Milne (*The Politician's Wife*) and directed by Antonia Bird (*Priest*), Brit interlopers in Hollywood, this has the elements of a '90s *Splendor in the Grass*, even a *Lilith*. When Barrymore says she likes 'rudeness, noise, honesty, danger' you tend to believe her, but sadly this movie has been Disneyed along the way, it's altogether too polite, quiet, false and safe. A disappointment. TCh

Mad Love

see L'Amour Fou

Mad Magician, The

(1954, US, 72 min, b/w)
d John Brahm. *p* Bryan Foy. *sc* Crane Wilbur. *ph* Bert Glennon. *ed* Grant Whytock. *ad* F Paul Sylos. *m* Arthur Lange. *cast* Vincent Price, Mary Murphy, Eva Gabor, John Emery, Donald Randolph, Lenita Lane, Patrick O'Neal.

●Originally shown in 3-D, this vigorous little shocker has another psychotic role for Price as a magic-trick inventor who goes over the edge when fellow magicians rip off his act and his wife runs off with a younger rival. There's much play with Vincent's latest gizmo (a chainsaw that seems to behead its victims) but the piece as a whole is a few notches down in content and style from the previous year's *House of Wax*. TJ

Mad Max

(1979, Aust, 100 min)
d George Miller. *p* Byron Kennedy. *sc* James McCausland, George Miller. *ph* David Eggby. *ed* Tony Paterson, Cliff Hayes. *ad* Jon Dowding. *m* Brian May. *cast* Mel Gibson, Joanne Samuel, Hugh Keays-Byrne, Steve Bisley, Tim Burns, Roger Ward, Vince Gill.
●George Miller's film is an outrageous exploiter drawing intelligently on everything from *Death Race 2000* to *Straw Dogs* for its JG Ballard-ish story about a future where cops and Hell's Angels stage protracted guerrilla warfare around what's left of a hapless civilian population. The tone sometimes wavers into self-parody, and there are occasional crude patches, but overall this edge-of-seat revenge movie marks the most exciting debut from an Australian director since Peter Weir. DP

Mad Max 2

(1981, Aust, 96 min)
d George Miller. *p* Byron Kennedy. *sc* Terry Hayes, George Miller, Brian Hannant. *ph* Dean Semler. *ed* David Stiven, Tim Wellburn, Michael Chirgwin. *m* Brian May. *cast* Mel Gibson, Bruce Spence, Vernon Wells, Emil Minty, Mike Preston, Kjell Nilsson, Virginia Hey, Syd Heylen, Moira Claux, Arkie Whiteley.
●Set a few years after *Mad Max* (which looks primitive by comparison), *Mad Max 2* concerns a strange post-industrial future where motorised warlords scour the deserts for fuel. Max, played in proper Eastwood style by Gibson, comes upon an oil fortress beleaguered by hordes of biker barbarians. The simple plot has the macho inspiration of a 2000 AD comic strip, and though the film can't quite sustain its length, it's kept alive by its humour and the sheer energy of its visuals. In fact, Miller's choreography of his innumerable vehicles is so extraordinary that it makes Spielberg's *Raiders of the Lost Ark* look like a kid fooling with Dinky Toys. DP

Mad Max Beyond Thunderdome

(1985, Aust, 107 min)
d George Miller, George Ogilvie. *p* George Miller. *sc* Terry Hayes, George Miller. *ph* Dean Semler. *ed* Richard Francis-Bruce. *pd* Graham Walker. *m* Maurice Jarre. *cast* Mel Gibson, Bruce Spence, Tina Turner, Helen Buday, Angelo Rossitto, Frank Thring, Rod Zuanic.
●Mad Mel is back on the job, cleaning up the dustbowls of post-apocalyptic Aussie. This time around, he's matched against Auntie (Turner) and the denizens of the pig-shit powered Bartertown in a rather erratic plot which rambles around the Outback before finally pulling itself together for the usual stunning chariots of fire and brimstone chase scene. En route, however, Miller unveils some marvellously original cinematic snaps (the lost city of the feral children; Master Blaster, the dwarf-powered giant; Thunderdome itself); and if the thrills and special effects lack a little of the punch of *Mad Max 2*, there's still enough imagination, wit and ingenuity to put recent Spielberg to shame. DAt

Mad Miss Manton, The

(1938, US, 80 min, b/w)
d Leigh Jason. *p* Pandro S Berman. *sc* Philip G Epstein. *ph* Nick Musuraca. *ed* George Hively. *ad* Van Nest Polglase, Carroll Clark. *m* Roy Webb. *cast* Barbara Stanwyck, Henry Fonda, Sam Levene, Frances Mercer, Stanley Ridges, Whitney Bourne, Hattie McDaniel, Penny Singleton.
●Gilt-edged performances from the two stars display something of the chemistry that exploded between them in *The Lady Eve*. Stanwyck's madcap heiress stumbles across a murder, only to have the body vanish and a dyspeptic cop (Levene) shrug it off as one of her notorious pranks, while journalist Fonda denounces her as an obnoxious example of the idle rich. Instantly on her mettle, Stanwyck rounds up her circle of equally scatty girlfriends and, ignoring a death threat or two, proceeds to solve the mystery with some help from the repentant Fonda. The whodunit tangles tend to overstay their welcome, but Nick Musuraca's dark-toned camerawork leavens the screwball comedy with genuine menace; and Philip G Epstein's dialogue provides a witty undertow of fun poked at the class war (what with Hattie McDaniel playing an anything but downtrodden black maid: 'In my home, the revolution is here,' Stanwyck grumbles). The final clinch even manages a neat subversion of 'correct' attitudes, when Fonda suggests an extended honeymoon since Stanwyck can afford it. 'I wanted to live on your income,' she coos meltingly. 'That's foolish,' he retorts, 'who's going to live on yours?' TM

Mad Monkey, The (El Mono loco)

(1990, Sp, 108 min)
d Fernando Trueba. *p* Andrés Vicente Gómez. *sc* Fernando Trueba, Manolo Matji. *ph* José Luis Alcaine. *ed* Carmen Frías. *ad* Pierre-Louis Thévenet. *m* Antoine Duhamel. *cast* Jeff Goldblum, Miranda Richardson, Anémone, Dexter Fletcher, Daniel Ceccaldi, Liza Walker, Arielle Dombasle.
●Relying more on atmosphere and serpentine plot twists than on button-pushing shock effects, this psychological thriller builds inexorably to a disturbing climax. Goldblum plays an American scriptwriter whose marital difficulties are exacerbated when he gets involved in a European movie project financed by a Paris-based producer (Ceccaldi). The precocious young English director (Fletcher) has only the flimsiest of outlines, a brief quotation from one of Goldblum's favourite books, *Peter Pan*. Nevertheless, after the writer's initially reluctant agent (Richardson) cuts him a good deal, he starts work with the director on an abstract, almost avant-garde script. Surrounding the project is a compelling web of sexual intrigue, at the centre of which is the director's androgynous 16-year-old sister (Walker), an adolescent femme fatale who catalyses all the participants' selfish desires. As the plot coils ever tighter, handled with smooth assurance by Trueba, sexual fantasy and hallucinatory dream sequences give way to a frighteningly complex psychological reality. NF

Mad Monster Party

(1967, US, 94 min)
d Jules Bass. *p* Arthur Rankin Jr. *sc* Len Korobkin, Harvey Kurtzman. *m/songs* Maury Laws. *cast* voices: Phyllis Diller, Boris Karloff, Gale Garnett, Ethel Ennis, Alan Swift.
●Horror spoof using stop-motion animation: the first meeting of the World Organisation of Monsters is attended by Frankenstein's creature, the Wolf Man, Dracula, King Kong and the Mummy. Not often removed from the vaults.

Madness of King George, The

(1994, GB/US, 110 min)
d Nicholas Hytner. *p* Stephen Evans, David Parfitt. *sc* Alan Bennett. *ph* Andrew Dunn. *ed* Tariq Anwar. *pd* Ken Adam. *m* George Fenton. *cast* Nigel Hawthorne, Helen Mirren, Amanda Donohoe, Rupert Everett, Ian Holm, Rupert Graves, Julian Wadham, Jim Carter, Geoffrey Palmer, Alan Bennett.
●The late 1780s: George III (Hawthorne), already disturbed by the loss of the American colonies, finds his ebullience further eroded by the onset of alarming mood swings: he jumps his wife's lady-in-waiting (Donohoe), disrupts concerts, and goes generally gaga. While doctors argue over stools and methodology, a wider crisis arises: Prime Minister Pitt vainly assures Parliament that the King is healthy; but his Whig rival Fox throws in with the disaffected Prince of Wales. The Queen (Mirren) alone remains absolutely loyal, and when Wales denies her access to her spouse, the monarch's only hopes lie with an equerry (Graves), a few wary courtiers, and Willis, an unconventional parson-turned-medic (Holm). This elegant adaptation by Alan Bennett of his own stage success is the best of his contributions to the big screen to date: sturdily performed and persuasively detailed, and with a beady delight in political in-fighting. The semi-heroic role afforded the disciplinarian Willis is perhaps a touch reactionary, and there's a nagging feeling that there's less here than meets the eye. But it's funny and moving. GA

Madonna of the Seven Moons

(1944, GB, 110 min, b/w)
d Arthur Crabtree. *p* RJ Minney. *sc* Roland Pertwee. *ph* Jack Cox. *ed* Lito Carruthers. *ad* Andrew Mazzei. *m* Hans May. *cast* Phyllis Calvert, Stewart Granger, Patricia Roc, Peter Glenville, Jean Kent, Nancy Price, John Stuart, Dulcie Gray.
●One of the main attractions of the early Gainsborough melodramas (*The Man in Grey*, *Fanny by Gaslight*) is Arthur Crabtree's atmospheric lighting. His touch is evident here, too, but doesn't really compensate for the mess he makes of directing this tale of schizoid sexuality and Florentine low-life. Calvert, the epitome of '40s respectability, displays a surprising sensuality as the woman raped in adolescence by a gypsy and subsequently developing a split personality, but the emotional impact of the scenes in the *Seven Moons* and its seedy environs is dissipated in subplots that are silly, clumsy and grindingly boring. Crabtree's melodrama collapses around his ears, but there are real gems among the debris. Just think of England while you wait for them to turn up. RMy

Madre Muerta, La

(1993, Sp, 111 min)
d/p Juanma Bajo Ulloa. *sc* Juanma Bajo Ulloa, Eduardo Bajo Ulloa. *ph* Javier Agirresarobe. *ed* Pablo Blanco. *pd* Satur Idarreta. *m* Bingen Mendizabal. *cast* Karra Elejalde, Ana Alvarez, Lio, Silvio Marsó, Elena Irueta.
●This follow-up to Ulloa's little-seen *Butterfly Wings* displays a notable aesthetic rigour and intellectual clarity. Without such formal discipline, this psychological thriller might have spilled over into dubious exploitation, but like his haunted protagonist, the director/co-writer always pulls back from the brink. Entering a house late one night, a thief shoots dead the mother of a child, who stares in silent witness to his crime. Ten years later, the thief, Ismael (Elejalde), spots a mute, seemingly autistic teenage girl in the garden of a Madrid hospital. Gripped by an irrational fear of disclosure, he abducts Leire (Alvarez) and holds her prisoner in the semi-derelict house he shares with his possessive girlfriend Maite (Lio). Jealous of their captive's womanly body, Maite favours walking her in front of a train, but the initially resolute Ismael suggests blackmail instead. The fact that Leire, a helpless child trapped in a woman's body, is fetishistically manacled to a bed lends a dangerous, almost perverse erotic edge to some scenes. Bound to her by guilt, however, Ismael is also paralysed by her innocence, a purity he cannot defile, which he believes may yet redeem him. Twisted and tender. NF

Madron

(1970, US/Isr, 93 min)
d Jerry Hopper. *p* Emanuel Henigman, Eric Weaver. *sc* Edward Chappell, Leo McMahon. *ph* Marcel Grignon, Adam Greenberg. *ed* Renzo Lucidi. *ad* Robert Ramsey. *m* Riz Ortolani. *cast* Richard Boone, Leslie Caron, Paul Smith, Gabi Amrani, Chaim Banai, Avraham Telya.
●There's Westerns, dull Westerns, and dull Richard Boone Westerns – here Boone joins up with gung-ho nun Leslie Caron to take on the Apaches. Shot in the Negev. TJ

Mad Room, The

(1968, US, 93 min)
d Bernard Girard. *p* Norman Maurer. *sc* Bernard Girard, AZ Martin. *ph* Harry Stradling Jr. *ed* Pat Somerset. *ad* Sydney Z Litwack. *m* David Grusin. *cast* Stella Stevens, Shelley Winters, Skip Ward, Carol Cole, Severn Darden, Beverly Garland.
●American Gothic: a remake of *Ladies in Retirement*, rather disastrously renovated for contemporary consumption. Shelley Winters is the wealthy widow, Stella Stevens the companion whose teenage brother and sister (released after years in a mental institution, suspected of hacking their parents to bits) come to stay. Skeletons in the cupboard, hacked-up bodies, and severed hands still can't make it anything more than routine. CPe

Mad Wednesday

see Sin of Harold Diddlebock, The

Maestro de Esgrima, El

see Fencing Master, The

Maestro, Il (The Maestro/ Double Game/Conductor)

(1989, Bel, 90 min)
d/sc Marion Hänsel. *ph* Acácio de Almeida. *ed* Susana Rossberg. *ad* Emita Frigato. *m* Frédéric Devresse. *cast* Malcolm McDowell, Charles Aznavour, Andréa Ferréol, Francis Lemaire, Pietro Pizzuti.

● Shot in English, writer/director Marion Hänsel's moody drama from the higher echelons of the European music scene has lots of ambition, but not quite the artistic clout to make the best of potentially interesting material. McDowell's a famous Jewish conductor who suffers a nervous breakdown when he returns to Italy for the first time in many years to work on a production of *Madame Butterfly*. It's left to impresario Lemaire to ferret out the his dark secret, tracing the maestro's life back to a wartime flight from the Nazis and a series of events that tied his destiny to charlatan Aznavour. Engrossing for classical music buffs, but finally somewhat superficial. TJ

Maeve

(1981, GB, 109 min)
d Pat Murphy, John Davies. *sc* Pat Murphy. *ph* Robert Smith. *ed* John Davies. *cast* Mary Jackson, Mark Mulholland, Brid Brennan, Trudy Kelly, John Keegan.

● 'Men's relationship to women is just like England's relationship to Ireland.' This assertion made to an ex-boyfriend by the heroine, on a return visit to her Catholic minority family in her native Belfast after a period of self-chosen exile in the (for her) liberating atmosphere of cosmopolitan London, signposts just what's wrong with this film. For, ambitious though it is, and largely successful in portraying the lived detail of the banality of bigotry operating in British Army-occupied Belfast, what *Maeve* conspicuously fails to do is to convincingly conflate its heroine's feminist concerns with those of the committed Republican boyfriend. Their dialogues finally find no point of intersection, and the film, like Maeve, seems to settle for its 'right not to know what (it's) doing'. An important effort, therefore, but a missed opportunity. RM

Mafu Cage, The

(1977, US, 101 min)
d Karen Arthur. *p* Diana Young. *sc* Don Chastain. *ed* Carol Littleton. *pd* Conrad E Angone. *cast* Lee Grant, Carol Kane, Will Geer, James Olson, Will Sherwood.

● A foray into the incestuous lives of two sisters, Karen Arthur's second feature is a slow, visually beautiful tale of sexuality and madness, with a haunting score by Roger Kellaway. Cissy (Kane, excellent) is creative and crazy. She's in love with her dead father and her doting older sister Ellen (Grant), and has turned their living-room into a claustrophobic jungle (they were brought up in Africa). At one end is 'The Mafu Cage', a home for primates – and a coffin if they go too far. For neither man nor ape (there's a lovely orang-utan involved) may touch her, Ellen, or their father's collection of phallic African treasures without violent consequences... At which point the film becomes problematic; the pace starts to drag; Ellen's relationship with a man is unconvincing; the two women's attitudes toward their own sexuality evolves in very unliberated fashion. Despite this, the hot-house aura remains enticing, and although the narrative comes close to exploitation, there's a surprisingly loving depth to the characters. HM

'Maggie', The (aka High and Dry)

(1953, GB, 92 min, b/w)
d Alexander Mackendrick. *p* Michael Truman. *sc* William Rose. *ph* Gordon Dines. *ed* Peter Tanner. *ad* Jim Morahan. *m* John Addison. *cast* Paul Douglas, Alex MacKenzie, Tommy Kearins, James Copeland, Abe Barker, Geoffrey Keen, Dorothy Alison.

● Here Ealing's foremost director was ostensibly making his statutory contribution to the studio's 'old crock' cycle that had begun the previous year with *The Titfield Thunderbolt*. But the cruel comedy of a rich Yank being slowly tormented by the canny crew of an ancient Scots cargo boat – it's transporting his furniture to a new holiday home, a commission undertaken only to save the boat from the scrapyard – gave Mackendrick and Ealing's resident American writer William Rose latitude to explore, in both autobiographical and wider cultural terms, the contradictions of the Old World and the New. Tradition and continuity become questionable values, the battle lines are blurred in comparison with those of *Whisky Galore!*, and typically of the director of the subsequent *High Wind in Jamaica* and *Sammy Going South*, it is the young cabin boy who is the most ambivalent character. PT

Magic

(1978, US, 107 min)
d Richard Attenborough. *p* Joseph E Levine, Richard P Levine. *sc* William Goldman. *ph* Victor J Kemper. *ed* John Bloom. *pd* Terence Marsh. *m* Jerry Goldsmith. *cast* Anthony Hopkins, Ann-Margret, Burgess Meredith, Ed Lauter, Jerry Houser, David Ogden Stiers.

● A hammed-up version of the old chestnut about the ventriloquist who is 'taken over' by his dummy, clumsily adapted by William Goldman from his own novel and infinitely better done in *The Great Gabbo* and *Dead of Night*. Hopkins starts over the top and soars even higher. Ann-Margret is wasted, and only Burgess Meredith (as the ventriloquist's ill-fated agent) comes out of the farrago with any honours. This is not a genre that suits Attenborough's 'epic' approach to movie-making. MA

Magic Bow, The

(1946, GB, 106 min, b/w)
d Bernard Knowles. *p* RJ Minney. *sc* Roland Pertwee. *ph* Jack Cox. *ad* Andrew Mazzei. *m* Henry Geehl. *cast* Stewart Granger, Phyllis Calvert, Jean Kent, Dennis Price, Cecil Parker, Felix Aylmer, Frank Cellier.

● The life and loves of violin virtuoso Paganini, heavily fictionalised to include a duel and the pawning of his beloved Stradivarius. Hokum, of course, but lent bravura by Knowles' vivid direction and camerawork (he also made the wonderful *Jassy* for Gainsborough), and just a touch of authenticity by having Yehudi Menuhin ghost the fiddling. GA

Magic Box, The

(1951, GB, 118 min)
d John Boulting. *p* Ronald Neame. *sc* Eric Ambler. *ph* Jack Cardiff. *ed* Richard Best. *pd* John Bryan. *m* William Alwyn. *cast* Robert Donat, Margaret Johnston, Maria Schell, John Howard Davies, Robert Beatty, Laurence Olivier, Michael Redgrave, Eric Portman.

● Written by Eric Ambler as a cinematic pageant for the 1951 Festival of Britain, this tale of William Friese-Greene, the British inventor who first patented a commercially viable motion picture camera (or did he?), is mainly of parochial interest for the cavalcade of household names. Lord Olivier turns up under a policeman's helmet to stare suspiciously at Donat's – 'But it moved!' – first triumphant screen projection. Then there's (among others) Jack Hulbert, Kathleen Harrison, Margaret Rutherford, Peter Ustinov, Stanley Holloway, Robertson Hare, Emlyn Williams, Ronald Shiner, Cecil Parker and most of the cast of *Radio Fun*, who all deferred most of their salaries. Dull stuff, though. BC

Magic Christian, The

(1969, GB, 95 min)
d Joseph McGrath. *p* Denis O'Dell. *sc* Terry Southern, Joseph McGrath, Peter Sellers. *ph* Geoffrey Unsworth. *ed* Kevin Connor. *pd* Assheton Gorton. *m* Ken Thorne. *cast* Peter Sellers, Ringo Starr, Richard Attenborough, Laurence Harvey, Christopher Lee, Spike Milligan, Yul Brynner, Roman Polanski, Raquel Welch, Dennis Price, John Cleese.

● An extravagant, undisciplined adaptation of Terry Southern's biting satire on the power of money – the plot is little but a stringing together of various hoaxes and practical jokes perpetrated by an eccentric multi-millionaire (Sellers) on a greedy populace – *The Magic Christian* is all too clearly representative of the impasse independent mainstream film-making found itself in when given its head by the industry in the '60s. The result is a variety concert of a film in which most of the acts/jokes fall flat. PH

Magic Donkey, The

see Peau d'Ane

Magic Flute, The (Trollflöjten)

(1974, Swe, 135 min)
d Ingmar Bergman. *p* Måns Reuterswärd. *sc* Ingmar Bergman. *ph* Sven Nykvist. *ed* Siv Lundgren. *ad* Henny Noremark. *cast* Josef Köstlinger, Irma Urrila, Håkan Hagegård, Elisabeth Eriksson, Ulrik Cold, Birgit Nordin, Ragnar Ulfung.

● The utopian imagery of Mozart's opera has pervaded Bergman's recent films; the 'ideal' couple Tamino and Pamina, united in the dawn of enlightenment and triumph over adversity, have haunted his angst-ridden couples since *Hour of the Wolf*. Made for Swedish TV, his film of the opera itself was obviously intended to popularise it. His strategy was to stage it in an 18th century theatre, complete with quaintly spectacular stagecraft, in front of a modern audience looking like delegates from a UNESCO conference; he introduces a few backstage gags, and lots of audience reaction shots, but mostly just films close-ups of the singers (doing their stuff in Swedish, incidentally). The trouble is that Bergman's ostensibly supportive tactics tend actually to subvert Mozart's conception, and so the result is a good deal less momentous than Bergman thinks. But it's still much livelier than most TV versions of operas. TR

Magic Hour, The (A Hora Mágica)

(1998, Braz, 101 min)
d Guilherme de Almeida Prado. *p* Sara Silvera. *sc* Guilherme de Almeida Prado. *ph* Jean-Benoît Crèpon. *ed* Cristina Amarac. *ad* Luis Rossi. *cast* Julia Lemmertz, Raul Gazolla, Maitê Proença, José Lewgoy, Tânia Alves, Walter Breda, John Herbert, David Cardoso.

● Similar in mood, tone and design to the same director's *Lady from the Shanghai Cinema*, this charts the love of Tito, a movie dubbing actor, for the mysterious Lucia amid the radio soap studios (he's the villain of 'The Murderer Is Amongst Us'), apartment corridors and bars of '30s Rio. It's an easily enjoyable, occasionally thought provoking, sometimes bemusing criss-cross of fantasy, parody, melodrama and reconstruction, filled with affectionate or ironic period references. WH

Magician, The

(1926, US, 77 min, b/w)
d/sc Rex Ingram. *ph* John F Seitz. *ed* Grant Whytock. *cast* Paul Wegener, Ivan Petrovich, Alice Terry, Firmin Gémier, Gladys Hamer, Stowitts.

● Adapted from the Somerset Maugham novel inspired by the life of Aleister Crowley, a bizarre melodrama which starts in Paris and moves to the Riviera: the sinister Dr Haddo (Wegener) uses hypnotism to kidnap a young woman (Terry) on the eve of her wedding, because he needs the blood from a virgin's heart to complete the formula for a homunculus. Ingram's strengths were mainly pictorial, and he here delivers plenty of high-flown images. Best of all is the sequence in which Haddo transports his victim into a Bosch-like vision and hands her over to a naked satyr for his nameless pleasures. Of great historical interest as the missing link between German expressionism and Hollywood fantasy. Michael Powell worked on it as assistant director. TR

Magician, The

see Ansiktet

Magician of Lublin, The

(1978, WGer/Isr, 114 min)
d Menahem Golan. *p* Menahem Golan, Yoram Globus. *sc* Irving S White, Menahem Golan. *ph* David Gurfinkel. *ed* Dov Hoenig. *pd* Hans-Jürgen Kiebach. *m* Maurice Jarre. *cast* Alan Arkin, Louise Fletcher, Valerie Perrine, Shelley Winters, Lou Jacobi, Warren Berlinger, Maia Danziger, Zachi Noy.

● Turn-of-the-century Warsaw: Yasha, an itinerant Jewish magician (Arkin), pursues the world, the flesh and the devil, and has enough spare hubris left over to want to fly; clearly the subject matter is rare enough to be beguiling. Unfortunately Golan's treatment, with its mixture of art house pretensions and vulgarity, founders at precisely those points where it departs from Isaac Bashevis Singer's original Yiddish novel. Where that used clear-eyed tender realism to point toward ambiguity of experience and mystery, Golan overdramatises, tips into hysteria, and substitutes a specious mysticism that is sadly literal. What survives (filmed in English) is sufficiently removed from mainstream cinema to be of interest – but not for Singer fans. CPea

Magic Night

see Goodnight Vienna

Magic of Lassie, The

(1978, US, 99 min)
d Don Chaffey. *p* Bonita Granville, William Beaudine Jr. *sc* Jean Holloway, Richard M Sherman, Robert B Sherman. *ph* Michael D Margulies. *ed* John C Horger. *ad* George Troast. *m* Richard M Sherman, Robert B Sherman. *cast* James Stewart, Mickey Rooney, Pernell Roberts, Stephanie Zimbalist, Michael Sharrett, Alice Faye, Gene Evans, Mike Mazurki.

● 'She's something that came from God!' James Stewart croaks in this monstrous musical adventure, which marks Lassie's comeback to the big screen after many years in TV. And he might be right, since everyone treats the dog with utmost sentimental reverence: when she's taken from her vineyard home by a nasty city slicker, even the sight of her empty food bowl makes people weepy. Diabetics and animal-haters should avoid, but for schlock addicts the film boasts Alice Faye (first film in 17 years) preparing eggs while singing a terrible song about roses and their 'scratchy, catchy thorns'. Unbelievable. GB

Magic Sword: Quest for Camelot, The

(1998, US, 86 min)
d Frederick Du Chau. *p* Dalisa Cooper Cohen. *sc* Kirk De Micco, William Schifrin, Jacqueline Feather, David Seidler. *ph* Mark Dinicola. ed Stanford C Allen. *pd* Steve Pilcher. *m* Patrick Doyle. *voices* Jessalyn Gilsig, Andrea Corr, Cary Elwes, Bryan White, Gary Oldman, Eric Idle, Don Rickles, Jane Seymour, Celine Dion, Pierce Brosnan.

● Warners' first fully animated feature is a disappointment – and this from the studio that fostered Chuck Jones and Tex Avery. There's no sign of those animators' anarchic style in this anodyne, PC tale from the table of King Arthur. Kayley, a cross between Pocahontas and Anastasia, longs to join the Knights of the Round Table, just like her dead father. Megalomaniac Ruber, however, has grander plans: he wants Arthur's sword, and dispatches his pet griffin to get it. The animation has little depth of field (galloping horses hover inches above the ground), the colours are watery, and there's not much Englishness in the settings. The characters, too, are unimaginative, with only bad boy Ruber (voiced by Oldman) providing any originality (his song and dance number is the one highlight). DA

Magic Town

(1947, US, 103 min, b/w)
d William Wellman. *p/sc* Robert Riskin. *ph* Joseph Biroc. *ed* Sherman Todd, Richard G Wray. *pd* Lionel Banks. *m* Roy Webb. *cast* James Stewart, Jane Wyman, Kent Smith, Ned Sparks, Wallace Ford, Regis Toomey, Ann Doran, Donald Meek.

● A fascinating companion piece (some would say antidote) to the films Robert Riskin wrote for Frank Capra. Riskin writes and produces here, and Capraesque elements seem well to the fore: Stewart's 'too much of a dreamer' hero, hoping for a 'miracle'; an idyllic small town called Grandview; a newspaper editor heroine (Wyman) trying to bring about positive change. But in fact there's an almost total reversal of Capraesque values, for director 'Wild Bill' Wellman is no old softie. Thus Stewart's dream (he's an independent opinion pollster) is to find the 'mathematic miracle' of a small town which will exactly represent America as a whole, and thus help him make a million at the expense of his big rivals with their cross-country sampling methods; while Wyman's idea of change might turn the idyllic community into another part of the rat race. There's a feeling of reserve and none of Capra's heart-rending; which of course makes for a less obviously involving experience, though Wellman's way of visually orchestrating his themes without drawing didactic attention to them is unique. CW

Magic Toyshop, The

(1986, GB, 107 min)
d David Wheatley. *p* Steve Morrison. *sc* Angela Carter. *ph* Ken Morgan. *ed* Anthony Ham. *pd* Stephen Finneren. *m* Bill Connor. *cast* Tom Bell, Caroline Milmoe, Kilian McKenna, Patricia Kerrigan, Lorcan Cranitch, Gareth Bushill.

● Like *The Company of Wolves*, an Angela Carter period piece. After the death of her parents, pubescent Melanie (Milmoe) is sent, along with younger brother and sister, to live with her tyrannical Uncle Philip (Bell), a toymaker who doesn't like children playing with his toys. The central relationship between the girl and her coeval Uncle Finn (McKenna) is touching and funny, but juvenile fantasy is an excuse for numerous not so special effects: a block of wood sprouting into leaf, a stone statue springing tears. These seem incongruous, which is not the same as being surreal. In sad contrast to *The Company of Wolves*, the nastiness is tame, the pace too laid-back, the sex not laid-back enough, and a magical atmosphere singularly lacking. MS

Magnet, The

see Comme un Aimant

Magnetic Monster, The

(1953, US, 76 min, b/w)
d Curt Siodmak. *p* Ivan Tors. *sc* Curt Siodmak, Ivan Tors. *ph* Charles Van Enger. *ed* Herbert L Strock. *pd* George Van Marter. *m* Blaine Sanford. *cast* Richard Carlson, King Donovan, Jean Byron, Leonard Mudie, Byron Foulger, Harry Ellerbe.

● One of the earnest 'menace to mankind' movies so beloved of sci-fi in the '50s, about an experimentally developed radioactive isotope that keeps consuming energy and doubling in size until it becomes a veritable monster. Crisply done and not at all bad, even though the climax is largely constructed out of footage borrowed from a 1934 German film, *Gold*. TM

Magnificent Ambersons, The

100

(1942, US, 88 min, b/w)
d/p/sc Orson Welles. *ph* Stanley Cortez. *ed* Robert Wise. *pd* Mark-Lee Kirk. *m* Bernard Herrmann. *cast* Joseph Cotten, Dolores Costello, Agnes Moorehead, Tim Holt, Anne Baxter, Ray Collins, Richard Bennett. *narrator* Orson Welles.

● Hacked about by a confused RKO, Welles' second film (from the novel by Booth Tarkington) still looks a masterpiece, astounding for its almost magical re-creation of a gentler age when cars were still a nightmare of the future and the Ambersons felt safe in their mansion on the edge of town. Right from the wryly comic opening, detailing changes in fashions and the family's exalted status, Welles takes an ambivalent view of the way the quality of life would change under the impact of a new industrial age, stressing the strength of community as evidenced in the old order while admitting to its rampant snobbery and petty sense of manners. With immaculate period reconstruction, and virtuoso acting shot in long, elegant takes, it remains the director's most moving film, despite the artificiality of the sentimental tacked-on ending. GA

Magnificent Doll

(1946, US, 95 min, b/w)
d Frank Borzage. *p* Jack H Skirball. *sc* Irving Stone. *ph* Joseph Valentine. *ad* Alexander Golitzen. *ed* Ted J Kent. *m* Hans J Salter. *cast* Ginger Rogers, Burgess Meredith, David Niven, Stephen McNally, Peggy Wood, Robert Barrat.

● Novelist Irving Stone scripted this stately pseudo-historical melodrama. Ginger Rogers is thoroughly miscast as the Virginia belle and Quaker widow Dolley Payne, who (unwittingly) held America's future in the balance as she prevaricated over her suitors Aaron Burr (Niven) and James Madison (Meredith). Fortunately, she chooses the latter, Thomas Jefferson's Secretary of State, destined to become the fourth President of the United States, while the cynical Burr tries and fails to declare himself Emperor. One of those biopics that substitute arrant nonsense for much more dramatic fact. TCh

Magnificent Obsession

(1954, US, 108 min)
d Douglas Sirk. *p* Ross Hunter. *sc* Robert Blees. *ph* Russell Metty. *ed* Milton Carruth. *ad* Bernard Herzbrun, Emrich Nicholson. *m* Frank Skinner. *cast* Jane Wyman, Rock Hudson, Barbara Rush, Otto Kruger, Agnes Moorehead, Paul Cavanagh.

● Sirk directed a number of films which say an awful lot about '50s America. A European who saw Americans more clearly than most, he found, in the 'women's weepies' producers often gave him, a freedom to examine contemporary middle class values. This one (from a novel by Lloyd C Douglas) has a preposterous plot: playboy Hudson takes up medicine again after being indirectly responsible for the death of a philanthropic doctor and directly responsible for his widow's blindness. Assuming the dead man's role, Hudson starts practising the same kind of secretive Christianity, but has to resort to an alias to win the widow herself. Sirk turns all this into an extraordinary film about vision: sight, destiny, blindness (literal and figurative), colour and light; the convoluted, rather absurd actions (a magnificent repression?) tellingly counterpointed by the clean compositions and the straight lines and space of modern architecture. Sirk's films are something else: can Fassbinder even hold a candle to them? CPe

Magnificent Seven, The

(1960, US, 138 min)
d/p John Sturges. *sc* William S Roberts. *ph* Charles Lang Jr. *ed* Ferris Webster. *ad* Edward Fitzgerald. *m* Elmer Bernstein. *cast* Yul Brynner, Steve McQueen, Robert Vaughn, Charles Bronson, Horst Buchholz, James Coburn, Eli Wallach, Brad Dexter, Vladimir Sokoloff, Whit Bissell.

● Sturges' remake of Kurosawa's *Seven Samurai* is always worth a look, mainly for the performances of McQueen, Bronson, Coburn and Vaughn. The theme of the group of professionals coming together to defend a cause or undertake a useless task, mainly as an exercise for their narcissistic talents, was one that would be constantly reworked during the '60s. Numerous set pieces, like Coburn's knife fight, Vaughn's fly-catching and McQueen's jokes, stay lodged in the mind. CPe

Magnificent Seven Deadly Sins, The

(1971, GB, 107 min)
d/p Graham Stark. *sc* Bob Larbey, John Esmonde ('Avarice'); Dave Freeman ('Envy'); Barry Cryer, Graham Chapham ('Gluttony', 'Wrath'); Graham Stark, Marty Feldman ('Lust'); Alan Simpson, Ray Galton ('Pride'); Spike Milligan ('Sloth'). *ph* Harvey Harrison. *ed* Rod Nelson-Keys, Roy Piper. *ad* Roger King. *m* Roy Budd. *cast* Harry Secombe, Spike Milligan, Bruce Forsyth, Harry H Corbett, Ronald Fraser, Leslie Phillips, Ian Carmichael, Alfie Bass, June Whitfield.

● A pitiful collection of burlesque sketches so laboriously scripted that Graham Stark's crude direction is like a kindly act of euthanasia. The comic talents involved, harping on their TV personalities with deadly monotony, hardly manage to raise a smile from beginning to end. At a pinch, one might make an exception for Ian Carmichael and Alfie Bass, mildly amusing as a couple of motorists illustrating the sin of pride when they meet bumper-to-bumper in a narrow lane, but it hardly seems worth while. TM

Magnificent Seven Ride!, The

(1972, US, 100 min)
d George McCowan. *p* William A Calihan. *sc* Arthur Rowe. *ph* Fred J Koenekamp. *ed* Walter Thompson. *ad* Red McCormick. *m* Elmer Bernstein. *cast* Lee Van Cleef, Stefanie Powers, Mariette Hartley, Michael Callan, Luke Askew, Pedro Armendariz Jr, James B Sikking, Ed Lauter.

● Fifth outing for the mercenary heroes who originated as the *Seven Samurai*, lagging a long way behind 1 and 2 (Kurosawa, Sturges), but a marked improvement on 3 and 4 (Kennedy, Wendkos). Set a little laboriously in 'changing times', with Chris now ageing, married and law-abiding, while likely candidates for his team are either dead or languishing in jail. But the characterisations are sharp, the script economical, and the strategy of the final confrontation set out almost as intriguingly as in *Seven Samurai*. TM

Magnificent Two, The

(1967, GB, 100 min)
d Cliff Owen. *p* Hugh Stewart. *sc* SC Green, RM Hills, Michael Pertwee, Peter Blackmore. *ph* Ernest Steward. *ed* Gerry Hambling. *ad* John Blezard. *m* Ron Goodwin. *cast* Eric Morecambe, Ernie Wise, Margit Saad, Cecil Parker, Isobel Black, Virgilio Teixeira, Martin Benson, Victor Maddern.
● Take Morecambe and Wise away from the stand-up TV routine and what do you have? A lame spoof adventure about travelling salesmen in a South American state torn by revolution (Eric, of course, resembles the revolution's dead figurehead and is persuaded to pose in his place, unaware of an assassination in the offing), in which the comedians' special talents are woefully misused. At least Cliff Owen keeps it pacy, making it the least awful of the trio of movies in which the duo failed to take the cinema by storm. GA

Magnifique, Le

see How to Destroy the Reputation of the Greatest Secret Agent

Magnolia (100)

(1999, US, 188 min)
d Paul Thomas Anderson. *p* Joanne Sellar. *sc* Paul Thomas Anderson. *ph* Robert Elswit. *ed* Dylan Tichenor. *pd* William Arnold, Mark Bridges. *m* Jon Brion. *cast* Tom Cruise, Julianne Moore, Jason Robards, Philip Seymour Hoffman, William H Macy, Melinda Dillon, Luis Guzmin, Philip Baker Hall, Alfred Molina, Michael Murphy, Henry Gibson.
● Anderson's meandering multi-story megasoap with a message is over-ambitious, self-conscious, self-indulgent, self-important and clumsy into the bargain. But it's also one of the most enthralling and exhilarating American movies in ages. Much in the style of *Nashville* and *Short Cuts* (though lacking Altman's light touch), this intimate epic charts the various fortunes, over a day or so, of various individuals living in the San Fernando Valley – including the dying Earl (Robards), his young wife Linda (Moore), and his nurse Phil (Hoffman); Frank Mackey (Cruise), prophet of machismo; and numerous people associated, past or present, with a TV quiz show – whose paths cross by design, destiny, chance or coincidence. Insofar as the film is about 'story', little happens save that Anderson initially conceals information, and then slowly scatters snippets so that we can piece the jigsaw together. For all the humour, it's a dark portrait of loss, lovelessness and fear of failure in contemporary America, and not a film that trades in understatement. As the lost souls make their way towards – what? – redemption? – a deus ex machina plot development occurs, as contrived, ludicrous, bold and grandly imaginative as any Biblical flood or plague. GA

Magnum Force

(1973, US, 122 min)
d Ted Post. *p* Robert Daley. *sc* John Milius, Michael Cimino. *ph* Frank Stanley. *ed* Ferris Webster. *ad* Jack T Collis. *m* Lalo Schifrin. *cast* Clint Eastwood, Hal Holbrook, Mitchell Ryan, David Soul, Felton Perry, Robert Urich, Kip Niven, Tim Matheson.
● Scripted by Milius and Cimino, this second *Dirty Harry* episode is both less violent and less morally ambivalent than its superb predecessor. Harry's back on the force after throwing away his badge in recognition of his illegal methods at the end of Siegel's movie, and here he's using his tough, no-nonsense approach to track down some rookie cops who, in emulation of his earlier vigilante deeds, are blasting the usual assortment of 'criminal scum'. While never as disturbing as the first film, it fails to convince because of the turnaround in Harry's character, and because it posits in facile fashion degrees of taking the law into one's own hands: Harry's acceptable, the gun crazy kids aren't. That said, it has some fine action sequences, and is far less objectionable than the later *Sudden Impact*. GA

Magus, The

(1968, GB, 116 min)
d Guy Green. *p* John Kohn, Jud Kinberg. *sc* John Fowles. *ph* Billy Williams. *ed* Max Benedict. *pd* Don Ashton. *m* John Dankworth. *cast* Michael Caine, Anthony Quinn, Candice Bergen, Anna Karina, Paul Stassino, Julian Glover, Takis Emmanuel, Corin Redgrave, Roger Lloyd Pack.
● A starry cast and flashily glossy location photography can't disguise the fact that this version of John Fowles' novel (from a screenplay by the author himself) is a muddled disaster. The rather silly, semi-mystical tale of humans on a Greek island being manipulated by Quinn's mysterious Doctor Conchis may have worked well enough in print, but on film (and only about half of the book is actually used) it seems pretentious, insubstantial, and sometimes barely comprehensible. GA

Mahabharata, Le (The Mahabharata)

(1989, Fr, 171 min)
d Peter Brook. *p* Michael Propper. *sc* Jean-Claude Carrière, Peter Brook, Marie-Hélène Estienne. *ph* William Lubtchansky. *ed* Nicholas Gaster. *pd* Chloe Oboloensky. *m* Toshi Tsuchitori, Djamchid Chemirani, Kudsi Erguner, Kim Menzer, Mahmoud Tabrizi-Zadeh. *cast* Urs Bihler, Ryszard Cieslak, Georges Corraface, Mamadou Dioumé, Miriam Goldschmidt, Jeffrey Kissoon.
● Based on a complex and subtle anonymously written Indian narrative 3,500 years old, *The Mahabharata* – originally adapted by Jean-Claude Carrière and Peter Brook for the latter's inspirational, widely praised stage production, also seen in a longer TV version – attempts nothing less than to tell the epic story of mankind. A fiery explosion of such rich Indian colours as saffron, ochre, crimson and white, the film is not just a record of the stage production, but a fine piece of work that has been completely rethought for the screen. Strangely, whereas in the theatre one was impressed with the *way* the story was told, on film the gripping tale – of the developing rivalry between the Pandavas and Kauravas, who provoke a war that brings the world to the brink of total destruction – comes over with greater intensity. Brook has created a film fantasy, a fascinating combination of the earthy and the spiritual which is never remotely folksy, and which is enriched by the vitality and diversity of its international cast. JE

Mahanagar (The Big City)

(1963, Ind, 131 min, b/w)
d Sayajit Ray. *p* RD Bansal. *sc* Satyajit Ray. *ph* Subrata Mitra. *ed* Dulal Dutta. *ad* Bansi Chandragupta. *m* Satyajit Ray. *cast* Madhabi Mukherjee, Anil Chatterjee, Haradhan Banerjee, Haren Chatterjee, Vicky Redwood.
● A funny and ambiguously ironic account of a young woman's progress from subdued, traditional housewife to wage earner, finally achieving equality when she resigns her job – a gesture of solidarity for a sacked friend – and joins her husband among the ranks of the lower middle class urban unemployed. Set in 1955 in a bank crash-ridden Calcutta, Ray's Ozu-like comedy about anglicised Indians who sprinkle their conversation with English phrases marks a step forward from the famous pastorales which made his name in the West. PW

Mahjong (Majiang)

(1996, Tai, 121 min)
d Edward Yang. *p* Yu Weiyen. *sc* Edward Yang. *ph* Li Yi-hsu. *ed* Chen Po-wen. *cast* Virginie Ledoyen, Tang Congsheng, Ke Yulun, Zhang Zhen, Wang Qizan, Elaine Jin, Carrie Ng, Wu Nianzhen.
● Edward Yang's brilliant dark comedy weaves together many characters in present-day Taipei. One desperate businessman faces ruin; another opts out of the rat race and finds a kind of serenity with a woman not his wife. A gang of street-smart boys breaks up. A lost French girl, looking for a man who said he loved her, get a crash course in emotional truths and lies. And one confused boy tries to figure out whether he should love his father or kill him. The various strands of plot are interwoven with phenomenal mastery, and Yang's images are as effortlessly precise as ever. It's his sharpest funny/sad vision of city life yet. TR

Mahler

(1974, GB, 115 min)
d Ken Russell. *p* Roy Baird. *sc* Ken Russell. *ph* Dick Bush. *ed* Michael Bradsell. *ad* Ian Whittaker. *cast* Robert Powell, Georgina Hale, Richard Morant, Lee Montague, Rosalie Crutchley, Benny Lee, Miriam Karlin, Angela Down, Ronald Pickup, Antonia Ellis, George Colouris.
● This musical biography, Russell-style, comes over like a cross between a comic strip and Life with the Mahlers (or the trials of bringing up and living with a genius). All the usual brashness and obsessions are there, which may well offend the purists, especially as the film is very much a reply to Visconti's *Death in Venice*. What he gives us is in fact one of the more successful excursions into the cinema of pantheism, a series of tableaux interpreting Mahler's music. Powell is suitably impressive as the composer, and Georgina Hale excellent as his wife (on its most serious level, the film is about her stifled creativity). Despite the low budget (maybe because of it), Russell has produced his most appealing work since his BBC *Omnibus* days.

Mahogany

(1975, US, 109 min)
d Berry Gordy. *p* Rob Cohen, Jack Ballard. *sc* John Byrum. *ph* David Watkin. *ed* Peter Zinner. *ad* Leon Ericksen, Aurelio Crugnola. *m* Michael Masser. *cast* Diana Ross, Billy Dee Williams, Anthony Perkins, Jean-Pierre Aumont, Beah Richards, Nina Foch, Marisa Mell.
● Much of the blame for the decline of Tamla-Motown as a source of great pop records has been allotted to founder Berry Gordy's ceaseless struggle for mainstream mass acceptance. The same glossy decadence permeates this Gordy produced/directed movie, wherein Motown's Diana Ross is the poor little black girl who achieves her fashion designer ambitions via a Rome-based modelling career – plus a golden-hearted sugar daddy – only to throw it all away for a return to the ghetto and Commitment in the form of her First Love. Total sacrifice to commerciality and the ethics of Dreamerica leave only the script's very occasional flash of wit and Anthony Perkins' deliciously loony fashion photographer on the credit side. GD

Maidens in Uniform

see Mädchen in Uniform

Maiden Work (Chunü Zuo)

(1997, China, 66 min)
d Wang Guangli. *p* Ye Rong, Li Dayu. *sc* Man Lin, Wang Guangli. *ph* Ma Xiaoming. *ed* Liu Qing. *pd* Ye You. *m* Zhang Guangtian. *cast* Ye You, Lou Ming, Meng Jinghui, Liu Bo, Ye Chengliang.
● Another curve ball from the Beijing 'underground', Wang's remarkable debut feature first tells a story and then wittily deconstructs it. Painter Jinian, undergoing eye surgery for wounds received in a bar fight, remembers or imagines his relationships with student journalist Xue and her lesbian lover Yu. On recovering, he sets about trying to write and direct a film about the three of them. His meetings with potential producers, actors and technicians eventually get the project moving, but not quite as he foresaw it. Wang smartly integrates material from society at large (old propaganda movies, a triumphalist TV report on military exercises in the Taiwan Strait, disco arrangements of old Maoist anthems) to build up a front-line bulletin from China's cultural wars of the late 1990s. TR

Maid for Pleasure (Filles Expertes en Jeux Clandestins)

(1974, Fr, 91 min)
d/p Guy Maria. *sc* Serge Mareuil, Georges Combret. *ph* Jacques Ledoux. *ed* Claude Guérin. *m* Bernard Gérard, Olivier Toussaint. *cast* Marcel Charvey, Olivier Mathot, Valérie Boisgel, Brigitte de Borghers, Bob Askloff.
● Maybe the maid was, but the movie isn't: it's liable to give a great deal of pain, particularly in the ear-drums. The heroine is a 'nurse' at an eerie château, full of ticking clocks, creaking doors and chirping crickets. She also has to contend with her master's leers, a major-domo with a hypnotic stare and a groping hand, and a 15th century witch. It's consistently repellent: ponderous, pretentious, and almost deafening. GB

Maids (Domésticas)

(2001, Braz, 85 min, b/w)
d Fernando Meirelles, Nando Olival. *p* Andrea Barata Ribeiro. *sc* Cecilia Homem de Mello, Fernando Meirelles, Renata Melo, Nando Olival. *ph* Laura Escorel. *ed* Deo Teixeira. *cast* Cláudia Missura, Graziela Moretto, Lena Roque, Olivia Araújo, Renata Melo.

●'You're born, you die… It's reincarnation… So why did I have to be born poor, dumb and uneducated' – such philosophical musings on the injustices of a maid's lot (including accusations of theft, laziness and heavy-handedness, which usually result in job loss), as well as individual hopes and disappointments, are the subject of this offbeat Brazilian comedy. The straight to camera, b/w 'video diary' treatment emphasises the vulnerability of the *domesticas*; while frenetic, fast-cut shots against the backdrop of a neon-lit São Paulo emulate the pace of these servants' frantic lives. Elsewhere the camaraderie and chutzpah of the women who support, listen to, and laugh with one another adds vibrancy and colour. Despite its sometimes morose social commentary, the overwhelmingly comic script gives the film a craziness worthy of Almodóvar. JFu

Maids, The

(1974, GB/Can, 95 min)
d Christopher Miles. *p* Robert Enders. *sc* Robert Enders, Christopher Miles. *ph* Douglas Slocombe. *ed* Peter Tanner. *ad* Robert Jones. *m* Laurie Johnson. *cast* Glenda Jackson, Susannah York, Vivien Merchant, Mark Burns.

●An appallingly castrated version of Genet's closeted, claustrophobic play about SM fantasies. Besides some silly attempts to 'open out' the proceedings (meaningless given the original's intention), the direction displays a disarming British sang froid and literalness towards the Gallic masterpiece. Worst offenders, however, are Jackson and York, prancing around like a couple of grandes dames of the theatre, and playing out their games of dominance and submission with all the conviction of a vicar's sisters feeling up the parrot.

Maidstone

(1970, US, 110 min)
d Norman Mailer. *p* Buzz Farber, Norman Mailer. *sc* Norman Mailer. *ph* Jim Desmond, Richard Leacock, DA Pennebaker, Sheldon Rochlin, Diane Rochlin, Jan Pieter Welt, Nicholas Proferes. *ed* Jan Pieter Welt, Lana Jokel, Norman Mailer. *m* Isaac Hayes, Wes Montgomery, Modern Jazz Quartet. *cast* Norman Mailer, Rip Torn, Beverly Bentley, Robert Gardiner, Carolyn McCullough, Lenny Morris, Ultra Violet, Harris Yulin.

●Mailer plays a 'character' called Norman T Kingsley, an avant-garde film-maker (he's also running for President) who harangues, provokes and debates with a number of people gathered as he's preparing his next movie. Despite a thin try at a story, some bluff spouting about exploring the nature of different 'realities', or about creating whirlpools of energy and then following them through, it's not really worth treating this farrago – in which the name of the game is 'let's play football with other people's psyches' – seriously as a film. Lawrence Durrell has treated the 'reality' theme much better in novel form; Cassavetes has coped far more honestly and delicately with the fine line between people acting themselves and projecting their abilities on to 'characters'; this is simply 110 minutes of pure Megalomailer. MV

Main Actor, The (Der Hauptdarsteller)

(1977, WGer, 91 min)
d Reinhard Hauff. *p* Eberhard Junkersdorf. *sc* Christel Buschmann, Reinhard Hauff. *ph* Frank Brühne. *ed* Stephanie Wilke. *ad* Winifried Hennig. *m* Klaus Doldinger. *cast* Mario Adorf, Vadim Glowna, Michael Schweiger, Hans Brenner, Rolf Zacher, Akim Ahrens, Doris Dörrie, Eberhard Hauff.

●This has something of the same hard-edged documentary authenticity as Hauff's earlier *Brutalisation of Franz Blum*, though a tone of autobiographical self-flagellation adds a slightly mawkish element. A teenage boy and his brutal father act in a film about their no-hope lives; at the end of the shooting, the boy runs away to the anguished middle class director, who unsuccessfully tries to help him start a new life. Hauff, it seems, actually had this experience with a non-professional actor whom he used in an earlier film. The movie doesn't get very deep beneath the skin of its wayward adolescent protagonist, but it registers as a thoroughly competent (if somewhat crude) example of second division New German Cinema. JPy

Main Event, The

(1979, US, 112 min)
d Howard Zieff. *p* Jon Peters, Barbra Streisand. *sc* Gail Parent, Andrew Smith. *ph* Mario Tosi. *ed* Edward A Warschilka. *pd* Charles Rosen. *m* Michael Melvoin. *cast* Barbra Streisand, Ryan O'Neal, Paul Sand, Whitman Mayo, Patti D'Arbanville, Chu Chu Malave, Richard Lawson, James Gregory, Rory Calhoun.

●This 'romantic screwball comedy/glove story', in which zany Streisand rescues failed boxer O'Neal, is awful – unless you're a devotee of the strident Streisand, who does at least deliver her lines with some punch. The script, however, assumes that the most powerful women are those who can beat men at their own game – a failed cosmetics queen, Streisand sets out to manipulate O'Neal so as to recoup her losses – but would be only too happy to throw in the towel to the right man.

Main Street

see Calle Mayor

Mairi Mhor

(1993, GB, 63 min)
d Mike Alexander. *p* John McGrath. *sc* John McGrath, Simon MacKenzie. *ph* Mark Littlewood. *ed* Bert Eeles. *pd* Graham Rose. *m* Jim Sutherland. *cast* Alyxis Daly, Ceit Kearney, Sim Mac Coinnich, Andrew Stanson, Pauline Lockhart, Artair Donald.

●In 1871, 'tired of the speakers of English', Mairi Mhor began writing resistance songs in Gaelic, protesting at the displacement of the Scottish Highland and Island folk by the Southern landlords. Unjustly imprisoned in Inverness at the age of 51, she expresses her anger in song, discovering a talent for music; these songs became central to the identity of the region and are still sung today. The achingly beautiful landscape of Skye, and the music it inspired, provide a haunting canvas for this valuable piece of historical research. FM

Maison de Jade, La

(1988, Fr, 98 min)
d Nadine Trintignant. *sc* Nadine Trintignant, Madeleine Chapsal. *ph* William Lubchansky. *ed* Joële van Effenterre. *ad* Michele Abbé. *m* Philippe Sarde. *cast* Jacqueline Bisset, Vincent Perez, Véronique Silver, Yves Lambrecht, Serge Marquand.

●Older woman falls for younger man and – we could have warned her – ends up alone, swigging from the Martell bottle as she sobs through their old camcorder footage. An adaptation by Trintignant and Madeleine Chapsal of the latter's allegedly autobiographical bestseller, this is all relentlessly subjective. In the early snog 'n' bonk stages, young Perez is presented as the epitome of charm and desirability, though many will yearn to see a custard pie collide with that would-be brooding pan. But after splitting, he is portrayed as a contemptible little coward, and again audience sympathies may reverse, with the reflection that no such all-round wonderful person as Bisset ever walked the earth. BBa

Maître de musique, Le

see Music Teacher, The

Maîtresse

(1976, Fr, 112 min)
d Barbet Schroeder. *p* Pierre Andrieux. *sc* Barbet Schroeder, Paul Voujargol. *ph* Nestor Almendros. *ed* Denise de Casabianca. *ad* Roberto Plate. *m* Carlos d'Alessio. *cast* Gérard Depardieu, Bulle Ogier, André Rouyer, Nathalie Kéryan, Roland Bertin, Tony Taffin, Holger Löwenadler.

●Schroeder's classic of underground love sits well alongside the masochistic undertones of *Last Tango in Paris*. Ogier is the professional *maîtresse* (or dominatrix) who conducts a straight romance with Depardieu at ground level, but has a dungeon below stairs where she entertains her compliant clients. The trick, of course, is that overground comes to mirror underground, but the whole thing is lent more than a little frisson from the knowledge that some of those clients were real. A wickedly funny fable on the more demanding side of love. CPea

Majdhar

(1984, GB, 76 min)
d/sc Ahmed A Jamal. *ph* Philip Chavannes. *ed* John Dinwoodie. *ad* Fay Rodrigues. *m* Ustad Imrat Khan. *cast* Rita Wolf, Tony Wredden, Feroza Syal, Andrew Johnson, Sudha Bhuchar, Daniel Foley, Julianne Mason, Tariq Yunus.

●Rita Wolf has a fine profile. Director Jamal thinks so too: any excuse serves for a close-up of her as Fauzia, a young middle class Pakistani who's caught in an uncomfortable mid-stream ('majdhar') when her husband deserts her for an Englishwoman. Fauzia copes, and emerges as a strong person after pensively staring at the wall and having an affair with a TV researcher who's after a bit of exotica. The film is an interesting 'worthy' experiment by Retake, an Asian collective anxious to redress the media stereotype image, etc. As collective efforts go, this is not bad. The plot is rich and full of possibilities, but the script is unfortunately thin and full of missed opportunities. Embarrassingly awkward (as opposed to meaningful) silences are broken by laborious and unnatural dialogue, which is rescued slightly by Ustad Imrat Khan's moving music. Both Wolf and Feroza Syal (playing her friend) are good, but more experienced direction would have helped. BB

Major and the Minor, The

(1942, US, 100 min, b/w)
d Billy Wilder. *p* Arthur Hornblower Jr. *sc* Charles Brackett, Billy Wilder. *ph* Leo Tover. *ed* Doane Harrison. *ad* Roland Anderson, Hans Dreier. *m* Robert Emmett Dolan. *cast* Ginger Rogers, Ray Milland, Rita Johnson, Robert Benchley, Diana Lynn, Frankie Thomas, Norma Varden.

●Wilder's first film as director begins brilliantly with Rogers as a New York career woman disillusioned to find her house calls offering scalp massage constantly subject to male misinterpretation – in particular from a lecherous Benchley pursuing 'a little drinkypoo, biteypoo, rhumbapoo' – who masquerades as a pigtailed 12-year-old innocent in order to avoid paying full adult fare on the train home to Iowa. Very funny stuff as she meets Milland's protective major, and finds ambiguous refuge in his sleeping compartment, although it later proves to be a one-joke situation as she is forced to accompany him to the military academy where he instructs, and becomes mascot to a horde of hopefully lecherous cadets. Pretty irresistible, nevertheless, with Rogers doing a beautiful job of dovetailing sexual provocation and demure innocence. TM

Major Barbara

(1941, GB, 121 min, b/w)
d Gabriel Pascal, Harold French, David Lean. *p* Gabriel Pascal. *sc* George Bernard Shaw. *ph* Ronald Neame. *ed* Charles Frend. *pd* Vincent Korda. *m* William Walton. *cast* Wendy Hiller, Rex Harrison, Robert Morley, Robert Newton, Emlyn Williams, David Tree, Marie Löhr, Sybil Thorndike, Deborah Kerr.

●George Bernard Shaw collaborated on the screenplay of this straightforward adaptation of his 1905 comedy about the daughter of a munitions tycoon (Hiller) who joins the army – the Salvation Army, that is – pursued by an amorous professor of Greek (Harrison). There is plenty to relish, notably Newton and Morley hamming it up (as, respectively, the rumbustious Bill Walker and the overbearing tycoon), and Deborah Kerr in her debut; but it does tend to just sit there. It was David Lean's first shot at directing, but producer Pascal helmed the bulk of it. TCh

Major Dundee

(1964, US, 134 min)
d Sam Peckinpah. *p* Jerry Bresler. *sc* Harry Julian Fink, Oscar Saul, Sam Peckinpah. ph Sam Leavitt. ed William A Lyon, Don Starling, Howard Kunin. ad Al Ybarra. m Daniele Amfitheatrof. cast Charlton Heston, Richard Harris, Jim Hutton, James Coburn, Michael Anderson Jr, Senta Berger, Mario Adorf, Brock Peters, Warren Oates, Ben Johnson, RG Armstrong, LQ Jones, Slim Pickens.

●Formally, this is barely recognisable as a Peckinpah movie (producers hacked out 20 minutes, distributors 14 more); yet many of his major thematic preoccupations (loyalty, betrayal, redemptive death) are clearly emerging here as Major Dundee, a Federal officer relegated to command of a prison camp, sets out to subdue a band of marauding Apaches at the head of a ragtag volunteer troop of thieves, renegades and paroled Confederate prisoners (the latter ambivalently headed by Harris). Of the many debts to Ford, the largest is Heston's Dundee, trading on his image of epic man of action but propelled, like Wayne in *The Searchers*, by racial hatred, worm-eaten by divided loyalties, and finally found wanting at the crunch. A fine if fractured Western, more subversive of conventional mythologies than it seems. CPea

Major League

(1989, US, 106 min)
d David S Ward. *p* Chris Chesser, Irby Smith. *sc* David S Ward. *ph* Reynaldo Villalobos. *ed* Dennis M Hill, Lou Lombardo. *pd* Jeffrey Howard. *m* James Newton Howard. *cast* Tom Berenger, Charlie Sheen, Corbin Bernsen, Margaret Whitton, James Gammon, René Russo, Wesley Snipes, Charles Cyphers, Dennis Haysbert.

● A baseball movie which crosses schoolboy fantasy with *Police Academy* slapstick and locker-room in-jokery. Its tale of a rags-to-riches rise by one of the sport's longest-standing jokes, the Cleveland Indians, is chock full of variably amusing gags and bit players, with Sheen as a wild punk pitcher raised in a series of prisons, and Berenger as an over-the-hill catcher who wins back the girl he loves. Whitton plays the new ex-showgirl owner, desperate to move the team to sunny Florida and herself to an exotic condo, who gathers together a bunch of players so ropey that their failure will enable her to convince the commissioners that the move is justified. Like so much of the film it's a daft but not too daft proposition; and what redeems it is that the action sequences are superbly filmed, climaxing with Sheen's bullish entry into the arena at make-or-break time, the crowd singing 'Wild Thing' in clamouring unison. SGr

Major League II

(1994, US, 105 min)
d David S Ward. *p* James G Robinson, David S Ward. *sc* RJ Stewart. *ed* Paul Seydor, Donn Cambern. *pd* Stephen Hendrickson. *m* Michel Colombier. *cast* Charlie Sheen, Tom Berenger, Corbin Bernsen, Dennis Haysbert, James Gammon, Omar Epps, Randy Quaid.

● The original *Major League* brought high jinks and low comedy to the baseball movie genre, and showcased the immense talents of Wesley Snipes. This sequel didn't cut it in the States, and it's hard to see why British audiences should show it any more respect, given that it's formula and lacks Snipes. True, most of the regulars return to the plate: Sheen as delinquent pitcher Rick 'Wild Thing' Vaughn; Berenger as Jake Taylor, the ageing catcher with dodgy knees; and the rest of the Cleveland Indians. RJ Stewart's screenplay highlights one of the great-in jokes of American team sports – how players are transformed during the close season by fame, fortune or adversity; here, the team is split asunder when Vaughn attempts to clean up his image and when Pedro Cerrano (Haysbert) switches bafflingly from voodoo to Buddhism. SGr

Make Mine a Million

(1959, GB, 82 min, b/w)
d Lance Comfort. *p* John Baxter. *sc* Peter Blackmore. *ph* Arthur Grant. *ed* Peter Pitt. *ad* Denis Wreford. *m* Stanley Black. *cast* Arthur Askey, Sidney James, Dermot Walsh, Olga Lindo, Bernard Cribbins, Kenneth Connor.

● Flimsy, dated, but not unenjoyable British farce. James is a soap-powder magnate. He wants promotion on the advert-free National Television service and hires Askey to interrupt transmissions with promo spots for his detergent, the delightfully named Bonko.

Making It

(1971, US, 97 min)
d John Erman. *p* Albert S Ruddy. *sc* Peter Bart. *ph* Richard C Glouner. *ed* Allan Jacobs. *m* Charles Fox. *cast* Kristoffer Tabori, Marilyn Mason, Bob Balaban, Joyce Van Patten, Lawrence Pressman, Louise Latham, Sherry Miles.

● The best thing about this piffling cautionary tale for teens is Tabori's cool and witty performance (his debut) as a 17-year-old high school kid (pushing drugs looms high on the curriculum) whose penchant for making it with anything in skirts stores up a load of grief for him. The unbelievably silly climax has Tabori procuring an abortion for his girlfriend (Miles) on a false alarm, finding the appointment coming in handy because his widowed mum (Van Patten) has got herself knocked up, and being forced to sit in on the operation because the doctor feels the experience may make a man of him. Cue for classic kitsch as mother and son gaze at each other with fond new understanding, murmuring 'It's been 17 years and I feel I'm just beginning to know you.' TM

Making It

see Valseuses, Les

Making Love

(1982, US, 112 min)
d Arthur Hiller. *p* Allen Adler, Daniel Melnick. *sc* Barry Sandler. *ph* David M Walsh. *ed* William H Reynolds. *pd* James D Vance. *m* Leonard Rosenman. *cast* Michael Ontkean, Kate Jackson, Harry Hamlin, Wendy Hiller, Arthur Hill, Nancy Olson, John Dukakis.

● Zack and Claire love Rupert Brooke, Gilbert & Sullivan, and each other. Till one day Zack meets Bart. Arthur *Love Story* Hiller, it seems, is a director possessed of what the French call a *thématique*. Note the subtle cultural references, substituting for the earlier film's Mozart and the Beatles, as well as the abiding interest in incurable conditions, whether leukaemia or, as here, homosexuality. Luckily, his hapless protagonists are deeply caring souls: Zack finds eventual fulfilment with a handsome, sensitive hunk; Bart, a novelist of the runny softboiled school, will write a sensitive bestseller about the affair; while Claire manages to land an overwhelmingly sensitive second husband (and even christens their son Rupert). This is a three-handkerchief movie, all right, but for the nose. It stinks. GAd

Making Mr Right

(1987, US, 98 min)
d Susan Seidelman. *p* Mike Wise, Joel Tuber. *sc* Floyd Byars, Laurie Frank. *ph* Ed Lachman. *ed* Andrew Mondshein. *pd* Barbara Ling. *m* Chas Jankel. *cast* John Malkovich, Ann Magnuson, Glenne Headly, Ben Masters, Laurie Metcalf, Polly Bergen, Hart Bochner.

● Seidelman's follow-up to *Desperately Seeking Susan* is a stylish, offbeat romantic comedy but lacks its predecessor's loopy charm. When PR consultant Frankie (Magnuson) is hired to create a human image for the Chemtech Corporation's latest android, Ulysses, she doesn't reckon on him losing his head over her, and vice versa, and ends up clashing with the android's maker, Dr Peters, who fears that Ulysses' exposure to love's irrationality will jeopardise his forthcoming space mission. Seidelman handles the romance with great sensitivity, contrasting Ulysses' innocent, non-manipulative affection with the self-centred immaturity of Frankie's senator boyfriend. Crucial weaknesses, however, are the miscasting of Malkovich as both Peters and Ulysses (he lacks charisma as the romantic lead), and the numerous distracting subplots. The flat, garish photography conjures up the shiny-clean future of '50s sci-fi movies, but the film's magpie borrowings are poorly integrated, resulting in inconsistencies of tone and pacing. Much to enjoy, though, not least the audaciously happy ending. NF

Making of Maps, The (Y Mapiwr)

(1995, GB, 90 min)
d Endaf Emlyn. *p* Pauline Williams. *sc* Endaf Emlyn. *ph* Nina Kellgren. *ed* Chris Lawrence. *pd* Venita Gribble. *m* Mark Thomas. *cast* Gavin Ashcroft, Catherine Tregenna, Maldwyn Pate, Abigail Creel, Lara Ward.

● Endaf Emlyn's third Welsh-language feature is a not entirely successful mood-piece set on the remote Welsh coast in the Cold War early '60s. An adolescent boy (Ashcroft, good) recalls the fateful months following the disappearance of his dancer sister. In the large family house by the dunes live his ex-ballerina mother, a bedridden 'hysteric'; his munitions-worker father, 'a bad man' who may have played too free with the young charges of the family dance school; and his other sister, 'all pain and no beauty'. The boy makes maps to hide his secrets and befriends an oddball Pole with secrets of his own. The story meanders on, meditating on unseen events (an accidental death, a suicide and a rape) to the neo-classical strains of Mark Thomas's score and the noise of sea birds, but to no discernible purpose. WH

Making Up (Abgeschminkt)

(1992, Ger, 54 min)
d Katja von Garnier. *p* Ewa Karlström. *sc* Benjamin Taylor, Katja von Garnier, Hannes Jaenicke. *ph* Torsten Breuer. *ed* Katja von Garnier. *ad* Irene Edenhofer, Nikolai Ritter. *m* Peter Wenke, Tillmann Höhn. *cast* Katja Riemann, Nina Kronjäger, Gedeon Burkhard, Max Tidof, Daniela Lunkewitz.

● An offbeat, sassy look at female friendship. Its 54 minutes tell a very slight story: Maischa (Kronjäger), a boy crazy nurse, has a dreary married boyfriend, but flips for a hunk at a party. The hunk, René, suggests a date, but has visitor Mark in tow. Maischa calls on her scruffy friend Frenzy (Riemann), whose despairing attempts to draw a newspaper comic-strip about a mosquito named Rubi are the backbone of the film, to find her suffering as usual from a creative block. Sulky Frenzy is paired off with Mark, facetious and childish, while Maischa swans off for dinner with gorgeous René. But things are not that simple. The two girls have a brilliant, silly chemistry. SFe

Mal (Evil)

(1999, Port/Braz/Ire/Sp, 85 min)
d Alberto Seixas Santos. *p* Amândio Coroado. *sc* Alberto Seixas Santos. *ph* Acácio de Almeida. *ed* Catarina Ruivo. *pd* Maria José Branco. *cast* Pauline Cadell, Rui Morrisson, Alexandro Pinto, Alicia Gomes Da Costa, Fábio Emanuel Silva, José Pinto, Luis Lima Barreto, Sofia Aparicio.

● Lisbon, 1999. Amid the bustle of a train station, an old man beseeches passers-by, 'Have you seen my daughter?' No one pays him any mind. Two junkie street kids live by night in an orgy of petty larceny, one, Daniel (Pinto), increasingly frustrated with their lack of haul. An Irish aid worker, Cathy (Cadell), celebrates her 20th anniversary with her native husband Pedro (Morrison), an influential lawyer with a finger in too many pies. If Portuguese films have a reputation for avant garde mysteriousness, this offering from film professor, public official, former critic and sometime film-maker Alberto Seixas Santos (his fifth film in 25 years, including joint efforts) certainly keeps the faith. It's a strange mixture of the portentous and the elusive: a fraught state-of-humanity address with a startlingly grandiose conclusion that keeps its meaning all too close to its chest. There are but pieces of stories here, only some connecting; the crux, in which the near-saintly Cathy discovers her husband's serial philandering the hard way, offers compelling glimpses of a blind but nourishing marriage. But Santos is less interested in developing his characters than in insinuating moral corruption through scattered references to broken relationships, political skulduggery, drugs, AIDS, race, immigration, the media and terrorism. NB

Maladie de Sachs, La

(1999, Fr, 107 min)
d Michel Deville. *p* Rosalinde Deville. *sc* Rosalinde Deville, Michel Deville. *ph* André Diot. *ed* Andrea Sedlackova. *ad* Isabelle Arnal, Denis Seiglan. *m* Jean-Féry Rebel. *cast* Albert Dupontel, Valérie Dréville, Dominique Reymond, Martine Sarcey.

● The big part of the film details the working life of Dr Sachs, small town physician. One after another his patients present their bad backs, tumours, neuroses, etc, for diagnosis and, maybe, cure. Deville resolutely declines to give the audience much of a break from this litany of dis-ease. Sachs himself fills sheets of paper with his feelings of revulsion and inadequacy. An encounter with an ex-patient blossoms into an affair, and we leave the doc soldiering on, a bit less angst in his heart. Hard to say whether all this – life, love, death, the basics – is banal or profound. Either way, Deville's careful orchestration of the minutiae of routine medical practice is utterly absorbing, and Dupontel is unimprovable as Sachs. From the novel by Martin Winckler. BBa

Mala Noche

(1985, US, 78 min, b/w & col)
d/p/sc Gus Van Sant. *ph* John Campbell. *ed* Gus Van Sant. *m* Creighton Lindsay. *cast* Tim Streeter, Doug Cooeyate, Ray Monge, Nyla McCarthy, Sam Downey, Bob Pitchlynn.

●Van Sant's winning feature debut (made on 16mm for an incredible $25,000) tells the tale of a shabby store-boy's brief encounter with two desperate wetbacks. Walt (Streeter, excellent) spends most of his time selling liquor to the bums of Portland, Oregon. He becomes obsessed with 16-year-old cock-tease Johnny, who doesn't speak a word of American but knows the difference between 15 and 25 dollars. Walt pursues him in his dreams and through the rainy nights, but only manages to put up (yes, that way too) his gun-toting friend Pepper, who is in his turn pursued by the cops. Walt's pawky commentary brings out the equivocal nature of his fragile relationship with the two boys: he may nurse Pepper when he's ill, let Johnny swipe food when he's hungry, but as a comparatively wealthy gringo Walt is nevertheless exploiting the situation. Even so – as one sweaty scene reveals – a Mexican can still make 'white butt squeal'. Offbeat, offhand, and at times off-the-wall, this sad and funny film recalls *Streetwise* and *Stranger Than Paradise*, but in its own unabashed way is better than either. MS

'Mala' Ordina, La

see Manhunt in Milan

Malaya (aka East of the Rising Sun)

(1949, US, 95 min, b/w)
d Richard Thorpe. *p* Edwin H Knopf. *sc* Frank Fenton. *ph* George Folsey. *ed* Ben Lewis. *ad* Cedric Gibbons, Malcolm Brown. *m* Bronislau Kaper. *cast* Spencer Tracy, James Stewart, Valentina Cortese, Sydney Greenstreet, Lionel Barrymore, Gilbert Roland, John Hodiak.

●A murky World War II actioner in which James Stewart and Spencer Tracy further the Allied cause by smuggling rubber out of Jap-infested Malaya with the help (sometimes given under 'persuasion') of the planters. Tracy does the rough stuff as an uncommitted adventurer; Stewart handles the message as a man with a score to settle (his brother was killed fighting in the Pacific). You'd think the film was still fighting the war, the way Stewart carries on, getting himself killed (Tracy too) while indomitably waving the flag. It's made, such as it is, by the excellent supporting cast which seems to have *Casablanca* vaguely in mind. TM

Malcolm

(1986, Aust, 86 min)
d/p Nadia Tass. *sc/ph* David Parker. *ed* Ken Sallows. *ad* Rike Kullack. *m* Simon Jeffes. *cast* Colin Friels, Lindy Davies, John Hargreaves, Chris Haywood, Charles Tingwell, Beverley Phillips, Judith Stratford.

●A would-be comic caper movie from the land of Oz. A wordly-witless but highly inventive simpleton (Friels) persuades his roomers, a laconic ex-con (Hargreaves) and his breasty 'sheila', to make use of his technical talents in a series of remote-controlled heists. If the set pieces don't exactly have you splitting your sides with mirth, the movie does engagingly stay true to its child-like vision, all gadgets and gleeful immorality, more than helped along by the perfectly pitched playing of Friels and Hargreaves. WH

Malcolm X

(1992, US, 201 min)
d Spike Lee. *p* Spike Lee, Marvin Worth, Ahmed Murad. *sc* Arnold Perl, Spike Lee. *ph* Ernest Dickerson, David Golia. *ed* Barry Alexander Brown. *pd* Wynn Thomas. *m* Terence Blanchard. *cast* Denzel Washington, Angela Bassett, Albert Hall, Al Freeman Jr, Delroy Lindo, Spike Lee, Theresa Randle, Kate Vernon, Lonette McKee, Debi Mazar.

●Lee's labour of love is arguably his most anonymous film to date, with fewer in-your-face stylistic flourishes or confrontational ideological statements than his earlier works. True, the scenes of young Malcolm (Washington) and his pal Shorty (Lee) at a Boston dance hall exhibit a fizzy choreographic flair; true, too, that the opening credits footage of the Rodney King beating hints at an anger none too shy of courting controversy. But mostly, while the film glides from Malcolm's early years as a hustler and petty criminal to his emergence in the Nation of Islam, it plays surprisingly safe as a solidly crafted trawl through the didactic/hagiographic conventions of the mainstream biopic. In short, it's a familiar tale of a man up against prejudice coming to see the light. If the first hour contains most of the drama, it's the later scenes that constitute the lesson: how to achieve black pride, power and dignity in the face of white oppression. Were it not for Washington's charismatic performance and the abiding fire of Malcolm's oratory, this didacticism might be tedious; but Lee's skill at playing to his strengths ensures that only the white-washing of NOI's attitude to women, and odd scenes such as Malcolm's prison visit by an apparition of Elijah Muhammad, come over as major flaws. GA

Maldone

(1927, Fr, 85 min approx, b/w)
d Jean Grémillon. *p* Charles Dullin. *sc* Alexandre Arnoux. *ph* Georges Périnal. *ad* André Barsacq. *cast* Charles Dullin, Annabella, Genica Athanasiou, André Bacqué, Marcelle Dullin.

●Dullin plays Maldone, a wandering womaniser summoned to run the family estate after his brother dies. He marries, struggles with his responsibilities, but you know he's not going to stay the course. This anecdote is used mainly as a shop window for the talents of Grémillon and Périnal, then both still in their twenties. In the first part, the tramp's life (lazy afternoons by the canal, harvesting, boozy nights at country inns), and in the second his despondency and frustration are all handled imaginatively and with panache. Interesting to see Dullin, one of France's great stage actors and forceful enough, but clearly too odd-looking to get far in the movies. BBa

Maldoror

(2000, GB/Ger, 100 min)
d Kerri Sharp, Filmgruppe Abgedreht, Duncan Reekie, Caroline Kennedy, Colette Rouhier, Filmgruppe Chaos, Steven Eastwood, Jenigerfilm, Andrew Coram, Hänt Film, Paul Tarrago, Jennet Thomas.

●Fearlessly disregarding cinema's hapless history of portmanteau films, this genuinely no-budget collaboration between members of Exploding Cinema and Filmgruppe Chaos – 'the no-torious no-bility of Underground Cinema' – takes a cleaver to the Comte de Lautréamont's 1868 pre-surrealist anti-novel *Maldoror*. Fifteen film-makers were dispatched into the night with but a chapter of the book (a vile, nightmarish poetic paean to the author's Satanic alter ego) and a Super-8 camera to their name; 12 have returned, and from the cauldron of their labours, delivered forth this wild and bewildering affront to common civilised cinema. Dissonant and depraved, it's a motley stew. The individual shorts are variously indigestible, inconsequential, inventive, evocative, comic, pornographic, illicit and ridiculous, linked only by an overload of narration from the book. Cumulatively, the effect's akin to both a good night at a film club, and a disorienting trip into the head of a stark raving misanthrope. NB

Maledetto Imbroglio, Un (A Sordid Affair/ The Facts of Murder)

(1959, It, 117 min, b/w)
d Pietro Germi. *p* Giuseppe Amato. *sc* Alfredo Giannetti, Ennio De Concini, Pietro Germi. *ph* Leonida Barboni. *ed* Roberto Cinquini. *ad* Carlo Egidi. *m* Carlo Rustichelli. *cast* Pietro Germi, Franco Fabrizi, Claudio Gora, Claudia Cardinale, Nino Castelnuovo, Saro Urzi, Eleanora Rossi Drago.

●A robbery in a Rome apartment block is followed a few days later by the murder of the robbery victim's neighbour. Are the cases linked? Inspector Ingravallo and his team investigate. This is a very Mediterranean sort of murder hunt, full of complicated disruptions and humorous asides, with everybody talking at once. Germi the actor (Ingravallo) is good at irascibility, his chief mode as he endures devious suspects, bumbling colleagues and a girlfriend (who we never see) demanding attention. Germi the director does his best to maintain narrative clarity against the compulsory obfuscations of the whodunit form. BBa

Malèna

(2000, It/US, 92 min)
d Giuseppe Tornatore. *p* Harvey Weinstein, Carlo Bernasconi. *sc* Giuseppe Tornatore. *ph* Lajos Koltai. *ed* Massimo Quaglia. *ad* Francesco Frigeri. *m* Ennio Morricone. *cast* Monica Bellucci, Giuseppe Sulfaro, Luciano Federico, Matilde Piana, Pietro Notarianni, Gaetano Aronica, Gilberto Idone.

●Picture Sicily, 1941: a beautiful spring day in the sleepy village of Castelcuto. In the wider world, Mussolini has declared war on France and Britain, but for narrator Renato Amoroso (Sulfaro), this was the day he got his first bicycle, caught sight of the irresistible Malèna (Bellucci) and fell in love. He was 13. Deposited in the village by her new husband (away fighting for the Fascists), the sultry siren becomes an object of desire for the local men – and scorn for the women – as she takes her daily strolls across the square in outfits designed to highlight every curve. Renato's lust and youthful imagination allow his cinematic fantasies to take over, and he secretly nominates himself as her protector, who will wreak vengeance on detractors. Tornatore's film resorts to shameless sentimentality even as it paints an unsympathetic portrait of small town cruelty and hypocrisy. But the voyeuristic fetishisation of Malèna – who hardly speaks, whether to defend herself or to offer a glimmer of personality – makes for uncomfortable viewing. On the plus side, the cinematography is beautifully executed. But Tornatore has yet to recapture the magic of *Cinema Paradiso*. JFu

Malena Is a Name from a Tango (Malena es un Nombre de Tango)

(1996, Sp, 109 min)
d Gerardo Herrero. *p* Gerrardo Herrero, Javier López Blanco. *sc* Senel Paz. *ph* Alfredo Mayo. *ed* Carmen Frias. *pd* Luis Valles, Alain Bainne. *m* Antoione Duhamel. *cast* Ariadna Gil, Marta Belaustegui, Carlos López, Luis Fernando Alvés, Isabel Otero, Marina Saura.

●A strangely detached and self-conscious, but surprisingly involving melodrama, which follows Malena (Gil) from childhood, through her adolescent obsession with a girl-chasing German cousin, and a raunchy but uncommitted relationship with a macho womaniser, to marriage to a loving but dull husband. Malena thinks there's bad blood in the family, and she's got it, unlike her well-behaved twin Reina. Is she too non-conformist ever to find happiness? An arresting take on the social and psychological obstacles faced by free-spirited women in a patriarchal world, it's helped no end by Ariadna Gil's versatile, charismatic performance. GA

Malevil

(1981, Fr/WGer, 119 min)
d Christian de Chalonge. *p* Claude Nedjar. *sc* Christian de Chalonge, Pierre Dumayet. *ph* Jean Penzer. *ed* Henri Lanoë. *ad* Max Douy. *m* Gabriel Yared. *cast* Michel Serrault, Jacques Dutronc, Robert Dhéry, Jacques Villeret, Hanns Zischler, Jean-Louis Trintignant.

●Vaguely reminiscent in mood of Polanski's *Cul-de-Sac*, this is a weird – but not weird enough – post-nuclear survival drama, with assorted members of a strong cast gathering at the eponymous castle and trying to keep civilisation going. After a decent start, the movie soon drifts into the usual set of dramatic options: illness, reproduction, farming, and of course the fascists in the forest. (From a novel by Robert Merle.) ATu

Malice

(1993, US, 107 min)
d Harold Becker. *p* Rachel Pfeffer, Charles Mulvehill, Harold Becker. *sc* Aaron Sorkin, Scott Frank. *ph* Gordon Willis. *ed* David Bretherton. *pd* Philip Harrison. *m* Jerry Goldsmith. *cast* Alec Baldwin, Nicole Kidman, Bill Pullman, Bebe Neuwirth, George C Scott, Anne Bancroft, Peter Gallagher, Josef Sommer.

●All appears normal in a tranquil college town in Massachusetts. Newly-weds Tracy and Andy Sarafian (Kidman and Pullman) are restoring their dream house. He teaches English, she does voluntary work at the hospital. Andy meets old chum, arrogant but brilliant surgeon Jed Hill (Baldwin) – who, to Tracy's chagrin, insinuates himself into their home. Surely he isn't the local serial rapist. A melodramatic thriller which did surprisingly well in the US given its implausible straight-to-video scenario. Undistinguished. TCh

Malicious

(1996, US, 90 min)
d Ian Corson. *p* Robert Vince, William Vince. *sc* George Saunders. *ph* Michael Slovis. *ed*

Richard Martin. *m* Graeme Coleman. *cast* Molly Ringwald, Patrick McGaw, John Vernon, Sarah Lassez.
● When sweetheart Laura departs for the weekend, Doug (McGaw) agrees against his better judgment to drop into a party. Slack teen fare thriller in the *Pacific Heights* and *Single White Female* mode (that is, psychopath in the the midst of cosy, homey perfection). Molly Ringwald has honed her rich-bitch routine since *The Breakfast Club*, but doesn't quite convince as Doug's malicious seductress. EP

Malizia

(1973, It, 97 min)
d Salvatore Samperi. *p* Silvio Clementelli. *sc* Salvatore Samperi, Ottavio Jemma, Alessandro Parenzo. *ph* Vittorio Storaro. *ed* Sergio Montanari. *ad* Ezio Altieri. *m* Fred Bongusto. *cast* Laura Antonelli, Turi Ferro, Alessandro Momo, Angela Luce, Pino Caruso, Tina Aumont, Lilla Brignone.
● Really no more than an extended joke revolving round the attitudes of Italian men towards *La Mama* and women in general. With the death of his wife, a businessman and his three sons find their lives disrupted by the arrival of a beautiful new maidservant. While father is trying to lay to rest the ghost of his wife and woo the maid into marriage, his middle son, aged 14, forces the girl through a series of sexual humiliations that culminate one stormy night on the eve of her wedding. Next day, after the ceremony, in front of a proud and unsuspecting father, he dutifully calls her 'Mother' and wishes every happiness. An Italian idyll: knocking off mother before father can. In spite of good moments, the film remains muddled and unsure, dividing itself between sharp observations and a 14-year-old's wet dream. CPe

Mallboy

(2000, Aust, 84 min)
d Vincent Giarrusso. *p* Fiona Eagger. *sc* Vincent Giarrusso. *ph* Brendan Lavalle. *ed* Mark Atkin. *cast* Kane McNay, Nell Feaney, Maxie Rickard, Brett Swain, Brett Tucker.
● Initially, this first feature comes over as stilted sub-Loachian study in youthful estrangement – it traces a couple of days in the life of 14-year-old Melbourne petty thief, Sean (McNay), at home from 'the centre' when his father gets out of jail. But it slowly grows in interest as writer/director Giarrusso shows his sympathy and understanding for the likeable young man's plight. If some of the comedy and drama feels a little staged, McNay's quietly affecting, natural performance eventually wins the day. WH

Mallrats

(1995, US, 96 min)
d Kevin Smith. *p* Sean Daniel, Jim Jacks, Scott Mosier. *sc* Kevin Smith. *ph* David Klein. *ed* Paul Dixon. *m* Ira Newborn. *cast* Shannen Doherty, Jason Lee, Jason Mewes, Kevin Smith, Renée Humphrey, Michael Rooker, Stan Lee, Claire Forlani.
● A depressing mess. Like *Clerks*, Smith's first film, it centres on a bunch of teen no-hopers, their lives dominated by sex and pop culture, but unlike *Clerks*, it never makes them seem any more interesting than the brats you'd find in a John Hughes' flick, just more obscene. 'Truth or Dare' is the TV show which provides the plot with an ostensible climax, but Smith seems to think they're synonymous – this is all dare, and precious little truth. The callow, sub-John Waters shock-comedy might be less tiresome if Smith didn't botch the timing so relentlessly. The funniest bit involves a topless palm reader with three nipples. TCh

Malou

(1980, WGer, 94 min)
d Jeanine Meerapfel. *p* Michael Boehm. *sc* Jeanine Meerapfel. *ph* Michael Ballhaus. *ed* Dagmar Hirtz. *ad* Rainer Schaper. *m* Peer Raben. *cast* Ingrid Caven, Helmut Griem, Grischa Huber, Ivan Desny, Peter Chatel, Marie Colbin.
● Meerapfel's first feature is a meandering but delicately engaging study of belonging and female self-discovery. The plot is deliberately simple, indeed almost non-existent. Spurred by the unearthing of certain glittering family heirlooms, a woman seeks out her family past. This device is used to create a tandem narrative, with her story of present marital uncertainty being set alongside the previous tragedy of her mother, Malou. Born around the turn of the century, Malou led a life entirely defined by men. When her husband leaves her, she is left without identity and even nationality, adrift in a strange country. With a hypnotic central performance from Dietrich lookalike Caven as the mother, Meerapfel's film makes its feminist points in ambiguous, even teasing fashion, and moves easily to a conclusion neatly poised between liberation and alienation. RR

Malpertuis

(1971, Bel/Fr/WGer, 104 min)
d Harry Kümel. *p* Pierre Levie, Paul Laffargue. *sc* Jean Ferry. *ph* Gerry Fisher. *ed* Richard Marden (English, French versions), Harry Kümel (Flemish version). *ad* Pierre Cadiou. *m* Georges Delerue. *cast* Orson Welles, Susan Hampshire, Michel Bouquet, Mathieu Carrière, Jean-Pierre Cassel, Sylvie Vartan, Walter Rilla, Johnny Hallyday.
● A fresh-faced blond sailor (Carrière) is shanghaied from a '20s port full of sleazy bars and art-nouveau mansions, and held captive in the endless corridors of a crumbling Gothic pile called Malpertuis: we don't discover why until the end, in a denouement as outrageous and devastating as any ever filmed. Kümel elaborates the mystery like a master, drawing much of his design and composition from Surrealist painting (Magritte, de Chirico), and weaving serpentine patterns from the intrigues between the many characters. Welles is at his most mountainous as the house's patriarch; Hampshire is a revelation, playing three contrasted women. This English-dialogue version is better than the French and Flemish originals (which run 22 minutes longer). From the novel by Jean Ray. TR

Malpractice

(1989, Aust, 91 min)
d Bill Bennett. *p* Tristram Miall. *sc* Jenny Ainge. *ph* Steve Arnold. *ed* Denise Hunter. *m* Michael Atkinson. *cast* Caz Lederman, Bob Baines, Ian Gilmour, Pat Thomson, Janet Stanley.
● This uncompromising, 'fly on the wall' Australian piece confronts medical malpractice and the aftermath suffered by an 'ordinary' family. Coral Davis goes into hospital to give birth to her third child, and misjudgments by the junior doctor who undertakes the delivery result in a brain-damaged baby. Bennett has produced an immensely impressive film which explores the emotional and legal consequences. Documentary camera techniques combine skilfully with credible performances, and dialogue which appears improvised underscores moments of great vulnerability. Strong and compelling. CM

Maltese Falcon, The (aka Dangerous Female)

(1931, US, 80 min, b/w)
d Roy Del Ruth. *sc* Maude Fulton, Brown Holmes. *ph* William Rees. *ed* George Marks. *ad* Robert M Haas. *m* Joseph A Burke. *cast* Bebe Daniels, Ricardo Cortez, Dudley Digges, Una Merkel, Robert Elliott, Thelma Todd, Dwight Frye.
● The first film version of Hammett's *The Maltese Falcon* (retitled *Dangerous Female* for TV): if it's not quite the solid classic of the Huston version (1941), the two adaptations are still remarkably similar, and it's fun to watch the earlier cast run through the characterisations that Bogey, et al, have made so familiar. Cortez, for instance, is a slightly sleeker Sam Spade, Daniels not quite as viper-ish as Mary Astor, while Digges makes good as 'the fat man', even if he doesn't really have the waistline. TJ

Maltese Falcon, The

(1941, US, 100 min, b/w)
d/sc John Huston. *ph* Arthur Edeson. *ed* Thomas Richards. *ad* Robert M Haas. *m* Adolph Deutsch. *cast* Humphrey Bogart, Mary Astor, Sydney Greenstreet, Peter Lorre, Elisha Cook Jr, Barton MacLane, Lee Patrick, Ward Bond, Gladys George.
● Huston's first film displays the hallmarks that were to distinguish his later work: the mocking attitude toward human greed; the cavalier insolence with which plot details are treated almost as asides; the delight in bizarre characterisations, here ranging from the amiably snarling Sam Spade ('When you're slapped, you'll take it and like it') who opened a whole new romantic career for Bogart, to Lorre's petulant, gardenia-scented Joel Cairo, Cook's waspishly effete gunsel, and Greenstreet's monstrously jocular Fat Man ('By gad, sir, you are a character'). What makes it a prototype *film noir* is the vein of unease missing from the two earlier versions of Hammett's novel. Filmed almost entirely in interiors, it presents a claustrophobic world animated by betrayal, perversion and pain, never – even at its most irresistibly funny, as when Cook listens in outraged disbelief while his fat sugar daddy proposes to sell him down the line – quite losing sight of this central abyss of darkness, ultimately embodied by Mary Astor's sadly duplicitous siren. TM

Mama

(1991, China, 90 min)
d Zhang Yuan. *p* Zhang Yuan, Huang Xing. *ph* Zhang Jian. *ed* Shuang Yuan. *ad* Shu Gang. *m* Wang Shi. *cast* Qing Yan, Huang Haibo, Pan Shaquan.
● Released in China only after a two-year ban, Zhang Yuan's debut feature looks at first glance like a Ken Loach 'social problem' movie. It centres on the plight of a woman librarian in Beijing who struggles to bring up her teenage son (retarded since a childhood accident) without help from her absent husband or the state, and juxtaposes that fiction with relevant documentary material. But Zhang isn't content with showing street-level realities for their own sake; he pushes his material towards expressionism, using the mother's inevitable mood swings as keys to the tone and texture of the images, a strategy that brings him within breathing distance of *film noir* by the end. China's 'Sixth Generation' film-makers couldn't have got off to a stronger start. TR

Mamá es boba

see My Silly Mother

Maman et la Putain, La

see Mother and the Whore, The

Mama's Dirty Girls

(1974, US, 80 min)
d John Hayes. *p* Ed Carlin, Gil Lasky. *sc* Gil Lasky. *ph* Henning Schellerup. *ed* Luke Porand. *m* Don Bagley, Steve Michaels. *cast* Gloria Grahame, Paul Lambert, Sondra Currie, Candice Rialson, Christopher Wines, Dennis Smith.
● For a while this looks promising, with Gloria Grahame laying down a fair and acrid parody of the bourgeois marriage ethos for the benefit of her daughters. 'When I was your age, I just wanted a man, but a man can go just as easy as a man can come. A man is only a man, but property is security'. Having murdered her husband with the aid of the two eldest girls, only to discover that he was unfortunately penniless, she tries again, but this time picks a man with the same idea. Meanwhile the daughters find men of their own... At which point the whole thing peters out into the drab flats of routine misogyny: the women become malevolent schemers, and it's up to the men to right things (violently). VG

Mamba

see Fair Game

Mambo Kings, The

(1992, US, 104 min)
d Arne Glimcher. *p* Arnon Milchan, Arne Glimcher. *sc* Cynthia Cidre. *ph* Michael Ballhaus. *ed* Claire Simpson. *pd* Stuart Wurtzel. *m* Robert Kraft, Carlos Franzetti. *cast* Armand Assante, Antonio Banderas, Cathy Moriarty, Maruschka Detmers, Roscoe Lee Browne, Desi Arnaz Jr, Celia Cruz.
● A spirited evocation of the mambo craze which swept post-war America, adapted from Oscar Hijuelos' Pulitzer Prize-winning novel. Cuban musicians César and Nestor Castillo (Assante and Banderas) arrive in New York to find love, greed and, ultimately, fame. César thrives on the success of their band, and relentlessly pursues sex and the Yankee dollar, while his mournful brother laments his lost love and homeland. First-time director Glimcher establishes a restless pace, from the opening violence through to the energetic, swirling musical sequences, while screenwriter Cynthia Cidre tones down some of the book's flamboyance and machismo, emphasising the eroticism of sudden passion and repressed desire; and there's a sure feel for period in both tone and technique. CM

Mame

(1974, US, 131 min)
d Gene Saks. *p* Roger Fryer, James Cresson. *sc* Paul Zindel. *ph* Philip H Lathrop. *ed* Maury Winetrobe. *pd* Robert Boyle. *m* Jerry Herman. *cast* Lucille Ball, Beatrice Arthur, Robert Preston, Bruce Davison, Kirby Furlong, Jane Connell, George Chiang, Joyce Van Patten.

●Starving fans of musicals won't live long on *Mame*, another paean to American matriarchy, or rather auntiarchy, and the swansong of the Queen of the B movie and TV sitcom. Lucille Ball, cast 20 years younger than she is, simply hasn't the drive and steel of a Rosalind Russell, an Angela Lansbury or a Ginger Rogers, all of whom played the part before her. And Mame is the Life Force. She can declare Christmas a month early and get snow with it. When he's not ogling his star in perpetual soft focus and a $300,000 fashion parade, Saks fails to get enough retakes, match his shots, or inject the essential vim. There's a preposterously smug put-down of the bourgeoisie, and some dull songs. SG

Mamma Roma

(1962, It, 114 min, b/w)
d Pier Paolo Pasolini. *p* Alfredo Bini. *sc* Pier Paolo Pasolini. *ph* Tonino Delli Colli. *ed* Nino Baragli. *ad* Flavio Mogherini. *m* Vivaldi. *cast* Anna Magnani, Ettore Garofolo, Franco Citti, Silvana Corsini, Luisa Loiano, Paolo Volponi, Luciano Gonini, Vittorio La Paglia.

●Pasolini's second feature jumps a class from the sub-proletarian milieu of *Accattone*, following the efforts of a prostitute, 'Mamma Roma' (Magnani), to make a petty-bourgeois life for herself and her teenage son in suburban Rome. It combines formal audacity, unflinching candour and heart-breaking compassion to produce a work of shattering beauty. Pasolini's was a cinema of contradictions. Nobody before – or since – had tried to marry stories about the underclass with a religious cinematic style normally reserved for the adoration of saints or the mysterious workings of God. The film is composed in the form of a lament, employing classical music (the 'populist' Vivaldi), painterly compositions (shot by Tonino Delli Colli to echo works by Caravaggio among others) and processional camera movements (a track through an apartment arch that suggests anything from a triumphal return to a descent through the gates of hell), in order to counterpoint the tragic trajectory of his story. For this Marxist sympathiser, radical poet and novelist, the peasantry was the fount of pre-religious grace, inevitably to be broken on the wheel of bourgeois conformity. Whatever Pasolini's intentions, what makes the film so distinctive is the passion he brings to the screen. Magnani is the only professional actress, but her iconic, larger-than-life persona, far from unsettling the film, balances it. WH

Man About Town

see Silence est d'Or, Le

Man Alive

(1945, US, 70 min, b/w)
d Ray Enright. *p* Robert Fellowes.*sc* Edwin Harvey Blum. *ph* Frank Redman. *ed* Marvin Coil. *ad* Albert S D'Agostino, Al Herman. *m* Leigh Harline. *cast* Pat O'Brien, Ellen Drew, Adolphe Menjou, Rudy Vallee, Fortunio Bonanova, Jonathan Hale, Jack Norton.

●A quite funny and charming minor comedy, with O'Brien as a neglectful husband who, reported drowned in a car accident while drunk, takes to posing as a ghost to prevent his wife from marrying an old flame. One particularly good sequence has O'Brien reviving after being fished out of the river, unaware that he is aboard a showboat, to be confronted by a 'Green Pastures'-style representation of heaven; convinced he is dead and distractedly going to the door, he this time finds himself in hell (the stokehold, given an added touch of conviction by the fortuitous presence of Menjou, sporting his Mephistopheles costume from the show). Invention flags latterly, though, as the lies and deceptions he gets up to instead of owning up (at Menjou's meddlesome suggestion) lead to rather tiresome complications. TM

Man Alone, A

(1955, US, 96 min)
d Ray Milland. p Herbert J Yates. *sc* John Tucker Battle. *ph* Lionel Lindon. *ed* Richard L Van Enger. *ad* Walter Keller. *m* Victor Young. *cast* Ray Milland, Mary Murphy, Ward Bond, Raymond Burr, Arthur Space, Lee Van Cleef, Alan Hale Jr.

●A lone gunslinger stranded in the desert (Milland) comes upon the corpse-strewn wreck of a stagecoach. With the finger of suspicion firmly pointed at him, he then holes up in town to play a lone hand (more or less, since he is befriended by sheriff's daughter Mary Murphy) against the corrupt citizen (Burr) using him as a cover-up for nefarious activities. At the film's heart is a persuasive though clumsily inserted consideration of the nature of corruption, occasioned when Ward Bond's sheriff, hitherto in Burr's pay, does some soul-searching on finally declaring himself on the side of the angels. Milland's direction (his debut) is sometimes a little too ponderously deliberate, but – like the performances – eminently watchable. TM

Man and a Woman, A

see Homme et une Femme, Un

Man, a Woman and a Bank, A

(1979, Can, 101 min)
d Noel Black. *p* Peter Samuelson, John D Bennett. *sc* Raynold Gideon, Bruce Evans, Stuart Margolin. *ph* Jack Cardiff. *ed* Carl Kress. *pd* Anne Pritchard. *m* Bill Conti. *cast* Donald Sutherland, Brooke Adams, Paul Mazursky, Allan Magicovsky, Leigh Hamilton, Nick Rice, Peter Erlich, Paul Rotherty.

●Oddly enough, the almost total failure to create suspense, laughs or even a credible technological heist (in what is supposed to be a comedy-suspense movie about a computer bank raid) doesn't matter much. A certain whimsical, old-fashioned charm refuses to be squashed by microchips or '80s cynicism; the relationship between the two men is touching; and the self-conscious 'romance' that develops for Sutherland and Adams provokes indulgent grins all round, not least from the principals themselves. There is also a truly sizzling scene involving Leigh Hamilton as a carefully luscious gameshow hostess demonstrating to lover Mazursky 'how Redford and Nicholson kiss' which is almost worth the price of a ticket alone. A difficult movie to get het up about: inoffensive, charming, and a bit like Banana Instant Whip. DSi

Man Between, The

(1953, GB, 101 min, b/w)
d/p Carol Reed. *sc* Harry Kurnitz, Eric Linklater. *ph* Desmond Dickinson. *ed* Bert Bates. *ad* Andre Andrejew. *m* John Addison. *cast* James Mason, Claire Bloom, Hildegard Neff, Geoffrey Toone, Aribert Wäscher, Ernst Schroeder, Dieter Krause, Hilde Sessak, Karl John.

●Very much a return to the world of Harry Lime, with the ruins of edgy, divided Berlin standing in for the sewers of Vienna. The drab, snow-clad city finds its human counterpart in Mason's sardonic, disreputable double agent, who stalks and then succumbs to the provocatively virginal Bloom. Cold war dogmatism is refreshingly muted, with free world heroes and Stalinist heavies merely a backcloth to the complexly ambiguous relations centred on Mason. The film's rambling, ramshackle construction drew unfavourable comparisons with *The Third Man*, but despite thematic similarities, it is more fruitfully seen as a forerunner to the down-at-heel spy stories of John Le Carré. RMy

Man Bites Dog (C'est arrivé près de chez vous)

(1992, Bel, 96 min)
d/p Rémy Belvaux, André Bonzel, Benoît Poelvoorde. sc Rémy Belvaux, André Bonzel, Benoît Poelvoorde, Vincent Tavier. ph André Bonzel. ed Rémy Belvaux, Eric Dardill. cast Benoît Poelvoorde, Rémy Belvaux, André Bonzel, Jacqueline Poelvoorde-Pappaert, Nelly Pappaert, Jenny Drye, Malou Madou.

●Mostly, Ben (Poelvoorde) is an ordinary sort of guy. One passion, however, is unusual: he regularly commits murder, not exactly at random, but certainly without malice or provocation. So intriguing is Ben's deadly charm that a film crew decide to make a documentary about him; and come to like him so much that they start facilitating, then collaborating in, his crimes. This spoof fly-on-the-wall documentary is funny, scary, provocative, and profoundly disturbing. While the body count is sky high and the violence explicit, it's neither a thriller nor, finally, a psychological study. Rather, it's a witty, uncompromising acknowledgment of both film-makers' and audiences' often unhealthy fascination with the spectacle of violence. Even as you admire its bravura, intelligence and seeming authenticity, such is its rigour that you are also forced to question just why you are watching it. Purely on a gut level, it may offend; but as an exploration of voyeurism, it's one of the most resonant, caustic contributions to the cinema of violence since *Peeping Tom*. GA

Man by the Shore, The (L'Homme sur les Quais)

(1992, Fr, 105 min)
d Raoul Peck. *p* Pascal Verroust. *sc* Raoul Peck, André Grail. *ph* Armand Marco. *ed* Jacques Comets. *pd* Gilles Aird. *m* Amos Coulanges. *cast* Jennifer Zubar, Toto Bissainthe, Jean-Michel Martial, Patrick Rameau, Mireille Metellus, François Latour.

●Political and social ferment in '60s Haiti as recalled by an innocent young girl. Initially too fragmented and arty – it comes on at times like a Caribbean *Spirit of the Beehive* – the film slowly settles down into an effectively understated portrait of a society beset by betrayal, fear and violence. Generally sturdy performances (though one character, wrecked after torture, seems a grotesque, metaphorical caricature) and sustained control of the unsettling mood make for a minor but intelligent entertainment. GA

Man Called Hero, A (Zhonghua Yingxiong)

(1999, HK, 105 min)
d Andrew Lau. *p* Manfred Wong, Barbie Tung. *sc* Manfred Wong. *ph* Andrew Lau. *ed* Danny Pang. *ad* Wong Ka-Nang. *m* Chan Kwong-Wing. *cast* Ekin Cheng, Kristy Yang, Nicholas Tse, Shu Qi, Francis Ng, Yuen Biao, Jerry Lamb, Anthony Wong.

●The follow-up to *Stormriders* is based on an earlier comic by Ma Wing-Shing (a 150-part graphic novel, the most influential ever published in HK), but it minimises the sword'n sorcery aspects in an apparent effort to go beyond the earlier film. Instead it goes for an Ellis Island storyline about indentured Chinese labourers in the New World and the struggle to establish a New York Chinatown, with a brief prologue in China and a flashback to Japan to cover the mystic kung-fu and clan leadership bases. But the script makes little geographical, chronological or dramatic sense and the digitally effected fight scenes are the only real reason to watch, although the climactic duel on the Statue of Liberty is less impressively visualised than two scraps with ninja. TR

Man Called Horse, A

(1970, US, 114 min)
d Elliot Silverstein. *p* Sandy Howard. *sc* Jack DeWitt. *ph* Robert B Hauser. *ed* Philip Anderson *pd* Dennis Lynton Clark. *m* Leonard Rosenman. *cast* Richard Harris, Judith Anderson, Jean Gascon, Manu Tupou, Corinna Tsopei, Dub Taylor, Eddie Littlesky, Michael Baseleon, Iron Eyes Cody.

●First of a series of Westerns in which Richard Harris seemed determined to outdo Brando's penchant for situations permitting a bit of sado-masochistic suffering. Here, as an English lordling captured by Sioux, he undergoes the particularly nasty trial-by-torture of the Sun Vow. Self-touted as an authentic picture of Sioux manners and customs, the film to some extent delivers the goods (despite sacrificing a great deal of credibility by absurdly casting Judith Anderson as a malevolent old crone). But the Sun Vow sequence, lingered on in enervatingly gloating detail, ultimately defines it as exploitative. (From a story by Dorothy M Johnson.)

Man Called Noon, The

(1973, GB/Sp/It, 95 min)
d Peter Collinson. *p* Euan Lloyd. *sc* Scot Finch. *ph* John Cabrera. *ed* Alan Pattillo. *ad* José Maria Tapiador. *m* Luis Enriquez Bacalov. *cast* Richard Crenna, Stephen Boyd, Rosanna Schiaffino, Farley Granger, Patty Shepard, Angel del Pozo, Aldo Sambrell.

●Instantly forgettable Western about a Dryden-quoting gunfighter who suffers from amnesia until he falls down a ravine at the end and –

surprise, surprise – remembers where the gold is and that he's not the villain everyone has accused him of being. The whole thing would be preposterous enough without Collinson's direction. He continually makes his actors compete with the flapping doors, wagon wheels, bites of driftwood and rock that he insists on placing between them and the camera. The only other shots in his repertoire are excessive close-up, zoom, and ground shots angled upwards at 45 degrees. Hardly surprising that you come out exhausted. (From a novel by Louis L'Amour.) CPe

Man Called Peter, A

(1955, US, 119 min)
d Henry Koster. *p* Samuel G Engel. *sc* Eleanore Griffin. *ph* Harold Lipstein. *ed* Robert Simpson. *ad* Lyle Wheeler, Maurice Ransford. *m* Alfred Newman. *cast* Richard Todd, Jean Peters, Marjorie Rambeau, Jill Esmond, Doris Lloyd, Emmett Lynn.

● Scots-born, American-trained Presbyterian minister Peter Marshall, who was to gain national prominence as the Chaplain to the US Senate, is the subject of this unstoppably earnest CinemaScope biopic, where faith is unshaken even by a heart attack in the pulpit. The combination of Richard Todd and Hollywood religiosity makes a potent argument for descaling the kettle. TJ

Manchurian Candidate, The

(1962, US, 126 min, b/w)
d John Frankenheimer. *p* George Axelrod, John Frankenheimer. *sc* George Axelrod. *ph* Lionel Lindon. *ed* Ferris Webster. *pd* Richard Sylbert. *m* David Amram *cast* Frank Sinatra, Laurence Harvey, Janet Leigh, Angela Lansbury, Henry Silva, James Gregory, Leslie Parrish, John McGiver, Khigh Dhiegh.

● Korean War veteran Major Marco (Sinatra) is troubled by a recurring nightmare in which Congressional Medal of Honor hero Raymond Shaw (Harvey) carries out Communist instructions to shoot fellow American PoWs. Working for Intelligence, Marco unravels a cunning Red plot to brainwash his old platoon and to turn Shaw into an assassin. Shaw's father-in-law is the ranting McCarthyite Senator Iselin (Gregory), a mouthpiece for Shaw's ambitious mother (Lansbury), a political background which gives the killer access to the highest in the land. Who is Shaw's American control, when and where are they going to aim him? Frankenheimer's version of Richard Condon's tragically prophetic novel looks even better now than it did then. It's greatest virtue lies in its brilliant balancing acts: political satire and nail-biting thriller, the twin lunacies of the Right and Left, and the outrageously funny dialogue during the parallel courtships set against the sadness of the unloveable Shaw's predicament. Among a marvellous cast – star-wattage Sinatra, hilariously dumb Gregory, the giggling Peking Institute brainwasher Khigh Dhiegh – Lansbury stands out. An Iron Lady to savour, for a change. A masterpiece. BC

Mandala

(1981, SKor, 112 min)
d Im Kwon-Taek. *cast* Chun Moo-Song, Ahn Song-Gi, Pang Hui, Ki Jong-Su.

● This breakthrough film by South Korea's best known director is a leisurely, chiefly lyrical account of the friendship between two notably different Buddhist monks – Pobun, a somewhat pessimistic young ascetic fleeing the commitment demanded by his girlfriend, and the old Jisan, whose unorthodox preference for alcohol and an active sex life belie an easy-going wisdom repressed by his stricter, seemingly more devout peers. The film also works as an unexpectedly tough appraisal of the tenets and practices of a living philosophy. Woolly mindedness and poetic overkill are, on the whole, avoided, while enlightenment is presented as often resulting from – or leading to – loneliness, masochism and self-denial. A film whose spiritual integrity is reflected in the mantric calm of its measured rhythms and elegant imagery, it's nevertheless rooted in a recognisably modern, material world, so that you don't need a special interest in Buddhism for its quiet virtues to work their spell. GA

Mandat, Le

see Money Order, The

Mandela

(1995, US, 123 min)
d Jo Menell, Angus Gibson. *p* Jonathan Demme, Edward Saxon, Jo Menell. *ph* Dewald Aukema, Peter Tischhauser, Edwin Wes, Siphiwo Ralo, Prospero Bailey. *ed* Andy Keir, Mona Davis. *m* Cedric Gradus Samson, Hugh Masekela. *with* Nelson Mandela, Mabel Mandela, Mandla Mandela, Walter Sisulu, Anthony Sampson, Joe Matthews, Evelyn Mandela, Nomzamo Winnie Mandela, Desmond Tutu.

● This two-hour 'official' biography, co-produced by Jonathan Demme, serves a double purpose. It's a populist résumé of the life of one of the 20th century's most remarkable men, tracing Mandela's days from his Xhosa village at the end of WWI to his Nobel Peace Prize in 1993 and his inauguration as President of South Africa in 1994. Mandela gives extensive studio and on-location interviews and narrates much of the film himself. Second, as a political work, it serves as a celebratory, if far from hagiographic tribute to the man, echoing to the sound of the 'revolutionary' voices and music, ancient and modern, of South Africa. WH

Mandingo

(1975, US, 126 min)
d Richard Fleischer. *p* Dino De Laurentiis. *sc* Norman Wexler. *ph* Richard H Kline. *ed* Frank Bracht. *pd* Boris Leven. *m* Maurice Jarre. *cast* James Mason, Susan George, Perry King, Richard Ward, Brenda Sykes, Ken Norton, Lillian Hayman, Ji-Tu Cumbaka.

● The tedious, emasculated stereotype of the Deep South circa 1840, with its stoical slaves and demure southern belles, is effectively exploded here. Fleischer utilises the real sexuality and violence behind slavery to mount a compelling slice of American Gothic which analyses, in appropriately lurid terms, the twists and turns of a distorted society. The plot (from a novel by Kyle Onstott) explores the declining years of a slave-breeding family, whose slaves are treated not so much like animals as humanoids: their physical intimacy with the master-race is total. Finally it is the sheer absurdity and incongruity of the various women's roles in this crazy set-up which cracks the society wide open. The story is basically Victorian melodrama with more than an echo of the Brontes, but it is acted with enormous gusto, by Perry King especially; and Richard Kline's highly atmospheric pictorialisation of the Falconhurst domain adds a great deal. Good to see Fleischer returning to the kind of psycho-pathological thriller that he can handle so well. DP

Mandragora

(1997, Czech Republic, 130 min)
d Wiktor Grodecki. *p* Miroslav Steinbach. *sc* Wiktor Grodecki, David Svec. *ph* Vladimir Holomek. *ed* Wiktor Grodecki. *pd* Martin Kurel. *m* Wolfgang Hammerschmid. *cast* Mirek Caslavka, David Sveck, Pavel Skripal, Kostas Zedraloglu, Jiri Kodes.

● Notwithstanding the elegant opening shot (of a shop window smashed and looted to the strains of choral music), this account of a teenage runaway who leaves his bullying father and boring home town for the streets of Prague, only to be pushed immediately by a ruthless pimp into a squalid, violent, druggy world of male prostitution and pornography, is pretty hackneyed by Western European standards. Despite the sombre tone, the film tends towards sensationalism, so that its manifest good intentions seldom result in anything more than trite stereotyping. GA

Mandy (aka Crash of Silence)

(1952, GB, 93 min, b/w)
d Alexander Mackendrick. *p* Leslie Norman. *sc* Nigel Balchin, Jack Whittingham. *ph* Douglas Slocombe. *ed* Seth Holt. *ad* Jim Morahan. *m* William Alwyn. *cast* Phyllis Calvert, Jack Hawkins, Terence Morgan, Mandy Miller, Godfrey Tearle, Marjorie Fielding, Patricia Plunkett, Dorothy Alison, Edward Chapman, Jane Asher.

● The only avowedly 'serious' film of Mackendrick's superb Ealing quintet, *Mandy* is also the first expression of his abiding fascination with the psychology and revealingly distorted perception of a child, developed later in *The Maggie* and, triumphantly, in *Sammy Going South* and *A High Wind in Jamaica*. Nevertheless, the director focuses as tightly on the emotional traumas and narrowed perspectives of the parents as he does on the deaf-and-dumb little girl of the title, revealing their senses to be almost as numbed as hers. Paradoxically, but with much justification, it has often been pointed out that the film's true theme is blindness. PT

Manèges (The Wanton)

(1949, Fr, 89 min, b/w)
d Yves Allégret. *p* Emile Natan. *sc* Jacques Sigurd. *ph* Jean Bourgoin. *ed* Maurice Serein. *ad* Auguste Capelier, Alexandre Trauner. *m* Paul Misraki. *cast* Simone Signoret, Bernard Blier, Jane Marken, Frank Villard, Jacques Baumer.

● A cynically sharpish script about a gold digger (Signoret) who marries a doting riding-master (Blier), leads him a wretched dance while bleeding him dry, then gets hoist with her own petard while looking for another rich sucker. Fussily structured as a complex of flashbacks sometimes covering the same scene from different viewpoints (with Allégret resorting to some irritatingly mannered optical effects to string them together), it's all pretty superficial. But the performances, especially Jane Marken as Signoret's brassily mercenary mother, are superb. TM

Man Escaped, A

see Condamné à mort s'est échappé, Un

Man for All Seasons, A

(1966, US, 120 min)
d/p Fred Zinnemann. *sc* Robert Bolt. *ph* Ted Moore. *ed* Ralph Kemplen. *pd* John Box. *m* Georges Delerue. *cast* Paul Scofield, Robert Shaw, Wendy Hiller, Leo McKern, Orson Welles, Susannah York, Nigel Davenport, John Hurt, Corin Redgrave, Colin Blakely, Cyril Luckham, Vanessa Redgrave.

● An agonisingly respectable, sincere film of Robert Bolt's literate play, with Scofield as Sir Thomas More, endorsing the divine right of the Pope over and above his King. McKern is Thomas Cromwell; Shaw, Henry VIII; Hiller, Mrs More. They're all fine, but Orson Welles alone relieves the boredom in a marvellous cameo as Cardinal Wolsey. If only they'd let him loose with the whole sorry history… TCh

Man Friday

(1975, GB, 115 min)
d Jack Gold. *p* David Korda. *sc* Adrian Mitchell. *ph* Alex Phillips. *ed* Anne V Coates. *pd* Peter Murton. *m* Carl Davis. *cast* Peter O'Toole, Richard Roundtree, Peter Cellier, Christopher Cabot, Joel Fluellen.

● Turning the familiar Crusoe/Man Friday story on its head, this version becomes a straightforward confrontation between instinctive, spontaneous, lithe and beautiful Black versus repressed, guilt-ridden and mottled White: a fable for our times. Crusoe's imperialism, individualism, competitiveness and other cornerstones of Western civilisation also fail to measure up alongside Man Friday's natural grace. But too seldom does this Crusoe become anything more than a one-dimensional, knock-down figure, and O'Toole's noisy, strangled performance is disastrously wide of the mark. The simple tone would be more acceptable if the general level of satire owed less to stock British comedy, and if attempts to leaven the message hadn't included interludes like the one where Crusoe and Friday go hang-gliding. CPe

Man from Africa and Girl from India

(1982, Trin, 138 min)
d Harbance Mickey Kumar. *cast* Sanam Suri, Bhalinder, Michael Walker, Kabir Bedi, Ralph Maraj, Grace Maraj, Ranji Ganase.

● Sexual repression, cultural alienation and religious fanaticism are only some of the ingredients in the extraordinary 'melting pot' of this movie from Trinidad. Parallel plots, stuck together with lots of calypso music, illustrate contrasting examples of extremism, with the black, virile macho-man Michael not getting enough, and his friend Shaam, the sensitive Indian boy, unable to kiss his beautiful bride without seeing devils. The complicated plot falls over itself trying to explain every moral twist and turn, while the actors (none of them professional) are endearingly theatrical. Apparently a huge success in the West Indies and parts of America, it's being aimed at an ethnic audience here who may be better able to appreciate its style and cultural intricacies. HR

Man from China

(1990, GB, 45 min)
d Zhang Tielin. *cast* Yang Ying Sheng, Marina Baker.

● A short feature by Zhang Tielin, a former movie star in China, now an exile in Britain. It charts the experiences of a young Chinese painter who comes to London soon after the Beijing massacre and decides to stay. His initial difficulties in adjusting and the misunderstandings are sketched succinctly, but the meat of the film is the account of the boy's psychological blocks: his determination to go it alone, and his almost pathological inability to accept help and affection. In other words, not the usual anecdotal guff, but an intense and demanding study of the 'inner wounds' that afflict so many Chinese from the PRC. A more than impressive debut. TR

Man from Colorado, The

(1948, US, 99 min)
d Henry Levin. *p* Jules Schermer. *sc* Robert Hardy Andrews, Ben Maddow. *ph* William Snyder. *ed* Charles Nelson. *ad* Stephen Goosson, A Leslie Thomas.*m* George Duning. *cast* William Holden, Glenn Ford, Ellen Drew, Ray Collins, Edgar Buchanan.

● An uncredited King Vidor allegedly shot some of this intriguing but not wholly achieved psychological Western (from a story by Borden Chase), which has twitchy cavalry officer Ford transformed by his Civil War experiences into a disturbed killer. The outlook is not good when he's appointed a noose-happy judge, leaving former adjutant Holden to rebel against his subsequent reign of terror. The scenario alludes to the homecoming traumas of WWII combatants, but the characterisation, regrettably, lacks the deftness to give the movie real punch. TJ

Man from Hong Kong, The

(1975, Aust/HK, 103 min)
d Brian Trenchard Smith. *p* Raymond Chow, John Fraser. *sc* Brian Trenchard Smith. *ph* Russell Boyd. *ed* Ron Williams. *ad* David Copping, Chien Shun. *m* Noel Quinlan. *cast* Jimmy Wang Yu, George Lazenby, Ros Spiers, Hugh Keays-Byrne, Roger Ward, Rebecca Gilling, Frank Thring.

● Wang Yu's Hong Kong super-cop arrives in Sydney on a case, mercifully not reduced to Chinese caricature status. Otherwise this is imitation late Bond stuff, larded with all the predictable ingredients: girls, car chases, less than pointed wit, fights (kung-fu and otherwise), hang-gliding as the novel twist, and a number of statutory Chinese martial arts movie ingredients lurking under the Western veneer. Directed with basic bash-and-smash competence. VG

Man from Island West, The (Xibu Lai de Ren)

(1990, Tai, 96 min)
d/p/sc/ed Huang Ming-Chuan. *cast* Wu Hongming, Chen Yiwen, Xiao Cuifen, Sharman Lanporan.

● Made on a shoestring, Taiwan's first ever indie feature breaks a lot of new ground: it focuses attention on the sad plight of survivors from Taiwan's aboriginal tribes (most of whom are now manual labourers or prostitutes), and it superimposes an ancient myth on its modern story to create an innovative twin-level structure. A stranger from Taipei turns up in a coastal village, founded by the Atayal tribe, in search of something he won't divulge. His visit catalyses contradictory local feelings about the place, but also mysteriously echoes an Atayal myth about the redeemer Yawi, who once led the tribe to deliverance. Strong elemental imagery plus startlingly raw emotions equals a minor classic. TR

Man from Laramie, The

(1955, US, 101 min)
d Anthony Mann. *p* William Goetz. *sc* Philip Yordan, Frank Burt. *ph* Charles Lang Jr. *ed* William A Lyon. *ad* Cary Odell. *m* George Duning. *cast* James Stewart, Arthur Kennedy, Donald Crisp, Cathy O'Donnell, Aline MacMahon, Wallace Ford, Alex Nicol, Jack Elam, John War Eagle.

● A magnificent, if slightly over-ambitious Western. Cattle baron Crisp, who is going blind, is obsessed with who will inherit his ranching empire: his psychopathic natural-born son Nicol, or the more reliable Kennedy, adopted by the old man to keep Nicol in line. Into this morass of sibling rivalry bursts a vengeful Stewart, bent on finding the gunrunner responsible for selling weapons to the Indians who slaughtered his younger brother's cavalry detachment. Visually impressive, psychologically complex and sometime brutally violent, it suffers slightly from the emphasis on the familial machinations at the expense of Stewart's tortured psyche. Otherwise, it's 24 carat stuff. NF

Man from Majorca, The (Mannen från Mallorca)

(1984, Swe/Den, 105 min)
d/sc Bo Widerberg. *ph* Thomas Wahlberg, Gunnar Nilsson, Hans Welin. *ed* Bo Widerberg. *ad* Jan Öquist. *m* Björn Jason Lindh. *cast* Sven Wollter, Tomas von Brömssen, Håkan Serner, Ernst Günther, Thomas Hellberg, Tommy Johnson, Johan Widerberg.

● A pair of Swedish vice cops stumble onto 'something big' when a routine post office raid turns out to be connected with a subsequent hit-and-run accident and the murder of a garrulous wino. They are beginning to get a whiff of high-level corruption, centering on the Minister of Justice's cavortings with a high-class prostitute, when their phlegmatic superior is ordered to drop the case. Widerberg keeps the action tight, dealing smoothly with the details of police routine and framing the most mundane objects in such a way as to lend them a strangely sinister aspect. The opening post office raid is a slickly handled set piece, setting the tone for a cleverly constructed script which contains enough suspense and red herrings to keep one gripped almost to the end. Unfortunately, the government cover-up having proved all too successful, there's no gratifying pay-off, leaving one with a slight sense of anti-climax. A neat thriller, but more satisfying than electrifying. NF

Man from Planet X, The

(1951, US, 70 min, b/w)
d Edgar G Ulmer. *p/sc* Aubrey Wisberg, Jack Pollexfen. *ph* John L Russell. *ed* Fred R Feitshans Jr. *ad* Angelo Scibetta, Byron Vreeland. *m* Charles Koff. *cast* Robert Clarke, Margaret Field, Raymond Bond, William Schallert, Roy Engel.

● Stuck with a lacklustre cast required to spout pages of inane gab, and sets so crude that his only option is to keep them shrouded in mist, 'never say die' Ulmer still manages to finesse a few glimmers of pulp poetry. The silent alien who's arrived for no clear reason on the Scottish moors (perhaps to justify the mist?) looks disconcertingly like a prissy schoolmaster, and his spaceship is quite stylish, even though it's clearly a diving bell with a flashing light on top. The general air of a bad dream is established from the start, as a bored-sounding physicist announces the end of the world three weeks from now. BBa

Man from Snowy River, The

(1982, Aust, 104 min)
d George Miller. *p* Geoff Burrowes. *sc* John Dixon. *ph* Keith Wagstaff. *ed* Adrian Carr. *ad* Leslie Binns. *m* Bruce Rowland. *cast* Kirk Douglas, Jack Thompson, Tom Burlinson, Sigrid Thornton, Lorraine Bayly, Terence Donovan, June Jago, David Bradshaw.

● Same name, but this movie based on an epic poem by one AB 'Banjo' Paterson, about a young mountain boy's efforts to tame a stallion, is not the work of the *Mad Max* director. This other Miller dolls up a routine passage-to-manhood saga with widescreen mountain locations and a camera that only moves to show off the expensive production values. The presence of Kirk Douglas in two roles (his scallywag performance and his gritted one) attempts to give the film the gloss of an American Western, fooling no one. CPe

Manganinnie

(1980, Aust, 90 min)
d John Honey. *p* Gilda Baracchi. *sc* Ken Kelso. *ph* Gary Hansen. *ed* Mike Woolveridge. *ad* Neil Angwin. *m* Peter Sculthorpe. *cast* Mawuyul Yathalawuy, Anna Ralph, Phillip Hinton, Elaine Mangan, Buruminy Dhamarrandji, Reg Evans.

● The last survivor of a doomed Aboriginal tribe goes walkabout with a little white girl, initiating her into the mysteries of the Dreamtime before finally falling victim to the guns of early European colonists in the infamous Black Drive. A Disney insistence on cute baby wombats and other assorted fauna mar the film, although the narrative itself is aeons away from the fresh-faced vigour of those ripping adventure yarns, at first seeming maddeningly slow, then assuming a dreamy, languid rhythm of its own. And despite the facile nature/culture clash turning on a Noble Savage stereotype of long lineage in Australian cinema, the fact that *Manganinnie* echoes history (the brutal 19th century genocide of the Tasmanian aboriginal race) lends this first project from the Tasmanian Film Corporation a curious poignancy as a small act of contrition. SJo

Mangler, The

(1994, US, 106 min)
d Tobe Hooper. *p* Anant Singh. *sc* Tobe Hooper, Stephen Brooks, Peter Welbeck. *ph* Amnon Salomon. *ed* David Heitner. *m* Barrington Pheloung. *cast* Robert Englund, Ted Levine, Daniel Matmor, Jeremy Crutchley, Vanessa Pike.

● One would expect a horror movie about a possessed laundry-press to put the audience through the wringer. Instead, this tedious Stephen King adaptation takes the two-dimensional characters of the source story and squashes them even flatter. Englund and Hooper last teamed up on the abysmal straight-to-video *Nightmare* (aka *De Sade*), on which this is no improvement. Levine fails to get inside the skin of his jaded cop, investigating a series of industrial accidents at the grim Blue Ribbon Laundry. The bone-crushing, limb-severing mayhem centres on an ancient machine jealously guarded by irascible owner Bill Gartley (Englund), who clanks around on stainless-steel leg braces following an earlier mishap of his own. Although the mechanical beast is a fearsome creation, and some of the mangling is gratifyingly gory, the bizarre ranting of the cop's veggie, mystic neighbour – about Faustian pacts and the sacrifice of 16-year-old virgins – takes some swallowing, as indeed do the stodgy plotting, scenery-chewing performances and dodgy sfx. NF

Mango Tree, The

(1977, Aust, 102 min)
d Kevin Dobson. *p/sc* Michael Pate. *ph* Brian Probyn. *ed* John Scott. *ad* Leslie Binns. *m* Marc Wilkinson. *cast* Christopher Pate, Geraldine Fitzgerald, Robert Helpmann, Gerard Kennedy, Gloria Dawn, Diane Craig.

● Written and produced by former Hollywood actor Michael Pate, and starring his son, this is yet another slice of Aussie nostalgia, with the wide-eyed lad about to come to manhood as he and the century move into their late teens. The inevitable acquisition of wisdom is aided by a collection of veteran Queensland small-town eccentrics, notably grandma (Fitzgerald) and a professor (former ballet star Helpmann). PT

Manhattan

(1979, US, 96 min, b/w)
d Woody Allen. *p* Charles H Joffe. *sc* Woody Allen, Marshall Brickman. *ph* Gordon Willis. *ed* Susan E Morse. *pd* Mel Bourne. *m* George Gershwin. *cast* Woody Allen, Diane Keaton, Michael Murphy, Mariel Hemingway, Meryl Streep, Anne Byrne, Karen Ludwig, Wallace Shawn.

● A milestone in Woody Allen's career as he dropped (temporarily, at least) the slavish imitation which undermined *Interiors* and found a tone of his own. The note of tragi-comedy is nicely judged as his hero, a TV comedy writer nervously contemplating a switch to serious literature, equally nervously frets over the women in his life and a pending betrayal of his best friend. An edgy social comedy framed as a loving tribute to neurotic New York, overlaid with an evocative Gershwin score, it's funny and sad in exactly the right proportions. Allen could well strive vainly ever to better this film. TM

Manhattan Melodrama

(1934, US, 93 min, b/w)
d WS Van Dyke. *p* David O Selznick. *sc* Oliver HP Garrett, Joseph L Mankiewicz. *ph* James Wong Howe. *ed* Ben Lewis. *ad* Cedric Gibbons, Joseph Wright, Edwin B Willis. *m* Max Axt. *cast* Clark Gable, William Powell, Myrna Loy, Leo Carrillo, Isabel Jewell, Mickey Rooney, Nat Pendleton.

● The last movie John Dillinger ever saw (he was fingered by the lady in red and shot as he left the cinema), this is an archetypal gangster movie of the period, a product of the moral backlash instigated by Hoover and the Hays Office in response to the dangerous ambivalence of *Little Caesar* and its ilk. Clark Gable (who was said to resemble Dillinger) is a thoroughly affable kind of gangster – not averse to a little wager, but essentially a good type who stumbled on to the wrong track when he was a lad (played by Mickey Rooney). Powell is his old pal from those bygone days, now a district attorney. Clark doesn't think twice about putting his life on the line if it will help Bill get elected governor. This Oscar-winning scenario inspired a hail of imitators over the next five years, and was thoughtfully resurrected by John Gregory Dunne in his novel *True Confessions*. TCh

Manhattan Murder Mystery

(1993, US, 107 min)
d Woody Allen. *p* Roger Greenhut. *sc* Woody Allen, Marshall Brickman. *ph* Carlo Di Palma. *ed* Susan E Morse. *pd* Santo Loquasto. *cast* Alan Alda, Woody Allen, Anjelica Huston, Diane Keaton, Jerry Adler, Joy Behar, Ron Rifkin.

● Like the Bob Hope movies which it alludes to, *Manhattan Murder Mystery* is as light and brazenly generic as Allen's early work. As a result, it is both unusually insubstantial, and, at least in the second half, extremely funny. Hope-like in his panicky cowardice, Larry worries not only about the feelings of his wife Carol (Keaton, refreshing) for his old friend Ted (Alda), but about her determination to investigate the death of a neighbour. At first, Larry thinks Carol is fantasising, but then he starts to witness strange events. Cue to a fast, ramshackle, thrill comedy as entertaining as it is removed from the realities of contemporary New York. A movie inspired by movie escapism. Minor, but surprisingly, almost defiantly upbeat. GA

Man Hunt

(1941, US, 105 min, b/w)
d Fritz Lang. *sc* Dudley Nichols. *ph* Arthur Miller. *ed* Allen McNeil. *ad* Richard Day, Wiard B Ihnen. *m* Alfred Newman. *cast* Walter Pidgeon, Joan Bennett, George Sanders, John Carradine, Roddy McDowall, Ludwig Stossel, Heather Thatcher.

● While far from Lang's finest, definitely a superior thriller, set on the eve of World War II. Sadly but inevitably jettisoning much of Geoffrey Household's superb novel (*Rogue Male*), it follows Pidgeon's big game hunter from his arrest by the Gestapo (after taking a 'practice' shot at Hitler), through his escape back to England, to his final, brutal conflict in the Dorset Hills where he has been pursued by Sanders' marvellously sinister Quive-Smith. The evocation of England is pure Hollywood nonsense, Bennett's prostitute is too coy and saddled with an atrocious Cockney accent, and the sequence with McDowall's cabin boy the stuff of *Boy's Own*. But the basic theme of hunter-and-hunted survives intact, beautifully expressed in taut scenes like Carradine's stalking of Pidgeon through the London Underground. Forget the shortcomings and the propagandistic finale, and you have a gripping *noir* thriller, bleak, complex and nightmarish. GA

Manhunt

see From Hell to Texas

Manhunter

(1986, US, 120 min)
d Michael Mann. *p* Richard Roth. *sc* Michael Mann. *ph* Dante Spinotti. *ed* Dov Hoenig. *pd* Mel Bourne. *m* Michael Rubini, Reds. *cast* William Peterson, Kim Greist, Joan Allen, Brian Cox, Dennis Farina, Stephen Lang, Tom Noonan, David Seaman.

● Mann hits top form with this splendidly stylish and oppressive thriller adapted from Thomas Harris' Red Dragon. The plot is complex and ingenious: FBI forensics expert Will Graham (Peterson), blessed (and tormented) by an ability to fathom the workings of the criminal mind through psychic empathy, is brought back from voluntary retirement to track down a serial killer, the 'Tooth Fairy'. Focused on the anxiety and confusion of the hunter rather than his psychotic prey, the film functions both as a disturbing examination of voyeurism, and as an often almost unbearably grim suspenser. Mann creates a terrifying menacing atmosphere without resorting to graphic depiction of the seriously nasty killings: music, designer-expressionist 'Scope photography, and an imaginative use of locations, combine with shots of the aftermath of the massacres to evoke a world nightmarishly perceived by Graham's haunted sensibility. The performances, too, are superior, most memorably Cox's intellectually brilliant and malevolent asylum inmate. One of the most impressive American thrillers of the late '80s. GA

Manhunt in Milan (La 'Mala' Ordina)

(1972, It/WGer, 92 min)
d Fernando Di Leo. *p* Lanfranco Ceccarelli. *sc* Fernando Di Leo, Augusto Finocchi, Ingo Hermes. *ph* Franco Villa. *ed* Amedeo Giomini. *ad* Francesco Cuppini. *m* Armando Trovaioli. *cast* Mario Adorf, Henry Silva, Woody Strode, Adolfo Celi, Luciana Paluzzi, Sylva Koscina, Cyril Cusack.

● Typically derivative Italian paranoid thriller about Mafia inter-gang feuding. A mishmash of formulary devices, decorated with the usual high ratio of lethal encounters, is perambulated around the statutory handful of 'thriller' locations: topless bar, hippie commune, boss' suite, prostitute-haunted roadside. The sole point of interest lies in the rise, some half way through, of one Luca Canalli, self-styled small-time pimp and Mafia stooge, to hero status. As played by Mario Adorf, Canalli is a character of literal bone-headedness – useful for smashing telephones, people and car windscreens – and patently soft-centred despite his profession. Adorf's two-dimensional performance gives the character a certain conviction; not enough to turn the film into a viable proposition, though. VG

Mania

see Flesh and the Fiends, The

Maniac Cop

(1988, US, 85 min)
d William Lustig. *p/sc* Larry Cohen. *ph* Vincent J Rabe. *ed* David Kern. *ad* Jonathan Hodges, Ann Cudworth. *m* Jay Chattaway. *cast* Tom Atkins, Bruce Campbell, Laurene Landon, Richard Roundtree, William Smith, Robert Z'Dar, Sheree North, Erik Holland, Jake La Motta, Sam Raimi.

● Had writer/producer Larry Cohen directed this low-budget thriller himself, it might have displayed more vitality and wit. As it is, despite abundant action and a start involving a fistful of murders, the overall effect is sluggish. There's a psycho killer in police colours terrorising New York. Detective McCrae (Atkins) reckons he's a member of the force, but his boss disagrees, until the wife of young officer Jack Forrest (Campbell) is found dead, leaving a diary and cuttings that implicate her faithless spouse. While Forrest and his policewoman girlfriend (Landon) struggle to establish his innonence, subplots snowball, peripheral characters proliferate, and the killings culminate in a none too imaginatively staged car chase. Only the odd line of dialogue and occasional bizarre detail hint at Cohen's quirky signature; performances and camerawork are solid enough, but both cutting and direction are formulary and flabby. EA

Maniac Cop 2

(1990, US, 88 min)
d William Lustig. p/sc Larry Cohen. ph James Lemmo. ed David Kern. pd Gene Abel. Charles Logola. m Jay Chattaway. cast Robert Davi, Claudia Christian, Michael Lerner, Bruce Campbell, Laurene Landon, Robert Z'Dar, Leo Rossi.

● Again scripted by Larry Cohen, this sequel is a lively if predictable romp, with unashamedly lowbrow ambitions and a budget to match. Returning from his watery grave to wreak further vengeance on the police force that stitched him up, zombiefied cop Matt Cordell (Z'Dar) teams up with serial killer Turkell (Rossi), a crazed degenerate on 'a crusade against the whores of the world'. Enter the sublimely acne-scarred Davi, stepping into Campbell's shoes (the star of the original is blown away after ten minutes) as substitute hero Lt McKinney, a gun-toting cynic who doesn't believe in the walking dead, psychiatrists, or guilt. Directed with workaday deftness by Lustig, who squeezes in a couple of rattlingly good car chases and some spectacular fiery special effects, the movie is notable mainly for the quirky black comedy of Cohen's script. Boasting some incredibly cheap gags about casually slaying traffic cops on parking patrol, this is bound to keep the exploitation cognoscenti more than happy. MK

Maniacs on Wheels

see Once a Jolly Swagman

Manic

(2001, US, 100 min)
d Jordan Melamed. *p* Trudi Callon, Kirk Hassig. *sc* Michael Bacall, Blayne Weaver. *ph* Nicholas Hay. *ed* Madeline Gavin, Gloria Rosa Vela. *pd* Carol Strober. *cast* Joseph Gordon-Levitt, Michael Bacall, Zooey Deschanel, Cody Lightning, Elden Henson, Sara Rivas, Don Cheadle.

● A teen *One Flew Over the Cuckoo's Nest* filmed like *The Idiots* (on DV, vérité-style), *Manic* confidently establishes its own tone and milieu through a calmly justified faith in its material. The setting is a juvenile psychiatric facility, a tentative, recreation centre limbo between the free world and permanent confinement – some inmates go one way, some the other. Most come with exaggerations of normal teen dysfunctions, typically revolving around a parent; Lyle (Gordon-Levitt) has anger and denial issues – he won't take responsibility for his violent outbursts. As their taxed warden and counsellor, Cheadle initially threatens to unbalance the film with his star baggage, but he gives a superlatively controlled, back-heel performance. The younger actors, too, really live their parts – it's an undemonstrative, vividly authentic film. NB

Manifesto

(1988, US, 96 min)
d Dusan Makavejev. *p* Menahem Golan, Yoram Globus. *sc* Dusan Makavejev. *ph* Tomislav Pinter. *ed* Tony Lawson. *pd* Viejko Despotovic. *m* Nicola Piovani. *cast* Camilla Soeberg, Alfred Molina, Simon Callow, Eric Stoltz, Lindsay Duncan, Rade Serbedzija.

● Makavejev's adaptation of a Zola short story has a vague period setting – Central Europe, 1920 – which augurs badly for the ensuing fuzziness of this self-conscious black comedy. Svetlana (pouting Danish discovery Soeberg) arrives in the village of Waldheim (well, one wonders…) with gun in garter ready for the assassination of the visiting King. Revolution may be in the air, but a lecherous police chief, a doting postman and an uptight schoolmistress all conspire to make her plans less well laid than her own person. Despite the presence of Molina, Stoltz and Duncan respectively in these roles, their various crazy performances render them both unrecognisable and oddly ineffective. There are glimpses of Makavejev's past exuberance, with dollops of wild sex and delicious photography, but the final impression is of a project too long delayed and heavily compromised. DT

Manila by Night (aka City After Dark)

(1980, Phil, 160 min)
d/sc Ishmael Bernal. *ph* Sergio Lobo. *cast* Charito Solis, Johnny Wilson, William Martinez, Rio Locsin, Bernardo Bernardo.

● Banned from export at the time by Imelda Marcos herself, this was Ishmael Bernal's masterpiece: a deeply truthful celebration of the night street-life he knew and loved in all its squalor, pain and joy. The characters are authentic flaming creatures (fags, dykes, bisexuals, hookers of all genders, dopers, plus assorted petty criminals), some played by big stars like Solis and Martinez, others by friends or bit-player favourites of Bernal's. There's no doubt that the fashions and lifestyles have dated, but it remains impressive for its honesty and candour, its daringly original structure, its Cassavetes-worthy improvisations and its complete lack of phoney compassion for its fraught and wasted characters. TR

Manila: In the Claws of Darkness (Maynila, sa mga Kuko ng Liwanag)

(1975, Phil, 125 min)
d Lino Brocka. *p* Severino Manotok Jr, Miguel de Leon. *sc* Clodualdo del Mundo Jr. *ph* Miguel de Leon. *ed* Edgardo Jarlego, Ike Jarlego Jr. *ad*

Socrates Topacio. *m* Max Jocson. *cast* Rafael Roco Jr, Hilda Koronel, Lou Salvador Jr, Lily Gamboa-Mendoza, Juling Bagabaldo.

●Gripped in the film's subtitular 'claws of darkness', country-boy Julio seeks his lost village sweetheart, lured to the big city by a procuress. Slitting the underbelly of Manila (Brocka's true protagonist), he moves through shanty towns, street markets, building sites, brothels, and cheap Chinese cafés, all throbbing with poisonous life: the sin and cynicism of poverty under President Marcos' regime, captured with a raw immediacy against which the golden, sun-splashed flashbacks of pastoral romance seem like the flimsiest of painted veils. SJo

Man I Love, The

(1946, US, 96 min, b/w)
d Raoul Walsh. *p* Arnold Albert. *sc* Catherine Turney, Jo Pagno. *ph* Sid Hickox. *ed* Owen Marks. *ad* Stanley Fleischer. *m* Max Steiner. *cast* Ida Lupino, Robert Alda, Bruce Bennett, Andrea King, Martha Vickers, Alan Hale, Dolores Moran, Warren Douglas, Don McGuire.

●At an after-hours session in a New York jazz club, resident singer Lupino joins in a heartfelt rendition of 'The Man I Love'. Homesick after an unhappy affair, she decides to visit her family in California: a married sister (King) and two younger siblings (Vickers, Douglas). All of them, not to mention the young married couple across the hall (Moran, McGuire), are either in or heading for trouble, mostly emotional, and much of it traceable to a lecherous night-club owner (Alda). Impulsively, driven by an awareness of her own bleak isolation, Lupino tries to help: with some success, but in the process getting snared in Alda's greasy clutches, while simultaneously grasping at the mirage of happiness with a former jazz pianist (Bennett) running away from an unhappy marriage and a burned-out talent. The dialogue is a mite pretentious at times, and the plot comes perilously close to soap at the end. But the performances are excellent, and Walsh's sympathetic direction, wonderfully flexible in negotiating the pin-ball effect as characters and problems interact, gives the whole thing the touching, kaleidoscopic flavour of a prototype Alan Rudolph movie. TM

Man I Married, The (aka I Married a Nazi)

(1940, US, 77 min, b/w)
d Irving Pichel. *p* Raymond Griffith. *sc* Oliver HP Garrett. *ph* Peverell Marley. *ed* Robert Simpson. *m* David Buttolph. *cast* Joan Bennett, Francis Lederer, Lloyd Nolan, Anna Sten, Otto Kruger, Maria Ouspenskaya.

●One of the movies that looks as though it was trying to prepare the American public for entry to the war in Europe, Fox's drama (from the novel *Swastika* by Oscar Shisgall) grafts a propaganda element on to a story of domestic discord. Bennett is the American wife left to battle for custody of her son when German husband Lederer's trip home winds him over to the Nazis and he decides to stay on. Although simplistic, the film's portrait of life under the Third Reich (where Czechs sweep the streets and beating drums whip up the crowds at public meetings) is unquestionably persuasive. TJ

Man in a Dream, A

see Homme qui Dort, Un

Man in Grey, The

(1943, GB, 116 min, b/w)
d Leslie Arliss. *p* Edward Black. *sc* Margaret Kennedy, Leslie Arliss. *ph* Arthur Crabtree. *ed* RE Dearing. *ad* Walter Murton. *m* Cedric Mallabey. *cast* Margaret Lockwood, Phyllis Calvert, James Mason, Stewart Granger, Harry Smith, Martita Hunt, Raymond Lovell.

●Mason was in fine caddish fettle for this Gainsborough bodice-ripper, a Regency romp (from Lady Eleanor Smith) chronicling the fortunes of old school chums Calvert and Lockwood, the latter eventually to seduce her pal's roguish husband, Mason's glacial Lord Rohan. The strangled vowels and heaving sighs play like the highest Cartland camp, but in its day this was raunchy stuff for the British screen. In fact, the low-cut dresses distressed the Americans so much, they asked for portions of the film to be reshot so they could get it past the censor.

Man in Love, A (Un Homme Amoureux)

(1987, Fr, 111 min)
d Diane Kurys. *p* Michel Seydoux, Diane Kurys. *sc* Diane Kurys, Olivier Schatzky. *ph* Bernard Zitzermann. *ed* Joële van Effenterre, Nathalie Le Guay, Michèle Robert, Valérie Longeville. *ad* Dean Tavoularis. *m* Georges Delerue. *cast* Peter Coyote, Greta Scacchi, Jamie Lee Curtis, Claudia Cardinale, Peter Riegert, John Berry, Vincent Lindon, Jean Pigozzi.

●Coyote plays an American film star, Steve Elliott, who falls for his young co-star (Scacchi) while in Rome to play the lead in a film about the writer Cesare Pavese. She, infatuated, walks out on her French fiancé, Elliott's suspicious wife (Curtis) threatens to turn up, the director throws tantrums, and Elliott's assistant (Riegert) engineers escape routes for his boss. It sounds farcical, but the opulent interiors, rousing score by Georges Delerue, and the embarrassment of unrestrained petting, give this tale of adultery a heavyweight romanticism it can't carry. The film (shot in English, incidentally) wins points on other scores: Riegert's wry detachment from the drama is wonderfully appropriate and often hilarious, and Pigozzi's bombastic director is perfect. EP

Man in My Life, The

see Homme de ma vie, L'

Man in the Glass Booth, The

(1975, US, 117 min)
d Arthur Hiller. *p* Ely Landau. *sc* Edward Anhalt. *ph* Sam Leavitt. *ed* David Bretherton. *pd* Joel Schiller. *cast* Maximilian Schell, Lois Nettleton, Luther Adler, Lawrence Pressman, Henry Brown.

●One of the unhappy 'American Film Theater' attempts to embalm theatrical performances. This version of Robert Shaw's play (from whose credits he requested his name be removed) works up a certain weight in its exploration of themes of guilt and forgiveness as a wealthy New York Jew is placed on trial, accused of being a former Nazi concentration camp commandant. But it still emerges as stagily verbose, with a self-indulgent performance from Schell. TM

Man in the Iron Mask, The

(1939, US, 110 min, b/w)
d James Whale. *p* Edward Small. *sc* George Bruce. *ph* Robert Planck. *ed* Grant Whytock. *ad* John DuCasse Schulze. *m* Lucien Moraweck. *cast* Louis Hayward, Joan Bennett, Warren William, Joseph Schildkraut, Alan Hale, Walter Kingsford, Bert Roach, Marion Martin, Albert Dekker, Peter Cushing.

●A stylish swashbuckler from the flamboyant James Whale, with Louis Hayward sharply distinguishing his twin roles, the tyrannical Louis XIV and his identical 'lost' brother. Warren William lends fine support as the fourth musketeer, D'Artagnan, and the film has a fine romantic arc to it, although it hasn't the bizarre wit of the director's most memorable pictures (except perhaps in the bizarre comeuppance that awaits the bad twin when he has to don the iron mask in his turn, and imagines himself strangling to death on his own ever-growing whiskers). TCh

Man in the Iron Mask, The

(1998, US, 132 min)
d Randall Wallace. *p* Randall Wallace, Russell Smith. *sc* Randall Wallace. *ph* Peter Suschitzky. *ed* William Hoy. *pd* Anthony Pratt. *m* Nick Glennie-Smith. *cast* Leonardo DiCaprio, Jeremy Irons, John Malkovich, Gérard Depardieu, Gabriel Byrne, Anne Parillaud, Judith Godrèche.

●The draw is fresh-faced DiCaprio in the dual role of the youthful despot Louis XIV and his wronged twin Phillippe, wearer of the cruel headgear. It then falls to older weightier thesps, Depardieu (Porthos), Irons (Aramis), Malkovich (Athos) and Byrne (D'Artagnan), to carry the action, as the standard ageing Musketeers. However, unable to impose any consistency of tone, writer/director Wallace (the scriptwriter of *Braveheart*) fails to reconcile the actors' diverse styles, leaving everyone costumed up but with no place to go. More comfortable with the emotional vulnerability of the imprisoned Phillippe than the vain cruelty of the tyrant monarch, DiCaprio again fails to convince as a worldly womanising adult. As the Musketeers who hatch a plot to replace the hated King with his identical twin, the others fare somewhat better. Only Depardieu, drunken and self-pitying, overplays his hand, his performance sliding into annoying farcical excess. NF

Man in the Moon, The

(1991, US, 99 min)
d Robert Mulligan. *p* Mark Rydell. *sc* Jenny Wingfield. *ph* Freddie Francis. *ed* Trudy Ship. *ad* Gene Callahan. *m* James Newton Howard. *cast* Sam Waterston, Tess Harper, Gail Strickland, Reese Witherspoon, Jason London, Emily Warfield, Bentley Mitchum.

●For this rites-of-passage drama, screenwriter Jenny Wingfield draws on personal recollections; but while she brings intelligence to the depiction of teen angst, her attempt to follow formula means that the heart-warming tone steadily becomes overheated. It's the late '50s, and 14-year-old Dani (Witherspoon) is on the verge of major discoveries about sex and family ties. There's a handsome new boy (London) in the neighbourhood who leaves both Dani and her older sister (Warfield) weak-kneed. As though uncertain of her material's quiet strengths, Wingfield resolves this tension and follows it up with a clichéd love scene, tear-jerking tragedy, and a chastening heart-to-heart on Dad's boat. More consistent are the fine performances which Mulligan draws from his cast: Harper as the level-headed mother, Waterston as the taciturn father, and Witherspoon in a striking debut. CM

Man in the Road, The

(1956, GB, 84 min, b/w)
d Lance Comfort. *p* Charles A Leeds. *sc* Guy Morgan. *ph* Stan Pavey. *ed* Jim Connock. *ad* Ray Simm. *m* Bruce Campbell. *cast* Derek Farr, Ella Raines, Donald Wolfit, Lisa Daniely, Karel Stepanek, Cyril Cusack.

●Cold War spy thriller with a stale storyline about communist agents trying to prise a secret formula from a brilliant amnesiac scientist (young writer Ella Raines to the rescue). Guy Morgan, who adapted the script from a popular novel of the day (Anthony Armstrong's *He Was Found in the Road*), was a former secretary of the British Screenwriters' Association and habitually complained about the lack of recognition screenwriters received. He protested too much, perhaps. GM

Man in the Silk Hat, The

see Homme au Chapeau de Soie, L'

Man in the Street, The (Sokaktaki Adam)

(1995, Tur, 89 min)
d Biket Ilhan. *cast* Metin Belgin, Suna Yildizoglu, Selda Özer.

●Sailing into Istanbul harbour, smuggling goods after a long sojourn away, come Yakub and Hasan. While Yakub's straight into the drinking dens and brothels, Hasan's losing control of the deal; except he hardly seems to care – he can't put away thoughts of Ayhan, his real love whom he abandoned here once before. There's an air of drunken melancholy about this film. At heart it seems to be a languorous dissertation on personal disquiet and disconsolation – there's some, slight sense of context (the dislocations of modern life and transient work, perhaps; every once in a while strangers stop as if in recognition of the camera, and regale us with observations, musings and wry remarks), but it makes little impression. Like a drunkard, Hasan seems governed by some foreign stimulus that we're not party to. NB

Man in the White Suit, The

(1951, GB, 85 min, b/w)
d Alexander Mackendrick. *p* Michael Balcon. *sc* Roger MacDougall, John Dighton, Alexander Mackendrick. *ph* Douglas Slocombe. *ed* Bernard Gribble. *ad* Jim Morahan. *m* Benjamin Frankel. *cast* Alec Guinness, Joan Greenwood, Cecil Parker, Michael Gough, Ernest Thesiger, Vida Hope, Howard Marion-Crawford, Patric Doonan.

●Certainly one of Guinness' best performances as the laboratory dishwasher in a textile mill who invents a fabric that never wears out and never gets dirty, thus incurring the wrath of both management and labour, satirically depicted as being hand-in-glove in their conservative reliance on restrictive practices. Typically, the Ealing formula for goodnatured whimsy prevents Mackendrick from pushing the darker aspects of the theme (eminently present in Thesiger's brooding old vulture of an industrialist) to their logical conclusion. But as David Thomson acutely observed, in a note about the extent to which the acid disenchantment of *Sweet Smell of Success* was already apparent in Mackendrick's earlier work, there is enough of Kafka in the film to lift it right out of the Ealing comedy tramlines. TM

Man in the Wilderness

(1971, US, 105 min)
d Richard C Sarafian. *p* Sanford Hopward. *sc* Jack DeWitt. *ph* Gerry Fisher. *ed* Geoffrey Foot. *pd* Dennis Lynton Clark. *m* Johnny Harris. *cast* Richard Harris, John Huston, Henry Wilcoxon, Percy Herbert, Dennis Waterman, Prunella Ransome, Norman Rossington.

● The team that had such a success with *A Man Called Horse* decided to try their luck again with this sensationalist bit of cod anthropology based on a true story. In the 1820s, the guide to a fur-trapping expedition in the great North West is left by his captain to die after being savaged by a grizzly. His desire for revenge is expiated after he faces the violence of nature and several gruelling Indian tribal rituals. Explicit, simplistic, and if you've seen *A Man Called Horse*, highly predictable. GA

Man Is a Woman (L'Homme est une femme comme les autres)

(1997, Fr, 100 min)
d Jean-Jacques Zilbermann. *p* Régine Conckier, Jean-Luc Ormières. *sc* Jean-Jacques Zilbermann, Gilles Taurand. *ph* Pierre Aïm. *ed* Monica Coleman. *ad* Valérie Grall, (NY) Stephen Beatrice. *cast* Antoine de Caunes, Elsa Zylberstein, Gad Elmaleh, Michel Aumont, Maurice Benichou, Judith Magre, Catherine Hiegel, Stéphane Metzger.

● The title is a reference to the Canadian novelist Robertson Davies' somewhat queer contention that every marriage involves a communion of four people – the man, the woman, plus the man in the woman and the woman in the man. Like, get outta here! Simon Eskenazy (de Caunes, unfamiliarly sober and bearded), an occasional clarinettist, might be a reasonably content gay man, but after his uncle offers him a grand inheritance to marry and propagate the family name, encouraged by his anxious mother, he decides to try his arm at a relationship with Rosalie (Zylberstein, ever reliable). She's an orthodox Jewish Klezmer singer, and saving herself for wedlock, but the way she takes a shine to his clarinet suggests this could yet make a marriage of inconvenience. The film's actually more concerned with the shifting sands of Simon's head and heart than with the physicalities of sexual incompatibility, which would be all very well if it weren't so muffed and muted. Director Zilbermann takes a relaxed, open approach to the material's possibilities, but no one manages to unearth any insights of note, and the result's pretty much a void. NB

Man Is Not a Bird (Covek nije Tica)

(1965, Yugo, 80 min, b/w)
d/sc Dusan Makavejev. *ph* Aleksandar Petkovic. *m* Petar Bergamo. *cast* Milena Dravic, Janez Vrhovec, Eva Ras, Stojan Arandelovic, Boris Dvornik.

● Makavejev's first feature is a delightful, typically eccentric concoction, centred very loosely indeed around a story about an engineer who visits a new town to assemble mining machinery. There his devotion to work fouls up his relationship with his beloved, while a fellow worker encounters problems when his wife discovers he has a mistress. A freewheeling kaleidoscope mixing comedy and social comment as it deals with both labour and sexual politics, not to mention many seemingly unrelated topics such as hypnotism and culture (there's a marvellous climactic scene with Beethoven performed in an enormous foundry while the heroine conjures her own ode to joy), it defies description but is extremely entertaining. GA

Man Is Ten Feet Tall, A

see Edge of the City

Mani sulla Città, Le (Hands Over the City)

(1963, It, 105 min, b/w)
d Francesco Rosi. *p* Lionello Santi. *sc* Francesco Rosi, Raffaele La Capria, Enzo Provenzale, Enzo Forcella. *ph* Gianni Di Venanzo. *ed* Mario Serandrei. *ad* Massimo Rosi. *m* Piero Piccioni. *cast* Rod Steiger, Guido Alberti, Carlo Fermariello, Salvo Randone, Dany Paris, Angelo D'Alessandro.

● Rosi on property development rackets and political manoeuvring in the Naples city council is every bit as tough and forthright as Rosi on Sicily (*Salvatore Giuliano*) and on oil diplomacy (*The Mattei Affair*). His film follows the irresistible rise of the speculator Nottola (Steiger, excellently cast) as he channels the public building programme on to his own land, shrugs off the collapse of a slum tenement in an area that needs redevelopment, and cold-bloodedly shifts the balance of power in the council to his own advantage. It's not only totally convincing as an analysis of civic corruption, but also one of the very few left wing movies that one can imagine actually reaching the mass audience it's aimed at. TR

Manitou, The

(1977, US, 105 min)
d/p William Girdler. *sc* William Girdler, Jon Cedar, Thomas Pope. *ph* Michel Hugo. *ed* Gene Ruggiero, Henry Asman. *pd* Walter Scott Herndon. *m* Lalo Schifrin. *cast* Tony Curtis, Michael Ansara, Susan Strasberg, Stella Stevens, Jon Cedar, Ann Sothern, Burgess Meredith, Paul Mantee, Jeanette Nolan.

● Burgess Meredith's splendid cameo of an eccentric anthropologist almost justifies the price of a seat for this *Exorcist* spin-off. The victim this time (Strasberg) develops a nasty lump on her neck which, growing at an astonishing rate, turns out to be the foetus of a 400-year-old medicine man. Medical science proves impotent, Indian magic a mere half-measure, requiring good old 'love' to weigh in on the final cosmic shootout. The special effects are superb, easy winners in an engaging inter-denominational free-for-all that blends Marvel Comics' Doctor Strange with Corman's *The Raven*. A successful excursion, spoiled only by the director's habit of plopping in postcard views of the Golden Gate Bridge instead of exteriors. (From a novel by Graham Masterton.) GD

Man Like Eva, A (Ein Mann wie Eva)

(1983, WGer, 89 min)
d Radu Gabrea. *p* Laurens Straub. *sc* Radu Gabrea, Laurens Straub. *ph* Horst Schier. *ed* Dragos-Emmanuel Witkowski. *ad* Herbert Buchenberger. *m* Loek Dikker. *cast* Eva Mattes, Lisa Kreuzer, Werner Stocker, Charles Régnier, Carola Regnier, Charly Muhamed Huber.

● That a woman plays the late German director Fassbinder is this film's trump card. For one thing, Mattes manages, miraculously, to look, talk and walk like the great man; for another, it lends the movie a psychosexual complexity that is highly suitable for dealing with Fassbinder's tortured bisexuality. Sexual power-games are the driving force behind both film and director as the Fassbinder figure's tormented jealousy and cruel whims play off friends, lovers, and actors against one another to disastrous effect. The movie's greatest strength is its manifest sincerity. You may not believe much of what happens here, but Fassbinder's life really was a chaotic can of worms, and this tells it like it was (though it is fiction, not documentary). No conventional biopic entertainment, it's a sad film about a sad man. GA

Man-Made Monster (aka The Electric Man)

(1941, US, 57 min, b/w)
d George Waggner. *sc* Joseph West. *ph* Woody Bredell. *ed* Arthur Hilton. *ad* Jack Otterson. *m* Charles Previn. *cast* Lionel Atwill, Lon Chaney Jr, Anne Nagel, Frank Albertson, Samuel S Hinds, William B Davidson, Ben Taggart.

● Minor but efficient little chiller, with Atwill doing his usual mad scientist bit and experimenting on the hapless Chaney who, after an accident, finds he is immune to electricity. Needless to say, things get nastily out of control as Chaney goes on the rampage. Nothing special, really, although Chaney (in his first horror movie) lends a touch of pathos to his role, and John Fulton's special effects are as good as ever. GA

Man Named John, A (E Venne un Uomo)

(1965, It, 90 min)
d Ermanno Olmi. *p* Vincenzo Labella. *sc* Vincenzo Labella, Ermanno Olmi. *ph* Piero Portalupi. *ed* Carla Colombo. *ad* Ennio Michettoni. *m* Franco Potenza. *cast* Rod Steiger, Adolfo Celi, Rita Bertocchi, Pietro Gelmi, Antonio Bertocchi.

● Not so much a biography of Angelo Roncalli as an attempt to evoke the aura of his life and the paths that led to his becoming the much-loved Pope John XXIII, Olmi's film uses Rod Steiger as a 'mediator'. Steiger, in other words, lends his presence as commentator, occasionally stands in for the Pope, gazes benignly at the small boy who represents the pontiff as a small boy. With Steiger reflecting a sort of conventional awe, it is perhaps small surprise that what emerges from this jigsaw portrait is pretty much a pious homage. Olmi's quirkish hand and eye as a film-maker are really evident only in the early sequences, shot in delicate colours almost like fairytale illustrations, which conjure the quaintly rustic surroundings in which the future Pope grew up. TM

Manneken Pis

(1994, Bel, 90 min)
d Frank Van Passel. *p* Dirk Impens. *sc* Frank Van Passel, Christophe Dirickx. *ph* Jan Vancaillie. *ed* Karin Vaerenberg. *pd* Johan Van Essche. *m* Noordcamp. *cast* Antje de Boeck, Frank Vercruyssen, Ann Petersen, Wim Opbrouck, Stany Crets.

● With its carefree blend of the off-beam and the everyday, this game Belgian first feature seems to tap the same vein of oddball whimsy mined by *Toto the Hero* and *The Sexual Life of the Belgians*. Sweet, bald, shy Harry is a humble dishwasher hiding a dark secret (his family were run over by a train while he was out of their car taking a leak), all of which makes him uncertain in his wooing of a comely Brussels tramdriver, whose elderly confidant pours scorn on the whole proceedings. Unafraid to switch from farce to grim foreboding in an instant, director Van Passel throws in a vibrant colour palette, but doesn't quite have the discipline to achieve the emotional impact intended. Refreshing, though. TJ

Mannequin

(1987, US, 90 min)
d Michael Gottlieb. *p* Art Levinson. *sc* Edward Rugoff, Michael Gottlieb. *ph* Tim Suhrstedt. *ed* Richard Halsey. *pd* Josan F Russo. *m* Sylvester Levay. *cast* Andrew McCarthy, Kim Cattrall, Estelle Getty, James Spader, GW Bailey, Carole Davis, Steve Vinovich.

● This pitifully unfunny comedy has only two things going for it: its theme song, Starship's 'Nothing's Gonna Stop Us Now', is a hit single; and it is short. Cattrall plays an Egyptian princess who, back in 2514 BC, is saved by the Gods from being married off to a dung-dealer, and turns up as a dummy in a Philadelphia department store window. McCarthy, a frustrated artist who had a hand in her fashioning, is enchanted to discover that she comes alive at night. In between dressing-up and undressing one another, the pair also dress a few of the ailing store's windows, thereby reviving its fortunes and thwarting the takeover plans of avaricious rivals. Incidental 'humour' is provided by a screaming gay black stereotype, a Rambo-fixated security guard and his cowardly bulldog, and McCarthy's jealous ex-girlfriend. A film about, by and for dummies. NF

Mannequin Two: On the Move (aka Mannequin on the Move)

(1991, US, 95 min)
d Stewart Raffill. *p* Edward Rugoff. *sc* Edward Rugoff, David Isaacs, Ken Levine, Betty Israel. *ph* Larry Pizer. *ed* Joan Chapman. *ad* Norman B Dodge Jr. *m* David McHugh. *cast* Kristy Swanson, William Ragsdale, Meshach Taylor, Terry Kiser, Stuart Pankin, Cynthia Harris, Andrew Hill Newman.

● This unwelcome sequel to *Mannequin* has neither the stars nor the director of the original. Only Taylor returns, reprising his offensive camp black stereotype. A thousand years ago in Hauptmann-Koenig, a prince's sweetheart is turned to wax by an evil enchanter (hooray!). Cut to the present: the girl awakens (boo!) in a department store, to be reunited with her inexplicably reincarnated lover. Young stars Swanson and Ragsdale are bland beyond belief, but worse still are the antics of the fiendish Count Spretzle's 'amusingly foreign' bodyguards. Raffill's heavy-handed direction is jam-packed with product placement, and interrupted every ten seconds with yet another plug for a boring MOR rock song. MK

Mann im Lift, Der

see Wild Games

Manny & Lo

(1996, US, 97 min)
d Lisa Krueger. *p* Dean Silvers. *sc* Lisa Krueger. *ph* Tom Krueger. *ed* Colleen Sharp. *pd* Sharon Lomofsky. *m* John Lurie. *cast* Mary Kay Place, Scarlett Johannson, Aleksa Palladino, Paul Guilfoyle, Glenn Fitzgerald, Cameron Boyd.

● After Mom dies, 11-year-old Manny is abducted by her 16-year-old sister Lo, an aggressively nihilist, petty criminal. They take off on a spree, ending up in a remote, deserted ski chalet. Trouble is, Lo's pregnant (though barely admits it), so they kidnap former nurse Elaine (Place), herself rather less stable than she first appears. This sweet if somewhat implausible first feature is a gentle, occasionally dark comedy-cum-coming-of-age drama, held together by strong interplay between the conflicting leads (Place is particularly good) and by a wry, pleasingly understated sense of humour. GA

Man of Africa

(1953, GB, 74 min)
d Cyril Frankel. *p* John Grierson. *sc* Montagu Slater. *ph* Denny Densham. *ed* Alvin Bailey. *m* Malcolm Arnold. *cast* Frederick Bijurenda, Violet Mukabureza, Mattayo Bukwirwa, Butensa, Seperiera Mpambara, Blaseo Mbalinda.

● A real oddity, shot by Frankel in deepest Uganda with an eight-man crew. Frequently revealing the shortcomings of the Flaherty/Grierson approach to fictionalised documentary, its story – about a tribe of Africans who resettle in pygmy country and face danger from malaria, elephants and internal strife – is thin, melodramatic and more than a little trite. But the film's curiosity value, plus the endearing grace and energy of the pygmies, make it worth a look. GA

Man of Aran

(1934, GB, 75 min, b/w)
d Robert Flaherty. *p* Michael Balcon. *sc* Robert Flaherty, Frances Flaherty, John Goldman. *ph* Robert Flaherty. *ed* John Goldman, John Monck. *m* John Greenwood. *cast* Colman King, Maggie Dirrane, Michael Dillane, Pat Mullen, Patch Ruadh.

● Flaherty was neither the documentary purist nor the victim of movie commerce that he has so often been called – more a talented exoticist. Here he quite happily places the Aran fishermen in a preconceived *mise en scène* of spartan struggle in order to arrive at his intended goal: images of stylised heroism. A film which remains – especially in its elemental images of sea and storm – mightily impressive. PT

Man of Flowers

(1983, Aust, 91 min)
d Paul Cox. *p* Jane Ballantyne, Paul Cox. *sc* Paul Cox. *ph* Yuri Sokol. *ed* Tim Lewis. *ad* Asher Bilu. *cast* Norman Kaye, Alyson Best, Chris Haywood, Sarah Walker, Julia Blake, Bob Ellis, Barry Dickins, Werner Herzog.

● A lonely, middle-aged art collector pays a young artist's model to ritually strip for his voyeuristic pleasure every week (to an aria from Donizetti's 'Lucia di Lammermoor'). Gradually he becomes unwillingly involved in her messy private life, and as his psychotherapy continues, we learn about the relationship of his fantasies to his obsession with his dead mother. Cox's film, handsome indeed for its modest budget, and not at all the dirty-old-man-buys-sex-object story the above suggests, is quite unlike any film to have emerged from Australia. Cox achieves a difficult balance between a quirkily individual sense of humour, and a more poignant, serious sense of purpose about the privacy of our fantasy lives and our essential loneliness, which is right on target. A genuine oddity. RM

Man of Iron

see Ferroviere, Il

Man of Iron (Czlowiek z Zelaza)

(1981, Pol, 152 min, b/w & col)
d Andrzej Wajda. *sc* Aleksander Scibor-Rylski. *ph* Edward Klosinski. *ed* Halina Prugar. *ad* Allan Starski. *m* Andrzej Korzynski. *cast* Jerzy Radziwilowicz, Krystyna Janda, Marian Opania, Irena Byrska, Wieslawa Kosmalska, Boguslaw Linda, Franciszek Trzeciak.

● Wajda's remarkable sequel to *Man of Marble* welds newsreel footage of the Solidarity strike to fiction in a strong investigative drama. A disillusioned, vodka-sodden radio producer is bundled off to Gdansk in a black limousine. His mission: to smear one of the main activists – who also happens to be the son of the hapless 'Marble' worker-hero. But, tempered by bitter experience of the failed reforms of '68 and '70, these new men of iron are more durable than their fathers, not as easily smashed. Media cynicism, censorship and corruption are again dominant themes, this time anchored through the TV coverage of the strike, though the conclusion hints with guarded optimism at a possible rapprochement between workers and intelligentsia. An urgent, nervy narrative conveys all the exhilaration and bewilderment of finding oneself on the very crestline of crucial historical change; and for the viewer, all the retrospective melancholy of knowing that euphoria shattered by subsequent events. SJo

Man of Marble (Czlowiek z Marmur)

(1976, Pol, 165 min, b/w & col)
d/p Andrzej Wajda. *sc* Aleksander Scibor-Rylski. *ph* Edward Klosinski. *ed* Halina Prugarowa. *pd* Allan Starski *m* Andrzej Korzynski. *cast* Jerzy Radziwilowicz, Krystyna Janda, Tadeusz Lomnicki, Jacek Lomnicki, Michael Tarkowski.

● A jaundiced regard for documentary practice pervades Wajda's slice of Polish history, which takes the form of an inquiry conducted by a young, aggressive film-school graduate into the fate, after reward, repudiation and rehabilitation, of a '50s Stakhanovite shock-worker, a record-breaking bricklayer. Film-as-evidence (monochrome flashbacks represent propagandist archive footage) is stripped of its authority just as inexorably as the investigative process meets an impasse at the point where preconceptions and actuality intersect. Wajda builds his own 'detection' story with complete assurance, though it's often difficult to decide whether his visual style is a parody of TV's (an ageing cameraman bemoans the constant use of hand-held shots and the wide-angle lens) or an accommodation of it. PT

Man of No Importance, A

(1994, GB/Ire, 99 min)
d Suri Krishnamma. *p* Jonathan Cavendish. *sc* Barry Devlin. *ph* Ashley Rowe. *ed* David Freeman. *ad* Frank Flood. *cast* Albert Finney, Brenda Fricker, Michael Gambon, Tara Fitzgerald, Rufus Sewell, Patrick Malahide, Anna Manahan, Michael Lally.

● A modest attempt at retelling the life of Oscar Wilde through the parallel experiences of a Dublin bus conductor. 1963: Alfie Byrne (Finney) enlivens the passengers on the Number 34 route by reciting poetry, but decides to stage Wilde's *Salome* after punching the ticket of a beautiful provincial girl, Adele (Fitzgerald). Alfie's sister (Fricker) senses matrimony in his new infatuation, though this is hardly likely as Alfie refers to his bus driver as 'Bosie' (Sewell), and diffidently frequents gay pubs. Soon the stage production is threatened by the local Queensberry in the form of a butcher (Gambon) outraged at being cast as Herod, and by Aubrey Beardsley's illustrations for the play. Rehearsals grind comically on while various hetero and homosexual revelations provoke a green carnation, an assault, a suicide attempt and a cautious, sexless entente. If the basic premise is far-fetched, the dialogue is often deftly literate. Finney is in fine form, but his accent is all over the place. BC

Man of the House

(1994, US, 97 min)
d James Orr. *p* Bonnie Bruckheimer, Marty Katrz. *sc* James Orr, Jim Cruickshank. *ph* Jamie Anderson. *ed* Harry Keramidas. *pd* Lawrence G Paull. *m* Mark Mancina. *cast* Chevy Chase, Farrah Fawcett, Jonathan Taylor Thomas, George Wendt, David Shiner, Art LaFleur.

● Excruciating Disney comedy in which Chase is a top DA and would-be step-dad to pubescent moppet Thomas. Junior doesn't want the newcomer disrupting the happy home he shares with artist mom Farrah Fawcett and a battle ensues to see just who's the real 'Man of the House'. On a YMCA programme father and son don Native American costumes to raindance together. Male bonding occurs. Come home, Herbie. TJ

Man of the Moment

(1955, GB, 88 min, b/w)
d John Paddy Carstairs. *p* Hugh Stewart. *sc* Vernon Sylvaine, John Paddy Carstairs. *ph* Jack Cox. *ed* John Shirley. *ad* Cedric Dawe. *m* Philip Green. *cast* Norman Wisdom, Lena Morris, Belinda Lee, Jerry Desmonde, Karel Stepanek.

● Foreign Office filing clerk Wisdom drops a washbasin on the head of one of the delegates to a Geneva conference and is forced to take his place. His unwitting efforts on behalf of a small island make him a major diplomatic figure and he is invited to visit the grateful islanders. Wisdom's cretinous humour is an acquired taste: fans speak highly of this one. NF

Man of the West

(1958, US, 100 min)
d Anthony Mann. *p* Walter Mirisch. *sc* Reginald Rose. *pd* Ernest Haller. *ed* Richard Heermance. *ad* Hilyard Brown. *m* Leigh Harline. *cast* Gary Cooper, Julie London, Lee J Cobb, Arthur O'Connell, Jack Lord, John Dehner, Royal Dano, Robert Wilke.

● A superb Western, exemplifying Mann's capacity for integrating his interest in spectacle with a resonant narrative fully deserving the adjective 'classic', in which Gary Cooper's ex-outlaw is under constant, ranting pressure from Cobb's gang-leader father-figure to return to the fold. The odyssey of Cooper (playing the emblematically named Link Jones) from pasture to desert to ghost town and back, and from settled present to tormented past and back, bridges the traditions of classical tragedy and classic Hollywood. Mann's synthesis of archetypal characters and generic iconography is seamless; and he manages to inscribe landscape, anxious voyeurism and fratricide within his narrative resolution. Textbook cinema, maybe, but Mann's work will remain rich for discovery and celebration. PT

Man of the Year

(1995, US, 86 min)
d Dirk Shafer. *p* Christian Moeyaert. *sc* Dirk Shafer. *ph* Stephen Timberlake. *ed* Barry Silver, Ken Solomon. *pd* Michael Mueller. *cast* Dirk Shafer, Vivian Paxton, Deidra Shafer, Michael Ornstein, Claudette Sutherland, Calvin Bartlett, Beth Broderick, Fabio, Mary Stein

● In 1992, Dirk Shafer was voted *Playgirl* magazine's man of the year. He was the incredible hunk, handsome, buff, built, yet sensitive and intelligent, sympathetic to the modern woman. Dirk worked *Playgirl* like he knew it was his big break, and *Playgirl* worked Dirk. They knew he was the best spokesman they could hope for. He manned the phone hotlines, and he did the TV talk show circuit. Only one problem. Dirk Shafer is, was and surely always will be…gay. A semi-documentary, this purports to be the work of film-makers who only stumble across Shafer's deception mid-shoot. This conceit doesn't come off: we never believe in the team behind the camera, let alone the eccentrics in front of it. The fake interviewees are fairly easy to spot, but the film gets the tone about right, touching lightly and wittily on issues of sexual orientation, pornography, 'outing' and popular self-deception. Dirk emerges as charming, naive and a little manipulative. He also wrote and directed this playful mea culpa. TCh

Manolito Four-Eyes (Manolita Gatofotas)

(1999, Sp, 85 min)
d Miguel Albaladejo. *p* Julio Fernández. *sc* Miguel Albaladejo, Elvira Lindo. *ph* Alfonso Sanz Aidúan. *ed* Pablo Blanco. *pd* Eduardo Cucatio. *m* Lucio Godoy. *cast* David Sánchez de Rey, Adriana Ozores, Roberto Alvarez, Antonio Gamero, Fedra Lorente, Marta Fernández Muro, Alejandro Martinez, David Martinez, Sergio del Pino, Laura Calabuig.

●Pitched as a family film, this light, winning comedy, set in the working class district of Madrid's Carabanchel Alto, traces the life of chubby, bespectacled primary school kid Manolo in the days before and during the summer holidays. Much of the gentle pathos and humour comes from the fact that events are viewed from the boy's quirky perspective – be they his travails with his kid brother ('the beast'), hanging with his gang of schoolmates, his spats with his time- and money-juggling mother, his phlegmatic grandpa or his all-too-often-absent but loving lorry-driver father. Part celebration of working class culture, part quirky comedy, part road movie, the able central performances and the film's evident affection, gentle charm and self-confidence make up for the occasional stray into sentimentality – not to mention the jolly/fairground umpa-pa-pa brass band score. WH

Man on a Tightrope

(1953, US, 105 min, b/w)
d Elia Kazan. *p* Robert L Jacks. *sc* Robert E Sherwood. *ph* Georg Kraus. *ed* Dorothy Spencer. *ad* Hans Kuhnert, Theo Zwirsky. *m* Franz Waxman. *cast* Fredric March, Gloria Grahame, Terry Moore, Cameron Mitchell, Adolphe Menjou, Richard Boone, Robert Beatty. Richard Boone.

●Cold War parable, decently acted and directed, but inevitably disappointing when compared to Kazan's other films of the era. There's no Brando or Dean to lift it above the ordinary – only Fredric March trying too hard to impress. The screenplay, by Robert E Sherwood from a story by Neil Paterson, concerns a struggling circus troupe in Communist Czechoslovakia who dream of escape to freedom in Austria. Apparently based on fact, but with little of the colour or energy of most big top tales. GM

Manon des Sources

(1986, Fr/It/Switz, 120 min)
d Claude Berri. *sc* Claude Berri, Gérard Brach. *ph* Bruno Nuytten. *ed* Geneviève Louveau, Hervé de Luze. *ad* Bernard Vézat. *m* Jean-Claude Petit. *cast* Yves Montand, Daniel Auteuil, Emmanuelle Béart, Hippolyte Girardot, Margarita Lozano, Elisabeth Depardieu, André Dupon.

●Essential viewing for anyone who enjoyed *Jean de Florette*. Ten years after Jean's death (in this continuation of Pagnol's novel *L'Eau des collines*), his 18-year-old daughter Manon (Béart) still haunts the hills overlooking the farm stolen from her father by the canny Soubeyran (Montand) and his dim-witted nephew Ugolin (Auteuil). Thousands of red carnations now flower there, but the Soubeyrans' blossoming fortunes are about to wither and die. Paradoxically, Ugolin has fallen in love with Manon, though his declarations fall on stony ground, leading in the end to tragedy. There is a satisfying symmetry to events, with Manon able to take her revenge on the Soubeyrans by stopping up the main village spring. However, in the final scenes, the film slides into a Hardyesque fatalism, with the loose ends tied up a little too neatly, resulting in an air of literary contrivance. It nevertheless succeeds, like the earlier film, in tapping the well-springs of one's emotions. NF

Man on Fire

(1987, Fr/It, 92 min)
d Elie Chouraqui. *p* Arnon Milchan. *sc* Elie Chouraqui. Sergio Donati. *ph* Gerry Fisher. *ed* Noëlle Boisson. *ad* Giantito Burchiellaro. *m* John Scott. *cast* Scott Glenn, Jade Malle, Joe Pesci, Brooke Adams, Jonathan Pryce, Paul Shenar, Danny Aiello, Laura Morante, Lou Castel.

●A thriller without a spark of imagination. As he is zipped into a body-bag, ex-CIA agent Creasy (Glenn) recalls how he was hired to babysit Sam (Malle), 12-year-old daughter of an Italian businessman. Sam's a cute kid, but she reminds him (in slo-mo flashback) of a dead child in war-torn Beirut. So he wants out, but things pick up when she compares him with Lenny in Steinbeck's *Of Mice and Men*, then serenades him with 'Someone to Watch Over Me'. Of course she gets kidnapped by reptilian criminals anyway; but with a subtlety typical of the film, he crashes a cement-mixer into the kidnappers' hideout and dies – or does he? – in his rescue bid. Borrowing wholesale from Scorsese, this inept thriller adds insult to injury with a risible voice-over, a sickly soundtrack, atrocious dubbing (though 'filmed in English'), and corny freeze frames. NF

Man on the Flying Trapeze, The

(1935, US, 65 min, b/w)
d Clyde Bruckman. *p* William Le Baron. *sc* Ray Harris, Sam Hardy, Jack Cunningham, Bobby Vernon. *story* Charles Bogle [WC Fields]. *ph* Alfred Gilks. *ed* Richard Currier. *cast* WC Fields, Mary Brian, Kathleen Howard, Grady Sutton, Vera Lewis, Carlotta Monti, Walter Brennan, Tor Johnson.

●A rich example of middle period Fields, when his films were squarely centred on the nightmare of American small town life and all the jokes had an extra edge. Fields' Ambrose Wolfinger suffers a termagant wife, a rude mother-in-law, her sponging son, and a job where he hasn't had any time off in 25 years. His only blessings are a very lovely daughter and a stock of applejack in the cellar. Director Clyde Bruckman worked on *The General*, but don't expect any cool control: it's just the usual helter-skelter style of all unpretentious comedies, with the kind of blatant back projection that only adds to the fun. GB

Man on the Moon

(1999, US, 119 min)
d Milos Forman. *p* Danny DeVito, Michael Shamberg, Stacey Sher. *sc* Scott Alexander, Larry Karaszewski. *ph* Anastas Michos. *ed* Christopher Tellefsen, Lynzee Klingman. *pd* Patrizia von Brandenstein. *m* REM. *cast* Jim Carrey, Danny DeVito, Courtney Love, Paul Giamatti, Tony Clifton, Vincent Schiavelli, Peter Bonerz, Jerry Lawler, Gerry Becker.

●In Britain, Andy Kaufman is best remembered as Latka in TV's *Taxi*. In the US, however, he won a controversial cult reputation as a genuinely bizarre stand-up/TV comedian. Carrey was the obvious choice to play a weirdo who never let his mask slip. As we're taken from Kaufman's early days playing a foreign simpleton and impersonating Elvis, to fame and infamy as a brazenly offensive wrestler of women, Carrey dons one persona after another while at the same time hinting that there may be a real Andy beneath the mimicry and mayhem. It's no more than a hint, however: at the close, one suspects that he remained as much an enigma for the film-makers as for us. That said, his plentifully recreated routines are mostly very funny, and the script wisely wrongfoots us as a regular ploy. Like Kaufman's manager (DeVito), his girl (Love), his partner in crime (Giamatti) and his public, we're constantly kept guessing as to what's real or false. Intriguing. GA

Man on the Roof, The (Mannen på Taket)

(1976, Swe, 113 min)
d Bo Widerberg. *p* Per Berglund. *sc* Bo Widerberg. *ph* Odd Geir Saether, Per Källberg, Lars-Åke Palén, Hans Welin. *ed* Sylvia Ingemarsson, Bo Widerberg. *ad* Alf Axén. *m* Björn J Lindh. *cast* Carl Gustaf Lindstedt, Gunnel Wadner, Håkan Serner, Sven Wollter, Eva Remaeus, Thomas Hellberg.

●A Swedish box-office hit, and a far cry from Widerberg's earlier *Adalen '31*: the lyrical feeling for landscape is replaced by the occasional aerial view of downtown Stockholm, and the visionary socialism by some trite sociologising. Based on a novel by Sjöwall and Wahlöö, it starts tough with a police inspector disembowelled in his hospital bed. But it swiftly undercuts its own suspense, with lengthy sections illustrating the equal tedium of police routine and cops' domestic lives. The idea of corruption on the force is evidently a shocking novelty in Sweden: the film is so busy explaining what turns a loyal civil servant into a psychopathic sniper that it's left without a villain. Keeping the killer's face off-camera causes more irritation than suspense. The few tense moments – like the helicopter lurching into a busy street – just aren't enough to make a thriller. JD

Manpower

(1941, US, 103 min, b/w)
d Raoul Walsh. *p* Hal Wallis.*sc* Richard Macaulay, Jerry Wald. *ph* Ernest Haller. *ed* Ralph Dawson. *ad* Max Parker. *m* Adolph Deutsch. *cast* Marlene Dietrich, Edward G Robinson, George Raft, Alan Hale, Walter Catlett, Eve Arden, Frank McHugh, Barton MacLane, Ward Bond.

●An overheated, *noir*-ish melodrama about a sexual triangle: stolid power-line worker Robinson has plucked Marlene Dietrich from a dance-hall dive and married her, but his sexier fellow-worker Raft fools around with her. The conflict naturally comes to a head on the power lines during a thunderstorm. This is the only American movie that doesn't label Dietrich as a foreigner, but its overall 'Frailty, thy name is woman' tone preserves her status as an object to be feared. TR

Man's Best Friend

(1993, US, 87 min)
d John Lafia. *p* Bob Engelman. *sc* John Lafia. *ph* Mark Irwin. *ed* Michael N Knue, Nancy Frazen. *pd* Jaymes Hinkle. *m* Joel Goldsmith. *cast* Ally Sheedy, Lance Henriksen, Robert Costanzo, John Cassini, Fredric Lehne.

●Mad scientist Henriksen transforms a cuddly Tibetan mastiff into MAX 3000, a genetically engineered 'psycho mutt' that can only be controlled with stabilising drugs. When scoop-seeking TV reporter Sheedy and her camerawomen break into the EMAX lab and escape with the pooch, the time bomb starts ticking. The police have no leads (ho ho), MAX is headed for a 'psychotic episode', and paperboys, mailmen and neighbourhood moggies are on the menu. Swerving arbitrarily from cute dog stuff that should carry an adult health warning to toned-down gore scenes that fail to deliver the necessary slavering savagery, this mongrel project lacks a pure horror pedigree. So by the time the genetically hybrid MAX starts camouflaging himself as a pile of garage junk, or scaling buildings with the agility of a gravity-defying leopard, you too may be climbing the walls. Hard to credit. NF

Man's Castle

(1933, US, 80 min, b/w)
d Frank Borzage. *sc* Jo Swerling. *ph* Joseph August. *ed* Viola Lawrence. *m* Frank Harling. *cast* Spencer Tracy, Loretta Young, Marjorie Rambeau, Arthur Hohl, Glenda Farrell, Walter Connolly.

●Borzage was responsible for some of the oddest Hollywood films of the '30s, and few can be more bizarre than *Man's Castle*, a heated Depression melodrama (from a play by Lawrence Hazard) with Tracy and Young as a pair of incurably optimistic lovers attempting to set up house together in shantytown. Their amoral romantic passion for each other is sufficient in Borzage's eyes to justify theft, even murder. The film ends with one of the director's most poetic images: the couple lying in each other's arms in a boxcar, she still in her wedding-dress. RM

Man's Favorite Sport?

(1963, US, 120 min)
d/p Howard Hawks. *sc* John Fenton Murray, Steve McNeil. *ph* Russell Harlan. *ed* Stuart Gilmore. *ad* Alexander Golitzen, Tambi Larsen. *m* Henry Mancini. *cast* Rock Hudson, Paula Prentiss, Maria Perschy, John McGiver, Charlene Holt, Roscoe Karns, Norman Alden, Regis Toomey.

●Dismissed by Robin Wood in his monograph on Hawks as 'tired' but championed by the French, *Man's Favorite Sport?* is in many ways the quintessential Hollywood auteur movie. Seen in isolation from the rest of Hawks' work, it seems to be merely an out-of-time slapstick comedy. Seen in context, it effortlessly demonstrates the auteur's ability to stamp his artistic identity on anything – in this case, the travails of an armchair expert (Hudson) forced to enter a fishing contest and confronted with a typically Hawksian superior woman (Prentiss). A marvellous film. PH

Mansfield Park

(1999, US/GB, 112 min)
d Patricia Rozema. *p* Sarah Curtis. *sc* Patricia Rozema. *ph* Michael Coulter. *ed* Martin Walsh. *pd* Christopher Hobbs. *m* Lesley Barber. *cast* Embeth Davidtz, Jonny Lee Miller, Alessandro Nivola, Frances O'Connor, Harold Pinter, Lindsay Duncan, Sheila Gish, Victoria Hamilton, James Purefoy, Justine Waddell.

●Rozema's fresh spin on Austen's most 'difficult' novel is not only her finest film to date, but one of the most ambitious – and successful – literary classic adaptations in recent memory. With the self-righteousness at the heart of Austen's heroine excised, Fanny Price becomes a bashful, even self-doubting figure, sidelined in the Bertram household by her lowly social status and her 'infallible judgment in matters of the heart', which consigns her to an indefinite spell in solitary before (perhaps) she finds her own happiness. The film riffs on the theme of moral rectitude and compromise, suggesting the rash, selfish or misguided actions which lead the other characters – often comically flawed, but never villainous – to fall from grace, and more generally the colonial crimes on which this 19th century gentility subsists. Delectably performed by a perfect cast, and beautifully measured by Rozema, whose light, fluid touch conveys the story along on a nod and a wink. NB

Man's Hope

see Espoir

Mansion of the Doomed (aka The Terror of Dr Chaney)

(1975, US, 89 min)
d Michael Pataki. *p* Charles Band. *sc* Frank Ray Perilli. *ph* Andrew Davis. *ed* Harry Keramidas. *ad* Roger Pancake. *m* Robert O Ragland. *cast* Richard Basehart, Trish Stewart, Gloria Grahame, Lance Henrikson, Al Ferrara, Jo Jo D'Amore, Vic Tayback.

● Hand a Franju-esque plot to an American Exploitation film maker, and you have to be prepared for pretty dire consequences. It's a pleasant surprise, therefore, to find that this rehash of *Les Yeux sans Visage* is a modest gem of pulp horror. Casting helps tremendously: Basehart is the eminent eye surgeon whose daughter loses her sight when his car crashes; Grahame the devoted assistant who helps him kidnap victims for transplant purposes, and acts as keeper to the unfortunates caged in the cellar, robbed blind. Pataki's direction has the courage of the script's grisly convictions, and he turns in a strong shocker, its relentless assault on the eyes aided by video close-ups of ocular surgery and some excellent make-up work. It's good to see an example of the genre without apocalyptic pretensions, and which doesn't feel the insecure need to send itself up. PT

Mansion of the Ghost Cat, The (Borei Kaibyo Yashiki)

(1958, Jap, 67 min, b/w & col)
d Nobuo Nakagawa. *p* Mitsugu Okura, Tatsuyoshi Shimamura. *sc* Yoshihiro Ishikawa, Jiro Fujishima. *ph* Tadashi Nishimoto. *ed* Toshio Goto. *ad* Hiroyasu Kurosawa. *m* Michiaki Watanabe. *cast* Toshio Hosokawa, Yuriko Ejima, Keinosuke Wada, Noriko Kitazawa, Ryuzaburo Nakamura, Shin Shibata, Fujie Satsuki.

● This *bakeneko-mono* (ghost-cat story) is one of the B-features that built the Nakagawa cult. Present day scenes in monochrome (a doctor takes his ailing wife to her Kyushu hometown for a rest cure; they rent Spiraea Mansion, where the wife is terrorised by a vengeful spook) frame a long flashback in colour to the Edo period, when the mansion was home to the clan warden Shogen (Shibata, giving the most outré performance). It turns out that Shogen killed his *go* teacher in a fit of rage and subsequently raped the man's blind mother. Before killing herself, the mother charged her beloved cat with avenging them both, creating a demonic hag with cat's ears to claw Shogen and his descendants into their graves. More amusing than scary, but it has some fine macabre touches and the 'Scope framing is lively. TR

Man's Neck, A

see Tête d'un Homme, La

Manson

(1972, US, 93 min)
d/p Robert Hendrickson, Laurence Merrick. *sc* Joan Huntington. *ph* Leo Rivers, Mike Thomas, Marvin Haskell, Joanne Wasserman, George Ryder, Norman Garmes, Margaret Kline, David Smythe-Richard. Henri Russell. *ed* Clancy Syrko. *ad* Michael Roberts. *m* Paul Watkins, Brooks Poston. *with* Charles Manson, members of his 'Family', DA Vincent Bugliosi. *narrator* Jess Pearson.

● This documentary compilation stretches a little material an awful long way (it's padded out with 'lyrical' song sequences and redundant multi-screen opticals), but it does include all the extant footage of Manson himself, and some fairly lengthy interviews with those members of the 'Family' who weren't arrested for the Sharon Tate/La Bianca killings. The approach of the reporting is earnestly middlebrow; the commentary is tendentious when it takes statements at face value (like Squeaky Fromm's bland assertion that she was influenced by TV violence), but it's thankfully never sensational. In truth, the material adds up to nothing very much, but it's undeniably discomforting to see acid-scarred hippies insisting on their continuing reverence for Manson, or discussing the experience of having a lover blow out his brains at the moment of climax as if it were nothing out of the ordinary. Many people won't need to see the film to come to terms with the fact of Manson's 'philosophy', and the compilers do very little to compel attention; a fictional treatment of the subject like Barry Shear's *The Todd Killings* works out a good deal more provocative and suggestive. TR

Man to Respect, A (Un Uomo da Rispettare/ aka The Master Touch)

(1972, It/WGer, 108 min)
d Michele Lupo. *p* Marina Cicogna. *sc* Mino Roli. *ph* Tonino Delli Colli. *ed* Tony Zila. *ad* Francesco Bronzi. *m* Ennio Morricone. *cast* Kirk Douglas, Giuliano Gemma, Florinda Bolkan, Reinhard Kolldehoff, Wolfgang Preiss, Romano Puppo.

● The old story of the professional thief pulling the ultimate job before getting out for good. The cast act like robots, and look as if they've been told to speak with their mouths shut to make dubbing easier. Underneath all the mechanics and violence lurks a shred of human feeling: Douglas' wife, understandably aggrieved by his behaviour, double-crosses him at the end, but it's the only human gesture in the whole film.

Man Trouble

(1992, US, 100 min)
d Bob Rafelson. *p* Bruce Gilbert, Carole Eastman. *sc* Carole Eastman. *ph* Stephen H Burum. *ed* William Steinkamp. *pd* Mel Bourne. *m* Georges Delerue. *cast* Jack Nicholson, Ellen Barkin, Harry Dean Stanton, Beverly D'Angelo, Michael McKean, Saul Rubinek, Viveka Davis, Veronica Cartwright, David Clennon, John Kapelos, Lauren Tom, Paul Mazursky.

● The last time Nicholson appeared in a film written by Carole Eastman and directed by Rafelson, the result was one of the definitive pictures of the early '70s, *Five Easy Pieces*. Here Nicholson is Harry Bliss, proprietor of the 'House of Bliss' guard-dog agency. A scuzzy charmer down on his luck, Harry isn't about to let a rich, beautiful and vulnerable client like Joan Spruance (Barkin) slip away from him. Her sister Andy (D'Angelo) owns the luxury mansion in the Hollywood hills, but she's been kidnapped by her boyfriend, one of the most powerful men in America (Dean Stanton); so Joan is all alone, and someone is trying to kill her. The trouble is, the film never seems to know where it's headed. Not quite a romance, a thriller or a comedy, it's a movie with an on-going identity crisis. Barkin, playing against type, produces a shrill caricature of femininity, while Rafelson indulges Nicholson's familiar soft-spoken laxity, another of his personable rogues. TCh

Manuela (aka Stowaway Girl)

(1957, GB, 95 min, b/w)
d Guy Hamilton. *p* Ivan Foxwell. *sc* William Woods, Guy Hamilton, Ivan Foxwell. *ph* Otto Heller. *ed* Alan Osbiston. *ad* John Hopwell. *m* William Alwyn. *cast* Trevor Howard, Elsa Martinelli, Pedro Armendariz, Donald Pleasence, Warren Mitchell, Jack McGowran.

● From the opening scene of ribaldry over a dead shipmate's coffin to the brutally off-hand dismissal of easement and affection at the end, this may prove too bleak a prospect for many temperaments. That such a despairing work emerged from where and when it did is one of the minor wonders of the cinema. The setting is a ramshackle freighter hauling cheap cargo around the Med, Howard the washed-up captain with a crew of averagely vicious malcontents, and Martinelli the fugitive teenager with whom Howard doesn't find love and redemption, though such is on offer. The treatment of religion as a silly nuisance is likewise unexpected, though adding to the general impression of hopelessness. The closing dialogue might have become one of the standard quotes of the movies, had not the tone of pervasive bitterness consigned the film to an isolation almost as complete as that of its hero. BBa

Manufacturing Consent: Noam Chomsky and the Media

(1992, Can, 165 min)
d Peter Wintonick, Mark Achbar. *p* Peter Wintonick, Mark Achbar, Adam Symansky. *ph* Mark Achbar, Francis Miquet, Barry Perles. *ed* Peter Wintonick. *m* Carl Schultz. *with* Noam Chomsky, Karl Meyers, William F Buckley, Tom Wolfe.

● The natural audience for this long but thoroughly engrossing documentary is North America, since it was made to give Chomsky and his radical ideas the kind of profile the US press and broadcast media routinely deny him. None the less, this is useful as an introduction to the man himself (his Depression childhood, his rise in linguistics, his radical activism) and even more valuable as an anthology of his political campaigns and major debating skirmishes. The film-makers avoid a 'voice-of-authority' commentary, allowing cutting and juxtapositions to carry the arguments and dialectics forward. More's the pity, then, that they sometimes fall back on tabloid-style gimmickry to get points across, none of which is necessary to bolster Chomsky's largely incontrovertible arguments. A decent, civilised piece of work. TR

Ma Nuit chez Maud

see My Night with Maud

Man Upstairs, The

(1958, GB, 88 min, b/w)
d Don Chaffey. *p* Robert Dunbar. *sc* Alun Falconer. *ph* Gerald Gibbs. *ed* John Trumper. *ad* William Kellner. *cast* Richard Attenborough, Bernard Lee, Donald Houston, Dorothy Alison, Kenneth Griffith, Patricia Jessel, Maureen Connell, Virginia Maskell.

● Attenborough as the quiet lodger who blows his cork, shoves a policeman down the stairs, and barricades himself into his room at the top. Very obviously a second-hand variation on *Le Jour se lève* but quite grippingly done, although Alun Falconer's script tends to run to stereotype in trying to extract significance from the reactions of police, welfare officer, and other tenants. The resolution, brought about by a sympathetic young mother (Alison), is dismayingly inadequate, to say the least. TM

Man Vanishes, A (Ningen Johatsu)

(1967, Jap, 130 min, b/w)
d Shohei Imamura. *ph* Kenji Ishiguro. *ed* Kunio Takeshige. *pd* Ichiro Takada. *cast* Yoshie Hayakawa. Shigeru Tsuyuguchi, Shohei Imamura.

● 'Please understand this is pure drama, a fictitious story.' Imamura's first 'documentary', an investigation (initially) of the social phenomenon of *'Johatsu'* – the disappearance of thousands of people in Japan every year – approached via a collaboration between the film-makers and one such missing man's abandoned fiancée. But their search gradually dissipates in the face of both the woman's own transference of interest to one of the crew, and the seemingly irreconcilable truths of conflicting witnesses. Eventually, the film grinds to a halt, turning in ever narrower circles of doubtfulness. The tone is scrupulously academic, with Imamura's cool anthropological eye skating over the woman's own story and the logistics of the search. By the time the director intervenes to demand our suspension of belief, we're left with only a disenchanted and a rather outdated essay in self-deconstruction. NB

Man Who Broke the Bank at Monte Carlo, The

(1935, US, 66 min, b/w)
d Stephen Roberts. *sc* Howard Ellis Smith, Nunnally Johnson. *ph* Ernest Palmer. *songs* Bert Kalmar, Harry Ruby. *cast* Ronald Colman, Joan Bennett, Colin Clive, Nigel Bruce, Montagu Love, Frank Reicher, Ferdinand Gottschalk.

●Brisk romantic comedy, co-scripted by Nunnally Johnson, with the debonair Colman as a White Russian aristocrat: at first, he earns his daily bread as a cabbie, but then strikes lucky on the Riviera gaming tables. Bennett's the vamp assigned to lure him back to the casino and make sure he loses what he's just won. GM

Man Who Came to Dinner, The

(1941, US, 116 min, b/w)
d William Keighley. *p* Hal Hallis. *sc* Julius J Epstein, Philip G Epstein. *ph* Tony Gaudio. *ed* Jack Kilifer. *ad* Robert Haas. *m* Frederick Hollander. *cast* Monty Woolley, Bette Davis, Ann Sheridan, Billie Burke, Jimmy Durante, Reginald Gardiner, Grant Mitchell, Mary Wickes.

●Scripted by Julius and Philip Epstein from Kaufman and Hart's play, a delightful comedy about a radio host (Woolley) and his chaotic sojourn, after accidental injury while on a lecture tour, at the suburban home of Billie Burke and family (who are expected to wait on him hand and foot while suffering a stream of insults). Based loosely on the character of theatre critic Alexander Woollcott, and thus peppered with caricatures of stage celebrities like Noël Coward (Gardiner), Harpo Marx (Durante) and Ann Sheridan's voracious actress (Gertrude Lawrence? Tallulah?), it's rather unimaginatively directed, but the performers savour the sharp, sparklingly cynical dialogue with glee. GA

Man Who Changed His Mind, The (aka The Man Who Lived Again)

(1936, GB, 70 min, b/w)
d Robert Stevenson. *p* Michael Balcon. *sc* L DuGarde Peach, Sidney Gilliat, John L Balderston. *ph* Jack Cox. *ed* RE Dearing, Alfred Roome. *ad* Alex Vetchinsky. *m* Louis Levy. *cast* Boris Karloff, Anna Lee, John Loder, Frank Cellier, Donald Calthrop, Cecil Parker, Lyn Harding.

●Stevenson's career followed exactly the same trajectory as that of Alfred Hitchcock – he was discovered by Michael Balcon, feted at home and then lured off to Hollywood by David O Selznick. (He went on to direct *Mary Poppins* and *The Love Bug*.) In the '30s, he was considered one of the most promising British talents around. This risible horror pic (co-scripted by Sidney Gilliat) does little to explain why. It's a far-fetched yarn about a scientist with an unlikely ability to transplant brains from one body to another. Stiff performances and creaking dialogue. GM

Man Who Could Work Miracles, The

(1936, GB, 82 min, b/w)
d Lothar Mendes. *p* Alexander Korda. *sc* HG Wells, Lajos Biro. *ph* Harold Rosson. *ed* Philip Charlot. *ad* Vincent Korda. *m* Mischa Spoliansky. *cast* Roland Young, Ralph Richardson, Ernest Thesiger, Joan Gardner, Edward Chapman, Sophie Stewart, George Zucco, George Sanders, Joan Hickson.

●Less well known than the other Korda/HG Wells collaboration *Things to Come*, this stands the test of time far better. Alexander Korda's anglophilia allows an endearing seriousness to settle round Wells' now clichéd visions, and the film's cosy view of the world doesn't entirely conceal a coldly pragmatic estimation of man's limitations. Roland Young, as a Mr Polly-like shop assistant, the unwitting guinea-pig in a divine experiment, succeeds marvellously in conveying the power-lust of the meek and righteous, and the wooden performances of the rest of the cast fail to rob the film of its resonance and charm. Certainly it's pedantic and disjointed, but its concerns for world peace, and meditations on the dangers and attractions of absolute power, make it a moving epitaph for Baldwin's Britain. RMy

Man Who Cried, The

(2000, GB/Fr/US, 100 min)
d Sally Potter. *p* Christopher Sheppard. *sc* Sally Potter. *ph* Sacha Vierny. *ed* Hervé Schneid. *pd* Carlos Conti. *m* Osvaldo Golijov. *cast* Christina Ricci, Cate Blanchett, John Turturro, Johnny Depp, Harry Dean Stanton, Miriam Karlin, Don Fellows.

●Potter comes unstuck with this misbegotten romance charting a Jewish girl's journey from Russian oppression, through schooling in England, to arrival in Paris as a dancer just in time to greet Hitler's armies. Yet for all her totalitarian encounters, English schools seem to be the most perfidious of these traumas. Potter adopts a heightened melodramatic language for her own ends, but the movie comes off as patronising kitsch, with a plodding chronological narrative and caricatures instead of characters. Among a clutch of miscast stars, Turturro probably gets the worst of it as an arrogant Italian opera singer, and Depp wisely keeps his trap shut as the soulful gypsy who rides his horse down the Champs-Elysées. At least the musical score has a degree of sophistication. TCh

Man Who Died Twice, The

see Silencieux, Le

Man Who Drove with Mandela, The

(1998, US/GB/SAf/Neth/Bel, 82 min)
d Greta Schiller. *p* Greta Schiller, Mark Gevisser, (One Man Show sequence) Simon Allen. *sc* Mark Gevisser. *ph* Michelle J Crenshaw, (One Man Show sequence) Tania Hoser. *ed* Prisca Swan. *pd* (One Man Show sequence) Sheba Phombeah. *m* Philip Miller. *cast* (One Man Show sequence) Corin Redgrave, (documentary sequence) Joseph Bale, Gavin Hayward, Robert Tsiesi, Ashley Brownlee, Adnaan Bassier. *with* Walter Sisulu.

●A documentary tribute to Cecil Williams, a leading theatre director in South Africa in 1950s and '60s who was also powerfully committed to the ANC. The fact that he was also gay may be a factor in the ANC's enlightened policies towards homosexuality. Schiller (who made *Before Stonewall*) combines archive news footage with interview testimony, and casts Redgrave as Williams, wandering a stage set recollecting his life and times. There's not a great deal of Mandela here, but it's a revealing record of wider social attitudes to race and sexuality in post-WWII South Africa. TCh

Man Who Fell to Earth, The 100

(1976, US, 138 min)
d Nicolas Roeg. *p* Michael Deeley, Barry Spikings. *sc* Paul Mayersberg. *ph* Anthony B Richmond. *ed* Graeme Clifford. *ad* Brian Eatwell. *cast* David Bowie, Rip Torn, Candy Clark, Buck Henry, Bernie Casey, Jackson D Kane.

●Roeg's hugely ambitious and imaginative film transforms a straightforward science fiction story (novel, Walter Tevis) into a rich kaleidoscope of contemporary America. Newton (Bowie), an alien whose understanding of the world comes from monitoring TV stations, arrives on earth, builds the largest corporate empire in the States to further his mission, but becomes increasingly frustrated by human emotions. What follows is as much a love story as sci-fi: like other films of Roeg's, this explores private and public behaviour. Newton/Bowie becomes involved in an almost pulp-like romance with Candy Clark, played out to the hits of middle America, that culminates with his 'fall' from innocence. Roeg, often using a dazzling technical skill, jettisons narrative in favour of thematic juxtapositions, working best when exploring the clichés of social and cultural ritual. Less successful is the 'explicit' sex Roeg now seems obliged to offer; but visually a treat throughout. CPe

Man Who Had His Hair Cut Short, The (De Man die Zijn Haar Kort Liet Knippen)

(1966, Bel, 94 min, b/w)
d André Delvaux. *sc* Anna de Pagter, André Delvaux. *ph* Ghislain Cloquet. *ed* Suzanne Baron. *ad* Jean-Claude Maes. *m* Frédéric Devreese. *cast* Senne Rouffaer, Beata Tyszkiewicz, Hector Camerlynck, Hilde Uitterlinden, Annemarie va Dijck, Hilda van Roose.

●This moving and remarkably original first feature from Delvaux (based on a novel by Johan Daisne) makes his subsequent excursions into 'Vogue' surrealism (*Un Soir…un Train, Rendez-vous à Bray*) look decidedly redundant. The man who has his hair cut short is Govert Miereveld (Rouffaer), a hopeless schoolteacher who develops a crush on a mature female pupil; the experience unhinges him, and his involuntary attendance at an autopsy is enough to push him right over the edge. Delvaux's main feat is to take his audience into Miereveld's manias without pretending to explain them, but he also manages to maintain an unsentimentally detached view of his character as an outsider, especially through the recurrent use of the Kurt Weill-esque 'Ballad of Real Life' on the soundtrack. The result is a mixture of psychological thriller and *noir* love story, and it's more than a little wonderful. TR

Man Who Had Power Over Women, The

(1970, GB, 90 min)
d John Krish. *p* Judd Bernard. *sc* Allan Scott, Chris Bryant. *ph* Gerry Turpin. *ed* Thom Noble. *ad* Colin Grimes. *m* Johnny Mandel. *cast* Rod Taylor, Carol White, James Booth, Penelope Horner, Charles Korvin, Alexandra Stewart, Keith Barron, Clive Francis.

●A Swinging London PR man (Taylor), having marital problems, gets so sickened by adulteries and abortion after shepherding round a nasty bisexual pop idol (Francis) that he punches the idol and quits his slick agency. It's an obvious Awful Warning to all those teenyboppers with too much stardust in their eyes. Disappointing, as Krish's earlier work looked good. RD

Man Who Knew Too Little, The

(1997, US/Ger, 94 min)
d Jon Amiel. *p* Arnon Milchan, Michael Nathanson, Mark Tarlov. *sc* Robert Farrar, Howard Franklin. *ph* Robert Stevens. *ed* Pamela Power. *pd* Jim Clay. *m* Christopher Young. *cast* Bill Murray, Peter Gallagher, Joanne Whalley, Alfred Molina, Richard Wilson, Geraldine James, John Standing, Anna Chancellor.

●When dumb video store assistant Murray arrives unexpectedly and inconveniently at the London home of his banker brother, Gallagher, the latter gets him out of the way for the evening by signing him up for an interactive role playing game – a fake thriller scenario – called 'Theatre of Life'. Trouble is Murray mistakenly answers a phone call intended for a hired killer, and is soon up to his neck in a real plot involving blackmail, murder, and a conspiracy engineered by Wilson to blow up a banquet held to mark an Anglo-Russian peace agreement. Cue misunderstandings, as Murray unwittingly finds himself in a life-threatening farce featuring callgirl Whalley, assassin Molina, cops, torturers, Morris dancers and Russian dolls. Despite the title, this fitfully very funny vehicle spoofs not Hitchcock but those tortuously silly British spy thrillers of the '60s, its depiction of London as risibly unreal as that of the movies it's guying. Unsophisticated but fun. GA

Man Who Knew Too Much, The

(1934, GB, 75 min, b/w)
d Alfred Hitchcock. *p* Michael Balcon. *sc* AR Rawlinson, Edwin Greenwood. *ph* Curt Courant. *ed* Hugh Stewart. *ad* Alfred Junge, Peter Proud. *m* Arthur Benjamin. *cast* Leslie Banks, Edna Best, Peter Lorre, Nova Pilbeam, Frank Vosper, Hugh Wakefield, Pierre Fresnay.

●Vintage Hitchcock, with sheer wit and verve masking an implausible plot that spins out of the murder of a spy (Fresnay) in an equally implausible Switzerland (all back-projected mountains), leaving a pair of innocent bystanders (Banks and Best) to track his secret – and their kidnapped daughter – in a dark and labyrinthine London. Where the remake had Doris Day maternally crooning with fateful foreboding, sharpshooting Best simply grabs a rifle and gets after the villains. Pacy, exciting, and with superb settings (taxidermist's shop, dentist's chair, mission chapel complete with gun-toting motherly body, shootout re-enacting the Sidney Street siege, terrific climax in the Albert Hall), it also has nice villainy from a scarred, leering Lorre (here making his British debut). At two-thirds the length of the remake, it's twice the fun. (From an original story by Charles Bennett and DB Wyndham Lewis.) TM

Man Who Knew Too Much, The

(1955, US, 120 min)
d Alfred Hitchcock. *sc* John Michael Hayes. *ph* Robert Burks. *ed* George Tomasini. *ad* Hal Pereira, Henry Bumstead. *m* Bernard Herrmann. *cast* James Stewart, Doris Day, Brenda de Banzie, Bernard Miles, Ralph Truman, Daniel Gélin, Alan Mowbray.
● The sole instance of Hitchcock actually remaking one of his earlier movies, this replaces the British version's tight, economic plotting and quirky social observations with altogether glossier production values and a typically '50s examination of the family under melodramatic stress. Stewart and Day are the complacent couple whose son is kidnapped by spies, and who wend their way through a characteristically Hitchcockian series of suspense set pieces (including a virtuoso crescendo at the Albert Hall) in their attempts to recover him. Starting slowly amid colourful but rather superfluous travelogue-style Moroccan footage, the film improves no end as it progresses, with anxiety about the boy's safety steadily undermining the apparent happiness of a marriage founded on habit and compromise. GA

Man Who Left His Will on Film, The (Tokyo Senso Sengo Hiwa/aka He Died After the War)

(1970, Jap, 94 min, b/w)
d Nagisa Oshima. *sc* Nagisa Oshima, Tsutomu Tamura, Mamoru Sasaki, Masataka Hara. *ph* Toichiro Narushima. *ed* Keichi Uraoka. *m* Toru Takemitsu. *cast* Kazuo Goto, Emiko Iwasaki, Sugio Fukuoka, Keiichi Fukuda, Hiroski Isogai, Kazuo Hashimoto.
● This is Oshima's post-1968 analysis of the failure and disillusionment of the student Left, and it's among his most biting and cautionary films. Like *Death by Hanging* and other movies, it starts with a riddle (the real or imaginary disappearance of a student militant), and then follows through all the implications with a remorseless logic. Another student sets out to trace the missing boy, fearing that he committed suicide; his only leads are conversations with the militant's estranged girlfriend and a roll of film shot by the boy just before he vanished. But it's less a mystery thriller than a series of provocative questions. What is militancy? Does 'struggle' mean violence? Is it really possible for an individual to identify with the interests of a group? And what part do sexual problems play in determining the feelings and actions of young people? TR

Man Who Lived Again, The

see Man Who Changed His Mind

Man Who Lived Twice, The

(1936, US, 73 min, b/w)
d Harry Lachman. *p* Ben Pivar. *sc* Tom Van Dyke, Fred Niblo Jr, Arthur Strawn. *ph* James Van Trees. *ed* Byron Robinson. *cast* Ralph Bellamy, Marian Marsh, Thurston Hall, Isabel Jewell, Nana Bryant, Ward Bond.
● Promising Columbia second feature in which Bellamy's the killer on the run who seeks refuge in a hospital, undergoes an op courtesy of neurosurgeon Hall, and begins a new career as a succesful doctor. But can the past be far behind? Implausible, perhaps, but there was enough in the idea to merit a 3-D remake, *Man in the Dark*, with Edmond O'Brien. TJ

Man Who Loved Cat Dancing, The

(1973, US, 114 min)
d Richard C Sarafian. *p* Martin H Poll, Eleanor Perry. *sc* Eleanor Perry. *ph* Harry Stradling Jr. *ed* Tom Rolf. *ad* Edward C Carfagno. *m* John Williams. *cast* Burt Reynolds, Sarah Miles, Lee J Cobb, Jack Warden, George Hamilton, Bo Hopkins, Robert Donner, Jay Silverheels.
● At first, after a chance encounter saddles a gang of train robbers with a refined lady, this looks as though it might develop into a reasonably engaging tale. But as the going gets harder and the gang fall out among themselves, the film reveals itself to be a thoroughly routine love story. The killing factor, however, is the supreme indifference that Burt Reynolds and Sarah Miles display towards their roles. CPe

Man Who Loved Women, The (L'Homme qui Aimait les Femmes)

(1977, Fr, 119 min)
d François Truffaut. *p* Marcel Berbert. *sc* François Truffaut, Michel Fermaud, Suzanne Schiffman. *ph* Nestor Almendros. *ed* Martine Barraque-Curie. *ad* Jean-Pierre Kohut-Svelko. *m* Maurice Jaubert. *cast* Charles Denner, Brigitte Fossey, Leslie Caron, Nelly Borgeaud, Geneviève Fontanel, Nathalie Baye, Sabine Glaser, Valérie Bonnier, Jean Dasté, Roger Leenhardt.
● Charmless tale of a man whose one interest in life is looking at, pursuing, and making love to women, an obsession leading him to a premature (for him, if not for the audience) death. Seen by some as a misogynist catalogue, by others as a mature, detached examination of an unsympathetic character's fatal passion for largely indifferent females, either way it irritates by its overwrought sense of literary-style paradox, by its insistence on eccentricity as its source of humour, and by its haphazard and gratuitous form: constructed largely in flashbacks, it nevertheless fails to explain or illuminate its central character's behaviour. GA

Man Who Loved Women, The

(1983, US, 110 min)
d Blake Edwards. *p* Blake Edwards, Tony Adams. *sc* Blake Edwards, Milton Wexler, Geoffrey Edwards. *ph* Haskell Wexler. *ed* Ralph E Winters. *pd* Rodger Maus. *m* Henry Mancini. *cast* Burt Reynolds, Julie Andrews, Kim Basinger, Marilu Henner, Cynthia Sikes, Jennifer Edwards, Sela Ward, Ellen Bauer.
● Edwards' muddled remake of one of Truffaut's less than happy movies involves a Hollywood layabout sculptor (Reynolds) whose sack-count seems about par for the course in LA. Far from his obsession with women seeming strange, his psycho-babble accounts of womanising to his shrink (an unlikely Andrews) sound like no more than the usual Anna Raeburn phone-in whingeing. But while the movie desperately lacks humour, and the right touch, it yet manages to be very good-natured in an unmalicious sort of way. CPea

Man Who Mistook His Wife for a Hat, The

(1987, GB, 75 min)
d Christopher Rawlence. *p* Debra Hauer. *sc* Michael Nyman, Christopher Rawlence, Michael Morris. *ph* Christopher Morphet. *ed* Howard Sharp. *pd* Jock Scott. *m* Michael Nyman. *cast* Emile Belcourt, Frederick Westcott, Patricia Hooper, John Tighe, Oliver Sacks.
● Michael Nyman's 'chamber opera' is based on neurologist Oliver Sacks' case history of a man suffering from agnosia: the inability to recognise everyday objects. As the Neurologist (Belcourt) questions and conducts tests upon music lecturer Dr P (Westcott), the story proper takes time out for interviews with both Sacks himself and a neurological surgeon, allowing librettist and director Rawlence to transform an individual case study into an investigation of problems of perception. Thanks to sensitivity and wit and to a subtle, sympathetic use of close-ups, the film finally becomes very moving. And Nyman's shimmering music, crisply sung by the three leads, is not only entirely appropriate to mood and meaning, but also memorable in its own right. GA

Man Who Saw Too Much, The (Nomu Mani Pon Sanai)

(2000, SKor, 100 min)
d Son Jae-Gon. *p* Ha Kwang-Hui. *sc* Son Jae-Gon. *ph* Jo Jae-Hyung. *ed* Son Jae-Gon, Kim Hyung-Joo. *m* Lee Young-Bae. *cast* Kim Sang-Hon, Kim Shin-Song, Lee Gye-Yong, Chong So-Yong, Kim Tae-Su.
● Son's terrific debut is in two parts because the first 52 minutes (made on a shoestring) ended with a joke caption promising more if anyone could be found to finance it. And since Part 1 is the smartest, most enjoyable riff on Hitchcock made by anyone, anywhere, the money to make Part 2 was soon on the table. A film-fan/voyeur secretly videotapes the young woman in the apartment opposite and one night finds himself recording her murder. By chance he tapes it over a boring Korean movie and manages to return the VHS to the rental shop before the killer gets him. Next day the killer faces a shopful of rental tapes and starts ploughing through them all in search of the one with the incriminating evidence. Before long he's become a film critic... In truth Part 2 (in which the killer tries to become a Hitchcockian director) is less funny and provocative than Part 1, which could easily stand alone. But the whole is still a paragon of what no-budget indie film-making can and should be. TR

Man Who Shot Liberty Valance, The

(1962, US, 121 min, b/w)
d John Ford. *p* Willis Goldbeck. *sc* James Warner Bellah, Willis Goldbeck. *ph* William H Clothier. *ed* Otho Lovering. *ad* Hal Pereira, Eddie Imazu. *m* Cyril J Mockridge. *cast* John Wayne, James Stewart, Vera Miles, Lee Marvin, Edmond O'Brien, Andy Devine, John Carradine, Jeanette Nolan, Woody Strode, Denver Pyle, Strother Martin, Lee Van Cleef.
● Ford's purest and most sustained expression of the familiar themes of the passing of the Old West, the conflict between the untamed wilderness and the cultivated garden, and the power of myth. Stewart plays a respected senator who returns on a train (in an opening echoing that of *My Darling Clementine*) to attend the funeral of his old friend Wayne. In one scene, Stewart wipes the dust off a disused stagecoach, marking in a simple gesture the distance between the Old West inhabited by Wayne and the new West which he himself represents. In the central flashback sequence, it is revealed that it was not Stewart who shot the outlaw Liberty Valance (Marvin) but Wayne, the gun law of the Old West paving the way for the development of a new civilisation. For Ford, the passing of the Old West is also the passing of an age of romantic heroism. The only link between the two worlds is the desert rose, a flowering cactus hardy enough to survive the harshness of the desert and humanise the wilderness. NF

Man Who Wasn't There, The

(2001, US, 115 min, b/w)
d Joel Coen. *p* Ethan Coen. *sc* Joel Coen, Ethan Coen. *ph* Roger Deakins. *ed* Roderick Jaynes [Joel Coen, Ethan Cohen], Tricia Cooke. *pd* Dennis Gassner. *m* Carter Burwell. *cast* Billy Bob Thornton, Frances McDormand, Michael Badalucco, James Gandolfini, Katherine Borowitz, Jon Polito, Scarlett Johansson, Tony Shalhoub.
● Set in post-war California and shot by Roger Deakins in ravishing, steely b/w, the Coens' predictably unpredictable crime movie – about an impassive, deeply internalised, reluctant barber whose doubts about his wife's fidelity lead him into a perilous realm of blackmail, homicide and obsessive feelings for a customer's teenage daughter – may be inspired in part by Cain, but it's neither *noir* nor thriller. Though it's touched by typically absurd or surreal moments of humour, it's otherwise quite meditative and arty. It's a brave and largely successful attempt to explore the inner workings of someone who simply doesn't feel the way most of us do. Indeed, he doesn't feel very much at all, and when he does, he doesn't get it. In this the Coens' sly script is helped no end by Billy Bob Thornton's supremely eloquent performance as the taciturn tonsor, lent terrific support from Frances McDormand as the wife. GA

Man Who Watched Trains Go By, The (aka Paris Express)

(1952, GB, 80 min)
d Harold French. *p* Raymond Stross. *sc* Harold French. *ph* Otto Heller. *ed* Vera Campbell. *ad* Paul Sheriff. *m* Benjamin Frankel. *cast* Claude Rains, Marius Goring, Herbert Lom, Marta Toren, Ferdy Mayne, Anouk Aimée, Eric Pohlmann, Felix Aylmer, Lucie Mannheim.
● Rains is perfectly cast as Simenon's mousy Dutch shipping clerk, Kees Popinga, outraged to find, after meticulously keeping the books for 18 years, that his boss (Lom) has besmirched his integrity by cooking those books, intending to make off with the proceeds. Unable to resist his wanderlust when fate takes a hand – Lom falls accidentally to his death – Rains skips impulsively out on his family with the loot and heads for Paris, romance and adventure. On the same train is his old chess crony from the police (Goring), sympathetic but suspicious and asking awkward questions. So far so good, even if the dialogue does make rather too free with pregnant chess metaphors. But when Rains gets away, to

find not the Paris of his dreams but a sordid nightmare of greed and murder, the film degenerates into crude, predictable melodrama (with Toren and Mayne hamming up the villainy, and Rains overdoing the naive bumpkin bit). TM

Man Who Would Be King, The

(1975, US, 129 min)
d John Huston. *p* John Foreman. *sc* John Huston, Gladys Hill. *ph* Oswald Morris. *ed* Russell Lloyd. *pd* Alexandre Trauner. *m* Maurice Jarre. *cast* Sean Connery, Michael Caine, Saeed Jaffrey, Christopher Plummer, Karroum Ben Bouih, Jack May, Shakira Caine.
●Huston first mooted his Kipling adaptation in the '40s (for Gable and Bogart), but the wait proved more than worthwhile, with the imperialist parody of two conmen's rise to Kafiristan kingship gaining in resonance from its director's maturity. Connery and Caine (both excellent) become classic Huston overreachers, and echoes of *The Treasure of the Sierra Madre* and *Moby Dick* permeate the mythic yarn. Almost too lively to be dubbed a meditation on power. PT

Man With a Cloak, The

(1951, US, 81 min, b/w)
d Fletcher Markle. *p* Stephen Ames. *sc* Frank Fenton. *ph* George Folsey. *ed* Newell P Kimlin. *ad* Cedric Gibbons, Arthur Lonergan. *m* David Raksin. *cast* Barbara Stanwyck, Joseph Cotten, Louis Calhern, Leslie Caron, Jim Backus, Margaret Wycherly, Joe DeSantis.
●Intriguing period melodrama/Gothic thriller set in 1840s New York, with Caron as a young Frenchwoman arriving from Paris to beg a financial favour of her curmudgeonly grandfather (Calhern), and discovering that his housekeeper and butler (Stanwyck and DeSantis) are planning to kill the old man for his money. But dashing stranger Cotten steps in to help. Peppered with literary allusions (Poe in particular), shot on elegant MGM sets, highly atmospheric, and endowed with fine performances from a strong cast, it's well worth a watch. GA

Man With a Million

see Million Pound Note, The

Man With a Movie Camera (Chelovek s Kinoapparatom)

(1929, USSR, 6,004 ft, b/w)
d/sc Dziga Vertov. *ph* Mikhail Kaufman. *ed* Dziga Vertoz, Elizaveta Svivlova.
●An analytical account of the State of the (Soviet) Union at a crucial transitional stage, this is one of the most seminal and therefore controversial films in the history of cinema. Vertov's exhilarating and often hilarious exploration of the relations between cinema, actuality and history opened up all the issues Godard, the avant-gardes, and political film-makers have been wrestling with ever since. The film cannot easily be slotted into any single tradition, because it poses all the questions about the status of representation which dominant cinema represses. A truly radical and liberating work. PW

Man Without a Face, The

(1993, US, 115 min)
d Mel Gibson. *p* Bruce Davey. *sc* Malcolm MacRury. *ph* Donald A McAlpine. *ed* Tony Gibbs. *pd* Barbara Dunphy. *m* James Horner. *cast* Mel Gibson, Nick Stahl, Margaret Whitton, Fay Masterson, Gaby Hoffman, Geoffrey Lewis, Richard Masur.
●A solidly crafted if ultimately unexceptional family film about the mentor-pupil relationship of a disfigured outcast and a fatherless 12-year-old boy. 'Hamburger Head' McLeod (Gibson) lives on an island, keeping visitors at bay with his Alsatian dog and his surly manner. Desperate to get into the military college attended by his missing father, Chuck Norstadt overcomes his fear and asks the former teacher to tutor him for the entrance exam. Nick Stahl is fine as the boy, but director Gibson could, perhaps, have dispensed with the redundant extracts from *Red River* and *The Merchant of Venice*. NF

Man Without a Past, The (Mies Vailla Menneisyyttä)

(2002, Fin, 97 min)
d/p/sc Aki Kaurismäki. *ph* Timo Salminen. *ed* Timo Linnasalo. *ad* Markku Pätilä, Jukka Salmi. *cast* Markku Peltola, Kati Outinen, Juhani Niemelä, Kaija Pakarinen, Sakari Kuosmanen, Annikki Tähti, Anneli Sauli.
●On arrival in Helsinki, a man (Peltola) is viciously mugged and given up for dead – but miraculously revives; without memory or any idea of who he is, the man wanders off into the city, moves in with the homeless living in freight containers around the harbour, and eventually begins to put his life (or someone else's?) back together after falling for a Salvation Army woman (Outinen) at the soup canteen. A typically droll, deadpan comedy from Kaurismäki, complete with nods to '50s B-movies, rock'n'roll, and fairytale romance, but also, like its predecessor *Drifting Clouds*, addressing social and political issues (unemployment, homelessness, welfare, heartless capitalism) with the lightest of touches. Beautifully tender, funny and idiosyncratic, right down to some lovely stuff featuring a predictably melancholy dog. GA

Man Without a Star

(1955, US, 86 min)
d King Vidor. *p* Aaron Rosenberg. *sc* Borden Chase, DD Beauchamp. *ph* Russell Metty. *ed* Virgil W Vogel. *ad* Alexander Golitzen, Richard H Riedel. *m* Joseph Gershenson. *cast* Kirk Douglas, Jeanne Crain, Claire Trevor, Richard Boone, Jay C Flippen, William Campbell, Mara Corday.
●A fine, edgy Western, handsomely shot by Russell Metty and beautifully paced by Vidor. A conventional range war plot is lent some of the sweaty unpredictability of *Duel in the Sun* by the love-hate relationship between Douglas, as the cowboy with a pathological hatred of barbed wire, and Crain as the cattle baroness whose cause he eventually abandons in defence of individual liberties. Fine performances, not least from Claire Trevor as the good-hearted saloon girl, and Boone as the villainous gunslinger. (From a novel by Dee Linford.) TM

Man With the Deadly Lens, The

see Wrong Is Right

Man With the Golden Arm, The

(1955, US, 119 min, b/w)
d/p Otto Preminger. *sc* Walter Newman, Lewis Meltzer. *ph* Sam Leavitt. *ed* Louis Loeffler. *pd* Joseph C Wright. *m* Elmer Bernstein. *cast* Frank Sinatra, Kim Novak, Eleanor Parker, Arnold Stang, Darren McGavin, Robert Strauss, Doro Merande.
●The first major Hollywood film on heroin addiction, a subject totally proscribed by the Hays Code. Sinatra is excellent as the ex-con junkie trying to make it as a jazz drummer but pulled into a world of pushing, and Kim Novak convinces as his enigmatic mistress; but the casting of Eleanor Parker as his supposedly wheelchair-ridden wife is miscalculated, and Preminger's evocation of the social milieu of the drug user/pusher shows little sign of first-hand observation. There are some great scenes, though, notably Sinatra's audition for a make-or-break drumming job, and the later scene where he suffers cold turkey in Novak's apartment. Notable for its jazz score, too. (From the novel by Nelson Algren.) RM

Man With the Golden Gun, The

(1974, GB, 125 min)
d Guy Hamilton. *p* Harry Saltzman, Albert R Broccoli. *sc* Richard Maibaum, Tom Mankiewicz. *ph* Ted Moore, Oswald Morris. *ed* John Shirley, Raymond Poulton. *pd* Peter Murton. *m* John Barry. *cast* Roger Moore, Christopher Lee, Britt Ekland, Maud Adams, Herve Villechaize, Clifton James, Marc Lawrence, Bernard Lee.
●Formula film-making that relies entirely on its set piece chases (land and water), fights (gun, fist and karate), and stunted gestures toward glamorous romance, played off against a variety of travel poster Far Eastern locations. The script is banal, the gags and double entendres barely up to *Carry On* standard, and the whole dismally lacking in the style that the 007 series so desperately needs. Roger Moore's interpretation of Bond is blandness personified. It is left to Christopher Lee, playing a kind of Westernised, Dracula-esque Fu Manchu, to lend some semblance of style and suavity as Scaramanga, the man with a hideout in Red China and a hankering after the status of gentleman. VG

Man With the Green Carnation, The

see Trials of Oscar Wilde, The

Man with the X-Ray Eyes, The

see X – the Man with X-Ray Eyes

Man With Two Brains, The

(1983, US, 93 min)
d Carl Reiner. *p* David V Picker, William E McEuen. *sc* Carl Reiner, Steve Martin, George Gipe. *ph* Michael Chapman. *ed* Bud Molin. *pd* Polly Platt. *m* Joel Goldsmith. *cast* Steve Martin, Kathleen Turner, David Warner, Paul Benedict, Richard Brestoff, James Cromwell, Gerge Furth.
●Played by Steve Martin with the mixture of flat cynicism and crazed childishness which makes him a near successor to Jerry Lewis, brilliant brain surgeon Dr Hfuhruhurr falls foul of a wicked husband-collector (Turner), while still carrying on an affair with the talking brain of his dead wife, conveniently stored in a jar of purple fluid. Also in there somewhere are the crazed 'elevator' killer who turns out to be a very famous American TV chat-show host, the even more crazed Dr Necessiter (Warner, on his usual bonkers form transferring human brains into gorillas), and a condo apartment with an interior as large as Frankenstein's castle. It's a patchy affair, often hilarious, often thin, but it does contain a bewildering array of underwear adorning Ms Turner which would make a corpse sit up and steam. And any movie which contains the line 'Into the mud, scum-queen' is surely not totally devoid of cultural merit. CPea

Man, Woman and Child

(1982, US, 100 min)
d Dick Richards. *p* Elmo Williams, Elliott Kastner. *sc* Erich Segal, David Zelag Goodman. *ph* Richard H Kline. *ed* David Bretherton. *pd* Dean Edward Mitzner. *m* Georges Delerue. *cast* Martin Sheen, Blythe Danner, Sebastian Dungan, David Hemmings, Craig T Nelson, Nathalie Nell.
●Drawn from an Erich (*Love Story*) Segal novel, this gives a predictably romantic account of the impact on a self-styled 'perfect marriage' of the existence of a 'love child'. The film is given an old-fashioned quality by making the child the progeny of a French dalliance by the husband, and falls into line by reserving the full weight of its carefully orchestrated poignancy for the 'lost' relationship of father and son. Sheen, as the père more or less manqué, bears up manfully. As the put-upon wife, Danner, a keenly stylish performer, is always a whole lot more than just watchable, and Hemmings is pudgily satyric as her chief temptation (she's a sucker for a Brit accent). VG

Manxman, The

(1928, GB, 8,163 ft, b/w)
d Alfred Hitchcock. *p* John Maxwell.*sc* Eliot Stannard. *ph* Jack Cox. *ed* Emile de Ruelle. *ad* C Wilfred Arnold. *cast* Carl Brisson, Anny Ondra, Malcolm Keen, Randle Ayrton, Clare Greet.
●A distinctly un-Hitchcockian melodrama (his last real silent, since *Blackmail* came next), based on a best-selling novel by Hall Caine written in the 1890s. Its story is accordingly old-hat (a love triangle that reaches crisis when the woman's fisherman husband – wrongly believed dead – returns to find her pregnant with his best friend's child); but Hitch makes the most of his locations (although the film is set on the Isle of Man, it was shot in Cornwall), while the frequent use of shots taken through windows anticipates the interest in voyeurism in his later work. GA

Mapantsula

(1988, SAf, 104 min)
d Oliver Schmitz. *p* Max Montocchio. *sc* Oliver Schmitz, Thomas Mogotlane. *ph* Rod Stewart. *ed* Mark Baard. *ad* Robyn Hofmeyr. *m* Ouens, Thapelo Khomo, Lloyd LeLosa, Nana Motijoane, Ian Osrin. *cast* Thomas Mogotlane, Marcel Van Heerden, Thembi Mtshali, Dolly Rathebe, Peter Sephuma, Darlington Michaels.

●At last, a South African movie about Panic in the streets! The streets are those of the suburbs, shantytowns and shopping malls of Johannesburg, and Panic is a small-time crook who keeps his nose out of politics. The trouble is that politics touches everyone on the streets of Jo'burg, as Panic discovers when he is picked up by the police for questioning and dumped in a cell with a bunch of township militants, precisely the people he most despises and fears. White director Schmitz and black co-writer/star Mogotlane wisely leave Panic's future to our imagination, and concentrate instead on getting inside the skin of a scuzzy but not dislikeable criminal. (The title, incidently, is the township argot for 'spiv'.) The result has much the same energy that Lino Brocka brings to his Filipino slum melodramas, and it gets far closer to the sights, sounds, smells and rhythms of Soweto life than an entire Attenborough of white liberal movies. Needless to say, it's banned from SA cinema screens. TR

Map of Sex and Love, The (Qingse Ditu)

(2001, HK/US, 130 min)
d Evans Chan. *p* Willy Tsao, Russell Freedman. *sc* Evans Chan. *ph* O Sing-Pui. *ed* Garret Sokoloff. *pd* Gill Wong. *m* Milos Raickovich, Peter Suart & The Eternalists. *cast* Bernardo Chow, Cherie Ho, Victor Ma, Lindzay Chan, Goh Boon-Ann.
●New York-based Wei Ming (Chow) returns to Hong Kong to make a documentary about the imminent opening of Disneyland. He rents a place on an outlying island, where his neighbours include the introvert Mimi (Ho), still not recovered from a bad sexual experience in her past, and the extrovert Larry (Ma), a promiscuous gay dancer with whom he gets into a relationship. Chan's film is an essay disguised as a narrative – or maybe vice versa. Each of its three chapters tackles the secret history of one of the protagonists, uncovering everything from homophobia in church schools to a cache of Nazi gold in Macau in the process. The film is discursive and occasionally flip, but more often seductive as it negotiates the spaces between desire and inhibition, between the troubled mind and the always troublesome body, between cruising and map-making. All three lead performances are charming. TR

Map of the Human Heart

(1992, GB/Aust/Fr/Can, 109 min)
d Vincent Ward. *p* Tim Bevan, Vincent Ward. *sc* Louis Nowra. *ph* Eduardo Serra. *ed* John Scott, Frans Vandenburg. *pd* John Beard. *m* Gabriel Yared. cast Jason Scott Lee, Patrick Bergin, Jeanne Moreau, Anne Parillaud, John Cusack.
●Ward's ambitious epic love story covers two continents and three decades and, its execution apart, could have sprung from one of those fat romantic chronicles written for the typing pool. But Ward has an extravagant visual imagination so that even the more outlandish scenes, like the hero and heroine finally consummating their passion on a half-deflated barrage balloon, linger in the mind. Where lack of money cramps his vision of WWII bombing raids on Germany, the director achieves a pleasing shorthand with lighting. Map-maker Bergin lands his biplane in Canada's Arctic Circle and befriends an Inuit boy with TB, flying him to a Montreal hospital, where he becomes best friends with a half-caste Indian girl on Moreau's ward. Ten years later, the friendship has blossomed into love. Fate intervenes at an indecent rate, serving up plenty of misunderstandings, but the mise-en-scène is stunning. Go with the floe. BC

Map of the World, A

(1999, US, 127 min)
d Scott Elliott. *p* Frank Marshall, Kathleen Kennedy. *sc* Peter Hedges, Polly Platt. *ph* Seamus McGarvey. *ed* Craig McKay, Naomi Geraghty. *pd* Richard Toyon. *m* Pat Metheny. *cast* Sigourney Weaver, Julianne Moore, David Strathairn, Arliss Howard, Chloë Sevigny, Louise Fletcher.
●Weaver leads a strong cast as the school nurse who's accused of abusing a pupil, shortly after a friend's child drowns in her care … but, alas! It's a brave, odd performance, mannered and cold, left high and dry by first time director Elliott's habit of putting the camera in the wrong place at the wrong time. Bizarrely, Jane Hamilton's novel views prison as a locus for personal growth. Indeed, it's a toss up which is more offensive, the film's muddled psychotherapy-think, or its 'TV movie of the week' designs on your handkerchief. TCh

Mar, El (The Sea)

(1999, Sp, 113 min)
d Augusti Villaronga. *p* Lluís Ferrando. *sc* Antonio Aloy, Biel Mesquida, Augustí Villaronga. *ph* Jaume Peracaula. *ed* Raúl Román. *ad* Francesc Candini. *m* Javier Navarrete. *cast* Bruno Bergonzini, Roger Casamajor, Antonia Torrens, Roger Casamajor, Angela Molina, Simón Andreu, Juli Mira, Hernán González.
●Of the Spanish films dealing with the traumas caused by the Civil War, many have followed what perhaps remains the finest of its kind – Erice's *The Spirit of the Beehive* – in filtering events through the sensibility of a child. This fifth feature by Villaronga initially looks like it belongs to the same line. In 1936, three kids see a pal kill a Francoist executioner's son and then himself. But the director evidently has something more unusual in mind, and soon leaps a decade to a sanatorium where Francisca (Torrens), now a nun, tends the all-male tubercular patients, including the almost fanatically religious Manuel (Bergonzini) and new arrival Andreu (Casamajor), whose boastful tales of sexual conquest and petty crime stir mixed emotions in his old friends. With its eye-catching bravura camerawork and editing, a prominent score and use of religious and sexual symbolism/metaphor, this takes a very different route from Erice's classic. Villaronga drums up neat pietàs and Crucifixion imagery, and there's even good dialogue on death and its approach. But it's too portentous, overheated, flashy, derivative and implausible for its own good. GA

Marathon Man

(1976, US, 126 min)
d John Schlesinger. *p* Robert Evans, Sidney Beckerman. *sc* William Goldman. *ph* Conrad Hall. *ed* Jim Clark. *pd* Richard MacDonald. *m* Michael Small. *cast* Dustin Hoffman, Laurence Olivier, Roy Scheider, William Devane, Marthe Keller, Fritz Weaver, Richard Bright, Marc Lawrence.
●Adapted by William Goldman from his own novel, this thriller is quite effective in its basic set pieces, even if the overall thrust seems a trifle ponderous. Hoffman plays a graduate student catapulted into a confrontation with grim former concentration camp Jew-killer Szell (Olivier, giving a rather circumscribed if impeccable performance). The pointlessly obscure construction and numerous loose ends make the triviality of the plot all the more annoying, and Schlesinger should have resisted the grossly over-used Central Park locations. Best moment is a compelling night sequence centering on the use of dentistry as a grisly method of torture. DP

Marat/Sade, The

see Persecution and Assassination of Jean-Paul Marat …

Maravillas

(1980, Sp, 95 min)
d Manuel Gutiérrez Aragón. *p* Luis Megino. *sc* Manuel Gutiérrez Aragón, Luis Megino. *ph* Teo Escamilla. *ed* José Salcedo. *ad* Félix Murcia. *m* Nina Hagen, Gustav Mahler. *cast* Fernando Fernan Gomez, Cristina Marcos, Enrique Sanfrancisco, Francisco Merino, Léon Klimovsky. Jorge Rigaud, Miguel Molina, José Manuel Cervino.
●An abrasive curio that begs anything but art-movie reverence from its audience, this slyly surreal patchwork stitches together 'problem pic' incidentals with provocative glee and no hint of a moralistic message. The culture-clash incongruity of Nina Hagen's 'African Reggae' and an image of walking along a precipice sets the tone for a narrative that attaches itself to a 16-year-old girl's encounters wth casual crime, a corrupt church, a charmed circle of godfatherly Jews, a father lazily resigned to porn and yoghurt, and a Judas identified with electric-chair icons Caryl Chessman and Gary Gilmore. Its inconsequentiality appearing alternately savage and absurd, with even the apocalypse conjured only in a kids' TV cartoon, the result is admirably irresponsible. PT

Marchands de Sable, Les

(2000, Fr, 105 min)
d Pierre Salvadori. *p* Philippe Martin, Gilles Sandoz. *sc* Pierre Salvadori, Nicolas Saada. *ph* Gilles Henry. *ed* Isabelle de Winck. *pd* Yan Arlaud, Sandrine Jarron. *m* Camille Baz Baz. *cast* Robert Castel, Mathieu Demy, Guillaume Depardieu, Serge Riaboukine, Marina Golovine.
●Compared to Salvadori's earlier films, *Wild Target* and *Les Apprentis*, this is a slight disappointment, but, nevertheless, it's a nifty thriller in its own right. It starts at the end, with a fire in Riaboukine's Café le Détour. Flashback to ex-con Golovine's arrival in Paris, and her brother Demy's involvement in a nefarious network of drug deals around the same little circus of cafés, the film's centre of gravity. It's taut and observant, but essentially familiar, and though the cast are credible enough, the characterisation's not so deep that the film really drags you in. (See also *Le Détour*.) NB

March Comes in Like a Lion (San-Gatsu no Lion)

(1990, Jap, 118 min)
d Hitoshi Yazaki. *p* Takashi Nishimura. *sc* Hitoshi Yazaki, Hiroshi Miyazaki. Sachio Ono, Takashi Nishimura. *ph* Isao Ishii. *ed* Ryuichi Takano. *m* The Bolivian Rockers. *cast* Yoshiko Yura, Bang-Ho Cho, Koen Okumura, Shoko Saito, Meika Seri, Takeshi Naito.
●Or, perhaps, love among the ruins. In present-day Tokyo, a waste land of tenements prey to decrepitude and demolition, 'Ice' (Yura) decides to collect Haruo (Cho), the young man she's set her heart on, from the hospital where he's being treated for amnesia. A little lie is needed to entice him back to the apartment she's found for them: she tells him she's his lover, neglecting to add that she's also his sister. With no recollections to suggest otherwise, he goes along with her – but how long before his memory returns? With its long, static, carefully composed takes, taciturn script and tantalisingly ambivalent tone, Yazaki's beautifully matter-of-fact study of incestuous longing is an engrossing, sexy and remarkably tender movie. Crucially, it eschews both easy judgments and fake sentimentality; indeed, there's a droll, deadpan humour at work, most noticeably in the frequent sight gags. At the same time, however, the evocative use of metaphors ensures that the general air of detachment makes not for a dry, academic exercise, but a poetic tale of a fragile, blossoming romance that's finally both subtly subversive and, thanks to the charismatic central performances, deeply affecting. GA

March or Die

(1977, GB, 107 min)
d Dick Richards. *p* Dick Richards, Jerry Bruckheimer. *sc* David Zelag Goodman. *ph* John Alcott. *ed* John C Howard, Stanford C Allen, O Nicholas Brown. *pd* Gil Parrondo. *m* Maurice Jarre. *cast* Gene Hackman, Terence Hill, Catherine Deneuve, Max von Sydow, Ian Holm, Marcel Bozzuffi, Jack O'Halloran.
●This uncertain conflation of *Morocco*, *Beau Geste* and *The Four Feathers* can't decide whether to take its Foreign Legion clichés at face value or to parody them. Hill's hard luck hero is OK, and Holm refines his oily Arab party piece, but as in so many Lew Grade confections, most of the cast are pure window-dressing. Despite Richards' helmsmanship, a yarn which obstinately refuses to rip. PT

Marcorelle Affair, The (L'Affaire Marcorelle)

(2000, Fr, 94 min)
d Serge Le Péron. *p* Vincent Roget. *sc* Serge Le Péron. *ph* Ivan Kozecka. *ed* Janice Jones. *pd* Patrick Durand. *m* Antoine Duhamel. *cast* Jean-Pierre Léaud, Irène Jacob, Mathieu Amalric, Dominique Reymond, Philippe Khorsand.
●An intriguing black comedy in the late-Buñuel mould. Léaud is a former '68 activist turned successful but neurotic prosecuting attorney who finds his guilt far from assuaged when he allows desire to lead him to the bedroom of Polish waitress Jacob. But is it the lust that torments him (he's married), or the fact that in the bedroom he kills a man who may or may not be her father? Conspiracy thriller, comic fantasy, psychological study and cinephile allusions combine in a shifting, unsettling narrative that never quite delivers on its initial promise. The casting, however,

is spot on, with Amalric weighing in as a young legal eagle on the lookout to make the most of Léaud's misfortune. GA

Margaret's Museum

(1995, Can/GB, 100 min)
d Mort Ransen. *p* Mort Ransen, Christopher Zimmer, Claudio Luca, Steve Clark-Hall. *sc* Gerald Wexler, Mort Ransen. *ph* Vic Sarin. *ed* Rita Roy. *pd* William Flemming (Canada), David McHenry (GB). *m* Milan Kymlicka. *cast* Helena Bonham Carter, Clive Russell, Craig Olejnik, Kate Nelligan, Kenneth Walsh, Andrea Morris.

●Nova Scotia, the late '40s: Margaret MacNeil (Bonham Carter), a child-woman, struggles against the inexorable pull of the coal mines. With father and one brother already gobbled up, Margaret and her mother (Nelligan) vow to preserve the youngest male in the family (Olejnik). And when Margaret falls in love with Neil (Russell) – a fiddle-tickling, Gaelic-crooning giant – she makes it her mission to safeguard him, too. Clearly attracted by all things Celtic, director/co-writer Ransen makes much of the siren call of the dead, Margaret's primitive wedding and Cape Breton's boozy yarn-spinning locals. Too much: he rubs our nose in lots of carefully placed grit, but essentially this is 'pixies skipping in the moonlight' territory. All in all, the enterprise seems embarrassingly amateurish. But lo! Half-an-hour before the end comes a miracle. As intricately Gothic, as sexually bizarre as a Leonora Carrington dreamscape, Margaret's final attempt to preserve her loved ones dismembers the emotions. Is she damned or blessed? You're too stunned to tell. Visceral details float glutinously and all the while a feverishly numb Bonham Carter finally achieves a level of concentration that makes the scenes between her and Nelligan electric. It's hard to imagine a more exhilarating testament to the reality of poverty and the utter impotence of love. CO'Su

Marge, La (The Streetwalker)

(1976, Fr, 91 min)
d Walerian Borowczyk. *p* Robert Hakim, Raymond Hakim. *sc* Walerian Borowczyk. *ph* Bernard Daillencourt. *ed* Louisette Hautecoeur. *ad* Jacques d'Ovidio. *cast* Sylvia Kristel, Joe Dallesandro, Mireille Audibert, Denis Manuel, André Falcon, Louise Chevalier.

●Saddled with an ungainly English title – even ignoring Barthes' specific use of *la marge* to denote the erotic midriff margin between two items of clothing, 'the edge' or 'on the fringe' would have been closer – Borowczyk's adaptation of an André Pieyre de Mandiargues novel works hard to create a private hallucinatory world out of modern Paris and the twilight district of the Rue St Denis. An unexpectedly well-groomed Dallesandro plays a happy husband who, learning of the sudden death back home of his wife and child, turns to the obsessive pursuit of a beautiful Dutch whore (Kristel). It's a frustrating battle of extraordinary details – the prostitutes' glistening wardrobe, the remarkable '70s soundtrack – over an unconvincing narrative and flat acting. Borowczyk delivers palpable moments of erotic fascination, but they surface fitfully in an environment over which the director clearly had insufficient control. DT

Margie

(1946, US, 94 min)
d Henry King. *p* Walter Morosco. *sc* F Hugh Herbert. *ph* Charles G Clarke. *ed* Barbra McLean. *ad* James Basevi, J Russell Spencer. *songs* Henry Davis, J Russell Robinson, Con Conrad. *cast* Jeanne Crain, Glenn Langan, Lynn Bari, Esther Dale, Hobart Cavanaugh, Alan Young, Barbara Lawrence, Conrad Janis, Hattie McDaniel.

●Harmless nostalgia as Crain passes on to her daughter tales of her own high school years in the Ohio of the late '20s, when the arrival of handsome French teacher Langan sent every girl's hormones into a tizzy. An unfortunate running gag involving knicker elastic, a crucial meeting at the skating rink, and much use of the popular songs of the time ease all and sundry towards an upbeat final reel. TJ

Mariachi, El

see El Mariachi

Mariage tardiff

see Late Marriage

Marian

(1996, Czech Republic, 109 min)
d Petr Václav. *p* Petr Václav, Kristina Petrova. *sc* Petr Václav, Jan Sikl. *ph* Stepán Kucera. *ed* Alois Fisarek, Jirí Václav. *pd* Ester Krumbachova, Ondrej Nevkasil. *m* Jirí Václav. *cast* Stefan Ferko, Milan Cifra, Radek Holub, Jaroslava Vyslouziklová.

●This moving first feature observes the institutionalisation of a gypsy boy, taken from his mother at the age of three, with a sharp realist's eye. Ferko (as the young Marian) and Cifra (as the older) give superb performances as 'the different boy' whose experiences made him first attempt suicide, and then the murder of a warden (who treated him as a temporary pet), before reform school, prison and then faltering steps into the equally cruel, outside world. The documentary roots of director and co-writer Václav are evident, but his emotionally expressionist use of landscape (the torrential river, the snow-bound woods) and mature, if demanding, use of narrative shorthand show him to be a film-maker of all-round talent. WH

Maria's Lovers

(1984, US, 109 min)
d Andrei Konchalovsky. *p* Bosko Djordjevic, Lawrence Taylor-Mortoff. *sc* Gérard Brach, Andrei Konchalovsky, Paul Zindel, Marjorie David. *ph* Juan Ruiz-Anchia. *ed* Humphrey Dixon. *pd* Jeannine Oppewall. *m* Gary S Remal. *cast* Nastassja Kinski, John Savage, Robert Mitchum, Keith Carradine, Anita Morris, Bud Cort, Karen Young, Tracy Nelson, John Goodman, Vincent Spano.

●Soldiers returning from the wars is a perennially hardy theme for revealing not only the mental ruinations of conflict, but also the way in which home is never quite the place you left behind. Savage, as the Slav soldier returning to his rural Pennsylvania home after World War II, is unable to face the reality of the woman he has kept stored in his dreams (Kinski), and he has to undergo further exile and debasement before he can return to his community once more whole. It may be Konchalovsky's own exile which makes some scenes waver on an edge of uncertainty, but there is still much to admire: filming the American heartlands so that they look like the Steppes is no mean achievement, nor is conjuring a very moving love scene between Mitchum and Kinski. CPea

Mari de la Coiffeuse, Le

see Hairdresser's Husband, The

Marie

(1985, US, 112 min)
d Roger Donaldson. *p* Frank Capra Jr. *sc* John Briley. *ph* Chris Menges. *ed* Neil Travis. *ad* Ron Foreman. *m* Francis Lai. *cast* Sissy Spacek, Jeff Daniels, Keith Szarabajka, Morgan Freeman, Fred Thompson, Lisa Banes, Trey Wilson.

●Marie is a single parent who supports her three kids and invalid mum through college, and braves the medical establishment in diagnosing her youngest child's illness; then, zooming to speedy prominence as chairwoman of the Tennessee parole board, she single-handedly purges the body politic of the sweaty parasites in its bosom. And it's all true. Blessed are the pure in heart, but also deadly dull. Spacek is competent as her usual embattled heroine, but Marie could use a few warts, and as hot political exposés go, local corruption in Tennessee seems of less than pressing concern. However, Donaldson directs with fluid, docudramatic urgency, and there are further compensations in the support performances. SJo

Marie – a Hungarian Legend

see Tavaszi Zápor

Marie Baie des Anges

see Angel Sharks

Mariée était en Noir, La

see Bride Wore Black, The

Marie in the City

see Marie s'en va-t-en ville

Marie-Jo and Her Two Loves (Marie-Jo et ses deux amours)

(2002, Fr, 124 min)
d Robert Guédiguian. *sc* Jean-Louis Milesi, Robert Guédiguian. *ph* Renato Berta. *ed* Bernard Sasia. *ad* Michel Vandestien. *cast* Ariane Ascaride, Jean-Pierre Darroussin, Gérard Meylan, Julie-Marie Parmentier, Jacques Boudet, Yann Tregouët, Frédérique Bonnal.

●Shot, like Guédiguian's other films, in and around Marseille and l'Estaque, and featuring his usual actors, this is otherwise rather atypical in jettisoning both the working-class milieu and a strong political context in favour of a straightforward tale of adultery. Ascaride plays an ambulance driver, still very much in love with builder husband Darroussin and devoted to her teenage daughter, but also passionately involved with harbour pilot Meylan. On the whole, until the absurd contrivance of the 'tragic' ending, the film is emotionally astute, striving to understand the characters in their difficult predicament, rather than pass easy judgment. At the same time, however, an uncharacteristic clumsiness – in the use of music, in the sometimes hackneyed notions of 'romance', in the daughter's dialogue – regularly disrupts the otherwise often intense mood, so that after a while, one simply begins to lose interest in the characters and their fate. GA

Marie-Jo et ses deux amours

see Marie-Jo and Her Two Loves

Marie, légende hongroise

see Tavaszi Zápor

Marie s'en va-t-en ville (Marie in the City)

(1987, Can, 75 min)
d Marquise Lepage. *p* François Bouvier. *sc* Marquise Lepage, François Bouvier, Pierre Fuglia, Micheline Lanctôt, Jacques Leduc. *ph* Daniel Jobin. *ed* Yves Chaput. *ad* Françoise Séguin. *m* Michel Rivard. *cast* Frédérique Collin, Geneviève Lenoir, Denis Lavasseur.

●A 13-year-old runaway holes up in the garish Montreal apartment of an out of luck, coke addicted hooker: no surprises here, but Lenoir, the tomboy determined not to show the knocks of life, and Collin, the middle aged professional determined not to hang up her wigs, add a dash of vinegar to a very sentimental script. JPy

Marigolds in August

(1979, SAf, 87 min)
d Ross Devenish. *p* Jonathan Joel Cohen, Mark Forstater. *sc* Athol Fugard. *ph* Mike Davis. *ed* Lionel Selwyn. *cast* Winston Ntshona, John Kani, Athol Fugard, Joyce Hesha, Abel Ntshinga, Nomonde Mhlobiso.

●An examination of the 'invisibility' of blacks in South Africa caused by conditioned white indifference; an invisibility which means poverty and unemployment. The film is set in and around Schoenmakerskop, an opulently sleepy, immaculately manicured whites-only seaside hamlet just outside Port Elizabeth, scriptwriter Athol Fugard's home town. Its central characters all have their real-life counterparts: Daan (Ntshona), the crafty, suspicious but fundamentally good-natured jobbing gardener, jealously protecting his economic lifeline; Melton (Kani), desperately and stubbornly courageous as he searches for work; and Paulus Olifant (Fugard), a nomadic snake-catcher, scavenger and bush-philosopher. All, in one way or another, are outlawed by white society, and gradually realise that this makes them brothers. A powerful, pessimistic, but bracing film. SC

Marilyn

(1963, US, 83 min, b/w & col)
d Henry Koster [Rock Hudson sequence]. *commentary* Don Medford. *narrator* Rock Hudson.

●A Fox compilation in which Rock Hudson turns up at a Hollywood projection room to show himself some clips from Marilyn Monroe's films. It's reasonably comprehensive, but there's one snag: Fox could use only their own material, so you won't see (or even hear any reference to), for example, UA's *Some Like It Hot* or MGM's *The Asphalt Jungle*. You will see *All About Eve*, *Monkey Business*, *Niagara*, *Gentlemen Prefer Blondes*, *River of No Return*, *Bus Stop*, and the unfinished *Something's Got to Give* (released with Doris Day as *Move Over, Darling*).

Marilyn – The Untold Story

(1980, US, 120 min)
d John Flynn, Jack Arnold, Lawrence Schiller. *p* Lawrence Schiller. *sc* Dalene Young. *ph* Terry K Meade, (New York) Sol Negrin, (Colorado) Jim Phalen. *ed* Jack Gleason, Patrick T Roark. *ad* Jan Scott, Sydney Z Litwack. *m* William Goldstein. *cast* Catherine Hicks, Richard Basehart, Frank Converse, John Ireland, Viveca Lindfors, Jason Miller, Sheree North.

●This made-for-TV movie (originally running 150 minutes) offers few fresh insights into the well-worn topic of Monroe's life and character. The depressingly familiar treatment portrays the stereotypical helpless dumb blonde, in search of a family she never had, vainly attempting to become a serious actress, with little suggestion either of her intelligence and courage, or of the destructive condescension of the men she lived and worked with. Catherine Hicks' performance is proficient enough, if woefully lacking in charisma. But the plodding script rarely transcends banality and ludicrous name-dropping ('Did Mr Kennedy ring?'), while many of the supporting cameos are downright embarrassing. GA

Mario and the Magician (Mario und der Zauberer)

(1994, Ger/Fr/Aus, 125 min)
d Klaus Maria Brandauer. *p* Jürgen Haase. *sc* Burt Weinshanker. *ph* Lajos Koltai. *ed* Tanja Schmidbauer. *ad* Peter Pabst. *m* Christian Brandauer. *cast* Julian Sands, Anna Galiéna, Klaus Maria Brandauer, Pavel Greco, Valentina Chico, Philippe Leroy.

●The '20s. A liberal German professor and his family holiday uneasily in Mussolini's Italy. They are ejected from their hotel in case their son's cough is catching and fined when their little girl is seen naked on the beach. Lurking violence surfaces during a performance by the hypnotist Cipolla, who inflicts increasingly sinister humiliations on his spellbound audience. As Cipolla, Brandauer underplays conspicuously. As director, he aims for not-quite-naturalism and a tone more suggestive of Kafka than Thomas Mann, whose 1929 fable is here revised and elaborated. Peculiar enough to warrant a look, despite its intermittent heavy-handedness and the Euro-mix casting. BBa

Marius

(1931, Fr, 122 min, b/w)
d Alexander Korda. *p/sc* Marcel Pagnol. *ph* Ted Pahle. *ed* Roger Spiri-Mercanton. *m* Francis Gromon. *cast* Raimu, Pierre Fresnay, Orane Demazis, Alida Rouffe, Fernand Charpin, Robert Vattier.

●The first of a trilogy set in Marcel Pagnol's home town of Marseilles (to be followed by *Fanny* and *César*), this centres on the decision of Marius (Fresnay) to answer the call of the sea, despite opposition from his father César (Raimu), and despite his love for Fanny (Demazis). Some sniffy critics thought that playwright Pagnol shouldn't have dabbled in celluloid at all: Richard Griffith, in *The Film Since Then*, considered his output 'not part of a purposeful cinema'. In place of purpose, these films display such old-fashioned virtues as truth to life and boundless humanity; they also contain some of the fruitiest acting under the sun, particularly from Raimu. This first instalment, notably more boisterous than the others, was directed by Korda on a whistle-stop tour of France; by the end of the year he had crossed the Channel, and the rest, as they say, is history. GB

Marius et Jeannette

(1997, Fr, 102 min)
d Robert Guédiguian. *p* Gilles Sandoz, Robert Guédiguian. *sc* Jean-Louis Milesi, Robert Guédiguian. *ph* Bernard Cavalié. *ed* Bernard Sasia. *ad* Karim Hamzaoui. *cast* Ariane Ascaride, Gérard Meylan, Pascale Roberts, Jacques Boudet, Frédérique Bonnal, Jean-Pierre Darroussin.

●Set in l'Estaque, an impoverished, industrialised area of Marseilles, this funny, tender, enchanting film starts as if it's going to be a familiar misfits-meeting-cute romance. Soon after her feisty temper costs her her supermarket job, single mother Jeannette (Ascaride, the writer/director's wife) embarks on a relationship with the equally wacky Marius (Meylan), a taciturn security guard at a disused cement works. He's accepted by her kids and friends, but when he disappears for a few days, Jeannette suspects his no-show is simply another example of male unreliability, and it's left to her neighbours to investigate. In fact, while the faltering central romance gives the film a semblance of narrative structure, Guédiguian's prime concern is how community and friendship make economic and emotional hardship bearable. That Marius is called 'Marius' is probably no accident, since the celebratory account of working class life in all its variety recalls Pagnol's classic Marseilles trilogy, albeit without the overheated theatricality and pathos. Less love story than love letter to a particular, Mediterranean way of life, this is peopled with credible individuals as proud, perverse and needy as they are brave, tolerant and likeable. GA

Marjoe

(1972, US, 88 min)
d/p Howard Smith, Sarah Kernochan. *ph* Ed Lynch, Ken Van Sickle, Richard Pearce, David Myers, Mike Shea. *ed* Lawrence Silk. *with* Marjoe Gortner, Sister Allie Taylor, the Rev. Ray Boatwright, Mrs Ruby Boatwright.

●Marjoe Gortner – the name's an amalgam of Mary and Joseph – began his career as a revivalist preacher at the age of four, broke off in his teens, but returned to the Church some years later, both eyes open and on the make. This documentary reveals that Marjoe really wants to belong to the Deity of Showbiz Rock; each night he preaches the word of the Lord to blue-rinsed motherly matrons who shudder in ecstasy and reach for their purses because he moves so sexily in the name of the Lord. Marjoe talks frankly, even cynically, to the camera about his profession: the gimmicks, the money, the qualms, the hypocrisy involved. Only gradually do we realise that he is manipulating us and the film-makers just as readily as he used his congregations. Marjoe wants to be famous and a star (he did get started, but never really made it). What better way of advertising than in this documentary where he shows himself the Lord's hipster putting down the squares, rejecting preaching and declaring himself up for offer? CPe

Marked for Death

(1990, US, 93 min)
d Dwight H Little. *p* Michael Grais, Mark Victor, Steven Seagal. *sc* Michael Grais, Mark Victor. *ph* Ric Waite. *ed* O Nicholas Brown. *pd* Robb Wilson King. *m* James Newton Howard. *cast* Steven Seagal, Basil Wallace, Keith David, Tom Wright, Joanna Pacula, Elizabeth Gracen, Bette Ford, Jimmy Cliff.

●'I've become what I most despise,' opines action-man Seagal in the risibly philosophical opening to this sub-standard bash-'em-up pic. A former narc agent, he makes a spiritual voyage home in search of his 'good side'. Unsurprisingly, his fascination for all things dark soon overwhelms his new-found pacifism, and he renews his struggle against the forces of evil: black dealers under the satanic influence of blue-eyed rasta Screwface (Wallace). The film is wretchedly incoherent; unable to orchestrate action sequences, Little leaves the knock-kneed nihilist flailing in impotent rage to a hideous score. As the climax approaches, the entire shebang ups stumps to Jamaica, where Jimmy Cliff makes a cameo appearance, and the hero's buddy (David) delivers a conciliatory speech about the native kids being driven to crime by their deprived upbringing. An ugly movie, with lousy wardrobe to match. MK

Marked Woman

(1937, US, 98 min, b/w)
d Lloyd Bacon. *sc* Robert Rossen, Abem Finkel. *ph* George Barnes. *ed* Jack Killifer. *ad* Max Parker. *m* Bernard Kaun, Heinz Roemheld. *cast* Bette Davis, Humphrey Bogart, Eduardo Ciannelli, Isabel Jewell, Allen Jenkins, Lola Lane, Jane Bryan, Mayo Methot.

●A markedly different sort of gangster movie, this is a *film à clef*, 'torn from the headlines' in the best Warners tradition. In 1936, Special Prosecutor Thomas E Dewey put Lucky Luciano behind bars on prostitution charges. The case hinged on the testimony of three 'working girls' who tied the mob boss directly to the vice operation. The names have been changed, and the less salubrious details swept under the carpet, but to all intents and purposes Bogart plays Dewey (a rare appearance on the right side of the law), Ciannelli is Luciano, and Davis is the prostitute 'Cokey Flo' (here, nightclub hostess Mary Dwight). What really makes the film stand out is its focus on the women, identifying Davis and her girlfriends as the unsung heroines of a cruel economic and social trap; even at their moment of triumph, the girls' future is defined by an uncertain and unsettling fog. Davis shows her mettle, smartly directed by Bacon, and there is strong support, right down to Bogie's wife at the time, Mayo Methot. The hardboiled screenplay is by Robert Rossen and Abem Finkel, who couldn't know that a year later Flo and the others would admit they had perjured themselves for money and legal protection. TCh

Markéta Lazarová

(1967, Czech, 162 min, b/w)
d Frantisek Vlácil. *sc* Frantisek Vlácil, Frantisek Pavlicek. *ph* Bedrick Batka. *ed* Miroslav Hájek. *ad* Oldrich Okác. *cast* Magda Vásáryová, Frantisek Velecky, Michal Kozuch, Zdenek Kryzanek, Pavla Polaskova, Zdenek Kutil, Josef Kemr, Nada Hejna, Jaroslav Moucka.

●An epic medieval meditation, filmed at some length from a purportedly unfilmable novel by Vladislav Vancura. Acting out the intrigue, suspicion and bloodlust of 13th century tribal rivalry, the plot, such as it is, is wilfully wayward and often close to impenetrable. As 'pure cinema', though, it's stark, daring and often astoundingly dynamic. Black and white 'Scope camerawork surveys a cruel, desolate landscape of plains, castles and forests populated by scavenging strays, strugglers, tyrants and wolf-men, while an eerily evocative sound design gives the picture a near hallucinatory quality. It's not so much a drama as an ancient litany – mystical and feral rather than spiritual or religious. NB

Mark of the Vampire

(1935, US, 61 min, b/w)
d Tod Browning. *p* Edward J Mannix. *sc* Guy Endore, Bernard Schubert. *ph* James Wong Howe. *ed* Ben Lewis. *ad* Cedric Gibbons. *cast* Lionel Barrymore, Elizabeth Allan, Bela Lugosi, Lionel Atwill, Jean Hersholt, Donald Meek, Carol Borland.

●A remake of Browning's own silent *London After Midnight* (transported to Czechoslovakia), this semi-parodic vampire thriller creaks here and there, but still has enough style to warrant an honoured place among early horror films. Lashings of lore and atmosphere (strange noises, dancing peasants, bats, spiders and cobwebs) embellish a far-fetched but amusing tale of strange deaths at a sinister castle. It's hard to decide who overacts the most, with Barrymore, Atwill and Lugosi all candidates, though the 'surprise' denouement provides Lugosi with an excuse of a sort. But a real touch of class is present in James Wong Howe's magnificent photography, not to mention Carol Borland's stunning apparition as a vampire. GA

Mark of Zorro, The

(1940, US, 93 min, b/w)
d Rouben Mamoulian. *p* Raymond Griffith. *sc* John Taintor Foote, Garrett Fort, Bess Meredyth. *ph* Arthur Miller. *ed* Robert Bischoff. *ad* Richard Day, Joseph C Wright. *m* Alfred Newman. *cast* Tyrone Power, Linda Darnell, Basil Rathbone, Gale Sondergaard, Eugene Pallette, J Edward Bromberg, Montagu Love.

●A superb swashbuckler, less athletic than the silent Fairbanks version but making up for it on the romantic side, and cleverly choreographing its action scenes until they whisk along like a ballet. Above all it looks terrific, with Mamoulian indulging his passion for shadows, while Arthur Miller's camerawork makes striking use of the contrasting white Spanish architecture and black of Zorro's cape and costume. Rathbone, rarely without a rapier in his hand and forever ferociously limbering up ('He's always stabbing at something' someone wearily complains) until he is summarily skewered in the magnificent final duel, is outstanding as Zorro's malevolent adversary. TM

MARKS (MARKS no Yama)

(1995, Jap, 139 min)
d Yoichi Sai. *sc* Yoichi Sai, Shoichi Maruyama, Renji Tazawa. *ph* Takeshi Hamada. *ed* Kenji Goto. *cast* Kiichi Nakai, Masato Hagiwara, Masato Furuoya, Ittoku Kishibe, Takuzo Kakuno.

● Bafflingly complex but totally assured in tone, style and pace, this adaptation of a celebrated novel by Kaoru Takamura starts out visceral, turns political and winds up metaphysical. The plot conflates a series of seemingly random murders in Tokyo with two dark histories: the fate of a young man orphaned when his parents killed themselves, and the secrets of a college mountaineering club which served as the front for a cell of gay right-wing fanatics. Nakai's down-at-heel detective gives it a very likeable centre. Full of images and scenes which stick in the mind, this is Korean-Japanese director Sai's best film to date. TR

Mark Twain

see Adventures of Mark Twain

Marlene

(1983, W Ger, 94 min, b/w & col)
d Maximilian Schell. *p* Peter Genée. *sc* Meir Dohnal, Maximilian Schell. *ph* Ivan Slapeta, Pavel Hispler, Henry Hauck. *ed* Heidi Genée, Dagmar Hirtz. *ad* Heinz Eickmeier, Zbynek Hloch. *m* Nicholas Economou. *with* Annie Albers, Bernard Hall, Marta Rakosnik, Patricia Schell, William von Stranz.

● How do you make a documentary about a legendary star who will talk but not be filmed (presumably because time has not been altogether kind to the celebrated image)? Schell takes no easy routes, and if the result borders on the pretentious, it rewards repeated viewings. As a starting point, he had twelve hours of taped conversations in which he and Dietrich can be heard arguing, eventually coming to verbal blows: throughout, Dietrich responds with defiant assertions, frequent dismissals of the past and her own performances, a reluctance to reveal much new. Schell supplies the necessary biography and film clips – plus some cruelly revelatory footage of her later stage performances – while brilliantly turning the documentary into a reflection on its own creation. DT

Marlene

(1999, Ger, 125 min)
d Joseph Vilsmaier. *p* Katharina M Trebitsch, Jutta Lieck-Klenke. *sc* Christian Pfannenschmidt. *ph* Joseph Vilsmaier. *ed* Barbara Hennings. *m* Harald Kloser. *cast* Katja Flint, Herbert Knaup, Hans-Werner Meyer, Heino Ferch, Armin Rhode, Cosma Shiva Hagen.

● How to conjure up a diva's fascination when it's embedded in her roles. Any portrait of Marlene Dietrich is bound to fall short of the phenomenon that arises in our heads when we put together *Morocco, Touch of Evil, Destry Rides Again*, etc. But it need not fall short quite so drastically as it does here. Was the woman who could portray the Scarlet Empress really the sentimental housewife this film would have us believe? SB

Marlowe

(1969, US, 95 min)
d Paul Bogart. *p* Gabriel Katzka, Sidney Beckerman. *sc* Stirling Silliphant. *ph* William H Daniels. *ed* Gene Ruggiero. *ad* George W Davis, Addison Hehr. *m* Peter Matz. *cast* James Garner, Gayle Hunnicutt, Carroll O'Connor, Rita Moreno, Sharon Farrell, William Daniels, Jackie Coogan, HM Wynant, Bruce Lee.

● Quite surprising that Chandler's *The Little Sister* – if memory serves, the only Marlowe novel to deal at all with the Hollywood film colony – had never been filmed before. This snappy and stylish update is certainly watchable, even if it lacks the definitive status of *The Big Sleep* (first version) and *The Long Goodbye*. Garner's rumpled charm is engaging enough as he takes on a missing persons case and finds himself sinking into ever more murky waters, while Paul Bogart's solid direction and some fine supporting performances (particularly O'Connor) help to create an atmosphere of almost universal corruptability. Surprisingly, even the inclusion of some fashionable martial arts – courtesy of Bruce Lee – actually works rather well. GA

Marnie

(1964, US, 130 min)
d/p Alfred Hitchcock. *sc* Jay Presson Allen. *ph* Robert Burks. *ed* George Tomasini. *pd* Robert Boyle. *m* Bernard Herrmann. *cast* Sean Connery, Tippi Hedren, Diane Baker, Martin Gabel, Louise Latham, Alan Napier, Mariette Hartley, Bruce Dern.

● Often criticised for its lack of suspense – a quality that underlines its similarity to *Vertigo* – this is neither thriller nor psychodrama, even though it deals with wealthy Connery's marriage to frigid, kleptomaniac Hedren. Rather, it's a perverse romance (from a novel by Winston Graham) which seeks less to explain its eponymous heroine's 'problems' than to examine a relationship based upon extraordinary motivations: Connery, in deciding to marry the woman who has stolen from him and betrayed his trust, is clearly as emotionally confused and unfulfilled as the woman whose mind and past he attempts to investigate. As such, it's as sour a vision of male-female interaction as *Vertigo*, though far less bleak and universal in its implications. That said, it's still thrilling to watch, lush, cool and oddly moving; though the claims of some devotees, arguing that the obviously artificial backdrops are a Brechtian device to make plain Marnie's alienation, are hard to swallow. GA

Marooned

(1969, US, 133 min)
d John Sturges. *p* MJ Frankovich. *sc* Mayo Simon. *ph* Daniel L Fapp. *ed* Walter Thompson. *pd* Lyle R Wheeler. *cast* Gregory Peck, Richard Crenna, David Janssen, James Franciscus, Gene Hackman, Lee Grant, Nancy Kovack, Mariette Hartley, Scott Brady.

● One of Sturges' better films, an extremely realistic space movie about a NASA accident, which had the misfortune to go out on release at precisely the time when the astronauts of Apollo 13 were battling with an exactly similar emergency. Faced with this real-life competition, the film was undeservedly buried. The widescreen effects are first-rate, as is Peck as the embattled controller, and the suspense builds remorselessly to a neat conclusion. DP

Marquis

(1989, Bel/Fr, 83 min)
d Henri Xhonneux. *sc* Roland Torpor, Henri Xhonneux. *ph* Etienne Fauduet. *ed* Chantal Hymans. *ad* Roland Torpor. *m* Reinhardt Wagner. *cast* Philippe Bizot, Bien de Moor, Gabrielle Van Damme, Olivier Dechaveau, Bernard Cogneaux, Pierre Decuypère.

● In this tribute to the Marquis de Sade, the original Mr Whippy of belles lettres is a dreamy-eyed spaniel who spends his time in the Bastille engaging in dispute with his winsome willy, an amiably philosophical member called Colin. French satirist and cartoonist Roland Topor designed and co-wrote this strange Revolutionary romp with Xhonneux. With the cast performing in half-animal, half-human panto drag, the film's principal novelty is to stage the events leading up to the fall of the Bastille as 'Carry On Beatrix Potter'. This the makers do very well, with disarmingly gruesome masks and atmospheric period decor. It's perhaps too burlesque to be disturbing, and there's a weary Gallic saltiness to the dream sequences. De Sade gets a rather easy ride, too, portrayed as content to scribble his sprawling libertine yarns rather than yield to Colin's priapic promptings. But it's a considerable oddity that manages to be witty, thoroughly obscene, and rather endearing all at once. JRo

Marquise

(1997, Fr/It/Switz/Sp, 117 min)
d Véra Belmont. *sc* Jean-François Josselin, Véra Belmont, Marcel Beaulieu. *ph* Jean-Marie Dreujou. *ed* Martine Giordano, Babak Karimi. *ad* Gianni Quaranta. *m* Jordi Savall, Marin Marais, Jean-Baptiste Lully, G Dumanoir, L Rossi. *cast* Sophie Marceau, Bernard Giraudeau, Lambert Wilson, Patrick Timsit, Thierry Lhermitte, Estelle Skornik.

● A lusty girl – 'a dancer, both vertical and horizontal,' as Marquise (Marceau) describes herself – is swept into the carnival atmosphere surrounding Molière's visiting touring company. Having married actor Gros-René, she travels with the troupe to Paris, where she is soon stealing the show with her interval tarantellas and drawing attention to herself with her sans-culottes cartwheels before Louis XIV (Lhermitte) and the bigwigs of Versailles. But, as the stagestruck Marquise forsakes Molière's boozy crew for the self-seeking charms of court favourite Racine (Wilson), will ambition or love prove her downfall? The theatrical whirl in which this whore's progress is set is that of the mid-1660s, the time of Molière's fall and Racine's rise. But the script uses both playwrights as mere agents in Marquise's melodrama, reducing them almost to caricature; only the acting skills of Wilson and, especially, Giraudeau, superb as Molière, make them sympathetic. Marceau dashes around with the brio of her D'Artagnan's Daughter, but as a stage actress she doesn't convince. WH

Marquise von O..., Die (The Marquise of O)

(1976, WGer/Fr, 107 min)
d Eric Rohmer. *p* Klaus Hellvig, Barbet Schroeder. *sc* Eric Rohmer. *ph* Nestor Almendros. *ed* Cécile Decugis. *ad* Rolf Kaden, Halo Gutschwager, Roger von Möllendorff. *m* Roger Delmotte. *cast* Edith Clever, Bruno Ganz, Peter Lühr, Edda Seippel, Otto Sander, Ezzo Huber, Bernhard Frey, Eric Rohmer.

● Based on a novella by Heinrich von Kleist set at the time of the Napoleonic Wars. A virtuous widow (Clever), saved from rape and then, while asleep, raped by her rescuer (Ganz), is cast off by her family when she gives birth to a child and proclaims her innocence, only to be then courted by her 'heroic rescuer', whom she doesn't know is the father of her child. In the course of the story, Kleist sets out in a most ironically literary fashion a series of arguments about the place of women in society. Rohmer's great achievement is that it is this, rather than merely the story, that he has brought to the screen, recreating and making even more ironic Kleist's literary written conversations, and opting, in his colour scheme, sets and camerawork, for a style that hovers between formalism and realism, and so further distances the viewer from the characters. PH

Marriage of Maria Braun, The (Die Ehe der Maria Braun)

(1978, WGer, 119 min)
d Rainer Werner Fassbinder. *p* Michael Fengler. *sc* Peter Märthesheimer, Pea Fröhlich. *ph* Michael Ballhaus. *ed* Juliane Lorenz, Franz Walsch [Rainer Werner Fassbinder]. *ad* Norbert Scherer. *m* Peer Raben. *cast* Hanna Schygulla, Klaus Löwitsch, Ivan Desny, Gottfried John, Gisela Uhlen, Günther Lamprecht, Hark Bohm. Elisabeth Trissenaar.

● Knowing in advance that Fassbinder considers the institution of marriage to be the most insidious trap that mankind has yet devised for itself doesn't prepare you for *The Marriage of Maria Braun*. It opens in 1943 as an air raid hits Maria and Hermann Braun's wedding ceremony, and closes with another explosion, highly ambiguous in effect and implication. In between, Hermann goes missing on the Russian front, serves years in jail, and emigrates to the States, while Maria sails through unruffled, acquiring wealth and position pending his return. It is at once Fassbinder's most conventional and elusive film: that final explosion keeps ricocheting long after it's over. TR

Marriage Story (Kyolhon Iyagi)

(1992, SKor, 101 min)
d Kim Ui-Seok. *cast* Choi Min-Su, Shim Hye-Jin.

● The 'honeymoon period' ends the night he asks her to give him a blow-job in the car. She realises that she's been getting less than him from the sex, and the marriage starts going downhill. Her professional progress (she graduates from dubbing foreign movies – Kim Novak in *Vertigo* – to working in radio plays) boosts her self-assurance. In Korea, though, a wife who puts herself at the same level as her husband is effectively ending the marriage. A key film for Korea's 'new cinema' (a huge domestic hit, it inspired a flood of imitations), this is an unerringly accurate account of feminist stirrings in a very patriarchal society. It's also really funny. TR

Married Couple, A

(1969, Can, 112 min)
d/p/sc Allan King. *ph* Richard Leiterman. *ed* Arla Saara. *m* Zal Yanofsky. *with* Billy Edwards, Antoinette Edwards, Bogart Edwards.

● Cinema not quite *vérité* as a camera crew camp out in a couple's house and watch their not quite every move. A frightening picture of the acquisitive society, but on the whole the bland camera fails to probe deep enough to make either good documentary or interesting escapism.

Married to the Mob

(1988, US, 104 min)
d Jonathan Demme. *p* Kenneth Utt, Edward Saxon. *sc* Barry Strugatz, Mark R Burns. *ph* Tak Fujimoto. *ed* Craig McKay. *pd* Kristi Zea. *m* David Byrne. *cast* Michelle Pfeiffer, Mathew Modine, Dean Stockwell, Mercedes Reuhl, Alec Baldwin, Trey Wilson, Joan Cusack, Todd Solondz.

● When philandering Mafia hitman 'Cucumber' Frank de Marco is killed by his boss Tony 'The Tiger' Russo, his widow Angela (Pfeiffer) decides to abandon her stockbroker-belt home (bursting with stolen goods) and start anew with a job and a dingy room on the Lower East Side. Easier said than done: obsessively amorous Tony (Stockwell) courts her with a vengeance, while FBI agent Mike Downey (Modine) suspects that she planned Frank's death with Tony. If the slim plot of Demme's romantic black comedy lacks the outrageous panache and exhilarating twists of *Something Wild*, the film nevertheless delights through its sheer good-humoured glee in all that is kitsch or off-the-wall, and its wealth of inventive incidental details. While it's all relentlessly shallow, the performances, music and gaudy visuals provide a fizzy vitality for which many other directors would give their right arm. Amazingly, for all its hip anarchy, it's finally an oddly old-fashioned slice of entertainment. Preston Sturges might have approved. GA

Married Woman, A

see Femme Mariée, Une

Marrying Kind, The

(1952, US, 92 min, b/w)
d George Cukor. *p* Bert Granet. *sc* Ruth Gordon, Garson Kanin. *ph* Joseph Walker. *ed* Charles Nelson. *ad* John Meehan. *m* Hugo Friedhofer. *cast* Judy Holliday, Aldo Ray, Madge Kennedy, Mickey Shaughnessy, Griff Barnett.

● A poignant little tragi-comedy, scripted by Ruth Gordon and Garson Kanin, about a lower middle-class couple (Holliday and Ray) whose marriage cannot withstand the pressures against them. The divorce court listens first to the husband's story, then to the wife's, and then the judge arrives at some notion of 'the truth'. It's contrived, but the film's critique of traditional gender roles within marriage is still sharp, and Judy Holliday shows an unexpected depth. TCh

Marrying Man, The (aka Too Hot to Handle)

(1991, US, 116 min)
d Jerry Rees. *p* David Permut. *sc* Neil Simon. *ph* Donald E Thorin. *ed* Michael Jablow. *pd* William F Matthews. *m* David Newman. *cast* Kim Basinger, Alec Baldwin, Robert Loggia, Elisabeth Shue, Armand Assante, Paul Reiser, Fisher Stevens.

● Handsome playboy Charley Pearl (Baldwin) has finally opted for stability, and is set to marry the respectable daughter (Shue) of a movie mogul. But on the way to his bachelor party, he is smitten by sultry nightclub singer Vicki (Basinger), and they embark on a tempestuous, on-off relationship which encompasses four marriages. It's hard to spot vintage Neil Simon in his screenplay for this indulgent comedy, which exhaustively examines the premise that no one lover can provide both passion *and* emotional security. The action kicks off in 1948, a period which throws up various characters supposed to remind us of real-life celebrity counterparts; such comparisons, however, are lost amid the clichéd dialogue uttered by Charley's adoring entourage of showbiz buddies, whose apparent function is to make the not-so-loving couple appear more exciting and glamorous. Alas, to little effect. CM

Marry Me! Marry Me!

see Mazel Tov ou le mariage

Mars Attacks!

(1996, US, 106 min)
d Tim Burton. *p* Tim Burton, Larry Franco. *sc* Jonathan Gems. *ph* Peter Suschitzky. *ed* Chris Lebenzon. *pd* Wynn Thomas. *m* Danny Elfman. *cast* Glenn Close, Michael J Fox, Pierce Brosnan, Danny DeVito, Annette Bening, Jack Nicholson, Martin Short, Sarah Jessica Parker, Rod Steiger, Tom Jones, Lukas Haas, Sylvia Sidney, Paul Winfield, Pam Grier, Joe Don Baker, Jerzy Skolimowski, Barbet Schroeder.

● Earth's in peril, yet again, and the US President must call the shots. This time, though, we're rooting for the space invaders. Tim Burton's film is the most subversive big-budget Hollywood production in years, a splenetic satire which gleefully trashes contemporary culture – politics, science and religion, the army, TV, food, music, even money. Unfortunately, it's not very good. The tacky design undoubtedly cost a fortune, and there's a real perversity in casting superstars to ham it up in homage to Ed Wood. The anarchy is sometimes inspired (Burton incinerates Congress, movie stars and doves with equal abandon – he loves playing Godzilla), but much of the film is flat and cripplingly indulgent. It feels nearly half an hour too long, and Nicholson, in a double role, is just too much. It's a personal work, but not a mature one. It didn't hit home at the US box-office, but the reviews have been surprisingly accommodating. In that sense, this sour, prefabricated cult movie has the last laugh – and I'm afraid the joke's on us. TCh

Marseillaise, La

(1937, Fr, 145, b/w)
d/p Jean Renoir. *sc* Jean Renoir, Carl Koch, N Martel Dreyfus. *ph* Jean Bourgoin, Alain Douarinou, Jean-Marie Maillols, Jean-Paul Alphen, Jean Louis. *ed* Marguerite Renoir. *ad* Léon Barsacq, Georges Wakhévitch, Jean Perrier. *m* Lalande, Grétry, Rameau, Mozart, JS Bach, Rouget de l'Isle. *cast* Pierre Renoir, Lise Delamare, Andrex, Edmond Ardisson, Nadia Sibirskaia, Louis Jouvet, Léon Larive, Gaston Modot, Julien Carette.

● A heroically romantic interpretation of the events leading up to the French Revolution; its postulation of an alternative to nationalism vs monarchism is obviously closely related to the Popular Front period during which the film was made. But this is also something that, along with Renoir's sweeping emotional populism, tends to distance us from much of the film. However, even if you're not particularly attuned to Renoir's values (simplicity, nature, etc), he is always sufficiently shrewd in his analysis of the aristocracy for those sections of the film to have an air of authentic and haunting decadence. It is a relief, too, to see the lingering archaism of the earlier sections of the film swept away in an astonishing last third of quiet power.

Marseille Contract, The

(1974, GB/Fr, 90 min)
d Robert Parrish. *p/sc* Judd Bernard. *ph* Douglas Slocombe. *ed* Willy Kemplen. *ad* Willy Holt. *m* Roy Budd. *cast* Michael Caine, Anthony Quinn, James Mason, Alexandra Stewart, Maureen Kerwin, Marcel Bozzuffi, Catherine Rouvel, Maurice Ronet, Gene Moskowitz.

● The old routine: tough cop, bent colleagues, dope shipment, hired killer…varied by moving the location to Paris and Marseille, by making Quinn a top US Embassy official, and by making his best buddy the contract killer out to get the untouchable 'respected member of society'. Despite the routine situation and the routine casting of Quinn, Caine and Mason (Caine actually perking the film into some semblance of interest), Parrish does manage to infiltrate a little intelligence into the proceedings from time to time. But he can't shift the nagging sense of numbing over-familiarity. VG

Martha

(1974, WGer, 95 min)
d Rainer Werner Fassbinder. *p* Peter Märthesheimer. *sc* Rainer Werner Fassbinder. *ph* Michael Ballhaus. *ed* Liesgret Schmitt-Klink. *pd* Kurt Raab. *cast* Margit Carstensen, Karlheinz Böhm, Gisela Fackeldey, Adrian Hoven, Barbara Valentin, Ingrid Caven. Peter Chatel.

● The everyday fascism Fassbinder dissects often rests on the simple observation that there are elements of sado-masochism even in such respectable bourgeois relationships as true romance and happy-ever-after marriage. Here, his script an adaptation of a story by Cornell Woolrich, he takes the staples of the Sirk melodrama (love at first sight, a big-dipper courtship, a honeymoon drive) and stands them on their heads, combining '40s costumes and movie references with recognisably real locations and high colour photography. He forces to their logical extremes the attitudes implicit in the woman's weepie and the little woman's traditional craving for a strong and competent man, pushing a sentimental romance into a high camp study of SM, full of images of vampirism, claustrophobia and haunted house genre movies. With no explicit references to a world beyond the screen, with indulgently aesthetic settings and outlandishly theatrical performances (notably from Carstensen as the perennially hapless victim), he creates a dazzling baroque abstraction with unsettling relevance to even the most mundane domestic partnerships. JD

Martha & Ethel

(1993, US, 77 min, b/w & col)
d Jyll Johnstone. *p* Jyll Johnstone, Barbara Ettinger. *ph* Joseph Friedman. *ed* Toby Shimin. *with* Martha Kneifel, Ethel Edwards.

● The nannies profiled in director Johnstone and co-producer Barbara Ettinger's absorbing documentary – Ethel, a black woman born in the Deep South, who worked for the Ettingers; and Martha, Johnstone's mother substitute, a former Rhine maiden who emigrated to the US in the mid-'30s – couldn't come from more different worlds, or embody more polarised values. Yet their lives ran curiously parallel. The film cuts between both them, incorporating archive footage (*Mädchen in Uniform* for Martha), photographs and contemporary music, together with extensive interviews and reflections from the nannies' now grown-up charges and employers. Ettinger takes Ethel back to South Carolina; Martha, likewise, is taken back to Oberkirch where, in an open carriage, she's feted by the mayor and dances a jig of joy that was a long time coming. The two women were born a couple of years apart in the first decade of the century; each struck out alone in her 30s, almost single-handedly raising someone else's large family. Seeing them in their 90s brings home very powerfully what can only be described as the workings of destiny in our lives. WH

Martha – Meet Frank, Daniel and Laurence

(1998, GB, 88 min)
d Nick Hamm. *p* Grainne Marmion. *sc* Peter Morgan. *ph* David Johnson. *ed* Michael Bradsell. *pd* Max Gottlieb. *m* Ed Shearmur. *cast* Monica Potter, Rufus Sewell, Tom Hollander, Joseph Fiennes, Ray Winstone, Deborah Weston.

● A love story in which three men take just two days to fall for the same woman. Martha (Potter), a blonde American, flies into London almost empty-handed, ready to start the rest of her life. The lads are childhood friends, now grown somewhat apart. Daniel (Hollander) is an unconvincingly successful but convincingly brazen music executive with a jet setting lifestyle and ego. Frank (Sewell) is an unemployed actor seemingly more motivated to spite Daniel than to find work. Caught in the middle, Laurence (Fiennes) is the shy, sensitive type, who teaches bridge to old ladies, finds his pals frustratingly self-absorbed, and generally looks flushed and uncomfortable as if wondering quite how he got into all this. Nothing special. NB

Martin

(1976, US, 95 min)
d George A Romero. *p* Richard Rubinstein. *sc* George A Romero. *ph* Michael Gornick. *ed* George A Romero. *m* Donald Rubinstein. *cast* John Amplas, Lincoln Maazel, Christine Forrest, Elyane Nadeau, Tom Savini, George A Romero.

● A dazzling opening sequence (not for the squeamish) as a teenage vampire of today (Amplas) satisfies his bloodlust in a railway sleeper compartment. Thereafter, Romero plays fascinating games with myth and reality as he balances traditional vampire lore against medically certifiable psychosis. Fundamentally a quite serious movie, relevant to contemporary personality problems and stresses, but shot through with a wicked streak of black humour. It doesn't always come off, but Romero makes stunning use of his Pittsburgh locations to create a desolate suburban wasteland, and at its best it is rivetingly raw-edged. TM

Martins, The

(2001, GB, 87 min)
d Tony Grounds. *p* Greg Brenman, Dixie Linder, Bruce Davey. *sc* Tony Grounds. *ph* David Johnson. *ed* Robin Sales. *pd* Michael Carlin. *m* Richard Hartley. *cast* Lee Evans, Kathy Burke, Linda Bassett, Eric Byrne, Terri Dumont, Frank Finlay, Lennie James, Jack Shepherd, Mark Strong, Ray Winstone.

●Unemployed layabout Robert Martin (Evans) always feels hard done by. Thinking he's a let-down to his wife Angie (Burke) and the kids, he enters competitions in the hope of winning the things he feels his dysfunctional family deserves. This time, it's a dream holiday. But when he finds he hasn't won – again – he decides he's had enough and, freaking out, sets out to steal the holiday instead. It would be misleading to judge this directorial debut by writer Grounds on the comic reputations of its stars. That's not to say the film isn't a comedy, because it's littered with scraps of absurd dark humour. But if you're banking on Evans' hilariously physical stand-up performance or expecting Burke to resurrect her Waynetta Slob persona, you'll be disappointed. And that – with due respect – is a good thing, because it's their talent for drama that makes the film. Grounds' screenplay strikes a yin-yang balance between realist drama and something more ridiculous. But Evans and Burke's superb performances, as a couple truly in love with each other and trying to make the best of what they have, make this a beautiful snapshot of life. AL

Marty

(1955, US, 90 min, b/w)
d Delbert Mann. *p* Harold Hecht. *sc* Paddy Chayefsky. *ph* Joseph La Shelle. *ed* Alan Crosland Jr. *ad* Ted Haworth, Walter M Simonds. *m* Roy Webb. *cast* Ernest Borgnine, Betsy Blair, Joe De Santis, Esther Minciotti, Karen Steele, Jerry Paris.

●Sentimental tale of a butcher from the Bronx, afraid he is too ugly to attract girls, who takes pity on a plain jane schoolteacher at a dance, then finds love sidling up crabwise. Overrated at the time, largely because its teleplay origins (by Paddy Chayefsky) brought a veneer of naturalism and close-up intimacy to the Hollywood of the day. But it does have doggy charm and a certain perceptiveness (the butcher's continuing doubts as to what his mates will think; his mother's jealousy despite constant nagging about marriage). TM

Martyrs of Love (Mucednící Lásky)

(1966, Czech, 73 min, b/w)
d Jan Nemec. *sc* Ester Krumbachová, Jan Nemec. *ph* Miroslav Ondricek. *ed* Miroslav Hájek. *ad* Oldrich Bosák. *m* Jan Klusák, Karel Mares. *cast* Petr Kopriva, Marta Kubisová; Hana Kuberová, Jan Klusák; Josef Konicek, Denisa Dvoráková.

●These three dreams of frustration date from the Prague Spring. A clerk is surrounded by sexuality, but he himself never manages to partake. A woman is driven to a country estate full of authority figures; fleeing, she encounters a guitarist on a train, but there the dream ends. A man is beckoned to join a garden party: fun, sex, friendship are on offer. But he has to leave, and can't find the place when he tries to go back. Shot in coal black and bleached white, this is a sympathetic but exasperating mish-mash of Freud, Magritte and old movies, with the justification that, after all, dreams *do* tend to be just such a mish-mash. Lindsay Anderson glowers on a staircase in the first episode. BBa

Marvin's Room

(1996, US, 98 min)
d Jerry Zaks. *p* Scott Rudin, Jane Rosenthal, Robert De Niro. *sc* Scott McPherson. *ph* Piotr Sobocinski. *ed* Jim Clark. *pd* David Gropman. *m* Rachel Portman. *cast* Meryl Streep, Diane Keaton, Leonardo DiCaprio, Robert De Niro, Hume Cronyn, Gwen Verdon, Hal Scardino, Dan Hedaya.

●Hairdresser and single mum Lee (Streep), struggling with rebellious teenager Hank (DiCaprio), gets an invitation to visit – after some 20 years – from her estranged sister Bessie (Keaton). On arrival in Florida, Lee finds that ditzy Dr Wally (De Niro) has not only diagnosed Bessie as having leukaemia, but her sister is also facing decisions about the care of their stroke-ridden father Marvin (Cronyn) and elderly aunt Ruth (Verdon), with whom Bessie shares her home. The movie's subject is how need and the imminence of death can be catalysts for growth, closer family feeling and love. First-time director Zaks has fashioned a restrained weepie, adapted by Scott McPherson from his own stage play, which doesn't so much open up the text as harness it to strong ensemble performances, with the actors investing power in restricted, even staple, roles: Streep gives her most credible blue-collar performance to date; Keaton sidesteps saintliness to mix vulnerability and small heroics. In concert with this, the film is shot with discreet professionalism, while Rachel Portman confirms her mastery of mildly melodramatic mood music. WH

Mary of Scotland

(1936, US, 123 min, b/w)
d John Ford. *p* Pandro S Berman. *sc* Dudley Nichols. *ph* Joseph H August. *ed* Jane Loring. *ad* Van Nest Polglase, Carroll Clark. *m* Max Steiner. *cast* Katharine Hepburn, Fredric March, Florence Eldridge, John Carradine, Donald Crisp, Douglas Walton, Robert Barrat, Moroni Olsen.

●A better film than its reputation would suggest, marvellously shot by Joe August, and with Ford making striking use of the imposing RKO sets even while remaining strangled by the arty ambitions of Maxwell Anderson's play (which contrives to reduce history to a novelette chronicling the jealous rivalry that drove Elizabeth Tudor to destroy Mary Stuart). One electric sequence – a hellfire sermon delivered by Moroni Olsen as John Knox – shows the extent to which Ford remained uninvolved elsewhere by the polite conventions of historical costume drama, but the performances are fascinating in their careful, slightly stilted way, and it looks terrific. TM

Mary Poppins

(1964, US, 139 min)
d Robert Stevenson. *p* Walt Disney. *sc* Bill Walsh, Don DaGradi. *ph* Edward Colman. *ed* Cotton Warburton. *ad* Carroll Clark, William H Tuntke. *songs* Richard M Sherman, Robert B Sherman. *cast* Julie Andrews, Dick Van Dyke, David Tomlinson, Glynis Johns, Hermione Baddeley, Karen Dotrice, Elsa Lanchester, Arthur Treacher, Reginald Owen, Ed Wynn.

●Compared to even 'sophisticated' juvenile fodder, the sheer exuberance of Disney's adaptation of PL Travers' children's classic should tickle the most jaded fancy. Indeed, the film can hardly contain itself with its catalogue of memorable songs, battery of dance routines, and strong supporting cast. As for the leads, Julie Andrews, after beating off other pretenders to the role (in part because Walt liked the way she whistled), produced an Academy Award-winning portrayal of the Edwardian nanny whose mad magic seethes beneath a patina of respectability that is, as Mary Poppins' references state, 'practically perfect in every way'. But oh, Dick Van Dyke's Cockney accent! You can hardly understand him with his mouth open – but you probably wouldn't recognise him with his mouth closed. FD

Mary, Queen of Scots

(1971, GB, 128 min)
d Charles Jarrott. *p* Hal B Wallis. *sc* John Hale. *ph* Christopher Challis. *ed* Richard Marden. *pd* Terence Marsh. *m* John Barry. *cast* Vanessa Redgrave, Glenda Jackson, Patrick McGoohan, Timothy Dalton, Nigel Davenport, Trevor Howard, Ian Holm, Daniel Massey, Maria Aitken.

●Meticulously schoolmarmish, John Hale's script lays out all the power plays behind Elizabeth Tudor's battle to keep Mary Stuart off her throne, but fails to provide much else. Redgrave (melting) and Jackson (tetchy) are head girls on the opposing teams, while Jarrott, who made a small corner for himself in this sort of coffee-table kitsch (*Anne of the Thousand Days, Lost Horizon*) before walking on the wilder side (*The Other Side of Midnight*), never lifts it much above the level of a village pageant. TM

Mary Reilly

(1996, US, 109 min)
d Stephen Frears. *p* Ned Tanen, Nancy Graham Tanen, Norma Heyman. *sc* Christopher Hampton. *ph* Philippe Rousselot. *ed* Lesley Walker. *pd* Stuart Craig. *m* George Fenton. *cast* Julia Roberts, John Malkovich, Glenn Close, George Cole, Michael Gambon, Michael Sheen, Linda Bassett, Ciaran Hinds, Moya Brady.

●Coppola's *Dracula*, Branagh's *Frankenstein*, Jordan's *Vampire*, and now Frears' *Jekyll and Hyde*. Will these horrors never cease? A more modest failure than the others, this lacks the vaulting artistic hubris to compensate for its over-produced, over-determined inertia. The film, adapted by Christopher Hampton from a novel by Valerie Martin, approaches Stevenson's characters from a new angle: the point of view of a scullery maid in Dr Jekyll's household. Such nifty cultural repackaging sounds intriguing, but comes a cropper as soon as it's apparent that Mary (Roberts) is missing all the action: she cleans up after the murders, watches while Jekyll goes into his lab and Hyde comes out, flirts timidly with both – and that's just the highlights. It's not all bad: cinematographer Philippe Rousselot enshrouds everything in a fine Victorian fog, and George Fenton contributes an atmospheric score, but Frears never seems to get a fix on the material. If her accent is all over the place, it's hardly Roberts' fault that her pale, gaunt Mary seems to have been sampling the doctor's concoctions. Columbia have grafted on a panicky blood-and-thunder climax, with a belated transformation scene, but the film remains obstinately decorous, about as scary as an episode of *Upstairs, Downstairs*. TCh

Mary Shelley's Frankenstein

(1994, US, 123 min)
d Kenneth Branagh. *p* Francis Ford Coppola, James V Hart, John Veitch. *sc* Steph Lady, Frank Darabont. *ph* Roger Pratt. *ed* Andrew Marcus. *pd* Tim Harvey. *m* Patrick Doyle. *cast* Robert De Niro, Kenneth Branagh, Helena Bonham Carter, Tom Hulce, John Cleese, Richard Briers, Aidan Quinn, Ian Holm, Robert Hardy, Celia Imrie, Cherie Lunghi.

●In returning to Mary Shelley's novel, Kenneth Branagh presumably intended to give his version of the much-told tale authenticity and depth. But the finished film, regrettably, for all it's romantic bombast, lacks the poetry and pathos of James Whale's 1931 classic, let alone the wit of the later *Bride of Frankenstein*. De Niro, as the hapless creature, is dependably sympathetic, eyes expressive beneath *Elephant Man*-style make-up. The rest of the cast, however, are pretty dismal: chest-baring Branagh, too earnest and dashing, as the obsessive Victor; Helena Bonham Carter, an inappropriately modern miss, as the doc's beloved Elizabeth; Cleese, ever the Python, a morose medical lecturer with a murky past; Briers as a blind peasant devoted to the good life. Equally uninspired is Steph Lady and Frank Darabont's often gratingly modern script and Branagh's far from light direction. Continuity seems all over the shop. Not frightening, just silly. GA

Masada (aka The Antagonists)

(1980, US, 121 min)
d Boris Sagal. *p* George Eckstein. *sc* Joel Oliansky. *ph* Paul Lohmann. *ed* Robert L Kimble. *pd* Jack Senter. *m* Jerry Goldsmith, Morton Stevens. *cast* Peter O'Toole, Peter Strauss, Barbara Carrera, Anthony Quayle, David Warner, Clive Francis, Giulia Pagano, Denis Quilley, Timothy West.

●A boiled down – but still interminable – version of the four-part TV series adapted from Ernest K Gann's novel, this is a sort of would-be Biblical epic with Zionist overtones. Set in Judea during the first century AD, it tells the tale of Masada, the fortress defiantly held against the might of Rome by a handful of Jews fighting to retrieve their freedom – and their homeland – after the sack of Jerusalem by Roman colonialists. In between lengthy bouts of scuffling, with rhubarbing Jews and Romans prodding each other with tinny swords, the Jewish leader Eleazar (Strauss) is as strong and silent as a good Zionist guerilla should be, while the Roman commander (O'Toole) ponders the ironies of good government and the loneliness of the long-distance colonial administrator. Terrible stuff, irretrievably scuttled by O'Toole's hollow, ranting performance. TM

Ma Saison Préférée (My Favourite Season)

(1993, Fr, 127 min)
d André Téchiné. *p* Alain Sarde. *sc* André Téchiné, Pascal Bonitzer. *ph* Thierry Arbogast. *ed* Martine Giordano. *ad* Carlos Conti. *m* Philippe Sarde. *cast* Catherine Deneuve, Daniel Auteuil, Marthe Villalonga, Jean-Pierre Bouvier, Chiara Mastroianni, Carmen Chaplin, Jean Bosquet, Ingrid Caven.
●Here is Gallic star power saving a standard domestic drama from mediocrity. Emilie (Deneuve) is a notary public in a small town in south-west France, her younger brother Antoine (Auteuil) a top Toulouse neurologist, while their widowed mother Berthe (Villalonga) lives alone, causing both offspring no little concern. Their ongoing confrontation over care plans for the old girl reveals the emptiness in their own personal lives. The performances bring these emotional entanglements to vivid, awkward life: Auteuil, as in *Un Coeur en Hiver*, manages to warm our sympathy for a fundamentally detached, even dislikeable character; and Deneuve glides elegantly through another two hours of screen time desired by all, but incapable of love herself. Before you know it you're affected. TJ

Masala

(1991, Can, 106 min)
d Srinivas Krishna. *p* Srinivas Krishna, Camelia Freiberg. *sc* Srinivas Krishna. *ph* Paul Sarossy. *ed* Michael Munn. *pd* Tamara Deverell. *m* The West India Company, Leslie Winston. *cast* Srinivas Krishna, Sakina Jaffrey, Zohra Segal, Saeed Jaffrey, Heri Johal, Madhuri Bhatia.
●From the opening of Srinivas Krishna's vibrant directorial debut, you know you're in for something different as an obviously model plane explodes and brightly coloured saris float down. Aboard are an Indian family returning home after emigrating to Canada, and the film recounts a bizarre chain of events among the extended family they leave behind. Rebel son Krishna (played by the director) returns to the fold, introducing one cousin to magic mushrooms, another to sex; his rich uncle harbours suspected terrorists in his sari shop while hobnobbing with the Minister of Multi-Culturalism; Grandma Tikkoo (the wonderfully expressive Segal) communicates with Lord Krishna via her video recorder; and Mounties ride around Toronto trying to keep the chaos under control. An uplifting, extremely funny film, this has some serious things to say about sexuality, race, religion and politics. It takes risks – drawing on Hindi musicals to convey the characters' inner lives isn't an unqualified success – but without them, *Masala* wouldn't be nearly as spicy. CO'S

Mascara

(1987, Bel/Neth/Fr/US, 98 min)
d Patrick Conrad. *p* Pierre Drouot, Rene Solleveld, Henry Lange. *sc* Hugo Claus, Patrick Conrad, Pierre Drouot. *ph* Gilberto Azevedo. *ed* Susana Rossberg. *ad* Dirk Debou, Misjel Vermeiren. *m* Egisto Macchi. *cast* Charlotte Rampling, Michael Sarrazin, Derek De Lint, Jappe Claes, Herbert Flack, Harry Cleven, Eva Robbins.
●At a performance of Gluck's *Orpheus and Eurydice*, twisted police chief Sanders (Sarrazin) and his incestuously beloved sister Gaby (Rampling) befriend the costume designer (De Lint). Gaby is enamoured of the designer's good looks, Sanders of one of his slinky creations, which he fancies for someone at a subterranean dive, where he and his cronies (straight off Genet's Balcony) amuse themselves listening to transvestite divas miming to Bellini, or watching chain-mailed leather boys swapping oysters mouth-to-mouth. Later discovering that the old (but unconsummated) flame for whom he had acquired the dress has something(s) in her panties, Sanders strangles her/him in disgust. The whole sordid affair dribbles on headlong to such a bathetic climax that even ardent searchers after nefarious enjoyment should draw seven veils over this one. WH

Maschera, La

see Mask, The

Maschera del Demonio, La (Black Sunday/Mask of the Demon/Revenge of the Vampire)

(1960, It, 88 min, b/w)
d Mario Bava. *p* Massimo De Rita, (US version) Lou Rusoff. *sc* Ennio De Concini, Mario Serandrei, Mario Bava, Marcello Coscia. *ph* Mario Bava. *ed* Mario Serandrei, (US version) Salvatore Billitteri. *ad* Giorgio Giovannini. *m* Roberto Nicolosi. *cast* Barbara Steele, John Richardson, Ivo Garrani, Andrea Cecchi, Ivo Garrani, Arturo Dominici, Enrico Olivieri.
●A classic horror film (from a story by Gogol) involving Barbara Steele as a resurrected witch who was burned to death in a small medieval town and seeks revenge on her persecutors. The exquisitely realised expressionist images of cruelty and sexual suggestion shocked audiences in the early '60s, and occasioned a long-standing ban by the British censor. The visual style still impresses, but the story beneath it has become too formularised for the film to retain all its original power. DP

Masculin Féminin (Masculine Feminine)

(1966, Fr/Swe, 110 min, b/w)
d/sc Jean-Luc Godard. *ph* Willy Kurant. *ed* Agnès Guillemot. *m* Francis Lai. *cast* Jean-Pierre Léaud, Chantal Goya, Catherine-Isabelle Duport, Marlène Jobert, Michel Debord, Birger Malmsten, Eva Britt Strandberg, Brigitte Bardot, Françoise Hardy.
●Godard offers '15 precise facts' about the children of Marx and Coca-Cola: a series of scattershot observations of young people in Paris in 1965. This is pre-political Godard, which means that it attacks on all cylinders without having any strong line of its own. But its parodies and satires are recklessly inventive, and its fundamental pessimism isn't as flip as it may at first seem. TR

M*A*S*H

(1969, US, 116 min)
d Robert Altman. *p* Ingo Preminger. *sc* Ring Lardner Jr. *ph* Harold Stine. *ed* Danford B Greene. *ad* Jack Martin Smith, Arthur Lonergan. *m* Johnny Mandel. *cast* Donald Sutherland, Elliott Gould, Tom Skerritt, Sally Kellerman, Robert Duvall, Jo Ann Pflug, Rene Auberjonois, Gary Burghoff, Fred Williamson, John Schuck, Bud Cort.
●Altman's idiosyncratic career received a dramatic boost when he took Ring Lardner Jr's script (already turned down by a dozen directors) and turned it into a box-office smash. Dealing with the crazily humorous activities of a Mobile Army Surgical Hospital's staff amid the carnage of the Korean (read Vietnam) war, it shows Altman's stylistic signature in embryonic form: a large number of fast-talking eccentric characters, a series of revealing vignettes rather than a structured plot, comparisons of real life with media versions purveyed by the camp's radio, and semi-audible, overlapping dialogue. It's frantic, clever fun, but in comparison with later works such as *Thieves Like Us* and *The Long Goodbye*, its cynical stance often rings hollow; its targets – military decorum, religious platitudes and sexual hypocrisy – are too easy, and there's little of the director's muted, unsentimental humanism in evidence. GA

Mask

(1985, US, 120 min)
d Peter Bogdanovich. *p* Martin Starger. *sc* Anna Hamilton Phelan. *ph* Laszlo Kovacs. *ed* Barbara Ford. *ad* Norman Newberry. *cast* Cher, Sam Elliott, Eric Stoltz, Estelle Getty, Richard Dysart, Laura Dern, Harry Carey Jr, Nick Cassavetes.
●Rocky Dennis (Stoltz), a boy with an appallingly deformed skull, at 16 has already far outlived doctors' predictions. The most effective scenes deal with Rocky's determined attempt to confront everyday problems: school, rows with parents and friends, growing up. Elsewhere the film becomes mawkish: the bike gang who act as Rocky's friends/occasional bodyguards seem idealised, while the romance between bike jock Gar (Elliott) and Rocky's mother (Cher) tends to curdle the stomach. Still, Bogdanovich invests the story with warmth, generosity and considerable power. RR

Mask, The (aka The Eyes of Hell)

(1961, Can, 83 min, b/w & col)
d/p Julian Roffman. *sc* Frank Taubes, Sandy Haber, (dream sequences) Slavko Vorkapich. *ph* Herbert S Alpert. *ed* Stephen Timar. *ad* David S Ballou, Hugo Wuehtrich. *m* Louis Applebaum. *cast* Paul Stevens, Claudette Nevins, Bill Walker, Anne Collings, Martin Lavut, Leo Leyden, Eleanor Beecroft.
●A totally banal murder plot is enlivened by sequences depicting the psychedelic nightmares induced by a magical burial mask, which impel first an archaeologist (Lavut), then the psychiatrist who refuses to believe him (Stevens), to murderous frenzies. When the mask is put on, the audience gets the cue to put on the cardboard specs. The 3-D process is tacky in the extreme, but some of the graphic effects (credited to Slavko Vorkapich) are quite unusual.

Mask, The (La Maschera)

(1988, It, 90 min)
d Fiorella Infascelli. *p* Lilia Smecchia, Ettore Rosboch. *sc* Adriano Aprà, Fiorella Infascelli, Ennio De Concini, Enzo Yngari. *ph* Acacio De Almeida. *ed* Francesco Melvestito. *pd* Antonello Geleng, Stefania Benelli. *m* Luis Bacalov. *cast* Michael Maloney, Helena Bonham Carter, Feodor Chaliapin Jr, Roberto Herlitzka, Michele de Marchi.
●Lush, if not mushy romance, in the 18th century Italian style, as playboy Maloney falls hard for travelling-player Bonham Carter. She promptly cold-shoulders him, but soon becomes fascinated by the enigmatic stranger who appears in her life. Decorative trappings, but the moth-eaten plot, regrettably, comes straight from the give-me-a-break file. TJ

Mask, The

(1994, US, 101 min)
d Charles Russell. *p* Bob Engelman. *sc* Mike Werb. *ph* John R Leonetti. *ed* Arthur Coburn. *pd* Craig Sterans. *m* Randy Edelman. *cast* Jim Carrey, Cameron Diaz, Peter Riegert, Peter Greene, Amy Yasbeck, Richard Jeni.
●Stanley Ipkiss is a likeable schmuck, a bank teller who wouldn't say 'boo' to a goose. Men don't give him a second glance, women look right through him – until, one night, Stanley happens across an ancient mask. Wearing it, he's transformed into a lime-faced bundle of mischievous energy, part man, part loony tune. 'I could be a superhero,' he muses, 'a force for good…' But first for some fun: he wreaks vengeful havoc at his local garage, robs the bank where he works, and sweeps lovely nightclub chanteuse Tina (Diaz) off her feet. This is a treat, a classic Jekyll and Hyde story for the '90s. Director Russell brings a lowbrow pulp rigour to the material that's reminiscent of vintage Roger Corman and pays lavish homage to animator Tex Avery. The design is bright as a button and the transformation scenes real eye-poppers, but the film's best special effect is putty-faced Carrey with his razzle-dazzle star turn as the affable Stanley and his manic alter ego. Hip, flip and fly. TCh

Mask of Dimitrios, The

(1944, US, 95 min, b/w)
d Jean Negulesco. *p* Henry Blanke. *sc* Frank Gruber. *ph* Arthur Edeson. *ed* Frederick Richards. *ad* Ted Smith. *m* Adolph Deutsch. *cast* Zachary Scott, Peter Lorre, Sydney Greenstreet, Faye Emerson, George Tobias, Victor Francen, Eduardo Ciannelli, Steve Geray, Florence Bates, Kurt Katch.
●A fine *noir*-ish thriller, adapted from Eric Ambler's novel (*A Coffin for Dimitrios*), and respecting its *Citizen Kane* structure as a mousy little mystery writer (Lorre), intrigued by the reported murder of a seedily nasty international criminal (Scott), begins to reconstruct his story by talking to people from his past. The result is superficial but stylishly atmospheric, with vivid characterisations (notably Greenstreet as a genial blackmailer who ambiguously and rather movingly befriends Lorre) and low-key lighting effects that bring subtle echoes of *The Maltese Falcon* (Arthur Edeson shot both films). TM

Mask of Fu Manchu, The

(1932, US, 72 min, b/w)
d Charles Brabin, [Charles Vidor]. *p* Hunt Stromberg. *sc* Irene Kuhn, Edgar Allan Woolf, John Willard. *ph* Tony Gaudio. *ed* Ben Lewis. *ad* Cedric Gibbons. *m* William Axt. *cast* Boris Karloff, Lewis Stone, Karen Morley, Myrna Loy, Charles Starrett, Jean Hersholt.
●Highly engaging if none too classy tale of Sax Rohmer's sophisticated and fiendishly brilliant Oriental villain, battling against Scotland Yard

in an attempt to obtain Genghis Khan's mask and sword, which he needs to conquer the world. Much depends on Karloff's tongue-in-cheek portrait of the sinister, sadistic anti-hero, although Tony Gaudio's camerawork, the surprisingly imaginative sets, the ingenious tortures, and Myrna Loy's gleeful performance as Fu Manchu's sado- nymphomaniac daughter help no end. GA

Mask of Fury

see First Yank into Tokyo

Mask of the Demon

see Maschera del Demonio, La

Mask of Zorro, The

(1998, US, 138 min)
d Martin Campbell. *p* Doug Claybourne, David Foster. *sc* John Eskow, Ted Elliott, Terry Rossio *ph* Phil Meheux. *ed* Thom Noble. *pd* Cecilia Montiel. *m* James Horner. *cast* Antonio Banderas, Anthony Hopkins, Catherine Zeta Jones, Stuart Wilson, Matt Letscher, Maury Chaykin, Tony Almendola.

● Los Angeles, the 1840s. Two decades after Spanish governor Montero (Wilson) threw him in jail, killing his wife and abducting his infant daughter, Zorro (Hopkins), the Mexican outlaw/freedom fighter, escapes. Meanwhile, bandit Alejandro (Banderas) wants revenge for the death of his own brother at the hands of Montero's aide Captain Love, a proto-Nazi. Zorro and Alejandro team to save Hispanic America from exploitative Europeans. The film is flawed by Hopkins' Connery-like eschewal of an appropriate accent, action movie bombast, a storyline short on logic and long on clichés, and that tiresome modern habit of proclaiming a character's heroism while undermining it with knowing winks and 'ironic' comedy. That said, it's also fun (if over-extended): the duels are colourful, the music and 'Scope camerawork touch in moments of romanticism, and Banderas and Zeta Jones (Zorro's daughter) cut a dash. GA

Masque of the Red Death, The

(1964, GB/US, 84 min)
d/p Roger Corman. *sc* Charles Beaumont, R Wright Campbell. *ph* Nicolas Roeg. *ed* Ann Chegwidden. *pd* Daniel Haller. *m* David Lee. *cast* Vincent Price, Hazel Court, Jane Asher, Skip Martin, David Weston, Patrick Magee, Nigel Green, John Westbrook.

● Less polished than *The Tomb of Ligeia*, but still the best and most ambitious of Corman's Poe cycle. Apart from a scruffy opening scene, it looks stunningly handsome, with Nicolas Roeg's camera providing alluring effects like the sudden switches from white to yellow, purple to black, as Jane Asher scurries through a sequence of rooms each designed in a different colour. It is also graced by an intelligent script (the admirable Charles Beaumont) which probes the concept of diabolism with considerable subtlety, even though the black magic scenes were removed in Britain by the censor. Where most films of this nature tend simply to pile on the blood, here there is a genuine chill of intellectual evil in the philosophical speculations of Price's 12th century Italian Prince Prospero, 'safely' immured in his castle while the plague rages outside, dreaming up fiendish ways of entertaining/tormenting his prisoner-guests. TM

Masquerade

(1964, GB, 102 min)
d Basil Dearden. *p* Michael Relph. *sc* Michael Relph, William Goldman. *ph* Otto Heller. *ed* John D Guthridge. *pd* Don Ashton. *m* Philip Green. *cast* Cliff Robertson, Jack Hawkins, Marisa Mell, Christopher Witty, Bill Fraser, Michel Piccoli, Tutte Lemkow, Charles Gray, John Le Mesurier.

● An early script collaboration from William Goldman produces a nicely understated satire on the spy movie boom, in which the Foreign Office despatch Hawkins and Robertson (old wartime buddies, not very up on the espionage thing) to kidnap a young Arab prince for his own protection prior to his coronation. The plot convolutions of Victor Canning's novel *Castle Minerva* are given a wryly cynical edge, and Dearden copes surprisingly well with the spectacle. PT

Masquerade

(1988, US, 91 min)
d Bob Swaim. *p* Michael I Levy. *sc* Dick Wolf. *ph* David Watkin. *ed* Scott Conrad. *pd* John Kasarda. *m* John Barry. *cast* Rob Lowe, Meg Tilly, Kim Cattrall, Doug Savant, John Glover, Dana Delany, Erik Holland, Brian Davies.

● Tilly (achingly vulnerable) plays a fragile young heiress who returns from college to find her loathsome stepfather (Glover) and his girlfriend monopolising her swanky Hamptons pile. She takes up with Lowe, whose professional yachtsman front masks his activities as a gigolo, and they marry, Tilly believing that he loves her for herself; but she is the target of a long-term conspiracy that results in double murder. Swaim has pulled together a dense, stylish, Hitchcockian thriller in *noir* vein which turns on the moral and sexual ambiguity of the Lowe character, beautifully shot in crisp, pristine tones that contrast effectively with the sordid goings-on. However, Swaim's analysis of American class structures is limited: the film finally sides with the rich as innocent victims of the criminally-embittered less privileged. EP

Masquerade (Marattom)

(1989, Ind, 90 min)
d G Aravindan. *sc* Kavalam Narayana Panicker. *ph* Shaji. *ed* KR Bose. *ad* Nambooderi. *songs* Kavalam Narayana Panicker. *cast* Urmilla Unni, Sadhanam Krishnan Kutty, Pulluvan Narayanan, Kalamandalam Keshavan.

● Financed by Indian national TV, Aravindan's film is a weird and sometimes wonderful meditation on the realities that may or may not underpin traditional Kathakali theatre. It centres on the climax of the play *Keechaka Vadham* – where the disguised protagonist Bhima kills the antagonist Keechaka – and posits a bumbling police investigation into the 'crime': was it the character who died or the actor? Or was it something *represented* by the character? And who actually carried out the killing? Despite helpful captions dividing the film into chapters, most western viewers will be too baffled by the forms of Kathakali itself to unravel these Brechtian complexities. Fortunately, the 'illusion' side of the conundrum is well served by the costumes and choreography of the original play, and so there's plenty to fill the eye. TR

Masques

(1987, Fr, 100 min)
d Claude Chabrol. *p* Marin Karmitz. *sc* Odile Barski, Claude Chabrol. *ph* Jean Rabier. *ed* Monique Fardoulis. *ad* Françoise Benoît-Fresco. *m* Matthieu Chabrol. *cast* Philippe Noiret, Robin Renucci, Bernadette Lafont, Monique Chaumette, Anne Brochet, Roger Dumas, Pierre-François Duméniaud.

● 'I'd kill my sister for a good pun,' says the hero of Chabrol's murder mystery; but it looks as if smarmy TV show host Christian Legagneur (Noiret) may already have knocked his chances, and his sister, on the head. Dressed in the sheep's clothing of biographer Roland Wolf, the hero insinuates himself into Legagneur's country house, where the latter's goddaughter (Brochet) languishes in a state of narcolepsy. Everyone in the house has a double identity, from the allegedly mute chauffeur/chef to the amorous masseuse/fortune-teller (Lafont). But it is what lies behind his host's polite mask that interests the snooping Roland. Noiret's slobbish screen persona is ill-suited to his role as a bourgeois manipulator with a gift for cerebral word games, and it is only when the facade cracks at the end that his more corporeal style of nastiness seems appropriate. Chabrol frames the verbal sparring with characteristic precision, but the subtle plot suffers from a surfeit of politesse and a dearth of red-blooded passion. NF

Massacre at Central High (aka Blackboard Massacre)

(1976, US, 88 min)
d Renee Daalder. *p* Harold Sobel. *sc* Renee Daalder. *ph* Bertram Van Munster. *ed* Harry Keramidas. *ad* Russell Tune. *m* Tony Leonetti. *cast* Derrel Maury, Andrew Stevens, Kimberly Beck, Robert Carradine, Ray Underwood, Steve Bond.

● An intriguing, diagrammatic example of subversive cinema. The action takes place in a lavish LA high school where authority is noticeable by its total absence, and where life exists only in the gaps between classes. This teen exploiter goes for nothing less than an entire allegory on society, power structures, and the failure of revolution. Despite a deceptively laid back style, the film's ambition, knowingness and surefootedness make it worth a look. VG

Massacre in Rome (Rappresaglia)

(1973, It/Fr, 104 min)
d George Pan Cosmatos. *p* Carlo Ponti. *sc* Robert Katz, George Pan Cosmatos. *ph* Marcello Gatti. *ed* Françoise Bonnot, Roberto Silvi. *pd* Morton Haack. *m* Ennio Morricone. *cast* Richard Burton, Marcello Mastroianni, Leo McKern, John Steiner, Robert Harris, Delia Boccardo, Peter Vaughan, Anthony Steel.

● Rome's Gestapo chief (Burton) and a Catholic priest (Mastroianni) size up over the problem of reprisals during the last days of the Nazi occupation in WWII. Although based on fact, the film invents Mastroianni's character for the dramatic purposes of face-to-face confrontation. The ensuing debate, cumbersome and full of doughty moralising about non-involvement and complicity, results in a hands down victory for Burton's well-modulated vowels over Mastroianni's limited machine-gun English. Cosmatos' cripplingly emphatic direction reveals every creak in the plot and displays no whit of faith in an audience's intelligence. CPe

Master and Margarita, The (Majstori i Margarita)

(1972, Yugo/It, 101 min)
d Aleksandar Petrovic. *p* Giorgio Papi, Arrigo Colombo. *sc* Aleksandar Petrovic, Barbara Alberti, Amedeo Pagani. *ph* Roberto Gerardi. *ed* Mihailo Ilic. *ad* Vlastimir Gavrik. *m* Ennio Morricone. *cast* Ugo Tognazzi, Mimsy Farmer, Alain Cuny, Bata Zivojinovic, Pavle Vujisic, Fabijan Sovagovic, Ljuba Tadic.

● An intriguing but rather half-baked adaptation of Mikhail Bulgakov's novel. The Master (Tognazzi) is a much revered writer whose new play about the life of Christ is threatened with withdrawal during rehearsals because it is considered ideologically unsound. He finds solace in Margarita (Farmer), a beautiful girl who mysteriously crosses his path, but becomes tortured to the point of insanity by conflicting hopes and fears when the sinister Professor Woland (Cuny, excellent) – the Devil, no less – uses his magical powers to ensure that rehearsals go forward, but also enlivens the première with a horrific display of illusions which drives the audience from the theatre in panic. Some pleasure is to be had from the loving recreation of Moscow in the '20s, and from the fantasy elements (though pedestrian by comparison with the novel). But despite literary allusions which dress up the narrative (evoking the tale of Faust and Marguerite, for example), the novel is still so boiled down that it emerges, anti-climactically, as just a plodding allegory about the repression of dissident artists. TM

Master Gunfighter, The

(1975, US, 121 min)
d Frank Laughlin [Tom Laughlin]. *p* Philip L Parslow. *sc* Harold Lapland. *ph* Jack Marta. *ed* William H Reynolds, Danford B Greene. *pd* Albert Brenner. *m* Lalo Schifrin. *cast* Tom Laughlin, Ron O'Neal, Lincoln Kilpatrick, Barbara Carrera, Geo Ann Sosa, Victor Campos, Hector Elias.

● The *Billy Jack* series (featuring a disillusioned half-breed Indian Vietnam veteran) was sufficiently successful in the States to produce this spin-off Western. Set in Spanish California, it has Laughlin alone in challenging a decadent aristocracy for exploiting the peaceful local Indians. The film could have worked but for an excess of formula ingredients and muddled preachings. Adapted from a Japanese film, the transposition dubiously retains much samurai swordfighting and semi-Oriental costumes. Meanwhile, the over-mannered camerawork pays its dues to the Italian Western. In the resulting cultural hash, the plot with its strong anti-religious theme is too often disregarded. Laughlin is spectacularly uncharismatic, his doughy features laughable in brooding close-up. Best are the superb Monterey coast locations, reminiscent of *One-Eyed Jacks*; a pity nothing else is. CPe

Master Musician, The

see Born of Fire

Master of Kung Fu, The

see Death Kick

Master of Love (Racconti Proibiti di Nulla Vestiti)

(1973, It, 109 min)
d Brunello Rondi. *p* Oscar Brazzi. *sc* Roberto Leoni, Gianfranco Bucceri, Brunello Rondi. *ph* Luciano Trasatti. *ed* Marcello Malvestito. *ad* Gianfrancesco Ramacci. *m* Stelvio Cipriani. *cast* Rossano Brazzi, Magali Noël, Arrigo Masi, Ben Eckland, Barbara Bouchet, Janet Agren, Tina Aumont.

● Carry On Decameron, with Pasolini's innocent doodlings sabotaged by a more leery, exploitative approach: nuns jump up and down in bathtubs, wearing just their wimples, and excruciating puns abound as the Master initiates his younger, more spiritual apprentice with the help of a number of tales. Tina Aumont makes a beguiling appearance as a witch in an otherwise silly episode, injecting more sense of fun into her role than the other ladies. The film does have its aspirations: stylistic references range as far afield as *Tom Jones*, and the church is lampooned rather heavy-handedly in a sketch about a 'miraculous' conception (the priest is behind a wooden screen doing his stuff). Another has the Master as a flagellating Christ in an amusing attempt to seduce a legendary virgin. The end sees the Master and Lady Death leaping through the fields, off for that Last Great Coupling in the sky.

Master of the World

(1961, US, 104 min)
d William Witney. *p* James H Nicholson, Anthony Carras. *sc* Richard Matheson. *ph* Gil Warrenton. *ed* Anthony Carras. *ad* Daniel Haller. *m* Les Baxter. *cast* Vincent Price, Charles Bronson, Mary Webster, Henry Hull, Wally Campo, Richard Harrison.

● A pleasantly ludicrous children's fantasy, with a talented production team making the most of a low budget (Richard Matheson, who was obviously having a holiday, adapted Jules Verne's *Master of the World* and *Robur, the Conqueror*). Vincent Price plays Robur, a mad inventor who has much the same anti-war hang ups as Captain Nemo, but who captains a giant flying machine rather than a submarine, and flies around the world trying to end war by the threat of mass destruction. Although the final message is pretty sickening, the film's imaginative use of stock shots and its garish line in 19th century hardware is admirable. DP

Master Race, The

(1944, US, 102 min, b/w)
d Herbert J Biberman. *p* Robert S Golden. *sc* Herbert J Biberman, Anne Froelick, Rowland Leigh. *ph* Russell Metty. *ed* Earnie Leadlay. *ad* Albert S D'Agostino, Jack Okey. *m* Roy Webb. *cast* George Coulouris, Stanley Ridges, Osa Massen, Nancy Gates, Lloyd Bridges.

● This wordy curiosity, made after D-Day in anticipation of a swift end to the war, serves mostly as a propaganda vehicle for the allied civilian rehabilitation programme. However, beneath the surface appeal to fundamentally decent values (and for a forgiveness amounting to an almost total eradication of memory), fear, hatred, suspicion and disruption are all conveyed with more conviction than the fragile brave new world for which the Americans (with help from the British and Russians) hope. A German general, aware that the war is lost, has gone undercover to stir up World War III, and even in the moment of victory, violence erupts again. CPe

Masters of the Universe

(1987, US, 106 min)
d Gary Goddard. *p* Menahem Golan, Yoram Globus. *sc* David Odell. *ph* Hanania Baer. *ed* Anne V Coates. *pd* William Stout. *m* Bill Conti. *cast* Dolph Lundgren, Frank Langella, Meg Foster, Billy Barty, Courteney Cox, James Tolkan, Christina Pickles.

● It must have seemed like a good idea at the time – to re-animate in live action the cartoon characters from the popular tots' TV series *He-Man*. Most of the action takes place on Earth, where the anorexic Skeletor (Langella) pursues with evil intention the squeaky clean He-Man (Lundgren). Each craves possession of the Cosmic Key, which – like a platinum Amex card – gets you wherever you want to go. A couple of dumb-ass kids become involved with the goodies and, in addition to some feeble lovey-dovey, provide the wherewithal for the stranded aliens to return to Eternia. There are lots of flashes and bangs, but the effects are neither special nor camp enough to be more than vaguely amusing. MS

Master Touch, The

see Uomo da Rispettare, Un

Matador

(1985, Sp, 106 min)
d Pedro Almodóvar. *p* Andrés Vicente Gómez. *sc* Pedro Almodóvar. *ph* Angel Luis Fernández. *ed* Jorge Salcedo. *ad* Roman Arango, José Morales, José Rosell. *m* Bernardo Bonezzi. *cast* Assumpta Serna, Antonio Banderas, Nacho Martinez, Eva Cobo, Julieta Serrano, Chus Lampreave, Carmen Maura.

● Ai No Corrida, literally. Death and Desire are inextricably linked in this Hispanic mix of sex, symbolism, violence and very chic design. A trainee bullfighter is driven by his guilt as a failed rapist to confess to the murder of a number of young men and women; but his maestro (retired from the corrida after being gored) and his lady lawyer are far guiltier than he, since the ultimate orgasm can only be achieved through killing. Not so much a maelstrom as a mess of contrived eroticism, pretentious dialogue, and voyeuristic sensationalism, Almodóvar's silly, cod-philosophical whodunit impresses only for its bravado (fans of Paul Verhoeven may love it). GA

Mata Hari

(1932, US, 88 min, b/w)
d George Fitzmaurice. *sc* Benjamin Glazer, Leo Birinski. *ph* William Daniels. *ed* Frank Sullivan. *ad* Cedric Gibbons. *cast* Greta Garbo, Ramon Novarro, Lionel Barrymore, Lewis Stone, C Henry Gordon, Karen Morley, Alec B Francis, Mischa Auer.

● Set in WWI France, the film is Garbo's even before she appears on screen to dazzle her willing audience; once there, it becomes impossible to dissociate the legend of the star from the myth of Mata Hari. Beautiful, charismatic and sublimely inaccessible, the miserable figure of history has become an irresistible spy, slavishly aided by her eager admirers. Staged almost entirely indoors and at night, the twilight melodrama of her mission is heightened by William Daniels' stunning visuals: shadows and lines which contrast her total strength with the pale imitations who surround her. And even when (romantically, inevitably) she's destroyed by the love of a young Russian pup, she remains as ever, laconic and riveting. HM

Mata Hari

(1984, GB, 108 min)
d Curtis Harrington. *p* Rony Yacov. *sc* Joel Ziskin. *ph* David Gurfinkel. *ed* Henry Richardson. *ad* Tivadar Bertalan. *m* Wilfred Josephs, (Indonesian) Sri Hastanto. *cast* Sylvia Kristel, Christopher Cazenove, Oliver Tobias, Gaye Brown, Gottfried John, William Fox, Vernon Dobtcheff, Tutte Lemkow.

● Emmanuelle on the Western Front: a screwy premise if ever there was one, though the period fashions do provide our heroine with something complicated to climb out of. A typically tacky Cannon production, shot in Hungary by a glum Harrington, the film's one interesting feat is the imperilment of its own reason for being, as Kristel lunges and parries her way through a topless fencing scene. BBa

Mata-Hari, Agent H.21

(1964, Fr/It, 99 min, b/w)
d Jean-Louis Richard. *p* Eugène Lepicier. *sc* Jean-Louis Richard, François Truffaut. *ph* Michel Kelber. *ed* Kénout Peltier. *ad* Claude Pignot. *m* Georges Delerue. *cast* Jeanne Moreau, Jean-Louis Trintignant, Claude Rich, Franck Villard, Albert Rémy, Georges Riquier, Henri Garcin, Marie Dubois.

● The first half is really rather irresistible, with period Paris lovingly recreated and Jeanne Moreau not afraid to present Mata Hari as a bourgeois homebody in between her bouts of glamorous slinkiness. Tongue at least partly in cheek, she is insidiously funny, not least while performing an idiotic Oriental dance in which the finger movements transmit a coded message. Then love raises its head (after some delightfully outrageous vamping): a drearily routine affair in which she and Trintignant are even subjected to the TV ad indignity of a rapturous romp in the country; and as the film founders, it becomes increasingly apparent that Richard's plodding direction has no way of keeping up with Truffaut's script. TM

Match, The

(1999, GB/US/Ire, 96 min)
d Mick Davis. *p* Allan Scott, Guymon Casady. *sc* Mick Davis. *ph* Witold Stok. *ed* Kate Williams. *pd* John Frankish. *m* Harry Gregson-Williams. *cast* Max Beesley, Isla Blair, James Cosmo, Laura Fraser, Richard E Grant, David Hayman, Ian Holm, Neil Morrissey, Bill Paterson, Hope Ross, Pierce Brosnan.

● Scottish milkman Wullie (Beesley) has worn a calliper since the accident that killed his brother. His only joy is a mouldy pub, Benny's Bar, but now evil winebar owner Gus (Grant) plans to destroy even that. Every year Gus's team defeats Benny's Bar at soccer – if they win again, Gus's fancy-nancy habits will swamp the village. Should Wullie take off for London with sussed Rosemary (Fraser) or fight to preserve his way of life? *Brassed Off* got away with this plot because Pete Postlethwaite's ability to warm the heart came with a chilly wind and Tara Fitzgerald was allowed a snooty sort of spark. There's no such distraction here. Ian Holm's turn as the beleaguered publican is wretchedly sentimental and Fraser has little to do but look pretty. That said, Hope Ross, as Wullie's grieving single parent Anna, brings a damp, dark-green misery to the proceedings. Mother and son's sitting room is like an impoverished aquarium: one from which Wullie can gaze but never hope to escape. CO'Su

Match Factory Girl, The (Tulitikkutehtaan Tytto)

(1990, Fin/Swe, 69 min)
d Aki Kaurismäki. *p* Aki Kaurismäki, Klas Olofsson, Katinka Farago. *sc* Aki Kaurismäki. *ph* Timo Salminen. *ed* Aki Kaurismäki. *pd* Risto Karilula. *cast* Kati Outinen, Elina Salo, Esko Nikkari, Vesa Vierikko, Reijo Taipale, Silu Seppälä.

● This final part of Kaurismäki's 'Working Class Trilogy' (which began with *Shadows in Paradise* and *Ariel*), has an affecting, fable-like simplicity. The tone is set by striking, almost abstract shots of the factory where shy, unattractive Iris (Outinen) sits checking matchbox labels on a production line. After handing over her hard-earned wages to her selfish mother and stepfather, Iris whiles away her spare time in a coffee bar, or waiting in vain to be asked to dance at the local disco. Her one attempt to break out – buying a pink dress, meeting a rich man, spending the night with him – inevitably ends in pregnancy and humiliation. Cheques, not feelings, are the currency of emotional exchange, left on bedside tables or sent with cursory notes saying 'Get rid of it'. Finally pushed over the edge, Iris plots a calm, methodical revenge on those who have poisoned her dreams. Despite the Bressonian overtones, the film has more in common with the radical proletarian pessimism of Fassbinder. Influences notwithstanding, Kaurismäki remains one of a kind. NF

Maternale

(1978, It, 95 min)
d Giovanna Gagliardo. *cast* Carla Gravina, Anna Maria Gherardi, Marino Masè, Francesca Muzio, Benedetta Fantoli.

● An affluent Italian family, an idyllic summer's day, a sumptuous villa, a destructive struggle for power between mother and daughter. Maternale is an intimate and – in its adherence to the unities of time, place and action – highly formalised exploration of 'female' themes: frustrated desires, mother-child rivalry, the regime of the domestic, manifested here in an almost sensual obsession with food. But despite Gagliardo's experimental intentions, it all seems curiously old-fashioned, with the luscious imagery, dreamlike mood, mannered mise en scène, and perhaps partly the 1960 setting, overlaying the film with the faded bloom of art cinema. SJo

Matewan

(1987, US, 133 min)
d John Sayles. *p* Peggy Rajski, Maggie Renzi. *sc* John Sayles. *ph* Haskell Wexler. *ed* Sonya Polonsky. *pd* Nora Chavooshian. *m* Mason

Daring. *cast* Chris Cooper, Mary McDonnell, Will Oldham, David Strathairn, Ken Jenkins, Kevin Tighe, Gordon Clapp, James Earl Jones, Josh Mostel.

● A lone stranger arrives in town to unite the locals against the heavies with guns: a scenario familiar from countless Westerns. When the Stone Mountain Coal Company, which owns virtually everything in the West Virginian town of Matewan, reduces its workers' pay and begins employing blacks and Italians against the wishes of the local whites, ex-Wobbly union rep Joe Kenehan (Cooper) is sent in to overcome dissidence and prevent violent conflict with the armed strike-breakers recently hired by the company. But tempers run high, racial contempt is rife, and betrayal looms. Set in the 1920s, Sayles' marvellously gripping movie never compromises its political content in its deployment, or up-ending, of Western conventions. It possesses a mythic clarity, yet there's also a welcome complexity at work, in the vivid characterisations and the unsentimental celebration of community and collective action. The result is witty, astute, and finally very moving. GA

Matilda

see Roald Dahl's Matilda

Matinee

(1993, US, 99 min)
d Joe Dante. *p* Michael Finnell. *sc* Charlie Haas. *ph* John Hora. *ed* Marshall Harvey. *pd* Steven Legler. *m* Jerry Goldsmith. *cast* John Goodman, Cathy Moriarty, Simon Fenton, Omri Katz, Lisa Jakub, John Sayles.

● In Key West during the 1962 Cuban Missile Crisis, 14-year-old Gene (Fenton) is preoccupied with the forthcoming visit by B-movie king Lawrence Woolsey (Goodman) to promote *Mant*, his new bargain-basement exploiter about a chap mutating into an ant. Plotwise that's about it in this engagingly affectionate satire on small-town American fears. As Gene, his brother and buddies prepare for the riotous excitement of Woolsey's Saturday matinee preview, it's the details of the string of visual and verbal gags that make the film so enjoyable. The clips from *Mant* are spot on, what with the cod-scientific expository dialogue, dreary design, deathless hamming and Cold War clichés. Goodman's schlock merchant displays just the right mix of con-man materialism and childlike glee at his own bogus movie magic; the customary in-jokes and cameos reinforce the mood of loving, wryly amused hommage, and the kids' stuff never cloys. Inspired chaos, and for anyone into the delirious absurdities of '50s sci-fi, a must. GA

Matinee Idol, The

(1928, US, 65 min, b/w)
d Frank Capra. *p* Harry Cohn. *sc* Elmer Harris. *ph* Philip Tannura. *ed* Arthur Roberts. *cast* Bessie Love, Johnnie Walker, Lionel Belmore, Ernest Hilliard, Sidney D'Albrook, David Mir.

● Long believed lost, until a print turned up in France and was beautifully restored with the aid of high definition video, Capra's silent comedy contains much that anticipates his later flair. A Broadway star stumbles on a travelling theatrical troupe of hilarious ineptitude, and hires them for a cheap laugh to appear in the big city. The cruelty of the conceit is happily defused by the exuberant playing of Bessie Love, one of the screen's great comediennes of the '20s and '30s. DT

Matrix, The (100)

(1999, US/Aust, 136 min)
d The Wachowski Brothers [Andy Wachowski, Larry Wachowski]. *p* Joel Silver. *sc* The Waxhowski Brothers. *ph* Bill Pope. *ed* Zach Staenberg. *pd* Owen Paterson. m Don Davis. *cast* Keanu Reeves, Laurence Fishburne, Carrie-Anne Moss, Hugo Weaving.

● Thomas (Reeves), a salaryman at a software company, leads a secret double life. As 'Neo' he's a computer hacker much in demand. But only when Trinity (Moss) introduces him to charismatic seer Morpheus (Fishburne) does Neo learn that the whole world's unwittingly in the same boat: life as we know it is merely virtual reality, a 'matrix' designed by mankind's overlords to hold us in unquestioning obeisance. Not only are Morpheus and his rebel crew fighting to regain our freedom, but the leader has a bee in his bonnet: might not Neo be the One, who'll lead us to salvation? For its first hour, the second feature by the Wachowskis works well enough as an ambitious if rather portentous dystopian fantasy in the vein of *eXistenZ* and *Blade Runner*. Though sometimes a little clumsy, the frequent switches between the different 'realities' are entertainingly ingenious, Bill Pope's camerawork and Owen Paterson's designs are slickly impressive, and the effects neatly embrace Cronenbergian body horror and comic strip panache. But the characters, too, are paper thin (Keanu, especially), while the promising premise is steadily wasted as the film turns into a fairly routine action pic, complete with facile Hollywood heroics, cod kung-fu homilies and computer enhanced martial arts scenes. Weaving is engagingly odd as the rebels' arch enemy Smith, but even he can't hold the attention in what's finally yet another slice of overlong, high concept hokum. GA

Mattei Affair, The (Il Caso Mattei)

(1972, It, 115 min)
d Francesco Rosi. *p* Franco Cristaldi. *sc* Francesco Rosi, Tonino Guerra. *ph* Pasqualino De Santis. *ed* Ruggero Mastroianni. *ad* Andrea Crisanti. *m* Piero Piccioni. *cast* Gian Maria Volonté, Luigi Squarzina, Peter Baldwin, Franco Graziosi, Gianfranco Ombuen, Elio Jotta, Edda Ferronao.

● An astonishingly powerful conspiracy thriller. Enrico Mattei, head of the state-owned oil firm AGIP and president of ENI, the man *Time* dubbed 'the most powerful Italian since Caesar Augustus', died in 1962 in a highly suspicious air crash. His death was followed by a wall of silence. In the light of his championship of the Italian economy against the machinations of international cartels, his death – in fact and in Rosi's masterful film – carries a sickening political inevitability. Rosi casts the film along the lines of an inquest, and pieces together not simply a picture of the man himself (Volonté, brilliantly cast), but of the dynamics of capital, the role of the media, and the traps to which the individualist hero can't help but fall prey. *The Mattei Affair* is *Point Blank* played out at the level of power politics and monopolistic economic intrigue. Essential viewing. VG

Matter of Heart

(1983, US, 106 min)
d/p Mark Whitney. *sc* Suzanne Wagner. *ph* Mark Whitney, William Neil, Hans Roderer, Rick Robertson, Robert Parker. *ed* Mark Whitney. M John Adams.*with* Marie-Louise von Franz, Barbara Hannah, Liliane Frey-Rohn, Laurens van der Post, Baroness Vera von der Heydt.

● A bio-doc about Jung, the man who took the sex out of psychoanalysis, put the supernatural in, and rechristened it Analytical Psychology. After brooding shots of Alpine mists and waterfalls, the stuff of Teutonic fairytale, the film is mostly well-heeled talking heads reminiscing about the man and expounding his teachings. Jung comes over like Dr Shorofsky in *Fame* – a loveable old grouch. For anyone coming from psychiatry, psychoanalysis, or just plain old messed-up common sense, the Jungian message may seem quite weird. But weird or not, it is quite well explored here as Jung's disciples, all quite old now of course, circle round selected themes – among them the role of the anima and animus in psychic life, the liberating and initiatory aspects of Jung's relationship with Toni Wolff, the power of the shadow side in human affairs, and Jung's apocalyptic visions of the end of the world. RI

Matter of Honour, A (Técnicas de duelo)

(1988, Col/Cuba, 92 min)
d Sergio Cabrera. *sc* Humberto Dorado. *ph* José Medeiros. *ed* Justo Vega. *ed* Enrique Linero. *m* Juan Marquez. *cast* Frank Ramirez, Humberto Dorado, Florina Lemaître, Vicky Hernández, Edgardo Roman.

● A film more about humour than honour. Set in a small town in the Colombian Andes, it concerns a feud between the local schoolteacher and the butcher – each of whom has a healthy and affectionate regard for the other, but is urged on by the differing factions determined not to spoil the chance of a fight. All the local characters and bureaucracies have their part to play: the mayor and the military, the priest and the police. They help to raise the temperature for the final duel, which is naturally assumed to settle every personal difference and show that might is right. But the scores the protagonists have to settle are those accumulated by long friendship and common politics, and these are the virtues that finally triumph. A touchingly funny film in the mould of post-war Italian cinema, pressing that most sensitive of Latin nerves, machismo. AH

Matter of Life and Death, A (aka Stairway to Heaven) 100 (100)

(1946, GB, 104, b/w & col)
d/p/sc Michael Powell, Emeric Pressburger. *ph* Jack Cardiff. *ed* Reginald Mills. *pd* Alfred Junge. *m* Allan Gray. *cast* David Niven, Kim Hunter, Roger Livesey, Raymond Massey, Marius Goring, Robert Coote, Abraham Sofaer, Kathleen Byron, Richard Attenborough, Bonar Colleano.

● One of Powell and Pressburger's finest films. Made at the instigation of the Ministry of Information, who wanted propaganda stressing the need for goodwill between Britain and America, it emerges as an outrageous fantasy full of wit, beautiful sets and Technicolor, and perfectly judged performances. The story is just a little bizarre. RAF pilot Niven bales out of his blazing plane without a chute and survives; but – at least in his tormented mind – he was due to die, and a heavenly messenger comes down to earth to collect him. A celestial tribunal ensues to judge his case while, back on earth, doctors are fighting for his life. What makes the film so very remarkable is the assurance of Powell's direction, which manages to make heaven at least as convincing as earth. (The celestial scenes are in monochrome, the terrestial ones in colour: was Powell slyly asserting, in the faces of the British documentary boys, the greater realism of that which is imagined?). But the whole thing works like a dream, with many hilarious swipes at national stereotypes, and a love story that is as moving as it is absurd. Masterly. GA

Matti di Slegare

see Fit to Be Untied

Mau Mau

(1992, Ger, 92 min)
d Uwe Schrader. *sc* Uwe Schrader, Daniel Dubbe. *ph* Peter Gauhe. *ed* Klaus Müller-Laue. *cast* Marlen Diekhoff, Peter Franke, Catrin Striebeck, Henryk Bista, Emanuel Bettencourt, Peter Gavadja.

● Uwe Schrader's third feature is a hand-held post-'Fall of the Wall' slice of low life, set in the immigrant area of a German city and following three interconnected couples. As city centres have filled with marginals, so Schrader makes marginals the centre of his extremely well acted film. Its focal point is the Mau Mau, a pastel kitsch, sleazy strip bar. Anyone old enough to have lost their way in life can drink here and toast their hard-won communality of defeat. Like a drink-sodden realist, Schrader hangs around and observes the pimps, gangsters, night-owls and lonely old bar flies. After an hour or so, you've got to know them, their interlocking destinies, and there you have it: a functioning model of a demi-monde! This is like a post-Fassbinder Fassbinder movie. It's non-judgmental and lacking in nihilism – but it also lacks Fassbinder's political acuity and gutter poetry. WH

Maurice

(1987, GB, 140 min)
d James Ivory. *p* Ismail Merchant. *sc* Kit Hesketh-Harvey, James Ivory. *sc* Pierre Lhomme. *ed* Katherine Wenning. *pd* Brian Ackland-Snow. *m* Richard Robbins. *cast* James Wilby, Hugh Grant, Rupert Graves, Denholm Elliott, Simon Callow, Billie Whitelaw, Ben Kingsley, Judy Parfitt, Mark Tandy, Phoebe Nicholls, Patrick Godfrey.

● In this adaptation of EM Forster's posthumously published novel, a gay man in Edwardian England is seen to have three choices. Like Durham (Grant), he can opt for frigid, respectable marriage; like Viscount Risley (Tandy), he can solicit soldiers in bars and be grateful for six months' hard labour; or, most bravely, like Maurice (Wilby), he can risk everything for requited love. It takes a long time for Maurice to reach this point; only in the arms of his game-keeping bit of rough (Graves) does he realise that he's been taught 'what isn't right'. The initial stages, set in Brideshead country, are jerky, but thereafter the original's social comedy and serious passion are superbly evoked. The performances are excellent, the period trappings, like the love scenes, in the best possible taste. MS

Mauvaise Conduite

see Improper Conduct

Mauvaise Passe

see Escort, The

Mauvais Sang (The Night Is Young)

(1986, Fr, 119 min)
d Léos Carax. *p* Philippe Diaz. *sc* Léos Carax. *ph* Jean-Yves Escoffier. *ed* Nelly Quettier. *ad* Michel Vandestien. *cast* Michel Piccoli, Juliette Binoche, Denis Lavant, Hans Meyer, Julie Delpy, Carroll Brooks, Hugo Pratt, Serge Reggiani.

●In his second feature (following *Boy Meets Girl*), Carax combines his personal concerns – young love, solitude – with the stylised conventions of the vaguely futuristic romantic thriller. Loner street-punk Alex (Lavant) joins a gang of elderly Parisian hoods whose plan to steal a serum that will cure an AIDS-like disease is complicated by the deadly rival strategies of a wealthy American woman, and by Alex falling for the young mistress of a fellow gang-member (Piccoli). Again Carax's virtues are visual and atmospheric rather than narrative; while the script may occasionally smack of indulgent pretension, there is no denying the exhilarating assurance of individual sequences, and the consistency of Carax's moodily romantic vision. Certainly he would do well to create stronger female characters and avoid lines lumbered with laconic poeticism. But the film is, finally, affecting, thanks to a seemingly intuitive understanding of colour, movement and composition, and to an ability to draw from earlier films without ever seeming plagiaristic. GA

Maverick

(1994, US, 127 min)
d Richard Donner. *p* Bruce Davey, Richard Donner. *sc* William Goldman. *ph* Vilmos Zsigmond. *ed* Stuart Baird, Mike Kelly. *pd* Tom Sanders. *m* Randy Newman. *cast* Mel Gibson, Jodie Foster, James Garner, Graham Greene, Alfred Molina, James Coburn, Dub Taylor, Geoffrey Lewis, Denver Pyle.

●Richard Donner's big-screen offshoot of the old TV Western series, from a *Butch Cassidy*-meets-*The Sting* script by William Goldman, is slick, cute, formula, and full of lazy gags. Gibson lobs in a narcissistic performance as card-sharp Brett Maverick, up to his neck in oater shenanigans with the likes of con-woman Annabelle (Foster, not a natural comic), 'Marshal' Zane Cooper (Garner, the original TV Maverick), bandido Angel (Molina), and Indian chief Joseph (Greene, in a turn that comes on as PC but seems somehow offensive). A financially successful exercise in target-marketing, but not much of a movie. GA

Ma Vie en Rose

(1997 Fr/Bel/GB/Switz, 89 min)
d Alain Berliner. *p* Carole Scotta. *sc* Chris Vander Stappen, Alain Berliner. *ph* Yves Cape. *ed* Sandrine Deegen. *pd* Véronique Melery. *m* Dominique Dalcan. *cast* Georges Du Fresne, Michèle Laroque, Jean-Philippe Ecoffey, Hélène Vincent, Daniel Hanssens, Laurence Bibot.

●Seven-year-old Ludovic's determined to grow up a girl, which is hard on his family, who face the scorn of locals made uneasy by a sudden outbreak of non-conformism. This Belgian first feature evolves into a domestic battle of wills. Will Ludo deny his feelings and put the household back on an even keel, or can the grown-ups find the courage to accept their child, even if it makes them the black sheep of the community? Child actor Georges Du Fresne's projection of innocence and absolute certainty drains away any suspicion that the film-makers might be using him to tell a story that's fundamentally about adult sexual confusions. It isn't. It's about a child's pre-sexual intimations of gender identity, as influenced by his favourite TV show, a pink extravaganza starring a sort of live-action Gallic Barbie doll. Wry comedy is certainly not precluded, while Laroque and the excellent Ecoffey make the parents' emotional confusion tell, but it's the film's combination of compassion and whimsical charm that makes it utterly disarming. TJ

Ma vie sexuelle (Paul Dedalus' Journey) (Comment je me suis disputé... ('ma vie sexuelle'))

(1996, Fr, 180 min)
d Arnaud Desplechin. *p* Pascale Caucheteux. *sc* Arnaud Desplechin, Emmanuel Bourdieu. *ph* Eric Gautier. *ed* François Gédigier. *ad* Antoine Platteau. *m* Krishna Lévy. *cast* Mathieu Amalric, Emmanuelle Devos, Emmanuel Salinger, Marianne Denicourt, Thibault de Montalembert, Chiara Mastroianni, Roland Amstutz.

●This subtle and startlingly imaginative film concerns the intersecting relationships between a group of 20 and 30-year-old Parisians, notably assistant university professor Paul (Amalric), who's torn between his long-term girl Esther (Devos), his best friend's girl (with whom he guiltily had a fling a couple of years ago), and another woman he meets at a party. Paul's problem is indecision, which is of little use to his friends, colleagues and lovers, and even more damaging to himself. What makes this intimate epic so fascinating is the depth of characterisation – it's beautifully acted – and the way both script and direction use small details to offer telling insights into the lives, emotions and aspirations of the group. Loneliness is economically but expertly evoked with a cup of coffee and Ravel on the soundtrack; a bizarre but highly original scene featuring a monkey, a radiator and an arrogant academic brilliantly blends black humour and psychological unease. GA

Maxie

(1985, US, 98 min)
d Paul Aaron. *p* Carter De Haven. *sc* Patricia Resnick. *ph* Fred Schuler. *ed* Lynzee Klingman. *pd* John J Lloyd. *m* Georges Delerue. *cast* Glenn Close, Mandy Patinkin, Ruth Gordon, Barnard Hughes, Valerie Curtin, Googy Gress, Michael Ensign, Michael Laskin.

●Much to husband Patinkin's dismay, spouse Close is periodically possessed by the spirit of one Maxie Malone, a fledgling silent movie star looking to make a screen comeback a mere 60 years after her death. Glenn gets to play both prim secretary and the flirtatious floozie she becomes when she isn't quite feeling herself, but the lightest of comic talents is not hers to boast of and this old-fashioned frolic (adapted from a novel by Jack Finney, of *Invasion of the Body Snatchers* note) never gets going as a result. Her erstwhile alter ego though, is represented by authentic vintage footage of Carole Lombard. Now there was an actress. TJ

Maximum Overdrive

(1986, US, 97 min)
d Stephen King. *p* Martha Schumacher. *sc* Stephen King. *ph* Armando Nannuzzi. *ed* Evan Lottman. *ad* Giorgio Postiglione. *m* AC/DC. *cast* Emilio Estevez, Pat Hingle, Laura Harrington, Yeardley Smith, John Short, Ellen McElduff, JC Quinn.

●Horror institution Stephen King's first shot at directing is a loud, obnoxious, single-idea schlocker. A malicious comet passes too close to Earth and sets all the mechanical objects in Wilmington, North Carolina, off on a bloody killing spree. Lawnmowers turn nasty, vending machines fire killer cans, and at the Dixie Boy Truck Stop only Emilio Estevez stands between the maniac rigs gathering force outside and the end of civilisation as we know it. There's carnage galore, but minimal interest. King himself described it as a 'wonderful moron picture', and he was half-right. TJ

Maximum Risk

(1996, US, 101 min)
d Ringo Lam. *p* Moshe Diamant. *sc* Larry Ferguson. *ph* Alexander Gruszynski. *ed* Bill Pankow. *pd* Steve Spence. *m* Robert Folk. *cast* Jean-Claude Van Damme, Natasha Henstridge, Jean-Hugues Anglade, Zach Grenier, Stéphane Audran, David Hemblen.

●A standard Van Damme pic, competently assembled but with little of the manic edge found in director Lam's Hong Kong movies. In the tradition of *Double Impact*, we get two action heroes for the price of one. Retired French soldier Alain discovers his unknown twin dead on the streets of their home town on the Côte d'Azur. The corpse, for reasons too convoluted to explain, is Mikhail, a runner for the gang bosses of New York's Russian community. To find the killer, Alain poses as Mikhail and probes the underworld of Little Odessa. Along for the ride is Henstridge, taking care of titillation as Mikhail's girl, while the likes of French law enforcer Anglade and Russian Mafia kingpin Hemblen ensure we never want for over-ripe supporting performances. TJ

Max Mon Amour (Max My Love)

(1986, Fr/US, 97 min)
d Nagisa Oshima. *p* Serge Silberman. *sc* Nagisa Oshima, Jean-Claude Carrière. *ph* Raoul Coutard. *ed* Hélène Plemiannikov. *pd* Pierre Guffroy. *m* Michal Portal. *cast* Charlotte Rampling, Anthony Higgins, Bernard-Pierre Donnadieu, Victoria Abril, Anne-Marie Besse, Nicole Calfan, Pierre Etaix, Fabrice Luchini, Diana Quick.

●Finding that his wife Margaret (Rampling) has been lying about her afternoon activities, Peter (Higgins) – a Brit diplomat in Paris – begins to suspect her of infidelity. But when he discovers that her lover is a chimpanzee, he is so taken aback that, instead of yielding to jealousy, he insists on Max moving into the plush apartment the couple share with their young son and a maid. As scripted by Buñuel's frequent collaborator Jean-Claude Carrière, Oshima's film bears more than a passing resemblance to the late master's sly, surreal satires on the charmless discretion of the bourgeoisie: eager to hide his shock and anger beneath a mantle of liberal sophistication, Peter merely engineers a situation of futile impasse, while Margaret's *amour fou* (or is it *amour bête*?) seems motivated less by passion than by a boredom born of indolence. That said, lumbered with stilted performances from Rampling and Higgins, clearly ill at ease with Anglo-French dialogue, Oshima never achieves Buñuel's cool but mordant tone: despite the potentially subversive material, the film frankly lacks bite. On one level, however, it succeeds: our sympathies rest throughout with Max who, despite his touchy irritability, deserves neither Peter's tolerant condescension nor – and this is perhaps more destructive – Margaret's love. GA

Max Wall – Funny Man

(1975, GB, 40 min)
d Jon Scoffield. *p* Ron Inkpen. *sc* Max Wall. *ph* James Boyers. *ed* Richard Hiscott. *ad* Vic Symonds. *with* Max Wall, Anne Hart, Bob Todd.

●An unfortunate title, for the great Max – 'man's answer to the peacock' – has to be seen in the flesh to be seen at his best. In this little movie (filmed with video cameras at the Richmond Theatre before a well-lubricated audience) he seems at his second best, simply because he relies so heavily on live audience response; when his gags and bits of business are edited together and framed in darkness on a cinema screen, they seem pale imitations of the originals. Still, this is a valuable celluloid record of Prof Wallofski doing his stuff, searching for the piano stool, swatting a fly, measuring up his arms, and pulling faces that you never knew existed. GB

Maxwell Street Blues

(1981, US, 56 min)
d Linda Williams, Raul Zaritsky. p Sandra Lieb, Linda Williams, Raul Zaritsky. *ph* Raul Zaritsky. *ed* Linda Williams, Raul Zaritsky. *with* Jim Brewer, Blind Arvella Gray, Coot 'Playboy' Venson, John Henry Davis, Pat Rushing.

●Blind ageing blacks playing the streets for a living and recounting hobo days seems like the stuff of Uncle Tom cliché; but it's a very real life for the musicians on Chicago's Maxwell Street, a poor Jewish market and blues buskers' venue since the beginning of the century. Williams and Zaritsky capture the blues as it was and still is played on the sidewalks which once hosted Big Bill Broonzy, Muddy Waters, Sleepy John Estes, Homesick James and others. Acoustic or electric, religious or rude, Maxwell Street is the untouched roots of the blues (although the absence of any youth on the street would seem to have set its expiry date). A heartening film, and a chastening experience for any rock fans who think their rock heroes thought up those licks themselves. JG

Maya

(2001, Ind, 105 min)
d Digvijay Singh. *p* Dileep Singh Rathore, Emmanuel Pappas. *sc* Digvijay Singh, Emmanuel Pappas. *ph* Mark Lapwood. *ed* Bridget Lyon. *pd* P Narayana Reddy. *m* Manesh Judge. *cast* Nitya Shetty, Anant Nag, Nikil Yadav, Mita Vasisht, Shilpa Navalkar, Virendra Saxenda.
● This social issue movie, beautifully shot in the extraordinary landscapes of rural India, follows the adolescence of the tomboy heroine (Shetty). Maya's parents are too poor to bring her up, so she finds security in her aunt's middle-class family, only to be rudely returned when she produces her first menstrual blood. The ensuing horrific events – namely, her initiation ceremony – are reputedly still common in the rural regions. They certainly come as a shock. The preparatory passages seem inadequate in this context, and offer too many mixed messages. Shame, for the performances are often touching and revealing. WH

Maybe Baby

see For Keeps

Maybe Baby

(2000, GB/Fr, 105 min)
d Ben Elton. *p* Phil McIntyre. *sc* Ben Elton. *ph* Roger Lanser. *ed* Peter Hollywood. *pd* Jim Clay. *m* Colin Towns. *cast* Hugh Laurie, Joely Richardson, Adrian Lester, James Purefoy, Tom Hollander, Joanna Lumley, Rowan Atkinson, Dawn French, Emma Thompson.
● Sam is out of touch at the all new BBC. Ewan, meanwhile, is successful. He's Scottish. He writes about drugs. (That's a *Trainspotting* reference.) But Sam's got Lucy. Lucy's great; stunning flat, scooter, bit like a trendy version of the original Madonna, only without the baby. They're both really sad about it. Sam says the London skyline 'makes you feel pretty damned insignificant, doesn't it?' and Lucy writes things down in her diary – you know, feelings, women's feelings. Sam 'suddenly' writes a brilliant film script (he copied the diary). Lucy's pretty angry, but some good does come out of the whole thing. The BBC goes back to making films about real people, and Ewan – who finally directs one – accepts that his writing is 'shite' (he's actually a positive character in the end). Rewind. A couple of loft-living media prats may or may not be infertile. One's a simpering idiot sicking up teenage twaddle into a pretty diary, the other – pitiable and emotionally retarded – still works at the BBC. Somehow getting it into his head that the twaddle in the diary is an authentic reflection of 'womanthink', the pitiable one turns twaddle into a script. Dazzled, the BBC wipes egg off its face for suspecting he was a middle class tosser and turns script into a film. Which a hotshot Scottish film-maker falls over his feet to direct. Pause. There is no 'Lucy' (that's just Joely Richardson, pretending). There is no 'Sam' (that's just Hugh Laurie, pretending to pretend). 'Authentic womanthink twaddle' is written by Ben (*Inconceivable*) Elton (he's not really a woman). Said twaddle does turn up in a film (this one). Elton directs it (in the mysterious absence of any hotshot Scottish director). The BBC funds it. (The BBC funds it.) SS

Maybe...Maybe Not

see Bewegte Mann, Der

Mayerling

(1935, Fr, 93 min, b/w)
d Anatole Litvak. *p* Seymour Nebenzal. *sc* Joseph Kessel. Irmgard von Cube. *ph* Armand Thirard. *ed* Henri Rust *ad* Serge Pimenoff, André Andréjew. *m* Arthur Honegger. *cast* Charles Boyer, Danielle Darrieux, Suzy Prim, Jean Debucourt, Vladimir Sokoloff, Jean Dax, Gabrielle Dorziat, Jean-Louis Barrault.
● A voluptuous romance, with Boyer as the Archduke Rudolf, tragically smitten with Darrieux' Maria Vetsera. Litvak is equally good at conveying the tidal wave of passion that drowned the heir to the throne, and the moral opprobrium that consumes the Hapsburg court. Of course it is novelettish, Barbara Cartland rubbish, but done with extraordinary skill and commitment. Boyer is ideal as the doomed and dissolute romancer who was never up to ruling anyway; and Darrieux is not only exquisitely beautiful, she's alive as well. The visual opulence rivals anything in Hollywood, where Litvak, a Jewish-Russian refugee, was hastily whisked, to produce wartime propaganda movies. This is his one really estimable picture, which he remade in 1957 for TV. ATu

May Fools

see Milou en mai

Mayor of Hell, The

(1933, US, 90 min, b/w)
d Archie Mayo. *sc* Edward Chodorov. *ph* Barney McGill. *ed* Jack Killifer. *ad* Esdras Hartley. *m* Leo F Forbstein. *cast* James Cagney, Madge Evans, Dudley Digges, Frankie Darro, Allen Jenkins, Arthur Byron, Harold Huber.
● Cloud nine tosh from the days when Warner movies preached that delinquents were just good kids in need of a helping hand. Cagney plays a ward-heeler rewarded with a political sinecure as Deputy Commissioner of a reform school. Up from the slums himself, horrified by the sadistic brutality of the director (Digges), Cagney takes over. Improving the food, relaxing the discipline, and replacing the warders with a system of self-government, he soon has the boys eating out of his hand. But unrest back in the ward ends with Cagney shooting the trouble-maker (Huber) in self-defence; and while he's in hiding, Digges restores his old regime. Jeopardising his freedom, Cagney rushes back in time to end a riot by the boys (a tubercular kid died after being locked in an unheated cell), though not before Digges falls to his death. The good angel Happy Ending tidies away all awkward questions, and Cagney is asked to stay on as director. Despite the risible script, Cagney is as watchable as ever, and Mayo directs sleekly. Remade as vehicles for the Dead End Kids: *Crime School* (1938) and *Hell's Kitchen* (1939). TM

Mazel Tov ou le mariage (Marry Me! Marry Me!)

(1968, Fr, 90 min)
d/p/sc Claude Berri. *ph* Ghislain Cloquet. *ed* Sophie Cossein. *ad* Georges Lévy. *m* Emily Stern. *cast* Claude Berri, Elizabeth Wiener, Luisa Colpeyn, Grégoire Aslan, Régine, Prudence Harrington, Betsy Blair.
● A comedy of manners which cocks a wryly amused eye at the pomp and circumstance attending preparations for the marriage of a nice Jewish boy (Berri himself) to a nice Jewish girl (Wiener). He is French, poor, a bit of a dreamer; she is Belgian, rich, practical and pregnant. Complications set in when she realises she truly loves him, but he goes starry-eyed about an English teacher (Harrington). All comes out in the wash, of course, though not without the caustic implication that a happy Jewish family in the hand is worth two grand passions in the bush. What makes the film, really, is its refusal to fall back on stereotypical characters and situations. Its constant alertness to eccentricities of behaviour make it both engaging and often very funny. TM

M. Butterfly

(1993, US, 101 min)
d David Cronenberg. *p* Gabriella Martinelli. *sc* David Henry Hwang. *ph* Peter Suschitzky. *ed* Ron Sanders. *pd* Carol Spier. *m* Howard Shore. *cast* Jeremy Irons, John Lone, Barbara Sukowa, Ian Richardson, Annabel Leventon, Vernon Dobtcheff.
● Despite initial surprise that Cronenberg was to film David Henry Hwang's play about an affair between a French diplomat and a she-male Chinese opera singer, links with the horrormeister's earlier work soon become clear. It's disappointing, however, that Cronenberg's dissection of the extremities of desire and the slippage of sex roles is less radical than in, say, *Dead Ringers* or *The Naked Lunch*. In pre-Cultural Revolution Beijing of the early '60s, René Gallimard (Irons), inspired by a performance of *Madame Butterfly*, projects on to singer Song Liling (Lone) a cultural imperialist fantasy of compliant Chinese womanhood. For reasons that remain obscure, he/she responds by recreating him/herself in this image, acting out a parody of submissive femininity and initiating a bizarre but mutually fulfilling charade. Blackmailed by a party official into obtaining political secrets, Song Liling later draws her lover into playing his own double role as a spy. Only when their espionage is revealed in a Paris court does Gallimard discover his lover's best-kept secret. NF

Me

see Enfance nue, L'

Me and Charly (Mig og Charly)

(1978, Den, 98 min)
d Morten Arnfred, Henning Kristiansen. *p* Steen Herdel. *sc* Morten Arnfred, Henning Kristiansen, Bent E Rasmussen. *ph* Henning Kristiansen. *ed* Anders Refn. *m* Kasper Winding. *cast* Kim Eduard Jensen, Allan Olsen, Helle Nielsen, Ghita Nørby, Jens Okking, Finn Nielsen, Karl Stegger.
● Teenage life '70s-style, this intimate study set in a provincial Danish town charts a young man's relationship with his girlfriend, widowed mother and his new, slightly delinquent friend Charly (Olsen) over the course of a summer. Engagingly acted, it's tentative and open ended in the realist mode, often intriguingly suggestive – not least a bed scene between the protagonist and his drunken mother – but finally understated to the point of inconsequentiality, and with a troublingly slippery ending. NB

Me and Marlborough

(1935, GB, 84 min, b/w)
d Victor Saville. *p* Michael Balcon. *sc* Marjorie Gaffney, Ian Hay, WP Lipscomb. *ph* Curt Courant. *ad* Alfred Junge. *songs* Noel Gay. *m* Jack Beaver. *cast* Cicely Courtneidge, Tom Walls, Barry Mackay, Alfred Drayton, Iris Ashley, Ivor McLaren, Gibb McLaughlinCecil Parker.
● A costume comedy which, despite the efforts of urbanely professional Saville, looks more like an English pantomime than the breakthrough to Hollywood it was intended as. Wooden old Tom Walls hasn't much to do as Marlborough, and his hangdog ragbag of an army is no match for ebullient Principal Boy Courtneidge. Strutting, pouting, singing, brawling, her woman soldier Kit Ross reduces the ruffianly riff-raff around her to a pack of sulky schoolboys. If the anti-patriotic populism of music hall songs like 'I'm Colonel Coldfeet Of The Coldstream Guards' is missing, there's still a slimy villain of a recruiting sergeant, and the film's cynicism about martial valour and the glories of war is refreshing. RMy

Me and My Brother

(1968, US, 95 min, b/w & col)
d Robert Frank. *p* Helen Silverstein. *sc* Robert Frank, Sam Shepard. *ph* Robert Frank. *ed* Helen Silverstein, Bob Easton. *with* Julius Orlovsky, Joseph Chaikin, Peter Orlovsky, John Coe, Allen Ginsberg, Roscoe Lee Browne, Christopher Walken, Otis Young, Gregory Corso.
● Frank's confusing, complex and ultimately exhilarating movie was one of the cinema's first serious attempts to deal with mental illness. It started out as a *cinéma-vérité* portrait of Julius Orlovsky, a catatonic schizophrenic removed from hospital by his poet brother Peter, and dragged along on a tour of campus poetry gigs with Allen Ginsberg. Partly because of Julius' own unresponsiveness (he's tranquillised up to the eyeballs), Frank decided during the shooting to introduce a second, fictional Julius (played by Chaikin) to act out some hypotheses about the real man's state of mind. The result is a daring mixture of fact and fiction, as Laingian as Peter Robinson's documentary *Asylum*: no statement is made or situation explored without immediately being challenged or confronted with an alternative reading. It's as sprawling and chaotic as it sounds, but it remains firmly (and movingly) anchored in its concern for Julius himself. TR

Me & My Matchmaker

(1996, US, 55 min)
d/p/sc/ph Mark Wexler. *ed* Robert DeMaio. *m* Mark Leggett. *with* Irene Nathan.
● When documentarist Mark Wexler (son of cinematographer Haskell) decided to make a film about traditional Jewish matchmaker Irene Nathan, he did not expect to find himself going out with some of her clients, whom he was interviewing, or to have Irene take such an interest in his own love life. The film's funny, fascinating, and finally faintly disturbing. How far is Wexler prepared to exploit the women he meets in order to 'improve' his movie? Or is he making it partly to meet women? And for all Irene's wit, charm

and good intentions, one can't help feeling by the end that she's something of a meddler and control freak. Creepily intriguing. GA

Mean Dog Blues

(1978, US, 109 min)
d Mel Stuart. *p* Charles A Pratt, George Lefferts. *sc* George Lefferts. *ph* Robert B Hauser. *ed* Houseley Stevenson. *ad* John S Poplin. *m* Fred Karlin. *cast* Gregg Henry, Kay Lenz, George Kennedy, Scatman Crothers, Tina Louise, Felton Perry, James Wainwright, William Windom, George Kennedy.
●Just an everyday story of an everyday prison farm containing the usual ingredients: sadistic guards, underfed Dobermann, and the obligatory framed innocent (Henry) whose survival rests with his choice to either 'Kiss ass, hard ass, or haul ass.' Guess what – he legs it. FF

Mean Machine

(2001, US/GB, 99 min)
d Barry Skolnick. *p* Matthew Vaughn. *sc* Charlie Fletcher, Chris Baker, Andrew Day. *ph* Alex Barber. *ed* Eddie Hamilton, Dayn Williams. *pd* Russell De Rozario. *m* John Murphy. *cast* Vinnie Jones, David Kelly, David Hemmings, Ralph Brown, Vas Blackwood, Robbie Gee, Geoff Bell, John Forgeham, Sally Phillips, Jason Flemyng, Danny Dyer, Jason Statham, Jake Abraham, Omid Djalili.
●This remake of the ballsy Robert Aldrich/Burt Reynolds prison drama *The Longest Yard* (released in Britain as *The Mean Machine*) substitutes soccer for American football, but otherwise retains the basic set-up: a disgraced sports star is incarcerated and compelled to lead his fellow inmates in a match against the warders for the entertainment of the governor. The Aldrich yarn was a hell of a movie: amid the crunching violence the director of *The Dirty Dozen* and *Kiss Me Deadly* mounted a characteristically no holds barred assault on authoritarianism and petty fascism. The remake is a joke. Fortunately director Skolnick has cottoned on that he was on a hiding to nothing, and after the dire first half hour, he essentially plays it for laughs. Vinnie Jones turns in a very decent performance (easily his most confident to date) as former England skipper Danny Meeham, a national villain after throwing a game. His rehabilitation comes reluctantly, finding some pride as he coaches a bunch of no-hopers for the game of their lives. The supporting cast give it a go too. TCh

Mean Machine, The

see Longest Yard, The

Mean Season, The

(1985, US, 104 min)
d Phillip Borsos. *p* David Foster, Lawrence Turman. *sc* Leon Piedmont. *ph* Frank Tidy. *ed* Duwayne Dunham. *pd* Philip M Jefferies. *m* Lalo Schifrin. *cast* Kurt Russell, Mariel Hemingway, Richard Jordan, Richard Masur, Joe Pantoliano, Richard Bradford, Andy Garcia, William Smith.
●A crime reporter is sucked deep into the story he is covering when the murderer chooses him as confidant. Russell is commanding as the burnt-out hack, but Hemingway (as his menaced girlfriend) is given no chance to do more than glow weakly beneath the darkening skies that herald Miami's 'mean season' of hurricanes. It is Jordan as the psychopath whose presence precipitates the gripping atmosphere already half achieved by Frank Tidy's photography of the humid closing of the weather. Based on the novel *In the Heat of the Summer* by one-time crime reporter John Katzenbach, and filmed in the actual newsroom of the 'Miami Herald', the film lacks nothing in verisimilitude. Only, perhaps, something in meaning: all the ingredients are assembled, but one leaves the cinema still waiting for someone to hand over the recipe. FD

Mean Streets 100

(1973, US, 110 min)
d Martin Scorsese. *p* Jonathan Taplin. *sc* Martin Scorsese, Mardik Martin. *ph* Kent Wakeford. *ed* Sidney Levin. *cast* Harvey Keitel, Robert De Niro, David Proval, Amy Robinson, Richard Romanus, Cesare Danova, Robert Carradine, David Carradine.
●The definitive New York movie, and one of the few to successfully integrate rock music into the structure of film: watch Keitel waking to the sound of the Ronettes, or De Niro dancing solo in the street to 'Mickey's Monkey'. *Mean Streets* is also pure Italian-American. Charlie (Keitel), a punk on the fringes of 'respectable' organised crime, ponders his adolescent confusions and loyalties. Beneath the swagger, he's embarrassed by his work, his religion, and by women and his friends, particularly Johnny Boy (De Niro), who owes everyone money. Scorsese directs with a breathless, head-on energy which infuses the performances, the sharp fast talk, the noise, neon and violence with a charge of adrenalin. One of the best American films of the decade. CPe

Meat

(1976, US, 112 min, b/w)
d/p Frederick Wiseman. *ph* William Brayne. *ed* Frederick Wiseman, Oliver Kool.
●Here Wiseman's normally astute and intelligent handling of documentary material for once falters. *Meat* never attempts to match Franju's descent to the slaughterhouse in *Le Sang des Bêtes*, it is true; but whatever one might expect from the director of *Hospital* and *Primate*, it surely would not be the bland and unenquiring advertisement for the US meat industry that emerges. The film does offer one eerie spectacle, however, as what Wiseman calls 'the Judas Goat' leads the other beasts to the slaughter before swiftly sidestepping the death chamber itself. VG

Meatballs

(1979, Can, 94 min)
d Ivan Reitman. *p* Daniel Goldberg. *sc* Len Blum, Daniel Goldberg, Janis Allen, Harold Ramis. *ph* Don Wilder. *ed* Debra Karen. *ad* David Charles. *m* Elmer Bernstein. *cast* Bill Murray, Harvey Atkin, Kate Lynch, Russ Banham, Kristine DeBell, sarah Torgov, Jack Blum, Keith Knight.
●This was apparently inspired by the experience of a Corman PR man who had a poignant moment once while watching *Animal House*. Filmed as light entertainment in the Canadian backwoods, *Meatballs* features a cast in search of a good time at summer camp. Camp counsellor Tripper (Murray) is a John Belushi clone whose 'charisma' dominates the film's standard wackiness and sentimental story (of a kid who doesn't fit). Learning to fit is what this dodo of a camp is all about, showing that the American Way is big and blowsy enough to take a few off-the-wall-style persons, once the ol' sexuality is straightened out. RP

Mechanic, The (aka Killer of Killers)

(1972, US, 100 min)
d Michael Winner. *p* Irwin Winkler, Robert Chartoff. *sc* Lewis John Carlino. *ph* Richard H Kline (US), Bob Paynter (Europe). *ed* Frederick Wilson. *ad* Rodger Maus (US), Herbert Westbrook (Europe). *m* Jerry Fielding. *cast* Charles Bronson, Jan-Michael Vincent, Keenan Wynn, Jill Ireland, Linda Ridgeway, Frank de Kova.
●In this case, mechanic means hired assassin. A glossy, violent, pointless movie from the team who later perpetrated *Death Wish*; mildly entertaining if you want to watch Bronson suggesting silent, brooding menace for the umpteenth time. VG

Mechanics of the Brain, The (Mekhanika Golovnova Mozga)

(1925, USSR, 95 min approx, b/w)
d/sc Vsevolod Pudovkin. *ph* Anatoli Golovnya.
●You need a cold scientific heart to appreciate this documentary of Pavlov's research into the 'conditioned reflex'. A series of agonising animal experiments is elucidated, this being a silent, by an onslaught of inter-titles, five consecutively at one point. Sights include dogs with their faces cut, so their saliva drips externally and measurably, dogs with bits of their brain removed, just to see what happens, chimps given electric shocks to confirm data that might be readily surmised. Pudovkin's chore (his first feature assignment) was to find a *mise-en-scène* to record these dismal tableaux – in theory an interesting challenge. In practice, except for lab-coat audiences, any screening is likely to be punctuated by the soft thud of the exit door. BBa

Medea

(1970, It/Fr/WGer, 118 min)
d Pier Paolo Pasolini. *p* Franco Rossellini, Marina Cicogna. *sc* Pier Paolo Pasolini. *ph* Ennio Guarnieri. *ed* Nino Baragli. *ad* Dante Ferretti, Nicola Tamburro. *cast* Maria Callas, Giuseppe Gentile, Laurent Terzieff, Massimo Girotti, Margareth Clementi, Anna Maria Chio.
●It's worth stressing the position of *Medea* in Pasolini's work, since it makes much the most sense when seen in context: it followed *Pigsty* (whose twin-level structure it duplicates, this time within a single narrative), and preceded the much-abused trilogy (whose rumbustious humour and sexuality were apparently a reaction against the outright nihilism evident here). That said, the film stands as Pasolini's most bizarre exploration of Freudian themes through Marxist eyes: a retelling of Medea's story (elopement, marriage, desertion, revenge) as a mixture of social anthropology and ritual theatre, with every incident given both a 'magic' and a 'rational' reading. Its splendours crystallise in the casting of Callas as Medea, a virtual mime performance with her extraordinary mask of a face bespeaking extremes of emotion; its weaknesses, equally, in the casting of Gentile as Jason, blandly butch, whose presence does nothing to fill out an ill-sketched, passive role. But the real achievement is that Pasolini's visual discourse is every bit as eloquent as the verbal one he puts in the mouth of Terzieff's centaur. TR

Medicine Man

(1992, US, 105 min)
d John McTiernan. *p* Andrew G Vajna, Donna Dubrow. *sc* Tom Schulman, Sally Robinson. *ph* Donald McAlpine. *ed* Michael R Miller. *pd* John Krenz Reinhart Jr. *m* Jerry Goldsmith. *cast* Sean Connery, Lorraine Bracco, José Wilker, Rodolfo de Alexandre, Francisco Tsirene Tsere Rereme.
●Deep in the heart of the rainforest, Dr Campbell (Connery) has discovered then lost a cure for cancer, so it's back to the drawing board in his rickety hut. Ignorant of his (near) findings, the university funding the research sends fellow biochemist Dr Crane (Bracco) to pull the plug. Once informed of the situation, she joins with Campbell in an attempt to repeat the formula *and* to beat the developers threatening the rainforest (which contains the crucial ingredient). Our couple argue and yell, in exchanges lent a humorous edge; national differences and eccentricities are endlessly flaunted (Connery as irascible Scot, Bracco as hard-nosed New Yorker); but the script utterly fails to create engaging sexual tension. A maestro of the action movie, McTiernan effectively captures the horrors of a climactic jungle fire, but at other times, the setting merely provides an exotic backdrop to bolshie posturing and feats of derring-do. If only they'd cast Schwarzenegger. CM

Mediterraneo

(1991, It, 90 min)
d Gabriele Salvatores. *p* Giovanni Minervini. *sc* Vincenzo Monteleone. *ph* Italo Pettriccione. *ed* Nino Baragali. *ad* Thalia Istikopoulos. *m* Giancarlo Bigazzi, Marco Falagiani. *cast* Diego Abatantuono, Claudio Bigagli, Giuseppe Cederna, Claudio Bisio, Gigio Alberti, Vanna Barba.
●Eight mismatched, unwilling Italian combatants and a donkey land on a tiny Greek island in 1941 in order to capture it for Mussolini. If the film hadn't been made by Italians, you might have thought it racist: the eight are alternately stupid, cowardly, lazy and libidinous. They scream, over-react, and fire at chickens by mistake. One night they shoot the donkey when it won't say the password. The wireless operator, whose beast it is, smashes the radio. Their battleship is blown up in the bay. No one knows where they are, and for them the war is over. Gradually, Attic transformation takes place. The hidden islanders emerge: compliant shepherdesses disrobe, the artistic lieutenant restores the frescoes in the church, breasts are bared physically and emotionally, and everyone tries Greek dancing. It isn't really together enough to be an anti-war film: there's no historical or philosophical background, no depth, nothing but sun, sand, saccharine and a stirring bouzouki score, and the surprisingly bitter epilogue doesn't begin to redress the balance. SFe

Medium, The

(1951, US, 84 min, b/w)
d Gian Carlo Menotti. *p* Walter Lowendahl. *sc* Gian Carlo Menotti. *ph* Enzo Serafin. *ed* Alexander Hammid. *pd* Georges Wakhévich. *m* Gian Carlo Menotti.*cast* Marie Powers, Anna Maria Alberghetti, Leo Coleman, Belver Kibler, Beverly Dame, Donald Morgan.

●The composer Menotti wandered only once into the world of cinema, splendidly directing (with the help of Alexander Hammid) this version of his tragic opera about a fake spiritualist thrust into spiralling madness by an unseen hand at her throat. This magnificent chimera, although without progeny, is perfectly realised as an eerie, claustrophobic chamber piece, with a musical style that exists somewhere between Beat and Bartok. With monstrous characters and images only conceivable in a fevered or an operatic mind (where else would one find Toby the deaf mute gypsy boy, or defiant eyelids sealed with hot candle wax), yet fully realisable nowhere else but the cinema, Menotti sucks one into his world of overwrought emotions, heightened by a libretto that makes the film as accessible as *West Side Story* yet perfectly demonstrates the power of the spoken word. FD

Medium Cool

(1969, US, 111 min)
d Haskell Wexler. *p* Tully Friedman, Haskell Wexler. *sc/ph* Haskell Wexler. *ed* Verna Fields. *ad* Leon Ericksen. *m* Mike Bloomfield. *cast* Robert Forster, Verna Bloom, Peter Bonerz, Marianna Hill, Harold Blankenship, Sid McCoy, Christine Bergstrom, Peter Boyle.

●Focusing on a news cameraman's responses and responsibilities to the world framed through his lens – in particular, the 1968 Chicago Democratic Convention and its attendant political riots, during which parts of the film were shot – ace liberal cinematographer Wexler's feature debut as director is a fascinating though not wholly successful fusion of *cinéma-vérité* and political radicalism. Already under the FBI's gaze for his civil rights and socialist documentaries, Wexler was actually accused of inciting the Chicago riots (the script was registered a year before); later he would again be subpoenaed over Emile de Antonio's film on the Weather Underground, which he shot. Recent movies owing a sizeable debt to *Medium Cool* include *Newsfront* and *Circle of Deceit*. PT

Medusa Touch, The

(1978, GB/Fr, 109 min)
d Jack Gold. *p* Jack Gold, Anne V Coates. *sc* John Briley. *ph* Arthur Ibbetson. *ed* Anne V Coates, Ian Crafford. *ad* Peter Mullins. *m* Michael J Lewis. *cast* Richard Burton, Lino Ventura, Lee Remick, Harry Andrews, Alan Badel, Marie-Christine Barrault, Jeremy Brett, Michael Hordern, Gordon Jackson.

●Gold's Midas touch with prestige TV material here for once transfers to the big screen with a full-blooded approach to the most implausible hokum. A skilful blend of the familiar (casting, English locations) and the outrageous (the script's mix of whodunit, disaster movie and telekinetic thriller) produces a beguiling entertainment in which half the fun's to be had from constructing a coherent synopsis out of the loony mess of flashback, foresight, eccentricity and even ecology. Ventura's a French sleuth on Common Market secondment to the Yard; Burton's a mysteriously troubled author with murderous mental powers. Watch for the bouncing cathedral bricks at the end. PT

Mee Pok Man

(1995, Singapore, 105 min)
d Eric Khoo. *p* Jacqueline Khoo. *sc* Foong Yu Lei. *ph* Ho Yoke Weng. *ed* Martyn See Tong Ming. *ad* Damien Brachet. *m* John Kompa. *cast* Joe Ng, Michelle Goh, Lim Kay Tong, George Chua, David Brazil.

●Hard to say if Khoo's splendid debut feature is an authentic tragedy of erotic obsession or the blackest of black comedies; either way, it scores brownie points for demolishing the vision of Singapore life put about by the island's tourist board. The Mee Pok Man (named after the flat noodles he makes and sells from a market stall) lives in the stern shadow of his late father and dotes from afar on the world-weary hooker Bunny. He gets his chance to 'save' this tarnished angel when he finds her bleeding after a hit-and-run accident and takes her home to nurse her. The plot may be *The Collector* with a twist, but the style is all Khoo's own: cool, tender and stoic, even in the face of extreme perversity. TR

Meetings of Anna, The

see Rendez-vous d'Anna, Les

Meeting Venus

(1990, GB, 120 min)
d István Szabó. *p* David Puttnam. *sc* István Szabó, Michael Hirst. *ph* Lajos Koltai. *ed* Jim Clark. *pd* Attila Kovacs. *m* Wagner. *cast* Glenn Close, Niels Arestrup, Moscu Alcalay, Macha Méril, Ildikó Bánsági, Dorottya Udvaros, Erland Josephson, Johanna Ter Teege, Maria de Medeiros.

●When Hungarian conductor Zoltan Szanto (Arestrup) arrives in Paris for rehearsals of Wagner's *Tannhäuser*, he is optimistic that this will be a big career break. The lavish production has brought together top European and American talent, and though this might mean that he is misunderstood in six different languages, Szanto hopes that everyone will share his dedication. Instead, passion among the musicians is confined to bedrooms and kitchens, and spirited debate saved for union meetings. Szabó based this story on his own experiences, along with producer David Puttnam's at Columbia, and personal affinities may have blinded both to the project's indulgences. Petty in-fighting might stir the creative juices, but the endless nationalistic jibes and egocentric displays do little to endear the characters. There's too much chaos and not enough comedy; if this is meant to mirror the new Europe, the future looks grim. CM

Meet Joe Black

(1998, US, 181 min)
d/p Martin Brest. *sc* Ron Osborn. Jeff Reno, Kevin Wade, Bo Goldman. *ph* Emmanuel Lubezki. *ed* Joe Hutshing, Michael Tronick. *pd* Dante Ferretti. *m* Thomas Newman. *cast* Brad Pitt, Anthony Hopkins, Claire Forlani, Jake Weber, Marcia Gay Harden.

●On the eve of his 65th birthday, media magnate William Parrish (Hopkins) feels heart tremors giving him notice to quit. In the meantime, he tells daughter Susan (Forlani) that her fiancé, his right-hand man Drew (Weber), is not quite right for her, which she too realises when sparks fly with a complete stranger in a New York café. After they part, she fails to notice him being run over and killed; even so, she's still surprised when he turns up at her father's house for dinner. In fact, Death (Pitt) has arrived in town for a look around. He's using the young man's body and has chosen Hopkins as his guide. Four writers have adapted Mitchell Leisen's 1934 film *Death Takes a Holiday* and spun it out to three hours. The result is seductively luxurious, with Hopkins bringing authority to his portrait of a man facing his end, and Pitt teasingly enigmatic as the force of mortality in human guise. But the drama's various elements – fantasy thriller, romantic fable, corporate shoot-out, family reconciliation – fail to pull together, and the interminable finale is simply soft in the head. TJ

Meet John Doe

(1941, US, 123 min, b/w)
d/p Frank Capra. *sc* Robert Riskin. *ph* George Barnes. *ed* Daniel Mandel. *ad* Stephen Goosson. *m* Dimitri Tiomkin. *cast* Barbara Stanwyck, Gary Cooper, Edward Arnold, Walter Brennan, James Gleason, Spring Byington, Regis Toomey, Ann Doran, Gene Lockhart.

●Stanwyck causes a sensation with an invented newspaper story about a tramp promising to kill himself to protest at the state of the world – and then she auditions plain-speaking hick Gary Cooper for the part. His goodwill campaign takes the nation by storm, but proves ripe for political manipulation. After a bright start, this hunkers down to serious hand-wringing… Coop's hick (none too convincingly hinted at as the new Messiah) turns out to be a bore, and Capra strains to accommodate political chicanery and his own half-baked idealism. TCh

Meet Me at the Fair

(1952, US, 87 min)
d Douglas Sirk. *p* Albert J Cohen. *sc* Irving Wallace. *ph* Maury Gertsman. *ed* Russell Schoengarth. *ad* Bernard Herzbrun. Eric Orbom. *m* Joseph Gershenson. *cast* Dan Dailey, Diana Lynn, Hugh O'Brian, Scatman Crothers, Carole Mathews, Chet Allen.

●The second of Sirk's 'trilogy' of witty, light-hearted musicals nostalgically evoking small-town America around the turn of the century, blessed with an engaging and lively performance from Dan Dailey as the travelling medicine show proprietor who hides out a runaway orphan (Allen) and woos the pretty delegate from the orphanage board (Lynn) who is supposed to bring him back. The song-and-dance numbers are adequate rather than inspired (although the backstage routine involving Dailey and Carole Mathews is staged and shot with astonishing virtuosity); but Sirk's customary concern with hypocrisy and intolerance is, given the genre and overall tone of the piece, surprisingly to the fore in a subplot about corrupt politicians (admirably headed by the darkly handsome O'Brian). GA

Meet Me in St Louis

(1944, US, 113 min)
d Vincente Minnelli. *p* Arthur Freed. *sc* Irving Brecher, Fred F Finklehoffe. *ph* George Folsey. *ed* Albert Akst. *ad* Cedric Gibbons, Lemuel Ayers, Jack Martin Smith. *songs* Ralph Blane, Hugh Martin, and others. *cast* Judy Garland, Margaret O'Brien, Leon Ames, Mary Astor, Tom Drake, Lucille Bremer, Marjorie Main, June Lockhart, Harry Davenport.

●Minnelli's captivating musical still comes up fresh as paint with each successive viewing, as charmingly, romantically nostalgic as an old valentine. One reason, quite apart from the wit and warmth of the characterisations or the skill with which Minnelli integrates the numbers, is that the seismic little shudders of dismay that shake the St Louis family of 1903 – threatened with a move to New York, where father has a better job waiting – seem to hint at the end of an era and the disappearance of a world where such uncomplicated happiness can exist. It's a feeling which the self-enclosed formality of the film encourages, with its division into four acts, each introduced by a filigreed tintype from the family album which gradually springs to life. One of the great musicals. TM

Meet Mr Lucifer

(1953, GB, 81 min, b/w)
d Anthony Pélissier. *p/sc* Monja Danischewsky. *ph* Desmond Dickinson. *ed* Bernard Gribble. *ad* Wilfrid Shingleton. *m* Eric Rogers. *cast* Stanley Holloway, Peggy Cummins, Jack Watling, Joseph Tomelty, Barbara Murray, Humphrey Lestocq, Kay Kendall, Gordon Jackson.

●Interesting more for its attitudes than for its execution, this satire on television sees Holloway as an unsuccessful panto actor taking out his grievance on the medium by dreaming he is the Devil, turning TV sets all over the country into a source of unhappiness for viewers. The attack is blunt-edged and the humour thin, though it does offer a chance to see a fascinating gallery of personalities from days long past (including such luminaries as Gilbert Harding, Philip Harben and MacDonald Hobley). GA

Meet the Applegates

(1990, US, 89 min)
d Michael Lehmann. *p* Denise Di Novi. *sc* Redbeard Simmons, Michael Lehmann. *ph* Mitchell Dubin. *ed* Norman Hollyn. *pd* Jon Hutman. *m* David Newman. *cast* Ed Begley Jr, Stockard Channing, Dabney Coleman, Bobby Jacoby, Cami Cooper, Glenn Shadix, Susan Barnes, Adam Biesk.

●The Applegates are highly evolved giant insects forced out of their Brazilian rain forest home by greedy land developers. With only a Dick and Jane school reader as guide, they show up in Median, Ohio, posing as a typical American family. Their plan is to infiltrate and blow up a nuclear power plant, irradiating the planet and making it safe again for bugs. But life in small-town Ohio is fraught with dangers: sonic bug repellents, date rapists, lethal Grasshopper cocktails, roaches of the marijuana variety. So while Jane Applegate (Channing) discovers hedonistic consumerism, neglected husband Dick (Begley) succumbs to fleshier pleasures, and the kids (Jacoby and Cooper) do the teenage thing. Soon they're your average, screwed-up American family, their mission forgotten, until fearsome Aunt Bea (Coleman in drag) turns up determined to kick some *homo sapiens* butt. While it never quite matches the sardonic bite, visual stylishness and ear-catching language of Lehmann's earlier *Heathers*, this wacky eco-comedy delivers plenty of laughs. NF

Meet the Feebles

(1989, NZ, 97 min)
d Peter Jackson. *p* Jim Booth Peter Jackson. *sc* Danny Mulheron, Frances Walsh, Stephen Sinclair, Peter Jackson. *ph* Murray Milne. *ed* Jamie Selkirk. *pd* Mike Kane. *m* Peter Dasent. *cast* voices: Danny Mulheron, Donna Akersten, Stuart Devenie, Mark Hadlow, Ross Jolly.
●This deliberately gross movie uses mangy muppets to send up the backstage musical. As the cast of the 'Meet the Feebles' variety show lurch towards a live performance that may land them a syndicated TV series, we are party to the egomaniac excesses, tribulations and jealousies that beset corrupt producer Bletch the Walrus, star singer Heidi the Hippo, star-struck new boy Robert the Hedgehog, and a host of talentless performers and backstage johnnies. Tacky song-and-dance numbers punctuate the action, but despite the attention to set and puppet design, the penning of seven original songs, and Murray Milne's often inventive camerawork, the question remains: why bother to go to all this trouble in order to make a string of gags about vomiting, pissing, shitting, jissom pressure, bunnilingus, and knicker-sniffing anteaters? More generous observers might cite the parallel with bad taste guru John Waters; but compared to this shallow crap, even the Baltimore Bard's offerings run deep. NF

Meet the Parents

(2000, US, 108 min)
d Jay Roach. *p* Nancy Tenenbaum, Jane Rosenthal, Robert De Niro, Jay Roach. *sc* Jim Herzfeld, John Hamburg. *ph* Peter James. *ed* Jon Poll. *pd* Rusty Smith. *m* Randy Newman. *cast* Robert De Niro, Ben Stiller, Blythe Danner, Teri Polo, James Rebhorn, Jon Abrahams, Owen Wilson, Nicole DeHuff.
●Astutely observed, subtly played and consistently hilarious, this family farce marks a change of pace for *Austin Powers* director Roach, who directs his perfectly matched stars, De Niro and Stiller, with a keen eye for comically exaggerated yet instantly recognisable human behaviour. For Jewish, cat-hating male nurse Greg Focker (Stiller), a visit to his girlfriend Pam's WASP family home quickly degenerates into a nightmarish series of gauche faux pas and embarrassing humiliations. His creepy prospective father-in-law, cat-loving ex-CIA operative Jack Byrnes (De Niro), cuts him no slack, using his specialist psychological profiling skills to keep eager to please Greg on the back foot at all times. It starts with lost luggage and ends with cat-painting, with plenty of foot in mouth and a little firestarting in between. De Niro has never been better; even so, Stiller's versatile and prodigious comic talent more than allows him to hold his own. If the screenplay has a fault, it's an over-emphasis on the Oedipal conflict between the two males, which often reduces Pam (Polo) and her likeable ditzy mother (Danner) to little more than spectators. As Pam's oh so perfect old flame Kevin, Wilson fares much better. NF

Meet Whiplash Willie

see Fortune Cookie, The

Meia Noite

see Midnight

Meilleure Façon de Marcher, La

see Best Way to Walk, The

Mein Krieg

see My Private War

Mein Liebster Fiend

see My Dearest Enemy

Mein Stern

see Be My Star

Me Ivan, You Abraham (Moi Ivan, Toi Abraham)

(1993, Fr, 105, b/w)
d Yolande Zauberman. *p* René Cleitman, Jean-Luc Ormières. *ph* Jean-Marc Fabre. *ed* Yann Dedet. *m* Ghedalia Tazartes. *cast* Roma Alexandrovitch, Sacha Iakovlev, Maria Lipkina, Vladimir Machkov, Hélène Lapiower.
●The first feature by documentary-maker Zauberman conjures up the culture of the Yiddish-speaking Jewish communities of pre-war Eastern Europe – specifically that of a schtetl near the Polish border, where two couples, a 12-year-old Orthodox Jew and his Gentile friend, and the Jew's sister and her communist boyfriend, are forced to flee the disintegrating town. These two friendships are examined with a strange, exultant mix of intimate lyricism and abstract physicality. The Jews' vanished world is seen through a glass darkly, with its ancient wooden interiors, markets, wild landscapes, and clashing generational, cultural and religious conflicts. The mood is hard to define – part gloomy pessimism, reminiscent of early Wajda, part the complex character-weaving of Alexei Gherman. Finally, perhaps, it has echoes of a Tarkovskian spiritual quest – but everything harmonises: Jean-Marc Fabre's saturated b/w imagery, the expressive acting, the evocative use of music (Arvo Pärt's 'Cantus'). A haunting auspicious film. WH

Mektoub

(1997, Mor/Fr, 90 min)
d/sc Nabil Ayouch. *ph* Vincent Mathias. *ed* Jean Robert Thomann. *m* Henri Agnel, Pierre Boscheron. *cast* Rachid El Ouali, Faouzi Bensaidi, Amal Chabli, Mohammed Miftah.
●In a plush Tangiers hotel, before a medical conference, young doctor Taoufik goes down with a stomach cramp; his wife is driven off and raped; and next day the couple are smuggled to the mountains – once the vengeful Taoufik has murdered a bent policeman. Why? It's unclear: sexual corruption in the Tangiers PD? Once under way, a taut if rather bare-bones road movie. NB

Melancholia

(1989, GB, 87 min)
d Andi Engel. *p* Colin MacCabe. *sc* Andi Engel, Lewis Rodia. *ph* Denis Crossan. *ed* Christopher Roth. *pd* Jock Scott. *m* Simon Fisher Turner. *cast* Jeroen Krabbé, Susannah York, Ulrich Wildgruber, Jane Gurnett, Kate Hardie, Saul Reichlin.
●Like writer/director Engel, the hero (or anti-hero) of this elegant existential/political thriller – successful art critic David Keller (Krabbé) – is a product of the radical '60s, a German now living in Britain. But his success is hollow: Dürer's engraving 'Melancholia' on his upmarket apartment wall, vodka on his desk, abandoned relationships (most notably with old flame York), angst and melancholy in his heart. This moral inertia is catalysed by an unexpected phone call: a voice from the German past tells him he has been chosen as the assassin of a Chilean ex-torturer, coming to London for a conference. Can he stay true to the ideals of his youth? Could he, should he, kill? Krabbe, rugged and taciturn (the clipped dialogue of the opening sounds echoes of the B thriller) gives an excellent performance, personalising moral and political issues with facial sensitivity, a palpable intellect, and physical restraint. There is much to enjoy: Hitchcockian tension and invention in the action sequences, a contemplative but fluid visual style and an evocative use of music. Good, too, to see London and Hamburg filmed as expressively as they are here by cameraman Denis Crossan. WH

Melancholic Chicken, The (Kure Melancholik)

(1999, Czech Rep, 116 min)
d Jaroslav Brabec. *sc* Jaroslav Brabec, Vladimír Körner. *ph* Jaroslav Brabec, Martin Cech. *ed* Filip Issa. *pd* Karel Vacek. *m* Jan Jirásek. *cast* Karel Roden, Anna Geislerová, Vlasta Chramostová, Lubomír Kostelka.
●A rather tortured rural tragedy that starts promisingly. A boy is born to a hilltop farmer and his lovely new bride. But, just as his chickens are attacked by an unwelcome bird of prey, so she is killed in a lightning storms. Her sister tries to fill her shoes, but is regarded as some sort of ogre by father and son, and she makes way for a lusty local barmaid with little patience for the boy, who brings out the worst in her new husband. It's impassioned stuff, but the characterisation's all over the place, and the lower and meaner the players fall, the more shrill and alienating the film becomes. Thumbs up to the stunt chicken in the finale, though. NB

Melinda

(1972, US, 109 min)
d Hugh A Robertson. *p* Purvis Atkins. *sc* Lonne Elder III. *ph* Wilmer C Butler. *ed* Paul L Evans. *ad* Edward C Carfagno. *m* Jerry Butler, Jerry Peters. *cast* Calvin Lockhart, Rosalind Cash, Vonetta McGee, Paul Stevens, Rockne Tarkington, Ross Hagen, Renny Roker.
●Directorial debut for the editor of *Midnight Cowboy* and *Shaft*. An entry in the short-lived blaxploitation genre, it features a hip, fast-jiving black DJ (Lockhart) who trains nights on karate at the Panther HQ and gives out ultracool sounds by day. He finds himself picking up lovely Melinda (McGee). They have two days of bliss before she's carved up. Turns out it's the Syndicate, an all-white band of nasties, and she has a tape incriminating the big boss which she has passed to our hero. Some scenes suggest that there's a strong eye somewhere behind the camera, but mostly the plot just meanders awkwardly along, not helped by similarly plodding dialogue.

Mélo

(1986, Fr, 110 min)
d Alain Resnais. *p* Marin Karmitz. *sc* Alain Resnais. *ph* Charlie van Damme. *ed* Jean-Pierre Besnard. *ad* Jacques Saulnier. *m* Philippe-Gérard. *cast* Sabine Azéma, Fanny Ardant, Pierre Arditi, André Dussollier, Jacques Dacqmine, Hubert Gignoux, Catherine Arditi.
●Resnais has preserved the theatrical conventions of Henry Bernstein's 1929 period piece, complete with interval curtains, stage lighting and enclosed sets. Why he chose this particular vehicle becomes clear as female anguish and the corrosive power of memory move centre stage. Settled hubby and violinist Pierre (Arditi) invites his more celebrated recitalist friend Marcel (Dussollier) to dinner. Pierre's wife Romaine (Azéma) falls for Marcel as he delivers a melancholy speech about faithless mistresses and the depths of his soul, and during their ensuing affair determines to prove him wrong. The grandly swooning passion, the petals of a rose pressed in a diary – the matter may be dated but the delivery is compelling. There is real pain and cruelty here among the Brahms duets. BC

Melodrama?

(1980, Greece, 93 min, b/w & col)
d Nikos Panayotopoulos. *p* Christos Mangos. *sc* Nikos Panayotopoulos. *ph* Stavros Hassapis. *ed* Andreas Andreadakis. *cast* Lefteris Voyatzis, Maria Xenoudaki, Kostas Kokakis, Aliki Georgouli, Eleonara Stathopoulou, Aleca Paizi.
●Yannis is a man in crisis. A emigrant returning after years away to his home on Corfu (no holiday island this – it's all de Chirico abandoned colonnades, rainswept piazzas and empty cafés) undergoes a profound testing of the limits of identity. He dictates numerous versions of his brief biography into a tape recorder, performs a vision of self reduced to essentials against almost mythic natural and urban landscapes. A brief affair with equally displaced music teacher Anna serves to magnify the problems (when he records their love-making, there is only silence). This vision of an ascetic personality plays out in a monochrome frame of bodies isolated in space, to a score of coded romanticism. Individuals walk, stand still, their faces tracked in thought. This is the poetry of provincial melancholy. But the ending, when it comes, is primal, cyclic and truly redemptive. An extraordinary meditation on the textures of isolation. GE

Melvin and Howard

(1980, US, 95 min)
d Jonathan Demme. *p* Art Linson, Don Phillips. *sc* Bo Goldman. *ph* Tak Fujimoto. *ed* Craig McKay. *pd* Toby Carr Rafelson. *m* Bruce Langhorne. *cast* Paul Le Mat, Jason Robards, Mary Steenburgen, Elizabeth Cheshire, Chip Taylor, Michael J Pollard, Denise Galik, Gloria Grahame, Elise Hudson.
●A beautifully observed, beautifully performed offbeat comedy. The story is slim: milkman Melvin Dummar (Le Mat) picks up a grouchy old

hobo in the Nevada desert one night, lends him a quarter while disbelieving his claim to be Howard Hughes, and then returns to a mundane life of work, divorce, remarriage, and failed songwriting attempts, until eight years later he appears to have been left a fortune by the dead tycoon. But this remarkable (factually based) plot is merely a hook on which to hang an unglamorous account of American working class life. Melvin and his wives' experiences are double-edged examples of the allure and failure of the American dream of success, fame and wealth, although Bo Goldman's script and Demme's understated direction never become overly serious or 'significant'. And the film's delightful humour derives – unusually in these days of brainless *Animal House* spoofs and one-liners – from the characters, who are affectionately observed but never patronised. GA

Melvin Van Peebles' Classified X

see Classified X

Memed My Hawk

(1984, GB, 110 min)
d Peter Ustinov. *p* Faud Kavur. *sc* Peter Ustinov. *ph* Freddie Francis. *ed* Peter Honess. *ad* Viejko Despotovic. *m* Manos Hadjidakis. *cast* Peter Ustinov, Herbert Lom, Denis Quilley, Michael Elphick, Simon Dutton, Leonie Mellinger, Rosalie Crutchley, Michael Gough.

● Set in Turkey in the 1920s, this tells the tale of young Memed (Dutton), a peasant who, to win his childhood sweetheart, heroically takes to the mountains as a brigand, incurring the wrath of his feudal master Abdi Agha (Ustinov) and the authorities. Beyond these bare bones, little remains of Yashar Kemal's fine novel (a stirring adventure and a persuasive indictment of injustice). Hopelessly mangled and confused, the film is little more than a vehicle for Ustinov (who stars, directs and wrote the screenplay) and his capacity for funny accents/camp comedy. It is left to Freddie Francis' photography of sun-bleached Yugoslavia (permission to film in Turkey was refused) to hold the attention during a trying two hours. FD

Memento

(2000, US, 113 min)
d Christopher Nolan. *p* Suzanne Todd, Jennifer Todd. *sc* Christopher Nolan. *ph* Wally Pfister. *ed* Dody Dorn. *pd* Patti Podesta. *m* David Julyan. *cast* Guy Pearce, Carrie-Anne Moss, Joe Pantoliano, Mark Boone Junior, Stephen Tobolowsky, Harriet Sansom Harris, Callum Keith Rennie, Larry Holden.

● Nolan's *Following* was one of the most original British films of the '90s, and this follow-up makes no compromise. It opens with reverse action: a Polaroid photo fading and sliding into the camera, a corpse returned to life, a gun pulled from the head, a bullet sucked into the barrel. The action thereafter plays forwards as usual – with Leonard Shelby (Pearce) out to track down and take revenge on whoever raped and killed his wife – save that the brief narrative chunks flash ever further backwards in time, so that we share Shelby's confused point of view. He suffers from a rare kind of memory loss whereby, while he remembers life before the murder, he's been unable since then to recall anything for more than a few minutes. Hence he's forever forced to fathom afresh everything he sees and hears. The photos he takes for future reference and words he tattoos into his flesh help, but life remains a mysterious, very risky business. This taut, ingenious thriller displays real interest in how perception and memory shape action, identity and, of course, filmic storytelling. Moreover, a plot strand featuring Stephen Tobolowsky even touches the heart. There's grade A work from all concerned, especially Pearce, but in the end this is Nolan's film. And he delivers, with a vengeance. GA

Memento Mori (Yeogo Goedam 2)

(1999, SKor, 94 min)
d Kim Tae-Yong, Min Kyu-Dong. *p* Oh Ki-Min. *sc* Kim Tae-Yong, Min Kyu-Dong. *ph* Kim Yun-Su. *ed* Kim Sang-Beom. *pd* Lee Dae-Hun. *m* Jo Seong-Woo. *cast* Kim Min-Seon, Park Ye-Jin, Lee Yeong-Jin, Kong Hyo-Jin, Baek Jong-Hak.

● When Park Ki-Hyung declined to make a sequel to his surprise hit *Whispering Corridors*, producer Oh had the smart idea of offering the challenge to two recent graduates from the Korean Film Academy who had already collaborated on the excellent shorts *Seventeen* and *Pale Blue Dot*. They came up with a very different take on a haunting in a high school for girls: a convoluted tale of teenage lesbian feelings, telepathy, sexual rivalry, spirit possession and unwanted pregnancy. Intricately structured and made with great technical brio, the film falters in its final reel in which the entire school is terrorised by the spirit of a wronged girl driven to suicide. But when it forgets about grandstanding and concentrates on the intimate feelings of its protagonists, it's quite something. TR

Mementos (Doea Tanda Mata)

(1985, Indon, 93 min)
d Teguh Karya. *p* Budi Prakoso. *sc* Teguh Karya, Alex Komang. *ph* George Kamarullah. *ed* Rizal Asmar. *pd* Thamrin Ludis, Benny Benhardi. *m* Idris Sardi. *cast* Alex Komang, Jenny Rachman, Hermín Chentini, Eka Gandara.

● Karya's film suffers from the *Hamlet* syndrome: a hero who spends the whole movie doing nothing but go through agonised introspections. The script problem (compounded by the shortcomings of Komang's performance in the lead) finally works the film into an impasse that no amount of beautiful period set-direction can relieve. Karya cunningly invests his story (of anticolonial resistance in the 1930s) with contemporary resonances, but his daring counts for little when the material is so uncompelling. TR

Mémoire des Apparences (Life Is a Dream)

(1986, Fr, 105 min)
d/sc Raúl Ruiz. *ph* Jacques Bouquin. *ed* Martine Bouquin, Rodolfo Wedeles. *pd* Christian Olivares. *m* Jorge Arriagada. *cast* Sylvain Thirolle, Roch Leibovici, Bénédicte Sire, Laurence Cortadellas, Jean-Bernard Guillard, Jean-Pierre Agazar.

● Ruiz at his densest and most oblique. Ostensibly a version of Calderón's Spanish Golden Age drama *Life Is a Dream*, it starts as a psychological detective story about a former Resistance fighter attempting to reconstitute the play and the details it conceals about an underground resistance network. Despairing, he ends up hanging around the local cinema, which doubles as a police station, as well as a playground for the excesses of memory and the imagination. The most explicitly dreamlike of Ruiz's fictions, with Magritte and Borges allusions foremost, it's also a good example of his tendency to overstate, to booby-trap his fictions with more false bottoms than the conscious mind can properly assimilate. But bearing in mind that sleep forms the main agenda here, you're probably safe to doze off from time to time. JRo

Memoirs of an Invisible Man

(1992, US, 99 min)
d John Carpenter. *p* Bruce Bodner, Dan Kolsrud. *sc* Robert Collector, Dana Olsen, William Goldman. *ph* William A Fraker. *ed* Marion Rothman. *pd* Lawrence G Paull. *m* Shirley Walker. *cast* Chevy Chase, Daryl Hannah, Sam Neill, Michael McKean, Stephen Tobolowsky, Jim Norton, Pat Skipper.

● Carpenter's sci-fi comedy is essentially a $40 million B movie, with remarkable special effects compensating for a thin storyline. A *noir*-ish opening, complete with voice-over and flashback, hints at a darker tone more in keeping with HF Saint's source novel. But once Chase has been rendered invisible, the plot consists of one endless chase scene, punctuated by inventive sight gags and the odd romantic interlude. After a freak accident at a research laboratory, Nick Halloway discovers that being invisible isn't the voyeur's dream he fantasised about as a child. Now 'the most exotic intelligence asset' available, he becomes the subject of a huge manhunt led by cynical CIA man Jenkins (Neill). Aided by anthropologist Alice (Hannah), he tries to evade his pursuers and find time to adjust to his invisibility. When played for laughs, this works well, while the action scenes generate an atmosphere of paranoia and menace; but failing to explore the pathos of Nick's predicament, the film becomes an inflated lightweight comedy whose shortcomings are all too visible. NF

Memoirs of a Survivor

(1981, GB, 115 min)
d David Gladwell. *p* Michael Medwin, Penny Clark. *sc* Kerry Crabbe, David Gladwell. *ph* Walter Lassally. *ed* William Shapter. *pd* Keith Wilson. *m* Mike Thorn. *cast* Julie Christie, Christopher Guard, Leonie Mellinger, Debbie Hutchings, Nigel Hawthorne, Pat Keen, Mark Dignam.

● Christie plays the diarist of Doris Lessing's novel, surviving in a not-too-distant future Britain resembling nothing so much as the landscape of Derek Jarman's 'Jubilee'. The depressing picture carefully detailed by Gladwell of a nation spiritually, politically and economically bankrupt – Thatcher's Britain, in fact – is one in which people queue in the streets for water rations, the corner newsvendor with no papers to sell speaks the news to impassive listeners, horses and dogs are set upon for food, packs of wild children huddle in the underground. Through all this Christie wanders with the comfort of her fantasies, too familiar by half to arthouse regulars. RM

Memories

(1995, Jap, 113 min)
d Katsuhiro Otomo, Koji Morimoto, Tensai Okamura. *p* Shigeru Watanabe. *sc* Satoshi Kon, Katsuhiro Otomi. *ed* Takeshi Seyama. *pd* Yuji Ikehata, Mitsuo Koseki, Akira Yamakawa, Nizou Yamakawa, Tatsuka Kushida, Katsuhiro Otomo. *m* Yoko Kanno, Jun Miyaka, Hiroyuki Nagashima, Takkyu Ishino. *cast* voices: Tsutumo Isobe, Hideyuki Hori, Isamu Hayashi.

● Not counting *Roujin Z*, for which he came up with a story and some designs, this is Otomo's first animation feature since *Akira*: a portmanteau film (based on three of his graphic short stories) which fully represents his range and at the same time fulfils his dream of providing real creative opportunities to young artists stuck in TV animation hell. *Magnetic Rose*, the first episode, is spectacular space opera: two intrepid scouts, a ghost ship and the story of a love without end, set in a cosmic Sargasso Sea. *Stink Bomb* is cautionary sci-fi comedy: a guy takes an untested drug in mistake for a cold cure and turns into a maximum security risk. And *Cannon Fodder*, directed by Otomo himself, is a bizarre parable of war, peace and expendability. All three episodes are cogent, provocative and superbly designed. TR

Memories of Duke

(1980, US, 85 min)
d/p Gary Keys. *ph* Ed Lachman, Urs Furrer, Bill Hudson. *ed* Jow Tripician, Janice Keuhnellan. *with* Duke Ellington, Cootie Williams, Russell Procope, the Duke Ellington Band.

● Black producer/director Gary Keys' monument to Ellington consists of concert footage of the band's 1968 tour, intercut with interview comments from long-time sidemen Cootie Williams and Russell Procope. If the sound quality of the numbers leaves something to be desired, the inclusion of Ellington-composed classics such as 'Take The A Train', 'Satin Doll' and 'Black And Tan Fantasy' (and information about long and satisfying sojourns of individual musicians with the band) more than attests to the Duke's stature as Jazz Giant. RM

Memories of Me

(1988, US, 105 min)
d Henry Winkler. *p* Alan King, Billy Crystal, Michael Hertzberg. *sc* Eric Roth, Billy Roth. *ph* Andrew Dintenfass. *ed* Peter E Berger. *pd* William J Cassidy. *m* Georges Delerue. *cast* Billy Crystal, Alan King, JoBeth Williams, Janet Carroll, David Ackroyd, Phil Fondacaro.

● Unreleased in the UK, this typical Billy Crystal offering, co-produced with fellow comic Alan King, is an uneasy blend of neurotic comedy and mawkish sentimentality. Its story of a heart surgeon whose recent coronary forces him to reassess his life and rebuild his relationship with his estranged dad is too eager to please, but Crystal mugs away with consummate professionalism and nightclub veteran King brings acerbity to the role of the curmudgeonly father.

Memories of Underdevelopment (Memorias del Subdesarrollo)

(1968, Cuba, 104 min, b/w)
d/sc Tomás Gutiérrez Alea. *ph* Ramón Suárez. *ed* Nelson Rodriguez. *m* Leo Brower. *cast* Sergio Corrieri, Daisy Granádos, Eslinda Nuñez, Beatriz Ponchora, Omar Valdés, René de la Cruz.
●The Cuban Film Institute (ICAIC) was founded in 1959, only months after Castro came to power. It was some years, however, before its fruits were exposed to European and US audiences; Alea's film, his fifth feature, was the breakthrough. The story is related in the form of a diary by a prosperous bourgeois who chooses to stay in Havana when his family leaves for the States in 1961. While he rejects many of the bourgeois ideals of his upbringing, he is unable to shake off either sexual neurosis or his European-based intellectual paralysis, continuing to live uncertainly as a rent-drawing property-owner. The 'underdevelopment' of the title is a complex pun describing both individual and national problems of the revolution in its infancy, though the film is anything but literary in its attack: Alea proceeds with dazzling and highly accomplished technique towards a perceptive and witty analysis. Many critics at the time were surprised by the strain of self-criticism running through a film produced by what is virtually a government ministry in a Marxist country. RM

Memories Within Miss Aggie

(1974, US, 69 min)
d Gerard Damiano. *sc* Ron Wertheim, Gerard Damiano. *ph* Harry Flecks. *ed* St Marks Place. *m* Rupert Holmes. *cast* Deborah Ashira, Patrick L Farrelly, Harry Reems, Kim Pope, Mary Stuart, Darby Lloyd Rains.
●Around 1974, US hardcore film-makers were getting over their first flush of triumph at simply putting the sex act on screen, and Damiano turns to psychological horror for this tale of a demented old woman reminiscing through a lifetime of romantic fantasy to a predictably macabre final revelation. In its hardcore form (running 78 minutes), the film's small momentum was generated by various sexual acts which served to disguise the sheer wretchedness of everything in between. This softcore version, from which the British censor removed nine minutes to eradicate any lingering traces, looks like some meandering American fringe theatre production in which everyone has swallowed too much Valium. Even the most diehard porno audience will be panting to get out of the cinema. DP

Memory of Justice, The

(1975, GB/WGer/US, 278 min, b/w & col)
d/p Marcel Ophüls. *ph* Mike Davis. *ed* Inge Behrens.*with* Yehudi Menuhin, Daniel Ellsberg, JK Galbraith, Albert Speer, Marcel Ophüls.
●An investigation of the impact of the Nuremberg trials on the German conscience, and a study of the implications of the moral and legal principles established there for events like Hiroshima and Vietnam, *The Memory of Justice* operates by steadily drawing the viewer into a situation that is forever expanding, as new ramifications and contexts are found by Ophüls in the course of his interviews and in the use he makes of library footage. The film is, accordingly, as important for its method of investigation as for the facts it reveals. In contrast to the tight narrative and fixed viewpoint of the run-of-the-mill TV documentary, Ophüls' film is so structured as to force the viewer to involve himself in the arguments presented in the actual process of watching the film, thus transforming a passive viewing into an active reading. (Originally broadcast in two parts, 'Nuremberg and the Germans' and 'Nuremberg and Other Places'.) PH

Memphis Belle

(1990, GB, 102 min)
d Michael Caton-Jones. *p* David Puttnam, Catherine Wyler. *sc* Monte Merrick. *ph* David Watkin. *ed* Jim Clark. *pd* Stuart Craig. *m* George Fenton. *cast* Matthew Modine, Eric Stoltz, Tate Donovan, DB Sweeney, Billy Zane, David Strathairn, John Lithgow, Jane Horrocks.
●In East Anglia, 1943, the crew of an American B17 bomber prepare for their 25th daylight mission: if they return alive, it'll be a record and they'll be whisked back to the States for a propaganda tour. Inspired by real-life events covered in Wyler's WWII documentary *The Memphis Belle*, this David Puttnam production may not be the most original movie around, but at least Caton-Jones steers through the stock situations with verve and panache. Aided by uniformly sturdy performances (Modine and Strathairn are particularly fine as the pilot and commanding officer), he even carries off such Hawksian moments as Modine's moonlit monologue to his plane, and achieves a genuine mood of claustrophobia, vulnerability and danger in the airborne scenes, while never giving way to bogus jingoism. Admittedly, one could do with less of the dog and 'Oh Danny Boy'; and towards the end, the story's sheer eventfulness risks tipping the tone into self-parody. For the most part, though, this is sensitive, gripping, oddly old-fashioned cinema. GA

Me, Myself & Irene

(2000, US, 116 min)
d Bob Farrelly, Peter Farrelly. *p* Bradley Thomas, Bobby Farrelly, Peter Farrelly. *sc* Peter Farrelly, Mike Cerrone, Bobby Farrelly. *ph* Mark Irwin. *ed* Christopher Greenbury. *pd* Sidney J Bartholomew Jr. *m* Peter Yorn, Lee Scott. *cast* Jim Carrey, Renée Zellweger, Chris Cooper, Robert Forster, Richard Jenkins, Rob Moran, Traylor Howard, Daniel Greene, Anthony Anderson.
●This offering lacks the sweet subtext and buried heart that marks the films of the Farrelly brothers from *Kingpin* to *There's Something About Mary*. It's dominated by Carrey as hyperbolically nice Rhode Island motorcycle cop Charlie who finally cracks, turns into alter ego Hank, and is diagnosed with 'advanced delusionary schizophrenia with involuntary narcissistic rage'. The brothers have tackled race, class, status, delinquency, sexual relations, social alienation, paranoia, disability and now madness through lavatory humour, cheap gags, crass offensiveness, pratfalls and all-round puerile goonery, hung together by ad hoc plotting and point the camera styling. And they've raised some of the richest, most uncomfortable, laughs in recent cinema. But what's a poor taboo breaker to do? Don't ask: here they ram one right up a character's arse. Their adolescent fear/idolisation of women is represented by the unpersuasive Zellweger as the fugitive Irene. But for turning positive discrimination – Charlie/Hank's delightful trio of overweight African-American sons, fruit of the congress of his wife and a Mensa-minded midget cab driver, are bright enough to fly a helicopter from first principles – into hilarious, affectionate comedy, they win my PC award. WH

Me Myself I

(1999, Fr/Aust, 104 min)
d Pip Karmel. *p* Fabien Liron. *sc* Pip Karmel. *ph* Graham Lind. *ed* Denise Haratzis. *pd* Murray Picknett. *m* Charlie Chan. *cast* Rachel Griffiths, David Roberts, Sandy Winton, Yael Stone, Shaun Loseby, Trent Sullivan, Rebecca Frith, Felix Williamson.
●This fanciful affair is Griffiths' first star vehicle, and although it's easy to understand why she opted for a light, mainstream(ish) domestic comedy, albeit one with an intriguing double role, she really is miles better than the material. Pamela (Griffiths), a lonely thirty-something journo, returns to an empty flat and wonders why she didn't marry college boyfriend Robert (Roberts). She gets her chance to discover what might have been after bumping into the Pamela (Griffiths two) who really did wed Robert. The latter then mysteriously disappears, leaving career girl Griffiths dumped in the middle of married life with children. The alternate reality schtick echoes *Sliding Doors*, but it's the weakest aspect of writer/director Karmel's first feature. Griffiths breezes through the proceedings, managing to keep the audience in tune with the rise and fall of her expectations, all the while presenting a facade which rather conveniently fools her new 'family'. TJ

Men (Männer)

(1985, WGer, 99 min)
d/sc Doris Dörrie. *ph* Helge Weindler. *ed* Raimund Barthelmes, Jeanette Magerl. *ad* Jörg Neumann, Gabriele Hochheim, Friedrich Natus. *m* Claus Bantzer. *cast* Heiner Lauterbach, Uwe Ochsenknecht, Ulrike Kriener, Janna Marangosoff, Dietmar Bär.
●Love me, love my double standards, that's what Julius (Lauterbach), a power hungry packaging magnate and habitual seducer of secretaries, expects from his wife. He gets it too, until their 12th anniversary, when a love bite on her neck suggests that an equaliser is at work. At this early point in Doris Dörrie's concise and sharply observed satire, you might be forgiven for thinking that a feminist attack is under way. Not so. Julius, who hasn't come to own a Maserati simply by waiting for things to happen, takes leave of absence to strike back. Concealing his identity, he persuades his wife's lover (Ochsenknecht) to accept him, first as a lodger in his squalid bachelor apartment, then as a partner in his low-achieving hippy life. It's the start of an unpredictable friendship that puts both men's motivation under the microscope. The screenplay requires a certain suspension of disbelief – would a wife be so easily deceived by a gorilla suit? – but she turns the tables neatly so that each gets his just deserts. Hers not to stick in the knife, rather to entertain with insight and mirth. MCR

Men, The

(1950, US, 85 min, b/w)
d Fred Zinnemann. *p* Stanley Kramer. *sc* Carl Foreman. *ph* Robert De Grasse. *ed* Harry Gerstad. *pd* Rudolph Sternad. *m* Dimitri Tiomkin. *cast* Marlon Brando, Teresa Wright, Everett Sloane, Jack Webb, Richard Erdman, Howard St John.
●Even in his first movie, Brando's ability to transcend mediocre material is very much in evidence. *The Men*, a ward full of war veteran paraplegics under the stern but loving care of Doctor Everett Sloane, struggle to come to terms with their predicament, hoping eventually to exchange their own tough bonhomie for the world outside. Although Stanley Kramer's typically soapy production focuses attention on Brando's tempestuous relationship (wrecked by his feelings of shame and inadequacy) with devoted fiancée Teresa Wright (all syrupy sincerity), the film timidly skirts problems of sexual frustration and impotence. It also almost totally ignores the cause of the paraplegics' disabilities: not one of them ever expresses regret at having ruined life and limb for Uncle Sam. Despite the worthy wetness, however, young Marlon manages to sidestep sentimentality; even confined to a wheelchair, the raw power underlying his controlled gestures and brooding glances is charismatic. GA

Menace II Society

(1993, US, 97 min)
d Allen Hughes, Albert Hughes. *p* Darin Scott. *sc* Tyger Williams. *ph* Jon Kranhouse. *ed* Christopher Koefoed. *pd* Penny Barrett. *m* QD III. *cast* Tyrin Turner, Jada Pinkett, Larenz Tate, Arnold Johnson, MC Eiht, Marilyn Coleman.
●Another tale from the 'hood, but, regrettably, the Hughes brothers' first feature is a compendium of clichés. Beginning with the murder of a Korean shopkeeper by two Watts teenagers, the film focuses on the dilemma faced by Caine (Turner), torn between the members of his 'posse' and his good girl Ronnie (Pinkett), who tries to persuade him from his violent ways. Photographed, scored and performed with more flair than the material deserves. GA

Men and Women (Nannan nünü)

(1999, China, 90 min)
d Liu Bingjian. *p* Li Jin Liang. *sc* Cui Zien. *ph* Luijiang Xujun. *ed* Ah Yi. *pd* Han Xiao. *cast* Qing Jie, Yu Bo, Zhang Kang, Yu Mengjie, Wei Jiangang, Cui Zien.
●The second film of a cinematographer turned indie director is a brave portrait of a country boy coming to Beijing and embarking on a homosexual lifestyle (to the chagrin of the lady who's taken him under her wing). It was written in less than a week, shot on the hoof, and indeed may never be seen in China. To Western sensibilities, it's low key with an earnest, observational style mixed haphazardly with some wacky, OTT comedy (mostly emanating from the character of a radio DJ carrying out a study of Beijing's public toilets). TCh

Men Are Children Twice

see Valley of Song

Men Are Not Gods

(1936, GB, 90 min, b/w)
d Walter Reisch. *p* Alexander Korda. *sc* Iris Wright, GB Stern. *ph* Charles Rosher, Robert Krasker. *ed* William Hornbeck, Henry Cornelius. *ad* Vincent Korda. *m* Geoffrey Toye. *cast* Miriam Hopkins, Gertrude Lawrence, Sebastian Shaw, Rex Harrison, AE Matthews, Val Gielgud, Laura Smithson, Lawrence Grossmith, Wally Patch.

●Producer Alexander Korda roped in Walter Reisch, an old pal from his Viennese days, to direct; hired top US cameraman Charles Rosher (who'd worked on Murnau's *Sunrise*); lured over Hollywood luminary Hopkins, and bolstered the cast with British stage stalwarts, but to no avail – this yarn about a stenographer who falls for a married actor (he contemplates strangling his wife during a performance of *Othello*) remains throwaway, novelettish nonsense. GM

Men at Work

(1990, US, 98 min)
d Emilio Estevez. *p* Cassian Elwes. *sc* Emilio Estevez. *ph* Tim Suhrstedt. *ed* Craig Bassett. *pd* Dins Danielsen. *m* Stewart Copeland. *cast* Charlie Sheen, Emilio Estevez, Leslie Hope, Keith David, Dean Cameron, John Getz, Hawk Wolinski, John Lavachielli, John Putch, Tommy Hinkley, Darrell Larson.

●Estevez scripted, directed and stars, alongside brother Sheen, in this comic thriller about two Californian garbage collectors who find a dead body in one of their bins. Estevez must take the blame for the overall cheery incompetence, although the film, like the average dustbin of affluence, contains many fresh elements amid the trash. There's a groansome conservation theme (toxic dumping off a premier surfing beach), and an amazingly lively corpse (Darrell Larson doesn't let a little detail like rigor mortis inhibit a performance of extraordinary animation). This snigger-snigger attitude to death is matched by a general tastelessness. Sheen gloatingly spies on the woman living opposite, and there's a nasty running gag whereby the boys outwit, disarm, strip and handcuff pairs of policemen in compromising positions. But the grotesque practical jokes perpetrated against two interfering bumblers are genuinely funny, while Estevez and Sheen remain cutely goofy even when indulging themselves in this adolescent idiocy. SFe

Men Don't Leave

(1990, US, 114 min)
d Paul Brickman. *p* Jon Avnet. *sc* Barbara Benedek, Paul Brickman. *ph* Bruce Surtees. *ed* Richard Chew. *pd* Barbara Ling. *m* Thomas Newman. *cast* Jessica Lange, Arliss Howard, Joan Cusack, Kathy Bates, Tom Mason, Chris O'Donnell, Charlie Korsmo.

●When her husband dies in an explosion, leaving her with massive debts, two young sons and no visible means of support, Beth Macauley (Lange) moves to a cramped apartment in the city, where she lands a thankless job in a gourmet foodstore. While her younger son (Korsmo) takes to petty burglary, and teenage Chris (O'Donnell) finds solace with a young nurse (Cusack), Beth starts an affair with a musician (Howard); but progress is impeded as she gives way to delayed shock and declines into depression. What distinguishes this weepie is its deglamorised approach: all-consuming angst is anchored in the minutiae of everyday life and wry observation. While not without its occasional lapses into over-long sob sessions, Barbara Benedek and Brickman's intelligent script offers strong characterisations, and the performances – particularly from Lange and Korsmo – are excellent. Absorbing, truthful, and full of tender insight. CM

Ménilmontant

(1924, Fr, 50 min, b/w)
d/p/sc Dimitri Kirsanoff. *ph* Léonce Crouan, Dimitri Kirsanoff. *ed* Dimitri Kirsanoff. *cast* Nadia Sibirskaia, Yolande Beaulieu, Guy Belmont, Jean Pasquier, Maurice Ronsard.

●Time has dealt much more kindly with Kirsanoff than with most of his contemporaries. A Russian émigré in Paris who enjoyed little contact with other film-makers, his extraordinary montages, dissolves and narrative ellipses nevertheless echo the tricks that became tics in so many early avant-garde experiments. But in Kirsanoff's work, such devices are overridden and firmly welded together by the romantic impressionism which casts a haunting aura of malevolent beauty over *Ménilmontant* and its suburban axe murderer.

Men in Black

(1997, US, 98 min)
d Barry Sonnenfeld. *p* Walter F Parkes, Laurie MacDonald. *sc* Ed Solomon. *ph* Don Peterman. *ed* Jim Miller. *pd* Bo Welch. *m* Danny Elfman. *cast* Tommy Lee Jones, Will Smith, Linda Fiorentino, Vincent D'Onofrio, Rip Torn, Tony Shalhoub, Siobhan Fallon.

●They're here – and they have social security numbers. Aliens are everywhere, just trying to get along like the rest of us, mostly, under the watchful eyes of an extra-governmental police agency, the Men in Black. Agent K (Jones) picks out a New York cop (Smith) to become his new partner, J, initiating him into the secrets of the universe: galactic weaponry, memory erasers and power dressing. At the same time, an unintegrated alien bug takes residence in the (loose-fitting) body of farmer D'Onofrio, with a plan that might mean curtains for the planet. Sonnenfeld's film is just good enough to remind us how lazy most blockbusters have become in the decade since *Gremlins* and *Ghostbusters* – hits with a similar hip, relaxed vibe.The personable well-paired stars make the most of a superior script by Ed Solomon ('He said the world was coming to an end.' 'Did he say when?'), and, taking eye-popping special fx in his stride, the director makes adroit use of out-of-this-world NY locations. It's so much fun, in fact, that it's almost over before you realise that you've been watching a great idea for a movie in desperate search of a plot. TCh

Men in War

(1957, US, 104 min, b/w)
d Anthony Mann. *p* Sidney Harmon. *sc* Philip Yordan. *ph* Ernest Haller. *ed* Richard C Meyer. *pd* Lewis Jacobs. *m* Elmer Bernstein. *cast* Robert Ryan, Aldo Ray, Robert Keith, Phillip Pine, Nehemiah Persoff, Vic Morrow, James Edwards, LQ Jones, Scott Marlowe.

●One of the best of the lost patrol movies, set in Korea in 1950, bleakly anti-heroic and prefiguring Milestone's *Pork Chop Hill* in the bitter irony of its climactic assault on a hill. Beautifully staged by Mann with his usual eye to landscape, and an intriguing sub-theme querying the nature of military authority as Ryan's lieutenant, wearily devoting himself to shepherding his men through alive, comes into conflict with – while forced to rely on the battle skills of – Aldo Ray's sergeant, whose sole interest, pursued with dog-like devotion, lies in trying to save a shellshocked colonel (mad but still a symbol of authority). TM

Men of Honor

(2000, US, 128 min)
d George Tillman Jr. *p* Robert Teitel, Bill Badalato. *sc* Scott Marshall Smith. *ph* Anthony B Richmond. *ed* John Carter. *pd* Leslie Dilley. *m* Mark Isham. *cast* Robert De Niro, Cuba Gooding Jr, Hal Holbrook, Charlize Theron, Aunjanue Ellis, Hal Holbrook, David Keith, Michael Rapaport, Powers Boothe, Joshua Leonard.

●You can't say Carl Brashear doesn't deserve this solid, old school biopic. With guts and pig headed determination this sharecropper's son signed up for the US Navy in the early '50s, and worked his way through the entrance exam to train as a salvage diver, becoming the first ever black man to qualify. If the institutional racism he has to overcome is hardly a surprise, this occasionally stodgy film offers the striking reminder of the terrifying conditions under which divers worked. Tough enough for any able-bodied man, but even the loss of half a leg in a shipboard accident doesn't deter Brashear from his dedication to duty. Gooding's central performance certainly does the man justice, embodying the strength of will never to take 'no' for an answer. Master Captain Billy Sunday (De Niro), the hard nosed training instructor under pressure to fail Brashear, understands what it means to work your way up, and the growing of respect between these two adversaries lends the proceedings its sturdy narrative fibre. Elsewhere the characterisation is less sure, with Holbrook's racist navy commander a too-obvious loony, and Theron's Mrs Sunday a masochistic puzzle. But when director Tillman takes his camera underwater we too are holding our breath. TJ

Men of Respect

(1990, US, 113 min)
d William Reilly. *p* Ephraim Horowitz. *sc* William Reilly. *ph* Bobby Bukowski. *ed* Elizabeth Kling. *pd* William Barclay. *m* Misha Segal. *cast* John Turturro, Katherine Borowitz, Dennis Farina, Peter Boyle, Lilia Skala, Steven Wright, Rod Steiger, Stanley Tucci.

●*Macbeth* as a mobland drama is no sillier than *The Tempest* in deep space; but the Scottish Play is so obviously a prototype for tales of young wiseguys slaying their way to *capo*-dom that to rewrite the original is simply stating the obvious. Young hood Mike Battaglia (Turturro), egged on by ambitious wife Ruthie (Borowitz), kills gang boss Steiger and gets to be *padrino*. But no sooner is the deed done than he starts hallucinating visits from slain buddy Bankie Como (Farina). Reilly rewrites the original in fustian *noir*, but shows too much respect for it, bending over backwards to fit in touches like catatonic comic Steven Wright in a slouch-on part as the Porter, pathetic fallacy galore, and lines like 'Not a man of woman born can do shit to me'. Turturro acts as though he can't believe what he's got into but is determined to have a field day anyhow; and Borowitz gives Ruthie a slinky gravitas, although she doesn't look the kind to freak out with the Ajax. JRo

Men of Two Worlds

(1946, GB, 109 min)
d Thorold Dickinson. *p* John Sutro. *sc* Thorold Dickinson, Herbert W Victor, Joyce Cary, E Arnot Robertson. *ph* Desmond Dickinson, Geoffrey Unsworth. *ed* Aben Jaggs. *ad* Tom Morahan. *m* Arthur Bliss. *cast* Eric Portman, Phyllis Calvert, Robert Adams, Cathleen Nesbitt, Orlando Martins, Cyril Raymond.

●Three years in the making, Dickinson's film survived the loss of filmstock and equipment when a U-Boat sunk their ship en route to locations in Tanzania. What remains is a well-intentioned, slightly musty drama exploring the clash of science and superstition in colonial East Africa, where a witch doctor refuses to let commissioner Portman evacuate his tribe to escape the sleeping sickness sweeping his village. These days though, it all looks a bit patronising. TJ

Menschen am Sonntag

see People on Sunday

Men's Club, The

(1986, US, 101 min)
d Peter Medak. *p* Howard Gottfried. *sc* Leonard Michaels. *ph* John Fleckenstein. *ed* Cynthia Scheider, David Dresher, Bill Butler. *pd* Ken Davis. *m* Lee Holdridge. *cast* Roy Scheider, Harvey Keitel, Richard Jordan, Craig Wasson, Frank Langella, Treat Williams, David Dukes, Stockard Channing, Marilyn Jones, Gwen Welles, Jennifer Jason Leigh.

●Californication. Six men meet in the home of a buddy psychotherapist to talk about themselves and women. The real estate agent (Keitel) remembers one who put her tongue in his mouth. The doctor (Williams) remembers the one who came between him and his strawberry dessert – he kicked her. Attorney Langella's wife, thanks to analysis, discovered herself and scarpered with the furniture. Blah blah blah. When they have eaten all the food, drunk all the wine, and wrecked the place throwing knives, they move on to an upmarket San Francisco brothel, where they all make out/up/mistakes. All, that is, except the shrink, rapped over the head with a casserole by his irate spouse. Flashes of genuine intelligence and wit in the writing only render the moral nihilism of the whole high-tack enterprise all the more inexcusable. MS

Men's Lives

(1975, US, 43 min)
d Josh Hanig, Will Roberts. *p* James Klein, Julia Reinchert. *ph* Josh Hanig. *ed* James Klein, Josh Hanig.

●With the rise of the women's movement in America, men have been forced to question, to some extent, male stereotypes and the roles they're expected to play. This rather twee documentary never gets much beyond asking very general questions, alternating between half-baked theorising and studying a variety of male groups, from the children's playground through to the student dance. The film largely ignores the gap between a male ideal and various interpretations of that ideal, and also skates over the implications of language and its emotional charges. When there's the curious contradiction of an 'effeminate' young male dancer defending himself in classic macho terms – 'A man is someone who will stand up for what he thinks is right' – the film fails to even notice the wires crossing. CPe

Mensonge

see Lie, The

Men Who Tread on the Tiger's Tail, The

see Tora no Oo Fumu Otokotachi

Men with Guns (aka Hombres armados)

(1997, US, 128 min)
d John Sayles. *p* R Paul Miller, Maggie Renzi. *sc* John Sayles. *ph* Slawomir Idziak. *ed* John Sayles. *pd* Felipe Fernández del Paso. *m* Mason Daring. *cast* Federico José Luppi, Damián Alcázar, Tania Cruz, Damián Delgado, Dan Rivera González, Iguandili López.

●Sayles' film echoes *The Secret of Roan Inish* in its fascination with storytelling, and *Lone Star* as an investigation of conspiracy and cover-up. In an unnamed Latin American country, eminent doctor Humberto Fuentes (José Luppi) decides to spend his vacation visiting students he trained to work in poor Indian villages in the mountains. Ignoring warnings that he's at risk from guerillas, his travels reveal that the medics have vanished. To his bewilderment he learns that the students – like many Indians – were taken away, tortured or killed by 'men with guns'. As his quest continues, he's joined by sundry unfortunates and outcasts who shatter his complacent liberal assumptions about his own position and responsibility. While the premise – that authoritarian states not only oppress their lowliest members but lay the blame elsewhere – is hardly original, Sayles elaborates his theme with rare sensitivity and intelligence. A film of beauty, integrity, power and compassion (in Spanish and Mayan, with English subtitles). GA

Men, Women: User's Manual (Hommes femmes Mode d'emploi)

(1996, Fr, 123 min)
d/p Claude Lelouch. *sc* Claude Lelouch, René Bonnell, Jean-Philippe Chatrier. *ph* Philippe Pavans. *ed* Hélène de Luze. *pd* Jacques Bufnoir. *m* Francis Lai. *cast* Fabrice Luchini, Bernard Tapie, Alessandra Martines, Pierre Arditi, Ticky Holgado, Daniel Gélin, Anouk Aimée, Claude Lelouch.

●After the international acclaim for his revisionist update of *Les Misérables* comes this offering from Lelouch, far more typical of the maverick film-maker's run of convoluted all-star melodramas that regularly boost the French box office and which, equally regularly, receive frosty treatment from the Paris critical elite. His major coup here, however, is casting business magnate Tapie, who served a prison sentence for tax evasion. He seems more or less to be playing himself, a charismatic rogue who receives his comeuppance from doctor Martines, a vengeful old flame who switches his unblemished medical reports with the gloomy verdict on twitchy undercover cop Luchini. The sick one soon comes over all glad-to-be-alive, and his perfectly healthy counterpart's on his way to Lourdes for a 'miracle' cure. Ever intent on gilding the lily, Lelouch weaves in some rather tiresome teenage romantic asides, and detains us further with the rags-to-riches story of a falsetto street singer. The main diversion is Lelouch's characteristically virtuoso camerawork, with sweeping helicopter shots and a luscious, blue-tinged Paris captivating the attention while you try to work out how elegant, sixty-something con-artist Anouk Aimée fits into the mazy grand design. Tapie is a surprisingly personable screen presence, but the film itself is decorative, mercurial and really rather mystifying. TJ

Mephisto

(1981, Hun, 144 min)
d Itsván Szabó. *sc* Péter Dobai. *ph* Lajos Koltai. *ed* Zsuzsa Csakany. *ad* József Romvari. *m* Zdenkó Tamassy. *cast* Klaus Maria Brandauer, Ildikó Bánsági, Krystyna Janda, Rolf Hoppe, György Cserhalmi, Péter Andorai, Karin Boyd, David Robinson.

●For all the retro art movie gloss recently applied to the cautionary spectacle of the pre-war rise of Nazism, there has been precious little incisive appraisal of the precise seductive allure of fascism, and certainly none to match that offered by Szabó's remarkable film. Adapted from Klaus Mann's more hysterically vindictive 1936 novel, Szabó's film delineates the self-deceiving ease with which a talented actor may rationalise the sort of radical careerist compromises that lead from committed exponency of Brecht towards impeccably Aryan readings of Goethe, and even the personal betrayals that doom friends and lovers to exile or elimination. A superbly modulated, fruitfully ambivalent central performance by Brandauer carries the emotional and intellectual weight of the political dilemma, while Szabó happily refuses to overstress the Faustian parallels of the perverse power-pact between the cultural icon and his Goebbels-like puppeteer. PT

Mephisto Waltz, The

(1971, US, 109 min)
d Paul Wendkos. *p* QuinnMartin. *sc* Ben Maddow. *ph* William W Spencer. *ed* Richard Brockway. *ad* Richard Y Haman. *m* Jerry Goldsmith. *cast* Alan Alda, Jacqueline Bisset, Barbara Parkins, Curd Jürgens, Bradford Dillman, William Windom, Kathleen Widdoes.

●A tale of diabolism with a plot familiar from *Rosemary's Baby*; but where Polanski's film developed into a complex investigation of doubt and fear as well as evil, this is anything but subtle. Alda plays an ex-musician turned writer of music ready to trade wife and child for a career, Bisset his down-to-earth, fearful wife who follows her man even into Satanism. The Devil-worshipping couple are a world famous concert pianist (Jürgens) dying of leukemia, and his daughter (Parkins), whose incestuous relationship is continued after her father's death through his usurping of the younger man's personality and hands. Wendkos seems prone to script troubles with his movies, and this is no exception; he goes all out to kill it, shooting with heavily greased lens from every conceivable angle, exiling normality to periphery. Bizarre and vulgar, certainly, but also very hard to follow. VG

Mépris, Le (Contempt)

(1963, Fr/It, 103 min)
d Jean-Luc Godard. *p* Georges de Beauregard, Carlo Ponti. *sc* Jean-Luc Godard. *ph* Raoul Coutard. *ed* Agnès Guillemot. *m* Georges Delerue, (Italian version) Piero Piccioni. *cast* Brigitte Bardot, Michel Piccoli, Jack Palance, Fritz Lang, Giorgia Moll, Jean-Luc Godard, Linda Veras, Raoul Coutard.

●A film about – among other things – integrity. The basic situation, faithfully adapted from Moravia's novel *A Ghost at Noon*, concerns a young woman (Bardot) who is gradually possessed by an overwhelming contempt for her husband (Piccoli), a writer beset by doubts when he is called in as script-doctor to a film of *The Odyssey*, being made by a director (Lang) who wants to capture the reality of Homer's world, and a crass producer (Palance) who just wants more mermaids. Yes, she agrees that the money will be useful; no, she doesn't feel he is selling out since he is interested in the subject; and which ever way he decides to jump is perfectly all right by her. But there still remains that tight knot of contempt which she won't explain and he doesn't understand. Around this Godard weaves subtle parallels with Homer's tale of patient Penelope, the statues of Minerva and Neptune which brood over the modern tragedy, locations which paradoxically set the airy spaces of a flat in Rome against the confines of the Homeric landscapes of Capri, and for good measure a stream of cinematic jokes. Magnificently shot by Raoul Coutard, it's a dazzling fable. TM

Mercedes Mon Amour (Fikrimin Ince Gülü)

(1992, Tur, 90 min)
d Tunc Okan. *p* Cengiz Ergun, Tunc Okan. *sc* Tunc Okan. *ph* Orhan Oguz. Vladimir Cosma. *cast* Iylas Salman, Valeria Lemoine, Micky Sebastian, Alexander Gittinger.

●Bit of a broad comedy with Bayram (Salman) as the nerd Everyman, a Munich street cleaner, who achieves his dream of buying a yellow 350SE Mercedes to show off at home. It's a long drive (believe me!): scratches, scrapes, troubles with hippy vans, aggressive lorry drivers and thieving parking-lot attendants dog his every kilometre. Turkey seems like bad car trouble: there's more crashed vehicles here than in Godard's French weekend. The music is French-style too: ding-dong disco seemingly from one of their '60s commercials. The film has a moral ('thinking about No 1' German-style can leave you stranded), but it's more interested in the drive. WH

Mercenaries, The (aka Dark of the Sun)

(1967, GB, 100 min)
d Jack Cardiff. *p* George Englund. *sc* Ranald MacDougall, Adrian Spies. *ph* Ted Scaife. *ed* Ernest Walter. *ad* Elliot Scott. *m* Jacques Loussier. *cast* Rod Taylor, Yvette Mimieux, Peter Carsten, Jim Brown, Kenneth More, Andre Morell, Olivier Despax, Guy Deghy, Calvin Lockhart.

●The Congo, 1960: soldier-of-fortune Taylor braves rebel-held territory to rescue the white folk and retrieve a fortune in diamonds for President Ubi. The political backgound is skated over so we can get on with a crude variation on the cowboy-and-injuns schtick and plenty of lip-smacking carnage. Tricked out with an ex-Nazi (Carsten) still sporting a swastika, a disheveled blonde Belgian refugee (Mimieux), a loyal African sergeant (Brown), and a dipso English doctor (More) who sacrifices himself for a woman in labour, the film has an exceptionally unsympathetic hero and a preposterous moral turn-round at the close. Adapted from a novel by Wilbur Smith. TJ

Mercenario, Il (The Mercenary/ A Professional Gun)

(1968, It/Sp, 105 min)
d Sergio Corbucci. *p* Alberto Grimaldi. *sc* Luciano Vincenzoni, Sergio Spina, Sergio Corbucci. *ph* Alejandro Ulloa. *ed* Eugenio Alabiso. *ad* Piero Filippone, Luis Vasquez. *m* Ennio Morricone, Bruno Nicolai. *cast* Franco Nero, Tony Musante, Jack Palance, Giovanna Ralli, Eduardo Fajardo, Bruno Corazzari, Remo De Angeles, Joe Kamel.

●During the Mexican Revolution, Nero, the mercenary Sergei Cowalski, is hired to transport silver to a mine in Texas, only to find that Musante and his co-workers have taken control. Switching sides, the hired gun finds himself teaching the rebel leader how to put his revolutionary ideas into practise, but his idealistic fervour is tested when the men's firepower gathers them a personal fortune. Plenty of baroque touches in this spaghetti Western, including Palance as Curly, a white-suited gay gunman (looking like 'a bewigged Burgess Meredith' as one contemporary reviewer had it). TJ

Mercenary, The

see Mercenario, Il

Merchant of Four Seasons, The (Händler der vier Jahreszeiten, Der)

(1971, WGer, 89 min)
d/p/sc Rainer Werner Fassbinder. *ph* Dietrich Lohmann. *ed* Thea Eymèsz. *pd* Kurt Raab. *cast* Hans Hirschmüller, Irm Hermann, Hanna Schygulla, Andrea Schober, Gusti Kreissl, Kurt Raab, Klaus Löwitsch, Ingrid Caven.

●Made before *Fear Eats the Soul*, which it resembles in many respects, this deceptively muted melodrama chronicles the 'rubbing out' of a character found oddly irrelevant by those around him: a man who dreamed of being an engineer, but had to settle for a fruit and vegetable stall, his aspirations constantly frustrated by his social circumstances. The film builds with remarkable power towards a concluding scene in which the process of Hans' destruction is revealed to be blindly self-perpetuating. Fassbinder's regular ensemble perform with enormous precision, and there's a remarkable dinner party scene in which, in a kind of mesmeric shorthand, the mechanics of destruction are revealed, working like clockwork. VG

Merci la vie (Thank You, Life)

(1991, Fr, 118 min, b/w & col)
d Bertrand Blier. *p* Bernard Marescot. *sc* Bertrand Blier. *ph* Philippe Rousselot. *ed* Claudine Merlin. *ad* Théobald Meurisse. *cast* Charlotte Gainsbourg, Anouk Grinberg, Gérard Depardieu, Michel Blanc, Jean Carmet, Catherine Jacob, Jean-Louis Trintignant, Annie Girardot.

● Wheeling a supermarket trolley full of seagulls, shy, sexually inexperienced Camille (Gainsbourg) comes across Joëlle (Grinberg), a none-too-virginal abandoned bride seen by Camille as a gift from heaven. The pair embark on a series of raucous, sometimes violent and often funny (mis)adventures with variously exploitative, lecherous and pathetic men: fathers, film-makers, a doctor (Depardieu), a Nazi officer (Trintignant). Is it all really happening, or just a movie, or simply Camille's dream? Snazzily shot, wittily performed and structured, Buñuel-fashion, according to the logic of a dream, this bizarre blend of road movie, comedy, psychodrama and various other genres shifts with wayward glee not only between times – the present (?) and WWII – but between colour, black-and-white and monochrome tints. Lending some coherence is a sense that every age has its crises (AIDS, the Holocaust), that life is shit; but Blier's precise intentions are finally unfathomable. GA

Merci pour le chocolat

(2000, Fr/Switz, 101 min)
d Claude Chabrol. *p* Marin Karmitz. *sc* Claude Chabrol, Caroline Eliacheff. *ph* Renato Berta. *ed* Monique Fardoulis. *ad* Yvan Niclass. *m* Matthieu Chabrol. *cast* Isabelle Huppert, Jacques Dutronc, Anna Mouglalis, Rodolphe Pauly, Michel Robin, Mathieu Simonet, Brigitte Catillon.

● A dark, velvety film which masks the rough with the smooth and coats a bitter pill in a veneer of decadent French polish. This has been Chabrol's way as often as not over the course of more than 50 films, and he's long since got it down to a fine art. Too fine, one suspects, for an audience accustomed to Hollywood overkill. Dutronc stars as the famous pianist André Polonski. Recently remarried to his first wife, Mika (Huppert), Polonski lives in Lausanne, along with Guillaume, a son by his second wife. Enter Jeanne Pollet (Mouglalis), born on the very same day and in the very same hospital as Guillaume, and a prodigy on the piano. Could it be there was some terrible mix-up 18 years ago? Plenty of material there, you'd have thought, for crazy farce or anguished melodrama. But Chabrol prefers a drily understated comedy of manners. These members of the *haute bourgeoisie* remain serenely implacable – intent on maintaining their own charades even as their dearest relationships unravel. You could call them sophisticated, or emotionally comatose. Either way, it takes a more macabre twist to shock them to their senses. Visually restrained and aurally elaborate, it's an old-fashioned, subtly deceptive film, the sort of thing Chabrol can turn out in his sleep. TCh

Mercury Rising

(1998, US, 112 min)
d Harold Becker. *p* Brian Grazer, Karen Kehela. *sc* Lawrence Konner, Mark Rosenthal. *ph* Michael Seresin. *ed* Peter Honess. *pd* Patrizia von Brandenstein. *m* John Barry. *cast* Bruce Willis, Alec Baldwin, Miko Hughes, Chi McBride, Kim Dickens, Peter Stormare.

● Autistic kid and washed-up FBI agent on the run from out-of-control government security outfit: such is the not very high concept which the fitfully interesting Becker has to dumb himself down to the point of ignominy to put over. Withholding wit, invention and style, he barely acknowledges life in the real world. John Barry's score, with its reiterated 'autistic kid' theme, would have sounded corny to Ivor Novello, though it's in keeping with the general principle of patronising the audience. BBa

Merlin: The Return

(2000, GB, 91 min)
d Paul Matthews. *p* Elizabeth Matthews, Paul Matthews. *sc* Paul Matthews. *ph* Vincent G Cox. *ed* Peter Davies. *pd* Edward Thomas. *m* Mark Thomas. *cast* Rik Mayall, Tia Carrere, Patrick Bergin, Adrian Paul, Craig Sheffer, Julie Hartley, Leigh Greyvenstein, Byron Taylor, Grethe Fox.

● This quasi-Arthurian fantasy, set mainly in the present, falls somewhere between slightly camp chainmail TV serial, dashing sword 'n' sorcery saga and sweetly naive Children's Film Foundation yarn. The wizard – a spectacularly bearded but otherwise restrained Mayall – teams up with a 14-year-old boy, recently arrived in leafy rural England from Idaho, to fight off Mordred (Sheffer), the evil sorcerer released from the netherworld into the present. Merlin, having in ancient times sent Arthur and his knights into the slumber of ages, must now re-awaken them in order to save the world. The attack on a steely oil-tanker by a befuddled band of knights is the one strictly humorous episode. Otherwise the fight 'twixt good and evil is a serious business. The film is mostly indifferently directed, but it's a harmless adventure that works best as a mild horror flick, with cheap but enjoyable special effects providing the biggest thrills. WH

Merlusse

(1935, Fr, 65 min, b/w)
d/p/sc Marcel Pagnol. *ph* Albert Assouad. *ed* Suzanne de Troeye. *m* Vincent Scotto. *cast* Henri Poupon, André Pollack, Thomeray, Rellys, Jean Castan.

● Merlusse, his face disfigured by shrapnel, is a *mutilé de guerre* – an everyday sight of the period. He's a teacher, cold and correct, as a defence against the routine nastiness of his boarding school charges. The substance of the film – Merlusse assigned to supervise those pupils with nowhere to go for the Christmas holidays – is strong enough to fuel a Disney melodrama or a grand, emotional Lloyd Webber aria. What's extraordinary is not that Pagnol declines the melodrama (a villain in a Pagnol movie is anyway unthinkable) but that he only casually dramatises the situation, making this perhaps the first do-it-yourself weepie. Discretion, a refusal to indulge poignant detail, to ironise or to produce a big finish – here's a film that clearly never imagined postmodernism. BBa

Mermaids

(1990, US, 110 min)
d Richard Benjamin. *p* Lauren Lloyd, Wallis Nicita, Patrick Palmer. *sc* June Roberts. *ph* Howard Atherton. *ed* Jacqueline Cambas. *pd* Stuart Wurtzel. *m* Jack Nitzsche. *cast* Cher, Bob Hoskins, Winona Ryder, Michael Schoeffling, Christina Ricci, Caroline McWilliams, Jan Miner.

● Charlotte (Ryder) has upped sticks eighteen times in her young life, and she's hoping to settle down with her mother and sister in Eastport, MA. Their new house borders a convent, allowing the Jewish teen to indulge in fantasies about handyman Joe (Schoeffling) and, perversely, about life as a nun. Loopy Mom (Cher) has neglected to tell her daughter about the facts of life, leaving Charlotte stranded between desire and fears of pregnancy. This self-conscious, eccentric comedy is set in 1963, a year which sees Charlotte's innocence fade in the wake of both sexual discovery and Kennedy's assassination. The film is burdened by curious details and observations, and its preoccupation with all things aquatic (little sister is an ace swimmer, Mom dresses up as a mermaid for New Year's Eve, etc) is overworked. Characterisation suffers, with Charlotte and her mother too self-absorbed to engage our sympathies. Crucially, they just aren't funny. CM

Merrill's Marauders

(1962, US, 98 min)
d Samuel Fuller. *p* Milton Sperling. *sc* Samuel Fuller, Milton Sperling. *ph* William Clothier. *ed* Folmar Blangsted. *ad* William Magginetti. *m* Howard Jackson. *cast* Jeff Chandler, Ty Hardin, Peter Brown, Andrew Duggan, Will Hutchins, Claude Akins, John Hoyt.

● Fuller's superb patrol movie – taut, bleak and damning – was a self-confessed 'rehearsal' for his long-gestating *The Big Red One*, following a World War II American platoon in Burma on a suicidal trek, suffering from what the unit doctor diagnoses as AOE – 'accumulation of everything' – and burdened by madness, exhaustion, and the demonstrable irrationality of their wasted energies. Fuller draws potent ironies from his casting of young cowboy 'heroes' (including Bronco and Tenderfoot), and mobilises his camera in violent sympathy with the men's physical and psychological effort. PT

Merrily We Go to Hell

(1932, US, 78 min, b/w)
d Dorothy Arzner. *sc* Edwin Justus Mayer. *ph* David Abel. *ed* Jane Loring. *ad* Hans Dreier. *cast* Fredric March, Sylvia Sidney, Adrienne Allen, Skeets Gallagher, Kent Taylor, Cary Grant, Esther Howard.

● Part voguish 'sophisticated' satire, part domestic melodrama, this film from the Lubitsch era at Paramount is a curious but highly entertaining hybrid. March, a journalist and would-be playwright with a heartbreak in his past and a liking for the bottle, woos and weds Sylvia Sidney's heiress, and we follow their 'matrimony modern style' through better and worse, richer and poorer, sickness and health, up to a dubiously happy ending of which Sirk would have been proud. As befits a film by Hollywood's foremost female 'auteur', all the male characters are hopelessly immature; yet the women rarely transcend movie types. PT

Merry Christmas Mr Lawrence

(1982, GB, 124 min)
d Nagisa Oshima. *p* Jeremy Thomas. *sc* Nagisa Oshima, Paul Mayersberg. *ph* Toichiro Narushima. *ed* Tomoyo Oshima. *pd* Jusho Toda. *m* Ryuichi Sakamoto. *cast* David Bowie, Tom Conti, Ryuichi Sakamoto, Takeshi [Takeshi Kitano], Jack Thompson, Johnny Okura, Yuya Uchida.

● For all the praise heaped upon Oshima's admittedly ambitious film about East-West relations in the microcosm of a Japanese PoW camp during World War II, it's far less satisfactory than most of his earlier work. It may go against Japanese taboos as it deals with commandant Sakamoto's obsessive love for prisoner Bowie, it may be stylishly shot, it may seem uncompromising in its depiction of the Japanese war ethic and the insistence on harakiri as a more honourable reaction to defeat than submission to imprisonment. But the web of relationships between English and Japanese is too schematic in its polarisation of characters, Oshima's handling of the narrative is not so much elliptical as awkward, and Bowie's performance is embarrassingly wooden. Add to that Sakamoto's turgid score and posing narcissism, some horrendous symbolism, and some pretty shoddy technical work (several of the pans are hurried and blurred), and you have a fair old mess. GA

Merry-Go-Round

(1923, US, 9,178 ft, b/w)
d Rupert Julian, [Erich von Stroheim]. *p* Irving Thalberg. *ph* William H Daniels, Charles Kaufman. *ed* Maurice Pivar, James C McKay. *ad* Richard Day, EE Sheeley. *cast* Norman Kerry, Dorothy Wallace, Mary Philbin, Cesare Gravina, Edith Yorke, George Siegmann, Dale Fuller.

● Stroheim was sacked by Irving Thalberg only a little way into the shooting of his last film for Universal, and it was completed by Rupert Julian. Sets and screenplay, however, remain Stroheim's personal achievement; and from the opening sequence, where his Viennese Count hero (Kerry) is observed going through his daily rituals in his leisured environment, it's possible to imagine what Stroheim himself would have done with the rest of the film. The fairground scenes, where the Count meets and falls for the heroine (Philbin), are mostly blown by Julian's direction of his actors. What remains, though, is a strong sense of contrast between the lavish Viennese court and the fairground low-life. If the contrived narrative lacks the conviction Stroheim's attention to detail might have given it, at least his sense of design remains dominant. (The script – uncredited on screen – is usually attributed to Stroheim, rewritten by Rupert Julian and Harvey Gates.) RM

Merry War, A

see Keep the Aspidistra Flying

Merry Widow, The

(1925, US, 12 reels, b/w)
d Erich von Stroheim. *p* Irving Thalberg. *sc* Erich von Stroheim, Benjamin Glazer, Marion Ainslee. *ph* Oliver T Marsh, Ben Reynolds, William Daniels. *ed* Frank E Hull. *ad* Cedric Gibbons, Richard Day. *m* William Axt, D Mendoza. *cast* John Gilbert, Mae Murray, Roy D'Arcy, Tully Marshall, George Fawcett, Josephine Crowell, Dale Fuller.

●Commissioned by MGM to film Franz Lehar's operetta, Stroheim characteristically tried to bury it within a larger framework of his own devising. He added a prologue that finally occupied more than half the total running time. Stroheim makes everything possible out of the grotesqueries, most notably the baron's foot fetishism and the sadist's ignominious death, but his elaborate scheme of erotic contrasts is finally engulfed by the frivolous artifice of the original operetta. The result is stylish and spasmodically witty, but rarely more. TR

Merveilleuse Visite, La (The Wonderful Visit)

(1974, Fr/It, 105 min)
d Marcel Carné. *p* Jacques Quintard, Roger Delpey. *sc* Marcel Carné, Didier Decoin, Robert Valey. *ph* Edmond Richard. *ed* Henri Rust. *ad* Bernard Evein, Louis le Barbenchon. *m* Alan Stivell. *cast* Gilles Kohler, Deborah Berger, Roland Lasaffre, Lucien Barjon, Jean-Pierre Castaldi, Yves Barsacq.

●HG Wells' second novel became Marcel Carné's penultimate movie. A beautiful young man is found naked on a beach; he says he's an angel fallen from the skies, though his difficulties with mirrors and cameras and the way he puts the wind up the locals are more indicative of Dracula. In fact, he's all too angelic, and his presence provokes nothing but unhappiness and violence, until finally he changes into a seagull and flies away. The late Victorian whimsy of Wells' misanthropic allegory, transplanted to a modern-day Breton village, has the charm of the incongruous, and permits Carné to create another of his little 'worlds', a rural one, as dreamily unreal as any in his big-city melodramas. The angel, sexy, absolutely unattainable, is also characteristic. BBa

Mery per sempre

see Forever Mary

Mésaventures de Margaret, Les

see The Misadventures of Margaret

Mes Petites Amoureuses

(1975, Fr, 123 min)
d Jean Eustache. *p* Pierre Cottrell. *sc* Jean Eustache. *ph* Nestor Almendros. *ed* Françoise Belleville, Alberto Yacelini, Vincent Cottrell. *m/songs* Charles Trenet, Théodore Botrel. *cast* Martin Loeb, Ingrid Caven, Jacqueline Dufranne, Dionys Mascolo, Henri Martinez, Marie-Paule Fernandez, Maurice Pialat.

●After *The Mother and the Whore*, Eustache turns his attention here to pubescence in provincial France. The tone is somewhat reminiscent of Malle (*Le Souffle au Coeur*, *Lacombe Lucien*) in its attempt at an unsentimental depiction of the sexual awakening of a 13-year-old boy; but ultimately it's more tough-minded, recognising as it does the effects of class and social status on the boy's development. More important is the continual stress on his essential aloneness in coming to terms with sexual experience; he rarely smiles, and finally comes across somewhat like a Bresson protagonist. A minor irritation is the relentless accumulation of short scenes, some with very little to add. RM

Message, The

see Al-Risalah

Message in a Bottle

(1999, US, 131 min)
d Luis Mandoki. *p* Denise Di Novi, Jim Wilson, Kevin Costner. *sc* Gerald DiPego. *ph* Caleb Deschanel. *ed* Steven Weisberg. *pd* Jeffrey Beecroft. *m* Gabriel Yared. *cast* Kevin Costner, Robin Wright Penn, Paul Newman, John Savage, Illeana Douglas, Robbie Coltrane, Jesse James, Bethel Leslie, Tom Aldredge.

●Lovelorn researcher Theresa (Wright Penn), a columnist's assistant on a Chicago newspaper, thinks she's found the man of her dreams when she reads a letter washed up on the shore, addressed to a Catherine and written in such heart-melting prose she instantly wants to track down the author. Thanks to her paper's best efforts, she homes in on the Carolina coast, where a fishing town delivers up its secret – Costner, softly-spoken shipwright and widower. Wright Penn ploughs a furrow of vulnerable earnestness, Costner delivers another quiet romantic, the screenplay tries to keep their relationship grounded in mutual need and lends it a modicum of credibility. It plays, up to a point. Best try and ignore Gabriel Yared's melisma of mush on the soundtrack, and enjoy Newman's masterclass in scene stealing. Clipped and wise, the old boy does ornery to perfection. TJ

Message to Love: The Isle of Wight Festival

(1970/94, US, 126 min)
d/p Murray Lerner. *ph* Murray Lerner, Andy Carchrae, Jack Hazan, Nic Knowland. *ed* Einar Westerlund, Stan Warnow, Greg Sheldon. *with* Jimi Hendrix, The Doors, Free, Kris Kristofferson, The Who, Miles Davis, Jethro Tull, Joan Baez, Joni Mitchell, Leonard Cohen, Ricki Farr.

●'I just woke up about two minutes ago,' quips Jimi Hendrix. He then launches into the title track of Lerner's often hilarious documentary on the biggest, grubbiest, most colourful, chaotic gathering of the masses since Jesus dished out the loaves. Shot on both 16 and 35mm, the film spends as much time rummaging through the backstage shenanigans as it does covering the sounds of the multitude of 'dadrockers' on the bill. And thank goodness it does, because here we have an event so haphazard and disorganised, you can only wonder how it continued to function beyond even the first few bars of music. Six hundred thousand 'brothers and sisters' rowed, shipped, and hitched their way across the watery divide, yet the organisers had sold just 50,000 tickets. 'The fence must die,' proclaimed graffiti painted by destitutes on 'desolation row'. The corrugated sheeting collapsed, and it was left to financially strapped MC/promoter Ricki Farr to cool things down, and to Joni Mitchell to lose her head by telling the rowdy crowds to 'stop behaving like tourists, man'. The music is exemplary stuff to anyone who heard it the first time around – The Doors, Free, Kris Kristofferson (who eventually stormed off stage), The Who, Miles Davis (silhouetted against the dusk), Jethro Tull – but it's the hilarity of the sound-bites that makes this *really* worth catching. DA

Messer im Kopf

see Knife in the Head

Messiah (Le Messie)

(1999, Fr, 111 min)
d William Klein. *p* Michel Rotman. *ph* William Klein, Pascal Marti, Paco Wiser. *ed* Sohie Henocq. *m* Handel. *cast* Lynne Dawson, Nicole Heaston, Magdalena Kozená, Charlotte Hellekant, Brian Asawa, John Mark Ainsley, Russell Smythe, Brian Bannatyne-Scott, Mark Minkowski.

●Handel's *Messiah* is an exultant declaration of religious faith. But does it still speak to us (and for us) in the same way, some 250 years after it was written? To find out, photographer and documentarian William Klein took his camera all around the world, from the United States to France, Israel and Russia, capturing images of devout choral groups, and a larger global culture which seems anything but spiritual. The soundtrack, meanwhile, is a new performance conducted by Marc Minkowski. It sounds like a great idea, but a lot of this film is pretty obvious. Klein begins in Las Vegas, for example, counterpointing shots of gambling with 'Behold Your God'. Nevertheless, for all its editorialising it does have some cumulative power. TCh

Messidor

(1978, Switz/Fr, 123 min)
d Alain Tanner. *p* Yves Gasser, Yves Peyrot. *sc* Alain Tanner. *ph* Renato Berta. *ed* Brigitte Sousselier, Laurent Uhler. *m* Arié Dzierlatka. *cast* Clémentine Amouroux, Catherine Retoré, Franziskus Abgottspon, Gérald Battiaz, Hansjorg Bedschard.

●A comparison between this and Terrence Malick's *Badlands* makes for an interesting contrast between American and European concepts of the cinema. Both films deal with a couple in flight, and the way in which a puzzled society becomes engrossed in their one-way journey. But there the similarities end. In Malick's film, the violence is within the central characters themselves. Tanner uses the progress of his female travellers to examine, not them but the harsh logic that underpins an 'exemplary' capitalist state like Switzerland. Thus, once Clémentine Amouroux and Catherine Retoré choose to become marginal characters – when they meet, they decide for a lark to see how long they can survive without money – they soon find that society has no place within it for them. PH

Messie, Le

see Messiah

Mestiere delle Armi, Il

see Profession of Arms, The

Metade Fumaça (Ban zhi Yan)

(1999, HK, 101 min)
d Riley Ip. *p* Claudie Chung, John Chong, Solon So. *sc* Riley Ip. *ph* Peter Pau. *ed* Maurice Li. *ad* Peter Wong. *m* Chiu Tsang-Hei. *cast* Nicholas Tse, Eric Tsang, Elaine Jin, Kelly Chen, Stephen Fung, Sam Lee, Shu Qi, Sandra Ng, Anthony Wong.

●Likeable, funny and finally quite touching, Ip's second feature is at heart an 'odd couple' movie. Roy (Tsang) returns to HK after living in Brazil for many years for a showdown with an old enemy, his rival for the affections of a beautiful girl. He enlists young street punk Smokey (Tse) to help and winds up staying in his apartment. It turns out that Roy has Alzheimer's and that his account of his 'exile' is a self-serving fantasy, but in the process of straightening matters out the film gives several characters small personal epiphanies and ends on a high note. (The title is Brazilian-Portuguese for 'Half a Cigarette', referring to a motif in Roy's memories.) TR

Metalstorm: The Destruction of Jared-Syn

(1983, US, 83 min)
d Charles Band. *p* Charles Band, Alan J Adler. *sc* Alan J Adler. *ph* Mac Ahlberg. *ed* Brad Arensman. *ad* Pamela B Warner. *m* Richard Band. *cast* Jeffrey Byron, Mike Preston, Tim Thomerson, Kelly Preston, Richard Moll, R David Smith, Mickey Fox.

●A dire cross between *Mad Max* and *Star Wars*, set on the futuristic desert planet of Lemuria, where a padded-leather-clad nasty called Jared-Syn (Mike Preston) is taking over the planet with the aid of a deadly crystal. Hero Jack Dogen (Byron), a Peacekeeping Ranger, sets out to destroy Jared-Syn, accompanied by a knowledgeable desert nomad (Thomerson, putting in the only decent performance). They stumble upon an ancient crystal mask which will give Jack sufficient power, but must first face Jared-Syn's son Baal, a half man/half machine that squirts green hallucinatory gunk at its victims. With vehicles and ideas left over from the *Mad Max* set, not even the 3-D effect can deflect attention from the naff performances and excruciatingly dull script. DA

Meteor

(1979, US, 107 min)
d Ronald Neame. *p* Arnold Orgolini, Theodore Parvin. *sc* Stanley Mann, Edmund H North. *ph* Paul Lohmann. *ed* Carl Kress. *pd* Edward C Carfagno. *m* Laurence Rosenthal. *cast* Sean Connery, Natalie Wood, Karl Malden, Brian Keith, Martin Landau, Trevor Howard, Richard Dysart, Henry Fonda.

●Shoddy, unspeakably inept sci-fi disaster movie, with America and Russia combining forces when a meteor on collision course threatens to destroy the earth. Shored up by tacky effects and a predictable hands-across-the-Iron-Curtain romance between Yank scientist (Connery) and Red interpreter (Wood). See it on peril of death by boredom. TM

Meteor Man, The

(1993, US, 100 min)
d Robert Townsend. *p* Loretha C Jones. *sc* Robert Townsend. *ph* John A Alonzo. *ed* Adam Bernardi. *pd* Toby Corbett. *m* Cliff Eidelman. *cast* Robert Townsend, Marla Gibbs, James Earl Jones, Robert Guillame, Don Cheadle, Luther Vandross, Bill Cosby.

●Meek black teacher (Townsend) is transformed into a green-garbed warrior after being struck by an emerald meteor. The teacher is the sort who tells pupils to run away from bullies. 'Meteor Man' walks the Washington, DC, 'hood and attends to gangsters who've spent too long at the hair salon – whenever you see a blond crop, trouble is never far away. Regrettably, writer/director Townsend spoils a promising idea (there aren't *that* many black masked avengers) by shamelessly milking every tear-jerking moment. RDo

Métisse (Cafe au Lait/Blended)

(1993, Fr, 101 min)
d Mathieu Kassovitz. *p* Christophe Rossignon. *sc* Mathieu Kassovitz. *ph* Pierre Aim. *ed* Colette Farrugia, Jean-Pierre Segal. *ad* Pierre André Roussotte. *m* Marie Daulne, Jean-Louis Daulne. *cast* Julie Mauduech, Hubert Koundé, Tadek Lokcinski, Mathieu Kassovitz, Vinceny Cassel, Jany Holt, Jean-Pierre Cassel.

● *Métisse*, the first film from the director of *La Haine*, is a (surprisingly) breezy and (unsurprisingly) brash comedy about a mulatto Parisienne torn between two boyfriends: a wealthy black (Koundé) and a laddish Jew (Kassovitz). The rivals reluctantly put their mutual antipathy on hold when their lover announces that she's pregnant, and won't reveal which of them's the father. If *La Haine* owed a debt to *Do the Right Thing*, here the key influence is *She's Gotta Have It* (at one point Koundé accuses the bike-mad Kassovitz of believing he's in a Spike Lee movie). This is a more benign than *La Haine*, and less assured, but it raises pertinent questions about gender and racial politics. TCh

Metro

(1997, US, 117 min)
d Thomas Carter. *p* Roger Birnbaum. *sc* Randy Feldman. *ph* Fred Murphy. *ed* Peter E Berger. *pd* William Elliott. *m* Steve Porcaro. *cast* Eddie Murphy, Michael Rapaport, Kim Miyori, Michael Wincott, Carmen Ejogo, Art Evans.

● An adept turn from Murphy as San Francisco hostage negotiator Scott Roper knits together a functional assembly of stock cop-movie elements. This is probably the closest to a genuine dramatic part Murphy's ever played, and his snappy patter is persuasively integrated into Roper's daily routine. It's a tailor-made role, balancing action highlights and the usual bit of lip. Unfortunately, there's little to be done with Randy Feldman's by-the-book plotting. Rapaport's SWAT team rookie proves his mettle as the main man's new partner; Wincott's ruthless jewel thief supplies the villainy; and Ejogo is the hero's vaguely feisty girlfriend-in-peril. TJ

Metroland

(1997, GB/Fr/Sp, 101 min)
d Philip Saville. *p* Andrew Bendel. *sc* Adrian Hodges. *ph* Jean-François Robin. *ed* Greg Miller. *pd* Don Taylor. *m* Mark Knopfler. *cast* Christian Bale, Lee Ross, Elsa Zylberstein, Emily Watson, John Wood, Rufus, Amanda Ryan.

● Chris (Bale) is vegetating in the commuter-belt: job, wife, baby, it's all horribly predictable. The sudden arrival of his old friend Toni (Ross) only makes matters worse. Toni is still living out their youthful dreams of freedom, sex and no strings attached. They go on the town for old time's sake, and Toni takes Chris to a punk gig – we're in the 1970s – where Chris only pretends to enjoy being spat at. Then the flashbacks start: Paris in the '60s. Chris is a young photographer in his own authentic atelier, with his own authentic French bohemian girlfriend who likes to make authentic bohemian love. Where did it all go wrong? It's hard to make the suburbs look sexy, and this production of Julian Barnes' novel never solves the problem. The script is gently amusing and not unintelligent, Bale captures a very English quality of befuddlement, and gets sensitive support from Ross, Watson (the wife), and Zylberstein (the girlfriend), but Chris's mild inertia slowly suffocates the material. You wouldn't necessarily switch it off on TV, but your finger might hover over the fast forward button. TCh

Metropolis (100)

(1926, Ger, 13,743 ft, b/w)
d Fritz Lang. *p* Erich Pommer. *sc* Fritz Lang, Thea von Harbou. *ph* Karl Freund, Günther Rittau. *ad* Otto Hunte, Erich Kettelhut, Karl Vollbrecht. *m* (original accompanying score) Gottfried Huppertz. *cast* Alfred Abel, Gustav Fröhlich, Brigitte Helm, Rudolf Klein-Rogge, Fritz Rasp, Heinrich George, Theodor Loos.

● UFA's most ambitious production, intended to rival Hollywood in its spectacular evocation of the 21st century city of Metropolis and its mechanised society founded on slavery. Thea von Harbou's script is a bizarre mixture of futuristic sci-fi and backward-looking Gothic horror; it's at best garbled, and its resolution is, to say the least, politically dubious. Fritz Lang's direction, on the other hand, is tremendously inventive and exhilarating: no director before (and not that many since) had worked so closely with cameramen and designers to achieve such dynamic visual and spatial effects. TR

Metropolis

(1926/1984, Ger/US, 83 min)
d Fritz Lang [director of the original], Giorgio Moroder. *p* Erich Pommer [original]. *sc* Fritz Lang, Thea von Harbou [original]. *ph* Karl Freund, Günther Rittau [original]. *colourisation/opticals* Jeff Matakovich. *ad* Otto Hunte, Erich Kettelhut, Karl Vollbrecht [original]. *m* Giorgio Moroder. *cast* Alfred Abel, Gustav Fröhlich, Brigitte Helm, Rudolf Klein-Rogge, Fritz Rasp, Heinrich George, Theodor Loos.

● Some balk in horror at Moroder's reduction in length of Lang's film (originally 137 minutes), and the addition of mush-rock songs (Pat Benatar, Adam Ant, Freddie Mercury, et al). Others praise the beautifully restored print, superb tinting, and the tautening induced by the removal of unnecessary intertitles and occasional substitution of subtitles. The political narrative – the city ruler's son reconciling his father's 'brain' with the 'hands' of the oppressed workers – remains highly suspect. But the swift tempo of Moroder's re-editing, combined with his feverish, disco-based score (the awful songs may prove easy to ignore), create the impression of a strip cartoon adventure directed by a genius. DT

Metropolis

(2001, Jap, 108 min)
d Rintaro. *sc* Katsuhiro Otomo. *ad* Shuichi Hirata. *m* Toshiyuki Honda. *cast* voices: Yuka Imoto, Kei Kobayashi, Kohki Okada, Taro Ishida, Kousei Tomita.

● This Japanese anime isn't merely a cartoon version of Fritz Lang's 1927 vision, with a screenplay by Katsuhiro Otomo (*Akira, Roujin Z*), it's actually adapted from the 1949 work of groundbreaking illustrator Osamu Tezuka. In Tezuka's dystopia, technology is both fetishised and reviled; rich megalomaniacs feud while disenchanted proles revolt against machines who ask: 'Why do humans use violence to resolve their problems?' Japanese detective Shunsaku Ban arrives in Metropolis with his nephew Kenichi, seeking to arrest corrupt scientist Dr Laughton. What they uncover, however, is Laughton's ultimate assignment: ethereal beauty Tima, built to control the Ziggurat ('the culmination of mankind's long history of scientific achievement'), and ultimately a tool of world domination. At first, the cute protagonists appear oddly out of place against the burnished Art Deco backgrounds. But Otomo's typically sophisticated script ensures slick pacing, combining humour, terror and pathos, particularly in the final scenes. Special mention goes to the vintage jazz and blues soundtrack. AHa

Metropolitan

(1989, US, 98 min)
d/p/sc Whit Stillman. *ph* John Thomas. *ed* Chris Tellefsen. *m* Mark Suozzo, Tom Judson. *cast* Carolyn Farina, Edward Clements, Christopher Eigeman, Taylor Nichols, Allison Rutledge-Parisi, Dylan Hundley, Isabel Gillies, Will Kempe, Elisabeth Thompson.

● When Tom (Clements), a quiet, middle class student with a distaste for privileged wealth, is unexpectedly adopted by a group of debs and escorts calling themselves the Sally Fowler Rat Pack, his pride and prejudice are rapidly eroded, not only by the glam sophistication of the soirées he attends in hired tux, but by the articulate, contentious conversations in which he takes part. Audrey (Farina), especially, seems a soul-mate, but Tom still nurses secret feelings for old flame Serena (Thompson), a socialite with too many strings to her beaux. Will he ditch the deb scene, find true love, or merely make it through the season unscathed? Writer-director Stillman's first feature is that rarity, a literate comedy of drawing-room manners which is at once civilised and *very* funny. Its nicely underplayed allusions to Jane Austen are wholly in keeping with Stillman's deft dialogue, ironic but sympathetic characterisations, and gentle probing of emotional and social nuance. The performances from a young, unknown cast are perfectly gauged, and wintry Manhattan is used as a gloriously seductive backdrop to the adolescent anxieties on view. GA

Me Without You

(2001, GB/Ger, 108 min)
d Sandra Goldbacher. *p* Finola Dwyer. *sc* Sandra Goldbacher, Laurence Coriat. *ph* Denis Crossan. *ed* Michael Ellis. *pd* Michael Carlin. *m* Adrian Johnston. *cast* Anna Friel, Michelle Williams, Oliver Milburn, Trudie Styler, Marianne Denicourt, Steve John Shepherd, Allan Corduner, Nicky Henson, Kyle MacLachlan.

● A girl's best friend is her girlfriend. Or is she? Marina and Holly grow up together in suburban London. Marina is bookish and a Jew, Holly is all face and a minx. They go through punk together, embrace the New Romantics in time for university in Brighton, and end up in bed with the same lecturer (MacLachlan), albeit at different times. Covering three decades – 1973 to the present day – with uncannily evocative and sometimes wincingly funny precision, Goldbacher's follow-up to *The Governess* has sophistication and intelligence – and an unrecognisable performance from Williams, American star of TV's *Dawson's Creek* – although it's ultimately too one-sided a declaration of independence. TCh

Mexican, The

(2001, US, 124 min)
d Gore Verbinsky. *p* Lawrence Bender, John Baldecchi. *sc* JH Wyman. *ph* Dariusz Wolski. *ed* Craig Wood. *pd* Cecilia Montiel. *m* Alan Silvestri. *cast* Brad Pitt, Julia Roberts, James Gandolfini, JK Simmons, Bob Balaban, Sherman Augustus, Michael Cerveris, Richard Coca, David Krumholtz, Gene Hackman.

● This hokey-jokey comic thriller doesn't add up to the proverbial hill o' beans, but it's an engaging curio all the same. Pitt is Jerry, American to the bone. The titular Mexican is actually a hand-wrought antique pistol. Jerry's mobster pals insist he stand up his girlfriend, Samantha (Roberts), head South of the Border, pick up the gun and bring it back home. Straightforward enough if Jerry wasn't such a loser. Meanwhile a hitman has kidnapped Sam as a little extra distraction. That the killer in question is played by Gandolfini suggests how loaded with stars the movie is. That might be a problem if audiences expect Brad and Julia to share 'quality time'; in fact they're apart for most of the film, and bickering when they're together. Gandolfini packs more emotional baggage. Screenwriter JH Wyman keeps the parallel storylines buzzing with smart dramatic zigzags and self-consciously tangy dialogue, but the whole thing gets a bit mired down with extraneous flashbacks. Director Verbinsky means to show you a good time, and he does, even if he sometimes he gets carried away. TCh

Mexico: The Frozen Revolution

(1970, US/Arg, 60 min, b/w & col)
d Raymundo Gleyzer. *p* Bill Susman, Sam Crane.

● Gleyzer's documentary analyses the betrayal of the 1910 revolution, incorporating rare newsreel footage of Villa and Zapata, not as historical decoration but as part of a dialectic that culminates in the massacre by troops of the present regime of some 400 students in one day during the Mexican Olympics. By being at all times specific, the film gains reverberations that reach well beyond its immediate subject, without letting that subject slide into second place. It's genuinely informative about Mexico as well as being a very gracefully made film. It also makes almost a virtue of the narrative voice-over, balancing it whenever possible against interviews with individuals – and if the level of political awareness of those individuals seems impressive, it's surely a comment on our own media. VG

Me You Them (Eu Tu Eles)

(2000, Braz, 107 min)
d Andrucha Waddington. *p* Leonardo M de Barros, Pedro B de Hollanda, Andrucha Waddington, Fávio R Tambelinni. *sc* Elena Soárez. *ph* Breno Silveira. *ed* Vicente

Kubrusly. *pd* Toni Vanzolini. *m* Gilberto Gil. *cast* Regina Casé, Lima Duarte, Stênio Garcia, Luiz Carlos Vasconcelos.
● Waddington's deliciously surprising second feature starts out incredibly bleakly, with its none-too-lovely pregnant heroine (Casé) leaving her cursing mother's home in the arid wastelands of north eastern Brazil, only to return with her son to find the old battle-axe dead, her elderly landlord proposing marriage and turning out to be an idle tyrant. Then gradually the film mutates into an unsentimental but uplifting comedy celebrating Casé's rise to power over not one but three husbands, all living under the same roof. Inspired by a true story, the film subtly observes how the woman plays on her suitors' jealousy, insecurity and pride, using her patience, good humour and earthy sexuality to place them in unlikely, unspoken but very real competition with each other. Heading a superb cast, Casé is simply extraordinary; Gilberto Gil's music is both lovely and entirely in keeping with the film's shifting moods; and Breno Silveira's 'Scope camerawork is both admirably to the point and visually stunning. A treat. GA

Miami Blues

(1990, US, 97 min)
d George Armitage. *p* Jonathan Demme, Gary Goetzman. *sc* George Armitage. *ph* Tak Fujimoto. *ed* Craig McKay. *pd* Maher Ahmad. *m* Gary Chang. *cast* Fred Ward, Jennifer Jason Leigh, Alec Baldwin, Nora Dunn, José Perez, Charles Napier, Paul Gleason, Martine Beswicke, Obba Babatunde.
● Armitage's adaptation of Charles Willeford's *Miami Blues* is a movie introduction to Hoke Moseley of the Miami Police Department, a middle-aged Homicide sergeant harried by alimony and sporting a set of dentures made for him on the cheap by the technician who makes false teeth for the Miami Dolphins. Like Elmore Leonard's, Willeford's world is very precise about economics; when Hoke is hospitalised by the blithe psychopath Junior Frenger (Baldwin) – who steals his gun, badge and, cruelly, his teeth – he has trouble settling his medical bill. Meanwhile Junior plays cop in the metropolis and house with an infantile hooker, while Hoke tries to trap him. Ward is physically fine for Hoke, Baldwin a wired Junior, and best of all is Leigh's hooker, but it doesn't quite translate to the screen. Willeford didn't write genre, and the film washes about a bit finding a tone. BC

Miami Rhapsody

(1995, US, 95 min)
d David Frankel. *p* Barry Jossen, David Frankel. *sc* David Frankel. *ph* Jack Wallner. *ed* Steven Weisberg. *pd* J Mark Harrington. *m* Mark Isham. *cast* Mia Farrow, Paul Mazursky, Sarah Jessica Parker, Antonio Banderas, Gil Bellows, Naomi Campbell, Kevin Pollak.
● We are in tropical Miami, but from the opening strains of Satchmo, Mia Farrow gabbling to her analyst, the infidelities, the talk and the whole damn *ronde*, we can sense that Woody Allen woz 'ere. Age has prompted ad-copywriter Gwyn (Parker) to accept the proposal of connubial whatsit from zoo-keeper Matt (Bellows), but the evidence of her family constitutes a caveat. First, dad tells her he suspects mum of a fling, and she finds mum (Farrow) is indeed romancing a nurse (Banderas); but then she finds dad (Mazursky, a director who cues another raft of associations) is himself sleeping with his secretary; brother Jordan is bonking Kaia (Campbell). As written, directed and produced by Frankel, this is a highly consumable product, a talky, breezy romantic comedy without particular insight, but filmed with pleasing brio. Mark Isham's score and the song soundtrack (mambo and jazz classics of the Porter/Ellington pedigree) give it the Rolls-Royce touch. But the acting's the thing. Parker's a sparky enough actress to hold the storm centre, and there are a half-dozen highly watchable performances, notably from Mazursky and Pollack. WH

Micha

(1992, Ire/Rus, 97 min)
d Gerard Michael MacCarthy. *p* Nicholas O'Neill. *sc* Gerard Michael MacCarthy. *ph* Valery Martynov. *ed* Sé Merry Doyle. *ad* Vladimir Yuzhakov. *m* Niall Byrne. *cast* Genya Korhin, Victoria Korhina, Igor Kostolevsky, Andrew Urgant, Inge Ilm, Sergey Koupriyanov.
● Filmed in St Petersburg and the old LenFilm Studios, Irish writer/director MacCarthy's ambitious first feature attempts to explore the harsh changing realities of living in that city through the experiences and mind of a young boy, Micha, whose father is in exile in Germany. It follows him from his anglophile school (where he's nevertheless chastised for reading American *Premiere*) and through the hours he spends exploring the city until his waitress mother finishes work. He is taken under the wing of the film crew surrounding the enigmatic Borodin (who plays a gangster in a TV soap), but everyday reality on the street seems equally unreal. Truth and fiction meld. Floating unsettlingly from stylisation to naturalism, from realism to expressionism, from dream to tough reality, the film is at times obscure, but it has a surreal, compulsive quality and is acted with melancholy conviction. WH

Michael

(1996, US, 105 min)
d Nora Ephron. *p* Sean Daniel, Nora Ephron, James Jacks. *sc* Nora Ephron, Delia Ephron, Pete Dexter, Jim Quinlan. *ph* John Lindley. *ed* Geraldine Peroni. *pd* Dan Davis. *m* Randy Newman. *cast* John Travolta, Andie MacDowell, William Hurt, Bob Hoskins, Robert Pastorelli, Jean Stapleton, Teri Garr, Calvin Trillin.
● Hollywood's perennial fascination with Earthbound angels gets a cornball comic twist in Ephron's shaggy-dog story about a pair of Chicago hacks and a self-professed 'angel expert' dispatched to *Field of Dreams* country to find a dotty old lady who claims the Archangel Michael is living at her Iowa motel. And yes, he has wings. What they find is a portly, stubble-chinned seraph (Travolta) who, in the course of a cross-country car journey to Chicago, reveals his God-given wisdom by smoking, drinking, brawling and seducing women. Since they work for a tabloid obsessed with alien invaders and human freaks, washed-up cynic Frank Quinlan (Hurt) and his feckless partner Huey Driscoll (Pastorelli) are unimpressed. But Michael isn't going to waste his last trip to Earth trying to convert non-believers. Instead, he redeems thrice-divorced, former romantic Dorothy (MacDowell) and ex-alcoholic Frank by helping them to fall in love with one another. Which leaves Huey to do what he does best: look after the paper's mongrel mascot Sparky and feed off the scraps of dialogue thrown to him by the other characters. One senses a tension between the original screenplay, by reporter Jim Quinlan and novelist Pete Dexter, and the whimsical gloss given it by Ephron and her sister/co-writer Delia. The result's a series of funny, sentimental, self-contained turns. The storyline, meanwhile, wanders aimlessly. NF

Michael (Mikaël)

(1924, Ger, 90 min approx, b/w)
d Carl Theodor Dreyer. *p* Erich Pommer. *sc* Thea von Harbou, Carl Dreyer. *ph* Karl Freund. *ad* Hugo Häring. *cast* Benjamin Christensen, Walter Slezak, Nora Gregor, Robert Garrison, Grete Mosheim, Karl Freund.
● The seasoned artist and the beautiful young man: it's Oscar and Bosie again, except here the artist, Zoret, is a painter and the 'Bosie' figure – Michael – jilts him for a Russian princess. Zoret's response is a giant canvas entitled 'Suffering' (an old guy wailing on a rock). At last, accepting it's all over, he wills his money to Michael, then takes to his bed and dies of love. Proposed: that on the basis of this horrible film Dreyer be frogmarched out of the Pantheon. True, Zoret looks so much like a Tony Hancock parody of the exquisite aesthete – smoking jackets à la mode and a three-foot long clay pipe – that it's possible guffaws are actually appropriate, the intention having been satirical. But that's unlikely: the self-pity, the adolescent concept of love, the view of women as bloody nuisances are consistent and entirely displeasing. BBa

Michael Collins

(1996, US, 132 min)
d Neil Jordan. *p* Stephen Woolley. *sc* Neil Jordan. *ph* Chris Menges. *ed* J Patrick Duffner, Tony Lawson. *pd* Anthony Pratt. *m* Elliot Goldenthal. *cast* Liam Neeson, Julia Roberts, Stephen Rea, Alan Rickman, Aidan Quinn, Ian Hart, John Kenny, Gerard McSorley, Michael Dwyer, Owen Roe.
● Writer/director Jordan's film tracing the career of Irish Republican hero Michael Collins, from the Easter Rising to his death in 1922, depicts a man whose belief in violence is finally transformed by the horrors of civil war into a desire for peace. It's a dense, stirring tale, with Collins (Neeson) under threat from both the English and his compatriots. Is Ned Broy (Rea) a spy or an ally working from within Dublin Castle? How serious is his split with Eamon De Valera (Rickman), who prefers to fight on for a Republic than settle temporarily for the Free State brokered by Collins? And what of bosom pal Harry Boland (Quinn), who feels personally betrayed when his girl Kitty (Roberts) transfers her affections to Collins? This is Jordan's most ambitious and satisfying movie a thriller with a real sense of scale, pace, menace and moral import. With the exception of Rickman's awesomely mannered De Valera, the performances are top notch (even Roberts makes a decent stab at the romantic interest, incarnating the ideological fall-out between Collins and Boland), while Chris Menges' camerawork and Anthony Pratt's designs perfectly evoke a country falling apart with no one, it seems, able to halt the tragedy. GA

Michael Kohlhaas

(1969, WGer, 95 min)
d Volker Schlöndorff. *p* Jerry Bick. *sc* Edward Bond, Clement Biddle-Wood, Volker Schlöndorff. *ph* Willy Kurant. *ed* Claus von Boro. *ad* Ivan Vanicek, Rudi Kovacs. *m* Stanley Myers. *cast* David Warner, Anna Karina, Relia Basic, Anita Pallenberg, Inigo Jackson, Michael Gothard, Anton Diffring, Kurt Meisel, Peter Weiss, Keith Richards.
● Schlöndorff's bizarre third feature was the first of a spate of adaptations from Kleist. Edward Bond wrote it (it's in English), and laboured mightily over the contemporary parallels in the story of a 16th century horse-dealer whose stand against a criminal landowner takes him outside the law himself. Schlöndorff films it as all-stops-out melodrama, complete with rioting peasants, rioting students, contrasts between righteous and non-righteous rebellion, and one of David Warner's least restrained performances. If the result evokes Ken Russell, it's because it shares some of Russell's visual strength as well as some of his dramatic weakness. TR

Michael Shayne Private Detective

(1941, US, 77 min, b/w)
d Eugene Forde. *p* Sol M Wurtzel. *sc* Stanley Rauh, Manning O'Connor. *ph* George Schneidermann. *ed* Al De Gaetano. *ad* Richard Day, Lewis Creber. *m* Emil Newman. *cast* Lloyd Nolan, Marjorie Weaver, Elizabeth Patterson, Joan Valerie, Walter Abel, Donald MacBride, Douglas Dumbrille.
● Nolan's 'keyhole dick' is ludicrously quick with his fists and has an annoying habit of twirling a keychain round his finger, he's also not above faking a murder (with a mickey finn and a bottle of catsup) to frighten the sense back into the headstrong girl (Weaver) he's supposed to be chaperoning. Based on a novel by Brett Halliday, *Dividend on Death*, this is the first in a series of 12 produced by Fox between 1940 and '47. It's an extremely convoluted betting and horse-swapping mystery, with a mildly diverting subplot featuring an elderly Ellery Queen fan (Patterson) who helps Shayne with this not terribly diverting 'baffle book' case. Nolan is a reliable player, and Bogart's Marlowe may have learned something from him, but he lacks ingrained world-weariness. JPy

Michael Strogoff

see Adventures of Michael Strogoff, The

Mickey Blue Eyes

(1999, US/GB, 102 min)
d Kelly Makin. *p* Elizabeth Hurley, Charles Mulvehill. *sc* Mark Lawrence, Adam Scheinman, Robert Kuhn. *ph* Donald E Thorin. *ed* David Freeman. *pd* Gregory P Keen. *m* Basil Poledouris. *cast* Hugh Grant, James Caan, Jeanne Tripplehorn, Burt Young, James Fox, Joe Viterelli, Gerry Becker, Maddie Corman.
● Grant's the dapper but reluctant English gent thrown in a flap when the discreet world of his NY auction house is spliced with the life of the

Mafia goon. Only when he proposes to girlfriend Tripplehorn does he discover that daddy (Caan) is a leading local mobster who, filled with family pride, now wants a piece of his prospective son-in-law. Thus Grant has to suffer dodgy paintings on his show floor, hapless Italian pronunciation practice, and the prospect of losing his bride before he's even won her. Comedy mobsters: don'tchaluv'em? The cartoon accents, the Old World family ties, the hackneyed juxtaposition of homeliness and casual violence, the impenetrable logic of their own codes and their feckless disregard for anyone else's. Fahgedaboudit. NB

Mickey One

(1964, US, 93 min, b/w)
d/p Arthur Penn. *sc* Alan Surgal. *ph* Ghislain Cloquet. *ed* Aram Avakian. *pd* George Jenkins. *m* Eddie Sauter. *cast* Warren Beatty, Alexandra Stewart, Hurd Hatfield, Franchot Tone, Teddy Hart, Jeff Corey, Kamatari Fujiwara.

● Mickey (Beatty) is a successful nightclub comedian, confused and neurotic about his life in general, and possibly suffering from a persecution complex: someone or something is threatening him, for something he may have done in the past. Exactly what he is afraid of – the Mob, America at large, his conscience? – and why remains all too obscure in Penn's most European movie, made with almost total artistic freedom; the result, at once his most infuriating and one of his most intriguing films, is a rather vague allegory about alienation, guilt and despair, structured as an elliptical narrative complete with jump-cuts and bizarre, symbolic images. A few scenes are truly disquieting – as when Beatty is auditioned in a silent, darkened auditorium – but the overall effect is too cerebrally self-conscious to be genuinely gripping. GA

Micki + Maude

(1984, US, 117 min)
d Blake Edwards. *p* Tony Adams. *sc* Jonathan Reynolds. *ph* Harry Stradling. *ed* Ralph E Winters. *pd* Rodger Maus. *m* Lee Holdridge. *cast* Dudley Moore, Amy Irving, Ann Reinking, Richard Mulligan, George Gaynes, Wallace Shawn, John Pleshette.

● After Edwards' hopeless *The Man Who Loved Women* comes this altogether more successful piece which might be subtitled 'The Man Who Loved Two Women'. Moore is married to careerist lawyer Micki (Reinking), and yearns for a child which she will not provide. He takes cellist Maude (Irving) for a mistress, impregnates and marries her, only to find Micki too is pregnant. The film's greatest moments of comedy spring from the bigamous Moore's escalating panic in the face of keeping two marriages together but separate, culminating in a double delivery in adjacent hospital wards of frantic delirium; Keystone cops meet *The Hospital*. It is none the worse for being resolutely old-fashioned in its virtues, and – in its compassion towards all parties – marked by a complete absence of the sour element which distinguished previous Edwards comedies like *'10'* and *S.O.B.* CPea

Microcosmos (Microcosmos: Le Peuple de l'herbe)

(1996, Fr/Switz/It, 75 min)
d Claude Nuridsany, Marie Pérennou. *p* Jacques Perrin, Christophe Barratier, Yvette Mallet. *ph* Claude Nuridsany, Marie Pérennou, Hugues Ryffel, Thierry Machado. *ed* Marie-Josèphe Yoyotte, Florence Ricard. *m* Bruno Coulais. *narrator* Kristin Scott Thomas.

● The close-up photography is stunning in this slightly (but not too cutely) anthropomorphic documentary on the lives of the inhabitants of a summer meadow. All insect and invertebrate life is here (ladybird with seven spots, swallowtail butterfly, burgundy snail, ang spider, rhinoceros beetle, red ants) in the daily round of sex, violence, work and conspicuous food consumption, but while the film's technically superb, the mainly wordless format ultimately wears a little thin. GA

Midaq Alley (El Callejon de los Milagros)

(1994, Mex, 140 min)
d Jorge Fons. *p* Alfredo Ripstein. *sc* Vicente Leñero. *ph* Carlos Marcovich. *ed* Carlos Savage. *pd* Carlos Gutiérrez. *m* Lucia Alvarez. *cast* Ernesto Gomez Cruz, Maria Rojo, Salma Hayek, Bruno Bichir, Delia Casanova, Damiel Giménez Cacho.

● Transposing a novel of Egyptian street life by the Nobel Prize-winning author Naguib Mahfouz to contemporary Mexico, director Fons splits the story into four episodes each told from a separate point of view: from the macho bar owner who seemingly turns gay in an afternoon, to the beautiful Alma (Hayek, star of Robert Rodriguez's *Desperado*), whose impatience for love leads her quickly to the local brothel. Although everything teeters on the edge of soap opera, and the intertwining of the stories reveals few surprises, the film scores with its strong pacing and gutsy humour. DT

Midas Run (aka A Run on Gold)

(1969, US, 103 min)
d Alf Kjellin. *p* Raymond Stross. *sc* James D Buchanan, Ronald Austin, Berne Giler. *ph* Ken Higgins. *ed* Fredric Steinkamp. *ad* Arthur Lawson, Ezio Cescotti. *m* Elmer Bernstein. *cast* Richard Crenna, Anne Heywood, Fred Astaire, Roddy McDowall, Ralph Richardson, Adolfo Celi, Cesar Romero, Maurice Denham.

● A crime-of-the-century caper, not high in the credibility stakes at the best of times, but pushed several rungs lower by the casting of Fred Astaire as a member of an aristocratic English family (his accent explained away by recalling that Sir Winston Churchill, too, had an American mother). A British secret service chief, Astaire masterminds a gold bullion robbery, then solves the crime himself, all in order to secure the knighthood that has so far escaped him. Crenna plays an expert in military strategy duped into helping (but ingeniously exculpated afterwards), and Richardson contributes a characteristic civil service cameo. Script, acting and direction are equally laboured. TM

Middle Age Crazy

(1980, Can, 95 min)
d John Trent. *p* Ronald I Cohen. *sc* Carl Kleinschmitt. *ph* Reginald Morris. *ed* John Kelly. *pd* Karen Bromley. *m* Matthew McCauley. *cast* Bruce Dern, Ann-Margret, Graham Jarvis, Deborah Wakeham, Eric Christmas, Helen Hughes, Geoffrey Bowes.

● Loosely based around a weepie sung by Jerry Lee Lewis, this should have you cringing in the aisles. Dern's Joe Suburbia appears to have everything – a wife (Ann-Margret) whose only consideration is her husband's satisfaction; a son who wants to be an architect; a business (building taco stands) that's thriving; and a ranch-styled villa with a jacuzzi. But in every dream home is a heartache, and Dern gets neurotic when he crosses the middle-age dateline of 39 to 40. All the popular US taboos suddenly strike: the quest for eternal youth ('The future sucks. Stay 18 for the rest of your lives'), the fear of death (Jessica Mitford for the '80s), male menopause (virility means you can score with a younger girl). Although Dern and Ann-Margret struggle valiantly, the cloying sentimentality, the repressive morality, the flabby direction and the scabrous script result in a slice of irredeemable cod. IB

Middleman, The (Jana-Aranya)

(1975, Ind, 131 min, b/w)
d Satyajit Ray. *p* Subir Guha. *sc* Satyajit Ray. *ph* Soumendu Roy. *ed* Dulal Dutta. *ad* Asok Bose. *m* Satyajit Ray. *cast* Pradip Mukherjee, Satya Banerjee, Dipankar Dey, Lily Chakravarti, Aparna Sen, Utpal Dutt.

● Although Ray's later films saw him moving away from his early gentle humanism towards something more concerned with the political and economic problems facing modern India, they remain primarily descriptive rather than works of intense political commitment. Here he deals with a university graduate forced to enter the world of commerce: his confidence eroded by the experience of being interviewed for jobs for which there are literally thousands of applicants, he eventually sets himself up as someone who buys and sells anything. Meanwhile he finds himself reduced to compromising his ideals more and more. Beautifully performed, blessed with Ray's customary sense of balance, and wittily satirising the absurdity of bureaucracy run riot, it makes absorbing viewing. GA

Middle of the World, The (Le Milieu du Monde)

(1974, Switz/Fr, 117 min)
d Alain Tanner. *p* Yves Peyrot. *sc* Alain Tanner, John Berger. *ph* Renato Berta. *ed* Brigitte Sousselier. *ad* Serge Etter. *m* Patrick Moraz. *cast* Olimpia Carlisi, Philippe Léotard, Juliet Berto, Denise Perron, Jacques Denis, Roger Jendly, Gilbert Bahon. *narrator* Claire Dominique.

● Tanner's most achieved film to date is also his most apparently conventional, the story of a love affair between a café waitress and an ambitious (married) local politician which comes to a catastrophic end. But the subject matter (a woman struggling for independence) and formal structure (including 'empty' shots of a bleak winter landscape) come together with breathtaking lucidity. The tone is compassionate, and for a truly '70s tragedy the ending is curiously upbeat. CA

Middle Passage, The (Passage du milieu)

(2000, Fr/Martinique, 88 min)
d Guy Deslauriers. *p* Yasmina Ho-You-Fat. *sc* Patrick Chamoiseau. *ph* Jacques Boumendil. *ed* Aïlo Auguste. *pd* Roland Fruytier. *m* Amos Coulanges. *narrator* Mako Kotto.

● *Amistad* showed that it's not enough to make an earnest film stating the obvious about slavery – that it's cruel, inhuman and totally wrong. But this far more modest movie actually does succeed in doing something new; using an anonymous narrator to evoke the experiences of Dahomey slaves on their terrible, most likely fatal boat trip across the Atlantic, the film is not only informative, it actually conveys something of the physical, spiritual and mental suffering involved. If the film is determinedly poetic and philosophical in both its images and narration, its artiness doesn't preclude truth, subtlety, imagination, even beauty. GA

Middleton's Changeling

(1997, GB, 96 min)
d/p/sc Marcus Thompson. *ph* Richard KJ Butland. *ed* Marcus Thompson. *ad* Rob Swinburn. *m* Brian Gray. *cast* Ian Dury, Amanda Ray-King, Colm Ó Maonlai, Billy Connolly, Campbell Morrison, Moya Brady, Richard Mayes, Guy Williams, Vivian Stanshall.

● Attempting a radical update of Middleton's Jacobean tragedy, with the iconoclastic intentions, but without the discipline or sense of Baz Luhrmann's *Romeo & Juliet*, writer/producer/director/editor Thompson throws in incongruous modern trappings amid a general sense of gothic medievalism. At court in Alicante, Beatrice (Ray-King), betrothed by her father Vermandero (Mayes) to marry Alonso (Williams), falls for dashing Alsemero (Ó Maonlaí). Their trysts are witnessed by Vermandero's servant De Flores (Dury), a toad-like villain who lusts after her and whom she abhors. In desperation she accepts his offer to dispose of Alonso; then, before she can marry Alsemero, De Flores reveals his price – Beatrice's virginity. Intercut are lengthy scenes of Connolly running a slave-trade circus of lunatics. Gary Moore's monotonous guitar lines soar across the soundtrack, attempting to evoke grand tragedy, while Thompson's camera indulges in similarly grandiloquent swoops. NB

Midnight

(1939, US, 94 min, b/w)
d Mitchell Leisen. *p* Arthur Hornblow Jr. *sc* Charles Brackett, Billy Wilder. *ph* Charles Lang Jr. *ed* Doane Harrison. *ad* Hans Dreier, Robert Usher. *m* Frederick Hollander. *cast* Claudette Colbert, Don Ameche, John Barrymore, Mary Astor, Francis Lederer, Hedda Hopper, Monty Woolley.

● An enchanting comedy which starts with Colbert, as an American chorine on the make, stranded in Paris in a gold lamé evening gown (what else?). She is befriended on the one hand by a poor taxi-driver who is really a Russian count (Ameche), and on the other by a wealthy socialite (Barrymore) who 'introduces' her to society so that she can oblige by luring a gigolo away from his wife. Uncanny coincidental parallels with *La Règle du Jeu* abound, and although the film echoes Renoir's bark more than his bite, it has a superbly malicious script by Brackett and Wilder, gorgeous sets and camerawork, and a matchless cast. All in all, probably Leisen's best film. TM

Midnight (O Primeiro Dia/ Le Premier Jour/aka Meia Noite)

(1998, Fr/Braz, 76 min)
d Walter Salles, Daniela Thomas. *p* Beth Pessoa, Elisa Tolomelli. *sc* João Emanuel Carneiro, José de Carvalho, Walter Salles, Daniela Thomas. *ph* Walter Carvalho. *ed* Felipe Lacerda. *m* Eduardo Bid, Antonio Pinto, Nana Vasconcelos. *cast* Fernanda Torres, Luís Carlos Vasconcelos, Matheus Nachtegaele, Nelson Sargento, Tonico Pereira, Aulio Ribeiro, Luciana Bezerra, Antonio Gomes.

● Rio de Janeiro, just before the start of the new millennium. Neither João nor Maria expect to join the massive celebrations: he's serving 30 years in a filthy jail, while she, a teacher of the deaf, simply wants to pass the time quietly at home with partner Pedro. Then everything changes. Maria wakes on the last day of the year to discover Pedro's farewell note. João takes advantage of an escape facilitated by guards who insist freedom has its price: he must kill an informer, who just happens to be his old friend Chico. This wonderful assured drama (intended originally for TV) is part gritty thriller, part psychological study of a woman on the verge of a nervous breakdown, and part discreet comment on the poverty, injustice and corruption permeating Brazil. Crucially, it all hangs together, thanks to vivid performances, exceptional 'Scope camerawork and the pace and flair with which the separate stories are intercut. As in Salles' earlier work, the metaphors and symbols are worn so lightly that even the Christian imagery never weighs down what is finally a tale of betrayal, sin, redemption and rebirth. Brief flashes of optimism notwithstanding, it's a remarkably tough, unsentimental film. GA

Midnight Clear, A

(1991, US, 108 min)
d Keith Gordon. *p* Dale Pollock, Bill Borden. *sc* Keith Gordon. *ph* Tom Richmond. *ed* Donald Brochu. *pd* David Nichols. *m* Mark Isham. *cast* Peter Berg, Kevin Dillon, Arye Gross, Ethan Hawke, Gary Sinise, Frank Whaley, John C McGinley.

● As the end of World War II approaches, a group of American soldiers settle in a deserted house on the Franco-German border in order to report on enemy movements. But their foe remains elusive, and after making contact with these young, nervous men, the Germans prove strangely unwilling to attack. Less war movie than psychological thriller, writer/director Gordon's absorbing, stylised adaptation of William Wharton's novel explores issues of faith and morality. The performances are uniformly excellent as the film moves inexorably towards bloody confrontation and spiritual reckoning. CM

Midnight Cowboy

(1969, US, 113 min)
d John Schlesinger. *p* Jerome Hellman. *sc* Waldo Salt. *ph* Adam Holender. *ed* Hugh A Robertson, Jim Clark. *pd* John Robert Lloyd. *m* John Barry. *cast* Jon Voight, Dustin Hoffman, Sylvia Miles, Brenda Vaccaro, John McGiver, Barnard Hughes, Ruth White, Jennifer Salt, Gil Rankin, Bob Balaban, Viva.

● Outrageously overrated at the cynical end of the Swinging Sixties, when the seedy New York milieu in which the pathetic buddy-buddy story takes place was thought to be truthfully depicted. Instead, as Voight's likeably dumb Texan hick hustler teams up with limping guttersnipe Hoffman in an effort to make enough money from the wealthy women of New York to fulfil dreams of living in sunny Florida, the film indulges in bland satire, fashionable flashiness, and a sodden sentimentality that never admits either to its homosexual elements or to the basic misogyny of its stance. Add to that a glamorisation of poverty and an ending that makes *Love Story* seem restrained, and you have a fairly characteristic example of Schlesinger's shallow talent. (From a novel by James Leo Herlihy.) GA

Midnight Dancers (Sibak)

(1994, Phil, 100 min)
d Mel Chionglo. *p* Richard Wong-Tang. *sc* Ricky Lee. *ph* George Tutanes. *ed* Jess Navaro. *pd* Edgar Martin Littaua. *m* Nonong Buencamino. *cast* Alex Del Rosario, Gandong Cervantes, Lawrence David, Luis Cortez, Richard Cassity, Danny Ramos, Perla Bautista.

● A sequel of sorts to Lino Broca's botched *Macho Dancer*, Chionglo's likeable melodrama offers a moral (but not moralistic) panorama of gay life in Manila. Young footballer Sonny, new in town from the sticks, is introduced to gay prostitution by his two elder brothers, both of whom already perform as G-stringed macho dancers in a gay bar and support their mother by turning tricks. The film is let down by some weak performances and feeble fight choreography, but its feeling for the vagaries of rent-boy life is palpably sincere. Its best scenes centre on eldest brother Joel, who has a wife and child and a male lover and manages to keep all of them happy. TR

Midnight Express

(1978, GB, 121 min)
d Alan Parker. *p* Alan Marshall, David Puttnam. *sc* Oliver Stone. *ph* Michael Seresin. *ed* Gerry Hambling. *pd* Geoffrey Kirkland. *m* Giorgio Moroder. *cast* Brad Davis, Randy Quaid, John Hurt, Irene Miracle, Bo Hopkins, Paolo Bonacelli, Paul Smith.

● A meaty anecdote, heavily fictionalised from a factual source, about an American kid on a dope charge going through Hell in a Turkish jail. Some of the performances (Hurt, Davis) give it an illusion of depth, but it's mostly expert in avoiding moral resonance and ambiguity: everything is satisfyingly clear-cut, just as every shot and every cut are geared to instant emotional impact. Political, moral and aesthetic problems arise when you try to superimpose the film on the 'truth' it purports to represent. As a head-banging thriller, though, it makes some of Hollywood's hoariest stereotypes seem good as new, and it panders to its audience's worst instincts magnificently. TR

Midnight Fear

(1990, US, 85 min)
d Bill Crain. *sc* Pat Tagliaferro, Bill Crain, Chuck Hughes, Craig Wasson, Shani S Grewal. *ph* Michael Crain. *pd* Pat Tagliaferro. *m* Steve Crain. *cast* David Carradine, Craig Wasson, August West, Page Fletcher, Evan Richards, Mark Carlton.

● Sheriff Carradine comes to the rescue in this minor shocker, a cheap variation on ye old psychos-menace-single-woman-in-remote-shack routine. There's a diabolically fiendish plot device (watch for it), but it's insufficient to make a proper movie out of nasty junk. TJ

Midnight in the Garden of Good and Evil

(1997, US, 155 min)
d Clint Eastwood. *p* Clint Eastwood, Arnold Stiefel. *sc* John Lee Hancock. *ph* Jack N Green. *ed* Joel Cox. *pd* Henry Bumstead. *m* Lennie Niehaus. *cast* Kevin Spacey, John Cusack, Jack Thompson, Irma P Hall, Jude Law, Alison Eastwood, Paul Hipp, The Lady Chablis, Kim Hunter, Geoffrey Lewis, Jo Ann Pflug.

● When New York journalist John Kelso (Cusack) arrives in Savannah, Georgia, to cover one of the lavish Christmas parties held by wealthy antique dealer Jim Williams (Spacey), he doesn't expect to get caught up in a murder trial. But after his host shoots volatile young employee Billy Hanson (Law), Kelso finds himself following the case with a view to writing a book, and making enquiries that might help substantiate Williams' self-defence plea – an investigation which, in introducing him to such locals as the transvestite nightclub artiste Lady Chablis and voodoo queen Minerva, uncovers a whole new world beneath the colourful but in many ways conservative veneer of Savannah society. Elegantly directed and beautifully performed, Eastwood's film of John Berendt's non-fiction best-seller is a warm, witty, consistently intriguing character study. Particularly successful are the funny, touching scenes shared by Cusack and the flirtatious Chablis, typical of the movie's fascination with questions of pretence, trust and tolerance. Also engaging, however, is the quirky wit and Eastwood's readiness, whenever the occasion arises, to deflect focus away from the crime on to other details in the social tapestry, subtly nudging at divisions involving race, class, gender and sexuality. GA

Midnight Man, The

(1974, US, 119 min)
d/p/sc Roland Kibbee, Burt Lancaster. *ph* Jack Priestley. *ed* Frank Morriss. *ad* James D Vance. *m* David Grusin. *cast* Burt Lancaster, Susan Clark, Cameron Mitchell, Morgan Woodward, Harris Yulin, Robert Quarry, Joan Lorring, Ed Lauter, Nick Cravat.

● Lancaster joins forces with screenwriting friend Kibbee (*The Crimson Pirate, Vera Cruz*) on an adaptation of David Anthony's thriller *The Midnight Lady and the Mourning Man*. The narrative is as abbreviated as the title, and for all the sense the plot makes, they might as well have called it 'The and The'. Even so, there's enough incident crammed in to fill columns. Suffice it to say that prominent parts are played by an ex-cop working as a college nightwatchman (Lancaster), a pretty parole officer with a taste for garish lipstick (Clark), the murdered daughter of a corrupt senator, a stolen tape of intimate confessions, an unfinished poem laced with Greek mythology, and a volume of Krafft-Ebing. Non-prominent parts are played by the two directors, who stage events with little flair. GB

Midnight Run

(1988, US, 126 min)
d/p Martin Brest. *sc* George Gallo. *ph* Donald Thorin. *ed* Billy Weber, Chris Lebenzon, Michael Tronick. *pd* Angelo Graham. *m* Danny Elfman. *cast* Robert De Niro, Charles Grodin, Yaphet Kotto, John Ashton, Dennis Farina, Joe Pantoliano, Richard Foronjy.

● That old formula, handcuffed captor and captive who become buddies on the run, gets an injection of new life from the playing of the cast. Bounty hunter Jack Walsh (De Niro) captures bail-jumping accountant Jon Mardukas (Grodin) in New York, but his problems really start when he tries to deliver him to the bail bondsman in LA. Mardukas, learning that his employer was a Mafia mobster, stole millions which he distributed among the poor, and Walsh has to run the gauntlet of the FBI, the Mob and a rival bounty hunter (Ashton), besides putting up with his captive's concern about smoking and morality. Both actors get off on each other, improvising routines and inhabiting the standard Odd Couple teaming so interestingly that at times the film touches a profundity. Here and there, director Brest succumbs to the car chase, but overall the movie is way above average for the genre. BC

Midnight Sting

see Diggstown

Midsummer Night's Dream, A

(1935, US, 132 min, b/w)
d Max Reinhardt, William Dieterle. *p* Henry Blanke. *sc* Charles Kenyon, Mary C McCall Jr. *ph* Hal Mohr. *ed* Ralph Dawson. *ad* Anton Grot. *m* Mendelssohn. *cast* James Cagney, Dick Powell, Olivia de Havilland, Joe E Brown, Mickey Rooney, Jean Muir, Verree Teasdale, Ian Hunter, Anita Louise, Victor Jory, Hugh Herbert.

● Perhaps not the most faithful of screen adaptations of Shakespeare, but certainly one of the most charming. The performances are surprisingly superb – notably Cagney as Bottom and a young Rooney as Puck – while visually the movie is a triumph of art direction and luminous photography. And although accusations of kitsch are perfectly justified, the scenes of the fairies wafting through the forest are beautiful enough to bring tears to the eyes. No wonder that the infant Kenneth Anger, playing the Changeling, would later turn to high camp and magic in his own movies. (Mendelssohn's music is arranged by Erich Wolfgang Korngold.) GA

Midsummer Night's Dream, A

(1984, GB/Sp, 77 min)
d Celestino Coronado. *p* Miguel Angel Pérez Campos. *sc* Celestino Coronado. *ph* Peter Middleton. *pd* Lindsay Kemp. *m* Carlos Miranda. *cast* Lindsay Kemp, Manuela Vargas, The Incredible Orlando, Michael Matou, François Testory, Neil Caplan, Atilo Lopez, José Luis Aguirre.

● This axes at least 75 per cent of Shakespeare's text and lets the images and score do the talking. It derives from a Kemp stage production, but is never stagy in the bad sense: its origins simply enhance the overall texture of the artifice, making it like a Richard Dadd painting come to life. Modest liberties are taken with the plot, so that the feuding couples switch sexual proclivities as well as partners, but it's surprisingly faithful to the spirit of the play, through lustrous photography and a memorably refined performance from Jack 'Orlando' Birkett as Titania. TR

Midsummer Night's Dream, A

(1996, GB, 103 min)
d Adrian Noble. *p* Paul Arnott. *sc* Adrian Noble. *ph* Ian Wilson. *ed* Peter Hodgson, Peter Hollywood. *pd* Anthony Ward. *m* Howard Blake. *cast* Lindsay Duncan, Alex Jennings, Desmond Barrit, Barry Lynch, Howard Crossley, Robin Gillespie, John Kane, Mark Letheren, Kenn Sabberton.

● Sadly, this cross-over to the screen of an acclaimed stage production by Adrian Noble, the Royal Shakespeare Company's artistic director, is a nightmare. What impressed about the original was the colour and energy. Here, the colours are chocolate-box garish. The women seem to be refugees from the wedding-gift counter at Peter Jones, and the men look like waiters in a haplessly themed King's Road restaurant. An attempt has been made to open the play out (and unify it) by letting loose a schoolboy in the action. The result's a baffling mix that leaves the action panting behind arch cinematic references to everything from *Peter Pan* and *The Wizard of Oz* to *ET*. SGr

Midsummer Night's Dream, A

(1999, US/Ger, 120 min)
d Michael Hoffman. *p* Leslie Urdang, Michael Hoffman. *sc* Michael Hoffman. *ph* Oliver Stapleton. *ed* Garth Craven. *pd* Luciana Arrighi. *m* Simon Boswell. *cast* Kevin Kline, Michelle Pfeiffer, Rupert Everett, Stanley Tucci, Calista Flockhart, Anna Friel, Christian Bale, Dominic West, David Strathairn, Sophie Marceau, Roger Rees, Max Wright, Gregory Jbara, Bill Irwin, Sam Rockwell, Bernard Hill, John Sessions.

● This 'Scope version of 'Bottom's Story' is placed in late 19th century Tuscany, with the tone set, most successfully, by Pfeiffer's recumbent, eroticised and shimmering Titania. Puck's mischief – pairing Friel's sweet petulant Hermia with Bale's dull Demetrius, and Flockhart's consternated Helena with West's posturing Lysander – brings an oh-so-sweet awakening, as the morning finds the lovers tumbled naked on the dewy sunlit grass. Such pleasurable moments make us forgive writer/director Hoffman his inability to reconcile the varied performances and readings of the international cast. More problematic are the provocative 'anachronisms': having characters, costumed out of pre-Raphaelite paintings, deport themselves on bicycles and listen to early gramophones, for instance, is unproductively Brechtian. Also irksome and claustrophobic is the design of the magic wood, all cardboard scenery and creaky contraptions. What shouldn't work, yet does, is the use of snippets of opera to add crescendos to the action: this *Dream* is middlebrow and unashamed of it. Injecting the film with fun and pathos, Kline makes a superb Bottom; it's his play and he acts it to the hilt. WH

Midsummer Night's Sex Comedy, A

(1982, US, 88 min)
d Woody Allen. *p* Robert Greenhut. *sc* Woody Allen. *ph* Gordon Willis. *ed* Susan E Morse. *pd* Mel Bourne. *cast* Woody Allen, Mia Farrow, José Ferrer, Julie Hagerty, Tony Roberts, Mary Steenburgen, Adam Redfield.

● Monogamous at heart, Allen has ended his brief affair with Fellini (*Stardust Memories* out of *8½*) and gone back to his first love Bergman. Allen's version of *Smiles of a Summer Night* keeps the period country house setting but reduces the characters to six: two medical swingers, an elderly academic and his much younger fiancée, and a long-married couple whose sex-life has ground to a halt. Allen, of course, plays the frustrated husband (he redirects his energies towards inventing flying bicycles, astral lamps and the like), and gives himself nearly all the funny lines. He spends the rest of the movie satirising the men and adoring the changing moods of the women. His best invention remains his own screen persona, and the Bergman borrowings here provide it with a warm, romantic and old-fashioned setting. TR

Midway (aka Battle of Midway)

(1976, US, 132 min)
d Jack Smight. *p* Walter Mirisch. *sc* Donald S Sanford. *ph* Harry Stradling Jr. *ed* Robert Swink, Frank J Urioste. *ad* Walter Tyler. *m* John Williams. *cast* Charlton Heston, Henry Fonda, James Coburn, Glenn Ford, Hal Holbrook, Toshiro Mifune, Robert Mitchum, Cliff Robertson, Robert Wagner, Robert Webber, Ed Nelson.

● 'This is the way it was,' drones the introduction to this massively extravagant account of America's WWII naval victory, a sure indication of the film's probable untrustworthiness. 'Dad, I've fallen in love with a Japanese girl. I need your help' – 'Six months after Pearl Harbor! You have one lousy sense of timing!' Saddled with such crass dialogue, the 'human' interest and the array of stars make predictably little impact against all the weaponry wheeled out to recreate the Pacific battle. Small wonder that Fonda wanders through the film looking as though he's holding a royal flush to Mifune's pair of twos. The rest is noisy, incomprehensible and lumberingly irrelevant, complete with shell-schlock Sensurround.

Midwinter Tale, A

see In the Bleak Midwinter

Miei Primi 40 Anni, I

see My First 40 Years

Mi Familia

see My Family

Mifune (Mifune sidste sang)

(1999, Den/Swe, 101 min)
d Søren Kragh-Jacobsen. *p* Brigitte Hald, Morten Kaufmann. *sc* Søren Kragh-Jacobsen, Anders Thomas Jensen. *ph* Anthony Dod Mantle. *ed* Valdís Óskarsdóttir. *cast* Iben Hjejle, Anders W Berthelsen, Jesper Asholt, Emil Tarding, Anders Hove, Sofie Gråbøl, Paprika Steen.

● The third Dogma release is at heart a very conventional romantic comedy, gussied up with 'provocative' anti-bourgeois elements carried over from *The Idiots* and *Festen*, and shot, as it were, in denial of any production restraints. Kresten (Berthelsen) hasn't told his new wife – the boss's daughter – about his moronic brother back home in the sticks. On the other hand he has told her that his father's dead, so it's a little embarrassing when he gets a phone call on their wedding night reiterating the fact and requesting his presence at the funeral. Off he goes, alone, to pick up the pieces on the farm where he grew up, and find some way of taking care of Rud (Asholt) – who has a mental age of eight. A prostitute fleeing a phone sex pest, Liva (Hjejle), answers Kresten's ad for a housekeeper, and shows up with her tearaway brother (Tarding). What follows would scarcely look out of place in a Garry Marshall film: in fact it's no stretch to imagine a Hollywood remake with Richard Gere, Julia Roberts and maybe Giovanni Ribisi as the idiot brother. True, they'd probably end up domesticating Rud (but then so does director Kragh-Jacobsen), cure the careerist Kresten of his misguided social pretensions (so does Kragh-Jacobsen), and neuter Livia's sexual threat (guess what?). Okay, so it's sailing under false colours and trying to have it both ways, but it is perfectly watchable schmaltz with just a soupçon of edge, right? Right! And camera noise! TCh

Mighty, The

(1998, US, 100 min)
d Peter Chelsom. *p* Jane Startz, Simon Fields. *sc* Charles Leavitt. *ph* John de Borman. *ed* Martin Walsh. *pd* Caroline Hanania. *m* Trevor Jones. *cast* Sharon Stone, Gena Rowlands, Harry Dean Stanton, Gillian Anderson, Kieran Culkin, Elden Henson, Meat Loaf.

● Cincinnati: Maxwell (Henson) has a hard time at school because he's huge for his age and his dad's in jail for murder. Kevin (Culkin) has it even worse, since a degenerative disease has left him hunchbacked and on crutches. Inspired by Kevin's love of Arthurian legend, they venture forth with Maxwell carrying his new chum around on his shoulders. Sounds heartwarming, yet the combination of not one but two children triumphing over harsh news from the doctors seems like a terribly calculated assault on our emotions. Chelsom struggles to make it quirky, but the mush factor remains. Good work from the two boys, though (especially Culkin jr), classy support from Rowlands and Stone as grandma and mom respectively. From the novel *Freak the Mighty* by Rodman Philbrick. TJ

Mighty Aphrodite

(1995, US, 95 min)
d Woody Allen. *p* Roger Greenhut. *sc* Woody Allen. *ph* Carlo Di Palma. *ed* Susan E Morse. *pd* Santo Loquasto. *cast* Woody Allen, Mira Sorvino, Helena Bonham Carter, Peter Weller, F Murray Abraham, Olympia Dukakis, Jeffrey Kurland, J Smith Cameron, Steven Randazzo, Claire Bloom, Michael Rapaport.

● Three years after sports writer Lenny (Allen) allowed his art dealer wife Amanda (Bonham Carter) to persuade him that they should adopt a child, a nagging curiosity about where young Max's brains came from leads Lenny to seek out the boy's natural mother, hooker Linda Ash (Sorvino), marginally better known as actress 'Judy Cum'. Horrified by, but sympathetic to Linda's plight, Lenny tries to better her life, pursuing his mission with such zeal that he barely notices when Amanda, encouraged by smooth Jerry Bender (Weller), starts to drift away from him. Lenny's another of Allen's nervy, intellectual, middle-class heroes, and most of the gags centre on the clash of social and cultural aspirations arising from his encounter with the dumb-blonde tart-with-a-heart. A make-weight Greek chorus is thrown in to comment on Lenny's hubristic do-gooding. Sorvino does her able best to transform her caricature into someone to care about; Bonham Carter copes respectably with a relatively minor role; and Rapaport contributes a fair turn as an unbelievably stupid boxer. But Allen's familiar device of juxtaposing sentiments and language, the lofty and the banal (one moment the Olympians, the next the nebbish protagonist), rapidly palls. GA

Mighty Barnum, The

(1934, US, 87 min, b/w)
d Walter Lang. *p* Darryl F Zanuck. *sc* Gene Fowler, Bess Meredith. *ph* Peverell Marley. *ed* Alan McNeil. *ad* Richard Day. *m* Alfred Newman. *cast* Wallace Beery, Adolphe Menjou, Virginia Bruce, Rochelle Hudson, Janet Beecher, Herman Bing.

● Wallace Beery, remembered for his disruptive scene-stealing in perennials *Dinner at Eight* and *Grand Hotel*, here plays showman PT Barnum in the period before his name was linked with that of Bailey. True to '30s biopic form, key moments and characters in Barnum's life are stitched together with improbable and entirely fictional romanticism, tracing his route from small-town con artist to international circus celebrity. DO

Mighty Ducks, The (aka Champions)

(1992, US, 103 min)
d Stephen Herek. *p* Jordan Kerner, Jon Avnet. *sc* Steven Brill. *ph* Thomas Del Ruth. *ed* Larry Bock, John F Link. *pd* Randy Ser. *m* David Newman. *cast* Emilio Estevez, Joss Ackland, Lane Smith, Heidi Kling, Josef Sommer, Joshua Jackson, Elden Ratliff.

● Very lame ice-hockey flick. Estevez is arrogant hot-shot lawyer Gordon Bombay, condemned to community service for drink-driving. He reckons he can go one-on-one with his troubled past and get back at his boss by coaching a team of little league no-hopers (cast from a cupboard marked 'brats, assorted'). Ackland lingers embarrassingly as a kindly sports-store owner. TJ

Mighty Joe Young

(1949, US, 94 min, b/w)
d Ernest B Schoedsack. *p* John Ford, Merian C Cooper. *sc* Ruth Rose. *ph* Roy Hunt. *ed* Ted Cheesman. *ad* James Basevi. *m* Roy Webb. *cast* Terry Moore, Ben Johnson, Robert Armstrong, Frank McHugh, Douglas Fowley, Paul Guilfoyle.

● King Kong for kids, with the great ape shorn of myth, tamely housebroken, and even required to be the hero of an orphanage fire. But he does have an engagingly dotty showbiz act, holding up a platform on which Terry Moore sits strumming 'Beautiful Dreamer' at a grand piano. The whole 'Golden Safari' nightclub show is rather a splendid piece of kitsch, complete with voodoo dancers, ten circus strongmen in leopard-skins pitted against Joe in a tug-of-war, and a spiritedly destructive rampage when three drunken revellers go backstage to ply the already resentful ape with a bottle. For all the sneers cast at the film, it's in fact surprisingly well crafted (Willis O'Brien, technical creator), with position of tongue in cheek perfectly judged. TM

Mighty Joe Young (aka Mighty Joe)

(1998, US, 114 min)
d Ron Underwood. *p* Ted Hartley, Tom Jacobson. *sc* Mark Rosenthal, Lawrence Konner. *ph* Don Peterman, Oliver Wood. *ed* Paul Hirsch. *pd* Michael Corenblith. *m* James Horner. *cast* Bill Paxton, Charlize Theron, Peter Firth, Rade Serbedzija, Regina King, Naveen Andrews, David Paymer.

● This Disney eco-flick about a huge gorilla may be as predictable as rain in a rainforest, but it's an enjoyable caper none the less. Mighty Joe is a freak of nature who lives in the fastness of Central Africa watched over by jungle girl Jill (Theron). Having both lost their mothers to poachers – during the film's only truly harrowing scene – the pair have become inseparable. Along stumbles zoologist Gregg (Paxton) who comes within inches of extinction following a surprise encounter with the fearsome but ultimately kind-hearted beast. Word spreads of Gregg's discovery, and before long the poachers are back. Jill and Gregg ship Joe to the deceptive safety of a Californian animal reserve and, eventually, to a cliff-hanging climax. Despite its longueurs, this is a welcome revamp of a genre that includes *King Kong*, *ET* and virtually every movie that pits misplaced creatures against evil humans. Most impressive, though, are the special effects. DA

Mighty Morphin Power Rangers: The Movie

(1995, US, 95 min)
d Bryan Spicer. *p* Haim Saban, Shuki Levy, Suzanne Todd. *sc* John Kamps, Arne Olsen. *ph* Paul Murphy. *ed* Wayne Wahrman. *pd* Craig Stearns. *m* Graeme Revell. *cast* Paul Freeman, Nicholas Bell, David Yost, Amy Jo Johnson, Jason David Frank, Karan Ashley, Johnny Yong Bosch, Steve Cardenas.

● The story goes thus: Angel Grove, California, is menaced by Ivan Ooze (Freeman), an ugly mug with a propensity for creating buckets of purple slime. Can the six all-American teenage superheroes overcome their new rubbery adversary? The TV series from which this is derived is notorious for its indifferent B-movie sfx; matters are improved here with some notably effective computer-generated graphics. The comic-book fight sequences, too, are a little more imaginative. But, like the series, the film is also corny as hell, with glaring continuity lapses, cringeworthy performances, silly monsters and laughable set-pieces. (Why, for instance, do the Rangers always perform somersaults diagonally across the screen whenever they yell, 'Okay, it's morphin' time'?) Kids will love it. DA

Mighty Mouse in the Great Space Chase

(1983, US, 87 min)
d Ed Friedman, Lou Kachivas, Marsh Lamore, Gwen Wetzler, Kay Wright, Lou Zukor. *p* Lou Scheimer, Norm Prescott, Don Christensen. *ph* RW Pope. *ed* James Blodgett, Ann Hagerman, Earl Biddle. *ad* Albert De Mello, James Fletcher. *m* Yvette Blaise, Jeff Michael. *cast* voices: Allen Oppenheimer, Diane Pershing.

● Mighty Mouse, the Patrick Swayze of Cartoonland, must save the cosmos from the schemes of a cat who was destined to be evil: his parents named him Harry the Heartless. Meanwhile, in a parallel universe, heartless Viacom schemed to milk a few extra dollars by crudely stitching together a bunch of TV episodes into a feature film of sorts. MM himself is not badly designed, but he showed poor taste in the company he kept. After saving the universe his career was downhill all the way. DO

Mighty Quinn, The

(1989, US, 98 min)
d Carl Schenkel. *p* Sandy Liberson, Marion Hunt, Ed Elbert. *sc* Hampton Fancher. *ph* Jacques Steyn. *ed* John Jympson. *pd* Roger Murray-Leach. *m* Anne Dudley. *cast* Denzel Washington, James Fox, Mimi Rogers, M Emmet Walsh, Sheryl Lee Ralph, Art Evans, Esther Rolle, Norman Beaton, Robert Townsend, Keye Luke.

● When a rich American is murdered on a Caribbean isle, the white community pins the blame on local ne'er-do-well Maubee (Townsend). They reckon without the new Chief of Police Xavier Quinn (Washington), crusader for Justice and Truth. The focus is firmly on the black cast: Townsend's deadpan patois, Washington playing the white man in a world gone sour, plus a posse of gutsy, gorgeous black gals. Which leaves a couple of stars with little to do: James 'Ice ay, get ite of hyar' Fox, and Rogers, who eschews acting and merely opens her eyes very wide to express intense sensuality. As if the plot weren't perfunctory enough (bags of Yankee dollars, corruption in high places, CIA asassins), we take extended breaks from it to contemplate Quinn's gradual recovery of his roots, culminating in the grateful islanders serenading him with a reggae version of the title song. SFe

Mignon Has Left (Mignon è partita)

(1988, It/Fr, 90 min)
d Francesca Archibugi. *p* Leo Pescarolo, Guido De Laurentiis. *sc* Francesca Archibugi, Gloria Malatesta, Claudia Sbarigia. *ph* Luigi Verga. *ed* Alfredo Muschietti. *ad* Massimo Spano. *m* Roberto Gatto, Battista Lena, Rita Marcotulli. *cast* Stefania Sandrelli, Jean-Pierre Duriez, Leonardo Ruta, Céline Beauvallet, Francesca Antonelli, Lorenzo De Pasqua.

● The posh Parisian life of 14-year-old Mignon (Beauvallet) is disrupted when her father is jailed and she is dispatched to Italy to visit relatives. Chaos reigns in the Forbicioni family: Dad is having an affair, Mum is pursued by her brother-in-law, and the five children are suffering growing pains. Particularly afflicted, Giorgio (Ruta) becomes infatuated with his snooty French cousin, neglects his schoolwork, and makes a botched suicide attempt. While the conflicts in Francesca Archibugi's first feature tend to soap opera (unrequited love, rebellion, teen pregnancy, terminal illness), there are compensations in the casual, affectionate portrayal of family life. More satisfying are the enfolding adult dramas, which receive less emphasis yet capture the sort of impulsiveness that eludes the depiction of teen angst. This has a great deal to do with Stefania Sandrelli's sensitive performance as the mother. CM

Mikado, The

(1939, GB, 91 min)
d Victor Schertzinger. *p* Geoffrey Toye, Joseph Somlo. *sc* Geoffrey Toye. *ph* Bernard Knowles, William Skall. *ed* Phili[Charlot, Gene Milford. *ad* Ralph Brinton. *cast* Kenny Baker, Jean Colin, Martyn Green, Constance Willis, Sydney Granville, John Barclay.

● England's answer to *The Wizard of Oz* proved to be another costly mistake for the man with the gong. Why shrewd businessmen CM Woolf and J Arthur Rank expected America to welcome this very English operetta is one of the unsolved mysteries of Wardour Street. Of course it's good, but casting an American crooner (the engaging and very pretty Baker) as Nanki-Poo hardly mitigates Gilbert & Sullivan's impenetrable insularity. For those with vague memories of 'Three Little Maids from School Are We' echoing through their childhood, however, this is a real treat. Enchantingly subtle Technicolor and the splendid ensemble playing of the D'Oyly Carte company make it a strangely evocative experience. RMy

Mikaël

see Michael

Mike Bassett England Manager

(2001, GB/US, 89 min)
d Steve Barron. *p* Neil Peplow, Steve Barron. *sc* Rob Spracking, JRN Smith. *ph* Mike Eley. *ed* Colin Green. *pd* John Reid. *m* Antony Genn. *cast* Ricky Tomlinson, Amanda Redman, Philip Jackson, Bradley Walsh, Phill Jupitus, Ulrich Thomsen, Pele, Terry Kiely, Dean Holness.

● To the modern game of English football, Mike Bassett ought to be an irrelevance, a lower league journeyman player turned lower league journeyman manager currently working fairly minor miracles at Norwich. So when Lancaster Gate's wise guys prevail upon Bassett to salvage the England team's fortunes – well, could you suspend disbelief? This mock doc sets up its hero as part Graham Taylor, part *Private Eye*'s Ron Knee, but for your average young Michael Owen fan it must look like a vérité-style *Walking with Dinosaurs*. This isn't really a football movie. Sure, it follows Bassett and his squad through thick and thicker, scraping into the Brazil World Cup Finals despite themselves. This one's about English self-image, going out to that inferiority complex that cherishes gallant failure. The film rollicks in the spirit of bulldogs and turnips, Dunkirk and Arthur Daley, while whizzing through the rare England victory with barely a glimpse of actual play. Perhaps fittingly, the film itself embodies this notion of the second-rate. In the spirit of Kevin Keegan, the film-making is enthused, artless and all over the park. NB

Mike's Murder

(1984, US, 97 min)
d/sc James Bridges. *ph* Reynaldo Villalobos. *ed* Jeff Gourson, Dede Allen. *pd* Peter Jamison. *m* John Barry, Joe Jackson. *cast* Debra Winger, Mark Keyloun, Darrell Larson, Paul Winfield, Brooke Alderson, William Ostrander, Robert Crosson, Daniel Shor.

● Shy bank worker Winger (*Winger* – shy?) is drawn out of her shell by a new romance, and, when the man of her dreams is brutally murdered, she turns 'tec to track down the culprits – uncovering some unpalatable home truths in the process. Two years in the editing, the makers' struggle to get the thing to make sense certainly shows. The dusty Joe Jackson soundtrack album is sometimes found in second-hand record stores. TJ

Mikey and Nicky

(1976, US, 106 min)
d Elaine May. *p* Michael Hausman. *sc* Elaine May. *ph* Victor J Kemper. *ed* John Carter. *pd* Paul Sylbert. *m* John Strauss. *cast* Peter Falk, John Cassavetes, Ned Beatty, Rose Arrick, Carol Grace, William Hickey, Sanford Meisner, Joyce Van Patten, M Emmet Walsh.

● Nicky (Cassavetes), cooped up in a dingy hotel room, dreading lethal reprisals from a mobster he's betrayed, calls upon Mikey (Falk) for help. But as they search the city's backstreets for sanctuary, it becomes clear that his buddy is less saviour than Judas (and that the sacrificial victim is no saint either). May's script simply observes the way old wounds are reopened as the pair reminisce about their past friendship, while allowing her actors ample space to emote with adolescent exuberance and paranoia. The *vérité* style, complete with itchy focus finger and rambling narrative, often seems less assured than in Cassavetes' own films. But with an imaginative use of locations, carefully controlled atmosphere, and superb performances all round, it's an often impressive, always watchable modern *noir* thriller, based on credible human motivations. GA

Mike Yokohama – A Forest with No Name (Hama Mike – Namae no nai Mori)

(2002, Jap, 71 min)
d Shinji Aoyama. *p* Hiroyuki Fujikado, Yoshinori Horiguchi, Yasuhisa Masuda, Takenori Sento, Shunsuke Koga, Akira Okano, Ayumi Hayashi. *sc* Shinji Aoyama. *ph* Masaki Tamura. *ed* Yuji Oshige. *ad* Takeshi Shimizu. *m* Dowser. *cast* Masatoshi Nagase, Kyoka Suzuki, Nene Otsuka, Yoshio Harada, Masashi Yamamoto.

● A misbegotten start for the project to revive Nagase's 'Mike Hama' character (introduced in a '90s trilogy by Kaizo Hayashi, here credited only with the story idea) in six made-for-video features, each by a different director. Mike is hired by an anxious father (Harada) to retrieve his daughter from a cult run by a woman doctor (Suzuki); Mike infiltrates by posing as a new recruit and discovers that adherents are turned into murderous and/or suicidal time-bombs by a secret buried deep in the forest adjacent to the cult's rural HQ. Aoyama directs this feeble variation on *Invasion of the Body Snatchers* with his usual half-assed pretensions, delivering neither a viable thriller nor a credible allegory of Japan's youth-identity problems. The only surprise is that the film's translators have renamed the hero 'Mike Yokohama' – presumably fearing legal action from the Mickey Spillane estate. TR

Milagro Beanfield War, The

(1987, US, 118 min)
d Robert Redford. *p* Robert Redford, Moctesuma Esparza. *sc* David S Ward, John Nichols. *ph* Robbie Greenberg. *ed* Dede Allen, Jim Miller. *ad* Joe Aubel. *m* David Grusin. *cast* Ruben Blades, Richard Bradford, Sonia Braga,

Melanie Griffith, John Heard, Carlos Riquelme, Daniel Stern, Chick Vennera, Christopher Walken, Jerry Hardin, M Emmet Walsh.
●A New Mexican handyman (Vennera), by a mix of magical intervention and carelessness, kicks down the sluice gate of a privatised water supply, which converts his parched ancestral patch into a potentially fertile field of beans. But a developer (Bradford) in cahoots with all the men-with-no-smiles from State Governor (Walsh) down, wants the water for a planned leisure valley. Battle is enjoined. Which cues stormy domestic quarrels, riotous community meetings, the re-illusionment of a hack (Heard), a chance for the local conscience (Braga) to look vital in jeans and crisp white blouse, and for the sheriff (Blades) to display his lopsided grin. A tragic accident threatens the happy ending, but hang on in. Ostensibly a celebration of the triumph of community over exploitation and injustice, Redford's film sustains a slow mood of simpatico amiability and photographs the landscape with moony or golden washes that are perhaps hard to dislike, but is slain by its adherence to an outdated populist mythology. WH

Milagro de P Tinto, El
see P Tinto's Miracle

Mildred Pierce
(1945, US, 113 min, b/w)
d Michael Curtiz. *p* Jerry Wald. *sc* Ranald MacDougall. *ph* Ernest Haller. *ed* David Weisbart. *ad* Anton Grot. *m* Max Steiner. *cast* Joan Crawford, Jack Carson, Zachary Scott, Eve Arden, Ann Blyth, Bruce Bennett, George Tobias, Veda Ann Borg.
●James Cain's novel of the treacherous life in (Crawford) against her own daughter (Blyth) in competition for the love of playboy Zachary Scott, is brought fastidiously and bleakly to life by Curtiz' direction, Ernest Haller's camerawork, and Anton Grot's magnificent sets. Told in flashback from the moment of Scott's murder, the film is a chilling demonstration of the fact that, in a patriarchal society, when a woman steps outside the home the end result may be disastrous. PH

Miles from Home
(1988, US, 108 min)
d Gary Sinise. *p* Frederick Zollo, Paul Kurta. *sc* Chris Gerolmo, Elliot Davis. *ph* Elliot Davis. *ed* Jane Schwartz Jaffe. *pd* David Gropman. *m* Robert Folk. *cast* Richard Gere, Kevin Anderson, Brian Dennehy, Penelope Ann Miller, Helen Hunt, John Malkovich.
●Sinise's opening sequence of Khrushchev paying an official visit to Iowa's most productive farm, shaking hands with the proud owner (Dennehy), and rumpling his small sons' hair, is so singular and promising that the film never really recovers from it. It settles for being the story of the two sons disillusionment as they are disinherited by the march of financial speculation, and forced into rebellion. In many ways, it's a late straggler in the brief farm genre, but the presence of Gere as the older brother, Frank, unbalances any attempt at airing agricultural grievances. Promp to resort to the gun, a hell-raising outlaw in a black hat, Frank is the stuff of Hollywood, and his relationship with his idolising brother, sensitive, circumspect Terry (Anderson), is practically a screen syndrome. The final shot of Frank's hat lying on a country road being taken up by another kid gives some idea of the deterioration that has taken place. BC

Milestones
(1975, US, 206 min)
d Robert Kramer, John Douglas. *p* Barbara Stone, David C Stone. *sc* Robert Kramer, John Douglas. *ph* John Douglas, Robert Kramer, Barbara Stone. *ed* Robert Kramer, John Douglas. *m* Bobby Buechler. *cast* Grace Paley, Mary Chapelle, Sharon Krebs, Jim Nolfi, Susie Solf, Joe Stork, Pacil Zimet, John Douglas, David C Stone.
●Shot as 'fictional' documentary, *Milestones* amounts to a three-and-a-half hour testament to a generation. Despite the *cinéma-vérité* style, the scope of the project is epic: the interconnecting lives and lifestyles of various young people scattered across America as a generation of white activists or dropouts ponder 'where they're at'. *Milestones* is almost entirely about people talking. Sometimes this compulsion to talk everything through – and an obsessive need for reassurance – amounts to moving in circles, not forward; what optimism there is seems almost wilfully naive and painfully fragile. The film refrains from judging its characters, which is why some may find it boring. But, as with Kramer's *Ice*, it's a film that will doubtless gain with age: posterity is left to decide whether the generation on view found a new future or lost its way. CPe

Milieu du Monde, Le
see Middle of the World, The

Militia Battlefield
(1975, GB, 61 min)
d Jana Bokova.
●This unusual documentary scores in two ways. One, it reveals a genuinely bizarre subculture of gay clubs and expatriate entertainers in London. Two, it builds its endearingly rambling philosophy into its own structure, so its focus remains suitably diffuse. A very promising debut. TR

Milk
(1999, GB, 96 min)
d William Brookfield. *p* George Duffield, Meg Thomson, Galt Niederhoff. *sc* William Brookfield. *ph* Peter Hannan. *ed* Peter Hollywood. *pd* Laurence Dorman. *m* Jools Holland. *cast* Joss Ackland, Francesca Annis, Clotilde Courau, James Fleet, Dawn French, Richard Johnson, Peter Jones, Phyllida Law, Lesley Manville, Judith Scott.
●An upmarket cast delivers mostly classy goods in this very English, dodgily conceived package. A middle-aged small farmer's apparent delight on the death of his racy old mum promises a black comedy which fails to materialise. Given the level of humour – dildo gags and an (admittedly) memorable accident with superglue – that's no great loss, as the film makes its serious points best. Poignancy is compromised, though, by the ludicrously dated conceit of the arty French sexpot turning up on the doorstep, and a mawkish ending. XS

Milk Money
(1994, US, 109 min)
d Richard Benjamin. *p* Kathleen Kennedy, Frank Marshall. *sc* John Mattson. *ph* David Watkin. *ed* Jacqueline Cambas. *pd* Paul Sylbert. *m* Michael Convertino. *cast* Melanie Griffith, Ed Harris, Michael Patrick Carter, Malcolm McDowell, Anne Heche, Casey Siemaszko, Philip Bosco.
●Melanie Griffith is V, a big-city tart with a heart, who's discovered by a group of schoolboys who've cycled in from the suburbs with the intention of paying a woman to take her clothes off. Motherless 12-year-old Frank (Carter) decides that V could be matched with his father, an absent-minded professor (Harris), and the girl finds herself strutting through the lawned suburbs of fictitious Middleton. Here no house has less than five bedrooms, and everyone says hello in the street. 'It looks like TV,' she observes. This feelgood romantic comedy is short on laughs, sexual chemistry, and the thriller subplot won't produce any white knuckles (McDowell is a pimp intent on tracking down his working girl). Like *Pretty Woman*, the major excitement comes from the wardrobe department. What'll V look like when gets out of that tacky brazen outfit? Answer: Jane Asher in a floral frock. JBa

Milk of Human Kindness, The (Le Lait de la tendresse humaine)
(2001, Fr/Bel, 93 min)
d Dominique Cabréra. *p* Philippe Martin. *sc* Dominique Cabréra, Cécile Vargaftig. *ph* Hélène Louvard. *ed* Francine Sandberg. *m* Béatrice Thiriet. *cast* Patrick Bruel, Maryline Canto, Dominique Blanc, Sergi López, Valéria Bruni-Tedeschi, Olivier Gourmet, Claude Brasseur.
●If the film as a whole never quite lives up to the promise of the opening few minutes, this is nevertheless an engrossing, perceptive study of a woman who suddenly cracks and mysteriously leaves home and baby; her husband has no idea where she's gone, and the people who take her in have no idea what's wrong with her. Director and co-writer Cabréra traces the effects of her actions on a variety of people with wit, subtlety and assurance, while her superb cast does the intelligent, credible script ample justice. GA

Milky Way, The
see Voie Lactée, La

Millennium
(1989, US, 105 min)
d Michael Anderson. *p* Douglas Leiterman. *sc* John Varley. *ph* René Ohashi. *ed* Ron Wisman. *pd* Gene Rudolf. *m* Eric N Robertson. *cast* Kris Kristofferson, Cheryl Ladd, Daniel J Travanti, Robert Joy, Lloyd Bochner, Brent Carver, David McIlwraith, Maury Chaykin, Albert S Waxman.
●Sci-fi writer John Varley adapted his own short story *Air Raid* for this screenwriting debut, but an intriguing concept ends up with all the credibility of speculation that the moon is made of green cheese. Plane crash expert Bill Smith (Kristofferson) is called in to investigate the mid-air collision of a 747 and a DC-10. But this is no ordinary catastrophe: watches found in the wreckage run backwards, and a futuristic stun-gun is unearthed. Bill soon meets Louise (Ladd), who heads a commando team from a thousand years in the future. These time travellers have urgent business in the 20th century, which helps sustain life among a dying race of humanoids subsisting on infusions of fluorocarbons. The film never really overcomes obvious budgetary constraints, with important moments drained of impact because the effects lack imagination. Kristofferson and Travanti (as a physicist) are effectively true to form, but Ladd is woefully inadequate. CM

Millennium Mambo (Qianxi Manbo)
(2001, Tai/Fr, 120 min)
d Hou Hsiao-Hsien [Hou Xiaoxian]. *p* Hou Xiaoxian, Eric Heumann. *sc* Chu Tien-Wen. *ph* Mark Lee [Li Pingbin]. *ed* Liao Qingsong. *pd* Hwarng Wern-Ying. *m* Lim Giong, Fish, Yoshihiro Hanno. *cast* Shu Qi, Jack Kao, Duan Chunhao, Jun Takeuchi, Ko Takeuchi.
●Vicky (Shu) came to Taipei as a teenager and lurched into an affair with the ultra-possessive Hao-Hao (Duan), who lived for DJ-ing but thought it would be uncool to play records for a living. She decided she'd leave him when her savings ran out but in the meantime gravitated into the orbit (not the bed) of small-time gangster Jack (Kao), who treated her like a best friend. But when she finally moved into Jack's place, he had a sudden money crisis and disappeared somewhere in Japan. This differs from Hou's earlier accounts of women around male riff-raff (*Daughter of the Nile*, the present-day parts of *Good Men, Good Women*) in two striking ways. First, it looks back at the present from a point ten years in the future, rendering it strange and distant. Second, Vicky is seen not as a marginalised onlooker but as a young woman coming into bloom, learning by experience how to build her own identity. The film is a virtual portrait of Shu Qi, in much the way that Godard once made films as pretexts for capturing the moods of Anna Karina. Extremely beautiful, as hypnotic as its trance-techno soundtrack, and (like *Flowers of Shanghai*) very, very druggy. TR

Miller's Crossing
(1990, US, 115 min)
d Joel Coen. *p* Ethan Cohen. *sc* Joel Cohen Ethan Cohen. *ph* Barry Sonnenfeld. *ed* Michael Miller. *pd* Dennis Gassner. *m* Carter Burwell. *cast* Gabriel Byrne, Albert Finney, Marcia Gay Harden, John Turturro, Jon Polito, JE Freeman, Mike Starr, Al Mancini, Richard Woods, Steve Buscemi.
●Like *Blood Simple* and *Raising Arizona*, this works both as a crime thriller and as an ironic commentary on that genre. With fast, sharp, witty dialogue and Byzantine plotting, it charts the gang war between Leo (Finney) and Caspar (Polito) in an American city during Prohibition. Tom (Byrne), Leo's loyal right-hand man, is the lover of Leo's mistress (Harden), whose brother (Turturro) Caspar wants killed. Exactly how this and other complications are sorted out forms the hugely inventive, enjoyable narrative core of the film. But it is also a tribute to the crime literature (notably Hammett) and movies of the '30s, artfully poised between 'realism' and a subtle acknowledgment of its own artifice. And there's yet another level, since it is composed – visually, verbally and structurally – as a series of

variations on the themes of 'Friendship, character, ethics'. At times the criss-crossing of abstract motifs recalls the formal complexity of a Greenaway film. It's arguably the US mainstream's first art movie since *Days of Heaven*; and quite wonderful. GA

Millhouse, a White Comedy

(1971, US, 92 min, b/w)
d/p/sc Emile de Antonio. *ph* Ed Emshwiller, Mike Gray, Bruce Shah, Richard Kletter. *ed* Mary Lampson. *m* Bridge.

● *Millhouse* follows the form of Antonio's earlier films in that it is almost entirely composed of carefully selected newsreel material that is allowed to speak for itself. Only the context in which the extracts are presented, and the occasional use of music to satirise a sequence, indicate Antonio's actual manipulation of his material. *Millhouse* is entirely concerned with Nixon's political career, backing up the early material with interviews with some of his opponents at the time. Most of the speeches he made then were terrifying in their implications, not merely for the content itself but for the cold-blooded way in which Nixon can be seen to support only those policies he reckons most popular (the death penalty for dope peddling, nuclear war as preferable to an American defeat in South East Asia, etc). It's certainly a funny film (commie-baiting Nixon 'discovering' microfilm in a bed of pumpkins), but the strength with which it reveals the full horror of Nixon's personality is devastating. JDuC

Million, Le

(1931, Fr, 89 min, b/w)
d René Clair. *p* Frank Clifford. *sc* René Clair. *ph* Georges Périnal. *ed* René Le Hénaff. *ad* Lazare Meerson. *m* Georges Van Parys, Armand Bernard, Philippe Parès. *lyrics* René Clair. *cast* René Lefèvre, Annabella, Louis Allibert, Vanda Gréville, Paul Ollivier, Odette Talazac, Raymond Cordy.

● Classic early René Clair, this is the one about a hunt for a lost lottery ticket which ends in a football scrimmage on an opera stage, foresh adowing *A Night at the Opera*. It features asynchronous sound and other experimental devices of the time. Luckily it's lively enough to survive the worst textbook bromides: the playing, the delightful music, and the dialogue (half-sung, half-spoken) all mesh together in a way no one but Clair ever quite matched. GB

Millionairess, The

(1960, GB, 90 min)
d Anthony Asquith. *p* Pierre Rouve. *sc* Wolf Mankowitz. *ph* Jack Hildyard. *ed* Anthony Harvey. *pd* Paul Sheriff. *m* Georges Van Parys. *cast* Sophia Loren, Peter Sellers, Alastair Sim, Dennis Price, Vittorio De Sica, Gary Raymond, Alfie Bass, Miriam Karlin.

● Absurd casting of Loren at the hands of husband Carlo Ponti and indifferent scripting by Wolf Mankowitz were poor beginnings for this turgid adaptation of Shaw's play. Millionairess in search of husband lights on poor humanitarian Indian doctor played by Sellers. The Shavian wit is dissipated somewhere between the glamorisation of Loren and the 'funny' Indian accent of Sellers which serves as mouthpiece for the familiar socialist message-mongering. RM

Million Dollar Hotel, The

(1999, Ger/US, 122 min)
d Wim Wenders. *p* Deepak Nayar, Bono, Nicholas Klein, Bruce Davey, Wim Wenders. *sc* Nicholas Klein. *ph* Phedon Papamichael. *ed* Tatiana S Riegel. *pd* Robert D Freed, Arabella A Serrell. *m* Jon Hassell, Bono, Daniel Lanois, Brian Edno. *cast* Milla Jovovich, Jeremy Davies, Mel Gibson, Jimmy Smits, Peter Stormare, Amanda Plummer, Gloria Stuart, Tom Bower, Donal Logue, Bud Cort, Julian Sands, Charlayne Woodard.

● *Buena Vista Social Club* profited from Ry Cooder's contacts book; this, however, stumbles at the first on a story originating with Wenders' other famous rock pal, Bono. It begins with a man leaping from the eponymous LA hostel. Why? To honour his friend Izzy, perhaps. Recalling his last days from beyond the grave, Tom Tom (Davies) expounds a tale in which his ex-pal's own skydive on to the same pavement stirs up a commotion among the denizens of this sanctuary for the down-and-out. What none of them knew was that Izzy was a slumming California golden boy, whose death attracts the attentions of the media and a hardnut FBI investigator called Skinner (Gibson in a neck-brace). Misjudgment abounds: the hotel jetsam are, one and all, rancorous 'wise fool' clichés; Gibson's obscure, obsessive stiffneck is alienating rather than intriguing; the plot goes nowhere, convolutedly; and the soundtrack's limp. One or two scenes evince the sort of cinematic dexterity Wenders might have exploited were he not set on floundering about with this witless material. NB

Million Pound Note, The (aka Man With a Million)

(1953, GB, 91 min)
d Ronald Neame. *p* John Bryan. *sc* Jill Craigie. *ph* Geoffrey Unsworth. *ed* Clive Donner. *ad* John Maxted, John Box. *m* William Alwyn. *cast* Gregory Peck, Jane Griffiths, Ronald Squire, Wilfrid Hyde-White, Joyce Grenfell, AE Matthews, Maurice Denham.

● An adaptation of Mark Twain's yarn about two wealthy brothers who pick on a penniless seaman to settle their bet as to whether someone could live on a million without spending anything. Scripted by Jill Craigie (Mrs Michael Foot), it emerges as a bland Technicolor sitcom that overstretches the short story ironies of everything coming to he who has. Squire and Hyde-White are the brothers, Peck the holder of the paper-money fortune who (initially) can't spend it for trying. PT

Millions Like Us

(1943, GB, 103 min, b/w)
d Frank Launder, Sidney Gilliat. *p* Edward Black. *sc* Frank Launder, Sidney Gilliat. *ph* Jack Cox, Roy Fogwell. *ed* RE Dearing, Alfred Roome. *m* Louis Levy. *ad* John Bryan. *cast* Eric Portman, Patricia Roc, Gordon Jackson, Anne Crawford, Joy Shelton, Basil Radford, Naunton Wayne, Valentine Dunn, Megs Jenkins.

● Launder and Gilliat's portrait of a family at war is remarkable not only for its breadth of social detail – Dad joins the Home Guard, Mum goes back to her old job as a telephonist, daughter joins the ATS, and son is sent overseas to fight – but also for its perceptive observation of the youngest daughter's experiences as a factory worker. Patricia Roc's life on the factory floor, and her relationships with the girls who share the dormitory accommodation, don't shy away – as many other films of the period did – from the class conflicts which still riddled wartime English society. The ending, too, with the working class foreman (Portman) rejecting the rich society girl (Crawford) who has fallen for him, and looking forward instead to a new kind of society (one with a Labour government), raises pertinent questions about what exactly is being fought for. Is it the restoration of the old order, or the foundation of a new one? Intelligent entertainment at its best. NF

1974, Une Partie de Campagne

(1974/2002, Fr, 90 min)
d Raymond Depardon. *p* Claudia Nougaret. *ph* Raymond Depardon. *ed* Bruno Zincone. *with* Valéry Giscard d'Estaing, Valérie-Anne Giscard d'Estaing, François Mitterrand, Michel Poniatowski, Charles Aznavour.

● Commissioned by the independent Gaullist Valéry Giscard d'Estaing as a record of his 1974 bid for the French presidency, Depardon's slice of *cinéma vérité* was immediately suppressed by the narrowly victorious Giscard, who deemed it 'irreverent'. Twenty-eight years later, he at last consented to the release of this perfectly innocuous document. Most of the footage consists of Giscard stepping out of cars and planes and delivering a few platitudes before speeding off again, or discussing tactics en route to another interview, another press conference. Depardon reckons it's all about 'power, solitude and the political process'. He might have added, without sarcasm, that it's also about monotony, *A Hard Day's Night* without the songs and jokes. Giscard personally comes across as quite sympathetic: driving his own car, teeth defiantly uncapped, his manner pitched artfully between the diffident and the remote. BBa

Milou en mai (May Fools/Milou in May)

(1989, Fr/It, 108 min)
d Louis Malle. *sc* Louis Malle, Jean-Claude Carrière. *ph* Renato Berta. *ed* Emmanuelle Castro. *ad* Willy Holt. *m* Stéphane Grappelli. *cast* Michel Piccoli, Miou-Miou, Michel Duchaussoy, Dominique Blanc, Harriet Walter, Bruno Carette, François Berléand, Martine Gautier, Paulette Dubost.

● Although this gentle country-house comedy is farcical in structure (with the various members of the Vieuzac family lapsing into indiscretion and conflict as they strive to sort out the estate after the death of the mother of Piccoli's sexagenarian aristocrat), genuine black humour is held at bay by Malle's refusal simply to condemn his characters' wealth, blinkered conservatism or selfishness. His huge, unsentimental affection for both bucolic milieu and characters is perhaps surprising given that the time is May 1968. Stranded by strikes and unable to hold a proper funeral for the corpse, the clan philander, fall out, and finally flee for the hills in absurd fear of Commie atrocities. It's less political satire, though, than a partly nostalgic evocation of an era; *La Règle du Jeu* and *Weekend* may be ancestors, but the tone is more akin to Goretta or Truffaut. The script (by Malle and Jean-Claude Carrière) never lives up to its promising premise, and the gags wear thin towards the end; but the performances and photography offer considerable pleasures, and the result has the same slight, poignant lyricism as its Stéphane Grappelli score. GA

Mimic

(1997, US, 106 min)
d Guillermo Del Toro. *p* Bob Weinstein, BJ Rack, Ole Bornedal. *sc* Matthew Robbins, Guillermo Del Toro. *ph* Dan Laustsen. *ed* Patrick Lussier, Peter Devaney Flanagan. *pd* Carol Spier. *m* Marco Beltrami. *cast* Mira Sorvino, Jeremy Northam, Alexander Goodwin, Giancarlo Giannini, Charles S Dutton, Josh Brolin, F Murray Abraham.

● The first US picture from the Mexican director of *Cronos* is a sci-fi thriller, fusing a dark, poetic allegory about the perils of genetic manipulation with grim, relentless, subterranean horror. Three years after scientists Sorvino and Northam save New York's children from a polio-like epidemic – by tampering with the DNA structure of the disease's main carrier, the ubiquitous cockroach – the results of their arrogant experiments come back to haunt them. Giant fast-evolving insects now lurk in the subway tunnels beneath the city, mimicking and preying upon their sometime predators, human beings. Uncompromising, subversive and occasionally perversely comic. NF

Minamata

(1971, Jap, 155 min, b/w)
d Noriaki Tsuchimoto. *p* Ryutaro Takagi. *sc* Noriaki Tsuchimoto. *ph* Koshiro Otsu.

● A documentary on the appalling tale of the Japanese village of Minamata, whose inhabitants were systematically poisoned by effluent from a nearby factory. It strips away the trendiness from the pollution issue, but makes it all too easy to localise the problem by concentrating on the victims of one primitive fishing village. What becomes plain is that the necessary area for investigation must be the firms and individuals who live off this degree of human agony, rather than primarily the victims.

Mina Tannenbaum

(1993, Fr, 128 min)
d Martine Dugowson. *p* Georges Benayoun. *sc* Martine Dugowson. *ph* Dominique Chapuis. *ed* Martine Barraqué, Dominique Gallieni. *ad* Philippe Chiffre. *m* Peter Chase. *cast* Romane Bohringer, Elsa Zylberstein, Florence Thomassin, Jean-Philippe Ecoffey, Nils Tavernier, Stéphane Slima, Hugues Quester.

● Cutting a swath through the personal histories of two young Jewish Parisians, aspiring painter Mina (Bohringer) and media wannabe Ethel (Zylberstein), this stylish, perceptive and wise film chronicles a friendship formed in childhood, strengthened by the romantic yearnings of adolescence, and tested by adulthood's inevitable parting of the ways. Reflective Mina is filled with anxiety, while Ethel can turn on the brash exterior – and though the mutual reliance forged in their teenage years has given these women shelter from their insecurities, it may not survive their common interest in the arrogant art dealer Dana (Ecoffey), whose own designs are cloaked beneath an abrasive exterior. Bohringer and Zylberstein work wonders, the chemistry of their relationship laying the foundation for the film's cumulative emotional impact. Its themes are the inescapable weight of the past, the damage unwittingly inflicted by the family's embrace; the betrayal involved when one dear friend who has been with you all your life is suddenly no longer there. TJ

Minbo Woman – Or the Gentle Art of Japanese Extortion (Minbo No Onna)

(1992, Jap, 125 min)
d Juzo Itami. *p* Seigo Hosogoe, Yasushi Tamaoki. *sc* Juzo Itami. *ph* Yonezo Maeda. *ed* Akira Suzuki. *pd* Shuji Nakamura. *m* Toshiyuki Honda. *cast* Nobuko Miyamoto, Akir Takarada, Takehiro Murata, Yasuo Daichi.

● After *Death Japanese Style*, *Tampopo* and *A Taxing Woman* had taken a freewheeling satiric approach to such established Japanese institutions as the family funeral, the quest for the perfect bowl of noodles, and the national tax agency,the internationally successful director Juzo Itami turned his attention to the country's yakuza in this courageous comic exposé. The film-maker's spouse Nobuko Miyamoto again features as a female lawyer who teams up with an anti-extortion expert to expel the gangster's influence from a luxury hotel business they threaten to overwhelm. Itami treats it all like the familiar genre story of the samurai coming to rescue the put-upon villagers, but his bravery was not without a price, for real-life yakuza stabbed the director near his home shortly after the film's release. TJ

Mind Games

see Agency

Mindwarp

(1990, US, 92 min)
d Steve Barnett. *p* Christopher Webster. *sc* Henry Dominic. *ph* Peter Fernberger. *ed* Adam Wolfe. *pd* Kim Hix. *m* Mark Governor. *cast* Bruce Campbell, Angus Scrimm, Marta Alicia, Elizabeth Kent, Mary Becker.

● A post-apocalyptic gore-fest funded by *Fangoria* magazine. Frustrated by the antiseptic underground environment of Inworld, with its narcotic, computer-induced fantasy images, Judy (Alicia) flees to the ravaged wasteland above. There, she teams up with post-apocalyptic Jeremiah Johnson figure Stover (Campbell), and together they confront The Seer (Scrimm), crazed leader of a religious cult based on salvaged scrap materials and human sacrifice. Eye-gouging, blood-spurting nastiness compensates for some ramshackle plotting. NF

Mine Own Executioner

(1947, GB, 108 min, b/w)
d Anthony Kimmins. *p* Anthony Kimmins, Jack Kitchin. *sc* Nigel Balchin. *ph* Wilkie Cooper. *ed* Richard Best. *ad* William C Andrews. *m* Benjamin Frankel. *cast* Burgess Meredith, Kieron Moore, Dulcie Gray, John Laurie, Christine Norden, Walter Fitzgerald, Michael Hordern.

● Two cases from the files of psycho-therapist Meredith. The first concerns a violently schizophrenic ex-PoW, the other relates to the shrink himself, and his compulsion to mistreat his wife. One case ends in provisional success, the other in utter disaster. Unlike most 1940s movies dealing with psychiatry, this refuses to be awe-struck by its subject or to put it to the service of melodrama. Kimmins, a middling, unexciting sort of director, at least had common sense, a virtue which this film exemplifies. He does allow himself one, quite successful, stylistic flourish, a subjectively shot flashback to the capture and torture of the PoW. Nigel Balchin scripted from his own novel. BBa

Miners' Film, The

(1975, GB, 45 min)
d/p/ph/ed Cinema Action.

● Cinema Action describe themselves as a non-profit-making collective of trade unionists dedicated to working class films. *The Miners' Film*, made around the 1974 strike, although necessarily partisan, avoids the distortions of so many seemingly 'honest' documentaries through its refusal to impose an overall viewpoint via a commentary. The miners are allowed to articulate for themselves the hardships of their recurring struggle and their strengthening solidarity. As a Welsh miner puts it: 'We're gradually understanding now that the greatest power, the most important people, are the people that produce. And I believe that 1974 was the turning point, when this power was realised for the first time.' CPe

Miniskirted Dynamo, The

(1996, Aust, 55 min)
d/p/sc Rivka Hartman. *ph* Jaems Grant. *ed* Julian Russell. *m* Nik Jeanes, Rachel Jeanes. *with* Dora Bialestock, Rivka Hartman.

● Rivka Hartman's highly personal portrait of her late mother, Dora, a leading pathologist-turned-pioneer in matters of child care and abuse, reveals a strong willed, self-motivated, immensely energetic Jewish woman whose warmth and generosity fell far short of reaching her daughter. Some of the family adored her, but they never stood up to her – for Rivka, who may end up as domineering as mom, it was an endless battle. Home movies, interviews with family and friends, and Hartman's reminiscences make for a surprisingly engrossing hour. GA

Ministry of Fear

(1944, US, 87 min, b/w)
d Fritz Lang. *p/sc* Seton Miller. *ph* Henry Sharp. *ed* Archie Marshek. *ad* Hans Dreier, Hal Pereira. *m* Victor Young. *cast* Ray Milland, Marjorie Reynolds, Carl Esmond, Hillary Brooke, Dan Duryea, Alan Napier, Percy Waram, Erskine Sanford.

● Forget the phony studio settings and the script's hesitancies in adapting Graham Greene's novel about a spy hunt in wartime London. This is a wonderfully atmospheric, almost expressionistic thriller, packed with memorable moments: the jolly village fête ominously taking place at night; the open door of the railway carriage and the muted tapping which heralds the arrival of the blind man out of a cloud of steam; the rat-like tailor using an enormous pair of cutting-shears to dial his call of warning moments before they are found plunged into his stomach. And right from the opening shot of Milland waiting alone in a darkened room for the stroke of midnight – the magic hour which will release him from one paranoiac nightmare (the mercy killing of his wife) into another – Lang sets his characteristic seal of fatality on the action. TM

Minnie and Moskowitz

(1971, US, 115 min)
d John Cassavetes. *p* Al Rubin. *sc* John Cassavetes. *ph* Arthur J Ornitz, Alric Edens, Michael D Margulies. *ed* Fred Knudtson. *m* Bob Harwood. *cast* Gena Rowlands, Seymour Cassel, Val Avery, Timothy Carey, Katherine Cassavetes, Elizabeth Deering, Lady Rowlands, Holly Near, John Cassavetes.

● An idiosyncratic romance, and a far lighter movie than is usual from Cassavetes. Detailing the problems that background and character bring to a relationship, he creates a captivatingly witty and sympathetic picture of a pair of misfits deciding to make a go of it together despite numerous incompatibilities and adversities. As always, it is the performances that dominate, with their sensitively-felt, naturalistic speech patterns and gestures; and for all its optimism, the film is still centred around a core of loneliness, while Cassavetes also contrasts the difficulties of real life with the idealised glamour purveyed by Hollywood (an attack on the system that could barely accommodate him?). The result is an understated and intimate view of two unexceptional people that is only sentimental when the characters themselves are sentimental. GA

Minotaur

(1993, US, 55 min)
d Dan McCormack. *p* Shelley Strong, Kris Krengel. *sc* Dan McCormack. *ph* Dan Gilham. *ed* Martin Hunter. *pd* Michael Krantz, Martha Rutan Fay. *m* William T Stromberg. *cast* Michael Faella, Ricky Aiello, Holley Chant, Willo Hausman.

● In a baroque room dominated by a champagne glass-shaped bath and the giggling beauty queen in it, the Minotaur, a balding, overweight, burnt-out '50s entertainer (Elvis with shades of John Belushi?), injects and ingests an insane cocktail of drugs and drink. The expensive camp setting points up the tawdriness of his behaviour, but his raw hysteria and explosive violence are punctuated by quieter reminiscences of his heyday and childhood. Stunningly designed, fluidly filmed and boldly acted, this provocative meditation on celebrity is both terrifying and exhilarating. NF

Mi Querido Tom Mix

see My Dear Tom Mix

Miracle (Mirakel)

(2000, Den, 80 min)
d Natasha Arthy. *p* Birgitte Hald, Morten Kaufmann. *sc* Kim Fupz Aakeson. *ph* Eric Kress. *ed* Kasper Leick. *pd* Peter de Neergaard. *m* Kåre Bjerkø, Frithjof Toksvig. *cast* Stefan Pagels Andersen, Sidse Babett Knudsen, Peter Frödin, Thomas Bo Larsen, Sebastian Jessen, Stephania Potalivo.

● This depicts the angst of schoolboy Dennis P (Andersen), who tries to come to terms with the death of his father by retreating into a *Grease*-meets-*Strictly Ballroom* fantasy life, inhabited by an all singing and dancing supporting cast. In truth, his mother blames Dennis for his father's suicide, his teacher considers him a no-hoper, and his two best friends, Mick and Karen Elise, share a secret that will break his heart. First time director Arthy handles the obsessions of youth well enough – the lack of pubic hair, compulsive swearing and unrequited love – but the 'three wishes' plotline and the level of absurdity involved in its telling slightly detract from an otherwise perfectly fine rites of passage film, adapted from a play by Kim Fupz Aakeson. MD

Miracle, The

(1990, GB, 97 min)
d Neil Jordan. *p* Stephen Woolley, Redmond Morris. *sc* Neil Jordan. *ph* Philippe Rousselot. *ed* Joke Van Wijk. *pd* Gemma Jackson. *m* Anne Dudley. *cast* Beverly D'Angelo, Donal McCann, Niall Byrne, Lorraine Pilkington, JG Devlin, Cathleen Delaney, Tom Hickey, Mikkel Gaup.

● In the small, nun-swept Irish seaside town of Bray, teenage would-be writers Rose (Pilkington) and Jimmy (Byrne) – the latter enjoying a strangely fraternal relationship with his saxophonist Dad (McCann), an alcoholic since his wife died before Jimmy could get to know her – spend their time speculating about the lives of the townsfolk. But only when glamorous American actress Renee (D'Angelo) turns up, do they really enter a world of romance and mystery, with Jimmy determining to seduce the older woman. But why is she holding back, and what is her interest in Jimmy's dad? Back on home ground after his spectacularly poor stabs at the American market, Jordan throws together, with some success, quite a few themes in this small-scale drama: the importance of memory, the problematically varied nature of love, issues of faith, and the relationship between reality, desire and literature. Although the film is overly literary in its use of symbolism and analogy, the performances are direct and affecting (D'Angelo, Byrne and Pilkington especially), and Jordan's affection for both characters and milieu is conspicuous throughout. GA

Miracle in Milan (Miracolo a Milano)

(1950, It, 101 min, b/w)
d Vittorio De Sica. *sc* Cesare Zavattini, Vittorio De Sica, Suso Cecchi D'Amico, Mario Chiari, Adolfo Franci. *ph* GR Aldo. *ed* Eraldo Da Roma. *ad* Guido Fiorini. *m* Alessandro Cicognini. *cast* Emma Gramatica, Francesco Golisano, Paolo Stoppa, Guglielmo Barnabò, Brunella Bovo, Anna Carena, Alba Arnova.

● Made the year after *Bicycle Thieves*, this is a less coherent but more exuberant film, with De Sica injecting a stiff dose of fantasy into what could have been another plangent tale of gentleman tramps and shantytown life: the humble down-and-outs threatened with eviction by business speculators escape – thanks to angelic intervention – to their reward in heaven. Outrageous sentimentality undercut by outrageous cheek. CA

Miracle in the Rain

(1956, US, 107 min, b/w)
d Rudolph Maté. *p* Frank P Rosenberg. *sc* Ben Hecht. *ph* Russell Metty. *ed* Thomas Reilly. *ad* Leo K Kuter. *m* Franz Waxman.

cast Jane Wyman, Van Johnson, Peggie Castle, Fred Clark, Eileen Heckart, Barbara Nichols, Alan King.

● Weepie in which plain Jane Wyman finds sweet romance with Johnson's wholesomely cheerful Southern soldier, only to have him killed in (WWII) action. Not a patch on Minnelli's *The Clock*, though much better than one might expect, thanks to a similar concern for humble detail and a nice array of New York locations. But the final 'miracle' – one of scriptwriter Ben Hecht's follies as Wyman is granted spiritual uplift in a vision of her late love – is a tough lump of goo to swallow. TM

Miracle Maker, The

(1999, GB/Rus, 91 min)
d Derek Hayes, Stanislav Sokolov. *p* Naomi Jones, Renat Zinnurov. *sc* Murray Watts. *ph* Alexander Vikhanski. *ed* William Oswald, John Richards. *ad* Helena Livanova. *m* Anne Dudley. *cast* voices: Ralph Fiennes, Michael Bryant, Julie Christie, Rebecca Callard, James Frain, Richard E Grant, Ian Holm, William Hurt, Anton Lesser, Daniel Massey, Tim McInnerny, Alfred Molina, Bob Peck, Miranda Richardson, Antony Sher, Ewan Stewart, Ken Stott, David Thewlis.

● From the company behind the successful animated TV Shakespeare, Chaucer and Old Testament series, this is an animated life of Christ (voiced by Fiennes), according to Luke, but told mainly from the point of view of Tamar, a sick 12-year-old Pharisee (Callard). On a trip to the doctor in Sepphoris, she witnesses the saving of Mary Magdalen and then follows the journey to the Crucifixion. A Welsh/Russian co-production, most of its 3-D animated, clay headed 'puppets' came from the Moscow team, while the pastel-crayon 'miracles' and flashbacks are from the Cartwn Cymru studio.The films eschews CGI techniques, producing an almost homely, handcrafted feel. The screenplay is a combination of simplicity and detail, its plenitude of characters and groupings doing justice to the religious, racial and social context. Christ is much the modest artisan carpenter, an Everyman lacking the dynamism and wrath of, say, Pasolini's Evangelist. Here, miracles are made manifest by dozens of minuscule rubber fish and everyone moves with the underwater slowness of entranced T'ai-chi practitioners. Strange – and strangely compelling. WH

Miracle Mile

(1989, US, 88 min)
d Steve DeJarnatt. *p* John Daly, Derek Gibson. *sc* Steve DeJarnatt. *ph* Theo Van De Sande. *ed* Stephen Semel, Kathie Weaver. *pd* Christopher Horner. *m* Tangerine Dream. *cast* Anthony Edwards, Mare Winningham, John Agar, Lou Hancock, Mykel T Williamson, Kelly Minter, Kurt Fuller, Denise Crosby, Robert Doqui.

● A nuclear thriller with a devastating narrative hook. Having arranged to meet a new girlfriend (Winningham) after her night shift at an LA diner, trombone-player and shy romantic Harry (Edwards) oversleeps and misses her. At 4.05 am, he picks up a ringing pay-phone outside the diner, and a voice screams 'It's happening! I can't believe it. We're locked into it…50 minutes and counting'. Is this some late-night freak's joke, or has a chance crossed line given Harry warning of impending nuclear Armageddon? With one deft stroke, writer-director DeJarnatt taps into the nightmare of being the first to know about the (possible) end of the world, and the awesome responsibility of having to communicate this news to others. The patrons of the Miracle Mile diner are understandably sceptical, but with less than an hour to live, Harry's personal priorities come sharply into focus. Cleverly written, authentically staged and sympathetically played, it's brave, uncompromising, and above all, frighteningly believable. NF

Miracle of Life, The

see Our Daily Bread

Miracle of Morgan's Creek, The

(1944, US, 99 min, b/w)
d/sc Preston Sturges. *ph* John F Seitz. *ed* Stuart Gilmore. *ad* Hans Dreier, Ernst Fegté. *m* Leo Shuken, Charles Bradshaw. *cast* Betty Hutton, Eddie Bracken, William Demarest, Diana Lynn, Porter Hall, Jimmy Conlin, Almira Sessions, Brian Donlevy, Akim Tamiroff, Almira Sessions.

● Characteristically hectic Sturges amalgam of satire and slapstick, hitting out at such sacred cows as Momism and religion as it tells of the predicament of Hutton, a lively smalltown girl who finds herself pregnant after a drunken binge during which she married one of six unknown soldiers. Enter the stuttering oaf Bracken who loves her, to help out as stand-in father and watch agog as the town itself gets caught up in an inexorable whirl of chaos. Great verbal gags and non-sequiturs, fast-paced action, and a thorough irreverence for all things deemed respectable – politicians, policemen and magistrates included – make it a lasting delight, not least when the lady finally gives birth…to sextuplets. GA

Miracle of the Bells, The

(1948, US, 120 min)
d Irving Pichel. *p* Jesse L Lasky, Walter MacEwen. *sc* Ben Hecht, Quentin Reynolds. *ph* Robert De Grasse. *ed* Elmo Williams. *ad* Ralph Berger. *m* Leigh Harline. *cast* Fred MacMurray, Frank Sinatra, Alida Valli, Lee J Cobb, Harold Vermilyea, Charles Meredith, Philip Ahn, Frank Ferguson.

● This over-extended and uncertain satire (adapted by Ben Hecht from a novel by Russell Janey) on fake religiosity has an ill-at-ease Sinatra as the priest persuaded by press agent MacMurray into offering his church for the funeral of late-lamented actress Valli, whose final film is due for imminent release. After three days of bell ringing, however, the girl is restored to life: Miracle or stunt? It's very hard to care. TJ

Miracle on 34th Street

(1994, US, 114 min)
d Les Mayfield. *p/sc* John Hughes. *ph* Julio Macat. *ed* Raja Gosnell. *pd* Douglas Kraner. *m* Bruce Broughton. *cast* Richard Attenborough, Elizabeth Perkins, Dylan McDermott, JT Walsh, Joss Ackland. James Remar.

● Padding the deluxe avenues of Manhattan, kindly gentleman Kriss Kringle (Attenborough) is first seen confirming to a child that he is in fact the real Father Christmas. Mr Reassuring he may be, but he's also possessed of a medieval guildsman's pride: seeing the Santa from Cole's department store swigging whisky on a street parade, he wrests the reins away from him and takes over his sleigh, so impressing a Cole's executive (Perkins) that she hires him for the duration. The queues grow legion, until finally he's charged with being an impostor. That's not his only trial: he also has to convince Perkins' precocious daughter, which means delivering her Christmas list of a father, a house and a brother. This is a philosophical movie. How do you prove Santa's existence? It's a shaky business – like this movie – based on trust. All the kids I took loved it. The appeal must lie in the Santa-as-fantasy-grandfather-figure – with bottomless pockets. WH

Miracles

(1985, US, 87 min)
d Jim Kouf. *p* Steve Roth, Bernard Williams. *sc* Jim Kouf. *ph* John Alcott. *ed* Susan E Morse, Dennis Virkler. *pd* Terence Marsh. *m* Peter Bernstein. *cast* Tom Conti, Teri Garr, Paul Rodriguez, Christopher Lloyd, Adalberto Martinez, Jorge Russek, Jorge Reynoso.

● Conti and Garr have just got divorced when they both, yes both, collide with a Mexican bankrobber on the run from the cops. He takes them hostage and flies off to his homeland, only to bale out when the plane runs out of fuel, leaving them to crash-land in the desert. But that's only the start of the non-stop, near-fatal disasters afflicting the couple. It's hard to win laughs with a script that is sitcom predictable; that aims for thrills with widespread destruction without ever making you care about its imperilled characters; that thinks kooks of all kinds saying 'sonofabitch' every half-minute and screaming at full volume are actually amusing. GA

Miracle Woman, The

(1931, US, 90 min, b/w)
d/p Frank Capra. *sc* Jo Swerling, Dorothy Howell. *ph* Joseph Walker. *ed* Maurice Wright. *cast* Barbara Stanwyck, David Manners, Sam Hardy, Beryl Mercer, Russell Hopton.

● Fascinating cautionary tale loosely inspired by the Aimee Semple Macpherson affair, with Stanwyck as a minister's daughter – seeking revenge against the faithful who hounded her father to his death – who teams up with a wily conman (Hardy) to become big business as an evangelist. Stunning camerawork from Joseph Walker makes a joy of the evangelistic razzmatazz (climaxed when Stanwyck does her preaching from a lion's cage), but is equal to the more delicate shading of the comeuppance in which Stanwyck sees the true light after bringing illumination to a blind songwriter. The end sees her a humble soldier in the Salvation Army, but – so beautifully do Stanwyck and Manners play out the love affair, and so perfectly does Capra direct it (with the tenderness, almost, of Borzage) – that you don't feel at all like laughing. (From the play *Bless You, Sister* by John Meehan and Robert Riskin.) TM

Miracle Worker, The

(1962, US, 106 min, b/w)
d Arthur Penn. *p* Fred Coe. *sc* William Gibson. *ph* Ernesto Caparros. *ed* Aram Avakian. *ad* George Jenkins. *m* Laurence Rosenthal. *cast* Anne Bancroft, Patty Duke, Victor Jory, Inga Swenson, Andrew Prine, Kathleen Comegys, Beah Richards.

● Penn's remarkable screen version of William Gibson's play about Helen Keller, which he directed on Broadway. It's a stunningly impressive piece of work, typically (for Penn) deriving much of its power from the performances. Patty Duke as the young girl born deaf and blind, and Anne Bancroft as the stubborn Irish governess who helps her overcome her inability to speak, spark off each other with a violence and emotional honesty rarely seen in the cinema, lighting up each other's loneliness, vulnerability, and plain fear. What is in fact astonishing is the way that, while constructing a piece of very carefully directed and intelligently written melodrama, Penn manages to avoid sentimentality or even undue optimism about the value of Helen's education, and the way he achieves such a feeling of raw spontaneity in the acting. GA

Miracolo a Milano

see Miracle in Milan

Mirage

(1965, US, 109 min, b/w)
d Edward Dmytryk. *p* Harry Keller. *sc* Peter Stone. *ph* Joseph MacDonald. *ed* Ted J Kent. *ad* Frank Arrigo, Alexander Golitzen. *m* Quincy Jones. *cast* Gregory Peck, Diane Baker, Walter Matthau, Leif Erickson, Kevin McCarthy, George Kennedy, Robert H Harris, Jack Weston, Walter Abel.

● Peck is an amnesiac in New York who traces his past back into the middle of a murder plot. Although the two leading players, Peck and Diane Baker, are shown up by their supporting cast, this remains one of the better thrillers of the '60s (adapted from a novel by Howard Fast). The harsh b/w photography, the various levels of reality, and the use of urban landscape, all contribute to the feeling of unease, building up an atmosphere that is perhaps better than the mechanics of the plot deserve. CPe

Miroir a deux faces, Le (Lo Specchi a due facce/ The Mirror Has Two Faces)

(1958, Fr/It, 97 min, b/w)
d André Cayatte. *p* Alain Poiré. *sc* Gérard Oury, André Cayatte. *ph* Christian Matras. *ed* Paul Cayatte. *ad* Jacques Colombier. *m* RS Louiguy. *cast* Michèle Morgan, Bourvil, Gérard Oury, Ivan Desny, Sandra Milo, Sylvie, Carette, Pierre Brice, Elisabeth Manet.

● Interesting to re-view this in the light of the Streisand 'remake', though any resemblance are so superficial as to appear coincidental. Bourvil, in one of his occasional dramatic roles, plays a mean, penny pinching, spoiled child of a man who deliberately seeks out a plain woman to marry, on the grounds she'll be less bother. Ten years later, a chance encounter with a cosmetic surgeon transforms the wife into Michèle Morgan, newly confident and socially in demand, whereupon Bourvil, deprived of his conveniently arranged world, goes spectacularly berserk. Cayatte shows his customary relish for the unpleasant: the nightmare honeymoon in Venice is richly detailed and Sylvie sketches in the quietly venomous mother-in-law with her usual economy. If Streisand's film was quintessential '90s Hollywood feel good, this is equally characteristic '50s French astringency. BBa

Mirror (Zerkalo) 100 *(100)*

(1974, USSR, 106 min, b/w & col)
d Andrei Tarkovsky. *p* E Waisberg. *sc* Andrei Tarkovsky, Alensandr Misharin. *ph* Georgi Rerberg. *ed* Lyudmila Feiginova. *ad* Nikolai Dvigubsky. *m* Eduard Artemiev, JS Bach, Pergolese, Purcell. *cast* Margarita Terekhova, Philip Yankovsky, Ignat Daniltsev, Oleg Yankovsky, Nikolai Grinko, Alla Demidova, Innokenti Smoktunovsky, L Tarkovskaya.
● Tarkovsky goes for the great white whale of politicised art – no less than a history of his country in this century seen in terms of the personal – and succeeds. Intercutting a fragmented series of autobiographical episodes, which have only the internal logic of dream and memory, with startling documentary footage, he lovingly builds a world where the domestic expands into the political and crisscrosses back again. Unique its form, unique its vision. CPea

Mirror, The (Der Spiegel/Ayna)

(1984, WGer/GB, 91 min)
d Erden Kiral. *p* Joachim von Vietinghoff. *sc* Erden Kiral. *ph* Kenan Ormanlar. *ed* Agape Dorstewitz. *ad* Nikos Perakis. *m* Brynmor Jones. *cast* Nur Sürer, Suavi Eren, Hikmet Celik, Vasilis Tsaglos, Nikos Skiadas.
● Based on *The White Ox* by Osman Sahin, this unrelenting Turkish moral tale (punctuated with many charged silences) was shot in Greece as a German-British co-production. Its theme is the mind-bending effects of extreme poverty. A rich young aga leaves the love gift of a mirror for the wife of a peasant. The husband murders the shy suitor with his wife's forced compliance, and buries his remains beneath the impacted earth of his ox's byre, which is half the couple's one-room home. However, the memory of the gift remains immovably lodged in the woman's mind. Spare, disquieting, and other-worldly. JPy

Mirror Crack'd, The

(1980, GB, 105 min)
d Guy Hamilton. *p* John Brabourne, Richard Goodwin. *sc* Jonathan Hales, Barry Sandler. *ph* Christopher Challis. *ed* Richard Marden. *pd* Michael Stringer. *m* John Cameron. *cast* Angela Lansbury, Edward Fox, Rock Hudson, Kim Novak, Elizabeth Taylor, Geraldine Chaplin, Tony Curtis, Charles Gray, Nigel Stock.
● Though it's obvious after five minutes that this is a complete no-no, the cinema equivalent of a bellyflop, it exercises a perverse fascination. You couldn't ask for a weirder exercise in whimsical English fantasy than a Miss Marple mystery masquerading as a Royal Command Performance in which all the American stars look stoned. Hingeing on death threats sent to the star (HRH Liz Taylor) of a visiting US movie, we are plunged into a timeless zone of the Home Counties, village lawns and pickled English character players where murders occur as inexplicably and as regularly as teatime. The main highlight is not the cheating plot but the rollcall of puffy, under-rehearsed stars: Hudson and Taylor as a neurotic couple in search of their cue cards, Tony Curtis stealing scenes as a bug-like movie producer, while a pink-clad, souped-up Kim Novak reappears as the legendary Kim Novak. The overall effect is of a holographed Madame Tussaud's. DMacp

Mirror Has Two Faces, The

see Miroir a deux faces, Le

Mirror Has Two Faces, The

(1996, US, 126 min)
d Barbra Streisand. *p* Barbra Streisand, Arnon Milchan. *sc* Richard LaGravenese. *ph* Dante Spinotti, Andrzej Bartkowiak. *ed* Jeff Werner. *pd* Tom John. *m* Marvin Hamlisch. *cast* Barbra Streisand, Jeff Bridges, Pierce Brosnan, George Segal, Mimi Rogers, Brenda Vaccaro, Lauren Bacall, Austin Pendleton.
● You want love against the odds? You've got it. Rose (Streisand) and Gregory (Bridges) are two brainy Columbia professors who wilt like lettuce in the presence of beauty. Greg hits on a plan. He and Rose will enter into a romance of the mind. He won't have to fight temptation, because Rose is homely as sin: no beauty, no sex, no worries. The only problem? Rose has already fallen in lust with Gregory and can't scramble out. The mirror may have two faces, but Streisand's happy with the one, still employing that riot of eye-rolls and lip-chews so disarming (once) in *Funny Girl*. Bridges does well as the bumbling nerd, his gulpingly shy exterior hiding a darkly fastidious core; and Bacall runs up and down the scale as Rose's haughty mother. Camp, but not much fun. CO'Su

Mirror Image (Ming dai ahui zhu)

(2000, Tai, 72 min)
d Hsiao Ya-chuan. *p* Hou Hsiao-hsien. *sc* Hsiao Ya-chuan. *ph* Lin Tse-chung. *ed* Chou Chia-chun. *ad* Hwang Wem-ying. *m* Hou Chih-chien. *cast* Lee Jiunn-jye. Fan Hsio-fan, Era Wang.
● This engagingly modest first feature finds its young protagonist tending to the family pawnshop while his dad is hospitalised by a stroke; there he passes the time amiably enough with his girlfriend, fascinated that an accident has scratched his palm and, he's been told, rendered his life unpredictable. Then an attractive young woman starts frequenting the joint, and things take a turn for the complicated and confusing. It's also, regrettably, when the film goes off the rails; for its first half, Hsiao uses the confines of the pawnshop imaginatively and amusingly, but when its reluctant young proprietor steps outside, narrative focus is lost. Still, the characters are deftly written and played, and if the film finally doesn't add up to much, it does show great promise. GA

Mirror Phase

(1978, GB, 47 min)
d/sc/ph/ed Carola Klein. *with* Leonie Klein, Carola Klein, Ewan Klein.
● When the child first catches sight of her image in a mirror, she sees herself as though she were another person. The 'recognition' of this framed coherent being as oneself is the first step in the creation of that fiction which is the Ego: the infant, as yet without full motor coordination, none the less perceives herself as a fully expressive whole. Carola Klein filmed her daughter Leonie in the process of such 'recognitions' in the early months of childhood. *Mirror Phase* is literally an analysed home movie, the 8mm print blown up into a perceptible 16mm grain. Choral voice-overs, dual camerawork, and the fractioning of the screen suggest that we also can misrecognise our relation to film: that cinema too can function as a 'specular ego'. Such work has obvious debts to Laura Mulvey's writing and film-making; and *Mirror Phase* is something like *Riddles of the Sphinx* from the child's perspective. But where *Riddles* attempted to question film's use of narrative and character, *Mirror Phase* is fixed within the actual fact of Leonie's development and her parents' evident personalities – a return to the charm of the home movie, but a crucial restraint on the film's analysis. MM

Misadventures of Margaret, The (Les Mésaventures de Margaret)

(1998, GB/Fr, 92 min)
d Brian Skeet. *p* Ian Benson. *sc* Brian Skeet. *ph* Romain Winding. *ed* Clare Douglas. *pd* Martin Childs. *m* James Shearman. *cast* Parker Posey, Jeremy Northam, Craig Chester, Elizabeth McGovern, Brooke Shields, Corbin Bernsen, Justine Waddell, Patrick Bruel, Stéphane Freiss.
● Seeking her maiden adventure in Paris, Margaret – nothing if not ditzy – contrives to hook up with an Englishman. Seven years later, marriage and NY literary success have not steadied her nerves, and in the glare of fortune Margaret (Posey) looks at herself and at Edward (Northam) and wonders: has this gentlemanly professor used up the best years of her life? Her next project offers a chance to vent her frustrations, especially on a research trip to France. Whatever the merits of Cathleen Schine's comic novel *Rameau's Niece*, this adaptation fails to fire up. The chief problem is the film's inability to gain any distance from its flighty heroine: people's interior lives may well be this inchoate, but simply replicating the confusion on screen is hardly art. Posey's doolally schtick is too much, and Northam's sweet but drippy hubbie hardly a foil. NB

Mischief Makers, The

see Mistons, Les

Misérables, Les

see Les Misérables (1935)

Miserables, Les

see Les Miserables (1952)

Misérables, Les

see Les Misérables (1998)

Misérables, Les

(1957, Fr, 217 min)
d Jean-Paul Le Chanois. *p* Paul Cadéac. *sc* René Barjavel, Michael Audiard, Jean-Paul Le Chanois. *ph* Jacques Natteau. *ed* Emma Le Chanois. *ad* Serge Pimenoff. *m* Georges Van Parys. *cast* Jean Gabin, Bernard Blier, Bourvil, Gianni Esposito, Serge Reggiani, Danièle Delorme, Silvia Monfort.
● A glossy CinemaScope classic, a film for all the family which does Victor Hugo proud. Back in 1957, directors didn't count for much, and it relies on clumsily edited, sluggish shots of an all-star cast, headed by a superb Gabin as the ex-convict turned do-gooding businessman struggling to atone for his past. In 1958, Truffaut made his first film. *Les Misérables* is, in other words, one of the last of the dinosaurs. For dinosaur, read splendidly moralistic melodrama, guaranteed to kill those Sunday afternoon blues. Bet it makes you cry. PHo

Misérables, Les (aka Les Misérables du vingtième siècle)

(1995, Fr, 174 min)
d/p/sc/ph Claude Lelouch. *ed* Hélène de Luze. *ad* Jacques Bufnoir. *m* Francis Lai, Philippe Servain, Erik Berchot, Michel Legrand, Didier Barbelivien. *cast* Jean-Paul Belmondo, Michel Boujenah, Alessandra Martines, Salomé (Lelouch), Annie Girardot, Philippe Léotard, Philippe Khorsand, Jean Marais, Micheline Presle.
● Following fate-tossed Henri Fortin's progress through unjust imprisonment, the boxing ring and two world wars, this vast and vastly enjoyable epic demonstrates how the hero's obsession with reaching the end of Hugo's novel makes him compare his plight to that of Jean Valjean, both men sticking to their moral integrity to get them through the very worst of times. In Fortin's case, he helps a Jewish family escape both the Gestapo and the anti-Semitic collaborators all too keen to sell them out, and it's Lelouch's unflinching depiction of France's shoddy wartime treatment of the Jews that puts a little iron in the movie's abundant soul. You could argue that such hard-edged drama sits ill beside the generally light-hearted tone of Belmondo's picaresque adventures and the imaginative dips in and out of Hugo, but it's part of the magic Lelouch has worked that his story-of-all-stories theme matches the catch-all inclusiveness of his old-fashioned celluloid showmanship. Although Boujenah's portrayal of the hard-pressed Jewish father Ziman sails close to caricature, elsewhere Léotard and Girardot make a marvellously grizzled rural couple, while Belmondo's performance sweeps the whole thing along with undemonstrative charisma. TJ

Misery

(1990, US, 107 min)
d Rob Reiner. *p* Andrew Scheinman, Rob Reiner. *sc* William Goldman. *ph* Barry Sonnenfeld. *ed* Robert Leighton. *pd* Norman Garwood. *m* Marc Shaiman. *cast* James Caan, Kathy Bates, Richard Farnsworth, Frances Sternhagen, Lauren Bacall, Graham Jarvis.
● The gore is toned down and the psychology played up in this darkly humorous adaptation of Stephen King's novel. Paul Sheldon (Caan) is a successful author of romantic fiction, but public demand for his heroine Misery Chastain has stifled his creativity; so after killing her off in a forthcoming final adventure, he writes a long-neglected personal novel. When a blizzard sends his car off the road on the drive home from his mountain retreat, his life is saved by nurse Annie Wilkes (Bates), who soon has the invalid tucked up in her home. It's a bonus that as his number one fan she's extremely attentive; and a definite minus that she's a psychopath who's looking forward to his next

'Misery' novel... William Goldman's intelligent script operates both as psycho-thriller and as sly comment on the sort of attitude towards celebrity which can enshrine and – in this case, literally – imprison the object of devotion. The casting is inspired: Caan oozes frustration at his physical disability, while Bates brings authority and an eerie naturalness to her demented character, her homespun expressions ('oogie', 'dirty birdy') providing a bizarre counterpoint to her increasingly cruel actions. Reiner captures *just* the right level of physical tension, but for the most part wisely emphasises the mental duels. Terrific. CM

Misfits, The

(1960, US, 125 min, b/w)
d John Huston. *p* Frank E Taylor. *sc* Arthur Miller. *ph* Russell Metty. *ed* George Tomasini. *ad* Stephen Grimes, Bill Newberry. *m* Alex North. *cast* Clark Gable, Marilyn Monroe, Montgomery Clift, Eli Wallach, Thelma Ritter, Estelle Winwood, James Barton, Kevin McCarthy.

● A superbly shot anti-Western, constantly dragged down by Arthur Miller's verbose, cloyingly glib script about emotional cripples searching for a meaning to life in the twilight of the American frontier, with Monroe as the Reno divorcee who becomes a sort of earth mother/conscience to a group of ex-cowboys scratching an unhappy living around the rodeos. Lent a testamentary (almost prophetic) gloss when it proved to be the end of the line for both Gable and Monroe, with Clift – giving the best performance in the film – to follow soon after. But it really comes good only in the mustang round-up at the end, an overly symbolic but nevertheless magnificent sequence. TM

Mishima: A Life in Four Chapters

(1985, US/Jap, 120 min, b/w & col)
d Paul Schrader. *p* Mata Yamamoto, Tom Luddy. *sc* Paul Schrader, Leonard Schrader, Chieko Schrader. *ph* John Bailey. *ed* Michael Chandler, Tomoyo Oshima. *pd* Eiko Ishioka. *m* Philip Glass. *cast* Ken Ogata, Masayuki Shionoya, Junkichi Orimoto, Naoko Otani, Go Riju.

● A fantasist recreating himself in his own image to perfection; a narcissist building his puny body into a muscled samurai; an ultra-rightist patriot raising a private army to restore Japan to its former glory; an artist achieving his spiritual redemption through the ritual disembowelling of *seppuku*. Schrader may have finally achieved the violent transfiguration that he seeks along with his protagonists: the movie has all the ritual sharpness and beauty of that final sword. Moreover it has a unique structure. Three of Mishima's most autobiographical novels are dramatised on sets of incandescent colour; flashbacks to Mishima's early life are in serene b/w; and the whole is bracketed by a Costa-Gavras style re-creation of the last day of his life. Confusing as it sounds, Schrader's grip never falters. Finally Philip Glass's insistent score virtually transforms the whole thing into opera. There is nothing quite like it. CPea

Miss Congeniality

(2000, US/Aust, 110 min)
d Donald Petrie. *p* Sandra Bullock. *sc* Marc Lawrence, Katie Ford, Caryn Lucas. *ph* Laszlo Kovacs. *ed* Billy Weber. *pd* Peter Larkin. *m* Edward Shearmur. *cast* Sandra Bullock, Michael Caine, Benjamin Bratt, Candice Bergen, William Shatner, Ernie Hudson, John Diresta, Heather Burns, Melissa De Sousa.

● Comedy targets don't come much easier than the American beauty pageant industry, and this Bullock vehicle milks the subject for every last joke. Her earnest clowning wins audience sympathy, and while there may not be many surprises, there's little to dislike either. Bullock plays Gracie Hart, a rookie FBI agent selected to go undercover at a beauty pageant threatened by a psychopathic arch-criminal, and pageant consultant Victor Melling (Caine) is called in to groom and turn the agent into what she disparagingly calls a 'bikini-stuffer'. Physically the transformation is sufficiently dramatic to convince colleague Eric Matthews (Bratt) that she's not just another one of the guys after all, but smoothing the rough edges of her personality proves rather more difficult. Caine phones in a lack-lustre performance, and as half of a romantic pairing Bratt is overshadowed by Bullock's undeniable screen presence. It's her movie, and for the most part she doesn't disappoint. WI

Miss Europe

see Prix de Beauté

Miss Firecracker

(1989, US, 103 min)
d Thomas Schlamme. *p* Fred Berner. *sc* Beth Henley. *ph* Arthur Albert. *ed* Peter C Frank. *pd* Kristi Zea. *m* David Mansfield, Homer Denison. *cast* Holly Hunter, Mary Steenburgen, Tim Robbins, Alfre Woodward, Scott Glenn, Veanne Cox, Ann Wedgeworth, Trey Wilson, Amy Wright, Bert Remsen.

● This adaptation of Beth Henley's play *The Miss Firecracker Contest* abounds with idiosyncratic detail and such familiar Henley ingredients as family madness; but the interplay is more emotionally complicated, the perspective less wilfully detached than, say, *Crimes of the Heart*. Carnells Scott (Hunter) is known as the loosest lady in her small Mississippi town. She plans to redeem her reputation by winning the Miss Firecracker beauty/talent contest (which, since she was orphaned as a child, assumes enormous importance as a sign of social acceptance), forging ahead with her ambitions both helped and hindered by her cousins, one-time Miss Firecracker Elaine (Steenburgen) and tormented Delmount (Robbins). Despite touches of enforced eccentricity, the story is redeemed by its observation of bittersweet relationships and self-deceptions. Amid notions of self-determination and individual enterprise, Henley is graciously compassionate, embracing human limitations and self-acceptance. Performances are carefully modulated, but this is Holly Hunter's movie. Her show-stopping tap dance to the strains of 'The Star-Spangled Banner' is worth the price of admission alone. CM

Missing

(1981, US, 122 min)
d Costa-Gavras. *p* Edward Lewis, Mildred Lewis. *sc* Costa-Gavras, Donald Stewart. *ph* Ricardo Aronovich. *ed* Françoise Bonnot. *pd* Peter Jamison. *m* Vangelis. *cast* Jack Lemmon, Sissy Spacek, Melanie Mayron, John Shea, Charles Cioffi, David Clennon, Jerry Hardin, Richard Bradford, Janice Rule.

● As darkness falls on a terrified city, taxis and buses refuse all passengers, trapped pedestrians beg strangers for sanctuary, even an earthquake cannot drive people onto the street. It may sound like apocalyptic science fiction, but it's Costa-Gavras' extraordinary first American movie, based on true events during the Chilean coup of 1973. It explores the disappearance of a young American writer, and prompted a furious rebuttal from the US State Department. Spacek and Lemmon are fine as the missing man's wife and father, but what makes the film so overwhelming in places is its unending night-time imagery of a society coming apart at the seams. Costa-Gavras underpins his campaigning content with all the electric atmosphere of a paranoid conspiracy thriller, and ensures that *Missing* will remain the cinematic evocation of a military coup for years to come. DP

Missing in Action

(1984, US, 101 min)
d Joseph Zito. *p* Menahem Golan, Yoram Globus. *sc* James Bruner. *ph* Joao Fernandes. *ed* Joel Goodman, Daniel Loewenthal. *ad* Ladislav Wilheim, (Philippines) Toto Castillo. *m* Jay Chattaway. *cast* Chuck Norris, M Emmet Walsh, Davis Tress, Leonore Kasdorf, James Hong, Ernie Ortega.

● This is so bad it defies belief. Norris, veteran of trashy but fun martial arts movies, plays Col Braddock, a gook-zapping 'Nam vet. Taking off his shirt at every opportunity, Norris hunks his way through the jungle to rescue a gang of unofficial PoWs, GIs imprisoned long after the end of the war. Cue lots of explosions, perfunctory action sequences, transparent gore, and 'all gooks are baddies' propaganda. Xenophobic, amateurish and extraordinarily dull, it nevertheless grossed $26m in the States. JCo

Missing Link

(1989, US, 90 min)
d David Hughes, Carol Hughes. *p* Dennis Kane, *sc* David Hughes, Carol Hughes. *cast* Peter Elliott.

● Michael Gambon's gruff tones lend weight to this offbeat Hollywood venture into pre-history, a slow quasi-documentary saga of the last ape-man left alone to confront the African landscape after his family is wiped out. Arresting location camerawork by the directors, and much hairy make-up by Rick (*American Werewolf in London*) Baker fail to fill the credibility gap. From *Batman* producers Peter Guber and John Peters. TJ

Mission, The

(1983, US/WGer, 108 min)
d/p/sc Parviz Sayyad. *ph* Reza Aria. *ed* Parviz Sayyad. *cast* Parviz Sayyad, Mary Apick, Houshang Touzie, Mohammad B Ghaffari, Hedyeh Anvar, Hatam Anvar.

● Well before Iranian cinema found international recognition, Sayyad's low budget thriller was distributed in the US and Europe. It didn't hurt that the film is set in New York. Here a representative of Ayatollah Khomeini's Islamic regime comes to assassinate an émigré, the Colonel (played by the multi-talented writer/director), formerly employed in the Shah's secret police. By a quirk of fate the would-be killer saves his target from a mugging, and is embraced by the unsuspecting Colonel and his family. Nuanced and even-handed. TCh

Mission, The

(1986, GB, 125 min)
d Roland Joffé. *p* Fernando Ghia, David Puttnam. *sc* Robert Bolt. *ph* Chris Menges. *ed* Jim Clark. *pd* Stuart Craig. *m* Ennio Morricone. *cast* Robert De Niro, Jeremy Irons, Ray McAnally, Aidan Quinn, Cherie Lunghi, Ronald Pickup, Chuck Low, Liam Neeson.

● In the 18th century, Spain and Portugal were at each other's throats over rights to territory in South America. Neither side suffered a great deal, the real victim being the native Indians. Here their only protection comes in the form of a Jesuit priest intent on giving God to the jungle (Irons), and a slave trader warring with the Jesuits who later joins their order (De Niro). The theme of Robert Bolt's script is the conflict between compassion and politics, at its moral centre the powerful church official (McAnally, marvellous) sent by the King of Portugal to decide whether the Jesuit missions, and the native communities which surround them, should survive. Enacted against the stunning backdrop of the Amazon jungle, the action has a rousing, epic quality. What it doesn't have, however, is passion. The climax is brutal, De Niro and Irons are impressive as the opponents who become soul mates; yet *The Mission* manages to be both magnificent and curiously uninvolving, a buddy movie played in soutanes. RR

Missionary, The

(1981, GB, 86 min)
d Richard Loncraine. *p* Neville C Thompson, Michael Palin. *sc* Michael Palin. *ph* Peter Hannan. *ed* Paul Green. *ad* Norman Garwood. *m* Mike Moran. *cast* Michael Palin, Maggie Smith, Trevor Howard, Denholm Elliott, Graham Crowden, David Suchet, Michael Hordern, Phoebe Nicholls, Roland Culver, Timothy Spall, Frances Barber.

● Along with *Local Hero*, this marks a return to the kind of gentle comedy drama that has more in common with the old Ealing films than with the zaniness of Monty Python. A naive missionary returns from colonial Africa to be sent among the Fallen Women of Edwardian London. From them he learns that missionary has another meaning, which he embraces with the fervour of a man finding his true vocation. Affectionate treatment of English eccentrics – choleric general (Howard), aristocratic nympho (Smith), dotty butler (Hordern), keep-fit bishop (Elliott) – maintains interest between the rather meagrely distributed comic set pieces. But despite stylish direction, Palin's artless vicar is too familiar and too supine to carry a full-length film, a personal project in which he seems oddly self-effacing. MB

Mission Impossible

(1996, US, 110 min)
d Brian De Palma. *p* Tom Cruise, Paula Wagner. *sc* David Koepp, Robert Towne. *ph* Stephen H Burum. *ed* Paul Hirsch. *pd* Norman Reynolds. *m* Danny Elfman, Lalo Schifrin. *cast* Tom Cruise, Jon Voight, Emmanuelle Béart, Henry Czerny, Jean Reno, Ving Rhames, Kristin Scott-Thomas, Vanessa Redgrave, Ingeborga Dapkunaite, Emilio Estevez.

● Twenty minutes into this big-budget update of the '70s spy series, half the cast has been wiped out, and Cruise's Ethan Hunt has been 'disavowed' by his employers, the CIA. To clear his name and avenge the death of his mentor Jim Phelps (Voight), Hunt assembles a crew of rogue agents to break in to CIA headquarters, playing a precarious double game with breathless self-assurance. 'Mission: Impenetrable': a bewildering, ludicrous, but mostly fun, sometimes even smart postscript to a genre that went out of fashion with the Cold War. There's more and less here than meets the eye. More, because De Palma, the cinematographer and the screenwriters have concocted an elaborate series of conceits and deceits, masks and trompe l'oeils, which slyly undermine the paranoid imperatives of the original series – and, indeed, the Cold War itself. Less, because De Palma is the most hermetic of American filmmakers; combine that with the pressure to deliver a mainstream blockbuster and you've got a recipe for superficiality. Despite the snags, De Palma remains a virtuoso puppet-master, pulling the strings taut in a nail-biting robbery sequence, switching from micro to macro with Hitchcockian panache, and finally letting rip with a hell-for-leather climax. TCh

Mission: Impossible II

(2000, US/Ger, 124 min)
d John Woo. *p* Tom Cruise, Paula Wagner. *sc* Robert Towne. *ph* Jeffrey L Kimball. *ed* Christian Wagner, Steven Kemper. *pd* Tom Sanders. *m* Hans Zimmer. *cast* Tom Cruise, Dougray Scott, Thandie Newton, Ving Rhames, Richard Roxburgh, John Polson, Brendan Gleeson, Rade Sherbedgia, Anthony Hopkins.

● 'This isn't *Mission: Difficult*, Mr Hunt,' cautions an incognito Hopkins. No, indeed. What would happen if Ethan Hunt ever choose to decline his assignment? Presumably we'd be left dangling, along with our hero, on some cliff face, while the world went to pot. It might make for a better movie, though, than this elaborately silly exercise in treading water. Screenwriter Towne tries to turn up the heat by teaming Ethan (Cruise) with cat burglar Nyrah (Newton) – setting a thief to catch a thief. Actually the model is closer to *Notorious*, what with Tom and Thandie getting it on, and her assuming pawn position to cosy up with her ex, renegade agent Ambrose (Scott). But Woo's hysterically hyper visuals and boytoy gimmickry can't camouflage the emptiness of the enterprise. Pumped up and sporting shoulder-length hair, Cruise endures love scenes, bike stunts and a smidgen of chop-socky with the same determination he used to survive Stanley Kubrick. TCh

Mission to Mars

(2000, US, 116 min)
d Brian De Palma. *p* Tom Jacobson. *sc* Jim Thomas, John Thomas, Graham Yost. *ph* Stephen H Burum. *ed* Paul Hirsch. *pd* Ed Verreaux. *m* Ennio Morricone. *cast* Gary Sinise, Don Cheadle, Connie Nielsen, Jerry O'Connell, Kim Delaney, Tim Robbins, Peter Outerbridge, Kavan Smith, Jill Teed, Elise Neal, Armin Mueller-Stahl.

● 2020: a manned mission to Mars has run into unexplained trouble on the red planet and a rescue team has the risky task of going in after them. With three of his colleagues dead and no radio contact, Cheadle draws the short straw. He has to hole up on the Martian surface, grow a beard and wait. The cavalry are coming, however, and they're the best that NASA's got, including ace helmsman Sinise and wise commander Robbins. All they have to do is align themselves to the correct orbit, but a dangerous fuel leak may be about to jeopardise their plans. De Palma's best stuff is in the middle of the movie, where he gets to grips with the nuts and bolts of the precarious rescue attempt and constructs a couple of flawless suspense sequences. The deliberate approach is most refreshing, but nothing else in the movie matches up to it – not the draggy set-up and certainly not the dismally unimaginative final half-hour, when we uncover the age old secrets of Mars. Given the glaring mismatch between the able performers, comic strip dialogue and monumental Morricone score, the whole thing reeks of a perversity unusual among today's machine tooled blockbusters, but that's hardly an unqualified recommendation. TJ

Mission to Moscow

(1943, US, 125 min, b/w)
d Michael Curtiz. *p* Robert Buckner. *sc* Howard Koch. *ph* Bert Glennon. *ed* Owen Marks. *ad* Carl Jules Weyl. *m* Max Steiner. *cast* Walter Huston, Ann Harding, Oscar Homolka, George Tobias, Gene Lockhart, Eleanor Parker, Helmut Dantine, Victor Francen, Henry Daniell, Maria Palmer, Lionel Stander, Cyd Charisse.

● Interesting either as an expressive object or as pure movie. Based on a bestselling memoir by Joseph E Davies, US ambassador to the USSR from 1936 to 1938, it makes an impassioned plea to John Doe to forget his fears about commies and embrace Russia as a comrade in arms against the Nazi peril. Subsequently an embarrassment, it was called in question by HUAC in 1947 (when studio head Jack Warner slid from under, since the film had seemingly been made at the request of the White House, but scriptwriter Howard Koch was thrown to the wolves). Presenting Stalin as everybody's favourite uncle, the infamous purges as mere matters of national security, and Reds as all-American Joes in furry hats sharing the same utopian dream, its thesis was rightly slated by Agee as 'a great glad two-million dollar bowl of canned borscht'. On the other hand, it's quite beautifully put together by Curtiz. TM

Mississippi Blues

(1993, Fr/US, 96 min)
d Robert Parrish, Bertrand Tavernier. *p* Bertrand Tavernier, Yannick Bernard. *ph* Pierre-William Glenn. *ed* Jean-Claude Vicquers. *with* Joe Cooper, Poppa Neale, Hayward Mills

● Tavernier, in pursuit of some Southland of the mind constructed from bits of Faulkner, Minnelli and Nick Ray, joins up with Parrish, whose own agenda has more to do with re-experiencing and communicating the flavour of his 1920s Georgia boyhood. Inevitably friction ensued, traces of which we are allowed to glimpse, but the fascinatingly lopsided result of the collaboration is really three overlapping movies, Parrish's, Tavernier's and the inadvertent one that emerges out of the obdurate individuality of the various interviewees. Those with low tolerance for gospel/blues should be aware that an awful lot of it goes on here – although we do get to see the director of *Saddle the Wind* sing 'Shall We Gather at the River', if that's your idea of a collector's item. BBa

Mississippi Burning

(1988, US, 127 min)
d Alan Parker. *p* Fred Zollo, Robert F Colesberry. *sc* Chris Gerolmo. *ph* Peter Biziou. *ed* Gerry Hambling. *pd* Philip Harrison, Geoffrey Kirkland. *m* Trevor Jones. *cast* Gene Hackman, Willem Dafoe, Frances McDormand, Brad Dourif, R Lee Ermey, Gailard Sartain, Stephen Tobolowsky, Michael Rooker.

● Parker's film, loosely based in fact, goes for the gut rather than the head in its assessment of Deep South racism. When three civil rights activists disappear from a small Mississippi town in 1964, the FBI responds (two of the missing men were white) by sending in agents Dafoe and Hackman, the former a by-the-book Yankee determined never to violate the rights of the interrogated, the latter a local boy who opines that to deal with scum you must sink to gutter level. Scum the villains certainly are: ugly, ignorant rednecks devoted to the Klan, and all too happy to punish blacks who protest against injustice or blab to interfering outsiders. In the film, the blacks are almost without exception seen as mute victims, and typically for a film by an Englishman, race hatred is defined in terms of class and economic envy. But Hackman is excellent, especially in his surprisingly tender scenes with McDormand, wife of sadistic deputy Dourif; and for once, Parker directs without depending on flashy visual tropes. The relative anonymity is a plus; only the end falls foul of hyperbole, and it's arguably the director's most controlled film to date. GA

Mississippi Masala

(1991, US, 113 min)
d Mira Nair. *p* Michael Nozik, Mira Nair. *sc* Sooni Taraporevala. *ph* Ed Lachman. *ed* Roberto Silvi. *pd* Mitch Epstein. *m* L Subramaniam. *cast* Denzel Washington, Sarita Choudhury, Roshan Seth, Sharmila Tagore, Charles S Dutton, Joe Seneca, Ranjit Chowdhry, Mira Nair.

● Nair's ambitious film examines a burdensome plurality of subjects associated with race and migration within the confines of a more-or-less conventional love story. Four-year-old Mina, her lawyer father and family, of Indian origin, are among those expelled from Uganda in 1972. Eighteen years later, we find them in Greenwood, Mississippi. Mina (Choudhury) has become, unlike her father (Seth), acclimatised if not entirely assimilated to her new country, and is employed as a cleaner at the local motel, hopeful but not impatient for greater things. She meets Afro-American Demetrius (Washington), a clean-cut, self-employed contract carpet cleaner, and their relationship unleashes the submerged rivalries, resentments and prejudices of their respective communities. An interesting if poorly constructed and self-contradicting drama, directed with something less than assurance, but given some appeal by the honesty of its performances. WH

Mississippi Mermaid

see Sirène du Mississipi, La

Miss Julie

(1999, GB/US, 101 min)
d Mike Figgis. *p* Mike Figgis, Harriet Cruickshank. *sc* Helen Cooper. *ph* Benoît Delhomme. *ed* Matthew Wood. *pd* Michael Howells. *m* Mike Figgis. *cast* Saffron Burrows, Peter Mullan, Maria Doyle Kennedy, Heathcote Williams.

● Figgis tackles Strindberg's chamber piece with rigour born of necessity. Shot in 16 days, the production is saddled with what looks like a flimsy hand-me-down BBC set (the action never leaves the kitchen of a large Swedish country house), and has only three principal speaking parts. But it's enthralling. Figgis asks us to listen and to watch as, one heady midsummer night, the young lady of the house, Miss Julie (Burrows), flirts with her father's footman Jean (Mullan). She is tipsy, depressed (her engagement has just been broken off) and reckless. He's wary, fiercely proud, angry about his lot and, once he gets the scent of opportunity, ravenous. This is a cold, cruel, eviscerating play. The lovers – if they can be called that – are poisoned by the class and power structures they recognise, but utterly fail to surmount. Yet the shifting power balance is what makes the drama so compelling. By filming in long, merciless takes, Figgis plugs us straight into the electricity between the performers, with Burrows haughty and vulnerable, towering over Mullan's white-knuckle fist of resentment and despair. TCh

Miss Mary

(1986, Arg/USA, 110 min)
d María Luisa Bemberg. *p* Lita Stantic. *sc* Jorge Goldenberg, María Luisa Bemberg. *ph* Miguel Rodriguez. *ed* Luis César d'Angiolillo. *ad* Esmeralda Almonacid. *m* Luis María Serra. *cast* Julie Christie, Nacha Guevara, Eduardo Pavlovsky, Luisina Brando, Gerardo Romano, Iris Marga.

● Miss Mary (Christie) is a lonely, starchy English governess whose recollections of her time in the employ of a wealthy Buenos Aires family provide insights into the type of spiritual malaise which is induced by an excess of cash. The father (Pavlovsky) spends much of the time at the billiard table; the mother (Guevara) is a fixture at the piano, playing melancholy Satie. The period is the late '30s/early '40s, and some acknowledgment of the shifting political scene as the Peron regime approaches filters through in after-dinner conversations or in the street disturbances which interrupt Miss Mary's thoughts. There's a sense of impending doom for the family, but the camera maintains a distance inhibiting our involvement, and even Miss Mary's testimony is thrown into question by the Catholic/Victorian upbringing which has left her almost as emotionally sterile as her employers. It's not an enjoyable film, rambling at times, but it deserves attention for its faithful reflection of the suffocating emptiness of a repressive way of life. EP

Miss Nobody (Panna Nikt)

(1996, Pol, 98 min)
d Andrzej Wajda. *sc* Radoslaw Piwowarski. *cast* Anna Wielgucka, Anna Mucha, Anna Powierza.

● A diffident 15-year-old girl from the countryside moves with her family to a high-rise apartment in Warsaw. As she tries to adjust to city life, she's befriended first by a wild, gypsy-like classmate, and then by the teenage daughter of entrepreneurial Poles. Miss Nobody clearly stands for Poland-in-miniature, caught between eastern mysticism and western materialism, but as political allegory, this is crude and heavy-handed. Wajda, seemingly taking his cue from Kieslowski, concentrates on the emotional lives of his characters, rather than on the social changes occurring around them. The strongest scenes are those in which the elements themselves seem torn by the heroine's anxieties (a climactic scene in the woods); but Wajda is no miniaturist by nature, and one suspects he'd prefer a much more epic canvas than this. Adapted from a novel by Tomas Tryzna. GM

Missouri Breaks, The

(1976, US, 126 min)
d Arthur Penn. *p* Elliott Kastner, Robert M Sherman. *sc* Thomas McGuane. *ph* Michael Butler. *ed* Jerry Greenberg, Stephen A Rotter, Dede Allen. *pd* Albert Brenner. *m* John Williams. *cast* Marlon Brando, Jack Nicholson, Randy Quaid, Kathleen Lloyd, Frederic Forrest, Harry Dean Stanton, John McLiam, John P Ryan, Richard Bradford.

● A wonderfully quirky Western, brilliantly scripted by Thomas McGuane, which strips all the cute whimsy away from the *Butch Cassidy* theme (outlaws on the run from a relentless lawman), replacing it with a kind of pixillated terror. Playing the 'regulator' as a camp Buffalo Bill with an Irish accent, Brando makes his entrance playing peekaboo from behind his horse, and at one point even stalks his prey in a dress and poke bonnet. But he is also a legalised killer, expert with a rifle but preferring (as the flail of God) to use a harpoon shaped like a crucifix. And as his gloating sadism shades into hints of bizarre perversion when he dedicates a love song and a kiss to his horse, the tone gradually darkens to a kind of horror. It's one of the few truly major Westerns of the '70s, with a very clear vision of the historical role played by fear and violence in the taming of the wilderness. TM

Miss Pinkerton

(1932, US, 66 min, b/w)
d Lloyd Bacon. *sc* Niven Busch, Lillian Hayward. *ph* Barney McGill. *ed* Ray Curtis. *cast* Joan Blondell, George Brent, John Wray, Ruth Hall, C Henry Gordon, Elizabeth Patterson, Holmes Herbert.

● Potboiling whodunit set in an old dark house, crammed with shots of menacing silhouettes and characters all behaving sinisterly. Blondell, as lively as usual, is the best thing in the film as a nurse sent to tend to Elizabeth Patterson, prostrated by the suicide – possibly murder – of her nephew. When Patterson goes the same way, done in by hypodermic, Blondell helps Brent's police inspector – for whom she naturally falls – uncover a dastardly legal plot. The supporting performances are indifferent. TM

Miss Robin Hood

(1952, GB, 78 min, b/w)
d John Guillermin. *p* Donald Wilson. *sc* Val Valentine, Patrick Campbell. *ph* Arthur Grant. *ed* Manuel Del Campo. *ad* Ray Simm. *m* Temple Abady. *cast* Margaret Rutherford, Richard Hearne, James Robertson Justice, Edward Lexy, Michael Medwin, Sidney James, Dora Bryan, Peter Jones, Reg Varney.

● Sub-Ealing whimsy finds shy children's writer Hearne unwittingly embroiled in a life of crime when eccentric youth club leader Rutherford enlists his help to swipe a whisky formula she claims was stolen from her ancestors. A jaunty but rather inane little number (co-written by Patrick Campbell), largely notable as one of the few films made by the short-lived Group 3 Productions, set up by the National Film Finance Corporation with the specific remit of making low budget pictures. TJ

Miss Sadie Thompson

(1953, US, 87 min)
d Curtis Bernhardt. *p* Jerry Wald. *sc* Harry Kleiner. *ph* Charles Lawton Jr. *ed* Viola Lawrence. *ad* Carl Anderson. *m* George Duning. *songs* Lester Lee, Ned Washington, Morris W Stoloff. *cast* Rita Hayworth, José Ferrer, Aldo Ray, Harry Bellaver, Charles Bronson, Russell Collins, Diosa Costello.

● A dire, updated, absurdly bloated 3-D version of Somerset Maugham's *Rain* – a tale of sin and redemption in the tropics – completely missing out on the dark, brooding intensity of Raoul Walsh's silent *Sadie Thompson*. Conviction never gets a look in, what with Ferrer wandering zombie-fashion through acres of pious platitudes as the religious bigot who turns out (surprise, surprise) to be a closet rapist, while Hayworth, mouthing a string of dubbed songs and cheerfully revving her motor as the good-time gal who is no better (and not much worse) than she should be, seems to be moulding her characterisation on Doris Day. Only Aldo Ray, as the bovine marine who falls for Sadie, and in so doing discovers the meaning of tolerance, emerges from the affair with any credit. TM

Miss Shumway jette un sort

see Rough Magic

Mr and Mrs Bridge

(1990, US, 125 min)
d James Ivory. *p* Ismail Merchant. *sc* Ruth Prawer Jhabvala. *ph* Tony Pierce-Roberts. *ed* Humphrey Dixon. *pd* David Gropman. *m* Richard Robbins. *cast* Paul Newman, Joanne Woodward, Margaret Welsh, Robert Sean Leonard, Kyra Sedgwick, Saundra McClain, Blythe Danner, Gale Garnett, Simon Callow, Austin Pendleton.

● In this adaptation of Evan S Connell's twin novels, Newman plays Mr Bridge, a distinguished Kansas City lawyer, and Woodward his wife. It is not a marriage of like minds: India Bridge is all caring and sharing, but hidebound Walter, though full of love for his family, dare not speak its name. The First World War is over and the second one coming, but Walter refuses to move with the times. In many ways the film is about disappointment: the disappointment children cause parents – fast-and-loose Ruth (Sedgwick) goes to New York to become an actress, and fails; Carolyn (Welsh) ends in divorce; Douglas (Leonard – the author Connell) cannot even bring himself to kiss mother – and the disappointment felt when spouses, friends and life itself fail to live up to expectation. The episodic outcome is disappointing, too. Newman is good and Woodward superb, but their moving portrayals exist in a vacuum of overpowering beauty. Stunningly photographed interiors and exteriors take the breath away, but their inhabitants seem almost irrelevant. MS

Mr and Mrs Smith

(1941, US, 95 min, b/w)
d Alfred Hitchcock. *sc* Norman Krasna. *ph* Harry Stradling. *ed* William Hamilton. *ad* Van Nest Polglase, LP Williams. *m* Edward Ward. *cast* Carole Lombard, Robert Montgomery, Gene Raymond, Jack Carson, Betty Compson, Philip Merivale.

● A gentle crazy comedy, with Lombard and Montgomery as a couple who discover that their marriage wasn't legal and go through courtship all over again. Less Hitchcock, however, than writer Norman Krasna, who at his best could twist conventional characters and plot patterns in such beguiling ways that you'd almost forget their antiquity. This comes near his best. GB

Mr Arkadin (aka Confidential Report)

(1955, Sp/Fr, 100 min, b/w)
d Orson Welles. *p* Louis Dolivet. *sc* Orson Welles. *ph* Jean Bourgoin. *ed* Renzo Lucidi. *ad* Orson Welles. *m* Paul Misraki. *cast* Orson Welles, Paola Mori, Robert Arden, Akim Tamiroff, Michael Redgrave, Patricia Medina, Mischa Auer, Katina Paxinou.

● Long unavailable for theatrical screening but finally resurfacing on TV in a version edited closer to Welles' cut than that originally released here, *Mr Arkadin* assumed an equivalent patina of myth and legend to that cultivated by its central character, non-naturalistically posited somewhere between Kane and God. Arkadin is the powerful financier who employs his own researcher to piece together his apparently forgotten past, to find a shabby Rosebud to dramatise his by-now bored puppeteering. Flamboyantly melodramatic, it's a playfully egocentric display of egocentrism and a magician's perverse revelation of his own trickery. Failure or not, it's irresistible. PT

Mr Baseball

(1992, US/Jap, 113 min)
d Fred Schepisi. *p* Fred Schepisi, Robert Newmyer, Doug Claybourne. *sc* Gary Ross, Kevin Wade, Monte Merrick. *ph* Ian Baker. *ed* Peter Honess. *ad* Ted Haworth. *m* Jerry Goldsmith. *cast* Tom Selleck, Ken Takakura, Aya Takanashi, Toshi Shioya, Dennis Haysbert.

● Hardly one of Schepisi's finest hours: Selleck mugs his way through the usual 'fish out of water' routine as a lippy American ball-player who joins a Japanese team, but, somewhat predictably, has difficulty adjusting to the confines of group mentality. It's fairly tame stuff, but Matsushita's take-over of Universal dumped the production into controversy, with the Japanese reckoning the script was anti-Japanese and the Yanks reckoning it anti-American. We Brits took one look and called it 'straight to video'. TJ

Mr Billion

(1977, US, 93 min)
d Jonathan Kaplan. *p* Steve Bach, Ken Friedman. *sc* Ken Friedman, Jonathan Kaplan. *ph* Matthew F Leonetti. *ed* O Nicholas Brown. *ad* Richard Berger. *m* David Grusin. *cast* Terence Hill, Valerie Perrine, Jackie Gleason, Slim Pickens, William Redfield, Chill Wills, Dick Miller, RG Armstrong, Kate Heflin.

● Chase comedy without the glamour of *Silver Streak* but with much pleasant and well-handled action. Italian garage mechanic (spaghetti Western star Hill in his American debut) inherits billion dollars from financier uncle in California; company hires Perrine to seduce him into handing over power of attorney; she falls for him instead, so the pair must be ambushed, shot at, handcuffed together etc, to prevent Hill claiming inheritance by specified date. He escapes, and naturally tangles with a whole crowd of eccentrics on his way across America. Like other Corman colts, Kaplan opts for a '30s approach, whose soft-centre no amount of flashy cutting can hide; but there is a nice tongue-in-cheek air ('Perverts are people too'), and a lot of Hollywood clichés are delivered fresh and with relish. AN

Mr Blandings Builds His Dream House

(1948, US, 93 min, b/w)
d HC Potter. *p/sc* Norman Panama, Melvin Frank. *ph* James Wong Howe. *ed* Harry Marker. *ad* Albert S D'Agostino, Carroll Clark. *m* Leigh Harline. *cast* Cary Grant, Myrna Loy, Melvyn Douglas, Reginald Denny, Sharyn Moffet, Connie Marshall, Louise Beavers, Jason Robards Sr.

● 'Mr Dreamings Builds His Bland House' would be a more accurate title for this distinctly quaint RKO comedy of Cary Grant's advertising man from Manhattan trying to set up a rural haven for his family in Connecticut, despite dry rot and all kinds of neighbourhood shysters. Naturally the dream comes true, and Blandings is probably the world's happiest commuter. The sweet, flimsy charm of all this would no doubt be indigestible without the personable performances of the stars, or the smug confidence of the script and direction. GB

Mister Cory

(1956, US, 92 min)
d Blake Edwards. *p* Robert Arthur. *sc* Blake Edwards. *ph* Russell Metty. *ed* Edward Curtiss. *ad* Alexander Golitzen, Eric Orbom. *m* Joseph Gershenson. *cast* Tony Curtis, Charles Bickford, Martha Hyer, Kathryn Grant, Henry Daniell, William Reynolds, Russ Morgan.

● Made just before *Sweet Smell of Success*, serving almost as a run-up to Curtis' characterisation as Sidney Falco, this mines the same vein of guttersnipe, braggart ambition, but to comic and rather less successful effect. Curtis plays a Chicago slum kid who, while employed as a waiter, makes it rich as a gambler among the country-club set, and ends up having to choose between classy Hyer (who likes him for his body) and her sister Grant (who likes him for himself). A glossy, almost-black comedy, it never really works as sharp social satire, despite the pointed irony of the sexually ambiguous relationship between Curtis and the ageing gambler (Bickford) with whom he goes into lucrative partnership. But Curtis' sense of timing, coupled with Edwards' solid professionalism, make for breezy if forgettable entertainment. GA

Mr Deeds Goes to Town

(1936, US, 115 min, b/w)
d/p Frank Capra. *sc* Robert Riskin. *ph* Joseph Walker. *ed* Gene Havlick. *ad* Stephen Goosson. *m* Howard Jackson. *cast* Gary Cooper, Jean Arthur, George Bancroft, Lionel Stander, Raymond Walburn, Walter Catlett, Douglas Dumbrille, HB Warner.

●Before Capra got down to Christmas card morals, he perfected the screwball comedy technique of pursuing common sense to logical ends in a lunatic situation. *Mr Deeds Goes to Town* is one of the best, with Cooper saying nope to a $20 million inheritance, and newshound Jean Arthur going for his 'inside story': and if you've seen *The Electric Horseman*, you'll see where it borrowed its ludicrous charm. DMacp

Mr Drake's Duck

(1950, GB, 85 min, b/w)
d Val Guest. *p* Daniel M Angel. *sc* Val Guest. *ph* Jack Cox. *ed* Sam Simmonds. *ad* Maurice Carter. *m* Bruce Campbell. *cast* Douglas Fairbanks Jr, Yolande Donlan, AE Matthews, Jon Pertwee, Reginald Beckwith, Wilfrid Hyde-White, Harry Fowler.

●Complications mount in this adaptation of a vintage radio play (by Ian Messiter) when nice American couple Fairbanks and Donlan start a new life in England and discover their recently purchased duck is laying solid uranium eggs. A light-hearted frolic from another age. Uranium eggs? Ho, ho! TJ

Mr Forbush and the Penguins (aka Cry of the Penguins)

(1971, GB, 101 min)
d Al Viola. *p* Henry Trettin. *sc* Anthony Shaffer. *ph* Ted Scaife (Antarctic), Harry Waxman. *ed* Bernard Gribble. *ad* Tony Masters. *m* John Addison. *cast* John Hurt, Hayley Mills, Dudley Sutton, Tony Britton, Thorley Walters, Judy Campbell, Joss Ackland.

●Filmed on location with the assistance of the Argentinian army and navy, and with Arne Sucksdorff responsible for the Antarctic animal sequences. Viola's version (Forbush alone in the Antarctic wastes) was pruned to make way for the inconsequential framing story (directed by an uncredited Roy Boulting) deemed necessary to get people into the cinema. So Graham Billing's novel emerges as a trite romantic fable about a rich young biologist who leaves home and his frigid girlfriend (Mills) for the warm-hearted beasties of the frozen South. There's a single sequence during the arrival of the penguins that makes the rest of the film just about worth sitting through.

Mister Freedom

(1968, Fr. 110 min)
d William Klein. *p* Guy Belfond, Michel Zemer, Christian Thivat. *sc* William Klein. *ph* Pierre Lhomme. *ed* Anne-Marie Cotret. *ad* Jacques Dugied, André Piltant. *m* Serge Gainsbourg. *cast* John Abbey, Delphine Seyrig, Jean-Claude Drouot, Philippe Noiret, Catherine Rouvel, Sami Frey, Serge Gainsbourg, Donald Pleasence, Yves Montand.

●The colossal Mr Freedom (Abbey) wears baseball gear, feverishly decorated – like so much else in this heavy-handed romp – with stars, stripes, red, white and blue. His mission is to rid France of America's ideological enemies, represented by Red-China-Man (a smoke-breathing yellow-tailed monster) and Moujik-Man (Noiret in a rather fetching inflated red costume). But Freedom overplays his hand, and blows up the whole country along with himself. Klein shows a parallel lack of restraint, going all out to slay American imperialism with sledgehammer irony and a comic strip style which soon becomes tiresome. Isolated things remain among the debris: a shot of a smiling girl with two boiled eggs and a strip of bacon on her chest in a heady montage on the delights of American life; the sight of Christ silencing the Virgin Mary with 'Mom, please!'; and of course Delphine Seyrig as a drum majorette/whore double agent. GB

Mister Frost

(1990, Fr/GB, 104 min)
d Philippe Setbon. *p* Xavier Gélin. *sc* Philippe Setbon, Brad Lynch. *ph* Dominique Brenguier. *ed* Ray Lovejoy. *ad* Max Berto. *m* Steve Levine. *cast* Jeff Goldblum, Alan Bates, Kathy Baker, Roland Giraud, Jean-Pierre Cassel, Daniel Gélin, Henri Serre, Charley Boorman.

●Setbon's second film as director, in a career which has encompassed cartoons, comics and the screenplay for Godard's *Détective*, is an odd affair. The eponymous anti-hero (Goldblum) is apprehended for a particularly hideous series of murders after a would-be burglar breaks into his garage and discovers a corpse with its throat cut. The question is: is Mister Frost, as detective Felix Detweiller (Bates) believes, the Devil himself; is he a vibrant, sexy, all-powerful healer in an institution for the helpless and insane; or is he just another heavy-duty nutter? The film does grip, despite the sometimes below-par quality of both the camerawork and the acting. The real weakness lies in the performance of Bates, who leaves much to be desired both as cop and as putative lover of a doctor played by the excellent Kathy Baker. Much of the narrative, moreover, is meandering, trying too hard to reconcile romance with horror pic and with theatre of the intellect. Different, though. SGr

Mr Hobbs Takes a Vacation

(1962, US, 115 min)
d Henry Koster. *p* Jerry Wald. *sc* Nunnally Johnson. *ph* William C Mellor. *ed* Marjorie Fowler. *ad* Jack Martin Smith, Malcolm Brown. *m* Henry Mancini. *cast* James Stewart, Maureen O'Hara, Fabian, John Saxon, Marie Wilson, Reginald Gardiner, Lauri Peters, John McGiver.

●A wholesome family comedy with Stewart and O'Hara as a couple whose quiet vacation becomes a noisy free-for-all for the kids. Fabian, one of the first rock singers to be created overnight by publicity hype (with hit songs like 'Tiger' and 'Turn Me Loose'), apart from singing one song, gives a performance so wooden it has to be seen to be believed. DP

Mr Holland's Opus

(1995, US, 143 min)
d Stephen Herek. *p* Ted Field, Michael Nolin, Robert W Cort. *sc* Patrick Sheane Duncan. *ph* Oliver Wood. *ed* Trudy Ship. *pd* David Nichols. *m* Michael Kamen. *cast* Richard Dreyfuss, Glenne Headly, Jay Thomas, Olympia Dukakis, WH Macy, Alicia Witt, Terrence Howard.

●It's Glenn Holland's first day at school: he's the reluctant new music teacher at John F Kennedy High. It's 1965, and Mr Holland (Dreyfuss) is anxious to get back to his real work, composition, but as time passes he rechannels his passion into the students, until one day he wakes up, 30 years later, and wonders what happened to his life. Although the avowed inspiration here is *It's a Wonderful Life*, this tear-jerker shares plenty of old school ties with such British counterparts as *The Browning Version* and *Goodbye, Mr Chips*. Screenwriter Patrick Sheane Duncan has created a dramatic arc that's also a learning curve: Holland starts off a stiff-shirt disciplinarian, but comes to realise that he gets better results when he mixes up the Ludwig Van with a little Ray Charles. The film soft-pedals the uglier realities of contemporary schools and Holland's last, most sentimental lesson is to appreciate his own worth. But sentimentality can have its heart in the right place and, in any case, this isn't the film's only message: Dreyfuss' exemplary performance shows how selfishly Holland neglects his own family in favour of his pupils, and it's clear how conservative politics impinge even on music classes. A middle-brow melodrama which functions as the thinking person's *Forrest Gump*. Music to my ears. TCh

Mr Hulot's Holiday

see Vacances de M. Hulot, Les

Mister Johnson

(1990, US, 101 min)
d Bruce Beresford. *p* Michael Fitzgerald. *sc* William Boyd. *ph* Peter James. *ed* Humphrey Dixon. *pd* Herbert Pinter. *m* Georges Delerue. *cast* Maynard Eziashi, Pierce Brosnan, Edward Woodward, Beatie Edney, Femi Fatoba, Denis Quilley, Bella Enahoro, Nick Reding.

●Another film about a white master and a black servant from the director of *Driving Miss Daisy*. Colonial West Africa, c.1920: Rudbeck (Brosnan) is a fastidious English District Officer, Johnson (Eziashi) his chief clerk, a native more English than the English. William Boyd, who adapted Joyce Cary's novel for the film, has compared Johnson to Falstaff and Candide; but a character who lived in his own right on the page picks up all kind of social baggage when projected on to the screen. Here, despite Eziashi's droll performance, Johnson comes to embody an offensive, regressive racial stereotype. A colonial sensibility runs through the film, despite the trite disavowals that pepper the script. It misfires drastically, but Beresford's anonymous direction at least apes some received notion of 'quality'. He photographs the landscape prettily, and the film is neatly turned. Eminently respectable, in fact. TCh

Mr Jolly Lives Next Door

(1987, GB, 52 min)
d Stephen Frears. *p* Elaine Taylor. *sc* Adrian Edmondson, Rik Mayall, Roiland Rivron. *ph* Oliver Stapleton. *ed* Rob Wright. *pd* Grant Hicks. *m* Roland Rivron. *cast* Adrian Edmondson, Rik Mayall, Peter Cook, Nicholas Parsons, Peter Richardson, Gerard Kelly, Granville Saxton.

●TV's Comic Strip in a niagara of blood, booze, saliva and sick, this has Edmondson and Mayall as a pair of bored escorts who, while taking no care of Nicholas Parsons, become involved with a hit-gang and an axe-man (Cook). The abuse is so gratuitous, the pace so riotous, that a kind of obscene serenity hovers over the mayhem. It's funny. Comic Strippers will adore it, and after a six-pack, so will anybody else. MS

Mr Jones

(1994, US, 114 min)
d Mike Figgis. *p* Alan Greisman, Debra Greenfield. *sc* Eric Roth, Michael Cristofer. *ph* Juan Ruiz Anchia. *ed* Tom Rolf. *pd* Waldemar Kalinowski. *m* Maurice Jarre. *cast* Richard Gere, Lena Olin, Anne Bancroft, Tom Irwin, Delroy Lindo, Bruce Altman, Lauren Tom.

●Mike Figgis's film began as a brooding account of the affair between Mr Jones (Gere), an erratic depressive, and Libbie (Olin), his dedicated, love-struck psychiatrist. But Gere, it seems, resisting typecasting and attempting to give his role some depth, started panic bells ringing in Hollywood executive offices. With the result that post-production tampering reduced an apparently sombre film – about (among other matters) whether the psychiatrist has the right to deprive Jones of his sometimes dangerous 'highs' – to an essentially empty, over-hyped, feel-good movie. In its present state, the film veers unsteadily between overblown romance and a portrait of a disturbed and pained man as a wacky guy who's fun to be with. Small wonder that the director has disowned the release version. NF

Mr Klein

(1976, Fr/It, 123 min)
d Joseph Losey. *p* Raymond Danon, Alain Delon, Robert Kuperberg, Jean-Pierre Labrande. *sc* Franco Solinas. *ph* Gerry Fisher. *ed* Henri Lanoe. *ad* Alexandre Trauner. *m* Egisto Macchi, Pierre Porte. *cast* Alain Delon, Jeanne Moreau, Suzanne Flon, Michel Lonsdale, Juliet Berto, Francine Bergé, Jean Bouise, Louis Seigner, Michel Aumont, Massimo Girotti, Roland Bertin.

●The action of Losey's film takes place against the Nazi deportation of French Jews – a set of circumstances which the film doesn't so much explore as get lost in. Klein (Delon), a Parisian art dealer, is delivered a copy of a Jewish newspaper. Investigating this, he becomes aware of a mysterious Jewish alter-ego bearing the same name. Though they do not meet, Klein finds the other impinging increasingly on his life, even living in his flat when he's not there. The confusion of identities forces Klein to defend himself against a charge of being Jewish. Predictably, the film ends with his deportation; quite unaccountably, Losey makes this a deliberate choice, as Klein purposely avoids the lawyers bringing the evidence which can release him, a piece of fatalism which resolves nothing whatsoever. Sadly, Losey's determinedly enigmatic treatment turns a potentially very interesting theme into cheap mystification. AS

Mr Lord Says No

see Happy Family, The

Mr Love

(1985, GB, 91 min)
d Roy Battersby. *p* Susan Richards, Robin Douet. *sc* Kenneth Eastaugh. *ph* Clive Tickner, John Davey. *ed* Alan J Cumner-Pryce. *ad* Adrienne Atkinson. *m* Willy Russell. *cast* Barry Jackson, Maurice Denham, Margaret Tyzack, Linda Marlowe, Christina Collier, Helen Cotterill, Julia Deakin.

●Set in crumbling Southport-on-Sea, where one Donald Lovelace (Jackson), a mild-mannered, fiftyish landscape gardener sows his wild oats among the town's lonely womenfolk in a last-ditch quest for romance and nooky. Both of which he reaps with astounding ease from a range of eccentric Lancastrian matrons, though poor Donald Juan ends up getting dumped on by all the ladies in his life from Queen Victoria downwards. An unashamedly old-fashioned little film with a dash of nostalgia and a touch of Ealing comic whimsy. SJo

Mr Majestyk

(1974, US, 103 min)
d Richard Fleischer. *p* Walter Mirisch. *sc* Elmore Leonard. *ph* Richard H Kline. *ed* Ralph E Winters. *ad* Cary Odell. *m* Charles Bernstein. *cast* Charles Bronson, Al Lettieri, Linda Cristal, Lee Purcell, Paul Koslo, Taylor Lacher, Frank Maxwell, Alejandro Rey.

●Charles Bronson, his eyes just about open, strides through this film as a paternalistic melon-grower in Colorado, anti-racist, tolerant of unions (well, you can tell, he gets the melon-picking union girl in the end; how does Cristal keep her hair so black and shiny after all that sweaty work?), who falls foul of local crooks and labour racketeers. But melon-grower beats ruthless psychopath, casting aspersions at the police force en route. Fleischer handles a heavy script and most of the acting like no one should handle a melon; but he really soars into competence at moments of tension, car chases, and general cinematic escapism. MV

Mr Mom (aka Mr Mum)

(1983, US, 91 min)
d Stan Dragoti. *p* Lynn Loring, Lauren Shuler Donner. *sc* John Hughes. *ph* Victor J Kemper. *ed* Patrick Kennedy. *pd* Alfred Sweeney. *m* Lee Holdridge. *cast* Michael Keaton, Teri Garr, Martin Mull, Ann Jillian, Christopher Lloyd, Carolyn Seymour.

●In these post-feminist times, you might have thought that the spectacle of men doing housework was a little played out as a subject for comedy. But this – in which unemployment forces Keaton to swop roles with his wife Garr – plays the usual trick of taking a '30s formula and pushing it far further than it has gone before. Keaton visibly disintegrates into an alcoholic, pill-popping soap opera addict, until he screams the final admission to his wife: 'My brain is like oatmeal. I never knew it was like this.' Written by ex-Lampoon regular John Hughes, the film is funniest when it is detailing the psychological horrors of housework, notably the awful pull of the soap opera which begins to merge with Keaton's domestic reality. The various props, like the voracious vacuum cleaner, are less successful, but Hughes still manages to play on the anxieties of middle America with fairly devilish skill. DP

Mr Moto's Gamble

(1938, US, 72 min, b/w)
d James Tinling. *sc* Charles Belden, Jerry Cady. *ph* Lucien Andriot. *ed* Nick De Maggio. *ad* Bernard Herzbrun, Haldane Douglas. *m* Samuel Kaylin. *cast* Peter Lorre, Keye Luke, Lynn Bari, Dick Baldwin, Harold Huber, Douglas Fowley, Harold Huber, Maxie Rosenbloom, Ward Bond, Lon Chaney Jr.

●Starting with *Think Fast, Mr Moto* in 1937, Lorre (sporting steel-rimmed glasses and buck teeth) starred eight times in an engaging characterisation as John P Marquand's inscrutable Japanese sleuth – expert in disguise, master of ju-jitsu – in a series discontinued in 1939 because of deteriorating relations between America and Japan. Fast, formulary and quite fun, the films are much of a muchness, and not unlike poor relations to the *Charlie Chan* series. *Mr Moto's Gamble* (third in the series) in fact started life as a Chan film, taken over (along with Keye Luke) on Warner Oland's death. Despite an equally engaging characterisation by Henry Silva, *The Return of Mr Moto*, an attempt to revive the series in 1965, remained a one-off. TM

Mr Mum

see Mr Mom

Mr Music

(1950, US, 114 min, b/w)
d Richard Haydn. *p* Robert L Welch. *sc* Arthur Sheekman. *ph* George Barnes. *ed* Doane Harrison. *ad* Hans Dreier, Earl Hedrick. *songs* Johnny Burke, James Van Heusen. *cast* Bing Crosby, Nancy Olson, Charles Coburn, Ruth Hussey, Marge and Gower Champion, Groucho Marx, Peggy Lee, Claude Curdle [Richard Haydn].

●Okay-ish Burke/Van Heusen musical has knitwear-clad Bing as a talented tunesmith who'd rather have another round of golf than write a hit Broadway show, but who, when the money runs low, has to turn to impresario Coburn for help. There are two conditions to the latter's offer of a substantial loan: that he come up with some new numbers, and that he take on super-secretary Olson. Crooning and romancing inevitably follow, but it's all a bit too relaxed to go down as one of the greats.

Mr Nanny

(1992, US, 84 min)
d Michael Gottlieb. *p* Robert Engelman. *sc* Ed Rugoff, Michael Gottlieb. *ph* Peter Stein. *ed* Earl Ghaffari, Michael Ripps. *pd* Don De Fina. *m* David Johansen, Brian Koonin. *cast* Hulk Hogan, Austin Pendleton, Sherman Hemsley, David Johansen, Robert Gorman, Madeline Zima.

●Cross *Home Alone* with *Kindergarten Cop* and you get 'Home Cop', which is basically what we have here. An American wrestling champ with two or three films under his belt, Hogan has an unusual combination of assets: brawn and an authentic American accent. He doesn't take himself too seriously either, which could prove his downfall – that and excruciating movies like this. He plays a genial ex-wrestler who accepts a job as a bodyguard, only to find that the bodies in question – Alex and Kate (Gorman and Zima), sorely neglected by their scientist father (Pendleton) since their mother's death – are both pre-pubescent and exceptionally vindictive. As the title implies, gender identity is at the heart of the movie. Kate teaches Hulk to be dainty by dressing him in a tutu; but come the crunch, the H-man – 'one tough mother' – helps father and son to bond by vanquishing their enemies. TCh

Mr Nice Guy (Yige Hao Ren)

(1996/8, HK, 96 min)
d Samo Hung [Hung Kam-Bo]. p Chua Lam. *sc* Edward Tang, Fibe Ma. *ph* Raymond Lam. *ed* Peter Cheung. *pd* Horace Ma. *m* Peter Kam. *cast* Jackie Chan, Richard Norton, Miki Lee, Karen McLymont, Gabrielle Fitzpatrick, Vince Poletto, Samo Hung.

●As Jackie Chan movies are fundamentally stunts in search of a plot, it's unsurprising he's become one of the most well-travelled stars, exporting his standard mix of thrills and gags to 'colourful' worldwide locations. Sadly, the metropolitan centres he favours appear to be virtually interchangeable; shopping malls, apartments, empty warehouses and building sites are his natural habitat. Though this casts him as a TV chef, his name, 'Jackie', hints at how indistinguishable the role really is from the happy-go-lucky cops Chan usually plays. Admittedly, he throws a mean noodle, but the recipe is beginning to taste a bit stale. This could have been made at any time over the last 15 years. Yet many of its multiple misunderstandings, chase and fight scenes are so dynamic and inventive they do in fact justify the enterprise. Director Samo Hung points the camera at the action and generally shies away from the saddest bunch of Australian bit-players you ever saw. TCh

Mr North

(1988, US, 93 min)
d Danny Huston. *p* Steven Haft, Skip Steloff. *sc* Janet Roach, John Huston, James Costigan. *ph* Robin Vidgeon. *ed* Roberto Silvi. *pd* Eugene Lee. *m* David McHugh. *cast* Anthony Edwards, Robert Mitchum, Lauren Bacall, Harry Dean Stanton, Anjelica Huston, Mary Stuart Masterson, Virginia Madsen, Tammy Grimes, David Warner, Hunter Carson, Christopher Durang.

●Danny Huston's first feature owes more to Frank Capra than to his dad John. Adapted from the Thornton Wilder novel *Theophilus North*, it's a gently moral fable about a young man (Edwards) who cycles into 1920s Newport (sun-dappled Gatsby territory) and roots out evil by virtue of his good nature, good sense and mysterious knack of dispensing static electricity at will. Kids call it magic, while adults call it faith healing and plague him with requests. Prime beneficiaries of Mr North's special powers are the town's wealthy elder (Mitchum), a shy debutante (Masterson), and a lively housemaid (Madsen). Also drifting in and out of the whimsical plot are Bacall's local madam, Stanton's fraudulent Cockney valet, and Anjelica Huston as Mitchum's loving daughter and North's heart's desire. Apart from a minor hiccup where sceptics initiate a witch hunt against our hero, there's never a moment's doubt that Good Will Out. Although delicately acted and lovingly shot, it adds up to little more than candy floss. EP

Mr Orchid

see Père Tranquille, Le

Mr Peabody and the Mermaid

(1948, US, 89 min, b/w)
d Irving Pichel. *p/sc* Nunnally Johnson. *ph* Russell Metty. *ed* Marjorie Fowler. *ad* Bernard Herzbrun, Boris Leven. *m* Robert Emmett Dolan. cast William Powell, Ann Blyth, Irene Harvey, Andrea King, Cliton Sundberg.

●Amorous amphibian antics as a staid Boston banker goes fishin' and catches comely mermaid Blyth. An inoffensive timepasser. TJ

Mister Quilp

(1974, GB, 119 min)
d Michael Tuchner. *p* Helen M Strauss. *sc* Louis Kamp, Irene Kamp. *ph* Christopher Challis. *ed* John Jympson. *pd* Elliot Scott. *m* Anthony Newley. *cast* Anthony Newley, David Hemmings, David Warner, Michael Hordern, Paul Rogers, Jill Bennett, Sarah-Jane Varley, Mona Washbourne, Philip Davis, Bryan Pringle.

●'I may be simple-hearted but I think the world is grand' trills winsome Little Nell in the opening minutes of this musical version of *The Old Curiosity Shop* sponsored by Reader's Digest. Well, the film is terrible: two solid hours of excruciating overacting from Newley as the vile and dwarfish Quilp, phony sets and costumes which look as though they've only just been removed from the wrapping-paper, botched songs (by Newley) and choreography, lackadaisical direction, and lots of good character actors going to waste. GB

Mr Reliable (a True Story)

(1996, Aust, 113 min)
d Nadia Tass. *p* Jim McElroy, Terry Hayes, Michael Hamlyn. *sc* Don Catchlove, Terry Hayes. *ph* David Parker, Greg Hunter. *ed* Peter Carrodus. *pd* Jon Dowding. *m* Philip Judd. *cast* Colin Friels, Jacqueline McKenzie, Paul Sonkkila, Frank Gallacher, Lisa Hensley, Aaron Blabey, Geoff Morrell, Neil Fitzpatrick.

●Recently released from prison, Wally Mellish (Friels) drives back into Sydney in the long hot summer of 1968. Having fallen for spunky single parent Beryl (McKenzie), Wally wins praise for his home-building skills in sleepy Glenfield, until he lets off a warning shotgun blast at a cop, who is hounding him unnecessarily, and finds himself at the centre of a lengthy siege – an open-air concert of emergency police squads, sniper units, back-up reserves with canteen facilities, journalists, camps of spectators, barbecue stalls – which becomes nationwide news. Ordinary and none too bright Wally may be, but his tenacity, self-awareness and inventive, if unconventional, manner make him suitable material for the media to fashion into a people's hero. An excess of nostalgic affection for the Australian Summer of Love results in a slight archness; and despite Friels' sympathetic performance and some engaging cameos (notably Sonkkila's sublimely second-rate Police Commissioner), a fluid pace and deft comic touches, the film ends up somewhat overloaded with whimsy and benevolence. WH

Mister Roberts

(1955, US, 120 min)
d John Ford, Mervyn LeRoy. *p* Leland Howard. *sc* Frank S Nugent, Joshua Logan. *ph* Winton C Hoch. *ed* Jack Murray. *ad* Arthur Loel. *m* Franz Waxman. *cast* Henry Fonda, James Cagney, William Powell, Jack Lemmon, Betsy Palmer, Ward Bond, Nick Adams, Harry Carey Jr.

●Trouble-bound adaptation of Thomas Heggen's Broadway hit about a WWII supply ship, its martinet captain, and the junior officer who finally makes the symbolic gesture required to liberate the pent-up tensions in the crew. Ford became diplomatically ill, LeRoy took over, and an uncredited Joshua Logan (responsible for the original stage show) directed bits as well. The fact that the picture is seamlessly anonymous testifies to the power of star performances rather than to any directorial engagement. The acting is the only reason to watch it: Fonda as the frustrated lieutenant who craves a go at the Japs; Cagney as the tyrannical captain; Powell as the cynical medico; and Lemmon as Ensign Pulver, the joker in the pack. ATu

Mr Saturday Night

(1992, US, 119 min)
d/p Billy Crystal. *sc* Billy Crystal, Lowell Ganz, Babaloo Mandel. *ph* Don Peterman. *ed* Kent Beyda. *pd* Albert Brenner. *m* Marc Shaiman. *cast* Billy Crystal, David Paymer, Julie Warner, Helen Hunt, Mary Mara, Jerry Orbach, Ron Silver, Sage Allen.

● A dream project for star, co-writer and first-time director Crystal, in which his affection for the characters and familiarity with the material sometimes prevent him from achieving sufficient distance. Stand-up comic Buddy Young Jr (Crystal), managed by his brother Stan (Paymer), was a household name in the '50s and '60s. Now he's just another has-been trying for a comeback, struggling to retain his dignity in the face of humiliating auditions and demeaning bit-parts in TV commercials. Flashbacks to Buddy's childhood and heyday strike the right balance between nostalgia and realism. Scenes of Jewish family life, jokes about food, and lovingly recreated borscht-belt shows evoke the atmosphere of the time; while the egocentric comic's difficult relationships with the self-sacrificing Stan and estranged daughter Susan (Mara) reveal a darker side to showbiz and familial ties. By contrast, the modern scenes are cloyingly sentimental. Even so, there are probably enough sharp one-liners, hilarious routines and clever mimicry to see most people through the soggier patches. NF

Mister Skeeter

(1985, GB, 78 min)
d Colin Finbow. *sc* Children's Film Unit. *ph* Daniel Ditch. *m* David Hewson. *cast* Peter Bayliss, Louise Rawlings, Orlando Wells, Rodney Dodds, Richard Bartlett, Rose Hill, Tim Page.

● Jamie and Lisa, on the run from a children's home, meet eccentric vaudevillian Mr Skeeter (Bayliss) in a seaside shelter; they exchange confidences, watch the sun rise, and share stolen food. As the police close in on the runaways, the film focuses on the brief encounter of this oddly innocent yet worldly-wise trio, and is closely observed, funny, and excellently photographed, with memorable performances and dialogue. Made by the Children's Film Unit. SMcA

Mr Skeffington

(1944, US, 146 min, b/w)
d Vincent Sherman. *p/sc* Philip G Epstein, Julius J Epstein. *ph* Ernest Haller. *ed* Ralph Dawson. *ad* Robert Haas. *m* Franz Waxman. *cast* Bette Davis, Claude Rains, Walter Abel, Richard Waring, George Coulouris, Jerome Cowan, Charles Drake.

● Take a large stock of hankies with you: this monumental soaper drips interminably on. It's a simple tale of a vain society gal (Davis, who else?) who secures a financially wonderful but loveless marriage to a Jewish stockbroker (Rains). After a stay in a concentration camp, he goes blind; then she catches diphtheria, and realises that he loves her after all, and… oh well, for the rest you can use your imagination, which is more than writers Julius and Philip Epstein (ex-*Casablanca*) did. Vincent Sherman cradles this arrant tosh with the tenderest of loving camera movements, and almost smothers it to death in the process. GB

Mr Smith Goes to Washington

(1939, US, 129 min, b/w)
d/p Frank Capra. *sc* Sidney Buchman. *ph* Joseph Walker. *ed* Gene Havelik, Al Clark. *ad* Lionel Banks. *m* Dimitri Tiomkin. *cast* James Stewart, Jean Arthur, Claude Rains, Edward Arnold, Guy Kibbee, Thomas Mitchell, Eugene Pallette, Beulah Bondi, HB Warner, Harry Carey, William Demarest.

● Stewart's young Wisconsin senator exposing corruption and upholding true American values in a Senate House riddled with graft is quintessential Capra – popular wish-fulfilment served up with such fast-talking comic panache that you don't have time to question its cornball idealism. Scriptwriter Sidney Buchman's crackling dialogue is also lent sharp-tongued conviction by Rains, as the slimy senior senator, Jean Arthur as the hard-boiled dame finally won over by Stewart's honesty, and Harry Carey as the Vice President. NF

Mr Vampire (Jiangshi Xiansheng)

(1986, HK, 92 min)
d Lau Kun Wai. *cast* Ricky Hui, Moon Lee, Chin Suit Ho, Lam Ching Ying, Pauline Wong, Billy Lau.

● A ditzy rewrite on vampire mythology as we know it. When a Chinese family is menaced by blood-craving zombies, they discover that the thing the creatures really hate is sticky rice, and that by holding your breath it's possible to stop the fiends in their tracks. How all this new-found knowledge filters into the narrative is wild, funny, and not a little strange.

Mr Wonderful

(1992, US, 97 min)
d Anthony Minghella. *p* Marianne Moloney. *sc* Anthony Minghella. *ph* Geoffrey Simpson. *ed* John Tintori. *pd* Doug Kraner. *m* Michael Gore. *cast* Matt Dillon, Annabella Sciorra, Mary-Louise Parker, William Hurt, Vincent D'Onofrio, Dan Heydaya.

● Writer/director Minghella's second feature brings ambivalence and a touch of realpolitik to the stuff of candyfloss romance as it charts the relationship between New York electrical worker Gus (Dillon) and his former wife Lee (Sciorra). Having achieved her long-suppressed wish to go to college, she's now the recipient of maintenance payments from her financially strapped ex-husband. If he could find someone to marry her pronto, it would solve all his money problems and let him pursue his new flame Rita (Parker) – but where to find such a Mr Wonderful? The answer, of course, is staring him in the mirror each morning, but the awkward corners of these emotional lives refuse to be subjugated within conventional movie plotting. Against an assured Italian-American background, Dillon adeptly conveys the inarticulate longings and confusion of a repairman who can't fix his own life, and the film's generosity of spirit is touching in itself. TJ

Mr Zhao (Zhao Xiansheng)

(1998, HK/China, 89 min)
d Lu Yue. *p* Yang Hongguang. *sc* Shu Ping. *ph* Wang Tianlin. *ed* Zhai Ru. *pd* Liu Xiaodian, Liu Xiaodong. *cast* Shi Jingming, Zhang Zhihua, Chen Yinan, Jiang Wenli.

● Best known as cinematographer on films by Tian Zhuangzhuang, Yim Ho and (especially) Zhang Yimou, Lu turns director with this tale of a bizarre love triangle. Zhao, a professor of Chinese medicine and part time doctor in Shanghai, is having an affair with a former student; his wife, a factory worker, finds out and confronts him. In the ensuing tug of love, Zhao's emotional immaturity and cowardice stand in contrast with the very different temperaments and attitudes of the two women. Within the basic storyline, Lu asked his actors to improvise dialogue and behaviour – with impressive and credible results. Westerners will see the ghost of Cassavetes hovering near, but this kind of work is new in China and the sense of aesthetic adventure is palpable. TR

Mistons, Les (The Mischief Makers)

(1957, Fr, 26 min, b/w)
d François Truffaut. *sc* François Truffaut, Maurice Pons. *ph* Jean Malige. *ed* Cécile Decugis. *m* Maurice Leroux. *cast* Bernadette Lafont, Gérard Blain.

● Five boys, themselves tormented by the first stirrings of adolescence, torment a young woman on whom they are fixated, trailing around after her as she tries to spend the summer holidays with her boyfriend. There's an overdone commentary, but the kids – hot, bothered and obnoxious with it – are the authentic article. Leroux's throbbing score and Lafont's physical presence – optimum femaleness, guaranteed to rattle any pubescent male – are just right. The startling slow-mo shot of a boy sniffing the saddle of Lafont's bicycle may be seen as, among other things, Truffaut's rude rejoinder to Old Wave sentimentalism. BBa

Mistress

(1991, US, 110 min)
d Barry Primus. *p* Meir Teper, Robert De Niro. *sc* Barry Primus, Jonathan Lawton. *ph* Sven Kirsten. *ed* Steven Weisberg. *pd* Phil Peters. *m* Galt MacDermot. *cast* Robert Wuhl, Martin Landau, Jace Alexander, Robert De Niro, Danny Aiello, Eli Wallach, Christopher Walken, Laurie Metcalf, Sheryl Lee Ralph, Jean Smart, Tuesday Knight, Ernest Borgnine, Stefan Gierasch.

● Despite sturdy acting from a starry cast, actor Barry Primus' directorial debut is a lacklustre affair, unsure of whether it's a satire or a morality play as it tells of down-at-heel producer (Landau) and has-been director (Wuhl) fighting to get the latter's movie script off the ground, intact and untainted by the financiers' desires to see their various mistresses become stars. The gags are too obvious; the conflict between art and money is hackneyed; and the plot goes badly off the rails in the later reels. De Niro, who produced, is surprisingly weak; Landau alone is excellent. GA

Mistress Pamela

(1973, GB, 91 min)
d/p/sc Jim O'Connolly. *ph* Arthur Ibbetson. *ed* Fergus McDonell. *pd* Disley Jones. *m* David Whitaker. *cast* Julian Barnes, Ann Michelle, Dudley Foster, Anna Quayle, Anthony Sharp, Rosemarie Dunham, Derek Fowlds, Jessie Evans, Fred Emney.

● Richardson's 18th century classic *Pamela* clearly dredged up for its bawdy possibilities. The self-satisfied and calculated middle class morality of his treatise on female virtue is transformed with much heavy-handed winking and nudging into an obsolete sitcom about the efforts of a beautiful servant (Michelle) to preserve her maidenhead from the insistent Lord Devenish (Barnes). A few wheezy jokes and some ripped clothing later, true love and a happy ending prevail. The supporting cast, notably Dudley Foster and Fred Emney, give some relief, but the two leading players offer little beyond their prettiness. About all the film has in common with the original is a notable lack of humour. CPe

Mrs Brown

(1997, GB/US/Ire, 104 min)
d John Madden. *p* Sarah Curtis. *sc* Jeremy Brock. *ph* Richard Greatrex. *ed* Robin Sales. *pd* Martin Childs. *m* Stephen Warbeck. *cast* Judi Dench, Billy Connolly, Antony Sher, Geoffrey Palmer, Richard Pasco, David Westhead, Gerard Butler.

● Madden's film owes its existence to the success of *The Madness of King George*, a period vehicle for a superb but cinematically under-appreciated actor. For Farmer George, substitute Widow Victoria, still immersed in grief four years after the death of Albert. For Nigel Hawthorne, substitute Judi Dench. Like Nicholas Hytner's film, *Mrs Brown* documents a period during which the monarchy was in crisis due to the government's unpopularity and the sovereign's emotional instability. For madness, substitute grief: Victoria was so inconsolable that she became known as the Widow of Windsor. Enter John Brown, a no-nonsense Highlander and devoted servant to Her Majesty; only he has the guts to wean her out of her sadness, to talk to her like a woman. Dench is magnificent as Victoria, a toy-sized, black-suited, dough girl of despair, a woman slowly recovering her wits and her expectations. But Connolly's Brown is hardly less fine, a cast-iron portrait of a man teetering on the edge of ridicule and disgrace but wishing to go the whole nine yards for the cause he serves. SGr

Mrs Dalloway

(1997, US/GB/Neth, 97 min)
d Marleen Gorris. *p* Lisa Katselas Paré, Stephen Bayly. *sc* Eileen Atkins. *ph* Sue Gibson. *ed* Michiel Reichwein. *pd* David Richens. *m* Ilona Sekacz. *cast* Vanessa Redgrave, Natascha McElhone, Michael Kitchen, Alan Cox, Sarah Badel, Lena Headey, John Standing, Rupert Graves, Margaret Tyzack, Robert Hardy.

● Clarissa Dalloway (Redgrave), the beautiful wife of an eminent MP, loves to give parties. A day in her life, however, is a serious affair, interwoven with the experiences of a WWI veteran, Septimus (Graves), and a flood of painfully pleasant memories. Eileen Atkins' adaptation of

Virginia Woolf's novel concentrates exclusively on Mrs Dalloway's ruminations. Thus, although we sympathise with Septimus, the originality of his experience is lost; and cousin Ellie, the 'invisible' spinster, brought so spikily to life in the novel – in the film remains a voiceless nobody. Unfortunately Redgrave chews up the scenery, and when she's meant to be ecstatic appears merely unhinged. The characters of Sally (Clarissa's best friend), and Peter (her first and most ardent suitor), make more sense and are well served by both young (Headey/Cox) and old (Badel/Kitchen) sets of actors. Peter's wimpish arrogance is wonderfully caught, as is Sally's casual, fox-like intelligence. Fascinated by Clarissa and also resentful, these two alone make us understand her appeal. Sue Gibson's visuals are excellent, and the depiction of London is perfect. CO'Su

Mrs Doubtfire

(1993, US, 125 min)
d Chris Columbus. *p* Marsha Garces Williams, Robin Williams, Mark Radcliffe. *sc* Randi Mayem Singer, Leslie Dixon. *ph* Donald McAlpine. *ed* Raja Gosnell. *pd* Angelo Graham. *m* Howard Shore. *cast* Robin Williams, Sally Field, Pierce Brosnan, Harvey Fierstein, Polly Holliday, Robert Prosky, Lisa Jakub.

●It's built like a Volvo, wears floral print dresses and affects a faint Scots burr: Robin Williams as Mrs Doubtfire – or, more accurately, divorced father-of-three Daniel as Mrs Doubtfire – is the sort of prosthetic-aesthetic nightmare you'd expect to encounter wielding a kitchen knife in a slasher movie. Not that this stops Daniel's ex-wife Sally Field from placing their winsome ones in his/her charge. Indeed, Mrs D soon begins to look like the perfect nanny, a hairy Poppins even the kids take a shine to. Williams has always been uncommonly in touch with his 'feminine', caring, nurturing side, so Daniel's all dressed up with no place to go. Instead, he/she has to learn some tried and trite lessons about parental responsibility and emotional maturity. Sit-com stuff, then, with laboured farcical interludes, and a mushy post-feminist sensibility. Funny notwithstanding. TCh

Mrs Miniver

(1942, US, 134 min, b/w)
d William Wyler. *p* Sidney A Franklin. *sc* Arthur Wimperis, George Froeschel, James Hilton, Claudine West. *ph* Joseph Ruttenberg. *ed* Harold F Kress. *ad* Cedric Gibbons, Urie McCleary. *m* Herbert Stothart. *cast* Greer Garson, Walter Pidgeon, Teresa Wright, Dame May Whitty, Reginald Owen, Henry Travers, Richard Ney, Henry Wilcoxon, Helmut Dantine.

●Hollywood's multi-Oscared tribute to the home front in wartime Britain. See Mrs Miniver disarm a German parachutist and hide his gun behind the teacups. See gallant hubby stiffen the old upper lip before sailing off to help with the Dunkirk evacuation. An average English couple, practising their little economies but housed in gracious splendour, they live in an England which may be at war but where the local flower show soldiers on. Classic soap opera in which good old British understatement has a field day, everybody is frightfully nice, and sentimentality is wrapped up in yards of tasteful gloss. TM

Mrs Parker and the Vicious Circle

(1994, US, 124 min, b/w & col)
d Alan Rudolph. *p* Robert Altman. *sc* Alan Rudolph, Randy Sue Coburn. *ph* Jan Kiesser. *ed* Suzy Elmiger. *pd* François Séguin. *m* Mark Isham. *cast* Jennifer Jason Leigh, Campbell Scott, Matthew Broderick, Andrew McCarthy, Tim McGowan, Nick Cassavetes, Matt Malloy, Sam Robards, Wallace Shawn, Keith Carradine, Gwyneth Paltrow.

●Alan Rudolph's *The Moderns* celebrated the American away team of the '20s – Hemingway and pals. This companion biopic of the mistress of the bon mot, Manhattanite Dorothy Parker, paints a similar mass portrait of the wits, wags and writers of the home team. All the Rudolph trademarks are here: the improvisatory feel, the overlapping dialogue, the ironic but celebratory tone, the vital performances from leads (Jennifer Jason Leigh as Parker and Broderick as Charles MacArthur, in particular) and cameos. Then there's the delight in design (François Séguin's low-lit speakeasies and hotel rooms), and the roving camera style (Jan Kiesser); the interest in art and artifice, genius and suffering. Rudolph and JJL manage to make this 'brilliant bitch' entirely fascinating, if not completely sympathetic. In perhaps the one scene where she looks radiantly happy, Parker says to MacArthur, 'Oh, Charlie, I'm going to wear my heart on my sleeve like a red wet stain.' She could be speaking for Rudolph. Absolutely superb. WH

Mrs Pollifax – Spy

(1970, US, 110 min)
d Leslie Martinson. *p* Frederick Brisson. *sc* CA McKnight [Rosalind Russell]. *ph* Joseph Biroc. *ed* Gene Milford, Fred M Bohanan. *ad* Jack Poplin. *m* Lalo Schifrin. *cast* Rosalind Russell, Darren McGavin, Nehemiah Persoff, Harold Gould, Albert Paulsen, John Beck, Dana Elcar.

●Witless, worthless spy comedy about a middle-aged matron's enlistment in the CIA. Martinson, a long-time TV series toiler who'd provided the drive-in market in the '50s with such treats as *Hot Rod Girl* and *Hot Rod Rumble*, had recently had his head turned by the unaccustomed success of the big-screen *Batman* and similar spy-spoof material in the Raquel Welch-starring *Fathom*. Ros Russell, pseudonymously scripting as well as starring, was old enough to have known better, but did the honourable thing and retired immediately after. PT

Mrs Soffel

(1984, US, 111 min)
d Gillian Armstrong. *p* Edgar J Scherick, Scott Rudin, David Nicksay. *sc* Ron Nyswaner. *ph* Russell Boyd, (Pittsburgh) Peter Norman, Darwin Dean. *ed* Nicholas Beauman. *pd* Luciana Arrighi. *m* Mark Isham. *cast* Diane Keaton, Mel Gibson, Matthew Modine, Edward Herrmann, Trini Alvarado, Jennie Dundas, Danny Corkill, Harley Cross.

●Mrs Soffel (Keaton), a good woman but victim of a cool marriage to the warden of Allegheny County jail in turn-of-the-century Pittsburgh, spends her days dispensing Christian comfort to the inmates: during the first hour there is more praying than regular dialogue. The answer to the lady's prayers turns up in Mel Gibson, a condemned murderer; they go on the run together, but without much success. It's a handsomely mounted period piece, but can't shake off a certain air of good manners; like the lady herself, stifled by law, custom and breeding, and unable to let rip on a bid for freedom. CPea

Mrs Winterbourne

(1996, US, 106 min)
d Richard Benjamin. *p* Dale Pollock, Ross Canter, Oren Koules. *sc* Phoef Sutton, Lisa-Maria Radano. *ph* Alex Nepomniaschy. *ed* Jacqueline Cambas, William Fletcher. *pd* Evelyn Sakash. m Patrick Doyle. *cast* Ricki Lake, Shirley MacLaine, Brendan Fraser, Loren Dean, Miguel Sandoval, Paula Prentiss.

●This adaptation of Cornell Woolrich's novel *I Married a Dead Man* (previously filmed as *No Man of Her Own*) begins with a seedy room, a corpse on the bed and an evangelist on the unwatched TV assuring of an astonishing future. The arrival of the cops trigger the flashbacks…so far, so *noir*. But then something truly nightmarish happens. The movie transforms somewhat unsuccessfully into a comedy about a loveable kook to whom awful things keep happening. It's as though ten minutes into *Phantom Lady*, June Allyson had entered the picture and staged a takeover. In principle, there's certainly no reason why a retro-*rosé*, neo-*noir*, postmodern genre stew shouldn't amuse, intrigue or innovate, but this crashes early on when it becomes clear that Lake is a rather chilly and distinctly unpersuasive presence. BBa

Mitchell

(1975, US, 97 min)
d Andrew V McLaglen. *p* R Ben Efraim. *sc* Ian Kennedy Martin. *ph* Harry Stradling Jr. *ed* Fred Chulack. *m* Larry Brown, Jerry Styner. *cast* Joe Don Baker, Martin Balsam, John Saxon, Linda Evans, Merlin Olsen, Morgan Paull, Harold J Stone, Robert Phillips.

●Baker's the big lumpy cop who won't take no and another assignment for an answer when he's told to lay off the gun-happy lawyer (Saxon) he suspects of cold-blooded murder, and to concentrate on the businessman with the coke connection (Balsam). He realises that in such a sparsely-populated cheapie they just have to be in collusion, as he punches and shoots his way to the final credits accompanied by vocal encouragement from one of those country singers with terminal cancer. Balsam and Saxon contribute no more than their required quota of urbane sneers before being bulldozed into oblivion by the golem hero of this irredeemably routine potboiler. GD

Mi Vida Loca

see My Crazy Life

Mixed Blood

see Cocaine

Mixed Company

(1974, US, 109 min)
d/p Melville Shavelson. *sc* Melville Shavelson, Mort Lachman. *ph* Stan Lazan. *ed* Walter Thompson, Ralph James Hall. *pd* Stan Jolley. *m* Fred Karlin. *cast* Barbara Harris, Joseph Bologna, Lisa Gerritsen, Tom Bosley, Dorothy Shay, Ruth McDevitt.

●A typically trite and sickly concoction by Shavelson, whose funnybone seemed much firmer when he was scripting Paramount comedies in the '40s. You can easily gauge its quality by the plot: when a basketball coach is rendered sterile through mumps, his wife urges the adoption of three cute but problematical kids – a semi-delinquent black, a Vietnamese orphan, and a Hopi Indian. All prejudices are ultimately overcome, and the result is a runaway victory for the upper class American liberal. The performers are far superior to their material, particularly Barbara Harris; but on the whole this movie gives a whole new meaning to the word 'yuck'. GB

Mixed Nuts

(1994, US, 97 min)
d Nora Ephron. *p* Paul Junger Witt, Tony Thomas, Joseph Hartwick. *sc* Nora Ephron, Delia Ephron. *ph* Sven Nykvist. *ed* Robert Reitano. *pd* Bill Groom. *m* George Fenton. *cast* Steve Martin, Rita Wilson, Madeline Kahn, Juliette Lewis, Anthony LaPaglia, Adam Sandler, Liev Schreiber, Rita Wilson, Rob Reiner.

●Oh, dear. Anyone who didn't appreciate the polished sophistication of *Sleepless in Seattle* should be made to watch Ephron's third outing as writer and director…until they submit. This remake of a 1982 French farce, *Le Père Noël est une Ordure!* (d Jean-Marie Poiré, not distributed in the UK), is a disaster. Ephron's timing and sensitivity have deserted her, leaving behind only the sentimentality. It's Christmas Eve at Martin's suicide hotline service – Lifesavers – but it's the staff (Wilson, Kahn) who seem most desperately in need of help. Ephron pitches for zany, which means we have to endure a pregnant Lewis at her most hysterical, LaPaglia as a gun-toting Santa, Sandler as a ukulele-playing tee-shirt writer ('Save the Dolphins – that's one of mine'), a lovelorn transvestite and a serial killer, while the leads alternately scream and faint, as well they might. TCh

Miyamoto Musashi (Musashi Miyamoto)

(1954, Jap, 93 min)
d Hiroshi Inagaki. *p* Kazuo Takimura. *sc* Hideji Hojo, Hiroshi Inagaki, Tokihei Wakao. *ph* Asushi Atumoto, Zazuo Yamada, Jun Yasumoto. *ad* Kisaku Ito, Hiroshi Ueda. *m* Ikuma Dan. *cast* Toshiro Mifune, Koji Tsuruta, Kaoru Yachigusa, Mariko Okada, Renataro Mikuni, Michiko Saga, Takashi Shimura.

●Part one of Inagaki's Samurai trilogy – rapturously received in the West in the first flush of enthusiasm for Japanese cinema in the 1950s (it was even awarded an honorary Oscar for Best Foreign Film), all but forgotten now. Inagaki actually made the trilogy twice, first in 1940, then again as Toho's first colour production. Perhaps that explains the somewhat murky visuals – a lot of the film looks a stop underexposed – and solemn pacing, which is not to deny that it's also strikingly atmospheric and occasionally beautiful. Mifune is Takezo, a peasant with a yen for adventure and excitement, who goes to fight in the civil war and ends up a wanted man, hunted even by his own family. An unconventional Buddhist priest became his saviour and mentor – by locking him in a room for three years with dozens of Zen manuscripts. The film lacks Kurosawa's dynamism, but is not without interest. TCh

Mob, The (aka Remember That Face)

(1951, US, 86 min, b/w)
d Robert Parrish. *p* Jerry Bresler. *sc* William Bowers. *ph* Joseph Walker. *ed* Charles Nelson. *ad* Cary Odell. *m* George Duning. *cast* Broderick Crawford, Betty Buehler, Richard Kiley, Otto Hulett, Matt Crowley, Neville Brand, Ernest Borgnine, Charles Bronson.

●Familiar gang-busting stuff set in *On the Waterfront* territory, with Crawford as a cop who, inadvertently goofing on duty, is officially reported as suspended and sent undercover to make good the damage by finding out who is masterminding the brutal extortion racket among longshoremen. William Bowers' script manages one or two genuine surprises – with Crawford at one point being hired to eliminate himself – but its main contribution is a nice line in sharp, waywardly witty dialogue. Given fast, flexible direction by Parrish, excellent camerawork (Joseph Walker) and a full house of vivid performances, the result is an unusually tense and enjoyable genre piece. Pity about the last reel, when everything collapses (though not too destructively) into routine histrionics. TM

Mo' Better Blues

(1990, US, 129 min)
d/p/sc Spike Lee. *ph* Ernest Dickerston. *ed* Sam Pollard. *pd* Wynn Thomas. *m* Bill Lee. *cast* Denzel Washington, Spike Lee, Wesley Snipes, Giancarlo Esposito, Robin Harris, Joie Lee, Bill Nunn, John Turturro, Dick Anthony Williams, Cynda Williams, Nicholas Turturro.

●It's clear from the opening that the way Lee sees jazz is as Art, sanitised and consequently a mite gutless. Indeed, as obsessive trumpeter Bleek (Washington) advances on his inevitable comeuppance – you *know* he's gotta get it – Lee's earnest parable proceeds to hit whole clusters of bad notes. First, the music is wrong: ghosted by Branford Marsalis, Terence Blanchard et al, Bleek's gigs range through an anachronistic array of styles, while Lee's underlining of mood with a handful of classics (Coltrane, Ornette, Miles) comes over as a showy hip parade of his own cultural credibility. But more damagingly, plot and characterisation are trite, perhaps even reactionary. If Bleek's errant attitude to his two lovers (Joie Lee, Cynda Williams) is symptomatic of an arrogant devotion to his art, the women rarely rise above schematic stereotypes (the Jewish club-owners fare even worse). Moreover, Lee's coda advocates submissive motherhood for a neglected lover and patriarchal domesticity for all concerned. Ideology apart (no drugs here), a messy, meandering script ensures that, despite stylish camerawork and sturdy acting, this lengthy indulgence succeeds neither as jazz movie nor as cautionary tale. GA

Mobster, The

see I, Mobster

Mobsters (aka Mobsters – The Evil Empire)

(1991, US, 121 min)
d Michael Karbelnikoff. *p* Steve Roth. *sc* Michael Mahern, Nicholas Kazan. *ph* Lajos Koltai. *ed* Scott Smith, Joe D'Augustine. *pd* Richard Sylbert. *m* Michael Small. *cast* Christian Slater, Patrick Dempsey, Richard Grieco, Costas Mandylor, F Murray Abraham, Lara Flynn Boyle, Michael Gambon, Christopher Penn, Anthony Quinn.

●This youth movie sees Slater leading a group of apprentice gangsters to the top of the bloody heap: *Young Guns* meets *The Untouchables* with a vengeance. But it has all the morals of the average clam: Slater plays the young Charlie 'Lucky' Luciano who, along with charming pals like Grieco's Bugsy Siegel and Dempsey's bookish Meyer Lansky, was a far more loathsome mobster than the Moustache Petes from the Old Country who came before him and his pals. In order to show these charmers in an attractive light as they scheme and plot and fight, Karbelnikoff makes sure that their wrinkly rivals, Don Masseria (Quinn) and Don Faranzano (Gambon) are depicted as, respectively, sadistic and pig-like, racist and rapacious. This is ageism with knobs on. A noisy, silly, rather immature film. (The US versions runs at 104 minutes.) SGr

Mobutu, King of Zaire (Mobutu, Roi du Zaïre)

(1999, Bel, 135 min)
d Thierry Michel. *p* Christine Pireaux. *sc* Thierry Michel. *ph* Alain Marcoen, Joël Marcipont, Didier Hill Derive. *ed* Marine Deleu.

●A comprehensively researched documentary history of the Congolese dictator who would be God, from his Stalin-like seizure and consolidation of power in the newly independent nation, through three decades of increasing corruption, brutality and megalomania, to his slightly shambolic fall from power in 1997. It's very much a personal study, meaning both that the passage of Zairean political, socio-economic and developmental change is detailed only insofar as it reflects on Mobutu himself, and that the insights into the self-styled leopard, notwithstanding much tantalising interview footage from down the years, are modest. Quite absorbing, despite the lengthy running time, but finally a rather familiar storyline. NB

Moby Dick

(1956, GB, 116 min)
d/p John Huston. *sc* Ray Bradbury, John Huston. *ph* Oswald Morris. *ed* Russell Lloyd. *ad* Ralph Brinton. *m* Philiph Stainton. *cast* Gregory Peck, Richard Basehart, Leo Genn, James Robertson Justice, Harry Andrews, Orson Welles, Friedrich Ledebur, Edric Connor, Bernard Miles.

●Easy to pick holes in Huston's brave stab at Melville's masterpiece, which opens with breathtaking boldness as a solitary wanderer appears over the brow of a hill, comes to camera to proclaim his 'Call me…Ishmael', then leaves it to follow in the wake of his odyssey. Granted the great white whale is significantly less impressive when lifting bodily out of the sea to crush the Pequod than when first glimpsed one moonlit night, a dim white mass of menace lurking in a black sea. Granted, too, a lightweight Ahab (Peck) and a pitifully weak Starbuck (Genn). But there are marvellous things here: Ishmael's alarming initiation into the whaling community at the tavern; Father Mapple's sermon (superbly delivered by Welles); Queequeg's casting of the bones and his preparation for death; nearly all the whaling scenes. Lent a stout overall unity by Ray Bradbury's intelligent adaptation, by colour grading which gives the images the tonal quality of old whaling prints, and by the discreet use of a commentary drawn from Melville's text which imposes the resonance of legend, it is often staggeringly good. TM

Model

(1980, US, 125 min, b/w)
d/p/sc Frederick Wiseman. *ph* John Davey. *ed* Frederick Wiseman.

●Models pose; Wiseman shoots. Photographers pose; Wiseman shoots. Wiseman shoots photographers shooting models. How objective can you get? Model intervenes in an image-making process whose variable components are objectification, exhibitionism and voyeurism: instead of analysis it offers us mere duplication. Not so much New York anthropology as a chic lifestyle commercial. Wiseman poses… PT

Model Shop

(1968, US, 92 min)
d/p/sc Jacques Demy. *ph* Michel Hugo. *ed* Walter Thompson. *pd* Kenneth A Reid. *m* Spirit, JS Bach, Schumann, Rimsky-Korsakov. *cast* Anouk Aimée, Gary Lockwood, Alexandra Hay, Carol Cole, Severn Darden, Tom Fielding, Neil Elliot, Jeanne Sorel.

●Demy's only – and underrated – American film may lack the fairytale charm of his finest French work, but the bitter-sweet delicacy of tone and acute feeling for place are at once familiar. Aimée's Lola, abandoned by her lover Michel, has now turned up in LA where, older and sadder, she works in a seedy photographer's shop, and brings brief respite to a disenchanted young drifter (Lockwood) with whom she has a one night stand. Unlike Antonioni with *Zabriskie Point*, Demy never even tries to deal with the malaise afflicting American youth in the '60s, but gives us yet another (relatively plotless) tale of transient happiness and love lost. It's also one of the great movies about LA, shown for once as a ramshackle, rootless sprawl, where movement on the freeways (accompanied by the sounds of West Coast band Spirit) is seemingly endless. GA

Modern Love

(1990, US, 109 min)
d/p/sc Robby Benson. *ph* Christopher Tufty. *ed* Gib Jaffe. *ad* Carl E Copeland. *m* Don Peake. *cast* Robby Benson, Karla DeVito, Burt Reynolds, Rue McClanahan, Frankie Valli, Louise Lasser.

●Producer/director/star Benson added this would-be comic tale of modern married life to his undistinguished screen canon while teaching a university film-making class in South Carolina. Karla DeVito, the shrink he visits to sort himself out then ends up marrying, is his real-life wife, and their daughter, too, ends up somewhere down the cast list. A vanity production with nothing to recommend it. TJ

Modern Romance

(1981, US, 93 min)
d Albert Brooks. *p* Andrew Scheinman, Martin Shafer. *sc* Albert Brooks, Monica Johnson. *ph* Eric Saarinen. *ed* David Finfer. *ad* Edward Richardson. *m* Lance Rubin. *cast* Albert Brooks, Kathryn Harrold, Bruno Kirby, Jane Hallaren, James L Brooks, George Kennedy, Bob Einstein.

●Writer/director Brooks casts himself as a neurotic, workaholic film editor who, unable to cope with his obsessive love for the beautiful Harrold, forces himself to give her up. He then adopts an equally compulsive regime of trying to forget her: taking up jogging, looking up old flames, and immersing himself in the editing of a low-budget sci-fi movie – made by his namesake James L Brooks (director of *Broadcast News*). None of this works, of course, but having wooed Harrold once more, he again falls prey to this perverse, self-destructive syndrome. Extremely funny, ultra-hip and alarmingly insightful. NF

Moderns, The

(1988, US, 126 min)
d Alan Rudolph. *p* Carolyn Pfeiffer, David Blocker. *sc* Alan Rudolph, Jon Bradshaw. *ph* Toyomichi Kurita, Jan Kiesser. *ed* Debra T Smith, Scott Brock. *pd* Steven Legler. *m* Mark Isham. *cast* Keith Carradine, Linda Fiorentino, Genevieve Bujold, Geraldine Chaplin, Wallace Shawn, John Lone, Kevin J O'Connor, Elsa Raven, Ali Giron.

●Rudolph's full-blown and unashamedly romantic evocation of the artistic life of '20s Paris – a playful, ironic, and affirmative meditation on life, love, and art – shows him at his most delightfully accessible. He relocates his resident ensemble players within the lusciously recreated cafés, galleries and salons of Montmartre and the Latin Quarter – truly 'a Paris of the mind' – where nothing can be taken at face value. Nick Hart, a poor painter-cum-*Chicago Tribune* caricaturist (Carradine, dazzlingly good), clashes with fellow American in Paris and rich art collector Stone (Lone, monolithic) over Rachel (Fiorentino, beautiful). His integrity is called into question when, thinking that money will enable him to reunite with Rachel, he is persuaded by predatory and fickle Nathalie de Ville (Chaplin), a wealthy collector of lovers, to forge a series of paintings. Hemingway is there, as are Gertrude Stein, Picasso, et al. It's Rudolph's most entertaining movie, elating, erotic, and full of life, colour, music, games, romance, dreams, and humour. Carradine could be Gary Cooper, and Rudolph turns fakery into an authenticated masterwork. WH

Modern Times

(1936, US, 85 min, b/w)
d/p/sc Charles Chaplin. *ph* Roland Totheroh, Ira Morgan. *ad* Charles D Hall, Russell Spencer. *m* Charles Chaplin. *cast* Charles Chaplin, Paulette Goddard, Henry Bergman, Chester Conklin, Tiny Sanford, Allan Garcia, Hank Mann.

●The last appearance of the Chaplin tramp, before Hitler, Monsieur Verdoux and other personae took over. Antics and situations from the earliest shorts are revived in a narrative framework designed to portray 'humanity crusading in the pursuit of happiness', as the opening title puts it; the tramp faces the perils of factory machinery, poverty, starvation and Depression unrest – and just about survives. Chaplin's political and philosophical naivety now seems as remarkable as his gift for pantomime. GB

Modesty Blaise

(1966, GB, 119 min)
d Joseph Losey. *p* Joseph Janni. *sc* Evan Jones. *ph* Jack Hildyard, (Amsterdam) Davis Boulton. *ed* Reginald Beck. *pd* Richard MacDonald. *m* John Dankworth. *cast* Monica Vitti, Dirk Bogarde, Terence Stamp, Harry Andrews, Michael Craig, Scilla Gabel, Clive Revill, Rossella Falk, Joe Melia, Alexander Knox.
●Coolly received by comparison with the more immediately accessible James Bond films which were then at the height of their popularity, *Modesty Blaise* is, like Rolls-Royces, built to last. Modelled on the cartoon strip, it plays the game up to the hilt with its op-art sets, its extravagant conceits, its outlandish violence, and its arch-fiend Gabriel (Bogarde having a ball in silvery wig and sinister glasses) daintily dreaming up ever more monstrous fancies. But under the non-stop stream of jokes lies a bitter edge of malice, directed not only against the genre itself but against a society which trusts its politicians and its generals. TM

Modulations

(1998, US, 75 min)
d Iara Lee. *p* George Gund. *sc* Peter Shapiro. *ph* Marcus Burnett, Paul Yates. *ed* Paula Heredia. *with* Arthur Baker, Afrika Bambaataa, Carl Cox, Derrick May, Moby, Robert Moog, Genesis P-Orridge, DJ Spooky, Karl-Heinz Stockhausen, Danny Tenaglia.
●One of the more curious upshots of the century's profusion of music technology has been how ideas and innovations once the preserve of avant gardists have found their way into every corner of dance music over the last two decades. Then again, as this documentary tracing the evolution of 'electronic' music makes abundantly clear, the crosscurrents and subcurrents of influence between musique concrète, elektronische musik, jazz fusion, ambient, techno, HipHop, house, jungle – the list goes on – are manifold and fascinating. Rightly rejecting a chronological approach, the film initially seems a little vague, but it soon becomes clear that Iara Lee has found a visual analogue for the music's collaging techniques. Her montage cuts back and forth across cities, decades, genres and performers – from Teo Macero, Giorgio Moroder, Kraftwerk and Africa Bambaataa to Future Sound of London and Prodigy, almost everyone's here, making it a must for anyone who loves any of this music. NB

Mogambo

(1953, US, 116 min)
d John Ford. *p* Sam Zimbalist. *sc* John Lee Mahin. *ph* Bruce Surtees, Frederick A Young. *ed* Frank Clarke. *ad* Alfred Junge. *cast* Clark Gable, Ava Gardner, Grace Kelly, Donald Sinden, Eric Pohlmann, Philip Stainton, Laurence Naismith, Denis O'Dea.
●Gable's performance in *Red Dust* alongside Jean Harlow had been one of his earliest hits; 21 years later he was still big enough at the box-office to star in this remake, re-scripted by original screenwriter John Lee Mahin, and re-sited from a studio-set Saigon to African locations. The insolent sex talk of the original is here toned down, and the relaxed rumbustiousness of the safari love triangle is wholly in keeping with Ford's holidaying inclinations at the time. Half-hearted, half-baked, and at least half-watchable. PT

Mogliamante

see Wifemistress

Mohammad, Messenger of God

see Al-Risalah

Mohawk

(1956, US, 79 min)
d Kurt Neumann. *p* Edward L Alperson. *sc* Maurice Geraghty, Milton Krims. *ph* Karl Struss. *ed* William B Murphy. *pd* Ernst Fegté. *m* Edward L Alperson Jr. *cast* Scott Brady, Rita Gam, Neville Brand, Lori Nelson, Allison Hayes, John Hoyt, Vera Vague, Mae Clarke, Ted de Corsia.
●One of only a handful of films that deal with New England's Mohawk Indians, this duff B Western re-uses battle and background footage from John Ford's *Drums Along the Mohawk*, and might have done well to borrow more, because the rest is quite ludicrous. Brady plays an artist whose charm captivates women as diverse as his fiancée Lori Nelson, barmaid Allison Hayes (the original 50-foot woman), and Native American Rita Gam. In between dalliances, he is instrumental in averting a wicked landowner's plot to provoke Indians and settlers into wiping each other out. TCh

Moi Ivan, Toi Abraham

see Me Ivan, You Abraham

Moindre des Choses, La

see Every Little Thing

Moine, Le (The Monk)

(1972, Fr/It/WGer, 92 min)
d Ado Kyrou. *p* Henry Lange. *sc* Luis Buñuel, Jean-Claude Carrière. *ph* Sacha Vierny. *ed* Eric Pluet. *ad* Max Douy. *m* Piero Piccioni. *cast* Franco Nero, Nathalie Delon, Nicol Williamson, Nadja Tiller, Eliana De Santis, Elisabeth Wiener, Denis Manuel.
●Buñuel had plans to film Matthew Gregory Lewis's controversial masterpiece, but finally handed the project over to his friend Kyrou. Buñuel is still credited as co-screenwriter (with Jean-Claude Carrière), and the production remains comparatively faithful to Lewis both in atmosphere and intention. The ending is more cynical (though much less horrific) in the film, while there are many simplifications and one very perverse interpolation; but the character of Ambrosio (a pious clerical superstar who is damned by a sudden all-engulfing sexual passion) remains the centrepiece. The problem with the film is that nobody can shoot a Buñuel script quite like Buñuel, and elements that might have become gold in the hands of the master tend to be flat. Still, there are few enough adaptations of Gothic novels, and this one is more intricate and intelligent than most. DP

Moi, Pierre Rivière, ayant égorgé ma mère, ma soeur et mon frère...

(1975, Fr, 130 min)
d René Allio. *p* René Feret. *sc* Pascal Bonitzer, Jean Jourdheuil, Serge Toubiana, René Allio. *ph* Nurith Aviv. *ed* Sylvie Blanc. *ad* Françoise Darne, François Vantrou, Denis Fruchaud. *cast* Claude Hébert, Jacqueline Millière, Joseph Leportier, Antoine Bourseiller, Jacques Debary, René Feret, Roland Amstutz.
●A naturalistic reconstruction of a 19th century peasant crime in Normandy: the young Pierre Rivière's 'inexplicable' murder of his mother, sister and brother. Rivière left behind a 50-page prison testament, recently published by Michel Foucault, and the film locates itself squarely within Foucault's questions about 'history' – about what is explicable and what is not. It's less impressive for Allio's quaintly French belief that nothing has changed in Normandy in the last 150 years (and that 'truth' in all its ambiguity was therefore waiting for the camera) than for the psychopathology of the case itself, and the interesting non-professional performances. TR

Mojo

(1997, GB, 90 min)
d Jez Butterworth. *p* Eric Abraham. *sc* Jez Butterworth. *ph* Bruno de Keyser. *ed* Richard Milward, Paul Green. *pd* Hugo Luczyc-Wyhowski. *m* Murray Gold. *cast* Ian Hart, Ewen Bremner, Aidan Gillen, Martyn Gwynn-Jones, Hans Matheson, Andy Serkis, Ricky Tomlinson, Harold Pinter.
●Jez Butterworth's viciously funny play (Royal Court, 1995) had the critics throwing Tarantino references like confetti. The movie, scripted by Jez and his brother Tom, is reminiscent of *Absolute Beginners*. It's set in 1958, in a Soho music club, the owner of which is killed by a rival gangster muscling in on a hot new singing sensation. Designed in bold, bright strokes, this has the kind of dizzy verve that mixes toffee apples with murder and revenge – a rock'n'roll freneticism that's never less than diverting. But the pinball structure may be too clever (the group power dynamics are unclear), and, for all the gloss, the movie still exists in the stunted half-world of theatrical adaptation. Fab performances, exuberance and style ensure that it works, but only in spurts. TCh

Mole, The

see Topo, El

Moll Flanders

(1996, US, 122 min)
d Pen Densham. *p* John Watson, Richard B Lewis, Pen Densham. *sc* Pen Densham. *ph* David Tattersall. *ed* Neil Travis, James R Symons. *pd* Caroline Hanania. *m* Mark Mancinia. *cast* Robin Wright, Morgan Freeman, Stockard Channing, John Lynch, Brenda Fricker, Geraldine James, Aisling Corcoran, Jim Sheridan, Jeremy Brett, Ardal O'Hanlon.
●As Robin Wright's (hardly unglamorous) Moll overcomes poverty, abuse, prostitution, drink, rich people's spite and the loss of her loved ones, her journal is recounted by Moll's fellow servant and ally Hibble (Freeman) to her orphaned daughter Flora (Corcoran). Many cut-out characters, and direction consisting largely of putting pictures against the words: a very basic historical tour of 18th century England. NB

Molly Maguires, The

(1969, US, 125 min)
d Martin Ritt. *p* Martin Ritt, Walter Bernstein. *sc* Walter Bernstein. *ph* James Wong Howe. *ed* Frank Bracht. *ad* Tambi Larsen. *m* Henry Mancini. *cast* Richard Harris, Sean Connery, Samantha Eggar, Frank Finlay, Anthony Zerbe, Bethel Leslie, Art Lund.
●Less simplistic than most Ritt movies, this is set in the Pennsylvania of 1876, where the miners, Catholic Irish and surly, are at the mercy of their predominantly Protestant employers after an ineffectual strike to improve conditions. The nub of the film comes in the odd, abrasive friendship that springs up between Connery, leader of a secret organisation committed to acts of terrorism until the bosses submit, and Harris as an informer equally disgruntled but out for his own interests. Essentially two facets of the same personality, the pair are cunningly used to explore areas of ambivalence in the extent to which the actions of each are justified. The trouble, as so often with Ritt films, is that the situation remains interesting rather than involving. But at least this detachment means that one has the leisure to savour the textures of Wong Howe's magnificent camerawork. TM

Moloch

(1999, Rus/Ger, 103 min)
d Aleksandr Sokurov. *sc* Yuri Arabov. *ph* Alexei Fyodorov, Anatoli Rodionov. *ed* Leda Semyonova. *ad* Sergei Kokovkin. *cast* Leonid Mosgovoi, Elena Rufanova, Leonid Sokoi, Elena Spridonova, Vladimir Bagdanov, Anatoli Schwederski.
●Alexei Fyodorov's gloomy, soft-focus photography, with its echoes of Riefenstahl and German Romantic paintings, is stunning. True, too, Sokurov and scriptwriter Yuri Arabov's intention – to understand a little more about Hitler the man through the self-sacrificing love of Eva Braun – is admirable. Despite one good scene between Hitler and a visiting priest, however, that's about all that can be said in favour of this far from illuminating chamber piece about a weekend at the Führer's Alpine retreat in 1942. Boorman smells of mustard gas, Goebbels screens his propaganda movies, and Adolf blathers on about food, death, responsibility, etc. Basically, the notion seems to be that the Nazis were buffoons who probably should have listened to Eva; inadequate, but not quite as dubious as the hint that Hitler may not even have heard of Auschwitz. GA

Molokai: The Story of Father Damien

(1999, Neth/Bel, 108 min)
d Paul Cox. *p* Tarsicius Vanhuysse, Griete Lammertyn, Andy Howard. *sc* John Briley. *ed* Kristina Hamilton, John Scott, Ludo Troch. *pd* Jan Petitjean. *m* Wim Mertens. *cast* David Wenham, Kate Ceberano, Derek Jacobi, Peter O'Toole, Kris Kristofferson, Alice Krige, Leo McKern, Sam Neill, Tom Wilkinson.

●Quite engrossing and often moving, this impressively mounted historical drama (from the book by Hilde Eynikel) is set in the late-Victorian era. It tells the story of a missionary from Flanders, Father Damien, who dedicated his life to the dying lepers on the colony of Kaluapapa on the Sandwich (now Hawaiian) island of Molokai – 'a place of terror and death,' as Leo McKern's bishop correctly calls it. The starry cast, including Kris Kristofferson as a rancher/admirer, are impressive, but Wenham's Roman Catholic priest is excellent, downplaying the man's awe-inspiring self-sacrifice, tenacity, courage and humanity. Director Cox plays it admirably straight, mostly, allowing the stark oppositions (beauty/ugliness, sacrifice/ self-seeking, etc) to speak for themselves, only weakening in the occasional use of emotive music. WH

Moment by Moment

(1978, US, 105 min)
d Jane Wagner. *p* Robert Stigwood. *sc* Jane Wagner. *ph* Philip H Lathrop. *ed* La Reine Johnstone. *pd* Harry Horner. *m* Lee Holdridge. *cast* Lily Tomlin, John Travolta, Andra Akers, Bert Kramer, Shelley R Bonus, Debra Feuer, James Luisi.
●Ostensibly a vehicle for John Travolta, the film documents a love story between an older woman and a young drifter. With totally unsympathetic characters set against a background of shrink-riddled, over-privileged Marin County society, and accompanied by some of the worst easy-listening muzak LA could dredge up. Yuk.

Moment d'Egarement, Un (In a Wild Moment/One Wild Moment/A Summer Affair)

(1977, Fr, 100 min)
d/sc Claude Berri. *ph* André Neau. *ed* Jacques Witta. *m* Michel Stelio. *cast* Jean-Pierre Marielle, Victor Lanoux, Christine Dejoux, Agnès Soral, Martine Sarcey, Robert Bahr, Tiburce Fauretto, Tessa Bouche.
●Computerised comedy: find two unappetisingly overweight hams (Marielle and Lanoux), cast them as a pair of menopausal mates adrift in St Tropez, let one of them be seduced by the other's nubile daughter. Should the need arise, through miscalculation, for an atom of real narrative invention (as here, with the film's denouement), just leave it fashionably 'open-ended' by resorting to a freeze-frame. Its sole interest is as a choice specimen of the complacent obsession of French film-makers with near-incestuous, near-paedophiliac liaisons. Remade equally blandly by Stanley Donen as *Blame It On Rio*. GAd

Moment of Innocence (Noon va Goldoon)

(1995, Iran/Fr/Switz, 78 min)
d Mohsen Makhmalbaf. *p* Abolfazl Alaghehband. *sc* Mohsen Makhmalbaf. *ph* Mahmoud Kalari. *ed* Mohsen Makhmalbaf. *ad* Reza Alaghehman. *m* Majid Entezami. *cast* Mirhadi Taiebi, Ali Bakhshi, Ammar Tafti, Mariyam Mohammad-Amini, Fariba Faghiri.
●Makhmalbaf's film elides fact and fiction, vérité and fantasy, and subtly points up the high esteem and selfish hopes invested in the director by his admirers. A former police officer travels to Tehran to audition for a role in director Makhmalbaf next film. The two recognise each other as pre-revolutionary opponents from the early '70s: the 17-year-old Makhmalbaf had attempted to disarm the policeman, stabbing him, and receiving a bullet wound and a prison sentence for his pains. Unlike Makhmalbaf's, the ex-cop's scars have yet to heal. Out of curiosity the two men agree to collaborate on a film about the incident, each casting, coaching and directing his own younger self in a series of turns which take on meaning for both sides and generations involved. A merry analogist, Makhmalbaf draws a wealth of parallels, between ages and eras, hopes and fears. His approach to narrative can appear cryptic, his metaphors dense, but it seems churlish to quarrel with a film that sends one character searching a bazaar, asking of bystanders, 'Have you seen a ray of sunlight here?' NB

Moment of Truth, The (Il Momento della Verità)

(1964, It/Sp, 110 min)
d Francesco Rosi. *p* Tonino Cervi, Francesco Rosi. *sc* Francesco Rosi. *ph* Gianni Di Venanzo, Aiace Parolin, Pasqualino De Santis. *ed* Mario Serandrei. *m* Piero Piccioni. *with* Miguel Mateo Miguelín, José Gomez Sevillano, Pedro Basauri Pedrucho, Linda Christian.
●The glare of the sun, the surge of flamenco, the roar of the crowd: Rosi's film about bullfighting is all this and more. On to a *Blood and Sand*-style story of an Andalusian boy abandoning his arid, poverty-stricken home for the supposed glamour of the urban corridas, is grafted an ambivalent, subtle analysis of the thorny byways bordering on the road to fame and fortune; exchanging hardship for the manipulative deals of entrepreneurial Dons and the contempt of bourgeois socialites, the hero's resolve to make good finally results in a blurred nightmare of disillusionment and death. Without glorifying the 'sport', the magnificent 'Scope compositions nevertheless display the matador's mesmeric grace and daring, while admitting the frenzied brutality that delights the bloodthirsty, callous crowds. It's a colourful, cruel world of senseless exploitation (of animals and humans alike) and tyrannical traditions, rendered with vivid brilliance by this uncommonly unsentimental director. GA

Moments

(1973, GB, 92 min)
d Peter Crane. *sc* Michael Sloan. *ph* Wolfgang Suschitzky. *ed* Roy Watts. *ad* Bruce Atkins. *m* John Cameron. *cast* Keith Michell, Angharad Rees, Bill Fraser, Jeannette Sterke, Donald Hewlett, Keith Bell.
●Figuratively, the story about the length of drop on the rope: a man in an Eastbourne hotel is seemingly rescued from suicide by a young girl. With the Grand Hotel setting, intermingling of past and present (real or imagined), shifting levels of 'reality', and the use of the out-of-season resort as a symbol for inner desolation, it is not hard to see the influence of Resnais. And such pretensions are surprisingly welcome after the sub-11 plus level of most British movies. It's all the more pity that the film's central relationship cannot sustain credibility: the plot depends on too much verbal exposition; explanations are too predictable for an essay on uncertainty; and the characters move from clichéd stodgy middle-age and freewheeling youth to stereotyped fugitives from deadening routine. CPe

Môme Pigalle, La (Scandal in Montmartre)

(1955, Fr, 90 min, b/w)
d Alfred Rode. *sc* Jacques Companeez. *ph* Marc Fossard. *ed* Louisette Hautecoeur-Taverna. *ad* Robert Bouladoux. *m* Roger-Roger. *cast* Claudine Dupuis, Jean Gaven, Dany Carrel, Philippe Nicaud, Jean Tissier, Dora Doll, Julien Carette.
●This tatty exploitation piece is simultaneously manic and repressed, silly and cynical, as paranoid as *Invasion of the Body Snatchers* and altogether a prime '50s artifact. Dupuis is the Pigalle Babe, a nightclub singer hoping to marry her nice young man (Nicaud), but falling into lust with a killer (Gaven) and confiding all to her best friend (Carrel). But the nice young man's a con artist, the killer's an undercover cop, and Carrel is an insurance sleuth posing as a stripper. Talk about the age of uncertainty… Quantities of nudes swan about, while Alfred Rode et Son Orchestre (that's right, a bandleader/cinéaste) rip through a couple of numbers. This was the fifth of eight titles from Rode-Dupuis, perhaps the cinema's least romantic husband-and-wife combo. BBa

Mommie Dearest

(1981, US, 129 min)
d Frank Perry. *p* Frank Yablans. *sc* Frank Yablans, Frank Perry, Tracy Hotchner, Robert Getchell. *ph* Paul Lohmann. *ed* Peter E Berger. *pd* Bill Malley. *m* Henry Mancini. *cast* Faye Dunaway, Diana Scarwid, Steve Forrest, Howard da Silva, Michael Edwards, Jocelyn Brando.
●Good intentions to redress the balance of Christina Crawford's vengeful mother-fucker of a bestseller bio are in evidence aplenty; but how else than as camp can you take Faye Dunaway's waxwork Joan Crawford screeching for an axe, or throwing a scenery-chewing fit over her daughter's use of wire coathangers in the wardrobe? Perry doesn't help, with his credit sequence tease withholding our first glimpse of the stellar visage, and his determination to pose 'Joan' in geometrical symmetry with the lines of her spotless deco domestic mausoleum. Really no dafter, perhaps, than some of Joanie's own Warner Bros melodramas; the trouble is, it thinks it's Art. PT

Mo' Money

(1992, US, 90 min)
d Peter Macdonald. *p* Michael Rachmil. *sc* Damon Wayans. *ph* Don Burgess. *ed* Hubert C de la Bouillerie. *pd* William Arnold. *m* Jay Gruska. *cast* Damon Wayans, Stacey Dash, Joe Santos, John Diehl, Harry J Lennix, Marlon Wayans, Mark Beltzman.
●This comedy-romance-thriller has the substance of a midnight snack. Writer and co-executive producer Wayans plays Johnny Stewart, a scam artist who works with his brother Seymour (Marlon Wayans), much to the despair of their dead father's ex-partner on the police force. Along strolls Amber (Dash), a glamorous careerist with a credit card company, and smitten Johnny lands a job in her firm's mailroom to pursue his courtship. His efforts to impress involve stealing credit cards with which to finance a fancy lifestyle; but once caught, he finds himself embroiled in blackmail and violence. Director Macdonald is comfortable with the action sequences, but tension dissipates well before the final bone-crunching shoot-out. Damon and Marlon are at their best in the opening comic sequences, which allow their chemistry to operate, but their pacing is disrupted by the ensuing formulaic thrills. CM

Mona Lisa

(1986, GB, 104 min)
d Neil Jordan. *p* Nick Cassavetti, Stephen Woolley. *sc* Neil Jordan, David Leland. *ph* Roger Pratt. *ed* Lesley Walker. *pd* Jamie Leonard. *m* Michael Kamen. *cast* Bob Hoskins, Cathy Tyson, Michael Caine, Robbie Coltrane, Clarke Peters, Kate Hardie, Zoe Nathenson.
●An assured London-set thriller about the need to love. An old friend (Caine, looking like a man who sweats horribly into his pyjamas) gives minor-league villain Hoskins a job as chauffeur to a dauntingly elegant prostitute (Tyson). This triggers one of the most affecting love stories in recent cinema, between a short, overweight racist and the 'thin black tart' who helps him adjust to a world he finds alien and asks him to find her friend, who has vanished in the mire of big city vice. Plotting a slow descent towards hell, the film deliberately invites comparison with Taxi Driver, though Hoskins, unlike Scorsese's solipsistic avenger, is an utterly ordinary hero, romantic, lost among the pimps and hoods, at ease only when listening to old Nat King Cole numbers. A wonderful achievement, a dark film with a generous heart in the shape of an extraordinarily touching performance from Hoskins. RR

Monday

(2000, Jap, 100 min)
d Sabu. *p* Lee Bong-Ou. *sc* Sabu. *ph* Kazuhiko Sato. *ed* Kumio Onaga. *pd* Tomoyuki Maruo. *m* Keiichiro Shibuya, Captain Funk, Twist & Shout. *cast* Shinichi Tsutsumi, Yasuko Matsuyuki, Ren Osugi, Masanobu Ando, Nanako Okochi, Hijiri Kojima.
●Once notorious for freezing the frame at the climax of a film to splash his own credit across the action, ex-actor Sabu is learning fast. *Monday* has exactly the same constituent parts as his three previous films – victims of circumstance, flaky yakuza, cruel humour – but it deploys them with far more control and finesse. Takagi (Tsutsumi, a Sabu regular) wakes in a hotel room one Monday morning with a packet of funeral salt in his pocket but no memory of the weekend. Gradually, flashbacks remind him of the awful truths: the exploding coffin, the sultry girl, the accidental shooting of the gangster, the police dragnet. All the funnier for being quite deliberately paced, and the elevator full of *butoh* dancers is just icing on the cake. TR

Monde du Silence, Le (The Silent World)

(1956, Fr, 86 min)
d Jacques-Yves Cousteau, Louis Malle. *ph* Edmond Séchan. *ph* Jacques-Yves Cousteau, Louis Malle, Frédéric Dumas, Albert Falco. *m* Yves Baudrier. with Jacques-Yves Cousteau.
●'The latest precision cameras…the deepest dive yet filmed…' Things change, though. Whereas this was regarded at the time as

irreproachable, improving, suitable for classroom bookings, the good Captain Cousteau and his all-male ensemble come across now, in 1998, as an aggravating lot, in their once natty '50s swimwear, amusing themselves by straddling giant turtles and turning them into agonising 'comic relief', or filling the screen with torrents of blood as they slaughter a passing school of sharks ('All sailors hate sharks'). On the other hand, the film-makers' intermittent poetic ambitions are strikingly justified as the cameras explore the wreck of a torpedoed freighter, the commentary becoming an elegy for the lost ship and her crew. The movie has acquired a further dimension as an apprentice work by co-director Louis Malle, though students of his oeuvre will need ingenuity to relate this to anything he made subsequently. BBa

Monde sans pitié, Un (Tough Life/A World Without Pity)

(1989, Fr, 88 min)
d Eric Rochant. *p* Alain Rocca. *sc* Eric Rochant. *ph* Pierre Novion. *ed* Michèle Darmon. *ad* Thierry François. *m* Gérard Torikan. *cast* Hippolyte Girardot, Mireille Perrier, Yvan Attal, Jean-Marie Rollin, Cécile Mazan, Aline Still, Paul Pavel, Anne Kessler, Patrick Blondel.

●Jobless, womanising Hippo (Girardot), who lives off his drug-dealing younger brother, is cynically devoted to no one but himself. Falling for Nathalie (Perrier), a rather bookish, professionally get-ahead woman, is the last thing he expects or thinks he needs. When Nathalie invites Hippo over for tea, his endless round of parties, poker games, petty crime and sleeping late suddenly seems less attractive. A simple story, this, but for his excellent feature debut, Rochant adopts a pacy, elliptical narrative style to create an enormously witty and likeable study of emotional alienation and commitment. Though dealing with 'serious' themes (the gulf between classes and generations, responsibility through influence, the need to be honest with oneself as well as with others), it never bogs down in solemn moralising, but paints a vivacious, uncommonly plausible portrait of the preoccupations of contemporary Parisian youth. Stylishly shot, it also benefits from very affecting performances by Perrier and Girardot. GA

Mondo Trasho

(1969, US, 95 min, b/w)
d/p/sc/ph/ed/ad John Waters. *cast* Divine, David Lochary, Mink Stole, Mary Vivian Pearce, Mark Isherwood.

●Everyone should see at least one early Waters film (this was his first feature); whether you can take two is a matter of personal bad taste. From the moment the picture wobbles reluctantly on to the screen, this clearly demonstrates that the Baltimore boy was ahead of his time when it came to punk aesthetics and shock for shock's sake. Especially in his next epic, *Multiple Maniacs*, inspired by the Sharon Tate killing, which has the obscene Divine as a mass murderer, delayed on her way to her final carnage by the Religious Whore (Mink Stole) who gives her a 'rosary job' before the altar. Less blasphemous, *Mondo Trasho* finds Divine lugging round the lifeless body of Mary Vivian Pearce, whom she has run over with her Cadillac convertible, all to the accompaniment of a tinny medley of '60s tunes. Both films are dreadful; bet they had a few laughs making them, though. JS

Money

see Argent, L'

Money Movers

(1978, Aust. 94 min)
d Bruce Beresford. *p* Matt Carroll. *sc* Bruce Beresford. *ph* Don McAlpine. *ed* William Anderson. *ad* David Copping. *cast* Terence Donovan, Ed Devereaux, Tony Bonner, Lucky Grills, Alan Cassell, Frank Wilson, Candy Raymond, Bryan Brown.

●Tautly paced and unpretentiously punchy, Beresford's heist thriller is an object lesson in mainstream narrative confidence and economy, detailing the ironic convergence of underworld, undercover and under-suspicion around a security firm vault containing $20 million. The question of who polices the police runs like a black comedy subtext through the film, but is never allowed articulation until the complex business at hand is out of the way in a generically inevitable blood-bath; while the prevalent assumption of universal corruption begins to play havoc with audience sympathies. PT

Money Order, The (Le Mandat)

(1968, Fr/Sen, 90 min)
d/p/sc Ousmane Sembéne. *ph* Paul Soulignac. *ed* Gilou Kikoïne, Max Saldinger. *cast* Makuredia Guey, Yunus Ndiay, Issen Niang, Mustafa Ture, Mustafa Ture, Farva Sar.

●A political film criticising the type of bureaucracy that has arisen in post-colonial Senegal. A money order is sent to an unemployed, illiterate relative by a hard-working lad seeking his fortune in Paris. But all attempts to cash the money order are frustrated: the man's illiteracy and ignorance of finance allow him to be exploited by those with education. The power is in the hands of the clerks and intellectuals, who use their knowledge for private advantage. Although the film can be criticised for the relative gentleness of its attack, Sembene succeeds in pointing up the divisiveness created by the colonial heritage. The French-colonised elite are now busy oppressing and colonising their own people. Shot in Wolof, the local language, the film asserts Senegalese culture against the rapacious way of the West. Not surprisingly it proved popular with the 'people', but was ignored by the bourgeois when originally released. JDuC

Money Pit, The

(1985, US, 91 min)
d Richard Benjamin. *p* Frank Marshall, Kathleen Kennedy. *sc* David Giler. *ph* Gordon Willis. *ed* Jacqueline Cambas. *pd* Patrizia von Brandenstein. *m* Michel Colombier. *cast* Tom Hanks, Shelley Long, Alexander Godunov, Maureen Stapleton, Joe Mantegna, Philip Bosco, Josh Mostel.

●As a yuppie nightmare, this is much safer than *After Hours*, but no less funny. Hanks is a successful lawyer, most of whose clients are 16 stone transvestite rock bands with names like 'The Cheap Girls'. When his girlfriend's ex-husband reappropriates their love nest, he is forced to buy a large amount of real estate out in the suburbs of New York. This is the money pit. Part of the pleasure is watching the house fulfil your worst expectations: doors come off hinges, wiring bums up like a powder trail, baths crash through ceilings, roofs leak. You can see it coming, but it still has the delicious anticipation of the slow burn. And it all gets much worse. Director Richard Benjamin has the rare gift of knowing just where the funnybone lies, a certain taste for Keaton-esque slapstick, and a very fine comic performer in Hanks. CPea

Money Talks

(1997, US, 96 min)
d Brett Ratner. *p* Walter Koblenz, Tracy Kramer. *sc* Joel Cohen, Alec Sokolow. *ph* Russell Carpenter, Robert Primes. *ed* Mark Helfrich. *pd* Robb Wilson-King. *m* Lalo Schifrin. *cast* Chris Tucker, Charlie Sheen, Heather Locklear, Gerard Ismaël, Damian Chapa, Veronica Cartwright, David Warner, Paul Sorvino.

●Tucker is an LA street hustler on the run from French diamond smugglers, and Sheen an ambitious TV journalist on the brink of an advantageous marriage, who has everything to gain (or lose) from helping him. Tucker's great in straight parts, but has modelled his funny man routine too closely on Eddie Murphy. Meanwhile, Sheen seems comfortable in a role that has only one angle (everything his character sees reminds him of an item he did for TV). Diversions are provided by the script, which comes from Alec Sokolow and Joel Cohen of *Toy Story*: Tucker makes a 'speech' at a posh, all-white gathering, which is in fact one long quote from a Barry White song, and (wrongly) assumes the palefaces won't recognise it. What we're being alerted to, over and over, is the cultural apartheid at work in America and the power to be gained from sneaking across the divide. CO'Su

Money Train

(1995, US, 110 min)
d Joseph Ruben. *p* Jon Peters, Neil Canton. *sc* Doug Richardson, David Loughery. *ph* John W Lindley. *ed* George Bowers. Bill Pankow. *pd* Bill Groom. *m* Mark Mancina. *cast* Wesley Snipes, Woody Harrelson, Jennifer Lopez, Robert Blake, Chris Cooper, Joe Grifasi, Scott Sowers, Skipp Sudduth.

●Ever since their successful teaming in *White Men Can't Jump*, Hollywood has wanted to reunite Snipes and Harrelson for a buddy picture. Directed with routine efficiency, this loco action comedy plays a one-joke, high-concept plot to the hilt, squandering cash and energy on a subway heist that takes forever to arrive and then goes nowhere. The comic twist is that Snipes and Harrelson are foster brothers; the set-up that they're New York transit cops who end up robbing the Money Train to pay Woody's gambling debts. With a fortune in fares at stake and hard-ass Money Train boss (Blake) on their case, Snipes once again digs his irresponsible white brother out of a hole. The pair obviously enjoyed ragging one another, and director Ruben finally puts the money on the screen with a *Taking of Pelham One Two Three*-style climax. As Snipes and Harrelson's fellow transit cop and mutual love interest, the smouldering Lopez mostly just stands around waiting for the boys to make up their minds about her. Hardly worth the four-year wait. NF

Mon Homme

(1996, Fr, 99 min)
d Bertrand Blier. *p* Alain Sarde. *sc* Bertrand Blier. *ph* Pierre Lhomme. *ed* Claudine Merlin. *pd* Willy Holt. *cast* Anouk Grinberg, Gérard Lanvin, Valéria Bruni-Tedeschi, Olivier Martinez, Dominique Valadié, Aurore Clément, Jean-Pierre Léaud, Sabine Azéma, Mathieu Kassovitz.

●This could be Blier's masterpiece, and/or his most disparaging work. For 25 years, he's been serving up provocative satirical dissections of French social, sexual and cultural mores. Here, again, he goes just too far. The pert Grinberg, the muse of his most recent films, is the tart with a heart: a $1,000-a-day girl, this woman has the gift and the appetite. Meeting homeless tramp Jeannot (Lanvin), she brings him to her apartment for succour and offers herself in a gesture of submission. She takes him as her pimp, shaving, suiting and smartening him, and enjoys the conventional (and conventionally ugly) life of the oldest profession, until 'her man' over-reaches himself, prostituting her neighbour (Bruni-Tedeschi), and the cops send him down. The merciless simplicity of Blier's method breaks the heart. His inscrutable stance and ironic distance from his characters is now so firmly entrenched that he feels free to blend moments of lyricism (a beautiful, dreamy drift of snowflakes worthy of Demy), jaundiced poetry (nodding toward Pialat) and melodrama, without teetering off the razor-edge path between offence and pathos. The Barry White songs and the 'Scope photography further emphasise the feeling of alienation. One senses an almost inhuman objectivity at work, which makes Blier seem more and more a compatriot of that arch misanthrope Henri-Georges Clouzot. WH

Monika

see Sommaren med Monika

Monk, The

see Moine, Le

Monk Dawson

(1997, GB, 107 min)
d/p Tom Waller. *sc* James Magrane. *ph* Teoh Gay Hian. *ed* Tom Waller. *pd* Harold Chapman. *m* Mark Jense. *cast* John Michie, Ben Taylor, Paula Hamilton, Martin Kemp, Rupert Vansittart, Frances Tomelty, Michael Cashman.

●Based on a Piers Paul Read novel about a defrocked monk's progress along the Via Dolorosa of trendy '70s Cheyne Walk, this sets up high expectations it's unable to satisfy. Michie's portrayal of the idealistic Benedictine Eddie Dawson is technically proficient, expressing well the man's vulnerability and angry, hurt consternation when he's expelled from the order for sheltering an unmarried mother. But as Dawson throws himself into the self-seeking cauldron of London society, reduced to hack journalism for a venal tabloid supremo (Kemp) in order to support an unwise marriage, Michie can't find the depth required to make palpable the complex feelings of alienation Dawson experiences, as he drowns in a sea of betrayal, broken ideals and misplaced affection. There's little at fault in the screenplay, and the cinematography lights the bleak Northumberland moors as effectively as the restaurants and houses of London SW3. But as a moral 'entertainment', the film has no enlightening core. WH

Monkeybone

(2001, US, 92 min)
d Henry Selick. *p* Michael Barnathan, Mark Radcliffe. *sc* Sam Hamm. *ph* Andrew Dunn, *ed* Mark Warner, Jon Poll, Nicholas C Smith. *pd* Bill Boes. *m* Anne Dudley. *cast* Ed Reif, Brendan Fraser, Bridget Fonda, Chris Kattan, Giancarlo Esposito, Rose McGowan, John Turturro, Dave Foley, Whoopi Goldberg, Megan Mullally.

●Directed by Henry Selick (*Tim Burton's Nightmare Before Christmas*) and based on Kaja Blakeley's graphic novel *Dark Town*, this is a bust, but at least it's different. Fraser is cartoonist Stu Miller, on the verge of hitting it big with his creation Monkeybone, a wisecracking simian monster from the id. Stu is too principled to cash in, but ends up in a coma after a freak accident, and his consciousness is transported to Dark Town, a purgatory from which Monkeybone escapes to wreak havoc with his body, not to mention his girlfriend's. The design is often brilliant, although the film is nowhere near as tasteless or funny as it ought to be. TCh

Monkey Business

(1931, US, 77 min, b/w)
d Norman Z McLeod. *sc* SJ Perelman, Will B Johnstone. *ph* Arthur Todd. *cast* The Marx Brothers, Thelma Todd, Ruth Hall, Harry Woods, Rockcliffe Fellowes, Tom Kennedy, Evelyn Pierce.

●The four Marx Brothers as stowaways trying to bull their way through immigration by pretending to be Maurice Chevalier (each hopefully doing an impersonation to prove it), then crashing a Long Island society party to sow havoc. With *Monkey Business*, their first screen original, the team cast caution to the winds, helped by a perky script ('Tell me, has your grandfather's beard got any money?' – 'Money? Why it fell hair to a fortune') and some lunatic sight gags. Thelma Todd provides Groucho with his most delectable and intelligent foil. GB

Monkey Business

(1952, US, 97 min, b/w)
p Howard Hawks. *p* Sol C Siegel. *sc* Ben Hecht, Charles Lederer, IAL Diamond. *ph* Milton Krasner. *ed* William B Murphy. *ad* Lyle Wheeler, George Patrick. *m* Leigh Harline. *cast* Cary Grant, Ginger Rogers, Charles Coburn, Marilyn Monroe, Hugh Marlowe, Henri Letondal, Robert Cornthwaite, George Winslow.

●Immaculate screwball comedy by its greatest practitioners, in which Cary Grant polishes up at least three previous roles as an absent-minded chemist in search of a youth drug. The chaos starts when a mischievous monkey accidentally mixes the magic formula into the water cooler, whereupon Grant and wife Ginger Rogers take turns to regress into childhood. For Grant, that means sex, speed, a crew-cut, checked jacket and socks, while Rogers wants to dance the hoochie-coochie in their honeymoon hotel. Monroe is on hand as the typist who can't type, while the timing of the gags can put most Hollywood comedies, never mind TV sitcoms, to shame. The classic inverted-world comedy, where kids and animals bring sexual anarchy into the demure adult world, leaving all inhabitants much refreshed and highly amused. DMacp

Monkey Grip

(1981, Aust, 102 min)
d Ken Cameron. *p* Patricia Lovell. *sc* Ken Cameron. *ph* David Gribble. *ed* David Huggett. *pd* Clark Munro. *m* Bruce Smeaton. *cast* Noni Hazlehurst, Colin Friels, Alice Garner, Harold Hopkins, Candy Raymond, Michael Caton, Tim Burns.

●Gloom settles quickly as Nora (Hazlehurst) launches into a portentous account of her emotional ups-and-downs. Thirtyish, separated from the father of her child, she is suffering almost stoically as a single parent in Sydney but still hoping to get fulfilled. Prospects look slim when, after discarding junkie number one, she falls for Javo (Friels), the sort of guy who needs a day's notice to tie his shoelaces. After much airing of thick-eared romantic problems in swimming-pools, squats and studies, Nora emerges, so she informs us, an older but infinitely wiser woman. What seems extraordinary is that this should have been held up (and apparently applauded) as the story of a woman fighting to control her life, when she's clearly making a dreadful mess of it. It's also unrelieved by the faintest glimmer of humour, except for one (unintentionally?) quite hilarious scene in which Javo's acting ambitions take a tumble when he heaves all over the footlights on his debut. Noni Hazlehurst is excellent, but it's an unrewarding plod. JP

Monkey Shines

(1988, US, 113 min)
d George A Romero. *p* Charles Evans. *sc* George A Romero. *ph* James A Contner. *ed* Pasquale Buba. *pd* Cletus Anderson. *m* David Shire. *cast* Jason Beghe, John Pankow, Kate McNeil, Joyce Van Patten, Christine Forrest, Stephen Root, Stanley Tucci, Janine Turner.

●Moving away from the apocalyptic horror of his 'Living Dead' trilogy, Romero reaffirms his equal aptitude for controlled chills, previously evident in *Martin*. Paralysed in a road accident, Allan Mann (Beghe) is provided with a trained Capuchin monkey, Ella, as home help. A research specimen before training, Ella had been injected with human brain tissue by Allan's mad scientist pal (Pankow) in the hope of increasing her learning ability. Now, as a result of a mysterious mind-meld, Ella responds to Allan's moods, violently enacting his frustrated rage against his bossy nurse (Forrest), fussing mother (Van Patten) and ex-fiancée (Turner), in nocturnal rampages which he experiences as hallucinatory nightmares seen through the monkey's eyes. Things build to a nasty climax when Allan falls in love with Ella's trainer Melanie (McNeil), triggering a violently jealous reaction from Ella. What sets this apart from most modern horror movies, besides a sparing use of special effects, is Romero's careful development of a credible emotional context for the pyromaniac madness and razor-wielding terror. Romero's is a formidable talent which others can only hope to ape. NF

Monkey's Mask, The (aka Poetry, Sex)

(2000, Aust/Fr/Jap/It, 93 min)
d Samantha Lang. *p* Robert Connolly, John Maynard. *sc* Anne Kennedy. *ph* Garry Phillips. *ed* Dany Cooper. *pd* Michael Philips. *m* Single Gun Theory. *cast* Susie Porter, Kelly McGillis, Marton Csokas, Deborah Mailman, Abbie Cornish, Jean-Pierre Mignon, Caroline Gillmer.

●Based on Dorothy Porter's acclaimed novel-in-poetry, this Australian production casts Porter as dyke dick Jill Fitzpatrick, whose latest missing-person case takes her into the seedy underbelly of Sydney's poetry scene. That's a good joke, played relatively straight. The search leads to the missing girl's poetry teacher Diana Maitland (McGillis); their shy, sly flirtation is nicely caught. The love story is allowed time and space, and the two fine actresses work well together. Close-cropped Porter just about comes up to McGillis' statuesque shoulders. The former is apparently more wordly-wise, but the older woman is really in the driving seat emotionally. McGillis' cool intellectual poise quite unbalances her more forthright lover. A shame, then, that the mystery is a bit ho-hum, and that director Lang fails to ratchet up the suspense in the crucial final third. Ultimately, what should have been sparky and unsettling comes off a bit flat and routine – at least, as routine as a literary lesbian private-eye thriller could ever be. TCh

Monkey's Tale, A (Le Château des singes/ A majmok kastélya)

(1999, Fr/GB/Ger/Hun, 79 min)
d Jean-François Laguionie. *p* Steve Walsh, Patrick Moine, Gerd Hecker. *sc* Norman Hudis, Jean-François Laguionie. *ph* Jean-Paul Rossard. *ed* Soizic Veillon, Ludovic Cassou, Yves Françon, Anke Schmidt. *pd* Zoltán Szilágyi Varga. *m* Alexandre Desplat. *cast* voices (English language version): Matt Hill, John Hurt, Michael York, Sally-Anne Marsh, Rik Mayall, Michael Gambon, Shirley Anne Field, Diana Quick.

●Centuries ago, a once happy tribe of monkeys was split asunder by a cataclysmic flood. Today, one half – the Woonkos – live in the jungle canopy, and other half – the Laankos – on terra firma. They despise each other. Then a gregarious young whippersnapper called Kom falls from the Woonkos' tree-top world into the hands of their arch enemy, charms the pants off them, and begins to sow a few seeds of peace, love and understanding. A happy reunion is inevitable. You can't knock the message – communication, racial harmony, interaction, oneness – but it's all so glaringly obvious, so contrived, so PC. Brits Hurt and Mayall do their darndest to inject some character into their parts, but truth is, the makers of this Euro production could have hired anyone. As for the naff animation, characters look like they're sketched in crayon, backgrounds like bleached-out watercolours. Even Westlife get a look in with an unappealing song called 'We Are One'. DA

Monkey Trouble

(1994, US, 96 min)
d Franco Amurri. *p* Mimi Polk, Heide Rufus Isaacs. *sc* Franco Amurri, Stu Krieger. *ph* Luciano Tovoli. *ed* Ray Lovejoy. *pd* Leslie Dilley. *m* Mark Mancina. *cast* Harvey Keitel, Mimi Rogers, Thora Birch, Christopher McDonald, Kevin Scannell, Alison Elliott.

●Like any nine-year-old, Eva (Birch) wants a dog. Stepdad is a cop with allergies to animal hair, and so he's no help. Mommy (Rogers) reckons that Eva isn't ready for the responsibility of a pet, since her room's a mess. Issues of trust, autonomy and self-realisation are at stake. Meanwhile, gypsy organ-grinder Shorty (Keitel) and his capuchin have attracted the attention of a pair of hoods who want the light-fingered monkey for a heist. The creature goes AWOL, hides in a tree and falls in Eva's lap. She keeps him, hides him, loves him, even puts a nappy on him. Very annoying. WH

Monolith

(1993, US, 91 min)
d John Eyres. *p* Geoff Griffiths, John Eyres. *sc* Stephen Lister. *ph* Alan Trow. *ed* Joel Goodman. *m* Frank Becker. *cast* Bill Paxton, Lindsay Frost, Louis Gossett Jr, John Hurt.

●Two mismatched Los Angeles detectives, thrown together after witnessing a Russian scientist shoot down an apparently 'possessed' child, discover a mysterious alien life-force that inhabits human bodies and shoots fireballs from their eyes. Ho-hum. NB

Monolith Monsters, The

(1957, US, 77 min, b/w)
d John Sherwood. *p* Howard Christie. *sc* Norman Jolley, Robert M Fresco. *ph* Ellis Carter. *ed* Sherman Todd. *ad* Alexander Golitzen, Bob Smith. *m* Joseph Gershenson. *cast* Lola Albright, Grant Williams, Les Tremayne, Phil Harvey, Trevor Bardette, William Flaherty, Linda Scheley.

●The original 'rocky horror': a Jack Arnold-originated, quite effective Universal sci-fi paranoia yarn featuring the alien-induced metamorphosis of men to stone, and a subsequent stampede of towering crystal structures across small-town America. Grant Williams (*The Incredible Shrinking Man*) is again dwarfed by his adversaries, though he plays the only possible hero: a geologist. PT

Mono loco, El

see Mad Monkey, The

Mon Oncle (My Uncle)

(1958, Fr, 116 min)
d Jacques Tati. *p* Louis Dolivet. *sc* Jacques Tati, Jacques Legrange. *ph* Jean Bourgoin. *ed* Suzanne Baron. *ad* Henry Schmitt. *m* Alain Romans, Franck Barcellini. *cast* Jacques Tati, Jean-Pierre Zola, Adrienne Servantie, Alain Bécourt, Lucien Fregis, Betty Schneider, Yvonne Arnaud.

●Tati's first film in colour. Yes, his contrast of the glorious awfulness of the Arpels' automated Modernistic house with Hulot's disordered Bohemianism is simplistic. Yes, Hulot as champion of the individual is oddly de-personalised. And one might even conclude that Tati is a closet misanthrope. Such text-book reservations come and go as this extraordinary film meanders like the Arpels' concrete garden path. But while some episodes are protracted, many are unforgettably funny, wonderfully observed, and always technically brilliant. Insane gadgets slam and roar, high heels click like metronomes, and even a depressed dachshund in a tartan overcoat obligingly submits to Tati's meticulous direction. JS

Mon Oncle Antoine (My Uncle Antoine)

(1971, Can, 110 min)
d Claude Jutra. *p* Marc Beaudet. *sc* Clément Perron, Claude Jutra. *ph* Michel Brault. *ed* Claude Jutra, Claire Boyer. *ad* Denis Boucher, Lawrence O'Brien. *m* Jean Cousineau. *cast* Jacques Gagnon, Lyne Champagne, Jean Duceppe, Olivette Thibault, Lionel Villeneuve, Claude Jutra, Monique Mercure.
●Taking a French-Canadian mining town, with all its feelings of dead-endedness, Jutra shows with some sympathy why people stay on. Events centre round one Christmas in the life of young Benoît (Gagnon), who works for his uncle, also the undertaker, in the general store. Against the background of communal festivities and the death of a boy, he becomes aware of the complexity of his own feelings and the fallibility and unhappiness of adults. A film of moments: Benoît's reaction to a girl first wearing make-up; glimpsing the notary's wife trying on a girdle; realising his uncle (Duceppe) is little more than a drunken sot; his revulsion at the dead boy's naked legs. Although sometimes lacking subtlety, the film avoids most of the clichés about adolescence and resists drawing conclusions. CPe

Mon Oncle d'Amérique (My American Uncle/My Uncle from America)

(1980, Fr, 126 min)
d Alain Resnais. *p* Philippe Dussart. *sc* Jean Gruault. *ph* Sacha Vierny. *ed* Albert Jurgenson. *ad* Jacques Saulnier. *m* Arié Dzierlatka. *cast* Gérard Depardieu, Nicole Garcia, Roger Pierre, Marie Dubois, Nelly Borgeaud, Pierre Arditi, Henri Laborit.
●After the disappointments of *Stavisky* and *Providence*, Resnais here retrieves his position as a great film innovator. *My American Uncle* takes three middle class characters (two of them from well-defined working class backgrounds) and leads them through a labyrinth of 'stress' situations. The tone hovers between soap opera and docudrama, consistently pleasurable if hardly gripping. Then it introduces its fourth major character, Henri Laborit, a bona fide behavioural scientist, who discusses his theories of biological and emotional triggers. Shortsighted critics seem to imagine that the fictional material merely illustrates what Laborit says, although Resnais inserts some jokey shots of 'human' mice to demolish any such notions. His triumph is to create a new kind of fiction: a drama that not only leaves room to think, but opens up fissures that thoughts flood into, some prompted by Laborit, others by personal reflections, yet others by dreams. Inevitably, it ends in a riddle, and one which proves that surrealism lives. TR

Mon Père, ce héros

(1991, Fr, 104 min)
d Gérard Lauzier. *p* Jean-Louis Livi. *sc* Gérard Lauzier. *ph* Patrick Blossier. *ed* Georges Klotz. ad Christian Marti. *m* François Bernheim. *cast* Gérard Depardieu, Marie Gillain, Patrick Mille, Catherine Jacob, Charlotte de Turckheim, Eric Berger.
●Proof positive that Depardieu is a star of international magnitude: even a pedestrian comedy like this warrants theatrical release in Britain. André (Depardieu), a divorced middle-aged businessman, takes daughter Véronique (Gillain) away for Christmas, but her bathing-suit makes him wonder whether Mauritius was such a good idea. At 14, she is not his little girl any more. Much smitten with one particular youth, Véronique impresses him with a tapestry of lies: she is a runaway, and André her sugar-daddy lover. Only when André is enveloped in the deceit do things perk up momentarily, and still the picture lumbers from laborious farce to shameless sentiment with all the grace of a beached whale (an image Depardieu brings to mind). The bovine sensibility of this tacky, tasteless blague is underscored with misogyny and a scurrilous hint of racism. TCh

Mon Premier Amour

(1978, Fr, 100 min)
d/sc Elie Chouraqui. *ph* Bernard Zitzermann. *ed* Marie-Josèphe Yoyotte. *ad* Hilton Mac Connico. *m* Michel Legrand. *cast* Anouk Aimée, Richard Berry, Gabriele Ferzetti, Nathalie Baye, Jacques Villeret.
●A young man falls in love with his mother (not hard if she's as agelessly radiant as Anouk) when he learns that she is dying of leukaemia. Not a case of necrophilia, alas, nor even of incest. Director Chouraqui obviously learned to distill pure mush with glitter sauce as assistant to Lelouch. TM

Monrak Transistor

(2002, Thai, 115 min)
d Pen-ek Ratanaruang. *p* Nonzee Nimibutr, Duangkamol Limcharoen. *sc* Pen-ek Ratanaruang. *ph* Chankit Chamniwikaipong. *ed* Patamanadda Yukol. *ad* Saksiri Chuntarangsri. *m* Amornbhong Methakunavudh, Chartchai Pongprapapan. *cast* Suppakorn Kitsuwan, Siriyakorn Pukkavesa, Black Pomtong, Somlek Sakdikul, Porntip Papanai, Ampol Rattanawong.
●Pen-ek's social/moral fable may have a slight Coen Brothers flavour, but it goes places no US movie has ever mapped. The first chapter celebrates the bucolic romance between Pan (Suppakorn, outstanding) and his village bride Sadaw (Siriyakorn, charming). Then, as Pan is sent off to do military service, the film's prison-guard narrator observes that what could have been a 'delightful short' still has a long way to go: Pan becomes a deserter to pursue a singing career, commits manslaughter while fending off his gay manager, and eventually winds up begging on the streets of Bangkok. Meanwhile the ever-loyal Sadaw gives up on him and allows herself to be seduced by a smooth-talking salesman of deworming pills. Not exactly a musical, the film integrates songs by Surapol Sombatcharoen, a Thai C&W star of the 1960s. (It also boasts a new song by Wisit, director of *Tears of the Black Tiger*, and pays a very sly homage to that film.) Great retro music, pop morality, social satire and absurdly potent drama. Wonderful, and one of a kind. TR

Monsieur Hawarden

(1968, Neth/Bel, 106 min, b/w)
d Harry Kümel. *p* Jacques Sitter, André Thomas, Rob du Meé. *sc* Jan Blokker, Harry Kümel. *ph* Eduard van der Enden. *ed* Suzanne Baron. *ad* Tom Payot, Stefania Unwin. *m* Pierre Batholomée. *cast* Ellen Vogel, Hilde Uitterlinden, Johan Remmelts, Dora Van Der Groen, Senne Rouffaer, Xander Fisher.
●Kümel's first feature is not much like his subsequent *Daughters of Darkness* or *Malpertuis*, although all three films centre on questions of sexual identity, and all three are bravura exercises in style. *Monsieur Hawarden* is an artily restrained melodrama about a Viennese lady around the turn of the century who kills one of her lovers and then retreats into hiding in masculine drag. It is hubristically dedicated to Sternberg, but in fact closely resembles Bergman's *The Face* in both its black-and-white chiaroscuro photography and its plotting. Relentlessly beautiful and sensitive, it clearly gave Kümel the chance to work a lot of 'art cinema' ideas out of his system before launching into his more commercial (and more imaginative) horror/fantasy films. TR

Monsieur Hire

(1989, Fr, 79 min)
d Patrice Leconte. *p* Philippe Carcassonne, René Cleitman. *sc* Patrice Leconte, Patrick Dewolf. *ph* Denis Lenoir. *ed* Joëlle Hache. *ad* Ivan Maussion. *m* Michael Nyman. *cast* Michel Blanc, Sandrine Bonnaire, Luc Thullier, André Wilms, Eric Berenger, Marielle Berthon, Philippe Dormoy.
●Prime suspect in the murder of a young girl, Monsieur Hire – a quiet, balding, middle-aged tailor – spends much of his time secretly gazing from his window at Alice, who lives in the apartment opposite. His solitude, however, is broken when Alice, having glimpsed his face in the light of a storm, visits him in his room and bluntly asks why he spies on her. In this oddly touching, enigmatic adaptation of Simenon's novel, Leconte focuses less on the murder mystery – Hire repeatedly proclaims his innocence, but how sinister is his voyeurism? – than on the unexpectedly tender relationship that develops between watcher and watched, gently manipulating audience sympathies to create a poignant study of *amour fou*. Appropriately in a film concerned with voyeurism and loneliness, restraint is the keynote, with Michel Blanc's playing of Hire especially intriguing in its cool, sensitive understatement. But it is Leconte's direction that steals the show. Opting for subtlety rather than suspense, slowly but surely piecing together a jigsaw of brief elliptical scenes which mirror the nervy hesitancy of Hire's emotions, Leconte's narrative economy contrives to say a great deal about his hapless protagonist. GA

Monsieur Hulot's Holiday

see Vacances de M. Hulot, Les

Monsieur Ripois

see Knave of Hearts

Monsieur Verdoux

(1947, US, 123 min, b/w)
d/p/sc Charles Chaplin. *ph* Roland Totheroh. *ed* Willard Nico. *ad* John Beckman. *m* Charles Chaplin. *cast* Charles Chaplin, Martha Raye, Isobel Elsom, Marilyn Nash, Mady Correll, Irving Bacon, William Frawley, Charles Evans.
●Chaplin's self-styled 'comedy of murders' (from an idea by Orson Welles) about a gent who marries short-lived wealthy women was generally disliked on its first appearance: people found it slow, cold, bitter and insufficiently funny. Now it shapes up as Chaplin's most startling, most invigorating movie: its icy temperature is positively bracing after the hot syrup of his earlier work (though a dollop of that survives in the waif character played by Marilyn Nash). Chaplin uses his customary fastidious gestures to emphasis human nastiness – typified by the brassy Martha Raye, who plays the most vulgar woman ever created, chattering away with her mouth full of croissant and laughing not like one drain but ten. GB

Monsignor

(1982, US, 121 min)
d Frank Perry. *p* Frank Yablans, David Niven Jr. *sc* Abraham Polonsky, Wendell Mayes. *ph* Billy Williams. *ed* Peter E Berger. *pd* John F DeCuir. *m* John Williams. *cast* Christopher Reeve, Genevieve Bujold, Fernando Rey, Jason Miller, Joe Cortese, Adolfo Celi, Leonardo Cimino, Tomas Milian, Robert Prosky, Joe Pantoliano.
●A movie seemingly predicated on the naive belief that audiences will be surprised that priests sleep with nuns, kill people (or Germans in World War II, at least), profit from the black market, and make deals with the Mafia to help the Vatican's cash flow problem. To its credit, there is commendably little wrestling with conscience over these minor doctrinal points; Christopher Reeve pauses only to square that mighty jaw and brush off his soutane, before plunging into the world of high finance, low sex, toppling dynasties, and Machiavellian in-fighting. Indeed, the movie's flat, TV-style matter-of-factness might even be said to correspond with a certain Pelagian pragmatism. Producer Frank Yablans was also guilty of *The Other Side of Midnight*, a 20-Hail Mary slice of epic schlock in roughly the same league as this: mortal sins, true confessions, purple stuff. CPea

Monsoon Wedding

(2001, US/It/Ger/Fr, 113 min)
d Mira Nair. *p* Caroline Baron, Mira Nair. *sc* Sabrina Dhawan. *ph* Declan Quinn. *ed* Allyson C Johnson. *pd* Stephanie Carroll. *m* Mychael Danna. *cast* Naseeruddin Shah, Lillete Dubey, Shefali Shetty, Vijay Raaz, Tilotama Shome, Vasundhara Das, Kulbhushan Kharbanda, Parvin Dabas, Roshan Seth.
●This big marquee movie – it portrays the preparations for an arranged-marriage wedding among an upper caste clan – is mostly a freewheeling celebration of Delhi bustle, middle-class mobility and an enlivening tension between tradition and modernity. A masala of Indian screen veterans, celebs and debutants mingle in the film's *mise-en-scène*, teeming with love torn characters. Among the most notable, Shah is a totem of vexed loyalty as the buffeted father of the bride; Shetty is defiant when her moment comes as the repressed writer-cousin with a secret; Raaz is the 'event manager' PK Dubey, who comes down with a precipitous crush on the family's servant girl Alice. So, like *The Philadelphia Story*, it justifies its focus on this enchanted class with an open-door social optimism, but finally shows its backbone when it comes to testing the limits of inclusiveness. A vibrant patchwork of people, colours and moods, the film's fluid, crowded and opaque in places, for a while leaving you wondering where it might be going. Then you find the pulse. The impression of cosmopolitan modern India, of diaspora lives thrown into collision

and collusion, is engaging in itself, but the emotional optimism here is the most heartening aspect of this vivacious film. NB

Monster
see Humanoids from the Deep

Monster and the Girl, The
(1941, US, 65 min, b/w)
d Stuart Heisler. *p* Jack Moss. *sc* Stuart Anthony. *ph* Victor Milner. ed Everett Douglas. *ad* Hans Dreier, Haldane Douglas. *m* Sigmund Krumgold. *cast* Ellen Drew, Robert Paige, Paul Lukas, Joseph Calleia, George Zucco, Rod Cameron, Onslow Stevens, Phillip Terry.
●No masterpiece, but an unusually lively B shocker, engagingly mixing ingredients as Drew, a girl tricked into white slavery prostitution by gangsters, is avenged by a gorilla into which her brother's brain has been transplanted (he was framed by the gang for murder and duly executed) by Zucco's mad doctor. It sounds wild and it is, but opening with a mesmerising shot of Drew looming up out of the mist to tell her story in flashback ('I'm Susan, the bad luck penny; I bought a million dollars' worth of trouble…for everybody'), it generates a bizarre conviction. Surprisingly well acted, it is also directed with real flair, notably in a sequence where the gorilla (constantly threatened with betrayal by a puzzled dog who recognises his master somewhere in there) stalks the rooftop in parallel with his gangster-prey strolling in the deserted nighttime street below. TM

Monster Club, The
(1980, GB, 97 min)
d Roy Ward Baker. *p* Milton Subotsky. *sc* Edward Abraham, Valerie Abraham. *ph* Peter Jessop. *ed* Peter Tanner. *pd* Tony Curtis. *cast* Vincent Price, John Carradine, Anthony Steel, Donald Pleasence, Stuart Whitman, Richard Johnson, Britt Ekland, Patrick Magee, Barbara Kellerman, Simon Ward.
●Scrapings of the horror-omnibus barrel in the Amicus tradition. The famous horror writer R Chetwynd-Hayes (Carradine), having donated some blood, is taken along by the grateful vampire (Price) to his club so that fellow-monster-members may provide him with material for future books. There follow three witlessly routine tales (adapted from stories by Chetwynd-Hayes), drearily executed and graced not at all by such luminaries as Pleasence, Magee and Whitman. Stultification is completed by assorted pop groups, presumably hired by the Monster Club to capture the teenage market, who are on hand to introduce each story with discordant squalls. TM

Monster from Green Hell
(1957, US, 71 min, b/w)
d Kenneth Crane. *p* Al Zimbalist. *sc* Louis Vittes, Endre Bohem. *ph* Ray Flin. *ed* Kenneth Crane. *pd* Ernst Fegté. *m* Albert Glasser. *cast* Jim Davis, Robert E Griffin, Barbara Turner, Eduardo Ciannelli, Vladimir Sokoloff, Joel Fluellen.
●A test rocket carrying various animals and insects goes off course and crash-lands in deepest Africa. Soon, scientists Davis and Griffin hear tell of giant wasps on the loose in the very area where the rocket went down. Could cosmic rays have brought about these grotesque mutations? Of course they could! Crane's monstrous film incorporates ingenious trick photography, model work and stop-motion animation, as well as extensive footage culled from the 1939 Spencer Tracy picture *Stanley and Livingstone*. The result is not so much a movie as a patchwork. TCh

Monster in a Box
(1991, US, 88 min)
d Nicholas Broomfield. *p* Jon Blair. *sc* Spalding Grey. *ed* Graham Hutchings. *ph* Michael Coulter. *m* Laurie Anderson. *with* Spalding Gray.
●As in *Swimming to Cambodia*, this is one man and his mouth, given free range; and again, against all odds, it's riveting. Here, Gray addresses the intimate business of writing a novel. Or not writing it. The opus in question – a huge, unwieldy chunk of his life, and the monster of the title – sits reproachfully on the table throughout, as Gray tells how he set out to write it in an attempt to exorcise the trauma of his mother's death. Gray's mastery of the art of digression is so compelling that the trimmings added by Broomfield are almost superfluous. Gray himself provides plenty to look at – the unearthly glow of his hair, his regrettable choice of shirt, those mystifyingly shaped eyebrows, and a repertoire of hand signals that makes it quite clear why he found it so hard to sit down and type. Whether you'd want to be stuck in a railway carriage with him is another matter, but on screen he is – as they say – unputdownable. JRo

Monster of Terror (aka Die, Monster, Die!)
(1965, GB/US, 81 min)
d Daniel Haller. *p* Pat Green. *sc* Jerry Sohl. *ph* Paul Beeson. *ed* Alfred Cox. *ad* Colin Southcott. *m* Don Banks. *cast* Boris Karloff, Nick Adams, Suzan Farmer, Freda Jackson, Terence de Marney, Patrick Magee, Leslie Dwyer.
●Haller's highly enjoyable debut as a director is a slow, moody, loose adaptation of HP Lovecraft's marvellous story *The Colour Out of Space*, with Karloff (excellent, as usual) as the scientist attempting, with the aid of a strange meteorite (it causes plant life to grow monstrously and organisms to mutate) to invoke the Dark Powers to return to rule the earth again. Not surprisingly, given that Haller served as art director on Corman's Poe cycle, his film features much the same battery of ground fogs, dank passageways, and vaulted stone chambers. He uses these effectively enough, but adds some even better effects of his own, notably the vision of desolate wasteland which surrounds the warlock's domain, and the greenhouse in which he secretes the monstrous, throbbing organisms he has created. TM

Monster on the Campus
(1958, US, 76 min, b/w)
d Jack Arnold. *p* Joseph Gershenson. *sc* David Duncan. *ph* Russell Metty. *ed* Ted J Kent. *ad* Alexander Golitzen. *m* Joseph Gershenson. *cast* Arthur Franz, Joanna Moore, Troy Donahue, Whit Bissell, Judson Pratt, Helen Westcott, Eddie Parker.
●'Is this fish really one million years old?' asks Troy Donahue, pointing at the new specimen at Professor Donald Blake's lab. It sure is, and what's more, if you get infected then you revert to primitive instinctual behaviour. With that in mind, Jack Arnold's hijacking of the Wolf Man plot onto a campus terror tale needs all his talent for making the incredible seem possible: giant dragonflies and million-year-old fish don't quite look so strange as the '50s finned creatures known as automobiles that glide down the campus and suburban avenues. DMacp

Monster's Ball
(2001, US, 111 min)
d Marc Forster. *p* Lee Daniels. *sc* Milo Addica, Will Rokos. *ph* Roberto Schaefer. *ed* Matt Chesse. *pd* Monroe Kelly. *m* Asche and Spencer. *cast* Billy Bob Thornton, Halle Berry, Peter Boyle, Heath Ledger, Sean Combs, Mos Def, Coronji Calhoun, Taylor Simpson, Gabrielle Witcher, Amber Rules.
●Leticia Musgrove (Berry) is the wife of a Death Row inmate (Combs) and mother of a troubled obese teenager. Hank Grotowski (Thornton) works, like his retired father Buck (Boyle) and his own boy Sonny (Ledger), as a guard at the pen, proudly professional to the bitter end. Leticia is imprisoned by hardship and disappointment, Hank by the steely reserve required for his job and by a disciplinarian machismo inherited from a racist dad. What brings them together is chance; what they have in common is death, pain, rage, loneliness. You'd expect this cast to produce fine performances, and Berry and Billy Bob are merely the laurel-stealing protagonists. Praiseworthy too is Schaefer's 'Scope camerawork and Addica and Rokos' tough but sensitive script. Director Forster doesn't hurry things; a hell of a lot happens before the leads meet, and even then it's not cute. Violence (familial and institutional), deep-seated distrust and hatred (this is the South) cast long shadows, and an electric-chair scene ensures we remember love's seldom simple. At the same time, Berry and Thornton play so well that the pitfalls of miserabilist chic are mostly avoided: hope is always felt as a presence or possibility. If certain heavier-handed sequences don't quite gel, the (un-Hollywood) ending is nevertheless perfectly judged, persuasive and unusually graceful. GA

Monsters, Inc.
(2001, US, 95 min)
d Pete Docter. *p* Darla K Anderson. *sc* Andrew Stanton, Daniel Gerson. *ed* Jim Stewart. *pd* Harley Jessup, Bob Pauley. *m* Randy Newman. *cast* voices: John Goodman, Billy Crystal, Mary Gibbs, Steve Buscemi, James Coburn, Jennifer Tilly, Bob Peterson, John Ratzenberger, Frank Oz.
●Pixar's computer-animated rumpus comes to you from Monstropolis, a pastel-coloured parallel world populated by largely peaceable beasts. Sure, some do victimise small children, but purely in a professional capacity: they're the scarers employed by Monsters Inc, the city's scream-fuelled power-generating corporation, to prospect kids' bedrooms and harvest their most piercing shrieks. Take James P Sullivan (voice: Goodman), a horned, shaggy-haired colossus, and the company's star scarer: off-duty you couldn't find a more genial creature, except perhaps for his assistant Mike Wazowski (Crystal), a green walking eyeball who's a hit with all the chicks. Life's smooth scaring, until the unthinkable happens: a small girl called Boo crosses the threshold into Monstropolis. It's common knowledge those things are toxic. A raucous underworld escapade, this is as vibrant and colourful as Orphean comedies come. It's unfailingly lively entertainment that doesn't stint on (earned) feeling. Ideas about fear of the unknown, industrial corruption, and the splendours of polymorphity are all taken in stride. The balance tilts towards action and gags, and does them gloriously. NB

Monster Squad, The
(1987, US, 82 min)
d Fred Dekker. *p* Jonathan A Zimbert. *sc* Shane Black, Fred Dekker. *ph* Bradford May. *ed* James Mitchell. *pd* Albert Brenner. *m* Bruce Broughton. *cast* André Gower, Robby Kiger, Stephen Macht, Duncan Regehr, Tom Noonan, Brent Chalem, Ryan Lambert.
●More of a clever comic parody than a jokey pastiche, this lively kiddies' horror pic delivers frights and laughs which are rooted in a sure and sympathetic grasp of Monster Movie mythology. To take advantage of a confluence of evil that occurs only once every hundred years, Count Dracula (Regehr) flies to America, then summons the Wolfman, Gill-Man, Mummy and Frankenstein's monster. Alerted to Dracula's evil plan, The Monster Squad – a gang of pre-teen kids and their slightly older tough-guy pal – fashion stakes in woodwork class, melt down their parents' cutlery to make silver bullets, and give the monsters hell. Confirming the promise of his debut feature *Night of the Creeps*, Dekker plays around imaginatively with the genre while delivering several nice touches. NF

Montagna del Dio Cannibale, La (Prisoner of the Cannibal God/Slave of the Cannibal God)
(1978, It, 99 min)
d Sergio Martino. *p* Luciano Martino. *sc* Cesare Frugoni, Sergio Martino. *ph* Giancarlo Ferrando. *ed* Eugenio Alabiso. *pd* Massimo Antonello Geleng. *m* Guido De Angelis, Maurizio De Angelis. *cast* Ursula Andress, Stacy Keach, Claudio Cassinelli, Antonio Marsina, Franco Fantasia, Lanfranco Spinola, Carlo Longhi.
●Kicking off with such gastronomic delights as the ingestion of live iguanas, snakes, toads and other wriggly things, this climaxes rather tamely with a main course of very dead human. In between, with Ursula Andress in New Guinea looking for her missing ethnologist husband, there is a fair helping of native bashing, alligator mauling, and the many ways Ursula can fall into the river, render her safari suit transparent, and display her waterproof mascara to full advantage. The flimsiest of plots and the crassest of ecological messages (uranium and capitalism versus nature and cannibalism) surround this general desire to disrobe the Andress form. FF

Montalvo et l'enfant (Montalvo and the Child)
(1988, Fr, 76 min, b/w)
d/sc Claude Mouriéras. *ph* Walther van den Ende. *ed* Monique Dartonne. *ad* Yves

Cassagne. *m* Arvo Pärt. *songs* Claudio Monteverdi. *cast* Mathilde Altaraz, Christophe Delachaux, Robert Seyfried, Jean-Claude Gallotta, Michel Ducret, Marceline Bertolot.
●De Sica with a difference; a gem that successfully wears its heart on its neo-realist sleeve, this coming-of-age tale is shot in a radiantly glowing black-and-white filled with deep shadows and pearly iridescence. Revolving around a boisterous working-class family's get-together, it links the separate stories of the Child (Ducret) and his hero Montalvo (Delachaux) through a series of short, telling incidents that are emotionally heightened by the subtle, imaginative choreography of Jean-Claude Gallotta, which integrates dance into the narrative with such skill that the dividing line between naturalism and stylisation seems to evaporate. Few such films allow us to believe so completely in the truth of their performers as real people; it is as if Mouriéras and Gallotta just happened to stumble across this family one Sunday afternoon. AR

Montand

(1994, Fr, 135 min)
d/sc Jean Labib. *ed* Bernard Josse. *with* Yves Montand.
●An 'auto-biopic' in that the commentary consists of the actor/singer's own reminiscences, recorded as he prepared material for his book, *You See, I Haven't Forgotten*, this is, inevitably, an affectionate look at a great French cultural icon. Moving from his impoverished childhood in Marseille, through music-hall and movies, and relationships with Piaf and Monroe, to his final disenchantment with communism and his sorrow and loneliness after the death of his wife Simone Signoret. Fascinating partly for the archive footage, and partly for the apparent honesty of Montand's revelations. GA

Monte Carlo

(1930, US, 90 min, b/w)
d Ernst Lubitsch. *sc* Ernest Vajda. *ph* Victor Milner. *ad* Hans Dreier. *m* Richard Whiting, L Franke Harling. *lyrics* Leo Robin. *cast* Jeanette MacDonald, Jack Buchanan, ZaSu Pitts, Claude Allister, Tyler Brooke, Jean Roche, Lionel Belmore.
●What can a penniless countess do when faced with the dilemma of true love vs class and financial expediency? She (Jeanette MacDonald) dithers: between Count Rudolf (Buchanan), known to her only in his masquerade as her hairdresser, and the monocled Prince Otto (Allister), who is 'Rich, wealthy, and has nothing but money'. Sumptuous sets, costumes, and a plethora of the titled and the wealthy combine to give *Monte Carlo* a fairytale quality which takes all the sting out of its assumptions about the mercenary nature of women, while preposterous songs and foolish romanticism make it gay, frivolous and thoroughly charming. (The screenplay was based on various sources, including *Monsieur Beaucaire* by Booth Tarkington.) FF

Montenegro

(1981, Swe/GB, 96 min)
d Dusan Makavejev. *p* Bo Jonsson. *sc* Dusan Makavejev. *ph* Tomislav Pinter. *ed* Sylvia Ingemarsson. *ad* Radu Boruzescu. *m* Kornell Kovach. *cast* Susan Anspach, Erland Josephson, Bora Todorovic, Per Oscarsson, John Zacharias, Svetozar Cvetkovic.
●If it begins deceptively, as though setting out to be your typically angst-ridden Swedish art movie, by the time it's reached its set of climaxes – fireworks exploding, couple orgasming, narrative resolving – Makavejev's film could not have strayed further from the beaten track. Anspach is the frustrated housewife taking her pleasure where she can find it; and where she finds it, after airport body searches and missed flight connections, is, Makavejev suggests, in an increasingly unstable landscape which may be interior (psychological) or exterior (the tacky, exotic Club Zanzi-Bar, local hangout for a community of immigrant workers). Funny, bizarre and horny, *Montenegro* may not be as extreme in conception as the suppressed *Sweet Movie*, but it certainly lives up to its producer's brief to Makavejev: 'high quality comedy with a popular appeal and measured eroticism'. What more do you want from a film? RM

Monterey Pop

(1968, US, 79 min)
d/sc DA Pennebaker. *ph* James Desmond, Barry Feinstein, Richard Leacock, Albert Maysles, Roger Murphy, DA Pennebaker, Nicholas Proferes. *ed* Nina Schulman. *with* Janis Joplin, Jefferson Airplane, The Who, Jimi Hendrix, Otis Redding, Ravi Shankar, The Mamas and the Papas, Hugh Masekala, Country Joe and the Fish, Booker T and the MGs.
●Quite simply one of the best rock concert films ever (distilling the 1967 International Pop Festival at Monterey, California), thanks not only to some great performances (towards the end, with Joplin, Redding, Hendrix, things really start cooking), but also to the way it sums up the spirit of the times (the Summer of Love) while never sentimentalising. Hang on to the end, however, when a small Indian man appears nursing a sitar: Ravi Shankar's exhilarating twenty-minute finale is the best thing in the entire movie. GA

Monte Walsh

(1970, US, 108 min)
d William A Fraker. *p* Hal Landers, Bobby Roberts. *sc* David Zelag Goodman, Lukas Heller. *ph* David M Walsh. *ed* Richard Brockway. *pd* Albert Brenner. *m* John Barry. *cast* Lee Marvin, Jack Palance, Mitch Ryan, Jeanne Moreau, Jim Davis, Bo Hopkins, Michael Conrad, GD Spradlin, Allyn Ann McLerie.
●A stunning debut Western for cameraman-turned-director Fraker, chronicling the death of an era as two cowboys (Marvin and Palance) ride into town to find that a bleak winter has brought hard times. Eastern capital has moved in with new methods, jobs are hard to come by, and the pair buckle down to the only work they can get, watching morosely as more and more men are laid off. Gradually the mood darkens. An old cowboy, ending his days in the humbling task of fence-mending, rides his horse crazily over a cliff. Old friends disappear, to return with the law on their heels as desperation drives them to rustling or robbery. Palance (brilliantly cast against type) decides to quit and become a storekeeper; and Marvin, after proving something to himself by taming a bronc no one else could handle, proves something else by rounding on the owner of a Wild West show who offers him a job ('I ain't spittin' on my whole life'). Thus far the film is relatively naturalistic, gently elegiac in tone; but after Marvin's nocturnal encounter with the horse, a strange twilight falls (the twilight of the gods, no less). Fate strikes twice at his life; he is forced to assume the traditional role of gunman; and in settings formally drained of colour, he embarks on his revenger's tragedy... A rare treat. TM

Month by the Lake, A

(1994, US/GB, 91 min)
d John Irvin. *p* Robert Fox. *sc* Trevor Bentham. *ph* Pasqualino De Santis. *ed* Peter Tanner. *pd* Giovanni Giovagnoni. *m* Nicola Piovani. *cast* Vanessa Redgrave, Edward Fox, Uma Thurman, Alida Valli, Carlo Cartier, Alessandro Gassman, Natalia Bizzi.
●Adapted from a romantic interlude by HE Bates, this is so flat and passionless that, without the warm glow of the cinematography and the deliriously romantic Italian settings, it would almost certainly have been consigned to video. Lake Como, 1939. Miss Bentley (Redgrave) is holidaying with her Italian friends on the shore of her favourite lake. Lonely and bored, she soon perks up when she notices the rugged looks of the only other English visitor present, Fox's starchy Major Wilshaw. The two meet, chat, play tennis, and romance might have blossomed, were it not for the arrival of fickle, flirtatious American nanny Miss Beaumont (Thurman, twitchy). Still, even though Miss Bentley feels rejected by the major's lack of interest in her, she's chuffed when she in turn attracts the attention of local youth Vittorio (Gassman). Thus unfolds a four-way tangle, age difference the theme. This day-by-day account of month-long holiday romances does not fit comfortably into 91 minutes, and after the fourth al fresco breakfast, your eyes wander past the characters to focus on the views behind. DA

Month in the Country, A

(1987, GB, 96 min)
d Pat O'Connor. *p* Kenith Trodd. *sc* Simon Gray. *ph* Kenneth MacMillan. *ed* John Victor Smith. *pd* Leo Austin. *m* Howard Blake. *cast* Colin Firth, Kenneth Branagh, Natasha Richardson, Patrick Malahide, Richard Vernon, Elizabeth Anson, Jim Carter, Tony Haygarth.
●In the summer of 1920, two traumatised victims of World War I meet in a Yorkshire village: Birkin (Firth), who stutters, has come to restore a mural in the local church, and Moon (Branagh), still tormented by nightmares, has come to excavate the land around it. Birkin falls for the beautiful wife (Richardson) of the uncharitable vicar (Malahide), and Moon falls for Birkin. Neither gets what he wants, but together they succeed in solving a minor mystery. O'Connor directs Simon Gray's script with great sensitivity. It's all taken at a gentle pace, but dullness is averted by a sly humour. The pretty-prettiness of Hovis commercials is not always avoided, and recurrent images of the apocalyptic painting, intended to give the rather pat plot a mystical resonance, don't; but all the performances are accomplished, and that of Firth is brilliant. MS

Montreal Main

(1974, Can, 88 min, b/w)
d Frank Vitale. *p* Frank Vitale, Allan Bozo Moyle. *sc* Frank Vitale, John Sutherland, Dave Sutherland, Ann Sutherland, Allan Bozo Moyle, Jackie Holden, Peter Brawley, Pam Marchant. *ph* Erich Bloch. *ed* Frank Vitale. *m* Beverley Glenn-Copeland. *cast* Frank Vitale, John Sutherland, Dave Sutherland, Ann Sutherland, Allan Bozo Moyle, Jackie Holden, Peter Brawley, Pam Marchant, Steve Lack, Anthony Booth.
●Vitale's first feature was the most honest film about male sexuality made to date...which is to say that it's both troubled and troubling, in the most positive sense. It centres on a character called Frank Vitale, an unemployed artist-photographer, and his circle of (predominantly gay) friends. Frank's closest friend is Bozo; they have a disastrously furtive attempt at sex together at one point, although neither considers himself gay. But their friendship, and Frank's life in general, threatens to fall apart when Frank meets the 12-year-old Johnny and in some sense falls in love with him. It's impossible to be more explicit about it, since the film itself isn't. In fact, hardly anything happens in the way of reportable incident: it plays as a stream of modest encounters and conversations, which seem like improvisations. Brilliant casting, photography, and especially editing, however, give the whole movie an acute psychological focus. TR

Monty Python and the Holy Grail

(1974, GB, 90 min)
d Terry Gilliam, Terry Jones. *p* Mark Forstater. *sc* Graham Chapman, John Cleese, Terry Gilliam, Eric Idle, Terry Jones, Michael Palin. *ph* Terry Bedford. *ed* John Hackney. *pd* Roy Smith. *m/songs* Neil Innes. *cast* Graham Chapman, John Cleese, Terry Gilliam, Eric Idle, Terry Jones, Michael Palin, Carol Cleveland, Connie Booth, Neil Innes, Bee Duffell.
●Python's delightful and, on the whole, consistent reductio ad absurdum of the Grail legend, in which the Knights forsake their chorus line can-can dancing at Camelot for a higher aim. The Pythons set up a 'historical' tale as the sum total of modern anachronisms and misconceptions about it, a format repeated in *The Life of Brian*. CPe

Monty Python's Life of Brian (100)

(1979, GB, 93 min)
d Terry Jones. *p* John Goldstone. *sc* Graham Chapman, John Cleese, Terry Gilliam, Eric Idle, Terry Jones, Michael Palin. *ph* Peter Biziou. *ed* Julian Doyle. *ad* Roger Christian. *m* Geoffrey Burgon. *cast* Terry Jones, Graham Chapman, Michael Palin, John Cleese, Eric Idle, Terry Gilliam, Carol Cleveland, Neil Innes, Spike Milligan, George Harrison.
●The Three Wise Men go to the wrong manger, thus foisting upon Brian Cohen a role for which he is eminently unprepared. More Carrying On than usual from the Pythons, but the use of a tried and tested storyline (Cleese: 'Yes, it has got a bit of shape, hasn't it?') results in their most sustained effort to date. Python successfully lampoon religious attitudes rather than religion itself, while the comedy relies mainly on memories of the classroom; which is apt enough, considering that most of the audience is likely to

associate knowledge of the Holy Writ with schooldays too. Jokes about Great Profits must have been hard to resist. CPe

Monty Python's The Meaning of Life

(1983, GB, 90 min)
d Terry Jones. *p* John Goldstone. *sc* Graham Chapman, John Cleese, Terry Gilliam, Eric Idle, Terry Jones, Michael Palin. *ph* Peter Hannan. *ed* Julian Doyle. *pd* Harry Lange. *cast* Graham Chapman, John Cleese, Terry Gilliam, Eric Idle, Terry Jones, Michael Palin, Carol Cleveland, Simon Jones, Patricia Quinn, Judy Loe.
● The Python swansong, a nostalgic return to the sketch format of the original TV shows, garnished with the 'explicit' sex and violence jokes that are deemed necessary to get bums on seats in cinemas in these depraved times. This is the one with the exploding Mr Creosote, the parody of *Zulu*, and the sketch about organ-snatching from live donors. The high point comes early, when a Catholic family in Yorkshire burst into song with 'Every Sperm Is Sacred'. TR

Moon and Sixpence, The

(1942, US, 85 min, b/w & col)
d Albert Lewin. *p* David L Loew. *sc* Albert Lewin. *ph* John F Seitz. *ed* George Hively, Richard L Van Enger. *ad* Gordon Wiles. *m* Dimitri Tiomkin. *cast* George Sanders, Herbert Marshall, Steve Geray, Doris Dudley, Elena Verdugo, Eric Blore, Florence Bates.
● Somerset Maugham's Gauguin-inspired novel is well and faithfully served by Lewin's characteristically literary direction; Sanders, especially, savours the elegant dialogue and cool ironies in his role as the quiet suburban broker who suddenly throws it all in, and leaves London and his family to embark upon a painting career in Paris. Indeed, the actor was the perfect choice for the part, his impeccably supercilious intelligence conveying both the self-centredness and the determination of a man with a private mission which he believes transcends social niceties. If the studio sets weaken the final scenes in Tahiti, Lewin's sensitivity to Maugham's moral nuances ensures unusually sophisticated Hollywood entertainment. GA

Moon and the Sledgehammer, The

(1971, GB, 65 min)
d Philip Trevelyan. *p* James Vaughan. *sc* Philip Trevelyan. *ph* Richard Stanley. *ed* Barrie Vince. *with* Mr Page, Jim Page, Peter Page, Kathy Page, Nancy Page.
● Engaging documentary about an eccentric family (old man, two sons, two daughters) living wild in a tumbledown house in the Sussex woods and doing their own thing (mainly music and tinkering with steam engines and other ancient machinery). Their lifestyle, expounded in fascinatingly wayward conversation which is allowed to make its own pace, embodies a weird cautionary logic about the miracles of modern technocracy. TM

Moonfleet

(1955, US, 87 min)
d Fritz Lang. *p* John Houseman. *sc* Jan Lustig, Margaret Fitts. *ph* Robert Planck. *ed* Albert Akst. *ad* Cedric Gibbons, Hans Peters. *m* Miklós Rózsa. *cast* Stewart Granger, Jon Whiteley, George Sanders, Viveca Lindfors, Joan Greenwood, Melville Cooper, Jack Elam, Dan Seymour, Ian Wolfe.
● A boy and a rakish smuggler search for a legendary lost diamond in a wonderfully stylised version of 19th century Cornwall. The characters are linked and haunted by the memory of the boy's dead mother, and their 'romance' is a journey through a dark world of gallows and graveyards. Lang disliked working in CinemaScope, a ratio he described in *Le Mépris* as 'only good for funerals and snakes', but uses it brilliantly. (From a novel by J Meade Faulkner.) SJ

Moon 44

(1989, WGer, 99 min)
d Roland Emmerich. *p* Dean Heyde, Roland Emmerich. *sc* Dean Heyde, Oliver Eberle. *ph* Karl Walter Undenlaub. *ed* Tony Wigand. *pd* Oliver Scholl. *m* Joel Goldsmith. *cast* Michael Paré, Lisa Eichhorn, Malcolm McDowell, Dean Devlin, Brian Thompson, Stephen Geoffreys, Leon Rippy, Jochen Nickel.
● Intergalactic hijackers are zapping our planets, and the next target is Moon 44, to be exploited for mineral wealth and already used as a training ground for hi-tech 'copter pilots. The mining corporation sends up investigator Felix Stone (Paré), who's *deep* undercover, pretending to be a fighter pilot while hunting a saboteur. The plot contains one potentially intriguing idea: the musclebound pilots, most of whom are criminals, are hamstrung without their navigators, weakling teen geniuses to a boy. The boys are beaten up and sexually abused by the pilots, who then wonder why they keep getting directed into cliff faces. A silly subplot concerns library books; and our worst fears are realised when McDowell bumbles into view as Major Lee, enigmatic station commander. The film looks nice but unoriginal (blue light, dry ice, flashing instrument panels); the model work is okay but laboured; the acting is stunningly mediocre. SFe

Moon Has Risen, The (Tsuki wa Noborinu)

(1955, Jap, 90 min, b/w)
d Kinuyo Tanaka. *sc* Yasujiro Ozu. *cast* Mie Kitahara, Shoji Yasui, Chishu Ryu, Hisako Yamane, Kinuyo Tanaka.
● A charming and vivid family drama, scripted by Ozu and directed by actress Tanaka, who also makes a cameo appearance as a put-upon servant. Kitahara plays spoilt and imperious Setsuko Asai, youngest daughter of a wealthy family from Nara. Together with handsome lodger Shoji, she plots to marry off her elder sister to a family friend who has long admired her; in a comic interlude, the inspired lovers begin to correspond in code, to the frustration of the plotters. But when Setsuko herself falls in love, she is not quite so adroit at manipulating matters. The relationship between the three sisters (the eldest a shy, widowed stay-at-home) is delicately drawn, as is the growing attraction between Setsuko and Shoji, which at first threatens to spoil their free-and-easy friendship. A delicate fable of growing up. SFe

Moonhunter, The (14 Tula, Songkram Prachachon)

(2001, Thai, 120 min, b/w & col)
d Bhandit Rittakol. *p* Charoen Iamphungporn, Thanit Jitnukul. *sc* Seksan Prasertkul, Bhandit Rittakol. *ph* Teerawat Rujintham. *ed* Sunit Asawanitkul. *ad* Bhandit Rittakol, Teekayu Thamnitayakul. *cast* Punu Suwanno, Pimpan Chanta, Kriangchai Fookasem, Supalak Chaowayuth, Pakachon Vo-onsri.
● Seksan Prasertkul was one of the student leaders of the 14 October 1973 protest that forced the heads of Thailand's ruling military junta into exile but failed to usher in real democracy. Like many others, Seksan became a guerilla; he spent six years in the jungle before disillusionment with the 'People's War' led him to surrender. Although co-scripted by Seksan himself (now a writer/academic), this dramatisation of the struggle lurches awkwardly between Pontecorvo-style political realism and lyrical adventure-romance. The best thing here is the account of the factional infighting in the jungle; you can always rely on the Left to tear itself apart. (Highlight: watching how the Maoists react to news of the fall of the Gang of Four in Beijing.) It was probably a mistake even to attempt this story as a mass-market film, but Bhandit puts it together with intelligence and shoots it with gusto. TR

Moon in the Gutter, The (La Lune dans le Caniveau)

(1983, Fr/It, 137 min)
d Jean-Jacques Beineix. *p* Lise Fayolle. *sc* Jean-Jacques Beineix, Olivier Mergault. *ph* Philippe Rousselot. *ed* Monique Prim, Yves Deschamps. *ad* Hilton Mac Connico. *m* Gabriel Yared. *cast* Gérard Depardieu, Nastassja Kinski, Victoria Abril, Vittorio Mezzogiorno, Dominique Pinon, Bertice Reading, Milena Vukotic.
● Like Beineix's debut feature *Diva*, this is a film of dazzling surface and equally dazzling superficiality; but where *Diva* was taut and full of action, *The Moon in the Gutter* is slow and portentous. Based on David Goodis' thriller about a bloodstain on a street and a stevedore obsessed with finding the man who raped his sister and prompted her suicide, the film expands the compressed plot of the novel into a catalogue of glossy images, all of it shot in the studio. The crux of the story is the relationship between the hulking stevedore (Depardieu) and a rich femme (Kinski) who, far from being fatale, represents the impossible dream at the end of his investigative quest. Beineix does manage to charge the affair with a sense of fierce anticipation; that aside, the film seems like an exercise in the non-development of narrative. In the end, though it's not the disaster the French press cracked it up to be, only the images stay in the memory as the Fabergé egg lies smashed on the floor, a pile of glittering fragments. RR

Moon in the Mirror, The (La Luna en el Espejo)

(1990, Chile, 75 min)
d/p Silvio Caiozzi. *sc* Silvio Caiozzi, José Donoso. *ph* Nelson Fuentes. *ed* Alvaro Ramirez, Silvio Caiozzi. *ad* Laura Gubelic, Guadelupe Bornand. *cast* Gloria Munchmeyer, Rafael Benavente, Ernesto Beadle, Maria Castiglione, Roberto Poblete, Loreto Valenzuela.
● A slight, but charming piece about a cantankerous, bedridden old bully and the deleterious effect he has on his shy, corpulent son's wooing of a neighbouring widow. At first the tone is light and semi-comic. Later, however, it shifts to a darker acknowledgement of complicitous emotional enslavement. Imaginatively shot, sensitively acted. GA

Moon Is Blue, The

(1953, US, 99 min, b/w)
d/p Otto Preminger. *sc* F Hugh Herbert. *ph* Ernest Laszlo. *ed* Otto Ludwig. *pd* Nicolai Remisoff. *m* Herschel Burke Gilbert. *cast* William Holden, David Niven, Maggie McNamara, Dawn Addams, Tom Tully, Fortunio Bonanova.
● Despite the fuss at the time, there's little blue about this except the title: a stage-bound adaptation of F Hugh Herbert's mildly amusing and mildly naughty romantic comedy – typical Broadway 'sophistication' – about a girl retaining her honour while snaring her man. McNamara is the pixie picked up by Holden on top of the Empire State Building (that's the 'opening out' bit), accepting a dinner invitation to his flat, and causing some tiresome altercations when the middle-aged and lecherous Niven (father of Holden's ex-fiancée Addams) happens to drop in. Amazing to think that the power of the Hollywood Production Code (not to mention the League of Decency) was effectively broken because Preminger insisted on retaining such shocking obscenities as 'virgin', 'seduce' and 'mistress' in the dialogue. TM

Moonlight and Valentino

(1995, US, 104 min)
d David Anspaugh. *p* Alison Owen, Eric Fellner, Tim Bevan. *sc* Ellen Simon. *ph* Julio Macat. *ed* David Rosenbloom, Paul Cichocki. *pd* Robb Wilson-King. *m* Howard Shore. *cast* Elizabeth Perkins, Whoopi Goldberg, Kathleen Turner, Gwyneth Paltrow, Jon Bon Jovi, Jeremy Sisto, Josef Sommer, Shadia Simmons.
● A women's film, '90s style. When her husband dies, Rebecca (Perkins) can't bring herself to pronounce the W-word, but she's immediately surrounded by an ad hoc support group – neighbour Goldberg, sister Paltrow, and mother-in-law Turner – all too ready to put her in her weeds. Each woman comes with a badge denoting her own special interest group: the widow, the wife, the virgin and the divorcee. It's like a convention. Grudges and recriminations surface, the inevitable 'intimacy issues', but nothing too disruptive, nothing that can't be put right with a cathartic group hug. You can gauge the sensitivity factor from Rebecca's creative writing assignment: write a poem without words. The film has a neat line in neat lines, gets a lift from Paltrow's palpable sexual anxiety, but works much too hard for its tears. In his first major role, Jon Bon Jovi plays a sex object, and he's every bit as anaemic as the rest. Based on an autobiographical play by Ellen Simon (Neil's daughter). TCh

Moonlighting

(1982, GB, 97 min)
d Jerzy Skolimowski. *p* Mark Shivas, Jerzy Skolimowski. *sc* Jerzy Skolimowski. *ph* Tony Pierce-Roberts. *ed* Barry Vince. *pd* Tony Woollard. *m* Stanley Myers. *cast* Jeremy Irons, Eugene Lipinski, Jiri Stanislav, Eugeniusz Haczkiewicz, Denis Holmes, Jenny Seagrove, Jerzy Skolimowski.

●Conceived and made with an urgency appropriate to the December 1981 military clampdown on Skolimowski's native Poland, this film is a characteristically oblique and quirky response. Displacement rather than confrontation is the key, with a group of Polish builders busy renovating their boss' London house when the axe falls at home. Irons plays their leader, the only English speaker, who is forced into a parody of twisted labour relations when he decides to conceal the news from his co-workers. But the tendency towards allegory is pleasingly offset by an alienated vision of the English daily round: a farcical and surreal mixture of frustration, deception and shoplifting. The result is as much about 'us' as 'them'; and constitutes a quietly disturbing, often sharply amusing, flip side to Wajda's men of marble and iron. SJ

Moon Over Harlem

(1939, US, 68 min, b/w)
d Edgar G Ulmer. *p* Edgar G Ulmer, Peter E Kassler. *sc* Sherle Castle, Mathew Mathews. *ph* J Burgi Contner, Edward Hyland. *ed* Jack Kemp. *ad* Eugene Wolk. *m* Donald Heywood. *cast* Bud Harris, Cora Green, Alec Lovejoy, Earl Gough, Izinetta Wilcox, Sidney Bechet, Christopher Columbus and his Swing Crew.

●According to Ulmer's widow, who rewrote the original script by Mathew Mathews, this mini-melodrama for the 'coloured' audience was made for $8,000 in four days, mostly in a disused cigar factory in New Jersey. It was Ulmer's only 16mm production, most likely the smallest of all the 'ethnic' pictures he made between his expulsion from Universal in 1934 and his arrival at PRC in 1942. Against the advice of friends, naive nightclub dresser Minnie (Green) marries protection racketeer Dollar Bill (Harris), estranging her daughter Sue (Wilcox). Minnie finally dies in crossfire and an angry rival rubs out Dollar. The message, personified by Sue's fiancé (Gough), is 'Clean up Harlem!' Given the production constraints, it's no surprise that most of it is hopelessly stagey. But there are flashes of Ulmer style in the nightclub scenes, and none other than Sidney Bechet blows clarinet at the wedding. TR

Moon Over Parador

(1988, US, 104 min)
d/p Paul Mazursky. *sc* Leon Capetanos, Paul Mazursky. *ph* Donald McAlpine. *ed* Stuart H Pappé. *pd* Pato Guzman. *m* Maurice Jarre. *cast* Richard Dreyfuss, Raul Julia, Sonia Braga, Jonathan Winters, Fernando Rey, Sammy Davis Jr, Marianne Sägebrecht, Reihard Kolldehoff, Paul Mazursky.

●This broad farce set in a fictional Latin American country has actor Dreyfuss, having finished work on a movie shot on location in Parador, expressing his desire to find the part of a lifetime. He little bargains for what follows: bearing a resemblance to the country's dictator, he is abducted by Chief of Police Julia and forced to impersonate the recently deceased tyrant in order to forestall revolution. Inevitably, after initial stage nerves, he takes to the part, revelling in deception and falling for the dead man's mistress (Braga), who persuades him to disobey his captors and involve himself in social reforms. Cameos by Mazursky himself (as the late dictator's mother) and Sammy Davis Jr only increase the impression that the whole thing is a lazy, self-indulgent home movie born of its creator's taste for theatricality. For one brief moment, with a malignant CIA introduced, the film looks a little more promising, but all too soon it slips back into soppy sentimentality. GA

Moon Over the Alley, The

(1975, GB, 102 min, b/w)
d Joseph Despins. *sc* William Dumaresq. *ph* Peter Hannan. *ed* Joseph Despins. *m* Galt MacDermot. *cast* Doris Fishwick, Peter Farrell, Erna May, John Gay, Sean Caffrey, Sharon Forester.

●About the lives of a number of dwellers in a rooming-house just off the Portobello Road, well within the Loach/Garnett tradition of environmental realism, but at the same time managing the infusion of poeticism implicit in the title by means of Kurt Weill-esque songs (music by *Hair* arranger Galt MacDermot). Though the characters initially come across as well-trodden kitchen sink stereotypes – frustrated adolescents, suspicious middle-aged parents, a young Jamaican couple, an Irish bartender, reclusive 'dirty old man' – the film quickly disarms with its quirky humour. Laughs aside, it's a far from complacent look at the problems of an increasingly squalid London. RM

Moonraker

(1979, GB/Fr. 126 min)
d Lewis Gilbert. *p* Albert R Broccoli. *sc* Christopher Wood. *ph* Jean Tournier. *ed* John Glen. *pd* Ken Adam. *m* John Barry. *cast* Roger Moore, Lois Chiles, Michel Lonsdale, Richard Kiel, Corinne Cléry, Emily Bolton, Toshiro Suga, Geoffrey Keen, Lois Maxwell.

●After one bravura *Superman* parody, one space battle, half-a-dozen seductions, and a host of gags, you feel that Bond has turned into a one-man variety show. But *Moonraker* is mercifully much better than recent Bondage, with fantastic special effects, some excellent buffery (cracks at *Star Wars*, *Close Encounters*, Clint Eastwood, to name but a few), and the usual location-hopping style that makes Versailles feel like Disneyland. The space-age plot is spread dangerously thin, the fights all tend to slapstick, and the wanton destruction has become rather too predictable. But it's held together by likeable performances (Kiel as 'Jaws', Lonsdale as a suitably urbane villain) and, above all, an overwhelming level of tongue-in-cheek. CA

Moonrise

(1948, US, 90 min, b/w)
d Frank Borzage. *p/sc* Charles Haas. *ph* John L Russell. *ed* Harry Keller. *pd* Lionel Banks. *m* William Lava. *cast* Dane Clark, Gail Russell, Ethel Barrymore, Allyn Joslyn, Harry Morgan, Rex Ingram, Lloyd Bridges, Selena Royle.

●Perhaps Borzage's greatest film, *Moonrise*, a brooding tale of a murderer's son (Clark) driven to violence by others harping on his past, is the perfect answer to those critics who have derided Borzage as a 'mere' romantic, a mere celebrator of the magic of love. Deeply melancholic, the film (from a novel by Theodore Strauss) creates a sense of physical reality with its low key lighting and harsh compositions that Borzage's lovers on the run cannot defeat: their 'Seventh Heaven' in an abandoned mansion is only temporary. PH

Moonrunners

(1974, US, 102 min)
d Gy Waldron. *p* Robert B Clark. *sc* Gy Waldron. *ph* Brian W Roy. *ed* Avrum Fine. *ad* Pat Mann. *m* Waylon Jennings. *cast* James Mitchum, Kiel Martin, Chris Forbes, Arthur Hunnicutt, Joan Blackman, George Ellis, Waylon Jennings, Spanky McFarland.

●Essentially an extended car chase laced with nuggets of wisdom dispensed by a moonshiner from way back (played by Arthur Hunnicutt, creating an island of watchability in the surrounding mishmash). *Moonrunners* assembles a crateful of familiar ingredients – the banjo-picking accompaniment, the car chases, some thick-ear rough stuff, a plot making gestures toward supporting the rugged individualist against the syndicate – all articulated with minimum atmosphere and maximum country-style mugging. It lacks even the slightly redeeming oddness of *The Lolly-Madonna War*, and James Mitchum gives an especially charmless performance in the lead, making his final words about 'going to Nashville to become a star' ring extremely hollow. VG

Moonshine War, The

(1970, US, 100 min)
d Richard Quine. *p* Martin Ransohoff. *sc* Elmore Leonard. *ph* Richard H Kline. *ed* Allan Jacobs. *ad* George W Davis, Edward C Carfagno. *m* Fred Karger. *cast* Patrick McGoohan, Richard Widmark, Alan Alda, Lee Hazlewood, Joe Williams, Will Geer, Melodie Johnson, Max Showalter, Harry Carey Jr, Teri Garr.

●Amiable caper adapted by Elmore Leonard from his own novel about whisky hijackers in hillbilly country just before the repeal of Prohibition, with McGoohan's scarecrow ex-revenue agent and Widmark's Rabelaisian struck-off dentist joining forces to lay siege to Alda's hidden cache of moonshine when money, guile and threats get them nowhere. Directing with one eye very much on *Bonnie and Clyde*, Quine makes heavy weather of the tone and style, but the characterisations – abetted by nice dialogue – make it more enjoyable than not. TM

Moonstruck

(1987, US, 102 min)
d Norman Jewison. *p* Patrick Palmer, Norman Jewison. *sc* John Patrick Shanley. *ph* David Watkin. *ed* Lou Lombardo. *pd* Philip Rosenberg. *m* Dick Hyman. *cast* Cher, Nicolas Cage, Vincent Gardenia, Olympia Dukakis, Danny Aiello, Julie Bovasso, John Mahoney, Feodor Chaliapin.

●Jewison's Italo-American movie mainly comprises the look of things: the family table, the homely Italian restaurant, Cher, the moon over Brooklyn Bridge. Widowed Loretta (Cher), engaged to dull Johnny (Aiello), contacts his brother Ronny (Cage) to invite him to the wedding; they fall in love. Her father (Gardenia), too, is having an affair. Both adulterer and suitor seem driven to passion by depression, though Cage's hammy performance convinces less than Gardenia's glooming over his glasses. Jewison gently mocks the old ways of formal respect and sexism. Stronger on mores than amore, a half smile for a summer night. BC

Moonwalker

(1988, US, 93 min)
d Colin Chilvers, Jerry Kramer. *p* Dennis Jones, Jerry Kramer. *sc* David Newman. *ph* John Hora, Thomas Ackerman, Bob Collins, Frederick Elmes, Crescenzo Notarile. *ed* David Blewitt, Mitchell Sinoway, Dale Beldin. *pd* Mike Ploog. *m* Bruce Broughton. *cast* Michael Jackson, Joe Pesci, Sean Lennon, Kellie Parker, Brandon Adams.

●What begins like a concert movie and ends with the dull whimper of a moralising fairytale for TV kids is, startlingly enough, a long and expensive pop video. The fact that it is a cut-and-paste job, interpolating chunks of Jackson history in with a sequence of rather feeble cartoon dominated 'episodes', lends the whole adventure the distinctly un-cinematic ambience of a fanzine, which is great for the fans. Mum and Dad and baby sibling, however, will be alarmed and bored by the spectacle – the former alarmed by the vast displacement of cash on so witless a project, and bored because it's boring, the latter frustrated because a human version of *My Little Pony* is not as entertaining as the real thing. Altogether a ghastly experience, which even the rabid 11-year-old in your life might well find patronising and unimaginative. NC

Moon Warriors (Zhan Shen Chuanshuo)

(1992, HK, 86 min)
d Samo Hung. *p* Andy Lau. *sc* Ching Siu-Tung. *cast* Andy Lau, Maggie Cheung, Anita Mui, Kenny Bee.

●A mythic tale of crossed swords and double-crossed allegiances, princes, peasants and killer bamboo, Samo Hung's film is a visually splendid, dramatically rich, but somewhat rarefied martial arts yarn. Andy Lau (*Days of Being Wild*) is Fei, a peasant fisherman who finds himself protecting the beautiful princess Yueh (Mui) and her betrothed, the rightful heir to the kingdom, who has been usurped by his evil younger brother. Taking refuge in an ancient subterranean palace, it becomes clear there's a traitor in their midst. Much imaginative staging, even if the romanticism sometimes topples into kitsch (Hei Wei the whale seems to have swum out of a Disney picture). The highly acrobatic fights, however, are oddly uninvolving. TCh

Mord und Totschlag

see Degree of Murder, A

More About the Language of Love (Mera ur Kärlekens Språk)

(1970, Swe, 97 min)
d Torgny Wickman. *p* Inge Ivarson. *ph* Lasse Björne. *ed* Carl-Olov Skeppstedt, Vic Kjellin. *m* Mats Olsson. *with* Inge Hegeler, Sten Hegeler, Maj-Briht Bergström-Walan, Ove Arström, Anna Berggren, Bengt Berggren.

●A follow-up to *The Language of Love* which is just as clumsily directed – all those round-the-coffee-table sex chats and unrelated street scenes! Stonily serious, the film is clearly informational (if on a grade school level) rather than exploitative, with the most detailed and basic demonstrations being the most successful sequences. Problems considered are homosexuality (male and female, superficially); VD (also superficially); sex and the handicapped; and impotence. One sequence deals with a repressive commune whose exploitation of its female members goes without comment by the pundits. VG

More American Graffiti

(1979, US, 111 min)
d BWL Norton. *p* Howard G Kazanjian. *sc* BWL Norton. *ph* Caleb Deschanel. *ed* Tina Hirsch. *ad* Ray Storey. *cast* Candy Clark, Bo Hopkins, Ron Howard, Paul Le Mat, Mackenzie Phillips, Charles Martin Smith, Cindy Williams, Anna Bjorn, Richard Bradford, Scott Glenn, Mary Kay Place, Rosanna Arquette, Delroy Lindo, Harrison Ford.
●Richard Dreyfuss' price proved too high, otherwise the whole gang returns for a sequel which builds its highly episodic narrative around a last reunion at a New Year's Eve drag race in 1964, used as an anchor from which to flash forward through the '60s; but the film's problems arise less from the confusing time structure than from the misguided determination to preserve the tone of the original at all costs. In the world of Vietnam, drugs and revolution, what was genuine innocence becomes glib farce, and Norton's refusal to register the darkening of the kids' world quickly makes that world itself less real. DP

More Bad News

(1987, GB, 53 min)
d Adrian Edmondson. *p* Simon Wright, Peter Richardson. *sc* Adrian Edmondson. *ph* John Metcalfe. *ed* Rob Wright. *ad* Denise Ruben*cast* Adrian Edmondson, Rik Mayall, Nigel Planer, Peter Richardson, Jennifer Saunders, Dawn French.
●A spoof rockumentary from TV's Comic Strip. It's 1987, four years after Bad News, the heavy alloy outfit, broke up in a welter of bitterness, apathy and prawn tandoori. Since then, Colin (Mayall) has become a bank clerk, Spider (Richardson) has retreated to rural hippiedom, and Den (Planer) has been getting by as a painter and decorator. Only Vim (Edmondson) has kept the faith, playing Mary Hopkins numbers in wine bars and lovingly transcribing songs sent to him from beyond the grave by John Lennon. Now they've been acrimoniously reunited to play the Castle Donnington Monsters of Rock festival, alongside Motorhead, Def Leppard et al. If you like the Comic Strip, and want to know what 100 pints of lager in the local Indian does to your deportment, this is for you. DAt

More the Merrier, The

(1943, US, 104 min, b/w)
d/p George Stevens. *sc* Robert Russell, Frank Ross, Richard Flournoy, Lewis R Foster. *ph* Ted Tetzlaff. *ed* Otto Meyer. *ad* Lionel Banks, Rudolph Sternard. *m* Leigh Harline. *cast* Jean Arthur, Joel McCrea, Charles Coburn, Bruce Bennett, Richard Gaines, Ann Savage, Ann Doran.
●The housing shortage in wartime Washington provides the pretext for this engaging post-screwball comedy, remade some two decades later as *Walk, Don't Run*. Prim Jean Arthur reluctantly agrees to take Coburn as a boarder, and the next thing she knows he has sublet his half of the apartment to handsome McCrea. Their *ménage à trois* is innocent enough, but inevitably Arthur's marriage plans come in for modification. Coburn won an Oscar for his supporting role as the mischievous old matchmaker Mr Dingle, but the real pleasure lies in the sympathetic ensemble playing: the trio trying to stick to Arthur's farcical morning schedule; sunbathing on the roof reading *Dick Tracy*; or the young lovers necking on the front steps. Shooting through and around doors, windows and paper-thin walls, Stevens achieves a credible sense of what it's like living in someone else's space. Despite a belated drift towards sentimentality, this remains a refreshingly intimate movie. TCh

Morgan, a Suitable Case for Treatment

(1966, GB, 97 min, b/w)
d Karel Reisz. *p* Leon Clore. *sc* David Mercer. *ph* Gerry Turpin, Larry Pizer. *ed* Tom Priestley. *ad* Philip Harrison. *m* John Dankworth. *cast* David Warner, Vanessa Redgrave, Robert Stephens, Irene Handl, Newton Blick, Nan Munro, Bernard Bresslaw, Arthur Mullard, Graham Crowden.
●Because it struggles to combine the Royal Court world of *Anger and After* playwrights (fantasising artist with Communist mother and rich wife in Kensington) with what Lester and Antonioni were doing to British cinema at the time, this version of David Mercer's TV play all but loses the theme of genuine madness underneath. Morgan, a part that suits David Warner down to the ground, sabotages his wife's second marriage, dressing up as a gorilla, rewiring her house, etc; but the character is itself short-circuited by being surrounded with eccentrics (Handl, Bresslaw, Mullard) as dotty as he is. *Morgan* sticks in the memory as a collection of funny moments, with the fatal habit (shared by *If…*, among others) of confronting issues, then farting around when the going gets rough. AN

Morgiana

(1972, Czech, 99 min)
d Juraj Herz. *sc* Juraj Herz, Vladimir Bor. *ph* Jaroslav Kucera. *m* Lubos Fisher. *cast* Iva Janzurova, Josef Abrham, Petr Cepek, Nina Diviskova, Josef Somr, Jiri Paluch, Jiri Lir, Václav Vondracek, Maria Drahokoupilova.
●Delirious gothic fairytale with Janzurova playing both the roles of 'good' and 'bad' sister in this adaptation of Alexandr Grin's Edwardian-set novel. Tom Hutchinson has called it 'living Aubrey Beardsley', which captures perfectly the ornate costume and set design, but not the hallucinatory Hammer-like atmospherics and the drenched colour. Often shot from the point of view of the cat (Morgiana), the film is an elegant, beautifully executed, post-'60s essay on sex and repression. WH

Morning After, The

(1986, US, 103 min)
d Sidney Lumet. *p* Bruce Gilbert. *sc* James Hicks, Jay Presson Allen, David Rayfiel. *ph* Andrzej Bartkowiak. *ed* Joel Goodman. *pd* Albert Brenner. *m* Paul Chihara. *cast* Jane Fonda, Jeff Bridges, Raúl Julia, Diane Salinger, Richard Foronjy, Geoffrey Scott, James Haake, Kathleen Wilhoite, Kathy Bates.
●Sometime promising actress turned lush Fonda wakes up to find, in her bed, a dead man with a knife through his heart. She panics and tries to flee the state, but thwarted by airport bureaucracy, ends up taking her chances with redneck excop Bridges. Focusing on the central character's struggle towards a tentative moral redemption, Lumet creates a film more intense than tense, more low-key character study than thriller. Fonda captures the duplicity of an actress playing a role, while Bridges' restraint provides the perfect foil for her neurotic mannerisms. But Lumet's narrative economy, sympathetic handling of actors, and superb eye never quite jell. It's as if a talented director has made the most of what he had, when what he had was never quite enough. NF

Morning Departure (aka Operation Disaster)

(1949, GB, 102 min, b/w)
d Roy Baker. *p* Jay Lewis. *sc* William Fairchild. *ph* Desmond Dickinson. *ed* Alan Osbiston. *ad* Alex Vetchinsky. *cast* John Mills, Helen Cherry, Richard Attenborough, Lana Morris, Nigel Patrick, George Cole, Bernard Lee, James Hayter, Kenneth More.
●Hit by a mine, a crippled submarine sinks to the sea floor, killing all but twelve of its crew – only eight of whom can escape. Stiff upper lips are brandished for'ard, aft and amidships, except by the always emotional Attenborough, who is reduced to a hysterical wreck by the thought of his slow demise. If the claustrophobia gets a bit too much for you, you might like to speculate upon the fact that this was originally a stage play. NF

Moroccan Chronicles (Chroniques Marocaines)

(1999, Mor, 80 min)
d/p/sc Moumen Smihi. *ph* Hélène Delale. *ed* Schéhérazade Saadi. *cast* Aïcha Mahmah, Tarik Jamil, Miloud Habachi, Soumaya Akaboune, Ahmed S Soussi, Miloud Timoud, Ahmed Simou.
●In Fez, traditional capital of N Morocco, a boy, recuperating from circumcision carried out too late due to his father's absence, is told three comforting stories by his mother. The first is a moral tale about three kids who torment a beggar and his performing monkey in Marrakesh; the second a sly fable about a sophisticated and beautiful young flirt leading an admirer a merry dance in Essaouira (where Welles, fittingly, shot *Othello*); the third a cautionary tale of an old Tangier fisherman determined, against all odds and advice from pals, to catch the monstrous whale he insists haunts the straits of Gibraltar. It's an odd little film, elusive, allusive, delicate, touching, and the final scenes are even more enigmatic. If it finally doesn't quite hang together, there's still plenty to intrigue and impress en route. GA

Morocco

(1930, US, 92 min, b/w)
d Josef von Sternberg. *p* Hector Turnbull. *sc* Jules Furthman. *ph* Lee Garmes. *ed* Sam Winston. *ad* Hans Dreier. *songs* Cremieux, Hajos, Leo Robin. *cast* Marlene Dietrich, Gary Cooper, Adolphe Menjou, Ulrich Haupt, Juliette Compton, Francis McDonald, Eve Southern, Emile Chautard.
●Sternberg's first Hollywood film with Dietrich looks like a deliberate reversal of their first collaboration on *The Blue Angel* the year before in Germany. Dietrich plays another sumptuous vamp, but this time one who is retreating from her past by taking a one-way ticket to Morocco… as although she runs delicately cruel rings around Menjou's affection for her, she ultimately sacrifices everything for the man she truly loves, legionnaire Gary Cooper. It's been customary to dismiss Sternberg's 'absurd' plots as mere vehicles for his experiments with lighting and decor, and his loving explorations of Dietrich's visual and emotional possibilities. The truth is that films like *Morocco* are completely homogeneous: the plotting and acting are in exactly the same expressionist register as everything else. Here, the highly nuanced portraits of men and a woman caught between the codes they live by and their deepest, secret impulses, remain very moving and 100 per cent modern. TR

Moro no Brasil

see Sound of Brazil

Morons from Outer Space

(1985, GB, 97 min)
d Mike Hodges. *p* Barry Hanson. *sc* Mel Smith, Griff Rhys Jones. *ph* Philip Meheux. *ed* Peter Boyle. *pd* Brian Eatwell. *m* Peter Brewis. *cast* Mel Smith, Griff Rhys Jones, Joanne Pearce, Jimmy Nail, Paul Bown, James B Sikking, Dinsdale Landen, Tristram Jellinek, Miriam Margolyes.
●This ineptly combines lamebrain comedy and sci-fi adventure, two of Hollywood's most popular genres of the last decade. Four dimwitted aliens get lost in space, crash on the M1, and are adopted by Rhys Jones, who immediately recognises their potential as pop stars and chat show persons. The whole mess ends with the rock concert now obligatory in a certain type of British movie. Both Hodges (*Get Carter*, *Pulp*) and Smith & Jones (*Not the Nine O'Clock News*), who also scripted, have promising track records; but here, despite straining every sinew desperately, they provide a minimal quotient of chuckles. RR

Mortal Kombat

(1995, US, 101 min)
d Paul Anderson. *p* Lawrence Kasanoff. *sc* Kevin Droney. *ph* John R Leonetti. *ed* Martin Hunter. *pd* Jonathan Carlson. *m* George S Clinton. *cast* Christopher Lambert, Robin Shou, Linden Ashby, Cary-Hiroyuki Tagawa, Bridgette Wilson, Talisa Soto, Trevor Goddard.
●As video-game-inspired movies go, this remains leagues ahead of last year's *Street Fighter*. Of course, there's only so much one can do with a game that never leaves the fighting arena, but British director Anderson does a fair job with what he was given: four good-looking leads, some very impressive sfx, Babylonian sets, a bone-crunching soundtrack, and a battery of well-choreographed fights. That the plot occasionally reaches areas so ambiguous as to be unfathomable is beside the point; this is about hand-to-hand combat, pure and simple. Lambert plays Rayden, a highly-charged friendly God from the mystical Outworld. Not so friendly is sorcerer Shang Tsung (Tagawa), host of Outworld's infamous tournament where groups of humans go into battle against unearthly

combatants and generally wind up getting thrashed. With Earth as the main prize, it's finally left to the skills of Rayden's three new hopefuls – Liu Kang (Shou), Johnny Cage (Ashby), and Sonya Blade (Wilson) – to wrest the fate of the planet from Outworld's grasp. DA

Mortal Kombat 2: Annihilation

(1997, US, 95 min)
d John R Leonetti. *p* Larry Kasanoff. *sc* Brent V Friedman, Bryce Zabel. *ph* Matthew F Leonetti. *ed* Peck Prior. *pd* Charles Wood. *m* George S Clinton. *cast* Robin Shou, Talisa Soto, Brian Thompson, Sandra Hess, Lynn Red Williams, Irina Pantaeva, Deron McBee.
●The ruler of Outworld, Shao-Khan, attempts yet again to merge his planet with Earth. It's a toss up which aspect of this drivel is worst: the pre-school performances; the elementary fantasy-speak; the design (purple and more purple); the lack of continuity (characters miraculously cleaned up following mud fights in the middle of nowhere); the action scenes (the cast spend most of their time somersaulting); the editing; the camerawork... DA

Mortal Storm, The

(1940, US, 100 min, b/w)
d Frank Borzage. *sc* Claudine West, Andersen Ellis, George Froeschel. *ph* William H Daniels. *ed* Elmo Veron. *ad* Cedric Gibbons, Wade B Rubottom. *m* Edward Kane. *cast* Margaret Sullavan, James Stewart, Robert Young, Frank Morgan, Irene Rich, Robert Stack, Bonita Granville, Maria Ouspenskaya, Dan Dailey, Ward Bond.
●One of Hollywood's invariably slightly embarrassing attempts to get to grips with the Nazi peril. Set in an all-American small town in Germany on the eve of Hitler's appointment as Chancellor of the Third Reich, with the narrator pontificating about 'the mortal storm in which man finds himself today', it constantly teeters on the brink of absurd naiveté, kept more or less on balance by skill, sincerity and good intentions. The film is almost retrieved by the touching Sullavan/Stewart love affair, shaping up to be one of those incandescent romantic visions transcending reality that is the mark of a Borzage film. The fact that it doesn't quite work that way is probably because almost the entire film was directed, uncredited, by Victor Saville. TM

Mortal Thoughts

(1991, US, 103 min)
d Alan Rudolph. *p* John Fiedler, Mark Tarlov. *sc* William Reilly, Claude Kerven. *ph* Elliot Davis. *ed* Tom Walls. *pd* Howard Cummings. *m* Mark Isham. *cast* Demi Moore, Glenne Headly, Bruce Willis, John Pankow, Harvey Keitel, Billie Neal, Frank Vincent.
●This intricate, intellectually satisfying and emotionally involving murder mystery risks falling between two stools. Neither an 'Alan Rudolph Film' nor a glossy star vehicle, it has a naturalistic tone, a conventional plot, measured pacing, and a serpentine narrative. It opens powerfully: Moore, giving evidence on her own free will, is questioned by detective Keitel. We flash back and forth in time as she relates events leading to an as yet unknown crime. Headly, who plays the happy-go-lucky owner of a hairdressing salon where Moore works, has a drunken, violent husband (Willis) whom she constantly jokes about bumping off. But Keitel senses that Moore's account of their volatile three-way relationship doesn't add up: who is she protecting, and from what? Rudolph makes excellent use of video technology, and coaxes outstanding performances from the three leads. NF

Mort de Mario Ricci, La

see Death of Mario Ricci, The

Morte a Venezia

see Death in Venice

Morte di un Operatore

see Death of a Cameraman

Mortelle Randonnée

see Deadly Run

Mort en ce Jardin, La (Evil Eden)

(1956, Fr/Mex, 97 min)
d Luis Buñuel. *p* Oscar Dancigers. *sc* Raymond Queneau, Gabriel Arout, Luis Alcoriza, Luis Buñuel. *ph* Jorge Stahl Jr. *ed* Marguerite Renoir, Denise Chardein. *ad* Edward Fitzgerald. *m* Paul Misraki. *cast* Georges Marchal, Simone Signoret, Charles Vanel, Michèle Girardon, Michel Piccoli, Tito Junco, Raúl Ramirez, Luis Aceves Castañeda.
●Buñuel uses an interesting genre: *The Wages of Fear* inspired left wing French film-makers to join Mexican producers and make very violent melodramas with Third Worldish themes. Here, in a Bolivia-type state, clashes between troops and striking miners force a jungle trek on an ill-starred gang: a prostitute (Signoret), a priest (Piccoli), a trader (Vanel), an adventurer (Marchal), a deaf-mute beauty (Girardon). Jungle hazards include snakes, thirst, toilet-paper problems, and the bourgeois joys of looting a wrecked plane. Its garish, vicious action beats Sam Fuller at his own game, and adds philosophical suspense, as jungle paranoia makes Marxist fraternity look as delirious as a Surrealist dream. Co-writer is Raymond Queneau, the Picasso of avant-garde writing. RD

Mortgage

(1989, Aust, 90 min)
d Bill Bennett. *p* Bruce Moir. *sc* Bill Bennett. *ph* Steve Arnold. *cast* Brian Vriends, Doris Younane, Bruce Venebles, Andrew Gilbert, Paul Coolahan.
●Australian director Bennett drafted in real solicitors and architects to stand in for the unsuspecting would-be home-owners in this documentary-style drama, which will draw groans of recognition from those who've been through the war zone of the housing market. Bennett used the same technique in *Malpractice* to explore the legal and medical ramifications following the delivery in hospital of a brain damaged baby. TJ

Morvern Callar

(2002, GB/Can, 97 min)
d Lynne Ramsay. *p* Robyn Slovo, Charles Pattinson, George Faber. *sc* Lynne Ramsay, Liana Dognini. *ph* Alwin Kuchler. *ed* Lucia Zucchetti. *pd* Jane Morton. *cast* Samantha Morton, Kathleen McDermott, Jim Wilson, Dolly Wells, Carolyn Calder, Andrew Flanagan.
●When Morvern (Morton), a supermarket assistant living in a small Scottish port, wakes to find her would-be-novelist boyfriend dead on the kitchen floor, she's unsure what to do, except carry on living. He's sent her a message hoping that posthumous publication of a book left on his computer might help her get by, but after the initial shock, Morvern finds she has ideas of her own. Ramsay's adaptation of Alan Warner's novel is as visually expressive, assured in its control of mood, and adept with its cast as was *Ratcatcher*. Morton is especially good (and given sterling support from newcomer Kathleen McDermott), making plausible some of the plot's more far-fetched moments, and really coming into her own (like the film itself) when Morvern takes a break in Spain and gets a better perspective on her options. A film that very clearly means a lot to its maker. GA

Moscow Distrusts Tears (Moskva Slezam ne Verit)

(1979, USSR, 148 min)
d Vladimir Menshov. *sc* Valentin Chernykh. *ph* Igor Slabnevich. *ed* E Mikhailovoi. *ad* Said Menyalshchikov. *m* Sergei Nikitin. *cast* Vera Alentova, Alexei Batalov, Irina Muraveva, Alexandr Fatiushin, Raisa Ryazanova, Natalya Vavilova, Oleg Tabakov.
●*Moscow Distrusts Tears*, maybe, but not Hollywood: incredibly, Menshov's jejune melodrama was awarded an Oscar for Best Foreign Language Film. By *The Three Sisters* out of *How to Marry a Millionaire* (or rather, in the Workers' State, a hockey champion or TV cameraman), its rambling plot involves a trio of provincial factory girls descending on the capital and setting their caps at every eligible member of the local intelligentsia. Twenty years later, predictability has set in with a vengeance: divorce, loneliness, intimations of mortality, as well as the providential apparition of a nice, virile hyper-sensitive mate for the most obviously sympathetic of the three. Well acted, occasionally amusing, but at over two hours, quite interminable. Heart warming assurance that escapism is the same the world over. GAd

Moscow on the Hudson

(1984, US, 117 min)
d/p Paul Mazursky. *sc* Paul Mazursky, Leon Capetanos. *ph* Donald McAlpine. *ed* Richard Halsey. *pd* Pato Guzman. *m* David McHugh. *cast* Robin Williams, Maria Conchita Alonso, Cleavant Derricks, Alejandro Rey, Savely Kramarov, Elya Baskin, Oleg Rudnik.
●When Russian saxophone player Vladimir (Williams) visits NY, his experiences back home lead him to defect, leaving family, friends and a familiar culture for the pursuit of pleasure and freedom. But after the initial delirium, he finds that the Big Apple is rife with poverty, racism, unemployment, and mugging. Mazursky's comedy may not exactly be politically profound, with its suggestion that freedom and happiness are relative concepts. But where it scores so highly is not only in its ability to evoke Vladimir's astonishment at the bizarre, sometimes brutal texture of New York life, but also in the generosity it extends to the musician's sad predicament. Even the absurdity and chaos of his department store defection (treated by the surrounding Americans as yet another media spectacle) becomes in Mazursky's hands a heroic moment of private, victorious self-assertion. Romantic humanism may not be fashionable in these cynical cinematic times, but few directors reveal the tragicomic lives of ordinary people with such sensitivity and humour. GA

Moses

(1975, It/GB, 141 min)
d Gianfranco De Bosio. *p* Vincenzo Labella. *sc* Anthony Burgess, Vittorio Bonicelli, Gianfranco De Bosio. *ph* Marcello Gatti. *ed* Gerry Hambling, Peter Boita, John D Guthridge, Alberto Gallitti, Frederick Wilson. *ad* Pierluigi Basile. *m* Ennio Morricone. *cast* Burt Lancaster, Anthony Quayle, Ingrid Thulin, Irene Papas, Aharon Ipalé, Yousef Shiloah, Marina Berti, Mariangela Melato, Laurent Terzieff, John Francis Lane. *narrator* (English version) Richard Johnson.
●'We must follow' – 'Follow? Where to?' – 'To the Promised Land – where else?' This long collection of edited highlights from the 360-minute Lew Grade TV series is sunk right from the start by some of the most pathetic 'epic' dialogue since Victor Mature said, 'Bring in a woman and you bring in trouble' during *Samson and Delilah*. But at least DeMille's splurges had cohesion and some sort of visual unity; *Moses* jumbles up half-formed ideas (the Egyptians as emaciated and verbose intellectuals, for example) with patches of realism, to produce something that is totally without style. The special effects are cut-price (directed by Mario Bava, so we might have expected better) and compare poorly with those of *The Ten Commandments*. So when the script finally becomes interesting, pitting Moses against an implacable God, the effect has already been sabotaged – by the second-rate manifestations of His vengeance, by an unsympathetic gang of Israelites/extras, and by Lancaster's wooden performance ('The punctilious observance of the Sabbath, as you so grandiloquently term it...'). AN

Moses and Aaron (Moses und Aron)

(1975, WGer/Fr, 110 min)
d/p/sc Jean-Marie Straub, Danièle Huillet. *ph* Ugo Piccone. *ed* Jean-Marie Straub, Danièle Huillet. *cast* Günter Reich, Louis Devos, Werner Mann, Eva Csapó, Roger Lucas, Richard Salter.
●As in Straub/Huillet's *Chronicle of Anna Magdalena Bach*, the soundtrack comes first: a performance, sung live on location, of Schönberg's passionately dialectical opera. The original is notoriously difficult to stage adequately, and Straub's 'materialist' approach serves it better than any theatrical production is ever likely to; the precise, ultra-concrete images are simple enough to permit concentration on the score, and (again like the Bach film) sufficiently charged to generate a passionate intensity of their own. TR

Mosquito Coast, The

(1986, US, 119 min)
d Peter Weir. *p* Jerome Hellman. *sc* Paul Schrader. *ph* John Seale. *ed* Thom Noble, (Australia) Richard Francis-Bruce. *pd* John Stoddart. *m* Maurice Jarre. *cast* Harrison Ford, Helen Mirren, River Phoenix, André Gregory, Dick O'Neill, Martha Plimpton, Conrad Roberts.

●Given that Paul Theroux's harrowing tale of jungle craziness is one of the least filmable properties of recent years, Weir's river journey to the heart of darkness works considerably better than one might imagine. Meticulously translated from the book, *Mosquito Coast* charts the mental decline and fall of idealistic inventor Allie Fox, who drags wife and family to the jungles of Central America in a doomed effort to bring ice to the natives. Although it's too long, with Weir attempting to negotiate too many psychological bends in Theroux's *River of No Return*, the director still manages to conjure out of the breathtaking landscape a genuine whiff of mental and physical hell, and in so doing draws from Harrison Ford a tour de force performance as mad Allie. Indeed, this is Ford's movie: Helen Mirren's flower-child-gone-to-seed wife and son Charlie (Phoenix), the heart and voice of the novel, are mere jungle shadows in comparison. Wherein lies the film's major flaw; for try as he might, after a lifetime playing the ultimate hero, Ford finally fails to convince as the ultimate villain, particularly when he's back battling natives à la Indiana Jones. A brave and serious piece of film-making, nevertheless. DAt

Mosquito Squadron

(1968, GB, 90 min)
d Boris Sagal. *p* Lewis J Rachmil. *sc* Donald S Sanford, Joyce Perry. *ph* Paul Beeson. *ed* John S Smith. *ad* Bill Andrews. *m* Frank Cordell. *cast* David McCallum, Suzanne Neve, David Buck, David Dundas, Dinsdale Landen, Charles Gray, Vladek Sheybal, Robert Urquhart.

●One of those WWII movies you'd thought they couldn't possibly make any more, with stiff-upper-lip quota filled to bursting as our brave boys in blue embark on low-level bombing raids to destroy V3 and V4 development installations in Germany. It means well, and stages the action competently enough, but that doesn't weigh much against the balance of a preposterously contrived script. McCallum is the squadron leader who falls for Neve, wife of his best friend (Buck) after the latter is reported missing, presumed killed in action. Then news comes that Buck is alive and being held hostage in the very château the squadron has orders to destroy. Cue for moral decision-making of the Boy's Own Paper variety. TM

Moss Rose

(1947, US, 82 min, b/w)
d Gregory Ratoff. *p* Gene Markey. *sc* Jules Furthman, Tom Reed. *ph* Joe MacDonald. *ed* James B Clark. *ad* Richard Day, Mark-Lee Kirk. *m* David Buttolph. *cast* Peggy Cummins, Victor Mature, Ethel Barrymore, Vincent Price, Margo Woode, George Zucco, Patricia Medina.

●Don't look too closely at the plot of this slice of Edwardian Gothic about a chorus girl (Cummins, not yet immortalised by *Gun Crazy*) who worms her way into an olde English household by blackmailing an invitation out of the young master (Mature, no less) who supposedly murdered her friend. Soon, silly girl, she is next in line to be done away with. Motivation is nobody's strong point, and poor Price's police inspector has to play singularly dumb (sitting on the fact that two murders are linked by a Bible and a pressed rose) to keep the pot boiling. Enjoyable, though, and beautifully shot by Joe MacDonald, with Ethel Barrymore rather splendidly doing her thing as a possessive matriarch. TM

Most Dangerous Game, The (aka The Hounds of Zaroff)

(1932, US, 63 min, b/w)
d Ernest B Schoedsack, Irving Pichel. *sc* James Ashmore Creelman. *ph* Henry Gerrard. *ed* Archie Marshek. *ad* Carroll Clark. *m* Max Steiner. *cast* Joel McCrea, Fay Wray, Leslie Banks, Robert Armstrong, Noble Johnson, Steve Clemento, James Flavin.

●By far the most chilling version of Richard Connell's much adapted and imitated short story, boasting an authentic touch of de Sade in Leslie Banks' performance as the world-weary big game hunter and connoisseur of arcane pleasures, possessor of a remote island fortress to which he ensures that passing ships are attracted and then wrecked on the reefs. 'First the hunt, then the revels' he purrs – with Fay Wray clearly destined to be the reluctant object of those revels – as he suavely entertains his guests while outlining the rules of the hunt against a human quarry he has devised to tickle his jaded palate, highly delighted to discover a worthy opponent in McCrea, a hunter almost his equal in celebrity. Still one of the best and most literate movies from the great days of horror, it is particularly effective in its measured graduation from words to action with the long, ferocious, beautifully choreographed hunt sequence, in which the human prey ironically wins the day by drawing on all his reserves of animal cunning. TM

Most Dangerous Man Alive

(1961, US, 82 min, b/w)
d Allan Dwan. *p* Benedict Bogeaus. *sc* James Leicester, Phillip Rock. *ph* Carl Carvahal. *ed* Carlos Lodato. *m* Louis Forbes. *cast* Ron Randell, Debra Paget, Elaine Stewart, Anthony Caruso, Gregg Palmer, Morris Ankrum.

●For the range and quantity of his output, Dwan has frequently been compared to Howard Hawks, and like Hawks he made one science fiction movie late in his career (his last film, in fact). But despite an interesting theme about a mobster who survives an atomic explosion to become a fugitive of steel, it's no *Thing from Another World*. Its bleak, uncompromising narrative and austere visuals are closer to a gangster B picture than sci-fi, and only three sequences (including a semi-nightmarish episode in which the heroine tries to arouse the metallic villain) are really memorable. The film does, however, contain one classic moment. The villain has been horribly mutilated by a nuclear explosion, has murdered five people, and is about to be incinerated by flame-throwers: 'If you tell the truth', the heroine shouts to him, 'there won't be anything to worry about'. This, incidentally, was the film being remade in Wim Wenders' *The State of Things*. DP

Most Desired Man, The

see Bewegte Mann, Der

Mostly Martha (Drei Sterne)

(2001, Aus/Ger/It/Switz, 107 min)
d Sandra Nettelbeck. *p* Karl Baumgartner, Christoph Friedel. *sc* Sandra Nettelbeck. *ph* Michael Bertl. *ed* Mona Bräuer. *pd* Thomas Freudenthal. *m* Keith Jarrett, Arvo Pärt, David Darling. *cast* Martina Gedeck, Sergio Castellitto, Maxime Förste, August Zirner, Ulrich Zirner, Sybille Canonica, Katja Studt, Idil Üner, Oliver Broumis, Antonio Wanneck.

●Slickly stylish if somewhat stale tale of a control-freak restaurant chef forced to reassess her life first when she's lumbered with the young son of her sister (who died in an accident), then again when an irrepressibly undisciplined Italian (aren't they all?) is appointed as her assistant. The stereotyping and predictability extend to the 'what this neurotic Northern bitch needs is a kid and a Southern stud' story structure, but Martina Gedeck's performance and discreet charm manage somehow to make it reasonably watchable. GA

Most Terrible Time in My Life, The (Waga Jinsei Saiaku no Toki)

(1993, Jap/Tai/China, 92 min, b/w)
d Kaizo Hayashi. *p* Yutaka Goto, Shunsuke Koga, Kaizo Hayashi, Yu Weiyen. *sc* Daisuke Tengan, Kaizo Hayashi. *ph* Yuichi Nagata. *ed* Nobuko Tomita. *ad* Takeo Kimura. *cast* Masatoshi Nagase, Shiro Sano, Kiyotaka Nanbara, Yang Haitin, Hou De Jian, Akaji Maro.

●*To Sleep, So As to Dream* and *Circus Boys* marked Kaizo Hayashi as an expert pasticheur of old movie styles, but this loving tribute to 'Scope thrillers of the Seijun Suzuki kind (complete with a Joe Shishido guest appearance) is something else again. Masatoshi Nagase stars as Yokohama private eye Mike Hama tangling with a gang of Chinese/Korean immigrants who call themselves 'The New Japs' and uncovering a plot to rearrange crime in East Asia. Cutting hard from laughs to gut-wrenching violence, featuring a cast of exceptionally beautiful hitmen and revelling in wicked subtexts, this is a rapturous entertainment. It comes with a recommendation from the Japan Detective Agency Association, so you know it makes sense. TR

Most Wanted

(1997, US, 99 min)
d David Hogan. *p* Eric Gold. *sc* Keenen Ivory Wayans. *ph* Marc Reshovsky. *ed* Michael J Duthie, Mark Helfrich. *pd* Jean-Philippe Carp. *m* Paul Buckmaster. *cast* Keenen Ivory Wayans, Jon Voight, Jill Hennessy, Paul Sorvino, Robert Culp, Wolfgang Bodison.

●Facing the hot seat after killing his commanding officer in a fight during the Gulf War, decorated marksman Sgt James Dunn (Wayans) is given one last, covert opportunity to redeem himself. Col Grant Casey (Voight) recruits him for the elite 'Black Sheep' hit squad, his first assignment being one Donald Bickhart (Culp), a biotechnology magnate accompanying the First Lady to a public dedication. Or so it seems. At any rate, Dunn doesn't have much choice. When another gun fires, however, just as he's taking aim, and the President's wife drops dead, he realises he's the fall guy for a political assassination. 'The First Lady…Wow!' surmises the CIA Deputy Director (Sorvino). Written by Wayans, this unexceptional chase movie takes itself rather seriously, but at least it knows the ground. NB

Motel

(1989, US/WGer, 86 min)
d/p/sc/ph Christian Blackwood. *ed* Monika Apsbacher. *m* Alwin Nikolais.

●Blackwood's free-wheeling documentary is actually a series of mini-films that suggest everything from Fred Wiseman to *Raising Arizona*. The first pitstop is The Silver Saddle, New Mexico, run by three redoubtable women. The most conventional of the sequences, it's still marked with expansive curiosity and grotesque humour. The guests at The Blue Mist – situated opposite the Arizona State Prison – are mostly wives of the inmates, and include a former guard, staying in the infamous room 22. Here a con on furlough chopped up his mother, before making the fundamental error of trying to sell the pieces to the local grocer. Then there's The Amargosa, complete with its own theatre, in a ghost town, pop. 4, and The Movie Manor, which backs on to a drive-in cinema. And why not? TCh

Motel Cactus (Motel Seoninjang)

(1997, SKor, 91 min)
d Park Ki-Yong. *p* Tcha Sung-Jai. *sc* Park Ki-Yong, Bong Joon-Ho. *ph* Christopher Doyle. *ed* Ham Sung-Won. *pd* Choi Jeeong-Hwa, Oh Jae-Won. *cast* Jin Hee-Kyung, Jung Woo-Sung, Kim Seung-Hyun, Han Woong-Soo, Lee Mi-Yeon, Park Shin-Yang.

●Thanks to Chris Doyle's typically fluid, sensuous camerawork, this never looks less than terrific; it is, however, a little low on narrative drive as it charts four sexual/emotional encounters in a Seoul 'love hotel'. Intriguingly, the couplings involve only six characters, so that the episodes are subtly (even obscurely) linked, but while Park is clearly adept at establishing and sustaining a variety of moods, there's nothing particularly original in what he has to say about male-female relationships. GA

Mother (Mat)

(1926, USSR, 5,906 ft, b/w)
d Vsevolod Pudovkin. *sc* Nathan Zarkhi, Vsevolod Pudovkin. *ph* Anatoli Golovnya. *ad* Serge Kozlovsky. *cast* Vera Baranovskaya, Nikolai Batalov, Alexander Chistyakov, Ivan Koval-Samborsky, Anna Zemtzova.

●A major work from the heroic age of radical experiment in Russian cinema, this is a much altered reworking of Gorki's novel, about a peasant woman becoming a political militant after betraying her son's cache of arms to the police. Pudovkin tightened the overall structure, introduced the character of the drunken reactionary husband, and drew masterly performances from members of the Moscow Art Theatre. TR

Mother

(1996, US, 104 min)
d Albert Brooks. *p* Scott Rudin, Herb Nanas. *sc* Albert Brooks, Monica Johnson. *ph* Lajos Koltai, (San Francisco) Bill Butler. *ed* Harvey Rosenstock. *pd* Charles Rosen. *m* Marc Shaiman. *cast* Albert Brooks, Debbie Reynolds, Rob Morrow, Vanessa Williams, Lisa Kudrow, John C McGinley, Isabel Glasser.
●Brooks is a sorely under-rated movie-maker in Britain. Andrew Sarris called *Mother* the best film of 1996, but here it is, a year later, sneaking out straight to video. That said, it doesn't lose much on the small screen, where its subtle, quietly devastating observations on dysfunctional families and male neuroses look right at home. *In Lost in America* Brooks hit the road in a camper van to 'touch Indians'; here, twice divorced, but still intrepid, he moves back in with mom to get to the root of his problems with women. He's aggressive; she's impassive. 'The Experiment' isn't very scientific, but it gradually gets (rather pat) results. There aren't many films which tackle the generation gap between middle-aged kids and their old folks with such unsentimental comic acuity – and Reynolds essays her best role in three decades with delectable good grace and charm. TCh

M/other

(1999, Jap, 147 min)
d Nobuhiro Suwa. *p* Takenori Sento. *sc* Nobuhiro Suwa, Makiko Watanabe, Tomokazu Miura. *ph* Masami Inomoto. *ed* Shuichi Kakesu. *pd* China Hayashi. *m* Haruyuki Suzuki. *cast* Tomokazu Miura, Makiko Watanabe, Ryudai Takahashi.
●Cleverly titled drama about a divorcé who shows up at the house he shares with his younger lover with his 8-year-old son in tow. His ex has had an accident, he explains, can Shun stay with them for a month? Unimpressed, Aki reluctantly agrees, and we imagine we know where it's headed as woman and child gradually form a bond. Grating discordant strings on the soundtrack hint that we might be wrong. Suwa shoots most of his lengthy, improvised scenes from a one camera set-up, but for all the apparent simplicity of this observational technique, his aesthetic is not averse to expressionist lighting effects. The result is a studied, cool and convincing examination of modern relationships struggling to come to terms with traditional gender roles. TCh

Mother Alone, A (Duwata Mawaka Misa)

(1997, Sri Lanka, 130 min)
d Sumitra Peries. *p* Milina Sumathipala. *sc* Tony Ranasinghe. *ph* KA Dharmasena. *ed* Gladwin Fernando. *ad* Manee Mendis. *m* Nimal Mendis. *cast* Sangeetha Weeraratne, Tony Ranasinghe, Sanath Gunathilake, Wasanthi Chathurani, Sriyani Amarasena.
●Jilted by her boyfriend as soon as she becomes pregnant, young Thushari is sent away to stay with her aunt; obviously, she can't now marry as her parents had arranged. It's pre-Independence Sri Lanka, and Thushari has already tried to induce a miscarriage. The problem is not all's well between aunt and uncle; Thushari comes home and is sent to another aunt. Adapted from a story by GB Senanayake, this rigidly episodic film conveys the stigma, confusion, helplessness and even tedium of being a single, young, disenfranchised mother. But for all its humanism, the plain storytelling never works in the film's favour; and at over two hours, it's very very slow. NB

Mother and Son (Mat i Syn/Mutter und Sohn)

(1997, Rus/Ger, 71 min)
d Aleksandr Sokurov. *p* Thomas Kufus. *sc* Iurii Arabov. *ph* Aleksei Fedorov. *ed* Leda Semenova. *ad* Vera Zelinskaia, Esther Rittersbusch. *m* Glinka, Otmar Nussio, Verdi. *cast* Gudrun Geyer, Aleksei Ananishnov.
●Aleksandr Sokurov's previous films have borne such titles as *The Lonely Voice of Man*, *The Degraded* and *Sad Insensitivity*, accompanied by documentary 'elegies' – *Elegy*, *Russian Elegy*, and *Simple Elegy*. 'Why can't America make cinema like this?' Scorsese has asked. The answer is not hard to find. This is not only slow (lyrical), serious (ambitious) and sombre (unironic), it's almost entirely free of narrative, conflict and character development, and manifests such a fundamental disengagement from the dramatic conventions of the medium as to make Peter Greenaway, or even Robert Bresson, look like naturals for the next Hollywood dinosaur picture. In other words, not a lot happens. In a stone cottage, the mother (Geyer) lies dying, old and hushed and frail, tended by her son (Ananishnov). They speak of shared dreams and fears, and he picks her up and carries her through the countryside; the next day he takes another such walk, alone. In place of drama, Sokurov's recourse and inspiration is art, landscape painting in particular. The walks take us through beach, forest and mountain country; Sokurov and his cameraman Aleksei Fedorov compose it in serene, stylised tableaux, sometimes hazy or luminous, sometimes stretched or skewed, emphasising the surface of the film until the locations resemble painted studio backdrops. As a pastoral tone poem, the film is stunning; there are images here as remarkable as any in cinema. NB

Mother and the Whore, The (La Maman et la Putain)

(1973, Fr, 219 min, b/w)
d Jean Eustache. *p* Pierre Cottrell. *sc* Jean Eustache. *ph* Pierre Lhomme, Jacques Renard, Michel Cenet. *ed* Jean Eustache, Denise de Casabianca. *cast* Jean-Pierre Léaud, Françoise Lebrun, Bernadette Lafont, Isabelle Weingarten, Jacques Renard, Pierre Cottrell, Bernard Eisenschitz, Jean Douchet, Jean Eustache.
●Three-and-a-half hours of people talking about sex sounds like a recipe for boredom; in Eustache's hands, it is anything but. There is no 'explicitness': the film is about attitudes to, and defences against, sex and the body. Using dialogue garnered entirely from real-life conversations and sticking entirely to a prepared script (no improvisation), Eustache has provided us with a ruthlessly sharp-eyed view of chic, supposedly liberated sexual relationships, revealing them to be no less a disaster area of tragic dimensions than their 'straighter' counterparts. Veronika (Lebrun) cripples herself by regarding herself entirely through male eyes; Alexandre (Léaud, playing a character eerily close to his standard screen persona) is revealed to be the victim of a greedy, self-regarding, and desperate chauvinism; Marie (the superb, strong Lafont) is a less fully delineated character, sadly allowed only two fierce rejoinders to Alexandre's blind demands. Each of the three holds part of the 'truth' about their situation; none can put the pieces together. *The Mother and the Whore* is an icy comment on the New Wave, informed throughout by Eustache's striking visual intelligence. VG

Mother Dao the Turtlelike

(1991, Neth, 85 min, b/w)
d Vincent Monnikendan.
●Subtitled 'a kinematographic picture of the Dutch East Indies 1912–c1933', this strange, luminous document conjoins and contrasts colonial propaganda footage with timeless indigenous creationist mythology. West of Sumatra, the islanders of Nias tell of Earth's creator Mother Dao, the ever-rejuvenating, the turtlelike, whose immaculate conception first begat man and woman. An atoll erupts, a chant begins, and we see local people and European settlers, segregated and increasingly intertwined as the progressive overhaul of the island's economic industry and cultural organisation takes shape. Natural resources, production, transportation, government, religion, education and health care are all developed in the imperialists' image. The director combed through 300,000 metres of documentary material in Dutch archives to compile these silent images: the spartan soundtrack employs only occasional native songs and poems alongside subdued ambient noises. The director's revisionist perspective of course complicates matters; still, the film is most impressive as a simple anthropological documentary, containing a few searingly memorable visions, such as a crocodile slaughter as calmly brutal as the rabbit hunt in *La Règle du Jeu*. NB

Mother India (Bharat Mata)

(1957, Ind, 172 min)
d/p Mehboob Khan. *sc* Vajahat Mirza, S Ali Raza. *ph* Faradoon A Irani. *ed* Shamsudin Kadri. *ad* VH Palnitkar. *m* Naushad. *cast* Nargis, Sunil Dutt, Rajendra Kumar, Raaj Kumar, Kumkum, Chanchal, Kanhaiyalal, Jiloo Maa, Azra, Master Saiid, Muqri, Sheela Nayak, Siddiqui, Geeta, Master Surendra.
●The success of such films as *Monsoon Wedding* and the increasing exposure of western audiences to a number of ambitious Bollywood epics has, perhaps, made many of us less snooty about the unabashed mix of melodrama, music and dance in Hindi cinema. One striking feature of this monumental landmark film is the skill with which the plot is unfolded (get out three if not four hankies), and underscored with a series of heartrending songs. Of course, we're not talking subtlety here, as the defiant heroine battles famine, flood, a fiendish moneylender and sundry tragic accidents in the ceaseless struggle to raise her sons and retain the family's few acres. True, there are dull spots and the overripe supporting cast pale beside Nargis' 'force of nature' central performance, but overall it's a wallowy treat. TJ

Mother, Jugs & Speed

(1976, US, 98 min)
d Peter Yates. *p* Peter Yates, Tom Mankiewicz. *sc* Tom Mankiewicz. *ph* Ralph Woolsey. *ed* Frank P Keller. *pd* Walter Scott Herndon. *cast* Bill Cosby, Raquel Welch, Harvey Keitel, Allen Garfield, Dick Butkus, Bruce Davison, LQ Jones, Larry Hagman, Valerie Curtin, Severn Darden.
●A totally inconsequential 'comedy-thriller' about rival freelance ambulance companies in LA. The film squanders its resources, both human (Cosby gets two funny lines, Keitel gets nothing) and automotive (the ambulances look like ice-cream vans) via a rambling, episodic excuse for a storyline and sub-minimal characterisation that makes *Crossroads* look like Ibsen. Incredible to think that Yates did *Bullitt* all those years ago, lamentable that a potential urban *M*A*S*H* should end up such an irredeemable, awesomely yawnsome farce. GD

Mother Küsters' Trip to Heaven (Mutter Küsters Fahrt zum Himmel)

(1975, WGer, 108 min)
d Rainer Werner Fassbinder. *sc* Rainer Werner Fassbinder, Kurt Raab. *ph* Michael Ballhaus. *ed* Thea Eymèsz. *pd* Kurt Raab. *m* Peer Raben. *cast* Brigitte Mira, Ingrid Caven, Margit Carstensen, Karlheinz Böhm, Irm Hermann, Gottfried John.
●One of Fassbinder's most provocative films, *Mother Küsters' Trip to Heaven* sets out to nail political exploitation on the left rather than the right. Factory worker Küsters, faced with the threat of redundancy, kills his boss and commits suicide. His widow (Mira) finds herself deserted by her family and friends…until a wealthy communist couple (Böhm and Carstensen) decide to make political capital from her plight. The film achieved the distinction of being banned from both the official Berlin Festival and its fringe event, the Forum. TR

Mother Night

(1996, US, 114 min)
d Keith Gordon. *p* Keith Gordon, Robert B Weide. *sc* Robert B Weide. *ph* Tom Richmond. *ed* Jay Rabinowitz. *pd* François Séguin. *m* Michael Convertino. *cast* Nick Nolte, Sheryl Lee, Alan Arkin, John Goodman, Kirsten Dunst, David Strathairn, Norman Rodway, Kurt Vonnegut.
●This stylish adaptation of Kurt Vonnegut's novel is an idiosyncratic mix of historical realism, rapt fantasy and offbeat humour. Nolte is Howard W Campbell Jr, an apolitical American playwright in Nazi Germany whose work as a conduit for US intelligence, concealing encoded communiqués in his Jew-baiting broadcasts on German radio, yields widely inspirational Nazi propaganda. Living incognito in New York after the war, his eventual exposure gathers a storm of interested parties – Israeli war-crimes investigators, white supremacists, his supposedly dead wife. An ambivalent meditation on deception, personal responsibility and commitment in an enigmatic world; some may find the studied, circumspect style unaffecting, but there's no denying the fascination of the material. NB

Mother of 1084 (Hazaar Chaurasi ki Maa)

(1997, Ind, 146 min)
d/p/sc/ph Govind Nihalani. *ed* Deepa Bhatia. *pd* Chokas Bharadwaj. *m* Debajyota Mishra. *cast* Jaya Bachchan, Joy Sengupta, Anupam Kher, Seema Biswas, Nandita Das, Melind Gunaji.

●Calcutta, the early '70s, and Bachchan's sheltered upper-middle class Calcutta housewife and mother slowly reacts to the shock of her favourite son's bloody death amidst the repression of the city's revolutionary Naxalite movement by piecing together the life she never knew. Not quite your average tale of consciousness-raising, Nihalani's lucid but slightly ponderous story makes its familiar points about the inter-relationship of revolutionary endeavour and female emancipation, and the fundamental need for human connection, with a certain calm authority. In places it strikes a profound note, but in all the story isn't enough to support the almost meditative length and pace. NB

Mother's Boys

(1993, US, 95 min)
d Yves Simoneau. *p* Jack E Freedman, Wayne S Williams, Patricia Herskovic. *sc* Barry Schneider, Richard Hawley. *ph* Elliot Davis. *ed* Michael Ornstein. *ad* David Bomba. *m* George S Clinton. *cast* Jamie Lee Curtis, Peter Gallagher, Joanne Whalley-Kilmer, Vanessa Redgrave, Luke Edwards, Joss Ackland.

●Just when you thought every conceivable permutation of the 'home invasion' plot had been worked, along comes this flashy, vapid variation. The twist here is that the 'happy family' consists of Gallagher, his three kids, and his schoolmarm girlfriend Whalley-Kilmer. And the intruder is not some scheming psycho home-wrecker but the children's 'natural' mother, Curtis, who walked out on them all three years earlier. Her revived claim on the family's affections at first seems genuine, but soon she's poisoning the boys' minds with lies about their father and surrogate mother. Curtis also makes a play for Gallagher and it's his refusal of her advances that precipitates the final all-out attack. Director Simoneau fills the screen with artificially lit images, over-dressed sets and immaculately designed costumes, while neglecting such essentials as pacing and suspense. NF

Mother Wore Tights

(1947, US, 107 min)
d Walter Lang. *p/sc* Lamar Trotti. *ph* Harry Jackson. *ed* J Watson Webb Jr. *ad* Richard Day, Joseph C Wright. *songs* Mark Gordon, Josef Myrow. *cast* Betty Grable, Dan Dailey, Mona Freeman, Connie Marshall, Vanessa Brown, Senor Wences.

●First teaming of Grable and Dailey, no Astaire-Rogers but the next best thing, and making the most of a nostalgic score ('Put Your Arms Around Me, Honey', 'Rolling Down to Bowling Green', 'You Do', 'Kokomo Indiana') as a pair of turn-of-the-century vaudevillains. Warm, colourful and a real charmer, despite tiresome complications latterly when the couple's eldest daughter grows up a snob ashamed of her background. TM

Mothman Prophecies, The

(2001, US, 119 min)
d Mark Pellington. *p* Tom Rosenberg, Gary Lucchesi, Gary Goldstein. *sc* Richard Hatem. *ph* Fred Murphy. *ed* Brian Berdan. *pd* Richard Hoover. *m* Tomandandy. *cast* Richard Gere, Laura Linney, Will Patton, Debra Messing, Lucinda Jenney, Alan Bates, David Eigenberg, Bob Tracey.

●Driving home, the wife of John Klein (Gere) crashes after seeing a vision. Following her death (from a 'temporal lobe tumour'), Klein, a *Washington Post* journo, discovers indecipherable, even 'possessed' drawings which hauntingly suggest the depth of her mute terror. Only years later, however, in a small town in West Virginia, does Klein begin to suspect a supernatural agency may be at work. Investigating with the help of local policewoman Connie (Linney), he uncovers a history of unexplained local events, the sinister nature of which is compounded by a series of anonymous, mocking phone calls boasting knowledge of future disasters. Director Pellington showed in *Arlington Road* that he can be a mischievous miner of paranoia and atmospherics. There are certainly strong moments and efficient set pieces here, too, but for all the claims that the film, adapted from a 1975 book by John Keel, is based on real events, Pellington fails to sustain credibility. The romance, too, seems tacked on, the ending predictably neat. WH

Motion and Emotion: The Films of Wim Wenders

(1990, GB, 90 min)
d Paul Joyce. *p* Chris Rodley. *with* Wim Wenders, Hanns Zischler, Samuel Fuller, Robby Müller, Dennis Hopper, Harry Dean Stanton, Peter Falk, Ry Cooder, Kraft Wetzel.

●Paul Joyce and producer Chris Rodley's thorough, intelligent documentary manages to celebrate Wenders' work, to contextualise it, and to question some of the assumptions he makes in his films. They use interviews (with Wenders, his actors, collaborators, and German critic Kraft Wetzel), clips, and music to explain and explore his output of the last two decades. Fuller is funny and colourful; Hopper, Falk, Stanton and Ry Cooder are anecdotal but perceptive; Zischler is Teutonically serious; and Wetzel provocative but often spot-on in his unsentimental assessment of Wenders' strengths and weaknesses (on his faintly adolescent attitude towards those he doesn't understand, for instance: 'Aren't women mysterious? Aren't kids wonderful in their innocent wisdom? Let's put on another record!'). The film, while justifiably admiring, never slips into hagiographic excess, and a judicious use of songs provides an uplifting, paean-like tone. GA

Motocyclette, La

see Girl on a Motorcycle

Motorist

(1989, US, 70 min)
d/p/sc Chip Lord. *ph* Jules Backus. *m* Terry Allen, The Residents. *cast* Richard Marcus, Jo Harvey Allen, Jules Backus, Sumi Nobuhara, Phil Garner, Toshi Onuki.

●Part fiction, part documentary essay, this wry, wacky road movie takes a driver (Richard Marcus) through the American Southwest to LA as he delivers a grey '62 Ford Thunderbird to a young Japanese. A Ford man with a respect for Cadillac, Richard talks to himself, the traffic, the radio and the car, lamenting the end of the Mechanical Age, offering an anecdotal history of himself and US dream cars, and commenting on the massive, mythic landscape around him. The few characters he meets – a mystic waitress, a gas attendant with a passion for franchise history – add vivid colour, but it's Richard's droll musings that fuel the film, providing a fascinating, often very funny semiology of '50s car culture to accompany ancient ads and documentary clips. The many references range from Henry Ford and Diego Rivera to McDonald's and UFOs, but the whole thing is lent coherence by Marcus' charismatic presence and Lord's assured control of mood. A small gem of a film. GA

Motor Psycho

(1965, US, 74 min, b/w)
d/p Russ Meyer. *sc* Russ Meyer, WE Sprague. *ph* Russ Meyer. *ed* Charles G Schelling. *m* Igo Kantor. *cast* Alex Rocco, Haji, Stephen Oliver, Holle K Winters, Joseph Cellini, Sharon Lee.

●It's the Battle of the Vets, as 'horse croaker' veterinarian Maddox (Rocco) takes on a biker whose mind, it seems, is on vacation after a tour of duty in Vietnam. Maddox, whose wife has been raped by the biker's gang, teams with Ruby (the pneumatic Haji) for an entertaining snakebite sequence and adequate finale, but otherwise it's hard to see what all the fuss is about. This is a rather tedious Western with whacked-out nutcases on bikes substituting for the Indians. Despite the disingenuous claims of Meyer fans that it's his editing and composition that mark him out, people only really watch his films for their parade of enormous breasts – though here they remain covered up. NRo

Mouchette

(1966, Fr, 90 min, b/w)
d Robert Bresson. *p* Anatole Dauman. *sc* Robert Bresson. *ph* Ghislain Cloquet. *ed* Raymond Lamy. *ad* Pierre Guffroy. *m* Monteverdi. *cast* Nadine Nortier, Marie Cardinal, Paul Hébert, Jean Vimenet, J-C Guilbert, Marie Susini, Liliane Princet, Raymonde Chabrun.

●Bresson's wholly austere study of the miseries of an inarticulate teenage peasant girl in provincial France, which culminates with her apathetic suicide, achieves an intense purity of a kind that few directors essay, let alone achieve. The simplicity is radical, not facile, and the result is an extraordinary spiritual meditation, not an exercise in gratuitous depression. TR

Moulin Rouge

(1952, US/Fr, 123 min)
d John Huston. *sc* Anthony Veiller, John Huston. *ph* Oswald Morris. *ed* Ralph Kemplen. *ad* Paul Sheriff. *m* Georges Auric. *cast* José Ferrer, Colette Marchand, Suzanne Flon, Zsa Zsa Gabor, Katherine Kath, Eric Pohlmann, Christopher Lee.

●Lumpish biopic, historically laughable as it pursues Hollywood's perennial view of the artist as solitary and star-crossed in both life and love. What taste can do, Huston does, abetted by Paul Sheriff's set designs and some fine colour camerawork from Oswald Morris. But playing Toulouse Lautrec on his knees, Ferrer could equally well be begging for mercy from the script. Best bit is the first reel, which evokes the spirit of Paris in the Naughty Nineties in a swirling mass of colour and movement. TM

Moulin Rouge (100)

(2001, US, 128 min)
d Baz Luhrmann. *p* Martin Brown, Baz Luhrmann, Fred Baron. *sc* Baz Luhrmann, Craig Pearce. *ph* Donald M McAlpine. *ed* Jill Bilcock. *pd* Catherine Martin. *m* Craig Armstrong. *cast* Nicole Kidman, Ewan McGregor, John Leguizamo, Jim Broadbent, Richard Roxburgh, Garry McDonald, Jacek Koman, Kylie Minogue.

●Another post-modern mix of myth, musical, comedy, romance and unfettered pastiche from the impressively inventive Luhrmann, here ransacking pop culture's iconographic archives – rather than the real Paris of 1900 – to mount a hyperkinetic update of the Orpheus myth. Naive, lovelorn writer/composer Christian (McGregor) is taken up by bohemians like Toulouse-Lautrec to put on a show at the scandalous showplace of the title, where courtesan/torch singer Satine (Kidman) will do anything – even sleep with a dodgy Duke – to further her acting career, especially if pressed by the club proprietor (Broadbent) – until, that is, she meets Christian, and her heart melts. A *Red Shoes*-style fable of love and art in conflict with commerce and power, it's luridly stunning to look at even if it's cut a little too quickly and insistently for its own good. It's also jam-packed with allusions and gags, and performed with enormous gusto. If it lacks the emotional punch of Luhrmann's earlier films, and drags towards the end, it is still great fun. GA

Mountains of the Moon

(1989, US, 136 min)
d Bob Rafelson. *p* Daniel Melnick. *sc* William Harrison, Bob Rafelson. *ph* Roger Deakins. *ed* Thom Noble. *pd* Norman Reynolds. *m* Michael Small. *cast* Patrick Bergin, Iain Glen, Richard E Grant, Fiona Shaw, John Savident, James Villiers, Adrian Rawlins, Peter Vaughn, Delroy Lindo, Bernard Hill, Roshan Seth, Anna Massey, Leslie Phillips.

●Because Rafelson's idiosyncratic account of Burton and Speke's search for the source of the Nile is concerned not with the destination but with the journey, he allows the narrative to be sidetracked by a series of colourful vignettes: a lion attack, the placating of wary tribesmen with swathes of cloth, and a menacing brush with camp Lord Ngola and his scheming advisor. These episodes reveal much about the Victorian explorers: Burton (Bergin) is a womanising adventurer and anthropologist; Speke (Glen) a shallow opportunist aristocrat with a book contract in his back pocket; and their relationship is further complicated by a hint that Speke harbours an unrequited love for his manly partner. Like any journey, it is more exciting going than coming back, a problem compounded here by a coda about Speke claiming full credit for their joint discoveries (though a lighter note is struck when Burton and Bernard Hill's Dr Livingstone strip off to compare battle scars). Unbounded praise for Roger Deakins' photography, equally at home with the sun-baked African vistas and the dark wood tones of the Royal Geographic Society. Despite longueurs, this handsome epic has a spark of intelligence and a pleasing wit. NF

Mourir à Tue-Tête (A Scream from Silence)

(1979, Can, 96 min)
d Anne-Claire Poirier. *p* Anne-Claire Poirier, Jacques Gagné. *sc* Anne-Claire Poirier, Marthe Blackburn. *ph* Michel Brault. *ed* André Corriveau. *m* Maurice Blackburn. *cast* Julie Vincent, Germain Houde, Paul Savoie, Monique Miller, Micheline Lanctôt, Pierre Gobeil, André Page.
●Harrowing rape movie (based on fact) in which the victim's life disintegrates as a result. It's dreadful as cinema (over-acted, obsessed with realism), but excellent as a case-example of Brownmiller's thesis – that rape is never the product of desire but a brutal and symbolic assertion of sexual oppression. Uncomfortable viewing for any man. CA

Mouse and His Child, The

(1977, US, 83 min)
d Fred Wolf, Charles Swenson. *p* Walt deFaria. *sc* Carol Mon Pere. *ph* Wally Bulloch. *ed* Rich Harrison. *pd* Vincent Davis, Sam Kirson, Bob Mitchell, Al Sheah. *songs* Roger Kellaway, Gene Lees. *cast* voices: Peter Ustinov, Neville Brand, Andy Devine, Sally Kellerman, Cloris Leachman.
●London crime figures are Toy Town statistics compared to the frog-mugging, mouse-napping and brazen treacle brittle heists in this animated feature based on author/illustrator Russell Hoban's fantasy classic. The graphics slog of more than 30 US animartistes is worth it, especially in the opening toyshop scene where we meet our heroes – a bland duo of wind-ups spot-welded together in an eternal last tango. The clockwork rule of 'doing what you're wound to do, not what you want to do' is topsy-turvied after the magic midnight hour; and the adventures of the mice meander to the rubbish dump empire of Manny the Rat (spivvy unctuous voice by Ustinov), their escape aided by a stagestruck parrot (high camp beak-work from Leachman). Hoban won't thank directors Wolf and Swenson for laying naff hands all over the finale of his whimsy and turning it into a homily. BPa

MouseHunt

(1997, US, 98 min)
d Gore Verbinski. *p* Alan Riche, Tony Ludwig, Bruce Cohen. *sc* Adam Rifkin. *ph* Phedon Papmichael. *ed* Craig Wood. *pd* Linda DeScenna. *m* Alan Silvestri. *cast* Nathan Lane, Lee Evans, Maury Chaykin, Christopher Walken, Vicki Lewis, Eric Christmas, Michael Jeter.
●Ernie and Lars Smuntz (Lane and Evans) are going through a bad patch. Their dying father's string factory is making a loss; Ernie's position as a chef has just been terminated; and dimwit Lars couldn't hold down a job even if he tried. Then father dies, leaving them the factory and a decrepit country mansion. As luck would have it, though, the house is worth a fortune, so the pair set about restoring it for auction. There's just one obstacle: a territorial mouse with an attitude problem. This film comes over as a mix of Laurel and Hardy, *Home Alone* and Tom and Jerry, and it works very well. Lane is especially funny, his deadpan Hardy-esque mannerisms working perfectly against Evans' winsome Laurel-inspired character, and there's a memorable cameo from Walken as a manic exterminator. It looks good, too, the generous use of wood and autumnal colours giving it an earthy, almost timeless appearance. Exceptional effects. DA

Mouse on the Moon, The

(1963, GB, 85 min)
d Richard Lester. *p* Walter Shenson. *sc* Michael Pertwee. *ph* Wilkie Cooper. *ed* Bill Lenny. *ad* John Howell. *m* Ron Grainer. *cast* Margaret Rutherford, Bernard Cribbins, Ron Moody, David Kossoff, Terry-Thomas, June Ritchie, Michael Crawford, Roddy McMillan, John Le Mesurier.
●Slightly desperate sequel to *The Mouse That Roared*, with the Duchy of Grand Fenwick beating the major powers in the space race, thanks to the happy discovery that the local wine is an excellent substitute for rocket fuel. No longer present in his triple role, Sellers is replaced by a busy horde of character actors, while Lester (just prior to his first Beatles film) works overtime on the jokes. TM

Mouse That Roared, The

(1959, GB, 90 min)
d Jack Arnold. *p* John Penington. *sc* Roger MacDougall, Stanley Mann. *ph* John Wilcox. *ed* Raymond Poulton. *ad* Geoffrey Drake. *m* Edwin Astley. *cast* Peter Sellers, Jean Seberg, David Kossoff, William Hartnell, Leo McKern, Macdonald Parke.
●Engaging Ealing-ish comedy about the Duchy of Grand Fenwick, a Lilliputian state which declares war on America on the principle that losers always boom economically. Sellers is brilliant as the graciously melancholy Duchess (less good in his other two impersonations as prime minister and army chief), but the script veers wildly between satire and slapstick. Taking it pretty much as it comes, Arnold (*Creature from the Black Lagoon*, *Incredible Shrinking Man*) seems most at home with moments of fantasy like the ten-man invading army's triumphal progress in clanking chain-mail through New York's deserted streets. TM

Mouth Agape, The (La Gueule Ouverte)

(1974, Fr, 82 min)
d Maurice Pialat. *p* André Genovès. *sc* Maurice Pialat. *ph* Nestor Almendros. *ed* Arlette Langmann, Bernard Dubois. *m* Mozart. *cast* Monique Mélinand, Hubert Deschamps, Philippe Léotard, Nathalie Baye, Alain Grestau.
●Pialat's third feature takes up a theme which, on the face of it, could not seem more uninviting: a middle-aged woman dying of cancer, and how this affects her husband and son. But what Pialat makes of this is so recognisable, embarrassing and moving – even, on occasion, funny – that he more than justifies his use of a forbidding subject. He has ideas about how emotions involving sex and death are intimately related – and about the clarity and lack of it that they shed on everything else, as son and father each go lusting after every woman in sight. He has ideas about cinema, too, and an expressive style that can encapsulate a lifetime of memories in a single shot. Without a trace of sentimentality or easy effect, this seemingly semi-autobiographical work is as intense in its way as *The Mother and the Whore*, and unforgettable. JR

Mouth to Mouth (Boca a Boca)

(1995, Sp, 96 min)
d Manuel Gómez Pereira. *p* Josian Gomez. *sc* Joaquín Oristrell, Juan Luis Iborra, Naomi Wise, Manuel Gómez Pereira. *ph* Juan Amoros. *ed* Guillermo Represa. *pd* Luis Valles. *m* Bernardo Bonezzi. *cast* Javier Bardem, Josep Maria Flotats, Aitana Sánchez-Gijón, Maria Barranco, Myriam Mézières.
●Bardem's a would-be Hollywood actor hoping to make it as a stereotype Spanish hunk, who falls for Sánchez-Gijón when she calls him up at the Madrid phone-sex company where he works. Things are difficult: she tells him she got his number from her husband, another of his clients, who's just decided he's gay. Complications ensue. Strangely similar in places to *Girl 6*, this is a stylish but none too funny slice of sub-Almodóvar farce, full of teasing, chic eroticism and absurd plot twists. GA

Mouth Wide Open – A Journey in Film with Ted Coubray

(1998, NZ, 55 min)
d Jonathan Dennis (Ted Coubray interview) John Anderson. *ph* Wayne Vinten. *ed* Annie Collins. *with* Ted Coubray.
●Interesting profile of inventor/film-maker Coubray who reminisces about his film viewing (from 1913) and film-making (from 1919) in the early days of the NZ industry. The nonagenarian handles his old Prestwick hand-ratchet camera with such affection and discusses his betrayal at the hands of Hungarian Alexander Markey in the early sound days so phlegmatically, you can't help but warm to him. WH

Movers and Shakers

(1985, US, 79 min)
d William Asher. *p* Charles Grodin, William Asher. *sc* Charles Grodin. *ph* Robbie Greenberg. *ed* Tom Benko. *ad* Donald Lee Harris. *m* Ken Welch, Mitzie Welch. *cast* Walter Matthau, Charles Grodin, Vincent Gardenia, Tyne Daly, Bill Macy, Gilda Radner, Steve Martin, Penny Marshall.
●Written and produced by Charles Grodin, this is a flat look at Hollywood madness from an insider who might have been expected to muster a little more sardonic zest. There's some mild fun to be had as mogul Matthau buys the rights to best-selling how-to guide *Love in Sex*, then hands hack writer Grodin the unenviable task of turning it into a movie. Cameos from Martin and Radner, but straight to video in the UK. TJ

Movie Crazy

(1932, US, 84 min, b/w)
d Clyde Bruckman. *p* Harold Lloyd. *sc* Vincent Lawrence. *ph* Walter Lundin. *ed* Bernard W Burton. *ad* Harry Oliver, William MacDonald. *cast* Harold Lloyd, Constance Cummings, Kenneth Thomson, Sydney Jarvis, Robert McWade, Louise Closser Hale.
●Patchy Lloyd talkie in which he rather drags out his all-American boy characterisation as an aspiring actor summoned to Hollywood by mistake but winning out in the end (discovered as a natural comedian during his disaster-prone attempts at being a heart-throb). Improving after a slow start, it has some fine sight gags, notably a cleverly sustained 10-minute elaboration of the magician's coat routine, inadvertently worn by Lloyd to a party and producing things that cause endless embarrassment. TM

Movie Days (Biodagar)

(1994, Ice, 85 min)
d Fridrik Thór Fridriksson. *p* Peter Rommel, Peter Aalbæk Jensen. *sc* Einar Már Gudmundsson, Fridrik Thór Fridriksson. *ph* Ari R Kristinsson. *ed* Steingrímur Karlsson. *pd* Arni Páll Johansson. *m* Hilmer Orn Hilmarsson. *cast* Örvar Jens Arnarsson, Orri Helgason, Rúrik Haraldsson, Sigrun Hjalmtysdottir, Asta Esper Andersen, Jon Sigurbjörnsson, Gudrün Asmundsdottir, Otto Sander.
●A semi-autobiographical film from the director of *Children of Nature* about a young movie addict banished for the summer to a relative's farm. There he is rewarded for his chores with an initiation into the ways of nature, and tales of trolls and ghosts from old man Toni. Stylised, but never particularly stylish, this is quiet, reflective and somewhat flimsy. TCh

Movie Movie

(1978, US, 106 min, b/w & col)
d/p Stanley Donen. *sc* Larry Gelbart, Sheldon Keller. *ph* Chuck Rosher Jr ('Dynamite Hands'), Bruce Surtees ('Baxter's Beauties of 1933'). *ed* George Hively. *ad* Jack Fisk. *m* Ralph Burns. *songs* Ralph Burns, Buster Davis, (lyrics) Larry Gelbart, Sheldon Keller. *cast* George C Scott, Harry Hamlin, Rebecca York, Trish Van Devere, Eli Wallach, Barbara Harris, Barry Bostwick, Art Carney, Red Buttons, Jocelyn Brando.
●Donen takes us back to the days 'when the only four-letter word in movie houses was EXIT' – to quote George Burns' explanatory prologue, nervously tacked on to this pastiche double feature of the 1930s in case any thickheads didn't get the joke. It's a useful word to know, too, considering the dire script, the flat performances from George C Scott and entourage, and the pointlessness of the entire exercise. The concluding Busby Berkeley-esque 'Baxter's Beauties of 1933' at least homes in on its genre far more sharply and sympathetically than the opening boxing melodrama 'Dynamite Hands' (in b/w), which loses its focus in a welter of cheap jokes. GB

Moving

(1988, US, 89 min)
d Alan Metter. *p* Stuart Cornfeld. *sc* Andy Breckman. *ph* Donald McAlpine. *ed* Alan Balsam. *pd* David L Snyder. *m* Howard Shore. *cast* Richard Pryor, Beverly Todd, Randy Quaid, Dave Thomas, Dana Carvey, Rodney Dangerfield.
●Pryor, in his unfunniest role to date, has just lost his long-standing engineering job, but has the good fortune to be offered the career opportunity of a lifetime. Less fortunately for his family, who like it where they are, it involves a 2,000 mile trek to relocate in Boise, Idaho. Still, anywhere to escape the wrath of neighbour Quaid, a manic slob who takes great pride in his postage-stamp lawn, trimming it

– and everyone else – with a souped-up industrial lawn-mower. The egg hits the fan when the removal men finally turn up and proceed to demolish the family's possessions, and when Pryor discovers that the delivery driver of his shiny new Saab is a schizo. A couple of funny moments, and that's it. DA

Moving (Ohikkoshi)

(1993, Jap, 117 min)
d Shinji Somai. *p* Hiroshisa Mukuju, Hiroyuki Fujikado. *sc* Satoko Okudera, Satoshi Okonogi, Satoru Kobiki. *ph* Toyomichi Kurita. *ed* Yoshiyuki Okuhara. *pd* Narinori Shimoizaka, H Yamazaki. *m* Yoshiyuki Okuhara, Nariaki Saegusa. *cast* Kiichi Nakai, Junko Sakurada, Tomoko Tabata, Shofukutei Tsurubei, Taro Tanaka.

●There are two unavoidable problems at the core of this film about the psychological impact of a couple's separation on their 11-year-old daughter. First, the 45-year-old male director seems to have no point of entry into the mind of his young protagonist, so that the entire film rings hollow. Second, the girl herself (newcomer Tomoko Tabata) is a most obnoxious spoiled brat, which makes it hard to care. TR

Moving Target, The

see Harper

Mozart in Love

(1975, US, 99 min)
d Mark Rappaport. *cast* Rich La Bonte.

●Funnier and altogether more assured than its predecessor, Rappaport's second feature respectfully lays waste to the inflexibility of grand opera. WA Mozart's casual/intense relations with the three Weber sisters are the pretext; Mozart's own arias are the soundtrack; the actors wear costumes, stand in front of backdrop projections, and mime to perfection. Inspired. TR

Ms .45 (aka Angel of Vengeance)

(1980, US, 84 min)
d Abel Ferrara. *sc* NG St John. *ph* James Momèl. *ed* Christopher Andrews. *ad* Ruben Masters. *m* Joe Delia. *cast* Zoë Tamerlis, Bogey, Albert Sinkys, Darlene Stuto, Helen McGara, Nike Zachmanoglou, Jimmy Laine [Abel Ferrara], Peter Yellen.

●Abel Ferrara opined that this made his previous film, *Driller Killer*, look like 'scratchings on the cave wall'. Who are we to disagree. Still working the gutter no-budget beat – a correlative to New York's no-wave punk music of the period – he brings a patina of slick visual sophistication to this rape/revenge thriller; more importantly, he allows a coherent, if extreme, feminist position to emerge. Nineteen-year-old Nastassja Kinski-lookalike Zoë Tamerlis plays Thana, a shy deaf-mute who works in New York's garment district. Raped twice within hours, she kills her second assailant and chops him up in the bathtub (an episode that finds its way into Alan Warner's novel *Morvern Callar*). Gaining confidence, she arms herself and woe to the chauvinist who crosses her path. It's a provocative, disreputable movie, well worth seeing. Regrettably, Tamerlis never really came through on her promise, though she co-wrote and appears in *Bad Lieutenant* as Zoe Lund. She died in 1999 of 'heart failure'. TCh

Much Ado About Nothing

(1993, GB/US, 111 min)
d Kenneth Branagh. *p* Stephen Evans, David Parfitt, Kenneth Branagh. *sc* Kenneth Branagh. *ph* Roger Lanser. *ed* Andrew Marcus. *pd* Tim Harvey. *m* Patrick Doyle. *cast* Kenneth Branagh, Emma Thompson, Michael Keaton, Ben Elton, Keanu Reeves, Denzel Washington, Imelda Staunton, Richard Briars, Kate Beckinsale, Robert Sean Leonard.

●If nothing quite matches the teeming, joyful, acrobatic opening high in the hills of Tuscany, there's much to commend in Branagh's pruned, international version of Shakespeare's troubling comedy. Washington is the well-meaning Duke to Reeves' splendidly imperious John the bastard, while Keaton and Elton are a suitably clueless Dogberry and Verges. Branagh and Thompson, as Beatrice and Benedick, seem on the whole happier with the romance than the comedy – but do a fair job with some of the best verbal jousting in the language. SGr

Muddy River (Doro no Kawa)

(1981, Jap, 105 min, b/w)
d Kohei Oguri. *p* Motoyasu Kimura. *sc* Takako Shigemori. *ph* Shohei Ando. *ed* Nobuo Ogawa. *ad* Akira Naito. *m* Kuroudo Mori. *cast* Nobutaka Asahara, Takahiro Tamura, Yumiko Fujita, Minoru Sakurai, Makiko Shibata, Mariko Kaga.

●The story of a necessarily short-lived friendship between children, set in a riverside suburb of Osaka in the mid-1950s, not yet witness to Japan's Economic Miracle. A war widow and her two kids moor their houseboat opposite a small restaurant, and the kids befriend Nobuo, the shy young son of the restaurateur. The woman surreptitiously carries out the only trade she can to support herself and her children. The film centres on Nobuo, the lower middle class boy, and observes (without undue sentimentality) his discoveries in rapid succession of class difference and sex. The movie is based on a novel, whence doubtless the metaphor that underpins the tale (the mud of experience), but Oguri's direction is not in the least literary: he trusts his sharp black-and-white images to dramatise the spaces between the characters, and gets performances of natural maturity from his young actors. Oguri's first feature, it's one from the heart. TR

Müde Tod, Der

see Destiny

Mudlark, The

(1950, GB, 97 min, b/w)
d Jean Negulesco. *p/sc* Nunnally Johnson. *ph* Georges Périnal. *ed* Thelma Myers. *ad* CP Norman. *m* William Alwyn. *cast* Alec Guinness, Irene Dunne, Andrew Ray, Anthony Steel, Finlay Currie, Beatrice Campbell, Wilfrid Hyde-White.

●This British-made Fox production wheels on a heavily made-up Irene Dunne as Queen Victoria and cuts in a lot of touristy footage in the service of a whimsical story about a young scamp who inveigles his way into Windsor Castle and gives the gloomy old monarch a good laugh in the process. Guinness is all fuss and business as Prime Minister Disraeli, pouncing on the incident to push his new Reform Bill through Parliament, but it's the boy, played by the 11-year-old son of comedian Ted Ray, who steals the movie.

Mueda – Memory and Massacre (Mueda – Memoria e Massacre)

(1980, Moz, 80 min, b/w & col)
d Ruy Guerra. *sc* Calisto Dos Lagos. *ph* Fernando Silva. *with* Filipe Gunoguacala, Romao Canapoquele, Baltasar Nchilem.

●Mueda was a massacre. The name is that of the village in Northern Mozambique where in 1960 it took place. The Portuguese colonial regime did the killing. In independent Mozambique, those inhabitants of Mueda who survived regularly re-enact the massacre *in situ*. They themselves play the roles of victims, assassins, and spectators. Ruy Guerra, now a Brazilian but born in Lourenço Marques (now Maputo, the capital of Mozambique), filmed this extraordinary creation of liberated popular culture, intercutting it with first-hand interviews on the massacre. The mix is compelling, and the grave yet joyous spectacle unique. SH

Muerte de un Burocrata

see Death of a Bureaucrat

Mugshot

(1996, US, 87 min)
d Matt Mahurin. *p* Sharon Oreck. *sc/ph/ed* Matt Mahurin. *m* Michael Montes. *cast* Robert Knepper, Michael Williams, Belinda Becker, Robert Walker, Willie Lassic, Maxine Joyner, Shevonne Tucker.

●Visually stylish it may be (like his two principal characters, writer/director Mahurin was a photographer), but this first feature is arty and pretentious as it explores the enigmatic relationship between an amnesiac white holed up in a derelict Harlem building, and the black guy ('Rumor') who offers to help in return for payment, but insists he stay put. As Rumor starts discovering aspects of his charge's life (including his black girlfriend), the film becomes increasingly stilted, symbolic and stultifying. New York is shot like some bleak sci-fi cityscape. GA

Muhammad Ali: The Greatest

(1975, Fr, 116 min, b/w & col)
d/ph William Klein. *ed* (US) Francine Grubert, Eva Zora, (Zaire) Isabelle Rathéry, Emmanuelle Le Ray. *m* (US) Mickey Baker, (Zaire) Umban, Le Wac. *with* Cassius Clay/Muhammad Ali, The Beatles, Sonny Liston, Angelo Dundee, Jack Nilon, Chris Dundee, Finlay Campbell, James X, Malcolm X, 'Jersey Joe' Walcott, James J Braddock, Floyd Patterson, Norman Mailer, Stepin Fetchit, Sam X, George Foreman, Don King, Mobutu Sese Seko, Joe Frazier, John Daly.

●This flawed but fascinating 1975 documentary adds yet another layer of insight and context to the world's greatest heavyweight champion. Focusing on the same events that top and tail Mann's *Ali*, it parallels the young Cassius Clay's shock 1964 triumphs over Sonny Liston, and the equally shocking Ali victory over George Foreman in Zaire in 1974. Klein's evocative b/w imagery and jumpy juxtapositions are sly and striking, giving revolutionary weight to our hero as Ali clowns, savages white supremacy and meets the Beatles, and everyone from drama students to Malcolm X has their say about the meaning of the phenomenon in their midst. Sadly, the film should have stopped right there. It suddenly jumps clumsily from '64 to '74, Maine to Kinshasa, b/w to colour, and moves through interminable tribal travelogue cut with some standard Ali media manipulation. In comparison to *When We Were Kings*, the footage is dull and undramatic, and Klein understandably struggles to shed light on Zaire with the same confidence and empathy he brings to American race relations. GMu

Mujer del puerto, La (Woman of the Port)

(1933, Mex, 76 min, b/w)
d Arcady Boytler, Raphael J Sevilla. *p* Servando C de la Garcia. *sc* Antonio Guzmán Aguilera, Raphael J Sevilla. *ph* Alex Phillips. *ed* José Marino *m* Manuel Esperón (songs), Max Urban. *lyrics* Ricardo López Méndez. *cast* Andrea Palma, Domingo Soler, Joaquin Busquets, Consuelo Segarra, Luisa Obregón, Elisa Soler, Arturo Manrique.

●Engagingly creaky Mexican melodrama, far from the glories of later work put together by the likes of Fernandez and Figueroa, but enjoyably excessive for all that. Palma – clearly, lookswise, a Latin riposte to Dietrich, but lacking her ironic cruelty – is the woman who turns to prostitution after dad dies and her fiancé flaunts his infidelity. Worse befalls her when, working a seedy sailors' bar in Vera Cruz, she falls for a kindly matelot who saves her from a drunkard. Then, too late, the truth dawns on them. The incestuous revelation is absurd icing on the spicy cake, rather than the stuff of tragedy, but Palma gives the closing moments all she's got and just about gets away with it. GA

Mujer más fea del mundo, La

see Ugliest Woman in the World, The

Mulan

(1998, US, 88 min)
d Barry Cook, Tony Bancroft. *p* Pam Coats. *sc* Rita Hsiao, Christopher Sanders, Philip Lazebnik, Raymond Singer, Eugenia Bostwick-Singer. *ed* Michael Kelly. *pd* Hans Bacher. *m* Jerry Goldsmith. *songs* Matthew Wilder, David Zippel. *cast* voices: Ming-Na Wen, Soon-Teck Oh, BD Wong, Eddie Murphy, Pat Morita, Miriam Margolyes.

●A feisty young go-getter rises above the male-dominated world in which she lives to survive the perils of war and, eventually, to bring honour to her family. The Huns have invaded China; hence the Emperor's call to arms demanding one male from every family. Mulan's father is too old and frail to fight, so Mulan shaves her head and, accompanied by a mythical dragon (a comic sidekick), takes her place in the Emperor's army, where she proceeds to inject inspiration into her fellow warriors. Using richly hued, angular animation, this vibrant, action-filled Disney offering is immensely entertaining. The script is mostly drum-tight and brimming with gags; there's even some amusing but sensitively illustrated play on the complexities of Oriental religious customs. If the songs are merely endurable, scenes like the amazing sight of the enemy charging down a mountain slope and Eddie Murphy's hilarious dragon help make this the cracker it is. DA

Mule Train

(1950, US, 60 min, b/w)
d John English. *p* Armand Shaefer. *sc* Gerald Geraghty. *ph* William Bradford. *ed* Richard Fantl. *ad* Charles Clague. *m* Mischa Bakaleinikoff. *cast* Gene Autry, Pat Buttram, Sheila Ryan, Robert Livingston, Frank Jaquet.

● When his pal's partner is killed in a dispute over mineral rights, Autry enters the fray by rigging up a wagon train to bring supplies to a dam under construction. The Museum of Modern Art, NY, chose this moderately pacy B-Western to represent Autry's homespun fare in their collection. TJ

Mulholland Dr.

(2001, US/Fr, 146 min)
d David Lynch. *p* Mary Sweeney, Alain Sarde, Neal Edelstein, Michael Polaire, Tony Krantz. *sc* David Lynch. *ph* Peter Deming. *ed* Mary Sweeney. *ad* Jack Fisk. *m* Angelo Badalamenti. *cast* Adam Kesher, Justin Theroux, Betty Elms, Naomi Watts, Rita Laura, Elena Harring, Coco Lenoix, Ann Miller, Robert Forster, Dan Hedaya.

● Originally intended for TV, *Mulholland Dr.* is much in the mould of *Twin Peaks* and *Lost Highway*, Lynch's characteristically bizarre *noir* focuses (probably too strong a word!) on a young beauty (Harring) who loses her memory after a car accident and hides out in a house where she's found and befriended by the absent owner's helpful niece (Watts), new to LA in the hope of becoming an actress. Meanwhile, a hot young film director (Theroux) is having trouble with the Mob trying to influence his choice of leading lady. Despite too many detours into nonsensical narrative cul-de-sacs, and too many shots that slowly travel towards corners down darkened corridors to the accompaniment of ominous rumbles, this works well enough as unsettlingly nightmarish suspense. That is, until it suddenly and stupidly decides to switch characters' identities, leaving one with a so-what feeling of déjà vu. GA

Mulholland Falls

(1995, US, 107 min)
d Lee Tamahori. *p* Richard D Zanuck, Lili Fini Zanuck. *sc* Pete Dexter. *ph* Haskell Wexler. *ed* Sally Menke. *pd* Richard Sylbert. *m* David Grusin. *cast* Nick Nolte, Melanie Griffith, Chazz Palminteri, Michael Madsen, Chris Penn, Andrew McCarthy, Treat Williams, John Malkovich, Ed Lauter, Daniel Baldwin, Bruce Dern.

● Meet the 'Hat Squad', a free-ranging unit of the LAPD comprising Detectives Hoover (Nolte), Coolidge (Palminteri), Hall (Madsen) and Relyea (Penn). It's the early '50s. A good-time gal is found embedded in six inches of sand, like a steamroller had a crush on her. Who knew her? Gay filmmaker Jimmy Fields (McCarthy), for starters; the chairman of the Atomic Energy Commission, General Timms (Malkovich), more intimately; and then there's the very married, very motivated detective Max Hoover. With cinematography by Haskell Wexler, production design by Richard Sylbert and a cast fleshed out with the likes of Treat Williams, Daniel Baldwin and Bruce Dern, this has the look down pat, but when it comes to substance, emotional complexity or narrative authority, forget it, Jake, this isn't Chinatown. Director Tamahori caught the eye with *Once Were Warriors*, but his first Hollywood feature falls flat with a hollow thud. It doesn't help that, after an intriguing opening, Pete Dexter's screenplay fails to construct a mystery which really connects, that too many supporting characters never come to life, and that Malkovich invests a pivotal role with his peculiar brand of terminal lethargy. TCh

Mullaway

(1988, Aust, 92 min)
d Don McLennan. *p* Howard Grigsby. *sc* Jon Stephens. *ph* Peter Friedrich. *ed* Peter Friedrich, Nick Lee. *pd* Paddy Reardon. *m* Michael Atkinson. *cast* Nadine Garner, Bill Hunter, Sue Jones, Craig Morrison, Brad Kilpatrick, Kymara Stowers.

● Mull, also confusingly known as Phoebe, has to leave school when her mother falls terminally ill, to look after her three siblings and her father who works nights. Her problems are just starting: she discovers her elder brother, who is trying to set up a rock band, shooting up; her younger sister is hair-wrenchingly precocious; and the younger brother, with a preference for the library rather than the beach like ordinary boys, has been inculcated into the ways of the Lord by their born-again father, who seems incapable of communicating with his children other than by reading them biblical quotes. Veering between the absorbing and the gauche, this is a gentle and at times poignant representation not only of teenagers and family life, but of someone young learning how to cope the hard way. JGl

Multiplicity

(1996, US, 117 min)
d Harold Ramis. *p* Trevor Albert, Harold Ramis. *sc* Chris Miller, Mary Hale, Lowell Ganz, Babaloo Mandel. *ph* Laszlo Kovacs. *ed* Pem Herring, Craig Herring, Marcelo Sansevieri. *pd* Jackson DeGovia. *m* George Fenton. *cast* Michael Keaton, Andie MacDowell, Harris Yulin, Richard Masur, Eugene Levy, Ann Cusack, John deLancie, Brian Doyle-Murray.

● Doug Kinney (Keaton) is running out of time. He's working all hours, barely sees the kids, and now wife Laura (MacDowell) wants to split domestic duties so she can return to her career. It seems too good to be true, then, when genetic scientist Dr Leeds (Yulin) offers to double Doug's capacity by making a clone, a facsimile identical in appearance and experience. Safely housed away above the garage, Doug 2 can handle business, while the original devotes himself to quality time with the family and the pursuit of happiness. Not quite a *Groundhog Day* replica, but a near-relative none the less, this is a mid-life crisis comedy about masculinity, mortality and the roads not taken. The development is funny and smart. Doug 2 has a mind of his own, and a libido, so he's soon dating his (their) secretary, eyeing the wife, and cloning himself for some additional home help. If Doug 2 embodies the original's repressed machismo, Doug 3 is his feminine side, swapping cooking tips with the bewildered, uncomprehending Laura. With the inevitable, infantile Doug 4 – a failed experiment, a third-generation copy – the movie comes close to genuinely anarchic subversion, even daring triple adultery in one night of passion. Unfortunately, in trying to rein in the material and impose some kind of closure, the film-makers plump for an inadequate, bourgeois sit-com mode and the movie evaporates before your eyes. Oh well, it was fun while it lasted, and hats off to Michael Keaton, Michael Keaton, Michael Keaton and – very funny in a supporting turn – Michael Keaton. TCh

Mummy, The

(1932, US, 72 min, b/w)
d Karl Freund. *p* Carl Laemmle Jr. *sc* John L Balderston. *ph* Charles Stumar. *ed* Milton Carruth. *ad* Willy Pogany. *m* Tchaikovsky. *cast* Boris Karloff, Zita Johann, David Manners, Edward Van Sloan, Arthur Byron, Noble Johnson, Leonard Mudie.

● Hardly a horror film in that it refuses to go for shock effects, this tale of Im-ho-tep, an ancient Egyptian priest brought back to life by an archaeologist, is a sombre and atmospheric depiction of eternal passion and occult reincarnation. The script throws up a heady mixture of evocative nonsense that bears little relation to the realities of Egyptian religion and history, but the whole thing is transformed by Karloff's restrained performance as the mummy who becomes, in his new life, an Egyptian archaeologist stalking Cairo in search of his beloved, a reincarnated princess; and by Freund's strong visual sense (he had previously been cameraman on Murnau's *The Last Laugh*, Lang's *Metropolis*, and the original *Dracula*). Not as great as Universal's earlier *Frankenstein*, but a fascinating instalment in the studio's series of classic fantasies. GA

Mummy, The

(1959, GB, 88 min)
d Terence Fisher. *p* Michael Carreras. *sc* Jimmy Sangster. *ph* Jack Asher. *ed* James Needs, Alfred Cox. *ad* Bernard Robinson. *m* Franz Reizenstein. *cast* Peter Cushing, Christopher Lee, Yvonne Furneaux, Eddie Byrne, Felix Aylmer, Raymond Huntley, George Pastell, John Stuart.

● One of the most fetching of Fisher's early Hammer movies, the third in the trilogy which comprises *The Curse of Frankenstein* and *Dracula*. Its qualities are almost entirely abstract and visual, with colour essential to its muted, subtle imagery. Christopher Lee looks tremendous in the title role, smashing his way through doorways and erupting from green, dream-like quagmires in really awe-isnpiring fashion. Yvonne Furneaux plays one of Fisher's most crucial heroines, Isobel Banning, who has let her hair down (literally) and become sensual in order to free her husband (Cushing) from the curse he invokes by opening an Egyptian tomb. DP

Mummy, The

(1999, US, 125 min)
d Stephen Sommers. *p* James Jacks, Sean Daniel. *sc* Stephen Sommers. *ph* Adrian Biddle. *ed* Rob Ducsay, Kelly Matsumoto. *pd* Allan Cameron. *m* Jerry Goldsmith. *cast* Brendan Fraser, Rachel Weisz, John Hannah, Arnold Vosloo, Kevin J O'Connor, Jonathan Hyde, Oded Fehr, Omid Djalili, Erick Avari, Aharon Ipalé, Carl Chase.

● A mix of *Raiders of the Lost Ark* and *Evil Dead II*, this is overlong and thematically meandering, and with mostly downmarket performances. Just as well, then, that writer/director Sommers chose to film it tongue-in-cheek. Egyptian high priest Imhotep (Vosloo) is caught in flagrante during a tryst with his lover, who then kills herself. Discovered trying to revive her in Hamunaptra, the forbidden City of the Dead, he's entombed alive, with obligatory curse and flesh-eating scarabs. In 1923, adventurer Rick O'Connell (Fraser), Egyptologist Evelyn (Weisz) and her wimpish brother (Hannah) take part in an international race to locate the lost city. Meanwhile, Imhotep's decomposing cadaver and curse are waiting to be unleashed. Though Fraser and Weisz look as if they've just stepped out of *Titanic*, the film aspires to *Raiders*: the settings, romantic interludes, the self-deprecating humour, the Cairo street chases, the creepy crawlies – they're all here. If you can swallow the hokum and ignore the plot implausibilities, you should find much to enjoy (the sfx are state of the art). But Spielberg it ain't. By the way, the Mummy's voice and soul shrieks were rattled off by Blixa Bargeld, from Einstürzende Neubauten and Nick Cave's Bad Seeds. DA

Mummy Returns, The

(2001, US, 129 min)
d Stephen Sommers. *p* James Jacks, Sean Daniel. *sc* Stephen Sommers. *ph* Adrian Biddle. *ed* Bob Ducsay. *pd* Allan Cameron. *m* Alan Silvestri. *cast* Brendan Fraser, Rachel Weisz, John Hannah, Arnold Vosloo, Oded Fehr, Patricia Velasquez, The Rock, Freddie Boath.

● It's archaelogical business as usual for Rick O'Connell (Fraser) and Egyptologist Evelyn (Weisz), who are now happily married with a gifted sand-building youngster called Alex (Boath). It's Alex who stirs it up this time round by inadvertently slipping on a gold bracelet his parents recovered on one of their numerous adventures. Big mistake. This very bracelet is the key to unleashing a chain of events that will obliterate the world. After being banished to the sands of time, the Scorpion King (The Rock) and his enormous army of dog soldiers are about to return. Meanwhile, the original mummy, Imhotep (Vosloo), has been re-resurrected and he wants control of the Scorpion's army. Where the original successfully integrated several different genres – lightweight horror, tongue-in-cheek kitsch, *Raiders*-style high adventure – the sequel goes overboard to please its target pre-teen audience with an indigestible plot that unfolds like a computer game. Still, it looks good and the battle sequences are well staged, even if the screenwriters have lost their sense of fun. DA

Mummy's Hand, The

(1940, US, 68 min, b/w)
d Christy Cabanne. *p* Ben Pivar. *sc* Griffin Jay, Maxwell Shane. *ph* Woody Bredell. *ed* Philip Cahn. *ad* Jack Otterson. *m* Hans J Salter. *cast* Dick Foran, Peggy Moran, Wallace Ford, George Zucco, Eduardo Ciannelli, Cecil Kellaway, Tom Tyler, Charles Trowbridge, Sig Arno.

● First of four '40s revivals for Universal's dreariest monster, who could do little but lurch around swathed in bandages, arms outstretched for another bout of mayhem. Western star Tom Tyler, dragging one useless leg behind him, at least brought a certain baleful menace to the role, whereas Lon Chaney Jr, taking over for *The*

Mummy's Tomb (1942), *The Mummy's Ghost* (1944) and *The Mummy's Curse* (1944), merely looked incongruously overweight. The sense of déjà vu is not helped by the cost-cutting habit of incorporating the famous flashback sequence from Freund's 1932 film explaining the historical circumstances of the mummy's fate (*The Mummy's Tomb* also includes a flashback to its predecessor, plus stock footage of torch-brandishing villagers from *Frankenstein*!). *The Mummy's Hand* and *The Mummy's Ghost* are the best in an uninspiring quartet. TM

Mummy's Shroud, The

(1966, GB, 84 min)
d John Gilling. *p* Anthony Nelson Keys. *sc* John Gilling. *ph* Arthur Grant. *ed* James Needs, Chris Barnes. *pd* Bernard Robinson. *m* Don Banks. *cast* Andre Morell, John Phillips, David Buck, Elizabeth Sellars, Maggie Kimberley, Michael Ripper, Richard Warner, Catherine Lacey, Dickie Owen.

● Writer/director Gilling collaborated on some of Hammer's most imaginative pictures (*The Plague of the Zombies* and *The Gorgon* among them), but this old bag of tricks does neither him nor the studio justice. In 1920 Stanley Preston, the usual swaggering imperialist (Phillips), orders the desecration of an Egyptian tomb and unleashes ancient evil. Vengeance comes in the shape of Prem (Owen), slave to a mummified pharaoh, occupant of the tomb. First to die is Sir Basil Walden (Morell), the honourable archaelogist committed to a lunatic asylum by Preston. Catherine Lacey performs entertainingly as a soothsayer. GM

Münchhausen

see Adventures of Baron Munchhausen, The

Mundo Grúa

see Crane World

Muppet Christmas Carol, The

(1992, US, 86 min)
d Brian Henson. *p* Brian Henson, Martin G Baker. *sc* Jerry Juhl. *ph* John Fenner. *ed* Micahel Jablow. *pd* Val Strazovec. *m* Miles Goodman. *cast* The Muppets, Michael Caine, Steven MacKintosh, Meredith Braun, Robin Weaver, Donald Austen.

● Acted to the parsimonious hilt by the human Scrooge (Caine), and framed by author-narrator Charles Dickens (the Great Gonzo) addressing his rodent audience (Rizzo the Rat), the story survives. Well, it would: it's the same story of redemption that powers Stallone movies. All the pen-pushing glovesters in Scrooge's office run on fear of dismissal, a topical note, with Bob Cratchit (Kermit the Frog) negotiating but nervous. Not so his wife Miss Piggy, ready to have a go at Scrooge, but mindful of the needs of their family, a brood as mixed as you would expect from pigs and frogs, which explains the medical condition of Tiny Tim, a froglet with a cough on crutches. The three ghosts of Christmas are wonderful. Elsewhere, Fozzie Bear bears a resemblance to Francis L Sullivan in the David Lean Dickens adaptations, and there's a shop called Micklewhite. As an actor, Kermit can corrugate his forehead vertically. Good fun. BC

Muppet Movie, The

(1979, GB, 97 min)
d James Frawley. *p* Jim Henson. *sc* Jerry Juhl, Jack Burns. *ph* Isidore Mankofsky. *ed* Chris Greenbury. *pd* Joel Schiller. *m* Paul Williams, Kenny Ascher. *cast* Charles Durning, Austin Pendleton, Milton Berle, Mel Brooks, James Coburn, Dom DeLuise, Elliott Gould, Bob Hope, Madeline Kahn, Carol Kane, Cloris Leachman, Steve Martin, Richard Pryor, Telly Savalas, Orson Welles, Paul Williams.

● First of the big-screen spin-offs, this unwisely ignores the successful formula of the TV shows. The Muppets travel to Hollywood and stardom; aimless aerial and American location footage replace the tight studio format; and Kermit is no longer a stand-up comic but a star in the making. Numerous guest stars make brief appearances instead of contributing to whole sketches built around their willingness to be lampooned by a bunch of puppets. Slapstick chases and weak movie references look tired, while the attitude towards Miss Piggy and Camilla the Chicken is, well, less than progressive. Somewhere the film loses sight of its origins and its audience (mainly children, one presumes); Mel Brooks' sinister, crazed Jewish Nazi surgeon looks particularly out of place. Even adults will have difficulty following the murky soundtrack. CPe

Muppets from Space

(1999, GB/US, 87 min)
d Tim Hill. *p* Brian Henson, Martin G Baker. *sc* Jerry Juhl, Joseph Mazzarino, Ken Kaufman. *ph* Alan Caso. *ed* Michael A Stevenson, Richard Pearson. *pd* Stephen Marsh. *m* Jamshied Sharifi. *cast* Jeffrey Tambor, F Murray Abraham, Rob Schneider, Josh Charles, Ray Liotta, David Arquette, Andie MacDowell, Kathy Griffin, Pat Hingle, Hollywood Hogan [Hulk Hogan].

● If you've ever wondered what sort of creature The Great Gonzo might be, the title of this latest Muppets frolic provides a much needed answer. Here, Gonzo himself learns he is not of this earth, and announces the same on Miss Piggy's cable TV show, 'UFO Mania', immediately attracting attention from government scientists investigating extra-terrestrial activity. But even as Gonzo's interplanetary brethren are zapping back down for a reunion, he's taken captive for experimental purposes by agent K Edgar Singer (Tambor). It's time for the rest of the Muppet family to spring him free, albeit at the risk of saying bye-bye to Gonzo forever. After some distinctive Muppet adaptations, the Henson company here suffer the perils of moving back to original material. Frankly, this half-hearted affair doesn't really make it. Not enough Kermit is one problem, dull songs and lacklustre humour also dampen the spirits. TJ

Muppets Take Manhattan, The

(1984, US, 94 min)
d Frank Oz. *p* David Lazer. *sc* Frank Oz, Tom Patchett, Jay Tarses. *ph* Bob Paynter. *ed* Evan Lottman. *pd* Stephen Hendrickson. *m* Jeff Moss, Ralph Burns. *cast* Art Carney, James Coco, Dabney Coleman, Gregory Hines, Linda Lavin, Joan Rivers, Elliott Gould, Liza Minnelli, Brooke Shields.

● After setting Hollywood alight, the Muppets take on another enduring rags to riches American myth: let's do a Broadway show. Only this time it's Frogway, and the musical, written and starring our own Kermit (natch), is only lacking one till-busting ingredient: there aren't enough frogs. During the 94 minutes of this delightful movie, the Muppets graduate from college, hit New York, are parted and reunited minutes before curtain-up, with Kermit saved from amnesia by a right hook from Miss Piggy. SGr

Muppet Treasure Island

(1996, US, 100 min)
d Brian Henson. *p* Martin G Baker, Brian Henson. *sc* Jerry Juhl, Kirk Thatcher, James V Hart. *ph* John Fenner. *ed* Michael Jablow. *pd* Val Strazovec. *m* Hans Zimmer, Harry Gregson-Williams. *cast* Tim Curry, Jennifer Saunders, Kevin Bishop, Billy Connolly, The Muppets.

● After the delightful *Muppet Christmas Carol*, this fourth Kermit and pals star vehicle comes as a slight disappointment, but it's a treat all the same. The format's unchanged. The pre-puppet warm-up, with black-toothed Saunders, slovenly 'kerchiefed Connolly and the rest of the sea dogs, is all slopped ale, menacing curses and roisterous yo-ho-ho, served up just short of Python-esque pastiche. The heart only leaps with the dockside arrival of Kermit's Capt Smollett and his kaleidoscopic crew of woolly friends as the movie sets sail for the usual ahistoric musical extravaganza. There's bad news. Kermit's role is upsettingly minor and underwritten. Worse, Miss Piggie's superstar status is becoming a crashing bore: her South Sea queen of the warthogs (Benjamina Gunn) favours ostentation over dignity. Yet Barry Mann and Cynthia Weil's musical numbers have more than enough goofy lyrics to cheer the cockles. Bishop comes off well, too, with his contemporary Jim Hawkins, sensible, winsome but thankfully not cute. The new star, and about time, is Rizzo the Rat. He's not as bright, witty or charismatic as Kermit, but what courage, what staying power! WH

Mur, Le

see Wall, The

Murder

(1930, GB, 108 min, b/w)
d Alfred Hitchcock. *p* John Maxwell. *sc* Alma Reville, Alfred Hitchcock, Walter C Mycroft. *ph* Jack Cox. *ed* Emile De Ruelle, Rene Harrison. *ad* John Mead. *cast* Herbert Marshall, Nora Baring, Phyllis Konstam, Edward Chapman, Miles Mander, Esmé Percy, Donald Calthrop.

● Perhaps the most provocative of all early British Hitchcocks, a whodunit (adapted from the novel and play by Clemence Dane) that transcends the limitations of its mystery plot by focusing on theatrical mediations of reality (courtesy of *Hamlet*). A girl silently accepts her prosecution for murder; the lone juror who believes in her innocence starts an investigation of his own; and winds up confronting the first negative gay stereotype in popular cinema. TR

MURDER and Murder

(1996, US, 113 min, b/w & col)
d/p/sc Yvonne Rainer. *ph* Stephen Kazmierski. *ed* Yvonne Rainer. *pd* Stephen McCabe. *m* Frank London. *cast* Joanna Merlin, Kathleen Chalfant, Catherine Kellner, Isa Thomas, Jennie Moreau, Rod McLachan.

● Doris, 63 and a grandmother, has recently fallen in love for the first time with a woman, Mildred, a life-long lesbian and well-to-do professor. Rainer's film examines the women's relationship in characteristically wide-ranging and often playful terms: it's about identity, memory, communication breakdown, role-playing, power-struggles, stereotypes, and performance. It's also not nearly as funny as it would like to be – much of the 'slapstick' is painfully tedious – and some of the vaguely experimental formal conceits seem a little pointless or dated. GA

Murder at 1600

(1997, US, 107 min)
d Dwight Little. *p* Arnold Kopelson, Arnon Milchan. *sc* Wayne Beach, David Hodgin. *ph* Steven Bernstein. *ed* Billy Weber, Leslie Jones. *pd* Nelson Coates. *m* Christopher Young. *cast* Wesley Snipes, Diane Lane, Alan Alda, Daniel Benzali, Ronny Cox, Dennis Miller, Diane Baker, Tate Donovan, Harris Yulin.

● That's 1600 Pennsylvania Avenue. A woman's found murdered at the White House and detective Snipes (average) is soon at loggerheads with secret service chief Benzali over jurisdictional privilege. Circumstantial evidence points to a cleaner, but Snipes knows a fall guy when he sees one, and special agent Lane reluctantly concurs. The script has President Cox trying to tough out a hostage crisis in North Korea without recourse to the military, while Snipes is understandably more concerned with the local bureaucracy about to flatten his house. Passable, but punches are pulled, and all suspense jettisoned some 20 minutes from home. TCh

Murder at the Vanities

(1934, US, 87 min, b/w)
d Mitchell Leisen. *p* E Lloyd Sheldon. *sc* Carey Wilson, Joseph Gollomb, Sam Hellman. *ph* Leo Tover. *ed* William Shea. *songs* Arthur Johnston, Sam Coslow. *cast* Carl Brisson, Victor McLaglen, Jack Oakie, Kitty Carlisle, Dorothy Stickney, Gertrude Michael, Jessie Ralph, Gail Patrick, Donald Meek, Duke Ellington and His Orchestra.

● Delightfully offbeat mixture of whodunit and musical, with McLaglen's cop called to the theatre to investigate the attempted murder of a singer during a run of Earl Carroll's 'Vanities' revue, then lingering to find the killer when a murder occurs. The mystery is merely conventional, but it's alternated with superbly staged musical sequences, spectacular but respecting the proscenium's limits and notable for their cheekily bizarre nature (scantily clad girls in suggestive routines, with the murder discovered when blood drips on to a posing chorine's bare shoulder during a rendition of 'Sweet Marijuana'). Duke Ellington makes a welcome appearance, and Leisen handles the whole thing with witty, typically lavish style. GA

Murder by Confession

see Absolution

Murder by Contract

(1958, US, 80 min, b/w)
d Irving Lerner. *p* Leon Chooluck. *sc* Ben Simcoe. *ph* Lucien Ballard. *ed* Carol Lodato. *ad* Jack Poplin. *m* Perry Botkin. *cast* Vince Edwards, Phillip Pine, Herschel Bernardi, Caprice Toriel, Michael Granger, Cathy Browne. Frances Osborne.
● A terrific, no-nonsense B movie which comes on like something by Jean-Pierre Melville: cool, calm and dispassionate. Edwards is Claude, a technician who goes into crime as a career move, to 'improve himself'. A series of hits later, he looks every inch the professional assassin, confident enough to take his time, competent enough not to fear detection. It isn't *entirely* his fault if something goes wrong on the big contract... Lerner and his superb cameraman, Lucien Ballard, make the most of a shoestring budget to produce a taut, spare, amoral film; it doesn't look restricted, it looks restrained. Well ahead of its time, too. TCh

Murder by Death

(1976, US, 95 min)
d Robert Moore. *p* Ray Stark. *sc* Neil Simon. *ph* David M Walsh. *ed* Margaret Booth, John F Burnett, Michael A Stevenson. *pd* Stephen Grimes. *m* David Grusin. *cast* Eileen Brennan, Truman Capote, James Coco, Peter Falk, Alec Guinness, Elsa Lanchester, David Niven, Peter Sellers, Maggie Smith, Nancy Walker, Estelle Winwood, James Cromwell.
● Essentially a filmed play (the world's most famous fictional sleuths summoned for a weekend by Capote's eccentric electronics wizard and invited to solve a murder due to happen at midnight), *Murder by Death* is entertaining enough, even though the joke wears a little thin. As plot loses importance and parody reigns supreme, Falk and Maggie Smith get the best lines. However, unlike *Murder on the Orient Express* – so stylised as to be virtually a parody – here director Moore and writer Neil Simon seem to have no real affection for either the characters they plunder mercilessly for laughs, or the locked room puzzle they turn on its head. Introductions over, the film slides downhill. PH

Murder by Decree

(1978, Can/GB, 112 min)
d Bob Clark. *p* René Dupont, Bob Clark. *sc* John Hopkins. *ph* Reginald Morris. *ed* Stan Cole. *pd* Harry Pottle. *m* Carl Zittrer, Paul Zaza. *cast* Christopher Plummer, James Mason, David Hemmings, Susan Clark, Anthony Quayle, John Gielgud, Frank Finlay, Donald Sutherland, Genevieve Bujold.
● Not entirely successful, but still an imaginative and ambitious attempt to combine historical speculation, conspiracy thriller, and the world of Conan Doyle. Treading much the same territory as Stephen Knight's book *The Final Solution*, it sees Sherlock Holmes and Dr Watson investigating the Jack the Ripper murders, and coming up with an answer that involves royalty, Parliament and the Masons. For a full account of the theory – largely convincing – read Knight's book; but this will give you an idea of what may have prompted the murder of five prostitutes in Victorian London. The different threads are neatly interwoven, suspense and explanation being carefully balanced, and the horror of the crimes evoked in suitably nightmarish images. The only drawbacks, in fact, lie in Sutherland's appearance as a loony visionary, and in Plummer's occasional adoption of ludicrous disguises. GA

Murderer Lives at Number 21, The

see Assassin Habite au 21, L'

Murder, He Says

(1945, US, 94 min, b/w)
d George Marshall. *p* ED Leshin. *sc* Lou Breslow. *ph* Theodor Sparkhul. *ed* LeRoy Stone. *ad* Hans Dreier, William Flannery. *m* Robert Emmett Dolan. *cast* Fred MacMurray, Helen Walker, Marjorie Main, Jean Heather, Porter Hall, Peter Whitney, Mabel Paige.
● A black farce with MacMurray as a public opinion pollster trapped in the backwoods home of a crazed hillbilly family while looking for a colleague who has disappeared. The family is alarming enough, with whip-cracking Ma (Main), half-witted twin giants with a gleeful taste for torture (Whitney), and murderous shenanigans which make *Cold Comfort Farm* look like child's play; but there's also a ferocious pistol-packin' mama newly busted out of jail (Walker), only she turns out to be a nice girl looking for the loot everyone is fussing about so that she can clear her innocent dad. Not always as subtle as it might be, but beautifully acted (MacMurray especially), nicely timed by Marshall, and really very funny. TM

Murder, Inc.

see Enforcer, The

Murder in the First

(1994, US, 122 min)
d Marc Rocco. *p* Mark Frydman, Mark Wolper. *sc* Dan Gordon. *ph* Fred Murphy. *ed* Russell Livingstone. *pd* Kirk M Petruccelli. *m* Christopher Young. *cast* Christian Slater, Kevin Bacon, Gary Oldman, Embeth Davidtz, Bill Macy, Stephen Tobolowsky, Brad Dourif, R Lee Ermey, Kyra Sedgwick, Ben Slack.
● In Alcatraz on a minor charge, gentle, granite-willed Henri Young (Bacon) ends in hellish solitary confinement for three punishing years that all but break his body yet leave him thirsting for revenge on the duplicitous inmate who put him away. Soon, there's a murder in the mess hall, and Young looks to be going down again for an even longer stretch. Yet when tyro lawyer Stamphill discovers the truth of his client's previous treatment, he decides to plead on the killer's behalf, thus shaking the prison service to the core. Bacon's extraordinary physical commitment powers this heartfelt, occasionally bombastic portrait of institutionalised injustice, compellingly adapted by Dan Gordon from a true story. A hyperactive camera and Chris Young's thunderous score lay on the emphasis. Slater's good as the lawyer and Oldman chilling as the razor-cropped associate warden, but it's Bacon's picture – and if he doesn't win an Oscar, there ain't no justice in the world. TJ

Murder in Thornton Square, The

see Gaslight

Murder Is a Murder...Is a Murder, A (Un Meurtre est un Meurtre)

(1972, Fr/It, 103 min)
d Etienne Périer. *p* André Guillet. *sc* Dominique Fabre, Etienne Périer. *ph* Marcel Grignon. *ed* Renée Lichtig. *m* Paul Misraki. *cast* Jean-Claude Brialy, Stéphane Audran, Robert Hossein, Michel Serrault, Catherine Spaak, Claude Chabrol, Madeleine Damien.
● In a seemingly undistinguished career, Périer at last came up with a fascinating thriller, a pure Hitchcock-Chabrol pastiche. The theme is essentially a reworking of *Strangers on a Train*, concerned with guilt rather than murder: guilt over the accidental death of the insufferable wife (Audran) of Paul Kastner (Brialy) which could so easily have been murder, and which a stranger (Hossein) subsequently claims his reward for arranging. Périer appears totally at ease with the Chabrol-like nuances: a sinister sister-in-law (also Audran) like a reincarnation from Poe's 'Ligeia', but who in reality is just nutty; or the carefully planned alibi that degenerates into pure farce when the railway commissionaire (Chabrol) breaks his glasses. Added to which he has set the protagonists in a sea of familiar Hollywood paraphernalia – rambling houses, wheelchair lifts, living-room chests – enhancing the gleefulness without destroying the menacing atmosphere. GSa

Murder My Sweet

see Farewell, My Lovely

Murder on Monday

see Home at Seven

Murder on the Orient Express

(1974, GB, 131 min)
d Sidney Lumet. *p* John Brabourne, Richard Goodwin. *sc* Paul Dehn. *ph* Geoffrey Unsworth. *ed* Anne V Coates. *pd* Tony Walton. *m* Richard Rodney Bennett. *cast* Albert Finney, Lauren Bacall, Martin Balsam, Ingrid Bergman, Jacqueline Bisset, Jean-Pierre Cassel, Sean Connery, John Gielgud, Wendy Hiller, Anthony Perkins, Vanessa Redgrave, Rachel Roberts, Richard Widmark, Michael York.
● The formula can't fail: a first class journey on the '30s Orient Express, meticulous detail, a murder with all suspects aboard. In fact, the most suspect thing is the comfortable complacency of it all, threatened only by the flashback beginning, a Lindbergh-type kidnapping recalled with dream-like intensity, and Richard Widmark's haunted performance. The script copes with the silliness of Agatha Christie's plot (whodunit is disappointingly obvious), and works best as an essay on the use of the English language by foreigners: the train's full of them, and their quirky phrases help provide the solution to the mystery. Lumet ensures a smooth ride, but as usual takes too long to say what he means and brings the Express in 20 minutes late. CPe

Murders in the Rue Morgue

(1932, US, 75 min, b/w)
d Robert Florey. *p* Carl Laemmle Jr. *sc* Tom Reed, Dale Van Every, Robert Florey, John Huston. *ph* Karl Freund. *ed* Maurice Pivar, Milton Carruth. *ad* Charles D Hall. *cast* Bela Lugosi, Sidney Fox, Leon Ames, Bert Roach, Arlene Francis, Noble Johnson, Brandon Hurst, Herman Bing.
● Very loosely based on a tale by Poe, this is a pedestrian but still highly enjoyable account of a mad scientist (Lugosi) scouring Paris for young female victims to prove his rather unusual theory of evolution: experiments involve mixing the blood of the women with that of a gorilla. The perverse and sordid sexual implications of the story are rarely made explicit, although there are a couple of genuinely unpleasant scenes. Stylistically (it's beautifully shot by Karl Freund) the whole thing owes more to *The Cabinet of Dr Caligari* than to Poe. GA

Murders in the Rue Morgue

(1971, US, 87 min)
d Gordon Hessler. *p* Louis M Heyward. *sc* Christopher Wicking, Henry Slesar. *ph* Manuel Berenguer. *ed* Max Benedict. *pd* José Luis Galicia. *m* Waldo de los Rios. *cast* Jason Robards, Herbert Lom, Christine Kaufman, Adolfo Celi, Lilli Palmer, Maria Perschy, Michael Dunn, José Calvo, Peter Arne.
● Chris Wicking's script takes the basic premise of a Grand Guignol theatre in Paris which is running an adaptation of Poe's story, and whose leading actress (Kaufman) is afflicted by weird nightmares involving elements of the play. The action slips back and forth bewilderingly from the play she is in to her dreams and then to her waking experience. It's a bold and complex structure for a horror film, and at times the thematic depth of the story doesn't hold up dramatically. But there's enough fascination and style in the dream sequences alone to hold the attention, and the action builds to a pleasingly obsessional – and genuinely Poe-like – climax, with the heroine completely isolated from reality. DP

Murders in the Zoo

(1933, US, 64 min, b/w)
d A Edward Sutherland. *sc* Philip Wylie, Seton I Miller. *ph* Ernest Haller. *cast* Lionel Atwill, Charlie Ruggles, Randolph Scott, Gail Patrick, Kathleen Burke, John Lodge.
● In a splendidly fiendish opening sequence, Atwill's millionaire sportsman disposes of a rival for his wife's affections by leaving him to die in the Indochinese jungle, having first carefully stitched up his lips. 'What did he say?' asks the anxious wife (Burke), told that her lover went on alone. 'He didn't say anything,' Atwill blandly replies. Back in America, Atwill carries on the good work, using the zoo to which he supplies animals as a convenient disposal ground: another rival succumbs to green mamba poison, and the suspicious Burke ends up in the alligator pit. Instead of exploring its Sadian motifs (the erotic charge Atwill gets from 'protecting' his wife, for instance), the script unfortunately opts for comedy relief (capably handled by Ruggles) and a slightly tiresome detection motif (Scott as a toxicologist who discovers that the mamba wasn't the culprit). Fine, macabre fun for all that, beautifully shot by Ernest Haller, and very capably directed (although a little more extravagance would have helped the finale: Atwill setting the big cats free to cover his escape, but ending in a boa constrictor's coils). TM

Muriel (Muriel, ou le Temps d'un Retour)

(1963, Fr/It, 116 min)
d Alain Resnais. *p* Anatole Dauman. *sc* Jean Cayrol. *ph* Sacha Vierny. *ed* Kénout Peltier, Eric Pluet. *ad* Jacques Saulinier. *m* Hans Werner Henze. *cast* Delphine Seyrig, Jean-Pierre Kérien, Nita Klein, Jean-Baptiste Thierrée, Claude Sainval, Jean Champion, Laurence Badie, Jean Dasté.
●Not the easiest of Resnais films, but certainly his wittiest exploration of the vagaries of memory (teasingly set in Boulogne, a city largely lost under post-war urban developments). A spellbinding mosaic of images preserving, destroying, falsifying or testifying to the past, it sets two attitudes in opposition. A woman (Seyrig) attempts to ward off present tedium by conjuring the memory of her first love. Her stepson (Thierrée), treasuring some film of an atrocity he witnessed in Algeria in which a girl called Muriel was tortured to death, is determined to allow no escape from actuality. What both forget is that things change, that memory must feed on reality and vice versa. If her remembered love proves disappointingly remote from actuality, so his celluloid actuality turns out to need memory to bring it alive again. Impasse. TM

Muriel's Wedding

(1994, Aust, 106 min)
d PJ Hogan. *p* Lynda House, Jocelyn Moorhouse. *sc* PJ Hogan. *ph* Martin McGrath. *ed* Jill Bilcock. *pd* Patrick Reardon. *m* Peter Best. *cast* Toni Collette, Bill Hunter, Rachel Griffiths, Jeanie Drynan, Gennie Nevinson, Matt Day, Belinda Jarrett, Chris Haywood.
●Rather too obviously aimed at the *Strictly Ballroom* feel-good market, this is nevertheless an engaging, funny and sometimes surprisingly tough romantic comedy about one Muriel Hislop, an unsophisticated plain Jane (Collette), who'll do anything – including lie – to leave her dull hometown of Porpoise Spit in pursuit of dreams fuelled by ABBA songs. It could do with a little more irony, not to say originality, but the perkiness of the script, production design and performances (notably Griffiths as Muriel's pal) carry it through with flying, gaudy colours. GA

Murmur of the Heart

see Souffle au Coeur, Le

Murmur of Youth (Meili zai Chang-ge)

(1997, Tai, 105 min)
d Lin Cheng-Sheng. *p* Hsu Li-Kong, Chiu Shun-Ching. *sc* Ko Shu-Ching, Lin Cheng-Sheng. *ph* Tsai Cheng-Hui. *ed* Chen Hsiao-Tong, Chen Li-Yu. *pd* Kuo Chuan-Chiu. *m* Chang Hong-Yee, Bobby Chen. *cast* Renée Liu, Tseng Tsing, Tsai Chin-Hsin, Lin Hsui.
●Two girls, coincidentally both named Meili, work side-by-side in a movie theatre box office and have a brief romantic fling – which means more to one of them than the other. Director/co-writer Lin Cheng-Sheng (*A Drifting Life*) takes his time getting them to this point; he spends more than an hour contrasting their home lives (one is from a middle-class family and gets no emotional support from her parents, the other is from an impoverished working-class family with a senile grandmother who was once a prostitute), turning the film into a meditation on changing values and morals in the ever-more-urbanised 1990s. Cool, calm and very assured. TR

Murphy's Law

(1986, US, 100 min)
d J Lee Thompson. *p* Pancho Kohner. *sc* Gail Morgan Hickman. *ph* Alex Phillips. *ed* Peter Lee-Thompson, Charles Simmons. *pd* William Cruise. *m* Marc Donahue, Valentine McCallum. *cast* Charles Bronson, Kathleen Wilhoite, Carrie Snodgress, Robert F Lyons, Richard Romanus, Angel Tompkins, Janet MacLachlan, Lawrence Tierney.
●Murphy's Law, if you recall, states that if anything can go wrong it will. For Bronson's Murphy, however, far more goes right than wrong. When reminded of that law, in fact, he snarls back his own variation: Don't fuck with Jack Murphy. It's a warning to be well heeded. Murphy's a tough LA cop, victim of a frame-up. So he goes on the run from his own colleagues, accompanied by a wily, recalcitrant gamine (Wilhoite) who happens to be handcuffed to his wrist, and who hot-wires cars and spews out more foul phrases than you may ever have heard at one time. Might and right ultimately prevail, of course, but not before nigh on a dozen reasonably inventive killings, the bulk of them utterly gratuitous. JCoh

Murphy's Romance

(1985, US, 108 min)
d Martin Ritt. *p* Laura Ziskin. *sc* Harriet Frank Jr, Irving Ravetch. *ph* William A Fraker. *ed* Sidney Levin. *pd* Joel Schiller. *m* Carole King. *cast* Sally Field, James Garner, Brian Kerwin, Corey Haim, Dennis Burkley, Georgann Johnson, Dortha Duckworth.
●The bridge drives and soda fountains of picturesque small-town Arizona offer interminable pretexts for meetings cute and heartwarming romance between Field's divorced mum and Garner's corner-store pharmacist who dispenses homespun advice along with his prescriptions. From the same writer/director/star team responsible for *Norma Rae*, this cornball comedy comes on more as a depressing barometer of contemporary Hollywood. Boo to Field's ex-husband (Kerwin), a no-good boyo who roars into town on an Easy Rider bike, strums '60s folk songs, enjoys *Friday the 13th*. Hooray for Murphy (Garner) with his purse-lipped work ethic, blue grass fiddle, and solid old jalopy (adorned with no-nukes stickers as a token nod to liberalism). Field ploughs her now over-familiar furrow of plucky independence, and it's only the abrasive charm of Garner and Kerwin that redeems the film from terminal whimsy. SJo

Murphy's War

(1971, GB, 106 min)
d Peter Yates. *p* Michael Deeley. *sc* Stirling Silliphant. *ph* Douglas Slocombe. *ed* Frank P Keller, John Glen. *pd* Disley Jones. *m* John Barry, Ken Thorne. *cast* Peter O'Toole, Siân Phillips, Philippe Noiret, Horst Janson, John Hallam, Ingo Mogendorf.
●Sole survivor of a British merchant vessel, sunk by torpedoes off the coast of Venezuela during the last days of World War II, conducts a one-man war against the U-boat responsible, all the way to a kamikaze end. But the potential of the storyline breaks down into a series of cliché scenes, characters and relationships, and neither Yates nor his lead actor Peter O'Toole has the inspiration to boost the level higher than mere competence. TR

Musashi Miyamoto

see Miyamoto Musashi

Muse, The

(1999, US, 96 min)
d Albert Brooks. *p* Herb Nanas. *sc* Albert Brooks, Monica Johnson. *ph* Thomas Ackerman. *ed* Peter Teschner. *pd* Dina Lipton. *m* Elton John. *cast* Albert Brooks, Sharon Stone, Andie MacDowell, Jeff Bridges, Mark Feuerstein, Steven Wright, Bradley Whitford, Cybill Shepherd.
●Like *Bowfinger*, this finds its writer/director-star (Brooks) searching his home turf for inspiration: he's a Hollywood writer stumped by a system that presents him with a humanitarian award of an evening, and the chop next morning; he's 'lost his edge' overnight. Counsel with a friend (Bridges) reveals a potential panacea in the form of Sarah (Stone), daughter of Zeus, and verily a Muse, freelancing in Tinseltown. Excitement gets the better of his frugal instincts and, after initial misunderstandings between writer, wife (MacDowell) and new girl, they get down to work. Hollywood-on-Hollywood satires might be two a nickel these days, but it's hard to think of anyone who'd slip in the knife so inconspicuously as Brooks. His comedy is gentle, occasionally sentimental, but never self-indulgent, and comes with a kick: what's madder than an entire industry built on the caprices of creative inspiration? The main joke, played wonderfully deadpan, extends to cameos from the likes of Cameron, Reiner and Scorsese, but it's the easy precision of Brooks' writing and timing is the real charm. His surreal conversation with an Italian waiter at Spago is the funniest thing I've seen all year. NB

Musicals Great Musicals: The Arthur Freed Unit at MGM

(1996, US, 85 min)
d David Thompson. *p* Margaret Smilow. *sc* David Thompson. *ph* Bill Megalos. *ed* Kate Hirson.*with* Leslie Caron, Cyd Charisse, Betty Comden, Stanley Donen, Adolph Green, Michael Kidd, Ann Miller, Andre Previn, Mickey Rooney.
●This lucid, lively and informative account of the lyricist-turned-producer who transformed the movie musical (from revue fare with contemporary hits and tap-dancing chorines, to lavish stories in which songs and dance furthered plot and characterisation) features terrific clips from all his hits and a raft of revealing interviews. Rare highlights include footage from the abandoned version of *Annie Get Your Gun* starring a less than capable Garland, and of the Broadway version of *On the Town*, with songs cut from the film. Best clip: the amazingly erotic blues section of the *American in Paris* ballet. GA

Music Box

(1989, US, 126 min)
d Costa-Gavras. *p* Irwin Winkler. *sc* Joe Eszterhas. *ph* Patrick Blossier. *ed* Joele Van Effenterre. *pd* Jeannine Claudia Oppewall. *m* Philippe Sarde. *cast* Jessica Lange, Armin Müller-Stahl, Frederic Forrest, Donald Moffat, Lukas Haas, Cheryl Lynne Bruce, Mari Töröcsik.
●Was Mike Laszlo (Müller-Stahl), a retired Hungarian blue-collar worker living in Chicago these last 37 years, once head of an SS death squad? War crimes investigator Burke (Forrest) thinks he was, and in the light of eye-witness reports of Nazi atrocities in Hungary, takes him to court to face extradition charges. Mike's attorney daughter Ann (Lange), defending him, successfully undermines the prosecution by suggesting that its Hungarian witnesses have been sent by a government keen to discredit anti-Commie Europeans…The film is a polished enough blend of courtroom thriller, domestic melodrama and political pot-boiler that asks us, like Ann, to judge Mike's claims of innocence for ourselves; but in its attempts to probe more deeply the gulf between filial loyalty and moral integrity, and the problem of how and why we serve justice on crimes committed half a century ago, it is often overly shallow and cautious. Costa-Gavras wisely avoids facile flashbacks, but the cool tone, fascination with architecture and visual symmetry, and sluggish pacing of the trial scenes preclude real emotional and intellectual involvement, sturdy performances from a solid cast notwithstanding. GA

Music for the Movies: Bernard Herrmann

(1992, US/Fr, 58 min)
d Joshua Waletzky. *p* Margaret Smilow, Roma Baran. *ph* Mark Daniels. *ed* Joshua Waletzky. *m* David Raksin. *with* Bernard Herrmann, Lucille Fletcher, James G Stewart, Martin Scorsese, Claudine Bouché, Alan Robinson, Claude Chabrol
●A fascinating documentary. A member of Aaron Copland's circle, Herrmann – after a stint in radio – made an auspicious start with the music for *Citizen Kane*, and went on to compose some fifty more scores before his last for Scorsese's *Taxi Driver*. In that time, he made his 'anti-Hollywood style' – he was all for the primacy of the expression of interior psychological states – a standard option. There are testimonies from his ex-wife and various other composers and critics (including Scorsese and Chabrol), and lots of his unforgettable music. Personally, he seemed to be an arsehole: irascible, egocentric and cold. He considered his film work second-rate by nature. He wanted to be a conductor of a major symphony orchestra, something he got to do only as an actor for Hitchcock in *The Man Who Knew Too Much*. WH

Music for the Movies: The Hollywood Sound

(1995, US/Fr/Jap, 85 min)
d Joshua Waletzky. *p* Yves Jeanneau, Margaret Smilow. *ph* Laurent Chevallier, Carlo Varini. *ed* Joshua Waletzky, Christine Le Goff. *m* David Raksin, Alfred Newman, Dimitri Tiomkin. *with* David Raksin, Jon Mauceri, Fred Steiner.

●With the aid (and occasional cheeky interference) of David Raksin, one of the few survivors of Hollywood's 'Golden Age' and the BBC National Orchestra of Wales under conductor John Mauceri playing to a big screen, this loving tribute to the great studio composers underlines the importance of their contribution to the success of so many classics. Such names as Alfred Newman, Max Steiner and Erich Wolfgang Korngold are mulled over and a number of key sequences recreated with live music for the camera (notably *The Adventures of Robin Hood*), but the real gem is Raksin's account of how he came to compose the *Laura* theme. Educational and really rather thrilling. DT

Music for the Movies: Toru Takemitsu

(1994, US, 58 min)
d Charlotte Zwerin. *p* Margaret Smilow, Peter Grilli. *ph* Toyomichi Kurita. *ed* Charlotte Zwerin, Bernadine Colish. *with* Hiroshi Teshigahara, Masaki Kobayashi, Masahiro Shinoda, Nagisa Oshima.
●Described by one of his co-workers as having a face 'like Jean-Louis Barrault with diarrhoea', Japan's Toru Takemitsu commands a unique position as a leading contemporary composer who also works prolifically on film soundtracks. Deploying well-chosen clips and a number of distinguished interviewees (directors Teshigahara, Kobayashi and Oshima), Zwerin's film concentrates on Takemitsu's association with the '60s new wave of Japanese cinema, introducing new freedom in musical form and breaking the mould with his use of traditional Japanese instruments. Sound stuff. TJ

Music Freelancers, The

see Cachetonneurs, Les

Music Lovers, The

(1970, GB, 123 min)
d Ken Russell. *sc* Melvyn Bragg. *ph* Douglas Slocombe. *ed* Michael Bradsell. *pd* Natasha Kroll. *m* Tchaikovsky. *cast* Richard Chamberlain, Glenda Jackson, Max Adrian, Christopher Gable, Izabella Telezynska, Kenneth Colley, Andrew Faulds.
●Little more than distorted *Omnibus* portraits, Russell's 'outrageous' musical musings have dated badly. This bombastic reading of Tchaikovsky as a guilty gay, disastrously over-compensating with Glenda Jackson, has by now acquired something approaching a patina of period charm. The '1812' sequence is pure Monty Python. PT

Music Machine, The

(1979, GB, 90 min)
d Ian Sharp. *p* Brian Smedley-Aston. *sc* James Kenelm Clarke. *ph* Philip Meheux. *ed* Alan Pattillo, Brian Smedley-Aston. *ad* Roger King. *m* Aaron Harry, Music Machine. *cast* Gerry Sundquist, Patti Boulaye, David Easter, Michael Feast, Ferdy Mayne, Clarke Peters, Brenda Fricker.
●Produced on a skin-tight budget, yet designed to contain every possible ingredient for mass commercial teen appeal. Its major source is *Saturday Night Fever*, transposed to Camden's Music Machine and its environs (with, incidentally, quite a good sense of location). The disco fairytale is pursued, with young hero (Sundquist) aided by two 'fairy godparents' (Boulaye and Peters) who embody the ideal qualities of the beautiful disco person. They're black, Americanised, and act rich. What disappoints is the limping naturalism of the style (which regrettably extends to the dancing), and the predictable bits of 'social realism' slotted in to explain the hero's disco-dream, like the scene at the Job Centre. JS

Music Man, The

(1962, US, 151 min)
d/p Morton Da Costa. *sc* Marion Hargrove. *ph* Robert Burks. *ed* William Ziegler. *ad* Paul Groesse. *songs* Meredith Willson. *cast* Robert Preston, Shirley Jones, Buddy Hackett, Hermione Gingold, Pert Kelton, Paul Ford, Timmy Everett, Susan Lucky, Ron Howard, Harry Hickox.
●Overlong but generally faithful and entertaining screen version of Meredith Willson's Broadway hit, with Preston in fine form as the con-man whose bogus music professor enlivens a small Iowa town by convincing the inhabitants they need a uniformed brass band, with himself on expenses. Zestily performed and choreographed, beautifully shot by Robert Burks, full of standards like '76 Trombones' and 'Till There Was You', and endowed with a warming nostalgia for old-fashioned ways. GA

Music of Chance, The

(1993, US, 98 min)
d Philip Haas. *p* Frederick Zollo, Dylan Sellers. *sc* Philip Haas, Belinda Haas. *ph* Bernard Zitzermann, (NY) Jean de Segonzac. *ed* Belinda Haas. *p* Hugo Luczyc-Wyhowski. *m* Phillip Johnston. *cast* James Spader, Mandy Patinkin, Charles Durning, Joel Grey, M Emmet Walsh, Samantha Mathis, Chris Penn.
●When fireman-turned-drifter Jim Nashe (Patinkin) offers to finance the next poker game of Jack Pozzi (Spader), a cardsharp he's found wandering dazed by a country road, he little bargains for the strange turn of events that follows. Pozzi looks a sure bet against old farts Bill and Willie (Durning and Grey), but suddenly his luck changes, and Jim and Jack, deep in debt, are forced to construct a medieval wall in the victors' garden, overseen by groundsman Calvin (Walsh). The first feature of documentarist Haas may be rather literary in tone, but for all its slightly studied air, it has many virtues. Most obviously, the actors are terrific, with Spader very successfully cast against type as a sleazeball, and Patinkin a small wonder of understatement. For the most part, Haas handles his droll, resonant parable admirably, balancing its philosophical and dramatic dynamics with assurance and wit. Crucially, he has a good eye for an element of mystery. Minor, but unexpectedly engrossing. GA

Music of the Heart

(1999, US, 124 min)
d Wes Craven. *p* Marianne Maddalena, Walter Scheuer, Allan Miller, Susan Kaplan. *sc* Pamela Gray. *ph* Peter Deming. *ed* Patrick Lussier, Gregg Featherman. *pd* Bruce Alan Miller. *m* Mason Daring. *cast* Meryl Streep, Aidan Quinn, Gloria Estefan, Angela Bassett, Jane Leeves, Cloris Leachman, Kieran Culkin, Charlie Hofheimer, Jay O Sanders.
●Sometimes real life turns out just like a TV movie. The story of music teacher Roberta Guaspari-Tzavaras is one such instance, where her dedication to the students on her East Harlem Violin Program produced such remarkable results that these slum kids ended up fiddling away on the stage of Carnegie Hall in a fund raising event. It's a rousing, inspirational tale all right, and a plum vehicle for Streep as the music tutor who simply would not take 'no' for an answer. But we sort of know that it's a rousing, inspirational tale before we go in, so the film has to be something rather special to make us experience that response anew. With the best will in the world, Craven's offering is merely decent, standout Streep aside. To be fair on Craven and his cast, it never gets too sickly, and it doesn't try and sell us any line about classical music ennobling the soul, choosing instead to give its young people something they can do which improves their self-esteem. Bassett (headmistress) and Estefan (fellow teacher) are clearly there to broaden the demographic, but Meryl dominates the proceedings. She simply disappears into the role, and the movie, for all its educational impulses, becomes about watching her do it. TJ

Music Room, The

see Jalsaghar

Music Teacher, The (Le Maître de musique)

(1988, Bel, 98 min)
d Gérard Corbiau. *p* Alexandre Pletser. *sc* Gérard Corbiau, André Corbiau. *ph* Walther Van Den Ende, Jean-Claude Neckelbrouck. *ed* Denise Vindevogel. *pd* Zouc Lanc. *m* Ronald Zollman. *cast* José Van Dam, Anne Roussel, Philippe Volter, Sylvie Fennec, Patrick Bauchau, Johan Leysen, Marc Schreiber.
●Van Dam (Leporello in Losey's *Don Giovanni*) plays a great baritone who retires at the height of his powers to teach two young pupils in his château: dewy-eyed Sophie (Roussel) and vulnerable street-thief Jean (Volter). Not since James Mason whisked schoolgirl Ann Todd to pianistic stardom in what seemed six months flat (*The Seventh Veil*) has the training of musical genius slipped by so smoothly, thanks to lyrical landscapes, sumptuous pre-WWI social swish, and doses of soundtrack Mahler. A showdown with the protégé of Van Dam's old enemy gives the chance of hearing tenors duel in a rare Bellini aria, well timed for a public apparently insatiable for the Domingo/Pavarotti/Carreras sound. Jerome Pruett's dubbed voice isn't in that league, and the film won't do for song competitions what *Breaking Away* did for bicycle races. MHoy

Mustang Country

(1976, US, 79 min)
d/p/sc John Champion. *ph* J Barry Herron. *ed* Douglas Robertson. *m* Lee Holdridge. *cast* Joel McCrea, Nika Mina, Robert Fuller, Patrick Wayne.
●Fourteen years on from Peckinpah's *Guns in the Afternoon*, McCrea's last movie was this mundane family Western in which a rancher comes out of retirement, teams up with Indian boy Mina and tames Montana's last wild mustang. Pleasant to see the old boy up and about, but there's little to it. TJ

Mustang...The House that Joe Built

(1975, US, 85 min)
d/p/sc Robert Guralnick. *ph* Robert Guralnick, Rick Wise. *ed* Irving Lerner, Howard Brock, Alan Gabelsky, Eugenia Morrison. *m* Carmine Coppola. *with* Joe Conforte, Sally Conforte.
●This does practically everything wrong. It's an extremely low-budget documentary (one man and a hand-held camera) filmed inside the Mustang Ranch in Storey County, Nevada, which in 1970 became America's first legalised brothel. Guralnick tracks after Mustang boss Joe Conforte long after it becomes painfully obvious the guy's sayin' nuttin'; and there's little in the way of hard information. But it doesn't matter. The extreme sleaziness of the environment (a prison-like compound surrounded by ten-foot wire), in contrast to the collective persona revealed by the women, is so evident that all Guralnick has to do is keep the camera rolling. There's no doubt about the women being exploited, or about their resilience; and it is they who manage to give the film its subversive force. VG

Mutant

see Forbidden World

Mutant

(1983, US, 99 min)
d John 'Bud' Cardos. *p* Igo Kantor. *sc* Peter Z Orton, Michael Jones, John C Kruize. *ph* Al Taylor. *ed* Michael Duthie. *ad* Tony Kupersmith. *m* Richard Band. *cast* Wings Hauser, Bo Hopkins, Jody Medford, Lee Montgomery, Marc Clement, Cary Guffey, Jennifer Warren, Danny Nelson.
●Slime-covered corpses litter the streets of Goodland; a dumping ground for toxic waste is soon implicated. *Mutant* lives comfortably within its slender indie means, using its budget with Lewton-like economy, building suspense with deep shadow and fidgety lighting. But it also incorporates every redneck cliché in the Stereotype Directory, with no attempt to subvert a single one. There are nice touches of humour – when, for instance, a teenager discovers that, yes, there really is something unpleasant lurking under the bed. The hard-drinking sheriff (Hopkins) straightens up and saves the day, though the script shirks the scene where he has to convince the state police that his town is overrun by vampiric zombies oozing toxic liquids. DO

Mutants, The (Os Mutantes)

(1998, Port, 113 min)
d Teresa Villaverde. *p* Jacques Bidou. *sc* Teresa Villaverde. *ph* Acácio de Almeida. *ed* Andrée Davanture. *pd* Sérgio Costa. *cast* Alexandre Pinto, Nelson Varela, Ana Moreira, Paulo Pereira, Teresa Roby, Helder Tavares.
●More taciturn tales of alienation, woe and suffering, this time focused on the shelters of Lisbon's homeless young. Like Pedro Costa's *Ossos*, it's a slow, elliptical and slightly pretentious affair. Right from the long, opening extreme close-up of hair blowing in the wind, Villaverde repeatedly pushes both imagery and sound to the brink of abstraction – an otherwise gratuitous

scene in a fairground becomes a truly extraordinary coup de cinéma. Fascinating and for the most part strangely beautiful. GA

Mutantes, Os

see Mutants, The

Mutations, The

(1973, GB, 92 min)
d Jack Cardiff. *p* Robert D Weinbach. *sc* Robert D Weinbach, Edward Mann. *ph* Paul Beeson. *ed* Russell Woolnough. *ad* Herbert Smith. *m* Basil Kirchin, Jack Nathan. *cast* Donald Pleasence, Tom Baker, Brad Harris, Julie Ege, Michael Dunn, Scott Antony, Jill Haworth, Olga Anthony.

●Tired sci-fi horror in which students live in Prince of Wales Drive and drive Jaguars, while their professor (Pleasence) uses human beings, procured for him by a grotesquely deformed Tom Baker, to further his experiments in plant-animal mutations. Shades of Tod Browning's *Freaks* as the results get hived off into Michael Dunn's sideshow. The moral stretches no further than don't carve up your own students: two in a week and everything starts to go wrong, including the plot. Scott Antony ends up a cross between a lizard and a Venus Flytrap; Julie Ege has a fair bash at acting, gives up in face of all the silliness, and takes off her clothes instead.

Mute Witness

(1995, GB/Ger/Rus, 96 min)
d Anthony Waller. *p* Alexander Buchman, Norbert Soentgen, Anthony Waller. *sc* Anthony Waller. *ph* Egon Werdin, Thomas Merker. *ed* Peter Adam. *pd* Matthias Kammermeier. *m* Wilbert Hitrsch. *cast* Marina Sudina, Fay Ripley, Evan Richards, Oleg Jankowskij, Igor Volkov, Alec Guinness.

●Billie (Sudina), the make-up artist on an American slasher-movie, is accidentally locked overnight in the rambling Moscow studio where the film is being made. She wanders into the basement looking for someone to let her out. What she finds, however, is a cameraman shooting a scene in which a masked actor stabs a woman to death – and it looks for real. Billie flees, though since she's mute, she can't scream or phone for help. What's more, will anyone ever believe her story? Waller's witty, action-packed thriller seldom lets up. He milks the murky Moscow locations and the heroine's isolated predicament for all they're worth – only Billie's sister Karen (Ripley) attempts to understand her sign-language, while brother-in-law Andy (Richards) is too obsessed by the film he's directing to attend to anyone but himself – while switching rapidly back and forth between straight suspense and black comedy, ironic excess and tiny telling details. Scary and great fun. GA

Mutiny on the Bounty

(1935, US, 132 min, b/w)
d Frank Lloyd. *sc* Talbot Jennings, Jules Furthman, Carey Wilson. *ph* Arthur Edeson. *ed* Margaret Booth. *ad* Cedric Gibbons, Arnold Gillespie. *m* Herbert Stothart. *cast* Charles Laughton, Clark Gable, Franchot Tone, Herbert Mundin, Eddie Quillan, Dudley Digges, Donald Crisp, Movita.

●An exotic and gripping piece of Hollywood mythology, made with all the technical skill and gloss one associates with Irving Thalberg's MGM. Frank Lloyd's direction and the literate screenplay constantly juxtapose the notions of 18th century naval service as an aristocrat's high adventure and an ordinary seaman's press-ganged misery, underlying the central clash between Captain Bligh and Fletcher Christian with a surprisingly sharp examination of British breadfruit imperialism. Unlike the 1962 remake, this version virtually deserts Christian after the mutiny, concentrating on Bligh's amazing 4,000 mile open boat voyage and the subsequent court-martial. Laughton scowls magnificently, and paints a remarkable portrait of Bligh's humourless character, while Gable injects a startling (and unintentional) bisexuality into the Tahitian sequences. ATu

Mutiny on the Bounty

(1962, US, 185 min)
d Lewis Milestone. *p* Aaron Rosenberg. *sc* Charles Lederer. *ph* Robert Surtees, Harold E Wellman. *ed* John McSweeney Jr. *ad* George W Davis, Joseph McMillan Johnson. *m* Bronislau Kaper. *cast* Marlon Brando, Trevor Howard, Richard Harris, Hugh Griffith, Richard Haydn, Tim Seely, Percy Herbert, Tarita, Gordon Jackson, Chips Rafferty.

●Milestone's overlong and frequently leaden version of the classic tale of sadism and revolt, set in the high-adventure world of an 18th century ship sailing to the South Pacific, is not a patch upon the 1935 Laughton and Gable version. Brando makes a total mess of his English accent, the romantic interlude in Tahiti goes on endlessly, and the visuals (perhaps the main point of interest in the movie) too often resort to travelogue vistas and picture postcard lighting. GA

Mutiny on the Buses

(1972, GB, 89 min)
d Harry Booth. *p/sc* Ronald Wolfe, Ronald Chesney. *ph* Mark McDonald. *ed* Archie Ludski. *ad* Scott MacGregor. *m* Ron Grainer. *cast* Reg Varney, Doris Hare, Anna Karen, Michael Robbins, Bob Grant, Stephen Lewis, Pat Ashton, Bob Todd.

●Much lower than these cretinous larks among London's bus crews comedy cannot get. The sole interest in this truly appalling spin-off from the TV sitcom series lies in wondering why the sweaty Varney – trying to play half his age as he gets engaged against his family's wishes – never got a better haircut to stop the greasy locks falling over his face. GA

Mutter und Sohn

see Mother and Son

Mutters Courage

see My Mother's Courage

My Ain Folk

see My Childhood

My American Cousin

(1985, Can, 95 min)
d Sandy Wilson. *p* Peter O'Brian. *sc* Sandy Wilson. *ph* Richard Leiterman. *ed* Haida Paul. *ad* Phil Schmidt. *cast* Margaret Langrick, John Wildman, Richard Donat, Jane Mortifee.

●A 12-year-old girl (Langrick) is stuck on a remote ranch in British Columbia in 1959 with her parents and five siblings. Her hormones play up when her American cousin (Wildman), 18, beautiful and very bored, comes to stay. The crunch comes when his folks turn up to take him home. A detailed, witty and highly sympathetic foray into the realm of adolescent sexuality, winner of six Genie awards in Canada. TJ

My American Uncle

see Mon Oncle d'Amérique

My Apprenticeship

see Childhood of Maxim Gorki, The

My Beautiful Laundrette

(1985, GB, 97 min)
d Stephen Frears. *p* Sarah Radclyffe, Tim Bevan. *sc* Hanif Kureishi. *ph* Oliver Stapleton. *ed* Mick Audsley. *pd* Hugo Luczyc-Wyhowski. *m* Ludus Tonalis. *cast* Saeed Jaffrey, Roshan Seth, Daniel Day Lewis, Gordon Warnecke, Derrick Branche, Shirley Anne Field, Rita Wolf.

●Not content with setting itself in London's Asian community, this also tells a gay love story. Daniel Day Lewis gives a luminous performance as the white ex-National Front hoodlum who befriends an Asian (Warnecke) and helps him create his commercial dream, a laundrette which glitters like a Hollywood picture palace. The fact that Lewis finds himself demoted in the ensuing suds war is typical of Hanif Kureishi's script, which refuses to push Asians into their customary dramatic role as victims. Instead, they're seen as rapacious businessmen, pedalling furiously on their Tebbitite cycles, and therefore puzzled, as well as angered, by the vicious prejudice they suffer at the hands of the establishment. Saeed Jaffrey is marvellous as the smoothest of the smooth operators, and Frears directs in his customarily unfussy style. But the strength of the film is its vision – cutting, compassionate and sometimes hilarious – of what it means to be Asian, and British, in Thatcher's Britain. RR

My Best Friend's Girl (La Femme de Mon Pote)

(1983, Fr, 100 min)
d Bertrand Blier. *p* Alain Sarde. *sc* Bertrand Blier, Gérard Brach. *ph* Jean Penzer. *ed* Claudine Merlin. *ad* Théobald Meurisse. *m* JJ Cale. *cast* Coluche, Isabelle Huppert, Thierry Lhermitte, Farid Chopel, François Perrot, Daniel Colas.

●Blier's films are a continuing chronicle of the male psyche, getting to the parts even Howard Hawks didn't often reach. Arriving at a ski resort in search of a new steady and the home that goes with him, Huppert seizes on the local romantic (Lhermitte). The latter's best buddy (Coluche), a slob heading towards a middle-age of confirmed bachelorhood, is designated as her daytime minder, and is disarmed by her guilt-free desire for an affair. Appalled at the discovery of his own vulnerability, he finds himself agonisingly torn between male loyalties and the emotional crutch of an affair. As ever, Blier's script is out of the top drawer, and French comic Coluche, atypically cast, is excellent as the racked 'mec'. A simple storyline belies a thoughful film with more than a hint of Buñuel's wit. BG

My Best Friend's Wedding

(1997, US, 105 min)
d PJ Hogan. *p* Jerry Zucker, Ronald Bass. *sc* Ronald Bass. *ph* Laszlo Kovacs. *ed* Garth Craven, Lisa Fruchtman. *pd* Richard Sylbert. *m* James Netwon Howard. *cast* Julia Roberts, Dermot Mulroney, Cameron Diaz, Rupert Everett, Philip Bosco, M Emmet Walsh, Rachel Griffiths.

●When Julianne (Roberts) hears that her best friend Michael (Mulroney) is getting married – this weekend! – she's horrified. The bride, Kimmy (Diaz), is beautiful, wealthy, smart, tasteful and sensitive. Obviously she'll have to go. Installed as maid of honour, Julianne has four days to win back her man and prevent the marriage. In *Muriel's Wedding*, director Hogan orchestrated sympathy for a perennial underdog obsessed with marriage; here, we're meant to empathise with a Machiavellian anti-hero – as Julianne humiliates her rival at a karaoke club, re-routes the honeymoon, and generally comes on like Glenn Close in *Fatal Attraction*. Roberts' fragile charm keeps it going for longer than you might imagine, but Mr Mulroney's magnetism must be taken entirely on faith, and the film's brazen amorality gradually freezes the smile on your face. Whenever invention fails, Hogan resorts to forced pratfalls, songs or camp farce – Everett easily steals the show as Julianne's gay colleague. TCh

My Blue Heaven

(1990, US, 95 min)
d Herbert Ross. *p* Herbert Ross, Anthea Sylbert. *sc* Nora Ephron. *ph* John Bailey. *ed* Stephen A Rotter, Robert Reitano. *pd* Charles Rosen. *m* Ira Newborn. *cast* Steve Martin, Rick Moranis, Joan Cusack, Melanie Mayron, William Irwin, Carol Kane, William Hickey, Deborah Rush, Ed Lauter.

●In this truly mind-numbingly awful movie, Steve Martin plays a mobster forced to move to San Diego from his New York stomping ground as part of a witness protection programme rap-beating deal. San Diego takes on the aura of some Pacific version of Milton Keynes: all little leagues, little boxes and little gardens, populated by so many of Martin's erstwhile criminal colleagues that life on the run turns into a nostalgic round of petty felonies and made-member hugs. Further dismay looms not only in co-star Rick Moranis' continuing obsession with misusing his talents by trying to play a straight man, but in the normally loveable Martin's gross and tedious portrayal of Mafia slobdom. If we must have parodies and comedies of crime, let them be funny, *capisce*? SGr

My Bodyguard

(1980, US, 96 min)
d Tony Bill. *p* Don Devlin. *sc* Alan Ormsby. *ph* Michael D Margulies. *ed* Stu Linder. *pd* Jackson de Govia. *m* David Grusin. *cast* Chris Makepeace, Adam Baldwin, Matt Dillon, Ruth Gordon, Martin Mull, John Houseman, Craig Richard Nelson.

●Alan Ormsby's script, about a new kid in a Chicago high school who hires the biggest guy in school to fend off a lunch money protection racket, is (unusually) directed not for nostalgia value but from a perspective of adolescent insecurity, and helped along by fresh performances from a cast of inexperienced young actors. Finally, though, the message that accompanies the central theme – Kids are basically Nice – is that Brute Force Rules. The only real refinement of that great American truth offered here is that it's likely to be most effective when employed intelligently.

My Brilliant Career

(1979, Aust, 100 min)
d Gillian Armstrong. *p* Margaret Fink. *sc* Eleanor Witcombe. *ph* Don McAlpine. *ed* Nick Beauman. *pd* Luciana Arrighi. *m* Nathan Waks. *cast* Judy Davis, Sam Neill, Wendy Hughes, Robert Grubb, Max Cullen, Pat Kennedy, Aileen Britton.
● Overrated though attractive slice of nostalgia, based on a novel published in 1901 about a girl from a poor farming family, stuck in the outback and undecided between expectations that she will marry a local landowner and her own resolve to become a writer. The period atmosphere is evoked with careful delicacy, but the characters rarely become more than stereotypes with performances (Judy Davis excepted) to match. TM

My Brother's Wedding

(1983, US, 116 min)
d Charles Burnett. *p* Charles Burnett, Gaye Shannon-Burnett. *sc/ph* Charles Burnett. *ed* Thomas M Penick. *cast* Everette Silas, Jessie Holmes, Gaye Shannon-Burnett, Ronald E Bell, Dennis Kemper, Sally Easter.
● A young working class black living in one of LA's seedier ghettos is having problems with his sense of duty to others, bothered by his brother's forthcoming marriage to a wealthy doctor's daughter, and hanging around with his wastrel ex-con pal against his family's wishes. Somewhere between domestic soap and *Mean Streets*, Burnett's low-budget film confronts a number of universal dilemmas without ever becoming turgidly heavy. Overlong, perhaps, but the witty script and generous characterisations often work wonders. GA

My Brother Talks to Horses

(1946, US, 94 min, b/w)
d Fred Zinnemann. *p* Samuel Marx. *sc* Morton Thompson. *ph* Harold Rosson. *ed* George White. *ad* Cedric Gibbons, Leonid Vasian. *m* Rudolph G Kopp. *cast* 'Butch' Jenkins, Peter Lawford, Beverly Tyler, Charlie Ruggles, Edward Arnold, Spring Byington, Paul Langton.
● An 11-year-old boy who converses with horses is popular with racetrack gamblers. Whimsical comic canter, drawn from a novel titled *Joe the Wounded Tennis Player*. NF

My Brother Tom

(2001, GB/Ger, 111 min)
d Dom Rotheroe. *p* Carl Schönfeld. *sc* Dom Rotheroe, Alison Beeton-Hilder. *ph* Robby Müller. *ed* David Charap. *pd* Isolde Sommerfeldt. *m* Annabelle Pangborn. *cast* Jenna Harrison, Ben Whishaw, Adrian Rawlins, Judith Scott, Richard Hope, Jonathan Hackett, Patrick Godfrey, Honeysuckle Weeks.
● Rosy Home Counties schoolgirl Jessica (Harrison) is unimpressed by most of her peers' standard acts of teenage unruliness, but intrigued by the boy who hides up trees from them and calls her 'Fee' – fi, fo, fum. This Tom (Whishaw), who shows her his favourite refuge beside a lake deep in the woods, has a hounded, feral quality, as if thoroughly unsocialised. But when Jessica herself experiences the adult world's depredations at the hands of her most trusted teacher, she rejects domestic respectability for the rare, primal intimacy offered by Tom in his sylvan sanctuary. This anti-fairytale is a fervent, effusive account of adolescent metamorphosis that's sharp but not pat on the claustrophobia of a middle-class family. It's almost pantheist out in the woods, where a religious anarchism confronts the complacent hypocrisy of Church and school chaplain with the kids' shows of suffering, communion and ecstasy. It's shot on handheld DV in an intimate go-go style with an urgent intensity; improvising like mad, the two young leads give vibrant, irrepressible performances. NB

My Childhood/My Ain Folk/My Way Home

(1972/1973/1978, GB, 48/55/78 min)
d Bill Douglas. *p* Geoffrey Evans; Nick Nascht; Richard Craven, Judy Cottam. *sc* Bill Douglas. *ph* Mick Campbell; Gale Tattersall; Ray Orton. *ed* Brand Thumin; Peter West; Mick Audsley. *cast* Stephen Archibald, Hughie Restorick, Jean Taylor-Smith, Helena Gloag, Bernard McKenna, Paul Kermack, Gerald James.
● Bill Douglas' trilogy succeeds in evoking a genuine sense of compassion for the characters in these harsh tales of his childhood in the Scottish mining village of Newcraighall in the '40s, without tipping the scales into mawkishness. Pared to essentials, the stark b/w images restore some freshness to a tired, unfashionable aesthetic. And shot over eight years, the cruelty and compulsiveness of the 'memories' still haunt the finished work. DMacp

My Cousin Rachel

(1952, US, 98 min, b/w)
d Henry Koster. *p/sc* Nunnally Johnson. *ph* Joseph La Shelle. *ed* Louis Loeffler. *ad* Lyle Wheeler, John F DeCuir. *m* Franz Waxman. *cast* Olivia de Havilland, Richard Burton, John Sutton, Audrey Dalton, Ronald Squire, George Dolenz, Tudor Owen.
● This Daphne du Maurier adaptation rather pales beside the earlier *Rebecca*, although the ingredients – death and a mysterious femme fatale – are not dissimilar. Burton was Oscar-nominated for his Hollywood debut as the young Englishman both distrustful of and attracted to de Havilland, the woman who may have fatally poisoned his foster father. Thick with studio atmospherics, but the resolution is weak. TJ

My Cousin Vinny

(1992, US, 119 min)
d Jonathan Lynn. *p* Dale Launer, Paul Schiff. *sc* Dale Launer. *ph* Peter Deming. *ed* Tony Lombardo, Stephen E Rivkin. *pd* Victoria Paul. *m* Randy Edelman. *cast* Joe Pesci, Ralph Macchio, Marisa Tomei, Mitchell Whitfield, Fred Gwynne, Lane Smith, Austin Pendleton, Bruce McGill, Maury Chaykin.
● Pesci plays Vincent La Guardia Gambini, proud Brooklyn attorney-at-law, who gets called South to Wahzoo City to defend his college-kid cousin (Macchio) and pal (Whitfield), falsely accused of a convenience store murder. Trouble is, Vinny ain't no expert on criminal law, having just completed his bar exams. Still, the majesty of the law doesn't over-impress this self-made guy; but then his shades, white shoes and total ignorance of procedure don't exactly impress by-the-book Judge Haller (Gwynne). Vinny fears he's gonna get found out, the kids fear they're gonna fry. Pesci's variation on New Jersey machismo (vulnerable in this case) isn't enough to fill a comedy; but Dale Launer's script luckily provides some fine routines for the supporting cast, notably the scene-stealing Marisa Tomei as Mona Lisa Vito, Pesci's sharp-tongued girlfriend. It's a small, surprisingly gentle affair, prone to fits and starts, but fun. WH

My Crasy Life

(1992, US, 92 min)
d Jean-Pierre Gorin. *p* Daniel Marks, Cameron Allan. *sc* Jean-Pierre Gorin. *voice* (of computer) Richard Masur.
● This portrait of Samoan street gangs in LA may appear to conform to fly-on-the-wall documentary criteria, but in fact it's highly manipulated, scripted and shaped by Gorin together with the gang members. There's little glamour or action: Gorin films the self-styled Original Gangsters sitting around, playing cards, reminiscing about getting stabbed, or talking chillingly about the revenge ethic. Essentially, they are playing their own parts, which casts an interesting light on their monotonous, almost ritualistic rhetoric: a language Gorin has called 'the music of survival'. As befits the co-founder with Godard of the radical Dziga Vertov Group, Gorin shakes up the structure by interspersing scenes that don't strictly integrate – notably, a LA patrol cop being talked at by his computer. *Anti-vérité* in the extreme, this is a hard film to watch, sometimes verging on the inscrutable; but at the very least it offers an antidote to the glamour that can seep into even the toughest Hollywood street fictions. JRo

My Crazy Life (Mi Vida Loca)

(1993, US, 95 min)
d Allison Anders. *p* Daniel Hassid, Carl-Jan Colpaert. *sc* Allison Anders. *ph* Rodrigo Garcia. *ed* Richard Chew, Kathryn Himoff, Tracy Granger. pd Jane Stewart. *m* John Taylor. *cast* Angel Aviles, Seidy Lopez, Jacob Vargas, Marlo Marron, Jessie Borrego, Magali Alvarado, Julian Reyes.
● With their men dead or in jail, a group of young Hispanic women from Echo Park, Los Angeles, struggle to raise their children, resorting to gangland tactics only to introduce some sense of identity or purpose into their difficult lives. The action revolves round five of these *locas* each with her own story to tell. Writer/director Anders mixes real gang members with up-and-coming Latin American actresses, but this ploy fails to lend the film authenticity or vitality. The tone seems, to put it kindly, misguidedly romantic. SFra

My Dad Is a Jerk (Dui-bu-qi, Dou Xie Ni)

(1997, HK, 101 min)
d Cheung Tung Cho. *cast* Lau Ching-Wan, Shu Qi.
● Dad makes a living parking cars, but his nine-year-old son thinks he's a racing driver – so the kid's in for a shock when they meet, dumped by his Americanised mom for a fortnight in Hong Kong. The concept might serve for, say, Bruce Willis and the latest Macaulay Culkin clone, but that's the best you can say. TCh

My Darling Clementine 100

(1946, US, 97 min, b/w)
d John Ford. *p* Samuel G Engel. *sc* Samuel G Engel, Winston Miller. *ph* Joseph P MacDonald. *ed* Dorothy Spencer. *ad* James Basevi, Lyle R Wheeler. *m* Cyril J Mockridge. *cast* Henry Fonda, Victor Mature, Linda Darnell, Walter Brennan, Cathy Downs, Tim Holt, Ward Bond, Alan Mowbray, John Ireland, Jane Darwell.
● Like many Hollywood directors, Ford's claims for his films are very modest. For him the key thing about *My Darling Clementine* is its authenticity: 'I knew Wyatt Earp…and he told me about the fight at the OK Corral. So we did it exactly the way it had been.' For viewers, however, the film's greatness (and enjoyability) rests not in the accuracy of the final shootout, but in the orchestrated series of incidents – the drunken Shakespearean actor, Earp's visit to the barber, the dance in the unfinished church – which give meaning to the shootout. Peter Wollen's comment on the significance of Earp's visit to the barber's and its outcome makes clear just how complex the ideas contained in these incidents are: 'This moment marks the turning point of Earp's transition from wandering cowboy, nomadic savage, bent on revenge, unmarried, to married man, settled, civilised, the sheriff who administers the law.' PH

My Dearest Enemy (Mein Liebster Fiend)

(1999, Ger/GB, 95 min)
d Werner Herzog. *p* Lucki Stipetic. *ph* Peter Zeitlinger. *ed* Joe Bini. *m* Popol Vuh. *with* Klaus Kinski, Werner Herzog, Claudia Cardinale, Eva Mattes, Beat Presser, Guillermo Rios, Andrés Vicente, Justo Gonzales, Benino Moreno Plácido, Baron v.d. Recke. *narrator* Werner Herzog.
● Not, agreed, one of Herzog's most distinctive, original or audacious documentaries, but given the crazed nature of his subject – former frequent collaborator Klaus Kinski – it's still a hugely entertaining foray into personal reminiscence and movie archaeology. Scattered among the interviews and Herzog's own deadpan stories of his altercations with the late actor (which, of course, confirm suspicions that the director himself is hardly the most conventional fellow on earth) is some marvellous behind-the-scenes archive footage. But it's also a fascinating document on the genesis of some extraordinary movies, with pristine clips reminding one of Herzog's own glorious past as a creator of visionary fictions. GA

My Dear Tom Mix (Mi Querido Tom Mix)

(1991, Mex, 120 min)
d Carlos Garcia Agraz. *p* Jorge Sanchez. *sc* Consuelo Garrido. *ph* Rodrigo Garcia. *ed*

Tlaceteotl Mata. *ad* Tere Pecanins. *m* Alberto Nuñez. *cast* Ana Ofelia Murgia, Federico Luppi, Damian Garcia Vasquez.

● A boy befriends his 60-year-old great aunt Joaquin in the Mexican town where she lives with her nephew and his wife. She a kind, generous soul, but somewhat crazy, with a fixation on Tom Mix Westerns. When bandits drive into town in a Model T, help comes from an unexpected quarter...well, not *that* unexpected, actually. A charming conceit, well acted but sluggishly paced, and as sentimental as the B Westerns it holds dear – developed through the Gabriel Garcia Marquez script workshop. TCh

My Dinner with André

(1981, US, 111 min)
d Louis Malle. *p* George W George, Beverley Karp. *sc* Wallace Shawn, André Gregory. *ph* Jeri Sopanen. *ed* Suzanne Baron. *pd* David Mitchell. *m* Allen Shawn. *cast* Wallace Shawn, André Gregory, Jean Lenauer, Roy Butler.

● Bring two New York intellectuals together and they'll beat each other's ears off swapping stories about their psychoanalysts. Here Malle celebrates just such an encounter, recreated by the original participants: a sad, never-quite-made-it playwright (Shawn) and a brilliantly successful director (Gregory) who dropped out to 'find himself in a quest ranging from Grotowski in Poland to Tibet, the Sahara and remoter Scotland. Just two people talking, shot mostly in close-up. But hammering against the wall of Shawn's pragmatism, sometimes pulled up short in awareness of its own absurdity, Gregory's account of his spiritual odyssey becomes a magical mystery tour of thoughts, dreams, fantasies and emotions. Riveting, exhilarating stuff. TM

My Dog Skip

(1999, US, 95 min)
d Jay Russell. *p* Mark Johnson, John Lee Hancock, Broderick Johnson, Andrew A Kosove. *sc* Gail Gilchriest. *ph* James L Carter. *ed* Harvey Rosenstock, Gary Winter. *pd* David J Bomba. *m* William Ross. *cast* Frankie Muniz, Diane Lane, Luke Wilson, Kevin Bacon, Mark Beech, Susan Carol Davis, David Pickens, Bradley Coryell.

● This adaptation of Willie Morris's autobiographical novel about growing up in small town Mississippi in WWII prominently features a Jack Russell, but mercifully the terrier is not allowed to steal the show. Rather, the dog serves as a bone of contention between eight-year-old Willie's parents: his mother – the optimistic Ellen (Lane) – thinks Skip will relieve the studious boy's social isolation; his lame, war veteran father Jack (Bacon) calls it 'a heartbreak waiting to happen'. For the boy (Muniz), Skip's a reliable companion, who somehow eases Willie's sometimes troubled path though a childhood dogged by fractious local boys and falling idols. The film manages psychological realism within its clearly defined bounds. Muniz makes a credible impression as the boy, his restraint reminding us of the reactive nature of childhood. The small victories he achieves aren't over-emphasised, and the role played by his resourcefulness, intelligence and fidelity play is left for the audience to infer. Moreover, although Willie gets his big day, proudly displaying to an impressed classroom the German helmet his hero/mentor Dink has sent him from a foreign field, the film allows Dink to return a fractured alcoholic. WH

My English Grandfather (Robinsonada anu Chemi Ingliseli Papa)

(1986, USSR, 76 min, b/w & col)
d Nana Dzhordzhadze. *sc* Irakly Kvirikadze. *ph* Levan Paatashvili. *ed* Nana Dzhordzhadze. *ad* Wachtang Kurna. *m* Enri Lolaschwili. *cast* Zhanri Lolashvili, Ninel Chankvetadze, Guram Pirtskhalava, Tiko Eliosidze, Elqudzha Burduli.

● Wacky and whimsical versions of the Russian revolution by Russians were hardly thick on the ground before glasnost, and if this film is sometimes too Comic Cuts to hold together, it tickles like a Flann O'Brien essay. A contemporary composer recalls his English grandfather, a telegraph engineer called Hughes who was stranded in Georgia by events in 1917. Legally, the 3m circumference of soil at the base of the telegraph posts belonged to Britain, so Hughes moved his brass bed and belongings away from the upheavals of history and became a species of Robinson Crusoe. Whether boxing with Bolsheviks, laying out rapists with flower vases, or courting the local leader's sister, our hero remains a rampant individualist of bumbling charm. A diverting curiosity. BC

My Fair Lady

(1964, US, 175 min)
d George Cukor. *p* Jack L Warner. *sc* Alan Jay Lerner. *ph* Harry Stradling. *ed* William Ziegler. *pd* Cecil Beaton. *m* Frederick Loewe. *lyrics* Alan J Lerner. *cast* Audrey Hepburn, Rex Harrison, Stanley Holloway, Wilfrid Hyde-White, Gladys Cooper, Jeremy Brett, Theodore Bikel, Isobel Elsom, Mona Washbourne, John Alderton, John McLiam.

● Lerner and Loewe's musical version of Shaw's *Pygmalion* transferred effectively to the screen by Cukor, the director who, thematically if not stylistically, would seem to be the perfect choice for the project (many of his films deal with the relationship between real life and assumed appearances, and *Born Yesterday* is a beautifully funny update of the story). The sets, costumes (by Cecil Beaton), photography, and Hermes Pan's choreography are all sumptuously impressive, and Harrison makes a fine, arrogant Professor Higgins; but Hepburn is clearly awkward as the Cockney Eliza in the first half, and in general the adaptation is a little too reverential to really come alive. GA

My Family (Mi Familia/aka East LA)

(1994, US, 126 min)
d Gregory Nava. *p* Anna Thomas. *sc* Gregory Nava, Anna Thomas. *ph* Edward Lachman. *ed* Nancy Richardson. *pd* Barry Robinson. *m* Mark McKenzie, (folkloric) Pepe Avila. *cast* Jimmy Smits, Edward James Olmos, Esai Morales, Eduardo Lopez Rojas, Elpidia Carrillo, Jenny Gago, Jennifer Lopez, Mary Steenburgen, DeDee Pfeiffer.

● Nava's first film since *A Time of Destiny*, written with his wife and collaborator Anna Thomas, and produced under the auspices of Francis Coppola, is an ambitious saga charting 60 years and three generations of the Sanchez family. Nava exacerbates the structural problems posed by the time-frame by relying too heavily on a folksy voice-over and by adapting his mise-en-scène to the decades, so that the 1920s sequence, in which paterfamilias Jose walks from Mexico to Los Angeles, is relayed in a mystic, misty-eyed style, complete with DW Griffith optical effects. Survive this (and it's a chore), and things come into sharper focus in the '50s, where scenes of teen angst – the death of young tearaway Chucho (Morales) at the hands of the police – are rendered in bold, saturated compositions which inevitably recall gang movies of the period. By the late '70s, the film's fragments of love, pain, anger and injustice are really beginning to add up, particularly in impassioned scenes between youngest son Jimmy (Smits) and illegal immigrant Isabel (Carrillo, a revelation here). It's shapeless, but there's iron in its soul. TCh

My Father Is Coming

(1991, Ger/US, 81 min)
d/p Monika Treut. *sc* Monika Treut, Bruce Benderson. *ph* Elfi Mikesch. *ed* Steve Brown. *ad* Robin Ford. *m* David Van Tieghem. *cast* Alfred Edel, Shelley Kästner, Annie Sprinkle, Mary Lou Graulau, David Bronstein, Michael Massee.

● Treut – a German director whose sex-pol essays like *Virgin Machine* and *Seduction: the Cruel Woman* have earned plenty of controversy and cult acclaim – here spins a tale of sexual awakening, presided over with ecstasy-aunt jollity by 'post-porn sex goddess' Sprinkle. Vicki (Kästner) is a sexually confused actress holding down a waitress job, and trying to persuade her visiting Bavarian papa (the marvellously shambling Edel) that she's happily married, although her 'husband' is fully occupied with vogueing Latin boys. Happily, La Sprinkle is on hand to distract papa with tender mercies and household appliances while Vicki makes her mark as a nightclub diva. A low-rent, loosely structured lesbian coming-out story that entertains a range of sexual orientations, Treut's film enshrines an engaging worldview – SoHo chic seen from a sort of polysexual Teutonic 'Carry On' perspective. JRo

My Father's Glory

see Gloire de mon père, La

My Father, the Hero

(1994, US, 90 min)
d Steve Miner. *p* Jacques Bar, Jean-Louis Livi. *sc* Francis Veber, Charlie Peters. *ph* Daryn Okada. *ed* Marshall Harvey. *pd* Christopher Nowak. *m* David Newman. *cast* Gérard Depardieu, Katherine Heigl, Emma Thompson, Dalton James, Lauren Hutton, Stephen Tobolowsky.

● A Hollywood remake of the French comedy *Mon Père, ce héros* in which Depardieu reprises his role as the discomforted father of a pubescent girl. André arrives at the apartment of his ex-wife (Hutton) to whisk daughter Nicole on a get-to-know-you vacation. In Nassau, Nicole (Heigl) is mortified at the idea of anyone suspecting he's her father and starts fabricating a lifestyle to impress heart-throb Ben (James). Meanwhile lonely André falls for the local manhunter Diana. Makes *Baywatch* seem intellectual. WH

My Favorite Blonde

(1942, US, 78 min, b/w)
d Sidney Lanfield. *sc* Don Hartman, Frank Butler. *ph* William C Mellor. *ed* William Shea. *ad* Hans Dreier, Robin Usher. *m* David Buttolph. *cast* Bob Hope, Madeleine Carroll, Gale Sondergaard, George Zucco, Victor Varconi, Otto Reichow, Edward Gargan, Dooley Wilson.

● Along with the later *My Favorite Brunette*, one of the funnier Hope vehicles, in which he plays a vaudeville entertainer (working with a trained penguin) who inadvertently becomes pulled into the world of espionage by British agent Carroll. With much cowardice and braggadocio in reaction to the threat of the pursuing Nazis, it's routine Hope, but the script sparkles with bright lines ('You got relatives out there?' he mutters when the penguin steals his applause. 'You and me will have to have a talk with a taxidermist') delivered with plenty of flair and gusto. GA

My Favorite Brunette

(1947, US, 87 min, b/w)
d Elliott Nugent. *p* Danny Dare. *sc* Edmund Beloin, Jack Rose. *ph* Lionel Lindon. *ed* Ellsworth Hoagland. *ad* Hans Dreier, Earl Hedrick. *m* Robert Emmett Dolan. *cast* Bob Hope, Dorothy Lamour, Peter Lorre, Lon Chaney Jr, John Hoyt, Reginald Denny, Charles Dingle, Frank Puglia, Ann Doran, Bing Crosby.

● Likeable parody of the hardboiled world of Hammett and Chandler. Hope goes through his familiar routine as a craven photographer, a specialist in baby portraiture, who takes over from an absent private eye (Alan Ladd in a trench-coated cameo appearance) to help out Lamour's damsel in distress. The wisecracks are a little thin on the ground, but the *noir* atmosphere is handled with a nice mixture of bizarrerie (Lorre, Chaney) and deadpan (such iconographic figures as Jack LaRue and Anthony Caruso). TM

My Favorite Wife

(1940, US, 88 min, b/w)
d Garson Kanin. *p* Leo McCarey. *sc* Samuel Spewack, Bella Spewack, Leo McCarey. *ph* Rudolph Maté. *ed* Robert Wise. *ad* Van Nest Polglase, Mark-Lee Kirk. *m* Roy Webb. *cast* Cary Grant, Irene Dunne, Gail Patrick, Randolph Scott, Ann Shoemaker, Donald MacBride, Scotty Beckett.

● Originally planned for Leo McCarey, but a car accident intervened. Directed by the mercurial Garson Kanin, it remains a relatively formulaic (though beautifully produced) bedroom comedy, with Grant as the husband whose wife, presumed dead after a shipwreck, returns to their Californian home only to find him remarried. Grant's habitual skill at playing the faint-hearted prig is such that one can almost overlook the moments of mawkish sentiment and gentle complacency about the country club milieu. The film was remade in 1963 as a Doris Day/James Garner vehicle (*Move Over, Darling*): some indication, perhaps, that it never really achieved the satirical bite of *Adam's Rib* (scripted by Kanin) or the giddy sexual risk-taking of Grant and Ginger Rogers in *Once Upon a Honeymoon*. CA

My Favorite Year

(1982, US, 92 min)
d Richard Benjamin. *p* Michael Gruskoff. *sc* Norman Steinberg, Dennis Palumbo. *ph* Gerald Hirschfeld. *ed* Richard Chew. *pd* Charles Rosen. *m* Ralph Burns. *cast* Peter O'Toole, Mark Linn-Baker, Jessica Harper, Joseph Bologna, Bill Macy, Lainie Kazan, Lou Jacobi, Cameron Mitchell.
●Fond nostalgia for that golden and not altogether mythical age (1954) when American television was live and innovative and came from New York City. Finding his feet in this buzz of hard work and talent is a young scriptwriter (Linn-Baker), suddenly assigned the heady task of nursemaiding an uproarious guest star through rehearsals and away from drink and trouble. The guest is a former screen idol in the Errol Flynn mould: a very funny performance from O'Toole, who throws himself into the drunk's pratfall routines like a lanky rag doll, coming up ever serene, debonair and with a suspicion of eye-liner. Richard Benjamin directs the smartish script and the chaotic tomfoolery quite brilliantly; but all concerned mishandle the soppy section where O'Toole gets misty-eyed about his discarded daughter. Still, the pace picks up for the magnificent comic climax. JS

My Favourite Martian

(1998, US, 94 min)
d Donald Petrie. *p* Robert Shapiro, Jerry Leider, Marc Toberoff. *sc* Deanna Oliver, Sherri Stoner. *ph* Thomas Ackerman. *ed* Malcolm Campbell. *pd* Sandy Veneziano. *m* John Debney. *cast* Jeff Daniels, Christopher Lloyd Elizabeth Hurley, Daryl Hannah, Christine Ebersole, Wallace Shawn, Michael Lerner, Ray Walston.
●Dire Disney effort, with competent sfx, inspired by the '60s TV series. Lloyd is Martin the Martian who crash-lands his spaceship, just as Daniels' struggling TV reporter, Tim O'Hara, is driving by. Tim befriends the gregarious, shape-changing alien, even as he begins to hatch a plan to expose his remarkable find on TV. Trouble is, wacky Martin (unknowingly) always seems to be one step ahead. Matters take a steeper nose dive with the introduction of Hannah as Tim's nutty neighbour, Hurley as his neurotic colleague, and a spacesuit that walks and cracks inane jokes. DA

My Favourite Season

see Ma Saison Préférée

My First 40 Years (I Miei Primi 40 Anni)

(1987, It, 107 min)
d Carlo Vanzina. *p* Mario Cecchi Gori, Vittorio Cecchi Gori. *sc* Enrico Vanzina, Carlo Vanzina. *ph* Luigi Kuveiller. *ed* Ruggero Mastroianni. *ad* Mario Chiari. *m* Umberto Smaila. *cast* Carol Alt, Elliott Gould, Jean Rochefort, Pierre Cosso, Massimo Venturiello, Riccardo Garrone, Capucine.
●This glitzy tale of ambition and sex Italian-style is like Fellini's *La Dolce Vita* rewritten by Jacqueline Susann on acid. It follows the beautiful Marina (Alt) in her sexual conquests and social climbing, from an early marriage to a handsome but penniless duke, through a spell as a millionaire's plaything, to a tempestuous affair with a mercurial communist artist who likes to slap her around. A romantic affair with married journo Nino (Gould) begins with champagne and roses, but also ends in disillusionment. The characters are vapid, the dubbing ludicrous, and the would-be evocative soundtrack merely bizarre (Paul Anka, Gilbert O'Sullivan, Mungo Jerry and '70s bubble gum pop). What it lacks in substance, it tries to make up for in sartorial accessories and exotic locations, achieving a perversely compelling trashiness. High camp fun or 24 carat kitsch, depending on your tolerance level. NF

My First Wife

(1984, Aust, 98 min)
d Paul Cox. *p* Jane Ballantyne, Paul Cox. *sc* Paul Cox. *ph* Yuri Sokol. *ed* Tim Lewis. *pd* Asher Bilu. *cast* John Hargreaves, Wendy Hughes, Lucy Angwin, David Cameron, Anna Jemison, Charles Tingwell, Betty Lucas.
●John (Hargreaves) introduces classical music over the late-night Melbourne air waves to pay his way as a composer. His wife Helen (Hughes) meanwhile indulges in some close harmony with a fellow choir member. One long painful night she comes clean about her adultery, and decides to leave John, taking their daughter with her. But John cannot cope with the separation. Standard soap on paper, but Cox fills the screen with luminous images of desires and anguish, and encourages his actors to portray emotional states of an almost embarrassing intensity. Rarely has the naked human body seemed so vulnerable, so raw; rarely has a simple shot – a girl and a dog – combined with a phrase of music seemed so potent. With its teasing, semi-autobiographical title, this is not always a comfortable film, but its compassion, wit and vigour are undoubtedly the real thing. DT

My Foolish Heart

(1949, US, 98 min, b/w)
d Mark Robson. p Samuel Goldwyn. sc Julius J Epstein, Philip G Epstein. ph Lee Garmes. ed Daniel Mandell. ad Richard Day. m Victor Young. cast Susan Hayward, Dana Andrews, Kent Smith, Lois Wheeler, Jessie Royce Landis, Gigi Perreau, Robert Keith.
●Loosely based on a story by JD Salinger (*Uncle Wiggily in Connecticut*, so travestied that it's no wonder Salinger subsequently kept Hollywood at arm's length), this Goldwyn production is a finely polished but drearily turgid example of the '40s weepie. Hayward plays a fallen college girl: cynical, selfish, alcoholic, married to a man she doesn't love, and expecting the child of a playboy pilot. The melodramatic situation is wrung for all it's worth and more, with the woman's final, inevitable realisation of the error of her ways only adding to the disaster of Robson's pedestrian direction and the mediocrity of the performances. GA

My Forbidden Past

(1951, US, 70 min, b/w)
d Robert Stevenson. *p* Robert Sparks, Polan Banks. *sc* Marion Parsonnet. *ph* Harry J Wild. *ed* George Shrader. *ad* Albert S D'Agostino, Al Herman. *m* Frederick Hollander. *cast* Robert Mitchum, Ava Gardner, Melvyn Douglas, Janis Carter, Lucile Watson.
●A Hughes RKO production dismissed as soapy claptrap by most critics, this steamy tale, set in 1890s New Orleans, of Ava Gardner's desperate plans to lure Mitchum away from his wife when she inherits a fortune, is terribly underrated. Nonsense it may be, and Mitchum's low key style is certainly at odds with the overheated emotionalism of the plot. But it is extremely entertaining, largely thanks to a marvellously cynical script (from Polan Banks' novel *Carriage Entrance*) which insists from start to finish on the basic selfishness of human interaction. Nasty fun. GA

My Friend Flicka

(1943, US, 88 min)
d Harold Schuster. *p* Ralph Dietrich. *sc* Lillie Hayward, Francis Edwards Faragoh. *ph* Dewey Wrigley. *ed* Robert Fritch. *ad* Richard Day, Chester Gore. *m* Alfred Newman. *cast* Roddy McDowall, Preston Foster, Rita Johnson, Jeff Corey, James Bell.
●Archetypal boy 'n' his hoss story (from the novel by Mary O'Hara), a Technicolor hit during the war and held in affection ever since. McDowall begs Foster, his rancher pa, for a colt of his own, then faces the trials and responsibilities of looking after it. All at once now, 'Aaah.' TJ

My Friend Ivan Lapshin (Moi Drug Ivan Lapshin)

(1986, USSR, 99 min, b/w & col)
d Alexei Gherman. *sc* Eduard Volodarsky. *ph* Valery Fedosov. *ed* L Semenovoi. *pd* Yuri Pugach. *m* Arkady Gagulashvili. *cast* Andrei Boltnev, Nina Ruslanova, Andrei Mironov, Aleksei Zharkov, Z Adamovich, A Filippenko, Yu Kuznetsov, V Filonov. *narrator* V Kuzin.
●Gherman's masterly film (his third) is framed as an autobiographical reminiscence of the 1930s, just before the Stalinist terror began to bite. Through the eyes of a nine-year-old we watch episodes from the life of a small town police chief: his home life in a ludicrously overcrowded apartment, his unsuccessful courtship of a glamorous actress, and his rather more successful campaign to hunt down the criminal fraternity of the Soloviev gang. There is nothing sinister about this Ivan, but the film is crammed with tiny suggestions of the horrors to come, designed to provoke disquieting speculations about the eventual fate of this potentially dangerous man. Gherman's methods are resolutely observational and low key, and his subject is the lull before the storm; the drama emerges as if by accident from a collage of resonant and deeply felt scenes from day-to-day life. Wonderfully vivid performances and amazingly original camerawork (mostly in elegantly faded monochrome) bring a vanished world to life with complete conviction. TR

My Generation

(2000, US, 103 min)
d/p Barbara Kopple. *ph* Tom Hurwitz. *ed* Tom Haneke. *with* The Allman Brothers, Country Joe McDonald, Cypress Hill, Janis Joplin, Jimi Hendrix, Joe Cocker, Melissa Etheridge, Metallica, Nine Inch Nails, Red Hot Chilli Peppers, Sheryl Crow, The Who
●This fascinating documentary from the director of *Wild Man Blues* shows how things have changed since the late '60s. Using the three Woodstock Festivals as an analogy for cultural and commercial change, Kopple focuses not only on the state of the kids who attended the gigs of 1969, '92 and '99, but also on the backstage shenanigans. Aside from drug choice and the love child's propensity for disrobing with alacrity, little appears to have changed in the concert-going fraternity. Noticeable, though, are the completely different working practices of just about everyone involved behind the scenes, so that by 1999, corporate sponsorship, product marketing and knee-jerk PC values have successfully hijacked the proceedings. Some snippets of good music from, among others, Joe Cocker and Red Hot Chilli Peppers. DA

My Giant

(1998, US, 103 min)
d Michael Lehmann. *p* Billy Crystal. *sc* David Seltzer. *ph* Michael Coulter. *ed* Stephen Semel. *pd* Jackson Degovia. *m* Marc Shaiman. *cast* Billy Crystal, Kathleen Quinlan, Gheorghe Muresan, Joanna Pacula, Zane Carney, Jere Burns, Harold Gould, Lorna Luft.
●Sammy (Crystal) is a regular Hollywood second-rater, separated from his wife (Quinlan) and son (Carney), and now reduced to scouting out his last promising client on a set in deepest Romania. Sacked on arrival, he subsequently crashes his car and is saved by a 7 foot 7 inch gentle giant called Max (basketball player Muresan). A reclusive literature buff, Max is still pining for the childhood sweetheart who left for America and hasn't replied to his letters these past 22 years; Sammy thus hatches a plan to escort Max back home, put him in the movies, reunite him with the old girl and prove his own true worth to the family happily ever after. This indolent family fare clasps old clichés (following your dreams, the guileless misfit, trust in family) to its breast like raggedy teddy-bears. NB

My Girl

(1991, US, 102 min)
d Howard Zieff. *p* Brian Grazer. *sc* Laurice Elehwany. *ph* Paul Elliott. *ed* Wendy Greene Bricmont. *pd* Joseph T Garrity. *m* James Newton Howard. *cast* Dan Aykroyd, Jamie Lee Curtis, Macaulay Culkin, Anna Chlumsky, Richard Masur, Griffin Dunne, Ann Nelson, Peter Michael Goetz.
●It's 1972, and 11-year-old Vada (Chlumsky) lives with her dotty granny and widowed mortician father (Aykroyd) in a house which doubles as a funeral parlour. Daily contact with corpses has produced a very odd child, given to pranks around the caskets, hypochondria and death-obsession, but shy Thomas (Culkin) proves a true and tolerant friend. Their knockabouts won't last forever, though: cosmetologist Shelly (Curtis) arrives to divide Dad's affections, and Vada experiences her first period, a make-up session, and bereavement... Zieff's direction is uninspired, but the film is considerably redeemed by screenwriter Laurice Elehwany's dark humour. Chlumsky gives a lively performance, which is more than can be said for Culkin. CM

My Girl 2

(1994, US, 99 min)
d Howard Zieff. *p* Brian Grazer. *sc* Janet Kovalcik. *ph* Paul Elliott. *ed* Wendy Greene Bricmont. *pd* Charles Rosen. *m* Cliff Eidelman. *cast* Dan Aykroyd, Jamie Lee Curtis, Anna Chlumsky, Austin O'Brien, Richard Masur, Christine Ebersole, John David Souther, Aubrey Morris, Gerrit Graham.

●After kissing Macaulay Culkin (in *My Girl*) only to see him stung to death by killer bees, Pennsylvania waif Vada Sultenfuss (Chlumsky) takes her pubertal trauma to Los Angeles. Assigned to write a school essay on 'someone very special…someone you've never met', mortician's daughter Vada opts for another stiff: her mother, who expired shortly after giving birth. She lived in Los Angeles, but nobody (including super-rotund dad Aykroyd) can remember anything about her. Maybe amiable Uncle Phil (Masur) and his unwed partner Rose (Ebersole) can help. It's hard to pinpoint what's so grisly about this film. Zieff's direction is far from his worst, Janet Kovalcik's script side-steps the mawkish, Chlumsky has shed her moppet-mouthed ghastliness, and new boyfriend O'Brien is one up on Culkin. Perhaps it's that the obsession with death sits so uneasily against the young-love backdrop. MK

My Girlfriend's Boyfriend (L'Ami de Mon Amie)

(1987, Fr, 103 min)
d Eric Rohmer. *p* Margaret Ménégoz. *sc* Eric Rohmer. *ph* Bernard Lutic, Sabine Lancelin. *ed* Maria-Luisa Garcia. *m* Jean-Louis Valero. *cast* Emmanuelle Chaulet, Sophie Renoir, Anne-Laure Meury, Eric Viellard, François-Eric Gendron.

●The sixth in Rohmer's glorious series of 'Comedies and Proverbs'. As ever, the plot is slight: shy civil servant Blanche escapes the loneliness of her new life in a Parisian suburb through her friendship with self-assured computer programmer Léa. When Léa goes on holiday, Blanche, who initially fancies herself enamoured of handsome engineer Alexandre, finds herself growing closer to her friend's lover Fabien. Questions of fidelity and betrayal, delusion and deceit lie at the film's heart, which is large indeed, extending ample compassion to the characters. Once again the performances of the young cast are miraculously naturalistic, and equally impressive is Rohmer's mastery of mood: a chaste and silent stroll along a canal towpath is tense with gentle eroticism, a summer party becomes fraught with embarrassment and unspoken feelings. Funny, moving, and full of insights that other directors barely dream of, it is quite simply an absolute charmer. GA

My Hero

see Southern Yankee, A

My Heroes Have Always Been Cowboys

(1991, US, 106 min)
d Stuart Rosenberg. *p* Martin H Poll, EK Gaylord II. *sc* Joel Don Humphreys. *ph* Bernd Heinl. *ed* Dennis M Hill. *m* James Horner. *cast* Scott Glenn, Kate Capshaw, Ben Johnson, Balthazar Getty, Tess Harper, Gary Busey, Mickey Rooney, Clu Gulager, Dub Taylor.

●Battered but unbowed, rodeo rider Glenn returns from the circuit dismayed to find pa Johnson in an old folks home, and running straight up against the rest of the family who reckon the old bastard should stay there. Glenn's world-weary performance brings a glimmer of real heart to this sagebrush saga, though the rekindling of romance with former high school sweetheart Capshaw and his eventual return to the bull ring are such contrivances that the characters don't stand much of a chance. TJ

My Hustler

(1965, US, 70 min, b/w)
d/p Andy Warhol. *sc* Chuck Wein. *ph* Andy Warhol. *cast* Paul America, Ed Hood, Joseph Campbell, John MacDermott, Genèvieve Charbon, Dorothy Dean.

●Made on Fire Island beach, this is vintage Warhol, with rather more structure than usual. The camera pans between a bronzed, blond hustler, statuesque on the sand, and an ageing queen talking on the verandah of a beach house. The queen provides most of the soundtrack: part monologue, part conversation in best New York camp style, witty, vicious, outrageous, etc. Dramatic interest of sorts is provided by the arrival of a female neighbour intent on seducing the hustler, and shortly after of the Sugar Plum Fairy, another hustler, also with a lustful eye on the beach. The three have a bet as to which one will succeed; and the second half is filmed with a static camera in the bathroom while they wash and shave. At the end, after they've all tried to pull him, offering variations on the wealth/possessions theme, we never get to know who wins out. But that's unimportant: the myth of the ending is a literary hangover. JB

My Journey, My Islam

(1999, Aust, 56 min)
d Kay Rasool. *p* Paul Humfress, Kay Rasool. *sc* Kay Rasool. *ph* Joel Peterson. *ed* Denise Hunter. *m* Avijit Sarkar. *with* Madiha, Nek Akhtar, Benazir Bhutto, Nina.

●This exploration of the role of the *Hijab* (the veil) in contemporary Muslim society takes a woman from her home in Sydney around the world to visit her dispersed family. Writer/director Kay Rasool questions her own commitment to her religion – hers is a pick 'n' mix approach – and ponders the wider cultural implications for Muslim women wherever they may find themselves. There are doubtless many complex and vital issues in here, somewhere, but Rasool is no film-maker. Her join-the-dots style is tiring; the endless voice-over grates and merely highlights the lack of rhythm to the film. As an example of documentary film-making, this couldn't be less exciting, as a polemic it is hardly more convincing. FM

My Learned Friend

(1943, GB, 76 min, b/w)
d Basil Dearden, Will Hay. *p* Michael Balcon. *sc* Angus Macphail, John Dighton. *ph* Wilkie Cooper. *ed* Charles Hasse. *ad* Michael Relph. *m* Ernest Irving. *cast* Will Hay, Claude Hulbert, Mervyn Johns, Ernest Thesiger, Charles Victor, Hy Hazell, Lloyd Pearson.

●A slightly desperate but surprisingly funny farce, agreeably tinged with black. Will Hay's last film, in which, as an incompetent barrister being kept till last as a bonne bouche by a criminal (Johns) determined to eliminate everyone connected with his trial, he frantically tries to forewarn the other victims in an attempt to stave off his own end. The dizzy climax, courtesy Harold Lloyd and/or Hitchcock, is a pursuit over the face and hands of Big Ben. TM

My Left Foot

(1989, GB, 103 min)
d Jim Sheridan. *p* Noel Pearson. *sc* Shane Connaughton, Jim Sheridan. *ph* Jack Conroy. *ed* J Patrick Duffner. *pd* Austen Spriggs. *m* Elmer Bernstein. *cast* Daniel Day Lewis, Ray McAnally, Brenda Fricker, Ruth McCabe, Fiona Shaw, Eanna MacLiam, Alison Whelan, Declan Croghan, Hugh O'Conor, Cyril Cusack, Adrian Dunbar.

●Day Lewis' re-creation of writer/painter Christy Brown's condition is so precise, so detailed and so matter-of-fact that it transcends the carping about casting an actor without cerebral palsy. He couldn't have done it better. More to the point, he does it with so little show that the character of Christy – cussed, frustrated, indulged, immature – comes through powerfully. Writers Shane Connaughton and Jim Sheridan take extraordinary liberties with Brown's autobiography, but they've caught the spirit of the man, and satisfied the family, who are presented as saintly, if chaotic. Brenda Fricker, wonderfully eloquent in her silences, and Ray McAnally, in his last screen role, make an utterly convincing Mam and Dad, stopping just the right side of sentimentality. Less happy is Fiona Shaw as the fictional Eileen Cole, an amalgam of several characters in the book. Sheridan gives us an atmospheric Dublin and the economy of the best TV drama; and 13-year-old Hugh O'Conor, playing Christy as a boy, makes an admirable job of holding the ring before the arrival of the main act. JMo

My Life

(1993, US, 117 min)
d Bruce Joel Rubin. *p* Jerry Zucker, Bruce Joel Rubin, Hunt Lowry. *sc* Bruce Joel Rubin. *ph* Peter James. *ed* Richard Chew. *pd* Neil Spisak. *m* John Barry. *cast* Michael Keaton, Nicole Kidman, Bradley Whitford, Queen Latifah, Michael Constantine, Haing S Ngor, Rebecca Schull.

●Bob and Gail Jones (Keaton and Kidman) are expecting their first child. Bob, though, has cancer and may not live to see the baby, so he starts to make a video journal about his life – thus embarking on a journey of self-discovery into the density of the human heart and the expansiveness of the human soul. The only thing dense and expansive, however, is the sentimentality. Ironically, we don't know much more about Bob after he's discovered himself than we knew before. He's angry and ashamed of his family, and angry and ashamed of himself because of it. Indeed, rather than examine Bob's life in any depth, the film chooses in the end to become the celebration of a baby. AO

My Life and Times with Antonin Artaud

see En Compagnie de Antonin Artaud

My Life as a Dog (Mit Liv som Hund)

(1985, Swe, 101 min)
d Lasse Hallström. *p* Waldemar Bergendahl. *sc* Lasse Hallström, Reidar Jönsson, Brasse Brännström, Per Berglund. *ph* Jörgen Persson. *ed* Susanne Linnmann, Christer Furubrand. *ad* Lasse Westfelt. *m* Björn Isfalt. *cast* Anton Glanzelius, Manfred Serner, Anki Lidén, Tomas von Brömssen, Melinda Kinnaman, Kicki Rundgren, Lennart Hjulström, Ing-Marie Carlsson.

●This charming, bitter-sweet evocation of childhood is something of a minor gem. Set in the Sweden of the 1950s, it describes the 400 blows suffered by a resourceful, twitchy and energetic 12-year-old boy who is farmed out to country relatives when his antics and demands for attention prove too much for his ailing mother. Hallström nurtures from his young star (Glanzelius) a performance of remarkable range and maturity, presenting a poignant picture of youthful tenacity struggling to come to terms with disappointments and events that may be beyond his comprehension, but which he manages to negotiate with his quirky, open-eyed optimism intact. Witty, touching and perceptive as he contrasts the rural village and its strange but generous-hearted eccentrics with the harsher realities of the city, Hallström makes it a seamless mix of tragedy and humour. WH

My Life's in Turnaround

(1993, US, 84 min)
d Eric Schaeffer, Donal Lardner Ward. *p* Daniel Einfeld. *sc* Eric Schaeffer, Donal Lardner Ward. *ph* Peter Hawkins. *ed* Susan Graff. *m* Reed Hays. *cast* Eric Schaeffer, Donald Lardner Ward, Dana Wheeler Nicholson, Lisa Gerstein, John Sayles, John Dore, Debra Klein.

●Schaeffer and Ward (writers, directors and stars of this first feature) play two struggling young film-makers scraping together the wherewithal to make a movie. Very droll, or it would be if the script had a bit more horsepower and the players a bit more screen presence. The best moment comes from John Sayles as a dodgy financier railing against so-called 'independent' movie-makers, but it's a very mild diversion. TJ

My Life So Far

(1998, US/GB, 98 min)
d Hugh Hudson. *p* David Puttnam, Steve Norris. *sc* Simon Donald. *ph* Bernard Lutic. *ed* Scott Thomas. *pd* Andy Harris. *m* Howard Blake. *cast* Colin Firth, Rosemary Harris, Irène Jacob, Tchéky Karyo, Mary Elizabeth Mastrantonio, Malcolm McDowell, Kelly MacDonald, Robert Norman, John Bett, Freddie Jones.

●David Puttnam's production signs off with an ill-advised flourish, a biographical notation to the effect that young Fraser, our pubescent hero, grew up to become a TV executive and serve on the board of the English National Opera. As CVs go, it's not exactly Olympic Gold medal material – especially as the preceding 90 minutes or so leave us in no doubt that the lad grew up in the most privileged surroundings in the Scottish Highlands. Still, if you can stomach a boy who clings to the skirts of 'Mumsy' and 'Gramma' to protect him from 'The Hairy Man' (a shell-shocked tramp), Sir Denis Forman's memoir serves well enough as the basis for a gently nostalgic coming-of-age story with a tourist-friendly 1920s setting. It centres on Fraser's relationship with his dad (Firth), an inventor who takes special pride in his spagnum moss, thinks Louis Armstrong plays the devil's music, and loses face when he becomes besotted with exotic Aunt Heloise (Jacob). This all causes great suffering to Mumsy, but at least affords Mastrantonio a couple of strong emotional scenes and relieves us momentarily from Fraser's not terribly exciting adventures in the library. Lasse Hallström might have dug out the human comedy in it, but director Hudson only manages to cloy. TCh

My Life to Live

see Vivre sa Vie

My Life Without Steve

(1986, Aust, 53 min)
d Gillian Leahy. *voice* Jenny Vuletic.

● Alone in a Sydney bedsit, a woman meditates on the loss of her lover to another woman. It's the usual thing: confusion, recrimination, guilt, fear, anger, loneliness. Finally, however, she takes a few tentative steps towards a rediscovery of her sense of self. It's structured as a monologue accompanied by crisp, painterly images of the narrator's apartment and its view over a bay, the rambling digressions (bursting with cultural references) clearly meant to represent an intensely relevant essay on romantic love and loss. But for all its worthy intentions, the movie suffers from fashionable, dilettante pretensions and from a dearth of humour that turns its narrator's liturgy of misery into a self-piteous wallow that fails to stir the emotions. Not a little irritating. GA

My Little Chickadee

(1940, US, 83 min, b/w)
d Edward F Cline. *p* Lester Cowan. *sc* Mae West, WC Fields. *ph* Joseph Valentine. *ed* Edward Curtiss. *ad* Jack Otterson, Martin Obzina. *m* Frank Skinner. *cast* Mae West, WC Fields, Joseph Calleia, Dick Foran, Ruth Donnelly, Margaret Hamilton, Donald Meek.

● Pairing West and Fields in one film was probably one of those ideas that seemed good at the time. But the two iconoclasts just don't mix. Fields has easily the best of it, working from his own script (though he diplomatically shared screen credit with his prickly co-star). He's in his element tossing off lunatic stories and choice aphorisms at the bar and card table of Greasewood City, a parody Western town, but time hangs heavy in his exchanges with the buxom Mae, who marries him for his non-existent money. And it hangs even heavier when Mae's by herself. GB

My Little Girl

(1986, US, 117 min)
d Connie Kaiserman. *p* Thomas F Turley. *sc* Connie Kaiserman, Nan Mason. *ph* Pierre Lhomme. *ed* Katherine Wenning. *pd* Dan Leigh. *m* Richard Robbins. *cast* James Earl Jones, Geraldine Page, Mary Stuart Masterson, Anne Meara, Pamela Payton Wright, Peter Michael Goetz, Peter Gallagher.

● Sixteen-year-old Franny (Masterson) is a poor little rich girl who spends some of her time as a volunteer helper at a centre for children in care. She befriends a pair of black sisters, but when one is transferred to a more secure institution, she become involved in helping her to escape. Connie Kaiserman's sententious debut aims to show the plight of criminal brats and circumstantial orphans and to reveal the dangers of do-gooding; as a director, unfortunately, she shares her central character's naivety and lack of judgment. The final half-hour is taken up with a wholly unnecessary and wholly awful talent night given by the centre's inmates. Still, the performances are good. MS

My Little Pony

(1986, US, 100 min)
d Michael Jones. *p* Joe Bacal, Tom Griffin. *sc* George Arthur Bloom. *ed* Steven C Brown, Mike DePatie. *m* Rob Walsh. *cast* voices: Danny DeVito, Madeline Kahn, Cloris Leachman, Rhea Perlman, Tony Randall.

● An animated feature hopefully plugging the *My Little Pony* line in toys. Pretty Ponyland is threatened with manic monochrome by the wicked witch Hydia and her evil slime, Smooze. Utter Flutter provides salvation, but don't ask what it is, because the queasy colours, screeching voices, and songs of staggering banality make paying attention difficult. Jejune in conception, devoid of talent in realisation, this painful dross perpetrates its own critique when Reeka (or was it Draggle? One of the witch's daughters, anyway) remarks on seeing her spell fail, 'How embarrassing, I'm going home.' MS

My Love Has Been Burning (Waga Koi Wa Moenu)

(1949, Jap, 84 min, b/w)
d Kenji Mizoguchi. *p* Hisao Itoya, Kiyoshi Shimazu. *sc* Yoshikata Yoda, Kaneto Shindo. *ph* Kohei Sugiyama, Tomotaro Nashiki. *ad* Hiroshi Mizutani, Dai Arakawa, Junichiro Osumi. *m* Senji Ito. *cast* Kinuyo Tanaka, Mitsuko Mito, Kuniko Miyabe, Eitaro Ozawa, Ichiro Sugai, Sadako Sawamura, Kuniko Miyake, Koreya Senda.

● A film that deserves the same kind of praise as *Ugetsu Monogatari* and *Sansho Dayu*. Drawn from the autobiography of a late 19th century pioneer for women's rights in Japan, the film is one woman's journey through an extremely complex, contradiction-laden phase of modern Japanese history: when notions of democratic party politics were cohering, for instance, although – as is devastatingly demonstrated – not even the most liberal-thinking male politician thought to extend the freedoms for which he was fighting to his own wife. Undoubtedly one of Mizoguchi's most violent films – the scenes in the silk mill and prison show some horrific brutalities – it's also notable for a wonderful performance from Mizoguchi's favourite actress, Kinuyo Tanaka. RM

My Lucky Star

(1938, US, 84 min, b/w)
d Roy Del Ruth. *p* Harry Joe Brown. *sc* Harry Tugend, Jack Yellen. *ph* John Mescall. *ed* Allen McNeil. *songs* Mack Gordon, Harry Revel. *cast* Sonja Henie, Richard Greene, Cesar Romero, Joan Davis, Buddy Ebsen, Arthur Treacher, Elisha Cook Jr, Louise Hovick.

● To boost sales in the sports department, Sonja Henie, a parcel-wrapper at a Fifth Avenue store, agrees to become an advertising mannequin at snowy Plymouth University, never suspecting this will rile her fellow co-eds. Skating, sleigh rides, and romance in the sweetshop (with Richard Greene) ensue. Mournful racoon-skin support from Buddy Ebsen and a notable ice finale, 'Alice in Wonderland Through the Looking Glass'. JPy

My Man Godfrey

(1936, US, 96 min, b/w)
d Gregory La Cava. *sc* Morrie Ryskind, Eric Hatch. *ph* Ted Tetzlaff. *ed* Ted J Kent, Russell Schoengarth. *ad* Charles D Hall. *cast* William Powell, Carole Lombard, Gail Patrick, Eugene Pallette, Alice Brady, Mischa Auer, Alan Mowbray, Franklin Pangborn, Grady Sutton, Jane Wyman.

● Heartless screwball classic, directed with clinical glee by the still undervalued La Cava and scripted by the mysterious Morrie Ryskind, who began with the Marx Brothers and later drifted into weepies and right wing politics. Godfrey (Powell) is the high-minded tramp found during a society 'scavenger hunt' and led back by the more than lovely Lombard into her household, full of profligate madcaps who duly become a little more civilised. The film has lost some of its allure over the years, but it's still streets and streets ahead of the addled whimsy favoured by latter-day Hollywood. GB

My Man Godfrey

(1957, US, 92 min)
d Henry Koster. *p* Ross Hunter. *sc* Everett Freeman, William Bowers, Peter Berneis. *ph* William H Daniels. *ed* Milton Carruth. *ad* Alexander Golitzen, Richard H Riedel. *m* Frank Skinner. *cast* June Allyson, David Niven, Jessie Royce Landis, Robert Keith, Martha Hyer, Eva Gabor, Jay Robinson, Jeff Donnell, Herbert Anderson.

● Wretched remake of La Cava's stinging screwball comedy about a scatterbrain socialite who 'collects' one of the Depression's forgotten men and adopts him as her butler. Apart from deficiencies on all other glitzy Ross Hunter fronts, the script tries to update by turning the down-and-out into an illegal immigrant. With the part of an ex-Luftwaffe pilot played by OW Fischer, as originally planned, it just might have worked; with Niven, it's disastrously bland. TM

My Memories of Old Beijing (Chengnan Jiushi)

(1983, China, 93 min)
d Wu Yigong. *sc* Yi Ming. *ph* Cao Weiye. *m* Lu Qiming. *cast* Shen Jie, Zheng Zhenyao, Zhang Min, Zhang Fengyi, Yan Xiang.

● Wu Yigong's almost dream-like re-creation of a young girl's Beijing childhood is often like memory itself, impressionistic, anecdotal and resonant in its initially disassociated detail; and because this framework eschews a direct, linear narrative, Wu neatly sidesteps the melodramatic conventions of much Chinese cinema. The result is an immensely accessible and often tender film, sometimes betrayed by its visual and stylistic ambition but nonetheless consistently evocative, and full of a diffuse, affecting melancholy. SM

My Mother's Castle

see Château de ma mère, Le

My Mother's Courage (Mutters Courage)

(1995, Ger/GB/Aus, 90 min)
d/p/sc Michael Verhoeven. *ph* Michaêl Epp, Theo Bierkens. *ed* David Freeman. *pd* Wolfgang Hundhammer, Javor Lorant. *m* Julian Nott, Simon Verhoeven. *cast* Pauline Collins, Ulrich Tukur, Natalie Morse, Robert Giggenbach, Günter Bothur, George Tabori.

● In 1994 the playwright George Tabori visits the set of a film being made from his mother's diaries. An encounter with the leading actress whisks him back to the past to place the story in context – a distancing framework that challenges us to consider our own connection with these images of terror. There's more time for reflection as the action moves on to Tabori's mother, a middle-aged housewife arrested while doing her shopping and dispatched to Budapest's main railway station, where the Gestapo punctiliously marshal hundreds of her fellow Jews into freight wagons. Surprising, maybe, to see Pauline Collins as Mrs Tabori (the film's shot in English), but she's superb as an essentially cheery woman numbed by the events around her and driven to make a stand for the first time in her life. Determined to avoid displaying emotion in front of her captors, Collins, in a key moment, chokes back the tears in a straining, desperate attempt to retain her dignity. A remarkable scene, and it says a lot for the power and intelligence of the film and its central performance, that its most haunting image is of a woman trying not to cry. TJ

My Name Is Joe

(1998, GB, 105 min)
d Ken Loach. *p* Rebecca O'Brien. *sc* Paul Laverty. *ph* Barry Ackroyd. *ed* Jonathan Morris. *pd* Martin Johnson. *m* George Fenton. *cast* Peter Mullan, Louise Goodall, David McKay, Anne Marie Kennedy, Gary Lewis, David Hayman.

● After coming into conflict over a young couple troubled by debt and drug-dependency, amateur soccer coach and recovering alcoholic Joe (Mullan) and health service worker Sarah (Goodall) find themselves embarking on a mutually wary but fulfilling romance; the trouble is, they have different ideas about how to deal with the problems posed by the unforgiving world around them. Very funny, typically insightful and authentic, and surprisingly sexy (for a Loach movie), this also proceeds to an emotionally quite devastating conclusion, where Renoir's thesis that 'everyone has their reasons' is put painfully to the test. The performances are uniformly superb (though Mullan is especially charismatic), and the direction discreet but wonderfully telling. GA

My Name Is Julia Ross

(1945, US, 65 min, b/w)
d Joseph H Lewis. *p* Wallace MacDonald. *sc* Muriel Roy Bolton. *ph* Burnett Guffey. *ed* Henry Batista. *ad* Jerome Pycha Jr. *m* Mischa Bakaleinikoff. *cast* Nina Foch, George Macready, Dame May Whitty, Roland Varno, Anita Bolster, Doris Lloyd, Leonard Mudie.

● Having toiled industriously on nonsense for years, B-movie king Lewis was at last given a chance, by Columbia's Harry Cohn, with a slightly higher budget and infinitely more malleable material. Taking a job as secretary to Whitty, Foch soon finds herself in deadly peril: drugged and removed to a remote Cornish manse, she awakes to discover that she has been given another woman's name, not to mention a husband in the shape of Whitty's psychotic son Macready. So far, so bad, but things worsen when she hears her incarcerators plotting her demise as a fake suicide. Handling the various plot twists with ease and eliciting superior performances from his three leads, Lewis repeatedly displays his ability to convey mood and meaning through visuals: Burnett Guffey's camera prowls nervously through shadowy interiors, Macready's madness is vividly evoked by his endless knife-playing. A small, dark gem in the *Rebecca* tradition, it may not be as startlingly original or adventurous as Lewis's later *Gun Crazy* or *The Big Combo*, but it knocks Penn's remake *Dead of Winter*, for six. (From Anthony Gilbert's novel *The Woman in Red*.) GA

My Name Is Nobody (Mio Nome è Nessuno, Il)

(1973, It/Fr/WGer, 130 min)
d Tonino Valerii. *p* Claudio Mancini. *sc* Ernesto Gastaldi. *ph* Giuseppe Ruzzolini, (US) Armando Nannuzzi. *ed* Nino Baragli. *ad* Gianni Polidori. *m* Ennio Morricone. *cast* Henry Fonda, Terence Hill, Jean Martin, Piero Lulli, Leo Gordon, RG Armstrong, Remus Peets.

●Produced by Sergio Leone and very much bearing his stamp, a Western which takes as its theme the alchemy whereby life is turned into legend. The year is 1899, and feared but fading gunfighter Jack Beauregard (Fonda) lives for the day he can lay down his deposit on a steamer berth to Europe. Instead he meets his angel of death, a young gunfighter calling himself Nobody who, in turn, lives for the legend of Beauregard and an obsessive vision of the ultimate confrontation: between Beauregard, alone on an immense plain, and the 150 men of the Wild Bunch. With superbly handled action sequences, excellent cinematography, and a Morricone score worthy of his *Man With No Name* efforts, it's a film to be seen. VG

My New Friends (Wo Xin Renshi de Pengyou)

(1995, Tai, 56 min)
d/with Tsai Ming-Liang.

●Tsai interrupted his pre-production for *The River* to make this pioneering documentary for Taiwan's nascent AIDS-awareness campaign. Ignoring instructions to 'play down the gay angle', he centres the film on his own very candid conversations with two HIV+ young men. Sadly the identities of the interviewees have to be concealed, and so the freewheeling camerawork focuses most often on Tsai himself; but the sense of rapport between the director and his 'new friends' is palpable and very moving, even to Western viewers already only too familiar with these issues. TR

My New Gun

(1992, US, 95 min)
d Stacy Cochran. *p* Michael Flynn. *sc* Stacy Cochran. *ph* Ed Lachman. *ed* Camilla Toniolo. *pd* Tony Corbett. *m* Pat Irwin. *cast* Diane Lane, James LeGros, Stephen Collins, Tess Harper, Bruce Altman, Maddie Corman, Bill Raymond.

●A deceptive, quirky and amusing black comedy from the independent sector. Set in upmarket wood-clad suburban New Jersey, it follows events when a housewife (Lane, in her best performance to date) is given a pearl-handled revolver by her nerd husband for her protection (and against her wishes). Attractive next door neighbour Skippy (Collins) asks to borrow the gun for unexplained reasons, she agrees, and the two become implicated. There are many questions. What, for instance, has Skippy's strange mother (Harper), a Country & Western singer, to do with all this? Cinematographer Ed Lachman gives it all a bright look, to augment the feeling of unsettling disingenuousness. For this is a film without explanations, more 'screw-loose' than 'screwball', with a pinch of Lynch. WH

My Nights with Susan, Sandra, Olga and Julie (Mijn Nachten med Susan Olga Albert Julie Piet & Sandra)

(1975, Neth, 100 min)
d Pim de la Parra. *p* Wim Verstappen. *sc* Charles Gormley, David Kaufman, Harry Kümel, Carel Donck, Pim de la Parra. *ph* Marc Felperlaan. *ed* Jutta Brandstaedter, Hans Van Dongen. *m* Elisabeth Lutyens. *cast* Willeke Van Ammelrooy, Hans Van der Gragt, Nelly Frijda, Franulka Heyermans, Marya de Heer, Jerry Brouer.

●The biggest mystery about this psycho-sexdrama is why it took five writers (including Harry Kümel, who should have known better) to cobble together dialogue that consists mainly of characters calling out the names in the title. Blond biker stays at farmhouse full of assorted weirdos, namely two murderous nymphets (Sandra and Olga), troubled heroine (Susan), sleeping beauty (Julie) and simpleton hag (Piet) who collects dead bodies and watches everyone spying on each other. Presumably intended as an adult fairytale, it takes itself ludicrously seriously but never overcomes the fundamental problem of so what and who cares.

My Night with Maud (Ma Nuit chez Maud)

(1969, Fr, 113 min, b/w)
d Eric Rohmer. *p* Pierre Cottrell. *sc* Eric Rohmer. *ph* Nestor Almendros. *ed* Cécile Decugis. *ad* Nicole Rachline. *cast* Jean-Louis Trintignant, Françoise Fabian, Marie-Christine Barrault, Antoine Vitez, Léonide Kogan, Anne Dubot, P Guy Léger.

●The third in Rohmer's series of 'Moral Tales' (though shot out of sequence after *La Collectionneuse*) was the film that sealed his international reputation. Exquisitely shot by Nestor Almendros in a chill and wintry Clermont-Ferrand, it tells – lightly, wittily and amazingly perceptively – of the long night of the soul of a Catholic engineer (Trintignant), smugly secure in his acceptance of Pascal's wager (it pays to believe in God, because if you win, you win eternity; if you lose, you lose nothing), who makes up his mind he is going to marry a girl (Barrault) he has seen only in church. His philosophy comes in for a rude shaking up during the teasing, tantalising, and ultimately chaste night he spends with the free-thinking divorcee Maud (Fabian), who opens his eyes to the fact that 'a choice can be heartbreaking'. Still one of Rohmer's best films. TM

My Own Private Idaho

(1991, US, 104 min)
d Gus Van Sant. *p* Laurie Parker. *sc* Gus Van Sant. *ph* Eric Alan Edwards, John Campbell. *ed* Curtiss Clayton. *pd* David Brisbin. *m* Bill Stafford. *cast* River Phoenix, Keanu Reeves, James Russo, Udo Kier, William Richert, Rodney Harvey, Chiara Caselli, Grace Zabriskie, Tom Troupe

●Van Sant's impressive third feature has enough ideas to fill three movies, a plenitude that threatens to blow the film apart (but never does). It's a road movie filmed mainly from the point of view of gay hustler Mike (Phoenix, superb), a narcoleptic who falls unconscious without warning at moments of stress. As Mike tours the Pacific Northwest doing 'dates', he meets up with mayor's son Scott (Reeves), and together they set off in search of Mike's mother. The disconcerting realities of the situation are punctuated by sequences of surreal, dreamlike beauty, 'documentary'-style inserts, and playful variations on Shakespeare, with Scott still playing Prince Hal to the Falstaffian Bob (Richert), a thief and ex-hustler, in the knowledge that he will soon be 'King'. Stunning to look at – the dawn and dusk landscapes are sublime – and seductively scored, the film's uniqueness lies in its remarkable emotional open-heartedness. WH

My Private War (Mein Krieg)

(1990, Ger, 90 min, b/w & col)
d Harriet Eder, Thomas Kufus. *p* Hans George Ullrich. *sc* Harriet Eder, Thomas Kufus. *ph* Johann Feindt. *ed* Harriet Eder, Thomas Kufus.

●The German army on the Russian front boasted six amateur cameramen in the ranks, whose footage comprised a fascinating blend of the ordinary and the horrendous. In place of the heel-clicking automata of war films, we see a young soldier in a swastika armband embarrassed by a visit from his mum; a Christmas tree stabbed into the frozen earth beside a machine-gun emplacement; the joy of shooting down a Russian plane with a rifle. In interview, the veterans display extreme agitation on the subject of the execution of peasants and Jews, and great pride in their old German cameras which performed so well at temperatures below zero. BC

Myra Breckinridge

(1970, US, 94 min)
d Michael Sarne. *p* Robert Fryer. *sc* Michael Sarne, David Giler, Gore Vidal. *ph* Richard Moore. *ed* Danford B Greene. *ad* Jack Martin Smith, Fred Harpman. *m* Lionel Newman. *cast* Mae West, John Huston, Raquel Welch, Rex Reed, Farrah Fawcett, Roger C Carmel, Jim Backus, John Carradine, Andy Devine, Grady Sutton, Tom Selleck.

●As an adaptation of Gore Vidal's novel, this is a major travesty. As a Hollywood comedy, it's a major disaster. As a 20th Century-Fox movie, it's the best argument yet for employing a director who can direct. But as a Raquel Welch movie, it's better than most. TR

My Silly Mother (Mamá es boba)

(1998, Sp, 92 min)
d Santiago Lorenzo. *p* Tomás Cimadevilla, Piluca Baquero. *sc* Santiago Lorenzo. *ph* Alfonso Parra. *ed* Antonio Lara. *pd* Victor Molero. *m* Malcolm Scarpa. *cast* Faustina Camacho, José Luis Lago, Adrián Gil, Eduardo Atuña, Cristina Garrigues, Mercedes Navarro, Juan Carlos Garcia.

●When the cynical programmers of a TV company are sent to the small town of Palencia, they take revenge on their employers and their new audience by promoting a naive, dumb cleaning lady to presenter. The story is related by her young son, himself already bullied at school and ashamed of his parents. An odd, and oddly dislikeable movie, which aims for black, cruelly amoral comedy but is actually deeply sentimental and moralistic, not to say implausible, patronising and predictable. Occasional hints that it may all be an allegory on God's cruelty don't help. GA

My Sister Eileen

(1955, US, 107 min)
d Richard Quine. *p* Fred Kohlmar. *sc* Blake Edwards, Richard Quine. *ph* Charles Lawton Jr. *ed* Charles Nelson. *ad* Walter Holscher. *m* George Duning. *songs* Jule Styne, Leo Robin. cast Janet Leigh, Jack Lemmon, Betty Garrett, Robert Fosse, Kurt Kasznar, Richard York, Horace McMahon.

●Two spirited Ohio girls, plain, forbearing Ruth (Garrett) and blonde, head-turning Eileen (Leigh), take a 30-day let on a Greenwich Village basement, determined to make their mark on Manhattan. Good-looking wide-screen musical (from the play by Joseph Fields and Jerome Chodorov, in turn an adaptation of short stories by Ruth McKenney – interestingly, not to say confusingly, the Leonard Bernstein stage musical *Wonderful Town* had the same provenance), with Bob Fosse as the unprepossessing soda jerk who wins Eileen against the opposition of a shipload of Brazilian naval cadets, and Jack Lemmon, as the magazine editor, an old-school sexual predator (essentially idiotic), who finally recognises Ruth for what she is, a real writer and a real stunner. Funny, innocent and light on its toes. JPy

My Sons (Musuko)

(1991, Jap, 121 min)
d Yoji Yamada. *p* Shigehiro Nakagawa, Hiroshi Fukazawa. *sc* Yoji Yamada, Yoshitaka Asama. *ph* Tetsuo Takaba. *ed* Iwao Ishii. *ad* Mitsuo Degawa. *m* Teizo Matsumura. *cast* Rentaro Mikuni, Emi Wakui, Masatoshi Nagase.

●Yamada, director of the endless 'Tora-san' series, called this his homage to Ozu, and it's true that the focus on parental expectations and filial obligations is Ozu-esque, as are a few of the images. Grizzled veteran Mikuni plays a cantankerous tobacco farmer from a village in Iwate Prefecture; his wife died a year ago, and he's getting too old to carry on. His two contrasted sons have moved to the outskirts of Tokyo, and the core of the film is the old man's visit to the capital to assess their futures and his own. This is not an example of what's happening in contemporary Japanese cinema, and it has the usual Yamada problem of being all surface and no depths; but it has sincere affection for its characters, and is very well acted and directed. Genuinely touching, its qualities make it Yamada's best film by far. TR

My Son the Fanatic

(1997, GB, 87 min)
d Udayan Prasad. *p* Chris Curling. *sc* Hanif Kureishi. *ph* Alan Almond. *ed* David Gamble. *pd* Grenville Horner. *m* Stephen Warbeck. *cast* Om Puri, Rachel Griffiths, Stellan Skarsgård, Akbar Kurtha, Gopi Desai, Moya Brady.

●Combining affecting romance with sharp political and psychological insights, Hanif Kureishi's script (from his own short story) centres on

Pakistani cabbie Parvez (Om Puri), whose respect and love for most things English – including local prostitute Bettina (Griffiths) – brings him into terrible conflict with his teenage son, an Islamic fundamentalist who contemptuously views the ways of his family's adopted northern English city as decadent, depraved and disposable. Thematically rich, and never opting for simplistic polarities in its exploration of the clash of cultures, generations and ethical beliefs, the film overcomes its initial uncertainties of tone to mount a very moving study of a man in crisis; Puri is terrific, especially in his scenes with the excellent Griffiths. GA

My Stepmother Is an Alien

(1988, US, 108 min)
d Richard Benjamin. *p* Ronald Parker, Franklin R Levy. *sc* Jerico [Jerico Stone], Herschel Weingrod, Timothy Harris, Jonathan Reynolds. *ph* Richard H Kline. *ed* Jacqueline Cambas. *pd* Charles Rosen. *m* Alan Silvestri. *cast* Dan Aykroyd, Kim Basinger, Jon Lovitz, Alyson Hannigan, Joseph Maher, Seth Green, Wesley Mann, Juliette Lewis.

● In a last-ditch attempt to save her planet from imminent destruction, alien Celeste (Basinger) arrives on earth to seek the help of widowed scientist Steve (Aykroyd). Her identity is a secret, which results in confusion when Steve falls for and marries what he believes to be a beautiful and naive European; his teenage daughter (Hannigan) is none too pleased with her conniving stepmother, particularly after catching her slurping on battery fluid and talking to an ugly creature in her handbag. The film offers several entertaining sequences, but *Splash* it ain't, for while that film took a similar scenario and beautifully conveyed romantic notions of innocence, this is marred by cruel and juvenile gags. Hence an overlong scene which introduces Celeste to the experience of kissing. Worse still, comedian Lovitz plays Steve's truly tedious playboy brother. With earthlings like him, intelligent forms of life would be better advised to stay in their own galaxy. CM.

Mystère Picasso, Le

(1956, Fr, 77 min, b/w & col)
d Henri-Georges Clouzot. *sc* Pablo Picasso, Henri-Georges Clouzot. *ph* Claude Renoir. *ed* Henri Colpi. *m* Georges Auric. *with* Pablo Picasso, Henri-Georges Clouzot.

● Picasso was famously reluctant to be filmed at work. But when persuaded in 1955 to sketch before the camera of Henri-Georges Clouzot, master (and miserabilist) film director, he evidently took to it with relish. Stripped to a pair of shorts, parading his square torso, the 75-year-old Pablo plays up to the camera, even turning out a sketch to a five-minute deadline. Because he was asked to work on transparent screens, allowing the camera fully to frame the emerging picture instead of having to peep over the artist's shoulder, we get to see the work develop, with Picasso's different styles accompanied by a soundtrack that moves from bebop to flamenco. RY

Mysterians, The (Chikyu Boeigun)

(1957, Jap, 89 min)
d Inoshiro Honda. *p* Tomoyuki Tanaka. *sc* Takeshi Kimura. *ph* Hajime Koizumi. *ad* Teruaki Aba. *m* Akira Ifukube. *cast* Kenji Sahara, Yumi Shirakawa, Momoko Kochi, Akihiko Hirata, Takashi Shimura, Susumu Fujita.

● The Mysterians come from an exploded planet and aren't the friendliest aliens: they start forest fires and landslides, and send up a galumphing robot monster. They ask for three kilometres of Japan, but really want the whole earth; most ghastly of all, they kidnap women to propagate their kind. Still, we humans aren't very nice in return, and it's not long before this lively sci-fi extravaganza from Inoshiro *Godzilla* Honda has turned into an out-and-out war film, with tanks and ray guns trundling and blasting away in the midst of lavish but variable special effects. GB

Mysterious Island

(1961, GB, 100 min)
d Cyril Endfield. *p* Charles H Schneer. *sc* John Prebble, Daniel B Ullman, Crane Wilbur. *ph* Wilkie Cooper. *ed* Frederick Wilson. *ad* Bill Andrews. *m* Bernard Herrmann. *cast* Joan Greenwood, Michael Craig, Herbert Lom, Michael Callan, Gary Merrill, Percy Herbert, Dan Jackson, Nigel Green.

● Ray Harryhausen's stop-motion animation effects are the best thing about this version of the oft-filmed Jules Verne yarn. Craig leads a gang of Union soldiers who flee a Confederate jail by balloon, only to be washed up on the isolated isle where Lom's Capt Nemo has been experimenting to solve the world's food crisis (hence the giant hen, huge bees and over-sized crabs which test the plucky escapees). Scripted by several hands, but Bernard Herrmann's score a decided plus. TJ

Mysterious Object at Noon (Dogfar Nai Mea Marn)

(2000, Thai, 85 min, b/w)
d Apichatpong Weerasethakul. *p* Gridthiya Gaweewong, Mingmongkol Sonakul. *sc* Villagers of Thailand, edited by Mingmongkol Sonakul, Apichatpong Weerasethakul. *ph* Prasong Klinborrom, Apichatpong Weerasethakul. *ed* Apichatpong Weerasethakul. *with* Somsri Pinyopol, Duangjai Hiransri, To Hanudomlapr, Kannikar Narong, Kongkiert Komsiri.

● Neither documentary nor fiction but something in between, this features interviews with real people, the rural poor, mostly. They talk about their lives, but also tell stories. And one story in particular emerges: a surreal tale of a crippled child whose teacher collapses, and out from under her skirts rolls a strange ball. Interviewees young and old take up this yarn and elaborate. Occasionally we get a dramatisation – or a traditional Thai opera version. Printed in ultra grainy monochrome, this perverse enterprise is certainly intriguing. What it all has to do with the price of fish, I can't imagine. TCh

Mystery Date

see Just Another Night

Mystery in Mexico

(1948, US, 66 min, b/w)
d Robert Wise. *p* Sid Rogell. *sc* Lawrence Kimble. *ph* Jack Draper. *ed* Samuel E Beetley. *ad* Gunther Gerzso. *m* Paul Sawtell. *cast* William Lundigan, Jacqueline White, Ricardo Cortez, Tony Barrett, Jacqueline Dalya, Walter Reed.

● You've seen every twist in this routine caper a thousand times before. Lundigan is the insurance agency detective sent to Mexico on the trail of a fellow-employee (Reed) who has disappeared along with a valuable necklace. White is the pretty blonde singer who may be an accomplice, but obviously isn't since Lundigan falls for her. She is actually Reed's sister, so he's obviously innocent too; and it only remains for Cortez' villain (who owns a nightclub, naturally) to get his comeuppance after demonstrating his nastiness. Wise directs neatly enough, but the half-hearted romantic byplay and wisecracking dialogue cry out for Mitchum and Russell. Only Dalya, as Cortez' disillusioned, man-hungry mistress, manages to give her lines any bite. TM

Mystery Men

(1999, US, 120 min)
d Kinka Usher. *p* Lawrence Gordon, Mike Richardson, Lloyd Levin. *sc* Neil Cuthbert. *ph* Stephen H Burum. *ed* Conrad Buff. *pd* Kirk M Petruccelli. *m* Stephen Warbeck. *cast* Hank Azaria, Claire Forlani, Janeane Garofalo, Greg Kinnear, William H Macy, Kel Mitchell, Lena Olin, Paul Reubens, Geoffrey Rush, Ben Stiller, Wes Studi, Tom Waits, Eddie Izzard, Jenifer Lewis.

● Usher's amiable spoof of superhero movies takes a brave stab at rewriting the mythology from the inside out, with lots of witty, mildly subversive stuff about working class heroes, commercial sponsorship of celebrities and casual depictions of violence. The Mystery Men are blue collar wannabes who live in the shadow of Captain Amazing (Kinnear). However, when the Amazing One's nemesis, Casanova Frankenstein (Rush), turns the tables on him, the proletarian underdogs recruit some new blood and bring their unique superpowers to bear on the situation. While commercials director Usher's visual style is polished, it is less frenetic than one might expect; indeed, the steady pacing and muddy storytelling are the movie's chief weaknesses. The lavish set designs are a little too busy, and the effects sequences sometimes more eye-dazzling than effective. But Usher's heart is in the right place, as is obvious from the flawed hero figures, pacifist undercurrents and likeable, downbeat performances. NF

Mystery of Alexina, The (Mystère Alexina)

(1985, Fr, 90 min)
d/p René Féret. *sc* Jean Gruault, René Féret. *ph* Bernard Zitzermann. *ed* Ariane Boeglin. *ad* Georges Stoll, Isabelle Manescau. *m* Anne-Marie Deschamps. *cast* Philippe Vuillemin, Valérie Stroh, Véronique Silver, Bernard Freyd, Marianne Basler, Philippe Clévenot, Isabelle Gruault.

● Set in mid-19th century provincial France, this tells of a young woman who arrives to teach at a girls' boarding school and falls in love with a colleague, only to discover to her own astonishment that she is in fact a man. It's excellently performed and shot, and Féret teases out the ironies of Alexina's predicament, denied the right to love either as woman or man, with sure, steady clarity. Finally, however, it never entirely escapes a certain dullness, while its portrait of oppression born of ignorance and fear is unduly one-dimensional. Fascinating, nevertheless, as a sensitive account of an extraordinary story based in historical fact. GA

Mystery of Edwin Drood, The

(1993, GB, 112 min)
d Timothy Forder. *p* Keith Hayley. *sc* Timothy Forder. *ph* Martin McGrath. *ed* Sue Alhadeff. *pd* Edward Thomas. *m* Kick Production. *cast* Robert Powell, Jonathan Phillips, Rupert Rainsford, Michelle Evans, Finty Williams, Freddie Jones, Peter Pacey, Nanette Newman, Ronald Fraser, Glyn Houston, Andrew Sachs, Gemma Craven.

● Dickens' final, tantalisingly unfinished novel, as adapted and directed by Forder, and filmed on a shoestring around the environs of Rochester Cathedral, hasn't supplied a particularly apt or satisfying development (in fact, there's a touch of Hammer about the finale). Too many scenes simply wobble about without registering much of pith or moment, and the absence of editing skills compounds the air of amateurism. The pity is that the central character of choirmaster John Jasper, who may or may not have done away with his eponymous nephew, is given great, brooding weight by Powell. Most Dickensian of all is Freddie Jones as local dignitary Mr Sapsea, a man both orotund and snuff-taking; while Finty Williams as Rosa presents the usual pale purity that Dickensian men pine after. BC

Mystery of Kaspar Hauser, The

see Jeder für sich und Gott gegen alle

Mystery of Rampo, The (Ranpo)

(1994, Jap, 100 min)
d Kazuyoshi Okuyama. *p* Kazuyoshi Okuyama, Yoshinobu Nishioka, Yoshihisa Nakagawa. *sc* Kazuyoshi Okuyama, Yuhei Enoki. *ph* Yasushi Sasakihara. *ed* Akimasa Kawashima. *pd* Kyoko Heya. *m* Akira Senju. *cast* Naoto Takenaka, Masahiro Motoki, Naoto Takenaka, Michiko Hada, Mikijiro Hira.

● This became a cause célèbre in 1994 when producer Okuyama objected to the work of director Rintaro Mayuzumi and remade it the way he wanted. The two versions were released side-by-side in Tokyo; the 1995 London Film Festival, predictably, showed only the producer's cut. Edogawa Ranpo ('Edgar Allan Poe') was the pen name of Hirai Taro (1894–1965), writer of erotic/fantastic mystery fiction; the wheeze behind this imaginary episode from his life is to trap him inside one of his own bizarre and enigmatic stories. Okuyama has cast and designed it expensively, and the animated prologue is quite cute. But it's basically piffle, founded on a lamentably dated idea of what images of Japan foreign suckers might pay to see. TR

Mystery of the Leaping Fish, The

(1916, US, 26 min, b/w)
d John Emerson. *p* DW Griffith. *sc* Tod Browning (*titles* Anita Loos). *ph* John Leezer. *cast* Douglas Fairbanks, Bessie Love, Allan D Sears, Alma Reubens, Benny Zeidman.

●This legendary comedy short is crude and ramshackle but lives up to its reputation for unorthodox content. Fairbanks, with his air of commotion and excitability, often seemed to be under the influence of something or other – a thought which was presumably the genesis of this picture. He plays private eye Coke Ennyday, who is festooned with hypodermics, keeps a bowl of cocaine on his desk as big as Pacino's in *Scarface*, and whose preferred tipple is a compound of laudanum and prussic acid. Humour, 1916. It's Coke vs a gang of opium smugglers who bring the stuff ashore in rubber fish inflated by a teenage Bessie Love. Billed as 'Inane, the little fish blower', she parodies the cliché of the helpless waif with great exuberance. BBa

Mystery of the Wax Museum

(1933, US, 78 min)
d Michael Curtiz. *p* Darryl F Zanuck. *sc* Don Mullaly, Carl Erickson. *ph* Ray Rennahan. *ed* George Amy. *ad* Anton F Grot. *m* Cliff Hess. *cast* Lionel Atwill, Fay Wray, Glenda Farrell, Allen Vincent, Frank McHugh, Gavin Gordon, Arthur Edmund Carewe, Matthew Betz.

●In the early '30s, when Universal were riding high with *Frankenstein* and *Dracula*, Warners hunted round for their own horror subject, and found one in the idea of a sculptor who murders his models and embalms them in wax to achieve death-in-life. It's an interesting Poe-like theme, full of bizarre implications, and has since been remade several times (once in 3-D); but this remains the classic. Filmed in one of the earliest two-tone Technicolor processes, it is beautiful to look at, full of muted green compositions and stunningly modulated colour effects. Interesting, too, to note that its tough, wise-cracking girl reporter (Farrell) and newspaper setting bear the unmistakable stamp of the Warner house style. There's a slightly cruel, almost fascist streak throughout, especially in the police's handling of things, and the shocks are a little sparse by present standards. But it holds up amazingly well, and its pale, shimmering images linger in the mind. DP

Mystery Street

(1950, US, 93 min, b/w)
d John Sturges. *p* Frank E Taylor. *sc* Sydney Boehm, Richard Brooks. *ph* John Alton. *ed* Ferris Webster. *ad* Cedric Gibbons, Gabriel Scognamillo. *m* Rudolph G Kopp. *cast* Ricardo Montalban, Sally Forrest, Marshall Thompson, Bruce Bennett, Elsa Lanchester, Jan Sterling, Edmon Ryan, Betsy Blair.

●A neat thriller, despite getting itself a little hung up on the contemporary vogue for documentary trimmings. The opening sequences, set in Boston for a change and magnificently shot by John Alton, are classic *film noir*, detailing the circumstances leading inexorably to the murder of Jan Sterling, a girl on the make and not above a bit of blackmail. Next comes the police procedural bit, featuring a didactic (but not uninteresting and cleverly integrated) sequence set in the Harvard Department of Legal Medicine. The temperature never fully recovers, although Sturges handles the rest (caught up in his own lies, the wrong man (Thompson) lands in the net; stoutly maintaining his innocence, his wife (Forrest) gets increasingly distraught; sympathetic cop (Montalban) begins to wonder if he could possibly have got it all wrong) with considerable deftness and some subtlety. Nice performances, too, especially from Montalban as the zealous but still self-questioning cop, while Elsa Lanchester revels in one of her inimitably batty, gin-swilling landladies. TM

Mystery Train

(1989, US, 110 min)
d Jim Jarmusch. *p* Jim Stark. *sc* Jim Jarmusch. *ph* Robby Müller. *ed* Melody London. *pd* Dan Bishop. *m* John Lurie. *cast* Masatoshi Nagase, Youki Kudoh, Screamin' Jay Hawkins, Cinqué Lee, Nicoletta Braschi, Elizabeth Bracco, Tom Noonan, Joe Strummer, Rick Aviles, Steve Buscemi, Tom Waits.

●A trilogy of off-beat, Beat-besotted tales, shot in gorgeous colour, set in and around a seedy Memphis hotel. On one level it's about passers-through: a Japanese teenage couple on a pilgrimage to Presley's grave and Sun studios; an Italian taking her husband's coffin back to Rome, forced to share a room with a garrulous American fleeing her boyfriend; and an English 'Elvis', out of work, luck in love and his head as he cruises round town with a black friend, a brother-in-law, and a gun. But on a deeper level, the film is about storytelling, about how we make connections between people, places, objects and time to create meaning, and how, when these connections shift, meaning changes. Only halfway through do we begin to grasp how the stories and characters relate to each other. Happily, Jarmusch's formal inventiveness is framed by a rare flair for zany entertainment: Kudoh and Nagase make 'Far From Yokohama' delightfully funny; Braschi brings the right wide-eyed wonder to 'A Ghost'; and Strummer proffers real legless menace in 'Lost in Space', which at least explains the cause and effect of a mysterious gun shot heard in the first two episodes. Best of all are Screamin' Jay Hawkins and Cinqué Lee as argumentative hotel receptionists hooked on Tom Waits' late night radio show. They, and Jarmusch's remarkably civilised direction, hold the whole shaggy dog affair together, turning it into one of the best films of the year. GA

Mystic Masseur, The

(2001, GB/Ind, 118 min)
d Ismail Merchant. *p* Nayeem Hafizka, Richard Hawley. *sc* Caryl Phillips. *ph* Ernie Vincze. *ed* Roberto Silvi. *pd* Lucy Richardson. *m* Richard Robbins, Zakir Hussain. *cast* Om Puri, James Fox, Aasif Mandvi, Sanjeev Bhaskar, Ayesha Dharkar, Jimi Mistry, Zohra Segal, Sakina Jaffrey, Albert Laveau, Grace Maharaj.

●Set midway through the 20th century within Trinidad's significant Indian population this is the first film adapted from the work of Nobel-winning author VS Naipaul. Following the death of his father, idealistic teacher Ganesh (Mandvi) strives to become a writer – but instead gains a reputation as a spiritual healer, and finds his fame propelled into national politics. Director Merchant is content to tackle pet issues: social airs, local eccentrics and a fetishised kind of nostalgia. The story begins via the memory of an Anglo-Indian Oxford student, 'cured' in childhood by Ganesh. The film's comic talent spans Mandvi and Sanjeev Bhaskar, speaking in unsteady patois as a boorish neighbour, both of whom share a background in stand-up, and veterans like Zohra Segal and Om Puri, who delivers indignant melodrama as Ganesh's unscrupulous father-in-law. But fitful gags and some clever incidental detail (a steel drums version of *Carmina Burana* on the radio; a gaudily ostentatious government dinner) can't compensate for the plot's lumpen pace. AHa

Mystic Pizza

(1988, US, 104 min)
d Donald Petrie. *p* Mark Levinson, Scott Rosenfelt. *sc* Amy Holden-Jones, Perry Howze, Randy Howze, Alfred Uhry. *ph* Tim Suhrstedt. *ed* Marion Rothman, Don Brochu. *pd* David Chapman. *m* David McHugh. *cast* Vincent Philip D'Onofrio, Annabeth Gish, William R Moses, Julia Roberts, Adam Storke, Lili Taylor, Conchata Ferrell, Porscha Radcliffe, Joanna Merlin, Arthur Walsh, Matt Damon.

●Jojo, Daisy and Kat are pizza-pushers who live in Mystic, on the Connecticut coast. Jojo (Taylor) is carrying on a stormy romance with a redneck fisherman. Daisy (Roberts), a bit of a social climber, is having an affair with the owner of a throbbing red Porsche. And good old Kat (Gish), soon to start studying astronomy at Yale, is about to have a bad case of babysitter blues. Each of these women, through being used and abused by men, achieves some kind of self-realisation. If the plot (by Amy Jones) sounds pedestrian and pat, it is. However, thanks to sensitive direction by Petrie, the result is a thoroughly involving movie that doesn't resort to violence, sex or schmaltz to pack an emotional punch. Petrie imbues the Portuguese-dominated fishing village with a real sense of place, and the three female leads (Gish in particular) are excellent. MS

My Sweet Lady

see Sunshine Part II

My Sweet Little Village (Vesnicko má Stredisková)

(1985, Czech, 100 min)
d Jirí Menzel. *p* Jan Suster. *sc* Zdenk Sverák. *ph* Jaromír Sofr. *ed* Jirí Brozek. *ad* Zbyner Hoch. *m* Jirí Sust. *cast* János Bán, Marian Labuda, Rudolf Hrusinsky, Petr Cepek, Milena Dvorská, Jan Hartl.

●In the village in question, a cooperatively-run community, live Pavek – who is short and fat – and his workmate Otik, who is long and thin. Because Otik's teeth outnumber his IQ, he is more hindrance than help, so when he directs the long-suffering Pavek's truck into a gatepost, their fraught friendship is threatened. As if this weren't catastrophic enough, a party bureaucrat sets his heart on Otik's cottage, and arranges for him to be rehoused in a high-rise honeycomb in Prague. Menzel directs a good-natured comedy in which pleasure is derived from such innocent pursuits as consuming beer and bangers in the sun, riding through the unremarkable countryside, and watching the desperate home-produced TV. The optimism, if indulgent, is infectious, and the Laurel and Hardski relationship is ultimately moving. MS

Myth of Fingerprints, The

(1996, US, 90 min)
d Bart Freundlich. *p* Mary Jane Skalski, Tim Perell, Bart Freundlich. *sc* Bart Freundlich. *ph* Stephen Kazmierski. *ed* Kate Williams, Ken J Sackheim. *pd* Susan Bolles. *m* David Bridie, John Phillips. *cast* Noah Wyle, Roy Scheider, Julianne Moore, Blythe Danner, James LeGros, Arija Bareikis, Hope Davis, Laurel Holloman, Brian Kerwin, Michael Vartan.

●Warren (Wyle) hasn't been home to Maine in three years, partly because he still hasn't got over being dumped by the love of his life. When he does turn up for Thanksgiving, however, it's not Daphne who's the problem, but his dad Hal (Scheider), who welcomes Warren, his other children – persistently angry Mia (Moore), non-committal Jake (Vartan), easy-going Leigh (Holloman) – and their various partners with an indifference verging on outright hostility. Somehow, Warren's mum Lena (Danner) keeps a fragile peace, though Mia's tantrums and Hal's icy disapproval repeatedly threaten to turn the reunion into an emotional bloodbath. While writer/director Freundlich's serio-comic study of a dysfunctional family is hardly original, it is a remarkably mature, assured and perceptive first feature. A superior cast give their best in a faintly old-fashioned, carefully crafted, very enjoyable movie from a young talent to watch. GA

My Tutor

(1982, US, 97 min)
d George Bowers. *p* Marilyn J Tenser. *sc* Joe Roberts. *ph* Mac Ahlberg. *ed* Sidney Wolinsky, George Berndt. *ad* Linda Pearl, Robert Lowy. *m* Webster Lewis. *cast* Caren Kaye, Matt Lattanzi, Kevin McCarthy, Clark Brandon, Bruce Bauer, Arlene Golonka, Crispin Glover.

●Poor little rich kid (Lattanzi) flunks his graduation French, so his father hires an attractive 29-year-old tutor (Kaye) who initiates him into rather more than the mysteries of *la plume de ma tante*. Both flap their eyelashes and flash their toothpaste smiles, but are insipid and boring as they go through the motions of nude swimming, clinging wet T-shirts, shared bubble baths and lyrical love scenes. Puerile dross which dares to speak with feeling of the value of sex while making such an obvious play for the soft porn market. JE

My 20th Century (Az én XX századom)

(1989, Hun/WGer/Cuba, 104 min, b/w)
d/sc Ildikó Enyedi. *ph* Tibor Mathé. *ed* Mária Rigó. *pd* Zoltán Lábas. *m* László Vidovszky. *cast* Dorothea Segda, Oleg Yankowski, Paulus Manker, Peter Andorai, Gábor Máté.

●East European whimsy is usually heavy-going, especially when most of the women are played by the same actress, and this feminist frolic through the political and technological birth-pangs of the present century has all the poetry of a dodo on downers. At the exact moment that Edison unveils the electric light bulb in a New York park, twin sisters are born in Budapest. This arbitrary conjunction leads into a collage of very loosely related scenes (crammed with allusions to movies, pulp fiction, etc, etc) in which the sisters' lives diverge and faithfully reconverge via a trip on the Orient Express. Chic b/w photography and relentless 'cleverness' won this wearying charade the Best First Feature prize at Cannes. TR

My Uncle

see Mon Oncle

My Uncle Antoine

see Mon Oncle Antoine

My Uncle from America

see Mon Oncle d'Amérique

My Universities

see Childhood of Maxim Gorki, The

My Way Home

see My Childhood

My Way Home (Igy Jöttem)

(1964, Hun, 109 min, b/w)
d Miklós Jancsó. *sc* Gyula Hernádi. *ph* Tamás Somló. *ed* Zoltán Farkas. *m* Zoltán Jenei. *cast* András Kozák, Sergei Nikonenko.

● This early (pre-*Round-Up*) Jancsó movie is apparently autobiographical in spirit if not in letter. Its young Hungarian protagonist wanders through the Russian-occupied Hungary of the final months of WWII, suffering a pointedly arbitrary round of arrests, internments and accusations. In a way that foreshadows Jancsó's later choreographic effects, he is sometimes the focus of our attention, and sometimes lost in larger patterns of landscape and movement. The film's centrepiece is its study of the one period when he comes to rest: he is assigned to help a wounded Russian soldier tend a herd of cows. Jancsó's portrait of the warm, doomed relationship between the two men is one of the most moving and clear-sighted analyses of male sensibilities and friendship in all cinema. TR

My Young Auntie (Zhangbei)

(1981, HK, 121 min)
d Lau Kar-Leung [aka Liu Jialiang]. *cast* Hui Yinghong, Lau Kar-Leung, Wang Longwei, Xiao Hou, Gordon Liu.

● The Shaw Bros policy of selling dubbed-only versions of their productions does no favours to Lau's over-extended kung fu comedy, first and foremost a showcase for the talents (martial and otherwise) of his then girlfriend Hui Yinghong. She plays an upright young widow from the Chinese hinterland, who finds herself in the 'cosmopolitan' Canton of the 1930s, trying to protect an inheritance from the black sheep of the family she married into. One set of repetitive jokes springs from her youth (she could be the daughter of her elderly nephew, played by Lau himself), and another from her joshing relationship with her nephew's son (played by Lau's real-life star pupil Xiao Hou), a boy her own age who has been 'westernised' by studying in Hong Kong. The dubbing kills all the 'Chinglish' language gags, and so the entertainment value rests squarely on the fight scenes – which are expectedly brilliant in choreography and execution. The UK video release is correctly letterboxed. TR

n

A Night at the Opera

Nach dem Fall

see After the Fall

Nada

(1974, Fr/It, 134 min)
d Claude Chabrol. *p* André Génoves. *sc* Jean-Patrick Manchette. *ph* Jean Rabier. *ed* Jacques Gaillard. *ad* Guy Littaye. *m* Pierre Jansen. *cast* Fabio Testi, Michel Duchaussoy, Maurice Garrel, Michel Aumont, Lou Castel, Didier Kaminka, Viviane Romance, Mariangela Melato.

● A chillingly cool political thriller, all the better for its non-partisan stance. No attempt is made to whitewash the activist group in Paris, calling themselves Nada in memory of the Spanish anarchists, who kidnap the American ambassador (at an exclusive brothel) in a welter of functional violence. A motley collection of malcontents and seasoned professionals, driven by absurd ideological confusions, they are for that reason a doubly dangerous time bomb likely to explode at any random moment. But against them Chabrol sets the cold calculation of the forces of order, wheeling, dealing, finally engineering a politic holocaust, and emerging as even less concerned with human life than the terrorists they are hunting down as a threat to society. Right is on their side, but it is the members of Nada, groping desperately to build little burrows of viable living in a world of expediency and corruption, who become the heroes in spite of everything. Powerful, pure *film noir* in mood, it's one of Chabrol's best films. TM

Nadia

(1984, US, 99 min)
d Alan Cooke. *p* James E Thompson. *sc* Jim McGinn. *ph* Frank Beascoechea. *ed* Raymond Bridgers. *pd* George Becket. *m* Christopher L Stone. *cast* Talia Balsam, Jonathan Banks, Joe Bennett, Simone Blue, Johann Carlo, Conchata Ferrell, Carrie Snodgress, Leslie Weiner.

●Inspirational, if not exactly inspired TV movie about the Romanian teen gymnast who swept aside the perennially victorious Russians at the 1976 Olympics with six 'perfect 10' scores. The film satisfies audience requirements for such biopics, picturing the triumphs and then the fall from grace. Nadia Comaneci had her 'fall': gaining weight, apparently attempting suicide, with nothing to reach for after those 10s. Nadia is played by an almost comparably gifted little girl, Leslie Weiner. Parental guidance: regardless of the cautionary aspects of the tale, show this to your daughters and you may be investing heavily in leotards. DO

Nadie conoce a nadie

see Nobody Knows Anybody

Nadine

(1987, US, 83 min)
d Robert Benton. *p* Arlene Donovan. *sc* Robert Benton. *ph* Nestor Almendros. *ed* Sam O'Steen. *pd* Paul Sylbert. *m* Howard Shore. *cast* Jeff Bridges, Kim Basinger, Rip Torn, Gwen Verdon, Glenne Headly, Jerry Stiller, Mickey Jones.

●Benton's lightweight romantic comedy has Nadine Hightower (Basinger) witness the murder of a photographer while trying to recover some candid nude pics. Having escaped with photos of a proposed road development instead, she tricks her soon-to-be-ex husband Vernon (Bridges) into helping her recover the right ones. However, when Vernon discovers the map photos, he decides to cash in on them. But first they must deal with their rightful owner, a ruthless businessman (Torn) and his two henchmen. Despite a plot with more twists than a rattlesnake, Benton plays the crime caper for laughs, concentrating on the couple's nervous edging towards a romantic reconciliation. Basinger is excellent as the flaky heroine, while Bridges exudes vulnerable charm as her two-bit loser of a husband. NF

Nadja

(1994, US, 100 min, b/w)
d Michael Almereyda. *p* Mary Sweeney, Amy Hobby. *sc* Michael Almereyda. *ph* Jim Denault. *ed* David Leonard. *pd* Kurt Ossenfort. *m* Simon Fisher Turner. *cast* Suzy Amis, Galaxy Craze, Martin Donovan, Peter Fonda, Jared Harris, Elina Löwensohn, Karl Geary, David Lynch.

●Highly stylised b/w camerawork and Pixelvision, moody poeticism, and farcical genre parody merge to tantalising if not altogether coherent effect in Almereyda's quirky New York update on the Dracula story. The heavily Mittel-European persona of Löwensohn is used effectively as the Count's enigmatic, doomy daughter who hopes to tempt Lucy (Craze) away from her husband (Donovan), while desperately trying to get in touch with her own estranged twin brother. About blood, blood ties and breakdown (of familes, relationships and, perhaps, an entire society), it's an idiosyncratic film, admired by many for its strong atmosphere, and by this writer for its absurd(ist) casting of a barely recognisable Fonda as Donovan's mad uncle Van Helsing. GA

Naked

(1993, GB, 131 min)
d Mike Leigh. *p* Simon Channing-Williams. *sc* Mike Leigh. *ph* Dick Pope. *ed* Jon Gregory. *pd* Alison Chitty. *m* Andrew Dickson. *cast* David Thewlis, Lesley Sharp, Katrin Cartlidge, Greg Cruttwell, Claire Skinner.

●Mike Leigh's film explores a form of male self-loathing manifesting itself in misogynist insults and violence. When Johnny (Thewlis), an out-of-work twenty-something given to manic rants and rough sex, visits ex-girlfriend Louise (Sharp) in London, it's hard to know whether or not he aims to persuade her to return with him to Manchester. Getting stoned and sleeping with her spaced-out flatmate Sophie (Cartlidge) is unlikely to endear her to such a prospect, as is his sudden decision to roam the streets of the capital, waxing philosophical to anyone he meets. But is he any worse than Jeremy (Cruttwell), a smooth sadist who claims a landlord's right to invade the girls' house and subject them to sexual humiliation? Hilarious, but sometimes hard to stomach, Leigh's picaresque tale is his most troubling and intriguing work since *Meantime*; it's also by far his most cinematic. The cast is outstanding – Thewlis, in particular, whose virtuoso performance gives the film its cruel energy, wit and power. GA

Naked and the Dead, The

(1958, US, 129 min)
d Raoul Walsh. *p* Paul Gregory. *sc* Denis Sanders, Terry Sanders. *ph* Joseph LaShelle. *ed* Arthur P Schmidt. *ad* Ted Haworth. *m* Bernard Herrmann. *cast* Aldo Ray, Cliff Robertson, Raymond Massey, William Campbell, Richard Jaeckel, James Best, Joey Bishop, LQ Jones, Robert Gist, Barbara Nichols.

●Just as Joseph Heller's *Catch-22* was to virtually defeat Hollywood a decade later, Norman Mailer's mighty (and mightily important) novel defeated director Walsh and screenwriters Denis and Terry Sanders. In fact, it owes hardly anything to Mailer, except for one or two episodes and the title. What we have is a routine war adventure about a platoon behind enemy lines, directed in Walsh's normal manner (he cares about the action and lets the rest dawdle). The tropical scenery is fine, and only Massey's performance as the fascist-minded general is memorable. ATu

Naked Are the Cheaters

(1971, US, 62 min)
d Derek Ashburne. *p* NE Shane. *sc* Derek Ashburne. *ph* Paul Hipp. *ed* NE Shane. *m* John Barth. *cast* Angela Carnan, Robert Warner, Vickie Carbe, Douglas Frey, Neola Graef, Vincent Mongol.

●Absolutely dire, farcically amateurish non-film about a Washington wheeler-dealer who runs a callgirl service on the side. Possibly stripped at some point of most of whatever rudimentary sex footage it contained; at any rate, tricked out with some incomprehensible flash-cutting, the perfunctoriness of the proceedings is impossible to describe. VG

Naked Cell, The

(1987, GB, 90 min)
d John Crome. *p* Georgina De Lacy. *sc* Berkeley Burdock. *ph* Brian Herlihy. *ed* Peter Dansie, David Howes. *pd* James Dillon. *m* Barrie Guard. *cast* Vicky Jeffrey, Richard Fallon, Jacquetta May, Yvonne Bonnamy, Jill Spurrier, Nicola Lamb.

●'Ere, wanna see a film about a woman who goes mad 'cos she can't get enough sex? Forget *Fatal Attraction* and all that glossy stuff, this is the real thing – serious bonking, filthy talk, you know, realistic. She's a career woman, see, and a bit of a lush, and we first meet her in the mental home where she's remembering episodes like this bloke with designer stubble giving her one on the sink. The guards question her repeatedly about why she keeps picking up strange blokes, but much of her memory is a blank. Known only as The Prisoner (Jeffrey), she spends much of her time f–ing and blinding and taking leaks in a bucket. We finally learn that she strangled a stranger while he was on the job. In short, she seems to be a Woman Trapped by her Desires. Crude, exploitative rubbish. NF

Naked Childhood

see Enfance nue, L'

Naked City, The

(1948, US, 96 min, b/w)
d Jules Dassin. *p* Mark Hellinger. *sc* Albert Maltz, Malvin Wald. *ph* William H Daniels. *ed* Paul Weatherwax. *ad* John F DeCuir. *m* Miklós Rósza, Frank Skinner. *cast* Barry Fitzgerald, Howard Duff, Dorothy Hart, Don Taylor, Frank Conroy, Ted de Corsia, Enid Markey, David Opatoshu, Paul Ford, Arthur O'Connell. *narrator* Mark Hellinger.

●Despite its reputation, a rather overrated police-procedure thriller which has gained its seminal status simply by its accent on ordinariness and by its adherence to the ideal of shooting on location. In organising the hunt for a brutal murderer, Fitzgerald's detective is too winsome and hammy, Taylor's assistant merely wooden; thanks be then to Ted de Corsia as the killer, adding a touch of real nastiness and urgency to the admittedly well-constructed final chase. GA

Naked Dawn, The

(1955, US, 82 min)
d Edgar G Ulmer. *sc* Nina Schneider, Herman Schneider. *ph* Frederick Gately. *ed* Dan Milner. *ad* Martin Lencer. *m* Herschel Burke Gilbert. *cast* Arthur Kennedy, Betta St John, Eugene Iglesias, Roy Engel, Charita.

●From the master of the B movie quickie, a rather studio-bound but compellingly tense Western. Kennedy plays a marauding bandit who, after the death of his sidekick, invades the home of a Mexican farmer (Iglesias), draws him into crime, and falls for his wife (St John). Unusually for Ulmer, it was shot in Technicolor, which is employed for some tellingly expressionistic effects. The film's romantic triangle was even an inspiration for Truffaut's *Jules and Jim*. DT

Naked Face, The

(1984, US, 106 min)
d Bryan Forbes. *p* Menahem Golan, Yoram Globus. *sc* Bryan Forbes. *ph* David Gurfinkel. *ed* Philip Shaw. *pd* William Fosser. *m* Michael J Lewis. *cast* Roger Moore, Rod Steiger, Elliott Gould, Anne Archer, David Hedison, Art Carney, Ron Parady, John Kapelos.

●Big Rog puts aside his James Bond image and dons a cardigan to play a wimpy psychiatrist who thinks that he's next on the list of those responsible for the murder of an ex-patient. Sidney Sheldon's pulp novel gets the Cannon treatment: numerous guest stars, shabby production values, and nil credibility. NF

Naked Gun, The

(1988, US, 85 min)
d David Zucker. *p* Robert K Weiss. *sc* Jerry Zucker, Jim Abrahams, David Zucker, Pat Proft. *ph* Robert Stevens. *ed* Michael Jablow. *pd* John J Lloyd. *m* Ira Newborn. *cast* Leslie Nielsen, Priscilla Presley, Ricardo Montalban, George Kennedy, OJ Simpson, Susan Beaubian, Nancy Marchand, John Houseman.

●Fans of the *Airplane* team (and especially of their short-lived TV series *Police Squad*, by which this gloriously tacky spoof cop-thriller is inspired) will know that corny old gags, hoary clichés, and downright silliness can, if delivered in the right spirit, provide far more fun than any amount of Merchant-Ivory *bons mots* or Woody Allen witticisms. As ever, sophistication is conspicuously absent as tactless, dim-witted Lt Frank Drebin (Nielsen) investigates the shooting of a cop during a ludicrously audacious drugs bust. One hesitates even to attempt a synopsis of the admirably perfunctory plot, other than that suspects include a delirously plastic Priscilla Presley and a magnificently corseted Montalban. Ineptitude rules throughout. Finally, though, it's Nielsen's show: with an unaccountable flair for the needlessly dramatic, he holds the entire shambling absurdity together by treating everything as if it were a matter of life or death. The endlessly tasteless juvenilia should make you ashamed of laughing yourself into a stupor. GA

Naked Gun 2½: The Smell of Fear, The

(1991, US, 85 min)
d David Zucker. *p* Robert K Weiss. *sc* David Zucker, Pat Proft. *ph* Robert Stevens. *ed* James Symons. Chris Greenbury. *pd* John J Lloyd. *m* Ira Newborn. *cast* Leslie Nielsen, Priscilla Presley, George Kennedy, OJ Simpson, Robert Goulet, Richard Griffiths, Jacqueline Brookes, Lloyd Bochner, Anthony James.

● In this deliriously silly sequel to the marvellously tasteless juvenilia of Lieutenant Frank Drebin's first chaotic outing on the big screen, Drebin (Nielsen) is out to foil a conspiracy designed to prevent wheelchair-bound conservationist Dr Meinheimer (Griffiths) from influencing George Bush's energy policy. The fact that the plotters' leader Hapsburg (Goulet) is dating Drebin's old flame Jane (Presley) only complicates matters further. Thus is the scene set for romantic agony, moral dilemma, profound ecological controversy, and the most tuneless caterwauling heard in a movie since the last instalment. A corny cornucopia of cop-saga clichés, Zucker's film is a sublimely free-wheeling parody of every ridiculous matter-of-life-and-death scene ever to appear in a crime thriller. A minor masterpiece of infantile idiocy. GA

Naked Gun 33⅓: The Final Insult

(1994, US, 83 min)
d Peter Segal. *p* Robert K Weiss, David Zucker. *sc* Pat Proft, David Zucker, Robert LoCash. *ph* Robert Stevens. *ed* James R Symons. *pd* Lawrence G Paull. *m* Ira Newborn. *cast* Leslie Nielsen, Priscilla Presley, George Kennedy, OJ Simpson, Fred Ward, Kathleen Freeman, Anna Nicole Smith, Ellen Greene.

● For all those fans desperate to find out what the Statesville Prison actually looks like, here's your chance. It's where Lt Frank Drebin (Nielsen) goes very conspicuously undercover when he's brought back from retirement, and a rough ride at the sperm bank, to monitor the activities of Rocco (Ward), a terrorist with grand plans. That's about it in terms of story (except for the usual heart-rending subplot detailing Drebin's efforts to win back the beloved Jane), but who cares? The spoof-policier series is about non-stop gags, pure and simple, and this third instalment, for all its lax plotting and ludicrous characterisation, remains infinitely more pleasurable than sticking you face in a fan. Indeed, the five minutes of the pre-credits sequence are quite possibly the funniest since the talkies came in. Thereafter, it's hit and miss, but the hits are so frequent and spot-on, you'd have to be dead (and buried) not to find the film painfully hilarious. Inspired, inspirational, gloriously inane. GA

Naked in New York

(1994, US, 91 min)
d Dan Algrant. *p* Fred Zollo. *sc* Dan Algrant, John Warren. *ph* Joey Forsyte. *ed* Bill Pankow. *pd* Kalina Ivanov. *m* Angelo Badalamenti. *cast* Eric Stoltz, Mary-Louise Parker, Ralph Macchio, Kathleen Turner, Tony Curtis, Timothy Dalton, Lynne Thigpen, Jill Clayburgh, Roscoe Lee Brown, Eric Bogosian, Quentin Crisp, William Styron, Whoopi Goldberg.

● This pseudo-autobiographical comedy, from a first-time writer/director, concerns a youthful playwright Jake Biggs (Stoltz), an aspiring angry young man with a Woody Allen line in romantic-neurotic confession straight to camera. Spurred by the absence of his father and the remoteness of his mother (Clayburgh), Jake's creativity wows his college classmates. But after graduation the spark falters when he settles down with Joanne (Parker). Picked up by a producer (Curtis), Jake hits the big time when a Broadway star (Turner) expresses interest in his work. The film begins brightly, but its agile, astute voice begins to flag as the plot becomes steadily more conventional, and the tone of wry self-effacement veers dangerously close to self-congratulation. An assured debut, nevertheless, scoring some satiric hits against the New York art scene, with Curtis and Turner enlivening matters no end. TCh

Naked Jungle, The

(1954, US, 95 min)
d Byron Haskin. *p* George Pal. *sc* Philip Yordan, Ranald MacDougall. *ph* Ernest Laszlo. *ed* Everett Douglas. *ad* Hal Pereira, Franz Bachelin. *m* Daniele Amfitheatrof. *cast* Charlton Heston, Eleanor Parker, William Conrad, Abraham Sofaer, Norma Calderon, John Dierkes, Douglas Fowley.

● A weird and wonderful combination of melodrama, sexual symbolism and exotic adventure. At the turn of the century, South American plantation-owner Heston battles both with an army of red ants and with his feelings of impotence and disgust towards the red-haired beauty he has married by proxy (Parker). Produced by George Pal, sumptuously shot by Ernest Laszlo, intelligently and literately scripted by Philip Yordan, it somehow, miraculously, holds absurdity at bay.

Naked Killer (Chiklo gouyeung)

(1992, HK, 92 min)
d Clarence Ford [Fok Yiu-Leung]. *p* Wong Jing. *sc* Wong Jing. *ph* Peter Pau, William Yim. *ad* Fong Nay Ngai. *m* Lowell Lo. *cast* Chingamy Yau, Simon Yam, Carrie Ng.

● A camp, high gloss and utterly incoherent conflation of *Nikita* and *Basic Instinct*. Yam plays Tinam, a cop under the spell of the lovely Kitty (Chingamy Yau), but when Kitty's father is murdered she joins a kind of finishing school for hit-women led by Sister Cindy (Ng). Although its titillating softcore sex has made the film something of a cult item in the West, it's actually rather tamer than the Verhoeven film, and the glassy look of it tends to magnify innumerable shortcomings in the credibility department. TCh

Naked Kiss, The

(1964, US, 93 min, b/w)
d/p/sc Samuel Fuller. *ph* Stanley Cortez. *ed* Jerome Thoms. *ad* Eugène Lourié. *m* Paul Dunlap. *cast* Constance Towers, Anthony Eisley, Michael Dante, Virginia Grey, Patsy Kelly, Betty Bronson, Marie Devereux.

● Not altogether the best of Fuller, despite an electrifying opening sequence in which a statuesque blonde (Towers) advances on her pimp, flailing out with her handbag as he staggers drunkenly until her wig falls off, revealing her to be totally bald. Subsequently seeking fresh fields in a small American town where vice is kept carefully screened behind locked doors, she instead becomes ministering angel in a children's orthopaedic hospital. It takes a little swallowing, but Fuller's grasp of character and milieu is so sure that the film gradually imposes itself as a scathing exposé of hypocrisy, unforgettable for the sharp savagery of scenes like the one in which Towers calmly marches into the local bordello and stuffs the madam's mouth full of dollar bills as retribution for trying to corrupt an innocent. TM

Naked Lunch

(1991, GB/Can, 115 min)
d David Cronenberg. *p* Jeremy Thomas. *sc* David Cronenberg. *ph* Peter Suschitzky. *ed* Ron Sanders. *pd* Carol Spiers. *m* Howard Shore. *cast* Peter Weller, Judy Davis, Ian Holm, Julian Sands, Roy Scheider, Monique Mercure, Nicholas Campbell, Michael Zelniker, Robert A Silverman, Joseph Scorsiani.

● Cronenberg's film of William Burroughs' novel fleshes out the plot with details from the junkie author's life. He casts Weller as Burroughs' alter ego, Bill Lee, a cockroach exterminator who experiments with injecting his own bug powder. An appointment with the sinister Dr Benway (Scheider), Lee's meeting with a strange creature, and the murder of his wife (Davis) precipitate Lee's flight to Interzone, more mental state than actual place, a decadent, nightmare world run by bureaucrats who control the market in a rare drug, The Black Meat. Under the hallucinatory influence of the drug, Lee's grasp of reality disintegrates as he uses a speaking insect typewriter to file obscure reports. Through his most complex and brilliant cinematic metaphor to date, Cronenberg links these drug-induced images with Lee's eventual salvation, as he comes to terms with his repressed homosexuality and discovers another, more permanent way of altering reality – the writing of his novel 'The Naked Lunch'. Burroughs purists may be disappointed, but this dark distillation of the novel's themes gets closer to its essence than any 'straight' adaptation could hope to do. NF

Naked Man, The

(1998, US, 98 min)
d J Todd Anderson. *p* Ben Baronholtz, Robert Graf.*sc* J Todd Anderson, Ethan Coen. *ph* Jeff Barklage.*cast* Joe Grifasi, Michael Rapaport, John Slattery, George R Willeman, Rachael Leigh Cook, Michael Jeter, Arija Bareikis, Traci Christofore, John Carroll Lynch.

● 'A Wacky New Comedy From the Co-Creator of *Fargo* and *The Big Lebowski*' splurges the video cover, over an appalling shot of what appears to be a skinned Michael Rapaport swinging across a wrestling ring. A chiropractor who moonlights as 'the naked man', Eddie Bliss loves the showmanship of the ring – then his family are gunned down by a psychotic drug-running cripple and his Elvis-lookalike cohort, and something snaps: The Naked Man goes on the rampage, combating evil, and preaching the virtues of 'spinal integrity'. Amazingly, Ethan Coen is credited as co-writer, along with first time director, J Todd Anderson – the Coens' storyboard artist. In as much as the Coens' comedies often play like they've been made up as they gone on, then this is truly Coenesque. It's also dismally unfunny – so unfunny you can imagine a cult audience getting off on it. Certainly I'll treasure the memory of Elvis, hypnotised into believing he's a drug enforcement officer, being shredded by a twin prop plane. TCh

Naked Night, The

see Gycklarnas Afton

Naked Runner, The

(1967, GB, 102 min)
d Sidney J Furie. *p* Brad Dexter. *sc* Stanley Mann. *ph* Otto Heller. *ed* Barrie Vince. *ad* Peter Proud. *m* Harry Sukman. *cast* Frank Sinatra, Peter Vaughan, Derren Nesbitt, Nadia Gray, Tony Robins, Cyril Luckham, Edward Fox.

● One of the complex spy games which proliferated in the mid-'60s: more Cold War crises of conscience in East Germany, with Sinatra as the wartime crack shot unwillingly reactivated for an assassination plot. A tortuously hollow narrative is further obfuscated by Furie's customarily flashy direction, which fragments the looking glass to the point of impenetrability. (From a novel by Francis Clifford.) PT

Naked Spur, The

(1953, US, 91 min)
d Anthony Mann. *p* William H Wright. *sc* Sam Rolfe, Harold Jack Bloom. *ph* William C Mellor. *ed* George White. *ad* Cedric Gibbons, Malcolm Brown. *m* Bronislau Kaper. *cast* James Stewart, Robert Ryan, Janet Leigh, Ralph Meeker, Millard Mitchell.

● The third Mann/Stewart Western was the simplest yet most effective of their collaborations, with the actor giving one of his most hysterical performances as a bounty hunter driven by naked greed. Unable to capture and bring back outlaw Ryan without help, Stewart enlists old-timer Mitchell and dishonourably discharged cavalryman Meeker. But having captured Ryan – who, they discover, is looking after a friend's young daughter (Leigh) – the ill-matched trio are played off against one another by the manipulative Ryan. Through strong, clear story-telling and tremendous use of landscape, Mann infuses the familiar scenario with a remarkable psychological complexity. NF

Naked Tango

(1990, US, 92 min)
d Leonard Schrader. *p* David Weisman. *sc* Leonard Schrader. *ph* Juan Ruiz-Anchia. *ed* Debra McDermott, Lee Percy. *pd* Anthony Pratt. *m* Thomas Newman. *cast* Vincent D'Onofrio, Mathilda May, Esai Morales, Fernando Rey, Cipe Lincovski, Josh Mostel, Constance McCashin.

● 1924. Sailing to Buenos Aires, tired of her ageing, possessive husband (Rey), Stephanie (May) impulsively exchanges identities with a suicide. The girl gone overboard was a mail-order bride, and Stephanie – now Alba – happily marries handsome Jewish groom Zico (Morales), only to find herself enslaved in a hellish world of prostitution, sexual abuse and murderous violence presided over by her hubby's underworld chum Cholo (D'Onofrio). As ever in such films, the heroine both abhors and comes to adore her captor-tormentor, mainly because of his passion for, and expertise in, the tango. The directing debut of screenwriter Leonard Schrader (brother of Paul) may be a slick study in baroque set design, costume and lighting; but the script's stilted clichés serve only to turn what was evidently intended as a homage to the films of Valentino and Louise Brooks into a sexist fantasy so inept it comes over as camp parody. GA

Naked Truth, The (aka Your Past is Showing!)

(1957, GB, 92 min, b/w)
d/p Mario Zampi. *sc* Michael Pertwee. *ph* Stan Pavey. *ed* William Lewthwaite. *ad* Ivan King. *m* Stanley Black. *cast* Terry-Thomas, Dennis Price, Peter Sellers, Peggy Mount, Shirley Eaton, Joan Sims, Miles Malleson, Kenneth Griffith, Wilfrid Lawson.

●Simply spiffing comedy about scandal-mongering, with smarmy Dennis Price playing a gutter press baron who plans to blackmail a number of public figures or smear them across page one unless they hand over their House of Lords luncheon vouchers. Much miffed, Terry-Thomas contacts other victims – Peggy Mount's romantic novelist, Peter Sellers' TV celeb – and lays plans to undo the beastly rotter. A period piece, maybe, but much funnier and arguably more authentic than *Scandal*. ATu

Naked Under Leather

see Girl on a Motorcycle

Name of the Rose, The (Der Name der Rose)

(1986, WGer/It/Fr, 131 min)
d Jean-Jacques Annaud. *p* Bernd Eichinger. *sc* Andrew Birkin, Gérard Brach, Howard Franklin, Alain Godard. *ph* Tonino Delli Colli. *ed* Jane Seitz. *pd* Dante Ferretti. *m* James Horner. *cast* Sean Connery, Christian Slater, Helmut Qualtinger, Elya Baskin, Michel Lonsdale, Volker Prechtel, F Murray Abraham.

●As intelligent a reductio of Umberto Eco's sly farrago of whodunnit and medieval metaphysics as one could have wished for. Just who is killing the monks of an isolated monastery in a variety of vile ways, and why? William of Baskerville is the Franciscan Holmes called upon to point the finger: a complex man, at once the great detective delighted with his own powers of deduction, and a man both defeated by the brutality of his age and enthralled by its mysteries (and it's to Sean Connery's credit that he portrays as much and more). In addition, the film simply looks good, really succeeds in communicating the sense and spirit of a time when the world was quite literally read like a book, with impressively claustrophobic sets, particularly the Escher-like labyrinth of a library with its momentous secret. The monks themselves are marvellous, a gallery of grotesques straight out of Brueghel, and if the film has faults, they are quibbles: the murder mystery is solved too soon, and rather too much plot is crammed into the available space. AMac

Namu, The Killer Whale

(1966, US, 89 min)
d/p Laslo Benedek. *sc* Arthur Weiss. *ph* Lamar Boren. *ed* Warren Adams. *ad* Eddie Imazu. *m* Samuel Matlovsky. *cast* Robert Lansing, John Anderson, Lee Meriwether, Richard Erdman, Robin Mattson, Joe Higgins.

●The usual 'boy and his killer whale' tale receives a slightly different spin in this superior family offering, with Lansing as the naturalist who gives sanctuary to the eponymous ocean-going predator in his own cove, only to meet strong opposition from fishermen worried about their salmon stocks. Not as glossy as the latter-day *Free Willy*, but it passes – quite attractively and unsentimentally. Laslo Benedek who began his career as a camera assistant at UFA in the early '30s is best remembered as the director of Marlon Brando's *The Wild One* (he was also responsible for a Frank Sinatra musical titled *The Kissing Bandit*). TJ

Nana

(1926, Fr, 144 min, b/w)
d/p Jean Renoir. *sc* Pierre Lestringuez [Pierre Philippe], Jean Renoir. *ph* Edmund Corwin, Jean Bachelet. *ed* Jean Renoir. *pd* Claude Autant-Lara. *cast* Catherine Hessling, Jean Angelo, Werner Krauss, Valeska Gert, Pierre Philippe, Claude Moore [Claude Autant-Lara], Pierre Champagne, André Cerf, Pierre Lestringuez, Raymond Guérin-Catelain.

●Renoir's rare 1926 adaptation of Zola's novel about a gamine's rise to riches and notoriety during the Second Empire, and widely regarded as the director's finest silent. True, the lead performance of Hessling is at the very least broad, eccentric and at odds with the overall naturalism of the piece, while for the first hour or so the film is rather static, mostly content simply to tell the story, record the performances, and lavish attention on Claude Autant-Lara's sumptuous sets. As the movie proceeds, however, with the amoral courtesan gleefully taking every opportunity to humiliate her various, rival suitors, the initially light-hearted satire gives way to a bleaker mood, admirably incarnated by the increasingly dark, shadowy images. Renoir's subtle way with detail, coupled with a beautifully restrained performance from Krauss as the Count Muffat, makes for an accumulation of psychological and emotional nuance that anticipates his (superior) later films. GA

Nana (aka Lady of the Boulevards)

(1934, US, 86 min, b/w)
d Dorothy Arzner. *p* Samuel Goldwyn. *sc* Willard Mack, Harry Wagstaff Gribble. *ph* Gregg Toland. *ed* Frank Lawrence. *ad* Richard Day. *m* Alfred Newman. *cast* Anna Sten, Phillips Holmes, Lionel Atwill, Muriel Kirkland, Richard Bennett, Mae Clarke, Reginald Owen.

●Conceived by Sam Goldwyn as a vehicle to launch his protégée Anna Sten, this is a very loose and inevitably bowdlerised version of Zola's classic novel about a *gamine* from the gutters who becomes the most celebrated whore in Paris. With the sex and syphilis gone, it becomes a somewhat stolid if sumptuously designed romantic melodrama about a music-hall actress torn apart by her liaisons with brothers Holmes and Atwill. But Arzner treats her heroine sympathetically, while Gregg Toland's lustrous photography makes a fair stab at exoticising her into a Garbo/Dietrich figure. And her lacklustre reputation notwithstanding, Sten – albeit rather too wholesome for the part – is surprisingly affecting. GA

Nana

(1982, It, 92 min)
d Dan Wolman. *p* Menahem Golan, Yoram Globus. *sc* Marc Behm. *ph* Armando Nannuzzi. *ed* Ursula West. *ad* Amedeo Mellone. *m* Ennio Morricone. *cast* Katya Berger, Jean-Pierre Aumont, Yehuda Efroni, Massimo Serato, Mandy Rice-Davies, Debra Berger.

●Cinephiles will pale at this travesty in which, in a sub-plot, Georges Méliès is depicted as the father not of cinematic fantasy but of cinematic pornography, the Zalman King of the *belle époque*. Predictably, this being a Cannon production, Nana's trail of sexual devastation across Parisian high society is given no social or moral dimension, but serves merely as framework for tepid erotica. Several talented artists are involved, the director emphatically not among their number. BBa

Nang Nak

(1999, Thai, 100 min)
d/p Nonzee Nimibutr. *sc* Wisid Sartsanatieng. *ph* Nattawut Kittikhun. *ed* Sunit Ussavinikul. *pd* Ek Eiamchurn. *m* Pakawat Waiwittaya, Chatchai Pongprapapun. *cast* Indhira Jaroenpura, Winai Kraibutr, Pramote Suksatid, Pachariya Nakbunchai, Bunsong Yuyangyuen, Pracha Tawornfia.

●A perennial Thai ghost story (filmed something like 30 times before) gets definitive treatment in this relatively big budget effort from the talented Nonzee Nimibutr. After Mak has reluctantly left his pregnant bride Nak to fight, he returns bearing the scars of battle. She greets him with all her heart, and they have a beautiful baby now, yet their old friends avoid the household. Nak died in childbirth, they tell him. The dialogue is rudimentary, but Nonzee goes to such pains to establish his characters and their love, the horror when it comes is as moving as it is grisly (and believe me, it's grisly!). TCh

Nanny, The

(1965, GB, 93 min, b/w)
d Seth Holt. *p/sc* Jimmy Sangster. *ph* Harry Waxman. *ed* Tom Simpson. *pd* Edward Carrick. *m* Richard Rodney Bennett. *cast* Bette Davis, Wendy Craig, Jill Bennett, James Villiers, William Dix, Pamela Franklin, Jack Watling, Maurice Denham, Alfred Burke.

●A spirited pot-boiler from the almost forgotten ex-editor Seth Holt (his *Station Six Sahara* is a stunner that deserves revival), with Davis as Nanny to a houseful of neurotics. In particular, there is a 10-year-old boy (Dix), just released from a psychiatric hospital, who believes Davis wants to murder him. Made for Hammer Films (with whom Davis subsequently starred in *The Anniversary*), it capitalises on the star's performance in *What Ever Happened to Baby Jane?*, and while no one will have any trouble figuring out what's going on, Holt's atmospheric direction and Davis' performance keep one thoroughly hooked. ATu

Nanou

(1986, GB/Fr, 110 min)
d Conny Templeman. *p* Simon Perry. *sc* Conny Templeman. *ph* Martin Fuhrer. *ed* Tom Priestley. *pd* Andrew Mollo. *m* John Keane. *cast* Imogen Stubbs, Jean-Philippe Ecoffey, Christophe Lidon, Valentine Pelka, Roger Ibanez, Anna Cropper, Patrick O'Connell, Daniel Day Lewis, Lou Castel.

●Nanou (Stubbs) is an awfully nice English rose, bent on adventure and experience during a summer in France. She takes up with political activist slob Luc (Ecoffey, clearly a would-be Depardieu), much to the dismay of old flame Max (Day Lewis, all brooding eyebrows and twitchy lips). Not only does Luc involve Nanou in dangerous acts of terrorism, he also treats her like a dog. Quite why the masochistic miss is so taken with him is unclear; first love never seemed so boring or unattractive. Conny Templeman's first feature is one of the most horrendously middle class movies in years. Seen through Nanou's irritatingly naive eyes, the French unemployed are a sorry bunch: unshaven, grubby male chauvinists who all eat like pigs. Only the evocation of place – the grim, grey villages and plains of Northern France – holds any interest, thanks no doubt to the work of production designer Andrew Mollo. GA

Naples Connection, The (Un Complicato Intrigo di Donne, Vicoli e Delitti)

(1985, It, 106 min)
d Lina Wertmüller. *p* Menahem Golan, Yoram Globus. *sc* Lina Wertmüller, Elvio Porta. *ph* Giuseppe Lanci. *ed* Luigi Zita. *pd* Enrico Job. *m* Tony Esposito. *cast* Angela Molina, Francisco Rabal, Harvey Keitel, Daniel Ezralow, Vittorio Squillante, Paolo Bonacelli, Elvio Porta.

●A back street sleaze job: someone is putting the frighteners on the Rocco clan by wasting their menfolk. The victims are found with their balls pricked by the needle of a syringe. Meanwhile an epicene bum-boy prances around in his redundant church dance studio with nothing on save a jockstrap. A bathetic script provides some unsavoury delicacies – 'let's take a walk in the drains'; 'the awesome vagina'; 'let's make hate' – and Harvey Keitel's gangster comes to a spectacular end. But at the conclusion, Wertmüller's ingenuous fem-moral cop-out fails to redeem this violent slapdash. As in all soft porn, the prurience is ultimately prudish, but even so this dip into depravity, with its druggery and buggery, its flirtations with lesbianism and transvestism, has something for everyone. Only dog-lovers will be disappointed. MS

Napoléon 100

(1927, Fr, 333 min)
d/p/sc Abel Gance. *ph* Léonce-Henry Burel, Jules Kruger, Jean-Paul Mindwiller, Fedor Bourgassoff, Alexandre Volkoff. *ed* Marguerite Beaugé, Abel Gance. *ad* Pierre Schildknecht, Alexandre Benois, Serge Pimenoff. *cast* Albert Dieudonné, Gina Manès,

Annabella, Nicolas Koline, Antonin Artaud, Edmond Van Daele, Pierre Batcheff, Wladimir Roudenko, Abel Gance.
●Bambi Ballard's latest restoration of cinema's supreme, grandiloquent epic (63 mins longer than the version premiered by Kevin Brownlow in 1979, tinted and with an extended three-screen climax) is the closest we're ever likely to get to Gance's original. Despite its simplistic view of Napoleon himself – seen from childhood to the fascistic start of his empire-building as a 'man of destiny', guided through hardships and loneliness by his 'inner eagle' – the film is completely vindicated by Gance's raving enthusiasm for his medium. All of the brilliant experiments with film language remain potent, from the montages of flash-frames to the bombastic poetry of the triptych finale; even the gags are still funny. The many highpoints include the hour-long siege of Toulon in torrential rain, won by strategies prefigured in the opening snowball fight, and Gance's own patrician performance as the cold-blooded Saint-Just. To see this with Carl Davis' score (lashings of Beethoven) played live is an almost unimaginably thrilling experience. TR

Napoléon

(1954, Fr, 193 min)
d Sacha Guitry. *p* Clément Duhour. *sc* Sacha Guitry. *ph* Pierre Montazel. *ed* Raymond Lamy. *ad* René Renoux. *m* Jean Françaix. *cast* Jean-Pierre Aumont, Pierre Brasseur, Danielle Darrieux, Jean Gabin, Daniel Gélin, Sacha Guitry, Jean Marais, Yves Montand, Michèle Morgan, Raymond Pellegrin, Micheline Presle, Serge Reggiani, Dany Robin, Maria Schell, Erich von Stroheim, Henri Vidal, Orson Welles.
●Halfway through, Gélin as the young Napoleon sits down for a haircut. Snip, snip, *et voilà*, 'he felt like a different man' – and the older Pellegrin now occupies the chair and the role. This easy way with a long, bumpy narrative is the best of Guitry. In the person of Talleyrand, he recounts admiringly, but with many a wry aside, Bonaparte's life and times. The interest level fluctuates, the staging is sedentary (Guitry delegated the battles to Eugène Lourié), the perspective is that of a French patriot. Still, the treats keep coming: Stroheim as Beethoven, Welles as the brutish Brit of St Helena, and Gabin as the mortally wounded Maréchal Lannes, gesturing feebly towards the heaps of corpses, then roaring into the Emperor's ear, *'Assez!'* BBa

Napoleon and Samantha

(1972, US, 91 min)
d Bernard McEveety. *p* Winston Hibler. *sc* Stewart Raffill. *ph* Monroe P Askins. *ed* Robert Stafford. *ad* John B Mansbridge, Walter M Simonds. *m* Buddy Baker. *cast* Michael Douglas, Will Geer, Arch Johnson, Johnny Whittaker, Jodie Foster, Henry Jones, Vito Scotti.
●Two kids, orphaned Whittaker and sidekick Foster (her first movie, aged nine), get the title roles in this mild Disney live-action offering: they embark across country (the Strawberry Mountains, Oregon) with their elderly pet lion, Major, to join college student pal Douglas, who's doing some goat-herding over the summer. Melodramatic 'kidnapping' angle (in the second half) fails to fire up the plot. TJ

Narrow Margin, The

(1952, US, 71 min, b/w)
d Richard Fleischer. *p* Stanley Rubin. *sc* Earl Felton. *ph* George E Diskant. *ed* Robert Swink. *ad* Albert S D'Agostino, Jack Okey. *cast* Charles McGraw, Marie Windsor, Jacqueline White, Gordon Gebert, Queenie Leonard, Paul Maxey, Don Beddoe.
●Fleischer has yet to have his critical day: with Blake Edwards, he is one of the last surviving classically trained American directors. Here is classic pulp premise (cops escorting hoodlum's widow to Grand Jury trial with a pack of killers bent on eliminating her before she talks); essence of B movie casting (the malevolently magnificent McGraw and the sleazy siren Windsor); and classic setting (transcontinental express train with every passenger, every stop a possibly malign menace). Teeming with incident, it is fashioned into a taut, breathtakingly fast and highly suspenseful 'sleeper' par excellence. CW

Narrow Margin

(1990, US, 97 min)
d Peter Hyams. *p* Jonathan A Zimbert. *sc* Peter Hyams. *ph* Peter Hyams. *ed* Beau Barthel-Blair. *pd* Joel Schiller. *m* Bruce Broughton. *cast* Gene Hackman, Anne Archer, James B Sikking, JT Walsh, M Emmet Walsh, Susan Hogan, Harris Yulin, Nigel Bennett, BA 'Smitty' Smith.
●A remake of Richard Fleischer's superb 1952 train thriller must be artistically redundant. But Hyams has always had a magpie tendency to borrow from the best, daring to make a sequel to *2001*, remaking *High Noon* as *Outland*, even fitting his original screenplays (*Capricorn One*, *Running Scared*) into prevailing cycles. Given this reliance on proven formula, Hyams is an ingenious craftsman who makes supremely watchable movies, and this one is a case in point. District Attorney Hackman is escorting a reluctant witness (Archer) to testify in a murder trial, but assassins are on the same train to make sure she doesn't. Hyams boosts the set-up with some heavy-duty action, but the journey follows essentially the same tracks as in '52 for an exciting ride. Hackman is boringly good, but Archer (like Marie Windsor before her) enjoys the more ambivalent role. Very good indeed, she offers sufficient reason to check out this update, even if it does run out of steam before the end of the line. TCh

Nashville

(1975, US, 161 min)
d/p Robert Altman. *sc* Joan Tewkesbury. *ph* Paul Lohmann. *ed* Sidney Levin, Dennis Hall. *songs* Richard Baskin, Karen Black, Keith Carradine, Gary Busey, Robert Altman and others. *cast* Ned Beatty, Karen Black, Ronee Blakley, Keith Carradine, Geraldine Chaplin, Shelley Duvall, Allen Garfield, Henry Gibson, Scott Glenn, Jeff Goldblum, Barbara Harris, Michael Murphy, Cristina Raines, Lily Tomlin, Gwen Welles, Keenan Wynn.
●Altman's country music epic, intertwining the lives and longings and lonelinesses of its twenty-four protagonists with exquisite free-form grace, can be faulted for trying to bring everything together at the end with an assassination making an arbitrarily resounding statement about showbiz and politics. Forget this and the film is a wonderful mosaic which yields up greater riches with successive viewings, not least in the underrated songs, the superlative performances, and the open-mindedness of Altman's approach to direction. Immensely, exhilaratingly enjoyable. TM

Nasty Girl, The (Das schreckliche Mädchen)

(1989, WGer, 94 min)
d Michael Verhoeven. *p* Michael Senftleben. *sc* Michael Verhoeven. *ph* Axel de Roche. *ed* Barbara Hennings, Daniela Paeper. *ad* Hubert Popp. *m* Mike Herting, Elmar Schloter, Billy Gortl, Lydie Auvray. *cast* Lena Stolze, Monika Baumgartner, Michael Gahr, Robert Giggenbach, Elisabeth Bertram, Fred Stillkrauth.
●Sonja (Stolze), a bright schoolgirl from a middle class Bavarian family, wins a Euro-essay prize and becomes the pride of her small town. Spurred by success, she embarks on a follow-up essay: 'My Town in the Third Reich'. Doors start slamming before anyone has time to formulate the usual lies and evasions, and Sonja is forced to abandon her project – although not before her parents suffer unpleasant social reprisals. Sonja grows up, marries her beloved teacher (Giggenbach) and has kids, but never forgets the time she was barred from access to the civic archives. Now a *very* determined adult, she picks up her old project… Verhoeven is far too smart to focus his movie on guilty secrets from the Nazi past; his target is the Germany of the present, and in particular the cosy way church and state work arm-in-arm to maintain a facade of bland social order. His script is based on a real-life woman, but his method couldn't be further from docudrama. He uses several types of stylisation to keep banality at bay, matching visual wit with scalpel-sharp dialogue. Stolze's highly engaging performance is the icing on the cake. TR

Nasty Habits

(1976, GB, 92 min)
d Michael Lindsay-Hogg. *p/sc* Robert J Enders. *ph* Douglas Slocombe. *ed* Peter Tanner. *ad* Robert Jones. *m* John Cameron. *cast* Glenda Jackson, Melina Mercouri, Geraldine Page, Sandy Dennis, Anne Jackson, Anne Meara, Susan Penhaligon, Edith Evans, Rip Torn, Eli Wallach.
●The appeal of this adaptation of Muriel Spark's novel *The Abbess of Crewe* rests precariously upon one slim idea: resetting Watergate in a nunnery. Once the initial idea has been planted – Glenda Jackson out to get elected abbess at all costs – the audience is made to look awfully hard for laughs. The 'political' gags, like Mercouri's Kissinger-type roving nun, are often abysmal (only Sandy Dennis' impersonation of John Dean deserves to escape criticism); and with increasing desperation, the humour depends on the nuns' monotonous displays of venal ways (smoking, swearing, boozing, even shacking up with the Jesuits down the road). It's all terribly predictable and tame. CPe

Nasty Neighbours

(2000, GB, 88 min)
d Debbie Isitt. *p* Christine Alderson. *sc* Debbie Isitt. *ph* Simon Reeves, Sam McCurdy. *ed* Nicky Ager. *pd* Tim Streater. *m* Jocelyn Pook. *cast* Ricky Tomlinson, Marion Bailey, Phil Daniels, Rachel Fielding, Hywel Bennett, Dawn Butler, Debbie Isitt.
●Playwright, stage director and actress Isitt makes her film directing debut with this adaptation of one of her own plays, a tragi-comic tale of jealousy, resentment and rancour in a quiet Middle England cul-de-sac. Tomlinson is magnificent as Mr Peach, both a curtain twitching busybody and a figure of tragedy, crushed by his failure to meet his wife's expectations. Initial distrust of his new neighbours, the brash, abrasive Chapmans (Daniels and Fielding) soon escalates into warfare when, increasingly frustrated and irrational in the face of a failing career and the threat of bankruptcy, Peach begins to hold them personally responsible for everything that's wrong with his life, mounting a one-man vigilante mission to spy on them at all hours. Isitt has an eye for absurdity and an ear for understated comic dialogue, while the actors turn in sound, believable performances. With its curious blend of straight drama and improvised mockumentary (reminiscent of TV's *Neighbours at War*), the film provides a footnote to television's current fascination with 'real-life' docu-drama. Neither spoof documentary nor conventional drama, however, the film can't quite decide what it wants to be, and the result is somewhat bewildering. WI

Nathalie Granger

(1972, Fr, 83 min, b/w)
d Marguerite Duras. *p* Luc Moullet. *sc* Marguerite Duras. *ph* Ghislain Cloquet. *ed* Nicole Lubtchansky. *m* Marguerite Duras. *cast* Jeanne Moreau, Lucia Bosé, Luce Garcia Ville, Gérard Depardieu, Dionys Mascolo, Nathalie Bourgeois, Valérie Mascolo.
●Duras' early feature gains much in atmosphere from the house where it was shot, the author's own home outside Paris (where, among other things, she wrote *Hiroshima, Mon Amour* with Resnais). It's the setting for a typically indefinable 'narrative' bringing together the brooding presence of two women, Moreau and Bosé, a sense of crisis surrounding daughter Nathalie's abandonment of her piano lessons and violent conduct at school, and a rather daffy tyro turn from Depardieu as a flailing washing machine salesman. The effect is as diffuse as it is compelling, a celluloid equivalent of atonal music or free verse, but Duras' avowedly instinctive approach pays dividends for the patient viewer. TJ

Nationale 7

see Uneasy Riders

National Health, The

(1973, GB, 97 min)
d Jack Gold. *p* Ned Sherrin, Terry Glinwood. *sc* Peter Nichols. *ph* John Coquillon. *ed* Ralph Sheldon. *pd* Ray Simm. *m* Carl Davis. *cast* Lynn Redgrave, Eleanor Bron, Sheila Scott-Wilkinson, Donald Sinden, Jim Dale, Colin Blakely, Clive Swift, Mervyn Johns, Bob Hoskins.
●A would-be blackly comic *Carry On Doctor* that never manages to work itself free from the deadly grip of Peter Nichols' script (from his own

stage play) about Britain as a terminal ward. Jack Gold really ought to be up there with Nicolas Roeg. His BBC films (*The World of Coppard*, *Mad Jack*, *Arturo Ui*, *Stocker's Copper*) show style and finesse. But his features have either lacked the identity to leap from a genre (*The Reckoning*), or been constricted by theatrical origins (*The Bofors Gun*, in the taut, burly mould of British film-making, and *The National Health*, too diffuse and fussy to satisfy). All three films betray TV's main bad influence – too much respect for the sanctity of the script. SG

National Lampoon Goes to the Movies (aka National Lampoon's Movie Madness)

(1981, US, 89 min)
d Henry Jaglom, Bob Giraldi. *p* Matty Simmons. *sc* Tod Carroll, Shary Flenniken, Pat Mephitis, Gerald Sussman, Ellis Weiner. *ph* Charles Correll, Tak Fujimoto. *ed* James Coblenz, Bud S Isaacs. *ad* Alexander A Mayer. *m* Andy Stein. *cast* Peter Riegert, Diane Lane, Candy Clark, Teresa Ganzel, Ann Dusenberry, Robert Culp, Robby Benson, Richard Widmark, Christopher Lloyd, Elisha Cook, Julie Kavner, Mary Woronov.
● A National Lampoon movie deemed unfit for US theatrical release. Dumb parodies of Harold Robbins-like soaps, cop movies and 'personal growth' educational fare. Very poor. TJ

National Lampoon's Animal House

(1978, US, 109 min)
d John Landis. *p* Matty Simmons, Ivan Reitman. *sc* Harold Ramis, Douglas Kenney, Chris Miller. *ph* Charles Correll. *ed* George Folsey Jr. *ad* John J Lloyd. *cast* John Belushi, Tim Matheson, John Vernon, Verna Bloom, Tom Hulce, Cesare Danova, Peter Riegert, Many Louise Weller, Stephen Furst, Karen Allen, Kevin Bacon, Donald Sutherland.
● Beer barrels shatter windows, rock'n'roll blares out, havoc rules in this sharp, college-campus-of-'62 crack at American Graffiti. An unashamed sense of its own fantasy is coupled with classically mounted slapstick; nostalgia mixes with cynicism in seductive proportions; and John Belushi's central performance as brain-damaged slob-cum-Thief of Baghdad is wonderful. CA

National Lampoon's Class Reunion

(1982, US, 85 min)
d Michael Miller. *p* Matty Simmons. *sc* John Hughes. *ph* Philip Lathrop. *ed* Richard C Meyer, Anne Mills. *pd* Dean Edward Mitzner. *m* Peter Bernstein, Mark Goldenberg. *cast* Gerrit Graham, Michael Lerner, Fred McCarren, Miriam Flynn, Stephen Furst, Marya Small, Shelley Smith, Zane Buzby.
● It's a dark and stormy night when a high school class reassembles in the now deserted classrooms of their alma mater. A murder is committed, and a mysterious doctor appears announcing that it's 'all about…mental illness'. A psychopath is lurking in the shadowy corridors of Lizzie Borden High: wimpish Walter seeking revenge upon his old classmates for a cruel joke once played on him. The characterisations and jokes remain as hackneyed as the plot and as primary as the film's garish colours. FD

National Lampoon's Loaded Weapon 1

(1992, US, 83 min)
d Gene Quintano. *p* Suzanne Todd, David Willis. *sc* Don Holley, Gene Quintano. *ph* Peter Dening. *ed* Christopher Greenbury. *pd* Jaymes Hinkle. *m* Robert Folk. *cast* Emilio Estevez, Samuel L Jackson, Jon Lovitz, Tim Curry, Kathy Ireland, William Shatner, F Murray Abraham, Charlie Sheen.
● A new low in lame spoofery, this half-cocked cop claptrap conjures up even fewer laughs than the *Lethal Weapon* series it's meant to be sending up. With Estevez and Jackson in the buddy-buddy Mel'n'Danny roles, we look set for a more contemporary spin on the *Naked Gun* routine, but this trigger-happy, chortle-shy effort is severely hampered by lack of comic invention. The mix isn't far from the similarly dismal fly-boy skit *Hot Shots!*: there ain't enough plot to sustain the action, so it's heigh-ho and on we go with embarrassed guest stars and meaningless sketches. Hence, rent-a-ham Shatner is a scenery-chewing Mr Big, Abraham lurks behind bars as Dr Hannibal Lecher, and Sheen wanders around under the impression that simply appearing uncredited with his bruv will just slay them out there. Wrong, wrong and wrong again; this *Loaded Weapon* fires only dumb-dumb bullets. TJ

National Lampoon's Movie Madness

see National Lampoon Goes to the Movies

National Lampoon's Vacation

(1983, US, 98 min)
d Harold Ramis. *p* Matty Simmons. *sc* John Hughes. *ph* Victor J Kemper. *ed* Paul Herring. *pd* Jack T Collis. *m* Ralph Burns. *cast* Chevy Chase, Beverly D'Angelo, Imogene Coca, Randy Quaid, Anthony Michael Hall, Dana Barron, John Candy, Eddie Bracken.
● National Lampoon takes on another stereotype of middle America: the family vacation. Chevy Chase, his face pinkened by the strain of having to be in control, plays the affluent suburban patriarch who leads his family on a summer jaunt from Chicago to Disneyland (here rechristened Walleyworld). The result is not so much a comedy about American values as a 2,500 mile skid on a banana skin. The visual gags come thick and fast, and are about as subtly signposted as the exit markers on a freeway. An exercise in the comedy of humiliation which is the stuff of shamefaced giggles. RR

National Velvet

(1944, US, 125 min)
d Clarence Brown. *p* Pandro S Berman. *sc* Theodore Reeves, Helen Deutsch. *ph* Leonard Smith. *ed* Robert J Kern. *ad* Cedric Gibbons, Urie McCleary. *m* Herbert Stothart. *cast* Mickey Rooney, Donald Crisp, Elizabeth Taylor, Anne Revere, Angela Lansbury, Reginald Owen, Norma Varden.
● Two children train a sorrel gelding, won in a village raffle, to win the Grand National. This is a charmer for boys and girls of all ages, with a captivating performance from the young Liz Taylor as Velvet, the butcher's daughter, and graceful, fluent direction by Clarence Brown. The National was actually filmed on a Pasadena golf course. (From the novel by Enid Bagnol.) TCh

Nattvardsgästerna (The Communicants/Winter Light)

(1962, Swe, 80 min, b/w)
d/sc Ingmar Bergman. *ph* Sven Nykvist. *ed* Ulla Ryghe. *ad* PA Lundgren. *cast* Ingrid Thulin, Gunnar Björnstrand, Max von Sydow, Gunnel Lindblom, Allan Edwall, Kolbjörn Knudsen, Olof Thunberg.
● The middle part of Bergman's trilogy about God's silence – it is flanked by *Through a Glass Darkly* and *The Silence* – and the most austere, *Winter Light* focuses on a small group of parishioners found at the beginning of the film attending Holy Communion. The village pastor (Björnstrand) is realising he has become an atheist since his wife's death. His faith is further tested by an offer of marriage from a schoolteacher (Thulin) tortured with eczema, and the solace demanded by a man (von Sydow) suicidally depressed by the threat of nuclear war. The pastor fails on both counts, and Bergman gives us an ambiguous ending back in the church service – what he himself called 'certainty unmasked'. Never a comfortable film, it's finely acted by a familiar Bergman ensemble, and the awesomely cold vistas form a perfect counterpoint to the spiritual freeze. DT

Natural, The

(1984, US, 137 min)
d Barry Levinson. *p* Mark Johnson. *sc* Roger Towne, Phil Dusenberry. *ph* Caleb Deschanel. *ed* Stu Linder. *pd* Angelo Graham (Los Angeles), Mel Bourne (New York). *m* Randy Newman. cast Robert Redford, Robert Duvall, Glenn Close, Kim Basinger, Wilford Brimley, Barbara Hershey, Robert Prosky, Richard Farnsworth, Joe Don Baker, Michael Madsen.
● This upbeat adaptation of Bernard Malamud's gritty allegory of the world of baseball is one of those test cases for the mood or generosity of the spectator: give yourself over completely to its wide-eyed brand of mythologising, and it will reward you with a tidal wave of emotion, hero-worship and strange medieval morality tale; a flicker of disbelief, however, and you'll see nothing but its faults. The Arthurian basis to Redford's rise to baseball stardom means that the narrative can include very un-Hollywoodlike devices such as an unexplained 16-year gap when he is out in the cold, expiating his fall from grace with a murderous femme fatale. Moreover, this mythological basis releases the cast from the necessity for naturalism (despite the title). There are also other things to enjoy: a great line up of supporting actors (especially Brimley and Farnsworth doing their grouchy old man double act), Caleb Deschanel's photography, Randy Newman's score. Let yourself go and be rewarded by the sight of a hero running home to victory through clouds of fire. CPea

Natural Born Killers

(1994, US, 119 min, b/w & col)
d Oliver Stone. *p* Jane Hamsher, Don Murphy, Clayton Townsend. *sc* David Veloz, Richard Rutowski, Oliver Stone. *ph* Robert Richardson. *ed* Hank Corwin, Brian Berdan. *pd* Victor Kempster. *cast* Woody Harrelson, Juliette Lewis, Robert Downey Jr, Tommy Lee Jones, O-Lan Jones, Tom Sizemore, Rodney Dangerfield, Yared Harris, Russell Means.
● Mickey (Harrelson) and Mallory (Lewis) are white-trash low-lifes who get their kicks from killin' just about anybody who gets in their way. Their antics are covered by scumbag talk-show host Wayne Gale (Downey) whose reports turn the pair into folk heroes. Meanwhile, detective Jack Scagnetti (Sizemore) is determined to put them behind bars. Trailing hype and tabloid hysteria in its wake, Stone's film is at once a phenomenon and unremarkable. True, it's technically extraordinary; with the director resorting to a frantic collage of film and video, b/w and colour, back- and front-projection, fast and slow motion to develop his thesis that crime and violence are fanned by sensationalist media attention. At least that's what he seems to be saying. Basically, the story is just a tarted up variation of the *Badlands/Wild at Heart* scenario, with ultra-broad swipes at media and authority figures tossed in for good measure. The actors are given no space to build up characters, and the film's main 'virtue' is that it's nowhere near as explicit as the tabloids suggested. Turgid. GA

Nature of the Beast, The

(1988, GB, 96 min)
d Franco Rosso. *p* Joanna Smith. *sc* Janni Howker. *ph* Nat Crosby. *ed* George Akers. *pd* Jamie Leonard. *m* Stanley Myers, Hans Zimmer. *cast* Lynton Dearden, Paul Simpson, Tony Melody, Freddie Fletcher, Dave Hill, Roberta Kerr, David Fleeshman.
● The beast is unemployment. There have been eight years of Thatcherism since Franco Rosso's *Babylon*, and as he turns from what it was to be working class, black and British in Brixton to what it is to be working class, white and unemployed in the distressed North of England, the effect of the intervening years can be detected in both the change of location to the colder, stonier climes of Lancashire, and the quieter but more desperate responses of his characters. The plainly allegorical tale is from the same school, if not the same class, as *Kes*. Fletcher (the hero's brother in Loach's film) plays the father of another troubled teenager and school truant, motherless wild-child Bill (Dearden), from whose point of view the narrative unfolds. There's trouble't mill. Grandad (Melody) is sacked, Dad joins the picket. Meanwhile a beast roams the moors, descending on the town to kill at night. Superstition is rife, and Bill takes a gun to kill it. The results may be uneven, but the restrained performances are truthful, and the sense of pain and frustration is genuinely moving. WH

Naufragos, Los (Shipwrecked)

(1994, Chile, 119 min)
d Miguel Littín. *p* Yvon Provost, Ely Menz. *sc* Miguel Littín, José Roman. *ph* Hans Burmann. *ed* Rodolfo Wedeles. *m* Jorge Arriagada. *cast* Marcelo Romo, Valentina Vargas, Luis Alarcon, Bastián Bodenhofer, Patricio Bunster, Tennyson Ferrada.

●This extraordinary dark and poetic movie is about a man who returns home to Chile after 20 years and finds himself in the cold grip of his own maddening ghost story. Littin layers his descent into the maelstrom in a series of scenes akin to Dante's *Divine Comedy* retold by Edgar Allan Poe: all the people the man encounters (old lovers, household retainers, his brother, who have stayed through the hurricane) reflect through a glass darkly his own guilt and despair. Here there's no boundary between the real and the imaginary. Hans Burmann's evocative camerawork suffuses the film in smoky mists and indelible images that achieve the same eery, alienating quality that Edmond Richard's did in Welles' *The Trial*. Except for the over-allegorical ending, it's a work of considerable power and originality. WH

Naughty but Nice

(1939, US, 89 min, b/w)
d Ray Enright. *p* Sam Bischoff. *sc* Richard Macaulay, Jerry Wald. *ph* Arthur L Todd. *ed* Thomas Richards. *songs* Harry Warren, Johnny Mercer. *cast* Ann Sheridan, Dick Powell, Gale Page, Helen Broderick, Ronald Reagan, ZaSu Pitts.

●Its title may make it sound like one of those saucy British sex comedies from the early 1970s, but in fact this is a squeaky clean Warner Bros musical. Powell's an ingenuous, clean-cut music professor from out in the sticks who heads for Manhattan hoping to sell his symphony. Smooth but untrustworthy shyster Ronald Reagan buys it, but then bowdlerises it, turning it into a popular song for oomph girl, Ann Sheridan. Wittily scripted by the prolific Jerry Wald, this takes a few sly digs at the world of music publishing before dribbling off into a conventional romantic ending. GM

Naughty Marietta

(1935, US, 106 min, b/w)
d WS Van Dyke. *p* Hunt Stromberg. *sc* John Lee Mahin, Frances Goodrich, Albert Hackett. *ph* William H Daniels. *ed* Blanche Sewell. *ad* Cedric Gibbons, A Arnold Gillespie, Edwin B Willis. *m* Victor Herbert. *lyrics* Rida Johnson Young, (additional) Gus Kahn. *cast* Jeanette MacDonald, Nelson Eddy, Frank Morgan, Elsa Lanchester, Douglas Dumbrille, Edward Brophy, Akim Tamiroff.

●The first MacDonald-Eddy vehicle, enormously popular in its day so somebody must have been able to stand this simpering duo. An adaptation of Victor Herbert's 1905 operetta (which perpetrated *Ah! Sweet Mystery of Life*), set in New Orleans, with MacDonald as the French princess running out on an arranged marriage, kidnapped by pirates, and falling for the stalwart backwoods scout who rescues her. Eddy, believe it or not, addresses her as 'Bright Eyes'. The fine supporting cast is a relief. TM

Navigator, The

(1924, US, 5,702 ft, b/w)
d Buster Keaton, Donald Crisp. *p* Joseph M Schenk. *sc* Jean Havez, Clyde Bruckman, Joe Mitchell. *ph* Elgin Lessley, Byron Houck. *ad* Fred Gabourie. *cast* Buster Keaton, Kathryn McGuire, Frederick Vroom, Noble Johnson, Clarence Burton.

●Gag for gag, one of the funniest of all Keaton's features as he copes with the snags involved in running a deserted ocean liner single-handed, philosophically accepting the fact that machinery has a malevolent will of its own. Prevented from becoming one of his best only because it (necessarily) lacks the lovingly detailed backgrounds and incredibly beautiful visual textures of films like *Our Hospitality*, *The General* and *Steamboat Bill Jr*. TM

Navigator: A Medieval Odyssey, The

(1988, Aust, 91 min, b/w & col)
d Vincent Ward. *p* John Maynard. *sc* Vincent Ward, Kely Lyons, Geoff Chapple. *ph* Geoffrey Simpson. *ed* John Scott. *pd* Sally Campbell. *m* Davood A Tabrizi. *cast* Bruce Lyons, Chris Haywood, Hamish McFarlane, Marshall Napier, Noel Appleby, Paul Livingston, Sarah Pierse.

●A bold fusion of history, myth, and futuristic fantasy, Ward's imaginitive medieval odyssey ravishes the eye, challenges the mind, and stirs the heart. When young Griffin's older brother Connor returns to their 14th century Cumbrian mining village with horrifying tales of the Black Death, the elders fear the small community is doomed. But in a prophetic dream, Griffin sees a religious pilgrimage by which a resolute band may triumph over the pestilence through an act of religious faith. Their quest, to erect a new spire on a distant church steeple, will take them deep into the bowels of the earth and make them strangers in a strange land, because they emerge from their tunnels into the glass towers, monstrous machinery and religious scepticism of modern-day New Zealand. There is a powerful allergorical undercurrent, too, which draws a parallel between the plague-threatened village and the modern city, itself living under the spectre of a nuclear Armageddon. NF

Navy Heroes

see Blue Peter, The

Navy Seals

(1990, US, 114 min)
d Lewis Teague. *p* Brenda Feigen, Bernard Williams. *sc* Chuck Pfarrer, Gary Goldman. *ph* John A Alonzo. *ed* Don Zimmerman. *pd* Guy J Comtois, Veronica Hadfield. *m* Sylvester Levay. *cast* Charlie Sheen, Michael Biehn, Joanne Whalley-Kilmer, Rick Rossovich, Cyril O'Reilly, Bill Paxton.

●Popularised by *The Abyss*, the Navy Sea, Air and Land commandos here go into action against an Arab terrorist who has his hands on a consignment of Stinger missiles. The film nevertheless avoids all mention of politics by pitching diligent team-leader Biehn, crazy Sheen and the other all-American sea-mammals against a fanatical splinter group dedicated to senseless violence rather than any specific ideological goal. Tipped off by half-Lebanese TV journalist Whalley-Kilmer, the SEALS parachute into the sea off Beirut and prepare to kick some Arab butt. Having played a psychotic SEALS officer in *The Abyss*, Biehn this time leaves the loony stuff to Sheen. Teague, meanwhile, is far too busy orchestrating the large-scale action sequences to make anything of the cardboard characters, episodic plotting, or clunking dialogue. NF

Nazarín

(1958, Mex, 94 min, b/w)
d Luis Buñuel. *p* Manuel Barbachano Ponce. *sc* Julio Alejandro, Luis Buñuel. *ph* Gabriel Figueroa. *ed* Carlos Savage. *ad* Edward Fitzgerald. *cast* Francisco Rabal, Marga López, Rita Macedo, Ignacio López Tarso, Ofelia Guilmain, Luis Aceves Castañeda, Noé Murayama, Rosenda Monteros.

●One of the least sardonic of all Buñuel's films. Father Nazarín, a non-denominational journeyman priest, wanders through the plagues, sins and poverty of the secular world, experiencing a number of episodes that echo incidents in the gospels...until he learns the momentous lesson that he can receive charity as well as give it. Buñuel never ridicules Nazarín's efforts to follow Christ's teachings, but instead stresses the priest's fundamental detachment, and observes how irrelevant most of his work is to the sinners he tangles with. To the extent that the open ending is optimistic, Nazarín is a true Buñuel hero. TR

Néa (A Young Emmanuelle)

(1976, Fr/WGer, 105 min)
d Nelly Kaplan. *p* André Génoves, Yvon Guezel. *sc* Nelly Kaplan, Jean Chapot. *ph* Andréas Winding. *ed* Hélène Plemiannikov. *ad* Bernard Evein. *m* Michel Magne. *cast* Sami Frey, Ann Zacharias, Nelly Kaplan, Françoise Brion, Micheline Presle, Heinz Bennent, Ingrid Caven, Martin Provost.

●Absurdly and opportunistically released here as *A Young Emmanuelle*, Nelly Kaplan's film in fact hovers in tone in the same range as Rohmer's moral fables, but its plot reveals the sexual-political drive that runs through all her work. The spoilt child of a rich Geneva family writes an erotic novel (for her own fantasy life). Oppressed by her bigoted father and by a hypocritical family life, she becomes wilfully determined – publishing the novel anonymously, encouraging her (gay) mother to leave home for her lover, and taking a lover herself to acquire the experience that she feels she lacks. The film's insistence on sexual liberation in itself makes it curious; but after a hesitant opening, the subject matter is matched by an enchanted tone, hanging between humour and cruelty, slim snatches of parody, heartache and eroticism. For once, a radical film that is generous, ingenious and alive. CA

Neapolitanische Geschwister

see Reign of Naples, The

Near Dark

(1987, US, 94 min)
d Kathryn Bigelow. *p* Steven-Charles Jaffe. *sc* Eric Red, Kathryn Bigelow. *ph* Adam Greenberg. *ed* Howard Smith. *pd* Stephen Altman. *m* Tangerine Dream. *cast* Adrian Pasdar, Jenny Wright, Lance Henriksen, Bill Paxton, Jenette Goldstein, Joshua Miller, Marcie Leeds, Tim Thomerson, James LeGros.

●A full-blooded vampire movie which gives the well-worn mythology a much-needed transfusion by stripping away the Gothic trappings and concentrating instead on a pack of nocturnal nomads who roam the sun-parched farmlands of the modern Midwest. Kissed by a pale, mysterious girl from out of town, it soon dawns on farmboy Caleb that Mae's love-bite has infected him with a burning desire – for blood. Subsequently snatched by Mae's vagabond pals, Caleb is gradually seduced by their exciting night-life. So, despite his reluctance to make a 'kill', Caleb is soon caught between his blood sister and his blood relatives – father and younger sister – who are in hot pursuit. Western iconography, *noir*-ish lighting, and visceral horror are fused with an affecting love story in this stylish 'Vampire Western', which (unlike Bigelow's rather static debut feature *The Loveless*) is driven forward at a scorching pace, a subtle study in the seductiveness of evil and a terrifying ride to the edge of darkness. NF

Nearly Wide Awake

(1977, GB, 65 min)
d David Hutt, Martin Turner. *p* Alan Bell, William Stair. *cast* Alex Cox, Suzy Gilbert, Liz Salmon, Niven Boyd, Glenys Gill.

●A wild and woolly tapestry woven from incidents in the novels of Knut Hamsun (including *Hunger*), this was shot on a frayed shoestring by two post-graduate film students at Bristol University – and looks very much like a student movie. Deliberately flouting any formal discipline and passing up no opportunity for visual or aural display inseeking to conjure up an outcast's hallucinating vision, it is often maddeningly uncoordinated, but intermittently packs a visceral punch. Budgetary limitations mean that the period setting sometimes goes awry, and the copper who appears at one point seems to have strayed in from Dock Green.

Near Room, The

(1995, GB, 89 min)
d David Hayman. *p* Len Crooks. *sc* Robert Murphy. *ph* Kevin Rowley. *ed* Martin Sharpe. *pd* Andy Harris. *m* James Grant, Paul McGeechan. *cast* Adrian Dunbar, David O'Hara, Julie Graham, Emma Faulkner, David Hayman, James Ellis, Robert Pugh.

●This Scottish thriller, developed by British Screen and written by Robert Murphy, is regrettably no advert for the future of small-budget, big-screen British product. Dunbar's a Glaswegian journo-turned-investigator whose search for a young girl (his daughter, unbeknownst to her) leads him into heavy-duty pressure, caught between hard-nosed editors, bent cops, prostitutes, paedophiles and power-hungry lawyers. 'The machinations of the secret state have been exposed,' says a character, but it's only a ruse. Hayman's stylised TV direction, the sountrack atmospherics, the over-use of red filters and circling overhead camera, and the formula performances detract from what could have been a topical *noir* drama. WH

Necessary Roughness

(1991, US, 108 min)
d Stan Dragoti. *p* Mace Neufeld, Robert Rehme. *sc* Rick Natkin, David Fuller. *ph* Peter Stein. *ed* John Wright, Steve Mirkovich, Wayne Wahrman. *pd* Paul Peters. *m* Bill Conti. *cast* Scott Bakula, Hector Elizondo, Robert Loggia, Harley Jane Kozak, Larry Miller, Sinbad, Fred Dalton Thompson.

●This tale of a 34-year-old quarterback's return to college football is marginally less funny than wearing a jock-strap on your head, and less original than putting Ralgex down your opponent's shorts. In Texas, former university league big-timers The Fighting Armadillos are decimated by charges of corruption, and forced to replenish their numbers with anaemic no-hoper academics. Only geriatric drop-out Paul (Bakula) can save the day, but to do so he must return to college and get his degree. Cue endless football montages, interspersed with a load of drivel about finding fulfilment, making real friends, and rediscovering the joys of pure sporting endeavour. Even the presence of reliably grimy stalwarts Elizondo and Loggia, and the inclusion of a naff sexual-equality subplot, can't alleviate the boredom. MK

Necronomicon (aka H.P. Lovecraft's Necronomicon)

(1993, US, 97 min)
d Christophe Gans, Shu Kaneko, Brian Yuzna. *p* Samuel Hadida, Brian Yuzna. *sc* ('The Library', 'Whispers') Brent V Friedman; ('The Drowned') Christophe Gans, Brent V Friedman; ('The Cold') Kazunori Ito, Brent V Friedman. *ph* Gerry Lively, ('The Drowned') Russell Brandt. *ed* ('The Drowned', 'The Cold') Christopher Roth; ('Whispers') Keith Sauter. *pd* Anthony Tremblay. *m* Tony LoDuca, Daniel Licht. *cast* ('The Library') Jeffrey Combs, Tony Azito; ('The Drowned') Bruce Payne, Richard Lynch, Belinda Bauer; ('The Cold') David Warner, Bess Myer, Millie Perkins; ('Whispers') Signy Coleman, Obba Babatunde, Don Calfa.
● A three-part portmanteau movie based on tales by the horror author HP Lovecraft. With its fluid camera style and lush score, French director Gans' 'The Drowned' is the most stylish segment, in which the inheritor of a 1920s cliff-top hotel, Payne, tries to resurrect his dead girlfriend. Gans' sure build-up emphasises atmosphere and character rather than effects, but the gloopy finale certainly makes up for it. By contrast, Japanese film-maker Kaneko's 'The Cold' is a torpid affair in which mad doctor Warner uses his victims' spinal fluid to sustain eternal life. Capping things off nicely is *Society* director Yuzna's 'Whispers', which makes a bloody spurt for the gorier end of the horror picture spectrum. Having pursued the furtive driver of a speeding car into a subterranean world, a male and female cop are lured to their fate by a sly old bum and his blind, religious-fanatic wife, who feed them to some flying flesh-eaters. While neither as subtle or stylish as Gans' segment, this certainly delivers old-fashioned gore-a-plenty. (Yuzna also directs a wrap-around segement, 'The Library', in which Lovecraft consults the Necronomicon, a book containing the secrets of the universe.) NF

Necropolis

(1970, It, 120 min)
d Franco Brocani. *p* Gianni Barcelloni. *sc* Franco Brocani. *ph* Ivan Stoinov. *ed* M Ludovica Barrani. *ad* Peter Steifel. *m* Gavin Bryars. *cast* Viva Auder, Tina Aumont, Carmelo Bene, Pierre Clémenti, Paul Jabara, Paolo Graziosa, Nicoletta Machiavelli, Louis Waldon.
● Brocani conjures together all your favourite European cultural and historical myth figures in order to attack the centuries of 'sublimation' that have produced our cities and their inhabitants. The gang's all here: Frankenstein's monster gropes towards the awareness that his mind is a universe; Attila, naked on a white horse, liberates his people from their ignominy; the ultra-caustic Viva bemoans the frustrations of married life and drifts into the elegiac persona of the Bloody Countess Bathory; Louis Waldon is a hip American tourist searching for the (missing) Mona Lisa. The range is extraordinary, from stand-up Jewish comedy to a kind of flea-market expressionism. Brocani's approach is contemplative rather than agitational, which confounds the impatient; Gavin Bryars' lovely Terry Riley-esque score matches the ambience exactly. TR

Ned Kelly

(1970, GB, 103 min)
d Tony Richardson. *p* Neil Hartley. *sc* Tony Richardson, Ian Jones. *ph* Gerry Fisher. *ed* Charles Rees. *pd* Jocelyn Herbert. *m/songs* Shel Silverstein. *cast* Mick Jagger, Allen Bickford, Geoff Gilmour, Mark McManus, Serge Lazareff, Peter Sumner, Ken Shorter, Frank Thring.
● Richardson's bushranger biopic merely applies a simplistic gloss to the 'outlaw' image already projected onto Jagger by the British media, and his role as the legendary Australian anti-hero emerges as little more than an uncomfortable displacement of his tabloid notoriety. The beard and iron mask Jagger assumes for the part obscure his specific rock/cultural persona as effectively as they do his features; and overall this outback Western comes a poor second to *Mad Dog*, the later Philippe Mora/Dennis Hopper outlaw movie also shot down under. PT

Needful Things

(1994, US, 120 min)
d Fraser C Heston. *p* Jack Cummins. *sc* WD Richter. *ph* Tony Westman. *ed* Rob Kobrin. *pd* Douglas Higgins. *m* Patrick Doyle. *cast* Max von Sydow, Ed Harris, Bonnie Bedelia, Amanda Plummer, JT Walsh, Ray McKinnon, Duncan Fraser, Valri Bromfield, Shane Meier, Lisa Blount.
● Better than most Stephen King adaptations, mainly because an exceptionally strong cast adds substance to the facile storyline about a mysterious stranger, Leland Gaunt (von Sydow), who opens the antique shop of the title in Castle Rock, Maine, and, by tapping into the inhabitants' acquisitive desires, sets them at one another's throats. As Fraser C Heston has observed, there are no supernatural beings here – the only monster is avarice. Little more than an EC Comics-style morality tale about the greedy getting their comeuppance, but the director has a strong eye for visual detail and expansive composition. NF

Negotiator, The

(1998, US/Ger, 139 min)
d F Gary Gray. *p* David Hoberman, Arnon Milchan. *sc* James DeMonaco, Kevin Fox. *ph* Russel Carpenter. *ed* Christian Wagner. *pd* Holger Gross. *m* Graeme Revell. *cast* Samuel L Jackson, Kevin Spacey, David Morse, Ron Rifkin, John Spencer, JT Walsh, Siobhan Fallon.
● Originally developed as a star vehicle for Sylvester Stallone, this mutated into a hybrid action-drama featuring the choreographed pyrotechnics of director Gray and a battle of words between contrasting hostage negotiators Jackson and Spacey. It scores on both counts, though the dovetailing of the explosive action and the verbal fireworks is not always as snug as it might be. Falsely accused of murder and embezzlement, Danny Roman (Jackson) buys time by taking hostage Commander Frost (Rifkin), head of the Chicago police's Internal Affairs Division, together with his administrative staff and an unlucky bystander. Suspecting an inside job, Roman demands that he deal with Chris Sabian (Spacey), a stranger from another district and reputedly the second best hostage negotiator in the city. Roman knows exactly how to manipulate the situation to his advantage, but his instinctive, improvisational approach is matched by Sabian's shrewd use of psychology and manipulative mind games. The draw for Spacey and Jackson fans is the chance to see two consummate actors engage in a subtle war of words, but for too much of the film they're either at separate ends of a telephone, or simply divided from one another by the plot logistics and action scenes. NF

Neige était sale, La (The Stain on the Snow/ The Snow Was Black)

(1953, Fr, 104 min, b/w)
d Luis Saslavsky. *p* F Bukofzer. *sc* André Tabet, Luis Saslavsky. *ph* André Bac. *ed* Isabelle Elman. *pd* René Moulaërt. *m* René Cloërec. *cast* Daniel Gélin, Marie Mansart, Daniel Ivernel, Nadine Basile, Jean-Pierre Mocky, Valentine Tessier, Bâlpetré, Véra Norman.
● The setting is a Nazi-occupied country (explicitly *not* France – *quelle suggestion!*) where Frank, the son of a blowsy brothel keeper, spends his days hanging out with the girls and their German clients, and his nights hanging out with the boys, stealing and black marketeering. Mired in self-disgust, he proceeds to ever greater atrocities – murdering an old lady who was kind to him as a child, arranging the rape of a naive neighbour who's in love with him – and finally, the depths plumbed, getting himself executed. The tone is non-sensational; indeed, from the start, the film seems as exhausted as its hero is by the finish: you wonder if the director even bothered to show up. Mostly, it induces gloom to no useful end. BBa

Neighbors

(1981, US, 96 min)
d John G Avildsen. *p* Richard D Zanuck, David Brown. *sc* Larry Gelbart. *ph* Gerald Hirschfeld. *ed* John G Avildsen, Jane Kurson. *pd* Peter Larkin. *m* Bill Conti. *cast* John Belushi, Kathryn Walker, Dan Aykroyd, Cathy Moriarty, Igors Gavon, Dru-Ann Chukron, Tim Kazurinsky.
● Belushi's final appearance, scripted by Larry Gelbart from Thomas Berger's novel, and detailing the purportedly hilarious chaos that befalls a quiet suburban couple (Belushi and Walker) when a pair of uninhibited nutters (Aykroyd, Moriarty) move in next door. In fact, ruthlessly ironing out Berger's subtleties of tone in favour of a rumbustious *Animal House* collision between Belushi and Aykroyd, it becomes increasingly tiresome, with few funny moments to leaven the proceedings. GA

Neil Simon's Lost in Yonkers

see Lost in Yonkers

Neil Simon's The Odd Couple II

see Odd Couple II, The

Neither by Day Nor by Night

(1972, US/Isr, 95 min)
d Steven Hilliard Stern. *p* Mordechai Slonim. *sc* Steven Hilliard Stern, Gisa W Slonim. *ph* Amnon Salomon. *ed* Alain Jakubowicz. *m* Vladimir Cosma. *cast* Zalman King, Miriam Bernstein-Cohen, Dalia Friedland, Edward G Robinson, Mischa Asheroff, Chaim Anitar, Eli Cohen.
● 'When I waited for light there came the darkness,' the pretty nurse reading from the Book of Job reminds us. And indeed it does in the shape of this peculiarly awkward story of a bitter-sweet relationship formed in hospital between a cynical expatriate American, a veteran of the Israeli war who is about to go blind, and a short-sighted old girl who mistakes him for a reincarnation of her former lover. Good intentions and a Yiddish flavour abound, but emotional toughness soon gets sacrificed for the sake of a good wallow. Strange that a film which preaches the virtues of 'insight' should handle the theme with such obtuseness. All that pulling in and out of focus, plus a particularly crass sub-Simon and Garfunkel soundtrack, and it's difficult to say whose trials are more gruelling, the characters' or the audience's. CPe

Neither the Sea Nor the Sand

(1972, GB, 94 min)
d Fred Burnley. *p* Jack Smith, Peter Fetterman. *sc* Gordon Honeycombe. *ph* David Muir. *ed* Norman Wanstall. *ad* Michael Bastow. *m* Nahum Heiman. *cast* Susan Hampshire, Michael Petrovitch, Frank Finlay, Michael Craze, Jack Lambert, Anthony Booth.
● Must qualify as one of the worst films of the decade. Girl, married, goes to Jersey in winter to 'work things out'. Bumps into enigmatic chap who keeps saying urgent things like 'Reality is truth…can you understand that?' She leaves her husband for him, but his prim brother objects. 'Let's go to Scotland.' They arrive at the cottage. 'It used to be the old bakery, you know.' Not before time, Adonis succumbs to a heart attack, and the film veers into ghost territory. The girl's love somehow keeps him alive (but at least he's dumb, so can't trot out any more pearls of wisdom). Eventually, back in Jersey, she accepts that decomposition can no longer be put off, and they wander into the sea to drown. And be together. Which is no more than they deserve. Gordon Honeycombe scripted this awful effort from his own novel.

Nela

(1980, WGer, 99 min)
d/p/sc Hans Conrad Fischer. *ph* Wolfgang Simon, Hans Conrad Fischer. *ed* Annemarie Reisetbauer. *narrators* Paul Rogers, Judi Dench.

● Far from being the great unmentionable, death seems to be a topic about which most people will witter on interminably at the drop of an armband. This death belongs to Nela (Cornelia), a painter of naive pictures in bold colour, and the daughter of the director (an Austrian documentary filmmaker). She died of leukemia at 22 – a death in itself no different from anyone else's (normal, tragic), but whose circumstances here prompt a panegyric of bland mediocrity. It tells us nothing about her whatever. Her paintings remain; they can stand or fall on their own merits. Here death were better honoured by a decent silence. CPea

Nell

(1994, US, 113 min)
d Michael Apted. *p* Jodie Foster, Renée Missel. *sc* William Nicholson, Mark Handley. *ph* Dante Spinotti. *ed* Jim Clark. *pd* Jon Hutman. *m* Mark Isham, Phil Marshall. *cast* Jodie Foster, Liam Neeson, Natasha Richardson, Richard Libertini, Nick Searcy, Robin Mullins, Jeremy Davies.

● Deep in the mountains of North Carolina, Dr Jerome Lovell (Neeson) discovers a grown wild child, Nell (Foster). She's had no contact with the outside world, having been raised entirely by her invalid mother, and can speak only in a strange onomatopoeic language. But can Nell continue to live her own life, as Lovell hopes, or is she too important for that, a unique subject for a scientific study, as psychologist Paula Olsen (Richardson) would have it? With a court hearing in the offing, the rival scientists camp out in the backwoods. This metaphor-movie is both touching and tasteful. It allows Foster to play scared and alone, traumatised and neurotic, and, most importantly, free and inspirational. She gets to 'commune with nature', speak in tongues, and bring Neeson and Richardson together. Nice photography; nonsensical courtroom speech at the close. TCh

Nell Gwyn

(1934, GB, 85 min, b/w)
d/p Herbert Wilcox. *sc* Miles Malleson. *ph* Freddie Young. *ed* Merrill G White. *ad* LP Williams. *m* Philip Braham. *cast* Anna Neagle, Cedric Hardwicke, Jeanne de Casalis, Muriel George, Esmé Percy, Moore Marriott, Miles Malleson.

● With King Charles II putting into practice his promise to restore the country 'to its old good nature, its old good manners and its old good humour' by leading a rollicking chorus in a 17th century musical hall, it is difficult not to warm to Wilcox's very democratic brand of royalism. Neagle is rather too hoydenish to be truly sexy, but she has a zest and brazenness breathtaking in its disregard for the conventions of polite society, and Hardwicke's king almost convinces one that there was a time when royalty wasn't synonymous with lily-livered mediocrity. Despite a script which is rather too hesitant at improving upon history, this is a worthy example of disreputable costume drama, a genre British cinema occasionally excelled in. RMy

Nelly & Monsieur Arnaud (Nelly and Mr Arnaud)

(1995, Fr, 106 min)
d Claude Sautet. *p* Alain Sarde. *sc* Claude Sautet, Jacques Fieschi. *ph* Jean-François Robin. *ed* Jacqueline Thiedot. *pd* Carlos Conti. *m* Philippe Sarde. *cast* Emmanuelle Béart, Michel Serrault, Jean-Hughes Anglade, Claire Nadeau, Françoise Brion, Michel Lonsdale, Charles Berling.

● When Nelly (Béart) informs husband Jérôme that a certain Monsieur Arnaud (Serrault), an elderly friend of a friend, has offered her a fortune to help ease their financial troubles, Jérôme seems so unsurprised at her acceptance that she ends their relationship. Only then does she actually take the money, along with temp work typing up Arnaud's memoirs of his life as judge and businessman. A barely acknowledged intimacy grows between the young woman and her generous but temperamental employer, an intimacy threatened by jealousy when she begins seeing his publisher Vincent (Anglade). An exquisitely witty, beautifully moving film, Sautet's follow-up to *Un Coeur en hiver* is a similarly understated study in adult emotions. As the film proceeds quietly towards its unsentimental, but piercingly sad conclusion, Sautet's sure, light touch even allows for comic scenes (Lonsdale provides a splendidly morose cameo as a mysterious visitor to Arnaud's apartment). Béart is subtle and restrained, Serrault fastidious, moody, waspish, but given to moments of startling warmth and honesty; together they produce a fragile mood of humour and heartbreaking melancholy. Classical French film-making par excellence. GA

Nelly's Version

(1983, GB, 100 min)
d Maurice Hatton. *p* Penny Clark. *sc* Maurice Hatton. *ph* Curtis Clark. *ed* Thomas Schwalm. *pd* Grant Hicks. *m* Michael Nyman. *cast* Eileen Atkins, Nicholas Ball, Anthony Bate, Barbara Jefford, Brian Deacon.

● An amnesiac with a suitcase full of cash checks in at a Home Counties hotel. A Michael Nyman score propels her wanderings with edgy B movie insistence. Her wake becomes littered with cross-purpose conversations, crime, accidents and arson. Is she an escapee or an escapist? A conspirator or a conspiracy victim? Is she Nelly Dean (who, remember, used to sit and dream) or is she really this Eleanor Wilkinson whom strangers claim as friend, mother and wife? Is *Nelly's Version* a feminist thriller, or a fiction about fiction? It's a mystery, certainly, and a damn good one; inventively playful in the filmic ambiguities piled on those of Eva Figes' novel by director Maurice Hatton. And all, of course, to be taken as seriously as the Freudianism of Hitchcock's *Spellbound*, which strays on screen here amid umpteen wryly allusive nods to the *cinéma d'auteur*. As the railway porter helpfully explains, apropos of plot, psychology or maybe just trains, it's all a matter of connections. PT

Nel Nome del Padre

see In the Name of the Father

Nel segno di Roma

see Sign of the Gladiator

Nelson Affair, The

see Bequest to the Nation

Nelson Touch, The

see Corvette K–225

Nemuri Kyoshiro: The Book of Killing-Rules (Nemuri Kyoshiro: Sappo Cho/aka Sleepy Eyes of Death: The Chinese Jade)

(1963, Jap, 82 min)
d Tokuzo Tanaka. *p* Hisakazu Tsuji. *sc* Seiji Hoshikawa. *ph* Jishi Makiura. *ed* Hiroshi Yamada. *ad* Koichi Goto. *m* Taichiro Kosugi. *cast* Raizo Ichikawa, Tamao Nakamura, Kenzaburo Jo, Katsuhiko Kobayashi, Keiko Ogimachi.

● Ichikawa, who died of cancer aged 37 in 1969, is the object of an enduring cult in Japan and the 12-film *Nemuri Kyoshiro* series is one of its cornerstones. This inaugural episode doesn't go into Kyoshiro's nefarious origins as the son of a lapsed missionary and a geisha (later films show satanic rituals around his birth) but presents him as an auburn-coiffed scourge of greed and corruption in late-Tokugawa Japan: a cynical ronin (a masterless samurai) who lives for adventure and responds only to sincerity in others. His trademark duelling technique (a circular sweep of the sword, invariably fatal) is here pressed into service for a deeply wronged woman and tested against the karate skills of a worthy foe. The plot uses real life figures of the 1840s such as the trade embargo-buster Zeniya as historical referents, but historiography comes second to the fetishisation of the saturnine anti-hero. (The US release title is a nonsense: the Buddha statuette which contains an incriminating receipt isn't made of jade, and it's not Chinese but Thai.) TR

Nénette et Boni

(1996, Fr, 103 min)
d Claire Denis. *p* Georges Benayoun. *sc* Clair Denis, Jean-Pol Fargeau. *ph* Agnès Godard. *ed* Yann Dedet. *ad* Arnaud de Moléron. *m* Tindersticks. *cast* Grégoire Colin, Alice Houri, Valéria Bruni-Tedeschi, Jacques Nolot, Vincent Gallo, Alex Descas, Jamila Farah.

● Boni (Colin) is a pizza cook who harbours obscene, even sociopathic fantasies about the local baker's wife; Nénette (Houri) is his younger sister who runs away from boarding school and asks the embarrassed, reluctant Boni to give her shelter. This fragmented, often overly enigmatic film is a study of the two siblings' mostly aggressive relationships with each other, their friends and their estranged father. There are odd, rather contrived fantasy scenes here which sit uneasily with the generally downbeat naturalism of the rest of the film; and since the script seems determined to tease rather than inform, it's a little hard in the end to fathom exactly what director and co-writer Denis is really getting at. The performances, however, are good, and the music appealing. GA

Neon Bible, The

(1995, GB, 91 min)
d Terence Davies. *p* Elizabeth Karlsen, Olivia Stewart. *sc* Terence Davis. *ph* Mick Coulter. *ed* Charles Rees. *pd* Christopher Hobbs. *cast* Gena Rowlands, Diana Scarwid, Denis Leary, Jacob Tierney, Leo Burmester, Frances Conroy, Peter McRobbie.

● This adaptation of John Kennedy Toole's novel returns to the concerns of Terence Davies' acclaimed autobiographical work: the joys and agonies of family life; the onset of adulthood; the oppressive hypocrisy of organised religion. Here, however, instead of Liverpool, the setting is small-town Georgia in the '40s: life is quiet for young Tierney, son of struggling farmer Leary and hyper-sensitive Scarwid, until the sudden and not entirely unwelcome arrival of his aunt (Rowlands), a has-been but eternally optimistic nightclub singer whose devil-may-care ways sit awkwardly with the town's conservatism. Though the writer/director is working abroad and telling a linear story, it's immediately apparent – from the measured pacing, the immaculate compositions and elegant camera movements, the audacious ellipses and the inspired use of music – that this is a hallmarked Davies film. As such, it is extraordinarily moving, notably in a simple, underplayed death scene. Gena Rowlands' performance is a marvel of subtle nuances. GA

Nephew, The

(1997, Ire, 105 min)
d Eugene Brady. *p* Pierce Brosnan, Beau St Clair. *sc* Jacqueline O'Neill, Sean P Steele. *ph* Jack Conroy. *ed* J Patrick Duffner. *pd* John DeCuir. *m* Stephen McKeon. *cast* Donal McCann, Pierce Brosnan, Sinéad Cusack, Aislín McGuckin, Niall Toibín, Phelim Drew, Hill Harper.

● Pierce Brosnan turns producer with this resolutely routine Irish saga about the bitter hold of the past. Harper's dreadlocked black New Yorker arrives on a remote Irish island to return his mother's ashes to the place where she was born. His arrival provokes surprise among the locals, and leaves the lad himself with quite a lot of adjusting to do, not the least of which is getting his head round the longstanding feud between his grumpy old uncle (McCann) and the community's smoothie barman (Brosnan, of course). Naturally, the new generation gets things moving, but not before a few bumps along the way give the accomplished cast something to chew on. Sturdy but unexciting. TJ

Neptune Factor, The

(1973, Can, 98 min)
d Daniel Petrie. *p* Sanford Howard. *sc* Jack DeWitt. *ph* Harry Makin. *ed* Stan Cole. *pd* Dennis Lynton Clark, Jack McAdam. *m* Lalo Schifrin. *cast* Ben Gazzara, Yvette Mimieux, Walter Pidgeon, Ernest Borgnine, Chris Wiggins, Donnelly Rhodes, Ed McGibbon, Stuart Gillard.

● An extremely half-hearted attempt to make an undersea *2001* and a film of monumental dullness. Leaden submarine sequences that are too slow to be funny finally begin to alternate, about an hour into the film, with unconvincing blow-ups of harmlessly attractive goldfish, anemones, sea eels and so forth, all supposedly deadly creatures ready to destroy the craft at a single wrong move from her crew. One to avoid.

Nest, The (El Nido)

(1980, Sp, 97 min)
d/sc Jaime de Armiñán. *ph* Teodoro Escamilla. *ed* José Luis Matesánz. *ad* Jean Claude Hoerner. *cast* Héctor Alterio, Ana Torrent,

Luis Politti, Agustín González, Patricia Adriani, Maria Luisa Ponte, Mercedes Alonso.
●Don Alejandro is a courtly, quixotic figure on a white steed, stigmatised as 'eccentric' for daring, at sixty, to harbour sexual desires. 13-year-old Goyita (Ana Torrent from *Spirit of the Beehive*), first seen as a school-play Lady Macbeth, is a sensual child-woman but no simple Hispanic Lolita, for she lives literally in the shadow of the law at the station of the local Guarda Civil. The story tells of their chaste but erotic love, with nothing of the whimsical or lubricious: it's the 'tragic show' of stifled dreams, illicit longings, acted out intricately by all the characters, male and female, old and young, and interwoven with a dense web of symbolic allusions – suggestively haunting bird imagery, exultant use of music (Haydn's *Creation*) and the Macbeth motif that ominously mirrors the main plot. A film of infinite tenderness, lyricism and passion. SJo

Nest of Gentlefolk, A (Dvorianskoe Gnezdo)

(1969, USSR, 106 min)
d Andrei Mikhalkov-Konchalovsky. *sc* Valentin Yezhov, Andrei Mikhalkov-Konchalovsky. *ph* Georgi Rerberg. *ed* L Pokrovskoi. *ad* A Boim, Nikolai Dvigubsky, Mikhail Romadin. *m* Vyacheslav Ovchinnikov. *cast* Leonid Kulagin, Beata Tyszkiewicz, Irina Kupchenko, A Kostomolotsky, Viktor Sergachov, V Kochurikhin, Nikita Mikhalkov.
●The first thing you notice about Konchalovsky's film is the vulnerability of its characters. Based on one of Turgenev's stories, it's all there – the travels abroad to remote and seductive but unsatisfying foreign capitals, the continuing dialogue on the meaning of Russianness, the feeling of gentlemanly melancholy…and those women. A man, a gentleman (even if his mother was a servant), reopens his old estate, a servant girl bobbing ahead of him opening doors, drawing back curtains – an excuse for some superb camerawork. Shown sumptuous portraits of his father's family, he asks to see his mother's portrait. In a sense the rest of the film is an attempt to piece together the picture, first of one woman – the wife who left him – then another, and to paint himself into their world. Not a bad aim, and one that isn't given a falsely easy solution either.

Nest of Vipers (Ritratto di Borghesia in Nero)

(1978, It, 105 min)
d Tonino Cervi. *p* Piero La Mantia. *sc* Tonino Cervi, Cesare Frugoni, Goffredo Parise. *ph* Armando Nannuzzi. *ed* Nino Baragli. *ad* Luigi Scaccianoce. *m* Vincenzo Tempera. *cast* Senta Berger, Ornella Muti, Capucine, Christian Borromeo, Paolo Bonacelli, Maria Monti, Eros Pagni, Giuliana Calandra, Stefano Patrizi.
●A heated sex melodrama set in Fascist Italy just before World War II, this isn't bad at all. About a provincial innocent who comes to Venice to study music, befriends a fellow student (gay), has an affair with the friend's mother (attractive), then casts her aside in favour of a millionaire's daughter (attractive and rich), it boasts handsome production values recalling the sunbathed settings of Bertolucci and of *The Garden of the Finzi-Continis*. The Fascist context may be incidental, but Cervi makes some headway against the sexploitation elements in his tale of a passionate and jealousy-driven bourgeoisie, keeping things the right side of interesting up to his Chabrol-style climax of brutal murder and complicity in its cover-up. RM

Net, The

(1995, US, 115 min)
d Irwin Winkler. *p* Irwin Winkler, Rob Cowan. *sc* John Brancato, Michael Ferris. *ph* Jack N Green. *ed* Richard Halsey. *pd* Dennis Washington. *m* Mark Isham. *cast* Sandra Bullock, Jeremy Northam, Dennis Miller, Diane Baker, Wendy Gazelle, Ken Howard, Ray McKinnon.
●A cod Hitchcockian thriller with Internet knobs on. Babe-next-door Bullock plays Angela, a nerdy freelance computer analyst who, after a top politician blows his brains out, gets caught up in a worldwide web of intrigue, murder and corruption. The night before she goes on holiday, a colleague mails her a mystery virus that provides access to reams of top-secret classified information; however, neither his plane crashing, nor a total computer meltdown at LA airport alerts Angela to danger. While sunning herself in Mexico, she meets an Englishman (Northam), who shares her love of computers and can quote lines from her favourite film, *Breakfast at Tiffany's*. This immediately alerts us to the fact that Jack is either (a) married, (b) gay, or (c) the bad guy. Angela, however, who doesn't get out much, misses all this. Pretty soon she's fleeing from her gun-wielding seducer, trying to recover an identity that's being systematically erased through alteration of her personal computer records, and dodging bullets on spinning carousels. NF

Network

(1976, US, 121 min)
d Sidney Lumet. *p* Howard Gottfried. *sc* Paddy Chayefsky. *ph* Owen Roizman. *ed* Alan Heim. *ad* Philip Rosenberg. *m* Elliot Lawrence. *cast* Faye Dunaway, William Holden, Peter Finch, Robert Duvall, Wesley Addy, Ned Beatty, Arthur Burghardt, Stanley Grover, Darryl Hickman. *narrator* Lee Richardson.
●Washed-up news anchorman (Finch) flips on air, finds God, and is gleefully exploited by his TV company to boost the ratings with his epileptic evangelic revivalism. *Network* gives a rather old-fashioned plot the '70s treatment: the result is slick, 'adult', self-congratulatory, and almost entirely hollow. Paddy Chayefsky's entrenched but increasingly desperate script parades its middle-aged symptoms to little effect: it's ulcerous, bilious, paranoid about youth, and increasingly susceptible to fantasy. Above all, it's haunted by fear of failing powers; presumably people telling each other what lousy lays they were is to be taken as indication of the film's searing honesty. Lumet's direction does nothing to contain the sprawl, and most of the interest comes in watching such a lavishly mounted vehicle leaving the rails so spectacularly. CPe

Never Been Kissed

(1999, US, 107 min)
d Raja Gosnell. *p* Sandy Isaac, Nancy Juvonen. *sc* Abby Kohn, Marc Silverstein. *ph* Alex Nepomniaschy. *ed* Debbie Chiate, Marcelo Sansevieri. *pd* Steven Jordan. *m* David Newman. *cast* Drew Barrymore, David Arquette, Michael Vartan, Garry Marshall, Molly Shannon, John C Reilly, LeeLee Sobieski.
●Josie Geller (Barrymore), copy editor on the *Chicago Sun-Times*, has led a sheltered life. All that may change, however, when her editor (Marshall) gives her a big writing break by sending her back to school for an exposé on errant youth. Her own teenage years, however, were a nightmare of humiliation, so what's to guarantee that things will improve second time around? Choosing the wrong clothes on the first day isn't an auspicious start, and history begins to repeat itself until her jock brother (Arquette) goes undercover to improve her popularity, and she catches the eye of the English teacher (Vartan). This could be her chance for romance, but how can she tell him she's actually 25 without blowing her story? There's a contradiction at the heart of the film which suggests that nerds are people too, before setting out to transform Barrymore from geekette to hip and groovy young person. Shameless contrivance the lot of it, but Barrymore again displays her remarkable ability to get the audience rooting for her singular blend of vulnerability and sunny optimism. TJ

Never Cry Wolf

(1983, US, 105 min)
d Carroll Ballard. *p* Lewis M Allen, Jack Couffer, Joseph Strick. *sc* Curtis Hanson, Sam Hamm, Richard Kletter. *ph* Hiro Narita. *ed* Peter Parasheles, Michael Chandler. *ad* Graeme Murray. *m* Mark Isham. *cast* Charles Martin Smith, Brian Dennehy, Zachary Ittimangnaq, Samson Jorah, Hugh Webster, Martha Ittimangnaq.
●Sent to the desolate northern reaches of Canada to prove that the wolves are destroying the herds of caribou, Tyler (Martin Smith) might be any one of us left to fend for ourselves in a bleak landscape. Ballard's film, produced by Disney and resembling the old nature films, tells of an engaging, fearful scientist who grows to admire the wolves he is sent to condemn, adopts their diet (mouse stew minus the tails), and learns from an ancient, mystical Inuit (the furclad local inhabitants) that in true Darwinian fashion the wolves only cull the weaker members of the herd. For the most part very absorbing, the film suffers from some embarrassingly obvious symbolism. JE

NeverEnding Story, The (Die unendliche Geschichte)

(1984, WGer, 94 min)
d Wolfgang Petersen. *p* Bernd Eichinger, Dieter Geissler. *sc* Wolfgang Petersen, Herman Weigel. *ph* Jost Vacano. *ed* Jane Seitz. *pd* Rolf Zehetbauer. *m* Klaus Doldinger, Giorgio Moroder. *cast* Barret Oliver, Noah Hathaway, Moses Gunn, Tami Stronach, Patricia Hayes, Sydney Bromley.
●A fairytale of the very best kind, with luscious effects which include a flying dragon, a rock monster, a fairy princess (mercifully grave and untwee), and a threat in whose vanquishing lies hope. Made at Munich's Bavaria Studios, the film concerns a withdrawn schoolboy, ignored by his businessman father and bullied at school, who steals a book and finds himself in thrall to the point where he is called upon to enter its world and save the magic land of Fantasia. Adapted from the novel by Michael Ende, the film is a mix of German Romanticism (complete with Wagnerian sets and a score in part by Giorgio Moroder) and Syberberg by way of Disney, or perhaps vice versa. There are even moments of moralising which give the twin heroes' quest someting of the steely tone of a Pilgrim's Progress. VG

NeverEnding Story II: The Next Chapter, The

(1989, Ger, 90 min)
d George Miller. *p* Dieter Geissler. *sc* Karin Howard. *ph* Dave Connell. *ed* Peter Hollywood, Chris Blunden. *pd* Bob Laing, Gotz Weidner. *m* Robert Folk. *cast* Jonathan Brandis, Kenny Morrison, Clarissa Burt, John Wesley Shipp, Martin Umbach, Alexandra Johnes.
●This sequel to Wolfgang Petersen's ambitious film finds young Bastian (Brandis) returning to the dream world of Fantasia to save the Childlike Empress and her kingdom from an expanding and engulfing 'Emptiness'. Reunited with his alter ego Atreyu, and aided again by a menagerie of creatures (flying dog Falkor and the mountainous Rockbiter are joined by man-sized twitchy bird Nimbly), Bastian is lured into the deceitful web of sorceress Xayide (Burt), unknowingly selling his soul as he trades memories for miracles. Directed with pedestrian ease by Miller (of *Man from Snowy River* not *Mad Max* fame), this lacks the clumsy charm of its predecessor, its ropey narrative woefully failing to lash together the visual set pieces. While the intriguing themes are present and correct – the death of imagination, the loss of memory and identity – they are so swathed in cynical schmaltz as to be rendered all but sterile. MK

NeverEnding Story III: Escape from Fantasia, The

(1994, Ger, 95 min)
d Peter Macdonald. *p* Dieter Geissler, Tim Hampton. *sc* Jeff Lieberman. *ed* Michael Bradsell. *pd* Rolf Zehetbauer. *m* Peter Wolf. *cast* Jason James Richter, Melody Kay, Jack Black, Tony Robinson, Carole Finn, Ryan Bollman, Freddie Jones, Julie Cox.
●This further instalment reverses the worlds: here Fantasia comes to earth. Troubled by a new stepsister (Kay) and the taunts of the 'Nasties', led by crop-haired Slip (Black), Bastian (Richter) slopes off to Fantasia, leaving behind his copy of the empowering *NeverEnding Story*. The interactive book falls into the hands of Slip and his gang, who use it to foment chaos. Bastian is ordered back to the real world by the Child Empress, but accidentally takes his Fantasia pals with him. They are scattered all over the US. Can he reunite them? The animatronic characters from the Henson Creature Shop are looking familiar by now, but this new old-fashioned feel is part of the charm. It's a weak story, but the sfx, sets, opticals, humans and product-placements are orchestrated with a light touch. WH

Never Give an Inch

see Sometimes a Great Notion

Never Give a Sucker an Even Break (aka What a Man!)

(1941, US, 70 min, b/w)
d Edward Cline. *sc* John Thomas Neville, Prescott Chaplin. *ph* Charles Van Enger. *ed* Arthur Hilton, Jack Otterson, Richard H

Riedel. *m* Frank Skinner. *cast* WC Fields, Gloria Jean, Leon Errol, Susan Miller, Franklin Pangborn, Margaret Dumont.
● WC Fields' last starring vehicle has to be seen to be believed, and even then it probably won't be; it's constructed like one of his tallest stories, drunkenly veering from improbability to improbability, and produced with loving carelessness as Fields' hopeful scriptwriter tries to sell a story to the long-suffering Franklin Pangborn. The itinerary takes in the Esoteric Film Studios, a Russian colony in Mexico, and a neighbouring mountain top inhabited by the man-eating Mrs Hemogloben, played by a very raucous Margaret Dumont. But Fields' true co-star is the horrid singing moppet Gloria Jean, and for all the master's visual and verbal nonsense, the total result is more perverse than funny. GB

Never Let Go

(1960, GB, 91 min, b/w)
d John Guillermin. *p* Peter De Sarigny. *sc* Alun Falconer. *ph* Christopher Challis. *ed* Ralph Sheldon. *ad* George Provis. *m* John Barry. *cast* Richard Todd, Peter Sellers, Elizabeth Sellars, Adam Faith, Carol White, Mervyn Johns, John Le Mesurier.
● Cosmetics salesman Todd has his car stolen and, without insurance or much assistance from the police, decides to track it down himself. The trail leads through youthful thug Faith (his first screen role) to gang boss Sellers (taking a rare tilt at a villainous role) in this stolid homegrown crime caper, considered very brutal in its day, with a self-consciously strident use of 'adult' language. Quite persuasive turns from Todd and Sellers. TJ

Never on Sunday (Pote tin Kyriaki)

(1960, Greece, 97 min, b/w)
d/p/sc Jules Dassin. *ph* Jacques Natteau. *ed* Roger Dwyre. *ad* Alekos Tzonis. *m* Manos Hadjidakis. *cast* Melina Mercouri, Jules Dassin, Georges Foundas, Titos Vandis, Dimitri Papamichael
● Ilya is the happy hooker of Piraeus. Her clients are all shy and handsome, her circle of friends and lovers innocent of jealousy or ill will. Along comes earnest American Homer who tries to reform Ilya's morals and introduce her to Culture. By the end, of course, he's swigging ouzo and smashing crockery with the rest of them. You can see how this might have felt joyful and liberating to audiences coming out of the uptight '50s. Decades on, the relentless Grecian gusto is wearing, and rangy, gravel-voiced Mercouri is a very specialised sort of sex goddess. But in its favour is Hadjidakis' foot-tapping music and Dassin's ploy of shooting this rosiest of fantasies like a gritty documentary. BBa

Never Say Die

(1938, US, 76 min, b/w)
d Elliott Nugent. *p* Paul Jones. *sc* Don Hartman, Frank Butler, Preston Sturges. *ph* Leo Tover. *ed* James Smith. *ad* Hans Dreier, Ernst Fegté. *cast* Bob Hope, Martha Raye, Andy Devine, Gale Sondergaard, Alan Mowbray, Sig Ruman, Ivan Simpson, Monty Woolley.
● One of Bob Hope's best early films, in which he plays a millionaire hypochondriac led to believe he is slowly digesting himself (his acidity test has been mixed up with a dog's) and who therefore disposes of the rest of his life with the usual complicated results. Scripted originally by Preston Sturges, with Hope's regular gagmen Hartman and Butler brought in to add trademark wisecracks; the familiar Hope persona is already evident but not entirely fixed, so the mix works quite well, with enough of the original surviving (the European health spa, the philosophical butler, the delight in verbal eccentricities) to make it something of an embryo Sturges film. Martha Raye is excellent, even rather touching, as the girl he marries when he thinks he has only two weeks to live, and the supporting cast is admirable. TM

Never Say Never Again

(1983, GB, 134 min)
d Irvin Kershner. *p* Jack Schwartzman. *sc* Lorenzo Semple Jr. *ph* Douglas Slocombe. *ed* Ian Crafford, Peter Musgrave. *pd* Philip Harrison, Stephen Grimes. *m* Michel Legrand. *cast* Sean Connery, Klaus Maria Brandauer, Max von Sydow, Barbara Carrera, Kim Basinger, Bernie Casey, Alec McCowen, Edward Fox, Rowan Atkinson.
● For all of us whose adolescence was entwined around a vision of a coral beach and Ursula Andress emerging from the foam in a white bikini, it's very comforting to return to the ambience; as the admirable Q has it, 'I hope this is a return to more gratuitous sex and violence, Commander Bond'. The plot is a *Thunderball* retread – the underwater hijacking of nuclear weapons, the holding of the world to ransom; routine stuff if your name is 'Bond...James Bond'. As usual, a hefty slice of the pleasure in watching late Bondage comes from the villains, in this case Bergman's chief angst-master von Sydow as the man with the fluffy white cat, Brandauer proving that a man may smile and smile and be a villain, and Carrera, she of the pneumatic balcony. The action's good, the photography excellent, the sets decent; but the real clincher is the fact that Bond is once more played by a man with the right stuff. Civilisation is safe in the hands of he who has never tasted quiche, and who, on the evidence here, at least, can perform a very passable tango. CPea

Never So Few

(1959, US, 124 min)
d John Sturges. *p* Edmund Grainger. *sc* Millard Kaufman. *ph* William H Daniels. *ed* Ferris Webster. *ad* Hans Peters, Addison Hehr. *m* Hugo Friedhofer. *cast* Frank Sinatra, Gina Lollobrigida, Peter Lawford, Steve McQueen, Richard Johnson, Paul Henreid, Brian Donlevy, Dean Jones, Charles Bronson, Philip Ahn, John Hoyt.
● Capt Sinatra (plus facial hair in the opening scenes) finds himself leading a handful of Kachin guerillas against Burma's 40,000 Japanese invaders in this slack WWII picture, adapted from Tom T Chamales' novel, which somehow manages to include his romance with La Lollo, the mistress of an oily profiteer (Henreid). Most of the novel's moral issues are sidestepped, while much is made of the Himalayan scenery. McQueen joined the cast when Sinatra fell out with Sammy Davis Jr, a fortunate break for the youngster who went on to make both *The Magnificent Seven* and *The Great Escape* with action specialist Sturges. Shot in 'Scope. TJ

Never Talk to Strangers

(1995, Can/US, 86 min)
d Peter Hall. *p* András Hamori, Jeffrey R Neuman, Martin J Wiley. *sc* Lewis Green, Jordan Rush. *ph* Elemér Ragalyi, Harry Lake. *ed* Roberto Silvi, Susan Shipton, Marcus Manton. *pd* Linda Del Rosario, Richard Paris. *m* Pino Donaggio. *cast* Rebecca DeMornay, Harry Dean Stanton, Antonio Banderas, Dennis Miller, Len Cariou, Eugene Lipinski, Martha Burns, Beau Starr.
● An adequate psychological thriller on a topical theme – Repressed Memory Syndrome – but with little special quality, few frills or thrills, and a relaxed, almost languid exposition. DeMornay is a New York criminal psychologist, traumatised in childhood by the death of her mother, and currently engaged on the examination of a serial killer (Stanton) to determine whether or not he has Multiple Personality Disorder. Despite a desire to avoid romantic attachment, she's seduced into a passionate affair with mysterious stranger Tony Ramires (Banderas), a sensitive charmer with a darker side. She has a darker side, too, or at least a risk-taking sexual appetite, staying with her Puerto Rican amour despite his suspicious lies and his tampering with her personal property. When a series of threats come her way, she becomes more certain of his guilt, though viewers might plump for the grudge-taking serial killer, her creepy father or even a seemingly innocent 'friend' suffering from unrequited passion. Peter Hall's vocabulary of suspense rarely goes beyond the shock increase in volume or the quick edit, and the belated rendering of threatening atmosphere betokens a more subtle analytical approach which never arrives. WH

Never Too Young to Rock

(1975, GB, 99 min)
d Dennis Abey. *p* Greg Smith, Ron Inkpen. *sc* Ron Inkpen, Dennis Abey. *ph* Harvey Harrison. *ed* Ray Lovejoy. *ad* Denis Gordon-Orr. *cast* Peter Denyer, Freddie Jones, Sheila Steafel, Joe Lynch, John Clive, Peter Noone.
● Update of those putting-on-a-show escapades of the '40s, featuring Scott Fitzgerald, Mud, The Glitter Band, The Rubettes, Slick. All are top of the pops, with the exception of Bob Kerr's Whoopee Band, who seem a race apart and predictably get the least exposure. For the first hour, unfunny comedy dominates, as Denyer and a reluctant Freddie Jones track down famous groups for a 'Pick of the Hits' concert; the final 30 minutes is music, music, music. Despite the title, it makes you feel at least 102. GB

New Adventures of Don Juan, The

see Adventures of Don Juan

New Age, The

(1994, US, 110 min)
d Michael Tolkin. *p* Nick Wechsler, Keith Addis. *sc* Michael Tolkin. *ph* John H Campbell. *ed* Suzanne Fenn. *pd* Robin Standefer. *m* Mark Mothersbaugh. *cast* Peter Weller, Judy Davis, Samuel L Jackson, Patrick Bauchau, Corbin Bernsen, Jonathan Hadary, Patricia Heaton, Audra Lindley.
● Peter Witner (Weller) quits his mega-salaried job as a Los Angeles copywriter at the same time that his wife Katherine (Davis), a graphic designer, loses a major account. Their marriage on the rocks, the couple follow the advice of a New Age guru (Bauchau) and stake everything on opening a super-luxurious shop, 'Hip-ocracy'. Though filled with its fair share of diverting ideas, Tolkin's film seems half-seduced by the surfaces it attempts to penetrate. Cinematographer John F Campbell ably captures the ritzy, elegant, but unrewarding milieu of art-bedecked apartments, Petronius-like SM clubs, and spiritual retreats, and Weller and Davis suggest well the psychological panic and brittle suffering, respectively, of these two emblematic victims of modern American materialism. As a moral fable, however, it loses its way, chiefly due to the use of heavy-handed symbolism and an unenlightening play with confusing psycho-sexual ideas of opposing male-female principles. A brave stab, nevertheless, with a finely executed finale as Peter sets about his ironic salvation. WH

New Babylon, The (Novyi Vavilon)

(1929, USSR, 7,218 ft, b/w)
d/sc Grigori Kozintsev, Leonid Trauberg. *ph* Andrei Moskvin, Yevgeni Mikhailov. *ad* Yevgeni Enei. *m* (original score) Shostakovich. *cast* Yelena Kuzmina, Pyotr Sobolevsky, Dimitri Gutman, Sophie Magarill, Sergei Gerasimov, S Gusev, Janina Jeimo, Vsevolod Pudovkin.
● One of the very few great Soviet silent directors to re-establish a reputation after the intervening years of social-realist dogma, Kozintsev first made his mark as a pioneer of the 'Eccentric' movement, co-directing with Trauberg a series of extravagant entertainments and satires. *The New Babylon* represented one of the most controversial examples: muting the formal anarchy, but almost iconoclastically viewing the fate of the 1871 Paris Commune through the eyes of a department store shopgirl. TR

New Barbarians, The (I Nuovi Barbari)

(1983, It, 91 min)
d Enzo G Castellari. *p* Fabrizio De Angelis. *sc* Tito Carpi, Enzo G Castellari. *ph* Fausto Zuccoli. *ed* Gianfranco Amicucci. *pd* Antonio Visone. *m* Claudio Simonetti. *cast* Fred Williamson, Timothy Brent [Giancarlo Prete], George Eastman [Luigi Montefiore], Anna Kanakis, Venantino Venantini, Enzo G Castellari, Massimo Vanni.
● The minestrone version of *Mad Max 2*. The new Barbarians rule the post-holocaust desert with a doddery death-cult philosophy, an inexhaustible arsenal, a fleet of tackily customised dune buggies, and a fetching SM wardrobe eventually explained away by the revelation that they're all gay. They kill Christians (a new Moses included) and rape our hero – an insipid automaton with all the charisma of Mel Gibson's big toe – before being blown away by Fred Williamson's exploding arrows, a wild child's slingshot, and our buggered road warrior's instrument of poetic revenge, a massive corkscrew up the rear. For aficionados of true dreck only. PT

New Centurions, The (aka Precinct 45: Los Angeles Police)

(1972, US, 103 min)
d Richard Fleischer. *p* Irwin Winkler, Robert Chartoff. *sc* Stirling Silliphant. *ph* Ralph Woolsey. *ed* Robert C Jones. *pd* Boris Leven. *m* Quincy Jones. *cast* George C Scott, Stacy Keach, Jane Alexander, Scott Wilson, Rosalind Cash, Erik Estrada, Clifton James, James B Sikking, William Atherton, Ed Lauter.
●A hack adaptation of Joseph Wambaugh's novel which makes you see why he subsequently bulldozed into control of his own work on the screen. Every symbol of social unease is grabbed and used with unbelievable crudity in throwing together a series of all-in-a-day's-work episodes: battered baby, rent extortionists, marital strife, gay entrapment (for a giggle), it's all there, except that the more you're supposed to sympathise with the cops, the more sympathy you in fact feel for their victims. It's sort of bound together by a strange initiation theme, in which an older cop teaches the young one all he knows before blowing his own head off.

New Face in Hell

see P.J.

New Game of Death, The

see Legend of Bruce Lee

New God, The (Atarashii Kami-sama)

(1999, Jap, 99 min)
d/p/sc Yutaka Tsuchiya. *ph* Yutaka Tsuchiya, Karin Amamiya, Hidehito Ito. *ed* Yutaka Tsuchiya. *m* Rebel Blue, Takeshi Kato. *with* Karin Amamiya, Hidehito Ito, Yutaka Tsuchiya.
●In which pinko 'media activist' Tsuchiya chronicles his *amour fou* for Karin Amamiya, punk chanteuse with the ultra-right-wing nationalist band The Revolutionary Truth. Their notional political differences drown in their shared hatred of US imperialism, and they get to know each other through conversations about race, history, group identity and so on, which achieve hitherto unquantified heights of absurdity and self-delusion. Eventually, Tsuchiya lends the woman a camcorder to document her disillusioning visit to North Korea. When she gets back, he steals her from her existing boyfriend, the band's leader Ito, provoking threats of violence. At least the title gets it right: these idiots can't begin to feel alive at all unless they have a deity to worship. TR

New Jack City

(1991, US, 100 min)
d Mario Van Peebles. *p* Doug McHenry, George Jackson. *sc* Thomas Lee Wright, Barry Michael Cooper. *ph* Francis Kenny. *ed* Steven Kemper, Kevin Stitt. *pd* Charles C Bennett. *m* Michel Colombier. *cast* Wesley Snipes, Ice T, Allen Payne, Chris Rock, Judd Nelson, Mario Van Peebles, Michael Michele, Bill Nunn, Russell Wong, Thalmus Rasulala.
●Touted as a ground-breaking addition to the crime-on-the-streets genre, Van Peebles' thriller is far more modest: a high-tech update on that old warhorse, a mobster's rise and fall. Ruthless Nino Brown (Snipes) lords it over a New York neighbourhood with an empire built on crack and violence. It's only when two disenchanted streetwise officers come together – African-American Scott Appleton (Ice T) and Nick Peretti (Nelson) – that his domain is effectively threatened. The movie pays lip service to social analysis while delighting in the paraphernalia of violence. As such, it's a superior example of what used to be called blaxploitation, with Van Peebles piling on corruption and carnage for all he's worth. GA

New Jersey Drive

(1995, US, 95 min)
d Nick Gomez. *p* Bob Gosse, Larry Meistrich. *sc* Nick Gomez. *ph* Adam Kimmel. *ed* Tracy S Granger. *ad* Lester Cohen. *cast* Sharron Corley, Saul Stein, Gabriel Casseus, Gwen McGee, Andre Moore, Donald Adeosun Faison.
●After his over-rated debut, *Laws of Gravity*, writer/director Gomez comes down to earth with a thud in this dispiriting slice-of-life-in-the-projects picture. The film (executive producer Spike Lee) does have an authentic tedium about it (monotonous dialogue, repetitive dramatic situations) which mirrors the hopelessness of its young characters' predicament. Gomez is good with actors (Corley is a find), but his naturalistic, hand-held style only takes you so far; there's none of the insight or passion which ignites such films as, say, *La Haine* and Lee's own *Clockers*. TCh

New Kind of Love, A

(1963, US, 109 min)
d/p/sc Melville Shavelson. *ph* Daniel L Fapp. *ed* Frank Bracht. *ad* Hal Pereira, Arthur Lonergan. *m* Leith Stevens. *cast* Paul Newman, Joanne Woodward, Thelma Ritter, Eva Gabor, Maurice Chevalier, George Tobias, Marvin Kaplan, Robert Clary, Robert F Simon.
●Director Shavelson cut his teeth as a writer for Bob Hope and Danny Kaye. He could have done with either of those comedians in this laboured, overdressed Parisian comedy. Instead, he ended up with Mr and Mrs Method, the always earnest Newman and Woodward. She's a fashion buyer, he's a lout of a journalist. He can't stand her short hair, but ends up falling for her when she's fitted with a wig. Saint-Laurent, Cardin and Dior provided the costumes, but the script could have been written by Andy Capp. GM

New Leaf, A

(1970, US, 102 min)
d Elaine May. *p* Joseph Manduke. *sc* Elaine May. *ph* Gayne Rescher. *ed* Fredric Steinkamp, Donald Guidice. *pd* Richard Fried. *cast* Walter Matthau, Elaine May, Jack Weston, George Rose, William Redfield, James Coco, Graham Jarvis, Renée Taylor, David Doyle.
●Browning a little round the edges, not least because Paramount subjected the film to fairly drastic re-editing, Elaine May's directorial debut still makes for cherishable comedy viewing precisely because she eschewed the modish flash her former cabaret partner Mike Nichols brought to his movie-making. May herself plays the frumpishly eccentric but wealthy botanist pursued with murderous intent by Matthau's ageing, financially embarrassed playboy. PT

New Life, A

(1988, US, 104 min)
d Alan Alda. *p* Martin Bregman. *sc* Alan Alda. *ph* Kelvin Pike. *ed* William Reynolds. *ad* Barbara Dunphy. *m* Joseph Turrin. *cast* Alan Alda, Ann-Margaret, Hal Linden, Veronica Hamel, Mary Kay Place, John Shea, Beatrice Alda.
●After 20 years of marriage, middle-class New Yorkers Alda and Ann-Margaret decide to call it a day, leaving each of them free to enter anew the wild and wonderful world of the single life – which has altered somewhat since last they encountered it. This is deep Woody Allen territory, and despite something of a change of image for Alda the actor (bearded, permed and obnoxious), Alda the writer/director isn't quite able to ring the changes on a familiar routine. Smoothly done, though. TJ

New Lot, The

(1943, GB, 42 min, b/w)
d Carol Reed. *p* Thorold Dickinson. *sc* Eric Ambler, Peter Ustinov. *ph* John Wilcox. *ed* Reginald Mills. *ad* Lawrence Broadhouse. *m* Richard Addinsell. *cast* Bernard Miles, Peter Ustinov, Raymond Huntley, John Laurie, Philip Godfrey, Geoffrey Keen, Robert Donat.
●This was produced by the Army for in-house consumption only, then remade for the general public as *The Way Ahead*. Believed to be lost until a print turned up in India in the mid-'90s, it deals with the training of five conscripts and their transformation from truculent civilians into efficient soldiers and team members. The comparison has to be with the first half of *Full Metal Jacket*: the films collide at every point, e.g. the antithetical depictions of authority (Keen here compared to Lee Ermey there). Both movies take as central the business of schooling people to kill (a theme displaced in *The Way Ahead*) – what has naively been called 'dehumanisation' in Kubrick's film. With a brisk tenderness, Reed represents the process as the conscious, willing sacrifice of something precious. Nothing less gung-ho could be imagined than this affecting, invaluable work. BBa

Newman's Law

(1974, US, 99 min)
d Richard Heffron. *p* Richard Irving. *sc* Anthony Wilson. *ph* Vilis Lapenieks. *ed* John J Dumas. *ad* Alexander A Mayer. *m* Robert Prince. *cast* George Peppard, Roger Robinson, Eugene Roche, Gordon Pinsent, Abe Vigoda, Louis Zorich, Michael Lerner, Victor Campos, Antony Carbone.
●Hardnosed but rigorously honest detective (Peppard) finds himself framed and suspended when he gets too close to the big dope king. Despite the routine plot, Anthony Wilson's script (for the first half anyway) manages to establish with some feeling the routine and bureaucratic nature of policework. Unfortunately, Heffron's direction is incapable of sustaining the necessary momentum. Although he manages well enough with a supermarket shoot-up, things fall to pieces once Peppard goes on the rampage. Peppard's downbeat performance survives along with a few other fringe benefits: a gangster with a nice line in Nixonian answers; the all-pervasive, slightly suspect masculine relationships; and the way the film ends up somewhere between *Dirty Harry* and *Serpico*. CPe

New Moon

(1940, US, 105 min, b/w)
d/p Robert Z Leonard. *sc* Jacques Deval, Robert Arthur. *ph* William H Daniels. *ed* Harold F Kress. *ad* Cedric Gibbons, Eddie Imazu. *m/lyrics* Sigmund Romberg, Oscar Hammerstein. cast Jeanette MacDonald, Nelson Eddy, Mary Boland, George Zucco, HB Warner, Grant Mitchell, Stanley Fields.
●The Romberg-Hammerstein operetta with its setting switched from Tsarist Russia to New Orleans in the hope that audiences would identify it with the hugely successful (and remarkably similar) *Naughty Marietta* as MacDonald's haughty aristocrat falls for Eddy's gallant bondslave (but he's really a French Duke, exiled for his egalitarian beliefs since the year is 1789). The score isn't bad, otherwise the mixture is as before, only stodgier. TM

New Morning of Billy the Kid, The (Billy the Kid no Atarashii Yoake)

(1986, Jap, 109 min)
d Naoto Yamakawa. *p* Akira Morishige. *sc* Genichiro Takahashi, Naoto Yamakawa. *ph* Kenji Takama. *ed* Kan Suzuki. *pd* Terumi Hosoishi. *m* Shuichi Chino, Zelda. *cast* Hiroshi Mikami, Shigeru Muroi, Renji Ishibashi, Yoshio Harada, Takashi Naito.
●Fresh from brilliant adaptations of two Haruki Murakami stories, Yamakawa teamed up with hip novelist Takahashi to reach for postmodern heaven. Billy (Mikami), aged 21, waits tables in the Schlächtenhaus Saloon, last refuge of humanity from marauding, nihilistic gangs; co-workers include a samurai, Marx-Engels, an artist and the Tokyo telephone enquiries number made flesh. This bastion of global history and culture is duly invaded (the heavies leave a hole in the roof where the rain gets in), clearing the decks for our spiritual and cultural rebirth. Yeah, right. But it's executed with great flair (it has the style and production values of a vintage studio movie) and it's rich in paradoxes: elegiac farce, tragic social satire, you name it. Dreamers, comics addicts and fans of all-girl rock bands such as Zelda will likely very much enjoy it. TR

New One-Armed Swordsman, The (Xin Dubi Dao)

(1970, HK, 102 min)
d Chang Cheh. *p* Runme Shaw. *sc* I Kuang. *ph* Kung Mu To. *ed* Kuo Ting-Hung. *ad* Tsao Chuang-sheng. *m* Chen Yung-huang. *cast* Li Ching, David Chiang, Ti Lung, Ku Feng, Chen Hsing, Wang Chung, Cheng Lei.
●Chang Cheh had been the leading director of swordplay and martial arts movies at Shaw Brothers for ten years or more before this. A few years later, especially since the break-up of his partnership with the martial arts choreographer Liu Chia-Liang, his career would be on the wane. But there's no denying that he has knocked off a number of minor classics over the years, and this is one of the best: a sombre, Gothic-toned saga of chivalry, denied but finally confirmed.

Excellent performances from David Chiang (as the hero who severs his own right arm when he loses a duel), Ti Lung (as his utterly charming buddy), and Ku Feng (as the relishably villainous baddie). TR

News Boys, The

see Newsies

News from Home

(1976, Fr/Bel, 90 min)
d Chantal Akerman. *p* Alain Dahan. *sc* Chantal Akerman. *ph* Babette Mangolte, Jim Asbell. *ed* Francine Sandberg. *narrator* Chantal Akerman.

● Akerman explores the disjunction between European myths about New York – with its monumental cityscapes and cinematic glamour – and the reality, a place of hopeless ghettos and monotonous suburbs. In counterpoint to cinema-photographer Babette Mangolte's powerful images of the city, the soundtrack consists of banal letters from a petit bourgeois Belgian mother to her daughter in New York. A considerable contribution to the hinterland area between narrative cinema and the avant-garde. LM

News from Nowhere

(1978, GB, 53 min)
d/p Alister Hallum. *sc* Philip Henderson, Alister Hallum. *ph* Jeremy Stavenhagen. *ed* Michael Audsley. *pd* Lyall Hallum. *m* Red Eye Band. *cast* Timothy West, Kika Markham, John Cater, Clive Swift, Theresa Streatfeild, Dave Hastings.

● An attractive little film sponsored by the Arts Council. William Morris, wife, friend, dog and boatman travel up the Thames in 1880, their journey interrupted by champagne breakfasts, expostulations on matters aesthetic and socialist, flashbacks to Rossetti and the Pre-Raphaelites, and glimpses of Morris stomping about Iceland. By filtering facts and quotations through a fictional framework, Alister Hallum and his co-writer Philip Henderson have brought their fascinating subject painlessly and vividly to life, retaining all his ambiguities. And Timothy West has all the beard and fire required for a convincing impersonation. GB

News from the Good Lord

see Des Nouvelles du Bon Dieu

Newsfront

(1978, Aust, 11 min, b/w & col)
d Phillip Noyce. *p* David Elfick. *sc* Phillip Noyce. *ph* Vince Monton. *ed* John Scott. *pd* Lissa Coote. *m* William Motzing. *cast* Bill Hunter, Chris Haywood, John Dease, Wendy Hughes, Gerard Kennedy, John Ewart, Angela Punch, Bryan Brown.

● An ambitious attempt at capturing the social history of a generation through the experiences of a newsreel cameraman, with brilliantly mounted set pieces, including debates finely tuned to fluctuations in a bigoted, rapidly changing socio-political climate. Easy to overlook such shortcomings as the lack of a strong narrative, the failure to develop the women characters adequately, and the risk of degenerating into mere nostalgia. It's never less than terrific to look at, and the seamless matching of new material with actual newsreel footage is truly remarkable. RM

Newsies (aka The News Boys)

(1992, US, 121 min)
d Kenny Ortega. *p* Michael Finnell. *sc* Bob Tzudiker, Noni White. *ph* Andrew Laszlo. *ed* William Reynolds. *ad* William Sandell. *m* Alan Menken. *songs* Alan Menken, Jack Feldman. *cast* Christian Bale, Bill Pullman, Ann-Margret, Robert Duvall, David Moscow, Ele Keats, Kevin Tighe, Michael Lerner, Charles Cioffi, Marc Lawrence.

● Directed by choreographer Ortega, this Disney musical is based on a strike of 1899, in which New York's newsboys rallied against press baron Joseph Pulitzer (Duvall). It espouses the Great Man theory of history, with dynamic young tearaway Jack Kelly (Bale) galvanising the masses with his sheer charisma, sullen jeans-ad looks, and middling ability to carry a tune. If you have a soft spot for feisty, back-talking *bambini* with cute squints, backwards caps and names like Crutchy, Dutchy and Bumlets, your heart will melt. Frighteningly adept attention-grabbers to a lad, these *nouveaux* Dead End Kids gambol to a brassy, forgettable score; the anachronistic proto-hip-hop touches rankle, though Jack Feldman's lyrics provide the odd witty touch. Not quite *Matewan* with tunes; more like *Oliver!* without them. JRo

New Skin, A

see Peau Neuve

New Tales of the Taira Clan

see Shin Heike Monogatari

Newton Boys, The

(1997, US, 122 min)
d Richard Linklater. *p* Ann Walker-McBay. *sc* Richard Linklater, Claude Stanush, Clark Lee Walker. *ph* Peter James. *ed* Sandra Adair. *pd* Catherine Hardwicke. *m* Edward D Barnes. *cast* Matthew McConaughey, Ethan Hawke, Skeet Ulrich, Vincent D'Onofrio, Dwight Yoakam, Julianna Margulies, Chloe Webb.

● After the 'day in the life' indie quartet (*Slacker, Dazed and Confused, Before Sunrise, SubUrbia*) this was supposed to be Linklater's breakout mainstream movie, a Texan gangster flick with a hot young cast. In the event, it bombed at the US box office and limps straight to video in Britain. Set in the '20s, it's the story of four brothers who graduate from cowboy hijinks to federal bank heists. There are echoes of *Once Upon a Time in America, Bonnie and Clyde* and *The Long Riders*, but overall this is a pale shadow of those genre classics. Except for McConaughey, the brothers are inadequately characterised, and despite such surefire ingredients as chases, shootouts and explosions, Linklater gets no narrative momentum going. Quite what attracted one of the more ambitious US independent film-makers to this tired material is hard to imagine – save for a fascinating end credit sequence culled from old TV chat shows where the real life Newton boys, now pensioners, recollect their crimes. It seems a couple of them pulled another job in their seventies. Now that would have been a movie worth seeing. TCh

New Year's Day

(1989, US, 92 min)
d Henry Jaglom. *p* Judith Wolinsky. *sc* Henry Jaglom. *ph* Joey Forsyte, Hanania Baer, Nesya Blue. *ed* Ruth Zucker Wald. *cast* Maggie Jakobson, Gwen Welles, Melanie Winter, Henry Jaglom, David Duchovny, Milos Forman, Michael Emil, Donna Germain, Tracy Reiner.

● Drew (Jaglom), wrestling with mid-life crisis, has left LA for a new life in New York. He arrives on New Year's Day, only to find that the lease allows the previous tenants an extra day in his apartment. By the time he's argued his way into the living-room, he knows their most intimate problems: Lucy (Jakobson) has a womanising boyfriend, Annie (Welles) is giving up 'compulsive behaviour', and childless Winona (Winter) is feeling broody. They're joined by Lucy's parents, boyfriend and psychiatrist, as well as mutual friends (including Milos Forman) and a psychosexologist (Emil, wonderful). Jaglom's opening monologue gives way to a loosely structured series of revelations, his camera roving among conversations which are by turns banal, touching and funny. Some characters are appealing, but there's not much emotional depth as Jaglom raises complex themes only to conclude that they leave him feeling 'moody and weird'. By the end, you'll know what he means. CM

New Year's Day

(1999, GB/Fr, 101 min)
d Suri Krishnamma. *p* Stephen Cleary, Simon Channing-Williams. *sc* Ralph Brown. *ph* John de Borman. *ed* Adam Ross. *pd* Eve Stewart. *m* Julian Nott. *cast* Marianne Jean-Baptiste, Anastasia Hille, Andrew Lee Potts, Bobby Barry, Michael Kitchen, Sue Johnston, Ralph Brown, Jacqueline Bisset, Gregg Prentice.

● A Britflick with a difference – and timely, given its concern with the angry, grief-stricken difficulties of finding anchorage in a world suddenly altered by major loss. When teenagers Jake (Potts) and Steven (Barry) wake up in an ethereal foreign ward as the only survivors of a school skiing trip disaster, they resolve to cheat fate and commit suicide in 12 months, after completing a series of tasks compiled from the video-filmed wishes of their dead friends. These are generally the black-humoured stuff of adolescent aspiration, but the pair soon raise the stakes, which puts them increasingly at odds with their counsellor and their families. It's an effective move to take a familiar youth mindset – the rebellious, death-inspired desire for liberation from conventional codes of behaviour – and situate it in a narrative where it's believably sustained as a response to crisis. But, wanting to play both as heightened realism and as parable, the film's texture is uneven and its tone is uncertain. GE

New York, New York

(1977, US, 153 min)
d Martin Scorsese. *p* Irwin Winkler, Robert Chartoff. *sc* Earl Mac Rauch, Mardik Martin. *ph* Laszlo Kovacs. *ed* Irving Lerner, Marcia Lucas, Tom Rolf, Bert Lovitt, David Ramirez. *pd* Boris Leven. *songs* John Kander, Fred Ebb, others. *cast* Liza Minnelli, Robert De Niro, Lionel Stander, Barry Primus, Mary Kay Place, Georgie Auld, George Memmoli, Dick Miller.

● Scorsese's tribute/parody/critique of the MGM musical is a razor-sharp dissection of the conventions of both meeting-cute romances and rags-to-riches biopics, as it charts the traumatic love affair between irresponsible but charming jazz saxophonist De Niro (dubbed by George Auld) and mainstream singer Minnelli. On an emotional level, the film is a powerhouse, offering some of the most convincingly painful rows ever shot; as a depiction of changes in American music and the entertainment world, it is accurate and evocative; and as a commentary on showbiz films, it's a stunner, sounding echoes of Minnelli's own mother's movies and career (particularly *A Star Is Born*) as well as other classics like *On the Town* and the first *A Star Is Born* (in which Stander also appeared). Superbly scored, beautifully designed by Boris Leven to highlight the genre's artificiality, and performed to perfection. GA

New York Nights

(1983, US, 111 min)
d Simon Nuchtern. *p/sc* Romano Vanderbes. *ph* Alan Dobeman. *ed* Victor Zimet. *ad* Frank Boros, Patrick Mann. *m* Linda Schreyer. *cast* Corrine Alphen, George Ayer, Bobbi Burns, Peter Matthey, Missy O'Shea, Jim Hunter, Willem Dafoe.

● Schnitzler's cunning form from *La Ronde* blagged to display a group of daisy-chaining demi-mondaines indulging in ten kinds of rumpy-pumpy all over town. All vile stuff, of course, but as usual there is a certain recherché pleasure to be had from incidentals: 1. Sample dialogue: 'I am 18' – 'Yeah? And I'm Roman Polanski'. 2. A husband who decks his wife up in a moustache and makes talent from the local gay club have her on the sofa while he plays martial music on a baby grand. 3. Plato's Retreat: a place where Socratic dialogues take place in a sauna. 4. The NY skyline with a dirigible above it. Warning: the Surgeon General has determined that watching this film will give you herpes. CPea

New York Stories

(1989, US, 124 min)
d Martin Scorsese, Francis Coppola, Woody Allen. 'Life Lessons': *p* Barbara DeFina. *sc* Richard Price. *ph* Nestor Almendros. *ed* Thelma Schoonmaker. *pd* Kristi Zea. *cast* Nick Nolte, Rosanna Arquette, Steve Buscemi, Patrick O'Neal, Deborah Harry. 'Life Without Zoe': *p* Fred Roos, Fredric S Fuchs. *sc* Francis Coppola, Sofia Coppola. *ph* Vittorio Storaro. *ed* Barry Malkin. *pd* Dean Tavoularis. *m* Carmine Coppola, Kid Creole and the Coconuts. *cast* Heather McComb, Talia Shire, Giancarlo Giannini, Carole Bouquet. 'Oedipus Wrecks': *p* Robert Greenhut. *sc* Woody Allen. *ph* Sven Nykvist. *ed* Susan E Morse. *pd* Santo Loquasto. *cast* Woody Allen, Mia Farrow, Mae Questel, Julie Kavner.

● Three directors, three featurettes. Co-written with his teenage daughter, Coppola's centerpiece, 'Life Without Zoe', is quite simply a mess. The story (poor little rich girl plots to reunite her separated parents and return a bangle to an exotic princess) is nonsense, nothing more than a maudlin, self-indulgent excuse to have horrid brats and members of the Coppola clan prance about in funny clothes to the strains of Francis' favourite music. Scorsese's opener, 'Life Lessons', which does make sense, centres on a muscular performance from Nolte as an immature, egocentric artist obsessed with assistant Arquette. The plot, inspired by Dostoevsky, seems meant as some sort of personal reflection on the links between artistic productivity and sexual/emotional frustration. The visuals, performances and superb music provide many pleasures, but the slight, anecdotal inevitability of the tale is a drawback, since the material promises something richer and deeper. Only Woody Allen seems to have understood what is possible in a featurette. Although 'Oedipus Wrecks' is only an extended variation on nagging Jewish momma gags, it's not only his funniest film in years, it also works beautifully: as it should in a short, every moment counts. GA

Next Best Thing, The

(2000, US, 108 min)
d John Schlesinger. *p* Tom Rosenberg, Leslie Dixon, Linne Radmin. *sc* Thomas Ropelewski. *ph* Elliot Davis. *ed* Peter Honess. *pd* Howard Cummings. *m* Gabriel Yared. *cast* Madonna, Rupert Everett, Bejamin Bratt, Michael Vartan, Josef Sommer, Malcolm Stumpf, Lynn Redgrave, Neil Patrick Harris, Illeana Douglas, Gavin Lambert.

● This is one long mess, but Madonna, as Abbie, a needy yoga teacher who decides having a baby with gay best friend Robert (Everett) is the closest she'll get to playing happy families, is only partly to blame. What she's brilliant at is insouciance, wax-museum kitsch and, in her pop videos, even weakness, of the blissfully OTT 'Baby Jane' kind. But honest to goodness vulnerability? Madonna looks the modern singleton's part, but she can't make the woundedness stick. One scene only is cause for celebration, wherein her bolshie body is allowed to do all the talking. It's the little boy's birthday and a wrung-out Abbie is glaring at Robert as he allows himself to be flirted with. It's not just panic and envy we see in her eyes, but lust, a real *noir* look, ablaze with neurotic life. But this lovely, dangly moment – one of the few times director Schlesinger lets himself sit back and observe – is soon a distant memory, for the film has a seizure and decides it wants to be *Kramer vs Kramer*. CO'Su

Next Friday

(2000, US, 98 min)
d Steve Carr. *p/sc* Ice Cube. *ph* Christopher J Baffa. *ed* Elena Maganini. *pd* Dina Lipton. *m* Terence Blanchard. *cast* Ice Cube, Mike Epps, Justin Pierce, John Witherspoon, Don 'DC' Curry, Jacob Vargas, Tamala Jones, Clifton Powell, Kirk Jones.

● Less a sequel to Ice Cube's 1995 cult movie *Friday*, more a joke for joke rehash. The scatological humour has not abated and the smoking of weed underlies most major plot points, with Craig (Ice Cube) and his sidekick Day-Day (Epps) coming on like a latter-day Cheech and Chong. The story, such as it is, begins four years after the fateful Friday when Craig bested local bully Debo. He's still living with his parents in the 'hood when news filters through that Debo has busted out of jail and is looking for revenge. He temporarily relocates in the suburbs with his lottery-winning uncle and nerdish cousin Day-Day. But even in here, there's plenty of trouble waiting to ruin his Friday. Despite the crass humour, Ice Cube's inert performance and the pre-adolescent attitude to women, this is a sporadically funny picture with a strong soundtrack. Like most stoner movie, it will probably find its niche as a video release. WI

Next of Kin

(1989, US, 108 min)
d John Irvin. *p* Les Alexander, Don Enright. *sc* Michael Jenning, Jeb Stuart. *ph* Steven Poster. *ed* Peter Honess. *pd* Jack T Collis. *m* Jack Nitzsche, Gary Chang, Todd Hayen. *cast* Patrick Swayze, Liam Neeson, Helen Hunt, Adam Baldwin, Andreas Katsulas, Bill Paxton, Michael J Pollard.

● When his brother is killed in a mob-style hit, Truman Gates (Swayze), an Appalachian hillbilly turned Chicago cop, is torn between his duty and family loyalty which requires that he opt for Old Testament revenge. But even if he can locate a black witness to the slaying, or prove that a smooth mobster's ambitious son (Baldwin) was implicated, can he do so before vengeful brother Briar (Neeson) takes the law into his own hands? On the loose with a shotgun and a belly full of hate, Briar is unwittingly setting the scene for a showdown between the urban mobsters, with their state-of-the-art firepower, and the good ol' country boys who favour crossbows, axes and snakes. Together with *Hamburger Hill*, this illustrates that Irvin probably couldn't stage an action scene if you held a gun to his head. Even more turgid and unconvincing are the quieter 'dramatic' scenes, which serve only to arrest the plot's minimal momentum and prolong the agony. NF

Next of Kin, The

(1942, GB, 102 min, b/w)
d Thorold Dickinson. *p* Michael Balcon. *sc* Thorold Dickinson, John Dighton, Angus Macphail, Basil Bartlett. *ph* Ernest Palmer. *ed* Ray Pitt. *ad* Tom Morahan. *m* William Walton. *cast* Mervyn Johns, John Chandos, Nova Pilbeam, David Hutcheson, Stephen Murray, Phyllis Stanley, Charles Victor, Basil Radford, Naunton Wayne.

● Originally intended as an army training film advising that 'Careless Talk Costs Lives', this was expanded by Ealing into a feature thriller. The switch shows in the didactic pacing, especially at the beginning, but like Cavalcanti's *Went The Day Well?* (though not as good), the film has a chillingly casual authenticity as it noses into seedy byways to uncover the chain of fifth columnists that includes an antiquarian bookseller (Murray), a stripper (Stanley) and an Irish sailor (Victor). Although the ending was softened when Churchill wanted to have the film banned as a threat to morale (the 'betrayed' commando raid succeeds, though only at the cost of heavy casualties), it still stands up pretty well. TM

Next Stop, Greenwich Village

(1976, US, 111 min)
d Paul Mazursky. *p* Paul Mazursky, Tony Ray. *sc* Paul Mazursky. *ph* Arthur J Ornitz. *ed* Richard Halsey. *pd* Philip Rosenberg. *m* Bill Conti. *cast* Lenny Baker, Shelley Winters, Ellen Greene, Lois Smith, Christopher Walken, Dori Brenner, Antonio Fargas, Lou Jacobi, Jeff Goldblum, Bill Murray.

● A middlebrow *American Graffiti*, minus the music and set in Greenwich Village, 1953. Aspiring young actor moves into the Village, thereby allowing writer/director Mazursky to render into clichés all the obvious ingredients of the period: coffee bars, suicide bids, Actors' Studio classes, cheap parties, the Rosenbergs, uncertain contraception, illegal abortions. Add Shelley Winters as a Jewish momma to give the movie heart, and Antonio Fargas as a misunderstood black gay to give it pathos, and you have a fair idea of the film's efforts to win its audience. Sadly, the pretensions of most of the characters are matched by Mazursky: pointed homages to 'Gadge' Kazan and Marlon, unnecessary dream sequences, and continuous endorsement for his rather tedious characters; one is only surprised that there wasn't a kid called Jimmy Dean at the party.

Next Stop Wonderland

(1997, US, 96 min)
d Brad Anderson. *p* Mitchell B Robbins. *sc* Brad Anderson, Lyn Vaus. *ph* Uta Briesewitz. *ed* Brad Anderson. *pd* Chad Detweiller. *m* Claudio Ragazzi *cast* Hope Davis, Alan Gelfant, Victor Argo, Jon Benjamin, Cara Buono, Larry Gilliard Jr, Phil Hoffman.

● An indie slice-of romance: Hope Davis is recently single Erin, a doctor trying to enjoy her newfound solitude while being pressured by everyone and especially her mom to commit to the dating scene; and Gelfant the similarly lonesome Alan, a student marine biologist caught up in a local mobster's misdemeanours. It's Boston, and their paths occasionally cross, fleetingly, throughout the film. In other words, this is protracted meeting-cute. But cynicism aside the subject matter is presumably as valid as the two characters' subsequent bust-up. It's elegantly observed and sometimes insightful, but finally rather too whimsical and inconsequential. NB

Next Voice You Hear..., The

(1950, US, 80 min, b/w)
d William Wellman. *p* Dore Schary. *sc* Charles Schnee. *ph* William C Mellor. *ed* John Dunning. *ad* Cedric Gibbons, Eddie Imazu. *m* David Raksin. *cast* James Whitmore, Nancy Davis, Gary Gray, Lillian Bronson, Art Smith, Tom D'Andrea, Jeff Corey.

● Beautifully scripted and directed, the first half of this Dore Schary production is a persuasive minimalist portrait of a lower middle class small-town family (factory worker Whitmore, wife Davis, and young son Gray): loving and reasonably contented, but showing signs of stretchmarks where the struggle to make ends meet doesn't quite match consumer aspirations. Much of it is both funny and pointed; and the moments of unease, escalating into a vague sense of guilty panic, are equally well handled as the voice on the radio (heard only in reported speech, since the divine voice doesn't record) proves to be God announcing a visit. The trouble is that God's message turns out to be the usual guff (love one another, count your blessings, nature and all that); and the only way the film can drum up any suitable conflict is by waxing melodramatic about the mother's pregnancy ('Talk about your miracle!' cries delighted dad when all goes without a hitch). Schnee's dialogue and Wellman's direction deserve better than this crowd-pleasing scenario. TM

Nez au Vent, Le (aka Scent of Deceit)

(1995, Bel/Fr, 90 min)
d Dominique Guerrier. *p* Marion Hänsel, Bertrand Dussart, Eric van Beuren. *sc* Dominique Guerrier, Jean-Louis Benoît. *ph* Jan Vancaillie. *ed* Ludo Troch. *ad* Véronique Mélery. *m* Serge Franklin. *cast* Yves Robert, Philippine Leroy-Baulieu, Olivier Ythier, Jean-Marc Roulot, Olivier Massart, Sabrina Leurquin, Jean Vercheval.

● An ingenious if not entirely satisfying fantasy in which elderly perfume-boffin Robert commits suicide, is admitted to the wrong neighbourhood of the beyond, and returns to this world, where he relives key moments from his life and helps sort out his grown son's troubled existence. The film shifts between past and present, makes some telling points about love, selfishness and commitment, but never quite manages to balance its black comedy with its more serious moments. GA

Niagara

(1953, US, 90 min)
d Henry Hathaway. *p* Charles Brackett. *sc* Charles Brackett, Walter Reisch, Richard L Breen. *ph* Joseph MacDonald. *ed* Barbara McLean. *ad* Lyle Wheeler, Maurice Ransford. *m* Sol Kaplan. *cast* Marilyn Monroe, Joseph Cotten, Jean Peters, Denis O'Dea, Casey Adams, Don Wilson, Richard Allan, Lurene Tuttle.

● Marilyn's first real starring vehicle, a steamily melodramatic thriller into which she fits a trifle uncomfortably: unbecomingly costumed, uneasy with dialogue, and exposed to acres of footage designed to ram her down the audience's throat as a heartless, lusting bitch, a sexpot honeymooner scheming to kill her husband (Cotten), a mentally disturbed war veteran who has his own ideas. Odd to realise (this was after all her eighteenth film) that Hollywood took so long to discover the vulnerability that became Monroe's distinctive quality. Worthseeing for Hathaway's superbly crafted direction, even if it needed a Hitchcock to merge the symbolism of the location (the falls, the belltower) with the themes of sexual domination and envy. TM

Nibelungen, Die

(1924, Ger, 115 min (Pt 1)/80 min (Pt 2), b/w)
d Fritz Lang. *p* Erich Pommer. *sc* Thea von Harbou. *ph* Carl Hoffmann, Günther Rittau. *ad* Otto Hunte, Erich Kettelhut, Karl Vollbrecht. *m* (orig accompanying) Gottfried Huppertz. *cast* Paul Richter, Margarete Schön, Hanna Ralph, Gertrud Arnold, Theodor Loos, Hans Adalbert von Schlettow, Bernhard Goetzke, Rudolf Klein-Rogge.

● *Siegfried*, the first part of Lang's epic, based on the same myth cycle that inspired Wagner's *Ring*, is a slow, grave pageant in the form of a ballad. The visual style is as monumental as the narrative, with forests and castles modelled on 19th century Romantic paintings, and the whole is based upon an intense pleasure in spectacle, compounded by the inspired trick-work: a magical dragon, fiery landscapes for Brunhilde's Northern home, and Walter Ruttmann's interpolated

Dream of the Hawks. In the second part, *Kriemhild's Revenge*, as Kriemhild and the Huns destroy the Burgundians who have murdered Siegfried, so the emphasis on fatalistic design, plotting and architecture is replaced by the furious, crowded movement of the battle which comprises most of this half. The mix of desire, death and revenge is common in Lang, but here, with the distance of myth, the concentration on violent spectacle, and – most important – the woman as focal point, the impression is of pure, passionate nihilism running riot. SJ

Nicaragua – No Pasarán

(1984, Aust, 74 min)
d/p David Bradbury. *ph* Geoffrey Simpson, Yves Breux. *ed* Stewart Young. *narrator* Mark Aarons.

● A detailed account of the inability of America to accept Nicaragua's non-client status. The Sandinistas emerge as well short of perfect, but clearly no sane Nicaraguan would trade them for the vile Somoza, and the whole atmosphere of the country is clearly different from its neighbours. Even the soldiers smile. JCo

Nice Time

(1957, GB, 18 min, b/w)
d Claude Goretta, Alain Tanner. *ph* John Fletcher.

● One of the BFI's Free Cinema productions, this impression of nightlife around Piccadilly Circus is much less scolding in tone (sarcastic title apart) than *O Dreamland*, with which it's often bracketed. Big city poetry is what its directors are reaching for, with their snatched images cut to numbers by the Chas McDevitt Skiffle Group: hookers on parade to a whistled 'Greenback Dollar', wee small hours shots coupled with 'She Moved Through the Fair'. It's pretty small beer, but full of absorbing sociological minutiae: the scarcity of black faces, the quantities of uniformed servicemen milling around, the enormous, sternly regimented cinema queues. BBa

Nicholas and Alexandra

(1971, US, 189 min)
d Franklin J Schaffner. *p* Sam Spiegel. *sc* James Goldman. *ph* Freddie Young. *ed* Ernest Walter. *pd* John Box. *m* Richard Rodney Bennett. *cast* Michael Jayston, Janet Suzman, Harry Andrews, Tom Baker, Timothy West, Jack Hawkins, Laurence Olivier, John McEnery, Eric Porter, Michael Bryant, John Wood, Ian Holm, Michael Redgrave, Curt Jürgens, Brian Cox.

● Old-fashioned, overlong costume epic, comfortably reactionary in its view of the Tsar Nicholas as a saint who knew not what he was doing to the Russian people, and of the revolutionaries as potential tyrants reaching hungrily for power. The first part is elegant and surprisingly affecting in detailing the love story of Nicholas and Alexandra (beautifully played by Jayston and Suzman), blighted when their son turns out to be a haemophiliac and Rasputin (Baker) erupts into their lives. The revolutionaries get shorter shrift. Two comrades exchange recollections of Siberia before introducing themselves – 'Josef Stalin…' 'My name is Lenin' – with the name-dropping becoming decidedly Goonish when Lenin then turns to a bystander to cry, 'Trotsky, you've been avoiding me!' Much cameo role-playing around here; and in the last part of the film, devoted to the decline and fall of the Romanovs, they seem to take an unconscionable time a-dying. TM

Nicholas Nickleby

(1947, GB, 108 min, b/w)
d Alberto Cavalcanti. *p* Michael Balcon. *sc* John Dighton. *ph* Gordon Dines. *ed* Leslie Norman. *ad* Michael Relph. *m* Lord Berners. *cast* Derek Bond, Cedric Hardwicke, Alfred Drayton, Aubrey Woods, Jill Balcon, Bernard Miles, Sally Ann Howes, Stanley Holloway, Sybil Thorndike, Fay Compton, Cathleen Nesbitt.

● For a director who dabbled in the avant-garde, Cavalcanti makes surprisingly little of the surreal possibilities of this convoluted Dickensian nightmare. As in *Champagne Charlie* he collaborated with art director Michel Relph to create an impressively atmospheric Victorian London, but stylish visuals hardly compensate for the flat, cursory rendering of some of Dickens' best drawn characters. Only Bernard Miles as Noggs and Cedric Hardwicke as wicked Uncle Ralph are given enough space to establish a proper presence. Meagre and one-dimensional, the film is finally smothered by Ealing's cosy sentimentality. RMy

Nichts als die Wahrheit

see After the Truth

Nicht Versöhnt (Not Reconciled)

(1965, WGer, 53 min, b/w)
d Jean-Marie Straub. *p* Danièle Huillet, Jean-Marie Straub. *sc* Jean-Marie Straub. *ph* Wendelin Sachtler. *ed* Jean-Marie Straub, Danièle Huillet. *m* Bartok, JS Bach. *cast* Heinrich Hargesheimer, Carlheinz Hargesheimer, Martha Ständner, Danièle Straub, Henning Hermssen, Ulrich von Thüna.

● Fifty years of German social and political history, from the anti-Communism of 1910 through the anti-semitism of the '30s to a political reprisal in 1960. Explored a-chronologically, in vignettes from the lives of three generations of a middle class family. Taken from Heinrich Böll's novel *Billiards at Half Past Nine*, but with all the mechanics of storytelling and the frosting of 'style' removed. Read the novel for the narrative; see Straub's movie for the steely precision of its ideas and images, enhanced by Brechtian acting and the absence of all redundancies. Difficult in ways that few films are, but necessarily difficult. TR

Nick Carter in Prague (Adela Jeste Nevecerela/ aka Adele Hasn't Had Her Supper Yet)

(1977, Czech, 102 min)
d Oldrich Lipsky. *sc* Jiri Brdecka. *ph* Jaroslav Kucera. *pd* Vladimir Labsky, Milan Nejedly. *m* Lubos Fiser. *cast* Michal Docolomansky, Rudolf Hrusinsky, Milos Kopecky, Ladislav Pesek, Neda Konvalinkova.

● A whimsical, hopelessly leaden comedy about American private eye Nick Carter breezing into Prague to foil legendary master criminal The Gardener. The central problems are the script, which lacks even a glimmer of mystery, suspense or poetry, and the direction, which reduces every gag and every baroque extravagance to the same bland level. TR

Nick Carter – Master Detective

(1939, US, 59 min, b/w)
d Jacques Tourneur. *p* Lucien Hubbard. *sc* Bertram Millhauser. *ph* Charles Lawton Jr. *ed* Elmo Veron. *ad* Cedric Gibbons, Howard Campbell. *m* Edward Ward. *cast* Walter Pidgeon, Rita Johnson, Henry Hull, Donald Meek, Stanley Ridges, Milburn Stone, Sterling Holloway, Martin Kosleck, Frank Faylen.

● The first of MGM's three Nick Carter B movies, in which he (not the period creation but a private eye in the contemporary mould) investigates espionage in an aircraft factory. Tourneur's second film in Hollywood, it's briskly and competently done, but the best thing about it is Donald Meek's performance as Bartholomew the Bee Man, a mousy little apiculturist who fancies himself as a private eye, keeps following Nick Carter (Pidgeon) around, and more than once proves to be the man on the spot. TM

Nickelodeon

(1976, US/GB, 122 min)
d Peter Bogdanovich. *p* Irwin Winkler, Robert Chartoff. *sc* WD Richter, Peter Bogdanovich. *ph* Laszlo Kovacs. *ed* William Carruth. *ad* Richard Berger. *cast* Ryan O'Neal, Burt Reynolds, Tatum O'Neal, Brian Keith, Stella Stevens, John Ritter, Jane Hitchcock, Brion James, M Emmet Walsh.

● To make a clinker out of a gift of a subject like silent movie-making is some feat, yet Peter Bogdanovich manages it with honours. Set between 1910 and 1915, *Nickelodeon* spends ages muddling the protagonists' lives and their suitcases before they settle down to make pictures. Despite some comic intentions, the film takes itself far too seriously as a *hommage* to the movie pioneers. But with Bogdanovich's yearning nostalgia totally lacking in perspective, this dreary recreation becomes entirely a work of the past tense; certainly there's no wit, pace or enthusiasm to suggest that it's alive. The direction is agonisingly pedantic for a comedy, and leaves O'Neal and Reynolds totally exposed, mugging away in charmless and clumsy fashion. CPe

Nickel Queen

(1971, Aust, 89 min)
d John McCallum. *p* John McCallum, Joy Cavill. *sc* Henry C James, John McCallum, Joy Cavil. *ph* John Williams. *ed* Don Saunders. *ad* Bernard Hides. *m* Sven Libaek. *cast* Googie Withers, John Laws, Alfred Sandor, Ed Devereaux, Peter Gwynne, Joanna McCallum, Ross Thompson.

● Totally appalling piece of Australiana, with hippies and socialites and nickel in them thar hills, and banality by the spadeful all around. Makes *The Adventures of Barry McKenzie* look like a refreshing can of Fosters.

Nick of Time

(1995, US, 89 min)
d/p John Badham. *sc* Patrick Sheane Duncan. *ph* Roy H Wagner. *ed* Frank Morriss, Kevin Stitt. *pd* Philip Harrison. *m* Arthur B Rubinstein. *cast* Johnny Depp, Christopher Walken, Marsha Mason, Charles S Dutton, Roma Maffia, Peter Strauss, Gloria Reuben, GD Spradlin.

● No sooner has accountant Depp disembarked at the Los Angeles railway station than he's separated from his infant daughter and presented with a gun, a photograph and a schedule. If he hasn't killed the woman in the picture – Governor of California Marsha Mason – within the next 80 minutes, then he'll never see his child again. It's a nifty pretext for a nail-biting thriller, but even on this abbreviated timescale the movie nags at your credulity. Given that the conspiracy ripples out alarmingly wide, it seems improbable that head honcho Walken should have concocted quite such a whimsical plan, and it's a long wait before the impassive Depp takes any resolute action. Written by the prolific, old-fashioned Patrick Sheane Duncan, the film's passably ingenious, but director Badham fluffs its central gimmick, the notion that the action is played out, *Rope*-style, in real time, by cutting away from his hard-pressed protagonist at convenient intervals. Even so, it's not a bad effort. Badham's sub-De Palma, not Hitchcock, but he's still fractionally above average. TCh

Nick's Movie

see Lightning Over Water

Nicky and Gino

see Dominick and Eugene

Nico

see Above the Law

Nico Icon

(1995, Ger, 72 min)
d Susanne Ofteringer. *p* Thomas Mertens, Annette Pisacane, Peter Nadermann. *sc* Susanne Ofteringer. *ph* Judith Kaufmann, Katarzyna Remin, Sibylle Stürmer, Martin Baer. *ed* Elfe Brandenburger, Guido Krajewski. *with* Alan Wise, James Young, Helma Wolff, Nico Papatakis, Carlos de Maldonado-Bostock, Edith Boulogne, Billy Name, Paul Morrissey, Jonas Mekas, John Cale, Viva, Sterling Morrison.

● One of those figures who elevate ennui into an art form, or at least a way of life, Nico had a kind of night-of-the-living-dead glamour which fascinated anyone (mostly men) who spent time with her. A teen model for *Vogue*, she landed a bit part in *La Dolce Vita*, had a son by Alain Delon, and hooked up with Andy Warhol and the Velvet Underground to cut one classic album. As a chanteuse, she made Marlene Dietrich sound girlish. As a performer, she was utterly opaque – but then that seems to have been her way off stage, too. She didn't have a career, she had an addiction. It was the only thing she shared. Bonding with her son, she introduced him to heroin, and later, when he was hospitalised in a drug-induced coma, she recorded the sound of the life-support machine as a backing track for one of her songs. This is a compelling portrait of an unlovely beauty, a fascinating void. Using extensive home movies, especially from the Factory period, interviews with the survivors (John Cale, Paul Morrissey, Sterling Morrison), and clips painfully contrasting the glacial ingenue with the elegantly ravaged junkie, writer/director Ofteringer probes the enigma without finding much of substance behind the surface. But what surface! The film's formal inventiveness – games with framing and superimposition – gives it some of the texture of '60s underground film, and there's a strong sense of that whole pseudo-bohemian scene. You don't come out feeling any warmer towards Nico, necessarily, or desperate to dig out those solo albums, but there's something haunting about her; she didn't so much make her mark as leave us the scars to remember her by. TCh

Nido, El

see Nest, The

Night After Night

(1932, US, 70 min, b/w)
d Archie Mayo. *sc* Vincent Lawrence, Kathryn Scola. *ph* Ernest Haller. *cast* George Raft, Constance Cummings, Wynne Gibson, Mae West, Roscoe Karns, Alison Skipworth, Louis Calhern.

● It seems strange to find the stately Mae West playing a jolly character called Maudie Triplett, and even stranger to find her fourth in the cast list, but after all this was her first film. Her scenes are few, yet she throws so much into them that the leading players in this comedy drama (cool Constance Cummings and icy George Raft, the Archie Andrews of gangsters) momentarily fade into oblivion. They soon come back, though, along with the muddled story (from a novel by Louis Bromfield) about a speakeasy proprietor's love for a Park Avenue dame. GB

Night Ambush

see Ill Met By Moonlight

Night and Day

(1946, US, 128 min)
d Michael Curtiz. *p* Arthur Schwartz. *sc* Charles Hoffman, Leo Townsend, William Bowers. *ph* Peverell Marley, William V Skall. *ed* David Weisbart. *ad* John Hughes. *m* Max Steiner. *cast* Cary Grant, Alexis Smith, Monty Woolley, Mary Martin, Ginny Simms, Jane Wyman, Eve Arden, Victor Francen, Dorothy Malone, Alan Hale.

● Weak biopic of Cole Porter in which Curtiz fights a losing battle with a conventional, highly sanitised, thoroughly sentimental script. Though unadventurously chosen, the songs (staged lushly if none too imaginatively by LeRoy Prinz) are at least worth listening to, especially when sung by Ginny Simms (though some swear by Mary Martin's rendition of *My Heart Belongs to Daddy* as the highlight of the film). TM

Night and Day (Nuit et Jour)

(1991, Fr/Bel, 96 min)
d Chantal Akerman. *p* Maurice Tinchant, Martine Marignac, Marilyn Watelet. *sc* Chantal Akerman, Pascal Bonitzer. *ph* Jean-Claude Neckelbrouck. *ed* Francine Sandberg, Camille Bordes-Resnais. *ad* Dominique Douret. *m* Marc Herouet. *cast* Guillaine Londez, Thomas Langmann, François Negret, Nicole Colchat, Pierre Laroche. *narrator* Delphine Seyrig.

● Akerman's lyrical chronicle of a heterosexual ménage-à-trois looks banality straight in the face. New to Paris, youngsters Julie (Londez) and Jack (Langmann) experience a summer of love broken only by his nightly taxi round, which leaves her free to wander the streets and strike up an equally sexual relationship with Joseph (Negret), who drives the same cab during the day. Without conscience, Julie flits between lovers, but her willingness to flaunt every morality threatens both liaisons. The performers are attractive, in an androgynous way, but their lack of distinctiveness typifies the film's anonymity. TJ

Night and the City

(1950, GB/US, 100 min, b/w)
d Jules Dassin. *p* Samuel G Engel. *sc* Jo Eisinger. *ph* Max Greene. *ed* Sidney Stone, (US version) Nick De Maggio. *ad* CP Norman. *m* Benjamin Frankel, (US version) Franz Waxman. *cast* Richard Widmark, Gene Tierney, Googie Withers, Francis L Sullivan, Herbert Lom, Hugh Marlowe, Mike Mazurki.

● Bizarre *film noir* with Widmark as a small time nightclub tout trying to hustle his way into the wrestling rackets, but finding himself the object of a murderous manhunt when his cons catch up with him. Set in a London through which Widmark spends much of his time dodging in dark alleyways, it attempts to present the city in neo-expressionist terms as a grotesque, terrifyingly anonymous trap. Fascinating, even though the stylised characterisations (like Francis L Sullivan's obesely outsized nightclub king) remain theoretically interesting rather than convincing. Inclined to go over the top, it all too clearly contains the seeds of Dassin's later – and disastrous – pretensions. TM

Night and the City

(1992, US, 104 min)
d Irwin Winkler. *p* Jane Rosenthal, Irwin Winkler. *sc* Richard Price. *ph* Tak Fujimoto. *ed* David Brenner. *pd* Peter Larkin. *m* James Newton Howard. *cast* Robert De Niro, Jessica Lange, Cliff Gorman, Alan King, Jack Warden, Eli Wallach, Barry Primus, Gene Kirkwood, Richard Price.

● Nothing to write home about in this remake. Richard Price's script is typically funny-tough, but the structuring is aimless and the characters psychologically nowhere. Motormouth shyster lawyer Harry Fabian (De Niro) is humiliated in court by big shot boxing promoter Boom Boom (King), and decides to take revenge by recruiting Boom Boom's retired brother Al (Warden) and promoting some bouts of his own. He turns to his married mistress, bartender Helen (Lange), for the financing, but everything he touches plunges him deeper into trouble. None of this makes any sense (Fabian cheats Helen with a bogus liquor licence, for instance, and she doesn't complain). Worst of all, Fabian is issued with all the inner depths of a DJ, and we're expected to care about his ambitions. The hopes of no-hopers in *film noir* rendered up a piteous bouquet, but there's none of that here. Even De Niro can't do much with the role, beyond yammering and dancing on the spot like a warmed-over version of his Johnny Boy in *Mean Streets*. (From the novel by Gerald Kersh.) BC

Night at the Golden Eagle

(2001, US, 110 min)
d Adam Rifkin. *p* Adam Rifkin, Steve Bing. *sc* Adam Rifkin. *ph* Checho Varesse. *ed* Peter Schink. *pd* Sherman Williams. *m* Tyler Bates. *cast* Donnie Montemarano, Vinny Argiro, Natasha Lyonne, Vinnie Jones, Ann Magnuson.

● Watchable but overflashy and cynical fable. An elderly criminal gets out of prison, is told by his best buddy that they should go to Vegas and turn straight, but blows it by falling for temptation in the form of a young whore he invites to his room, which causes things to get very messy. The characters are relentlessly lowlife and/or eccentric (including Jones as a pimp, and Sam Moore and one of the Nicholas Bros cameoing as hotel guests), the camerawork and cutting are redundantly emphatic, and the treatment of the whore quite callous. Guy Ritchie might like it. GA

Night at the Opera, A

(1935, US, 94 min, b/w)
d Sam Wood. *p* Irving G Thalberg. *sc* George S Kaufman, Morrie Ryskind. *ph* Merritt B Gerstad. *ed* William LeVanway. *ad* Cedric Gibbons, Ben Carré, Edwin B Willis. *m* Herbert Stothart. *cast* The Marx Brothers, Kitty Carlisle, Allan Jones, Margaret Dumont, Sig Ruman, Walter Woolf King, Edward Keane, Robert Emmet O'Connor, Lorraine Bridges.

● The Marx Brothers at the turning point, just before their gradual descent into mediocrity at the hands of MGM, who wanted their comedy to be rationed and rationalised. It's a top budget job, opulent and meticulous, with its fair share of vices: this is the first Marx Brothers film where you really feel like strangling the romantic leads. But it has even more virtues: there's no Zeppo, the script's generally great (Kaufman and Ryskind), Dumont's completely great, and the Brothers get to perform some of their most irresistible routines – the stateroom scene and all. GB

Night at the Roxbury, A

(1998, US, 82 min)
d John Fortenberry. *p* Lorne Michaels, Amy Heckerling. *sc* Steve Koren, Will Ferrell, Chris Kattan. *ph* Francis Kenny. *ed* Jay Kamen. *pd* Steve Jordan. *m* David Kitay. *cast* Will Ferrell, Chris Kattan, Dan Hedaya, Molly Shannon, Richard Grieco, Loni Anderson.

● Shun this witless showcase for the *Saturday Night Live* double act of Ferrell and Kattan. The 'Roxbury Guys', brothers Steve and Doug Butabi, are improbable twenty-something Angelenos, thoroughbred inadequates who live for the dancefloor but struggle to get on and stay on it. Steve (Ferrell) at least achieves a degree of bathos; Doug (Kattan), however, is simply reptilian. As summarised by their permanently contemptuous father (Hedaya, the only recognisable human being in the movie), one son has his head in the clouds, the other his head up his ass. NB

Night Beauties

see Belles de nuit, Les

Nightbreed

(1990, US, 102 min)
d Clive Barker. *p* Gabriella Martinelli. *sc* Clive Barker. *ph* Robin Vidgeon. *ed* Richard Marden, Mark Goldblatt. *pd* Steve Hardie, (LA) Mark Haskins. *m* Danny Elfman. *cast* Craig Sheffer, Anne Bobby, David Cronenberg, Charles Haid, Hugh Quarshie, Hugh Ross, Doug Bradley, Oliver Parker, Nicholas Vince.

● Psychotic shrink Decker (Cronenberg) and racist police chief Eigerman (Haid) are icons of modern evil; the Nightbreed are a variegated tribe of shape-shifters, whose subterranean lair is attacked and overrun by the genocidal forces of law and order. Caught in the cultural crossfire are confused, colourless hero Boone (Sheffer) and transparently doomed love interest Lori (Bobby). Convinced by Decker that he is a serial killer, Boone panics, escapes from custody and heads for Midian, a mythical necropolis to which he feels drawn by an inexorable fate. Pursued by Decker's homicidal alter ego, Boone unwittingly fulfils an ancient prophecy... In adapting his own novella *Cabal*, Barker aims for a carnival feel, a breathless ghost-train ride through a fantastical world of grotesquely glamorous monsters. For all their dangerous exoticism, however, none of the myriad monsters has an identity that is more than skin deep. Barker calls his shambolic, uninvolving narrative 'scattershot'; put less kindly, it's as explosive and directionless as a blunderbuss. NF

Night Caller, The (aka Blood Beast from Outer Space)

(1965, GB, 84 min, b/w)
d John Gilling. *p* Ronald Liles. *sc* Jim O'Connolly. *ph* Stephen Dade. *ed* Philip Barnikel. *ad* Harry White. *m* Johnny Gregory. *cast* John Saxon, Maurice Denham, Patricia Haines, Alfred Burke, John Carson, Warren Mitchell, Robert Crewdson.

● Minor but not unintelligent British sci-fi thriller (from a novel by Frank Crisp) with imported star Saxon looking as though he hasn't quite found his bearings yet. The plot involves a UFO (an energy valve for transmuting matter), a female scientist (Haines, persuasive) who succumbs at the close to chief alien Medra (Crewdson), and sundry young women who answer the advertisements of Medra's modelling agency, only to be spirited away to planet Ganymede for genetic jiggery-pokery. TJ

Night Caller (Peur sur la Ville)

(1975, Fr/It, 125 min)
d/p Henri Verneuil. *sc* Henri Verneuil, Jean Laborde, Francis Verber. *ph* Jean Penzer. *ed* Pierre Gillette, Henri Lanoë. *ad* Jean André. *m* Ennio Morricone. *cast* Jean-Paul Belmondo, Charles Denner, Catherine Morin, Adalberto-Maria Merli, Lea Massari, Rosy Varte, Jean Martin.

● Belmondo plays super-cop on the tops of Paris buildings and undergound trains, piling stunt on daredevil stunt and risking his neck for a particularly silly story. Like *The Eiger Sanction*, there's some mileage in seeing a star so blatantly performing his own stunts, crashing through plate-glass windows of high rise buildings while suspended from a helicopter, etc. But desperately little of the film's energy goes into a plot that combines a settling of an old score with a hunt for a one-eyed killer who strangles loose women. CPe

Nightcleaners

(1975, GB, 90 min)
d/p/ph/ed Berwick Street Film Collective.
● This documentary started out as a conventional agit-prop project in support of the 1972 campaign to unionise women nightcleaners in London. In the three years that it took to complete, it turned into something very much more complex and challenging: a film that places the nightcleaners' campaign within a series of broader political discussions formulated as an 'open text' which asks as many questions about its own status as a film as it does about the socio-political issues that are its subject. No engaged person should overlook its challenge. TR

Nightcomers, The

(1971, GB, 96 min)
d/p Michael Winner. *sc* Michael Hastings. *ph* Bob Paynter. *ed* Frederick Wilson. *ad* Herbert Westbrook. *m* Jerry Fielding. *cast* Marlon Brando, Stephanie Beacham, Thora Hird, Harry Andrews, Verna Harvey, Christopher Ellis, Anna Palk.
● A film crass enough to have the outraged ghost of Henry James haunting Wardour Street with flashing eyes and gnashing teeth. Purporting to explain how Peter Quint and Miss Jessel became the ghostly presences of *The Turn of the Screw*, it has Brando mumbling endless Irish blarney, and Stephanie Beacham roped naked to her bed at frequent intervals, as the pair corrupt the two innocents in their care with sado-masochist goings-on. Michael Hastings' dialogue is evidently designed to echo the hieratic Jamesian flavour, but tends to sound embarrassingly like a Cockney nanny doing her best to be genteel. TM

Night Crossing

(1982, US, 106 min)
d Delbert Mann. *p* Tom Leetch. *sc* John McGreevey. *ph* Tony Imi. *ed* Gordon D Brenner. *pd* Rolf Zehetbauer. *m* Jerry Goldsmith. *cast* John Hurt, Jane Alexander, Beau Bridges, Glynnis O'Connor, Ian Bannen, Anne Stallybrass. Klaus Löwitsch, Kay Walsh.
● Scrapings of the Disney barrel in this true story of two East German families (supplied in best Disney tradition with two kids apiece) perilously escaping to the West in a flimsy, homemade hot-air balloon. Despite valiant efforts by the cast to overcome unimaginative stereotyping, didactic moralising makes the film largely unpalatable, and the excitement, although piled on, never really mounts. It's hard to care whether the families make it or not. FD

Night Digger, The

see Road Builder, The

Nightfall

(1956, US, 79 min, b/w)
d Jacques Tourneur. *p* Ted Richmond. *sc* Stirling Silliphant. *ph* Burnett Guffey. *ed* William A Lyon. *ad* Ross Bellah. *m* George Duning. *cast* Aldo Ray, Brian Keith, Anne Bancroft, James Gregory, Jocelyn Brando, Frank Albertson, Rudy Bond.
● In this superb adaptation of David Goodis' novel, a man (Ray), evidently on the run in California, befriends a girl (Bancroft) in a bar, but thinks (wrongly) she has set him up for two men on his tail. Dogging his footsteps for some months now, an insurance investigator (Gregory) wearily mulls over the case with his wife (Brando): the man is wanted for murder back in Chicago, but… 'he grows on you; it's almost like he needs protection'. A series of flashbacks, as beautifully placed and paced as in *Out of the Past*, prove the aptness of this description of the characteristic Goodis hero, perfectly incarnated by Ray as a large, friendly dog baring its teeth under threat. He was, we learn, an innocent bystander framed for murder by two bank-robbers – one sadistically trigger-happy (Bond), the other curiously ambivalent (Keith) – who think he knows the whereabouts of the $350,000 which went astray somewhere in the mountains of Wyoming. With nicely unforced symbolism (Burnett Guffey's camerawork is terrific throughout), the dark urban streets give way to wide open snowscapes as he embarks on a desperate quest for his lost innocence. A minor film compared to *Out of the Past*, perhaps, but no less gripping. TM

Nightfall (Abendland)

(1999, Ger, 140 min)
d Fred Kelemen. *p* Alexander Ris. *sc/ph* Fred Kelemen. *ed* Fred Kelemen, Anja Neraal, Nicola Undritz Cope. *pd* Ralf Küfner, Anette Kuhn. *m* Rainer Kirchmann. *cast* Verena Jasch, Wolfgang Michael, Adolfo Assor, Isa Hochgerner, Urs Redmond, Thomas Baumann, Daniela Roque-Magalhaes.
● Kelemen is an acquired taste. The little-seen *Frost* has acquired a near-mythic status among intellectual cinephiles. But *Fate*, his first (student) feature was mittel-European angst by the numbers: seedy Teutonic nihilism with an aesthetic borrowed equally from Angelopoulos and Tarkovsky. This is more of the same. Technically impressive, with its long, concerted travelling shots, slow reveals and morbid fades to black, the film still smacks of a strictly academic alienation. If someone puts a song on the radio, God knows we're going to hear it all. Every scene is an endurance test. (Sample dialogue: 'I've just raped my budgie.') TCh

Night Falls on Manhattan

(1996, US, 113 min)
d Sidney Lumet. *p* Thom Mount, Josh Kramer. *sc* Sidney Lumet. *ph* David Watkin. *ed* Sam O'Steen. *pd* Philip Rosenberg. *m* Mark Isham. *cast* Andy Garcia, Richard Dreyfuss, Lena Olin, Ian Holm, James Gandolfini, Colm Feore, Ron Liebman, Sheik Mahmud-Bey.
● Lumet has made 40-odd films, some classic, some lousy. This isn't by any means the biggest Lumet dog (it's from Robert Dailey's novel *Tainted Evidence*), but it's definitely barking in the big one at Cruft's. Promising Assistant DA Casey (Garcia) is son of veteran cop Liam (Holm). Liam's seriously injured during a raid on brutal drug dealer Washington (Mahmud-Bey). With the deranged New York DA at risk of losing his job, Casey prosecutes his father's assailant. He mysteriously acquires, within seconds, the hand of a beautiful, well connected woman (Olin) and is catapulted from crappy little Assistant DA to head of the whole shebang. Dreyfuss shines as a radical defence attorney. SGr

Night Fighters

see Terrible Beauty, A

Night Games

(1979, US, 107 min)
d Roger Vadim. *p* André Morgan, Roger Lewis. *sc* Anton Diether, Clarke Reynolds. *ph* Denis Lewiston. *ed* William Carruth. *pd* Robert Laing. *m* John Barry. *cast* Cindy Pickett, Barry Primus, Joanna Cassidy, Paul Jenkins, Mark Hanks, Gene Davis.
● Cindy Pickett plays an ageing anorexic narcissist, freaked by flashbacks to a childhood rape whenever her Hollywood tycoon husband attempts to penetrate one of her Janet Reger negligees. He soon departs, leaving our heroine to her fantasies, which concern a very silly lesbian *thé dansant* and a succession of square-jawed chaps in feather boas. In no way funny or erotic, the only nice thing about it is that after 107 minutes, it ends.

Night Hair Child (La tua presenza nuda/aka What the Peeper Saw)

(1971, GB/It/WGer/Sp, 89 min)
d James Kelly. *p* Graham Harris. *sc* Trevor Preston. *ph* Luis Cuadrado, Harry Waxman. *ed* Nicholas Wentworth. *m* Stelvio Cipriani. *cast* Mark Lester, Britt Ekland, Hardy Krüger, Lilli Palmer, Harry Andrews, Conchita Montez.
● The sight of kids in adult situations is unfailingly embarrassing, and *Night Hair Child* (whatever that means) is no exception. In it Mark Lester plays a 12-year-old voyeur who touches up Britt Ekland, and later joins her for some purpose or other (even he seems uncertain) between the sheets. Everyone involved blunders along, seemingly unaware of the sensitivity necessary to develop this story of a young newlywed who finds that she is living in the same house as a pubescent sex maniac, who may also be plotting to murder her. The casting is crazy, with Ekland hardly the actress for this sort of thing; and the script meanders all over the place, with a long psychiatric interview and a dream sequence seemingly interpolated just for the hell of it, before finally falling to bits. Still, at least Lester gets his deserts, the little brat. (Andrea Bianchi is credited as director on foreign language versions.) DMcG

Night Has a Thousand Eyes

(1948, US, 81 min, b/w)
d John Farrow. *p* Endre Bohem. *sc* Barré Lyndon, Jonathan Latimer. *ph* John F Seitz. *ed* Eda Warren. *ad* Hans Dreier, Franz Bachelin. *m* Victor Young. *cast* Edward G Robinson, Gail Russell, John Lund, Virginia Bruce, William Demarest, Jerome Cowan, John Alexander.
● Aside from the fine opening sequence – Lund's rescue of Gail Russell from the brink of suicide, and discovery of her mortal terror of the stars – a disappointing adaptation of Cornell Woolrich's superb novel, which is systematically emasculated and stripped of its darkly obsessional drive. On its own more conventional level, though, a reasonably gripping psychological thriller, with a fine performance from Edward G Robinson as a man haunted by his ability to foresee the future. Farrow makes it reasonably atmospheric (abetted by very fine camerawork from John F Seitz), but the script is marred by tiresome discussions as to whether extrasensory perception is rationally or scientifically accountable, and by a silly plot twist which allows for a (partly) happy ending. TM

Night Has Eyes, The (aka Terror House)

(1942, GB, 79 min, b/w)
d Leslie Arliss. *p* John F Argyle. *sc* Leslie Arliss. *ph* Günther Krampf. *ad* Duncan Sutherland. *m* Charles Williams. *cast* James Mason, Joyce Howard, Mary Clare, Wilfrid Lawson, Tucker McGuire, John Fernald.
● Mason is his usual interestingly ambivalent self as a shellshocked composer in this unremarkable but efficient little thriller (adapted from a novel by Alan Kennington) in which he plays host one dark and stormy night to a young woman (with whom he falls in love) searching for her missing friend, presumed murdered on the foggy Yorkshire Moors. No more than a question of did he or didn't he, but handled with gusto and some style. GA

Nighthawks

(1978, GB, 113 min)
d/p/sc Ron Peck, Paul Hallam. *ph* Joanna Davis. *ed* Richard Taylor, Mary Pat Leece. *ad* Jan Sendor. *m* David Graham Ellis. *cast* Ken Robertson, Tony Westrope, Rachel Nicholas James, Maureen Dolan, Stuart Craig Turton, Clive Peters, Derek Jarman.
● Undoubtedly worthy, Britain's first major gay movie is nevertheless often excruciatingly dull, and in many ways highly pessimistic. Dealing with a schoolteacher who cruises the discos endlessly but remains in the closet at work – until, that is, a revelatory discussion with his pupils – the film fails through its sluggish pace and awkward amateur performances. Worst of all, however, is that it presents its hero as such a miserable sod; anyone tempted toward his own sex would surely be deterred after watching Robertson's endlessly unsmiling face. GA

Nighthawks

(1981, US, 99 min)
d Bruce Malmuth. *p* Martin J Poll. *sc* David Shaber. *ph* James A Contner. *ed* Christopher Holmes, Stanford C Allen. *pd* Peter Larkin. *m* Keith Emerson. *cast* Sylvester Stallone, Billy Dee Williams, Rutger Hauer, Lindsay Wagner, Persis Khambatta, Nigel Davenport, Joe Spinell.
● A terrorist hijacking a cable car, even in New York, is a mildly ludicrous idea – were no 747s handy? The plot of *Nighthawks* makes no sense. Its thrills are strictly visual: the thriller as TV commercial? Stallone (the cop) gives a restrained performance for once, and Rutger Hauer (the terrorist) shows why he was to make it big in Hollywood. MB

Nighthawks II

see Strip Jack Naked

Night Holds Terror, The

(1955, US, 84 min, b/w)
d/p/sc Andrew L Stone. *ph* Fred Jackman Jr. *ed* Virginia Stone. *m* Lucien Calliet. *cast* Jack Kelly, Hildy Parks, Vince Edwards, John Cassavetes, David Cross, Edward Marr, Jack Kruschen, Joel Marston.

● Tense thriller, based on an actual incident, follows husband and wife Kelly and Parks as they're held hostage by a gang led by Edwards and an especially nasty Cassavetes. Low-key and unsensationalised, it takes an effective grip on the nerves and predates the likes of *In Cold Blood* by a decade or more. TJ

Night in Casablanca, A

(1946, US, 85 min, b/w)
d Archie L Mayo. *p* David L Loew. *sc* Joseph Fields, Roland Kibbee. *ph* James Van Trees. *ed* Gregg G Tallas, Grace Baughman. *pd* Duncan Cramer. *m* Werner Janssen. *cast* The Marx Brothers, Sig Ruman, Lisette Verea, Charles Drake, Lois Collier, Dan Seymour.

● 'I'm Beatrice Reiner, I stop at the hotel,' says Verea as the slinky spy; 'I'm Ronald Kornblow, I stop at nothing,' leers Groucho, manager of the said hotel in Casablanca mainly because previous incumbents have been mysteriously murdered. Independently produced, the Marx Brothers' penultimate vehicle is a vast improvement on their last four rapidly degenerating efforts for MGM. Lightweight, saddled with too much plot about spies and a hunt for hidden loot; but with Groucho enjoying a liberal supply of one-liners and Harpo very much at the heart of things, it is funny if hardly as subversive as their best work. Frank Tashlin contributed some of the brighter ideas, notably the opening gag of the building collapsing when Harpo obligingly stops leaning against it in response to a cop's enquiry as to whether he thinks he's holding it up, and the sequence in which all three Marxes delay spy-master Ruman's getaway by surreptitiously emptying his trunks as fast as he packs them. TM

Night in Havana: Dizzy Gillespie in Cuba, A

(1989, US, 84 min)
d John Holland. *with* Dizzy Gillespie.

● John Birks ('Dizzy') Gillespie, trumpeter, bebop confederate of Charlie Parker, champion of Afro-Cuban rhythms in the American jazz mainstream, in Cuba to headline Havana's Fifth International Jazz Festival, is filmed at official receptions (including an audience with Castro), walkabouts, interviews, rehearsals, jam sessions and in performance. The result is an entertaining mixture of documentary, travelogue, concert and historical music lesson. The last is fascinating, illustrating the difference in the development of rhythm in the Caribbean and South America and in the US (slaves shipped to South America and the Caribbean were allowed to keep their percussive instruments – their common 'language' – and those sold to the US were not). The music is a unifying thread. He plays 'A Night in Tunisia', duets with fast and flashy Cuban trumpeter Arturo Sandoval, rehearses a big band, finales with 'Manteca'. In view of the current hipness of Cuban music, a timely film. GBr

Night in the Life of Jimmy Reardon, A (aka Jimmy Reardon)

(1988, US, 93 min)
d William Richert. *p* Russell Schwartz. *sc* William Richert. *ph* John Connor. *ed* Suzanne Fenn. *pd* Norman Newberry. *m* Elmer Bernstein. *cast* River Phoenix, Ann Magnuson, Meredith Salenger, Ione Skye, Louanne, Matthew L Perry, Paul Koslo, Jane Hallaren.

● William (*Winter Kills*) Richert's rites of passage movie is based on a novel he wrote 20 years ago when he was 19. Set in Chicago in 1962, it's narrated by the eponymous hero (Phoenix), a socially-ambitious 17-year-old from the wrong side of the tracks, who models himself on Dean, Kerouac and Casanova. The film charts a crucial few days, between school and college, in which his boyhood illusions of a glittering campus career, and an idyllic romance with virginal Ivy Leaguer Salenger, succumb to a manly assumption of responsibility. The trouble starts when he is conned by an ex into paying for her abortion with money intended for college; then, planning to elope with Salenger, he falls foul of his own libido, bedding everyone from his best friend's girl to a divorcee acquaintance of his mother. While the film has the charm of rose-tinted retrospect and is often very funny, the pacing is wrong (it seems much longer than it is) and the sex scenes fail to convince. EP

Night into Morning

(1951, US, 86 min, b/w)
d Fletcher Markle. *p* Edwin H Knopf. *sc* Karl Tunberg, Leonard Spigelgass. *ph* George Folsey. *ed* George White, Robert Watts. *ad* Cedric Gibbons, James Basevi. *m* Carmen Dragon. *cast* Ray Milland, Nancy Davis, John Hodiak, Lewis Stone, Jean Hagen, Rosemary de Camp, Dawn Addams.

● A distant boom momentarily disturbs Professor Ainley's English class – in fact, the sound of a boiler exploding in the professor's house, killing his wife and son. The film charts the bereaved man's progress from bewildered rage to, finally, a sort of acceptance. Low key, naturalistic, never descending into melodrama, the film seems tangibly to embody somebody or other's – one of the writers? – lived experience. Despite a zero reputation and a scarcely thrilling cast and credits, this is well worth seeking out, a fine example of the offbeat stuff coming out of MGM during Dore Schary's too brief tenure. BBa

Night in Versailles, A

see Versailles rive gauche

Night Is Ending, The

see Paris After Dark

Night Is Young, The

see Mauvais Sang

Night Journey (Gece Yolculugu)

(1987, Tur, 107 min)
d Ömer Kavur. *cast* Aytaç Arman, Macit Koper, Zuhal Olcay, Sahika Tekand.

● Sombre (possibly cautionary) tale of a man's retreat from the world. Director Ali and his writer scout locations for their next feature. They find the perfect set, an archaic ghost town abandoned in 1923, whereupon Ali, already feeling uncommunicative, is so struck by the forsaken buildings that he withdraws from the film project and moves in to the empty church with just a candle and his typewriter, to the bewilderment of everyone who knows him. The town's an arresting presence, but Ali's a real mystery. NB

Nightmare

(1942, US, 82 min, b/w)
d Tim Whelan. *p/sc* Dwight Taylor. *ph* George Barnes. *ed* Frank Gross. *ad* John Goodman, Martin Obzina. *m* Frank Skinner. *cast* Brian Donlevy, Diana Barrymore, Gavin Muir, Henry Daniell, Hans Conreid, Arthur Shields.

● Based on a story by Philip MacDonald, a cheap but reasonably effective little Universal thriller, with gambler Donlevy stumbling across a murder, getting involved with a girl (of course), and finding himself up against Nazi agents. George Barnes' photography of a Hollywoodian London is nicely atmospheric, while Daniell is as marvellously sour and sinister as ever. GA

Nightmare

(1956, US, 89 min, b/w)
d Maxwell Shane. *p* William C Thomas, Howard Pine. *sc* Maxwell Shane. *ph* Joseph Biroc. *ed* George A Gittens. *ad* F Paul Sylos. *m* Herschel Burke Gilbert. *cast* Edward G Robinson, Kevin McCarthy, Connie Russell, Virginia Christine, Rhys Williams, Gage Clarke, Marian Carr.

● Everyone knows the dream from which you wake up convinced you've committed a murder. Here Kevin McCarthy finds evidence that suggests the nightmare was in fact reality, and brings his detective brother-in-law (Robinson) in to investigate. McCarthy's good at paranoia – remember him in *Invasion of the Body Snatchers*? – and Robinson is as dependable as ever as the sleuth. The story is by Cornell Woolrich, and the superb *noir* atmosphere is the work of cinematographer Joseph Biroc. A jumpy jazz score by Herschel Burke tightens the strings on this taut little thriller. Shane had nevertheless filmed the same story before, to greater effect, as a 1947 cheapie, *Fear in the Night*. MA

Nightmare

(1963, GB, 82 min, b/w)
d Freddie Francis. *p/sc* Jimmy Sangster. *ph* John Wilcox. *ed* James Needs. *pd* Bernard Robinson. *m* Don Banks. *cast* David Knight, Moira Redmond, Jennie Linden, Brenda Bruce, George A Cooper, Irene Richmond, John Welsh, Clytie Jessop.

● The fourth of Hammer's psychological thrillers, made to capitalise on the success of films like *Psycho* and *Les Diaboliques*. It is one of Freddie Francis' most imaginative films, making the most of a patchy Jimmy Sangster script. Knight (a faceless Hammer lead) is the suspect hero, and Linden the tormented young heroine haunted by the fear of hereditary insanity who, as the film begins, is plagued by a recurring nightmare in which her mother lures her into a mental asylum. Normally the Hammer psychological strain has a disconcertingly contemporary tone, but here the apparatus (who is trying to drive the girl out of her mind?) is truly Gothic: old country house, absent guardian, white phantom, etc. DP

Nightmare Alley

(1947, US, 111 min, b/w)
d Edmund Goulding. *p* George Jessel. *sc* Jules Furthman. *ph* Lee Garmes. *ed* Barbara McLean. *ad* Lyle R Wheeler, J Russell Spencer. *m* Cyril J Mockridge. *cast* Tyrone Power, Joan Blondell, Colleen Gray, Helen Walker, Mike Mazurki, Taylor Holmes, Ian Keith, James Flavin.

● Though perhaps it tries too hard to be 'respectable' and downplays its tawdry trash vulgarity a little too much (the film is tough, but William Lindsay Gresham's superb novel is even tougher), this is still a mean, moody, and well-nigh magnificent melodrama. Power excels as the hick fairground huckster who rises to society celebrity as a fake spiritualist, only to have fickle fortune arc him back to the midway as the boozed-up, live-chicken-eating geek. Blondell, Gray and the strange Helen Walker are the women he uses/abuses to grease his path. Lee Garmes' camerawork, Jules Furthman's script, and Goulding's direction make this one of the most oddball and enduring of the decade's Hollywood highspots. CW

Nightmare Before Christmas, The (aka Tim Burton's The Nightmare Before Christmas)

(1993, US, 76 min)
d Henry Selick. *p* Tim Burton, Denise Di Novi. *sc* Caroline Thompson. *ph* Pete Kozachik. *ed* Stan Webb. *ad* Deane Taylor. *m* Danny Elfman. *cast* voices: Danny Elfman, Chris Sarandon, Catherine O'Hara, William Hickey, Glenn Shadix.

● A treat from Hollywood's most unlikely Midas: an original fairy tale, screenplay by Caroline Thompson from a story and characters created by Tim Burton, adapted by Michael McDowell and told in stop-motion animation with a lively score by Danny Elfman. Jack Skellington, the Pumpkin King, is bored with his annual Halloween triumph. A chance visit to nearby Christmastown gives him an idea: he and his spooky friends will stand in for Santa this Christmas! This beautifully realised confection will delight grown-ups of all ages. TCh

Nightmare on Elm Street, A

(1984, US, 91 min)
d Wes Craven. *p* Robert Shaye. *sc* Wes Craven. *ph* Jacques Haitkin. *ed* Rick Shaine. *pd* Greg Fonseca. *m* Charles Bernstein. *cast* John Saxon, Ronee Blakley, Heather Langenkamp, Amanda Wyss, Nick Corri, Johnny Depp, Robert Englund, Charles Fleischer.

● The Elm Street kids are having the same bad dream in which a malicious bogeyman in a stripey jumper with a hideously scarred face is terrorising them with knives attached to his fingers. The dream becomes reality when Tina (Wyss) is cut to ribbons in the locked bedroom she's sharing with boyfriend Rod (Corri). Nancy (Langenkamp) sets out to discover the truth by trying to draw the bogeyman out of the dream. Hard though it is to divorce the image of Fred Krueger (Englund) from the farrago of a franchise that we now know was to follow, there are some genuinely frightening dream sequences – and some throwaway black humour. 'It's dreadful up there. You need a mop,' advises a cop after the fountain-of-blood scene in Glen's (Depp's) bedroom. The subtext wanders around a bit – one minute Krueger is a Christlike figure, the next he's a boyfriend substitute – but it's all good scary fun. NRo

Nightmare on Elm Street Part 2: Freddy's Revenge, A

(1985, US, 85 min)
d Jack Sholder. *p* Robert Shaye. *sc* David Chaskin. *ph* Jacques Haitkin. *ed* Arline Garson. *pd* Clifford Searcy. *m* Christopher Young. *cast* Mark Patton, Kim Myers, Robert Rusler, Clu Gulager, Hope Lange, Marshall Bell, Robert Englund.

● An adequate follow-up, although Freddy the freak's claw-flexing is nowhere near as gory. This time he possesses the body of young Jesse Walsh (Patton), a lad who moves into that house five years on from the earlier killings. The plotline has more holes than a tea bag, and is essentially no more than an excuse for a series of well executed special effects. Nevertheless, the film hangs reasonably well together, not least because of good performances from all concerned. DPe

Nightmare on Elm Street 3: Dream Warriors, A

(1987, US, 96 min)
d Chuck Russell. *p* Robert Shaye. *sc* Wes Craven, Bruce Wagner, Chuck Russell, Frank Darabont. *ph* Roy H Wagner. *ed* Terry Stokes, Chuck Weiss. *ad* Mick Strawn, CJ Strawn. *m* Angelo Badalamenti. *cast* Heather Langenkamp, Patricia Arquette, Larry Fishburne, Priscilla Pointer, Craig Wasson, Brooke Bundy, John Saxon, Robert Englund.

● This time, Old Pizza Face terrorises a bunch of 'sleep-disturbed' kids whose doctors believe they share a group delusion. Langenkamp, heroine of the original film and now a specialist in dream disorders, helps sceptical psychiatrist Wasson wake up to the truth. A particularly nice touch is the ability of one of the teenagers to pull people into her dreams, allowing Langenkamp and the threatened kids to gang up against Freddie. The neat script also fills in a little more of the Freddie mythology, including a suitably tasteless account of his conception. A creepy score and Russell's sure grasp of the skewed logic of nightmares helps to sustain the ambiguity between the 'real' and 'dream' worlds, while Englund's Freddie now fits like a glove. NF

Nightmare on Elm Street, 4: The Dream Master, A

(1988, US, 93 min)
d Renny Harlin. *p* Robert Shaye, Rachel Talalay. *sc* Brian Helgeland, Scott Pierce. *ph* Steven Fierberg. *ed* Michael N Knue, Jack Weiss. *pd* Mick Strawn, CJ Strawn. *m* Craig Safan. *cast* Robert Englund, Rodney Eastman, Danny Hassel, Andras Jones, Tuesday Knight, Toy Newkirtk, Lisa Wilcox.

● The dislocated nightmare logic of Wes Craven's original has now been reduced to a black comic carnival ride designed to showcase cult-hero Freddy's stand-up act and some variable special effects. Before that, the negligible script has to explain how Old Pizza Face can extend his stalking-ground to a new generation of kids. In brief, he reaches out into the darkness to embrace shy, teenage Alice (Wilcox) who, once tainted by her knowledge of Freddy's existence, unwittingly forms a link between the two generations. There are a few genuinely inspired moments – notably the Roach Motel joke, and the extraordinary body-ripping climax. But while some of the monotonous effects are strikingly surreal, Harlin's direction creates an atmosphere which is more morbid than scary. NF

Nightmare on Elm Street 5: The Dream Child, A

(1989, US, 89 min)
d Stephen Hopkins. *p* Robert Shaye, Rupert Harvey. *sc* Leslie Bohem. *ph* Peter Levy. *ed* Chuck Weiss, Brent Schoenfeld. *pd* CJ Strawn. *m* Jay Ferguson. *cast* Robert Englund, Lisa Wilcox, Kelly Jo Minter, Danny Hassel, Erika Anderson, Nick Mele, Whitby Hertford.

● A flimsily plotted but visually impressive addition to the endless Freddy Krueger saga, with an unsavoury gynaecological flavour. Teenage Alice (Wilcox) is terrorised by a reborn Freddy (Englund), who is attempting to massacre her Springwood High chums by stalking them through the dreams of Alice's unborn child. Retreading old ground, the chaotic storyline flashes back to the now legendary rape of Amanda Krueger by a throng of maniacs, and the subsequent birth of Old Pizza Face. 'It's a breech-birth…It's backwards!' screams a nurse as a frog-legged Freddy foetus (courtesy David Miller) hightails it out of the womb. Later, director Hopkins goes one step further and takes us *inside* Alice's womb, where her unborn child is being fed the souls of Krueger's victims by a flesh-faced Freddy, functioning as a decidedly suspect intrauterine device. The rest is a series of disjointed but nevertheless diverting special effects set pieces. Leslie Bohem's script dishes up the requisite helping of one-liners, and all the usual quasi-religious mythical tosh is present and correct. MK

Nightmares

(1983, US, 99 min)
d Joseph Sargent. *p* Christopher Crowe. *sc* (ep 1, 2, 3) Christopher Crowe, (ep 4) Jeffrey Bloom. *ph* (ep 1, 2) Gerald Perry Finnerman, (ep 3, 4) Marie Di Leo. *ed* Roy Stephens, Michael Brown. *pd* Dean Edward Mitzner. *m* Craig Safan, X, Black Flag, Rik L Rik, Fear. *cast* Cristina Raines, Emilio Estevez, Lance Henriksen, Richard Masur, Veronica Cartwright, Moon Zappa.

● A portmanteau of four stories, three of them scripted by Christopher Crowe, the fourth by Jeffrey Bloom, hopefully in the *Twilight Zone* manner. The best of them has Emilio Estevez as a computer whizkid, obsessed with a space combat game, who finds himself engaged in a real battle that alarmingly ends in another world. Here Sargent makes effectively febrile use of the bustling activity of the arcades and the rock pouring from the hero's walkman in counterpoint to the video game imagery. In general, though, the scripting is unimaginative, derivative, and desperately predictable as the film limps through its jokily cautionary tales of a housewife who narrowly escapes a homicidal maniac when she insists on a late-night shopping trip because she's out of cigarettes, a priest restored to his faith and duty by an encounter with a demonic car, and a suburban family busy exterminating rats who find themselves confronted by a monster looking for its baby. TM

'Night, Mother

(1986, US, 96 min)
d Tom Moore. *p* Aaron Spelling, Alan Greisman. *sc* Marsha Norman. *ph* Stephen M Katz. *ed* Suzanne Pettit. *pd* Jack De Govia. *m* David Shire. *cast* Anne Bancroft, Sissy Spacek, Ed Berke, Carol Robbins.

● Overwrought adaptation by Marsha Norman of her own Pulitzer Prize-winning play which fails to make the most of its leading ladies. Bancroft in her familiar role as the long-suffering mother is dignified, severe and utterly humourless, and her character sets the movie's tone. Spacek likewise seems a little self-important as her suicidal middle-aged daughter. Director Moore presumably thought his main task was simply to provide a platform for his bravura stars. Unfortunately, by plumping for an inert shooting style, he leaves the actresses looking smug and stolid. GM

Night Moves

(1975, US, 99 min)
d Arthur Penn. *p* Robert M Sherman. *sc* Alan Sharp. *ph* Bruce Surtees. *ed* Dede Allen. *pd* George Jenkins. *m* Michael Small. *cast* Gene Hackman, Jennifer Warren, Edward Binns, Harris Yulin, Kenneth Mars, Janet Ward, James Woods, Anthony Costello, John Crawford, Melanie Griffith, Susan Clark.

● A truly enigmatic thriller and a key film of the '70s, brilliantly scripted by Alan Sharp. Hackman is the private eye torn apart from within, unable to come to terms either with his father or his errant wife, but doggedly, almost pointlessly, pursuing a wayward daughter for an equally wayward mother. Sharp's elusive, fragmented script precisely catches the post-Watergate mood, while Penn's direction brilliantly parallels the interior/exterior investigation. A very pessimistic film, it ends exactly at the moment that Hackman understands what has happened but can do nothing about it. Essential viewing. PH

Night Must Fall

(1937, US, 116 min, b/w)
d Richard Thorpe. *p* Hunt Stromberg. *sc* John Van Druten. *ph* Ray June. *ed* Robert J Kern. *ad* Cedric Gibbons. *m* Edward Ward. *cast* Robert Montgomery, Rosalind Russell, Dame May Whitty, Alan Marshal, Kathleen Harrison, EE Clive, Beryl Mercer.

● Montgomery, skilfully suggesting a sickly veneer that belies his matinée idol charm, is surprisingly effective as the psychopathic pageboy with a hat-box in which he treasures the grisly trophies of his penchant for decapitation. The trouble with Emlyn Williams' stage play is that, having established Danny's character and the basic situation – Danny closeted with the rich old lady he wants as his next victim (Whitty, wonderfully skittish and foolish), and the frustrated young companion who wants *him* (Russell, miscast) – it resorts to pure melodramatic contrivance. The creakiness is exacerbated in this barely opened-out adaptation, with a series of stagy exits and entrances conveniently helping the plot along, but frittering away what tension there is as the consummation of Danny's desire is forever delayed while the police bumble absurdly and Russell agonises as she realises the truth. TM

Night Must Fall

(1964, GB, 101 min, b/w)
d Karel Reisz. *p* Albert Finney, Karel Reisz. *sc* Clive Exton. *ph* Freddie Francis. *ed* Fergus McDonell, Philip Barnikel. *pd* Timothy O'Brien. *m* Ron Grainer. *cast* Albert Finney, Mona Washbourne, Susan Hampshire, Sheila Hancock, Michael Medwin, Martin Wyldeck, Joe Gladwin.

● Mindful, perhaps, of the way a straightforward approach exposed the limitations of Emlyn Williams' play in 1937, this adaptation by Clive Exton and Reisz not only adds a good deal of flummery psychological detail, but abandons the narrative approach in favour of a choppy, static style, with jagged direct cuts between scenes and the emphasis often on close-ups of heads awkwardly (symbolically ?) poised at the edge of the screen. The idea, it seems, is to evoke the *aura* of the psychopath rather than the narrative excitements of his story. But with old-fashioned cross-cutting coming back with a vengeance to provide some suspense for the climax, nothing really hangs together. Finney brings off a few memorable moments (notably a hypnotically horrible little ritual with the hatbox), but the one unqualified success of the film is Freddie Francis' dreamy yet diamond-sharp camerawork. TM

Night My Number Came Up, The

(1955, GB, 94 min)
d Leslie Norman. *p* Michael Balcon. *sc* RC Sherriff. *ph* Lionel Banes. *ed* Peter Tanner. *ad* Jim Morahan. *m* Malcolm Arnold. *cast* Michael Redgrave, Alexander Knox, Sheila Sim, Denholm Elliott, Ursula Jeans, Michael Hordern, Nigel Stock, Bill Kerr, Alfie Bass, Victor Maddern.

● RC Sherriff turned a newspaper article by Air Marshal Sir Victor Goddard (a leading spiritualist and communicator with the Other Side) into this suspenseful Ealing aerial drama. Redgrave grows progressively more uptight on a long-haul flight to Japan as events in a nightmare he's experienced begin to come true. Clever plot construction, a plane-load of top British thesps, and smooth handling from director Leslie Norman (Barry's dad) all give good value. TJ

Night Nurse

(1931, US, 72 min, b/w)
d William Wellman. *sc* Oliver HP Garrett, Charles Kenyon. *ph* Barney McGill. *ed* Edward M McDermott. *ad* Max Parker. *cast* Barbara Stanwyck, Ben Lyon, Joan Blondell, Clark Gable, Charlotte Merriam, Charles Winninger, Blanche Frederici.

● A wonderfully pacy thriller, with sparkling dialogue, a nice line in blackish humour, an undertow of pre-Hays Code eroticism, and

Stanwyck in full-hard-bitten cry as a nurse foiling a plot to kill two little girls for their inheritance. With neither she nor Gable (in support as a villainous chauffeur; Lyon makes little impact as the nominal hero) worrying about niceties of image, it's tough, taut and fun. TM

Night of Counting the Years, The (El Mumia)

(1969, UAR, 102 min)
d/sc Shadi Abdelsalam. *ph* Abdel Aziz Fahmy. *ed* Kamal Abou El Ella. *ad* Salah Marei. *m* Mario Nascimbene. *cast* Ahmed Marei, Zouzou El Hakim, Ahmad Hegazi, Nadia Loutfy, Gaby Karraz.
●An impressive directorial debut by ex-art director Shadi Abdelsalam, *The Night of Counting the Years* is an examination of cultural imperialism in reverse: instead of selling Coca-Cola to Egypt, Western merchants are stealing rarities from Egyptian tombs. At first posed in moral terms – should the new chief of an Egyptian tribe allow his people to earn money by selling the antiquities from 'officially' undiscovered tombs, or stop the trade at the cost of stopping the flow of money to his poverty-stricken people – the film develops into a study of the importance of defending the past from would-be cultural exploiters. Slow-moving but absorbing, and quite beautifully shot. PH

Night of San Juan, The

see Coraje del Pueblo, El

Night of San Lorenzo, The (La Notte di San Lorenzo)

(1981, It, 107 min)
d Paolo Taviani, Vittorio Taviani. *p* Giuliani G De Negri. *sc* Paolo Taviani, Vittorio Taviani. *ph* Franco Di Giacomo. *ed* Roberto Perpignani. *ad* Gianni Sbarra. *m* Nicola Piovani. *cast* Omero Antonutti, Margarita Lozano, Claudio Bigagli, Massimo Bonetti, Norma Martelli, Enrica Maria Modugno.
●On the Night of San Lorenzo, the night of falling stars when wishes come true, a woman recalls for her loved one another such night long ago, when a group of peasants fled the Nazis through the Tuscan countryside and exploding shells shot through the sky instead of stars. The Taviani brothers have transformed this story from their own childhood into a collective epic handed down orally through the decades, but wildly embellished in the re-telling. It's at once more ambitious in its sweep and more Utopian than their previous *Padre Padrone*, more romantic in its desire to recapture a lost, breathless intensity of experience. SJo

Night of the Big Heat (aka Island of the Burning Damned

(1967, GB, 94 min)
d Terence Fisher. *p* Tom Blakeley. *sc* Ronald C Liles. *ph* Reginald Wyer. *ed* Rod Keys. *ad* Alex Vetchinsky. *m* Malcolm Lockyer. *cast* Christopher Lee, Peter Cushing, Patrick Allen, Sarah Lawson, Jane Merrow, William Lucas, Kenneth Cope.
●Hammer mainstay Terence Fisher made three movies for the cheapjack Planet outfit of which this (from a sci-fi novel by John Lymington) was the last. It's mighty hot for winter on the small island of Fara where scientist Lee has rigged up a lab in the security of the White Swan hotel. He believes the heat's caused by energy starved aliens. Cushing, the local doctor, is frazzled to death. Dynamite proves ineffective against the invaders, but as all seems lost a saving thunderstorm breaks. Even less exciting than it sounds. TJ

Night of the Comet

(1984, US, 95 min)
d Thom Eberhardt. *p* Andrew Lane, Wayne Crawford. *sc* Thom Eberhardt. *ph* Arthur Albert. *ed* Fred Stafford. *pd* John Muto. *m* David Richard Campbell. *cast* Robert Beltran, Catherine Mary Stewart, Kelli Maroney, Sharon Farrell, Mary Woronov, Geoffrey Lewis, Peter Fox.
●A passing comet turns almost everyone in LA into piles of red dust. Survivors include a pair of cheerleaders who respond to the end of the world by shopping for disco clothes in a disco-free town. But these girls can handle the occasional zombie – another comet-related effect – with automatic weapons and karate moves. Meanwhile very camp scientists emerge from their low-budget bunker to reveal that the turn-to-dust thing is accelerating and they need to drain the blood of uncontaminated survivors. Suspecting that all this plus the cheerleaders might fail to excite, the film-makers also pack in twenty songs. DO

Night of the Creeps

(1986, US, 88 min)
d Fred Dekker. *p* Charles Gordon. *sc* Fred Dekker. *ph* Robert C New. *ed* Michael N Knue. *pd* George Costello. *m* Barry DeVorzon. *cast* Jason Lively, Steve Marshall, Jill Whitlow, Tom Atkins, Wally Taylor, Bruce Solomon.
●Egged on by frat house jock Brad, nerds Chris and JC thaw out the freeze-dried body of a guy who got 'slugged' back in 1959. Meanwhile, the axe-man who offed his girlfriend on the same night comes up through the floorboards and starts cutting people down to size. The careworn cop on the case thinks he's Hammett, the kids just ham it. Neither Dekker's sloppy direction nor the cheapo make-up and effects do justice to the hand-me-down but sporadically lively script. Not the most sophisticated or scary horror film of the year, perhaps, but enjoyable enough in a ramshackle sort of way. NF

Night of the Demon (aka Curse of the Demon)

(1957, GB, 82 min, b/w)
d Jacques Tourneur. *p* Frank Bevis, Hal E Chester. *sc* Charles Bennett, Hal E Chester. *ph* Ted Scaife. *ed* Michael S Gordon. *pd* Ken Adam. *m* Clifton Parker. *cast* Dana Andrews, Peggy Cummins, Niall MacGinnis, Maurice Denham, Athene Seyler, Liam Redmond, Reginald Beckwith.
●One of the finest thrillers made in England during the '50s, despite the fact that the final cut was tampered with against the director's wishes. Tourneur had used MR James's short story *Casting the Runes* as the basis for a marvellous cinematic dialogue between belief and scepticism, fantasy and reality. His intrepid rational hero (Andrews) is a modern scientist who is gradually persuaded that his life is threatened by a black magician. The director employed a number of e normously skilful devices to ensure that the audience experiences the hero's transition from confident scepticism to panic, and the process is observed with such subtlety that, in the original version at least, the interpretation of the plot was left open (i.e. the hero may simply be the victim of a conspiracy and/or his own imagination). The producer decided that the film lacked substance (in fact it was far more terrifying than most horror films), and added special effects of the 'demon' very near the beginning, which of course missed the whole point of what Tourneur had been attempting. Even so, the rest is so good that the film remains immensely gripping, with certain sequences (like the one where Andrews is chased through the wood) reaching poetic dimensions. DP

Night of the Demons

(1988, US, 89 min)
d Kevin S Tenney. *p* Joe Augustyn, Jeff Geoffray, Walter Josten. *sc* Joe Augustyn. *ph* David Lewis. *ed* Daniel Duncan. *ad* Ken Aichele. *m* Dennis Michael Tenney. *cast* Lance Fenton, Cathy Podewell, Alvin Alexis, Hal Havins, Mimi Kinkade, Linnea Quigley.
●A gang of thoroughly objectionable teenagers party Halloween away in a haunted house. Some of them get possessed by evil spirits, and the frequent foulness of language is then replaced by nastiness of a different sort. A girl dances around a room with a bodiless arm clamped to her ankle (severed while a couple copulate in a coffin); a boy gets his eyes squished out by the bimbo who's putting him up; but the best bit is when a somewhat distraught young lady pushes her lipstick *inside* her left breast. You feel for her. MS

Night of the Eagle (aka Burn, Witch, Burn!)

(1961, GB, 87 min, b/w)
d Sidney Hayers. *p* Albert Fennell. *sc* Charles Beaumont, Richard Matheson, George Baxt. *ph* Reginald Wyer. *ed* Ralph Sheldon. *ad* Jack Shampan. *m* William Alwyn. *cast* Janet Blair, Peter Wyngarde, Margaret Johnston, Kathleen Byron, Anthony Nicholls, Colin Gordon, Reginald Beckwith, Norman Bird.
●Made on a comparatively low budget and adapted from Fritz Leiber's novel *Conjure Wife*, this is about a hardheaded psychology lecturer in a provincial university who gradually discovers that his wife Tanzie and some of his closest colleagues are practising witchcraft (in furtherance of campus politics). From the opening sequences in which Tanzie (Blair) scrambles frantically round her house searching for a witch-doll left by one of the faculty wives, the whole thing takes off into a kind of joyous amalgam of *Rosemary's Baby* and *Who's Afraid of Virginia Woolf?* There are one or two irritations in the phony Americanised look of the college students, and in the miscasting of Janet Blair; but Sidney Hayers shoots the whole thing with an almost Wellesian flourish, and the script (by Charles Beaumont and Richard Matheson) is structured with incredible tightness as the sane, rational outlook of the hero (Wyngarde) is gradually dislocated by the world of madness and dreams. DP

Night of the Following Day, The

(1968, US, 93 min)
d/p Hubert Cornfield. *sc* Hubert Cornfield, Rodney Phippeny. *ph* Willy Kurant. *ed* Anne Vogler. *ad* Jean Boulet. *m* Stanley Myers. *cast* Marlon Brando, Richard Boone, Rita Moreno, Pamela Franklin, Jess Hahn, Gérard Buhr, Al Lettieri.
●Cornfield is one of the more enigmatic filmmakers of post-war Hollywood, an industry insider from an early age, whose occasional movies are quirky, innovative and well worthseeking out. This one is a gripping account of a kidnapping that goes wrong, and the script takes its dreamlike narrative structure from – of all things – Ealing's *Dead of Night*. Its other major asset is an expert cast, with Brando giving one of his most gutsy, enjoyable, least mannered performances of the '60s, and Boone outstanding as a sadistic thug. DP

Night of the Generals, The

(1966, GB/Fr, 147 min)
d Anatole Litvak. *p* Sam Spiegel. *sc* Joseph Kessel, Paul Dehn. *ph* Henri Decae. *ed* Alan Osbiston. *pd* Alexandre Trauner. *m* Maurice Jarre. *cast* Peter O'Toole, Omar Sharif, Tom Courtenay, Donald Pleasence, Joanna Pettet, Philippe Noiret, Charles Gray, Coral Browne, Harry Andrews, Christopher Plummer, JulietteGréco.
●Outraged Nazi general to German major: 'Are you wearing perfume?' 'I occasionally wear a light after-shave, sir.' O'Toole and Sharif utter lines like these with absolutely straight faces in what is ostensibly about the generals' plot to assassinate Hitler. There's also a subplot involving a prostitute murderer (quite obviously O'Toole, since he's nutty as a fruitcake). O'Toole's performance is as over the top as it was in *The Ruling Class*, but this film (also an analysis of the elite) is far funnier since it takes itself so seriously. Ignore the plot, just revel in the clichés. (From the novel by Hans Helmuth Kirst.) CPe

Night of the Ghouls (aka Revenge of the Dead)

(1959, US, 69 min, b/w)
d/p/sc Edward D Wood Jr. *ph* William C Thompson. *ad* Kathleen O'Hara Everett. *cast* Criswell, Tor Johnson, Keene Duncan, Valda Hansen, Maila 'Vampira' Nurmi, Duke Moore, John Carpenter.
●If you thought cult 'artiste' Edward D Wood Jr's ironically celebrated astro-turkey *Plan 9 from Outer Space* was transcendently awful, you'd better brace yourself for this, deemed too shambolic to unleash on unsuspecting cinema audiences. Scenery-chewing psychic Criswell and majestically talentless ex-wrestler Johnson return in this no-budget farrago about a fake medium unwittingly resurrecting the dead. Expect yet more of the 'neo-Brechtian panache' (i.e. complete technical incompetence) that secured Wood his rep as the very worst of the worst. TJ

Night of the Hunter, The

(1955, US, 92 min, b/w)
d Charles Laughton. *p* Paul Gregory. *sc* James Agee. *ph* Stanley Cortez. *ed* Robert Golden. *ad* Hilyard Brown. *m* Walter Schumann. *cast* Robert Mitchum, Lillian Gish, Shelley Winters, Billy Chapin, James Gleason, Sally Ann Bruce, Peter Graves, Evelyn Varden.

● Laughton's only stab at directing, with Mitchum as the psychopathic preacher with 'LOVE' and 'HATE' tattooed on his knuckles, turned out to be a genuine weirdie. Set in '30s rural America, the film polarises into a struggle between good and evil for the souls of innocent children. Everyone's contribution is equally important. Laughton's deliberately old-fashioned direction throws up a startling array of images: an amalgam of Mark Twain-like exteriors (idyllic riverside life) and expressionist interiors, full of moody nighttime shadows. The style reaches its pitch in the extraordinary moonlight flight of the two children downriver, gliding silently in the distance, watched over by animals seen in huge close-up, filling up the foreground of the screen. James Agee's script (faithfully translating Davis Grubb's novel) treads a tight path between humour (it's a surprisingly light film in many ways) and straight suspense, a combination best realised when Gish sits the night out on the porch waiting for Mitchum to attack, and they both sing 'Leaning on the Everlasting Arms' to themselves. Finally, there's the absolute authority of Mitchum's performance – easy, charming, infinitely sinister. CPe

Night of the Iguana, The

(1964, US, 118 min, b/w)
d John Huston. *p* Ray Stark. *sc* Anthony Veiller, John Huston. *ph* Gabriel Figueroa. *ed* Ralph Kemplen. *ad* Stephen Grimes. *m* Benjamin Frankel. *cast* Richard Burton, Ava Gardner, Deborah Kerr, Sue Lyon, Skip Ward, Grayson Hall, Cyril Delevanti, Mary Boylan.

● Films of Tennessee Williams' plays now often look very artificial and overwrought, but with this Huston came up with one of the best. Williams is treated with respect rather than reverence, and Huston injects his own sly humour. The film, which perambulates around Burton as the clergyman turned travel courier after a sex scandal, and the effects of his various crises of faith on the coachload of women teachers he is escorting (with assorted provocations from Lyon's nymphet, Gardner's blowsy hotel proprietor, Kerr's artist) is all the more interesting in the light of *Wise Blood*, Huston's later descent into the maelstrom of religious obsessions. PH

Night of the Lepus

(1972, US, 88 min)
d William F Claxton. *p* AC Lyles. *sc* Don Holliday, Gene R Kearney. *ph* Ted Voigtlander. *ed* John McSweeney. *pd* Stan Jolley. *m* Jimmie Haskell. *cast* Stuart Whitman, Janet Leigh, Rory Calhoun, DeForest Kelley, Paul Fix, Melanie Fullerton, Henry Wills, Robert Hardy.

● The countryside is being terrorised by packs of giant man-eating – well, rabbits actually. Who thought this one up? Step forward Russell Braddon, Aussie author of *Year of the Angry Rabbit*, which producer AC Lyles recklessly decided to turn into a movie. The Lyles policy (see his numerous B-Westerns) of packing the cast with fading middle-aged stars has a certain gloomy fascination, as does the whole idea of rampaging bunnies emitting leopard-like growls as they bound along in slow-motion, intent on devouring the likes of DeForest Kelley. Impossible not to admire the total withholding of irony in Claxton's approach to this kamikaze project. BBa

Night of the Living Dead

(1968, US, 96 min, b/w)
d George A Romero. *p* Russell Streiner, Karl Hardman. *sc* John A Russo. *ph* George A Romero. *cast* Judith O'Dea, Duane Jones, Karl Hardman, Keith Wayne, Judith Ridley, Marilyn Eastman, Russell Streiner.

● With its radical rewriting of a genre in which good had always triumphed over evil, Romero's first feature shattered the conventions of horror and paved the way for the subversive visions of directors like David Cronenberg, Tobe Hooper and Sam Raimi. The film's opening scene immediately signals its own subversiveness. In broad daylight, a brother and sister visit their father's grave; seeing a tall man lumbering towards them, Johnny tries to frighten Barbara with a daft Boris Karloff impersonation; suddenly the figure lurches forward and kills him. With the presumed hero dead within the first few minutes, the inexorable logic of the modern 'nightmare movie' is set in motion, and from this moment on the terror never lets up. Together with a small group of fellow survivors, Barbara holes up in a nearby farmhouse, besieged by an ever-swelling tide of flesh-eating zombies. Trapped inside the house, they fight for their lives, but nothing works out as it should; whenever it seems there might be a glimmer of hope, Romero cruelly reverses our expectations. The nihilistic ending, in particular, has to be seen to be believed. Chuckle, if you can, during the first few minutes; because after that laughter catches in the throat as the clammy hand of terror tightens its grip. NF

Night of the Living Dead

(1990, US, 96 min)
d Tom Savini. *p* John A Russo, Russell Streiner. *sc* George A Romero. *ph* Frank Prinzi. *ed* Tom Dubensky. *pd* Cletus R Anderson. *m* Paul McCollough. *cast* Tony Todd, Patricia Tallman, Tom Towles, McKee Anderson, William Butler, Katie Finnerman.

● This surprisingly successful colour remake of George Romero's seminal zombie movie, scripted by Romero himself and directed by make-up effects man Savini, uses the audience's familiarity with the original to indulge, frustrate and subvert its expectations. Savini himself has said: 'It's not a remake so much as retelling… There are lots of twists and turns that aren't in the original. And, in a way, it's almost a sequel: sixty minutes into this movie you're getting, in a way, another film.' Yet despite its knowingness, there is genuine horror here, as a party of terrified survivors are trapped in a remote country house by a relentless horde of flesh-eating zombies. NF

Night of the Party, The

(1934, GB, 61 min, b/w)
d Michael Powell. *p* Jerome Jackson. *sc* Ralph Smart. *ph* Glen MacWilliams. *ad* Alfred Junge. *cast* Leslie Banks, Malcolm Keen, Jane Baxter, Ian Hunter, Ernest Thesiger, Viola Keats, Muriel Aked.

● 'The script was a stinker,' was Powell's justifiable comment in his autobiography. A whodunit in the most antiquated sub-Agatha Christie mode, it has a lecherous newspaper baron (Keen) try to blackmail an indiscreet girl (Keats), daughter of the Commissioner of Police (Banks), into submitting to his unwelcome attentions. During a game of 'Murder' at a society party, the lecher, unsurprisingly, is murdered. The routine expository labour of setting everybody up with a motive (there's even a sinister butler) is leavened by Powell's willingness to give the actors time and space; he makes a mini bravura triumph of the party sequence by shooting the 'Murder' game in darkness, with intermittent illumination by firelight and a flickering neon sign; and the final court scene, after the usual routine of police interrogation and politic confessions, is enlivened by a magnificently dotty performance from Ernest Thesiger at his most malignantly epicene. The end result is much more fun than it has any right to be. TM

Night on Earth

(1991, US, 129 min)
d/p/sc Jim Jarmusch. *ph* Frederick Elmes. *ed* Jay Rabinowitz. *m* Tom Waits. *cast* Winona Ryder, Gena Rowlands, Giancarlo Esposito, Armin Müller-Stahl, Rosie Perez, Isaach De Bankolé, Béatrice Dalle, Roberto Benigni, Paolo Bonacelli, Matti Pellonpää, Kari Väänänen.

● LA, 7.07 pm: chain-smoking Ryder gets movie agent Rowlands in the back of her cab, and inadvertently persuades her she'd be right for a role Rowlands is casting. At the very same time, taxi drivers across the world are also having seemingly inconsequential encounters with passengers: in New York, inept East German exile Müller-Stahl hands over the wheel to young black Esposito; in Paris, Ivory Coaster De Bankolé discusses sight and sex with blind, belligerent Dalle; in Rome, raving Benigni confesses a carnal past to priest Bonacelli; and in Helsinki, melancholy Pellonpää calms three drunks with a tale of infinite sadness. As ever with Jarmusch, as the five sequential stories proceed toward their unexpectedly poignant conclusion, there's a touch of the experimental at play; but it's also a film of great warmth. Character prevails throughout, and with the exception of a miscast Ryder, the performances are terrific. Though it may take a while to get Jarmusch's gist, hang in there; by the time Tom Waits growls his lovely closing waltz over the credits, Jarmusch has shown us moments most film-makers don't even notice. GA

Night on the Terrace (Noche en la Terraza)

(2001, Arg, 87 min)
d/p/sc Jorge Zima. *ph* Teddy Kearney. *ed* Miguel Sumaria. *m* Jorge Zima. *cast* Soledad Alloni, Diego Freigedo, Gabriel Fernandez.

● Stagnating couple in third-party crisis: a tired tale receives no new spin except for some early rooftop voyeurism. This is in itself suspect, given that Paula goes for the poetic calls and tapes of her mysterious admirer and throws her life into freefall. Feeling like a graduation film and lacking any real authority (the fact that it's shot on tape, while it shouldn't interfere, does underline this absence), it's well meaning and all involved are energetic enough, but it's underwritten and doesn't move beyond the initial premise. GE

Night on the Town, A

see Adventures in Babysitting

Night Passage

(1957, US, 90 min)
d James Neilson. *p* Aaron Rosenberg. *sc* Borden Chase. *ph* William H Daniels. *ed* Sherman Todd. *ad* Alexander Golitzen, Robert Clatworthy. *m* Dimitri Tiomkin. *songs* Ned Washington. *cast* James Stewart, Audie Murphy, Dan Duryea, Brandon de Wilde, Dianne Foster, Elaine Stewart, Jay C Flippen, Robert J Wilke.

● This minor (and obscurely titled) Stewart Western was to have been directed by Anthony Mann, who pulled out at the last minute because he felt Borden (*Winchester '73*) Chase's script wasn't up to scratch. Stewart plays a railroad worker who discovers that the robbers bent on stealing the payroll with which he has been entrusted are being led by his brother (Murphy). Neilson wades through the good brother/bad brother plot like an ox through mud, Stewart whiling away the time by playing accordion. NF

Night Paths (Wege in der Nacht)

(1979, WGer, 97 min)
d Krzysztof Zanussi. *p* Hartwig Schmidt. *sc* Krzysztof Zanussi. *ph* Witold Sobocinski. *ed* Liesgret Schmitt-Klink. *pd* Tadeusz Wybult, Wolfgang Schünke, Maciej Putowski. *m* Wojciech Kilar. *cast* Mathieu Carrière, Maja Komorowska, Horst Frank, Zbigniew Zapasiewicz, Irmgard Först, Diana Körner.

● Working for German TV in exile from his native Poland, Zanussi seems curiously uninvolved in this return to the well-worn theme of uneasy relationships between victor and vanquished during World War II. A Polish baroness (Komorowska), whose estate has been commandeered, at first resists the attentions of a young German officer (Carrière), then exploits them on behalf of the partisans. Mournfully attractive visually (the chateau, the lowering forest), but the conflict remains largely theoretical. TM

Night Porter, The (Il Portiere di Notte)

(1973, It, 118 min)
d Liliana Cavani. *p* Robert Gordon Edwards. *sc* Liliana Cavani, Italo Moscati. *ph* Alfio Contini. *ed* Franco Arcalli. *ad* Nedo Azzini, Jean-Marie Simon. *m* Danièle Paris. *cast* Dirk Bogarde, Charlotte Rampling, Philippe Leroy, Gabriele Ferzetti, Giuseppe Addobbati, Isa Miranda, Piero Vida, Nora Ricci.

● Like *Last Tango in Paris*, an operatic celebration of sexual disgust, set in 1957 in a Viennese hotel where Bogarde (maintaining a low profile as a porter) and Rampling (a guest while her conductor husband embarks on a concert tour) meet and recreate their former relationship as sadistic SS officer and child concentration camp inmate;

a sexuality that can only end in degradation and self-destruction. Somewhere along the way, the film's handling of serious themes, and its attempts to examine the Nazi legacy in terms of repression and guilt, both sexual and political, get lost amid all the self-conscious decadence. The English language version is terrible. CPe

Night Shift

(1982, US, 106 min)
d Ron Howard. *p* Brian Grazer. *sc* Lowell Ganz, Babaloo Mandel. *ph* James Crabe. *ed* Robert J Kern Jr, Daniel P Hanley, Mike Hill. *pd* Jack Collis. *m* Burt Bacharach. *cast* Henry Winkler, Michael Keaton, Shelley Long, Gina Hecht, Pat Corley, Bobby DiCicco, Nita Talbot, Clint Howard, Joe Spinell, Kevin Costner, Shanen Doherty.

● All credit to Howard, Winkler and co-writer Lowell Ganz for bucking their *Happy Days* TV formula to cast Winkler as a shy, sad sack Wall Street wizard who runs away from the pressures into a job as night attendant at the morgue. Very funny he is too, whether cosseting his pet rubber plant, fighting a running duel with a ferociously neighbourly dog, or trying to make love with a girlfriend whose neuroses make coitus interruptus a way of life. Even brighter is his odd couple pairing with Michael Keaton in the Fonz role as a manic ideas man who bounces in, takes one look round at the mortuary drawers – 'What's in here? Stiffs and stuff? Neat!' – and soon has the bewildered Winkler turning his sanctum into a cooperative sanctuary for harassed prostitutes. Thereabouts the script begins to lose momentum, opting for frantic farce rather than pointed satire. Likeable, though. TM

Nightshift

(1981, GB, 67 min)
d Robina Rose. *p* Mary Rose. *sc* Robina Rose, Nicola Lane. *ph* Jon Jost. *ed* Janet Revell, Robina Rose. *m* (Hoover) Simon Jeffes, (lounge) Eye Level, (bar) Stroke, Famous Names. *cast* Jordan, Anne Rees-Mogg, Mitch Davies, Jon Jost, Max Handley, Mike Lesser, Heathcote Williams.

● An evocation of Resnais' *Marienbad* in a West London hotel where the nocturnal residents inexplicably walk and talk in slow motion and the receptionist sits silently watching the world drift by from behind an impassive white Noh mask. Heathcote Williams does a conjuring trick, Jon Jost impersonates an American (movie?) tycoon, and three girls re-enact the pillow fight from *Zéro de Conduite*. A few odd arresting images fail to stifle the tedium of watching a succession of post-punk Knightsbridge poseurs going through their art film number. MA

Nightshift (Trois Huit)

(2000, Fr, 97 min)
d Philippe Le Guay. *p* Alain Rocca. *sc* Philippe Le Guay. *ph* Jean-Marc Fabre. *ed* Emmanuelle Castro. *ad* Jimmy Vansteenkiste. *m* Yann Tiersen. *cast* Gérald Laroche, Marc Barbé, Bernard Ballet, Michel Cassagne, Alexandre Carrière, Jean-François Lapalus, Sabri Lahmer, Luce Mouchel, Maria Verdi, Philippe Frécon.

● Hard-working family man Pierre (Laroche) transfers to the night shift in a French provincial bottle factory only to meet hostility from co-worker Fred (Barbé). What starts out as mean-spirited but harmless joshing soon escalates to something more threatening; and though Pierre does his best to understand his tormentor's troubled background, he can't quite face a physical confrontation with a much more powerful rival. Le Guay's film displays steely reserve as it aims straight for the modern male's sensitive parts. New Man reasonableness is all very well, but what if you have to punch your way towards self-respect? Would your so-called friends lift a finger to help you? What does it do to a father-son relationship when the latter sees the bully as the 'real man'? This never pretends there are easy answers to any of these questions; as tension builds towards confrontation, subtle erotic longings flicker between ostensibly heterosexual males, and workplace solidarity comes under scrutiny. The cast (no big names here) inhabit their roles beautifully, while there are enough unexpected deviations to keep things interesting. A thoughtful nail-biter. TJ

Nights of Cabiria

see Notti di Cabiria, Le

Night Sun (Il Sole anche di notte)

(1990, It/Fr/Ger, 113 min)
d Paolo Taviani, Vittorio Taviani. *p* Giuliani G De Negri. *sc* Paolo Taviani, Vittorio Taviani, Tonino Guerra. *ph* Giuseppi Lanci. *ed* Roberto Perpignani. *ad* Gianni Sbarra. *m* Nicola Piovani. *cast* Julian Sands, Charlotte Gainsbourg, Nastassja Kinski, Massimo Bonetti, Margarita Lozano, Patricia Millardet, Rüdiger Vogler.

● In 18th century southern Italy, favoured by the king, promising young soldier Baron Sergio Giuramondo (Sands) is to marry a duchess (Kinski), but finds that she was previously the monarch's lover. Proudly turning his back on court life, he becomes a monk; but such is his disillusionment with society, that he presently elects to live alone in a desolate hermitage on Mount Petra. Even there, however, his quest for truth and spiritual perfection comes under threat, both from an adventuress bent on seducing him, and from the priests and pilgrims who believe him a worker of miracles. In their characteristically sensitive, imaginative adaptation of Tolstoy's *Father Sergius*, the Tavianis again address philosophical and political questions (the value and perils of retreat, the place of pride in idealism) in a simple, lucid style that lends the story the magical power of myth. Though Giuseppe Lanci's camerawork is consistently elegant, the way the Tavianis pare down composition, dialogue, narrative and performance to essentials ensures a clarity of purpose and effect rarely encountered in contemporary cinema. GA

Night to Remember, A

(1958, GB, 123 min, b/w)
d Roy Baker. *p* William MacQuitty. *sc* Eric Ambler. *ph* Geoffrey Unsworth. *ed* Sidney Hayers. *ad* Alex Vetchinsky. *m* William Alwyn. *cast* Kenneth More, Laurence Naismith, Michael Goodliffe, Frank Lawton, David McCallum, Honor Blackman.

● It's going to be years before this can be watched in a spontaneous way, without measuring pro and con against *Titanic* (1997). This earlier account of the sinking differs first in methodology: declining to superimpose any trivial business about unsuitable marriages or missing jewels, it proceeds via a series of vignettes to relate the facts as researched in Walter Lord's best-seller – although still retaining a few unshakeable myths (the cowardly transvestite, the playing of 'Nearer My God to Thee'). Some artfully carpentered plywood in the Pinewood tank (with extras bussed to the local lido for jumping-in-the-water shots) can hardly compare with the prodigiousness of Cameron's reconstruction, although the mere sight of the actors' breath, an effect available free of charge to Baker, is arguably more eloquent than all the digital composition in the world. Certainly, this is the version for grown ups. The characterisation of the ship's officers, for example, as representatives of an indefensible system, yet individually honourable and brave, proved too tough a concept for Cameron, strictly a heroes and villains man. And much is made here (and nothing there) of the role of the *Californian*, the Mr Magoo of maritime history, which lay a few miles off the wreck, her crew perfectly unable to grasp what was happening in front of them. Kenneth More may not measure up to Leonardo DiCaprio in terms of erotic impact, but his personification of brisk, cheerful efficiency is just the job. BBa

Night Train

(1998, Ire, 92 min)
d John Lynch. *p* Tristan Orpen Lynch, Derek Ryan. *sc* Aodhan Madden, *ph* Seamus Deasy. *ed* Pat Duffner. *pd* Alan Farquharson. *m* Adam Lynch. *cast* John Hurt, Brenda Blethyn, Pauline Flanagan, Rynagh O'Grady, Paul Rose, Lorcan Cranitch, Cathy White.

● This quirky romantic drama with thriller trimmings sees gentle ageing ex-con Hurt, an English northerner with a lonely passion for toy trains, holing up in a middle class Dublin lodging house to escape the hired killers of his old boss (Cranitch). There, he falls for Graham Greene-reading spinster (Blethyn) to the consternation of her embittered mother (Flanagan). Performances are good, with Hurt, especially, dignifying the rather pedestrian script, and the romance is handled delicately and humorously, but the gangsters' cardboard characterisations and periodic brutalities we could do without. Though it's often well observed and nicely shot by Seamus Deasy, it's spoilt by clumsily edited thriller sequences, predictable plotting and a lacklustre climax set on the Venice-bound Orient Express. WH

Night Train to Munich

(1940, GB, 95 min, b/w)
d Carol Reed. *p* Edward Black. *sc* Frank Launder, Sidney Gilliat. *ph* Otto Kanturek. *ed* RE Dearing, Michael Gordon. *ad* Alex Vetchinsky. *m* Charles Williams. *cast* Margaret Lockwood, Rex Harrison, Paul Henreid, Basil Radford, Naunton Wayne, Felix Aylmer, Raymond Huntley.

● In terms of cast, plot and scriptwriters (Launder and Gilliat), this bears a deliberate resemblance to Hitchcock's *The Lady Vanishes* as it merges comedy and thrills with propaganda in its tale of a Czech scientist's daughter escaping from a concentration camp, only belatedly to discover that she's been allowed to get away to reveal the whereabouts of her father. And though the action bats along at a furious pace, especially during the train scenes and the cable-car climax, the film only serves to show the importance of the director in the film-making process; the cast and script are fine, but Reed fatally lacks Hitchcock's light, witty touch and his effortless ability to create suspense out of ordinary circumstances. GA

Night Watch

(1973, GB, 98 min)
d Brian G Hutton. *p* Martin H Poll, George W George, Bernard Straus. *sc* Tony Williamson. *ph* Billy Williams. *ad* Peter Murton. *m* John Cameron. *cast* Elizabeth Taylor, Laurence Harvey, Billie Whitelaw, Robert Lang, Tony Britton, Bill Dean.

● Tired, old-fashioned thriller, with Elizabeth Taylor as that old stand-by: a woman recovering from a nervous breakdown who sees dead bodies in the boarded-up house across the garden, but naturally they have disappeared by the time the police arrive. Based on a stage play, it has a gratuitously bloody climax and a kick-yourself ending, but its amoebic plot is stretched almost to snapping point over 98 minutes. DMcG

Nightwatch (Nattevagten)

(1994, Den, 107 min)
d Ole Bornedal. *p* Michael Obel. *sc* Ole Bornedal. *ph* Dan Laustsen. *ed* Camilla Skousen. *ad* Soren Krag Sorensen. *m* Joachim Holbek. *cast* Nikolai Coster Waldau, Ulf Pilgaard, Kim Bodnia, Sofie Graaboel, Lotte Andersen, Ulf Pigaard.

● Danish writer/director Bornedal exploits the peculiarly horrifying and portentous atmosphere of a hospital mortuary to the full in this classy psychological thriller. While law student Martin (Waldau) moonlights as a nightwatchman at the city's hospital morgue, a sex killer stalks the streets, leaving behind a string of scalped female bodies. Martin has barely started his new job when one of the victims is brought in and laid out between the serried ranks of corpses. The sly insinuations of Chief Insp Wörmer (Pilgaard) increase his edginess, as the policeman implicates first his old friend Jens (Bodnia) and then Martin himself in the murders. Tightly scripted, with just a drop of wicked black humour, the film delivers creepy hints of necrophilia, visceral shocks and heart-racing suspense. The one unconvincing note is the parallel between these murderous events and rehearsals for an amateur theatrical production of *Mephisto*. Otherwise, this is the kind of superior genre movie-making where the eerie fluttering of moths in a glass lampshade is as chilling as the screaming, hysterical violence that follows. NF

Nightwatch

(1998, US, 97 min)
d/p Ole Bornedal. *sc* Ole Bornedal, Steven Soderberg. *ph* Dan Lausten. *ed* Sally Menkel. *pd* Richard Hoover. *m* Joachim Holbek. *cast* Ewan McGregor, Nick Nolte, Patricia Arquette, Josh Brolin, Brad Dourif, Lauren Graham.

● Ewan McGregor straight to video shocker! Danish director Bornedal was tempted by Miramax to remake his stylish 1994 chiller with American accents, and despite a screenplay credit to Steven Soderbergh, that's just what he's done. If it isn't shot-for-shot, it's near as makes no odds. McGregor is the law student who takes a job working nights as a guard in the city morgue, just as a psycho killer starts terrorising the community, and falls suspect himself. Creepy atmospherics and lots of dead meat make for a tense opening, but significant problems soon surface: McGregor's friendship with misogynist daredevil Brolin is not only a glaringly contrived red herring, but also effectively precludes our sympathy. Nice guys just don't allow themselves to be jerked off by hookers in public – not in America; and there's a nasty whiff about the treatment of women – dead or alive – that goes beyond grisly genre requirements. TCh

Night Watch, The

see Trou, Le

Night We Never Met, The

(1993, US, 89 min)
d Warren Leight. *p* Michael Peyser. *sc* Warren Leight. *ph* John A Thomas. *ed* Camilla Toniolo. *pd* Lester Cohen. *m* Evan Lurie. *cast* Matthew Broderick, Annabella Sciorra, Kevin Anderson, Jeanne Tripplehorn, Justine Bateman, Michael Mantell, Christine Baranski.

●You can live with someone without knowing them, but in most cases at least the co-habitants have been properly introduced. Not so in writer/director Leight's first film. When stockbroker Brian (Anderson) moves in with his fiancée, he assures his drinking buddies he'll keep his Greenwich Village bachelor pad for a couple of nights a week. He instructs his secretary to sublet it on the free days. That suits Sam (Broderick) just fine. He can't afford a place of his own, but craves escape from his crowded flatshare, even if only at weekends. Then there's Ellen (Sciorra), a frustrated housewife looking for a pied-à-terre in the city. She gets Mondays and Fridays. Brian and Sam swap nights, unbeknown to Ellen, who assumes that the former is the sensitive, tasteful gourmet who leaves her presents, and that Sam is the slob who treats the flat like a tip. When she decides to have an affair, she chooses the wrong man. The film has three amiable leads and doesn't overstay its welcome. TCh

Nightwing

(1979, Neth, 105 min)
d Arthur Hiller. *p* Martin Ransohoff. *sc* Steve Shagan, Bud Shrake, Martin Cruz Smith. *ph* Charles Rosher Jr. *ed* John C Howard. *pd* James D Vance. *m* Henry Mancini. *cast* Nick Mancuso, David Warner, Kathryn Harrold, Steven Macht, Strother Martin, George Clutesi, Ben Piazza, Charles Hallahan.

●Despite the fluttering efforts of its many thousand leathery predators, *Nightwing* (based on Martin Cruz Smith's first novel) never really takes off. It does inspire one or two moments of nausea, as the itinerant vampire bat colony emerges from a canyon on an American Indian reservation to dine on the living bodies of local campers. But Hiller's direction simply plods to a corny and unsatisfactory ending after getting bogged down in subplots concerning whale-oil prospectors, Indian religious mumbo-jumbo, and inter-tribal rivalries. MPl

Night Zoo (Un Zoo la Nuit)

(1987, Can, 115 min)
d Jean-Claude Lauzon. *p* Roger Frappier, Pierre Gendron. *sc* Jean-Claude Lauzon. *ph* Guy Dufaux. *ed* Michel Arcand. *ad* Jean-Baptiste Tard. *m* Jean Corriveau. *cast* Gilles Maheu, Roger Le Bel, Lynne Adams, Lorne Brass, Germain Houde, Corrado Mastropasqua, Jerry Snell, Denys Arcand.

●This unconvincing French-Canadian thriller is a dawdler, with outbreaks of nastiness followed by listlessly arty longeurs. Marcel (Maheu) gets out of prison and goes to retrieve his loot, but a couple of bent cops are determined on their cut. Meanwhile, Marcel's girl Julie (Adams) has gone on the game, and his dad Albert (Le Bel) has a weak ticker which makes family reconciliation yet another priority, and our hero spends a lot of time blasting about on his motorbike. Dad's birthday party apart, it is determinedly sleazy. We are treated to Marcel getting forcibly sodomised in prison at the start, blown in an insanitary lav by one of the cops, Marcel's labouring rump as he attempts to reunite with Julie, and an improbable scene in a porno peep show in which the bad guys threaten Julie with a syringe. There are lots of empty threats featuring gunshots across the bows, and Marcel's loft is so spacious you wonder why he needs the money anyway. BC

Nijinsky

(1980, US, 125 min)
d Herbert Ross. *p* Nora Kaye, Stanley O'Toole. *sc* Hugh Wheeler. *ph* Douglas Slocombe. *ed* William H Reynolds. *pd* John Blezard. *m* Borodin, Debussy, Rimsky-Korsakov, Schumann, Stravinsky, Weber. *cast* Alan Bates, George de la Peña, Leslie Brown, Alan Badel, Carla Fracci, Colin Blakely, Ronald Pickup, Ronald Lacey, Jeremy Irons, Anton Dolin, Janet Suzman.

●At the very least, *Nijinsky* is the best gay weepie since *Death in Venice*. It chronicles the last fraught year or so in the dancer's romance with Ballets Russes impresario Diaghilev, and is thus the first major studio film to centre on a male homosexual relationship (albeit a doomed one) without being moralistic. Director Ross and writer Hugh Wheeler betray their subject by presenting Nijinsky's choreographic experiments as deranged, and by associating his madness with Stravinsky's discords; they also give short shrift to the one woman involved, Romola de Pulsky, the go-getting heiress who seduced and married Nijinsky, thereby alienating Diaghilev from his protégé forever. But they do right by their male characters (Alan Bates, in particular, is a plausibly adult Diaghilev), their grasp of the historical reconstructions seems more than competent, and their dialogue and exposition are unusually adroit. Best of all, they never show ballet for its own sake, and have the courage to keep emotional dynamics in the forefront throughout. TR

Nikita

(1990, Fr/It, 117 min)
d Luc Besson. *p* Jérôme Chalou. *sc* Luc Besson. *ph* Thierry Arbogast. *ed* Olivier Mauffroy. *pd* Dan Weil. *m* Eric Serra. *cast* Anne Parillaud, Jean-Hugues Anglade, Tchéky Karyo, Jeanne Moreau, Jean Reno, Roland Blanche, Jean Bouise.

●Starting with a bloody tour de force – a drugstore robbery – this seldom lets up. The eponymous heroine, a punk-junkie sociopath, is given a life sentence for killing a cop, but after being drugged by her captors, wakes up believing herself dead. And so she is, officially: held in a secret government establishment which trains undercover assassins, she is given a new identity; and on her eventual release, she turns her violent tendencies to patriotic use, sporadically abandoning both her new-found respectability and her law-abiding lover to earn her keep with a gun. While Besson's relentlessly stylish *noir*-thriller suffers from occasionally implausible plotting and an increasing lack of clarity in its later scenes, it benefits enormously from a memorably assured, intense performance from Anne Parillaud. Her scenes with her prison boss/Svengali (Karyo) and her gullible lover (Anglade) are surprisingly touching, so that there is for once an emotional undertow to Besson's visual pyrotechnics, even if the film finally doesn't add up to anything very profound. GA

Nil by Mouth

(1997, GB, 124 min)
d Gary Oldman. *p* Luc Besson, Douglas Urbanski, Gary Oldman. *sc* Gary Oldman. *ph* Ron Fortunato. *ed* Brad Fuller. *pd* Hugo Luczyc-Wyhowski. *m* Eric Clapton. *cast* Ray Winstone, Kathy Burke, Charlie Creed-Miles, Laila Morse, Edna Doré, Chrissie Cotterill, Jon Morrison, Jamie Forman.

●The actor Gary Oldman's debut as writer/director is so uncompromisingly honest, it makes other portraits of working-class life look like sour caricature or misplaced idealism. Oldman grew up in south east London, the setting for this tale of macho violence, drunkenness, drug addiction and petty crime, and very clearly knows what he's talking about. He's helped, of course, by stunning performances from his entire cast, most notably Winstone as the volatile but self-pitying Ray, given to beating up his long-suffering wife (Burke) and threatening her irresponsible junkie brother (Creed-Miles). There's no sermonising or romanticising here, just a sad, clear-eyed acknowledgement that domestic abuse and crime create a vicious circle from which many barely even try to escape. Shot and scripted in a deceptively casual, bleakly 'realist' style, it's the closest Britain has produced to a Cassavetes film, and as such, profoundly humane. GA

Nina Takes a Lover

(1993, US, 100 min)
d Alan Jacobs. *p* Jane Hernandez, Alan Jacobs. *sc* Alan Jacobs. *ph* Phil Parmet. *ed* John Nutt, Marjorie L Hagar. *pd* Don DeFina. *m* Todd Boekelheide. *cast* Laura San Giacomo, Paul Rhys, Michael O'Keefe, Cristi Canway, Fisher Stevens.

●Bored and neglected, Nina (San Giacomo) falls under the spell of a Welsh photographer (Rhys) she meets in a San Francisco park. Their affair is revealed in flashbacks, a series of confessions and confidences, as a journalist investigating 'marriage in the '90s' gently probes the whys and wherefores. The device is a little obvious, but director Jacobs gives the film an ingenious structure, and it's charmingly played by two attractive leads. 'This story is different than what you've heard before,' Nina promises at the start, and within the familiar confines of the sex-and-lies genre, she's absolutely right. TCh

Nine ½ Weeks

(1985, US, 117 min)
d Adrian Lyne. *p* Anthony Rufus-Isaacs, Zalman King. *sc* Patricia Knop, Zalman King, Sarah Kernochan. *ph* Peter Biziou. *ed* Caroline Biggerstaff, Tom Rolfe. *pd* Ken Davis. *m* Jack Nitzsche, Michael Hoenig. *cast* Mickey Rourke, Kim Basinger, Margaret Whitton, David Margulies, Christine Baranski, Karen Young.

●Adrian (*Flashdance*) Lyne's steamy saga of *amour fou* hardly bears up to the inevitable *Last Tango* comparisons. He, a slimline, ultracool Mickey Rourke, is a self-satisfied commodities broker. She, sultry yet sweet Kim Basinger, is a recently divorced art gallery gal. She believes love is unimportant until meeting him, and then his teasing request, 'Will you do this for me?', cues a decorative series of sexual variations in search of a theme. Lyne works hard to give their naughty games a glossy veneer – streams of light and water, jagged editing, rock music to seduce by – but prefers to leave the audience to work out the psychology. The film has evidently gone through innumerable revisions, and little remains that is truly daring for the jaded '80s. Bump and grind for the Porsche owner. DT

Nine Lives (Ni Liv)

(1957, Nor, 96 min, b/w)
d/p/sc Arne Skouen. *ph* Ragnar Sørensen. *ed* Bjorn Breigutu. *ad* HC Hansen. *m* Gunnar Sønstevold. *cast* Jack Fjeldstad, Henny Moan, Alf Malland, Joachim Holst-Jensen, Lydia Opøien, Edvard Drabløs, Sverre Hansen, Rolf Søder.

●Skouen's Oscar-nominated film, based on David Howarth's book *We Die Alone*, tells the story of Jan Baalsrud, the only survivor of a betrayed commando raid in Northern Norway who made a daring escape to Sweden. Baalsrud was wounded in the foot, suffered from frost bite and snow blindness, and nearly starved. He hid out in a snow cave for over a month and ended up lopping off his own toes to stop the gangrene spreading. With the help of doughty, Nazi-hating Norwegians he keeps ahead of his pursuers, swimming across fjords, clambering up mountains and skiing cross country. It's an extraordinary tale of courage and resilience. Ironically, the more extreme the conditions, the more beautiful the landscapes become. Skouen, an acclaimed journalist as well as a film-maker, treats his material in terse, phlegmatic fashion. The understatement here makes Scott of the Antarctic look like an exhibitionist. GM

Nine Lives of Fritz the Cat, The

(1974, US, 76 min)
d Robert Taylor. *p* Steve Krantz. *sc* Fred Halliday, Eric Monte, Robert Taylor. *ph* Ted C Bemiller, Gregg Heschong. *ed* Marshall M Borden. *m* Tom Scott and LA Express. *cast* voices: Skip Hinnant, Reva Rose, Bob Holt, Robert Ridgley.

●Without director Ralph Bakshi, and now bearing almost no resemblance to Robert Crumb's original, this animated sequel to *Fritz the Cat* is woefully inept. A stoned Fritz fantasises his way out of his welfare and tenement existence. Kissinger makes a telling appearance; but Hitler as an anaemic-looking Pink Panther, and a time-filling photo montage sequence are better indications of the film's true level. CPe

Nine Lives of Tomas Katz, The

(1999, Ger/GB, 86 min, b/w)
d Ben Hopkins. *p* Caroline Hewitt. *sc* Ben Hopkins, Thomas Browne. *ph* Julian Court. *ed* Alan Levy. *pd* Gideon Davey. *m* Dominik Scherrer. *cast* Tom Fisher, Ian McNeice, Tony Maudsley, Will Keen, Andrew Melville, Janet Henfrey, Tim Barlow.

● For this second feature, Hopkins mounts a semi-experimental, part-improvised, multi-stock, German Expressionism-influenced, b/w sci-fi black comedy about London's countdown to the coming apocalypse. It's a wacky, fun, febrile concoction, full of verbal and visual styles, jibes, jokes and puns, po-faced prognostications and gnomic utterances, with wildly eclectic scoring, surreal asides and occasional sublime cinematic coups. The sallow-faced Fisher stars as the protean Mr No – whom we first meet, decked out like an 18th century ghoul, emerging backwards from a cavernous hole by the M25. No has the ability to swap places with the souls he encounters and, by inhabiting their bodies and taking their powers, wreaks havoc in London and the world. His only capable adversary is the blind, mystic Dr Mabuse-like chief of police (McNeice), who senses the danger when, as he says, 'the pale child in the astral plane seems to be dying!' It's plain loopy, often awkward, clumsy and overdigressive, but rarely dull. Hopkins' gleeful melange of styles might feel like a nightmare, were it not for his undercutting playfulness, irony and humour. WH

Nine Months (Kilenc Hónap)

(1976, Hun, 93 min)
d Márta Mészáros. *sc* Gyula Hernádi, Ildikó Kóródy, Márta Mészáros. *ph* János Kende. *ed* Adrásné Kármentó. *ad* Tamás Banovich, *m* György Kovacs. *cast* Lili Monori, Jan Nowicki, Gyula Szersén, Roszich Dzsoko, Kati Berek, Géza Bodó.

● Márta Mészáros is the wife of Miklós Jancsó, though it is hard to see any family resemblance in this direct, appealing and humanly complex account of a young woman's quest for (or rather, gradual acceptance of) independence. The options, between marriage to a likeable but repressive foundry foreman and life on her own with a child by a former lover, are presented in equally unenviable light. The film's case comes to rest, in the end, on which kind of life the heroine is most prepared to sacrifice herself to. Crisply filmed and politically less a matter of special pleading than much recent East European cinema. MA

Nine Months

(1995, US, 103 min)
d Chris Columbus. *p* Anne François, Chris Columbus, Mark Radcliffe, Michael Barnathan. *sc* Chris Columbus. *ph* Donald McAlpine. *ed* Raja Gosnell. *pd* Angelo P Graham. *m* Hans Zimmer. *cast* Hugh Grant, Julianne Moore, Tom Arnold, Joan Cusack, Jeff Goldblum, Robin Williams, Mia Cottet.

● An extraordinarily naff concoction from writer/director Columbus, which confirms the near certain perils of remaking French comedies (here *Neuf mois*, 1994). Grant plays Englishman Sam Faulkner who's happily coupled with Moore's Rebecca – until, that is, she announces she's pregnant. His painful memories of their would-be romantic tryst on the beach being broken up by the noxious kids of the parents-from-hell, car-trader Marty (Arnold) and wife Gail (Cusack), the philosophical counsels of confirmed bachelor Sean (Goldblum, the only vaguely recognisable human in the film), and his fear of trading in his beloved Porsche for a four-wheel drive, push Sam the way of the true cad: off out of it. But, of course, being a Columbus movie, transgression is only a learning curve, here a pretty reactionary one, and smug to boot. When Williams did his turn as an émigré Russian gynaecologist facing his first delivery, I felt a chuckle building. But by the time Grant emotes before the ultrasound scan, my goodwill had been all used up. WH

Nine Queens (Nueve Reinas)

(2000, Arg, 115 min)
d Fabián Bielinsky. *p* Pablo Bossi. *sc* Fabián Bielinsky. *ph* Marcelo Camorino. *ed* Sergio Zottola. *pd* Marcelo Salvioli. *m* Cesar Lerner. *cast* Ricardo Darín, Gastón Pauls, Leticia Brédice, Tomás Fonzi.

● Another impressive lob out of Argentina, this gleaming, tricksy thriller is pure accomplished entertainment with a sting in its tail worthy of *The Usual Suspects* – equal parts brilliant and ridiculous. Juan (Pauls) and Marcos (Darín) are a 'student and master' con-artist couple, paired for a day when the opportunity of a lifetime lands in their laps: the chance to flog a forged sheet of rare stamps (the Nine Queens) to a rich tycoon collector who's about to be deported. But can they trust each other or anyone else? First-time director Bielinsky snaps through this Mamet-like construct with justified confidence: the plot twists are sharp, the pacing sprightly (meaning fast subtitles at times), and the two leads completely convincing. And the ending, which suggests you can beat 'em if you join 'em, also contrives to redeem the rest of the film's amoral gusto. Crafty. NB

976-Evil

(1988, US, 100 min)
d Robert Englund. *p* Lisa M Hansen. *sc* Rhet Topham, Brian Helgeland. *ph* Paul Elliot. *ed* Stephen Myers. *ad* David Brian Miller. *m* Thomas Chase, Steve Rucker. *cast* Stephen Geoffreys, Patrick O'Bryan, Sandy Dennis, Jim Metzler, Maria Rubell, Robert Picardo, Lezlie Deane.

● The directorial debut of *Nightmare on Elm Street* anti-hero Robert ('Freddie') Englund is a sloppily scripted horror pic which takes far too long to get started and then fails to deliver the goods. 976-Evil is a toll-free phone number providing a daily horrorscope, an offer which connects with rebellious teenager Spike (O'Bryan); but it's his nerdy cousin Hoax (Geoffreys) whose attention is really engaged. Hooked up to the diabolical forces on the other end of the line, Hoax undergoes a physical and mental transformation. Little happens for the first hour, after which Hoax starts taking revenge on his religious fanatic Aunt Lucy (Dennis), Spike's new girlfriend (Deane), and the school bully. Englund says the film is about filial envy and the dangers of hero worship, but really it's just a reworking of the revenge-of-the-nerd scenario, with an underdeveloped familial twist. So by the time the Ice and Fire pits open up inside and outside Aunt Lucy's house, it's difficult to care about who will plummet into the frozen abyss or plunge to a fiery death. Odd scenes suggest that Englund has a good eye for visual set pieces. NF

1988: The Remake

(1978, US, 97 min, b/w & col)
d Richard R Schmidt. *sc* Henry Bean, William Farley, Nick Kazan, Richard R Schmidt. *ph/ed* Richard R schmidt *cast* Ed Nylund, Skip Covington, Carolyn Zaremba, Willie Boy Walker, Dickie Marcus, Bruce Parry.

● Bizarre, overlong low-budget independent depicting the auditions held by a dying librarian who wants to remake *Showboat* as 'a musical comedy with the stench of death'. Patchily amusing as it wheels on freaks, eccentrics and talentless no-hopers – with all references to the MGM classic bleeped out (resulting in a dreadful Gong Show-style cacophony) – it's all a little indulgent. GA

Nineteen Eighty-Four

(1984, GB, 110 min)
d Michael Radford. *p* Simon Perry. *sc* Michael Radford, Jonathan Gems. *ph* Roger Deakins. *ed* Tom Priestley. *pd* Allan Cameron. *m* Dominic Muldowney, Eurythmics. *cast* John Hurt, Richard Burton, Suzanna Hamilton, Cyril Cusack, Gregor Fisher, James Walker, Andrew Wilde, Phyllis Logan, Shirley Stefox.

● Sensibly realising that science fiction is always a distortion of the time at which it was written rather than a prediction of the future, Radford aligns himself with Anthony Burgess' suggestion that the book only makes sense as *1948*, with its food rationing, its housing shortages, bad cigarettes and Churchillian slogans. The look of the film certainly achieves the right rubble-strewn, monochrome period feel with precision and genuinely cinematic scope. Perhaps the greatest hurdle cleared, however, is the problem of incident. Radford's achievement is to have incorporated the impossible preaching and crazed ideas into the fabric with hardly any loose threads. The locations look very like modern Britain; and Burton at last found the one serious role for which he searched all his life. CPea

1941

(1979, US, 118 min)
d Steven Spielberg. *p* Buzz Feitshans. *sc* Robert Zemeckis, Bob Gale. *ph* William A Fraker. *ed* Michael Kahn. *pd* Dean Edward Mitzner. *m* John Williams. *cast* Dan Aykroyd, Ned Beatty, John Belushi, Lorraine Gary, Murray Hamilton, Christopher Lee, Tim Matheson, Toshiro Mifune, Warren Oates, Robert Stack, Treat Williams, Nancy Allen, Bobby DiCicco, John Candy, Elisha Cook Jr, Slim Pickens, Lionel Stander, Penny Marshall, Sam Fuller, Mickey Rourke.

● Spielberg's extravagant folie de grandeur, a madcap comedy recreation of an allegedly true story, with Hollywood suffering from mass panic when it's thought that a Japanese submarine is about to lead an invasion force into California. The period sets are wonderful, the cast full of bright talent, and Spielberg's expertly choreographed slapstick is wondrous to behold. There is a problem, however, in that it isn't actually very funny: one feels that Spielberg was concentrating his powers so much on the mechanics of timing, cause and effect, that he forgot that what makes the best comedies funny is human reaction. Here the characters are too cartoon-like ever to win our attention (though Stack's military bigwig obsessed with Disney's *Dumbo* is the touching exception who proves the rule). GA

1900 (Novecento)

(1976, It/Fr/WGer, 320 min)
d Bernardo Bertolucci. *p* Alberto Grimaldi. *sc* Bernardo Bertolucci, Franco Arcalli, Giuseppi Bertolucci. *ph* Vittorio Storaro. *ed* Franco Arcalli. *ad* Ezio Frigerio. *m* Ennio Morricone. *cast* Burt Lancaster, Robert De Niro, Gérard Depardieu, Dominique Sanda, Donald Sutherland, Sterling Hayden, Stefania Sandrelli, Francesca Bertini, Romolo Valli, Laura Betti, Alida Valli.

● International tensions and discords are often mainsprings of interest in a film, and the fundamental contradiction between political line and status as glossy commodity might have made Bertolucci's *1900* fascinating. But whether one takes the two-part movie as a glamorous epic or as a lengthy advertisement for the Italian communist party, it still looks like a major catastrophe. Even leaving aside the questions about its sexual politics, the film is crippled by its ineptitude as 'popular' drama (the dynastic rivalries spanning the years, the convulsive deaths, the messy marriages are all strictly sub-Jacqueline Susann) and its manifest inadequacy as political argument (Donald Sutherland is established as Fascism incarnate and then metamorphosed into something like a Disney cartoon villain). The mannered elegance of the camerawork and lighting cocoons the whole sad mess within a veneer of utterly spurious 'style'. (Also shown in a 250-minute version.) TR

Nineteen Nineteen

(1984, GB, 99 min)
d Hugh Brody. *p* Nita Amy. *sc* Hugh Brody, Michael Ignatieff. *ph* Ivan Strasburg. *ed* David Gladwell. *ad* Caroline Amies. *m* Brian Gascoigne. *cast* Paul Scofield, Maria Schell, Frank Finlay, Diana Quick, Clare Higgins, Colin Firth, Sandra Berkin.

● For Sophie (Schell), the past is literally a foreign country; when she flies from New York to Vienna to see Alexander Scherbatov (Scofield), it is to explore that forgotten territory. For in 1919 they were both patients of Dr Freud. Together they dredge their memories, and map out not only the confessions of the couch, but also the huge historical shifts that separated them; like Freud himself, they were victims of the Nazi arrival. The film operates in much the same way as the talking cure itself; Freud's skilful probings are heard (Finlay's voice) though he is never seen; and the film makes sense of the past by the same shifting, organic, inexplicable process. A sensitive, interior film, with all the restorative power that Freud must have hoped for. CPea

1999 Madeleine

(1999, Fr, 85 min)
d Laurent Bouhnik. *p* Jean Cottin, Etienne Comar, Laurent Bouhnik. *sc* Laurent Bouhnik. *ph* Gilles Henry. *ed* Clémence Lafarge. *pd* Yvon Fustec. *m* Jérôme Coullet. *cast* Véra Briole, Manuel Blanc, Anouk Aimée, Jean-Michel Fête, Jean-François Gallotee, Michel Goudouin, Aurélia Petit, Emmanuelle Rozes.

●Confirming the promise of *Sélect Hôtel*, his debut *vérité*-style examination of Parisian marginals, Laurent Bouhnik's second feature has echoes of Godard in its sympathetic study of a lonely but proud/bold dressmaker, Madeleine (Briole, open and dignified). 'My Life's fucked – but I'm not part of it,' says the alienated, thirty-something woman, in a series of interior monolgues. She embarks on a run Lonely Hearts encounters, observed by with acute but non-judgmental detail. A film of subtle discretion, formal vigour and delight in the still rich humanist-realist cinematic tradition. WH

1974, Une Partie de Campagne

see 1974, Une Partie de Campagne [as 'Mil Neuf Cent Soixante Quatorze…']

1969

(1988, US, 95 min)
d Ernest Thompson. *p* Daniel Grodnik, Bill Badalato. *sc* Ernest Thompson. *ph* Jules Brenner. *ed* William Anderson. *pd* Marcia Hinds. *m* Michael Small. *cast* Robert Downey Jr, Kiefer Sutherland, Bruce Dern, Mariette Hartley, Winona Ryder, Joanna Cassidy.

●Thompson's evocation of the spirit of the '60s protest is most moving when it abandons the soapbox and concentrates on domestic discord. We follow the fortunes of college buddies Ralph (Downey) and Scott (Sutherland), opposed in temperament but united in ideals. They both despise American involvement in Vietnam, but Scott's the one with a social conscience, while Ralph likes to get stoned and strip down to his underwear. Inevitably the two rebels clash with their parents, inspiring support from their mothers (splendid perfomrances from Cassidy and Hartley) and hostility from Scott's gung-ho father (played with conviction by Dern). The film effectively recreates the fear and defiance which accompanied Nixon's support of the draft lottery, with 19-year-olds designated as the first for the slaughter. CM

Nine to Five

(1980, US, 109 min)
d Colin Higgins. *p* Bruce Gilbert. *sc* Colin Higgins, Patricia Resnick. *ph* Reynaldo Villalobos. *ed* Pembroke J Herring. *pd* Dean Edward Mitzner. *m* Charles Fox. *cast* Jane Fonda, Lily Tomlin, Dolly Parton, Dabney Coleman, Sterling Hayden, Elizabeth Wilson, Henry Jones, Lawrence Pressman.

●Despite an excellent and promising cast, this Hollywood attempt at a mainstream feminist comedy is flabby and bland. Fonda is the new secretary in the office, Tomlin and Parton are the veterans who teach her to cope with and combat chauvinistic male oppression, incarnated by embezzling boss Coleman. As one might expect, the three club together in a plot to exact revenge, but as soon as their plans get underway, the film degenerates still further into toothless satire and wish-fulfilment slapstick (notably a fantasy involving Coleman's death). And the climax simply underlines the film's lack of courage in its convictions: the trio's tangle of problems are resolved (happily, of course) by a man. Complacent, and even worse, not very funny, despite the efforts of the ever-excellent Tomlin. GA

90 Days

(1985, Can, 99 min)
d Giles Walker. *p/sc* David Wilson, Giles Walker. *ph* Andrew Kitzanuk. *ed* David Wilson. *m* Richard Gresko. *cast* Stefan Wodoslawsky, Christine Pak, Sam Grana, Fernanda Tavares, Daisy De Bellefeuille, Katy de Volpi.

●Blue is shy, sincere, a little surly; his friend Alex, conversely, is a full-blooded philanderer, ludicrously unable to comprehend why his wife has thrown him out and his mistress won't see him. So far so simple, but Giles Walker's gently probing comedy of masculine manners soon breaks away from such polarities. The self-centred Blue invites over from Korea a woman he's never met, courtesy of a mail-order catalogue, but is too hung-up to come clean about their relationship; while Alex's macho pride softens into confusion and fear as soon as he is approached by a mysterious young woman offering $10,000 for his sperm. *90 Days* – the visa period the Canadian authorities allow Blue and Hyang-Sook to make up their minds about marriage – avoids making judgments; Walker is content simply to observe his creations with warmth and honesty. It is all largely charming, and the quiet performances ensure involvement. GA

99 and 44/100% Dead (aka Call Harry Crown)

(1974, US, 98 min)
d John Frankenheimer. *p* Joe Wizan. *sc* Robert Dillon. *ph* Ralph Woolsey. *ed* Harold F Kress. *ad* Herman A Blumenthal. *m* Henry Mancini. *cast* Richard Harris, Edmond O'Brien, Bradford Dillman, Ann Turkel, Chuck Connors, Constance Ford, David Hall, Max Kleven.

●A further chapter in the decline of a brilliant '60s director, with Frankenheimer here aping the more surefire gangland milieu treats of Siegel and Boorman. Harris, with O'Brien and Dillman as rival bosses, plays a hitman contracted to sort out a gangland war in a coyly futuristic environment of urban decay. Snappily edited chase and crash sequences, shot with Frankenheimer's familiar command of distorting lenses, make for the best moments in a film which looks as if it had been designed by Hugh Hefner, inflatable women and all. Harris goes through his usual long-suffering trauma as the peerless protagonist. RM

92 in the Shade

(1975, US, 93 min)
d Thomas McGuane. *p* George Pappas. *sc* Thomas McGuane. *ph* Michael C Butler. *ed* Ed Rothkowitz. *m* Michael J Lewis. *cast* Peter Fonda, Warren Oates, Margot Kidder, Burgess Meredith, Harry Dean Stanton, Sylvia Miles, Elizabeth Ashley, William Hickey, Joe Spinell.

●Adapted from his own superb, blackly comic novel of eastern seabord eccentrics, macho mythology and the ultimate Florida face-off, McGuane's sole film as director is one of the most enjoyable messes ever to be suppressed as unsaleable. His literary talent lionised and his film reputation secure on scripts for *Rancho Deluxe*, *Missouri Breaks* and *Tom Horn*, McGuane here exhibits a totally appealing incompetence as director: the movie's got all the coherence of an amiable narrative jam-session. Storywise, Fonda wants to set up as a Key West fishing guide; Oates claims a monopoly and threatens to kill him if he does. That's it…except for the crazy-quilt interaction of cultishly-cast fringe characters, mouthing idiosyncratically lively dialogue and obviously having a ball. Jimmy Buffet's songs might give you some hook for what's going on, but the fun's infectious anyway. PT

'92 The Legendary La Rose Noire (Heimeigui dui Heimeigui)

(1992, HK, 100 min)
d Joe Chan. *p* Laura Fu. *sc* Jeff Lau. *ph* Chan Yuen Kai. *ed* Kai Kit Wai. *ad* Joe Chan. *m* Lowell Lo. *cast* Tony Leung, Maggie Shiu, Bo Bo Fung, Wan Sze Wong.

●As its ineffably pretentious Anglo-French title suggests, this looks back to the '60s, when costumed crime-busters, mysterious private eyes and vicious master criminals crowded the screen in low-budget Cantonese movies. Joe Chan (with substantial uncredited assistance from Wong Kar-Wai's then partner Jeff Lau) lifts characters, dialogue and sometimes entire scenes from these movies in parody of material that was pretty far gone to begin with. Highbrow critics in Hong Kong and Taiwan were charmed out of their pants and raved about post-modernism. Westerners may be reminded of Losey's *Modesty Blaise*. TR

Ninja III – The Domination

(1984, US, 95 min)
d Sam Firstenberg. *p* Menahem Golan, Yoram Globus. *sc* James R Silke. *ph* Hanania Baer. *ed* Michael J Duthie. *ad* Elliot Ellentuck. *m* Arthur Kempel (orchestral), Udi Harpaz, Misha Segal (synthesizer). *cast* Sho Kosugi, Lucinda Dickey, Jordan Bennett, David Chung, Dale Ishimodo, James Hong, Bob Craig.

●Telephone engineer and aerobics wiz Christie (Dickey) becomes possessed by a demon ninja who, leaving her when the plot requires, hides in the fridge or under the sink. What the ninja's masterplan could be is anyone's guess, but he has previously run amok on an Arizona golf course, so it may not be immediate world domination. Rather than golfers, Ninja-Christie kills the cops who doubled the previous incarnate's body-weight in bullets. This sequel to *Enter the Ninja* and *Revenge of the Ninja* rapidly auto-sequels itself, as plot and duels repeat every few minutes. It being a Golan/Globus product, smoke and strobes are as special as the effects get, and helicopters crash inexpensively, behind hills. For the necromantically inclined, there's a vocal-only appearance by Diamanda Galas. DO

Niño Llamado Muerte, Un

see Jory

Niños Abandonados, Los

(1975, US, 63 min)
d Danny Lyon.

●Although its obvious point of reference is *Los Olvidados*, there are few similarities between Lyon's film and Buñuel's, other than the subject: the homeless children of South America. *Los Niños Abandonados* is the simplest and most basic documentary, avoiding embroidery, refusing commentary, and largely choosing to avoid judgment or easy answers. Its observation of the children in their pathetic round of begging and cruel games, ignored by the world around them, is essentially pictorial (Lyon was a photographer before he started making films). If Lyon opts for compassion rather than analysis, it is nevertheless hard to sidestep an awareness of the church's impotence and hypocrisy. SM

Ninotchka

(1939, US, 110 min, b/w)
d/p Ernst Lubitsch. *sc* Charles Brackett, Billy Wilder, Walter Reisch. *ph* William H Daniels. *ed* Gene Ruggiero. *ad* Cedric Gibbons, Randall Duell. *m* Werner R Heymann. *cast* Greta Garbo, Melvyn Douglas, Ina Claire, Bela Lugosi, Sig Ruman, Felix Bressart, Alexander Granach, Gregory Gaye, Rolfe Sedan.

●This was the first time since 1934 that Garbo had been seen in the 20th century, and the first time ever that her material was predominantly comic (though it was hardly the first time she'd laughed, as the ads insisted). But her character still had an icy aura, at least at the outset – she plays a Russian comrade staying in Paris on government business, a situation providing writers Wilder, Brackett and Walter Reisch with rich material for impish political jokes ('The last mass trials were a great success. There are going to be fewer but better Russians'). Then she meets the acceptable face of Capitalism in the form of Melvyn Douglas, and like many a lesser MGM star before her, succumbs completely to his suave looks and honeyed voice. The film's not quite the delight history says it is – by the late '30s, the famed Lubitsch touch was resembling a heavy blow, the elegant sophistication turning crude and cynical. Yet it's still consistently amusing, and Garbo throws herself into the fray with engaging vigour. GB

Ninth Configuration, The (aka Twinkle, Twinkle, Killer Kane)

(1979, US, 118 min)
d/p/sc William Peter Blatty. *ph* Gerry Fisher. *ed* T Battle Davis, Peter Lee-Thompson, Roberto Silvi. *pd* Bill Malley, J Dennis Washington. *m* Barry DeVorzon. *cast* Stacy Keach, Scott Wilson, Jason Miller, Ed Flanders, Neville Brand, George DiCenzo, Moses Gunn, Robert Loggia, Joe Spinell, Alejandro Rey, Tom Atkins.

●It's easy to see why *Exorcist* author William Peter Blatty's debut effort as a director stayed on the shelf for a year. This unfathomable yarn about an ace US Army psychiatrist, at work in an isolated military nuthouse populated by a gallery of service fruitcakes (from cowardly astronauts and Congressional Medal winners to Vietnam war malingerers) has the same tortured

Christian iconography as Blatty's bestseller, but is altogether more pretentious on the level of reflection about the Problem of Evil and the question Is God Dead (or is he just living in sin?). A kind of *Invasion of the Body Snatchers* meets *Catch-22*, or maybe Fuller's *Shock Corridor* set as an episode from *The Twilight Zone*. Sounds interesting enough, but isn't. RM

Ninth Gate, The

(1999, Fr/Sp, 133 min)
d/p Roman Polanski. *sc* Enrique Urbizu, John Brownjohn, Roman Polanski. *ph* Darius Khondji. *ed* Hervé Deluze. *pd* Dean Tavoularis. *m* Wojciech Kilar. *cast* Johnny Depp, Lena Olin, Frank Langella, James Russo, Jack Taylor, Emmanuelle Seigner.

●When Dean Corso (Depp), a cunning and accomplished New York rare book dealer, agrees to do a little job for rich publisher and demonologist Boris Balkan (Langella), he little suspects what's coming. Balkan already owns a copy of the 17th-century Satanic text, *The Nine Gates of the Kingdom of Shadows* – reputedly an aid in summoning the Prince of Darkness – but fears it's not authentic. Corso is to track down the other two extant copies and compare their engravings. But Balkan's not the only one after the book, as Corso's encounters with a mysterious girl who seems to be following him (Seigner) and the widow of a previous owner of the text (Olin) make clear. Polanski's film is as elegantly assembled as one would expect, and there's an engagingly understated irony to a number of scenes that suggests the director didn't see the story – from Arturo Pérez-Reverte's novel *The Dumas Club* – as fodder for a serious study in metaphysical evil. That said, for the most part Polanski plays by the rules, refusing to show anything explicitly supernatural despite the superstitions of everyone involved (save Corso, of course), and preferring to rely on old-fashioned mood and telling details for effect. Fun, but a pale shadow of *Rosemary's Baby*. GA

Nixon

(1995, US, 192 min)
d Oliver Stone. *p* Clayton Townsend, Oliver Stone, Andrew G Vajna. *sc* Stephen J Rivele, Christopher Wilkinson, Oliver Stone. *ph* Robert Richardson. *ed* Brian Berdan, Hank Corwin. *pd* Victor Kempster. *m* John Williams. *cast* Anthony Hopkins, Joan Allen, Powers Boothe, Ed Harris, Bob Hoskins, EG Marshall, David Paymer, David Hyde Pierce, Paul Sorvino, Mary Steenburgen, JT Walsh, James Woods, Kevin Dunn.

●Centred on a storm-tossed night in 1973, with President Nixon slipping into embittered reverie and recollection as he sits in the Lincoln Room at the White House listening to the tapes that may prove his undoing, Stone's film flashes back to Nixon's childhood in '20s California before meandering on to modern times and ending with his funeral. Though fragmented and using various styles and filmstocks, this is more engrossing than most of the duds in the director's ambitious but frustrating career, partly because it focuses squarely on such a tantalising protagonist. As played (not mimicked) by Hopkins, Tricky Dick is a maelstrom of emotions: convinced he's universally misunderstood and hated; haunted by guilt over the dead Kennedys and his own TB-afflicted brothers; alternating between idealism and despair, honesty and lies; scared, stubborn, erratic. It's a rich conception, well supported by muscular performances from Boothe (Al Haig), Sorvino (Kissinger), Hoskins (Hoover) and, especially, Allen (Nixon's wife Pat). With Watergate dominating the third and final hour, however, the narrative becomes more familiar, predictable and prone to bathos and bombast: as wayward and self-regarding as its subject, the film long overstays its welcome. GA

Nô

(1998, Can, 85 min, b/w & col)
d Robert Lepage. *p* Bruno Jobin. *sc* Robert Lepage, André Morency. *ph* Pierre Mignot. *ed* Aube Foglia. *ad* Monique Dion. *m* Michel F Côté, Bernard Falaise. *cast* Marie Brassard, Anne-Marie Cadieux, Richard Fréchette, Alexis Martin, Marie Gignac, Eric Bernier.

●Set in 1970, Lepage's offbeat blend of farce and socio-political satire cuts between Canada, where a none-too-together group of terrorists belonging to the Quebec Liberation Front squabble among themselves while under police surveillance, and Osaka, where one of the activists' girlfriends. is performing in a Feydeau play for the World Expo. So depressed at finding herself pregnant, she has a drunken fling with the Canadian cultural attaché, virtually under the snobby, suspicious nose of his wife. It's a cool, drily amusing, determinedly unromantic roundelay (based on a segment of Lepage's play *The Seven Branches of the River Ota*), which doesn't quite succeed as a comment on various kinds of commitment, but passes the time quite agreeably. GA

Noah's Ark

(1929, US, 135 min, b/w)
d Michael Curtiz. *p* Darryl F Zanuck. *sc* Darryl F Zanuck, Anthony Coldeway, De Leon Anthony. *ph* Hal Mohr, Barney McGill. *ed* Harold McCord. *m* Louis Silvers. *cast* Dolores Costello, George O'Brien, Noah Beery Sr, Louise Fazenda, Guinn Williams, Paul McAllister, Myrna Loy.

●A spectacular and ambitious part-talkie epic which marries a Biblical theme (the Flood) with a romance set on the eve of the Great War. Each actor doubles parts in the Biblical and contemporary stories, and the Warners special effects department has a beano: train wrecks, battles, deluges, and a cast of thousands. Whether it makes any sense as an historical parallel seems somehow beside the point. What matters is that they spent $1.5m on the production, and the money, as they say, is on the screen. A much-trimmed version running 75 minutes (the intertitles and dialogue sequences were eliminated, and a new sound effects track added) was issued in 1957. MA

No Answer from F.P.1 (F.P.1 antwortet nicht)

(1932, Ger, 114 min, b/w)
d Karl Hartl. *p* Erich Pommer. *sc* Walter Reisch, Curt Siodmak. *ph* Günther Rittau, Konstantin Tschet, Otto Baecker. *ed* Willi Zeyn Jr, Rudolf Schaad. *ad* Erich Kettelhut. *m* Allan Gray. *cast* Hans Albers, Sybille Schmitz, Paul Hartmann, Peter Lorre, Herrmann Speelmans, Georg August Koch.

●F.P.1 is an artificial island in mid-Atlantic, and it's not answering because there's a saboteur on board: the designer has been shot, the crew have been gassed, and the structure is sinking… This German sci-fi melodrama aspires to something of the grandeur of *Metropolis*, but its roots really lie in penny dreadful comics and early movie serials. As such, it's rather pedestrian in its exposition (it takes forever to get the plot moving), but fair value once the panics and alarms start multiplying. The stock performances are rather good, especially from Albers as the aviator-hero soaked in booze and self-pity, and Lorre as a bizarrely masochistic photographer. And Curt Siodmak's storyline manages to cross the epic adventure elements with a romantic triangle without either getting in the way of the other. Specialists may care to note the early associations of flying with sexual virility. TR

No Blade of Grass

(1970, GB, 96 min)
d/p Cornel Wilde. *sc* Sean Forestal, Jefferson Pascal. *ph* HAR Thomson. *ed* Frank Clarke, Eric Boyd-Perkins. *ad* Elliot Scott. *m* Burnell Whibley. *cast* Nigel Davenport, Jean Wallace, John Hamill, Lynne Frederick, Patrick Holt, Anthony May, Wendy Richard, George Coulouris.

●An account of an English family's struggle for survival in the new world created by a virus that has destroyed virtually all earth's crops, *No Blade of Grass* lacks the primitive power of Wilde's earlier films *The Naked Prey* and *Beach Red*. Moreover, in its social attitudes and theorising, it exposes the shallowness of Wilde's conception of man as an animal dressed in civilised trappings that can, all too easily, be slipped off. (From a novel by John Christopher.) PH

Nobody Knows Anybody (Nadie conoce a nadie)

(1999, Sp, 108 min)
d Mateo Gil. *p* Gustavo Ferrada, Antonio P Pérez. *sc* Alejandro Amenábar, Mateo Gil. *ph* Javier G Salmones. *m* Alejandro Amenábar. *cast* Jordi Mollà, Eduardo Noriego, Natalia Verbeke, Paz Vega, Pedro Alvarez-Ossorio, Mauro Ribera, Jesús Olmedo, Críspulo Cabezas.

●Ambitious but finally botched thriller. It starts with mysterious murders during Seville's Holy Week, turning preposterously apocalyptic as it proceeds into silly sci-fi territory. Glossy but too comic-strippy for its own good. GA

Nobody Lives Forever

(1946, US, 100 min, b/w)
d Jean Negulesco. *p* Robert Buckner. *sc* WR Burnett. *ph* Arthur Edeson. *ed* Rudi Fehr. *ad* Hugh Reticker. *m* Adolph Deutsch. *cast* John Garfield, Geraldine Fitzgerald, Walter Brennan, Faye Emerson, George Coulouris, George Tobias.

●Garfield is the New York con-man, semi-reformed by wartime service as an army NCO, who goes to Los Angeles to 'rest', but is there tempted to swindle the innocent Fitzgerald of the inheritance left to her by her late husband. Predictable but well-acted Warners yarn, scripted by WR Burnett, with a horribly sugary conversion scene in a chapel at Capistrano, but a memorable finish on a fogbound pier in which the radiantly beautiful Fitzgerald, kidnapped by jibberingly psychotic Coulouris, seems somehow to transcend her oil-stained surroundings. JPy

Nobody Loves Me

see Keiner Liebt Mich

Nobody Ordered Love

(1971, GB, 87 min)
d/p Robert Hartford-Davis. *sc* Robert Shearer. *ph* Desmond Dickinson. *ed* Alan Pattillo. *ad* Hayden Pearce. *m* Tony Osborne. *cast* Ingrid Pitt, Judy Huxtable, John Ronane, Tony Selby, Peter Arne, Mark Eden, David Lodge.

●Dreadful 'exposé' of the movie scene, involving a hustling opportunist (Selby) who wheels and lays his way through a completely phony version of the British film industry. The film in production that all the fuss is about, a challenging anti-war epic that supposedly ends up as a big success, looks every bit as abysmal as the rest.

Nobody Runs Forever (aka The High Commissioner)

(1968, GB/US, 101 min)
d Ralph Thomas. *p* Betty E Box. *sc* Wilfred Greatorex. *ph* Ernest Steward. *ed* Ernest Hosler. *pd* Tony Woollard. *m* Georges Delerue. *cast* Rod Taylor, Christopher Plummer, Lilli Palmer, Camilla Sparv, Daliah Lavi, Clive Revill, Lee Montague, Derren Nesbitt, Burt Kwouk, Franchot Tone, Leo McKern.

●Limp Rank thriller from Jon Cleary's novel *The High Commissioner*, with Taylor as the Aussie cop who tracks the eponymous diplomat (Plummer) to London to investigate his first wife's murder, and finds himself involved in a political assassination intrigue. A lamentable waste of a good cast. PT

Nobody's Fool

(1986, US, 105 min)
d Evelyn Purcell. *p* James C Katz, Jon S Denny. *sc* Beth Henley. *ph* Mikhail Suslov. *ed* Dennis Virkler. *pd* Jackson De Govia. *m* James Newton Howard. *cast* Rosanna Arquette, Eric Roberts, Mare Winningham, Jim Youngs, Louise Fletcher, Gwen Welles, Stephen Tobolowsky.

●The opening track on Cassie (Arquette), in drifty Thrift shop layers puffing at a dandelion clock, may activate fears that Frodo is in the offing, but hang in there. Buckeye Basin – motto: to be or not to be ain't much of a choice – is a cartoon of tank-town half-life. Seen through this perspective, Cassie's kookiness is a touching attempt to keep her dreams alive. Happily, a travelling Shakespeare theatre comes to town, along with hunky set designer Riley (Roberts, improved). The film, full of extraordinary images, seldom slips off its playful perch, and when it does there's always Arquette to cope with the Brautigans. A Shelley Duvall for the '80s, her blend of vulnerability and physical comedy could charm you into believing anything. Delightful. BC

Nobody's Fool

(1994, US, 110 min)
d Robert Benton. *p* Scott Rudin, Arlene Donovan. *sc* Robert Benton. *ph* John Bailey. *ed* John Bloom. *pd* David Gropman. *m* Howard Shore. *cast* Paul Newman, Melanie Griffith,

Bruce Willis, Jessica Tandy, Dylan Walsh, Pruitt Taylor Vince, Philip Bosco, Josef Sommer.
● Around North Bath, upstate New York, Don 'Sully' Sullivan (Newman) is notorious as something of a wastrel. He left his family years ago, he's not averse to a spot of petty crime – especially in his run-ins with construction boss Carl (Willis), with whose wife (Griffith) Sully has a barely platonic relationship – and his cronies include the town idiot and a one-legged lawyer who's never won Sully a case. Only his landlady (Tandy) really believes in him. Still, Sully is a die-hard optimist, and when his estranged son and grandson turn up, a chance arises to make amends to his family. Benton's quietly superb adaptation of Richard Russo's novel is one of those movies you thought they didn't make any more. It succeeds on several levels: as a wry hymn to community and long-term familiarity, a Hawksian fable about responsibility, an elegiac portrait of an endangered way of American life, and a quixotic celebration of unfounded optimism as embodied in Newman's supremely easy playing. GA

Nobody Someday

(2001, GB, 99 min, b/w & col)
d Brian Hill. *p* Caroline Levy. *sc* Brian Hill. *ph* Simon Niblett, Michael Timney. *ed* Stuart Briggs. *m* (incidental/arranger) Guy Chambers. *with* Robbie Williams, Guy Chambers, Gary Nuttall, Fil Eisler, Yolanda Charles, Chris Sharrock, Claire Worall, Tessa Niles, Katie Kissoon.
● Who wants to delve into the psyche of pop star Robbie Williams? No one more than the 27-year-old who commissioned this on the road rockumentary, namely Robbie Williams. He's got the means – and some potentially interesting material: his hugely successful graduation from boy band Take That, the much publicised battles with addiction, the self-deprecating cheekiness. Unfortunately, while pre-concert prayers to Elvis are a nice touch, the central tour itself is drearily uninspired. Shot for TV, the grainy, choppily edited, b/w live scrapbook doesn't particularly impress on the big screen. Various revelations include Robbie playing 'Uno' backstage, Robbie buying a sofa, amusingly sententious bodyguards, and Robbie vacillating over how ace being famous is. Which means, unless you're a devotee satiated by the mere sight of your crush, that the 'wow' factor is barely tangible; the monotone voice-over from director Hill doesn't help. AHa

Nobody Will Speak of Us When We're Dead (Nadie Hablará de Nosotras cuando Hayamos Muerto)

(1995, Sp, 105 min)
d Agustín Díaz Yanes. *p* Edmundo Gil Casas. *sc* Agustín Díaz Yanes. *ph* Francisco Femenia. *ed* José Salcedo. *pd* Benjamin Fernández. *m* Bernardo Bonezzi. *cast* Victoria Abril, Federico Luppi, Pilar Bardem, Daniel Giménez Cacho, Ana Ofelia Murgia.
● This breathtakingly assured film begins in Tarantino mode with Abril caught in the crossfire between Mexican gangsters and DEA agents. She heads back to Spain with details of the Mob's local money-laundering operation; unfortunately, she's a total flop as a cat burglar, and falls off the wagon with a bump. A thriller with a difference: we're concerned, for instance, as much about Abril's fish dinner as the gangsters' reprisals. An acute, witty dissection of machismo in Spanish culture, a disquisition on the existence of God, and an advertisement for adult education. TCh

Noce, La

see Wedding, The

Noce blanche

(1989, Fr, 92 min)
d Jean-Claude Brisseau. *p* Margaret Ménégoz. *sc* Jean-Claude Brisseau. *ph* Romain Winding. *ed* Maria-Luisa Garcia. *m* Jean Musy. *cast* Vanessa Paradis, Bruno Crémer, Ludmilla Mikael, François Negret, Jean Dasté, Véronique Silver.
● This pessimistic romance, a vehicle for teenage French pop star Paradis, is a self-conscious and occasionally nauseating tale of *amour fou*, assembled with some skill from a collection of clichés both banal and exploitative. Paradis plays a troubled (but brilliant) 17-year-old school truant who becomes passionately involved with a 50-year-old married philosophy teacher. There are reasons for her moody, distracted personality: her psychiatrist dad has absented himself to Paris, leaving her alone amid the soulless concrete modernity of St Etienne; her mother is suicidal; her brothers are hardened delinquents; and she herself has a murky history of child prostitution. Paradis doesn't have to act much: the emphasis is on penetrating glances, pulling on jeans, coquettish pawing and petulant tantrums. Crémer provides the film's backbone, bringing intelligence and feeling to the role of a man swamped by an impossible, unwanted, but irresistible passion. WH

Noces de lune

see Wedding Moon

Noces de Papier, Les

see Paper Wedding, A

Noces Rouges, Les (Blood Wedding/Red Wedding/ Wedding in Blood)

(1973, Fr/It, 90 min)
d Claude Chabrol. *p* André Génoves. *sc* Claude Chabrol. *ph* Jean Rabier, *ed* Jacques Gaillard, Monique Gaillard. *ad* Guy Littaye. *m* Pierre Jansen. *cast* Michel Piccoli, Stéphane Audran, Claude Piéplu, Eliana De Santis, Clotilde Joano, François Robert, Daniel Lecourtois.
● Coinciding with the French elections, *Les Noces Rouges* was banned ostensibly because it was about a real murder case, but obviously also for the broad portrayal of its Gaullist villain – a man with a sly plan for purchasing property and developing it as factory-workers' high-rise dwellings plus plastics factory which, while benefiting the town, will end up pouring a small fortune into his own pocket. Sadly, although there is more positive vulgarity around than ever, Chabrol doesn't seem to know how to take his errant couple. As more or less critically approached figures of fun, they're great; it's when he falls in love with them that the film goes awry. Should have been sly and funny, or dark and tragic; ends up neither one nor the other. VG

Noche en la Terraza

see Night on the Terrace

Nocturna

(1978, US, 83 min)
d Harry Tampa [Harry Hurwitz]. *p* Vernon P Becker. *sc* Harry Tampa. *ph* Mac Ahlberg. *ed* Ian Maitland. *ad* Jack Krueger, Steve De Vita. *m/songs* Reid Whitelaw, Norman Bergen. *cast* Yvonne De Carlo, John Carradine, Nai Bonet, Brother Theodore, Sy Richardson, Tony Hamilton.
● And now, suckers – Dracula…disco version. The Count's statuesque granddaughter Nocturna (played with unusual zomboid quality by executive producer Nai Bonet) runs away to the New York disco scene with what she calls 'my boyfriend', a friendly blond hulk who had been doing a gig in Transylvania. There are a few ideas which wouldn't disgrace a Mel Brooks movie: Dracula (Carradine) wearing dentures, a lady vamp sleeping in curlers and coffin, and her exasperated complaints about the quality of urban blood through 'pollution, drugs and preservatives'. It's all terrible, but there's no indication that it's meant to be anything else. Only see it when you feel very, very silly. JS

Nocturne

(1946, US, 88 min, b/w)
d Edwin L Marin. *p* Joan Harrison. *sc* Jonathan Latimer. *ph* Harry J Wild. *ed* Elmo Williams. *ad* Albert S D'Agostino, Robert Boyle. *m* Leigh Harline. *cast* George Raft, Lynn Bari, Virginia Huston, Joseph Pevney, Myrna Dell, Mabel Paige.
● Scripted by Jonathan Latimer and treading similar ground to *Laura*, *Nocturne* turns investigation (the search for a composer's murderer) into obsession, largely through Raft's understated performance. He follows a typically fetishistic trail: spurred on by photographs of the victim's lovers, and looking for 'Dolores', just a name in a song by a dead man… SJ

No Deposit, No Return

(1976, US, 112 min)
d Norman Tokar. *p* Ron Miller. *sc* Arthur Alsberg, Don Nelson. *ph* Frank Phillips. *ed* Cotton Warburton. *ad* John B Mansbridge, Jack Senter. *m* Buddy Baker. *cast* David Niven, Darren McGavin, Don Knotts, Herschel Bernardi, Barbara Feldon, Kim Richards, Brad Savage, John Williams, Charlie Martin Smith.
● Lukewarm Disney comedy about two kids – plus pet skunk, natch – mistakenly kidnapped by a pair of bungling crooks. Millionaire grandpa Niven, normally pestered out of his life at hols time, is highly delighted and does his best to see they stay kidnapped. The kids/crooks scenes are fair enough, with Darren McGavin milking his part for every resigned look it's worth. There are also some good Harold Lloyd antics in pursuit of the skunk, and a funny car chase. But the rest is sacrificed to the bland presence of Niven, looking throughout as if he's doing everyone a favour. He isn't. AN

No Drums, No Bugles

(1971, US, 85 min)
d/p/sc Clyde Ware. *ph* Richard McCarty, Peter Bartlett. *ed* David Bretherton, Richard Halsey. *m* Lyle Ritz. *cast* Martin Sheen, Davey Davison, Rod McCary, Denine Terry.
● Virtually a solo piece for Sheen, as the legendary Ashby Gatrell, sitting out the Civil War in a Virginia cave. Surprisingly watchable for what boils down to a long interior monologue, and retrospectively resonant as one of Sheen's trio of key military portraits: his pacifist here shading into his deserter in *The Execution of Private Slovik* and his uncomprehending Willard in *Apocalypse Now*. Sheen and Ware later reunited on the telemovie *Story of Pretty Boy Floyd*. PT

No End (Bez Konca)

(1984, Pol, 107 min)
d Krzysztof Kieslowski. *sc* Krzysztof Kieslowski, Krzysztof Piesiewicz. *ph* Jacek Petrycki. *ed* Krystyna Rutkowska. *ad* Allan Starski. *m* Zbigniew Preisner. *cast* Grazyna Szapolowska, Maria Pakulnis, Aleksander Bardini, Jerzy Radziwilowicz, Artur Barcis, Michal Bajor.
● A film not seen outside Poland until 1986 because of its pro-Solidarity stance. It opens with its hero (Radziwilowicz) explaining that he is already dead; he spends his time, unseen, patiently observing the actions of his wife, child and lawyer colleagues, and just occasionally intervening from his spirit world. He was a lawyer who specialised in representing victims of Poland's martial law, but now he watches helpless as one of his clients is persuaded by his survivors to renounce his principles in order to remain free. Interwoven in the knotty debates on law, freedom and *realpolitik*, is the growing despair of his wife, who discovers too late that she loved him more than she thought. Western cinema has the luxury of being politically apathetic if it wishes; it is heartening to find that a film burning with a passionate engagement with the system can still emerge from a closed world. And one, moreover, which still has space for tenderness, quiet, and an excursion into the realms of the spirit. CPea

No Escape

(1994, US, 115 min)
d Martin Campbell. *p* Gale Anne Hurd. *sc* Michael Gaylin, Joel Gross. *ph* Philip Meheux. *ed* Terry Rawlings. *pd* Allan Cameron. *m* Graeme Revell. *cast* Ray Liotta, Lance Henriksen, Stuart Wilson, Kevin Dillon, Kevin J O'Connor, Don Henderson, Jack Shepherd.
● This futuristic prison movie takes place on an island where civilisation has broken down, to be replaced by a violent struggle between two primitive factions. The anarchic Outsiders, led by the charismatic Marek (Wilson), have 'gone native', wearing fearsome masks and launching repeated attacks on the peace-loving Insiders' fenced-off commune. Presided over by their spiritual leader, the Father (Henriksen), these born-again New Age hippies grow crops, wear hand-knits and try to recover their self-esteem. Meanwhile,

the prison island's sadistic warder rubs his hands at the prospect of the factions wiping each out. Ex-Marine Captain Liotta is the wild card who may shift the balance of power. Impressive production values, but, regrettably, the robust action scenes and human drama are too often dwarfed by the stunning landscapes and imaginative sets, or clouded by the script's baggy philosophising. NF

No Exit

see Huis Clos

No Fear, No Die

see S'en fout la mort

No Highway (aka No Highway in the Sky)

(1951, GB, 99 min, b/w)
d Henry Koster. *p* Louis D Lighton. *sc* Alec Coppel, RC Sherriff, Oscar Millard. *ph* Georges Périnal. *ed* Manuel Del Campo. *ad* CP Norman. *m* Malcolm Arnold. *cast* James Stewart, Marlene Dietrich, Glynis Johns, Jack Hawkins, Elizabeth Allan, Janette Scott, Ronald Squire, Niall MacGinnis, Kenneth More.

●Flying to Labrador to investigate an air crash, scientist Jimmy Stewart works out that the plane he is travelling in (with Dietrich as a glamorous fellow-passenger) is due to disintegrate at any minute. The drama (based on Nevil Shute's novel) strains credibility; but sly comic touches from the leads effectively give us a nod and a wink, while Koster milks the suspense for all it's worth. TCh

Noire de..., La

see Black Girl

Noir et Blanc

(1986, Fr, 80 min, b/w)
d/sc Claire Devers. *ph* Daniel Desbois, Christopher Doyle, Alain Lasfargues, Jean-Paul de Costa. *ed* Fabienne Alvarez, Yves Sarda. *ad* Claire Devers. *cast* Francis Frappat, Jacques Martial, Joséphine Fresson, Marc Berman, Claire Rigollier, Benoît Régent, Isaach de Bankolé.

●Accountant Antoine (Frappat) is so shy that his health club boss suggests a massage to reduce tension. Thus he takes his first steps into a secret life of self-discovery, shame and pain. Devers' debut, adapted from Tennessee Williams' short story *Desire and the Black Masseur*, is a compelling look at an asexual sado-masochistic relationship between two utterly ordinary men. Shot, rightly, in black-and-white, the film never romanticises the tender emotions that grow in a climate of sinister ritual and silent desire, nor does it fall prey to easy moralising or racial stereotypes. Until the enigmatic final scene, Devers' quiet observations are lucid, often touching and funny. Most impressively, the handling of potentially sensationalist subject matter is discreet but tough. The performances, too, are admirably understated. GA

Noises Off

(1992, US, 104 min)
d Peter Bogdanovich. *p* Frank Marshall. *sc* Marty Kaplan. *ph* Tim Suhrstedt. *ed* Lisa Day. *pd* Norman Newberry. *cast* Carol Burnett, Michael Caine, Denholm Elliott, Julie Hagerty, Marilu Henner, Mark Linn-Baker, Christopher Reeve, John Ritter, Nicollette Sheridan.

●Another theatrical metaphor fails to transfer to the screen. This adaptation of Michael Frayn's stage hit undoubtedly has its moments, but will still disappoint those who laughed themselves silly at the original. Frayn's play is literally a set piece: the humour derives from the way his cast of *farceurs* eminently succeed in tripping over the furniture, and suffering havoc from every prop, every technical and personal nightmare known to the business. Bogdanovich's film neither reproduces the tableau immediacy of the original, nor opens it up sufficiently as Peter Yates did with *The Dresser*. The result is almost always frustrating, the camera often cutting away from the point of a scene or an exchange, and the early part of the film flags badly before the giddy mayhem of the climax. Reeve (as a squeamish matinee idol) and Elliott (as the veteran drunk) turn in top-rate performances. Not good or fun enough, though. SGr

Noi Tre (We Three/ The Three of Us)

(1984, It, 90 min)
d Pupi Avati. *p* Antonio Avati. *sc* Pupi Avati, Antonio Avati. *ph* Pasquale Rachini. *ed* Amedeo Salfa. *ad* Giancarlo Basili, Leonardo Scarpa. *m* Riz Ortolani. *cast* Christopher Davidson, Lino Capolicchio, Dario Parisini, Carlo Delle Piane, Gianni Cavina, Ida Di Benedetto.

●It's idyllic summer-interlude time for the 14-year-old Mozart. To prepare for examinations for Bologna's Accademia Filarmonica, spunky young Amadé comes with his father to the country villa of Count Pallavicini. It is not a welcoming household: the Count is a curmudgeon with a distant young wife, a diffident son Giuseppe (who pisses on their bed) and a mad cousin. Avati's interest is in showing Mozart as a common-or-garden spotted youth, sneaking in a quick adolescence (fights with local roughnecks, romance with a neighbour's daughter, bonding with Giuseppe) between music lessons, exam pressure, overbearing parental encouragement, and the damnable, insistent call of genius. It's not an engaging tale, shot with the restraint of Straub but with hardly a note of music to relieve the deathly monotony. Framed as a poetic imagining, in the present, of two old men taking a walk in the woods, the film is entirely true to their dull inspiration. WH

Noi vivi

see We the Living

No Man of Her Own

(1932, US, 81 min, b/w)
d Wesley Ruggles. *sc* Maurine Watkins, Milton H Gropper. *ph* Leo Tover. *cast* Clark Gable, Carole Lombard, Dorothy Mackaill, Grant Mitchell, J Farrell MacDonald, Charley Grapewin.

●Gable's the boss of a gang of cardsharps, Lombard's the small town librarian who marries him on a bet. Lightly brushing at least three separate genres, this good-natured yarn (from a story by Edmund Goulding and Benjamin Glazer) eschews conflict at every turn. The henchmen are supportive, the rejected girlfriend rallies round, the cop's kind-hearted: the film resolutely refuses to admit a villain. Besides, Ruggles was a famously one-take director who relished spontaneity, e.g. the scene where Gable asks Grapewin for directions. It's also a reminder of how relaxed Hollywood movies were before the enforcement of the Production Code, in their sexual references and in the casual disrobings by their leading ladies. BBa

No Man of Her Own

(1949, US, 98 min, b/w)
d Mitchell Leisen. *p* Richard Maibaum. *sc* Sally Benson, Catherine Turney. *ph* Daniel L Fapp. *ed* Alma Macrorie. *ad* Hans Dreier, Henry Bumstead. *m* Hugo Friedhofer. *cast* Barbara Stanwyck, John Lund, Jane Cowl, Phyllis Thaxter, Richard Denning, Lyle Bettger, Henry O'Neill, Milburn Stone.

●Based on a Cornell Woolrich novel (*I Married a Dead Man*) that bears many similarities to his *Waltz Into Darkness* (filmed by Truffaut as *La Sirène du Mississipi*), this is an excellent little thriller, tautly directed by Leisen and with a powerhouse performance from Stanwyck as a pregnant woman who assumes the identity of a young bride killed with her husband in a train crash. Just as she is enjoying the fiscal fruits of deception, her lover (Bettger) shows up and blackmails her. Apart from John Lund's predictable performance as the romantic lead – he's as anaemic here as in Wilder's *A Foreign Affair* – the film is constantly surprising and deliriously implausible. ATu

No Man's Land

(1985, Switz/Fr/WGer/GB, 110 min)
d Alain Tanner. *p* Alain Tanner, Marin Karmitz. *sc* Alain Tanner. *ph* Bernard Zitzermann. *ed* Laurent Uhler. *pd* Alain Nicolet. *m* Terry Riley. *cast* Hughes Quester, Myriam Mézières, Jean-Philippe Ecoffey, Betty Berr, Marie-Luce Felber.

●A very inconsequential yarn about a group of disenchanted small time smugglers (a cowman, an Algerian girl, a couple who run a club with a small dance-floor) in a village somewhere on the frontier of France and Switzerland. A gold run seems to offer the prospect of the freedom they all crave, but oddball characters, some torrid clinical sex and a lot of coming and going through the woods and across the mountains fails, regrettably, to add up to anything either significant or diverting. JPy

No Man's Land

(1987, US, 106 min)
d Peter Werner. *p* Joseph Stern, Dick Wolf. *sc* Dick Wolf. *ph* Hiro Narita. *ed* Steve Cohen, Daniel Hanley. *pd* Paul Peters. *m* Basil Poledouris. *cast* DB Sweeney, Charlie Sheen, Lara Harris, Randy Quaid, Bill Duke, RD Call, Arlen Dean Snyder, M Emmet Walsh, Brad Pitt.

●Great to watch experts at work, but one of the things that militates against this portrait of professional car thieves is that they daren't show you how they do it (after *Rififi*, there was a rash of burglars sticking umbrellas through ceilings to catch falling plaster). Beyond carrying a posh shopping-bag to allay suspicion, there are no tips about ripping off Porsches. Rookie cop Benjy (Sweeney) is sent to infiltrate a bent garage owned by Ted Varrick (Sheen), who may have been implicated in the killing of a cop. Varrick lives the high life, and is so personable that Benjy falls for his spell and his sister (Harris, toneless and wilting), besides getting off on stealing cars. Will the cop in him rise up in time to intercept the evil in Varrick? Surface stuff, with neither actor up to the ambiguities, but entertaining enough around the car chases. BC

No Man's Land

(2001, Fr/It/GB/Bel/Slovenia, 98 min)
d Danis Tanovic. *p* Frédérique Dumas-Zajdela, Marc Baschet, Cedomir Kolar. *sc* Danis Tanovic. *ph* Walther Vanden Ende. *ed* Francesca Calvelli. *pd* Dusko Milavec. *m* Danis Tanovic. *cast* Branko Djuric, Rene Bitorajac, Filip Sovagovic, Georges Siatidis, Serge-Henri Valcke, Sacha Kremer, Simon Callow, Katrin Cartlidge.

●Bosnian Tanovic's taut, witty script is the secret of this film's success in mounting a darkly comic but very suspenseful satirical attack on the absurdity of war. By a cruel twist of fate, three soldiers – two Bosnians, one Serb – find themselves trapped in a trench between lines, with one of the Bosnians wounded and lying on a mine that will explode if he so much as moves; a UN sergeant tries to help him, but repeatedly faces obstacles in the form of his own superiors, the press, and the mutual hatred of the two other soldiers. The performances are uniformly good, the direction conventionally slick but very efficient. It's Tanovic's ear for dialogue, however, and firm grasp of dramatic structure that impress most as the situation spirals out of control. Admirably, it's pretty even-handed, too. GA

No Maps on My Taps

(1979, US, 60 min)
d George T Nierenberg. *cast* Chuck Green, Sandman Sims, Buster Brown, Bunny Briggs.

●Can blue men sing the whites? Can Fred Astaire tap dance? Well – yes; but the top-hat-and-tails routine, like the Clapton solo, sho' nuff got black roots. This lively showcase for veteran Harlem hoofers delightedly lets them show. A spirited tap 'contest' in front of the Lionel Hampton Band and an enthusiastic audience caps a unique retrospective portrait of the art, featuring amazing clips from both mainstream and 'race' movies of the '30s heyday, and fixing tap as another enduring expression of black American culture. PT

No Mercy

(1986, US, 108 min)
d Richard Pearce. *p* D Constantine Conte. *sc* Jim Carabatsos. *ph* Michel Brault. *ed* Jerry Greenberg, Bill Yahraus. *pd* Patrizia von Brandenstein. *m* Alain Silvestri. *cast* Richard Gere, Kim Basinger, Jeroen Krabbé, George Dzundza, Gary Basaraba, William Atherton, Ray Sharkey.

●His partner murdered by hoodlums, tough Chicago cop Eddie Jillette (Gere) takes a trip to New Orleans on a mission of vengeance against gangster Losado (Krabbé). Trouble is, the sole witness to the crime – a sultry, pouting blonde named Michel (Basinger) – is also Losado's slave-cum-mistress. To complicate matters, they do things different down South, and pretty soon Eddie's at loggerheads not only with Losado's lot but with the New Orleans cops. What matter, though, when a sweaty stint fleeing through the Bayou swamps with Michel brings at long last love into Eddie's life? Richard Pearce's thriller suffers from near-total predictability, with a script that careers headlong through clichéd situations, calculatedly coarse dialogue, and cardboard characters. That said, Pearce reveals a strong feel for lurid locations and spectacular set pieces, and makes the film look stylish, too much so in the case of the three leads. Indeed, taken straight it's all a little risible; but as fast-paced hokum pitted with plot-holes, it's polished fun – no more, no less. GA

No Mercy, No Future (Die Berührte)

(1981, WGer, 108 min)
d/p Helma Sanders-Brahms. *sc* Helma Sanders-Brahms, Rita G. *ph* Thomas Mauch. *ed* Ursula West, Hanni Lewerenz. *m* Manfred Opitz, Harald Grosskopf. *cast* Elisabeth Stepanek, Hubertus von Weyrauch, Irmgard Mellinger, Nguyen Chi Danh, Erich Koitzsch-Koltzack, Curt Curtini, Carola Regnier.

● Based on a letter received from a schizophrenic woman, this is not about treatment or clinical causes, but – as Sanders-Brahms puts it – about 'madness from within'. Called Veronika, the woman trudges through Berlin, lank-haired and grey faced, giving herself to society's castoffs (the old, the disabled, the immigrants) in the hope of finding Christ. Elisabeth Stepanek's performance is faultless, her heavy yet mobile face always interesting. But it's questionable whether the film is successful at exploring emotions 'from within'. The hallucinations are mere effects, the stroboscopic sequence is physically unbearable; while the sex and suicide attempts are more curious than moving. But detachment is continually challenged by urgent evidence of the madness on the outside: the tawdriness of Berlin (the paradigmatic schizoid city), the radio news reports, the shadowy figures of the girl's crabby parents living in uncomfortable, rococo splendour. If it's miserable being mad, it's pretty tough being ordinary. JS

None But the Brave

(1965, US/Jap, 105 min)
d/p Frank Sinatra. *sc* John Twist, Katsuya Susaki. *ph* Harold Lipstein. *ed* Sam O'Steen. *ad* LeRoy Deane. *m* John Williams. *cast* Clint Walker, Tatsuya Mihashi, Frank Sinatra, Tommy Sands, Brad Dexter, Takeshi Kato, Tony Bill, Sammy Jackson.

● Sinatra's sole attempt at direction prefigures Boorman's *Hell in the Pacific* by stranding a World War II planeload of American marines on the same tiny island in the Solomons as a band of marooned survivors from a Japanese battalion. The carefully constructed mood as the two groups warily circle each other – spasmodically clashing in battle, tentatively setting up lines of contact, gradually establishing an all too brief time out of war – is stupidly fractured by two flashbacks obviously designed to provide a love interest; and the anti-war message is naively overplayed. Nevertheless, Sinatra displays great competence as an action director, and a sequence where the Americans attempt to capture a boat laboriously built by the Japanese is beautifully choreographed, ending with a memorable shot of both sides staring in silence as a hand-grenade destroys their only means of escape. Excellent performances, too (with the Japanese mercifully allowed to speak Japanese). TM

None But the Brave

see Kung Fu Girl, The

None But the Lonely Heart

(1944, US, 113 min, b/w)
d Clifford Odets. *p* David Hempstead. *sc* Clifford Odets. *ph* George Barnes. *ed* Roland Gross. *ad* Albert S D'Agostino, Jack Okey. *m* Hanns Eisler. *cast* Cary Grant, Ethel Barrymore, June Duprez, Barry Fitzgerald, Jane Wyatt, Dan Duryea, George Coulouris.

● A fascinating but dissatisfying adaptation by Odets of Richard Llewellyn's tale of a Cockney wastrel, living in the London slums of the '30s, who mends his selfish ways when he realises that his mum (Barrymore) is dying. Bogus poetry wrecks the Cockney dialogue, dripping sentimentality and a distinctly Hollywoodian East End soften the darker shadows of the piece. The performances, however, and George Barnes' camerawork are worth watching. GA

None Shall Escape

(1944, US, 86 min, b/w)
d André De Toth. *p* Sam Bischoff. *sc* Lester Cole. *ph* Lee Garmes. *ed* Charles Nelson. *ad* Lionel Banks. *m* Ernst Toch. *cast* Alexander Knox, Marsha Hunt, Henry Travers, Richard Crane, Dorothy Morris, Trevor Bardette.

● Scripted by Lester Cole (later one of the HUAC 'Hollywood Ten'), this anticipates the end of WWII and the Nuremberg Trials to stage an International War Crimes Commission in Warsaw. The case under consideration is that of Wilhelm Grimm (Knox), former Reichs Commissioner of the Western Region of Poland. Fascinatingly, although 'leniency' is not the order of the day (as the title suggests), and no punches are pulled in detailing his crimes (the term 'extermination camp' is not used, but the script is unique for the period in making it quite clear that Grimm's regime in Warsaw is to implement the final solution), the film is not concerned with zomboid Nazis and their horrors. Rather, tracing Grimm's career in flashback from 1919, when he returned after WWI minus a leg and plus a bitter resentment of Germany's humiliation in defeat, it attempts to probe the psychology of the man; and in so doing, without in any way condoning or sympathising, it manages to elicit a glimmer of understanding. There are naiveties, and the film now suffers from a certain déjà vu; but script, direction and acting all remain impressive. TM

Nonhosonno

see Sleepless

No Nukes

(1980, US, 103 min)
d Julian Schlossberg, Danny Goldberg, Anthony Potenza. *p* Julian Schlossberg, Danny Goldberg. *ph* Haskell Wexler. *ed* Joel Goodman, Neil Kaufman, Dennis O'Connor, Ahmad Shirazi, Stan Warnow, (music sequences) Ed Rothkowitz, (documentary sequences) Anthony Potenza. *with* James Taylor, Carly Simon, Bonnie Raitt, Graham Nash, John Hall, David Crosby, Stephen Stills, Jackson Browne, The Doobie Brothers, Bruce Springsteen, Phoebe Snow, Ralph Nader, Jane Fonda.

● First the good news: 20 minutes of Springsteen. The bad news is a further 80 minutes of concert and behind-the-scenes footage which, unless you're a fan of the soft rock icons of the late '60s, looks like a catalogue of aged hippies reliving their former glory. Filmed during five concerts performed for free and organised by Musicians United for Safe Energy (MUSE), it's a pity that the movie builds so obviously towards Springsteen's appearance, defusing the very real political message of the MUSE team (Nuclear Energy is BAD for you) and turning Springsteen into nothing more than a crowd-puller. (Haskell Wexler directed the documentary footage, and Barbara Kopple the Madison Square Garden sequence and Battery Park Rally.) FF

No Orchids for Miss Blandish

(1948, GB, 104 min, b/w)
d St John L Clowes. *p* AR Shipman. *sc* St John L Clowes. *ph* Gerald Gibbs. *ed* Manuel Del Campo. *ad* Harry Moore. *m* George Melachrino. *cast* Jack LaRue, Hugh McDermott, Linden Travers, Walter Crisham, Lily Molnar, Zoe Gail, Charles Goldner, Percy Marmont, Sidney James.

● 'The most sickening exhibition of brutality, perversion, sex and sadism ever to be shown on a cinema screen,' squawked the *Monthly Film Bulletin*. 'Nauseating muck', 'about as fragrant as a cesspool', 'a wicked disgrace to the British film industry' echoed the national press. The film's 'hero' – a down-at-heel newspaperman – is indeed a nasty piece of work, and as insensitive as his colleagues in the real world to the fondly passionate relationship between Miss Blandish and her morbidly introverted kidnapper. But the critical hysteria over this confident, well-crafted homage to Hollywood is puzzling. The sets, the acting, the smoothly effective direction are all remarkably good, redolent of a short-lived maturity attained by British cinema in the late '40s. James Hadley Chase's novel was remade in 1971 as *The Grissom Gang*. RMy

Noose

(1948, GB, 95 min, b/w)
d Edmond T Gréville. *p* Edward Dryhurst. *sc* Richard Llewellyn. *ph* Hone Glendining. *ed* Dpuglas Robertson, David Newhouse. *ad* Bernard Robinson. *m* Charles Williams. *cast* Carole Landis, Joseph Calleia, Derek Farr, Stanley Holloway, Nigel Patrick, Ruth Nixon, Carol Van Derman, Hay Petrie, John Slater.

● Richard Llewellyn's adaptation of his own play is something of a transatlantic compromise. Calleia, a vicious Mafia-style gangster nastier than Edward G Robinson ever was in his heyday, heads a profitable black market racket in post-war Soho, throwing vicious tantrums and pursuing his hedonistic pleasures (ex-girlfriends get knuckledustered and dumped in the Thames) while his partner, a cheery Cockney wide-boy (Patrick), takes care of the business end. His comeuppance – brought about when an intrepid girl reporter (Landis) stirs up trouble, and her ex-army husband (Farr) leads troops of local workers in a pugilistic rescue – is very British and slightly risible. But taking the whole thing by the scruff of the neck, the talented Gréville turns it into something rich, strange and rather wonderful. His boldly stylised direction, backed by Hone Glendining's expressionistic lighting and the daringly over-the-top performances (Calleia and Patrick are both marvellous), gives this grippingly black yet bleakly funny thriller an almost Wellesian edge. TM

No Pets

(1994, US, 79 min)
d Tony Buba. *p* Tony Buba, M Meather Hartley. *sc* Jim Daniels. *ph* John Rice. *ed* John Stuart Bick. *cast* John Amplas, Lori Cardihle, Ben Tatar, Rick Applegate.

● Shot on a shoestring budget in Pittsburgh, this is a perceptive, unpatronising and compassionate study of a blue-collar worker struggling through in the face of inevitable disappointments. Episodic in structure, it follows Eddie (Amplas), a factory machinist, a single man, and owner of a mongrel that his landlady wants shot of. What happens to a guy like this, stuck in a dead-end job when his high-school pals went off to college, left to contemplate the might-have-beens over a beer with the guys from work? There are no false promises or fake uplift here, just an honest stare into the face of some uncomfortable home truths. TJ

No Place to Go (Die Unberührbare)

(2000, Ger, 100 min, b/w)
d Oskar Röhler. *p* Ulrich Caspar, Käte Ehrmann. *sc* Oskar Röhler. *ph* Hagen Bogdanski. *ed* Isabel Meier. *ad* Birgit Kniep. *m* Martin Todsharow. *cast* Hannelore Elsner, Vadim Glowna, Jasmin Tabatabai, Lars Rudolph, Michael Gwisdek, Nina Petri, Tonio Arango, Claudia Giesler.

● The spirit of RW Fassbinder presides over this intense, personal drama. Hanna Flanders might be a distant cousin to Lola or Maria Braun, except that she's based on director Röhler's mother, novelist Giseta Elsner. Like Fassbinder, Röhler links his tragic heroine's psyche to the political sphere. The film's set in 1989, as the Berlin Wall comes down. Germany is high on freedom and truth – in fact, almost everyone Hanna meets on her pilgrimage to Berlin is literally drunk – but the novelist is in despair. A Leninist to her core, long ago rejected by publishers in the West, she mourns the victory of consumerism over the Communist ideal. A woman of a certain age and then some, she's formidable, articulate, and a bag of neuroses, teetering on the high heels of collapse. Röhler gets a brave, brittle performance out of Hannelore Elsner (no relation): together, they don't soften this often ridiculous, lost and unlovely woman, but make us grateful for the small kindnesses she encounters on her way. Shot in stark, sometimes lovely monochrome, and directed with impressive assurance and sensitivity, this is a tough, intelligent film of a kind not often encountered. TCh

No quiero volver a casa

see I Won't Go Back Home

Nora

(1999, GB/Ire/Ger/It, 106 min)
d Pat Murphy. *p* Bradley Adams, Damon Bryant, Tracey Seaward, (Volta Films) Tiernan MacBride. *sc* Pat Murphy, Gerard Stembridge. *ph* Jean-François Robin. *ed* Pia Da Ciaula. *pd* Alan MacDonald. *m* Stanislas Syrewicz. *cast* Ewan McGregor, Susan Lynch, Peter McDonald, Roberto Citran, Andrew Scott, Vincent McCabe, Veronica Duffy, Alan Devine.
●Great films about great writers are few and far between, and any portrait of James Joyce as a young man inevitably has too much to live up to. Nevertheless, director Murphy and her co-writer Gerald Stembridge have a go, and at least they make a fist of it. Wisely, they focus on Nora Barnacle, the chambermaid Joyce became obsessed with, and who inspired his most vivid writing. On their first date he comes in her hand. 'It was sacred for me,' he tells her. 'Have you a handkerchief?' she wants to know. As Nora, Lynch is remarkable: thick lipped and long faced, she's a constant adventuress in love; bold, earthy and every inch her own woman. As Joyce, McGregor combines bookish absorbency with raffish self-conviction, but he doesn't spring to life in the same way. Their love is pornographic and spiritual, jealous and pure. Joyce discovers everything through Nora, and when the well is dry, he engineers his own betrayal for new material. Although it's an intelligent effort, it is an effort all the same. TCh

Nora Helmer

(1973, WGer, 101 min)
d/sc Rainer Werner Fassbinder. *ph* Willi Raber, Wilfried Mier, Peter Weyrich, Gisela Loew, Hans Schlugg. *ed* Anne-Marie Bornheimer, Friedrich Niquet. *pd* Friedrich Boehm. *cast* Margit Carstensen, Joachim Hansen, Barbara Valentin, Ulli Lommel, Klaus Löwitsch.
●Fassbinder's version of Ibsen's *A Doll's House* for television develops a radical yet scrupulous reading of the play. Stripped of sentimentality and giving Nora (Carstensen) self-assurance from the start, this studio production delivers its critique of bourgeois marriage with a force rarely matched even in the theatre. The brutal prose, harshly delivered, is complemented by the unique visual spectacle which Fassbinder manages to wring from a videotape studio. Achieving effects of lighting and framing which British TV directors have never dreamed of, he makes the oppressiveness of Nora's home as concrete as a tank-trap. Almost every scene is shot through latticework, net curtains, cut glass, ornate mirrors, so that the characters are perhaps visually obscured but always intellectually focused. All the BBC's producers of tele-classics should be chained to chairs and forced to watch it. JW

Nord (North)

(1991, Fr, 96 min)
d Xavier Beauvois. *p* Bernard Verley. *sc* Xavier Beauvois, Arlette Langmann, Sophie Fillières. *ph* Fabio Conversi. *ed* Agnès Guillemot. *m* Philippe Chatiliez. *cast* Xavier Beauvois, Bulle Ogier, Bernard Verley, Agnès Evrard, Thomas Langmann, Pierre Richard, Raoul Billerey.
●Despite an (acknowledged) debt to the films of Maurice Pialat, this feature debut by Xavier Beauvois is a pretty distinctive achievement, not only for the authenticity of its observations (it's set in Calais, where the writer/director/lead actor grew up), but for the raw honesty of its emotional content. At first you think it's Beauvois, as the teenager bored out his box by provincial life, who's on the slippery slope; then it transpires it's his pharmacist dad (Verley) who's into substance abuse; then mum (Ogier), hitherto apparently the voice of reason, gets in on the dysfunctional act. Aided by superb performances, Beauvois shows us the potential (and all too common) horrors of everyday family life without moralising or sensationalism; as in his even more ambitious follow-up (*Don't Forget You're Going to Die*), there's real depth, insight and truth here. GA

No Retreat, No Surrender

(1985, US, 84 min)
d Corey Yuen. *p* Ng See Yuen. *sc* Keith Strandberg. *ph* John Huneck, David Golia. *ed* Alan Poon, Mark Pierce, James Melkonian. *m* Paul Gilreath. *cast* Kurt McKinney, Jean-Claude Van Damme, JW Fails, Kathie Sileno, Kim Tai Chong, Kent Lipham.
●McKinney, a Bruce Lee freak, is disappointed when his karate instructor dad opts out of a confrontation with some dumb heavies and moves the family to Seattle. There McKinney chums up with break dancer RJ (Fails), who shows him the town's most famous slab of marble, covering the grave of the late Bruce Lee; and as the new boy in town, he becomes a choice victim for the bully boys who frequent the hamburger bars. Drawing upon the spirit and skills of his deceased mentor to quell the local populace, he also gets even with the bad guys who chop-sueyed his father. *No Retreat, No Surrender* borrows heavily from the likes of *The Last Dragon*, *Karate Kid* and even *Rocky IV*, but makes them look like masterpieces by comparison. Some fancy dan karate and a good cameo performance from Van Damme as a Russian heavy might have made an enthralling ten-minute video; otherwise it's just more proof that the real thing died with Bruce Lee in 1973, even though the corpse keeps twitching. CB

No Return Address (Sin Remitente)

(1994, Mex, 97 min)
d Carlos Carrera. *p* Gabriela Obregon. *sc* Ignacio Oritz, Silvia Pasternac. *ph* Xavier Pérez Grobet. *ed* Sigfrido Barjau. *pd* Gloria Carrasco. *m* Juan Cristobel Pérez Grobet. *cast* Tiaré Scanda, Fernando Torre Laphame, Guillermo Gil, Luisa Huertas, Luis Filipe Tovar, Gina Morett, Gerardo Moscoso.
●An impressive and melancholy drama, finely lit in dark tones by Xavier Perez Grobet, which sees an old bachelor postal clerk teased into a sad last go at love by an equally 'lost' upstairs neighbour, a twenty-something female photo-journalist who writes him anonymous notes, supposedly from an admirer. It's fascinating to watch Carrera's mordant humanism at work: no character – the clerk, the prostitutes, the modern neighbour, the clerk's unreconstructed friend, especially – is without faults, delusions or reasons. It's this attention to detail, observation and even-handedness that distinguishes the movie. The mood is ably sustained and Laphame (as the clerk) gives a performance that recalls the master Emil Jannings in its old-fashioned pathos. WH

Normal Life

(1995, US, 102 min)
d John McNaughton. *p* Richard Maynard. *sc* Peg Haller, Bob Schneider. *ph* Jean de Segonzac. *ed* Elena Maganini. *pd* Rick Paul. *m* Robert McNaughton, Ken Hale. *cast* Luke Perry, Ashley Judd, Bruce Young, Jim True, Dawn Maxey, Scott Cummins, Kate Walsh, Penelope Milford, Tom Towles.
●This 'true life' crime drama may not view love as a form of pathological delusion, but it sure paints a cynical portrait of suburban alienation, particularly within marriage. The film straddles the territory between freewheeling 'couple on the lam' actioner and darker domestic drama, but isn't settled in either. There are three main characters. Perry is rookie cop Chris, a neat and sober, military moustachioed man who falls for stargazing, self-mutilating, probably suicidal wild card Pam (Ashley Judd, playing it like she's in an Abel Ferrara movie). The third character (as in *My New Gun*) is an automatic weapon, introduced to Pam by Chris on their first date at the Chicago cops' indoor shooting range. As the film traces the arc of Chris and Pam's relationship – an at times bloody battle of diametrically opposed aspirations, coursing through credit card debt, housekeeping arguments and bank-robbing methods – the gun increasingly becomes the third member in a destructive ménage-à-trois, not least in terms of sexual symbolism. The flattened non-judgmental style pays dividends in some highly evocative scenes – the cold discomfort of a marriage ceremony echoing to the sound of Pam's dying father's cough – but in most it seems clumsy and over-emphatic. WH

Norman...Is That You?

(1976, US, 92 min)
d/p George Schlatter. *sc* Ron Clark, Sam Bobrick, George Schlatter. *ph* Gayne Rescher. *ed* George Folsey Jr. *ad* Stephen M Berger. *m* William Goldstein. *cast* Redd Foxx, Pearl Bailey, Dennis Dugan, Michael Warren, Tamara Dobson, Vernée Watson, Jayne Meadows, Wayland Flowers.
●Betrayed by his wife, the boorish manager of an Arizona dry-cleaning establishment is dealt a second blow when he discovers his son Norman living in a hideous Los Angeles apartment with a camp boyfriend. After ninety minutes of shouting, pouting, door-slamming and homespun philosophising – adapted with a black cast from a Broadway flop – one can only marvel at the continuing, condescending, sitcom attitude to homosexuality. Foxx and Bailey bluster helplessly as the parents; the statuesque Dobson, as a hooker brought in to straighten Norman out, looks on in saucer-eyed incomprehension; only Wayland Flowers, a manic puppeteer, manages to transcend the material with an energetic display of self-parody. JPy

Norman Loves Rose

(1982, Aust, 98 min)
d/p/sc Henri Safran. *ph* Vince Monton. *ed* Don Saunders. *pd* Darrell Lass. *m* Mike Perjanik. *cast* Carol Kane, Tony Owen, Warren Mitchell, Myra De Groot, David Downer, Barry Otto, Sandy Gore.
●An ill-conceived Frankenstein's monster of second-hand jokes and worn-out caricatures, this is a disappointment after Safran's earlier *Storm Boy*. While preparing for his bar mitzvah, Norman discovers sacred encouragement for his profane interest in sister-in-law Rose, and seizes the opportunity presented by his mother's absence and his brother Michael's low sperm count. Rose becomes pregnant, but refuses to reveal Norman as the father. Norman is not happy. Only Warren Mitchell's unerring sense of comic timing instils any humour into this banal film; the other characters cast only pale shadows upon the stifling Sydney suburbs. FD

Norma Rae

(1979, US, 114 min)
d Martin Ritt. *p* Tamara Asseyev, Alex Rose. *sc* Irving Ravetch, Harriet Frank Jr. *ph* John A Alonzo. *ed* Sidney Levin. *pd* Walter Scott Herndon. *m* David Shire. *cast* Sally Field, Beau Bridges, Ron Leibman, Pat Hingle, Barbara Baxley, Gail Strickland, Morgan Paull, Robert Broyles, John Calvin.
●Ritt's usual simplistic liberalism certainly dampens the labour relations angle to this tale of a Southern millworker finding herself as a union activist protesting against working conditions. Sentimental and facile, the film allows her far too easy a path to success in terms of her almost universal acceptance by fellow-workers, give or take a few token blacklegs. But far more successful is the way the film stresses her development as an independent woman; finding it painful as she undermines her husband's expectations of her simply as a washing, cooking, ironing, maternal sex-machine, she nevertheless ploughs firmly ahead, while never being portrayed as in any way an incomplete, irresponsible mother and wife. Nicely performed by a strong cast, especially Field and Leibman, it's often mawkishly soft, but surprisingly touching. GA

Norseman, The

(1978, US, 90 min)
d/p/sc Charles B Pierce. *ph* Robert Bethard. *ed* Stephen Dunn, Shirak Khojayan, Aladar Klein, Sarah Legon, Robert Bell. *pd* John Ball, Henry 'Pete' Peterson. *m* Jaime Mendoza-Nava. *cast* Lee Majors, Cornel Wilde, Mel Ferrer, Jack Elam, Christopher Connelly, Kathleen Freeman, Denny Miller, Seamon Glass.
●'Wizard, what say your signs about this New Land?' asks Lee Majors – playing a permed Bionic Bjorn of a Viking prince – of soothsayer Jack Elam in AIP's idea of Norsespeak. The New Land is Vineland (America), and the Six Million Dollar Viking and his crew have rowed across in AD 1006 in search of his father who, it turns out, has been captured and blinded by cartoon Indians who resemble Grateful Dead roadies given the freedom of the make-up department. From then on, even Mel Brooks couldn't have improved on it: hilarious dialogue, eccentrically filmed battle scenes, Cornel Wilde and Mel Ferrer both in beards behind which to hide their embarrassment. AC

North

see Nord

North

(1994, US, 87 min)
d Rob Reiner. *p* Rob Reiner, Alan Zweibel. *sc* Alan Zweibel, Andrew Scheinman. *ph* Adam Greenberg, (Alaska) Mark Vargo. *ed* Robert Leighton. *pd* J Michael Riva. *m* Marc Shaiman. *cast* Elijah Wood, Matthew McCurley, Dan Aykroyd, Kathy Bates, Kelly McGillis, Bruce Willis.

● Tired of suffering neglect and endless rows, bright, popular, eight-year-old North (Wood) makes history by divorcing his parents; the catch is he has to find acceptable replacements by Labor Day, or he'll end up in an orphanage or back with Mom and Dad. Cue a frantic odyssey to Texas, Hawaii, Alaska, Africa where sundry would-be parents fail to live up to his dreams. And what if he decides to go home? Would his pal Winchell (McCurley), riding high on the nationwide fervour he's whipped up in kids against their folks, allow North to abandon the cause? Reiner is undecided just how fantastically he should treat this ludicrous plotline. Added to which there's a dire musical number, a silly thriller subplot, and much maudlin didacticism from narrator Willis in various guardian angel (dis)guises. Misery. GA

North Avenue Irregulars, The (aka Hill's Angels)

(1978, US, 99 min)
d Bruce Bilson. *p* Ron Miller. *sc* Don Tait. *ph* Leonard South. *ed* Gordon D Brenner. *ad* John B Mansbridge, Jack T Collis. *m* Robert F Brunner. *cast* Edward Herrmann, Barbara Harris, Susan Clark, Karen Valentine, Michael Constantine, Cloris Leachman, Patsy Kelly, Douglas Foley.

● The British release title, *Hill's Angels*, may be misleading but it's no misprint: the hero is Presbyterian minister Mike Hill, the angels are his nutty female parishioners, and they all have some cutesy, badly-plotted fun battling against a horrid crime syndicate. The style is the norm for late '70s Disney: low on kids and animals, high on limp satire of contemporary fads (citizens' radio) and car-mangling. The cast is a weird mix of Hollywood veterans and younger talents who deserve far better parts; the director's a recruit from TV; the result is just about bearable. GB

North by Northwest 100 (100)

(1959, US, 136 min)
d/p Alfred Hitchcock. *sc* Ernest Lehman. *ph* Robert Burks. *ed* George Tomasini. *pd* Robert Boyle. *m* Bernard Herrmann. *cast* Cary Grant, Eva Marie Saint, James Mason, Leo G Carroll, Jessie Royce Landis, Leo G Carroll, Josephine Hutchinson, Philip Ober, Martin Landau, Adam Williams, Ed Platt.

● From the glossy '60s-style surface of Saul Bass' credit sequence to Hitchcock's almost audible chortle at his final phallic image, *North by Northwest* treads a bizarre tightrope between sex and repression, nightmarish thriller and urbane comedy. Cary Grant is truly superb as the light-hearted advertising executive who's abducted, escapes, and is then hounded across America trying to find out what's going on and slowly being forced to assume another man's identity. And it's one of those films from which you can take as many readings as you want: conspiracy paranoia, Freudian nightmare (in which mothers, lovers, gays and cops all conspire against a man), parable on modern America in which final escape must be made down the treacherous face of Mt Rushmore (the one carved with US Presidents' heads). All in all, an improbable classic. HM

North Dallas Forty

(1979, US, 118 min)
d Ted Kotcheff. *p* Frank Yablans. *sc* Frank Yablans, Ted Kotcheff, Peter Gent. *ph* Paul Lohmann. *ed* Jay Kamen. *pd* Alfred Sweeney. *cast* Nick Nolte, Mac Davis, Charles Durning, Dayle Haddon, Bo Svenson, John Matuszak, Steve Forrest, GD Spradlin, Dabney Coleman, Savannah Smith.

● Something of a mess, both in terms of the wayward plot which rambles all over the place, and in terms of the rather muddled juggling of audience sympathies. Nolte is the pro-football player who is disgusted on the one hand by the ruthless machinations of the team management, and on the other by the brute macho behaviour of his fellow-players. The trouble is that his confusion is mirrored by the film-makers in that they seem undecided as to whether the sports biz and the hulks it enlists are charismatically exciting or morally bankrupt. But Nolte ambles through it all with naturalistic conviction, and Durning is his usual reliable self. GA

Northerners, The (Der Noorderlingen)

(1992, Neth, 107 min)
d Alex Van Warmerdam. *p* Laurens Geels, Dick Maas. *sc* Alex Van Warmerdam, Aat Ceelen. *ph* Marc Felperlaan. *ed* René Wiegmans. *pd* Rikke Jelier. *m* Vincent Van Warmerdam. *cast* Leonard Lucieer, Jack Wouterse, Rudolf Lucieer, Alex Van Warmerdam, Annet Malherbe, Loes Wouterson.

● Van Warmerdam's bizarre but not unappealing comedy inhabits a world of its own. Set in a remote village in the latter half of 1960, the film observes the oddball antics of the few villagers through the eyes of a 12-year-old boy so obsessed with news from the Congo that he wanders the woods in blackface calling himself Lumumba. Evidently, this is a form of escape from his parents' bickering: his fanatically religious mother is unhappy about the sexual demands made by his butcher father. The neighbours, meanwhile, are a woman desirous of a child and her infertile forest-warden husband, arch-enemy of the postman, who habitually steams open everyone's mail. What all this signifies is unclear. Certainly, the village is presented as a hotbed of hypocrisy, veiled racism, dysfunctional sexuality, and all-round nosiness, but Van Warmerdam isn't one for the explicit touch. That said, there are moments of deadpan charm, and the offbeat tone holds the attention surprisingly well. GA

Northern Lights

(1978, US, 93 min, b/w)
d/p John Hanson, Rob Nilsson. *sc* John Hanson, Harry Nilsson. *ph* Judy Irola. *ed* John Hanson, Harry Nilsson. *ad* Marianna Åström-DeFina, Richard Brown. *m* David Ozzie Ahlers. *cast* Robert Behling, Susan Lynch, Joe Spano, Marianna Åström-DeFina, Ray Ness, Helen Ness, Thorbjorn Rue, Nick Eldridge.

● Extraordinary film-making: vast, looming close-ups of faces in b/w, a landscape gripped by winter, and behind it all a fictional re-creation of the struggle by a handful of Dakota farmers toward political organisation during WWI. The pseudo-documentary tone is maddeningly naive, but the stubborn, passionate images survive. CA

Northern Star, The

see Etoile du Nord, L'

North of Vortex

(1991, GB, 58 min)
d Constantine Giannaris.

● A superbly composed and strikingly evocative film. Skyscrapers, freight trains, desert roads: we are in the midst of an American mood piece distilled from road movies, Kerouac, junk and all that jazz. A (gay) poet picks up a (bi) sailor and a (desperate) waitress. Taking turns behind the wheel, they drive west across the radio dial. Shot in a grainy monochrome you could get lost in, the film never quite arrives at the ironic nonchalance Giannaris is aiming for, but his cool eye for emotional byways makes it a proposition worth exploring. TCh

North Sea Hijack

(1979, GB, 100 min)
d Andrew V McLaglen. *p* Elliott Kastner. *sc* Jack Davies. *ph* Tony Imi. *ed* Alan Strachan. *pd* Maurice Carter. *m* Michael J Lewis. *cast* Roger Moore, James Mason, Anthony Perkins, Michael Parks, David Hedison, Jack Watson, George Baker, Jeremy Clyde, David Wood, Faith Brook.

● It's a wonder that the SNP ('It's Scotland's oil') never thought of this one, it's so simple: hold HM Government to ransom by threatening to blow up a drilling rig and a production platform. Where *North Sea Hijack* fails is that it takes a potentially convincing idea, then completely undermines it by subjecting it to shallow treatment. The Navy, represented by tired Admiral James ('I wish I sailed') Mason, is beaten before it starts, and it's left to free enterprise (Moore) to save the coffers of the nation. He is a freelance commando chappie, against whose ice-cool nerve (he does petit-point) the hijackers haven't a chance…and neither does the film. With more imagination, more of Faith Brook's send-up of a well-known lady PM, and less of Moore's excruciatingly smug misogyny, this might just have made it to comic levels. FF

North Star, The (aka Armored Attack)

(1943, US, 105 min, b/w)
d Lewis Milestone. *p* Samuel Goldwyn. *sc* Lillian Hellman. *ph* James Wong Howe. *ed* Daniel Mandel. *ad* William Cameron Menzies. *m* Aaron Copland. *cast* Anne Baxter, Dana Andrews, Walter Huston, Ann Harding, Erich von Stroheim, Farley Granger, Walter Brennan, Dean Jagger.

● Heroic Russian villagers fight off Nazi invaders in this hokey pro-Soviet flag-waver, which was later to embarrass the Goldwyn studio and just about everybody who'd worked on it, when McCarthy's commie-hunting investigators started prying. Lillian Hellman adapted the dire screenplay from her own book – and, yes, that is Walter Brennan as a Russky.

North to Alaska

(1960, US, 122 min)
d/p Henry Hathaway. *sc* John Lee Mahin, Martin Rackin, Claude Binyon. *ph* Leon Shamoy. *ed* Dorothy Spencer. *ad* Duncan Cramer, Jack Martin Smith. *m* Lionel Newman. *cast* John Wayne, Stewart Granger, Ernie Kovacs, Fabian, Capucine, Mickey Shaugnessy, Karl Swenson, Joseph Sawyer, Kathleen Freeman.

● Wayne's on good-natured, cussin' and brawlin' form for this frontier adventure (from a play by Laszlo Fodor) in which he and partner Granger strike gold in Alaska, then spend the rest of the movie fighting over Capucine and battling it out with swindler Kovacs. Two-fisted 'Scope barnstormer. TJ

North West Frontier (aka Flame Over India)

(1959, GB, 129 min)
d J Lee Thompson. *p* Marcel Hellman. *sc* Robin Estridge. *ph* Geoffrey Unsworth. *ed* Frederick Wilson. *ad* Alex Vetchinsky. *m* Mischa Spoliansky. *cast* Kenneth More, Lauren Bacall, Herbert Lom, Wilfrid Hyde-White, IS Johar, Ursula Jeans, Ian Hunter.

● An excellent adventure film which turns the Raj into an apposite backdrop for the British equivalent of a Western ('based on a script by Frank Nugent'). Kenneth More is a British officer who must aid the escape of a Hindu prince from a city besieged by the Muslims. This he does by means of a decrepit steam train, with a handful of Western passengers on board, one of them an enemy agent. It's exciting stuff, with reams of incident, confident dialogue, and impeccable 'Scope photography by Geoffrey Unsworth. TCh

Northwest Passage

(1940, US, 125 min)
d King Vidor. *p* Hunt Stromberg. *sc* Laurence Stallings, Talbot Jennings. *ph* Sidney Wagner, William V Skall. *ed* Conrad A Nervig. *ad* Cedric Gibbons, Malcolm Brown. *m* Herbert Stothart. *cast* Spencer Tracy, Robert Young, Ruth Hussey, Walter Brennan, Nat Pendleton, Robert Barrat, Lumsden Hare, Donald MacBride, Isabel Jewell, Regis Toomey, Montagu Love.

● Subtitled 'Rogers' Rangers' and intended as the first instalment in a two-part true-life adventure (the second film was never made because Tracy and Vidor didn't get on), this 18th century frontier saga follows Tracy's Major Rogers and mapmaker Young into Canada to quell the Indian tribes who'd been striking across the border at the colonists. Vidor certainly plays up the hardships they endure en route, but it's hard for modern viewers to look on in approval as Tracy and his men set fire to a sleeping Indian village, treated as just another testing obstacle like the torrential river bridged by the teamwork of a human chain. It's never suggested that his heroes emerge from all this unscathed, but they are certainly made stronger and wiser by the experience. The early Technicolor gives the film the look of a children's storybook. TJ

No Sad Songs for Me

(1950, US, 89 min, b/w)
d Rudolph Maté. *p* Buddy Adler. *sc* Howard Koch. *ph* Joseph Walker. *ed* William A Lyon. *ad* Cary Odell. *m* George Duning. *cast* Margaret Sullavan, Wendell Corey, Viveca Lindfors, Natalie Wood, John McIntire, Ann Doran, Richard Quine, Jeanette Nolan.

●In her last film, Margaret Sullavan plays a housewife diagnosed as suffering from terminal cancer. Keeping the news from her husband (Corey), at first because she is panicky, later because he is at a crucial stage in his career as a surveyor, she gradually starts putting her house in order: teaching her small daughter (Wood) to be self-reliant, and befriending her husband's assistant (Lindfors) – whom he has hovered on the brink of falling in love with while working together – in the hope that the gap she leaves behind will soon be filled. Despite the soapy scenario, and a cosmetic illness that allows Sullavan to fade out as gracefully as the Lady of the Camellias, this is a much better film than it sounds. Howard Koch's script is a miracle of delicacy, psychological insight and quiet humour; the performances are superb; and Maté's precise, perfectly controlled direction obstinately refuses to indulge any slush. TM

No Scandal

see Pas de Scandale

No Secrets! (aka Touch of the Sun)

(1982, GB, 80 min)
d Peter Curran. *p* Elizabeth Curran. *cast* Oliver Reed, Sylvaine Charlet, Peter Cushing, Keenan Wynn, Bruce Boa, Edwin Manda, Sylvaine Charlet, Wilfrid Hyde White.

●Dismal would-be comedy laden with patronising post-colonial attitudes (the characters have names like Miss Funnypenny and President P Nutts). When an American spacecraft crash lands in Africa and its crew members are held captive by local tribesmen, officer Reed and commissioner Cushing (looking particularly weary) are the bumbling response despatched by the West. From the lost battalion of unreleased British features, it seems. TJ

No se lo digas a nadie

see Don't Tell Anyone

Nosferatu a Venezia

see Vampires in Venice

Nosferatu the Vampyre (Nosferatu: Phantom der Nacht)

(1979, WGer/Fr, 107 min)
d/p/sc Werner Herzog. *ph* Jörg Schmidt-Reitwein. *ed* Beate Mainka-Jellinghaus. *pd* Henning von Gierke. *m* Popol Vuh, Florian Fricke, Wagner, Gounod. cast Klaus Kinski, Isabelle Adjani, Bruno Ganz, Roland Topor, Walter Ladengast, Dan Van Husen, Jacques Dufilho.

●Stylish, sombre, owing little to the Murnau classic and nothing to Hammer or Hollywood, Herzog's foray into Dracula territory is the story of an inhabitant of 18th century Delft (Ganz, striving hard to expand the limits of his part), whose encounter with the weary, jealous Count (Kinski, indescribable) brings doom to his marriage, home town and self. Unfortunately, Herzog's inspired seriousness creates serious problems, for the film is too aware of its cultural dimensions (the Plague, Faust, Freud), too lacking in narrative drive, to work as a horror story. And the impressively detailed historical recreation tends to undermine – not underline – the deliberate silent-screen formality of acting and (minimal) dialogue. It's an error of conception which clouds over the luminous photography and excellent performances with an intermittent failure of style: fascinating, but flawed. CA

Nosferatu – eine Symphonie des Grauens

(1922, Ger, 6,453 ft, b/w)
d FW Murnau. *p* Albin Grau, Enrico Dieckmann. *sc* Henrik Galeen. *ph* Fritz Arno Wagner. *ad* Albin Grau. *m* (restored version) James Bernard. *cast* Max Schreck, Alexander Granach, Gustav von Wangenheim, Greta Schröder, GH Schnell, Ruth Landshoff, John Gottowt, Gustav Botz.

●Murnau's classic vampire movie, though not his best film, remains one of the most poetic of all horror films. Its power derives partly from Schreck's almost literally sub-human portrayal of the Count, respelendent with long ears and fingers and a wizened, skeletal face, partly from the sexual undercurrents coursing through the movie which suggest that the vampire is a threat not only to bougeois society and its emphasis upon scientific rationality, but also to the very marriage of the Harker couple. A film that survives repeated viewings. GA

No Skin Off My Ass

(1990, Can, 75 min, b/w)
d Bruce LaBruce. *cast* Klaus von Brucker, Bruce LaBruce, GB Jones.

●A punk hairdresser (LaBruce) takes time off from watching Altman's *That Cold Day in the Park* on TV and picks up a surly skinhead (von Brucker), taking him home to bed, board and bondage fantasies. The sullen object of his desire isn't about to stick around and listen to the Carpenters, though, and hightails it to the apartment of his lesbian film-maker sister (Jones), who's busy casting for her new production, 'Girls of the SLA'. Jones is undoubtedly the star of this exceptionally cut-price venture, with the sassiest delivery and by far the best lines ('I wonder if this is how Agnès Varda got started?' she sighs). LaBruce's film has been compared to Kuchar and Warhol, but both would be hard pressed to beat the longueurs and economy measures. One of the tackier highlights of the new wave of Queer Cinema, it's patchily enjoyable and pretty endearing. JRo

No Smoking

see Smoking/No Smoking

Nostalgia (Nostalghia)

(1983, It, 126 min, b/w & col)
d Andrei Tarkovsky. *p* Francesco Casati. *sc* Andrei Tarkovsky, Tonino Guerra. *ph* Giuseppe Lanci. *ed* Erminia Marani, Amedeo Salfa. *ad* Andrea Crisanti. *cast* Oleg Jankovsky, Erland Josephson, Domiziana Giordano, Patrizia Terreno, Laura De Marchi, Delia Boccardo, Milena Vukotic.

●Another of Tarkovsky's strange, hauntingly beautiful meditations on man's search for self. The film may forsake the run-down space station of *Solaris* or the miraculous Zone of *Stalker* for the hilltop villages of Tuscany, but its framework is familiar (flashbacks in spectral black-and-white, the use of rich sepia alongside pastel colour to blur distinctions between dream and reality), and so are its themes (memory, melancholia, disenchantment with the material world, dogged stumbling after salvation). An appropriately haggard academic, Gorchakov (Jankovsky), has come to Italy to research the life of an obscure Russian composer. Brooding over familial traumas and his compatriot's eventual suicide, he's incapable of communicating with his statuesque young interpreter (Giordano), let alone having an affair with her. In the meantime he meets Domenico (Josephson), a recluse whom the locals dismiss as mad. Each man recognises something of himself in the other, and they embark upon the most absolute of alliances…Tarkovsky remains as much a metaphysician as anything else, and *Nostalgia* isn't an entertainment but an article of faith. AMac

Nostalgia for Countryland (Thuong Nho Dong Que)

(1995, Vietnam/Jap, 116 min)
d/sc Dang Nhat Minh. *ph* Nguyen Huu Tuan. *ed* Tran Anh Hoa. *pd* PhamLuoc Trung. *m* Hoang Luong. *cast* Ta Ngoc Bao, Thuy Huong, Lê Vân.

●With four excellent movies behind him, there's no doubt that Dang Nhat Minh is Vietnam's foremost director and one of the best in South-East Asia as a whole. But this Japanese-financed film about a farm boy's crush on a woman émigrée who revisits her home village in North Vietnam lacks almost all the qualities which have distinguished his early work: it's soft-edged, easily sentimental, poorly acted and full of obvious padding. This is not the first time that money from NHK (Japan's BBC) has thrown a talented director off course, but it's the saddest example of recent years. The single most interesting moment – the young hero's astonishment when he has his first spontaneous orgasm in the fields – was too much for the Vietnamese censor. TR

Nostradamus

(1993, GB/Ger, 120 min)
d Roger Christian. *p* Edward Simons, Harald Reichebner. *sc* Knut Boeser. *ph* Denis Crossan. *ed* Alan Strachan. pd Peter J Hampton. *m* Barrington Pheloung. *cast* Tchéky Karyo, F Murray Abraham, Rutger Hauer, Amanda Plummer, Julia Ormond, Assumpta Serna, Anthony Higgins, Diana Quick, Michael Gough.

●As the millennium approaches, interest in the writings of the 16th century visionary Nostradamus has revived. Played with effective restraint, Karyo's Nostradamus is a man tormented by dreams and drug-fuelled visions, frustrated by the ignorance of his fellow medical practitioners, and persecuted by religious zealots. Although the film hedges its bets regarding the veracity of Nostradamus's predictions, there is much to admire here. Director Christian successfully evokes the historical period, and Karyo conveys the intellectual turmoil of a religious man driven by a hunger for truth. The only off-key note is sounded by Hauer's eccentric turn as a mystic monk. NF

No Such Thing

(2001, US/Ice, 101 min)
d Hal Hartley. *p* Hal Hartley, Fridrik Thór Fridriksson, Cecilia Kate Roque. *sc* Hal Hartley. *ph* Michael Spiller. *ed* Steve Hamilton. *pd* Árni Páll Jóhannsson. *m* Hal Hartley. *cast* Sarah Polley, Robert John Burke, Helen Mirren, Julie Christie, Annika Peterson, Ilene Bergelson, Peter O'Hara, Damian Young.

●Ambitious but, perhaps, misguided, Hartley's latter-day fairytale-cum-monster fable has innocent but brave young Polley (a lowly secretary on a TV news show run by ratings-crazed Mirren) head off to the Icelandic wilderness when it's reported that a camera crew (her boyfriend included) had been killed by a monster. When she eventually meets the misanthropic, resentfully immortal beast (Burke), she gets on so well with him that she persuades him to accompany her to New York, to meet a boffin who could finish him off. Polley and Burke work well alone and together, but the scenes satirising media sensationalism are too heavy-handed to be funny. Good, intriguing ideas about the death of fear, mystery and difference, are executed with an uncharacteristic forthrightness which forgoes the engagingly offbeat subtleties of his earlier work; clearly, allegory and genre are not Hartley's strong points. GA

No Surrender

(1985, GB/Can, 104 min)
d Peter Smith. *p* Mamoun Hassan. *sc* Alan Bleasdale. *ph* Michael Coulter. *ed* Rodney Holland. *pd* Andrew Mollo. *m* Daryl Runswick. *cast* Michael Angelis, Avis Bunnage, James Ellis, Tom Georgeson, Bernard Hill, Ray McAnally, Mark Mulholland, Joanne Whalley, JG Devlin.

●An acerbic, frequently very funny farce scripted by Alan Bleasdale, here bringing with him Angelis, Hill and Ellis from *The Boys from the Black Stuff.* It's the same slightly surreal allegory on contemporary Britain: a seedy Liverpool nightclub, where Angelis takes over as manager to find that his predecessor – a practical joker – has booked a gaggle of appalling acts to perform at a New Year's Eve binge, attended by two parties of OAPs, one Protestant, the other devout Irish Catholics. Mayhem ensues, of course, amid a collection of excellent performances and witty one-liners. No masterpiece, to be sure, but highly enjoyable, for all its underlying bleakness. GA

Not a Love Story

(1981, Can, 68 min)
d Bonnie Sherr Klein. *p* Dorothy Todd Hénaut. *sc* Bonnie Sherr Klein. *ph* Pierre Letarte. *ed* Anne Henderson. *m* Ginette Bellavance. *with* Bonnie Sherr Klein, Linda Lee Tracey, Marc Stevens, Ed Donnerstein, Kate Millett.

● A crusading attack on pornography by concerned mother Klein, seconded by a Montreal stripper (Tracey) with a cute comedy act and increasing doubts about her profession. Klein's pretty depressing view that porn is not culturally determined, but born of some 'inherently male' drive to hurt and defile, seems almost oblivious to basic and much-debated questions such as how to find the thin blue line between hardcore and misogyny in 'respectable' representations of women, or the potentially enlightening effect of porn's explicitness about female sexuality (both points raised by Kate Millett in an all-too-brief sequence). Most disturbing of all is that Klein's own camera is itself often compulsively and rather unpleasantly voyeuristic. SJo

Not a Pretty Picture

(1975, US, 83 min)
d/p/sc Martha Coolidge. *ph* Don Lenzer, Fred Murphy. *ed* Suzanne Pettit, Martha Coolidge. *m* Tom Griffith. *cast* Michele Manenti, Jim Carrington, Anne Mundstuk, John Fedinatz, Amy Wright, Stephen Laurier, Martha Coolidge.

● Written, directed and produced by Coolidge, this is a film within a film. Part narrative reconstruction of her own rape at 16, part documentary footage of director and actors, it seems more of a cathartic exercise for those participating than an instruction to its audience (Michele Manenti, who plays Martha, was also an adolescent rape victim). Their tremendous emotional involvement proves inadvertently alienating: watching the director's distress at seeing her narrative self being raped is disturbing, not because of what it says about rape, but because it's so intensely personal. Also, the 1962 high school scenario is culturally distancing, particularly for a British audience. A film which never really manages to confront us with the enormity of its subject, nor with any kind of analysis as to why rape occurs. HM

Not As a Stranger

(1955, US, 135 min, b/w)
d/p Stanley Kramer. *sc* Edna Anhalt, Edward Anhalt. *ph* Franz Planer. *ed* Frederick Knudtson. *pd* Rudolph Sternard. *m* George Antheil. *cast* Robert Mitchum, Olivia de Havilland, Frank Sinatra, Charles Bickford, Gloria Grahame, Broderick Crawford, Lee Marvin, Lon Chaney.

● Typically well-meaning slice of Kramerkitsch, based on a bestseller by Morton Thompson (what else, with that title?) about a medical student (Mitchum) driven by a sense of vocation which makes him use people – notably de Havilland's improbably blonde Swedish nurse – with the kind of alienating selfishness that means his comeuppance is on the way. The exceptional cast helps to while away the platitudes and pieties, provided you can accept the likes of Mitchum, Sinatra and Marvin as somewhat wrinkly students. TM

Notebook on Cities and Clothes (Aufzeichnungen zu Kleidern und Städten)

(1989, WGer, 81 min)
d/sc Wim Wenders. *ph* Robbie Müller, Muriel Edelstein, Uli Kudicke, Wim Wenders, Masatoshi Nakajima, Masashi Chikamori. *ed* Dominique Auvray, Lenie Savietto, Anne Schnee. *m* Laurent Petitgand. *with* Yohji Yamamoto, Wim Wenders. *narrator* Wim Wenders.

● After the dizzy heights of *Wings of Desire*, Wenders came down to earth with this scribble-pad of a documentary, comprised of sundry video doodles and 16mm jottings. Invited by the Georges Pompidou Centre to make a film 'in the context of fashion', he overcame his initial scorn, and decided to fly from Berlin to Paris and Tokyo on the trail of clothes designer guru Yohji Yamamoto. There is footage of the black-clad genius of the cutting-shears spluttering about his love for cities from the roof of the Pompidou, circling and snipping in his Tokyo studio, and sitting with Buddha-like serenity amid the chaos of his Paris show. Through it all, Wenders drones on with a series of either banal or tenuous links and meditations on the similarities between film-making and clothes-designing, the suitability of video to the ephemerality of fashion, and how he had been *aching* to meet Yamamoto ever since purchasing one of his creations. The result has all the panache of a hastily-assembled jumble of out-takes from a *Clothes' Show* filler. WH

Not Forgotten (Wasurerarenu Hitobito)

(2000, Jap, 121 min)
d Makoto Shinozaki. *p* Yuji Sadai, Naoki Kai, Katsuichi Sawai. *sc* Makoto Shinozaki, Ryo Yamamura. *ph* Kazuhiro Suzuki. *ed* Nobuko Tomita. *ad* Koichi Kanekatsu. *m* Little Creatures. *cast* Tatsuya Mihashi, Minoru Oki, Keiko Utsumi, Tomio Aoki, Saburo Shinoda, Akiko Kazami, Masumi Sanada, Masashi Endo.

● Swing low, sweet chariot… The central characters in this highly engaging film are elderly men, former soldiers in the Pacific War, one of whom is still haunted by guilt for abandoning a wounded colleague to die. But what starts as a study of the problems faced by Japan's rapidly ageing population turns into something very different when the 'religious' cult Utopia turns up and starts swindling old people out of their savings and homes. Suddenly these veterans on the cusp of death are confronted with a new and very contemporary threat; they are goaded into action one last time. Ex-critic Shinozaki casts some of Japan's finest character actors (in some cases, unseen in movies for years) and consciously echoes genre movies of the past in crafting a story balanced between pathos and anger, nostalgia and innovation. TR

Not for Publication

(1984, US, 87 min)
d Paul Bartel. *p* Anne Kimmel. *sc* John Meyer, Paul Bartel. *ph* George Tirl. *ed* Alan Toomayan. *pd* Robert Schulenberg. *m* John Meyer. *cast* Nancy Allen, David Naughton, Laurence Luckinbill, Alice Ghostley, Barry Dennen, Richard Paul, Paul Bartel.

● The career trajectory that took Bartel from extremist satire to comfortable retro pictures with unthreatening undercurrents of outré humour (prefiguring a similar shift in John Waters' career) snapped into focus with this benign but anodyne pastiche of the Preston Sturges approach to screwball comedy. Lois (Allen, pert but vacuous) writes for a sleazy tabloid and dreams of turning it back into the crusading paper her father founded. Aided by an out-of-his-depth photographer (Naughton), she stumbles through exposés of a porn-baron and a bestiality club before uncovering evidence of the mayor's involvement in organised crime. Plenty of viable gags, but the tone is too innocuous and the performances are too one-dimensional for the film to work as anything more than a remembrance of comedies past. All Bartel and no bite. TR

Nothing But the Best

(1964, GB, 99 min)
d Clive Donner. *p* David Deutsch. *sc* Frederic Raphael. *ph* Nicolas Roeg. *ed* Fergus McDonell. *pd* Reece Pemberton. *m* Ron Grainer. *cast* Alan Bates, Denholm Elliott, Harry Andrews, Millicent Martin, Pauline Delany, Godfrey Quigley, Alison Leggatt, Nigel Stock, James Villiers, Willie Rushton.

● An echo from a time when social mobility looked easy and 'A-type ladies in E-type Jags' were the goal of every bright young man. If, despite Nic Roeg's lush photography, the glittering prizes look horribly tarnished, that only deepens the black comedy. Jimmy Brewster's climb to the top comes without angst or guilt or tragic sacrifice; he doesn't sell his working class soul, but merely steals one with a better pedigree. Frederic Raphael's witty script and Donner's tricksy direction superbly capture a world where image is everything. Trumpeting that robust contempt for the establishment that was the essence of TV's *That Was the Week That Was* satire, they hack their way through social conventions to expose the grubbily materialist heart of 'Swinging London'. Salutarily un-nostalgic. RMy

Nothing But the Night

(1972, GB, 90 min)
d Peter Sasdy. *p* Anthony Nelson Keys. *sc* Brian Hayles. *ph* Ken Talbot. *ed* Keith Palmer. *ad* Colin Grimes. *m* Malcolm Williamson. *cast* Christopher Lee, Peter Cushing, Diana Dors, Georgia Brown, Keith Barron, Gwyneth Strong, Fulton Mackay, Michael Gambon.

● Strange tale of a series of murders of trustees of an orphanage on a Scottish island, revealed as having supernatural causes. Something has obviously come fatally adrift with the film, which wavers between Chabrol-like touches, a bit of Truffaut in his *Bride Wore Black* mood, and some straight British MI5 stuff. The script seems mostly at fault, and often the acting is just that little bit over-emphatic, which doesn't help. Not Sasdy at his best. DP

Nothing in Common

(1986, US, 119 min)
d Garry Marshall. *p* Alex Rose. *sc* Rick Podell, Michael Preminger. *ph* John A Alonzo. *ed* Glenn Farr. *pd* Charles Rosen. *m* Patrick Leonard. *cast* Tom Hanks, Jackie Gleason, Eva Marie Saint, Hector Elizondo, Barry Corbin, Bess Armstrong, Sela Ward, Cindy Harrell, John Kapelos.

● Hanks plays David Basner, slick creative director of an advertising agency. Trying to land a lucrative account, he negotiates with the irascible client while unwittingly falling into bed with his daughter. Meanwhile, David's grouchy father (Gleason) announces that David's mother (Saint) has left him after 33 years of marriage. As the familial crisis becomes increasingly intrusive, it not only affects David's work but forces him to reassess his relationship with his parents. This curiously broken-backed film begins as a hilarious satire on high-power advertising, but ends as a *Terms of Endearment*-style weepie about intergenerational conflicts. Thanks to Hanks and a razor-sharp script, the early scenes make the most of the frenetic, cutthroat action. When the film slips into a more serious vein, however, it simply treads water while threatening to drown in its own tears. NF

Nothing Lasts Forever

(1984, US, 82 min, b/w & col)
d Tom Schiller. *p* Lorne Michaels. *sc* Tom Schiller. *ph* Fred Schuler. *ed* Kathleen Dougherty, Margot Francis. *ad* Woods MacKintosh. *cast* Zach Galligan, Apollonia van Ravenstein, Lauren Tom, Dan Aykroyd, Imogen Coca, Eddie Fisher, Sam Jaffe, Paul Rogers, Mort Sahl, Bill Murray.

● *Saturday Night Live* alumnus Schiller wrote and directed this oddball first feature, a glimpse of a future where the Port Authority now rules New York City with an iron hand, and where young Galligan, having failed the regulatory artist's test, is sent to the traffic department. The film soon descends underground (where veteran Sam Jaffe holds sway) before heading to the moon for further adventures. Not all of the invention hits the target, but the film's determination to go its own way is not unendearing, and there's a succession of star cameos to prick the interest. TJ

Nothing Personal

(1995, GB/Ire, 85 min)
d Thaddeus O'Sullivan. *p* Jonathan Cavendish, Tracey Seaward. *sc* Daniel Mornin. *ph* Dick Pope. *ed* Michael Parker. *pd* Mark Geraghty. *m* Philip Appleby. *cast* Ian Hart, John Lynch, James Frain, Michael Gambon, Gary Lydon, Ruaidhri Conroy, Maria Boyle Kennedy, Gerard McSorley, BJ Hogg.

● One dark night in Belfast, 1975. Trapped on the wrong side of the sectarian divide, Liam (Lynch) finds himself at the mercy of a Loyalist paramilitary group, while his young daughter roams the streets looking for him. Confidently mounted by O'Sullivan, working in a very different register from his mainstream feature debut, *December Bride*, this humanist drama is engaging enough, and very well acted with a tooth-and-nails psycho turn from Ian Hart, but it's too schematic, one of those films where you can read the third act in the first ten minutes. TCh

Nothing Sacred

(1937, US, 75 min)
d William Wellman. *p* David O Selznick. *sc* Ben Hecht. *ph* W Howard Greene. *ed* Hal C

Kern, James E Newcom. *ad* Lyle Wheeler. *m* Oscar Levant. *cast* Carole Lombard, Fredric March, Charles Winninger, Walter Connolly, Sig Ruman, Maxie Rosenbloom, Frank Fay.
●Irresistible performance from Lombard as the small town girl, supposedly dying of radium poisoning but well aware that she isn't, who determines to grab all she can get when a newspaper brings her to New York for a last fling as a publicity stunt. Ben Hecht's sparkling script occasionally loses its way between the satire and the screwball romance, but is even more caustic about newspapermen than *The Front Page* ('The hand of God reaching down into the mire couldn't elevate one of 'em to the depths of degradation'), and provides a welcome antidote to Capracorn in its view of small towns as hell-holes to be got out of where an intruder is likely to be stoned or bitten by small boys. Some marvellous digs at the morbid sentimentality of the crowd, too, in particular a scene where a wrestling match is held up for ten seconds in tribute to the doomed girl while the bell solemnly tolls ten times. Quite attractively shot in colour, although prints tend to be suffused by an unpleasant pinkish wash. TM

Nothing to Lose

(1997, US, 98 min)
d Steve Oedekerk. *p* Martin Bregman, Dan Jinks, Michael Bregman. *sc* Steve Oedekerk. *ph* Donald Thorin. *ed* Malcolm Campbell. *pd* Maria Caso. *m* Robert Folk. *cast* Tim Robbins, Martin Lawrence, John C McGinley, Giancarlo Esposito, Michael McKean, Susan Barnes, Rebecca Gayheart, Kelly Preston, Steve Oedekerk.
●Nick (Robbins) and Ann (Preston) play husband-and-wife games in bed. He thinks she's a fat pig; she wants a divorce. Who can spin it out longest? Anyway, next day Nick gets off a late working assignment, only to catch Ann in bed with his boss (McKean). Stunned, he drives away, anywhere – to a hold-up at a red light in slumtown. It's T Paul (Lawrence) wanting Nick's wallet, waving a gun in his face. With a manic laugh and his foot on the gas, Nick defenestrates the money and drives the hapless sometime criminal to the Arizona desert for a round of mismatched comic capers. No surprises here. There are nods to the race issue, but this isn't exactly Tom Wolfe, and though some jokes work, more don't. NB

No. 3

(1997, SKor, 108 min)
d Song Neung-Han. *cast* Han Suk-Kyu, Lee Mi-Yeon, Choi Min-Sik.
●A brilliantly inventive, off-the-wall satire on the gangster mentality. Tae-Ju (Han) joins a gang in 1990, when economic times are hard, and finds himself stuck at No 3 in the hierarchy – essentially a low grade hatchet man. His efforts to get ahead are not helped by his wife's infidelity (she aspires to a literary career and starts taking lessons) or by the attentions of a cynical, bad mannered prosecutor who dogs his steps. The action leapfrogs through the years until Tae-Ju finally settles his rivalry with the gang's No 2 (Ashtray, named after his weapon of choice) in a night-club called Chaos; a coda whisks the characters into the future to see what becomes of them after the millennium. First-time director Song, previously best known as the writer of *Taebaek Mountains*, reportedly based it on his encounters with a real-life gang boss. TR

Not I

(2000, Ire/GB, 14 min)
d Neil Jordan. *p* Stephen Woolley. *sc* Samuel Beckett. *ph* Roger Pratt. *ed* Tony Lawson. *cast* Julianne Moore.
●In Jordan's frenetic version of Beckett's monologue, the screen is filled with a woman's mouth. It happens to be Moore's pouty bow and this close-up vision of lips, teeth and tongue as Julianne spits out the words gives the viewer a sense of her character's state of mind, the overwhelming disarray of thoughts and the struggle between the pressing intrusiveness of life versus instinctive attempts at control. EPe

No Time for Tears

(1957, GB, 86 min)
d Cyril Frankel. *p* WA Whittaker. *sc* Anne Burnaby. *ph* Gilbert Taylor. *ed* Gordon Pilkington. *ad* Robert Jones. *m* Francis Chagrin. *cast* Anna Neagle, George Baker, Sylvia Syms, Anthony Quayle, Flora Robson, Michael Hordern, Joan Hickson, Rosalie Crutchley, Joan Sims, Angela Baddeley.
●Maybe there's a note of irony in the title, for this children's hospital drama spends nearly all its efforts bathing us in sentimentality of the starchy, received-pronunciation Home Counties kind. Anna Neagle's the all-seeing matron who saves two slum kids from their slovenly mother, while doctor Baker tries out his bedside manner on nurse Syms. Predictable and fairly patronising, but it certainly gives an insight into prevailing health attitudes of the day. TJ

Not Now, Comrade

(1976, GB, 90 min)
d Harold Snoad, Ray Cooney. *p* Martin C Schute. *sc* Ray Cooney. *ph* Jack Hildyard. *ed* Peter Thornton. *ad* Edward Marshall. *m* Harry Robinson. *cast* Leslie Phillips, Lewis Fiander, Carol Hawkins, Roy Kinnear, Windsor Davies, Don Estelle, Michele Dotrice, June Whitfield, Ray Cooney, Ian Lavender.
●Or ever. Leslie Phillips capers as one Rimmington of the Defence Ministry (in naval beard and yellow Bentley), hot on the trail of defecting Russian ballet dancer Fiander, the KGB who're tailing him, and accompanying stripper Hawkins whose purpose seems to be to add a whiff of titillation. From the darkest days of British cinema, a farrago which began life as Cooney's Whitehall farce, *Chase Me, Comrade*. TJ

Not of This Earth

(1956, US, 67 min, b/w)
d/p Roger Corman. *sc* Charles Griffith, Mark Hanna. *ph* John Mescall. *ed* Charles Gross Jr. *m* Ronald Stein. *cast* Paul Birch, Beverly Garland, Morgan Jones, William Roerick, Jonathan Haze, Dick Miller, Ann Carroll, Pat Flynn.
●Low budgets give little reason for regret when the often tacky effects are surrounded by so much imagination, good humour, and sheer joy in film-making as here. *Not of This Earth* is a minor sci-fi gem, with an alien (Birch; you can tell he's an ET by his briefcase and dark glasses, establishing him as infinitely superior to the moronic middle Americans on view) terrorising Earth (or a small backlot) in his quest for blood for the folks back home. GA

Not One Less (Yi Ge Duo Bu Neng Shao)

(1998, China, 102 min)
d Zhang Yimou. *p* Zhao Yu. *sc* Shi Xiangsheng. *ph* Hou Yong. *ed* Zhai Ru. *pd* Cao Jiuping. *m* San Bao. *cast* Wei Minzhi, Zhang Huike, Tian Zhenda, Gao Enman, Sun Zhimei, Feng Yuying, Li Fanfan, Xu Zhanqing.
●The 1999 Golden Lion winner at Venice (after being denied a competition slot at Cannes), Zhang's film is a real audience pleaser. Shot in his *vérité* style, on real locations and using non-professionals, it tells of a 13-year-old substitute teacher drafted in to take over at a village school in the mountains, despite her obvious lack of qualifications. Promised a bonus if she keeps her class numbers up for a month, she determines to retrieve one pupil when he disappears to work in the city. The result is funny, heartwarming, and, frankly, sentimental – but it's not without some steel in its depiction of poverty and persistence. A pity Columbia insisted on a mawkish end-title card to ram the point home. TCh

Not on Your Life

see Verdugo, El

Notorious 100

(1946, US, 102 min, b/w)
d/p Alfred Hitchcock. *sc* Ben Hecht. *ph* Ted Tetzlaff. *ed* Theron Warth. *ad* Albert S D'Agostino, Carroll Clark. *m* Roy Webb. *cast* Cary Grant, Ingrid Bergman, Claude Rains, Louis Calhern, Leopoldine Konstantin, Reinhold Schunzel, Moroni Olsen, Ivan Triesault, Alexis Minotis.
●One of Hitchcock's finest films of the '40s, using its espionage plot about Nazis hiding out in South America as a mere MacGuffin, in order to focus on a perverse, cruel love affair between US agent Grant and alcoholic Bergman, whom he blackmails into providing sexual favours for the German Rains as a means of getting information. Suspense there is, but what really distinguishes the film is the way its smooth, polished surface illuminates a sickening tangle of self-sacrifice, exploitation, suspicion, and emotional dependence. Grant, in fact, is the least sympathetic character in the dark, ever-shifting relationships on view, while Rains, oppressed by a cigar-chewing, possessive mother and deceived by all around him, is treated with great generosity. Less war thriller than black romance, it in fact looks forward to the misanthropic portrait of manipulation in *Vertigo*. GA

Notorious Gentleman

see Rake's Progress, The

Not Quite Jerusalem (aka Not Quite Paradise)

(1984, GB, 114 min)
d/p Lewis Gilbert. *sc* Paul Kember. *ph* Tony Imi. *ed* Alan Strachan. *pd* John Stoll. *m* Rondo Veneziano, Gian Reverberi. *cast* Joanna Pacula, Sam Robards, Todd Graff, Kevin McNally, Gary Cady, Selina Cadell, Zafrir Kochanovsky.
●In the play from which this is adapted, the tough desert life of the kibbutzniks lent them an air of curt self-sufficiency, while the working class English volunteers who had come for a working holiday displayed a vicious, heartfeld hatred for England. Here, this strong material (adapted by playwright Paul Kember himself) has been caramelised. Gilbert has created a toffee-apple with the apple removed: bite through the sweet crust of romantic Holy Land locations, handsome Israelis, dashing Arab terrorists and corny jokes, and what remains is sheer emptiness. The characters are caricatures, the situations clichés, and the production leaden. One saving grace: Polish actress Joanna Pacula, who alone manages to invest her role with a patina of plausibility, radiates a heat that marks the ascension of a star. MH

Notre Dame des assassins

see Our Lady of the Assassins

No Trees in the Street

(1958, GB, 96 min, b/w)
d J Lee Thompson. *p* Frank Godwin. *sc* Ted Willis. *ph* Gilbert Taylor. *ed* Richard Best. *ad* Robert Jones. *m* Laurie Johnson. *cast* Sylvia Syms, Herbert Lom, Joan Miller, Melvyn Hayes, Stanley Holloway, Liam Redmond, Lana Morris.
●Released at a time when kitchen sink drama was all the rage, this is an unremarkable 'we had it tough' chronicle from another age (Ted Willis adapted his own play), set in the backstreets of 1938 London. Joan Miller's the desperate mum who tries to get sultry daughter Sylvia Syms married off to crooked turf accountant Lom, while young Melvyn Hayes – latterly remembered for his stint on TV's *It Ain't Half Hot Mum* – tries hard to convince as the ne'er-do-well son. TJ

Not Reconciled

see Nicht Versöhnt

Notre Histoire (Our Story/ Separate Rooms)

(1984, Fr, 111 min)
d Bertrand Blier. *p* Alain Sarde. *sc* Bertrand Blier. *ph* Jean Penzer. *ed* Claudine Merlin. *ad* Bernard Evein. *cast* Alain Delon, Nathalie Baye, Michel Galabru, Geneviève Fontanel, Jean-Pierre Darroussin, Gérard Darmon, Sabine Haudepin, Norbert Letheule, Vincent Lindon, Jean-François Stévenin, Jen Réno.
●Blier kicks off with a dream that must be uppermost in the male psyche: Nathalie Baye entering your railway carriage and demanding a fast one from the luggage rack. The trouble here is that she picks on Delon, a drunken old romantic, who just won't let her go. She is intent on being a short story; he clearly prefers Russian novels. There are glorious scenes of the town's male population shuttling from house to house in dressing gowns, their coitus forever interrupted, which bring to mind the anarchy and nightmare of Buñuel. But the ending looks like a shaky conclusion to a film with nowhere to go. However, Baye grows more and more beautiful, while at 50 Delon looks like he hasn't slept for years. CPea

Notte, La

(1961, It/Fr, 121 min, b/w)
d Michelangelo Antonioni. *p* Emanuele Cassuto. *sc* Michelangelo Antonioni, Ennio Flaiano, Tonino Guerra. *ph* Gianni Di Venanzo. *ed* Eraldo Da Roma. *ad* Piero Zuffi. *m* Giorgio Gaslini. *cast* Jeanne Moreau, Marcello Mastroianni, Monica Vitti, Bernhard Wicki, Maria Pia Luzi, Rosy Mazzacurati, Guido Ajmone Marsan.

●The middle section of Antonioni's trilogy on bourgeois alienation, *La Notte* covers twenty-four hours in the breakdown of a 'typical' middle class marriage. The husband (Mastroianni) is a novelist with a block, spineless, out of touch with his own instincts; the wife (Moreau) is a bored socialite who understands her own predicament but doesn't know how to get past it. Scene after scene is introduced solely to make laboured points about their emotional/social/philosophical problems; Antonioni's intimations of a broader political context are startlingly shallow. It's impossible to discern the relevance of this kind of film-making, which is doubtless why nobody (including Antonioni) practises it any more. TR

Notte di San Lorenzo, La

see Night of San Lorenzo, The

Notti Bianche, Le

see White Nights

Notti di Cabiria, Le (Cabiria/Nights of Cabiria)

(1956, It/Fr, 117 min, b/w)
d Federico Fellini. *p* Dino De Laurentiis. *sc* Federico Fellini, Ennio Flaiano, Tullio Pinelli. *ph* Aldo Tonti. *ed* Leo Catozzo. *ad* Piero Gherardi. *m* Nino Rota. *cast* Giulietta Masina, François Périer, Amedeo Nazzari, Franca Marzi, Dorian Gray, Aldo Silvana, Mario Passante, Pina Gualandri.

●In 1957, Fellini was still as indebted to neo-realism as to surrealism, and this melancholy tale of a prostitute working the outskirts of Rome is notable for its straightforward depiction of destitution. It may come as a surprise to those who know only Fellini's later work. It's easy to appreciate how Bob Fosse, Neil Simon and Peter Stone found a musical in it (*Sweet Charity*): Fellini orchestrates his story in waves of simple, pure emotion, telegraphed with silent screen gusto by Giulietta Masina. With her Noh eyebrows and white bobby socks, Masina is the missing link between Charlie Chaplin and Shirley MacLaine. One of life's eternal optimists, Cabiria one day meets the man of her prayers (Périer), and what follows is scarcely unexpected, but heartbreaking for all that. This new (1999) print features a seven minute sequence not seen since the film's Cannes premiere – Cabiria's encounter with a stranger delivering food parcels to the poor. Censored apparently at the behest of the Catholic Church, it underlines the severity of the social context, deepens Cabiria's character and serves as a poignant harbinger of things to come. TCh

Notting Hill

(1999, US/GB, 124 min)
d Roger Michell. *p* Duncan Kenworthy. *sc* Richard Curtis. *ph* Michael Coulter. *ed* Nick Moore. *pd* Stuart Craig. *m* Trevor Jones. *cast* Julia Roberts, Hugh Grant, Hugh Bonneville, Emma Chambers, James Dreyfus, Rhys Ifans, Tim McInnerny, Gina McKee.

●While it's hard to forget the cool, calculating mind set that shapes every second of this upfront attempt to repeat and enlarge on the box office success of *Four Weddings and a Funeral*, there's no denying that, as a romantic comedy playing up to our naivest, most innocuous fantasies, it *is* very enjoyable. The latter-day fairytale plotting is simple. When shy Portobello Road bookshop owner William Thacker (Grant) accidentally spills fruit juice over browsing Hollywood star Anna Scott (Roberts), it's the start of a tentative, faltering, on/off relationship. Nothing very unpredictable occurs as they wonder whether their deeply different lives might come together for more than a few moments, but enough neat conceits, nuances and gags ensure polished, engaging entertainment throughout. True, both Richard Curtis' well-honed script and Roger Michell's solid if somewhat academic direction depict W11 life from a complacently white, well-to-do perspective; true, also, that there are too many over-extended moments. Overall, however, it's an agreeably slick affair, with decent support performances, elegant camerawork, and several impressive set pieces. GA

Not Without My Daughter

(1990, US, 116 min)
d Brian Gilbert. *p* Harry J Ufland, Mary Jane Ufland. *sc* Brian Gilbert, David Rintels. *ph* Peter Hannan. *ed* Terry Rawlings. *pd* Anthony Pratt. *m* Jerry Goldsmith. *cast* Sally Field, Alfred Molina, Sheila Rosenthal, Roshan Seth, Sarah Badel, Mony Rey, George Corraface.

●According to her Iranian-born husband Moody (Molina), Betty Mahmoody (Field) is as American as apple pie. Certainly Moody's family reunion in Tehran ain't her idea of a holiday, and no sooner have they stepped on foreign soil than Betty is accosted by shrieking women beseeching her to cover her head. Things get worse. She's informed that Moody plans to stay in Iran and raise their little girl as a Muslim. The law strips Betty of all her rights, while Moody prevents her from leaving the house. Based on Betty Mahmoody's real-life story, the film emphasises her isolation, surrounded by an incomprehensible language and culture, and by vehement anti-American sentiments. Field captures the sense of outrage to perfection, puffy-eyed, screaming and plotting escape. Appropriately enough, the film is strictly deglamorised; combined with the lack of sympathetic characters, it all adds up to difficult, compelling viewing as we're drawn into the deepening nightmare. CM

Not Yet

see Madadayo

N'oublie pas que tu vas mourir (Don't Forget You're Going to Die)

(1995, Fr, 121 min)
d Xavier Beauvois. *p* Pascal Caucheteux. *sc* Xavier Beauvois. *ph* Caroline Champetier. *ed* Agnès Guillemot. *ad* Denis Barbier. *m* John Cale. *cast* Xavier Beauvois, Chiara Mastroianni, Roschdy Zem, Bulle Ogier, Jean-Louis Richard, Emmanuel Salinger, Jean Douchet, Pascal Bonitzer, Cédric Khan, Stanislas Nordey.

●Xavier Beauvois won admirers for *Nord*, his memorable debut; here, in his even better and more unsettling follow-up, he plays an art student whose desperate attempts to avoid military service reveal that he's HIV positive, whereupon he begins systematically to immerse himself in the realm of the senses. Despite a finished technique, there's a rawness here – evident not only in the explicit scenes of sex and drugs, but in the dark, edgy humour that repeatedly and unexpectedly bubbles to the surface – that lends the film an emotional punch. Great performances and a strong John Cale score. GA

Nous Etions Tous des Noms d'Arbres

see Writing on the Wall, The

Nous Etions un Seul Homme

see We Were One Man

Nous Irons Tous au Paradis

see Pardon Mon Affaire, Too

Nouvelle Eve, La

(1998, Fr, 94 min)
d Catherine Corsini. *p* Paulo Branco. *sc* Catherine Corsini, Marc Syrigas. *ph* Agnès Godard. *ed* Sabine Mamou. *ad* Solange Zeitoun. *cast* Karin Viard, Pierre-Loup Rajot, Catherine Frot, Sergi López, Laurent Lucas, Mireille Roussel, Nozha Khouadra, Valentin Vidal.

●In this, her third feature, Corsini brings a maturity and lightness of touch to an amusing exploration of the complexity of modern relationships and of the search for love and freedom of expression. Camille (Viard) is a feisty, volatile 30-year-old stressed out by her current lifestyle: by day, strife with the kid at the pool where she's a lifeguard, and by night, increasingly unfulfilling sexual encounters with strangers. She seems independent and emotionally self-sufficient; in truth, her life lacks tenderness, which becomes apparent when she's overwhelmed by a gesture from Alexis (Rajot), a man she meets in the street. That he's married and clearly not interested in an affair makes little difference to her and she sets out to win him over. This then, according to Corsini, is 'the new Eve': a woman doing the chasing in a very direct, even quite aggressive, way. Perfectly cast, Viard portrays with verve and energy a character as selfish and contrary as she is endearing, and captures the frustration of a woman struggling to reconcile her need for independence with her need for closeness. KW

Nouvelle Vague

(1990, Fr/Switz, 89 min)
d Jean-Luc Godard. *p* Alain Sarde. *sc* Jean-Luc Godard. *ph* William Lubtchansky. *ad* Anne-Marie Miéville. *cast* Alain Delon, Domiziana Giordano, Roland Amstutz, Laurence Cote, Jacques Dacqmine, Christophe Odent, Laurence Guerre, Joseph Lisbona, Laure Killing.

●As the rather obvious storyline progresses – a woman kills a lover, whose exact double (his brother?) comes back to haunt her – Godard's script and soundtrack make interminable use of quotations to offer thoughts (?) on almost everything under the sun. It looks nice enough, in an elegant, posh-car-commercial kind of way, but Delon, in the dual role, looks unhappily as if he had strayed in from another movie, and the whole thing comes over as inconsequential intellectual wank. Stillborn stuff from a former *enfant terrible* who seems to be suffering from terminal regression, it is vague rather than *nouvelle*. GA

November Days Voices and Choices

(1990, GB/Ger, 130 min, b/w & col)
d/p Marcel Ophuls. *ph* Peter Boultwood. *ed* Sophie Brunet, Albert Jurgenson, Catherine Zins. *with* Marcel Ophuls, Egon Krenz, Günther Schabowski, Stefan Hermlin, Heiner Muller, Kurt Masur, Barbara Brecht.

●November '89, when the Wall came tumbling down. Ophuls showed up not long after, tracking down ordinary citizens caught on camera during those initial joyous hours, questioning them about their lives before, their expectations now. And he gently grills former members of what had been the East German political and artistic establishment, who prove variously rueful, defiant or evasive about their roles in the GDR. Ophuls is perhaps overly attentive to the minutiae of Honecker's downfall – who did what when – and the parallels he draws with Julius Caesar seem inappropriate for so shabby a bunch. Mostly though this is valuable, moving film-journalism, with Ophuls himself – courteous, committed, playful – a most sympathetic guide. BBa

November 1828

(1979, Indon, 135 min)
d Teguh Karya. *cast* Slamet Rahardjo, Jenny Rachman, Miruli Sitompul, El Manik, Rahmat Hidayat, Sunarti Rendra, Herman Pelani.

●Celebrations of anti-colonial struggles are par for the course for cinema from emerging countries, but Teguh Karya's mini-epic about the Javan resistance against the Dutch in the early 19th century isn't just another 'worthy' Third World entry. Apart from the fact that it looks and sounds very accomplished, the movie displays an intelligent grasp of the dynamics of melodrama (there are 'family' tensions on both sides of the clash), and presents traditional Javan culture without recourse to folksy stereotypes. TR

November Men, The

(1993, US, 98 min)
d Paul Williams. *p* Rodney Byron Ellis, Paul Williams. *sc* James Andronica. *ph* Susan Emerson. *ed* Chip Brooks. *m* Scott Thomas Smith. *cast* Paul Williams, James Andronica, Leslie Bevis, Beau Starr, Rod Ellis, Robert Davi, Lexie Shine, Coralissa Gines.

●Following the 1992 Bush/Clinton presidential campaign with an unauthorised (and undetected) camera, Paul Williams' thriller draws on the legacy of 1960s assassinations, fusing conspiracy fact and fiction. An egotistical guerilla filmmaker (Andronica) recruits a seriously disaffected band of citizens to film a fake assassination attempt on a very real George Bush. The stakes appear to be raised when individual factions emerge and are incorporated into an ever-changing script, to the point where the camerawoman (Bevis) alerts the Secret Service. Shot as low-budget realism with an improvised air, the film unsettles, using dreams and shifting narrators, while exploring the reality behind the 'seeing is believing' myth. A multilayered, twisting denouement supports Lyndon Johnson's belief that there's no need to worry about the left, they'll never pick up a gun – 'It's the right you have to worry about; it they don't get what they want, they'll blow you fucking head off.' FM

November Moon (Novembermond)

(1984, WGer/Fr, 107 min)
d Alexandra von Grote. *p* Ottokar Runze. *sc* Alexandra von Grote. *ph* Bernard Zitzermann. *ed* Susann Lahaye. *ad* Holger Gross, Jean-Pierre Bazerolle. *m* Egisto Macchi. *cast* Gabriele Osburg, Christiane Millet, Danièle Delorme, Stéphane Garcin, Bruno Pradal, Louise Martini, Gerhard Olschewski, Maria Krasna, Werner Stocker.

●A wartime romance in which the two lovers just happen to be women. When November, a German Jewess, arrives in Paris in 1939, she captures the heart of a young man, but falls for his sister Férial. As the Occupation looms, November is forced to flee into the countryside, where she is sheltered by gentle peasants, but is shopped to the authorities and set to work in an officers' brothel. She manages to return to Paris, the bottom of the sofa acting as hidey-hole when anyone comes to call. With another mouth to feed, Férial has no choice but to work for the collaborationist press, bringing the mistaken but inevitable peacetime retribution. Both Osburg (November) and Millet (Férial) give powerful performances, and thanks to von Grote's sensitive direction, this gripping slice of herstory achieves a quiet grandeur. MS

November Plan, The

(1976, US, 103 min)
d Don Medford. *p* Roy Huggins. *sc* Stephen J Cannell. *ph* Ric Waite. *ed* Larry Lester, Edwin F England, Ronald Lavine. *ad* John W Corso. *m* Nelson Riddle. *cast* Wayne Rogers, Elaine Joyce, Philip Sterling, Clifton James, Diane Ladd, Meredith Baxter Birney, Laurence Luckinbill, Stephen Elliott, Jack Kruschen, Dorothy Malone, Lloyd Nolan, GD Spradlin.

●Occasionally interesting private eye thriller, set in '30s LA, with Rogers investigating the murder of a starlet's lover and uncovering a plot to overthrow Roosevelt's government. With the film cobbled out of three episodes of a TV series called *City of Angels*, the weakly wisecracking, sub-Chandleresque script poses problems, as does Rogers' bland performance. But the political insights are intriguing in their tentative equation of the more conservative elements in American society with similar tendencies in Fascist Italy. GA

Novia que te Vea

see Like a Bride

Novocaine

(2001, US, 95 min)
d David Atkins. *p* Paul Mones, Daniel M Rosenberg. *sc* David Atkins. *ph* Vilko Filac. *ed* Melody London. *pd* Sharon Seymour. *m* Steve Bartek, (theme) Dany Elfman. *cast* Steve Martin, Helena Bonham Carter, Laura Dern, Elias Koteas, Scott Caan, Keith David, Lynne Thigpen, Kevin Bacon.

●Hmm, dentistry *noir*. Martin plays Frank Sangster, an easy-going LA tooth doctor with a cornball hygienist-girlfriend (Dern), an occasionally irritating deadwood brother (Elias Koteas), and, it proves, a regulation-issue manipulable libido, exposed by grungy mystery patient Bonham Carter. Enter her mad bad brother Scott Caan, and soon Frank's on the run from hard evidence of murder most gruesome. A tongue-in-cheek comedy thriller riffing on the usual nefarious high jinks, Atkins' debut starts with some neat ideas ('lying is a lot like tooth decay'), but they don't play out; the characters are too shallow, the storytelling too standardised and self-amused, and the visual sensibility that bit too slap-happy for it to take. NB

Now and Then

(1995, US, 102 min)
d Lesli Linka Glatter. *p* Suzanne Todd, Demi Moore. *sc* I Marlene King. *ph* Ueli Steiger. *ed* Jacqueline Cambas. *pd* Gershon Ginsburg, Anne Kuljian. *m* Cliff Eidelman. *cast* Demi Moore, Melanie Griffith, Rosie O'Donnell, Rita Wilson, Christina Ricci, Thora Birch, Gaby Hoffmann, Ashleigh Aston Moore, Willa Glen, Bonnie Hunt, Janean Garofalo, Lolita Davidovich, Cloris Leachman.

●Producer Demi Moore intended, it seems, a coming-of-age tale in the *Stand by Me* mould. What she ended up with was a syrupy dose of boyfriends and female bonding – in short, yet another uninspired 'women's film'. Fulfilling a childhood promise to 'always be there for each other', bohemian writer Samantha (Moore), actress Teeny (Griffith), and doctor Roberta (O'Donnell) return to their hometown, the bizarrely named Gaslight Addition, as Chrissy (Wilson) prepares for the birth of her first child. As they reflect on the pact which brought them together, the film reverts to 1970 and the start of their friendship. Director Glatter cut her teeth of *NYPD Blue*, but she brings none of that TV series' realism and punch to her feature debut, favouring instead a pastel-hued mise-en-scène. For a film which defines its characters entirely in relation to each other, there's a curious lack of chemistry between the leads. Only in the childhood sequences are the undercurrents and tensions of the various relationships explored. KM

No Way Home

(1996, US, 93 min)
d Buddy Giovinazzo. *p* Lisa Bruce, Robert Nickson. *sc* Buddy Giovinazzo. *ph* Claudia Raschke. *ed* Stan Warnow. *pd* Phyllis Cedar. *m* Rick Giovinazzo. *cast* Tim Roth, James Russo, Deborah Kara Unger, Joseph Regno, Catherine Kellner, Saul Stein, Bernadette Penotti, Gareth Williams.

●As Joey Larabito leaves prison, we glimpse the scars cut into his back: cue flashback to the moment they were inflicted. In the same way, what develops as a subtle low-key character piece eventually descends into an OTT criminal melodrama. Six years in arrears – his wits damaged by a childhood accident – Joey (Roth) arrives home to see his older brother Tommy (Russo). His knock is answered by a dishwater blonde, Lorraine, a sister-in-law he knew nothing about (Unger). She's reluctant to let a murderer stay, but Joey's quiet manner wins her over, and he becomes a useful ally as her husband digs himself ever deeper into debt. Roth negotiates the tricky business of mental deficiency with unsentimental deliberation. Unger – so cool and distant in *Crash* – emerges as a fine actress, shading from suspicion of Joey to trust with real emotional delicacy, going the opposite route with Russo, and hinting at a suburban fatigue that's eating away at her insides. Writer/director Giovinazzo gives us an authentic whiff of the sunny, slummy streets of Staten Island, but undercuts the good work which has gone before with an ill-judged bloody denouement. TCh

No Way Out

(1950, US, 101 min, b/w)
d Joseph L Mankiewicz. *p* Darryl F Zanuck. *sc* Joseph L Mankiewicz, Lesser Samuels. *ph* Milton Krasner. *ed* Barbara McLean. *ad* Lyle Wheeler, George W Davis. *m* Alfred Newman. *cast* Richard Widmark, Sidney Poitier, Linda Darnell, Stephen McNally, Ruby Dee, Ossie Davis, Mildred Joanne Smith, Harry Bellaver.

●Poitier's first – and best – film, *No Way Out* is also one of the most honest films dealing with racial conflict. Widmark plays the bigoted petty criminal who holds Poitier's doctor responsible for the death of his friend, and nearly incites a race riot in his search for revenge. While undoubtedly it fudges some of the issues, Mankiewicz's literate script makes this one of the few movies from the past dealing with racial issues that are still viewable today. PH

No Way Out

(1986, US, 115 min)
d Roger Donaldson. *p* Laura Ziskin, Robert Garland. *sc* Robert Garland. *ph* John Alcott, (NZ) Alun Bollinger. *ed* Neil Travis. *pd* J Dennis Washington, (NZ) Kai Hawkins. *m* Maurice Jarre. *cast* Kevin Costner, Gene Hackman, Sean Young, Will Patton, Howard Duff, George Dzundza, Jason Bernard, Iman, Fred Dalton Thompson.

●A gripping update on John Farrow's 1947 *The Big Clock*, its parallel duplicities relocated to the Pentagon. The mistress (Young) of devious Secretary of Defence Brice (Hackman) has been murdered, and Lt Farrell (Costner) is called in to catch the killer without stirring up the headlines. The problem is that Brice himself did the deed accidentally, while Farrell is the unknown man who had roused his jealousy by sharing her favours. Farrell's mission becomes a quicksand of double bluffs, concealments, and attempts to sabotage the clues in order to avoid the Pentagon fingering him for the murder. A very convincing nightmare, and if Hackman gives too rounded a performance to approach the omniscient evil of Laughton's original, Patton assumes the mantle as Brice's henchman, while Costner confirms his arrival as a star. Clearly, they can remake 'em like that any more. BC

No Way to Treat a Lady

(1967, US, 108 min)
d Jack Smight. *p* Sol C Siegel. *sc* John Gay. *ph* Jack Priestley. *ed* Archie Marshek. *ad* Hal Pereira, George Jenkins. *m* Stanley Myers. *cast* Rod Steiger, Lee Remick, George Segal, Eileen Heckart, Murray Hamilton, Michael Dunn, Barbara Baxley, Ruth White, David Doyle.

●A scathingly funny black comedy satirising movie psychopathology. Steiger is brilliant as a sort of Boston strangler, son of a great actress who has left her boy with a mother fixation, a taste for impersonation, and a thirst for applause. Genuinely funny as he sets out to satisfy all three urges through murder, meanwhile making a special telephone confidant out of a reluctant cop (Segal, also brilliant) with Jewish momma problems of his own. Smight directs uncertainly, especially in some statutory love scenes, but the script (based on William Goldman's novel) is unstoppably witty. Difficult to resist a film in which a dwarf hopefully confesses to the killings, only to be told that eyewitness accounts point to a taller killer. 'See what I mean?' he cries, 'I'm a master of disguises!' TM

Nowhere

(1996, US/Fr, 82 min)
d Gregg Araki. *p* Andrea Sperling,Gregg Araki. *sc* Gregg Araki. *ph* Arturo Smith. *ed* Gregg Araki. *pd* Patti Podesta. *cast* James Duval, Rachel True, Nathan Bexton, Chiara Mastroianni, Debi Mazar, Kathleen Robertson, Scott Caan, Christina Applegate, Shannen Doherty, Rose McGowan.

●Araki's previous film, *The Doom Generation* (1994), never got a release in Britain. A lurid orgy of sex and violence, it was genuinely provocative, shocking and erotic, and it would have been sport watching the censor trying to grapple with it. *Nowhere* does have a UK distributor, but it's a piece of shit. Teen nihilism of the cheapest kind, it's as pretentious as Jean-Luc Godard, as tacky as one of those Z grade turkeys by Ted V Miklas, and at least twice as boring as that sounds. The hero (Duval) is a confused bisexual called 'Dark'. Araki persuaded a bunch of hot young actors to appear around him – True, Caan, Applegate, Mastroianni, Doherty, McGowan, an Alien Bodysuit – but he forgot to give them anything to do or say. TCh

Nowhere Man (Muno no Hito)

(1991, Jap, 110 min)
d Naoto Takenaka. *p* Shozo Ichiyama, Hirotsugu Yoshida. *sc* Toshiharu Maruuchi. *ph* Yasushi Sasakihara. *ed* Yoshiyuki Okuhara. *pd* Iwao Saitoh. *m* Gontiti. *cast* Naoto Takenaka, Jun Fubuki, Kotaro Saito, Miyako Yamaguchi, Hiroshi Kanabe, Ren Ohsugi, Tatsumi Kumashiro.

●Adapted from an avant-garde comic-strip by Yoshiharu Tsuge, this debut feature by the actor Naoto Takenaka is like a Japanese answer to the average 'Film on Four': earnest, quirky, overemphatic and a little preachy. The meandering plot, a shaggy-dog story without the punchline, follows a down-at-heel comic-strip author whose work no longer sells; he tries to support his family by selling 'aesthetic' stones, tangles with the crook who controls the stone market, gets new inspiration from a mysterious bird-man, and winds up doing the lowliest work he can think of. As protests against materialism and the Japanese work ethic go, this is on the weak side, but it has a certain languorous charm. TR

Nowhere to Hide (Injong Sajong Polkot Opta)

(1999, SKor, 108 min)
d Lee Myung-Se. *p* Chung Tae-Won. *sc* Lee Myung-Se. *ph* Jeong Kwang-Seok, Song Haeng-Ki. *ed* Go Im-Pyo. *pd* Lee Myung-Se. *m* Cho Sung-Woo. *cast* Park Joong-Hoon, Ahn Sung-Ki, Jang Dong-Kun, Choi Ji-Woo.
●There's a carefully researched police procedural underpinning Lee's breakthrough movie (a huge success at home and widely sold abroad), but its tone, texture and rhythms could not be less naturalistic. It's a work of committed and often dazzling artifice. Druglord Sungmin (Ahn playing a villain for once) kills a rival on the Forty Steps in Inchon, sparking a dogged manhunt led by the violent and scrofulous Detective Woo (Park at his best ever). Ruthless and ingenious, Sungmin slips repeatedly through the dragnet; Woo is on the case for 72 days, more often than not in pouring rain. Even without the odd discreet touches of CGI embellishment, Lee's work on the images is original enough to confirm that he's a world class talent. TR

Nowhere to Run

(1993, US, 95 min)
d Robert Harmon. *p* Craig Baumgarten, Gary Adelson. *sc* Joe Eszterhas, Leslie Bohem, Randy Feldman. *ph* David Gribble. *ed* Zack Staenberg, Mark Helfrich. *pd* Dennis Washington. *m* Mark Isham. *cast* Jean-Claude Van Damme, Rosanna Arquette, Kieran Culkin, Joss Ackland, Ted Levine, Tiffany Taubman.
●When fugitive jailbird Van Damme holes up with widowed mother Arquette, he not only charms his way into her kids' affections and her bed, but ends up protecting her from avaricious speculator Ackland. Based on a story by Joe Eszterhas and Richard Marquand, this ham-fisted thriller from Mark (*The Hitcher*) Harmon was intended to transform Van Damme from muscle bound action star to mainstream Hollywood hero. When Van Damme is doing what he does best – narcissistically displaying his body and thumping the bad guys – the film works reasonably well. By contrast his attempts to lighten up and play quieter dramatic scenes offer an embarrassing array of boyish smiles, dumb looks and stilted dialogue. NF

Now, Voyager

(1942, US, 117 min, b/w)
d Irving Rapper. *p* Hal B Wallis. *sc* Casey Robinson. *ph* Sol Polito. *ed* Warren Low. *ad* Robert M Haas. *m* Max Steiner. *cast* Bette Davis, Paul Henreid, Claude Rains, Bonita Granville, Gladys Cooper, John Loder, Ilka Chase, Lee Patrick, Janis Wilson, Franklin Pangborn.
●Davis, impeccable as usual, turns the sow's ear of Hollywood's notion of a repressed spinster (remove the glasses and lo! a beauty) into something like a silk purse. Great stuff as a worldly-wise psychiatrist (Rains at his smoothest) recommends a cruise, and bitter-sweet shipboard romance soars with an unhappily married architect (Henreid, suavely performing the archetypal two-cigarette trick). The women's weepie angle gets to be a bit of a slog later on, but it is all wrapped up as a mesmerically glittering package by Rapper's direction, Sol Polito's camerawork, and Max Steiner's lushly romantic score. (From a novel by Olive Prouty.) TM

Nude Bomb, The (aka The Return of Maxwell Smart)

(1980, US, 94 min)
d Clive Donner. *p* Jennings Lang. *sc* Arne Sultan, Bill Dana, Leonard B Stern. *ph* Harry Wolf. *ed* Walter Hannemann, Phil Tucker. *pd* William Tuntke. *m* Lalo Schifrin. *cast* Don Adams, Sylvia Kristel, Vittorio Gassman, Rhonda Fleming, Dana Elcar, Pamela Hensley, Andrea Howard, Norman Lloyd, Bill Dana.
●From the production team that gave us TV's *Get Smart* – part of that post-McCarthy tradition in spy series intent on demonstrating that the individualist bungling West could defeat the starkly mechanical East. For the big screen, though, the producers have turned post-Watergate: corporate business is now the object of paranoia. The flimsy plot is built around a Mafia-style designer (Dana) whose organisation (KAOS) broadcasts worldwide the fact that it has the power to destroy all known fabrics. Unless ransom is paid it will unleash its device: will Agent 86 (Adams) and his female companions be able to save the world from nakedness? 'From a character conceived by Mel Brooks', reads the blurb, and there are various nods to his style of humour throughout this bitty spoof. But the rest relies more on technology than style, and on mediocre effects that can't carry the plot. RW

Nueve Reinas

see Nine Queens

Nuit Américaine, La

see Day for Night

Nuit de Varennes, La

see That Night in Varennes

Nuit du Carrefour, La

(1932, Fr, 73 min, b/w)
d Jean Renoir. *sc* Jean Renoir. *ph* Marcel Lucien, Georges Asselin. *ed* Marguerite Renoir. *ad* William Aguet. *cast* Pierre Renoir, Georges Terof, Winna Winfried, Georges Koudria, Dignimont, GA Martin, Jean Gehret, Jane Pierson, Michel Duran.
●The screen's first Simenon adaptation, a wonderfully impenetrable mystery in which a series of murders and murder attempts gradually unravel a tale of star-crossed love and stolen diamonds, centring on a lonely crossroads, a sleazy garage, and a semi-derelict house harbouring an enigmatic, drug-stupefied femme fatale. Shot almost entirely on location and in direct sound, with most of the action taking place at night or in permanently shrouding mists, the whole film is seen and heard as through a glass, darkly. Myth (perpetuated by Godard) has it that three reels were lost; in fact nothing is missing, except that the money ran out and undoubtedly left gaps and rough edges. The mystification is an integral part of Renoir's conception: scenes are constantly being shot past Maigret or over his shoulder, as if to focus concentration on the mysterious person or object he is contemplating, but which is seen only hazily in the background, leaving us intrigued, tantalised and little the wiser until Pierre Renoir's Maigret ('Simple! Why didn't I think of it before?') condescends to explain. Weird, hallucinating and oddly poetic, it prefigures the treacherous perspectives of the later *film noir*. TM

Nuit et Jour

see Night and Day

Nuit fantastique, La (The Fantastic Night)

(1942, Fr, 89 min, b/w)
d Marcel L'Herbier. *sc* Louis Chavance, Maurice Henry, Marcel L'Herbier, Henri Jeanson. *ph* Pierre Montazel. *ed* Emilienne Nélissen, Suzanne Catelain. *ad* René Moulaert. *m* Maurice Thiriet. *cast* Fernand Gravey, Micheline Presle, Saturnin Fabre, Charles Granval, Jean Parédes, Bernard Blier.
●Better known for his silent films, L'Herbier here essayed a wartime escapist fantasy. A young man (Gravey) prefers his dream world to daytime reality, where he pursues his obsession, a mysterious goddess in white named Irène (Presle), who inhabits a small surreal world dominated by her father, a conjuror (Fabre). As in Woody Allen's *Purple Rose of Cairo*, the dreamer remains conscious of his edifying fiction, preferring it to reality. A bit rough around the edges: let's call it a semi-precious jewel. SGo

Nuits de la Pleine Lune, Les

see Full Moon in Paris

Nuits Fauves, Les

see Savage Nights

Nuits Rouges (Shadowman)

(1973, Fr/It, 105 min)
d Georges Franju. *p* Raymond Froment. *sc* Jacques Champreux. *ph* Guido Renzo Bertoni. *ed* Gilbert Natot. *ad* Robert Luchaire, Charles Finelli. *m* Georges Franju. *cast* Jacques Champreux, Gayle Hunnicut, Gert Fröbe, Ugo Pagliai, Josephine Chaplin, Patrick Préjean, Clément Harari, Raymond Bussières.
●This is the movie version of *L'Homme sans Visage*, a pilot for a TV series shot simultaneously but separately: a hugely beguiling tribute to the world of the pulp thriller, in which bizarre and ornate secret societies emerge from their mysterious labyrinths to do battle on the streets and rooftops of contemporary Europe. Feuillade, the early master of the French serial, is a major visual influence, but *Shadowman* broadens to take in the twilit worlds of Sax Rohmer (signalled by the character Petrie, the English antiquarian) and Jean Ray, with nods even in the direction of Von Daniken and *The Dawn of Magic*. The plot feasts itself on remote contol taxis piloted by waxworks, occult ceremonies, staring zombies, ancient charts, and mass assassinations: no one uses a revolver when a poison blowpipe or an animated sculpture will do, and Franju leavens the brew with his own style and wit, achieving some effects of startling visual beauty. DP

Number One

(1984, GB, 106 min)
d Les Blair. *p* Mark Forstater, Raymond Day. *sc* GF Newman. *ph* Bahram Manocheri. *ed* Jon Gregory. *pd* Martin Johnson. *m* David Mackay. *cast* Bob Geldof, Mel Smith, Alison Steadman, PH Moriarty, Phil Daniels, Alfred Molina, James Marcus, Ian Dury, Alun Armstrong, Kate Hardie Ray Winstone.
●Lots of street cred, low-rent locations, a plot based around snooker, and a nice big dollop of London villainy; add an unlikely, bumpy love story between Geldof's budding Hurricane Higgins and Steadman's tart with heart of gold, plus Smith on top form, and you could almost shout 'Frame and Match!' to all concerned. Sadly, though, what lets the film down is its preposterous ignorance of the game in question, which goes so deep that it will appal or amuse anyone who has managed two consecutive editions of *Pot Black*. When it steers clear of snooker, there's much to enjoy, but any film which lurches from grainy realism to outrageous cartoon with such abandon simply can't be number one. SGr

Number One (aka Pro)

(1969, US, 105 min)
d Tom Gries. *p* Walter Seltzer. *sc* Dan Moessinger. *ph* Michel Hugo. *ed* Richard Brockway. *ad* Arthur Loel. *m* Dominic Frontiere. *cast* Charlton Heston, Jessica Walter, Bruce Dern, John Randolph, Diana Muldaur, Al Hirt, GD Spradlin.
●As his fortieth year approaches, American footballer Heston finds his marriage falling apart and his playing career with the New Orleans Saints in its twilight, an odd role for one of the monolithic heroes of the Hollywood screen, and one that he doesn't seem to be able to do much with. Pretty banal, for Heston completists only. TJ.

Number Seventeen

(1932, GB, 64 min, b/w)
d Alfred Hitchcock. *p* Leon M Lion. *sc* Alma Reville, Alfred Hitchcock, Rodney Ackland. *ph* John Cox, Bryan Langley. *ed* AC Hammond. *ad* Wilfred Arnold. *m* A Hallis. *cast* Leon M Lion, Anne Grey, John Stuart, Donald Calthrop, Barry Jones, Ann Casson, Hugh Caine, Garry Marsh.
●This Bulldog Drummond-style yarn about a cop, a femme fatale and a gang of jewel thieves was made on one of Hitchcock's off-days. He didn't think much of the source material, a ropey stage play by Jefferson Farjeon, and he and his collaborators approached the film with their tongues firmly in their cheeks. There are occasional flourishes that testify to the director's ingenuity and ability – Expressionist lighting, faces looming over spiral staircases, hats blown off in the wind – and Hitch throws in plenty of knockabout English humour, but the plotting is half-baked and the special effects are so crude that they make the back projection in *Marnie* look like the last word in verisimilitude. GM

Number 3

See No. 3

Numéro Deux (Number Two)

(1975, Fr, 88 min)
d Jean-Luc Godard. *p* Anne-Marie Miéville, Jean-Luc Godard. *sc* Jean-Luc Godard. *ph*

William Lubtchansky. *cast* Sandrine Battistella, Pierre Oudry, Alexandre Rignault, Rachel Stéfanopoli.
●Despite its experimental format (video images of varying proportions and numbers superimposed on a 35 mm image), Godard's film is wholly lucid. It examines three generations of a working class French family living together, and argues against traditional concepts of eroticism, instead referring the characters' sexual parameters to a whole series of complex emotions which in turn relate to any number of separate factors, political and social. The result was Godard's richest film in years. CPe

Nun and the Devil, The (Le Monache di Sant'Arcangelo)

(1973, It/Fr, 102 min)
d Paolo Dominici [Domenico Paolella]. *p* Tonino Cervi. *sc* Paolo Dominici, Tonino Cervi. *ph* Giuseppe Ruzzolini. *ed* Nino Baragli. *ad* Claudio Cinini. *m* Piero Piccioni. *cast* Anne Heywood, Duilio Del Prete, Ornella Muti, Martine Brochard, Pier Paolo Capponi, Luc Merenda, Claudio Gora, Muriel Catala.
●Based on a story by Stendhal and 16th century records, this ostensibly offers a tale of intrigue and power politics in a Naples nunnery, caused by the death of the Mother Superior, whose appointment carries a charter for rifling gold mines in the New World. A mood of Jacobean intensity is occasionally promised as the plot dwells on obsession, lust and deceit, developing a sufficiently disenchanted view of humanity. But instead the film opts for much close-up goggling at nuns' habits, and heavy breathing as stockings are unfurled and feet kissed. Hence any attempt to convey the petty jealousies, frictions and sexual frustrations of convent life becomes so obtuse as to discourage much interest in what's going on.

Nuns on the Run

(1990, GB, 92 min)
d Jonathan Lynn. *p* Michael White. *sc* Jonathan Lynn. *ph* Michael Garfath. *ed* David Martin. *pd* Simon Holland. *m* Hidden Faces. *cast* Eric Idle, Robbie Coltrane, Camille Coduri, Janet Suzman, Doris Hare, Lila Kaye, Robert Patterson, Robert Morgan.
●Is there something intrinsically humorous about an old man (Idle) and a fat man (Coltrane) dressed up as nuns? To be honest, yes, but not enough to carry a whole film. For the rest, writer/director Lynn serves up a glossary of British film gags: incompetent rival gangsters, mistaken identities, a car chase, a nurse stripped to her black lace undies, right down to a girl who says 'There's nothing wrong with my eyesight', and walks straight into a lamppost. There's even a nod or two towards Monty Python in the cod theological debates, and in Coltrane appropriating Idle's wink-wink nudge-nudge say-no-more routine. The mystery is how the co-writer of *Yes, Minister* could produce such a string of clichés and pass it off as a film. That said, there is a comic chemistry between Idle and Coltrane, Camille Coduri (the blind blonde) makes the most of a limited part, and Janet Suzman plays a deliciously no-nonsense nun. DW

Nun's Story, The

(1959, US, 149 min)
d Fred Zinnemann. *p* Henry Blanke. *sc* Robert Anderson. *ph* Franz Planer. *ed* Walter Thompson. *ad* Alexandre Trauner. *m* Franz Waxman. *cast* Audrey Hepburn, Peter Finch, Edith Evans, Peggy Ashcroft, Dean Jagger, Mildred Dunnock, Patricia Collinge, Colleen Dewhurst, Lionel Jeffries, Niall MacGinnis.
●An adaptation of Kathryn Hulme's factually based bestseller about a Belgian girl, a surgeon's daughter whose dream always was to serve in the Congo as a nurse, and who later finds fulfilment doing just that as a missionary nun; but who simultaneously realises, forbidden by her vows to act on her attraction to Finch's handsome, agnostic doctor, that she is not by nature endowed with the self-denying humility that is the stuff of which nuns are made. Not as awful as you might expect, since the nun's training is shown in fascinating detail and the later doubts are quite subtly expressed. Solid performances, too, but it's still a long haul (made no lighter by Franz Waxman's abominably insistent score) for anyone not committed to theological problems of faith, conscience and obedience. TM

Nuovo Cinema Paradiso

see Cinema Paradiso

Nurse Betty

(2000, US, 110 min)
d Neil LaBute. *p* Gail Mutrux, Steve Golin. *sc* John C Richards, James Flamberg. *ph* Jean Yves Escoffier. *ed* Joel Plotch, Steven Weisberg. *pd* Charles Breen. *m* Rolfe Kent. *cast* Renée Zellweger, Morgan Freeman, Chris Rock, Greg Kinnear, Tia Texada, Aaron Eckhart, Pruitt Taylor Vince, Crispin Glover.
●Kansas waitress Zellweger is already obsessed, like most of her friends, with a hospital soap and its leading man (Kinnear); but after witnessing her awful husband's murder at the hands of drug dealers Freeman and Rock, she's so traumatised that she sets off for LA determined to reunite with her long-lost love – the fictional doctor – while killers, cops and pals follow her tracks in none too hot pursuit. A slick, clever, heartless satire on a society whose dreams, ambitions and mores are influenced at every turn by the deceptive blandishments of TV culture, LaBute's third feature, though scripted by others, is as cynical as its predecessors. Almost every emotion and action on view is presented as false, idiotic or superficial. There are more clichés than meet the eye too (viz the arguing, philosophising hitmen), and despite some very funny moments, only the truly horrific murder scene rings true. GA

Nutcracker

(1982, GB, 101 min)
d Anwar Kawadri. *p* Panos Nicolaou. *sc* Raymond Christodoulou. *ph* Peter Jessop. *ed* Max Benedict. *m* Simon Park. *cast* Joan Collins, Carol White, Paul Nicholas, Finola Hughes, William Franklyn, Leslie Ash, Murray Melvin, Anna Bergman.
●Collins, Britain's most durable nutcracker, plays the head of an international ballet company; an unlikely establishment, more suggestive of a discreet casino or hairdressing salon than anything terpsichorean, but lending itself nicely to a handful of desultory shower scenes and the machine-washable eroticism of Lycra and leg warmers. Nicholas plays a leather-jacketed photojournalist out to scoop a shot of a defecting Russian dancer (Hughes) who has holed up at Madame C's...but the minutiae of the plot are, to put it kindly, elusive. JS

Nutcracker, The (aka George Balanchine's The Nutcracker)

(1993, US, 85 min)
d Emile Ardolino. *p* Robert A Krasnow, Robert Hurwitz. *ph* Ralf D Bode. *ed* Girish Bhargava. *m* Tchaikovsky. *narrator* Kevin Kline. *cast* Macaulay Culkin, Bart Robinson Cook, Jessica Lynn Cohen, Darci Kistler, Damian Woetzel, Kyra Nichols, Wendy Whelan, the Company of the New York City Ballet.
●This version of an American stage production will do little to thrill most movie buffs. Though handsomely filmed and drenched with colours as saturated as wet paint, it has just three indoor locales and no exteriors. It's true market is as a festive TV event or a video where connoisseurs can play favourite bits over and over (the stupendously confident Kyra Nichols leading 'The Waltz of the Flowers') while fast forwarding through much of the rest. One reason George Balanchine's original choreography of the ballet is so special for Americans is that over the past 40 years it has become an annual New York tradition. Many of the participants, including director Ardolino, are graduates of the long-running TV series 'Dance in America'. They opted for as little gimmickry as possible, though they did add a voice-over (by Kevin Kline). The use of Macaulay Culkin isn't actually a gimmick – he was in the stage version in 1989 and '90, and his father did the same in the '50s, when he was paired with Bonnie Bedelia. AR

Nutcracker – the Motion Picture

(1986, US, 85 min)
d Carroll Ballard. *p* Willard Carroll, Donald Kushner, Peter Locke, Thomas L Wilhite. *ph* Stephen H Burum, Hiro Narita. *ed* John Nutt, Michael Silvers. *pd* Maurice Sendak. *m* Tchaikovsky. *with* Hugh Bigney, Vanessa Sharp, Patricia Barker, Wade Walthall, Dancers of the Pacific Northwest Ballet. narration Julie Harris.
●Not just a children's' dance film. Ballard invests this perennial Christmas treat with rapture, and aided by Maurice Sendak's gargoyle-in-the-candybox designs, he transforms this usually sugar-coated tale into a pubescent girl's nocturnal dream fantasy. He charts young Clara's overnight rite of passage from child to adult through her ambiguous feelings for godfather Drosselmeier, creator of the toy soldier that is Clara's most cherished Christmas gift. Her diffident response to this bright-eyed old codger adds an incipient Lolita angle for adult viewers, an approach typical of author/illustrator Sendak, whose books masterfully evoke simultaneous moods of malevolence and benevolence by mixing childhood's monstrous fears with heroic courage. The choreography is adequately serviceable, and the film's occasional visual muddiness and homespun narration both qualify the Freudian-tinged magic. AR

Nuts

(1987, US, 116 min)
d Martin Ritt. *p* Barbra Streisand. *sc* Tom Topor, Darryl Ponicsan, Alvin Sargent. *ph* Andrzej Bartkowiak. *ed* Sidney Levin. *pd* Joel Schiller. *m* Barbra Streisand. *cast* Barbra Streisand, Richard Dreyfuss, Maureen Stapleton, Karl Malden, Eli Wallach, Robert Webber, James Whitmore, Leslie Nielsen.
●A star vehicle in the tradition of those Susan Hayward biopics featuring major emotions and an unironed wardrobe. The question before the court is whether Claudia (Streisand) is nuts, and thus unfit to stand trial for manslaughter, or just bristlingly independent. A high-price hooker, she killed a client in self-defence, but her rich parents want her committed rather than risk a trial. She resists, snarling at shrink, counsel, and due process alike through matted hair. Lawyer Levinsky (Dreyfuss) is assigned the case, and grudgingly they work together towards getting Claudia her day in court, though she gets the big speech which wins the day. Why she is like she is gets explained, and it's plenty neat; Streisand's a star, which means your complicity is on call at all times. In the shade, Dreyfuss is terrific, banking down his natural cockiness. At the risk of sounding like the guy who went to *Cleopatra* to see the snake, Wallach, Whitmore, Webber, Malden and Stapleton lay on limousine service. BC

Nutty Professor, The

(1963, US, 107 min)
d Jerry Lewis. *p* Ernest D Glucksman. *sc* Jerry Lewis, Bill Richmond. *ph* W Wallace Kelley. *ed* John Woodcock. *ad* Hal Pereira, Walter Tyler. *m* Walter Scharf. *cast* Jerry Lewis, Stella Stevens, Del Moore, Kathleen Freeman, Med Flory, Norman Alden, Howard Morris, Elvia Allman, Henry Gibson.
●Surreal off-the-wall masterpiece, with Lewis again playing 7-stone cretin, this time a campus chemistry professor who woos his dream girl by inventing a magic potion that turns him (on and off) into a he-man of the Dean Martin school (hip, brylcreemed, offensive). The Technicolor blazes and swirls with manic energy, while the Jekyll-and-Hyde plot hustles its way through a minefield of gags, and sneers eloquently at the joys of the New America (a popular off-limits bar called The Purple Pit). Parody and nostalgia: pure alchemy. CA

Nutty Professor, The

(1996, US, 95 min)
d Tom Shadyac. *p* Brian Grazer, Russell Simmons. *sc* David Sheffield, Barry W Blausten, Tom Shadyac, Steve Oedekerk. *ph* Julio Macat. *ed* Don Zimmerman. *pd* William Elliott. *m* David Newman. *cast* Eddie Murphy, Jada Pinkett, James Coburn, Larry Miller, Dave Chappelle, John Ales, Patricia Wilson.
●In the original, a potion transformed a geeky chemistry teacher into a Dean Martin-style womaniser. In this unsubtle remake, Murphy is Professor Klump, a shy, 28-stone geneticist who uses his 'fat gene' formula to change himself into svelte ladies' man Buddy Love. He also plays the Prof's flatulent father, hard-ass brother, indulgent mother and eccentric grandmother. The Klump family's get-togethers are a tour de force. For all Murphy's comic energy and inventiveness,

however, the action remains predictable. The clumsy Prof falls for wafer-thin graduate student Carla Purty (Pinkett), but, after being humiliated by an abrasive night-club comedian (Chappelle), she opts for the testosterone-charged Buddy. To add to Klump's troubles, the potion has a tendency to wear off at embarrassing moments. Every fat gag, fart joke and crude piece of misogyny is played to the hilt. NF

Nutty Professor II: The Klumps

(2000, US, 107 min)
d Peter Segal. *p* Brian Grazer. *sc* Barry W Blaustein, David Sheffield, Paul Weitz, Chris Weitz. *ph* Dean Semler. *ed* William Kerr. *pd* William Elliott. *m* David Newman. *cast* Eddie Murphy, Janet Jackson, Larry Miller, John Ales, Richard Gant, Anna Maria Horsford, Melinda McGraw.

● Portly professor Sherman Klump returns, with his svelte alter ego Buddy Love and his bickering family: grouchy papa, indulgent mama, bellicose bro, nympho granny and Ernie Jr. All but the last of these are played by Murphy. Last time out, the Klumps featured in just two dinner table scenes. Here they're fleshed out big time. Jada Pinkett's graduate student gives way to Jackson's insipid scientist, who, like her predecessor, loves the tubster for his mind. Enough, in fact, to marry him. The nuptials are imminent and only Buddy Love can prevent little and large from walking down the aisle. The original was an effects heavy kids' movie with some risqué adult situations and borderline dialogue. This sequel edges towards the grown-ups: the 'youth juice' has a startling effect on papa's drooping member. A damaging technical problem with the layers of latex and/or poor sound recording renders much of the family dialogue inaudible. NF

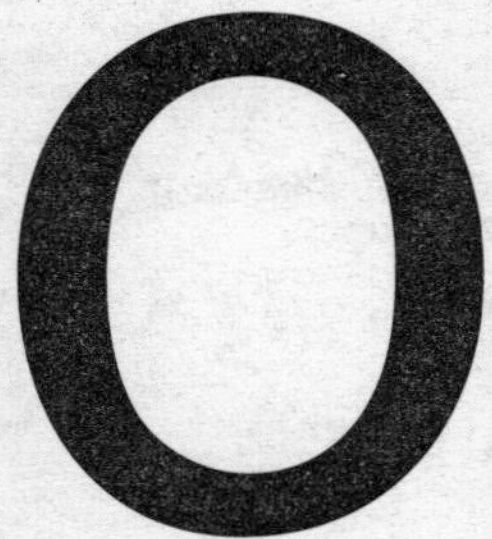

The Others

O Amor Natural

(1996, Neth, 76 min)
d Heddy Honigmann. *p* Pieter van Huystee. *sc* Heddy Honigmann. *ph* Jose Guerra. *ed* Marc Nolens.

● This feature length documentary was inspired by the erotic poetry of the Brazilian writer Carlos Drummond de Andrade. The poetry was never published during Drummond's lifetime – he was worried that readers would find it pornographic. The director interviews elderly Brazilians from all walks of life, inviting them to recite Drummond's verse and to reminisce about their own erotic adventures. The poetry itself is tremendous – full of ripe, carnal imagery – and there's something touching and humorous in seeing the dessicated old timers read it aloud. The film works both as a social document, charting a generation's attitudes toward love, sex and marriage, and as a lyrical celebration of Drummond's life and work. GM

Oberwald Mystery, The (Il Mistero di Oberwald)

(1980, It/WGer, 129 min)
d Michelangelo Antonioni. *p* Sergio Benvenuti, Alessandro von Normann, Giancarlo Bernardoni. *sc* Michelangelo Antonioni, Tonino Guerra. *ph* Luciano Tovoli. *ed* Michelangelo Antonioni, Francesco Grandoni. *ad* Mischa Scandella. *cast* Monica Vitti, Franco Branciaroli, Luigi Diberti, Elisabetta Pozzi, Amad Saha Alan, Paolo Bonacelli, Silvano Tranquilli.

● An oddly misjudged attempt by the master of Italian alienation to film Jean Cocteau's melodramatic play *The Eagle Has Two Heads*, previously filmed by Cocteau himself (*L'Aigle à Deux Têtes*, 1948). Ten years after the assassination of her husband Prince Ferdinand, the lonely internal exile of the queen (Vitti) of a middle European country is broken when she gives refuge to a fugitive anarchist poet. Shot on video and transferred to film, this features muddy visuals and suffers badly from the predictable mismatch of Cocteau's flamboyant aestheticism and Antonioni's emotionally distanced formalism. NF

Objective Burma!

(1944, US, 142 min, b/w)
d Raoul Walsh. *p* Jerry Wald. *sc* Ranald MacDougall, Lester Cole. *ph* James Wong Howe. *ed* George Amy. *ad* Ted Smith. *m* Franz Waxman. *cast* Errol Flynn, William Prince, James Brown, George Tobias, Henry Hull, Warner Anderson.

● A classic Hollywood platoon movie (from a story by Alvah Bessie), with Flynn and his men parachuting into Burma to wipe out a key Japanese radio station. The taut action, sparse dialogue, and faultless technique keep things moving so fast that there's no time to reflect upon the morality of war or the miraculous way in which Flynn and his men survive against such overwhelming odds. Very much in the time-honoured 'war is hell' tradition, with plenty of gritty detail but the implicit suggestion that those who survive such carnage are somehow ennobled by it. Prickly reading of the film as suggesting that Errol Flynn and the Americans won the Burma Campaign single-handed provoked a massive outburst of popular and critical vilification when the film was first released in this country, and following a full-scale diplomatic incident the distributor kept it under wraps until 1952. NF

Object of Beauty

(1991, US/GB, 103 min)
d Michael Lindsay-Hogg. *p* Jon S Denny, Alex Gohar. *sc* Michael Lindsay-Hogg. *ph* David Watkin. *ed* Ruth Foster. *pd* Derek Dodd. *m* Tom Bähler. *cast* John Malkovich, Andie MacDowell, Lolita Davidovich, Rudi Davies, Joss Ackland, Bill Paterson, Ricci Harnett, Peter Riegert, Jack Shepherd.

● An enervated American couple in London, Jake (Malkovich) and Tina (MacDowell) find their funds running out and their hotel bill mounting. He pressures her to sell her valuable Henry Moore sculpture, she resists, and its disappearance widens the mistrust between them. In fact, it has been stolen by deaf-mute chambermaid Jenny (Davies), who appreciates it for its beauty. This, on paper, contrasts with the futility of their values. Few who sit through the film will need the signpost, though they may wonder why Jenny, her punk brother, and their milieu seem to have strayed in out of Mayhew. Lindsay-Hogg wrote and directed this dull, static flounder, which exposes both MacDowell's limitations and Malkovich's withdrawal of labour. Shepherd, Ackland and Paterson go for little in cameo roles. BC

Object of My Affection, The

(1998, US, 111 min)
d Nicholas Hytner. *p* Laurence Mark. *sc* Wendy Wasserstein. *ph* Oliver Stapleton. *ed* Tariq Anwar. *pd* Jane Musky. *m* George Fenton. *cast* Jennifer Aniston, Paul Rudd, John Pankow, Alan Alda, Tim Daly, Nigel Hawthorne, Joan Copeland.

● Nina meets George at a dinner party and tells him how sorry she is to hear about his break-up with Robert – which comes as news to George. Despite her boyfriend Vince's misgivings, Nina invites George to move in with her and they become fast friends – so much so that when Nina conceives, she decides she'd rather raise t he kid with her nice gay lodger than with Vince. Hey, what are friends for? On some level, I suppose you might call this a radical film – but then how to account for its many longueurs? Perhaps it's because those confessional talk shows have effectively domesticated polymorphous sexuality, so that we mix-and-match gender roles almost as a matter of course. Hytner's right-on film of Stephen McCauley's novel works out the complications with a degree of intelligence and sensitivity, but it feels laborious and underwhelming. It never persuades you it belongs on the big screen. The central performances are fine – Aniston as Nina, Rudd as George, Pankow as Vince – but a lonely, philosophical Nigel Hawthorne registers most strongly in a supporting role. TCh

Obligation

see Forfaiture

Oblomov (Neskolko Dnei iz Zhizni I.I. Oblomova)

(1979, USSR, 140 min)
d Nikita Mikhalkov. *sc* Alexander Adabashian, Nikita Mikhalkov. *ph* Pavel Lebeshev. *ed* E Praksinoi. *ad* Alexander Adabashian, Aleksandr Samulekin. *m* Eduard Artemiev, (extracts) Bellini, Rachmaninov. *cast* Oleg Tabakov, Yuri Bogatyriov, Elena Solovei, Andrei Popov, Elena Solovei, Avangard Leontiev, Evgeni Steblov, Evgenia Glushenko. narrator A Romashin.

● Cross the two-hour barrier with a film about inertia and ennui – albeit a gentle period comedy – and you've automatically got a problem: how to convey the feelings without inducing them? Mikhalkov can't totally stave off drooping eyelids, but this engagingly adapted parable (from Goncharov's novel) of a privileged recluse being reluctantly dragged towards light, life and love produces its share of helpful wry nudges. Still, it has to be admitted that as the tardily socialised, eternally indecisive Oblomov, Tabakov invests sloth with a winning seductiveness. PT

Oblong Box, The

(1969, GB, 91 min)
d/p Gordon Hessler. *sc* Lawrence Huntington, Christopher Wicking. *ph* John Coquillon. *ed* Max Benedict. *ad* George Provis. *m* Harry Robinson. *cast* Vincent Price, Christopher Lee, Alastair Williamson, Hilary Dwyer, Peter Arne, Maxwell Shaw, Michael Balfour, Godfrey James, Rupert Davies.

● A loose adaptation of Poe's story *The Premature Burial*, set in 19th century England, with Price as the lord of the manor whose brother (Williamson), kept locked away after being mysteriously mutilated in Africa, escapes and seeks revenge after being inadvertently buried alive in an attempt to spirit him away from prying eyes. The first half-hour or so has a really enigmatic quality as Hessler's camera prowls through the sombre mansion, using subjective camera to convey the alienated and animal-like existence of the strange Sir Edward. By keeping Sir Edward behind the camera for so long, his evil is exaggerated enormously, giving him a kind of sub-human aura long after the device has been discontinued. After this cryptic opening, however, the script rapidly begins to disintegrate (Chris Wicking, alas, is confined to 'additional dialogue'). Begun by Michael Reeves, the film was taken over by Hessler after the former's death.

O Brother, Where Art Thou?

(2000, US, 102 min)
d Joel Coen. *p* Ethan Coen. *sc* Ethan Coen, Joel Coen. *ph* Roger Deakins. *ed* Roderick Jaynes, Tricia Cooke. *pd* Dennis Gassner. *m* T Bone Burnett. *cast* George Clooney, John Turturro, Tim Blake Nelson, Holly Hunter, John Goodman, Chris Thomas King, Charles Durning.

● The title alludes to Preston Sturges and evokes the engagingly anarchic, almost throwaway tone and setting of the Coens' shaggy Deep South Depression-era semi-musical road-comedy. The story, however, as announced with gleeful idiocy (but honesty!) in the opening credits, is loosely 'Based on Homer's Odyssey'. Clooney is perfectly cast as Everett Ulysses McGill, a somewhat vainglorious Mississippi charmer who breaks from a chain gang, dragging two none-too-bright buddies (Turturro and Nelson) in his wake, purportedly to retrieve his booty, but actually to try to tempt his less than faithful Penelope (Hunter) away from her new suitor. En route, there are adventures with latter-day lotus eaters, sirens, a Bible-bashing Polyphemus (Goodman), a Robert Johnson-like bluesman, a public enemy, corrupt politicians and the Klan, accompanied by a wealth of terrific blues, bluegrass and gospel music. Great dialogue, superb 'Scope camerawork from Roger Deakins, and a genuinely wondrous deus ex machina are among the delights. GA

Obsession (aka The Hidden Room)

(1949, GB, 98 min, b/w)
d Edward Dmytryk. *p* NA Bronsten. *sc* Alec Coppel. *ph* CM Pennington-Richards. *ed* Lito Carruthers. *ad* Duncan Sutherland. *m* Nino Rota. *cast* Robert Newton, Phil Brown, Sally Gray, Naunton Wayne, Michael Balfour, Olga Lindo, Ronald Adam.

● Certainly Dmytryk's best British film, made after his blacklist exile and before freedom from the Hollywood system led him into the pretensions of *Give Us This Day*. Adapted by Alec Coppel from his own novel, it's an intriguing 'perfect murder' thriller in which an obsessively jealous husband lures his rival to a cellar on a bomb site, keeping him chained there until the coast is clear and his own grimly meticulous preparations for disposing of the body in an acid bath are complete. Perhaps only Buñuel could have done justice to the flavour as the avenger sadistically torments his victim during the wait, and an odd intimacy starts to spring up between them. Here both dialogue and performances (with Newton doing much less eye-rolling than usual) stay a little too close to the surface, but it has much the same narrative grip as Dmytryk's earlier Hollywood movies like *Murder My Sweet*, *Cornered* and *Crossfire*. TM

Obsession

(1976, US, 98 min)
d Brian De Palma. *p* George Litto, Harry N Blum. *sc* Paul Schrader. *ph* Vilmos Zsigmond. *ed* Paul Hirsch. *ad* Jack Senter. *m* Bernard Herrmann. *cast* Cliff Robertson, Genevieve Bujold, John Lithgow, Sylvia Williams, Wanda Blackman, Patrick McNamara, Stanley J Reyes, Nick Krieger.

● Schrader and De Palma's tribute to Hitchcock's *Vertigo* may lack the misogyny and bloodbath sensationalism of De Palma's later work, but it's still dressed up in a mortifyingly vacuous imitation of the Master's stylistic touches. Virtuoso gliding camera movements do not necessarily a good film make. The main problem with the film, in fact, is the excruciatingly slow pace; although if you've seen *Vertigo*, the story itself – of a businessman haunted by guilt about his wife's death, and getting involved years later with her lookalike – will fail to yield the narrative surprises and suspense required in a thriller. GA

Obsession, An (Tsumetai Chi)

(1997, Jap, 109 min)
d Shinji Aoyama. *p* Naoki Kai, Katsuaki Takemoto, Tsutomu Kuno. *sc* Shinji Aoyama. *ph* Isao Ishii. *ed* Shinji Aoyama. *ad* Takeshi

Shimizu. *m* Shinji Aoyama, Isao Yamada. *cast* Ryo Ishibashi, Kazuma Suzuki, Kyoko Toyama, Eiko Nagashima, Taro Suwa. Yurei Yanagi.
● Cool, distinctive, borderline pretentious thriller about a cop who loses his gun, a lung, his wife and his grip in a shooting incident. The case itself is frankly mystifying, but the manner in which the director layers and textures the film is reward in itself, especially the highly expressive use of sound. Not quite in the Takeshi Kitano league, however. TCh

O.C. & Stiggs

(1987, US, 109 min)
d Robert Altman. *p* Robert Altman, Peter Newman. *sc* Donald Cantrell, Ted Mann. *ph* Pierre Mignot. *ed* Elizabeth Kling. *pd* Scott Bushnell. *m* King Sunny Adé and His African Beats. *cast* Daniel H Jenkins, Neill Barry, Paul Dooley, Jane Curtin, Jon Cryer, Ray Walston, Dennis Hopper, Melvin Van Peebles, Martin Mull, Melvin Van Peebles, Nina Van Pallandt.
● Altman's one major studio picture between *Popeye* and *The Player* was a complete misfire. As scripted by *National Lampoon*'s Tod Carroll and Ted Mann, it's a peculiarly juvenile foray into teen anarchy, as the two pranksters of the title set about harassing Phoenix, Arizona, in general, and the Schwab family (racist, materialistic, dumb and ugly) in particular. As satire, it falls flat, partly because Altman gets the sub-*Popeye* comic-strip tone all wrong (with the notable exception of Dooley's Randall Schwab), partly because the kids are so snide and smart-ass. Small wonder it only achieved video release. GA

Occasional Work of a Female Slave (Gelegenheitsarbeit einer Sklavin)

(1973, WGer, 91 min, b/w)
d/p Alexander Kluge. *sc* Alexander Kluge, Hans Drawe, HD Müller. *ph* Thomas Mauch. *ed* Beate Mainka-Jellinghaus, Christina Warnck. *cast* Alexandra Kluge, Franz Bronski, Sylvia Gartmann, Traugott Buhre, Ursula Dirichs, Walter Flamme, Ulrike Laureze.
● That rarest of movies: a left wing comedy which doesn't hang itself up in questions of 'realism' but does involve itself very closely with the everyday flux of political and social pressures. Alexandra Kluge (the director's sister) plays a young housewife and mother who works as a part-time abortionist; her cynical complacency gives way to a bright-eyed 'activism' when she's forced out of the job and starts waging a one-woman war against the authorities, the bosses, and the tyranny of the family. Kluge charts her hopeless campaign through documentary (an unblinking look at the fact of abortion) and witty fiction alike, his methods recalling both Brecht and Godard; everything is informed by a kind of wry humour that keeps the plot in perspective without tempering its immediacy. It's hard to think of another film that's as honest, relevant and yet not disillusioned as this. TR

Occupation in 26 Pictures, The (Okupacija u 26 Slika)

(1978, Yugo, 116 min)
d Lordan Zafranovic. *sc* Mirko Kovac, Lordan Zafranovic. *ph* Karpo Godina. *m* Alfi Kabiljo. *cast* Frano Lasic, Boris Kralj, Milan Strljic, Stevo Zigon.
● An exquisitely photographed, excessively 'choreographed' picture-book study of the impact, on three initially gilded youths (Jew, radical and staunch patriot) of Yugoslavia's fascist occupation. It progresses at a self-indulgent pace from idyll to nightmare – indeed, to scenes of unwatchably sadistic repression. JD

Occupied Palestine

(1981, US, 86 min)
d David Koff.
● The opening credit on this documentary reads 'Vanessa Redgrave Productions presents…', but those expecting the cause-mongering propaganda of a crank will be disappointed. For Koff's film does allow the opposition's apologists to defend Israel and Zionism. *Occupied Palestine* has sufficient perspective to be able to see the 'repossession' of land by the Israelis both as a cultural fulfilment of Zionism and as an economic strategy since, as one witness shrewdly observes, 'the separation of the Arab from his land provided a mobile labour force in the service of the Zionist economy'. The catalogue of atrocities attributed to the Israeli army makes it very difficult to dismiss the Palestinian case out of hand. RM

Occupy!

(1976, GB, 55 min)
d Gael Dohany. *ph* HB Trevelyan, Peter Chappell, Joan Churchill, Pasco MacFarlane, Richard Mordant. *ed* Michael Zimbrich. *m* Sally Wizard. *with* CG Bond, Allan Dosser, Bernard Dunleavy, Clive Odom, Peter Postlethwaite, Julie Walters.
● 'You can't fight redundancy with strike action. It can't be done.' So the Fisher-Bendix factory workers in Kirkby, Liverpool, occupied – twice, both times literally chasing management off the premises. Their struggle against a succession of asset-stripping owners, grotesque mismanagement, and their own gender and occupational divisions, is unusually well portrayed here. Three media are interwoven – the workers' own recollections on film; the Liverpool Everyman's theatrical reconstruction of the work-in; and Granada TV's news footage – enabling the film to avoid the turgidity of British documentary exegesis and to counterpoint different styles of 'reality'. The strategy gives the agitational work an ironical portent, and links it wonderfully well with another Kirkby film, *Behind the Rent Strike*. MM

Ocean's 11

(1960, US, 127 min)
d/p Lewis Milestone. *sc* Harry Brown, Charles Lederer. *ph* William H Daniels. *ed* Philip W Anderson. *ad* Nicolai Remisoff. *m* Nelson Riddle. *songs* Sammy Cahn, James Van Heusen. *cast* Frank Sinatra, Dean Martin, Sammy Davis Jr, Peter Lawford, Angie Dickinson, Richard Conte, Cesar Romero, Patrice Wymore, Akim Tamiroff, Henry Silva, Joey Bishop, Ilka Chase.
● The Rat Pack plus sundry others, playing ex-army buddies, plan a grand heist in Las Vegas, relieving five casinos simultaneously of their loot. The antics of Sinatra & Co (complete with guest spots for the likes of Shirley MacLaine, George Raft and Red Skelton) become rather hard to bear, and the evocation of Las Vegas as a neon nightmare may possibly be unintentional, since the film was made by Sinatra's own company as an extended advertisement for the Clan's shows there. The heist itself, though, is a superb piece of movie-making. ATu

Ocean's Eleven

(2001, US/Aust, 116 min)
d Steven Soderbergh. *p* Jerry Weintraub. *sc* Ted Griffin. *ph* Peter Andrews [Steven Soderbergh]. *ed* Steve Mirrione. *pd* Philip Messina. *m* David Holmes. *cast* George Clooney, Matt Damon, Andy Garcia, Brad Pitt, Julia Roberts, Casey Affleck, Scott Caan, Elliott Gould, Bernie Mac, Carl Reiner, Don Cheadle.
● What possessed Soderbergh to remake a flabby '50s heist movie best remembered as a vanity project for the Rat Pack? Fair question – except this isn't really a remake. Yes, it's set in Vegas, concerns a robbery and has a starry cast, but that's it, resemblance-wise. Ted Griffin's script persuaded Soderbergh there was a chance for audiences, himself and the cast to have some fun. You know you're in safe hands from the start: twinkly-eyed Danny Ocean (Clooney) reassuring a prison board of his determination to stay clean outside. Cut: the ex-con's conman talents are immediately on display as he assembles a crew of partners old and new – a strategist (Pitt), a pickpocket (Damon), a Cockney explosives man (Cheadle), a veteran fraudster (Reiner), a financier (Gould) – for the most daring robbery yet attempted of a Nevada casino. It'll be fun (but risky) taking shady Vegas tycoon Terry Benedict (Garcia) for $150m, especially as he has a thing going with Danny's ex-wife, Tess (Roberts). Performed, choreographed, shot and directed with deceptive ease, this wholly enjoyable entertainment sees Soderbergh setting himself a new challenge – the hi-tech robbery procedural – and relishing the clichés even as he freshens them with a dab of polish, wit, pace and a light touch of irony. GA

October

see Oktyabr

October Man, The

(1947, GB, 98 min, b/w)
d Roy Baker. *p* Filippo Del Giudice. *sc* Eric Ambler. *ph* Erwin Hillier. *ed* Alan L Jaggs. *ad* Alex Vetchinsky. *m* William Alwyn. *cast* John Mills, Joan Greenwood, Kay Walsh, Edward Chapman, Joyce Carey, Felix Aylmer, Catherine Lacey, Patrick Holt.
● Good old amnesia has another outing, with Mills as a murder suspect none too sure of his own innocence when a model (Walsh) to whom he has lent some money is found strangled, but eventually able to unmask the (glaringly obvious) real killer. Lethargically paced, stiffly scripted by Eric Ambler, the film's most attractive features are Joan Greenwood as the girl who believes in our hero, and the setting in a gently decaying hotel. TM

October Sky

(1999, US, 107 min)
d Joe Johnston. *p* Charles Gordon, Larry Franco. *sc* Lewis Colick. *ph* Fred Murphy. *ed* Robert Dalva. *pd* Barry Robison. *m* Mark Isham. *cast* Jake Gyllenhaal, Chris Cooper, William Lee Scott, Chris Owen, Chad Lindberg, Natalie Canerday, Elya Baskin, Chris Ellis, Laura Dern, Scott Miles, Randy Stripling.
● This adaptation of Homer H Hickam's best selling memoir *Rocket Boys* is set in a working class corner of the Appalachians, where life for the young folk follows a depressingly familiar pattern: after high school, down the mine. Young Homer (Gyllenhaal) however, gazes up at Sputnik in the night sky and is inspired to join the '50s space race by experimenting with his own homemade rockets. Encouraged by a teacher (Dern), Homer and his pals look to the state and national school science fairs, where college scholarships are up for grabs, thinking the unthinkable for mining town lads. Still, Hickam senior (Cooper, never better), pit foreman, disapproves of such foolishness. Even if Homer were to build a successful rocket, would it create a permanent rift between him and his dad? Director Johnston plays this archetypal tale of small town endeavour straight and simple. Such plainspeaking sincerity might be mistaken for mere slush, but the TV movie subject matter is infused with genuine feeling for the value of learning as a passport to freedom, and an authentic regard for the honest graft of working men. TJ

Octopussy

(1983, GB, 131 min)
d John Glen. *p* Albert R Broccoli. *sc* George MacDonald Fraser, Richard Maibaum, Michael Wilson. *ph* Alan Hume. *ed* Peter Davies, Henry Richardson. *pd* Peter Lamont. *m* John Barry. *cast* Roger Moore, Maud Adams, Louis Jourdan, Kristina Wayborn, Kabir Bedi, Steven Berkoff, David Meyer, Anthony Meyer, Vijay Amritraj, Desmond Llewelyn, Lois Maxwell.
● This finds Bond on better form than he's been for some time. The action sequences are tighter, the visual gags more inventive, and if the plot is no great shakes, the whole thing is served up with a decent approximation to the old panache. Predictably, the Red Menace is hammered even harder than usual. No mileage in hanging around dreary old East Berlin though, so quick switch to the exotic sunbaked vistas of India, where Maud Adams presides over an international smuggling gang. Hot in pursuit via balloon, folding mini-jet and supercharged rickshaw comes Bond to try to tie up a few plot strands. If age has done nothing to sap Old Moore's ability to emerge shamelessly into close-up once the stunt double has done his stuff, his potency is showing signs of wear and tear with only two cursory scenes *en sack*. He even looks vaguely abashed when Ms Adams calls him a hired assassin. Could Bond finally be falling prey to the superspy's most dreaded malady – introspection? JP

Odd Angry Shot, The

(1979, Aust, 92 min)
d Tom Jeffrey. *p* Sue Milliken, Tom Jeffrey. *sc* Tom Jeffrey. *ph* Donald McAlpine. *ed* Brian Kavanagh. *pd* Bernard Hides. *m* Michael Carlos. *cast* Graham Kennedy, John Hargreaves, John Jarratt, Bryan Brown, Graeme Blundell, Richard Moir, Ian Gilmore.
● The odd angry shot was just about all the Aussies managed in their own ignominious Vietnam war adventure. The film's title, though,

might as well refer to the barbed sentiments the 'poor bloody infantry' reserve for the local politicos who sent them there and then conveniently forgot them. The movie, like the slim autobiographical novel on which it's closely based, raised something of a ruckus at home. But away from the controversy, its message of class-conscious disenchantment sits uneasily atop an episodic, post-*M*A*S*H* tragi-comedy featuring everybody's stereotype of the boozy, brawling, macho Aussie group. A brave gesture, maybe (and one in terms of narrative economy from which *Gallipoli* could have learned), but hidebound by its respect for generic clichés. PT

Odd Couple, The

(1967, US, 105 min)
d Gene Saks. *p* Howard W Koch. *sc* Neil Simon. *ph* Robert B Hauser. *ed* Frank Bracht. *ad* Hal Pereira, Walter Tyler. *m* Neal Hefti. *cast* Jack Lemmon, Walter Matthau, John Fiedler, Herbert Edelman, Monica Evans, Carole Shelley.

● An irresistible double act from Lemmon and Matthau as a pair of divorced husbands who set up house together for companionship, and in so doing discover exactly what it was that made them impossible to live with in the first place. Lemmon is the neurotic one who tries to throw himself out of a window but can't get it open, and who clears his sinuses by barking like a seal in the middle of the night; Matthau is the placid slob determined on a good time who can't understand why his flatmate threatens to burst into tears if he suggests a bit of fun and female companionship. Chief bone of contention is the apartment itself, which Matthau likes to keep swilling in a poker-playing atmosphere of ash and empties, while Lemmon rushes home each evening to wield an obsessively fastidious vacuum-cleaner. Saks takes Neil Simon's play pretty much as it comes, but with Lemmon and Matthau to watch, and a generous quota of one-liners, who needs direction? TM

Odd Couple II, The (aka Neil Simon's The Odd Couple II)

(1998, US, 96 min)
d Howard Deutch. *p* Neil Simon, Robert W Cort, David Madden. *sc* Neil Simon. *ph* Jamie Anderson. *ed* Seth Flaum. *pd* Dan Bishop. *m* Alan Silvestri. *cast* Jack Lemmon, Walter Matthau, Christine Baranski, Barnard Hughes, Jonathan Silverman, Jean Smart, Lisa Waltz.

● When it comes to jokes, the old ones can be the best; be it re-release, remake or repackaged videos, the market for superannuated comedy is stronger than ever. No reason, then, why Neil Simon shouldn't resurrect Oscar Madison (Matthau) and Felix Unger (Lemmon) from his 30-year-old film script to see where life has led them. The sequel reunites them to witness the occasion of their respective son and daughter's LA wedding. Despite initial reticence, Felix and Oscar travel to the ceremony together, but a series of mishaps holds them up along the way. But for a lame start and a painful scene where Oscar tries to pick up two much younger women and subsequently becomes embroiled in a domestic with their hammy husbands, this is an entertaining oldie road movie, with the humour hotting up in the desert where the pair inflict multiple fractures on the long arm of the law. MD

Odd Job, The

(1978, GB, 87 min)
d Peter Medak. *p* Mark Forstater, Graham Chapman. *sc* Bernard McKenna, Graham Chapman. *ph* Ken Hodges. *ed* Barrie Vince. *ad* Tony Curtis. *m* Howard Blake. *cast* Graham Chapman, David Jason, Diana Quick, Simon Williams, Edward Hardwicke, Bill Paterson, Michael Elphick, Richard O'Brien.

● The preconceptions surrounding the Monty Python team and their particular brand of lunacy do not marry well with this solo venture from Graham Chapman. Playing the straight man Arthur, who hires a bungling odd job man (Jason) to perpetrate his 'suicide', Chapman is in need of an outrageous cast in order to reduce the plot to the level of absurdity that this type of humour demands. From his opposite number Diana Quick (as the wife whose desertion provokes the quest for – and subsequent flight from – suicide), all he gets as a foil is over-dramatic acting without the required degree of parody. Hardly rolling in the aisles stuff, but there are some chuckles. Watch for a brilliant performance from Bill Paterson as Morningside Mull of Scotland Yard, and Richard O'Brien's cameo as a gay/bike leather heavy. FF

Odd Man Out

(1947, GB, 116 min, b/w)
d/p Carol Reed. *sc* FL Green, RC Sherriff. *ph* Robert Krasker. *ed* Fergus McDonell. *pd* Roger Furse. *m* William Alwyn. *cast* James Mason, Robert Newton, Cyril Cusack, FJ McCormick, William Hartnell, Fay Compton, Robert Beatty, Daniel O'Herlihy, Kathleen Ryan.

● Mason's wounded, haunted, hunted IRA gunman staggers through expressive and suspenseful encounters with the pavement sages, barroom poets and angel artists of the urban landscape of Guinness-soaked legend; through a *noir*-ish, nightmarish purgatory whose heady atmosphere was conjured by Reed out of the (oh so) thin air of British cinema and reconstructed two years later for the better-known *The Third Man*. Based on the novel by FL Green; an eccentric masterpiece. PT

Odds Against Tomorrow

(1959, US, 96 min, b/w)
d/p Robert Wise. *sc* John O Killens, Nelson Gidding, [Abraham Polonsky]. *ph* Joseph Brun. *ed* Dede Allen. *ad* Leo Kerz. *m* John Lewis. *cast* Harry Belafonte, Robert Ryan, Shelley Winters, Ed Begley, Gloria Grahame, Will Kuluva.

● A taut, downbeat, New York-shot bank heist thriller, with the traditional dishonour among thieves revolving around the openly racial conflict between Ryan and Belafonte. Developed originally by Belafonte's own company after he'd picked up the rights to the William McGivern novel, the script was rewritten at Wise's suggestion to turn around the optimistic 'kin-under-the-skin' conclusion and provide a stunning shoot-out finale (in which the two corpses, ironically, become indistinguishable). PT

Odessa File, The

(1974, GB/WGer, 129 min)
d Ronald Neame. *p* John Woolf, John R Sloan. *sc* Kenneth Ross, George Markstein. *ph* Oswald Morris. *ed* Ralph Kemplen. *pd* Rolf Zehetbauer. *m* Andrew Lloyd Webber. *cast* Jon Voight, Maximilian Schell, Maria Schell, Mary Tamm, Derek Jacobi, Peter Jeffrey, Klaus Löwitsch, Kurt Meisel, Hannes Messemer.

● Adapted from Frederick Forsyth's bestseller, a straightforward slice of investigative journalism that has Young Germany trying to reconcile itself to the evils of Nazism as Voight hunts down a protected war criminal (Schell) now high up in industry. Voight's performance gives credibility to his character's obsession, but even that cannot overcome the discrepancy between the deeper themes (mass execution and the expiation of guilt) and the routine nature of this piece of box-office action adventure.

Ode to Billy Joe

(1976, US, 106 min)
d Max Baer. *p* Max Baer, Roger Camras. *sc* Herman Raucher. *ph* Michel Hugo. *ed* Frank Morriss. *ad* Philip M Jefferies. *m* Michel Legrand. *cast* Robby Benson, Glynnis O'Connor, Joan Hotchkis, Sandy McPeak, James Best, Terence Goodman.

● Based on Bobbie Gentry's caustic pop classic, *Ode to Billy Joe* fleshes out the narrative ambiguities and implications of the song with surprising success. Through sensitive use of some beautiful locations (Tallahatchie Bridge is always central to, but never overwhelms, the proceedings), sympathetic attention to the flavour of the period (like the excited reaction to a first flush toilet), and an unusually sinewy script from Herman Raucher (it only dissolves into sticky Rod McKuen territory towards the close), Baer convincingly depicts the smalltown mores of a Mississippi backwater in the early '50s. Virtually all the performances are winners, but most impressive are the star-crossed teenage lovers, Benson and O'Connor, who catch the joys, fears and fantasies of adolescence with ingenuous authenticity. Only the last half-hour becomes laboured, and in one sequence hideously sentimental, which is not improved by the intrusively slushy score from Michel Legrand. IB

Ode to Cologne (Viel Passiert – Der BAP Film)

(2001, Ger, 96 min)
d Wim Wenders. *p* Olaf Wicke. *sc* Wim Wenders. *ph* Phedon Papamichael. *ed* Moritz Laube. *m* BAP. *with* BAP, Marie Bäumer, Joachim Król, Willi Laschet, Anger 77, Wolf Biermann.

● Wolfgang Niedecken's pub-rock-style band BAP, formed in the '70s in Cologne, has been through many changes in size, shape, ethnicity and repertoire over the years, but never strays far from social commentary and always performs its originals in the local dialect 'Kölsch'. This rockumentary uses archive and newsreel clips to show the band evolving in response to social/political changes and features highlights from a 'retrospective' concert in an old picture-palace in Essen; Niedecken emerges as a fine, committed writer with a likeable penchant for Bob Dylan and Kinks covers. Wenders brings very little to the party: just a couple of Steadicam operators and the hopelessly lame idea of having three actors sleepwalk through pretentious little dramatisations of some of the songs. Oh, and one of the worst English titles ever. TR

Odette

(1950, GB, 123 min, b/w)
d/p Herbert Wilcox. *sc* Warren Chetham-Strode. *ph* Max Greene. *ed* William Lewthwaite. *ad* William C Andrews. *m* Anthony Collins. *cast* Anna Neagle, Trevor Howard, Peter Ustinov, Marius Goring, Bernard Lee, Alfred Shieske, Gilles Quéant.

● Neagle portraying another Great Lady, this time Odette Churchill, the French wife of an Englishman, who spied for the French Resistance during World War II, was captured and tortured by the Nazis, but survived to be awarded the George Cross. Neagle acquits herself reasonably well, but the whole film is bogged down by a surfeit of respect and patriotism. The kind of film in which you know in advance exactly what will happen next. GA

Odeur de la Papaye Verte, L'

see Scent of Green Papaya, The

O Dreamland

(1953, GB, 13 min, b/w)
d/p/sc Lindsay Anderson. *ph* John Fletcher. *ed* Lindsay Anderson.

● Dreamland Amusement Park, Margate in Coronation year. Tacky mechanical dummies depict tortures and executions; people in daft hats mill around, lose on the slot machines, gawp at animals in tiny cages, scoff greasy food; in the background slushy ballads vie with bingo callers and the demented shrieks of a Laughing Sailor. Yes, these proles are certainly a grisly lot. Okay, eating mushy peas and listening to Frankie Laine may not be very edifying, but Anderson's snotty attitude towards it all, his withholding of any affection or empathy, is a sight less so. At one point, some women spot the camera and break into an impromptu can-can. Presumably, Anderson included the shot because he thought they looked silly. BBa

Oedipus Rex (Edipo Re)

(1967, It, 104 min)
d Pier Paolo Pasolini. *p* Alfredo Bini. *sc* Pier Paolo Pasolini. *ph* Giuseppe Ruzzolini. *ed* Nino Baragli. *ad* Luigi Scaccianoce, Andrea Fantacci. *cast* Franco Citti, Silvana Mangano, Carmelo Bene, Julian Beck, Alida Valli, Ninetto Davoli, Pier Paolo Pasolini.

● Pasolini's working of the Sophocles tragedy, though not wholly successful, has its very definite strengths. Citti's Oedipus is intuitive and primitive rather than intellectual; the myth itself is treated as a dream set in the Moroccan desert in parenthesis between 'Oedipal' scenes in modern Bologna; and visually it's often astonishing, the harsh desert sunlight and dry buildings isolating the characters effectively. RM

Oedipus the King

(1967, GB, 97 min)
d Philip Saville. *p* Michael Luke. *sc* Michael Luke, Philip Saville. *ph* Walter Lassally. *ed* Paul Davies. *ad* Yannis Migadis. *m* Yannis Christou. *cast* Christopher Plummer, Lilli

Palmer, Richard Johnson, Orson Welles, Cyril Cusack, Roger Livesey, Donald Sutherland, Friedrich Ledebur.
● Screamingly tedious version of the Sophocles tragedy in which the cast progress from poetic mouthing to ferocious ranting as they shuffle around the ruins of a Greek amphitheatre. Even Welles, looking like Santa Claus on leave from a disreputable department store in woolly wig and sackcloth nightie, seems subdued in his brief appearance as Tiresias. TM

Oeufs de l'Autruche, Les

see Ostrich Has Two Eggs, The

Of a Thousand Delights

see Vaghe Stelle dell'Orsa

Off and Running

(1991, US, 90 min)
d Edward Bianchi. *p* Aaron Russo, William C Carraro. *sc* Mitch Glazer. *ph* Andrzej Bartkowiak. *ed* Rick Shaine. *ad* Norman E Weber. *m* Mason Daring. *cast* Cyndi Lauper, David Keith, Johnny Pinto, David Thornton, Richard Belzer, José Perez, Anita Morris, Hazen Gifford.
● Although not up to the standard of Madonna in *Desperately Seeking Susan*, Cyndi Lauper (in her second feature) isn't bad at playing a version of herself: a tough cookie with a soft centre. Would-be actress Cyd (Lauper) has got as far as playing a mermaid in a Miami Beach hotel bar. After witnessing her boyfriend's murder, she hightails it out of town and hooks up with an unlikely lover (Keith) and a streetwise kid (Pinto). With the killer on their trail, the mismatched family jumps the Manhattan train for a predictably madcap adventure. For Lauper fans only. CO'S

Off Beat

(1986, US, 92 min)
d Michael Dinner. *p* Joe Roth, Harry J Ufland. *sc* Mark Medoff. *ph* Carlo Di Palma. *ed* Dede Allen, Angelo Corrao. *pd* Woods MacKintosh. *m* James Horner. *cast* Judge Reinhold, Meg Tilly, Cleavant Derricks, Joe Mantegna, Jacques D'Amboise, James Tolkan, Amy Wright, John Turturro, Anthony Zerbe, Harvey Keitel, Fred Gwynne, Austin Pendleton, Penn Jillette, Mark Medoff.
● Librarian Reinhold (moonlighting for a cop friend) falls for law-enforcer Tilly in this impossibly mellow-yellow comedy: writer Mark Medoff (*Children of a Lesser God*) turns up as a police sergeant, mingling with a first-division supporting cast, which includes illusionist Penn Jillette. Did they show Mantegna, Keitel, Gwynne, et al, another script? TJ

Offence, The

(1972, GB, 113 min)
d Sidney Lumet. *p* Denis O'Dell. *sc* John Hopkins. *ph* Gerry Fisher. *ed* John Victor Smith. *ad* John Clark. *m* Harrison Birtwistle. *cast* Sean Connery, Trevor Howard, Vivien Merchant, Ian Bannen, Derek Newark, Peter Bowles, John Hallam.
● Adaptation of a stage play (*This Story of Yours*) by John Hopkins (of *Z Cars*). Discreet as it is, the opening-out process (effected by Hopkins himself) has sabotaged the strange, claustrophobic duel in which a suspected child-molester (Bannen) and the cop obsessively convinced of his guilt (Connery) find themselves subtly changing places during the course of interrogation. Embedded in a 'realistic' police scene, dialogue and situations now have a ring of arty melodrama. Fascinating, nevertheless, with outstanding performances from Connery and (especially) Bannen. TM

Offending Angels

(2000, GB, 93 min)
d/p Andrew Rajan. *sc* Andrew Rajan, Tim Moyler. *ph* Alvin Leong. *ed* Roger Burgess, Catherine Fletcher. *pd* Annie Gosney. *m* Martin Ward. *cast* Susannah Harker, Andrew Lincoln, Shaun Parkes, Andrew Rajan, Paula O'Grady, Marion Bailey, Michael Cochrane, Sophie Dix, Sean Gallagher.
● Guardian angels Zeke (Parkes) and Paris (Harker) are incarnated in human form and ordered to look out for drifters Baggy (Rajan) and Sam (Lincoln). All goes fine until Paris and Baggy fall for each other. A neat idea – who wouldn't marvel at a beautiful mystery someone sent to ensure future happiness? – but not enough to sustain a feature. Layabout Baggy is meant to be a charming babe magnet and thus an irritant to bachelor flatmate Sam. But when has anybody who deliberately pisses his pants ever been a serious contender? Meanwhile, Lincoln reprises his roles in TV's *Teachers* and *This Life* as an emotionally retarded kidult, too blind to realise the love of his life is already there in the shape of dour Alison (O'Grady). CF

Officer and a Gentleman, An

(1981, US, 124 min)
d Taylor Hackford. *p* Martin Elfand. *sc* Douglas Day Stewart. *ph* Donald Thorin. *ed* Paul Zinner. *pd* Philip M Jefferies. *m* Jack Nitzche. *cast* Richard Gere, Debra Winger, Louis Gossett Jr, David Keith, Robert Loggia, Lisa Blount, Lisa Eilbacher, David Caruso, Victor French.
● *Pace* all those swooning fans of gorgeous Gere, but Hackford's hymn to rampant individualism in Reagan's America is an exploitative no-no. While the immaculately garbed and coiffed hero goes through the paces of training under a sadistic black (natch) sergeant to be a military pilot (we all find it admirable to want to drop bombs and kill, don't we?), he discovers that self is the sole person worth bothering about, and that women are really only after men for their status and money. Macho, materialistic, and pro-militarist, it's an objectionable little number made all the more insidious by the way Hackford pulls the strings and turns it into a heart-chilling weepie. GA

Officers' Ward, The

see Chambre des officiers, La

Official Version, The (La Historia Oficial)

(1985, Arg, 115 min)
d Luis Puenzo. *p* Marcelo Piñeyro. *sc* Aida Bortnik, Luis Puenzo. *ph* Felix Monti. *ed* Juan Carlos Macias. *ad* Abel Facello. *m* Atilio Stampone. *cast* Héctor Alterio, Norma Aleandro, Chela Ruiz, Chunchuna Villafañe, Hugo Arana, Patricio Contreras, Guillermo Battaglia.
● Alicia (Aleandro) happily disseminates doctored Argentinian history to her pupils, and dutifully tolerates a husband who unashamedly boasts of his entrepreneurial expediency. But the suspicion begins to grow that her adopted daughter might be the child of one of 'The Disappeared', which prompts not only a reappraisal of her non-political stance, but also of her marriage. Surprisingly muted and not without lapses into sentimentality, the result nevertheless packs a massive emotional punch. JP

Off Limits (aka Saigon)

(1988, US, 102 min)
d Christopher Crowe. *p* Alan Barnette. *sc* Christopher Crowe, Jack Thibeau. *ph* David Gribble. *ed* Doug Ibold. *pd* J Dennis Washington. *m* James Newton Howard. *cast* Willem Dafoe, Gregory Hines, Fred Ward, Amanda Pays, Kay Tong Lim, Scott Glenn, David Alan Grier, Keith David, Raymond O'Connor.
● Not another Vietnam War film but a pacy, violent thriller set in the sleazy red light district of Saigon in 1968. Two US Army cops (Dafoe and Hines) think a serial prostitute killer may be one of their own top brass. A previous investigator and key witnesses have been frightened into silence or simply killed off. Backed up by their staff sergeant (Ward), they whittle the suspects down to five, but pressure from above squashes the investigation, forcing them to go it alone. Later, with the help of a streetwise nun (Pays), they locate a vital eye-witness who has disappeared into the VC tunnel complex on the outskirts of the city. Like these labyrinthine tunnels, the plot twists and turns, but Crowe never loses his sense of direction, sustaining the suspense and staging the action scenes with admirable vigour; the result, although the Saigon setting is simply a seedily exotic backdrop, is an auspicious first feature. NF

Of Freaks and Men (Pro Ourodov i Lioudiei)

(1998, Rus, 93 min, b/w & col)
d Alexei Balabanov. *p* Sergei Selyanov, Oleg Botogov. *sc* Alexei Balabanov. *ph* Sergei Astakhov. *ed* Marina Lipartia. *pd* Vera Zelinskaya. *cast* Sergei Makovetsky, Dinara Drukarova, Victor Sukhorukov, Alyesha Dî, Chingiz Tsydendabayev.
● St Petersburg in the first years of the century and an illicit operation specialising in spanking photos swiftly graduates to moving pictures of the same activities. Gradually, the families of a doctor and a railway engineer find their destinies intertwined with that of Johann, the sinister porn merchant, though the enigmatic plotting seems to matter less than the film's parade of eccentricities. There are Siamese twins who play the accordion and sing to huge music hall crowds, repeated shots of vintage locomotives and identical tartan suitcases carried by practically everyone in the city. Although deeply puzzling, Balabanov's film certainly creates its own unique world, and makes the valid point that audiences merely want to see the same thing all the time. In this case, bare bottoms. TJ

Off the Dole

(1935, GB, 81 min, b/w)
d Arthur Mertz. *p* John E Blakeley. *sc* John E Blakeley, Arthur Mertz. *ph* Sydney L Eaton. *ed* Denis Cantley. *ad* Frank P Atherton. *cast* George Formby, Beryl [Formby], Constance Shotter, Cyril McLaglen, Wally Patch, Tully Comber.
● There's more than a whiff of the music halls about this 'merry musical burlesque', as Formby, assorted comic pals, plus The Twelve London Babes and The Twilight Blondes run through their routines in front of a cameraman evidently in a state of rigor mortis. Formby's persona – aggressive, smart alec – is quite different from the one he developed later at Ealing, though his ditties ('With My Little Ukulele in My Hand') sound familiar. The title is catchpenny: after an opening number in a labour exchange, 'The Poor Old Working Man', the film degenerates into a nonsense about Formby running a detective agency. Mainly for students/devotees of the period. BBa

Off to the Revolution by 2CV (Alla Rivoluzione sulla Due Cavalli)

(2001, It, 95 min)
d Maurizio Sciarra. *p* Rosanna Sergni, Monica Venturini. *sc* Marco Ferrari, Enzo Monteleone, Maurizio Sciarra. *ph* Arnaldo Catinari. *ed* Claudio Cormio. *pd* Giada Calabria. *m* Lele Marchitelli. *cast* Adriano Giannini, Gwenaëlla Simon, Andoni Gracia, Francisco Rabal, Georges Moustaki, Oscar Ladoire.
● This celebration of car and comradeship is set during the peaceful 1974 Portuguese revolution. The heady days of politically idealistic youth are well evoked in a buddy movie of the road. Two friends in Paris decide to join the Lisbon uprising and en route pick up a now uneasily settled mutual former girlfriend. Adventures of the body and spirit ensue, but it's all attractively played and enjoyably watchable. GE

Of Great Events and Ordinary People (De Grands Evénements et des Gens Ordinaires)

(1978, Fr, 63 min)
d Raúl Ruiz. *p* Martine Durand. *sc* Raúl Ruiz. *ph* Jacques Bouquin, Dominique Forgue, Alain Salomon. *ed* Valeria Sarmiento.
● Ruiz has the gaze of an exile and a mind brimming with Cartesian wit. Detached, demanding, often scintillating, his films are conundrums without simple answers. But in *Of Great Events* (which starts out as a documentary on the '78 French presidential elections), Ruiz seems curiously uninterested in the documentary discourse he uses and confronts. Its meanderings are, none the less, a pleasing antidote to the moral fervour of the Griersonian documentary tradition. SH

Of Mice and Men

(1939, US, 106 min, b/w)
d/p Lewis Milestone. *sc* Eugene Solow. *ph* Norbert Brodine. *ed* Bert Jordan. *ad* Nicolai Remisoff. *m* Aaron Copland. *cast* Lon Chaney Jr, Burgess Meredith, Betty Field, Charles Bickford, Bob Steele, Roman Bohnen, Noah Beery Jr.
● Impressive adaptation of Steinbeck's novel, made at the same time as *The Grapes of Wrath* (though released earlier) and matching Ford's harsh lyricism in its evocation of the Depression,

the desperation of the migrant farmworkers, their pipedreams of a little place of their own some day. Terrific performances mask much of the novel's naive social philosophy: Chaney as Lenny, the half-witted gentle giant with a fondness for soft, furry things and a tendency to pet too hard when panicked; Field as the bored young farmer's wife who provokes tragedy by playing the sex kitten; Meredith as Lenny's friend and minder, who is forced to turn executioner rather than let society's notions of justice loose on his charge. TM

Of Mice and Men

(1992, US, 111 min)
d Gary Sinise. *p* Russ Smith, Gary Sinise. *sc* Horton Foote. *ph* Kenneth MacMillan. *ed* Robert L Sinise. *pd* David Gropman. *m* Mark Isham. *cast* John Malkovich, Gary Sinise, Ray Walston, Casey Siemaszko, Sherilyn Fenn, John Terry, Alexis Arquette, Joe Morton, Noble Willingham.

● Sinise's second crack at directing, with a Horton Foote adaptation of the John Steinbeck Depression era novel – about innocently lethal retard Lenny (Malkovich) and his increasingly despairing protector George (Sinise) – which seems doomed to remain a period piece. Big Lenny likes stroking soft things, and nags George to describe life on their fantasy farm while they labour as ranch-hands under the tyrannical Curly (Siemaszko). Lenny crunches Curly's fist to pulp in his paw, and over-responds to the come-ons from Curly's wife (Fenn). It's hard not to snigger at her arching about and complaining of the heat, and harder still to believe Malkovich's shamble and gape, a simian variant on Dustin Hoffman's Rain Man. Both are strictly Dogpatch caricatures, while Sinise seems plain vain. BC

O for Oblomov (O wie Oblomov)

(1982, Switz, 85 min)
d/p/sc Sebastian C Schroeder. *ph* Hans Liechti. *ed* Fee Liechti. *m* Benedikt Jeger. *cast* Erhard Koren, Olga Strub, Daniel Plancherel, Sebastian C Schroeder.

● Almost a documentary about a documentary, which cleverly avoids the tedium often inherent in film about film and fiction about fiction (the reference point is Goncharov's novel about a well-intentioned but slothful Russian nobleman). Two film crews (documentary and TV live show) arrive simultaneously to interview a likeable but pseud eccentric, Niklaus Nepro, whose chaotic disposition proves infectious: the crews each shoot each other, the live show disintegrates into utter muddle. Witty and intelligent, the film preaches something; but peeling away the fragile layers of irony, sparing no one, it's hard to see quite what. SFr

Oggi a me...domani a te!

see Today It's Me...Tomorrow You!

Ohayo (Good Morning)

(1959, Jap, 94 min)
d Yasujiro Ozu. *p* Shizuo Yamanouchi. *sc* Yasujiro Ozu, Kogo Noda. *ph* Yuharu Atsuta. *ed* Yoshiyasu Hamamura. *ad* Tatsuo Hamada. *m* Toshiro Mayuzumi. *cast* Chishu Ryu, Kuniko Miyake, Yoshiko Kuga, Koji Shidara, Masahiko Shimazu, Keiji Sada, Haruo Tanaka, Haruko Sugimura.

● An enchanting update of Ozu's own silent *I Was Born, But...*, dedicated to the proposition that small talk, however tedious and repetitious, is a necessary lubricant for the wheels of social intercourse. The setting is a residential suburb of Tokyo, in the process of transition to Western consumerism, where two small boys send the entire world to Coventry because their parents, fearing TV will breed idiocy (killing the conversation that the boys cruelly dismiss as small talk), refuse to have a set in the house. Radiating out from the resulting tensions and resentments in the community comes an extraordinary cross-section of tragi-comic incident. An old man gets drunk because he cannot get a job; a middle-aged man is brought face to face with his approaching retirement; a young couple are inspired to declare their love entirely in terms of the weather; an unwanted grandmother broods about filial ingratitude; a kindly woman is forced to move by neighbourly doubts as to her morals. A brimming sense of life, in other words, gradually transforms the small talk into a richly devious portrait of humanity being human. TM

Oh! Calcutta!

(1972, US, 100 min)
d Jacques Levy. *p* Guillaume Martin Aucion. *sc* Jules Feiffer, John Lennon, Leonard Melfi, Robert Benton, Sherman Yellen, Dan Greenburg, Jacques Levy, Sam Shepard. *ph* Jerry Sarcone, Frank Biondo, Arnold Giordano. *ed* Frank Herold. *ad* Eugene Gurlitz. *m/lyrics* Robert Dennis, Peter Schickele, Stanley Walden. *cast* Raina Barrett, Mark Dempsey, Samantha Harper, Patricia Hawkins, Bill Macy, Mitchell McGuire, Gary Rethmeier, Margo Sappington, Nancy Tribush, George Welbes.

● An unqualified disaster, repudiated by Kenneth Tynan as a travesty of his censor-challenging stage revue. Sketches contributed by Jules Feiffer, John Lennon, Robert Benton and Sam Shepard, among others, are staged by Levy on a stage, complete with canned audience reactions; and one watches in bemusement and mounting boredom as theatrical timing and delivery kill what little wit there is. Even worse are the 'opened out' passages where the cast coyly assemble in the nude by a lake, there to prance amid the pastoral scene. TM

O. Henry's Full House (aka Full House)

(1952, US, 117 min, b/w)
d Henry Koster, Henry Hathaway, Jean Negulesco, Howard Hawks, Henry King. p André Hakim. *sc* (1 'The Cop and the Anthem') Lamar Trotti, (2 'The Clarion Call') Richard L Breen, (3 'The Last Leaf') Ivan Goff, Ben Roberts, (4 The Ransom of Red Chief') Nunnally Johnson, Howard Hawks, (5 'The Gift of the Magi') Walter Bullock. *ph* (1) Lloyd Ahern, (2) Lucien Ballard, (3, 5) Joseph MacDonald, (4) Milton Krasner. *ed* (1, 2, 3) Nick De Maggio, (4) William B Murphy, (5) Barbara McLean. *ad* Lyle Wheeler, Chester Gore, Joseph C Wright, Richard Irvine, Addison Hehr. *m* Alfred Newman. *cast* (1) Charles Laughton, David Wayne, Marilyn Monroe, (2) Richard Widmark, Dale Robertson, Joyce MacKenzie, (3) Anne Baxter, Jean Peters, Gregory Ratoff, (4) Fred Allen, Oscar Levant, Lee Aaker, Kathleen Freeman, (5) Jeanne Crain, Farley Granger.

● John Steinbeck, looking and sounding disconcertingly like Ward Bond, hosts five tales by O Henry, of which only Hathaway's segment ('The Clarion Call') is devoid of interest. Negulesco and King both contribute sentimental valentines ('The Last Leaf' and 'The Gift of the Magi') in which love transcends the miseries of illness and poverty respectively. Hawks' 'The Ransom of Red Chief' is about two child-kidnappers who end up paying their victim's dad to take the little horror off their hands. It's noteworthy for the casting of the two most mournful comics of the day as a double act; and for the fact that the adventures of such unprofessional no-hopers interested someone like Hawks in the first place. At the front of the movie, Laughton characteristically generates his own atmosphere of benign fantasy, playing a bum trying to get himself jailed for the winter. This episode ('The Cop and the Anthem') also includes an encounter between two sacred monsters – Laughton's hobo and Monroe's hooker meeting on a windy street corner for a brief demonstration of the virtues of kindliness and respect. BBa

Oh! For a Man

see Will Success Spoil Rock Hunter?

Oh, God!

(1977, US, 104 min)
d Carl Reiner. *p* Jerry Weintraub. *sc* Larry Gelbart. *ph* Victor J Kemper. *ed* Bud Molin. *ad* Jack Senter. *m* Jack Elliott. *cast* George Burns, John Denver, Teri Garr, Donald Pleasence, Ralph Bellamy, William Daniels, Barnard Hughes, Paul Sorvino, Barry Sullivan, Dinah Shore.

● The title's no idle blasphemy, for God really does feature in Reiner's highly bizarre, mostly delightful comedy – and in the avuncular shape of George Burns, too, dressed for the golf course. He appears before supermarket manager Denver (more weird casting), determined to tell mankind that he's still around and watching. The result plays like an over-extended version of the Reiner/Mel Brooks 2000-Year-Old Man sketches, where world history is seen through the eyes of a grouchy Jewish old-timer. So here we have God's views on most things from TV to avocados, all enunciated in Burns' inimitably crisp'n'dry manner. Fun ultimately falters with some routine satire, but when the Devil's having such a time at the box-office, this comes as a welcome comic riposte from the other side. Two indifferent sequels followed: *Oh, God! Book II* (1980) and *Oh, God! You Devil* (1984). GB

Oh, Men! Oh, Women!

(1957, US, 90 min)
d/p/sc Nunnally Johnson. *ph* Charles G Clarke. *ed* Marjorie Fowler. *ad* Lyle Wheeler, Maurice Ransford. *m* Cyril J Mockridge. *cast* Ginger Rogers, David Niven, Dan Dailey, Barbara Rush, Tony Randall, Natalie Schafer.

● Oh, crikey! Debonair shrink Niven finds his personal and professional life in a spin when he learns from patient Rogers that his fiancée Rush is carrying on with her movie-star husband Dailey. His feelings of shock and dismay are further compounded when no-hoper Randall announces from the couch that he too is having a much-anticipated fling – also with Rush, of course. Writer/director Johnson's jolly farce isn't what you'd call challenging, but thanks to willing performers it's very light on its feet. Niven's as elegant as ever, Randall's suitably klutzy in his first screen bow. Shot in CinemaScope, because there's a whole lot of reclining going on.

Oh, Mr Porter!

(1937, GB, 84 min, b/w)
d Marcel Varnel. *p* Edward Black. *sc* John Orton, Val Guest, Marriot Edgar. *ph* Arthur Crabtree. *ed* RE Dearing, Alfred Roome. *ad* Alex Vetchinsky. *m* Jack Beaver. *cast* Will Hay, Moore Marriott, Graham Moffatt, Sebastian Smith, Agnes Laughlan, Percy Walsh, Dave O'Toole, Dennis Wyndham.

● You either love or loathe Will Hay, though this is by far his finest moment and might well convert unbelievers. As the garrulous, officious and totally incompetent station master of the isolated and sleepy Irish village of Buggleskelly, he tries desperately to modernise facilities and meanwhile gets involved with gun-runners. Some of the humour is rather dated now, but the atmospheric creation of a quaintly antiquated rural Britain – that never in reality existed – holds plenty of charm. (From an original story by Frank Launder.) GA

O.H.M.S. (aka You're in the Army Now)

(1937, GB, 87 min, b/w)
d Raoul Walsh. *p* Geoffrey Barkas. *sc* Lesser Samuels, Ralph Bettinson. *ph* Roy Kellino. *ed* Charles Saunders. *ad* Edward Carrick. *m* Jack Beaver. *cast* Wallace Ford, John Mills, Anna Lee, Grace Bradley, Frank Cellier, Peter Croft, Frederick Leister, Lawrence Anderson, Athol Fleming.

● A brisk Warners-style gangster thriller rapidly turns into a plodding British military drama: Wallace Ford is the American hoodlum who flees the States after being tagged for a murder he didn't commit in a Chinese gambling den. Arriving in Britain, he pretends he's Canadian and enrols in the army. Fresh-faced recruit John Mills becomes his best friend, and they both vie for the attention of the Sgt-Major's daughter. Some neat jokes about the differences between Yank and Limey culture don't atone for all the shots of British military parades and postcard village scenes. Nor does the *Boy's Own* ending carry anything like the charge of one of director Walsh's Hollywood thrillers. GM

Oh Rosalinda!!

(1955, GB, 101 min)
d/p/sc Michael Powell, Emeric Pressburger. *ph* Christopher Challis. *ed* Reginald Mills. *pd* Hein Heckroth. *m* Johann Strauss Jr. *lyrics* (new) Dennis Arundell. *cast* Anton Walbrook, Michael Redgrave, Anthony Quayle, Ludmilla Tcherina, Dennis Price, Mel Ferrer, Anneliese Rothenberger, Richard Marner, Oskar Sima.

● 'They should have been forcibly suppressed,' spluttered one early review of Powell and Pressburger's update of the Strauss operetta *Die Fledermaus*, set in four-power occupied Vienna; even the title's two exclamation marks betrayed an unseemly excess. The blatant artifice, sugar-candy sets, and preposterous plot, once deplored by the critical establishment, are now cherished by connoisseurs: what better way to pass a disgracefully self-indulgent Sunday afternoon? SJo

Oh! What a Lovely War

(1969, GB, 144 min)
d Richard Attenborough. *p* Brian Duffy, Richard Attenborough. *sc* [Len Deighton]. *ph* Gerry Turpin. *ed* Kevin Connor. *pd* Don Ashton. *m* Alfred Ralston. *cast* Joe Melia, Colin Farrell, Paul Shelley, Angela Thorne, Mary Wimbush, Corin Redgrave, Maggie Smith, Michael Redgrave, Laurence Olivier, John Mills, Vanessa Redgrave, Ralph Richardson, John Gielgud, Dirk Bogarde, Kenneth More.

● Joan Littlewood's Theatre Workshop play on the excesses and follies of war got misplaced in transition, and producer Len Deighton ended up removing his name from the credits. It remains an often too-clever, sometimes moving piece which never effectively reconciles its lampooning of the WWI General Staff (Haig playing leapfrog; conducting battles from a helter-skelter; losses reflected on cricket scoreboards) with its sincerity towards the salt-of-the-earth working class who were the ones who copped it. Lots of contemporary songs, scores of well-known faces. CPe

Oh, You Beautiful Doll

(1949, US, 94 min)
d John M Stahl. *p* George Jessel. *sc* Albert Lewis, Arthur Lewis. *ph* Harry Jackson. *ed* Louis Loeffler. *ad* Lyle Wheeler, Maurice Ransford. *songs* Fred Fisher. *cast* June Haver, Mark Stevens, SZ Sakall, Charlotte Greenwood, Jay C Flippen, Gale Robbins, Andrew Tombes, Eduard Franz.

● Purporting to be a biopic of Fred Fisher, composer of such '20s song hits as 'Come Josephine in My Flying Machine' and 'Who Paid the Rent for Mrs Rip Van Winkle', this is a stock Fox musical featuring Cuddles Sakall as a would-be classical composer distressed to have his operatic efforts turned into popular songs. Stahl's last film, it's something of a come-down from the glories of *Leave Her to Heaven*, made four years earlier; full of charm and attractive touches, all the same. TM

Okaeri

(1995, Jap, 99 min)
d Makoto Shinozaki. *p* Tsutsui Takefumi. *sc* Makoto Shinozaki, Ryo Yamamura. *ph* Osamu Furuya. *ed* Tsutsui Takefumi. *cast* Susumu Terajima, Miho Uemura, Shoichi Komatsu.

● Shinozaki's debut feature (the deliberately Ozu-esque title is the set expression for welcoming someone home) argues speciously that it takes something as grave as a mental crack-up to bring warmth and sincerity into a 'typical' Japanese marriage. Kitazawa is a primary school teacher, an average neglectful husband; his childless wife Yuriko has a part-time job but spends most of her days pining for her lost career as a concert pianist...until she slips into paranoid delusions and starts to behave with alarming oddity. The woman's unexplained lack of relatives or friends to turn to tips you the wink that this version of Japanese home life is phoney from the word go, and the endless elaboration of her schizophrenia is a repellently cruel way of conveying her need for tenderness and love. Pretentious and ugly. TR

O-Kay for Sound

(1937, GB, 87 min, b/w)
d Marcel Varnel. *p* Edward Black. *sc* Marriott Edgar, Val Guest. *ph* Jack Cox. *ed* RE Dearing. *ad* Alex Vetchinsky. *songs* RP Weston, Bert Lee, Noel Gay, Michael Carr, Jimmy Kennedy. *cast* Bud Flanagan, Chesney Allen, Jimmy Nervo, Teddy Knox, Charlie Naughton, Jimmy Gold, Graham Moffatt, Fred Duprez, Enid Stamp-Taylor.

● The Crazy Gang (street buskers) are signed up as extras for a film, but when they arrive on set in natty pinstripes and bowlers they're mistaken for the financier's emissaries and given control of the production. Chaos ensues plus some of the boys' favourite stage routines. Made in the same year as *Oh, Mr Porter!*, director Marcel Varnel's best-remembered British picture. TJ

Oklahoma!

(1955, US, 145 min)
d Fred Zinnemann. *p* Arthur Hornblow Jr. *sc* Sonya Levien, William Ludwig. *ph* Robert Surtees. *ed* George Boemler. *pd* Oliver Smith. *m* Richard Rodgers. *lyrics* Oscar Hammerstein II. *cast* Gordon MacRae, Shirley Jones, Charlotte Greenwood, Rod Steiger, Gloria Grahame, Eddie Albert, James Whitmore, Gene Nelson, Barbara Lawrence, Jay C Flippen, Roy Barcroft.

● Rodgers and Hammerstein's musical about the growth of love in the farmlands where the corn stands as high as an elephant's eye, transferred to the screen with stolid respect rather than verve. The story's threadbare (and rather overbalanced by Steiger's Method intensity as the sinister Jud), the visual aspects are uninspired; but some of the performances are delightful (notably Gloria Grahame singing 'I Cain't Say No'), and the choreography by Agnes DeMille is suitably ebullient. GA

Oklahoma Crude

(1973, US, 111 min)
d/p Stanley Kramer. *sc* Marc Norman. *ph* Robert Surtees. *ed* Folmar Blangsted. *pd* Alfred Sweeney. *m* Henry Mancini. *cast* George C Scott, Faye Dunaway, John Mills, Jack Palance, William Lucking, Harvey Jason, Cliff Osmond, Rafael Campos.

● Crude oil, that is, with Faye Dunaway back in 1913 – hair dyed black and talking so like Jane Fonda that Kramer could be excused for thinking he had perhaps signed her up – reluctantly allowing Pa John Mills and hobo George C Scott to defend her one oil well against the big and nasty Pan Okie oil company, led by Jack Palance. Dunaway, a rabid man hater, nevertheless determined for some reason to succeed in a man's world, fights them all off with a virginal intensity before implausibly succumbing to Scott's embraces in the face of box-office demands. In spite of a couple of attempts (thanks mainly to the script) to venture outside routine comedy-adventure, things remain hampered by the curious casting, blatant overacting, and Big Country theme music. However if the sight grabs you of Scott delivering the 'message' of the film by literally pissing on Palance, with the news that it's what businessmen do to each other all the time, then this might be your movie. CPe

Oklahoma Woman, The

(1956, US, 73 min, b/w)
d/p Roger Corman. *sc* Lou Rusoff. *ph* Frederick E West. *ed* Ronald Sinclair. *m* Ronald Stein. *cast* Richard Denning, Peggie Castle, Cathy Downs, Mike Connors, Martin Kingsley, Tudor Owen, Dick Miller, Bruno Ve Sota.

● Corman made four lively B-Westerns at the start of his career as a producer/director, of which this is probably the best. Peggie Castle, 'queen of the outlaws', stands between reforming ex-con Denning and his dubious past, so Cathy Downs grabs the reins and sets her man back on the straight and narrow. TJ

Okoge

(1992, Jap, 120 min)
d Takehiro Nakajima. *p* Yoshinori Takazawa, Masashi Moromizato. *sc* Takehiro Nakajima. *ph* Yoshimasa Hakata. *cast* Misa Shimizu, Takehiro Murata, Takeo Nakahara, Atsushi Fukazawa.

● The best of a sudden surge of gay movies from Japan, this second feature by veteran scriptwriter Nakajima is all about compromise and accommodation. Two gay men, with nowhere to go to make love, avail themselves of a bedroom offered by an obliging young woman. But one of them is married with a family, and his vengeful wife tears his secret life to shreds, along with his designer shirts. With its emotional cataclysms, its graphic sex scenes, and its chorus of drag queens, *Okoge* is one of the year's prime guilty pleasures. TR

Oksutan (3pm Paradise/Bath House)

(1997, SKor, 90 min)
d Kwak Kyung-Taek.

● A somewhat tiresome and predictable allegorical 'satire', with representatives of a microcosmic contemporary Korea – a monk, a hood, whores, a politician's wife, a voyeur, a soldier – hanging out at a bath house with lame comic consequences. The humour is generally flabby, the humanism soggy, and the only notable element is the (within limits) frank depiction of human anatomy. GA

Oktyabr (October/Ten Days That Shook the World)

(1927, USSR, 9,317 ft, b/w)
d Sergei Eisenstein, Grigori Alexandrov. *sc* Sergei Eisenstein. *ph* Eduard Tissé. *ed* Sergei Eisenstein. *ad* Vladimir Kovrigin. *cast* Vasili Nikandrov, Nikolai Popov, Boris Livanov, Eduard Tissé, Nikolai Podvoisky.

● Commissioned to celebrate the tenth anniversary of the 1917 revolution, Eisenstein came up not with a rousing spectacle that might please the proletariat, but with an experimental film aimed at exemplifying his theory of 'intellectual montage'. The result, for all its spectacular set pieces (notably the raising of the Petrograd bridges and the storming of the Winter Palace), is sometimes hard to follow, since human actions and motivations tend to be neglected in favour of the overall, rather abstract design of the film, and the narrative is regularly interrupted by montage shots of metaphorical and symbolic value. As a result, the film remains an interesting oddity rather than entertaining or illuminating. Indeed, watching it today can seem hard work. GA

Old Acquaintance

(1943, US, 110 min, b/w)
d Vincent Sherman. *p* Henry Blanke. *sc* John Van Druten, Lenore Coffee. *ph* Sol Polito. *ed* Terry Morse. *ad* John Hughes. *m* Franz Waxman. *cast* Bette Davis, Miriam Hopkins, John Loder, Gig Young, Dolores Moran, Roscoe Karns, Phillip Reed.

● Based on a play by John Van Druten, remade by Cukor in 1981 as *Rich and Famous*, this has Davis (sweet) and Hopkins (sour) as two novelists maintaining a professional and personal love-hate rivalry over twenty years. Arrant nonsense, with Davis (though Hopkins is the despicable one who writes for money) living in fabulously opulent circumstances and required to carry her noble self-sacrifice on into the next generation. Sherman and the stars somehow contrive to make it riveting. TM

Old and New

see General Line, The

Old Boyfriends

(1978, US, 103 min)
d Joan Tewkesbury. *p* Edward R Pressman, Michele Rappaport. *sc* Paul Schrader, Leonard Schrader. *ph* William A Fraker. *ed* William H Reynolds. *ad* Peter Jamison. *m* David Shire. *cast* Talia Shire, Richard Jordan, John Belushi, Keith Carradine, John Houseman, Buck Henry, Bethel Leslie, Joan Hotchkis, Gerrit Graham.

● First feature for Joan Tewkesbury, an Altman associate who scripted *Thieves Like Us* and *Nashville*. Hesitating between its Old Hollywood ambitions and soap opera climax, it definitively blows a promising road movie story – of fucked-up West Coast psychologist Dianne Cruise (Shire) visiting three old boyfriends on a compulsive trip down memory lane. The failure owes something to slack direction, and probably more to the misogyny of Paul and Leonard Schrader's script, which contrives a distinctly reactionary mix of sentiment, morality, and melodrama. CA

Old Crook, The

see Vieille Canaille

Old Curiosity Shop, The

(1934, GB, 90 min, b/w)
d Thomas Bentley. *p* Walter C Mycroft. *sc* Margaret Kennedy, Ralph Neale. *ph* Claude Friese-Greene. *ed* Leslie Norman. *ad* Cedric Dawe. *m* Eric Coates. *cast* Ben Webster, Elaine Benson, Hay Petrie, Beatrix Thompson, Gibb McLaughlin, Reginald Purdell, Lily Long, Polly Ward.

● Thomas Bentley built his entire career out of Dickens: prior to 1921, he had filmed *Oliver Twist*, *David Copperfield*, *Hard Times*, *The Pickwick Papers*, and even managed a remake of his 1914 version of *The Old Curiosity Shop*. His third version of the novel, photographed by Claude Friese-

Greene (the son of the bankrupted camera inventor) is a lovingly butchered rendition of the story of the moneylender Quilp (Petrie) and the tragic Little Nell (Benson). It's cloyingly sentimental, and in its style still shows the primitive glow of early British movie-making of the 1910s. More of an artifact than an adaptation. ATu

Old Dark House, The

(1932, US, 71min, b/w)
d James Whale. *p* Carl Laemmle Jr. *sc* Benn W Levy, RC Sherriff. *ph* Arthur Edeson. *ed* Maurice Pivar, Clarence Kolster. *ad* Charles D Hall. *m* Heinz Roemheld. *cast* Boris Karloff, Melvyn Douglas, Charles Laughton, Gloria Stuart, Ernest Thesiger, Raymond Massey, Lilian Bond, Eva Moore.

● Alongside *The Bride of Frankenstein*, Whale's greatest film, a masterly mixture of macabre humour and effectively gripping suspense. A very simple story – a group of travellers stranded by a storm take shelter in the sinister, unwelcome Femm household, a gloomy mansion peopled by maniacs and murderers – allows Whale to concentrate on quirky characters (Laughton's brash, boorish Yorkshire mill-owner, blessed with a near-incomprehensible accent, is particularly delightful) and thick Gothic atmosphere to stunning effect. But what is perhaps most remarkable is the way Whale manages to parody the conventions of the dark house horror genre as he creates them, in which respect the film remains entirely modern. (Frm JB Priestley's novel *Benighted*.) GA

Old Dracula

see Vampira

Old Enough

(1983, US, 92 min)
d Marisa Silver. *p* Dina Silver. *sc* Marisa Silver. *ph* Michael Ballhaus. *ed* Mark Burns. *pd* Jeffrey Townsend. *m* Julian Marshall. *cast* Sarah Boyd, Rainbow Harvest, Neill Barry, Alyssa Milano, Danny Aiello, Susan Kingsley, Roxanne Hart, Fran Brill, Gerry Bamman.

● An exceptional delight, this first feature from Joan Micklin Silver's daughter brings together two girls during a hot New York summer: Lonnie (Boyd), twelve, well-behaved, a little innocent, from a wealthy, sophisticated family; and Karen (Harvest), fourteen, seemingly more mature, sassy in the knowledge of the streets handed down from working class parents and elder brother. Little happens: but with its precise, perceptive observation and performances, and wry, gently ironic humour, the whole thing rings remarkably true. GA

Old-Fashioned Way, The

(1934, US, 74 min, b/w)
d William Beaudine. *p* William LeBaron. *sc* Garnett Weston, Jack Cunningham. *ph* Benjamin Reynolds. *ad* John Goodman. *m* Harry Revel. *cast* WC Fields, Judith Allen, Joe Morrison, Jan Duggan, Nora Cecil, Baby LeRoy, Jack Mulhall, Joe Mills.

● Old-fashioned indeed: this wonderful Fields vehicle, set at the end of the last century, includes the song 'A Little Bit of Heaven Known as Mother' and a performance of the renowned melodrama *The Drunkard*. For all his pose of misanthropy, Fields has a heart as wide as the Grand Canyon, and he poured into this one film all his love for the gaslight era and the vaudeville life. As the Great McGonigle, leader of a travelling theatre troupe, he fights heroically against a sea of troubles, including an interfering sheriff and a doting old ham called Cleopatra Pepperday. Beaudine's direction is on the slow side, but this at least allows the laughs to be fully savoured. GB

Old Flames

(1989, GB, 86 min)
d Christopher Morahan. *p* Kenith Trodd. *sc* Simon Gray. *ph* David Feig. *cast* Simon Callow, Stephen Fry, Miriam Margolyes, Clive Francis.

● Simon Gray's dark spoof in which sundry fucked-up ex-public school yuppies 'disappear', features those noble stalwarts of the system, Fry and Callow, battling to stop their middle age being wrecked by an old 'Amplesider' with an obscure grudge. Full of the usual social-sexual frumpery that lends itself so admirably to that unremarkable genre of London-based thrillers in which smarmy city types get their comeuppance. Morahan's film, made for the BBC, will no doubt carve some morbid niche for itself on late night television. The moral? Don't lock up a promising violinist in the school music rooms if he's going to turn up 25 years later as an asthmatic, toupee-troubled neurotic by the name of Mr Quass. JCh

Old Gringo

(1989, US, 120 min)
d Luis Puenzo. *p* Lois Bonfiglio. *sc* Aída Bortnik, Luis Puenzo. *ph* Felix Monti. *ed* Juan Carlos Macias, William Anderson, Glenn Farr. *pd* Stuart Wurtzel, Bruno Rubeo. *m* Lee Holdridge. *cast* Jane Fonda, Gregory Peck, Jimmy Smits, Patricio Contreras, Jenny Gago, Gabriela Roel, Sergio Calderon, Pedro Armendariz Jr.

● Novelist Carlos Fuentes' speculation about what actually befell writer Ambrose Bierce when he joined Pancho Villa's revolution down Mexico way in 1913 makes a fascinating story, rich in character, relationships and cultural clashes. The film, though it doesn't look particularly good and often sounds rather literary, certainly bulges with content, and the principals, Bierce (Peck), middle-aged spinster Harriet Winslow (Fonda) and revolutionary general Arroyo (Smits) grab the dramatic opportunities with both hands. Bierce's predicament, cynical, self-disgusted and seeking a meaningful death, echoes that of the hero in *The Petrified Forest*. In the autumn of his years, he finds a surrogate family, a daughter, and a satisfying quietus. The Fonda part – besides carrying the voice-over – is something of a stereotype, initially brittle and later melted by love. The film can't substantiate its claim to play out the personal drama in terms of this turbulent period of history, but it's a worthy project, and will probably send people back to the book and – even better – to Bierce. BC

Old Lady Who Walked in the Sea, The (La Vieille qui Marchait dans la Mer)

(1992, Fr, 94 min)
d Laurent Heynemann. *p* Gérard Jourd'hui. *sc* Dominique Roulet. *ph* Robert Alazraki. *ed* Jacques Comets. *pd* Valérie Grall. *m* Philippe Sarde. *cast* Jeanne Moreau, Michel Serrault, Luc Thuillier, Géraldine Danon, Jean Bouchaud, Marie-Dominique Aumont, Hester Wilcox.

● Moreau is growing old disgracefully – and clearly enjoying every minute of it. That famously haughty countenance is somewhat weather-beaten now, but the imperious demeanour is still very much intact. As inveterate con-artist and incorrigible jewel thief Lady M, Moreau combines instinctive class with learned disdain for social convention, elegant diction with a singularly vituperative tongue, rampant egoism with painful infirmity. She enjoys challenging the conceits of the world, she says. Heynemann's mainstream comedy has surprisingly dark undercurrents – it's a caper movie which dares to ebb from time to time. Given her head, Moreau wrings every drop of pathos, pride and passion from the proceedings. Serrault just about holds up his end as her antiquated accomplice Pompilius, but Thuillier is out of his depth as the bronzed toyboy she adopts as her *dauphin*. Fleetingly, Moreau makes you think of an earlier ménage-à-trois, when she consorted with Jules and Jim so happily. But things are more complicated in old age and neither man is really a match for her. TCh

Old Man and the Sea, The

(1958, US, 86 min)
d John Sturges. *p* Leland Hayward. *sc* Peter Viertel. *ph* James Wong Howe, Floyd Crosby, Tom Tutwiler, (underwater) Lamar Boren. *ed* Arthur P Schmidt. *ad* Arthur Loel, Edward Carrere. *m* Dimitri Tiomkin. *cast* Spencer Tracy, Felipe Pazos, Harry Bellaver.

● A painfully sincere, meticulously faithful, and pitifully plodding adaptation of Hemingway's novel about the symbolic struggle between an old Mexican fisherman and a giant marlin. At its most embarrassing in the endless monologues where Tracy has to mouth Hemingway's notion of a poetic patois ('You're a fine fish, Fish, you fight a brave good fight'). The pity of it is that some fine camerawork (from a team that included James Wong Howe and Floyd Crosby) is sabotaged by clumsy back-projection and hideous colour-matching. Hemingway himself can be briefly glimpsed in a bar scene towards the end. TM

Old Well (Lao Jing)

(1987, China, 130 min)
d Wu Tianming. *sc* Yi Zheng. *ph* Cheng Wancai, Zhang Yimou. *ed* Chen Dali. *pd* Yang Gong. *m* Xu Youfu. *cast* Zhang Yimou, Liang Yujin, Xie Yan, Lu Liping

● This chronicles decades of ill-fated attempts to dig for water in an arid village in the Taihang mountains, and like some Chinese answer to *Padre Padrone*, tells the story of the village's first college graduate and his struggle to bring a measure of rationality to a bizarre and backward community. The result is not the standard tract on Third World problems, but a quite remarkable warts-and-all portrait of the strengths and weaknesses of the Chinese people, shot through with memorable characters and moments of heart-stopping intensity. At its core is a stunning performance from first-time actor Zhang Yimou, the brilliant young cinematographer of *Yellow Earth*. TR

Oleanna

(1994, US/GB, 89 min)
d David Mamet. *p* Patricia Wolff, Sarah Green. *sc* David Mamet. *ph* Andrzej Sekula. *ed* Barbara Tulliver. *m* Rebecca Pidgeon. *cast* William H Macy, Debra Eisenstadt.

● Mamet's film of his controversial play sensibly resists the temptation to 'open out' the material for the screen; it stays a two-hander and the focus remains on the switchback of argument and counter-argument. Macy's the slightly pompous college professor accused by angry student Eisenstadt of sexual misconduct, yet the issue is directed less toward the actual physical detail of the incident, rounding more on the whole male/female nexus of elitism, authority and power that's almost a given in our everyday experiences. Are the conventions of social interaction harmless, or are they to be picked apart by the revisionist ethics of political correctness? Mamet shows both sides of the coin and allows the audience to continue to argue it out among themselves – which they did, frequently, in theatre foyers. Expect this straightforward, compelling adaptation to provoke just the same level of domestic debate. As ever, the writing is rich, flexible, masterly. TJ

Oliver!

(1968, GB, 146 min)
d Carol Reed. *p* John Woolf. *sc* Vernon Harris. *ph* Oswald Morris. *ed* Ralph Kemplen. *pd* John Box. *m* Lionel Bart. *cast* Ron Moody, Shani Wallis, Oliver Reed, Harry Secombe, Hugh Griffith, Jack Wild, Clive Moss, Mark Lester, Peggy Mount, Leonard Rossiter, Kenneth Cranham, Megs Jenkins.

● From *The Third Man* to *Oliver!* is a pretty vertiginous collapse, even for twenty years in the British film industry. Reed is craftsman enough to make an efficient family entertainment out of Lionel Bart's musical, but not artist enough to put back any of Dickens' teeth which Bart had so assiduously drawn. SG

Oliver & Company

(1988, US, 74 min)
d George Scribner. *sc* Jim Cox, Timothy J Disney, James Mangold. *ph* (anim) Ed Austin, John Aardal, John Cunningham, Brandy Hill, Dan Larsen, Jim Pickel, Dean Teves, Errol Aubry, Roncie Hantke, Dave Link, Lindsay Rogers, Chuck Warren. *ed* Jim Melton, Mark Hester. *ad* Dan Hansen. *m* JAC Redford. *cast* voices: Joey Lawrence, Billy Joel, Cheech Marin, Richard Mulligan, Roscoe Lee Browne, Sheryl Lee Ralph, Dom DeLuise, Taurean Blacque, Robert Loggia, Bette Midler.

● This animation feature from Disney is a bestial rehash of *Oliver Twist*, wherein cute kitten Ollie, abandoned in New York, falls into 'baaaad' (i.e. good) canine company. Swindled out of a meal by streetwise hound Dodger, our hero asserts his virility by debunking the rogue mutt in front of his comrades. Accepted as 'one of the boys', Ollie is sent out with his new chums as they scavenge for pickings with which their amiable master Fagin can pay off a debt to fiendish Mr Sykes. Much cornball adventure ensues, punctuated by healthy helpings of singing, dancing and general merriment. Billy Joel provides the voice of Dodger, and despite having made some unpleasant records, turns in a few tolerable foot-tapping numbers. Midler's larynx is its usual gargantuan self, handling the steamy vocal chores for pampered pooch Georgette, but top marks go to Cheech Marin as Tito, the diminutive chihuahua with a man-sized ego who wins Georgette's heart by challenging everything that moves to a fight. MK

Oliver's Story

(1978, US, 90 min)
d John Korty. *p* David V Picker. *sc* Erich Segal, John Korty. *ph* Arthur J Ornitz. *ed* Stuart H Pappé. *ad* Robert Gundlach. *m* Lee Holdridge. *cast* Ryan O'Neal, Candice Bergen, Nicola Pagett, Edward Binns, Benson Fong, Charles Haid, Kenneth McMillan, Ray Milland, Josef Sommer, Sully Boyar, Swoosie Kurtz.

●It's been 18 months since Jenny's death (nearer 8 years for the paying public). A decent enough period for mourning, but now Oliver must 'get out and meet people'. Equally manipulative in its intentions, the sequel to *Love Story* is less *Oliver's Story* than a neo-conservative tribute to 'life involvement'. 'Tangible incentive' murmurs his therapist when O'Neal's permanent angst at last fetches up against Candice Bergen (beautiful… liberated…rich), and his musings turn once more to love and exploitation. As far as it goes, all perfectly competently handled, aside from the occasional masochistic hilarity ('Is that how you know it's good? When it hurts?'). What really hurts is that the prodigal's final return to his father's wealth and business is seen as more life-enhancing than his community law practice. CPea

Oliver Twist

(1948, GB, 116 min, b/w)
d David Lean. *p* Ronald Neame. *sc* David Lean, Stanley Haynes. *ph* Guy Green. *ed* Jack Harris. *ad* John Bryan. *m* Arnold Bax. *cast* John Howard Davies, Alec Guinness, Robert Newton, Kay Walsh, Francis L Sullivan, Henry Stephenson, Mary Clare, Anthony Newley, Kathleen Harrison, Diana Dors.

●David Lean's second Dickens adaptation, perhaps marginally less beguiling than *Great Expectations*, but still a moving and enjoyable account of Dickens' masterpiece, which gets off to a memorable start with Oliver's pregnant mother battling through the storm to reach the safety of the workhouse. The film tellingly recreates the horrors of Victorian slum life (the attractive if artificial sets atmospherically lit and shot by Guy Green), and is particularly noteworthy for Guinness' striking Fagin.

Oliver Twist

(1982, GB, 102 min)
d Clive Donner. *p* Ted Childs, Norton Romsey. *sc* James Goldman. *ph* Norman Langley. *ed* Peter Tanner. *pd* Tony Curtis. *m* Nick Bicât. *cast* George C Scott, Tim Curry, Michael Hordern, Timothy West, Eileen Atkins, Cherie Lunghi, Oliver Cotton, Richard Charles, Martin Tempest.

●Writer James Goldman has in the past come up with imaginative slants on familiar figures (Sherlock Holmes, Robin Hood) but nothing very original seems to have occurred to him as regards Fagin, Bill Sikes and the rest. If the picture has an auteur it's the corporate one of Trident Television, and the enterprise registers as perfunctory, flavourless and underproduced, in the way of conventional TV adaptations. Unfair to all concerned, especially the audience, to allow such feeble stuff on to the big screen. BBa

Olivia

(1950, Fr, 94 min, b/w)
d Jacqueline Audry. *p* Jean Velter. *sc* Colette Audry, Pierre Laroche. *ph* Christian Matras. *ed* Marguerite Beaugé. *ad* Jean d'Eaubonne. *m* Pierre Sancan. *cast* Edwige Feuillère, Simone Simon, Marie-Claire Olivia, Yvonne de Bray, Suzanne Dehelly, Marina de Berg, Lesley Maynard, Rita Roanda, Danièle Delorme.

●Based on the novel by Dorothy Bussy (originally published pseudonymously), *Olivia* is set in a French girls' boarding school late in the 19th century, and deals with suppressed love, idolatry and inner conflict, a million miles away from infantile crushes on 'Miss'. Perhaps a little long, it narrowly misses being maudlin and hammy thanks to the performance by Edwige Feuillère as the charismatic head teacher, Mademoiselle Julie, on whom Olivia more than dotes. Although the main theme is self-control and self-will, references and innuendoes point to lesbian love, and it's not hard to imagine that in the '50s the censors' eyebrows would have shot up (eleven minutes were in fact cut on its first release in this country). Today it seems perfect viewing for a quiet Sunday afternoon. LS

Olivier Olivier

(1991, Fr, 109 min)
d Agnieszka Holland. *p* Marie-Laure Reyre. *sc* Agnieszka Holland. *ph* Bernard Zitzermann. *ed* Isabelle Lorente. *ad* Hélène Bourgy, Benoît Clémenceau. *m* Zbigniew Preisner. *cast* François Cluzet, Brigitte Roüan, Jean-François Stévenin, Grégoire Colin, Marina Golovine, Frédéric Quiring.

●Olivier, the coddled nine-year-old son of a provincial French family, disappears; and despite the promises of a well-meaning police inspector (Stévenin), fails to reappear. The loss breaks up his already tension-torn family – older sister Nadine, vet father (Cluzet) and over-protective mother (Roüan) – and in a storm of recriminations, Papa hightails it to Africa. Then, six years later, the unthinkable happens… Based, unimaginably, on a true story, the film begins with a picture of rural bliss, but then turns the conventions upside down. Six years on, the drama focuses on the older Nadine (a sensitive, fiery performance by Golovine) and the young seed of discord who enters the family nest, played with disarming charisma by Colin. Cluzet, Roüan and Stévenin are excellent too. Part intimate melodrama, part mystery story, the film delves with confidence into some dark areas, and takes the scalpel to the nuclear family as pitilessly as anything since Bergman's heyday. JRo

O Lucky Man!

(1973, GB, 174 min)
d Lindsay Anderson. *p* Michael Medwin, Lindsay Anderson. *sc* David Sherwin. *ph* Miroslav Ondricek. *ed* David Gladwell. *pd* Jocelyn Herbert. *m* Alan Price. *cast* Malcolm McDowell, Ralph Richardson, Rachel Roberts, Arthur Lowe, Helen Mirren, Mona Washbourne, Dandy Nichols, Graham Crowden, Peter Jeffrey, Anthony Nicholls, Michael Medwin, Warren Clark, Alan Price.

●A modern *Pilgrim's Progress*, with Malcolm McDowell (reprising the name, if not the character, of the hero of *If…*) as the young man in search of fame and the better things of life, *O Lucky Man!* is a disappointment. Lacking the specificity of either *If…* or *This Sporting Life*, it's an undisciplined (at nearly three hours long) humanist shriek of anger at what 'They' are doing to 'Us', lashing out wildly without purpose. The result is a film that approaches its material not in the manner of a Swift or an Orwell, but as the *Carry On* team might under the temporary influence of surrealism. In short, all puff and no thought. None the less interesting, with Alan Price's songs punctuating and informing the film's episodic action. PH

Olvidados, Los (The Young and the Damned)

(1950, Mex, 88 min, b/w)
d Luis Buñuel. *p* Oscar Dancigers. *sc* Luis Buñuel, Luis Alcoriza. *ph* Gabriel Figueroa. *ed* Carlos Savage. *ad* Edward Fitzgerald. *m* Gustavo Pitaluga. *cast* Alfonso Mejia, Roberto Cobo, Estela Inda, Miguel Inclán, Alma Delia Fuentes, Francisco Jambrina.

●Buñuel's return to the public eye after nearly 20 years in the critical wilderness came with this superbly caustic account of poverty, delinquency and crime in the slums of Mexico City. Basically he took a then popular genre, a major force in both Hollywood and Italian neo-realism – the liberal social conscience picture – and transformed it into a brilliantly acidic vision of human desires, fears and foibles. The story concerns the tragedies that befall a couple of members of a violent gang of kids who go round mugging, robbing and generally inflicting cruelty on everyone around them. But Buñuel, unlike his peers, is not content to lay all the blame for their acts and predicament on an abstract society: individuals also have inner motivations. Thus there is a poetic and precise emphasis on dreams and sexuality, and characters are far from being stereotypes: a blind man, frequently tormented by the kids, can hardly arouse our pity when Buñuel also shows him to be a hypocrite and a paedophile. A wonderfully lucid film that refuses to allow us to indulge in blinkered sentimentality or narrow ideology. GA

Olympische Spiele 1936 (Olympiad)

(1938, Ger, 118 min (Part 1)/107 min (Part 2), b/w)
d/p Leni Riefenstahl. *ph* Willy Zielke, Hans Ertl, Walter Frentz, Guzzi Lantschner, Heinz von Jaworsky, Kurt Neubert, Hans Scheib. *ed* Leni Riefenstahl, Max Michel, Johannes Lüdke, Arnfried Heyne. *m* Herbert Winde

●Masterwork – or vicious propaganda for the master race? Riefenstahl's films haunt the liberal imagination and its belief in the ennobling function of Art. Orchestrated like *Triumph of the Will* around a historical mass gathering, this record of the 1936 Berlin Olympics is another display of epic showmanship, where documentary information is placed a very poor second to sheerly spectacular effects. Here, though, the human body is eroticised in a paean to physical beauty that suggests how compatible fetishism and fascism can be. SJo

Ombre du Doute, L' (A Shadow of Doubt)

(1992, Fr, 106 min)
d Aline Issermann. *sc* Aline Issermann, Martine Fadier-Nisse, Frédérique Gruyer. *ph* Darius Khondji. *ed* Hervé Schnéid. *pd* Cyr Boitard. *m* Reno Isaac. cast Mireille Perrier, Alain Bashung, Sandrine Blancke, Emmanuelle Riva, Michel Aumont, Roland Bertin, Thierry Lhermitte, Josiane Balasko.

●Questioned by a teacher over her tendency to rewrite fairy-tales with unhappy endings, 12-year-old Alexandrine (Blancke) timidly admits that her father Jean (Bashung) has been sexually abusing her. Unsurprisingly, he denies the accusation, rightly confident that, like the sceptical legal authorities, his wife Marie (Perrier) will believe him rather than her daughter. Nevertheless, social worker Sophia (Balasko) feels sure the girl isn't lying or even the victim of an over-ripe imagination, and goes ahead with the investigation… Happily resorting neither to stale Hollywood-style homily, nor to the dour grainy 'realism' of most British social-problem movies, this fictional case-study blends a cool, almost scientifically objective approach to a notoriously difficult issue with a visual and narrative style that's distinctly poetic. Crucially, writer/director Issermann avoids sensationalism and sentimentality, allowing for a dramatic balance that's enhanced by the uniform excellence of the performances. Tough, intelligent, compelling and – remarkably – not at all grim. GA

Omega Connection, The

see London Connection, The

Omega Man, The

(1971, US, 98 min)
d Boris Sagal. *p* Walter Seltzer. *sc* John William Corrington. *ph* Russell Metty. *ed* William Ziegler. *ad* Arthur Loel, Walter M Simonds. *m* Ron Grainer. *cast* Charlton Heston, Anthony Zerbe, Rosalind Cash, Paul Koslo, Lincoln Kilpatrick, Eric Laneuville.

●This second screen adaptation of Richard Matheson's classic sci-fi novel *I Am Legend* (the first was *The Last Man on Earth*, 1964) still doesn't succeed in conveying the exultant paranoia of its original as effectively as (for example) *Night of the Living Dead*. In Matheson's story, the last man on earth was besieged by vast numbers of vampires, the victims of an apocalyptic plague; but this version substitutes a few albino mutants for the vampires, and reduces the original's brilliant cross-fertilisation of Gothic myth and doomsday fantasy to an averagely competent exercise in comic strip sci-fi. DP

Omen, The

(1976, US, 111 min)
d Richard Donner. *p* Harvey Bernhard. *sc* David Seltzer. *ph* Gilbert Taylor. *ed* Stuart Baird. *ad* Carmen Dillon. *m* Jerry Goldsmith. *cast* Gregory Peck, Lee Remick, David Warner, Billie Whitelaw, Harvey Stephens, Leo McKern, Patrick Troughton, Martin Benson, Robert Rietty.

●Although this tale of a satanic child was as successful at the box-office as *The Exorcist*, there's not a drop of green vomit in sight. Instead, this apocalyptic movie mostly avoids physical gore to boost its relatively unoriginal storyline with suspense, some excellent acting (especially from Warner and Whitelaw), and a very deft, incident-packed script. There is not a single original theme in *The Omen*, but its makers are so resolute in avoiding padding, and so deceptively accomplished in their use of emotional triggers, that you come out wondering how the film succeeds so well. The secret lies partly in the hermetically tight construction which, among other things, veers the action to a spooky chase across Europe just when other horror movies are getting bogged down in what dumb effect to produce next. DP

Omen IV: The Awakening

(1991, US, 97 min)
d Jorge Montesi, Dominique Othenin-Girard. *p* Harvey Bernhard. *sc* Brian Taggert. *ph* Martin Fuhrer. *ed* Frank Irvine, Bruce Giesbrecht. *pd* Richard Wilcox. *cast* Faye Grant, Michael Woods, Michael Lerner, Madison Mason, Ann Hearn, Jim Byrnes, Asia Vieira.

●'You have won…*nothing!*' gurgled Antichrist Damien Thorn ten years ago, as he expired at the feet of a gigantic Jesus in *The Final Conflict*. No idle threat, for Damien had a child (surprise!) in whose hands rests the future of evil. Adopted by a rising statesman and his twitchy wife, young Delia is soon enjoying all the fiendish fun befitting the devil's daughter (throwing nannies out of windows, etc). Directed in workaday fashion by Montesi (who was dragged in to sort out the mess made by Othenin-Girard), this misguided TV mini-series turned big-screen blow-out boasts the silliest script since *Exorcist II: The Heretic*. 'I couldn't believe we had two strange deaths in one day,' mumbles Mom with completely straight face, before launching into yet another tiresome tirade about the apocalpyse, intercut with baffling footage of ex-nuns frolicking with live snakes. MK

On a Clear Day You Can See Forever

(1970, US, 130 min)
d Vincente Minnelli. *p* Howard W Koch. *sc* Alan Jay Lerner. *ph* Harry Stradling. *ed* David Bretherton. *pd* John F DeCuir. *m* Burton Lane. *lyrics* Alan Jay Lerner. *cast* Barbra Streisand, Yves Montand, Bob Newhart, Larry Blyden, Simon Oakland, Jack Nicholson, John Richardson, Pamela Brown, Irene Handl, Roy Kinnear.

●Fashioned from a Broadway half-success of 1965, this can be strongly recommended to all who like curate's eggs, good tunes, and nice colours. On the surface, Alan Jay Lerner's libretto could have been made to measure for Minnelli, with its emphasis on lavish imagined worlds juxtaposed with reality (under hypnosis a Brooklyn girl reveals a past life as a Regency dazzler called Melinda – and guess who the hypnotist falls in love with?). And Minnelli is able to decorate his material with beguiling visual conceits – the opening time-lapse photography, the colour contrasts between past and present. But he can do nothing to combat the script's length and shallowness, and there are some thumb-twiddling moments in between Burton Lane's delightful songs. The two star performers make an odd team, with their varying kinds of professionalism and vowel sounds. GB

On Any Sunday

(1971, US, 89 min)
d/p/sc Bruce Brown. *ph* Bob Bagley, Don Shoemaker, Bruce Brown, Allan Seymour, Gordon Brettelle, Bob Collins, Dan Wright, Richard Carrillo, Nelson Tyler, Mark Zavad, James Odom, Mark Brelsford. *ed* Don Shoemaker. *m* Dominic Frontière. *lyrics* Sally Stevens. *cast* Mert Lawwill, Steve McQueen, Malcolm Smith, Bruce Brown. *narrator* Bruce Brown.

●A bike movie with a difference: no Hell's Angels, no sex, no drugs. Instead, all-rounder Bruce Brown (who made the surfing documentary *The Endless Summer*) has come up with a feature-length commercial for good, clean motorcycling fun depicting just about every conceivable permutation of motorised two-wheel sport from ice-racing, enduro, moto-cross and road racing to the spectacular, crash-ridden American speciality, dirt-track racing. Spending some time following the progress of Mert Lawwill, one of America's top dirt-trackers, the film also has considerable footage of Steve McQueen playing at moto-cross and desert racing. It abounds with intelligently applied stop-frame, slow motion and colour treatment knick-knacks which heighten the excitement and visual impact. Though a schlocky Country 'n' Western soundtrack and facile narration irritate after a while, this is an imposing essay compared to which the outlaw biker pics are tame travesties of what the two-wheel trip's all about. MW

On Approval

(1944, GB, 80 min, b/w)
d Clive Brook. *p* Clive Brook, Sydney Box. *sc* Clive Brook. *ph* Claude Friese-Greene. *ed* Fergus McDonell. *ad* Tom Morahan. *m* William Alwyn. *cast* Clive Brook, Beatrice Lillie, Roland Culver, Googie Withers, OB Clarence, Lawrence Hanray, Eliot Mason, Hay Petrie, Marjorie Rhodes.

●Though plays dealing with the amorous and other vagaries of the idle rich may no longer dominate the West End stage, the species is by no means extinct, and with this version of Frederick Lonsdale's hit of the '20s we have a good opportunity to examine the animal. Brook plays a penurious duke wooing an American pickle heiress (Withers), but – after a twin 'trial marriage' on a remote Scottish island – being rejected in favour of his dog-eared companion (Culver) and ending up with Beatrice Lillie, whose selfish cynicism dwarfs even his own. Though Brook's deliberately 'cinematic' approach was highly praised at the time (according to Lindsay Anderson it was 'the funniest British comedy ever made'), it is the performances, Lonsdale's deft craftsmanship, and the presence of the semi-mythical Lillie which now holds interest. RMy

On Boys, Girls and the Veil (Sobyan Wa Banat)

(1995, Egypt, 72 min)
d/sc Yousry Nasrallah. *ph* Samir Bahsan. *ed* Tamer Ezzat. *with* Bessem Saura.

●This documentary on contemporary attitudes to the wearing of the *hijab* (the veil) among Egypt's youth seems deceptively simple at first: he follows Bessem Saura, a 24-year-old teacher and would-be actor, as he chats to friends, family and colleagues about their lives. However these relaxed discussions constantly throw up fragments of historical, social, and political information which gradually fit together to present an image of a non-fundamentalist Islamic society which undermines and challenges many of the assumptions too easily vocalised in the West. Not only that, but the interaction between the members of the Saura family provides a wonderfully engrossing central narrative. FM

Once a Jolly Swagman (aka Maniacs on Wheels)

(1948, GB, 100 min, b/w)
d Jack Lee. *p* Ian Dalrymple. *sc* William Rose, Jack Lee. *ph* HE Fowle. *ed* Jack Harris. *ad* Fred Pusey. *m* Bernard Stevens. *cast* Dirk Bogarde, Renee Asherson, Moira Lister, Bill Owen, Bonar Colleano, Thora Hird, James Hayter, Patric Doonan, Cyril Cusack, Sidney James.

●In America, in anticipation of Roger Corman, this twee little film was called *Maniacs on Wheels*. Bogarde plays a factory worker who becomes a speedway star. His Aussie mate (Owen) flies off the handlebars and suffers brain damage (hence the original title). But this does not deter Dirk from racing – and enlisting for WWII – while fiancée Renee Asherson gets all worried for his safety. ATu

Once Around

(1991, US, 115 min)
d Lasse Hallström. *p* Amy Robinson, Griffin Dunne. *sc* Malia Scotch Marmo. *ed* Andrew Mondshein. *ph* Theo van de Sande. *pd* David Gropman. *m* James Horner. *cast* Holly Hunter, Richard Dreyfuss, Danny Aiello, Laura San Giacomo, Gena Rowlands, Roxanne Hart, Danton Stone, Tim Guinee, Griffin Dunne.

●Hallström's first Hollywood feature went belly-up at the US box office (it opened the weekend the Gulf War erupted) and emerged gingerly on video in Britain, but this rather overbearing romantic comedy is by no means a disaster. Hunter's the inexperienced heroine who travels to the Caribbean for a much-needed break after being dumped by her boyfriend, but the rebound brings brash salesman Dreyfuss her way, sweeping her off her feet and soon causing a deep rift with her close-knit family. Dreyfuss is even more obnoxious here than he was in *Tin Men*, but intentionally so, his eagerness to please driving everyone but Hunter nuts. TJ

Once a Thief (Zongheng Sihai)

(1991, HK, 108 min)
d John Woo. *p* Linda Kuk, Terence Chang. *sc* John Woo, Clifton Ko, Janet Chun. *ph* Poon Hang-Sang. cast Chow Yun Fat, Leslie Cheung, Cherie Chung.

●Lighter in tone than most Woo thrillers, this begins – disconcertingly – far away from the mean streets of Hong Kong as three master thieves plan to steal a Modigliani masterpiece outside Paris. The opening stunt, involving car, motorcycle and parachute, is slickly handled but bloodless. Only when the thieves become involved in an epic seafront shoot-out does Woo really get into his customary kinetic groove. Back in Hong Kong, the pace quickens, but the attempt to combine comedy with hardboiled action doesn't convince. Nor do the director's usual musings on friendship and family loyalty carry much resonance. GM

Once in Paris...

(1978, US, 100 min)
d Frank D Gilroy. *p* Frank D Gilroy, Manny Fuchs, Gerard Croce. *sc* Frank D Gilroy. *ph* Claude Saunier. *ed* Robert Q Lovett. *m* Mitch Leigh. *cast* Wayne Rogers, Gayle Hunnicutt, Jack Lenoir, Clément Harari, Tanya Lopert, Doris Roberts.

●No more and no less than a tale of American-alone-in-Paris seducing the lady in the hotel room next door. All the ritual stages of courtship are trotted out, on down to a bitter-sweet parting. A certain gay undertone in the subplot (concerning the roguish chauffeur who comes between them) does little to rescue the film from being absolutely average. CPea

Once in the Life

(2000, US, 107 min)
d Laurence Fishburne. *p* David L Bushell, Laurence Fishburne, Helen Sugland. *sc* Laurence Fishburne. *ph* Richard Turner. *ed* Bill Pankow. *pd* Charles Beal. *m* Branford Marsalis. *cast* Eamonn Walker, Gregory Hines, Laurence Fishburne, Anabella Sciorra, Michael Paul Chan, Dominic Chianese, Paul Calderon, Andres Titus, Titus Welliver.

●Fishburne's directorial debut is based on his own stage play, *Riff Raff*. The opening has a credible street feel, but everything turns very wordy and theatrical when hustlers Michael and Billy hole up in an abandoned loft space, and Michael's old friend Tony T struggles with the dilemma, to off or not to off. A pity, because there are some fun performances going on. TCh

Once Is Not Enough

see Jacqueline Susann's Once Is Not Enough

Once There Was a War (Der var engang en Krig)

(1966, Den, 94 min, b/w)
d Palle Kjaerulff-Schmidt. *sc* Klaus Rifbjerg. *ph* Claus Loof. *ed* Ole Steen. *ad* Henning Bahs. *m* Leo Mathiesen. *cast* Ole Busck, Yvonne Ingdal, Kjeld Jacobsen, Astrid Villaume, Katja Miehe Renard, Birgit Bendix Madsen, Jan Heinig Hansen.

●A calm, doggily funny study of a young boy growing up in the suburbs of Copenhagen during WWII. In this child's eye view of war, there is scarcely a German to be seen, except for the odd embarrassed sentry, considered as fair game for mockery. RAF bombers fly overhead, eagerly watched because they drop mysterious strips of tinfoil, to be collected and hoarded away as treasures. Adults, huddled in corners muttering about the Gestapo, impinge chiefly as nuisances because they worry, they forbid excursions. There are airy fantasies of heroism ('Hello, Winston' begins his report to London, 'it's me'), and occasional nightmares in which his family is tortured to death. Mostly, though, he is too busy poring over dirty books and worrying about girls to think too much about the war. Beautifully shot on location in soft, naturalistic tones, with witty high-contrast lighting for the fantasy sequences, it's a strangely haunted and haunting film, all the more effective for its insouciant air of being miles removed from the realities of war. TM

Once Upon a Forest

(1992, US, 71 min)
d Charles Grosvenor. *p* David Kirschner, Jerry Mills. *sc* Mark Young, Kelly Ward. *ed* Pat A Foley. *pd* Carol Holman Grosvenor, Bill Proctor. *m* James Horner. *cast* voices: Michael Crawford, Ben Vereen, Ellen Blain, Ben Gregory, Paige Gosney, Elizabeth Moss.

● Toxic gas contaminates an idyllic wood. Three youngsters – woodmouse, mole and hedgehog – seek a rare herbal remedy for their irradiated badger friend. Sage Cornelius (Crawford) watches over the sick infant. Eco-friendly animated co-production between Hanna-Barbera and HTV Cymru/Wales which makes one long for animals whacking each other with sticks of dynamite. MK

Once Upon a Honeymoon

(1942, US, 115 min, b/w)
d Leo McCarey. *sc* Sheridan Gibney. *ph* George Barnes. *ed* Theron Warth. *ad* Albert S D'Agostino, Al Herman. *m* Robert Emmett Dolan. *cast* Ginger Rogers, Cary Grant, Walter Slezak, Albert Dekker, Albert Basserman, Ferike Boros, Harry Shannon.

● The year is 1938, the setting a beleaguered Europe in which Cary Grant plays roving radio reporter to Ginger Rogers' Bronx-born gold-digger (with Viennese baron Slezak for a husband). A nonsense plot and bizarre soundtrack (continuous waltzes) can't disguise the fact that this is really three movies in one (love story, spy drama, anti-Nazi polemic), but the whole thing is saved by its irreverence, mixing the romance (and newsreel footage) with moments of outrageously tasteless kitsch: Rogers' Nazi husband cutting up a cake-map of Czechoslovakia, clocks with swastika hands. Splendid, eccentric tragi-comedy. And the erotic undertow of the Grant-Rogers partnership is just incredible. CA

Once Upon a Time

(1944, US, 88 min, b/w)
d Alexander Hall. *p* Louis Edelman. *sc* Lewis Meltzer, Oscar Saul. *ph* Franz Planer. *ed* Gene Havlick. *ad* Lionel Banks, Edward Jewell. *m* Frederick Hollander. *cast* Cary Grant, Janet Blair, James Gleason, Ted Donaldson, William Demarest, Howard Freeman, Art Baker.

● Light-hearted Hollywood fairytale (adapted from Norman Corwin and Lucille Herrmann's radio play *My Client Curley*) has Broadway producer Grant looking for new talent after mounting three flops in a row, and hitting pay-dirt with young Donaldson's dancing caterpillar, a remarkable creature that performs only to 'Yes Sir, That's My Baby' on the harmonica. Success beckons, a deal with Disney is struck, and then our many-legged friend vanishes without trace. That's showbiz, huh? TJ

Once Upon a Time in America 100 (100)

(1983, US, 229 min)
d Sergio Leone. *p* Arnon Milchan. *sc* Leo Benvenuti, Piero De Bernardi, Enrico Medioli, Franco Arcalli, Franco Ferrini, Sergio Leone. *ph* Tonino Delli Colli. *ed* Nino Baragli. *ad* Carlo Simi, (NY) James Singelis. *m* Ennio Morricone. *cast* Robert De Niro, James Woods, Elizabeth McGovern, Treat Williams, Tuesday Weld, Burt Young, Joe Pesci, Danny Aiello.

● In 1968, Noodles (De Niro) returns to New York an old man after 35 years of exile, ridden by guilt. His cross-cut memories of the Jewish Mafia's coming of age on the Lower East Side in 1923, their rise to wealth during Prohibition, and their *Götterdämmerung* in 1933, provide the epic background to a story of friendship and betrayal, love and death. While Leone's vision still has a magnificent sweep, the film finally subsides to an emotional core that is sombre, even elegiac, and which centres on a man who is bent and broken by time, and finally left with nothing but an impotent sadness. CPea

Once Upon a Time in China (Huang Feihong)

(1991, HK, 135 min)
d Tsui Hark. *p* Raymond Chow. *sc* Tsui Hark, Kai Chi Yuen, Yiu Ming Leung, Pik Yin Tang. *ph* Bill Wong, Arthur Wong, Lam Kwok-Wah, Tung Chuen Chan, Pui Kai Chan. *ed* Chi Sin Mak. *pd* Man Hung Lau. *m* Wong Mak. *cast* Jet Li, Yuen Biao, Jacky Cheung, Rosamund Kwan.

● Tsui Hark has been trawling his childhood memories of Hong Kong for years, looking for stories to remake and heroes to revive, and this is his most impressive catch to date. It brings back one of South China's perennial favourites, martial artist and bone-setter Wong Fei Hung, and imagines him as a young man in 1875, battling renegade Chinese in cahoots with the unscrupulous British. Tsui spends far too much time trying to freshen up the mythology surrounding the character (he has a rather tiresome stable of disciples); as usual, he comes into his own in the action set pieces, especially a fight atop flailing ladders. Underlying it all is a Peckinpah-esque lament for dying traditions and values, but its real strengths are its choreography, its flashes of wit, and its all-round exuberance. TR

Once Upon a Time in China II (Huang Feihong zhi Er: Nan'r Dang Zi Qiang)

(1993, HK, 123 min)
d Tsui Hark. *p* Tsui Hark, Ng See-Yuen. *sc* Tsui Hark, Hanson Chan, Carbon Cheung. *ph* Arthur Wong. *ed* Mak Chi-Sin. *pd* Cho King Man. *m* Richard Yuen, Johnny Jio. *cast* Jet Li, Rosemond Kwan, Max Mok, Zhang Tielin, David Chiang, Yen Chi Tan, Xiong Xin Xin.

● Episode Two in Tsui Hark's project to do for late 19th century China what Sergio Leone did for the American West is a blast. This is the best action-adventure-comedy that Tsui has ever made, hence one of the year's most exhilarating entertainments. Young hero Wong Fei Hung travels from Hong Kong to Guangzhou in 1895 to attend a medical conference, and finds himself caught between Sun Yat-Sen's struggle to overthrow imperial rule and the hysterical xenophobia of the White Lotus Clan, a mystical 'boxer' sect. The entire film is a riff on East-West relations, and it implicitly questions China's present-day political competence and stability, but choreographer Yuen Woo-Ping's action set pieces are its true *raison d'être*. TR

Once Upon a Time in the Midlands

(2002, GB, 104 min)
d Shane Meadows. *p* Andrea Calderwood. *sc* Paul Fraser, Shane Meadows. *ph* Brian Tufano. *ed* Peter Beston, Trevor Waite. *pd* Crispian Sallis. *m* John Lunn. *cast* Robert Carlyle, Rhys Ifans, Kathy Burke, Shirley Henderson, Ricky Tomlinson, Finn Atkins.

● Irresponsible charmer Carlyle returns to the wife and child he left behind on a Nottingham estate, partly to hide from the partners in petty crime he's just betrayed, partly with the idea of winning back his ex (Henderson) from loving but cowardly nerd Ifans. Thus the scene is set for a big showdown (hence the title and much of the music), and one of Meadows' affectionate serio-comic studies of East Midlands manners and mores. The director seems a less assured with a comparatively starry cast (Burke and Tomlinson are part of the extended family at the heart of the story) than with the unknowns of his earlier films, and the final moments fall a little flat; but on the whole his facility in shifting between mirth and menace, 'realism' and something less easily categorisable still remains marvellously evident. GA

Once Upon a Time in the West (C'era una Volta il West) 100 (100)

(1968, It, 165 min)
d Sergio Leone. *p* Sergio Leone, Fulvio Morsella. *sc* Sergio Leone, Sergio Donati, Mickey Knox. *ph* Tonino Delli Colli. *ed* Nino Baragli. *ad* Carlo Simi. *m* Ennio Morricone. *cast* Henry Fonda, Claudia Cardinale, Jason Robards, Charles Bronson, Frank Wolff, Gabriele Ferzetti, Keenan Wynn, Paolo Stoppa, Lionel Stander, Jack Elam, Woody Strode.

● The Western is dead, they tell us. Long live Leone's timeless monument to the death of the West itself, rivalled only by Peckinpah's *Pat Garrett and Billy the Kid* for the title of best ever made. We're talking favourite films here, so only superlatives will do. Worth starting at the beginning: a stakeout at a deserted station, Jack Elam and a fly – the most audacious credit sequence in film history. A soundtrack never bettered by any Dolby knob-twiddlers – unnatural sounds of 'silence' and Morricone's greatest score, handing Bronson his identity with a plangent, shivery harmonica riff, carrying Leone's crane shots upwards over a railhead township, clip-clopping Robards into the rigorous good/bad/ugly schema. Countercasting (sadist Fonda) and location choice (Monument Valley) that render an iconic base for Leone and collaborators (Bertolucci and Argento, no less) to perform their revisionist/revolutionary critique of the Classic American (i.e. Fordian) Creation Myth. And more, too. Critical tools needed are eyes and ears – this is Cinema. PT

Once Upon a Time in Triad Society (Wangjiao Cha-fit-ren)

(1996, HK, 92 min)
d Cha Chuen-Yee. *sc* Chung Kai-Cheong. *ph* Peter Ngor. *ad* Lam Wai-Sum. *m* Johnny Yeung. *cast* Francis Ng, Lee Lai-Chun, So Chi-Wai, Allen Ting, Chan Wai-Man, Pauline Chan.

● Knocked off in ten days by an ex-TV director with nine previous quickies to his credit, this is a spirited and remarkably witty demolition of the myth of 'righteousness' in triad gangs as expressed in the hit *Young and Dangerous* series. Kwan (Francis Ng, villain in the first *Young and Dangerous* movie) is a housing estate kid who sets out to become 'the worst guy in triad society' after suffering a series of let-downs, betrayals and beatings. Director Cha provides alternative versions of his story (one Kwan's idealised fantasy, the other supposedly real), but both are full of parodies of other movies and cynical subversions of cops-and-robbers conventions. Pitched somewhere between Monty Python and Roger Corman, this shows what can be achieved by a film-maker with more talent than money. TR

Once Upon a Time in Triad Society 2 (Qu ba! Cha-fit-ren Bingtuan)

(1996, HK, 92 min)
d Cha Chuen-Yee. *sc* Chung Kai-Cheong. *ph* Ko Chiu-Lam. *ed* Angie Lam. *ad* Lam Wai-Sum. *m* Johnny Yeung. *cast* Francis Ng, Roy Cheung, Cheung Tat-Ming, Ivy Leung, Ada Choi, Angie Cheung, Spencer Lam.

● Less a sequel – it has the same director, writer and star as the first movie, but new characters and an unrelated storyline – than an even more inventive follow-up. This time Ng plays a compulsive gambler and congenital coward; unluckily for him, his need to present a macho front wins him a starring role in a battle to save control of Mongkok from a marauding Mainland China gang. His bathetic exploits (mostly with a gay prostitute friend getting in the way) are intercut with the lives of a tough-but-sensitive triad foot-soldier (Roy Cheung) and an out-of-his-depth cop (Cheung Tat-Ming) whose pregnant wife goes shopping in the wrong place at the wrong time. Funny, emotive and really quite exciting, this was one of the best Hong Kong movies of its year. TR

Once Upon a Time – the Revolution

see Giù la Testa

Once Upon a Time...This Morning (Kala Krangnung Mua Shao Ni)

(1994, Thai, 135 min)
d Bhandit Rittakol. *p* Chareon Iamphungporn. *sc* Chaninthon Prasertprasat, Bhandit Rittakol. *ph* Leng-Eiu Wanchai. *ed* Poonsakdi Uthaiphant. *cast* Santisuk Promsiri, Jintara Sukkapat, Ronnarong Buranat, Martang Jantranee, Poramatti Thammamon.

● Ex-critic and screenwriter Bhandit Rittakol updates a Thai fairy tale about a family in peril into the terms of a mid-1990s thriller. Mum and Dad are divorced and the three kids (much to their disgust) live with Mum in her new Bangkok apartment. After one of their frequent rows with Mum, the kids run away to look for Dad – unaware that the baby's cot contains a bag of pure heroin hidden there by a kid courier on the run. Cue an extended chase in which the fast-learning kids are pursued by both their distraught parents, the police and the drug lords and their hired street kids. A lot happens on the way to the admirably unsentimental climax, much of it genuinely gripping. TR

Once Upon a Time... When We Were Colored

(1996, US, 112 min)
d Tim Reid. *p* Mike Bennett, Tim Reid. *sc* Paul Cooper. *ph* Johnny Simmons. *ed* David Pincus. *cast* Al Freeman Jr, Phylicia Rashad, Paula Kelly, Leon, Richard Roundtree, Salli Richardson, Isaac Hayes, Polly Bergen. *narrator* Phil Lewis.

●This adaptation of Clifton Taulbert's novel details a young boy's post-WWII rites of passage in the segregated Mississippi Delta. Basically anecdotal – the Joe Louis title defeat; the 'ice wars' as the NAACP campaign began to bite – it celebrates a community who were 'never beat down', surviving days in the cotton fields on a diet of pride, resolution, family and community solidarity and sweet potato pie. The period reconstruction is flawless, the camerawork glowing, and the affirmation of the progressive role of education effulgent and endearing. WH

Once Were Warriors

(1993, NZ, 103 min)
d Lee Tamahori. *p* Robin Scholes. *sc* Riwai Brown. *ph* Stuart Dryburgh. *ed* Michael Horton. *pd* Michael Kane. *m* Murray Grindlay, Murray McNabb. *cast* Rena Owen, Temuera Morrison, Mamaengaroa Kerr-Bell, Julian Arahanga, Taungaroa Emile, Rachel Morris Jr, Joseph Kairau, Clifford Curtis, Pete Smith.

●An emotionally raw, visually stylish first feature, with the intensity of the best social melodrama, about the indomitable spirit of battered Maori wife Beth Heke (Owen) as she struggles to hold together her disintegrating family. Husband Jake (Morrison) is a violent yet charismatic bully, the sullen eldest son is already a gang member, the youngest is in care, and only gifted daughter Grace (Kerr-Bell) offers hope for the future. A gritty human drama evoking the residual vibrancy of a threatened culture. NF

On Company Business

(1980, US, 180 min)
d Allan Francovich. *p* Howard Dratch, Allan Francovich. *ph* Kevin Keating. *ed* Veronica Selver. *with* Phillip Agee, James Wilcott, William Colby, Victor Marchetti, John Stockwell.

●Francovich's three-hour documentary on the CIA may seem a daunting prospect, but don't be put off: it's an exemplary piece of documentary construction which makes full use of archive material and rarely loses its sense of pace or humour. The film's real strength lies in its interviews with CIA personnel and ex-personnel – from bureau chiefs to mercenaries – who behave increasingly like the cast of a Hollywood film about the CIA. It's frightening on several counts: the openness of those involved in naked political aggression and interference, and the overwhelming feeling that everyone interviewed is telling only part of the truth. An indictment of American foreign policy, of several administrations, and of an entire social structure, the film also raises the interesting speculation that a similar examination would never be possible in this country. SM

On connaît la chanson

see Same Old Song

On Dangerous Ground

(1951, US, 80 min, b/w)
d Nicholas Ray. *p* John Houseman. *sc* AI Bezzerides. *ph* George E Diskant. *ed* Roland Gross. *ad* Albert S D'Agostino, Ralph Berger. *m* Bernard Herrmann. *cast* Robert Ryan, Ida Lupino, Ward Bond, Ed Begley, Cleo Moore, Charles Kemper, Sumner Williams.

●A superb *noir* thriller with a difference. Ray's second film with producer John Houseman (the first being *They Live By Night*) starts off in the sinister urban jungle, with Ryan's cop increasingly brutalised by the 'garbage' he is forced to deal with. Finally, his methods become so violent that he is sent to cool off in snowy upstate New York, where his search for a sex killer brings him into contact with Lupino's blind woman and her mentally retarded brother (Williams). It's a film about the violence within us all, about the effects of environment and family upon character (Lupino, peaceful and a healing force, even has a tree in her living room), and about the spiritual redemption of a fallen man. If it sometimes seems a little schematic, there is no denying the power of the performances (Ryan in particular is ferociously effective, a true precursor to Siegel's *Dirty Harry*), nor the eloquence of Ray's poetic but tough direction. Aided enormously by George Diskant's high contrast camerawork and by Bernard Herrmann's stunning score, which emphasises the hunt motif in Ryan's quest, it's a film of frequent brilliance. GA

On Dangerous Ground

see Choke Canyon

On Deadly Ground

(1994, US, 100 min)
d Steven Seagal. *p* Steven Seagal, Julius R Nasso, A Kitman Ho. *sc* Ed Horowitz, Robin U Ruscin. *ph* Ric Waite, (Alaska) Theo Van de Sande. *ed* Robert A Ferretti, Don Brochu. *pd* William Ladd Skinner. *m* Basil Poledouris. *cast* Steven Seagal, Michael Caine, Joan Chen, John C McGinley, R Lee Ermey, Shari Shattuck, Billy Bob Thornton, Richard Hamilton.

●Seagal has made a name for himself knocking the stuffing out of low life scumbags – here, in his directorial debut, his victims are rich, ecologically unsound scumbags. Caine's snaked-eyed, snakeskin-booted oil magnate knows he must get his rig on-line, or drilling rights will revert to the 'Eskimos'. Following the death of the rig foreman and an oil spill, trouble-shooter Forest Taft (Seagal) is set up as the fall guy for an alleged sabotage plot. Through contact with the Inuits, Taft learns he is a spirit warrior who must teach the oil men to 'fear the bear'. When the crud hits the fan, however, Taft eschews cosmic dream energy in favour of 'cold, hard reality' – i.e. a familiar arsenal of weapons. In contrast to his short, sharp fighting style, Seagal's presentation of the human conflicts and underlying issues consists of vague, sweeping gestures. NF

Ondeko-za on Sado, The

(1975, Jap, 55 min)
d Masahiro Shinoda.

●The 'Ondeko-za' is an extraordinary group of young Japanese who have exiled themselves to virtually complete isolation on Sado Island in the Japan Sea in order to preserve and/or recreate various Japanese folk arts, especially so-called 'demon drumming'. Shinoda's documentary provides a good deal of useful background information about their motives and the range of their activities. Founder/leader Tagayasu Den turns out to be a veteran of the '50s student riots, and many of the 17-strong group are dropouts or otherwise alienated kids; it's clear that the strenuous physical discipline of training for and performing in the Ondeko-za programme provides all of them with more constructive solutions to contemporary problems than most self-willed exiles achieve. TR

Ondergronds Orkest, Het

see Underground Orchestra, The

One, The

(2001, US, 87 min)
d James Wong. *p* Glen Morgan, Steven Chasman. *sc* Glen Morgan, James Wong. *ph* Robert McLachlan. *ed* James Coblentz. *pd* David L Snyder. *m* Trevor Rabin. *cast* Jet Li, Delroy Lindo, Carla Gugino, Jason Statham, James Morrison, Dylan Bruno, Richard Steinmetz, Harriet Sansom Harris.

●The international success of *The Matrix* opened a portal for numerous lower budget imitators – of which this Jet Li double role action-fantasy is one. It pivots shakily on the notion of a 'multiverse', where everyone has an alter ego in other worlds. Rebellious investigator Gabriel Yulaw (Li) has illegally trawled 123 dimensions, murdering his other personae and absorbing their strength. Now a final opponent – kindly, unwitting LA Sheriff Gabe (Li again) – stands in the way of his becoming 'The One'. Jet's forte, and the film's draw, is physical expression: he's most charismatic when he's kicking ass. In the edgy showdown between Yulaw and Gabe, Jet employs two martial art techniques, providing the only convincing contrast between his dual characters. A full-throttle nu-metal soundtrack and the probability of a sequel target an adolescent male audience. With its camp good humour, it's altogether unoriginal, but divertingly daft. AHa

One and a Two..., A (Yi Yi)

(2000, Tai/Jap, 173 min)
d Edward Yang. *p* Shinya Kawai, Naoko Tsukeda. *sc* Edward Yang. *ph* Yang Wei-Han. *ed* Chen Bo-Wen. *pd/m* Peng Kai-Li. *cast* Wu Nianzhen, Elaine Jin, Issey Ogata, Kelly Lee, Jonathan Chang, Adrian Lin, Ko Su-Yun.

●Yang's most fully achieved film since *A Brighter Summer Day* offers a detailed and very moving account across three generations of a family of the ways people cope with crises and emotional setbacks. The problems, it humorously suggests, may change as one grows older, but the means of coping don't change much. The central focus is on family head NJ (Wu, a fine screenwriter and director in his own right), who bumps into his long-lost first love on the very day his mother-in-law goes into a coma, and finds himself wondering if he can erase the last 20 years and start over. This is one film which justifies a three-hour running time: each character is drawn with warmth and complexity, and each has to deal with issues which are all too recognisably real. The interweaving of story threads and the ability to keep larger perspectives in sight while not stinting on specifics both bespeak a true mastery. TR

One and One (En och En)

(1978, Swe, 90 min)
d Erland Josephson, Sven Nykvist, Ingrid Thulin. *p* Erland Josephson, Sven Nykvist, Bengt Forslund. *sc* Erland Josephson. *ph* Sven Nykvist, Charlie Nykvist. *ed* Peter Falck. *pd* Marik Vos. *cast* Ingrid Thulin, Erland Josephson, Björn Gustafsson.

●One and one makes two: the message of this study of the social relationship between an odd couple (middle-aged woman artist and her bachelor cousin) is that good maths is bad psychology. From a script by Josephson, shot by Nykvist, and directed by Josephson, Nykvist and Thulin, the package just oozes prestige made in Bergmanland, but the film is full of silences and whispers signifying nothing, except perhaps Bergman's absence. In this case, one and one and one make zero. SH

One and Only, The

(1977, US, 98 min)
d Carl Reiner. *p* Steve Gordon, David V Picker. *sc* Steve Gordon. *ph* Victor J Kemper. *ed* Bud Molin. *pd* Edward C Carfagno. *m* Patrick Williams. *cast* Henry Winkler, Kim Darby, Gene Saks, William Daniels, Harold Gould, Polly Holliday, Hervé Villechaise, Richard Karron.

●'The One and Only' is Andy Schmidt, a hopeful actor setting out in the '50s with a Texas-sized ego, a bottomless barrel of jokes, and a WASP wife called Mary Crawford, only to find himself in the wrestling branch of showbiz, his fighting persona variously a hypnotist, Adolf Hitler, and an outrageous gay. And Andy Schmidt is Henry Winkler, whose ingratiating style certainly helps to make this comedy flabby round the edges. However, Reiner obviously loves the subject, and his direction is pointed but unfussy, while Steve Gordon's script balances the soppy looks and exchanges with many lunacies and acid cracks, often aimed at Winkler's dwarf sidekick ('Why don't you take three months off and change a light bulb?'). If only the madcap strain had been strengthened, the film might have achieved more momentum; as it is, with good performances all round, it's pleasant but so-so. GB

One Arabian Night

see Sumurun

One Armed Boxer (Dubi Quan Wang)

(1973, HK, 97 min)
d Wang Yu. *p* Raymond Chow. *sc* Wang Yu. *ph* Mo Shen Ku. *ed* Cheng Hung Min. *m* Wang Fu Ling, Wang Ping. *cast* Wang Yu, Tang Shin, Tien Yeh, Lung Fei, Wu Tung Choo, Pan Chun Lin.

●Here the tournament-dominated martial arts film intersects interestingly with the more folkloric magic aspects of the sword film. Wang Yu, directing with an eye to the Italian Western, plays his own hero, perhaps the most masochistic, impetuous and fight-loving of the lot, subjecting himself to the ultimate in dispossession before, through pain and self-punishment, coming back from the as-good-as-dead to wreak havoc. Wang Yu pits his hero against a genuinely fantastic array of fighters, including a fanged karate expert with a lank black mane, given to perching in the corners of rooms between the wall and ceiling like some malevolent bat, and two inflatable Tibetan lamas (who are able to arrest their own circulation). Distributor cuts make nonsense of the care taken to build up to the fight scenes by paying scrupulous attention to the rites attached to the various arts. VG

One Born Every Minute

see Flim-Flam Man, The

One by One

(1974, US, 94 min)
d Claude DuBoc. *p* Peter Leavell. *ph* Jacques Kargayan, Michael Delaney, René Guissart, Jamie Shourt, Bill Shourt, Claude DuBoc, Steve Fauth, Doug Hodge. *ed* Jean Bruce Gree. *m* Stomu Yamash'ta's Kargayan. *with* Jackie Stewart, Mike Hailwood, Peter Revson, François Cevert. *narrator* Stacy Keach.

●A very boring documentary indeed about Grand Prix racing: you don't know what dullness is until you've been talked round the Nurburgring by Jackie Stewart. Everything in it is touched with banality, from the camera being pointed at everything in range, to Stacy Keach's narration, which gives every bromide the ring of Eternal Truth ('The car is a thoroughbred with a soul of its own, brought to life by sorcerers' apprentices called…Mechanics'). But the main complaint is more fundamental: it's impossible to tell what's going on, as we cut from Monaco to the pile-up at Silverstone (good footage of the latter, but the BBC's was better). And a lot of the title's irony is thrown away, as it's never made clear to the less informed that the interviews with Revson and Cevert are being shown after their deaths. AN

One Day in September

(1999, GB, 95 min)
d Kevin Macdonald. *p* John Battsek, Arthur Cohn. *ph* Alwin Küchler, Neve Cunningham. *ed* Justine Wright. *m* Alex Heffes. *with* Ankie Spitzer, Jamal Al-Gashey. Gerald Seymour, Alex Springer, Gad Zabari, Shmuel Lalkin, Manfred Schreiber, Walther Troger, Ulrich K Wegener, Hans-Dietrich Genscher, Schlomit Romajo, Magdi Gahary, Zvi Zamir. *narrator* Michael Douglas.

●A worthy winner of an Oscar for Best Documentary, this dynamic, polemical account of the Black December terrorist attack on Israeli athletes during the 1972 Munich Olympics – which left 11 Israeli dead – is a bold attempt to pump new energy into documentary storytelling. The film-makers have gathered an impressive list of witnesses, including Ankie Spitzer (widow of the murdered fencing coach), Hans-Dietrich Genscher (the government negotiator, subsequently Foreign Minister), Zvi Zamir (chief of Mossad) and, not least, the last surviving member of the terrorist team, Jamal Al-Gashey. Innovative editing and multi-perspective techniques, plus computer modelling and graphics, and the excellent camerawork of Alwin (*Ratcatcher*) Küchler result in a fascinating documentary in thriller mode, accompanied by a varied, tension-boosting rock score. The film manages to take full account of the sensibilities of the victims' family and friends, while also fashioning a compelling condemnation of the sorry record of incompetence, callousness and double-standards, if not inadvertent racism and outright illegality, on the part of the German authorities. WH

One Day in the Life of Andrei Arsenevitch (Une Journée dans la Vie d'Andrei Arsenevitch)

(1999, Fr, 55 min)
d/sc/ph Chris Marker.

●A documentary on one of cinema's masters by one of cinema's masters. This homage to Tarkovsky incorporates video footage Marker shot while the Russian lay dying in Paris in 1986, and a lengthy sequence from a year earlier, on location for the six-minute take at the climax of *The Sacrifice*. Marker is evidently enthralled by the orchestration of men, machines and elements. This brilliant, penetrating piece of film criticism won over even a Tarkovsky agnostic like myself as an illumination of the metaphysics of movie-making. TCh

One Day in the Life of Ivan Denisovich

(1971, GB/Nor, 100 min)
d/p Caspar Wrede. *sc* Ronald Harwood. *ph* Sven Nykvist. *ed* Thelma Connell. *ad* Per Schwab. *m* Arne Nordheim. *cast* Tom Courtenay, Espen Skjonberg, James Maxwell, Alfred Burke, Eric Thompson, John Cording, Wolfe Morris, Sverre Hansen.

●Worthy, faithful version of Solzhenitsyn's novel about the difficulties of life in a Siberian labour camp. Courtenay is superb as Ivan, struggling to survive to the end of his ten-year sentence, and the whole thing is conscientiously put together – shot in sub-zero temperatures near the Arctic Circle in Norway, with gaunt, haunted faces and the drab buildings and landscapes evocatively shot by the great Sven Nykvist (Bergman's regular cameraman). The problem, however, is that in his efforts to be accurate and restrained, Wrede forsakes passion, and creates a film as cold and clinical as the environment it observes. GA

One Deadly Summer (L'Eté Meurtrier)

(1983, Fr, 133 min)
d Jean Becker. *p* Christine Beytout. *sc* Sébastien Japrisot. *ph* Etienne Becker. *ed* Jacques Witta. *ad* Jean-Claude Gallouin. *m* Georges Delerue. *cast* Isabelle Adjani, Alain Souchon, Suzanne Flon, Jenny Clève, Michel Galabru, François Cluzet, Manuel Gélin, Roger Carel, Edith Scob.

●For the first twenty minutes or so, this looks like an all too familiar chirpy French rural comedy: wiggly, pert-buttocked coquette-cum-slut Adjani arrives in a small French village and sets the local manhood afire with lust and rumour. Then the tone shifts and we're all set to discover that she's out for revenge for some outrage inflicted on her in childhood. Things still look predictable, but as the film progresses, become more and more complex; events are related in differing ways by the various characters, and Adjani's role takes on deepening and more disturbing perspectives. Just as beneath the glossy visuals there lie murky and enigmatic themes of exploitation, treachery and falsehood, so the initial stereotypes are gradually peeled away to reveal confused characters played with an increasing intensity by a fine cast, none more so than Adjani herself. Directed with verve, the film rarely departs from the commercial mainstream, but within those conventions it operates with assurance, subtlety and plenty of surprises. GA

One Eight Seven

(1997, US, 119 min)
d Kevin Reynolds. *p* Bruce Davey, Stephen McEveety. *sc* Scott Yagemann. *ph* Ericson Core. *ed* Stephen Semel. *pd* Stephen Storer. *cast* Samuel L Jackson, John Heard, Kelly Rowan, Clifton Gonzalez Gonzalez, Tony Plana, Karina Arroyave, Lobo Sebastian, Jack Kehler.

●Brooklyn. Teacher Trevor Garfield (Jackson) finds '187' scrawled across his notebook – the California penal code number for homicide. It's a death threat from (he thinks) a pupil he's just failed, but the principal won't take heed. Garfield's stabbed by an unseen assailant in the school corridor. A year later and physically healed, he takes a job in South Central LA, with fellow teachers Rowan and Heard. It's another rundown institution. Goaded by another macho homeboy, Cesar (Gonzalez), Garfield decides to play it Cesar's way. Thus far, that Hollywood rarity: an intelligent issue film with a social conscience and a sense of dramatic control. Echoing the trip-hoppy soundtrack, the visuals owe too much to pop video, yet exercise a certain pull. Jackson bears the weight of the film in a constrained, introverted role (terrorised, pertinacious, innocent passion squandered), but a grand resolution and some melodramatic twists and set-pieces undercut the hard-nosed tone. NB

One-Eyed Jacks

(1961, US, 141 min)
d Marlon Brando. *p* Frank P Rosenberg. *sc* Guy Trosper, Calder Willingham. *ph* Charles Lang Jr. *ed* Archie Marshek. *ad* Hal Pereira, Joseph McMillan Johnson. *m* Hugo Friedhofer. *cast* Marlon Brando, Karl Malden, Pina Pellicer, Katy Jurado, Ben Johnson, Slim Pickens, Larry Duran, Sam Gilman, Timothy Carey, Miriam Colon, Elisha Cook Jr, Rodolfo Acosta.

●Fascinating to see Brando directing this revenge Western – double-crossed by Malden, his outlaw partner, he erupts from the past to haunt the older man, now a lawman and proud father – exactly as he acts, so that the whole movie smoulders in a manner that is mean, moody and magnificent. At its origin is a novel by Charles Neider which, though changing the names, retold the story of Pat Garrett and Billy the Kid. Brando's further changes (Rio/Billy now kills rather than is killed by Dad Longworth/Garrett) were evidently made with a view to indicting shifty, mendacious society as the real villain. The Freudian intentions lurking in the character conflicts and the card symbolism, the homosexual and Oedipal intimations, are underpinned by the extraordinary settings. Surely uniquely in a Western, the key scenes are played out against the rocky Monterey sea coast, with waves crashing portentously in the background, so that nature echoes the Romantic agony of a hero much given to brooding in corners or gazing out into space shrouded in his Byronic cape. The result, laced with some fine traditional sequences and stretches of masochistic violence, is a Western of remarkable though sometimes muddled power. TM

One False Move

(1991, US, 105 min)
d Carl Franklin. *p* Jesse Beaton, Ben Myron. *sc* Billy Bob Thornton, Tom Epperson. *ph* James L Carter. *ed* Carole Kravetz. *pd* Gary T New. *m* Peter Haycock, Derek Holt. *cast* Bill Paxton, Cynda Williams, Billy Bob Thornton, Jim Metzler, Michael Beach, Earl Billings, Natalie Canerday.

●A superb modern thriller in the ultra-hard-boiled Jim Thompson mould, in which a trio of criminals, wanted for a brutally murderous drugs heist, converge on a small, quiet Arkansas township where the local cop, treated with contempt by the LA officers in charge of the case, looks forward to a *High Noon*-style showdown. The asides on racial and sexual inequality are made subtly and succinctly; the performances and pacing are nigh perfect; the violence is explicit, disturbing but never gratuitous; and Franklin – a black actor whose directing debut this is – achieves a consistency of mood that other far more experienced film-makers would give their right arms for. One of the finest American movies in recent years. GA

One Fine Day

(1996, US, 109 min)
d Michael Hoffman. *p* Lynda Obst. *sc* Terrel Seltzer, Ellen Simon. *ph* Oliver Stapleton. *ed* Garth Craven. *pd* David Gropman. *m* James Newton Howard. *cast* Michelle Pfeiffer, George Clooney, Mae Whitman, Alex D Linz, Charles Durning, John Robin Baitz, Ellen Greene, Joe Gifasi, Pete Hamill.

●More a mobile-phone movie than an old-fashioned romantic comedy, this irksomely frenetic love story sees single mother Melanie (Pfeiffer, not glamorous but with all modern Hollywood's ersatz PC trimmings) and divorced weekend dad Jack (arch-mugger Clooney) meeting cute all over touristy New York City. It's a tease. Melanie falls in hate at first sight, as Jack's lateness at the school gates means their respective five-year-olds will miss the Circle Line ferry trip. But necessity makes strange bedfellows – though it could hurry up! – as the two are forced to care for each other's kids in rotation while she races to close an architectural project and he hurtles about to support a City Hall corruption piece he's written. WH

One Fine Spring Day (Bomnal eun Ganda)

(2001, SKor/Jap/HK, 113 min)
d Hur Jin-Ho. *p* Tcha Sung-Jai, Kim Seon-Ah, Hideshi Miyajima, Peter Ho-Sun Chan. *sc* Ryu Jang-Ha, Lee Sook-Yeon, Shin Jun-Ho, Hur Jin-Ho. *ph* Kim Hyung-Gu. *ed* Kim Hyun. *ad* Park Il-Hyun. *m* Cho Seong-Woo. *cast* Yoo Ji-Tae, Lee Young-Ae, Baek Sung-Hee, Park In-Hwan, Shin Shin-Ae.

●Young sound recordist Sang-Woo (Yoo) lives in Seoul with his father, aunt and senile grandmother; he accepts a gig recording natural sounds for a radio series which takes him to Gangleung City and introduces him to divorcée Eun-Soo (Lee). They meet-cute (he has her mobile phone to wake her in the station waiting room), and so it's no surprise that they drift into a sexual relationship. But as winter shades into spring, she tires of her toy-boy and calls it all off – whereupon he falls to pieces. The emphasis on male vulnerability could be seen as a reaction against the gains in social/sexual status made by Korean women in recent years, except that the film's identification with the hapless Sang-Woo is so obviously heartfelt and personal. In its low key, contemplative way, this well-acted and observed movie offers a modern counterpoint to von Sternberg's *The Devil Is a Woman*. TR

One Flew Over the Cuckoo's Nest

(1975, US, 134 min)
d Milos Forman. *p* Saul Zaentz, Michael Douglas. *sc* Lawrence Hauben, Bo Goldman. *ph* Haskell Wexler, Bill Butler, William A Fraker. *ed* Lynzee Klingman, Sheldon Kahn. *pd* Paul Sylbert. *m* Jack Nitzsche. *cast* Jack Nicholson, Louise Fletcher, William Redfield, Will Sampson, Brad Dourif, Sydney Lassick, Christopher Lloyd, Danny De Vito, Delos V Smith Jr, Marya Small, Louisa Moritz, Dean R Brooks, Scatman Crothers.

●A strictly realistic approach to Ken Kesey's novel confines the horizons of the original into a saner, less delirious tragi-comedy. Set in an insane asylum, the film involves the oppression of the individual, a struggle spearheaded by an ebullient Nicholson, turning in a star performance if ever there was one as he leads his fellow-inmates against the sinisterly well-meaning Nurse Ratched (Fletcher). For all the film's painstaking sensitivity and scrupulous chartings of energies and repressions, one longs for more muscle, which only Nicholson consistently provides. CPe

One From the Heart

(1982, US, 107 min)
d Francis Coppola. *p* Gray Frederickson, Fred Roos. *sc* Armyan Bernstein, Francis Coppola. *ph* Vittorio Storaro, Ronald V Garcia. *ed* Anne Goursaud, Rudi Fehr, Randy Roberts. *pd* Dean Tavoularis. *m* Tom Waits. *cast* Frederic Forrest, Teri Garr, Raúl Julia, Nastassja Kinski, Lainie Kazan, Harry Dean Stanton, Allen Garfield.

●Apparently Coppola got his inspiration while wandering the back streets of Tokyo with a copy of Goethe's *Elective Affinities*, pondering the Kabuki and his alimony payments. He saw a sequence of brilliant tableaux: a hoary yarn about love lost and refound, spun with high-tech artifice and elaborate theories about colour. Fortunately the movie outgrew its origins with barely a stretch mark in sight, to become a likeable, idiosyncratic musical, its few remaining pretensions (dud symbolism just when you most expect it) so bare-faced they're almost winning. The human element keeps the film modest. Coppola shows an affection for the commonplaceness of his new romantic couple (Forrest and Garr) surprising after his previous ones from the heart of darkness: they smooch, quarrel, cheat on each other (respectively with Kinski and Julia), and live to smooch again over a long Fourth of July weekend in a Las Vegas confected entirely in the sets and mixing-boards of Zoetrope studios. The result, crafted with the help of cinematographer Vittorio Storaro, looks terrific: walls dissolve, scenes play in wry tandem, and the dance routines move nimbly into neon-tinged fantasies. At times the project seems in danger of being scuppered by its own lavishness; the saving grace is a light heart. KJ

One Full Moon (Un Nos Ola Leuad)

(1991, GB, 98 min)
d Endaf Emlyn. *p* Pauline Williams. *sc* Gwenlyn Parry, Endaf Emlyn. *ph* Ashley Rowe. *ed* Chris Lawrence. *ad* Ray Price. *m* Mark Thomas. *cast* Dyfan Roberts, Tudor Roberts, Betsan Llwyd, Delyth Einir, Cian Ciaran, Dilwyn Vaughn Thomas, Robin Griffith, Endaf Emlyn.

●This subtitled Welsh language drama, the second feature from Ffilm Cymru, is based on a novel by Caradog Prichard dealing with a harrowing remembered childhood in a remote slate-mining community in the 1920s, and is essentially of the poetic naturalism school. It cuts back and forward from the '50s to the '20s as a man (D Roberts) revisits the village where he spent his traumatic, fatherless adolescence with his hard-pressed mother. Past and present begin to meld. The film shows their hard daily lives, conducted under the vigilant, sin-watching eye of the church, with matter-of-fact honesty and no little humour. The bright, imaginative boy (T Roberts) – angels are no strangers to him – has a warm relationship with his mother. But she is vulnerable: when she is assaulted by a mad itinerant tinker, her frenzied need for expiation pushes her over the edge, and unbalances the boy. Emlyn's attitude to redemption is as enigmatic as the recurring images – scudding skies over green hills, cleansing water, the impassive face of the Virgin. How much does heaven allow? WH

One Generation of Tattoos (Irezumi Ichidai)

(1965, Jap, 87 min)
d Seijun Suzuki. *sc* Kinya Naoi, Kei Hattori. *ph* Kurataro Takamura. *ed* Ko Suzuki. *cast* Hideki Takahashi, Kotobuki Hananomoto, Akira Yomauchi, Hiroko Ito, Masako Izumi, Ken Yamanouchi, Kayo Matsuo.

●A somewhat more straight-ahead yakuza yarn than Suzuki was later to come up with, but still a perfect example of how gangster histrionics can be wedded with flights of emotional and spiritual fancy. A mob executioner, desperate to protect his sensitive younger brother from his treacherous boss, takes him on the road, only to find endless moral complications and divided loyalties, all of which culminate in a chance to make the supreme sacrifice. The climactic fight, filmed through a battery of sliding doors, offers all the aesthetic brilliance you'd desire, but the film's real strength lies in its depiction of a cathartic confrontation with destiny. AP

Onegin

(1998, GB/US, 106 min)
d Martha Fiennes. *p* Ileen Maisel, Simon Bosanquet. *sc* Peter Ettedgui, Michael Ignatieff. *ph* Remi Adefarasin. *ed* Jim Clark. *pd* Jim Clay. *m* Magnus Fiennes. *cast* Ralph Fiennes, Liv Tyler, Toby Stephens, Lena Headey, Martin Donovan, Alun Armstrong, Harriet Walter, Irene Worth, Francesca Annis.

●A family affair for the Fiennes clan. Ralph serves as producer as well as playing the tragic hero in this handsome and moving, if finally, enigmatic, version of Pushkin's great verse novel; his sister quite assuredly makes her directorial debut; and Magnus Fiennes composed the score. Languorous Evgeny Onegin is first spotted in the St Petersburg salons of the 1820s barely hiding his distaste for his foppish, dissolute fellows, before the inheritance of a country estate brings him into contact with the invigorating poet Lensky (Stephens), his fiancée and her pretty sister Tatyana (Tyler). That Tatyana falls for this elegant paragon of non-commitment will have dramatic consequences for all three. Shot partly in Russia, this is quality costume drama with a difference. Adapting Pushkin demands sustaining a slow agonising burn, finding a visual correlative for the inflections, the subtlest of cruel ironies, much of which must be read in the face, demeanour and diction of Onegin. Ralph suffers and disdains (himself) with authority, but his efforts to mute stuffed-shirt romanticism merely draw attention to it. The film suffers from some lapses of emotional tension, some over-emphatically edited contrasts and unnecessary effects. But, even if grand pathos isn't achieved, Martha Fiennes makes a brave and welcome stab at it. WH

One Good Cop

(1991, US, 105 min)
d Heywood Gould. *p* Laurence Mark. *sc* Heywood Gould. *ph* Ralf D Bode. *ed* Richard Marks. *ad* Sandy Veneziano. *m* David Foster, William Ross. *cast* Michael Keaton, Rene Russo, Anthony LaPaglia, Kevin Conway, Rachel Ticotin, Tony Plana, Benjamin Bratt, Charlayne Woodard.

●Out of the Batsuit, Keaton has run up and down the register, playing a drug addict (*Clean and Sober*), succumbing to a fatal illness (*My Life*), or Relating to Children, which he does in a big way here as a caring NYC police officer. When his partner's killed in the line of duty, Keaton adopts his offspring. Still time, though, to track down the bad guys in this bland, uninvolving thriller, one of those films that seems to be speaking to two mutually exclusive audiences: the junior schmaltz crowd and cop movie completists. Straight to video in Britain. TJ

One Hamlet Less (Un Amleto di Meno)

(1973, It, 65 min)
d Carmelo Bene. *p* Anna Maria Papi. *sc* Carmelo Bene. *ph* Mario Masini. *ed* Mauro Contini. *ad/m* Carmelo Bene. *cast* Carmelo Bene, Lydia Mancinelli, Alfiero Vincenti, Luigi Mezzanotte, Franco Leo, Pippo Tuminelli, Sergio Di Giulio, Isabella Russo.

●A parody of Shakespeare with Hamlet as a frustrated playwright, Polonius as a bumbling Freudian psychologist, Ophelia and Gertrude as half-naked fantasy figures. Carmelo Bene's film (derived from one of Jules Laforgue's *Moralités Légendaires*) begins with some striking visual ideas – pure white backdrops, outlandishly overblown and opulent costumes – and then proceeds to repeat these motifs to the point of monotony and way beyond. JR

One Heavenly Night

(1931, US, 82 min, b/w)
d George Fitzmaurice. *sc* Sidney Howard. *ph* George Barnes, Gregg Toland. *ed* Stuart Heisler. *ad* Richard Day. *songs* Nacio Herb Brown, Bruno Granichstaedten, Edward Elisen, Clifford Grey. *cast* Evelyn Laye, John Boles, Leon Errol, Lilyan Tashman, Hugh Cameron, Henry Kolker, Marion Lord.

●Hopes for this Goldwyn musical are raised by a stylish opening in which Tashman – as Fritzi, toast of Budapest night life – belts out her number, then gleefully provokes a riot among her admirers. Alas, she is rusticated by the police for scandalous behaviour; and Laye, making her Hollywood debut as a flower-seller with dreams of stardom, is persuaded to serve Fritzi's stint of rustic exile while she holes up with her current lover. Some very sub-Stroheim sex-play ensues as Count Mirko (Boles), the country magistrate responsible for Fritzi's good behaviour, confidently expects to bed the pseudo-Fritzi, while the dismayed innocent sets a romantic snare intended to leave him panting with frustration. True love naturally brings matrimonial bliss, and boredom for the viewer. The songs are standard operetta stuff, moonily sung; there are acres of unfunny comedy for Errol and Cameron (in servant/confidant roles); but the camerawork (George Barnes and Gregg Toland) is gorgeous. TM

One Hour With You

(1932, US, 80 min, b/w)
d Ernst Lubitsch, George Cukor. *sc* Samson Raphaelson. *ph* Victor Milner. *ed* William Shea. *ad* Hans Dreier. *m* Richard Whiting, Oscar Straus. *cast* Maurice Chevalier, Jeanette MacDonald, Genevieve Tobin, Roland Young, Charlie Ruggles, George Barbier, Josephine Dunn.

●Directed first by Cukor under Lubitsch's supervision, and then largely re-shot by the latter, this is in many ways a typical piece of sophisticated, smug fluff from Lubitsch and his regular screenwriter Samuel Raphaelson. A remake of the 1924 *The Marriage Circle*, it presents Chevalier as a philandering Paris doctor, flaunting his thick-accented charm at MacDonald. Songs, verse, snappy dialogue, and asides to the audience make it likeable and clever. But Cukor, interviewed about the film's authorship, put his finger on its problem: 'It's really a Lubitsch picture, and if you think you can detect what I did in it, you're imagining things. Lubitsch's pictures were brilliant, even if they lacked feeling. He didn't want his comedies to have any feeling. Now, my idea of comedy is that they should always touch you unexpectedly.' GA

One Hundred and One Dalmatians

(1960, US, 79 min)
d Wolfgang Reitherman, Hamilton Luske, Clyde Geronimi. *sc* Bill Peet. *ed* Donald Halliday, Roy M Brewer Jr. *pd* Ken Anderson. *m* George Bruns. *songs* Mel

Leven. *cast* voices: Rod Taylor, J Pat O'Malley, Betty Lou Gerson, Martha Wentworth, Ben Wright,Cate Bauer.

●One hundred and one little bundles of fun; enormous quantities of bog-roll spring to mind. This is Disney at his finest, and not until *The Prisoner* was there a work of such intense numerological significance. Sure it's wonderful to see spots on the screen, but why so many spots and why 101 Dalmatians? This version of Dodie Smith's dognapping classic has a voice-over by Pongo the Dog to keep a tight lead on the activities of his cute human pets, the screechingly evil Cruella de Vil and her voguishly Cockney minions, Jasper and Horace. Beyond this sublimely simple alienation effect, deeper thematic concerns are run with theological significance: when to start a litter, the slaughter of animals for fur coats, the deadly opiate of TV commercials, and even a pre-echo of the cable debate (the 'twilight bark') turn and re-turn to the conclusion that we're all in some sense 'spotted', if not actually Dalmatians. There is probably not enough violence for it to be a profoundly moral film, but it is brilliant entertainment none the less. RP

101 Dalmatians

(1996, US, 103 min)
d Stephen Herek. *p* John Hughes, Ricardo Mestres. *sc* John Hughes. *ph* Adrian Biddle. *ed* Trudy Ship, Larry Bock. *pd* Assheton Gorton. *m* Michael Kamen. *cast* Glenn Close, Jeff Daniels, Joely Richardson, Joan Plowright, Hugh Laurie, Mark Williams, John Shrapnel, Tim McInnerny, Hugh Fraser.

●Live-action remake of Disney's enduring classic scripted by John Hughes – and the final act is pretty much a retread of *Home Alone*. Pongo starts well, turning on the shower for his 'pet' human (Daniels) and engineering his meeting with an attractive member of the opposite sex (Richardson), but soon abandons any pretence of being an intelligent protagonist. The film has two main things going for it: Glenn, and Close, whose outlandish, cartoonish, monstrously coiffed performance as Cruella gives it life and breath. Plaudits are also due to McInnerny's sadly underused flunky, a breathtaking dalmatian-powered bike chase around London, and the first-rate costume designs. Delightfully dotty in places, but mostly patchy. DW

102 Dalmatians

(2000, US, 100 min)
d Kevin Lima. *p* Edward S Feldman. *sc* Kristen Buckley, Brian Regan, Bob Tzudiker, Noni White. *ph* Adrian Biddle. *ed* Gregory Perler. *pd* Assheton Gorton. *m* David Newman. *cast* Glenn Close, Ioan Gruffudd, Alice Evans,Tim McInnerny, Ian Richardson, Gérard Depardieu, Jim Carter, Timothy West.

●Stephen Herek's live-action remake of the Disney animated classic had bite and dash. The four writers of this sequel haven't, however, struck many new notes. With her outrageous coiffure and array of polka dot creations, Close is again good value as the rehabilitated, if not reprogrammed, Dalmatian furcoat collector, buying her way into Gruffudd's ramshackle London dog sanctuary. But the chimes of Big Ben cause a relapse. Gruffudd's girlfriend, probation officer Evans, is a very modern Miss; and with the addition of Depardieu's mad, bad couturier, Le Pelt, the film feels only tokenistically updated, and all the more absurd for it. Given that pacing and plotting are so misconceived – one frenetic scene follows another – you concentrate on the endless cute puppies. The limitless patience of the Evans and Gruffudd characters with the messy pooches makes you want to bark out loud. There's a lively sequence featuring a balloon rescue in London Zoo, good stunts, and designer Gorton pulls out all the stops for the finale inside the creaking machinery of an ancient Parisian cake factory, but the romance and humour are really quite perfunctory. WH

101 Reykjavík

(2000, Ice/Den/Nor/Fr/Ger, 88 min)
d Baltasar Kormákur. *p* Ingvar H Thórdarson, Baltasar Kormákur. *sc* Baltasar Kormákur. *ph* Peter Steuger. *ed* Sigvaldi J Kárason, Skule Eriksen, Steingrímur Karlsson. *ad* Árni Páll Jóhannsson. *m* Damon Albarn, Einar Örn Benediktsson. *cast* Victoria Abril, Hilmir Snær Gudnason, Hanna María Karlsdóttir, Thrúdur Vilhjalmsdóttir, Baltasar Kormákur, Ólafur Darri Ólafsson, Thröstur Leó Gunnarsson.

●Actor Baltasar Kormákur's first feature as director is an Icelandic slacker comedy with a quirky, lackadaisical, thrown-together feel. The most arresting image is of young Hlynur (Gudnason) prone on a mountain top, cigarette in mouth, as the snow settles to give him a light crust; not a picture of twenty-something ennui you'd turn up in Austin, Texas, then. Hlynur's anti-charisma (prescription specs, pudding-basin haircut) works for him – or maybe it's just lack of competition. Still living with his mother, he's already looking forward to drawing a pension, and struggles only to fend off the girls. Then his mother invites her Spanish flamenco teacher to stay over Christmas. Lola (Abril) is a sexy free spirit whose lesbian inclinations don't preclude a drunken fuck with Hlynur on New Year's. Only later does he realise that he's cheated on his mother. Worse, Lola may be pregnant with both his brother and his de facto son. Above and beyond his anti-hero's 'do nothing' vibe, Kormákur entertains some hazy notions about male redundancy, and how that might suit men more than they like to admit. The film's in danger of disappearing up its own inertia, but Abril's feisty, and you have to say it's a doozy of a hole Hlynur digs for himself. TCh

100 Days Before the Command (Sto Dnei Do Prikaza...)

(1990, Rus, 68 min)
d Khusein Erkenov. *sc* Iurii Poliakov, Vladimir Kholodov. *ph* Vladimir Menshikov. *ed* Vladimir Portnov. *ad* Sergei Filenko, Sergei Serebriannikov. *m* JS Bach. *cast* Vladimir Zamanskii, Armen Dzhigarkhanian, Elena Kondulainen, Aleksandr Chislov, Oleg Vasilikov, Roman Grekov.

●Shot in 1990, but not seen outside Russia until the director took a print to the 1994 Berlin Film Festival, this expressive anti-militarist collage must have come as quite a shock to the Gorky studio which funded it and to the local army barracks which offered manpower and facilities. Both were apparently duped by a fake script, concealing the film's swingeing assault on the brutality, dehumanisation and outright despair that was the ordinary Russian soldier's lot. The film's non-linear narrative encompasses a wider field of concern, however, than the strictly political. While one might rank director Erkenov's work beside that of such mavericks as Tarkovsky and Paradjanov, the Uzbeki-born director is more directly confrontational in using the Russian realist tradition to his own ends, revealing harsh poetic truths about a country whose troops have served in the Afghan war and a recent series of internal conflicts. If the obfuscatory construction makes it hard-going at times, the film has a burning commitment and a forthright individuality that's hard not to admire. Recommended to those with a strong constitution. TJ

One Hundred Men and a Girl

(1937, US, 84 min, b/w)
d Henry Koster. *p* Joe Pasternak, Charles Rogers. *sc* Bruce Manning, Charles Kenyon, James Mulhauser, Hans Kraly. *ph* Joseph Valentine. *ed* Bernard W Burton. *pd* John W Harkrider. *m* Frederick Hollander. *cast* Deanna Durbin, Leopold Stokowski, Adolphe Menjou, Eugene Pallette, Mischa Auer, Alice Brady, Billy Gilbert, Alma Kruger, Jameson Thomas.

●Tugging at conductor Stokowski's sleeve a few years before the Mickey Mouse of *Fantasia* pulled the same trick, Universal teen-star Durbin here had the object of getting him to lead her orchestra of unemployed musician friends, including papa Menjou, in a programme of suitably cloying classics. By happy circumstance, those friends happen to comprise the Philadelphia Symphony Orchestra. PT

100 Years of Polish Cinema (100 Lat w Kinie)

(1996, Pol, 61 min)
d Pawel Lozinski. *p* Ryszard Strasewski. *sc* Kryzysztof Kieslowski. *ph* Arthur Reinhart. *ed* Dorota Wardeszkiewicz.

●Conceived by Kieslowski and executed by his assistant on *Three Colours: White*, this is the only film in the British Film Institute's 'Century of Cinema' series which focuses on the viewer rather than the cinéaste: film-goers of all ages are invited to recall the Polish movies which have meant most to them. The conjunction of their words and their favourite images not only brings the film clips to life but also says a lot about the fundamental appeal of cinema itself. Highly engaging throughout, it becomes immoderately moving when two of the interviewees explain how Kieslowski films changed their lives. TR

One in a Million

(1937, US, 95 min, b/w)
d Sidney Lanfield. *p* Raymond Griffith. *sc* Leonard Praskins, Mark Kelly. *ph* Edward Cronjager. *ed* Robert Simpsons. *songs* Sidney Mitchell, Lew Pollack. *cast* Sonja Henie, Adolphe Menjou, Don Ameche, Ned Sparks, Jean Hersholt, the Ritz Brothers, Borrah Minevitch, Arline Judge.

●Sonja Henie figure skates to victory for her Swiss papa (Hersholt) at the 1936 Garmisch Winter Olympics (only one uniformed German soldier in sight). At the 1908 Games father was stripped of *his* title for naively taking money for a new pair of skates. The Norwegian world champion skater made her unaffected US debut for Fox in this musical concoction enlivened by Ned Sparks' lugubrious asides and a robust showstopper by Borrah Minevitch and his Harmonica Rascals. JPy

One Life Stand

(2000, GB, 118 min, b/w)
d/p/sc/ph/ed May Miles Thomas. *pd* Ewen Duncan. *cast* Gary Lewis, Maureen Carr, John Kielty, Archie Lal, Alyson Orr, Rohanna Law, Ros McCue.

●This micro-budget Scottish drama is allegedly Britain's first DV feature. Thomas concentrates her unflinching gaze on Trise, the single mother of an 18-year-old son living on the poverty line in Glasgow. While John Paul gets a job as a 'model' (read: male escort), his mam starts working in a call centre reading tarot cards down the phone. Befriending young colleague Justine, Trise deludes herself that she might be a suitable girlfriend for her lad. The cards don't hold up any such hope. Slightly overlong, the film nevertheless maintains a grim and memorable composure, and Thomas is evidently a talent to watch. TCh

One Lost Year (Un Año Perdido)

(1993, Mex, 100 min)
d Gerardo Lara. *p* Dulce Kuri. *sc* Patricio Ruffo. *ph* Luis Manuel Serrano. *cast* Vanessa Bauche, Tiaré Scanda, Marco Muñoz, Ada Carrasco.

●Sensitive if somewhat drawn-out account of the sentimental education of a 16-year-old girl from a Mexican village, who, against the wishes of father and childhood sweetheart, goes to high school in the city of Toluca in 1976. Strong on her friendship with another girl, and fine, if predictable, on her experiences with various macho types, the film is weakest in its pretension towards wider social comment. GA

One Man Mutiny

see Court-Martial of Billy Mitchell, The

One Man's War (La Guerre d'un Seul Homme)

(1981, Fr/WGer, 109 min, b/w)
d Edgardo Cozarinsky. *p* Jean-Marc Henchoz. *sc* Edgardo Cozarinsky. *ed* Christine Aya, Véronique Auricoste. *m* ('Aryan') Hans Pfitzner, Richard Strauss, ('Degenerate') Arnold Schoenberg, Franz Schreker. *narrators* (German text) Peter Chatel, (Jünger's voice) Niels Arestrup.

●A representation of Occupied France through the diaries of Ernst Jünger, German military commandant in Paris, *One Man's War* brings World War II into focus not with the lying lens of the deadpan documentary, but through a series of highly original techniques which gain all the more brilliance by their obliqueness. The diaries are not accompanied by pictures representing the events Jünger describes, but by contemporary newsreels, and by painstakingly chosen music which challenges words, images and their assumptions. The effect is to produce a moving, gripping document which raises profound questions about the war, and indeed all wars: the interaction of individuals and events; the definitions of propaganda and collaboration; and the weakness of ideologies in the face of gigantic forces equipped with their own superhuman logic. Jünger's beliefs, a strange mix of futurism and Junker chivalry, start by imposing a bizarre, philosophical unity on the film, but they end in dissolution. A genuine *tour de force*. DRo

One Million Years B.C.

(1966, GB, 100 min)
d Don Chaffey. *p/sc* Michael Carreras. *ph* Wilkie Cooper. *ed* Tom Simpson. *ad* Robert Jones. *m* Mario Nascimbene. *cast* John Richardson, Raquel Welch, Percy Herbert, Robert Brown, Martine Beswick, Jean Wladon, Lisa Thomas, Malya Nappi, William Lyon Brown.

●A loose remake of the 1940 special effects extravaganza with Victor Mature, Hammer's version of the life and times of cavemen and women again cheerfully neglects a few million years of evolution and has our antecedents living side by side with the brontosauri. There's a simple story about lovers from different tribes, and Welch grunts beautifully clad only in a few bits of bunny fur, but the real stars are Ray Harryhausen's superbly animated dinosaurs. It was Hammer's biggest box-office hit and inaugurated a cycle, but the more cheaply made sequels were no match for the ferocious reptile fights on display here. DT

One Minute to Zero

(1952, US, 106 min, b/w)
d Tay Garnett. *p* Edmund Grainger. *sc* Milton Krims, William Wister Haines. *ph* William Snyder. *ed* Sherman Todd. *ad* Albert S D'Agostino, Jack Okey. *m* C Bakaleinikoff. *cast* Robert Mitchum, Ann Blyth, William Talman, Richard Egan, Charles McGraw, Margaret Sheridan, Eduard Franz.

●RKO didn't waste much time in getting this Korean War drama on screen, and the documentary footage used to fill in the background is far more striking than anything the scriptwriters could come up with. Mitchum's strictly on autopilot as the US colonel charged with evacuating all American citizens from Korea, which means persuading comely UN official Blyth that she has to go too. The blend of action and romance never amounts to much. TJ

One More Kiss

(1999, GB, 102 min)
d Vadim Jean. *p* Vadim Jean, Paul Brooks. *sc* Suzie Halewood. *ph* Mike Fox. *ed* Joe McNally. *pd* Simon Hicks. *m* David A Hughes, John Murphy. *cast* Gerard Butler, James Cosmo, Valerie Edmond, Valerie Gogan, Carl Proctor, Danny Nussbaum, Dilys Miller.

●Sam (Butler) and Charlotte (Grogan) seem blissfully happy, operating a smart restaurant in Berwick upon Tweed. Then Sam's old girlfriend, Sarah (Esmond), returns from her high flying career in the States and drops a bombshell: she has inoperable cancer, and a favour to ask – she wants to spend her last months in the company of the only man she ever loved. Charlotte isn't amused. Sam is stunned, flattered, and quite keen to have it both ways. Admittedly, the prospect of watching a terminal disease movie by Vadim Jean sounds dicey, but don't be too hasty; this is a very decent effort, and Jean's directorial authority grows every time at the crease. With her first feature script, Suzie Halewood has come up with a juicy emotional dilemma, and offsets the inevitable cancer movie clichés with acute, witty dialogue. Grogan and Esmond especially relish their dynamic, rounded characters, though Sam seems too painfully wishy washy for either. The film certainly doesn't avoid all the pitfalls – there's blatant prettification going on, and some of the development is a bit sketchy – but given the degree to which the film wears its heart on its sleeve, it's surprising how often it hits a raw nerve. TCh

One More River (aka Over the River)

(1934, US, 90 min, b/w)
d James Whale. *p* Carl Laemmle Jr. *sc* RC Sherriff. *ph* John Mescall. *ed* Ted Kent. *ad* Charles D Hall. *m* W Franke Harling. *cast* Diana Wynyard, Colin Clive, Frank Lawton, Mrs Patrick Campbell, Jane Wyatt, Reginald Denny, C Aubrey Smith, Lionel Atwill.

●A glowing example of how to turn English drawing-rooms and stiff upper lips into the stuff of tragedy, adapted by RC Sherriff from the last volume in Galsworthy's *Forsyte Saga* (which made a forceful plea for a change in the divorce laws). Wynyard and Lawton are perfect as the unhappily married lady and the nice young man kept apart by the barriers of convention, and finding their love for each other cruelly put through the wringer when (though blameless) they are dragged through the mire by her odious husband (Clive). It's not unlike *Brief Encounter*, raised a couple of rungs in the social ladder to the milieu of noblesse oblige and the proper thing, pride, privilege and Tory victories at the polls; but what astonishes is the skill and sensitivity with which Whale manages to suggest the still waters of passion slowly coming to the boil under the surface. A polished, elegant gem of a movie. TM

One More Time

(1969, GB, 93 min)
d Jerry Lewis. *p* Milton Ebbins. *sc* Michael Pertwee. *ph* Ernest Steward. *ed* Bill Butler. *pd* Jack Stevens. *m* Les Reed. *cast* Sammy Davis Jr, Peter Lawford, Maggie Wright, Leslie Sands, John Wood, Sydney Arnold, Esther Anderson, Moultrie Kelsall.

●A film to leave egg on the faces of Jerry Lewis' staunchest admirers is this London-set Rat Pack farce in which the man himself doesn't appear. A sequel to Richard Donner's equally inept *Salt and Pepper*, it shifts Davis and Lawford from Soho clubland into the criminal environs of the landed gentry when Lawford undertakes the impersonation of his late, lorded twin brother. Absolutely appalling. PT

One Night at McCool's

(2001, US, 92 min)
d Harald Zwart. *p* Michael Dougals, Allison Lyon Segan. *sc* Stan Seidel. *ph* Karl Walter Lindenlaub. *ed* Bruce Cannon. *pd* Jon Gary Steele. *m* Marc Shaiman. *cast* Liv Tyler, Matt Dillon, John Goodman, Paul Reiser, Michael Douglas, Reba McEntire, Andrew Silverstein, Mary Jo Smith, Richard Jenkins.

●Randy (Dillon) is minding the bar and his own business, when in comes Jewel (Tyler), the sort of vamp he could only dream about. She's so fast he barely has time to think – so when the post-coital conversation turns into a murder inquiry, Randy finds himself taking the rap for shooting Jewel's ex in self-defence. Well, that's *his* perspective. Police detective Dehling (Goodman) sees only an abused, sensitive young woman terrified to speak in front of a self-confessed killer, a woman who reminds him uncannily of his late, lamented wife, God rest her soul. Then there's Carl (Reiser), Randy's cousin, a lawyer so in love with himself he can only assume Jewel loves him too. No wonder hired hitman Burmeister (Douglas) has such trouble making head or tail of it. 'A Harald Zwart Film', no less, this imagines itself much smarter, sexier and funnier than it really is. Its gimmick is an overlapping story structure courtesy of three male narrators, but it's a tiresome and pointless conceit, given that these guys only ever have one thing on their mind. At least the film's sexism cuts both ways. As the object of all this desire, poor Liv Tyler is forced to dress like a tart, speak in a breathless Marilyn lisp, and care about nothing but sex and home furnishings – not necessarily in that order. TCh

One Night Stand

(1997, US, 103 min)
d Mike Figgis. *p* Mike Figgis, Annie Stewart, Ben Myron. *sc* Mike Figgis. *ph* Declan Quinn. *ed* John Smith. *pd* Waldemar Kalinowski. *m* Mike Figgis. *cast* Wesley Snipes, Nastassja Kinski, Kyle MacLachlan, Ming-na Wen, Robert Downey Jr, Amanda Donohoe, John Ratzenberger.

●On a trip to New York, commercials director Snipes bumps into and spends the night with UN employee Kinski. Thus is set in train a series of feelings, emotions and events driven by a logic of their own. Figgis has refashioned a bonkfest outline by Joe Eszterhas into a script focused evenly on the experience and motivations of its five main characters. Snipes, cast against type, is notable as a decent guy, happily married with two kids, for whom the affair constitutes a trigger for a quiet reassessment of both his marriage and his lost '60s idealism. Downey is affecting as the gay choreographer, still idealistic and still suffering for his art (AIDS, inevitably), with whom Snipes rekindles a friendship; and Kinski enlivens all her scenes. WH

One of Our Aircraft Is Missing

(1942, GB, 106 min, b/w)
d/p/sc Michael Powell, Emeric Pressburger. *ph* Ronald Neame, Robert Krasker. *ed* David Lean. *ad* David Rawnsley. *cast* Godfrey Tearle, Eric Portman, Hugh Williams, Bernard Miles, Hugh Burden, Googie Withers, Pamela Brown, Emrys Jones, Robert Helpmann, Peter Ustinov.

●Though not top-notch Powell & Pressburger, an ambitious low-key wartime thriller that totally transcends any propaganda considerations, thanks to sharp characterisation and imaginative scripting. The crew of a British bomber sent out on a mission to Europe (by air controller Powell, making a symbolically revealing guest appearance) are forced to bale out and make their way back overland through the Low Countries. No simple task, given that – as so often in Powell's movies – the enemy is not merely external but also internal: tensions mount among the Brits, while distrust abounds in their dealings with apparently sympathetic Dutchmen. Rather like *49th Parallel* without the epic sweep, an impressively directed and beautifully performed piece of work. GA

One of Our Dinosaurs Is Missing

(1975, US, 94 min)
d Robert Stevenson. *p/sc* Bill Walsh. *ph* Paul Beeson. *ed* Peter Boita. *ad* Michael Stringer. *m* Ron Goodwin. *cast* Peter Ustinov, Helen Hayes, Clive Revill, Derek Nimmo, Joan Sims, Andrew Dove, Max Harris, Bernard Bresslaw, Roy Kinnear, Joss Ackland, John Laurie, Max Wall.

●A delight: old pro Stevenson invests a sketchy story with the same flair for mysterious smoky visuals he brought to the neglected *Bedknobs and Broomsticks* and to *Jane Eyre* twenty-seven years earlier. This is a further Disney return to the picturesque England of fog, milords and crimped nannies, with every foreigner a villain – it's the Chinese this time, led by Peter Ustinov, who turns a straightforward part into an acting showcase. The English cast, too, bats right down in a way happily reminiscent of Ealing comedy. Given all these assets, the plot hardly matters. AN

One of Those Things (Haendeligt Uheld)

(1970, Den, 88 min)
d/p Erik Balling. *sc* Erik Balling, Anders Bodelsen. *ph* Jørgen Skov, Claus Loof. *ed* Ole Steen Nielsen, Robert Lovett. *ad* Henning Bahs. *m* Bent Fabricius-Bjerre. *cast* Roy Dotrice, Judy Geeson, Zena Walker, Frederick Jaeger, Ann Firbank, Geoffrey Chater, Yvette Dotrice.

●Watchable Danish thriller, shot in English for the international market, has Dotrice as a car company exec who tries to conceal that he ran over and killed a cyclist. Geeson is the minx who uses her knowledge of the incident to worm her way into a job and threaten his marriage, but are her motives sexual, or financial. or mere perversity? The complications are well worked out, and there's even a trip to Japan to test a new car and make love on the train from Tokyo to Fujiyama. TJ

One of Us (Echad Mi'Shelanu)

(1989, Isr, 110 min)
d Uri Barbash. *p* Zvi Spielman, Shlomo Mograbi. *sc* Benny Barbash. *ph* Amnon Salomon. *ed* Tova Asher. *ad* Etyan Levi. *m* Ilan Virtzberg. *cast* Sharon Alexander, Alon Aboutboul, Dahlia Shimko, Dan Toren, Arnon Tzadok, Eli Yatzpan.

●Conflicting loyalties come to the boil in this passionately felt Israeli drama when military policeman Alexander has to investigate his former pals in an elite paratroop unit, accused of murdering the Arab who blew up one of their comrades. The treatment is well-judged, pointed but never hectoringly didactic, in a screenplay by the director's brother Benny Barbash, a soldier in the Yom Kippur War, who later turned peace activist and playwright. TJ

One on One

(1977, US, 97 min)
d Lamont Johnson. *p* Marty Hornstein. *sc* Robby Benson, Jerry Segal. *ph* Donald M Morgan. *ed* Robbe Roberts. *ad* Sherman Loudermilk. *songs* Charles Fox, Paul Williams.

cast Robby Benson, Annette O'Toole, GD Spradlin, Gail Strickland, Melanie Griffith, James G Richardson, Hector Morales, Cory Faucher, Lamont Johnson.

● Attractive if soft-centred basketball story, a sort of junior *Rocky*. High-school star Benson is wooed with a sports car into taking an athletics scholarship, finds himself chased by the randy college secretary, falls hopelessly for his teacher, is persecuted by a tyrannical coach, almost flunks, resolves to make the team, does so, gets the (right) girl, wins the match, then tells the coach where to stick his scholarship. The most interesting scene involves Lamont Johnson himself, as the mysterious alumnus who sponsors Benson, and who stands for the corrupt recruiting dwelt on at greater length in the original script (written by Benson and his father) which caused two universities to forbid filming on their premises. AN

One Plus One (aka Sympathy for the Devil)

(1968, GB, 99 min)
d Jean-Luc Godard. *p* Michael Pearson, Ian Quarrier. *sc* Jean-Luc Godard. *ph* Anthony B Richmond. *ed* Kenneth F Rowles. *m* The Rolling Stones. *cast* The Rolling Stones, Anne Wiazemsky, Iain Quarrier, Frankie Dymon Jr, Danny Daniels, Illarrio Pedro, Françoise Pascal, Joanna David.

● Like *Le Gai Savoir*, though more extreme in its abandonment of narrative forms, one of Godard's attempts to 'start again at zero'. Originally conceived literally as one plus one: a theme of construction (the Rolling Stones rehearsing 'Sympathy for the Devil'), and one of destruction (the suicide of a white revolutionary when her boyfriend deserts to Black Power). Endless production problems and disgruntlement on Godard's part turned it into a random collage which the viewer is supposed to 'edit' himself. A daunting task, but the images are often riveting. In the version called 'Sympathy for the Devil', producer Iain Quarrier tacked the completed recording of the Stones' number on to the end of the film (and in an incident at the 1968 London Film Festival that has become legend, was assaulted by an infuriated Godard for his pains). TM

1 + 1 = 3

(1979, WGer, 85 min)
d/sc Heidi Genée. *p* Peter Genée. *ph* Gernot Roll. *ed* Helga Beyer. *ad* Peter Grenz. *m* Andreas Köbner. *cast* Adelheit Arndt, Dominik Graf, Christoph Quest, Helga Storck, Dietrich Leiding, Charlotte Witthauer, Kelle Riedl, Hark Bohm.

● A modestly engaging, low-key feminist movie about an unmarried actress in Munich who becomes pregnant but decides against marrying the child's father, and eventually moves in with a more agreeable man she meets on a winter sports holiday. In the end she determines to live and raise her child alone, a decision which, considering the men in the movie, seems eminently reasonable. Don't get the impression that this movie has it in for men; it's much harder on the parental generation, and very sympathetic to kids who find themselves unwitting victims of middle class domestic unrest. Heidi Genée worked as an editor with the first wave of new German directors (Kluge, Sinkel), and has a keen eye for the absurdities of domestic life as well as a good ear for comic lines. MA

One PM

(1969, US, 90 min)
d/sc DA Pennebaker. *ph* Richard Leacock, DA Pennebaker. *ed* DA Pennebaker. *cast* Jean-Luc Godard, Richard Leacock, Eldridge Cleaver, Tom Hayden, Jefferson Airplane, LeRoi Jones, Tom Luddy, Paula Madder, Rip Torn, Anne Wiazemsky.

● In 1968, Godard began work on a film in America (*One AM* or *One American Movie*) dealing with aspects of resistance and revolution. Dissatisfied with what he had shot, he abandoned the project. Pennebaker here assembles the Godard footage, together with his own coverage of Godard at work (*One PM* standing for either *One Parallel Movie* or *One Pennebaker Movie*). Although it may be dubious to show stuff that Godard had rejected, the film does manage to convey how he got his results. You can draw your own conclusions about his approach and why he abandoned the film.

On Equal Terms (Kosh Ba Kosh)

(1993, Tajikistan/Switz/Jap, 98 min)
d Bakhtiar Khudojnazarov. *p* Bakhtiar Khudojnazarov, Christa Saredi. *sc* Bakhtiar Khudojnazarov. *ph* Georgy Dzalaiev. *ed* Bakhtiar Khudojnazarov. *ad* Negmat Jouraiev. *m* Achmad Bakaev. *cast* Paulina Galvez, Daler Madjidav, Alisher Kasimov.

● Planned as a not-quite-love story but adapted to take account of the Tajik civil war which erupted during production, Khudojnazarov's second feature is a much more assertive and confident film than *Brothers*. The setting is Dushanbe, capital of Tajikistan. Feckless dreamer Daler (Madjidav), who operates an almost redundant cable-car system, impulsively carries off Mira (Spanish actress Galvez) when she is used as a pawn in a dispute over a gambling debt between her loser father and another man. Their relationship is abrasive until Mira overhears Daler fighting for her honour, but the local tradition of treating women as men's chattels is finally too much for her. The film's hard-edged romanticism is crystallised in its wonderful poetic imagery – most especially the scenes in, on and hanging from the cable-car. TR

One Rainy Afternoon

(1936, US, 79 min, b/w)
d Rowland V Lee. *sc* Stephen Morehouse Avery, Maurice Hanline. *ph* Peverell Marley. *ed* Margaret Clancy. *ad* Richard Day. *m* Ralph Irwin*cast* Francis Lederer, Ida Lupino, Hugh Herbert, Mischa Auer, Erik Rhodes, Roland Young, Joseph Cawthorn.

● Lederer causes consternation when he arrives in a cinema after the show has started, sits in the wrong seat, and kisses Lupino (very much the wrong girl) who isn't at all happy about it. That's the set-up in this bubble-headed piece of tosh (from a script by Emeric Pressburger and René Pujol, *Monsieur Sans-Gêne*, directed by Karl Anton, 1935) which needed a higher voltage cast than the one on offer to charm the viewer in the manner intended. Quite sweet though. TJ

One Sings, the Other Doesn't (L'Une Chante, l'Autre Pas)

(1976, Fr/Bel/Cur, 120 min)
d/sc Agnès Varda. *ph* Charlie van Damme. *ed* Joële van Effenterre. *ad* Frankie Diago, (Iran) Marguerite Yazdanparazt. *m* François Wertheimer. *songs* Agnès Varda. *cast* Valérie Mairesse, Thérèse Liotard, Gisèle Halimi, Ali Raffi, Jean-Pierre Pellegrin, Mona Mairesse, Francis Lemaire, Marion Hänsel.

● Varda's film about the changing but deep friendship between two women from 1962 to 1976 is also the story of the transformation of their attitudes towards being women in a patriarchal culture. But two distinct elements – a stylistic approach and a sense of nostalgia – make this a very different kind of feminist film, in which reality, though present, never leaves any real scars on an essentially romantic fable. The film's ambience remains that of the '60s dream rather than the harsh reality of the '70s; but as such, it at least provides a considered escapist identification that mainstream cinema has traditionally denied women in its male-dominated fantasies. SM

One That Got Away, The

(1957, GB, 111 min, b/w)
d Roy Baker. *p* Julian Wintle. *sc* Howard Clewes. *ph* Eric Cross. *ed* Sidney Hayers. *ad* Edward Carrick. *m* Hubert Clifford. *cast* Hardy Krüger, Michael Goodliffe, Terence Alexander, Alec McCowen, Colin Gordon, Jack Gwillim, Andrew Faulds, Stratford Johns.

● Here's the seemingly authentic story of Oberleutnant Franz von Werra, shot down in 1940, author of two unsuccessful attempts to escape from England and a third, successful one from Canada. In national terms one can read this as British self-abasement (hard to imagine the Germans making *The Wooden Horse*), as self-confidence (no problem about acknowledging a resourceful enemy) or as unblushing commercialism (Rank determined to crack the German market). But the strongest impression is of an incredibly glamorous Krüger, with Dean haircut and black leather jacket, against whom the home side have fielded such dubious sexpots as McCowen and Alexander – this no doubt a token of the self-image of the British male in 1957. Worth noting that the film was regarded as piquant rather than as offensive; it's still worth watching, despite too many scenes of Krüger lurching across muddy fields and frozen rivers. A laconic end title states that von Werra was killed in action a few months after getting back to Germany. BBa

1,000 Plane Raid, The

(1968, US, 94 min)
d Boris Sagal. *p* Lewis J Rachmil. *sc* Donald S Sanford. *ph* William W Spencer. *ed* Henry Batista, Jodie Copelan. *ad* Harold Michelson. *m* Jimmie Haskell. *cast* Christopher George, Laraine Stephens, JD Cannon, Gary Marshall, Michael Evans, James Gammon, Gavin MacLeod, Henry Jaglom.

● George has the task of training up a thousand new pilots for a massed raid on a Nazi aeronautics factory in this routine WWII actioner. Along the way he begins to wonder whether saturation bombing is justified…but by that time the mission is fixed. Doubtful whether the budget actually stretched to the demands of the title. TJ

One Touch of Venus

(1948, US, 82 min, b/w)
d William A Seiter. *p* Lester Cowan. *sc* Harry Kurnitz, Frank Tashlin. *ph* Franz Planer. *ed* Otto Ludwig. *ad* Bernard Herzbrun, Emrich Nicholson. *m* Kurt Weill. *lyrics* Ogden Nash. *cast* Ava Gardner, Robert Walker, Dick Haymes, Eve Arden, Olga San Juan, Tom Conway, James Flavin, Sara Allgood.

● Despite the rude deletion of over half the score and less than ecstatic renditions of the remaining songs, a pleasantly witty adaptation of the Kurt Weill/SJ Perelman/Ogden Nash musical. The gaps are only patchily filled by zany comic business presumably supplied by Frank Tashlin as co-screenwriter; but Robert Walker, excellent as the timid store clerk in love with a statue of Venus which comes alive as the predatory Gardner (dubbed in the songs by Eileen Wilson) is backed by a sterling cast. TM

One-Trick Pony

(1980, US, 98 min)
d Robert M Young. *p* Michael Tannen. *sc* Paul Simon. *ph* Dick Bush. *ed* Edward Beyer, Barry Malkin, David Ray. *pd* David Mitchell. *m* Paul Simon. *cast* Paul Simon, Blair Brown, Rip Torn, Joan Hackett, Lou Reed, Allen Goorwitz [Allen Garfield], Mare Winningham, The Lovin' Spoonful, The B-52's, Sam and Dave, Tiny Tim.

● Shambling, self-obsessed and extremely irritating bleat of a film, written and starring Paul Simon, about how terrible it is to be a huge rock star when your personal life is falling apart. Plenty of muso spotting to be done. TJ

One True Thing

(1998, US, 127 min)
d Carl Franklin. *p* Harry Ufland, Jesse Beaton. *sc* Karen Croner. *ph* Declan Quinn. *ed* Carole Kravetz. *pd* Paul Peters. *m* Cliff Edelman. *cast* Meryl Streep, Renée Zellweger, William Hurt, Tom Everett Scott, Lauren Graham, Nicky Katt.

● Not quite a weepy despite its drippy score and feel-good ending, this adaptation of Anna Quindlen's novel is less about bereavement than the preliminaries thereto. Its theme is the sheer inconvenience which a dying family member, no matter how loved, represents. When it becomes clear that Mother (Streep) has terminal cancer, her son seems to fade from the scene, her college professor husband clings stubbornly to his routine, and it's left to the daughter (Zellweger) to put her life on hold for the duration. The script shifts audience sympathies about quite adroitly, though it's a pity all the men had to be such humbugs. Franklin's lyrical evocation of small town life and Streep's lavishly mannered performance disrupt the project in not uninteresting ways. BBa

One, Two, Three

(1961, US/WGer, 115 min, b/w)
d/p Billy Wilder. *sc* Billy Wilder, IAL Diamond. *ph* Daniel Fapp. *ed* Daniel Mandell. *ad* Alex Trauner. *m* André Previn. *cast* James Cagney, Horst Buchholz, Pamela Tiffin, Arlene Francis, Lilo Pulver, Howard St John, Hanns Lothar, Leon Askin, Red Buttons.

●Coarse Cold War satire, structured largely as farce, with Cagney as the aggressive Coca-Cola executive in West Berlin, trying desperately to win advancement by selling the beverage to Russia, and simultaneously required to prevent his boss from discovering that the latter's bird-brained daughter has married a rabid Commie from East Berlin. Marvellous one-liners, of course, and Cagney, spitting out his lines with machine-gun rapidity in his final film until his belated appearance in 'Ragtime', is superb (and superbly backed by a fine cast). But the targets of Wilder's satire – go-getting, up-to-the-minute, consumer America versus the poverty and outdatedness of Communist culture – are rather too obvious. GA

1, 2, 3, Sun

see Un Deux Trois Soleil

One Way or Another (De Cierta Manera)

(1977, Cuba, 73 min, b/w)
d Sara Gomez Yera. *p* Camilo Vives. *sc* Sara Gomez Yera, Tomás Gonzalez Perez. *ph* Luis Garcia. *ed* Ivan Arocha. *pd* Roberto Larrasure. *m* Sergio Vitier, Sara Gomez Yera. *songs* Sara Gonzalez. *cast* Mario Balmaseda, Yolanda Cuéllar, Mario Limonta, Isaura Mendoza, Bobby Carcases, Sarita Reyes, Guillermo Diaz.

●The ostensible subject of this remarkable film is the jive-talking, toe-tapping, good-for-nothing class of slum-dwelling lumpens known as 'marginals': 'a worldwide economic stratum of very defined characteristics – principally unemployment.' But the actual subject turns out to be a rather different delinquency: the misogyny and anti-social codes of Cuban machismo. Back in '74, the year of her tragic death (left unfinished, the film was completed by Tomás Alea and Julio Garcia Espinosa), Sara Gomez Yera was already combining documentary, fiction, samba music and droll voice-over lectures to examine the transformations wrought by revolution on a generation of Cuban men. As the title indicates, contradiction is the name of the game, and the film brilliantly counterposes macho cruelties and loyalties, socialist change and intractable traditions, revolutionary fervour and political authoritarianism. MM

One Wild Moment

see Moment d'Egarement, Un

One Woman's Story

see Passionate Friends, The

On Golden Pond

(1981, US, 109 min)
d Mark Rydell. *p* Bruce Gilbert. *sc* Ernest Thompson. *ph* Billy Williams. *ed* Robert L Wolfe. *pd* Stephen Grimes. *m* David Grusin. *cast* Katharine Hepburn, Henry Fonda, Jane Fonda, Doug McKeon, Dabney Coleman, William Lanteau, Chris Rydell.

●Generation gap tearjerker with Fonda and Hepburn as a septuagenarian married couple visiting their lakeside New England bungalow for their 48th summer together. When middle-aged daughter Jane arrives with boyfriend and his teenage son in tow, the scene is set for the artificial befriending across the generations – Fonda teaches the boy to fish, to read *Treasure Island* (a 'real' life alternative to chasing girls and television). This adaptation of Ernest Thompson's immensely calculated 1978 play leaves you wishing Jane Fonda's IPC production company had never become involved as she regrets (the relationship she never had with her father), Hepburn flutters, and the elder Fonda mutters (the four-letter words that are supposed to endear him to us as a salty old 'character'). Two of Hollywood's best-loved veterans deserved a far better swan song than this sticky confection. RM

On Guard!

see Bossu, Le

On Her Majesty's Secret Service

(1969, GB, 140 min)
d Peter Hunt. *p* Harry Saltzman, Albert R Broccoli. *sc* Richard Maibaum. *ph* Michael Reed. *ed* John Glen. *pd* Syd Cain. *m* John Barry. *cast* George Lazenby, Diana Rigg, Telly Savalas, Ilse Steppat, Gabriele Ferzetti, Yuri Borienko, Bernard Horsfall, George Baker, Baernard Lee, Lois Maxwell, Desmond Llewelyn, Julie Ege, Joanna Lumley, Bessie Love.

●The Bond films were bad enough even with the partially ironic performances of Connery. Here, featuring the stunning nonentity Lazenby, there are no redeeming features. The 'plot' (a series of glossy set pieces) is the one about 007 tracking down a loony Swiss villain (Savalas) who's (guess what?) threatening the world with some scientific thingamyjig. GA

Onibaba (The Hole)

(1964, Jap, 105 min, b/w)
d/sc Kaneto Shindo. *ph* Kiyomi Kuroda. *ed* Toshio Enoki. *ad* Kaneto Shindo. *m* Hikaru Hayashi. *cast* Nobuko Otowa, Jitsuko Yoshimura, Kei Sato, Taiji Tonomura, Jukichi Uno.

●A tale, apparently based on legend, about two women, one elderly and the other her daughter-in-law, who survive by killing samurai and selling their armour to buy rice. When the girl begins to lust after a neighbour, the older woman becomes jealous, and tries to frighten the girl by wearing a demon mask at night. No masterpiece by any means, it's at times overplayed, but it's striking visually, handling swift horizontal movement – and using the claustrophobic body-high reeds among which the women live – very well. It's also genuinely erotic, and the treatment in detail of the women's lives as essentially bestial is interesting so long as Shindo stops short of portentous allegorising about the human condition. RM

Onion Field, The

(1979, US, 126 min)
d Harold Becker. *p* Walter Coblenz. *sc* Joseph Wambaugh. *ph* Charles Rosher Jr. *ed* John W Wheeler. *pd* Brian Eatwell. *m* Eumir Deodato. *cast* John Savage, James Woods, Franklyn Seales, Ted Danson, Ronny Cox, David Huffman, Christopher Lloyd, Diane Hull, Priscilla Pointer.

●An expertly performed adaptation of Joseph Wambaugh's novel, based on the real-life case history of an LA Cop (Danson) murdered by two hijackers he tries to arrest (Woods, Seales), and the effect of the killing on his partner (Savage). It's the usual heavy Wambaugh brew: police procedure closely observed without a trace of romanticism, suggesting simply that life in the force is psychological hell. So far, so good. But that very insistence on authenticity is followed by the film to the detriment of the narrative's dramatic structure; half way through, the whole thing begins to ramble badly. Engrossingly sordid, nevertheless. GA

Only Angels Have Wings

(1939, US, 121 min, b/w)
d Howard Hawks. *sc* Jules Furthman. *ph* Joseph Walker. *ed* Viola Lawrence. *ad* Lionel Banks. *m* Dimitri Tiomkin. *cast* Cary Grant, Jean Arthur, Richard Barthelmess, Rita Hayworth, Thomas Mitchell, Allyn Joslyn, Sig Ruman, Victor Kilian, John Carroll, Don Barry, Noah Beery Jr.

●Take Hollywood's idea of a small banana republic in Central America, move in on its bar cum rooming-house cum airstrip, focus on the group of people living and working there, and you've got the basic elements of Hawks' terrific *Only Angels Have Wings*, or Only Mad People Want to Fly Mail Planes Over the Andes. Hemmed in by impassable mountains (all the time) and fog and blizzards (most of the time), the personal and work ethics of this little crew become magnified to epic proportions. But it's an epic played out in the confined space of the Dutchman's bar; the more claustrophobic because these men are flyers and need the open sky. If it sounds improbable, it is. Mythical cinema at its best. JCl

Only Game in Town, The

(1969, US, 113 min)
d George Stevens. *p* Fred Kohlmar. *sc* Frank D Gilroy. *ph* Henri Decae. *ed* John W Holmes, Williams Sands, Pat Shade. *ad* Herman A Blumenthal, Auguste Capelier. *m* Maurice Jarre. *cast* Elizabeth Taylor, Warren Beatty, Charles Braswell, Hank Henry, Olga Valéry.

●Stevens' last film, a hoarily old-fashioned romantic comedy about a Las Vegas chorus girl and a compulsive gambler who find the courage to face life in their love for each other. Based on a play and always looking the part, it has occasional moments of life injected by Taylor and Beatty. Characteristic of the general soft-centredness is the fact that the title evidently refers not to gambling or prostitution – as one might expect of the Las Vegas setting – but to marriage. TM

Only the Brave

(1995, Aust, 60 min)
d Ana Kokkinos. *p* Fiona Eager. *sc* Ana Kokkinos, Mira Robertson. *ph* Jaems Grant. *ed* Mark Atkin. *ad* Georgina Campbell. *m* Philip Brophy. *cast* Elena Mandalis, Dora Kaskanis, Maude Davey, Bob Bright.

●Four girls smoke joints and torch trees. Another saga of wild, nihilistic teenagers? Not quite. While her friend Vicki is disruptive at school, seemingly an easy score for the local blokes, and keen to try her luck as a singer, Alex is more introspective: wary of losing her virginity, fascinated by literature, and haunted by the fact that her mum abandoned herself and her dad to go and live in Sydney. Neither girl has much of a life; both, in the end, are determined to get out of town, separately or together, depending on whether their friendship can withstand the tensions that arise when Alex develops an interest in the woman who teaches her English. Tough and unsentimental, the film nevertheless suffers from slightly awkward performances and from the fact that, for the first half at least, its two leads are not as sympathetically drawn as they might be. GA

Only the Lonely

(1991, US, 104 min)
d Chris Columbus. *p* John Hughes, Hunt Lowry. *sc* Chris Columbus. *ph* Julio Macat. *ed* Raja Gosnell, Peter Teschner. *pd* John Muto. *m* Maurice Jarre. *cast* John Candy, Maureen O'Hara, Ally Sheedy, Kevin Dunn, Milo O'Shea, Bert Remsen, Anthony Quinn, James Belushi, Macaulay Culkin.

●Chicago policeman Danny Muldoon (Candy) is bored. His working day is spent with a loutish partner (Belushi), while evenings are devoted to his cantankerous mother (O'Hara). Even this is more exciting than the existence suffered by Theresa (Sheedy), who spends her day making-up corpses in the local morgue. She overcomes painful shyness, and the unlikely couple fall in love, much to the annoyance of Danny's mother. It's ultimatum time: move with Mom to Florida, or marry his girlfriend. Writer-director Columbus never really hits his stride (is this a drama about overcoming loneliness, or a comedy about a domineering mother?). Worse, he can't resist indulging in overwrought fantasy sequences which, far from being funny, serve to undermine the prevailing tender mood. The performances, at least, are fine, particularly the exchanges between O'Hara and Quinn as her patient suitor. CM

Only the Strong

(1993, US, 99 min)
d Sheldon Lettich. *p* Samuel Hadida, Stuart S Shapiro, Steven G Menkin. *sc* Sheldon Lettich, Luis Esteban. *ph* Edward Pei. *ed* Stephen Semel. *pd* J Mark Harrington. *m* Harvey W Mason. *cast* Mark Dacascos, Stacey Travis, Geoffrey Lewis, Paco Christian Prieto, Todd Susman, Jeffrey Anderson Gunter, Roman Cardwell.

●A paean to the Brazilian martial art of *capoeira* harks back to those break-dancing quickies. The plot is the usual. Louis (kung-fu champ Dacascos) learns kicking ass to samba in Brazil with the US Army Special Forces, returns to Miami to find drug-dealers all over his old high school, kicks ass, converts a squad of delinquents to *capoeira*, takes on bossman Silverio (Prieto) in an ass-kick-up, and gets the green light for ass-kicking to samba on the syllabus. This martial art requires chaps to go into slow motion a lot and to be ethnically vague about the moves. In this context an average actor like Geoffrey Lewis, playing the defeated old schoolteacher, hums like a dynamo. Avoid like El Plagueo. BC

Only Two Can Play

(1961, GB, 106 min, b/w)
d Sidney Gilliat. *p* Leslie Gilliat. *sc* Bryan Forbes. *ph* John Wilcox. *ed* Thelma Connell. *ad* Albert Witherick. *m* Richard Rodney Bennett.

cast Peter Sellers, Mai Zetterling, Virginia Maskell, Kenneth Griffith, Raymond Huntley, John Le Mesurier, Graham Stark, Richard Attenborough.

● Peter Sellers is at his most controlled in this biting, rather sad farce, adapted from the Kingsley Amis novel *That Uncertain Feeling*. He's embarrassingly good as an anxiously lecherous Welsh librarian, married with kids, living in a gloomy apartment with peeling wallpaper and the plumbing up the spout. Enter Mai Zetterling, the delicious, bored wife of a local dignitary… It's well-observed, dry, and just a tad smutty. TCh

Only When I Larf

(1968, GB, 103 min)
d Basil Dearden. *p* Len Deighton, Brian Duffy. *sc* John Salmon. *ph* Anthony B Richmond. *ed* Fergus McDonell. *ad* John Blezard. *m* Ron Grainer. *cast* Richard Attenborough, David Hemmings, Alexandra Stewart, Nicholas Pennell, Melissa Stribling, Terence Alexander, Edric Connor.

● Richard Attenborough dons assorted disguises and is sometimes brilliant – notably as a manically jolly psychiatrist. Otherwise this is a plodding adaptation of Len Deighton's jokey novel about a trio of confidence tricksters (Attenborough, Hemmings, Stewart), which opens with a lengthy pre-credits sequence detailing their method of operation, repeats this twice over with variations, and ends on a note of hollow laughter. TM

Only When I Laugh (aka It Hurts Only When I Laugh)

(1981, US, 120 min)
d Glenn Jordan. *p* Roger M Rothstein, Neil Simon. *sc* Neil Simon. *ph* David M Walsh. *ed* John Wright. *pd* Albert Brenner. *m* David Shire. *cast* Marsha Mason, Kristy McNichol, James Coco, Joan Hackett, David Dukes, John Bennett Perry, Kevin Bacon.

● Expertly reworked by Neil Simon from his play *The Gingerbread Lady*, *Only When I Laugh* is positively profligate with its witty dialogue, yet resolves itself into something of dramatic weight. In his first film as producer, Simon assembles a trio of New Yorkers who, like all his best characters, are smart enough to know which part they are playing, and support each other via a droll orgy of facetious self-mockery. Coco is the fat, gay actor who feels he should be a star but is turned down for haemorrhoid commercials; Hackett, the placid beauty anxiously approaching her fortieth birthday; Mason, the central character, a Broadway actress who comes home from the boozers' clinic, a little wan but puckish glamour restored. Though full of good intentions re daughter (McNichol) and career, we know she's going to take that fatal drink sometime in the next three reels. JS

Only Yesterday

(1933, US, 106 min, b/w)
d John M Stahl. *p* Carl Laemmle Jr. *sc* Arthur Richman, George O'Neill. *ph* Merritt B Gerstad. *ed* Milton Carruth. *ad* Charles D Hall. *cast* Margaret Sullavan, John Boles, Edna May Oliver, Billie Burke, Benita Hume, Reginald Denny, George Meeker, Jane Darwell, Franklin Pangborn.

● An incredible opening sequence, offering a crash course on the Wall Street disaster of October 29, 1929 as the camera cruises lingeringly from stock exchange through society party, shows Stahl at his very best. On the day that ruins him, the dispirited tycoon hero (Boles) has his conscience coincidentally prodded by a letter from the girl (Sullavan) he ruined in the days of his youth, and he remembers… A pleasing conceit, reminiscent of *Letter from an Unknown Woman*, but developed on lines that run more to sentimentality than to the incandescent romantic despair of Ophüls' film. Some remarkable sequences, nevertheless, with unfailingly elegant direction from Stahl and a radiant performance from Sullavan (her debut) making up for the stodgy Boles. TM

Only You

(1994, US, 108 min)
d Norman Jewison. *p* Norman Jewison, Cary Woods, Robert N Fried, Charles Mulvehill. *sc* Diane Drake. *ph* Sven Nykvist. *ed* Stephen Rivkin. *pd* Luciana Arrighi. *m* Rachel Portman. *cast* Marisa Tomei, Robert Downey Jr, Bonnie Hunt, Joaquim de Almeida, Fisher Stevens, Billy Zane, Adam LeFevre, John Benjamin Hickey.

● Though convinced by a childhood ouija game that she's destined to marry a man named 'Damon Bradley', incorrigible romantic Faith Corvatch (Tomei) is now betrothed to a dull podiatrist. Until, that is, she answers a phone call from one of her fiancé's school chums who's passing through Pittsburgh en route to Venice, Italy – his name, Damon Bradley. She dashes to the airport, misses him, then sets off in quest of her soulmate. Damon, however, proves elusive, and in Rome Faith is wooed by shoe-salesman Peter (Downey), who tries to persuade her that he, Mr Wright, is a better bet than her fantasy Mr Right. With smitten Peter now in pursuit, Faith persists in her quest, scouring the Tuscan countryside and coastline for the man of her dreams. For a veteran director, Jewison is surprisingly light on his feet, though he tends to wander off forgetfully at times, leaving the plot to advance without him. Even so, the ravishing visuals, some swooning love songs, and the strains of Verdi should see you through to the predictably moist ending. NF

On Moonlight Bay

(1951, US, 95 min)
d Roy Del Ruth. *p* William Jacobs. *sc* Melville Shavelson, Jack Rose. *ph* Ernest Haller. *ed* Thomas Reilly. *ad* Douglas Bacon. *cast* Doris Day, Gordon MacRae, Jack Smith, Leon Ames, Rosemary DeCamp, Mary Wickes, Ellen Corby, Billy Gray.

● A pleasantly nostalgic period musical, set in small town Indiana on the eve of America's involvement in World War I, based on Booth Tarkington's marvellous *Penrod* stories but largely ditching his monstrously funny small boy to provide a vehicle for big sister Doris Day and her budding romance with MacRae. Very much in the manner of *Meet Me in St Louis*, though nowhere near as good. The charming golden oldie score, featuring an array of hummable standards to go with the title song, is a definite plus. TM

On ne Meurt que 2 Fois

see He Died with His Eyes Open

On Our Land

(1981, GB, 55 min)
d/p Antonia Caccia. *ph* Jeff Perks. *ed* Chris Thomas.

● As a catalogue of the officially sanctioned iniquities and inequities of the Israeli government against the state's one in six citizens who are Palestinian Arabs, Antonia Caccia's documentary is efficient enough. What it achieves by means of its conventional interviews with dispossessed Palestinians (in Arab villages on the West Bank and Gaza Strip) is a persuasive profile of a state pursuing welfare policies which, whether intentionally or by default, amount to racism. Housing, employment, education and medicine are all areas where the Arabs are shown as suffering blatant discrimination. But most telling of all are laws which forbid Arabs to own or build on land they've occupied for generations. What diminishes the film's value to the viewer who is not so much uncommitted to either side as simply uninformed, is a partisanship which doesn't even allow the official Israeli position the opportunity to condemn itself out of its own mouth. RM

On purge Bébé

(1931, Fr, 62 min, b/w)
d Jean Renoir. *p* Charles David. *sc* Jean Renoir. *ph* Theodore Sparkuhl. *ed* Jean Mamy. *ad* Gabriel Scongnamillo. *m* Paul Misraki. *cast* Louvigny, Marguerite Pierry, Michel Simon, Olga Valéry, Sacha Tarride, Nicole Fernandez, Fernandel.

● Undertaken by Renoir to prove his efficiency as a director of talking pictures, this droll adaptation of a slight, one-act farce by Feydeau is chiefly memorable for the relaxed performances and the then revolutionary sound effect of a flushed toilet. The plot revolves around a porcelain manufacturer (Louvigny) vainly trying to sell a supposedly unbreakable line in chamber-pots to a supplier (Simon) for the French army. Meanwhile, the manufacturer's idle wife (Pierry), drifting casually about their apartment in her dressing-gown, struggles to persuade their son to take a laxative. Aside from the inimitable Michel Simon as the slow-witted supplier, the film also features the first screen performance by Fernandel. DT

On the Beach

(1959, US, 134 min, b/w)
d/p Stanley Kramer. *sc* John Paxton, James Lee Barrett. *ph* Giuseppe Rotunno, (auto race) Daniel L Fapp. *ed* Frederick Knudtson. *pd* Rudolph Sternad. *ad* Fernando Carrere. *m* Ernest Gold. *cast* Gregory Peck, Ava Gardner, Fred Astaire, Anthony Perkins, John Meillon, Donna Anderson, John Tate, Lola Brooks, John Meillon.

● Heavy going indeed as Mr Liberal Conscience himself, Stanley Kramer, wades turgidly through Nevil Shute's story of the aftermath of nuclear apocalypse. Set in Australia, where the radiation effects of war in the Northern hemisphere have still to take effect, it follows a group of characters as they wait for death to arrive. Fine photography, but the script is a typically numbing affair, and the cast, aside from Peck and Meillon (whose part was considerably cut), seem totally out of their depth. GA

On the Beat

(1962, GB, 105 min, b/w)
d Robert Asher. *p* Hugh Stewart. *sc* Jack Davies. *ph* Geoffrey Faithfull. *ed* William Lewthwaite. *ad* Bert Davey. *m* Philip Green. *cast* Norman Wisdom, Jennifer Jayne, Raymond Huntley, David Lodge, Esma Cannon, Eric Barker, Eleanor Summerfield.

● You may not believe this, but an otherwise totally sensible and widely respected British film director, not altogether unconnected with *Time Out*'s past, has a soft spot for Norman Wisdom. Phooey! The man's humour is of the most cretinous nature imaginable. Here he appears as a dimwit car park attendant at Scotland Yard who sees his dream of becoming a copper like dad come true after he accidentally catches a bunch of crooks. Embarrassingly unfunny, it just shows that being a film comic is a most unsuitable job for a moron. GA

On the Black Hill

(1987, GB, 117 min)
d Andrew Grieve. *p* Jennifer Howarth. *sc* Andrew Grieve. *ph* Thaddeus O'Sullivan. *ed* Scott Thomas. *ad* Jocelyn James. *m* Robert Lockhart. *cast* Mike Gwilym, Robert Gwilym, Bob Peck, Gemma Jones, Jack Walters, Nesta Harris, Geoffrey Hutchings, Benjamin Whitrow, Patrick Godfrey, Mark Dignam.

● Our countryside, in this adaptation of Bruce Chatwin's novel which crams 80 years into less than two hours, hasn't looked so ravishingly lovely since *Far From the Madding Crowd*. Hardy, without his overview, crops up a bit in Chatwin's characters too, with Amos Jones (Peck), a stubbly and splenetic son of the soil, belonging to the same bloodline as the Mayor of Casterbridge ('wrong-headed as a buffalo'), and further enraged by being a Welsh tenant on marcher land. His tender courtship of English middle class Mary (Jones) leads to a miserable marriage. They rent a farm, he's out in all weathers, and only fiddle-playing granddad (Walters) provides much companionship for gifted Mary. Twins are born (Mike and Robert Gwilym) who prove constitutionally inseparable, World War I conscription and the possibilities of romance notwithstanding. Amos feuds irreconcilably with his neighbour, and dies regretting his expulsion of a pregnant daughter. The bachelor twins celebrate their 80th birthday with a flight over the terrain they have toiled so long upon. Grieve's film may portray baffled lives in which chances of joy are stifled by a mixture of stiff-necked pride and chapel religion, but it is the look of it all you remember. BC

On the Bridge

(1992, US, 95 min)
d/p/sc Frank Perry. *ph* Kevin Keating. *m* Toni Childs. *with* Frank Perry.

● A documentary account, surprisingly non-depressing, of veteran director Perry's own reaction to being diagnosed as having prostate cancer and, perhaps, other related, possibly terminal symptoms. We see him trying out various treatments (both conventional and alternative), arguing with his doctor, visiting counsellors and faith-healers, and generally coping with an admirable blend of courage, wit and determination. Still fighting the disease with an unexpected degree of success, he has made a film which, besides being fascinating in its own right, may well give heart to other sufferers and their loved ones. GA

On the Buses

(1971, GB, 88 min)
d Harry Booth. *p/sc* Ronald Woolfe, Ronald Chesney. *ph* Mark McDonald. *ed* Archie Ludski. *pd* Scott MacGregor. *m* Max Harris. *cast* Reg Varney, Doris Hare, Michael Robbins, Anna Karen, Stephen Lewis, Bob Grant, Andrea Lawrence, Pat Ashton, Brian Quilton.
●Dire spin-off from the stultifyingly unfunny TV series, with the lads at the local bus depot peeved to find women being brought in as drivers, and cracking a lot of awful sexist jokes as a result. Just to add to the insult, the film is extraordinarily badly made: flat, paceless and technically shoddy. GA

On the Game

(1973, GB, 87 min)
d Stanley Long. *p* Stanley Long, Barry Jacobs. *sc* Suzanne Mercer. *ph* Mike Boultbee. *ed* Patrick Foster. *cast* Pamela Manson, Charles Hodgson, Suzy Bowen, Nicola Austine, Allen Morton, Peter Duncan, Louise Pajo, Fiona Victory. *narrator* Charles Gray.
●Listless 'documentary' about prostitution through the ages, with lots of hammy recreations from different periods (presumably a follow-up to Long's *Naughty!* of 1971, a 'report on pornography and erotica through the ages'). It is neither informative nor provoking on any level. All the women have exceptionally large breasts.

On the Hunting Ground (Liechang Zhasa)

(1985, China, 66 min)
d Tian Zhuangzhuang. *sc* Jiang Hao. *ph* Lü Le, Hou Yong. *cast* Tigen Yiwai, Laxi, Bawaltu, Sewang Dalgi.
●Tian's portrait of the herdsmen of the Inner Mongolian steppes centres on the ancient code (the *zasag*) which governs their lives as hunter gatherers. Much of the film could easily pass for documentary, alternating domestic scenes with hunting scenes in which numerous small, furry animals are blasted with shotguns. The very minimal plot concerns a huntsman who infringes the code and is required to do both social and religious penance; the complete absence of explanations has rendered the film opaque to most audiences. But it's clear enough that Tian is (as in *Horse Thief*) interested in the contrast between living by a code and trangressing it – and it's not much of a stretch to see this as an alienated metaphor for his own generation's faith in, and later rejection of, Maoism. TR

On the Nickel

(1979, US, 96 min)
d/p/sc Ralph Waite. *ph* Ric Waite. *ed* Wendy Greene Bricmont. *m* Fred Myrow. *song* Tom Waits. *cast* Ralph Waite, Donald Moffat, Penelope Allen, Hal Williams, Jack Kehoe, Daniel Ades, Paul Weaver, Arthur Space, Tom Mahoney, Lane Smith, Ellen Geer.
●Waite, himself openly a former alcoholic, took time off from playing Dad in TV's *The Waltons* to make and star in this hopelessly sentimentalised picture of life on Los Angeles' Skid Row. Most of the cast came from Waite's own Los Angeles Actors' Theatre company. TR

On the Old Roman Road

(2001, Armenia/Neth, 76 min)
d Don Askarian. *p* René Goossens, Don Askarian. *sc* Don Askarian. *ph* Rudolf Vatinyan. *ed/ad* Don Askarian. *cast* Pavel Sahakyantz, Anna Bassentyan, Ohan Askarian, Piet van Dijk. Sylvia Gettar.
●Somewhat impenetrable and very pretentious poetic hodge-podge which links at least two separate narratives through the figure of an Armenian writer living in Rotterdam (the source of the film's funding). One strand concerns his childhood memories of Kurds, Turks, concubines and camel-drivers; the other deals with his present predicament on the fringes of a terrorist conspiracy. Hard to say more than that, since it's all so wilfully arty, solemn and obscure. GA

On the Town

(1949, US, 98 min)
d Stanley Donen, Gene Kelly. *p* Arthur Freed. *sc* Adolph Green, Betty Comden. *ph* Harold Rosson. *ed* Ralph E Winters. *ad* Cedric Gibbons, Jack Martin Smith. *m* Leonard Bernstein. *lyrics* Adolph Green, Betty Comden, Leonard Bernstein. *cast* Gene Kelly, Frank Sinatra, Jules Munshin, Betty Garrett, Ann Miller, Vera-Ellen, Florence Bates, Alice Pearce, George Meader.
●In 1948, Jules Dassin used New York as one big location for *The Naked City*. The following year, to Louis B Mayer's incredulity, producer Arthur Freed turned the city into a sound stage for the movie of the Broadway musical of the Leonard Bernstein/Jerome Robbins ballet *Fancy Free*. Taking as its premise 'New York, New York, it's a wonderful town', the show looses three 'gobs' on the women (including the imperishable Alice Pearce), the sights, and the nightlife of the town. The most cinematic of film musicals and the one most given to dance, *On the Town* is exhilarating, brash spectacle, all rip-snorting, wisecracking attack, and maybe just a teensy bit unlikeable. SG

On the Waterfront

(1954, US, 108 min, b/w)
d Elia Kazan. *p* Sam Spiegel. *sc* Budd Schulberg. *ph* Boris Kaufman. *ed* Arthur E Milford. *ad* Richard Day. *m* Leonard Bernstein. *cast* Marlon Brando, Eva Marie Saint, Karl Malden, Lee J Cobb, Rod Steiger, Pat Henning, Leif Erickson, James Westerfield, John Heldabrand, Rudy Bond, John Hamilton, Martin Balsam.
●Superb performances (none more so than Brando as Terry Malloy, the ex-boxer unwittingly entangled in corrupt union politics), a memorably colourful script by Budd Schulberg, and a sure control of atmosphere make this account of Brando's struggles against gangster Cobb's hold over the New York longshoremen's union powerful stuff. It is undermined, however, by both the religious symbolism (that turns Malloy not into a Judas but a Christ figure) and the embarrassing special pleading on behalf of informers, deriving presumably from the fact that Kazan and Schulberg named names during the McCarthy witch-hunts. Politics apart, though, it's pretty electrifying. GA

On the Wire

(1990, GB, 85 min)
d Elaine Proctor. *p* Laurie Borg. *sc* Elaine Proctor. *ph* Yoshi Tezuka. *ed* David Freeman. *pd* Carmel Collins. *m* Lucien & Erik Windrich. *cast* Michael O'Brien, Aletta Bezuidenhout, Valerie Gozo, Laurens Seliye, Gys de Villiers, Marie Human.
●In this riveting study of mental and social disintegration, Michael O'Brien plays Wouter Fourie, an Afrikaner major in the South African Defence Force, desperately trying to equate his experiences in the bush with the strict God-fearing Calvinist community at home. The fences are going up around him, while he and his wife fall prey to a frankly dangerous sexuality. Provocatively linking sex, repression and violence with the forces of religion and apartheid, this is powerful film-making, an immensely bold, accomplished debut for writer/director Elaine Proctor of the National Film and Television School. TCh

On Top of the Whale (Het Dak van de Walvis)

(1981, Neth, 90 min, b/w & col)
d Raúl Ruiz. *p* Monica Tegelaar, Kees Kasander. *sc* Raúl Ruiz, Roland Kay. *ph* Henri Alekan, Theo Bierkens. *ed* Valerie Sarmiento. *ad* Jan de Winter. *cast* Willeke van Ammelrooy, Jean Badin, Fernando Bordeu, Herbert Curiel, Amber De Grauw.
●The most minimalist of Ruiz's extended fictions, this is a linguistic fantasy set – supposedly – in the depths of Patagonia, although the action is quite patently shot in a non-descript house in Holland. Some time in a barely recognisable future, two Dutch anthropologists visit a mysterious socialist millionaire on an island where only two members remain of a legendary tribe. As the action unfolds, so does the Indians' strange, paradoxically limited language. One of Ruiz' most Babel-like fictions, hopping from language to language almost arbitrarily, it's also among his richest in visual terms. Not altogether convincing as the disquisition on colonialism that it's been seen as, it's more a scrambled shaggy dog story, but austere with it. (Apparently it's Jim Jarmusch's third favourite film ever; make of that what you will.) JRo

Onze Mille Verges, Les

see Bisexual

Ooh...You Are Awful (aka Get Charlie Tully)

(1972, GB, 97 min)
d Cliff Owen. *p* EM Smedley Aston. *sc* John Warren, John Singer. *ph* Ernest Stewart. *ed* Bill Blunden. *ad* Geoffrey Tozer. *m* Christopher Gunning. *cast* Dick Emery, Derren Nesbitt, Ronald Fraser, Pat Coombs, William Franklyn, Cheryl Kennedy, Norman Bird, Liza Goddard, Ambrosine Phillpotts, Brian Oulton, Sheila Keith.
●All TV comic Emery's favourite creations (the naughty vicar, the gay stereotype, the thick-as-a-plank skinhead) are present and correct in this tawdry screen adventure, where he plays a conman in line for a fortune if he can locate the mystery woman who has the combination to a Swiss bank account tattooed on her bottom. TJ

Open City

see Roma, Città Aperta

Open Doors (Porte aperte)

(1989, It, 109 min)
d Gianni Amelio. *p* Angelo Rizzoli. *sc* Gianni Amelio, Vincenzo Cerami. *ph* Tonino Nardi. *ed* Simona Paggi. *ad* Franco Velchi, Amedeo Fago. *m* Franco Piersanti. *cast* Gian Maria Volonté, Ennio Fantastichini, Renato Carpentieri, Renzo Giovampietro.
●Fascist Palermo, 1937. Scalia (Fantastichini), sacked accountant of the Confederation of Workers and Artists, slips a bayonet into its chief, Councillor Spadafora, and leaves him face down on a bloodied map of Italy. In the accounts office, he similarly despatches his successor. Then he rapes his wife and shoots her dead in front of an altar to her blessed Virgin. At home with his young son, he calmly awaits arrest. The heart of the film consists of the efforts of a liberal judge (Volonté) to investigate, despite pressure, the facts behind the case – a tale of all-pervasive corruption – in order to save the entirely unsympathetic Scalia. Despite the period trappings – it's adapted from a factually based book by Leonardo Sciascia – the left wing Amelio is more interested in universal concerns, especially the role of a cultured mind in societies where political expediency is the order of the day. The film's glory, accordingly, is Volonté's massive, remarkably sensitive performance: he makes thought palpable. A leisurely, thoughtful political drama, its sophistication and depth rewardingly confound expectations at every turn. WH

Opening Night

(1977, US, 143 min)
d John Cassavetes. *p* Al Ruban. *sc* John Cassavetes. *ph* Al Ruban. *ed* Tom Cornwell. *ad* Bryan Ryman. *m* Bo Harwood. *cast* Gena Rowlands, Ben Gazzara, John Cassavetes, Joan Blondell, Paul Stewart, Zohra Lampert, Laura Johnson, John Tuell, Ray Powers.
●Since *Minnie and Moskowitz*, Cassavetes has preoccupied himself with qualifying traditional genre material through emphasis on the intuitive and improvised aspects of the actor-as-auteur. In *Opening Night*, this essentially stylistic approach takes on an additionally playful thematic resonance. For here we are in the realm of backstage drama; the casting of Joan Blondell and distant echoes of *All About Eve* locate the film squarely within that tradition. And Cassavetes gives us several levels of 'performance' to contend with as he parallels the 'real' problems of ageing star Gena Rowlands with those of the character she plays onstage in the appropriately titled *The Second Woman*. Overlong, but intelligent and intriguing. PT

Open Season (Los Cazadores)

(1974, Sp/Switz, 104 min)
d Peter Collinson. *p* José Sainz de Vicuña. *sc* David Osborn, Liz Charles-Williams. *ph* Fernando Arribas. *ed* Alan Pattillo. *ad* Gil Parrondo. *m* Ruggero Cini. *cast* Peter Fonda,

Cornelia Sharpe, John Phillip Law, Richard Lynch, Albert Mendoza, William Holden, Helga Liné, Did Sherman.

● A cross between *Straw Dogs* and *Deliverance*, although its references are considerably wider and the plot itself is another reworking of *The Hounds of Zaroff*. Fonda, Law and Lynch – three clean-cut American boys who played football and served in Vietnam together – like to prove they are men two weeks in the year by going into the mountains to indulge in a little swimming, hunting, drinking, comradeship, murder and rape. Unfortunately Collinson is no Peckinpah or Boorman; so he has to rely on self-indulgent camerawork (soft focus and telephoto), ironic music, and overstressed dialogue ('Your licence to kill ran out after the war...but they forgot to tell you') to make sure the message gets across. And the hamfisted structure – fatal to this type of movie – makes even the Hitchcockian techniques fall flat. But there is plenty of nastiness, if that's what turns you on. GSa

Open Your Eyes (Abre los ojos/Ouvre les yeux/ Apri gli occhi)

(1997, Sp/Fr/It, 119 min)
d Alejandro Amenábar. *sc* Alejandro Amenábar, Mateo Gil. *ph* Hans Burmann. *ed* Maria Elena Sainz de Rozas. *ad* Wolfgang Burmann. *m* Alejandro Amenábar, Mariano Marin. *cast* Eduardo Noriega, Penélope Cruz, Chete Lera, Fele Martinez, Najwa Nimri, Gérard Barray, Jorge de Juan, Miguel Palenzuela.

● You might think seeing is believing, but tell that to Amenábar, writer/director of this dazzling thriller, which toys with our perceptions to exquisitely torturous effect. Initially, it appears that playboy César (Noriega) has it all: money, looks, girls. One night at a party, however, eager to escape jealous Nuria (Nimri), he strikes up a conversation with Sofia (Cruz), and soon realises he's in love. After one chaste evening together, it all goes wrong: Nuria is waiting outside, offers a lift, then deliberately drives off the road. She's killed, but he survives with a face so horribly disfigured he needs a mask. His hopes of getting back together with Sofia seem slim, especially since he's now facing a possible murder charge. Will this nightmare never end? Actually, it's only just beginning, as Amenábar adds layers of information overload, altering the picture from *noir*-ish poser to latter-day *Beauty and the Beast*, and eventually to head spinning sci-fi mode. What holds us through the revelations are the sheer chutzpah with which Amenábar and his cast deliver them, the emotional imperative of the material and the fascinating way it touches on concepts of interior/exterior worth, personal responsibility and phenomenology. This is so smart, mischievous and stylish, you'll instantly want to see it again. TJ

Opera (Terror at the Opera)

(1987, It, 95 min)
d/p/sc Dario Argento. *ph* Ronnie Taylor. *ed* Franco Fraticelli. *pd* Davide Bassan. *m* Brian Eno. *cast* Cristina Marsillach, Urbano Barberini, Daria Nicolodi, Ian Charleson, Coralina Cataldi Tassoni, Antonella Vitale, William McNamara, Barbara Cupisti.

● The Visconti of Violence goes straight for the throat (and eyes) in this stylishly sick thriller about a young diva – the setting is a production of *Macbeth* at La Scala opera house – terrorised by a psycho killer. All the trademarks are here: minimal plot, striking set pieces, baroque camera movements, misogynist violence. As always, though, the most horrific thing is the dubbing. See it, if you must, on the big screen, because its swirling camerawork and imaginative nastiness will be completely lost on video. NF

Opera do Malandro

(1986, Fr/Braz, 108 min)
d Ruy Guerra. *p* Marin Karmitz, Ruy Guerra. *sc* Chico Buarque, Orlando Senna, Ruy Guerra. *ph* Antonio Luiz Mendes. *ed* Mair Tavares, Idê Lacreta, Kénout Peltier. *ad* Mauro Monteiro, Irenio Maia. *m* Chico Buarque. *cast* Edson Celulari, Claudia Ohana, Elba Ramalho, Ney Latorraca, Fabio Sabag, JC Violla, Wilson Grey, Maria Silvia.

● Take *The Threepenny Opera*, relocate in Rio, replace Kurt Weill's score with Brazilian sambas, and embellish with dancing and dreamy decor... In this loose adaptation of Brecht's classic, Guerra tells a tale of fairytale simplicity: the year is 1941, and the Brazilian government is backing the Nazis against the wishes of the US-obsessed population at large, one of whom – white-suited pimp Max – is developing his own capitalistic practices. Between pool-room rumbles, black-market deals, and living off the earnings of faithful Margot (ex-mistress of corrupt cop Tiger), Max devises a plan to seduce the apparently innocent daughter of his arch-enemy, nightclub-owner Otto Strüdell, which has unexpected consequences. The pleasure to be had from Guerra's elegant, robustly physical movie derives not only from Chico Buarque's lilting, swinging score and the colourfully extravagant dancing, but from Guerra's deceptively playful tone, bewitchingly pitched somewhere between realism and filmic fantasy. Hollywood ancestors – notably Hawks' *Scarface* and Gene Kelly musicals – are refracted through a double prism of Brechtian modernism and traditional Brazilian culture. Political satire and lusty melodrama are imaginatively merged, with Guerra's camera deftly juggling various tropes of cinematic illusion. All in all, an astonishing offering of wit, verve and imagination. GA

Operation Amsterdam

(1959, GB, 104 min, b/w)
d Michael McCarthy. *p* Maurice Cowan. *sc* Michael McCarthy, John Eldridge. *ph* Reginald Wyer. *ed* Arthur Stevens. *ad* Alex Vetchinsky. *m* Philip Green. *cast* Peter Finch, Eva Bartok, Tony Britton, Alexander Knox, Malcolm Keen, Tim Turner, John Horsley, Melvyn Hayes.

● Brisk, no-nonsense British war movie (from Rank), tersely directed by McCarthy (whose background was in documentary) and full of unfussy, businesslike performances. Tony Britton leads a mission to Amsterdam in the summer of 1940 (the eve of the Nazi invasion) to prevent a valuable stash of industrial diamonds falling into enemy hands. Time is short – the Germans are only hours from town – but Britton and his crew make sure they get the job done. The one real casualty here is characterisation – there's such an onus on keeping the narrative moving that we get precious little chance to learn what makes the heroes tick. Adapted by the director and John Eldridge from the book *Adventure in Diamonds* by David E Walker. GM

Operation Crossbow

(1965, GB/It, 116 min)
d Michael Anderson. *p* Carlo Ponti. *sc* Richard Imrie [Emeric Pressburger], Derry Quinn, Ray Rigby. *ph* Erwin Hillier. *ed* Ernest Walter. *ad* Elliot Scott. *m* Ron Goodwin. *cast* George Peppard, Jeremy Kemp, Tom Courtenay, Sophia Loren, Trevor Howard, John Mills, Richard Johnson, Anthony Quayle, Helmut Dantine, Richard Todd, Lilli Palmer, Paul Henreid, Sylvia Syms.

● Standard World War II 'mission impossible' adventure in which three Allied officers with scientific training (Peppard, Kemp, Courtenay) are parachuted into Holland, posing as Dutch or German scientists reported missing, in order to locate – and help destroy, at the cost of their lives – the V2 rocket base at Peenemunde. Much ado about background authenticity is nullified by the cardboard characters, but the starry cast makes it all relatively painless. A Carlo Ponti production, so Sophia Loren came with the package and gets shot for her pains. TM

Operation Daybreak

(1975, US, 119 min)
d Lewis Gilbert. *p* Carter De Haven Jr. *sc* Ronald Harwood. *ph* Henri Decaë. *ed* Thelma Connell. *ad* Bill McCrow, (Czechoslovakia) Bob Kulic. *m* David Hentschel. *cast* Timothy Bottoms, Martin Shaw, Joss Ackland, Nicola Pagett, Anthony Andrews, Kika Markham, Anton Diffring, Carl Duering, Timothy West, Nigel Stock.

● As with other war films around this time, the problems of dramatic reconstruction are never reconciled with those of historical perspective. Based on the assassination in 1941 of Reinhard Heydrich (the Nazi leader in Czechoslovakia) and the subsequent German reprisals, the film unhappily mixes scrupulous accuracy with too much shoddily-rendered suspense. Apart from Anton Diffring's Heydrich, the characters are painted in black and white, so that the film falls apart when one of the freedom fighters unconvincingly becomes a turncoat. Only in the last ten minutes or so, with the final shootout and death of the last two assassins, does the film get to grips at all. Otherwise an over-routine journey.

Operation Disaster

see Morning Departure

Operation Petticoat

(1959, US, 124 min)
d Blake Edwards. *p* Robert Arthur. *sc* Stanley Shapiro, Maurice Richlin. *ph* Russell Harlan. *ed* Ted J Kent, Frank Gross. *ad* Alexander Golitzen, Robert E Smith. *m* David Rose. *cast* Cary Grant, Tony Curtis, Joan O'Brien, Dina Merrill, Gene Evans, Arthur O'Connell, Richard Sargent, Virginia Gregg.

● Despite the fortuitous teaming of Grant and Curtis – as the commander of a creaking World War II submarine determined to get it back in action by fair means or foul, and as the con-man lieutenant who obligingly wheels, deals and steals the necessary materials – this is a very thin comedy indeed. Not unpleasant, but the situations (including the inevitable invasion of women aboard the sub) are horribly familiar, and the dialogue none too inspired. GA

Operation Scorpio

see Scorpion King, The

Operation Thunderbolt (Mivtza Yonatan/aka Entebbe: Operation Thunderbolt)

(1977, Isr, 117 min)
d Menahem Golan. *p* Menahem Golan, Yoram Globus. *sc* Clarke Reynolds. *ph* Adam Greenberg. *ed* Dov Henig. *ad* Kuli Sander. *m* Dov Seltzer. *cast* Yehoram Gaon, Assaf Dayan, Ori Levy, Arik Lavi, Klaus Kinski, Sybil Danning, Oded Teomi, Mark Heath.

● Who needs another Entebbe raid film? Following *Raid on Entebbe* and *Victory at Entebbe*, this official Israeli version does rather have the look of yesterday's news despite Golan's efforts to build an immediacy through use of reaction shots and fast editing. The script wisely concentrates on the general plight of the hijacked instead of opting for the usual disaster movie composition of individual experiences. The result at least has more cohesion than *Victory at Entebbe*. Two strikes against it are its dreadful score and Mark Heath's Idi Amin; compensation comes with Kinski's haunted, cryptic performance as the hijack leader, giving the film a much-needed dramatic centre. CPe

Operation Undercover

see Report to the Commissioner

Oporto of My Childhood (O Porto da Minha Infância/ La Porte de mon enfance)

(2001, Port/Fr, 62 min)
d Manoel de Oliveira. *p* Paulo Branco. *sc* Julia Buisel. *ph* Emmanuel Machuel. *ed* Valérie Loiseleux. *with* Jorge Trêpa, Ricardo Trêpa, Maria De Medeiros, Manoel de Oliveira, José Wallenstein, Rogério Samoras, Jose Maria Vaz da Silva, David Cardoso, Agustina Bessa-Luís, Leonor Silveira.

● This Proustian documentary, made when Oliveira was 93 years old, explores the great Portuguese film-maker's relationship with his home town, Oporto, the place which inspired his first film *Douro, Faina Fluvial* way back in 1931. Using old photographs and newsreels with dramatic reconstructions, he offers a vivid portrait of a city caught between the old and the new. When he was a child, Oporto didn't even have proper cinemas, film shows were improvised in sheds, Oliveira (born 1908) recalls. Most of the landmarks familiar from his youth have vanished. The brothels and cafés where he and his artist friends used to while away their days are long since closed. Even the house where he grew up is in ruins. The city I remember only remains alive in my sad memory, he sadly reflects. Poignant and playful, this is one of the old master's most accessible late films. GM

Opportunists, The

(1999, US, 95 min)
d Myles Connell. *p* Tim Perell, John Lyons. *sc* Myles Connell. *ph* Teodoro Maniaci. *ed* Andy Keir. *pd* Debbie De Villa. *m* Kurt Hoffman. *cast* Christopher Walken, Peter McDonald, Cyndi Lauper, Vera Farmiga, Donal Logue, Jose Zuniga, Jerry Grayson, Chuck Cooper, Tom Noonan.
●A great actor who has settled for scene-stealing eccentricity in recent years, Walken switches registers to do excellent, controlled work here as an ex-con turned mechanic. His efforts to go straight are hindered by the arrival of a dubious cousin from Ireland (McDonald) just as the bills are mounting. Admittedly we've seen this before, but writer/director Connell's low key authenticity has its charms, not least a very credible supporting turn from Lauper as the long suffering barkeep in Walken's life. TCh

Opposite of Sex, The

(1998, US, 101 min)
d Don Roos. *p* David Kirkpatrick, Michael Besman. *sc* Don Roos. *ph* Hubert Taczanowski. *ed* David Codron. *pd* Michael Clausen. *m* Mason Daring. *cast* Christina Ricci, Martin Donovan, Lisa Kudrow, Lyle Lovett, Johnny Galecki, William Lee Scott.
●Selling itself as a transgressive black comedy, a kind of 18-rated *Clueless*, this runs out of ideas an hour in and proceeds to beat a suitably red-faced retreat from its more outrageous contentions. Ricci consolidates her newfound teen cred as the amoral Dedee, our unreliable narrator, who throws herself on the mercy of half-brother Bill (Donovan) only to seduce his boyfriend Matt (Sergei). She then persuades him to rip off Bill's savings and takes off for a new life in LA. Sadly, the highly resistible Kudrow has more screen time as Bill's drippy, repressed 'friend'. The movie has attitude, all right, but there are no likeable characters (they're either boring or obnoxious), and when you get down to it, it's a pretty conventional AIDS movie manqué. TCh

Opposite Sex, The

(1956, US, 116 min)
d David Miller. *p* Joe Pasternak. *sc* Fay Kanin, Michael Kanin. *ph* Robert Bronner. *ed* John McSweeney Jr. *ad* Cedric Gibbons, Daniel B Cathcart. *m* George Stoll. *songs* Nicholas Brodszky, Sammy Cahn. *cast* June Allyson, Joan Collins, Dolores Gray, Ann Sheridan, Leslie Nielsen, Jeff Richards, Agnes Moorehead, Charlotte Greenwood, Joan Blondell.
●Cukor's 1939 sparkling conversation piece, *The Women*, had an all female cast. This low voltage remake adds songs, CinemaScope and (gulp) men, in the shape of philandering Nielsen, who's married to ex-chanteuse Allyson but fooling around with chorine Collins. 'Young Man With a Horn' remains the most memorable title from an undistinguished set of tunes. TJ

Optimists of Nine Elms, The

(1973, GB, 110 min)
d Anthony Simmons. *p* Adrian Gaye, Victor Lyndon. *sc* Tudor Gates, Anthony Simmons. *ph* Larry Pizer. *ed* John Jympson. *ad* Robert Cartwright. *m* George Martin. *cast* Peter Sellers, Donna Mullane, John Chaffey, David Daker, Marjorie Yates, Patricia Brake.
●Two kids form a quirky relationship with an eccentric old busker (Sellers). Despite there being a host of things (like songs and music by Lionel Bart) that should have crippled this venture, it has, on the contrary, a lot going for it. With the help of the two kids and some fine location work, Simmons sketches a suitably hard-edged and realistic portrait of a drab existence south of the river. Father is aggressive and mother run-down, reduced to having a quick one Sunday mornings when the children are out. Conditions at home are poor and crowded, but the 'better life' of a promised new council flat is shown up for what it is. At least you feel that Simmons has continually avoided the easy way out, and that should be enough to counteract any feelings of unease. CPe

Orca (aka Orca... Killer Whale)

(1977, US, 92 min)
d Michael Anderson. *p* Luciano Vincenzoni. *sc* Luciano Vincenzoni, Sergio Donati. *ph* Ted Moore, (whale squences) J Barry Herron, (shark sequences) Ron Taylor. *ed* Ralph E Winters, John Bloom, Marion Rothman. *pd* Mario Garbuglia *m* Ennio Morricone. *cast* Richard Harris, Charlotte Rampling, Will Sampson, Bo Derek, Keenan Wynn, Scott Walker, Robert Carradine.
●Yet another attempt to poach in the profitable waters of *Jaws*. The threat this time is the eponymous whale, supposedly a killer species. The threatened include Richard Harris in a one-dimensional performance as the shark hunter turned whale-killer, Charlotte Rampling as a marine biologist studying the species, and a townful of fisherfolk. There is some startling footage, but Anderson's direction dithers perceptibly, and finally opts for an unpleasant mish-mash of phony ecological concern and meretricious sensationalism. The ultimate indignity the beast suffers is to become a simple extension of Harris' threadbare macho image. VG

Orchestra Rehearsal (Prova d'Orchestra)

(1978, It/WGer, 72 min)
d Federico Fellini. *sc* Federico Fellini, Brunello Rondi. *ph* Giuseppe Rotunno. *ed* Ruggero Mastroianni. *pd* Dante Ferretti. *m* Nino Rota. *cast* Balduin Baas, Clara Colosimo, Elisabeth Labi, Ronaldo Bonacchi, Ferdinando Villella, Giovanni Javarone, David Mauhsell, Francesco Aluigi.
●Too much art, too little substance, kills Fellini's modern parable of an orchestra intent on anarchy – confessing their passions, protesting their individuality, and collectively dismissing their boss conductor. A satirical made-for-TV vignette, it makes you marvel at what can be done with one gag, one set, and a swollen reputation. DMacp

Orchestra Wives

(1942, US, 98 min, b/w)
d Archie Mayo. *p* William Le Baron. *sc* Karl Tunberg, Darrell Ware. *ph* Lucien Ballard. *ed* Robert Bischoff. *ad* Richard Day. *songs* Mack Gordon, Harry Warren. *cast* George Montgomery, Ann Rutherford, Cesar Romero, Lynn Bari, Carole Landis, Jackie Gleason, Glenn Miller and his Band.
●Second and by far the best of (surprisingly) only two movies graced by the Glenn Miller band, with some great numbers strung out on a slender plot enlivened by bright dialogue as the wives do a lot of loving and bitching while following the band tour. A moment to treasure is the specialty dance to 'I've Got a Gal in Kalamazoo' by the marvellous Nicholas Brothers. TM

Ordeal by Innocence

(1984, GB, 88 min)
d Desmond Davis. *p* Jenny Craven. *sc* Alexander Stuart. *ph* Billy Williams. *ed* Timothy Gee. *pd* Ken Bridgeman. *m* Dave Brubeck. *cast* Donald Sutherland, Faye Dunaway, Christopher Plummer, Sarah Miles, Ian McShane, Diana Quick, Annette Crosbie, Michael Elphick, Phoebe Nicholls, Michael Maloney, Brian Glover.
●In this adaptation of what was reputedly Agatha Christie's favourite among her own novels, a scientist (Sutherland) turns up with evidence which would have cleared a tried murderer. Alas, the boy has been hanged, and the family seems more interested in covering up the past than rehabilitating his reputation. Set in the '50s, the film succeeds admirably in catching a feeling of repression and social conformity, and the idea of murder as a means of maintaining respectability rather than for gain or passion. Agatha Christie's creation is finally recovered from Cluedo territory, and provides British cinema with a genuine '50s black thriller. CPea

Order of Death (L'Assassino del Poliziotti/aka Corrupt)

(1983, It, 101 min)
d Roberto Faenza. *p* Elda Ferri. *sc* Ennio De Concini, Hugh Fleetwood, Roberto Faenza. *ph* Giuseppe Pinori. *ed* Nino Baragli. *ad* Giantito Burchiellaro. *m* Ennio Morricone. *cast* Harvey Keitel, John Lydon, Nicole Garcia, Leonard Mann, Sylvia Sidney, Carla Romanelli.
●Keitel is a cop whose secret world of high living (financed by illicit side-dealing) is invaded by Lydon, who not only confesses to a spate of cop-killings, but seems to know more about Keitel than is comfortable. Two little balls of poison, they become locked together in sadistic games in which the captor needs his victim as much as the victim needs his confessor. The film (shot in English) is very much in line with the Continental habit of turning genres around – like Leone with the Western, this is a spaghetti thriller – and it uses the hard-nosed framework as a prop for its greater interest in the moral complexities of guilt, punishment and transference, rather than the traditional gestures of its US models. Keitel is his usual ineffable self, his features glassy with repressed anxiety and violence; the only miscalculation is the casting of Lydon (aka Johnny Rotten), who seems as threatening as a wet poodle. CPea

Orders

see Ordres, Les

Orders Are Orders

(1954, GB, 78 min, b/w)
d David Paltenghi. *p* Donald Taylor. *sc* Donald Taylor, Geoffrey Orme, Eric Sykes. *ph* Arthur Grant. *ed* Joseph Sterling. *ad* Ray Simm. *m* Stanley Black. *cast* Margot Grahame, Maureen Swanson, June Thorburn, Raymond Huntley, Bill Fraser, Peter Sellers, Brian Reece, Sidney James, Tony Hancock, Donald Pleasence, Eric Sykes.
●Crude farce in which an American film unit descends on an army barracks to make a sci-fi movie, with the buxom actresses sowing predictable havoc. Based on a 1932 play, previously filmed (as *Orders Is Orders*) in 1933, with jokes just as antiquated. Just about worth suffering to see Tony Hancock in his film debut as the harassed bandmaster. TM

Orders to Kill

(1958, GB, 111 min, b/w)
d Anthony Asquith. *p* Anthony Havelock-Allan. *sc* Paul Dehn. *ph* Desmond Dickinson. *ed* Gordon Hales. *ad* John Howell. *m* Benjamin Frankel. *cast* Paul Massie, Irene Worth, Lillian Gish, Eddie Albert, Leslie French, James Robertson Justice, John Crawford, Lionel Jeffries, Sandra Dorne, Jacques Brunius.
●A way above average Asquith film, this is a WWII drama, with Massie sent to Occupied Paris to kill a Resistance leader (French) suspected of being a Nazi collaborator. But his target turns out to be a mild-mannered family man with Lillian Gish for a mother. Despite his doubts (later proved to be well-founded), the deed is done, and the movie starts to focus on Massie's later life. Working well in the first half as a thriller, it then turns into a Graham Greene-like, intensely Catholic study of the conflict between conscience and duty. ATu

Order to Kill (El Clan de los Inmorales)

(1973, Sp/It/Dom, 95 min)
d/p José G Maesso. *sc* Santiago Moncada, Eugenio Martin, Massimo De Rita, José G Maesso. *ph* Aice Parolini. *ed* Angel Serrano. *ad* Rafael Ferri. *m* Adolfo Waitzman. *cast* Helmut Berger, Sydne Rome, José Ferrer, Kevin McCarthy, Elena Berrido, Claudio Chea, Juan Luis Galiardo.
●This extraordinarily tacky offering does at least have some interesting undercurrents. Shot in Santo Domingo (of all places), and featuring Helmut Berger (of all people) toting a machine-gun (of all things), the film on one level is a catalogue of ineptness: crude establishing shots, irrelevant music, jerky editing, and a plot (which has Berger blackmailed into working for a renegade police chief) that warrants little attention. What holds it together beneath the surface mess is a distinctly homosexual aura of sadism and masochism. Since this has nothing to do with the plot, one is surprised at the relentlessness of the smouldering looks and rippling torsos. In addition to some crude emphasis on phallic gunplay, the utter disposability of the women, and trials of strength and endurance, the film goes to outrageous lengths to have its star look disarranged or be beaten up.

Ordet (The Word) 100

(1954, Den, 125 min, b/w)
d/sc Carl Dreyer. *ph* Henning Bendtsen. *ed* Edith Schlüssel. *ad* Erik Aaes. *m* Poul Schierbeck. *cast* Henrik Malberg, Emil Hass Christensen, Preben Lerdorff Rye, Cay Kristiansen, Birgitte Federspiel, Ann Elizabeth.

●Dreyer's penultimate feature (*Gertrud* followed a full decade later) is another of his explorations of the clash between orthodox religion and true faith. Based with great fidelity on a play by Kaj Munk, it's formulated as a kind of rural chamber drama, and like most of Dreyer's films it centres on the tensions within a family. Its method is to establish a scrupulously realistic frame of reference, then undercut it thematically with elements of the fantastic and formally with a film syntax that demands constant attention to the way meaning is being constructed. The intensity of the viewer's relationship with the film makes the closing scene (a miracle) one of the most extraordinary in all cinema. TR

Ordinary Decent Criminal

(1999, Ire/Ger/US/GB, 94 min)
d Thaddeus O'Sullivan. *p* Jonathan Cavendish. *sc* Gerard Stembridge. *ph* Andrew Dunn. *ed* William Anderson. *pd* Tony Burrough. *m* Damon Albarn. *cast* Kevin Spacey, Linda Fiorentino, Peter Mullan, Stephen Dillane, Helen Baxendale, David Hayman, Patrick Malahide, Gerard McSorley, David Kelly, Gary Lydon.

●With Irish gangster Martin Cahill's life and crimes already filmed twice (as John Boorman's *The General* and David Blair's superior TV movie *Vicious Circle*), this third version of the same events is belated and superfluous. Pitched between cartoonish caper and knockabout farce, it also suffers from an uneven tone compounded by Damon Albarn's relentlessly jaunty soundtrack. Renamed Michael Lynch (Spacey, ludicrously miscast), the Cahill character goes through the motions as before, dividing his affections between his wife and her sister, robbing banks and relishing his status as public irritant No. 1. But his decision to taunt the police with the theft of an unsellable Caravaggio painting is an act of hubris that undermines his Robin Hood persona, alienates his loyal gang members and stresses him out. Occasional topical allusions aside, this could be taking place anywhere, especially as the stripping away of the social and political context extends to playing fast and loose with the facts. Fiorentino flounders in the thinly written role of Lynch's wife, leaving the supporting players such as Baxendale (as her sister) and Mullan (as his increasingly disenchanted henchman) to anchor the centrifugal action. NF

Ordinary Heroes (Qianyan Wanyu)

(1999, HK, 128 min)
d/p Ann Hui. *sc* Chan Kin-Chung. *ph* Yu Lik-Wai. *ed* Kwong Chi-Leung. *pd* Elbut Poon, Ringo Fung. *m* Clarence Hui, Chiu Tsang-Hei. *cast* Rachel Lee, Lee Kang-Sheng, Anthony Wong, Tse Kwan-Ho, Augustine Mok.

●Hui's sprawling, difficult film expresses very complex feelings about Hong Kong as a place and its people. Its core is a kind of 'rough guide' to recent social and political activism. Hui frames the film with sequences from a street play about the late Ng Chung-Yin, an agit-prop pioneer in the 1970s, and focuses on the few individuals who in the 1980s lobbied the government on China-related issues and campaigned for social reforms – activities cut short by events in Tiananmen Square in June 1989. Some of the characters are close to their real life prototypes (the Maoist-Catholic priest Ah Kam, superbly played by Wong) while others are more or less fictional (the boy who joins Ah Kam to get near a girl he fancies), but all of them are 'heroic' losers. In their lonely, principled struggles, cold shouldered by society, Hui pinpoints something which could be a key to Hong Kong identity. TR

Ordinary People

(1980, US, 124 min)
d Robert Redford. *p* Donald L Schwary. *sc* Alvin Sargent. *ph* John Bailey. *ed* Jeff Kanew. *ad* Phil Bennett, J Michael Riva. *cast* Donald Sutherland, Mary Tyler Moore, Judd Hirsch, Timothy Hutton, M Emmet Walsh, Elizabeth McGovern, Dinah Manoff, James B Sikking.

●Any movie starring the all-American dream mum Mary Tyler Moore as a neurotic, domineering mother, papering over the cracks as her husband and son go to pieces, should get ten out of ten. Unfortunately, Robert Redford's super-tasteful movie (from the novel by Judith Guest) uses her pixie grin as its only effective irony. For the rest, it's a scrupulously observed affluent American psychodrama that wishes it was Chekhov: tinged with autumn leaves, and following the cocktail party, the golfing holiday, the school swimming race, it peels away the happy smile of these 'ordinary people', plunged into misery after the death of one son and the breakdown of another. An actors' movie and an advert for therapy, extremely bitter, but handsomely directed in its elegant pretentiousness, it leaves you the impression that Redford is, despite it all, as cuddly as a teddy-bear. DMacp

Ordinary Tenderness

see Tendresse Ordinaire

Ordres, Les (Orders)

(1974, Can, 107 min, b/w & col)
d/sc Michel Brault. *ph* Michel Brault, François Protat. *ed* Yves Dion. *ad* Normand Sarrazin. *song* Philippe Gagnon. *cast* Jean Lapointe, Hélène Loiselle, Claude Gauthier, Louise Forestier, Guy Provost, Amulette Garneau, Louise Latraverse.

●Brault's film not only doesn't provide answers to the political questions it throws up in its reconstruction of the effects of Canada's 1970 War Measures Act, it scarcely even seems aware of the true questions. Brault's sifting of the case histories of 450 Quebec citizens, arrested and detained without charge under virtual martial law which arose from two political kidnappings, is absorbing enough as 'Kafkaesque' dramatic reconstruction. And the persecution of five of them invites all of the expected audience empathy. But ultimately the film merely becomes a prolonged liberal wank over the summary loss of civil liberties, when it should be getting at the question of how this state of authoritarian paranoia became possible in a supposedly democratic society. RM

Orfeu

(1999, Braz, 110 min)
d Carlos Diegues. *p* Renata de Almeida Magalhães, Paula Lavigne. *sc* Carlos Diegues, Hermano Vianna, Hamilton Vaz Pereira, Paulo Lins, João Emanuel Carneiro. *ph* Affonso Beato. *ed* Sergio Mekler. *pd* Clóvis Bueno. *m* Caetano Veloso. *cast* Toni Garrido, Patricia França, Murilo Benício, Zezé Motta, Milton Gonçalves, Isabel Fillardis.

●In veteran Diegues' colourful update of the Greek myth – not to mention Marcel Camus' 1959 classic *Orfeu Negro*, also set during the Rio carnival – Orfeu is a top samba composer and Euridice a beautiful if innocent hick from the sticks, who tempts the womanising songster away from the adoring and voluptuous Mira and from Death (a drug-dealing gang). Nothing very original in any of that, especially if you've seen Camus' film, but the carnival scenes are spectacular, the music is mostly lovely (though one wishes the characters would actually burst into song and dance more often), and the performances charming. When compared, however, to Luhrmann's *Romeo & Juliet*, which Diegues has surely been watching, it looks a little staid and obvious. GA

Orfeu Negro

see Black Orpheus

Organ

(1996, Jap, 105 min)
d Kei Fujiwara. *p* Binbun Furusawa, Koichi Toda. *sc/ph* Kei Fujiwara. *ed* Kenji Nasa. *pd* Binbun Furusawa, Koichi Toda. *m* Kei Fujiwara. *cast* Kimihiko Hasegawa, Kenji Nasa, Kei Fujiwara, Ryo Okubo, Shozo Tojima, Yosiaki Maekawa.

●Diminishing returns hit splatter movies faster than most other genres, and this starts straining for effect and repeating itself within its first hour – with a turgid 45 minutes of blood-letting and grotesquerie to go. Director/writer/star Fujiwara (she played the mutilated girlfriend in *Tetsuo*) kicks it off in neo-*noir* mode: undercover cops investigate a yakuza-financed trade in body parts ripped from murder victims for transplant surgery. But the weird brother and sister doing the murdering and organ-extractions turn out to have histories as hideously abused kids, which twists the film in the direction of pop psycho-drama. TR

Organization, The

(1971, US, 107 min)
d Don Medford. *p* Walter Mirisch. *sc* James R Webb. *ph* Joseph Biroc. *ed* Ferris Webster. *pd* James F McGuire. *m* Gil Mellé. *cast* Sidney Poitier, Gerald S O'Loughlin, Barbara McNair, Sheree North, Raúl Julia, Ron O'Neal, Lani Miyazaki, Allen Garfield, bernie Hamilton, Daniel J Travanti.

●Poitier's third (and final) appearance as Lt Virgil Tibbs, now risen beyond the good black cop idea to regular good cop, with all the hagiography this implies (good looks, boyish charm, nice wife, happy kids; against him the villains are unpleasant, faceless, childless, ruthless). The organization is a world-wide heroin combine operating behind the façade of big business. None too convincing (since the film is torn between the need to make them ridiculous and the need to have us rooting for them) is the group of good-hearted liberals who, distressed by the fuzz's lack of action, decide to take on the organization themselves. Tibbs, needless to say, does an exemplary job. In spite of everything, the climactic action sequences are genuinely intriguing and totally involving. VG

Organized Crime and Triad Bureau (Zhong'an Shilu O-ji)

(1993, HK, 90 min)
d Che Kirk Wong. *sc* Winky Wong. *ph* Wong Wing-Hang, Chan Kwong-hung. *ed* Choi Hung. *m* Tsung Ding-yat. *cast* Danny Lee, Anthony Wong, Cecilia Yip, Elisabeth Lee, Cheung Yiu-yeung.

●The perennial bad boy of Hong Kong cinema, Kirk Wong (trained in Croydon) has left behind the SM perversities of his early movies and found a niche directing hard-man thrillers much closer to street-level realities than anything John Woo ever did. This one's about an oddball cop (Danny Lee, who also produced) tracking a villain to his island hideaway to arrest him, only to lose him in a break-out. The fact that the bad guy was about to flee into Mainland China hints at political references, but what this is really about is staging running battles between cops and criminals in everyday locations, from the island backwater to the crowded streets of central Kowloon. As such, it's a blast. TR

Orgasmo

see Paranoia

Orgazmo

(1997, US, 94 min)
d Trey Parker. *p* Fran Rubel Kuzui, Jason McHugh, Matt Stone. *sc* Trey Parker. *ph* Kenny Gioseffi. *ed* Trey Parker, Michael R Miller. *pd* Tristan Paris Bourne. *m* Paul Robb. *cast* Trey Parker, Dian Bachar, Robyn Lynne, Michael Dean Jacobs, Ron Jeremy, Andrew W Kemler, David Dunn.

●Trey Parker, creator of TV's *South Park*, knocked out this cheap 'n' cheerful comedy while his animated delinquents were little more than a gleam across his cherubic face. The plot is pure silliness: pretty Mormon boy Joe Young (Parker) comes to the city and winds up starring in a porn flick under the dastardly direction of Maxxx Orbison (Jacobs), meets with national acclaim, but subsequently turns the tables on his scheming Svengali with the help of his screen sidekick Ben, aka 'Choda Boy' (Bachar), and the Orgazmatron, a home-invented ray gun which induces instant orgasm. Parker's humour is essentially sarcastic, but inventive as well as obvious: the *South Park* sensibility is easily discernible, though far from perfected. What's missing is the animation's juvenile irony: instead of ten-year-olds' artwork and humour produced to an adult standard, this is just boy's fare produced by boys – the production values don't even merit evaluation. Easily scorned, just as easily forgotten, but not without a certain crude charm. NB

Orgueilleux, Les (The Proud Ones)

(1953, Fr/Mex, 104 min, b/w)
d Yves Allégret. *sc* Jean Aurenche, Yves Allégret, Pierre Bost, Jean Clouzot. *ph* Alex Phillips. *ed* Claude Nicole. *ad* Auguste Capelier, Gunther Gerzso. *m* Paul Misraki. *cast* Gérard Philipe, Michèle Morgan, Carlos L Moctezuma, Victor M Mendoza, Michèle Cordoue, André Toffel.

●One of those sub-Graham Greene tales of redemption in exotic climes (actually based on a story by Sartre, *L'Amour Rédempteur*), with Morgan as a chic tourist stranded in a Mexican village when her husband suddenly dies of meningitis, and Philipe as the drink-sodden doctor regaining his self-respect in the ensuing epidemic (not to mention her arms). Busily atmospheric, it strains mightily after a sort of sweaty eroticism (a key scene being one in which Philipe has to give Morgan an extremely painful lumbar injection), with the bleak and dusty locations often strikingly shot by Alex Phillips; but despite the valiant efforts of both leads, the central relationship and redemption theme are ludicrously spurious. TM

Original Gangstas

(1996, US, 99 min)
d Larry Cohen. *p* Fred Williamson. *sc* Aubrey Rattan. *ph* Carlos Gonzalez. *ed* David Kern, Peter B Ellis. *pd* Elayn Ceder. *m* Vladimir Horunzhy. *cast* Fred Williamson, Jim Brown, Pam Grier, Paul Winfield, Isabel Sanford, Ron O'Neal, Robert Forster, Charles Napier, Wings Hauser, Richard Roundtree.

●Gary, Indiana: a dying steeltown. A young basketball hopeful is killed by hoodlums. An elderly cornerstore proprietor tells the cops who did it. The Rebels shoot him. The man's football-coach son (Williamson) returns from LA and, with the help of angry oldies, including the dead boy's mum (Grier) and estranged, ex-boxer father (Brown), sets about cleaning up the town. He declares war on the Rebels – ironic, given that two decades earlier he'd been a founder of the gang. Despite its standard formula, this belated blaxploitation picture is something of an oddity. First, it attempts to frame its story of ghetto warfare within an economic and political context; second, it pits '70s stars against the kind of younger, more heavily armed and more nihilistic characters familiar from '90s fare. In siding so explicitly with the old-timers in their outrage at mindless murder, it flirts with sentimentality, but at least it's not seduced by the gangstas' macho posturing; moreover, Williamson and Brown's own former irresponsibilities – abandoning families and struggling communities – are presented as being at least partly to blame for the chaos and carnage now on the streets. As an action-thriller the film never quite delivers; sociologically, however, it's not without interest. GA

Original Kings of Comedy, The

(2000, US, 116 min)
d Spike Lee. *p* Walter Latham, David Gale, Spike Lee. *ph* Malik Sayeed. *ed* Barry Alexander Brown. *pd* Wynn P Thomas. *with* Steve Harvey, DL Hughley, Cedric the Entertainer, Bernie Mac.

●The Kings, for the uninitiated, are four black stand-ups, who toured together to sell out audiences across the States. Spike Lee's concert film shows each in turn doing his thang, with occasional, brief backstage chat as punctuation between the routines. The on-screen audience, in Charlotte, N Carolina, is predominantly black and wildly enthusiastic. So is it exclusively a black thing, or does comedy cross colour boundaries? Well, colour difference figures large as a subject. A subversive routine imagining a black *Titanic* hits home, but the opening riff on a local NFL player will bemuse most British audiences. When two of the comics fix on the incongruous thought of a black man flipping out and going on a gun-crazy killing spree, you have to think that colour might be less of a barrier than social difference. American culture rarely seems parochial, but judicious pruning for international audiences could have sharpened the effect. As for that 'original' tag, only Bernie Mac brings anything very different to the table, with his confrontational persona and insistence on saying the unsayable. This is comedy with a sense of showmanship, and Lee cuts shrewdly to the rhythm of the jokes. TCh

Original Sin (Péché originel)

(2000, US/Fr, 116 min)
d Michael Cristofer. *p* Denise Di Novi, Kate Guinzburg, Carol Lees. *sc* Michael Cristofer. *ph* Rodrigo Prieto. *ed* Eric Sears. *pd* David J Bomba. *m* Terence Blanchard. *cast* Antonio Banderas, Angelina Jolie, Thomas Jane, Jack Thompson, Gregory Itzin, Allison Mackie, Joan Pringle, Cordelia Richards.

●Early 20th century Cuba. Luis (Banderas) eagerly awaits the arrival of his mail-order bride. But when he meets the woman, Julia (Jolie), she's a knockout, not the homely maid of her photo. She didn't want him to like her for her looks, she says – which is okay because Luis, in turn, admits that he's actually a coffee tycoon, not the lowly clerk he'd described in his correspondence. Julia reveals incredible sexual skills and quickly puts Luis under her spell and keeps him there, even after he knows she's actually a con artist. Adapted from Cornell Woolrich's novel *Waltz into Darkness*, the film wallows in overblown acting and an insufferably long and convoluted narrative. Inconsistencies in Julia's story pop up like jack in the boxes as soon as she steps on to the island; the second half is especially painful to watch. In return, however, we're treated to several long shots of the nude, impossibly attractive leads. Don't feel bad about taking a prurient interest. They owe you. NKee

Orion's Belt (Orions Belte)

(1985, Nor, 103 min)
d Ola Solum. *p* Dag Alveberg, Petter Borgli. *sc* Richard Harris [Harald Paalgard, Ola Solum]. *ph* Harald Paalgard. *ed* Bjørn Breigutu. *ad* Harald Egede-Nissen. *m* Geir Bøhren, Bent Åserud. *cast* Helge Jordal, Sverre Anker Ousdal, Hans Ola Sørlie, Kjersti Holmen, Vidar Sandem, Nils Johnson, Jon Eikemo.

●A Norwegian thriller, and it ain't half bad. Actually, it's half pretty good, and the rest is average. Three sailors, who make a living doing less than legal things with their broken-down boat, are quite happy roaming the stormy Arctic seas until they stumble on a secret Russian surveillance post. Chaos ensues as the Russians discover them and try to kill them off, notably in a fine helicopter attack. Towards the end, the suspense drops a little as the film becomes more conventional, but the first hour is gripping, intelligent, and unusual, both in terms of characterisation and story. And the location shooting, predictably, is superb. GA

Orlando

(1992, GB/Rus/Fr/It/Neth, 93 min)
d Sally Potter. *p* Christopher Sheppard. *sc* Sally Potter. *ph* Alexei Rodionov. *ed* Hervé Schneid. *pd* Ben Van Os, Jan Roelfs. *m* David Motion, Sally Potter. *cast* Tilda Swinton, Billy Zane, John Wood, Lothaire Bluteau, Charlotte Valandrey, Heathcote Williams, Quentin Crisp, Dudley Sutton.

●There are lots of intellectual traditions vying for ascendancy in Potter's adaptation of Virginia Woolf's 1928 modernist novel, but the joy is that the film comes over simply: a beautiful historical pageant of 400 years of English history, full of visual and aural pleasures, sly jokes, thought-provoking insights, emotional truths – and romance. It begins at the opulent court of Virgin Queen Elizabeth (Crisp), where the male immortal Orlando receives favour and an estate; and thence follows his quest for love in 50-year jumps through the Civil War, the early colonial period, the effete literary salons of 1750 (by which time Orlando is a woman), the Victorian era of property, and finally a 20th century postscript added by Potter. The fine, stylised performances from an idiosyncratic international cast are admirably headed by Swinton's magnificent Orlando, who acts as the film's complicitous eyes and ears; and there's little to fault in Alexei Rodionov's cinematography, which renders the scenes with rare sensitivity. It's a critical work – in the sense that it comments wryly on such things as representations of English history, sexuality/androgyny and class – but made in the spirit of a love poem to both Woolf and the England that made us. WH

Orlovs, The (Suprugi Orlovy)

(1978, USSR, 85 min)
d Mark Donskoi. *p* Mark Aizenberg. *sc* Mark Azov, Mark Donskoi, Valery Mikhailovsky. *ph* Viacheslav Egorov. *ed* O Bachorunoi. *ad* Olga Kravchenya. *m* Raphil Khozak. *cast* Nina Ruslanova, Anatoly Semyonov, Seryozha Tegin, Danil Sagal, Yuri Kamorny, Pyotr Merkuryev, Pavel Vinnik.

●A friend of Gorki, Eisenstein's assistant, Civil War Red soldier: Mark Donskoi's extraordinary career spans a century of Russian history, and includes making the three famous *Gorki* films in the '30s which more recently influenced Bill Douglas in his own autobiographical trilogy. *The Orlovs*, taken from another Gorki story, is fashioned in the same style as his earlier films: a close Dickensian focus on everyday village life which pre-dates the later unacceptable face of Soviet Social Realism. The central couple are given the chance of transcending the general misery of their lives by working in a hospital during a cholera outbreak. She responds, he regresses, they part; a moral tale with its typical Gorkian emphasis on the necessity of striving for a better existence. Heartening to find a social vision of such clear-eyed optimism from a 78-year-old. CPea

Ornette: Made in America

(1985, US, 80 min)
d Shirley Clarke. *p* Kathleen Hoffman. *ph* Ed Lachman, (additional) Baird Bryant, Hilary Harris, John M Heller, Bob Elfstrom. *ed* Shirley Clarke. *with* Ornette Coleman, Demon Marshall, Gene Tatum, Prime Time, John Giordano, Fort Worth Symphony Orchestra.

●Not surprisingly, the musical content in this documentary about modern jazz's greatest iconoclast is superb: much of it revolves around a 1983 performance of Ornette Coleman's 'Skies of America' suite, with orchestra and the harmolodic Prime Time band. Clarke's film, however, is something else: with updated psychedelic visual tricks, and little info on the master's life or career, it fails to do him or his music justice. But for the sight and sound of the man in action (including some fine archive footage from the early '70s), it's essential viewing for any jazz aficionado. GA

Orphan of Anyang, The (Anyang Ying'er)

(2001, China, 84 min)
d Wang Chao. *p* Fang Li. *sc* Wang Chao. *ph* Zhang Xi. *ed* Wang Chao, Wang Gang. *ad* Wang Chao. *cast* Zhu Jie, Sun Guilin, Yue Senyi, Liu Tianhao, Miao Fuwen.

●The dirt-town setting and non-pro cast mean that Wang Chao's debut stands somewhat in the shadow of *Xiao Wu*, a beacon for an entire generation of underground directors in China. Middle-aged, unmarried and now unemployed, Yu Dagang comes upon an abandoned baby with a note from its mother promising a stipend to anyone willing to raise it. The mother turns out to be ex-nightclub hostess Yanli; they meet and eventually start living together, he repairing bicycles and she working as a hooker. But then another prospective parent shows up: gang-boss Side (probably the biological father), terminally ill and looking for an heir. It all ends badly, but Wang sweetens the pill with a closing wish-fulfilment fantasy. The numerous sequence-shots evidence a good cinematic eye: two extended fixed-angle shots of Yanli in a noodle shop show exactly how less can yield more. TR

Orphans

(1987, US, 120 min)
d/p Alan J Pakula. *sc* Lyle Kessler. *ph* Donald McAlpine. *ed* Evan Lottman. *pd* George Jenkins. *m* Michael Small. *cast* Albert Finney, Matthew Modine, Kevin Anderson, John Kellogg, Anthony Heald, Novella Nelson.

●Adapting his own play, Lyle Kessler has ventured out from the clapped-out clapboard in Newark where Phillip (Anderson) is kept in thrall to his brother Treat (Modine). An opening sequence, showing Treat as a compassionate mugger, establishes the violent conflict of emotions within the robbing hood, but otherwise the few external excursions don't add much. Fortunately, the pressure-cooker atmosphere of the central arena is by no means dissipated. Phillip believes he will die if he goes outside, so while his keeper is out providing for them, he prowls the house like a mangy caged animal or (though Treat thinks he's illiterate) reads in the attic. This precarious state of interdependence is upset when Treat brings back Harold (Finney), a gangster who is drunk and rolling in dodgy dollars, in a ransom bid defeated when Harold, a fellow-orphan, offers these dead end kids his affection. Under Harold's munificent guidance, the lonesome sons rehabilitate both their home and themselves...until Treat's inability to control his feelings precipitates disaster. Pakula's direction extracts every ounce of energy from this ferocious tragedy, with Finney and Anderson, repeating their acclaimed performances from the London stage production, eclipsed by Modine, in stunning form. It's funny, fearsome, and finally very moving. MS

Orphans

(1997, GB, 95 min)
d Peter Mullan. *p* Frances Higson. *sc* Peter Mullan. *ph* Grant Scott Cameron. *ed* Colin Monie. *pd* Campbell Gordon. *m* Craig Armstrong. *cast* Douglas Henshall, Gary Lewis, Stephen McCole, Rosemarie Stevenson, Frank Gallagher, Alex Norton, Dave Anderson, Deirdre Davis.

● Their mother dead, the Flynns – Thomas (Lewis), Michael (Henshall), John (McCole), Sheila (Stevenson) – gather in a pub on the eve of her funeral. When Michael is stabbed in a fight with a local who mocks Thomas's maudlin sung tribute, it's the start of a long, dark night of the soul, as the siblings separately wander Glasgow trying to come to terms with feelings of grief, pride, rage and revenge: Thomas stubbornly staying in church with the coffin, disabled Sheila left to fend for herself after her wheelchair gets stuck, Michael delaying hospital treatment in order to profit by pretending his wound was caused by a work accident, and John going in search of a gun to kill his brother's attacker. Mullan's first feature as writer/director is a tough mix of searing drama and black comedy, an imaginative, sometimes surreal account of lives so afflicted by boozily confused, aggressive self-assertiveness that there seems little room left for mercy, hope or compassion. GA

Orphans of the Storm

(1921, US, 143 min (21 fps), b/w (tinted))
d/p/sc DW Griffith. *ph* Hendrik Sartov, Paul Allen, Billy Bitzer. *ed* James Smith, Rose Smith. *ad* Charles M Kirk, Edward Scholl. *m* (original accompanying) Louis F Gottschalk, William Frederick Peters. *cast* Lillian Gish, Dorothy Gish, Creighton Hale, Joseph Schildkraut, Frank Losee, Catherine Emmett, Morgan Wallace.

● Griffith's neglected epic stars the Gish sisters as victims of the chaos that hits Paris during the French Revolution. Authentic down to real champagne at an aristocratic bacchanal, the film depicts the storming of the Bastille with spectacular flair. While the director's handling of humour (clumsy) and pathos (heavily milked) demands some generosity from the audience, the eternal radiance of Lillian Gish shines through everything. The restored print under review (in 1998), from New York's Museum of Modern Art, is fine on detail but suffers from excessive tinting. DT

Orphée (Orpheus)

(1950, Fr, 112 min, b/w)
d Jean Cocteau. *p* André Paulvé. *sc* Jean Cocteau. *ph* Nicolas Hayer. *ed* Jacqueline Sadoul. *ad* Jean d'Eaubonne. *m* Georges Auric. *cast* Jean Marais, Maria Casarès, François Périer, Marie Déa, Edouard Dermithe, Juliette Gréco, Henri Crémieux, Roger Blin.

● Marais (Cocteau's companion) plays the '40s poet (alias Cocteau) who's won fame, fortune and the hatred of Left Bank youth. Desperate for inspiration, he follows an imperious Princess flanked by Fascist (or 'Cruising') type police. Her rubber-gloved hand leads through the looking-glass to a slow-motion night kingdom. This *Sur-Noir* fantasy has more meanings than the Book of Revelations. It's an allegory for Poetry. It's the Confessions of a Gay Opium-Eater. Its mirrors and misogyny, optical tricks and enigmatic phrases, mark it as prime meat for Lacanians and feminists. With its Resis-tance Band radios and brutal militiamen it catches the terrors of Occupation life. Its tight cross-lacing of paranoid dreaming and poetic realism grips like a bondage corset. When Alain Resnais in Japan couldn't get the crew of *Hiroshima, Mon Amour* to understand, he'd refer to *Orphée,* whose weird myth fascinated them all. RD

Ortliebschen Frauen, Die

see Josephine

Osaka Elegy (Naiwa ereji)

(1936, Jap, 71 min, b/w)
d Kenji Mizoguchi. *p* Masaichi Nagata. *sc* Yoshikata Yoda. *ph* Minoru Miki. *m* Koichi Takagi. *cast* Isuzu Yamada, Seichi Takegawa, Chiyoko Okura, Shinpachiro Asaka, Benkei Shiganoya, Yoko Umemura.

● Mizoguchi's first collaboration with long-time screenwriting colleague Yoshikata Yoda tells of a company telephone operator who, out of a desire to help her impoverished father and student brother, embarks on an affair with her boss, with disastrous results. A tale of lecherous, exploitative businessmen, ungrateful families, and a feisty but self-sacrificing woman, with a savage sting in its tail, the film prefigures Mizoguchi's later work in its angry emphasis on double standards, its visual precision and its engaged but never preachy tone. GA

Osaka Story

(1994, GB, 75 min)
d/sc Toichi Nakata. *ph* Simon Atkins. *ed* Toichi Nakata.

● A compulsive account of Toichi Nakata's return to Osaka to tell his Japanese-Korean family, who want him home and married, that he plans to stay in the West as a film-maker. An illuminating look at Japanese family life (dad is a misanthropic tyrant) and a study of the difficult relationship between Japanese and Koreans, the film has an almost confrontational frankness that belies some of the conventionally polite behaviour on view. GA

Oscar

(1991, US, 109 min)
d John Landis. *p* Leslie Belzberg. *sc* Michael Barrie, Jim Mulholland. *ph* Mac Ahlberg. *ed* Dale Beldin, Michael R Miller. *pd* Bill Kenney. *m* Elmer Bernstein. *cast* Sylvester Stallone, Ornella Muti, Kirk Douglas, Peter Riegert, Chazz Palminteri, Vincent Spano, Marisa Tomei, Tim Curry, Don Ameche, Harry Shearer, Martin Ferrero, Yvonne De Carlo, Richard Romanus, Eddie Bracken, William Atherton.

● Landis transposes Claude Magnier's French farce to Prohibition-era America in homage to the screwball comedies of the '30s. The script is sharp, if formulaic, but the film suffers from several contradictions: this is a farce without sexual tension, a family film with Stallone in the lead, a Landis comedy without vulgarity. At the centre of a deliciously convoluted plot involving mislaid suitcases and never-laid suitors is the plight of Snaps (Stallone), a gangster who promised his dying father to go straight, only no one believes him. Which is the reverse of Stallone's plight: he's trying to go into comedy, only we can't quite believe him. It's a demanding role which calls for more than he can give. Only an eye-poppingly camp Tim Curry, and Harry Shearer and Martin Ferrero's bickering Finucci Brothers, inject life into the proceedings. Landis orchestrates the action with military precision, but forgot to tell his troupe to go over the top. DW

Oscar, The

(1966, US, 121 min)
d Russell Rouse. *p* Clarence Greene. *sc* Harlan Ellison, Russell Rouse, Clarence Greene. *ph* Joseph Ruttenberg. *ed* Chester W Schaeffer. *ad* Hal Pereira, Arthur Lonergan. *m* Percy Faith. *cast* Stephen Boyd, Elke Sommer, Tony Bennett, Eleanor Parker, Milton Berle, Joseph Cotten, Jill St John, Edie Adams, Ernest Borgnine, Ed Begley, Walter Brennan, Broderick Crawford.

● Tacky Tinseltown soaper, logging the unscrupulous rise to stardom of an Academy-nominated actor in a succession of flashbacks, featuring numerous stellar walk-ons and dreadful dialogue. Co-scripted by sci-fi hero Harlan Ellison, based on the novel by Richard Sale, and directed by gimmick-master Rouse, whose *The Thief* contains not one line of dialogue, but who himself had a moment of true glory in co-scripting *DOA*. PT

Oscar and Lucinda

(1997, US/Aus, 132 min)
d Gillian Armstrong. *p* Robin Dalton, Timothy White. *sc* Laura Jones. *ph* Geoffrey Simpson. *ed* Nicholas Beauman. *pd* Luciana Arrighi. *m* Thomas Newman. *cast* Ralph Fiennes, Cate Blanchett, Ciaran Hinds, Tom Wilkinson, Richard Roxburgh, Clive Russell, Bille Brown, Josephine Byrnes. *narrator* Geoffrey Rush.

● In this exquisite adaptation of Peter Carey's novel, gambling is more than an obsession – it's a leap of faith. For eccentric Anglican cleric Oscar Hopkins, winning on the horses is God's way of providing financial support for him and the Oxford poorhouse, while Australian heiress Lucinda Leplastrier's evenings around the card table are just one expression of the scandalous individualism that has already seen this single woman running her own glass factory. As we follow their personal histories from troubled childhood to awkward maturity, the pair seem destined to meet, even though they have grown up on opposite sides of the world. An ocean voyage from Portsmouth to Sydney allows fate to play its hand, but can such emotionally fragile individuals take advantage of their chance combination? Fiennes and Blanchett's expertly judged performances stand at the centre of this tantalising narrative, which conjures a touching love story from the silences of its protagonists' halting vulnerability. For director Armstrong, it marks another wise portrait of resilient Victorian womanhood to match even *My Brilliant Career,* but here she goes beyond her usual classical economy. Everything a costume drama should be. TJ

Osmosis Jones

(2001, US, 95 min)
d Peter Farrelly, Bobby Farrelly, (animation) Piet Kroon, Tom Sito. *p* Bradley Thomas, Peter Farrelly, Bobby Farrelly, Zak Penn, Dennis Edwards. *sc* Marc Hyman. *ph* Mark Irwin. *ed* Lois Freeman-Fox, Stephen R Schaffer, Sam Seig. *pd* (animation) Steve Pilcher, (live action) Sidney Jackson Bartholomew Jr. *m* Randy Edelman. *cast* Bill Murray, Molly Shannon, Chris Elliott, Elena Franklin, Danny Murphy; voices: Chris Rock, Laurence Fishburne, David Hyde Pierce, Brandy Norwood, William Shatner, Ron Howard, Bill Murray.

● The Farrelly brothers take a cartoonish turn. The concept is basically The Numbskulls (the *Beano* comic strip about the little folk who run your head), scaled up to US proportions: an entire body politic organised per representative democracy and the division of labour. And, as Hollywood teaches, when such a system becomes corrupted, it takes a maverick cop and his fat buddy to save the day. Meet jive-talking white blood cell Osmosis Jones, and his new partner in infection-fighting, a 12-hour cold suppressant capsule. The corrupt constitution in question belongs to zoo janitor Frank (Murray), who's not doing his immune system any favours eating boiled eggs off the monkey cage floor. Enter Thrax, a virus of rare toxic intent. The film is remarkably versatile, even if the Farrellys' live footage looks like the chimps commandeered the camera. The plot's so much old rote, and the characters have all the personality of protoplasm; but the anthropomorphising of this microcosmic metropolis is wonderfully imaginative, and the dialogue decidedly spiffy. NB

Ososhiki (Death Japanese Style/Funeral Rites)

(1984, Jap, 124 min, b/w & col)
d Juzo Itami. *p* Seigo Hosogoe. *sc* Juzo Itami. *ph* Yonezo Maeda, (b/w) Shinpei Asai. *ed* Akira Suzuki. *ad* Hiroshi Tokuda. *m* Joji Yuasa. *cast* Tsutomu Yamazaki, Nobuko Miyamoto, Kin Sugai, Shuji Otaki, Ichiro Zaitsu, Nekohachi Edoya, Koen Okumura.

● Another film about food, sex and death from Itami, inspired by his own participation in the funeral of his wife's father. Yamazaki and Miyamoto play a married couple who are hauled out of their dopey work in a TV studio and plunged into the exceedingly expensive business of co-ordinating the burial rites of the wife's cantankerous father. The three-day wake turns out to be a succession of absurd mishaps, family squabbles and unwelcome surprises, reaching its spiritual nadir when an uninvited woman guest drunkenly insists on having sex with Yamazaki before she'll agree to leave. A light-black satire, this is less a Japanese *The Loved One* than a rather feebly wishful attempt to revive the Ozu spirit in Japanese cinema. Invoking Ozu (and there are direct visual quotes from *The End of Summer* and other movies) is to invite comparisons, and that's unwise, given the film's uncertainty of tone and structure. The stand-out sequence is probably also the most realistic: the head of the family struggling to master funeral etiquette from an instructional video. TR

Ossessione

(1942, It, 139 min, b/w)
d Luchino Visconti. *sc* Luchino Visconti, Mario Alicata, Giuseppi De Santis, Gianni Puccini, Antonio Pietrangeli. *ph* Aldo Tonti, Domenico Scala. *ed* Mario Serandrei. *ad* Gino Franzi. *m* Giuseppe Rosati. *cast* Clara Calamai, Massimo Girotti, Juan De Landa, Dhia Cristiani, Elio Marcuzzo, Vittorio Duse, Michele Riccardini.

● Visconti's stunning feature debut transposes *The Postman Always Rings Twice* to the endless, empty lowlands of the Po Delta. There, an itinerant labourer (Girotti) stumbles into a tatty roadside trattoria and an emotional quagmire. Seduced by Calamai, he disposes of her fat, doltish husband (De Landa), and the familiar Cain litany – lust, greed, murder, recrimination – begins. *Ossessione* is often described as the harbinger of neo-realism, but the pictorial beauty (and astute use of music, often ironically) are pure Visconti, while the bleak view of sexual passion poaches on authentic *noir* territory, steeped, as co-scriptwriter Giuseppe De Santis put it, 'in the air of death and sperm'. SJo

Ossos (Bones)

(1996, Port/Fr/Den, 98 min)
d Pedro Costa. *p* Paulo Branco. *sc* Pedro Costa. *ph* Emmanuel Machuel. *ed* Jackie Bastide. *ad* Ze Branco. *m* Wire, Subura. *cast* Nuno Vaz, Maria Lipkina, Vanda Duarte, Isabel Ruth, Inês de Medeiros, Miguel Sermao, Berta Susana Teixeira.

●An initially enigmatic but finally pretty forthright account of extreme angst, alienation and poverty in contemporary Lisbon. It's all fairly extreme, from the lengthy close-ups of silent, haggard, miserable faces to the sequence in which one of the dispossessed tries to get rid of a baby in a busy square, but it's made with conviction and great visual and narrative assurance. GA

Osterman Weekend, The

(1983, US, 105 min)
d Sam Peckinpah. *p* Peter S Davis, William N Panzer. *sc* Alan Sharp. *ph* John Coquillon. *ed* Edward Abroms, David Rawlins. *ad* Robb Wilson-King. *m* Lalo Schifrin. *cast* Rutger Hauer, John Hurt, Meg Foster, Dennis Hopper, Craig T Nelson, Helen Shaver, Cassie Yates, Burt Lancaster, Chris Sarandon.

●Adapted from Robert Ludlum's thriller, this trails a McGuffin about an un-American spy ring, but really revolves around a top brass CIA man with his eye on dictatorship (Lancaster), a disgruntled agent whom the aforesaid bastard has doublecrossed (Hurt), and a flag-waving investigative reporter (Hauer) whom Hurt manipulates into a game of unmask the spy from three candidates (Hopper, Nelson, Sarandon) that has a much more sinister purpose. It all raises the question: who needs another mess of espionage and post-Watergate paranoia? Not Peckinpah, certainly, since he shows scant interest in the convolutions of the plot (neatly enough set out in Alan Sharp's script). Instead, he toys with the agent's name (Fassett) as an excuse to explore facets of reality, fascinatingly turning the screen into a multi-purpose surveillance device. There's a neat trick involving a prerecorded 'live' TV show, a precision-timed shootout round a swimming-pool, some flickers of dark humour. Not a hell of a lot to come away with, except that (sadly, Peckinpah's last film) it is directed with such dazzling skill. TM

Ostrich Has Two Eggs, The (Les Oeufs de l'Autruche)

(1957, Fr, 82 min, b/w)
d Denys de la Patellière. *p* Maurice Teyssier. *sc* Frédéric Grendel, Denys de la Patellière, Shervan Sidery, André Roussin. *ph* Pierre Petit. *ed* Robert Isnardon, Monique Isnardon. *ad* Paul-Louis Boutié. *m* Henri Sauguet. *cast* Pierre Fresnay, Simone Renant, Georges Poujouly, André Roussin, Yoko Tani.

●'My wife's cheating on me, my son's got a boyfriend… *Vive la famille!*' ironises Fresnay in the gruff bark he favoured for comedies. This adaptation of a play by André Roussin (who also fancied himself as an actor) has zero entertainment value or cinematic interest, but it remains significant sociologically for having, mid-century, a leading character who is gay *and* sympathetic. Not only that, but the traditional 'heavy' figures (e.g. the womanising younger brother) all accept Lolo's gayness and try to help him; even Dad comes around when one of his son's frock designs wins a big cash prize. Who plays this phenomenon? No one. In a virtuoso job of construction, Lolo is kept off-screen from start to finish, evidently on the calculation that audiences would be more inclined to accept an abstract sympathetic gay. Still, as incremental progress goes, this counted as a moderate increment. BBa

Otello

(1986, It, 123 min)
d Franco Zeffirelli. *p* Menahem Golan, Yoram Globus. *sc* Franco Zeffirelli. *ph* Ennio Guarnieri. *ed* Peter Taylor, Franca Silvi. *ad* Gianni Quaranta. *m* Verdi. *cast* Placido Domingo, Katia Ricciarelli, Justino Diaz, Petra Malakova, Urbano Barberini, Massimo Foschi, Edwin Francis, Sergio Nicolai, Remo Remotti, Antonio Pierfederici.

●Zeffirelli's lavish Verdi production will annoy the purists (in comes ballet music written for the Paris premiere, plus the odd surprise flashback, out goes Desdemona's plaintive 'Willow' song), but it does enshrine Domingo's magnificent Moor, one of the great characterisations of the past decade or so, for those of us unlikely ever to see him do it in the opera house. The settings are lavish rather than particularly imaginative, and Zeffirelli sometimes loses the surging power of the tragedy behind ever-bustling foreground detail. Yet the singing's the thing, and the principals have been able to translate their stage performances for the camera in a way that will captivate old hands, but won't put off newcomers to filmed opera. TJ

Otesánek

(2000, Czech Rep, 127 min)
d Jan Svankmajer. *p* Keith Griffiths, Jaromír Kallista, Jan Svankmajer. *sc* Jan Svankmajer. *ph* Juraj Galvánek. *ed* Marie Zemanova. *ad* Eva Svankmajerová, Jan Svankmajer. *m* Carl Maria von Weber. *cast* Veronika Zilková, Jan Hartl, Kristina Adamcová, Jaroslava Kretschmerová, Pavel Novy.

●A wonderfully wicked comedy, this is adapted from a traditional Czech folktale about the destructive aspects of humanity's procreative urges. Unable to have a child, a couple become so desperate that the husband decides to amuse his wife by carving a garden tree stump into a baby-like shape. Hilariously, her inability to distinguish the twiggy monstrosity from the real thing at first causes further tensions, but then proves infectious. With folktale inevitability, the thing comes to life and develops a murderously insatiable appetite – but still the parents will protect their offspring, however destructive he gets. Dark, dreamlike and very subversive, it is yet again distinguished by Svankmajer's dazzling blend of animation and live action. GA

Othello

(1951, Mor, 91 min, b/w)
d/p/sc Orson Welles. *ph* Anchise Brizzi, GR Aldo, George Fanto, Oberdan Trojani, Roberto Fusi. *ed* John Shepridge, Jean Sacha, Renzo Lucidi, William Morton. *ad* Alexandre Trauner. *m* Angelo Francesco Lavagnino, Alberto Barberis. *cast* Orson Welles, Micheál MacLiammóir, Suzanne Cloutier, Robert Coote, Hilton Edwards, Michael Lawrence, Fay Compton, Nicholas Bruce, Jean Davis, Doris Dowling. *narrator* Orson Welles.

●Welles' sixth feature (made directly after his avant-garde *Macbeth*) was shot in fits and starts over a period of four years, on a dozen locations in Morocco and Italy, often without money. Naturally, Welles turned the limitations into strengths. When the costumes didn't show up, he filmed in a Turkish bath. When an actor couldn't make it, he used a stand-in and changed his camera angle. When challenged to match footage shot in Mogador and Venice, he contrived dazzling webs of montage. This is Shakespeare filmed with love and powerhouse enthusiasm, never with reverence. The visual rhetoric is synchronised with the verbal imagery: they hit sensory overload together. A very great *film noir*. TR

Othello

(1965, GB, 166 min)
d Stuart Burge. *p* Anthony Havelock-Allan, John Brabourne. *ph* Geoffrey Unsworth. *ed* Richard Marden. *pd* Jocelyn Herbert. *cast* Laurence Olivier, Maggie Smith, Frank Finlay, Joyce Redman, Derek Jacobi, Robert Lang, Kenneth Mackintosh, Anthony Nicholls, Sheila Reid, Michael Turner, Edward Hardwicke.

●Fortunately, Shakespeare's most compressed, most domestic tragedy is here not 'opened out', but kept in its place as a claustrophobic chamber piece. But the basic, very evident fault of the film lies in its initial conception: an apparent desire simply to record Olivier's justly famous stage performance (at the National Theatre, directed by John Dexter). His bravura 'school of semaphore' style will not translate to a subtler, less literary medium, and comes across as such gross hamming as to leave a lingering impression of Othello as some demented nigger minstrel. Yet further evidence (as if more were needed) of the fundamental differences between theatre and film. Great theatre performances need great critics; not some enthusiast with a camera and an eye for posterity. CPea

Othello

(1995, GB, 123 min)
d Oliver Parker. *p* Luc Roeg, David Barron. *sc* Oliver Parker. *ph* David Johnson. *ed* Tony Lawson. *pd* Tim Harvey. *m* Charlie Mole. *cast* Laurence Fishburne, Irène Jacob, Kenneth Branagh, Nathaniel Parker, Michael Maloney, Anna Patrick, Indra Ove, Nicholas Farrell, Michael Sheen.

●Though purists may decry the number of textual excisions and accent-watchers balk at the mix of French, Italian, English and tidied-up Brooklyn on offer here, Parker's first feature is a highly engaging attempt at Shakespeare's most domestic tragedy. Set in various Italian locations, the film obeys the cardinal rule which helps Iago to ensnare the jealous Moor and allows us to forget much of the play's innate absurdity: speed in all things. Using the camera well to explore reactions from onlookers and the main participants, Parker allows Branagh to assume the ring-master role in what is the actor's finest screen performance to date: an Iago rooted in reality, torn and muddied by the art of warfare, but still determined to work his poisonous will; a villain inspired by sexual jealousy but also by a banal, inexplicable malice, superbly hinted at in several perky asides. Fishburne is exotic, proud, bald and more than usually violent. The flashbacks and bed-scenes work, and the idea of having Cassio (Nathaniel Parker) slip Othello his suicide weapon is typically intelligent. But most importantly, everyone gets better as the film progresses, especially Fishburne whose early reserve explodes into passion, violence and moving sorrow. SGr

Other, The

(1972, US, 100 min)
d/p Robert Mulligan. *sc* Tom Tryon. *ph* Robert Surtees. *ed* Folmar Blangsted, O Nicholas Brown. *pd* Albert Brenner. *m* Jerry Goldsmith, Don Bassman. *cast* Uta Hagen, Diana Muldaur, Chris Udvarnoky, Martin Udvarnoky, Norma Connolly, Victor French, Loretta Leversee, Lou Frizzell, John Ritter.

●Scripted by Tom Tryon from his own novel, Mulligan's supernatural foray into the troubled world of childhood mercifully avoids the gory excesses of superficially similar films like *The Exorcist*, made the following year. It might have been mere mumbo-jumbo: his already fertile imagination further stimulated by the promptings of a wise old Russian-born grandmother (Hagen), who teaches him how to empathise totally with other creatures (human and animal), a young boy refuses to believe in the death of his twin brother, whom he blames for a series of mysterious killings. If the level of suspense is lowered by the fact that we soon realise who is responsible, Mulligan none the less produces a genuinely unsettling atmosphere, undermining the idyllic veneer of his '30s pastoral setting by refusing to romanticise his characters and stressing the claustrophobic elements of living in a close-knit community. As so often with this director's work, the film is craftsmanlike rather than brilliant, but the performances, Robert Surtees' lush camerawork, and Mulligan's solid psychological insights make for thoughtful, sometimes even chilling, entertainment. GA

Other, The

see Autre, L'

Other Halves

(1984, NZ, 105 min)
d John Laing. *p* Tom Finlayson, Dean Hill. *sc* Sue McCauley. *ph* Leon Narbey. *ed* Harley Oliver. *pd* Robert Gillies. *m* Don McGlashan. *cast* Lisa Harrow, Mark Pilisi, Fraser Stephen-Smith, Paul Gittins, John Bach, Clare Clifford, Bruce Purchase.

●Laing deserves a medal for his attempts to negotiate the minefield of sensibilities laid by fellow New Zealander Sue McCauley in this adaptation of her controversial novel: the tale of a despairing, middle class Auckland housewife

(Harrow) who falls in love with a teenage Polynesian offender (Pilisi) while receiving psychiatric care for attempted suicide. Treating every taboo, not to mention cliché, associated with race, class and age, it could so easily have led to disaster. But Laing's documentarist's eye, used so effectively in his earlier *Beyond Reasonable Doubt*, manages to give enough sense of the reality behind the contrasted urban nightmares experienced by the two principals to make up for the inevitable infelicities involved. Using a quiet, unemphatic style, he concentrates on the fine performances of Harrow and Pilisi; and what emerges is an honest and affecting tribute to the courage of two outsiders struggling to find some private place of their own in the hostile world. WH

Other Men's Women (aka Steel Highway)

(1931, US, 70 min, b/w)
d William Wellman. *sc* Maude Fulton, William K Wells. *ph* Barney McGill. *ed* Edward M McDermott. *m* Louis Silvers. *cast* Grant Withers, Mary Astor, Regis Toomey, James Cagney, Joan Blondell.

● Reminiscent of Renoir's *La Bête Humaine* (and not shamed by the comparison), this kicks off as fast, fluid, wisecracking comedy, then unexpectedly turns into a touching little tragedy about three people caught up in an unhappy triangle. The outcome is familiar, even conventional, with one rival being heroic and the other outdoing him; but the treatment is so rooted in reality and the acting so good (a bizarre trio of Astor, Withers and Toomey) that the result is a small masterpiece. Above all it is a film to be revelled in for its documentary detail: the sleepy little town with its quiet suburbia, its grimy hash-joint and steamy dance hall (where Cagney, in a supporting role, has a characteristically marvellous moment), and its vast, smoky complex of railway lines, shunting yards and railway sheds, always a major character in the film and swelling to malevolent proportions for the dark, rain-soaked finale. TM

Other One, The (Conversa Acabada)

(1981, Port, 100 min)
d João Botelho. *p* Antonio Pedro Vasconelos. *sc* João Botelho, Helena Domingos. *ph* Acácio d'Almeida. *ed* Manuel Viegas. *ad* Ana Jotta. *m* Jorge Arriagada. *cast* Fernando Cabral Martins, André Gomes, Juliet Berto, Jorge Silva Melo.

● 'I am neither I nor the other one/I am something in between.' So wrote the Portuguese poet Mário de Sá-Carneiro, whose friendship with fellow-poet Fernando Pessoa during 1912–16 forms the 'documentary' material of this Syberbergian first feature by Botelho. The political and moral crisis in early 20th century Portugal, the impasse of exile and the seduction of death, are the key themes in this richly stylised, quasi-theatrical attempt to put poetry on the screen. Stylish, and not short of substance. MA

Other People's Money

see Argent des Autres, L'

Other People's Money

(1991, US, 101 min)
d Norman Jewison. *p* Norman Jewison, Ric Kidney. *sc* Alvin Sargent. *ph* Haskell Wexler. *ed* Lou Lombardo, Michael Pacek, Hubert de la Bouillerie. *pd* Philip Rosenberg. *m* David Newman, Angelo Badalamenti. *cast* Danny DeVito, Gregory Peck, Penelope Ann Miller, Piper Laurie, Dean Jones, RD Call, Mo Gaffney, Tom Aldredge, Ric Kidney.

● The wiles of Wall Street may have been the stuff of '80s entertainment, but this adaptation of an off-Broadway play seems distinctly dated. Still, DeVito gives a wonderfully hammy, vindictive performance as wheeler-dealer 'Larry the Liquidator', whose latest target is a family-run, debt-free company. But chief executive Peck, his companion (Laurie) and her lawyer daughter (Miller) are determined to fight tooth and nail against the onslaught. Jewison does an impressive job with the sexually-charged scenes between DeVito and Miller. Other passages fall flat: the relationship between Peck and Laurie lacks impetus, and there's a sense of déjà vu about the constant references to Japanese knowhow. What Peck is doing in such an underwritten role is something of a mystery. CM

Others, The (Los Otros)

(2001, Sp/US, 104 min)
d Alejandro Amenábar. *p* Fernando Bovaira, José Luis Cuerda, Sunmin Park. *sc* Alejandro Amenábar. *ph* Javier Aguirresarobe. *ed* Nacho Ruiz Capillas. *pd* Benjamin Fernández. m Alejandro Amenábar. *cast* Nicole Kidman, Fionnula Flanagan, Christopher Eccleston, Alakina Mann, James Bentley, Eric Sykes, Elaine Cassidy, Keith Allen, Renée Asherson.

● There are 50 doors in the house. Grace (Kidman) locks each one behind her, and insists the servants do the same. The curtains must be kept closed at all times. Her two children, Anne and Nicholas, are photo-sensitive, Grace explains: allergic to the sun. They live in an isolated Jersey manse, praying for the day Grace's husband will return from WWII, with only the domestic help for company: Lydia (Cassidy) is a mute, Mr Tuttle (Sykes) busies himself around the grounds, while Mrs Mills (Flanagan) seems unimpressed with her new employer's ways. It's to the redoubtable Mrs Mills that Anne turns when her mother refuses to countenance her stories of a mystery interloper, a lodger who makes himself at home without ever showing his face. Reminiscent of Jack Clayton's Henry James adaptation *The Innocents*, this intelligent chiller relies on atmosphere and suggestion rather than gross-out gore. It's a surprise just how confident and controlled Amenábar's first Hollywood venture turns out to be. Subtle, too. Absence makes the heart beat faster: the absence of light, the corporeal absence of loved ones. Shrewdly cast, Kidman is pitch perfect. It's a clammy, ingenious film, one of the best studio movies of the year. TCh

Other Side of Midnight, The

(1977, US, 166 min)
d Charles Jarrott. *p* Frank Yablans. *sc* Herman Raucher, Daniel Taradash. *ph* Fred J Koenekamp. *ed* Donn Cambern, Harold F Kress. *pd* John F DeCuir. *m* Michel Legrand. *cast* Marie-France Pisier, John Beck, Susan Sarandon, Raf Vallone, Clu Gulager, Christian Marquand, Michael Lerner, Sorrell Booke, Charles Cioffi, Josette Banzet.

● *The Other Side of Midnight* gloriously restores the era of *Now, Voyager* – right down to the nonsense title; expert schlocksmiths Daniel Taradash (*Doctors' Wives*) and Herman Raucher (*Summer of '42*) have adapted Sidney Sheldon's bestseller into the movie equivalent of a good long bad read. Pisier aborts herself with a (wire) coathanger as World War II breaks out, sleeps her way across Europe, winds up mistress to a Greek tycoon, and deviously hires the pilot who jilted her back in 1940. The only let-downs are Jarrott's usual stuffy direction and John Beck's boring performance as the pilot. AN

Other Side of Sunday, The (Søndagsengler)

(1996, Nor, 97 min)
d Berit Nesheim. *p* Grete Rypdal, Oddvar Bull-Tuhus. *sc* Berit Nesheim. *ph* Arne Borsheim. *ed* Lillian Fjellvaer. *pd* Grete Heier. *m* Geir Bøhren, Bent Åserub. *cast* Marie Theisen, Hildegun Riise, Bjørn Sundquist.

● Rural Norway, 1959: Maria (Theisen), eldest of three children born to a stern parson, finds there's little of God's love in either her own life or the town's conformist Christian ethos; everything remotely pleasurable – lipstick, cafés, rock'n'roll, boys – is out of bounds. Only the verger, Mrs Tunheim, seems to share Maria's frustration and love of nature. Slight, but well-observed and ably performed. GA

Other Side of the Mountain, The (aka A Window to the Sky)

(1975, US, 102 min)
d Larry Peerce. *p* Edward S Feldman. *sc* David Seltzer. *ph* David M Walsh. *ed* Eve Newman. *m* Charles Fox. *cast* Marilyn Hassett, Beau Bridges, Belinda J Montgomery, Nan Martin, William Bryant, Dabney Coleman.

● Embarrassing tearjerker wrung out of the real-life tragedy of a girl paralysed by a fall on the eve of selection as an Olympic skier. Shaken out of her self-pity by another skier (Bridges), she (Hassett) finds that she can still live a useful life (teaching in an Indian reservation school), and at last feels able to accept the love offered by Bridges – only to have fate tragically intervene once more. Accompanied by a slushy number sung by Olivia Newton-John, ending on a note of bitter-sweet resignation, it's as unbearably fulsome as its sequel (*The Other Side of the Mountain Part 2*, 1978). TM

Other Sister, The

see Otra, La

Other Sister, The

(1999, US, 130 min)
d Garry Marshall. *p* Mario Iscovich, Alexandra Rose. *sc* Gary Marshall, Bob Brunner. *ph* Dante Spinotti. *ed* Bruce Green. *pd* Stephen J Lineweaver. *m* Rachel Portman. *cast* Juliette Lewis, Diane Keaton, Tom Skerritt, Giovanni Ribisi, Poppy Montgomery, Sarah Paulson, Linda Thorson, Joe Flanigan, Juliet Mills, Hector Elizondo.

● Formerly a reliable purveyor of glossy tear-jerkers (*Beaches*, *Frankie & Johnny*) and polished romantic comedies (*Pretty Woman*, *Overboard*), director Garry Marshall has been through a rocky spell recently. *Exit to Eden* was universally panned; *Dear God* went straight to video, and immediately after shooting *The Other Sister*, Marshall covered his back with *Runaway Bride*. Here the mentally challenged daughter of upper middleclass parents (Keaton and Skerritt), Carla requires Juliette Lewis to accentuate all her most irritating mannerisms: the nervous tics, slack-jawed naivety and mangled speech patterns. Carla is, literally, barking. Mrs Tate doesn't want to allow her 24-year-old out into the world, and when she relents, Carla immediately goes and falls in love with the similarly 'challenged' Danny (Ribisi). Next thing you know they're planning to have sex. Marshall has always taken his emotions straight, but there's something so shameless about a man who'd pep up his 'sensitive' drama with a musical montage to the Fine Young Cannibals' 'She Drives Me Crazy', the appropriate response can only be awe. A touchy-feely hotchpotch of good intentions, dishonourable manipulation, smug laughs and uncomfortable half-truths. TCh

Other Voices Other Rooms

(1995, US, 98 min)
d David Rocksavage. *p* Peter Wentworth, David Rocksavage. *sc* Sara Flanigan, David Rocksavage. *ph* Paul Ryan. *ed* Cynthia Scheider. *pd* Amy McGary. *m* Chris Hajian. *cast* Lothaire Bluteau, Anna Thomson, David Speck, April Turner, Frank Taylor, Leonard Watkins, Audrey Dollar, Elizabeth Byler.

● Truman Capote's broadly autobiographical first novel reads like a Gothic cross between *Great Expectations* and Tennessee Williams. In 1938, 13-year-old Joel (Speck) is recalled to a crumbling Deep Southern manse by his father, from whom he has been separated for ten years; there he finds a morbid, effete household languishing in sufferings of the heart or mind, and is denied access to his 'sick' father, mysteriously secreted upstairs. A rites of passage tale of deep psycho-sexual import follows, and debut director Rocksavage, ably assisted by his costume and production designers and cinematographer, has done well in suggesting the almost opiate atmosphere of faded grandeur, outmoded gentlemanly etiquette and otiose regret that suffuses this lonesome house of secrets and compromised nostalgia. The casting seems perfect, too. But something is missing. The script has room for other voices but finds no place for all the symbolic tales and cautionary histories that, in the novel, fill the boy's head and give poignant context to the story's revelations. In moving away from the adolescent's point of view, Rocksavage reduces a ghost-ridden flight of the mind into a claustrophobic chamber piece. WH

Othon (Les Yeux ne peuvent pas en tout temps se fermer)

(1969, WGer/It, 83 min)
d Jean-Marie Straub, Danièle Huillet. *p* Klaus Hellwig. *ph* Ugo Piccone. *ed* Jean-Marie Straub, Danièle Huillet. *cast* Adriano Aprà, Anne Brumagne, Ennio Lauricella, Olimpia Carlisi, Anthony Pensabene, Jean-Claude Biette, Jubarithe Semaran [Jean-Marie Straub].

● Straub examines the process by which events enter our cultural mainstream, and the process by which their use as part of a communications system is transformed into Culture. Corneille's play of political intrigue in Late Empire Rome is used as a base. The text speaks of individual power games outside any social context. Straub perches his actors in togas on the Capitoline Hill in broad daylight. He treats Corneille's words as an undifferentiated block of sound (the actors gabble expressionlessly), and interweaves it with birdsong, traffic noises, the loud splashing of a fountain. A dialectic is set up between the abstraction of the actors' speech and the intimacy of their presence on screen; and between the actors as actors and the actors as play characters, between the actuality of the past and our use of it, with light and colour changes taking on some of the functions of intonation in speech. The film can be mesmeric or irritating: irritating if one tries to force it into fulfilling preconceived notions of plot and character, mesmeric if one trusts the film-maker to lead one into fresh areas of perception.

Otley

(1968, GB, 91 min)
d Dick Clement. *p* Bruce Cohn Curtis. *sc* Ian La Frenais, Dick Clement. *ph* Austin Dempster, Brian West. *ed* Richard Best. *ad* Carmen Dillon. *m* Stanley Myers. *cast* Tom Courtenay, Romy Schneider, Alan Badel, James Villiers, Leonard Rossiter, James Bolam, Fiona Lewis, Freddie Jones.

●Scripted by Clement and Ian La Frenais, this vastly entertaining – if occasionally bewildering – comedy thriller stars Courtenay as the cowardly Otley, an innocent (though none too honest) Portobello Road layabout caught in a muddle of murder, mayhem and espionage. The plot never stops in its search for new ways to embarrass Otley: in one scene he seeks refuge in a crowd, only to find himself the only white man in a Black Power demonstration. More importantly, Otley's petty but human wheeling-and-dealing (lifting the odd art object for resale to the antique stalls) is consistently counterpoised to the slick inhumanity of his forever changing allies/friends, who only think of him as a tool to be used and then thrown away. PH

Otra, La (The Other Sister)

(1946, Mex, 104 min, b/w)
d/sc Roberto Gavaldón. *m* Raul Lavista. *cast* Dolores del Rio, Agustín Irusta, Victor Junco, José Baviera.

●If it weren't for the frequent pauses for morbid pseudo-poetic philosophising, this might be a Warners melodrama, Bette Davis vintage. (Indeed, it bears some resemblance to Bernhardt's *A Stolen Life*.) Desperate, impoverished del Rio murders her wealthy, unsympathetic, identical twin sister, and adopts her identity, only to experience doubts over abandoning her own loyal lover and confusion over the hitherto unknown facets of her sibling's existence. Fine *noir*-style camerawork and a taut if over-schematic narrative are let down by clumsy dialogue and the star's hammy double performance. Hitchcock might have enjoyed the fascination with guilt and its transference, but not, probably, the execution. GA

Otros, Los

see Others, The

Our Daily Bread

see City Girl

Our Daily Bread (aka The Miracle of Life)

(1934, US, 75 min, b/w)
d/p King Vidor. *sc* King Vidor, Elizabeth Hill, (dialogue) Joseph L Mankiewicz. *ph* Robert Planck. *ed* Lloyd Nosler. *m* Alfred Newman. *cast* Karen Morley, Tom Keene, Barbara Pepper, Addison Richards, John Qualen, Lloyd Ingraham, Sidney Bracey, Henry Hall, Nellie V Nichols.

●'Inspired by the Headlines of Today', or at least, the headlines of 1934, this is a fascinating time capsule from the New Deal period, and a rare instance of an 'independent' American movie of the time. An established film-maker with two significant critical hits to his name, *The Crowd* and *The Big Parade*, King Vidor paid for this picture out of his own pocket when the studios told him it was 'too down to earth'. It's the story of a young couple with no money to their name who are given an abandoned farm by a relative. John (Keene) knows nothing about farming, but hits upon the idea of establishing a cooperative. He's inundated with volunteers. The politics are actually pretty confused ('We've got a big job here, we're gonna need a big boss!' they decide), and as drama it's pretty shaky, but the powerful illustration of collective action in the climactic ditch digging sequence holds up. The Connoisseur Academy release under review comes with a brief introduction by Vidor himself (circa 1983) and propaganda newsreels sponsored by Irving Thalberg. TCh

Our Girl Friday (aka The Adventures of Sadie)

(1954, GB, 87 min)
d Noel Langley. *p* George Minter, Noel Langley. *sc* Noel Langley. *ph* Wilkie Cooper. *ed* John Seabourne. *ad* Fred Pusey. *m* Ronald Binge. *cast* Joan Collins, Kenneth More, George Cole, Robertson Hare, Hermione Gingold, Walter Fitzgerald, Hattie Jacques.

●Shipwrecked on an island in the Pacific with jolly Irish stoker More, hardbitten journo Cole and stuffy economics lecturer Hare, millionaire's daughter Joan Collins clung to her 'U' certificate in this British sex comedy of 1954 (from Norman Lindsay's novel *The Cautious Amorist*). TJ

Our Hospitality

(1923, US, 6,220 ft, b/w)
d Buster Keaton, John Blystone. *p* Joseph M Schenck. *sc* Clyde Bruckman, Jean Havez, Joseph Mitchell. *ph* Elgin Lessley, Gordon Jennings. *cast* Buster Keaton, Natalie Talmadge, Joe Roberts, Joseph Keaton, Leonard Chapman, Craig Ward, Ralph Bushman, Edward Coxon, Jean Dumas, Monty Collins, James Duffy.

●The main reason why Keaton is funnier and infinitely more 'modern' than Chaplin is that his movies are written, directed and shot as movies, never as excuses for comedy and/or pathos. This was his second feature and first full-length masterpiece, a story about the innocent inheritor of an old feud between Southern families, who carelessly starts dating the girl from the other family. The period setting (1831, the early days of rail travel) is made integral to the action, and all the laughs spring directly from the narrative and the characters. Buster's climactic rescue of his sweetheart from a waterfall is one of his most daringly acrobatic (and most celebrated) gags. TR

Our Lady of the Assassins (Notre Dame des assassins/ La Virgen de los Sicarios)

(2000, Fr/Col, 101 min)
d Barbet Schroeder. *p* Jaime Osorio Gomez, Margaret Ménégoz. *sc* Fernando Vallejo. *ph* Rodrigo Lalinde. *ed* Elsa Vasquez. *ad* Monica Marulanda. *m* Jorge Arriagada. *cast* German Jaramillo, Anderson Ballesteros, Juan David Restrepo, Manuel Busquets.

●Novelist Fernando (stage actor Jaramillo) comes home to Medellín 'to die' after spending most of his life abroad. He's introduced to Alexis (Ballesteros) at a gay soirée and becomes the boy's sugar daddy – until Alexis is killed in one of the city's countless, everyday street hits, whereupon Fernando replaces him with the assassin (Restrepo). Vallejo's adaptation of his own (autobiographical?) novel provides Schroeder with a way of tackling life and, more particularly, death under the drug cartels. The main body of the film has Fernando revisiting sites he remembers from childhood and commenting on their decline and decay. Shot on high-definition video to minimise the crew's time in dangerous locations, the film certainly underlines how cheap life has become in Medellín. But by focusing on such an acquiescent protagonist and failing to question the sleazy gay soap-opera mechanics of the plot, the film looks more like part of the problem than part of the solution. TR

Our Man in Havana

(1959, GB, 111 min, b/w)
d/p Carol Reed. *sc* Graham Greene. *ph* Oswald Morris. *ed* Bert Bates. *ad* John Box. *cast* Alec Guinness, Burl Ives, Maureen O'Hara, Ernie Kovacs, Noël Coward, Ralph Richardson, Paul Rogers, Jo Morrow, Grégoire Aslan.

●A real 'winds of change' film, with traditional values crumbling in the heat of pre-revolutionary Cuba. Guinness is wonderful. Discovering an unexpected ability to recognise the real in the game of make-believe, he emerges as master of the situation through the boldness of his fantasies. This mad world, where fictional characters die real deaths and even the Clean-Easy man can't be trusted, has little in common with Le Carré's Circus, but as Guinness' vacuum-cleaner salesman/spy sheds his innocence, he becomes dimly recognisable as an early incarnation of molecatcher Smiley. Graham Greene's 'entertainment' is only gently macabre and the threats never quite materialise, but the film cleverly captures the confusion of optimism, cynicism and money-grubbing greed of the 'never had it so good' years. RMy

Our Man in Marrakesh

see Homme de Marrakech, L'

Our Mother's House

(1967, GB, 105 min)
d/p Jack Clayton. *sc* Jeremy Brooks, Haya Harareet. *ph* Larry Pizer. *ed* Tom Priestley. *ad* Reece Pemberton. *m* Georges Delerue. *cast* Dirk Bogarde, Margaret Brooks, Pamela Franklin, Louis Sheldon Williams, John Gugolka, Mark Lester, Sarah Nicholls, Gustav Henry, Parnham Wallace, Yootha Joyce.

●In this matter of fact tale of the macabre, seven children, the eldest aged 13, stick together to carry on as normal after their mother's death. With the old girl safely buried in the garden, all looks to be going smoothly, until ne'er-do-well Bogarde turns up claiming he's their long-lost dad. Intriguing material (adapted from the novel by Julian Gloag), but it's not quite as persuasive as it could have been since all the brats seem to speak with different accents and Bogarde is notably uneasy as the passing Cockernee rogue. TJ

Our Relations

(1936, US, 74 min, b/w)
d Harry Lachman. *p* Stan Laurel. *sc* Richard Connell, Felix Adler. *ph* Rudolph Maté. *ed* Bert Jordan. *ad* Arthur I Royce, William L Stevens. *m* LeRoy Shields. *cast* Stan Laurel, Oliver Hardy, Sidney Toler, James Finlayson, Daphne Pollard, Iris Adrian, Alan Hale, Betty Laurel, James Finlayson, Lona Andre.

●The first of only two of their films produced by Stan Laurel – the other is *Way Out West* – *Our Relations* is a key Laurel and Hardy movie, polished in its production values and spared any interference from Hal Roach. Stan and Ollie play two respectable citizens confronted with their disreputable and irresponsible twin brothers in the most tightly plotted and structured of their films. Abounding in comic moments, it has been both praised as a masterpiece (by Borde and Perrin) and attacked (by Charles Barr) for being too neat and structured. PH

Our Republic

see Repubblica Nostra

Our Story

see Notre Histoire

Our Town

(1940, US, 90 min, b/w)
d Sam Wood. *p* Sol Lesser. *sc* Thornton Wilder, Frank Craven, Harry Chandlee. *ph* Bert Glennon. *ed* Sherman Todd. *ad* William Cameron Menzies, Harry Horner. *m* Aaron Copland. *cast* Thomas Mitchell, Fay Bainter, Frank Craven, William Holden, Martha Scott, Guy Kibbee, Beulah Bondi.

●An amiable, slightly expurgated adaptation of Thornton Wilder's play celebrating the homespun values of a 'typical' small town in New Hampshire. Kicking off with a senior citizen (Craven) buttonholing the camera to act as our guide, it proceeds (by way of some hokey philosophising) to a tolerably banal account of humble humanity facing up to the everyday experience of living, loving and dying. Set in a studio-built town, attractively designed by William Cameron Menzies but not exactly conducive to the required 'realistic' atmosphere, the film is rescued from insufferable cosiness by pleasant performances, Aaron Copland's score, and Wood's meticulous attention to detail. TM

Our Twisted Hero (Uridleui Ilgureojin Youngung)

(1992, SKor, 119 min)
d Park Chon-Won. *p* Do Dong Hwan. *sc* Chang Hyun Soo, Rho Hyo Chung. *ph* Chung Kwang-Suk. *ed* Lee Kyuung Ja. *m* Song Byong Jun.

cast Kyung In Hong, Jung Il Ko, Min Sik Choi.
● Park Chon-Won began his career with a dire pseudo-Marxist agit-prop movie about workers' rights. This second feature is a considerable improvement, but the director hasn't yet fully outgrown a reliance on melodramatic cliché or a tendency to hammer home elementary lessons. His subject here is a school in 1959–60 (a microcosm of the state) and the focus is on a new boy's discovery of the collusion between the class bully and the corrupt teacher. TR

Our Vines Have Tender Grapes

(1945, US, 105 min, b/w)
d Roy Rowland. *p* Robert Sisk. *sc* Dalton Trumbo. *ph* Robert Surtees. *ed* Ralph E Winters. *ad* Cedric Gibbons, Edward Carfagno. *m* Bronsialau Kaper. *cast* Edward G Robinson, Margaret O'Brien, James Craig, Agnes Moorehead, Butch Jenkins, Frances Gifford, Morris Carnovsky, Sara Haden.
● Hollywood was never at its best describing rustic simplicities and folksy values, as in this account of the humble lives of a Norwegian farming community in Wisconsin. Good performances (Moorehead in particular) and a fair feel for the pace of country life, but the film's better moments (the kids squabbling over a pair of roller-skates, the arrival of the circus in town) have to be offset against the crampingly studio-bound atmosphere and an intrusively conventional love interest. TM

Our Wall (Duvarimiz)

(1993, Cyp, 112 min)
d Panicos Chrysanthou.
● The Berlin Wall may be gone, but Europe still endures its wire-mesh curtains: 22 years after Turkey's invasion, Cyprus is yet a nation divided. This grand-standing documentary conveys the history at a multiform, personal level, capturing the individual tragedies on both sides with accounts of Greek and Turkish speakers, friends and families, riven by the partition. Memories and archive footage recall 40 years of disintegration since – surprise! – the colonial machinations of British rule, and there are troubling allusions to other, contemporary outbreaks of nationalistic madness ('Cyprus Will Not Become Yugoslavia,' peace marchers proclaim). NB

Out

(1982, US, 85 min)
d/p Eli Hollander. *sc* Eli Hollander, Ronald Sukenick. *ph* Robert Ball. *ed* Eli Hollander. *pd* Antony Chapman. *m* David Cope. *cast* Peter Coyote, O-Lan Shepard, Jim Haynie, Danny Glover, Scott Beach, Semu Haute.
● Coyote sets off on a spiritual odyssey through a series of explosive and paranoid scenarios which, as well as providing him with a bewildering range of different identities (terrorist, drugs dealer, vice squad agent, healer), serve to parody both movie genres and 'significant' situations. Taken seriously, this offbeat road movie looks like so much late '60s counter-culture codswallop. But what saves the film from accusations of horrendous pretentiousness is its bizarre and often very funny sense of the absurd (presumably intentional). Political plotters derive plans from letters fished out of alphabet soup; intensely meaningful dialogues degenerate into hilariously banal banter; a wise old Indian intersperses words of cosmic insight with glowing appreciations of his new boots. Infuriating and amiable at the same time, it's so far out it's almost in. GA

Outback

see Wake in Fright

Outbreak

(1995, US, 128 min)
d Wolfgang Petersen. *p* Arnold Kopelson, Wolfgang Petersen, Gail Katz. *sc* Laurence Dworet, Robert Roy Pool. *ph* Michael Ballhaus. *ed* Neil Travis, Lynzee Klingman, William Hoy. *pd* William Sandell. *m* James Newton Howard. *cast* Dustin Hoffman, Rene Russo, Morgan Freeman, Kevin Spacey, Cuba Gooding Jr, Donald Sutherland, Patrick Dempsey, Zakes Mokae, Malick Bowens.
● Imagine a disease that makes the bubonic plague look like measles, and is spread in the air like a common cold: so deadly, so rapacious that within a matter of days a sub-continent the size of America is consumed. It's rather too easy to see the film as a metaphor for AIDS panic in the same way that '50s alien B-movies mirrored fears of the Red Menace: viruses as deadly as the one in the film already exist, and apocalyptic non-fiction best-sellers like Laurie Garrett's *The Coming Plague* have already softened up audiences for a film that its makers have touted as a *Jaws* for the '90s. Petersen's thriller does have its moments, most of them in the first half, which shows the painstaking methods by which such viral monsters are tracked and identified, and touches on the ethical problems presented by military intelligence and germ warfare, represented here by Sutherland's beribboned baddie, Gen McClintock. It's a pity, then, that the second half degenerates somewhat into a barely credible rescue mission involving dinky Hoffman and his estranged wife Russo. Entertaining, but not fatally attractive. SGr

Outcast of the Islands

(1951, GB, 102 min, b/w)
d/p Carol Reed. *sc* William Fairchild. *ph* John Wilcox, Ted Scaife. *ed* Bert Bates. *ad* Vincent Korda. *m* Brian Easdale. *cast* Trevor Howard, Ralph Richardson, Kerima, Wendy Hiller, Robert Morley, George Coulouris, Wilfrid Hyde-White, Frederick Valk, Betty Ann Davies, AV Bramble.
● With all its faults, still one of the cinema's sharpest stabs at Conrad. Chief problem is the script, which tends to turn the whole thing towards picaresque tropical adventure by introducing character after character without ever quite pinning down the moral conflicts illuminated by their interaction. The recurring Conrad theme (clash between noble and ignoble) was probably doomed anyway, since Richardson gives a bizarrely stilted performance as Lingard, thereby depriving Willems (superbly played by Howard) of the sounding-board that measures his descent into moral degradation. A pity, since individual scenes have a power rare in Reed's work, and the last shot – of Aissa, the sultry beauty who both destroys and is destroyed by Willems, squatting balefully in the rain and seeming to melt back into the earth – perfectly encapsulates Conrad's ambivalent view of the man who is hopelessly wrong in all his actions yet represents a bold gesture towards life. TM

Outcasts, The

(1982, Ire/GB, 104 min)
d/p/sc Robert Wynne-Simmons. *ph* Seamus Corcoran. *ed* Arthur Keating. *pd* Bertram Tyrer. *m* Stephen Cooney. *cast* Mary Ryan, Mick Lally, Don Foley, Tom Jordan, Cyril Cusack, Brenda Scallon, Bairbre Ni Chaoimh, Mairtín Ó Flathearta.
● Mystery and magic from the mists of Erin in which a shy and awkward girl, Maura (Ryan), finds friendship and maybe more with an itinerant, half-legendary fiddler called Scarf Michael (Lally) on the night of a rural wedding. Thereafter, Maura is no longer a figure of fun and abuse, but a woman suspected of black magic by the superstitious villagers. The film is strong on 'atmosphere' (which means it pisses with rain most of the time and everyone struggles through the bog on their way to various dramatic encounters), but predictably slack in dialogue and characterisation. Mary Ryan works hard at making Maura a sympathetic central character, but this is another 'romantically Irish' film that has little of the power and articulacy of Neil Jordan. MA

Outer Way, The (Gedo)

(1998, Jap, 99 min)
d Rokuro Mochizuki. *m* Koji Endom. *cast* Haku Ryu, Amiko Kanetani, Akaji Maro, Atsushi Narasaka, Shiro Shimomoto.
● Only Mochizuki could have come up with a Buddhist deconstruction of the yakuza movie. Himuro (Haku Ryu at his best since Kitano's *Violent Cop*) is fired by his police superiors as a scapegoat for their complicity with *sokaiya* racketeers. This pale rider fetches up in a small town by the sea and soon figures out what makes the community tick: a mix of bent politics, dodgy religion, Internet porn, disorganised crime and a little marijuana cultivation on the side. He befriends the mysterious local 'garbageman' Kuwata (*butoh* star Maro) and the self-hating Mika (Kanetani), who becomes his lover. With an assist from Kuwata, Himuro does weed the yakuza patch and sort out the scumbag politician who is the centre of the local moral vacuum. But he's no angelic scourge, being as mired in corruption as anyone else. As ambiguous moral fables go, this is in the same league as Pasolini's *Theorem*. The amazing score (based on Buddhist music and chants) is by Koji Endo. TR

Outfit, The

(1973, US, 103 min)
d John Flynn. *p* Carter De Haven Jr. *sc* John Flynn. *ph* Bruce Surtees. *ed* Ralph E Winters. *ad* Tambi Larsen. *m* Jerry Fielding. *cast* Robert Duvall, Karen Black, Joe Don Baker, Robert Ryan, Timothy Carey, Richard Jaeckel, Sheree North, Felice Orlandi, Marie Windsor, Jane Greer, Elisha Cook.
● Excellent adaptation of a novel by Richard Stark (Donald E Westlake), who also provided the source material for *Point Blank*, *The Split* and Godard's *Made in USA*. A taut, grim thriller, it sees Duvall, just out of prison and with revenge burning in his heart for the murder of his brother, taking on the Syndicate with the help of heavy Joe Don Baker. Tightly scripted by Flynn himself, sharply shot by Bruce Surtees, it's a cool, exciting thriller in the Siegel tradition, paying more than passing reference to classic *film noir* with its host of character actors (Cook, Windsor, Greer, Carey), a cruel performance from Ryan as the mob leader, and its vision of people caught up in a chaotic, confused and treacherous world. GA

Out for Justice

(1991, US, 91 min)
d John Flynn. *p* Steven Seagal, Arnold Kopelson. *sc* David Lee Henry. *ph* Ric Waite. *ed* Robert A Ferretti, Donald Brochu. *ad* Gene Rudolf. *m* David Michael Frank *cast* Steven Seagal, William Forsythe, Jerry Orbach, Jo Champa, Shareen Mitchell, Sal Richards, Gina Gershon.
● Hollywood bodyguard turned producer/star, Seagal sees this as a progression from the foundation of his action films (*Above the Law*, *Hard to Kill*, *Marked for Death*) to the higher ground of 'art'. If his career wasn't built on brawn and *aikido* skills, it would be tempting to challenge him on this. Okay, so the plot is 'character-driven' to the extent that his tough New York cop Gino has a problem: he's too busy beating up the baddies who whacked his best friend/partner to find a moment to patch up his rocky marriage. But if you cut the beatings, you wouldn't be left with much. Fans of unnecessarily graphic violence will love it, but if you're looking for 'art', look elsewhere. CO'S

Outland

(1981, GB, 109 min)
d Peter Hyams. *p* Richard A Roth. *sc* Peter Hyams. *ph* Stephen Goldblatt. *ed* Stuart Baird. *pd* Philip Harrison. *m* Jerry Goldsmith. *cast* Sean Connery, Peter Boyle, Frances Sternhagen, James B Sikking, Kika Markham, Clarke Peters, Steven Berkoff, John Ratzenberger, Hal Galili.
● *High Noon* re-located on sunless Io, Jupiter's third moon, with Connery as the upright federal marshal posted to the mining base where a death-dealing black market in drugs is tacitly sanctioned by the profiteering authorities. Because both dialogue and direction are none too exciting, one's tired eyes wander endlessly over the space base sets, where there has been an overuse of that potent sci-fi movie convention which conveys 'realism' by showing that life on the outer limits will be as dingy and badly lit as a suburban subway, with all the usual vices. JS

Outlaw, The

(1941, US, 116 min, b/w)
d/p Howard Hughes. *sc* Jules Furthman. *ph* Gregg Toland. *ed* Wallace A Grissell, Otho Lovering. *ad* Perry Ferguson. *m* Victor Young. *cast* Jane Russell, Jack Beutel, Walter Huston, Thomas Mitchell, Joe Sawyer, Mimi Aguglia.
● A film more joked about than seriously considered after its notorious production problems (director Hawks walked off the set), censorship difficulties (centering on Jane Russell's cleavage), and Hughes' usual obsessive tinkering with details. By no means as bad as its detractors would have it, it remains a fascinating (if minor) Western with a determinedly offbeat story about Doc Holliday, Pat Garrett and Billy the Kid coming to conflict over Holliday's stolen horse and half-breed Russell. Jules Furthman's script is often disarmingly tongue-in-cheek, Gregg Toland's photography is characteristically ravishing, and there is a quirky eroticism to the

proceedings, manifest in Russell's performance and in some surprising undertones suggesting homosexuality. GA

Outlaw and His Wife, The (Berg-Ejvind och hans Hustru)

(1917, Swe, 9,124 ft, b/w)
d Victor Sjöström. *sc* Victor Sjöström, Sam Ask. *ph* Julius Jaenzon. *cast* Victor Sjöström, Edith Erastoff, John Ekman, Nils Arehn, Artur Rolén, Jenny Tchernichin-Larsson.
●Sjöström's performance may disappoint those familiar with his marvellous contribution many years later to Bergman's *Wild Strawberries*, but there is still much to admire in this tale, set in 19th century Iceland, of a sheep-stealer finding work and love with a rich widow (the director's wife), and then being hounded by society into the freezing wilderness. If the story tends to aim too self-consciously for grand passions (often resulting in an unfortunately melodramatic tone), there is no denying the film's visual beauty, with Sjöström's use of the sparse farm sets and the monumental landscape serving to ensure that Nature, as opposed to the humans on view, takes precedence as the most forceful character. GA

Outlaw Blues

(1977, US, 101 min)
d Richard T Heffron. *p* Steve Tisch. *sc* BWL Norton. *ph* Jules Brenner. *ed* Danford B Greene, Scott Conrad. *ad* Jack Marty. *m* Charles Bernstein. *cast* Peter Fonda, Susan Saint James, John Crawford, James Callahan, Michael Lerner, Steve Fromholz, Richard Lockmiller, Matt Clark, Jan Rita Cobler.
●'You'll never catch me alive – except on KVET,' boasts country-singing ex-con Peter Fonda in a tone both romantic and expedient, which sums up the genial anecdote that is *Outlaw Blues*. His song is ripped off after a prison visit by the local Johnny Cash, so the paroled Fonda goes after him, shoots him in the leg, and hides out in Susan Saint James' shed. She sees the main chance, negotiates a recording contract, and makes Fonda a celebrity by smuggling him into record stores and radio stations and then calling the cops. Heffron and writer BWL Norton might have taken the story to its logical conclusion (posthumous superstardom) instead of spending so much time on chase sequences. But as it is there are many interesting ironies, not least that an indifferent title song, poorly sung by Fonda, can be made so effective by judicious use. AN

Outlaw Josey Wales, The

(1976, US, 134 min)
d Clint Eastwood. *p* Robert Daley. *sc* Philip Kaufman, Sonia Chernus. *ph* Bruce Surtees. *ed* Ferris Webster. *pd* Tambi Larsen. *m* Jerry Fielding. *cast* Clint Eastwood, Chief Dan George, Sondra Locke, Bill McKinney, John Vernon, Paula Trueman, Sam Bottoms, Geraldine Keams, Woodrow Parfrey, Joyce Jameson, Sheb Wooley, Royal Dano, Matt Clark, Will Sampson.
●A remarkable film which sets out as a revenge Western: Eastwood sees his family massacred and joins the Confederate guerillas; after the Civil War, he is hunted by Union soldiers while he pursues his family's slayer and a friend apparently turned traitor. But slowly the film changes direction, until through a series of comic interludes it becomes the story of a man who (re)discovers his role as family man, as he befriends Indians and various strays and leads them to a paradise of sorts where they can forget their individual pasts. If that seems like a rewrite of Hawks' *Red River*, visually *The Outlaw Josey Wales* is closest to Anthony Mann in its breathtaking survey of American landscapes (and seasons). Most importantly, after a period of directorial uncertainty, the film demonstrated Eastwood's ability to recreate his first starring role, as the mythic Man with No Name of the Italian Westerns, and to subtly undercut it through comedy and mockery. PH

Out of Africa

(1985, US, 162 min)
d/p Sydney Pollack. *sc* Kurt Luedtke. *ph* David Watkin. *ed* Frederick Steinkamp, William Steinkamp, Pembroke Herring, Sheldon Kahn. *pd* Stephen Grimes. *m* John Barry. *cast* Meryl Streep, Robert Redford, Klaus Maria Brandauer, Michael Kitchen, Malick Bowens, Joseph Thiaka, Stephen Kinyanjui, Michael Gough, Suzanna Hamilton, Rachel Kempson, Graham Crowden, Leslie Phillips.
●Aptly described in *TO* as a Safari Park movie; it's hard to imagine how even an untalented director could make the landscape here look less than ravishing, and Pollack is certainly better than untalented. As to the rest: Meryl gets to try a Danish accent this time as Karen Blixen, the author whose accounts of farming in Africa are the basis of the film. In Brandauer, as her pox-ridden husband, she has met her match in the ham stakes. And in Redford, as the Etonian adventurer who becomes her lover, she is bettered by the 'blank sponge' effect; for once his bland charm actually has a use. For all that it may come out of Africa, the film's final destination is not many miles from Disneyland. CPea

Out of an Old Man's Head (I Huvet på en Gammal Gubbe)

(1968, Swe, 76 min)
d Tage Danielsson. *p* Gunnar Karlsson. *sc* Hasse Alfredson, Tage Danielsson. *ph* Conny Marnelius, Bo Wanngård. *ed* Lars Ögenklev. *m* Gunnar Svensson. *cast* Hasse Alfredson, Fatima Ekman, Monica Nielsen, Ernst Günther, Gus Dahlström, Rolf Bengtsson.
●Recuperating from an injury in an old folk's home, widower Johan Björk (the comedian Hasse Alfredson) runs through the incidents of his life: from childhood japes in the countryside, through his first visit to a whore house, to the running-away to sea of his son Erik – all expressed in a curious dreamlike mix of animation and live action. The tone and content of Per Åhlin's often inventive animation styles (two-dimensional cut-outs, crayon drawings, photographic collages, realist line-drawings, etc) veers between sophisticated erotic surrealism, notably in the whore house episode, and the standard sentiments of a children's cartoon. Over-extended and uneven, but a genuine oddity none the less. JPy

Out of Depth

(1998, GB, 99 min)
d Simon Marshall. *p* Stephen Cranny. *sc* Simon Marshall. *ph* Adam Suschitzky. *ed* St John O'Rorke. *pd* Philip Robinson. *m* Barry Adamson. *cast* Sean Maguire, Danny Midwinter, Nicholas Ball, Phil Cornwell, Josephine Butler, Leigh Lawson, Clive Russell, Rita Tushingham.
●This first feature can hardly be faulted for its sincerity, since it's based on the tragic case of the writer/director's boyhood friend who was killed in a still unsolved gangland shooting. You get the sense, too, that there's a genuine personal investment in its story of a South London lad making his way in the design world, yet drawn inexorably back into the clutches of the villainry he hoped he'd left behind. A shame, then, that the result is so poorly written, cliché packed, overacted and flatly directed. For go-ahead Paul (Maguire), the trouble all starts when his barmaid mum (Tushingham) is assaulted by a local heavy (comic Phil Cornwell). He's ready for revenge himself, but his old schoolmate Steve (Midwinter), now a hustling dealer, suggests it might be wiser instead to have a quiet word with notorious hardman Pussy Cat Lenny (Ball). From which point on, we can more or less forecast the gap widening between the protagonist's trendy new West End milieu and the dodgy terrain he grew up in, with drugs and firearms speeding the decay. TJ

Out of Life

see Hors la vie

Out of Order (Abwärts)

(1984, WGer, 88 min)
d Carl Schenkel. *p* Thomas Schühly, Mathias Deyle. *sc* Carl Schenkel, Frank Göhre. *ph* Jacques Steyn. *ed* Norbert Herzner. *ad* Toni Lüdi. *m* Jacques Zwart. *cast* Götz George, Renée Soutendijk, Wolfgang Kieling, Hannes Jaenicke, Klaus Wennemann, Ralph Richter, Kurt Raab.
●It's the office worker's ultimate nightmare: being stuck in a lift that's going nowhere, unless it's down and fast, too fast, with oblivion waiting at the bottom. Not only that, but your last moments are to be spent listening to the creak of fraying wires. The four unlucky elevator riders in this tense shocker are an accountant, a punky youth, an attractive young woman and a mysterious third man. Long-term frustrations clash with instant rivalries: in extremis the truth will out. One by one, the cables snap. Think *Huis Clos* without the existentialism. Director Schenkel went on to make, among other things, *Tarzan and the Lost City*: what is it with him and swinging from ropes? Not one for claustrophobes. NRo

Out of Order

(1987, GB, 98 min)
d Jonnie Turpie. *p* Lucy Hooberman, Roger Shannon. *sc* Dead Honest Soul Searchers. *ph* Terry Flaxton. *cast* Sharon Fryer, Gary Webster, Pete Lee-Wilson, Cheryl Maiker, The Wee Papa Girl Rappers, George Baker, Peter Cellier, Glynn Edwards.
●Jaz (Fryer) and Anthony (Webster) are a couple of layabout lovebirds roosting in the telegenic town of Telford. Glynis and Kerry (The Wee Papa Girl Rappers) run pirate station Radio Giro. When Anthony decides to climb out of the rut and become a rookie rozzer, teenage trauma looms. Meanwhile Billy (Lee-Wilson), a BT phone fetishist, gets fired but discovers that he has the ability to tap into the network without using the receiver, i.e. he is tele-pathic. One way or another they all end up in the cells, and Anthony has to decide which side he's on. This offering from the Birmingham Film and Video Workshop gleefully rips off the good bits of TV, video and cinema techniques, and stirs them up into a tangy salmagundi of styles. The soundtrack, a basic mix of Rap, Disco and Funk, manages to splice The Smiths, Robert Palmer and Smiley Culture with Frank Sinatra. The result doesn't say anything new about the joys of living in Thatcher's Britain, but the means by which the message is put across is both witty and wacky. MS

Out of Rosenheim

see Bagdad Café

Out of Season

(1975, GB, 90 min)
d Alan Bridges. *p/sc* Reuben Bercovitch, Eric Bercovitch. *ph* Arthur Ibbetson. *ed* Peter Weatherley. *ad* Robert Jones. *m* John Cameron. *cast* Vanessa Redgrave, Cliff Robertson, Susan George, Edward Evans, Frank Jarvis.
●After relishing the nuances of the master-servant relationship in *The Hireling*, the super-smooth Alan Bridges finds himself landed with an impossible project. The dire script wrings every possible cliché out of the situation (mother and daughter while winter away in their deserted seaside hotel, until they're interrupted by the arrival of an intruder from the past). The biggest mystery is why this stagey stuff (all brooding desire, jealousy and intimations of incest) was filmed at all, and why a cast of this calibre should have bothered. VG

Out of Sight

(1998, US, 123 min)
d Steven Soderbergh. *p* Danny DeVito, Michael Shamberg, Stacey Sher. *sc* Scott Frank. *ph* Elliot Davis. *ed* Anne V Coates. *pd* Gary Frutkoff. *m* Cliff Maretinez. *cast* George Clooney, Jennifer Lopez, Ving Rhames, Don Cheadle, Dennis Farina, Albert Brooks, Steve Zahn, Michael Keaton, Samuel L Jackson.
●A splendid reminder of just how assured, intelligent and involving Soderbergh's movies can be. Working from Scott Frank's exemplary adaptation of Elmore Leonard's novel, the director deftly mixes suspense, comedy and romance, and generates considerable erotic tension. Bank robber Clooney and ambitious federal marshal Lopez – whose first brush with each other comes when he holds her hostage in a car trunk while escaping from prison – circle one another irresistibly but warily, both knowing she'll put him away if she can. This evidently ill-starred relationship is the pulsating heart of the film, but there are more than enough subplots involving a host of vividly drawn characters to prevent the unlikely pair's courtship from becoming cute, obvious or overbearingly smart. All the performances are first rate, while the pace, wit and low key concern with questions of honour, professionalism and loyalty are wholly in keeping with Leonard's perky, deceptively effortless style. Most impressive, though, is how Soderbergh keeps every ingredient simmering enticingly while sacrificing none of his storytelling subtlety. The finest Leonard adaptation to date, and a rare example of a Hollywood film that's adult, ambitious and terrific entertainment. GA

Out of the Blue

(1980, Can, 93 min)
d Dennis Hopper. *p* Leonard Yakir, Gary Jules Jouvenat. *sc* Leonard Yakir, Brenda Nielson. *ph* Marc Champion. *ed* Doris Dyck. *ad* David Hiscox. *m* Tom Lavin. *cast* Linda Manz, Dennis Hopper, Sharon Farrell, Raymond Burr, Don Gordon, Eric Allen, Fiona Brody, David Crowley.

●From its horrific opening – truckdriver Hopper drunk at the wheel with daughter Manz ploughs into a school bus full of screaming children – you're left in no doubt that you're in for an edgy experience. The teenage Manz, in a quite sensational performance under Hopper's direction, embodies the nihilistic ethos of punk in a way that other mainstream projects (*Foxes, Times Square*) couldn't begin to achieve. Manz impassively (and why not, with mum a junkie and dad an incestuous paedophile) observes life in small-town America's roadhouses and bowling alleys, embittered by the death of Elvis and Sid Vicious, and interested only in the drum kit at which she flails away in her bedroom. If ever there was a movie about Sex and Drugs and Rock'n'Roll, this is it, a film of and about extremes, directed by an extremist. RM

Out of the Dark

(1988, US, 89 min)
d Michael Schroeder. *p* Zane W Levitt. *sc* James DeFelice, Zane W Levitt. *ph* Julio Macat. *ed* Mark Manos. *pd* Robert Schulenberg. *m* Paul F Antonelli, David Wheatley. *cast* Cameron Dye, Karen Black, Lynn Danielson, Karen Witter, Starr Andreeff, Karen Mayo-Chandler, Angela Robinson, Teresa Crespo, Tracey Walter, Silvana Gallardo, Bud Cort, Geoffrey Lewis, Divine, Paul Bartel.

●A straight re-run of those '70s slasher pics in which a string of attractive young women are bludgeoned, strangled or stabbed to death by a mystery assailant whose identity is obvious after about ten minutes. This time, it's the employees of the Suite Nothings phone-sex business (presided over by Karen Black) who are being terrorised by a killer in a clown mask. As a gesture towards sexual equality, a Hispanic male gets a spade through his head, while the sleaze quotient is constantly upped by the woman's breathy phone-talk about throbbing love muscles (what's never explained is why they dress and make-up like hookers to talk on the phone). Candidates for whodunit include the hunky photographer (Dye) with a previous conviction for assaulting his girl, the dorky assistant (Cort) with a stash of SM mags, and the prostitute-killer whom LA cop Divine (in his last film) is tracking in a parallel investigation. NF

Out of the Fog

(1941, US, 85 min, b/w)
d Anatole Litvak. *p* Henry Blanke. *sc* Robert Rossen, Jerry Wald, Richard Macaulay. *ph* James Wong Howe. *ed* Warren Low. *ad* Carl Jules Weyl. *m* Leo Forbstein. *cast* Ida Lupino, John Garfield, Thomas Mitchell, Eddie Albert, John Qualen, George Tobias, Aline MacMahon, Leo Gorcey.

●Oddly atmospheric mixture of *noir* melodrama and semi-comic parable (based on Irwin Shaw's play *The Gentle People*), in which Garfield's tinpot Dillinger terrorises a small wharfside community by extracting protection money. Problems arise when Lupino, daughter of Mitchell – who eventually plots with Qualen to combat their oppressor – falls for the hood. Originally intended by Shaw as an anti-fascist statement, the film's message is inevitably confused by the fact that Mitchell and Qualen finally take the law into their own hands. Nevertheless, the vivid performances, the occasionally poetic dialogue (by a team of writers that included Jerry Wald and Robert Rossen), and James Wong Howe's excellent moody photography lend it a professionalism that the story barely warrants. GA

Out of the Past (aka Build My Gallows High) 100

(1947, US, 97 min, b/w)
d Jacques Tourneur. *p* Warren Duff. *sc* Daniel Mainwaring. *ph* Nick Musuraca. *ed* Samuel E Beetley. *ad* Albert S D'Agostino, Jack Okey. *m* Roy Webb. *cast* Robert Mitchum, Jane Greer, Kirk Douglas, Rhonda Fleming, Richard Webb, Steve Brodie, Virginia Huston.

●The definitive flashback movie, in which our fated hero Mitchum makes a rendezvous with death and his own past in the shape of Jane Greer. Beguiling and resolutely ominous, this hallucinatory voyage has two more distinctions: as the only movie with both a deaf-mute garage hand and death by fishing-rod, and as one of the most bewildering and beautiful films ever made. From a traditionally doomed and perversely corrupt world, the mood of obsession was never more powerfully suggestive: Mitchum waiting for Greer in a Mexican bar beneath a flashing neon sign sums it up – nothing happens, but everything is said. Superbly crafted pulp is revealed at every level: in the intricate script by Daniel Mainwaring (*Phenix City Story, Invasion of the Body Snatchers*), the almost abstract lighting patterns of Nick Musuraca (previously perfected in *Cat People* and *The Spiral Staircase*), and the downbeat, tragic otherworldliness of Jacques Tourneur (only equalled in his *I Walked with a Zombie*). All these B movie poets were under contract to RKO in the winter of 1946, and produced the best movie of everyone involved – once seen, never forgotten. (The source novel was by Mainwaring writing as Geoffrey Homes.) DMacp

Out of the Present

(1995, Ger/Fr/Bel/Rus, 100 min)
d Andrei Ujica. *p* Elke Peters. *sc* Andrei Ujica. *ph* Vadim Yusov. *ed* Ralf Henninger, Heidi Leihbecher. *with* Anatoli Artsebarski, Sergei Krikalev, Helen Sharman, Viktor Afanasiev, Musa Monarov, Aleksandr Volkov, Franz Viehböck, Toktar Aubakirov, Aleksandr Viktorenko, Aleksandr Kaleri, Klaus-Dietrich Flade, Vladimir Soloviev, Aleksei Leonov.

●It could have been called '1991: A Space Odyssey'; in fact, that would have highlighted one of the fascinating features of Ujica's odd but engrossing documentary on the MIR Space Station's Ozon mission. The portrait provided here of the cramped, comparatively messy, human-sized reality of space travel makes a striking contrast to the grandeur and galactic sweep of fictionalised accounts familiar from films by Kubrick and others. Ozon took two cosmonauts, pilot Sergei Krikalev and commander Anatoli Artsebarski, and (briefly) British scientist Helen Sharman on a more or less routine mission. It hit the headlines following the aborted Moscow putsch which consigned Gorbachev's Soviet Union to the history books, leaving Krikalev stranded in space for an unprecedented ten months – only, on his return, to have journalists' microphones stuffed in his face for comments on Yeltsin and the new Russia. Krikalev shot 35mm footage with the mission's on-board camera, and to this has been added video link material, amateur film and TV news cuttings. Narrated by Artsebarski, it is edited to run as long as the MIR's earth orbit. Ujica has remarked that a 'comedy of manners' rather than an 'odyssey' is a more appropriate description of his film; and it's true there's a strange aimlessness at play here. Viewing 'earth shattering' events from the perspective of space confers on them an eerie calm: instead, our attention is focused on the almost surreal movements and banal comments of weightless men, prompting philosophical musings on our place in the cosmos. Stranger than fiction. WH

Out-of-Towners, The

(1969, US, 97 min)
d Arthur Hiller. *p* Paul Nathan. *sc* Neil Simon. *ph* Andrew Laszlo. *ed* Fred Chulack. *ad* Charlie Bailey. *m* Quincy Jones. *cast* Jack Lemmon, Sandy Dennis, Anne Meara, Ann Prentiss, Ron Carey, Sandy Baron, Phil Bruns, Carlos Montalban, Paul Dooley, Billy Dee Williams.

●Lemmon and Dennis undergo the unexpurgated Manhattan melodrama: arriving from Iowa for a job interview, the couple run into a transit strike, a blizzard, a hotel which hasn't honoured their reservation, a mugging, and other New York specialities. Then, when they are flying home again happily, their plane is hijacked by Cuban revolutionaries. Neil Simon cranks out this kind of fluff before breakfast, but it *is* enjoyable. Lemmon suffers the mounting indignities with the skill acquired from playing urban neurotics for most of his career. Sandy Dennis, whose '*Oh my Gaards*' punctuate the film like fingernails on a blackboard, gets everything she asks for. ATu

Out-of-Towners, The

(1999, US, 92 min)
d Sam Weisman. *p* Robert Cort, David Madden, Robert Evans, Teri Schwartz. *sc* Marc Lawrence. *ph* John Bailey. *ed* Kent Beyda. *pd* Ken Adam. *m* Marc Shaiman. *cast* Steve Martin, Goldie Hawn, John Cleese, Mark McKinney, Oliver Hudson, Valerie Perri, Steve Mittleman, Randall Arney, Carlease Burke, William Duell, JP Bumstead, Peggy Mannix, Anne Haney.

●In this half-hearted revamp of Arthur Hiller's 1969 comedy of mishaps, as penned by Neil Simon, *Housesitter* duo Martin and Hawn are reunited as a happily married Midwestern couple, who decide to embark on a simple business trip to New York. For 24 long hours, Nancy and Henry live to regret it: they're relieved of their money by an Andrew Lloyd Webber impersonator, go hungry and inadvertently find themselves in a group therapy session full of wankers. Worse, on arrival at their NY hotel, their reservation is declined by the manager, a condescending cross-dresser played, predictably, by John Cleese (embarrassing). Hawn and Martin make a likeable enough couple and their unexpected 'adventure' does throw up a few very funny set-pieces. But from the opening scene, it's clear director Sam Weisman has neither the desire nor, for that matter, the talent for turning what is essentially mere melodramatic Hollywood fluff into something a little less, well, lazy. DA

Out 1: Spectre

(1972, Fr, 255 min)
d Jacques Rivette. *p* Stéphane Tchalgadjieff. *sc* Jacques Rivette, Suzanne Schiffman. *ph* Pierre-William Glenn. *ed* Nicole Lubtchansky, Deirdre de Casabianca, Claire Pinheiro. *cast* Jean-Pierre Léaud, Bulle Ogier, Michel Lonsdale, Juliet Berto, Françoise Fabian, Bernadette Lafont, Jean Bouise.

●Jacques Rivette's grandest and boldest experiment to date (based on Balzac's *L'Histore des Treize*) enrages some spectators because it gives them so much to cope with: 255 minutes of improvisation by at least half of the best New Wave actors, edited and arranged so that sometimes it's telling a complex mystery story – about thirteen conspirators, two theatre groups, and a couple of crazed outsiders – while the rest of the time it's telling a realistic story about the same people that deliberately makes no sense at all. Not so much a digest of Rivette's legendary 12-hour version (hardly ever screened, its title is *Out 1: Noli Me Tangere*) as a ghost and a reworking of some of the same material ('a critique', Rivette himself says), it's a challenging and terrifying journey for all who can bear with it. As Richard Roud put it: 'Cinema will never be the same, and neither will I.' JR

Outrageous!

(1977, Can, 98 min)
d Richard Benner. *p* William Marshall, Henk van der Kolk. *sc* Richard Benner. *ph* James B Kelly. *ed* George Appleby. *ad* Karen Bromley. *m* Paul Hoffert. *cast* Craig Russell, Hollis McLaren, Richert Easley, Allan Moyle, David McIlwraith, Gerry Salsberg, Andrée Pelletier, Helen Shaver.

●'Isn't anybody straight any more?' wonders Robin (Russell) as he arrives in New York to make his club debut as a drag artiste, having left his flatmate Liza (McLaren) back in Toronto struggling with her schizophrenia and an awkward pregnancy. As in the best vintage Warhol movies, everything rests on the characters, and hence the performances: McLaren's inwardness connecting improbably with Russell's brashness in a funny/serious relationship that is often touching. Plus, of course, the wicked drag impersonations of Dietrich, the Bettes (Davis and Midler), Garland, Streisand and others. It's technically very rough-and-ready, but consistently very funny in its off-the-wall humour. CPe

Outrageous Fortune

(1987, US, 99 min)
d Arthur Hiller. *p* Ted Field, Robert W Cort. *sc* Leslie Dixon. *ph* David M Walsh. *ed* Tom Rolf. *pd* James D Vance. *m* Alan Silvestri. *cast* Bette Midler, Shelley Long, Peter Coyote, Robert Prosky, John Schuck, George Carlin, Anthony Heald.

●Lauren (Long) and Sandy (Midler) share the same two-timing lover (Coyote), a fact they only discover after he has skipped town, hotly pursued by the CIA over some stolen toxin. The stick-sisters join the chase, the script's mistaken assumption being the more the merrier. Lauren is classy and cultured, Sandy ain't, and their initial rivalry resembles a duet for the disdainful nostril and the gob. As a vehicle for their considerable comic talents, the enterprise is wheelclamped by type casting. Both identify a mutilated corpse as not being their man, but of course it is Bette who gets to spell out in clear that the clue was the size of his dick. Once the chase is on, there are reels of escapes down laundry chutes and madcap rides on baggage carts and motorbikes, and no shortage of threshing gams. It's the sort of comedy in which captives' bonds are thick and new as ropes aboard pirate films, while outbursts of C & W underline the fun of the chase. BC

Outside In

(1981, GB/WGer, 115 min)
d Steve Dwoskin. *p* Rebecca Dobbs, Madeleine Shaer. *sc* Steve Dwoskin. *ph* Steve Dwoskin, Robert Smith, Bernard Trude. *ed* Brian Trenerry, Steve Dwoskin. *ad* Bernard Trude. *m* Ben Mason. *cast* Olimpia Carlisi, Steve Dwoskin, Merdelle Jordine, Derek O'Connor, Tony Haygarth, Marie Manet.

●For his eighth feature, Dwoskin focuses on his own disablement by polio, and its hazards to his emotional and sexual life. It's a strange, riveting mixture of Hal Roach slapstick, vivid confessions, open-hearted self-reflexivity, and Dwoskin's own highly formalist aesthetic of the unblinking look (which had some English feminists hopping mad but reached their European sisters). Dwoskin reinvents the cinema from where Straub left off. The cast ranges through Carlisi from Fellini-land to Jordine from TV's*Crossroads*. A haunting documentation of a strange, difficult life; its pratfalls and fetishes, triumphs and disasters. Crutches of fire? RD

Outside Man, The (Un Homme est Mort)

(1972, Fr/It, 104 min)
d Jacques Deray. *p* Jacques Bar. *sc* Jean-Claude Carrière, Jacques Deray, Ian McLellan Hunter. *ph* Terry K Meade, Silvano Ippoliti. *ed* Henri Lanoë, William Chulack. *m* Michel Legrand. *cast* Jean-Louis Trintignant, Ann-Margret, Roy Scheider, Angie Dickinson, Georgia Engel, Michel Constantin, Umberto Orsini. Ted de Corsia, Talia Shire.

●Perfect casting for Trintignant as a French hitman imported to America and efficiently executing his contract, only to discover that there appears to be a contract out on him. Deray's thrillers often go sadly astray, but this one was co-scripted by Jean-Claude Carrière (Buñuel's latter-day collaborator), and wittily fashions a dark variation on *Through the Looking-Glass* out of the hit man's bafflement as he becomes the hunted in a country where he doesn't understand the language (the dialogue is in English, with occasional subtitled French) and where tribal customs seem alarmingly bizarre. Los Angeles becomes the quirky central character, and although Dickinson is rather wasted, there are memorable supporting performances from Ann-Margret, Scheider, Engel and de Corsia (the latter summarily rubbed out as subject of the contract, but presiding – embalmed and seated on a funeral parlour throne) over a shootout at his own wake. TM

Outsider, The

see Guinea Pig, The

Outsider, The

(1979, Neth, 128 min)
d/sc Tony Luraschi. *ph* Ricardo Aronovich. *ed* Catherine Kelber. *m* Ken Thorne. *ad* Franco Fumagalli. *cast* Craig Wasson, Sterling Hayden, Patricia Quinn, Niall O'Brien, TP McKenna, Niall Toibin, Frank Grimes, Elizabeth Begley, Bosco Hogan, Ray McAnally, Joe Lynch, Allan Cuthbertson, Geoffrey Palmer, Gabriel Byrne.

●Grimly authentic by all accounts about life in 1973 Belfast, this first feature about Northern Ireland still seems more a piece of crusading Americana: a young, war-scarred American idealist enlists in the IRA only to find he is worth more to them dead than alive. From there it trades on the sensationalism and realism of its material: torture, bitterness, and sudden violent death. More confusing than illuminating, it's a film which will rely more on its reputation than its achievement; at a time when 'anything goes', is this one of the limits? DMacp

Outsiders, The

see Bande à part

Outsiders, The (Oka Oorie Katha)

(1977, Ind, 114 min)
d Mrinal Sen. *p* A Parandhama Reddy. *sc* Mrinal Sen, Mohit Chattopadhyay. *ph* KK Mahajan. *ed* Gangadhar Naskar. *ad* B Kalyan. *m* Vijay Raghav Rao. *cast* Vasudeva Rao, Narayana Rao, Mamata Shankar, AR Krishna, Pradeep Kumar.

●Though Sen is often touted as the more corrosively political counterpart of his compatriot Satyajit Ray, the evidence of a film like this tends to suggest that he merely draws from a deeper well of despair. A study of 'marginals' – a low-caste father and son whose response to rural poverty is an extremist passivity, shading into idle parasitism – it manages a modicum of black humour from the old man's half-baked self-justifications, but slides inexorably towards tragedy and into a deadlock position of presenting defeatism as revolt. The anger's real enough, but its direction is uncertain, and sadly ineffectual. PT

Outsiders, The

(1983, US, 91 min)
d Francis Coppola. *p* Fred Roos, Gray Frederickson. *sc* Kathleen Knutsen Rowell. *ph* Stephen H Burum. *ed* Anne Goursaud. *pd* Dan Tavoularis. *m* Carmine Coppola. *cast* C Thomas Howell, Matt Dillon, Ralph Macchio, Patrick Swayze, Rob Lowe, Emilio Estevez, Tom Cruise, Glenn Withrow, Diane Lane, Leif Garrett, Tom Waits, SE Hinton.

●Like the Corleones, like Kurtz in *Apocalypse Now*, and like Hank and Frannie in *One From the Heart*, the kids in *The Outsiders* (adapted from SE Hinton's novel) are looking for a better world. The street life of teenage Tulsa is divided into the 'socs' (pronounced soches) who go to college and wear Brut, and the greasers from the other side of the tracks, who don't. When a soc is knifed, three greasers go on the run to a rural idyll, turn tragic heroes, and finally return to try to cement a tenuous truce: like so much teenage Americana, it's about the rites of passage from adolescence to adulthood. Surprisingly for Coppola, it's a modest, prosaic, rather puritan drama with a MORAL, which, if you want to be uncharitable, is a last-ditch attempt to prove he can turn in a well-crafted piece without contracting elephantiasis of the budget. Lightly likeable, but the kids at whom it's aimed would probably rather be leaping in the aisles to Duran Duran, while their parents would opt for a rerun of *Rebel Without a Cause*. CPea

Outskirts (Okraina)

(1998, Rus, 95 min, b/w)
d Petr Lutsik. *p* Lew Kagno, Petr Lutsik. *sc* Petr Lutsik, Alexei Samoryadov. *ph* Nikolai Ivasiv. *ed* Svetlana Guralskaya. *ad* Andrei Bessolitsin. *m* Georgi Sviridov, Gavril Popov. *cast* Yuri Dubrovin, Nikolai Olyalin, Alexei Pushkin, Rimma Markova.

●Named after the 1933 Boris Barnet classic (of which it's the rueful shadow remake), Lutsik's sparky debut is a cruel, comic fable about grim peasant vigilantes going on a killing spree to reclaim their land rights. Shot deadpan in glacial monochrome, it has an earnest absurdity fully worthy of Monty Python: grizzled kulaks forming human igloos to survive the cold during overnight stops, a neo-capitalist gangster executive whose all white office has shelves stacked to the ceiling with oil samples from the fields he has pillaged. As the violence escalates, so does the underlying vehemence, underscored by the use of music recycled from Stalinist propaganda warhorses of the 1930s. Highly original, and probably as accurate an account of current social chaos in Russia as any other. TR

Outward Bound

(1930, US, 85 min, b/w)
d Robert Milton. *p* Jack l Warner. *sc* J Grubb Alexander. *ph* Hal Mohr. *ed* Ralph Dawson. *m* Louis Silvers. *cast* Leslie Howard, Douglas Fairbanks Jr, Helen Chandler, Beryl Mercer, Alec B Francis, Alison Skipworth, Dudley Digges.

●An allegorical Broadway play (by Sutton Vane) from the mid-'20s became a mildly intriguing early talkie. Howard's a passenger on a sombre ocean liner bound who-knows-where, lost souls heading for their final destination. The dialogue is heavy going and primitively recorded, but Hal Mohr did an evocative job with the ghostly visuals. TJ

Ouvre les yeux

see Open Your Eyes

Overboard

(1987, US, 112 min)
d Garry Marshall. *p* Alex Rose, Anthea Sylbert. *sc* Leslie Dixon. *ph* John A Alonzo. *ed* Dov Hoenig, Sonny Baskin. *ad* James Shanahan, Jim Dultz. *m* Alan Silvestri. *cast* Goldie Hawn, Kurt Russell, Edward Herrmann, Katherine Helmond, Michael Hagerty, Roddy McDowall, Jared Rushton, Hector Elizondo.

●This hilarious and touching romantic comedy recalls the integrated plotting and sophisticated dialogue of '30s Hollywood. Spoiled heiress Joanna (Hawn) and her husband (Herrmann) sail their luxury yacht into a tiny Oregon fishing village to effect some repairs. Joanna hires hunky local carpenter Dean Proffitt (Russell) to fit some cupboards, but when his handiwork fails to satisfy, tosses him overboard and sails away. Shortly after, Joanna herself falls overboard and lands in hospital with amnesia. Seizing his chance, Dean claims the rich bitch as his lost wife, mother to four uncontrollable kids. Russell is excellent as overgrown kid Dean; Hawn gives her best performance to date as the hapless heiress turned gutsy wife and mother (the kids aren't just cutely naughty, they're truly obnoxious); and Marshall's faultless timing makes the most of Leslie Dixon's neatly contrived situations and snappy dialogue. NF

Over Her Dead Body

see Enid Is Sleeping

Overlanders, The

(1946, GB, 91 min, b/w)
d Harry Watt. *p* Michael Balcon. *sc* Harry Watt. *ph* Osmonde Borradaile. *ed* Leslie Norman, EM Inman Hunter. *m* John Ireland. *cast* Chips Rafferty, John Nugent Hayward, Daphne Campbell, Jean Blue, Helen Grieve, John Fernside, Peter Pagan, Frank Ransome.

●Ealing's plans to dramatise the Australian contribution to the war effort didn't mature until after hostilities ceased, but the success of this epic reconstruction of a 1942 cattle-drive (virtually a displaced Western, but given an emphatic political context – the drive is occasioned by a 'scorched earth' policy in face of the advancing Japanese threat – at odds with a counterpart like 'Red River') ensured a continuity of antipodean production that lasted until the home studio itself folded in 1959. Watt brought both a documentarist's research and eye to the project, exposing the outback as a viable location and incidentally elevating Rafferty to the status of a national icon. PT

Overlord

(1975, GB, 83 min, b/w)
d Stuart Cooper. *p* James Quinn. *sc* Stuart Cooper, Christopher Hudson. *ph* John Alcott. *ed* Jonathan Gili. *ad* Michael Moody, Barry Kitts. *m* Paul Glass. *cast* Brian Stirner, Davyd Harries, Nicholas Ball, Julie Neesam, Sam Sewell, John Franklyn-Robbins, Stella Tanner.

●Set against the build-up to D-Day, a grainy fictional account of a young man's call-up, his life on and off duty while training, and the final vindication of his premonitions of death on the beaches of Normandy, is juxtaposed with contemporary footage. Made with the cooperation of various military establishments, the result is predictably restricted. With a script of little beyond stock phrases, and uninspired handling of the well-worn tale of the private's progress, the film does little to allay its endorsement of a passive acceptance of death to a point where it's elevated into a falsely poetic notion. More problematic is the handling of documentary footage, edited in such a way as to convey a hallucinatory and grotesque beauty: shots of a night raid intercut with daylight dead; a plane's camera recording the strafing of a train; the pattern of exploding bombs. Such aerial scenes are disturbing for their eerie remoteness, but they also bear little relation to the leaden-footed human story. CPe

Over Our Dead Bodies

(1991, GB, 84 min)
d Stuart Marshall.

●This documentary (an extended version of the one televised in Channel 4's *Out* series) traces the response to AIDS of gay activist groups in America and Britain. The film itself is also activist, giving platform to ACT UP, Queer Nation and Outrage, organisations fighting to keep AIDS and all the issues surrounding the disease in the public consciousness. Interviews are intercut with footage of meetings, demos and kiss-ins. The messages come hard and fast, with serious allegations levelled at church, state and health bodies. British lesbians and gays are criticised for failing to use grief and anger as political weapons for change. The opinions and statistics that dominate the film provoke a detached, intellectual response; only the few personal stories, and the scenes of demos where AIDS patients are manhandled by butch NYPD officers, encourage emotional involvement. CO'S

Over the Brooklyn Bridge

(1983, US, 106 min)
d Menahem Golan. *p* Menahem Golan, Yoram Globus. *sc* Arnold Somkin. *ph* Adam Greenberg. *ed* Mark Goldblatt. *ad* John Lawless. *m* Pino Donaggio. *cast* Elliott Gould, Margaux Hemingway, Sid Caesar, Burt Young, Shelley Winters, Carol Kane, Jerry Lazarus, Francine Beers.

●From the deep end of Gould's career decline, this is the tale of Alby, a small-time Jewish café owner who dreams of becoming a Manhattan restaurateur. The only means of achieving this, a loan from his uncle (Caesar), seems unavailable as long as Alby persists in his long-term affair with Catholic Elizabeth (Hemingway). A tasteless snack from the Golan/Globus greasy-spoon on a street later visited to much greater effect by Joan Micklin Silver in *Crossing Delancey*. DO

Over the Edge

(1979, US, 94 min)
d Jonathan Kaplan. *p* George Litto. *sc* Charlie Haas, Tim Hunter. *ph* Andrew Davis. *ed* Robert Barrere. *pd* Jim Newport. *m* Sol Kaplan. *cast* Michael Kramer, Matt Dillon, Pamela Ludwig, Vincent Spano, Tom Fergus, Harry Northrup, Andy Romano, Ellen Geer, Lane Smith.

●New Granada: a typically neat and neighbourly new town for middle class families, offering all mod cons. Except, that is, for the kids, left to find the usual entertainment of drugs, drink and sex in a run-down prefab 'rec'. When this last haven is threatened with demolition, adolescent high spirits and bad behaviour result in nihilist rage and rebellion. Kaplan's terrific movie – nervously held back from distribution here for five years – is one of the best movies to date about the generation gap. Although the parents and teachers are never reduced to uncaring stereotypes, their blind, status-oriented decisions and actions provide adequate fuel for the justly frustrated kids, who must be the most credible bunch of youngsters to make it onto celluloid. Script, photography and performances (including Dillon before he decided to become a teenage Stallone) are all top notch, while Kaplan directs with pace, imagination, and a fine ear for dialogue and music. GA

Over the Hill

(1992, Aust, 101 min)
d George Miller. *p* Robert Caswell, Bernard Terry. *sc* Robert Caswell. *ph* David Connell. *ed* Henry Dangar. *cast* Olympia Dukakis, Sigrid Thornton, Derek Fowlds, Bill Kerr, Steve Bisley, Pippa Grandison, Martin Jacobs.

●Imported leading lady Dukakis takes centre stage in this well-meaning but uninspired road movie. A 60-year-old widow flies back from America to stay with her daughter in Sydney. Unfortunately, the welcome there isn't as warm as she'd hoped, so she makes an escape with her granddaughter and heads off across country in a flashy '59 Chevvy. TJ

Over the Top

(1986, US, 93 min)
d Menahem Golan. *p* Menahem Golan, Yoram Globus. *sc* Stirling Silliphant, Sylvester Stallone. *ph* David Gurfinkel. *ed* Don Zimmerman, James R Symons. *pd* James Schoppe. *m* Giorgio Moroder. *cast* Sylvester Stallone, Robert Loggia, Susan Blakely, Rick Zumwalt, David Mendenhall, Chris McCarty.

●Machismo with schmaltz. Stallone plays some dumb trucker, into arm-wrestling, whose cab is a mobile gym. Twelve years ago – for some never-explained reason – he deserted his wife and kid, and now that his spouse is dying, he comes to collect his son from a military academy. An evil plutocratic grandfather doesn't like it; neither does the stuck-up cadet, but gradually his stand-offishness turns to love. Pop-promo tactics are resorted to only some of the time, and this enables the persistent humour and compassion of the script to shine through. Inevitably there is a bicep-bursting climax in Vegas, and even though he does wear clip-on ties, it is impossible not to root for the New Yorkie Bar man. What next, caber-tossing? MS

Owd Bob (aka To the Victor)

(1938, GB, 78 min, b/w)
d Robert Stevenson. *p* Edward Black. *sc* Michael Hogan, JB Williams. *ph* Jack Cox. *ed* RE Dearing, Alfred Roome. *ad* Alex Vetchinsky. *m* Louis Levy. *cast* Will Fyffe, John Loder, Margaret Lockwood, Moore Marriott, Graham Moffatt, Elliott Mason, Edmund Breon, Wally Patch, Alf Goddard.

●One of the great sheepdog trial films and a clear hint that Stevenson (who went on to make many similar saccharine fables for Disney) was obsessed with sentimental comedy even in his British days. Fyffe is tremendous value as the wheezing avaricious Cumberland shepherd whose prize-winning dog attacks other folk's sheep. John Loder is the handsome newcomer to the valley with the temerity to challenge Fyffe's authority. Margaret Lockwood, soon to become Gainsborough's brightest light, is largely wasted as Fyffe's sweet natured daughter, but many of the studio's most rambunctious character actors (including Will Hay's two stooges, Moffatt and Marriott) are on parade. Hearty, rustic fun. GM

Owl and the Pussycat, The

(1970, US, 96 min)
d Herbert Ross. *p* Ray Stark. *sc* Buck Henry. *ph* Harry Stradling, Andrew Laszlo. *ed* Margaret Booth, John F Burnett. *pd* Ken Adam, John Robert Lloyd. *m* Richard Halligan. *cast* Barbra Streisand, George Segal, Robert Klein, Allen Garfield, Roz Kelly, Jacques Sandulescu, Jack Manning, Grace Carney.

●Buck Henry's skilful adaptation of Bill Manhoff's Broadway hit about the abrasive encounter (mental and physical) between an illiterate tart and an intellectual pseud. Neil Simon territory, sometimes tiresomely raucous and treading well-worn paths, but any tendency to sentimental whimsy is kept firmly at arm's length by the verbal fireworks. Brilliant performances from Streisand and Segal, each timing their lines with the knife-edge precision that used to be the glory of the Tracy-Hepburn partnership. TM

Ox, The (Oxen)

(1992, Swe, 92 min)
d Sven Nykvist. *p* Jean Doumanian. *sc* Sven Nykvist, Lasse Summanen. *ph* Dan Myhrman. *ed* Lasse Summanen. *ad* Peter Høimark. *m* JS Bach, Lubos Fisor. *cast* Stellan Skarsgård, Ewa Fröling, Lennart Hjulström, Max von Sydow, Liv Ullmann, Erland Josephson, Björn Granath.

●A subtitle introduces this harrowing, but finally uplifting film as 'a true story as told by Sven Nykvist'. This is rural southern Sweden, in the middle of the catastrophic crop failures and famine of the late 1860s. Skarsgard, his wife Fröling, and their young child face certain starvation; ox meat is the only desperate solution. Without the beast, the man's employer's smallholding cannot function, and the penalty for its slaughter is as harsh as that for murder. Disconcertingly straightforward, veteran cinematographer Nykvist's film is an essentialist delineation of a society under severe strain, held together only by the strictest religious and social codes. By focusing on the couple's story, themes of crime and punishment, suffering and redemption, suspicion and fidelity, are made manifest. The acting (not least von Sydow's pastor) matches the overall mood, restrained and expressive; and shot with varying colour tones to reflect inner states of mind, the film unfolds like the four seasons, ending with a spring-like scene of reconciliation. WH

Ox-Bow Incident, The (aka Strange Incident)

(1943, US, 75 min, b/w)
d William Wellman. *p/sc* Lamar Trotti. *ph* Arthur Miller. *ed* Allen McNeil. *ad* Richard Day, James Basevi. *m* Cyril J Mockridge. *cast* Henry Fonda, Dana Andrews, Mary Beth Hughes, Anthony Quinn, William Eythe, Henry Morgan, Jane Darwell, Frank Conroy, Francis Ford.

●A sombre, somewhat simplistically liberal Western from a novel by Walter Van Tilburg Clark in which three drifters (Andrews, Quinn and Ford), lynched as rustlers on the flimsiest of evidence, are posthumously proven innocent by good guy Fonda (interestingly, the film's dynamics and characterisations can be seen to prefigure *Twelve Angry Men*). But for all the obviousness of its 'message' (which once made it seem a landmark in the genre), the movie is impressively taut, not merely because of Wellman's tersely economic pacing of his material, but because Fox's decision to cut costs by shooting it entirely on a studio set serves, ironically, to increase the mood of claustrophobic tension. Indeed, its affinity to *film noir* is evident not only in the dark shadowy photography, but in the gallery of grotesques that populates this decidedly uncelebratory portrait of the frontier spirit. GA

Oxford Blues

(1984, US, 97 min)
d Robert Boris. *p* Cassian Elwes, Elliott Kastner. *sc* Robert Boris. *ph* John Stanier. *ed* Patrick Moore. *pd* Terry Pritchard. *m* John Du Prez. *cast* Rob Lowe, Ally Sheedy, Amanda Pays, Julian Sands, Julian Firth, Alan Howard, Gail Strickland, Michael Gough, Aubrey Morris, Cary Elwes.

●Or 'A Wank in Oxford'. An obtuse, obsessed Las Vegas car lot attendant (Lowe), thanks to a little computer hacking, gets to go to an Oxford of perpetual wintry sunrises and sunsets and where, God help us, cicadas still chirp at night. He manages to take the virginity of fellow-student Lady Victoria (Pays, beautiful), but not her hand in marriage. His American brashness riles fuddy-duddy academia and the mafia of the Oriel Rowing Club. They instil him with 'character'. He rows and grows up to indulge in such adult activities as wrecking rooms and sloshing Moët & Chandon everywhere. Funny and moral? Nah. Tiresome? You bet. MS

Oyster and the Wind, The (A ostra e o vento)

(1997, Braz, 115 min)
d Walter Lima Jr. *p* Flávio R Tambellini. *sc* Walter Lima Jr. *ph* Pedro Farkas. *ed* Sergio Mekler. *pd* Vera Hamburger. *m* Wagner Tiso. *cast* Leandra Leal, Lima Duarte, Fernando Torres, Floriano Peixoto, Castrinho, Debora Bloch.

●This reverie-cum-mystery (beautifully shot by Pedro Farkas) concerns the inhabitants of one of Brazil's remote Downed Islands – 'where the days go backwards and forwards like the waves' – populated only by a 60-year-old lighthouse keeper, his jealously guarded daughter Marcela, and a crew of sailors who bring provisions once a month. Unfolding through flashbacks (Marcela is played by three actresses), it's a tale of troubled sexual awakening, repressed passions and mysterious pasts, in which nothing is made explicit. Marcela's disembodied voice is invoked as one sailor reads her journal, conjuring up the story of the mysterious Saulo and 'The Idiot' boy Roberto – but what's truth? what fiction? A mature, distinctively directed work, oneiric and powerful, but also a touch warped and darkly obsessive. WH

p

The Public Enemy

Pace That Kills, The

see Cocaine Fields, The

Pacific Heights

(1990, US, 104 min)
d John Schlesinger. *p* Scott Rudin, William Sackheim. *sc* Daniel Pyne. *ph* Amir Mokri. *ed* Mark Warner, Steven Ramirez. *pd* Neil Spisak. *m* Hans Zimmer. *cast* Melanie Griffith, Matthew Modine, Michael Keaton, Mako, Nobu McCarthy, Laurie Metcalf, Carl Lumbly, Dorian Harewood, Luca Bercovici, Tippi Hedren, Sheila McCarthy, Dan Hedaya, Miriam Margolyes, Beverly D'Angelo.

●Carter Hayes (Keaton) is *not* the ideal tenant: he trifles with razor blades, cultivates cockroaches, and doesn't pay the rent. It's a sign of the times when the landlord gets all our sympathy, but that's the general idea. Live-in lovers Drake and Patty (Modine and Griffith) buy a sprawling Victorian house in San Francisco. To pay for renovations, they rent out apartments to a quiet Japanese couple and to the psychopathic Hayes, who proceeds to strip the fittings and terrorise everyone in the house. But the law is firmly on his side. Schlesinger stages the action with smooth assurance, gradually building tension until Hayes goes completely round the bend. The problem lies in Daniel Pyne's script: the relationship between Drake and Patty is half-realised, while Hayes' motivations remain strangely muddled. That said, Keaton is chillingly convincing. CM

Pack, The

(1977, US, 99 min)
d Robert Clouse. *p* Fred Weintraub, Paul Heller. *sc* Robert Clouse. *ph* Ralph Woolsey. *ed* Peter E. Berger. *m* Lee Holdridge. *cast* Joe Don Baker, Hope Alexander-Willis, Richard B Shull, RG Armstrong, Ned Wertimer.

●Dogs left by summer vacationers gang together, run wild, and terrorise an out-of-season island resort. Somewhere inside *The Pack* a modestly good movie struggles to find expression. But Robert Clouse's script (from Dave Fisher's novel) is almost indecently hasty in turning the characters into dog food, and his direction is monotonously relentless in its pursuit of the requisite thrills. Occasional set pieces work – a woman trapped in a car, for instance – but little is done to string them together. It's a pity that Joe Don Baker's strangely reticent hero isn't allowed greater dimension, and that stalwarts like Shull and Armstrong are given so little to do. CPe

Package, The

(1989, US, 108 min)
d Andrew Davis. *p* Beverly J. Camhe, Tobie Haggerty. *sc* John Bishop. *ph* Frank Tidy. *ed* Don Zimmerman, Billy Weber. *ad* Michael Levesque. *m* James Newton Howard. *cast* Gene Hackman, Joanna Cassidy, Tommy Lee Jones, John Heard, Dennis Franz, Reni Santoni, Pam Grier, Chelcie Ross, Ron Dean, Kevin Crowley, Thalmus Rasulala.

●Soviet intelligence has nasty plans for the American President. This time their plot is assisted by neo-Nazis who are none too happy with feelings of East-West accord, but they haven't reckoned on Sergeant Johnny Gallagher (Hackman), an army veteran at loggerheads with young(ish) Colonel Whitaker (Heard). A court-martialled serviceman (Jones) escapes from Gallagher's custody, and it transpires that the man had adopted a false identity. Gallagher gets his ex-wife (Cassidy), a personnel officer, to help his private investigation, which uncovers military and police corruption… The plot is reasonably entertaining, and Davis handles the action sequences well, but where the film transcends a lingering sense of *déjà vu* is in its intelligent performances: Hackman and Cassidy make a strong, unsentimental couple, hints of romance and reconciliation lurking beneath their businesslike exchanges. But this is hardly groundbreaking stuff, the main difference from earlier Red Threat thrillers being that the enemy is less clearly defined. CM

Package Tour, The (Társasutazás)

(1985, Hun, 73 min)
d Gyula Gazdag. *p* György Marx. *ph* Elemér Ragályi. *ed* Julia Sivó.

●A documentary which follows a coach party of former inmates on a trip to Auschwitz. As a subject it has a certain built-in success factor; the uncontained grief of these people is inevitable, though none the less moving. But while the camera's presence often proves unbearably intrusive upon its subjects' emotions, there is a far more telling interview, intercut with the journey, from a woman who was forced to stay at home, thanks to a recurrent illness brought on by the attentions of the camp doctor. She speaks in tranquil recollection about the arbitrary nature of the death queues, and who might or might not survive the ovens. Because of her cool and her distance, it is her one remembers when the agony of the visitors is long forgotten. CPea

Pack Up Your Troubles

(1932, US, 68 min, b/w)
d George Marshall, Raymond McCarey. *p* Hal Roach. *sc* HM Walker. *ph* Art Lloyd. *ed* Richard Currier. *cast* Stan Laurel, Oliver Hardy, Donald Dillaway, Mary Carr, Charles Middleton, Tom Kennedy, Billy Gilbert, James Finlayson, George Marshall.

●The second Laurel and Hardy feature, admittedly patchy but generally underrated. Perhaps because, after the rumbustious army farce of the beginning, it switches to a quieter vein of sentimental comedy as the boys fulfil a promise to deliver a dead comrade's little daughter to the care of her wealthy grandparents (only clue, the family name is Smith). Best moment is when Stan tries to tell the child a bedtime story and finds himself sleepily on the receiving end. Look out for director Marshall's cameo as a bad-tempered army cook. TM

Pacte des loups, Le

see Brotherhood of the Wolf

Padre Padrone

(1977, It, 113 min)
d Paolo Taviani, Vittorio Taviani. *p* Giuliani De Negri. *sc* Paolo Taviani, Vittorio Taviani. *ph* Mario Masini. *ed* Roberto Perpignani. *m* Egisto Macchi. *cast* Omero Antonutti, Saverio Marconi, Marcella Michelangeli, Fabrizio Forte, Marino Cenna.

●A Sardinian shepherd manages to free himself from his family, educate himself, then return home to fight an overdue battle with the figure who oppressed him, his father. *Padre Padrone* is a terrific subject, a true story that illuminates a universal problem: how can one man make a positive stand against his own patriarchal society? The boy's acquisition of language is a key factor, and the film's triumph is that it actualises this in an extraordinarily emotive way: after a consciously theatrical introduction, it presents fragments of experience (landscape, sounds, routines) which cohere into a vision of nature and human society as the boy matures. TR

Pagemaster, The

(1994, US, 75 min)
d Maurice Hunt (animation), Joe Johnston (live action). *p* David Kirschner, Paul Gertz. *sc* David Casci, David Kirshner, Ernie Contreras. *ph* Alexandra Gruszynski. *ed* Roy Forge Smith. *ad* Gay Lawrence, Valeria Ventura. *m* James Horner. *cast* Macaulay Culkin, Christopher Lloyd, Ed Begley Jr, Mel Harris, Whoopi Goldberg.

●Mediocre, really, this mixture of real actors and animation. Richard (Culkin) is a kid who learns courage after being exposed to the world of books. Sheltering from a storm in the library, Richard encounters the Merlin-like librarian (Lloyd), slips and is knocked unconscious, after which he's conducted on a tour of Adventure fiction (voice of Patrick Stewart), Horror (Frank Weller) and Fantasy (Whoopi Goldberg). These three are books with arms, and are as imaginatively drawn as Mr Sugar Lump. Dr Jekyll and Mr Hyde, Moby Dick and Ahab, Long John Silver and Alice in Wonderland thrust their more visceral moments at the lad, forcing him to overcome his fear of heights and confrontation. BC

Page Miss Glory

(1935, US, 90 min, b/w)
d Mervyn LeRoy. *sc* Delmer Daves, Robert Lord. *ph* George Folsey. *ed* William Clemens. *ad* Robert M. Haas. *m* Leo F Forbstein. *cast* Marion Davies, Pat O'Brien, Dick Powell, Mary Astor, Frank McHugh, Patsy Kelly, Barton MacLane.

●Although more famous for being newspaper tycoon William Randolph Hearst's mistress than an actress in her own right, Marion Davies gives a fair performance here as a small-town girl who comes to New York and works as a chambermaid. Until, that is, con-men O'Brien and McHugh, who've won a beauty contest with a fake composite photo, talk her into putting flesh on their latest scam. NF

Page of Madness, A (Kurutta Ippeiji)

(1926, Jap, 60 min, b/w)
d/p Teinosuke Kinugasa. *sc* Yasunari Kawabata. *ph* Konei Sugiyama. *ad* Chiyo Ozaki. *cast* Masao Inoue, Yoshie Nakagawa, Ayako Iijima, Hiroshi Nemoto.

●Acted by an avant-garde theatre group, conceived and directed by one-time kabuki female impersonator Kinugasa, *A Page of Madness* remains one of the most radical and challenging Japanese movies ever seen here. An old sailor works as a janitor in an asylum to stay close to his insane wife and to help her to escape, except that she doesn't want to go… Kinugasa deploys a battery of expressionist distortions and otherwise stylised images to plunge his audience into 'irrational' experience, always withdrawing to a 'saner' perspective, and then undercutting that with another visual or dramatic shock. This version has music added by Kinugasa when he rediscovered the print in 1970. TR

Pagliacci (aka A Clown Must Laugh)

(1936, GB, 92 min, b/w & col)
d Karl Grune. *p* Max Schach. *sc* Monckton Hoffe, Roger Burford. *ph* Otto Kanturek. *ed* Editor. *pd* Oscar F Werndorff. *m* Ruggiero Leoncavallo. *cast* Richard Tauber, Steffi Duna, Diana Napier, Arthur Margetson, Esmond Knight, Jerry Verno, Gordon James.

●Rudimentary adaptation of Leoncavallo's one-act opera, which gives brawny Austrian tenor Tauber (who'd emigrated to England in 1933) the chance to belt out the big number (in English) 'On with the Motley'. Duna's the unfaithful spouse, Knight (who lost much of his sight during WWII but successfully continued his screen career right up until Lars von Trier's startling 1984 debut *Element of Crime*) her soldier lover. It switches to experimental Chemicolour for a couple of scenes. TJ

Painful Pair, A (Itai Futari)

(2001, Jap, 112 min)
d Hisashi Saito. *p* Yutaka Suzuki. *sc* Hisashi Saito. *ph* Katsuyuki Hirano. *ed* Kumi Okada. *ad* Tamiko Tomioka, Yoshifumi Tsubota, Haruka Kikuchi. *m* Shinichi Kanazawa. *cast* Hidetoshi Nishijima, Miako Tadano, Takuji Suzuki, Yuho Tadano, Kazuo Hara, Ryuichi Hiroki.

●DV-shot Japanese indie with an interesting premise (a young husband and wife literally feel each other's pain) – which it squanders on a mixture of farce and comedy of embarrassment. The husband Ryo (Nishijima) is a teacher, stalked by an overweight female pupil; the wife Natsu (Tadano) is an office worker harassed by a gloomy, no-hoper colleague (Suzuki, reprising a persona established in his *One Piece!* shorts). It aims for a kind of kooky charm, but it's clumsily directed and the underlying attitudes seem deeply misanthropic. The supporting cast includes two other indie directors, Hara and Hiroki, neither very funny. TR

Pain in the A**, A

see Emmerdeur, L

Painted Angels

(1997, Can/GB, 110 min)
d Jon Sanders. *p* Ann Scott, Christina Jennings, Stephen Onda. *sc* Anna Mottram, Jon Sanders. *ph* Gerald Packer. *ed* Maysoon Pachachi. *pd* Hayden Griffin. *m* Douglas Finch. *cast* Brenda Fricker, Kelly McGillis, Meret Becker, Bronagh Gallagher, Lisa Jakub, Anna Mottram.

●A British feminist Western? It's not a recipe to tickle the palette, and indeed, Sanders' film is scrupulously miserable. A portrait of life in a frontier brothel, where half-a-dozen whores ply their trade, this is a long way from the inane adventures of Jonathan Kaplan's *Bad Girls* or the diffuse poetics of Altman's *McCabe and Mrs Miller*. Sanders and co-writer Mottram strip away the phoney romance of the West to put the focus squarely on the women. The coupling is brusque, or brutal, or both, and the whores are no more than the chattels of the unsentimental madam (Fricker). Underneath inches of historically accurate slap, the performances just about carry it. Yes, the film serves as a stern historical corrective, yes, it scores still relevant points about the prostitution of women and refuses to stoop to melodramatic manipulation – but the narrow tonal range is forbidding, and for vast stretches nothing much happens at all. TCh

Painted Boats (aka The Girl on the Canal)

(1945, GB, 63 min, b/w)
d Charles Crichton. *p* Michael Balcon. *sc* Stephen Black. *ph* Douglas Slocombe. *ed* Leslie Allen. *ad* Jim Morahan. *m* John Greenwood. *cast* Jenny Laird, Robert Griffith, Bill Blewett, May Hallatt, Grace Arnold, Harry Fowler.

●Ealing docu-drama portrait of English canal life, modestly charting the lives of two boat families with the aid of a Louis MacNeice commentary, and examining the demands of tradition and change in the immediate postwar world. The sole product of a proposed studio series to consolidate the wartime fusions of fiction and documentary, elsewhere sustained only intermittently until TV stepped wholeheartedly into the breach. PT

Painted Desert

(1993, US, 96 min)
d Masato Harada. *p* Tikki Goldberg. *sc* Masato Harada, Rebecca Ross. *ph* David Bridges, Bernard Salzmann. *ed* Rebecca Ross. *pd* Rae Fox. *m* Masahiro Kawasaki. *cast* James Gammon, Kazuya Kimura, Nobu McCarthy.

●The Shochiku company's first English-language production has the slightly clammy air of something pulled out of a film buff's closet (that's what comes from getting Hollywood obsessive Masato Harada to direct and co-write it), but it plays remarkably well. A heavily guarded Mafia *capo* holes up in a desert villa fearful of assassination. The only visitor allowed in is the chef from the rundown local diner – a handsome young Japanese man recently found dying in the desert, who turns out to have his own secret agenda. Some of the plot's Japanese baggage is clumsily integrated, but the dialogue is witty and the playing absolutely charming. Best of all is James Gammon, plucked from character-actor obscurity and pushed centre stage as a grizzled, seen-it-all gangster with old-time manners out of a John Ford movie. TR

Painted Heart

(1992, US, 90 min)
d Michael Taav. *p* Mark Pollard, Randall Poster. *sc* Michael Taav. *ph* Robert Yeoman. *ed* Nancy Richardson. *pd* Mark Friedberg. *m* John Wesley Harding. *cast* Will Patton, Bebe Neuwirth, Robert Pastorelli, Casey Siemaszko, Mark Boone Jr, Jayne Haynes.

●Taav's first feature occupies the same setting and psychological territory as David Lynch's visions of small-town America. About a love triangle, involving house painter Wesley (Patton), his boss Willie (Pastorelli) and Willie's sensitive, vulnerable wife Margaret (Neuwirth), the film turns into a picture of hidden desires, romantic dreams and dangerous obsessions. A boy is saved from his drunken father by his mother's offer of sex; using her lipstick he colours a newspaper ad that reads, 'With these clothes you'll have no problems.' Thirty years later, an agitated Wesley breaks into Margaret's house and, before leaving lipstick as a present, tells her, 'I've got some ideas I don't know what to do with.' An affair develops: Margaret projects years of romantic longing on to her new lover, while the paranoid Wesley, fearing discovery, spies on Willie's own clandestine activities. At this stage, it's not clear whose disturbing childhood we've seen. The consequences, though, are alarmingly clear – 'The Lipstick Killer' is on the loose. An unsettling film in which ideas, tone and texture unite with quietly confident storytelling. NF

Painted Veil, The

(1934, US, 83 min, b/w)
d Richard Boleslawski. *p* Hunt Stromberg. *sc* John Meehan, Salka Viertel, Edith Fitzgerald. *ph* William Daniels. *ed* Hugh Wynn. *ad* Cedric Gibbons. *m* Herbert Stothart. *cast* Greta Garbo, Herbert Marshall, George Brent, Warner Oland, Jean Hersholt, Keye Luke.

●Typically lush MGM vehicle for Garbo, drawn from Somerset Maugham's novel and set in Hollywood's China, in which she manages to sail through a clichéd plot – neglected by overworked medical missionary husband (Marshall), she succumbs to unworthy diplomat lover (Brent), but redeems herself during a cholera epidemic – and still light up the screen with her ever-sensuous, charismatic presence. The production values are characteristically sumptuous, William Daniels' photography is lustrous, and Boleslawski directs with suitable flair, although his interest in the acting theories and practices of Stanislavsky is hardly apparent from the performances. GA

Painters Painting

(1972, US, 116 min, b/w & col)
d/p/sc Emile de Antonio. *ph* Ed Emshwiller, Marc N Weiss. *ed* Mary Lampson, Cinda Firestone. *with* Willem de Kooning, Helen Frankenthaler, Hans Hoffman, Jasper Johns, Bob Rauschenberg, Andy Warhol.

●Uncharacteristically for de Antonio, this takes the form of a homage rather than a critique. An apparently non-evaluative selection of auspicious interviewees (long-time friends of the film-maker, we're told) holding forth on postwar American art and its fashionable New York heyday, in fact take their validity as spokespeople from the commercial terms of the art market, and the only analytical correlatives invoked are those of the contemporary critics, dealers and buyers who decreed their 'importance' in the first place. The interviews are almost conspiratorially cosy, although still mystificatory next to the colour shots of the paintings in question, and one is left grasping at anecdotal material to sustain interest. While fans of Rauschenberg, Stella, Johns, Koons, de Kooning, et al, might love it, it's a decided aberration in de Antonio's important oeuvre. PT

Paint Your Wagon

(1969, US, 165 min)
d Joshua Logan. *p* Alan Jay Lerner. *sc* Alan Jay Lerner, Paddy Chayefsky. *ph* William A Fraker. *ed* Robert C Jones. *pd* John Truscott. *m* Frederick Loewe. *cast* Lee Marvin, Clint Eastwood, Jean Seberg, Harve Presnell, Ray Walston, Tom Ligon.

●Logan's rotund version of Lerner and Loewe's musical Western may lack actors (Presnell excepted) who can actually sing, but that's compensated for by a solid plot involving a farcical discovery of gold, and the growth of a mining town (No Name City) that develops from amoral shantydom to respectability and a holocaust. When the novelty wears off of watching Eastwood (as one of Seberg's two husbands in a variant on a Mormon ménage) singing *I Talk to the Trees* like a cross between Roy Rogers and Bobby Vee, you'll have a wavering but consistently interesting performance from Marvin, hamming away as the other husband. VG

Paisà

(1946, It, 124 min, b/w)
d Roberto Rossellini. *p* Roberto Rossellini, Rod E Geiger, Mario Conti. *sc* Federico Fellini, Roberto Rossellini, Sergio Amidei. *ph* Otello Martelli. *ed* Eraldo Da Roma. *m* Renzo Rossellini. *cast* Maria Michi, Gar Moore, Carmela Sazio, Dots M Johnson, Harriet White, Bill Tubbs, Dale Edmonds.

●Rossellini recounts the liberation of Italy during WWII in six distinct episodes. The film's style is the foundation on which the whole aesthetic of neo-realism was built: endless establishing shots, and long 'neutral' takes that allow each viewer to make up his own mind about the characters. But the choked-back sentimentality of much of the action (GI doesn't recognise prostitute as the girl he once loved, etc) belongs to a very much older tradition than the visual style. Only the long, final episode in the Po Valley remains wholly impressive: its view of the sheer arbitrariness of warfare anticipates some of Jancsó's abstractions. TR

Pajama Game, The

(1957, US, 101 min)
d George Abbott, Stanley Donen. *p* George Abbott. *sc* George Abbot, Richard Bissell. *ph* Harry Stradling. *ed* William Ziegler. *ad* Malcolm Bert. *songs* Richard Adler, Jerry Ross. *cast* Doris Day, John Raitt, Carol Haney, Eddie Foy Jr, Barbara Nichols, Reta Shaw.

●A truly joyous screen adaptation of the Broadway musical, with Doris Day heading the union in a clothing factory. The real star of the show is arguably Bob Fosse's stunning choreography, in particular the *tour de force* sequence of the workers' picnic. No opportunity to use the bright colours and props offered by the setting is missed, and the songs by Richard Adler and Jerry Ross are memorable ('Hey, There' and 'There Once Was a Man'). An enthusiastic young Jean-Luc Godard dubbed it 'the first left-wing operetta'. DT

Pakeezah

(1972, Ind, 150 min)
d/p/sc Kamal Amrohi. *ph* Joseph Wirshing. *ed* DN Pai. *ad* NB Kulkarni, DS Malwankar. *m* Gulam Mohammed. *cast* Ashok Kumar, Meena Kumari, Raaj Kumar, Veena, Kamal Kapoor.

●This popular musical suggests that, at its best, the much-scorned commercial product of 'Hollywood-Bombay' is equally extraordinary in its own way. A byzantine story (of star-crossed lovers) that proceeds fitfully through the fabulous logic of dreams; luscious colour-scope photography, and a febrile camera craning and tracking restlessly through fairytale locations and sets; and never even a single screen kiss, but instead some of the most brazenly erotic songs and dances you'll ever see on film. SJo

Paleface, The

(1948, US, 91 min)
d Norman Z McLeod. *p* Robert L Welch. *sc* Edmund Hartmann, Frank Tashlin. *ph* Ray Rennahan. *ed* Ellsworth Hoagland. *ad* Hans Dreier, Earl Hedrick. *m* Victor Young. *cast* Bob Hope, Jane Russell, Robert Armstrong, Iris Adrian, Robert Watson, Clem Bevans.

●Hope in perhaps his finest role as Painless Potter, a quack dentist travelling the Old West and getting into deep waters when he meets and is married by the trouble-shooting Calamity Jane as a cover for her secret activities as a government agent. The gags centre as always around his bluff bravado, but he was rarely given a better script (to which Frank Tashlin contributed) or a more responsive partner than the wittily seductive, sardonic and deceitful Jane Russell. GA

Pale Rider

(1985, US, 116 min)
d/p Clint Eastwood. *sc* Michael Butler, Dennis Shryack. *ph* Bruce Surtees. *ed* Joel Cox. *pd* Edward C Carfagno. *m* Lennie Niehaus. *cast* Clint Eastwood, Michael Moriarty, Carrie Snodgrass, Christopher Penn, Richard Dysart, Sydney Penny, Richard Kiel, John Russell.

●One of the oldest Western themes: an enigmatic knight errant rides into town, sides with the poor but decent folk against the robber barons, then rides back to the horizon leaving the West won for the forces of good. This is shot in classical style, with much less of the baroque, mystical flourish which characterised *High Plains Drifter*. But there are sufficient question-marks inserted to lift it out of the routine: Eastwood's preacher man seems to carry the stigmata of a ghost; and he arrives as the answer to a maiden's prayer. Furthermore, his care for the landscape puts him in the Anthony Mann class. It's good to be back in the saddle again. CPea

Palermo or Wolfsburg (Palermo oder Wolfsburg)

(1980, WGer/It, 175 min)
d Werner Schroeter. *p* Thomas Mauch, Eric Franck. *sc* Werner Schroeter, Giuseppe Fava. *ph* T Mauch. *ed* Werner Schroeter, Ursula West. *pd* Albert Barsacq, Roberto Lagana, Magdalena Montezuma, Edwin Wengobowski. *cast* Nicola Zarbo, Calogero Arancio, Padre Pace, Cavaliere Comparato, Brigitte Tilg, Gisela Hahn.

●The story of a Sicilian boy from Palermo who arrives as a guest-worker at the Volkswagen factory in Wolfsburg. He meets a pretty German girl, settles a debt of honour by murder, and as a final surprise becomes a Christ-like martyr at his trial. Operatic and naturalistic in turn, Schroeter's tale of helplessness and outrage seems too convinced of its own importance to really work; and after nearly three hours, that matters. DMacp

Pal Joey

(1957, US, 111 min)
d George Sidney. *p* Fred Kohlmar. *sc* Dorothy Kingsley. *ph* Harold Lipstein. *ed* Viola Lawrence, Jerome Thoms. *ad* Walter Holscher. *songs* Richard Rodgers, Lorenz Hart. *cast* Frank Sinatra, Kim Novak, Rita Hayworth, Barbara Nichols, Elizabeth Patterson, Bobby Sherwood.
●Columbia's Harry Cohn snapped up the rights to the Rodgers and Hart musical on its first appearance, no doubt feeling a strong kinship with its heel of a hero, and then had a pig of a job casting the leads. By the mid-'50s he'd got it nailed – showing off his new sex symbol Kim Novak as the young innocent eyed by Sinatra's nightclub entertainer, and providing a final chance for his old sex symbol Rita Hayworth to sing (dubbed) and shake those legs as her experienced rival. In other films, George Sidney cultivated his dubious taste to the point of a fine art, but here his glossy vulgarity ultimately serves to smother the bite of the original material. The result is a musical externally lavish but somehow hollow inside; a musical with electric moments but dull scenes. GB

Pallieter

(1975, Bel/Neth, 90 min)
d Roland Verhavert. *p* Jan van Raemdonck, JE Lauwers, Gerrit Visscher. *sc* Hugo Claus. *ph* Pim Heytman. *ed* Ine Schenkkan, Peter Simons. *ad* Ludo Bex, Philippe Graff. *cast* Eddy Brugman, Jacqueline Rommerts, Sylvia De Leur.
●Plot is nothing and atmosphere is all in this Belgian oddity based on a famous novel by Felix Timmermans. A turn-of-the-century degenerate townie transforms himself into a childlike rural hero who blows soap-bubbles, puts mirrors round the outside of his house, champions nature against the bespoilers ('Oh tree, my brother' he declaims), marries a charming girl, and sets out round the world in a cart to avoid the century's horrid future. All of which is captured in radiant photography, accompanied by the inevitable bursts of Vivaldi's *Four Seasons* (eat your heart out, *Elvira Madigan*). It's far too simpering and flaccid for lasting pleasure, but there is something relaxing about the film's relaxed pace and indulgent moods. Provided you're in an indulgent mood yourself, of course. GB

Palm Beach Story, The

(1942, US, 90 min, b/w)
d Preston Sturges. *sc* Preston Sturges. *ph* Victor Milner. *ed* Stuart Gilmore. *ad* Hans Dreier, Ernst Fegté. *m* Victor Young. *cast* Claudette Colbert, Joel McCrea, Rudy Vallee, Mary Astor, Sig Arno, Robert Warwick, William Demarest, Franklin Pangborn.
●Sturges was riding high in the early '40s, writing and directing comedies of such density and wit that a moment's inattention might make an audience miss six great one-liners, five amazing bits of business, four eight-syllable words, and three crowd scenes. And few of his films were as smoothly accomplished as *The Palm Beach Story*, a knowing satire on the driving forces of sex and money, with Colbert fleeing from her righteous and penniless husband into the ridiculous arms of yachtsman billionaire Rudy Vallee. Hilarious, irresistible, impeccably cast. GB

Palmetto

(1998, US/Ger, 113 min)
d Volker Schlöndorff. *p* Matthias Wendlandt. *sc* E Max Frye. *ph* Thomas Kloss. *ed* Peter Przygodda. *pd* Claire Jenora Bowin. *m* Klaus Doldinger. *cast* Woody Harrelson, Elisabeth Shue, Gina Gershon, Rolf Hoppe, Michael Rapaport, Chloe Sevigny.
●Somewhat embittered after spending two years in prison for a crime he didn't commit, journo Harry Barber (Harrelson) returns to his Florida hometown and his artist girlfriend Nina (Gershon) feeling the world owes him. So when an apparently chance meeting with millionaire's wife Rhea Malroux (Shue) leads to steamy sex and an offer of $50,000 in return for making a phonecall and a ransom pick-up in a bogus kidnap involving her stepdaughter Odette (Sevigny), he's not averse to the proposal. Trouble is, genre convention dictates that all Harry's precautions against becoming a fall guy are in vain, and soon he's up to his neck in trouble. Despite decent credentials (script from James Hadley Chase's *Just Another Sucker*), this is a banal contribution to that very variable modern subgenre, 'neo-*noir*'. For all the sweaty, fatalistic ambience and frequent, if predictable, narrative twists, it's finally just a string of hard-boiled clichés, churned out with insufficient conviction to succeed as a thriller and not enough irony to work as parody. GA

Palms

see Hands

Palmy Days

(1931, US, 77 min, b/w)
d Edward Sutherland. *p* Samuel Goldwyn. *sc* Eddie Cantor, Morrie Ryskind, David Freedman. *ph* Gregg Toland. *ed* Sherman Todd. *ad* Richard Day, Willy Pogany. *songs* Con Conrad, Harry Akst. *cast* Eddie Cantor, Charlotte Greenwood, Barbara Weeks, Charles Middleton, George Raft.
●This pre-Code musical opens with a surreal sequence featuring a bakery staffed entirely by flimsily clad Goldwyn Girls. Next, a ducky young man orders a chocolate cake 'with a pansy on top', whereupon the Girls return, wearing even less, for a Busby Berkeley number entitled 'Bend Down, Sister'. After that, things get less libidinous as zany india-rubber man Eddie Cantor takes over the movie. Charles Middleton, later to find fame as Ming the Merciless, is a pantomime villain, but cold-eyed George Raft as his henchman is the real thing. Berkeley's contributions are unmistakable, overhead shots and all, his camera ogling the chorus girls' faces almost as intensely as it does their bodies. BBa

Palookaville

(1995, US, 92 min)
d Alan Taylor. *p* Uberto Pasolini. *sc* David Epstein. *ph* John Thomas. *ed* David Leonard. *pd* Anne Stuhler. *m* Rachel Portman. *cast* William Forsythe, Vincent Gallo, Adam Trese, Gareth Williams, Lisa Gay Hamilton, Bridgit Ryan, Kim Dickens, Frances McDormand.
●Russ, Sid and Jerry are at wit's end: they're broke, unemployed, and prepared to turn a blind eye to legal niceties. Yet burglary may not be for them. They over-shoot the local jewellery store and break into the pastry shop next door – a sticky situation, especially for Russ, whose brother-in-law's a cop. An armoured car robbery suggests itself, if only they can work up the necessary gumption, but these guys may be too good to be bad – or just too bad at being bad. A gentle comic fable, this follows the trials of three not-so wiseguys and finds them fundamentally innocent. It's hardly an original idea – that criminal negligence can be funny – but Taylor, his screenwriter David Epstein and a winning cast headed by Gallo (Russ), Trese (Jerry) and Forsythe (Sid) find a fresh angle on it, fruitfully exploiting the discrepancy between a macho gun culture and the impotence of these men's lives. The film makes time for a handful of delicious, delicately observed comic digressions; and Taylor captures an eloquent slice of New Jersey lowlife: Springsteen with laughs. All very nice. But Gallo's charged, explosive presence spikes the punch – he gives the whimsy some kick. TCh

Paltoquet, Le

(1986, Fr, 93 min)
d Michel Deville. *p* Rosalinde Damamme. *sc* Michel Deville. *ph* André Diot. *ed* Raymonde Guyot. *ad* Thierry Leproust. *m* Antonín Dvorák, Leos Janácek. *cast* Fanny Ardant, Daniel Auteuil, Richard Bohringer, Philippe Léotard, Jeanne Moreau, Michel Piccoli, Claude Piéplu, Jean Yanne, An Luu.
●There's been a death in a French flophouse, but virtually all of the film takes place in a deserted factory which Moreau has turned into a gloomy café of sorts. Here four men play bridge while the Dior-draped Ardant languishes in a hammock. One of them is a killer. The barman (Piccoli in fine whimsical form) is the 'nonentity' of the title; he presides over the game-playing, and cues bursts of loud music: Janacek, for example, serves to herald the entrance of the detective (Yanne) determined to unravel the murder mystery. When not being abused by the customers, Piccoli reads a copy of the thriller by Franz-Rudolph Falk on which the film is based: its subject, in other words, is nothing but itself. This is Robbe-Grillet intertextualised with Greenaway, and the result is an enthralling tediousness. MS

Pandaemonium

(2000, GB/US, 124 min)
d Julien Temple. *p* Nick O'Hagan. *sc* Frank Cottrell Boyce. *ph* John Lynch. *ed* Niven Howie. *pd* Laurence Dorman. *m* Dario Marianelli. *cast* John Hannah, Linus Roache, Samantha Morton, Emily Woof, Emma Fielding, Andy Serkis, Samuel West, Clive Merrison, Dexter Fletcher.
●Temple has had an uneven career since smashing on to the scene with *The Great Rock'n'Roll Swindle*. Once compared to Tashlin, he's now turned his graphic skills to the costume drama with this Ken Russell-like Romantik romp in the company of Coleridge, Wordsworth, Byron, Southey, et al – with disappointing results. There's no doubt where the sympathies of Temple and his scriptwriter lie; Roache is allowed loose rein in his wilful characterisation of impulsive genius Coleridge, whereas Hannah's envious tightwad Wordsworth is reduced to playing treacherous Salieri to Roache's Mozart. Coleridge's progressive laudanum dependency (his 'Kubla Khan' writing frenzy is interrupted by Wordsworth, not the person from Porlock) provides Temple's aesthetic justification for the anachronisms, flashback structure (from 1816 back to 1795), and subjective shots, but too often to trite effect. Cinematographer John Lynch's experiments occasionally pay dividends– witness the affecting moonlit sequence with Coleridge, Sarah (Samantha Morton, enjoying her malapropisms) and baby, when he reads 'Frost at Midnight' – but is more often alienating in all the wrong ways. It's the old problem of theatrical performances trouncing any hope of subtlety or insight.WH

Pandemonium (Shura)

(1970, Jap, 134 min, b/w)
d Toshio Matsumoto. *sc* Shuji Ishizawa, Toshio Matsumoto. *ph* Tatsuo Suzuki. *ed* Toshie Iwasa. *ad* Setsu Asakura. *m* Fumikazu Nishimatsu. *cast* Katsuo Nakamura, Yasuko Sanjo, Juro Kira, Masao Imafuku, Tamotsu Tamura.
●Conceived as a lacerating attack on the Japanese film industry's typical 'heroic' samurai movies, this Japanese independent adapts an 18th century kabuki play to remarkably provocative effect. The plot, as schematic and stylised as a Jacobean tragedy, deals with a would-be samurai's descent into a hell of his own making as he seeks revenge on a couple who trick him. Matsumoto couldn't have realised the psychological passions or the violence with more terrifying force, but his aim is exorcism, not indulgence: the reflective, ultra-formal shooting style, and strategies like the use of captions as 'chapter headings', force the audience to read the film as a complex web of metaphors. The integrity and aesthetic daring of the result are doubtless what caused the British censor to ban it. TR

Pandora and the Flying Dutchman

(1950, GB, 122 min)
d Albert Lewin. *p* Albert Lewin, Joseph Kaufman. *sc* Albert Lewin. *ph* Jack Cardiff. *ed* Ralph Kemplen. *pd* John Bryan. *m* Alan Rawsthorne. *cast* James Mason, Ava Gardner, Nigel Patrick, Sheila Sim, Harold Warrender, Mario Cabré, Marius Goring, John Laurie.
●Lewin's extraordinary film is based on the story of the unfortunate sailor doomed to travel the oceans for all time until he finds a woman who loves him so much that she will sacrifice her own life for his salvation. The legend is updated to a Spanish village in the '30s where various men compete for the affections of Pandora, a beautiful young American (Gardner), and where Mason's mysterious yacht puts into harbour. Lewin combines a script of exuberant literacy with a visual splendour often bordering on the surreal. Mason is his usual impeccable self, while Gardner is gloriously believable as a woman for whom any man would be prepared to suffer eternal damnation. Occasionally absurd, always bold, the film tells a lushly romantic story so skilfully that it possesses the inevitability of myth. RR

Pandora's Box 100 (Die Büchse der Pandora)

(1928, Ger, 10,676 ft. b/w)
d GW Pabst. *p* George C Horsetzky. *sc* Ladislao Vajda. *ph* Günther Krampf. *ed* Joseph R Fliesler. *ad* Andre Andrejew. *cast* Louise Brooks, Fritz Kortner, Franz Lederer, Carl Goetz, Krafft Raschig, Alice Roberts, Gustav Diessl.
● A masterful adaptation/compression of Wedekind's *Lulu* plays, the most humanely tragic portrait of obsession that the cinema has to boast. Lulu's guilelessly provocative sexuality leads her from a gaggle of Berlin lovers and admirers (a lesbian countess, a newspaper editor, the latter's son, etc) to a squalid garret in London, where she finds her Thanatos in the shape of Jack the Ripper. Louise Brooks' legendary performance and Pabst's brilliantly acute direction both remain enthralling. TR

Pane e Cioccolata

see Bread and Chocolate

Pane e Tulipani

see Bread and Tulips

Panic in Needle Park, The

(1971, US, 110 min)
d Jerry Schatzberg. *p* Dominick Dunne. *sc* Joan Didion, John Gregory Mills. *ph* Adam Holender. *ed* Evan Lottman. *ad* Murray P Stern. *cast* Al Pacino, Kitty Winn, Alan Vint, Richard Bright, Kiel Martin, Michael McClanathan, Warren Finnerty, Marcia Jean Kurtz, Raúl Julia.
● A gruelling but highly responsible film about the influence of heroin on a New York street romance. Schatzberg moves with considerable force over the urban territory of *Midnight Cowboy,* using hand-held cameras and a sustained editing rhythm to convey the couple's gradual descent into hell as mercilessly as he shows the needles entering his characters' veins (in close-up). Pacino, as the boy, proves that he didn't need Coppola to make him act, but Kitty Winn is less satisfactory, and the film is finally subject to an iron law of diminishing returns after its plot plumbs the depths and can find nothing to do except batter us some more. In fact, the anti hard drugs message comes on so strong and so realistically that the British censor's ban (lifted in 1975) seems positively malicious: it's precisely this kind of suppression of information which results in junkie mythologies. DP

Panic in the Parlor

see Sailor Beware

Panic in the Streets

(1950, US, 93 min, b/w)
d Elia Kazan. *p* Sol C Siegel. *sc* Richard Murphy. *ph* Joseph MacDonald. *ed* Harmon Jones. *ad* Lyle Wheeler, Maurice Ransford. *m* Alfred Newman. *cast* Richard Widmark, Paul Douglas, Barbara Bel Geddes, Jack Palance, Zero Mostel, Alexis Minotis.
● A classy thriller, much less laden with significance than most Kazan movies. *Film noir* and the Method go remarkably well together as the panic-stricken manhunt gets under way when a victim of a gangland killing is found to be riddled with pneumonic plague. Explicitly identified as rats to be exterminated, the menace – two killers (Palance, Mostel) who may be plague-carriers – is tracked through a pullulating garbage dump marvellously conjured out of some sweaty dockland locations in New Orleans. Some awkward psychologising early on about the police chief (Douglas) and his obstructive attitude as Widmark's Public Health Service officer tries to get things moving, otherwise it's all go, heightened realism, and first-rate performances. TM

Panic in Year Zero

(1962, US, 95 min, b/w)
d Ray Milland. *p* Lou Rusoff, Arnold Houghland. *sc* Jay Simms, John Morton. *ph* Gilbert Warrenton. *ed* William Austin. *ad* Daniel Haller. *m* Les Baxter. *cast* Jean Hagen, Frankie Avalon, Mary Mitchell, Joan Freeman, Richard Garland, Richard Bakalyan.
● *Panic in Year Zero,* about the aftermath of the devastation of Los Angeles by nuclear attack, stands as an extraordinary reminder of just how close avant-garde and popular movies can get in times of social upheaval. The first half-hour, consisting of an endless series of half-wrecked cars streaming across the screen, close-ups of a meaningless radio dial, and the characters' frantic attempts to think the 'unthinkable', could almost be an experimental short rather than an AIP exploitation movie. Frankie Avalon is about the only difference. There are perhaps some naivetés as Milland (actor) realises that the law of the jungle now holds sway in trying to protect his family, but a remarkable effort from Milland (director) all the same. DP

Panic Room

(2002, US, 112 min)
d David Fincher. *p* Gavin Polone, Judy Hofflund, David Koepp, Ceán Chaffin. *sc* David Koepp. *ph* Conrad W Hall, Darius Khondji. *ed* James Haygood, Angus Wall. *pd* Arthur Max. *m* Howard Shore. *cast* Jodie Foster, Forest Whitaker, Dwight Yoakam, Jared Leto, Kristen Stewart, Ann Magnuson, Ian Buchanan, Patrick Bauchau.
● Meg (Foster) is rich, recently divorced and rock-solid, save for occasional bouts of claustrophobia, and she's devoted to diabetic, but likewise feisty daughter Sarah (Stewart). You'd think they'd be safe in their huge new brownstone, especially as a former owner had installed a panic room: a well-hidden hi-tech priest's hole complete with a surveillance system covering the house. The very night Meg and Sarah move in, three burglars turn up expecting a clear run. Suddenly mother and daughter must fight for their lives. Never averse to glistening darkness, meaty metaphor or grandiloquent technical display, Fincher is also surprisingly at home with hokum. Less far-fetched than *The Game,* this is at once less imaginative and more routine. It's a tight, very efficient reworking of women-in-peril motifs, notably from *Wait Until Dark,* with a number of nods to Hitchcock's *Dial M for Murder* and *Rear Window.* Fincher handles the contours of the script as smoothly as the camera passes through plumbing and keyholes; while Jodie ably conveys the tight-lipped anxiety, resourcefulness and lithe strength familiar from her later roles. GA

Panther

(1995, US, 124 min)
d Mario Van Peebles. *p* Mario Van Peebles, Melvin Van Peebles. *sc* Melvin Van Peebles. *ph* Edward Pei. *ed* Earl Watson. *pd* Richard Hoover. *m* Stanley Clarke. *cast* Marcus Chong, Courtney B Vance, Kadeem Hardison, Bokeem Woodbine, James Russo, Tyrin Turner.
● 1966. The Disunited States of America. Huey Newton (Chong) and Bobby Seale (Vance) form the Black Panther Party for Self-Defense. Initially little more than a community self-help programme, the organisation soon becomes a popular movement with a radical political agenda, and enough militancy to terrify J Edgar Hoover, who labels the Panthers 'Public Enemy Number One'. When Judge (Hardison) is approached by the FBI, the Panther leadership convinces him to act as a double agent, and the stakes become a matter of life and death, for Judge himself and for subsequent generations of black Americans. Working from a screenplay by his father Melvin (taken from his own novel), Mario Van Peebles recreates the turbulence of the period, and makes a convincing case on behalf of the Panthers. Less happily, fictional paranoia-thriller elements are clumsily integrated: Judge's story doesn't ring true, and it distracts from more absorbing, documented facts. Time will tell whether the Van Peebles' theory that the FBI collaborated with the Mob to flood the ghettos with drugs holds up as history, but here it's a hysterical, dramatically suspect conclusion to an often stimulating, stylish movie. TCh

Paolozzi Story, The

(1980, WGer/GB, 120 min)
d Al Lauder. *with* Eduardo Paolozzi.
● Just as collage is central to Eduardo Paolozzi's art, so this fascinating documentary about the rebellious, versatile Italo-Scot interprets his life and work through a collage of disparate but carefully juxtaposed references. Figures invoked in illuminating his style and ideas include (to name but a few) Léger, Disney, Wittgenstein, Icarus and St Sebastian; while his mixed cultural inheritance, his love of nature and distaste for industrialised society, are lucidly demonstrated as we view his creations and are led through his varied history. If Paolozzi's verbal abilities are rarely as eloquent as the enormous range of his vividly intelligent castings, graphics and totems to mechanised man, the film nevertheless successfully presents his work in a socio-political as well as an aesthetic context. And it's good, too, to see in detail the physical processes of artistic work, rather than simply its finished products. GA

Pao of the Jungle

see Paw

Papa, les Petits Bateaux...

(1971, Fr, 102 min)
d Nelly Kaplan. *sc* Nelly Kaplan, Claude Makovski, René Guyonnet. *ph* Ricardo Aranovich. *ed* Noëlle Boisson, Nelly Kaplan. *pd* Michel Landi. *m* André Popp. *cast* Michel Bouquet, Sheila White, Michel Lonsdale, Sydney Chaplin, Pierre Mondy, Marcel Dalio, Bernard Musson.
● Very much a film of its time, this is Nelly Kaplan's oblique tribute to Tex Avery and Betty Boop (and Jerry Lewis), a comedy melodrama that aspires to animation with its utterly improbable fantasy of an incorrigible millionaire heiress kidnapped by comic strip gangsters, and held to ransom in a suburban house where she picks them off one by one, seeding little squabbles, encouraging greed, and carrying out the occasional murder (funniest of these: a Corsican mobster, inflamed by lust for the héroine, demonstrates his macho tour de force, the Death Leap, only to be impaled on his own knife). It's Snow White and the Seven Dwarfs as much as anything, with all seven eventually laid to rest in the garden and she their wide-eyed victor. The tone (insistent fake-naiveté) is occasionally irritating, but at its best rather resembles the charmed craziness of *Céline and Julie.* CA

Paper, The

(1994, US, 112 min)
d Ron Howard. *p* Brian Grazer, Fred Zollo. *sc* David Koepp, Stephen Koepp. *ph* John Seale. *ed* Michael Hill, Daniel Hanley. *pd* Todd Hallowell. *m* Randy Newman. *cast* Michael Keaton, Glenn Close, Robert Duvall, Marisa Tomei, Randy Quaid, Jason Robards, Spalding Gray.
● Director Howard's attempt to recycle the classic '30s newspaper comedy is busy, busy, busy. Keaton's in his element as Henry Hackett, city editor of the New York *Sun.* Today's top story is the controversial arrest of two black youths in a race murder. But while Henry and his bitchy colleague Alicia (Close) debate tabloid semantics, he's equally preoccupied with a job offer from a rival, editor Duvall's health, and his wife's great expectations (Tomei, eight and a half months pregnant)...the suspects' rumoured innocence is almost an afterthought. A perennial innocent himself, Howard responds to the blunt professionalism of the hack pack with as much enthusiasm as Billy Wilder and Howard Hawks before him – but spoils it by insisting that somehow the tabloids have integrity. He likes his sincerity straight. It's come to something when a newspaper movie casts the cynical journalist as the villain, and the big moral dilemma here would scarcely support a sit-com. Even so, quite watchable, with whip pans and fast tracks, and one eye constantly on the clock. TCh

Paperback Hero

(1972, Can, 94 min)
d Peter Pearson. *p* James Margellos, John Bassett. *sc* Les Rose, Barry Pearson. *ph* Don Wilder. *ed* Kirk Jones. *ad* Tony Hall. *m* Ron Collier. *cast* Keir Dullea, Elizabeth Ashley, John Beck, Dayle Haddon, Franz Russell, George R Robertson.
● Not at all a bad film, Pearson's portrait of a small-town Midnight Cowboy is precise and convincing. The background of the wheat and cattle town in Saskatchewan is drawn with a conscientiousness that gives the film a rare three-dimensionality; and Dillon (Dullea) is a persuasive hero/victim, a totally unsympathetic character who has swallowed the Big Country myth whole, and is increasingly puzzled to find the world around him oddly out of phase with his 'Marshal Dillon' self-image. Pearson has expertly judged the distance between Dillon in his circumscribed world and the townsfolk in their not

unattractive one, never falling into the trap of caricature; his faults are a tendency towards over-explicitness, plus a certain lack of emotional directness and vitality. Visually, the film is almost too seductive, but Elizabeth Ashley is excellent as the ever-waiting girlfriend, and all the smaller parts are uniformly well filled. VG

Paperback Hero

(1998, Aust, 96 min)
d Antony J Bowman. *p* Lance W Reynolds, John Winter. *sc* Antony J Bowman. *ph* David Burr. *ed* Veronika Jenet. *pd* Jon Dowding. *m* Burkhard Dallwitz. *cast* Hugh Jackman, Claudia Karvan, Angie Milliken, Bruce Venables, Andrew S Gilbert, Jeanie Drynan.

●Jack (Jackman) is an Aussie truck driver who writes a romantic novel under the name of his pal Ruby (Karvan) and neglects to tell her about it. So when Ziggy Keane (Milliken) shows up in the outback with a lucrative contract and big ideas for a publicity tour, it's the non-plussed owner of the Boomerang cafe she talks to. An accommodation is reached: Ruby will maintain the masquerade in return for a cut of the profits – and Jack will pay for her wedding to his best mate Hamish (Venables). This romantic comedy fails to capitalise on a serviceable plot set-up. Writer/director Bowman knows he's dabbling with gender roles and, to his credit, comes up with both a believably tough heroine (Ruby swings a mean punch when it's called for), and a hero who's understandably a little sheepish about revealing his sensitive side in the macho culture of the Australian hinterland. But while the movie affects a vaguely literate air, it's never what you'd call a page turner. TCh

Paperback Vigilante

(1975, US, 75 min)
d Peter Davis, Steffan Lam. *with* Howard Hunt.

●Howard Hunt was a crook. His biggest job was the break-in at the Democratic Party headquarters in the Watergate building, a crime which eventually toppled a President. He was also a prolific writer of spy stories in which the agents of Western capitalism blackmail and subvert – and don't get caught. *Paperback Vigilante* is a documentary which exploits this paradox, tracing Hunt's life from university to White House against the fantasy backdrop of his novels. The film isn't just biography, though. Hunt's career in the CIA, through the Guatemala coup ('a clean and surgical-like operation'), the ill-fated Bay of Pigs invasion of Cuba, to his plucking from retirement to join Nixon's 'plumber's unit', is shown as a classic example of a son of the American ruling class being heavily financed to subvert 'international communism'. 'If you cut off the head of a chicken, you can do with the body what you will' says Hunt about his own plan to assassinate Castro (the interview which interlaces the film is excellent). EPr

Paper Chase, The

(1973, US, 111 min)
d James Bridges. *p* Robert C Thompson, Rodrick Paul. *sc* James Bridges. *ph* Gordon Willis. *ed* Walter Thompson. *pd* George Jenkins. *m* John Williams. *cast* Timothy Bottoms, Lindsay Wagner, John Houseman, Graham Beckel, James Naughton, Edward Herrmann, Craig Richard Nelson.

●A muddled and slick 'youth' film. Worth seeing because it says a lot more than the makers intended about how hustlers like John Mitchell and Ehrlichman were turned out by the 'best' law school. Bottoms plays a small-town Minnesota kid who wants to make it into the upper echelon via Harvard Law School. Excellent sequences of his quarrelsome study group tearing one another apart under fierce competitive strain – and a fine performance by Houseman as their olympian, sadistic professor – make the film watchable. Writer-director Bridges seems totally unaware that his ambitious young hero, not the professor, is the villain. CSi

Paperhouse

(1988, GB, 92 min)
d Bernard Rose. *p* Tim Bevan, Sarah Radclyffe. *sc* Matthew Jacobs. *ph* Mike Southon. *ed* Dan Rae. *pd* Gemma Jackson. *m* Hans Zimmer, Stanley Myers. *cast* Charlotte Burke, Ben Cross, Glenne Headley, Elliot Spiers, Gemma Jones, Sarah Newbold.

●An 11-year-old girl succumbs to fainting fits, is put to bed, and draws an imaginary house with an imaginary friend. Through dreams, she enters this otherworld of her own creation. Down these Elm Streets a young girl must go, you might think, but Bernard Rose's striking movie debut has more art (and heart) up its sleeve than the usual bogeyman/ teenagers routine. This time the monster is the girl's estranged father, and the shocks are more to do with primary fears of a violent adult world. Matthew Jacobs' script also manages to convey atmospheric banality without dealing with naturalistic characters, while the design department succeeds in turning infantile sketches into near-apocalyptic landscapes, often to shatttering effect. Ultimately, where the film scores over the current gore market is in its return to the values of emotion and psychology within fantasy. There are production compromises (an-over inflated score, a miscast Glenne Headly); but Rose, veteran of that banned Frankie Goes To Hollywood video, directs with exhilarating assurance, and Charlotte Burke makes an excellent heroine. DT

Paper Marriage

(1991, Pol/GB, 90 min)
d Krzysztof Lang. *p* Mark Forstater, Raymond Day. *sc* Krzysztof Lang, Marek Kreutz. *ph* Grzegorz Kedzierski. *m* Stanislas Syrewicz. *cast* Gary Kemp, Joanna Trepechinska, Rita Tushingham, Richard Hawley.

●Alicjia (Trepechinska) comes from Warsaw to Newcastle to marry an accommodating Englishman, only he isn't so accommodating this side of the channel. Being, she says, resourceful and emancipated, she sets about finding work and a husband. Aiden (Kemp) fits the bill: he's a British citizen and desperate for money. Although their marriage is a sham, circumstances contrive to keep the couple together, for richer, for poorer, for better, for worse. Peter Weir made essentially the same story with a New York setting and a French star; but in contrast to *Green Card*'s lush romanticism, this is cold and depressing. Lang and his Polish crew obviously felt no compulsion to prettify Newcastle, and it's no surprise when Alicjia starts to gaze longingly at flight offers to the US. By the same token, there's no warmth in the relationship. Trepechinska gives a fair account of herself without ever reconciling the contradictions inherent in the role, while Kemp proves so soft-spoken he barely registers. That's one trouble with a marriage of convenience: there's no meaningful long-term engagement. TCh

Paper Mask

(1990, GB, 105 min)
d Christopher Morahan. *p* Christopher Morahan, Sue Austin. *sc* John Collee. *ph* Nat Crosby. *ed* Peter Coulson. *pd* Caroline Hanania. *m* Richard Harvey. *cast* Paul McGann, Amanda Donohoe, Frederick Treves, Tom Wilkinson, Barbara Leigh-Hunt, Jimmy Yuill, Mark Lewis Jones.

●Dissatisfied as a lowly hospital porter, Matthew Harris (McGann) decides to step into the shoes of a recently deceased doctor in an attempt to up his social status, and bluffs his way into a job in a Bristol hospital. One disastrous night in casualty later, the administrators are on his case, and Harris is ready to give up. However, inspired by lust for lithesome nurse Christine (Donohoe), he decides to bash on, resulting in fatal blunder, grand illusions, and murderously misguided covert operations. Written with flair by ex-medic John Collee, this competent thriller-cum-melodrama is held together by Donohoe's endearingly edgy performance as the love-struck Christine. There are equally rewarding scenes set in the world of dinner parties and of boorish professional bonhomie. Where the screenplay falls down, however, is in its failure to establish Harris' ability to carry off such an audacious hoax, leaving the movie with a major credibility problem. MK

Paper Moon

(1973, US, 102 min, b/w)
d/p Peter Bogdanovich. *sc* Alvin Sargent. *ph* Laszlo Kovacs. *ed* Verna Fields. *pd* Polly Platt. *cast* Ryan O'Neal, Tatum O'Neal, Madeline Kahn, John Hillerman, PJ Johnson, Randy Quaid.

●A charming mixture of Hawksian comedy and Fordian lyricism imbues Bogdanovich's not-too-sentimental meeting-cute between a conman (Ryan O'Neal) busy bamboozling widows into buying bibles during the Depression, and the 9-year-old wily brat who may or may not be his daughter (Tatum O'Neal). Modern cynicism and efficient acting hold the potential mushiness at bay, and the pair's picaresque odyssey through the Kansas dustbowl, during which they vie for control over their increasingly bizarre partnership, is admirably served by Laszlo Kovacs' marvellous monochrome camerawork. After *Targets* and *The Last Picture Show*, Bogdanovich's best movie. GA

Paper Tiger

(1974, GB, 99 min)
d Ken Annakin. *p* Euan Lloyd. *sc* Jack Davies. *ph* John Cabrera. *ed* Alan Pattillo. *pd* Herbert Smith. *m* Roy Budd. *cast* David Niven, Toshiro Mifune, Hardy Kruger, Ando Kazuhito, Ivan Desny, Irene Tsu, Ronald Fraser.

●Niven does an ageing Billy Liar with a wavering upper lip, spinning tall stories to the crushingly winsome little brat, son of a Japanese diplomat, whom he tutors in some unspecified Far Eastern country plagued with cretinous revolutionaries. In so far as the film has any serious themes, they are entirely retrospective, with their roots in WWII: Kruger (the German), Mifune (the Jap) and Niven (the Englishman) all conform to desperate type. Niven, of course, despite all his blustering, still proves capable (it's that Dunkirk spirit) of acquitting himself when the chips are down (in the form of a listless kidnapping plot). CPe

Paper Wedding, A (Les Noces de Papier)

(1989, Can, 90 min)
d Michel Brault. *p* Aimée Danis. *sc* Jefferson Lewis, Andrée Pelletier. *ph* Sylvain Brault. *ed* Jacques Gagné. *ad* François Laplante. *cast* Genevieve Bujold, Manuel Aranguiz, Dorothée Berryman, Monique Lepage.

●Claire (Bujold) is 39 and, despite the matchmaking efforts of her mother, still a spinster, with only a (married) lover for security. When her lawyer sister asks her to marry political exile Pablo Torres (Aranguiz) to prevent his deportation, Claire grudgingly agrees, only to find herself under investigation by the Immigration Department. With only three days to spare before the official hearing to determine whether the marriage is genuine, the newly-acquainted newly-weds set about discovering enough about each other to present a passable imitation of *bona fide* lovers. Less overtly political than his previous work, Brault's gently observed drama still manages to tackle the corruption of immigration laws while wistfully fantasising about the productive coalition of alien cultures. The elfin-like Bujold is excellent, and the interesting use of stop-frame and flashback make this an intriguing cinematic exercise. MK

Papillon

(1973, US, 150 min)
d Franklin J Schaffner. *p* Robert Dorfmann. *sc* Dalton Trumbo, Lorenzo Semple Jr. *ph* Fred J Koenekamp. *ed* Robert Swink. *pd* Tony Masters. *m* Jerry Goldsmith. *cast* Steve McQueen, Dustin Hoffman, Victor Jory, Don Gordon, Anthony Zerbe, Robert Deman, Woodrow Parfrey, Bill Mumy, George Coulouris.

●Based on Henri Charrière's bestselling epic about life imprisonment in a French penal colony, *Papillon* begins atmospherically with the heat and deprivation well conveyed. But with Schaffner unable to find the necessary perspective to prevent the film from becoming unevenly episodic, it ends up looking as if it were tacked together by at least three different directors. Jerry Goldsmith's insistent music doesn't help much either. Consequently McQueen's escape bids and subsequent doses of solitary take on the proportions of a masochist's marathon. He battles manfully against miscasting and a script that remains content merely to celebrate his prowess. He almost carries it off, apart from one romantic dalliance, true Hollywood South Seas style, and the totally perfunctory final half-hour. CPe

Parade

(1974, Fr/Swe, 85 min)
d/sc Jacques Tati. *ph* Jean Badal, Gunnar Fischer. *ed* Sophie Tatischeff, Aline Asseo, Per Carlesson, Siv Lundgren, Jonny Mair. *ad* Ulla

Malmer-Lagerkvist. *m* Charles Dumont. *with* Jacques Tati, Karl Kossmayer and His Mule, Les Williams, Les Vétérans, Les Sipolo.
● An eccentric slice of light entertainment ring-mastered by Tati. He contributes a couple of superlative mime routines, and even briefly resurrects Hulot as a klutzy angler battling with slippery fish and a folding stool. But the show, and its host, are not the main thing. *Les clowns, c'est vous* announces Tati: contributions from the floor are invited and (thanks to judicious plants) are forthcoming, with scuffles erupting in the orchestra, a hatcheck girl surrounded by crash helmets, and a myriad other behind-the-scenes incongruities and calamities. This was Tati's valediction, made for Swedish TV the year he went bankrupt. Shot live, and on video, it can't aspire to the meticulous *mise en scène* of his big screen work; and one feels saddened that this great director should have found no other outlet for his genius. SJo

Parade of the Planets (Parad Planyet)

(1984, USSR, 96 min)
d Vadim Abdrashitov. *sc* Alexander Mindadze. *ph* Vladimir Shevtsik. *ed* R Rogatkina. *pd* A Klimenko. *m* Vyacheslav Ganelin. *cast* Oleg Borisov, Sergei Nikonenko, Sergei Shakurov, Alexei Zharkov, Pyotr Zaichenko.
● A strangely dreamlike tale, perhaps symbolic. The narrative is straightforward enough: a group of Red Guard veterans are unexpectedly 'killed' during a weekend of manoeuvres, and finding themselves with ample free time, set off on an odyssey into an increasingly disturbing landscape: a town populated only by women, deserted lakeland forests, a sinister old people's home. Some of it is almost embarrassingly reminiscent of Hollywood's hippy '60s allegories (notably the skinny-dipping to the strains of Beethoven); other moments have an elusive poetry. It's supposedly about the ghosts that haunt the contemporary Russian psyche: quite what they are isn't exactly clear. GA

Paradine Case, The

(1947, US, 115 min, b/w)
d Alfred Hitchcock. *p* David O Selznick. *sc* David O Selznick, Alma Reville. *ph* Lee Garmes. *ed* Hal C Kern. *pd* J McMillan Johnson. *m* Franz Waxman. *cast* Gregory Peck, Alida Valli, Ann Todd, Louis Jourdan, Charles Laughton, Charles Coburn, Ethel Barrymore, Leo G Carroll.
● In no sense a 'wronged innocent' thriller, *The Paradine Case* sets out to be a morality tale on the dangers of Strong Emotion. A happy marriage is threatened when rising young barrister Peck falls hopelessly in love with the woman (Valli) he is defending on a murder rap. Blinded by passion, he can see neither her guilt, nor that her obsession lies elsewhere – with the man (Jourdan) whom he would destroy in her stead. Bleak in its message (those who love passionately inevitably destroy the object of their desire), the movie only half works; Peck is rather half-hearted, Valli coldly cat-like, Ann Todd as the rejected wife too self-sacrificing and loyally forgiving to be true. And the intricate, triangular plot is finally overburdened by the courtroom setting from which it tries to draw a laborious analogy between the perversion of love and justice. FF

Paradise

(1991, US, 111 min)
d Mary Agnes Donoghue. *p* Patrick Palmer, Scott Kroopf. *sc* Mary Agnes Donoghue. *ph* Jerzy Zielinski. *ed* Eva Gardos, Debra McDermott. *ad* Evelyn Sakash. *m* David Newman. *cast* Melanie Griffith, Don Johnson, Elijah Wood, Thora Birch, Sheila McCarthy, Eve Gordon, Louise Latham, Greg Davis.
● This Hollywood remake of *Le Grand Chemin* is altogether slicker, revelling less in strange and simple provincial goings-on than in the star pairing of real-life couple Johnson and Griffith. Unhappily married, Ben and Lily Reed are plunged into bitter reflection on the death of their son when they are left in charge of ten-year-old Willard (Wood). The city boy has his own problems: he's uncertain why his pregnant mother (Gordon) has dumped him with country bumpkins, and bewildered about his father's prolonged absence from home. Amid the domestic dramas, sentimentality is never very far away. Johnson is nowhere near as flawed or interesting as his French counterpart, but at least he and Griffith are credibly loveless and joyless. They're helped by writer-director Donoghue's jaded observations and sensitive direction, though such attention is at the expense of the children, who are sometimes painfully stilted in their exchanges. Alas, the quirks which enlivened the original are missing: no peeing into gargoyles here. CM

Paradise Alley

(1978, US, 109 min)
d Sylvester Stallone. *p* John Faunce Roach, Ronald A Suppa. *sc* Sylvester Stallone. *ph* Laszlo Kovacs. *ed* Eve Newman. *pd* John W Corso. *m* Bill Conti. *cast* Sylvester Stallone, Lee Canalito, Armand Assante, Frank McRae, Anne Archer, Kevin Conway, Aimée Eccles, Tom Waits.
● Nominally set in 1946, in the poverty-trap of Hell's Kitchen, but pitched waveringly between *Rocky*, *Guys and Dolls*, and some prototype Warner Brothers Depression drama of the preceding decade, Stallone's hit-and-miss directorial debut (he also writes, stars and sings the theme song) maps the classic escape route via the ring (wrestling this time) with a unique style of baroque excess. The plot (Stallone scheming himself and his two brothers uptown on the tails of ambitious gimmickry) is shot full of sentimental holes; but the creation of a floridly fantasticated netherworld of low-life high-rollers and their inevitably multi-coloured circumlocutions is irresistible. PT

Paradise – Hawaiian Style

(1965, US, 91 min)
d Michael Moore. *p* Hal B Wallis. *sc* Allan Weiss, Anthony Lawrence. *ph* W Wallace Kelley. *ed* Warren Low. *pd* Hal Pereira, Walter Tyler. *songs* Bill Giant, Sid Tepper, Bernie Baum. *cast* Elvis Presley, Suzanna Leigh, James Shigeta, Donna Butterworth, Marianna Hill, Irene Tsu, Linda Wong.
● A desperate attempt to revive Presley's by then flagging film career with a brazen action replay of *Blue Hawaii*. Irredeemably awful, it displays an enervated, paunchy Elvis ambling through familiar locations against which dreary adolescent tiffs are played out. AC

Paradise Lagoon

see Admirable Crichton, The

Paradise Road

(1997, US/Aust, 121 min)
d Bruce Beresford. *p* Sue Milliken, Greg Coote. *sc* Bruce Beresford. *ph* Peter James. *ed* Tim Wellburn. *pd* Herbert Pinter. *m* Ross Edwards. *cast* Glenn Close, Frances McDormand, Pauline Collins, Cate Blanchett, Jennifer Ehle, Julianna Margulies, Wendy Hughes, Elizabeth Spriggs.
● The Fall of Singapore. A boat evacuating women and children is strafed and sunk. The survivors swim ashore to be met by the Japanese forces in Sumatra and herded into a remote internment camp. For the various women – a dignitary's wife (Close), a missionary (Collins), a model (Ehle), a grande dame (Spriggs), an Aussie nurse (Blanchett), and a lone American (Margulies) – those who can endure will face three years' hard labour. A feminised PoW movie, writer/director Beresford's ensemble film describes downbeat, recalcitrant heroism: the loss of family, serfdom, disease, the threat of rape and prostitution. The 'twist' is the women's choice of succour. Based on Betty Jeffrey's diaries *White Coolies*, the film documents how inmates formed a 'vocal orchestra' and performed their own arrangements of symphonic classics. Finely acted, opulently produced, old-fashioned, unadventurous and emotionally hidebound. NB

Paradise View

(1985, Jap, 113 min)
d Go Takamine. *p* Mitsuzo Anan. *sc* Go Takamine. *ph* Takao Toshioka. *ed/ad* Go Takamine. *m* Haruomi Hosono. *cast* Kaoru Kobayashi, Jun Togawa, Haruomi Hosono, Hiroko Taniyama, Shizuko Osemi, Tomi Heira.
● Takamine's first theatrical feature was a pioneering attempt to confront the Japanese public with the fact of Okinawa's cultural difference from Japan. Reishu (yakuza movie star Kobayashi) quits a job on a US military base; while mulling over his future he catches snakes, sticks numbers on ants and gets village girl Nabi (pop star Togawa) pregnant. But then he is 'hidden by God' (= mislays his *mabui* or soul) and in this enfeebled condition is savaged by a wild rainbow pig. The film is as laidback and idiosyncratic as its misfit characters. Instead of melodrama it strings its plot-lines on eccentric detail, part-invented folklore, psychedelic digressions and creative modifications to Okinawa's indigenous fauna and flora. Shot almost entirely in Okinawan dialect, it's a languid tropical fantasy with concealed political teeth. TR

Paradis Perdu

(1939, Fr, 88 min, b/w)
d Abel Gance. *sc* Abel Gance, Joseph Than, Stève Passeur. *ph* Christian Matras, Robert Juillard. *ed* Léonide Azar. *ad* Henri Mahé. *m* Hans May. *cast* Fernand Gravey, Micheline Presle, Robert Pizani, Elvire Popesco, Robert Le Vigan, Alerme, Jane Marken.
● *Napoléon* made Gance, at 38, the youngest Grand Old Man of French cinema. Thereafter his career, a sequence of theatrical adaptations and historical romances relieved only by some grandiose (and mostly doomed) projects, described a precipitously downward spiral similar to that of L'Herbier. Not much extravagance, then, in this film, the sentimental chronicle of a World War I widower overly troubled by his daughter's physical resemblance to her late mother. Academic and impersonal, its sole asset is a youthfully ingenuous Micheline Presle. GAd

Paragraph 175

(2000, GB/Ger/US, 80 min)
d Rob Epstein, Jeffrey Friedman. *p* Janet Cole, Michael Ehrenzweig, Rob Epstein. *sc* Sharon Wood. *ph* Bernd Meiners. *ed* Dawn Logsdon. *m* Tibor Szemzö. *narrator* Rupert Everett.
● After *The Celluloid Closet*, Epstein and Friedman continue their survey of 20th century homophobia with this unadorned account of the impact of the Holocaust on Germany's once thriving gay culture. Paragraph 175 was the clause in the 1871 German Penal Code criminalising 'unnatural sex acts' between persons of the male sex (or with animals). Though it remained unrepealed by both post-war German states for some 25 years, there was a period, amidst the determined gaiety and hedonism of the Weimar Republic, when gay and lesbian culture blossomed. Then came the Brown Shirts, and the pink stars, and the camps. Fewer than ten people are still known to be alive – and they've gone on suppressing their experiences for 50 years afterwards, silenced by a society that didn't wanted to know. Now the film-makers and their researcher/interviewer Klaus Müller have persuaded most of them to open up, and their individual testimonies here colour the broad historical overview with discretion and sensitivity. The film's lack of technical finesse works to its advantage. NB

Parallax View, The

(1974, US, 102 min)
d/p Alan J Pakula. *sc* David Giler, Lorenzo Semple Jr. *ph* Gordon Willis. *ed* John W Wheeler. *pd* George Jenkins. *m* Michael Small. *cast* Warren Beatty, Paula Prentiss, William Daniels, Walter McGinn, Hume Cronyn, Kelly Thordsen, Chuck Waters.
● A thriller about a journalist, alerted to the mysterious deaths of witnesses to the assassination of a presidential candidate, who embarks on an investigation that reveals a nebulous conspiracy of gigantic and all-embracing scope. It sounds familiar, and refers to or overlaps a good handful of similar films, but is most relevantly tied to *Klute*. Where *Klute* was an exploration of claustrophobic anxiety, *The Parallax View* is inexorably agoraphobic. Its visual organisation is stunning as the journalist (Beatty) is drawn into an increasingly nightmarish world characterised by impenetrably opaque structures, a screen whited out from time to time, or meshed over with visually deceptive patterns. It is some indication of the area the film explores that in place of the self-revealing session with the analyst in *Klute*, *The Parallax View* presents us with the more insecurity-inducing questionnaire used by the mysterious Parallax Corporation for personality-testing prospective employees. Excellent performances; fascinating film. VG

Parallel Worlds (Paralelní svety)

(2001, Czech Rep/Fr, 98 min)
d Petr Václav. *p* Katerina Cerna, Petr Václav. *sc* Petr Václav, Marie Desplechin. *ph* Stepan Kucera. *ed* Luba Durkovicova. *pd* Ondrej Nekvasil. *m* Jiri Václav. *cast* Lenka Vlasáková, Karel Roden, Jitka Schneiderová.
●Designing status projects for the newly wealthy while vaguely pursuing an affair, a successful but frustrated architect loses sight of his listless wife's depression until she is forced to take radical steps to repair her selfhood. There's no real surprise in the narrative premise of this Franco-Czech production, but its limpid mood, charged atmosphere of often unvoiced conflicts, and dream sequences of disquieting, symbolic authority (London conjured as desert; living houses and the like) ensure that it speaks truthfully about the emotional silences of modern life and relationships, despite an unpersuasive finish. GE

Paranoia (Orgasmo)

(1969, It/Fr, 91 min)
d Umberto Lenzi. *p* Salvatore Alabiso.*sc* Ugo Moretti, Umberto Lenzi, MarieClaire Sollenville. *ph* Guglielmo Mancori.*ed* Enzo Alabiso. *ad* Giorgio Bertolini.*m* Piero Umiliani. *cast* Carroll Baker,Lou Castel, Colette Descombes, Tino Carraro, Lilla Brignone.
●Luridly dotty yarn in which an American lady (Baker) holes up in a lonely Italian villa, suffering from drink and some sort of guilt complex about the elderly husband who died in a car crash leaving her a sizeable fortune. Enter a smooth young man (Castel), calling to her from the bushes and holding out dirt-encrusted arms into which she ecstatically rushes ('Oh, yes! Dirty me!'). Joined by his so-called sister (Descombes) and getting rid of the Mrs Danvers-like housekeeper (Brignone), Castel proceeds to inveigle the poor lady into a mad-making programme of swinging music, drugs and three-way sex. No prizes for guessing that money is the root of all evil, and that the victim, reduced to crawling haggardly from one empty whisky bottle to the next, wends her way to the attic for an agreeably ruthless finale. Good performances keep it watchable, but Lenzi's swinging direction (a mass of hideous mannerisms) keeps it well short of achieving orgasmo. TM

Parapluies de Cherbourg, Les (The Umbrellas of Cherbourg)

(1964, Fr/WGer, 92 min)
d Jacques Demy. *p* Mag Bodard. *sc* Jacques Demy. *ph* Jean Rabier. *ed* Monique Teissure. *ad* Bernard Evein. *m* Michel Legrand. *cast* Catherine Deneuve, Nino Castelnuovo, Anne Vernon, Ellen Farner, Marc Michel, Mireille Perrey, Jean Champion.
●A novelettish story that in the hands of most directors would be no more than trivial is transformed by Demy into something rather wonderful: a full-scale all-singing musical whose inspiration is Hollywood but whose tone and setting are resolutely Gallic. Shopgirl Deneuve loves a poor mechanic who leaves her pregnant when he departs for military service. During his absence, she is courted by a diamond merchant and nudged into marriage by her ambitious mother… This bittersweet romance – whose underlying message would seem to be that people invariably marry the wrong person – is lavished with affection. Vivid colours and elegant camera choreography are bound together by Michel Legrand's sumptuous score. And never has an Esso station looked so romantic. CPe

Para Recibir el Canto de los Pajaros

see Bird's Singing, The

Parasite

(1982, US, 85 min)
d/p Charles Band. *sc* Alan Alder, Michael Shoob, Frank Levering. *ph* Mac Ahlberg. *ed* Brad Arensman. *ad* Pamela B Warner. *m* Richard Band. *cast* Robert Glaudini, Demi Moore, Luca Bercovici, James Davidson, Al Fann, Cherie Currie, Vivian Blaine.
●When a scientist arrives in an arid, futuristic landscape largely inhabited by 'Fickies' (predictably resembling Hell's Angels), he unfortunately brings with him two lethally ravenous lumps of slime: one in his stomach, one in a thermos. These of course attack all and sundry in repetitively gory set pieces which lack any of the intelligence, wit or style of Cronenberg's superficially similar *Shivers*. Uninspired actors intone a banal script, reduced by clumsy pacing to a minimum of suspense. The use of 3-D is presumably meant to lift this cinematic sludge above its peers; but apart from the obligatory objects placed in the foreground or – just occasionally – hurled at the camera, it's visually as uninteresting as a catfood commercial. GA

Parasite Murders, The (aka Shivers/They Came from Within)

(1974, Can, 87 min)
d David Cronenberg. *p* Ivan Reitman. *sc* David Cronenberg. *ph* Robert Saad. *ed* Patrick Dodd. *ad* Erla Gliserman. *cast* Paul Hampton, Joe Silver, Lynn Lowry, Allan Migicovsky, Susan Petrie, Barbara Steele.
●This first commercial feature by a former underground film-maker offers a heady, if finally muddled, combination of globs of horror and social criticism. Despite its exploitation format, even the British censor discerned a moral to the tale and passed it uncut. Best is the way Cronenberg deliberately manipulates his synthetic cast and bland visuals, whose plastic surfaces erupt to reveal their repressions and taboos beneath; slug-like parasites (a mix of aphrodisiac and venereal disease) rampage through a luxury tower block, turning the inhabitants into sex-craving zombies. But exactly what is its moral? One suspects Cronenberg is laughing up his sleeve, as some (like the censor) read *Shivers* as an attack on permissiveness, while others take it as an indictment of the whole of modern society. Often, however, the film stops little short of wholesale disgust at the human condition. Misanthropic, indeed, but the black humour and general inventiveness place it high above most contemporary horror pictures. CPe

Par-delà les Nuages

see Beyond the Clouds

Pardners

(1956, US, 90 min)
d Norman Taurog. *p* Paul Jones. *sc* Sidney Sheldon. *ph* Daniel L Fapp. *ed* Archie Marshek. *pd* Hal Pereira, Roland Anderson. *m* Frank De Vol. *cast* Dean Martin, Jerry Lewis, Lori Nelson, Jackie Loughery, Agnes Moorehead, John Baragrey, Jeff Morrow, Lon Chaney Jr.
●Despite the title, the Martin and Lewis partnership was nearing breaking point on this spoof Western, a loose remake of Taurog's *Rhythm on the Range*, made 20 years earlier with Bing Crosby. Lewis is the especially maladroit millionaire son of a former rancher, who is persuaded to go west once again by the saddle-happy son (Martin) of his father's old partner, to regain the family seat and clean up the town. There is more singing than gunslinging, and Lewis is at his most worryingly infantile; but overall it's an amiable enough romp scripted by, of all people, bestseller Sidney Sheldon. DT

Pardon Mon Affaire (Un éléphant ça trompe énormément)

(1976, Fr, 108 min)
d Yves Robert. *p* Daniel Deschamps. *sc* Jean-Loup Dabadie, Yves Robert. *ph* René Mathelin. *ed* Gérard Pollicand. *ad* Jean-Pierre Kohut-Svelko. *m* Vladimir Cosma. *cast* Jean Rochefort, Daniele Delorme, Claude Brasseur, Guy Bedos, Victor Lanoux, Annie Duperey, Martine Sarcey.
●Middle-aged, married Rochefort is stricken with lust for model Duperey. His pals Brasseur (closet gay), Bedos (mother-ridden) and Lanoux (failed he-man) offer encouragement from the sidelines, in between coping with their own problems. The plot is the bare minimum required to string together a bunch of fairly amusing, occasionally hilarious sketches, which contrive a few unexpected riffs on the stereotypes involved. Gene Wilder liked it enough to cook up his own Hollywoodisation, *The Woman in Red*. BBa

Pardon Mon Affaire, Too (Nous Irons Tous au Paradis)

(1977, Fr, 112 min)
d Yves Robert. *p* Alain Poiré, Yves Robert. *sc* Jean-Loup Dabadie, Yves Robert. *ph* René Mathelin. *ed* Pierre Gillette. *ad* Jean-Pierre Kohut-Svelko. *m* Vladimir Cosma. *cast* Jean Rochefort, Claude Brasseur, Guy Bedos, Victor Lanoux, Danièle Delorme, Marthe Villalonga, Jenny Arasse.
●Sprawling comic saga of four middle-aged lads about Paris; and very typical fare from Yves Robert, who bestrides MOR French cinema like a colossus, at least in terms of quantity and popularity. Robert isn't short of good gags; unfortunately he isn't short of bad ones, either, and seems unable or unwilling to fit his horde into any coherent shape or maintain any coherent tone. Rochefort is always watchable as the would-be rake, while Danièle Delorme's performance as his spirited wife saves the film from being unpleasantly chauvinist. All in all, it's bearable. GB

Pardon Us

(1931, US, 55 min, b/w)
d James Parrott. *p* Hal Roach. *sc* HM Walker. *ph* George Stevens. *ed* Richard Currier. *cast* Stan Laurel, Oliver Hardy, Wilfred Lucas, June Marlowe, James Finlayson, Walter Long.
●The first Laurel and Hardy feature (if one excludes *Rogue Song*, in which they were merely featured), shot on the sets of *The Big House* and parodying prison breakout movies. Too slow and rambling to rank with their best, but full of things to treasure like Laurel's raspberry-blowing tooth, and the wonderful blackface musical interlude when the boys hide out in a cotton-picking shantytown. TM

Parenthood

(1989, US, 124 min)
d Ron Howard. *p* Brian Grazer. *sc* Lowell Ganz, Babaloo Mandel. *ph* Donald McAlpine. *ed* Michael Hill, Daniel Hanley. *pd* Todd Hallowell. *m* Randy Newman. *cast* Steve Martin, Mary Steenburgen, Dianne Wiest, Jason Robards, Rick Moranis, Tom Hulce, Martha Plimpton, Keanu Reeves, Harley Kozak, Dennis Dugan, Leaf Phoenix.
●The first ten minutes of this comedy about families is terrific, but after that it's hit-and-miss peppered with very funny one-liners. Probably only Robert Altman has the narrative grip to keep such a mosaic moving, and several stories here merely take up space. Steve Martin's manically over-conscientious dad steals the film, whether chewing the pitch as his small son fumbles at baseball, or entertaining a kids' party as an unconvincing cowboy. All this is in reaction against his own dad (Robards), who neglected him in favour of ever-feckless Hulce. Divorcee Wiest's fruity teenage offspring (Plimpton and Phoenix) barely communicate with her, except to hurl insults about her vibrator, while Rick Moranis' toddler is force-fed a flash-card education in Kafka and karate. At bottom, it's squashy old Dodie Smith's *Dear Octupus* with a top dressing of hard, smart-ass gags – very much the American TV sitcom formula. But if it's all a bit of a cop-out, there's enough to chortle at, and Martin at least is bang on. BC

Parents

(1988, US, 82 min)
d Bob Balaban. *p* Bonnie Palef-Woolf. *sc* Christopher Hawthorne. *ph* Ernest Day, Robin Vidgeon. *ed* Bill Pankow. *ad* Andris Hausmanis. *m* Angelo Badalamenti, Jonathan Elias. *cast* Randy Quaid, Mary Beth Hurt, Sandy Dennis, Bryan Madorsky, Juno Mills-Cockell, Kathryn Grody, Deborah Rush.
●Balaban's grisly feature debut deals with both the stultifying bad-taste conformism of Eisenhower's America and the theme of mutual distrust between adults and offspring, and turns them into the stuff of everyday horror. Nick and Lily Laemle (Quaid an td Hurt) are new arrivals in a small Indiana town; everything about their life together stresses their normality. If there is a fly in the ointment, it's their young son Michael (Madorsky), a moody, introspective brat who has macabre fantasies derived from his horrific Oedipal nightmares. As the film progresses, however, we come to wonder whether it's the adults, rather than the progeny, who are loopy and cruel…If the film finally fails

to shock or surprise, it's nevertheless both imaginatively shot and wittily scripted, and strikes a nice balance between gentle parody and a queasy unease associated with *bona fide* genre suspense. Superior performances by Quaid, Hurt and Madorsky. GA

Parents Terribles, Les (The Storm Within)

(1948, Fr, 98 min, b/w)
d Jean Cocteau. *p* Francis Cosne. *sc* Jean Cocteau. *ph* Michel Kelber. *ed* Jacqueline Douarinon. *pd* Christian Bérard, Guy de Gastyne. *m* Georges Auric. *cast* Yvonne de Bray, Jean Marais, Gabrielle Dorziat, Marcel André, Josette Day.
●*Les Parents Terribles* is the opposite pole to a film like *Orphée*: Cocteau the airy purveyor of fantasy proving that he could keep his feet on the ground with the best of them in a gut-wrenching tale of incestuous emotional rivalries destroying a family from within. Simply transposing his play intact (two sets, five characters, no exteriors), stressing the theatricality (credits imposed on a stage curtain; the *trois coups* sounded; the division into acts marked), Cocteau nevertheless translates it into claustrophobically cinematic terms. Subtle changes in perspective, metronomically precise editing, clinical use of close-up (like the justly famous shot – his smiling mouth, her agonised eyes – as the son confidingly whispers into possessive mum's ear that he has fallen in love), make this not only an astonishingly dynamic film, but melodrama of the highest order. Stunning ensemble performances, but Yvonne de Bray (the mother) is out of this world. TM

Parent Trap, The

(1998, US, 128 min)
d Nancy Meyers. *p* Charles Shyer. *sc* David Swift, Nancy Meyers, Charles Shyer. *ph* Dean Cundey. *ed* Stephen A Rotter. *pd* Dean Tavoularis. *m* Alan Silvetsri. *cast* Dennis Quaid, Natasha Richardson, Lindsay Lohan, Lisa Ann Walter, Elaine Hendrix, Simon Kunz, Ronnie Stevens.
●Another stab at Erich Kästner's story of separated identical twins conniving to unite their parents by swapping places. Bright spark Lohan is engaging enough as both the 11-year-olds, thrown together by accident at American summer camp: she sports classy hairbands and a faux-British middle class accent as Anna, adored moppet of London fashion designer Richardson, and a Barbie-inspired wardrobe as Hallie, likewise relished little princess of rich Napa Valley vintner Quaid. Hendrix as Quaid's gold-digging, spanner-in-the-works fiancée makes venality almost endearing; her fish-out-of-water act on a backpacking trip, lizard-swallowing and all, gets the biggest laugh and momentarily dilutes the saccharine suspense. Quaid exudes an almost smug self-satisfaction nurtured by slippers and tweeds; Richardson looks like she's using her role to audition for more parts demanding class and orthodox femininity. For all that, the light comedy is sweetly timed, the direction smart and assured, and the visuals bright, colourful, unobtrusive and faultless. WH

Parfait Amour! (Perfect Love!)

(1996, Fr, 115 min)
d Catherine Breillat. *p* Georges Benayoun. *sc* Catherine Breillat. *ph* Laurent Dailland. *ed* Agnès Guillemot. *pd* Michel Vandestien. *m* Alexandre Desplat. *cast* Francis Renaud, Isabelle Renauld, Laura Saglio, Alain Soral, Delphine de Malerbé.
●Breillat's provocative drama charts how an idyllic affair between a divorcee – an optician with two kids – and a feckless, womanising twenty-something leads to brutal murder. Though some may find the woman's increasingly masochistic reactions to her young lover's behaviour questionable, the film is psychologically astute; just watch how the boy's early curiosity about the woman's greater experience slowly turns to insecurity and a determination to take control. The performances are unsentimental, the tone uncompromising, and if the film ends up too schematic for its own good, there's no denying its emotional punch or the intelligence of its dark insights. GA

Parfum d'Yvonne, Le

(1994, Fr, 89 min)
d Patrice Leconte. *p* Thierry de Ganay. *sc* Patrice Leconte. *ph* Eduardo Serra. *ed* Joëlle Hache. *ad* Ivan Maussion. *m* Pascale Esteve. *cast* Jean-Pierre Marielle, Hippolyte Girardot, Sandra Majani, Richard Bohringer, Paul Guers, Corinne Marchand.
●Summer on Lake Geneva in the '50s finds Girardot's would-be writer hiding out from military service and the Algerian War. For a youthful wastrel of enigmatic means, the holiday atmosphere keeps the rest of the world at bay, perfectly setting the scene for a moment of sensual adventure when into his life walks glacial beauty Yvonne (Majani), and fez-wearing associate, the mysterious Dr Meinthe (Marielle). Erotic fascination and a giddy whirl of socialising fill the days that follow, all of it undercut by the realisation of life's fleeting evanescence. Typically succinct and joyously using the 'Scope format, Leconte's film is diaphanous in content but rich in visual and aural atmospherics. There's a heady whiff of pleasure to be gained from its piquant bouquet. TJ

Paris After Dark (aka The Night Is Ending)

(1943, US, 85 min, b/w)
d Léonide Moguy. *p* André Daven. *sc* Harold Buchman. *ph* Lucien Andriot. *ed* Nick De Maggio. *ad* James Basevi, John Ewing. *m* Hugo Friedhofer. *cast* George Sanders, Philip Dorn, Brenda Marshall, Madeleine LeBeau, Marcel Dalio, Robert Lewis, Henry Roland.
●Stock WWII tub-thumper about the need for resistance to Nazism. Dorn plays a factory worker who limps home to occupied Paris. Having suffered terrible brutality while a PoW (he is in fact dying), he is determined to keep his nose clean; but his wife (Marshall) is helping the society doctor (Sanders) for whom she works as a nurse to organise sabotage at the factory. Instead of exploring this dilemma (or the hint of class conflict between factory worker and aristocratic doctor), Howard Buchman's script opts for a woozy plot in which Dorn thinks Marshall and Sanders are lovers. After young brother shows that it's better to die than live as a slave, Dorn comes round and makes the good sacrifice to get the Gestapo off his wife's tail. Dalio hovers as the local barber, a perfumed poodle who – to no one's surprise but the cast's – turns out to be a collaborator. TM

Paris Awakens

see Paris s'éveille

Paris Belongs to Us

see Paris Nous Appartient

Paris by Night

(1988, GB, 103 min)
d David Hare. *p* Patrick Cassavetti. *sc* David Hare. *ph* Roger Pratt. *ed* George Akers. *pd* Anthony Pratt. *m* Georges Delerue. *cast* Charlotte Rampling, Michael Gambon, Robert Hardy, Iain Glen, Jane Asher, Andrew Ray, Niamh Cusack, Robert Flemyng.
●Writer/director Hare could hardly have anticipated the topicality of this study in Thatcherite morality released amid Tory debate over a 'united' Europe. The heroine of this thriller is ambitious Euro MP Clara Paige (a riveting performance by Rampling), whose swift rise within the Conservative ranks has been paralleled by growing neglect of her relationships with drink-sodden MP husband (Gambon) and young son. On assignment in Paris, Clara's life is devastated by hitherto untapped emotions. She has a passionate affair with entrepreneur Wallace (Glen), and – suspecting a blackmail attempt – commits murder with horrifying efficiency. For all her advocacy of self-determination, Clara is quick to try to evade the consequences of her misdeed. Hare avoids preachiness, thanks largely to taut, sparse dialogue, and brooding visuals from cinematographer Roger Pratt; the look and themes are those of a modern-day *film noir*, with the plot conjuring a nighmarish world of deception, sexual manipulation, and extortion. CM

Paris Does Strange Things

see Eléna et les Hommes

Paris Express

see Man Who Watched Trains Go By, The

Paris France

(1993, Can, 105 min)
d Gérard Ciccoritti. *p* Eric Norlen. *sc* Tom Walmsley. *ph* Barry Stone. *ed* Roushell Goldstein. *pd* Marian Wihak. *m* John McCarthy. *cast* Leslie Hope, Peter Outerbridge, Victor Ertmanis, Dan Lett.
●Blocked wife and bored writer Lucy Quick (Hope) is an acolyte of Anaïs Nin's brand of author-erotica, so when she finds Sloan, the latest discovery of Michael, her publisher husband, rifling through her drawers, she of course invites him in for a closer look. Sloan (Outerbridge) is a hot young bisexual with a book on serial killer Ed Gein under his belt. His arrogant, ambiguous pose also excites Michael's business partner William (Lett). This movie resembles a nightmare collaboration between Philip Kaufman's shrink and the National Film Board of Canada: lots of liberal, literary huffing and puffing interspersed with recherché avant garde-ism. The stew is overcooked and then some. TCh

Paris Is Burning

(1990, US, 78 min)
d/p Jennie Livingston. *ph* Paul Gibson. *ed* Jonathan Oppenheim.
●Made over three years (and also seen in Britain on TV in a shortened version in the BBC's *Arena* slot in 1990), Jennie Livingston's documentary is the original fly-on-the-ball vogueing spectacular. Long before Madonna tightened up that basque, the black and Hispanic queens of Harlem and Brooklyn were striking all manner of poses. Bound by poverty and prejudice, these material girls staged their own world of high fashion and fantasy, costume and competition. 'Giving good face' is only part of the challenge; it's whether you can pass as something other than your 'real' self that determines how well you score. This is queer culture's revenge on the world that surrounds and excludes it. Drag queens compete for the accolade of Real Woman, butch queens for the title of Real Man, which would all be rather tiring were it not for the varying combinations of enthusiasm and irony the competitors invest in the proceedings. 'If everyone did more balls and less drugs, it would be a sweet world,' proclaims one. Now who could possibly throw shade at that? PBur

Paris Mil Neuf Cent Chronique de 1900 à 1914 (aka Paris 1900)

(1948, Fr, 91 min, b/w)
d Nicole Védres. *p* Pierre Braunberger. *sc* Nicole Védres. *ed* Myriam Borsoutzky. *m* Guy Bernard. *narrator* Claud Dauphin.
●A charming compilation which broke new ground in its day with its breezily impressionistic portrait of *La Belle Epoque*, all fun and frolic but ending with a trainload of fodder setting off for the front in 1914. It may have been overtaken by more recent efforts on TV, but the marvellous footage is wittily used: Blériot's triumph after flying the channel, Eiffel and his tower (plus the birdman who sadly plopped from the top), the great flood of Paris, a street round-up of anarchists, snippets of a whole host of personalities from Monet, Renoir and Rodin to Bernhardt, Réjane, Melba, Mistinguett, Colette, Willy and Buffalo Bill. Pity that in the American version, which was cut to 50 mins, Monty Woolley's phrasing of the commentary is so archly facetious. TM

Paris 1900

see Paris Mil Neuf Cent Chronique de 1900 à 1914

Paris Nous Appartient (Paris Belongs to Us)

(1961, Fr, 140 min, b/w)
d Jacques Rivette. *p* Roland Nonia. *sc* Jacques Rivette, Jean Grualt. *ph* Charles L Bitsch. *ed* Denise de Casabianca. *m* Philippe Arthuys. *cast* Betty Schneider, Gianni Esposito, Françoise Prévost, Daniel Crohem, François Maistre, Jean-Claude Brialy.
●Ex-*Cahiers du Cinéma* critic Rivette now makes stupendously long (and good) films that tend to get shown only at festivals. This was his first,

made with the traditional shoestring budget and Claude Chabrol's camera. As in most Rivette films, the action centres around a ritual or theatrical event: here, a troupe of actors rehearse *Pericles*, only to fall apart under the burden of various kinds of angst. It's a bracing experience, though the movie is ultimately too hermetic and mysterious for its own good; when he gives himself a longer time span – as in the magnificent four-hour *L'Amour Fou* – Rivette shows he can orchestrate his themes to perfection. GB

Paris qui Dort (The Crazy Ray)

(1923, Fr, 5,500 ft, b/w)
d René Clair. *p* Maurice Diamant-Berger. *sc* René Clair. *ph* Maurice Desfassiaux. *ed* René Clair. *ad* André Foy. *cast* Henri Rollan, Madeleine Rodrigue, Marcel Vallée, Albert Préjean, Charles Martinelli.

●The first feature of director-writer-novelist-Dadaist René Clair resembles his better-known short 'Entr'acte' in its manic comic invention and its all-round energetic absurdity. It starts out with a crazed inventor perfecting a ray that suspends animation throughout Paris, and then has a great deal of fun tracing the paths of a handful of 'survivors' through the frozen city. The prolific jokes about motion and stasis are fundamentally movie concept gags, and they relate directly to contemporary avant-garde film concerns. TR

Paris s'éveille (Paris Awakens)

(1991, Fr, 95 min)
d Olivier Assayas. *p* Bruno Pesery. *sc* Olivier Assayas. *ph* Denis Lenoir. *ed* Luc Barnier. *m* John Cale. *cast* Judith Godrèche, Jean-Pierre Léaud, Thomas Langmann.

●This third feature by former *Cahiers du Cinéma* critic Assayas is his best to date, and one of the few French movies about middle-class relationships that is neither precious nor airily detached from social realities. It's essentially a triangle drama: father (Léaud, playing his real age, for once), much younger second wife (Godrèche, fetching), and semi-estranged son (Langmann, son of Claude Berri). Fluently written and played with palpable enthusiasm by the entire cast, it works outwards from small details. Everything is precisely judged, from the hang of an art-class model's scrotum to the bearing of a waitress in a Chinese restaurant. TR

Paris, Texas

(1984, WGer/Fr/GB, 148 min)
d Wim Wenders. *p* Don Guest, Anatole Dauman. *sc* Wim Wenders, Sam Shepard. *ph* Robby Müller. *ed* Peter Przygodda. *ad* Kate Altman. *m* Ry Cooder. *cast* Harry Dean Stanton, Dean Stockwell, Aurore Clément, Hunter Carson, Nastassja Kinski, Bernhard Wicki.

●A man in a red baseball cap comes stumbling over the Mexican border and into the Texan desert, mute, bowed but driven by an obsessive quest. When his brother (Stockwell) drives him (Stanton) home to LA, the shards of his broken life are painfully pieced together in fits and starts of talk. Four years ago he 'lost' his family; now he has returned to find them. Reunited with his 7-year-old son, he travels to Houston, where he finds his wife (Kinski) working in a peep-show. Wenders once more finds himself on the borders of experience, finally achieving an unprecedented declaration of the heart, even if man and wife can only perceive each other through a glass darkly. Wenders' collaboration with writer Sam Shepard is a master-stroke, wholly beneficial to both talents; if Wenders' previous film, *The State of Things*, was on the very limits of possibility, this one, through its final scenes, pushes the frontier three steps forward into new and sublime territory. CPea

Paris Trout

(1991, US, 99 min)
d Stephen Gyllenhaal. *p* Frank Konigsberg, Larry Sanitsky. *sc* Pete Dexter. *ph* Robert Elswit. *ed* Harvey Rosenstock. *ad* Richard Sherman. *m* David Shire. *cast* Dennis Hopper, Barbara Hershey, Ed Harris, Ray McKinnon, Tina Lifford, Darnita Henry, Eric Ware, Ronreaco Lee, Gary Bullock.

●The eponymous protagonist of Gyllenhaal's rather superb first feature is a repellent, racist loanshark (played to the tight-lipped hilt by Hopper) who rules the roost in a late '40s Southern community. When a young black (Ware) welshes on the agreement after borrowing money to buy a car, Trout dispenses the only kind of justice he feels comfortable with; then, confronted by his wife (Hershey) about his crime, he starts down a road to total insanity by first humiliating, then subjecting her to horrible sexual abuse. Pete Dexter's script from his own novel is tough, often disturbing stuff, with a whiff of small-town Southern life that takes in everything from a John Lee Hooker TV commercial to William Faulkner and Harper Lee. Sometimes the pace is as slow as watching cotton grow, but at others the rage and bigotry on Hopper's face spills out dreadfully across the screen. Excellent performances from Hopper, Hershey and Ed Harris (as Hershey's lawyer-lover), some languorous photography from Robert Elswit, and a package of big issues inside a small frame, make this a film not to be missed. SGr

Paris vu par... (Six in Paris)

(1964, Fr, 98 min)
d Jean Douchet, Jean Rouch, Jean-Daniel Pollet, Eric Rohmer, Jean-Luc Godard, Claude Chabrol. *p* Barbet Schroeder. *sc* Jean Douchet, Georges Keller, Jean Rouch, Jean-Daniel Pollet, Eric Rohmer, Jean-Luc Godard, Claude Chabrol. *ph* Nestor Almendros, Etienne Becker, Alain Levent, Albert Maysles, Jean Rabier. *ed* Jacqueline Raynal. *cast* Joanna Shimkus, Nadine Ballot, Barbet Schroeder, Micheline Dax, Claude Melki, Claude Chabrol, Stéphane Audran.

●A disappointingly lightweight collection of sketches, filmed in 16mm (blown up to 35mm) in an attempt to encourage experiment by reducing costs. Godard's contribution elaborates a story told in *Une Femme est une Femme* (about a girl who posts letters to her two lovers, then agonises that she got the envelopes mixed), interestingly but not very successfully shot *cinéma-vérité* style with Albert Maysles as cameraman.Rohmer and Rouch are desperately cramped for space; Douchet's episode is routine *Nouvelle Vague* sexual sparring; Pollet's is neatly observed but conventional. By far the best sketch is Chabrol's ruthlessly funny caricature of a bourgeois couple (played by himself and Audran) whose constant nagging, quarrelling and platitudinising drive their young son to resort to ear-plugs, with the result that he is blithely unaware of his mother's desperate cries for help when… TM

Paris Was a Woman

(1995, GB, 75 min)
d Greta Schiller. *p* Frances Berrigan, Greta Schiller, Andrea Weiss. *sc* Andrea Weiss. *ph* Greta Schiller, Nurith Aviv. *ed* Greta Schiller. *m* Janette Mason.

●Greta Schiller is best known for her 1986 documentary on early women jazz musicians, *International Sweethearts of Rhythm*. Ten years may have passed, but this appraisal of the women involved in the Left Bank scene shares a similar mix of marvellous archive footage and testimony. Schiller contends that the creative women living in Paris during the early decades of this century have been overlooked in favour of their more famous male contemporaries, and that Gertrude Stein, Sylvia Beach, Adrienne Monnier, Janet (Genet) Flanner and Djuna Barnes deserve recognition for their contributions to the modernist movement. The problem is that, with the possible exception of Stein, the achievements of the group compared to those of, say, Picasso, Hemingway or Joyce do seem relatively minor. In fact, it soon becomes clear that it's the way these women led their lives, as much as what they chose to do, that interests Schiller. The obvious, if never overtly stated connection is that they were all lesbians (the commentary's constant use of the term 'friends' grates horribly) who, by distancing themselves sexually from contemporary mores, also released themselves from other conventional expectations. FM

Paris: XY

(2000, Fr, 80 min, b/w)
d/p/sc Zeka Laplaine. *ph* Octavio Espirito Santo. *ed* Sarah Taouss Matton, Chaty Chamorey. *pd* Thierry Tourant. *m* Papa Monteiro. *cast* Zeka Laplaine, Sylvia Vaudano, Pilou Ioua, Lisa Edmonson, Kudzo Do Tobias, Moussa Sene Absa.

●Max is a Congolese tailor with a business in Paris, a smart, white, middle-class wife and two kids, and a flirtatious way with the women he meets in bars. He's also a workaholic, and when he cancels a Christmas break with the family, his wife leaves with the children for her dad's. Thereafter, Max desperately tries to save his marriage. That's about it, plotwise, but writer/director Laplaine makes for an engaging protagonist, and he's surrounded himself with a decent cast. While some of the editing's a touch clumsy, there's an air of spontaneity about the b/w camerawork. GA

Parker

(1984, GB, 97 min)
d Jim Goddard. *p* Nigel Stafford-Clark. *sc* Trevor Preston. *ph* Peter Jessop. *ed* Ralph Sheldon. *ad* Andrew McAlpine. *m* Richard Hartley. *cast* Bryan Brown, Cherie Lunghi, Kurt Raab, Bob Peck, Beate Finkh, Gwyneth Strong, Hannelore Elsner.

●An Australian toy manufacturer (Brown) has a charming English wife (Lunghi), a high-class German whore as mistress (Elsner), and a suitably comfortable life-style which crumbles after he is kidnapped and then mysteriously released on a business trip to Germany. Parker's experiences begin to obsess not only him, but also the German investigator (Raab) and the wife, who suspects the worst, and whose loyalty finally cracks as her husband bizarrely returns to images of the crime while recuperating back in London. Though arrestingly shot on location and with a tense, restless performance from Brown, both direction and script are just too fussy for their own good, more interested in lots of confusing and enervating cutting about than in establishing the initial premise of the story: a man suddenly at odds with both himself and all he surveys. SGr

Parking

(1985, Fr, 95 min)
d/sc Jacques Demy. *ph* Jean-François Robin. *ad* Patrice Mercier. *m* Michel Legrand. *cast* Francis Huster, Keiko Ito, Hugues Quester, Marie-France Pisier, Jean Marais.

●Demy's career peaked early, the references, tone, sentiments all fixed and fully explored by the end of the '60s. His later movies all seemed to misfire in one way or another, not least this passing strange musical adaptation of Greek myth, in which Orpheus is represented as a French pop star of Eurovision-esque vapidity, performing a Michel Legrand score which veers from the characteristically inventive to the characteristically saccharine. The scenes in the Underworld (reached via doward spiralling car park) have some force, and it would be worth knowing whether the director, who died in 1990, had already felt the touch of mortality when he embarked on this project. The hero's upfront bisexuality indicates a buried motif running through much of Demy's work. BBa

Park Row

(1952, US, 83 min, b/w)
d/p/sc Samuel Fuller. *ph* Jack Russell. *ed* Philip Cahn. *pd* Theobold Holsopple. *m* Paul Dunlap. *cast* Gene Evans, Mary Welch, Bela Kovacs, Herbert Heyes, Tina Rome, JM Kerrigan.

●This early Fuller drama matches his tabloid style to the story of a newspaper war between two proprietors in 1886. It's compulsive for its insider's knowledge, and passion for the press, but is mostly memorable for a roller-coaster type tracking shot of a fight scene that is pure cinema. The mood is set early: a guy in a bar jumps off Brooklyn Bridge to provide a front page story. When he returns from the jump (alive), the journalist in question has been sacked. A tough world. DMacp

Parlor, Bedroom and Bath (aka Romeo in Pyjamas)

(1931, US, 75 min, b/w)
d Edward Sedgwick. *p* Buster Keaton. *sc* Richard Schayer, Robert Hopkins. *ph* Leonard Smith. *ed* William Le Vanway. *cast* Buster Keaton, Charlotte Greenwood, Reginald Denny, Cliff Edwards, Dorothy Christy, Joan Peers, Sally Eilers, Edward Brophy.

●After a marvellous start with *The Cameraman*, Keaton's features for MGM went steadily downhill. Convinced that slapstick was not only finished but infra dig for a major star, Thalberg saddled him here with a Broadway farce from 1917, ploddingly handled in the 'photographed stage play' manner. Buster plays a gormless billposter who stumbles into a household of rich young things, and in a plot to further romance, is persuaded to pretend to be a mysterious Lothario. Hopelessly backward with girls, he is sent to an experienced female tutor (Greenwood), but a mix-up finds him closeted instead with the young wife (Peers) of a violently jealous man. Bogged down in acres of plot and witless dialogue that prevents him from developing a single gag (slapstick or otherwise), Keaton simply goes through the motions. Pitiful to watch. TM

Parole de Flic

see Cop's Honour

Parole Officer, The

(2001, GB, 94 min)
d John Duigan. *p* Duncan Kenworthy, Andrew Macdonald, Callum McDougall. *sc* Steve Coogan, Henry Normal. *ph* John Daly. *ed* David Freeman. *pd* Tom Brown. *m* Alex Heffes. *cast* Steve Coogan, Lena Heady, Om Puri, Steven Waddington, Ben Miller, Jenny Agutter, Emma Williams, Stephen Dillane.

●Messrs Partridge and Calf are conspicuous by their absence from Coogan's first feature, which at least deserves credit for opting not to rehash the comedy star's brightest TV moments. Instead, Coogan and his co-writer have come up with an Ealing-style crime caper shaped around the exploits of an inept, irritating but cheerily well-meaning probation officer. Transferred from Blackpool to Manchester, Coogan's title character drops out of the service after tangling with corrupt police inspector Dillane, who's ready to pin a gangland murder on him – unless Coogan can retrieve a surveillance video from a bank vault, proving the cop is the killer. The tape's existence allows Coogan to set up a daring heist with a team of misfits (bigamist Puri, computer whiz Miller, hardman Waddington) drawn from former clients. With the bland policewoman Heady popping up as the routine love interest, it's easy to see where the rest is going. For the most part it chugs along pleasantly. TJ

Parsifal

(1982, Fr/WGer, 255 min)
d Hans-Jürgen Syberberg. *ph* Igor Luthor. *ed* Jutta Brandstaedter, Marianne Fehrenberg. *ad* Werner Achmann. *m* Richard Wagner. *cast* Michael Kutter, Karin Krick, Edith Clever, Armin Jordan, Robert Lloyd, Aage Haugland.

●Set in medieval times, around the temple of the Holy Grail, *Parsifal* offers its director more than just the possibility of interpreting Wagner's seductive last opera. He reduces the central Christian theme and refocuses it on a decaying Europe, while simultaneously confronting past with present, myth with reality, the rational with the romantic. Filmed exclusively within a studio – a practice which Syberberg has practically reinvented – it's all staged within a gigantic set of Wagner's death mask, with constantly shifting projected backgrounds. Among a mixed cast of actors and singers, Edith Clever gives a particularly impressive expressionist performance as Kundry (sung by Yvonne Minton). Wagner, as the most radical dramatist of his age, is matched by Syberberg's vision, confirming that he is one of the most visually distinctive film-makers of his time. Continually surprising, provocative, probably infuriating for purists, *Parsifal* is compulsive viewing for both music and movie enthusiasts. KG

Partie de Campagne, Une 100

(1936, Fr, 45 min, b/w)
d Jean Renoir. *p* Pierre Braunberger. *sc* Jean Renoir. *ph* Claude Renoir. *ed* Marinette Cadix. *m* Joseph Kosma. *cast* Sylvia Bataille, Georges Darnoux, Jane Marken, André Gabriello, Jacques Brunius, Paul Temps, Jean Renoir.

●Supposedly left unfinished, but filming was in fact completed, except that the producers wanted Renoir to expand to feature length; he was reluctant, other things intervened, then the war, and the film was finally released in 1946 with the addition of a couple of titles. It may be only a featurette, but this masterly adaptation of a Maupassant story is rich in both poetry and thematic content. On an idyllic country picnic, a young girl leaves her family and fiancé for a while, and succumbs to an all-too-brief romance. The careful reconstruction of period (around 1860) is enhanced by a typically touching generosity towards the characters and an aching, poignant sense of love lost but never forgotten. And, as always in Renoir, the river is far, far more than just a picturesque stretch of water. Witty and sensuous, it's pure magic. GA

Partie de Plaisir, Une (Love Match)

(1974, Fr/It, 101 min)
d Claude Chabrol. *p* André Genoves. *sc* Paul Gégauff. *ph* Jean Rabier. *ed* Jacques Gaillard. *ad* Guy Littaye. *m* Ludwig van Beethoven, Johannes Brahms, Franz Schubert. *cast* Paul Gégauff, Danièle Gégauff, Paula Moore, Michel Valette, Pierre Santini, Giancarlo Sisti, Clémence Gégauff.

●One of Chabrol's most maligned films. A cool and elegiac study of the canker destroying a family from within, it is given bizarre overtones – part confession, part game – as well as a peculiar poignancy by the fact that the script is modelled by Chabrol's regular scriptwriter Paul Gégauff, who plays the lead opposite his former wife Danièle, on his own marital troubles. Accusations galore of chauvinism were levelled at the film, of course, as the man, having fashioned the woman in his image of perfection, then simultaneously encourages and resents her independence to the point of brutality and even murder. But what emerges from the heart of the film, undercutting the Pavlovian response, is the sense of bitter despair underlying the man's full awareness that he had found paradise, but because of his own intransigently idealistic nature, was unable to find peace and harmony there. TM

Parting Glances

(1985, US, 90 min)
d Bill Sherwood. *p* Yoram Mandel, Arthur Silverman. *sc* Bill Sherwood. *ph* Jacek Laskus. *ed* Bill Sherwood. *pd* John Loggia. *cast* Richard Ganoung, John Bolger, Steve Buscemi, Adam Nathan, Kathy Kinney, Patrick Tull.

●On the surface, Sherwood's first feature looks like the Gay Yuppie Movie it was rumoured to be. Its beautiful characters inhabit covetable NY apartments and lofts, and Fire Island and the Area club are on their social circuit. Yet crucially they lack the cocaine-charged solipsism which renders such things Yuppoid. Sherwood brings a notable grace and droll humour to his story of two male lovers parting against the backdrop of a friend dying of the Big A. At times it errs towards MGM production values, but it has a tenderness, warmth, humour and, despite that looming Big A, a lightness of heart that will win it many friends. The romantic close stretches belief, but it's a film of subtle and elegant musicality. JG

Parting Shots

(1998, GB, 98 min)
d/p Michael Winner. *sc* Michael Winner, Nick Mead. *ph* Ousama Rawi. *ed* Chris Barnes, Arnold Crust [Michael Winner]. *pd* Crispian Sallis. *m* Les Reed. *cast* Chris Rea, Felicity Kendal, Bob Hoskins, Ben Kingsley, Joanna Lumley, Oliver Reed, Diana Rigg, John Cleese, Gareth Hunt, Peter Davison, Patrick Ryecart, Nicholas Gecks, Caroline Langrishe, Nicky Henson, Sheila Steafel.

●A self-styled 'feelgood' version of *Death Wish*: Harry (Rea), a put-upon photographer, discovers he has only six weeks to live, and the worm turns. He's going to be avenged on all those who ever put him down, and first on the hit list is his evil ex-wife Lisa (Rigg). This should be offensive, but isn't. It was Charles Bronson's sensual, enigmatic presence that made *Death Wish* so repellent. Rea is impossible to take seriously, and so the nastiness of the idea – that people we don't like deserve to die – implodes on a spectacular scale. Like one of those Alan Bennett monologues that slowly expose the speaker as completely potty, *Parting Shots* dangles us in two places at once. The strangulated acting by Winner's friends and neighbours, the ugly zooms, the feckless dubbing, the barmy dialogue all add to the strange, otherworldly atmosphere. A touch of genuine surrealism. CO'Su

Partner

(1968, It, 105 min)
d Bernardo Bertolucci. *p* Giovanni Bertolucci. *sc* Bernardo Bertolucci, Gianni Amico. *ph* Ugo Piccone. *ed* Roberto Perpignani. *ad* Francesco Tullio-Altan. *m* Ennio Morricone. *cast* Pierre Clémenti, Stefania Sandrelli, Tina Aumont, Sergio Tofano, Giulio Cesare Castello.

●In all of Bertolucci's movies, there's a central conflict between the 'radical' impulses and a pessimistic (and/or willing) capitulation to the mainstream of bourgeois society and culture. It's a contradiction that takes on juggernaut proportions in '1900', but it stands as a major source of tension and interest in many of the earlier films. Both *Before the Revolution* and *Partner* try to examine it head-on. *Revolution* is about a middle class 20-year-old who 'discovers' Marxism and tries – for a while – to change his life; *Partner* is an exuberant response to the student riots of '68, with Clémenti as a timid drama student confronting his anarchic revolutionary alter ego. The first is mostly 'classical' in style, the second aggressively 'new wave', but both are full of interruptions and digressions: they throw out ideas and allusions (usually to other movies) with reckless enthusiasm, and they remain invaluable aids to an understanding of the '60s. TR

Partners

(1982, US, 98 min)
d James Burrows. *p* Aaron Russo. *sc* Francis Veber. *ph* Victor J Kemper. *ed* Danford B Greene, Stephen Lovejoy. *pd* Richard Sylbert. *m* Georges Delerue. *cast* Ryan O'Neal, John Hurt, Kenneth McMillan, Robyn Douglass, Jay Robinson, Denise Galik, Rick Jason.

●Sent into the decadent underworld in a lilac VW convertible, odd couple O'Neal (womanising cop masquerading – unconvincingly – as a dumb gay stud) and Hurt (given a bum deal as his partner, an unhappy closet case) skid to a halt in a welter of stupidly sexist stereotypes and a scrappy murder investigation plot. The way O'Neal is confirmed in his macho piggishness, and Hurt finds fulfilment in proving himself an ideal housewife, suggests that the average American male, his privileges eroded by feminism, can still get his dinner cooked and his slippers warmed by the fire if he turns gay. But the film seems less interested in exploring this intriguing (if offensive) idea than in setting up situations where we can ogle O'Neal's body. RMy

Parts: the Clonus Horror (aka Clonus)

(1978, US, 90 min)
d Robert S Fiveson. *p* Myrl A Schreibman, Robert S Fiveson. *sc* Myrl A Schreibman. *ph* Max Beaufort. *ed* Robert Gordon. *ad* Steve Nelson. *m* Hod David Schudson. *cast* Tim Donnelly, Dick Sargent, Peter Graves, Paulette Breen, Keenan Wynn, David Hooks.

●Competent and engrossing sci-fi thriller in the *Coma* vein, concerning a human transplantation top-security unit, in which clones of top people are carefully nurtured before being suspended in plastic bags to await their medical fate. Interesting on ethics, and boasting nice cameos from Hollywood vets Keenan Wynn (as a retired journalist) and Peter Graves (a corrupt senator). SGo

Party, The

(1968, US, 98 min)
d/p Blake Edwards. *sc* Blake Edwards, Tom Waldman, Frank Waldman. *ph* Lucien Ballard. *ed* Ralph E Winters. *pd* Fernando Carrere. *m* Henry Mancini. *cast* Peter Sellers, Claudine Longet, Marge Champion, J Edward McKinley, Fay McKenzie.

●Sellers gets to do his funny accent as an accident-prone Indian actor brought to Hollywood, fired for inadvertently sabotaging the movie (a briefly hilarious parody of *Gunga Din*), and invited in error to a posh party at the studio chief's home. From there on, Blake Edwards flexes his Jacques Tati muscles, spinning an elaborate garland of gags around one rather drawn-out situation as Sellers – seconded by a drunken waiter and a baby elephant – innocently reduces the party by degrees to an apocalyptic shambles and his hosts to gibbering wrecks. Quite a few very funny moments, but one doesn't laugh so much as admire the ingenuity. TM

Party and the Guests, The (O Slavnosti a Hostech)

(1966, Czech, 71 min, b/w)
d Jan Nemec. *sc* Ester Krumbachová. *ph* Jaromir Sofr. *ed* Miroslav Hajek. *ad* Oldrich Bosak. *m* Karel Mares. *cast* Ivan Vyskocil, Jan Klusák, Jiri Nemec, Zdenka Skvorecká.

●An acute piece of historical foresight, with a marvellous basic idea. A group of picnickers wandering in a summery wood change into evening-dress, emerge into the grounds of a stately mansion, and are rescued from a band of roving thugs by their host, who ushers them to a magnificent banquet laid out under the stars. Then a man is reported to have left the party; the urbanity vanishes; tracker dogs can be heard howling in the distance. The allegory is obvious, of course, with the avuncular dictator mouthing platitudes, his brutish minions straining at the leash, and the guests submitting like patient sheep to the pointless show of the party. But once one has grasped the message and admired the glittering camerawork, that's about it (although the dialogue may well have carried more hidden charges for Czech audiences). TM

Party Girl

(1958, US, 99 min)
d Nicholas Ray. *p* Joe Pasternak. *sc* George Wells. *ph* Robert Bronner. *ed* John McSweeney. *ad* William A Horning, Randall Duell. *m* Jeff Alexander. *cast* Robert Taylor, Cyd Charisse, Lee J Cobb, John Ireland, Kent Smith.

●Or the optimistic version of *Johnny Guitar*, set in Prohibition Chicago. Robert Taylor has the limp, Cyd Charisse is the dancer, and both are prostitutes of a kind (he a gangster's lawyer, she a party girl) who use each other as emotional crutches before achieving mutual independence and trust. Although the script is poor, Ray's handling of colour and scope is as masterful as ever. Too often consigned to the 'fabulous but flawed' bin, *Party Girl* is far better than that. As in all Ray's films, ideas and emotions are transformed into stunning visuals, as when Lee J Cobb's gangster shoots up a portrait of Jean Harlow after he discovers that she's recently got married. PH

Party – Nature Morte, The

(1991, Ger, 89 min, b/w)
d Cynthia Beatt. *p* Alfred Hürmer. *sc* Cynthia Beatt. *cast* Tilda Swinton, Féodor Atkine.

●Beatt's first feature centres on a staggering performance from Swinton: part Diva, part Harpy, part woman struggling to cope and make sense of it all. She plays Queenie, married to a German and living in Germany; the marriage has reached one of its periodic crises, and Queenie's way out of the impasse is to throw a big all-night party. During it, she humiliates her husband by flirting with a handsome French stranger (Atkine). She succeeds in making a drama out of a crisis. Shot in steely monochrome, this is a small triumph for high-concept film-making. It's structured as a flow of vignettes, with an ever-changing cast of party guests in the background; dozens of people get their minute or two of prominence, but everything turns around the central triangle of wife, husband and potential lover. The only real weakness is the dialogue, far too much of which is quoted from literature and poetry. But the grasp of mood and rhythm is spot on. TR

Party Party

(1983, GB, 98 min)
d Terry Winsor. *p* Davina Belling, Clive Parsons. *sc* Daniel Peacock, Terry Winsor. *ph* Syd MacCartney. *ed* Eddy Joseph. *ad* Deborah Gillingham. *cast* Daniel Peacock, Karl Howman, Perry Fenwick, Sean Chapman, Phoebe Nicholls, Gary Olsen.

●Sold as a sassy young British film ('lotta skirt, lotta geezers, lotta class…') with a passable compilation soundtrack, and directed/co-scripted by National Film School graduate Winsor, this comedy of adolescent errors and angst comes across as disappointingly arthritic. The plot – New Year's Eve jollities, expanded from a student short – seems too insubstantial for a full-length feature. It's impossible to sympathise or identify with this charmless assembly of wimps, vamps, wallflowers, fast flash womanisers, piss artists, comic bobbies, vicars, and – that ultimate figure of *Carry On* hilarity – the horny middle-aged male. You feel Winsor doesn't much like his desperate party people; and that, surely, is unforgivable. SJo

Pascali's Island

(1988, GB, 104 min)
d James Dearden. *p* Eric Fellner. *sc* James Dearden. *ph* Roger Deakins. *ed* Edward Marnier. *pd* Andrew Mollo. *m* Loek Dikker. *cast* Ben Kingsley, Charles Dance, Helen Mirren, Stefan Gryff, George Murcell, Nadim Sawalha, TP McKenna.

●Set during the death throes of the Ottoman Empire on an island uneasily divided between Greeks and Turks, Barry Unsworth's tragic tale of deceit makes an ambitious subject for Dearden's debut. Pascali (Kingsley) is a Turkish spy increasingly troubled that his reports are unread. Into this stalled society of spies and lies comes a new development when Bowles (Dance), a bogus English archaeologist, unearths an ancient bronze statue, risks all to bear it off, and places Pascali in a position where he has to initiate action. Fez, Levantine shiftiness and all, Kingsley strips away the facile associations with Lorre, Ustinov, Greenstreet & Co, and justifies a tragic destiny for his character. The milieu may seem remote but the performances illuminate, and the story has an originality that compensates for the modest budget. BC

Pas de Scandale (Keep It Quiet/No Scandal)

(1999, Fr, 106 min)
d Benoît Jacquot. *p* Philippe Carcassone, Georges Benayoun. *sc* Benoît Jacquot, Jérôme Beaujour. *ph* Romain Winding. *ed* Pascale Chavance. *pd* Sylvain Chauvelot. *cast* Fabrice Luchini, Isabelle Huppert, Vincent Lindon, Vahina Giocante, Sophie Aubry, Andréa Parisy, Thérèse Liotard, Ludovic Bergery.

●This wry, low key satirical comedy benefits from a wonderful performance by Luchini as a disgraced businessman just out of jail. The one time captain of industry has completely reassessed his priorities. He's more interested in chatting to his chauffeur, his wife's hairdresser or ex-prison colleagues than in justifying his previous cut throat behaviour. Jacquot's trick is to take a cynical, sophisticated capitalist and turn him into a holy innocent. At times, as he bumbles around Paris, he evokes memories of Peter Sellers' gardener in *Being There*. The businessman's wife (Huppert) and family are perplexed by the transformation. Audiences, too, are likely to be a little baffled by a film which focuses so intently on such a quizzical, inscrutable character. GM

Pasolini's 120 Days of Sodom

see Salò o le Centoventi Giornate di Sodoma

Pasolini, un Delitto Italiano (Pasolini, an Italian Crime)

(1995, It/Fr, 100 min)
d Marco Tullio Giordana. *p* Claudio Bonivento. *sc* Stefano Rulli, Sandro Petraglia, Marco Tullio Giodana. *ph* Franco Lecca. *ed* Cecilia Zanuso. *pd* Gianni Silvestri. *m* Ennio Morricone. *cast* Carlo de Filippi, Nicoletta Braschi, Tony Bertorelli.

●Driven by a pulsing Morricone score, this forthright investigative thriller re-examines the murder of the great Italian director and poet Pier Paolo Pasolini in Ostia in 1975, and the subsequent, inadaquate police inquiry (the case was reopened in light of the evidence presented in the film and the book which inspired it). While Giordana's comparatively conventional style has nothing in common with Pasolini's, the film's mode of address serves as a powerful, moving testament to the esteem in which the film-maker was (and still is) held, and a devastating critique of the society which couldn't accommodate his integrity. TCh

Pasqualino Settebellezze

see Seven Beauties

Passage, The

(1978, GB, 98 min)
d J Lee Thompson. *p* John Quested. *sc* Bruce Nicolaysen. *ph* Michael Reed. *ed* Alan Strachan. *ad* Jean Forestier, Constantin Mejinsky. *m* Michael J Lewis. *cast* Anthony Quinn, James Mason, Malcolm McDowell, Patricia Neal, Kay Lenz, Christopher Lee, Michel Lonsdale, Marcel Bozzuffi.

●Anthony Quinn, in yet another portrait from his gallery of craggy, loveable peasants, plays a Basque shepherd who ferries an escaping scientist and his family across the Pyrenees into Spain during WWII, pursued by a tenacious SS officer (Malcolm McDowell with supercilious swagger). McDowell's comically histrionic performance is, in fact, the single redeeming feature in this lamentably simplistic and unpleasant piffle. File under *Carry On Garrotting* and forget. AC

Passage du milieu

see Middle Passage, The

Passage Home

(1955, GB, 102 min, b/w)
d Roy Baker. *p* Julian Wintle. *sc* William Fairchild. *ph* Geoffrey Unsworth. *ed* Sidney Hayers. *ad* Alex Vetchinsky. *m* Clifton Parker. *cast* Anthony Steel, Peter Finch, Diane Cilento, Cyril Cusack, Geoffrey Keen, Hugh Griffith, Duncan Lamont, Gordon Jackson, Michael Craig.

●This is the one about the martinet captain (Finch) and the mutinous crew. But given that the setting is the Depression year of 1931, that the captain of the merchant ship feeds his crew rotten potatoes to cut down on expenses, and that the film is told in flashback from the moment when the merchant company offers a grateful eulogy on his retirement, it is by no means uninteresting. Brightly scripted and well acted (aside from the colourless Anthony Steel), it takes some sharpish digs at exploitation and the class system, only partly negated by the cop-out ending. MA

Passager de la Pluie

see Rider on the Rain

Passagers, Les

see Shattered

Passages (Langer Gang)

(1992, Ger, 90 min)
d Yilmaz Arslan. *p* Frank Löprich, Katrin Schlösser. *sc* Yilmaz Arslan. *ph* Izzet Akkay. *ed* Bettina Böhler. *m* Ralph Graf. *cast* Nina Kunzendorf, Dieter Resch, Martin Seeger, Marco Neumeier, Tarik Senouci.

●Semi-autobiographical, semi-documentary debut from a Turkish-German director. Arslan constructs an almost plotless panorama of life inside Germany's biggest rehab centre for physically disabled kids, a characterless, over-large facility which inevitably creates more problems than it solves. The film's vignettes detail most aspects of the kids' lives: boredom, dreams of escape, fights, sexual approaches (straight and gay). The grim conclusion is that the place is full of passages leading nowhere. The visual flair and formal control justify comparisons with early Herzog movies. TR

Passage to India, A

(1984, GB, 163 min)
d David Lean. *p* John Brabourne, Richard Goodwin. *sc* David Lean. *ph* Ernest Day. *ed* David Lean. *pd* John Box. *m* Maurice Jarre. *cast* Judy Davis, Victor Banerjee, Peggy Ashcroft, James Fox, Alec Guinness, Nigel Havers, Richard Wilson, Antonia Pemberton, Saeed Jaffrey.

●This proves a curiously modest affair, abandoning the tub-thumping epic style of Lean's late years. While adhering to perhaps 80 per cent of the book's incident, Lean veers very wide of the mark over EM Forster's hatred of the British presence in India, and comes down much more heavily on the side of the British. But he has assembled his strongest cast in years. Particularly fine is Judy Davis as the foolish hysteric, Miss Quested, who gives the crux of the film (was she or was she not raped in the Marabar caves by her Indian host?) its strongest moments. And once again Lean indulges his taste for scenery, demonstrating an ability with sheer scale which has virtually eluded British cinema throughout its history. Not for literary purists, but if you like your entertainment well tailored, then feel the quality and the width. CPea

Passage to Marseille

(1944, US, 110 min, b/w)
d Michael Curtiz. *p* Hal Wallis. *sc* Casey Robinson, John Moffit. *ph* James Wong Howe. *ed* Owen Marks. *ad* Carl Jules Weyl. *m* Max Steiner. *cast* Humphrey Bogart, Michèle Morgan, Claude Rains, Philip Dorn, Sydney Greenstreet, Peter Lorre, George Tobias, Helmut Dantine, John Loder, Victor Francen, Eduardo Ciannelli.

●Something of a follow-up to *Casablanca*, but without that movie's deft and evocative script. Bogart plays Jean Matrac, a journalist converted, by a confrontation at sea with Greenstreet's elegant fascism (shades of Huston's *Across the Pacific*), from bitterness against a France that has wronged him to self-destructive patriotism with the Free French. The movie is brought to earth by its unnecessary complexity – at one point we're in a flashback from a flashback from a flashback – but the central scenes on Devil's Island have a cogency and atmosphere, particularly Bogart's spell in solitary, which demonstrate the movie it might have been. The last reel quivers with the sort of emotionalism that wartime audiences adored. Bogart hasn't much to do beyond gritting his teeth, Rains typically holds the plot together, and Michèle Morgan is thanklessly cast as the wife waiting at home 'till we meet again'. SG

Passenger, The (Professione: Reporter)

(1975, It/Fr/Sp, 119 min)
d Michelangelo Antonioni. *p* Carlo Ponti. *sc* Mark Peploe, Peter Wollen, Michelangelo Antonioni. *ph* Luciano Tovoli. *ed* Franco Arcalli, Michelangelo Antonioni. *ad* Piero Poletto. *cast* Jack Nicholson, Maria Schneider, Jenny Runacre, Ian Hendry, Steven Berkoff, Ambrose Bia.

●Despite the burdensome presence of Runacre in a relatively minor role, this is Antonioni's finest film for years. With a terse, imaginative script by Peter Wollen (betraying both his interest in structure/structuralism and his past experiences as a political correspondent abroad) that delves into Graham Greene-ish territory, it concerns a TV reporter (Nicholson) who exchanges identity with an acquaintance he finds dead in a North African hotel room, only to find himself hunted not just by mystified wife and friends, but by some rather threatening strangers. At times obscure, the film certainly sags in the middle, while the relationship Nicholson strikes up with Schneider in his bid to escape to a new life seems both a little perfunctory and gratuitous to the central theme. But the film's opening, charting the burnt-out journalist's progress through an endless desert, and the final twenty minutes – including a virtuoso seven-minute single take – are stunning. GA

Passenger 57

(1992, US, 84 min)
d Kevin Hooks. *p* Lee Rich, Dan Paulson, Dylan Sellers. *sc* David Loughery, Dan Gordon. *ph* Mark Irwin. *ed* Richard Nord. *pd* Jaymes Hinkle. *m* Stanley Clarke. *cast* Wesley Snipes, Bruce Payne, Tom Sizemore, Alex Datcher, Bruce Greenwood, Robert Hooks, Elizabeth Hurley, Michael Horse.

●This routine hijack drama lacks the budget and class to match the *Die Hard* films it seeks to emulate. It's lifted, however, by a top-flight performance by Wesley Snipes, whose fast-talking airline security expert enlivens the plot with his screen presence, physical grace and devastating martial arts skills. 'Always bet on black,' Snipes advises feisty flight attendant Datcher, after Payne, freed from his FBI captors by fellow terrorists, takes over a domestic flight to Los Angeles. The plot soon nose dives; but what it lacks in logic, it makes up for in relentless action. An efficient, entertaining time-waster, but Snipes deserved better for his first solo starring role. NF

Passe ton bac d'abord

(1979, Fr, 80 min)
d/sc Maurice Pialat. *ph* Pierre-William Glenn. *ed* Arlette Langmann, Sophie Coussein, Martine Giordano. *m* Pierre-Alain Dahan, Slim Pezin. *cast* Sabine Haudepin, Philippe Marlaud, Bernard Tronczyk, Anik Alane, Michel Caron.

●Best known in Britain for *La Gueule Ouverte* and *Loulou*, Pialat is a major, though unfortunately marginalised, French talent whose realist eye here lights on provincial teenage life, producing something like a cross between Ken Loach and a Gallic *Gregory's Girl*. The non-professional kids, on communal holiday from the title's exhortation to concentrate on their school exams, show a lively disregard for any notion of adolescent angst, despite dead-end prospects, while Pialat never indulges the exploitative clichés of the native genre of 'nostalgic' teen-sex low comedy. PT

Passion

(1982, Fr/Switz, 88 min)
d Jean-Luc Godard. *p* Alain Sarde. *sc* Jean-Luc Godard. *ph* Raoul Coutard. *ed* Jean-Luc Godard. *ad* Serge Marzolff, Jean Bauer. *m* Maurice Ravel, Gabriel Fauré, Ludwig van Beethoven, Antonín Dvorak, Wolfgang Amadeus Mozart. *cast* Isabelle Huppert, Hanna Schygulla, Jerzy Radziwilowicz, Michel Piccoli, Laszlo Szabo, Jean-François Stévenin.

●For the '60s generation, Godard effectively reinvented cinema, but for many who came to movies in the '70s he trailed a reputation as a verbose, didactic, doctrinaire apologist for the 'lost causes' of May '68. *Passion* brought a chance to (re)discover what all the fuss was about. Reunited with cameraman Raoul Coutard after 16 years, and with a trio of great actors (Huppert, Schygulla, Piccoli), he orchestrates his personal passions for classical music, romantic painting, and the business of film-making around his favourite theme of how life relates to love. In a film studio, a Polish director is recreating in tableaux vivants a series of celebrated paintings by Goya, Ingres, Delacroix, Rembrandt and El Greco (breathtakingly lit and framed by Coutard), but the backers complain that there's no story. Outside, at the hotel, are many stories, but none is allowed to assume centre stage and focus your vision on a single narrative. Godard asks you to look everywhere at once, offering sounds and images that astonish the senses and tease the mind. It's a film you'll need – and want – to see several times. MA

Passion (Szenvedély)

(1997, Hun, 136 min, b/w)
d György Fehér. *p* Jolan Arvai, Ferenc Kardos, Eva Schulze. *sc* György Fehér, Bela Tarr. *ph* Miklós Gurbán, Tibor Mathé. *ed* Maria Czeilik. *pd* Tamas Vayer. *cast* Ildiko Bansagi, Janos Dezsi, Dzsoko Rozics, Peter Hauman.

●Fehèr follows Visconti, Tay Garnett and Bob Rafelson in tackling *The Postman Always Rings Twice*, James M Cain's classic pulp tale of infidelity, murder and recrimination in which a hired hand makes a fateful move on his employer's wife. Here the cast grunt in Hungarian monosyllables, the action moves at glacier pace, and the b/w print has been specially processed to look like someone just dug it up. After an hour or so, it does, however, begin to exert a certain hold, especially when the insurance company investigator (who looks like Georg Solti crossed with something out of George Grosz) gets on the trail of the guilty couple. We finish with a quotation from the Book of Revelation reminding us that we're all going to hell. TJ

Passion, A (En Passion)

(1969, Swe, 100 min)
d/sc Ingmar Bergman. *ph* Sven Nykvist. *ed* Siv Lundgren. *ad* PA Lundgren. *cast* Liv Ullmann, Bibi Anderson, Max von Sydow, Erland Josephson, Erik Hell, Sigge Forst.

●All Bergman's films in the late '60s centre on isolated social groups (often the partners of a marriage) and show them under attack from both inside and out: Laingian fissures and cracks open up between the characters, and their precarious security is challenged by irruptions from the outside world. Bergman preserves and extends his private mythologies (witness the way that images and names recur from film to film), but in a broader (less precious, more honest) context. Liv Ullmann says it all in *The Shame* when she dreams of 'living in the truth'. Here, another bold step forward in Bergman's analysis of human isolation, the public and private manias of *Hour of the Wolf* are brought down to earth among middle class intruders in an island community. TR

Passionate Friends, The (aka One Woman's Story)

(1948, GB, 95 min, b/w)
d David Lean. *p* Ronald Neame. *sc* Eric Ambler, David Lean, Stanley Haynes. *ph* Guy Green. *ed* Geoffrey Foot. *pd* John Bryan. *m* Richard Addinsell. *cast* Trevor Howard, Ann Todd, Claude Rains, Betty Ann Davies, Isabel Dean, Arthur Howard, Wilfrid Hyde White.

●Adapted by Eric Ambler from the novel by HG Wells, this triangular romance is one of three films Lean made in the late '40s with his then wife Ann Todd and reckoned by critic David Thomson as his piece 'most deserving rediscovery'. Todd and husband Rains are on holiday in Switzerland when she runs into her former lover Howard for the first time in nine years, causing a rift in her present relationship when her other half misreads the by-now platonic relationship between the two old pals. As ever the craft of the piece (an intrictae flashback structure, Guy Green's beautiful cinematography) seems to carry all before it, but there's a degree of emotional subtlety here that often went missing in the director's later work. TJ

Passion Béatrice, La

(1987, Fr, 131 min)
d Bertrand Tavernier. *p* Adolphe Viezzi. *sc* Colo Tavernier O'Hagan. *ph* Bruno De Keyzer. *ed* Armand Psenny. *ad* Guy-Claude François. *m* Ron Carter. *cast* Bernard-Pierre Donnadieu, Julie Delpy, Nils Tavernier, Monique Chaumette, Robert Dhéry, Jean-Claude Adelin.

●The usually temperate Tavernier veers towards the dark side in this catalogue of medieval cruelty. Lord of the manor Donnadieu returns from the wars in a state of rage, seeking nothing but bloodshed and harm. He rapes his daughter, dresses his insufficiently macho son in a frock and sets the hunt on him, and plunders the neighbourhood. Just the situation for a hero to set right, but none is forthcoming. This monster only dies when he himself wills it. Tavernier has enjoyed recreating the detail of this cheerless world, with its contending superstitions. But it's relentlessly brutal and extremely long. What were they again, the rewards of Tragedy? BBa

Passione, La

see La Passione

Passion de Jeanne d'Arc, La (The Passion of Joan of Arc) 100

(1928, Fr, 7,251 ft, b/w)
d Carl Dreyer. *sc* Carl Dreyer, Jospeh Delteil. *ph* Rudolph Maté, Goestula Kottula. *ed* Carl Dreyer. *ad* Jean-Victor Hugo, Hermann Warm. *cast* Renée Jeanne Falconetti, Eugène Silvain, Maurice Schutz, Michel Simon, Antonin Artaud.

●Dreyer's most universally acclaimed masterpiece remains one of the most staggeringly intense films ever made. It deals only with the final stages of Joan's trial and her execution, and is composed almost exclusively of close-ups: hands, robes, crosses, metal bars, and (most of all) faces. The face we see most is, naturally, Falconetti's as Joan, and it's hard to imagine a performer evincing physical anguish and spiritual exaltation more palpably. Dreyer encloses this stark, infinitely expressive face with other characters and sets that are equally devoid of decoration and equally direct in conveying both material and metaphysical essences. The entire film is less moulded in light than carved in stone: it's magisterial cinema, and almost unbearably moving. TR

Passione d'Amore

(1981, It/Fr, 119 min)
d Ettore Scola. *p* Franco Committeri. *sc* Ruggero Maccari, Ettore Scola. *ph* Claudio Ragona. *ed* Raimondo Crociani. *ad* Fiorenzo Senese. *m* Armando Trovaioli. *cast* Bernard Giraudeau, Valeria D'Obici, Laura Antonelli, Jean-Louis Trintignant, Massimo Girotti, Bernard Blier.

●An Italian costume drama set in the 19th century, about a dashing young cavalry officer and his love. *Senso*, alas, it is not. After interminable mopings when the lovers are separated by his transfer to a remote frontier post, things brighten up momentarily with the appearance of a mysterious woman bearing a marked resemblance to Murnau's *Nosferatu*. Her looks apparently suffered in an illness following an early amorous deception. Now, requiring to be treated with the forbearance befitting an officer and a gentleman, she battens onto our hero's affections like a vampire on heat. Probably only Buñuel could have got away with the grotesque romantic tushery whereby the enormity of her passion finally conjures a response, and the pair soar together in a bout of *amour fou*. Po faced nonsense with cardboard characters, it has excellent camerawork and nicely dry supporting performances from Trintignant and Blier. TM

Passion Fish

(1992, US, 135 min)
d John Sayles. *p* Sarah Green, Maggie Renzi. *sc* John Sayles. *ph* Roger Deakins. *ed* John Sayles. *pd* Dan Bishop, Dianna Freas. *m* Mason Daring. *cast* Mary McDonnell, Alfre Woodard, Vondie Curtis-Hall, Angela Bassett, David Strathairn.
●Tetchy and bitter after a car crash which has left her paralysed from the waist down, daytime soap star May-Alice (McDonnell) returns to her late parents' Louisiana home to drown her sorrows. Only with the arrival of Chantelle (Woodard), a determinedly unservile black from Chicago, does the reluctant patient meet her match in obstinacy. It's a spiky, volatile relationship, but when Chantelle helps May-Alice get rid of some unwelcome visitors, a fragile link is forged between the two equally proud but very different women. Sayles' most warmly perceptive, touching movie to date, *Passion Fish* delivers far more than its generic roots would suggest. The director's witty, understated script and relaxed, classical direction may touch on issues of sickness, race and sexual politics, but do so in ways that are never laboured, schematic or sentimental. Marvellously nuanced performances, effortlessly superior film-making. GA

Passion in the Desert

(1994, US, 93 min)
d/p Lavinia Currier. *sc* Lavinia Currier, Martin Edmunds. *ph* Alexei Rodionov. *ed* Nick Gaster. *pd* Amanda McArthur. *m* José Nieto. *cast* Ben Daniels, Michel Piccoli, Paul Meston, Kenneth Collard.
●Set in 1798, at the time of Napoleon's failed attempts to conquer Egypt, this blazingly ridiculous yarn (from a Balzac novella) follows French soldier Augustin (Daniels), a rational child of the Enlightenment who views Egypt as little more than physical geography, and Venture (Piccoli), a romantic artist and scholar who's been commissioned to record the country's monuments and terrain. When they're separated from their platoon and get lost in the desert, things look rocky for the unlikely heroes. Dehydrated and delirious, Augustin searches for aid, his path crossing with that of a wild leopard who leads him to a pool. While the meditative, sober pace and uncluttered visual aesthetic reflect first time film-maker Currier's uncompromising vision, the awkward dialogue and two-dimensional characterisation render the film little more than a silly schoolboy adventure, hankering for the 'glory' days of the Empire. HK

Passion of Darkly Noon, The (Die Passion des Darkly Noon)

(1995, GB/Ger/Bel, 101 min)
d Philip Ridley. *p* Dominic Anciano, Frank Henschke, Alain Keytsman. *sc* Philip Ridley. *ph* John de Borman. *ed* Leslie Healey. *pd* Hubert Pouillé. *m* Nick Bicât. *cast* Brendan Fraser, Ashley Judd, Viggo Mortensen, Loren Dean, Grace Zabriskie, Lou Myers, Kate Harper.
●Ridley's slow-burning fable builds to a shocking finale, part apocalyptic religious vision, part intellectual slasher movie. Darkly Noon (Fraser), sole survivor of a Waco-like siege, is given refuge by beautiful forest dweller Callie (Judd), whose lover Clay (Mortensen) later returns for a passionate reunion. Egged on by crazy hermit Roxy (Zabriskie), Darkly cranks himself up into a state of violent delirium. As the vengeful innocent wraps barbed wire around his chest, one recalls the disturbing weirdness of *The Reflecting Skin* and fears the worst. NF

Passion of Remembrance, The

(1986, GB, 82 min)
d Maureen Blackwood, Isaac Julien. *p* Martina Attille. *sc* Maureen Blackwood, Isaac Julien. *ph* Steven Bernstein, Nina Kellgren. *ed* Nadine Marsh-Edwards. *m* Tony Rémy. *cast* Anni Domingo, Joseph Charles, Antonia Thomas, Carlton Chance, Jim Findley, Ram John Holder.
●This montage of documentary footage and representational dramatic episodes from London's Sankofa Collective offers a series of individual reflections, each bearing a potential for further development. The focal point is the confrontation between a young man and woman, attempting to rationalise the gap which has separated them as they stand before a barren landscape. 'Man' is accused of forsaking 'Woman' in his struggle to raise the consciousness of the black community. Over-extended in scope and tied down by its own rhetoric, the film nevertheless succeeds as it catches the conflicts of gender and generation within the community itself, with visions of a 'black experience' giving way to the more nominal insights of black experiences. SGo

Passport (Paszport)

(2001, Hun, 70 min, b/w)
d Péter Gothár. *p* József Berger, István Kardos. *sc* Péter Gothár. *ph* Tamás Babos. *ed* Agnes Ostoros, Zoltán Vida. *m* György Orbán. *cast* Enikö Börcsök, Gergely Kocsis, Mari Nagy, István Medgyesi, Eva Fehér.
●An account of a happily arranged marriage that goes badly wrong, set against the backdrop of severe economic transitions in post-Soviet Europe and focusing on a brick factory, this b/w video drama is probably not for everyone. But the skid-row budget is employed to convey the grimness and quasi-medieval rituals of life in the new market reality of the East. The final scene, of renegade mother and daughter literally in limbo between earth and sky, is as good an image as any of the region's uncertain future. GE

Passport to Fame

see Whole Town's Talking, The

Passport to Pimlico

(1949, GB, 85 min, b/w)
d Henry Cornelius. *p* Michael Balcon. *sc* TEB Clarke. *ph* Lionel Banes. *ed* Michael Truman. *ad* Roy Oxley. *m* Georges Auric. *cast* Stanley Holloway, Margaret Rutherford, John Slater, Barbara Murray, Betty Warren, Hermione Baddeley, Paul Dupuis, Raymond Huntley, Jane Hylton, Basil Radford, Naunton Wayne.
●Perhaps the most Ealingish of the Ealing comedies, celebrating the cosy sense of wartime togetherness recaptured when the inhabitants of Pimlico, discovering their hereditary independence from Britain, set up a restriction-free (but soon beleaguered and ration-hit) state. A brilliant idea whose satirical possibilities are never really explored. The film is nevertheless carried along on a wave of zany inventiveness (hit by sanctions, the 'Burgundians' promptly respond by having customs officers patrol the tube trains passing through their territory), while an amiable cast does well by TEB Clarke's genial script (especially Margaret Rutherford as the history don quivering with ecstasy over the historical significance of the discovery of the ancient Burgundian charter). TM

Password Is Courage, The

(1962, GB, 116 min)
d Andrew L Stone. *p* Andrew L Stone, Virginia Stone. *sc* Andrew L Stone. *ph* Davis Boulton. *ed* Noreen Ackland. *ad* Wilfred Arnold. *cast* Dirk Bogarde, Maria Perschy, Alfred Lynch, Nigel Stock, Reginald Beckwith, Richard Marner, Ed Devereaux, Colin Blakely, Ferdy Mayne.
●Although frequent sticklers for authenticity (they sank a real ship for *The Last Voyage*), writer/ director Andrew Stone and his producer wife Virginia turned English villages into enemy Germany in this unexpected take on the true-life WWII heroism of a certain Sgt-Maj Coward, the scourge of Nazi PoW camps (he bartered, at one point, to save prisoners in Auschwitz). Often played for fun, it doesn't quite come off, but at least it's a variation on the usual stiff-upper-lip routine. Based on John Castle's biography of Charles Coward. TJ

Pasternaks, The

(1978, GB, 50 min)
d Nick Gifford. *with* Josephine Pasternak, Lydia Pasternak.
●Nick Gifford's fine, slow-burning documentaries all work by the same set of principles: to get as close to the subjects as possible, but not to use them; and to allow them to speak for themselves – no spurious manufacture of narrative or 'telling' structuralising. *The Pasternaks* is an extended interview with Boris Pasternak's two surviving septuagenarian sisters, who share a house in Oxford. They reminisce wonderfully about their father Leonid (a painter who seems to have crossed the subject matter of Millet with Impressionist techniques) and the family, via a collection of photographs, paintings and drawings. What emerges from Gifford's most 'conventional' documentary subject is a Jamesian pastel portrait of a rather respectable artistic family, living through extraordinary times. The description of Boris' funeral, where thousands flocked to the unannounced ceremony, is most moving. CPea

Pasteur

(1935, Fr, 74 min, b/w)
d Sacha Guitry. *p* Fernand Rivers. *sc* Sacha Guitry. *ph* Jean Bachelet, René Ribault. *ed* Pierre Schwab. *ad* Robert Gys. *m* Louis Beydts. *cast* Sacha Guitry, Jean Périer, José Squinquel, Henry Bonvallet.
●Guitry was meticulous about his credits, and when this movie announces itself as '*réalisé par Sacha Guitry, sous la direction de Fernand Rivers*' – Rivers was the producer – we may assume that Guitry expects us to infer he was not entirely a free agent here. And indeed, it is all rather uncharacteristic. The film is a series of highlights from a brilliant life: experiments, obstruction by pig-headed establishment, rabid child cured, ideas embraced, venerated old age. Guitry could never be dull, but this is undemanding stuff by his standards. However, it's notable for the opening, in which the author summarises Pasteur's career, shows us some photos, analyses his handwriting and reads the admirable letter by the scientist that moved him to make the film. A common sense biopic opening, but can anyone think of another film-maker who's had the self-confidence to attempt anything similar? BBa

Pastorale

(1978, USSR, 95 min)
d Otar Ioselliani. *sc* Rezo Inanichvili, Otar Mekschrichvili, Otar Yoseliani. *ph* Abbesalom Maishradze. *m* Corelli. *cast* Rezo Tsarchalachvili, Lia Tokkadse-Djiegueli, Marina Kartzevadse, Tamara Gabarachvili, Nana Ioselliani, Nukri Davitashvili, Mikhail Naneashvili, Zeinab Marsaberidse.
●A turgid and occasionally twee account of a string quartet holidaying in (Soviet) Georgia. A hint of romance, a touch of the travelogues, a surfeit of lyrical shots, and a lot of chamber music. Running into trouble, apparently because of its 'formalist aesthetic', it was not released to the West until 1982, when it was shown at the Berlin and London festivals: not the best of choices, even considering the generally dismal contemporary output of Soviet cinema. MA

Pastoral Hide-and-Seek (Denen ni Shisu)

(1974, Jap, 102 min)
d Shuji Terayama. *p* Eiko Kujo, Hiroko Govaers. *sc* Shuji Terayama. *ph* Tatsuo Suzuki. *ed* Sachiko Yamaji, Takasuke Otsubo, Hiroshi Asai. *pd* Kazuichi Hanawa. *m* JA Seazer. *cast* Kantaro Suga, Hiroyuki Takana, Chigusa Takayama, Keiko Niitaka, Kaoru Yachigusa.
●Terayama's second feature recapitulates some of the main themes of *Throw Away Your Books* in more directly personal terms: it's a film about a film-maker's re-examination (and attempted revision) of his own childhood. His boyhood self is an unprepossessing lad who lives with his monstrous, widowed mother, fantasises about the desirable girl-next-door, and finds the visiting circus a touchstone for his dreams of escape. With passion, wit and a genuinely engaging charm, Terayama poses the burning question: Does murdering your mother constitute a true liberation? The autobiographical stance and the circus motif have evoked countless comparisons with Fellini, but they're very wide of the mark: the film isn't burdened with bombast or rhetoric, but it is rich in (authentically Japanese) poetry, and its modernist approach is challenging in the best and most accessible sense. TR

Pastor Hall

(1940, GB, 97 min, b/w)
d Roy Boulting. *p* John Boulting. *sc* Leslie Arliss, Anna Reiner, Haworth Bromley. *ph* Max Greene. *ed* Roy Boulting. *ad* James Carter. *m* Charles Brill, Mac Adams. *cast* Nova Pilbeam, Seymour Hicks, Wilfrid Lawson, Marius Goring, Percy Walsh, Brian Worth, Bernard Miles.

● Although its production was halted for reasons of political expediency by the censors during the Chamberlain era, after war erupted this treatment of Pastor Martin Niemöller's principled stand against the Nazis in 1934 reached the screen with its portrayal of camp atrocities intact. Roy Boulting turns rural Germany into a mirror for little England, which ups the propaganda factor. Adapted by Leslie Arliss, Haworth Bromley and Anne Reiner from the play by the German revolutionary poet and dramatist Ernst Toller. A bit creaky, but fascinating. TJ

Pas très Catholique (A Dubious Business)

(1993, Fr, 101 min)
d/sc Tonie Marshall. *p* Michel Propper, Frédéric Bourboulon. *ph* Dominique Chapuis. *ed* Jacques Comets. *ad* Marie-Pierre Bourboulon. *cast* Anémone, Roland Bertin, Grégorie Colin, Bernard Verley, Christine Boisson, Micheline Presle.

● In a great lollipop of a star role, Anémone plays Maxime, a scruffy, chain-smoking, bisexual private eye and dedicated loner, who is beginning to feel the chill of early middle age. She is uncertain about her new lover and apprehensive about the teenage son she abandoned as a baby and who is now trying to make friends with her. But having invented an intriguing character, Marshall is unable to find much of interest for her to do, and disappointingly Maxime's big investigation turns out to intersect her own private life in an excessively coincidental, convenient way. The talk is non-stop, the action is non-start and there is no compelling reason why this should be a movie, rather than a novel or a radio play. Even so, Maxime is worth meeting. BBa

Past Tense

(1994, US, 87 min)
d Graeme Clifford. *cast* Scott Glenn, Anthony LaPaglia, Lara Flynn Boyle.

● A hardbitten cop has dreams (and dreams within dreams) about a mysterious femme fatale, the sort of stuff parodied in Altman's *The Player*. Director Clifford strains for psychological symbolism, but the stylised photography and design are simply silly, as is the script. And with Glenn and Flynn Boyle failing to be James Stewart and Kim Novak, that leaves a 'thriller' which is very vaguely Hitchcockian, but lacks an ounce of the Master's art – though making sex and violence this tedious is, perhaps, an art in itself. AO

Pat and Mike

(1952, US, 95 min, b/w)
d George Cukor. *p* Lawrence Weingarten. *sc* Garson Kanin, Ruth Gordon. *ph* William H Daniels. *ed* George Boemler. *ad* Cedric Gibbons, Urie McCleary. *m* David Raksin. *cast* Spencer Tracy, Katharine Hepburn, Aldo Ray, William Ching, Jim Backus, Sammy White, Charles Bronson, Chuck Connors.

● Written, like several other Cukor films of the period, by Ruth Gordon and Garson Kanin, and charting the conflict between what Carlos Clarens called 'the redneck paternalism of Spencer Tracy and Katharine Hepburn's outraged liberal sensibilities', this is a lazy, episodic, conventional but strangely charming variation on the old comedy formula of initially hostile misfits falling in love (here platonic). Hepburn gets to show off her considerable athletic talents as the bright, upper middle class sporting all-rounder; Tracy gets to be gruffly loveable as the rough-diamond promoter-manager who finally becomes her protector. There are far too many shots featuring real-life sports stars, but the sparring leads, and Ray's dim boxer, work superbly together under Cukor's deceptively effortless, always elegant direction. GA

Patch Adams

(1998, US, 115 min)
d Tom Shadyac. *p* Barry Kemp, Mike Farrell, Marvin Minoff, Charles Newirth. *sc* Steve Oedekerk. *ph* Phedon Papamichael. *ed* Don Zimmerman. *pd* Linda DeScenna. *m* Marc Shaiman. *cast* Robin Williams, Monica Potter, Daniel London, Philip Seymour Hoffman, Bob Gunton, Josef Sommer, Harve Presnell, Peter Coyote.

● This slushy comedy drama, set in 1969, tells the 'true story' of misfit Hunter Doherty Adams who, having spent time in a mental home, enlists in medical school and proceeds to shake up the US medical system by being his 'excessively happy' self. He cheers up terminally ill kids by wearing an enema bulb on his nose. The film is all about the healing qualities of laughter and generally getting on an equal level with others. Admirable, of course – except, this being a Williams vehicle, there's also an overdose of sentimental claptrap, underscored by Marc Shaiman's clichéd string arrangements. DA

Patch of Blue, A

(1965, US, 105 min, b/w)
d Guy Green. *p* Pandro S Berman. *sc* Guy Green. *ph* Robert Burks. *ed* Rita Roland. *ad* George W Davis, Urie McCleary. *m* Jerry Goldsmith. *cast* Sidney Poitier, Shelley Winters, Elizabeth Hartman, Wallace Ford, Ivan Dixon.

● Shelley Winters won an Oscar for being perfectly horrible as the harridan mom in this dated, but not too sentimental fable in which blind daughter Hartman is brought out of her shell and given a sense of self-worth by her burgeoning friendship with Poitier, unaware throughout that he's a black man. In hindsight, it all looks like a rather tentative Hollywood essay at the race angle, but the actors do mesh together convincingly despite the obvious narrative contrivances, and debut girl Hartman's persuasive account of the everyday travails of the sightless is engrossing without overdoing the self-pity. That, unfortunately, is left to Jerry Goldsmith's insistently 'sensitive' score, plaintive woodwinds to the fore. TJ

Paternity

(1981, US, 93 min)
d David Steinberg. *p* Lawrence Gordon, Hank Moonjean. *sc* Charlie Peters. *ph* Bobby Byrne. *ed* Donn Cambern. *pd* Jack T Collis. *m* David Shire. *cast* Burt Reynolds, Beverly D'Angelo, Norman Fell, Paul Dooley, Elizabeth Ashley, Lauren Hutton, Juanita Moore.

● Reynolds tones down the Southern accent that goes with his popular redneck image for the part of New York's most eligible bachelor, just turned 44 and realising that his life is empty without progeny. The decision that he wants to be a father, and the recruitment of waitress Beverly D'Angelo as the mother (she needs the money for her music studies), sets the scene for a lightweight sex comedy, with her whiling away her pregnancy in his luxurious Manhattan apartment while he continues to womanise. Any notion that a topical social issue will be taken as seriously as it deserves is decisively scotched long before the thoroughly predictable romantic ending; but *Paternity* is difficult to actually dislike, largely because of its engaging duo of stars. RM

Pat Garrett and Billy the Kid

(1973, US, 121 min)
d Sam Peckinpah. *p* Gordon Carroll. *sc* Rudy Wurlitzer. *ph* John Coquillon. *ed* Roger Spottiswoode, Garth Craven, Robert L Wolfe, Richard Halsey, David Berlatsky, Tony De Zarraga. *ad* Ted Haworth. *m* Bob Dylan. *cast* James Coburn, Kris Kristofferson, Bob Dylan, Richard Jaeckel, Katy Jurado, Slim Pickens, Chill Wills, Jason Robards, RG Armstrong, Luke Askew, Jack Elam, Charlie Martin Smith, Harry Dean Stanton, Barry Sullivan.

● Restored and reassembled, this is the full and harmonious movie that Peckinpah wanted to be remembered by before the butchers at MGM got their hands on it. Starting with a framing sequence from 1909 which shows Coburn's aged Garrett being gunned down by the same men who hired him to get Billy the Kid back in 1881, the additional 15 minutes introduce the menacing figure of Barry Sullivan's Boss Chisum, a frolicsome brothel scene ('Last time Billy was here it took four to get him up and five to get him down again'), some engaging Wild West cameos, and a less obtrusive use of Bob Dylan's soundtrack. All in all the film is more playful, more balanced, and very much an elegy for the old ways of the West, rather than a meandering bloodthirsty battle between Kristofferson's preposterously likeable outlaw and Coburn's ambivalent survivor, Garrett. Like Ford's *The Man Who Shot Liberty Valance*, it both records and condemns the passage of time and the advent of progress; and there is a sombre, mournful quality which places the film very high up in the league of great Westerns. SGr

Pather Panchali 100

(1955, Ind, 115 min, b/w)
d/sc Satyajit Ray. *ph* Subrata Mitra. *ed* Dulal Dutta. *ad* Banshi Chandra Gupta. *m* Ravi Shankar. *cast* Kanu Bannerjee, Karuna Bannerjee, Uma Das Gupta, Subir Bannerjee, Chunibala Devi.

● Ray's first film, and the first instalment of what came to be known as *The Apu Trilogy*, completed by *Aparajito* (*The Unvanquished*, 1956, 113 min, b/w) and *Apur Sansar* (*The World of Apu*, 1959, 106 min, b/w). The first Indian film to cause any real stir in Europe and America, it is still something to wonder at: a simple story of country folk told with all the effortless beauty, drama and humanity which seem beyond the grasp of most Western directors. The plot is nothing more than a string of ordinary events, focused on the experiences of Apu, child of a small family eking out an existence in a ramshackle Bengal village: a train thunders by across the plains, a frugal meal is prepared, the rains and the wind flatten and drench the landscape, someone dies. The two later films show Apu's development in more 'civilised' societies – particularly Calcutta, where he pursues his studies until money runs out, falls into an arranged marriage, painfully lives through the deaths of his parents and wife, loses direction, and pulls through chastened but undefeated. There are three changes of actor (Apu at different ages), and Ray's narrative methods sometimes veer distractingly from the episodic to the linear. What doesn't change is his remarkably natural way with symbolism (spot all those trains!), his eye for the visual poetry of both raw nature and industrial squalor, and his faith in the human ability to grow with experience. *Pather Panchali*, in particular, retains a fresh and pellucid beauty. GB

Pathfinder (Veiviseren)

(1987, Nor, 86 min)
d Nils Gaup. *p* John M Jacobsen. *sc* Nils Gaup. *ph* Erling Thurmann-Andersen. *ed* Niels Pagh Andersen. *pd* Harald Egede-Nissen. *m* Nils-Aslak Valkeapää, Marius Müller, Kjetil Bjerkestrand. *cast* Mikkel Gaup, Ingvald Guttorm, Ellen Anne Buljo, Inger Utsi, Svein Scharffenberg.

● An epic adventure set in Lapland a thousand years ago, this fuses the mythic simplicity of a folk tale with the kind of lean action that would not disgrace a Kurosawa film. The battle between Good and Evil here involves the peace-loving Lapps and savage black-clad invaders, the Tchudes. When 16-year-old Aigin (Mikkel Gaup) sees his family wiped out by a Tchude raiding party, he flees to a nearby village. The villagers make for the safety of the coastlands, but the vengeful Aigin stays to confront the raiders, only to be captured and forced to act as their pathfinder. Will he lead them to the Lapp settlement, or will he succeed in tricking them into a vital mistake? Shot against a frozen landscape of breathtaking beauty, Nils Gaup's film is supported by a strangely appropriate electronic soundtrack, and although the sudden climax doesn't quite fulfil expectations, has a rivetingly economical narrative development. NF

Path of the Brave (Vittee Khon Kla)

(1991, Thai, 133 min)
d Euthana Mukdasanit. *ph* Vichten Danakkaew. *cast* Narin Tongkum, Thisawan Suwanpho, N-hatai Pichitra, Puthichai Amatayakul.

● The handsome young Jopa is inspired by the legends of heroes past to challenge what he sees as the declining virility of his people (a hill-tribe in Northern Thailand). He claws his way to victory in the tribe's ritual tests of strength and then demands to choose his own bride rather than accepting the reigning 'Earth Mother'. Before long, having trampled on rivals and critics, he is making warlike noises at a neighbouring tribe. Euthana's folk epic is an Orwellian political fable with up-to-date resonance in Thailand. It's a touch didactic, but interestingly stylised performances and a great score make it impressive overall. TR

Paths of Glory

(1957, US, 86 min, b/w)
d Stanley Kubrick. *p* James B Harris. *sc* Stanley Kubrick, Calder Willingham, Jim Thompson. *ph* Georg Krause. *ed* Eva Kroll. *ad*

Ludwig Reiber. *m* Gerald Fried. *cast* Kirk Douglas, Adolphe Menjou, Ralph Meeker, George Macready, Wayne Morris, Timothy Carey, Joseph Turkel, Richard Anderson.
●Unusually trenchant for its time, adapted from Humphrey Cobb's factually based novel, Kubrick's first 'prestige' movie bitterly attacks the role of the French military authorities in World War I through an account of the court-martial and execution of three blameless privates. The critique of military hypocrisy and misguided strategy is laid out in an ultra-lucid exposition, full of almost diagrammatic tracking shots that are much more self-consciously virtuoso in camera style than anything in later Kubrick. The film is politically and emotionally anchored in Kirk Douglas' astonishingly successful performance as the condemned men's defender. One measure of the film's effectiveness is that it was banned in France on political grounds for eighteen years. TR

Patlabor – The Movie

(1989, Jap, 99 min)
d Mamoru Oshii. *p* Headgear. *sc* Kazunori Ito. *character design* Akemi Takada. *mechanical design* Yutaka Izubuchi. *m* Kenji Kawai.
●'Labors' are giant, driver-operated robots used to enhance industrial strength, speed and productivity and essential to the Babylon Project, an urban renewal scheme in Tokyo Bay. Criminal appropriation of some Labors has prompted the creation of a special police division equipped with Patrol Labors (Patlabors). Ace animator Oshii used these premises (from *manga* by Masami Yuuke) for six made-for-video shorts; their success led to this feature, more ambitious in scale and scope and much darker in tone. The designer of a new operating system for Labors has committed suicide after implanting a computer virus which causes them to run riot. The police have to find out what activates the virus – as a huge typhoon bears down on the hi-tech Ark in Tokyo Bay. Oshii assumes knowledge of the shorts (the main characters are taken as already established), but doesn't stint on spectacle or fears of technological disaster. TR

Patlabor 2 – The Movie

(1993, Jap, 113 min)
d Mamoru Oshii. *p* IG Tatsunoko. *sc* Kazunori Ito. *ph* Akihiko Takahashi. *ed* Shuichi Kakesu. *ad* Hiromasa Ogura. *m* Kenji Kawai.
●The most overtly political *anime* ever made in Japan, this apocalyptic coda to the *Patlabor* series asks if the concept of an unjust peace is any more tenable than the concept of a just war. Some years after the disbandment of the Patlabor police unit, a series of terrorist attacks (the first real, the second virtual, the third…) panics the government, sets the police against the army and opens the way to a civil war or a pre-emptive coup by the Americans. Captain Goto comes out of semi-retirement to figure out what it all has to do with the near-annihilation of a UN Labor team in a SE Asian jungle – and with sightings of unidentified bright yellow blimps in the sky over Tokyo. There are none of the usual *manga* heroics, just an expert deconstruction of the 'peace' and 'stability' Japan has enjoyed since the end of the Pacific War. A genre masterpiece. TR

Patrick

(1978, Aust, 110 min)
d Richard Franklin. *p* Antony I Ginnane. *sc* Everett de Roche. *ph* Donald McAlpine. *ed* Edward McQueen-Mason. *ad* Leslie Binns. *m* Brian May. *cast* Susan Penhaligon, Robert Helpmann, Rod Mullinar, Bruce Barry, Julia Blake, Helen Hemingway, Robert Thompson.
●An Australian thriller concerning a comatose patient with telekinetic powers (Thompson) who looks a lot like Marty Feldman. There are a few interesting ideas, and at least one good shock, but they're buried by some dreadful script and production errors: the setting is a hospital in which everyone spends their time shouting at each other for no reason at all except the writer's eccentric idea of dramatic construction, and even the shock sequences are interrupted by long phone calls discussing what's happened so far. DP

Patriot, The

(2000, US/Ger, 165 min)
d Roland Emmerich. *p* Dean Devlin, Mark Gordon, Gary Levinsohn. *sc* Robert Rodat. *ph* Caleb Deschanel. *ed* David Brenner. *pd* Kirk M Petruccelli. *m* John Williams. *cast* Mel Gibson, Heath Ledger, Joely Richardson, Jason Isaacs, Chris Cooper, Tchéky Karyo, René Auberjonois, Lisa Brenner, Donal Logue, Leon Rippy, Adam Baldwin, Tom Wilkinson, Mary Jo Deschanel.
●Gibson plays Benjamin Martin, bloodied veteran of the French and Indian Wars and, a few years later, conscientious objector to the War of Independence. His pacificism owes as much to pragmatism as conviction – he's a widower father of seven who inclines against British rule – but, more interestingly, it's also born of shame at the violence he knows within himself. At least on some level, *The Patriot* attempts to harness this rage. Perhaps it's to the credit of this violently idealistic film that it doesn't entirely succeed. You can approach it from many angles. It's written by Robert Rodat of *Saving Private Ryan*, and shares that film's anxiety about 'fighting the good fight'; it's directed by Emmerich and, after *Independence Day* and *Godzilla*, you could say it's his third American war movie; or it's Mad Mel up to his old tricks, learning to channel anger to socially productive ends. The intimate and domestic scenes tend to be stuffy and forced, but Emmerich does convey a sense of war encroaching across the land. It looks ravishing, too. But isn't there something obscene about a film which parades a very modern knowledge of atrocity and evil, only to tub the trite rhetoric of Stars and Stripes forever? Often impressive, but stirring and stomach churning in equal measure. TCh

Patriot, The (Die Patriotin)

(1979, WGer, 120 min, b/w & col)
d/p/sc Alexander Kluge. *ph* Thomas Mauch, Jörg Schmidt-Reitwein, Werner Lüring, Günther Hörmann. *ed* Beate Mainka-Jellinghaus. *cast* Hannelore Hoger, Alfred Edel, Alexander von Eschwege, Hans Heckel, Beate Holle.
●The mocking intelligence which has pricked so many German bubbles in Kluge's films for once seems to have overreached itself. *The Patriot* is Gabi Teichert (Hoger), the history teacher first seen excavating the past in *Germany in Autumn*. Here her symbolic quest for a counter-history, expanded to inordinate length, is presented as a whimsical collage of documentary footage, interview material, and fairytale interludes, all supposedly seen from the viewpoint of a knee belonging to a German corporal who died at Stalingrad. Itself a joint but unable to make connections, the knee leaves the spectator to draw his own conclusions while remembering that the casualties of war still deserve their say. The idea is that reading between the lines of these impressions of Germany past and present might – as in Syberberg's *Hitler* – yield a new concept of history. But Kluge's lesson, muffled by some laborious humour, emerges as pretty banal. TM

Patriot Game, The

(1978, Fr, 97 min)
d/sc Arthur Mac Caig. *ph* Théo Robichet, Arthur Mac Caig. *ed* Arthur Mac Caig, Dominique Creussay. *m* Horslips. *cast* Rev Ian Paisley, Bernadette Devlin, Lord Chichester Clark, Brian Faulkner, Joe Austin.
●By denying the premise of the British media's treatment of Ulster as an insoluble religious conflict, Mac Caig's documentary restores a historical and political context to Republican struggle for a united, socialist Ireland. Unashamedly propagandist, it gives a coherent voice to the Provisionals, and re-runs the TV headlines of the past eleven years to frame rare scenes of contemporary life in the nationalist ghettos. Not only does it succinctly analyse the roots of the 'troubles' (Britain's economic and military oppression) and offer a rationale for Republican strategy (from the Civil Rights movement to IRA bombing campaigns), but it presents a 'hidden', and in many ways inspirational, portrait of life under occupation, of a besieged but organised working class, and of pervasive grass roots resistance. PT

Patriot Games

(1992, US, 117 min)
d Phillip Noyce. *p* Mace Neufeld, Robert Rehme. *sc* Peter Iliff, Donald Stewart, Steven Zaillian. *ph* Donald McAlpine. *ed* Neil Travis, William Hoy. *pd* Joseph Nemec III. *m* James Horner. *cast* Harrison Ford, Anne Archer, Patrick Bergin, Sean Bean, Thora Birch, James Fox, Samuel L Jackson, Polly Walker, James Earl Jones, Richard Harris.
●So duff that you wonder why they didn't ask Roger Moore to star. Jack Ryan (Ford) has retired from his CIA job as an analyst, but finds himself dragged back into that world after foiling an IRA assassination attempt on a Brit royal. He kills a terrorist, whose brother Sean (Bean) vows vengeance on Ryan and his family. In fact, Sean becomes an uncontrollable menace to terrorist organiser Kevin (Bergin), though this is sabotaged by plaintive Irish jigs whenever he dons the ski-mask. Attempts on the lives of Ryan's wife (Archer) and daughter (Birch) force him to sign up again with avuncular Admiral Greer (Jones). Between the implausibilities – Lord Holmes (Fox) decorates Ryan on behalf of Britain in Ryan's front room – the loose ends, and the climactic speedboat duel, one might be forgiven for seeing it as a Saturday Morning Picture Club serial. BC

Patrullero, El

see Highway Patrolman

Patsy, The

(1964, US, 101 min)
d Jerry Lewis. *p* Ernest D Glucksman. *sc* Jerry Lewis, Bill Richmond. *ph* W Wallace Kelley. *ed* John Woodcock. *ad* Hal Pereira, Cary Odell. *m* David Raksin. *cast* Jerry Lewis, Ina Balin, Everett Sloane, Keenan Wynn, Peter Lorre, John Carradine, Phil Harris, Hans Conreid, Rhonda Fleming, Hedda Hopper, George Raft, Ed Sullivan, Mel Tormé, Ed Wynn.
●Who but Jerry Lewis would have dreamed up this pot-pourri of comic fears as a bellboy is chosen to take the place of a dead comedian by his scriptwriters? Explicitly quoting Chaplin-style routines, Lewis bends the sentimentality into shape to produce a witty and magical essay on comedy, illusionism and fear. DMacp

Patsy, The

see Addition, L'

Patterns (aka Patterns of Power)

(1956, US, 83 min, b/w)
d Fielder Cook. *p* Michael Myerberg. *sc* Rod Serling. *ph* Boris Kaufman. *ed* Dave Kummins, Carl Lerner. *pd* Duane McKinney. *cast* Van Heflin, Everett Sloane, Ed Begley, Beatrice Straight, Elizabeth Wilson.
●Adapted by Rod *Twilight Zone* Serling from his own TV play, this is a tense and claustrophobic melodrama which demonstrates the price of professional ambition. Heflin is the recently hired company man who is forced, by his boss Sloane, to come into conflict with ageing executive Begley, the man he is supposed to replace. Reminiscent of *Executive Suite* (though much less sleek and slick), it's a little dated now, but the well-crafted performances of the strong cast (especially Begley as the disintegrating man) work wonders. GA

Patterns of Power

see Patterns

Patti Rocks

(1987, US, 87 min)
d David Burton Morris. *p* Gwen Field, Gregory M Cummins. *sc* David Burton Morris, Chris Mulkey, John Jenkins, Karen Landry. *ph/ed* Gregory M Cummins. *ad* Charlotte Whitaker. *m* Doug Maynard. *cast* Chris Mulkey, John Jenkins, Karen Landry, David L Turk, Stephen Yoakum.
●More sex, lies and celluloid. Morris' independent feature is less conspicuously smart and neat than Soderbergh's *sex, lies and videotape*, delivering instead a confrontational, dirty, blue-collar realism. In the first of two clearly opposed halves, Billy (Mulkey) convinces Eddie (Jenkins) to accompany him on a long journey to meet his mistress; he wants to persuade her to have an abortion. They drive through the night, Billy sustaining an endless tirade of pussy jokes and cock fantasies, while his more mature, lonely friend laughs, argues, listens. This provocative glimpse of 'real men' at large, written and acted with rare conviction, proved too much for some; but rest assured, further up the road waits Patti Rocks. Played with enormous affection by Karen Landry, she is compassionate, responsible, and much more than a match for the guys. It is a beau-

tifully judged, stimulating film, full of risks and verve, and worked through with rare intelligence and humour. TCh

Patton (aka Patton: Lust for Glory)

(1969, US, 171 min)
d Franklin J Schaffner. *p* Frank McCarthy. *sc* Francis Ford Coppola, Edmund H North. *ph* Fred J Koenekamp. *ed* Hugh S Fowler. *ad* Urie McCleary, Gil Parrondo. *m* Jerry Goldsmith. *cast* George C Scott, Karl Malden, Michael Bates, Stephen Young, Michael Strong, James Edwards, Frank Latimore.

● As a study of power, neither Coppola's script nor Schaffner's direction are precise enough to merit the praise that has been heaped upon them. As an exercise in biography, however, Schaffner and Coppola's character study of General George S Patton is marvellous, especially in its sideways debunking of the American Hero. The film lays bare the roots of Patton's lust for power in his willingess to sacrifice everything to his vaunting ego, a trait which is mirrored in George C Scott's superb performance. PH

Patty Hearst

(1988, US/GB, 108 min)
d Paul Schrader. *p* Marvin Worth. *sc* Nicholas Kazan. *ph* Bojan Bazelli, Stewart Barbee. *ed* Michael R Miller. *pd* Jane Musky. *m* Scott Johnson. *cast* Natasha Richardson, William Forsythe, Ving Rhames, Frances Fisher, Jodi Long, Olivia Baraash, Dana Delany, Marek Johnson.

● Schrader's biopic covers well-documented events: the kidnapping of newspaper heiress Hearst by the Symbionese Liberation Army, her transformation into an urban guerrilla, her capture by the FBI, and subsequent trial. Schrader, interested in how she survived, accepts her version and stands clear of the nagging doubts that most of us entertained at the time. There's a Bressonian rigour to this portrayal of the process of brainwashing. Bound, gagged, and blindfolded, Patty is kept in a tiny cupboard for days, after which sensory deprivation is gradually reduced, so that her impressions grow from voices and changes in light to distinctions between her captors. And what a Spartist crew they are – all revolutionary claptrap and middle clas guilt. Reborn as Tania, she takes part in a bank raid, during which she is photographed on security video, gun in hand. Later she takes part in a shootout at a sports store. The SLA are wiped out in a police swoop, but she escapes, living with underground groups till her arrest. It's a lot for trauma to account for. Richardson brings terrific dedication to the role including a perfect American accent, but it's an airless, exhausting film. BC

Patu!

(1983, NZ, 112 min)
d/p Merata Mita. *ph* Barry Harbert. *ed* Annie Collins.

● A record of the anti-apartheid protests against the South Africans' 1981 rugby union tour of New Zealand. The received image of the country as a land in which harmonious interracial relationships have been worked out is profoundly undermined by this documentary (its director is a Maori woman; its title is a Maori word for 'kill' or 'hit'). Their police, looking identical to the British copper, turn out to be expert at cracking the skulls of unarmed, peaceful protesters as the extent and determination of the protests increase (it comes as a relief when they eventually don crash helmets). And the sport itself is represented not by players, but by supporters who are rampantly racist (they really do say 'Would you want your sister to marry one?'). As a record of mobilisation of public opinion in the face of immense propaganda (through the collusion of the media with Muldoon's right wing government in misrepresenting the aims of the protest), it's a wholly successful and convincing tribute. GBr

Pau and His Brother (Pau i el seu Germa)

(2001, Sp/Fr, 110 min)
d Marc Recha. *p* Antonio Chavarrias. *sc* Marc Recha. *ph* Hélène Louvart. *ed* Ernest Blasi. *m* Geronación, Xavier Turull, Fred Vilmar, Toni Xucià, El Gitano. *cast* David Selvas, Nathalie Boutefeu, Marieta Orozco, Luis Hostalot, Alicia Orozco, Juan Márquez.

● Pau and his mother leave Barcelona for a Pyrenean village where his brother, who's unexpectedly committed suicide, had been living for some years; there they meet his lover and friends, and in so doing discover more about him, themselves and each other. A quiet, gentle, contemplative film, it lacks focus, so that it's often hard to know how the characters are related to each other, let alone to take any great interest in their emotional or psychological predicament. The film's strength lies in the sure sense of time, weather and place: seldom have the distinctive light, hues, shapes and sounds of the Pyrenees been conveyed so authentically. GA

Paul and Michelle (Paul et Michelle)

(1974, Fr/GB, 105 min)
d/p Lewis Gilbert. *sc* Angela Huth, Vernon Harris. *ph* Claude Renoir. *ed* Thelma Connell. *ad* Pierre Guffroy. *m* Michel Colombier. *cast* Anicée Alvina, Sean Bury, Keir Dullea, Ronald Lewis, Catherine Allégret.

● Sequel to the soppy *Friends* (1971), in which a pair of neglected Parisian kids (aged 15 and 14) mooned through a romantic idyll in the Camargue which ended in the birth of a child. Now, leaving school three years later, Paul sets off in search of Michelle and their young daughter, and wins her away from an American airline officer (Dullea). Summer together, followed by life at the Sorbonne, conjures up flashbacks from the earlier film, much gamboling, a contrived student riot, and a gratuitous abortion. Claude Renoir's photography and Alvina's looks help some, but Dullea's air of constant embarrassment is comment enough on this extremely awkward film.

Paulie

(1997, US, 92 min)
d John Roberts. *p* Mark Gordon, Gary Levinsohn, Allison Lyon Segan. *sc* Laurie Craig. *ph* Tony Pierce-Roberts. *ed* Bruce Cannon. *pd* Dennis Washington. *m* John Debney. *cast* Gena Rowlands, Tony Shalhoub, Cheech Marin, Bruce Davison, Jay Mohr, Buddy Hackett, Hallie Kate Eisenberg, Trini Alvarado.

● To call this the best parrot film ever is to damn with faint praise; neither Rowlands nor Davison is so washed-up that they must play opposite a parrot, and both have attributed their presence to the excellent script. We first meet Paulie the parrot in the basement of an experimental centre. How did he wind up there, asks the cleaner, Misha (Shalhoub). It's a long story, replies Paulie. 'I am Russian. We love long stories,' says Misha. Fledgling Paulie was given as a present to little Marie (Eisenberg) to help her over her stutter, and in the process not only became preternaturally verbal and literate, but also evolved beyond mere mimicry. He is parted from her and spends the rest of the film trying to find her again, but it's the digressive meetings that register. There's none of the usual chase-and-destruction thought indispensable to tots, and everybody's given time to develop. Jolly good. BC

Paulina 1880

(1972, Fr, 105 min)
d Jean-Louis Bertuccelli. *p* Albina de Bois Rouvray. *sc* Albina Du Boisrouvray, Jean-Louis Bertuccelli. *ph* Andréas Winding. *ed* Françoise Ceppi. *ad* Emilio Carcano. *m* Nicolas Nabokov. *cast* Eliana de Santis, Olga Karlatos, Maximilian Schell, Michel Bouquet, Sami Frey, Romolo Valli.

● As a result of a highly repressive upbringing, super-sensual Paulina is brought to the extreme pitch of murdering her married lover. The critique of Catholicism and the late 19th century *haute bourgeoisie* intended by Bertuccelli (who made his debut the previous year with the impressive *Ramparts of Clay*) is unfortunately smothered by a blandly 'beautiful' treatment and an insistent glamorisation of victim Paulina. It hovers on the edge of good film-making, but never quite makes the grade. VG

Pauline à la Plage (Pauline at the Beach)

(1982, Fr, 95 min)
d Eric Rohmer. *p* Margaret Ménégoz. *sc* Eric Rohmer. *ph* Nestor Almendros. *ed* Cécile Decugis. *m* Jean-Louis Velero. *cast* Arielle Dombasle, Amanda Langlet, Pascal Greggory, Feodor Atkine, Simon de la Brosse, Rosette.

● Rohmer, in the third of his 'Comedies and Proverbs', may still be tiptoeing delightfully through the same verbose ground that he's covered for years, but no other director so clearly reveals the distances between words and meaning, thought and action. Here his 15-year-old heroine (Langlet) goes on holiday, and instead of fun finds a perverse, sometimes painful lesson in the emotional games of the adult world: as her older cousin (Dombasle) rejects a boring old flame and lurches into an affair with a sly advocate of freedom in relationships, she witnesses the trio's discussions, double standards, and deceit. Dispensing with heavy plotting as he coolly observes and dissects well-meaning but frequently cruel human interaction, Rohmer yet again proves his ability to merge poignancy and humour by means of delicately nuanced performances and naturalistic but pointed dialogue. GA

Pauline & Paulette

(2001, Bel/Neth/Fr, 78 min)
d Lieven Debrauwer. *p* Dominique Janne. *sc* Lieven Debrauwer, Jaak Boon. *ph* Michel van Laer. *ed* Philippe Ravoet. *ad* Hilde Duyck. *m* Frédéric Devreese. *cast* Ann Petersen, Dora van der Groen, Rosemarie Bergmans, Idwig Stéphane, Julienne de Bruyn, Camilia Blereau, Nanda Buyl, Magda Cnudde, Jef Demedts.

● The moral of this homely fable concerns not its retarded heroine – could she absorb a lesson? it would be good to find out – but her mentally normal sister, charged with mild hubris. Pauline, a childlike septuagenarian (van der Groen), worships her sister Paulette (Petersen), the local florist. The feeling isn't mutual, but Pauline is left on Paulette's hands when their eldest sister Martha cops it at the outset: Martha's will dictates that one of her surviving sisters keep Pauline out of a home – and fourth sister Cécile (Stéphane) lives with a Frenchman in faraway Brussels. Writer/director Debrauwer has some gentle fun with visual contrasts – the drab browns of Martha's cottage; Paulette's florid pinks and reds; clean, hard Brussels – and with the usual misunderstandings and embarrassments wrought by Pauline's blithe behaviour. It's a sweet, pat film, a hit on home territory, that doesn't exactly gloss over its questions, but never deeply probes them either. NB

Paura, La

see Fear

Paura e amore

see Three Sisters

Paura nella Città dei Morti Viventi (City of the Living Dead/The Gates of Hell)

(1980, It, 93 min)
d Lucio Fulci. *p* Giovanni Masini. *sc* Lucio Fulci, Dardano Sacchetti. *ph* Sergio Salvati. *ed* Vincenzo Tomassi. *pd* Massimo Antonello Geleng. *m* Fabio Frizzi. *cast* Christopher George, Janet Agren, Katriona MacColl, Carlo De Mejo, Antonella Interlenghi.

● Low-grade actors wander Salem and one by one become victims, then members, of a group of mouldy, maggotty corpses performing motiveless murders. It's laughably awful; though with its nonsensical 'plot' randomly constructed according to the illogic of fear, and its grotesque emphasis on physical mutability, fragmentation and decay, it could just conceivably be the sort of disreputable movie the Surrealists would have loved. GA

Pavlova – A Woman for All Time (aka Anna Pavlova)

(1983, GB/USSR, 133 min)
d/sc Emil Lotianou. *ph* Evgeni Guslinsky, Vladimir Nakhabtsev *ed* I Kalatikova, E Galkina, Jim Connock. *ad* Boris Blank. *m* Evgeny Dogas. *cast* Galina Beliaeva, James Fox, Sergei Shakourov, Vsevolod Larionov, Martin Scorsese, Bruce Forsyth, Roy Kinnear.

● A rendering of highlights from the life of the celebrated dancer, this is less an entertainment than the by-product of a dotty Western/Soviet trade deal. The film was in negotiation for years before it went before the cameras and then, very briefly, before a few unenthusiastic spectators. All that keeps its memory alive is the footnote it adds to the career of Michael Powell, nominally supervising the film's suitability for anglophone audiences. During the diplomatic cosying up on the project, wildly improbable casting options were aired, including Brando as Diaghilev. As it turned out, the cast was fairly improbable anyway – Scorsese, Bruce Forsyth, Roy Kinnear, none of whom, alas, plays Diaghilev either. DO

Paw (Boy of Two Worlds/ The Lure of the Jungle/ Pao of the Jungle)

(1959, Den, 93 min)
d Astrid Henning-Jensen. *p* Mogens Skot-Hansen. *sc* Torry Gredsted, Astrid Henning-Jensen, Bjarne Henning-Jensen. *ph* Henning Bendtsen, Niels Carstens, Arthur Christiansen. *ed* Anker Sørensen. *cast* Jimmy Sterman, Edvin Adolphson, Ebba Amfeldt, Asbjørn Andersen, Svend Billie, Ego Brønnum-Jacobsen, Helge Kjærulff-Schmidt, Karen Lykkehus, Preben Neergaard, Freddy Pedersen, Karl Stegger, Ninja Tholstrup, Sacha Wamberg.

●The orphaned Paw (Sterman), 'a Boy of Two Worlds,' is imported to Denmark from the West Indies to live with his aunt. His natural inclination for the Great Outdoors is bolstered by the bullying and misunderstanding he meets in his new rural community, and after an apprenticeship with the local poacher, he goes to ground like a fox. Partly a plea for innocence, tolerance and reconciliation, the film is determined to find common ground for its various village factions, but its ambivalence about the natural order of hunter and prey makes intriguing drama, and the director's nature documentary approach, constantly cutting away to local animal life, adds a certain contemplative depth. NB

Pawnbroker, The

(1964, US, 115 min, b/w)
d Sidney Lumet. *p* Roger H Lewis, Philip Langner. *sc* David Friedkin, Morton Fine. *ph* Boris Kaufman. *ed* Ralph Rosenblum. *pd* Richard Sylbert. *m* Quincy Jones. *cast* Rod Steiger, Geraldine Fitzgerald, Jaime Sanchez, Brock Peters, Thelma Oliver, Baruch Lumet, Juano Hernandez, Raymond St Jacques.

●An uneasy mixture of European art movie (the Resnais-like flashbacks that punctuate the narrative) and American *ciné-vérité* (it was shot on the streets of New York), *The Pawnbroker* never achieves the intensity its subject matter threatens. It's almost as though Lumet was unsure as to whether he wanted to shock or move his audience with the story of a Jewish pawnbroker (Steiger) who is finally forced to leave the world of his concentration camp memories as the pressures of living in Harlem force themselves upon him. PH

Paws

(1997, GB/Aust, 84 min)
d Karl Zwicky. *p* Andrena Finlay, Vicki Watson. *sc* Harry Cripps. *ph* Geoff Burton. *ed* Nick Holmes. *pd* Steven Jones-Evans. *m* Mario Millo. *cast* Billy Connolly (voice), Nathan Cavaleri, Emilie Francois, Joe Petruzzi, Caroline Gillmer, Rachael Blake, Sandy Gore.

●Connolly's voice-over is the one redeeming feature of this Australian oddity. 'PC' is a Jack Russell with above-average intelligence – when connected to a crude portable computer system (old circuit boards, elastic bands and a plastic lunch box), he's able to speak. After the mysterious murder of his elderly owner, PC shows up at the Feldman household in suburban Sydney and types commands into the computer of teenage Zac (Cavaleri). It transpires that the dog's former owner had salted away a fortune, leaving clues to its whereabouts on a floppy disk. DA

Payback

(1998, US, 101 min)
d Brian Helgeland. *p* Bruce Davey. *sc* Brian Helgeland, Terry Hayes. *ph* Ericson Core. *ed* Kevin Stitt. *pd* Richard Hoover. *m* Chris Boardman. *cast* Mel Gibson, Maria Bello, Kris Kristofferson, William Devane, James Coburn, David Paymer, Deborah Kara Unger.

●Porter (Gibson) is the sort of guy who'll steal the notes from a blind beggar. Ripped off in a heist and left for dead by his wife and best friend, he's not about to take such treachery lying down. Director/co-writer Helgeland had a hand in *LA Confidential*, so there's a certain amount of pedigree here (the source novel is Richard Stark's *The Hunter*, previously filmed by John Boorman as *Point Blank*). Helgeland also co-scripted Mel Gibson's *Conspiracy Theory*, a paranoia thriller in the 1970s mode – but with a happy ending. Though there are no explicit date references, *Payback* is styled as a '70s movie manqué: dial phones and chunky automobiles; desaturated colour palette; funky soul/jazz score. The conceit even extends to the supporting roles, with such veterans as Kristofferson, Devane and Coburn representing 'the Outfit'. Sadly, it doesn't have the courage of its convictions. Where even a fair-to-middling '70s thriller like *Hustle* took its nihilism straight, this feels like a put-on. TCh

Payday

(1972, US, 103 min)
d Daryl Duke. *p* Martin Fink, Don Carpenter. *sc* Don Carpenter. *ph* Richard C Glouner. *ed* Richard Halsey. *cast* Rip Torn, Ahna Capri, Elayne Heilveil, Michael C Gwynne, Jeff Morris, Cliff Emmich.

●For the most part this is an accurate and observant movie about a country and western singer on the road. Doubts about the commercial viability of such a project are reflected in the introduction of overly dramatic elements into the script (a manslaughter and a last-scene death). But it remains one of those welcome movies made by people with genuine knowledge of their subject, on the assumption that their audience is going to be reasonably knowledgeable and interested in the first place. Rip Torn makes a credible middle-weight country star…petulant, arrogant and vulnerable; and the support players are well cast (particularly Gwynne as the band's manager, whose job involves immediately converting every incident into commercial terms). Not a total success, but anyone in any way fascinated by the music business should be stimulated. JC

Pay It Forward

(2000, US, 123 min)
d Mimi Leder. *p* Steven Reuther, Peter Abrams, Robert L Levy. *sc* Leslie Dixon. *ph* Oliver Stapleton. *ed* David Rosenbloom. *pd* Leslie Dilley. *m* Thomas Newman. *cast* Kevin Spacey, Helen Hunt, Haley Joel Osment, Jay Mohr, James Caviezel, Jon Bon Jovi, Angie Dickinson.

●This soft-boiled sub-Spielbergian mush is a children's film for grown-ups who never grew up. In a scurrilous bid to muscle in on Robin Williams' territory, Spacey plays social studies teacher Eugene Simonet, a virgin with bad skin and a preposterous vocabulary. Mr Simonet sets a class project: to think of an idea to change our world and act on it. Lonely, serious Trevor (Osment) comes up with an inspired wheeze. He brings home a tramp (Caviezel), gives him a place to stay for the night, and sets him straight on a few things. Don't return the favour to me, he tells him, pay it forward to three strangers, and tell each to do the same. Only a hardcore cynic would diss such an altruistic daydream but somewhere along the line the message gets scrambled. A singularly ill-judged, suspense-crushing subplot has reporter Mohr tracing the phenomenon from its tentacles in Chicago, where one man has given a perfect stranger his Jaguar. The script's relatively realist Las Vegas milieu is ill-served by director Leder's sentimental overkill, while Spacey and Hunt (as Trevor's alcoholic waitress mom) make heavy weather of being normal. (From the novel by Catherine Ryan Hyde.) TCh

Payroll

(1961, GB, 105 min)
d Sidney Hayers. *p* Norman Priggen. *sc* George Baxt. *ph* Ernest Steward. *ed* Tristram Cones. *ad* Jack Shampan. *m* Reg Owen. *cast* Michael Craig, Françoise Prévost, Billie Whitelaw, Kenneth Griffith, William Lucas, Tom Bell, Barry Keegan, Joan Rice.

●Treading Tyneside territory a decade before *Get Carter*, this crime thriller features a gang of unlikely Geordies as the target of the vengeance-seeking widow of a security guard killed in a factory payroll heist. Nerve-ends snap a little too patly on cue as the noose tightens, but the fresh use of provincial backdrops (part of the British cinema's belatedly sudden discovery of 'the North') and the oddly assorted casting exercise their own fascination. PT

Peacemaker, The

(1997, US, 124 min)
d Mimi Leder. *p* Walter F Parkes, Branko Lustig. *sc* Michael Schiffer. *ph* Dietrich Lohmann. *ed* David Rosenbloom, Paul Cichocki. *pd* Leslie Dilley. *m* Hans Zimmer. *cast* George Clooney, Nicole Kidman, Armin Mueller-Stahl, Marcel Iures, Alexander Baluev.

●When an explosive train-collision in deepest Russia results in radioactive fallout, spunky boffin Kidman and shit kickin' Colonel Clooney (briefly at odds) are despatched East to trace terrorists suspected of smuggling Soviet nuclear weapons into countries less stable, safe and, dammit, less civilised and cherishable than the USA. The ultimate horror arises when the man behind it all (Iures), seemingly a meek Bosnian music professor, arrives armed and dangerous in NY. If this sounds cynical, maybe that's unfair on the action sequences, mostly well directed (albeit often at excessive length) by Mimi Leder, an *ER* veteran whose first feature this is. It's also a little harsh on the efficient, attractive Kidman and Clooney; on Iures, who lends the prof a modicum of dignity (though his principles are explained only in terms of vengeful grief); and on Mueller-Stahl, whose good Russian – the movie's best performance – disappears all too soon. But Michael Schiffer's half-hearted liberal script remains riddled with the xenophobic stereotyping mistaken by Hollywood fat cats for an accurate depiction of the world. That said, fair fireballs. GA

Peach-Blossom Land, The (Anlian Taohuayuan)

(1992, Tai, 107 min)
d Stan Lai. *p* Ding Nai-Chu. *sc* Stan Lai. *ph* Christopher Doyle. *ed* Chen Po-Wen. *pd* William Chang Suk-Ping. *m* Fumio Itabashi, Kazutoki Umezu. *cast* Brigitte Lin, Jin Shijie, Li Lijun, Ismene Ting.

●Based on his own stage play, Stan Lai's feature debut is a textbook lesson in finding cinema within and beyond theatre. A rehearsal space has been double booked. One troupe wants to work on *Hidden Love*, a sob story about an old man's memories of his one great love in old Shanghai. The other is shambling through a farcical parody of the classical *Peach-Blossom Land*, in which a cuckolded peasant stumbles into utopia but cannot get past his earthly woes. It's predictable that the two plays will intersect to produce new meanings, but not so obvious that those meanings turn out to be working notes for an analysis of key problems in modern Chinese culture. Lai sensibly hired the creative team from *Days of Being Wild* (cameraman Chris Doyle, designer William Chang) to help him hone a credible cinematic style. TR

Peaches

(2000, Ire/GB, 85 min)
d Nick Grosso. *p* Ronan Glennane, Max Stubblefield. *sc* Nick Grosso. *ph* Brendan Galvin. *ed* Niamh Fagan. *pd* Jessica Coyle. *cast* Matthew Rhys, Kelly Reilly, Justin Salinger, Matthew Dunster, Sophie Okonedo, Emily Hillier, Stephanie Bagshaw.

●Frank is looking forward to another summer of boozing and screwing – vaguely aware that this could be his last downtime before he's sucked into a job. He's got a rent-free flat with a mate in Kentish Town, N London, but he's scoring poorly with the girls, and doesn't know how he feels about Cherry, who might at least improve his average. Grosso's adaptation of his laddish play shows promise, but he's no director. Too often the actors are marooned in front of a static, unreceptive camera, and he has no idea how to end a scene (or a movie). Still, if you can stomach the excesses of boys behaving badly, it provides larks, a top soundtrack and further proof that Kelly Reilly is someone to watch. TCh

Pearl Harbor

(2001, US, 180 min)
d Michael Bay. *p* Jerry Bruckheimer, Michael Bay. *sc* Randall Wallace. *ph* John Schwartzman. *ed* Chris Lebenzon, Steven Rosenblum, Mark Goldblatt, Roger Barton. *pd* Nigel Phelps. *m* Hans Zimmer. *cast* Ben Affleck, Josh Hartnett, Kate Beckinsale, Cuba Gooding Jr, Tom Sizemore, Jon Voight, Colm Feore, Mako, Alec Baldwin, Ewen Bremner, Dan Aykroyd.

●Bay and Bruckheimer's previous movie, the action-fest *Armageddon*, is crudely rehashed here, with the Japanese bombing of Pearl Harbor, Hawaii, in December 1941 standing in for global holocaust – but at inflated cost and length, and with added romance. Is the money on the screen? Yes, because massive WWII-style air attacks are astronomically expensive to mount these days. And on a purely technical level, the team's thrilling mastery of the cinematic kinesis of exploding matter is reaffirmed (though Hans Zimmer's martial-romantic noise is acceptably muted). Visually, the alternating paradise-island gloss and nuclear-fallout chic drips money like one long advertisement. The plot endlessly strings out a standard love triangle – Tennessee crop-duster's son turned ace pilot Rafe (Affleck, overawed) and his childhood pal and fellow pilot Danny (Hartnett, cute as fuck) set their caps in turn at nurse Evelyn (Beckinsale) – you know won't be over by next Christmas. Bare grace notes include the stately procession of standing officers in dress whites through the carnage, accompanied by a Barber-esque adagio; and Gooding's 'Dorie' Miller, the cook who understates his conspicuous bravery. Otherwise this bunk is history. WH

Pearl of Death, The

(1944, US, 69 min, b/w)
d/p Roy William Neill. *sc* Bertram Millhauser. *ph* Virgil Miller. *ed* Ray Snyder. *ad* John Goodman, Martin Obzina. *m* Paul Sawtell. *cast* Basil Rathbone, Nigel Bruce, Evelyn Ankers, Miles Mander, Dennis Hoey, Rondo Hatton.
●Holmes and Watson on the trail of the Borgia pearl, hastily hidden after its theft in a plaster bust of Napoleon, and simultaneously sought by the criminal's horrific henchman, the Creeper. Neill does his usual neat job on this adaptation of *The Six Napoleons*, with the atmosphere considerably enhanced by the introduction of the monstrous, silently prowling Creeper. Rondo Hatton, who played the part, suffered from a rare glandular deformity and became a sinister horror movie heavy before his disease killed him in 1946. PT

Pearls of the Crown, The

see Perles de la Couronne, Les

Pearls of the Deep (Perlicky na dne)

(1965, Czech, 107 min, b/w & col)
d Jirí Menzel, Jan Nemec, Vera Chytilová, Jaromil Jires, Evald Schorm. *sc* Bohumil Hrabal, Jirí Menzel, Jan Nemec, Ewald Schorm, Vera Chytilova, Jaromil Jires. *ph* Jaroslav Kucrea. *ed* Jirina Lukesova, Miroslav Hajek. *ad* Oldrich Bosak. *m* Jan Klusak, Jirí Sust. *cast* Pavla Marsálková, Ferdinand Kruta, Josefa Pecháltová, Vera Mrázková.
●This episode film from the days of the New Wave, based on stories by the writer of *Closely Observed Trains* (Bohumil Hrabal), provides a heady reminder of Czech fashions. The thing closely observed here is death, seen at work in locations like a geriatric hospital (Nemec's episode), a Grand Prix motor race (Menzel), and a self-service restaurant (Chytilová). But the mood is the customary one of ironic contemplation, shading into overt fantasy; sometimes the mixture is clumsily handled (Chytilová and Schorm are the main culprits), yet it's mostly successful. GB

Peasants of the Second Fortress, The (Sanrizuka: Daini Toride no Hitobito)

(1971, Jap, 143 min, b/w)
d/p/sc Shinsuke Ogawa. *ph* Masaki Tamura. *ed* Shinsuke Ogawa.
●The fourth film of six devoted to the peasant communities of Sanrizuka, giving a complete documentation of an important political struggle in Japan. Excellently photographed, it records a six-year battle (thus far successful) between peasants and the State over farmland which the government wished to take over for a new airport: a useful reminder that the forces of pollution can be stemmed by concerted action. Ogawa has the fortunate ability to let people and events speak for themselves, while remaining evidently compassionate, curious, and carefully selective in his handling of the material. An admirable political film. JDuC

Peau d'Ane (The Magic Donkey)

(1970, Fr, 89 min)
d Jacques Demy. *p* Mag Bodard. *sc* Jacques Demy. *ph* Ghislain Cloquet. *ed* Anne Marie Cotret. *ad* Jacques Dugied, Jim Léon. *m* Michel Legrand. *cast* Catherine Deneuve, Jean Marais, Jacques Perrin, Delphine Seyrig, Micheline Presle, Fernand Ledoux, Sacha Pitoeff, Henri Crémieux.
●Even on paper this couldn't have seemed such a terrific idea, and Demy's attempt to fuse Cocteau with Disney via one of Perrault's less endearing conceits (a gold-shitting donkey) contrives to be both garish and coyly tasteful. Deneuve sings four Michel Legrand ballads whose resemblance to each other is matched by their resemblance to the composer's earlier work, while a soppy Perrin emerges as more Prince Charles than Prince Charming. To its credit are Delphine Seyrig as a chic, malicious Fairy Godmother, and Marais as the genuinely Cocteau-esque King. GAd

Peau d'homme coeur de bête

see Skin of Man, Heart of Beast

Peau Douce, La (Silken Skin/The Soft Skin)

(1964, Fr, 118 min, b/w)
d François Truffaut. *sc* François Truffaut, Jean-Louis Richard. *ph* Raoul Coutard. *ed* Claudine Bouché. *m* Georges Delerue. *cast* Jean Desailly, Françoise Dorléac, Nelly Bénédetti, Daniel Ceccaldi, Laurence Badie, Jean Lanier.
●A superb tragi-comedy of adultery in which a middle-aged intellectual ducking out from under a demanding wife tries to turn a casual affair with an air hostess into the love of his life, but succeeds only in triggering a calamitous *crime passionel*. Wry, disenchanted, directed with an astonishingly acute eye for the disruptions of modern urban living (the film is punctuated by gears changing in cars, lights being switched on and off), it is rather as though the airily fantastic triangle of *Jules and Jim* had been subjected to a cold douche of reality. Between the two films, Truffaut had been preparing his book on Hitchcock, and the lesson of the master, evident in the rigour of Truffaut's direction, is even more pleasingly applied in the irony whereby the hero's chosen mistress turns out to be a cool, teasingly uninvolved blonde, while all the passion lurks in the dark wife's libido. TM

Peau Neuve (A New Skin)

(1999, Fr, 96 min)
d Emilie Deleuze. *p* Carole Scotta. *sc* Emilie Deleuze, Laurent Guyot, Guy Laurent. *ph* Antoine Héberlé. *ed* Fabrice Rouaud. *pd* Jimmy Vansteenkiste, Moundji Gaceb Couture. *m* L'Attirail, Supersonic. *cast* Samuel Le Bihan, Marcial Di Fonzo Bo, Catherine Vinatier, Claire Nebout, Fabien Lucciarini.
●The kind of film perhaps only the French would make, would want to make, and would carry off so subtly. It focuses on a bored video-game tester who, much to the puzzlement of his wife and four-year-old daughter, decides – at the suggestion of a careers officer he's had a fling with – to throw it all in and take a four-month course training to operate bulldozers. Miles from the home he now visits only occasionally at weekends, he is befriended by, among others, a dimwitted bulldozer fanatic whose obsession, sadly, doesn't provide him with the ability to drive the machines. The film simply assesses the pressures exerted on the protagonist's home life by his new relationships, interests and aspirations, with a low key realism wholly lacking in Loachian didacticism; for all its lack of sentimentality, this is a warm, witty, perceptive and utterly credible study of the kind of ordinary people seldom found in western movies. GA

Pebble and the Penguin, The

(1995, US, 74 min)
d Don Bluth. *p* Russell Boland. *sc* Racheal Koretsky, Steve Whitestone. *m* Barry Manilow, Mark Watters. *cast* voices: Martin Short, James Belushi, Tim Curry, Shani Wallis.
●The bold, Technicolor palette used against Antarctic white is pleasurable, and the film fair rattles through its formula set-pieces. And if the coat-tailed penguins resemble puff-cheeked (Yogi) bears and (Minnie) mice more than true *sphenisciformes*, that's par for the cartoon course. But the romantic plot is excruciating. Dork penguin Hubie falls for flutter-eyed babe Marina in the run-up to the match-making 'Full Moon Ceremony', but nasty Drake pushes him out of the way – into a half-hour of escapades on the high seas. Can he make it back with the requisite pebble (part of the real-life mating ritual of the Adeli penguins, it seems) before she meets a fate worse than death? The characterisations are weak and unendearing. Worse, the big 'action' sequences turn up with the pacing and predictability of clock chimes. And, in what is perhaps the last great medium for musicals, the perfunctoriness of Barry Manilow's songs and arrangements seem guaranteed to put off yet another generation. WH

Peccato Veniale

see Venial Sin

Péché originel

see Original Sin

Pecker

(1998, US, 86 min)
d John Waters. *p* John Fiedler, Mark Tarlov. *sc* John Waters. *ph* Robert Stevens. *ed* Janice Hampton. *pd* Vincent Peranio. *m* Stewart Copeland. *cast* Edward Furlong, Christina Ricci, Bess Armstrong. Mark Joy, Mary Kay Place, Martha Plimpton, Mink Stole, Lili Taylor, Patricia Hearst.
●There was never much of a centre to Waters' films, and now he's lost his edge too. Occasional burger bar chef and full-time photo enthusiast Pecker (Furlong) stalks his local Baltimore backwater, ceaselessly snapping his colourful, spaced-out and/or degenerate family, friends (including laundromat-tyrannising girlfriend Ricci) and neighbours. One greasy spoon exhibition later and Taylor's NY art dealer snaps up this documentarist of the 'culturally challenged' for her own nefarious metropolitan purposes – only for Pecker to take his camera to the Big Apple and turn the tables. That's the sum of the kitsch concoction, Waters' cutest, most homely fluff yet. Nowadays the Farrelly Bros do tastelessness, low-life empathy and crap camera angles with far more wit and verve. NB

Peddler, The (Dastforoush)

(1987, Iran, 95 min)
d/sc/ed Mohsen Makhmalbaf. *ph* Homayun Payvar, Mehrdad Fakhini, Ali R Zarindast. *m* Majid Entezam. *cast* Zohreh Saramadi, Esmail Saramadian, Morteza Zarrabi, Behzad Behzadpoor.
●A trilogy of low-key misery set in the poor quarters and shanty suburbs of modern Teheran, *The Peddler* plumbs depths of unhappiness usually the territory of David Lynch, with none of his redeeming humour. From the title shot – of a pickled foetus revolving slowly in a bottle – onwards, the stories are grisly viewing. Babies are abandoned to the mercies of grinning lunatics; sheep are slaughtered in protracted detail; the elderly are left to rot. Mankind lives in terror, courting death; the overall effect is numbing. RS

Pedestrian, The (Der Fussgänger)

(1973, WGer/Switz, 97 min)
d Maximilian Schell. *p* Maximilian Schell, Zev Braun. *sc* Maximilian Schell. *ph* Wolfgang Treu, Klaus Koenig. *ed* Dagmar Hirtz. *m* Manos Hadjidakis. *cast* Gustav Rudolf Sellner, Maximilian Schell, Peter Hall, Gila von Weitershausen, Peggy Ashcroft, Elisabeth Bergner, Lil Dagover, Françoise Rosay
●A strange excursion into writing, producing and directing for actor Schell, with a depressing tale of an elderly German industrialist whose life falls apart after he is banned from driving due to an accident in which his son is killed. The press claims he is a war criminal, workers at his factory get restless, and confusion sets in with a vengeance. Notable mainly for its weird casting: the gaggle of grandes dames; Sellner, in the lead part, was head of the Berlin Opera; and yes, it is the Peter Hall, playing a scandal-mongering newspaper editor. GA

Peeper

(1975, US, 87 min)
d Peter Hyams. *p* Irwin Winkler, Robert Chartoff. *sc* WD Richter. *ph* Earl Rath. *ed* James Mitchell. *pd* Albert Brenner. *m* Richard Clements. *cast* Michael Caine, Natalie Wood, Kitty Winn, Thayer David, Liam Dunn, Dorothy Adams, Timothy Carey.
●A lame spoof of the '40s private eye thriller. Doubts set in with the credits, read off by 'Humphrey Bogart' (impersonator Jerry Lacy) standing in a dark alley, although what follows could have worked if only the director and cast had found the right pace and inflection for WD Richter's script, a satisfying pastiche which has the nice touch of not having anyone killed. In addition, the depth of the sets, period detail, and richly dark photography all conspire against the film's stars. Wood makes a distinctly un-fatale contribution, and Caine looks totally miscast as a Cockney private eye in California; even Segal and Audran, so disappointing in *The Black Bird*, outclass them. Like that film, this comedy reworking of the detective thriller, a type of film that often carried enough wit of its own, invites only detrimental comparisons. CPe

Peeping Tom

(1960, GB, 109 min)
d/p Michael Powell. *sc* Leo Marks. *ph* Otto Heller. *ed* Noreen Ackland. *ad* Arthur Lawson. *m* Brian Easdale. *cast* Karl Böhm, Anna Massey, Maxine Audley, Moira Shearer, Esmond Knight, Michael Goodliffe, Shirley Anne Field, Brenda Bruce.
●In the early '60s, there was one brave film (which had nothing to do with kitchen sinks or working class tragedies) which struggled single-handed to drag the British cinema into the present tense: Michael Powell's phenomenal *Peeping Tom*. It centres on scoptophilia (voyeurism, or the morbid desire to watch), and so the central character naturally works in movies; but his obsessions are compounded by his childhood experiences at the hands of his father, a psychologist interested in the mechanisms of human fear, and he grows up with a helpless compulsion to kill. Mark Lewis (Böhm, later rediscovered by Fassbinder for *Fox*) is the most gentle of psychopaths, an eternal victim whose crimes are cries of rage against his father and stepmother, and at the same time pathetic rehearsals for his own inevitable death. A Freudian script of notable maturity teases limitless implications from this premise, while maintaining a healthy sense of humour. First-timers may care to note that Daddy in this Oedipal riddle is played by Michael Powell. TR

Pee-Wee's Big Adventure

(1985, US, 91 min)
d Tim Burton. *p* Robert Shapiro, Richard Gilbert Abramson. *sc* Phil Hartman, Paul Reubens [Paul Reubenfeld], Michael Varhol. *ph* Victor J Kemper. *ed* Billy Weber. *pd* David L Snyder. *m* Danny Elfman. *cast* Paul Reubens, Elizabeth Daily, Mark Holton, Diane Salinger, Judd Omen, Tony Bill, James Brolin.
●Fed by comic tributaries perhaps, but Pee-Wee Herman comes over as a delightful original. It's a balancing act, and he doesn't put a '50s preppy white buckskin wrong. He lives in a house which is a Heath Robinsonish turn in itself, and responds to his environment with all the restraint of a streaker in a carwash. A nasty boy steals his beloved bicycle. Pee-Wee gives chase, taking in a lot of America's tourist map and winding up in Hollywood (which buys his adventure, and we see their version too). Dreamlike situations hover on the edge of unease (a meeting with a waitress in the mouth of a model dinosaur, pursuit by her giant boyfriend waving a caveman's bone), and there's a wonderfully sustained gag in which Pee-Wee rescues animals from a burning pet shop, nervously stalling the snakes. The score works edgily against the comedy, and the dream sequences are just this side of Dali. Pee-Wee himself comes from the school of acting that usually sits under a bubble – Rage, Foiled, Idea – in a cartoon. Truly weird and wonderfully addictive. BC

Peggy Sue Got Married

(1986, US, 103 min)
d Francis Coppola. *p* Paul R Gurian. *sc* Jerry Leichtling, Arlene Sarner. *ph* Jordan Cronenweth. *ed* Barry Malkin. *pd* Dean Taoularis. *m* John Barry. *cast* Kathleen Turner, Nicolas Cage, Barry Miller, Catherine Hicks, Joan Allen, Barbara Harris, Don Murray, Maureen O'Sullivan, Leon Ames, Jim Carrey.
●More relaxed – sloppy, even – than any of Coppola's usual busy films, this explores that universal fantasy of getting a second chance at your youth: a 40-year-old Turner faints at her high school reunion, and wakes 20 years earlier in 1960 during her last schooldays. The crux of her return is to sort out what later became a less-than-successful marriage to her feckless husband (Cage in endearingly dopey form). The movie is unfortunately bound to be compared with the much slicker *Back to the Future*. Ignore the ridiculous happy ending of this film, and you have a much more fatalistic exercise in which Coppola eschews easy laughs in favour of the exposure of feeling and the fact that these people's lives, however empty, matter to them. Turner is in the Oscar class. CPea

Peg of Old Drury

(1935, GB, 77 min, b/w)
d/p Herbert Wilcox. *sc* Miles Malleson. *ph* Freddie Young. *ed* Merril G White. *ad* LP Williams. *m* Roy Robertson. *cast* Anna Neagle, Jack Hawkins, Cedric Hardwicke, Hay Petrie, Margaretta Scott, Mairie O'Neill, Arthur Sinclair, Sara Allgood.
●Biopic of 18th century Irish actress Peg Woffington. With curly hair, gypsy earrings and an excruciating Irish accent, Neagle's Peg is intended as a warm earthy hussy. 'That David Garrick, sure he's the broth of a man,' is typical of her banter (script by Miles Malleson from the play *Masks and Faces* by Charles Reade and Tom Taylor). But there's not a hint of spontaneity or passion about her performance. Even when she's swilling beer with the male members of the Steak and Kidney Club, or dressed as a young swell, fighting a duel in the Vauxhall Gardens, there's always a Home Counties reserve, a coldness, about her. When she sings, she sounds suspiciously like Vera Lynn. Even stiffer is Sir Cedric Hardwicke as Garrick, a pompous, porcine figure with a ridiculous bellow of a voice. Wilcox is so determined to remind us of his high art credentials that he continually slows up the action with dreary static scenes of his stars reciting Shakespeare on stage. GM

Peking Opera Blues (Dao Ma Dan)

(1986, HK, 105 min)
d/p/pd Tsui Hark. *sc* To Kwok-wai. *ph* Poon Hung-seng. *ed* David Wu. *m* James Wong. *cast* Brigitte Lin, Cherie Chung, Sally Yeh, Mark Cheng, Wu Ma.
●You need a fairly thorough-going grasp of the political and factional fall out from China's 1911 revolution to make sense of the plot (in which two undercover revolutionaries set out to foil warlord Yuan Shikai's plan to expand his territory), not to mention a working knowledge of traditional Peking Opera. Happily, the plot doesn't matter. The film is a speed-crazed riff on what happens when a spy melodrama meets a backstage comedy: Feydeau with blood at 150 beats per minute. Everyone in it is sparky (especially Brigitte Lin, in male drag for the first time), and most of the gags are pretty funny. But Tsui's kinetic dazzle is the main thing. TR

Pelican Brief, The

(1993, US, 141 min)
d Alan J Pakula. *p* Alan J Pakula, Pieter Jan Brugge. *sc* Alan J Pakula. *ph* Stephen Goldblatt. *ed* Tom Rolf, Trudy Ship. *pd* Philip Rosenberg. *m* James Horner. *cast* Julia Roberts, Denzel Washington, Sam Shepard, John Heard, Tony Goldwyn, James B Sikking, Robert Culp, John Lithgow.
●The assassination of two Supreme Court justices has bewildered the nation, but not coltish, flame-haired law student Darby Shaw (Roberts), whose unofficial conspiracy theory is shockingly vindicated by anonymous hitmen. Exit Darby's sozzled mentor Callahan (Shepard), enter crusading reporter Grantham (Washington). Writer/director Pakula's adaptation of John Grisham's potboiler is a classy but transparent reintroduction to Roberts' sympathetic spunky/vulnerable screen presence (and also, regrettably, to her limited range). Washington, on the other hand, breathes composure and self-assurance, despite finding himself fighting with his impatient news editor, clarifying the plot with a sketchy flow-diagram, and other clichés from the thriller-hack's manual. An old hand at this sort of thing, Pakula goes through the motions, but not much more. TCh

Pelle the Conqueror (Pelle Erobreren)

(1987, Den/Swe, 150 min)
d Bille August. *p* Per Holst. *sc* Bille August. *ph* Jörgen Persson. *ed* Janus Billeskov Jansen. *pd* Anna Asp. *m* Stefan Nilsson. *cast* Max von Sydow, Pelle Hvenegaard, Astrid Villaume.
●The moralistic plot of August's literary adaptation (it's based on the first part of Martin Andersen Nexo's four-volume novel) revolves around the adventures of turn-of-the-century Swedish emigrants Lasse (von Sydow) and his son Pelle (Hvenegaard), who seek their fortunes in Denmark. But life's no better abroad, with employment and lodgings secured under back-breaking conditions at a large farm. Underdog labourers find comfort in each other's company, while their rich employers in the big house can trust no one. Against the backdrop of the changing seasons, wide-eyed Pelle is on hand to witness relationships form and flounder. Despite occasional lapses into sentimentality, the film is saved by its performances and its uncluttered depiction of harsh impoverished lives. Von Sydow towers above the rest of the cast with an immensely moving, tender depiction of a man cowed by age and servitude. Some dramatic intensity is nevertheless dissipated by the sheer number of conflicts contained within the two-and-a-half hours running time. CM

Pelvis

(1977, US, 83 min)
d RT Megginson. *p* Lew Mishkin, RT Megginson. *sc* Straw Weisman. *ph* Lloyd Freidus. *ed* RT Megginson *ad* John Lawless. *cast* Luther 'Bud' Whaney, Mary Mitchell, Cindy Tree, Bobby Astyr, Billy Pagett.
●Hick musician Purvis (Whaney) leaves his Southern sweetheart Betty-Lou (Mitchell), comes to New York, and meets up with agent Suzie Starmonger (Tree), who changes his name to Pelvis and puts him on the road to success: he sings bad-taste songs like 'Nazi Lady' and ends up dressed completely in silver (face and all), flying as high as a kite. This crude, frantic parody has very little to do with Presley himself (though the star won fame as an impersonator), and concentrates instead on giving the whole myth of showbiz success a swift and childish kick below the belt. There are a few dotty moments, and Pelvis himself has a certain gormless charm, but in general – fergettit! GB

Pelvis of J.W., The

see Hips of John Wayne, The

Penelope 'Pulls It Off'

(1975, GB, 84 min)
d Peter Curran. *p* Elizabeth Curran, Rosemarie Walter. *sc* Jonathan Walters. *ph* Jost Graf von Hardenberg. *ed* Karl Brauer. *ad* Kathrin Kegler. *cast* Linda Marlowe, Anna Bergman, Nicholas Day, George Murcell, Horst G Fleck, Benno Hummer, Ron Kitchen Jr, Judith de la Couronne.
●Lady Charterley (Marlowe) and daughter Penelope (Ingmar's sprog Anna) meet the debts of the ancestral pile by selling forged Old Masters, and taking their clothes off (quite cheerfully). 'It's rubbish, it's rubbish,' a green parrot squawks. Filmed in West Germany. JPy

Penitentiary

(1979, US, 99 min)
d/p/sc Jamaa Fanaka. *ph* Marty Ollstein. *ed* Betsy Blankett. *ad* Adel Mazen. *m* Frankie Gaye. *cast* Leon Isaac Kennedy, Thommy Pollard, Hazel Spears, Donovan Womack, Floyd Chatman.
●A second wave blaxploitation flick, *Penitentiary* is still bedevilled by the uncomfortable contradictions of its mucho macho forebears. It's basically the serviceable yarn of the young stranger on a bum rap, sentenced to an institutional hell-hole, and eventually bucking the terror regime with two righteous fists. And daubed onto the screen with the vitality of all-round excess, teetering crazily between heavy gore and

outright farce, it works effectively as back row cheer-a-minute stuff. But its assumptions stink. Stomp the gays, screw the women, and everyone else make way for the superspade swagger. Black cinema's standing still while it merely swaps one stereotype for another, and any brothers'n'sisters routine will just have to wait till a man's done what a man's gotta do. Consciousness here is as low as the budget. A sequel, *Penitentiary II*, followed in 1982. PT

Pennies from Heaven

(1981, US, 108 min)
d Herbert Ross. *p* Nora Kaye, Herbert Ross. *sc* Dennis Potter. *ph* Gordon Willis. *ed* Richard Marks. *ad* Fred Tuch, Bernard Cutler. *m* Marvin Hamlisch, Billy May. *cast* Steve Martin, Bernadette Peters, Christopher Walken, Jessica Harper, Vernel Bagneris, John McMartin, John Karlen, Tommy Rall.

● Dennis Potter's remarkably intelligent transatlantic adaptation of his BBC serial turns the pitfalls of 'Hollywoodisation' into profit, now stressing the 'pennies' over the 'heavenly' symbolism by specifically locating Arthur Parker's grubby melodrama in the Chicago of the Depression, and culling his liberating daydreams from not only the era's popular music, but its even more culturally resonant musicals, recreated with both MGM opulence and biting Brechtian wit. Parker's search for sexual and spiritual silver linings takes him (Martin) through the dark worlds of Edward Hopper and Walker Evans, as he and fallen angel Bernadette Peters become true nighthawks whose epiphanies are those of the glitzy sound-stage production number, and who re-problematise every earnest thesis on the evils of escapism by confronting economic and emotional recession with Holmlywood's eternal currency. Let's face the music and dance, indeed. PT

Penny Gold

(1973, GB, 90 min)
d Jack Cardiff. *p* George H Brown. *sc* David Osborn, Liz Charles-Williams. *ph* Ken Hodges. *ed* John Trumper. *ad* Bert Davey. *m* John Scott. *cast* Francesca Annis, James Booth, Nicky Henson, Una Stubbs, Joseph O'Conor, Joss Ackland.

● A brilliant opening sequence, otherwise this flat-footed British thriller is hampered by something like the world's worst script, including flashbacks no one would ever conceivably flash back to, and by a cumbersome storyline about big league stamp trading. A couple of incipient themes are visible: one lingers in the juxtaposition of traveloguish footage (shot round Windsor Castle) with the *Blow-Up* style investigation into the jet set life of a girl found dead in a studio; the other is the air of evil alter ego that hangs about the dead girl's twin sister, and is dismissed in one badly written scene.

Penny Serenade

(1941, US, 125 min, b/w)
d/p George Stevens. *sc* Morrie Ryskind. *ph* Joseph Walker. *ed* Otto Meyer. *ad* Lionel Banks. *m* W Franke Harling. *cast* Irene Dunne, Cary Grant, Edgar Buchanan, Beulah Bondi, Ann Doran.

● A classic 'women's picture' in every sense: an emotional/sentimental switchback, nostalgically framed (Dunne, on the point of leaving Grant, reminisces the family-romance narrative to gramophone accompaniment), and a construction of the 'ideal' woman (fulfilled in motherhood, naturally) so upfront as to be almost disarming – though not, as in similar work by Douglas Sirk, pushed quite so far that it might be construed as being critical. Either with it or at it, or more likely both, you'll weep. PT

Pension Mimosas

(1934, Fr, 109 min, b/w)
d Jacques Feyder. *sc* Jacques Feyder, Charles Spaak. *ph* Roger Hubert. *ed* Jacques Brillouin. *ad* Lazare Meerson. *m* Armand Bernard. *cast* Françoise Rosay, Paul Bernard, Alerme, Lise Delamare, Raymond Cordy, Ila Meery, Arletty.

● Phaedra hits the Côte d'Azur in this tale of a hotel proprietor (Rosay, wife of the director) in love with her foster child, who's grown up to be a self-pitying gambling addict. A cleverly contrived darkening of mood extends from the comic opening, in which casino staff are briefed on how to handle suicides, to the despairing finale in which Rosay sets out to win a fortune for her beloved, wayward boy. The world of gambling and petty crooks and that of the happily humming little hotel are nicely counterpointed; and Arletty, with one scene only, is clearly on an unstoppable course for stardom. Feyder's detached, precisely detailed style results in a film that essentially has hardly dated at all. BBa

Penthesilea: Queen of the Amazons

(1974, GB, 99 min)
d/p/sc Laura Mulvey, Peter Wollen. *ph* Louis Castelli. *cast* Northwestern University Mime Company, Peter Wollen, Grace McKeaney.

● Mulvey and Wollen's film opens with a mime performance of Kleist's play about the Queen of the Amazons, and then proceeds through a suite of four further sequences designed to tease out some of the main implications in this opening 'statement'. Feminist issues loom large, not surprisingly, but the film embraces many other things, from Kleist's bizarre personal history to the way an actor feels in assuming a role. It's constructed as an exploration of relationships, real or potential, rather than as an argument or a single line of thought: it's interested in the link that may exist between a Greek vase-painting of a warrior woman and the Suffragettes, or, more formally, between a specific sound and a specific image. As such, it's a kind of scrapbook with a polemic kick. And it's also something of a milestone in dragging the moribund British cinema into an era long inhabited by Godard and Straub. TR

People Next Door, The

(1970, US, 93 min)
d David Greene. *p* Herbert Brodkin. *sc* JP Miller. *ph* Gordon Willis. *ed* Arline Garson. *ad* Charles Bailey. *m* Don Sebesky. *cast* Eli Wallach, Julie Harris, Deborah Winters, Stephen McHattie, Hal Holbrook, Cloris Leachman, Nehemiah Persoff.

● Heartless soap opera with good actors given no time to develop any character in depth as they are hurtled on from crisis to crisis to crisis. Much soul-searching among the over-thirties about where they went wrong as they try to bridge the generation gap. Much is made of the question of just who is the nigger in the staid, suburban woodpile – organ-playing son, tripped-out daughter, killer father, chainsmoking mum? There's even a mum-knows-best miracle cure.

People of France, The

see Vie est à nous, La

People of the North Sea (Vester-Vov-Vov)

(1927, Den, 92 min, b/w)
d Lau Lauritzen. *p* Svend Nielsen. *sc* Lau Lauritzen. *ph* Hugo Fisher. *m* (1933) Victor Cornelius. *cast* Fyrtårnet ['Long' – Carl Schenstrøm], Bivognen ['Short' – Harald Madsen], Kate Fabian, Karl Jørgensen, Jørgen Lund, Karin Nellemose, Erling Schroeder, Christian Schøder, Petrine Sonne, Emma Wiehe, Viggo Wiehe.

● This droll silent comedy set among a windswept beach community headlines the odd couple act of Fyrtårnet and Bivognen (a sort of Danish Laurel and Hardy), aka abroad as 'Long and Short' and 'Pat and Patachon'. The over-extended carryings-on are enlivened by some exotic comic touches and an inspired eccentric dance sequence from Long and Short. NB

People on Sunday (Menschen am Sonntag)

(1929, Ger, 89 min. b/w)
d Robert Siodmak, Edgar G Ulmer. *p* Seymour Nebenzal. *sc* Robert Siodmak, Kurt Siodmak. *ph* Eugen Schüfftan. *ad* Moritz Seeler. *cast* Erwin Splettstosser, Wolfgang von Waltershausen, Brigitte Borchert, Christl Ehlers, Annie Schreyer.

● There are two reasons why a modest, silent German movie like this is still in circulation today. One is a matter of its authorship: all four of the unknown young men who wrote and directed it (Fred Zinnemann and Billy Wilder in addition to Siodmak and Ulmer) went on to have more or less distinguished careers in Hollywood. The other is a matter of style: it was one of the earliest movies to renounce stars, drama and the other paraphernalia of commercial cinema in favour of a non-professional cast and an unmomentous, everyday storyline. Amazingly, its variety of 'realism' has hardly dated at all. Most of it centres on a Sunday excursion from the bustle of Berlin to a countryside lake, where a bachelor and his married friend drift in and out of flirtations with two young women. Hardly anything happens, but the play of gazes, emotions and counterpoints becomes deeply engrossing. You end up not only learning a lot about life in 1929, but also realising how little sexual mores have changed. TR

People That Time Forgot, The

(1977, GB, 90 min)
d Kevin Connor. *p* John Dark. *sc* Patrick Tilley. *ph* Alan Hume. *ed* John Ireland, Barry Peters. *pd* Maurice Carter. *m* John Scott. *cast* Patrick Wayne, Sarah Douglas, Dana Gillespie, Thorley Walters, Shane Rimmer, Doug McClure, Tony Britton.

● A lame sequel to Connor's earlier Edgar Rice Burroughs adaptation, *The Land That Time Forgot*, which was at least occasionally lively. This time it's a dreary trudge through perfunctory adventures (prehistoric monsters, hostile natives, erupting lava) as Patrick Wayne leads an expedition back to the mysterious island where Doug McClure has been stranded since last time. Even the dinosaurs seem dozy.

People Under the Stairs, The

(1991, US, 102 min)
d Wes Craven. *p* Marianne Maddalena, Stuart Besser. *sc* Wes Craven. *ph* Sandi Sissel. *ed* James Coblentz. *pd* Bryan James. *m* Graeme Revell. *cast* Brandon Adams, Everett McGill, Wendy Robie, AJ Langer, Ving Rhames, Sean Whalen, Bill Cobbs.

● Craven aims for an archetypal confrontation between childlike innocence and wicked step-parent cruelty, but the results are more grim than Grimm. Black ghetto child Fool (Adams) joins a pair of neighbourhood burglars planning to steal a legendary hoard of gold coins from the Old Dark House of weirdo couple McGill and Robie. Once inside, things go badly wrong: Rottweilers go for the throat, mutant children lurk beneath the stairs, and while maniacal Robie invokes the wrath of the Lord, wigged out McGill rampages in leather fetish gear, firing a shotgun at the brats in the walls. Trapped with tongue-less mutant Roach (Whalen) and abused stepdaughter Alice (Langer), Fool barely escapes being fed to the voracious People Under the Stairs. There are a few push-button frights, but a total dearth of mind-disturbing terror; the humour, too, is broad, crowd-pleasing stuff. NF

People vs. Larry Flynt, The

(1996, US, 130 min)
d Milos Forman. *p* Oliver Stone, Janet Yang, Michael Hausman. *sc* Scott Alexander, Larry Karaszewski. *ph* Philippe Rousselot. *ed* Chris Tellefsen. *pd* Patrizia von Brandenstein. *m* Thomas Newman. *cast* Woody Harrelson, Courtney Love, Edward Norton, James Cromwell, Crispin Glover, James Carville, Brett Harrelson, Donna Hanover.

● When Larry Flynt (Woody Harrelson), a Cincinnati strip-club proprietor, decides to improve business by putting out an explicitly illustrated newsletter, even his shrewd business sense can't predict that, as publisher of *Hustler* magazine, he'll end up a millionaire. Nor does he foresee the trials and tribulations his notoriety will bring in the shape of prosecutions for obscenity, contempt of court and libel. Fortunately, Flynt has the support of both his wife Althea (Love) and his lawyer Alan Isaacman (Norton) whose devotion to civil liberties outweighs his distaste for his client's life style. Since Flynt's real-life saga is colourful enough to ensure compelling drama, Forman's film is never less than fun: the irrepressible pornographer's courtroom antics make lively comedy. The performances, too, are winning: Love, gradually succumbing to drug-addiction and AIDS, is all too credible; Harrelson engagingly roguish; and Norton steals the show. But Forman and scriptwriters Scott Alexander and Larry Karaszewski are so keen to render Flynt a populist hero that they skate over the issues: the exploitative misogyny of Flynt's output is never examined, the prurient hypocrisy and intolerance of his persecutors seriously overplayed, plus Larry and Althea's odd romance lacks bittersweet conviction. GA

People Will Talk

(1951, US, 110 min, b/w)
d Joseph L Mankiewicz. *p* Darryl F Zanuck. *sc* Joseph L Mankiewicz. *ph* Milton Krasner. *ed* Barbara McLean. *ad* Lyle Wheeler, George W Davis. *m* Alfred Newman. *cast* Cary Grant, Jeanne Crain, Walter Slezak, Finlay Currie, Hume Cronyn, Sidney Blackmer.

●A bracingly bilious and loquacious Mankiewicz film that turns a highly esteemed gynaecologist (Grant) into a mouthpiece for the director's State of the Union address. The US of A is in a terrible state, and Grant's treatment of an unmarried mother (Crain) is heavily symbolic: her apparent immorality (Mankiewicz was amazed that the Hays Office approved the script) is set against the darker crimes and hypocrisies of American society. The man who made Crain pregnant dies in Korea; a university professor (Cronyn) stands in for Senator McCarthy; and there are pungent swipes at tax evasion and the crass materialism of the postwar boom. The fact that Mankiewicz can contain all this within the context of a romantic comedy testifies to his immense sophistication, and Grant's performance is one of his very best. ATu

Pépé le Moko

(1936, Fr, 93 min, b/w)
d Julien Duvivier. *p* Robert Hakim, Raymond Hakim. *sc* Julien Duvivier, Ashelbé [Henri La Barthe], Henri Jeanson. *ph* Jules Kruger, Marc Fossard. *ed* Marguerite Beaugé. *pd* Jacques Krauss. *m* Vincent Scotto, Mohamed Yguerbouchen. *cast* Jean Gabin, Mireille Balin, Line Noro, Lucas Gridoux, Fernand Charpin, Saturnin Fabre, Marcel Dalio, Gaston Modot.

●A touchstone film for cinema historians trading in literary labels like 'poetic realism' and often mistakenly said to be a transposition of the Hollywood gangster movie, *Pépé le Moko* deserves to be reassessed for what it is – a vigorous thriller about a French gangster hiding out in the Algiers Casbah. Full of sinuous camerawork, dingy sets, deep shadows, and even darker motives, this is also the film that fixed Gabin's image for keeps as the outsider condemned to a life in the underworld. See it for the edgy, suspenseful climax where Gabin, tempted out of hiding by his femme fatale, runs to meet death. *Film noir* as we know (and love) it is just around the corner from here. MA

Pepi, Luci, Bom... (Pepi, Luci, Bom y otras chicas del montón)

(1980, Sp, 80 min)
d Pedro Almodóvar. *p* Pepón Corominas. *sc* Pedro Almodóvar. *ph* Paco Femenia. *ed* Pepe Salcedo. *cast* Carmen Maura, Félix Rotaeta, Olvido 'Alaska' Gara, Eva Siva, Diego Alvarez, Pedro Almodóvar.

●Almodóvar's first feature shows how many of his obsessions and themes sprang fully formed from the start. Some scabs he feels compelled to pick at: drugs, adverts, musical numbers, sexual violence, and that dodgy topic, female masochism. Pepi (Maura), after inviting a neighbouring cop to fondle rather than bust her, is raped in her trashy flat and vows revenge, introducing the policeman's wife to the pleasures of golden showers and lesbian SM. Set during Madrid's punk era, the film shows in embryo Almodóvar's technique of alternating pleasurable humour with wanton offensiveness. Some scenes are hard to stomach, plotting is chaotic, and the budget and film quality are so low that the king of kitsch can make only a brave stab at his favourite acid colours and tacky interiors. The costumes are fab. SFe

Peppermint

(1999, Greece, 105 min)
d/sc Costas Kapakas. *ph* Yannis Daskalothanasis. *ed* Takis Yannopoulos. *cast* Georges Corraface, Giorgos Gerontidakis-Sempetadelis, Anny Loulou, Alexandros Mylonas, Tassos Paltzidis, Markella Pappa, Nikoletta Vlavianou.

●Aircraft engineer Stefanos is invited to a party by an old friend, which makes him cast his mind back to his upbringing with his pretty cousin Marina (his love for whom he was dimly aware of at the time, but in retrospect it takes on far greater significance), his adored grandmother Venetia and others. Cue a kaleidoscope of genial, affectionate and well mounted reminiscences of protected middle class life. The movie's attention to detail, keen sense of observation and lack of bombast and false nostalgia add up to a pleasant reverie from what would be familiar material. WH

Peppermint Candy (Bakha Satang)

(1999, SKor, 129 min)
d Lee Chang-Dong. *p* Myung Kay-Nam, Jeon Jae-Young, Jay Jeon. *sc* Lee Chang-Dong. *ph* Kim Hyung-Koo. *ed* Kim Hyun. *ad* Park Il-Hyun. *m* Lee Jae-Jin. *cast* Sol Kyung-Gu, Moon So-Ri, Kim Yeo-Jin.

●As in *Green Fish*, Lee uses his protagonist's life as a sounding-board for Korea's modern history – here, the 20 years from the eve of the Kwangju Massacre to the film's present. Twenty years which see Young-Ho (newcomer Sol, electric) turn from a fresh-faced innocent into a self-hating, suicidal jerk via traumatic experiences during his military service and a thoroughly dehumanising stint in the police force. Well aware that his pessimistic analysis of Korea's trajectory could be a pill too bitter for most audiences to swallow, Lee has had the smart idea of telling the story backwards: the film opens in the present and ends 20 years earlier with Young-Ho looking forward hopefully to his future. Thanks to fine writing and performances and subtle use of recurring imagery, the film is dramatically powerful and highly emotive. TR

Peppermint Frappé

(1967, Sp, 94 min)
d Carlos Saura. *p* Elias Querejeta. *sc* Rafael Azcona, Angelino Fons, Carlos Saura. *ph* Luis Cuadrado. *ad* Emilio Sanz de Soto. *m* Luis de Pablo. *cast* Geraldine Chaplin, José Luis López Vásquez, Alfredo Mayo, Emiliano Redondo.

● *Vertigo* via Buñuel. Saura's ambitions may have been a bit loftier than his talent back in 1967, but this slice of art house surrealism insinuated itself past Franco's censors to give a welcome glimpse of a Spanish film culture dominated by the shadow of its absent master. The engagingly provocative yarn of erotic obsession, in which plain-Jane Chaplin is 'remoulded' by her unhinged boss into the image of his brother's foxy wife (also Chaplin) isn't obstructed overmuch by Saura's reverential 'homages', and its roots in a script by Rafael Azcona (subversive plotsmith for Berlanga and Ferreri) ensure that sufficient black comedy incisiveness penetrates the flashy surface. PT

Peppermint Freedom (Peppermint Frieden)

(1984, WGer, 112 min, b/w & col)
d/sc Marianne SW Rosenbaum. *ph* Alfred Tichawsky. *ed* Gérard Samaan. *ad* Franz Tyroller. *m* Konstantin Wecker. *cast* Peter Fonda, Saskia Tyroller, Hans Brenner, Hans Peter Korff, Cleo Kretschmer.

●Marianne Rosenbaum's first feature returns to the well-thumbed time of Germany, year zero, as seen through the eyes of a little girl (Tyroller), living in US-occupied Bavaria, for whom postwar freedom is as palpable as the tastes of peppermint and fresh-ground coffee. Her fantasies focus on Mr Frieden/Freedom (Fonda), a larger-than-life American soldier with a great big black sedan, a huge toothpaste ad grin, infinite supplies of Wrigley's spearmint gum, and the hots for one of the local women. All *streng verboten* by the village priest, whose awful warnings of the red peril, hellfire and nuclear holocaust blur and balloon in the little girl's mind to the point of nervous breakdown. The kids emerge, refreshingly, not as cute moppets but as beings with a sense of wonder, scepticism and implacable logic that shows up the adult world as absurd and impoverished. And while Rosenbaum comes to some melancholy conclusions, her arresting, grainy images and sharp eye for the incongruous take her there with considerable astringency and wit. SJo

Peppermint Soda

see Diabolo Menthe

Pequeños Milagros

see Little Miracles

Perceval le Gallois

(1978, Fr, 138 min)
d Eric Rohmer. *p* Margaret Ménégoz. *sc* Eric Rohmer. *ph* Nestor Almendros. *ed* Cécile Decugis. *ad* Jean-Pierre Kohut-Svelko. *m* Guy Robert. *cast* Fabrice Luchini, André Dussollier, Marc Eyraud, Gérard Falconetti, Arielle Dombasle, Clémentine Amouroux, Michel Etcheverry, Marie-Christine Barrault.

●Rohmer's adaptation of Chrétien de Troyes 12th century Arthurian poem is a unique film, combining cinema, theatre, medieval music, iconography, mime and verse to create a stylised and surprisingly coherent spectacle: shot totally in the studio, its sets alone are worth the price of a ticket. But more astonishing, perhaps, is the way in which Rohmer translates the text into a moral investigation which frequently resembles his contemporary comedies as selfish young innocent Perceval, whose very naiveté literally disarms his enemies, undergoes a sentimental education in the codes of Chivalry, Courtship, and Faith. His odyssey is observed with ironic wit and revealing distance; not surprisingly for Rohmer, a key stage in his development occurs when he learns the dangers of talking too much or too little. Far more accessible and entertaining than Bresson's *Lancelot du Lac* or Syberberg's *Parsifal,* and relevant in a sense undreamed of by *Excalibur*, the film marries medieval passion with modern perspective and sires its own special magic. GA

Percy

(1971, GB, 103 min)
d Ralph Thomas. *p* Betty E Box. *sc* Hugh Leonard. *ph* Ernest Steward. *ed* Roy Watts. *ad* Robert Jones. *m* Ray Davies. *cast* Hywel Bennett, Denholm Elliott, Elke Sommer, Britt Ekland, Cyd Hayman, Janet Key, Adrienne Posta.

●Excruciating comedy in the *Carry On* mould, with Bennett as the hapless recipient of the world's first penis transplant. When it isn't leeringly dragging in nudge-nudge images (like the Post Office Tower) or dredging up every phallic gag known to schoolboy smut, the film laboriously records the bemused hero's attempts to come to terms with 'Percy' by tracing the donor (a notorious philanderer killed in the accident that caused his own dismemberment) and interviewing the female witnesses to its prowess.

Percy's Progress

(1974, GB, 101 min)
d Ralph Thomas. *p* Betty E Box. *sc* Sid Colin. *ph* Tony Imi. *ed* Roy Watts. *ad* Albert Witherick. *m* Tony Macauley. *cast* Leigh Lawson, Elke Sommer, Denholm Elliott, Judy Geeson, Harry H Corbett, Vincent Price, Adrienne Posta, Julie Ege, Barry Humphries.

●One would have thought that *Percy* had pretty well worn out the already thin gag about the man who has a nine-inch penis transplant. But no, we are regaled with a second episode in which, with Lawson taking over the lead from Hywel Bennett, Percy is left (temporarily) the sole sexually active organ on the planet. British sex comedies are nothing if not prurient, and Percy (the name is now the hero's) isn't allowed so much as a bulge in his trousers. Incredibly, someone has blackmailed all sorts of big names into appearing in cameo parts. VG

Perdita Durango

(1997, Sp/Mex/US, 124 min)
d Alex de la Iglesia. *p* Andrés Vicente Goméz. *sc* Barry Gifford, Jorge Guerricaechevarría, David Trueba, Alex de le Iglesia. *ph* Flavio Mntz Labiano. *ed* Teresa Font. *pd* Biaffra, José Luis Arrizabálaga. *m* Simon Boswell. *cast* Rosie Perez, Javier Bardem, Don Stroud, Harley Cross, Aimee Graham, James Gandolfini, Screamin' Jay Hawkins, Alex Cox.

●Spanish director Alex de la Iglesia tackles the further adventures of the Tex-Mex femme fatale, Perdita Durango, who was first incarnated by Isabella Rossellini in *Wild at Heart*. The David Lynch film effectively played on hallucinatory weirdness, but de la Iglesia's English-language debut (shot in the US) is so hesitant that, despite lashings of sexual abandon, violence and sleazeball local colour, it barely quickens the pulse. Perez flashes her don't-mess-with-me look as Perdita, but meets her match in Bardem's butch Romeo Dolorosa, dangerous exponent of the voodoo-like cult *santero*. The plot kicks in when Bardem has to transport a lorryload of live foetuses across the border. He and Perez nevertheless find time along the way to take a couple of teens for a forced march on the wild side. The fantasy-fuelled intercutting of footage from Aldrich's wonderful Mexican Western *Vera Cruz* is little short of unforgivable. TJ

Père Goriot, Le

(1944, Fr, 96 min, b/w)
d Robert Vernay. *p* Pierre O'Connell, Arys Nissotti. *sc* Charles Spaak, Bernard Zimmer. *ph* Victor Arménise. *ed* Suzanne de Troeye. *ad* René Renoux. *m* Jean Wiener. *cast* Pierre Renoir, Georges Rollin, Pierre Larquey, Claude Genia, Sylvie, Jean Desailly.

●Balzac's 1835 novel was allegedly the first, but not the last, to use a boarding house setting to present a cross section of humanity. This crowded canvas is made more intricate for the adaptor by several characters whose histories were developed in later Balzac tales. In the event scriptwriter Charles Spaak opts to focus on Rastignac, gauche young man on the make at the start, disillusioned opportunist at the end. His rough handling by jovial corrupter Vautrin and by the two poisonous daughters of Old Goriot are the substance of the film. Sometimes the staging seems rather flat, while other sequences are startlingly good, a discrepancy explained by the film's date. But it's further confirmation, along with *Fantômas contre Fantômas*, that Vernay deserves better than the obscurity into which he's fallen. The acting is uneven, ranging from mesmerising (Renoir) to amateurish (Larquey). BBa

Père Tranquille, Le (Mr Orchid)

(1946, Fr, 97 min, b/w)
d René Clément. *sc* Noël-Noël. *ph* Claude Renoir. *ed* Henriette Wurtzer. *ad* Lucien Carré. *m* René Cloërec. *cast* Noël-Noël, Nadine Alari, Claire Olivier, Paul Frankeur, Marcel Dieudonné, Howard Vernon.

●Sub-titled 'The life of a French family during the Occupation', this low key melodrama sets out to tell the French a story they were anxious to hear in 1946. Middle-aged insurance agent M. Martin seems to lead a dull life, caring only for his family and his orchids. Secretly though, he's leader of the local Resistance cell. The reputations of Clément and writer/star Noël-Noël may have faded, but such scenes as the killing of a Gestapo spy, or the moment when Martin's daughter realises the truth indicate that their cinematic reflexes used to be pretty sharp. But overall it's too tendentious to take seriously. BBa

Perez Family, The

(1995, US, 113 min)
d Mira Nair. *p* Michael Nozik, Lydia Dean Pilcher. *sc* Robin Swicord. *ph* Stuart Dryburgh. *ed* Robert Estrin. *pd* Mark Friedberg. *m* Alan Silvestri. *cast* Marisa Tomei, Anjelica Huston, Alfred Molina, Chazz Palminteri, Trini Alvarado, Celia Cruz, Bill Sage, Vincent Gallo.

●There's something about Hispanic culture which has film-makers swinging their hips. Although based on the Mariel boatlift of 1980, this is no less a rose-tinted spectacle than, say, *Don Juan DeMarco* or *The Mambo Kings*. It's crammed with histrionic performances and ersatz *mise en scène*, and it looks like a musical after all the songs have been cut out. Tomei is Cuban prostitute Dottie Perez, Molina political prisoner Juan Raul Perez (they're erroneously recorded as husband and wife by US immigration officials); Huston is his real wife Carmela, who escaped to Miami 20 years before, and token Hispanic Alvarado their daughter Teresa. Tomei gets the worst of it. Coming to the States with a passion for Elvis, a long line in cocktail dresses, and the ambition to 'fok' John Wayne, she shakes her money-maker, amasses an extended misfit family, and generally carries on like Rita Moreno with ants in her pants. TCh

Perfect

(1985, US, 120 min)
d/p James Bridges. *sc* Aaron Latham, James Bridges. *ph* Gordon Willis. *ed* Jeff Gourson. *pd* Michael Haller. *m* Ralph Burns. *cast* John Travolta, Jamie Lee Curtis, Jann Wenner, Anne De Salvo, Stefan Gierasch, Laraine Newman, Marilu Henner.

●Muddled saga of journalistic ethics puts *Rolling Stone* reporter Travolta in a spin when he falls for Curtis, the aerobics instructor he's about to trash in an exposé article. Director Bridges' main interest, however, seems to be the leotarded contours of the interminable aerobics sequences. A second storyline concerns a computer company chairman who's been arrested on drug offences, but claims in an interview that Washington is after him for selling his products to the Eastern Bloc. This demonstration of journalistic integrity sits uneasily beside the unscrupulous methods Travolta deploys in his health club story, and if that's the point, the movie certainly meanders towards it. *Rolling Stone* editor Jann Wenner plays himself in an extended plug for the magazine. TJ

Perfect Alibi

(1994, US, 96 min)
d Kevin Meyer. *p* Bruce Cohn Curtis. *sc* Keven Meyer. *ph* Doyle Smith. *cast* Teri Garr, Hector Elizondo, Charles Martin Smith, Kathleen Quinlan, Alex McArthur.

●Your basic *Hand That Rocks the Cradle* knock-off. French au pair, employed by wealthy Americans, takes charge of kids, husband, house and car, edging the wife and mother out of the picture and rubbing out anyone in the way. Family friend Garr investigates, helped by sympathetic cop Elizondo and sleazy private eye Smith, leading to a highly uninteresting conclusion. With its boring, high-key TV-movie look, banal script, and comatose performances, it makes Curtis Hanson's creaky Rebecca De Mornay vehicle seem the pinnacle of the genre. AO

Perfect Blue

(1997, Jap, 80 min)
d Satoshi Kon. *p* Masao Maruyama, Hiroaki Inoue. *sc* Sadayuki Murai. *ph* Hisao Shirai. *pd* Mitsusuke Hayakawa. *m* Masahiro Ikumi.

●Based on a novel by Yoshikazu Tekeuchi, this unusual animé follows Polanski's *Repulsion* into some fairly grown-up areas: the vulnerability of one's sense of self, the flimsiness of a public persona, the price to be paid for female complicity with male fantasies. Mima, lead singer with a teen-idol group which has had its statutory 15 minutes, as usual submits to her manager's instructions by going solo and taking a 'bad girl' role in a TV soap. But then she finds her private diary posted on the Internet, imagines herself stalked by a slasher movie monster and is harassed by her own shadow double, a malign version of her popstar self. The old *Diaboliques* question arises: is she 'merely' cracking up, or is someone really out to get her? The denouement isn't very surprising or enlightening, but at its best this works as both a critique of Japan's pop culture system and an effective woman-in-peril psycho-thriller. (The animation director was Hideki Hamazu.) TR

Perfect Circle (Savresni Krug)

(1997, Fr, 108 min)
d Ademir Kenovic. *p* Ademir Kenovic, Ismet Arnautalic, Dana Rotberg. *sc* Ademir Kenovic, Abdulah Sidran, Pjer Zalica. *ph* Milenko Uhenko. *ed* Christel Tanovic. *pd* Kemal Hrustanovic. *m* Esad Arnautalic, Ranko Rihtman. *cast* Mustafa Nadarevic, Almedin Leleta, Almir Podgorica, Josip Pejakovic, Jasna Diklic.

●This is the Bosnian Muslim take on the siege of Sarajevo. Quieter than *Welcome to Sarajevo* (and a million miles from *For Ever Mozart*), it adopts a low key, humanist perspective which might be termed 'old fashioned', both in a pejorative and complimentary sense. A little like *Kolya*, it has an older man reluctantly adopting a couple of orphaned boys, one of them a deaf mute. There's a strong feeling for ordinary life in extraordinary circumstances (circumstances shared by the film-makers), which renders the occasional explosions of senseless horror all the more effective. TCh

Perfect Couple, A

(1979, US, 112 min)
d/p Robert Altman. *sc* Robert Altman, Allan Nicholls. *ph* Edmond L Koons. *ed* Tony Lombardo. *ad* Leon Ericksen. *m* Tom Pierson, Tony Berg. *cast* Paul Dooley, Marta Heflin, Titos Vandis, Belita Moreno, Henry Gibson, Dimitra Arliss, Ted Neeley, Heather MacRae.

●Altman hits a note of surprising magic here, commenting on cinematic traditions of romantic comedy even as he updates them. The lovers (Dooley, Heflin) meet through an LA video-dating service. He's an ageing antique dealer, driven to the bureau by his entombment in a repressive Greek-American family; she's an aimless waif who lives and sings in a communal rock group tyrannised by its lead singer. Music is as focal as it was in *Nashville*: the classics in which Dooley's family are steeped, versus the Easy-Listening raunch which Heflin peddles. Though both commune and traditional family are shown to be equal parts alluring and lethal, the search for togetherness is treated with a satirical sympathy, so that the happy ending – clearly recognised when it comes as a slyly structured fantasy – works as a real reward for both lovers and audience. CR

Perfect Friday

(1970, GB, 95 min)
d Peter Hall. *p* Jack Smith. *sc* Anthony Greville-Bell, C Scott Forbes. *ph* Alan Hume. *ed* Rex Pyke. *pd* Terence Marsh. *m* John Dankworth. *cast* Ursula Andress, Stanley Baker, David Warner, Patience Collier, TP McKenna, David Waller.

●Straightforward thriller in which a staid bank clerk (Baker) becomes aware of brighter horizons when he meets the invitingly luscious Andress, who is more or less estranged from her impecunious husband, a layabout peer of the realm (Warner). He therefore evolves a plan, in which all three members of the triangle take part, to rob his own bank. Familiar stuff, right down to the airport finale in which all foregather for a last ironic flourish; but it's competently staged (after a queasily 'stylish' beginning) and well performed. TM

Perfect Love!

see Parfait Amour!

Perfectly Normal

(1990, GB/Can, 105 min)
d Yves Simoneau. *p* Michael Burns. *sc* Eugene Lipinski, Paul Quarrington. *ph* Alain Dostie. *ed* Ronald Sanders. *pd* Anne Pritchard. *m* Richard Gregoire. *cast* Robbie Coltrane, Michael Riley, Deborah Duchene, Eugene Lipinski.

●Coltrane plays garrulous con-man-cum-chef Turner. Arriving in an Ontario town, he inveigles his cab driver into sharing a meal. Five minutes of fast food and patter later, the driver – a retiring brewery-operative, hockey-player and all-round nonentity named Renzo (Riley), clearly a soupçon less than the full salami himself – finds Turner has invited himself back to his flat, where he takes over the spare room, prepares a lavish Italian meal, and proceeds to elaborate his grandiose scheme to open a restaurant with a grand opera theme. Before you can shout Puccini, shy Renzo – throw off those inhibitions! – is donning prima donna outfit and warbling with the best of them down at the packed-out Ristorante Bel Canto. Canadian director Simoneau plays out this liberationist tosh with ne'er a qualm of self-consciousness. His uneasy mix of Capra-esque whimsy, camp sensibility and oddball romance is so absolutely ingenuous that words fail. The lead performances, both curiously winning, hold the film together, after a fashion. WH

Perfect Murder, A

(1998, US, 107 min)
d Andrew Davis. *p* Arnold Kopelson, Anne Kopelson, Christopher Mankiewicz, Peter MacGregor-Scott. *sc* Patrick Smith Kelly. *ph* Dariusz Wolski. *ed* Dennis Virkler, Dov Hoenig. *pd* Philip Rosenberg. *m* James Newton Howard. *cast* Michael Douglas, Gwyneth Paltrow, Viggo Mortensen, David Suchet, Sarita Choudhury, Michael P Moran.

●Douglas is perfectly cast as a predatory 'control freak' in this classy, intelligent remake of Hitchcock's dramatically flat 3-D thriller, *Dial M for Murder*. The script's contemporary update complicates the central triangular relationship between Douglas's cuckolded industrialist, Mortensen's struggling artist and Paltrow's sleek, highly intelligent 'trophy wife'. Free of the 'helpless victim' role given to Grace Kelly, Paltrow achieves a far more credible complexity: by turns passionate, naive, vulnerable and smart, her character ultimately finds the strength to confront the truth about the web of deceitful, mercenary relationships in which she has become entangled. Though better known for action pics like *The Fugitive*, director Davis displays an equal facility for seamless plotting, taut suspense and scenes of twisted intimacy. NF

Perfect Murder, The

(1988, Ind, 93 min)
d Zafar Hai. *p* Wahid Chowhan. *sc* HRF Keating, Zafar Hai. *ph* Walter Lassally. *ed* Charles Rees. *pd* Kiran Patki, Sartaj Noorani. *m* Richard Robbins. *cast* Naseeruddin Shah, Stellan Skarsgard, Amjad Khan, Madhur Jaffrey, Ratna Pathak Shah, Sakina Jaffrey.
●Someone tries to bump off Mr Perfect, you see, private secretary to a building tycoon. He survives – which is more than can be said for this Bombay duck. Inspector Ghote (Shah) is called in to investigate. The malignant millionaire (Khan) doesn't like it; nor does his wife (Madhur Jaffrey); nor, for that matter, does anybody else. Ghote's wife wants him home with her; his boss wants him to solve the case of a Minister's missing ring; and he is expected to look after a visiting Swedish criminologist. Nothing goes according to plan. HRF Keating's adaptation of his own novel, though shot in English, must surely have been originally intended for home consumption in India. A mixture of cack-handed slapstick and schmaltz, it seems primarily a tribute to *Carry On Up the Khyber*. An Indian throwaway. MS

Perfect Storm, The

(2000, US, 130 min)
d Wolfgang Petersen. *p* Paula Weinstein, Wolfgang Petersen, Gail Katz. *sc* Bill Wittliff. *ph* John Seale. *ed* Richard Francis-Bruce. *pd* William Sandell. *m* James Horner. *cast* George Clooney, Mark Wahlberg, John C Reilly, Diane Lane, William Fichtner, John Hawkes, Allen Payne, Karen Allen, Bob Gunton, Michael Ironside, Rusty Schwimmer, Mary Elizabeth Mastrantonio.
●Petersen's movie of Sebastian Junger's best-seller chronicles the last voyage of the *Andrea Gail*, a swordfishing boat out of Gloucester, Massachussetts, lost at sea in October 1991. In his foreword, Junger admits any attempt to recreate the crew's experience can only be a matter of conjecture: 'I toyed with the idea of fictionalising, but that risked diminishing the value of whatever facts I was able to determine.' No such scruples for the movie-makers, of course, but given that they're making it up, there's no excuse for lines as corny as 'I wanna catch some fish – it's what I do!' It doesn't much matter though. This is one of those films where actions speak louder than words. Regular guy Clooney may be too intuitively smarmy to play your straight-ahead skipper, but the authentically grizzled beard helps, and Petersen loads the boat with plausible working-man types. And this is what's striking about the movie. It's the first blockbuster in recent memory to hold faith with everyday heroes just doing their jobs. More impressive still, their heroism is a kind of unconscious blunder, a macho bluff compelled by hard economic choices. The special effects are staggering and the last hour builds from sinking dread to exhilarating defiance and, finally, remorseful exhaustion. TCh

Perfect Strangers (aka Vacation from Marriage)

(1945, GB, 102 min, b/w)
d/p Alexander Korda. *sc* Clemence Dane, Anthony Pélissier. *ph* Georges Périnal. *ed* EB Jarvis. *pd* Vincent Korda. *m* Clifton Parker. *cast* Robert Donat, Deborah Kerr, Glynis Johns, Ann Todd, Roland Culver, Elliot Mason.
●Meet the Drabs – Donat and Kerr – and watch how the war gives their marriage a little excitement and a well-deserved holiday: he goes into the Navy, she becomes a Wren, and each enjoys a fling. The movie was made by MGM British in the manner of *Mrs Miniver*, and was to have been directed by Wesley Ruggles. Divided into three 'acts', with a script by Clemence Dane, it is a reasonably acted, authentically staged evocation of British resolve under stress. The eagle-eyed may spot Roger Moore in a walk-on. ATu

Perfect Weapon, The

(1991, US, 112 min)
d Mark DiSalle. *p* Mark DiSalle, Pierre David. *sc* David Campbell Wilson. *ph* Russell Carpenter. *ed* Wayne Wahrman. *pd* Curtis A Schnell. *m* Gary Chang. *cast* Jeff Speakman, John Dye, Mako, James Hong, Dante Basco, Mariska Hargitay, Seth Sakai.
●On the sliding scale of high-kicking action heroes, Jeff Speakman chops in a long way beneath the Chuck Norrises and Jean-Claude Van Dammes of the martial arts world. He's a nifty enough mover, but boasts rather less charisma than the average PE instructor. Here, he's one of those quiet loner types. When his spiritual guru is murdered by a rampaging gang of Koreans, he takes instant revenge in the usual fashion. GM

Perfect Woman, The

(1949, GB, 89 min, b/w)
d Bernard Knowles. *p* George Black, Alfred Black. *sc* George Black, Bernard Knowles, JB Boothroyd. *ph* Jack Hildyard. *ed* Peter Graham Scott. *ad* J Elder Wills. *m* Arthur Wilkinson. *cast* Patricia Roc, Stanley Holloway, Nigel Patrick, Miles Malleson, Irene Handl, Anita Sharp-Bolster, Fred Berger.
●When Prof Malleson models a revolutionary robot on niece Roc, Messrs Patrick and Holloway take the creation to the West End to prove just how convincing 'she' is. Unfortunately, the tin woman's flesh-and-blood counterpart gets wind of the wheeze, leading to much complication when the boys book 'her' into the bridal suite of a snazzy hotel. Hardly your PC vision of womanhood, but this British farce breezes along happily enough on its own terms. TJ

Perfect World, A

(1993, US, 138 min)
d Clint Eastwood. *p* Mark Johnson, David Valdes. *sc* John Lee Hancock. *ph* Jack N Green. *ed* Joel Cox, Ron Spang. *pd* Henry Bumstead. *m* Jeff Wexler. *cast* Kevin Costner, Clint Eastwood, Laura Dern, TJ Lowther, Keith Szarabajka, Leo Burmeister.
●While this lacks the class and assured blend of genre traditions and subversion that marks Eastwood's best work, it *is* very entertaining. In some respects, the film looks formulaic: an escaped con (Costner) flees with a child hostage (Lowther), pursued by Texas Ranger Eastwood, criminologist Dern, a trigger-happy FBI sniper and assorted redneck assistants. To an extent, all goes predictably. Costner gets to like the kid, his essential goodness underlined by contrast with the psycho sadist who is briefly his fugitive partner, while Clint's conservative but well-meaning law enforcer discovers a measure of empathy with both the pragmatic Dern and his prey. Among the familiar stuff, however, there are very fine moments. It's just a pity that Costner never really comes alive. That said, the director manages mostly to avoid the enormous maudlin pitfalls of his material, at least until the over-extended final scene. As usual with Eastwood, little is overstated – and the accent is on humour. GA

Performance 100

(1970, GB, 105 min)
d Nicolas Roeg, Donald Cammell. *p* Sandy Lieberson. *sc* Donald Cammell. *ph* Nicolas Roeg. *ed* Antony Gibbs, Brian Smedley-Aston. *ad* John Clark. *m* Jack Nitzsche. *cast* James Fox, Mick Jagger, Anita Pallenberg, Michèle Breton, Ann Sidney, Johnny Shannon, Anthony Valentine.
●Roeg's debut as a director is a virtuoso juggling act which manipulates its visual and verbal imagery so cunningly that the borderline between reality and fantasy is gradually eliminated. The first half-hour is straight thriller enough to suggest a Kray Bros documentary as Fox, enforcer for a London protection racket, goes about his work with such relish that he involves the gang in a murder and has to hide from retribution in a Notting Hill basement. There, waiting to escape abroad, he becomes involved with a fading pop star (Jagger) brooding in exile over the loss of his powers of incantation. In what might be described (to borrow from Kenneth Anger) as an invocation to his demon brother, the pop star recognises his lost power lurking in the blind impulse to violence of his visitor, and so teases and torments him with drug-induced psychedelics that the latter responds in the only way he knows how: by rewarding one mind-blowing with another, at gunpoint. Ideas in profusion here about power and persuasion and performance ('The only performance that makes it, that makes it all the way, is one that achieves madness'); and the latter half becomes one of Roeg's most complex visual kaleidoscopes as pop star and enforcer coalesce in a marriage of heaven and hell (or underworld and underground) where the common denominator is Big Business. TM

Péril en la Demeure

see Death in a French Garden

Péril Jeune, Le (Good Old Daze)

(1994, Fr, 101 min)
d Cédric Klapisch. *p* Aïssa Djabri, Fred Lahouassa. *sc* Cédric Klpasch, Santiago Amigorena, Alexis Galmot, Daniel Thieux. *ph* Dominique Colin. *ed* Francine Sandberg. *ad* François Emmanuelli. *cast* Romain Duris, Julien Lambroschini, Nicolas Koretzky, Vincent Elbaz, Joachim Lombard.
●Four thirty-something men await the birth of a child fathered by their dead pal; as they reminisce, we're taken back to their schooldays in the early '70s, when picking up girls, political demos, squats and drugs seemed more important than settling down or thinking about the future. The film's a bitter-sweet tribute to the trials and joys of friendship, distinguished less by its final stance on drugs and irresponsibility than by its energetic, wry and affectionately vivid re-creation of what now, 20 years on, seems an unfashionable decade. It could be tougher and subtler, but it's highly watchable all the same. GA

Period of Adjustment

(1962, US, 112 min, b/w)
d George Roy Hill. *p* Lawrence Weingarten. *sc* Isobel Lennart. *ph* Paul C Vogel. *ed* Fredric Steinkamp. *ad* George W Davis, Edward C Carfagno. *m* Lyn Murray. *cast* Jane Fonda, Tony Franciosa, Jim Hutton, Lois Nettleton, John McGiver, Mabel Albertson, Jack Albertson.
●Light comedy mixes with more intimate material in Isobel Lennart's adaptation of the Tennessee Williams play, with newly-wed Fonda dismayed to find that macho Korean vet husband Jim Hutton won't be winning any medals for services between the sheets, and taking their problem to more established couple Franciosa and Nettleton, who have in-law trauma of their own. All in all, it's an appealing mix, even if the shifts in tone seem to unsettle cast and director alike. First-rate performances, though, especially from Fonda, as a wide-eyed Southern belle. TJ

Perles de la Couronne, Les (The Pearls of the Crown)

(1937, Fr, 118 min, b/w)
d Sacha Guitry, Christian-Jaque. *sc* Sacha Guitry. *ph* Jules Kruger. *ed* William Barache, Myriam. *ad* Jean Perrier. *m* Jean Françaix. *cast* Sacha Guitry, Raimu, Jacqueline Delubac, Arletty, Jean-Louis Barrault, Lyn Harding, Marguerite Moréno, Renée Saint-Cyr, Marcel Dalio, Claude Dauphin, Cécile Sorel.
●Guitry's trilingual (French, English, Italian) toast to the *Entente Cordiale* is a tale of the adventures of seven pearls, four of them safe in the English crown, three of them lost from a necklace at the time of Mary Queen of Scots. Perhaps little more than the sum of its parts – but what parts! Raimu, Marguerite Moréno (Giraudoux's *Madwoman of Chaillot*), Arletty as an Abyssinian snake-charmer, Jean-Louis Barrault as Napoleon, and the maestro himself in a quintet of roles. Irresistibly effervescent dialogue, a sprightly 'modern' visual style – one could go on forever about a film that comes to an end all too soon. GAd

Permanent Record

(1988, US, 91 min)
d Marisa Silver. *p* Frank Mancuso Jr. *sc* Jarre Fees, Alice Liddle, Larry Ketron. *ph* Frederick Elmes. *ed* Robert Brown. *pd* Michel Levesque. *m* Joe Strummer. *cast* Alan Boyce, Keanu Reeves, Michelle Meyrink, Jennifer Rubin, Pamela Gidley, Richard Bradford, Barry Corbin, Kathy Baker.

●This second feature from the director of *Old Enough* must be counted a disappointment. A well-intentioned study of high-school kids coping (and not coping) with the pressures of adolescence, its naturalistic style only makes the more overt dramatic elements look forced and clichéd. Basically a non-starter, it does showcase a sympathetic performance from the very happening Keanu Reeves. The music is by Joe Strummer, and Lou Reed has a cameo, but it's par for the course that Gilbert and Sullivan get more of a look in. TCh

Permanent Vacation

(1981, US, 65 min)
d/p/sc Jim Jarmusch. *ph* Jim Lebovitz, Tom DiCillo. *ed* Jim Jarmusch. *m* Jim Jarmusch, John Lurie. *cast* Chris Parker, Leila Gastil, Maria Duval, John Lurie.
●Jim Jarmusch's 16mm feature debut, made not long after the writer/director graduated from film school, is an oblique study of a young man (Parker) adrift on the streets of New York. As he roams, he has chance encounters with a car thief, a saxophone player and a grizzled war veteran, among others. Learning their stories, he begins to seem more and more isolated. Even his relationship with his girlfriend (Gastil) is coming under strain. Perhaps the film doesn't have quite the charm of its successor, *Stranger Than Paradise*, but Jarmusch's freewheeling episodic approach to storytelling is already evident. GM

Permis de Conduire, Le (The Driving Licence)

(1974, Fr, 90 min)
d Jean Girault. *p* Simone Allouche. *sc* Jacques Vilfrid. *ph* Etienne Szabo. *ed* Michael Lewin. *ad* Sydney Bettex. *m* Raymond Lefèvre. *cast* Louis Velle, Pascale Roberts, Paul Prébois, Sandra Julien, Jacques Jouabbeau.
●Appalling Gallic sitcom about a provincial bank manager's automotive and amorous misadventures when posted to Paris. The insulting script and slap-happy direction stall as often as Velle's ingratiating *naif* on their collective way through every second-hand learner-driver/driving test gag you've ever seen before, and the going actually gets harder as the film goes further downhill with our 'hero' plunging into a 'misunderstood' affair. *Merde*, in any language. PT

Permission to Kill

(1975, US/Aus, 97 min)
d Cyril Frankel. *p* Paul Mills. *sc* Robin Estridge. *ph* Freddie Young. *ed* Ernest Scott. *pd* Elliot Scott. *m* Richard Rodney Bennett. *cast* Dirk Bogarde, Ava Gardner, Bekim Fehmiu, Timothy Dalton, Nicole Calfan, Frederic Forrest.
●This limp spy story should have been prefaced by a caption saying: actors at work. A goodish cast demonstrates little more than the fact that actors, too, sometimes have to take on jobs to pay the rent. The film also indulges Bogarde's weakness for inferior espionage thrillers. At his most fastidious (the pursed lips vs the raised eyebrow), he plays a security officer attempting to prevent a political exile (Fehmiu) from returning to lead his people. Various skeletons from the hapless man's past are manipulated into Bogarde's service and wheeled on in an attempt to make him stay. As one of them says towards the end: 'There are no words adequate to describe what we've just seen'. A fair demonstration of the script's lack of any awareness. CPe

Per Qualche Dollari in più

see For a Few Dollars More

Persecution

(1974, GB, 96 min)
d Don Chaffey. *p* Kevin Francis. *sc* Robert B Hutton, Rosemary Wooten. *ph* Ken Talbot. *ed* Michael Campbell. *ad* Jack Shampan. *m* Paul Ferris. *cast* Lana Turner, Ralph Bates, Olga Georges-Picot, Suzan Farmer, Mark Weavers, Patrick Allen, Ronald Howard, Trevor Howard.
●Routine attempt at a psychological thriller, given more weight than it deserves by a good performance from Ralph Bates as the pawn in his pathologically domineering mother's game. Lana Turner, as the rich American widow living in London and haunted by a richly murky past, labours to hold her head high and bear up despite the Grand Guignol all round her tipping into embarrassing silliness. Trevor Howard makes a fleeting guest appearance, and Chaffey's direction lapses into the tic of concealing the camera behind whatever comes to hand (leaves, a balustrade, fire…). VG

Persecution and Assassination of Jean-Paul Marat as Performed by the Inmates of the Asylum of Charenton Under the Direction of the Marquis de Sade, The

(1966, GB, 116 min)
d Peter Brook. *p* Michael Birkett. *sc* Adrian Mitchell. *ph* David Watkin. *ed* Tom Priestley. *pd* Sally Jacobs. *m* Richard Peaslee. *cast* Ian Richardson, Patrick Magee, Glenda Jackson, Michael Williams, Robert Lloyd, Clifford Rose, John Steiner, Freddie Jones.
●Straightforward 'theatrical' version of Peter Weiss' fascinating play, a brilliantly analytical Brechtian epic with tortuous play-within-play convolutions. In the asylum, de Sade (Magee) has written a play, to be performed by inmates under his own direction and staged before an invited audience: a dialectic on revolution argued between Marat (Richardson) and de Sade himself, its performance continually interrupted by the director of the asylum (Rose) demanding certain excisions. There was much critical hostility to the film when it was first released, based on the premise that Brook had ruined his own stage production by isolating details for emphasis at the expense of an overall tableau effect. In fact the film works very well, right up to the audience-entrapping finale. RM

Persona 100

(1966, Swe, 81 min, b/w)
d Ingmar Bergman. *p* Lars-Owe Carlberg. *sc* Ingmar Bergman. *ph* Sven Nykvist. *ed* Ulla Ryghe. *ad* Bibi Lindström. *m* Lars Johan Werle. *cast* Liv Ullmann, Bibi Andersson, Margaretha Krook, Gunnar Björnstrand, Jörgen Lindström.
●Bergman at his most brilliant as he explores the symbiotic relationship that evolves between an actress suffering a breakdown in which she refuses to speak, and the nurse in charge as she recuperates in a country cottage. To comment is to betray the film's extraordinary complexity, but basically it returns to two favourite Bergman themes: the difficulty of true communication between human beings, and the essentially egocentric nature of art. Here the actress (named Vogler after the charlatan/artist in *The Face*) dries up in the middle of a performance, thereafter refusing to exercise her art. We aren't told why, but from the context it's a fair guess that she withdraws from a feeling of inadequacy in face of the horrors of the modern world; and in her withdrawal, she watches with detached tolerance as humanity (the nurse chattering on about her troubled sex life) reveals its petty woes. Then comes the weird moment of communion in which the two women merge as one: charlatan or not, the artist can still be understood, and can therefore still understand. Not an easy film, but an infinitely rewarding one. TM

Personal Best

(1982, US, 127 min)
d/p Robert Towne. *sc* Robert Towne. *ph* Michael Chapman. *ed* Ned Humphreys, Jere Huggins, Jacqueline Cambras, Walt Mulconery. *pd* Ron Hobbs. *m* Jack Nitzsche, Jill Fraser. *cast* Mariel Hemingway, Scott Glenn, Patrice Donnelly, Kenny Moore, Jim Moody, Kari Gosswiller.
●The sort of nerve required to produce an excellent screenplay like *Chinatown* seems to have deserted Towne in this, his directorial debut. A hesitation in dealing fully with the central relationship, coupled with an over-reliance on slow-motion photography, finds the film losing momentum almost before it leaves the starting blocks. Having set up a lesbian relationship between two athletes preparing for the Olympics (Hemingway and Donnelly) which promises to explore the effect of competition and rivalry in the context of physical surrender and gentle intimacy, it trickles away, foundering on such scenes as a first evening spent arm-wrestling, boozing, belching and farting, too reminiscent of the rugby locker room to be a convincing prelude to any sort of love affair. The thesis collapses into banal presumptions as jarring as the superfluous close-ups of undulating thighs and quivering crotches. HR

Personal Choice

see Beyond the Stars

Personal Column

see Lured

Personal History of the Australian Surf, A

(1981, Aust, 52 min)
d Michael Blakemore. *p* Jeremy Cornfold. *sc* Michael Blakemore. *ph* Tony Wilson. *ed* David Pulbrook. *m* Peter Best. *cast* Michael Blakemore, Leaf Nowland, Mathew Watkin, Daniel Matz, Michael Shearman.
●Basically a home movie in which theatre director Blakemore traces his graduation from Bondi Beach to National Theatre. Wryly subtitled 'the confessions of a straight poofter', it focuses on what seems to be Australia's national hang-up: dad's macho indoctrinations versus sonny's artistic leanings. Engaging enough, and mercifully (or sadly, depending on point of view) short on surfing spectacle. TM

Personal Services

(1987, GB, 105 min)
d Terry Jones. *p* Tim Bevan. *sc* David Leland. *ph* Roger Deakins. *ed* George Akers. *pd* Hugo Luczyc-Wyhowski. *m* John Du Prez. *cast* Julie Walters, Alec McCowen, Danny Schiller, Shirley Stelfox, Victoria Hardcastle, Tim Woodward, Dave Atkins.
●Waitress Christine Painter (Walters) sublets seedy bedsits to local prostitutes, by whose lifestyle she is at once appalled and fascinated. Inevitably, one thing leads to another, and pretty soon CP is catering to the oddly innocuous fantasies of middle-aged, middle class clients. The opening disclaimer, offering safe assurance that the film is not about, only inspired by Cynthia Payne, seems symptomatic of its overall timidity. For although one can applaud the emphasis on everyday ordinariness and the almost matter-of-fact portrait of sexual diversity, what begins as a sporadically astute examination of one woman's drift into a secret and forbidden life, soon degenerates into cliché (what she truly wants is a real man) and an embarrassingly celebratory 'all the world's a pervert' stance. Some good performances (notably Walters, McCowen and Stelfox), but the film itself finally remains toothless, cosy, and (in the saddest sense) very, very English. GA

Persons Unknown

see Soliti Ignoti, I

Persons Unknown

(1996, US, 99 min)
d George Hickenlooper. *p* David Lancaster. *sc* Craig Smith. *ph* Richard Crudo. *ed* Suzanne Pettit. *pd* Jerry Fleming. *m* Ed Tomney. *cast* Joe Mantegna, Kelly Lynch, Naomi Watts, JT Walsh, Xander Berkeley, Jon Favreau.
●Jim Holland (Mantegna), an ex-cop nursing an ailing Long Beach security business, knocks the beautiful Amanda (Lynch) off her feet, but has no idea what he's getting into. He wakes to find she's made herself at home in his filing cabinet. Next time they meet, Amanda's ripped off a sackful of drugs money, and he's stolen it right back. By now he's more interested in her sister Molly (Watts). There's something about a woman in a wheelchair. The breezy set-up promises a thriller in the Elmore Leonard vein: snappy dialogue, strong sense of place, quirky character detail. It's a shame that an hour in, just as everything's shaping up nicely, Hickenlooper's film regroups, resettles and rethinks. In essence, this consists of throwing away the plot and getting to know Jim, Amanda and Molly a whole lot better as they hole up in the High Sierras. Worse, the longer we spend in their company, the less interesting they seem, but at least JT Walsh is on hand with his trademark brand of shameless opportunism. TCh

Persuasion

(1995, GB, 107 min)
d Roger Michell. *p* Fiona Finlay. *sc* Nick Dear. *ph* John Daly. *ed* Kate Evans. *pd* William Dudley. *m* Jeremy Sams. *cast* Amanda Root,

Ciaran Hinds, Sam West, Corin Redgrave, Phoebe Nicholls, Susan Fleetwood.
●A TV Jane Austen which enjoyed considerable theatrical success in the US. Anne Elliot (Root, working wonders with an array of awkward, furtive glances) is the one sensible, unselfish member of the family of a foolish baronet, forced by debt to abandon their mansion for Bath. A decade earlier, she suffered an enduring 'disappointment': she reluctantly gave up her intended, deemed by her family and friends to have few prospects or connections. Now, however, Capt Wentworth (Hinds) is back in England, having made his fortune on the high seas; society being what it is, their paths soon cross. But will he succumb to the young Musgrove girl who's set her cap at him? And what of Anne's hitherto estranged cousin (West), whose charm, money and affections would seem to make him a perfect catch? Overall, the film, adapted by Nick Dear, is strong on psychological insights, feminist asides and the social relevance of place; if the dominant look remains televisual, John Daly's fluid camera (particularly mobile in the whirl of Bath), and some careful colour coding lend a level of invention seldom seen in TV costumers. GA

Per un Pugno di Dollari

see Fistful of Dollars, A

Pétain

(1992, Fr, 135 min)
d Jean Marboeuf. *p* Jacques Kirsner. *sc* Alain Riou, Jean Marboeuf, Jean-Pierre Marchand. *ph* Dominique Bouilleret. *ed* Anne-France Lebrun. *pd* Jérôme Clément. *m* Georges Garvarentz. *cast* Jacques Dufilho, Jean Yanne, Jean-Pierre Cassel, Jean-Claude Dreyfus, Antoinette Moya, Julie Marboeuf, Ludwig Haas.
●Marboeuf's meticulous history lesson on Vichy France is unlikely to win fans anywhere. The French won't thrill to his re-creation of their shameful period of collaboration with the Nazis, while foreigners will prate about moral fibre. Having lost the war, most Frenchmen wanted to keep in with the victors to limit the damage, and this meant obeying orders and rounding up the Jews. The aged WWI hero Marshal Pétain (Dufilho) was wheeled on-stage as the fig leaf of Third Reich absolutism, but the political running was made by Laval (Yanne) who managed to trick the octogenarian into a public handshake with Hitler. Most of the action occurs in the Hôtel du Parc in Vichy where the French puppet government trim and twist their principles. It's an extraordinarily hermetic work. None of the stuff going on outside the hotel room is involving. Dufilho is wonderfully cast, while Yanne chiefly picks on Laval's cartoon characteristic and smokes incessantly as he signs away his nation. A plod. BC

Petal, A (Kkotyip)

(1996, SKor, 101 min)
d Jang Sun-Woo. *p* Byoung-Joo Ahn. *sc* Jang Sun-Woo. *ph* Yoo Young-Kil. *ed* Yang-il Kim. *m* Won Il. *cast* Moon Sung-Kuen, Lee Jung-Hyun, Lee Young-Ran, Sul Kyoung-Ku, Park Chul-Min, Nah Chang-Jin.
●The first mature attempt in Korean culture to come to terms with the Kwangju Massacre of 1980, an unhealed wound comparable with the Tiananmen Square massacre in the minds of Chinese. A young woman, nameless and mentally disturbed, wanders the countryside looking for her brother; she runs into a heavy-drinking labourer and starts tagging along behind him. He tries to get rid of her by insulting, abusing and finally raping her, but she stays with him. Through flashbacks (two of them animated) we learn what the man doesn't know: how the girl's brother and mother died, why she cracked mentally. The girl is perhaps too fragile a symbol to personify the entire nation's trauma, but Jang's shattering film none the less sets a new benchmark for the serious treatment of politics and sex in Korean cinema. TR

Pete Kelly's Blues

(1955, US, 95 min)
d/p Jack Webb. *sc* Richard L Breen. *ph* Harold Rosson. *ed* Robert M Leeds. *pd* Harper Goff. *m* Sammy Cahn, Ray Heindorf, Arthur Hamilton, Matty Matlock. *cast* Jack Webb, Janet Leigh, Peggy Lee, Edmond O'Brien, Andy Devine, Lee Marvin, Ella Fitzgerald, Martin Milner, Jayne Mansfield.
●Opens stunningly with a New Orleans jazz funeral which puts the similar sequences in *Young Man with a Horn* and *Imitation of Life* to shame both musically and atmospherically. Perhaps a little too pedantic in its recreation of Kansas City speakeasies during Prohibition days, and inclined to strain after effect in its depiction of gangster violence (the final shootout in a deserted dance hall, with coloured lights flashing and player piano rattling away, is just a shade too much). Enormously likeable all the same as one of the few films to take jazz seriously. The soundtrack, with Ella Fitzgerald a real knockout as she sings 'Hard Hearted Hannah' and the title song, is a treat. TM

Pete 'n' Tillie

(1972, US, 100 min)
d Martin Ritt. *p/sc* Julius J Epstein. *ph* John A Alonzo. *ed* Frank Bracht. *ad* George Webb. *m* John Williams. *cast* Walter Matthau, Carol Burnett, Geraldine Page, Barry Nelson, Rene Auberjonois, Lee H Montgomery, Henry Jones, Kent Smith.
●This starts out as one of those hard-boiled romances in which Matthau and Burnett, performing with characteristic professionalism, graduate from affair to marriage while Julius J Epstein's script supplies them with suitably grudging wisecracks. But then it gets taken over by a series of soap-style catastrophes: he screws his secretary, their baby dies, they separate, she's in a 'rest home'...but everything's really all right, of course. There's even a moment when you think she's going to marry campy Rene Auberjonois – unfortunately not. Often incidentally funny, though.

Peter and Pavla (Cerny Petr)

(1964, Czech, 85 min, b/w)
d Milos Forman. *sc* Milos Forman, Jaroslav Papousek. *ph* Jan Nemecek. *ed* Miroslav Hajek. *ad* Karel Cerny. *m* Jiri Slitr. *cast* Ladislav Jakim, Pavla Martinková, Jan Ostrcil, Bozena Matusková, Vladimir Pucholt.
●Like *Il Posto,* Forman's first film is about a boy's bemused encounter with the world in his first job, in this case as a trainee supermarket detective; and like Olmi, Forman displays a sympathetically quizzical eye for human failings. Urged by pompous dad to make good, the slow-witted Peter doggedly shadows a suspect (the wrong man, as it happens) through the shelves and the streets, but never quite summons up the resolution to do anything; prodded by fond mum about marriage prospects, he falls for the adorable Pavla, but remains too bashfully hesitant to realise how available she is. No messages here, simply an irresistibly wry and witty look at life's little pitfalls, full of affection for every last one of the characters. TM

Peter Ibbetson

(1935, US, 88 min, b/w)
d Henry Hathaway. *p* Louis D Lighton. *sc* Vincent Lawrence, Waldemar Young. *ph* Charles Lang Jr. *ed* Stuart Heisler. *ad* Hans Dreier, Robert Usher. *m* Ernst Toch. *cast* Gary Cooper, Ann Harding, Ida Lupino, John Halliday, Douglas Dumbrille, Virginia Weidler, Dickie Moore.
●Reputedly 'discovered' by Paul Eluard in a suitably aleatory fashion by following a woman into the Paris cinema at which it was playing, this adaptation of George du Maurier's novel was hailed by André Breton and other Surrealists as the cinematic embodiment of their magnificent obsession with *l'amour fou* – the love that transcends all known obstacles. In fact it is a gentler and more romantic channelling of the libidinal surges of *L'Age d'Or*. A young architect, played with understated intensity by Cooper, meets in adult life his lost childhood love, and is subsequently falsely imprisoned for the murder of her husband. Undeterred by physical separation, the couple continue to meet in their own world, preserved in their youth, until the lasting reunion of death. The film's boldness and continuing appeal lie in its unhesitating and exultant acceptance of the primacy of love, and in its seamless transitions between the worlds of reality and dream. NA

Peter Pan

(1953, US, 76 min)
d Hamilton Luske, Clyde Geronimi, Wilfred Jackson. *sc* Ted Sears, Bill Peet, Joe Rinaldi, Erdman Penner, Winston Hibler, Milt Banta, Ralph Wright. *m* Oliver Wallace. *songs* Sammy Fain, Sammy Cahn, Ted Sears, Erdman Penner, Winston Hibler, Frank Churchill. *cast* voices: Bobby Driscoll, Kathryn Beaumont, Hans Conried.
●Having annoyed Carroll purists in 1951 with his cartoon version of *Alice in Wonderland*, Disney went on to exasperate Barrie fans by using American boy star Bobby Driscoll's voice for Peter Pan, modelling the usually unseen Tinkerbell on Marilyn Monroe, and employing the Sammys Cahn and Fain to compose songs like 'What Makes the Red Man Red'. If you can view it without thinking of Disney fucking about with yet another children's classic and relax in the studio's last decent use of Technicolor, then you're in for a treat. PM

Peter Rabbit and Tales of Beatrix Potter

see Tales of Beatrix Potter

Petersen

(1974, Aust, 107 min)
d/p Tim Burstall. *sc* David Williamson. *ph* Robin Copping. *ed* David Bilcock. *ad* Bill Hutchinson. *m* Peter Best. *cast* Jack Thompson, Jacki Weaver, Joey Hohenfels, Amanda Hunt, George Mallaby, Arthur Dignam, Wendy Hughes.
●Petersen (Thompson), another in the *Alvin Purple* brigade of Australian superstuds, is a peculiarly repulsive anti-hero who grunts his way acquiescently through various encounters and a baffling mish-mash of middle class observation and incident. The fact that the film has some well-observed moments (the script is by David Williamson) only makes its overall effect all the more inconsequential. We are whirled from the sterility of academic life, via the hypocrisy of marriage, to the crude vulnerability of a lower middle class party menaced by Hell's Angels. But each reasonable scene is promptly knocked on the head by idiotic drinking bouts and repulsive leers in the direction of women's lib, abortion, etc. The fact that the softcore sex is less tedious than usual remains something of an achievement in view of the hero's corpse-like demeanour. DP

Peter's Friends

(1992, GB, 101 min)
d/p Kenneth Branagh. *sc* Rita Rudner, Martin Bergman. *ph* Roger Lanser. *ed* Andrew Marcus. *pd* Tim Harvey. *m* Gavin Greenaway. *cast* Hugh Laurie, Imelda Staunton, Stephen Fry, Emma Thompson, Kenneth Branagh, Alphonsia Emmanuel, Rita Rudner, Tony Slattery, Richard Briers.
●Six old friends from the Cambridge Footlights are reunited after a decade for New Year's Eve, and take stock of what happened to their dreams, characters and relationships. The witty script isn't pitched much above a sitcom, but a couple of the turns are terrifically good. Maggie (Thompson) is in publishing, palpably lonely, and so desperate for a lover that she bounds at prospects like a puppy, while Sarah (Emmanuel) has a turnover rate that approximates Catherine the Great's. Peter (Fry), now a Lord and hosting the party at his stately home, never fulfilled his literary promise, nor did Andrew (Branagh), who sold out to Hollywood and has returned with a laminated LA wife (Rudner). Roger (Laurie) and Mary (Staunton) live lives of quiet desperation after the death of a child. Acting honours go to Staunton for her extraordinary emotional depths, and to Thompson for her super-gawky eccentricity. Branagh's drunk scene doesn't work, and most will guess the pay-off, but it's an amiable enterprise. BC

Pete's Dragon

(1977, US, 134 min)
d Don Chaffey. *p* Ron Miller, Jerome Courtland. *sc* Malcolm Marmorstein. *ph* Frank Phillips. *ed* Gordon D Brenner. *ad* John B Mansbridge, Jack Martin Smith. *m* Al Kasha, Joel Hirschhorn. *cast* Sean Marshall, Helen Reddy, Jim Dale, Mickey Rooney, Red Buttons, Shelley Winters, Jim Backus.
●Pete (Marshall) is orphaned and freckly; the dragon is animated and pale green. As a pair they're technically unconvincing and emotionally unpalatable, particularly when they snuggle together in close-up or when the dragon uses a gentle finger to lift a tear from his pal's eye. But the film's sentimentality is mostly contained in the trite and foolish songs; the remainder is familiar Disney knockabout comedy, depending for

much of its appeal on the mugging of mountebank Jim Dale, his assistant Red Buttons, and Mickey Rooney's cuddly drunk of a lighthouse keeper. The dragon itself grunts, grins and goofs around, but isn't half as appealing as its creators obviously hoped. More character and better animation would have helped. GB

Petite chérie

see Little Darling

Petite Marchande d'allumettes, La (The Little Matchgirl)

(1928, Fr, 29 min, b/w)
d/p Jean Renoir, Jean Tedesco. *sc* Jean Renoir. *ph* Jean Bachelet. *ad* Eric Aes. *m* Franz Schubert, Johann Strauss Jr, Richard Wagner, Felix Mendelssohn. *cast* Catherine Hessling, Jean Storm, Manuel Raaby, Amy Wells.

●All too often, Renoir has been simplistically characterised as a 'realist', poetic or otherwise. This little gem from his silent period, based on the Hans Christian Andersen story, gives the lie to both that categorisation and to the director's own oft-quoted assertion that he had only made one film over and over again. For here, as the little match girl (Hessling, then his wife) lies dreaming in the snow – her would-be customers and a gendarme become toy soldiers and a jack-in-the-box – Renoir revels both in various optical effects and in the fantastic nature of the dying girl's delirium. The imagery, an extraordinarily potent blend of impressionism and expressionism, creates a genuinely poignant magic, confirming the director's origins in the avant-garde. (The film under review is the sonorised version. The considerably longer silent version has been lost.) GA

Petite Vendeuse de Soleil, La

see Little Girl Who Sold the Sun, The

Petite Voleuse, La

(1988, Fr, 109 min)
d Claude Miller. *p* Jean-José Richer. *sc* François Truffaut, Claude de Givray. *ph* Dominique Chapuis. *ed* Albert Jurgenson. *ad* Jean-Pierre Kohut-Svelko. *m* Alain Jomy. *cast* Charlotte Gainsbourg, Didier Bazace, Simon de la Brosse, Raoul Billerey, Chantal Banlier.

●Originally a project nurtured by Truffaut over many years, this also had some late input from Claude de Givray. The array of authors could in part account for the somewhat uneven quality of the film's opening third, which focusses at length upon the heroine's delinquency and her stumbling attempts to lose her virginity. Gradually, however, a greater sense of direction emerges. The setting is post-war France, and precocious teenager Janine (Gainsbourg) is keen to enter the adult world. Initial successes are thwarted when a background in petty theft catches up with her. From provincial tolerance to punitive austerity, the mood shifts to encompass Janine's fortunes. It's difficult not to become interested in the perverse twist of her life, but her strange detachment divests the film of some emotional impact. Given such constraints, Gainsbourg delivers an appropriately low-key performance which boasts maturity way beyond her years. References to the romantic allure of cinema, and Janine's blossoming interest in photography (read film-making), add up to something of a homage to Truffaut. CM

Petit Matin, Le (The Virgin and the Soldier)

(1970, Fr, 115 min)
d Jean-Gabriel Albicocco. *p* Paul Cadéac d'Arbaud. *sc* Pierre Kast, Jean-Gabriel Albicocco. *ph* Quinto Albicocco. *ed* Georges Klotz. *ad* David Louradour, Jacques Duguid. *m* Francis Lai. *cast* Catherine Jourdan, Mathieu Carrière, Madeleine Robinson, Jean Vilar, Christian Baltauss, Margo Lion.

●A coyly maudlin romance set in Occupied France during WWII, all about an adolescent girl, much given to riding dreamily around on a white horse, and her love affairs – of varying degrees of intensity and fulfilment – with said horse, a childhood playmate who turns out to be gay (Baltauss), and a handsome young German soldier (Carrière), also much addicted to galloping about. Always a prettifier, Albicocco drenches the whole thing in a pale green tint, so that even shots of Jewish deportees look like chocolate-box tops. There's a fulsome Francis Lai score to match the decoratively swirling mists prevailing in the area, and despite a would-be tragic ending, the whole thing is marshmallow through and through. TM

Petit Prince a dit, Le

(1992, Fr/Switz, 106 min)
d Christine Pascal. *p* Robert Boner. *sc* Christine Pascal, Robert Boner. *ph* Pascal Marti. *ed* Jacques Comets. *m* Bruno Coulais. *cast* Richard Berry, Anémone, Marie Kleiber, Lucie Phan, Mista Prechac, Claude Muret.

●This movie treats with restraint the emotive subject of a little girl diagnosed with a fatal illness – and its effect on her parents. But don't turn the page yet. The film is no horror ride, and watching it is by no means depressing. Violette (Kleiber) is a pudgy, well-adjusted, rather awkward ten-year-old, whose recent blackouts and lack of manual co-ordination arouse concern in her mother Mélanie, a divorced actress (Anémone), who arrives on a visit while the girl's father Adam (Berry) is away on a trip. On his return, Mélanie berates him: how can he, a medical man, be so blind to his daughter's problems? After seeing scans of Violette's brain and overhearing the diagnosis of a tumour, he whisks her away in an effort to forestall the truth. For Violette the trip is just an unexplained holiday, and much of the film's specialness resides in its invitation to reflect anew on the everyday pleasures and pastimes of life, and on the moving father-daughter relationship. WH

Petits Frères, Les

(1999, Fr, 92 min)
d Jacques Doillon. *p* Marin Karmitz. *sc* Jacques Doillon. *ph* Manuel Téran. *ed* Jacques Doillon. *m* Oxmo Puccino. *cast* Stéphanie Touly, Iliès Sefraoui, Mustapha Goumane, Nassim Izem,Rachid Mansouri, Dembo Goumane, Sabrina Mansar.

●For all the welcome developments in the French cinema's return to realism, not to mention its growing interest in the hitherto neglected immigrant inhabitants of the *banlieux*, the 'kids in the hood' saga is fast becoming a cliché, and Doillon, despite fine performances from his young cast, does little to avoid it. A 13-year-old girl, tired of abuse from her stepfather, leaves home with her pitbull to see a pal in the suburbs; soon four Arab boys trick her out of the dog, which is in turn taken away by their older brothers for dogfights. The film charts the girl's efforts to get the dog back, and the boys' deceits and crises of conscience, but the documentary tone never really allows Doillon to delve beneath the surface of gestures and social ritual. Well-meaning but trite and repetitive. GA

Petit Soldat, Le (The Little Soldier)

(1960, Fr, 88 min, b/w)
d Jean-Luc Godard. *p* Georges de Beauregard. *sc* Jean-Luc Godard. *ph* Raoul Coutard. *ed* Agnès Guillemot, Nadine Marquand. *m* Maurice Le Roux. *cast* Michel Subor, Anna Karina, Henri-Jacques Huet, Paul Beauvais, Laszlo Szabo, Georges de Beauregard, Jean-Luc Godard.

●Godard introduces his 'little soldier' as a man turning from action to reflection: Bruno Forestier (Subor) is some kind of secret agent working against Algerian terrorists in France, but he doesn't believe in his fight, and his mind is full of aesthetic and philosophical questions. In fact, he's in many ways a prototype for *Pierrot le Fou*. Bruno, too, falls in love with Anna Karina, and worries whether her eyes are Velazquez-grey or Renoir-grey; he suffers torture for her, and is finally betrayed, not by her but by the lousy political machine, in which Left and Right are mirror faces of each other. Looked at in the context of Godard's later, militant work, this film's analysis is at once naive and fascinating. TR

Petit Théâtre de Jean Renoir, Le (The Little Theatre of Jean Renoir)

(1969, Fr/It/WGer, 100 min)
d/p/sc Jean Renoir. *ph* Georges LeClerc. *ed* Geneviève Winding. *ad* Gilbert Margerie. *m* Joseph Kosma, Jean Wiener. *cast* Fernand Sardou, Jeanne Moreau, Françoise Arnoul, Jean Carmet, Marguerite Cassan, Milly, Nino Formicola, Andrex, Dominique Labourier.

●Renoir's last film, made for TV, displays all the effortlessness of a master, with Renoir introducing his four sketches as anecdotes that have amused him. In lesser hands, they might have become sentimental or misguided, rather than the light, deft pieces they are, full of charm and an awareness of civilised virtues. An old tramp and his wife retain their dignity and love in the face of hardship; a husband falls victim of his wife's electric waxer in a satire on some of the dehumanising aspects of city life; Jeanne Moreau sings a song from the *Belle Epoque*; an old man learns to accept his young wife's infidelity in a piece that affirms the positive virtues of country life as strongly as the second episode condemns city ways. Renoir proves once again that he is among the easiest and most relaxing of directors to watch. CPe

Petit Voleur, Le

see Smalltime Thief

Petomane, Il (The Windbreaker)

(1983, It, 101 min)
d Pasquale Festa Campanile. *p* Luigi De Laurentiis, Aurelio De Laurentiis. *sc* Leo Benvenuti, Piero De Barnardi. *ph* Alfio Contini. *ed* Franco Fraticelli. *ad* Dario Cecchi. *m* Carlo Rustichelli, Paolo Rustichelli. *cast* Ugo Tognazzi, Mariangela Melato, Vittorio Caprioli, Riccardo Tognazzi, Gianmarco Tognazzi, Flavio Colusso.

●Joseph Pujol, *Le Pétomane*, was a real-life character who had an astonishing range of bowel sounds: 'not every zephyr is alike'. In *Belle Epoque* Paris, he earned a fortune with his show at the Moulin Rouge, where he performed to musical accompaniment by his sons and blew smoke-rings from both ends at once. He is shown mixing with the likes of Gide and Satie, and Schönberg writes a piece for his sphincter (which, if true, says a lot about 'the great dodecaphonist'). Tognazzi, in marvellous form, plays the fartiste as a fastidious, rueful man who falls in love with an orphaned countess cellist, and goes to great lengths to conceal his profession, with predictable results. He also rouses the wrath of moralists who, having failed to deter him with heckling, brand 'TACI' (silence) on his right buttock. Festa Campanile's leisurely film includes the obscenity trial where Dante, no less, is cited in his defence ('And he made of his arse a trumpet'), and a bum-blasting finale in front of royalty. It's entirely inoffensive, and such handsome light comedy is not to be sniffed at. MS

Petrified Forest, The

(1936, US, 83 min, b/w)
d Archie Mayo. *p* Henry Blanke. *sc* Charles Kenyon, Delmer Daves. *ph* Sol Polito. *ed* Owen Marks. *ad* John Hughes. *m* Bernard Kaun. *cast* Leslie Howard, Bette Davis, Humphrey Bogart, Genevieve Tobin, Dick Foran, Charley Grapewin, Porter Hall.

●Based on a play by Robert Sherwood rather than Maxwell Anderson, but otherwise astonishingly similar to *Key Largo*, and for a time almost as good as the setting is established (a rundown desert roadhouse) and the characters introduced (dissatisfied girl dreaming of escape, her garrulous grandfather, pouter pigeon father, ox-like hired hand admirer). But all too soon the insufferable literary pretensions creep in, mainly centering on Howard's vagrant poet, who stumbles in from the desert nursing some sort of existential grievance against a world which has no place for Art; and who begs the on-the-run gangster who turns up to hold them hostage ('the last great apostle of rugged individualism') to put him out of his misery. 'Sure I'll do it', Bogart laconically drawls (thereby earning the audience's gratitude). As the darkly brooding Duke Mantee, spared the speechifying because his lines are monosyllabic, Bogart wipes the floor with Howard, and the rest of the cast are fine. TM

Pet Sematary

(1989, US, 103 min)
d Mary Lambert. *p* Richard P Rubinstein. *sc* Stephen King. *ph* Peter Stein. *ed* Michael Hill, Daniel Hanley. *pd* Michael Z Hanan. *m* Elliot Goldenthal. *cast* Dale Midkiff, Fred Gwynne, Denise Crosby, Brad Greenquist, Michael Lombard, Miko Hughes, Blaze Berdahl, Susan Blommaert.

●Like its predecessors (though this time scripted by the author himself), Lambert's leaden, morbid, rather nasty adaptation of Stephen King's novel fails to solve the problem of visualising his complicated internal narratives: stripped of inner lives, the ordinary people who populate his books take on a flat cartoon-like quality. The story of Dr Louis Creed (Midkiff) and his efforts to revive his three-year-old son (Hughes), killed by one of the giant trucks that thunder past their new Maine home, is more like a sketchy outline than a finished work. No film about a scalpel-wielding three-year-old psycho zombie could be entirely devoid of shocks. But reams of tedious exposition, about a children's pet 'sematary' and the magical resurrecting properties of an Indian burial ground, stretch patience and credulity to their limits, while Lambert fails to exploit the potential of the novel's best set pieces. The stories told in flashback by Creed's wife (Crosby) and their elderly neighbour (Gwynne) also seem hopelessly contrived, arresting the book's page-turning plot without adding emotional or psychological depth. NF

Pett and Pott

(1934, GB, 33 min, b/w)
d Alberto Cavalcanti. *p* John Grierson. *sc* uncredited [Alberto Cavalcanti, Stuart Legg]. *ph* John Taylor. *ed* Alberto Cavalcanti. *ad* Humphrey Jennings. *m* Walter Leigh. *cast* Barbara Nixon, Eric Hudson, JM Reeves, Bruce Winston, Valeska Gert, Humphrey Jennings, Basil Wright, Stuart Legg, Alberto Cavalcanti.

●If you can imagine *Un Chien Andalou* reworked by Gilbert and Sullivan, you'll have the flavour of this unlikely product of the Grierson-supervised GPO Film Unit. Subtitled 'A fairy story of the suburbs', it's a satirical-ironical-irrational reverie, which contrasts the virtuous Pett family (who have a phone) with the disgraceful Potts (who don't). The latter are gleefully portrayed as the embodiment of everything un-suburban, with their libidinous continental ways and laxity with the hired help. Made for a pittance, it's radical, fun and probably left its sponsors aghast. (In bit parts: Humphrey Jennings as a grocer, Basil Wright as a parson and Cavalcanti himself as a showman.) BBa

Petticoat Pirates

(1961, GB, 87 min)
d David MacDonald. *p* Gordon LT Scott. *sc* Lewis Schwartz, Charlie Drake. *ph* Gilbert Taylor. *ed* Ann Chegwidden. *ad* Robert Jones. *m* Don Banks. *cast* Charlie Drake, Anne Heywood, Cecil Parker, John Turner, Maxine Audley, Thorley Walters, Victor Maddern, Dilys Laye, Anton Rodgers, Murray Melvin.

●Undistinguished British farce (in Technicolor and CinemaScope). Stoker Charlie (the diminutive Drake) helps 150 Wrens under Superintendent Maxine Audley, who've hijacked a frigate, HMS 'Huntress', to prove they're the equal of their male counterparts. Hardly a feminist masterpiece, but fans will relish the nightmare court-martial in which Drake plays all the parts. TJ

Petulia

(1968, GB, 105 min)
d Richard Lester. *p* Raymond Wagner. *sc* Lawrence B Marcus. *ph* Nicolas Roeg. *ed* Antony Gibbs. *pd* Tony Walton. *m* John Barry. *cast* Julie Christie, George C Scott, Richard Chamberlain, Arthur Hill, Shirley Knight, Pippa Scott, Joseph Cotten, Kathleen Widdoes, Richard Dysart.

●Did Nicolas Roeg have a hand in directing *Petulia*? He's credited as the cinematographer, and the visual style is unmistakably his, but the film's 'Roegian' currents run deeper than that. There's the splintered narrative, full of cuts back and forward through time. There's the structure based on visual 'rhymes' and other correspondences. There's the mixture of muted melodrama and neurotic psychology. There's even a 'psychic' association between Julie Christie and a child in danger, like a flash-forward to *Don't Look Now*. The actual subject remains typical of Dick Lester, with its funny/sad storyline (the 'kooky' Petulia is torn between her bizarre in-laws and her own whims, the latter including a flirtation with a divorced doctor) and its backdrop of 'psychedelic' San Francisco (complete with the Grateful Dead and Janis Joplin). Overall, though, the film leads into *Performance* much more than it harks back to *Help* and *The Knack*. TR

Peu de Soleil dans l'Eau Froide, Un (Sunlight on Cold Water)

(1971, Fr, 110 min)
d Jacques Deray. *p* Gérard Beytout. *sc* Jean-Claude Carrière, Jacques Deray. *ph* Jean Badal. *ed* Henri Lanoe. *ad* François de Lamothe. *m* Michel Legrand. *cast* Claudine Auger, Marc Porel, Bernard Fresson, Barbara Bach, Judith Magre, Gérard Depardieu, Jean-Claude Carrière.

●A fatuous tale (adapted from a novel by Françoise Sagan) about a young journalist, on the verge of nervous breakdown, who is sent away to the country to recuperate. There he meets – wouldn't you know? – a married lady who falls in love with him at first sight. Complications follow, merely multiplying the incredulity. Porel gives one of the most boring, suburban, asexual performances imaginable, and Auger comes on with all the discretion of a Kotex ad. How did Jean-Claude Carrière come to get mixed up in this as co-scriptwriter? VG

Peur sur la Ville

see Night Caller

Peyton Place

(1957, US, 162 min)
d Mark Robson. *p* Jerry Wald. *sc* John Michael Hayes. *ph* William C Mellor. *ed* David Bretherton. *ad* Lyle Wheeler, Jack Martin Smith. *m* Franz Waxman. *cast* Lana Turner, Hope Lange, Arthur Kennedy, Lloyd Nolan, Lee Philips, Terry Moore, Russ Tamblyn, Betty Field, Mildred Dunnock, Diane Varsi.

●Tasteful adaptation of Grace Metalious' best-selling novel detailing the lives and loves of 'ordinary folk' in a small New England town. It comes with its full quota of sex, conspiracy and violence, but the story is told in such circumspect fashion that next to nobody was offended. Turner, whose own private life was one long soap opera, plays a widow with a teenage daughter. Nobody knows why she treats the lass quite so sternly. Nor can they understand why she doesn't want to marry the dashing new high school principal. Nominated for just about every Oscar going, the film spawned a dreary sequel and an immensely popular TV series. GM

Phaedra

(1961, US/Greece, 116 min, b/w)
d/p Jules Dassin. *sc* Jules Dassin, Margarita Liberaki. *ph* Jacques Natteau. *ed* Roger Dwyre. *ad* Max Douy. *m* Mikis Theodorakis. *cast* Melina Mercouri, Anthony Perkins, Raf Vallone, Elizabeth Ercy, Olympia Papadouka, Jules Dassin.

●A risibly misbegotten attempt to update Euripides' *Hippolytus*, and not a patch upon Dassin's best Hollywood work. Mercouri is characteristically overbearing as the wife of a shipping magnate (Vallone) who falls in love with her stepson (Perkins, hopelessly miscast). But the main problem is that the transposition from ancient to modern Greece simply won't wash: gone are the poetry, psychological insights, and dramatic single-mindedness of the original, while the horror of incest seems horribly overblown when applied to a stepson in the modern world. Thus the final car crash is less tragic than wholly unnecessary, and what one takes away from the film is the impression of a classic travestied. GA

Phantasm

(1978, US, 89 min)
d/p/sc/ph/ed Don Coscarelli. *pd* S Tyer. *m* Fred Myrow, Malcolm Seagrave. *cast* Angus Scrimm, Michael Baldwin, Bill Thornbury, Reggie Bannister, Kathy Lester, Terrie Kalbus.

●A film that somehow manages to disregard all known standards of suspense and narrative without paying the price. For twenty minutes it's recognisable horror pic stuff, with a flimsy youngster-discovers-shady-doings-up-at-funeral-parlour plot. But that's before the revelation that the local morgue is actually an assembly line for some incredibly mixed-up creatures who stop living, get crushed to a height of 3ft 2in, packed in garbage cans, and shipped off as dwarf slaves to somewhere in outer space. Simply has to be seen to be (dis)believed.

Phantasm II

(1988, US, 97 min)
d Don Coscarelli. *p* Roberto Quezada. *sc* Don Coscarelli. *ph* Daryn Okada. *ed* Peter Teschner. *pd* Peter Duffin. *m* Fred Myrow, Christopher L Stone, Malcolm Seagrave. *cast* James Le Gros, Reggie Bannister, Angus Scrimm, Paula Irvine, Samantha Phillips, Kenneth Tigar.

●The only valid reason for seeing this belated sequel is that it goes some way towards explaining the incomprehensible plot of its predecessor. Now 19, Mike (Le Gros) emerges from seven solid years of psychoanalysis to discover – surprise, surprise – that it wasn't all in his disturbed mind. The ensuing action again pits Mike and 'bald, middle-aged ex-ice cream vendor Reg' (Bannister) against the cadaverous Tall Man (Scrimm) and his malevolent dwarf slaves. Clammy stuff, with a few spirited gore sequences, such as flying spheres which attach themselves to the victim's forehead and drill their way into the brain. There are a few good jokes, and patches of gruesome inventiveness, but no cumulative tension. NF

Phantom, The

(1996, US/Aust, 100 min)
d Simon Wincer. *p* Robert Evans, Alan Ladd Jr. *sc* Jeffrey Boam. *ph* David Burr. *ed* O Nicholas Brown. *pd* Paul Peters. *m* David Newman. *cast* Billy Zane, Treat Williams, Kristy Swanson, Catherine Zeta Jones, James Remar, Casey Siemaszko, Samantha Eggar, Patrick McGoohan.

●Created by cartoonist Lee Falk in 1936 and still running, The Phantom has some claims to being the original comic-strip superhero, but this belated, albeit decorative adaptation looks tamely second-hand. Deep in the jungle island of Bengalla, the Ghost Who Walks is an immortal masked figure who watches over the native tribespeople, but closer inspection reveals that this purple-clad crusader is actually 21st in a family line whose mission has remained constant through the generations: revenge against the Sengh pirate brotherhood, now vying with power-crazed magnate Xander Drax to reunite the four deadly Skulls of Touganda and unleash an ancient and deadly force of evil. Little expense has been spared in putting this adventure fantasy on screen, with vintage planes and automobiles by the yard, striking Art Deco production design and breathtaking Thai coastal locations. A pity that the performers are so uncharismatic, with leading man Billy Zane plastic and soulless in Lycra, and not much more winning when he switches to playboy mode to woo free-spirited politico's daughter Kristy Swanson (pertly anonymous). Treat Williams barks as bully-boy Drax to numbing effect and Catherine Zeta Jones proves remarkably boring as a dyke-vixen villainess. TJ

Phantom Baron, The

see Baron Fantôme, Le

Phantom India (L'Inde Fantôme)

(1968, Fr, 378 min – 7 parts, each 54 min)
d Louis Malle. *p* Elliott Kastner. *sc* Louis Malle. *ph* Etienne Becker. *ed* Suzanne Baron. *narrator* Louis Malle.

●A very personal labour and a densely informative account of its subject. Though the film opens with the avowed intention of 'not making up one's mind…of just following the camera', Malle's own commentary continually betrays a need to interpret what he sees, to tease out symbols from his visual impressions (a blinkered horse endlessly circling a mill as an image of a society unchanging and blind to the necessity of change, for instance). This compulsion seems limiting, but is always counteracted by a deliberate sense of irony at Malle's own expense, and the reminder that in India there are always at least two ways of looking at things. Seen together, the seven episodes provide an excellent picture of a very complicated society in its several aspects: the religion, predominantly Hindu but accommodating 50 million Muslims, as well as minority sects; the caste system, officially abolished in 1947 but still all-pervasive; the rival cultures of the North and South, Aryan and Dravidian; and political differences, ranging from xenophobic and racist minority groups preaching persecution of the Muslims to Communist parties operating in societies without trade union consciousness even in industrialised communities. Well worth seeing if you've any interest in India at all. RM

Phantom Lady

(1944, US, 87 min, b/w)
d Robert Siodmak. *p* Joan Harrison. *sc* Bernard C Schoenfeld. *ph* Woody Bredell. *ed* Arthur Hilton. *ad* John Goodman, Robert Clatworthy. *m* Hans Salter. *cast* Ella Raines, Franchot Tone, Alan Curtis, Thomas Gomez, Elisha Cook Jr, Aurora, Fay Helm, Andrew Tombes, Regis Toomey.

●Siodmak's first American success, a moody thriller from a Cornell Woolrich novel which set the mould for a string of dark classics. The wife of an engineer (Curtis) is murdered, his female alibi's very existence is denied by every witness, and he faces the chair. His secretary (Raines) and a curious off-duty cop (Gomez) investigate… Siodmak's angled compositions and dramatic lighting might be uncharitably ticked off as genre staples, but his manipulation of the film's key motif is masterly. He concentrates on the tangible and psychological evidence – the 'records' – of absence: the wife's portrait, the messages on the office dictaphone, the court transcript, the dead witness' typed address, the hat that recalls a dead fiancé. And the film's quest is for a woman who exists only in the memories of the condemned man and the audience. PT

Phantom Light, The

(1935, GB, 75 min, b/w)
d Michael Powell. *p* Michael Balcon. *sc* Ralph Smart. *ph* Roy Kellino. *ed* Derek Twist. *ad* Alex Vetchinsky. *m* Louis Levy. *cast* Gordon Harker, Ian Hunter, Binnie Hale, Milton Rosmer, Donald Calthrop, Reginald Tate.

●A creaky stage play is transformed by Powell into a cheap but splendidly atmospheric comedy thriller. Gordon Harker stars as a Cockney lighthouse-keeper who, with the aid of an insurance investigator (Hale) and a naval officer (Hunter), sees off a gang of wreckers intent on no good. The leader of the wreckers is one 'Dr Carey', the setting is Wales, and the climactic confrontation is intercut with a ship heading for the rocks. Any party, even the Welsh Nationalists, could interpret this allegory to their own ends. TCh

Phantom Lover, The (Xin Yeban Gesheng)

(1995, HK, 102 min)
d Ronny Yu. *p* Michael Ng. *sc* Roy Szeto, Raymond Wong Bak-Ming, Ronny Yu. *ph* Peter Pan. *ed* David Wu Dai-Wai. *ad* Eddie Ma. *m* Lelie Cheung. *cast* Leslie Cheung, Wu Qian Lian, Huang Lei, Liu Lin.

●This grandiose vehicle for Leslie Cheung was intended to launch his comeback from a few years of 'retirement' as a singer, but neither the movie nor the soundtrack CD impressed the justifiably cynical HK public. Shot in China and based on a much more interesting 1937 melodrama made in Shanghai, it's a thinly plotted riff on the Phantom of the Opera story: Cheung plays the acid-scarred tenor who's reduced to warbling to his true love from behind a curtain while a surrogate beau mimes his words on stage. Awesomely insincere, the film piles on the romantic imagery and hopes the anachronistic score will glutinise the viewer's natural resistance. TR

Phantom of Liberty, The

see Fantôme de la Liberté, Le

Phantom of the Opera, The

(1925, US, 8,460 ft. b/w & col)
d Rupert Julian. *p* Carl Laemmle. *sc* Elliott J Clawson. *ph* Charles van Enger, Virgil Miller, Milton, Bridenbecker. *ed* Gilmore Walker. *ad* EE Sheeley, Sidney M Ullman, Ben Carré. *cast* Lon Chaney, Mary Philbin, Norman Kerry, Snitz Edwards, Gibson Gowland, Arthur Edmund Carewe.

●There were many fingers in this pie during production, most of them no longer on the credits, which doubtless accounts for its hobbling exposition and the pathetic scenes that separate its highpoints. But the highs are way up there with the best in the tradition of Gothic fantasy: Chaney's best ever phantom, his face scarred to hell by acid, unmasked at the organ by the timorous heroine; the phantom stopping a costume ball when he appears as the Red Death; the phantom shrouded in the most romantic cape ever seen, perched on top of the statue of Apollo to eavesdrop on the lovers. And the sustained crescendo of the end is still unrivalled. TR

Phantom of the Opera

(1943, US, 92 min)
d Arthur Lubin. *p* George Waggner. *sc* Eric Taylor, Samuel Hoffenstein. *ph* Hal Mohr, W Howard Greene. *ed* Russell Schoengarth. *ad* John Goodman, Alexander Golizten. *m* Edward Ward. *cast* Claude Rains, Susanna Foster, Nelson Eddy, Edgar Barrier, Jane Farrar, J Edward Bromberg, Hume Cronyn, Leo Carrillo, Miles Mander.

●Very pretty to look at, with lush Technicolor, handsome sets, and even a fetchingly sculptured mask to give Claude Rains' rather benign Phantom the look of a contented feline. The accent is more on musical extravaganza than horror, with endless operatic snippets for Eddy and Foster to warble, making it all a somewhat tiresome waste of Rains' performance. TM

Phantom of the Opera, The

(1962, GB, 84 min)
d Terence Fisher. *p* John Elder [Anthony Hinds]. *sc* John Elder. *ph* Arthur Grant. *ed* James Needs, Alfred Cox. *ad* Bernard Robinson, Don Mingaye. *m* Edwin Astley. *cast* Edward de Souza, Heather Sears, Herbert Lom, Michael Gough, Thorley Walters, Ian Wilson, Martin Miller, Renee Houston, Miles Malleson.

●A peculiarly low-keyed film, containing very little violence by Hammer's standards (it didn't even get an X certificate), with the whole Phantom theme handled remarkably tamely (and Lom suffering from a particularly unimaginative make-up and mask). But Fisher's direction is as accomplished as ever, and there are several good flourishes in the opera house auditorium. Because of its restraint and a fairly thin plot, the overall effect of the film is curiously abstract, evolving into a series of nice sets and compositions. DP

Phantom of the Opera

(1989, US, 93 min)
d Dwight H Little. *p* Menahem Golan, Harry Alan Towers. *sc* Duke Sandefur. *ph* Elemér Ragalyi. *ed* Charles Bornstein. *ad* Tivadar Bertalan. *m* Misha Segal. *cast* Robert Englund, Jill Schoelen, Alex Hyde-White, Bill Nighy, Terence Harvey, Stephanie Lawrence.

●Knocked unconscious while auditioning for a Broadway musical, aspiring starlet Christine Day (Schoelen) awakens to find herself mysteriously transported to Victorian London, where she is understudying for objectionable prima donna Carlotta (Lawrence). When Carlotta is struck dumb by the discovery of a freshly peeled stagehand in her wardrobe, Christina is manoeuvred into the spotlight by the shadowy figure of deformed and demented composer Erik Destler (Englund). Soon the temporally displaced diva finds herself the centre of a murder investigation as all who slight her are swiftly and stickily dispensed with by her pathological paramour. Little's rehashing of the well-worn melodrama (with added sub-Faustian angle) pays half-hearted visual homage to Hammer's 1962 Herbert Lom vehicle. It also chucks in gruesome skin-grafting special effects for good measure. Englund romps around doing his standard 'hideously deformed anti-hero' routine, but the rest of the cast remain resolutely wooden. Sporadically interesting, occasionally inept, and not a little uncalled for. MK

Phantom of the Paradise

(1974, US, 91 min)
d Brian De Palma. *p* Edward R Pressman. *sc* Brian De Palma. *ph* Larry Pizer. *ed* Paul Hirsch. *pd* Jack Fisk. *m* Paul Williams. *cast* Paul Williams, William Finley, Jessica Harper, George Memmoli, Gerrit Graham.

●Despite the dread MOR dirges given to Harper's crooning ingenue, arguably De Palma's finest film. A highly inventive updating of the *Phantom of the Opera* story to the rockbiz world – complete with borrowings from *Faust* and *The Picture of Dorian Gray* – it tells of rock composer Finley's desire for revenge after he is cheated by a nightclub and record label mogul (Williams). Nothing that remarkable about the plot in itself, but De Palma employs his love of gadgetry to imaginative effect (making terrific use of split screens and video technology), and casts a satirically beady eye upon the money-hungry foibles of the music industry. Best, in fact, is the cameo by Gerrit Graham as the camp, 'Producers'-style glamrock star, although Memmoli's world-weary manager and the piss-take of Alice Cooper are also memorable. GA

Phantom President, The

(1932, US, 78 min, b/w)
d Norman Taurog. *sc* Walter de Leon, Harlan Thompson. *ph* David Abel. *songs* Richard Rodgers, Lorenz Hart. *cast* George M Cohan, Claudette Colbert, Jimmy Durante, George Barbier, Sidney Toler.

●Not exactly sharp political satire, this tells of a stodgy banker who's running for the American presidency, and of the lookalike silver-tongued medicine man who is drafted in to take his place and add zest to the campaign. But it does offer a rare chance to see Cohan ('Mr Broadway') in action. Whether he's as wonderful as Cagney's impersonation of him in *Yankee Doodle Dandy* is a matter of opinion, but the double role certainly allows him ample space to demonstrate his versatility. Not, however, his song-writing skills: the mediocre tunes were supplied, surprisingly, by Rodgers and Hart. GA

Phantom Strikes, The

see Gaunt Stranger, The

Phantom Tollbooth, The

(1969, US, 89 min)
d Chuck Jones, Abe Levitow (animation), Dave Monahan (live action). *p* Abe Levitow, Les Goldman. *sc* Chuck Jones, Sam Rosen. *ph* Lester Shorr. *ed* Jim Faris. *ad* George W Davis, Charles K Hagedon. *m* Dean Elliott. *cast* voices: Mel Blanc, Laws Butler, Candy Candido, Hans Conreid.

●MGM's first feature-length cartoon is about a bored child who drives through a magic turnpike and learns from the (too) many strange characters he meets that the world is really a very interesting place. The Norton Juster book it's based on obviously aspired to become a children's classic, being a very moral tale indeed. But although all its teaching is sensible (learning words and numbers can be useful, mistakes don't matter as long as you try), there are just too many lessons here for most kids to take in, and not enough conventional cartoon humour to sugar the pill. But there are some very nice ideas to get older children's imaginations working, particularly the professor who conducts the sunrise from a podium, and a well-directed live action prologue and epilogue.

Phar Lap

(1983, Aust, 118 min)
d Simon Wincer. *p* John Sexton. *sc* David Williamson. *ph* Russell Boyd. *ed* Tony Paterson. *pd* Larry Eastwood. *m* Bruce Rowland. *cast* Tom Burlinson, Martin Vaughan, Judy Morris, Celia de Burgh, Ron Liebman, Vincent Ball, John Stanton.

●Reluctant sportsters may empathise with Phar Lap, the ugly duckling of the 1930s Australian horse-racing scene. Despite a pedigree bloodline, the horse is unwilling to put any effort into racing, until a young 'strapper' dishes a little love into training sessions and hey presto, a winner is born. Trouble follows when he becomes too big to race in Australia and is shipped abroad, where disaster strikes…Based on fact, Wincer's film leaves a lot of unanswered questions concerning Phar Lap's fate, and echoes the horse's pace: slow start, pick up in the middle, a blinkered rush to the finishing post. The sight of the animal racing, shot in slow motion, fully reveals the beauty of the power and effort needed to win; less enjoyment, however, is to be had from the human characters, with only Leibman and Vaughan standing out as a pair of stubborn toughs. JWil

Phase IV

(1973, GB, 84 min)
d Saul Bass. *p* Paul Radin. *sc* Mayo Simon. *ph* Dick Bush. *ed* Willy Kemplen. *ad* John Barry. *m* Brian Gascoigne. *cast* Nigel Davenport, Lynne Frederick, Michael Murphy, Alan Gifford, Helen Horton, Robert Henderson.

●The ants is coming! Anyone who has ever watched an army of ants streaming back and forth along their 'motorways', defying the elements to accomplish their world-conquering task, knows this story well. Too well. Humankind's fate is left in the hands of several unusually inept and colourless scientists, the ants get the works from the special effects department, and original ideas (so often a casualty in sci-fi cinema) take a back seat. Only the opening titles really grab you, but then they should: Bass is the man who gave you the cat crawl for *Walk on the Wild Side*. As a director he's still got a lot of bugs to iron out. MA

Phenix City Story, The

(1955, US, 100 min, b/w)
d Phil Karlson. *p* Samuel Bischoff, David Diamond. *sc* Crane Wilbur, Daniel Mainwaring. *ph* Harry Neumann. *ed* George White. *ad* Stanley Fleischer. *m* Harry Sukman. *cast* Richard Kiley, Edward Andrews, John McIntire, Kathryn Grant, Biff McGuire, John Larch, James Edwards.

●Behind the bland title lies a barnstorming semi-hysterical thriller which pulls few punches in its attempt to chronicle the true story of an Alabama town which was founded in the early 1800s by runaway blacks and renegade whites, and by the 1950s had become a kind of supermarket for every conceivable criminal activity, from black market babies to elections rigged by crime syndicates. Eventually the military moved in and laid waste most of the vice area. Karlson's film follows this extraordinary story with newsreel-type relish, and the militaristic ending may be the closest any American film ever got to advocating a domestic coup. DP

Phenomena

see Creepers

Phenomenon

(1996, US, 124 min)
d Jon Turteltaub. *p* Barbara Boyle, Michael Taylor. *sc* Gerald DiPego. *ph* Phedon Papamichael. *ed* Bruce Green, David Rennie. *pd* Garreth Stover. *m* Thomas Newman. *cast* John Travolta, Kyra Sedgwick, Forest Whitaker, Robert Duvall, David Gallagher, Ashley Buccille.

●Despite an intriguing premise and a strong opening, this allegory about the limits of human intelligence goes seriously pear-shaped in the middle. Struck by heavenly (or is it alien?) light, auto mechanic George Malley acquires a voracious intellect and an ability to absorb facts and ideas. At first these gifts provide trivial entertainment and practical solutions to everyday problems, but once the novelty wears off, his small-town neighbours start to worry. As with his Jamaican bobsled comedy, *Cool Runnings*, director Turteltaub's film soon slips into inspirational mode, allowing subtle performances to be overshadowed by a hyperbolic score and a desperate straining for cosmic significance. Not even Travolta's bold performance as the brilliant but bewildered George, skillfully treading the line between affecting naivety and cloying sentimentality, can survive this deluge of mawkishness. NF

Philadelphia

(1993, US, 125 min)
d Jonathan Demme. *p* Edward Saxon, Jonathan Demme. *sc* Alice Hoffman, Ron Nyswaner. *ph* Tak Fujimoto. *ed* Craig McKay. *pd* Kristi Zea. *m* Howard Shore. *cast* Tom Hanks, Denzel Washington, Jason Robards, Mary Steenburgen, Antonio Banderas, Ron Vawter.

●Hollywood's first major movie about AIDS is, at the very least, as good as we had any right to expect. The plot is simple: Andrew Beckett (Hanks), a gay lawyer with AIDS, is fired for 'incompetence' and sues his bosses, hiring a homophobic attorney (Washington) to represent him. Less a portrait of gay life or the effects of AIDS, the story serves as a framework to examine associated issues. Why do Beckett's bosses sack him and not a woman employee with AIDS? Should people with fatal or contagious diseases tell their employers about their condition? Is there any occasion when we don't have the right to remain silent about our sexuality? Such questions constitute the film's backbone. More importantly, most of the 'big' emotional scenes we'd expect to see are omitted. Thus, we never feel we're being manipulated into shedding easy tears. The movie is defined by a tone of quiet restraint. Safe and apolitical it may be, but *Philadelphia* succeeds as a deeply affecting humanist drama. GA

Philadelphia Experiment, The

(1984, US, 101 min)
d Stewart Raffill. *p* Joel B Michaels, Douglas Curtis. *sc* William Gray, Michael Janover. *ph* Dick Bush. *ed* Neil Travis, William Hoy. *ad* Chris Campbell. *m* Ken Wannberg. *cast* Michael Paré, Nancy Allen, Eric Christmas, Bobby DiCicco, Louise Latham, Kene Holliday, Joe Dorsey.

●A time-travel yarn of the 'past arrives in the present' persuasion. Two WWII sailors involved in some early radar experiment tumble through the decades into 1984. The 'what the hell's happened?' passages are, as usual, more diverting than the 'what the hell can we do about it?' scenes, the latter involving merely flashing lights, showers of sparks and talk of imploding vortexes. Much more fun is the spectacle of Young 1943 trying to work out why the US President looks vaguely familiar, and how come the folks in the diner are hardly glancing at a television, on which a noisy monster is assaulting a bare-breasted starlet. BBa

Philadelphia Story, The 

(1940, US, 112 min, b/w)
d George Cukor. *p* Joseph L Mankiewicz. *sc* Donald Ogden Stewart. *ph* Joseph Ruttenberg. *ed* Frank Sullivan. *ad* Cedric Gibbons. *m* Franz Waxman. *cast* Katharine Hepburn, Cary Grant, James Stewart, Ruth Hussey, Roland Young, John Howard, Virginia Weidler, Henry Daniell.

●Cukor and Donald Ogden Stewart's evergreen version of Philip Barry's romantic farce, centring on a socialite wedding threatened by scandal, is a delight from start to finish, with everyone involved working on peak form. Hepburn's the ice maiden, recently divorced from irresponsible millionaire Grant and just about to marry a truly dull but supposedly more considerate type (Howard). Enter Grant, importunate and distinctly sceptical. Also enter Stewart and Hussey, snoopers from *Spy* magazine, to cover the society wedding of the year and throw another spanner in the works. Superbly directed by Cukor, the film is a marvel of timing and understated performances, effortlessly transcending its stage origins without ever feeling the need to 'open out' in any way. The wit still sparkles; the ambivalent attitude towards the rich and idle is still resonant; and the moments between Stewart and Hepburn, drunk and flirty on the moonlit terrace, tingle with a real, if rarely explicit, eroticism. GA

Philosoph, Der

see 3 Women in Love

Philosopher's Stone, The (Paras Pathar)

(1957, Ind, 111 min, b/w)
d Satyajit Ray. *p* Promod Lahiri. *sc* Satyajit Ray. *ph* Subrata Mitra. *ed* Dulal Dutta. *ad* Bansi Chandragupta. *m* Ravi Shankar. *cast* Tulsi Chakravarti, Kali Bannerjee, Ranibala, Gangapada Bose, Haridhan, Jahar Roy.

●A comic fantasy about an elderly clerk who finds a stone which has the property of turning base metals into gold, this was something of a potboiler slipped into Ray's schedule because of delays on *The Music Room*. Losing out against the promptings of conscience, the downtrodden hero decides to use the stone to acquire the comforts he and his wife have never known, only to find his troubles merely beginning as he is swept into a wealthy social whirl. Shot in the neo-realist style, it has something of the same doggy charm as Rossellini's *Miracle in Milan*, though much more crudely made. If the political and social satire sometimes seems a little obvious, it is also evident that there are many allusions which tend to escape Western audiences. TM

Phoelix

(1979, GB, 47 min)
d/sc Anna Ambrose. *ph* Peter Harvey, Stephen Dwoskin. *ed* Charles Rees, Anna Ambrose. *ad* Miranda Melville, Mary Hobden. *m* Ronnie Leahy, Iggy Quail Jazz Combo, Steve Norbert Trio. *cast* Philip Beaumont, Angela Coles, Amber Teran, Cozey Fanni Tutte, Robert Hornery.

●An aged art connoisseur (Beaumont) and his young female neighbour (Coles), who has a job posing naked in a club, meet and exist in fantasy and reality. Although this raises certain much-discussed questions about the nature of representation, and about the construction of narrative and daydreams in films, 'Phoelix' tends to treat these as just pretty and pertinent issues, opting instead for a mannered concentration on detail. HM

Phone Call from a Stranger

(1952, US, 96 min, b/w)
d Jean Negulesco. *p/sc* Nunnally Johnson. *ph* Milton Krasner. *ed* Hugh Fowler. *ad* Lyle Wheeler, J Russell Spencer. *m* Franz Waxman. *cast* Shelley Winters, Gary Merrill, Keenan Wynn, Michael Rennie, Bette Davis.

●A decent, but hardly outstanding dramatic compendium. Having survived an air crash, Merrill visits the bereaved families of three of the fellow passengers with whom he had become friendly during the fateful flight. Davis, then Merrill's husband, appears in a subordinate role as Wynn's bedridden spouse, and moves things up a gear or two. Written and produced by Nunnally Johnson. TJ

Phörpa

see Cup, The

Photographing Fairies

(1997, GB, 106 min)
d Nick Willing. *p* Michele Carmarda. *sc* Nick Willing, Chris Harrald. *ph* John de Borman. *ed* Sean Barton. *pd* Laurence Dorman. *m* Simon Boswell. *cast* Toby Stephens, Emily Woof, Frances Barber, Phil Davis, Ben Kingsley, Rachel Shelley, Edward Hardwicke.

●Devastated by the death of his true love, photographer Charles Castle (Stephens) withdraws into a life of rational scepticism, calmly plying his trade through the trenches of WWI and its aftermath. When a woman brings him a photograph of her two girls playing with little winged creatures, it seems genuine; and upon investigation, Charles awakens to new possibilities and discovers a flower which, when consumed, provides sensory access to a world of fairies. This first feature (from the book by Steve Szilagyi) is a resolutely modern period drama, a grown-up fairytale for the '90s. One can quibble with the overly precise, determined dialogue, and the dramatic weight Emily Woof's character (Charles' potential real-world lover) must bear in a secondary but pivotal role, but these are minor failings, and director Nick Willing otherwise shows a sure sense of judgment. Aided by a fine cast (notably Kingsley as the girls' vicar father) and, appropriately, stunning photography by John de Borman, it's a fresh, rewarding film, intelligent and very beautiful. (See also *FairyTale – A True Story*.) NB

Physical Evidence

(1988, US, 99 min)
d Michael Crichton. *p* Martin Ransohoff. *sc* Bill Phillips. *ph* John A Alonzo. *ed* Glenn Farr. *pd* Dan Yarhi. *m* Henry Mancini. *cast* Burt Reynolds, Theresa Russell, Ned Beatty, Kay Lenz, Ted McGinley, Tom O'Brien, Kenneth Welsh, Ray Baker.

●Reynolds used to snap out a smart line, hold the audacity for a close-up, then cinch a zip or slam in a magazine. In this hopelessly muddled thriller, he is denied his routine, and what his fans make of the resulting penny-plain actor is anybody's guess. Script-heavy, improbable, and with a thrown-together plot, the movie doubtless started out as a gloss on the complications of '40s *film noir*. Framed for a killing, drunken cop Joe Paris (Reynolds) is assigned up-market attorney Jenny Hudson (Russell) to defend him. He can't remember what he did on the night in question, won't implicate his married lover (Lenz), and they go through the usual period of mutual resentment. Jenny lives with a bracered yuppie (McGinley) who says things like 'I thought we were gonna spend some quality time together'. The case is crazy with clues, fights, new characters who fail to detain the attention, and all-important tapes containing something or other. The resolution is rubbish. BC

Piaf (aka Piaf – The Early Years/The Sparrow of Pigalle)

(1974, Fr, 105 min)
d Guy Casaril. *p* Cy Feuer, EH Martin. *sc* Françoise Ferley, Guy Casaril, (English-language version) Marc Behm. *ph* Edmond Séchan. *ed* Henri Taverna, Louisette Taverna. *ad* François de Lamothe. *m* Ralph Burns. *cast* Brigitte Ariel, Pascale Christophe, Guy Tréjean, Pierre Vernier, Jacques Duby, Anouk Ferjac.
● She was born in a gutter (literally) and raised in a brothel, went blind in infancy and 'miraculously' recovered her sight, lost her own child to tuberculosis, and ultimately triumphed on the music hall stage: Edith Piaf's early life, as potential biopic material, is simply too crude to be true. Yet, if rendered as a popular song by a director like Demy, it could have been extraordinarily poignant. By infallibly homing in on every available cliché, and dubbing the lugubrious Ariel with the voice of an imitator rather than Piaf's own, Casaril has made a movie worthy of inclusion in the catalogue of indignities which befell its subject during her lifetime. GAd

π [Pi]

(1997, US, 84 min, b/w)
d Darren Aronofsky. *p* Eric Watson. *sc* Darren Aronofsky. *ph* Matthew Libatique. *ed* Oren Sarch. *pd* Matthew Maraffi. *m* Clint Mansell. *cast* Sean Gullette, Mark Margolis, Ben Shenkman, Pamela Hart, Stephen Pearlman, Samia Shoaib.
● Holed up in his Chinatown apartment, electronics whiz Max (Gullette, who, with the director and producer, came up with the film's story) is obsessed with finding the underlying numerical pattern behind the global stock market, since he believes everything in the universe can be expressed in purely mathematical terms. Is he staring into the mysteries of creation? Or is he just a disturbed loner whose off-kilter psychosis has spurred him to find patterns of meaning where none exist? Aronofsky's startlingly original debut recalls the inspirational fervour of *Eraserhead*, as it constructs a paranoid vision from b/w cinematography, a pounding score, and flashes of sheer hallucinatory weirdness. We share Max's feelings of imminent psychological disintegration as the film probes our own insecurity in the face of the eternal. Maths meets millennial doom in one of the decade's true originals. TJ

Pianist, The

(2002, Fr, 148 min)
d Roman Polanski. *p* Roman Polanski, Robert Benmussa, Alain Sarde. *sc* Ronald Harwood. *ph* Pawel Edelman. *ed* Hervé de Luze. *pd* Allan Starski. *m* Wojciech Kilar. *cast* Adrien Brody, Emilia Fox, Michal Zebrowski, Ed Stoppard, Maureen Lipman, Frank Finlay, Jessica Kate, Julia Rayner.
● An adaptation of concert pianist Wladyslaw Szpilman's memoirs about his experiences in Nazi-occupied Warsaw, Polanski's cinematic return to the ravaged world of his childhood starts inauspiciously, lumbered with the clichés of Ronald Harwood's script. The actors (mostly from British TV) who play the musician's doomed family squabble to order about how to react to events. Once Szpilman is left behind, however, and forced to hide in empty apartments in the ever more unrecognisable city, his struggle simply to survive is rendered with increasing subtlety, and Brody's lead performance steadily comes into its own. Old-fashioned in both visual and narrative style and in its overall restraint, the film clearly benefits from the director's first-hand knowledge of the territory. GA

Pianiste, La

see Piano Teacher, The

Piano, The 100

(1993, Aust, 120 min)
d Jane Campion. *p* Jan Chapman. *sc* Jane Campion. *ph* Stuart Dryburgh. *ed* Veronika Jenet. *pd* Andrew McAlpine. *m* Michael Nyman. *cast* Holly Hunter, Harvey Keitel, Sam Neill, Anna Paquin, Kerry Walker, Tungia Baker.
● Nineteenth century Scotland: Ada (Hunter) hasn't spoken since she was six. She communicates with hand signs, and doesn't consider herself silent, thanks to the joy she takes in playing her piano. But when she arrives in New Zealand for an arranged marriage, her husband (Neill) insists the piano is too unwieldy to be carried from the beach. So, when Baines (Keitel), a neighbouring settler turned half-Maori, buys it, Ada agrees to give him piano lessons, unaware that he intends eventually to give her the instrument in return for small but illicit sexual favours. Campion's Gothic romance is notable for its performances and Michael Nyman's score. The writer/director offers something more starkly, strangely beautiful than most costume dramas, and the whole film puts a fresh spin on the traditional love story. The characters are stubborn and inward-looking, and it's the refusal to sentimentalise that makes this harsh tale of obsession so moving. Campion never underestimates the power physical obsession exerts over human souls, and, for once, a modern film treats erotic passion honestly. GA

Piano Teacher, The (La Pianiste)

(2001, Aus/Fr, 130 min)
d/sc Michael Haneke. *ph* Christian Berger. *ed* Monika Willi, Nadine Muse. *pd* Christoph Kanter. *cast* Isabelle Huppert, Benoît Magimel, Annie Girardot, Anna Sigalevitch, Susanne Lothar, Udo Samel.
● Haneke's adaptation of a novel by Elfriede Jelinek may be shot, edited and performed rather more conventionally than most of his work, but in many ways it's no less confrontational or transgressive than, say, *The Seventh Continent* or *Funny Games*. If the latter was a chaste but provocative variation on the violent thriller, this puts the porn movie through much the same paces, refusing to provide explicit titillation even as it explores the psychopathology of a professor of music, touching 40 but still so oppressed by her tyrannical mother, with whom she still lives, and by the disciplines of her vocation, that her only acquaintance with emotion and eroticism comes from watching porn. Then, into her sad life comes a young student, who falls for her. No conventional redemption ensues, as the pair slide slowly but inexorably into a relationship so painfully twisted it would be implausible, were it not for Haneke's rigorous intelligence and Huppert's controlled and courageous performance. Ambitious, profoundly articulate, and despite its avoidance of sentimentality and sermonising, very compassionate. GA

Piccadilly

(1929, GB, 106 min, b/w)
d EA Dupont. *sc* Arnold Bennett. *ph* Werner Brandes. *ad* Alfred Junge. *cast* Anna May Wong, Jameson Thomas, Gilda Gray, Cyril Ritchard, King Ho Chang, Charles Laughton, Ellen Pollock, Ray Milland.
● Big silent buses, spilling light out onto an incongruously familiar West End, display the film's credits and introduce us to Dupont's glitteringly sinister London. Descending from the palatial dance-floor of a Piccadilly nightclub, we pass through the kitchen and the scullery to a world of roughhouse pubs and seamy Chinese emporia. Anna May Wong has a wiry strength which belies expectations of lotus-flower passivity. She distracts the dishwashers with her table-top dancing, and snares her all-powerful boss (Thomas) with her serpentine sensuality. The melodramatic machinations of the plot may be weak, but Dupont's assured direction, Alfred Jünge's art direction, and Werner Brandes' lighting create an atmosphere so hauntingly evocative as to be satisfying in itself. RMy

Piccadilly Third Stop

(1960, GB, 90 min, b/w)
d Wolf Rilla. *p* Norman Williams. *sc* Leigh Vance. *ph* Ernest Steward. *ed* Bernard Gribble. *ad* Ernest Archer. *m* Philip Green. *cast* Terence Morgan, Yoko Tani, John Crawford, Mai Zetterling, William Hartnell, Dennis Price, Clement Freud.
● At a London society wedding, small-time thief Dominic Colpoys-Owen (Morgan, eyes twinkling) charms Fina (Tani), daughter of a Far Eastern ambassador who keeps a £100k in the diplomatic safe. Tired of running errands for (and cuckolding) American smuggler Preedy (Crawford), Dominic plots with Fina's help to rob her father's safe. Dominic, Preedy and top cracksman the Colonel (Hartnell) enter the embassy's basement via Belgravia (now Knightsbridge) tube station and a disused tunnel branching off the Piccadilly line, but getting out with the loot is never going to be as straightforward. Agreeably showing its age, with its references to scrubbers and chisellers and furniture by G-Plan (as credited in the opening titles), Rilla's feature, which came out the same year as his better known *Village of the Damned*, is most notable for its thrilling underground sequences. NRo

Pickpocket 100

(1959, Fr, 75 min, b/w)
d Robert Bresson. *p* Agnès Delahaie. *sc* Robert Bresson. *ph* Léonce-Henry Burel. *ed* Raymond Lamy. *ad* Pierre Charbonnier. *m* Jean-Baptiste Lully. *cast* Martin Lassalle, Marika Green, Pierre Leymarie, Jean Pelegri, Kassagi, Pierre Etaix.
● Bresson is the dark Catholic of French cinema. Here a young man, unwilling/unable to find work, flirts with the idea of pickpocketing: an initial, almost disastrous attempt leads him on. Theft follows theft, on the Paris Métro, in the streets. for the activity occupies an obsessive, erotic position in his daily life. Increasing skill leads to increasing desire, and so to alienation from his only friend, and from the moral counsel of the detective who watches over him with paternal concern. Black-and-white images in the summer sun…of hands flexing uncontrollably, of eyes opaque to the camera's gaze…all part of a diary/flashback that is in the process of being 'written' by the thief himself in prison. Read it as an allegory on the insufficiency of human reason; as a tone poem on displaced desire; as Catholic first cousin to Camus' *The Outsider* (written about the same time): one of the few postwar European films that is both cerebral (an essay on The Human Condition) and resolutely sensual (the constant, restless evaporation of our daily lives). CA

Pickup on South Street

(1953, US, 80 min, b/w)
d Samuel Fuller. *p* Jules Schermer. *sc* Samuel Fuller. *ph* Joseph MacDonald. *ed* Nick DiMaggio. *ad* Lyle Wheeler, George Patrick. *m* Leigh Harline. *cast* Richard Widmark, Jean Peters, Thelma Ritter, Richard Kiley, Murvyn Vye, Willis Bouchey.
● A superb thriller dismissed by many critics as a McCarthyist tract on its first appearance. Nominally about the hunting of Commie spies, it broadens to probe the hysterical New York underworld of the '50s, effortlessly capturing the feel of the milieu. The character Fuller seems to admire most is Widmark's pickpocket, a petty criminal who finally helps the FBI not because of any political commitment, but to settle a personal score; and although there are patriotic lines in the film, like Ritter's 'What do I know about Commies? Nothing. I just know I don't like them', they usually have an ironical slant in that they stem from private rather than public motives. Perhaps finally flawed by its overt political assumptions, but the film remains a desperate kind of masterpiece.

Picnic

(1955, US, 113 min)
d Joshua Logan. *p* Fred Kohlmar. *sc* Daniel Taradash. *ph* James Wong Howe. *ed* Charles Nelson, William A Lyon. *pd* Jo Mielziner. *m* George Duning. *cast* William Holden, Rosalind Russell, Kim Novak, Betty Field, Cliff Robertson, Susan Strasberg, Arthur O'Connell, Nick Adams.
● An enormously tedious and overblown adaptation of William Inge's successful play about a drifter (Holden) who arrives in a Kansas town, a brawny sexual presence who changes some of the people's lives. It is typical of the kind of histrionic, slightly daring, small-town stories which always got rave reviews in the '50s on account of their 'dramatic authenticity'. There are admittedly some reasonable performances (Holden, Robertson and Strasberg, in particular), but Kim Novak in a crucial central role is completely flat. DP

Picnic at Hanging Rock

(1975, Aust, 115 min)
d Peter Weir. *p* Hal McElroy, Jim McElroy. *sc* Cliff Green. *ph* Russell Boyd. *ed* Max Lemon. *ad* David Copping. *m* Bruce Smeaton. *cast* Rachel Roberts, Dominic Guard, Helen Morse, Jacki Weaver, Vivean Gray, Kirsty Child, Margaret Nelson.

●Three girls and a teacher from an exclusive Australian academy unaccountably vanish while visiting a local beauty spot. Set in the Indian summer of the Victorian era, the film is dominated in turns by vague feelings of unease, barely controlled sexual hysteria, and a swooning lyricism. As for the mystery, we're left to conclude that it can only be explained in terms beyond human understanding. As such, the film is rooted in a tradition of sci-fi and horror cinema, depicting the school as a privileged elite, gradually contaminated and destroyed from within by its inability to understand the mystery which confronts it. But in the final count, nothing is satisfactorily resolved because tensions remain unexplored. while the atmospherically beautiful images merely entice and divert. The result is little more than a discreetly artistic horror film. CPe

Picnic on the Grass

see Déjeuner sur l'Herbe, Le

Picture Bride

(1995, US, 95 min)
d Kayo Hatta. *p* Lisa Onodera, Cellin Gluck. *sc* Kayo Hatta, Mari Hatta. *ph* Claudio Rocha. *ed* Lynzee Klingman, Mallory Gottlieb. *pd* Paul Guncheon. *m* Mark Adler. *cast* Youki Kudoh, Tamlyn Tomita, Akira Takayama, Toshiro Mifune, Yoko Sugi.

●The sugar trade with the US brought many Japanese labourers to the fields of Hawaii from the later part of the 19th century on. The most they could look forward to was saving enough for a mail-order wife from back home, and suitable payment brought thousands of single young 'picture brides' to the new frontier. The first feature of Hawaiian-born Kayo Hatta is drawn from an amalgam of real-life testimony and follows the fortunes of Riyo (Kudoh from *Mystery Train*), who arrives in Honolulu in 1918 to find that her husband Matsuji (Takayama) is 20 years older than his photo, and that she faces a married life dominated by toil on the plantation. We're left in no doubt as to the fortitude of these women or the burden placed on their menfolk, yet the film-makers' determination to see the best in everyone feels forced. Tamlyn Tomita is sound as the heroine's supportive best friend and there's a noteworthy cameo from Mifune as a silent-cinema narrator, but a subplot about industrial agitation is left unresolved and a sidestep into the supernatural misfires. TJ

Picture of Dorian Gray, The

(1945, US, 110 min, b/w & col)
d Albert Lewin. *p* Pandro S Berman. *sc* Albert Lewin. *ph* Harry Stradling. *ed* Ferris Webster. *ad* Cedric Gibbons, Hans Peters. *m* Herbert Stothart. *cast* Hurd Hatfield, George Sanders, Angela Lansbury, Peter Lawford, Donna Reed, Lowell Gilmore, Richard Fraser, Morton Lowry.

●Generally underrated version of Oscar Wilde's Faustian tale about a young Victorian gentleman who sells his soul to retain his youth, directed with loving care by the equally underrated Lewin (best known, perhaps, for *Pandora and the Flying Dutchman*). Hatfield – cool, beautiful, and effortlessly suggesting the corruptibility of Dorian's dark soul – is excellent, though even he is overshadowed by the cynical, epigrammatic brilliance of Sanders as Lord Henry. With elegant *fin de siècle* sets superbly shot by Harry Stradling, and the ironic Wildean wit understated rather than overplayed, it's that rare thing: a Hollywoodian literary adaptation that both stays faithful and does justice to its source. GA

Picture Perfect

(1997, US, 102 min)
d Glenn Gordon Caron. *p* Erwin Stoff. *sc* Arleen Sorkin, Paul Slansky, Glenn Gordon Caron. *ph* Paul Sarossy. *ed* Robert Reitano. *pd* Larry Fulton. *m* Carter Burwell. *cast* Jennifer Aniston, Jay Mohr, Kevin Bacon, Olympia Dukakis, Illeana Douglas, Kevin Dunn, Anne Twomey.

●Aniston's a thrusting advertising exec who gets passed over for promotion because she doesn't quite fit in with the corporate ethic – married is good, married and mortgaged even better. Best pal Illeana Douglas reckons that if she can at least pretend to be engaged to some rich Bostonian, then the bosses might change their minds. The only Bostonian she can lay hands on, however, is Jay Mohr, a bloke who videotapes weddings. She wants to pay him to pose as her fiancée, but he has already fallen in love with her. And so on, until the director suddenly has one more sub-plot than he knows what to do with. Still, Aniston (from TV's *Friends*) has the rare gift of getting you to root for her in the most trying of circumstances, a quality that will stand her in good stead when she progresses to better material. TJ

Pictures

(1981, NZ, 87 min)
d Michael Black. *p* John O'Shea. *sc* Robert Lord, John O'Shea. *ph* Rory O'Shea. *ed* John Kiley. *ad* Russell Collins. *m* Jan Preston. *cast* Kevin J Wilson, Peter Vere-Jones, Helen Moulder, Elizabeth Coulter, Terence Bayler, Matiu Mareikura, Ron Lynn.

●A pensive, oddly querulous tribute to New Zealand's 19th century pioneer stills photographers, the Burton Brothers, this is weighed down with a gravely simple lesson in political history that sacrifices both character and drama to sketchy schematics. In the aftermath of the Maori wars, idealistic settler Walter Burton (Vere-Jones) documents the misery of a dying culture while becoming increasingly estranged from his own: he's less the misunderstood artist, though, than one all too well understood by the colonial authorities bent on censoring him. Brother Alfred (Wilson) arrives later, trading on his reputation as a society portraitist and landscape romanticist to give the governmental patrons the images they want. Supporting stereotypes abound, and the ironies are trowelled on. It's handsome and well-meaning enough, but there's hardly a spark of cinema to it. PT

Picture Show Man, The

(1977, Aust, 98 min)
d John Power. *p/sc* Joan Long. *ph* Geoff Burton. *ed* Nicholas Beauman. *ad* David Copping. *m* Peter Best. *cast* Rod Taylor, John Meillon, John Ewart, Harold Hopkins, Judy Morris, Sally Conabere, Garry McDonald, Patrick Cargill.

●A cutely nostalgic portrait of the early years of movie exhibition in Australia, charting the tragi-comic rivalries of travelling film showmen in the '20s. If the scenery and period 'charm' don't grab you, you could try reading the narrative as a metaphor on the contemporary Aussie cinema's production boom, and the conflicting demands for an indigenous or 'international' focus (the latter represented by Taylor's outsider/competitor). Not, however, particularly recommended. PT

Picture Snatcher

(1933, US, 77 min, b/w)
d Lloyd Bacon. *sc* Allen Rivkin, PJ Wolfson. *ph* Sol Polito. *ed* William Holmes. *ad* Robert M Haas. *m* Leo F Forbstein. *cast* James Cagney, Ralph Bellamy, Patricia Ellis, Alice White, Ralfe Harolde, Robert Emmett O'Connor, Robert Barrat.

●Cagney's in typically ebullient shape for this zippy little melodrama as an ex-con who turns Weegee-style 'picture snatcher', grabbing shots of camera-shy underworld figures and selling them to the newspapers. He uses his skills to get in with the police lieutenant father of latest flame Patricia Ellis, but his copybook is soon severely blotted when he smuggles a camera in up his trouser leg to snap a notorious murderer in the electric chair. Cagney's energy keeps it going, though there's also an early bow for Ralph Bellamy as a feisty newspaper editor. TJ

Piece of the Action, A

(1977, US, 135 min)
d Sidney Poitier. *p* Melville Tucker. *sc* Charles Blackwell. *ph* Donald M Morgan. *ed* Pembroke J Herring. *pd* Alfred Sweeney. *m* Curtis Mayfield. *cast* Sidney Poitier, Bill Cosby, James Earl Jones, Denise Nicholas, Hope Clark, Tracy Reed, Titos Vandis, Frances Foster, Jason Evers, Marc Lawrence.

●Poitier and Cosby, successful thieves and pointedly more honest than the organisations they rob, suddenly acquire a social conscience when blackmailed by a retired cop (Jones) into doing time at the local community centre and using their knowhow to prepare a bunch of dead end kids for society. Instead of usefully contemplating the subversive implications of such an arrangement, *A Piece of the Action* abandons the idea that society's there for the taking in favour of wholesale sincerity and homespun philosophy. The result is best described as integration comedy: a kind of black version of Dale Carnegie's *How to Win Friends and Influence People*. CPe

Pieces of Dreams

(1970, US, 99 min)
d Daniel Haller. *p* Robert F Blumofe. *sc* Roger O Hirson. *ph* Charles F Wheeler. *ed* William Chulack. *ad* Herman A Blumenthal. *m* Michel Legrand. *cast* Robert Forster, Lauren Hutton, Will Geer, Ivor Francis, Richard O'Brien, Edith Atwater.

●Soapy melodrama about a priest who gives up the priesthood after meeting Hutton's long-legged and embarrassingly rich social worker divorcee. Sole surprise is the presence as director of Haller, who almost manages to erect quite another kind of film within the general skeleton of this smooth escapist vehicle by having our Father fall victim to the very 'vice' against which he is seen holding forth – 'Beware the flesh, above all beware the flesh' – in the confessional. VG

Pied Piper, The

(1942, US, 86 min, b/w)
d Irving Pichel. *p/sc* Nunnally Johnson. *ph* Edward Cronjager. *ed* Allen McNeil. *ad* Richard Day, Maurice Ransford. *m* Alfred Newman. *cast* Monty Woolley, Roddy McDowall, Anne Baxter, Peggy Ann Garner, Otto Preminger, J Carrol Naish.

●A world-weary misanthrope (Woolley, an unlikely star) finds himself escorting young master McDowall and his brattish sister across France by train to escape the Nazi occupation. Baxter falters as the mademoiselle who comes to their aid, but the film does well by an obviously contrived scenario. Highlight: Woolley squaring up to Nazi major Preminger in the interrogation room. Scripted by Nunnally Johnson from a Nevil Shute novel. TJ

Pied Piper, The

(1971, GB, 90 min)
d Jacques Demy. *p* David Puttnam. *sc* Andrew Birkin, Jacques Demy, Mark Peploe. *ph* Peter Suschitzky. *ed* John Trumper. *pd* Assheton Gorton. *m* Donovan. *cast* Donovan, Donald Pleasence, Jack Wild, Michael Hordern, John Hurt, Cathryn Harrison, Roy Kinnear, Peter Vaughan, Diana Dors.

●Pleasence, as the *nouveau riche* burgomeister of Hamelin, attempts to evade the plague of rats by perching his chair of office in tubs of boiling water; behind him – pulling the strings? – the Church struggles on a knife edge for power. *The Pied Piper* has everything wrong with it; yet over and over again it will toss up images that take it towards what must have been Demy's intentions. The film is strongest when dealing in his characteristic language of images: the corpse left by the Black Death nestling in the midst of apparent rural bliss, the cathedral-shaped cake that explodes obscenely with live rats. Too often Demy has seemed to be doing little but produce cinematic candy floss; this admittedly imperfect film of Browning's poem is at least trying for more. VG

Pied Piper, The (Krysar)

(1985, Czech/WGer, 57 min)
d Jiri Barta. *p* Rudolf Gráf, Klára Stoklasová. *sc* Kamil Pixa. *pd* Jiri Barta. *m* Michael Kocáb.

●Barta's cruel Gothic version of the classic medieval legend once again demonstrates the continuing excellence of Czech animation. Hamelin is a grey Caligariesque mountain of sloping hovels and palaces, its burghers obscene figures whose sole motivation is the acquisition of filthy lucre; the Piper, cheated by the corrupt council after clearing the city of rats, is a gaunt incarnation of Death whose flute conjures idyllic visions of verdant landscapes totally at odds with Hamelin's stony monotones. An impressive film, notable not only for its richly imaginative juxtapositions of visual textures, but for its resolutely grotesque account of a society's lemming-like race towards self-annihilation. GA

Pièges (Personal Column/Snares)

(1939, Fr, 115 min b&w)
d Robert Siodmak. *p* Michel Safra. *sc* Jacques Companeez, Ernest Neuville, Simon Gantillon. *ph* Michel Kelber, Jacques Mercanton, Marcel Fradetal. *ed* Yvonne Martin. *ad* George

Wakhévitch, Maurice Colasson. *m* Michel Levine [Michel Michelet]. *cast* Maurice Chevalier, Pierre Renoir, Marie Déa, Erich von Stroheim, André Brunot, Jean Temerson, Jacques Varennes.
● A likeable *policier*, with Déa as a taxi-dancer persuaded by the police to act as a decoy when a friend falls victim to a serial killer who snares his prey through lonely hearts ads. Her adventures while responding to likely ads are a trifle too picaresque (they include taking down a gang of white slavers), but they do hang together in mood and manner until Chevalier turns up as romantic lead and chief suspect: in effect playing himself with repellent complacency, indulged with *two* trademark songs, he very nearly destroys the ambience. At its best, though, the film captures the same sense of brooding menace as Siodmak's later work in *film noir*, with terrific performances from Stroheim (as a pathetically batty couturier, ruined by a rival, who stages fashion shows for imaginary audiences) and Pierre Renoir (as the enigmatic *éminence grise* behind Chevalier's business interests). TM

Piel

see Colour of Love, The

Pierre dans la Bouche, Une (aka Le Fugitif)

(1983, Fr, 104 min)
d Jean-Louis Leconte. *sc* Gérard Brach, Jean-Louis Leconte. *ph* Henri Alekan. *ed* Geneviève Letellier. *ad* Jean-Pierre Bazarolle, Colombe Anouilh. *m* Egisto Macchi. *cast* Harvey Keitel, Michel Robin, Catherine Frot, Richard Anconina, Hugues Quester.
● If this seems vaguely familiar, bear in mind that Gérard Brach also co-scripted Polanski's *Cul-de-Sac*, and there's a distinct feeling of early drafts resurrected and rejigged, as another American gangster in Europe, wounded and on the run, erupts into another strange household by the sea. What's lacking here is the sexual tension, the equivocal power games, the humour and the cinematic flair. In other words, Polanski is what's lacking. Instead, we have the distinctly under-matched Keitel befriending a blind old actor (Robin), seeing off the actor's creepy nephew (Anconina) and getting the nephew's girlfriend (Frot) fatally plugged by a couple of ludicrous hit men. Keitel's franglais and Alekan's lighting are the most salvageable aspects. BBa

Pierrot le Fou 100 (100)

(1965, Fr/It, 110 min)
d Jean-Luc Godard. *p* Georges de Beauregard. *sc* Jean-Luc Godard. *ph* Raoul Coutard. *ed* Françoise Collin. *ad* Pierre Guffroy. *m* Antoine Duhamel. *cast* Jean-Paul Belmondo, Anna Karina, Dirk Sanders, Raymond Devos, Graziella Galvani, Samuel Fuller, Laszlo Szabo, Jean-Pierre Léaud.
● 'Put a tiger in my tank' says Belmondo to an outraged Esso pump attendant...and the voyage begins. *Pierrot le Fou* was a turning-point in Godard's career, the film in which he tried to do everything (and almost succeeded). It's the tragic tale of a last romantic couple fleeing Paris for the South of France. But then again it's a painting by Velazquez (says Godard); or the story of a bourgeois hubby eloping with the babysitter; a musical under the high-summer pine trees; or a gangster story (with Karina the moll and Belmondo the sucker). She was never more cautious about her love; he was never more drily self-aware; and the film agonises for two hours over a relationship that is equal parts nonsense and despair. In desperation he finally kills her and himself while the camera sweeps out over a majestic Mediterranean sea. And a voice mockingly asks: 'Eternity? No, it's just the sun and the sea'. CA

Pier, The

see Jetée, La

Pig Across Paris

see Traversée de Paris, La

Pigs

(1984, Eire, 79 min)
d Cathal Black. *p* David Collins. *sc* Jimmy Brennan. *ph* Thaddeus O'Sullivan. *ed* Sé Merry Doyle. *ad* Frank Conway. *m* Roger Doyle. *cast* Jimmy Brennan, George Shane, Maurice O'Donoghue, Liam Halligan, Kwesi Kay, Joan Harpur.
● 'Home Sweet Home' mutters Jimmy (Brennan), screwing a bulb into a naked socket in the derelict Georgian pile where he has decided to take up residence, soon joined by a motley crew of other squatters. Set on the subcultural fringes of Dublin's not-so-fair inner city, *Pigs* starts out as everyone's worst nightmare of house-sharing, with the inhabitants variously subsisting on diets of cider and Complan, a pair of false teeth pressed into service as pastry cutters, and a pan of pigs' trotters festering on the stove. Gradually it darkens into a sardonic comedy of despair as the little household falls apart under the pressures of violence, harassment and urban decay. Black's first feature is a small film and a bit raggedy round the edges, but possessed of an angry and pungent eccentricity that carries the day. SJo

Pigs and Battleships (Buta to Gunkan/aka The Flesh Is Hot)

(1961, Jap, 108 min, b/w)
d Shohei Imamura. *sc* Hisashi Yamauchi. *ph* Shinsaku Himeda. *ad* Kimihiko Nakamura. *m* Toshiro Mayuzumi. *cast* Hiroyuki Nagato, Jitsuko Yoshimura, Masao Mishima.
● Imamura's fifth film kicks off with hordes of uniformed American sailors running rampant through the neon lit streets of Yokosuka, and closes with a stampede of pigs doing much the same: a rather wonderful bracketing device pinpointing the twin poles of the slum town's economic life. Kinta (Nagato), like every other young punk in town, has his heart set on making a favourable impression with the gangsters, whose main racket involves exploiting the local pig trade. By contrast his girlfriend Haruko (Yoshimura) is one of the few women to think twice about prostituting herself to the steady influx of Yanks flush with money and booze. She wants them both to quit town while they can. Around this familiar set-up Imamura spins a hectic, furious portrait of a melting pot of deadend low-lives, which, with its restless tracking and panning shots, high contrast 'Scope photography and gothic secondary characters, recalls the corrupt, sweaty universe captured by Welles in *Touch of Evil*. Imamura plays fast and loose with the plotting (he likes his films 'messy'), but if some of the finer narrative details are opaque, the over-arching vision of life as a meat market is abundantly clear. NB

Pigskin Parade (aka The Harmony Parade)

(1936, US, 93 min, b/w)
d David Butler. *p* Bogart Rogers. *sc* Harry Tugend, Jack Yellen, William Conselman. *ph* Arthur Miller. *ed* Irene Morra. *ad* Hans Peters. *m* David Buttolph. *songs* Sidney Mitchell, Lew Pollack. *cast* Stuart Erwin, Judy Garland, Patsy Kelly, Jack Haley, Johnny Downs, Betty Grable, Elisha Cook Jr, Alan Ladd.
● Grid-iron musical caper in which Texas college no-hopers take on Yale's finest. Major train-spotting points if you already knew that 15-year-old Judy Garland made her big screen entrance here, billed ninth and singing 'It's Love I'm After', but that the Oscar-nominated Erwin stole the show as a hick melon-thrower who comes in handy when the Texas quarterback gets injured. TJ

Pigsty (Porcile)

(1969, It/Fr, 100 min)
d Pier Paolo Pasolini. *p* Gian Vittorio Baldi. *sc* Pier Paolo Pasolini. *ph* Tonino Delli Colli, Armando Nannuzzi. *ed* Nino Baragli. *ad* Danilo Donati. *m* Benedetto Ghiglia. *cast* Pierre Clémenti, Jean-Pierre Léaud, Alberto Lionello, Ugo Tognazzi, Anne Wiazemsky, Margarita Lozano, Marco Ferreri, Franco Citti, Ninetto Davoli.
● To accompany screenings of Buñuel's short feature *Simon of the Desert*, Pasolini wanted to make *Orgy*, a fairytale about an 'innocent' (Clémenti) who roams the volcanic wastes of Etna devouring people. But then he added a second story mirroring the themes of *Orgy*, called *Pigsty*. A savage parody of Godard, Resnais and ...Pasolini, ironically chronicling the 'existential anguish' of the children of the bourgeoisie, it features Léaud as a mystic youth whose being finally merges with 'nature': he gets eaten by the pigs he loves. *Porcile* is not only an exquisitely revolting satire, it is also Pasolini's most fascinating piece of cinema. PW

Pill, The

see Test Tube Babies

Pillars of Society (Stützen der Gesellschaft)

(1935, Ger, 84 min, b/w)
d Detlef Sierck [Douglas Sirk]. *p* Ernst Krüger, Hans Herbert Ulrich. *sc* Georg C Klaren, Karl Peter Gillmann. *ph* Karl Drews. *ed* Friedel Buckow. *ad* Otto Gülstorff, Hans Minzloff. *m* Franz R Friedl. *cast* Heinrich George, Maria Krahn, Horst Teetzmann, Albrecht Schoenhals, Suse Graf, Oskar Sima.
● Hypocrisy, opportunist exploitation, small-town gossip and greed: the ills infecting the bourgeoisie in the sublime '50s weepies of Douglas Sirk were already deliciously apparent in his German films of the '30s. Characteristically dissecting a decadent middle-class family, his *Pillars of Society* – adapted from Ibsen – employs the homecoming of black sheep brother-in-law Johann (Schoenhals) to exhume the buried sins of corrupt capitalist Councillor Bernick (George). Just as illicit desire and deceit fester beneath Bernick's respectable facade, so lucid detachment and acute psychological detail underlie Sirk's smooth, shimmering visuals: Brechtian songs and discreet symbolism keep things cool and clear until the repressed passions finally erupt in a cathartic sea-storm. GA

Pillow Book, The

(1995, Neth/Fr/GB, 126 min)
d Peter Greenaway. *p* Kees Kasander. *sc* Peter Greenaway. *ph* Sacha Vierny. *ed* Chris Wyatt, Peter Greenaway. *pd* Wilbert van Dorp, Andrée Putman, Emi Wada. *cast* Vivian Wu, Yoshi Oida, Ken Ogata, Hideko Yoshida, Ewan McGregor, Judy Ongg, Ken Mitsuishi, Yutaka Honda.
● A Japanese calligrapher marks his daughter Nagiko's every birthday with two rituals: he paints a greeting on her face, and then his sister reads from Sei Shonagon's 'Pillow Book', a 10th century diary of reminiscences, observations, and list upon list of exquisite, precious and graceful things. Nagiko (Vivian Wu) grows up with a fetish for calligraphy – demanding that her lovers paint hieroglyphics on her flesh. She keeps a pillow book, too, but her lists reflect a growing frustration. Then an affair with a bisexual British translator, Jerome (McGregor), opens up possibilites. Jerome's scribbling cannot satisfy her, but he offers his own body as her canvas. They fall in love, and he strips to present her texts to his gay lover, a publisher. This is as defiantly esoteric as any of Greenaway's films, and as visually dense as *Prospero's Books*, with frames within frames, computer graphics, subtitles, projections and superimpositions all vying for the eye in a sumptuous, seamless collage of gold, red and black. The result is ravishingly gorgeous, but such aestheticism is itself a kind of perversion, an idea embodied in Nagiko. The actors are models, fetishised objects, and sometimes they seem utterly at a loss, but, by way of counterpoint, this is also both a very intimate, sensual film, and a torrid, lurid melodrama, full of passion, jealousy, hatred and revenge. TCh

Pillow Talk

(1959, US, 105 min)
d Michael Gordon. *p* Ross Hunter, Martin Melcher. *sc* Stanley Shapiro, Maurice Richlin. *ph* Arthur E Arling. *ed* Milton Carruth. *ad* Alexander Golitzen, Richard H Riedel. *m* Frank De Vol. *cast* Doris Day, Rock Hudson, Tony Randall, Thelma Ritter, Nick Adams, Marcel Dalio, Allen Jenkins, Lee Patrick.
● Long disparaged as a reactionary, prudish symbol of virginal womanhood, Doris Day was hopefully reclaimed by certain British feminist film critics as a woman who chose to say no to the manipulations of Don Juans. A fair point, but did she have to be quite so clean and wholesome, verging on the stereotype of the 'good girl'? At any rate, this, the first of her romantic comedies with Rock Hudson – chaste Doris shares a party line with philandering Rock and with predictable results – is frothily enjoyable, although in comparison with (say) the battle-of-the-sexes comedies of Hawks, it often seems complacent and shallow. GA

Pimpernel Smith

(1941, GB, 121 min, b/w)
d/p Leslie Howard. *sc* Anatole De Grunwald. *ph* Max Greene. *ed* Douglas Myers. *ad* Duncan Sutherland. *m* John Greenwood. *cast* Leslie Howard, Francis L Sullivan, Mary Morris, Hugh McDermott, Raymond Huntley, Manning Whiley, David Tomlinson.

●Leslie Howard was among the British actors based in Hollywood who returned home during World War I to do their bit for the war effort, and this tale of a reincarnated Scarlet Pimpernel smuggling people out from under the Nazi's noses typifies the star's attitude to traditionally English values. Deftly directed and imaginatively edited, the film may nevertheless be just too restrained and Anglo-Saxon for its own good (especially Howard's characterisation of the absent-minded archaeology professor setting out to disprove the existence of an Aryan civilisation). Stiff-upper-lip it ain't, though. MA

Piñero

(2001, US, 103 min, col & b/w)
d Leon Ichaso. *p* John Penotti, Fisher Stevens, Tim Williams. *sc* Leon Ichaso. *ph* Claudio Chea. *ed* David Tedeschi. *pd* Sharon Lomofsky. *m* Kip Hanrahan. *cast* Benjamin Bratt, Giancarlo Esposito, Talisa Soto, Nelson Vasquez, Michael Irby, Rita Moreno, Mandy Patinkin.

●Muddled biopic of lowlife Latino actor/writer Miguel Piñero – a drug addict, petty thief and vagrant who left a trail of chaos in his wake, but won awards for his plays in the early '70s, and is now seen as one of the precursors of rap. To write good, I've got to live bad, Piñero states, summing up the drama in a nutshell. Writer/director Ichaso can't help romanticising his subject, but whatever gloss he puts on Piñero's story, the man still comes across as a monster. Flashily but irritatingly shot, full of unmotivated switches from colour to b/w, sudden flashbacks, mannered slow mo and jump cuts, this is hardly a subtle evocation of its subject's life. Its trump card is Bratt who brings a febrile intensity to his role as the gutter poet, rekindling memories of the equally dynamic Al Pacino in his '70s heyday in *Serpico* and *Dog Day Afternoon*. GM

Ping Pong

(1986, GB, 100 min)
d Po Chih Leong. *p* Malcolm Craddock, Michael Guest. *sc* Jerry Liu. *ph* Nic Knowland. *ed* David Spiers. *pd* Colin Pigott. *m* Richard Harvey. *cast* David Yip, Lucy Sheen, Robert Lee, Lam Fung, Victor Kan, Barbara Yu Ling, Ric Young.

●At last a Chinatown movie, distinguished by its lively pace and quirky humour, that's about Gerrard Street, not San Francisco: the British-born director has made a dozen or more features in Hong Kong, but this is his first on home ground. It's about Elaine Choi (Sheen, excellent), a junior clerk in a law office, who is plucked from the typing pool to execute a Chinese will she can't even read. But there are strings attached to restaurateur Sam Wong's bequests that the beneficiaries cannot accept; and Elaine finds herself at the centre of a mystery thriller – or is it a farce? Finally, inspired by the legend of the Woman Warrior, she begins to discover reserves of inner strength she never knew she had. Aside from the ever-reliable David Yip, most of the faces are unfamiliar. Not in the least inscrutable, though: these are engaging characters whose confusions and doubts testify to the problems of being foreigners in a strange (but largely benign) land. TR

Pink Flamingos

(1972, US, 95 min)
d/p/sc/ph/ed John Waters. *ad* Vincent Peranio. *cast* Divine, David Lochary, Mary Vivian Pearce, Mink Stole, Danny Mills, Edith Maney, Channing Wilroy, Cookie Mueller.

●Waters' exercise in deliberately appalling taste is not for the sensitive, needless to say, offering a series of more or less disgusting gags (a messy copulation involving the killing of a chicken, loads of scatological references, a close-up of a scrawny youth spectacularly flexing his anus) deployed around a plot in which a villainous couple attempt to wrest from Divine 'her' claim to be the most disgusting person alive. The cast camp it up as if auditioning for some long-gone Warhol project. Waters raids de Sade in pursuit of extremes, but the difference between him and Warhol (or that other arch-exponent of extreme disgust, Otto Muehl) is that Waters' grotesquerie is decidedly trivial. VG

Pink Floyd Live at Pompeii (Pink Floyd à Pompéi)

(1971, Fr/Bel/WGer, 85 min)
d Adrian Maben. *p* Michèle Arnaud. *sc* Adrian Maben. *ph* Gabor Pogany. *ed* Adrian Maben. *ad* José Pinheiro. *m* Pink Floyd. *with* David Gilmour, Roger Waters, Richard Wright, Nick Mason.

●Technically excellent, this raises the question whether documentary is the most suitable cinematic form in which to present rock music. Although Pompeii and its geography are used along with split screen and rhythmic editing to evoke atmosphere, the unnecessary interviews with the group – and even the images of the band playing – tend to detract from the pleasure the music arouses, simply because the music is constructed not to conjure images of musicians but to provide scope for the listener's imagination. The film may be a brilliant visual record of the Floyd playing, but sadly the music works on you more if you just close your eyes. SM

Pink Floyd: The Wall

(1982, GB, 95 min)
d Alan Parker. *p* Alan Marshall. *sc* Roger Waters. *ph* Peter Biziou. *ed* Gerry Hambling. *pd* Brian Morris. *m* Pink Floyd. *cast* Bob Geldof, Christine Hargreaves, James Laurenson, Eleanor David, Kevin McKeon, Bob Hoskins.

●'We don't need no education' – cue inevitable shots of blank-faced schoolkids on a conveyor-belt to the dead-end mincer. It's hard to see where the much-rumoured creative clashes between Floydian self-analyst Roger Waters and director Parker arose, since the movie is a matter of such stunning literalism: it's little more than kinetic sleeve art keyed slavishly to a slim concept-album narrative. Neither Parker's bombastic live action sequences (carrying Geldof's mute Pink from a war-baby context of military carnage towards neo-fascist rallying, via the turbulence of rock stardom) nor Gerald Scarfe's animation offer more than pictorial italicising of Waters' lyrics; and the autobiographical pain is laid on so thick it emerges looking more like misogynist petulance. Crossing *Privilege* with *Tommy* couldn't result in anything shallower. All in all, it's just another flick to appal. PT

Pink Narcissus

(1971, US, 70 min)
d/p/sc/ph Anonymous (James Bidgood). *ed* Martin Jay Sadoff. *m* Martin Jay Sadoff, Gary Goch. *cast* Bobby Kendall.

●For years, *Pink Narcissus* was a film shrouded in mystery, known only to the most ardent fans of underground/gay cinema after a brief outing in the early '70s, and from a few awed reviews in the press. Now that it has resurfaced in a rediscovered print, it's pleasing to report that the film's wicked reputation is fully justified. It's a hugely overblown sexual fantasy centering around one boy, a dark-haired, pouting young thing who drifts through various sets (sleazy street, club, Arabian Nights-style orgy), dressing up and dressing down, cruising and being cruised. It's all massively erotic, healthily funny and visually impressive, reminiscent of Lindsay Kemp, Kenneth Anger and their ilk. RS

Pink Panther, The

(1963, US, 114 min)
d Blake Edwards. *p* Martin Jurow. *sc* Maurice Richlin, Blake Edwards. *ph* Philip H Lathrop. *ed* Ralph E Winters. *ad* Fernando Carrere. *m* Henry Mancini. *cast* David Niven, Peter Sellers, Robert Wagner, Capucine, Claudia Cardinale, Brenda de Banzie, John Le Mesurier.

●First in the popular series that has repeatedly sidetracked Edwards ever since, with Sellers' death not even staunching the flow. Live action cartoonery had been underworked since Tashlin mapped its possibilities with Jerry Lewis, but the novelty value of Sellers' disaster-prone Inspector Clouseau, funny French accent and all, wore off quicker than its commercial value. The eponymous diamond, which reappeared in 1974's *The Return of the Pink Panther* – and was here sought by suave thief Niven – was symptomatically forgotten in subsequent efforts which still bore its name. PT

Pink Panther Strikes Again, The

(1976, GB, 103 min)
d/p Blake Edwards. *sc* Frank Waldman, Blake Edwards. *ph* Harry Waxman. *ed* Alan Jones. *pd* Peter Mullins. *m* Henry Mancini. *cast* Peter Sellers, Herbert Lom, Colin Blakely, Leonard Rossiter, Lesley-Anne Down, Burt Kwouk, André Maranne, Richard Vernon.

●The fifth Pink Panther effort might seem marginally disappointing even to diehard Clouseau fans, with slapstick gags for the pratfalling clown hung very loosely on increasingly implausible jetsetting plot antics. Lom's former Chief Inspector Dreyfus, driven mad by Clouseau's bungling and now a master criminal plotting manic, twitching revenge, shifts the series into the realm of mad scientist fantasy, full-scale exploding Bavarian castle finale and all. Added to a score of movie references, it's just enough to keep one's critical faculties anaesthetised. RM

Pink String and Sealing Wax

(1945, GB, 89 min, b/w)
d Robert Hamer. *p* Michael Balcon. *sc* Diana Morgan, Robert Hamer. *ph* Richard S Pavey. *ed* Michael Truman. *ad* Duncan Sutherland. *m* Norman Demuth. *cast* Googie Withers, Mervyn Johns, Gordon Jackson, Sally Ann Howes, Mary Merrall, Garry Marsh, John Carol, Catherine Lacey.

●Hamer spins his melodrama between two parallel worlds in Victorian Brighton: a suffocatingly middle-class household dominated by bullying patriarch Johns, and a glitteringly sordid tavern queened over by the magnificently bosomed Withers. As Johns' repressed son (Jackson) becomes infatuated with Withers and implicated in a plot to poison her husband, Hamer unfortunately dissipates the central conflict between these two worlds in a plethora of marginal subplots. Brilliant scenes round the bourgeois dinner table, bitchy confrontations in the bar, add some classy realism to the film, but the parallel between Johns' repressive sadism and Withers' destructive amorality is not pursued. In a distinctly hurried denouement, arrogant Googie is reduced far too easily to a crumpled mass of guilt and tears while the bourgeois family lives happily ever after. RMy

Pink Telephone, The (Le Téléphone Rose)

(1975, Fr, 93 min)
d Edouard Molinaro. *p* Alain Poiré. *sc* Francis Veber. *ph* Gérard Hameline. *ed* Robert Isnardon, Monique Isnardon. *ad* François de Lamothe. *m* Vladimir Cosma. *cast* Mireille Darc, Pierre Mondy, Michel Lonsdale, Daniel Ceccaldi, Gérard Hérold, Françoise Prévost.

●A sadly predictable satire about the French small businessman: a naive, middle-aged and paternal managing director (Mondy), subject to takeover by a wily American conglomerate, becomes besotted with Darc, supposedly the PR man's niece but actually a callgirl hired as an inducement for the night. Unfortunately, the film follows the man's lumbering innocence through to its logical conclusion (he decides to give up everything for her), ignoring the more interesting implications of his ruined marriage and striking work force. Even the humour at the expense of business ethics isn't as sharp as it might have been.

Pinocchio

(1911, Italy, appx 50 min)
d Gant [Giulio Antamoro]. *cast* Ferdinando Guillaume, Augusto Mastripietri, Lea Giunchi, Natalino Guillaume.

●An enchanting silent produced by Cines – and perhaps, even, the earliest extant Italian feature – this live-action version of Collodi's story may be saddled with a stationary camera and intertitles announcing what one is about to see, but it never feels turgidly staged or predictable. The costumes, sets, picturesque locations and the performance of comedian Ferdinando Guillaume (then hugely popular for the Tontolini series) all contribute to a warm, lively, tongue-in-cheek sense of fun, while the wayward narrative – expanded a little from the original to include encounters with Redskins and the Canadian army – is so gleefully eccentric as to seem surreal. GA

Pinocchio

(1940, US, 88 min)
d Ben Sharpsteen, Hamilton Luske. *sc* Ted Sears, Webb Smith, Joseph Sabo, Otto Englander, William Cottrell, Aurelius Battaglia, Erdman Penner. *m* Leigh Harline, Paul J Smith, Ned Washington. *cast* voices: Dickie Jones, Christian Rub, Cliff Edwards, Evelyn Venable, Walter Catlett, Frankie Darro.
●Disney's second cartoon feature is a rum old mixture of the excellent and the awful. The story itself has the harsh morality and cruelty of Victorian children's literature, but Disney orchestrates his queasy material with some stunning animation of a monster whale thrashing about and much delightful background detail (the candle-holders and clocks in the toymaker's shop). However, one also has to suffer the cavortings of a cute goldfish called Cleo, and several appearances of an odious fairy. *Pinocchio*, in fact, probably shows Disney's virtues and vices more clearly than any other cartoon. GB

Pinocchio

see Adventures of Pinocchio

Pinocchio and the Emperor of the Night

(1987, US, 87 min)
d Hal Sutherland. *p* Lou Scheimer. *sc* Robby London, Barry O'Brien, Dennis O'Flaherty. *ed* Jeffrey Patch, Rick Gehr. *pd* Gerland Forton, Tenny Henson, Rick Maki, Phil Ortiz, Connie Schurr, Cliff Voorhees, Pat Wong, Ray Aragon, Rex Barron, T Bird, Frank Frezzo, Tom Shannon. *m* Anthony Marinelli, Brian Banks. *cast* voices: Edward Asner, Tom Bosley, Scott Grimes, James Earl Jones, Rickie Lee Jones, Don Knotts.
●Likeable, if predictably pale, sequel to Disney's *Pinocchio*, which replaces Jiminy Cricket with a glowbug called Gee Willikers. Pinocchio is whisked off to sea on a passing magic carnival ship commanded by the Emperor of the Night, who gets his power from living puppets like Pinocchio or he dies. 'The music is cheerful and bouncy although it was very loud, and the voices are good too, particularly the Good Fairy, who reminded me of Margaret Thatcher. Overall, I'd say it was an enjoyable film' (Keiron Pim, aged eight). DA

Pin Up Girl

(1944, US, 83 min)
d Bruce Humberstone. *p* William LeBaron. *sc* Robert Ellis, Helen Logan, Earl Baldwin. *ph* Ernest Palmer. *ed* Robert Simpson. *ad* James Basevi, Joseph C Wright. *songs* James V Monaco, Mack Gordon. *cast* Betty Grable, John Harvey, Martha Rae, Joe E Brown, Eugene Pallette, Mantan Moreland, Skating Vanities, Condos Brothers, Charlie Spivak and His Orchestra.
●A peppy Washington stenographer (Grable) becomes entangled by chance with a Navy hero of Guadalcanal (Harvey), and to maintain the romance takes a night job as a singer in a swanky new club (run by Brown). Her fantasising past catches up with her, however, in the shape of one of her 500 'fiancés', a soldier to whom she gave a pin-up photo of herself when she was a service waitress back home in Missouri. Harvey's a vapid hero, and the script is nothing special (it's one of those stories where the hero fails to recognise his true love when she puts on a pair of spectacles and looks at him cross-eyed), but Grable and singing rival Rae, both engaging troupers despite the mugging, do their best to liven up the proceedings, and there's a rousing uniformed finale in which Sgt Grable puts the female chorus through their parade ground paces. JPy

Pippi Longstocking (Pippi Långstrump)

(1999, Swe/Ger/Can, 78 min)
d Clive Smith. *p* Waldemar Bergendahl, Hasmi Giakoumis, Merle-Anne Ridley, Michael Schaack. *sc* Catharina Stackelberg. *ph* (camera supervisor) Graham Tiernan. *ed* Noda Tsamardos. *pd* (supervisors) Dermot Walshe, Paul Riley. *m* Anders Berglund. *cast* voices: Catherine O'Hara, Dave Thomas, Gordon Pinsent, Wayne Robson, Melissa Altro. Carole Pope.
●Traditional style (read old fashioned) animation returns with this amiable adaptation of Astrid Lindgren's children's books. The heroine is pretty sussed on all fronts. She's tough as a boot, speaks several languages, is loaded with doubloons, and wears odd stockings. Indeed, she's an archetypal feisty young non-conformist who rubs the local villagers up the wrong way. Returning home from another of her round the world sea voyages, Pippi longs to hear from her father, who sadly fell overboard. Meanwhile, Mrs Prysselius wants to ship her off to an orphanage, and a couple of robbers are after her money. Think Disney's *One Hundred and One Dalmatians* meets *Home Alone* and you get the gist. Jokes are scarce and the songs horrendous. Worse, Pippi's singing voice sounds like Shirley Temple's, and it doesn't take long to drive you round the twist. DA

P.I. Private Investigations

(1987, US, 91 min)
d Nigel Dick. *p* Steven Golin, Sigurjon Sighvatsson. *sc* John Dahl, David Warfield. *ph* David Bridges. *ed* Scott Chestnut. *pd* Piers Plowden. *m* Murray Munro. *cast* Clayton Rohner, Ray Sharkey, Paul LeMat, Talia Balsam, Phil Morris, Martin Balsam, Anthony Zerbe, Robert Ito, Vernon Wells.
●First feature from pop video impresario Nigel Dick, keeping an eye on the critical success of *After Hours* and *Something Wild*. Joey (Rohner) is the uncool yuppie who stumbles into someone else's trauma and emerges a more together person, his tormentors this time a gang of bent cops. The humour stems from a series of seemingly fated coincidences. After being unfairly passed over for promotion at work, he returns to his apartment to find a body in the shower and an alien tape on his answering machine, which contains information that could help Joey's journalist father (Zerbe) expose police corruption, and turns Joey into a marked man. Razor-faced Ryan (Sharkey) is the crooked detective assigned the job, but he consistently bungles his opportunities and degenerates into a cop of the Keystone variety. Similarly, as our hero is relentlessly pursued against a soundtrack of Dick's video hits, the film slides into self-parody, despite some outrageous moments and inspired twists. EP

Piranha

(1978, US, 94 min)
d Joe Dante. *p* Jon Davison, Chako Van Leeuwen. *sc* John Sayles. *ph* Jamie Anderson. *ed* Mark Goldblatt, Joe Dante. *ad* Bill Mellin, Kerry Mellin. *m* Pino Donaggio. *cast* Bradford Dillman, Heather Menzies, Kevin McCarthy, Keenan Wynn, Dick Miller, Barbara Steele, Belinda Balaski, Melody Thomas, Bruce Gordon, Barry Brown, Paul Bartel.
●Engaging tongue-in-cheek exploitation pic from the Corman stable, in which Menzies and Dillman stumble upon an army camp where mad scientist McCarthy has been developing a mutant strain of man-eating piranha fish for use in the Vietnam war. Things get worse when the finned flesh-eaters escape into a local river. John Sayles' witty script plays the action for laughs rather than chills, stealing wholesale from the plot of Spielberg's *Jaws*, while director Dante piles on the cinematic in-jokes and cheap shock effects. NF

Piranha II: Flying Killers

(1981, Neth, 95 min)
d James Cameron. *p* Chako Van Leeuwen, Jeff Schechtman. *sc* HA Milton. *ph* Roberto D'Ettorre Piazzoli. *ed* Roberto Silvi. *ad* Vincenzo Medusa, Stefano Paltrinieri. *m* Stelvio Cipriani. *cast* Tricia O'Neil, Steve Marachuk, Lance Henricksen, Ricky G Paull, Ted Richert.
●A copy rather than a sequel, this has none of the intelligence, wit or tempo that graced the first swarm of hungry fish. With ruthless resort-owners again refusing to jeopardise their dollars for the sake of their guests' safety, the film relies unimaginatively on the puritanical notion that pleasure invites punishment. Tanned flesh is appetisingly displayed, to be torn to shreds by appallingly squeaky fish-models, and the drunken lechery of the holidaymakers seems far more responsible than profit lust for the final bloodshed. That bare-breasted women and a young black deaf-mute are on the menu makes it very clear who is considered fit to survive and who isn't. RB

Piranha Women in the Avocado Jungle of Death

see Cannibal Women in the Avocado Jungle of Death

Pirate, The

(1948, US, 102 min)
d Vincente Minnelli. *p* Arthur Freed. *sc* Albert Hackett, Frances Goodrich. *ph* Harry Stradling. *ed* Blanche Sewell. *ad* Cedric Gibbons, Jack Martin Smith. *songs* Cole Porter. *cast* Judy Garland, Gene Kelly, Walter Slezak, Gladys Cooper, Reginald Owen, George Zucco, the Nicholas Brothers.
●A dazzling Caribbean cod-swashbuckler of a musical, with acting as its very theme and the imaginative projection of illusionism its self-referential life-blood. Strolling player (Kelly) woos sheltered but romantic girl (Garland) in the guise of the notorious pirate Macoco, while her dull fiancé (Slezak) desperately hangs on to his own concealed identity. Cole Porter songs, a choreographed camera, vivacious performances, and Minnelli's customarily camp colour scheme and decor are wonderfully seductive vehicles for the themes that run obsessively through almost all the director's films, be they musicals, comedies or melodramas. PT

Pirates

(1986, Fr, 124 min)
d Roman Polanski. *p* Tarak Ben Ammar. *sc* Gérard Brach, Roman Polanski. *ph* Witold Sobocinski. *ed* Hervé de Luze, William H Reynolds. *pd* Pierre Guffroy. *m* Philippe Sarde. *cast* Walter Matthau, Cris Campion, Damien Thomas, Ferdy Mayne, David Kelly, Charlotte Lewis, Richard Pearson, Olu Jacobs, Roy Kinnear, Bill Fraser.
●Polanski won the Palme d'Or at Cannes with *The Pianist* in 2002. The last time he was in competition there was with *Pirates*. Few would disagree that he won with the right film. In genre terms, *Pirates* is undoubtedly a pirate movie, not a mystery film, yet it's a mystery why Polanski swapped urban paranoia for the skull and crossbones. Polanski and Gérard Brach had collaborated on scripts for *Repulsion* and *The Tenant*, but their sure touch deserted them on the high seas. Shipwrecked Captain Red (Matthau) and his sidekick the Frog (Campion) are picked up by a Spanish vessel and clapped in irons, but Cap'n Red foments unrest in the crew by smuggling a rat into the men's soup. Cue swashbuckling and choreographed scrapping. It's fun intermittently, but a bit of a stretch at two hours, and Matthau's Cockney accent is about as convincing as the rubber sharks. Perhaps the key to understanding what it's about lies in considering Polanski's displacement: of Polish extraction, exiled in Paris, faced with arrest should he return to the US. The only flag he could comfortably wrap himself in was the Jolly Roger. NRo

Pirates of Penzance, The

(1982, GB, 112 min)
d Wilford Leach. *p* Joseph Papp. *sc* Wilford Leach. *ph* Douglas Slocombe. *ed* Anne V Coates. *pd* Elliot Scott. *m* AS Sullivan. *cast* Kevin Kline, Angela Lansbury, Linda Ronstadt, George Rose, Rex Smith, Tony Azito.
●Not so much a movie as a straight lift from Joe Papp's Broadway stage production, this should of course be awful – a couple of Yankee pop stars (Ronstadt, Smith) camping up Gilbert and Sullivan. In fact, taken on its own terms, it's a near unqualified success, ironically because the camera illuminates the parts footlights fail to reach. Consequently, the show is strewn with throwaway sight gags absent from the stage version which, while mercifully never quite sliding into camp, serve to apply a much needed cattle prod to Messrs G & S. The sets are superb. La Ronstadt – despite a more than casual resemblance to Miss Piggy – makes Pamela Stephenson sound like Arthur Mullard; and Pirate King Kline is definitely the most dashing thing since Errol Flynn swung from his last chandelier. DAt

Piravi (The Birth)

(1988, Ind, 110 min)
d Shaji. *sc* Raghunath Paleri, Shaji. *ph* Sunny Joseph. *m* G Aravindan. *cast* Premji, SV Raman, Chandran Nair, Mullaneyi, Kottara Gopalakrishnan.

●An unusual first film in many ways, centered around an absent hero, an engineering student at the state capital. His father, who lives in a remote coastal village, expects his son's imminent return, and journeys each evening to the bus stop, only to be disappointed. Following a report of police arrest, the old man makes a painful trip to the city, but discovers nothing.It becomes clear that the son will not be coming back. Writer/director Shaji and his 83-year-old star Premji make the father's pain and confusion heartbreakingly authentic in what is a profoundly sensual film: the sheer effort of walking, the abrasive physical presence of the elements. At the same time, it addresses current political concerns: the infringement of the modern world on traditional beliefs; establishment corruption; the role of women; education. A master of nuance and mood, Shaji values grace and the human spirit, but the film ends on a tragically ambivalent note. Quiet and contemplative in conception, it is deeply moving in effect. TCh

Pirosmani

(1971, USSR, 85 min)
d Georgy Shengelaya. *sc* Giorgi Shengelaja, Erlom Akhvediani. *ph* Konstantin Apryatin. *ed* M Karalashvili. *ad* Avtandil Varazi, V Arabidze. *m* V Kukhianidze. *cast* Avtandil Varazi, David Abashidze, Zurab Kapianidze, Teimuraz Beridze.
●A slow and sensitive portrait of the great Georgian primitive artist who died in 1918 and whose work is still not widely known outside Russia, *Pirosmani* effectively keeps its distance from the central character. Proud and lonely, Pirosmani forsakes all security to paint, exchanging his work in city bars for food, drink and a bed. His isolation is conveyed through composition and image, while his private life (alcoholism and an inability to make contact with a singer he silently worships) is hinted rather than stressed. A restrained film, possibly too non-involving for some, beautifully shot in muted colours, and composed of studies with the subjects often looking posed and self-conscious, as the artist must have seen them. It's not often that an artist gets the film he deserves. CPe

Pistol, The (Pistolen)

(1973, Swe, 79 min)
d Jiri Tirl. *p* Bengt Forslund. *sc/ph* Jiri Tirl. *ed* Lasse Hagström. *ad* Jiri Kotlar. *m* Ture Rangström. *cast* Inga Tidblad, Gunnar Björnstrand, Håkan Westergren, Nils Eklund, Berndt Lundquist, Bertil Norström.
●A spry old lady (Tidblad), tired of living alone for 30 years in a servantless but immaculately clean mansion, decides to commit suicide. Setting about repairing an antique pistol which is a family heirloom, she temporarily regains the will to live through the friendship of a gentlemanly antique-dealer (Westergren), and in gratitude makes him a present of the now fully-functioning pistol. When he unaccountably puts the piece up for sale, she smashes his shop window and steals it back. Written, directed and photographed by Jiri Tirl, a Czech-born cameraman, *The Pistol* aspires to the tone of a Chekhov chamber-drama, but turns out as little more than a pretty, but essentially empty, photo-essay on an old lady and a stately home. JPy

Pistolero of Red River, The

see Last Challenge, The

Pistol Opera

(2001, Jap, 112 min)
d Seijun Suzuki. *p* Satoru Ogura, Ikki Katashima. *sc* Kazunori Ito. *ph* Yonezo Maeda. *ed* Akira Suzuki. *ad* Takeo Kimura. *m* Kazufumi Kodama. *cast* Makiko Esumi, Sayoko Yamaguchi, Kan Hanae, Masatoshi Nagase, Kenji Sawada, Tomio Aoki, Mikijiro Hira.
●Encouraged by the recent 'Deep Seijun' tribute in Tokyo, Suzuki emerges from directorial retirement with a kind-of-remake of *Branded to Kill*, the film that ended his career as a studio director in 1967. From the first moments (a pre-credits cameo by Sawada, falling off Tokyo Station), it's obvious that this is a mistake. This time the No. 3 Killer is a woman (Esumi, last seen in *Maboroshi*), as is the agent who lines up her jobs (Yamaguchi, mostly encased in a white/purple fashion *burka*). As one outré, over-designed hit follows another, the film touches every cultural base it can think of, from reggae to Art Deco; but there's no narrative momentum, the genre foundations have collapsed and there's nothing for the actors to do but pose. The free-floating virtuoso images (some of which reference Suzuki's Greatest Hits of the 1960s) soon become excruciating. If *Branded to Kill* had been anything like this, Nikkatsu would have been justified in firing him. TR

Pit and the Pendulum, The

(1961, US, 85 min)
d/p Roger Corman. *sc* Richard Matheson. *ph* Floyd Crosby. *ed* Anthony Carras. *pd* Daniel Haller. *m* Les Baxter. *cast* Vincent Price, Barbara Steele, John Kerr, Luana Anders, Anthony Carbone, Patrick Westwood.
●Corman at his intoxicating best, drawing a seductive mesh of sexual motifs from Poe's story through a fine Richard Matheson script. Vincent Price is superbly tormented as the 16th century Spanish nobleman obsessed by the fear that his wife was entombed alive in his castle's torture chamber, a repetition of family history that entails his takeover by the personality of his dead father, the Inquisitor who built the fiendish dungeon. And Barbara Steele, as the faithless wife who faked her own death, embodies all the contradictions of Poe's quintessential female to perfection.

Pit and the Pendulum, The

(1990, US, 92 min)
d Stuart Gordon. *p* Albert Band. *sc* Dennis Paoli. *ph* Adolfo Bartoli. *ed* Andy Horvitch. *ad* Giovanni Natalucci. *m* Richard Band. *cast* Lance Henriksen, Roma de Ricci, Jonathan Fuller, Francis Bay, Mark Margolis, Jeffrey Combs, Tom Towles, Oliver Reed.
●A gruesome adaptation of Edgar Allan Poe's classic horror story which, while lacking the subtlety of Richard Matheson's script for Roger Corman's 1961 version, lays on the cruelty and horror with relish. During the Spanish Inquisition, the pious fiancée of a baker attends an *auto-da-fe* and unwittingly incurs the wrath of Henriksen's ruthless Grand Inquisitor. While Maria is interrogated and tortured, her lover sneaks into the castle and tries to rescue her, only to end up on the wrong end of a razor-sharp pendulum. The scene in which inquisitor Henriksen willingly surrenders himself to a whipping by a man he previously crucified as a heretic – meanwhile enjoying erotic visions of the Virgin Mary's face superimposed onto the heroine's voluptuous body – is especially memorable, perversely combining violent spectacle, religious asceticism, masochism and blasphemy. Sadly, Gordon throws away the poorly staged pendulum scene at the end, resulting in a slight anti-climax. NF

Pitch Black

(2000, US/Aust, 110 min)
d David Twohy. *p* Tom Engelman. *sc* Jim Wheat, Ken Wheat, David Twohy. *ph* David Eggby. *ed* Rick Shaine. *pd* Graham 'Grace' Walker. *m* Graeme Revell. *cast* Vin Diesel, Radha Mitchell, Cole Hauser, Keith David, Lewis Fitz-Gerald, Claudia Black, Rhiana Griffith, John Moore.
●A smart, suspenseful sci-fi movie from director Twohy, whose underrated 1996 film, *The Arrival*, also brought visual imagination and intelligence to the genre. When an interstellar spacecraft collides with a meteor shower, passengers and crew awake from cryo-sleep to find the captain dead and the ship spinning out of control. Inexperienced docking pilot Mitchell crashlands on a planet, scorched by three suns that never set. This is particularly bad news for psycho prisoner Diesel, whose surgically altered eyes are adapted for night vision. It also gives a vital edge to his captor, hardass lawman Hauser. With help from the game but guiltridden Mitchell, Hauser tries to rally the survivors, who include an antiques collector, a Moslem cleric and a shy boy. Despite the modest budget, the visualisation of the parched planet and voracious creatures is credible and spectacular. But it's the skilful handling of the tense, shifting group dynamics that seizes your attention. If the film has a weakness, it is perhaps that Diesel's intense psycho totally outshines Hauser's bland, handsome hero and Mitchell's Ripley-like heroine. NF

Pitfall

(1948, US, 86 min, b/w)
d André De Toth. *p* Samuel Bischoff. *sc* Karl Lamb. *ph* Harry Wild. *ed* Walter Thompson. *ad* Arthur Lonergan. *m* Louis Forbes. *cast* Dick Powell, Lizabeth Scott, Jane Wyatt, Raymond Burr, Byron Barr, John Litel, Ann Doran.
●Rather flatly scripted, but a not uninteresting clash between moral tale and *film noir*. Powell plays the archetypal suburban man, blessed with family, home and job, but suffering a vague itch of awareness that life hasn't lived up to expectations. His work as an insurance claims agent lures him into involvement with a siren (Scott) and the inevitable aftermath of violence, deceit, and sudden death. From this he is rescued by the exercise of a double standard (Scott pays for her murder, Powell gets away with his); but the film still contrives a troubled intimation that things ain't quite what they used to be in suburbia. Burr, modelling himself on Laird Cregar (who would have made more of the role), gives one of his better performances as the hulking yet oddly pathetic private eye who digs the pitfall in trying to pursue his own hopeless infatuation. TM

Pit of Darkness

(1961, GB, 76 min, b/w)
d/p/sc Lance Comfort. *ph* Basil Emmott. *ed* John Trumper. *ad* John Earl. *m* Martin Slavin. *cast* William Franklyn, Moira Redmond, Bruno Barnabe, Leonard Sachs, Nigel Green, Anthony Booth, Nanette Newman.
●British B-pic, adapted by director Lance Comfort from Hugh McCutcheon's novel *To Dusty Death*, spinning a tortuous yarn about a honest man with memory loss who seems to have done something villainous in the past. Moira Redmond's the concerned wife trying to get husband Franklyn (as smooth as he always is) to remember the details of a jewel heist from a safe he personally designed. TJ

Pixote (Pixote a lei do mais fraco)

(1981, Braz, 127 min)
d Hector Babenco. *p* Paulo Francini, José Pinto. *sc* Hector Babenco, Jorge Duran. *ph* Rodolfo Sanches. *ed* Luis Elias. *ad* Clovis Bueno. *m* John Neschling. *cast* Fernando Ramos da Silva, Jorge Juliao, Gilberto Moura, Edilson Lino, Zenildo Oliveira Santos, Marilia Pera.
●Not since Buñuel's *Los Olvidados* has the plight of kids in Third World urban poverty been so acutely affecting; and not since Truffaut's *400 Blows* has a child actor (da Silva) so etched his tragic delinquency on the memory of middle-class audiences. Even allowing for the institutional horrors depicted in *Scum*, nothing in recent cinema comes close to the devastating account of brutalisation and exploitation offered in Babenco's film about a 10-year-old boy who somehow survives the vicious oppression of the reform school, to escape and find his way into dope-dealing, prostitution and murder in the Brazilian underworld. Originally labelled a 'denunciation' film in Brazil for its critique of a social system that fails to prevent the majority of the country's three million homeless kids from turning to crime, *Pixote* arrived here laden with art cinema awards for its exposé of a problem which, for all its cultural remoteness, carves into your conscience with the sudden thrust of a flick knife in a street fight. MA

Pizza Triangle, The

see Dramma della Gelosia

P.J. (aka New Face in Hell)

(1967, US, 109 min)
d John Guillermin. *p* Edward J Montague. *sc* Phil Reisman Jr. *ph* Loyal Griggs. *ed* Sam E Waxman. *ad* Alexander Golitzen, Philip Harrison. *m* Neal Hefti. *cast* George Peppard, Raymond Burr, Gayle Hunnicutt, Coleen Gray, Susan Saint James, Brock Peters, Jason Evers, Wilfrid Hyde-White, Severn Darden, Bert Freed.
●Peppard plays PJ Detweiler, down-at-heel shamus, in this unmemorable addition to the largely unmemorable private eye cycle of the late '60s. Hired (after undergoing a toughness test) by tycoon Raymond Burr – you know *he's* up to no good because he hoards his cigar butts – PJ gets to go to a murkily exotic island in the Bahamas as bodyguard to the tycoon's mistress (Hunnicutt) because someone has been trying

to kill her. Beatings-up, attempted murders and red herrings proliferate before he solves the case. Gracelessly directed with a huge close-up to underline every plot point, it goes through the routine motions, offering very little apart from the odd wisecrack and a lot of thick-ear violence. TM

Place, The

see Platz, Der

Place in the Sun, A

(1951, US, 122 min, b/w)
d/p George Stevens. *sc* Michael Wilson, Harry Brown. *ph* William C Mellor. *ed* William Hornbeck. *ad* Hans Dreier, Walter Tyler. *m* Franz Waxman. *cast* Montgomery Clift, Elizabeth Taylor, Shelley Winters, Anne Revere, Keefe Brasselle, Raymond Burr, Fred Clark.

● Typically slow and stately in the later Stevens manner, this is a shameless travesty of Theodore Dreiser's monumental (if ponderous) *An American Tragedy*. Most of the book's acid social comment is elided, turning Dreiser's hero's attempt to better himself by latching onto a snobbish society girl into something like a starry-eyed romance; what is left is rendered meaningless by being ripped out of period context into a contemporary setting. Although all three leads are excellent, only the scenes with Winters (the pregnant mill girl who gets in the way, and of whose murder – willed if not actually committed – Clift is found guilty) really work. TM

Place in the World, A

(1992, Arg, 120 min)
d/p/sc Adolfo Aristarain. *ph* Ricardo De Angelis. *ad* Abel Facelloi. *m* Patricio Kauderer. *cast* Jose Sacristan, Federico Luppi, Leonor Benedetto, Cecilia Roth.

● An entirely winning and deceptively unassuming portrait of life in a 'frontier' town – some hundreds of miles down the railway tracks from the Argentine capital – with an only son revisiting the small sheep-rearing community of his late adolescence and recalling both his remarkable family and the turn of events during a particular autumn some eight years before. His father, a one-time sociology professor, his mother, a doctor, and a no-nonsense nun in civvies are the three 'progressive' figures who minister to the families of the local collective they've fought to set up. But when a mysterious Spanish geologist arrives to work for the town's venal landowner, it slowly emerges that radical change is on the way. Directror Aristarain lavishes this unremarkable scenario with highly nuanced attention to character, mood and structure, and produces a film of quiet profundity, laced with gentle regret and something of the elegiac glow of some late Westerns. Evocative camerawork from Ricardo de Angelis, a fine Copland-esque score by Patricio Kauderer, and highly impressive performances. Thoughtful, informed, perfectly judged. WH

Place Nearby, A (Her i Nærheden)

(2000, Den, 100 min)
d Kaspar Rostrup. *p* Tina Dalhoff. *sc* Kaspar Rostrup. *ph* Eric Kress. *ed* Grete Møldrup. *pd* Søren Gam. *m* Fuzzy. *cast* Ghita Nørby, Frits Helmuth, Henning Moritzen, Thure Lindhardt, Magnus Stahl Jacobsen, Hannah Bjarnhof, Thomas Bo Larsen, Sarah Boberg.

● Rostrup's third feature film, from a novella by Martha Christensen, explores the relationship of devoted Fru Nielsen (Nørby) and her autistic adult son Brian (Lindhardt), who becomes a suspect in a murder enquiry. Investigating officer Jespersen (Helmuth), renowned as a man who always gets his prey, is frustrated by the mother's desperate attempts to cover up or destroy evidence which might implicate her son. Exemplary camerawork and an arresting use of light underscore the tensions between the apparent innocence of the protagonists and the darker possibility of a more sinister scenario. The film is peppered with memorable cameos: an eccentric bag lady, the junkies living upstairs, and the charmingly camp family friend, the Baron (Moritzen, odious patriarch of *Festen*), who provide relief from the charged interaction between Nørby and Lindhardt. JFu

Place of One's Own, A

(1945, GB, 92 min, b/w)
d Bernard Knowles. *p* RJ Minney. *sc* Brock Williams. *ph* Stephen Dade. *ed* Charles Knott. *ad* John Elphick. *m* Hubert Bath. *cast* Margaret Lockwood, James Mason, Barbara Mullen, Dennis Price, Dulcie Gray, Ernest Thesiger, Helen Haye, Moore Marriott.

● Tame but occasionally effective ghost story (an adaptation from Osbert Sitwell), set in Edwardian times, with Lockwood as the young secretary haunted by a murdered woman when she goes to live with an elderly couple (Mason and Mullen) in an elegant country house. Not a patch upon Knowles' loony but marvellous *Jassy*, although Lockwood and Mason are as effortlessly professional as ever. GA

Places in the Heart

(1984, US, 111 min)
d Robert Benton. *p* Arlene Donovan. *sc* Robert Benton. *ph* Nestor Almendros. *ed* Carol Littleton. *pd* Gene Callahan. *m* John Kander. *cast* Sally Field, Lindsay Crouse, Ed Harris, Amy Madigan, John Malkovich, Danny Glover, Lane Smith, Bert Remsen.

● A winner in the cardiac stakes. Field is the smallholding farmer, recently widowed, who takes in a blind veteran (Malkovich) and desperately tries to farm her cotton crop with the help of a black itinerant farmhand (Glover). Friendships quicken, love hardens, the constant toil is made endurable by the small town ethic of communal feelings. Much is unemphatic, but all of it carries the moving weight of conviction. And it ends on a healing grace-note which passeth all understanding. CPea

Place Vendôme

(1998, Fr/Bel/GB, 118 min)
d Nicole Garcia. *p* Alain Sarde. *sc* Nicole Garcia, Jacques Fieschi. *ph* Laurent Dailland. *ed* Luc Barnier, Françoise Bonnot. *ad* Thierry Flammand. *m* Richard Robbins. *cast* Catherine Deneuve, Jean-Pierre Bacri, Emmanuelle Seigner, Jacques Dutronc, Bernard Fresson, François Berléand, Philippe Clévenot, László Szabó.

● Behind the glitzy façades of the Paris square, Place Vendôme, Vincent's (Fresson) jewellery company founders. His brother and other board associates suspect a history of gambles and dextrous semi-legal deals – involving Mafia connections and illicit gem cutting – but sit on their hands. His wife Marianne (Deneuve), showing all the tics and tropes of the long term alcoholic, once shared his profession, but now rarely shares even his bed. She keeps mainly to the shadows, until his untimely death forces her into a stocktaking which sees her confront not only duplicitous figures like Vincent's onetime lover Nathalie (Seigner), but also ghosts from her own past, including the dangerous Battistelli (Dutronc). Nicole Garcia's edgy psychological thriller doesn't succeed on every level, but offers many pleasures, notably the performances of the hangdog Bacri as Nathalie's cohort, the superb, Gabin-like Fresson, and Deneuve in a prize-winning study in dignity regained. The 'Scope camerawork is nuanced and varied, alternating Marianne's sombre chambers with the gleaming hi-tech of the boardroom. It's a Rolls-Royce entertainment of the old school with an intriguing modernist edge, glorying in a plot as tortuous (but sadly in the end as enervating) as a salesman's patter. As a suspenser, it's weak: Garcia's direction vacillates, but she often snaps back and grabs you. WH

Placido Rizzotto

(2000, It, 110 min)
d/sc Pasquale Scimeca. *ph* Pasquale Mari. *ed* Babak Karimi. *pd* Luisa Taravella. *m* Agricantus. *cast* Marcello Mazzarella, Vincenzo Albanese, Carmelo Di Mazzarelli, Gioia Spaziani, Arturo Todaro, Biagio Barone, Franco Catalano.

● A startling opener, of partisan resistance to Nazi brutality, sets the scene for this exploration of personal moral responsibility amidst community oppression. Young Placido Rizzotto returns to Sicily from the mainland and WWII to find a fresh campaign of violence directed against the peasants by the Corleone Mafia. Organising the dispossessed to occupy the land, he himself is inevitably targeted for assassination. The film then moves into a multi-faceted analysis of the 'versions' of his last hours. Crafting both an insightful historical reconstruction and a timeless fable of resistance, writer/director Scimeca has taken a true story to explore the necessary dialogue between individual action and social cohesion. With a powerful central performance from Mazzarella (light years from his delicate Proust for Ruiz's *Time Regained*), striking photography and an air of authenticity in the mise-en-scène, supporting cast and evocative score, this is regional film-making without a whiff of the provincial. GE

Plaff! or Too Afraid of Life (Plaf – Demasiado miedo a la vida)

(1988, Cuba, 110 min)
d Juan Carlos Tabio. *p* Ricardo Avila. *sc* Juan Carlos Tabio, Daniel Chavarria. *ph* Julio Valdés. *ed* Roberto Bravo, Osvaldo M Donatien. *ad* Raúl Oliva. *m* Nicolás Reynoso. *cast* Daisy Granados, Thais Valdés, Luis Alberto Garcia, Raúl Pomares.

● Tabio's screwball soap opera takes us into the lives and loves of a family in the middle-class suburbs of Havana. It's tacky, it's wacky, it's, well, serious too. Widowed Concha (Granados) distrusts the alliance of brawn and brain when her beloved baseball-player son marries a girl engineer with her own ideas (about bureaucratic impedimenta, the role of women, and Concha). Concha has problems enough: made wary of men by the philandering of her dear departed, she distrusts the charms of taxi-driver Tomas, so is forced to take comfort in the spells of a Santeria-cult priestess. When the young marrieds move in, splat! – eggs start to fly. Tabio leaves no doubt that this is *farce*, not so much admitting the presence of the camera as flaunting it. Every mirror reveals the camera crew, props are thrown onto the set, the film cranks to a halt for apologies about missing scenes. The sight gags, absurd histrionics and hyperbolic use of sound communicate an infectious sense of fun, but the film can't quite hide a deathly conventional morality which, sadly, hauls it back into sanity and nauseating good faith. WH

Plague Dogs, The

(1982, US, 103 min)
d/p/sc Martin Rosen. *ph* James Farrell, Marlyn O'Connor, Ron Jackson, Ted Bemiller Jr, Bill Bemiller, Robert Velguth, Thane Berti. *ed* Richard Harkness. *pd* Gordon Harrison. *m* Patrick Gleeson. *cast* voices: John Hurt, Christopher Benjamin, James Bolam, Nigel Hawthorne, Warren Mitchell, Bernard Hepton.

● The uncharitable might claim that the same heavy hands which mauled *Watership Down* four years earlier have beaten *The Plague Dogs* back into the dreary pack of animal tales that Richard Adams' books towered head and shoulders above. Certainly the story of Snitter (a pathetic fox terrier who believes himself responsible for the death of his master and much else besides), his friend (an embittered Labrador), and their escape from an animal research centre into the Lake District and the company of a worldly fox, gains nothing from animation more closely resembling painting-by-numbers than the Disney-type high quality it aspires to. Similarly, Adams' succinct complaint about animal exploitation is reduced to a mute whine. However, the point is at least made, and the sugary coating may make it easier for some to swallow. FD

Plague of the Zombies, The

(1966, GB, 91 min)
d John Gilling. *p* Anthony Nelson Keys. *sc* Peter Bryan. *ph* Arthur Grant. *ed* Chris Barnes. *pd* Bernard Robinson. *m* James Bernard. *cast* Andre Morell, Diane Clare, Brook Williams, Jacqueline Pearce, John Carson, Alex Davion, Michael Ripper.

● Perhaps a little tame these days, compared with modern gore-shock, but Gilling's Hammer chiller about zombies being exploited by a Cornish tin-mine owner (echoes of the classic *White Zombie*) is highly atmospheric. Often imaginatively directed (in particular a splendid, nightmarishly green-tinted vision of the undead rising from the graveyard earth), it boasts really classy photography (Arthur Grant) and an outstanding performance from Jacqueline Pearce (the admirable snake-woman from *The Reptile*, here being beheaded to save her from untimely zombification). GA

Plainsman, The

(1936, US, 113 min, b/w)
d Cecil B DeMille. *sc* Waldemar Young, Harold Lamb, Lynn Riggs. *ph* Victor Milner. *ed* Anne Bauchens. *ad* Hans Dreier, Roland Anderson. *m* George Antheil. *cast* Gary Cooper, Jean Arthur, James Ellison, Charles Bickford, Porter Hall, Victor Varconi, John Miljan, Gabby Hayes, Anthony Quinn.
●A little too self-consciously epic (it begins with Mrs Lincoln reminding the President that they'll be late for the theatre) and much too reliant on back-projection, but still an enjoyably spectacular Western which rambles through the familiar parade of gun-runners, Indian uprisings and figures from history (ruthlessly telescoped to get them all in, including a nobly heroic Custer). Cooper's fine, sombre portrayal of Wild Bill Hickok (lumbered with a skittishly romantic Calamity Jane, but nevertheless allowed to meet his death at the hands of Jack McCall) seems to come from another, altogether less trivial movie. TM

Plaisir, Le (House of Pleasure)

(1951, Fr, 95 min, b/w)
d Max Ophüls. *sc* Jacques Natanson, Max Ophüls. *ph* Christian Matras, Philippe Agostini. *ed* Léonide Azar. *ad* Jean D'Eaubonne. *m* Joe Hajos, Maurice Yvain. *cast* Claude Dauphin, Gaby Morlay, Madeleine Renaud, Danielle Darrieux, Ginette Leclerc, Jean Gabin, Pierre Brasseur, Daniel Gélin, Simone Simon.
●Ophüls' second French film following his return from the USA was adapted from three stories by Maupassant. *Le Masque* describes how an old man wears a mask of youth at a dance hall to extend his youthful memories. *La Maison Tellier*, the longest episode, deals with a day's outing for the ladies from a brothel, and a brief romance. In *Le Modéle*, the model in question jumps from a window for love of an artist, who then marries her. Although Ophüls had to drop a fourth story intended to contrast pleasure and death, these three on old age, purity and marriage are shot with a supreme elegance and sympathy, and the central tale in particular luxuriates in the Normandy countryside. The whole is summed up by the concluding line, that 'happiness is no lark'. DT

Plan 9 from Outer Space

(1956, US, 79 min, b/w)
d/p/sc Edward D Wood Jr. *ph* William C Thompson. *ed* Edward D Wood Jr. *ad* Tom Kemp. *m* Gordon Zahler. *cast* Gregory Walcott, Mona McKinnon, Bela Lugosi, Maila 'Vampira' Nurmi, Tor Johnson, Lyle Talbot, Tom Keene, Criswell.
●Crowned 'The Worst Film Ever Made' at New York's Worst Film Festival in 1980, this deserves its niche in history for featuring the last screen performance of Bela Lugosi, as a ghoul resurrected by space visitors for use against scientists destroying the world with their nuclear tests. Two minutes of Lugosi in his Dracula outfit, shot for another Wood film abandoned when Lugosi died, are supplemented by footage of an unemployed chiropractor hired as a double; a good foot taller than Lugosi, he of course keeps his face wrapped in a cape. But that's nothing: we also learn that top-level Pentagon offices are furnished with one lamp and two telephones each, while the bedroom furniture of one character is exactly the same as his patio furniture of the previous scene. It all ends with famous psychic Criswell asking the audience, 'Can you prove it didn't happen? God help us in the future'. Prophetic. CR

Planes, Trains and Automobiles

(1987, US, 92 min)
d/p/sc John Hughes. *ph* Don Peterman. *ed* Paul Hirsch. *pd* John W Corso. *m* Ira Newborn. *cast* Steve Martin, John Candy, Laila Robbins, Michael McKean, Larry Hankin, Edie McClurg.
●When their flight is grounded by snow, suave advertising exec Neal Page (Martin) finds himself stuck with travelling shower-curtain-ring salesman Del Griffith (Candy), the human equivalent of a Double Whopper. Griffith offers the benefit of his wide-ranging travel experience, and the pair set off overland on an odyssey of disasters. Sympathy, initially with the exec, shifts to the salesman, who is revealed as a vulnerable and lonely misfit, while his companion proves an intolerant bully and foul-tempered snob. A couple of overgrown brats seems an appropriate focus for John *The Breakfast Club* Hughes first adult movie, but if his direction is slick, his script lacks wit and perception. Essentially, it's the stars' keenly observed nuances of character that make this comedy amiable enough. EP

Planète Sauvage, La

see Fantastic Planet

Planet of the Apes

(1967, US, 112)
d Franklin J Schaffner. *p* Arthur P Jacobs. *sc* Michael Wilson, Rod Serling. *ph* Leon Shamroy. *ed* Hugh S Fowler. *ad* Jack Martin Smith, William J Creber. *m* Jerry Goldsmith. *cast* Charlton Heston, Roddy McDowall, Kim Hunter, Maurice Evans, James Whitmore, James Daly, Linda Harrison.
●Four sequels and a TV series bred contempt, but this first visit to Pierre Boulle's planet, bringing a welcome touch of wit to his rather humourlessly topsy-turvy theory of evolution, remains a minor sci-fi classic. The settings (courtesy of the National Parks of Utah and Arizona) are wonderfully outlandish, and Schaffner makes superb use of them as a long shot chillingly establishes the isolation of the crashed astronauts, as exploration brings alarming intimations of life (pelts staked out on the skyline like crucified scarecrows), and as discovery of a tribe of frightened humans is followed by an eruption of jackbooted apes on horseback. The enigma of the planet's history, juggled through Heston's humiliating experience of being studied as an interesting laboratory specimen by his ape captors, right down to his final startling rediscovery of civilisation, is quite beautifully sustained. TM

Planet of the Apes

(2001, US, 120 min)
d Tim Burton. *p* Richard D Zanuck. *sc* William Broyles Jr, Lawrence Konner, Mark Rosenthal. *ph* Philippe Rousselot. *ed* Chris Lebenzon. *pd* Rick Heinrichs. *m* Danny Elfman. *cast* Mark Wahlberg, Tim Roth, Helena Bonham Carter, Michael Clarke Duncan, Kris Kristofferson, Estella Warren, Paul Giamatti, David Warner, Charlton Heston.
●If Franklin Schaffner's rather prosaic 1968 adaptation of Pierre Boulle's novel now appears as an iconic allegory of its time, it's worth remembering that, along with four sequels and a live action TV series, it also spawned a cartoon series, Halloween masks, bubblegum cards and a patina of self-parody. Burton's facetious and forgettable remake – 're-imagining' if you must – owes as much to such pop ephemera as it does to woolly liberal sentiments. It's a cliché to praise Burton's visual élan and bemoan his lack of narrative sophistication, but these attributes are all part of the same sketchy, knowing and naive aesthetic. The film's jerky B-movie theatricality is as integral to Burton's peculiar design as Rick Baker's incredibly lifelike apes: part of the intermittent joy of the movie is to recognise the stars underneath their costumes, and a lot of the comedy is impish caricature of human vanities reflected through the crazy mirror of gorilla affectation. Naturally the best performances come from the hairier cast members, notably Roth as the dyslexic Gen Thade. Burton is understandably unimpressed by Wahlberg's astronaut and utterly bored by the human slaves he encounters – which may explain the slapdash, outrageous and irrational climax. TCh

Platform, The (Zhantai)

(2000, HK/Fr/Jap, 193 min)
d Jia Zhangke. *p* Li Kit-Ming, Shozo Ichiyama, Joel Farges, Elise Jalladeau. *sc* Jia Zhangke. *ph* Yu Lik-wai. *ed* Kong Jinglei. *ad* Qiu Sheng. *m* Yoshihiro Hanno. *cast* Wang Hongwei, Zhao Tao, Liang Jingdong, Yang Tianyi, Wang Bo.
●Fenyang in Shanxi Province, Jia's hometown and already the setting for *Xiao Wu*, provides the anchor for an epic account of the changes in China's pop culture in the 1980s, as seen across the lives of four friends. In 1979 all four are members of a state-run variety troupe, presenting Maoist propaganda shows to passive audiences in the sticks. By the mid-1980s, when state support is withdrawn and the troupe tries to reform as a private enterprise, everything is different: the Maoist repertoire is buried, Taiwanese pop is ubiquitous, ideas of personal wealth and independence are on the rise – and old friendships are under strain. And by the end of the decade the couple seemingly made for each other have gone separate ways, while the joker/live wire Mingliang (Wang Hongwei) has become a somnolent husband and father. Jia uses large-scale vignettes, filmed in sequence shots, to chart ten years of far-reaching social changes and their psychological repercussions. A masterly achievement. (A 'streamlined version' cut by some 35 minutes also exists.) TR

Platinum Blonde

(1931, US, 98 min, b/w)
d Frank Capra. *p* Harry Cohn. *sc* Jo Swerling, Robert Riskin. *ph* Joseph Walker. *ed* Gene Milford. *cast* Jean Harlow, Loretta Young, Robert Williams, Reginald Owen, Walter Catlett, Halliwell Hobbes.
●Although finally saddled with a somewhat banal message about the value of good hard work and the evils of inherited wealth, this lively comedy is infinitely preferable to the turgid, reactionary sermonising of the director's later Capracorn epics (*Mr Deeds Goes to Town, Mr Smith Goes to Washington*, etc). The plot – Williams' journalist falls for a wealthy but fickle socialite, rather than his tough colleague, only to discover the error of his ways – is predictable but fast-moving, with some delightfully cynical wisecracks contributed by Capra's regular writer Robert Riskin. But it's finally Williams, in his last performance before dying from a ruptured appendix, who steals the show; though both Harlow and Young are efficient and ravishing, they are strangely miscast – Harlow as the heiress, Young as the down-to-earth news hound. GA

Platoon

(1986, US, 120 min)
d Oliver Stone. *p* Arnold Kopelson. *sc* Oliver Stone. *ph* Robert Richardson. *ed* Claire Simpson. *pd* Bruno Rubeo. *m* Georges Delerue. *cast* Tom Berenger, Willem Dafoe, Charlie Sheen, Forest Whitaker, Francesco Quinn, John C McGinley, Richard Edson, Johnny Depp.
●Stone's Vietnam film is a savage yet moving account of a 19-year-old's baptism under fire: clambering out of a transport plane, Sheen is soon plunged into the bloody chaos of combat. The use of his letters home as a commentary establishes personal experience as the core of the film; but broader political issues do manifest themselves when, unable to make any headway against the elusive Vietcong, the grunts turn their anger and weaponry on one another, the platoon splitting into warring factions that reflect peacetime social divisions. Two conflicting impulses appear in the movie: a desire to assault the audience with searing images that will cauterise the Vietnam wound once and for all; and a wish for a more artistically distanced elegy, given its purest expression in Georges Delerue's plaintive score. Perhaps it is this unresolved tension that allows *Rambo* fans to relish the violence while concerned liberals ponder the horror. That said, Stone's eye-blistering images possess an awesome power, which sets the senses reeling and leaves the mind disturbed. NF

Platz, Der (The Place)

(1997, Ger, 52 min)
d Uli M Schüppel.
●A video documentary about a German building site may not sound exciting. Rest assured: it isn't. I suppose you could say Schüppel's film draws on the tradition of Walter Ruttmann's 1927 *Berlin, Symphony of a Great City* and Wenders' *Wings of Desire*, but all it really boils down to is monochrome footage of construction work at the Potsdamer Platz, with voice-over reminiscences from the labourers, reflecting on their own special places – pastoral, to a man. Music by former Einstürzende Neubauten musician FM Einheit. TCh

Play

(2000, Ire/GB, 16 min)
d Anthony Minghella. *p* Tim Bricknell; Michael Cologan, Alan Moloney. *sc* Samuel Beckett. *ph* Benoît Delhomme. *ed* Lisa Gunning. *pd* Roy Walker. *cast* Alan Rickman, Juliet Stevenson, Kristin Scott Thomas.

●Three characters sit trapped in urns in a purgatorial limbo, forever condemned to replay the sordid details of their bitter, triangular love affair. Of all the plays in the 'Beckett on Film' project, Minghella's aroused the most negative feelings when it premiered in Dublin, where purists accused the director of betraying the author's intentions by adding lots of other urn-people and by generally privileging style over content. Certainly the cinematic apparatus is heavily foregrounded (whirring noises accompany camera moves, frenetic cutting), but these experiments seem apt in the light of Beckett's own preoccupations with form. A bold if not entirely successful attempt to reinvent the play for a different medium. KC

Playbirds, The

(1978, GB, 94 min)
d/p Willy Roe. *sc* Bud Topin, Robin O'Connor. *ph* Douglas Hill. *ed* Jim Connick. *ad* Peter Williams. *m* David Whitaker. *cast* Mary Millington, Glynn Edwards, Gavin Campbell, Alan Lake, Windsor Davies, Derren Nesbitt.
●Tatty sex thriller named after the magazine of the same title and characteristics, a down-market 'Men Only' competitor. It's not surprising, then, that the movie – featuring mascot Mary as the policewoman who becomes bait for the centre-spread murderer – is dreary yawn-a-minute stuff. GD

Playboys, The

(1992, GB, 109 min)
d Gillies MacKinnon. *p* Simon Perry, William P Cartlidge. *sc* Shane Connaughton, Kerry Crabbe. *ph* Jack Conroy. *ed* Humphrey Dixon. *pd* Andy Harris. *m* Jean-Claude Petit. *cast* Albert Finney, Aidan Quinn, Robin Wright, Milo O'Shea, Alan Devlin, Niamh Cusack, Ian McElhinney, Adrian Dunbar.
●In a remote Irish border village in 1957, unwed mother Tara (Wright) is lectured by the womenfolk and priest on the wages of sin, while the men, notably Police Sergeant Hegarty (Finney) hover like moths around a flame, only to meet with rejection. The situation worsens when she finally yields to Tom (Quinn), tale-spinning member of a troupe of travelling players led by the irrepressibly optimistic Freddie (O'Shea)... Directed by MacKinnon with great pace and a minimum of moralising or sentimentality, Shane Connaughton and Kerry Crabbe's tale of passion threatened by a repressed, close-knit society makes for a superior period drama, as tough, touching and witty as Connaughton's *My Left Foot*. Much credit is due to the cast, particularly Finney, who brings a melancholy gravity to a film which elsewhere steers sensibly clear of solemnity (the troupe's hammy renditions of *Othello* and *Gone With the Wind* are especially funny). With time, place and mood sensitively evoked, this is solid, intelligent entertainment, mercifully free of the usual 'Oirish' clichés. GA

Play Dirty

(1968, GB. 117 min)
d André De Toth. *p* Harry Saltzman. *sc* Lotte Colin, Melvyn Bragg. *ph* Edward Scaife. *ed* Alan Osbiston. *ad* Tom Morahan. *m* Michel Legrand. *cast* Michael Caine, Nigel Davenport, Nigel Green, Harry Andrews, Bernard Archard, Daniel Pilon.
●A workmanlike rip-off of *The Dirty Dozen*, with Caine leading a group of ex-criminals in an attack on a German supply dump in North Africa during WWII. The script, by Lotte Colin and a certain Melvyn Bragg, aims for grand anti-war rhetoric. De Toth keeps the action going well, and the end is great – forgetting that they are wearing German uniforms, our surviving lads break cover to take a bow and get mown down by friendly fire. Ironic, huh? ATu

Player, The

(1992, US, 124 min)
d Robert Altman. *p* David Brown, Michael Tolkin, Nick Wechsler. *sc* Michael Tolkin. *ph* Jean Lépine. *ed* Geraldine Peroni. *pd* Stephen Altman. *m* Thomas Newman. *cast* Tim Robbins, Greta Scacchi, Fred Ward, Whoopi Goldberg, Peter Gallagher, Brion James, Cynthia Stevenson, Vincent D'Onofrio, Dean Stockwell, Richard E Grant, Sydney Pollack, Lyle Lovett, Dina Merrill.
●Shrewd Hollywood exec Griffin Mill (Robbins) is already paranoid that a rival may join the studio; but what of the anonymous postcards he's getting from a scriptwriter whose pitch he hasn't followed up? Rattled by the death threats, he decides (wrongly) that the likely sender is David Kahane (D'Onofrio). But when Kahane is found dead after a meeting with Mill and it becomes known that Mill is dating the writer's ungrieving lover (Scacchi), his troubles multiply... Altman turns Michael Tolkin's thriller into the most honest, hilarious Hollywood satire ever, even persuading some 60 celebs to play themselves. Besides the superb performances, photography, music and seamless blend of comedy and tension, what's finally so special about the film is its form. Altman refines his open, 'democratic' style of the '70s, to show an untidy world from numerous shifting perspectives, yet the film is far from chaotic. With its many movie references and film-within-a-film structure, it's forever owning up to the fact that it's only a movie. Only? Were more films as complex and revealing about people, society and the way we watch and think about films, today's Hollywood product would be far more interesting than it is. GA

Players

(1979, US, 120 min)
d Anthony Harvey. *p* Robert Evans. *sc* Arnold Schulman. *ph* James Crabe. *ed* Randy Roberts. *pd* Richard Sylbert. *m* Jerry Goldsmith. *cast* Ali MacGraw, Dean-Paul Martin, Maximilian Schell, Pancho González, Steve Guttenberg, Melissa Prophet, Guillermo Vilas.
●At Wimbledon's Centre Court, the men's singles finalists emerge, Dan Maskell's commentary sets the scene, and the heartaches (ie. flashbacks) begin. Finalist Martin, we learn, likes having sex beside Mexican swimming-pools with MacGraw, the wealthy designer he rescued from a burning car; but she keeps jetting to the side of her Italian millionaire/yachtsman (Schell), who in turn seems to be quite into his glamorous secretary. The soapy plot is so incredibly old-fashioned that it might be forgiven if the script didn't keep hitting so many lines straight into the net: exchanges like 'How old are you?' – 'Don't ask' are only matched by unashamedly pulpy love scenes ('Tell me everything...like how you got so beautiful'). A pity, because the tennis relationships, including a cameo from Pancho González, ring far more true; and the last set of the Wimbledon final, when we are allowed to get to it, comes close to Hollywood adrenalin-pumping at its best. DP

Players Club, The

(1997, US, 103 min)
d Ice Cube. *p* Patricia Charbonnet, Carl Craig. *sc* Ice Cube. *ph* Malik Sayeed. *ed* Suzanne Hines. *pd* Dina Lipton. *m* Frank Fitzpatrick. *cast* Bernie Mac, LisaRaye, Chrystale Wilson, Adele Givens, Monica Calhoun, AJ Johnson, Ice Cube.
●Ice Cube's first foray behind the camera as writer/director combines a cautionary tale of greed, folly and brutality at a Southern black strip club with an account of one fresh intern's triumph over the joint's stacked odds. The 'girls' occupy centre frame: Diana 'Diamond' Armstrong (LisaRaye), using the night work to support a young son and pay her way through journalism college, and Ronnie (Wilson) and Tricks (Givens), sour lifers who amuse themselves corrupting new recruits, including Diamond's gullible young cousin Ebony (Calhoun). For the most part, the film follows Spike Lee's *Girl 6* and the post-feminist consensus in defending sex workers' professional choices according to the control they maintain over their acts while acknowledging at least some of the constant sexual, economic and personal pressures involved. Sympathetic it may be, but it never cuts deep; moreover, the camera spends far longer gazing at the women's stage acts than it does recording their feelings of degradation. That said, there are strong performances and two or three house-raising comic set pieces. NB

Playgirl Gang

see Switchblade Sisters

Playing Away

(1986, GB, 102 min)
d Horace Ové. *p* Brian Skilton, Vijay Amarnani. *sc* Caryl Phillips. *ph* Nic Knowland. *ed* Graham Whitlock. *ad* Pip Gardner. *m* Simon Webb. *cast* Norman Beaton, Robert Urquhart, Helen Lindsay, Nicholas Farrell, Brian Bovell, Gary Beadle, Sheila Ruskin, Patrick Holt.
●Monocle, pipe in clenched jaw, retired colonel and vicar showing slides of the Masai in the village hall for Third World Week – all this lacks is Basil Radford and Naunton Wayne for a picture of the Home Counties in the '30s according to Agatha Christie. The trouble is, it's set in the present. The annual cricket match between a Suffolk village and Brixton begins with a phone call from Derek (Farrell) – almost lockjawed with good breeding – to Willie Boy (Beaton), loveably demonstrative captain of the partying Brixton XI. Willie Boy dreams of returning to Jamaica, and his experiences in chilly Sneddington help him make up his mind. Most of the cultural exchanges are on the obvious level of introducing the whites to the herb, a bit of fancying, and the odd racist remark. The cricket match turns into a shambles, Brixton wins, but Sneddington discourteously fails to lay on an end-of-play 'Spot of lunch, old boy?' celebration. Miss Marple would have served tea and Osbornes at least. BC

Playing by Heart

(1998, US, 121 min)
d Willard Carroll. *p* Willard Carroll, Meg Liberman, Tom Wilhite. *sc* Willard Carroll. *ph* Vilmos Zsigmond. *ed* Pietro Scalia. *pd* Missy Stewart. *m* John Barry. *cast* Sean Connery, Gena Rowlands, Gillian Anderson, Jon Stewart, Dennis Quaid, Ellen Burstyn, Anthony Edwards, Angelina Jolie, Jay Mohr, Ryan Phillippe, Gena Rowlands, Madeleine Stowe.
●First-time writer/director Willard Carroll has marshalled quite a cast for this ensemble piece about life and love in contemporary Los Angeles. There's Sean Connery and Gena Rowlands as the long-married couple bickering about past infidelities. There's Gillian Anderson as a theatre director insecure about men until Jon Stewart comes along. Dennis Quaid has a recurring role as a barfly whose tales of misfortune grow ever more baroque with each retelling; Madeline Stowe and Anthony Edwards find some satisfaction in their strictly physical affair; while Ellen Burstyn is the mum facing up to son Jay Mohr's terminal AIDS. Providing the keynote line for all of them is clubber Angelina Jolie, who, having landed bewitched and bewildered Ryan Phillippe, informs him that 'talking about love is like dancing about architecture'. Although the screenplay's resourcefulness in threading it all together is to be admired, it's the cast who provide the pleasures, what with Connery and Rowland's luxurious ease on screen together, the sheer Day-Glo energy emanating from Jolie, and Anderson's expertly judged portrait of a smart woman who can't figure out why her life's such a mess. The trouble is that all of these characters are more interesting when things are going badly for them than when the tide has turned, and Carroll's determination to make the final reel an extended bout of audience tummy tickling is disappointingly conventional. Compared to Alan Rudolph's exotic, tantalising meditations on a similar theme, it's all a bit meat-and-potatoes. TJ

Playing for Keeps

(1984, US, 106 min)
d Bob Weinstein, Harvey Weinstein. *p* Alan Brewer, Bob Weinstein, Harvey Weinstein. *sc* Bob Weinstein, Harvey Weinstein. *ph* Eric van Haren Noman. *ed* Gary Karr, Sharyn L Ross. *pd* Steve Miller. *m* George Acogny, Daniel Bechet. *cast* Daniel Jordano, Matthew Penn, Leon W Grant, Mary B Ward, Marisa Tomei, Jimmy Baio, Harold Gould.
●Danny (Jordan) inherits an old run-down estate, and with the help of his friends, sets out to build the first hotel run by and for teenagers. The townsfolk oppose their plans, but Chloe Hatcher (Ward), Farmer Hatcher's daughter, decides to help them out – she's fallen for Danny. Disappointingly, Danny's opening night festivities at the Rock Hotel do not include a surprise performance by the ever-loveable Einstürzende Neubauten. SGo

Playing from Plates (Grajacy Z Talerza)

(1995, Pol/Fr, 107 min)
d Jan Jakub Kolski. *p* Grzegorz Warchol. *sc* Jan Jakub Kolski. *ph* Piotr Lenar. *ed* Ewa Pakulska. *m* Zygmunt Konieczny. *cast* Dojnica

Paladiuk, Krzysztof Pieczynski, Mariusz Saniternik, Franciszek Pieczka, Grazyna Blecka-Kolska.

● Kolski's enigmatic mix of fantastic allegory, mystic fairytale, and bucolic comedy tosses together a crew of peasant weirdos – an elderly farmer visited by the Angel of Death, a dwarf would-be nurse whom he saves from suicide, a two-faced 'monster' who lives at the bottom of his well, and a mad fiddler who 'reads' shards of crockery as inspiration for his fatally hypnotic rhapsodies – to create a meandering Beauty and the Beast-style parable about the transforming power of love. Ludicrous, for sure, and not, as far as one can gather, politically correct or progressive; still, the sheer, wayward inventiveness of the whole thing ensures a certain oddball appeal. GA

Playing God

(1997, US, 94 min)
d Andy Wilson. *p* Marc Abraham, Laura Bickford. *sc* Mark Haskell Smith. *ph* Anthony B Richmond. *ed* Louise Rubacky. *pd* Naomi Shohan. *m* Richard Hartley. *cast* David Duchovny, Timothy Hutton, Angelina Jolie, Michael Massee, Peter Stormare, Gary Dourdan.

● Struck off for killing a woman under his care, junkie doctor Eugene (Duchovny) reverts to healing type when a man is shot. His action attracts the attention of gangster Raymond (Hutton), who proposes a deal. In return for keeping quiet about Raymond's activities, Eugene can practise as much medicine as he wants. The film starts with a whimper, first time director Wilson (of TV's *Cracker*) alloxwing the Bacardi-ad sets and sub-*Pulp Fiction* dialogue to float free of personality, while Duchovny wears the pained expression of a man trying to have an out-of-body experience. It flares into life, however, with the appearance of Hutton. No longer an angry innocent, he resembles Anthony Perkins, gaunt and ravaged. When Eugene asks, 'Are you going to hurt me?' and Raymond hisses, sensuously, 'Do you say that 'cos you're frightened or 'cos you want me to?' – for the first time Eugene looks intrigued. Flawed nonsense, but quite lively. CO'Su

Play It Again, Sam

(1972, US, 86 min)
d Herbert Ross. *p* Arthur P Jacobs. *sc* Woody Allen. *ph* Owen Roizman. *ed* Marion Rothman. *pd* Ed Wittstein. *m* Billy Goldenberg. *cast* Woody Allen, Diane Keaton, Tony Roberts, Jerry Lacy, Susan Anspach, Jennifer Salt, Joy Bang, Viva.

● Allen's neurosis is not to everyone's taste, but this movie – based on his own stage play about a film critic with seduction problems who takes Bogart as a role model – shows him at his best, exploring the gap between movie escapism and reality. It's not really as pretentious as that, and anyway, in contrasting his chaotic life with the Bogart image, Allen forgets the contrast between his chaos and our prosaic lives. No doubt someone somewhere takes Woody as his mentor and fails to be funny, just as Woody here stumbles after Bogey's cool. Still, the working out of the parallels with *Casablanca* are masterly, and there are plenty of good sight gags and one-liners. Much better than Allen's previous self-directed effort, *Everything You Always Wanted to Know About Sex*. SG

Play It Cool

(1962, GB, 81 min, b/w)
d Michael Winner. *p* Julian Wintle, Leslie Parkyn. *sc* Jack Henry. *ph* Reginald Wyer. *ed* Tristam Cones. *ad* Lionel Couch. *m* Norrie Paramor, Richard B Rowe, Bernard Jewry. *cast* Billy Fury, Michael Anderson Jr, Dennis Price, Richard Wattis, Anna Palk, Maurice Kaufmann, Peter Barkworth, Helen Shapiro, Shane Fenton, Bobby Vee, Danny Williams, Lionel Blair.

● Rich business type Price is the titled old square who wants to keeps daughter Anna Palk out of the clutches of dodgy popster Kaufmann, but is powerless to prevent romance spawning when she meets up with hunky singing sensation Billy Universe (Fury) and embarks on a tour of London nightlife. Minor fresco of '60s Britpop frippery: Helen Shapiro, Shane Fenton and The Fentones, an imported Bobby Vee and Lionel Blair all in the same movie. Blimey, pass the Tizer. TJ

Play It to the Bone

(1999, US, 124 min)
d Ron Shelton. *p* Stephen Chin. *sc* Ron Shelton. *ph* Mark Vargo. *ed* Paul Seydor. *pd* Claire Jenora Bowin. *m* Alex Wurman. *cast* Antonio Banderas, Woody Harrelson, Lolita Davidovich, Tom Sizemore, Robert Wagner, Lucy Liu, Richard Masur, Willie Garson, Cylk Cozart, Aida Turturro.

● Inspired by a locker room boxing legend, this concerns two low rent never-coulda-beens who land an invitation to fight each other as the warm-up bout for a championship match. Presumably because the drama hinges on the opponents' friendship, writer/director Shelton opts to follow them on the road from LA to Vegas. They take the scenic route, and this first hour and a half should have been a chance to savour the salty comic dialogue that sports mythologiser Shelton does so well. But Vince Boudreau (Harrelson) and Cesar Dominguez (Banderas) don't seem to know anything about each other – and nor does Grace (Davidovich), supposedly Vince's ex and Cesar's current girlfriend. It's by far Shelton's weakest film, badly in need of a rewrite, with such a flatfooted camera style that the road sections look like back projection. On the positive side, Cesar's admission of homosexual experimentation is an unexpected touch and, as usual, Shelton supplies his female lead with an amusing intellectual superiority. Still, it's only when you get down to the fight that the movie begins to make sense: you want both of them to win. That's an interesting and original dynamic for a boxing movie. TCh

Playmaker, The

(1994, GB, 91 min)
d Yuri Zeltser. *p* Thomas Baer, Marc Samuelson, Peter Samuelson. *sc* Yuri Zeltser. *ph* Ross Berryman. *ed* John Rosenberg. *ad* Philip Vasels, Diane Hughes. *m* Mark Snow. *cast* Colin Firth, Jennifer Rubin, John Getz.

● On advice from barman Eddie (Getz), aspiring actress Jamie (Rubin) takes on a $5,000 one-to-one acting course with Talbert (Firth) in his isolated Los Angeles eyrie (like the pad in *North by Northwest*). First, she undergoes a bit of personality stripping, then he dresses her as a harridan/femme fatale and ropes her into a wheelchair. And that's only lesson two. The tables are later turned by some very implausible plot twists. A movie veering unsteadily from psycho-sexual power play to naturalistic horror thriller, with some finely achieved, but far from saving moments of tension and sexual *frisson*. WH

Play Me Something

(1989, GB, 72 min, b/w & col)
d Timothy Neat. *p* Kate Swan. *sc* John Berger, Timothy Neat. *ph* Chris Cox, Timothy Neat. *ed* Russell Fenton. *ad* Annette Gillies. *m* Jim Sutherland. *cast* Lucia Lanzarini, Charlie Barron, John Berger, Hamish Henderson, Tilda Swinton, Stewart Ennis, Robert Carr.

● John Berger here collaborates with Neat to bring one of his own short stories to the screen, also appearing as the mysterious story teller. A handful of men and women await the plane for Glasgow on the Hebridean island of Barra: visitors, a girl (Swinton) setting off for a job on the mainland, locals who have charge of the airport, and in their midst, Berger. Jaunty, vibrant and expansive, he makes a mesmerising storyteller; and his tale, on the face of it a simple yarn of a peasant (Brumo) on a weekend trip to Venice, becomes a complex exploration of people and places, factories and farms, sex, politics, music…ways of being. The film quite naturally takes on myriad textures: colour and black-and-white, 35mm and blown-up 16mm footage, and for the story-within-the-story, still photographs by the exemplary Jean Mohr. Berger and Neat have discovered that there is a useful application for post-modernism after all, the better to tell a tale. TCh

Play Misty for Me

(1971, US, 102 min)
d Clint Eastwood. *p* Robert Daley. *sc* Jo Heims, Dean Riesner. *ph* Bruce Surtees. *ed* Carl Pingitore. *ad* Alexander Golitzen. *m* Dee Barton. *cast* Clint Eastwood, Jessica Walter, Donna Mills, John Larch, Jack Ging, Irene Hervey, Donald Siegel.

● Eastwood's first film as director, and first exploratory probe for the flaws in his macho image as outlined in Siegel's *The Beguiled*. A highly enjoyable thriller made under the influence of Siegel (who contributes a memorable cameo as a bartender), it casts Eastwood as a late-night Californian DJ who, flattered by the persistent attentions of a mysterious fan (Walter), lets himself be picked up for a one night stand before going back to his true love (Mills). Before long, blandly assuming an on-going relationship, Walter reveals herself to be a suicidal hysteric who won't take no for an answer; and poor Eastwood is driven into a corner like a mesmerised rabbit, unable to find a way out of the impasse without driving one of his two jealous women over the edge. From there it's but a step to the watcher in the bushes, the carving knife glittering in a darkened room, and a splendid all-stops-out finale. TM

Playtime

(1967, Fr, 152 min)
d Jacques Tati. *p* René Silvera. *sc* Jacques Tati, Jacques Lagrange. *ph* Jean Badal, Andréas Winding. *ed* Gérard Pollicand. *pd* Eugène Roman. *m* Francis Lemarque. *cast* Jacques Tati, Barbara Dennek, Jacqueline Lecomte, Valérie Camille, France Rumilly.

● Tati's Hulot on the loose in a surreal, scarcely recognisable Paris, tangling intermittently with a troop of nice American matrons on a 24-hour trip. Not so much a saga of the individual against an increasingly dehumanised decor, it's more a semi-celebratory symphony to Tati's sensational city-set, all reflections and rectangles, steel, chrome, gleaming sheet metal and *trompe l'oeil* plate glass. Shot in colour that looks almost like monochrome, recorded in five-track stereo sound with scarcely a word of speech (the mysterious language of objects echoes louder than words), this jewel of Tati's career is a hallucinatory comic vision on the verge of abstraction. SJo

Plaza Suite

(1970, US, 114 min)
d Arthur Hiller. *p* Howard W Koch. *sc* Neil Simon. *ph* Jack Marta. *ed* Frank Bracht. *ad* Arthur Lonergan. *m* Maurice Jarre. *cast* Walter Matthau, Maureen Stapleton, Barbara Harris, Lee Grant, Jennie Sullivan, Tom Carey.

● Harmless piece of Neil Simon fluff, rather flattened by Hiller's steamroller direction: three playlets, set in the same hotel room, with the gimmick that all three male leads are played by Matthau. The first is the best, with Matthau beautifully partnered by Maureen Stapleton as a couple celebrating their 24th wedding anniversary, she waxing all nostalgic, he itching to get away to his mistress, and a history of marital irritation charted by their absurdist dialogue. The rest is thumb-twiddling time, with Matthau as a Hollywood producer seducing a happily married old flame (the delightful Harris, wasted)) with his big-time act, and as the father of a hysterical bride (Sullivan) who has locked herself in the loo with the wedding waiting. TM

Pleasantville

(1998, US, 124 min)
d Gary Ross. *p* John Kilik, Robert J Degus, Steven Soderbergh, Gary Ross. *sc* Gary Ross. *ph* John Lindley. *ed* William Goldenberg. *pd* Jeannine Oppewall. *m* Randy Newman. *cast* Tobey Maguire, Jeff Daniels, Joan Allen, Reese Witherspoon, Don Knotts, William H Macy, JT Walsh.

● It's 1998, a time of liberal homilies, and two youngsters from a broken home plainly need spiritual guidance: while Jennifer (Witherspoon) wraps herself in the attentions of the opposite sex, brother David (Maguire) finds comfort in the nostalgia of a '50s soap, 'Pleasantville', offering 'a flashback to kinder, gentler times'. Enter the fairy godfather: Knotts' slightly misguided TV repair man, who, reading David's wish for refuge literally, whisks the pair inside the show's b/w world, where they're welcomed into the Parker family, and life is simple, happy, regular, insular, sexless. An ingenious fable, screenwriter Ross's directorial debut playfully spoofs the small-minded lifestyle idealised by 'family values' advocates, and the intolerance and insecurity underlying that ideal. The introduction of colour to the original monochrome palette, marking the spread of disturbing new ideas imported by the '90s teens, is a concise cinematic device and gloriously watchable. NB

Please Don't Eat the Daisies

(1960, US, 111 min)
d Charles Walters. *p* Joe Pasternak. *sc* Isobel Lennart. *ph* Robert Bronner. *ed* John McSweeney Jr. *ad* George W Davis, Hans Peters. *m* David Rose. *cast* Doris Day, David Niven, Janis Paige, Spring Byington, Richard Haydn, Patsy Kelly, Jack Weston.
● Urbane, thoroughly frivolous comedy about a drama critic, his wife, their four squabbling sons, and pet sheepdog (adapted by Isobel Lennart from Jean Kerr's best-seller about life with the *NY Herald-Tribune*'s Walter Kerr). There's not much in the way of plot (a slap in the face from an actress he's panned precipitates a family move from New York to the safety of the country), but the interplay between the stars is mildly diverting: Doris Day, prim and fragrant, bustles around the house; Niven smiles and wriggles his tache in his usual louche way. And that's about it. Good performance from the dog. GM

Pleasure Principle, The

(1991, GB, 100 min)
d/p/sc David Cohen. *ph* Andrew Spellar. *ed* Joe McAllister. *pd* Cecilia Brerton. *m* Sonny Southon. *cast* Peter Firth, Lynsey Baxter, Hadyn Gwynne, Lysette Anthony, Sara Mair-Thomas, Ian Hogg.
● Freelance journalist Dick (Firth) can't resist dames, and dames can't resist him. Causing him varying degrees of hormonal distress are Sammy (Baxter), a dippy divorcee just waiting for Dick to come and free her sexuality; ex-wife Anne (Mair-Thomas), now a born-again radical lesbian; and two women whose elegance and sophistication are signalled by their coffee-ad eyebrow-arching: brain surgeon Judith (Gwynne) and lawyer Charlotte (Anthony). The theme of the improbable Don Juan has been thoroughly overhauled by the likes of Truffaut and Woody Allen, and this adds nothing new. It knee-jerks smugly at all the right themes, acknowledging its hero's new-man machismo, but the voice-over continually invites the male viewer to share its wide-eyed bewilderment at the Mystery That Is Woman. The women are stereotyped and manipulative, perverse harridans or cuddlesome love-bunnies. More pain than pleasure. JRo

Pleasure Seekers, The

(1964, US, 107 min)
d Jean Negulesco. *p* David Weisbart. *sc* Edith Sommer. *ph* Daniel L Fapp. *ed* Louis Loeffler. *ad* Jack Martin Smith, Edward Carrere. *m* Lionel Newman, Alexander Courage. *cast* Ann-Margret, Tony Franciosa, Carol Lynley, Gardner McKay, Pamela Tiffin, Gene Tierney, Vito Scoti, Brian Keith, Antonio Gades.
● The box-office recipe for *Three Coins in the Fountain* (three American gals, a glitzy European location, romantic complication) doesn't quite hold good the second time around when director Negulesco tries to repeat the trick in Madrid instead of Rome. Ann-Margret gets most screen time (and has a socko dance number, 'Everything Makes Music When You're in Love', on a Spanish beach) as she pines for a local medic, while Lynley falls for her boss and Tiffin makes a play for aloof playboy Franciosa. Smoothly done in lush CinemaScope, but so contrived its sundry dramatic crises exist in an emotional vacuum. TJ

Pledge, The

(2001, US, 124 min)
d Sean Penn. *p* Michael Fitzgerald, Sean Penn, Elie Samaha. *sc* Jerzy Kromolowski, Mary Olson-Kromolowski. *ph* Chris Menges. *ed* Jay Cassidy. *pd* Bill Groom. *m* Hans Zimmer, Klaus Badelt. *cast* Jack Nicholson, Benicio Del Toro, Aaron Eckhart, Helen Mirren, Tom Noonan, Robin Wright Penn, Vanessa Redgrave, Mickey Rourke, Sam Shepard, Lois Smith, Harry Dean Stanton.
● Adapted from a book by Friedrich Dürrenmatt, Penn's cop thriller-cum-psycho-drama is ambitious but deeply flawed. Nicholson is mostly impressive as the cop whose retirement is effectively blown by the news of the horrendous killing of an eight-year-old girl. But Penn's occasionally flashy direction of a contrived, often clichéd script all too happy to toss in a shoal of red herrings progressively undermines his efforts as the story (literally) unravels. It's just about credible that the cop would stand by his promise to the dead girl's mother to solve the mystery, but by the time he encounters Del Toro's retarded redskin (dubious indeed) and Mirren's psychologist (who profiles the murderer and his probable future actions after looking at the child's painting!), we're deep into movie madness, and the rest is hokum. Chris Menges' camerawork, however, remains effective. GA

Pleins Feux sur l'assassin (Spotlight on Murder)

(1960, Fr, 88 min, b/w)
d Georges Franju. *sc* Pierre Boileau, Thomas Narcejac, Georges Franju. *ph* Marcel Fredetal. *ed* Gilbert Natot. *ad* Roger Briancourt. *m* Maurice Jarre. *cast* Pierre Brasseur, Pascale Audret, Jean-Louis Trintignant, Jean Babilée, Dany Saval, Marianne Koch, Philippe Leroy-Beaulieu.
● Characteristically, Franju's adaptation of a story by Boileau-Narcejac (the creators of *Vertigo* and *Les Diaboliques)* negates suspense in favour of a highly pleasurable succession of strange images. An eccentric château-owner (Brasseur) dies, peacefully encased with his favourite wind-up miniature ballerina behind a mirror. With his body unaccounted for, the greedy heirs are legally obliged to wait five years, and devise a *son-et-lumière* to raise funds for the upkeep of the expensive château. Meanwhile, a murderer in their midst begins eliminating future rivals... Franju creates some wonderfully atmospheric monochrome textures, extracts another haunting score from Maurice Jarre, and throws in plenty of absurd humour, as well as a typically fetishistic line-up of doll-like women. The actors are encouraged into striking attitudes, so that emotional conviction is sacrificed for surreal effect. With its unconventional blend of narrative pulp and visual sophistication, the film was a commercial flop, rarely to be seen outside France, until eventually the rediscovery of the original negative gave it a new lease of life. DT

Plein Soleil (Delitto in pieno sole/Blazing Sun/ Purple Noon)

(1959, Fr/It, 119 min)
d René Clément. *p* Robert Hakim, Raymond Hakim. *sc* Paul Gégauff, René Clément. *ph* Henri Decaë. *ed* Françoise Javet. *ad* Paul Bertrand. *m* Nino Rota. *cast* Alain Delon, Marie Laforêt, Maurice Ronet, Elvire Popesco, Erno Crisa, Frank Latimore, Bill Kearns, Romy Schneider.
● René Clément and Chabrol's collaborator Paul Gégauff got hold of Patricia Highsmith's *The Talented Mr Ripley* decades before Wim Wenders laid hands on the novelist's psychopathic protagonist in *The American Friend.* In his third film appearance, 24-year-old Delon exudes icy charm as Ripley, the emissary sent by an American industrialist to rescue his son (Ronet, sublimely dissolute) from yachting decadence. Delon, though, has a killer scheme of his own – murder the guy, pocket the loot, and steal his girl (Laforêt). Easy. It just takes a thread of steel in the nerves – and a director with the stealth and patience to wind up the tension and avoid rushing the pay-off. Audiences weaned on switchback cutting and adrenalin pace will have to adjust, but even the admittedly clunky first 30 minutes make sense in retrospect. Delon's determined chill aside, there's much to enjoy: a narrative stitched together with old school expertise; vivid marine camerawork by Henri Decaë; a startling rinky-dink piano score by Nino Rota. TJ

Plenty

(1985, US, 124 min)
d Fred Schepisi. *p* Edward R Pressman, Joseph Papp. *sc* David Hare. *ph* Ian Baker. *ed* Peter Honess. *pd* Richard MacDonald. *m* Bruce Smeaton. *cast* Meryl Streep, Sam Neill, Charles Dance, John Gielgud, Tracey Ullman, Sting, Ian McKellen, André Maranne.
● David Hare has been laying into the British for so long now, one begins to wonder what they ever did to him. When *Plenty* was first produced on the stage, its compelling vision of our postwar decline, seen through the eyes of a wartime heroine, had its edge dulled by a hectoring moral righteousness. Balance is restored in Schepisi's film, largely by the obvious filmic process of shifting the point of view among the characters. The life of Susan Traherne (Streep) suffers a steady decline alongside the more retrograde incidents of our history (Festival of Britain, Suez), until her only option is to take to the road as a vagrant to try and recapture her former glory as a spy in World War II France, when the world seemed young. Performances all round are excellent, especially Dance as her long-suffering boyfriend, and Gielgud as the last exponent of decency at the Foreign office. Whether or not you buy the message, it's a work that qualifies as epic, and reveals Hare as a great Romantic. CPea

Pleure Pas la Bouche Pleine

see Spring into Summer

Plot

see Attentat, L'

Plot Against Harry, The

(1970, US, 81 min, b/w)
d Michael Roemer. *p* Robert Young, Michael Roemer. *sc* Michael Roemer. *ph* Robert Young. *ed* Maurice Schell. *ad* Howard Mandel. *m* Frank Lewin. *cast* Martin Priest, Ben Lang, Maxine Woods, Henry Nemo, Jacques Taylor, Jean Leslie.
● Described by the *Village Voice* as 'a deadpan, post-Jarmusch comedy made when Jarmusch was still in grammar school', shot on the streets in black-and-white with sly camera movements and naturalistic sound, Roemer's film is comedy out of *cinéma-vérité*. It looks and feels like Jarmusch, a seriously oblique, cool look at Jewish aspirations and social morality: this perhaps explains why it was shelved until 1989, since no one in 1970 thought it merited release. A two-bit New York Jewish racketeer, Harry Plotnick is released after a 12-month 'vacation' to find his affairs in disarray. The Mob has muscled in on his turf, the tax man is auditing his books, a parole officer is hovering, and his sister's staying over...all this before Harry has even crashed into his ex-wife's car and met a daughter he didn't know he had. It may sound frantic, but in fact the plot takes a back seat to ironic observation. Through it all wanders Martin Priest's magnificently non-plussed Harry, an outsider stoically trying to work his way back in. TCh

Ploughman's Lunch, The

(1983, GB, 107 min)
d Richard Eyre. *p* Simon Relph, Ann Scott. *sc* Ian McEwan. *ph* Clive Tickner. *ed* Dean Martin. *pd* Luciana Arrighi. *m* Dominic Muldowney. *cast* Jonathan Pryce, Tim Curry, Rosemary Harris, Frank Finlay, Charlie Dore, David De Keyser, Nat Jackley, Bill Paterson.
● Ian McEwan must have whooped for joy when the Falklands war erupted, transforming his script from an examination of the Suez affair into a much spicier story of shabby English values, set during the Falklands crisis but filtered through the perspective of Suez. Sadly, the resulting film veers wildly in quality, and fails to cast much illumination on either past or present. Pryce turns in a creepingly accurate performance as an ambitious BBC newsroom hack who is commissioned to write a book on Suez while the Falklands war is in progress; but much of the film is concerned with his pursuit of a rich bitch (Dore), whom he fancies precisely because she is (literally) out of his class. It all culminates neatly, but with typically facile signposting of its political analysis, at the 1982 Conservative Party Conference, with the old guard (for which read resurgent Tory traditionalism) triumphing over the middle class upstart (opportunistic liberalism). It's all far too literary for its own good (McEwan indulges himself by including portraits of his bookish mates), and these aren't people you love to hate, they're just people you hate. RR

Plow That Broke the Plains, The

(1936, US, 28 min, b/w)
d/sc Pare Lorentz. *ph* Paul Strand, Ralph Steiner, Leo Hurwitz, Paul Ivano, Dorothea Lange. *ed* Pare Lorentz, Leo Zochling. *m* Virgil Thomson. *narrator* Thomas Chalmers.
● The didactic side of this classic documentary has to do with how over-cultivation plus drought were turning millions of acres of the Midwest into a dust bowl. But not to worry – the government is on the case. The desolated farmsteads, the procession of heavy-laden jalopies along the highway, the migrant camps: this is *The Grapes of Wrath*, actuality version. Lorentz's self-consciously poetic manner and the declamatory style

of his commentary ('Blown out! Baked out! And broke!') now seem the very essence of the New Deal '30s. But the most forceful element is the music, with Thomson reworking such hackneyed material as 'Streets of Laredo' and 'Mademoiselle from Armentières' into one of the greatest and most influential of film scores. BBa

Plumbum, or a Dangerous Game (Plyumbum, ili opasnaya igra)

(1986, USSR, 90 min)
d Vadim Abdrashitov. *sc* Alexander Mindadze. *cast* Anton Androsov, Yelena Yakovleva, Aleksandr Feklistov, Elena Dmitrieva.

● A Soviet teenager adopts a code name based on the Latin word for lead, worms his way into the city's underworld gangs, and sets himself up as a supergrass. The special police squad to which Plumbum attaches himself are happy to use him, but when he turns in his own father for poaching, the zealousness with which he is pursuing his clean-up campaign raises some perplexing questions about his methods and motives. Is Plumbum an exemplary citizen, or simply the product of a repressive regime, which delegates only a distorted image of power to one who, like his fellow citizens, had so long been denied it? This was the subject of much controversy and heated debate when first released in the USSR. GA

Plunder

(1930, GB, 98 min, b/w)
d Tom Walls. *p* Herbert Wilcox. *sc* WP Lipscomb. *ph* Freddie Young. *ed* Duncan Mansfield. *ad* LP Williams. *cast* Tom Walls, Ralph Lynn, Robertson Hare, Winifred Shotter, Mary Brough, Doreen Bendix.

●Ben Travers' farces, which were immensely popular in the '20s, were filmed at the time with the original casts. *Plunder* (revived at the National Theatre in 1978) is as fine an example of the farceur's art as you will find anywhere, though unusually it contrives to include a violent death. Filmically naive, it nevertheless offers considerable pleasure, not only as the historical recreation of a '20s Aldwych farce, but principally as a showcase for the exemplary acting of Ralph Lynn as the monocled ass, and Tom Walls as a Raffles-type jewel thief of unusually sombre suavity. As the plotting escalates to the correct pitch of frenzy, their interplay and timing remain consistently immaculate. There's also a neat Art Deco set. CPea

Plunder of Peach and Plum (Tao Li Jie)

(1934, China, 101 min, b/w)
d Ying Yunwei. *p* Ma Dejian. *sc* Ying Yunwei. *ph* Wu Weiyun. *ed* Ying Yunwei. *ad* Zhang Yunqiao. *m* Nie Er. *cast* Yuan Muzhi, Chen Bo'er, Tang Kuaiqiu, Zhang Zhixun, Zhou Boxun, Wang Yizhi, Zhu Mingxian.

●China's first sound-on-film talkie, made for the covert communist company Denton (Diantong), offers a grim picture of the fate awaiting honest job-seekers in the Shanghai of the mid-'30s. Tao (Yuan) graduates, marries Li (Chen) and takes a prime white-collar job with a shipping company. But he quits rather than endanger life by knowingly overloading a ship, and then finds himself on a downward slope which eventually reduces him to labouring in a metal foundry. Meanwhile, his wife becomes a secretary but quits after her boss (Zhou) tricks her to a hotel and tries to rape her. Told in flashback from Death Row, where Tao awaits execution for murder, this is unremittingly pessimistic. But the director and lead actor (both first-timers) were huge talents, and their skills make for a compulsive, even enjoyable movie. The sequence in which Tao scours four floors of the Taishan Hotel for his missing wife, shot with an amazingly mobile camera, is a classic. TR

Plunkett & Macleane

(1999, GB, 101 min)
d Jake Scott. *p* Tim Bevan, Eric Fellner, Rupert Harvey. *sc* Robert Wade, Neal Purvis, Charles McKeown. *ph* John Mathieson. *ed* Oral Norrie Ottey. *pd* Norris Spencer. *m* Craig Armstrong. *cast* Robert Carlyle, Jonny Lee Miller, Liv Tyler, Ken Stott, Michael Gambon, Alan Cumming, Terence Rigby.

●London, 1748. Notorious highwayman Plunkett (Carlyle) is on the run from ruthless Thief-Taker General Chance (Stott). Meanwhile, Capt Macleane (Lee Miller), who has the manners of an aristo but none of the financial wherewithal, faces a spell in debtors' prison. Criminal partnership between the men will help both with their money problems and throw the law off the scent. Gaining instant notoriety as 'the Gentlemen Highway-men', they attract the attention of Rebecca (Tyler), niece of Lord Gibson (Gambon). Scott's first feature is an enticing set-up but with little inspiration in the follow through. Of course, we root for the boys, since Carlyle and Miller have an easy rapport, but the plotting's fumbled, Tyler is given little to do, Stott's sideline villainy is fudged, and the frenetically upbeat last reel is almost nonsensical. TJ

Plutonium Circus, The

(1994, US, 73 min)
d/p George Whittenburg Ratliff. *ph* Judd Metni. *ed* George Whittenburg Ratliff.

●A documentary canvassing opinion on the safety, or otherwise, of the Pantex Plant outside Amarillo, Texas, a Cold War nuclear weapons factory – now devoted to dismantling the weapons. As in Errol Morris's work, what's fascinating here is the sheer eccentricity of so many of Ratliff's subjects: best, probably, is Stanley Marsh III, owner of the Cadillac ranch, crackpot conceptual artist and acerbic wordsmith. GA

Poachers (Furtivos)

(1975, Sp, 83 min)
d/p José Luis Borau. *sc* Manolo Gutierrez. *ph* Luis Cuadrado. *ed* Ana Romero. *ad* Mario Ortiz. *m* Vainica Doble. *cast* Lola Gaos, Ovidi Montllor, Alicia Sánchez, Ismael Merlo, José Luis Borau, Felipe Solano.

●A local Spanish governor, still impetuous and spoilt in middle age, hunts with his cronies in a forest where his former nurse runs an inn. Such insolences as seeing this figure of authority in relation to his childhood nanny underlie much of this muted and beautifully observed film. Spanish publicity for *Furtivos* challenged Franco's description of Spain as 'a peaceful forest' by asking 'What is rotting beneath the silence of a peaceful forest?' Thus, the family tragedy at the film's centre is related on several levels: individual, generational, political, and religious. The nurse, bitter and perhaps incestuous, is usurped by a runaway girl brought to stay by her only son. After years of repression and forced servility, she finally cracks when presented with her son's spontaneous, guilt-free relationship with the girl. Strong performances, photographed with beautiful precision. CPe

Pocahontas

(1995, US, 81 min)
d Mike Gabriel, Eric Goldberg. *p* James Pentecost. *sc* Carl Binder, Susannah Grant, Philip Lazebnick. *ed* H Lee Petersen. *ad* Michael Giaimo. *m* Alan Menken. *cast* voices: Irene Bedard, Mel Gibson, David Ogden Stiers, Billy Connolly, Christian Bale, Linda Hunt.

●Disney's *Pocahontas* can't get stirred dramatically for political correctness, the finale will please nobody, and the songs are duff. That said, there are enough incidental felicities to pass the time pleasantly. A great deal of care went into the depiction of the Native Americans, in particular the gorgeous heroine, but the whites and various pet animals – Meeko the racoon, Flit the hummingbird – come from stock. Given the pompous colonialist views that John Smith has to express, it's just as well they requisitioned the endearingly jivey tones of Gibson for the hero. Pocahontas shows him that the natives live harmoniously in primitive Paradise. He takes her point and they fall in love. The British settlers only want gold, but whether they're all as villainous (Connolly voices one) as mustachioed Gov Ratcliffe and his decadent pug isn't clear. Smith is captured by Pocahontas' father, Chief Powhatan, but she saves his life by offering hers. He then stops a British bullet intended for the Chief. All this self-abnegation carries over into a *Casablanca*-style ending. BC

Pocket Money

(1972, US, 102 min)
d Stuart Rosenberg. *p* John Foreman. *sc* Terrence Malick. *ph* Laszlo Kovacs. *ed* Robert Wyman. *ad* Tambi Larsen. *m* Alex North. *cast* Paul Newman, Lee Marvin, Strother Martin, Wayne Rogers, Christine Belford, Kelly Jean Peters, Fred Graham, Hector Elizondo, Terrence Malick.

●Third of the Rosenberg/Newman collaborations, and a wry, leisurely relief after the heavyweight experiences of *Cool Hand Luke* and *WUSA*. The lazily incongruous character studies of naive Newman, hard-drinking, slow-witted Marvin, and a strong support cast, come from a script by Terrence Malick, revving up on this and the equally off-the-wall *Gravy Train* for his own *Badlands*; while the barest bones of plot (the ill-suited pair stumble through Mexico on a crooked cattle-dealing assignment) are down to the source novel, JPS Brown's *Jim Kane*. PT

Po di Sangui

(1996, Fr/Port/Guinea-Bissau, 90 min)
d Flora Gomes. *p* Jean-Pierre Galepe. *sc* Anita Fernandez, Flora Gomes. *ph* Vincenzo Marano. *ed* Christiane Lack. *pd* Joseph Kpobly. *m* Pablo Cueco. *cast* Ramiro Naka, Bia Gomes, Edna Evora, Dadu Cissé.

●When the nomad Dou returns to his Guinea-Bissau village to find his twin has died, he's reluctant to take on, according to tradition, his brother's widow and daughter. Things get worse: the village is stricken by drought, and the witch doctor advises his people to abandon their birthplace. Though visually elegant (even if the slow, ornate camera-movements soon begin to irritate), Gomes' film is too obscure for non-African audiences. Included somewhere is an ecological message about the need to preserve trees (which, apparently, contain the villagers' souls), but quite what some scenes in the snail-paced narrative actually mean is likely to remain, for most, a mystery. GA

Poetic Justice

(1993, US, 109 min)
d John Singleton. *p* Steve Nicolaides, John Singleton. *sc* John Singleton. *ph* Peter Lyons Collister. *ed* Bruce Cannon. *m* Stanley Clarke. *cast* Janet Jackson, Tupac Shakur, Khandi Alexander, Regina King, Joe Torry, Maya Angelou, Ché J Avery, Lloyd Avery II, Lori Petty.

●Singleton's follow-up to *Boyz N the Hood* is an honorable failure, a flawed attempt to take black film out of the macho gangsta ghetto. It's the tale of a hairdresser, Justice (Jackson), and a mailman, Lucky (Shakur). Fate throws them together with mutual friends, bickering lovers Iesha (King) and Chicago (Torry), on a road trip up the coast from LA to Oakland. In classic Hollywood style they loathe each other at first, but slowly come to fall in love. Singleton has a feel for the rhythms of black lives and the movie begins promisingly. Intermittent forays into subjectivity are, however, less persuasive: notably the interior monologues in which we hear Justice's poetry. Actually the work of Maya Angelou, these mature, proud declamations don't belong in Justice's mouth (the nadir finds the camera ogling Jackson's curves as she 'writes' Angelou's 'Phenomenal Woman'). But it's when the movie hits the road that trouble really starts. The stop-go motion of the mail van is an appropriate image for the film's lack of momentum, as both couples repeatedly fight and make up, with an alternative image of black experience at each pit stop. Too much cultural baggage for so slight a scenario. TCh

Poetry, Sex

see Monkey's Mask, The

Point, The

(1970, US, 75 min)
d Fred Wolf. *p* Harry Nilsson, Jerry Good, Fred Wolf, Larry Gordon. *sc* Norman Lenzer. *ed* Rich Harrison. *pd* Gary Lund. *m* Harry Nilsson. *cast* voices: Alan Barzman, Mike Lookinland, Paul Frees, Lenny Weinrib.

●A patchy one-man-band attempt by rock-'n'crooner Harry Nilsson at a children's animated musical fantasy, about a father who tears his son away from watching TV by reading a story about the Pointed Village, where everything has a point until the birth of a round-headed boy... Made originally for TV, the animation is excellent, and many of the images are given a shot in the arm by a tailor-made score ('the pointless forest' especially), but the whole thing is weighed down by the doughy morality (dare one say 'point'?). Adults who ferret out readings in Puffins will love it; children will probably be reasonably entertained. IB

Point Blank

(1967, US, 92 min)
d John Boorman. *p* Judd Bernard,Robert Chartoff. *sc* Alexander Jacobs,David Newhouse, Rafe Newhouse.*ph* Philip H Lathrop. *ed* Henry Berman.*ad* George W Davis, Albert Brenner. *m* Johnny Mandel. *cast* Lee Marvin, Angie Dickinson, Keenan Wynn, Carroll O'Connor, Lloyd Bochner, Michael Strong, John Vernon, Sharon Acker, James B Sikking.

●One of the definitive films to emerge from Hollywood in the late '60s, this hard-nosed adaptation of Richard Stark's *The Hunter* owed much to the European influences that Boorman brought with him from England. People have noted the influence of Resnais behind the film's time lapses and possible dream setting, but Godard's *Alphaville* offers a more rewarding comparison. Both films use the gangster/thriller framework to explore the increasing depersonalisation of living in a mechanised urban world. Just as Constantine's Lemmy Caution was a figure from the past stranded in a futuristic setting, so Marvin's bullet-headed gangster is an anachronism from the '50s transported to San Francisco and LA of the '60s, a world of concrete slabs and menacing vertical lines. Double-crossed and left to die, Marvin comes back from the dead to claim his share of the money from the Organization, only to become increasingly puzzled and frustrated when he finds there is no money, because the Organization is the world of big business run by respectable men with wallets full of credit cards. CPe

Point Break

(1991, US, 122 min)
d Kathryn Bigelow. *p* Peter Abrams, Robert L Levy. *sc* Peter Iliff. *ph* Donald Peterman. *ed* Howard Smith, Scott Conrad, Burt Lovitt. *pd* Peter Jamison. *m* Mark Isham. *cast* Patrick Swayze, Keanu Reeves, Gary Busey, Lori Petty, John McGinley, James Le Gros, John Philbin.

●Undercover FBI agent Reeves strips for action and gets into some serious male bonding when he infiltrates the Californian surfing fraternity in search of a gang of bank robbers who call themselves the Ex-Presidents. During the course of the investigation, however, Reeves is seduced by 'spiritual' surfer Swayze's cosmic talk about oneness with the sea, and becomes addicted to the adrenalin rush of life on the edge. Despite this theme of Faustian redemption, the distinction between good and evil is far from black and white, Swayze's reckless craving for danger filling an elemental void in Reeves' hollow soul. There are times when the dialogue is a shade comic, others when the brilliantly staged action set pieces become almost abstract. Plausibility, though, has never been director Bigelow's strong suit, and there's precious little to be found here. Even so, there's enough high-octane, heart-racing excitement for a dozen movies. NF

Point Is to Change It, The (Es Kommt drauf an, sie zu verändern)

(1973, WGer, 54 min, b/w)
d Claudia Alemann.

●A documentary made at a time when feminist theory on unequal pay was in its infancy, this gets at the heart of the problem with considerable precision. For instance: why are women workers often employed in declining industrial sectors? Answer: cheap labour and minimal plant investment go together. 'It's more profitable to employ women than to automate a plant. It's cheaper to sack a woman than to keep a machine idle'. With Britain in the throes of 'de-industrialisation', there are lessons here for more than just women. MM

Point of No Return (aka The Assassin)

(1992, US, 108 min)
d John Badham. *p* Art Linson. *sc* Robert Getchell, Alexandra Seros. *ph* Michael Watkins. *ed* Frank Morris. *pd* Philip Harrison. *m* Hans Zimmer. *cast* Bridget Fonda, Gabriel Byrne, Dermot Mulroney, Anne Bancroft, Harvey Keitel, Geoffrey Lewis.

●Bland Hollywood remake of Luc Besson's *Nikita*: Fonda plays Maggie, a junkie who kills a cop and is offered the choice of dying or selling her soul to the Government. She chooses the latter, and under the eye of agent Bob (Byrne) retrains as a killer with feminine wiles. Bob is infatuated with his creation, but can't mix business with pleasure, so, when Maggie emerges as a glamorous hitwoman, he has to stand by while she falls for photographer JP (Mulroney). In the original, stylish direction and committed acting diverted attention from the espionage hocus-pocus. Here we have MTV slickness, bigger-budget action and a Nina Simone soundtrack. CO'S

Point of Order

(1963, US, 97 min, b/w)
d Emile de Antonio. *p* Emile de Antonio, Daniel Talbot. *sc* Emile de Antonio. *ed* Robert Duncan.

●Rejected by the 1963 New York Film Festival because it wasn't 'a real film', de Antonio's debut feature is perhaps the purest expression of his analytical approach to documentary and the 'media-event'. To the raw material of hours of video footage of the 1954 US Army-McCarthy hearings, he brought a radical collagist's technique: constructing an inquiry into the phenomenon of McCarthyism without moving from his editing bench, taking up a camera, or adding a word of commentary; re-democratising the historical documents once dominated by the authority of McCarthy's 'performance'; and opening up an early oppositional direction to *cinéma-vérité*. PT

Pointsman, The (De Wisselwachter)

(1986, Neth, 96 min)
d Jos Stelling. *p* Stanley Hillebrandt. *sc* George Brugmans, Hans de Wolf, Jos Stelling. *ph* Frans Bromet, Theo van de Sande, Paul van den Bos, Goert Giltaij. *ed* Rimko Haanstra. *ad* Gert Brinkers. *m* Michel Mulders. *cast* Jim Van Der Woude, Stéphane Excoffier, John Kraaykamp, Josse De Pauw, Ton Van Dort.

●Accidentally stepping off a train in the remote Scottish Highlands, a chic Frenchwoman finds herself stranded with a Dutch railway points-operator who leads a lonely, basic existence. Winter falls; as the pair become increasingly isolated, lacking a common language, an intricate, near-silent mating ritual is enacted. The woman, sophisticated and worldly, wears her most provocative clothes to tease never-felt emotions from her virgin acquaintance, until she becomes a captive of his awakened passion. Taking no account of plausibility, Stelling's exploration of the uses and abuses of power is art house fare, but neither obscure nor elitist. Enthralling performances generate a claustrophobic tension, but there's humour too. The director is merciless with the pointsman's few visitors: a leering, randy postman with transparent courtship tactics, an engine driver whose scepticism about the whole affair anticipates that of the audience. EP

Poison

(1990, US, 85 min)
d Todd Haynes. *p* Christine Vachon. *sc* Todd Haynes. *ph* Maryse Alberti. *ed* James Lyons, Todd Haynes. *pd* Sarah Stollman. *m* James Bennett. *cast* Edith Meeks, Scott Renderer, James Lyons, John R Lombardi, Larry Maxwell, Susan Norman.

●Inspired by Jean Genet, Haynes' enigmatic movie interweaves three apparently unconnected stories. In 'Hero' (shot in the style of a vox-pop TV documentary on suburban life), a young boy's mother (Meeks), schoolmates and neighbours relate how he disappeared, miraculously, after killing his father; in 'Horror' (reminiscent of '50s B movie sci-fi fantasies), a scientist (Maxwell) isolates the human sex-drive in a serum which turns him into a lethally infectious, grotesque mutant; and 'Homo', a mix of pastoral lyricism and claustrophobic grittiness, portrays the cruel, obsessive love felt by an imprisoned thief (Renderer) for an inmate he first met at reform school. The disparate styles and the absence of clear links between the stories make for unusually provocative viewing, because their shared themes (deviancy, alienation, persecution, monstrousness) are merely *implied* through the cutting. Compelling and quirkily intelligent; Genet, one feels, would have been impressed. GA

Poison Ivy

(1992, US, 89 min)
d Katt Shea Ruben. *p* Andy Ruben. *sc* Andy Ruben, Katt Shea Ruben. *ph* Phedon Papamichael. *ed* Gina Mittleman. *pd* Virginia Lee. *m* Aaron Davies. *cast* Drew Barrymore, Sara Gilbert, Tom Skerritt, Cheryl Ladd.

●Although marketed as a 'home invasion' thriller in the *Single White Female* vein – teenage nymphette Ivy (Barrymore) wreaks havoc in the home of rich kid Cooper (Gilbert) by seducing her ex-alcoholic father (Skerritt), supplanting her ailing mother (Ladd), and generally ruining Coop's life – there is more to *Poison Ivy* than meets the eye. Distanced from the over-heated emotions and events by Coop's naive voice-over narration ('I guess you have to give up certain things when you take on a friendship'), we witness much of what happens at one remove. In this and other ways, Ruben subverts the salacious subject matter, while exploring the dangerously ambiguous relationship between anarchic wild child Ivy and emotionally neglected rich kid Coop (an understated, moody performance from Gilbert). Its willingness to take risks, and its insights into the frailties and confusions of teenage friendships ('She might have been lonelier than I was', reflects Coop at the end), lift the film right out of the rut. NF

Pokémon – The First Movie: Mewtwo Strikes Back

(1999, Jap/US, 74 min)
d Kunihiko Yuyama, Michael Haigney. *p* Norman J Grossfeld, Choji Yoshikawa, Tomoyuki Igarashi, Takemoto Mori. *sc* Takeshi Shudo, (English adaptation) Norman J Grossfeld, Michael Haigney, John Touhey. *ph* Hisao Shirai. *ed* Toshio Henmi, Jay Film, Yutaka Ito. *ad* Katsuyoshi Kanemura. *m* Ralph Schuckett, John Loeffler. *cast* voices: Veronica Taylor, Philip Bartlett, Rachael Lillis, Eric Stuart, Addie Blaustein, Ikue Otani.

●The 'Americanised' version of Kunohiko Yuyama's primitively animated, samurai-influenced, 'quest and battle' epic (derived from Nintendo's 'Pocket Monster' game) boasts digitally enhanced backgrounds, a new score, a new rock soundtrack and, excepting the favoured baby-ish Pikachû, new voice talents. The story is a humourless retread of a Bond-style world domination yarn with a Frankenstein theme. From a DNA sample, scientists engineer a superclone, 'Mewtwo', who, angry at his genesis, swears to achieve world domination. So Kids ('trainers', in the film's parlance) Ash and pals voyage to Mewtwo's island to do battle. Parents struggle to stay awake, children are spellbound – proof of the film's fidelity to the puerile, bloodless play-fighting, collecting and eye-spying nature of the game's appeal. WH

Pokémon 2: The Power of One (Gekijôban Poketto Monsutâ: Maboroshi no Pokemon Ekkusu – Rugia Bakudan)

(1999, Jap [2000, US], 82 min)
d Kunihiko Yûyama. *p* Chôji Yoshikawa, Yukako Matsusako, Takemoto Mori. *sc* Takeshi Shudô. *ph* Hisao Shirai. *ed* Jay Film, Toshio Henmi, Yutaka Itô. *ad* Katsuyoshi Kanemura. *m* Shinji Miyazaki. *cast* voices: Rika Matsumoto, Ikue Ôtani, Mayumi Iizuka, Tomokazu Seki; (US version) Veronica Taylor, Rachael Lillis, Ted Lewis, Eric Stuart, Addie Blaustein.

●Surprisingly, this turns out to be marginally more coherent than the first movie. Of course, it's still fantasy codswallop for any parent forced to sit through it, but at least the story makes some sense. In a nutshell, spiky-haired young Pocket Monster-trainer Ash Ketchum is called on to save planet Earth from the hands of a power-crazed Pokémon collector who plans to unleash the combined forces of three of his latest acquisitions. What grates about these *Pokémon* movies is the appalling animation. This time around, the makers have at least put a little more depth into the visuals, even squeezing in some fairly impressive computer generated imagery. This minor improvement doesn't make the film any better, just a mite more bearable. DA

Pokémon 3: Spell of the Unown

(2001, Jap, 73 min)
d Kunihiko Yuyama, Michael Haigney. *p* Norman J Grossfeld, Choji Yoshikawa, Yukako Matsusako, Takemoto Mori. *sc* Takeshi Shudo, Hideki Sonoda. *ph* Hisao Shirai. *ed* Jay Film, Toshio Henmi, Yutaka Ito, (Pikachu and Pichu) Toshio Henmi. *ad* Katsuyoshi Kanemura, (Pikachu and Pichu) Shichiro Kobayashi. *m* Ralph Schuckett, (Pikachu and Pichu) Hirokazu Tanaka, Ken Shima. *cast* voices: Veronica Taylor, Eric Stuart, Rachael Lillis, Addie Blaustein, Ikue Otani.

●Three Poké flicks in 12 months – which suggests how little work goes into these confounding Japanese creations. As usual, the quality of the animation is abysmal: lead characters hardly move as they speak, while those towards the edge of the frame remain resolutely motionless. There are many things which we, as parents, simply cannot understand. Why are the films often saddled with two or more titles (this one's subtitled 'Spell of the Unown' [sic] – or should that be 'Entei', as listed on the press invitation)? Why is the dire accompanying short called *Pikachu & Pichu*, when it features not two but three lead characters? And then – a small but perhaps not insignificant matter – why have the characters' eyes changed from animé-style horizontal to a more Westernised vertical? However, the film is a shade more coherent than its predecessors, which is saying something. Addressing darker elements of loss and loneliness, it finds young hero Ash on a quest to reunite Molly with her missing parents after a brush with the mysterious Unown, whatever that is. DA

Pola X

(1999, Fr/Jap/Ger/Switz, 134 min)
d Leos Carax. *sc* Leos Carax, Lauren Sedofsky, Jean-Pol Fargeau. *ph* Eric Gautier. *ed* Nelly Quettier. *pd* Laurent Allaire. *m* Scott Walker. *cast* Guillaume Depardieu, Katernia Golubeva, Catherine Deneuve, Delphine Chuillot, Petruta Catana, Laurent Lucas, Sharunas Barta.

●Carax's long-awaited follow-up to *Les Amants du Pont-Neuf* is a misguided and narcissistic update of Melville's *Pierre, or the Ambiguities*. A well-to-do Normandy writer, Depardieu, abandons his carefree life with his adoring mother and girlfriend after meeting a ghostly refugee from the Balkans, who may or may not be his sister. Taking off for Paris and a life of frenzied, impoverished creativity (in a grim commune peopled by artistic types who wouldn't look out of place as the Nihilists in *The Big Lebowski*), he retreats further and further from society. The first part is merely dull and vacuous; thereafter the film slides into absurdly pretentious bluster (or a 'raging morass, full of plagiarism', as the hero's publishers would put it) which, it seems, has far less to do with modern realities than with Carax's nonsensically romanticised vision of himself. Woeful. (In the end, perhaps, it is most notable for securing an increasingly rare Scott Walker recording for its soundtrack.) GA

Police

(1985, Fr, 113 min)
d Maurice Pialat. *p* Emmanuel Pialat. *sc* Catherine Breillat, Sylvie Danton, Jacques Fieschi, Maurice Pialat. *ph* Luciano Tovoli. *ed* Yann Dedet. *ad* Constantin Mejinsky. *m* Henryk Gorecki. *cast* Gérard Depardieu, Sophie Marceau, Richard Anconina, Pascale Rocard, Sandrine Bonnaire, Franck Karoui, Jonathan Leina.

●A superficially genial cop (Depardieu) cross-examines a Tunisian drug-dealer. The can of worms is opened, and Depardieu plunges in, laying about the Parisian Arab community, doing deals with their corrupt lawyer, and with a woman (Marceau) who has stolen a suitcase of money. It is all going tougher and more furious than any other recent policier, when the film abruptly changes gear and becomes the chronicle of Depardieu's ill-fated amour for Marceau, a chronic liar, and deep in sin. Pialat is heir to the misanthropic strain in French culture, and dwells at great length on the uncomfortably real. There is no one else who pushes his actors to such uncomfortable extremes. If you want a thriller, then you're in for a rough ride; this is about tension, conflict and hostility, and almost all of it between man and woman. CPea

Police Academy

(1984, US, 96 min)
d Hugh Wilson. *p* Paul Maslansky. *sc* Neal Israel, Pat Proft, Hugh Wilson. *ph* Michael D Margulies. *ed* Robert Brown, Zach Staenberg. *pd* Trevor Williams. *m* Robert Folk. *cast* Steve Guttenberg, Kim Cattrall, GW Bailey, Bubba Smith, Donovan Scott, George Gaynes, Andrew Rubin, David Graf, Michael Winslow, Georgina Spelvin.

●This is where it all began: to increase recruitment levels, police entry restrictions are lowered, and out come the freaks. The barrage of sheerly vulgar humour, leaping on sexual and racial stereotypes with ideologically dubious gusto, is enough to take you aback, with the casting of hardcore star Georgina Spelvin for a comedy fellatio gag (it doesn't help commander Gaynes' concentration as he addresses VIP guests) not inappropriate in the circumstances. The hit-and-mostly-miss humour proves so cringeworthy, however, your real amazement will be reserved for that fact that they sprang six sequels and three different TV series out of this. Marginally better than the others perhaps, but what isn't? TJ

Police Academy 2: Their First Assignment

(1985, US, 87 min)
d Jerry Paris. *p* Paul Maslansky. *sc* Barry W Blaustein. *ph* James Crabe. *ed* Robert Wyman. *pd* Trevor Williams. *m* Robert Folk. *cast* Steve Guttenberg, Bubba Smith, David Graf, Michael Winslow, Bruce Mahler, Marion Ramsey, Colleen Camp, Howard Hesseman, Art Metrano, George Gaynes, Bobcat Goldthwait.

●Toning down the smut for a PG-rating, and bringing in veteran comedy director Paris, who made his feature debut with 1968's Jerry Lewis vehicle *Don't Raise the Bridge, Lower the River*, ensured slightly more in the way of comic consistency for this modest sequel. The local commander of a precinct swamped by a crimewave drafts in a sextet of raw recruits from the police training academy run by his brother, with predictably chaotic consequences. Guttenberg again has little to do but wonder where his career's going after the likes of *Diner* and *Cocoon*, yet newcomer Goldthwait's bizarre falsetto and singular body language announce the arrival of a genuinely eccentric presence. TJ

Police Academy 3: Back in Training

(1986, US, 84 min)
d Jerry Paris. *p* Paul Maslansky. *sc* Gene Quintano. *ph* Robert Saad. *ed* Bud Molin. *pd* Trevor Williams. *m* Robert Folk. *cast* Steve Guttenberg, Bubba Smith, David Graf, Michael Winslow, Marion Ramsey, Leslie Easterbrook, Art Metrano, Bobcat Goldthwait, George Gaynes.

●Due to budget cuts, one of the two police academies in the state has to close, so Lassard's graduates come back to help out. The slim plot is a feeble excuse for a series of set pieces, some of which can be seen coming even before the opening credits roll, and a handful that are genuinely funny. Guttenberg (who cut his teeth on *Diner*) is a natural comedian, but it's Goldthwait who impresses most with a truly awesome performance as Zed, the acid casualty cadet. DPe

Police Academy 4: Citizens on Patrol

(1987, US, 87 min)
d Jim Drake. *p* Paul Maslansky. *sc* Gene Quintano. *ph* Robert Saad. *ed* David Rawlins. *pd* Trevor Williams. *m* Robert Folk. *cast* Steve Guttenberg, Bubba Smith, Michael Winslow, David Graf, Tim Kazurinsky, Sharon Stone, Leslie Easterbrook, Marion Ramsey, GW Bailey, Bobcat Goldthwait, George Gaynes.

●More of the same from the wackiest police force on the streets, and their newly recruited civilian helpers. Goldfish-loving Commandant Lassard institutes a new community policing programme, and slimy Captain Harris (Bailey) tries to sabotage the operation. Plenty of pigeon-shit, superglue and squirting ketchup sight gags, plus the usual smutty verbal innuendo. Highlights again include Goldthwait's strangulated vocal ejaculations, a couple of Ninja movie naff-dubbing jokes, and a signposted life-saving gag featuring the chesty Easterbrook in a wet T-shirt. NF

Police Academy 5: Assignment Miami Beach

(1988, US, 90 min)
d Alan Myerson. *p* Paul Maslansky. *sc* Stephen J Curwick. *ph* James Pergola. *ed* Hubert C de la Bouillerie. *pd* Trevor Williams. *m* Robert Folk. *cast* Bubba Smith, David Graf, Michael Winslow, Leslie Easterbrook, Marion Ramsey, Janet Jones, GW Bailey, George Gaynes, Rene Auberjonois.

●With Guttenberg and Goldthwait having taken their engaging charm and strangulated vocal chords elsewhere, this plumbs new depths of puerile humour. Commandant Lassard having reached retirement age, the devious Captain Harris wants to step into his shoes. Meanwhile, the whole gang flies to Miami to see Lassard receive an award. En route, Lassard unwittingly swaps bags with a trio of bungling jewel thieves, and is later kidnapped by them. The *Apocalypse Now*-style Wagnerian soundtrack that accompanies the air boat chase across the Everglades almost raises a smile. Otherwise it's business as usual: fart jokes. NF

Police Academy 6: City Under Siege

(1989, US, 84 min)
d Peter Bonerz. *p* Paul Maslansky. *sc* Stephen J Curwick. *ph* Charles Rosher. *ed* Hubert C de la Bouillerie. *pd* Thomas E Azzari. *m* Robert Folk. *cast* Bubba Smith, David Graf, Michael Winslow, Leslie Easterbrook, Marion Ramsey, Lance Kinsey, Matt McCoy, Bruce Mahler, GW Bailey, George Gayns, Kenneth Mars, Gerrit Graham.

●Surely the nadir of the rehash genre, a string of unconnected party pieces by a cast whose world weariness would imply that they know exactly how cynical this whole venture has become. With Guttenberg long gone and his space duly filled by a lookalike cutie, the gang are hot on the trail of a mastermind villain knee-deep in burglary and real estate fraud. One by one, the scriptwriters manoeuvre each wacky funster into position to perform his or her zany turn. The finest moment features a rap performed by three 'dudes' who have clearly recorded the vocals *a cappella*, over which the Neanderthals in post-production have dubbed some backing music. The fact that said music is in a different time signature to the rapping hasn't occurred to anyone, so we are treated to a surrealist fusion of rap and morse code: the only arresting moment in a mind-numbingly tedious film. MK

Police Academy 7: Mission to Moscow

(1994, US, 82 min)
d Alan Metter. *p* Paul Maslansky, Leonid Vereshchagin. *sc* Randolph Davis, Michele Chodos. *ph* Ian Jones. *ed* Denise Hill, Suzanne Hines. *m* Robert Folk. *cast* George Gaynes, Michael Winslow, David Graf, GW Bailey, Leslie Easterbrook, Christopher Lee, Ron Perlman.

●Maybe the stringent environmental protection laws in the States prevented the producers from filming their dirty work on home territory, but this time they fled to Russia, where the boys and girls in blue have been called in by Lee's desperate Moscow cop to take on Perlman's rampant Mafia mobster and generally kick butsky. Lame, sloppy, cack-handed, utterly redundant – put succinctly, the very worst of the series. TJ

Police Story

(1973, US, 100 min)
d William Graham. *p* David Gerber. *sc* E Jack Nauman. *ph* Robert L Morrison. *ed* Rita Roland. *ad* Ross Bellah, Robert Peterson. *m* Jerry Goldsmith. *cast* Vic Morrow, Edward Asner, Diane Baker, Sandy Baron, Chuck Connors, Harry Guardino, Ralph Meeker, John Bennett Perry, Ina Balin.

●LA cop Joseph Wambaugh turned writer to tell it like it was/is, and his first books, *The New Centurions* and *The Blue Knight*, quickly became movie and (award winning) TV mini-series respectively. Wooed some more by the small screen, he created *Police Story* and served on the often marvellous series as consultant. This is the pilot, released here as a movie. Directed with his usual authority by Graham, arguably the most subtle and mature of small screen specialists, it offers a chance to see Asner in pre *Lou Grant* days, teamed with such excellent but unsung actors as Morrow,

Guardino and Meeker. Disturbed by the way Hollywood treated his novels, Wambaugh turned producer for *The Onion Field*, but the result was more meaningful than muscular. CW

Police Story (Jingcha Gushi)

(1985, HK, 100 min)
d Jackie Chan. *p* Leonard Ho. *sc* Edward Tang. *ph* Cheung Yiu Joe. *ed* Peter Cheung. *ad* Oliver Wong. *m* Kevin Bassinson. *cast* Jackie Chan, Brigitte Lin, Maggie Cheung, Chua Yuen, Bill Tung, Kenneth Tong.

●In Jackie Chan-land vehicles are for trashing small buildings, while big buildings are for falling off or sliding down. Umbrellas are grappling hooks to fasten Jackie on to speeding buses. Bad guys have armies larger and better equipped than most sovereign nations. The plot here is essentially recycled from *Narrow Margin*, but serves principally as an excuse for the trademark demolitions, death-defying leaps, bone-crunching scraps and noise (plus a little unserious romance). The likeable and graceful Chan directs, sings and performs jaw-dropping stunts. Few of his American or Austrian rivals attempt a fraction of that. DO

Policewoman, The (Die Polizistin)

(1999, Ger, 98 min)
d Andreas Dresen. *p* Norbert Sauer, Christian Granderath. *sc* Laila Stieler. *ph* Michael Hammon. *ed* Monika Schindler. *cast* Gabriela Maria Schmeide, Axel Prahl, Jevgenif Sitochin, Katrin Sass, Horst Krause, Martin Seifert.

●Another tragi-comic view of street life from Dresen and his scriptwriter Laila Stieler. Here a novice policewoman (Schmeide) finds that compassion and law enforcement don't mix. The roving documentary style perfectly suits the director's customary themes of people living hand to mouth, involved in petty crime or generally unable to cope. While not so original as *Night Shapes*, it's worth seeing for Schmeide alone, whose moving portrayal of the beleagured cop lends a poignancy to the recognition that policing is not a solution for the dispossessed. SB

Polish Bride, The (De Poolse Bruid)

(1998, Neth, 90 min)
d Karim Traidia. *p* Mar Barry, Jeroen Beker. *sc* Kees van der Huls, Frans van Gestel, Ilana Netiv. *ph* Jacques Laureys, Daniel Reeves. *ed* Chris Teerink. *ad* Annie Winterink. *m* Fons Merkies. *cast* Jaap Spijkers, Monic Hendrickx, Roef Ragas, Rudi Falkenhagen.

●Algerian-born director Traidia may not seem an obvious choice to helm a small-scale love story set in rural Holland, but he deals with unpromising material deftly enough. The two main characters are seemingly incompatible: one is a phlegmatic Dutch farmer, the other a Polish refugee on the run from the pimps who forced her into prostitution. The cultural differences separating them may be immense, but, inevitably, they overcome their wariness and slowly fall in love. Traidia captures the beauty and the monotony of country life, and only marring the quietly affecting story with a bombastic and violent denouement. GM

Polizistin, Die

see Policewoman, The

Pollock

(2000, US, 123 min)
d Ed Harris. *p* Fred Berner, Ed Harris, John Kilick, James Francis Trezza. *sc* Barbara Turner, Susan Emshwiller. *ph* Lisa Rinzler. *ed* Kathryn Himoff. *pd* Mark Friedberg. *m* Jeff Beal. *cast* Ed Harris, Marcia Gay Harden, Tom Bower, Jennifer Connelly, Bud Cort, Val Kilmer, Robert Knott, David Leary, Amy Madigan, Jeffrey Tambor.

●1941: an artist on the verge of a nervous breakthrough. When Lee Krasner sidles through Jackson Pollock's door, he's nursing an apparently permanent hangover. She's interested in his work, and in him – reflecting his own priorities perfectly. Krasner takes him in hand, introducing him to the people who will break him: the critics , the dealers, the patrons. Pollock will piss in Peggy Guggenheim's fireplace – and she will love him for it. He will become the first modern American art star, embodying all the contradictions buried in those words. This impressive and absorbing film is evidently a labour of love for Ed Harris, who spent ten years and his own money getting *Pollock* to the screen. The result is a watchful patient movie, more interested in observation than explanation – less a biopic than a portrait. The approach is in keeping with Pollock's pronouncements, if not abstract expressionism per se: 'Paint is paint, surface is surface.' Harden invests all manner of subtleties in Krasner (winning an Oscar in the process), and the support from Tambor, Madigan and Connelly is first rate – but the film is at its best regarding the artist's relationship to the canvas: Pollock sizing up a frame, his super-confident approach to a line, or that cold winter morning when a dollop of white paint drips from his brush. TCh

Pollux et le Chat Bleu

see Dougal and the Blue Cat

Poltergeist

(1982, US, 114 min)
d Tobe Hooper. *p* Steven Spielberg, Frank Marshall. *sc* Steven Spielberg, Michael Grais, Mark Victor. *ph* Matthew F Leonetti. *ed* Michael Kahn. *pd* James H Spencer. *m* Jerry Goldsmith. *cast* JoBeth Williams, Craig T Nelson, Beatrice Straight, Dominique Dunne, Oliver Robbins, Heather O'Rourke, Michael McManus, Zelda Rubinstein.

●Credited to Hooper, but every inch a Spielberg film, this is a barnstorming ghost story, set in one of the small suburban houses Spielberg knows and loves, where the family canary is called Tweety, and the kids read Captain America comics and eat at the Pizza Hut. Gradually this impossibly safe world is (in a truly ingenious plot development) invaded by something inside the family television. Soon the plot takes off into a delirious fight with demonic forces suggestive of nothing so much as a Walt Disney horror movie; and although the sub-religious gobbledegook (including a tiresome midget medium) is hard to take, it is consistently redeemed by its creator's dazzling sense of craft. For this one, Spielberg has even contrived a structural surprise which leaves the audience spinning like one of his house's haunted rooms, and arguably matches the opening of *Psycho* in its impudent virtuosity. DP

Poltergeist 2: The Other Side

(1986, US, 91 min)
d Brian Gibson. *p/sc* Mark Victor, Michael Grais. *ph* Andrew Laszlo, Bill Neil. *ed* Thom Noble. *pd* Ted Haworth. *m* Jerry Goldsmith. *cast* JoBeth Williams, Craig T Nelson, Heather O'Rourke, Oliver Robins, Zelda Rubinstein, Will Sampson, Julian Beck, Geraldine Fitzgerald.

●Some people never learn. The Freeling family sensibly quit their hole in the ground at Cuesta Verde and take refuge with Granma Jess, who recognises a fellow clairvoyant in little Carol Anne. Soon the psychic forces are shaking up their domestic life, and a cadaverous stranger seems determined to take the blonde moppet back into the other world. Enter Munchkin medium Tangina (Rubinstein) and an all-wise Red Indian (Sampson) to join in the battle, and the old tug-of-war is noisily enacted again. This sequel, *sans* Spielberg but obedient to his spirit, simply fails to regenerate the original's gut-grinding fears that make you dread ever scratching a spot again. And the contribution of Giger's design work has only added one near-unwatchable sequence. DT

Poltergeist III

(1988, US, 98 min)
d Gary Sherman. *p* Barry Bernardi. *sc* Gary Sherman, Brian Taggert. *ph* Alex Nepomniaschy. *ed* Ross Albert. *pd* Paul Eads. *m* Joe Renzetti. *cast* Tom Skerritt, Nancy Allen, Heather O'Rourke, Zelda Rubinstein, Lara Flynn Boyle, Kip Wentz, Richard Fire, Nathan Davis.

●A low-budget sequel which tries, and fails, to make a virtue out of adversity by substituting cheap mechanical effects for the expensive light and magic of Parts I and II. Little Carol Anne (O'Rourke), now living with her uncle (Skerritt) and aunt (Allen) in an ultra-modern Chicago condominium, attends a school for exceptionally gifted but emotionally disturbed children. But the Preacher of Pain is still on her trail, so her guardians team up with diminutive psychic Tangina (Rubinstein), who says it's all done with mirrors. Small consolation for those trapped in the iced-over swimming pool or the building's increasingly erratic lifts! A couple of choice moments cannot compensate for a threadbare scenario bereft of attention-grabbing visual effects. Sadly, talented young O'Rourke passed over to the other side herself shortly after the film was completed: a shame that this mundane movie will be her celluloid epitaph. NF

Polyester

(1981, US, 86 min)
d/p/sc John Waters. *ph* David Insley. *ed* Charles Roggero. *ad* Vincent Peranio. *m* Chris Stein, Michael Kamen. *cast* Divine, Tab Hunter, Edith Massey, Mink Stole, David Samson, Joni Ruth White, Mary Garlington, Ken King.

●Likely to be criticised for being less than murky Waters, even with its 'Odorama' card to scratch for olfactory pleasures/displeasures; but then it's clear from an opening helicopter shot that bad taste has found the budget to go middle of the road. Divine, as a Baltimore housewife with the cultural aspirations of Mary Whitehouse on speed, is now virtually indistinguishable from the Liz Taylor of *The Mirror Crack'd*. Spurned in family life by an unfaithful husband, a contemptuous disco-queen daughter, and a glue-sniffing son with a vicious bent towards foot fetishism – but undeterred by her dog's suicide – she relives the dreams of all '50s queens and finds solace in the arms of Tab Hunter. OK, so it's not *The Cherry Orchard*, but who can resist a film where a massive drive-in billboard proclaims 'Now showing – Three Great Marguerite Duras Hits'. SM

Polygraph, The (Le Polygraphe)

(1996, Can/Fr/Ger, 104 min)
d Robert Lepage. *p* Bruno Jobin. *sc* Robert Lepage, Marie Brassard. *ph* Guy Dufaux. *ed* Emmanuelle Castro, Jean-François Bergeron. *ad* Monique Dion. *m* Robert Caux. *cast* Patrick Goyette, Marie Brassard, Peter Stormare, Maria de Medeiros, Josée Deschênes.

●Do memories – or lie-detectors – always reveal the truth? That's just one of questions raised by Lepage's ambitious but occasionally clumsy follow-up to *The Confessional.* Did François murder his lover two years ago? His neighbour, Lucie – playing, as it happens, the dead woman in a film being made by the latter's friend – finds him gentle and supportive, but then she's too busy with her own new, mysterious lover (Stormare, the psycho from *Fargo*) to realise that François was once a prime suspect. If this complex, visually adventurous exploration of memory, guilt and the strange connections between apparently unconnected people and events may be seen as another oddball Hitchcockian pastiche, it's also rather too contrived for its own good. Very watchable, nevertheless. GA

Ponette

(1996, Fr, 97 min)
d Jacques Doillon. *p* Alain Sarde. *sc* Jacques Doillon. *ph* Caroline Champetier. *ed* Jacqueline Lecompte. *pd* Henri Berthon. *m* Philippe Sarde. *cast* Victoire Thivisol, Matiaz Bureau Caton, Delphine Schiltz, Léopoldine Serre, Xavier Beauvois, Claire Nebout, Marie Trintignant.

●Four-year-old Victoire Thivisol won the best actress award at the 1996 Venice Festival for the title role, a prize which probably belonged more to writer/director Jacques Doillon. Nevertheless, the jury's decision is understandable: Thivisol represents what is pure and honest in the movie, but one may have doubts about the work as a whole. The film begins shortly after the death of Ponette's mother in a car accident. The girl, her own arm in a sling, has only a limited understanding of what death means. At the funeral, one of her pals places gifts in the coffin; another kisses her gently; a third explains that they place heavy stones on top to keep you down. Called away on business for a few days, Ponette's father (Beauvois) leaves her in the country with her aunt (Nebout) and her cousins, but her loneliness is only intensified. Taking her aunt's words of solace literally, she stands vigil, willing her mother to reappear before her.

Doillon is after a sense of mortality from the four-year-old's perspective. The result is touching, but not always convincing. TCh

Pont du Nord, Le

(1981, Fr, 131 mins)
d Jacques Rivette. *p* Margaret Ménégoz. *sc* Jacques Rivette, Suzanne Schiffman, Bulle Ogier, Pascale Ogier, Jérôme Prieur. *ph* William Lubtchansky. *ed* Nicole Lubtchansky. *m* Astor Piazzola. *cast* Bulle Ogier, Pascale Ogier, Jean-François Stévenin, Pierre Clémenti, Mathieu Schiffman.
●A movie that pushes the conspiratorial playfulness of Rivette's *Céline and Julie* in directions both maddening and magical. Ogier and her daughter Pascale are here the crossed-paths comrades impulsively taking up the silent challenge of the city's codes: hopscotching the map of Paris' arrondissements and turning it into a life-size outdoor board game. As ever in Rivette's labyrinthine re-imaginings of the urban obstacle course, the rules and goals are obscure while the allusive clues, keys and signposts multiply alarmingly. Underworld and wonderland merge in the open air; joyous whimsy blurs with justified worry; and Rivette risks exploring the scarifying powers of fantasy and paranoia with a panning, punning documentary eye. With so many oblique strategies, a little irritation is inevitable…but if you could possibly imagine a pre-micro *Tron*, the leaps of faith needed here shouldn't be difficult. PT

Pony Soldier (aka MacDonald of the Canadian Mounties)

(1952, US, 82 min)
d Joseph M Newman. *p* Samuel G Engel. *sc* John C Higgins. *ph* Harry Jackson. *ed* John McCafferty. *ad* Lyle Wheeler, Chester Gore. *m* Alex North. *cast* Tyrone Power, Cameron Mitchell, Thomas Gomez, Robert Horton, Penny Edwards.
●Unexceptional Western with Power as the Mountie on a mission to the US to stop Mitchell and his Cree Indians from launching an all out attack. There are white captives to be rescued, too, in a movie that builds to a finale patched together from borrowed bits of Wellman's *Buffalo Bill* (1944). TJ

Poodle Springs

(1998, US, 96 min)
d Bob Rafelson. *p* Tony Mark. *sc* Tom Stoppard. *ph* Stuart Dryburgh. *ed* Steven Cohen. *pd* Mark Friedberg. *m* Michael Small. *cast* James Caan, Dina Meyer, David Keith, Brian Cox, Joe Don Baker.
●First the Bard, and now Marlowe.Having bastardised Shakespeare, to Oscar-winning effect, jobbing screenwriter Tom Stoppard has fun dicking with Raymond Chandler for this HBO production of Chandler's last, unfinished novel (completed posthumously by Robert B Parker). Caan is hardly many people's idea of Philip Marlowe, but then this is a Marlowe with a difference: grey haired, worn out and paunch-drunk, he's definitely seen better days, even if he still carries his integrity intact. He's also got a brand new wife in tow after a whirlwind romance in Mexico. She's a knockout, loaded, and keen to retire to Daddy's wedding present home in Poodle Springs – when is Hollywood going to wake up to Dina (*Starship Troopers*) Meyer? The plot is satisfyingly opaque, drawing on those Chandler staples of dirty pictures, spoiled rich girls and philandering husbands, and Stoppard/Rafelson/Parker work a nifty new angle by playing up the early '60s timeframe. It's *Chinatown*-lite, and as Elliott Gould's more jaded Marlowe would say, 'It's okay with me.' TCh

Pookie

see Sterile Cuckoo, The

Pool of London

(1950, GB, 85 min, b/w)
d Basil Dearden. *p* Michael Balcon. *sc* Jack Whittingham, John Eldridge. *ph* Gordon Dines. *ed* Peter Tanner. *ad* Jim Morahan. *m* John Addison. *cast* Bonar Colleano, Susan Shaw, Renee Asherson, Earl Cameron, Moira Lister, Max Adrian, Joan Dowling, James Robertson Justice, Alfie Bass, Leslie Phillips, George Benson, Victor Maddern.
●After the success of the police drama *The Blue Lamp* (1949), Basil Dearden and Ealing studios continued in what passed for a realist vein with this tale of merchant seaman Colleano's involvement in a diamond smuggling racket and his subsequent flight when he becomes chief suspect in a murder investigation. Few surprises in the story, but the location work in the bustling Docklands captures a time and place now gone forever. TJ

Poolse Bruid, De

see Polish Bride, The

Poor Cow

(1967, GB, 101 min)
d Kenneth Loach. *p* Joseph Janni. *sc* Nell Dunn, Kenneth Loach. *ph* Brian Probyn. *ed* Roy Watts. *ad* Bernard Sarron. *m* Donovan. *cast* Carol White, Terence Stamp, John Bindon, Kate Williams, Queenie Watts, Geraldine Sherman.
●Not a patch upon Loach's best work, largely because he falls into all the usual traps of kitchen sink realism as he follows the fortunes of a dismal teenage girl (White), saddled with a criminal husband (Bindon, typecast), living with a prostitute aunt (Watts) while he's inside, falling for the husband's mate (Stamp), then going back to the aunt and further troubles when he gets nicked too. Relentlessly sordid, and not helped by the unusual move (for Loach) of using name actors. GA

Pop and Me

(1999, US, 91 min)
d Chris Roe. *p* Walter Buckley, Tony Kiernan. *sc* Erik Arnesen, Juliann Jannus, Mark Kornweibel, Jesse Negron, Chris Roe, Richard Roe. *ph* Erik Arnesen, Chris Roe. *ed* Jesse Negron, Chris Roe. *m* Stephen Edwards, Mazatl Galindo. *with* Richard Roe.
●When Richard Roe, a retired Wall St banker, decides to repeat the big trip of his youth, he invites one of his three sons along, documentary filmmaker Chris, who records the entire thing. This fascinating travelogue is filmed over the six months that father and son spent travelling, interviewing and filming other fathers and sons, across 26 countries in five continents. The diversity of the subjects, and their struggle to express themselves is eloquently captured, and made all the more intimate by the fact that, against this backdrop, the pair are working out their own relationship. JFu

Popdown

(1968, GB, 98 min)
d/p/sc Fred Marshall. *ph* Oliver Wood. *ed* Dateline Editorial Services. *m* Michel Hausser. *cast* Diane Keen, Jane Bates, Zoot Money, Carol Rachell, Debbie Slater, Bill Aron.
●An embarrassingly dated and tedious tour of Swinging '60s London (mini-skirts and Hank Marvin glasses everywhere), as bizarrely undertaken by two camera-clicking aliens, Aries and Sagittarius (Bates, Money). Crazy, man. Though not enough so to prevent it from being rapidly cut down to 54 minutes for release. IB

Pope Joan

(1972, GB, 132 min)
d Michael Anderson. *p* Kurt Unger. *sc* John Briley. *ph* Billy Williams. *ed* Bill Lenny. *pd* Elliot Scott. *m* Maurice Jarre. *cast* Liv Ullmann, Olivia de Havilland, Lesley-Anne Down, Trevor Howard, Jeremy Kemp, Patrick Magee, Franco Nero, Maximilian Schell.
●Based on a legend about a woman who became Pope in the 9th century in the guise of a man, and who was torn apart by an angry crowd when her deception was discovered, this was stripped here of the contemporary frame (shown in America) in which Joan reappears as a modern lass who believes herself to be the reincarnation of the 9th century Pope. What's left is a rough and often painfully clumsy costume epic with the usual love story underneath it all, and chauvinistic presumptions abounding. Against all odds, Ullmann gives a remarkable performance, and it could have been a gem of a subject had it been handled by a woman director. VG

Pope Must Die, The

(1991, GB, 99 min)
d Peter Richardson. *p* Stephen Woolley. *sc* Peter Richardson, Pete Richens. *ph* Frank Gell. *ed* Katharine Wenning. *pd* John Ebden. *m* Anne Dudley, Jeff Beck. *cast* Robbie Coltrane, Beverly D'Angelo, Herbert Lom, Alex Rocco, Paul Bartel, Balthazar Getty, William Hootkins, Robert Stephens, Annette Crosbie, Salvatore Cascio, John Sessions, Peter Richardson, Adrian Edmondson.
●Coltrane plays a portly priest appointed Pope due to a clerical mix-up: Father Albini is a smiling front-man for the masons, mafiosi and gun-runners who run the Vatican Bank, while Father Albinizi (Coltrane) is a rock'n'rolling, really rather useless priest holed up in a rural orphanage filled with photogenic *bambini*. Like John Goodman's King Ralph, Pope Dave I must locate reserves of greatness beneath his unpromising exterior; discover that the love of a good woman is incompatible with his office; and finally waddle back to obscurity. The Vatican he inherits is staffed by chain-smoking, poker-playing prelates with hip-flasks under their robes. Coltrane manages his few moments of Papal grandeur with something approaching true dignity, whether it's sweeping out the money-lenders from the Bank, delivering an impromptu sermon on the hellfire awaiting a jobsworth, or administering extreme unction. There are many good laughs, albeit of a rather simple-minded nature, but even by its own ludicrous standards the plot unravels helplessly towards the end. A pontiff's egg. SFe

Pope of Greenwich Village, The

(1984, US, 120 min)
d Stuart Rosenberg. *p* Gene Kirkwood. *sc* Vincent Patrick. *ph* John Bailey. *ed* Robert Brown. *pd* Paul Sylbert. *m* David Grusin. *cast* Eric Roberts, Mickey Rourke, Daryl Hannah, Geraldine Page, Kenneth McMillan, Tony Musante, M Emmet Walsh, Burt Young, Val Avery.
●A sad re-run of the *Mean Streets* idea (awkwardly adapted by Vincent Patrick from his own admirable novel): the excellent Mickey Rourke, dipping in and out of the New York Italian underworld, just can't keep tabs on his wild young protégé (Roberts, in a performance about five miles over the top). It lacks virtually everything that made Scorsese's film great, although there is a characteristically fine performance from Burt Young as Bedbug Eddie, the local Mafia boss. The final confrontation, in which Bedbug threatens to remove Rourke's right hand, gives the right chill, which the rest can't match. CPea

Popeye

(1980, US, 114 min)
d Robert Altman. *p* Robert Evans. *sc* Jules Feiffer. *ph* Giuseppe Rotunno. *ed* John W Holmes, David Simmons. *pd* Wolf Kroeger. *m* Harry Nilsson. *cast* Robin Williams, Shelley Duvall, Ray Walston, Paul Dooley, Paul L Smith, Richard Libertini, Donald Moffat.
●With neither production companies (Paramount and Disney, for heaven's sakes!) nor critics able to make up their minds what a maverick iconoclast like Altman was doing turning EC Segar's comic strip into a live-action musical, this film was virtually doomed to failure and neglect. Certainly, with Williams giving a virtuoso fast-mumbling performance as the hero, and gags ranging from expertly choreographed slapstick to subtle verbal infelicities (Popeye muttering about 'venerable disease'), it is far too sophisticated to function merely as kids' fodder. Nor is its story – in which Popeye searches for his lost Pappy while courting Olive Oyl – any less discursive, fragmented or off-the-wall than Altman's finest work. Indeed, the film may be seen as a weird and wonderful variation on the *McCabe and Mrs Miller* theme, with the immaculately designed township of Sweethaven, the vividly drawn characters, and Harry Nilsson's songs of inarticulacy all contributing to a portrait of a bizarre society at once recognisably human and fantastically dreamlike. Often, watching the actors contorting themselves into non-human shapes, you wonder how on earth Altman did it; equally often, you feel you are watching a wacky masterpiece, the like of which you've never seen before. GA

Pop Gear

(1965, GB, 68 min)
d Frederic Goode. *p* Harry Field. *sc* Roger Dunton. *ph* Geoffrey Unsworth. *ed* Frederick Ives. *ad* Peter Moll. *with* Matt Monro, Susan

Maughan, The Animals, The Honeycombs, The Rockin' Berries, Herman's Hermits, The Nashville Teens, The Four Pennies, Billy J Kramer and the Dakotas.
● An end-of-'64 round-up of fab numbers introduced by Jimmy Savile, sung one after another under conditions of extreme commercial duress, and bookended with Beatles clips. It's the moment when the Beat Boom has just been co-opted: each pancake-encrusted group pouts and plays to the camera, allowed only neutered movement and looking confused all round. For hipster and historian alike it's fascinating (The Four Pennies perform Leadbelly's *Black Girl*, which they've obviously just discovered for themselves; Tommy Quickly does a novelty version of early ska classic *Humpty Dumpty*; Eric Burdon looks menacing among the Christmas decorations; and Stevie Windwood is obviously under the age of consent). It also demonstrates to the rock fashionmonger of today the reactionary context from which those stilettoes and stretch pants really evolved. CR

Porcile

see Pigsty

Pork Chop Hill

(1959, US, 97 min, b/w)
d Lewis Milestone. *p* Sy Bartlett. *sc* James R Webb. *ph* Sam Leavitt. *ed* George Boemler. *pd* Nicolai Remisoff. *m* Leonard Rosenman. *cast* Gregory Peck, Harry Guardino, George Shibata, Woody Strode, Rip Torn, James Edwards, George Peppard, Robert Blake.
● A film that might have been an only slightly lesser echo of Milestone's marvellous *A Walk in the Sun* in its concern for the individual soldier and the collective pointlessness of war (Korea in this case). It details (quite brilliantly) the bloody assault on a hill of no particular strategic value (no sooner taken than it's abandoned) except that winning it will mean that the general staff will be speaking from strength at the truce talks already under way. Compromise is evident in the way Peck plays the lead as a gung-ho John Wayne (in the real action on which the story is based, the lieutenant commanding the assault was apparently untried and more than fallible); but pre-release tampering also introduced a note of jingoism into Peck's final voice-off after the carnage ('Millions live in freedom today because of what they did') which was contrary to Milestone's intentions and contrary to the tone of the film itself. Impressive, nevertheless, and with fine performances. TM

Porky's

(1981, Can, 98 min)
d Bob Clark. *p* Don Carmody, Bob Clark. *sc* Bob Clark. *ph* Reginald Morris. *ed* Stan Cole. *pd* Reuben Freed. *m* Carl Zitter, Paul Zaza. *cast* Dan Monahan, Mark Herrier, Wyatt Knight, Roger Wilson, Cyril O'Reilly, Tony Ganios, Kaki Hunter, Kim Cattrall, Susan Clark, Alex Carras.
● Writer/director Clark shifts the *American Graffiti* formula to a '50s Florida high school to mount a runaway farce fuelled by the agonies of adolescent sexual frustration. The resulting American box-office bonanza made it the *Animal House* of 1982, and Clark convincingly captures a tone of masochistic agony as his randy kids are derided, exploited and generally humiliated by the adults around them. There are plenty of sexual gags, but the basic plot is as innocently Oedipal as *Jack the Giant Killer* as the gang desperately attempt to defeat nightclub owners, parents, and policemen armed with glistening truncheons in their quest for sexual experience. Despite its thinly liberal veneer, it's as reactionary as a smash-and-grab raid, but it's vulgar enough to be fascinating even while you hate it, and it's certainly the most revealing American success since *Taps*. DP

Porky's II: The Next Day

(1983, Can, 98 min)
d Bob Clark. *p* Dan Carmody, Bob Clark. *sc* Roger E Swaybill, Alan Ormsby. *ph* Reginald H Morris. *ed* Stan Cole. *ad* Fred Price. *m* Carl Zittrer. *cast* Dan Monahan, Wyatt Knight, Mark Herrier, Roger Wilson, Cyril O'Reilly, Tony Ganios, Kaki Hunter.
● Masquerading as a brainless assembly of lavatory and graveyard gags, this often reveals itself as a charming and witty farce, far closer to the British music hall tradition than the Carry On series ever managed to get. The high school jocks are unfashionably conformist, their chief project being a 'Scenes from Shakespeare' festival. Even the humiliation of bible-bashers, Klansmen and oily politicians stops short of outright cruelty. The set-piece finale of misery being heaped upon a lecherous councillor belongs to the girl of the group, the inexhaustible Kaki Hunter. Only an opening montage of clips binds this movie to its inferior parent, though we're clearly presumed to have seen it. DO

Porky's Revenge

(1985, Can, 92 min)
d James Komack. *p* Robert L Rosen. *sc* Ziggy Steinberg. *ph* Robert Jessup. *ed* John W Wheeler. *pd* Peter Wooley. *m* Dave Edmunds. *cast* Dan Monahan, Wyatt Knight, Tony Ganios, Mark Herrier, Kaki Hunter, Scott Colomby, Nancy Parsons.
● It's graduation time, and the oldest bunch of high school kids since *Grease*, still in search of the true nature of sex, are together again in a series of witless capers, tenuously linked with attempts to win the interstate basketball championship and put one over on their old adversary, den-of-vice owner Porky. It's all surprisingly tame, with raunch and humour conspicuous by their absence; and structurally it's a mess, nothing more than a series of unconnected events thrown together in no particular order. GO

Pornographer, The (Le Pornographe)

(2001, Fr/Can, 111 min)
d Bertrand Bonello. *p* Carole Scotta. *sc* Bertrand Bonello. *ph* Josée Deshaies. *ed* Fabrice Rouaud. *ad* Romain Denis. *m* Laurie Markovitch. *cast* Jean-Pierre Léaud, Jérémie Rénier, Dominique Blanc, Catherine Mouchet, Thibault de Montalembert, André Marcon, Alice Houri, Ovidie, Laurent Lucas.
● A long, dark boogie-night of the soul – trust the French to turn porno into a rumination on the male menopause! Anyone hoping for jollies will be climbing the walls within minutes – especially since the British censor has seen fit to protect us from 11 seconds of the blue movie Jacques (Léaud) is directing. The decision is regrettable, not least because it's probably the most eloquent scene in the film. A contemporary of the New Wave, Jacques aspires to make a purely artistic fuck-film, but his producer, disgusted (or bored?) by the performers' Bressonian restraint, intervenes mid-coitus to pep up the action. Fired and burnt out, Jacques retires home to lick his wounds, but finds little solace. For reasons he can't articulate, he's out of love with his wife. A subplot involving a meeting with estranged son Joseph (Rénier) turns out to be little more than a condescending putdown with trite romantic strings attached. Solemn and pretentious, the film is more or less redeemed by Léaud's incontrovertibly morose presence. Carrying a paunch like a ghost pregnancy and looking several generations seedier than he did even in *Irma Vep*, Truffaut's old alter ego makes Bonello's arty angst all too real. TCh

Porridge

(1979, GB, 93 min)
d Dick Clement. *p* Allan McKeown, Ian La Frenais. *sc* Dick Clement, Ian La Frenais. *ph* Bob Huke. *ed* Alan Jones. *ad* Tim Gleeson. *m* Terry Oates. *cast* Ronnie Barker, Richard Beckinsale, Fulton MacKay, Brian Wilde, Peter Vaughan, Julian Holloway, Geoffrey Bayldon, Christopher Godwin.
● 'I'm used to this kind of food, I went to Harrow' admits a disgraced dentist over his lunch. Prison life as conceived in *Porridge* is indeed about as punishing an ordeal as boarding school, and because links with a tougher and nastier reality are very, very tenuous, the film is in fact unobjectionable and quite funny. Far funnier and better constructed than the dread phrase 'TV spin-off' would imply, and still firmly under the control of screenwriters Dick Clement and Ian La Frenais (also credited, respectively, as director and producer). Beckinsale and Barker are excellent as the Laurel and Hardy duo of cons who find themselves breaking in, rather than out of the nick. Another definite plus is the use of Chelmsford Prison (empty since a fire the previous year) as principal location. JS

Portaborse, Il

see Footman, The

Port Alamo

see Alamo Bay

Porte aperte

see Open Doors

Porte de mon enfance, La

see Oporto of My Childhood

Porte des Lilas (Gates of Paris/Gate of Lilacs)

(1957, Fr, 95 min, b/w)
d René Clair. *p* Jacques Plante. *sc* René Clair, Jean Aurel. *ph* Robert Le Febvre. *ed* Louisette Hautecoeur. *ad* Léon Barsacq. *m* Georges Brassens. *cast* Pierre Brasseur, Georges Brassens, Henri Vidal, Dany Carrel, Raymond Bussières, Annette Poivre.
● An alcoholic stumblebum (Brasseur) befriends a dashing but amoral young hoodlum (Vidal) with predictably sombre results. The absolute last gasp of French poetic realism, engulfed only two years later by the tidal New Wave, whose airy location shooting made Clair's suffocating studio-bound 'realism' hard to differentiate from the so-called 'poetry'. Of interest, though, as the sole venture into film of the bardic guitarist Brassens. GAd

Portes de la Nuit, Les (Gates of the Night)

(1946, Fr, 106 min, b/w)
d Marcel Carné. *sc* Jacques Prévert. *ph* Philippe Agostini. *ad* Alexandre Trauner. *m* Joseph Kosma. *cast* Pierre Brasseur, Yves Montand, Nathalie Nattier, Serge Reggiani, Jean Vilar, Saturnin Fabre, Mady Berry, Raymond Bussières, Julien Carette.
● Perhaps unwisely, despite Vilar's fine performance, Destiny is personified in this tail-end example of the Carné-Prévert collaboration, offering doom-laden warnings which the characters ignore as they rush to meet their fates. Carné wasn't too happy about Prévert's dated populism, evident here in the suggestion that France's legacy from the Occupation was a heroic working class and a bourgeoisie of collaborators or profiteers. Stemming from this, the film's main problem is its contrived characters, not helped by Brasseur at his most hysterical, with Montand and Nattier hopelessly inadequate in roles written for Gabin and Dietrich. Only Reggiani really impresses as a young collaborator tormented by self-loathing. The evocation of nocturnal Paris (the action takes place from dusk to dawn) is hauntingly beautiful, but this is a hollow film. TM

Portes tournantes, Les

see Revolving Doors, The

Portland Street Blues (Hongxing Shisan Mei)

(1998, HK, 114 min)
d Raymond Yip. *cast* Sandra Ng, Kristy Yeung, Alex Fong, Shu Qi, Ng Mang-Tat, Noel Chik.
● A spin off from the *Young and Dangerous* series, telling the life story of Sister 13 (Sandra Ng, terrific), the Hung Hing gang's lesbian branch leader in Mongkok, a character introduced in *Young and Dangerous IV*. Sister 13 has 'felt like a boy' since childhood, but went through a quasi-hetero phase when she and a girlfriend had to flee into China and found themselves rivals for the attention of gang-member/boxer Coke (Fong, authentically dishy). But the constant struggle to compensate for her father's endless mistakes and a friendship with the vengeful junkie prostitute Scarface (Shu, amazing) helped her to realise her true sexuality – and won her status in the gang. The flashback structure and back-story elements are a touch over complicated, but nothing matters much other than Sister 13 herself: a plausible, non-iconic dyke at the centre of a broadly realistic thriller. Three cheers. TR

Porto da Minha Infância, O

see Oporto of My Childhood

Port of Shadows
see Quai des Brumes, Le

Portrait of a Lady, The
(1996, GB/US, 144 min)
d Jane Campion. *p* Monty Montgomery, Steve Golin. *sc* Laura Jones. *ph* Stuart Dryburgh. *ed* Veronika Jenet. *pd* Janet Patterson. *m* Wojciech Kilar. *cast* Nicole Kidman, Barbara Hershey, John Malkovich, Martin Donovan, Mary Louise Parker, Shelley Winters, Richard E Grant, Shelley Duvall, Christian Bale, Viggo Mortensen, John Gielgud.
●Henry James' masterpiece has long been deemed impossible to translate successfully into film; Jane Campion and screenwriter Laura Jones have, however, produced an adaptation as cinematically intelligent as it is faithful to the original. Beginning, adventurously but wisely, with Isabel Archer (Kidman) rejecting Lord Warburton's proposal of marriage, the film charts the changes in its young American heroine's fortunes when, after inheriting a fortune put her way by ailing English cousin Ralph Touchett (Donovan), she travels to Italy, where she's introduced by her mentor Madame Merle (Hershey) to widowed aesthete Gilbert Osmond (Malkovich). Though a friend advises her to wed a long-time admirer who's followed her from America, and Ralph would prefer her to remain true to her free-spirited ideals, Isabel is tempted by Osmond's courtship. Besides the uniformly fine performances, what makes the film so rewarding – and challenging – is its refusal to soften or sentimentalise James' study of New World innocence unprotected against Old World experience. With Stuart Dryburgh's stunning 'Scope camerawork, and a number of audaciously imaginative sequences (notably Isabel's erotic fantasy, and a Dali-esque, b/w 'silent' short to evoke her Grand Tour), this is as far from heritage flummery as you can get. GA

Portrait of a '60% Perfect' Man: Billy Wilder (Portrait d'un Homme 'à 60% Parfait': Billy Wilder)
(1980, Fr, 58 min)
d Annie Tresgot. *p* Klaus Hellwig. *ph* Gary Graver. *ed* Françoise Ceppi. *with* Billy Wilder, Jack Lemmon, Walter Matthau, IAL Diamond, Michel Ciment.
●This is Wilder on Wilder, really, even though he's intelligently interviewed by Michel Ciment (film critic from Positif), affectionately talked about by Lemmon and Matthau, and the whole is filmed with style by Annie Tresgot. Because the cunning old professional knows exactly where he wants the film to go: he's as capable of directing, with humour, from in front of as from behind the camera. Lovely stuff. HM

Portrait of a Young Girl at the End of the '60s in Brussels
(1993, Fr, 59 min)
d Chantal Akerman. *cast* Circé, Julien Rassam, Joelle Marlier, Cynthia Rodberg.
●A semi-autobiographical portrait of a young girl's final day at school – she quits, that is – in 1968, which she spends playing hookie with a young army deserter she meets at a cinema, and later partying with him and her best pal Danièle (who may be her secret love). It's a talky movie, shot on the hoof through the streets of Brussels. Fresh, gentle and touching, not at all 'minimalist'.

Portrait of Jason
(1967, US, 100 min, b/w)
d/p Shirley Clarke. *ph* Jeri Sopanen. *ed* Shirley Clarke. *cast* Jason Holliday [Aaron Paine].
●Shirley Clarke's third feature is almost as straightforward as its title. It picks up the passionate interest in ghetto subcultures that Clarke established in *The Connection* and *The Cool World*, but this time without feeling any need to create a fiction: *Portrait of Jason* is simply a two-hour conversation with a middle-aged, black, homosexual prostitute. The new simplicity of approach reflects the enormous influence of Andy Warhol on independent film-making in the '60s: a new trust in basic film-making techniques, and a new distrust of 'artifice' like editing. Jason himself certainly provides enough artifice to keep any audience engrossed: his colourful, self-mocking account of his life reveals a great deal about the situation of a ghetto boy with 'white-boy fever'. The moral catch is that by fulfilling Jason's dreams of himself as a 'performer', the movie deliberately pushes him out of his own control… TR

Portrait of Jennie
(1948, US, 86 min, b/w & col)
d William Dieterle. *p* David O Selznick. *sc* Paul Osborn, Peter Berneis. *ph* Joseph August. *ed* Gerard Wilson. *pd* Joseph McMillan Johnson, Joseph B Platt. *m* Dimitri Tiomkin. *cast* Jennifer Jones, Joseph Cotten, Ethel Barrymore, Lillian Gish, Cecil Kellaway, David Wayne, Henry Hull, Florence Bates.
●A companion piece to the Dieterle/Selznick *Love Letters*, also starring Jones and Cotten; but where the earlier film remained rooted in superior romantic hokum, this one takes wing into genuine romantic fantasy through its tale of a love that transcends space and time as Cotten's struggling artist meets, falls in love with, and is inspired by a strangely ethereal girl (Jones) whom he eventually realises is the spirit of a woman long dead. Direction and performances are superb throughout, but the real star is Joseph August's camera, which conjures pure magic out of the couple's tender odyssey, from the gravely quizzical charm of their first encounter in snowy Central Park (when she is still a little girl, strangely dressed in clothes of bygone days) through to the awesome storm at sea that supernaturally heralds their final parting. Buñuel saw it and of course approved: 'It opened up a big window for me'. TM

Portrait of Teresa (Retrato de Teresa)
(1979, Cuba, 103 min)
d Pastor Vega. *p* Evelio Delgardo. *sc* Ambrosio Fornet, Pastor Vega. *ph* Livio Delgado. *ed* Rolando Diaz. *ad* Luis Lacosta. *m* Carlos Fariñas. *cast* Daisy Granados, Adolfo Llaurado, Alina Sanchez, Alberto Molina.
●Havana housewife and mother, textile worker and convener of her factory's cultural group: Teresa has to balance the demands of an exhausting triple day, coping all the while with conspicuous lack of cooperation from her husband and other Cuban heels. Notable among their number is a television interviewer whose oily machismo is an acute indictment of the female image projected by the media. The archaic attitudes and insulting assumptions that confront working women, even after a revolution, are sketched in with a skilful lightness of touch. Vega directs in bright primary colours, and with a fine eye for the minute but revealing moments and movements of daily life. SJo

Portrait of the Artist as a Young Man, A
(1977, GB, 92 min)
d/p Joseph Strick. *sc* Judith Rascoe. *ph* Stuart Hetherington. *ed* Lesley Walker. *pd* Wendy Shea. *m* Stanley Myers. *cast* Bosco Hogan, TP McKenna, John Gielgud, Rosaleen Linehan, Maureen Potter, Niall Buggy, Brian Murray.
●A prosaic and reverential treatment of the didactic high points of James Joyce's novel, which provides at best an occasional reminder of his gleeful contempt for that uniquely Irish blend of political and religious duplicity. But Strick's view of Ireland as the subject of a coffee table movie gives no sense of 'the sow that eats her farrow'. JPy

Portraits Chinois
(1996, Fr/GB, 123 min)
d Martine Dugowson. *p* Georges Benayoun. *sc* Martin Dugowson, Peter Chase. *ph* Antoine Roch. *ed* Martine Barraque-Curie, Noëlle Boisson. *ad* Pierre Guffroy. *m* Peter Chase. *cast* Helena Bonham Carter, Romane Bohringer, Marie Trintignant, Elsa Zylberstein, Yvan Attal, Jean-Philippe Ecoffey, Miki Manojlovic, Jean-Claude Brialy.
●A flat-warming party on the Left Bank brings together design assistant Bonham Carter, her partner, screenwriter Ecoffey, vain movie director Attal, his womanising producer Manojlovic, shy couture assistant Bohringer, and even more neurotic Zylberstein, who winds up tearful in the loo. The presence of the last two reminds us of writer/director Dugowson's startling debut *Mina Tannenbaum*, but her approach here takes in a wider ensemble, eases up on the melodrama, and develops its insights cumulatively. We see how these friends and co-workers negotiate their relationships through a swath of infidelities, creative rivalries and secret romances, each remaining true only to him or herself. While the tone's predominantly light, some of the actors take their chances better than others. Unfortunately, Bonham Carter's central performance (in creditable French) is too busy and bitty, in the process filleting the emotional core from the film. Even so, Dugowson's deft attentiveness to her characters' inner lives shows the instinctive flair of a film-maker who will doubtless continue to get better and better. TJ

Portuguese Goodbye, A (Um Adeus Português)
(1985, Port, 85 min, b/w & col)
d/p Joao Botelho. *sc* Leonor Pinhao, Joao Botelho. *ph* Acácio de Almeida. *ed* Joao Botelho, Leandro Ferreira, Leonor Guterres. *pd* António Lima. *m* Música Popular Angolana, Conjunto Monte Cara, Anamar. *cast* Rui Furtado, Isabel de Castro, Maria Cabral, Fernando Heitor, Cristina Hauser.
●In Portuguese Africa in 1973, a small platoon of soldiers is stranded, prey both to an unseen guerrilla enemy and to their own doubts about the war they are waging. Twelve years on, an elderly couple, still mourning the death of their son in the African campaign, make one last visit to their surviving children, now grown up and living in Lisbon. Botelho's delicately mesmerising film interweaves these two simple stories, and achieves a contemplative serenity not unlike that of Ozu; hardly surprising or inappropriate in that the contemporary story is indeed a Portuguese update of the Japanese master's *Tokyo Story*. As the reunion gives rise to painful memories and barely expressed tension, the film charts the family's disappointments and losses with a dry-eyed melancholy, gently proposing a stoic resignation as a response to life's vicissitudes. Botelho never quite matches the emotional power of his mentor. Nevertheless, this is one fine film; watch it peacefully and patiently, and be moved. GA

Poseidon Adventure, The
(1972, US, 117 min)
d Ronald Neame. *p* Irwin Allen. *sc* Stirling Silliphant, Wendell Mayes. *ph* Harold Stine. *ed* Harold F Kress. *pd* William J Creber. *m* John Williams. *cast* Gene Hackman, Ernest Borgnine, Red Buttons, Carol Lynley, Roddy McDowall, Stella Stevens, Shelley Winters, Jack Albertson, Leslie Nielsen.
●The Big Upturned Ship film, with God and the Rev Gene Hackman leading a motley crew to the top – no, sorry, to the bottom – of the SS *Poseidon*, capsized by high waves in one of Irwin Allen's sea-tanks. They mount an outsize Christmas tree, clamber through kitchens, wriggle along ventilator shafts, battling all the while with personal crises and water, water, water. It's a terrific piece of junk: the top-notch screenwriters (Stirling Silliphant and Wendell Mayes) never let a cliché slip through the net, and Neame's anaemic direction ensures that every absurdity is treated at face value. GB

Positively True Adventures of the Alleged Texas Cheerleader-Murdering Mom, The
(1993, US, 105 min)
d Michael Ritchie. *p* James Manos Jr. *sc* Jane Anderson. *ph* Gerry Fisher. *ed* Eric A Sears. *pd* Stephen Hendrickson. *m* Lucy Simin. *cast* Holly Hunter, Beau Bridges, Swoosie Kurtz, Gregg Henry, Matt Frewer, Fred Koehler, Frankie Ingrassia.
●This sharply satirical slice of true-life Americana is a gift for *Smile* director Ritchie, whose films and themes it uncannily parallels. Hunter is by turns charming, chilling and oddly sympathetic as the ambitious Baptist mother ruthlessly promoting her daughter's ill-fated campaign to become a high-school cheerleader. Flatly lit TV interview footage after the incident is intercut with dramatisations of the lead-up to Hunter's arrest and trial for solicitation to murder her

daughter's rival. Ritchie captures the texture of small-town Texan life and the mad scramble for TV rights to the story. (Made for cable.) NF

Posse

(1975, US, 93 min)
d/p Kirk Douglas. *sc* William S Roberts, Christopher Knopf. *ph* Fred J Koenekamp. *ed* John W Wheeler. *pd* Lyle Wheeler. *m* Maurice Jarre. *cast* Kirk Douglas, Bruce Dern, Bo Hopkins, James Stacy, Luke Askew, David Canary, Alfonso Arau, Katharine Woodville.
● A post-Watergate Western reflecting a profound mistrust of the motives of politicians, and framing its story within the ironic cry: 'To the polls, ye sons of freedom!' The small township is shown to be as much a prey to Douglas' ambitious, uptight marshal, bucking for the US Senate, as it is to the man he's tracking down, a 'ruthless' outlaw (Dern, being generously allowed to steal the film). With its picture of America in the making (on the make) – early baseball, carefully conspicuous ads for Bulova and Schlitz, and the ubiquitous photographer recording everything for posterity – the film painstakingly attempts to locate the roots of contemporary malaise. That it doesn't work, as such, is a result of the general *naiveté* of its reversals of the standard good guy/bad guy format. But what emerges is a likeable Western, pleasantly subversive, crisply photographed, and despite some padding, engagingly put together. CPe

Posse

(1993, US, 111 min)
d Mario Van Peebles. *p* Jim Steele, Preston Holmes. *sc* Dario Scardapane, Sy Richardson. *ph* Peter Menzies Jr. *ed* Mark Conte. *ad* Catherine Hardwicke. *m* Michel Colombier. *cast* Mario Van Peebles, Stephen Baldwin, Billy Zane, Charles Lane, Salli Richardson, Melvin Van Peebles.
● This 'New Jack' Western shoots off in all directions but never hits home. There's much historical revisionism on offer – one third of cowboys were black, apparently – but the only source material that really counts here is old movies (*The Wild Bunch*, *The Magnificent Seven*, and, especially, Leone). A refugee from the Spanish-American war, Mario Van Peebles' Jessie Lee leads a band of deserters west to Cutter's Town, where he has a score to settle. On his tail is sadistic Colonel Graham (Zane) and his 'Iron Brigade'. The jarring 1990s sensibility of this over-directed, under-written movie extends to style as well as content. Worst of all is the blatantly fetishistic attitude the director adopts towards his posturing macho star. TCh

Possessed

(1947, US, 108 min, b/w)
d Curtis Bernhardt. *p* Jerry Wald. *sc* Ranald MacDougall, Silvia Richards. *ph* Joseph Valentine. *ed* Rudi Fehr. *ad* Anton Grot. *m* Franz Waxman. *cast* Joan Crawford, Van Heflin, Raymond Massey, Geraldine Brooks, Stanley Ridges, John Ridgely, Moroni Olsen.
● Crawford may play a nurse, but she'd need a warehouse of Phensics to clear up her troubles in this one. Madly in love with nogoodnik Heflin, she chooses to marry her wealthy employer (Massey) after his own ailing wife has tottered into insanity and suicide. Joan totters the same way soon after, and no one in the '40s could do it with such steely eyes or tautened shoulders. And she's helped every inch of the way by the Warners melodrama machine, working at fever pitch under the direction of German émigré Bernhardt, revelling in the expressionist tradition of morbid fantasy and psychological anguish. Compelling viewing, then, and a film even madder than most of its characters. GB

Possession

(1981, Fr/WGer, 127 min)
d Andrzej Zulawski. *p* Marie-Laure Reyre. *sc* Andrzej Zulawski, Frederic Tuten. *ph* Bruno Nuytten. *ed* Marie-Sophie Dubus. *ad* Holger Gross. *m* Andrzej Korzynski. *cast* Isabelle Adjani, Sam Neill, Margit Carstensen, Heinz Bennent, Johanna Hofer, Shaun Lawton, Carl Duering.
● Self-exiled Polish directors – like Walerian Borowczyk – who wind up doing art movies in Paris tend over the years to go over the top in the sex/horror stakes. But Zulawski goes Grand Guignol in one leap with an outrageously sick story, filmed in English, about a schizoid housewife (Adjani, acting like a terminal rabies victim) who deserts husband and lover for an affair in a deserted Berlin apartment with a piece of fungus that grows into a many-tentacled monster and eventually metamorphoses into her husband's *doppelgänger*. Confused? Don't look for logic, don't ask why Adjani mutilates herself with an electric knife, or why Carstensen (playing a hooker) affects a clubfoot, don't expect any relief from the miscarriage scene (buckets of oozing blood and pus), and above all don't see this on a full stomach. Turkey of the year, even though the main ingredient is pure ham. MA

Possession of Joel Delaney, The

(1971, US, 108 min)
d Waris Hussein. *p* George Justin. *sc* Matt Robinson, Grimes Grice. *ph* Arthur Ornitz. *ed* John Victor Smith. *pd* Peter Murton. *m* Joe Raposo. *cast* Shirley MacLaine, Perry King, Michael Hordern, David Elliott, Lisa Kohane, Barbara Trentham, Lovelady Powell, Miriam Colon.
● MacLaine plays a wealthy New York divorcée who is beastly to her Puerto Rican maid, and gets her comeuppance when her brother (King) – whom she dotes on with more than sisterly warmth – becomes possessed by the spirit of a Puerto Rican sex murderer. There is some slick racial moralising (rich white New Yorkers shouldn't be beastly to their less privileged neighbours). But stir in some mumbo-jumbo in which shrieking Puerto Ricans try to exorcise the devil, and a climax in which MacLaine and her children are tortured at knife-point by the spirit of racial vengeance, and what you come away with is an alarmist message saying 'Keep New York White'. Even as melodrama it's distinctly sluggish. TM

Possible Worlds

(2000, Can, 94 min)
d Robert Lepage. *p* Sandra Cunningham, Bruno Jobin. *sc* John Mighton. *ph* Jonathan Freeman. *ed* Susan Shipton. *pd* François Séguin. *cast* Tilda Swinton, Tom McCamus, Sean McCann, Gabriel Gascon, Rick Miller, Griffith Brewer, Daniel Brooks.
● 'Imagination rules the world': Napoleon's compelling observation underpins Quebecois director Robert Lepage's fourth (but first English language) feature, adapted by John Mighton from his own play. The result of their collaboration is simultaneously an intellectual murder mystery, a philosophical poem about identity and the nature of consciousness, and a luminous romance that embraces different versions of desire as it searches for the unpredictable kernel of affection. Narrative pace derives from an unconventional investigation into the removal – for uneasy scientific ends – of particularly gifted brains from their host skulls. This genre riff threads among encounters between George Barber (McCamus, memorably obsessive in *I Love a Man in Uniform*) and Joyce (Swinton, with all her familiar and welcome ambiguity) as they meet in different lives, testing intimacy and rejection, marriage and strangerhood. Add mathematical memory games and a community with a three word language ('slab', 'block', 'hilarious') and it's clear the cerebral stakes are high. Tiers of meaning cross-fertilise in an open, associative approach to storytelling, as the sublime cinematography and design tease out a heightened Möbius strip reality that challenges unthinking naturalism. But it's the keen yearning at the film's core (with a marine motif suggesting the oceanic possibilities of the human heart and mind) that anchors the whole conception. Allusive, mysterious and moving, with the ambition of its assembly amplified by the calm beauty of its surface, the film shows Lepage at the peak of his art. GE

Postcards from America

(1994, GB/US, 93 min)
d Steve McLean. *p* Christine Vachon, Craig Paull. *sc* Steve McLean. *ph* Ellen Kuras. *ed* Elizabeth Gazzara. *pd* Thérèse Deprez. *m* Stephen Endelman. *cast* Olmo Tighe, Michael Tighe, James Lyons, Michael Imperioli, Michael Ringer, Maggie Low.
● New York multi-media artist and gay activist David Wojnarowicz died in 1992, but his faith in writer/director McLean, the adapter of his autobiographical writings, is vindicated by this arresting first feature. Framing three periods in the life of an American outsider, the film moves nimbly between a troubled New Jersey childhood as young David (Olmo Tighe) finds himself caught between an abusive father and long-suffering mother; an adolescence spent on sidewalks where the teenage David (Michael Tighe) hustles for a living; and anguished maturity in which the adult David (Lyons) discovers the thrill of anonymous sex on the open road, before facing the shadow of AIDS. With its feel for the American landscape pitched between Kerouac and Gus Van Sant, the film's immersion in low-life Americana seems so authentic it's a surprise to learn that this is the work of a British movie-maker – McLean's background in music video and art direction tells in the sheer visual assurance. Piercing and provocative, McLean's determinedly cinematic vision announces him as, potentially, a key British independent of the '90s. TJ

Postcards from the Edge

(1990, US, 101 min)
d Mike Nichols. *p* Mike Nichols, John Calley. *sc* Carrie Fisher. *ph* Michael Ballhaus. *ed* Sam O'Steen. *pd* Patrizia von Brandenstein. *m* Carly Simon. *cast* Meryl Streep, Shirley MacLaine, Dennis Quaid, Gene Hackman, Richard Dreyfuss, Rob Reiner, Mary Wickes, Conrad Bain, Annette Bening, Simon Callow, Gary Morton, CCH Pounder.
● Carrie Fisher has successfully adapted her semi-autobiographical novel about a Hollywood actress' battle with drug addiction, broadening the conflict in order to accommodate family strife between brassy showbiz all-rounder Doris Mann (MacLaine) and her addictive daughter Suzanne (Streep). While the film works partly on the level of exposé, this relationship dominates; as a result, Dreyfuss (kindly doctor), Quaid (unreliable lover) and Hackman (avuncular director) have an almost functional status. Fisher's intelligence and humour turn what might have been movie brat indulgence into something much sharper and involving. Nichols has a sure feel for the material, and he's blessed with two great performances from his leads (particularly a gutsy MacLaine). Despite the serious themes, the film remains essentially lightweight, with an uplifting resolution. This is Hollywood, after all. CM

Postino, Il (The Postman)

(1995, It/Fr, 108 min)
d Michael Radford. *p* Mario Cecchi Gori, Vittorio Cecchi Gori, Gaetano Daniele. *sc* Anna Pavignano, Michael Radford, Furio Scarpelli, Giacomo Scarpelli, Massimo Troisi. *ph* Franco di Giacomo. *ed* Roberto Perpignani. *ad* Lorenzo Baraldi. *m* Luis Enrique Bacalov. *cast* Massimo Troisi, Philippe Noiret, Maria Grazia Cucinotta, Linda Moretti, Renato Scarpa, Anna Bonaiuto.
● When, in 1952, the exiled Chilean poet and diplomat Pablo Neruda (Noiret) takes up residence in a house on a quiet little island off the Neapolitan coast, the fan mail he receives is so copious that the postmaster hires Mario (Troisi), the none too bright son of a local fisherman, to deliver the celebrity's mail. At first, Mario is simply star-struck by Neruda, who responds with understandable wariness to the postman's gauche attempts at conversation; soon, however, he's teaching Mario about metaphors, and when the postman falls for Beatrice (Cucinotta), a lovely but rather aloof barmaid, the poet agrees to try to help him win her with words. Inspired by an incident in Neruda's life, the story's engaging blend of easy humour and sunny romance takes hold from the start and never lets go. Much of its seductive charm derives from the excellence of the leads: Noiret does his gruff but malleable turn to perfection, while Troisi (who died soon after filming finished) exudes a simplicity of heart, mind and soul that never seems excessively sentimental. Mercifully, Radford avoids making the small peasant community too glamorously Arcadian. Old-fashioned it may be, but it knocks the spots off pap like *Cinema Paradiso*. GA

Postman (Youchai)

(1995, China, 90 min)
d He Jianjun. *p* Shu Kei. *sc* He Yi, You Ni. *ph* Wu Di. *ed* Liu Xiaojing. *cast* Feng Yuanzheng.

●The second independent film by He Jianjun (aka He Yi) marks a new level of achievement for Beijing's seemingly uncrushable independent film-makers. The introverted Xiao Dou is promoted from installing post-boxes to the job of delivering mail when an old postman is arrested for stealing letters. Before long he too is intercepting other people's mail, a habit that makes him privy to their secrets and leads him to make furtive sorties into their lives. He comes to know a woman who was sucked into prostitution when her singing career stalled, a gay junkie pining for his dead lover, and an elderly lover whose son has decided to kill himself. Meanwhile Xiao Dou's relationship with his own sister begins to shift from emotional to sexual intimacy. Nothing here can be reduced to symbolism or allegory, but the *Dekalog*-like story yields any number of provocative implications for Chinese urban society in the 1990s. The core issues here are privacy (a concept so alien it's hard to express in Chinese) and the way that people's inner lives remain beyond the reach of even the most rigorous state control. TR

Postman, The

see Postino, Il

Postman, The

(1997, US, 178 min)
d Kevin Costner. *p* Jim Wilson, Steve Tisch, Kevin Costner. *sc* Eric Roth, Brian Helgeland. *ph* Stephen Windon. *ed* Peter Boyle. *pd* Ida Random. *m* James Newton Howard. *cast* Kevin Costner, Will Patton, Larenz Tate, Olivia Williams, James Russo, Tom Petty.

●A sense of déjà vu pervades this self-directed, over long and outsized Costner project. In a post-apocalyptic, anarchic wilderness, a semi-fascist goon squad terrorises the surviving populace. Costner, a loner scavenging on the fringe of society, instigates and leads a just and glorious resistance. The film aims for an uncomfortable compromise between the dramatic sincerity of *Dances with Wolves* and the epic spectacle of *Waterworld*, but lacks the explanatory detail and narrative fluency to achieve either. Only Costner's character is at all remarkable. It's his charlatan side that switches on the story: chancing across a crashed mail truck, he assumes the dead postman's uniform and talks his way into the next walled town, improvising a tale in which a reconstituted US government is slowly re-establishing its infrastructure. He gets his food, and thus inspires a true, rookie mail service – an audacious social enterprise which outrages Patton's feudal tyrant. There's no discernible irony in the eventual glorification of the hero. NB

Postman Always Rings Twice, The

(1946, US, 113 min, b/w)
d Tay Garnett. *p* Carey Wilson. *sc* Harry Ruskin, Niven Busch. *ph* Sidney Wagner. *ed* George White. *ad* Cedric Gibbons, Randall Duell. *m* George Bassman. *cast* Lana Turner, John Garfield, Cecil Kellaway, Hume Cronyn, Audrey Totter, Leon Ames, Alan Reed.

●In many ways a more striking reading of Cain's novel than the Rafelson remake, even though required to pussyfoot on the sexual side. With the opening shot of a sign announcing 'Man Wanted', and Turner's first appearance heralded by a lipstick teasingly rolling across the floor to Garfield's feet, no bed is needed to show what she is selling. A drifter passing through, paralysed by her black widow sting, Garfield becomes a man without a will, immobilised in the bleak little California backwater and gradually mired in a cesspit of lust, betrayal and murder that turns too late into love. The plot gathers slack latterly; but this is only a minor flaw in a film, more grey than *noir*, whose strength is that it is cast as a bleak memory in which, from the far side of paradise, a condemned man surveys the age-old trail through sex, love and disillusionment. TM

Postman Always Rings Twice, The

(1981, US, 123 min)
d Bob Rafelson. *p* Charles Mulvehill, Bob Rafelson. *sc* David Mamet. *ph* Sven Nykvist. *ed* Graeme Clifford. *pd* George Jenkins. *m* Michael Small. *cast* Jack Nicholson, Jessica Lange, John Colicos, Michael Lerner, John P Ryan, Anjelica Huston, William Traylor.

●An honourable effort to be faithful to James M Cain's novel about a hobo and a waitress who murder her husband in Depression-era America. Nicholson and Lange make a class act, and the film does restore the overt sexuality missing from the 1946 version. But, disappointingly given his excellent track record with films like *Five Easy Pieces, The King of Marvin Gardens* and *Stay Hungry*, Bob Rafelson tries to make art out of high-grade pulp, with a resultant loss of energy. MB

Postman Blues (Posutoman burusu)

(1997, Jap, 110 min)
d Sabu [Hiroyuki Tanaka]. *p* Hidemi Satani. *sc* Hiroyuki Tanaka. *ph* Shuji Kuriyama. *m* Daisuke Okamoto. *cast* Shinichi Tsutsumi, Kyôko Tohyama, Ren Ohsugi, Keisuke Horibe, Tomoro Taguchi, Susumu Terajima.

●Tsutsumi is Sawaki, a postman who finds himself making a delivery to an old school chum, Noguchi (Horibe). Noguchi doesn't look at all well. In fact, he's just chopped off his little finger. Being a yakuza is 'one big thrill after another,' he claims. 'And when was the last time your heart pumped like when you were a boy?' Sawaki isn't entirely convinced, but ripping open some mail, he comes across a letter from Kyôko (Toyama), a girl hospitalised with cancer. Moved, he goes to visit her, and befriends another patient, Joe (Ohsugi), who happens to be a professional hitman. Meanwhile the cops come to believe this unassuming postman must be Public Enemy No. 1. Peppered with homages to Wong Kar-Wai, Luc Besson and the samurai masters, this chipper action comedy keeps puncturing the pomposity of the tradition, but it never breaks out of its own cinephilic world view. When any film-maker resorts to pretty cancer victims for romantic interest, you know caution is in order. That said, the film's escalating comedy of errors includes plenty of nice touches, and there's an underlying innocence about its conception which is likeable enough. TCh

Post Mortem

(1999, Can, 92 min)
d Louis Bélanger. *p* Lorraine Dufour. *sc* Louis Bélanger. *ph* Jean-Pierre St-Louis. *ed* Lorraine Dufour. *ad* Colombe Raby. *m* Guy Bélanger. *cast* Sylvie Moreau, Gabriel Arcand, Hélène Loiselle, Sarah Lecompte-Bergeron. Ghislain Taschereau, Pierre Collin, Roger Léger.

●Perhaps it's a formal conceit, an overriding subtlety, that the first hour of this movie plays like a sub-standard TV thriller. For, after lulling us into contemptuous familiarity, the writer/director in effect begins the picture all over again, but this time with a wallop. Single mom Linda allows herself to turn tricks for money – stealing the customer's wallet at the earliest opportunity. She gets in over her head, however, and winds up in the morgue, where creepy Art Garfunkel-type Arcand falls in love at first sight. You could say what happens next is tasteless, or risible, or provocative (or all three), but it certainly gives the movie a third act when it seemed to be DOA. TCh

Posto, Il (The Job/ The Sound of Trumpets)

(1961, It, 90 min, b/w)
d Ermanno Olmi. *p* Alberto Soffientini. *sc* Ermanno Olmi. *ph* Lamberto Caimi. *ed* Carla Colombo. *ad* Ettore Lombardi. *cast* Sandro Panzeri, Loredano Detto, Tullio Kezich.

●Olmi's modern classic, his second feature, has a hero of Keatonesque ingenuousness – a Candide loosed on the big city (Milan), and surviving in spite of the roaring alienation and enclaves of privilege apparently designed to defeat him. Olmi keeps the scenario firmly anchored in a humane realism, and builds a comedy of feeling based upon the implicit observation of the minutest detail, the subtle shifts of emotion on the human face, the shared memories of adolescent embarrassment. If exercises in applied sadism like *10* pall, go and see a genuine master extract as much sexual charge from the sharing of a coffee spoon, and then real humour from the problem of how to dispose of the cups. A delight, no less acute for being gentle. CPea

Pot Luck

(1936, GB, 71 min, b/w)
d Tom Walls. *p* Michael Balcon. *sc* Ben Travers. *ph* Roy Kellino, Arthur Crabtree. *ed* Alfred Roome. *ad* Walter Murton. *m* Louis Levy. *cast* Tom Walls, Ralph Lynn, Robertson Hare, Diana Churchill, Gordon James, Martita Hunt, Sara Allgood.

●The 'funniest team of comedians on any screen today' have aged less well than contemporaries like Claude Hulbert and Will Hay. Hare is still marvellous as the incarnation of timid bourgeois respectability, but Walls – here afflicted by an awful Oirish brogue – is terribly hammy, and the appeal of Lynn's silly-ass antics defies comprehension. That said, the Aldwych farces, enormously popular in the inter-war years, are a part of English history, and this one is a relatively painless introduction to their standard routines and characterisations. Walls is an appalling director, but with one of Ben Travers' few original screenplays, and the photography of Arthur Crabtree and Roy Kellino – two of Britain's most gifted cameramen – the moonlit meanderings around Wrotten Abbey look refreshingly unstagebound. RMy

Poto and Cabengo

(1979, WGer/US, 73 min)
d/p/sc Jean-Pierre Gorin. *ph* Lee Blank. *ed* Greg Durbin. *cast* Grace Kennedy, Virginia Kennedy, Jean-Pierre Gorin, Dr Elissa Newport.

●A fascinating if only partly successful film by Godard's former collaborator. A documentary about six-year-old twins, Grace and Virginia Kennedy, who for years spoke in their own private, impenetrable language, it frustrates partly because, by the time the film was being made, the girls were already losing their own language and beginning to speak in broken English. But Gorin's open depiction of his own effect on the girls' lives while making the film, his portrait of sterile lower middle class American family life, and the innate interest of his subject still make it highly absorbing. GA

Poulet au Vinaigre

see Cop au Vin

Pourquoi pas moi? (Why Not Me?)

(1998, Fr/Sp/Switz, 94 min)
d Stéphane Giusti. *p* Marie Masmonteil, Caroline Adrian. *sc* Stéphane Giusti. *ph* Antoine Roch. *ed* Catherine Schwartz. *ad* Rosa Ros. *cast* Amira Casar, Julie Gayet, Bruno Putzulu, Alexandra London, Carmen Chaplin, Johnny Hallyday, Marie-France Pisier, Brigitte Roüan, Assumpta Serna.

●This light gay/lesbian comedy follows the escapades of a group middle class youngsters who work at a small publishing house in Barcelona and culminates in a swanky, nerve-wracking 'coming out' party to which the friends' parents are invited. Popstar Johnny Hallyday is typical of the casting. He plays ex-bullfighter El Rubio, whose initially shocked reaction to his daughter's 'revelation' eventually turns into sympathy. In effect, he functions as an index of the film's wish-fulfilling optimism about overcoming prejudice. WH

Poussière d'Ange

see Angel Dust

Powaqqatsi

(1988, US, 99 min)
d Godfrey Reggio. *p* Mel Lawrence, Godfrey Reggio, Lawrence S Taub. *sc* Godfrey Reggio, Ken Richards. *ph* Graham Berry, Leonidas Zourdoumis. *ed* Iris Cahn, Alton Walpole. *m* Philip Glass.

●Like its predecessor *Koyaanisqatsi*, Reggio's wordless eco-doc is visually stunning, but undermined by a fairly serious flaw. Where *Koyaanisqatsi* looked at the madness of First World civilisation, and ended up criticising the very technology that enabled the film to be made, *Powaqqatsi* (Hopi for a parasitic life force) directs the same technology at the Third World. The result is even more dubious than its predecessor. Once again Philip Glass supplies the soundtrack, infiltrated here by choirs and Third World instrumentation; and where *Koyaanisqatsi* was edited into a progressively steeper climax, this has little sense of rhythmic flow. At best the message is a fairly obvious criticism of First World domination of the Third, and at worst a hippy celebration of the Dignity of Labour. JG

Powder

(1995, US, 112 min)
d Victor Salva. *p* Roger Birnbaum, Daniel Grodnik. *sc* Victor Salva. *ph* Jerry Zielinski. *ed* Dennis M Hill. *pd* Waldemar Kalinowski. *m* Jerry Goldsmith. *cast* Sean Patrick Flanery, Mary Steenburgen, Lance Henriksen, Jeff Goldblum, Brandon Smith, Bradford Tatum, Susan Tyrrell.

●When his guardian grandparent cops it, 'Powder' (Flanery), a traumatised, telepathic teenage albino, is dragged from his cellar into the unknown world of rural Texas. His frightened-rabbit appearance is only intensified by the hostile reception he encounters. Still, some folk are kindlier: Jessie (Steenburgen), for instance, principal of the kids' home he is taken to, or Sheriff Barnum (Henriksen), converted to the cause after Powder provides a medium to his comatose mother's final wishes. Then there's Goldblum's chipper science teacher, sufficiently intrigued to make reference to Einstein's forecast of a more evolved, more enlightened future humankind. It's astonishing how far writer/director Salva's film takes its ideas of innocence, beauty and goodness versus all that is false and ugly: thoroughly OTT and yet apparently straight-faced, with nary a wink of self-recognition. Impassioned nonsense, really, but something to behold. NB

Powder Keg, The

see Cabaret Balkan

Power

(1986, US, 11 min)
d Sidney Lumet. *p* Reene Schisgal, Mark Tarlov. *sc* David Himmelstein. *ph* Andrzej Bartkowiak. *ed* Andrew Mondshein. *pd* Peter Larkin. *m* Cy Coleman. *cast* Richard Gere, Julie Christie, Gene Hackman, Denzel Washington, Kate Capshaw, EG Marshall, Beatrice Straight, Fritz Weaver, Michael Learned, JT Walsh.

●What Lumet did for American broadcasting in *Network*, he tries to do here for the political campaign trail, with Gere – media consultant to American political hopefuls – to personify the transference of power from candidates and parties to those experts who can best manipulate the tube. Although it puts him in direct competition with his former mentor (Hackman), Gere takes up a suspicious newcomer (Walsh) at the request of a Washington lobbyist (Denzel Washington) whose underhanded dealings eventually reawaken his own political convictions. Despite making use of Hackman, Christie and Marshall in supporting roles, and actual US newscasters to cover the election results, the film is still a complete mess. Barely held together by Cy Coleman's powerful score, it finally falls apart thanks to the embarrassing amateurism of the party political broadcasts the characters produce, and the Vidal Sassoon world they inhabit. SGo

Power, The

(1967, US, 108 min)
d Byron Haskin. *p* George Pal. *sc* John Gay. *ph* Ellsworth J Fredricks. *ed* Thomas J McCarthy. *ad* George W Davis, Merrill Pye. *m* Miklós Rozsa. *cast* George Hamilton, Suzanne Pleshette, Michael Rennie, Nehemiah Persoff, Earl Holliman, Arthur O'Connell, Aldo Ray, Barbara Nichols, Yvonne De Carlo, Richard Carlson, Gary Merrill.

●An underrated sci-fi thriller, based on the novel by Frank M Robinson. Set in a research institute, the plot concerns the hunt for a mysterious, murderous super-brain who is evidently one of the scientists. The investigation, led by Hamilton, whose mind becomes increasingly tampered with by his quarry's power, takes him through a cross-section of contemporary America in search of the killer's past. More than once the film seemingly goes off at a tangent, only to return chillingly to the matter at hand: as when a woman kisses one of the researchers during a party into which the film has become sidetracked, only to discover that he's dead. George Pal's special effects are excellent, and Hamilton's performance is surprisingly good. DP

Power and the Glory, The

(1933, US, 76 min, b/w)
d William K Howard. *p* Jesse L Lasky. *sc* Preston Sturges. *ph* James Wong Howe. *ed* Paul Weatherwax. *ad* Max Parker. *m* Louis De Francesco. *cast* Spencer Tracy, Colleen Moore, Ralph Morgan, Helen Vinson, Clifford Jones, Henry Kolker, Sarah Padden.

●As scripted by Preston Sturges (who impressed the producers at Fox so much they ordered director Howard to shoot his screenplay word for word), this story of a railway tycoon's rise and fall looks like a dry run for *Citizen Kane*, even though Sturges allows himself a little more sentiment on the matter than Welles ever did. Tracy, previously a villainous supporting player, grabbed his first lead and never looked back, but the movie as a whole is more significant for its place in the history books than as a living, breathing, viewing experience. TJ

Power of Kangwon Province, The (Kangwon-do ui Him)

(1998, SKor, 110 min)
d Hong Sang-Soo. *p* Ahn Byung-Joo. *sc* Hong Sang-Soo. *ph* Kim Young-Cheoul. *ed* Hahm Sung-Won. *m* Wong Il. *cast* Paik Jong-Hak, Oh Youn-Hong, Kim You-Suk, Jun Jae-Hyun, Park Hyun-Young, Im Sun-Young.

●Less assertively 'new' than *The Day a Pig Fell into the Well* but more complex in structure and subtler in effect, Hong's second film tells two seemingly distinct stories (one after the other) and leaves the viewer to grapple with two disconcerting revelations: first, that the two protagonists are ex-lovers who have never got over each other, and second, that their stories happen *not* sequentially but within the *same* time frame. The first centres on Jisook, a young woman from Seoul who takes a trip to Kangwon with two girlfriends and meets a nice-but-married cop with whom she stays in touch. The second centres on Cho, a between-jobs teacher with a wife and kid; he, too, takes a short break in Kangwon with an old schoolfriend, who already has tenure in a university teaching post. The twist of lemon is that the two stories are also virtual mirror images of each other, as if both were variations on some larger meta-narrative. Virtuoso film-making, but not in the least high flown; Hong's targets are the ways people trap themselves in routines of all kinds, and the ways people hide truths from themselves and each other behind desultory small talk. TR

Power of Men Is the Patience of Women, The (Die Macht der Männer ist die Geduld der Frauen)

(1978, WGer, 80 min)
d/p Cristina Perincioli. *sc* Cristina Perincioli. *ph* Katia Forbert Petersen, Henrietta Loch. *ed* Helga Schmirre. *m* Flying Lesbians. *cast* Elisabeth Walinski, Eberhard Feik, Dora Kürten, Christa Gehrmann.

●A docu-drama on battered wives, reconstructing the very painful experiences of Addi (Walinski), a young working mother, at the hands of her husband (and of the patriarchal powers-that-be). A strange hybrid of narrative and documentary realism, the film is sometimes hard to watch, but the use of Addi's voice-over, commenting and analysing her situation, widens it out to demand involvement. Made on a slim budget by a largely female crew, it's a sincere if distressing film which contrives to end on a positive note: women can be strong, especially when they act together. HM

Power of One, The

(1991, US, 127 min)
d John G Avildsen. *p* Arnon Milchan, Steve Ruether. *sc* Robert Mark Kamen. *ph* Dean Semler. *pd* Roger Hall. *m* Hans Zimmer. *cast* Stephen Dorff, Armin Müller-Stahl, Morgan Freeman, John Gielgud, Fay Masterson, Robbie Bulloch, Clive Russell, Alois Moyo, Marius Weyers.

●A glossy adaptation of Bryce Courtenay's novel, set in '30s South Africa, where orphaned PK (latterly played by Dorff) experiences both the privileges and privations of his strife-ridden society. Set upon in boarding-school because he is the only English boy among Afrikaners, he falls back on the friendship of kindly German composer/botanist Doc (Müller-Stahl). But the outbreak of war brings further conflict: the British imprison Doc, and PK's visits introduce him to the brutality inflicted on black prisoners. It's there that proud, resourceful Geel Piet (Freeman) takes the boy in hand, teaching him to box and transforming him into a champion. Avildsen draws good performances from the three actors who play PK, as well as from the ever-reliable Freeman and Müller-Stahl, but subtlety is abandoned when he focuses on the ring and teen romance. The climax is a slugging match between PK and a former school bully which would make Rocky proud. CM

Power Play

(1978, Can/GB, 102 min)
d Martyn Burke. *p* Christopher Dalton. *sc* Martyn Burke. *ph* Ousama Rawi. *ed* John Victor Smith. *pd* Karen Bromley. *m* Ken Thorne. *cast* Peter O'Toole, David Hemmings, Donald Pleasence, Barry Morse, Jon Granik, Marcella Saint-Amant, Dick Cavett.

●Tedious, glib and reactionary, this hovers in CIA fantasy land (*Mission Impossible* time warp). In an anonymous European banana republic, an idealistic young WASP military junta overthrow a corrupt and fascistic civilian government of Balkan villains. Despite O'Toole's endearingly ironic performance as the double-crosser in the pack, the moral remains objectionably circular: 'change breeds reaction, so join the reactionaries'. Miss it. CA

Powwow Highway

(1988, GB, 91 min)
d Jonathan Wacks. *p* Jan Wieringa. *sc* Janet Heaney, Jean Stawarz. *ph* Toyomichi Kurita. *ed* Hilarie Roope. *pd* Cynthia Sowder. *m* Barry Goldberg. *cast* A Martinez, Gary Farmer, Joanelle Nadine Romero, Geoff Rivas, Roscoe Born, Wayne Waterman.

●In Santa Fe, a Cheyenne woman is arrested on a trumped-up drugs charge. A few hundred miles north, her brother, Buddy Red Bow (Martinez), leaves the land hearings he is contesting for his tribe and sets off to bail her out. By chance, he meets old schoolmate Philbert Bono (Farmer) in his 'war pony', a beat-up '64 Buick. Together, they head down the Powwow Highway. Martinez makes Buddy an urgent, charismatic militant, but the thrust of the movie – like *Kiss of the Spider Woman* – is to deepen the activist's understanding of his own people and undercut his assumptions of superiority. Farmer's Philbert is a wonderful creation: a huge, lumbering totem-pole of a man whose heart matches his enormous appetite, and whose easygoing nature softens a determination quite as strong as Buddy's. They drive through wintry Montana, Philbert quietly digressing to do homage at spiritual picnic spots, until the open space gives way to 'condo-land' and the end of their quest comes into view. It's an odd, breezy picture, crisply directed by *Repo Man* producer Wacks; Farmer and Martinez are funny and warm, though their sensitivity is too often swamped by a wailing rock score, and the ideas, finally, are replaced by movie clichés. TCh

Practical Magic

(1998, US, 104 min)
d Griffin Dunne. *p* Denise Di Novi. *sc* Robin Swicord, Akiva Goldsman, Adam Brooks. *ph* Andrew Dunn. *ed* Elizabeth Kling. *pd* Robin Standefer. *m* Alan Silvestri. *cast* Sandra Bullock, Nicole Kidman, Dianne Wiest, Stockard Channing, Aidan Quinn, Goran Visnjic, Evan Rachel Wood.

●Sisters Sally and Gillian Owens (Bullock and Kidman) come from a long line of New England witches under an ancestral curse: any man who loves an Owens woman must die. While aunts Jet and Frances (Wiest and Channing) live happily without romance, serious Sally wants more and ends up with a beloved corpse. Sexy Gillian, meanwhile, settles for Jimmy (Visnjic), a charismatic drifter who mistreats her. Sally comes to the rescue – sort of – and a handsome police officer (Quinn) is soon on her trail. This is a film with neither heart nor mind. Adapted from Alice Hoffman's bestseller, it substitutes set pieces for drama and music for dialogue. Bullock and Kidman are in hammy overdrive as the chalk-and-cheese siblings; ditto the talented team of Wiest and Channing. Poor Quinn, though, is stuck playing a sensitive bimbo. CO'Su

Prague

(1991, GB/Fr, 89 min)
d Ian Sellar. *p* Christopher Young. *sc* Ian Sellar. *ph* Darius Khondji. *ed* John Bloom. *pd* Jiri Matolin. *m* Jonathan Dove. *cast* Alan

Cumming, Sandrine Bonnaire, Bruno Ganz, Raphael Meiss, Henri Meiss, Hana Gregorová.

●The opening scenes of Sellar's film – in which young Scot Alex Novak (Cumming) arrives in Prague in search of a snippet of film that supposedly shows his family swimming in the river back in 1941 – suggest a distinct improvement upon the indulgent, woolly poeticism of *Venus Peter*. Unfortunately, the sub-Forsythian comedy of this prologue soon gives way to arty obscurantism. As the increasingly unsympathetic Alex becomes embroiled in a bizarre *ménage à trois* with film archive clerk Elena (Bonnaire) and her boss Josef (Ganz), the script degenerates into frustratingly enigmatic dialogue and a series of scenes whose precise import is unclear. Characters are insufficiently fleshed out, and Prague is reduced to a picturesque backdrop to a story that doesn't seem to be able to decide whether it's a full-blown romance, a satire on East European bureaucracy, a comedy of errors, or a meditation on the legacy of time, memory and history. The cast does its best, to no avail, with a portentous, contrived script. GA

Praise

(1998, Aust, 98 min)
d John Curran. *p* Martha Coleman, Helen Scott. *sc* Andrew McGahan. *ph* Dion Beebe. *ed* Alexandre de Franceschi. *pd* Michael Philips. *cast* Peter Fenton, Sacha Horler, Marta Dusseldorp, Joel Edgerton, Tyvette Duncan, Winston Bull, Gregory Perkins, Loene Carmen.

●Adapted from a hit novel by Andrew McGahan, this superb, challenging film is the kind of unorthodox love story we've come to expect from the Australians: an oddballs' romance transfigured by cumulative, surreal domestic insights, an audacity of technique – which gently suggests avant garde borrowings – and a canny use of landscape to contextualise the dark farce of human strivings. Director Curran encourages such brave, rich performances from his two main actors – Fenton playing chain-smoking asthmatic Gordon, and Horler as sexual and substance addict Cynthia – that the movie takes on the nature of an enquiry into sexual politics. There's a lot of pain, love, sex and laughter going down here, but the movie's daring honesty, easy pace and courage in staying with these two right to the bitter end makes it feel like a breakthrough 'male' feminist movie: *Betty Blue* revisited with the advertising chic ripped out. Cinematographer Dion Beebe puts gutter poetry into the Brisbane flophouse interiors and makes the big blue horizons oddly mysterious. If this sounds like miserabilism, that isn't the whole story. Curran's movie is also funny, moving and thought provoking, edited like a dream and I can't wait for his next one. WH

Praise Marx and Pass the Ammunition

(1968, GB, 90 min)
d/p/sc Maurice Hatton. *ph* Charles Stewart. *ed* Eduardo Guedes, Tim Lewis. *ad* Nick Pollock. *m* Carl Davis. *cast* John Thaw, Edina Ronay, Louis Mahoney, Anthony Villaroel, Helen Fleming.

●Very much a product of the revolution in the air of 1968, Hatton's first feature has rather dated in its attempts to state a case for radical social change in Britain. More than a little muddled anyway when trying to be serious, it was always much better at digging satirically into areas of bad faith as its hero, a 30-year-old Marxist-Leninist of working class origins (sharply played by a pre-*Sweeney* Thaw), seduces a string of bourgeois beauties in the hope of also impregnating them with his revolutionary message. As in *Long Shot*, Hatton's quirkish sense of humour is the thing. TM

Pram (Barnvagnen)

(1963, Swe, 95 min)
d/sc Bo Widerberg. *ph* Jan Troell. *ed* Wic Kjellin. *ad* C Friberg. *m* Jan Johansson. *cast* Inger Taube, Thommy Berggren, Lars Passgard.

●Bo Widerberg had just scandalised his native industry with a book criticising Ingmar Bergman's domination of the Swedish cinema when he turned out his first feature as writer/director. This story of a female drifter vacillating between two lovers, an intellectual and a pop singer, has, it could be said, a more contemporary feel than Bergman's work from the same period. But really – a mouse scraping at the cathedral door. TJ

Pravda

(1969, Fr, 58 min)
d Jean-Luc Godard, Dziga Vertov Group. *p* Claude Nedjar.

●Put together as crudely and urgently as an agit-prop poster, this analysis of Czechoslovakia after Dubcek finds Godard's Dziga Vertov Group beginning its struggle to formulate an uncompromised, revolutionary, theoretical film practice. On the soundtrack, the voices of 'Vladimir' and 'Rosa' argue dialectically in an attempt to arrive at the 'truth' about Dubcek revisionism and Russian imperialism. Meanwhile the images are what Godard has since called 'political tourism' in post-'68 Czechoslovakia, giving way to a blank screen whenever the country cannot furnish a politically correct signifier. A self-confessed failure on its own terms, the film is none the less vital as a step towards a valid form of political cinema. TR

Prayer for the Dying, A

(1987, GB, 108 min)
d Mike Hodges. *p* Peter Snell. *sc* Edmund Ward, Martin Lynch. *ph* Mike Garfath. *ed* Peter Boyle. *pd* Evan Hercules. *m* Bill Conti. *cast* Mickey Rourke, Bob Hoskins, Alan Bates, Sammi Davis, Christopher Fulford, Liam Neeson, Leonard Termo.

●It would be nice to say that Hodges' movie about an IRA man – chopped about by other hands, laden with opprobrium after Enniskillen – is a noble ruin. Actually, it is so preposterously melodramatic that you can relish every minute. Sickened by killing, IRA hit man Fallon (Rourke, great accent) flees to England, contacting crime boss Meehan (Bates, camp) to get a new passport. Meehan's price is one more hit, but in carrying out the contract Fallon is seen by Father Da Costa (Hoskins, ludicrously miscast). To silence the priest, Fallon tricks him into hearing his confession, but the police and an IRA hit team are closing in. There is still time, however, for Fallon to fall in love with the priest's blind, organ-playing niece, and for ex-SAS Father DaCosta to go berserk and flatten three heavies with a dustbin lid. Will Fallon manage to rescue priest and niece, who are tied to the top of the belfry tower with a time-bomb, and thereby save his soul, if not his ass? BC

Prayer of the Rollerboys

(1990, US, 94 min)
d Rick King. *p* Robert Mickelson. *sc* Peter Iliff. *ph* Phaedon Papamichael. *ed* Daniel Loewenthal. *ad* Jay Klein. *m* Stacy Wideltiz. *cast* Corey Haim, Patricia Arquette, Christopher Collet, JC Quinn, Julius Harris, Devin Clark, Mark Pellegrino, Morgan Weisser.

●A tame, teen-movie rip-off of – among others – *Red Dawn*, *A Clockwork Orange* and *Surf Nazis Must Die*, this is a sci-fi pic for the computer-games generation. *RoboCop*-style media images present a paranoid vision of a future where the economic superpowers of Germany and Japan have bankrupted the United States, decimating its adult population and forcing the abandoned children to live in camps. Teen heart-throb Haim plays Griffin, a pizza delivery boy dedicated to saving both his country and his impressionable younger brother from the fascist New Order promised by Gary Lee (Collet) and his racist Rollerboy army (with the aid of an addictive drug). The only opposition is from the Freaks, a motley collection of Blacks, Hispanics and bikers, unsuitable allies for our clean-cut hero. Instead, he teams up with an adult cop (Quinn) and a young, attractive undercover agent (Arquette). The violence is toned down, the sex innocuous, the interest level zero. NF

Preacher's Wife, The

(1996, US, 124 min)
d Penny Marshall. *p* Samuel Goldwyn Jr. *sc* Nat Mauldin, Allan Scott. *ph* Miroslav Ondricek. *ed* Stephen A Rotter, George Bowers. *pd* Bill Groom. *m* Hans Zimmer. *cast* Whitney Houston, Denzel Washington, Gregory Hines, Courtney B Vance, Jenifer Lewis, Loretta Devine, Lionel Ritchie.

●Christmas is here, but for the Rev Henry Biggs (Vance) it's hard to be jolly. A life-long do-gooder, he's reached a mid-life crisis of faith: he's no longer convinced he's making a difference to his community, is failing to put in that quality time with his gospel-singing wife Julia (Houston) and son Jeremiah, and is tempted to sell up the run-down church he inherited from Julia's father to a smarmy property developer (Hines). Not only that, but he's even disbelieving when the Lord answers his prayers by sending down the Angel Dudley (Washington). A surprisingly tolerable remake of the 1947 Cary Grant vehicle *The Bishop's Wife*, thanks chiefly to the casting of Washington, who lends a vital blend of wit, pathos and self-effacement. A pleasingly uncynical film, too, about halfway real people and problems, however two-dimensional and trite. But, beware, if you can't abide Hollywood platitudes, if you're allergic to syrup, and if you object to a movie designed partly to showcase Whitney's new album. NB

Preaching to the Perverted

(1997, GB, 100 min)
d/p/sc Stuart Urban. *ph* Sam McCurdy. *ed* Julian Rodd. *pd* James Hendy. *m* Maya Fiennes, Magnus Fiennes. *cast* Guinevere Turner, Christien Anholt, Tom Bell, Julie Graham.

●Pity poor Peter (Anholt). A virginal computer boffin, he thinks he's bound for glory when Henry Harding MP (Bell) sends him undercover, on a mission from God to infiltrate the House of Thwax fetish club. The idea is to record evidence for a public prosecution, but for Peter this entails gross private humiliation at the hands of American dominatrix Tanya Cheex (Turner). She's only too happy to whip this puppy lover into shape, but when he comes clean, will she turn the other Cheex? Writer/director Urban is known for his BBC TV work, including the BAFTA-winning Falklands drama *An Ungentlemanly Act*, but his first feature is more in line with late-night satellite broadcasting at its starkest. The shock tactics, however, are nowhere near as offensive as the tissue-thin characterisation, stiff performances, anti-climactic script, and a half-cocked stylisation – play-school Almodóvar – which basically boils down to pink and purple production design. A movie for masochists. TCh

Precinct 45: Los Angeles Police

see New Centurions, The

Predator

(1987, US, 106 min)
d John McTiernan. *p* Lawrence Gordon, Joel Silver, John Davis. *sc* Jim Thomas, John Thomas. *ph* Donald McAlpine. *ed* John F Link, Mark Helfrich. *pd* John Vallone. *m* Alan Silvestri. *cast* Arnold Schwarzenegger, Carl Weathers, Elpidia Carrillo, Bill Duke, Jesse Ventura, Kevin Peter Hall.

●Big Arnie straps on the fetishistic military hardware for a rumble in the jungle with a merciless, camouflaged alien (Hall). A routine operation to rescue a cabinet minister captured by South American guerrillas turns into a fight to the death when Arnie's crack platoon is picked off one by one by an invisible adversary, which then makes itself visible, removes its protective helmet, and challenges him to a fair (!) fight. With its stilted dialogue and hammy acting, the film has the look of an expensive production but the feel of a B movie, delivering the sort of undemanding monster mayhem Arnie's fans have come to expect. NF

Predator 2

(1990, US, 108 min)
d Stephen Hopkins. *p* Joel Silver, Lawrence Gordon, John Davis. *sc* Jim Thomas, John Thomas. *ph* Peter Levy. *ed* Mark Goldblatt. *pd* Lawrence G Paull. *m* Alan Silvestri. *cast* Kevin Peter Hall, Danny Glover, Gary Busey, Ruben Blades, Maria Conchita Alonso, Bill Paxton, Adam Baldwin, Robert Davi, Calvin Lockhart.

●Showing little of the flair that distinguished its predecessor, this sequel lacks two winning ingredients: a suspenseful plot and Schwarzenegger. It's 1997, ten years since the invisible alien's last appearance, and the conflict has shifted to a different kind of jungle: futuristic Los Angeles, where the police battle against powerful drug lords. The law enforcers get unexpected help from the predator (Hall), who shimmers into view and rips out a villain's spinal column. Maverick cop Harrigan (Glover) is on his trail, but so is Federal Agent Keyes (Busey), heading a special task force. Attempting an uneasy alliance of genres, the film ends up rudderless, leaving the bewildered heroes with merely functional roles as they chart the indiscriminate behaviour of their foe. Harrigan and Keyes clash wardrobes and fall to ceaseless bickering over jurisdiction. CM

Prejudice

(1989, Aust, 115 min)
d Ian Munro. *p/sc* Pam Williams. *cast* Patsy Stephen, Grace Parr, Vic Hawkins, Penny Stehli, Robert Burns, Allan McFadden.

● Docu-drama exposing the discrimination faced by two women. Jessica is a photographer on a daily paper. She's good at her job, but her Barry McKenzie-like colleagues harass and denigrate her. Letitia's a highly qualified Filipino nurse, ostracised by her patients and passed over for promotion because of her race. The women fight back. Earnest, self-righteous, but powerful in patches. GM

Prelude to a Kiss

(1992, US, 106 min)
d Norman René. *p* Michael Gruskoff, Michael Levy. *sc* Craig Lucas. *ph* Stefan Czapsky. *ed* Stephen A Rotter. *pd* Andrew Jackness. *m* Howard Shore. *cast* Alec Baldwin, Meg Ryan, Kathy Bates, Ned Beatty, Patty Duke, Sydney Walker, Stanley Tucci.

● Straight-as-a-die Peter (Baldwin) and ditzy bartender Rita (Ryan) are introduced at a party, fall swiftly in love and, despite differences, marry after a few months. At the wedding things start to go really wrong, for the couple and for us: after a congratulatory kiss from an old codger (Walker), Rita undergoes a massive personality change which first manifests itself on the honeymoon. For Peter, it's almost as if the body-snatchers have invaded, but when he bumps into the mysterious old buffer in the bar, it becomes clear that the scenario is less a study in sci-fi paranoia, more a matter of maudlin hokum. Very sticky. GA

Premature Burial, The

(1961, US, 81 min)
d/p Roger Corman. *sc* Charles Beaumont, Ray Russell. *ph* Floyd Crosby. *ed* Ronald Sinclair. *ad* Daniel Haller. *m* Ronald Stein. *cast* Ray Milland, Hazel Court, Richard Ney, Heather Angel, Alan Napier, Dick Miller.

● The third of Corman's generally impressive Poe cycle suffers from the fact that Milland, rather than Vincent Price (lead in most of the other entries in the series), stars as the cataleptic medical student haunted by fantastic fears of being buried alive like his father before him. Needless to say, nightmare becomes reality and revenge is meted out; indeed, the predictability of the plotting clearly led Corman to focus his attention, somewhat decoratively, on conjuring up a gloomy Gothic atmosphere that, while effective, too often seems an end in itself, rather than a means of creating horror. The film does have its macabre moments, however, notably Milland proudly showing friends around a tomb he has devised for himself, complete with a variety of exits should his worst dreams come true. GA

Premier Jour, Le

see Midnight

Premonition, The (Svart Lucia)

(1992, Swe, 114 min)
d Rumle Hammerich. *p* Waldemar Bergendahl. *sc* Carina Rydberg. *ph* Jens Fischer. *ed* Camilla Skousen. *pd* Gert Wibe. *m* Jacob Groth. *cast* Tova Magnusson, Figge Norling, Lars Green, Björn Kjellman, Niklas Hjulström, Malin Berghagen.

● This slow-burning and finally rather unsatisfying genre offering teases the viewer with a smorgasbord of doomy portentousness. Having confided numerous sexual fantasies to her diary and a subsequent, rather daring academic assignment, schoolgirl Mikaela (Magnusson) is understandably alarmed when the bespectacled Swedish teacher (Green), who's the object of her adolescent desire, appears to act out her innermost sado-masochistic dreams. The narrative looks set to burst into carnage when Mikaela's mind conjures an ominously threatening set of images. Hammerich keeps us waiting an age before anything definitively bloody occurs and his movie hits the rocks as soon as he has to put away the fancy flummery and come up with a pay-off. TJ

Prénom Carmen

see First Name: Carmen

Préparez Vos Mouchoirs (Get Out Your Handkerchiefs)

(1977, Fr/Bel, 109 min)
d Bertrand Blier. *p* Georges Dancigers, Alexandre Mnouchkine. *sc* Bertrand Blier. *ph* Jean Penzer. *ed* Claudine Merlin, Elisabeth Moulinier, Sylvie Quester. *ad* Eric Moulard. *m* Georges Delerue. *cast* Gérard Depardieu, Patrick Dewaere, Carole Laure, Riton, Michel Serrault, Sylvie Joly, Eléonore Hirt.

● An inspired attack on 'real life' melodramas of the soppy kind capped by *Kramer vs Kramer*. Depardieu, all solicitude and whispers, is the ham-fisted husband, worried by his wife's elusive 'dizzy spells'; Dewaere is the first of several men he invites into their marriage to 'cheer her up'; Riton is the schoolboy-lover she finally adopts to complete a bizarre *ménage-à-quatre*. Somewhere in all this chaos, the movie firmly puts the boot into mainstream French comedy, substituting absurd and amiable bad taste for the intellectual rigor mortis of which Parisians are so proud. An erratic, often hilarious movie. CA

Présence réelle, La

(1984, Fr, 60 min)
d Raúl Ruiz. *p* Jean Lefaux, Maya Feuillette. *sc* Raul Ruiz. *ph* Jacques Bouquin. *ed* Martine Bouquin. *cast* Franck Oger, Nadège Clair, Camila Mora, Catherine Oudin, Louis Castel, Jean-Loup Rivière.

● A good example of how Ruiz, given a perfectly straightforward commission, will deliver anything but the expected. Ostensibly an essay on the Avignon Festival, it starts off with an actor puzzling over his 'virtual' presence on a videodisc about a Festival that hasn't happened yet, but where he can nevertheless be seen. If this sort of meditation on real and imaginary presence – on the differences between film, theatre, filmed theatre and theatrical cinema – had been developed more cohesively, it would have been a much more gripping film. But then it wouldn't have been Ruiz. As it is, the Gothic horror imagery, run-of-the-mill Magritte allusions, and staggeringly cut-rate special effects – felt pen on glass – are so many prodigal throwaways from a man who's often plagued with too many ideas for his own good. JRo

President, The (Praesidenten)

(1919, Den, 90 min, b/w)
d/sc Carl Theodor Dreyer. *ph* Hans Vaagø. *ad* Carl Theodor Dreyer. *cast* Halvard Hoff, Elith Pio, Carl Meyer, Olga Raphael-Linden, Betty Kirkebye, Richard Christensen, Peter Nielsen, Axel Madsden, Jacoba Jessen.

● Dazzlingly restored in 1999 with the original colour tinting, Dreyer's first feature is, like much of his work, a tale of love, bigotry, cruelty and (mostly female) suffering. A sophisticated interlocking narrative tells of the fates of three 'commoners' made pregnant by aristos of high repute; since patriarchal tradition and self-interest outweigh honour, the seducers, willingly or otherwise, tend to abandon the women to their fates. Familiar melodramatic material, then, but Dreyer mostly underplays things, with naturalistic but intense acting, elegant but stark designs, and a keen eye for cruel irony and moral nuance. Very watchable, and often very beautiful: a torchlight procession is especially impressive. GA

President's Analyst, The

(1967, US, 103 min)
d Theodore J Flicker. *p* Stanley Rubin. *sc* Theodore J Flicker. *ph* William A Fraker. *ed* Stuart H Pappé. *pd* Pato Guzman. *m* Lalo Schifrin. *cast* James Coburn, Godfrey Cambridge, Severn Darden, Joan Delaney, Pat Harrington, Barry McGuire, Eduard Franz, Will Geer, William Daniels, Joan Darling.

● A neglected satire whose premise is the secrets to which the US President's shrink is privy, and the ways in which these endanger him. Pursued by everyone from foreign agents to security organisations like the FBI and the CIA, Coburn quickly becomes a picaresque hero on the run through an America whose psychological landscape is every bit as absurd as Hunter Thompson's Las Vegas. Inevitably, in a paranoid conspiracy-theory movie about ten years before its time, some sequences – like a psychedelic sojourn with a hippy group – are now badly dated. But overall it's hilarious stuff, held together by Coburn's tongue-in-cheek performance, one of his best. RM

Presidio, The

(1988, US, 98 min)
d Peter Hyams. *p* D Constantine Conte. *sc* Larry Ferguson. *ph* Peter Hyams. *ed* James Mitchell, Diane Adler, Beau Barthel-Blair. *pd* Albert Brenner. *m* Bruce Broughton. *cast* Sean Connery, Mark Harmon, Meg Ryan, Jack Warden, Mark Blum, Dana Gladstone, Jenette Goldstein.

● Hyams' *Running Scared* was a crime thriller about a pair of ill-matched cops, one black, the other white; this one is a crime thriller about a pair of ill-matched cops, one military, the other civilian: one can have too much of a goodish thing. Set on the eponymous San Francisco military base, it opens promisingly with a break-in at an officers' club culminating in the killing of a military policewoman, a car chase, and the shooting of a civilian cop. The resulting joint investigation teams seasoned, by-the-book military policeman Connery and young civilian cop Harmon. They have crossed swords before, and just to complicate things, Connery's daughter (Ryan) starts making advances to Harmon to wind up her dad. Meanwhile, the investigation dribbles along, with links between former CIA agents, Vietnam veterans, and a missing water bottle pointing to some kind of criminal conspiracy. As usual, Hyams makes good use of the locations, and stages the stunt sequences with great skill, but his handling of the romance and father/daughter conflicts is at best uncertain, at worst embarrassing. NF

P..... Respectueuse, La (The Respectful Prostitute/The Respectable Prostitute)

(1952, Fr, 97 min, b/w)
d Marcel Pagliero, Charles Brabant. *sc* Jacques-Laurent Bost, Alexandre Astruc, Jean-Paul Sartre. *ph* Eugen Shuftan. *ed* Monique Kirsanoff. *ad* Maurice Colasson. *m* Georges Auric. *cast* Barbara Laage, Ivan Desny, Walter Bryant, Marcel Herrand.

● Is Sartre still taken seriously? This barbarous melodrama (based on his play, which he helped adapt) should sow misgivings in the heart of even the staunchest admirer. It's set in an American South where all the blacks are saintly and passive and all the whites, except the title *putain*, do nothing but seethe with racist venom. Enter the movie at any point and it offends – musically, via Auric's whining arrangement of 'Swing Low Sweet Chariot', and dramatically through the author's inability even to compose a scene in which two people in a room behave plausibly. Cameraman Shuftan does his best to reproduce Dixie in the Courbevoie studios, but is hampered by Laage's willowy mannequin looks, as wrong here as the signs telling motorists to 'honck' for service. BBa

Presque rien

(2000, Fr/Bel, 98 min)
d Sébastien Lifshitz. *p* Christian Tison. *sc* Sébastien Lifshitz, Stéphane Bouquet. *ph* Pascal Poucet. *ed* Yann Dedet. *ad* Roseanna Sacco. *m* Perry Blake. *cast* Jérémie Elkaïm, Stéphane Rideau, Marie Matheron, Dominique Reymond, Laetitia Legrix, Nils Öhlund, Réjane Kerdaffrec.

● A queer, elusive slip of a film, this before and after tale of a failed first gay love affair effaces drama, motivation, and ultimately itself, rather. More Proust-lite than Soderbergh, it slips to and fro in time – between breezy summer and bluesy winter, coming out and fall-out – not for fun or show, but simply perhaps to compound and contextualise emotions. Still, it's something of a puzzle. Director Lifshitz's aesthetic control is so tantalising, he leaves the impression there are secrets he's not quite relinquishing. Playful summer days on the Brittany coast are recalled by Mathieu (Elkaïm), returning alone a year and a half later in decidedly sobered mood. He's hardly the extrovert type anyway, but whereas the silent allure of a vacationing local man, Cédric (Rideau), initially elicits a sense of adventure, some subsequent untold derailment has taken him to the brink of suicide. Quietly composed of discreet disclosures, the film is mainly about moment-to-moment impressions which Lifshitz lets unfold from a respectful distance. It's beautifully inscribed, so far as it goes, but the understatement is overwrought. Even the title ('Almost Nothing') seems evasive. NB

Press for Time

(1966, GB, 102 min)
d Robert Asher. *p* Robert Hartford-Davis, Peter Newbrook. *sc* Norman Wisdom, Eddie Leslie. *ph* Peter Newbrook. *ed* Gerry Hambling. *ad* Bruce Grimes. *m* Mike Vickers. *cast* Norman Wisdom, Derek Bond, Angela Browne, Derek Francis, Noel Dyson, Frances White, Peter Jones, Allan Cuthbertson.
●Gormless Norman is the Prime Minister's grandson, a newspaper-seller kicked upstairs (because grandfather is embarrassed) to a journalist's post in a seaside town (where he wreaks much havoc). Based on a novel by *Evening Standard* hack Angus McGill, this features Wisdom in three roles, spreading his creepy persona too thinly for comfort. His humour was very much a product of the conscription years; by 1966, it had worn hopelessly thin, and after this film, he attempted to update his style with Swinging Sixties fare like *What's Good for the Goose* – a disastrous step, it transpired. JRo

Pressure

(1975, GB, 100 min)
d Horace Ové. *p* Robert Buckler. *sc* Horace Ové, Samuel Selvon. *ph* Mike Davis. *ed* Alan J Cumner-Pryce. *cast* Herbert Norville, Oscar James, Frank Singuineau, Lucita Lijertwood, Sheila Scott-Wilkinson, Ed Devereaux.
●Britain's first 'black' feature, co-scripted by Ové and Samuel Selvon, deals honestly and realistically with what life is like for a school-leaver who is black: the futile job interviews, the patronising platitudes, people's simple inability to comprehend that black can be not only beautiful but also English. Although it fudges its ending, there's enough honesty and entertainment along the way to place the Dickensian jokes of 'Black Joy' firmly back in their fairytale. SM

Presumed Innocent

(1990, US, 127 min)
d Alan J Pakula. *p* Sydney Pollack, Mark Rosenberg. *sc* Alan J Pakula, Frank R Pierson. *ph* Gordon Willis. *ed* Evan Lottman. *pd* George Jenkins. *m* John Williams. *cast* Harrison Ford, Brian Dennehy, Raúl Julia, Bonnie Bedelia, Paul Winfield, Greta Scacchi, John Spencer, Joe Grifasi, Tom Mardirosian.
●Pakula and Frank Pierson faced a difficult task in adapting Scott Turow's novel. The dense, first-person narrative – told from the perspective of an alleged murderer – has been simplified and tightened, its psychological subtleties jettisoned, the emphasis shifted to legal and forensic investigation. Rusty Sabich (Ford) is a prosecuting attorney whose life is thrown into turmoil after a colleague (Scacchi) is raped and murdered. They had enjoyed a brief affair, and suspicion falls on Sabich, who finds himself hiring a defence attorney (Julia). Even stripped down, the plot provides suspense and intellectual fascination, but the film quickly runs into problems of characterisation. In Turow's novel, the victim is viewed from Sabich's vantage point; here, the emotional distortion has been lost, and her role is merely functional. To a lesser degree, Sabich also loses in the translation, but he's given dimension via his relationship with his tormented, mathematician wife (Bedelia, excellent) and through Ford's earnest intensity. In a welcome return to suspense, Pakula effectively conveys the claustrophobia of domesticity and courtroom procedure. CM

Prêt-à-Porter

see Ready to Wear

Pretty as a Picture: The Art of David Lynch

(1997, US, 95 min)
d/p Toby Keeler. *ph* Vince Dyer. *ed* Toby Keeler. *with* David Lynch, Barry Gifford, Angelo Badalamenti, Jennifer Lynch, Jack Nance, Dean Stockwell.
●Essentially 'The Making of *Lost Highway*', this covers various stages of the shoot, the music recording in Prague and the premiere at Sundance and contains interviews with all the key people, most of them going well beyond promo-speak. A mini history of Lynch as both a film-maker and a painter is rather awkwardly spliced in (but who's complaining?). We learn from family members and friends how real life experiences were turned into images and motifs in the films, get a guided tour of the *Eraserhead* sets and hear from Mel Brooks why he hired 'a young Charles Lindbergh' to direct *The Elephant Man*. Topped by increasingly improbable hair, Lynch is remarkably forthcoming. Best revelation: the origins of Bob in *Twin Peaks*. The DVD release adds 15 minutes of out-takes from the interviews, including Jack Fisk on the young Lynch's visits to the Philadelphia morgue. TR

Pretty Baby

(1977, US, 110 min)
d/p Louis Malle. *sc* Polly Platt, Louis Malle. *ph* Sven Nykvist. *ed* Suzanne Fenn. *pd* Trevor Williams. *m* Jerry Wexler. *cast* Brooke Shields, Keith Carradine, Susan Sarandon, Frances Faye, Antonio Fargas, Matthew Anton, Diana Scarwid, Barbara Steele, Gerrit Graham.
●Despite the scandalised yelps about child pornography, a film of disarmingly subversive innocence, set in a New Orleans bordello (1917 vintage) where the pretty baby of the title eagerly awaits her twelfth birthday and the deflowerment which will inaugurate her career. All red plush, ragtime and Renoir nudes, it would be candy confection except that vice is viewed here partly through the enchanted eyes of the child (Shields), partly through the candid camera of a photographer (Carradine) who sees flesh and its desires as the stuff of art and beauty. The Nabokovian relationship between these two asks some very pertinent questions about the hypocrisy of conventional morality. TM

Pretty in Pink

(1986, US, 97 min)
d Howard Deutch. *p* Lauren Schuler Donner. *sc* John Hughes. *ph* Tak Fujimoto. *ed* Richard Marks. *pd* John W Corso. *m* Michael Gore. *cast* Molly Ringwald, Harry Dean Stanton, Jon Cryer, Annie Potts, James Spader, Andrew McCarthy.
●A pretty superior teen angst movie, with John Hughes (executive-producing and scripting but not directing this time) completing the series he began with *Sixteen Candles* and *The Breakfast Club*. Being young, Hughes tells us, isn't easy. Red-haired Ringwald has no mother in sight, Harry Dean Stanton for a downbeat father, and an unfortunate high school rep. She wears odd clothes, tools round in a clapped-out Beetle, and works in a record store at weekends (cue Psychedelic Furs, The Smiths, etc). Still, she's got lots of spirit, and by the end even the Nice, Unbelievably Rich Kid with the BMW is beginning to recognise what we've known all along: that she's the best thing around. It's a plea on behalf of upward mobility, and – more remarkable – revolves around a single question: will Molly make it to the high school prom? To be able to give this kind of stuff new and sympathetic twists is a tribute to Hughes' skill with narrative, and to Ringwald's magnetism as a performer. RR

Pretty Maids All in a Row

(1971, US, 95 min)
d Roger Vadim. *p/sc* Gene Roddenberry. *ph* Charles Rosher. *ed* Bill Brame. *ad* George W Davis, Preston Ames. *m* Lalo Schifrin. *cast* Rock Hudson, Angie Dickinson, Telly Savalas, John David Carson, Roddy McDowall, Keenan Wynn, William Campbell.
●Somebody's knocking off girls at the high school in this sex-comedy-thriller, which doesn't get far in any of these directions. The sex is an updated equivalent of the kind indulged in by Rock Hudson in innumerable bedroom comedies. The comedy consists largely of Telly Savalas wearing his dark glasses on the top of his bald head, plus a few gags about embarrassing erections. And the thriller aspect derives from a couple of close-ups of Hudson looking dangerously manic. In one shot, the boom microphone hovers in full view for several seconds; an indication of the general sloppiness and pointlessness of Vadim's first American-made feature.

Pretty Poison

(1968, US, 89 min)
d Noel Black. *p* Marshal Backlar, Noel Black. *sc* Lorenzo Semple Jr. *ph* David Quaid. *ed* William Ziegler. *ad* Jack Martin Smith, Harold Michelson. *m* Johnny Mandel. *cast* Anthony Perkins, Tuesday Weld, Beverly Garland, John Randolph, Dick O'Neill, Clarice Blackburn.
●Ever since this corrosive tale of insidious madness and deceptive innocence in Small Town USA, buffs have sought out Noel Black's other work (mainly for TV), vainly hoping to find something as good. The film is blithely written by Lorenzo Semple Jr, who suddenly proved at a stroke that he was worthy of more than the script consultant's job on *Batman*. And the performances are great. Perkins' role, as a dedicated fantasist employed at a chemical factory, treads on *Psycho* ground without ever causing the usual feelings of *déjà vu*; but Tuesday Weld is the film's linch-pin, brilliantly playing a girl whose drum-majorette demeanour hides the most amazing emotions. In a word, recommended. GB

Pretty Village, Pretty Flame (Lepa sela lepo gore)

(1996, Serbia, 129 min)
d Srdjan Dragojevic. *p* Goran Bjelogrlic, Dragan Bjelogrlic, Nikola Kojo, Milko Josifov. *sc* Vanja Bulic, Srdjan Dragojevic, Nikola Pejakovic. *ph* Dusan Joksimovic. *ed* Petar Markovic. *pd* Milenko Jeremic. *m* Aleksandar Sasa Habic. *cast* Dragan Bjelogrlic, Nikola Kojo, Velimir Bata Zivojinovic, Dragan Maksimovic, Zoran Cvijanovic.
●A harrowing response to the Bosnian conflict, this war drama disarms preconceptions and prejudices by adopting a strategy of temporal dislocation. Cutting from 1980 to 1992 (the first day of the war) and to 1994 (a bloody hospital ward), and back again, it reveals its secrets with no little care. A Muslim and a Serb grow up and work together, but inevitably find themselves on opposite sides when a Serb unit is trapped inside a disused tunnel with no food or water. Boldly shot and edited, the film quite rightly puts you through the wringer. TCh

Pretty Woman

(1990, US, 119 min)
d Garry Marshall. *p* Arnon Milchan, Steven Reuther. *sc* JF Lawton. *ph* Charles Minsky. *ed* Priscilla Nedd. *ad* Albert Brenner. *m* James Newton Howard. *cast* Richard Gere, Julia Roberts, Ralph Bellamy, Jason Alexander, Laura San Giacomo, Alex Hyde-White, Hector Elizondo.
●Vivian (Roberts) is not a happy hooker. She looks the part, but unlike her feisty friend Kit (San Giacomo) she retains a *core of vulnerability*. So does workaholic Edward (Gere), even though he's a millionaire take-'em-and-break-'em tycoon. In LA for the week, he hires Vivian to act as a beautiful, disarming escort while he dines the opposition, grooming and schooling her in the process. Before you know it, she's discovering a sense of self-worth, while he's taking shoes and socks (and time) off to stroll in the park and overhaul his ethics. This is predictable *Pygmalion* stuff, but with plenty of laughs along the way. Roberts can act, and Gere, though not renowned for his comic skills, is more than a smoochy foil to kooky Vivian, and just about manages to look like a man who has channelled all his sexual energy into corporate ball-crushing. Retch-making moments (he thinks she's doing drugs in the bathroom, she's really – *aaawww!* – flossing her teeth) are kept to a minimum and the sex scenes sweetly restrained. But for a film that attempts to satirise snooty materialism, it focuses too pantingly on the designer labels, and comes down firmly on the side of 'rich is better'. SFe

Prey of the Chameleon

(1991, US, 85 min)
d Tex Fuller. *cast* James Wilder, Alexandra Paul, Daphne Zuniga.

●*The Hitcher* with a twist. A dumb psychological suspense picture in which ex-mercenary Wilder, back home in middle America, picks up a housewife stranded by her broken-down car. His passenger (Zuniga, best known for Rob Reiner's *The Sure Thing*) is not what she seems; in fact, she's an escapee from a mental institution, who befriends her victims, kills them, and then assumes their identities. TJ

Price Above Rubies, A

(1997, US/Fr/GB, 116 min)
d Boaz Yakin. *p* Lawrence Bender, John Penotti. *sc* Boaz Yakin. *ph* Adam Holender. *ed* Arthur Coburn. *pd* Dan Leigh. *m* Lesley Barber. *cast* Renee Zellweger, Christopher Eccleston, Allen Payne, Glenn Fitzgerald, Julianna Margulies, Kim Hunter, John Randolph, Edie Falco.

●Sonia (Zellweger) is in trouble. Her husband Mendel (Fitzgerald) is a Jewish religious scholar who makes love 'under the eyes of God', that is shamefully and infrequently. Meanwhile Sonia's turned on even by the baby at her breast. She doubts it is in her heart to be the wife of a holy man. There's little sympathy for her within NYC's Orthodox community, so when her brother-in-law Sender (Eccleston) fucks her against the wall and then asks her to buy jewels for his basement store, she goes with it. But in finding herself, must Sonia lose everything else? This tyro effort is a disappointment, a stilted emancipatory drama which neither illuminates its milieu nor transcends it. The tone is sober and subdued, but writer/director Yakin risks derisory laughter when Sonia confesses her frustration to the venerable Rebbe, inadvertently waking his dormant libido – followed by a cut to the elder's funeral. The film is every bit as phony as Hollywood pap, but with its excruciatingly high-minded penchant for symbolism, metaphor and speechifying, it is altogether too precious to permit the lowly pleasures of melodrama. TCh

Price of Glory

(2000, US, 117 min)
d Carlos Avila. *p* Moctesuma Esparza, Robert Katz, Arthur E Friedman. *sc* Phil Berger. *ph* Affonso Beato. *ed* Gary Karr. pd Robb Wilson King. *m* Joseph Julián González. *cast* Jimmy Smits, Jon Seda, Clifton Collins Jr, Ernesto Hernández, Maria Del Mar, Sal López, Louis Mandylor, Danielle Camastra, Ron Perlman.

●Set in Mariposa, California, this debut film has a fit-looking Jimmy Smits as Latino patriarch, Arturo Ortega, an ex-boxer whose brilliant career was cut short by a crooked manager. Determined to protect his sons from a similar fate, Ortega coaches the three boys in the noble art himself. Hard work and determination bear fruit as sons Jimmy (Collins) and Sonny (Seda) do well, but it's younger brother, Johnny (Hernández), who catches the eye of professional promoter, Nick Everson (Perlman). A combination of pride, vanity and sheer bloody mindedness, however, see Ortega turn down Everson's offer, and pretty soon his single-mindedness starts to look more like bullying. The story follows a standard 'struggling path to fame and fortune' route, in the *Rocky* mould, with the inter-familial relationships offering limited and fairly two-dimensional side interest but the climactic bout delivers. JFu

Prick Up Your Ears

(1987, GB, 110 min)
d Stephen Frears. *p* Andrew Brown. *sc* Alan Bennett. *ph* Oliver Stapleton. *ed* Mick Audsley. *pd* Hugo Luczyc-Wyhowski. *m* Stanley Myers. *cast* Gary Oldman, Alfred Molina, Vanessa Redgrave, Wallace Shawn, Lindsay Duncan, Julie Walters, James Grant.

●Artists have usually had a cardboard time of it on film. What writers do is not cinematic, so Frears' film on Joe Orton concentrates elsewhere. The finally tragic 16-year relationship between Orton (Oldman) and his lover Kenneth Halliwell (Molina), and their defiant isolation from conventional society are the central themes here, but neither is particularly illuminating. The clumsy distancing device of a narrative by literary agent Peggy Ramsay (Redgrave) prevents one from caring about the doomed pair, or from feeling Halliwell's anguish. Orton was formed in opposition to the prevailing moral climate, and his plays were his revenge. They were distinguished by a gleeful vindictiveness that seems disproportionate to the Establishment targets presented here as caricatures. The main failure to get to grips with the subject lies in Alan Bennett's script: his familiar comic cadences and inspired mismatches hijack the proceedings. Line by line, it's outrageously funny, but like the collage on the wall of the Islington flat, it doesn't add up to more than the sum of its parts. BC

Pride and Prejudice

(1940, US, 119 min, b/w)
d Robert Z Leonard. *p* Hunt Stromberg. *sc* Aldous Huxley, Jane Murfin. *ph* Karl Freund. *ed* Robert J Kern. *ad* Cedric Gibbons, Paul Groesse. *m* Herbert Stothart. *cast* Greer Garson, Laurence Olivier, Edna May Oliver, Edmund Gwenn, Mary Boland, Maureen O'Sullivan, Melville Cooper, Marsha Hunt, Heather Angel, Ann Rutherford, Karen Morley.

●An adaptation of the Helen Jerome play based on Jane Austen's novel, which may well make Austenites quiver at its infidelities and occasional insensitivities (not to mention the perhaps inevitable blurring of the subtler social ironies), but is surprisingly dry and droll. Aldous Huxley's contribution to the script undoubtedly helped, but it is the cast which carries it: marvellous performances all round, with Garson's cool prejudice perfectly matched against Olivier's chill pride, and only minor reservations (Mary Boland's Mrs Bennett is a little too tiresomely tiresome). TM

Pride and the Passion, The

(1957, US, 132 min)
d/p Stanley Kramer. *sc* Edna Anhalt, Edward Anhalt. *ph* Franz Planer. *ed* Frederick Knudtson, Ellsworth Hoagland. *ad* Fernando Carrere. *m* George Antheil. *cast* Cary Grant, Frank Sinatra, Sophia Loren, Theodore Bikel, John Wengraf, Jay Novello.

●Spectacularly solemn and silly epic based on CS Forester's novel about Napoleon's Iberian campaign (*The Gun*), full of sound and fury (and heaving bodies) signifying nothing. If you can believe in Sinatra as an 1810 vintage Spanish guerrilla, you can believe anything, but it's still a slog through a platitudinous script as (with Grant and Loren looking on while providing the love interest) he struggles to lug a vast cannon within range of the Napoleonic invaders. TM

Pride of St Louis, The

(1952, US, 93 min, b/w)
d Harmon Jones. *p* Jules Schermer. *sc* Herman J Mankiewicz. *ph* Leo Tover. *ed* Robert Simpson. *ad* Lyle Wheeler, Addison Hehr. *m* Arthur Lange. *cast* Dan Dailey, Joanne Dru, Richard Hylton, Richard Crenna, Hugh Sanders, James Brown, Chet Huntley.

●Full enjoyment of this sports biopic depends on actually having heard of baseball giant Dizzy Dean, the hillbilly pitcher who won stardom with the St Louis Cardinals before injury almost ended his involvement with the sport. Dailey, usually seen in Hollywood musicals, makes him a cheerily sympathetic type, but it's one for the aficionados of the game and *Citizen Kane* obsessives looking for another movie where screenwriter Herman J Mankiewicz gives a real-life figure fictional treatment. TJ

Pride of the Marines (aka Forever in Love)

(1945, US, 120 min, b/w)
d Delmer Daves. *p* Jerry Wald. *sc* Albert Maltz, Marvin Borowsky. *ph* Peverell Marley, Robert Burks. *ed* Owen Marks. *ad* Leo Kuter. *m* Franz Waxman. *cast* John Garfield, Eleanor Parker, Dane Clark, John Ridgely, Rosemary DeCamp, Ann Doran.

●The true story of Al Schmid, a young soldier blinded by a Japanese grenade in the heroic defence of Guadalcanal, allows Garfield to produce a performance of well-modulated intensity that draws upon his understanding of ordinary people, their eager but simple ambitions, and the courage they often find in adversity and despair. The cloying patriotism – although mitigated in part by a confrontation of the social problems facing the US in the aftermath of World War II – is hard to stomach. But the thoughtful script (notice in particular the characters' reaction to the news of Pearl Harbor), the fine direction (you'll either love or hate the bizarre dream sequence), and above all Garfield, make this a film that's always watchable, sometimes riveting. FD

Priest

(1994, GB, 109 min)
d Antonia Bird. *p* Josephine Ward, George Faber. *sc* Jimmy McGovern. *ph* Fred Tammes. *ed* Susan Spivey. *pd* Raymond Langhorn. *m* Andy Roberts. *cast* Linus Roache, Tom Wilkinson, Cathy Tyson, Robert Carlyle, James Ellis, Lesley Sharp, Robert Pugh.

●When Father Greg (Roache) arrives at his new Liverpool parish, he's appalled at what he regards as the lax morals of his more experienced colleague, Father Matthew (Wilkinson), who shares a bed with their housekeeper Maria (Tyson). The priests are utterly at odds, temperamentally, politically and doctrinally. However, it soon emerges that Greg's fierce conservatism covers a turmoil of self-doubt: one evening he swaps his dog collar for a leather jacket and picks up a lover in a gay bar (Carlyle). The film calls on the traditions of the best radical TV drama. Wickedly sardonic and very moving, with an outstanding performance from Roache at the centre of a fine cast, it clearly works a treat for cinema audiences. In the opening sequence a priest uses a large crucifix as a battering ram, which gives a fair idea of the level of ecclesiastical debate. The film's true subject, however, is emotional courage, and that it has in spades. TCh

Priest of Love

(1980, GB, 125 min)
d Christopher Miles. *p* Christopher Miles, Andrew Donally. *sc* Alan Plater. *ph* Ted Moore. *ed* Paul Davies. *pd* Ted Tester. *m* Joseph James. *cast* Ian McKellen, Janet Suzman, Ava Gardner, Penelope Keith, Jorge Rivero, Maurizio Merli, John Gielgud, James Faulkner, Sarah Miles.

●High in the running for the year's dumbest art movie, opening on a shot of burning books, this launches into the life story of DH Lawrence with all the naive lyricism of an early Ken Russell biopic. Suzman struggles to toughen up the role of Frieda, but succumbs to the script early on when required to describe sex as 'the only way to reach the soul of man'. McKellen has the 'look of genius' in his eyes, the twang of Nottingham in his speech, and TB in his lungs. On the interminable route to his deathbed, Lawrence experiences lurid sunsets and a generous helping of flashbacks, and sees his manuscripts blown away in the wind so often you wonder how he ever published a single word. Directed like the most twee of travelogues, it's not worth staying with even for the closing moment of sublime silliness when the remains of the dead novelist return to New Mexico in a terracotta chicken brick. Desperate … although subsequent re-editing down to a 99-minute version did help slightly. MA

Prima della Rivoluzione

see Before the Revolution

Primal Fear

(1996, US, 129 min)
d Gregory Hoblit. *p* Gary Lucchesi. *sc* Steve Shagan, Ann Biderman. *ph* Michael Chapman. *ed* David Rosenbloom. *pd* Jeannine C Oppewall. *m* James Newton Howard. *cast* Richard Gere, Laura Linney, Frances McDormand, Edward Norton, John Mahoney, Alfre Woodard, Terry O'Quinn, Joe Spano, Tony Plana.

●Suave, womanising top Chicago attorney Martin Vail (Gere) is arrogant enough to demand the cover for any magazine interview he grants. In fact, he's such a publicity fiend, that when he catches a newsflash of young Aaron Stampler (Norton) attempting to escape from the scene of an ugly murder, he drops everything to be the first to offer his services – gratis. The stuttering Southern ex-hobo's accused of killing his guardian, the city's beloved archbishop. The DA, an old foe of Vail, and a friend of the victim, is insisting on the death penalty; and, to spice things up, Vail's embittered ex (Linney), a prosecutor in the DA's department, is detailed to the case. Despite a talky script (based on a book by William Diehl) full of hanging ethical, procedural and social conundrums, first-time director Hoblitt seems at ease in this two-act movie. The first hour, detailing the city's scummy realpolitik, is a smooth, predictable preamble to the ably executed trial-scene second half. There are twists, but few surprises. Gere speechifies grandly, and dashes around manfully in his tailor-made role, and Norton shows notable range, but unfortunately in an environment too mechanical for it to prove much. WH

Primary Colors

(1998, US, 143 min)
d/p Mike Nichols. *sc* Elaine May. *ph* Michael Ballhaus. *ed* Arthur Schmidt. *pd* Bo Welch. *m* Ry Cooder. *cast* John Travolta, Emma Thompson, Adrian Lester, Kathy Bates, Billy Bob Thornton.

● Travolta looks the spitting image of Bill Clinton – from the rear. This *film à clef* about Clinton's 1990 campaign for the Democratic Presidential nomination offers plenty of food for thought on the corruption of the political process, but despite the absorbing material – Elaine May sticking close to the novel by Anonymous (actually political correspondent Joe Klein) – Nichols comes off as the perennial wavering voter. As satire, it's toothless and indulgent; as drama of conscience, it's not a patch on real life (see DA Pennebaker's documentary *The War Room*). The performances are pitched all over the place, but the real problem is Travolta's avowedly sympathetic, yet distractingly uncharismatic, intellectually light-weight impersonation of the President – Bill gives much better sincerity than this. TCh

Primate

(1974, US, 105 min, b/w)
d/p/sc Frederick Wiseman. *ph* William Brayne. *ed* Frederick Wiseman.

● 'We get erection at one frequency, and ejaculation at another' a researcher says to a colleague. In this case the scientists are talking about apes, but as behaviour researchers discover and refine new methods of electronic control, it's perhaps only a matter of time before human beings are routinely implanted with electrodes and their sexuality controlled by electronic impulses. Wiseman spent a great deal of time filming these types of investigations at a well-known primate research centre in America. Unfortunately, his style is not to inform but simply to record. We are shown an endless series of experiments on chimpanzees, orang-utangs and gorillas, executed with cold, heartless efficiency; but the images of operations and dissections, as brutal as they sometimes appear, are meaningless unless we are provided with basic information on why this particular research is being conducted. This lack of viewpoint is particularly disappointing in a slow, rambling documentary that could have given us a purposeful look into the mechanics of behaviour and the frightening implications suggested by scientific research. LR

Prime Cut

(1972, US, 86 min)
d Michael Ritchie. *p* Joe Wizan. *sc* Robert Dillon. *ph* Gene Polito. *ed* Carl Pingitore. *ad* Bill Malley. *m* Lalo Schifrin. *cast* Lee Marvin, Gene Hackman, Angel Tompkins, Gregory Walcott, Sissy Spacek, Janit Baldwin, William Morey.

● Ritchie's inexplicably underrated second feature is a superb amalgam of pulp gangster thriller and fairytale, in which white knight/ Chicago syndicate enforcer (Marvin) visits recalcitrant black knight/Kansas boss (Hackman), rescuing damsel in distress (Spacek, making her debut) while there. Underneath a surface that constantly juxtaposes opposites, *Prime Cut* concerns a curious, fundamental *naiveté* underlying America's corruption: that allows Hackman to give the country the dope and flesh it wants; that permits Marvin to attempt to live out his Beauty and the Beast romance; that implies, in the fairground shootout, an America totally oblivious to what is going on in front of its eyes. In his round-trip of bars, hotels, flophouses, ranches, cities and countryside, Ritchie demonstrates a truly fine handling of locations, best realised in two classic Hitchcock-like chases, through the fairground, and across a cornfield pursued by a combine harvester. CPe

Prime Gig, The

(2000, US, 97 min)
d Gregory Mosher. *p* Cary Woods, Gina Mingacci, Elliot Lewis Rosenblatt, William Wheeler. *sc* William Wheeler. *ph* John A Alonzo. *ed* James Kwei. *pd* Richard Hoover. *m* David Robbins. *cast* Vince Vaughn, Julia Ormond, Ed Harris, Rory Cochrane, Wallace Shawn, George Wendt, Stephen Tobolowsky, Jeannetta Arnette.

● Theatre director Mosher is a longstanding collaborator of David Mamet; and presumably that made him a natural choice for this sting movie, written by former telesales op William Wheeler, which resembles *Glengarry Glen Ross* crossed with *The Spanish Prisoner*. Vaughn is well cast as the gifted spieler who warily enlists in what he knows deep down must be a scam, selling shares in a goldmine at the behest of legendary con-man Kelly Grant (Harris). None of this is quite as sharp as it might be, but Mosher has a feel for the seedy milieu of these moneygrubbers, and it ends on just the right note of sour self-disgust. TCh

Primeiro Dia, O

see Midnight

Prime luci dell'alba, Le

see First Light of Dawn

Prime of Miss Jean Brodie, The

(1968, GB, 116 min)
d Ronald Neame. *p* Robert Fryer. *sc* Jay Presson Allen. *ph* Ted Moore. *ed* Norman Savage. *pd* John Howell. *m* Rod McKuen. *cast* Maggie Smith, Robert Stephens, Pamela Franklin, Gordon Jackson, Celia Johnson, Diane Grayson, Jane Carr, Shirley Steedman, Helena Gloag.

● Muriel Spark's wonderful slip-sliding novella is narrowed down and heightened in Jay Presson Allen's adaptation for Fox of her own stage play (drawn from Spark's book), which omits much sense of the wider, crueller world of the '30s outside the Marcia Blaine School for Girls in Edinburgh, where Miss Brodie imparts her own rarefied, romantic view of life to her chosen 'set'. Nevertheless, Maggie Smith is handed a part in the eccentric, trite, purposeful and finally pathetic Jean Brodie which allows her to play to all her considerable strengths. Her performance is ably counterpointed by Stephens as the knowing, married art teacher Teddy Lloyd (to whose bed she attempts to send one of her girls, in her own place), and Celia Johnson as the pursed headmistress determined to sack her. Good support, too, from the girls, notably Jane Carr, as Mary McGregor, the new girl who dies on her way to fight against Miss Brodie's hero Franco, and Pamela Franklin, as Sandy, who finally puts paid to her teacher by denouncing her fascism. JPy

Primrose Path, The

(1940, US, 93 min, b/w)
d/p Gregory La Cava. *sc* Allan Scott, Gregory La Cava. *ph* Joseph H August. *ed* William Hamilton. *ad* Van Nest Polglase, Carroll Clark. *m* Werner Heymann. *cast* Ginger Rogers, Joel McCrea, Marjorie Rambeau, Miles Mander, Henry Travers, Joan Carroll.

● A likeable social comedy from the talented La Cava (for whom Rogers had given such a fine performance in the earlier *Stage Door*). Ginger's the girl from the wrong side of the tracks – morally rather than financially, coming as she does from a family of prostitutes and drunkards – who loses her respectable hubby McCrea, ambitious proprietor of a hamburger stand, when he finally gets to meet her parents. The romance and the attempts at seamy realism don't really mesh smoothly enough, but the performances and civilised direction make the unusual subject highly watchable. GA

Prince and the Pauper, The (aka Crossed Swords)

(1977, Pan, 121 min)
d Richard Fleischer. *p* Pierre Spengler. *sc* George MacDonald Fraser. *ph* Jack Cardiff. *ed* Ernest Walter. *pd* Anthony Pratt. *m* Maurice Jarre. *cast* Oliver Reed, Raquel Welch, Mark Lester, Ernest Borgnine, George C Scott, Rex Harrison, David Hemmings, Charlton Heston, Harry Andrews, Murray Melvin, Sybil Danning.

● Produced under the same flag of convenience as the Salkinds had employed for their earlier pair of Dick Lester *Three Musketeers* films, this hid its status as a redundant remake (of a Warners/Errol Flynn romp of 1937, which cast genuine twins in the double-lead role) under the title *Crossed Swords* in America. Fleischer's anonymous direction and Mark Lester's lack of range (as the urchin/prince lookalikes) throw the weight of Mark Twain's cross-cut yarn of confused identities onto a series of lumbering star cameos (Heston as Henry VIII, Scott as a Cockney villain, etc). Princely sets, but a debilitating poverty of wit and imagination. PT

Prince and the Showgirl, The

(1957, GB, 117 min)
d/p Laurence Olivier. *sc* Terence Rattigan. *ph* Jack Cardiff. *ed* Jack Harris. *pd* Roger Furse. *m* Richard Addinsell. *cast* Laurence Olivier, Marilyn Monroe, Sybil Thorndike, Richard Wattis, Jeremy Spenser, Jean Kent, Esmond Knight, Maxine Audley.

● Flimsy Ruritanian whimsy adapted from Terence Rattigan's damp coronation year divertissement, *The Sleeping Prince*. A rather condescending vehicle for Monroe, who had demonstrated astonishing range and skill the previous year in *Bus Stop*, with Olivier's leaden direction constantly conveying the impression that real actors are graciously propping up the pretty novice. Few sparks fly, but Olivier's Teutonically humourless Regent of Carpathia – in Britain for the 1911 coronation of George V – is nicely played off against Marilyn's innocently saucy showgirl. TM

Prince of Darkness

(1987, US, 101 min)
d John Carpenter. *p* Larry Franco. *sc* John Carpenter. *ph* Gary B Kibbe. *ed* Steve Mirkovich. *pd* Dan Lomino. *m* John Carpenter, Alan Howarth. *cast* Donald Pleasence, Jameson Parker, Victor Wong, Lisa Blount, Dennis Dun, Susan Blanchard, Anne Howard.

● Carpenter's first low-budget horror pic for some time. Summoned to an abandoned church by a frightened priest (Pleasence), Prof Birack (Wong) finds a basement shrine dominated by a canister of green fluid. A manuscript reveals the existence of the Secret Brotherhood of Sleep, worshippers of Satan, who was entombed in the canister by his father, the evil anti-God, millions of years ago. Birack is sceptical until jets of liquid from the canister transform some of his team into malevolent zombies. Meanwhile, the embryonic Satan is struggling to release himself, and his father's power has begun to manifest itself. Refracting the traditional conflict of Good and Evil through quantum mechanics and sub-atomic physics, the sometimes talky script remains engrossing thanks to Carpenter's chilling atmospherics. The claustrophobic terror generated by fluid camerawork and striking angles is reinforced by a narrative which builds slowly but surely towards a heart-racing climax. NF

Prince of Egypt, The

(1998, US, 99 min)
d Brenda Chapman, Simon Wells, Steve Hickner. *p* Penney Finkelman Cox, Sandra Rabins. *sc* Philip Lazebnik. *ed* Nick Fletcher. *pd* Darek Gogol. *m* Hans Zimmer. *cast* voices: Val Kilmer, Ralph Fiennes, Michelle Pfeiffer, Sandra Bullock, Jeff Goldblum, Helen Mirren, Steve Martin.

● DreamWorks' animated version of the story of Moses sticks to the Bible and eschews the Disney tradition of having a cute comic sidekick on board. The film is visually sumptuous, but scenes like the chariot race, or even the parting of the Red Sea, look no more impressive than the David Lean-style action in Disney's *Mulan*. Nor is it a comforting film for the very young – the 'death of the first born' plague is especially harrowing, albeit stunningly realised – and kids may even find God's use of violence to defeat the Egyptians excessive. But as epic, emotionally satisfying spectacle, it's way up there with the very best in mainstream animation. It's a pity that some of the more wondrous moments are spoiled by mundane songs. DA

Prince of Foxes

(1949, US, 107 min, b/w)
d Henry King. *p* Sol C Siegel. *sc* Milton Krims. *ph* Leon Shamroy. *ed* Barbara McLean. *ad* Lyle Wheeler, Mark-Lee Kirk. *m* Alfred Newman. *cast* Tyrone Power, Wanda Hendrix, Orson Welles, Everett Sloane, Felix Aylmer, Marina Berti, Katina Paxinou.

● In one of his enforced breaks from filming *Othello*, Welles contributed a bold outline sketch for Cesare Borgia to this strikingly handsome historical drama, filmed in Italy on actual locations wherever possible. Alas, his is virtually a cameo performance, and the plot focuses less happily on Power as a soldier of fortune, determined to bury his peasant origins, who agrees to serve as Cesare's ruthless hatchet man. Much of the film is given over to his drearily prolonged crisis of conscience, resolved when he is taught a lesson in selfless humanity by the elderly duke (Aylmer) whose domain he is committed to destroy and whose young wife (Hendrix) he is busily seducing. It nevertheless remains visually splendid throughout; there's a fascinatingly detailed siege sequence (courtesy of Leonardo Da Vinci); and Everett Sloane chips in with a lively display of roguishly amoral villainy. TM

Prince of Homburg, The (Il Principe di Homburg)

(1996, It, 89 min)
d Marco Bellocchio. *p* Piergiorgio Bellocchio. *sc* Marco Bellocchio. *ph* Giuseppe Lanci. *ed* Francesca Calvelli. *pd* Giantito Burchiellaro. *m* Carlo Crivelli. *cast* Andrea Di Stefano, Barbora Bobulova, Toni Bertorelli, Anita Laurenzi.
●A staid, uninvolving adaptation of Kleist's story about a high-born cavalry general (Di Stefano) who faces execution after disobeying orders and leading a charge that results in victory. As the film proceeds to examine his crisis of faith, it confronts questions of honour, courage, heroism and responsibility with clarity but little dramatic force. It's a slow, elegant, lifeless costume drama, and its stylistic conservatism only adds to its aura of redundancy. GA

Prince of Jutland

(1994, Fr/GB/Den/Neth/Ger, 100 min)
d Gabriel Axel. *p* Kees Kasander, Denis Wigman, Sylvaine Sainderichin, Terry Glinwood. *sc* Gabriel Axel, Erik Kjersgard. *ph* Henning Kristiansen. *ed* Jean-François Naudon. *pd* Sven Wichman. *m* Per Norgaard. *cast* Gabriel Byrne, Helen Mirren, Christian Bale, Tom Wilkinson, Brian Cox, Freddie Jones.
●A major disappointment after the delightful *Babette's Feast*, Axel's version of the Hamlet story (in English) is taken not from Shakespeare but an earlier source. Bale is the prince who goes literally barking mad (or does he?) after witnessing the murder of the king his father (Wilkinson). By the time we reach the scene in which the murderer (Byrne) 'consoles' the coveted queen (Mirren), the stilted script, half-hearted acting and overall poverty (financial and imaginative) raise the question: Is it some sort of parody? Indeed the later skirmishes are so small and scrappy they look not unlike the Pythons' glorious sketch of famous battles staged by the Batley Townswomen's Guild. GA

Prince of Pennsylvania, The

(1988, US, 93 min)
d Ron Nyswaner. *p* Joan Fishman. *sc* Ron Nyswaner. *ph* Frank Prinzi. *ed* William Scharf. *pd* Toby Corbett. *m* Thomas Newman. *cast* Fred Ward, Keanu Reeves, Bonnie Bedelia, Amy Madigan, Jeff Hayenga, Tracey Ellis.
●The problem with small town movies is that story and characters can seem as inconsequential as the place itself. Nyswaner's episodic script counters this by playing up the idiosyncrasies of his horizontally mobile mining family, presided over by domineering patriarch Ward. Oppressed by Ward's narrow pursuit of the American Dream, his wife (Bedelia) turns to obsessive consumerism and clandestine nookie with Ward's best pal, while his eldest son (Reeves) indulges in Heath Robinson inventions and unrequited love for the world-weary ex-hippy owner of a rundown ice-cream joint (Madigan). Determined to avoid a life of quiet desperation, Reeves hatches a bizarre plot to kidnap his own father and split the ransom (a jealously-guarded family nest-egg) with his mother. The quirky charm soon wears thin as the shrewd observations of small town frustration give way to a more strained oddball humour. By the time Reeves dons a Freddy Krueger mask to abduct his father, one feels the desperation has begun to affect the film itself. NF

Prince of the City

(1981, US, 167 min)
d Sidney Lumet. *p* Burtt Harris. *sc* Jay Presson Allen, Sidney Lumet. *ph* Andrzej Bartkowiak. *ed* John J Fitzstephens. *pd* Tony Walton. *m* Paul Chihara. *cast* Treat Williams, Jerry Orbach, Richard Foronjy, Don Billett, Kenny Marino, Carmine Caridi, Tony Page, Lindsay Crouse, Bob Balaban, James Tolkan.
●Dealing with drugs, cops and corruption, this is *Serpico* all over again, but revised, enlarged and immeasurably improved. All moral certainties have gone, leaving instead a can of worms where questions of friendship, loyalty and honesty are redefined in the ambiguous light of corruption as a NY police officer (Williams), inspired by an indefinable mixture of reformist zeal, guilty self-loathing, and sheer delight in the opportunity for headline exploits, turns informer on behalf of the DA's commission of enquiry. An astonishing in-depth portrait of the interlocking worlds of police and hoodlum results, with no punches pulled and no easy solutions. Lumet isn't noted as the most cinematic of directors; but here the intricate mosaic structure he developed in *Dog Day Afternoon* generates a dynamism entirely its own, with the invisible *mise en scène* guaranteed by the galvanising interplay of New York locations and a brilliant ensemble cast. TM

Prince of Tides, The

(1991, US, 132 min)
d Barbra Streisand. *p* Andy Karsch, Barbra Streisand. *sc* Becky Johnston, Pat Conroy. *ph* Stephen Goldblatt. *ed* Don Zimmerman. *pd* Paul Sylbert. *m* James Newton Howard. *cast* Nick Nolte, Barbra Streisand, Blythe Danner, Kate Nelligan, Jeroen Krabbé, Melinda Dillon, George Carlin, Jason Gould, Brad Sullivan.
●Pat Conroy's novel of tears, treacle and trauma cries out for the Sirk treatment, but gets, thanks to Streisand, the sort of over-the-top endorsement Joan Crawford brought to *Mildred Pierce*. South Carolina football coach Tom Wingo (Nolte) is called to New York by his suicidal sister's shrink, Dr Lowenstein (Streisand), to help unearth the childhood trauma. He's been bent out of shape by it, too, and can't get in touch with his love centres. During psychoanalytical sessions, his trauma surfaces in flashbacks. These are yeasty indeed. We glimpse Tom, his sister and brother underwater, where they congregate to avoid their parents. Dad (Sullivan) could give Freddy Kreuger a run for his money; Mom (Nelligan, brilliant) plays all emotional ends against the middle; but the capper comes when a pack of slavering convicts descends upon the household. Better at last, Tom makes it with Lowenstein, who seems to get a costume change in every frame. They do make 'em like it any more. BC

Princes, Les (The Princes)

(1982, Fr, 100 min)
d Tony Gatlif. *p* Ken Legargeant, Romaine Legargeant. *sc* Tony Gatlif. *ph* Jacques Loiseleux. *ed* Claudine Bouché. *ad* Denis Champenois. *m* Tony Gatlif. *cast* Gérard Darmon, Muse Dalbray, Dominique Maurin, Hagop Arslanian, Tony Gatlif, Tony Librizzi, Céline Militon.
●Inhabiting a squalid slum, along with his obstinate old mother and his daughter, Nara (Darmon) has problems. He is forever threatened with eviction; his job, to say the least, is less than secure; and he is the constant victim of contempt and prejudice emanating from 'respectable' society, whose guardians are the surly gendarmes. For Nara is a gypsy, and as such is automatically relegated to the lower echelons of French society. Gatlif's episodic study of the *gitanes* of modern France carries plentiful conviction, thanks no doubt to the fact that the director is himself of Romany stock. The grim options afforded his nomadic heroes are depicted with grainy realism (Jacques Loiseleux's muted, sombre photography providing countless evocative images of a France rarely shown on film), and Gatlif rarely sentimentalises: the gypsies' macho, patriarchal culture is viewed critically, while moments of humour alleviate the film's downbeat thrust. GA

Princesa

(2001, GB/Fr/Ger/It/Sp, 93 min)
d Henrique Goldman. *p* Rebecca O'Brien. *sc* Ellis Freeman, Henrique Goldman. *ph* Guillermo Escalon. *ed* Kerry Kohler. *pd* Andrea Melo. *m* Giovanni Venosta. *cast* Ingrid de Souza, Cesare Bocci, Lulu Pecorari, Mauro Pirovano, Biba Lerhue, Sonia Morgan, Alessandra Acciai.
●From Ken Loach's regular producers at Parallax Pictures, this is a highly effective amalgam of gritty social document and emotive melodrama. Set among Brazilian transvestite prostitutes working the streets of Milan, it follows newcomer de Souza as her dreams of family life edge closer when (s)he begins a relationship with a married Italian businessman. Ultimately, though happiness may be built upon securing a sense of sexual identity. Is a full sex-change operation the answer? Filled with raucous humour and memorable non-professional performers, Goldman's film shows a powerfully moving humanity by revealing universal dilemmas in the seediest of surroundings. TJ

Prince – Sign o' the Times

(1987, US, 85 min)
d Prince. *p* Robert Cavallo, Joseph Rufallo, Steven Fargnoli. *ph* Peter Sinclair. *ed* Steve Purcell. *pd* Leroy Bennett. *m* Prince. *cast* Prince, Cat, Sheila E, Sheena Easton.
●Shot in Rotterdam and the Paisley Park Studios in Minnesota, this is the film of Prince's 1987 tour. It also includes the promo video for the single 'U Got The Look', featuring Sheena Easton, who is obviously a trouper but a loser in the raw sex/pure energy stakes to Cat, Prince's co-star in the sexual slapstick routines that constitute a good part of the film's visual appeal. Musically, it's a matter of opinion, but from the sparse funk of the title tune to the bebop blow-out around Charlie Parker's *Now's the Time*, this guiltless grooving in Eden fizzes with brilliantly choreographed wit and invention. MC

Prince Valiant (Prinz Eisenherz)

(1997, Ger/GB/Ire/US, 91 min)
d Anthony Hickox. *p* Carsten HW Lorenz. *sc* Michael Beckner, Anthony Hickox, Carsten HW Lorenz. *ph* Roger Lanser. *ed* Martin Hunter. *pd* Crispian Sallis. *m* David Bergeaud. *cast* Stephen Moyer, Katherine Heigl, Thomas Kretschmann, Edward Fox, Udo Kier, Joanna Lumley, Ron Perlman, Anthony Hickox.
●The Camelot squire Segue (Moyer) jousts in the armour of Sir Gawain (Hickox) in defence of his fallen master's reputation: watching the display is King Arthur (Fox) and his charge, slender Princess Ilene of Wales (Heigl). Bu then villains escape with Excalibur. Blaming the Scots, Arthur dispatches his lieutenants to do battle, and entrusts Segue with Ilene's safe passage home. The real culprits, however, are the Barbarians of Thule, in league with exiled Morgan Le Fey (Lumley), who's hell-bent on world domination. Directed by horror specialist Hickox with his customary visual panache – the opening is a marvel of heady whip pans, close-ups and jump cuts – this is a very contemporary, '90s timepiece. Characters and language are given a modern, revisionist sheen. Sources are sported like a coat of arms, from the story's origins (comic-strip frames interrupt/develop the narrative), to a Pythonesque pseudo-*Jabberwocky* and a *Lancelot du Lac*-like focus on detail. That said, this is hardly junior Bresson. Very silly towards the end. NB

Princess, The (Adj Király Katonát!)

(1982, Hun, 113 min, b/w)
d/p Pál Erdöss. *sc* Istvan Kardos. *ph* Ferenc Pap, Lajos Koltai, Gabor Szabo. *ed* Klara Majoros. *pd* Andras Gyurki. *cast* Erika Ozsda, Andrea Szendrei, Dénes Diczházi, Arpád Tóth.
●Fresh from school, 15-year-old Jutka and several friends leave rural Hungary for what they hope will be a better life in Budapest. But alongside the joys of boys, coffee-bars, concerts and a little money, they also discover a harsh adult world of betrayal, violence and endless compromise. With its catalogue of disasters that turn the girls' dreams into nightmares, *The Princess* might seem like a resolutely pessimistic foray into *vérité*-style naturalism; the overwhelming final impression, however, is of its characters' ability to survive against all odds. Central to the movie's faith in humanity is Erika Ozsda's glowing performance as Jutka, as she slowly but steadily is transformed from surly orphan to responsible, worldly-wise young woman. For once the realist style illuminates rather than irritates. GA

Princess + the Warrior, The (Der Krieger und die Kaiserin)

(2000, Ger, 135 min)
d Tom Tykwer. *p* Stefan Arndt, Maria Köpf. *sc* Tom Tykwer. *ph* Frank Griebe. *ed* Mathilde Bonnefoy. *pd* Uli Hanisch. *m* (Pale 3) Tom

Tykwer, Johnny Klimek, Reinhold Heil. *cast* Franka Potente, Benno Fürmann, Joachim Król, Lars Rudolph, Melchior Besion, Ludger Pistor, Marita Breuer.

● Wuppertal, Germany. When Sissi (Potente), a psychiatric nurse, is run over by a tanker on her way to the bank, Bodo (Fürmann), ex-army, saves her life with an improvised tracheotomy – an act she believes will bind them together for ever. Thanks to a blind patient, tracking down her saviour proves easy; what's more difficult is persuading him to join in her obscure plans for their future. He slams the door in her face. His brother explains that Bodo is wedded to the past, still brooding over the day his wife perished in an explosion while he cheated Death sitting on the toilet. Tykwer's imaginative follow-up to *Run Lola Run* adopts the tone of a more contemplative, emotionally mature work – mostly in vain. Fine performances notwithstanding, this is a contrived-to-oblivion nonsense exercise in pretending that the notion of two outsiders having to save each other's lives before they can share each other's love is something more than deeply sentimental. The film's interest in psychiatry goes no further than the alienation effects afforded by a sterile clinic and the usefulness of its patients, while a lacklustre heist goes not so much wrong as nowhere. SS

Princess Bride, The

(1987, US, 98 min)
d Rob Reiner. *p* Andrew Scheinman, Rob Reiner. *sc* William Goldman. *ph* Adrian Biddle. *ed* Robert Leighton. *pd* Norman Garwood. *m* Mark Knopfler. *cast* Cary Elwes, Mandy Patinkin, Chris Sarandon, Christopher Guest, Wallace Shawn, Andre the Giant, Robin Wright, Peter Falk, Carol Kane, Peter Cook, Mel Smith.

● A fairytale as told to a bedridden boy: the willowy Buttercup (Wright), destined as consort to the wicked Prince Humperdinck (Sarandon), is abducted and whisked through a series of life-threatening exploits and miscast comic cameos. The story, adapted from William Goldman's book, is partly a traditional fantasy, with a damsel in distress, dashing lover, evil villains, and lotsa monsters and swordfights, but also a knowing commentary on the conventions of all such tales. The tone falls disconcertingly between straight action adventure and anachronistic Jewish spoof; the leads are vacuous; the absurdities sometimes forced and obvious. Only Guest's sadistic Count Rugen and Patinkin's vengeful Spanish swordsman inject any real enthusiasm into the proceedings; but the film does exude a certain innocent, unassertive charm, and kids will probably love it. GA

Princess Caraboo

(1994, US, 97 min)
d Michael Austin. *p* Simon Bosanquet, Andy Karsch. *sc* Michael Austin, John Wells. *ph* Freddie Francis. *ed* George Akers. *pd* Michael Howells. *m* Jupiter Sen. *cast* Phoebe Cates, Jim Broadbent, Wendy Hughes, Kevin Kline, John Lithgow, Stephen Rea, John Sessions, John Wells, Roger Lloyd Pack, Murray Melvin.

● Based on a true story, this decorative social satire relates the case of a beautiful vagabond picked up near Bristol in 1817, who claims to be Princess Caraboo, escaped from a slave ship. Roundly mocked as an impostor, she winds up in court, but her composure commands respect and a wealthy woman takes her in. While insecure Mrs Worrall (Hughes) detects true quality, her husband (Broadbent) is more sceptical, but once dreams of lucrative trade beckon, he's as ready as his wife to parade their enigmatic guest. Caraboo lives it up in Regency society, but the servants, convinced that 'one of them' is pulling a fast one, plot to unmask her. Phoebe Cates's intriguing Caraboo transcends all tests. Called on to convince an ethnographer, she flunks badly, but he leaves in tears, touched by her grace. An everyday story of social-climbing and neo-classicism, this is a winner. SFe

Princess Charming

(1934, GB, 78 min, b/w)
d Maurice Elvey. *p* Michael Balcon. *sc* L Dugarde Peach. *ph* Max Greene. *ad* Ernö Metzner. *m* Ray Noble. *cast* Evelyn Laye, Henry Wilcoxon, Yvonne Arnaud, Max Miller, George Grossmith, Finlay Currie, Ivor Barnard, Francis L Sullivan.

● As a princess escaping from revolutionaries, in disguise and married to the handsome captain of the guard (although already promised to a neighbouring ruler), Laye finds her singing brutally curtailed by a bunch of ersatz Bolsheviks and Max Miller's machine-gun humour. Elvey's direction is, to say the least, erratic; but the Gainsborough emphasis on speed and economy prevents the film from plunging into embarrassing longueurs. Continuity and plot plausibility become increasingly irrelevant as Miller indelicately tramples upon the conventions of Ruritanian musical romance, in the end galvanising the rest of the cast enough to transform the film into a gloriously funny pantomime. RMy

Princess Diaries, The

(2001, US, 115 min)
d Garry Marshall. *p* Whitney Houston, Debra Martin Chase, Mario Iscovich. *sc* Gina Wendkos. *ph* Karl Walter Lindenlaub. *ed* Bruce Green. *pd* Mayne Berke. *m* John Debney. *cast* Julie Andrews, Anne Hathaway, Heather Matarazzo, Hector Elizondo, Mandy Moore, Caroline Goodall, Robert Schwartzman, Erik von Detten, Sean O'Bryan.

● A passable 'make-over' movie from the director of *Pretty Woman*, this introduces Hathaway as a San Francisco schoolgirl shocked to hear that she's in line for the throne of Genovia. It's fast track Pygmalion time, as Queen Renaldi, her new royal grandmother (Andrews), sets about teaching deportment, etiquette and waving to commoners. But wasn't she happy enough sharing the wacky ex-fire station with her artist single mother in their balanced post-hippy paradise? And isn't the timing bad, now that her best pal's sweet-natured brother Michael (Schwartzman) has started making bashful eyes at her from beneath his Beatles mop? Marshall has described Hathaway as a 'combination of Audrey Hepburn, Judy Garland and Julia Roberts', alluding, presumably, to her somewhat erect elegance, singing ability and piano keyboard set of teeth. Notions of responsibility, surrogacy, rites of passage and the value of friendship are gone through, but the highlighting of modern tropes merely serves to emphasise the film's conventionality. WH

Princesse Tam Tam

(1935, Fr, 76 min, b/w)
d Edmond T Gréville. *sc* Pepito Abatino, Yves Mirande. *ph* Georges Benoît. *ed* Jean Feyte. *ad* Guy de Gastyne, Lazare Meerson. *m/songs* Jacques Dallin, Elixo Grenet, Walter Goehr, Al Romans. *cast* Josephine Baker, Albert Préjean, Robert Arnoux, Germaine Aussey, Viviane Romance, Jean Galland.

● Gréville had a cinematically adventurous side, but principally he was one of the most dedicated crumpeteers ever to direct even a French movie, and his horrible predicament here was to be assigned a spectacularly sexual leading lady who, because she was black, he was required to de-eroticise. Baker plays a Bedouin beggar taken up, rather as a pet, by wealthy novelist Préjean (a straight-looking Edward Everett Horton, of scant appeal today). He introduces her to the glamorous complications of Paris, she falls unrequitedly (well, of course) in love, ho-hum. From first shot (close-up of a slapped face) to last (a donkey munching a copy of *Civilisation*) Gréville keeps things on the boil, but still – a no-win situation from everybody's point of view. BBa

Princess Mononoke (Mononoke Hime)

(1997, Jap, 133 min)
d Hayao Miyazaki. *p* Toshio Suzuki. *sc* Hayao Miyazaki. *ph* Atsushi Okui. *m* Joe Hisaishi. *cast* voices: Yoji Matsuda, Yuriko Ishida, Akihiro Maruyama, Kaoru Kobayashi, Masahiko Nishimura, Tsunehiko Kamijyo.

● Miyazaki was already a culture hero in Japan when this animated mythic adventure raised him to a status approaching living national treasure. The young warrior Ashitaka is infected by poison while saving his village from a demonic giant boar; he rides his elk to the west (where the boar came from) in the hope of finding a cure. He stumbles into a three-way battle between a woman chieftain in a fortified encampment (built to protect the secret of smelting iron from ore), a clan of samurai eager to take control of the iron – and the creatures (chiefly wolves and boars) of the surrounding forest, enraged by all the human damage to their natural habitat. Fighting on the side of the animals is Mononoke, a girl raised by the wolves, who hates and distrusts all humans, including Ashitaka. The samurai are pretty unredeemed, but Miyazaki insists that there are things to be said for both the Iron Age settlers and the animals and their deities: rather than a *Lord of the Rings*-style showdown between good and evil, this argues for peaceful co-existence. Superbly imagined and visually sumptuous, it's let down only by Hisaishi's sub-Miklos Rosza score. (An uncut English language dub also exists, with dialogue by Neil Gaiman and a voice cast including Gillian Anderson, Billy Crudup, Claire Danes, Minnie Driver and Billy Bob Thornton.) TR

Principe di Homburg, Il

see Prince of Homburg, The

Princípio da Incerteza, O

see Uncertainty Principle, The

Prinz Eisenherz

see Prince Valiant

Priscilla Queen of the Desert

see Adventures of Priscilla Queen of the Desert, The

Prise de Pouvoir par Louis XIV, La (The Rise to Power of Louis XIV)

(1966, Fr, 102 min)
d Roberto Rossellini. *p* Pierre Gout. *sc* Philippe Erlanger. *ph* Georges LeClerc. *ed* Armand Ridel. *ad* Maurice Valay. *m* Betty Willemetz. *cast* Jean-Marie Patte, Raymond Jourdan, Silvagni, Katharina Renn, Dominique Vincent, Pierre Barrat.

● 'Power is shared by too many hands': the Sun King ponders problems of maintaining monarchic strength in the face of hungry peasants and conniving nobility. Rossellini displays the king's bizarre but effective methods of minimising the threat of insurgence: reserving every governmental decision for himself, assembling the aristocrats full-time at Versailles away from parliament, and forcing them into debt through emulation of his own extravagant tastes in fashion. Brilliantly marshalling performance, colour, dialogue, and above all claustrophobic space, Rossellini reveals the customs, atmosphere and ideology of Louis' reign with an unrivalled lucidity and honesty; at the same time he creates a new moral cinema of history. Draining his account of distracting dramatic artifice, he constructs a cinema of ideas, didactic without being propagandistic, cerebral but highly accessible. It's as inventive as Syberberg's tableaux, but endowed with infinitely greater clarity. GA

Prison

(1987, US, 103 min)
d Renny Harlin. *p* Irwin Yablans. *sc* C Courtney Joyner. *ph* Mac Ahlberg. *ed* Andy Horvitch. *pd* Philip Duffin. *m* Richard Band, Christopher L Stone. *cast* Viggo Mortensen, Chelsea Field, Lane Smith, Lincoln Kilpatrick, Tom Everett, Ivan Kane, Andre De Shields.

● Way out in the Wyoming wastes, a rotting concrete hell-hole, once Creedmore Penitentiary, condemned these 20 years, is re-commissioned to ease overcrowding. In charge is illiberal Warden Sharpe (Smith), one-time Creedmore guard with a guilty secret: back then an innocent man was given a 60,000 volt goodbye in the execution chamber, and Sharpe kept stumm. Unluckily for Sharpe, the victim's spirit decided to hang around to exact gruesome revenge. With an assured visual style, Harlin stokes up the temperature to near-riot conditions before exploding the screen with electrifying special effects mayhem – floors glow red hot, barbed wire is vivified, the very pipes take on murderous life. The staple array of cons and screws are interestingly characterised, and the woman-reformer-to-the-rescue plot is neatly integrated with the supernatural effects. A tough, entertaining, intelligent hybrid of hard-ass prison drama and horror-shocker exploiter from Charles Band's Empire Pictures. WH

Prisoner, The

(1955, GB, 91 min, b/w)
d Peter Glenville. *p* Vivian A Cox. *sc* Bridget Boland. *ph* Reginald Wyer. *ed* Frederick Wilson. *ad* John Hawkesworth. *m* Benjamin Frankel. *cast* Alec Guinness, Jack Hawkins, Raymond Huntley, Wilfrid Lawson, Jeannette Sterke, Ronald Lewis, Kenneth Griffith.

● Bridget Boland's play has been opened out slightly to emphasise a context of social unrest in an unspecified totalitarian (Eastern bloc?) state, but as with other works about inquisition, the suspect's ordeal becomes the audience's. Glenville stands back from time to time so that we can really appreciate the performances of Guinness, as a Cardinal subjected to torture for his beliefs, and Hawkins as his inquisitor; but in boxing parlance, he might have broken up more of the clinches. TCh

Prisoner of Rio

(1988, Braz, 105 min)
d Lech Majewski. *p* Juliusz Kossakaowski, Mark Slater. *sc* Lech J Majewski, Ronald Biggs, Julia Frankel. *ph* George Morradian. *ed* Darren Kloomok. *ad* Oscar Ramos. *m* Luiz Bonfa. *cast* Steven Berkoff, Paul Freeman, Peter Firth, Florinda Bolkan, José Wilker, Zezé Mota, Desmond Llewelyn.

● The fact that Ronnie Biggs co-wrote this fiasco (filmed in English) may explain the portrait of the Great Train Robber as a sharp-witted charmer, his sole real concern in life his son. The story recounts the less-than-legal efforts of cop Berkoff (macho, variable accent) to bring Biggs (Freeman, larger-than-life Londoner) back to Blighty and prison. The intrigue is messily and murkily conceived, involving undercover agents, swarthy thugs, shady fixers, and much predictable ado about Carnival. Majewski renders entire scenes devoid of dramatic point or meaning by the sort of editing that makes you wonder what's happening, why, and where; the pacing is listless, the camera invariably wrongly placed, the whole stitched with leering shots of skimpily clad revellers and travelogue padding. Risible throughout. GA

Prisoner of Second Avenue, The

(1975, US, 105 min)
d/p Melvin Frank. *sc* Neil Simon. *ph* Philip H Lathrop. *ed* Robert Wyman. *ad* Preston Ames. *m* Marvin Hamlisch. *cast* Jack Lemmon, Anne Bancroft, Gene Saks, Elizabeth Wilson, Florence Stanley, Maxine Stuart, Ed Peck, Sylvester Stallone.

● A promising opening, with Lemmon pitting his nervous energy against a New York heat wave. But a glance at the credits gives rise to a stifling feeling of over-familiarity: director from *A Touch of Class*, author (Neil Simon) of numerous well-oiled Broadway hits, guest actor (Saks) better known for directing film versions of those hits. It all adds up to one of those wisecracking comedies that move smoothly and predictably through set pieces dwelling on the frustrations of urban life and the toll exacted on Lemmon and Bancroft's middle class marriage. At least it confirms Anne Bancroft's latent talent for comedy, but otherwise there's little more than routine jokes like the day in the country, the relations, the buckets of water, the burglary, the TV dinners, and the glib touches of sentimentality that warn you the ending's coming up. CPe

Prisoner of Shark Island, The

(1936, US, 95 min, b/w)
d John Ford. *p* Darryl F Zanuck. *sc* Nunnally Johnson. *ph* Bert Glennon. *ed* Jack Murray. *ad* William Darling. *m* Louis Silvers. *cast* Warner Baxter, Gloria Stuart, Joyce Kay, Claude Gillingwater, Harry Carey, Paul Fix, John Carradine.

● One of Ford's least dated films from the '30s, even though its attitude towards the blacks it portrays is (understandably, given the times) undeniably racist. Inspired by historical reality, it begins with the assassination of the director's beloved, almost Godlike Lincoln by John Wilkes Booth, before proceeding to focus on the harsh fate dealt by destiny and an unforgiving America to Dr Samuel A Mudd, imprisoned for treating Booth's wounded leg. If the quasi-liberal message is undermined not only by a nostalgia for the Old (ie slave-owning) South but also by the over-emphatic assertions of Mudd's innocence, the film is nevertheless for the most part tautly scripted (by Dudley Nichols), vividly shot, and blessed with muscular performances. Baxter excels himself as the good doctor whose selfless integrity finally ensures his pardon, while Carradine's sadistic prison guard is terrific. GA

Prisoner of the Cannibal God

see Montagna del Dio Cannibale, La

Prisoner of the Mountains (Kavkazski Plennik)

(1996, Kazakhstan/Rus, 99 min)
d Sergei Bodrov. *p* Boris Giller, Sergei Bodrov. *sc* Arif Aliev, Sergei Bodrov, Boris Giller. *ph* Pavel Lebeshev. *ed* Olga Grinshun, Vera Kruglova, Alan Baril. *pd* Valerii Kostrin. *m* Leonid Desiatnikov. *cast* Oleg Menshikov, Sergei Bodrov Jr, Djemal Sikharulidze, Susanna Mekhralieva, Alexei Zharkov, Valentina Fedotova.

● Two Russian soldiers (one experienced, one a rookie) are ambushed and taken hostage by a Chechen village chieftain who intends to trade them for his son, imprisoned by the Russian authorities. That's about it in terms of plot, with the two soldiers falling out and getting to know each other, trying to work out a means of escape, and coming to some sort of uneasy, suspicious understanding of their captors. Bodrov's clear-eyed, unsentimental, but engrossing film is impressive for many reasons: its genuinely unromanticised sympathy for the Chechens, its awareness of the absurd futility of war, its insistence that despite cultural differences we share a common humanity, the use of landscape, and the marvellous performances (with the director's son terrific as the novice Russian). GA

Prisoner of Zenda, The

(1937, US, 101 min, b/w)
d John Cromwell. *p* David D Selznick. *sc* John L Balderston, Wells Root. *ph* James Wong Howe. *ed* James E Newton. *ad* Lyle Wheeler. *m* Alfred Newman. *cast* Ronald Colman, Madeleine Carroll, Douglas Fairbanks Jr, Raymond Massey, Mary Astor, C Aubrey Smith, David Niven, Montagu Love.

● Easily the best version of Anthony Hope's perennial Ruritanian adventure, often cited as one of the great swashbucklers. It's certainly impeccably cast, with Colman at his dashingly romantic best doubling as the King and the English lookalike who helps to save his throne, while Fairbanks revels in Rupert of Hentzau's charming villainy, Carroll provides a sweetly melting princess, and Massey is iconographically perfect as Black Michael the usurper. Lots of pomp and splendour (especially in the over-indulged Coronation sequence) make Cromwell's elegant direction incline to stateliness, but the swordplay is ripping and Wong Howe's camerawork superb. TM

Prisoner of Zenda, The

(1952, US, 100 min)
d Richard Thorpe. *p* Pandro S Berman. *sc* John L Balderston, Noel Langley. *ph* Joseph Ruttenberg. *ed* George Boemler. *ad* Cedric Gibbons, Hans Peters. *m* Alfred Newman. *cast* Stewart Granger, Deborah Kerr, James Mason, Louis Calhern, Jane Greer, Lewis Stone, Robert Douglas, Robert Coote.

● Lush but rather leaden remake of Anthony Hope's Ruritanian romance, establishing some sort of continuity by casting Lewis Stone, star of the 1922 version, in a supporting role as the Cardinal. Entertaining enough, though Granger is merely competent by comparison with Colman in the 1937 version, and Thorpe hasn't a tenth of Cromwell's style. Mason, though basically miscast, runs away with the acting honours as a Teutonically villainous Rupert of Hentzau, and Joseph Ruttenberg contributes some attractive Technicolor camerawork.

Prisoner of Zenda, The

(1979, US, 108 min)
d Richard Quine. *p* Walter Mirisch. *sc* Dick Clement, Ian La Frenais. *ph* Arthur Ibbetson. *ed* Byron "Buzz" Brandt. *pd* John J Lloyd. *m* Henry Mancini. *cast* Peter Sellers, Lynne Frederick, Lionel Jeffries, Elke Sommer, Gregory Sierra, Jeremy Kemp, Catherine Schell, Norman Rossington, John Laurie.

● A limp and shoddy farce in which neither Sellers' lifeless double-role mugging, nor a dire fish-out-of-water script by Dick Clement and Ian La Frenais, encourage anything more than a deepening nostalgia for the straightfaced swashbuckling of previous adaptations of Anthony Hope's novel. Here the intrigues of Ruritanian royalty are conveyed with all the comic panache of an overlong Christmas variety show sketch on TV. PT

Prison Girls

(1973, US, 94 min)
d Thomas de Simone. *p* Nicholas J Grippo, Burton C Gershfield. *sc* Lee Walters. *ph* Gerhard Hentschel. *ed* Paul Young. *ad* Robinson Royce. *m* Christopher Huston. *cast* Robin Whitting, Angie Monet, Tracy Handfuss, Maria Arrold, Liz Wolfe.

● Various girls undergo sexual rehabilitation during a two-day parole from prison (a plot is hastily added at the very end: the authorities have let the girls out in the hope that one of them will lead the police to a notorious hoodlum). Thanks to the censor, the episodes range in quality from the pretty dire to the abysmal. An Angels' gang-bang survives more or less intact, while a sequence involving a woman being brought to climax for the first time is cut almost into non-existence. Two points of interest: no one makes it as far as a bed (sofas and floors draw at two apiece); and although characters drag hard on the occasional joint, no one thinks of actually lighting it.

Prison Stories: Women on the Inside

(1990, US, 90 min)
d Donna Deitch, Joan Micklin Silver, Penelope Spheeris. *p* Gerald T Olson. *sc* Martin Jones, Jule Selbo, Dick Beebe, Marlane Meyer. *ph* Robert Elswit, Jamie Thompson. *ed* Virginia Katz, Earl Watson, Janice Hampton. *pd* J Rae Fox. *m* J Peter Robinson, Stanley Clarke, Jack Hues. *cast* Rae Dawn Chong, Lolita Davidovich, Annabella Sciorra, Talisa Soto, Rachel Ticotin, Silvana Gallardo, Grace Zabriskie, Francesca Roberts.

● Made for cable, this three-part film by women, about women in prison and its effect upon their families, is less convincing than the average TV documentary. Outwardly swaggering but inwardly crushed, the subjects gradually progress towards rehabilitation and remorse to save their children. Prison authorities come across as tough but fair, with the exception of the members of Silver's 'Parole Board' – easily the best of the trio – who have trouble understanding that a pregnant battered wife who sees her daughter attacked might resort to firearms. BC

Private Affairs of Bel Ami, The

(1946, US, 112 min, b/w)
d Albert Lewin. *p* Ray Heinz. *sc* Albert Lewin. *ph* Russell Metty. *ed* Albrecht Joseph. *ad* F Paul Sylos. *m* Darius Milhaud. *cast* George Sanders, Angela Lansbury, Ann Dvorak, Frances Dee, Albert Basserman, Hugo Haas, Katherine Emery, Warren William, John Carradine.

● A lovingly literate adaptation of Guy de Maupassant's novella about a soldier (Sanders) returning from the wars without prospects, persuaded to capitalise on the good looks that seem irresistible to women, and finding it difficult to get off the roundabout even when he falls genuinely in love (with the wonderful Lansbury). Set in a stylish evocation of 19th century Paris partly based on contemporary paintings, and partly (like the London of *The Picture of Dorian Gray*) a vivid product of the imagination, the film fascinatingly refuses to stigmatise its hero as he becomes increasingly and tragically mired. If there is a villain, it is a society so dependent on the appearances of success that everyone in it is encouraged to adopt a facade to reap their just rewards. In a series of elliptical asides that combine into a wry comment on the non-status of the career woman at that time, Lewin even contrives to suggest that the widow of a distinguished journalist who helps Sanders on his way to success not only secretly writes his copy, but had done the same for her husband for years. A sadly neglected film. TM

Private Benjamin

(1980, US, 110 min)
d Howard Zieff. *p/sc* Nancy Meyers, Charles Shyer, Harvey Miller. *ph* David M Walsh. *ed* Sheldon Kahn. *pd* Robert Boyle. *m* Bill Conti. *cast* Goldie Hawn, Eileen Brennan, Armand Assante, Robert Webber, Sam Wanamaker, Barbara Barrie, Mary Kay Place, Harry Dean Stanton, Albert Brooks.

●Before he fell victim to the debilitating Hollywood law that demands comedy star vehicles be written by committee, Zieff showed in *Slither* and *Hollywood Cowboy* a real flair for enhancing off-the-wall fun material. But *Private Benjamin*, concocted by no less than three scribes from a collective semi-consciousness bounded by re-runs of *M*A*S*H* and *No Time for Sergeants*, lodges gracelessly alongside *House Calls* and *The Main Event* as an anonymous chore for its director. Another depressing example of the big-screen gag-string sitcom, it turns exclusively on a plot that grew from a concept that developed from an idea that somebody should never have had – Goldie Hawn joins the army. PT

Private Club (Club Privé pour Couples Avertis)

(1974, Fr, 90 min)
d/p Max Pécas. *sc* Max Pécas, Michel Vocoret. *ph* Robert Le Febvre. *ed* Max Pécas. *m* Derry Hall. *cast* Philippe Gasté, Eva Stroll, Patrick Lachaume, Chantal Arondel, Michel Vocoret.

●Sometimes funny, often inept story of a Parisian taxi-driver who goes over the top when he discovers that his fiancée works in an exclusive brothel (whose wares he nevertheless samples without scruple). Some characterisation seeps in at the edges, and there's even a twist to the plot, such as it is. But it of course turns out that the fiancée was being blackmailed, so a rather abrupt true-love ending wins out over the 'liberated' hedonism preached elsewhere in the film. It's notable mainly for the curious blessing given by implication to the audience in one scene: as the bushes fill up with snoopers trying to see what's going on with a trio on the back seat of a taxi, someone announces that such people are quite harmless, being there only to pay 'their respects to these lovely goddesses – it's a time-honoured ritual'. Which is one way of putting it.

Private Conversation, A (Bez Svidetelei)

(1983, USSR, 93 min)
d Nikita Mikhalov. *sc* Nikita Mikhalov, Sofia Prokofieva, Ramiz Fataliyev. *ph* Pavel Lebeshev. *ed* Elenora Praksina. *ad* Alexander Adabashian, Igor Makarov, Aleksander Samulekin. *m* Eduani Artemiev. *cast* Irina Kupchenko, Mikhail Ulyanov.

●An ex-husband unexpectedly returns to his former wife's flat. He is boozy and belligerent, elated with the success of his daughter's concert; she timid, dowdy and anxious about their son. Appearances are inevitably not what they seem, and an intricate power game commences to the ironic accompaniment of romantic schmaltz on the TV. Worth seeing for the acting alone, especially for Ulyanov as he exposes the pathetic justifications of a paranoid failure who knows he has gone off the rails. JE

Private Enterprise, A

(1974, GB, 78 min)
d/p Peter K Smith. *sc* Peter K Smith, Charles Rees. *ph* Ray Orton. *ed* Peter K Smith, Charles Rees. *ad* Matthew Knox, Charles Rees. *m* Ram Narayan. *cast* Salmaan Peer, Marc Zuber, Ramon Sinha, Yehye Saeed, Diana Quick, Subhash Luthra.

●A nicely quirky and human-scaled study of a young Birmingham Asian undergoing cultural dislocations as he tries to come to terms with trade union activity at work and the prospect of a prearranged marriage within his ethnic community. Smith's occasionally absurdist eye, and Peer's performance as the low-key hero determined to become an individual citizen rather than an immigration statistic, lift this low-budget first feature out of the problem pic rut. PT

Private Files of J Edgar Hoover, The

(1977, US, 112 min)
d/p/sc Larry Cohen. *ph* Paul Glickman. *ed* Chris Lebenzon. *pd* Cathy Davis. *m* Miklós Rozsa. *cast* Broderick Crawford, José Ferrer, Michael Parks, Ronee Blakley, Rip Torn, Celeste Holm, Michael Sacks, Dan Dailey, Raymond St Jacques, Howard da Silva, June Havoc, Lloyd Nolan, John Marley.

●Rattling compulsively along through myth and history like some factoid TV mini-series, but constantly informed by a radical intelligence and humour, Cohen's analytical biopic surprisingly resolves into a complex investigation of the forces of realpolitik and sexual politics which created an arch-villain/monster from a moralist boy-scout lawyer. The movie may have the look of tabloid sleaze, but it never trades in the simplistic put-down or facile political optimism. If the idea of Hoover as a tragic figure hardly squares with the '70s consensus, then the playing, especially of Broderick Crawford as Hoover, does much to shift the prejudice; while at the point where post-Watergate cinema would usually present us with a revelatory crusader, Rip Torn's uptight FBI agent (our narrator) peters out into confused impotence. Genre fans can take comfort, however, since some expectations are happily served… Dillinger dies again. PT

Private Function, A

(1984, GB, 94 min)
d Malcolm Mowbray. *p* Mark Shivas. *sc* Alan Bennett. *ph* Tony Pierce-Roberts. *ed* Barrie Vince. *pd* Stuart Walker. *m* John Du Prez. *cast* Michael Palin, Maggie Smith, Denholm Elliott, Richard Griffiths, Tony Haygarth, John Normington, Bill Paterson, Liz Smith, Alison Steadman.

●Set in a small Yorkshire town in 1947, this first feature scripted by Alan Bennett is a pig-movie, about the smells they make and the lengths to which people went to steal one in austerity Britain, when there really was an illicit trade in the animals. Onto this thin premise, Bennett and Mowbray layer a subplot of middle class social warfare as timid chiropodist Palin and his wife Maggie Smith, a Lady Macbeth of the aspidistras, try to scale the heights of Northern society by nicking a porker secretly earmarked for the town's celebration of the coming marriage of Princess Elizabeth. Too downbeat for farce, too whimsical to be an effective observation of the reality of ration-book Britain, the movie seems a mess, despite fine performances. RR

Private Hell 36

(1954, US, 81 min, b/w)
d Don Siegel. *p* Collier Young. *sc* Collier Young, Ida Lupino. *ph* Burnett Guffey. *ed* Stanford Tischler. *ad* Walter Keller. *m* Leith Stevens. *cast* Ida Lupino, Steve Cochran, Warren Duff, Dean Jagger, Dorothy Malone.

●Minor by Siegel standards, but still an admirably neat, tight B thriller from Lupino's Filmakers company (she also co-scripted), with Cochran and Duff as two LA cops who accidentally stumble on the loot during a robbery investigation, the latter reluctantly playing along with the former's impulsive decision to keep it for themselves. Familiar stuff, with conscience and comeuppance dogging their every move (the title refers to the trailer park where their guilty secret is stashed), but given a vivid edge by the characterisations (Cochran the likeable good-timer, Duff the dour family man) and the plausible motivations. A fellow cop is killed in the line of duty, and the latent resentment of men risking their lives for too little pay is given a turn of the screw because Duff now has a baby to provide for, and Cochran falls hard for a singer (Lupino) who loves him but asks for the moon. Siegel's direction (the opening sequence in particular, with an off-duty Cochran stumbling perilously in on a store robbery while on his way home, is a gem) is impeccable. TM

Private Lesson, The (Lezioni Private)

(1975, It, 93 min)
d Vittorio De Sisti. *p* Enzo Doria. *ph* Mario Masini. *ed* Angelo Curi. *ad* Gisella Longo. *m* Franco Micalizzi. *cast* Carroll Baker, Renzo Montagnani, Rosalina Cellamare, Leonora Fani, Emilio Lo Curcio, Leopoldo Trieste.

●Determined not to let personal feelings hamper her career, matronly music teacher Carroll Baker grits her teeth and submits to the unconventional demands of a teenage homosexual blackmailer. De Sisti opts for an over-familiar evocation of the '50s and a conventional loss-of-virginity sexploiter, hampered by the customary contrivances and caricatures of the genre. JPy

Private Lessons

(1980, US, 87 min)
d Alan Myerson. *p* R Ben Efraim. *sc* Dan Greenburg. *ph* Jan De Bont. *ed* Fred Chulack. *ad* Linda Pearl. *cast* Sylvia Kristel, Howard Hesseman, Eric Brown, Patrick Piccininni, Ed Begley Jr, Pamela Bryant.

●Anyone who enjoyed *Steelyard Blues* and waited patiently for Myerson's second big screen venture, might be tempted by this; but unless you're also a 15-year-old male virgin dreaming of being sexually initiated by your father's housekeeper, who just happens to be Sylvia Kristel, then forget it. This particular wet dream is wrapped in a vacuous blackmail plot (which enables the young hero to fantasise that he's fucked Sylvia to death, and her to reveal her heart of gold) and padded with lots of horrible Adult Oriented Rock (Clapton, Rod Stewart, etc). But Teen Oriented Voyeurism rules as the protagonist (Brown) stalks his prey (and her stand-in) armed with cameras, binoculars, and an overtly Oedipal mix of fear and desire. SJ

Private Life (Chastnaya Zhizn)

(1982, USSR, 104 min)
d Yuli Raizman. *sc* Anatoly Grebnyev, Yuli Raizman. *ph* Nikolai Olonovsky. *ed* Valeria Belova. *ad* Tatyana Lapshina. *cast* Mikhail Ulyanov, Iya Savvina, Irina Gubanova, Tatyana Dogileva, Aleksei Blokhin.

●About the spiritual desolation of a workaholic factory manager (Ulyanov) who finds himself retired early, and finds suddenly that he has no friends and can no longer talk to anyone in his family. The languorous pace and utter obviousness of every point encourages the mind to wander, and it ultimately runs for the cover of easy sentimentality. Hard to dislike, though, since its main quality is its burning sincerity. TR

Private Life, A

(1988, GB, 93 min)
d/p Francis Gerard. *sc* Andrew Davies. *ph* Nat Crosby. *ed* Robin Sales. *pd* Mark Wilby. *m* Trevor Jones. *cast* Bill Flynn, Jana Cilliers, Kevin Smith, Ian Roberts, Anthony Fridjhon, Joanna Weinberg.

●Based on the true story of Jack and Stella Dupont, who waged a 30-year fight against South African apartheid and its laws forbidding marriage across the colour bar. Gerard's film traces the couple's relationship from their first meeting, when policeman Jack wanders into the café where Stella (of mixed race background but untraced birth registration) works; after he leaves the force, the emphasis is on their efforts to maintain domestic harmony while contesting Stella's classification as coloured. The focus is almost exclusively on tension within the family rather than the broader context of confrontation, which produces an emotional force that is direct and uncluttered; but Jack's position as a solid, stable force is too literally conveyed, a fault due in part to the fact that Bill Flynn offers only modest support to Jana Cilliers' sensitive performance. Worthy and at times moving, but with a soppy and intrusive score. CM

Private Life of Henry VIII, The

(1933, GB, 96 min, b/w)
d Alexander Korda. *p* Alexander Korda, Ludovico Toeplitz. *sc* Arthur Wimperis, Lajos Biro. *ph* Georges Périnal, Osmond Borradaile. *ed* Harold Young. *ad* Vincent Korda. *m* Kurt Schroeder. *cast* Charles Laughton, Binnie Barnes, Robert Donat, Elsa Lanchester, Merle Oberon, Wendy Barrie, Everley Gregg, John Loder.

●'Am I a king or a breeding bull?' Laughton sulkily roars down the dinner table in what is probably the most commercially successful British film ever made. Throughout the film, he manages to hold in tension Henry's greedy enjoyment of the trappings of power and his weary loathing for a life where everything, especially his sexual performance, is a matter of public interest. Laughton's transformation from bullying womaniser to henpecked glutton is a masterly study of a man's decline into dotage, but it is still only the icing on the cake of an amazing exploration of the morbid doubts and fears underlying a seemingly virile masculinity. RMy

Private Life of Sherlock Holmes, The

(1970, GB, 125 min)
d/p Billy Wilder. *sc* Billy Wilder, IAL Diamond. *ph* Christopher Challis. *ed* Ernest Walter. *pd* Alexandre Trauner. *m* Miklós Rozsa. *cast* Robert Stephens, Colin Blakely, Irene Handl, Christopher Lee, Tamara Toumanova, Genevieve Page, Clive Revill, Catherine Lacey, Stanley Holloway.
●A wonderful, cruelly underrated film. Although there are some terrifically funny moments, and on one level the Wilder/Diamond conception of Conan Doyle's hero does tend to debunk the myth of the perfect sleuth (there are allusions to his misogyny and cocaine addiction), this alternative vision of Holmes sets up a stylish and totally appropriate story (concerning dwarfs, dead canaries, and the Loch Ness monster) as a context in which to explain the reason for Holmes' forsaking of his emotional life to become a thinking machine. Betrayal and lost love are the elements that catalyse this process, turning Holmes from a fallible romantic into a disillusioned cynic. With a stunning score by Miklós Rozsa, carefully modulated performances, lush location photography, and perfect sets by Trauner, it is Wilder's least embittered film and by far his most moving. GA

Private Lives of Elizabeth and Essex, The

(1939, US, 106 min)
d Michael Curtiz. *sc* Norman Reilly Raine, Aeneas MacKenzie. *ph* Sol Polito, W Howard Greene. *ed* Owen Marks. *ad* Anton F Grot. *m* Erich Wolfgang Korngold. *cast* Bette Davis, Errol Flynn, Olivia de Havilland, Donald Crisp, Vincent Price, Henry Daniell, Nanette Fabray, Alan Hale, Robert Warwick, Leo G Carroll.
●Not so much a swashbuckler as a costume romance, kept high-toned (not to say strangled) by its source in a Maxwell Anderson play. Dominated by historical inaccuracies and a tightly controlled performance from Davis as the waspish queen, all too conscious of her fading charms and her favourite Flynn's roguishly roving eye. Some spectacular pageantry too in what was, oddly enough, the only colour film in which Davis appeared until the '50s. TM

Private Parts

(1972, US, 87 min)
d Paul Bartel. *p* Gene Corman. *sc* Philip Kearney, Les Rendelstein. *ph* Andrew Davis. *ed* Morton Tubor. *pd* John Retsek. *m* Hugo Friedhofer. *cast* Ayn Ruymen, Lucille Benson, John Ventantonio, Laurie Main, Stanley Livingstone, Charles Woolf, Ann Gibbs.
●Bartel's first feature is a version of his perennial theme: caricatured straight middle class values brought up against caricatured sexual excesses. The heroine is a teenage runaway (straight out of a *Beach Party* movie) who takes refuge in a seedy San Francisco hotel populated with freaks, perverts, and nuts. The funniest of the latter is the guilty leather queen with a secret phallic shrine in his room; the most inventively conceived is the transvestite photographer who uses a hypo as a phallic substitute and has a thing about dirty bath-water. Bartel himself doesn't remember it too fondly, probably because the plot's demands sometimes get in the way of the humour, but it is in exceptionally poor taste, and the tone is quintessential Bartel. TR

Private Parts

(1997, US, 109 min)
d Betty Thomas. *p* Ivan Reitman. *sc* Len Blum, Michael Kalesniko. *ph* Walt Lloyd. *ed* Peter Teschner. *pd* Charles Rosen. *m* Van Dyke Parks. *cast* Howard Stern, Robin Quivers, Mary McCormack, Fred Norris, Michael Murphy.
●Given US 'shock jock' Howard Stern's most conspicuous qualities – the ultra-nerdy appearance, the unrepentant egotism, the arrested adolescent obsession with breast and penis size – you'd be forgiven for expecting this loose adaptation of his best-selling 'autobiography' to be embarrassing and annoying in equal measure. Nor do the opening scenes bode well. But once the film flashes back to trawl through his life and career – from staging salacious puppet shows for OAPs as a kid, through the endless battles with station bosses angered by his determination to say and do whatever he wants on-air, to his final vindication, in 1985, as America's top radio personality – it's hard to resist his rude, gleeful determination to rid himself of the taboos, predictability and tedium of conventional radio. Though Betty Thomas's movie tones down some of Stern's more troubling takes on sensitive issues and plays up his enduring relationship with his astonishingly supportive wife (McCormack), it still has more than enough outrageous moments to sustain hilarity until the end credits. No one could seriously take Stern for a people's hero – he's too crass, conceited and self-serving – but here at least, as a non-PC mirth-monger, he has what it takes, no shit. GA

Private Pleasures (I Lust och Nöd)

(1976, Swe, 96 min)
d Paul Gerber. *p* Göran Sjöstedt. *sc* Paul D Gerber. *ph* Lasse Björne, Jack Churchill, Paul D Gerver. *ed* Thomas Holewa. *m* Anders Henriksson. *cast* Elona Glenn, Ulf Brunnberg, Per-Axel Arosenius, Marie Ekorre, Caroline Christensen.
●This somewhat pretentious Swedish sex offering about a young woman's discovery of her 'duality' displays a lot of ostentatious camerawork and arty editing which will probably go unnoticed by most patrons. Essentially a rather stolid reworking of the *Emmanuelle* themes, the film nevertheless makes some effort with its psychological mystery plot and attention to detail. Occasional sequences deserve a place in a much better movie (a drowsy conversation in the bright sun, for instance), and Elona Glenn adds distinction. The rest scarcely lives up to its rather over-inflated estimation of its own 'significance'.

Private Popsicle (Sapiches)

(1982, Isr/WGer, 100 min)
d Boaz Davidson. *p* Menham Golan, Yoram Globus. *sc* Boaz Davidson. *ph* Adam Greenberg. *ad* Ariel Roshko. *m* Paul Fishman. *cast* Iftach Katzur, Zachi Noy, Jonathan Segal, Sonia Martin, Menache Warshawsky.
●Or, 'Carry On Up the Golan Heights'. The fourth episode in the seemingly inexhaustible spew of puerile sexual antics, scatological language, and inappropriately used '50s pop soundtrack, has the *Lemon Popsicle* trio called up for National Service. Amid tried, tested and worried-to-death clichés of the army training camp (including ignorant ranting sergeant, visiting dignitaries, and mistaken rank identities), Eckel, Meckel and Schmeckel descend beyond the limits of bad taste to literally end up covered in excreta. The plot is as fresh as an Italian's armpit, the dubbing was seemingly done by a blind deaf mute, and the jokes are as funny as bubonic plague. FL

Private Road

(1971, GB, 89 min)
d Barney Platts-Mills. *p* Andrew St John. *sc* Barney Platts-Mills. *ph* Adam Barker-Mill. *ed* Jonathan Gili. *pd* Andrew Sanders. *m* George Fenton, Michael Feast, David Dundas. *cast* Susan Penhaligon, Bruce Robinson, Michael Feast, George Fenton, Robert Brown, Kathleen Byron, Patricia Cutts.
●Platts-Mills' second feature steps up a class from working to middle, but remains as quietly and sympathetically observant as *Bronco Bullfrog*, though this time using professional actors and a bolder visual stylisation. Very much of its time in its account of a girl's attempt to escape the cosy suburbanism of her family in Esher – by way of an affair with a classless writer who introduces her to the dropout world – it remains as engagingly unclassifiable as *Bronco Bullfrog*. Well worth a look for its odd mixture of romanticism and scepticism about society's future. TM

Privates on Parade

(1982, GB, 113 min)
d Michael Blakemore. *p* Simon Relph. *sc* Peter Nichols. *ph* Ian Wilson. *ed* Jim Clark. *pd* Luciana Arrighi. *m* Denis King. *cast* John Cleese, Denis Quilley, Michael Elphick, Nicola Pagett, Bruce Payne, Joe Melia, David Bamber, Simon Jones, Patrick Pearson.
●An adaptation of Peter Nichols' play which continues the strange British love affair with National Service, the Far East, and tatty theatrical camp, rolling them all together in a thin excuse for a plot: a troupe of virgin soldiers trek around up-country Malaysia, doing Carmen Miranda impressions to audiences of blank-faced Gurkhas, and getting caught in the cross-fire between Communists, the locals, and their own sergeant's gun-running activities. A few laughs, a few tears; something palatable is being said about the state of the nation. Through it all strides Cleese, barking his familiar brand of pop-eyed, cheerful racism to cover the unmistakable air of a man fighting a losing battle. But it's all rather wan; the sensibilities remain stubbornly theatrical, and the English countryside resolutely refuses to stand in for the Malaysian jungle. CPea

Private's Progress

(1956, GB, 102 min, b/w)
d John Boulting. *p* Roy Boulting. *sc* Frank Harvey, John Boulting. *ph* Eric Cross. *ed* Anthony Harvey. *ad* Alan Harris. *m* John Addison. *cast* Ian Carmichael, Richard Attenborough, Dennis Price, Terry-Thomas, William Hartnell, Peter Jones, Victor Maddern, Jill Adams, Thorley Walters, Ian Bannen, John Le Mesurier, Kenneth Griffith, George Coulouris.
●A delightful Boulting Brothers comedy about a mild, innocent undergraduate (Carmichael) drafted into the army, falling in with a bunch of spivs, and being sent to Germany disguised as a Nazi to steal art treasures. The absurdly irreverent attitude towards everything – army routines, class snobbery, official protocol, and corruption – is the stuff of amiable, nostalgic farce rather than biting satire, but it's beautifully performed by a host of character actors and often very funny. GA

Private Vices & Public Virtues (Vizi Privati, Pubbliche Virtù)

(1976, It/Yugo, 104 min)
d Miklós Jancsó. *p* Monica Venturini, Giancarlo Marchetti. *sc* Giovanni Gagliardo. *ph* Tomislav Pinter. *ed* Roberto Perpignani. *ad* Zeljko Senecic. *m* Francesco De Masi. *cast* Lajos Balázsovits, Pamela Villoresi, Franco Branciaroli, Teresa Ann Savoy, Laura Betti.
●This continues Jancsó's attack on paternalist authority, but its dreamily languorous pace is about all it has in common with its predecessors. Filmed in Italy, it uses the Mayerling story as the basis for a political fable about an act of rebellion: a young prince refuses to bend to his father's will, by staying on his country estate and by debauching the sons and daughters of local landowners to create a scandal in the capital. Apart from the cruel but inevitable pay-off, that's really all that happens, but Jancsó elaborates it into an extraordinary multi-sexual erotic rhapsody, using dancers rather than actors to turn the pastoral drama into something like an Elizabethan masque. The sexual aspect manages to be completely forthright (it centres on the figure of a hermaphrodite) but not at all prurient; as if Freud's 'polymorphous perversity' were the ultimate weapon against patriarchal tyranny. TR

Privilege

(1967, GB, 103 min)
d Peter Watkins. *p* John Heyman. *sc* Norman Bogner. *ph* Peter Suschitsky. *ed* John Trumper. *ad* Bill Brodie. *m* Mike Leander. *cast* Paul Jones, Jean Shrimpton, Mark London, Max Bacon, Jeremy Child, William Job, James Cossins.
●There's no denying Watkins' ambition and intelligence in this satire of the rock world being used by the Establishment as a force for keeping the masses quiet in times of hardship and fascism; but much of the acting is poor, while the tone is frequently far too hysterical for its own good. That said, Johnny Speight's story, of an enormously successful pop idol (Jones) being manipulated by the government for their own devious purposes, did allow Watkins to make some pertinent points anticipating both the Festival of Light, and the way that rock culture has been absorbed and rendered harmless by the society it is supposed to be rebelling against. GA

Privilege

(1990, US, 103 min, b/w & col)
d Yvonne Rainer. *p* Yvonne Rainer, Kathryn Colbert. *sc* Yvonne Rainer. *ph* Marc Daniels. *cast* Alice Spivak, Novella Nelson, Blaire Baron.
● Rainer's meditative film on the menopause has a mock-documentary framework: 'Yvonne', a black American film-maker, conducts a series of interviews with middle-aged women. Intespersed are clips from hilarious black-and-white educational films with pompous male doctors. The camera also watches a computer screen, scrolling up provocative texts, messages from the real or the fictional documentary-maker. The menopause is rather left behind as we follow the story of Jenny, a white friend of the fictional Yvonne. Her experiences with a lesbian neighbour and two repellent local men serve to muddle the central issue. In the end the message seems simply to be that we often disparage people who are older or darker-skinned than us, and that men in general aren't very nice to women. SFe

Privileged

(1982, GB, 96 min)
d Michael Hoffman. *p* Rick Stevenson, Andy Paterson. *sc* Michael Hoffman, David Woollcombe, Rupert Walters. *ph* Fiona Cunningham Reid. *ed* Derek Goldman. *ad* Peter Schwabach. *m* Rachel Portman. *cast* Robert Woolley, Diana Katis, Hughie Grant, Victoria Studd, James Wilby.
● The story of the making of *Privileged* would make a good film: a group of Oxford students under the avuncular eye of John Schlesinger make a film. Instead, the students have opted for undergraduate melodrama, which rather tiresomely echoes Schlesinger's '60s-style narcissism. Edward (Woolley), who's generously endowed with arrogance, leads an attractive quartet of fellow-students through the travails of love, during rehearsals for a production of *The Duchess of Malfi* which acts as an arena and a mirror for their emotional ups and downs. Curiously, for a first film, this is well acted, well paced, and made with considerable style (perhaps too much, as punts float by lazily and all too familiarly), but the content is so light that it has all but blown away before the credits roll. LU

Prix de Beauté (Miss Europe)

(1930, Fr, 94 min, b/w)
d Augusto Genina. *sc* Augusto Genina, Bernard Zimmer, Alessandro De Stefani, René Clair. *ph* Rudolph Maté, Louis Née. *ed* Edmond T Gréville. *ad* Robert Gys. *m* Wolfgang Zeller, René Sylviano, Horace Shepherd. *cast* Louise Brooks (dubbed by Hélène Regelly), Georges Charlia, Jean Bradin, H Bandini, Alex Bernard.
● Forget the obscure Genina, this is a photographer's movie, from the fluid location shooting at the start to the strikingly lit finale of murder in a preview theatre. Most beguiling is the camera's love affair with the face of Louise Brooks, whose eyes retain their sparkle no matter how faded the print. She plays a typist whose progress from beauty queen to film star alienates her working class boyfriend, who kills her with his ignominiously tiny pistol. Although beset by a possessive lover, by showbiz exploiters and, in a remarkable funfair scene, by humanity generally, Brooks is so sheerly, dominatingly vivacious that oppression hardly seems an issue. The ending – Brooks dead in the stalls, her image alive on screen – will be more resonant now than in 1930. BBa

Prize of Arms, A

(1961, GB, 105 min, b/w)
d Cliff Owen. *p* George Maynard. *sc* Paul Ryder. *ph* Gilbert Taylor, Gerald Gibbs. *ed* John Jympson. *ad* Jim Morahan, Bernard Sarron, Fred Carter. *m* Robert Sharples. *cast* Stanley Baker, Tom Bell, Helmut Schmid, John Westbrook, John Phillips, Fulton MacKay, Patrick Magee, Geoffrey Palmer.
● Cashiered army officer Baker, dismissed from the service for black marketeering, teams with Tom Bell and Polish explosives expert Schmid to steal a military payroll bound for North Africa in this watchable selection of heist-goes-wrong plot manoeuvres. Atmospheric and authentic army camp-life photography by Gilbert Taylor; based on a story co-credited to Nicolas Roeg. TJ

Prize of Peril, The (Le Prix du Danger)

(1983, Fr/Yugo, 98 min)
d Yves Boisset. *p* Norbert Saada. *sc* Yves Boisset, Jean Curtelin. *ph* Pierre-William Glenn. *ed* Michelle David. *pd* Serge Douy. *m* Vladimir Cosma. *cast* Gérard Lanvin, Michel Piccoli, Marie-France Pisier, Bruno Cremer, Andréa Ferreol, Jean Rougerie.
● A desperately dumb variation on the thesis that all the world's a telly channel, life (and death) just another game show. Unemployment is rising, ratings are falling, when a TV executive comes up with a show that pits a solitary volunteer contestant against a team of armed hunters in a once-a-week chase across the city, filmed live up to and including the moment of death. The show wins Christians vs Lions popularity. Everyone is happy: the producer (Pisier, just bitching it in the absence of a scripted character), the presenter (Piccoli, in Daz-white suit and slipping hair-piece), and the advertisers. Until Lanvin, playing The Hero (remember heroes? they're supposed to win), makes his bid for the million-dollar prize and discovers (you don't say) the game is rigged. Plot weaknesses apart, there's something culturally unreal about this cheapie Paris production with second-rate stuntwork that tries to be (the dubbing doesn't help) mid-Atlantic or universal. MA

Prizzi's Honor

(1985, US, 129 min)
d John Huston. *p* John Foreman. *sc* Richard Condon, Janet Roach. *ph* Andrzej Bartkowiak. *ed* Rudi Fehr, Kaja Fehr. *pd* J Dennis Washington. *m* Alex North. *cast* Jack Nicholson, Kathleen Turner, Robert Loggia, John Randolph, William Hickey, Lee Richardson, Michael Lombard, Anjelica Huston, Lawrence Tierney, CCH Pounder.
● When hit man Nicholson, a thick lieutenant for the Prizzi mob, falls for unknown beauty Turner, it's bad luck that she too turns out to be a highly paid, if freelance, assassin. She's also brainy enough to take the Prizzi clan for a financial ride; so it's only a matter of time before it's a case of till death do them part. The movie's success lies in Huston's very sure manipulation of mood and tone, somehow connecting black comedy, tongue-in-cheek acting, heavy irony, and even high camp into a coherent story. For all the coast-to-coast jetting, the action is largely composed of faces talking in rooms; the period could be '50s, could be '80s; and Nicholson's thick-upper-lip impersonation of Burt Young has him moving perilously close to Brando, both in mannerism and sheer size. It is, however, a very stylish walk with love and death. CPea

Pro

see Number One

Problem Child

(1990, US, 81 min)
d Dennis Dugan. *p* Robert Simonds. *sc* Scott Alexander, Larry Karaszewski. *ph* Peter Lyons Collister. *ed* Daniel Hanley, Michael Hill. *pd* George Costello. *m* Miles Goodman. *cast* John Ritter, Jack Warden, Michael Oliver, Gilbert Gottfried, Amy Yasbeck, Michael Richards.
● For this story to work (wealthy, shallow but well-meaning parents adopt nightmare child), the audience should identify with the boy, or at least feel a sneaking admiration for his antics. But Michael Oliver's snotty, fakesy-cutesy, grating, whining brat is a fatal turn-off. A film this bad just has to have a mushy message, and it's this: unloved and unwanted, it isn't until he meets Ben Healy (Ritter) and experiences unconditional love, that the unspeakable Junior attains a sense of self-worth. This isn't so much a film about parenting as *fathering;* the bitch-wife who wants a child purely as a lifestyle accessory is finally and humiliatingly removed from the scene so that Dad and his lad can march off into the happy sunset of mutual regard. Enough to make you gag. SFe

Problem Child 2

(1991, US, 91 min)
d Brian Levant. *p* Robert Simonds. *sc* Scott Alexander, Larry Karaszewski. *ph* Peter Smokler. *ed* Lois Freeman-Fox, Robert P Seppey. *pd* Maria Caso. *m* David Kitay. *cast* John Ritter, Michael Oliver, Jack Warden, Laraine Newman, Amy Yasbeck, Ivyann Schwan, Gilbert Gottfried.
● The sorry crew are back again, except that Amy Yasbeck, unable to reprise her role as the humiliated mother, plays the simpering school nurse who steals Ritter's heart. The wicked witch here is heiress LaWanda Dumore (Newman), who improbably sets her Calvin Klein cap at pop-eyed, pudgy Ritter. A faint heh-heh might escape your lips at the antics of an Ellen Barkin lookalike tot (Schwan), but mostly it's predictable, hopelessly over-extended stuff: the pissing-in-lemonade joke, the lengthy projectile vomit scene, fun with farts, and the exploding toilet gag. SFe

Procès de Jeanne d'Arc (Trial of Joan of Arc)

(1962, Fr, 65 min, b/w)
d Robert Bresson. *p* Agnès Delahaie. *sc* Robert Bresson. *ph* Léonce-Henry Burel. *ed* Germaine Artus. *ad* Pierre Charbonnier. *m* Francis Seyrig. *cast* Florence Carrez, Jean-Claude Fourneau, Marc Jacquier, Roger Honorat, Jean Gillibert.
● Based on the minutes of Joan of Arc's trial, this can be seen as Bresson's essay in sadomasochistic voyeurism. Joan (Carrez) is manacled, spied at through peepholes, genitally scrutinised, and forced (by the director) to squat on a wooden stool as if on a toilet seat. The tension generated by juxtaposing such humiliation with the serenely beautiful text (from the transcription of the trial) resolves itself in the unforgettable final image of Joan's charred remains like a burnt-out firework. GAd

Producers, The

(1967, US, 88 min)
d Mel Brooks. *p* Sidney Glazier. *sc* Mel Brooks. *ph* Joseph Coffey. *ed* Ralph Rosenblum. *pd* Charles Rosen. *m* John Morris. *cast* Zero Mostel, Gene Wilder, Kenneth Mars, Estelle Winwood, Renee Taylor, Dick Shawn, Lee Meredith.
● Brooks' first feature, an absolutely hilarious and tasteless New York Jewish comedy about Broadway. Mostel plays a producer determined to clean up by staging the worst flop in history, first making sure that it's over-backed by all of the rich widows hot for him. Mostel and Wilder (as his bumbling Portnovian accountant) ham outrageously, and some of the humour falls flat. But the all-time flop itself could serve as a definition of kitsch, its centrepiece being the number 'Springtime for Hitler', all tits, pretzels and beer steins, in the best tradition of gaudy American burlesque. RM

Professional, The

see Leon

Professional Gun, A

see Mercenario, Il

Professionals, The

(1966, US, 123 min)
d/p/sc Richard Brooks. *ph* Conrad Hall. *ed* Peter Zinner. *ad* Ted Haworth. *m* Maurice Jarre. *cast* Burt Lancaster, Lee Marvin, Robert Ryan, Jack Palance, Claudia Cardinale, Ralph Bellamy, Woody Strode, Joe De Santis.
● Bellamy: 'You bastard!' Marvin: 'In my case an accident of birth, but you, sir, are a self-made man'. Brooks could certainly write a line and direct action, but his taut and disillusioned yarn of American mercenaries intruding into the Mexican revolution to 'rescue' Cardinale had only a couple of years in critical favour before it was comprehensively eclipsed by Peckinpah's ostensibly similar *The Wild Bunch.* PT

Professione: Reporter

see Passenger, The

Profession of Arms, The (Il Mestiere delle Armi)

(2000, It/Fr/Ger, 105 min)
d/sc Ermanno Olmi. *ph* Fabio Olmi. *ed* Paolo Cottignola. *ad* Luigi Marchione. *m* Fabio Vacchi. *cast* Hristo Jivkov, Sergio Grammatico, Dimitar Ratchkov, Fabio Giubbani, Sasa Vulicevic, Dessy Tenekedjieva, Sandra Ceccarelli, Giancarlo Belelli.

●To follow the first half of Olmi's dense narrative – charting developments in the 16th century war between the Papal army and an invading German force – it'd be wise to do some historical research beforehand: so swiftly and persistently are we bombarded by names, dates, facts and figures, that the only theme to emerge with any clarity is that of war, the world and our view of life and our fellow men having been transformed (for the worse, naturally) by the development of firearms. Thereafter, however, things slow down to focus more closely on the heroic captain Giovanni de' Medici, wounded by a cannonball and bravely facing amputation; here,Olmi's historical rigour still pertains, but, in being applied to an individual's experiences, rather than that of society at large, allows for a more accessible meditation on courage, mortality, love and loyalty. A very fine film, then, but also, for a while, extremely, even excessively demanding. GA

Profound Desire of the Gods: Tales from a Southern Island, The (Kamigami no Fukaki Yokubô/aka Legend from Southern Island/ Kuragejima – Legends from a Southern Island)

(1968, Jap, 172 min)
d Shohei Imamura. *sc* Shohei Imamura, Keiji Hasebe. *ph* Masao Tochizawa. *ed* Mutsuo Tanji. *ad* Takeo Kimura. *m* Toshiro Mayuzumi. *cast* Rentaro Mikuni, Chôichorô Kawarazaki, Hideko Okiyama, Kanjuro Arashi, Yasuko Matsui, Yoshi Kato, Kazuo Kitamura, Jun Hamamura.
●Sex, God and Greed play their parts in one of Imamura's most ambitious and powerful films, a rich earthy fable set on a Pacific island where ancient beliefs come head-to-head with 20th century capitalism. The company engineer sent from Tokyo to build an airport exhorts the peasants to 'Forget the Gods!', but goes native himself when he's seduced by a half-witted harpy. It all ends badly. TCh

Profundo carmesí

see Deep Crimson

Proiezionista, Il

see Inner Circle, The

Project A (A Jihua)

(1984, HK, 102 min)
d Jackie Chan. *p* Leonard KC Ho. *sc* Jackie Chan. *cast* Jackie Chan, Samo Hung, Yuen Baio, Dick Wei, Mars, Isabela Wong.
●Famous for the scene in which the acrobatic Chan, cornered by pirates, is left hanging by a clock's minute hand, this is a rumbustiously entertaining caper set in Hong Kong at the turn of the century. Chan's a navy daredevil up against the most ruthless buccaneers and con artists of the South Seas. There's little sign of the effort it took to achieve the startling and always fluid effects. It's reported that after one vertiginous stunt went wrong writer/director/star Chan landed head first and was lucky to escape with his life. GM

Projected Man, The

(1966, GB, 90 min)
d Ian Curteis. *p* John Croydon, Maurice Foster. *sc* John C Cooper, Peter Bryan. *ph* Stan Pavey. *ed* Derek Holding. *ad* Peter Mullins. *m* Kenneth Jones. *cast* Bryant Halliday, Mary Peach, Norman Wooland, Ronald Allen, Derek Farr, Sam Kydd.
●British sci-fi yarn cloned from *The Fly*. A push-back-the-frontiers-of-knowledge scientist uses himself as a guinea pig in a laser-power experiment. He emerges a frazzled monster. Anyone who touches his electrically charged body dies. Low voltage. GM

Projectionist, The

(1970, US, 88 min)
d/p/sc Harry Hurwitz. *ph* Victor Petrashevic. *ed* Harry Hurwitz. *m* Igo Kantor, Erma E Levin. *cast* Chuck McCann, Ina Balin, Rodney Dangerfield, Jara Kohout, Harry Hurwitz, Robert Staats.
●An affectionately scatty though uneven low-budget independent chronicling the numerous fantasies of a slobbish projectionist (McCann), given to retreating into movie-inspired fantasies and meanwhile waging a running battle against his tyrannical theatre manager (Dangerfield). The film is unhappiest in its attitude towards its hero, the archetypal fat man whom we're half-expected to sympathise with, half-expected to laugh at. But anyone with a fondness for Hollywood will find much to enjoy: trailers for *The Terrible World of Tomorrow*, the Judeo-Christian Good-Guy kit, impersonations of Bogart, Wayne and Greenstreet. Less successful are the collages using contemporary footage, the visit to Rick's Café in *Casablanca*, and the running battle involving Captain Flash (McCann's alter ego) and The Bat which culminates with the heroes of Hollywood (Errol Flynn, Sergeant York, Flash Gordon etc.) pounding the forces of Fascism, Hitler and Mussolini included.

Project X

(1987, US, 108 min)
d Jonathan Kaplan. *p* Walter F Parkes. Lawrence Lasker. *sc* Stanley Weiser. *ph* Dean Cundey. *ed* O Nicholas Brown, Brent A Schoenfeld. *pd* Lawrence G Paull. *m* James Horner. *cast* Matthew Broderick, Helen Hunt, Bill Sadler, Johnny Ray McGhee, Jonathan Stark, Robin Gammell.
●Broderick is assigned to work on a US military programme using chimps to test flight simulators, but becomes so attached to the primates that he's soon railing against their treatment. Disney-ish drama with a conscience.

Promesse, La

see Promise, The

Prometheus

(1998, GB, 126 min)
d Tony Harrison. *p* Andrew Holmes. *sc* Tony Harrison. *ph* Alistair Cameron. *ed* Luke Dunkley. *pd* Jocelyn Herbert. *m* Richard Blackford. *cast* Walter Sparrow, Michael Feast, Fern Smith, Jonathan Waistnidge, Steve Huison, Audrey Haggerty.
●This ciné-poem is locked in the tradition of the poet-playwright Tony Harrison's TV work, with a creaky, old-fashioned feel to the visuals and a slight over-earnestness of performance that distracts from the 'message' – the despoliation of the environment, our misuse of the gift of technology and the imperative need for us to wake up to our power to change things for the better by co-operation rather than competition. In this free-form modernisation of Aeschylus's *Prometheus Unbound*, Feast's Hermes ('spin-doctor' of Zeus) scorns human futility and frailty in endless rhyming couplets, as the golden 'souls' of Yorkshire miners are smelted in Germany, before a 30ft gold statue of Prometheus is driven through Eastern Europe to its combustion in Greece. There's pleasure to be had in the dexterity, humour and robustness of the prose, but as drama, it's turgid. WH

Promise (Ningen no Yakusoku)

(1986, Jap, 123 min)
d Yoshihige Yoshida. *p* Yusuyo Saito, Matsuo Takahashi. *sc* Yoshihige Yoshida, Fukiko Miyauchi. *ph* Yoshihiro Yamazaki. *ed* Akira Suzuki. *pd* Yoshie Kikukawa. *m* Haruomi Hosano. *cast* Rentaro Mikuni, Sachiko Murase, Choichiro Kawarazaki, Orie Sato, Tetsuta Sugimoto.
●An old woman is found dead: hubby confesses to murdering her. What starts out as a whodunit thriller evolves into a flashback meditation on the effects of senility, both on the victim and on the family that tries to support its elders. All very sensitive, and quite powerful in its tentative argument in support of euthanasia, but it's relentlessly grim, over-reliant on symbolism (water, mirrors), and often tediously repetitive. But the performances and imaginative, precisely composed photography work wonders in counteracting boredom. GA

Promise, The (Das Versprechen/ La Promesse)

(1994, Ger/Fr, 116 min)
d Margarethe von Trotta. *p* Eberhard Junkersdorf. *sc* Peter Schneider, Margarethe von Trotta. *ph* Franz Rath. *ed* Suzanne Baron. *pd* Benedikt Herforth. *m* Jürgen Knieper. *cast* Meret Becker, Corinna Harfouch, Anian Zollner, August Zirner, Susann Ugé, Eva Mattes, Hark Bohm.
●In tracing the love affair of two bright young East Germans – Konrad (played in gauche youth by Zollner, in soulful maturity by Zirner) and Sophie (Becker in her rock'n'rollin' days, Harfouch in her svelte designer mode) – separated from the outset when she escapes to the West, Margarethe von Trotta, a doyenne of the leftist New German Cinema of the '70s and '80s, seems to be attempting too much: a history, in personal terms, of the two Germanys from the building of the Wall, in 1961, to its fall. When the couple meet up in Prague, in the spring, you know the tanks of '68 will crush their chances of being re-united; their son's sole function seems to be as a symbolic bond between the two states; and when Konrad becomes an eminent scientist, specialising in the periodicity of sunspots, one wearily suspects yet another ironic metaphoris on offer. On the plus side, there's a bold, eclectic blend of *vérité*-style footage, still photographs and straightforward narrative, while Jürgen Knieper's sub-Georges Delerue strings often evoke a sympathetic mournfulness. WH

Promise, The (La Promesse)

(1996, Belg/Fr/Luxembourg, 93 min)
d Jean-Pierre Dardenne, Luc Dardenne. *p* Luc Dardenne. *sc* Jean-Pierre Dardenne, Luc Dardenne. *ph* Alain Marcoen. *ed* Marie Hélène Dozo. *ad* Igor Gabriel. *m* Jean-Marie Billy, Denis M'Punga. *cast* Jérémie Renier, Olivier Gourmet, Assita Ouedraogo, Rasmané Ouedraogo.
●An impressively tough, raw realist drama, set in and around the drabber areas of Liège, in which a 15-year-old comes into conflict with his single parent father after a tragedy forces the boy to confront the moral implications of the pair's exploitative business in smuggling and housing illegal immigrants. Having made a promise to a dying African that he'll look after his wife and kid, young Igor is torn between filial duty and growing affection for his impoverished 'charges', between fear of his dad's bouts of drunken violence and his desire to keep his word. The performances are superb, the interplay between father and son extraordinarily well observed, and the whole thing at once wholly unsentimental and deeply moving. GA

Promised Land

(1987, US, 102 min)
d Michael Hoffman. *p* Rick Stevenson. *sc* Michael Hoffman. *ph* Ueli Steiger, Alexander Gruszynski. *ed* David Spiers. *pd* Eugenio Zanetti. *m* James Newton Howard. *cast* Jason Gedrick, Tracy Pollan, Kiefer Sutherland, Meg Ryan, Goofy Gress, Deborah Richter, Oscar Rowland, Sandra Seacat.
●The American Dream hasn't a prayer in the small town of Ashville. Of the four teenage protagonists, Hancock (Gedrick) slides from the pinnacle of high school basketball hero to local cop, and looks like losing his cheerleader girlfriend (Pollan) to college as well; and sensitive Danny (Sutherland) drops out and takes off, but returns with nothing but a prison record and a delinquent tattooed wife (Ryan). Friends at school, sweet Danny and soured Hancock are manipulated into a tragic confrontation, but it hardly proves the case against American ethics. On the debit side – 'Look Homeward Angel'? – winged symbols abound, Ryan's zany Bev is a spin-off from *Something Wild*, and the police force seems altogether too young. The film has a lot going for it though, with its beautiful snowy landscapes, empty highways, and committed playing from the cast. BC

Promised Lands

(1974, Fr, 87 min)
d Susan Sontag. *p* Nicole Stéphane. *sc* Susan Sontag. *ph* Jen Sopanen. *ed* Annie Chevallay, Florence Bocquet.
●A marked advance on Sontag's first two films (*Duet for Cannibals* and *Brother Carl*) in terms of imagination and cogency, this personal essay about contemporary Israel reflects much of the same passion and intelligence to be found in her non-fictional prose. Addressing itself to tragic and contradictory elements in the state of Israel itself rather than a broader consideration of the Arab-Israeli conflict, it intermittently suggests

the influence of Russian documentary film-maker Dziga Vertov in its use of sound and grasp of visual syntax. But while many of Vertov's works are songs of celebration, *Promised Lands* – through statements by a novelist, physicist, psychiatrist, and a harrowing final sequence of a soldier being 'treated' for shock – is closer to the feeling of a scream. Like some of Sontag's other work, it may suffer from an attraction to morbidity that detracts from a wholly lucid exposition. JR

Promise Her Anything

(1965, GB, 97 min)
d Arthur Hiller. *p* Stanley Rubin. *sc* William Peter Blatty. *ph* Douglas Slocombe. *ed* John Shirley. *pd* Wilfrid Shingleton. *m* Lyn Murray. *cast* Warren Beatty, Leslie Caron, Robert Cummings, Hermione Gingold, Keenan Wynn, Lionel Stander, Cathleen Nesbitt, Bessie Love, Donald Sutherland.

●Shot in Britain but set in the supposedly wacky Bohemian world of Greenwich Village, this dull attempt at an offbeat and sophisticated romantic comedy falls flat on its face, thanks largely to the usual sluggish direction from Arthur (*Love Story*) Hiller. Opportunis-tically cast (Beatty had just been cited as co-respondent in the Peter Hall-Leslie Caron divorce), Beatty and Caron try hard as the down-at-heel 'adult' movie-maker and the French widow looking for a father for her baby son, while the rest of the cast do their best; but a dismal script by William Peter Blatty leaves them flailing in the dark. GA

Promises

(2001, US, 106 min)
d Justine Shapiro, BZ Goldberg, Carlos Bolado. *p* BZ Goldberg, Justine Shapiro. *ph* Ilan Buchbinder, Yoram Millo. *ed* Carlos Bolado.

●Moishe wants to be the first religious military commander-in-chief. Taking us on a tour of his neighbourhood in the occupied West Bank, he points out an army firing range which backs on to a Palestinian district. If they miss the targets, well, maybe there will be one less Palestinian to worry about, he smirks. Of course he's just a kid, but he knows Israel belongs to the Jews, and he can prove it: what better evidence than the word of God? Then there's Sanabel, a young Palestinian girl whose father has been imprisoned without charge for the past two years. This award-winning documentary explores the political faultlines tearing up Israel by focusing on the experiences of seven children, aged 9 to 13. The kids are Palestinian and Jewish, religious and secular, and live within 20 minutes of each other – yet in this deeply segregated society it's only when the film-makers intervene that there's any interaction between them. Shot between 1997 and the summer of 2000, this clear, cogent documentary is a useful primer on the roots of the conflict, and, despite its explicit liberal-humanist agenda, ultimately a depressing warning sign of more trouble ahead. It's impossible not to be moved by the injustices inflicted on the Palestinians. TCh

Prom Night

(1980, US, 95 min)
d Paul Lynch. *p* Peter R Simpson. *sc* William Gray. *ph* Robert New. *ed* Brian Ravok. *ad* Reuben Freed. *m* Carl Zittrer, Paul Zaza. *cast* Leslie Nielsen, Jamie Lee Curtis, Casey Stevens, Eddie Benton, Antoinette Bower, Michael Tough, Robert Silverman.

●It looks promising: a sincere *Halloween* rip-off which takes time out to milk *Carrie, Saturday Night Fever*, and all those B feature 'lust and rivalry' high school sagas. The masked axeman terror here coincides with the anniversary of the death of a small girl, caused accidentally by four older kids who swear to keep their guilty secret. Corny, but not enough for Lynch, who also throws in the escape of a homicidal maniac wrongly imprisoned for the child's murder, and a confusion of red herring conflicts which mark the plot as a poor imitation of John Carpenter's patient terrorism of good by evil. But if you forget motivation, the visual trick-or-treat of slow revenge is entertaining enough: a weirdo janitor dribbling at the window; the victim's year book photos pinned with shards of shattered mirror. Jamie Lee Curtis is superb as Miss Naturally Popular and Prom Queen-to-be, isolated in empty high school corridors: if you like your psychologising loose and edited to that unstoppable disco beat, it's a night out, just.

Promoter, The

see Card, The

Proof

(1991, Aust, 90 min)
d Jocelyn Moorhouse. *p* Lynda House. *sc* Jocelyn Moorhouse. *ph* Martin McGrath. *ed* Ken Sallows. *pd* Patrick Reardon. *m* Not Drowning, Waving. *cast* Hugo Weaving, Genevieve Picot, Russell Crowe, Heather Mitchell, Jeffrey Walker.

●Writer/director Moorhouse's striking first feature deals with blindness, but the opening shot of dark glasses, a white stick and a camera immediately signals its unorthodox approach. Although its main character is a blind photographer, its true subject is emotional security, the need to have faith in what we cannot see, to trust without proof. When 32-year-old Martin (Weaving) befriends amiable kitchen-hand Andy (Crowe), he asks him to describe photographs he has taken but never seen. In this way, he uses his photographs to test people's honesty. But his young housekeeper Celia (Picot), secretly in love with Martin and fiercely jealous, seduces Andy, thereby forcing him to lie to Martin... Moorhouse's deceptively simple snapshot aesthetic, and bold juxtaposition of harrowing and humorous scenes, are both powerful and original. Like the Hockney-style collage Celia creates from photo fragments of Andy's body, the edges don't fit neatly, but a truth emerges from the composite whole. As Andy says, 'Everybody lies, but not all the time'. NF

Proof of Life

(2000, US/GB, 135 min)
d Taylor Hackford. *p* Taylor Hackford, Charles Mulvehill. *sc* Tony Gilroy. *ph* Slawomir Idziak. *ed* John Smith, Sheldon Kahn. *pd* Bruno Rubeo. *m* Danny Elfman. *cast* Meg Ryan, Russell Crowe, David Morse, Pamela Reed, David Caruso, Anthony Heald, Stanley Anderson, Gottfried John, Alun Armstrong, Michael Kitchen.

●Peter Bowman, husband of Alice (Ryan), is kidnapped by corrupt, cocaine-financed South American guerillas. A gritty, semi-documentary style often pays dividends and the film is strongest on the mercenary cynicism of the kidnap business, its well-oiled procedures and poker-faced bluffing games contrasting sharply with the true emotional cost to the victims. The protracted negotiations are complicated by many factors, not least that the Bowmans' marriage was on the verge of collapse. Negotiator and ex-SAS commando Terry Thorne (Crowe) is professional to the point of coldness: when the insurance company pulls the financial plug, he leaves. Alice's pushy sister-in-law strikes a deal with a dodgy local 'co-ordinator', but then Thorne shows his mettle, returning to finish the job at his own expense. The charismatic Crowe's steely restraint pulls us through this melodramatic mudslide, even as we question his professional and personal motives. Morse is excellent as the pragmatic engineer pushed to the limits, and Gottfried John has a fine cameo as a 'crazy' fellow prisoner. Compromising all this solid work, however, is Ryan's idealistic 'hippie' wife, whose immaculate make-up and pink lipstick are as incongruous as her teary-eyed histrionics. NF

Prophecy

(1979, US, 102 min)
d John Frankenheimer. *p* Robert L Rosen. *sc* David Seltzer. *ph* Harry Stradling Jr. *ed* Tom Rolf. *pd* William Craig Smith. *m* Leonard Rosenman. *cast* Talia Shire, Robert Foxworth, Armand Assante, Richard Dysart, Victoria Racimo, George Clutesi.

●Based on the intrinsically arresting idea that mercury poisoning has populated a huge area of American wilderness with numerous rampaging mutations, but somehow no one has noticed. Unfortunately, the film never integrates its eco-horror plot with the cardboard shocks, and the whole venture stops dead with the script's inane assumption that the heroine will put motherhood above all to nurse an ailing monster. It's a small relief when it finally turns round and bites her.

Prophecy, The

see God's Army

Proposition, The (Y Fargen)

(1996, Wales, 100 min)
d Strathford Hamilton. *p* Elizabeth Matthews, Paul Matthews. *sc* Paul Matthews. *ph* David Lewis. *ed* Peter Davies. *pd* Roger Cain. *m* Heneghan & Lawson. *cast* Nicola Beddoe, Aneirin Hughes, Richard Lynch, Richard Harrington, Jennifer Jones, Owen Garmon.

●Made-for-Welsh-TV period drama, with a recently widowed (and recently indebted) bourgeois wife forced to take her herd of cattle south-east to Gloucester to sell them to the army to save her ancient pile. It was billed as a Wales-ian Western and, true, the shots of the landscape are impressively handled, but its Napoleonic War background is just so much red-coated colour. The dramatic triangle (she takes brawling and boozing bastard Rhys along as drover; his legit brother Huw, the sheriff, a demented and murderously insane man, clearly suffering from unrequited love, follows on) is too standard to generate genuine emotion or frisson. WH

Proposition, The

(1998, US, 111 min)
d Lesli Linka Glatter. *p* Ted Field, Diane Nabatoff, Scott Kroopf, *sc* Rick Ramage. *ph* Peter Sova. *ed* Jacqueline Cambas. *pd* David Brisbin. *m* Stephen Endelman. *cast* Kenneth Branagh, Madeleine Stowe, William Hurt, Neil Patrick Harris, Robert Loggia, Blythe Danner, Josef Sommer.

●Boston, 1935: a lawyer (Hurt) discovers he's infertile and proposes to pay a law student (Harris) to impregnate his novelist wife (Stowe). Still without child and on the brink of a major family scandal, the wife seeks solace with the student's uncle, Fr McKinnon (Branagh, miscast), their friendship swiftly developing into a liaison. This flimsy exploration of sexual surrogacy and East Coast materialism between the wars is not improved by director Glatter (remember the syrupy *Now and Then*?) coating each scene with tacky glamour. HK

Proprietor, The (Le Propriétaire)

(1996, US/GB/Fr, 113 min)
d Ismail Merchant. *p* Humbert Balsan, Donald Rosenfeld. *sc* Jean-Marie Besset, George Swift Trow. *ph* Larry Pizer. *ed* William Webb. *pd* Bruno Santini, Kevin Thompson. *m* Richard Robbins. *cast* Jeanne Moreau, Sean Young, Sam Waterston, Nell Carter, Austin Pendleton, Pierre Vaneck, Christopher Cazenove, Jean-Pierre Aumont, Marc Tissot.

●This long, intricately woven film concerns Adrienne Mark, a famous French writer, long resident in New York, who renews her flagging self-belief through the reacquisition of her old family house in Paris, stolen by a Nazi collaborator whom her mother had trusted. On its deepest level this is an oblique tribute by Ismail Merchant to his scriptwriter of 35 years, the author Ruth Prawer Jhabvala, who as a child quit her native Cologne, as the earth began to shake in the prelude to WWII, for the start of what was to become a life marked by a sense of 'dispossession'. Written by George Trow, who worked on the surreal *Savages* for Merchant Ivory in 1972, and Jean-Marie Besset, the story discourses on the necessity of not standing still, following your heart and not compromising your principles. Above all, however, it's about the duties of friendship, which take precedence over even the custodianship of true works of art: exemplified here by a portrait of Adrienne as a child, given by the author to her New York maid (Carter, superb), as a parting present and then returned to enable Adrienne to reclaim her past. The film is unified by the calm, regal presence of Jeanne Moreau, who keeps her head while all about her seem close to losing theirs in a scrabble of intrigue, crossed love affairs, and the hurly burly of a contentious film remake of one of Adrienne's books. Delightful and, at the close, very affecting. JPy

Prospero's Books

(1991, Neth/Fr/It, 120 min)
d Peter Greenaway. *p* Kees Kasander. *sc* Peter Greenaway. *ph* Sacha Vierny. *ed* Marina Bodbyl. *pd* Jan Roelfs. *m* Michael Nyman. *cast* John Gielgud, Michael Clark, Michel Blanc, Erland Josephson, Isabelle Pasco, Tom Bell, Kenneth Cranham.

●Though faithful to the text of Shakespeare's *The Tempest*, Greenaway's characteristically dense film could hardly differ more from literal adaptations like Branagh's *Henry V*. Structuring its motifs around the 24 books Prospero took into exile (as imagined by Greenaway, they dealt with water, cosmology, pornography, ruins, hell, music, etc), the director conveys the arcane knowledge the Duke needs to take his magical revenge. By having Prospero 'invent' the other characters and their lines (all spoken by Gielgud until the final act), he equates him with the Bard, lending the play a modernist dimension as an exploration of creative processes. The movie serves not only as an acknowledgment of the imminent end of Gielgud's career, but as a demonstration of how new technology has expanded film's potential, its superimposed images offering an almost unprecedented complexity of information. To some degree, the relentless proliferation of ideas smothers the dramatic highs and lows, but this is a minor quibble compared to the sheer ambition and audacity of the overall conception. GA

Prostitute

(1980, GB, 98 min)
d/p Tony Garnett. *sc* Tony Garnett. *ph* Charles Stewart, Diane Tammes. *ed* Bill Shapter. *ad* Martin Johnson. *m* Gangsters. *cast* Eleanor Forsythe, Kate Crutchley, Kim Lockett, Nancy Samuels, Richard Mangan, Phyllis Hickson.
●Producer Tony Garnett's first stab at direction was obviously made for the best of motives: a concern about the harassment of prostitutes by police and courts. But his style (TV docu-drama) and line of argument (prostitution is a job like any other) leave a lot to be desired. Just as important as the day-to-day reality of sex for sale is the imaginative role that it plays in the Western world; and with his tale of a Birmingham prostitute and her unhappy move to London, Garnett seems determined to exclude that whole area of debate. Fine as a campaign film; but a major disappointment as anything else.

Prostitution Racket, The (Storie di Vita e Malavita)

(1975, It, 91 min)
d Carlo Lizzani. *p* Adelina Tattilo. *sc* Carlo Lizzani, Mino Giarda. *ph* Lamberto Caimi. *ed* Franco Fraticelli. *pd* Franco Fumagelli. *m* Ennio Morricone. *cast* Cinzia Mambretti, Cristina Moranzoni, Lidia Di Corato, Danila Grassini, Anna Curti.
●Sad to see Lizzani, a not inconsiderable talent from the days of Italian neo-realism, reduced to scripting and directing this standard exploitation-exposé stuff. On the basis of 'research' (that dead hand), we are subjected to gritty but uniformly overheated episodes purporting to show how poverty and boredom force women to turn tricks. Quite so, but the relentless villainy of all the pimps, and the submissive foolishness of all the women, makes the whole exercise implausible. JPy

Protagonists, The

(1999, It, 92 min)
d Luca Guadagnino. *p* Massimo Vigliar, Fulvio Colombo. *sc* Luca Guadagnino. *ph* Paolo Bravi. *ed* Walter Fasano. *pd* Roberto de Angelis. *m* Andrea Guerra. *cast* Tilda Swinton, Fabrizia Sacchi, Andrew Tiernan, Claudio Gioé, Paolo Briguglia, Michelle Hunziker, Chiara Conti, Laura Betti.
●Oh dear. No doubt Swinton and Guadagnino meant well. This experimental documentary attempts to get to grips with the motiveless murder of a London waiter by two schoolboys in 1994 by deconstructing itself as it goes along. What is it that fascinates us so about crime? How can we explain such irrational impulses? Does it help to recreate murder, and if so, how graphic should we be? All valid questions, but the movie is horribly ill-judged and not a little offensive. There's more than a hint of amateur theatricals about it, with Tilda and pals dressing up in wigs to stage the court scenes in her back garden, totally gratuitous female nudity, and a yawning gap between intention and result. It doesn't make your film more honest to incorporate a boom in the shot, just more self-conscious. TCh

Proteus

(1995, GB, 97 min)
d Bob Keen. *p* Paul Brooks. *sc* John Brosnan. *ph* Adam Rodgers. *ed* Liz Webber. *pd* Mike Grant. *m* David Hughes. *cast* Craig Fairbrass, Toni Barry, William Marsh, Jennifer Calvert, Doug (Pinhead) Bradley.
●A sci-fi action picture based on the novel *Slimmer* by John Brosnan (alias Harry Adam Knight), this first feature by sfx wizard Keen wisely allows only glimpses of its mutant creature before delivering a monstrous finale. Stranded on an oil rig, six shipwrecked drug smugglers stumble on a secret DNA manipulation lab. Roaming the rig is the resultant abomination, a protean creature that absorbs its victims and their characteristics. Gung-ho hero Fairbrass plays the action scenes to the hilt; scary atmosphere sustained by watery images and gloopy effects. NF

Protocol

(1984, US, 95 min)
d Herbert Ross. *p* Anthea Sylbert. *sc* Buck Henry. *ph* William A Fraker. *ed* Paul Hirsch. *pd* Bill Malley. *m* Basil Poledouris. *cast* Goldie Hawn, Chris Sarandon, Richard Romanus, André Gregory, Gail Strickland, Cliff De Young, Keith Szarabajka, Ed Begley Jr, Kenneth Mars, Kenneth McMillan.
●Snoozeworthy diplomatic lark in which the ditsy star's a cocktail waitress who stops a bullet meant for Middle Eastern potentate Romanus, then gets a job with the US State Department, whose scheming mandarins reckon she might be helpful in persuading the aforementioned sheikh to let the Yanks build a military base on his soil. With its innocent, smiley heroine running rings round Capitol Hill cynicism, then learning about the US Constitution for the first time, Buck Henry's screenplay borrows freely from both *Mr Smith Goes to Washington* and *Born Yesterday*, but its populist approximations carry no hint of a specifically Reagan-era political context. Instead, Goldie affirms 'government by the people, for the people' with such big-eyed sincerity you'll not know whether to laugh or throw up. TJ

Proud and Profane, The

(1955, US, 111 min, b/w)
d George Seaton. *p* William Perlberg. *sc* George Seaton. *ph* John F Warren. *ed* Alma Macrorie. *ad* Hal Pereira, Earl Hedrick. *m* Victor Young. *cast* William Holden, Deborah Kerr, Thelma Ritter, Dewey Martin, William Redfield, Marion Ross.
●Lucy Hendon Crockett's turbulent novel of WWII romance, *The Magnificent Bastards*, underwent a title change on its way to the screen, though the producers almost settled for *The Magnificent Devils* before ending up with this one. Nurse Kerr is a widow who tangles emotionally with colonel Holden while on a mission to visit the place where her husband died, but her ensuing pregnancy and his invalid wife complicate matters. The ghost of *From Here to Eternity* is never far away, but in this instance the credibility factor is a good deal lower. TJ

Proud Ones, The

(1956, US, 94 min)
d Robert D Webb. *p* Robert L Jacks. *sc* Edmund H North, Joseph Petracca. *ph* Lucien Ballard. *ed* Hugh S Fowler. *ad* Lyle Wheeler, Leland Fuller. *m* Lionel Newman. *cast* Robert Ryan, Jeffrey Hunter, Virginia Mayo, Robert Middleton, Walter Brennan.
●Unusual Western in which the oedipal themes are writ large. Ryan's a marshall trying to keep order in a violent frontier town, but he's prey to recurring fits of blindness. Moreover, the son of a desperado has vowed to kill him, and Mayo, tired of life in a lawless backwater, won't wait for him forever. 'Scope photography by Lucien Ballard. GM

Proud Ones, The

see Orgueilleux, Les

Proud Ones, The

see Cheval d'Orgueil, Le

Proud to Be British

(1973, GB, 40 min, b/w & col)
d Nicholas Broomfield. *ph* Nicholas Broomfield, Dennis Burrow. *ed* Nicholas Broomfield. *with* interviewer: Ben Lewin.
●A National Film School documentary in which residents of the small town of Beaconsfield reveal appallingly ingrained attitudes on such subjects as Britain's imperialistic benevolence, the natural superiority of the British race, the necessity of class and the status quo. Interviewees range over several generations, and from working to ruling class. Broomfield has eschewed all commentary and allowed the subjects to speak for themselves. The irony is blunt but effective. RM

Prova d'Orchestra

see Orchestra Rehearsal

Providence

(1977, Fr/Switz, 107 min)
d Alain Resnais. *p* Klaus Hellwig, Yves Gasser, Yves Peyrot. *sc* David Mercer. *ph* Ricardo Aronovich. *ed* Albert Jurgenson. *ad* Jacques Saulnier. *m* Miklós Rozsa. *cast* John Gielgud, Dirk Bogarde, Ellen Burstyn, David Warner, Elaine Stritch, Denis Lawson, Samson Fainsilber.
●At the centre of David Mercer's tendentious, scatological and wordy screenplay is the figure of a dying writer (Gielgud), a protean spider weaving his final malevolent fiction from the tangled fabric of patriarchal feelings and retributive fantasies about his family's independent lives. In the gentler and more sensitive hands of Resnais, eschewing as always absolutes and glib moral equations, this hackneyed central device leads, not into a predictable reality vs fantasy narrative, but into a haunted, haunting journey through the corridors of the unconscious mind. A painted backdrop against which real waves break; Saint Laurent-clothed characters posed theatrically in rooms so totally given over to deco chic that their three-dimensional reality seems cardboard; scrambled identities (one character taking on another's dialogue or face): through such devices Resnais creates the steps and sets of a kind of Freudian ballet that is also pure cinema. Past and future dissolved into a totally compelling present tense that can, paradoxically, only be approached through memory and imagination. JD

Provinciale, La

see Girl from Lorraine, A

Prowler, The

(1950, US, 92 min, b/w)
d Joseph Losey. *p* Sam Spiegel. *sc* Hugo Butler [Dalton Trumbo]. *ph* Arthur Miller. *ed* Paul Weatherwax. *ad* Boris Leven. *m* Lyn Murray. *cast* Van Heflin, Evelyn Keyes, John Maxwell, Katherine Warren, Emerson Treacy, Madge Blake.
●A rivetingly cool, clean thriller about the trap which inexorably closes on a woman unhappily married to a rich husband, and the cop on the make for the better things in life who, summoned to deal with a prowler, lingers to get rid of the husband and take both wife and money for himself. Superb performances from Evelyn Keyes and Van Heflin, equally superb art direction (with the white Spanish house, a symbol of affluence and its emptiness, surrounded by the night of the hunter), and direction which grips like a steel claw, loosening only in the rather melodramatic final sequences. Even here, with the lovers guiltily holed up in a derelict shack to keep her pregnancy secret from awkward questioning, and their relationship boiling to a fraught climax over the difficult birth, Losey rises magnificently to the occasion in his use of the Mojave Desert ghost town location. TM

Prowler, The (aka Rosemary's Killer)

(1981, US, 88 min)
d Joseph Zito. *p* Joseph Zito, David Streit. *sc* Glenn Leopold, Neal F Barbera. *ph* Raoul Lomas. *ed* Joel Goodman. *pd* Lorenzo Mans. *m* Richard Einhorn. *cast* Vicky Dawson, Christopher Goutman, Lawrence Tierney, Farley Granger, Cindy Weintraub, Lisa Dunsheath.
●Mad axeman action yet again, cravenly conformist in every department. Hitchcock connoisseurs may be mildly interested to see the hero of *Strangers on a Train* finally getting to play the homicidal role. BBa

Psychic Killer

(1975, US, 89 min)
d Raymond Danton. *p* Mardi Rustan. *sc* Greydon Clark, Mikel Angel, Raymond

Danton. *ph* Herb Pearl. *ed* Michael Brown. *ad* Joel Leonard. *m* William Kraft. *cast* Paul Burke, Jim Hutton, Julie Adams, Nehemiah Persoff, Neville Brand, Aldo Ray, Whit Bissell, Rod Cameron, Della Reese.

●Although not up to sophisticated John Carpenter standards, *Psychic Killer* – with Hutton released from an asylum in possession of a mysterious medallion which enables him to wreak revenge on those responsible for his wrongful commitment – wouldn't disgrace the Corman stable. A good, cheap, diverting horror exploiter with a reasonably developed sense of its own ridiculousness (a couple of funny, bloody murders), and a cast of old hands (Adams, Ray, Brand) who know a hilt when they see one, and boy, do they play up to it. Ray Danton used to act in films just like this, and if not inspired, his handling of the grotesque is both sure-footed and fun. SM

Psycho (100)

(1960, US, 109 min, b/w)
d/p Alfred Hitchcock. *sc* Joseph Stefano. *ph* John L Russell. *ed* George Tomasini. *ad* Joseph Hurley, Robert Clatworthy. *m* Bernard Herrmann. *cast* Anthony Perkins, Janet Leigh, Vera Miles, John Gavin, Martin Balsam, John McIntire, Simon Oakland, John Anderson.

●No introduction needed, surely, for Hitchcock's best film, a stunningly realised (on a relatively low budget) slice of Grand Guignol in which the Bates Motel is the arena for much sly verbal sparring and several gruesome murders. But it's worth pointing out that Hitch was perfectly right to view it as fun; for all its scream of horror at the idea (and consequences) of madness, it's actually a very black comedy, titillating the audience with its barely linear narrative (the heroine disappears after two reels), with its constant shuffling of audience sympathies, and with its ironic dialogue ('Mother's not quite herself today'). Add the fact that we never learn who's buried in Mrs Bates' coffin, and you've got a stunning, if sadistic, two-hour joke. The cod-Freudian explanation offered at the conclusion is just so much nonsense, but the real text concerning schizophrenia lies in the tellingly complex visuals. A masterpiece by any standard. GA

Psycho

(1998, US, 104 min)
d Gus Van Sant. *p* Brian Grazer, Gus Van Sant. *sc* Joseph Stefano. *ph* Chris Doyle. *ed* Amy Duddleston. *pd* Tim Foden. *m* Bernard Herrmann. *cast* Vince Vaughn, Julianne Moore, Viggo Mortensen, William H Macy, Anne Heche, Robert Forster, Philip Baker Hall, Rita Wilson, James LeGros.

●As original, and as personal, as a Warhol screen print, Van Sant's shot-for-shot remake of Hitchcock's seminal shocker takes an established text and recontextualises it 38 years on. The choice of *Psycho* is a shrewd one; the original hasn't a shot out of place. It stands as the first truly modern American film: Hollywood movies lost their innocence here, in the ruthless brutality of Marion Crane's murder. Van Sant allows himself only about half-a-dozen fractional variations from Hitchcock's storyboard – most blatantly during the murders – though in some respects the mise-en-scène is quite distinct, and in colour (out goes the black lingerie, in comes orange nail varnish). Fascinating to watch Heche and Moore riff on Marion and Lila Crane, though Vaughn has an impossible job supplanting Anthony Perkins' indelible performance. Appropriately, given the schizophrenia theme, you end up watching it in mental split-screen, and of course the b/w version in your head is far superior to the intermittently effective academic exercise playing before your eyes. Hitchcock probably wouldn't tell this story if he was making films today, and he certainly wouldn't tell it this way, with internal 'voices', back projection, minimal nudity and violence. TCh

Psycho II

(1983, US, 113 min)
d Richard Franklin. *p* Hilton A Green. *sc* Tom Holland. *ph* Dean Cundey. *ed* Andrew London. *pd* John W Corso. *m* Jerry Goldsmith. *cast* Anthony Perkins, Vera Miles, Meg Tilly, Robert Loggia, Dennis Franz, Hugh Gillin, Claudia Bryar.

●With Norman Bates judged sane and released from mental hospital 22 years after the Crane shower murder, things revert to abnormal at the old Gothic house: Norman takes in a sweet young house guest (Tilly), and jealous Mother rears her murderous head again. But who's the real killer? Norman? Marion Crane's revenge-mad sister (Miles)? The fired motel manager (Franz), incensed by Norm's puritan attitude to his turning the place into a vice-house? While the film lacks the thematic depth and darkness – and the virtuoso style – of Hitchcock's, it does a fair job of recreating the exhilarating blend of horror and black humour, with a fair quota of outrageous narrative digressions and perplexing twists along the way. Franklin manages to pay homage to the Master's style without ever falling into the redundantly baroque excesses of, say, De Palma. Scary and fun, it's as worthy a sequel as one might reasonably expect. GA

Psycho III

(1986, US, 96 min)
d Anthony Perkins. *p* Hilton A Green. *sc* Charles Edward Pogue. *ph* Bruce Surtees. *ed* David Blewitt. *pd* Henry Bumstead. *m* Carter Burwell. *cast* Anthony Perkins, Diana Scarwid, Jeff Fahey, Roberta Maxwell, Hugh Gillin, Lee Garlington, Gary Bayer.

●Business as usual at the Bates motel as a runaway nun with the same initials as Marion Crane triggers Norman first into a mental replay of the showerbath murder, then to a tender case of mooncalf love. Nice idea to revive Norman's taxidermy hobby, so that his real mum of *Psycho II* (an impostor, it transpires) is now stuffed and directing operations from upstairs just as Mother used to, ensuring that the course of true love is anything but smooth. Sadly, the slashings have become distinctly déjà vu, and the plot is as full of holes as Janet Leigh's corpse. As Norman, Perkins gives another superb exhibition of controlled hysteria, with the fetching hint of a macabre wink lurking in the background; but in his role as director (his debut), he sets too much store by Hitchcock's Catholic apologists. Kicking off with a suicidal nun in a recreation of the bell-tower scene from *Vertigo*, he lumbers the film with some religious ironies which simply get in the way. It's not unenjoyable, but it isn't half the pastiche that *Psycho II* was. TM

Psycho-Circus

see Circus of Fear

Psycho Killers

see Flesh and the Fiends, The

Psychomania

(1972, GB, 91 min)
d Don Sharp. *p* Andrew Donally. *sc* Arnaud d'Usseau. *ph* Ted Moore. *ed* Richard Best. *ad* Maurice Carter. *m* David Whitaker. *cast* George Sanders, Beryl Reid, Nicky Henson, Mary Larkin, Roy Holder, Robert Hardy, Patrick Holt.

●The first British Hell's Angels pic, and just about the blackest comedy to come out of this country in years. It features a bike gang called The Living Dead, whose leader (Henson) discovers the art of becoming just that. So he kills himself and is buried along with his bike, until he guns the engine and shoots back up through the turf; two victims later, he drives to a pub and calls his mother (Reid), a devil worshipper ensconced in her stately old dark house with Sanders as her sinisterly imperturbable butler, to say he's back. This level of absurdity could be feeble, but Sharp knows how to shoot it straight, without any directorial elbows-in-the-ribs. Consequently, much of the humour really works, even though the gang as individuals are strictly plastic. DP

Psychotherapy

see Don't Get Me Started

Psych-Out

(1968, US, 88 min)
d Richard Rush. *p* Dick Clark. *sc* E Hunter Willett, Betty Ulius. *ph* Laszlo Kovacs. *ed* Ken Reynolds. *ad* Leon Ericksen. *m* Ronald Stein. *cast* Susan Strasberg, Dean Stockwell, Jack Nicholson, Bruce Dern, Adam Roarke, Max Julien, Henry Jaglom, Barbara London.

●A typical AIP quickie put together in an instant bid to cash in on the 'Summer of Love', its action eventually amounting to a slam-bang compendium of every hippy cliché from the bad trip to the redneck rumble. The plot, which has a deaf girl (Strasberg) scouring San Francisco's Haight Ashbury for her missing brother (a crazed Dern), is hard to take. But if you can accept the clichés and archaisms, as well as some third-rate acid rock from The Seeds and Strawberry Alarm Clock, there are compensations: some beautifully baroque performances (Dern and Stockwell in particular), Laszlo Kovacs' effective visualisation of Strasberg's bad STP trip, the spectacle (as irresistible as it is preposterous) of Jack Nicholson sporting lead guitar at the Filmore. DP

P'Tang, Yang, Kipperbang

(1982, GB, 80 min)
d Michael Apted. *p* Chris Griffin. *sc* Jack Rosenthal. *ph* Tony Pierce-Roberts. *ed* John Shirley. *ad* Jeff Woolbridge. *m* David Earl. *cast* John Albasiny, Abigail Cruttenden, Maurice Dee, Alison Steadman, Mark Brailsford, Robert Urquhart.

●The first in Channel 4's *First Love* telemovie series (unwisely given a theatrical release after being seen on TV), this has its roots in the boyhood memories of writer Jack Rosenthal. We're back in postwar England, an age of unbounded optimism buoyed by the prospect of peace and the promises of a Labour government. Our schoolboy hero, 'Quack Quack' Duckworth (Albasiny) has only two ambitions: to score the winning run for England in a test match against Australia, and to kiss a girl in his class (the enchanting Cruttenden). Such is the flimsy premise of this all-too-easily nostalgic movie, whose production values and period detail are overstated to the point of cliché. Apted's direction is precise but unremarkable, and though Rosenthal's script triggers some long-buried memories, like classroom catchwords (hence the title) and furtive fumblings towards sexual awareness, it's an empty film that leaves you with little besides a Heinz soup glow. MA

P Tinto's Miracle (El Milagro de P Tinto)

(1998, Sp, 106 min)
d Javier Fesser. *p* Luis Manso. *sc* Javier Fesser, Guillermo Fesser. *ph* Javier Aguirresarobe. *ed* Guillermo Represa. *pd* César Macarrón. *m* Suso Saiz. *cast* Luis Ciges, Silvia Casanova, Pablo Pinedo, Javier Aller, Emilio Gavira, Janfri Topera, Germán Montaner, Tomás Sáez, Carlos Soto, Goizalde Núnez.

●Somewhere between the stylish fantasy of *Delicatessen* and the brainless gusto of *Dumb & Dumber*, this comedy makes up in pizzazz what it lacks in subtlety. P Tinto is an imbecile who inherits a business in communion wafers somewhere in the middle of nowhere. He has with him his wife, who is blind ('No woman had ever looked at me like that before'), and who is as ignorant of sex as he is. Their attempts to procreate are fruitless, until a couple of Martians crashland in their backyard. What follows is very silly, outrageous, and (if you're so inclined) unreasonably funny. TCh

PT Raiders

see Ship That Died of Shame, The

Puberty Blues

(1981, Aust, 87 min)
d Bruce Beresford. *p* Joan Long, Margaret Kelly. *sc* Margaret Kelly. *ph* Donald McAlpine. *ed* William Anderson, Jeanine Chialvo. *pd* David Copping. *cast* Nell Schofield, Jad Capelja, Geoff Rhoe, Tony Hughes, Sandy Paul, Leander Brett.

●Nothing more than the overrated *Getting of Wisdom* updated and transposed to beach-movie territory, this replaces period prettiness with an equally crass teenage formula imported from countless cheap Californian quickies. The trouble is that Beresford is determined both to have his cake and to eat it, as he adopts the viewpoint of two schoolgirl surfer-gang apprentices on the codes and rituals of their Aussie peers, parading the sex'n'drugs'n'sand staples of the genre at grating length before finally turning round with his heroines to dismiss it all as boys' play kidstuff. And even then the message comes down to a wimpy 'don't beat 'em, join 'em' compromise. PT

Public Access

(1993, US, 90 min)
d Bryan J Singer. *p* Kenneth Kokin. *sc* Bryan J Singer, Christopher McQuarrie. *ph* Bruce Douglas Johnson. *ed* John Ottman. *pd* Jan Sessler. *m* John Ottman. *cast* Ron Marquette, Dina Brooks, Burt Williams.

●An impressive debut from writer/director Singer, this chilly little parable taps into the poisonous well-springs of the middle-American psyche. When Whiley Pritcher (Marquette) arrives in Brewster, it's a quiet, complacent, no-account kind of place. He rents a room by the week and then sets about booking four slots of prime-time public access TV on the local cable TV station: Sunday, 7pm, 'family hour'. He calls the show 'Our Town' and asks, 'What's wrong with Brewster?' Before too long it's '*Who's* wrong?' It's obvious from the way Whiley scrubs the bath naked that something's amiss, but as Singer probes his soft-spoken anti-hero, it becomes clear he'll stop at nothing to achieve his enigmatic ends. The film is overly measured, with lots of slow zooms and slow motion (even the actors seem to be on go-slow), but it's engrossing, and Marquette is a genuinely scary customer, a dry-cleaned all-American sociopath. TCh

Public Enemy, The

(1931, US, 84 min, b/w)
d William Wellman. *p* Dev Jennings. *sc* Harvey Thew, Kubec Glasman, John Bright. *ph* Dev Jennings. *ed* Edward M McDermott. *ad* Max Parker. *m* David Mendoza. *cast* James Cagney, Jean Harlow, Edward Woods, Donald Cook, Joan Blondell, Mae Clarke, Beryl Mercer.

●Hard to believe that it was the aptly named Woods and not Cagney who was originally slated for the lead role of Tom Powers, the part that rocketed Cagney to stardom and typecast him as a trigger-happy punk. Now, of course, the film seems the archetypal Cagney vehicle as he graduates from petty theft to big-time bootlegging and murder, but it's fairly seminal for other reasons: the acknowledgment that crime is at least partly the product of poor social conditions, the emphasis on booze as the mainspring for the Mob's illegal income, the deployment of events and characteristics from the lives of real-life gangsters (in this case Hymie Weiss) to create myth from fact. Best known for the rampantly misogynist scene in which Cagney plunges a grapefruit into Mae Clarke's nagging face over the breakfast table, the film is badly let down by the performances of Harlow as a classy moll, and Cook and Mercer as Cagney's brother and mother (the latter coming across as a simpering moron). But Cagney's energy and Wellman's gutsy direction carry the day, counteracting the moralistic sentimentality of the script and indelibly etching the star on the memory as a definitive gangster hero. GA

Public Enemy Number One

(1980, Aust, 58 min)
d David Bradbury. *p* David Bradbury, Stewart Young. *with* Wilfred Burchett. *narrator* Richard Oxenburgh.

●A documentary on Australia's veteran radical journalist Wilfred Burchett. Returning to his beloved SE Asia in the wake of Pol Pot's holocaust and in the midst of a war between former comrades, Burchett exhibits much the same devastated incomprehension he had to conquer as the first Western newsman to file a report from Hiroshima. Burchett's unique experience between these two cataclysms – 30 years of reporting from the communist position on Korea, Vietnam and Cambodia, which earned him close friendship with Ho Chi Minh and an 'enemy's' exile from his Australian homeland – more happily form the major focus of this remarkable inspirational film memoir. PT

Public Eye, The

(1992, US, 99 min, col)
d Howard Franklin. *p* Sue Baden-Powell. *sc* Howard Franklin. *ph* Peter Suschitzky. *ed* Evan Lottman. *pd* Marcia Hinds-Johnson. *m* Mark Isham. *cast* Joe Pesci, Barbara Hershey, Stanley Tucci, Jerry Adler, Jared Harris, Richard Riehle.

●The main virtue of screenwriter Franklin's debut as director is Pesci's portrayal of Weegee, the famous low-life tabloid photographer of urban disaster, lightly concealed as Bernstein, The Great Bernzini. Watching this isolated character in his nocturnal environment, cursing and kicking corpses into patterns for the shot, seeing the scene freeze into black-and-white for the famous photo – this is the heart of the film. When we track the uncouth artist to a publisher where his work is rejected again, leaving his ego undented, veterans may be reminded of the painter Gulley Jimson in *The Horse's Mouth*, with the swearing left in. Pesci is unstoppably *on* throughout. Both the tentative romance with nightclub-owner Kay Levitz (Hershey) – though finely played – and the plot, which concerns a government gas-rationing scandal, seem uneasily grafted on in an attempt to qualify for *film noir*, though Bernstein does get an incredible live action shot out of it. Good dialogue, nice period recreation, great performances. BC

Puen-Paeng

(1983, Thai, 131 min)
d Cherd Songsri. *p* Chantana Songsri. *sc* Thom Thatrae. *ph* Kawee Kiattinan. *ed* Kacha Rajapratarn. *pd* Narong Phuenprapai. *cast* Sorapong Chatri, Kanungnit Rerksasarn, Chanuteporn Visitsophon.

●Quite unlike the mainstream of Thai movies (but a little too similar to the same director's masterly *The Scar*), this is an elegiac rural melodrama about two contrasted sisters in love with the same cowherd. It's set in the '30s, and lovingly detailed period touches strike an optimum balance between nostalgic escapism and serious reconstruction of traditions that are already almost extinct. At its heart are magical images of life in a Thai village: a brazen girl propositioning a naked boy as he bathes in the river, a romance pursued on the backs of water buffalo. TR

Puerto Escondido

(1993, It, 110 min)
d Gabriele Salvatore. *p* Maurizio Totti, Mario Cecchi Gori, Vittorio Cecchi Gori. *sc* Gabriele Salvatores, Enzo Monteleone, Diego Abatantuono. *ph* Italo Petriccione. *ed* Nino Baragli. *ad* Marco Belluzzu, Alejandro Olmas. *m* Mauro Pagani, Federico de Robertis. *cast* Diego Abatantuono, Valeria Golino, Claudio Bisio, Renato Carpentieri.

●Surprisingly, from the maker of *Mediterraneo*, this opens with an edgy comic menace as self-important Milan banker Mario (Abatantuono) is blasted at close range by a smiling serial killer. He survives, but is visited in hospital by his assailant – a police commissioner investigating the case. It's like *The Trial* meets *Man Bites Dog* until Mario, having anxiously befriended the killer cop, dumps him and flees to South America. As his designer suit frays and money fails, he falls in with fellow Italians, a peyote-loving beach bum (Bisio) and his girl (Golino), who find their already incompetent scams hopelessly compromised by their lazy, cowardly house guest. The film's all over the place and has its longueurs, but succeeds thanks to Abatantuono's performance. Full marks, too, for the dark, unpatronising picture of Mexico, throwing into deeper relief the merry antics of the protagonists. SFe

Pugni in Tasca, I

see Fists in the Pocket

Pull My Daisy

(1959, US, 50 min)
d/p Robert Frank, Alfred Leslie. *sc* Jack Kerouac. *ph* Robert Frank. *ed* Leon Prochnick, Robert Frank, Alfred Leslie. *m* David Amram. *cast* Allen Ginsberg, Jack Kerouac, Larry Rivers, Delphine Seyrig.

●Those who know Frank's stark, dispassionate pictures of blank-faced Americans will be surprised by the zany humour of this film. A group of Frank's friends (Ginsberg and painter Larry Rivers) loon about in a New York loft improvising round a scene from a Kerouac play about the Beat Generation. Straight society is represented by the bishop, his disapproving mother and prim sister, who are entertained with drinking, cussing, poetry and jazz. Kerouac provides an insane voice-over commentary which distances the audience by emphasising the artificiality and self-parody of the play-acting. The uneasy mix of informality and posturing makes the film a forerunner of Warhol's 'home movies'.

Pull-Over Rouge, Le (The Red Sweater)

(1979, Fr, 107 min)
d/p Michel Drach. *sc* Michel Drach, Ariane Litaize. *ph* Jean Boffety. *ed* André Gaultier. *m* Jean-Louis d'Ondrio. *cast* Serge Avédikian, Michèle Marquais, Reine Bartève, Roland Blanche.

●Christian Ranucci was arrested in 1974 for the kidnap and murder of a little girl, Elisa Garcia. This is an adaptation of Gilles Perrault's book about the affair, beginning with the reports of Elisa's disappearance (taken away by a man in a red pull-over, according to her brother) and ending on a freeze frame of Ranucci's agonized face as he is strapped to the guillotine. Drach takes it as read that Ranucci was innocent, the investigation and trial having been grotesquely mismanaged. Adopting a severe, resolutely non-dramatic style, he presents a compelling case. Still, this is pamphleteering, not cinema. On the other hand, it made its point: Ranucci's was the last execution carried out in France. BBa

Pulp

(1972, GB, 95 min)
d Mike Hodges. *p* Michael Klinger. *sc* Mike Hodges. *ph* Ousama Rawi. *ed* John Glen. *pd* Patrick Downing. *m* George Martin. *cast* Michael Caine, Mickey Rooney, Lionel Stander, Lizabeth Scott, Nadia Cassini, Al Lettieri, Dennis Price.

●Writer/director Hodges took his abrasive, mordant style from the Newcastle of *Get Carter* to the Mediterranean for this, his second feature. Caine plays a pithy author of pulp fiction hired to ghost some secret memoirs. So inevitably he becomes an amateur sleuth, a wisecracking sore thumb in the impenetrable murk of fringe mafioso. There's a touch of hommage here, a dash of indulgence there, but *Pulp* deserved a kinder critical reception than it received, if only for Rooney's exuberant send-up of himself. One of those movies that's a laugh a line after a pint or three. SG

Pulp Fiction (100)

(1994, US, 154 min)
d Quentin Tarantino. *p* Lawrence Bender. *sc* Quentin Tarantino. *ph* Andrzej Sekula. *ed* Sally Menke. *pd* David Wasco. *cast* John Travolta, Samuel L Jackson, Uma Thurman, Bruce Willis, Harvey Keitel, Tim Roth, Rosanna Arquette, Amanda Plummer, Eric Stoltz, Steve Buscemi.

●A sprawling, discursive fresco: three stories bookended by a prologue and epilogue. In the first story, a mobster (Travolta) is charged with looking after the irresponsible wife (Thurman) of his vengeful boss. In the second, a washed-up boxer (Willis) tries to trick the Mob by failing to throw a fight. And in the third, two hitmen (Travolta and Jackson) carry out a job, only to call on the services of a 'cleaner' (Keitel) when it gets messier than planned. It's the way Tarantino embellishes and, finally, interlinks these old chestnuts that makes the film alternately exhilarating and frustrating. There's plenty of sharp, sassy, profane dialogue, and there are plenty of acute, funny references to pop culture, though the talk sometimes delays the action, and the references sometimes seem self-consciously arch. And there are, too, the sudden lurches between humour and violence – shocking, but without moral depth. What writer/director Tarantino lacks, as yet, is the maturity to invest his work with anything that might provoke a heartfelt emotional response to his characters. Very entertaining, none the less. GA

Pulse

(1988, US, 91 min)
d Paul Golding. *p* Patricia A Stallone. *sc* Paul Golding. *ph* Peter Lyons Collister. *ed* Gib Jaffe. *pd* Holger Gross. *m* Jay Ferguson. *cast* Joey Lawrence, Cliff De Young, Roxanne Hart, Charles Tyner, Myron Healey.

●This tense little thriller with a touch of the Stephen Kings shows what happens when a series of power surges turns an ordinary Los Angeles household into a death-trap. An uneasy exposition with well-handled effects gives way to a disappointing resolution. As tends to be the case in these affairs, the film-makers can't think up much of a reason why the electrics should go berserk in the first place. TJ

Pumping Iron

(1976, US, 86 min)
d George Butler, Robert Fiore. *p* George Butler, Jerome Gary. *sc* George Butler. *ph* Robert Fiore. *ed* Lawrence Silk, Geof Bartz. *m* Michael Small. *with* Arnold Schwarzenegger, Louis Ferrigno, Matty Ferrigno, Victoria Ferrigno, Mike Katz, Ken Waller.
●'Pumping iron is a great feeling… like coming, but coming continuously,' smiles Arnold Schwarzenegger, relaxed in the confidence that he's demolishing another popular prejudice against bodybuilding. *Pumping Iron* in fact starts knocking preconceptions sideways in its opening moments – with a sequence showing Schwarzenegger taking ballet lessons to improve his posing style – and it goes on to demonstrate convincingly that bodybuilders are as 'normal' in their vanities, foibles and rivalries as any other group of nuts. The movie is a very shrewd mixture of documentary and realistic fiction, put together with both eyes and ears on entertainment value; it has, for example, an extremely agreeable LA session-rock score. Its strongest card is the outrageously charismatic Schwarzenegger, but its view of musclemen and physique contests in general has a charm not unlike *Rocky*. TR

Pumping Iron II: The Women

(1984, US, 107 min)
d/p/sc George Butler. *ph* Dyanna Taylor. *ed* Paul Barnes, Susan Crutcher. *m* David McHugh, Michael Montes. *with* Bev Francis, Rachel McLish, Lori Bowen Rice, Carla Dunlap, Steve Michalik.
●A drama doc on the run-up and final for the 1983 Caesar's Cup in Las Vegas which proves even more engaging than *Pumping Iron*. The line-up of well-oiled beauties includes one controversial Australian, Bev Francis, who powerlifts 500 pounds for breakfast, and whose musculature defies rational analysis. The crux of the tournament then comes down to whether the judges, blind fools to a man, will accept something so obviously superior or opt for the safety of a body more 'traditionally feminine' such as gorgeous pouting Rachel McLish, who is discovered to have illegal padding in her unmuscled bits, oh the shame of it all. Ironically, the winner turns out to be the one with the firmest grasp of the political undercurrents. Huge fun. CPea

Pumpkin Eater, The

(1964, GB, 118 min, b/w)
d Jack Clayton. *p* James Woolf. *sc* Harold Pinter. *ph* Oswald Morris. *ed* Jim Clark. *ad* Edward Marshall. *m* Georges Delerue. *cast* Anne Bancroft, Peter Finch, James Mason, Cedric Hardwicke, Rosalind Atkinson, Richard Johnson, Maggie Smith, Eric Porter.
●Harold Pinter penned one of his superior scripts in this fastidious adaptation of Penelope Mortimer's novel about a compulsive child-bearer and her unfaithful screenwriter husband. The influence of European cinema (in particular Antonioni) is evident in the delineation of despair among the middle classes, and there is something peculiarly self-parodic in the heroine enduring a nervous breakdown in Harrods. Fine performances notwithstanding, the world of the Hampstead soap opera now seems so far away as to almost rate as science fiction. DT

Pumpkinhead (aka Vengeance, the Demon)

(1987, US, 86 min)
d Stan Winston. *p* Howard Smith, Richard C Weinman. *sc* Mark Patrick Carducci, Gary Gerani. *ph* Bojan Bazelli. *pd* Cynthia Kay Charette. *m* Richard Stone. *cast* Lance Henriksen, John DiAquino, Jeff East, Florence Schauffler, Kimberly Ross, Joel Hoffman, Cynthia Bain.
●When Pennsylvanian country-dweller Ed Harley's kid gets (accidentally) killed by a group of marauding young townies on motorbikes, the aggrieved father (Henriksen) seeks justice, or more precisely, vengeance. Aided by the mythically wizened old crone from Black Ridge (Schauffler), he invokes the rampaging form of Pumpkinhead, a 15-foot monstrosity who doesn't believe in penal reform and with whom one does not mess lightly. From there on it's stiff-city for the unfortunate kids, as well as some hellish rewards for Harley himself. Having established himself in make-up before moving to directing, Winston eschews the usual frustratingly fleeting glimpses of 'monster-in-very-poorly-lit-surroundings', and – with the help of the creature-effects team that brought you *Aliens* and *Predator* – delivers more than ample amounts of full-bodied fantasy. Henriksen is superbly anguished throughout, his pectorals and cheekbones competing for the most exciting on-screen spectacle award. MK

Pump Up the Volume

(1990, US, 102 min)
d Allan Moyle. *p* Rupert Harvey, Sandor Stern. *sc* Allan Moyle. *ph* Walt Lloyd. *ed* Wendy Bricmont, Ric Keeley, Kurt Hathaway. *pd* Bruce Bolander. *cast* Christian Slater, Scott Paulin, Ellen Greene, Samantha Mathis, Anthony Lucero, Andy Romano, Annie Ross.
●By night, shy student Mark Hunter (Slater), resentful because his family has moved from New York to an Arizona backwater, retires to the basement to become pirate radio DJ Hard Harry, so named because he pretends to masturbate on air. Mixing outrage, Leonard Cohen and social commentary, his show becomes compulsory for the youngsters at Hubert Humphrey High School. They phone and write in with problems ranging from teen pregnancy to loneliness, but when one listener commits suicide, Hard Harry is charged with criminal solicitation. Now all they have to do is find him… Writer/director Moyle turns what could have been a wallow in teen angst into something altogether more forceful. The perfectly cast Slater effectively propels the film, his intensity and dry delivery giving it a definite edge, as does a soundtrack which includes Ice T, Concrete Blonde and the Cowboy Junkies. CM

Punch and Judy Man, The

(1962, GB, 90 min, b/w)
d Jeremy Summers. *p* Gordon LT Scott. *sc* Philip Oakes, Tony Hancock. *ph* Gilbert Taylor. *ed* Gordon Pilkington. *ad* Robert Jones. *m* Derek Scott, Don Banks. *cast* Tony Hancock, Sylvia Syms, Ronald Fraser, John Le Mesurier, Hugh Lloyd, Barbara Murray, Hattie Jacques.
●Hancock's finest celluloid hour-and-a-half has the doleful comic as a seaside children's entertainer whose marriage to ambitious Syms is under threat due to his continuing lowly rank in the town's social strata. Written by Hancock and Philip Oakes, it's an understated, melancholy tale with a rather personal tone, and good work from the likes of Le Mesurier and Hugh Lloyd as Hancock's fellow beach-front artistes. TJ

Punch-Drunk Love

(2002, US, 91 min)
d Paul Thomas Anderson. *p* Joanne Sellar, Daniel Lupi, Paul Thomas Anderson. *sc* Paul Thomas Anderson. *ph* Robert Elswit. *ed* Leslie Jones. *pd* William Arnold. *m* Jon Brion. *cast* Adam Sandler, Emily Watson, Luis Guzman, Philip Seymour Hoffman.
●Essentially an unremittingly arty update of those Jerry Lewis-style romantic comedies where a geeky beast-figure (here, Sandler's nerdy salesman) is improbably courted by a cute, uncommonly understanding beauty (Watson, friend of one of the hero's seven bossy sisters). In this case, the protagonist's feral characteristics extend to a physically ferocious volatile temper, thus allowing him to prove his manhood by taking on a phone-sex blackmailing outfit led by Hoffman (the best thing in the movie despite scant screen-time). The film looks good and has its funny moments, but too often one senses Anderson straining to impress, whether by purloining (and misusing) a Harry Nilsson song from Altman's *Popeye*, or by tossing in yet another surreal, surprising or seemingly inexplicable narrative idiosyncrasy. GA

Punchline

(1988, US, 122 min)
d David Seltzer. *p* Daniel Melnick, Michael Rachmil. *sc* David Seltzer. *ph* Reynaldo Villalobos. *ed* Bruce Green. *pd* Jackson De Govia. *m* Charles Gross. *cast* Sally Field, Tom Hanks, John Goodman, Mark Rydell, Kim Greist, Paul Mazursky.
●One problem here is that the jokes aren't funny; another is that Sally Field is funny by mistake. It's saved by Tom Hanks' portrayal of Steven Gold, flunking seedy medical student by day and ambitious trainee stand-up by night. Admiration (hero worship) arrives in the shape of Lilah Krytsick (Field), a downtrodden housewife so sweetly caring, so maternally smothering, that even boiling oil couldn't be good enough. Lilah, alas, wants to be a comic too. Under Gold's tutelage she becomes one; the rule, he explains, is that you don't get on by telling someone else's haggard gags, but by spieling from experience. Her experience consists of Polish roots and her husband's personal habits, and the punters learn to love it. Worse, Krytsick learns to love Gold, and vice versa. The talent contest climax is the equivalent of a badly engineered courtroom drama, tantrums, tears and all. It's to Hanks' credit that *Punchline* remains grimly watchable. SGa

Punch Me in the Stomach

(1996, NZ/Can, 72 min)
d Francine Zuckerman. *p* Francine Zuckerman, Jonathan Dowling. *sc* Francine Zuckerman, Deb Filler. *ph* Rudolph Blahacek. *ed* Nicola Smith. *pd* Joey Shiner. *m* Joey Miller. *cast* Deb Filler.
●A barely cinematic 'opening out' of stand-up comic Deb Filler's one-woman show, inspired by her own experiences growing up as a Jew in New Zealand, and those of her father, a survivor of the death camps. A bold attempt to turn unlikely material into comedy, but really, it just ain't funny. GA

Punisher, The

(1989, Aust, 89 min)
d Mark Goldblatt. *p* Robert Mark Kamen. *sc* Boaz Yakin, Robert Mark Kamen. *ph* Ian Baker. *ed* Tim Wellburn. *pd* Norma Moriceau. *m* Dennis Dreith. *cast* Dolph Lundgren, Louis Gossett Jr, Jeroen Krabbé, Kim Miyori, Bryan Marshall, Nancy Everhard, Barry Otto.
●Renegade cop Frank Castle (Lundgren) goes underground after his wife and kiddies are killed by the Mafia, emerging leather-clad and steel-eyed as the Punisher. After offing 125 hoods in five years, a feat he describes as 'work in progress', it looks like he can hang up his crossbow when the Yakuza muscle in on New York to finish off the rest of the Family. But when the fiendish Japs kidnap the capo's children, soft-hearted Mr P intervenes on behalf of his erstwhile enemies. Villains are offed, guns go blam, and inarticulate Oriental cries fill the air. Almost worse than the storyline's hackneyed idiocy is the psychological improbability of the characters (though Krabbé wrestles heroically with his numb role as the head Don). A little more fetishism wouldn't go amiss, and we get nowhere near enough kinky weaponry, crotch shots and masochism (despite a neat bit of auto-cauterising). Set against this is the blithe humour of the proceedings, a welcome shortage of love interest, Dolph's minimalist wit, and two arch-villainesses attired in black plastic and other form-fitting fabrics. Destructive, reprehensible, and marvellous fun. SFe

Punishment Park

(1971, US, 89 min)
d Peter Watkins. *p* Susan Martin. *sc* Peter Watkins. *ph* Joan Churchill. *ed* Peter Watkins, Terry Hodel. *ad* David Hancock. *m* Paul Motian. *cast* Carmen Argenziano, Stan Armsted, Jim Bohan, Frederick Franklyn, Gladys Golden, Sanford Golden.
●A futuristic pseudo-documentary in which political dissenters can choose Federal prison or the three-day ordeal of Punishment Park. Watkins reconstructs Greening of America political confrontations with a grainy realism and a pretence of impartiality. The trouble is that as the film progresses, his own political intentions become increasingly obscure, unless what we have here is merely an indulgence of the naive polarisation of the American left in the late '60s – Us (the righteous) versus Them (the pigs), with nothing in between. RM

Punk and the Princess, The (aka The Punk)

(1993, GB, 96 min)
d Mike Sarne. *p* Mike Sarne, Robin Mahoney. *sc* Mike Sarne. *ph* Alan Trow. *ed* Gwyn Jones, Matthew Salkeld. *m* Claudia Sarne, Charlie Creed-Miles, Nigel Powell. *cast* Charlie Creed-Miles, Vanessa Hadaway, David Shawyer, Jess Conrad, Jacqueline Skarvellis.

●An adaptation of 14-year-old Gideon Sams' cult novel *The Punk*, made 15 years after publication by 53-year-old singer/sometime-director Mike Sarne (who also co-produced and wrote the screenplay). David (Creed-Miles), the disaffected son of an odious copper, wanders the streets of Notting Hill. One day he stumbles backstage during rehearsals for a fringe production of *Romeo and Juliet*. There he meets spoilt rich-girl Rachel (Hadaway), and amid the sniffing, spliffing, squalor and squats of West London, the star-cross'd lovers experience the usual coming-of-age problems. Very poor in all departments. NF

Punk in London

(1977, WGer, 106 min)
d/sc Wolfgang Büld. *ph* Helge Weindler, Willy Brunner, Sven Kirsten. *ed* Wolfgang Büld. *with* The Sex Pistols, Stranglers, Clash, X-Ray Spex, Boomtown Rats, Adverts, Jolt, Electric Chairs, Subway Sect, Jam.

●Earnest young German TV director: 'Why don't you want to appear in our movie?' Jean-Jacques Burnel: 'Because I'm not a prostitute'. *Punk in London* makes all the mistakes that visiting film crews with sociological briefs usually make, especially when they're headed by earnest young directors. It pretends that its superficial observations are in-depth analyses; it contents itself with interviewing peripheral figures because it can't get near the nazz. Büld doesn't help himself by worrying about the sound quality, and sometimes dubbing recorded versions of songs over images of the same song in performance, to absurd effect. No musical highlights, but a couple of the interviews are fun: one with the disarmingly honest roadie Rodent, the other with The Lurkers' bassist and his elderly parents, conducted in their home over a TV set relaying a disco track on *Top of the Pops*. TR

Punk Rock Movie, The

(1977, GB, 45 min)
d Don Letts. *with* The Sex Pistols, Clash, Siouxsie and the Banshees, Generation X, X-Ray Spex, Heartbreakers, Subway Sect.

●The directness of the title sums it up sweetly: after nine years this still emerges as the most faithful and wittiest punk documentary ever made. Filmed largely during the famed 100 days of the Roxy in early '77 by resident DJ Letts, it captures the smell and rush of the phenomenon at its chaotic peak, and the jitter of Super-8 shoots most of the prime movers as the spirit of the thing befits; video would have been disastrous. Priceless and highly embarrassing highlights include pre-Pogue Jam fan Shane McGowan pogoing fitfully during the opening credits, a confused Siouxsie applauding herself at the end of 'Bad Shape', assorted Clash persons making dicks of themselves outside a cafe (reminiscent in part of Dezo Hoffman's home movies of the Beatles), and a splendidly explicit Wayne County sticking his head into the bass drum at the end of 'Cream in My Jeans'. Best of all, Rotten's performance on stage and off is magnificent. In pre-punk terminology, it's all eminently groovy.

Puppetmaster, The (Ximeng Rensheng)

(1993, Tai, 141 min)
d Hou Xiaoxian. *p* Chiu Fu-Sheng. *sc* Wu Nien-jen, Zhu Tianwen. *ph* Li Ping-Bin. *ed* Liao Ch'ing-sung. *pd* John Myhre. *m* Chen Ming-Chang. *cast* Li Tianlu, Lin Qiang, Chen Kuizhong, Zuo Juwei, Hong Liu, Bai Minghua.

●This hallucinatory biopic covers the first 36 years of Li Tianlu's life story. The film shows a life buffeted every which way by family, work and politics (Taiwan was a Japanese colony for the whole period shown here, and things got rough in the war years), but Li survived each chapter of accidents by turning himself into a true folk-artist, retelling myths and legends on his puppet theatre stage. Li appears several times as a funny and very laid-back raconteur, but mostly we see reconstructed episodes from his memoirs. The film covers much ground, from the collapse of feudal society to the defeat of the Japanese, but the overall pace is slow and contemplative, and the focus is deliberately narrow. Hou Xiaoxian has been moving towards this storytelling style for years, and it's probably too minimalist to make new converts. But long-term admirers (and dope heads) will come out of the film with a vivid sense of Chinese folk-culture and an agreeably blurred vision of the relations between an individual and his society. TR

Puppet Masters, The (aka Robert A. Heinlein's The Puppet Masters)

(1994, US, 109 min)
d Stuart Orme. *p* Ralph Winter. *sc* David S Goyer, Ted Elliot, Terry Rossio. *ph* Clive Tickner. *ed* E William Goldenberg. *pd* Daniel Lomino. *m* Colin Towns. *cast* Donald Sutherland, Eric Thal, Julie Warner, Will Patton, Richard Belzer, Tom Mason.

●Aliens land in Iowa and take over humans. Sutherland has been this way before (*Invasion of the Body Snatchers*, 1978) and it shows. There's no suspense (ETs rampage from the word go); no frissons (loud hailers telegraph the shocks); and it's insufficiently bright to be an *hommage*. AO

Puppet on a Chain

(1970, GB, 98 min)
d Geoffrey Reeve. *p* Kurt Unger. *sc* Alistair MacLean. *ph* Jack Hildyard, Skeets Kelly. *ed* Bill Lenny. *pd* Peter Mullins. *m* Piero Piccioni. *cast* Sven-Bertil Taube, Barbara Parkins, Alexander Knox, Patrick Allen, Vladek Sheybal, Ania Marson.

●A half-baked thriller set in Amsterdam, and wearily flaunting the familiar backdrop of canals and barrel-organs while struggling to extract some excitement from a limp Alistair MacLean adventure about an American narcotics agent (Taube) and a drug ring whose nastiest habit is getting rid of meddlers by hanging them from meathooks. Reeve's direction serves up spasmodic lumps of violence in lieu of suspense, and the one tolerable sequence – an extended speedboat chase through the canals – was contributed by Don Sharp. TM

Pure Formality, A (Una Pura Formalità)

(1993, It/Fr, 108 min)
d Giuseppe Tornatore. *p* Mario Cecchi Gori, Vittorio Cecchi Gori. *sc* Giuseppe Tornatore. *ph* Blasco Giurato. *ed* Giuseppe Tornatore. *m* Ennio Morricone. *cast* Gérard Depardieu, Roman Polanski, Sergio Rubini, Nicola di Pinto.

●Essentially a stagey two-hander in which, in a strangely sinister, seemingly timeless police station, inspector Polanski interrogates the partly amnesiac Depardieu, who claims he's a famous author but who may in fact be responsible for a murder committed near the novelist's home. Emphatically metaphorical and full of thumpingly obvious symbolism, Tornatore's film depends heavily on the two leads for effect – Polanski's sly, shrewd performance outshines Depardieu's broader turn – but even they can't distract from the ludicrous contrivance of the film's threadbare central conceit. GA

Pure Hell of St Trinian's, The

(1960, GB, 94 min, b/w)
d Frank Launder. *p* Sidney Gilliat, Frank Launder. *sc* Frank Launder, Val Valentine, Sidney Gilliat. *ph* Gerald Gibbs. *ed* Thelma Connell. *ad* Wilfrid Shingleton. *m* Malcolm Arnold. *cast* Cecil Parker, Joyce Grenfell, George Cole, Thorley Walters, Eric Barker, Irene Handl, Dennis Price, Liz Fraser, Sidney James.

●Third in the Ronald Searle series. After they have burned down the school, the girls are shipped off to the Middle East, where – with the inevitable harem and secret agents lurking – inspiration seems to have deserted the St Trinian's scriptwriters. Some bright moments, but on the whole very disappointing. Irene Handl replaced Alastair Sim as the headmistress, otherwise the crew remained the same. DMcG

Pure Luck

(1991, US, 96 min)
d Nadia Tass. *p* Lance Hool, Sean Daniel. *sc* Herschell Weingrod. *ph* David Parker. *ed* Billy Weber. *pd* Peter Wooley. *m* Jonathan Sheffer. *cast* Martin Short, Danny Glover, Sheila Kelley, Sam Wanamaker, Scott Wilson, Harry Shearer, Jorge Russek.

●Hollywood remake of a French farce has private eye Glover on the trail of klutzy heiress Kelley, who's been kidnapped on vacation in Mexico. Concerned dad Wanamaker comes up with the notion of unleashing accountant Short on the case, a man so encumbered by ill fortune he's somehow bound to stumble across the girl. A misfire. TJ

Purely Belter

(2000, GB, 99 min)
d Mark Herman. *p* Elizabeth Karlsen. *sc* Mark Herman. *ph* Andy Collins. *ed* Michael Ellis. *pd* Don Taylor. *m* Ian Broudie, Michael Gibbs. *cast* Charlie Hardwick, Tim Healy, Roy Hudd, Kevin Whately, Chris Beattie, Greg McLane, Jody Baldwin, Kerry Ann Christiansen.

●Gerry (Beattie) and Sewell (McLane) are apprentice foot soldiers in the Toon Army – meaning that, as low expectation truants, they haven't a prayer of finding the £1,000 needed for a season ticket to see their beloved Newcastle United FC. Indomitable, they lay off the tabs and the glue, and start fund raising. They tout scrap metal, try robbing 'Everything's-a-Pound' stores, even beseech Alan Shearer. Mostly, though, real life intrudes in the form of simple or sickly parental figures, brutal errant dads, useless social workers, scornful teachers, fickle girls and street psychos. Given the growing inequities between big showbiz football clubs and their old proletarian fans, you'd not blame writer/director Herman for expounding the sort of angry polemic that gave his *Brassed Off* its biting edge. That's implicit in this lively adaptation of Jonathan Tulloch's novel *The Season Ticket*, but Herman couches his social judgment in broadminded comic observation. The comedy is patchily successful, but it's the immediate affection and empathy for the wayward leads that really plays. There's none of the triumphalism of most sports movies here, just a whole lot of mixed-up life. NB

Puritan, The (Le Puritain)

(1937, Fr, 87 min, b/w)
d/sc Jeff Musso. *ph* Curt Courant. *ed* Emilienne Nelissen. *ad* Serge Pimenoff, Henri Ménessier. *m* Jeff Musso, Jacques Dallin. *cast* Jean-Louis Barrault, Pierre Fresnay, Viviane Romance, Mady Berry, Jean Tissier.

●Apparently the centre of considerable controversy when it was made, *The Puritan* still looks cogently argued and provocative. Based on a novel by Liam O'Flaherty, it's basically the old chestnut about puritanism masking an inferno of repressed lusts. What makes it interesting is partly Barrault's terrific performance as the moral vigilante who kills a girl and clumsily tries to frame her lover; and partly the plotting, which leaves the police in no doubt about Barrault's guilt from the start, and allows Barrault to understand his own problems as the effect of his crime sinks in. The result is a rather well-crafted study of a pathetic figure who achieves personal freedom only at the moment that the cell door closes on him. Musso isn't another Buñuel, and nobody could consider the film especially subversive; but its fundamental intelligence is nicely complemented by the warmth of Musso's feeling for his characters, especially in the low-life bars and clubs. TR

Purple Haze

(1982, US, 104 min)
d David Burton Morris. *p* Thomas Anthony Fucci. *sc* Victoria Wozniak. *ph* Richard Gibb. *ed* Dusy Dennison. *ad* James Johnson. *cast* Peter Nelson, Chuck McQuary, Bernard Baldan, Susanna Lack, Bob Breuler, Joanne Bauman.

●Magenta Fogg writes: 'Sometimes life is really too much, I mean, I just saw this incredibly deep and meaningful movie about this guy called Caulfield (like in *Catcher in the Rye*) who gets thrown out of school back in 1968, and he trucks on home to Straight City, and his mum and dad lay a heavy trip on him, and his chick freaks out over *The Graduate*, and everyone is giving off very negative vibes, except these two amazing friends, one's into frying his brains on all kinds of dynamite stuff, and the other is this really cool disc jockey who spins Procul Harum and Steppenwolf and The Byrds and other beautiful sounds into the universe, and they all go to this party full of groovy flower girls flashing their titties and making good karma, but then the first friend gets drafted and freaks out and the whole scene turns very, very heavy, I mean, a load of straights think this movie is a total and complete bummer full of stupid clichés about the 'Age of Aquarius', and only for 'Book of the Dead' heads and other geriatric hippies, but they are just part of the breadhead conspiracy and should be left inside their boring fascist reality.' SJo

Purple Noon

see Plein Soleil

Purple Rain

(1984, US, 111 min)
d Albert Magnoli. *p* Robert Cavallo, Joseph Ruffalo, Steven Fargnoli. *sc* Albert Magnoli, William Blinn. *ph* Donald Thorin. *ed* Albert Magnoli. *pd* Ward Preston. *m* Michel Colombier. *cast* Prince, Apollonia Kotero, Morris Day, Olga Karlatos, Clarence Williams III.

●Since Prince first appeared on stage caressing the long neck of his guitar and sucking at its quivering head, he has been a man to watch. And if at first it was just to check that he did not creep up from behind, it burgeoned into something else…respect, earned by his raunchy, inventive brand of funk and the sense that here was someone who could be truly great. The considerable appeal of the film depends upon his presence, and luckily the man sweats charisma, for the plot is at best predictable, at worst incomprehensible. Partly autobiographical, part fiction, it tells of The Kid (Prince), product of a broken home and an impregnable ego, struggling to the top of the rock heap. His girlfriend Apollonia loves him but is attracted by his arch-enemy, lead singer with rival band The Time (it gets very reductionist). But this is all no more than fancy padding around the film's heart, which only starts to really pump when Prince is up on stage: a teasing, hot amalgam of Marc Bolan, Nijinsky and the Scarlet Pimpernel, as electric as his guitar. FD

Purple Rose of Cairo, The

(1985, US, 82 min)
d Woody Allen. *p* Robert Greenhut. *sc* Woody Allen. *ph* Gordon Willis. *ed* Susan E Morse. *pd* Stuart Wurtzel. *m* Dick Hyman. *cast* Mia Farrow, Jeff Daniels, Danny Aiello, Irving Metzman, Stephanie Farrow, Van Johnson, Dianne Wiest, Zoe Caldwell, John Wood, Milo O'Shea, Edward Herrmann.

●During the Depression, downtrodden housewife Farrow so inflames a film's leading man (an explorer-poet) that he climbs down from the screen, and entices her into a chaotic but charming love affair. Woody Allen's deft script investigates every nook and cranny of the couple's bizarre relationship, the irate Pirandellian reactions of the illusory characters left up on the screen, and the bewilderment of the actor whose movie persona has miraculously gone walkies. As the star-struck couple, Farrow and Daniels work wonders with fantastic emotions, while Allen's direction invests enough care, wit and warmth to make it genuinely moving. GA

Purple Storm (Ziyu Fengbao)

(1999, HK, 113 min)
d Teddy Chen. *p* John Chong, Solon So. *sc* Lam Oi-Wah, Jojo Hui, Clarence Yip. *ph* Arthur Wong. *ed* Kong Chi-Leung. *ad* Kenneth Mak. *m* Peter Kam. *cast* Daniel Wu, Emil Chow, Kam Kwok-Keung, Josey Ho, Joan Chen, Theresa Lee, Huang Jianxin.

●Crammed with fights, pyrotechnics and CGI effects, this is a mildly spectacular polit-thriller let down by formula plotting, slack writing and a bathetic ending. Soong (Kam, bleached blond) is a fanatical Khmer Rouge terrorist stranded in Hong Kong with an apocalyptic bio-toxin up his sleeve; his US-educated son Todd (Wu), a key member of his team, is an amnesiac in the hands of cop Ma (Chow) and a psychiatrist (Joan Chen in a cameo, defeated by the script's idea of doctor-speak). The plot hinges on parallel races against time to de-program Todd and decode the CD-ROMs which contain details of Soong's planned strike, a belated fulfilment of Pol Pot's 'Year Zero' project. There's one surprise: a guest spot at the start for mainland director Huang Jianxin as a Khmer Rouge commandant. TR

Purple Taxi, The (Le Taxi Mauve)

(1977, Fr/It/Ire, 120 min)
d Yves Boisset. *sc* Michel Déon, Yves Boisset. *ph* Tonino Delli Colli. *ed* Albert Jurgenson. *ad* Arrigo Equini, Franco Fumagalli. *m* Philippe Sarde. *cast* Peter Ustinov, Charlotte Rampling, Fred Astaire, Philippe Noiret, Edward Albert, Agostina Belli.

●Filmed in Ireland, with Boisset not the only French director of his generation to be seduced into making a mystery movie with a whimsical flavour, this is one of the worst French movies of the decade: a confused attempt at creating intrigue out of the lives of several expatriates trying to escape their past. None of the English-speaking stars look like they know what's going on, especially Astaire, bowling round the Irish countryside in the taxi of the title. Thank God the best French film-makers have realised that making an English-language movie is not as easy as it seems; pity it took a disaster like this to ram home the message. MA

Pursued

(1947, US, 101 min, b/w)
d Raoul Walsh. *p* Milton Sperling. *sc* Niven Busch. *ph* James Wong Howe. *ed* Christian I Nyby. *ad* Ted Smith. *m* Max Steiner. *cast* Robert Mitchum, Teresa Wright, Judith Anderson, Dean Jagger, John Rodney, Alan Hale, Harry Carey Jr.

●A superb Western *film noir*, with Mitchum pursued through near-epic landscapes of the mind by the indistinct demons of childhood trauma, and the narrative boldly structured around flashback insights which gradually provide both a key to his identity and the inexorable impetus for a violent catharsis. Walsh's intelligent handling of Oedipal themes here and in *White Heat* gives the definitive lie to his self-cultured image as merely an adventuresome Hollywood primitive, while the film proves that the late '40s *noir* sensibility spread way beyond the bounds of the urban crime thriller. PT

Pursuit of Happiness, The

(1970, US, 98 min)
d Robert Mulligan. *p* David Susskind. *sc* Sidney Carroll, George L Sherman. *ph* Dick Kratina. *ed* Folmar Blangsted. *ad* George Jenkins. *m* David Grusin. *cast* Michael Sarrazin, Barbara Hershey, Robert Klein, Sada Thompson, Ralph Waite, Arthur Hill, EG Marshall.

●Too shapeless, too drawn out, too much reliance on symbols – that is part of what is wrong with Mulligan's entry in the youth movie stakes. The plot is melodramatic but not incredibly so: the hero (Sarrazin) finds himself college boy one moment, prisoner (by virtue of a collision with an old lady who steps out in front of his car on a dark and rainy night) and prosecution witness in a prison murder trial the next. Mulligan seems to have intended exploring his innocent hero's 'pursuit', or rather flight, on a physical level – his opting out of student politics to indulge his model boat hobby is merely the first step – but instead the subject escapes, losing itself in getting Sarrazin from A to B rather than really looking at why. There is a serious point to it all – it shouldn't look faintly silly, but it does. VG

Pursuit of the Graf Spee

see Battle of the River Plate, The

Pursuit to Algiers

(1945, US, 65 min, b/w)
d/p Roy William Neill. *sc* Leonard Lee. *ph* Paul Ivano. *ed* Saul A Goodkind. *ad* John B Goodman, Martin Obzina. *m* Edgar Fairchild. *cast* Basil Rathbone, Nigel Bruce, Marjorie Riordan, Rosalind Ivan, Martin Kosleck, John Abbott, Frederick Worlock, Morton Lowry.

●Twelfth in the Rathbone/Bruce Sherlock Holmes series, with only two more to go and energies beginning to flag. After an intriguingly mysterious opening in a typically foggy London, Holmes and Watson are bogged down in a shipboard adventure, fending off would-be assassins of the young European monarch they are escorting. Pretty stale stuff, through Nigel Bruce makes his singing debut with 'Loch Lomond'. GA

Pusher

(1996, Den, 110 min)
d Nikolas Winding Refn. *p* Henrik Danstrup. *sc* Nikolas Winding Refn. *ph* Morten Soborg. *ed* Anne Osterud. *pd* Kim Lovetand Julebæk. *cast* Kim Bodnia, Zlatko Buric, Laura Drasbæk, Slavko Labovik.

●This is the worst week in Frank's life – and very possibly the last. Deep in debt, he fixes up a complicated heroin deal involving his skinhead pal Tony and Balkan dealer Milo. The exchange is a bust, and Frank loses both the money and the merchandise. By Thursday, Tony's out of the picture and Milo's putting on the squeeze. By Friday, Saturday might never happen. Using available light, spasmodic handheld camerawork, and improvised dialogue, write/director Refn goes out of his way (in his first feature) to create an everyday world of extraordinary circumstance – then piles on a pounding thrash guitar score and punchy editing to create a kind of electric realism. Scorsese is a touchstone, but it's a long time since he achieved this kind of blistering intensity. It's a rough ride, for sure: Tony's idea of small talk scorches the ear; the music's loud enough to feel; and a series of violent confrontations are so near-the-knuckle it's a relief not to come out bleeding. Yet this is much more than an assault on the senses. As Frank, Bodnia's baleful tough guy stoicism masks an emotional constipation which even precludes physical contact with his hooker girlfriend (Drasbæk). Wheeling and dealing for all he's worth, he can only conclude that he's not worth much; and if Copenhagen comes to resemble hell on earth, it's definitely a hell of Frank's own making. TCh

Pushing Hands (Tui Shou)

(1991, Tai, 105 min)
d Ang Lee. *p* Ted Hope, James Schamus, Hsu Li-Kong. *sc* Ang Lee. *ph* Lin Liang-Chung. *ed* Ang Lee. pd Scott Bradley. *m* Xiao Song Qu. *cast* Sihung Lung, Lai Wang, Deb Snyder, Bo Z Wang.

●This first feature by a Taiwanese graduate from the NYU Film School has a crippling central flaw. The film is about an elderly tai chi master from Beijing who clashes with his all-American daughter-in-law when he retires to his son's home in up-state New York. The culture gap is so extreme (and on her side, so vehemently expressed) that you wonder why on earth she married a Chinese guy in the first place – a question the script blithely ignores. That said, this is a reasonably amiable comedy-drama with a strong streak of sentimentality. It falls a long way short of Wayne Wang's Chinatown movies. TR

Pushing Tin

(1999, US, 124 min)
d Mike Newell. *p* Art Linson. *sc* Glen Charles, Les Charles. *ph* Gale Tattersall. *ed* Jon Gregory. *pd* Bruno Rubeo. *m* Anne Dudley. *cast* John Cusack, Billy Bob Thornton, Cate Blanchett, Angelina Jolie, Jake Weber, Vicki Lewis, Matt Ross, Kurt Fuller, Jerry Grayson, Michael Willis.

●Working from a quick-fire screenplay, by *Cheers* writers Glen and Les Charles, Newell meanders through a two hour-plus mix of macho melodramatics, romantic entanglements and comedy, uncertain whether he's making a desktop version of *Only Angels Have Wings*, a Buñuelian black farce, or a Tony Scott picture. Cusack, however, is good value as über-yuppie Nick Falzone, top gun of NY's Air Traffic Control facility (TRACON), whose chair spinning self-congratulation takes a dive with the arrival of Zen-lite country poke Russell Bell (Thornton). A cross between Iron John, Sitting Bull and Sam Shepard, Bell is a man without a pulse for whom 'thought is your enemy – you have to let go'. Newell encourages Thornton to have fun with the part, pushing it to the edge of self-parody – possibly the only option, given that Bell's idea of kicks is laying in front of jumbo jets. Satire, you think. And confirmation seems to come in the way Newell deals with Falzone's seduction of Bell's wife (Jolie) and his subsequent tremulous showdown with Bell. Maybe that's just the director having fun. In any event, we're whipped straight back into the control room – with its flashing screens, technobabble and adrenalin, indistinguishable from a Hollywood war room – for the standard issue climactic bonding between Falzone and Bell. WH

Push! Push! (San-bu In-gwa)

(1997, SKor, 95 min)
d Park Chul-Soo.

●After a technically smart but seemingly uninvolving first 20 minutes, this ambitious, fragmented comedy drama, charting the experiences of doctors, patients, family and friends in a busy maternity ward, kicks in with a vengeance. Covering all manner of medical, ethical, political and psychological issues to do with pregnancy, the film embraces slapstick, satire, social comment, suspense, melodrama and even documentary footage, as it mounts an unexpectedly affecting tribute to the courage and determination of women, whatever their take on motherhood. GA

Pussy Talk (Le Sexe qui Parle)

(1975, Fr, 91 min)
d Frédéric Lanzac. *p* Francis Leroi. *sc* Claude Mulot. *ph* Roger Fellous. *ed* Gérard Kikoine. *m* Mike Steitheson. *cast* Pénélope Lamour, Béatrice Harnois, Sylvia Bourdon, Ellen Earl-Coupey, Nils Hortzs.

● Men! Are you afraid of women? Are you weighed down by their insatiable sexual demands? Are you embarrassed by their behaviour in public? Do they humiliate you? Do you have nightmares about their furry little snatches concealing vicious little teeth? Then here at last is a film made with you, only you, in mind! And all those nasty hardcore sex scenes have been cut out in the 65 minute British release version, so you won't be distracted from the message you want to hear! TR

Putney Swope

(1969, US, 88 min, b/w & col)
d/sc Robert Downey. *ph* Gerald Cotts. *ed* Bud Smith. *ad* Gary Weist. *m* Charley Cuva. *cast* Arnold Johnson, Antonio Fargas, Laura Greene, Eric Krupnik, Pepi Hermine, Ruth Hermine, Allen Garfield, Mel Brooks.

● A satire on American ways of life, written and directed by Downey and misfiring on most cylinders. The idea is promising enough: the token black member of a big business board of directors is elected chairman because everybody votes for him on the assumption that no one else will. After some good lines in the opening scene, however, it all fizzles out in a series of damp squibs aimed indiscriminately at capitalism, Black Power, TV commercials, etc. TM

Puzzle of a Downfall Child

(1970, US, 104 min)
d Jerry Schatzberg. *p* John Foreman. *sc* Adrien Joyce [Carole Eastman]. *ph* Adam Holender. *ed* Evan Lottman. *ad* Richard Bianchi. *m* Michael Small. *cast* Faye Dunaway, Barry Primus, Viveca Lindfors, Barry Morse, Roy Scheider.

● Written by Adrian Joyce, who scripted the infinitely superior *Five Easy Pieces*, this emerges as an overwrought and soapy psychodrama in which top fashion model Dunaway, in an attempt to recover from a nervous breakdown, retires to a beach cottage and looks back into the events, both real and imaginary, that have caused her predicament. Vacuously stylish, pretentious, and poorly performed, this dud marked the debut of the often overrated Schatzberg, a former fashion photographer. GA

Pygmalion

(1938, GB, 96 min, b/w)
d Anthony Asquith, Leslie Howard. *p* Gabriel Pascal. *sc* George Bernard Shaw, WP Lipscomb, Cecil Lewis, Ian Dalrymple. *ph* Harry Stradling. *ed* David Lean. *ad* John Bryan. *m* Arthur Honegger. *cast* Leslie Howard, Wendy Hiller, Wilfrid Lawson, Marie Lohr, Scott Sunderland, Jean Cadell, David Tree, Everley Gregg, Esmé Percy.

● While the British film industry tumbled into one of the more serious of its periodic crises, an unlikely bunch of radicals and adventurers set out to breathe life into GBS's pre-First World War excursion into language and materialism. They produced a very radical – if still very male – film. Unlike the later *My Fair Lady*, the stress here is on Higgins' creation of a princess from 'a heap of stuffed cabbage leaves'. There is no Cinderella story: Eliza's transformation is forced and painful, and Higgins' final 'Where the devil are my slippers?' a refusal to forget, sentimentally, the enduring reality of patriarchy. Above all, the film is remarkable in that it strengthens rather than dilutes Shaw's insistence on language as the vital instrument of power and oppression. RMy

Pyrates

(1991, US, 95 min)
d Noah Stern. *p* Johnathan Furie. *sc* Noah Stern. *ph* Janusz Kaminski. *ed* Gib Jaffe. *pd* Sherman Willams. *m* Peter Himmelman. *cast* Kevin Bacon, Kyra Sedgwick, Bruce Martin Payne, Kristin Datillo, Buckley Norris.

● Groovy photographer Bacon and free-spirited cellist Sedgwick find their passions causing havoc when fires keep breaking out as they do the nasty. The first time a lava lamp explodes, the second time round though, and the joke's already gone too far. Presumably, real-life couple Kev 'n' Kyra had a few giggles making it, but a match carefully placed under the script would have saved everyone a lot of trouble. TJ

Pyromaniac's Love Story, A

(1995, US, 94 min)
d Joshua Brand. *sc* Morgan Ward. *ph* John Schwartzman. *ed* David Rosenbloom. *pd* Dan Davis. *m* Rachel Portman. *cast* William Baldwin, John Leguizamo, Sadie Frost, Erika Eleniak, Joan Plowright, Armin Mueller-Stahl, Mike Starr, Julio Oscar Mechoso.

● Be warned by the 'once upon a time' opening: this film serves up sugar and ham in a reduced-plot dressing, and has the nerve to call it cute salad. Sergio (Leguizamo) is the pastry boy with the light and fluffy head whose hopeless love for the waitress across the street (Frost) is to be edged towards fruition by the mysterious fire that destroys the cake shop where he works. His fate at the hands of a convoluted plot is exacerbated by a stupidity so infuriating that that you begin to find the very sight of him intensely annoying. Enter the other young lovers. Baldwin, almost overwhelmed by his kook-signifiers (walking stick, beard, overcoat), plays the real pyromaniac, who's burnt down the shop in a fit of pique with his own object of desire. Outrageously overdone, this character arrives far too late to add much interest or shed much light; and by the time Eleniak (the super-rich super-bitch Baldwin's in love with) enters the fray to sort out the nonsense from the rubbish, you're long since ready to wash your hands of the lot of them. LMu

q

Quo Vadis?

Q & A

(1990, US, 132 min)
d Sidney Lumet. *p* Arnon Milchan, Burtt Harris. *sc* Sidney Lumet. *ph* Andrzej Bartkowiak. *ed* Richard Cirincione. *pd* Philip Rosenberg. *m* Ruben Blades. *cast* Nick Nolte, Timothy Hutton, Armand Assante, Patrick O'Neal, Lee Richardson, Luis Guzman, Charles Dutton, Jenny Lumet, Paul Calderon.

●Few film-makers have dealt with American police corruption as effectively as Lumet; but while this tough, fundamentally sound New York thriller has its moments, it's no *Prince of the City*. Ambitious, idealistic assistant DA Reilly (Hutton) investigates a homicide case in which Lt Mike Brennan (Nolte), one of the NYPD's finest, shot a Hispanic dope dealer. The focus shifts towards racial tension as the Irish fall prey to old animosities against blacks and Hispanics, including crime baron Texador (Assante). Despite a redundant romantic subplot, much of the film is tightly written and directed, embellishing its conflicts with a wealth of telling detail; but it does remain earnest and faintly predictable. Although the performances are mostly solid (Assante particularly fine throughout), it never quite achieves the harsh, convincing tone it aims for. GA

Q – the Winged Serpent

see Winged Serpent, The

Quadrophenia

(1979, GB, 120 min)
d Franc Roddam. *p* Roy Baird, Bill Curbishley. *sc* Dave Humphries, Martin Stellman, Franc Roddam. *ph* Brian Tufano. *ed* Sean Barton, Mike Taylor. *pd* Simon Holland. *m* The Who. *cast* Phil Daniels, Leslie Ash, Philip Davis, Mark Wingett, Sting, Raymond Winstone, Toyah Wilcox, Michael Elphick.

●Fine as long as it sticks to recreation of period and place, and stays with a simple enough plot – 1964 mod Daniels' Brighton beach battles with the Rockers, and his on/off love affair with Ash. But as the film progresses, it becomes bogged down in silly moralising and metaphysics, struggling to accommodate itself to the absurd story of The Who's rock opera. Good performances, though, and directed with admirable energy for the first half. GA

Quai des Brumes, Le (Port of Shadows)

(1938, Fr, 89 min, b/w)
d Marcel Carné. *p* Grégor Rabinovitch. *sc* Jacques Prévert. *ph* Eugen Schüfftan. *ed* René Le Hénaff. *ad* Alexandre Trauner. *m* Maurice Jaubert. *cast* Jean Gabin, Michèle Morgan, Michel Simon, Pierre Brasseur, Le Vigan, Aimos, Perez.

●One reason the French picked up on American *film noir* so quickly in the late '40s was that they'd had their own *films noirs* a decade earlier: romantic crime thrillers in low-life settings, fatalistic in mood and fog-grey in atmosphere. *Pépé le Moko* launched the cycle in 1937 and made Gabin a star. *Quai des Brumes* clinched every last detail of the genre the following year. Gabin plays an army deserter who tries to protect Morgan from the criminal intentions of Simon and Brasseur. Shot almost entirely on its main studio set, a waterfront bar, the visuals have the same downbeat poetry as Jacques Prévert's dialogue. Those who know Gabin's glowering silences only from the clips in *Mon Oncle d'Amérique* have a revelation in store. TR

Quai des Orfèvres

(1947, Fr, 105 min, b/w)
d Henri-Georges Clouzot. *p* Roger de Venloo. *sc* Henri-Georges Clouzot, Jean Ferry. *ph* Armand Thirard. *ed* Charles Bretoneiche. *ad* Max Douy. *m* Francis Lopez. *cast* Louis Jouvet, Suzy Delair, Bernard Blier, Simone Renant, Charles Dullin, Pierre Larquey.

●It's unfortunate that *The Wages of Fear* is virtually the only Clouzot film that anyone remembers, since his real background lies in a much more traditional French thriller vein, of which *Quai des Orfèvres* is a fine example. The plot is suitably marginal: a hard-times couple (Blier, Delair) whose marriage is crumbling find themselves implicated in a murder. Clouzot doesn't waste a moment over the rampant implausibilities, but devotes all his energies to a romantically bleak evocation of the low-life settings: run-down music-halls, squalid apartments and gloomy police stations, peopled with lonely hookers, lesbians and pornographers. Jouvet's Maigret-esque cop gets all the best lines, and gives the film its human, tragic focus. TR

Quante Volte...Quella Notte (Four Times That Night)

(1969, It/WGer, 85 min)
d Mario Bava. *p* Alfredo Leone. *sc* Mario Moroni. *ph* Antonio Rinaldi. *ed* Otello Colangeli. *ad* Romeo Costantini. *m* Lallo Gori. *cast* Daniela Giordano, Brett Halsey, Dick Randall, Pascale Petit, Michael Hinz, Brigitte Skay.

●Imagine *Rashomon* remade as a tame and frivolous '60s sex comedy and shot with the zoom happy, retina-challenging elan characteristic of the director. We're offered four accounts of the same evening out: she describes a farcically failed rape, he a seduction; the lewd night porter tells of another couple and a same-sex pairing off, while a psychiatrist infers chaste abstention. The audience may prefer a fifth version where the cast is massacred by one of Bava's mad axemen; though let's spare Pascale Petit, a starlet ten years earlier and about to become surplus to requirements, still spirited and good humoured in her final role. BBa

Quantrill's Raiders

(1958, US, 68 min)
d Edward Bernds. *p* Ben Schwalb. *sc* Polly James. *ph* William Whitley. *ed* William Austin. *ad* David Milton. *m* Marlin Skiles. *cast* Steve Cochran, Diane Brewster, Leo Gordon, Gale Robbins.

●Brisk little Western. Bernds has a knack for action and keeps matters galloping along. Set in Kansas during the Civil War, the story concerns a Confederate outlaw's attempt to blow up a Yankee ammunition dump. Gordon, fresh from playing Dillinger in *Baby Face Nelson*, is as mean a varmint as anybody could wish to find on the open plains. Cochran, who'd just appeared in Antonioni's *Il Grido*, is the Gary Cooper-like hero. GM

Quarry, The (La Faille)

(1998, Bel/Fr/Neth/Sp, 112 min)
d Marion Hänsel. *p* Marion Hänsel, Jeremy Nathan. *sc* Marion Hänsel. *ph* Bernard Lutic. *ed* Michèle Hubinon. *ad* Thierry Leproust. *cast* John Lynch, Oscar Petersen, Sylvia Esau, Jody Abrahams, Serge-Henri Valcke, Jonathan Phillips.

●This religious thriller, based on a novel by Damon Galgut, is set in a one-car township in Nowheresville, South Africa. Lynch stars as a (presumed) prison escapee who accidentally kills a Baptist minister who sexually propositions him. Dumping the body in a quarry, in desperation he assumes the man's identity in a new ministry. When two dope-growing blacks steal his luggage, the ruse is revealed, but they are banged in stir by racist cop Phillips. Subsequently, a body is found near their dope patch and they're charged with murder. How will the 'minister' react? With nice visuals, a patient, leisurely pace and a strong performance by Lynch, this riff on conscience and justice would have been more convincing were it not for its over-reliance on coincidence. WH

Quartet

(1948, GB, 120 min, b/w)
d Ralph Smart, Harold French, Arthur Crabtree, Ken Annakin. *p* Antony Darnborough. *sc* RC Sherriff. *ph* Ray Elton, Reginald Wyer. *ed* Jean Barker. *ad* George Provis, Cedric Dawe. *m* John Greenwood. *cast* Basil Radford, Jack Watling, Mai Zetterling, Dirk Bogarde, Françoise Rosay, George Cole, Susan Shaw, Mervyn Johns, Hermione Baddeley, Cecil Parker, Nora Swinburne.

●First of three Somerset Maugham portmanteaux (its success engendered *Trio* and *Encore*), introduced by the old boy himself. Predictably enough, the beady-eyed Maugham cynicism has been smoothed away in RC Sherriff's adaptation of the four carefully assorted stories, leaving 'civilised' entertainment that is rescued from typically glossy but indifferent Gainsborough packaging (sets and music are particularly bad) by the performances. Parker and Swinburne are outstanding in the last (and best) story, directed by Annakin, about a pukka colonel baffled by the discovery that his placid wife has a reputation as a passionate poetess. TM

Quartet

(1981, GB/Fr, 101 min)
d James Ivory. *p* Ismail Merchant, Jean-Pierre Mahot de La Querantonnais. *sc* Ruth Prawer Jhabvala. *ph* Pierre Lhomme. *ed* Humphrey Dixon. *ad* Jean-Jacques Caziot. *m* Richard Robbins. *cast* Isabelle Adjani, Anthony Higgins, Maggie Smith, Alan Bates, Pierre Clémenti, Daniel Mesguich, Suzanne Flon.

●An adaptation of Jean Rhys' semi-autobiographical novel (for another angle on the affair, see Ford Madox Ford's *The Good Soldier*), in which a victim of circumstances, stranded in the Paris of the '20s when her con-man husband is jailed, becomes subject to the predatory help of a hedonistic upper class English couple. Maggie Smith and Alan Bates successfully personify the cold spirit that Rhys held to be pre-war England, but Adjani manages merely to reduce Marya's fatalism to spinelessness. The direction, intimate yet retaining a sense of distance, is true both to Rhys and to Ivory. FD

Quatermass Experiment, The

(1955, GB, 82 min, b/w)
d Val Guest. *p* Anthony Hinds. *sc* Richard Landau, Val Guest. *ph* Walter J Harvey. *ed* James Needs. *ad* J Elder Wills. *m* James Bernard. *cast* Brian Donlevy, Richard Wordsworth, Jack Warner, Margia Dean, David King-Wood, Gordon Jackson, Harold Lang, Thora Hird, Lionel Jeffries.

●It was the enormous success of this Hammer version of Nigel Kneale's TV series which began the whole horror boom in Britain. As a result of its popularity, the company decided to tackle the Frankenstein monster, and subsequently discovered that the public's appetite for myth and fantasy was practically insatiable. The theme of the film (man returns from space as a kind of monster) is by now fairly stereotyped, but it's amazing how impressive Richard Wordsworth's performance remains. Phil Leakey's make-up manages to convey the idea of a whole body in the process of decomposition; and staggering over bombsites, his deformed arm wrapped pathetically in an old overcoat, Wordsworth's Victor remains one of the most sympathetic monsters in movie history. Perhaps the most remarkable thing about the film, in retrospect, is the way in which its opening sequence mirrors so precisely the intrusion of Hammer into the cosy middle class domesticity of British cinema in the late '50s. Two insipid lovers are sent screaming from their haystack bower as a huge tubular rocket ship (looking less like a spacecraft than an enormous phallus) plunges into the ground where they have been lying... DP

Quatermass II

(1957, GB, 85 min, b/w)
d Val Guest. *p* Anthony Hinds. *sc* Nigel Kneale, Val Guest. *ph* Gerald Gibbs. *ed* James Needs. *ad* Bernard Robinson. *m* James Bernard. *cast* Brian Donlevy, John Longden, Sidney James, Bryan Forbes, Vera Day, William Franklyn, Charles Lloyd Pack, Michael Ripper.

●An eerie political fable on the lines of Siegel's *Invasion of the Body Snatchers*, and despite some clumsy moments that have not worn well, it remains one of the more bizarre and impressive of the early British horror pictures. Photographed by Gerald Gibbs in a sombre monochrome that nicely evokes an aura of muted hysteria and despair, it describes Quatermass' discovery that virtually the whole of Britain has been taken over by things from another world, and that the government has already begun laying waste the countryside. Provided you steel yourself against the familiar faces (like Bryan Forbes and Sidney James), the chill is still there. CPe

Quatermass and the Pit

(1967, GB, 97 min)
d Roy Ward Baker. *p* Anthony Nelson Keys. *sc* Nigel Kneale. *ph* Arthur Grant. *ed* Spencer Reeve. *pd* Bernard Robinson. *m* Tristram Cary. *cast* James Donald, Andrew Keir,

Barbara Shelley, Julian Glover, Duncan Lamont, Bryan Marshall, Peter Copley, Edwin Richfield.
●The third and most interesting of Nigel Kneale's *Quatermass* parables, scripted without interference by Kneale himself from his original TV series, so that his richly allusive web of occult, anthropological, religious and extraterrestrial speculation emerges intact as excavations at a London underground station turn up what appears to be an unexploded Nazi bomb, but proves to be a mysterious space craft. Hammer unfortunately delayed filming for several years, partly because of the sheer elaborateness of the subject matter, and partly because the plot did not lend itself to instant monster treatment. By the time the project came to be filmed, the company had moved from Bray and much of the atmosphere of their productions had been lost; but the brilliant pre-Von Daniken anthropological theme of Kneale's script still guarantees interest. DP

Quatorze Juillet (July 14th)

(1932, Fr, 90 min, b/w)
d/sc René Clair. *ph* Georges Périnal. *ed* René le Hénaff. *ad* Lazare Meerson. *m* Maurice Jaubert. *cast* Annabella, Georges Rigaud, Raymond Cordy, Pola Illéry, Paul Olivier, Raymond Aimos.
●The opening shot, in which Périnal's camera cranes sinuously around Meerson's distillation of a Paris *quartier* to the accompaniment of Jaubert's gently lyrical score (what a team!) is followed by a series of vignettes introducing the principal characters as they prepare for the 14th July festivities. It's lovely but, oh dear, you think, I bet there's going to be a story. In fact, there isn't much of one. Taxi driver Rigaud and flower girl Annabella (emblematic '30s occupations) are lovers. They fall out, spend some time being separately unhappy, until Clair contrives a whimsical reunion for the finale. It's the most Borzage-like of Clair's romances, with such incidents as the death of the heroine's mother lending unaccustomed weight to the proceedings. BBa

Quatre Aventures de Reinette & Mirabelle

see 4 Adventures of Reinette & Mirabelle

Quatre Cents Coups, Les (The 400 Blows) *(100)*

(1959, Fr, 101 min, b/w)
d/sc François Truffaut. *ph* Henri Decaë. *ed* Marie-Josèphe Yoyotte. *ad* Bernard Evein. *m* Jean Constantin. *cast* Jean-Pierre Léaud, Albert Rémy, Claire Maurier, Patrick Auffay, Georges Flamant, Guy Decomble.
●Truffaut's first feature, and although not his best, infinitely better than the self-indulgent, increasingly compromised work he was turning out towards the end of his career. Revealing a complicity with downtrodden, neglected and rebellious adolescence that is intensely moving but never mawkish, shot on location in Paris with a casually vivid eye that is almost documentary, it still has an amazing freshness in its (quasi-autobiographical) account of 13-year-old Antoine Doinel's bleak odyssey through family life, reform school, and an escape whose precarious permanence is questioned by the final frozen image of the boy's face as he reaches the sea – freedom or point of no return? Still one of the cinema's most perceptive forays into childhood, and fun for spotting the guest appearances of such *nouvelle vague* luminaries as Jeanne Moreau, Jean-Claude Brialy, Jacques Demy and (in the funfair scene) Truffaut himself. TM

Quatre Nuits d'un Rêveur

see Four Nights of a Dreamer

Quattro dell'Ave Maria, I (Ace High/Revenge in El Paso)

(1968, It, 137 min)
d Giuseppe Colizzi. *p* Bino Cicogna, Giuseppe Colizzi. *sc* Giuseppe Colizzi. *ph* Marcello Masciocchi. *ed* Marcello Malvestiti. *ad* Gastone Carsetti. *m* Carlo Rustichelli. *cast* Eli Wallach, Terence Hill [Mario Girotti], Bud Spencer [Carlo Pedersoli], Brock Peters, Kevin McCarthy, Livio Lorenzon.
●Second pairing of the Hill/Spencer team (later to sustain the 'Trinity' series) in a spaghetti spoof that has Wallach parodying his 'Ugly' persona as a roguish Mexican bandit, playing cat-and-mouse with Hill and Spencer over some stolen money while plotting revenge against the four men who framed him into jail. In a suitably cockeyed homage to Leone and Morricone, the climactic Wallach/McCarthy confrontation uncoils to the strains of a waltz. Apparently nothing but coincidentally, the Hill character is named Cat Stevens. PH

Queen, The

(1968, US, 68 min)
d Frank Simon. *p* Si Litvinoff, Don Herbert. *ph* Frank Simon, Ken Van Sickle, Robert Elfstrom, Alfonse Schilling, Joseph Zysman. *ed* Fred Shore, Geraldine Fabrikant. *with* Jack Doroshow, Richard Finochio, Crystal, Andy Warhol, Larry Rivers, Edie Sedgewick, Terry Southern.
●An outlandish documentary which follows the arrival, preparation for, and participation in the 1967 Drag Miss All American Beauty Queen Contest of a bunch of international hopefuls. The men come into town, lounge about, then dress up and sally out on stage as girls. Breasts created by flesh-cramping sellotape squeeze out of swim-suits; rivalries created by a pursuit for the title shriek around backstage; Sylvia goes bananas and the audience go wild. A rocky horror show indeed. HM

Queen Christina

(1933, US, 100 min, b/w)
d Rouben Mamoulian. *p* Walter Wanger. *sc* HM Harwood, Salka Viertel, SN Behrman. *ph* William Daniels. *ed* Blanche Sewell. *ad* Alexander Toluboff, Edwin B Willis. *m* Herbert Stothart. *cast* Greta Garbo, John Gilbert, Ian Keith, Lewis Stone, Elizabeth Young, C Aubrey Smith, Reginald Owen, Gustav von Seyffertitz, Akim Tamiroff.
●On the face of it, this is the usual historical hogwash, made to the traditional recipe (prepare a literate but daft script around the concepts of love, honour and duty; stir in two gooey-eyed stars, one of whom may be miscast and a bad wearer of costumes; bring to the boil, stirring in teaspoonfuls of C Aubrey Smith, rhubarbing peasants, snow, ducks, and Gothic lettering; serve with naive music). But *Queen Christina* is lifted far above its origins, partly by Mamoulian (who moulds potentially stodgy scenes with his finicky regard to detail), and partly by Garbo herself: she turns her character into a living entity, extracts real emotion from the script's purple clumps ('Snow is like a wild sea. One can go and get lost in it…'), and glides through Mamoulian's winding camera movements with grace, wit and beauty. She plays the 17th century Queen of Sweden, whose career comes unstuck when she falls for the Spanish Ambassador (a touching but inadequate performance from John Gilbert, her old cohort from the silents). GB

Queenie in Love

(2001, US, 98 min)
d/p/sc Amos Kollek. *ph* Ed Talavera. *ed* Ron Len. *ad* Brook Yeaton. *m* David Carbonara. *cast* Victor Argo, Valerie Geffner, Louise Lasser.
●Kollek's determinedly eccentric, New York-set comedy-drama comes across like a franker, more bawdy version of *Annie Hall*. The statuesque Geffner plays Queenie, a spoilt little rich girl who's trying without much success to be an actress while living in a rundown apartment and paying the bills by working with disadvantaged children. Rather than marry any of the wealthy types lined up by her parents, she sets out to seduce near neighbour Victor Argo, a gruff, chain-smoking old-timer with a very weak heart. There are some tremendous comic set pieces (if you like watching pensioners with an appetite for S/M, this is the film for you), as well as some flamboyant character performances, but it's hard to keep patience with the wilful, meandering narrative or to warm to the unctuous psychoanalyst who turns out to be pulling all the strings behind the scenes. GM

Queen Kelly

(1931/1985, US, 100 min, b/w)
d Erich von Stroheim. *p* Joseph P Kennedy, Gloria Swanson. *sc* Erich von Stroheim. *ph* Ben Reynolds, Gordon Pollock, Paul Ivano. *ed* Viola Lawrence. *ad* Richard Day, Harold Miles. *m* Adolph Tandler. *cast* Gloria Swanson, Walter Byron, Seena Owen, Wilhelm von Brinken, Madge Hunt, Tully Marshall, Florence Gibson.
●Bearing even less resemblance, as it stands, to Stroheim's original conception than did his earlier masterpieces, this tale of an innocent convent girl courted and corrupted by a dissolute prince engaged to a Ruritanian queen, simultaneously delights and frustrates. Transforming the hackneyed melodramatic plot into an audaciously slow spectacle of lush decor and delirious lighting, the Von conjured up a sensuously detailed world of misguided romanticism and seductive cynicism, where monarchs wield jealous whips and kindness conceals cunning strategies. But with only half the script filmed, and a dissatisfying ending tacked on by other, insensitive hands, Swanson's original 1931 release inevitably betrayed the balance, epic scope and tragic irony one would expect from this giant among filmmakers. The present version, deleting the tacked on 'suicide' ending, incorporates the two edited reels of African footage (on which Stroheim was working when he was fired) which were rediscovered in 1965, fleshed out by the use of titles and stills. The result is a profoundly flawed vision of what might have been, but riveting none the less. GA

Queen of Hearts

(1989, GB, 112 min)
d Jon Amiel. *p* John Hardy. *sc* Tony Grisoni. *ph* Mike Southon. *ed* Peter Boyle. *pd* Jim Clay *m* Michael Convertino. *cast* Vittorio Duse, Joseph Long, Anita Zagaria, Eileen Way, Vittorio Amandola, Roberto Scateni, Ian Hawkes.
●A winning debut for Amiel, working from a script by Tony Grisoni about the experience of Italian immigrants to London circa the '50s (although it seems to waver in period). It's told from the point of view of imaginative ten-year-old Eddie (Hawkes), son of Rosa and Danilo (Long, excellent), elopers from Central Italy (where the first section is set). It's a family affair, centering on the East End café which waiter Danilo buys after a gambling windfall. Relatives arrive; the four children quarrel and grow up; grandma grumbles about the old ways; a shining new Espresso machine arrives; a wedding is celebrated; Eddie's brother takes to crime. Then jilted Barbariccia, 'King of the Knives', to whom Rosa was promised back in Italy, arrives bent on revenge. It's a modest film, but rich in human relationships – their scams, aspirations and myths – and true to the fantastic spirit of the boy narrator. The strong cast (some of the actors unprofessional) makes up for the rough edges. It plays like a mix of Ealing kids' fantasy and a gentle, naive pastiche of *The Godfather*. WH

Queen of Outer Space

(1958, US, 80 min)
d Edward Bernds. *p* Ben Schwalb. *sc* Charles Beaumont. *ph* William Whitley. *ed* William Austin. *ad* David Milton. *m* Marlin Skiles. *cast* Zsa Zsa Gabor, Eric Fleming, Laurie Mitchell, Paul Birch, Barbara Darrow, Dave Willock.
●Standout 'Best Worst' movie in which astronauts crash-land on Venus and discover that women are ruling the planet. It takes the earthlings a while to grasp the feminine superiorities ('Even if a woman could build a gizmo like that, she'd never know how to aim it!'), and rather longer to locate the leader (Gabor) of those subversives who feel that 'vimmin cannot live vizout men'. The Place may be Venus, but the Time looks more like cocktail hour than the future; everyone's wearing vintage Swanky Modes and ice-skating skirts. There's also a fine display of '50s sublimated sexuality in the endless kissing scenes – which may have you pondering, along with the expedition's professor, 'How ironic that our lives and the lives of millions on Earth should depend on the sex appeal of our Captain'. CR

Queen of Spades, The

(1949, GB, 95 min, b/w)
d Thorold Dickinson. *p* Anatole de Grunwald. *sc* Rodney Ackland, Arthur Boys. *ph* Otto Heller. *ed* Hazel Wilkinson. *ad* Oliver Messel. *m* Georges Auric. *cast* Anton Walbrook, Edith Evans, Yvonne Mitchell, Mary Jerrold, Ronald Howard, Anthony Dawson, Miles Malleson, Athene Seyler, Michael Medwin.

● A pleasingly macabre fantasy, brilliantly designed by Oliver Messel, whose sets show rare imagination in evoking the suffocating decadence of imperial Russia. Expansion of Pushkin's short story, about an impecunious young officer's obsessive attempts to wrest the secret of winning at cards from a diabolical old countess, means that the first half never seems to be getting anywhere (there are cast problems, too, with Walbrook at his most sibilantly melodramatic, Evans coated in rubberised make-up, and the support variable to say the least). Yet Dickinson's elegantly prowling, darting camera, and his marvellously eerie sound effects (like the rustle of silk and the tapping stick that herald the ghostly presence of the countess) pull it all together in an impressive crescendo. TM

Queen of the Damned

(2002, US/Aust, 101 min)
d Michael Rymer. *p* Jorge Saralegui. *sc* Scott Abbott, Michael Petroni. *ph* Ian Baker. *ed* Dany Cooper. *pd* Graham 'Grace' Walker. *m* Richard Gibbs, Jonathan Davis. *cast* Stuart Townsend, Marguerite Moreau, Aaliyah, Vincent Perez, Paul McGann, Lena Olin, Christian Manon, Claudia Black, Bruce Spence, Matthew Newton, Tiriel Mora, Megan Dorman.

● This Anne Rice adaptation sees vampire Lestat (Townsend) roused from a century of elegant ennui by the power of rock'n'roll – or nu-metal goth, to be precise. As the world's first openly vampiric rock singer, he recklessly enrages fellow bloodsuckers by blowing their cover with coded messages in his lyrics. His unearthly pallor, shiny trousers and blood-curdling wails attract the attention of mortal woman and vampire-stalker Jesse (Moreau); more worryingly, he also awakens Akasha (the late Aaliyah), mother of all vampires, who desires him as her new king and partner in carnage. Rice's complex, sprawling novel is rendered virtually incomprehensible by a combination of lacklustre direction, risible dialogue and shoddy effects. The narrative pointlessly and confusingly globetrots from New Orleans through London and Los Angeles, to 'Glastonbury, West England'. The acting's rarely at fault. Townsend's heavy-lidded sensuality works well, while Aaliyah is a brittle, voracious goddess, a memorable presence in a tiny role. WI

Queen's Guards, The

(1961, GB, 110 min)
d/p Michael Powell. *sc* Roger Milner. *ph* Gerald Turpin. *ed* Noreen Ackland. *ad* Wilfrid Shingleton. *m* Brian Easdale. *cast* Daniel Massey, Robert Stephens, Raymond Massey, Ursula Jeans, Judith Stott, Elizabeth Shepherd, Duncan Lamont, Ian Hunter, Jess Conrad, Jack Watling, Andrew Crawford, Nigel Green.

● Powell's sad farewell to British features was, by his own admission, crippled by lack of any conviction in the script. In a series of flashbacks from a Trooping the Colour ceremony, a young officer (Daniel Massey) remembers the abiding family problem: his dead brother is forever held up to him as an example by their military father, who is totally obsessed with the pride of the service. Despite an imposing performance by Raymond Massey in this role, neither the period frolics (which include a visit to a 'beat' club) nor the ponderous heroics carry much conviction, with only the faintest whiff of the flair or emotion that infused *The Life and Death of Colonel Blimp*. DT

Queens of the Big Time

(1996, US, 74 min)
d Adriana Trigiani.

● Roseto, Pennsylvania, is a small town populated almost entirely by people of Italian stock, whose forefathers recreated their hometown, Roseto Valforte, in Foggia, upon emigrating to America in the 1890s. 'The Big Time' is the annual festival honouring the town's patron saint, Our Lady of Mt Carmel, and begins with a car procession of teenage 'princesses' and the crowning of the new 'queen'. This first film, complete with the home movies of the director's grandfather, covers the centennial celebration, when all the living queens (from the most recent to her 1926 counterpart) gathered together. A warm, amusing, uncritical look at tradition, friendship and community. GA

Queens Logic

(1991, US, 112 min)
d Steve Rash. *p* Stuart Oken, Russel Smith. *sc* Tony Spiridakis. *ph* Amir Mokri. *ed* Patrick Kennedy. *pd* Esward Pisoni. *m* Joe Jackson. *cast* Kevin Bacon, Linda Fiorentino, John Malkovich, Joe Mantegna, Ken Olin, Tony Spiridakis, Chloe Webb, Tom Waits, Jamie Lee Curtis, Ed Marinaro, Kelly Bishop.

● Fabulous cast, so-so idea. This is yet another post-*Big Chill* way-we-were movie: a bunch of buddies hang out remembering the good times, the bad times, the godawful records. What's testing their communal ability to grow up here is marriage: the impending one between painter Olin and hairdresser Webb, and the crumbling one between Mantegna's mouthy fishmonger and Fiorentino. The rest of the gang is on hand to provide moral or alcoholic support. Steve Rash handles the slightly diffuse business with sensitivity, but the film coasts mainly on the acting. Mantegna stands out for sheer bravado; Chloe Webb just about contrives to steal the show with a lipful of feistiness. But, as usual, it's really a boys' film, about leering, beering and losing your swim-shorts, and for straight boozy larking, *Hangin' with the Homeboys* has it licked by a mile. JRo

Queer Story, A (Jilao Sishi)

(1997, HK, 112 min)
d Shu Kei. *p* Clifton Ko. *sc* Shu Kei, Abe Kwong. *ph* Bill Wong. *ed* Wong Yee-Shun. *ad* Bill Lui. *m* Danny Chung. *cast* George Lam, Jordan Chan, Francis Ng, Christine Ng, Fredric Mao.

● Marriage guidance counsellor Law Kar-Sing (Lam) has a stable relationship with his younger boyfriend Sonny (Chan), but remains so deeply closeted that he has never broken the news to his childhood sweetheart that he's gay. Nor has he ever told his ultra-conservative father. The crunch comes when Sonny tires of his lover's evasions and walks out, forcing Law to rethink his life. The only real problem with Shu Kei's enjoyable comedy-drama is its insufficiently hidden agenda: too many scenes seem designed solely to set up common Chinese homophobic prejudices, only to knock 'em down. As Hong Kong's first overtly pro-gay movie, though, it's a credible piece of work. Its biggest asset is Jordan Chan, clearly a huge star-to-be. TR

Queimada! (Burn!)

(1968, It/Fr, 132 min)
d Gillo Pontecorvo. *p* Alberto Grimaldi. *sc* Franco Solinas, Giorgio Arlorio. *ph* Giuseppe Bruzzolini, Marcello Gatti. *ed* Mario Morra. *pd* Piero Gherardi. *m* Ennio Morricone. *cast* Marlon Brando, Evaristo Marquez, Renato Salvatori, Norman Hill, Tom Lyons.

● Pontecorvo's memorable sequel to *Battle of Algiers* sees Brando in finely ambiguous form as the drunken, cynical Sir William Walker, a British agent sent to the Caribbean island of Queimada in the mid-1800s to stir up a native rebellion against the Portuguese sugar monopoly; ten years later, he is forced to return there to destroy the leader he himself created, in order to open up trade with Britain. Falling between epic adventure and political allegory, the film is occasionally clumsily structured and poorly focused; but Pontecorvo, working from a script by Franco Solinas, provides a sharp, provocative analysis of colonialism, full of telling irony, bravura set pieces, and compelling imagery, while Brando's stiff-lipped performance, emphasising his character's confused mixture of dignity and deceit, intelligence and evil, determination and disillusion, never allows the allegory to dominate the human content. A flawed but fascinating film. GA

Que la Bête Meure (Killer!)

(1969, Fr/It, 110 min)
d Claude Chabrol. *p* André Génovès. *sc* Paul Gégauff. *ph* Jean Rabier. *ed* Jacques Gaillard. *ad* Guy Littaye. *m* Pierre Jansen. *cast* Michel Duchaussoy, Caroline Cellier, Jean Yanne, Anouk Ferjac, Marc Di Napoli, Maurice Pialat, Guy Marly, Lorraine Rainer, Dominique Zardi.

● Chabrol's most Langian film – the end is a virtual recreation of that of *Moonfleet* – *Que la Bête Meure*, like Lang's *Rancho Notorious* and *The Big Heat*, is dominated by the themes of revenge and destiny. However, in contrast to those films, whose heroes are trapped within their desire for revenge, Chabrol's protagonist (Duchaussoy), at first determined to kill the murderer (Yanne) of his son in a hit-and-run accident, finds his self-imposed task less and less appealing as he closes in on his prey. Finally, after Yanne's son kills his boorish, tyrannical father, Duchaussoy claims responsibility for the murder in order not to lose this second, substitute son. A masterful film, all the more powerful for the fact that so much of its meaning is contained in the camera's perspective of what happens rather than simply what happens. PH

Que la Fête Commence (Let Joy Reign Supreme)

(1975, Fr, 120 min)
d Bertrand Tavernier. *p* Michele de Broca. *sc* Jean Aurenche, Bertrand Tavernier. *ph* Pierre William Glenn. *ed* Armand Psenny. *ad* Pierre Guffroy. *m* Philippe D'Orleans. *cast* Philippe Noiret, Christine Pascal, Jean Rochefort, Jean-Pierre Marielle, Marina Vlady.

● Tavernier's second film, made during the period when the rewriting of history on film was the key issue in French cinema, never released in Britain but a hit in the US under the ironic title *Let Joy Reign Supreme*. Spectacular as French costume movies go, but never extravagant for its own sake, this is a subtle exploration of power politics in the court of the Regent Philippe of Orleans in 1719, taking in the revolutionary cause of Breton secessionists and the commerce in sex that provokes intrigues. Noiret is compelling as the Regent, and Pascal fleshes out the peasant girl from whose perspective the narrative is argued. Here 'Winstanley' meets 'Casanova', and it works. MA

Que no quede huella (Without a Trace/Leaving No Trace/aka Sin dejar huella)

(2000, Mex/Sp, 105 min)
d María Novaro. *p* Dulce Kuri. *sc* María Novaro. *ph* Serguei Saldívar Tanaka. *ed* Ángel Hernández Zoido. *ad* Patrick Pasquier. *cast* Aitana Sánchez-Gijón, Tiaré Scanda, Jesús Ochoa, Martín Altomaro, Juan Manuel Bernal.

● Marilu aka Ana (Sánchez-Gijón) crosses the US/Mexican border the wrong way. Arriving in the Sonora desert from Arizona, she's picked up by sleazy border officer Mendizabel (Ochoa). Her crime? Dealing in fake Mayan artefacts – and repeatedly refusing Mendi's advances. She escapes and hitches a ride with mother-of-two Aurelia (Scanda), who's just run off with the proceeds of her dealer boyfriend's stash. Journeying through towns called No Turning Back and Shifting Sands, they bond – while the federales and drug dealers close in. The women give solid performances and the car radio provides a quirky, surreal soundtrack featuring folk songs of iguanas with tits, and news reports of serial killers, sweatshop workers, floods and the like. 'Thelma y Luisa' – *sin los cojones*. JFu

Quentin Durward

see Adventures of Quentin Durward, The

Querelle

(1982, WGer/Fr, 108 min)
d Rainer Werner Fassbinder. *p* Dieter Schidor. *sc* Rainer Werner Fassbinder. *ph* Xaver Schwarzenberger, Josef Vavra. *ed* Juliane Lorenz. *pd* Rolf Zehetbauer. *m* Peer Raben. *cast* Brad Davis, Franco Nero, Jeanne Moreau, Günther Kaufmann, Laurent Malet, Hanno Pöschl.

● More a dream about than a dramatisation of Genet's novel, this is glorious and infuriating in equal parts. The port of Brest is built and lit more like one of Burroughs' Cities of the Red Night, murderous deity Querelle's ambisexual encounters are suffused with a sweaty, tangible eroticism, and Fassbinder's 'version' stays faithful to Genet's nightmare poetry. But its narrative detachment, weighty monologues, Resnais-like anachronisms, and (most irritating of all) listless rationale turn it into a lurid hymn to teenybop nihilism. All in all, perhaps an entirely appropriate parting shot from a drug-crazed German faggot. JG

Quest, The

(1996, US, 95 min)
d Jean-Claude Van Damme. *p* Moshe Diamant. *sc* Steven Klein, Paul Mones. *ph* David Gribble. *ed* John F Link, William J Meshover. *pd* Steve Spence. *m* Randy Edelman. *cast* Jean-Claude Van Damme, Roger Moore, Janet Gunn.

● Lord Edgar Dobbs (Moore), a roguish con-man, first rescues fugitive New York street criminal Chris Dubois (Van Damme) from sea-borne gunrunners, then sells him into bondage. But all this 1920s *Boy's Own* stuff is just window-dressing for the main event, the Ghan-gheng, a winner-takes-all contest featuring the world's greatest fighters. Dobbs' bumbling efforts to steal the prize, a Golden Dragon, are no more diverting than the drippy romance between Dubois and society-girl reporter Carrie (ex-stuntwoman Janet Gunn who, like first-time director Van Damme, should have stuck to her day job). The risible fight scenes showcase the stereotyped sartorial and imaginary fighting styles of the international contestants: the Orientals are treated with some respect, but the Spanish contestant prances Flamenco-style in frilly shirts and bum-hugging trousers, while his Scottish counterpart sports a kilt and eschews the traditional head-butt for a similarly terpsichorean approach. NF

Qu'est-ce qui fait courir David?

see What Makes David Run?

Quest for Fire

(1981, Can/Fr, 100 min)
d Jean-Jacques Annaud. *p* John Kemeny, Denis Héroux. *sc* Gérard Brach. *ph* Claude Agostini. *ed* Yves Langlois. *pd* Brian Morris. *m* Philippe Sarde. *cast* Everett McGill, Ron Perlman, Nameer El-Kadi, Rae Dawn Chong.

● 'Body Language and Gestures by Desmond Morris; Special Languages Created by Anthony Burgess'. With these eye-catching credits, *Quest for Fire* boldly states its claims to dance along the abyss of the ridiculous. That it manages not to fall in is something of an achievement, but not a sufficient one to justify 100 minutes of grunts and hand-waving in the service of an otherwise unremarkable story. What watchability the film does have is probably due to a screenplay by Gerard Brach, Polanski's regular co-writer. Still, if you have a weakness for exotic scenery (filmed in Canada, Scotland, Kenya), and some curiosity about the everyday life of prehistoric humankind, you will probably take some mild pleasure in this saga of the Ulam tribe's search for a way to light their fire. MH

Quest for Love

(1971, GB, 91 min)
d Ralph Thomas. *p* Peter Eton. *sc* Terence Feely. *ph* Ernest Steward. *ed* Roy Watts. *ad* Robert Jones. *m* Eric Rogers. *cast* Joan Collins, Tom Bell, Denholm Elliott, Laurence Naismith, Lyn Ashley, Neil McCallum, Ray McAnally.

● An adaptation of a story by John Wyndham, but as directed by Ralph Thomas and 'acted' by Joan Collins, it emerges as a puerile sci-fi romance in which a scientist (Bell) is transported into a parallel world. The year is the same, but in his new world, Vietnam hasn't happened, nor the conquest of Everest, nor the surgery of heart transplants. Making little of this premise, the film plunges forthwith into a moony romance where his lady of the camellias (Collins) dies of a heart condition, and he races off in search of her counterpart in the other world to save her from a similar fate. TM

Question of Silence, A (De Stilte Rond Christine M)

(1982, Neth, 96 min)
d Marleen Gorris. *p* Matthijs van Heijningen. *sc* Marleen Gorris. *ph* Frans Bromet. *ed* Hans van Dongen. *ad* Harry Ammerlaan. *m* Lodewijk de Boer, Martijn Hasebos. *cast* Edda Barends, Nelly Frijda, Henriette Tol, Cox Habbema, Eddy Brugman, Hans Croiset.

● Three strangers brutally murder the inoffensive manager of an Amsterdam boutique, but the case is less straightforward than it seems. Told in flashback via the investigation of a criminal psychiatrist brought in to certify insanity, the film convincingly shows the motive behind the killing as intolerable male oppression of various kinds, the twist in this thriller/courtroom drama being that the muggers – and their psychiatrist – are very ordinary women and their victim a man. The story is told with an astonishing assurance and visual flair that belie the small budget and debutant director Gorris' lack of experience. Her feminism is uncompromising, but of a disarmingly undogmatic kind. The result is at once accessible and deeply unsettling: the upbeat ending, for instance, has the male way of looking at the world literally laughed out of court, with a cathartic laughter that explodes out of the women's earlier silent isolation, and goes on echoing long after the film is over. SJo

Questo è il giardino

see This Is the Garden

Quick

(1932, Ger, 98 min, b/w)
d Robert Siodmak. *p* Erich Pommer. *sc* Hans Müller. *ph* Günther Rittau. *ed* Viktor Gertler. *ad* Erich Kettelhut. *m* Hans-Otto Borgmann, Gérard Jacobson. *cast* Lilian Harvey, Hans Albers, Willy Stettner, Paul Hörbiger, Albert von Kersten.

● No intersections whatever between this and the distinguished *films noirs* Siodmak made in the '40s. Albers is Quick the singing clown, Harvey a rich divorcée living in a health clinic (cue some mild satire). She is a fan of the clown but doesn't recognise him out of character and he, for no better reason than that he's in a comedy, pretends to be Herr Direktor Henkel – and so on, and on. The contrast between Albers/Henkel, beefy Germanic he-man, and Albers/Quick, epicene refugee from *Cabaret*, is more spooky than funny. Quick's big number, in which he skids down the neck of a giant banjo then cavorts around the auditorium, is well staged. But the appeal of Harvey, who combined Home Counties prettiness with the manic manner of early Mickey Rooney, seems to have been mislaid over the years. BBa

Quick and the Dead, The

(1995, US, 108 min)
d Sam Raimi. *p* Joshua Donen, Allen Shapiro, Patrick Markey. *sc* Simon Moore. *ph* Dante Spinotti. *ed* Pietro Scalia. *pd* Patrizia von Brandenstein. *m* Pietro Scalia. *cast* Sharon Stone, Gene Hackman, Russell Crowe, Leonardo DiCaprio, Lance Henriksen.

● This engagingly OTT homage to the style and revenge fantasies of the spaghetti Western centres on a deadly tournament – organised by Hackman, boss of the township Redemption – to find the fastest gun in the West. Enter a motley crew, among them Sharon Stone's Eastwood-like interloper, who has a secret agenda of her own… A deadpan black comedy, Sam Raimi's fast-paced movie looks and sounds like a Leone oater but more so. The violence is heightened by an intelligent, often hilarious use of special effects. Stone, who co-produced, is surprisingly effective in the lead, and Hackman's Herod is wonderfully, unrepentantly villainous. Terrific fun. GA

Quick Change

(1990, US, 88 min)
d Howard Franklin, Bill Murray. *p* Robert Greenhut, Bill Murray. *sc* Howard Franklin, Bill Murray. *ph* Michael Chapman. *ed* Alan Heim. *pd* David Gropman. *m* Randy Edelman. *cast* Bill Murray, Geena Davis, Randy Quaid, Jason Robards, Bob Elliott, Philip Bosco, Phil Hartman, Jack Gilpin.

● New York is the central character in this quirky comedy, which brings Murray, Davis and Quaid together as an unlikely trio of bank-robbers, pulling off the neatest heist imaginable before going adrift on the rocks of Big Apple chaos. It's Murray and screenwriter Franklin's joint first directorial effort – based on Jay Cronley's novel – and does have much to recommend it, notably some superb set pieces from a collection of redoubtable character actors (particularly cherishable is a scene with a hopelessly lost Central American cab driver), a feisty show from Robards as the cop who has to crack the case, and a tailing-down of Murray's usual smart-ass character into someone who has to achieve a cool equilibrium under pressure. There are also some useful street locations, climaxing with a very accurate conjuration of all the hell that is Times Square. Not likely to set the world alight, but a neat and engaging little comedy of bad manners. SGr

¿Quién Puede Matar a un Niño? (Death Is Child's Play/Island of the Damned/ Would You Kill a Child?)

(1975, Sp, 112 min)
d Narciso Ibáñez Serrador. *p* Manuel Pérez. *sc* Luis Peñafiel, Narciso Ibañez Serrador. *ph* José Luis Alcaine. *ed* Juan Serra, Antonio Ramirez de Loaysa. *m* Waldo de los Rios. *cast* Lewis Fiander, Prunella Ransome, Maria Druille, Lourdes de la Cámara, Roberto Nauta.

● Horror films are almost by definition so full of plagiarism and revamped ideas that it's always exciting to find real originality in a plot. While this is influenced by *Night of the Living Dead* and *Lord of the Flies*, its twist is inventive and, potentially, highly relevant: the children of a remote Spanish island are afflicted by a kind of supernatural plague, and slaughter the adult population. Finally, though, the film fails to take advantage of its own idea. Hints over the credits that the children of the human race may be exacting revenge for war atrocities are undercut by a gratuitous *Rosemary's Baby* subplot. DP

¿Quién sabe?

see Bullet for the General, A

Quiet American, The

(1958, US, 120 min, b/w)
d/p/sc Joseph L Mankiewicz. *ph* Robert Krasker. *ed* William Hornbeck. *ad* Rino Mondellini. *m* Mario Nascimbene. *cast* Audie Murphy, Michael Redgrave, Claude Dauphin, Giorgia Moll, Bruce Cabot, Richard Loo.

● Graham Greene was incensed by the way his novel's anti-American bias was shifted into anti-Communism as his quiet American arrives in Indo-China in 1952 with naive notions about a moral 'third force' helping to resolve the conflict. Vietnam history may have proved Greene right, but this remains a superior, strikingly intelligent film. Locations in Saigon help in lending an amazingly convincing atmosphere, and Mankiewicz is very nearly at his best in probing the murky relationship between Murphy's American Candide and Redgrave's tormentedly cynical British war correspondent, with sexual rivalry and unwanted personal obligations providing a quicksand basis for their ideological clash. Much underrated at the time. TM

Quiet Days in Clichy (Stille Dage i Clichy)

(1969, Den, 96 min, b/w)
d Jens Jorgen Thorsen. *p* Klaus Pagh. *sc* Jens Jorgen Thorsen. *ph* Jesper Hom, Teit Jorgensen. *ad* Elith Nykjaer Jorgensen. *m* Country Joe McDonald, Ben Webster, Young Flowers, Andy Sundstrom, Papa Blue's Viking Jazz Band. *cast* Paul Valjean, Wayne John Rodda, Ulla Lemvigh-Müller, Avi Sagild, Susanne Krage.

● Joey and Carl fuck, suck and eat their way through Henry Miller's Paris, the last frontier for the American hero to conquer. There's lots of women, and the studs waste no time getting them on the bed, in the bath, on the floor, anytime, anywhere, anyhow. Cartoon bubbles, subtitles, and Country Joe's music fill in the thoughts and keep it moving. Rodda's bad acting defies description. You might dismiss the whole thing as a superior skinflick; nevertheless it goes a long way towards conveying what Miller was about, giving the feel of Paris behind the feel of the crack. It's also often quite funny, which should be sufficient recommendation for those who have sat through one dour sex film too many. CPe

Quiet Days in Clichy (Jours Tranquilles à Clichy)

(1989, Fr/It/Ger, 104 min)
d Claude Chabrol. *sc* Ugo Leonzio, Claude Chabrol. *ph* Jean Rabier. *ed* Monique Fardoulis. *ad* Marco Dentici. *m* Matthieu Chabrol, Luigi Ceccarelli, Jean-Michel Bernard. *cast* Andrew McCarthy, Nigel Havers, Stephanie Cotta, Barbara De Rossi, Anna Galiéna, Stéphane Audran, Mario Adorf.

●Any Chabrol character who washes his oysters down with a pint of beer is probably in directorial disfavour, and indeed the director does seem to find Joey – Henry Miller's alter ego – a bit of a creep. The film opens with Joey shrivelled and impotent, living in desolation. The flashbacks to '30s Paris are a fantasia of florid decor, nudity and uncomplicated pleasure. Left and right clash in the streets but at the fabulous Club Melody the fun goes on. 'I want to stay here forever,' cries Joey, fastening onto a symbolic nipple, even as the image fades to dry, embittered old age. It's hardly profound and the *Jules et Jim* references are misplaced. But as a subversion of its source material the film is on a par with *Kiss Me Deadly*. BBa

Quiet Desperation, A

(2001, GB, 90 min)
d Shakila Taranum Maan. *ph* Koutaiba Al-Janabi. *cast* Shiv Grewal Gurpreet Bhatti, Dev Sagoo.
●When, prompted by the death of his brother, Shammi returns home to Southall, he reignites a number of unfinished stories, while provoking mixed emotions by his significant time away. Indifference, isolation, prostitution and murder all lead to major confrontations and reassessments. Atmospheric and effectively scored, its too literal voice-over aside, this tale of one man's journey through a quasi-deserted city and the past nevertheless provides an insight into a little known London community. GE

Quiet Earth, The

(1985, NZ, 91 min)
d Geoffrey Murphy. *p* Don Reynolds, Sam Pillsbury. *sc* Bill Baer, Bruno Lawrence, Sam Pillsbury. *ph* James Bartle. *ed* Michael Horton. *pd* Josephine Ford. *m* John Charles. *cast* Bruno Lawrence, Alison Routledge, Peter Smith, Anzac Wallace, Norman Fletcher, Tom Hyde.
●Zac Hobson finds himself the planet's sole reluctant survivor of a catastrophic error in the secret energy project on which he's been engaged, and the combination of guilt and self-delusion soon sends him off his rocker. Murphy starts to develop this idea with a series of delightfully inventive scenes, with Zac proclaiming himself world dictator, trying a little transvestism, and finally challenging God to a duel. But what promises initially to become an SF spoof of genuine oddity, soon degenerates into a merely conventional thriller with the arrival of two fellow survivors. Still, compensation is provided by desolate Auckland locations, some fine sight gags, and the ebullient Lawrence as Zac. The moral: 'Don't fuck with the infinite'. WH

Qui êtes-vous Polly Maggoo?

see Who Are You Polly Maggoo?

Quiet Man, The 100

(1952, US, 129 min)
d John Ford. *p* John Ford, Merian C Cooper. *sc* Frank S Nugent. *ph* Winton C Hoch. *ed* Jack Murray. *ad* Frank Hotaling. *m* Victor Young. *cast* John Wayne, Maureen O'Hara, Victor McLaglen, Barry Fitzgerald, Mildred Natwick, Arthur Shields, Ward Bond, Jack MacGowran.
●Ford's flamboyantly Oirish romantic comedy hides a few tough ironies deep in its mistily nostalgic recreation of an exile's dream. But the illusion/reality theme underlying immigrant boxer Wayne's return from America to County Galway – there to become involved in a *Taming of the Shrew* courtship of flame-haired O'Hara, and a marathon donnybrook with her truculent, dowry-withholding brother McLaglen – is soon swamped within a vibrant community of stage-Irish 'types'. Ford once described it gnomically as 'the sexiest picture ever made'. PT

Quiet Please, Murder

(1942, US, 70 min, b/w)
d John Larkin. *p* Ralph Dietrich. *sc* John Larkin. *ph* Joe MacDonald. *ed* Louis Loeffler. *ad* Richard Day, Joseph C Wright. *m* Arthur Lange. *cast* George Sanders, Gail Patrick, Richard Denning, Sidney Blackmer, Lynne Roberts, Kurt Katch.
●Cheapo thriller enhanced by an unusual plot and location, with Sanders as a manic book collector who will do anything to get his hands on rare editions. Mainly set in a library, it takes off when Sanders kills while stealing a Shakespeare folio, and becomes more complicated when an evil Nazi art collector gets in on the act. Lively, blessed by a typically cool performance from Sanders, and helped no end by Joe MacDonald's stylish camerawork. GA

Quiet Room, The

(1996, Aust, 90 min)
d Rolf de Heer. *p* Domenico Procacci, Rolf de Heer. *sc* Rolf de Heer. *ph* Tony Clark. *ed* Tania Nehme. *pd* Fiona Paterson. *m* Graham Tardiff. *cast* Chloe Ferguson, Phoebe Ferguson, Paul Blackwell, Celine O'Leary.
●The fascination with perception and communication that characterised de Heer's *Bad Boy Bubby* again dominates this look at a couple's deteriorating relationship as witnessed (with confusion and misunderstanding) by their seven-year-old daughter, who simply refuses to speak – though we hear her thoughts in voice-over. Without ramming the point home, de Heer shows the well-meaning parents' insensitivity, their desperation and their occasional readiness to use the child as a pawn in their power games; and while it's basically a one-idea movie, and perhaps too concerned with formal originality, as opposed to emotional content, it still offers acute insights into a child's inner world. GA

Quigley Down Under

(1990, US, 120 min)
d Simon Wincer. *p* Stanley O'Toole, Alexandra Rose. *sc* John Hill. *ph* David Egby. *ed* Peter Burgess. *pd* Ross Major. *m* Basil Poledouris. *cast* Tom Selleck, Laura San Giacomo, Alan Rickman, Chris Haywood, Ron Haddrick, Tony Bonner, Jerome Ehlers.
●To date, the '90s Westerns suggest a return to the revisionist oaters of 20 years earlier: anti-Westerns, or at any rate anti-colonial. If this Selleck vehicle about an American cowboy in Australia is hardly 'Dances with Dingoes', it is a pleasant surprise to see the predictably jokey signs of dislocation – koalas and roos – make way for the moral issues the genre thrives on. Sharpshooter Quigley goes down under to shoot dingoes for rancher Marston (Rickman) – or so he thinks. When it transpires that he is to eliminate aborigines, a feud develops, and he becomes a champion of the native tribes. Unfortunately, his status as righter of wrongs is mirrored to some extent by the script, which shows a particularly heavy hand in exposition. But Selleck's easy charm carries it through the sticky patches. Aussie director Wincer handles the action convincingly, and Rickman's splendidly snide villain is a real treat. TCh

Quiller Memorandum, The

(1966, GB/US, 103 min)
d Michael Anderson. *p* Ivan Foxwell. *sc* Harold Pinter. *ph* Erwin Hillier. *ed* Frederick Wilson. *ad* Maurice Carter. *m* John Barry. *cast* George Segal, Alec Guinness, Max von Sydow, Senta Berger, George Sanders, Robert Helpmann, Robert Flemyng, Peter Carsten.
●The thinking man's spy thriller, in as much as Harold Pinter wrote the script. Although the whole thing is ill-served by Michael Anderson's direction, it remains perversely likeable precisely because it is rather long-winded and enigmatic: it gets closer to the feel of Len Deighton's novels far better than any of the three Harry Palmer films. The acting, with George Segal versus neo-Nazi Max von Sydow, is excellent, the Berlin locations so-so. CPe

Quills

(1999, US/Ger, 124 min)
d Philip Kaufman. *p* Julia Chasman, Nick Wechsler, Peter Kaufman. *sc* Doug Wright. *ph* Rogier Stoffers. *ed* Peter Boyle. *pd* Martin Childs. *m* Stephen Warbeck. *cast* Geoffrey Rush, Kate Winslet, Joaquin Phoenix, Michael Caine, Billie Whitelaw, Patrick Malahide, Amelia Warner, Jane Menelaus, Stephen Moyer, Edward Tudor-Pole.
●It's true that the Marquis de Sade was held at the Charenton asylum, diagnosed with 'Libertine dementia', that he wrote plays there, and came into contact with a laundry maid (Winslet), the Abbé Coulmier (Phoenix) and Dr Royer-Collard (Caine). But scenarist Wright, adapting his own play, has freely imagined what passed between them in terms of ribald comedy and Grand Guignol horror. Rush has a whale of a time as Sade, a debauched rake with a permanent hard-on, playing sly devil's advocate to the Abbé's zealous innocent. The hypocritical Royer-Collard ups the ante when he institutes a new, repressive regime, confiscating the Marquis's writing instruments. Announcing itself as 'a naughty little tale', the film cultivates an air of sardonic detachment beneath a lascivious leer. It pokes at sexual taboos – it's pretty subversive, considering – but sexuality and creativity are indelibly linked, and its true subject is expression, repression and catharsis. If that sounds schematic, the script's frank libertarian agenda is muddied by Sade's perversity. On some bedrock level he relishes his own degradation. But it's the artist's irrefutable compulsion to write which fuels the most powerful sequence, as Sade turns in on himself for material in the basest sense of the word, bringing body and soul together at the last. TCh

Quince Tree Sun, The (El Sol del Membrillo)

(1991, Sp, 137 min)
d Victor Erice. *sc* Antonio López, Victor Erice. *ph* Javier Aguirresarobe, Angel Luis Fernàndez. *ed* Juan Ignacio San Mateo. *m* Pascal Gaigne. *cast* Antonio López, Maria Moreno, Enrique Gran, José Carrtero.
●A truly magnificent film from the maker of *Spirit of the Beehive* and *The South*, which effortlessly transcends the term 'documentary'. Basically, it follows Madrileño painter Antonio López as he meticulously and slowly labours over a painting of a quince tree in his garden. That the task takes him months is of interest in itself, but where the film scores is in its fleshing out of its subject through conversation with friends, wife, admirers, and builders at work on his house, a strategy that simultaneously contextualises López and puts his bizarre, even limited conception of artistic endeavour into perspective. Don't worry about a lengthy, fairly banal dialogue about half-an-hour into the film; the rest is visually extraordinary, funny, touching, and quite unlike anything else. GA

Quintet

(1979, US, 118 min)
d/p Robert Altman. *sc* Frank Barhydt, Robert Altman, Patricia Resnick. *ph* Jean Boffety. *ed* Dennis M Hill. *pd* Leon Ericksen. *m* Tom Pierson. *cast* Paul Newman, Vittorio Gassman, Fernando Rey, Bibi Andersson, Brigitte Fossey, Nina Van Pallandt, David Langton.
●While certainly not one of Altman's most successful movies, this excursion into the sci-fi genre was unfairly criticised or neglected upon release. Set in a bleak landscape during a tough, inhospitable ice-age, it concerns a seal trapper (Newman) and his wife (Fossey) who wander into a strange, desolate city where they meet a group of people playing a mysterious game, for which the stakes gambled are life and death. Slow, humourless, and occasionally over-emphatic in its use of symbolism, it's nevertheless a fascinating film, which manages to work thanks to its absolute mastery of atmosphere. GA

Quitting (Zuotian)

(2001, China, 118 min)
d Zhang Yang. *p* Peter Loehr. *sc* Zhang Yang, Hou Xin. *ph* Wang Yu, Cheng Shouqi. *ed* Yang Hongyu. *ad* An Bin. *m* Zhang Yadong. *cast* Jia Hongsheng, Jia Fengsen, Chai Xiuling, Wang Tong, Shun Xing.
●The *Shower* team changes direction with a dramatised re-creation of a screwed-up junkie's agonising steps towards rehab. Jia Hongsheng was a movie star in China before he got into 'new wave' film-making (Lou Ye's *Weekend Lover*, Wang Xiaoshuai's *Frozen*) and discovered heroin. He quickly became a junkie recluse, ripping off his friends, obsessed with Beatles music and convinced he was John Lennon's son. His anxious parents moved in to try to cure him, but gave up when he assaulted his father. Hospital care eventually helped him enough to resume acting (*Suzhou River*), but his future remains insecure. Zhang Yang directed Jia on stage ten years ago, which must be why he was able to persuade him and his family and friends to re-enact these painful episodes. But the film isn't docu-drama for its own sake; Zhang introduces Brechtian moments to stress that it *is* a re-enactment, and uses the story to reflect on a turbulent, self-destructive period in Chinese culture. TR

Quiz Show

(1994, US, 132 min)
d Robert Redford. *p* Robert Redford, Michael Jacobs, Julian Krainin, Michael Nozik. *sc* Paul Attanasio. *ph* Michael Ballhaus. *ed* Stu Linder. *pd* Jon Hutman. *m* Mark Isham. *cast* John Turturro, Rob Morrow, Ralph Fiennes, Paul Scofield, Elizabeth Wilson, Mira Sorvino, Martin Scorsese, Barry Levinson.

● In America in the '50s, TV quiz shows were watched by more than half the viewing public. When handsome Ivy League lecturer Charles Van Doren became reigning champ of *Twenty One*, he found himself a national celebrity. Then a defeated former champion, Herbie Stempel, a working-class Jew from Queens, New York, claimed the show was fixed. Redford has fashioned (from Paul Attanasio's brilliant screenplay) an impeccably nuanced Faustian drama which aspires to capture America's fall from grace: that point at the end of the '50s when the country first lost faith in itself. Poised, patrician and with a genius IQ, Van Doren (Fiennes) appears to be the perfect role model. Instead, he is a victim of the values of the times and his own greed for approval. In an investigation which evokes (or prefigures) *All the President's Men*, Congressional agent Dick Goodwin (Morrow) sniffs out the conspiracy. He's intent on putting television on trial, but deeply reluctant to believe that Van Doren could be implicated. Perfectly pitched, the film brims with insight and wit. Highly recommended. TCh

Quo Vadis?

(1951, US, 171 min)
d Mervyn LeRoy. *p* Sam Zimbalist. *sc* John Lee Makin, Sonya Levien, SN Behrman. *ph* Robert Surtees, William V Skall. *ed* Ralph E Winters. *ad* William A Horning, Cedric Gibbons, Edward C Carfagno. *m* Miklós Rozsa. *cast* Robert Taylor, Deborah Kerr, Peter Ustinov, Leo Genn, Patricia Laffan, Finlay Currie, Abraham Sofaer, Buddy Baer, Marina Berti, Felix Aylmer.

● At the time, *Quo Vadis?* was the highest grosser for MGM after *Gone With the Wind*. Between the acres of heaving muscle in the arena, half of Italy starring as the Roman troops, and sets that dwarf even Ustinov, you may detect a story about a Roman commander under Nero who falls in love with a Christian girl and gets them both thrown to the lions. It does last virtually three hours, and along the way does have stretches of tedium, but LeRoy invests most of it with pace, true spectacle, and not a little imagination (like the camera craning acrobatically over thousands of festive Romans before coming to rest on Robert Taylor's face; or an 'orgy' viewed by Nero through a piece of red glass). They won't make them like this any more. MSu

r

The Royal Tenenbaums

Rabid

(1976, Can, 91 min)
d David Cronenberg. *p* John Dunning. *sc* David Cronenberg. *ph* René Verzier. *ed* Jean LaFleur. *ad* Claude Marchand. *m* Ivan Reitman. *cast* Marilyn Chambers, Frank Moore, Joe Silver, Howard Ryshpan, Patricia Gage, Susan Roman, J Roger Periard

● As a maker of sci-fi/horror movies, Cronenberg seems obsessed with the links between sex and violence as well as the *Body Snatchers* theme of a possessed community. His earlier combination of the two strains in *Shivers* was too mechanically lurid and derivative to be very effective, but *Rabid* is far more successful. This time Cronenberg has opened up his story so that it literally portrays the panic and slow devastation of a whole Canadian city: a new strain of rabies reduces its victims to foaming murderous animals, and Cronenberg examines the mysterious sexual agency behind the plague with bewitching ambiguity. *Rabid* is also far better staged than its predecessor, and the best scenes, including one classic episode in a chicken takeaway, are pitched ingeniously between shock and parody, never quite succumbing to farce. None of the other recent apocalypse movies has shown so much political or cinematic sophistication. DP

Rabid Grannies

(1989, Bel, 88 min)
d Emmanuel Kervyn. *p* James Desert, Jonathan Rambert. *sc* Emmanuel Kervyn. *ph* Hugo Labye. *ed* Philippe Ravoet. *pd* Luc Bertrand. *m* Pierre-Damien Castelain. *cast* Elie Lison, Catherine Aymerie, Danielle Daven, Anne-Marie Fox, Jack Mayar, Françoise Moens.

● An opportunistically retitled Belgian horror pic, courtesy of Troma Inc, in which a group of mercenary nephews and nieces gather for their aged aunts' annual birthday party. Half way through dinner, the two old girls are transformed by a surprise present into grotesque, vengeful crones, who vomit green slime and are a little short on familial affection. Crucifixes, holy water and pump-action shotguns prove useless as the vicious oldsters rip, slice and hack their way through the assembled relatives. The cheapskate special effects are reasonably effective, but the characters are cardboard, the plot negligible, and the dubbed 'English' dialogue literally unspeakable. The fact that the old ladies are neither rabid nor grannies – they are in fact Possessed Aunties – is conveniently ignored. NF

Racconti di Canterbury, I

see Canterbury Tales, The

Racconti Proibiti di Nulla Vestita

see Master of Love

Race for Life

see Si tous les gars du monde…

Race for the Yankee Zephyr

(1981, NZ/Aust, 108 min)
d David Hemmings. *p* Antony I Ginnane, John Barnett, David Hemmings. *sc* Everett De Roche. *ph* Vincent Monton. *ed* John Laing. *pd* Bernard Hides. *m* Brian May. *cast* Ken Wahl, Lesley Ann Warren, Donald Pleasence, George Peppard, Bruno Lawrence, Grant Tilly, Robert Bruce.

● The Yankee Zephyr of this amiable treasure hunt yarn is a US Navy cargo plane, missing since 1944, with a shipment of medals, a crate of Old Crow, and 50 million dollars in gold bullion aboard. The race to claim the salvage rights involves jet boats, beat-up helicopters, and mechanical abortions of the latter's parts, with Pleasence as a wheezy old sot who discovers the wreck. Pitting him and his macho partner (Wahl) against the suave penthouse chic of Peppard's businessman, Hemmings operates the race at a stop/start pace that leaves you feeling genial enough to forgive the stereotyping and the thin running jokes. It's all so lightweight that the action has to be anchored into place by a picaresque script involving crocodiles and their various genitalia. FL

Race, the Spirit of Franco (Raza, el Espíritu de Franco)

(1977, Sp, 80 min, b/w & col)
d Gonzalo Herralde. *with* Pilar Franco, Alfredo Mayo.

● A fascinating demolition operation on Franco's imaginatively autobiographical exercise in cinematic myth-making, the 1941 *Race*, this juxtaposes sections of that notorious piece of melodramatic propaganda with the more prosaic testimonies of Franco's surviving sister, Pilar, and the actor Alfredo Mayo, who incarnated the role of the Franco surrogate 36 years earlier. The distance between fact and the romantic image is naturally comic, and the inherent interest of the previously inaccessible film is immense. The whole goes entertainingly beyond mere posthumous point-scoring. PT

Race with the Devil

(1975, US, 88 min)
d Jack Starrett. *p* Wes Bishop. *sc* Lee Frost, Wes Bishop. *ph* Robert Jessup. *ed* John F Link. *m* Leonard Rosenman. *cast* Peter Fonda, Warren Oates, Loretta Swit, Lara Parker, RG Armstrong, Clay Tanner, Jack Starrett, Wes Bishop.

● Less a race than a chase, with holidaymaking Fonda, Oates and wives fleeing a bunch of Texas Satanists whose human sacrifice they've barged into. A crescendo of near-miss car smashes, horrible discoveries in the caravan, and out-of-order telephones, convinces the quartet that the whole state's bent; by which time we think so too, and dread the outcome. A wittily efficient quickie, the film is a winner all the way – a surprise, since Starrett's career thus far had been the movie director's equivalent of a criminal record. But it was scripted by Lee Frost and Wes Bishop, who produced another jolly horror, *The Thing With Two Heads* and who started classically by making sex films in a garage. AN

Rachel and the Stranger

(1948, US, 93 min, b/w)
d Norman Foster. *p* Richard H Berger. *sc* Waldo Salt. *ph* Maury Gertsman. *ed* Les Millbrook. *ad* Darrell Silvera, John Sturtevant. *m* Constantin Bakeleinikoff. *cast* Loretta Young, William Holden, Robert Mitchum, Gary Gray, Tom Tully, Sara Haden.

● A film about homesteaders which has the lazy rhythm of a ballad in telling its tale of the widower (Holden), the bondswoman (Young) he marries but treats as a servant, and the roving cowboy friend (Mitchum) who opens his eyes by seeing – and treating – her as a woman. Although slightly marred by an Indian raid dragged in as an unnecessary catalyst (but very well done), it's a real charmer, held together by Mitchum's electric presence as the laconic interloper with a gently roving eye and a winning way with his guitar and songs. TM

Rachel Papers, The

(1989, GB, 95 min)
d Damian Harris. *p* Andy Karsch. *sc* Damian Harris. *ph* Alex Thomson. *ed* David Martin. *pd* Andrew McAlpine. *m* Chaz Jankel. *cast* Dexter Fletcher, Ione Skye, Jonathan Pryce, James Spader, Bill Paterson, Shirley Anne Field, Michael Gambon, Lesley Sharp.

● Despite certain changes – it is updated from the early '70s to the late '80s, for instance – Martin Amis' clever, shallow first novel, the tale of teenager Charles Highway, eager to sleep with an older woman before he is 20, is rendered with some fidelity. The book's first person narrative finds a clumsy correlative in the brat's direct-to-camera confessions; and the humour is as smug, adolescent and misogynist as it was in the novel. The flaws lie less in the performances (Fletcher's Highway and Skye's Rachel, primary object of his self-serving affections, are both insubstantial, overshadowed by Pryce's crowd-pleasing cameo as Highway's irreverent hippy brother-in-law) than in the direction. Working from his own script, Harris shows no sense of detail; characters barely develop, London becomes a topographical mess, and each time the plot falters, we get long '60s-style interludes with no dialogue, cut to bland pop. The result is without dramatic or moral weight, despite Highway's contrived comeuppance, and it's impossible to care about the characters. GA

Rachel, Rachel

(1968, US, 101 min)
d/p Paul Newman. *sc* Stewart Stern. *ph* Gayne Rescher. *ed* Dede Allen. *ad* Robert Gundlach. *m* Jerome Moross. *cast* Joanne Woodward, Estelle Parsons, James Olson, Kate Harrington, Bernard Barrow, Donald Moffat, Geraldine Fitzgerald, Nell Potts.

● An impressive directorial debut for Newman, *Rachel, Rachel* stars his wife, Joanne Woodward, and their daughter Nell Potts. An account of a spinster striving to break out of her frustrating job as a teacher and her demanding home life, looking after her mother, the film's virtues lie in the wry observation of Rachel's slipping into a second childhood when James Olson appears on the scene as a possible saviour. While in no way as powerful as Barbara Loden's Wanda, Newman's film none the less captures the quiet desperation of enforced life in sleepytown America. PH

Rachel's Man

(1975, Isr, 111 min)
d Moshe Mizrahi. *p* Michael Klinger. *sc* Moshe Mizrahi, Rachel Fabien. *ph* Ousama Rawi. *ed* Dav Hoenig. *ad* Ariela Vidzer. *m* Georges Moustaki. *cast* Mickey Rooney, Rita Tushingham, Leonard Whiting, Michal Bat-Adam, Avner Hiskiyahu, Dalia Cohen.

● The biblical saga of Jacob (Whiting), who received his father's blessing instead of Esau, ran away and fell in love with Rachel (Bat-Adam), courted her for seven years, but then got fobbed off with her elder sister (Tushingham). Lots of simple sunny visuals, combined with some flashy photography, make the film look like a cross between a Russell Flint watercolour and a Pirelli calendar. Attempts to beef up a desperately slim story include much emphasis on Jacob and Rachel's love story, some discreet nudity, a couple of songs 'Smother Me With Kisses For Ya Love Is Sweeter Than Wine', and an outrageously hammy (but thankfully diverting) performance from Rooney, offering his interpretation of the original Jewish businessman. Overall, the film's attempts to capture the measured pace of the Old Testament are terribly laboured, making it seem twice as long as it actually is.

Racing with the Moon

(1984, US, 108 min)
d Richard Benjamin. *p* Alain Bernheim, John Kohn. *sc* Steve Kloves. *ph* John Bailey. *ed* Jacqueline Cambas. *pd* David L Snyder. *m* David Grusin. *cast* Sean Penn, Elizabeth McGovern, Nicolas Cage, John Karlen, Rutanya Alda, Max Showalter, Crispin Glover.

● Yuletide 1942 in a small Californian coastal town, and local boy Penn is hoping to step out with McGovern (who, unlike him, comes from the right side of the tracks) before induction into the Marines. This conflates a number of currently modish themes: coming of age in small-town USA; the last fling before manhood and possible death; nostalgia; and the crossing of social barriers. What it doesn't do, however, is give sufficiently dramatic incident; very little seems to happen in this social vacuum, and none of it is memorable. CPea

Racket, The

(1951, US, 89 min, b/w)
d John Cromwell. *p* Edmund Grainger. *sc* William Wister Haines, WR Burnett. *ph* George E Diskant. *ed* Sherman Todd. *ad* Albert S D'Agostino, Jack Okey. *m* Constantin Bakaleinikoff. *cast* Robert Ryan, Robert Mitchum, Lizabeth Scott, William Talman, Ray Collins, Joyce MacKenzie, Robert Hutton, Virginia Huston, William Conrad.

● The omens were good. Howard Hughes had produced the silent version of *The Racket* that sparked Hollywood's gangster cycle. John Cromwell had won his first movie chance with his performance in a Broadway revival of the original play. Mitchum plus Ryan looked a fail-safe powerhouse confrontation. But…Hughes' RKO was slowly running down; Cromwell was under greylist pressure from HUAC; and Mitchum got himself cast as a cop – representing goddam Society, no less! Softer than it should have been, then, but still dark enough to lose yourself in. PT

Radiance

(1998, Aust, 83 min)
d Rachel Perkins.*p* Ned Lander, Andrew Myer. *sc* Louis Nowra. *ph* Warwick Thornton. *ed* James Bradley. *pd* Sarah Stollman. *m* Alistair Jones. *cast* Rachel Maza, Deborah Mailman, Trisha Morton-Thomas.

●This first feature, adapted by Louis Nowra from his own play, reunites three estranged Aboriginal sisters for their mother's funeral, and travels a somewhat familiar road as it explores the women's similarities and differences, hopes and memories, tensions and reconciliations. But the performances are energetic, witty and likeable; the revelations, while specifically reflecting on certain aspects of the Aboriginal experience, are sufficiently frequent and dramatic to grab and hold the attention; and the director does manage to offset the staginess by vivid images and sharp editing. GA

Radio Days

(1987, US, 88 min)
d Woody Allen. *p* Robert Greenhut, Gail Sicilia. *sc* Woody Allen. *ph* Carlo Di Palma. *ed* Susan E Morse. *pd* Santo Loquasto. *m* Dick Hyman. *cast* Seth Green, Julie Kavner, Michael Tucker, Dianne Wiest, Josh Mostel, Mia Farrow, Wallace Shawn, Kenneth Mars, Jeff Daniels, Danny Aiello, Tony Roberts, Diane Keaton.

●Woody Allen is always weakest when nostalgic: indulgence leads to caricature and overstatement. Set at the start of World War II, the film follows the fortunes of a family of Jewish underachievers. Against the backdrop of their predictably colourful obsessions, a glimmer of a story charts the progress of Farrow from Manhattan nightclub cigarette-girl to celeb of the airwaves. The real star, however, is radio itself, that pre-TV purveyor of everyday unreality against which wartime America measured its dreams. It's a great idea for a movie, but Allen fatally opts for a *Fellini: Amarcord* approach of formless narrative, larger-than-life coincidence, and rambling ruminations on what times there used to be. GA

Radio Flyer

(1993, US, 101 min)
d Richard Donner. *p* Lauren Schuler-Donner. *sc* David Mickey Evans. *ph* Laszlo Kovacs. *ed* Stuart Baird, Dallas Puett. *ad* J Michael Riva. *m* Hans Zimmer. *cast* Lorraine Bracco, John Heard, Elijah Wood, Joseph Mazello, Adam Baldwin, Ben Johnson.

●'History is all in the mind of the teller; the truth is in the telling' – so Tom Hanks instructs his young son by way of a preamble to this fanciful coming-of-age tale, which failed to find a theatrical distributor in Britain after bombing in the States. You can see why the script attracted big bucks: it has an accentuated literary air that must have read like 'class', a serious angle – child abuse – and it's all couched in the magic juvenilia of a Spielberg (Donner directed *Goonies*). It's the story of two brothers, their mother (Bracco), and the violent alcoholic who becomes their stepfather (Adam Baldwin in a pitiless role, photographed Spielberg-style from the waist down). It's not a total loss, but the voice-over is infuriatingly overdone, as if the film-makers didn't trust the visuals, the kids are resistible and the tone's discomfortingly cute. TCh

Radioland Murders

(1994, US, 112 min)
d Mel Smith. *p* Rick McCallum, Fred Roos. *sc* Willard Huyck, Gloria Katz, Jeff Reno, Ron Osborn. *ph* David Tattersall. *ed* Paul Trejo. *pd* Gavin Bocquet. *m* Joel McNeely. *cast* Mary Stuart Masterson, Brian Benben, Ned Beatty, Michael Lerner, Christopher Lloyd, Scott Michael Campbell, Corbin Bernsen, Candy Clark, Rosemary Clooney.

●It's 1939 and Radio WBN Chicago is on air, but amid the melee of performers and technicians lurks a dastardly killer. Did anyone control this cross between *Radio Days* and *Rocketeer*, or was it just left to freewheel? George Lucas, once the director of *Star Wars*, now an effects guru and shadowy executive producer, apparently had the idea long long ago. As an *hommage* to the screwball comedies of yesteryear it fails, with obvious one-liners and mistimed pratfalls, but as kitsch farce it succeeds, with an attractive cast, breathless pace, and lavish visuals. AO

Radio On

(1979, GB/WGer, 102 min, b/w)
d Christopher Petit. *p* Keith Griffiths. *sc* Christopher Petit. *ph* Martin Schäfer. *ed* Anthony Sloman, Stefna Smal, Stuart De Jong, *ad* Susannah Buxton. *cast* David Beames, Lisa Kreuzer, Sandy Ratcliff, Andrew Byatt, Sue Jones-Davies, Sting, Sabina Michael.

●A first feature written and directed by Petit, this is an apparently simple road movie (with an extraordinary soundtrack that runs from Bowie to Kraftwerk and Wreckless Eric) in which a man travels from London to Bristol by car to clarify the mysterious death of his brother. But his private journey also stands for an excursion back into the sour '70s, and his failure to communicate with those he meets on the road – an army deserter, a garage mechanic, a woman in search of her child – becomes a rambling commentary on the obsessive, ironic disenchantment of living in Britain now. A rare, almost eerie attempt at mythic British cinema, which ends with its hero stalled in his battered old Rover at a quarry edge, his questions still unanswered, forced to move on (into the '80s). *'We could be heroes, just for one day...'* – and the time is up. CA

Radio On (Remix)

(1998, GB, 24 min, b/w & col)
d Chris Petit. *p* Keith Griffiths. *ed* Emma Matthews.

●Petit's digital remix of his debut feature came out of a desire, prompted by Gareth Evans and Ben Slater (credited as associate producers) of *Entropy* magazine, to revisit some of the original Bristol locations with editor Matthews at a time of change in the city. There's much here that fans of *Radio On* will enjoy: Bruce Gilbert's reworking of the soundtrack; all sorts of 1979/98 split-screen fun, mixing Hi-8 video with Super-8 and original footage; contact sheets, stills, shots of the making of the original. Look out for the dismantling of the Victoria Street flyover, which means that a retake of the languid drive-by shot of the Grosvenor Hotel, with its lonely Edward Hopper figures in bedroom windows, is, sadly, not possible. NRo

Rafferty and the Gold Dust Twins

(1975, US, 91 min)
d Dick Richards. *p* Michael Gruskoff, Art Linson. *sc* John Kaye. *ph* Ralph Woolsey. *ed* Walter Thompson. *ad* Joel Schiller. *m* Artie Butler. *cast* Alan Arkin, Sally Kellerman, Mackenzie Phillips, Alex Rocco, Charlie Martin Smith, Harry Dean Stanton, John McLiam, Arch Johnson.

●A road movie which teams three unlikelies – two female vagrants, one of them a spiky 15-year-old, and a washed-up ex-sergeant – and gives them no particular destination. As with many similar films, it substitutes character study for narrative. At first the film's low-key approach is deceptive. But for all the oblique humour, engaging peripheries, and surface toughness, *Rafferty* is a fundamentally warm-hearted movie which gradually beseeches us to love its oddball characters. During the last third, by which time the film has started to wear its heart on its sleeve, it all starts to come together; it's a long wait, though. Mackenzie Phillips, as the girl, gives a strong natural performance which offsets Arkin's studious acting. Really the entire film should have been about their relationship, rather than just the ending, which has them exiting for Uruguay just as things were getting interesting. CPe

Raffles

(1930, US, 72 min, b/w)
d Harry D'Abbadie D'Arrast, George Fitzmaurice. *p* Samuel Goldwyn. *sc* John Van Druten, Sidney Howard. *ph* George Barnes, Gregg Toland. *ed* Stuart Heisler. *ad* William Cameron Menzies, Park French. *m* Victor Young. *cast* Ronald Colman, Kay Francis, Bramwell Fletcher, Frances Dade, David Torrence, Alison Skipworth.

●EW Hornung's 'Raffles' helped fix the ideal of the gentleman amateur, the handsome urbane sportsman with a hankering for illicit adventure. In this caper, scripted by Sidney Howard, Raffles romances Lady Gwen Manders (Francis), hobnobs with royalty, and pinches a priceless necklace for a suicidal friend who can't honour a debt. John Barrymore had played the hero a few years before, David Niven was to play him a few years later, but neither matched Colman's effortless, brilliantined charm. GM

Raga

(1971, US, 96 min)
d/p Howard Worth. *sc* Nancy Bacal. *ph* Jimmy Allen. *ed* Merle Worth. *m* Ravi Shankar. *with* Ravi Shankar, Alla Rakha, Yehudi Menuhin, Lakshmi Shankar, Usted Allaudin Khan, George Harrison.

●A very reasonable documentary about Ravi Shankar, very uncritical about him and very critical about some of the ways the West has assimilated his music. Full rein is given to Shankar's belief in the importance of authority, tradition, the guru in music, with some good footage of Indian 'culture' to back it all up. Thankfully you get to hear a sizeable amount of music in different contexts, from Western pop and classical to Indian traditional. All in all, an adequate delve into a musician who deserves a lot of respect. The clichés are there, but are pleasantly unobtrusive. George Harrison can't be too happy with the way he comes over, though. JDuC

Ragazza di Trieste, La

see Girl from Trieste, The

Rage

(1999, GB, 120 min)
d Newton I Aduaka. *p* Maria-Elena L'Abbate, Newton I Aduaka. *sc* Newton I Aduaka. *ph* Carlos Arango. *ed* Marcela Cuneo. *pd* Kathryn Bates, Tone Emblemsvaag. *cast* Fraser Ayres, Shaun Parkes, John Pickard, Shango Baku, Wale Ojo, Alison Rose.

●'Tell me about your reality.' Rage (or Jamie to his mum) dreams of cutting a rap record with his friends Thomas (a DJ), and Godwin, a talented pianist. They're each struggling in their own way to grapple with questions of identity and race on the streets of south London. Rage, the most rebellious, is also walking a moral knife-edge, trying to help an elderly mentor out of his drug debts, but feeling the pressure to cross the law himself. Aduaka's independent, improvised feature isn't a smooth ride ('This ain't no Hollywood movie'), but it feels real, and it has something important to say about where young people are at right now. It's made with sincerity, but more than that, with integrity. TCh

Rage: Carrie 2, The

(1999, US, 105 min)
d Katt Shea. *p* Paul Monash. *sc* Rafael Moreu, Howard A Rodman. *ph* Donald M Morgan. *ed* Richard Nord. *pd* Peter Jamison. *m* Danny B Harvey. *cast* Amy Irving, Emily Bergl, Jason London, Dylan Bruno, J Smith-Cameron. Zachery Ty Bryan, John Doe, Gordon Clapp, Rachel Blanchard, Charlotte Ayanna, Justin Ulrich, Mena Suvari.

●You might think using clips from the original *Carrie* would add a postmodern tremor to this sequel. Wrong. In this latest outing, set 20 years on, secretly romantic Goth Rachel (Bergl) meets sensitive jock Jessie (London), whose friends take the piss, then pretend to accept her, inviting her to a booby-trapped party. There is something to engage the brain, however. And it's not just astonishment that Irving's career is in such a bad way that she's agreed to reprise her role as Sue Snell (still traumatised by her part in Carrie's death, she's become a caring, sharing teacher). Rachel's friend Lisa (Suvari) sets the horror rolling by sleeping with Jessie's bullish friend Mark. When he dumps her, she kills herself, and as part of her newfound altruism, Snell tries to get him arrested for statutory rape. Setting aside the issue of why an intelligent Shirley Manson clone would fall for a cleancut idiot, this also raises ethical questions, in taking desire and individual responsibility right out of the equation. The film-makers obviously decided the original *Carrie* lacked riot grrrl oomph. Paradoxically, in Lisa, they've created a far more dubious sacrificial lamb. A stinker – but as a gender-studies footnote, it's a must-see. CO'Su

Rage in Harlem, A

(1991, GB/US, 115 min)
d Bill Duke. *p* Stephen Woolley, Kerry Boyle. *sc* John Toles-Bey, Bobby Crawford. *ph* Toyomichi Kurita. *ed* Curtiss Clayton. *pd* Steven Legler. *m* Elmer Bernstein. *cast* Forest Whitaker, Gregory Hines, Robin Givens, Zakes Mokae, Danny Glover, Badja Djola, John Toles-Bey, Screamin' Jay Hawkins.

●Duke's snappy, stylish, relentlessly pacy comedy-thriller, lighter than Chester Himes' source novel, is mostly very enjoyable. It charts the farcical situation that develops when Imabelle (Givens) arrives in mid-'50s Harlem with bullion stolen by her presumed-dead lover Slim (Djola). Hoping to do a deal with fence Easy Money (Glover) and needing a hideaway, she moves in with naive, pious undertaker's assistant Jackson (Whitaker), who reluctantly enlists the help of his criminal brother Goldy (Hines) when Slim turns up to regain both loot and Imabelle. The scene is thus set for funny, bloody intrigue involving hoodlums, cops, club-owners, and other cartoon-thin inhabitants of an improbably colourful Harlem; but for all the explicit violence, the film is less gritty *noir* than ebullient, good-natured fantasy. GA

Rage in Heaven

(1941, US, 85 min)
d WS Van Dyke. *p* Gottfried Reinhardt. *sc* Christopher Isherwood, Robert Thoeren. *ph* Oliver T Marsh. *ed* Harold F Kress. *ad* Cedric Gibbons. *m* Bronislau Kaper. *cast* Robert Montgomery, Ingrid Bergman, George Sanders, Lucile Watson, Oscar Homolka.

●Co-scripted by Christopher Isherwood from a novel by James Hilton, but still boasting a plot as murkily unconvincing as the English setting. Montgomery, blandly repeating his *Night Must Fall* characterisation (though further up the social scale), is a wealthy scion who goes all funny at full moon, marries his mama's companion (Bergman in her third Hollywood movie), and conceives a dotty revenge plot when he thinks he has grounds for jealousy. Even a strong cast can't make much headway on such soggy ground. TM

Raggedy Man

(1981, US, 94 min)
d Jack Fisk. *p* Burt Weissbourd, William Wittlife. *sc* William Wittliff. *ph* Ralf Bode. *ed* Edward Warschilka. *ad* John J Lloyd. *m* Jerry Goldsmith. *cast* Sissy Spacek, Eric Roberts, Sam Shepard, William Sanderson, Tracey Walter, RG Armstrong, Henry Thomas.

●Spacek's extraordinary ability to portray a specific kind of American innocence gives life to a fairly ordinary plot about a frustrated 1940s rural telephonist – the mother of two children – who becomes involved with a passing sailor. Eventually the film erupts into small-town violence, but it is essentially a period piece directed with quiet impressiveness by Spacek's husband, former art director Fisk, who has extracted good performances from all of the principals (including Thomas as one of the kids, soon to appear as the boy in *E.T.*). Spacek herself is given free rein, and turns in all that you'd expect and more, including a number of marvellous little insights from her own Texas childhood. Something as slight as this could never have got off the ground without her, but she makes you glad it did. DP

Raggedy Rawney, The

(1987, GB, 103 min)
d Bob Hoskins. *p* Bob Weis. *sc* Bob Hoskins, Nicole de Wilde. *ph* Frank Tidy. *ed* Alan Jones. *pd* Jiri Matolin. *m* Michael Kamen. *cast* Bob Hoskins, Dexter Fletcher, Zoe Nathenson, Zoe Wanamaker, Dave Hill, Ian Dury, Ian McNeice, Veronica Clifford.

●Hoskins' first outing as a director, a World War I tale of Romany Folk, is set somewhere unspecific in the East European theatre. Fletcher plays a drafted boy soldier who escapes the carnage by donning woman's clothing and taking to the countryside. Port in a storm is provided by a passing band of gypsies, led by the ever-the-cockney Hoskins, who mistake Fletcher for a rawney – a traveller's word meaning a kind of vagabond female fortune-teller – and take him/her into their company. From here on in, Hoskins' darkening tale focuses on the lives of this less than merry band, with various set pieces – a traditional wedding, a ritual burial – strung together by a meandering plot concerning the group's various sexual and social rivalries and problems. The film suffers from disconcerting shifts of tone, mood, and focus, and threatens to become a case of paving over with good intentions; but its themes – the warts-and-all humanity of the travellers culture, the all pervasive destructiveness of war, the survival instinct – are delivered with sufficient sympathy and commitment to overcome the doubts. WH

Raging Bull 100 (100)

(1980, US, 129 min, b/w & col)
d Martin Scorsese. *p* Irwin Winkler, Robert Chartoff. *sc* Paul Schrader, Mardik Martin. *ph* Michael Chapman. *ed* Thelma Schoonmaker. *pd* Gene Rudolf. *cast* Robert De Niro, Cathy Moriarty, Joe Pesci, Frank Vincent, Nicholas Colasanto, Theresa Saldana, Mario Gallo.

●With breathtaking accuracy, *Raging Bull* ventures still further into the territory Scorsese has mapped in all his films – men and male values; in this case through the story of 1949 middleweight champion Jake La Motta. De Niro's performance as the cocky young boxer who gradually declines into a pathetic fat slob forces you to question the rigid and sentimental codes of masculinity which he clings to even as they destroy him, like a drowning man clutching a lead weight. The anti-realism of the fights prevents them sinking back into the narrative, and instead creates a set of images which resound through Jake's personal confrontations: their smashing, storyless violence is relentlessly cut with domestic scenes until you learn to flinch in anticipation. This film does more than make you think about masculinity, it makes you see it – in a way that's relevant to all men, not just Bronx boxers. JWi

Raging Moon, The (aka Long Ago, Tomorrow)

(1970, GB, 111 min)
d Bryan Forbes. *p* Bruce Cohn Curtis. *sc* Bryan Forbes. *ph* Tony Imi. *ed* Timothy Gee. *ad* Robert Jones. *m* Stanley Myers. *cast* Malcolm McDowell, Nanette Newman, Georgia Brown, Barry Jackson, Gerald Sim, Michael Flanders, Bernard Lee.

●A sincere attempt to portray a love affair between two paraplegics without undue sentimentality. It's not quite as awful as it sounds, mainly because McDowell and Newman perform well, convincingly scoffing at do-gooders. Meanwhile, Bryan Forbes' screenplay often has an acid joke up its sleeve to cut the cuteness. ATu

Ragman's Daughter, The

(1972, GB, 94 min)
d Harold Becker. *p* Harold Becker, Souter Harris. *sc* Alan Sillitoe. *ph* Michael Seresin. *ed* Anthony Gibbs. *ad* David Brockhurst. *m* Kenny Clayton. *cast* Simon Rouse, Victoria Tennant, Patrick O'Connell, Leslie Sands, Rita Howard, Brenda Peters, Brian Murphy, Jane Wood.

●A sloppy slice of social realism, adapted from Alan Sillitoe's novel but not bothering to reproduce the period detail that goes with its archetypal '60s message about regional dead ends. Good performance by Rouse as the working class chap with council flat, two kids, and no job after being fired from the cheese factory for pilfering, who looks back in nostalgia to his youth of carefree petty criminality in the company of a nouveau riche girlfriend. But the already rootless narrative is further sabotaged by camerawork which drains all character from the Nottingham locations. TM

Ragtime

(1981, US, 155 min)
d Milos Forman. *p* Dino De Laurentiis. *sc* Michael Weller. *ph* Miroslav Ondricek. *ed* Anne V Coates, Antony Gibbs, Stan Warnow. *pd* John Graysmark. *m* Randy Newman. *cast* James Cagney, Brad Dourif, Moses Gunn, Elizabeth McGovern, Kenneth McMillan, Pat O'Brien, Donald O'Connor, James Olson, Mandy Patinkin, Howard E Rollins, Mary Steenburgen.

●EL Doctorow's overrated bestseller, a panoramic epic of the melting-pot America of 1906, made its way to the screen shorn of Doctorow's central conceit, that his 'Ordinary People' warrant equal time alongside major historical figures: Henry Ford, J Pierpont Morgan, Emma Goldman, Harry Houdini, all are written out of the script. It's also clear that the dementia which animates each of the important fictional characters in the novel simply doesn't work when rendered in flesh-and-blood. Forman nevertheless handles the diverse strands of the complicated plot well enough to suggest that the film's central weakness – black pianist Coalhouse Walker's attempt to obtain satisfaction for the racially-motivated vandalism of his shining new car – is inherent in the novel. The siege of the Pierpont Morgan Library which ensues is protracted and boring. Good performances, though, from Cagney as the persuasively authoritative police chief Waldo, and (especially) James Olson, a pillar of quiet Waspish dignity as the self-appointed conscience interceding between the massing police and the militant Coalhouse. RM

Raid, The

(1954, US, 83 min)
d Hugo Fregonese. *p* Robert L Jacks. *sc* Sydney Boehm. *ph* Lucien Ballard. *ed* Robert Golden. *ad* George Patrick. *m* Roy Webb. *cast* Van Heflin, Anne Bancroft, Richard Boone, Lee Marvin, Peter Graves, Tommy Rettig, James Best, John Dierkes, Claude Akins.

●Excellent, factually based Civil War Western, in which Heflin's Confederate officer leads a group of soldiers, with whom he has escaped from a Union prison camp, in a plan to avenge the destruction of Southern communities by first taking over, and then sacking, a Northern town close to the Canadian border. Tension is slowly but surely built up as the men try to infiltrate the township; conflicting emotions arise with Heflin's growing respect for the widow with whom he lodges (Bancroft); and the final, savage massacre is powerfully staged by Fregonese, who makes superb use throughout of Lucien Ballard's typically moody photography. This was the film that served as a springboard for John Arden in writing his play *Serjeant Musgrave's Dance*. GA

Raider, The

see Western Approaches

Raiders of the Lost Ark (100)

(1981, US, 115 min)
d Steven Spielberg. *p* Frank Marshall. *sc* Lawrence Kasdan. *ph* Douglas Slocombe. *ed* Michael Kahn. *pd* Norman Reynolds. *m* John Williams. *cast* Harrison Ford, Karen Allen, Paul Freeman, Ronald Lacey, John Rhys-Davies, Denholm Elliott, Alfred Molina, Wolf Kahler.

●Hollywood's chutzpah whizzkids Spielberg and Lucas team up to bring the audiences who flocked to *Star Wars* and *Close Encounters* a replay of the innocent pleasures of Saturday serials, but done at two hours length with a much larger budget than the old cliffhangers could command. Spielberg's evasion of present day realities in an effort to recapture the sheer childlike fun of moviegoing is as perverse as was his previous film, *1941*. What he offers is one long, breathtaking chase of a plot as his pre-World War II superhero, outsize and Bogartian, races to prevent the omnipotent Ark of the Covenant from falling into the hands of Hitler's Nazis. Whether you swallow it or not, see it for a handful of totally unexpected visual jokes, worth the price of admission alone. RM

Raid on Entebbe

(1976, US, 118 min)
d Irvin Kershner. *p* Edgar J Scherick, Daniel H Blatt. *sc* Barry Beckerman. *ph* Bill Butler. *ed* Bud S Isaacs, Nick Archer, Arthur Seid. *pd* W Stewart Campbell. *m* David Shire. *cast* Peter Finch, Martin Balsam, Horst Buchholz, John Saxon, Sylvia Sidney, Jack Warden, Yaphet Kotto, Charles Bronson, Tige Andrews, Eddie Constantine, Warren Kemmerling, Robert Loggia, David Opatoshu, James Woods.

●Heroic jingoism and some sentimental moments aside, this version of the Israeli raid on Entebbe airport (shot as a TV special and considerably better than *Victory at Entebbe*), catches a good deal of the breathless excitement of the first media reports of that made-for-the-movies military operation. Predictably, no time is wasted on the PFLP's version of events, though suave Horst Buchholz, leader of the unattractive kidnappers, is allowed one moment of humanity when he finally declines to blow up the prisoners. Resisting his recent propensity for effects, Kershner adopts a sensibly straightforward approach to Barry Beckerman's boiled-down and politically low-key narrative. In this he is self-effacingly assisted by his well-cast stars (avoiding caricature, Yaphet Kotto gives a notably intelligent and charismatic impersonation of Amin). JPy

Railroad Man, The

see Ferroviere, Il

Railway Children, The

(1970, GB, 108 min)
d Lionel Jeffries. *p* Robert Lynn. *sc* Lionel Jeffries. *ph* Arthur Ibbetson. *ed* Teddy Darvas. *ad* John Clark. *m* Johnny Douglas. *cast* Dinah Sheridan, Bernard Cribbins, William Mervyn, Iain Cuthbertson, Jenny Agutter, Sally Thomsett, Peter Bromilow, Gordon Whiting.

●Jeffries displays miraculous tact in adapting E Nesbit's children's classic as an affectionate homage to those golden Edwardian days when God was in his heaven and all right with the world. Christmas festivities are under way at a cosy suburban home when Father (Cuthbertson) is spirited away by two suspiciously flat-footed visitors; it's all right really, of course, but meanwhile, Mother (Sheridan) and her three children are exiled to genteel poverty in a cottage on the Yorkshire moors. There the children take over, forming a secret pact with the railway which runs sleepily past the bottom of the garden, and responding gravely to wryly funny encounters with such characters as the portly businessman from the train (Mervyn) who is delighted to be adopted as 'the nicest old gentleman we know', or the stationmaster (Cribbins) who never quite manages to shed his air of stuffy resentment while becoming their best friend. Events are not lacking – mother falls ill, they save the train from derailment, they harbour an unhappy Bolshevik refugee – but above all the film perfectly captures the timeless, magical world of childhood where grief, joy and adventure are solemn, entirely personal affairs, quite unexplainable to adults. It is…almost…another *Meet Me in St Louis* TM

Rain

(1932, US, 93 min, b/w)
d Lewis Milestone. *p* Joseph Schenck. *sc* Maxwell Anderson. *ph* Oliver T Marsh. *ed* Duncan Mansfield. *ad* Richard Day. *m* Alfred Newman. *cast* Joan Crawford, Walter Huston, William Gargan, Beulah Bondi, Matt Moore, Guy Kibbee, Walter Catlett.

●Crawford was released by MGM to United Artists for this second screen adaptation of Somerset Maugham's steamy short story about a missionary bigot and prostitute Sadie Thompson, locked in an implacable battle of wills amid the pounding of tomtoms and tropical rain. Feeling herself in the shadow of distinguished previous Sadies on both stage and screen, Crawford was later to pronounce herself 'lousy', as did contemporary critics and fans. Their judgment in retrospect seems unkind: Crawford's Sadie is a mature, gutsy performance; she and Huston, as the repressed zealot, strike sparks off each other, an electricity that Milestone's stolid direction is seldom able to match. (An adaptation of the play *Rain* by John Colton and Clemence Randolph, itself an adaptation of Maugham's short story *Miss Thompson*.) SJo

Rainbow

(1995, GB/Can, 101 min)
d Bob Hoskins. *p* Robert Sidaway, Nicolas Clermont. *sc* Ashley Sidaway, Robert Sidaway. *ph* Freddie Francis. *ed* Ray Lovejoy, Melissa Kampschroder. *pd* Claude Paré. *m* Alan Reeves. *cast* Willy Lavendal, Bob Hoskins, Saul Rubinek, Dan Aykroyd, Jacob Tierney, Jonathan Schuman.

●Plants need light to photosynthesise; rainbows give colour (thence light) to the world; without rainbows the world would turn monochrome and everyone would suffocate. Circulating within the rainbow are gold nuggets providing energy. If the nuggets are removed the rainbow will feel sick and lose interest. Were someone to find a way into the rainbow, one brief moment of greed could trigger global apocalypse – a harsh, fading world ravaged by fatal illness and social breakdown, where hordes of incompetent supporting actors roam the streets. That's the scenario envisioned in Hoskins' geo-fable. Bob's an 'offbeat' magician whose 10-year-old son Mike (Lavendal) discovers the end of the rainbow behind Hudson Harbor, NJ, and jumps in, only to be followed by sulky adolescent brother Steven (Tierney), who pockets the gold. There's comic relief with Aykroyd's paedophobic Kansan police chief, before matters enter the realm of pre-millennial kids' apocalypse movie. Despite sterling cinematography, the special effects look like computer games. NB

Rainbow, The

(1988, GB, 111 min)
d/p Ken Russell. *sc* Ken Russell, Vivan Russell. *ph* Billy Williams. *ed* Peter Davies. *pd* Luciana Arrighi. *m* Carl Davis. *cast* Sammi Davis, Paul McGann, Amanda Donohoe, Christopher Gable, David Hemmings, Glenda Jackson, Dudley Sutton.

●Russell's second bash at DH Lawrence is either evidence of a fizzled-out talent or a sad, cliché-ridden attempt to make his film subservient to (part of) the text. He focuses on the later chapters: the story of Ursula Brangwen, wilful, intelligent and independent daughter of Anna (Jackson, who played an older Ursula in *Women in Love)* and artisan Will (Gable). Ursula engages in an uninhibited, exploratory relationship with her swimming teacher Winifred (cue skinny-dipping and intimate, glowing rub-downs on the hearth rug); falls for the dashing, if rough, charms of army officer Skrebensky (McGann); and, breaking the familial bonds, strives to make her way as a teacher in a school stifled by sexual harrassment and formality. The film reeks of mediocrity, floundering in banal imagery (kisses against boughs, rushing waterfalls, etc). Many essentials in what is a masterful three-generation novel have been jettisoned, and Carl Davis' score is formulary in the extreme. Saving graces are Sammi Davis' earthy, matter-of-fact portrayal of Ursula, and Amanda Donohoe's sensitive Winifred. WH

Rainbow Jacket, The

(1954, GB, 99 min)
d Basil Dearden. *p* Michael Relph. *sc* TEB Clarke. *ph* Otto Heller. *ed* Jack Harris. *ad* Tom Morahan. *m* William Alwyn. *cast* Bill Owen, Fella Edmonds, Kay Walsh, Edward Underdown, Robert Morley, Wilfrid Hyde-White, Charles Victor, Honor Blackman, Sidney James.

●The first collaboration between Dearden and TEB Clarke after *The Blue Lamp* follows the career of a middle-aged jockey (Owen) who, having forfeited his own career by taking a bribe, lives again through the success of a young protegé (Edmonds), whom he rescues from corruption at the vital moment. Despite its intriguing subject, the film offers little but the cosy, sentimental view of life that is typical of late Ealing films. PH

Rainclouds Over Wushan (Wushan Yunyu/aka In Expectation)

(1995, China, 96 min)
d Zhang Ming. *p* Han Sanping. *sc* Zhu Wen. *ph* Yao Xiaofeng. *cast* Zhang Xianmin, Zhong Ping, Wang Wenqiang, Yang Liu, Li Bing, Xiu Zongdi, Wang Shengguo.

●Shot as an unauthorised indie production but finally released under the Beijing Film Studio banner, Zhang's excellent first feature has been in trouble with the Film Bureau ever since it began winning prizes abroad. Wushan is a small town on the Yangtze which will be submerged when the Three Gorges Dam comes into service. In this doomed setting, Zhang traces three disparate but intersecting lives: a river-station watchman, a hotel clerk and a young cop, all currently single but two expecting to marry soon. All three central characters are selfish but lack self-awareness; Zhang's funny/sad emphasis is on their sexual desires, frustrations and (often misplaced) hopes. TR

Raining in the Mountain (Kong Shan Ling Yu)

(1978, HK, 120 min)
d King Hu. *cast* Hsu Feng, Sun Yueh, Shih Chun, Tien Feng, Tung Lin.

●Stylised gesture, pantomime humour, flurries of colour and fighting: King Hu's tale of a power struggle in a Ming dynasty monastery has all the abrupt magic of a fairy story, with its villains, good guys, and secret treasure. An immaculately made, inscrutable, and eventually frustrating play of forms. CA

Raining Stones

(1993, GB, 91 min)
d Ken Loach. *p* Sally Hibbin. *sc* Jim Allen. *ph* Barry Ackroyd. *ed* Jonathan Morris. *pd* Martin Johnson. *m* Stewart Copeland. *cast* Bruce Jones, Julie Brown, Gemma Phoenix, Ricky Tomlinson, Tom Hickey.

●Despite the unemployment, petty crime and crack that afflict their Lancashire housing estate, Bob (Jones) and wife Anne (Brown) remain staunch Catholics. Bob does odd jobs to put food on the table, but also because he's determined to buy their daughter her communion dress, rather than accept a loan from the priest. He's soon in hock to loan-sharks. Though the subject of Loach's film is as dark as ever, the movie is funnier than *Riff-Raff*, thanks to another delicious performance from Ricky Tomlinson as Bob's pal Tommy. The gags range from deadpan Northern banter to slapstick and scatology, but they don't overshadow the political acuity of Jim Allen's script , or the narrative's inexorable progress into the stuff of everyday nightmare. This is no rant, but a warm, unsentimental tribute to the working-class spirit. Superbly acted, as always, and a hugely enjoyable example of the cinema of commitment. GA

Rainmaker, The (aka John Grisham's The Rainmaker)

(1997, Ger/US, 135 min)
d Francis Ford Coppola. *p* Michael Douglas, Steven Reuther, Fredric S Fuchs. *sc* Francis Ford Coppola. *ph* John Toll. *ed* Barry Malkin, Melissa Kent. *pd* Howard Cummings. *m* Elmer Bernstein. *cast* Matt Damon, Claire Danes, Jon Voight, Mary Kay Place, Mickey Rourke, Danny DeVito, Dean Stockwell, Teresa Wright, Virginia Madsen, Johnny Whitworth, Danny Glover.

●This competent, anonymous legal drama (scripted by Michael Herr) is the best John Grisham adaptation yet. We're back in ingenue Southern lawyer territory, following law school grad Rudy Baylor (Damon) through his inaugural case to a mercurial triumph against the odds. So far, so insipid; thankfully, the story is less the usual addled potboiler than a diary of civil litigation – centring on Rudy's pursuit of a giant insurance company accused of stalling on health claims arising from policies marketed to the poor and unrepresented, such as his client Donny Ray Black (Whitworth). Rudy describes the dilemma of his calling in voice-over, musing over ideals and corruptions, compromises and lawyer jokes. His pilgrim's progress leads us through an entertaining gallery of lawyerly archetypes. There's the cynic, Rudy's long sold-out adversary Leo F Drummond (Voight); the corrupt, his low-life employer Bruiser Stone (Rourke); and the merely ignoble, his 'paralawyer' assistant Deck Schifflet (DeVito). There's a wider perspective on the legal action, too, counterpointing Rudy's 'rainmaking' lawsuit with both a damp squib of another case, and a subplot involving Danes' abused wife which suggests the limitations of the law. NB

Rain Man

(1988, US, 133 min)
d Barry Levinson. *p* Mark Johnson. *sc* Ronald Bass, Barry Morrow. *ph* John Seale. *ed* Stu Linder. *pd* Ida Random *m* Hans Zimmer. *cast* Dustin Hoffman, Tom Cruise, Valeria Golino, Jerry Molen, Jack Murdock, Michael D Roberts, Ralph Seymour, Lucinda Jenney.

●Seeing the finished product, you can see why there was such a turnover of directors and writers. There is no story, no motor, and given the nature of the premise, nothing much can happen; so it's lucky that Levinson, a fine observer of human behaviour washing about, was signed to make this increasingly costly dramatic standoff look busy. Hoffman does a self-contained turn, Cruise does Handsome Classes, though people say he's getting better. Charlie Babbitt (Cruise), a two-bit hustler trading cars, learns that Raymond (Hoffman), the brother he's forgotten, is to inherit three million dollars, and zones in to chisel him out of it. Raymond is autistic and institutionalised, but in their time together on the road, Charlie learns Raymond's limitations and windfall gifts – he can memorise numbers – and discovers his own decency. Raymond is a fixed point for Charlie to develop against, and just to amplify that Charlie is a stranger in a strange land, even his girlfriend Susanne (Golino) exists more fully in another language. Basically, it is a two-hander in which one side is stalled and stays stalled, devoid of an overview which might illuminate. Hard to do, though. BC

Rain or Shine

(1930, US, 92 min, b/w)
d Frank Capra. *p* Harry Cohn. *sc* Dorothy Howell, Jo Swerling. *ph* Joe Walker. *ed* Maurice Wright. *cast* Joe Cook, Louise Fazenda, Joan Peers, William Collier Jr, Dave Chasen, Tom Howard.

●Capra's early sound effort was intended as a showcase for Broadway comic Cook, whose mercurial slapstick talent made him a top draw on stage, but rarely translated into screen craft. Here he's running a circus hit by bad weather, declining audiences, a recalcitrant owner and performers about to go on strike. He manages to keep the show on the road, however, with a one-man display of clowning that (literally) brings the house down. Capra upped his directorial reputation by filming the climactic conflagration in one take, a risky undertaking given rudimentary early talkie technology, even if he did use several cameras for coverage. TJ

Rain People, The

(1969, US, 101 min)
d Francis Ford Coppola. *p* Bart Patton, Ronald Colby. *sc* Francis Ford Coppola. *ph* Wilmer C Butler. *ed* Barry Malkin. *ad* Leon Ericksen. *m* Ronald Stein. *cast* Shirley Knight, James Caan, Robert Duvall, Tom Aldredge, Marya Zimmet, Laurie Crews, Andrew Duncan.
●Coppola's fourth feature, a fascinating early road movie made entirely on location with a minimal crew and a constantly evolving script. Never very popular by comparison with *Easy Rider* probably because it suggested that dropping out was mere escapism, it has far greater depth and complexity to its curious admixture of feminist tract and pure thriller. Knight is outstanding (in a superb cast) as the pregnant woman who runs away in quest of the identity she feels she has lost as a Long Island housewife, and finds herself increasingly tangled in the snares of responsibility through her encounters with a football player left mindless by an accident (Caan) and a darkly amorous traffic cop (Duvall). Symbolism rumbles beneath the characterisations (Caan as the baby she is running from and with, Duvall as the sexuality and domination she is trying to deny) but it is never facile; and the rhythms of the road movie (leading through wonderfully bizarre locations to a resonantly melodramatic finale) confirm that Coppola's prime talent lies in choreographing movement. TM

Rains Came, The

(1939, US, 104 min, b/w)
d Clarence Brown. *p* Darryl F Zanuck. *sc* Philip Dunne, Julien Josephson. *ph* Arthur Miller. *ed* Barbara McLean. *ad* William Darling, George S Dudley. *m* Alfred Newman. *cast* Myrna Loy, Tyrone Power, George Brent, Brenda Joyce, Nigel Bruce, Maria Ouspenskaya, Joseph Schildkraut, HB Warner, Laura Hope Crews.
●Skilful direction, superlative camerawork from Arthur Miller, but the script is precious twaddle about a strangled romance between a titled English coquette (Loy) and a bashful Hindu doctor (Power in tasteful brownface). Honour is saved when the monsoon comes (with spectacular earthquake to boot), bringing self-sacrifice and redemption among the suffering plague victims. TM

Rains of Ranchipur, The

(1955, US, 104 min)
d Jean Negulesco. *p* Frank Ross. *sc* Merle Miller. *ph* Milton Krasner. *ed* Dorothy Spencer. *ad* Lyle Wheeler, Addison Hehr. *m* Hugo Friedhofer. *cast* Richard Burton, Lana Turner, Fred MacMurray, Joan Caulfield, Eugenie Leontovich, Michael Rennie.
●Redundant colour/'Scope remake of Clarence Brown's overrated *The Rains Came* (itself not much more than a transposition of Ford's *The Hurricane*), with forbidden interracial romance (memsahib Turner and unlikely Hindu Burton) metaphorically stirring the monsoon and worse as the elements turn censorious. PT

Raintree County

(1958, US, 168 min)
d Edward Dmytryk. *p* David Lewis. *sc* Millard Kaufman. *ph* Robert Surtees. *ed* John Dunning. *ad* William A Horning, Urie McCleary. *m* Johnny Green. *cast* Elizabeth Taylor, Montgomery Clift, Eva Marie Saint, Nigel Patrick, Lee Marvin, Agnes Moorehead, Rod Taylor, Walter Abel, Tom Drake.
●MGM's attempt to repeat the success of *Gone With the Wind* turned out to be an elephantine bore. Set in the Civil War, with Taylor as a tough Southern belle doing anything to win Yankee teacher Monty Clift for a husband, only to get bored with him, it offers up the usual stew of sordid goings on, but never brings it to the boil. The performances, surprisingly given the cast, don't help either; even Clift, wrecked by drink and the emotional problems (the car accident came during production), fails to convince. GA

Rainy Dog (Gokudo Kuro Shakai – Rainy Dog)

(1997, Jap, 94 min)
d Takashi Miike. *p* Tsutomu Tsuchikawa, Toshiki Kimura, Zhang Huakun. *sc* Seigo Inoue. *ph* Li Sixu. *ed* Taiji Shimamura. *ad* Zheng Hongzhan. *m* Sound Kids. *cast* Sho Aikawa, Gao Mingjun, Chen Xianmei, Li Liqun, Zhang Shi, Tomoro Taguchi.
●Miike's crush on Taiwan runs wild in this location-shot thriller about a yakuza hitman working for a triad gang boss in Taipei. Yuji (Aikawa) is in his bare apartment being cool and moody when an ex-girlfriend barges in to dump a boy she says is his son; the kid is left to fend for himself in the alley outside, and discovers what daddy does only when he tags along and sees Yuji shoot someone. The minimal plot is fleshed out by everyone's favourite Taiwanese character actors (including two of Hou Xiaoxian's original *Boys from Fengkuei*), and it never stops raining. Not only the definitive bad-parenting movie but also very likely the coolest rainsoaked lonely hitman movie ever made. TR

Raise Ravens

see Cría Cuervos

Raise the Red Lantern (Dahong Denglong Gaogao Gua)

(1991, HK, 125 min)
d Zhang Yimou. *p* Chiu Fu-Sheng. *sc* Ni Zhen. *ph* Zhao Fei. *ed* Du Yuan. *ad* Cao Jiuping, Dong Huamiao. *m* Zhao Jiping. *cast* Gong Li, Ma Jingwu, He Caifei, Cao Cuifeng, Jin Shuyuan, Kong Lin.
●Northern China, the 1920s. Having agreed – to spite both her stepmother and fate – to become the fourth wife of an ageing, wealthy clan-leader, 19-year-old Songlian (Gong Li) finds herself immured in a palatial complex plagued by paranoia, jealousy and intrigue. The red lanterns, hung outside the suite of whichever wife is currently the object of the master's attentions, are an index of power; and Songlian, determined to wrest control from her rivals, feigns pregnancy. But the real power, of course, lies with the master, and the women's in-fighting yields tragic results. Dealing, like *Red Sorghum* and *Ju Dou*, with a young woman married to an older man and struggling to survive in a society defined by oppressive patriarchal tradition, Zhang's film elicits a strong sense of *déjà vu*. The lavish, schematic colours hold considerable appeal, while the atypical symmetry and stillness of the compositions stress the strait-jacket mores of a stagnant feudal culture. The acting is excellent, too, but one can't help but feel that Zhang has said it all before and more imaginatively. GA

Raise the Roof

(1930, GB, 77 min, b&w)
d Walter Summers. *sc* Walter Summers, Philip MacDonald. *songs* Jay Whidden, Idris Lewis, Tom Helmore. *m* Tom Helmore. *cast* Betty Balfour, Maurice Evans, Jack Raine, Sam Livesey, Ellis Jeffreys, Arthur Hardy.
●A refreshingly unpretentious backstage musical, set among the lower reaches of the theatre world, where a tatty revue company that makes Hamlet seem like a perishing pantomime battles valiantly against the catcalls and rotten tomatoes. Fortunately it has the inestimable advantage of silents star Betty Balfour, trembling on the brink of love with a bizarre mixture of worldly vulgarity and little girl charm. Like a ruffled cockatoo, she bullies her fellow players into dropping their costumes and their actorly aspirations and giving the public what it wants: 'Laughter and legs…mostly legs'. Nice to know Britain has a musical tradition to be proud of. RMy

Raise the Titanic!

(1980, US, 114 min)
d Jerry Jameson. *p* William Frye. *sc* Adam Kennedy. *ph* Matthew F Leonetti. *ed* J Terry Williams, Robert F Shugrue. *pd* John F DeCuir. *m* John Barry. *cast* Jason Robards, Richard Jordan, David Selby, Anne Archer, Alec Guinness, Norman Bartold, M Emmet Walsh.
●One of the floppiest of Lord Grade's expensive flops, a would-be blockbuster limply adapted from Clive Cussler's bestseller about a secret operation to recover a haul of 'byzanium', reportedly in the hold of the 'Titanic' when it sank in 1912, and now urgently sought to fuel a defence system codenamed 'The Sicilian Project'. Naturally the Commies get in on the act, and apart from a brief perk-up during the actual raising of the ship, the whole thing founders dismally in a welter of ludicrous dialogue, routine love triangle, and desperately dull action. PG

Raising Arizona

(1987, US, 94 min)
d Joel Coen. *p* Ethan Coen. *sc* Ethan Coen, Joel Coen. *ph* Barry Sonnenfeld. *ed* Michael R Miller. *pd* Jane Musky. *m* Carter Burwell. *cast* Nicolas Cage, Holly Hunter, Trey Wilson, John Goodman, William Forsythe, Sam McMurray, Randall 'Tex' Cobb, M Emmet Walsh.
●The superbly labyrinthine plotting of *Blood Simple* must have been a hard act to follow; praise be, then, to the Brothers Coen for confounding all expectations with this fervently inventive comedy. Sublimely incompetent convenience-store robber Hi McDonnough (Cage, at his best yet) seems doomed to return repeatedly to the same penitentiary until true love hoves in view in the form of prison officer Edwina (Hunter). Spliced in a trice, the frustratedly infertile couple kidnap one (surely he won't be missed?) of the celebrated Arizona quintuplets, heirs to an unpainted-furniture fortune. But happiness being evanescent, complications ensue when a pair of Hi's old cellmates turn up in search of sanctuary; and then there's the problem of a rabbit-shooting biker of hellish hue, hired by Arizona Senior to find his missing brat. What makes this hectic farce so fresh and funny is the sheer fertility of the writing, while the lives and times of Hi, Ed and friends are painted in splendidly seedy colours, turning Arizona into a mythical haven for a memorable gaggle of no-hopers, halfwits and hasbeens. Starting from a point of delirious excess, the film leaps into dark and virtually uncharted territory to soar like a comet. GA

Raising Cain

(1992, US, 92 min)
d Brian De Palma. *p* Gale Anne Hurd. *sc* Brian De Palma. *ph* Stephen H Burum. *ed* Paul Hirsch, Bonnie Koehler. *pd* Doug Kraner. *m* Pino Donaggio. *cast* John Lithgow, Lolita Davidovich, Steven Bauer, Frances Sternhagen, Gregg Henry, Tom Bower, Mel Harris, Teri Austin.
●Dealing here with the potentially juicy subject of multiple-personality disorder, De Palma provides an irresistible vehicle for Lithgow in a variety of parts stemming from child psychologist Dr Carter Nix. The first half-hour is deliberately unnerving and confusing before the plot settles down to examine why and how a number of children and a few adults have disappeared. There's a great deal of humour, not least in the persons of Carter's evil alter ego Cain, and their equally nasty father, a psycho-scientist who thinks nothing of driving his own kin completely round the twist in the name of research. And Sternhagen is superb as a cancer-stricken doctor who first sparks off suspicions about the aforementioned Lithgow brood. More to the point, De Palma, as an avowed disciple of Hitchcock, is back at his chilling best with a series of real seat-ejectors. Lithgow is consistently brilliant, while Davidovich makes a good fist as his wife. A really exciting 90 minutes worth, so long as you don't take it too seriously. SGr

Raising the Wind

(1961, GB, 91 min)
d Gerald Thomas. *p* Peter Rogers. *sc* Bruce Montgomery. *ph* Alan Hume. *ed* John Shirley. *ad* Carmen Dillon. *m* Bruce Montgomery. *cast* James Robertson Justice, Leslie Phillips, Kenneth Williams, Sidney James, Liz Fraser, Paul Massie, Eric Barker, Jennifer Jayne.
●The Doctor in the House formula recycled, with music replacing medicine, but otherwise incorporating the usual college pranks, overbearing but golden-hearted authority figure (yes, James Robertson Justice again) and U-certificate sex. It must have seemed like a museum piece even while it was being edited. BBa

Rake's Progress, The (aka Notorious Gentleman)

(1945, GB, 123 min, b/w)
d Sidney Gilliat. *p/sc* Frank Launder, Sidney Gilliat. *ph* Wilkie Cooper. *ed* Thelma Myers. *pd* David Rawnsley. *m* William Alwyn. *cast* Rex Harrison, Lilli Palmer, Griffith Jones, Margaret Johnston, Jean Kent, Godfrey Tearle, Guy Middleton, Marie Lohr.
●A memorable performance from Harrison as the quintessential upper class cad, scion of a family which traditionally breeds Tories for Westminster. Sent down from Oxford after crowning the Martyrs' Memorial with a chamberpot, he is packed off to a South American coffee plantation, rebels against the idiocies of the colonial way, and returns for a brief period of glory as a racing driver. From there on it's downhill, pursuing a shabby love 'em and leave 'em attitude to women, causing his father's death with his drunken driving, and drifting from selling used cars to selling himself as a professional dancing partner. Consistently enjoyable and often caustically witty; but the satirical overview of upper class decadence is rather undercut by the script's implication that all the boy needs is a good war to make him pull his socks up. With his sins already excused by his reckless courage and devilish charm, he naturally redeems himself by getting blown up in World War II. TM

Rally 'round the Flag, Boys!

(1958, US, 106 min)
d/p Leo McCarey. *sc* Claude Binyon, Leo McCarey. *ph* Leon Shamroy. *ed* Louis Loeffler. *ad* Lyle Wheeler, Leland Fuller. *m* Cyril J Mockridge. *cast* Paul Newman, Joanne Woodward, Joan Collins, Jack Carson, Dwayne Hickman, Tuesday Weld, Gale Gordon, Murvyn Vye.
●A roundly botched farce about the uproar in a small community when a missile base is planned in the area. A good example of Hollywood's hesitant efforts to get with it in the late '50s, with fashionable subject matter (sex and the bomb), hip stars (Newman, struggling in the days before he learned to play comedy), and unwarranted CinemaScope fittings. It backfires grandly, of course. TCh

Rambling Rose

(1991, US, 112 min)
d Martha Coolidge. *p* Renny Harlin. *sc* Calder Willingham. *ph* Johnny Jensen. *ed* Steven Cohen. *pd* John Vallone. *m* Elmer Bernstein. *cast* Laura Dern, Robert Duvall, Diane Ladd, Lukas Haas, John Heard, Kevin Conway, Robert Burke, Lisa Jakub.
●Though her employers, the ever-genteel Daddy and Mother (Duvall and Ladd) welcome her with open arms, 19-year-old housekeeper Rose (Dern) proves a difficult addition to their household. Thirteen-year-old Buddy (Haas) is hopelessly smitten; and Rose develops a crush on Daddy. She's out to find Mr Right, which involves wearing skimpy dresses and sleeping with one boyfriend after another. Calder Willingham's adaptation of his own novel is set in the pre-war South of his youth; instead of prompting jealousy, Rose's promiscuous behaviour causes Mother to rail against the South's tradition of oppression; and when the terrible truths of Rose's past are revealed, Mother's defence of the girl provides an electrifying climax. The performances are first-rate as emotions shift between confusion and confrontation; and Willingham's intelligent script combines humour, idiosyncratic observation, and lingering tenderness. CM

Rambo: First Blood, Part II

(1985, US, 96 min)
d George Pan Cosmatos. *p* Buzz Feitshans. *sc* Sylvester Stallone, James Cameron. *ph* Jack Cardiff. *ed* Mark Goldblatt, Mark Helfrich; Gib Jaffe, Frank E Jimenez, Larry Bock. *pd* Bill Kenney. *m* Jerry Goldsmith. *cast* Sylvester Stallone, Richard Crenna, Julie Nickson, Charles Napier, Steven Berkoff, Martin Kove, Andy Wood, George Kee Cheung.
●Rehabilitating the reactionary outsider John Rambo from *First Blood*, the sequel sends him back to happier hunting grounds: Vietnam, on a rescue mission for American PoWs. The body count is rising, Sly's pecs are blowing up, and Rambo himself is becoming more of a brand-name than a character, a mascot for masochism and murderous self-assertion. TCh

Rambo III

(1988, US, 102 min)
d Peter MacDonald. *p* Buzz Feitshans. *sc* Sylvester Stallone, Sheldon Lettich. *ph* John Stanier. *ed* James R Symons, Andrew London, O Nicholas Brown, Edward A Warschilka. *pd* Bill Kenney, Austin Spriggs. *m* Jerry Goldsmith. *cast* Sylvester Stallone, Richard Crenna, Marc de Jonge, Kurtwood Smith, Spiros Focas, Sasson Gabai, Doudi Shoua.
●Stallone, up against the Soviet Union, caught in a casuistical interchange between good guy Crenna and Red hammer of Afghanistan de Jonge about the unwisdom of superpowers attempting to crush freedom-loving peasant patriots. Huh? Not for Rambo such abstractions. He is only persuaded to break off his crash course in Buddhist meditation by the capture of his buddy, and his commitment to liberating Afghanistan comes after a manly variant of polo with the tribesmen and a dead goat. Then there's spunky orphan Hamid, though quite what depths of empathy their lingering looks are meant to imply remains a tantaliser. Rambo fights his way into the Russian fortress, fights his way out, and fights his way in again. He doesn't award pay-off lines, but he does explain that he's no tourist, and displays risible stoicism in removing a spike from his stomach and cauterising the hole with a charge of gunpowder. Saturday Morning Picture Club stuff, only dearer. BC

Rampage

(1963, US, 98 min)
d Phil Karlson. *p* William Fadiman. *sc* Robert I Holt, Marguerite Roberts. *ph* Harold Lipstein. *ed* Gene Milford. *ad* Herman A Blumenthal. *m* Elmer Bernstein. *cast* Robert Mitchum, Elsa Martinelli, Jack Hawkins, Sabu, Cely Carillo.
●On assignment in the Malaysian jungle at the behest of a German zoo, hunters Mitchum and Hawkins tussle over female prey Martinelli as they stalk the trail of a fearsome feline. Standard action romp amid variably convincing greenery. Sabu, who died later that year, looks especially weary, a shadow of his younger self. TJ

Ramparts of Clay (Remparts d'Argile)

(1970, Fr/Alg, 86 min)
d/p Jean-Louis Bertuccelli. *sc* Jean Duvignaud. *ph* Andréas Winding. *ed* Françoise Ceppi. *cast* Leila Schenna, the inhabitants of the village of Tehouda, Algeria.
●A slow, often fascinating, documentary-like study of an alien and primitive existence in a remote North African village, based on the book *Change at Shebika* by Jean Duvignaud. Only gradually, as the ways of 'civilisation' intrude, does the theme of rebellion emerge. The village men strike over their wages, bringing in the military; on a more personal level, an illiterate orphan girl's frustrations increase. At the film's centre lies an awareness both of the villagers' simple dignity (endorsed by almost every shot) and of the hopelessly stultifying impositions of a primitive culture upon the individual. Civilisation does offer knowledge, but with it comes exploitation and destruction.

Ramrod

(1947, US, 94 min, b/w)
d André De Toth. *p* Harry Sherman. *sc* Jack Moffitt, Graham Baker, Cecile Kramer. *ph* Russell Harlan. *ed* Sherman A Rose. *pd* Lionel Banks. *m* Adolph Deutsch. *cast* Joel McCrea, Veronica Lake, Donald Crisp, Don DeFore, Preston Foster, Arleen Whelan, Charlie Ruggles, Lloyd Bridges.
●Despite an enigmatic opening reel, the issues soon sort themselves out in this striking 'psychological' Western. Veronica Lake (excellent) is the strong-willed daughter of a rancher (Ruggles) who wants her to marry the man *he* admires, a ruthless, up-and-coming cattle baron (Foster). Clearly opting for a man she can dominate, Lake rebelliously elects to marry an out-of-town sheepman provided he re-locates on land she owns, careless of the fact that a range war will probably ensue. When the sheepman is scared off by Foster's threats, Lake defiantly decides to go it alone; and violence escalates as Foster, with her father's tacit blessing, sets out to bring her to heel. Caught in the middle as her reluctant ramrod is McCrea, just emerging from a bout of alcoholism after losing his wife and child. McCrea insists on doing things by the law, but finds himself sucked in as evil breeds evil, with Lake gradually emulating Foster, dirty trick for dirty trick. The stark little tragedy whereby Lake wins her war but forfeits McCrea's love is surprisingly persuasive; and all the performances are first-rate, with several minor characters (Crisp's ageing but indomitable sheriff, DeFore's happy-go-lucky opportunist, Whelan's patient 'other woman') adding their strands to the complex moral weave. TM

Ran 100

(1985, Fr/Jap, 160 min)
d Akira Kurosawa. *p* Serge Silberman, Masato Hara. *sc* Akira Kurosawa, Hideo Oguni, Masato Ide. *ph* Takao Saito, Masaharu Ueda. *ed* Akira Kurosawa. *pd* Yoshiro Muraki, Shinobu Muraki. *m* Toru Takemitsu. *cast* Tatsuya Nakadai, Akira Terao, Jinpachi Nezu, Daisuke Ryu, Mieko Harada, Yoshiko Miyazaki.
●Kurosawa established himself as the best cinematic interpreter of Shakespeare with his recasting of Macbeth as a samurai warlord in *Throne of Blood*. That he should in his later years turn to *King Lear* is appropriate, and the results are all that one could possibly dream of. *Ran* proposes a great warlord (Nakadai), in a less than serene old age, dividing his kingdoms up between his three sons. True to the original, the one he dispossesses is the only one faithful to him, and *ran* (chaos) ensues as the two elder sons battle for power, egged on by the Lady Kaede (an incendiary performance from Mieko Harada). The shift and sway of a nation divided is vast, the chaos terrible, the battle scenes the most ghastly ever filmed, and the outcome is even bleaker than Shakespeare's. Indeed the only note of optimism resides in the nobility of the film itself: a huge, tormented canvas, in which Kurosawa even contrives to command the elements to obey his vision. A Lear for our age, and for all time. CPea

Rancho Deluxe

(1974, US, 94 min)
d Frank Perry. *p* Elliot Kastner. *sc* Thomas McGuane. *ph* William A Fraker. *ed* Sidney Katz. *ad* Michael Haller. *m* Jimmy Buffett. *cast* Jeff Bridges, Sam Waterston, Elizabeth Ashley, Charlene Dallas, Clifton James, Slim Pickens, Harry Dean Stanton, Richard Bright, Patti D'Arbanville.
●Despite a preoccupation with puncturing the myths of the modern West, *Rancho Deluxe* operates most noticeably, and in the main successfully, as a slickly packaged youth movie. Although given a narrative about cattle rustling, the film is just as much a present day generation gap comedy, about the romps of two 'cowboys' (one white, one Indian), whose disdain of establishment values and notions of the 'freedom' of the West bring them into perpetual confrontation with reactionary elders. In keeping with the audience it is aimed at, the film is self-consciously cynical and insolent, and at the same time fundamentally romantic and seeking to be liked. The combination works surprisingly well, thanks to good ensemble acting, even if Thomas McGuane's script sometimes veers towards sentiment and smart-ass observations. CPe

Rancho Notorious

(1952, US, 89 min)
d Fritz Lang. *p* Howard Welsch. *sc* Daniel Taradash. *ph* Hal Mohr. *ed* Otto Ludwig. *ad* Robert Priestley. *m* Emil Newman. *cast* Marlene Dietrich, Arthur Kennedy, Mel Ferrer, Lloyd Gough, Gloria Henry, Jack Elam, William Frawley, Dan Seymour.
●The old Lang story of Hate, Murder and Revenge…this time in the form of his last and most unusual Western. Arthur Kennedy, obsessed with avenging his murdered fiancée, falls in with gunslinger Ferrer and crime queen Dietrich, and gradually, inexorably, becomes indistinguishable from the men he was hunting. The fateful moral, the complete avoidance of naturalism, and the integration of an ongoing ballad into the plot, all make the movie quintessential Lang; add an overt political stance and it would be quintessentially Brechtian too. TR

Rancid Aluminium

(2000, GB, 91 min)
d Edward Thomas. *p* Mike Parker, Mark Thomas, (Poland) Teresa Dworzecka. *sc* James Hawes. *ph* Tony Imi. *ed* Chris Lawrence. *pd* Hayden Pearce. *m* John Hardy. *cast* Rhys Ifans,

Joseph Fiennes, Tara Fitzgerald, Sadie Frost, Steven Berkoff, Keith Allen, Dani Behr, Andrew Howard, Barry Foster.

●This probably sounded like a good idea at the time: put Ifans and Fiennes in a caper thriller from cult author James Hawes, mix in Frost and Fitzgerald for the sex, and a Russian Mafia plot should supply cold steel. Might have been semi-watchable, too, until you factor in a director who's too intent on flinging the camera around, laying on jazzy lighting effects and over-indulging a sub-Morricone score to notice that he's left the actors to their own devices, while the audience wonder what on earth is going on. The story has something to do with Ifans inheriting daddy's company, and Fiennes, his accountant, plotting with Russki bad guys to get control of the business himself. Frost is Mrs Ifans and they're going through fertility problems, which push hubby into the accommodating arms of Fitzgerald, daughter of Russian mob king-pin Steven Berkoff (dire). The freefalling quandary into which this drives gung-ho Ifans leaves him with the taste of 'less than nothing, like rancid aluminium' in his mouth, until he devises a way of striking back. TJ

Random Harvest

(1942, US, 124 min, b/w)
d Mervyn LeRoy. *p* Sidney Franklin. *sc* Claudine West, George Froeschel, Arthur Wimperis. *ph* Joseph Ruttenberg. *ed* Harold F Kress. *ad* Cedric Gibbons, Randall Duell. *m* Herbert Stothart. *cast* Ronald Colman, Greer Garson, Susan Peters, Philip Dorn, Reginald Owen, Henry Travers, Margaret Wycherly, Edmund Gwenn.

●Colman is a shell-shocked WWI amnesiac who meets and marries music hall singer Garson; a collision with a taxi makes him forget he's married to her and return to his pedigreed family background; but she becomes his secretary, and eventually another shock…Eclipsed at the time only by the adjacent Garson-starring *Mrs Miniver* for both tosh-value and box-office receipts, this remarkably contrived delve into the here-today-gone-tomorrow memory of lovelorn Colman drew from critic James Agee the oft-quoted but irresistible line: 'I would like to recommend this film to those who can stay interested in Ronald Colman's amnesia for two hours and who could with pleasure eat a bowl of Yardley's shaving soap for breakfast'. Of course, you get froth both ways, but it doesn't taste that bad. PT

Random Hearts

(1999, US, 132 min)
d Sydney Pollack. *p* Sydney Pollack, Marykay Powell. *sc* Kurt Luedtke, Darryl Ponicsan. *ph* Philippe Rousselot. *ed* William Steinkamp. *pd* Barbara Ling. *m* Dave Grusin. *cast* Harrison Ford, Kristin Scott Thomas, Charles S Dutton, Bonnie Hunt, Dennis Haysbert, Richard Jenkins, Paul Guilfoyle, Susanna Thompson, Lynne Thigpen, Sydney Pollack, Peter Coyote, Edie Falco, Jack Gilpin, M Emmet Walsh.

●Dutch (Ford) is a greying, aggressive Internal Affairs officer in the Washington, DC, force. Shocked to hear his wife has died in a Miami-bound plane crash; his own investigation reveals she was booked on the flight as one half of a fictitious married couple, with the now-dead husband of Congresswoman Kay Chandler (Scott Thomas). Contacting the woman, he tells her his life seems a lie; she, meanwhile, wishes to preserve a professional silence. Adapted from a Warren Adler novel, this might have been tailor-made by director Pollack to ease Ford into more straightforwardly romantic territory. In that sense, there must have been a failure of nerve, since the film involves the increasingly edgy Ford in an over-elaborate police corruption subplot angled to present the actor's undiminished physical powers as vividly as Dutchy's stubborn yet vulnerable character, and the chasm between his life and that of his lover-to-be. The director's evident intention to etch detail and emotional power into the conventional Hollywood template with strokes of East Coast psychological realism – seen best in the tense scene of the leads' first encounter, worst in the spontaneous eruption of passionate fumbling in an airport limousine – is inadequately realised, leaving the performers exposed but not revealed. WH

Randonneurs, Les (The Back-Packers)

(1996, Fr, 100 min)
d Philippe Harel. *p* Adeline Lecallier. *sc* Philippe Harel, Nelly Ryher, Eric Assous. *ph* Gilles Henry, Olivier Raffet. *ed* Bénédicte Teiger. *m* Philippe Eidel. *cast* Benoît Poelvoorde, Karen Viard, Géraldine Pailhas, Philippe Harel, Vincent Elbaz.

●Five friends (3m/2f), all with troubles of their own, get on each other's nerves during a walking holiday in Corsica. Ever since Monsieur Hulot, French cinema has held to the maxim that taking vacations is seldom a good idea, and Harel's film also derives quiet amusement from observing the discomforts of its little group: tantrums from the one who can't keep up, getting lost, discovering their food has been eaten by 'wild pigs'. Full marks to the ensemble playing, especially Poelvoorde as the teeth-grittingly hearty group leader and the lugubrious Harel, whose character spends his time fretting over a possessive girlfriend back home. Stick around till after the end credits for a melancholy coda, a series of titles recounting what did, and didn't, happen subsequently. BBa

Randy Rides Alone

(1934, US, 53 min, b/w)
d Harry Fraser. *p* Paul Malvern. *sc* Lindsley Parsons Sr. *ph* Archie J Stout. *ed* Carl Pierson. *cast* John Wayne, Alberta Vaughn, George Hayes, Yakima Canutt, Earl Dwire, Arthur Artego, Tex Phelps.

●Marvin Black (Hayes), a desperado, otherwise a mild, hunch-backed storekeeper known as 'Matt the Mute', is determined to gain control of Peyote Pass by murdering the owner of the Half-Way House saloon and buying the property from his niece (Vaughn). Wayne, speaking his few lines with the dry tone and slow inflection which was to be his trademark as a star, puts matters right and blows the blackhat to smithereens with his own dynamite. (Poor sound recording on the print under review, from the UCLA Film Archive.) JPy

Ranpo

see Mystery of Rampo, The

Ransom

(1974, GB, 98 min)
d Casper Wrede. *p* Peter Rawley. *sc* Paul Wheeler. *ph* Sven Nykvist. *ed* Thelma Connell. *ad* Sven Wickman. *m* Jerry Goldsmith. *cast* Sean Connery, Ian McShane, Norman Bristow, John Cording, Isabel Dean, William Fox, Richard Hampton, Robert Harris.

●A modest British thriller, in the same mould as *The Internecine Project*, which seems similarly intent on dealing with issues of contemporary relevance. The action is set in Scandinavia, and concerns two terrorist actions: the kidnap of the British ambassador at his residence; and the hijack of a passenger plane on the tarmac of a nearby airport. Law and order security chief Colonel Tahlvik (Connery) is given the task of handling the situations – only to discover that all is not what it seems. Although Wrede and his photographer Sven Nykvist are more than competent, the movie nevertheless has a distinct air of triviality, due mainly to the made-for-TV ethos that seems to surround the whole production. Some stock characters and formula dialogue don't help either. GSa

Ransom

(1996, US, 121 min)
d Ron Howard. *p* Scott Rudin, Brian Grazer, B Kipling Hagopian. *sc* Alexander Ignon, Richard Price. *ph* Piotr Sobocinski. *ed* Daniel Hanley, Michael Hill. *pd* Michael Corenblith. *m* James Horner. *cast* Mel Gibson, Rene Russo, Brawley Nolte, Gary Sinise, Delroy Lindo, Lili Taylor, Liev Schreiber, Donnie Wahlberg.

●They want $2m – chump change to a NY entrepreneur like Tom Mullen (Gibson) when his son's life is on the line. He goes to the FBI, and they advise him to pay. But the drop-off is botched, and Mullen's not so sure he can trust these kidnappers to hold up their end of the bargain. To pay or not to pay? Such dilemmas make for edgy suspense, if not equitable marital relations, and Mullen's audacious solution here only ups the ante, leaving wife Russo hoarse with rage and horror. Unless you're familiar with an obscure 1955 Glenn Ford movie, also called *Ransom*, you'll likely be quite taken aback too. Yet this twist is as nothing compared to the truly mind-boggling claim in the credits, that this tough, penetrating thriller was directed by Ron Howard. In popular, sentimental movies from *Splash* through *Apollo 13*, Howard has proved himself a reliably competent but unerringly fatuous craftsman. How he's grown up overnight! Much of the credit must go to screenwriter Richard Price, who brings an insidious, vitriolic class-consciousness to bear. The film doesn't just trade on Gibson's dangerous, lunatic machismo, it unearths a colder, more callous and more complex narcissism. His nemesis knows him so much better than his wife. Howard pushes and probes this rich tension with expert casting, restless camerawork and a fractured editing style. The result is overwrought, but riveting. TCh

Rapa Nui

(1994, US, 106 min)
d Kevin Reynolds. *p* Kevin Costner, Jim Wilson. *sc* Kevin Reynolds, Tim Rose Price. *ph* Stephen Windon. *ed* Peter Boyle. *pd* George Liddle. *m* Stewart Copeland. *cast* Jason Scott Lee, Esai Morales, Sandrine Holt, George Hanares, Eru Potaka-Dewes, Rena Owen.

●Rapa Nui is what the natives call Easter Island: 'the navel of the world'. Here the Long Ears lord it over the Short Ears, forcing them to carve huge, monolithic statues – the *moai* – for the gods. Noro (Lee), the Long Ears' champion, will compete against his childhood friend Make (Morales) to decide who will be clan 'birdman' this year – and for the hand of a Short Ear, Ramana (Holt). A labour of love for director Reynolds (*Robin Hood*), and co-produced by Kevin Costner, this is a curious Hollywood project, but not a successful one. The leads are okay, but the English-language Polynesian dialogue, containing such lines as, 'I don't need this, I have chicken entrails to read,' does not help matters; and the script settles for the kind of cod anthropology found in Disney animations. Shot on Easter Island, the movie looks impressive – the *National Geographic* in 'Scope – but perhaps the makers should have followed the example of the *moai* and kept their mouths shut. TCh

Rape, The (Niet voor de Poesen)

(1973, Neth/Bel, 93 min)
d/p Fons Rademakers. *sc* Hugo Claus. *ph* Eduard van der Enden. *ed* Ton Aarden. *ad* Jean-Paul Vroom. *m* Rund Bos. *cast* Bryan Marshall, Alexandra Stewart, Alex Van Rooyen, Leo Beyers, Martin Van Zundert, George Baker, Sylvia Kristel, Edward Judd.

●An interesting little movie adapted from Nicolas Freeling's novel *Because of the Cats*, *Rape* is an intelligent thriller masquerading as a sex film. The sex is there – in an extended rape sequence and a bit of underwater fucking – but the thrust of the film is the investigation by Inspector Van der Valk (Marshall) of a series of senseless robberies, culminating in a rape and a murder, that leads him to a confrontation with the Ravens, a group of adolescent rich kids. A Dutch/Belgian co-production shot in English, the stilted conversations meld perfectly with the static, non-dramatic visuals which forever have Van der Valk's slightly puritanical presence calling into question the luxurious surroundings he is caught up in. PH

Rape of Malaya, The

see Town Like Alice, A

Rape Squad

see Act of Vengeance

Rapid Fire

(1992, US, 95 min)
d Dwight H Little. *p* Robert Lawrence. *sc* Alan McElroy. *ph* Ric Waite. *ed* Gib Jaffe. *pd* Ron Foreman. *m* Christopher Young. *cast* Brandon Lee, Powers Boothe, Nick Mancuso, Raymond J Barry, Kate Hodge, Tzi Ma, Tony Longo.

●The kicks and jinks are high in this jolly martial arts movie. Jake Lo (Lee), brought up in the States, is briefly at Tiananmen Square when his Chinese father, working for the US Government, is run over by a tank. Back at college in the States, he angrily refuses to endorse the Democracy movement (the depiction of Chinese immigrants is thoughtful and unstereotypical), then witnesses a Mafia hit against a Chinese drug baron. He chops his way outta that one, but the FBI want him to testify, and suddenly everyone's on his tail… The fight scenes are brilliant, and though Lee lacks the animal grace of his father Bruce or the comic skills of Jackie Chan, he has cheerful wit and timing, plus the bod of a Chippendale. Like a good spring roll, this is crisp, tasty, and full of good things. SFe

Rappin'

(1985, US, 92 min)
d Joel Silberg. *p* Menahem Golan, Yoram Globus. *sc* Robert Litz, Adam Friedman. *ph* David Gurfinkel. *ed* Andy Horvitch, Bert Glatstein. *pd* Steve Miller. *cast* Mario Van Peebles, Tasia Valenza, Charles Flohe, Eriq La Salle, Kadeem Hardison, Richie Abanes, Leo O'Brien.

●John 'Rappin' Hood (Van Peebles) and his band of merry poets take on the baddies, a stop-at-nothing property development corporation and the gang recruited to terrorise the tenants they wish to evict; it seems that all Hood & Co have to do is break into verse and everything is suddenly right as rain. Peppered with offensive stereotypes, the only light relief comes when the hip crew succumb to another rapattack. It's not an unmitigated disaster, but the absurd grand finale, at the crucial public hearing where the power of rap conquers all, pushes it irrevocably over the edge. PG

Rappresaglia

see Massacre in Rome

Rapture, The

(1991, US, 102 min)
d Michael Tolkin. *p* Nick Wechsler, Nancy Tanenbaum, Karen Koch. *sc* Michael Tolkin. *ph* Bojan Bazelli. *ed* Suzanne Fenn. *pd* Robin Standefer. *m* Thomas Newman. *cast* Mimi Rogers, David Duchovny, Patrick Bauchau, Kimberly Cullum, Terri Hanauer, Dick Anthony Williams, Will Patton.

●Directorial debut for Tolkin, best known as the novelist who wrote *The Player*. Unfortunately, it is loony stuff, rising to a cherishable risibility in the final third. Sharon (Rogers) is a telephone operator who spends her nights partying with three-in-a-bed pick-ups until self-disgust turns her to God, after which disgustingness becomes the least of her problems. When her husband is randomly murdered, she takes her little daughter into the desert to await the Last Trumpets of Armageddon. A caring cop (Patton) turns up with food, but is unable to prevent an almost unwatchable tragedy. In jail, the prophecies of the Book of Revelations come to pass, the bars fall away, and she scoots off on the cop's motorbike pursued by the First Horseman of the Apocalypse, after which the shit gets plenty astral. Disquietingly, America seems to be leaping with these evangelistic Born Agains, but quite where Tolkin stands is obscured by shoddy plotting. Rogers puts her all into it. BC

Rapunzel Let Down Your Hair

(1978, GB, 78 min)
d/p/sc Susan Shapiro, Esther Ronay, Francine Winham. *ph* Diane Tammes. *ed* Esther Ronay. *ad* Diana Morris. *m* Laka Koc, Benni Lees, Ruthie Smith. *cast* Margaret Ford, Suzie Hickford, Jessica Swift, Laka Koc, Lydia Blackman.

●From the Grimm Brothers' story (immediate inquiry into the nature of fairytales – eternal truths or patriarchal fantasies?) emerges a very attractive, perceptive film, which encompasses several knotty problems relevant to feminism today. Breaking with a traditional narrative, Rapunzel's story is retold and reinterpreted, each version using a different movie genre accompanied by a wonderful music score. Thus the superseductive animation of dream and symbolism; the opportunist male voyeur as *film noir* detective; a raunchy cartoon Venus, her roots firmly in witchcraft; the family melodrama of menopausal angst; and finally Rapunzel's own tale, a live-action narrative which completes the film's substructure of the stages of womanhood, and leads firmly out of an urban desert to a finale of feminist celebration. Fairytales were always appealing, but they never made quite so much sense. HM

Rare Breed, The

(1965, US, 108 min)
d Andrew V McLaglen. *p* William Alland. *sc* Ric Hardman. *ph* William H Clothier. *ed* Russell Schoengarth. *ad* Alexander Golitzen, Alfred Ybarra. *m* John Williams. *cast* James Stewart, Maureen O'Hara, Brian Keith, Juliet Mills, Don Galloway, David Brian, Jack Elam, Ben Johnson, Harry Carey Jr.

●Born into the Ford/Wayne axis as the son of Victor, McLaglen was steeped in Western lore from an early age, and graduated through teleseries like *Gunsmoke* and *Have Gun – Will Travel* to a string of features hymning the old generic simplicities in their twilight. His features with Wayne tended to be as reactionary as the Duke himself (a predilection subsequently confirmed in work like *The Wild Geese*), but this effort about O'Hara's attempts to cross a Hereford bull with Texas longhorn stock is innocuously banal. And the human supporting cast just about make it worthwhile. PT

Rashomon 100

(1951, Jap, 88 min, b/w)
d Akira Kurosawa. *p* Jingo Minoura. *sc* Akira Kurosawa. *ph* Kazuo Matsuyama. *ad* H Motsumoto. *m* Takashi Matsuyama. *cast* Toshiro Mifune, Machiko Kyo, Masayuki Mori, Takashi Shimura, Minoru Chiaki, Fumiko Homma.

●If it weren't for the closing spasm of gratuitous, humanist optimism, *Rashomon* could be warmly recommended as one of Kurosawa's most inventive and sustained achievements. The main part of the film, set in 12th century Kyoto, offers four mutually contradictory versions of an ambush, rape and murder, each through the eyes of one of those involved. The view of human weaknesses and vices is notably astringent, although the sheer animal vigour of Mifune's bandit is perhaps a celebration of a sort. The film is much less formally daring than its literary source, but its virtues are still plentiful: Kurosawa's visual style at its most muscular, rhythmically nuanced editing, and excellent performances. TR

Raskolnikow

(1923, Ger, 6,992 ft, b/w)
d/p/sc Robert Wiene. *ph* Willy Goldberger. *ad* Andre Andrejew. *cast* Gregory Chmara, Maria Germanowa, Sergei Kammissaroff, Pawel Pawloff, Maria Krishanovskaja.

●*The Cabinet of Dr Caligari* is almost unique among silent 'classics' in that nobody attributes its qualities to its director; Robert Wiene has never seemed more than a peripheral figure, and his later attempts to repeat his one-off success never won him any real reputation. He both directed and scripted this adaptation of Dostoevsky's *Crime and Punishment*, and seems to have had grandiose artistic ambitions for the project, drawing his cast from Stanislavsky's Moscow Art Theatre, and commissioning 'expressionist' sets from Andrei Andreiev. The result poses fascinating questions. Was the disjunction between the naturalistic acting and the artificial decor deliberate, or simply inept? And was the 'expressionism' (the sets and a scattering of dream sequences) an attempt to visualise the moral/theological dimension of the novel, or simply a matter of fashion? There are no ready answers, but the film certainly sustains the questions. TR

Rasputin

see Agony

Rasputin and the Empress

(1932, US, 133 min, b/w)
d Richard Boleslawski. *p* Irving Thalberg. *sc* Charles MacArthur. *ph* William Daniels. *ed* Tom Held. *ad* Cedric Gibbons, Alexander Tobuloff. *m* Herbert Stothart. *cast* John Barrymore, Ethel Barrymore, Lionel Barrymore, Diana Wynyard, Ralph Morgan, Edward Arnold, Gustav von Seyffertitz, Jean Parker.

●The one and only time that the Barrymore family appeared together on screen, Lionel as Rasputin, Ethel as the Tsarina, John as Prince Chegodieff (ie. Youssoupoff). This curio – the subject of litigation brought against MGM by the Prince and Princess Youssoupoff, who claimed it was historically inaccurate – is often strangely dull in its depiction of the last days of the Czar's court, although one can't deny the attraction of its impressive sets and costumes. GA

Rat, The

(1925, GB, b/w, 7323 ft)
d Graham Cutts. *p* Michael Balcon. *sc* Graham Cutts. *ph* Hal Young. *ad* Charles W Arnold. *cast* Ivor Novello, Mae Marsh, Isobel Jeans, Robert Scholtz, James Lindsay, Marie Ault.

●Swaggering adaptation of Novello's own play, co-written with Constance Collier. Novello plays Pierre Boucheron, a 19th century Parisian jewel thief and vagabond. The picture opens in exhilarating fashion, with Boucheron leading the gendarmes on a chase through the back streets before escaping down a manhole. Much of the story unfolds in the White Coffin, a demi-monde bar full of sultry looking prostitutes, all of them in love with Boucheron, and assorted knife brandishing ruffians. (At one stage, in an attempt to show he's easily a match for Valentino and Novarro, the star dances a tango, ripping his partner's skirt at the hip so she can move more easily.) The subplot, about his fling with a bored aristocratic woman whose diamonds he steals, is purely routine. But Cutts directs the chases and fights with verve, the Gallic underworld is imaginatively evoked, and Novello makes a suitably louche, charismatic anti-hero. GM

Ratas, Ratones, Rateros

see Rodents

Ratboy

(1986, US, 104 min)
d Sondra Locke. *p* Fritz Manes. *sc* Robert Thompson. *ph* Bruce Surtees. *ed* Joel Cox. *pd* Edward C Carfagno. *m* Lennie Niehaus. *cast* Sondra Locke, Robert Townsend, Christopher Hewett, Larry Hankin, Sydney Lassick, Gerrit Graham, Louie Anderson, SL Baird.

●Once upon a time in Hollywood a young actress, with the help of her friend Clint Eastwood and his Malpaso company, made a modern fairytale about a little boy who looked like a rat. Locke plays the good ol' country girl who rescues the bewhiskered rubbish-tip recluse to transform him into a star. Unfortunately, however, Locke's 'very black, funny and sad comedy' is neither funny nor sad, and the only thing black about it is its stereotypical depiction of Blacks as conmen and Uncle Toms. Give it a miss. SGo

Ratcatcher

(1999, GB, 94 min)
d Lynne Ramsay. *p* Gavin Emerson. *sc* Lynne Ramsay. *ph* Alwin Kuchler. *ed* Lucia Zucchetti. *pd* Jane Morton. *m* Rachel Portman. *cast* William Eadie, Tommy Flanagan, Mandy Matthews, Leanne Mullen, John Miller.

●Set in and around a Glasgow tenement block during a dustman's strike in the mid-'70s, Ramsay's astonishingly assured feature debut centres on a 12-year-old (Eadie, excellent) who, haunted by the (secret) role he played in a pal's accidental death by drowning, gradually retreats into a private world of solitude, strange friendships and consoling dreams of a new home for his family. That's about it, story-wise, but Ramsay's bold visual sense, droll wit and tender but unsentimental take on the various characters and their relationships makes for a distinctly poetic brand of gritty realism, and one of the most impressive first features by a British director in some years. GA

Rate It X

(1985, US, 93 min, b/w & col)
d Paula de Koenigsberg, Lucy Winer. *p* Lynn Campbell, Claudette Charbonneau, Paula de Koenigsberg, Lucy Winer. *ph* Paul de Koenigsberg. *ed* Lucy Winer. *m* Elizabeth Swados.

●In what the production notes describe as 'a bitingly funny and disarming journey through the landscape of American sexism', the (women) filmmakers have collated some fifteen or so interviews with men involved in some way or another in what is called the 'consumer zone'. Quite what this grisly assortment of wits and raconteurs thought they were letting themselves in for is a mystery. It is not a pretty sight. The interviews range from 'Ugly George', he of the successful cable TV show – the travelling Mr Camera who persuades passing 'pieces of ass' to strip in alleyways for a quiet bit of nationwide exposure – through Madison Avenue lingerie execs boasting of overcoming the bra-burning threat, to a gang of gaga war vets, given the opportunity to enlarge on their perception of traditional sex roles. Sexism? Nah, we can't spell it, but heck, we's can do it anyway! There's ample evidence in this film to confirm that some 15 years after what has been called the 'second feminist wave', the nasty extremes of sexism are only too alive and well.

But what of the ethics of documentary film-making? The poor damn fools who people this document may have been too obtuse to comprehend the intentions of its makers if it was spelled out to them. But was it? And does it matter? WH

Rat Race

(2001, US, 112 min)
d Jerry Zucker. *p* Jerry Zucker, Janet Zucker, Sean Daniel. *sc* Andy Breckman. *ph* Thomas Ackerman. *ed* Tom Lewis. *pd* Gary Frutkoff. *m* John Powell. *cast* Rowan Atkinson, John Cleese, Whoopi Goldberg, Cuba Gooding Jr, Seth Green, Jon Lovitz, Breckin Meyer, Kathy Najimi, Amy Smart, Kathy Bates.

● Avaricious Las Vegas casino tycoon Donald Sinclair (Cleese) will do anything to fulfil the whims of his high-rolling clientèle. But his latest wager is his most imaginative yet. Concealed in a station locker several hundred miles away is a duffel bag containing $2m cash. Expounding his distaste for the low-rollers who also frequent his casino, he places six unique coins in the casino's slots and invites the winners to go forth and seek out the booty. The first one to open the locker gets to keep the cash. Yet, unbeknown to this gaggle of gullibles, Sinclair and his classy clients will be tracking their every move, *Truman Show*-style, and betting high stakes on the outcome. Roll on a madcap *Cannonball Run* across several states. Director Zucker is best known for his contributions to zany comedies like *Airplane!* and *The Naked Gun*. Yet, incoherently stupid, more than it is funny, only one scene here – with Kathy Bates and a bunch of squirrels – gets close to the hilarity of those films. Still, there are some humourous allusions to the new compensation culture, and the soppy feelgood finalé could be deemed a fitting end to its sarcastic swipe at capitalism. DA

Rats, The (aka Deadly Eyes)

(1982, US, 93 min)
d Robert Clouse. *p* Paul Kahnert, Charles Eglee. *sc* Charles Eglee. *ph* René Verzier. *ed* Ron Wisman. *m* Anthony Guefen. *cast* Sam Groom, Sara Botsford, Scatman Crothers, Lisa Langlois, Cec Linder.

● Silly film about a plague of giant cat-size rats that can gnaw through a human hand more viciously than a Great Dane. Hunky schoolteacher (Groom) falls for the local public health inspector (Botsford), who is concerned about the frequent sightings of rats in and around the sewage system. With the opening of a new public subway system under way, she orders the sewers to be fumigated, but these tough critters are immune to such trivial things. From then on, it's rodent on the rampage. Clouse uses the Steadicam technique (as employed by Carpenter in *Halloween*), but unfortunately it doesn't work for rats, and only gives the impression that they are huge, slow-moving creatures. A short but wonderful performance from Scatman Crothers is the only thing that lifts the film out of the sewers for a few moments. DA

Rat-Trap (Elippathayam)

(1981, Ind, 121 min)
d Adoor Gopalakrishnan. *p* Ravi. *sc* Adoor Gopalakrishnan. *ph* Mankada Ravi Varma. *ed* M Mani. *ad* Sivan. *m* MB Srinivasan. *cast* Karamana, Sarada, Jalaja, Rajam K Nair, Prakash, Sonan.

● A middle-aged rural landowner, who has never had to do a thing for himself, loses the female relatives who wait on him, one after another, and watches helplessly as his estate, already ravaged by thefts and mismanagement, falls into decay. Not a fresh subject, but the treatment is extraordinary: using rats as his governing metaphor, Gopalakrishnan constructs his film like a cinematic rondo, making every composition and every camera movement count. TR

Raven, The

(1935, US, 62 min, b/w)
d Louis Friedlander [Lew Landers]. *p* David Diamant. *sc* David Boehm. *ph* Charles Stumar. *ed* Albert Akst. *ad* Albert S D'Agostino. *m* Gilbert Harland. *cast* Bela Lugosi, Boris Karloff, Irene Ware, Lester Matthews, Samuel S Hinds.

● A second teaming for Karloff and Lugosi after the success of *The Black Cat*. This time round Bela has the upper hand as a surgeon obsessed by Poe, frustrated in his passion for a beautiful dancer (Ware) after repairing the damage when her face is scarred in a car crash, and mutilating Karloff's ugly criminal even further when he arrives for a face job, in order to force his cooperation in pursuing his ugly designs on the girl. An absurd script, without a hint of self-parody, and a nicely equipped set (moving walls, a razor sharp pendulum that slowly lowers itself on to victims) make for entertaining if undemanding viewing. GA

Raven, The

see Corbeau, Le

Raven, The

(1963, US, 86 min)
d/p Roger Corman. *sc* Richard Matheson. *ph* Floyd Crosby. *ed* Ronald Sinclair. *pd* Daniel Haller. *m* Les Baxter. *cast* Vincent Price, Boris Karloff, Peter Lorre, Hazel Court, Olive Sturgess, Jack Nicholson, Connie Wallace.

● The humour of Richard Matheson's well-calculated send-up of Poe's gruesome *The Black Cat* – as the middle story in Corman 's *Tales of Terror* – went down so well that Matheson here used Poe's poem *The Raven* as the basis for a full-length parody. With Price, Karloff and Lorre superbly funny as rival magicians – and Jack Nicholson turning up to give the most atrocious performance of his career as the juvenile lead – *The Raven* is one of the few fantasy comedies that hangs together as happily as a fairytale, and it climaxes with a suitably splendid duel of marvels between Karloff and Price. DP

Ravenous

(1999, US/GB, 101 min)
d Antonia Bird. *p* Adam Fields, David Heyman. *sc* Ted Griffin. *ph* Anthony Richmond. *ed* Neil Farrell. *pd* Bryce Perrin. *m* Michael Nyman, Damon Albarn. *cast* Guy Pearce, Robert Carlyle, Jeremy Davies, Jeffrey Jones, John Spencer, Stephen Spinella, Neal McDonough.

● This peculiar, funny addition to the already out-there cannibal sub-genre is your basic black-comedy horror Western with metaphorical overtones. Call it *Dances with Werewolves*. The year is 1847. Fresh from the Mexican American war, Capt John Boyd (Pearce) is transferred to a remote, sparsely populated army fort in the high Nevadas. Hot on his heels comes the stricken figure of a Scot, Colqhoun (Carlyle), with a cannibal tale to chill even the bravest of them. Colqhoun escaped, hoping to save the last of the women, so Boyd and Colonel Hart (Jones) lead a rescue party with Colqhoun as guide. What they encounter is more terrifying than they ever imagined. Antonia Bird (*Priest*) was the third director on what was evidently a troubled shoot, and it's not a neat and tidy piece of work. But whoever wanted a neat, tidy comic horror Western? Carlyle acts his socks off, Pearce endures against terrible odds, and the action is confidently handled. As bizarre as its Michael Nyman-Damon Albarn bluegrass score, this is a gourmet dish for midnight movie ghouls. TCh

Raw Deal

(1948, US, 82 min, b/w)
d Anthony Mann. *p* Edward Small. *sc* Leopold Atlas, John C Higgins. *ph* John Alton. *ed* Alfredo Gaetano. *ad* Edward Ilou. *m* Paul Sawtell. *cast* Dennis O'Keefe, Claire Trevor, Marsha Hunt, Raymond Burr, John Ireland, Chili Williams, Curt Conway, Whit Bissell.

● A fine *noir* thriller, product of the dream marriage between Mann's direction and John Alton's camera. O'Keefe's escape from jail is arranged by the racketeer (Burr) for whom he is serving a rap, and who confidently expects him to be killed, thus shutting his mouth and eliminating the need to pay him off. Along for the ride is Trevor, who loves him, and as hostage, the girl from the lawyer's office (Hunt) who has become interested in his case. The action is sharp, the characterisation vivid (Burr gets to anticipate *The Big Heat* by hurling a bowl of flaming brandy over a girl who annoys him; Ireland is memorable as a cool hood who gets his kicks by needling the nervous Burr while patiently building card houses). But what gives the film its wholly distinctive flavour is the voice-over narration by Trevor. 'She's getting under his skin,' she sadly comments as Hunt's initial flirtatiousness turns to disgust, thereby sparking a yearning in O'Keefe for his own lost innocence; throughout, her despairing efforts to understand the romantic ramifications in which the three of them get caught lend the film an unusual emotional depth. TM

Raw Deal

(1986, US, 105 min)
d John Irvin. *p* Martha Schumacher. *sc* Gary M DeVore, Norman Wexler. *ph* Alex Thomson. *ed* Anne V Coates. *pd* Giorgio Postiglione. *m* Tom Bahler, Albhy Galuten, Chris Boardman, (addit) Jerry Hey, Randy Kerber. *cast* Arnold Schwarzenegger, Kathryn Harrold, Sam Wanamaker, Paul Shenar, Robert Davi, Ed Lauter, Darren McGavin, Joe Regalbuto.

● Stone-faced shoot-'em-up in the implacable Chuck Norris/Steven Seagal mode. Arnie's recruited by his old FBI boss McGavin to break up crimelord Wanamaker's Chicago drugs gang, which he does by inveigling himself into the role of Mr Big's bodyguard and routing the villains from the inside. There follows the machine-guns in both hands trick, dumb wisecracks, and the requisite drive-the-truck-through-the-building set piece. None of it delivered with *Commando*'s tongue-in-cheek sense of the absurd. TJ

Rawhide (aka Desperate Siege)

(1950, US, 86 min, b/w)
d Henry Hathaway. *p* Samuel G Engel. *sc* Dudley Nichols. *ph* Milton Krasner. *ed* Robert Simpson. *ad* Lyle Wheeler, George W Davis. *m* Sol Kaplan. *cast* Tyrone Power, Susan Hayward, Hugh Marlowe, Dean Jagger, Edgar Buchanan, Jack Elam, George Tobias, Jeff Corey.

● A competent Western, not improved by a redundant voice-over and a corny score, very similar in plot to the later *The Desperate Hours* (actually, it's based on a 1935 gangster movie, *Show Them No Mercy*). Power is a young Easterner, sent by his father to learn the Overland Mail business, who finds himself fighting for survival – along with a woman (Hayward) and her dead sister's little daughter – when four escaped convicts, led by the well-bred but ruthless Marlowe, take over his way station to wait for the stage carrying a shipment of gold. The action follows pretty predictable lines, but Marlowe's three henchmen are nicely characterised and played: Tobias, bovine and stolidly obedient; Jagger, grizzled and amiable, forever muttering crazily into his beard; Elam, leering, lecherously sadistic, gleefully potting off shots at the child (he misses, of course). By contrast, the three leads tend to declaim Dudley Nichols' stiff dialogue as though it were holy writ. TM

Raw Meat

see Death Line

Rayon Vert, Le

see Green Ray, The

Razorback

(1984, Aust, 95 min)
d Russell Mulcahy. *p* Hal McElroy *sc* Everett De Roche. *ph* Dean Semler. *ed* William Anderson. *pd* Bryce Walmsley. *m* Iva Davies. *cast* Gregory Harrison, Arkie Whiteley, Bill Kerr, Chris Haywood, David Argue, Judy Morris, John Howard, John Ewart.

● Mulcahy went from Duran Duran videos (the epochal 'Rio' among them) to a rampaging boar in this souped-up eco shocker of a movie debut. Searching for his wife, an animal activist missing in the outback while investigating the slaughter of kangaroos, Harrison comes across a mysterious meat-canning plant, sundry male chauvinist psychos and a malevolent razorback porker with a dingo-like penchant for baby-snatching. While grizzled hunter Kerr merrily chomps away at the equivalent of Robert Shaw's role in *Jaws*, Mulcahy directs with a mixture of self-conscious artiness (exaggerated lighting effects, brief surrealist flourishes) and B-picture zip. He's badly let down by the effects team's dismayingly mechanical killer beastie, but the charnel house of the Petpak Cannery is certainly a good spot for a gruesome final-reel showdown. TJ

Razor Blade Smile

(1998, GB, 102 min)
d Jake West. *p* Jake West, Robert Mercer. *sc* Jake West. *ph* James Solan. *ed* Jake West. *pd* Neil Jenkins. *m* Richard Wells. *cast* Eileen Daly, Christopher Adamson, Jonathan Coote, Kevin Howarth, David Warbeck.
● A low budget British vampire flick in which Lilith, a hitwoman in a leather catsuit (Daly), has been plying her trade, poor dear, for some 150 years to assuage the tedium of immortality. But when old flame Platinum (Howarth) sets her on a series of assassinations of members of a shadowy, sinister supernatural cult called the 'Illuminati', things almost get exciting. And when the police, led by uninspiring Inspector Price (Coote), close in and Platinum is kidnapped, she must turn avenger. West aims squarely at the late-night fetish/horror crowd, playing it surprisingly straight and soft-peddling the camp – notwithstanding the pre-neck-sucking routines with Daly – in favour of gunplay. Visually, it's a mish-mash, shifting from boringly lit interiors to flash computer-generated psychedelic effects, via speeded up London night shots and b/w and splash-red historical flashbacks. But despite the mad switches in tone, the implausibility, the frequently poor sound and the actors' often shamateurish 'in-quotes' delivery, there's a no-nonsense, unapologetic mood that makes the film hard to dislike. WH

Razor's Edge, The

(1946, US, 146 min, b/w)
d Edmund Goulding. *p* Darryl F Zanuck. *sc* Lamar Trotti. *ph* Arthur Miller. *ed* J Watson Webb. *ad* Richard Day, Nathan Juran. *m* Alfred Newman. *cast* Tyrone Power, Gene Tierney, John Payne, Anne Baxter, Clifton Webb, Herbert Marshall, Elsa Lanchester, Fritz Kortner.
● A kind of *Lost Horizon* for the Lost Generation as a soldier returning from the First World War shrugs off his wealthy background to search for spiritual fulfilment. Starting among the smart set in Europe (Paris and the Riviera created in the studio), it then moves rather less persuasively to India. Classic Hollywood kitsch, with the shallow sophistication of Somerset Maugham's novel well matched by the glossiest glitter that Fox could buy. But somehow Goulding (an erratic but underrated director) manages to dominate it all with an almost Premingerian *mise en scène*, aided by some superb performances (Tierney in particular). TM

Reach for the Sky

(1956, GB, 135 min, b/w)
d Lewis Gilbert. *p* Daniel M Angel. *sc* Lewis Gilbert. *ph* Jack Asher. *ed* John Shirley. *ad* Bernard Robinson. *m* John Addison. *cast* Kenneth More, Muriel Pavlow, Lyndon Brook, Lee Patterson, Alexander Knox, Dorothy Alison, Sydney Tafler.
● Chocks away, Smithy. Maudlin, overlong, hero-worshipping stuff, with More waddling pathetically around on artificial legs impersonating Douglas Bader, symbol of everything stiff-upper-lipped and jolly good show about Britain and the RAF boys during the war. If you haven't seen this, you're probably the saner for it. GA

Reaching for the Moon

(1931, US, 90 min, b/w)
d Edmund Goulding. *sc* Irving Berlin, Elsie Janis, Edmund Goulding. *ph* Ray June, Robert Planck. *ed* Lloyd Nosler, Hal C Kern. *ad* William Cameron Menzies. *m* Irving Berlin. *cast* Douglas Fairbanks, Bebe Daniels, Edward Everett Horton, Claud Allister, Jack Mulhall, Bing Crosby.
● This was, or would have been, Berlin's first Hollywood musical, but in a fit of early-talkie jitters United Artists cut out all the numbers but one. What survives is an awkward comedy-drama featuring an aging but still energetic Fairbanks as a bumptious tycoon humbled by glamorous aviator Daniels and then by the Wall Street crash. Surprisingly, coming from old pro Goulding, some scenes look more like rehearsals than the real thing. But there are engaging elements: the fantasia of Menzies' Art Deco sets, bursts of mike-defying camera movement and lashings of pre-Code innuendo involving, who else, Edward Everett Horton. BBa

Ready to Rumble

(2000, US, 106 min)
d Brian Robbins. *p* Bobby Newmyer, Jeffrey Silver. *sc* Steven Brill. *ph* Clark Mathis. *ed* Ned Bastille, Cindy Mollo. *pd* Jaymes Hinkle. *m* George S Clinton. *cast* David Arquette, Oliver Platt, Scott Caan, Bill Goldberg, Rose McGowan, Diamond Dallas Page, Joe Pantoliano, Martin Landau, Richard Lineback, Chris Owen, Steve 'Sting' Borden.
● Heaven knows when wrestling became cinema's *sport du mode*, but this cheerily corpulent comedy follows close on the heavy heels of Barry Blaustein's documentary *Beyond the Mat*, and toes much the same philosophical line. These glitzy grunt 'n' groan shows may be entertainment by fuck-ups for fuck-ups, it concedes – but hell, we do love 'em. You may beg to differ. The film profiles two cretinous, reality-challenged late adolescents, Gordie (Arquette) and Sean (Caan), who haul sewage and obsess about wrestling. Their idol and guiding light is unvanquished WCW champ Jimmy King (Platt) – but it turns out Jimmy's more of a WCW chimp, and it's on the very 'Monday Nitro Night' the duo choose to make their pilgrimage that tassled tournament supremo Titus Sinclair (Pantoliano) ordains that his other fighters put their boots in. All this is intellectually unacceptable to the boys, however, so they drag the King out of hiding – and women's clothing – and kickstart a grudge rematch with an enthusiasm he can't quite share. NB

Ready to Wear (aka Prêt-à-Porter)

(1994, US, 133 min)
d/p Robert Altman. *sc* Robert Altman, Barbara Shulgasser. *ph* Pierre Mignot, Jean Lépine. *ed* Geraldine Peroni. *pd* Stephen Altman. *m* Michel Legrand. *cast* Kim Basinger, Richard E Grant, Tim Robbins, Julia Roberts, Marcello Mastroianni, Sophia Loren, Anouk Aimée, Tracey Ullman, Michel Blanc, Jean-Pierre Cassel, Linda Hunt.
● One of the world's finest film-makers, Robert Altman is also one of the most erratic, with an alarming tendency to aim his satirical barbs at easy targets. It's no surprise, then, that he should opt for this smug, unfocused, facile swipe at the follies of the fashion world. Much has been made of the authentic location shooting and the starry cast, but there's a world of difference between the carefully interwoven vignettes and deft portraiture of *Nashville* and *Short Cuts* and what passes for narrative and characterisation here. There's no story to speak of and no centre. Ironically, the only halfway decent moments involve the emotional sparring between journos Robbins and Roberts, and the gentle comic style of Mastroianni's furtive fugitive. Otherwise, it's a meaningless, meandering babble of broad grotesquerie. GA

Real Blonde, The

(1997, US, 105 min)
d Tom DiCillo. *p* Marcus Viscidi, Tom Rosenberg. *sc* Tom DiCillo. *ph* Frank Prinzi. *ed* Camilla Toniolo, Keiko DeGuchi. *pd* Christopher Nowak. *m* Jim Farmer. *cast* Matthew Modine, Catherine Keener, Daryl Hannah, Kathleen Turner, Maxwell Caulfield, Elizabeth Berkley, Buck Henry, Christopher Lloyd, Denis Leary, Steve Buscemi.
● This attempt at combining satirical comedy with deeply felt emotional drama is only fitfully successful. One minute, he's mocking the inanities of the New York film, fashion and music industries. The next, he's scratching over the relationship between his antagonists, struggling actor Modine and make-up artist Keener, with Bergman-like intensity. There are some wonderful moments along the way – Keener beating up her martial arts tutor (Leary) or Modine as a pimpled, white-skinned extra in a Madonna video. Caulfield is sardonic and funny as the louche young seducer/soap opera star who shrivels up when he has the chance to make love with a real blonde (Hannah). Modine is enjoyably sanctimonious as the Arthur Miller-spouting young thesp, but, bizarrely, director DiCillo, while mocking everybody else, seems to take him at face value. GM

Real Cool Time (Ce vieux rêve qui bouge)

(2001, Fr, 50 min)
d Alain Guiraudie. *p* Jean Philippe Labadie, Nathalie Eybrard, Lilie Lê-liêu. *sc* Alain Guiraudie. *ph* Emmanuel Soyer. *ed* Philippe Ramos. *cast* Pierre Louis-Calixte, Jean Marie Combelles, Jean Segani, Yves Dinse, Serge Ribes, Jean-Claude Montheil.
● A young guy turns up at a rundown factory to dismantle some kind of machine before the place closes in a week. In the process, he gets to talk to the understandably morose staff about how they plan to face the future. About work, economics, class, sex, money, happiness and a whole lot more, this unassuming, sometimes funny and always surprising film has been hailed by Godard – perhaps the most sensible thing he's done in years. It's near perfect, without an ounce of narrative fat or stylistic gristle, and utterly relevant. GA

Real Genius

(1985, US, 106 min)
d Martha Coolidge. *p* Brian Grazer. *sc* Neal Israel, Pat Proft, Peter Torokvei. *ph* Vilmos Zsigmond. *ed* Richard Chew. *pd* Josan F Russo. *m* Thomas Newman. *cast* Val Kilmer, Gabe Jarret, Michelle Meyrink, William Atherton, Patti D'Arbanville, Robert Prescott, Louis Giambalvo, Jonathan Gries, Ed Lauter.
● Coolidge's career progressed from personal independent documentaries on rape and drug abuse, through an ill-fated brush with Coppola's Zoetrope, and eventually moved towards the mainstream with the engaging off-kilter teen flick *Valley Girl*. This, her first Hollywood feature, was co-written by the *Police Academy* team, and mainly plays like it. Supersmart college boffins Kilmer and Jarret are recruited by teacher Atherton to work on a new laser project, but the kids eventually turn rebellious when they discover the device's covert military implications. It's a change to see young folk are more obsessed with technology than the promptings of the trouser department, but the gizmo-heavy hi-jinks (fun with helium, frozen gas and other science-class materials) do outstay their welcome. It does make you wonder if the drive of the US education system is ultimately to develop better weapons of mass-destruction, though Coolidge's movie is too hazily good-natured to capitalise on the tougher aspects of the material. TJ

Real Glory, The

(1939, US, 95 min, b/w)
d Henry Hathaway. *p* Samuel Goldwyn. *sc* Jo Swerling, Robert Presnell. *ph* Rudolph Maté. *ed* Daniel Mandell. *ad* James Basevi. *m* Alfred Newman. *cast* Gary Cooper, David Niven, Broderick Crawford, Reginald Owen, Andrea Leeds, Kay Johnson, Vladimir Sokoloff, Henry Kolker.
● Shades of *Gunga Din* and *Lives of a Bengal Lancer* as three soldiers of fortune (Cooper also being an army doctor) join a suicide mission to stamp out Moro terrorism in the Philippines in 1906. Dubious historically and politically, and inclined to overdo the heroism (especially when the colonel's daughter bravely joins the fight against cholera after refusing to leave for safety). But Hathaway is second to none at this sort of boy's own adventure. The action, virtually non-stop, is terrific. TM

Real Howard Spitz, The

(1997, GB/Can, 98 min)
d Vadim Jean. *p* Paul Brooks, Christopher Zimmer. *sc* Jurgen Wolff. *ph* Glen Macpherson. *ed* Pia Di Ciaula. *pd* Chris Townsend. *m* David A Hughes, John Murphy. *cast* Kelsey Grammer, Amanda Donohoe, Joseph Rutten, Patrick McKenna, Genevieve Tessier.
● A British movie with an American setting, but shot in Nova Scotia, this perfectly pitched family film is a winning vehicle for the deadpan comic talents of Grammer, star of TV's *Cheers* and *Frasier*. He plays Howard, an unshaven, alimony-paying, frequently blocked pulp writer who is forever arguing with his Jewish agent Lou (Rutten). Out of frustration he takes to children's books, and hits paydirt. Sam (Tessier) is the straight-talking kid with razor-sharp literary insight he meets doing research on the floor of the children's library; and Laura (Donohoe), Sam's single mum, an English florist with whom he strikes up a relationship to provide romantic interest. The film's teasing pleasure derives from the easy charm of the playing, the unpatronising, slightly risqué dialogue, the robust, unpretentious mood, and the light comic touch of Jean's direction. Moreover, in a world of paedophile scares, it's good to see a film in which a lone man

with a dirty raincoat and untied sneakers plays so unselfconsciously and naturally with children not his own. WH

Reality Bites

(1994, US, 99 min)
d Ben Stiller. *p* Danny DeVito. *sc* Helen Childress. *ph* Emmanuel Lubezki. *ed* Lisa Churgin. *pd* Sharon Seymour. *m* Karl Wallinger. *cast* Winona Ryder, Ethan Hawke, Ben Stiller, Janeane Garofalo, Steve Zahn, Swoosie Kurtz, Joe Don Baker, Harry O'Reilly.
●Almost inevitably, as the first mainstream Hollywood movie to focus on post-college 'Generation X'-ers, actor Stiller's directorial debut sets up all sorts of youth-cred expectations it then has a hard time fulfilling. Ryder plays recent graduate Lelaina Pierce, given the heave-ho by a Houston TV station and left to fend for herself in the harsh economic climate of the '90s. Luckily, though, love is there – but can she choose between muso Troy (Hawke), a goatee-sporting wastrel, or will it be smarmball MTV executive Michael (Stiller)? There's probably a moderate little romantic comedy crying to get out here, but the film's vain striving for casual hip proves suffocatingly obtrusive. TJ

Real Life

(1983, GB, 93 min)
d Francis Megahy. *p* Michael Dineen. *sc* Francis Megahy, Bernie Cooper. *ph* Peter Jessop. *ed* Peter Delfgou. *ad* John White. *m* David Mindel. *cast* Rupert Everett, Cristina Raines, Norman Beaton, Warren Clarke, Isla Blair, James Faulkner, Catherine Rabett.
●Calling a film *Real Life* and subtitling it *A Romantic Comedy* suggests a certain coyness of approach, which as it turns out is not far wrong. The material is such that, in comparison, Mills & Boon look positively Wagnerian. A young man of faultless profile (Everett – no prizes for guessing) is given to much whimsical fantasising, something that renders him inept both professionally and personally, until he meets an older woman (Raines) and, the richer for the experience, gets his girl. Paper-thin, and sadly lacking either the brittle/crisp scripting or the lightness of touch needed to make it acceptable escapism. Megahy, veteran of TV's *Minder* and *The Professionals* as well as numerous documentaries, signally fails to suggest that he has found a new vocation. VG

Real McCoy, The

(1993, US, 105 min)
d Russell Mulcahy. *p* Martin Bregman, Michael Bregman, Willi Baer. *sc* William Osborne, William Davies. *ph* Denis Crossan. *ed* Peter Honess. *pd* Kim Colefax. *m* Brad Fiedel. *cast* Kim Basinger, Val Kilmer, Terence Stamp, Gailard Sartain, Zach English.
●Part old-fashioned caper, party vanity project for Basinger, this yarn about a reformed cat burglar trying to go straight aims for the lightweight appeal of something like *To Catch a Thief* but is burdened with a sentimental subplot about the heroine's relationship with her estranged son. Having served six years for an aborted bank robbery, Karen McCoy (Basinger) returns to Atlanta, Georgia, where sometime associate Schmidt (Stamp) coerces her into one last job. Kilmer is the getaway driver (and love interest). Pretty lifeless. NF

Realm of the Senses, The

see Ai No Corrida

Re-Animator

(1985, US, 86 min)
d Stuart Gordon. *p* Brian Yuzna. *sc* Dennis Paoli, William J Norris, Stuart Gordon. *ph* Mac Ahlberg. *ed* Lee Percy. *ad* Robert A Burns. *m* Richard Band. *cast* Jeffrey Combs, Bruce Abbott, Barbara Crampton, David Gale, Robert Sampson, Gerry Black.
●When cleancut med student Dan Cain (Abbott) advertises for a roommate, little does he suspect how spectacularly his life – and the laws of creation – are about to be turned upside down. He soon wishes he'd heeded the caution of girlfriend Megan (Crampton), who can obviously spot a crazed re-animator when she sees one. In no time at all, Herbert West (Combs) has brought Dan's dead cat twitching back to life with a syringe full of green gloop. The dean (Sampson) fails to see the beneficial side and expels Dan and West, who promptly turn Burke and Hare in the university morgue. Mayhem ensues as the dead run amok. Dr Hill (Gale), a rival for Megan's affections, loses his head – and then finds it again. The injection of humour into HP Lovecraft's 1922 tale is what saves this splatterfest from being mere fodder for gorehounds. NRo

Re-Animator 2

(1989, US, 96 min)
d/p Brian Yuzna. *sc* Woody Keith, Rick Fry. *ph* Rick Fichter. *ed* Peter Teschner. *pd* Philip JC Duffin. *m* Richard Band. *cast* Jeffrey Combs, Bruce Abbott, Claude Earl Jones, Fabiana Udenio, David Gale, Kathleen Kinmont, Mel Stewart.
●Five years after the 'Miskatonic Massacre', mad scientist West (Combs) conducts Frankensteinian experiments in creating human life: mixing re-animating serum with an iguana's amniotic fluid, he bypasses the brain to inject new life into autonomous body parts. Sadly, the film has the same quality, its spastic, sloppily assembled plot jerking around with no hint of governing intelligence. After an hour, some semblance of direction is achieved as West and his partner Cain (Abbott) graduate from limb grafts to produce a splendidly ghoulish 'bride' (dead patient's head, metal-clasped torso, dancer's feet, hooker's legs, the heart of Cain's dead lover) as the object of Cain's perverse desire. Meanwhile a maniac cop, assorted loons and hordes of mausoleum mutants besiege the basement lab, and West's arch-rival Dr Hill (Gale) – undeterred by the loss of his body – plans a flying visit. The excessive blood-spurting gruesomeness and cartoonish stop-motion effects trivialise the horror and undercut the would-be black humour in this travestied sequel to Stuart Gordon's hugely enjoyable film. NF

Rear Window 100 (100)

(1954, US, 112 min)
d Alfred Hitchcock. *sc* John Michael Hayes. *ph* Robert Burks. *ed* George Tomasini. *ad* Hal Pereira, Joseph McMillan Johnson. *m* Franz Waxman. *cast* James Stewart, Grace Kelly, Wendell Corey, Thelma Ritter, Raymond Burr, Judith Evelyn.
●Of all Hitchcock's films, this is the one which most reveals the man. As usual it evolves from one brilliantly plain idea: Stewart, immobilised in his apartment by a broken leg and aided by his girlfriend (Grace Kelly at her most Vogue-coverish), takes to watching the inhabitants across the courtyard, first with binoculars, later with his camera. He thinks he witnesses a murder… There is suspense enough, of course, but the important thing is the way that it is filmed: the camera never strays from inside Stewart's apartment, and every shot is closely aligned with his point of view. And what this relentless monomaniac witnesses is everyone's dirty linen: suicide, broken dreams, and cheap death. Quite aside from the violation of intimacy, which is shocking enough, Hitchcock has nowhere else come so close to pure misanthropy, nor given us so disturbing a definition of what it is to watch the 'silent film' of other people's lives, whether across a courtyard or up on a screen. No wonder the sensual puritan in him punishes Stewart by breaking his other leg. CPea

Reason Over Passion (La Raison avant la Passion)

(1969, Can, 82 min, b/w & col)
d Joyce Wieland.
●Not quite a structural film, *Reason Over Passion* nevertheless aggressively incorporates its own sense of space (the film almost literally traverses the vast expanse of Canada) and time (80 minutes metronomically click by as computer-generated anagrams of the title flash across the screen). As in all basically formalist work, the political sympathies remain ambiguous, but the film is clearly grounded in an ironic attitude toward the colonial status of Canada (the title is a phrase invoked by Pierre Trudeau), and perhaps even the colonial status of women. The way those sympathies are formulated – re-situating the subject in space, playing on language versus image, raising the notion of a patriotic (sic) ideology – is what gives the film a continuing freshness and surprising relevance. DD

Reason to Live, a Reason to Die, A (Una Ragione per Vivere e Una per Morire)

(1972, It/Fr/Sp/WGer, 96 min)
d Tonino Valerii. *p* Michael Billingsley, Alfonso Sansone, Enrico Chroscicki. *sc* Tonino Valerii, Ernesto Gastaldi. *ph* Alejandro Ulloa. *ed* Franklin Boll, Franco Fraticelli, Maruja Soriano. *ad* Rafael Ferri. *m* Riz Ortolani. *cast* James Coburn, Telly Savalas, Bud Spencer, Ralph Goodwin, Joseph Mitchell, Robert Burton.
●One of the worst Westerns in years, curious only for the way it mixes standard motifs from Western and war film. The beginning owes everything to *The Dirty Dozen*; and the finale, the attack on the fortress (after an extremely plodding journey across familiar terrain) has commander Telly Savalas' uniform looking more like field grey than Confederate blue. There's some wholesale carnage at the end, but even that fails to revive flagging spirits. CPe

Rebecca

(1940, US, 130 min, b/w)
d Alfred Hitchcock. *p* David O Selznick. *sc* Robert E Sherwood, Joan Harrison. *ph* George Barnes. *ed* Hal C Kern. *ad* Lyle Wheeler. *m* Franz Waxman. *cast* Laurence Olivier, Joan Fontaine, George Sanders, Judith Anderson, Nigel Bruce, Gladys Cooper, Reginald Denny, C Aubrey Smith, Florence Bates, Melville Cooper, Leo G Carroll.
●Hitchcock's first Hollywood film (made for David O Selznick) was also his only one to receive a 'best picture' Oscar: all the financial advantages of America meant that for the first time he could really explore his technical imagination and create a gripping blend of detective story, gothic romance, and psychological drama. Daphne Du Maurier's fairly lightweight bestseller (about a naive young woman who marries an aristocratic patriarch, then finds her life dominated by his dead wife Rebecca) became a tale of fear and guilt, power and class. What makes the film doubly interesting is Hitchcock's fear of women, and the way it goes beyond the simple limits of narrative. The blindly loyal Mrs Danvers (Rebecca's former maid) is an almost immobile, leech-like figure. Rebecca, as malevolence personified, is never seen and therefore more dangerous. The 'pure' innocent central character (Fontaine, excellent by being totally infuriating) is treated as a pathetic victim of circumstance, her *gaucherie* and anguish trapped by a circling camera whose measured, taunting pace revels in her 'female' masochism. A riveting and painful film. HM

Rebecca's Daughters

(1991, GB/Ger, 97 min)
d Karl Francis. *p* Chris Sievernich. *sc* Guy Jenkin. *ph* Russ Walker. *ed* Roy Sharman. *m* Rachel Portman. *cast* Peter O'Toole, Paul Rhys, Joely Richardson, Keith Allen, Simon Dormandy, Dafydd Hywel, Sue Roderick.
●Based on a screenplay by Dylan Thomas, with updatings by Guy Jenkin, this rural romp is *The Scarlet Pimpernel* out of Gainsborough Studios via Ealing. Set in Wales in 1843 and drawing upon historical fact, it has handsome heir Anthony Raine (Rhys) joining forces with a rabble of local farmers and labourers against avaricious drunk Lord Sarn (O'Toole) and the Turnpike Trust. Called in to protect the owners' interests, priggish Captain Marsden (Dormandy) and his dragoons are outwitted by Rebecca's Daughters, marauding gangs of men who dress as women to attack the hated turnpikes. Anthony's fiancée (Richardson) naturally prefers the cross-dressed avenging Rebecca to the seemingly ineffectual Anthony. Hints of an underlying seriousness are reinforced by Welsh director Francis' obvious affinity with both the material and the locations. For the most part, though, the tone is set by the fist fight between Anthony and a 'son of the soil' (Hywel) which predictably spills over into a pigsty. NF

Rebel

(1985, Aust, 93 min)
d Michael Jenkins. *p* Phillip Emanuel. *sc* Michael Jenkins, Bob Herbert. *ph* Peter James. *ed* Michael Honey. *pd* Brian Thomson. *m* Chris Neal. *cast* Matt Dillon, Debbie Byrne, Bryan Brown, Bill Hunter, Ray Barrett, Julie Nihill, John O'May, Kim Deacon.
●The year is 1942: the Japanese are on the run at Guadalcanal, and Matt Dillon's libido is advancing on Sydney, Australia. The well-defined object of his desire is Kathy (Byrne), lead singer of an all-girl band, who's doing her bit by entertaining the troops on leave. Persistence pays off, and though married, Kathy is won over by young Sgt Rebel's humanity, sensitivity and high cheek bones: he's

a deserter determined never to fight again, and willing to sock several people in the jaw to emphasise the point. With an anti-war stance at heart, *Rebel* deserves some praise amid the current onslaught of bellicose films. But instead of confronting the complex issues and emotions plausibly inherent in the scenario, it falls back on clichés and one-dimensional characters, less a musical than a comic strip punctuated by verse. SGo

Rebel, The

(1960, GB, 105 min)
d Robert Day. *p* WA Whittaker. *sc* Alan Simpson, Ray Galton. *ph* Gilbert Taylor. *ed* Richard Best. *ad* Robert Jones. *m* Frank Cordell. *cast* Tony Hancock, George Sanders, Dennis Price, Irene Handl, John Le Mesurier, Paul Massie, Margit Saad, Grégoire Aslan, Liz Fraser.

●The first and best of two attempts to turn Hancock into a screen star, scripted by his regular TV writers Ray Galton and Alan Simpson, this is an only partially successful film. The first half, with Hancock turning from a bowler hat and the City to an artist's beret and the Left Bank – and ordering 'snails, egg and chips' as a compromise – is fine. But Day labours over Hancock's unexpected success as the leader of the Infantile school of painting, and breaks the golden rule of Hancock's comic art by allowing him an unqualified victory over life's circumstances. PH

Rebellion (Joi-Uchi)

(1967, Jap, 121 min, b/w)
d Masaki Kobayashi. *p* Tomoyuki Tanaka. *sc* Shinobu Hashimoto. *ph* Kazui Yamada. *ad* Yoshiro Muraki. *m* Toru Takemitsu. *cast* Toshiro Mifune, Takeshi Kato, Yoko Tsukasa, Tatsuya Nakadai, Tatsuyoshi Ehara, Michiko Otsuka.

●A fine movie from the team that gave you *Harakiri*, though this is much easier on the stomach. Again the spotlight is on Japan's code of honour – the rebellion is Mifune's, tired of having his family life mucked around by his Shogun overlords (the date is 1725). Characters spend much time talking, sitting cross-legged and frozen while their passions rise to boiling-point; everything erupts, however, in the finale, in which long grass, glistening sword blades and bloody bodies elegantly fill the Tohoscope frame. Compare or contrast with the French classical drama of Corneille and Racine (and don't write on both sides of the paper). GB

Rebel Nun, The (Flavia la Monaca Musulmana)

(1974, It/Fr, 99 min)
d Gianfranco Mingozzi. *p* Raniero di Giovanbattista. *sc* Gianfranco Mingozzi, Sergio Tau, Fabrizio Onofri, Bruno Di Geronimo. *ph* Alfio Contini. *ed* Ruggero Mastroianni. *ad* Guido Josia. *m* Nicola Piovani. *cast* Florinda Bolkan, Maria Casarès, Claudio Cassinelli, Antony Corlan, Spiros Focas.

●Most Italian movies dealing with naughty nuns are fairly decorous (like *The Nun and the Devil*, which wouldn't make anyone's wimple flutter), but here is an exception: it's packed to bursting with naughty happenings, and all beautifully photographed too. The heroine, moreover, is portrayed as a fervent Women's Libber, born five centuries too early, who is enraged that Father, Son, Holy Ghost and all twelve apostles are masculine. To prove that women can outdo males in senseless brutality, she joins forces with an invading army of Moslems, and takes revenge by aiming a spiked ball at the eyes of her convent's male patron saint. Any sign of intelligence or serious thinking is welcome in this cesspool realm of cinema, but the results here seem very hollow. GB

Rebel Rousers

(1970, US, 78 min)
d/p Martin B Cohen. *sc* Abe Polsky, Michael Kars, Martin B Cohen. *ph* Leslie Kovacs, Glen Smith. *ed* Thor Brooks. *m* William Loose. *cast* Cameron Mitchell, Jack Nicholson, Bruce Dern, Diane Ladd, Harry Dean Stanton.

●Shot in 1967 and shelved for three years before it was allowed to escape, this dim entry in the '60s slew of biker pictures is as tawdry as they come, but at least the makers had the good fortune to catch a young cast on the cusp of bigger and better things. When Nicholson's gang rides into town, architect Mitchell's girlfriend becomes a race trophy. TJ

Rebels of the Neon God (Qing Shaonian Nezha)

(1992, Tai, 106 min)
d Tsai Ming-Liang. *p* Jiang Feng-Chyi, Hsu Li-Kong. *sc* Tsai Ming-Liang. *ph* Liao Pen-Jung. *ed* Wang Chyi-yang. *ad* Lee Pao-Lin. *m* Huang Shu-chun. *cast* Chao-Jung Chen, Yu-Wen Wang, Kang Sheng Lee, Chang-Bin Jen.

●Hsiao Kang doesn't really believe his superstitious mother's notion that he might be a reincarnation of the mischievous god Nezha, but it does give him ideas: he drops out of cram school, pockets the refund and gets hung up on the slightly older crook Ah Tze. His confused feelings for Ah Tze find suitably confused expression – he tries to get to know him by vandalising his motorbike and daubing it with the word 'AIDS'. No director since Fassbinder has such insight into the lives of lost young men in crumbling inner cities as Tsai Ming-Liang delivers in this devastating first feature. Brilliantly observed, with dialogue kept to a minimum, and as tender as a Lou Reed elegy. TR

Rebel Without a Cause

(1955, US, 111 min)
d Nicholas Ray. *p* David Weisbart. *sc* Stewart Stern. *ph* Ernest Haller. *ed* William Ziegler. *ad* Malcolm Bert. *m* Leonard Rosenman. *cast* James Dean, Natalie Wood, Sal Mineo, Jim Backus, Ann Doran, Corey Allen, Edward Platt, Dennis Hopper, Nick Adams, William Hopper.

●Dean's finest film, hardly surprisingly in that Ray was one of the great '50s directors. The story, much imitated since, might sound like nothing much – unsettled adolescent from good home can't keep himself out of trouble, and gets involved with bad sorts until tragedy takes over – but what makes the film so powerful is both the sympathy it extends towards all the characters (including the seemingly callous parents) and the precise expressionism of Ray's direction. His use of light, space and motion is continually at the service of the characters' emotions, while the trio that Dean, Wood and Mineo form as a refuge from society is explicitly depicted as an 'alternative family'. Still the best of the youth movies. GA

Recess: School's Out

(2000, US, 83 min)
d Chuck Sheetz. *p* Joe Ansolabehere, Paul Germain, Stephen Swofford. *sc* Jonathan Greenberg. *ed* Tony Mizgalski. *ad* Eric Keyes. *m* Dennis M Hannigan. *cast* voices: Rickey D'Shon Collins, Jason Davis, Andy Lawrence, Ashley Johnson, Courtland Mead, Pam Segall, Dabney Courtland, James Woods.

●This Disney make-over of a kids' TV cartoon series offers no cinematic surprises, and plainly strains by imposing upon itself a preposterous save the world adventure. Yet its well characterised comedy of playground manners and teasing social awareness rings confidently through. The sole flashy effect is an opening CGI 'helicopter' zoom into the urban, mixed race playground of Third Street Junior, where reverse-capped, freckled hero TJ realises that everyone but him is going to camp for summer vacation. So big deal! Meanwhile, a reformed-hippie former principal (hilariously voiced by Woods), embittered by his holiday-shortening plans being thwarted, has set up a laser machine in Third Street to alter Earth's orbit – it could happen! – and TJ has to recall the gang to fight the foe. The under-11s nostalgia ('This is the last summer we will get to do stuff!') catches the throat, and Marvin Gaye, Nilsson and Hendrix play on the soundtrack. That'll educate 'em. WH

Reckless Moment, The 100

(1949, US, 81 min, b/w)
d Max Ophüls. *p* Walter Wanger. *sc* Henry Garson, Robert W Soderberg, Mel Dinelli, Robert Kent. *ph* Burnett Guffey. *ed* Gene Havlick. *ad* Cary Odell. *m* Hans J Salter. *cast* James Mason, Joan Bennett, Geraldine Brooks, Henry O'Neill, Shepperd Strudwick.

●Having concealed her daughter's accidental killing of her seedy older lover, upper middle class housewife Bennett finds herself being blackmailed by a loan shark; fortunately for her, the man he sends – small-time crook and loner Mason – becomes infatuated with Bennett, and ends up killling his partner. Ophüls' *noir* melodrama, like his previous film, *Caught*, can be seen as a subtle, subversive critique of American ambitions and class-structures: in committing the moral and legal transgression of concealing a corpse, Bennett is merely protecting the comfort and respectability of her family life, and the irony is that Mason's self-sacrifice, made on her behalf, simply serves to preserve the status quo that has relegated him to the role of social outcast. This sense of waste, however, is implied rather than emphasised by Ophüls' elegant, low key direction, which counterpoints the stylisation of Burnett Guffey's shadowy photography with long, mobile takes that stress the everyday reality of the milieu. A marvellous, tantalising thriller, it also features never-better performances from Mason and Bennett. GA

Recluse, La

see Anchoress

Recollections of the Yellow House (Recordacões da Casa Amarela)

(1989, Port, 122 min)
d João César Monteiro. *p* Joaquim Pinto, João Pedro Bénard. *sc* João César Monteiro. *ph* José Antonio Loureiro. *ed* Elena Alves, Claudio Martinez. *ad* Luis Monteiro. *m* Schubert, Vivaldi. *cast* Manuela de Freitas, João César Monteiro, Sabina Sacchi, Inéz de Medeiros, Teresa Calado.

●The impoverished tenant of a Lisbon boarding-house, João de Deus (played to perfection by the writer/director) is one of *the* great miseries of the movies. He muses, in a dispassionate but doomy voice-over, on death, illness, solitude, and the bedbugs that make a nightly attack on his testicles. As the seedy, sexually frustrated, but occasionally kindly protagonist proceeds towards a pathetic, cracked assault on his harridan landlady's daughter, it's hard to know whether to laugh, weep or simply slit your wrists. In the end, it's that wry, detached sense of comic absurdity that saves the film from plunging into maudlin miserabilism. Using long, often static takes, an elliptical narrative, and stark but stylish compositions, Monteiro sidesteps psychodrama to produce something altogether cooler, more thought-provoking, and more perverse. The film makes its slow way towards the appallingly rundown mental hospital of the title, and a denouement as fantastic as it is subversive. A fascinating, quietly caustic critique of the outmoded mores of Portugal's *petite bourgeoisie*. GA

Record of a Tenement Gentleman (Nagaya Shinshiroku)

(1947, Jap, 72 min, b/w)
d Yasujiro Ozu. *sc* Yasuhiro Ozu, Tadao Ikeda. *ph* Yuharu Atsuta. *ed* Yoshi Sugihara. *ad* Tatsuo Hamada. *m* Ichiro Saito. *cast* Choko Iida, Hohi Aoki, Eitaro Ozawa, Mitsuko Yoshikawa, Sokichi Kawamura, Hideko Mimura, Chishu Ryu.

●A widow, Tane, reluctantly shelters a young boy for the night when her neighbour discovers him lost and alone in the city. On further investigation, it seems that the boy's father, a carpenter, has abandoned him out of poverty. Tane tries to do the same, but the boy will have none of it. They strike a deal – as long as he stops wetting his bed, he can stay. This is Ozu in optimistic mood, which is not to say that loss and resignation don't figure in large part (no film-maker ever had a surer grasp of the melancholy of everyday things), just that here the generosity of spirit seems irresistible – and irresistibly comic. (And Chishu Ryu sings!) TCh

Recuperanti, I (The Scavengers)

(1969, It, 97 min)
d Ermanno Olmi. *sc* Mario Rigoni Stern, Tullio Kezich, Ermanno Olmi. *ph/ed/ad* Ermanno Olmi. *m* Gianni Ferrio. *cast* Antonio Lunardi, Andreino Carli, Alessandra Micheletto, Pietro Tolin, Marilena Rossi.

●A curiously exact echo of Olmi's first feature, *Time Stood Still*, with its quietly funny exploration of the relationship between two men, one young and one old, who have nothing in common but their work. High up in the mountains, amid past battlefields, they scavenge for old shells and hidden ammunition dumps, dreaming of the day of El Dorado when they will find the armoured car which supposedly lies buried somewhere, lost and forgotten. Shot in documentary style, with amateur actors and a minimum of plot, it may not sound too enticing; but one has to reckon with Olmi's extraordinary ability to make bricks without straw, and here he constructs an entire drama out of the conflict between two lifestyles. Deceptively simple, it speaks volumes about our rat-race civilisation in its vivid, quizzically funny way. TM

Red and the White, The (Csillagosok, Katonák)

(1967, Hun/USSR, 90 min, b/w)
d Miklós Jancsó. *sc* Gyulam Hernadi, Georgi Mdivani, Miklós Jancsó. *ph* Tamas Somlo. *ed* Zoltan Farkas. *ad* Boris Chebotarev. *cast* Jószef Madaras, András Kozák, Tibor Molnár, Jácint Juhász, Anatoli Yabbarov.

●The setting is the aftermath of the Russian Revolution: the 'reds' are the revolutionaries, the 'whites' the government forces ordered to suppress them. Jancsó focuses on a young Hungarian fighting with the reds, and charts the arbitrary pattern of arrests, imprisonments and escapes that he goes through. As in *The Round-Up,* Jancsó is here primarily interested in the mechanisms of power, seen as virtual abstractions: the characters have political status, not personal identity, and the lengthy arabesques described by the camera classify their struggles for supremacy as an endless cycle of gain and loss. The effect is a precise ambivalence: a celebration of revolutionary heroism, and an icily detached recognition that both sides in a war can be mirror images of each other. TR

Red Badge of Courage, The

(1951, US, 69 min, b/w)
d John Huston. *p* Gottfried Reinhardt. *sc* John Huston. *ph* Harold Rosson. *ed* Ben Lewis. *ad* Cedric Gibbons, Hans Peters. *m* Bronislau Kaper. *cast* Audie Murphy, Bill Mauldin, Arthur Hunnicutt, John Dierkes, Royal Dano, Andy Devine, Douglas Dick.

●By the time MGM had finished chopping and re-editing Huston's footage in quest of a more conventional war movie, the interior logic of Stephen Crane's account of a terrified boy's baptism of fire during the American Civil War had been rudely cast overboard. The fragments that remain, linked by a voice-over commentary drawn from the novel, nevertheless exhibit a remarkable delicacy and depth of feeling that sometimes (as in the death of the Tall Soldier) approximates the visionary quality of the novel. And visually, with Harold Rosson's camerawork lovingly recreating the harsh, dustily faded textures of Matthew Brady's Civil War pictures, it looks absolutely superb. TM

Red Baron, The

see Von Richthofen and Brown

Red Beads (Xuan Lian)

(1993, HK/China, 90 min)
d He Yi. *p* Xiao Ming. *sc* Liu Xiaojing, Yiu Ni. *ph* Yu Xiao Yang. *ed* Liu Xiaojing. *pd* Wang Yongsheng. *m* Gho Iahong. *cast* Liu Jiang, Shi Ke.

●He Yi (aka He Jianjun) raised money privately to make this underground feature without official approval, and the film fully reflects the resulting freedom from constraints. A pallid guy waiting for his date in a noisy restaurant daydreams a situation in which he works as a lonely orderly in a mental hospital. He grows obsessed with the young woman patient who is already dreaming of red beads and gradually enters her delusions – if that's what they are. Hard to say if this is jet-black comedy or expressionist nightmare. Either way, it's an amazingly provocative vision by Chinese standards. It's also highly atmospheric, persuasively felt and eerily erotic. TR

Red Beard (Akahige)

(1965, Jap, 185 min, b/w)
d Akira Kurosawa. *p* Tomoyuki Tanaka, Ryuzo Kikushima. *sc* Masato Ide, Hideo Oguni, Ryuso Kikushima, Akira Kurosawa. *ph* Asakazu Nakai, Takao Saito. *ad* Yoshiro Muraki. *m* Masaru Sato. *cast* Toshiro Mifune, Yuzo Kayama, Yoshio Tsuchiya, Tatsuyoshi Ehara, Reiko Dan, Kyoko Kagawa, Takashi Shimura.

●A monumental hospital soap opera which looks exactly as though Kurosawa had taken a long look at *Ben Casey* and *Dr Kildare*, and decided that anything they could do he could do better. One has to reckon, however, with the fact that the Japanese Dr Gillespie, alias Red Beard, is played by Toshiro Mifune, and that Kurosawa really can do things better than most. While Red Beard busily demonstrates to his reluctant young intern that caring for the poor is more rewarding than a society practice, the film bowls along magnificently in a weird mixture of genuine emotion, absurdity and poetic fantasy. Perhaps only Kurosawa could have brought off the scene in which Red Beard, thwarted in one of his good works, erupts into a samurai frenzy, knocks out some 20 men, breaks arms and legs like matchsticks, and ends with a gravely shamefaced mutter: 'I think I've gone too far'. TM

Red Circle, The (Le Cercle Rouge)

(1970, Fr/It, 150 min)
d Jean-Pierre Melville. *p* Robert Dorfmann. *sc* Jean-Pierre Melville. *ph* Henri Decaë. *ed* Jean-Pierre Melville. *ad* Théo Meurisse. *m* Eric de Marsan. *cast* Alain Delon, André Bourvil, Yves Montand, François Périer, Gian Maria Volonté, André Eykan, Pierre Collet, Paul Crauchet.

●Melville's special achievement was to relocate the American gangster film in France, and to incorporate his own steely poetic and philosophical obsessions. He described this, his penultimate film, as a digest of the nineteen definitive underworld set-ups that could be found in John Huston's picture of doomed gangsters, *The Asphalt Jungle.* Darker, more abstract and desolate than his earlier work, this shows, set piece by set piece, the breakdown of the criminal codes under which Melville's characters had previously operated. Even in the butchered version distributed in Britain (dubbed and cut to 102 minutes) it's worth seeing: the mood remains, as does the film's central sequence, a superbly executed silent jewel robbery in the Place Vendôme. CPe

Red Corner

(1997,US, 122 min)
d Jon Avnet. *p* Jon Avnet, Jordan Kerner, Charles Mulvehill, Rosalie Swedlin. *sc* Robert King. *ph* Karl Walter Lindenlaub. *ed* Peter E Berger. *pd* Richard Sylbert. *m* Thomas Newman. *cast* Richard Gere, Bai Ling, Peter Donat, Byron Mann, Tsai Chin, Bradley Whitford, Robert Stanton.

●A fundamental circumstance of the 20th century: the unjustly accused prisoner shut up in some vast, unknowable totalitarian penal system. Not really a predicament to be exploited as a vehicle for a film star (Gere, playing a media executive under arrest in contemporary China), nor one to be crudely decked out as melodrama, complete with heroine, bad guy and final courtroom shootout that puts everything to rights. But if you're curious to see what *Darkness at Noon* might have been like had Koestler written it for Mills & Boon… BBa

Red Dawn

(1984, US, 114 min)
d John Milius. *p* Buzz Feitshans, Barry Beckerman. *sc* Kevin Reynolds, John Milius. *ph* Ric Waite. *ed* Thom Noble. *pd* Jackson De Govia. *m* Basil Poledouris. *cast* Patrick Swayze, C Thomas Howell, Lea Thompson, Charlie Sheen, Darren Dalton, Ben Johnson, Harry Dean Stanton, Powers Boothe, Ron O'Neal, Vladek Sheybal.

●This imagines a Russo/Cuban invasion of the American heartland by crack airborne troops. Despite scrupulously reconstructed tank battles and partisan raids, its military thesis is patently ridiculous: why would the Russians ignore the massive lessons they learned against Napoleon and Hitler to instigate a suicidal conventional invasion of the American mainland? They wouldn't, but any other scenario, including the obvious nuclear one which Milius ducks, leaves no room for the patriotic struggle he wants to show. Paranoia can of course be an excellent dynamic for movie-makers, and within its own dream-like structure, *Red Dawn* is both compelling and witty (the town's drive-in becomes a 're-education camp'). But it also contains moments that are repulsive in the grand right wing tradition, all the more so since Milius, who once held the fascination of a rebel, is here voicing sentiments that the Reagan administration actually believes. DP

Red Desert, The (Deserto Rosso)

(1964, It/Fr, 116 min)
d Michelangelo Antonioni. *p* Antonio Cervi. *sc* Michelangelo Antonioni, Tonino Guerra. *ph* Carlo Di Palma. *ed* Eraldo Da Roma. *ad* Piero Poletto. *m* Giovanni Fusco. *cast* Monica Vitti, Richard Harris, Carlo Chionetti, Xenia Valderi, Rita Renoir, Aldo Grotti.

●Perhaps the most extraordinary and riveting film of Antonioni's entire career; and correspondingly impossible to synopsise. Monica Vitti is an electronics engineer's neurotic wife, wandering in bewilderment through a modern industrial landscape (the film is set in Ravenna) which Antonioni has coloured in the most startling and original way imaginable. The film is an aesthetic feast, but don't let that distract you from the haunting intricacy of the plot and the performances. Only Richard Harris, as Corrado, the mining engineer who becomes her refuge but who is just passing through, seems uneasy; despite what so many critics said at the time, Vitti's portrayal of the confused girl, alienated from the stark technological landscape around her, is among her very best. DP

Red Detachment of Women (Hongse Niangzijun)

(1960, China, 113 min)
d Xie Jin. *cast* Zhu Xijuan, Wang Xin'gang, Xiang Mei, Jin Naihua, Wang Li, Tie Niu.

●The original tropical-gothic melodrama whose storyline was co-opted during the Cultural Revolution for both a dance drama and a 'model revolutionary opera'. Apparently there really was a women's militia which rebelled against local tyrants in Hainan Island in the 1930s. But this script is an outright fantasia, part *Caged Heat* (women in chains in torture dungeons) and part Maoist dogma (underground communists guide the uprising and the heroine's greatest moment is signing her application for Party membership). Xie Jin delivers the propaganda but doesn't disguise his nostalgia for an older current in romantic film-making; the film looks like a cousin of *Black Narcissus*, complete with the dishy Wang Xin'gang in the David Farrar role. TR

Red Detachment of Women (Hongse Niangzijun)

(1970, China, 105 min)
d Collective. *cast* Ching Ching-hua, Lo Sing Siang, members of the China Ballet Troupe.

●This showpiece of the Cultural Revolution now functions as a virtual documentary of an ideological 'moment'. Objectively it's a straightforward transposition from the stage of a balletic narrative detailing the heroic exploits of a peasant's daughter with a women's battalion of Communist guerillas during the '30s. But the staging, score and shooting together stridently attest to a highly specific, transparently limited view of the parameters of revolutionary art. PT

Red Dust

(1932, US, 83 min, b/w)
d/p Victor Fleming. *sc* John Lee Mahin. *ph* Harold Rosson. *ed* Blanche Sewell. *ad* Cedric Gibbons, A Arnold Gillespie. *cast* Clark Gable, Jean Harlow, Mary Astor, Donald Crisp, Gene Raymond, Tully Marshall, Willie Fung.

●The archetypal steamy melodrama, with Gable as the boorish-but-sexy manager of a rubber plantation in Indo-China who falls for platinum prostitute Harlow, despite a moment of adulterous lust for cool-but-I'm-burning-up-inside Mary Astor. So excessive that some of it turns camp, and rampantly sexist, but you can see why the Depression audiences flocked. CA

Red Firecracker, Green Firecracker (Paoda Shuang Deng)

(1994, HK/China, 111 min)
d He Ping. *p* Chan Chun-Keung, Yong Naiming. *sc* Da Ying. *ph* Yang Lun. *ed* Yuan Hong. *ad* Qian Yunxiu. *m* Zhao Jiping. *cast* Ning Jing, Wu Gang, Zhao Xiarui, Gao Yang.

●He Ping's overdue follow-up to *The Swordsman in Double-Flag Town* is one of the few Chinese films to have absolutely no subtext: all its phallic play, gender subversion and castration fantasies are right up there on screen. Set in the 1920s, it's about a macho painter hired to produce New Year pictures for a fireworks company headed by a woman who's been forced to dress and behave like a man. She, however, finds the presence of a louche male in the house curiously disturbing and starts paying him private visits. Ructions of the explosive sort ensue, culminating in a hair-raising fireworks contest orchestrated by the vengeful elders of the clan. No great leap forward for Fifth Generation cinema, but a lot of fun. TR

Redheads

(1992, Aust, 107 min)
d Danny Vendramini. *p* Richard Mason. *sc* Danny Vendramini. *ph* Steve Mason. *ed* Marc Van Burren. *pd* Ross Wallace. *m* Felicity Foxx. *cast* Claudia Karvan, Catherine McClements, Alexander Petersons, Sally McKenzie, Anthony Phelan.

●This thriller, set in Brisbane, kills two good ideas with one movie. The first is to tell a realist story of the developing relationship between two young women from either side of the tracks: of how sisterly friendship gives them the courage to face up to the chauvinistic, corrupt and unjust system surrounding them. The other is to deliver a slick crime thriller with a high paranoia factor. The one elbows out the other. The script has its origins in a play directed by Vendramini, where the main characters were a Maori girl and a female social worker. Here they've been replaced by a teenage white offender, Lucy (Karvan), and a rookie legal-aid lawyer, Diana (McClements). Lucy has been secretly sleeping with Diana's boss, and when he's gunned down by an anonymous assailant, she fears for her life as the web of cops, lawyers and detention-centre employees close in. A ponderous script is not helped by self-conscious video and sound effects and jarring *noir* lighting. A plus is Karvan's sparky performance. WH

Red Heat

(1988, US, 104 min)
d Walter Hill. *p* Walter Hill, Gordon Carroll. *sc* Harry Kleiner, Walter Hill, Troy Kennedy Martin. *ph* Matthew F Leonetti. *ed* Freeman Davies, Carmel Davies, Donn Aron. *pd* John Vallone. *m* James Horner. *cast* Arnold Schwarzenegger, James Belushi, Peter Boyle, Ed O'Ross, Larry Fishburne, Gina Gershon, Richard Bright.

●A partial return to form for slam-bang Hill, this is the *48 HRS* formula crossed with *Gorky Park*. Unstoppable unorthodox Russian cop Danko (Schwarzenegger) arrives in the US on the trail of Soviet pusher and cop-killer Viktor (O'Ross), and is assigned to reluctant, wisecracking, unorthodox Chicago cop Ridzik (Belushi). 'We're parked in the Red Zone, no offence' says Ridzik at the airport: perhaps the only passably witty line in a canon of crass national jibes. Big Arnie plays the Soviet the way he plays all his juggernauts, only more taciturn again, but the relationship grows as he breaks a suspect's fingers and generally bypasses Miranda-Escobedo. 'Who is Dirty Harry?' goes a gag, after the cops have compared firepower. The most visually interesting stuff occurs in Moscow; hugely amplified biffs accompany the pell-mell punch-ups; and the ending, a suicidal confrontation between large vehicles, may be intended as a parody of *Rambo III*. Surface stuff, moderately contemptuous, but entertaining enough. BC

Red House, The

(1947, US, 100 min, b/w)
d Delmer Daves. *p* Sol Lesser. *sc* Delmer Daves. *ph* Bert Glennon. *ed* Merrill White. *ad* McClure Capps. *m* Miklós Rózsa. *cast* Edward G Robinson, Lon McCallister, Allene Roberts, Judith Anderson, Rory Calhoun, Julie London, Ona Munson.

●If you go down to the woods today, you're bound for a big surprise: you won't find a picnic, however, but necrophilia, madness, incestuous longings, tyrannical possessiveness, and murder. Impossible to give an effective synopsis of the incredibly heavy plotting; but basically, when one-legged farmer Robinson's adopted daughter brings home a potential boyfriend, all manner of mysteries, scandals and sinister goings-on are let loose as Robinson resorts to violence to keep the young ones away from his nasty secret down in the nearby forest. Warped relationships are the norm in his weird but hardly wonderful world, and indeed even the film itself boasts a perverse pedigree: it's a pastoral, *noir*-inflected psychodrama with supernatural overtones, dealing chiefly with the thin line between healthy and sick sexuality. All very Freudian, in fact, and often very frightening, with Robinson in superb form as the patriarch tormented by his past. GA

Red Inn, The

see Auberge Rouge, L'

Red Line 7000

(1965, US, 110 min)
d/p Howard Hawks. *sc* George Kirgo. *ph* Milton Krasner. *ed* Stuart Gilmore, Bill Brame. *ad* Hal Pereira, Arthur Lonergan. *m* Nelson Riddle. *cast* James Caan, Laura Devon, Gail Hire, Charlene Holt, John Robert Crawford, Marianna Hill, James Ward, Norman Alden.

●Hawks' most *maudit* film: a motor-racing melodrama with a cast of then-unknowns who have (with the exception of Caan) remained unknown. There is undoubtedly a certain classical finesse to Hawks' dovetailing of thrills on the track with spills in the boudoir. But even the most devoted Hawksians have acknowledged that this rehash of favourite characters and situations is strictly Formula One…and non-Hawksians were thinking out their emotional problems in rather different terms by the mid-1960s. TR

Red Lotus Society, The (Feixia A-Da)

(1994, Tai, 120 min)
d Stan Lai. *p* Wang Ying-Hsiang. *sc* Stan Lai. *ph* Christopher Doyle. *ed* Chen Bowen. *cast* Ying Zhaode, Chen Wenming, Na Weixun, Li Tongcun, Li Lijin.

●More cinematic but less sure-footed than Lai's first film *The Peach-Blossom Land*, this anatomy of the Chinese obsession with keys to 'secret knowledge' suggests that the whole city of Taipei has lost the plot. A young language tape salesman decides to find someone to teach him 'vaulting' – the art of achieving weightlessness, as described in countless martial arts movies and novels – and scours the city for three surviving masters from the legendary Red Lotus Society who are rumoured to be living ordinary lives under assumed identities. Very beautifully shot by Chris Doyle, but not persuasive enough as a vision of reality for the characters' superstitions and paranoias to seem justified. TR

Red Monarch

(1983, GB, 100 min)
d Jack Gold. *p* Graham Benson. *sc* Charles Wood. *ph* Mike Fash. *ed* Laurence Méry-Clark. *pd* Norman Garwood. *cast* Colin Blakely, David Suchet, Carroll Baker, Ian Hogg, Jean Heywood, David Threlfall, Nigel Stock, Brian Glover.

●In this jet black comedy about the end of Stalin, scripted by Charles Wood from stories by the well-placed Kremlin-watcher Yuri Krotkov, the dictator (Blakely) is a ghastly paranoid prankster, while Beria (Suchet), his lecherous police chief, rolls with the jokes and abuses himself like a terrified jester when his master seems about to dispense with his services. This quicksilver double act is a tour de force (the two Georgians are represented as distrustful Ulstermen), and the film runs confidently up and down the comic scale, from the absurdity of Mao Tse-tung's visit for Stalin's 70th birthday (unable to communicate, the two dictators stuff themselves on hard-boiled eggs), to the macabre finale when the Politburo gathers outside Stalin's door hoping against hope he may be dead (opening his eyes to see his marionettes jigging for joy, the tyrant spits out the one word 'Idiot!' – a judgment on himself perhaps – before Beria sinks to his knees and throttles him). The film ends with a line from Yevtushenko: the poet will never feel safe until Stalin's heirs cease to occupy the Kremlin. JPy

Red Nightmare

(1962, US, 29 min)
d George Waggner. *p* William L Hendricks, Jack Webb. *cast* Jack Webb, Jack Kelly, Jeanne Cooper, Peter Breck, Robert Conrad.

●This slice of Hollywood paranoia, never actually released, dates from the Red Scare period following the Cuban missile crisis, and was 'personally supervised' by Jack L Warner for the Department of Defence, to remind every American not taking sufficient interest in their local PTA that 'responsibilities are a privilege'. With an omnipresent Jack Webb acting as thought-control personified, the film hilariously scuttles its own thesis all the way down the line. The uniformed Reds who actually turn up in some poor Mid-Town Joe's dream not only take over his community, but turn his family into automatons, march his daughter off to work farm, close the Sunday School, up his piecework quota, and – final straw – claim to have invented the telephone! Tantrums inevitably lead to a show trial and a quick bullet. Awakening, on the other hand, brings everyday American sweetness and light – and just as inevitably, another cautionary lecture from Webb. Hysterical, indeed. PT

Red Peony Gambler: Flower-cards Match (Hibotan Bakuto: Hanafuda Shobu)

(1969, Jap, 98 min)
d Tai Kato. *p* Koji Shundo, Goro Kusakabe. *sc* Norifumi Suzuki, Motohiro Torii. *ph* Shin Furuya. *ed* Shintaro Miyamoto. *ad* Jiro Tomita. *m* Takeo Watanabe. *cast* Junko Fuji, Ken Takakura, Kanjuro Arashi, Tomisaburo Wakayama.

●'Red Peony' is Ryu Yano (Fuji, exquisite), a woman yakuza roaming the gambling dens of 1890s Japan, righting wrongs as she goes. This was the third film (of eight) in an enjoyable but very formulary series – but the first directed by Kato, who plays these games at their highest level. Red Peony shows up in Nagoya, lodges with the righteous Nishi Clan and helps her hosts meet a challenge from the thoroughly dishonourable Kimbara Clan; she also finds time to deal with a cheat operating under her name. All the series' constants are present and correct, from Wakayama's brief appearance as a comic deus ex machina to the guest star role for a strong, silent yakuza torn between duty and humanity (here Takakura, riveting as usual). The blend of violence, card game suspense, sentimentality and melancholy is silky. TR

Red Planet

(2000, US/Aust, 106 min)
d Antony Hoffman. *p* Mark Canton, Bruce Berman, Jorge Saralegui. *sc* Chuck Pfarrer, Jonathan Lemkin. *ph* Peter Suschitzky. *ed* Robert K Lambert, Dallas S Puett. *pd* Owen Paterson. *m* Graeme Revell. *cast* Val Kilmer, Tom Sizemore, Carrie-Anne Moss, Benjamin Bratt, Simon Baker, Terence Stamp, Jessica Morton, Caroline Bossi.

●The portentous opening voice-over by Moss – about an ecologically ravaged Earth and the terra-forming colonisation of Mars with oxygen producing algae – does not bode well. Nor does the interminable journey to the planet itself, during which we learn precious little about Moss's mission commander and her motley crew of pragmatic systems engineer Kilmer, arrogant geneticist Sizemore, truthseeking philosopher Stamp, macho flyboy Bratt and terra-forming expert Baker. Once the male crew's exploration module crashlands on Mars, though, destroying most of their equipment, we're on familiar, inhospitable ground. Alone aboard their orbiting, damaged spaceship, Moss makes repairs and finally establishes radio contact with her stranded crew. If they don't make it back, Earth and its inhabitants are doomed. The pedestrian script lurches from dull exposition to large scale action and low key exchanges of dialogue. But Peter Suschitzky adds texture and atmosphere with his stunning cinematography. One for diehard genre fans in a forgiving mood. NF

Red Planet Mars

(1952, US, 87 min, b/w)
d Harry Horner. *p* Anthony Veiller. *sc* John L Balderston, Anthony Veiller. *ph* Joseph Biroc. *ed* Francis D Lyon. *ad* Charles D Hall. *m* Mahlon Merrick. *cast* Peter Graves, Andrea King, Herbert Berghof, Marvin Miller, House Peters, Vince Barnett.

●A candidate for the nuttiest sci-fi pic of all time, this incredible Cold War relic rolls out a barnstorming plot in which TV transmissions from Mars, revealing that the planet's ruled by a god-like supreme being, cause global revolution on Earth. But that's just the set-up. It then transpires that the messages were faked by a mad scientist hoping to topple capitalism. But that's just the twist. There follows a further bona fide transmission from Mars, proclaiming that its leader is God himself, which stirs up a worldwide religious revival and a resolve for all to live in harmony. From another age, if not another planet. TJ

Red Psalm (Még Kér a Nép)

(1971, Hun, 88 min)
d Miklós Jancsó. *sc* Gyula Hernadi. *ph* János Kende. *ad* Tamás Banovich. *m* Ferenc Sebo. *cast* Lajos Balázsovits, András Bálint, Gyöngyi Bürös, Andrea Drahota, József Madaras.

● Where Jancsó's *Agnus Dei* was opaque and difficult, this is crystal clear and involving: looking for a language in that film, he found it here and uses it with dazzling precision. Like his earlier films, *Red Psalm* is centred on a specific period in Hungarian history: the turn-of-the-century uprising of landless agricultural workers. It was a socialist uprising, and songs of the period – including a remarkable socialist *Lord's Prayer* – are woven into the film. A work of amazing and totally uncosmetic beauty, it's a folk tale around the belief of the people in their own ultimate victory, and the symbol Jancsó has chosen is the wounded palm that's also a rosette of hope. VG

Red Rings of Fear (Enigma Rosso)

(1978, It/Sp/WGer, 85 min)
d Alberto Negrín. *p* Antonio Mazza. *sc* Marcello Coscia, Franco Ferrini, Massimo Dalamano, Alberto Negrin, Stefano Ubezio, Peter Berling. *ph* Carlo Carlini, Eduardo Noé. *ed* Paolo Boccio. *m* Riz Ortolani. *cast* Fabio Testi, Christine Kaufmann, Ivan Desny, John Taylor, Fausta Avelli, Brigitte Wagner.

● A dire cheapo thriller which relies on confusion for suspense, schoolgirl nymphets for titillation, and Fabio Testi's five o'clock shadow for a sense of adventure. A girl gets murdered, Testi's the flat-footed gumshoe who investigates, convent school inmates are under siege and suspicion, and there's a complicated sideline about a jeans shop. The *denouement* is just about discernible from the surrounding detail – abortions, arson, art forgeries – but hardly worth waiting for. HM

Red River

(1948, US, 133 min, b/w)
d/p Howard Hawks. *sc* Borden Chase, Charles Schnee. *ph* Russell Harlan. *ed* Christian I Nyby. *ad* John Datu Arensma. *m* Dimitri Tiomkin. *cast* John Wayne, Montgomery Clift, Walter Brennan, Joanne Dru, John Ireland, Noah Beery Jr, Paul Fix, Coleen Gray, Harry Carey Jr, Harry Carey Sr.

● Hawks' leisurely adaptation of Borden Chase's story about the establishing of the Chisholm Trail by Wayne and Clift's cattle train is a sheer delight that works on many levels. Firstly, it's an examination of Wayne's heroic image, here shown to be needlessly authoritarian and stubborn as he comes into conflict with his more liberal surrogate son Clift, gradually coming in for more and more criticism from garrulous Greek-chorus figure Brennan for his repeated killing of deserters. Secondly, it's yet another variation on Hawks' perennial concern with the theme of self-respect and professionalism, and being part of 'the group'. Finally, it's an intimate epic celebrating the determination to establish civilisation in the wilderness, with Clift's refusal to resort to the gun viewed as an essential improvement upon Wayne's trigger-happy rough justice. Immaculately shot by Russell Harlan, perfectly performed by a host of Hawks regulars, and shot through with dark comedy, it's probably the finest Western of the '40s. GA

Red Rock West

(1992, US, 98 min)
d John Dahl. *p* Steve Golin, Sigurjon Sighvatsson. *sc* John Dahl, Rick Dahl. *ph* Marc Reshovsky. *ed* Scott Chestnut. *pd* Robert Pearson. *m* William Olvis. *cast* Nicolas Cage, JT Walsh, Lara Flynn Boyle, Dennis Hopper, Craig Reay.

● When Michael Williams (Cage) drifts into the hick town of Red Rock, he's surprised when barowner Wayne Brown (Walsh) assumes he's a hitman and hands over five grand as down payment on killing his wife Suzanne (Boyle). Having told Suzanne about the contract, Williams accepts $10,000 from her to kill Brown. Free to skedaddle, he thinks he's struck lucky. But fate steps in when he runs over a man, takes him back to hospital and finds that *sheriff* Brown wants to nail him. And that's just the first 20 minutes of this well-played, highly entertaining and playfully ingenious thriller. GA

Red Rose, White Rose (Hong Meigui Bai Meigui)

(1994, HK/Tai, 110 min)
d Stanley Kwan. *p* Wong Hoi. *sc* Liu Heng, Edward Lam. *ph* Christopher Doyle. *ed* Brian Schwegmann. *pd* Pan Lai. *m* Johnny Chen. *cast* Winston Chao, Joan Chen, Veronika Yip.

● Stanley Kwan, director of the sublime *Rouge* and *Actress*, has adapted the most famous Chinese account of the war between men and women, a novella by the late Eileen Chang, preserving every ounce of the book's irony and sarcasm. In pre-communist Shanghai a western–educated man (Chao) runs away from his torrid mistress (Chen, never better) and marries a traditionally submissive girl (Yip)...and proceeds to turn her into a neurotic wreck. Easy to imagine Fassbinder liking this story, and he'd have loved the way Chris Doyle's hallucinatory cinematography accentuates the plot's twists of the knife. TR

Reds

(1981, US, 196 min)
d/p Warren Beatty. *sc* Warren Beatty, Trevor Griffiths. *ph* Vittorio Storaro. *ed* Dede Allen, Craig McKay. *pd* Richard Sylbert. *m* Stephen Sondheim. *cast* Warren Beatty, Diane Keaton, Edward Herrmann, Jerzy Kozinski, Jack Nicholson, Paul Sorvino, Maureen Stapleton, Nicolas Coster, M Emmet Walsh, Gene Hackman, Ian Wolfe, Bessie Love.

● Maybe not three hours to shake the world, but mightily impressive in its creative grasp of the inbuilt contradictions of 'epic' political cinema and historical representation, *Reds* intriguingly yokes romance and revolution to produce a timely monument to dissent. While veteran witnesses to the lives and impact of activist journalists John Reed and Louise Bryant offer conflicting memories in documentary inserts, Beatty and co-writer Trevor Griffiths construct a heroic love story textured as a dialectical biopic. The Russian October stands as an emotively agitational centrepiece, but the film's focus remains on the American socialist heritage and radical tradition: a deliberately patterned weave that acknowledges provocative contrasts – between Greenwich Village intellectualism and the rank-and-file labour struggles of the Wobblies, between organisation and 'culture', between vying CP factions, between enlightened patriarchy and early feminism. Beatty's Reed and Keaton's Bryant observe, criticise, swim against and participate in their times, maintaining a steady fascination through the plausibility of their erratically developing relationship, emphasising that history begins at home, in every sense. PT

Red Shoes, The 100

(1948, GB, 133 min)
d/p/sc Michael Powell, Emeric Pressburger. *ph* Jack Cardiff. *ed* Reginald Mills. *pd* Hein Heckroth. *m* Brian Easdale. *cast* Anton Walbrook, Moira Shearer, Marius Goring, Leonid Massine, Albert Basserman, Robert Helpmann, Esmond Knight, Ludmilla Tcherina, Frederick Ashton.

● In outline, a rather over-determined melodrama set in the ballet world: impresario (Walbrook) 'discovers' dancer (Shearer), and makes her a slave to her art, until young composer (Goring) turns up to offer her a lifeline back to reality. But in texture, it's like nothing the British cinema had ever seen: a rhapsody of colour expressionism, reaching delirious heights in the ballet scenes, but never becoming too brash and smothering its own nuances. And if the plot threatens to anchor the spectacle in a more mundane register, it's worth bearing in mind the inhibition on which it rests: the central impresario/dancer relationship was modelled directly on Diaghilev and Nijinsky, and its dynamic remains 'secretly' gay. TR

Red Sky at Morning

(1970, US, 112 min)
d James Goldstone. *p* Hal B Wallis. *sc* Marguerite Roberts. *ph* Vilmos Zsigmond. *ed* Edward A Biery, Richard M Sprague. *ad* Alexander Golitzen, Walter Tyler. *m* Billy Goldenberg. *cast* Richard Thomas, Catherine Burns, Desi Arnaz Jr, Richard Crenna, Claire Bloom, John Colicos, Harry Guardino, Strother Martin, Nehemiah Persoff, Victoria Racimo.

● 1944, and off Dad (Crenna) goes into the Navy after taking wilting Southern Mum (Bloom, slipping into Vivien Leigh's shoes) and son (Thomas) to a Mexican hideaway mansion. From there develops an unusually blatant mixture of voyeuristic wish-fulfilment as teeny high school petting and chicken games are laid aside by sons who follow their fathers, unquestioning, to the battlefront. As if by sympathetic magic, for instance, the moment Thomas actually screws his girlfriend, the moment he takes over his father's ritual manly tasks (such as helping an artist friend lug yet another of his hero-busts up to his private Mount Rushmore where Bogart, Chuchill and DiMaggio rub shoulders), comes the news that Dad has been blown up. Any number of loving, lying shots of tousselled heads windblown against the sky, gamely tearful faces saying goodbye. The only good thing is that Vilmos Zsigmond's photography manages to wring a grain or two of realism from those faces.

Red Sonja

(1985, US, 89 min)
d Richard Fleischer. *p* Christian Ferry. *sc* Clive Exton, George MacDonald Fraser. *ph* Giuseppe Rotunno. *ed* Frank J Urioste. *pd* Danilo Donati. *m* Ennio Morricone. *cast* Arnold Schwarzenegger, Brigitte Nielsen, Sandahl Bergman, Paul Smith, Ernie Reyes Jr, Ronald Lacey, Pat Roach.

● Dim *Conan* style comic strip adventure about some prehistoric bint from Hyborea (Nielsen) wandering around seeking revenge on the evil Princess whatsername (Bergman), who's nicked some powerful talisman and is bent on destroying the world as rotten set designers know it. Big Arnie flexes his muscles but not his thespian talents, Nielsen (Stallone's friend) delivers her lines at two words a minute, and poor Ronald Lacey is forced to reprise his *Raiders of the Lost Ark* Nazi villain bit in exceedingly silly costumes and hats. Worst of all, there's a charmless brat prince for Sonja to take under her wing. Pap, and Fleischer – who at least brought a touch of humour to *Conan the Destroyer* – should know better. GA

Red Sorghum (Hong Gaoliang)

(1987, China, 92 min)
d Zhang Yimou. *p* Li Changqing. *sc* Chen Jianyu, Zhu Wei, Mo Yan. *ph* Gu Changwei. *ed* Du Yuan. *ad* Yang Gang. *m* Zhao Jiping. *cast* Gong Li, Jiang Wen, Teng Rujun, Liu Ji, Qian Ming, Ji Chunhua.

● The stuff of legend, Zhang Yimou's film satisfies both as straight folk tale and as a subversive tribute to the vitality and endurance of Chinese peasant culture. Set in a remote Northern province in the '20s and '30s, the story is narrated by a man who remembers the lives and times of his grandparents. A girl is waylaid and ravished in a field, en route to an arranged marriage with an elderly, leprous winemaker. He mysteriously dies, and her ravisher eventually lives with her so that together they may make the red sorghum wine. As the film develops, the tone shifts from light to dark, humour giving way to horror and sacrifice with the arrival of Japanese forces. Formerly a cameraman, Zhang fills the 'Scope screen with rich, sensuous images that illuminate and celebrate peasant life (waving sorghum fields, an eclipse of the sun), and uses actors, music and colour in a deeply expressive way. This, his debut as a director, confirms him as one of the finest and most versatile of China's 'Fifth Generation' film-makers. WH

Red Squirrel, The (La Ardilla Roja)

(1993, Sp, 104 min)
d Julio Medem. *p* Ricardo Garcia Arrojo. *sc* Julio Medem. *ph* Gonzalo Berridi. *ed* Maria Helena Sainz de Rozas. *m* Alberto Iglesias. *cast* Nancho Novo, Emma Suárez, Maria Barranco, Carmelo Gómez, Karra Elejalde, Cristina Marcos.

● Abandoned by his girl, washed up as a rock singer, Jota (Novo) is on the brink of suicide when he sees a biker skidding off the road. First on the scene, he discovers a young woman (Suárez), physically unharmed, but without memory or ID. Improvising wildly, Jota claims she is his girlfriend Lisa and steals her away from hospital to a remote campsite ('The Red Squirrel') where, he says, they will become reacquainted. As 'Lisa's' old personality begins to reassert itself, events take a dark turn, and it becomes clear Jota's got a lot more than he bargained for. Funny in both senses, the movie is improbable, melodramatic and overblown, yet utterly compelling and entirely persuasive. The Basque writer/director Julio Medem (*Vacas*) addresses psycho-sexual power plays, the nature of identity, lies and surprises. A fervid romantic mystery, forever flying off in new and unexpected directions. TCh

Red Sun (Soleil Rouge)

(1971, Fr/It/Sp, 112 min)
d Terence Young. *p* Robert Dorfmann. *sc* Laird Koenig, Denne B Petitclerc, W Roberts, L Roman. *ph* Henri Alekan. *ed* John Dwyre. *ad* Paul Apoteker. *m* Maurice Jarre. *cast* Charles Bronson, Toshiro Mifune, Alain Delon, Ursula Andress, Capucine, Bart Barry, Lee Burton.
●Samurai (Mifune) meets gunslinging hero (Bronson) meets black-gloved fascist (Delon) in the old West, with touches of the *Dollar* syndrome. Young, of *Dr No*, *Thunderball* and *Mayerling*, can't keep the over-inflated production values together, and it all disintegrates into individual performances. A wasted opportunity.

Red Sweater, The

see Pull-Over Rouge, Le

Red Violin, The (Il Violino Rosso)

(1998, Can/It/US/GB, 130 min)
d François Girard. *p* Niv Fichman. *sc* Don McKellar, François Girard. *ph* Alain Dostie. *ed* Gaëtan Huot. *pd* François Séguin. *m* John Corigliano. *cast* Carlo Cecchi, Irene Grazioli, Jean-Luc Bideau, Christoph Koncz, Clothilde Mollet, Jason Flemyng, Greta Scacchi, Sylvia Chang, Liu Zifeng, Samuel L Jackson.
●Cremona, 1693: master violin maker Nicolo Bussotti (Cecchi) loses both wife and child to a difficult birth and adds their blood to the varnish on his latest and finest instrument. The tarot cards had, however, foretold a long life for the mother, a prediction with an element of truth as we follow the violin's across continents and centuries. In 1990s Montreal, Charles Morritz (Jackson) is appraises a collection of instruments for auction. He is about to stumble across the find of his career, the original, fabled 'Red Violin', but can he really bear to see it sold off for millions of dollars? From the team of Girard and McKellar, this is almost as rigorously structured as their earlier film, *Thirty Two Short Films About Glenn Gould*. While the soundtrack playing of Joshua Bell and the keening, multifaceted orchestral score provide a connecting thread, the individual vignettes are rarely powerful enough to create a cumulative emotional pull. However, just when the proceedings seem in danger of drifting into exquisite academicism, along comes Jackson's intensely focused performance to demonstrate just why the enduring power of musical expression matters so much. TJ

Red Wedding

see Noces Rouges, Les

Reed: Insurgent Mexico (Reed: México Insurgente)

(1971, Mex, 106 min, b/w)
d Paul Leduc. *p* Salvador Lopez, Berta Navarro. *sc* Paul Leduc, Juan Tovar. *ph* Alexis Grivas. *ed* Giovanni Korporaal, Rafael Castanedo. *cast* Claudio Obregón, Eduardo López Rojas, Ernesto Gómez Cruz, Juan Angel Martínez, Carlos Castañón.
●American journalist John Reed became world famous through his reporting of the Russian Revolution in *The Ten Days That Shook the World*. This deals with his earlier conversion to the cause of social upheaval, a result of his observation of the Mexican Revolution. The strength of Paul Leduc's dramatised reconstruction lies in its authenticity (the sepia wash is suitably appropriate) and its refusal to indulge in myth-making. Instead, the struggle is presented in terms of the people involved, and reflected in Reed's own crisis of conscience and gradual commitment (via a somewhat Hemingway-like path) to the uprising.

Reefer and the Model

(1988, Ire, 93 min)
d Joe Comerford. *p* Lelia Doolan. *sc* Joe Comerford. *ph* Breffni Byrne. *ed* Sé Merry. *pd* John Lucas. *m* Johnny Duhan. *cast* Ian McElhinney, Eve Watkinson, Carol Scanlan, Birdy Sweeney, Sean Lawlor, Ray McBride.
●Reefer, Spider and Badger eke out a living on a dilapidated trawler, having renounced (provisionally, at least) their lawless past. When the homeless, pregnant 'Model' (Scanlan) – returning from London to kick a heroin habit – joins the crew and begins a hesitant relationship with Reefer (McElhinney), the men's complacent beliefs and faded ideals come in for reappraisal…but one last caper proves inevitable. This sharp thriller sparks with vitality and wit, artfully playing its macho hero off against the innate authority of the pregnant Model, and discovering refreshing variations on the 'underdogs against the world' formula. Comerford is strong on spiky characterisation and political nuance, but uneasy when it comes to the mechanics of narrative development (the time scale is particularly erratic) and stylistic treatment. Disarmingly balancing elements of Ealing-esque whimsy and violent realism, the ending comes perilously close to incoherence, arguably romanticising the very mentality it attempts to undercut. Even so, the film has a relevance and resonance you won't find in many a more polished effort. TCh

Reefer Madness

(1936, US, 67 min, b/w)
d Louis Gasnier. *p* George A Hirliman. *sc* Arthur Hoerl, Paul Franklin. *ph* Jack Greenhalgh. *ed* Carl Pierson. *ad* Robert Pristley. *m* Abe Meyer. *cast* Dave O'Brien, Dorothy Short, Kenneth Craig, Carleton Young, Lillian Miles, Thelma White, Pat Royale.
●Vintage camp in the form of an outrageous anti-dope film, this begins with a pompous teacher warning his startled parents' association that the killer weed, more dangerous than any other drug, is spreading through the land like an evil disease, sapping the cream from our upstanding youth. An exemplary tale unfolds, where maniacal creatures seduce a handsome lad, with the best grades and a fine eye for the tennis ball, into the abhorrent looseness of the reefer game. Horror of horrors, he fucks a lady of ill virtue, and ends accused of murdering his girlfriend. Another murder and a suicide later, the villain is caught, justice vindicated, and the drug gang cleaned up. It's basically a lousily made film, but the one-dimensional 'vice' and portentous didacticism more than make up for that. One of the most absurdly earnest exercises in paranoia you'll ever have the good fortune to see. JDuC

Ref, The (aka Hostile Hostages)

(1994, US, 97 min)
d Ted Demme. *p* Richard LaGravenese, Jeff Weiss, Ron Bozman. *sc* Richard LaGravenese, Marie Weiss. *ph* Adam Kimmel. *ed* Jeffrey Wolf. *pd* Dan Davis. *m* David A Stewart. *cast* Denis Leary, Judy Davis, Kevin Spacey, Glynis Johns, Robert J Steinmiller Jr, Raymond J Barry, Christine Baranski.
●It's Christmas Eve in Connecticut and for the Chasseurs (Davis and Spacey), Santa arrives a few hours early in the unconventional form of cat burglar Gus (Leary), an armed desperado who takes them hostage when his get-away falls apart. This is a vindictive affair, a truly nasty-minded black comedy at the expense of your upper-middle-class dysfunctional American family. Director Ted Demme (Jonathan's nephew) never applies the scalpel where a blunt instrument will do, and the screenplay by Richard LaGravenese and Marie Weiss does become a mite repetitive. Nevertheless the film has a caustic edge and energy which keeps the laughs flowing. In his first starring role, comedian Leary makes his ranting career criminal strangely sympathetic, but he's more than matched in the vituperation stakes by Spacey, Davis, and especially Glynis Johns, as a demurely monstrous mother-in-law. Naturally, the ordeal gravitates towards gun-point group therapy, but there's bite here as well as bark. TCh

Reflecting Skin, The

(1990, GB, 95 min)
d Philip Ridley. *p* Dominic Anciano, Ray Burdis. *sc* Philip Ridley. *ph* Dick Pope. *ed* Scott Thomas. *ad* Rick Roberts. *m* Nick Bicat. *cast* Viggo Mortensen, Lindsay Duncan, Jeremy Cooper, Sheila Moore, Duncan Fraser, Evan Hall.
●Set amid the golden corn of the '50s Midwest, Ridley's directorial debut (he scripted *The Krays*) confronts 'the nightmare of childhood'. Virtually ignored by his neurotic mother and ineffectual father, eight-year-old Seth (Cooper) creates a world of his own, imagining that reclusive English-woman Dolphin Blue (Duncan) is a vampire, and that the foetus he finds in a barn is his dead friend transformed into an earth-bound angel. Reality begins to seep in when Seth's father is accused of murdering children who have gone missing in the area, and Seth's older brother (Mortensen) returns from the Pacific with tales of a bomb that explodes like a second sun. The complex, non-linear narrative is almost operatic in its visual and emotional excess, employing exaggerated camera angles, saturated colours and an ultra-loud soundtrack to create a heightened, sometimes dangerously portentous reality. Admirably ambitious but, one suspects, a little overripe for English sensibilities. NF

Reflections

(1983, GB, 100 min)
d Kevin Billington. *p* David Deutsch, Kevin Billington. *sc* John Banville. *ph* Mike Molloy. *ed* Chris Ridsdale. *ad* Martin Johnson. *m* Rachel Portman. *cast* Gabriel Byrne, Donal McCann, Fionnula Flanagan, Harriet Walter, Gerard Cummins, Niall Tobin.
●A pompous young academic (Byrne) rents a cottage on a dilapidated Irish estate in order to finish off his book on Isaac Newton. The days are hot, the grass is high, and the folks in the Big House soon prove a whole lot more interesting than Newton: drunken stumblebum husband (McCann), valiumed-up wife (Flanagan), and exceedingly playful niece (Walter). Scripted by novelist John Banville, Billington's film certainly looks engaging enough, but it gets increasingly bogged down in its own languor. Art and Life grapple rather solemnly, and the surface gloss only points up the lack of dramatic bite. Yet almost all reservations pale beside Harriet Walter's superb performance as the niece. Tender, understated, generous, this is film acting of a very high calibre, and makes the film well worth a spin. JP

Reflections in a Golden Eye

(1967, US, 109 min)
d John Huston. *p* Ray Stark. *sc* Chapman Mortimer, Gladys Hill. *ph* Aldo Tonti. *ed* Russell Lloyd. *pd* Stephen Grimes. *m* Toshiro Mayuzumi. *cast* Marlon Brando, Elizabeth Taylor, Brian Keith, Julie Harris, Robert Forster, Zorro David.
●A veritable hothouse of strange desires and bizarre fancies, what with Taylor and Brando brooding moodily, brandishing whips, and galloping round on symbolic stallions. Stuck in the married quarters of a Deep South army base, she is carrying on with another officer (Keith), while he hopefully dogs a virginal young soldier (Forster) with a penchant for riding nude in the woods. The soldier meanwhile takes to sneaking into Taylor's room to watch her sleep, and Keith's neurotic wife (Harris) consoles herself in a motherly affair with a cuddly Filipino houseboy. It all ends predictably in murder, but isn't nearly so risible as it sounds. For one thing, Huston's quirkish sense of humour is way ahead of anybody, while the unusually literate script (based on the Carson McCullers novel) manages to lend genuine depth and credibility to the characters. For another, the sense of tranquil summer stagnation is beautifully sustained; the lectures on military history in stifling classrooms, the afternoons spent riding in the forest, the evening drinks and endless card games, and at night the boredom, the frustrations, and the loneliness which make anything possible. All in all, a superbly controlled exercise in the malevolent torments of despair. TM

Refrigerator, The

(1991, US, 86 min)
d Nicholas Jacobs. *p* Christopher Oldcorn. *sc* Nicholas Jacobs. *ph* Paul Gibson. *ed* PJ Pesce, Suzanne Pillsbury, Christopher Oldcorn, Nicholas Jacobs. *pd* Therese Duprez. *m* Don Peterkofsky, Chris Burke. *cast* Julia McNeal, David Simonds, Angel Caban.

●A wry slice of domestic horror, in which Ohio newlyweds Eileen and Steve Bateman move into a seedy New York apartment and dream of making it in the big city. But the apartment's ancient refrigerator exerts a strange influence over their lives. Steve is consumed by a desire to consume, while Eileen is haunted by memories of her mother's domestic enslavement. The malevolent appliance also frustrates her efforts to start an independent career as an actress. The cheapo special effects (a man-eating fridge, flying fans, and a foot-eating pedal-bin) are perfectly suited to an offbeat, Kafkaesque horror comedy which, while sympathetic to Eileen's female plight, satirises her husband's yuppie aspirations. NF

Refusal, The (Die Verweigerung)

(1972, Aus, 94 min, b/w)
d Alex Corti. *p* Günther Köpf. *sc* Hellmut Kindler. *ph* Walter Kindler. *ed* Erika Geiger. *ad* Gabriel Bauer. *cast* Kurt Weinzierl, Julia Gschnitzer, Hugo Gottschlich, Helmut Wlasak, Fritz Schmiedl.

●A dramatised documentary about Franz Jägerstetter, perhaps the least understandable type of our times: the man who dies for his religious principles. Austria, 1943: the Catholic Church and the local community have adopted the line of least resistance towards the Nazis. Against everyone's advice, Jägerstetter refuses to do military service, accepting execution rather than serve a country in which he has no rights, only obligations. Only secondarily, however, is the film concerned with one man's martyrdom; primarily it deals with the very ordinary people party to it. Much has been made of the human body's capacity for deprivation and abuse (reinforced by a soldier talking of Stalingrad) at the expense of the mind's faculty for the same. Jägerstetter's exception points to the rule: crises like living under Nazi regimes do little to formulate people's attitudes. Life is a matter of prevarication and endurance, and afterwards forgetting. Thirty years later, the villagers interviewed in this film had little opinion either way about the whole business.

Regarde la Mer (See the Sea)

(1997, Fr, 50 min)
d François Ozon. *p* Olivier Delbosc, Marc Missonnier. *sc* François Ozon. *ph* Yorick Le Saux. *m* Eric Neveux. *cast* Sasha Hails, Marina de Van, Samantha, Paul Raoux.

●On the surface the story seems slight. Set on Ile d'Yeu, one of the French Atlantic islands, it concerns Sasha (Hails), a lonely English housewife – abandoned for the week by her businessman husband – and their screaming baby. Happy to have the company, she allows a French backpacker to pitch her tent in the yard. Tatiana (de Van) is sulky and taciturn, but is she also dangerous? Ozon builds an overwhelming sense of nightmarish unease from seemingly banal detail; every composition, every cut signals a startling, disquieting talent. The scene in which Tatiana 'borrows' Sasha's toothbrush is worthy of *Repulsion*. TCh

Regarde les hommes tomber (See How They Fall)

(1993, Fr, 100 min)
d Jacques Audiard. *p* Didier Haudepin. *sc* Alain Le Henry, Jacques Audiard. *ph* Gérard Sterin. *ed* Juliette Welfling. *pd* Jacques Rouxel. *m* Alexandre Desplat. *cast* Jean Yanne, Jean-Louis Trintignant, Mathieu Kassovitz, Bulle Ogier.

●The first feature of the screenwriter Jacques Audiard is a clever thriller that fascinates as much for its ingenious, elliptical structure as for its *noir*-derived insights into obsession, loyalty and betrayal. Yanne's the salesman whose midlife crisis coincides with his inadvertent involvement in the murder of a cop; as he sets out to trace the killer, his life begins to fall apart. At the same time, we witness the faltering growth of the friendship between seedy, aggressive con-man Trintignant and slow-witted innocent Kassovitz. Inexorably, but in surprising ways, the two stories gradually converge. And because it ends up admitting to the homo-erotic dynamics of the Trintignant-Kassovitz relationship, it's also, finally, rather more moving than the enigmatic early scenes lead one to expect. GA

Regarding Henry

(1991, US, 108 min)
d Mike Nichols. *p* Mike Nichols, Scott Rudin. *sc* Jeffrey Abrams. *ph* Giuseppe Rotunno. *ed* Sam O'Steen. *pd* Tony Walton. *m* Hans Zimmer. *cast* Harrison Ford, Annette Bening, Bill Nunn, Mikki Allen, Donald Moffat, Aida Linares, Elizabeth Wilson.

●This contrived, custom-built drama for the caring '90s seeks to manipulate every cliché about the greedy '80s. Henry Turner (Ford) is a rich New York lawyer who has pursued his career at the expense of relationships with his wife (Bening) and young daughter (Allen). He throws tantrums over petty domestic details, bolsters wealthy clients, and kicks the underdog when he's down. Then one night he is shot during a robbery, and the resulting brain damage renders him utterly dependent on the goodwill of others. He learns to read again, re-evaluates relationships, and upon returning to work, realises his old, evil ways. There's no subtlety of characterisation, and despite the severity of Henry's injuries, little to disconcert the viewer. Bening and Ford give the material all they've got, but they're fighting an uphill battle. CM

Regeneration

(1915, US, 6 reels, b/w)
d Raoul Walsh. *sc* Raoul Walsh, Carl Harbaugh. *ph* Georges Benoit. *cast* Rockliffe Fellowes, Anna Q Nilsson, Carl Harbaugh, William A Sheer, James A Marcus.

●The problems and pitfalls of film history are well illustrated by the case of Walsh's feature debut for Fox. Long feared lost until rediscovered by the Museum of Modern Art, this first feature-length gangster picture emerges as a fast-moving melodrama; an energetic account of the rise of a slum kid (Fellowes) to gang leader, and his subsequent dilemma when torn between the code of loyalty of his gang and his good, mission-running sweetheart (Nilsson). Intriguingly, its eventful plotline is revealed as flatly contradicting the accepted synoptic account provided by Walsh in his autobiography. There the eventual fates of Nilsson and Fellowes are reversed, and an ending is transposed from another film entirely. None the less, a distinctly major rediscovery, distinguished by a remarkable approach to physical casting, a robust treatment of violent action, and a sheer narrative pace to shame contemporary ponderousness. PT

Regeneration

(1997, GB/Can, 114 min)
d Gillies MacKinnon. *p* Allan Scott, Peter R Simpson. *sc* Allan Scott. *ph* Glen MacPherson. *ed* Pia Di Claula. *pd* Andy Harris. *m* Mychael Danna. *cast* Jonathan Pryce, James Wilby, Jonny Lee Miller, Stuart Bunce, Tanya Allen, David Hayman, Dougray Scott, John Neville.

●Near the end of WWI, the poet Siegfried Sassoon (Wilby) arrives at Craiglockhart Castle, Edinburgh, a military hospital where pioneering psychiatrist William Rivers (Pryce) tends shell-shocked victims of the trenches. Not that Sassoon needs treatment: having published a pamphlet opposing the war, he's been diplomatically dispatched to hospital rather than prison. His 'convalescence' brings him into contact with another writer, Wilfred Owen (Bunce), whose poetry Sassoon encourages. Rivers, meanwhile, is heading for a breakdown of his own, brought on less by overwork than his empathy with traumatised patients like Billy Prior (Miller), a working class officer rendered mute by his battlefield experiences. Adapted by Allan Scott from Pat Barker's acclaimed novel, MacKinnon's film is subtle, elegant and sharply intelligent. Aided by marvellous performances all round, MacKinnon has fashioned a profoundly moving film that never resorts to manipulative cliché. The trenches are impressively recreated in flashback, but even more affecting are those intimate scenes which suggest that such horrors will never lose their grip on those who have survived them. GA

Reggae

(1970, GB, 60 min)
d/p/sc Horace Ové. *ph* Nic Knowland, Alan Moore, Bill Prayne, Mike Davis. *ed* Franco Rosso. *with* The Pyramids, Pioneers, Maytals, Desmond Dekker, Black Faith, John Holt, Count Prince Miller, Millie.

●Ové's documentary record of the 1970 Caribbean Music Festival at Wembley is now inevitably dated by somewhat sententious political and social claims. Nevertheless, it remains a fascinating and indispensable key to understanding this originally very derivative form. And latter-day converts, uninterested in anything but the excitement generated by the music itself, will want to catch the movie for individual performances. RM

Reggae Sunsplash II

(1979, WGer, 109 min)
d/p/sc Stefan Paul. *ph* Hans Schalk, Peter Rees, Rainer Heinzelmann. *ed* Hildegard Schröder. *with* Burning Spear, Third World, Peter Tosh, Bob Marley and the Wailers, Clancy Eccles.

●A travel-fodder tableau of young lovers silhouetted against a Caribbean beach, with an accompaniment of 10cc's *Dreadlock Holiday*, strikes the first discordant note. Nearly two hours and much well-intentioned but naive politicising later, all credibility is gone. The film chronicles the Reggae Sunsplash II festival at Montego Bay, with the proceedings interrupted by apparently random interviews with Rastafarians and by unguarded shots of locals where the prying camera produces a distinctly uncomfortable air. Unfortunately there is little here for the reggae connoisseur: a passable performance from Marley; some flaccid disco from Third World; and probably the best of the bunch, silken vocals from one of reggae's gentlemen, Winston Rodney (Burning Spear). LW

Règle du Jeu, La 100 (100) 10 (The Rules of the Game)

(1939, Fr, 110 min, b/w)
d Jean Renoir. *sc* Jean Renoir, Carl Koch. *ph* Jean Bachelet. *ed* Marguerite Renoir, Marthe Huguet. *ad* Eugène Lourié, Max Douy. *m* Mozart, Monsigny, Saint-Saëns, Johann Strauss. *cast* Marcel Dalio, Nora Gregor, Jean Renoir, Roland Toutain, Mila Parély, Gaston Modot, Julien Carette, Paulette Dubost, Pierre Magnier.

●Banned on its original release as 'too demoralising', and only made available again in its original form in 1956, Renoir's brilliant social comedy is epitomised by the phrase 'everyone has their reasons'. Centreing on a lavish country house party given by the Marquis de la Chesnaye and his wife (Dalio, Gregor), the film effects audacious slides from melodrama into farce, from realism into fantasy, and from comedy into tragedy. Romantic intrigues, social rivalries, and human foibles are all observed with an unblinking eye that nevertheless refuses to judge. The carnage of the rabbit shoot, the intimations of mortality introduced by the after-dinner entertainment, and Renoir's own performance are all unforgettable. Embracing every level of French society, from the aristocratic hosts to a poacher turned servant, the film presents a hilarious yet melancholic picture of a nation riven by petty class distinctions. NF

Reigen

see Dance of Love

Reign of Naples, The (Neapolitanische eschwister)

(1978, WGer/It, 125 min)
d Werner Schroeter. *p* Christoph Hotch. *sc* Werner Schroeter. *ph* Thomas Mauch. *ed* Werner Schroeter, Ursula West-Messinger. *ad* Francesco Calabrese. *m* Roberto Pregadio. *cast* Liana Trouché, Roméo Giro, Tiziana Ambretti, Antonio Orlando, Renata Zamengo.

●Most films show people's personal lives as if they were outside history, and History as a dry document of political events. *The Reign of Naples* breaks down this comfortable separation in its telling of history – Naples from 1944 to '69 – as everyday existence. And not, as in so many Italian art films (*The Damned* for example) as the everyday existence of the upper middle class; Schroeter follows the lives of a few families in the poor quarter, and shows us post-war Italy in the flesh. The young girl trying to keep her dignity and earn a living, her brother working for the Party, the woman whose daughter dies from lack of penicillin – all are shown with as much passion as if this were a romantic melodrama. In contrast, standard historical information is cursorily sketched in at intervals over shots of posters, documentary footage, old stills: standard images for 'History'. It is rare that politics is shown to be the substance of real life: this film achieves it. JWi

Reign of Terror (aka The Black Book)

(1949, US, 89 min, b/w)
d Anthony Mann. *p* William Cameron Menzies. *sc* Philip Yordan, Aeneas Mackenzie. *ph* John Alton. *ed* Fred Allen. *ad* Edward L Ilou. *m* Sol Kaplan. *cast* Robert Cummings, Arlene Dahl, Richard Basehart, Richard Hart, Norman Lloyd, Arnold Moss, Charles McGraw, Jess Barker, Beulah Bondi.

●Co-scripted by Philip Yordan – who wrote *Johnny Guitar* as well as Mann's two great epics, *El Cid* and *The Fall of the Roman Empire* – this is a French Revolutionary drama made on the lines of Mann's *films noirs* like *T-Men*, with atmospheric camerawork by John Alton and ambitious art direction (the producer was William Cameron Menzies, who made *Things To Come* and designed *Gone With the Wind*). History is thrown to the wolves as Robert Cummings impersonates a public prosecutor and tries to overthrow the dictatorship of Robespierre (Basehart), whose incriminating 'Black Book' (furnishing the British release title) has been stolen. Historians will scoff and the casting is hardly French, but on its own terms the movie works very well. ATu

Reincarnation of Peter Proud, The

(1974, US, 104 min)
d J Lee Thompson. *p* Frank P Rosenberg. *sc* Max Ehrlich. *ph* Victor J Kemper. *ed* Michael F Anderson. *ad* Jack Martin Smith. *m* Jerry Goldsmith. *cast* Michael Sarrazin, Jennifer O'Neill, Margot Kidder, Cornelia Sharpe, Paul Hecht, Tony Stephano.

●A psychical sex thriller totally lacking in thrills, sex or psychic phenomena, this takes its proud place in that tiny elite of features with scenarios so atrocious that their entire action has to unfold before the title premise can even be established: in other words, that the reincarnation of Peter Proud is indeed Peter Proud's reincarnation. Sarrazin moves prosaically through the proceedings as the man whose recurring nightmare turns out to be a memory of his former life, but the plot is so minimal that the proceedings constantly have to be padded out with hideous travelogue footage and emoting-by-numbers from a shifting and evidently uncertain cast. At one point, in what is supposed (God help us) to be a climactic suspense sequence involving cross-cutting, Thompson interpolates lengthy footage of Sarrazin and girlfriend doing a lolloping square dance to a vocal which endlessly intones 'Better is to come'. This is by far the film's most fantastic assertion. DP

Reindeer Games (aka Deception)

(2000, US, 104 min)
d John Frankenheimer. *p* Marty Katz, Bob Weinsten, Chris Moore. *sc* Ehren Kruger. *ph* Alan Caso. *ed* Tony Gibbs, Michael Kahn. *pd* Barbara Dunphy. *m* Alan Silvestri. *cast* Ben Affleck, Gary Sinise, Charlize Theron, Dennis Farina, James Frain, Donal Logue, Clarence Williams III, Dana Stubblefield, Mark Acheson, Isaac Hayes.

●Frankenheimer's twisty thriller feels like a film from the mid-'60s, albeit one with a '50s B *noir* set-up and a Runyon-esque turns: it's Yuletide and there are several dead Santas. The widescreen, deep focus compositions and long takes give free rein to the actors, whose natural performances are curiously at odds with the arch clever-cleverness of the screenplay. Too complicated to summarise, the plot has Affleck leaving prison and being lured into an amateurish casino heist by Theron, a femme fatale masquerading as a wholesome blue collar girl. Affleck is too lightweight and likeable to convince as a hardened criminal, but Theron shows her claws as the white trash wildcat and, as her violent, psychotic 'brother', Sinise adds a nasty edge. There are enjoyable moments, not least the hungry lovemaking of Affleck and Theron shortly after his release. Filmed with handheld cameras and edited as jump cuts, the scene is far from explicit but looks and feels like two people having raunchy sex. By contrast, the action scenes are flaccid, while all the snappy dialogue sounds just that: snappy movie dialogue. NF

Reine Margot, La

(1994, Fr/Ger/It, 162 min)
d Patrice Chéreau. *p* Claude Berri. *sc* Patrice Chéreau, Danièle Thompson. *ph* Philippe Rousselot. *ed* François Gédigier, Hélène Viard. *pd* Richard Peduzzi, Olivier Radot. *m* Goran Bregovic. *cast* Isabelle Adjani, Daniel Auteuil, Jean-Hugues Anglade, Vincent Perez, Virna Lisi, Pascal Greggory, Jean-Claude Brialy, Barbet Schroeder.

●Centred on the intrigues leading up to and following the St Bartholomew's Day Massacre of 1572, this historical drama begins with the arranged, loveless wedding of the Roman Catholic Marguerite de Valois (Adjani) – sister to eccentric King Charles IX (Anglade), daughter of the scheming Catherine de Medici – and the Huguenot Henri de Navarre (Auteuil). Despite Catherine's hope that the marriage may unite France, the mutual hatred felt by Catholics and Protestants soon degenerates into carnage; and Margot, who has learned to tolerate her husband while falling for young Huguenot La Môle (Perez), finds herself caught in a deadly trap. Chéreau's film is a fast-moving and savagely ironic yarn. It's also visceral, with a high gore-factor, a pervasive whiff of filth, and a compelling percussive score. The performances are top-notch, while the dark, rich photography is painterly but never lifeless. GA

Reines d'un jour

see Hell of a Day, A

Reise der Hoffnung

see Journey of Hope

Reise nach Lyon, Die

see Blind Spot

Reise zur Sonne

see Journey to the Sun

Reivers, The

(1969, US, 111 min)
d Mark Rydell. *p* Irving Ravetch. *sc* Irving Ravetch, Harriet Frank Jr. *ph* Richard Moore. *ed* Tom Stanford. *ad* Charles Bailey, Joel Schiller. *m* John Williams. *cast* Steve McQueen, Sharon Farrell, Will Geer, Rupert Crosse, Mitch Vogel, Michael Constantine, Lonny Chapman, Juano Hernandez, Clifton James, Dub Taylor, Allyn Ann McLerie.

●Period charm accounts for much of the mild enjoyment to be had from this sunnily nostalgic adaptation of William Faulkner's novel about an unholy trio – small boy (Vogel), dimwitted young buck (McQueen) and wily black (Crosse) – who 'borrow' a 1905 Winton Flyer and drive triumphantly off to Memphis for three days of illicit pleasure. The message about how his experiences help the boy to grow up is a little hard to take in this winsome reading of Faulkner, but the settings are first rate and so are the performances, though Rydell's direction tries just too hard, drenching itself in 'style'. TM

Réjeanne Padovani

(1973, Can, 90 min)
d Denys Arcand. *p* Marguerite Duparc. *sc* Jacques Benoit, Denys Arcand. *ph* Alain Dostie. *ed* Denys Arcand, Marguerite Duparc. *m* Walter Boudreau. *cast* Luce Guilbeault, Jean Lajeunesse, Roger Lebel, Margot MacKinnon, René Caron.

●Municipal corruption vaguely echoing *Hands Over the City* led some critics to align Arcand's second feature with the political dossiers of Francesco Rosi. In fact, Arcand uses a more detached, observational style, rooted in the documentary background he shares with better-known Quebecois directors like Perrault and Brault, and his finely-nuanced portrait of capitalist conspiracy is strained only by some belated, over-wrought melodrama. By which time you'll believe anything, anyway. PT

Relative Values

(2000, GB/US, 89 min)
d Eric Styles. *p* Christophern Milburn. *sc* Paul Rattigan, Michael Walker. *ph* Jimmy Dibling. *ed* Caroline Limmer. *pd* Humphrey Jaeger. *m* John Debney. *cast* Julie Andrews, Edward Atterton, William Baldwin, Colin Firth, Stephen Fry, Sophie Thompson, Jeanne Tripplehorn, Stephanie Beacham, Gaye Brown.

●Director Styles follows *Dreaming of Joseph Lees* with another '50s British setting and, more broadly, another depiction of the complications of romance and marriage. The eligible Earl of Marshwood (Atterton) is expected to marry within his class. His plan, therefore, to wed Hollywood starlet Miranda Frayle (Tripplehorn) is met with consternation. His doting mother, the Countess (Andrews), is advised by friends not to allow her corner of England to be sullied; her personal maid reveals that she's Miranda's long-lost sister and terrified lest their disparate circumstances be made plain; and the staff of Marshwood Hall are dizzy at the prospect of meeting a Hollywood actress. Near-hysteria builds when Don Lucas (Baldwin), a bigshot actor and Miranda's former lover, turns up wanting her back. Based on Noël Coward's satire of class-ridden post-war Britain, this is undemanding, but somewhat enlivened by sharp moments of contemporary relevance. Unfortunately, the hidden depth and compassion of Coward's play only occasionally surfaces. KW

Relentless

(1989, US, 93 min)
d William Lustig. *p* Howard Smith. *sc* Jack TD Robinson. *ph* Jack Lemmo. *ed* David Kern. *pd* Gene Abel. *m* Jay Chattaway. *cast* Judd Nelson, Robert Loggia, Leo Rossi, Meg Foster, Patrick O'Bryan, Ken Lerner.

●Nelson, the coolly rebellious type from *The Breakfast Club*, turns psycho in this unimaginative serial-killer number. Abused as a child and turned down for entry to the police force, he becomes the randomly motivated 'Sunset Killer', leaving buddy cop duo Loggia and Rossi to track him down. Straight to video in Britain, but successful enough on homeground to spawn a couple of sequels. TJ

Relic, The

(1996, US, 110 min)
d Peter Hyams. *p* Gale Anne Hurd, Sam Mercer. *sc* Amy Holden-Jones, John Raffo, Rick Jaffa. *ph* Peter Hyams. *ed* Steven Kemper. *pd* Philip Harison. *m* John Debney. *cast* Penelope Ann Miller, Tom Sizemore, Linda Hunt, James Whitmore, Clayton Rohner, Chi Muoi Lo, Thomas Ryan.

●This surprisingly nasty horror picture fuses elements of the haunted-house, serial-killer and monster-mayhem sub-genres into a hybrid creature that grabs you and won't let go. A gala evening is disrupted and police lieutenant Vincent D'Agosta (Sizemore) clashes with the director of the Chicago natural history museum when a violent murder suggests a psycho killer is loose in the building. Evolutionary scientist Margo Green (Miller) shares the cop's fears, but her investigations suggest that a genetically mutating mythical creature, Kothoga (effects Stan Winston), is about to chew its way through some of the city's wealthiest benefactors. It's not hard to spot who'll be next to suffer the beast's wrath, but it's difficult to resist the relentless bombardment of knee-jerk shocks, genetic gobbledygook, South American mythology and head-ripping gore. NF

Religieuse, La (aka Suzanne Simonin, La Religieuse de Denis Diderot)

(1966, Fr, 140 min)
d Jacques Rivette. *p* Georges de Beauregard. *sc* Jean Gruault, Jacques Rivette. *ph* Alain Levent. *ed* Denise de Casabianca. *ad* Jean-Jacques Fabre. *m* Jean-Claude Eloy. *cast* Anna Karina, Liselotte Pulver, Micheline Presle, Francine Bergé, Francisco Rabal, Christiane Lenier.

●Unlike the shadowy, possibly non-existent conspirators of *Paris Nous Appartient*, the heavies in Rivette's second feature are all too identifiable. An adaptation of Diderot's novel of the 1750s, its litany of woe begins with poor Suzanne being rejected by her parents and forced to become a nun. She's beaten, starved and pestered by lesbians, but eventually manages to flee the convent with the aid of a rapist priest. She winds up in a brothel, where she ends it all by jumping out of a high window. Visually uninteresting, with a 'bars' motif that's so redundant as to become irritating, it's further handicapped by Karina's depthless, unaffecting portrayal. The French censors banned the film for over a year, thus generating both notoriety and goodwill, neither justified. BBa

Remains of the Day, The

(1993, US, 134 min)
d James Ivory. *p* Mike Nichols, John Calley, Ismail Merchant. *sc* Ruth Prawer Jhabvala.

ph Tony Pierce-Roberts. *ed* Andrew Marcus. *pd* Luciana Arrighi. *m* Richard Robbins. *cast* Anthony Hopkins, Emma Thompson, Peter Vaughan, James Fox, Ben Chaplin, Christopher Reeve.

● Who else but Merchant Ivory to give the big-screen treatment to Ishiguro's Booker Prize-winning novel about class, fascism and the stiff upper lip? Hopkins plays Mr Stevens the butler, a man so fanatically devoted to selfless service that he carries on pouring the port while his father lies dying, and refuses to question the Nazi sympathies of his titled master (Fox). Yet love steals unawares into even the hardest of hearts, and his stern warnings to female staff cannot protect him from falling slowly for the new housekeeper, Miss Kenton (Thompson). That the film works is down to Hopkins, who plays his face like a lyre – a tic here, an inflected eyebrow there. It's an astonishing performance, but the viewer is still hard-pressed to commit to him emotionally. It's Thompson we really feel for, trying to get some reaction from the man she too comes secretly to love. In these scenes of repartee, where politeness is a weapon and every honorific twists in the gut like a knife, the film finally comes alive. DW

Rembrandt

(1936, GB, 85 min, b/w)
d/p Alexander Korda. *sc* Arthur Wimperis, Carl Zuckmayer, June Head. *ph* Georges Périnal. *ed* Francis D Lyon, William Hornbeck. *ad* Vincent Korda. *m* Geoffrey Toye. *cast* Charles Laughton, Elsa Lanchester, Gertrude Lawrence, Edward Chapman, Walter Hudd, Roger Livesey, John Clements, Marius Goring.

● Less successful at the time than the earlier *Private Life of Henry VIII*, but a far better film, thanks to a subtle, touching performance from Laughton as the ageing painter coming to terms with both the death of his beloved Saskia (Lanchester) and an increasing hostility to his work. Surprisingly sombre, it lacks a tight plot, but appeals through its vivid characterisation, superb Vincent Korda sets, and Georges Périnal's lovely camerawork. GA

Remember Last Night?

(1935, US, 81 min, b/w)
d James Whale. *p* Carl Laemmle Jr. *sc* Harry Clark, Doris Malloy, Dan Totheroh. *ph* Joseph Valentine. *ed* Ted J Kent. *ad* Charles D Hall. *m* Franz Waxman. *cast* Edward Arnold, Robert Young, Constance Cummings, Sally Eilers, Arthur Treacher, Edward Brophy, Robert Armstrong, Reginald Denny, Gustav von Seyffertitz.

● Delightful screwball parody of the detective thriller, where the discovery of a corpse among inert revellers after a wild party triggers a sparkling cascade of gags eventually taking off into surrealist fantasy. Cheerfully annexing ice-cubes from the packs on their hungover heads to mix a hair of the dog, faltering only momentarily as they discover another body sleeping it off ('Steady! They can't all be dead'), the hero and heroine (beautifully played by Young and Cummings) are clearly derived from the Nick and Nora Charles of *The Thin Man*. But Whale's use of elisions, non-sequiturs and unexpected stresses creates what is virtually a blueprint for the style developed by Robert Altman in and after *M*A*S*H*. TM

Remember Me?

(1996, GB, 77 min)
d Nick Hurran. *p* Alan Shallcross, Alan Wright. *sc* Michael Frayn. *ph* David Odd. *ed* John Wilson. *pd* Christopher Bradshaw. *m* Michael Kamen. *cast* Robert Lindsay, Rik Mayall, Imelda Staunton, Brenda Blethyn, James Fleet, Haydn Gwynne.

● Mired in suburbia and a stale marriage, and engaged in a vicious territorial dispute with her two teenagers, Lorna (Staunton) hates her life. So when old college beau Jamie (Lindsay) shows up on the doorstep, well, it has to be an improvement. He has a Rolls outside, but no petrol and no ready cash. Perhaps Lorna could spare a few bob? She can't, but she will, if Jamie stays for dinner – and never mind her sadsack husband Ian (Mayall), he's just feeling sorry for himself. This is essentially a modest British domestic comedy remoulded as Chekhovian farce. Screenwriter Michael Frayn doesn't let the mechanics overshadow character; the humour here springs from heartfelt hope and despair. Wisely resisting the temptation to caricature, the actors retain straight faces even as their world is invaded by gangsters, rampaging ex-wives and preposterous in-laws. Restrained, sour and stooped, Mayall is all grey defeat; and you can see how Lindsay's blithe charm rekindles something in Staunton's breast. The film's melancholy hysteria couldn't be more British – it is subtle but exact on the unwitting effrontery of the rich, and the sorry, ingrained subservience of the rest. And very funny too. TCh

Remember My Name

(1978, US, 94 min)
d Alan Rudolph. *p* Robert Altman. *sc* Alan Rudolph. *ph* Tak Fujimoto. *ed* Thomas Walls, William A Sawyer. *m* Alberta Hunter. *cast* Geraldine Chaplin, Anthony Perkins, Moses Gunn, Berry Berenson, Jeff Goldblum, Timothy Thomerson, Alfre Woodard, Marilyn Coleman.

● Largely successful update of the *noir*-inflected melodramas of the '40s, with Chaplin playing the Stanwyck-style role as the vengeful but sympathetic woman who gets out of prison and returns to her former husband (Perkins) to wreak havoc upon his new marriage. What really distinguishes the film are the tremulous, nervy performances, although Rudolph's direction – while occasionally too arty – is imbued with an admirable generosity towards the characters. Also endowed with a fine blues score by (and performed by) Alberta Hunter, and crisp photography from Tak Fujimoto, it's well worth seeing. GA

Remember That Face

see Mob, The

Remember the Day

(1941, US, 85 min, b/w)
d Henry King. *p* William Perling. *sc* Tess Schlesinger, Frank Davis, Allan Scott. *ph* George Barnes. *m* Alfred Newman. *cast* Claudette Colbert, John Payne, John Shepperd, Ann Todd, Anne Revere, Douglas Croft.

● Somewhat reminiscent of a female American *Goodbye, Mr Chips*, this expertly crafted school story has Colbert as the teacher who inspires future presidential candidate Croft during his formative years, but who shatters his youthful crush on her by falling for fellow tutor Payne. It's all told in nostalgic flashback, and controls the ebb and flow of laughter and tears with old-school command. TJ

Remember the Night

(1940, US, 94 min, b/w)
d/p Mitchell Leisen. *sc* Preston Sturges. *ph* Ted Tetzlaff. *ed* Doane Harrison. *ad* Hans Dreier, Roland Anderson. *m* Frederick Hollander. *cast* Barbara Stanwyck, Fred MacMurray, Beulah Bondi, Elizabeth Patterson, Sterling Holloway, Georgia Caine.

● Taken from a script by Preston Sturges (his last before he graduated to directing), a winning romantic comedy-drama from the ever-elegant Leisen, who elicits a superb performance from Stanwyck as the hardboiled shoplifter faced with staying in jail over Christmas, but given bail by prosecuting attorney MacMurray and taken to visit his family for the holiday. Playing superbly on the personae of his leads, Leisen creates a movie of warmth and immense style, which never quite trips over into excessive sentimentality. GA

Remember the Titans

(2000, US, 113 min)
d Boaz Yakin. *p* Jerry Bruckheimer, Chad Oman. *sc* Gregory Allen Howard. *ph* Philippe Rousselot. *ed* Michael Tronick. *pd* Deborah Evans. *m* Trevor Rabin. *cast* Denzel Washington, Will Patton, Donald Faison, Wood Harris, Ryan Hurst, Ethan Suplee, Nicole Ari Parker, Hayden Panettiere.

● Alexandria, Virginia, 1971: in an act of positive discrimination aimed at soothing a divided community, the authorities have appointed a black football coach at a newly integrated high school. Enter Washington, with Patton, the much admired previous incumbent, agreeing to play second fiddle. The pair hope that success on the field will demonstrate that the races can work in harmony. This Disney production proves predictably positive and a little too cute, despite its basis in a true story. Get past all that, however, and it's also a pretty decent sports movie. Washington, of course, is as commanding as ever, his decidedly Spartan training regime overcoming resistance as he fashions his disparate players into a cohesive unit by making it compulsory for the different races to get to know each other. The gradual thawing of suspicions on both sides holds few surprises, but the confidence of the football sequences is perhaps unexpected in Boaz (*Fresh*) Yakin's first studio picture. The emphasis on the players' developing mutual trust, is absorbing to watch and cleanly directed. TJ

Remembrance

(1982, GB, 117 min)
d/p Colin Gregg. *sc* Hugh Stoddart. *ph* John Metcalfe. *ed* Peter Delfgou. *ad* Jamie Leonard. *cast* David John, Gary Oldman, Martin Barrass, Kenneth Griffith, Ewan Stewart, John Altman, Sally Jane Jackson.

● An episodic slice-of-life drama (the last 24 hours in port of a group of young naval ratings) cut with muted suspense (a search for the identity of the comatose victim of a disco bouncer's brutality), this Channel 4-commissioned feature occupies an unhappy middle ground between the distinctive approaches of Loach and Hines (*Looks and Smiles*) and Frears and Poliakoff (*Bloody Kids*). Opportunistically and inappropriately lumbered with a 'Falklands factor' promotional emphasis during its cinema release, the film subsequently took a major prize at the Taormina festival – presumably awarded more for good intentions than achievements. PT

Remembrance (Kyoshu)

(1987, Jap, 115 min)
d Takehiro Nakajima. *p* Hiroshi Ishikawa., Tetsuo Konda, Shinsuke Achida. *sc* Takehiro Nakajima. *ph* Junchiro Hayashi. *ed* Kiyoaki Saito. *ad* Osamu Kameoka. *m* Toshinori Kondo. *cast* Hiroshi Nishikawa, Sairi Komaki, Masahiro Tsugawa, Takaki Enomoto, Masashi Fujita.

● This plotless movie, obviously autobiographical in origin, charts a young man's coming-of-age in a small country town in the early 1950s: familiar territory for anyone who has seen films like *Muddy River* and *Warming Up for the Festival* (the latter scripted by Nakajima, here a first-time director at the age of 53). It's thoroughly amiable, and persuasively acted by its young lead Nishikawa, but fatally lacks the underlying toughness and sense of larger perspectives found in an equivalent Chinese movie like *The Time to Live and the Time to Die*. TR

Reminiscences of a Journey to Lithuania

(1972, US, 82 min)
d Jonas Mekas.

● In 1972, Jonas and Adolfas Mekas returned to visit their family in Lithuania for the first time since they had emigrated to America 27 years earlier. Both brothers made films of the event. Jonas Mekas' version is his most formally ambitious work to date: a film in three dissimilar parts designed to explore the relationship between residence, exile, and the experience of visiting a 'foreign' place. It begins somewhat like a conventional documentary, with material examining the ghettoes of New York in the '50s, where the Mekas immigrants first made their homes, then shifts into a less predictable 'diary' mode for the reunion with the family in Lithuania itself, and then moves on to self-questioning footage shot in Europe on the way back to America. The basic romanticism is patently sincere, but sometimes looks like a defensive pose, which makes it all the more poignant. TR

Remorques (Stormy Waters)

(1941, Fr, 85 min, b/w)
d Jean Grémillon. *sc* Jacques Prévert, André Cayatte. *ph* Armand Thirard. *ed* Yvonne Martin. *ad* uncredited [Alexandre Trauner]. *m* Roland-Manuel. *cast* Jean Gabin, Michèle Morgan, Madeleine Renaud, Fernand Ledoux, Charles Blavette, Jean Dasté.

● A number of cross-references apply: Reed's *The Key*, likewise a melancholy tale of doomed love set against a background of rough seas and salvage vessels; *Le Quai des Brumes*, the two stars' initial pairing, Gabin here reprising his blend of the tender and the explosive, and Morgan again entering the movie trailing clouds of sadness behind her; and Fassbinder's *Querelle*

– though this one's set in the real Brest, grey and wind-lashed, but still, cinematically, one of the capital cities of desolation. *Remorques* was begun in summer '39, shut down when war was declared and finished during the Occupation. Sometimes, as when Morgan contemplates the dead starfish which Gabin has given her, it feels precisely like the last European movie of the 1930s. BBa

Remo Williams: The Adventure Begins (aka Remo – Unarmed and Dangerous)

(1985, US, 121 min)
d Guy Hamilton. *p* Larry Spiegel. *sc* Christopher Wood. *ph* Andrew Laszlo. *ed* Merk Melnick. *pd* Jackson De Govia. *m* Craig Safan. *cast* Fred Ward, Joel Grey, Wilford Brimley, JA Preston, George Coe, Charles Cioffi, Kate Mulgrew, Patrick Kilpatrick, Michael Pataki.

● Adolescent actioner in which NYC cop Ward is spirited away after a brutal mugging, given a facelift, and taught Eastern martial art skills by a heavily made-up Grey (yes, the *Cabaret* master of ceremonies here dubiously done up as a Korean), just so he can right wrongs, dodge bullets and generally hang by his fingertips off very tall Ferris wheels. Dodgy business magnate Cioffi is up to no good in the armaments world, but even he can't ship an extra consignment of charisma to a picture that suffers from able character performer Ward's lack of leading-man presence or physique. Adapted from *The Destroyer* series of comics, it also seems caught in two minds over whether it's an escapist fantasy (compare director Hamilton's track-record on the Bond films), or the rather tougher fare suggested by the viciousness of some of the combat scenes. In the event, Remo's adventure began and ended here. TJ

Rempart des Béguines, Le (The Beguines)

(1972, Fr/It, 90 min)
d Guy Casaril. *p* Robert Hakim, Raymond Hakim. *sc* Guy Casaril, Françoise Mallet-Joris. *ph* Andréas Winding. *ed* Louisette Haudecoeur. *ad* François de Lamothe. *m* Michel Delpech, Roland Vincent. *cast* Nicole Courcel, Anicée Alvina, Venantino Venantini, Jean Martin, Ginette Leclerc, Harry-Max, Yvonne Clech.

● A self-consciously 'artistic' film about lesbianism, so coy that one spends much of the time wondering whether the older woman is 'bohemian' – she wears kimonos and has a taste for black Russian cigarettes – or just a high class tart. The story's about a poor little rich girl, only child of a widowed politician, whose furtive emotions blossom at the hands of his mistress, around which Casaril is content merely to weave pretty pictures. They're such an unsympathetic bunch – cold fish of a father (Martin), the mistress (Courcel) overbearing and tetchy, and the daughter (Alvina) spoilt – that with Casaril prepared to take them at face value, it's difficult not to lose interest fast and resign oneself to yet another sex movie. CPe

Remparts d'Argile

see Ramparts of Clay

Renaissance Man

(1994, US, 128 min)
d Penny Marshall. *p* Sara Colleton, Elliot Abbott, Robert Greenhut. *sc* Jim Burnstein, Nat Maudlin. *ph* Adam Greenberg. *ed* George Bowers, Battle Davis. *pd* Geoffrey Kirkland. *m* Hans Zimmer. *cast* Danny DeVito, Gregory Hines, Cliff Robertson, James Remar, Lillo Brancato Jr, Stacey Dash, Kadeem Hardison, Richard T Jones, Khalil Kain.

● Unemployed ad exec Bill Rago (DeVito) lands a civilian posting at a US Army base. He's to teach basic comprehension to eight 'squeakers' – the slowest new recruits. Armed only with an intuitively unmilitary intelligence and a well-thumbed copy of *Hamlet*, he does just that. Penny Marshall's film couldn't be more sincere. But don't let the poster fool you: this is no comedy, it's a two-hour-plus English lesson. Very much a product of the Clinton era, the movie has serious political intentions. It's an exhortation to America to face up to her social and spiritual malaise with a sense of responsibility, discipline and humanity. Too bad the director's such a lousy propagandist. In essence, a painfully earnest sit-com. TCh

Renaldo & Clara

(1977, US, 235 min)
d Bob Dylan. *sc* Bob Dylan. *ph* David Myers, Paul Goldsmith, Howard Alk. *ed* Bob Dylan, Howard Alk. *with* Bob Dylan, Sara Dylan, Joan Baez, Ronnie Hawkins, Ronee Blakley, Jack Elliott, Harry Dean Stanton, Bob Neuwirth, Mel Howard, Allen Ginsberg, Helena Kallianiotes, Joni Mitchell, Sam Shepard, Arlo Guthrie.

● Dylan's endlessly long attempt at a personal feature intercuts excellent concert footage from the Rolling Thunder tour with some pretentious but quite enjoyable play-acting from his retinue (Baez, wife Sarah, Allen Ginsberg) which capitalises on the rumours and mysteries surrounding Dylan's love life. Not nearly as bad as its vitriolic US reception suggested, but if you don't like Dylan you won't be converted. DP

Rendez-vous à Bray (Rendezvous at Bray)

(1971, Fr/Bel/WGer, 93 min)
d André Delvaux. *p* Mag Bodard. *sc* André Delvaux. *ph* Ghislain Cloquet. *ed* Nicole Berckmans. *ad* Claude Pignot. *m* Frédéric Devreese. *cast* Anna Karina, Bulle Ogier, Mathieu Carrière, Roger Van Hool, Martine Sarcey, Pierre Vernier.

● On the surface, Delvaux's excursions into the ambiguous territory lying between fact and fantasy, past and present, may appear similar to the dry and difficult puzzles offered in the films of Resnais. But the Belgian seems a much warmer director, concerned with the emotional impulses behind dreams, combining dread and desire in both images and narrative. The result is a genuinely beautiful surrealism exploring the pains and joys of the human mind. Here the setting is a lonely country house during the First World War. Summoned to a rendezvous there by the owner, a friend serving at the front in the air force, a young pianist (Carrière) arrives to find the friend mysteriously absent and no explanation forthcoming from the enigmatically beautiful housekeeper (Karina). Fearing his friend dead, he relives their relationship, stimulated by erotic yearnings that span past (the friend's girl, Ogier) and present (the housekeeper), conjuring ghostly shadows of guilt... GA

Rendez-vous d'Anna, Les (The Meetings of Anna)

(1978, Fr/Bel/WGer, 127 min)
d Chantal Akerman. *p* Alain Dahan. *sc* Chantal Akerman. *ph* Jean Penzer. *ed* Francine Sandberg. *ad* Philippe Graaf, André Fonteyne Coyotte. *cast* Aurore Clément, Helmut Griem, Magali Noël, Lea Massari, Hanns Zischler, Jean-Pierre Cassel.

● A quietly moving odyssey: an itinerary of train journeys, hotel rooms, and chance meetings that relates the past to a present lack of confidence among Europeans. A series of train rides, a series of tales. Only once do film and central character overcome their emotional reticence: when Anna (hitherto a passive listener), in a scene both surprising and logical, lies in bed with her mother and 'confesses' her love for another woman. A chaste refusal to supply easy answers means that the film is primarily descriptive; what emerges most strongly is a moving eroticism stemming from the everyday. HM

Rendez-vous de juillet

(1949, Fr, 98 min, b/w)
d Jacques Becker. *sc* Jacques Becker, Maurice Griffe. *ph* Claude Renoir. *ed* Marguerite Renoir. *ad* Robert-Jules Garnier. *m* Jean Wiener. *cast* Daniel Gélin, Nicole Courcel, Brigitte Auber, Maurice Ronet, Pierre Trabaud, Louis Segner, Claude Luter and his Band.

● Hard to believe that a movie about a bunch of affluent 20-year-olds ever seemed a welcome novelty. Evidently it did, though, in the context of sullen post-war French cinema. But a lot of acetate has gone through the gate since then. Allowing that the film's milieu and range of situations had not yet become hackneyed, Becker's characters are still very thin (the dreamer, the schemer, the cheeky comic relief), the tone rather uncertain. And Gélin's aspiring ethnologist is a fatally humourless and disagreeable hero, what with slapping his girlfriend around and fretting about his expedition to Brazzaville. The sharp-eyed will spot Alexandre Astruc at a jazz club and Capucine as a backstage visitor. BBa

Rendez-vous de Paris, Les (Rendez-vous in Paris)

(1995, Fr, 98 min)
d Eric Rohmer. *p* Françoise Etchegaray. *sc* Eric Rohmer. *ph* Diane Baratier. *ed* Mary Stephen. *ad* Claire Champion. *m* Sébastien Erms. *cast* Clara Bellar, Antoine Basler, Mathias Megard, Judith Chancel, Malcolm Conrath, Cécile Pares.

● Three short stories chart the effects of chance encounters of the amorous kind in contemporary Paris. In the first, a student, doubtful of her lover's fidelity, is chatted up in a market by a youth who may or may not be a thief; in the second, a teacher's attempts to seduce a woman already in a long-term relationship are both stimulated and frustrated by her feelings about the public places in which they are forced to meet; in the third, an artist playing host to a Swedish visitor decides to ignore her in favour of a woman he follows through the streets to the Picasso Museum. Slight tales, perhaps, but Rohmer turns a seemingly inconsequential confection into yet another of his subtle studies of modern love. What gives this particular piece a lift is that Rohmer shot it so casually, on 16mm and a minimal budget, so it's something of a return to the ideals of the *nouvelle vague*; and that it's very much a love-letter to Paris. The acute feeling for milieu is not decorative but crucial, in that the relationships we see are profoundly affected by the mood, population and topography of the places in which they develop. Witty, touching, perceptive, this is a film that belies Rohmer's 70-odd years. GA

Renegades

(1989, US, 106 min)
d Jack Sholder. *p* David Madden. *sc* David Rich. *ph* Phil Meheux. *ed* Caroline Biggerstaff. *pd* Carol Spier. *m* Michael Kamen. *cast* Kiefer Sutherland, Lou Diamond Phillips, Clark Johnson, Peter MacNeill, John Di Benedetto, Joe Griffin, Floyd Westerman, Jami Gertz, Rob Knepper, Bill Smitrovich.

● Young guns Sutherland and Phillips team up again, this time as a renegade cop and a Lakota Indian thrown together by tangentially related crimes. Working undercover to expose a bent cop, Sutherland participates in a heist that goes wrong; the fleeing gang members duck into a museum, where they kill Phillips' brother and make off with a priceless Lakota spear. Subsequently left for dead, Sutherland is saved by Phillips, and the two embark on a joint quest, suppressing their mutual hostility as they pursue the murderers down Philadelphia's mean-ish streets. Sholder's robust staging of the car chases, punch-ups and shootouts recalls the kinetic energy of his earlier *The Hidden*. His handling of the quieter familial and buddy-buddy realtionships, on the other hand, is hopelessly leaden, serving only to stop the action-packed narrative in its tracks. The sadly under-used Jami Gertz turns up briefly as a beauty parlour bimbo with 'disposable love interest' written all over her. NF

Rentadick

(1972, GB, 94 min)
d Jim Clark. *p* Ned Sherrin, Terry Glinwood. *sc* John Cleese, Graham Chapman. *ph* John Coquillon. *ed* Martin Charles. *pd* Seamus Flannery. *m* Carl Davis. *cast* James Booth, Richard Briers, Julie Ege, Ronald Fraser, Donald Sinden, Tsai Chin, Kenneth Cope, John Wells, Richard Beckinsale, Michael Bentine, Spike Milligan.

● Written by John Cleese and Graham Chapman, with help from satire-generation veterans John Wells and John Fortune, and produced by Ned Sherrin, this ought to be a cut above the level suggested by the 'oo-er missus' title and the presence of a character called Madame Greenfly. It isn't quite, but a fairly scattershot approach to its spoof spy formula – inept 'tec Booth caught up in a nerve gas scam – at least keeps it moving briskly. A touch of exotic strangeness comes from the likes of Sinden, Bentine, Milligan, and that tackiest of early '70s sex symbols, Julie Ege. But the film's single weirdest asset has to be the theme song by Dave Dee and the Kings Singers. JRo

Repentance (Monanieba)

(1984, USSR, 150 min)
d Tengiz Abuladze. *sc* Nana Janelidze, Tengiz Abuladze, Rezo Kveselava. *ph* Mikhail

Agranovich. *ed* Guliko Omadze. *pd* Georgis Mikeladze. *m* Nana Janelidze. *cast* Avtandil Makharadze, Iya Ninidze, Merab Ninidze, Zeynab Botsvadze, Ketevan Abuladze.

● A Soviet movie about the traumas of the Stalinist years: the tyranny, the betrayals, the persecutions, and the unexplained disappearances, mounted by Georgian director Abuladze as a weird phantasmagoria of dreams and nightmares, absurdist drama and black comedy. He starts from the ceremonial burial of a town mayor, and the subsequent repeated disinterment of the corpse by the daughter of two of the late tyrant's victims. Flashbacks show his rise to power and growing megalomania. Varlam the mayor was a paranoid secret policeman, a brutal bully-boy. The character is not just an amalgam of Stalin and Beria, but a compendium of every conceivable fascistic trait; and Abuladze tries to underline this desperately literal 'universality' by setting him in a context outside history and culture, where knights in armour stand alongside black-shirted thugs and Boney M vies with Debussy on the soundtrack. The result is neither as minatory nor as moving as it thinks it is, despite some arresting surrealist images and the performance of Makharadze as Varlam. TR

Replacement Killers, The

(1998, US, 87 min)
d Antoine Fuqua. *p* Brad Grey, Bernie Brillstein. *sc* Ken Sanzel. *ph* Peter Lyons Collister. *ed* Jay Cassidy. *pd* Naomi Shohan. *m* Harry Gregson-Williams. *cast* Chow Yun-Fat, Mira Sorvino, Michael Rooker, Jürgen Prochnow, Carlos Gomez, Frank Medrano, Kenneth Tsang.

● With his looks, easy charm and devastating close combat skills, Chow Yun-Fat became one of the world's coolest stars, despite never having made an American movie. He was iconic in John Woo's *The Killer* and *Hard-Boiled*; and perhaps inevitably, the US majors signed him up in the wake of Woo's Hollywood success. Several English lessons later, with Woo as watchful exec producer, Chow gets his big break, but, regrettably, it's a lifeless copy of his HK pictures. In a virtual rerun of *The Killer*, he plays a hitman, whose debt to the Chinese mob will be paid off if he carries out one last job on detective Rooker's small son. Lining up his sights, he finds himself unable to eliminate his target, and soon the mob are out to replace him with someone who can. The formula is so wearisome, the viewer has plenty of time to muse on the incidentals: Chow's uncanny facility for returning fire in mid-dive; Mira Sorvino's no nonsense re-invention of the clichéd squealing bimbo role; director Antoine Fuqua's striking repertory of sinuous camera moves. Next time maybe they'll trust the star with more than three words of dialogue at a time. TJ

Repo Man

(1984, US, 92 min)
d Alex Cox. *p* Jonathan Wacks, Peter McCarthy. *sc* Alex Cox. *ph* Robby Müller. *ed* Dennis Dolan. *ad* J Rae Fox, Linda Burbank. *m* Tito Larriva, Steven Hufsteter. *cast* Harry Dean Stanton, Emilio Estevez, Tracey Walter, Olivia Barash, Sy Richardson, Susan Barnes, Fox Harris, Tom Finnegan, Vonetta McGee.

● When LA punk Otto (Estevez) loses both girl and job, he's hardly prepared for an adventure of mind-blowing proportions when he's conned into helping out a repo man (Stanton). Not only does he find himself in mortal danger while repossessing cars from irate owners, he also gets caught up in a manic world populated by knitting cops, CIA clones, lobotomised nuclear scientists, drippy hippies, UFO freaks, and the roguish Rodriguez Brothers, all in search of a '64 Chevy carrying a lethal cargo. Cox's weird and wonderful first feature defies description, with a plot and characters at once grounded in the seedy reality of Reagan's America and effortlessly enhanced by flights of pure, imaginative fantasy. What distinguishes the movie is its offbeat, semi-satirical sense of humour, seamlessly woven into its wacky thriller plot. But there are endless things to enjoy, from Robby Müller's crisp camerawork to a superb set of performances, from witty movie parodies to a tremendous punk soundtrack. GA

Report to the Commissioner (aka Operation Undercover)

(1974, US, 112 min)
d Milton Katselas. *p* MJ Frankovich. *sc* Abby Mann, Ernest Tidyman. *ph* Mario Tosi. *ed* David Blewitt. *pd* Robert Clatworthy. *m* Elmer Bernstein. *cast* Michael Moriarty, Yaphet Kotto, Susan Blakely, Hector Elizondo, Tony King, Michael McGuire, Dana Elcar, William Devane, Richard Gere.

● 'It's happened – they've sent us a hippy', Yaphet Kotto cries on sighting his latest recruit, the zombie-like Bo (Moriarty) framed in the precinct doorway. And one's heart goes out to him, for nothing is quite as stodgy (even obnoxious) as a slice of basic Hollywood action that tries to persuade us of its social concern. Cursed with a weighty script by Abby (*Judgement at Nuremberg*) Mann and Ernest Tidyman based on James Mills' novel, the film makes very heavy weather indeed of its inane tale about a hippy-liberal who joins the (undercover) force. Katselas injects what sentimentality he can into the patently contrived affair. VG

Repossessed

(1990, US, 84 min)
d Bob Logan. *p* Steve Wizan. *sc* Bob Logan. *ph* Michael D Margulies. *ed* Jeff Freeman. *pd* Shay Austin. *m* Charles Fox. *cast* Linda Blair, Ned Beatty, Leslie Nielsen, Anthony Starke, Thom J Sharp, Lana Schwab, Robert Fuller.

● Suburban housewife Nancy Aglet's childhood ordeal of demonic possession is becoming a recurring nightmare. Beset by demons emerging from her TV set, Nancy (Blair) starts spewing green vomit over her children, writhing on vibrating beds, and threatening the neighbourhood priest in a gruff voice. The kids suspect PMT, but Nancy knows better, as does retired exorcist Father Mayii (Nielsen). Originally conceived as a spoof of *The Exorcist*, this was extensively re-edited when test screenings showed that 15-year-olds simply didn't understand the references. Afraid of losing the teen market, writer/director Logan excised the subtler humour and pasted in a batch of unrelated and (supposedly) crowd-pleasing bawdy gags, notably a lengthy gym sequence wherein Father Mayii gets fit to fight the devil, allowing Nielsen to wander into women's showers, gaze at women pumping up their bosoms, play with brassières, etc. The result may be worth a few cheap pubescent laughs, but *Exorcist* fans will doubtless feel cheated. MK

Reptile, The

(1966, GB, 91 min)
d John Gilling. *p* Anthony Nelson-Keys. *sc* Anthony Hinds. *ph* Arthur Grant. *ed* James Needs, Roy Hyde. *pd* Bernard Robinson. *m* Don Banks. *cast* Noel Willman, Jennifer Daniel, Ray Barrett, Jacqueline Pearce, Michael Ripper, John Laurie, Marne Maitland.

● Down in remoter Cornwall, courtesy of Hammer horror, a doctor is busily experimenting and villagers are foaming at the mouth, turning black, and dying of snake venom. Made back-to-back with *Plague of the Zombies* and shot on the same sets, it's slower and moodier than its companion-piece but strikingly Conan Doyleish in its stately costume horrors. Jacqueline Pearce is terrific as the unfortunate cobra-girl, victim of her father's pursuit of forbidden knowledge. TM

Repubblica Nostra (Our Republic)

(1995, It, 78 min)
d Daniele Incalcaterra.

● A skilfully edited documentary with minimum of directorial intervention about the 'charismatic' media tycoon Silvio Berlusconi, his foundation of Forza Italia (which swept to power in February 1994), his rise to become Italy's prime minister, and his fall from power. The film cross-cuts, primarily, between two political candidates, one from the broad left Progressive Alliance, the other a Berlusconi employee (a director of the Diakron polling company); the 'clean hands' investigating magistrates Davigo and Di Pietro; and various media representatives. For those who like to draw their own conclusions. WH

Republic of Sin

see Fièvre Monte à El Pao, La

Repulsion

(1965, GB, 104 min, b/w)
d Roman Polanski. *p* Gene Gutowski. *sc* Roman Polanski, Gérard Brach. *ph* Gilbert Taylor. *ed* Alastair McIntyre. *ad* Seamus Flannery. *m* Chico Hamilton. *cast* Catherine Deneuve, Yvonne Furneaux, John Fraser, Ian Hendry, Patrick Wymark, Valerie Taylor, Helen Fraser, Renee Houston, James Villiers.

● Still perhaps Polanski's most perfectly realised film, a stunning portrait of the disintegration, mental and emotional, of a shy young Belgian girl (Deneuve) living in London. When she's left alone by her sister in their Kensington flat, she becomes reclusive and retreats into a terrifying world of fantasies and nightmares which find murderous physical expression when she is visited by a would-be boyfriend (Fraser) and her leering landlord (Wymark). Polanski employs a host of wonderfully integrated visual and aural effects to suggest the inner torment Deneuve suffers: cracks in pavements, hands groping from walls, shadows under doors, rotting skinned rabbits, and – as in *Rosemary's Baby* – the eerie, ever-present sound of someone practising scales on a piano. And despite the fact that the girl's manically destructive actions derive from a terror of sexual contact, Polanski never turns his film into a misogynist binge: the men she meets are far from sympathetically portrayed, and we are led to understand her fear and revulsion by the surreal expressionism used to portray her mental state. All in all, one of the most intelligent horror movies ever made, and certainly one of the most frighteningly effective. GA

Requiem for a Dream (100)

(2000, US, 101 min)
d Darren Aronofsky. *p* Eric Watson, Palmer West. *sc* Hubert Selby Jr, Darren Aronofsky. *ph* Matthew Libatique. *ed* Jay Rabinowitz. *pd* James Chinlund. *m* Clint Mansell. *cast* Ellen Burstyn, Jared Leto, Jennifer Connelly, Marlon Wayans, Christopher McDonald, Louise Lasser, Hubert Selby Jr.

● Refused a US censor's rating, this adaptation of Hubert Selby's 1978 novel is as visually experimental and thematically uncompromising as director Aronofsky's first feature *Pi*. A relentless sensory assault threatens to overwhelm the viewer, but the visceral images and frantic editing capture the euphoric 'highs' and repetitive rituals of drug blighted lives, while drawing clear parallels between the characters' different forms of addiction. Aronofsky interweaves the tales of four Coney Island residents, each desperate to escape a dull existence. Burstyn gives a fearless, heartbreaking performance as Sara Goldfarb, a widow who shrugs off lethargy when promised an appearance on her favourite TV game show; but an amphetamine-based crash diet slowly disconnects her from reality. Her junkie son Harry (Leto) dreams of becoming a bigtime dealer with his friend Tyrone (Wayans). With the profits, Harry plans to open a clothes shop, based on his girlfriend Marion's designs. Burnished camerawork and ex-Pop Will Eat Itself head Mansell's part-punchy, part-elegiac score reinforce and counterpoint the increasingly nightmarish visuals. NF

Requiem for a Vampire

see Requiem pour un Vampire

Requiem for a Village

(1975, GB, 68 min)
d David Gladwell. *p* Michael Raeburn. *sc* David Gladwell. *ph* Bruce Parsons. *ed* David Gladwell. *m* David Fanshawe. *cast* Vic Smith, the villagers of Witnesham and Metfield, Suffolk.

● Here the dead quite literally arise, and an old man follows them into church where, his youth regained, he relives his wedding in a sleepy Suffolk village, now under siege from ice-cream vans, motorcycles and excavators. The film proceeds, within the framework of the old man's working day, slowly and with scrupulous detail, to build a picture of the village as it was in his youth. What separates the movie, however, from a mere wistful lament for happier times, is the way in which its parts cohere around the central conceit that, through memory, the past and present merge to form a bond which proves stronger than death itself. JPy

Requiem for Dominic

(1990, Aus, 91 min)
d Robert Dornhelm. *p* Norbert Blecha. *sc* Michael Kohlmeier, Felix Mitterer. *ph* Hans Selikovsky. *ed* Ingrid Koller, Barbara Heraut. *m* Harald Kloser. *cast* Felix Mitterer, Viktoria Schubert, August Schmölzer, Angelica Schütz.

●Not since *Circle of Deceit* – perhaps even *Battle of Algiers* – have the deadly chaos and white-knuckled fear of political turmoil been as convincingly conveyed as in this docu-thriller about the lies, violence and anger of the 1989 Romanian revolution. Shot on location in Timisoara just months after Ceausescu's demise, it interweaves newsreel and video footage with fictional material inspired by the fate of Dornhelm's childhood friend Dominic Paraschiv, with a fictional Paul Weiss (Mitterer) standing in for Dornhelm as an exile returning to seek out the truth behind Paraschiv's arrest and imprisonment as a Securitate terrorist allegedly guilty of murdering 80 factory workers. Despite its autobiographical aspects, the factually-based investigative plot serves primarily not to clear the late Paraschiv's name, but to demonstrate how the paranoia and bloodlust born of such a repressive regime merely serve to produce further fear and mindless brutality: humane ideals are in short supply, and anyone who threatens to expose the deceptions of an already unstable system finds his life in peril. Dornhelm films with a gut-wrenching immediacy, but never sinks to simplistic agit-prop.GA

Requiem pour un Vampire (Requiem for a Vampire/ Virgins and Vampires)

(1971, Fr/Ger, 95 min)
d Jean Rollin. *p* Sam Selsky. *sc* Jean Rollin. *ph* Renan Polles. *ed* Michel Patient. *m* Pierre Raph. *cast* Marie-Pierre Castel, Mireille D'Argent, Philippe Gasté, Dominique, Louise Dhour.

●Although rarely seen, this faintly surreal sex-vampire movie achieved a minor cult reputation thanks to its blend of vampirism and sado-eroticism. With almost all of the latter removed at the censor's behest (cut running time, 78 minutes), what remains is a mildly distracting tale of two fugitive teenagers who stumble upon a castle inhabited by an aged vampire and his cohorts. Attempts to initiate the girls conveniently entail the loss of their virginity, but when one fails to follow through and the other refuses to reveal the whereabouts of her handsome seducer, their captors threaten cruel reprisals. Much sought in its original form. NF

Rescuers, The

(1977, US, 77 min)
d Wolfgang Reitherman, John Lounsbery, Art Stevens. *p* Wolfgang Reitherman. *sc* Larry Clemmons, Ken Anderson, Vance Gerry, Frank Thomas, David Michener, Ted Berman, Fred Lucky, Burny Mattinson, Dick Sebast. *ed* James Melton, Jim Koford. *ad* Don Griffith. *m* Artie Butler. *cast* voices: Bob Newhart, Eva Gabor, Geraldine Page, Joe Flynn, Jeanette Nolan, John McIntire.

●Two members of the all-mouse Rescue Aid Society go to the help of an orphan girl being held captive by the horribly evil Medusa in her riverboat home at the Devil's Bayou. But the people who really need rescuing are the Disney animators and storymen, who seem uncertain whether to keep up the old studio traditions of cute characters and plush settings, or to branch out into contemporary urban satire. *The Rescuers* dabbles in both styles, most unsatisfyingly, and the handful of sappy songs don't improve things. There is one lovely character, though – Orville the albatross, who runs an airline service armed with goggles, scarf, and a sardine tin for his passengers to sit in. GB

Rescuers Down Under, The

(1990, US, 77 min)
d Hendel Butoy, Mike Gabriel. *p* Thomas C Schumacher. *sc* Jim Cox, Karey Kirkpatrick, Byron Simpson, Joe Ranft. *ed* Michael Kelly. *ad* Maurice Hunt. *m* Bruce Broughton. *cast* voices: Bob Newhart, Eva Gabor, John Candy, Tristan Rogers, Adam Ryan, George C Scott, Peter Firth.

●Thirteen years after the Mouse Rescue Aid Society packed off Bernard and Bianca on their first mission, they're back. A young boy has been kidnapped, deep in the Australian outback: an evil poacher is holding him until he reveals the whereabouts of a rare eagle's nest, so this is a double quest – to save the child and the eagle eggs. It's surprising that *The Rescuers* should be the first Disney animated feature to merit a sequel. Inoffensive as they are, humble Bernard and the aristocratic Bianca are not the studio's most memorable creations; and for all the quaintly old-fashioned romance and desperately broad comedy, this is nothing if not an adventure film (clearly testifying to the influence of Spielberg). As for the animation, computer technology invests contemporary features with sometimes breathtaking dynamism, but outback flora being what it is, this isn't the most colourful Disney movie. TCh

Reservoir Dogs (100)

(1991, US, 99 min)
d Quentin Tarantino. *p* Lawrence Bender. *sc* Quentin Tarantino. *ph* Andrzej Sekula. *ed* Sally Menke. *pd* David Wasco. *m* Karyn Rachtman. *cast* Harvey Keitel, Tim Roth, Michael Madsen, Chris Penn, Steve Buscemi, Lawrence Tierney, Randy Brooks, Kirk Baltz, Eddie Bunker, Quentin Tarantino.

●Tarantino's powerful homage/reworking of the heist-gone-wrong thriller – stealing ideas from Kubrick's *The Killing* and Scorsese's *Mean Streets*, among others – is probably the final word (or frame) on the subject. A bunch of colour-coded crooks (Mr White, Mr Pink, etc), previously unknown to each other, chosen and named by ageing *capo* Joe Cabot (Tierney) and his son Nice Guy Eddie (Penn), execute a jewellery robbery. The job done, the getaway fucked up, they reassemble at a warehouse to get what's coming to them. Tarantino engineers their demise from the interaction of their character flaws – there is certainly no honour among these talkative thieves – with the inexorable logic of a chess grandmaster. Despite the clockwork theatrical dynamics – most of the action is restricted to the warehouse – the film packs a massive punch. It's violent, intelligent, well written (by Tarantino) and acted (Buscemi, Roth and Penn take the prizes). A *tour de force*. WH

Respectable Prostitute, The

see P..... Respectueuse, La

Respectful Prostitute, The

see P..... Respectueuse, La

Ressources Humaines

see Human Resources

Restless Breed, The

(1957, US, 81 min)
d Allan Dwan. *p* Edward L Alperson. *sc* Steve Fisher. *ph* John W Boyle. *ed* Merrill G White. *ad* Ernst Fegté. *m* Edward L Alperson Jr. *cast* Scott Brady, Anne Bancroft, Jay C Flippen, Rhys Williams, Jim Davis, Scott Marlowe, Evelyn Rudie.

●Dwan made his first picture in 1911, invented the dolly shot around 1915, and was still working in his seventies on a series of low-budget Westerns, much admired by connoisseurs like Martin Scorsese for their supreme economy of form, the gesture of a true master. In this instance, money was obviously tight, but Dwan's craftmanship is well in evidence in the simplest of revenge stories, with Brady as the lawyer out to get his father's killer, Davis the villainous gunrunner, and a youthful Bancroft as the half-breed Indian who proves her mettle along the way. Roundly satisfying. TJ

Restless Natives

(1985, GB, 89 min)
d Michael Hoffman. *p* Rick Stevenson. *sc* Ninian Dunnett. *ph* Oliver Stapleton. *ed* Sean Barton. *ad* Adrienne Atkinson. *m* Stuart Adamson. *cast* Vincent Friell, Joe Mullaney, Teri Lally, Ned Beatty, Robert Urquhart, Bernard Hill, Rachel Boyd, Mel Smith, Bryan Forbes.

●Truly dire attempt to reproduce the whimsical charm of Bill Forsyth, in which two Edinburgh teenagers tackle the problem of unemployment by turning to highway robbery, relieving coachloads of tourists of cash and jewellery as they buzz around the Highlands on a moped, disguised in joke-shop masks and armed with toy guns loaded with sneezing powder. Dreadfully unfunny, it soon becomes embarrassing as fantasy takes over, and the pair are lauded as modern-day Rob Roys, legends in their own lifetime. Syrupy, silly, and not a mite objectionable in its closet patriotism. GA

Restoration

(1996, US, 118 min)
d Michael Hoffman. *p* Andy Paterson, Cary Brokaw, Sarah Ryan Black. *sc* Rupert Walters. *ph* Oliver Stapleton. *ed* Garth Craven. *pd* Eugenio Zanetti. *m* James Newton Howard. *cast* Robert Downey Jr, Sam Neill, Polly Walker, David Thewlis, Meg Ryan, Ian McKellen, Hugh Grant.

●This adaptation (by Rupert Walters) of Rose Tremain's brilliant Booker-shortlisted novel is a lot better than rumours about its frantic, lengthy post-production might have suggested. Downey is Robert Merivel, a rakish physician invited to the court of Charles II and favoured for curing one of the king's spaniels. He's a callow, hedonistic young man torn between the rigours of knowledge, the wealth of preferment, and the sexual intemperance of an age quickly forgetting the puritanism of the Cromwells. He weds one of the king's best mistresses in a lavish court ceremony, but is deflated to find Charles ready to take his place in the marriage bed. Out of favour and tricked by court painter Finn (Grant), Merivel journeys through 1660s England, taking refuge in a Quaker community that includes his sickly friend Pearce (Thewlis) and mad, Irish Katharine (Ryan). Ryan, with legs waxed and lipstick in place, is a striking example of how the film goes astray as soon as it plays the star casting game; but at least the doomed Katharine and the survivor Merivel have their baby, the major stepping stone on the physican's path to maturity and virtue. Engaging if uneven. SGr

Resurrected

(1989, GB, 92 min)
d Paul Greengrass. *p* Tara Prem, Adrian Hughes. *sc* Martin Allen. *ph* Ivan Strasburg. *ed* Dan Rae. *pd* Chris Burke. *m* John Keane. *cast* David Thewlis, Tom Bell, Rita Tushingham, Michael Pollitt, Rudi Davies, William Hoyland, Ewan Stewart, Christopher Fulford, David Lonsdale.

●Combining a Falklands story with the broader theme of institutionalised bullying within the armed forces, this provocative and punchy drama attacks both issues with fierce intelligence. The basis is the true story of a young British soldier who went missing during battle, was presumed dead, and accorded a memorial service with full military honours. Some weeks later, Private Deakin (Thewlis) turned up alive. The name has been changed, but fiction takes over properly when Deakin, an awkward embarrassment for his Lancashire village community, returns to barracks. Their hatred fuelled by tabloid stories of Deakin's alleged desertion, two fellow soldiers (Fulford, Lonsdale) organise a kangaroo court martial. Although Greengrass' direction is a shade televisual, Martin Allen's tough, polemical screenplay confronts the core issues without losing sight of the characters' individual psychology. Most tellingly, Allen demonstrates that the soldiers' systematic brutalisation of Deakin is provoked partly by their own insecurity, their realisation that the dividing line between heroism and desertion is wafer thin. Thewlis is superb as the confused Deakin, with excellent support from Bell (his father) and Fulford. NF

Resurrection

(1980, US, 103 min)
d Daniel Petrie. *p* Renée Missel, Howard Rosenman. *sc* Lewis John Carlino. *ph* Mario Tosi. *ed* Rita Roland. *pd* Paul Sylbert. *m* Maurice Jarre. *cast* Ellen Burstyn, Sam Shepard, Richard Farnsworth, Roberts Blossom, Clifford David, Pamela Payton-Wright, Eve LeGallienne, Lois Smith.

●Despite strong performances, particularly from Burstyn and Shepard, a rather embarrassing look at the subject of faith-healing, with Burstyn finding she has the power after she survives a car crash which kills her husband. Problems develop with her Bible-thumping parents (she insists it's love, not God, that helps her heal), and with Shepard, a beneficiary of her gift who treats her with erratic, tormented reverence after romance develops between them. The film is let down by Petrie's bland, prettified direction, and by a script from Lewis John Carlino which is forever going on hippy-style about the Power of Love. GA

Resurrection Man

(1997, GB, 102 min)
d Marc Evans. *p* Andrew Eaton. *sc* Eoin McNamee. *ph* Pierre Aim. *ed* John Wilson.

pd Mark Tildesley. *m* David Holmes, Gary Burns, Keith Tenniswood. *cast* Stuart Townsend, Geraldine O'Rawe, James Nesbitt, John Hannah, Brenda Fricker, James Ellis, Sean McGinley.

●Notwithstanding a sterling central performance from the up-and-coming Townsend, this account of the deeds of the Shankhill Butchers (adapted by Eoin McNamee from his book) leaves a pretty nasty taste in the mouth. The problem lies in the film-makers' seeming inability to decide whether it's a political work, a genre thriller, or a study of violent psychopaths (in which case it doesn't tell us much about them). Regardless of the fact that the killers' contribution to the Belfast Troubles of the '70s was not politically motivated (though their capacity for carnage was used by the terrorists), and despite director Marc Evans' insistence that this is a fiction, the makers seem to want to have their cake and eat it, leaving the movie open to charges of sensationalist exploitation. Polished but dodgy. GA

Resurrection of Zachary Wheeler, The

(1971, US, 100 min)
d Bob Wynn. *p* Robert W Stabler. *sc* Jay Simms, Tom Rolf. *ph* Bob Boatman. *ed* Jerry Greene. *ad* Herman Zimmerman. *m* Marlin Skiles. *cast* Leslie Nielsen, Bradford Dillman, James Daly, Angie Dickinson, Robert J Wilke, Jack Carter.

●Yesterday's sci-fi meets today's 'heart-snatchers' headlines in this pre-*Coma* medical thriller. As dogged reporter Nielsen searches for the senator he's seen whisked away from hospital after a near-fatal car crash, the politician himself (Dillman) wakes in a New Mexico clinic with a whole new set of internal organs, plundered from clone-like captive 'somas', bred specifically as transplant donors. This low-budget curio (itself seamlessly transferred from video to film) treads an engaging path through the genre clichés and asks most of the right questions about the selective application of medical high-tech, without ever quite sparking. But if it ends with an evasive whimper, at least it's a politically outrageous one. PT

Retour d'Afrique, Le (Return from Africa)

(1973, Switz/Fr, 109 min, b/w)
d/p/sc Alain Tanner. *ph* Renato Berta, Carlo Varini. *ed* Brigitte Sousselier, Marc Blavet. *ad* Yanko Hodjis. *m* Johann Sebastian Bach. *cast* Josée Destoop, François Marthouret, Juliet Berto, Anne Wiazemsky, André Schmidt.

●Stifled by the alienating dead weight of Genevan conventions, a young Swiss couple hatch heady plans to move to Africa and 'work for the Third World'. A last-minute hitch, however, leaves them stuck in their own stripped flat, to come to terms with their own world. Their articulate self-awareness precludes the sort of instinctive, freewheeling revolt of Tanner's *La Salamandre*, but never leads them into the mere cypher roles of Godard's analogous couple in *Le Gai Savoir*. Instead, they explore a claustrophobic environment of ideas which is the landscape of *Messidor* in miniature, and emerge with an optimistic vision of personal politics of the sort worked through later in *Jonah Who Will Be 25 in the Year 2000*. Surprisingly warm didacticism. PT

Retour de Martin Guerre, Le (The Return of Martin Guerre)

(1982, Fr, 123 min)
d/p Daniel Vigne. *sc* Jean-Claude Carrière, Daniel Vigne. *ph* André Neau. *ed* Denise de Casabianca. *ad* Alain Negre. *m* Michel Portal. *cast* Gérard Depardieu, Nathalie Baye, Stéphane Peau, Sylvie Méda, Bernard-Pierre Donnadieu, Maurice Barrier, Isabelle Sadoyan, Roger Planchon, Maurice Jacquemont.

●Rural France, 1542: after several years of unhappiness in his village, a young man suddenly disappears, leaving his wife and farm. Nine years later he returns from the war, a changed man; his story is convincing, his wife accepts him wholeheartedly, and his farm prospers. But doubts about his true identity are sown. The storyline is a legend which the French hold dear, and even inspired Montaigne to write an essay on its curiosity. For quite aside from the obvious interest over a possible impostor in the wrong bed, the story strikes deep at a philosophic knot: what constitutes human identity, or soul? And is a woman's love necessarily exclusive? Unfortunately the film lets the questions go hang, in favour of some admittedly successful courtroom drama, in which Depardieu reprises his role from *Danton*, where he has to talk as if his life depended on it (which it does). The decor is dripping with research from some university's medieval department: mud-caked codpieces and pigs rooting among the worzels, all filmed in glorious Squalorama. But there are enough courtroom reversals to keep Perry Mason fans more than happy. CPea

Retreat, Hell!

(1952, US, 95 min, b/w)
d Joseph H Lewis. *p* Milton Sperling. *sc* Milton Sperling, Ted Sherdeman. *ph* Warren Lynch. *ed* Folmar Blangsted. *ad* Edward Carrere. *m* William Lava. *cast* Frank Lovejoy, Richard Carlson, Russ Tamblyn, Anita Louise, Ned Young, Lamont Johnson.

●A curious Korean War propaganda assignment, perversely hymning the American art of attacking in the wrong direction. Lewis can't (for once) do a great deal with the well-worn yarn of an army unit being blooded and battling forth-and-back to rearguard heroism. But beyond his characteristically telling handling of violence, several incidentals push up the interest quotient: the most capable soldier is played by McCarthy blacklist victim Ned Young, while Lamont Johnson, later a director of note, is also in the cast. PT

Retribution

(1987, US, 109 min)
d/p Guy Magar. *sc* Guy Magar, Lee Wasserman. *ph* Gary Thieltges. *ed* Guy Magar, Alan Shefland. *pd* Robb Wilson-King. *m* Alan Howarth. *cast* Dennis Lipscomb, Leslie Wing, Suzanne Snyder, Jeff Pomerantz, George Murdock, Pamela Dunlap.

●Though often scary, this patchy horror pic is handicapped by embarrassment about its tawdry terror tactics, its hyperventilated hysteria all too often tempered by an undue attention to redundant 'human interest' stuff. Tortured artist (Lipscomb) takes a dive from a high window, but his suicidal impulses are frustrated when his body is possessed at the moment of death by the vengeful spirit of a murdered gambler, and he is transformed into a telekinetic maniac hunting down the culprits (and subjecting them to grisly deaths). Tart-with-a-heart (Snyder) tries to console him with soppy romantic love, while psychatrist (Wing) wrestles with his schizophrenia. Hampered by some hideous dialogue, it's about 20 tedious minutes too long, though Magar's stylish handling of the telekinetic mayhem just manages to sustain one's wavering interest. NF

Retroactive

(1997, US, 90 min)
d Louis Morneau. *p* David Bixler, Michael Nadeau, Brad Krevoy, Steve Stabler. *sc* Michael Hamilton-Wright, Robert Ian Strauss, Philip Badger. *ph* George Mooradian. *ed* Glenn Garland. *pd* Philip Duffin. *m* Tim Truman. *cast* Shannon Whirry, Jesse Borrego, Jim Belushi, Kylie Travis, Frank Whaley, M Emmet Walsh.

●Returning to Texas after a botched hostage crisis, police psychologist Travis crashes her car in the middle of nowhere. Accepting a lift from redneck Belushi and his girl Whirry, she little suspects he's a petty criminal with a murderous temper. When the ride turns into a nightmare, with corpses scattered across the desert, Travis takes refuge in a government lab where lone boffin Whaley is experimenting in time reversal. Trouble is, when Travis travels back to forestall the havoc wreaked by Belushi, the situation deteriorates. With its explosive action, black comedy and far-fetched sci-fi imposed on an otherwise vaguely plausible crime thriller, this modest indie film is reminiscent of such low budget '80s exploiters as *Tremors* and the work of Charles Band. Like the most memorable of these, it's lifted out of the rut by a quirky, imaginative script. True, Belushi's performance is overbearing and M Emmet Walsh turns in yet another sweaty cameo; true, too, that the frequent visual emphasis on Travis' cleavage flags the movie's compromised ambitions. Nevertheless, there's more than enough energy, bravado and invention to engage the attention throughout. GA

Return, The

(1988, GB, 85 min)
d/p/sc Phil Mulloy. *ph* Thaddeus O'Sullivan. *ad* Lia Cramer, Miranda Melville. *m* Donal Lunny. *cast* Tony Guilfoyle, Oengus Macnamara, Lesley Nightingale.

●First feature in ages (since *Give Us This Day* in 1982, in fact) from one of Britain's most talented independent film-makers: a powerful, claustrophobic drama that uncovers Oedipal passions in the mind of a desperate Irishman facing eviction from his docklands slum. Literate writing and magnificent performances wring maximum intensity from a plot sprung on flashbacks and fantasies. It sounds like the usual social-realist guff, but it plays more like a Borges condundrum. TR

Return, The (Tro' Vé)

(1994, Vietnam, 110 min)
d/sc Dang Nhât Minh. *ph* Nguyen Huu Tuan. *ed* Nguyen Quoc Dung. *pd* Pham Quoc Trung. *m* Xuan Ho. *cast* Nguyên Thu Hiên, Tran Luc, Manh Cuong, Duong Viêt Bát, Minh Tiêp.

●Using the idiom of melodrama but not the clichés, Dang explores the regrets and contradictions provoked by the new materialism which has swept Vietnam with the government's economic reforms. As a schoolteacher, Loan lost the man she loved; already married, he left on an illegal boat to seek his fortune overseas. Three years later she's unhappily married to a go-getting nouveau riche businessman when her first love comes back. Vastly more accomplished than most Vietnamese films, this is original and sincerely felt. And its ending is a real surprise. TR

Return Engagement

(1983, US, 89 min)
d Alan Rudolph. *p* Carolyn Pfeiffer. *ph* Jan Kiesser. *ed* Tom Walls. *m* Adrian Belew. *with* Dr Timothy Leary, G Gordon Liddy, Carol Hemingway.

●'You sound like an old married couple' a journalist tells acid guru Timothy Leary and Watergate master-plumber G Gordon Liddy, as they squabble drunkenly over supper between engagements. Leary? Liddy? Engagements? America really is a wonderful country: two of the wildest cards in its pack became the highest-paid act on the college lecture circuit, debating each other. Liddy is the straight man – patriotism, loyalty, law & order, guns and the flag; Leary is the soft-shoe-shuffling joker – youth, consciousness expansion, evolution, the individual. *Return Engagement* – Liddy arrested Leary 16 years before – follows them on the road, on and off stage, with their wives, Liddy with a Hell's Angels chapter, Leary lecturing alfresco at Esalen. By the end it's hard to decide which is flakier than the other, though some of the debate audiences are weirder than either. A fascinating portrait of seeming opposites locked together by mutual self-interest, and in some twisted way, by history. JCo

Return from Africa

see Retour d'Afrique, Le

Return from the River Kwai

(1988, GB, 101 min)
d Andrew V McLaglen. *p* Kurt Unger. *sc* Sargon Tamimi, Paul Mayersberg. *ph* Arthur G Wooster. *ed* Alan Strachan. *pd* Michael Stringer. *m* Lalo Schifrin. *cast* Edward Fox, Denholm Elliott, Christopher Penn, Tatsuya Nakadai, George Takei, Nick Tate, Timothy Bottoms, Michael Dante, Richard Graham.

●This definitive 'non-fictional' account of the rescue of Allied troops from a Japanese PoW camp features an unspectacular line-up of actors whose sole point of reference is the implicit understanding that they've all had better parts. Leading our heroes is well-known American fighter pilot Christopher Penn, followed hotly by Edward Fox, commander of the Brit contingent of the prisoners, the Australian Commander Nick Tate, and Colonel Denholm Elliott, who makes a virtue of playing the fall guy in life's rich tapestry of war films. Pitted against these awesome odds are evil Lieutenant Tanaka (played with traditional sadistic relish by George Takei) whose plan is to ship the PoWs to various Japanese car factories, and a thinly disguised Hirohito-style Major Harada (Nakadai). A tacky lager lout view of war. JCh

Return from Witch Mountain

(1978, US, 93 min)
d John Hough. *p* Ron Miller, Jerome Courtland. *sc* Malcolm Marmorstein. *ph* Frank Phillips. *ed* Bob Bring. *ad* John B Mansbridge, Jack Senter. *m* Lalo Schifrin. *cast* Kim Richards, Ike Eisenmann, Bette Davis, Christopher Lee, Jack Soo, Denver Pyle.
● With its early scenes set in LA's urban wasteland and superior music from Lalo Schifrin, Disney's belated sequel to *Escape to Witch Mountain* seems promising for a while. But it rapidly gets stuck in the same groove as the original: the two kids with supernatural powers fall prey to Lee's villainous scientist, and constantly display their gift for 'molecular mobilisation', levitating (among many other things) wine casks, museum exhibits, gold bars, trash cans, security guards, and the Board of Education's bus for rounding up truants. There's also a helpful goat called Alfred, and it's a moot point who does the most bleating – the goat or Bette Davis as Lee's sidekick. OK family fun, at a pinch. GB

Return of a Man Called Horse, The

(1976, US, 129 min)
d Irvin Kershner. *p* Terry Morse Jr. *sc* Jack DeWitt. *ph* Owen Roizman. *ed* Michael Kahn. *pd* W Stewart Campbell. *m* Laurence Rosenthal. *cast* Richard Harris, Gale Sondergaard, Geoffrey Lewis, Bill Lucking, Jorge Luke, Claudio Brook, Enrique Lucero, Jorge Russek.
● Surprisingly, this sequel eclipses *A Man Called Horse* in every way. The action resumes six years on, with Lord John Morgan (Harris, as ardently inscrutable as ever) chafing against a lame aristocracy in England. He returns to Dakota and his Yellow Hand Indians, only to find them routed from their sacred burial grounds by unscrupulous trappers and living, physically and spiritually blighted, in the badlands. By painfully rediscovering his own sense of identity, he helps bring about the rebirth of the tribe. The sumptuous locations and seasonal variations skilfully complement this meticulous recreation of the early 19th century Indian lifestyle. Interestingly, the emotional peak comes half way through with the harrowing Sun Vow ritual, which culminates in a cathartic thunderstorm of epic proportions. Thereafter the film shifts into a lower but still effective key. IB

Return of Captain Invincible, The

(1982, Aust, 91 min)
d Philippe Mora. *p* Andrew Gaty. *sc* Steven E De Souza, Andrew Gaty. *ph* Mike Molloy. *ed* John Scott. *pd* David Copping. *m* William Motzing. *cast* Alan Arkin, Christopher Lee, Kate Fitzpatrick, Bill Hunter, Michael Pate, David Argue, John Bluthal, Chelsea Brown, Arthur Dignam, Chris Haywood.
● Years after the McCarthy tribunal questioned his 'premature anti-fascist' good deeds and a suspiciously red cape, Capt Invincible (Arkin), superhero champion of the underdog, is living as a washed-up drunk in Sydney. When crisis calls in the form of his resurrected arch-enemy, Lee's Mr Midnight, and his heinous plans for New York City, he dons the old uniform once more – trouble is, he's just a bit knackered after all that time out of action. The stars are clearly enjoying themselves in this charmingly ramshackle affair, which makes a virtue of its modest resources by integrating clever use of stock footage, cheapo props and cheesy costumes into an affectionate take-off of yesteryear's quickie serials. Adeptly pitched songs by the *Rocky Horror* duo of Richard Hartley and Richard O'Brien add to the entertainment value of a movie that really ought to be remembered more often. TJ

Return of Captain Marvel, The

see Adventures of Captain Marvel, The

Return of Captain Nemo, The

see Amazing Captain Nemo, The

Return of Count Yorga, The

(1971, US, 97 min)
d Bob Kelljan. *p* Michael Macready. *sc* Bob Kelljan, Yvonne Wilder. *ph* Bill Butler. *ed* Fabien Tordjmann, Laurette Odney. *ad* Vince Cresceman. *m* Bill Marx. *cast* Robert Quarry, Mariette Hartley, Roger Perry, Yvonne Wilder, George Macready.
● Witty and suspenseful sequel to *Count Yorga, Vampire*, with Quarry's ruthless, hypnotic, modern-day bloodsucker offing a family in order to lay his fangs into a new bride, only to meet resistance from the girl's fella. Moments of inventively chilling horror. TJ

Return of Doctor X, The

(1939, US, 62 min, b/w)
d Vincent Sherman. *p* Bryan Foy. *sc* Lee Katz. *ph* Sid Hickox. *ed* Thomas Pratt. *ad* Esdras Hartley. *m* Bernhard Kaun. *cast* Wayne Morris, Rosemary Lane, Dennis Morgan, Humphrey Bogart, John Litel, Lya Lys, William Hopper, Huntz Hall.
● A brisk B horror, not so much a sequel to *Dr X* as an imitation of *The Walking Dead*, with Bogart replacing Karloff as the executed man brought back to zombie life, this time with vampiric lusts to boot, by a doctor (Litel) made up to look like Leslie Banks in *The Most Dangerous Game*. Directed with some style by Sherman (his first film), but saddled with the usual lame script and designed too much as a vehicle for the routinely breezy reporter hero (Morris), it's worth watching mainly for Bogart's baleful performance. The best moment is his unsettling first appearance, emerging from the depths of Litel's laboratory, pallid in pince-nez, with a white streak in his hair and a white rabbit in his arms. TM

Return of Dracula, The (aka The Fantastic Disappearing Man)

(1958, US, 77 min)
d Paul Landres. *p* Jules V Levy, Arthur Gardner. *sc* Pat Fielder. *ph* Jack MacKenzie. *ed* Sherman A Rose. *ad* James D Vance. *m* Gerald Fried. *cast* Francis Lederer, Norma Eberhardt, Ray Stricklyn, Jimmie Baird, John Wengraf, Virginia Vincent.
● Little known, apparently (since Carlos Clarens and Les Daniels both ignore it in their key books on the horror genre), but a surprisingly 'deep' piece of schlock, ignoring most of the drive-in requirements of the time and building up a flat, grey, joyless picture of vampire Lederer searching for 'love' in Middle America – and thus the regeneration which only the New World can give his dying 'culture'. Mucho cheapo, and probably for devotees only, but they ought to find it quietly remarkable. CW

Return of Frank James, The

(1940, US, 92 min)
d Fritz Lang. *p* Darryl F Zanuck. *sc* Sam Hellman. *ph* George Barnes, William V Skall. *ed* Walter Thompson. *ad* Wiard B Ihnen, Richard Day. *m* David Buttolph. *cast* Henry Fonda, Gene Tierney, Jackie Cooper, Henry Hull, John Carradine, Donald Meek, J Edward Bromberg.
● Fox's follow-up to *Jesse James* was Lang's first Western and his first film in colour; if it's more conventional than the later *Rancho Notorious*, it nevertheless displays the director's interest in the psychology (and indeed the pitfalls) of revenge. At the start of the film, Frank (Fonda) is happy to let the law pronounce sentence on the Ford brothers, who killed Jesse; but when they are pardoned, he begins a deadly hunt that alienates him from society, imperils not only his own life but those of his friends, and threatens to destroy his long-held ideas of justice. For all its fine photography and sturdy performances, the film is finally little more than efficient and routine, with Lang rarely probing beyond the ironic if superficial twists of the narrative. Though it bears some slight thematic resemblance to the earlier *Fury* and *You Only Live Once*, he's clearly not as comfortable with dusty townships and baked landscapes as with the *noir*-like ambience of his contemporary crime movies. GA

Return of Godzilla

see Gojira 1984

Return of Martin Guerre, The

see Retour de Martin Guerre, Le

Return of Maxwell Smart, The

see Nude Bomb, The

Return of Sabata (E'Tornato Sabata...Hai Chiuso un' Altra Volta)

(1971, It/Fr/WGer, 107 min)
d Frank Kramer [Gianfranco Parolini]. *p* Alberto Grimaldi. *sc* Renato Izzo, Gianfranco Parolini. *ph* Sandro Mancori. *ed* Gianfranco Parolini, Salvatore Aventario. *ad* Luciano Puccini. *m* Marcello Giombini. *cast* Lee Van Cleef, Reiner Schöne, Annabella Incontrera, Gianni Rizzo, Gianpiero Albertini.
● Standard Italian Western starring an invincible Van Cleef, armed with a battery of fancy weapons, up against an over-complicated plot and a cast that shows a lot of teeth in an unsuccessful attempt to cover up some appalling dubbing. As usual, greed and hypocrisy are the themes, and gold is the real reason for a ruthless Irishman's exploitation of the local people. Until Van Cleef rides into town, that is. He recruits his assistants from a travelling circus; lots of sleight-of-hand and acrobatics, therefore, but the rest is routine.

Return of the Big Cat

(1974, US, 70 min)
d Tom Leetch. *p* Ron Miller, James Algar. *sc* Herman Groves. *ph* Frank Phillips. *ed* Ray de Leuw. *ad* John B Mansbridge, Walter Tyler. *m* Buddy Baker, Franklyn Marks. *cast* Jeremy Slate, Pat Crawley, Jeff East, Kim Richards, Christian Juttner, David Wayne.
● In a homestead in the timberland of Northern California, a small girl (Richards) has not spoken since encountering a cougar two years before. Now the mountain lion's back. Amy's two brothers have tamed a wild yellow dog, Boomer, which at the Thanksgiving Day climax sees justice done. A Disney programmer (little seen after its initial release) in which ageless old timers enact an undiluted fundamentalist parable and a graceful big cat is regarded as nothing less than a 'heathen devil'. JPy

Return of the Cisco Kid, The

(1939, US, 70 min, b/w)
d Herbert I Leeds. *p* Kenneth Macgowan. *sc* Milton Sperling. *ph* Charles G Clarke. *ed* James B Clark. *ad* Richard Day. *m* Cyril Mockridge. *cast* Warner Baxter, Lynn Bari, Cesar Romero, Henry Hull, Kane Richmond, C Henry Gordon, Robert Barrat.
● Baxter won an Oscar as the do-gooding bandit the Cisco Kid ten years previously for *In Old Arizona*, and here he's back under the sombrero for a third time, falling for Bari and helping her old dad get back at the swindler who cheated them out of their nest-egg. Pretty creaky, but the public enjoyed it enough to warrant a string of sequels with sidekick Romero assuming the title role. TJ

Return of the Dragon

see Way of the Dragon

Return of the Dragon (Qisha Jie/aka Infernal Street)

(1973, Tai, 93 min)
d Shen Jiang. *p* Huang Ya Pai. *sc* Shen Jiang. *ph* Wang Sun. *ed* Sung Ming. *ad* Ku Yi. *m* Chen Yung Yu. *cast* Yu Tien Lung, Chao Chien, Wang Yen Pin, Miao Tien, Sun Yueh.
● An example of the middle phase martial arts film. No longer attached to the depiction of tournaments, it retains from those earlier films the teenage rebel hero chafing against the restraints of a compromised adult world paying its dues to imperialism. The film is set around an opium rehabilitation clinic (in the early '30s), whose doctors notice a dramatic increase in patients following the opening of a club as an underhand means of paving the way for a Japanese invasion. Yu Tien Lung, looking all of 17, plays the adopted helper at the clinic with exemplary directness, illustrating the concept of the everyman protagonist who can assume heroic dimensions, even – as a kind of gag – invincibility. Formula stuff that runs like clockwork. VG

Return of the Fly

(1959, US, 80 min, b/w)
d Edward Bernds. *p* Bernard Glasser. *sc* Edward Bernds. *ph* Brydon Baker. *ed* Richard C Meyer. *ad* Lyle Wheeler, John Mansbridge. *m* Paul Sawtell, Bert Shefter. *cast* Vincent Price, Brett Halsey, David Frankham, John Sutton, Danielle De Metz.
● Virtually a re-run of the original shocker, with surviving brother Price issuing dire warnings before young master Halsey reassembles his late dad's matter transference equipment and swiftly ends up in the same half-man/half-fly state himself. Passable enough for genre addicts, but watching it straight after the first film probably isn't a good idea. TJ

Return of the Idiot (Návrat Idiota)

(1999, Czech Republic, 100 min)
d Sasa Gedeon. *p* Petr Oukropec. *sc* Sasa Gedeon. *ph* Stepán Kucera. *ed* Petr Turyna. *pd* Petr Fort. *m* Vladimir Godár. *cast* Pavel Liska, Anna Geislerová, Tatiana Vilhelmová, Jirí Langmajer, Jirí Machácek, Zdena Hadrbolcová.
● A faintly sentimental but beautifully observed film inspired by the hero of Dostoevsky's novel, this charts the serio-comic experiences of Dean Stockwell-lookalike Liska, recently released from psychiatric therapy, who visits distant relatives in a small town and finds himself involuntarily immersed in romantic intrigue involving two sisters and two brothers. Starting from an eloquent, wordless opening, the film slowly unravels to reveal a core of emotional confusion and dissatisfaction, while subtly establishing the innocence and unwitting goodness of the protagonist. Immaculately acted and controlled, and a modest but quite lovely gem. GA

Return of the Jedi

(1983, US, 132 min)
d Richard Marquand. *p* Howard G Kazanjian. *sc* Lawrence Kasdan, George Lucas. *ph* Alan Hume. *ed* Sean Barton, Marcia Lucas, Duwayne Dunham. *pd* Norman Reynolds. *m* John Williams. *cast* Mark Hamill, Harrison Ford, Carrie Fisher, Billy Dee Williams, Anthony Daniels, Peter Mayhew, Sebastian Shaw, Frank Oz, Dave Prowse, Alec Guinness, Kenny Baker.
● At the opening of this third instalment of the *Star Wars* saga in the States, an audience rioted, convinced that someone had switched reels on them, so baffled were they by the shifts in the narrative. It is confusing. All the old gang are there, older, wiser and tinnier: Luke Skywalker is looking more like Han Solo, who is looking more like Ben Kenobi; Princess Leia seems almost Queenly; and in the concentration on sub-Muppet gothic, impressive aerial combat effects, and occasional attempts at 'love me, love my monster' humour, it's not surprising that Billy Dee Williams' Lando Calrissian has little chance to re-establish his *Empire Strikes Back* persona in all the toing-and-froing. But try telling that to the kids and the parents who have come, not to riot, but to wonder. To wonder at the teddy-bear tribes, the monstrous Tenniel-style Jabba the Hutt, and the way in which heroes and heroines can fall off high-speed motorbikes without a stain on their 25th century jockstraps. The rest of us might be wondering if it isn't about time George Lucas tried his hand at universes new. SGr

Return of the Jedi: Special Edition

(1983/1997, US, 132 min)
d Richard Marquand. *p* Howard G Kazanjian. *sc* Lawrence Kasdan, George Lucas. *ph* Alan Hum. *ed* Sean Barton, Marcia Lucas, Duwayne Dunham. *pd* Norman Reynolds. *m* John Williams. *cast* Mark Hamill, Harrison Ford, Carrie Fisher, Billy Dee Williams, Anthony Daniels, Peter Mayhew, Sebastian Shaw, Frank Oz, Dave Prowse, Alec Guinness, Kenny Baker.
● This reissue accentuates the film's disengaged, almost perfunctory air. Tonal continuity isn't at fault. Director Marquand surrendered most of his post-production responsibilities to executive producer George Lucas, so the result isn't exactly idiosyncratic. It's just that in scope and ambition, *Jedi* resembles nothing so much as the next level of a computer game, with a new environment, new gadgets and new creatures. The first hour is deathly slow, a problem the 'Special Edition' compounds by inserting new footage into the singing-and-dancing scenes at Jabba's palace, where Leia, Lando and the droids have gone to rescue the carbon-frozen Han. Things liven up once Luke, having reached the peak of his Jedi powers, tries to coax his father, Darth Vader, from the dark side of the Force. Their subsequent confrontation, culminating in the removal of Vader's mask, is the film's strongest moment. Most people's biggest *Jedi* gripe can be summed up in one word: Ewoks. Do you think they're cute lickle lifesavers? Or do you, like me, simply wonder what they taste like barbecued? The debate will run and run. JO'C

Return of the Living Dead, The

(1984, US, 91 min)
d Dan O'Bannon. *p* Tom Fox. *sc* Dan O'Bannon. *ph* Jules Brenner. *ed* Robert Gordon. *pd* William Stout. *m* Matt Clifford. *cast* Clu Gulager, James Karen, Don Calfa, Thom Mathews, Beverly Randolph, John Philbin, Jewel Shepard.
● Any film which features a dead, bald and very hungry punk lurching towards the camera screaming '*More Brains!*' gets my vote. Directed by O'Bannon courtesy of George Romero, this is an energetic cross-referencing of genre: not just a horror movie, but a comic apocalyptic zombie horror movie. O'Bannon has his cake, eats it, and then throws it up in the face of the audience. Warehousemen unwittingly release a zombie interred by the CIA (of course) along with a nifty gas which ensures that local graveyards are bursting at the seams with brain-peckish corpses. Most of the film froths and bubbles merrily: there is a deeply artistic sequence where a punkette dances naked on a tombstone before being transformed into a zombie, and another moving bit where para-meds get their heads munched. Finally, however, O'Bannon runs short on the bad taste gags. Matters conclude, anti-climactically, with the death of civilised life as we know it. RR

Return of the Living Dead Part II

(1987, US, 89 min)
d Ken Wiederhorn. *p* Tom Fox. *sc* Ken Wiederhorn. *ph* Robert Elswit. *ed* Charles Bornstein. *ad* Dale Allan Pelton. *m* J Peter Robinson, Vladimir Horunzhy. *cast* James Karen, Thom Mathews, Dana Ashbrook, Marsha Dietlein, Suzanne Snyder, Philip Bruns, Michael Kenworthy.
● Not even a nuclear explosion, it seems, can prevent a sequel to a tongue-in-cheek zombie pic. A surviving canister of zombiefying fumes rolls off an army truck and is punctured by a pair of teenage meatheads, once again releasing a weird fog that revives the occupants of an adjacent graveyard. The rest is a virtual re-run, with 12-year-old Jesse (Kenworthy), his older sister Lucy (Dietlein), and handsome cable TV-installer Tom (Ashbrook) enjoying such edifying experiences as a bunch of zombies turning a pet shop into a brain emporium. Karen and Mathews, heroes of Part I, are also resurrected for guest appearances as a pair of grave-robbers; fortunately they get theirs early on. Unlike O'Bannon's film, this is merely repetitive and dull, the tedium relieved only by the graphic brain-eating and Philip Bruns' deliciously OTT performance as the mad Doctor Mandel. NF

Return of the Living Dead III

(1993, US, 97 min)
d Brian Yuzna. *p* Gary Schmoeller, Brian Yuzna. *sc* John Penney. *ph* Gerry Lively. *ed* Chris Roth. *pd* Anthony Tremblay. *m* Barry Goldberg. *cast* J Trevor Edmond, Mindy Clarke, Kent McCord, Sarah Douglas, Mike Moroff, Sal Lopez.
● Retaining the jokiness of Dan O'Bannon's original, and a marked improvement on Ken Weiderhorn's lame sequel, Yuzna gets back to basics with a mutated Romeo and Juliet storyline, an anti-military theme, some fetishistic zombie make-up, and a surprisingly bleak ending. Unable to cope with the death of new girlfriend Julie (Clarke), army brat Kurt (Edmond) employs the experimental methods developed by his scientist father for use on captive zombies to bring her back from the dead. Yuzna and fx maestro Steve Johnson put human flesh on the plot's bare bones, without ever losing sight of the central offbeat romance. NF

Return of the Magnificent Seven

see Return of the Seven

Return of the Musketeers, The

(1989, GB/Fr/Sp, 101 min)
d Richard Lester. *p* Pierre Spengler. *sc* George MacDonald Fraser. *ph* Bernard Lutic. *ed* John Victor Smith. *pd* Gil Parrondo. *m* Jean-Claude Petit. *cast* Michael York, Oliver Reed, Frank Finlay, C Thomas Howell, Kim Cattrall, Geraldine Chaplin, Roy Kinnear, Christopher Lee, Philippe Noiret, Richard Chamberlain, Eusebio Lazaro, Alan Howard, Bill Paterson, Jean-Pierre Cassel.
● Those boisterous idealists are back behind the reins, and despite the prolonged rest since the last in Lester's series of Dumas adaptations, they're looking pretty saddle-sore. Twenty years on, after a parting of ways, the musketeers are reunited – following initial skirmishes which divide loyalties – by France's Queen Anne (Chaplin) in a bid to save King Charles (Paterson) from the chop. Laying siege to their plan is the avenging Justine (Cattrall), daughter of their old enemy Milady. Howell acquits himself well enough as the bookish adopted son of Athos (Reed), while old troopers York, Finlay, Chamberlain and Kinnear (his last performance) coast lazily through their roles. The most glaring weakness lies in the needless complexity of the action, which at times threatens to overwhelm what little coherence exists as subplots tumble into each other until a speedy resolution in the final frames. Only undemanding fans of preceding instalments will find something to enjoy. CM

Return of the Pink Panther, The

(1974, GB, 113 min)
d/p Blake Edwards. *sc* Frank Waldman, Blake Edwards. *ph* Geoffrey Unsworth. *ed* Tom Priestley. *pd* Peter Mullins. *m* Henry Mancini. *cast* Peter Sellers, Christopher Plummer, Catherine Schell, Herbert Lom, Peter Arne, Peter Jeffrey, Grégoire Aslan, David Lodge, Graham Stark, Eric Pohlmann, Burt Kwouk, Victor Spinetti, John Bluthal, Peter Jones.
● Fourth in the series, promisingly reuniting Edwards and Sellers with their respective careers not exactly buoyant since *A Shot in the Dark* ten years earlier, *The Return of the Pink Panther* delivers a good deal of that promise, from Richard Williams' ultra-ritzy animated credits to the four or five brilliantly timed set pieces of Clouseau-engineered mayhem. Things are shakier whenever Sellers is off-screen, and especially whenever Plummer's debonair jewel thief is on; and the movie wastes time on its jet-set locations, has too many British character actors in unfunny bit parts, and cries out for a devastating finale which never comes. But the occasional misfires, with the verbal gags rarely as inspired as the visual ones, are forgiveable in the context of Clouseau's running battles with swimming pools, a vacuum cleaner, false moustaches, gear levers that come away in the hand, and his oriental factotum-cum-sparring partner. TR

Return of the Secaucus Seven

(1979, US, 110 min)
d John Sayles. *p* Jeffrey Nelson, William Aydelott. *sc* John Sayles. *ph* Austin de Besche. *ed* John Sayles. *m* Guy Van Duser, Bill Staines, Timothy Jackson, Mason Daring. *cast* Bruce MacDonald, Adam Lefevre, Gordon Clapp, Karen Trott, David Strathaim, Maggie Renzi, Maggie Cousineau, Jean Passanante, Mark Arnott, John Sayles, Amy Schewel.
● A motley group of '60s survivors reunite ten years on in a New Hampshire cottage to mull over the implications of reaching thirty – shuffling counter-culture nostalgia and fragmenting future perspectives between themselves during a weekend of low-key stocktaking, love-making and laughter. Sayles' fascinating debut as a writer/director, produced independently on the modest earnings from his witty genre screenplays for Roger Corman, returns him to the naturalistically observed world and characters of his fiction. Intelligently applying the virtues of necessity, Sayles concentrates on dialogue and editing to construct a spider's web of intricate personal

politics and emotions, and a warm, unmannered comedy of character and connections. No amens, no emblems, and no excess; just a variant on Alain Tanner's *Jonah Who Will Be 25 in the Year 2000* which laughs with its 'greened' Americans rather than at them. PT

Return of the Seven (aka Return of the Magnificent Seven)

(1966, US, 96 min)
d Burt Kennedy. *p* Ted Richmond. *sc* Larry Cohen. *ph* Paul Vogel. *ed* Bert Bates. *ad* José Alguero. *m* Elmer Bernstein. *cast* Yul Brynner, Robert Fuller, Julian Mateos, Warren Oates, Jordan Christopher, Claude Atkins.
●Actually, only Brynner returns for this okay-ish sequel in which the requisite number of gunslinging types, among them a pre-Peckinpah Warren Oates, saves another Mexican village, though this time Larry Cohen's script has the unfortunate peasants toiling under the yoke of a crazed visionary. Bubblegum stuff. TJ

Return of the Soldier, The

(1982, GB, 102 min)
d Alan Bridges. *p* Ann Skinner, Simon Relph. *sc* Hugh Whitemore. *ph* Stephen Goldblatt. *ed* Laurence Mery Clark. *pd* Luciana Arrighi. *m* Richard Rodney Bennett. *cast* Alan Bates, Ann-Margret, Glenda Jackson, Julie Christie, Jeremy Kemp, Edward De Souza, Frank Finlay, Jack May, Ian Holm.
●Coming home. Ulysses, Napoleon, Travis Bickle, they all suffered from the same problem of returning from the wars to a prosaic home life, which is not quite the place they left behind them. In this adaptation of Rebecca West's novel, Bates returns from the First World War, his mind in ruins, to a starchy wife (Christie), an adoring female cousin (Ann-Margret), and his modest Palladian pile. After the trenches, what he now faces is the pain of an arid marriage and the weight of the past, so he opts for an old and dowdy flame (Jackson) and leaves the trick cyclist (Holm) to sort out the *ménage à quatre*. It's a glossy, respectful costume drama about the upper class habit of strangling the heart, but over it all hovers that certain, unmistakable air of irrelevance. Now, if it had been a soldier returning from Ulster, that would have been something. CPea

Return of the Swamp Thing, The

(1989, US, 87 min)
d Jim Wynorski. *p* Benjamin Melniker, Michael Uslan. *sc* Derek Spencer, Grant Morris. *ph* Zoran Hochstatter. *ed* Leslie Rosenthal. *pd* Robb Wilson-King. *m* Chuck Cirino. *cast* Louis Jourdan, Heather Locklear, Sarah Douglas, Dick Durock, Joey Sagal, Ace Mask, Chris Doyle.
●Having accidentally created his own arch-enemy in Wes Craven's 1982 *Swamp Thing*, Dr Arcane (Jourdan) is now perfecting an immortality serum, in which his late wife's rare blood group was to be a vital ingredient. Enter estranged daughter Abigail (Locklear), full of questions about mother, and, more importantly, full of the requisite red stuff. Soon the only thing standing between dad and daughter's main artery is the vegetating form of Dr Alec Holland (Durock), victim of a 'bio-restorative' chemical accident which turned his body into Hampstead Heath on legs. 'You're a plant, aren't you?' Abigail observes astutely as she's whisked to safety by the he-man hedgerow, with whom she soon falls in love. Apprenticed under Corman, Wynorski is well-versed in double-bluffing his audience, denying them the chance of balking at dreadful special effects by implying that the ineptitude is deliberate. He opts for cheap nostalgic laughs and camp '50s sci-fi scenery; depending on whether you find this funny, you'll either smile knowingly or gasp in disbelief. MK

Return of the Vampire, The

(1943, US, 69 min, b/w)
d Lew Landers. *p* Sam White. *sc* Griffin Jay. *ph* John Stumar, L William O'Connell. *ed* Paul Borofsky. *ad* Lionel Banks. *m* Mario Castelnuovo-Tedesco. *cast* Bela Lugosi, Nina Foch, Frieda Inescort, Matt Willis, Gilbert Emery, Miles Mander, Roland Varno.
●Verbose but appealingly tatty little horror movie which is given a facelift by excellent performances (Foch did well enough in this debut to earn a starring role as the splendidly lycanthropic gypsy queen in *Cry of the Werewolf*). Dracula (Lugosi in his first genuine vampire role since the original *Dracula*), now known as Armand Tesla since Columbia had filched him from Universal, is unearthed by a bomb during the London blitz, and goes about his usual depredations with the aid of a werewolf (Willis) whose presence was obviously inspired by *Frankenstein Meets the Wolf Man*. Soon after, monster rallies assembling all the old favourites became two a penny as the ailing horror genre went into almost terminal decline. MA

Return to Me

(2000, US, 116 min)
d Bonnie Hunt. *p* Jennie Lew Tugend. *sc* Bonnie Hunt, Don Lake. *ph* Laszlo Kovacs. *ed* Garth Craven. *pd* Brent Thomas. *m* Nicholas Pike. *cast* David Duchovny, Minnie Driver, Carroll O'Connor, Robert Loggia, Bonnie Hunt, David Alan Grier, Joely Richardson, Eddie Jones, James Belushi.
●Driver needs a new heart; building supervisor Duchovny is happily married to zoologist Richardson; signpost – Joely's got the 'marked for death' role. A car crash later, and guess who's going to benefit from a heart transplant and new romance. Hollywood gush in the classic mould it is too, though this semi-charming romantic comedy plays like it was the most natural thing in the world, an approach which happens to be the movie's strength and weakness. It's pleasing to see a movie rolling out its central idea so straightforwardly, avoiding Nora Ephron-ish superslick one-liners, and allowing Duchovny and Driver to do what they do best. Writer/director Bonnie Hunt performs onscreen heroics in the wise best-friend role, all the while sharing house with amiable spouse Belushi in a warmly convincing sketch of messy but true two-point-four child domesticity. We like them, we're rooting for Dave 'n' Minnie, we'll even forgive the thick Oirish ham served by her old dad O'Connor, but it's all because we're waiting for a triple-hankie surrender which, regrettably, never fully materialises. TJ

Return to Never Land

(2000, US/Can/Aust, 72 min)
d Robin Budd. *p* Christopher Chase, Michelle Robinson, Dan Rounds. *sc* Temple Mathews. *ed* Anthony F Rocco, Daniel Lee. *pd* John Kleber. *m* Joel McNeely. *cast* voices: Harriet Owen, Blayne Weaver, Corey Burton, Jeff Bennett, Kath Soucie, Andrew McDonough, Roger Rees.
●Disney has been churning out sequels to its recent animated hits for a while and quietly releasing them straight to video. Now the studio has started plundering the classics, and this *Peter Pan* retread is the first to reach cinema screens. Hardly an act of sacrilege, but still a pale shadow of the original, it's the story of Wendy's 12-year-old daughter Jane, who grew up too fast during the Blitz and consequently could use a revivifying spell in Never Land. Capt Hook duly kidnaps her to lure Pan out of hiding. Unsurprisingly, this ploy doesn't work. Though the graphic style stays true to the original, the storytelling lacks colour and vibrancy. Pan himself isn't so much fun second time round, and Jane's conversion to the lost boys' cause is disappointingly perfunctory. TCh

Return to Oz

(1985, US, 109 min)
d Walter Murch. *p* Paul Maslansky. *sc* Walter Murch, Gill Dennis. *ph* David Watkin. *ed* Leslie Hodgson. *ad* Charles Bishop. *m* David Shire. *cast* Nicol Williamson, Jean Marsh, Fairuza Balk, Piper Laurie, Matt Clark, Michael Sundin, Tim Rose.
●Dorothy (Balk) slips back into the dreamworld of Oz, where she finds a crumbling Yellow Brick Road and Oz itself deserted and desolate. In restoring order, she has to contend with the likes of the Nome King (Williamson), part-human, part-avalanche, and Princess Mombi (Marsh), a decapitation hobbyist with her eye on Dorothy's Christmas pudding of a head. Despite the presence of Billina the talking hen, the emphasis on insecurity and peril harks back to the treat-'em-rough days of children's fiction, and the disturbing/comforting ratio tilts conclusively towards the former. Some startling visuals (Will Vinton's Clay-mation effects) and streaks of gruesome whimsy will perhaps be best appreciated by grown-up sensibilities. BBa

Return to Paradise

(1998, US, 112 min)
d Joseph Ruben. *p* Alain Bernheim, Steve Golin. *sc* Wesley Strick, Bruce Robinson. *ph* Reynaldo Villalobos. *ed* Andrew Mondshein, Craig McKay. *pd* Bill Groom. *m* Mark Mancina. *cast* Vince Vaughn, Anne Heche, Joaquin Phoenix, David Conrad, Jada Pinkett Smith, Vera Farmiga, Nick Sandow.
●This remake of the 1990 French film *Force Majeure* has one notable dramatic bombshell. Picking up three college grads having a ball in Malaysia, the film dispassionately observes them as unself-consciously ugly Americans screwing and smoking their way through a Third World 'paradise'. Two years on, we're forced to reassess the trio's 'innocent' hijinks. A lawyer, Beth (Heche), tracks down first Sheriff (Vaughn), then Tony (Conrad). Breaking to them that she represents their old pal Lewis (Phoenix), she chills them with the news that, unbeknown to them, he was imprisoned by the Malay authorities the morning they left for home – for possessing drugs they all three shared. He's sentenced to hang in a week, unless his friends return to accept their share of the punishment. It's a painful prospect, to be sure, and Sheriff, in particular, insists he's no hero, but the next hour or so of handwringing conjures little suspense. TCh

Return to the Blue Lagoon

(1991, US, 98 min)
d/p William A Graham. *sc* Leslie Stevens. *ph* Robert Steadman. *ed* Ronald J Fagan. *pd* Jon Dowding. *m* Basil Poledouris. *cast* Milla Jovovich, Brian Krause, Lisa Pelikan, Courtney Phillips, Garette Patrick Ratliff.
●Having touched a voyeuristic nerve with *The Blue Lagoon*, H de Vere Stacpoole promptly banged out a few follow-ups, one of which (*The Garden of God*) inspired this movie sequel in which the infant son of the deceased couple from *The Blue Lagoon* is castaway along with a girl child whose mother (Pelikan) dies of pneumonia after raising both kids to puberty. This spectacularly contrived plot allows director Graham to put his strapping stars (Krause and Jovovich) through their pubescent paces while simply re-running the sexy set pieces for which Randal Kleiser's tacky 1980 movie was famed. Things begin boldly, with bloody evidence of menstruation and talk of masturbation and copulation; but when mating time arrives, the pair merely snog, simper, fall writhing to the ground, then proceed to an impromptu wedding ceremony, perpetuating the myth that babies come from marriage. Like a sex education film made by semi-liberated nuns, the movie keeps its sticky truths hidden beneath a veneer of leering cleanliness. MK

Return to the Edge of the World

see Edge of the World, The

Reuben, Reuben

(1982, US, 101 min)
d Robert Ellis Miller. *p* Walter Shenson. *sc* Julius J Epstein. *ph* Peter Stein. *ed* Skip Lusk. *pd* Peter Larkin. *m* Billy Goldenberg. *cast* Tom Conti, Kelly McGillis, Roberts Blossom, Cynthia Harris, E Katherine Kerr, Joel Fabiani, Lois Smith.
●With his crumpled tweed suit and his apparently irresistible Highland brogue, writer Gowan McGland is soon worming his way into the pants of neighbourhood New England wives while mourning the expiry of his muse. Since the stuff he wrote when he was on top form sounds like Patience Strong in especially lyrical vein, this might not be too much of a blow. Nevertheless, McGland/Conti is a worried man, and well he might be as he has to try to straddle a plot cannibalised out of a Peter DeVries novel and an unrelated Broadway play, which threatens constantly to come apart at the seams. Director Miller seems quite unable to decide whether he's making a portrait of maudlin self-absorption or an eccentric-on-the-loose comedy, and has a habit of turning glutinous whenever the cracks start to appear. Conti is impressively dissolute, and turns on the charm with great gusto, but against odds like these all he can do is go down fighting. JP.

Reunion (L'Ami retrouvé)

(1989, Fr/WGer/GB, 110 min)
d Jerry Schatzberg. *p* Anne François. *sc* Harold Pinter. *ph* Bruno de Keyzer. *ed* Martine Barraque. *pd* Alexandre Trauner. *m* Philippe Sarde. *cast* Jason Robards, Christian Anholt, Samuel West, Françoise Fabian, Maureen Kerwin, Barbara Jefford.
●This moving rendition of Fred Uhlman's novel, about boyhood friendship betrayed under the destructive momentum of Nazism, shows Schatzberg at his (albeit limited) best. Jewish New York lawyer Henry Strauss (Robards) revisits Stuttgart to claim the remaining effects of the family he left in 1933. Cue a flashback to the body of the film: his time at the elite Gymnasium and his deep but never easy friendship with a fellow outsider, the aristocratic Konradin. The film is dominated by remembrance: the tricks it plays, the pain it involves. Schatzberg encourages his young actors – Anholt as the adolescent 'Hans', West as Konradin – to personalise, and thus to universalise – their relationship. It's a staple situation, but their sharing (Konradin proudly showing a coin collection in his grand house on the hill; Hans introducing his politically naive parents; the soon-to-be-shattered idyll of trips to the Black Forest) speaks volumes of cumulative small truths. Harold Pinter's tight and unobtrusive script, Trauner's fine production design and Philippe Sarde's muted but expressive score ensure a feeling of all-round professionalism. WH

Revelation

(2001, GB, 111 min)
d Stuart Urban. *p* Jonathan Woolf, Stuart Urban. *sc* Stuart Urban. *ph* Sam McCurdy. *ed* Julian Rodd. *pd* James Merifield. *cast* Terence Stamp, James D'Arcy, Natasha Wightman, Liam Cunningham, Heathcote Williams, Derek Jacobi, Celia Imrie, Ron Moody, Udo Kier, Charlotte Weston, Vernon Dobtcheff.
●Billionaire industrialist Magnus Martel (Stamp) has devoted his life to tracking down the Loculus, a knick-knack of enormous historical importance and power. When he hears it's been found in the Middle East, he sends estranged son Jake (D'Arcy) and alchemy student Mira (Wightman) to retrieve it. But a murderous secret society led by a satanic immortal (Kier) have other ideas. Writer/director Urban makes the fatal mistake of playing the whole thing relentlessly straight; Kier should have told him the only way to make drivel like this bearable is to camp it up. It's painful to see Stamp, Jacobi and Moody reduced to mouthing such inane dialogue; and as Jake's mother, Imrie has perhaps the most undignified death scene in recent movie history. NY

Revenge

(1989, US, 124 min)
d Tony Scott. *p* Hunt Lowry, Stanley Rubin. *sc* Jim Harrison, Jeffrey Fiskin. *ph* Jeffrey Kimball. *ed* Chris Lebenzon. *pd* Michael Seymour, Benjamin Fernandez. *m* Jack Nitzsche. *cast* Kevin Costner, Anthony Quinn, Madeline Stowe, Tomas Milian, Sally Kirkland.
●Recently retired fighter pilot Cochran (Costner) enjoys an idyllic break at the Mexican ranch of old friend and tennis partner Tibey Mendez (Quinn). Despite a sense of loyalty and hints of Tibey's ruthlessness, Cochran becomes involved in a passionate affair with his beautiful wife Miryea (Stowe). When their treachery is discovered, Tibey's revenge is cold, calculated and vicious; but Cochran survives to even the score...Scott manages the shift from tremulous romance to violent retribution very well, but his efficient handling of some surprisingly tough action scenes is compromised by a surfeit of pop promo clichés: billowing net curtains, clouds of fluttering doves, an excessive use of coloured filters. What emotional intensity there is therefore derives from the two central performances. Always comfortable as a romantic lead, Costner here displays a more menacing side, his obsession laced with a dangerously uncontrolled violence; and his conviction is matched by Quinn's formidable portrayal of the autocratic Mendez. With more dramatic depth and less visual flash, this might have captured some of the poetic fatalism of Jim Harrison's original novella. NF

Revenge (aka Inn of the Frightened People)

(1971, GB, 89 min)
d Sidney Hayers. *p* George H Brown. *sc* Jack Kruse. *ph* Ken Hodges. *ed* Tony Palk. *ad* Lionel Couch. *m* Eric Rogers. *cast* Joan Collins, James Booth, Ray Barrett, Sinead Cusack, Tom Marshall, Kenneth Griffith, Zuleika Robson, Donald Morley, Patrick McAlinney.
●A barnstorming melodrama in which two grieving fathers (Booth and Barrett) kidnap the slimy recluse (Griffith) they suspect of being the rapist who murdered their pre-teen daughters. Having beaten him up somewhat over-enthusiastically, they stash the corpse in the cellar of Booth's pub pending disposal, only to find that he is still alive and an acute embarrassment, since they dare neither let him go nor despatch him in cold blood. Cue for some wild loony tunes as everybody concerned gets hysterically caught up in rape and violence. 'I don't know what's come over us' says Booth's wife (Collins), as she eagerly submits to sexual assault by her stepson. Done with deadly solemnity and a truly atrocious script (the characters are forever asking each other if they're all right, suggesting nice cups of tea, and saying 'I'll think of something' as the problems escalate), it's almost as hilarious as a Joe Orton farce. Poor Sidney Hayers can do nothing but go along for the ride. TM

Revenge in El Paso

see Quattro dell'Ave Maria, I

Revenge of Frankenstein, The

(1958, GB, 89 min)
d Terence Fisher. *p* Anthony Hinds. *sc* Jimmy Sangster. *ph* Jack Asher. *ed* James Needs, Alfred Cox. *pd* Bernard Robinson. *m* Leonard Salzedo. *cast* Peter Cushing, Michael Gwynn, Francis Matthews, Eunice Gayson, John Welsh, George Woodbridge, Lionel Jeffries, Oscar Quitak, Richard Wordsworth, Michael Ripper.
●A strange, blackly comic reworking of the Frankenstein myth, which was Fisher and Hammer's follow-up to their initial *The Curse of Frankenstein* of 1956. In one of his best performances, Cushing plays on the ambiguity of the central character, so that the Baron becomes a kind of Wildean martyr, alternating between noble defiance and detached cruelty. Much of the action is set in a poor hospital reminiscent of *The Marat/Sade*, and there is an extraordinary climax which irresistibly suggests the forces of chaos erupting into a repressive community as a monstrously deformed experimental subject crashes through a window into a smart society ball. DP

Revenge of the Creature

(1955, US, 82 min, b/w)
d Jack Arnold. *p* William Alland. *sc* Martin Berkeley. *ph* Charles S Welbourne. *ed* Paul Weatherwax. *ad* Alexander Golitzen, Alfred Sweeney. *m* Herman Stein. *cast* John Agar, Lori Nelson, John Bromfield, Nestor Paiva, Grandon Rhodes, Robert B Williams, Ricou Browning, Clint Eastwood.
●The official sequel to *The Creature from the Black Lagoon*, also shot in 3-D, this is a quirky fusion of subterranean imagery and social anxiety which has weathered as well as its predecessor. Here the Amazon gill-man is captured by a research team and taken to a huge tank in Marineland, Florida, from which it eventually escapes. Far from being a monster, it emerges as a strange, beautiful alien which the humans torment with crude behavioural experiments. The story of captivity and the creature's gradual reassertion of its identity is arresting enough, but in a flash of unconscious insight, the film also throws up a link between the creature's otherness and the identity confusion of the heroine. This is not just a question of beauty-and-the-beast sexual suggestion (though there's plenty of that). The two keep staring at each other through the glass tank as she begins to express doubts about abandoning science for motherhood; although fleeting, this notion of creature and woman as strangers in a male colony is something you won't find in *King Kong*. If the monster hunt at the end proves a little disappointing, it's only because, unlike so much of the rest, it has become familiar through imitation. DP

Revenge of the Dead

see Night of the Ghouls

Revenge of the Dead

(1975, US, 87 min)
d Evan Lee. *p* Ray Atherton. *sc* Keith Burns, Ray Atherton. *ph* Guerdon Trueblood. *ed* Miklós Gyulai. *m* Joe Azarello, Ed Scannell, Gary Ray, Steve Singer, Jay Stewart. *cast* Larry Justin, J Arthur Craig, James Habif, Robert Clark, Doug Senior, Christopher Lee.
●This wreck could best be summarised as a really bad episode of *Night Gallery*, endlessly protracted. The makers appear to have dabbled in cinema in much the same way that their characters dabble in the occult: ineptly, and with horrendous results. Christopher Lee has been enlisted to give a pre-credits pep talk, but surely he couldn't have seen what follows: a cut-rate catalogue of amateur acting, botched continuity, mismatched footage, and all-embracing incompetence. Purporting to portray a paralysis victim's psychically-conjured monster, the filmmakers feel obliged to spike the mess with derivative, adolescent 'humour' and a dose of prurient sex. Not even the aesthetic of trash could be used to defend this saddening spectacle. PT

Revenge of the Nerds

(1984, US, 90 min)
d Jeff Kanew. *p* Ted Field, Peter Samuelson. *sc* Steve Zacharias, Jeff Buhai. *ph* King Baggot. *ed* Alan Balsam. *pd* James Schoppe. *m* Thomas Newman. *cast* Robert Carradine, Anthony Edwards, Tim Busfield, Andrew Cassese, Curtis Armstrong, Julie Montgomery.
●Of all movie genres, the Yankee hi-jinks college comedy, populated by nauseating stereotypes (the hunky super-bonker sportsman, the outrageous but loveable slob, the token black man with riddim, girls with huge busty substances) is surely one of the most expendable. Kanew's film takes a timely hatchet to them all, with a bunch of nerds, fed up with being dumped on by the star fraternity, deciding on all-out confrontation to seek retribution. The resulting mêlée occasionally degenerates to utter filth (the belching contest has to be heard to be believed), but most of the time is a fine balance of send-up and superior slapstick. The only worthy successor to *Animal House*. DPe

Revenge of the Pink Panther

(1978, GB, 100 min)
d/p Blake Edwards. *sc* Frank Waldman, Ron Clark, Blake Edwards. *ph* Ernest Day. *ed* Alan Jones. *pd* Peter Mullins. *m* Henry Mancini. *cast* Peter Sellers, Herbert Lom, Dyan Cannon, Robert Webber, Burt Kwouk, Paul Stewart, Robert Loggia, Graham Stark, Alfie Bass.
●The best things about the previous two Clouseau movies were brilliantly orchestrated set pieces of Clouseau's mechanical incompetence, and Herbert Lom's psychotic Chief Inspector Dreyfus. In this, the sixth in the series, Edwards forsakes these two strengths almost completely in favour of a flurry of lame racial jokes (inscrutable Chinese, Italian mafiosi, that outrageous French accent), and a plot which has Clouseau involved with the French connection, resorting to a string of strictly one-joke disguises. The part of the Chinese manservant Cato (Kwouk) is built up to little effect, and Dyan Cannon is mostly wasted. The laughs come, but they're pretty hollow. RM

Revenge of the Vampire

see Maschera del Demonio, La

Revengers, The

(1972, US/Mex, 112 min)
d Daniel Mann. *p* Martin Rackin. *sc* Wendell Mayes. *ph* Gabriel Torres. *ed* Walter Hannemann, Juan José Marino. *ad* Jorge Fernandez. *m* Pino Calvi. *cast* William Holden, Ernest Borgnine, Woody Strode, Susan Hayward, Roger Hanin, Jorge Luke, Warren Vanders.
●Respectable rancher (Holden) hires six convicts from a Mexican chain gang to help track down the renegade white man (Vanders) who led the raiding party of Indians which massacred his family. The body of the story concerns the highly dubious relationship between the rancher, who is rapidly becoming corruptible, and the ex-cons, expressing varying degrees of corruption, integrity and loyalty. All of which culminates in a morally-charged confrontation with the comanchero; but relying heavily on (useless) action for want

of ideas, it's mainly a matter of guys galloping through forests, over mountains, and through blizzards to the point of exhausting boredom. JPi

Reversal of Fortune

(1990, US, 111 min)
d Barbet Schroeder. *p* Oliver Stone, Edward R Pressman. *sc* Nicholas Kazan. *ph* Luciano Tovoli. *ed* Lee Percy. *pd* Mel Bourne. *m* Mark Isham. *cast* Glenn Close, Jeremy Irons, Ron Silver, Annabella Sciorra, Uta Hagen, Fisher Stevens, Jack Gilpin, Christine Baranski.

●Claus von Bülow's trial in 1982 for the attempted murder of his wealthy wife Sunny had it all: sex, drugs, nobility and betrayal. She had lapsed into an irreversible coma and her husband was found guilty; but an appeal, in which his case was handled by Alan Dershowitz (from whose book the film is adapted), led to acquittal. *Reversal of Fortune* intersperses flashbacks of the von Bülow marriage with a reconstruction of legal investigations for the second trial. Under Schroeder's direction, the social comparisons are by no means subtle; and a detached approach to characterisation is most acute in the case of comatose Sunny (Close) – 'brain dead, body never better' – whose disembodied voice provides commentary. That said, the performances from Irons (as von Bülow) and Silver (Dershowitz) hit the right pitch within a rather difficult scenario. But this is a strange, unsatisfactory mixture of satire and docudrama which engages the mind and leaves the emotions intact. CM

Revolt of Mamie Stover, The

(1956, US, 93 min)
d Raoul Walsh. *p* Buddy Adler. *sc* Sydney Boehm. *ph* Leo Tover. *ed* Louis Loeffler. *ad* Lyle Wheeler, Mark-Lee Kirk. *m* Hugo Friedhofer. *cast* Jane Russell, Richard Egan, Joan Leslie, Agnes Moorehead, Jorja Curtright, Jean Willes.

●William Bradford Huie's novel about the production-line life of a Honolulu prostitute came to the screen (adapted by Sidney Boehm) virtually unrecognisable thanks to the good offices of the Production Code. Here the emphasis is on Russell's romantic travails as a dance hall 'hostess' and her ill-starred relationship with wealthy writer Egan, though Agnes Moorehead does inject a sliver of hard reality as the madam who runs the joint. The star looks good in CinemaScope and Technicolor, but as a movie it rarely convinces. TJ

Revolution

(1985, GB, 125 min)
d Hugh Hudson. *p* Irwin Winkler. *sc* Robert Dillon. *ph* Bernard Lutic. *ed* Stuart Baird. *pd* Assheton Gorton. *m* John Corigliano. *cast* Al Pacino, Donald Sutherland, Nastassja Kinski, Joan Plowright, Dave King, Steven Berkoff, John Wells, Annie Lennox, Richard O'Brien.

●An almost inconceivable disaster which tries for a worm's eye view of the American Revolution, the worm in question being Pacino as a son of the good earth who is pushed into the fight by the taunts of Kinski and motivated by the sadism of British sergeant Sutherland. Maybe the original script had a shape and a grasp of events. If so, it has gone. There has clearly been drastic cutting, and nothing is left but a cortege of fragments and mismatched cuts. It's also the first 70 mm movie that looks as if it was shot hand-held on 16 mm and blown up for the big screen. Director? I didn't catch the credit. Was there one? TR.

Revolutionary, The

(1970, US, 101 min)
d Paul Williams. *p* Edward R Pressman. *sc* Hans Koningsberger. *ph* Brian Probyn. *ed* Henry Richardson. *pd* Disley Jones. *m* Michael Small. *cast* Jon Voight, Jennifer Salt, Seymour Cassel, Robert Duvall, Collin Wilcox-Horne, Lionel Murton.

●Adapted from Hans Koningsberger's novel, this is the classic story of a youth (Voight, excellent) seeking change but unsure how to bring it about, set within the context of revolutionary politics in a seedy and deliberately anonymous London that might be taken as any major city. Paul Williams' film is a masterful piece of social observation. Although the issues raised by *The Revolutionary* are the age-old ones of means-versus-ends, it achieves a certain integrity by its determinedly low-key approach to its subject. PH

Revolving Doors, The (Les Portes tournantes)

(1988, Can/Fr, 102 min)
d Francis Mankiewicz. *p* René Malo, Francyne Morin. *sc* Jacques Savoie, Francis Mankiewicz. *ph* Támas Vamos. *ed* André Corriveau. *pd* Anne Pritchard. *m* François Dompierre. *cast* Monique Spaziani, Gabriel Arcand, Miou-Miou, François Méthé, Jacques Penot.

●From New York, sensitive Quebecoise Celeste (Spaziani) sends her memoirs – spanning 50 years or so in her journey from provincial '20s immaturity to Big City jazz life – to her abandoned middle-aged son, taciturn painter Blaudelle (Arcand). Most of the action, or inaction, takes place in his flat as he stares into space – ah, memory! Blaudelle's son Antoine (Méthé) is a lonely, bright boy, disturbed by his parents' estrangement (there are explanatory scenes in parks with Miou-Miou as his mother); intrigued, he sets off to find his grandmother in the mean bars of New York. Mankiewicz directs this dull essay on memory and generational separation with an enervating sensitivity that borders on obscurity. Symptomatic is a lengthy, central flashback set in and around a local silent cinema where Celeste, a classically inclined musician, takes a job providing piano accompaniment; presumably intended to illuminate the broadening of her musical, intellectual and emotional horizons, it explains nothing. WH

Reward, The

(1965, US, 91 min)
d Serge Bourguignon. *p* Aaron Rosenberg. *sc* Serge Bourguignon, Oscar Millard. *ph* Joseph MacDonald. *ed* Robert Simpson. *ad* Jack Martin Smith, Robert Boyle. *m* Elmer Bernstein. *cast* Max von Sydow, Gilbert Roland, Emilio Fernandez, Yvette Mimieux, Efrem Zimbalist Jr, Henry Silva.

●French director Bourguignon won the Oscar for Best Foreign Language Film with 1962's *Sundays and Cybele*, his first feature, then went to Hollywood and swiftly blew his chances with this lackadaisical South-of-the-Border thriller. The price on accused killer Zimbalist's head becomes the source of much friction between von Sydow, the crop-duster who fingers him, and Roland, the cop leading the hunt. The point about the malign influence of money is made early on, leaving the rest of the film to fizzle to a surprisingly underwhelming conclusion. 'Where's the beef?' you're tempted to ask. TJ

Rhapsody in August (Hachigatsu no Kyoshikyoku)

(1990, Jap, 97 min)
d Akira Kurosawa. *p* Toru Okuyama. *sc* Akira Kurosawa. *ph* Takao Saito, Masaharu Ueda. *ad* Yoshiro Muraki. *m* Shinichiro Ikebe. *cast* Sachiko Murase, Hisashi Igawa, Narumi Kayashima, Tomoko Ohtakara, Mitsumori Isaki, Toshie Negishi, Richard Gere.

●If Kurosawa's execrable *Dreams* ended up as a moron's guide to the Green manifesto, here we are presented with a child's primer to the evils of war. Four children are spending the summer at their grandma's home near Nagasaki while their parents are visiting the old lady's long-lost brother in Hawaii. Thanks to grandma's tales of 1945, when America's atomic bomb killed her husband, the kids learn the importance of never forgetting the lessons of the past, and of blaming war itself rather than foreigners. All's well until Clark (Gere) – the old lady's Japanese-American nephew – announces his imminent arrival: will he imagine that his Japanese cousins hate him for the Bomb, and so dash the kids' parents' dreams of an easier life? Who cares would be a tempting response, were it not for the often touching performances. There's more narrative movement here than in *Dreams*, but the pedagogic humanism still gets bogged down in facile simplification. GA

Rhapsody in Blue

(1945, US, 139 min, b/w)
d Irving Rapper. *p* Jesse L Lasky. *sc* Howard Koch, Elliot Paul. *ph* Sol Polito. *ed* Folmar Blangstead. *ad* John Hughes, Anton Grot. *songs* George Gershwin, Ira Gershwin. *cast* Robert Alda, Joan Leslie, Alexis Smith, Oscar Levant, Charles Coburn, Julie Bishop, Albert Basserman, Al Jolson, Paul Whiteman, Hazel Scott.

●Biopic with all the usual faults plus Alda, as George Gershwin, at one point looking hilariously like a Frankenstein monster as he sits at the piano while protruding arms clearly not his own tinkle the ivories. Still, it's something of a musical feast, with a slew of old favourites and an outstanding all-black number on 'Blue Monday Blues'. When the music fails, there's always Sol Polito's lushly impressive camerawork. TM

Rhubarb

(1951, US, 95 min, b/w)
d Arthur Lubin. *p* William Perlberg, George Seaton. *sc* Dorothy Reid, Francis Cockrell. *ph* Lionel Lindon. *ed* Alma Macrorie. *ad* Hal Pereira, Henry Bumstead. *m* Van Cleave. *cast* Ray Milland, Jan Sterling, Gene Lockhart, William Frawley, Elsie Holmes, Taylor Holmes, Donald MacBride,

●An eccentric millionaire (Lockhart), soured by his daughter's lack of affection, leaves his empire – including a baseball team – to a stray cat called Rhubarb, appointing the team's publicity manager (Milland) as the cat's guardian. A nice opening sequence has Lockhart watching gleefully as the disrespectful stray drives the VIP members of an exclusive golf club crazy by stealing balls from under their noses. After that it's downhill all the way as Milland fights off escalating problems: the disgruntled daughter (Elsie Holmes) tries to discredit Rhubarb in court as an impostor, then to have him eliminated; Milland's wedding has to be postponed several times because his fiancée (Sterling) seems to be allergic to Rhubarb; and worried bookies kidnap the cat when the baseball team, convinced he is a good luck charm, unexpectedly starts winning. Laboriously written, directed and acted (apart from Lockhart and the splendid cat), the comedy obstinately refuses to fizz. TM

Rhythm Thief

(1995, US, 84 min, b/w)
d Matthew Harrison. *p* Jonathan Starch. *sc* Matthew Harrison, Christopher Grimm. *ph* Howard Krupa. *ed* Matthew Harrison. *ad* Daniel Fisher. *m* Danny Brenner. *cast* Jason Andrews, Kimberley Flynn.

●Simon (Andrews) plays his cards close to his chest and seems to think he's in control: since arriving in New York from the sticks, he's built a kind of career selling bootleg music tapes on the streets, embarked on a casual relationship with a woman who, despite herself, can barely resist him, and his cool demeanour has earned the respect of local low-lifes. Well, not quite all. The musos whose sounds he steals are ready to get heavy, while Marti (Flynn), a dreamy girl with mystical-poetic pretensions who's followed him from back home, seems quietly determined to crack his tough emotional shell. Maybe city life isn't all it's made out to be. Harrison's grainy b/w, $11,000 second feature may have won the Best Director Prize at 1995's Sundance festival, but that doesn't mean it's not a pretty trite tale of redemption. True, the direction has a certain raw energy and terse economy, but the slim, stretched-out storyline is laden with clichés both ancient (the waifish would-be saviour, a seaside idyll) and modern (endless inarticulate street talk, seedily offbeat behaviour). Hard going. GA

Riaba Ma Poule (Ryaba My Chicken)

(1993, Rus/Fr, 117 min)
d/p Andrei Konchalovsky. *sc* Andrei Konchalovsky, Victor Merejko. *ph* Evgueni Gouslinski. *ed* Hélène Gagarin. *pd* Leonid Platov, Andrei Platov. *m* Boris Basourov. *cast* Inna Churikova, Alexander Surin, Guennadi Iegoritchev, Guennadi Nazarov.

●O tempora! O mores! Not only has Russian peasant life altered somewhat since Konchalovsky made *Asya's Happiness* back in '67, his talent has changed dramatically too – and not for the better. Here, he returns to the kolkhoz of the earlier and far superior film (featured, unwisely, in brief clips), and uses the same villagers to act out a bizarre, supposedly comic fable about the moral and social turmoil caused when Asya's chicken lays a golden egg. A broad, sour farce, that seems to argue that democracy can't succeed because the Russian peasants are so idle, greedy and stupid. Which wouldn't be so bad if it were funny or touching. But it's not. Awful. GA

Ricco (Un Tipo con una Faccia Strana Ti Cerca per Ucciderti)

(1973, It/Sp, 93 min)
d Tullio Demicheli. *p* José G Maesso. *sc* Santiago Moncade, José G Maesso, Mario Di Nardo. *ph* Francisco Fraile. *ed* Angel Serrano. *m* Nando De Luca. *cast* Christopher Mitchum, Barbara Bouchet, Arthur Kennedy, Malisa Longo, Paola Senatore.

●New Turin Mafia chief Don Vito enjoys immersing enemies in caustic soda and turning them into bars of soap, but this won't wash with Ricco, whose dad, the previous chief, was rubbed out in Vito's bid for top position. Back in 1962, Demicheli tried to launch Sean Flynn in *The Son of Captain Blood* as natural swashbuckling successor to dad Errol, and failed miserably. Here he tries the same trick with Robert Mitchum's second son Chris and succeeds, if only because it's far easier to walk around half-asleep than it is to leap up a ship's mast. Arthur Kennedy as Vito lends a small measure of reliable respectability, but it's not enough to get this superordinary revenge movie off the rocks. PM

Rice People

see Gens de la rizière, Les

Rich and Famous

(1981, US, 117 min)
d George Cukor. *p* William Allyn. *sc* Gerald Ayres. *ph* Don Peterman. *ed* John F Burnett. *pd* Jan Scott. *m* Georges Delerue. *cast* Jacqueline Bisset, Candice Bergen, David Selby, Hart Bochner, Steven Hill, Meg Ryan, Matt Lattanzi, Daniel Faraldo.

●Considering neither Bisset nor Bergen had ever shown the slightest acting ability before in movies, their performances in the Bette Davis/Miriam Hopkins roles in this loose reworking of *Old Acquaintance* are very capable. They play two college friends in a story spanning the years 1959–81. Liz (Bisset) develops into a formidable, prickly New York literary figure (Calvin Klein wardrobe, Algonquin, Greenwich Village), while southern belle Merry Noel (a surprisingly comic Bergen) turns from Malibu housewife into wealthy trash novelist (Chanel, gold-chain handbags, Waldorf Astoria, Beverly Hills). Of course much of the credit must go to Cukor, the veteran 'woman's director'; but the film disappoints in its unconfident handling of the secondary characters: the Rolling Stone journalist who lays Liz, Merry's daughter, and the daughter's unsuitable Puerto Rican boyfriend. So many young people in a very old man's film (his last, in fact). JS

Rich and Strange

(1932, GB, 92 min, b/w)
d Alfred Hitchcock. *p* John Maxwell. *sc* Alma Reville, Val Valentine. *ph* John Cox, Charles Martin. *ed* Rene Marrison, Winifred Cooper. *ad* Wilfred Arnold. *m* Hal Dolphe. *cast* Henry Kendall, Joan Barry, Betty Amann, Percy Marmont, Elsie Randolph, Aubrey Dexter.

●Hitchcock's career is full of unexpected patterns and internal correspondences, but none are more bizarre than the comparison between this modestly ambitious drama of 1932 and his Cold War spy movie. *Torn Curtain* of 1966. Both are about couples abroad (in this case, middle class suburbanites who come into money and take a disastrous world cruise), and both are extraordinarily scathing about the timidity and emotional reserve of their central characters: innocence, of the most banal and compromised kind confronts experience in the form of exotic strangers and risks, and responds by retreating further into its shell. It wasn't well received at the time, but Hitchcock himself retained enthusiasm for it. TR

Richard Pryor Here & Now

(1983, US, 95 min)
d Richard Pryor. *p* Bob Parkinson, Andy Friendly. *sc* Richard Pryor. *ph* Vince Singletary, Kenneth A Patterson, Joe Epperson, Tom Geren, John Simmons, Dave Landry. *ed* Raymond M Bush. *pd* Anthony Sabatino, William Harris. *with* Richard Pryor.

●Filmed in front of a wildly partisan crowd in New Orleans who are clearly going to crease themselves at every 'motherfucker' he utters, Pryor tries to swing into his accustomed groove and finds it eluding him at every turn. The material is weak, the delivery uncertain, and the manic depressive behind the quickfire patter is more clearly revealed than ever. Interspersed with variations on the old routines are plaintive assurances that he's straightened himself out, with Pryor seeming pathetically eager to immerse himself in the glow of goodwill emanating from the faithful. While the general embarrassment is not entirely untempered by flashes of brilliance, the abiding memory is of a once great comedian brought (literally) to his knees. JP

Richard Pryor Live in Concert

(1979, US, 78 min)
d Jeff Margolis. *p* Del Jack, J Marktravis. *sc* Richard Pryor. *ph* Tom Schamp. *ed* Steve Livingston. *with* Richard Pryor.

●The film that introduced British audiences to Richard Pryor's real forte – acidic and self-damning humour – after his appearance in a relatively straight role in *Blue Collar*, and his 'clean' parts in *California Suite* and *The Wiz*. This record of one of his gigs in 1978 at Long Beach, California, may be technically imcompetent, but it just can't mar his vulgar and ebullient attacks on everything from Richard Pryor to police brutality, from God to sexual chauvinism. Politics, humour and sex in a great combination.

Richard Pryor Live on the Sunset Strip

(1982, US, 81 min)
d Joe Layton. *p/sc* Richard Pryor. *ph* Haskell Wexler. *ed* Sheldon Kahn. *pd* Michael Baugh. *m* Harry Betts. *with* Richard Pryor.

●Pryor is a one-man comic circus: mime artist, piss artist, wisecracker and, briefly in 1981, human firecracker. His freebasing accident gives him the chance to get one back at his fans when he strikes a match at the end of his gig and waves it at the audience: 'Richard Pryor running down the street, huh? I know all that shit you have been saying while I was away'. But nothing's burned out inside him. The jokes still go off like repeater fireworks, a second punchline catching you unawares just when you thought your sides were splitting for real. Pryor's act (and the filming of it) is so smoothly articulated , one subject detouring into another, that it's impossible to isolate favourite individual routines. But you have to see it – a couple of times – to savour the satire and relish the wit of the solo stand-up comic who's so slick and smartassed he makes Alexei Sayle look like a glove puppet and George Burns a dinosaur. MA

Richard III

(1955, GB, 161 min)
d/p Laurence Olivier. *sc* Alan Dent, Laurence Olivier. *ph* Otto Heller. *ed* Helga Cranston. *pd* Roger Furse. *m* William Walton. *cast* Laurence Olivier, John Gielgud, Claire Bloom, Ralph Richardson, Cedric Hardwicke, Stanley Baker, Alec Clunes, Norman Wooland, Laurence Naismith, Pamela Brown, John Laurie, Michael Gough.

●Olivier's third film as actor/director, and his third 'personal' Shakespeare adaptation. Whether you take his central performance on its own terms (as a 'definitive' reading of the part) or as high camp, it's undoubtedly interesting as a phenomenon. Less debatable, unfortunately, is his ability as a director: his approach is for the most part tediously staid and conservative, and it becomes almost laughable when it tries to transcend its own timidity in the dramatic climaxes. TR

Richard III

(1995, GB, 104 min)
d Richard Loncraine. *p* Stephen Bayly, Lisa Katselas Paré, Ellen Dinerman Little. *sc* Ian McKellan, Richard Eyre, Richard Loncraine. *ph* Peter Biziou. *ed* Paul Green. *pd* Tony Burrough. *m* Trevor Jones. *cast* Ian McKellen, Annette Bening, Kristin Scott-Thomas, Jim Broadbent, Robert Downey Jr, Maggie Smith, Nigel Hawthorne, Jim Carter, Dominic West, Bill Paterson, Adrian Dunbar, Edward Hardwicke, Michael Elphick.

●This triumphant take on the Crookback king is as different from Olivier's '50s historical pageant as chalk is from malmsey. It starts in some vague, post-WWI civil-war period: a ritzy function, a jazz band, a crooner belting out lines from the wrong author – Marlowe! But the ambience soon assumes the fractured pomp of the original, superbly realised in the remastered southern landscapes: Brighton Pavilion, St Pancras turned into a seaside palace, the Armageddon of Bosworth Field played out with Battersea Power Station as a backdrop. The reasoning behind the film was to bring classical actor McKellen together with a director who has avoided the Bard; the result is a fresh, unified vision which may add lines and make cuts, but does a fine job of turning Shakespeare's grand design into a veritable world at war. With Scott-Thomas' loveless Lady Anne fixing up in the back of a Rolls; Downey and Bening as out-of-favour American Nevilles; Broadbent as a pucker, pissed-off Buckingham; and Hawthorne as a sonorous Clarence pacing his last steps amid rain and concrete, the piece is awash with talent and imagery. McKellen is a marvellous demon king: unctuous, snarling, taking the throne like Hitler at a Nuremberg rally. A seamless, high-octane thriller of power and politics, one for today and tomorrow. SGr

Richie Rich

(1994, US, 94 min)
d Donald Petrie. *p* Joel Silver, John Davis. *sc* Tom S Parker, Jim Jennewein. *ph* Don Burgess. *ed* Malcolm Campbell. *pd* James Spencer. *m* Alan Silvestri. *cast* Macaulay Culkin, Jonathan Hyde, John Larroquette, Michael McShane, Edward Herrmann, Christine Ebersole, Claudia Schiffer.

●Richie, heir to billions, must defeat villainous Van Dough (Larroquette) who's taken over the benevolent family business and plans to murder the parents. Happily, Richie (Culkin) is a rebellious Little Lord Fauntleroy, and has buddied with a bunch of tough ethnically mixed street kids. Aided by a laser gun and inventor Prof Keenbean (McShane), the youngsters rout the baddies. Richie's faithful British butler (Hyde) does the usual with the role and, like Gielgud before him, is demoted to leathers. Unendurable. BC

Rich in Love

(1992, US, 105 min)
d Bruce Beresford. *p* Richard D Zanuck, Lili Zanuck. *sc* Alfred Uhry. *ph* Peter James. *ed* Mark Warner. *pd* John Stoddart. *m* Georges Delerue. *cast* Albert Finney, Jill Clayburgh, Kathryn Erbe, Kyle MacLachlan, Piper Laurie, Ethan Hawke, Suzy Amis, Alfre Woodard.

●Another sub-literary Deep South coming-of-age snoozer, in which 17-year-old Lucille (Erbe) has a bit of growing up to do when Mom (Clayburgh) leaves to start 'a second life'. There's bullish paterfamilias Warren (Finney) to guide through the trauma of being on his own again, a task so time-consuming that Lucille has to put her own life (upcoming exams, tentative steps towards romance) on hold a while. Then the surprise return of vivacious, pregnant, married sister Rae (Amis) with her Yankee husband Billy (MacLachlan) livens up the whole household, particularly when that little glint in Billy's eye starts to do strange things to a girl's adolescent hormones. We've been here many times before, but rarely with such an unprepossessing junior heroine: Erbe's such a prissy li'l missy that the sympathy vacuum at its core kills the movie stone dead. For the rest, reuniting Beresford and writer Alfred Uhry from *Driving Miss Daisy*, it's all lengthy *vaawel* sounds, Charleston summer sun, Georges Delerue firmly in the key of saccharine, and absolutely no surprises. TJ

Rich Kids

(1979, US, 101 min)
d Robert M Young. *p* George W George, Michael Hausman. *sc* Judith Ross. *ph* Ralf D Bode. *ed* Edward Beyer. *ad* David Mitchell. *m* Craig Doerge. *cast* Trini Alvarado, Jeremy Levy, Kathryn Walker, John Lithgow, Terry Kiser, David Selby, Roberta Maxwell, Paul Dooley.

●Exec produced by Robert Altman but set in Woody Allen country, this is the mild-mannered story of a 12-year-old boy and girl whose friendship is strengthened by the common bond of screwed-up, wealthy, divorcing parents. What at first looks like a critical and obsessively detailed chronicle of the families' lifestyle (high energy consumers), opts instead for a faintly funny, more than faintly stereotyped treatment of anxious and well-meaning child/parent relations – and is consequently less interesting. Alvarado and Levy, as the wise pre-teens, have much the best scenes, and sense exactly what is expected of children pretending to be children. JS

Rich Kids (Chicos Ricos)

(2000, Arg, 87 min)
d Mariano Galperin. *sc* Sergio Bisio. *ph* Magdalena Ripa Alsina, Jorge Cano, Ezequiel Fernández, Alejandro Giuliani, Cesar Iguiñez, Luis Lattanzi, Carlos Lermett, Hector Santillan. *ad* Paula Abramovich, Maria Battaglia, Mauro Do Porto, Mariana Estela, Marlene Lievendag, Sebastián Serra, Tania Waisberg. *m* E Flavius. *cast* José María Monje, Iván González, Victoria Onetto, Martín Adjemián, Erasmo Olivera, Déborah de Corral, Divina Gloria, Luis Ziembrowsky, Sebastián Borensztein.

● Two successful advertising directors get a couple of prostitutes around to their flash suburban pad, only for their night of drug-fuelled S/M and general debauchery to be thwarted by an old-style father and son burglar duo. The intended quick steal soon becomes a long night of sweating as two cops sit on night patrol outside, engaged in *Pulp Fiction*-informed conversation. Power ebbs and flows and things get very bloody. Setting itself up as a satirical analysis of a certain moral void in the affluent younger generation, this quickly becomes more exploitation than exploration. Crude, explicit and tasteless, but with a degree of unpleasant energy. GE

Ricochet

(1991, US, 102 min)
d Russell Mulcahy. *p* Joel Silver, Michael Levy. *sc* Steven E De Souza. *ph* Peter Levy. *ed* Peter Honess. *pd* Jay Hinkle. *m* Alan Silvestri. *cast* Denzel Washington, John Lithgow, Ice T, Kevin Pollak, Lindsay Wagner, Mary Ellen Trainor, Josh Evans, Victoria Dillard.

● Mulcahy's slasher-thriller manages to be as entertaining as it is improbable and violent. Washington, in a refreshingly unpolitical role, plays Nick Styles, a cop who becomes a hero when he pulls down his pants in order to arrest a street psycho. The event, recorded on amateur video, catapults Styles into the big time as an assistant district attorney and role model, but also makes him an implacable enemy in the shape of the demonic psycho (Lithgow). He is the stuff of which nightmares are made, and Washington's mental and physical destruction is the driving force behind his escape from prison and assumption of a new identity. *Ricochet* has some dodgy moments – a scene where Washington is doped and then infected with VD by a hired prostitute leaves a nasty taste in the mouth – but it runs a fascinating line between cartoon fantasy and big city chiller. If you don't take it seriously, it's a lot of fun. SGr

Riddle of the Sands, The

(1978, GB, 102 min)
d Tony Maylam. *p* Drummond Challis. *sc* Tony Maylam, John Bailey. *ph* Christopher Challis. *ed* Peter Hollywood. *pd* Hazel Peiser. *m* Howard Blake. *cast* Michael York, Jenny Agutter, Simon MacCorkindale, Alan Badel, Jürgen Andersen, Michael Sheard, Hans Meyer.

● First published in 1903, Erskine Childers' novel is one of the great adventure classics of English fiction, a *tour de force* (long a favourite project of Michael Powell's) in which two eccentric young Englishmen manoeuvre a 30-foot yacht around the North Sea German coastline and stumble on a demonic Hun scheme for the invasion of England. Rank's version is faithful enough, but founders on the considerable production difficulties involved: without the resources of *Jaws*, how do you portray violent storms, wrecks, sea chases, and the whole eerie desolation of dangerous coastal navigation? Although it works hard for authenticity (locations rather than a studio tank), the film is just too pretty to convey a real sense of danger, and too glossy to capture subtleties of atmosphere and characterisation. DP

Riddles of the Sphinx

(1977, GB, 92 min)
d/p/sc Laura Mulvey, Peter Wollen. *ph* Diane Tammes. *ed* Carola Klein, Larry Sider. *m* Mike Ratledge. *cast* Dinah Stabb, Merdelle Jordine, Rhiannon Tise, Clive Merrison, Marie Green, Paula Melbourne.

● Mulvey and Wollen's second film places the simple story of a mother/child relationship in the wholly unexpected context of the myth of Oedipus' encounter with the Sphinx; its achievement is to make that context seem both logical and necessary. First off, the story: a broken marriage, an over-possessive mother, a growing awareness of feminist issues, a close female friend, and a newly questioning spirit of independence. Then, underpinning it, the myth, which introduces a set of basic questions about the female unconscious. The mixture of feminist politics and Freudian theory would be enough in itself to make the film unusually interesting, but various other elements make it actively compelling: the beautiful, hypnotic score by Mike Ratledge, the tantalising blend of visual, aural and literary narration in the telling of the story, and the firm intelligence that informs the film's unique and seductive overall structure. TR

Ride, The (Jísda)

(1994, Czech, 88 min)
d/p Jan Sverák. *sc* Jan Sverák, Martin Dostal. *ph* Frantisek A Brabec. *ed* Alois Fisarek. *m* Radek Pasternák. *cast* Anna Geislerová, Radek Pasternák, Jakub Spalek.

● Mercifully less obscure – and indeed less ambitious – than Sverák's previous *Accumulator 1*, this is a good-looking road movie in which two friends buy a second-hand car (from a shady dealer, natch), drive out into the country, and give a lift to strange, distracted woman whose presence fuels tensions between the two men. Snappily edited and consummately stylish, it's nevertheless a somewhat hollow, formula affair, interesting more for what it shows of the current mindset of the Czech Republic than for any inherent drama. GA

Ride a Wild Pony

(1975, US, 91 min)
d Don Chaffey. *p* Jerome Courtland. *sc* Rosemary Anne Sisson. *ph* Jack Cardiff. *ed* Mike Campbell. *ad* Robert Hilditch. *m* John Addison. *cast* Robert Bettles, Eva Griffith, Michael Craig, John Meillon Sr, Alfred Bell, Melissa Jaffer, John Meillon Jr.

● A Disney film set in Australia with two kids (one rich, paralysed and pampered, the other poor, gap-toothed and cheeky) fighting for the ownership of a wild white pony. Sounds irredeemably yucky? Well, you're wrong – the pony gets very few close-ups, and the script makes a point of presenting the paralysed girl as a real toffee-nosed stinker, thus giving a welcome acerbic tinge to the drama. Jack Cardiff's photography is radiantly crisp, and all the actors, young or old, seem to believe in what they're doing. Even the moral homilies ('If you keep running away from the big people, you just make yourself small') ring true. The only blight is provided by Chaffey's mannered direction, liable to induce vertigo or a permanent squint. GB

Ride in the Whirlwind

(1966, US, 82 min)
d Monte Hellman. *p* Monte Hellman, Jack Nicholson. *sc* Jack Nicholson. *ph* Gregory Sandor. *ad* James Campbell. *m* Robert Drasnin. *cast* Cameron Mitchell, Jack Nicholson, Millie Perkins, Harry Dean Stanton, George Mitchell, Tom Filer.

● Shot back-to-back with *The Shooting*, this Jack Nicholson-scripted effort is considerably less ambiguous and weird than its celebrated sibling Western. Most of the action takes place in a ranch-house, where three cowboys wrongly accused of being outlaws wait out their fate. Incidental laughs aside, the resulting *ennuis* don't always seem intentional. DT

Ride Lonesome

(1959, US, 73 min)
d/p Budd Boetticher. *sc* Burt Kennedy. *ph* Charles Lawton Jr. *ed* Jermome Thoms. *ad* Robert Peterson. *m* Heinz Roemheld. *cast* Randolph Scott, Karen Steele, Pernell Roberts, James Coburn, James Best, Lee Van Cleef.

● One of the best of the Boetticher/Scott Westerns, bleaker but not too distant in mood from the autumnal resignation of Peckinpah's *Ride the High Country*, as Scott's ageing lawman lets time catch up with him and foregoes (even as he achieves) the vengeance he had planned on the man who hanged his wife so long ago that the killer, taxed with it, says 'I 'most forgot'. It's deviously structured as an odyssey of cross-purposes in which Scott captures a young gunman (Best) and proceeds to take him in, ostensibly for the bounty on his head. Actually, Scott hopes to lure Best's brother (Van Cleef), the man who killed his wife, into a rescue bid; two outlaw buddies (Roberts and Coburn) tag along, biding their time, desperate to collect the amnesty that goes with Best's capture; the presence of a pretty widow (Steele) stokes a measure of sexual rivalry; and there are Indians about. Beautifully scripted by Burt Kennedy, with excellent performances all round as the characters evolve through subtly shifting loyalties and ambitions, it's a small masterpiece. TM

Rider on the Rain (Passager de la Pluie)

(1969, Fr/It, 119 min, b/w)
d René Clément. *p* Serge Silberman. *sc* Sébastien Japrisot. *ph* Andréas Winding. *ed* Françoise Javet. *ad* Pierre Guffroy. *m* Francis Lai. *cast* Marlène Jobert, Charles Bronson, Annie Cordy, Jill Ireland, Gabriele Tinti, Jean Gaven, Corinne Marchand, Marika Green

● A promising start with a girl going home to a lonely house, unaware that she has a sex maniac in the boot of her car. He rapes her, she shoots him, and the film spirals into a mad Hitchcockian mystery (the dead man's name is finally revealed, in tribute to the Master, to be MacGuffin), which is rather nullified by the fact that nobody behaves with any sort of credibility. Good performances from Jobert and Bronson, though, and glossy direction from Clément. TM

Riders of Destiny

(1934, US, 60 min, b/w)
d Robert North Bradbury. *p* Paul Malvern. *sc* Robert North Bradbury. *ph* Archie Stout. *ed* Carl Pierson. *cast* John Wayne, Cecilia Parker, George Hayes, Yakima Canutt.

● First of the 16 Westerns produced by the Lone Star outfit for the B-studio Monogram Pictures and starring the young John Wayne, this has particular curiosity value because the Duke's undercover agent Singin' Sandy does just that (though the voice is dubbed by the director's son). Stuntman Canutt wears the black hat, pilfering the water supply from beneath the noses of honest farmers, while he and Wayne worked out between them the slick fight choreography. Surprisingly good, considering. TJ

Riders of the Storm

see American Way, The

Ride the High Country (aka Guns in the Afternoon)

(1961, US, 93 min)
d Sam Peckinpah. *p* Richard E Lyons. *sc* NB Stone Jr. *ph* Lucien Ballard. *ed* Frank Santillo. *ad* George W Davis, Leroy Coleman. *m* George Bassman. *cast* Randolph Scott, Joel McCrea, Ronald Starr, Mariette Hartley, James Drury, RG Armstrong, Edgar Buchanan, LQ Jones, Warren Oates.

● Peckinpah's superb second film, a nostalgic lament for the West in its declining years, with a couple of great set pieces (the bizarre wedding in the mining camp, the final shootout among the chickens). Affectionately funny as Scott and McCrea, once more hired and temporarily in harness, creak rheumatically while climbing off their horses, turn aside from the trail to bathe aching feet, and sport long woolly combinations for bed. But also achieving an almost biblical grandeur as the two oldtime lawmen, fallen upon hard times and suddenly realising that the world has left them behind, contrive not to fall from grace and self-respect when a tempting gold shipment comes between them. Truly magnificent camerawork from Lucien Ballard. TM

Ride with the Devil

(1999, US, 138 min)
d Ang Lee. *p* Ted Hope, Robert F Colesberry, James Schamus. *sc* James Schamus. *ph* Frederick Elmes. *ed* Tim Squyres. *pd* Mark Friedberg. *m* Mychael Danna. *cast* Skeet Ulrich, Tobey Maguire, Jewel, Jeffrey Wright, Simon Baker, Jonathan Rhys Meyers, James Caviezel, Thomas Guiry, Tom Wilkinson, Jonathan Brandis, Matthew Faber.

● Building on the qualities of *Wedding Banquet*, *Sense and Sensibility* and *The Ice Storm*, director Lee here tackles a far grander subject – the American Civil War. About a unit of young 'Bushwhackers' – Southern guerillas tackling Yankee platoons – it focuses on the experiences of two friends: plantation owner's son Jack Bull (Ulrich) and Jake (Maguire), both basically liberal on the issue of slavery but driven by vengeance and proud loyalty to bear arms for the Confederacy. Steadily, however, as altercations with volatile colleague Pitt (Rhys Meyers), Jack's encounter with the widow Sue Lee (Jewel), and Jake's deepening friendship with ex-slave Daniel (Wright) take effect, the pair find themselves rebels without a cause. Truly epic in scale yet full of beautifully observed details, the film benefits hugely from sturdy yet exquisite performances, Frederick Elmes' typically meaty camerawork and yet another intelligent and incisive James Schamus script. The social and ethical issues are treated with depth, but there's no sermonising; the light touch extends to a gentle humour interspersed amid the carnage. Like *The Outlaw Josey Wales* and *Once Upon a Time in America*, it's a tale of hatred transformed by disillusionment into a redemptive desire to abandon bloodlust and look to the future. GA

Ridicule

(1996, Fr, 102 min)
d Patrice Leconte. *p* Gilles Legrand, Frédéric Brillion, Philippe Carcassonne. *sc* Remi Waterhouse. *ph* Thierry Arbogast. *ed* Joëlle Hache. *pd* Ivan Maussion. *m* Antoine Duhamel. *cast* Fanny Ardant, Charles Berling, Bernard Giraudeau, Judith Godrèche, Jean Rochefort, Carlo Brandt, Bernard Dhéran, Albert Delpy.

●Leconte's costumer, detailing the deceit and moral destitution of pre-Revolutionary Versailles, is an idiosyncratic, but never self-indulgent caricature of aristocratic *belle esprit*, as the 18th century lobbying system secures political advancement through finely wrought dirty gibes. To the court comes Ponceludon de Malavoy (Berling), a hydrologist seeking royal sponsorship for a scheme to drain his marshes. Though struck by the alien ways of the courtly class, with his rapier tongue he could profit in a world where 'wit opens every door'. He finds an ally in the Marquis de Bellegarde (Rochefort), and in Bellegarde's daughter, the buxom Mathilde (Godrèche). But does he have the force of character to survive the self-serving designs of his competitors, typified by the Comtesse de Blayac (Ardant) and her lover, the Abbé de Vilecourt (Giraudeau)? And can he preserve his sense of mission amid the temptations of self-glory? Leconte was never in danger of succumbing to the trappings of period drama, but it's remarkable how distinct in tone this is from such flamboyant extravagances as *The Hairdresser's Husband* or *Tango*. Rather than indulging the eccentric rebelliousness of his characters, this is a more sober, mature work, a disquisition on personal corruption, the duplicity of social graces and the malignancy of self-enclosed elites. Rather deliberately paced, and mired in archaic and abstruse puns, the film is perhaps more interesting than enjoyable. Still, Leconte's customary zest and mordant humour are there, lurking behind the claustrophobic production design and free-spirited camerawork. NB

Riding in Cars with Boys

(2001, US, 131 min)
d Penny Marshall. *p* James L Brooks, Julie Ansell, Richard Sakai, Sara Colleton, Laurence Mark. *sc* Morgan Upton Ward. *ph* Miroslav Ondricek. *ed* Richard Marks, Lawrence Jordan. *pd* Bill Groom. *m* Hans Zimmer, Heitor Pereira. *cast* Drew Barrymore, Steve Zahn, Brittany Murphy, Adam Garcia, Lorraine Bracco, James Woods, Sara Gilbert, Desmond Harrington.

●Based on Beverly Donofrio's memoir about her struggles to juggle fun, family, and her ambition to become a writer – sidetracked by an unplanned teenage pregnancy – this begins in the mid-1980s with thirty-something Beverly (Barrymore) on the verge of success, then cuts back two decades to the point where it all began to go wrong. Enter amiable doofus Ray (Zahn). He's sweet, but not exactly husband material. Trouble is, her strict religious father (Woods) sees things differently – that oh so eloquently penned confession note only makes things worse – and before she knows it, Bev is a mother and housewife deadended just a couple of blocks from where she grew up. The film is not without its curious aspects. Most conspicuously, it's narrated by Bev's grown son (Garcia), which is odd, given the source material. It's almost as if director Marshall decided halfway through that she didn't like her heroine after all. She's clearly revealed to be a lousy mother, though she does get the hell away from Ray eventually. It begins breezily enough, in girls behaving badly mode, but Marshall is more adept at light comedy than drama. The longer Bev's marriage limps on, the duller it gets. TCh

Rien à Faire (Empty Days)

(1999, Fr, 100 min)
d Marion Vernoux. *p* Alain Rozanes, Pascal Verroust. *sc* Marion Vernoux, Santiago Amigorena. *ph* Dominique Colin. *ed* Jennifer Augé. *pd* Emmanuel Duplay. *m* Alexandre Desplat. *cast* Valéria Bruni Tedeschi, Patrick Dell'Isola, Sergi López, Florence Thomassin, Kelly Hornoy, Alexandre Carrière, Marco Cherqui, Chloe Mons, Marion Desfachelles.

●Vernoux takes a remarkably fresh look at adultery and comes up with a small masterpiece. Bruni Tedeschi, superb as ever, plays an unemployed housewife living on a modern council estate; Dell'Isola is a likewise jobless executive from the same company where she once toiled in the store rooms. First meeting in a supermarket, they find that shopping at the same time alleviates boredom, reduces the social divide between them – and gives rise to something that may be love. Vernoux rightly realises that socio-economic circumstance is what makes the affair possible and inevitably limits its potential; at the same time, she never underestimates the emotional traumas and confusions experienced by the lovers, but, thanks to Dominique Colin's amazing 'Scope close-ups, to some marvellous music, and to an authentic feeling for time and milieu, she makes us empathise with and respect their passion. GA

Rien ne va plus

(1997, Fr/Switz, 106 min)
d/sc Claude Chabrol. *ph* Eduardo Serra. *ed* Monique Fardoulis. *ad* Françoise Benoît-Fresco. *m* Matthieu Chabrol. *cast* Isabelle Huppert, Michel Serrault, François Cluzet, Jean-François Balmer, Jackie Berroyer, Jean Benguigui, Mony Dalmes.

●When you're a con artist, how can you really trust your lifepartner if they're also your professional partner – a trickster, like you? And at what point does a small-time scam become dangerously big-time? When is the game no longer a game? How, in fact, after years of living a lie, can you tell what's real any more? These are the questions raised by Chabrol's eccentrically clever concoction, situated in that treacherous territory between sly comedy and something rather nastier. Betty (Huppert) and Victor (Serrault) have been happily conning convention guests for years, until she sets her cap at Maurice (Cluzet) – is she simply out to swindle him, really attracted, or out to make Victor jealous? And is Maurice as innocent as he seems? Chabrol's movie is mostly a slight, elegant jape, enjoyable but undemanding save in the way it asks us to keep pace with the Mamet-style twists. It's all very playful, with an ironic, irreverent take on national stereotypes, and motives kept admirably ambiguous. Then, along comes a killer twist and a climax of authentically operatic cruelty, as baroque, brilliantly unsettling and casually brutal as almost anything he's done; proof that after 50 movies the old magic's still there. GA

Rien sur Robert

(1998, Fr, 107 min)
d Pascal Bonitzer. *p* Jean-Michel Rey, Philippe Liégeois. *sc* Pascal Bonitzer. *ph* Christophe Pollock. *ed* Suzanne Koch. *ad* Emmanuel de Chavigny. *cast* Fabrice Luchini, Sandrine Kimberlain, Valentina Cervi, Michel Piccoli, Bernadette Lafont, Laurent Lucas, Denis Podalydès, Natalie Boutefeu.

●Despite the cast, which perhaps suggests a cross between Rohmer and Buñuel, this bizarre farce is rather more like a misbegotten Gallic intellectual rehash of *After Hours*. Luchini is a neurotic writer, forever at war with tetchy lover Kimberlain, his family and his own paranoia about another acclaimed young author. The latter turns up for dinner on the wrong night at his former professor's place, with disastrous consequences. At first it looks like being an odd but engaging comedy of embarrassment, but as Luchini gets involved with weird waif *fatale* Cervi, and the sexual intrigues thicken, it becomes increasingly turgid, precious and even, for all its posturing, moralistic. GA

Riff-Raff

(1990, GB, 95 min)
d Ken Loach. *p* Sally Hibbin. *sc* Bill Jesse. *ph* Barry Ackroyd. *ed* Jonathan Morris. *pd* Martin Johnson. *m* Stewart Copeland. *cast* Robert Carlyle, Emer McCourt, Jimmy Coleman, George Moss, Ricky Tomlinson, David Finch, Richard Belgrave, Derek Young.

●Loach lightens up for this documentary-style comedy about the scams, laughs, dangers and camaraderie of work on a London building site. Newcomer Carlyle plays Stevie, a Scottish ex-con teenager who gets a job tearing the guts out of a closed-down hospital. His workmates are a mixed bunch: Irishmen, West Indians and Scousers with a healthy disrespect for their idle ganger, a talent for ducking and diving, and a keen eye for the main chance. The company's cavalier disrespect for basic safety standards eventually brings tensions on the site to a head. Bill Jesse's pointedly funny script skilfully evokes the texture of working life; Loach's handling of Stevie's tentative romance with would-be singer Susan (McCourt), on the other hand, wavers between the touchingly simple and curiously off-key. There are times, too, when the lively spontaneity of the improvised scenes slips into inaudible chaos. Sadly, Bill Jesse died without seeing the finished film, but this is as good an epitaph as he could have hoped for. NF

Rififi

see Du Rififi chez les Hommes

Rififi in Paris

see Du Rififi à Paname

Rift, The (La Grieta)

(1988, Sp, 89 min)
d Juan Piquer-Simon. *p* José Escriva, Juan Piquer Simon. *sc* Juan Piquer Simon. *ph* Manuel Rojas. *ed* Isaac Sehayek, Earl Watson. *pd* Gonzalo Gonzalo. *m* Joel Goldsmith. *cast* Jack Scalia, R Lee Ermey, Ray Wise, Deborah Adair.

●A by-the-numbers submarine pic which steals its every idea and re-floats the usual stuff about a missing craft, a government conspiracy, an on-board saboteur (*Alien*), and a big mother of a monster (*Aliens*). The captain (Ermey) is a hardass, the crew is multi-ethnic, and the hero's estranged wife is on board (*The Abyss*) to up the tension level. When Siren One, a state-of-the-art nuclear sub, goes missing at a depth of 27,000 feet, the vessel's hunky designer (Scalia) joins a NATO team sent down to investigate. Tracking a 'black box' signal to the deep Dannekin rift, the crew discovers a vast underwater cavern populated by mutant life forms, apparently the result of some secret government experiments in gene splicing and accelerated evolution. Pretty soon, the seaweed hits the fan, and the crew are faced by monsters without and an enemy within. The wooden characterisations are predictably shallow, but the dodgy monster effects and model work plumb new depths of ineptitude. NF

Right Out of History: The Making of Judy Chicago's Dinner Party

(1980, US, 75 min)
d Johanna Demetrakas. *p* Thom Tyson. *ph* Baird Bryant. *ed* Johanna Demetrakas. *m* Catherine Macdonald.

●A documentary about the creation of an elaborate work of art: 'The Dinner Party', made not only by Judy Chicago but by 400 volunteers, is an immense table with place settings designed to commemorate great women from history whose achievements have been pushed 'right out of it' (hence the title). The film is perhaps even more interesting than the finished 'Dinner Party', since it raises some tricky questions about the relations of production on this 'cooperative project', and reveals the complexity of its history. Skilled women with no pretensions to being 'artists', such as china painters and embroiderers, slave away on a labour of love; but even more fascinating than the vast and detailed organisation of traditionally feminine skills is the enormity of Judy Chicago's ego, as she hectors mild-looking co-workers about their ignorance, clinging to her authorship to the end. JWi

Right Stuff, The

(1983, US, 193 min)
d Philip Kaufman. *p* Irwin Winkler, Robert Chartoff. *sc* Philip Kaufman. *ph* Caleb

Deschanel. *ed* Glenn Farr, Lisa Fruchtman, Stephen A Rotter, Douglas Stewart, Tom Rolf. *pd* Geoffrey Kirkland. *m* Bill Conti. *cast* Sam Shepard, Scott Glenn, Ed Harris, Dennis Quaid, Fred Ward, Barbara Hershey, Kim Stanley, Veronica Cartwright, Pamela Reed, Scott Paulin, Mary Jo Deschanel, Levon Helm, Scott Wilson, Jeff Goldblum.
●From the opening moments it is clear that we have the nearest modern equivalent to a Western: men of quiet virtue going skyward, leaving the tawdry world of log-rolling politicians behind. John Ford might have made it, and director Kaufman matches up to the master of this kind of poetic hero worship. Beginning with Chuck Yeager's breaking of the sound barrier in the late '40s, he uses the great test pilot as a counterpoint to the training and eventual missions of the seven astronauts chosen for America's first space programme. Kaufman (like Tom Wolfe, whose book *The Right Stuff* this is taken from) is well enough aware of the media circus surrounding the whole project, but still celebrates his magnificent seven's heroism with a rhetoric that is respectful and irresistible. CPea

Rigolboche

(1936, Fr, 90 min, b/w)
d Christian-Jaque. *p* Jean-Pierre Frogerais. *sc* Jean-Henri Blanchon, Jacques de Bénac. *ph* Marcel Lucien, André Germain. *ed* William Barache. *ad* Jacques Gotko. *m* Casimir Oberfeld, Jacques Simoneau. *cast* Mistinguett, Jules Berry, André Lefaur.
●Aged 61, gallantly described as a young lady and supposedly capturing the heart of a noticeably bored Jules Berry, the fabled Mistinguett delivers all her close-up lines gazing soulfully skywards (presumably it helped to keep the dewlaps from sagging). Fleeing from a shady past in Dakar, she becomes a star in Paris, finding time to croon to her boarded-out child along the way. Gracelessly tedious, but there is one nice thing about the film : it was solemnly banned during the WWII Occupation because the Germans thought the title (actually the name of Mistinguett's character) was making fun of 'les Boches'. TM

Rigoletto

(1989, It, 118 min)
d Jean-Pierre Ponnelle. *cast* Luciano Pavarotti, Ingvar Wixell, Edita Gruberova.
●Guzzling dwarfs, bedizened courtesans, Pavarotti draped in gilded fruit and garlands: Ponnelle's film of Verdi's melodious blood-and-thunder – about a hunchbacked jester, his ravished daughter, and vengeance that goes terribly wrong – is taken at full-frontal face value. Marvellous locations – mouldering palaces, riverside slums – make up for Ponnelle's filmic clumsiness and occasional over-emphasis. As Rigoletto, Wixell is spiteful, tender and ferocious, Gruberova sings like an angel except when stretched by the 'Tremenda vendetta' duet, and Pavarotti's libertine Duke photographs well, acts dashingly, and ends 'La donna è mobile' with a ringing high B. Riccardo Chailly conducts the Vienna Philharmonic Orchestra in a sleek, surging performance. Handsome to see and hear. MHoy

Ring 0 – Birthday

see Ring 0 – Birthday [as 'Ring Zero – Birthday']

Ring

(1998, Jap, 95 min)
d Hideo Nakata. *p* Shinya Kawai, Takashige Ichise, Takenori Sento. *sc* Hiroshi Takahashi. *ph* Ichiro Hayashi. *m* Kenji Kawai. *cast* Nanako Matsushima, Miki Nakatani, Hiroyuki Sanada, Yuko Takeuchi, Hitomi Sato.
●See it and die! The agent of evil in *Ring* (based on a hit novel by Koji Suzuki) is a mysterious videotape. Exactly one week after watching it, the viewer is visited by the implacable, murderous wraith Sadako, unless... but that would be telling. TV journalist Reiko recklessly watches the tape and enlists the help of her ex-husband Ryuji to solve the mystery of its origin while racing the clock (and rushing from Izu to Oshima Island and back to newspaper files from the 1950s) to save their own lives. More cod science in the Cronenberg vein than part of the old Japanese tradition of vengeful Buddhist ghosts, this well-mounted, well-acted thriller builds up a real frisson en route to its grim conclusion. The moment when Reiko grasps that her father will have to die to save her young son Yoichi is the scariest in a generally scary movie. TR

Ring 2

(1999, Jap, 99 min)
d Hideo Nakata. *p* Takashige Ichise, Makoto Ishihara. *sc* Hiroshi Takahashi. *ph* Hideo Yamamoto. *ed* Nobuyuki Takahashi. *m* Kenji Kawai. *cast* Miki Nakatani, Hitomi Sato, Kyoko Fukada, Fumiya Kohinata, Kenjiro Ishimaru.
●Rare case of a sequel living up to (and in some ways even improving on) the original. The quest for answers about the killer videotape – now understood to be a kind of psychic virus – is taken up by Ryuji's girlfriend Mai (Nakatani), a marginal character in the original *Ring*. There are more grisly revelations about Sadako (including a hint that her father was Not Of This Earth), more dodgy brain chemistry and a doomed scientific attempt to channel the destructive energy into a pool of water. Unlike equivalent American movies, this feels no need to provide a redemptive ending: the threat appears unstoppable, and the isolation cell awaits. TR

Ring, The

(1927, GB, b/w, 8,007 ft)
d Alfred Hitchcock. *p* John Maxwell. *sc* Alma Reville, Alfred Hitchcock, Eliot Stannard. *ph* Jack Cox. *ad* C Wilfred Arnold. *cast* Ian Hunter, Carl Brisson, Lillian Hall-Davies, Forrester Harvey, Gordon Harker, Billy Wells.
●Arguably the finest of Hitchcock's silent films, this tale of a fairground boxer (Brisson) whose wife takes a shine to the far more socially sophisticated new champion (Hunter), sees the young director completely confident in his control of the medium. The title is ambivalent, referring not only to the boxing-ring (scene of Brisson's first humiliation), to the wedding-ring and to the bracelet Hunter secretly gives to his rival's wife, but also to the circular shape of the story, which stresses the philanderer's apathy when his adulterous affair comes to nothing. Impressive, too, is Hitchcock's keen eye for social detail, and his command of expressionist visual devices to suggest his characters' states of mind, perhaps most memorably a shot which 'melts' off the screen to evoke the cuckold's drunken slide into oblivion. GA

Ring of Bright Water

(1969, GB, 107 min)
d Jack Couffer. *p* Joseph Strick. *sc* Jack Couffer, Bill Travers. *ph* Wolfgang Suschitzky. *ed* Reginald Mills. *ad* Ken Ryan. *m* Frank Cordell. *cast* Bill Travers, Virginia McKenna, Peter Jeffrey, Roddy McMillan, Jean Taylor-Smith, Helena Gloag.
●Civil servant Travers and pet otter Mij forsake their cramped London flat for the wide-open spaces of the Scottish Highlands and the tender care of Dr McKenna in this much-loved everyday story of furry folk (from the book by Gavin Maxwell). Accomplished wildlife photography, and solid work from the cast, who are old hands at this sort of thing. The 'aahhh' factor is not insubstantial. TJ

Ring 0 – Birthday

(2000, Jap, 98 min)
d Norio Tsuruta. *p* Masato Hara, Shinji Ogawa, Masao Nagai, Takashige Ichise. *sc* Hiroshi Takahashi. *ph* Takahide Shibanushi. *ed* Hiroshi Sunaga. *ad* Shu Yamaguchi. *m* Shinichiro Ogata. *cast* Yukie Nakama, Seiichi Tanabe, Kumiko Aso, Yoshiko Tanaka, Takashi Wakamatsu.
●Hideo Nakata wisely declined to make this prequel, no doubt because the producers were intent on slavish fidelity to ideas from Koji Suzuki's original novel – rather than developing the sci-fi/body-horror implications of *Ring 2*. This plod through the virginal Sadako's adolescence as a member of a theatre group in the 1950s is an anthology of theatre-mystery clichés: the corpse discovered in mid-performance, imploding flashbulbs, stage machinery that animates itself, dark rumours, nagging nightmares. All of the more intriguing questions about Sadako's true parentage are sidestepped in favour of the 'relevation' that this innocent girl has an evil twin who causes all the trouble. Dull and extremely disappointing, this was none the less a hit in Japan. Straight to DVD everywhere else, of course. TR

Rio Bravo 100

(1959, US, 141 min)
d/p Howard Hawks. *sc* Jules Furthman, Leigh Brackett. *ph* Russell Harlan. *ed* Folmar Blangsted. *ad* Leo K Kuter. *m* Dimitri Tiomkin. *cast* John Wayne, Dean Martin, Angie Dickinson, Walter Brennan, Ricky Nelson, Ward Bond, Claude Akins, John Russell, Bob Steele, Harry Carey Jr.
●Arguably Hawks' greatest film, a deceptively rambling chamber Western made in response to the liberal homilies of *High Noon*. Here the marshal in need of help is Wayne, desperately fending off a clan of villains determined to release the murderer he's holding in jail until the arrival of the state magistrate. Unlike Cooper, however, he rejects rather than courts offers of help, simply because his supporters are either too old (Brennan), too young (Nelson), female (Dickinson) or alcoholic (Martin). Thus the film becomes an examination of various forms of pride, prejudice and professionalism, as the various outcasts slowly cohere through mutual aid to form one of the director's beloved self-contained groups. Little of the film is shot outdoors, with a subsequent increase in claustrophobic tension, while Hawks peppers the generally relaxed and easy narrative – which even takes time out to include a couple of songs for Dino and Ricky – with superb set pieces: Dino's redemptory shooting of a fugitive villain; the explosive finale in which Duke realises he needs all the help he can get. Beautifully acted, wonderfully observed, and scripted with enormous wit and generosity, it's the sort of film, in David Thomson's words, which reveals that 'men are more expressive rolling a cigarette than saving the world'. GA

Rio Conchos

(1964, US, 107 min)
d Gordon Douglas. *p* David Weisbart. *sc* Joseph Landon, Clair Huffaker. *ph* Joseph MacDonald. *ed* Joseph Silver. *ad* Jack Martin Smith, William J Creber. *m* Jerry Goldsmith. *cast* Richard Boone, Stuart Whitman, Anthony Franciosa, Edmond O'Brien, Wende Wagner, Jim Brown, Rodolfo Acosta, Timothy Carey.
●This borrows a star (Whitman), a screenwriter (Clair Huffaker) and the plot of another Fox Western, *The Comancheros* (1961). A stolen shipment of repeater rifles forces an unlikely – and severely tested – alliance between a Yankee Captain (Whitman), his black sergeant (Brown), an Indian-hating Rebel (Boone), and a Mexican killer (Franciosa). Their common foe: a megalomaniac Southern Colonel (O'Brien) who plans to revive the Civil War and strike back at the Union by arming the Apaches. While it shares the earlier film's taste for the picaresque, this version is in far darker register: Gordon Douglas directs with a blistering vehemence Michael Curtiz never dreamed of. It begins with the massacre of an Indian burial party, and ends with an extraordinarily baroque conflagration: a voyage from dust to ashes only one of the men will survive. TCh

Río Escondido (Hidden River)

(1947, Mex, 99 min, b/w)
d Emilio Fernández. *p* Raúl de Anda. *sc* Emilio Fernández. *ph* Gabriel Figueroa. *ed* Gloria Schoemann. *pd* Manuel Fonatnais. *m* Francisco Dominguez. *cast* María Félix, Domingo Soler, Carlos López Moctezuma, Fernando Fernández, Arturo Soto Rangel.
●Interesting primarily for Gabriel Figueroa's predictably ravishing b/w camerawork, but also for the way it melds typically overheated Mexican melodrama with political propaganda, inflecting both with distinctly religious overtones. Félix is the virginal (!) but idealistic teacher sent by the country's new, godlike president to a remote rural hellhole terrorised by a sadistic, woman-hating, Indian-hating local tyrant. Very much a didactic nationalistic parable highlighting the need for self-sacrifice in the fight against corruption, it's mostly pretty clunky, especially in comparison with, say, Fernández's gorgeous *Enamorada*, but the exquisite images do make up for the pious solemnities. GA

Río Escondido (Hidden River)

(1999, Arg, 88 min)
d/p/sc Mercedes García Guevara. *ph* Esteban Sapir. *ed* Alejandro Brodersohn. *pd* Diego Dubcovsky. *cast* Paola Krum, Juan Palomino, Maria José Gabin, Matias Del Pozo, Pablo Cedrón, Elias Carrasco, Inés Baum.
●A woman finds a letter written by a complete stranger to her husband, and fears that his many working trips may be covering up a secret life. Leaving Buenos Aires for a small town in the

remote Mendoza Valley, she meets the woman in question – the first stap in a sometimes painful, often bewildering voyage of (self-)discovery. This is perhaps a little overstretched and a touch too solemn for its own good, but the performances are strong, the air of ambiguity and mystery is well sustained, the use of landscape is superb, and the compositions and camera movements are strangely reminiscent of late Hitchcock. A delicate parable about the need for trust and courage in a world where lives are often built on lies. GA

Rio Grande

(1950, US, 105 min, b/w)
d John Ford. *p* John Ford, Merian C Cooper. *sc* James K McGuinness. *ph* Bert Glennon. *ed* Jack Murray. *ad* Frank Hotaling. *m* Victor Young. *cast* John Wayne, Maureen O'Hara, Ben Johnson, Harry Carey Jr, Claude Jarman Jr, Victor McLaglen, J Carrol Naish, Chill Wills.

● Wayne's Captain York from *Fort Apache* has become a Colonel by the time *Rio Grande* closes the Ford cavalry trilogy, but is still much exercised by troubled notions of authority in both the mirrored families of home life (O'Hara and estranged son Jarman) and command (hamstrung by the inconveniently close Mexican border while keeping down marauding Apaches). A bit wordy, a bit plot-heavy, and with an unfortunate tendency to saccharine musical excess (the Sons of the Pioneers), it's fairly minor but still resonant Ford. PT

Rio Lobo

(1970, US, 114 min)
d/p Howard Hawks. *sc* Leigh Brackett, Burton Wohl. *ph* William H Clothier. *ed* John Woodcock. *pd* Robert E Smith. *m* Jerry Goldsmith. *cast* John Wayne, Jorge Rivero, Jennifer O'Neill, Jack Elam, Victor French, Chris Mitchum, Susana Dosamantes, Mike Henry, David Huddleston, Bill Williams, Sherry Lansing, Jim Davis.

● Though Hawks' last film moves away from the claustrophobic night-time interiors of *Rio Bravo* and the second half of *El Dorado*, the third Western in this loose trilogy scripted by Leigh Brackett retains many similarities with its predecessors. Wayne is the Union cavalry officer who, after the Civil War, joins forces with a couple of Confederates he once captured, in an effort to hunt down a treacherous bootlegger. Rambling, relaxed (though with several superbly staged set pieces), and often shot through with laconic humour, it's another of Hawks' fascinating portraits of disparate individuals brought together into a cohesive moral force by a mutual sense of respect, responsibility, and physical and emotional needs. If it lacks the formal perfection of *Rio Bravo* and the moving elegy for men grown old of *El Dorado*, it's still a marvellous film. GA

Riot in Cell Block 11

(1954, US, 80 min, b/w)
d Don Siegel. *p* Walter Wanger. *sc* Richard Collins. *ph* Russell Harlan. *ed* Bruce Pierce. *ad* David Milton. *m* Herschel Burke Gilbert. *cast* Neville Brand, Emile Meyer, Frank Faylen, Leo Gordon, Robert Osterloh, Paul Frees, Don Keefer, Dabbs Greer, Whit Bissell.

● A classic of the genre, almost documentary in approach – low budget, no stars, Folsom Prison locations, inmates as extras – and boiling up an explosive violence kept under perfect control. Not looking for cosy answers (in fact, final victory shades ironically into defeat), the script's prime concern is less to establish the need for reform than to demonstrate the fallibilities that militate against its accomplishment: Brand's riot leader and Meyer's warden are men of integrity in essential agreement as to what needs to be done, but each is attended by an evil genius – one psychopathic, the other corrupt – so that simple issues mutate into an entirely different ball game. A riveting movie. TM

Ripa Hits the Skids (Ripa Ruostuu)

(1993, Fin, 80 min)
d Christian Lindblad. *p* Aki Kaurismäki, Klaus Heydemann. *sc* Christian Lindblad. *ph* Ilkka Ruuhuärvi. *ed* Ulli Enckell. *ad* Marjaana Rantama. *m* Björn B Lindström. *cast* Sam Huber, Mari Vainio, Merja Larivaara, Leena Votila.

● Another dour sub-Kaurismäki comedy-drama from Finland, with the slobby, drunken hero of the title, a none-too-promising would-be film-maker, getting up to his neck in trouble thanks to his professional ambitions and easy-going promiscuity. With its vaguely Chandler-esque voice-over, it's clearly meant to be a *noir* parody – but mostly it's just tiresome. GA

Ripoux, Les

see Le Cop

Ripoux contre ripoux

see Le Cop 2

Ripples Across Stagnant Water (Sishui Wei Lan)

(1992, HK/China, 95 min)
d Ling Zifeng. *p* Tam Wing-chuen, Wu Baowen. *sc* Han Lanfang. *ph* Sun Tongtian. *ed* Pan Sufei. *ad* Yang Zhanjia. *m* Mo Fan. *cast* Xu Qing, You Yong, Zhao Jun, Cheng Xi.

● Ten years ago, when he made *Rickshaw Boy*, veteran director Ling Zifeng began a shift from Communist propaganda cinema to much more personal film-making: idiosyncratic adaptations from his favourite literature of the '30s and '40s, centred on strong-willed, independent women, and formed by his interests in visual art, history and sexuality. Much of the present film is as vivid and youthful as anything by Léos Carax. A young woman stuck in a Sichuan backwater town at the turn of the last century marries a grocer but then openly takes a lover; can she hold her own when enemies in the community strike at her and the men in her life? The closing scenes seem choppy and over-compressed, but the film as a whole is clear-sighted, gripping and very beautiful. TR

Rise and Fall of a Little Film Company from a novel by James Hadley Chase (Grandeur et Décadence d'un Petit Commerce de Cinéma d'après un roman de J H Chase)

(1986, Fr, 90 min)
d Jean-Luc Godard. *p* Pierre Grimblat. *sc* Jean-Luc Godard. *ph* Caroline Champetier. *ed* Jean-Luc Godard. *cast* Jean-Pierre Léaud, Jean-Pierre Mocky, Marie Valéra, Jean-Luc Godard.

● Characteristically, Godard's contribution to the TV thriller series *Série Noire* retains only the most rudimentary trappings of the thriller (mysterious voice-overs, secretive assignations, random shootings). He focuses his attentions on the nuts-and-bolts process of TV production as a neurotic genius (Léaud) and his harassed producer (Mocky) swallow their auteur pride and get down to the business of casting for a James Hadley Chase flick. In one long sequence after another, director Léaud attempts to resurrect theories and images from the great days of the French cinema, torturing actors, chucking out references to everyone from Stanislavsky to Cocteau, until the appearance of Godard himself, a shuffling, nicotine-stained cynic whose pragmatism debunks the mystique of movie-making too much for all concerned. The movie ends with a dead producer, a starving director, and Godard shuffling off to retirement in Iceland, as a new generation of video darlings swamp their efforts in the high gloss pop-promo pouting and posturing. Any criticism that this is too much a movie about a movie about a movie is understandable, but *Rise and Fall* goes further into that territory than anyone (including Godard) has gone before. RS

Rise and Fall of Idi Amin

see Amin, the Rise and Fall

Rise and Fall of Legs Diamond, The

(1960, US, 101 min, b/w)
d Budd Boetticher. *p* Milton Sperling. *sc* Joseph Landon. *ph* Lucien Ballard. *ed* Folmar Blangsted. *ad* Jack Poplin. *m* Leonard Rosenman. *cast* Ray Danton, Karen Steele, Warren Oates, Elaine Stewart, Jesse White, Simon Oakland.

● Quite the equal of Boetticher's classic B-Western series starring Randolph Scott, this ferocious gangster biopic indulges in none of the nostalgia for the Depression or glamorisation of its anti-heroes so prevalent in most such movies. As incarnated by Danton, Diamond is a bundle of pure, destructive energy, so ruthless in his sexual, social and financial ambitions that he'll do *anything* to increase or protect his criminal domain; even to the point of agreeing to his brother's death as insurance that the law doesn't reach him through his inevitably softer sibling. With superb *noir* photography from Lucien Ballard, the tone is almost existential: wisely, Boetticher defines his protagonist not through psychology but through action. Indeed, the very form of the film mirrors the speed, intelligence, and amoral cunning of its hell-bent mobster. GA

Rise and Rise of Michael Rimmer, The

(1970, GB, 94 min)
d Kevin Billington. *p* Harry Fine. *sc* Peter Cook, John Cleese, Graham Chapman, Kevin Billington. *ph* Alex Thomson. *ed* Stanley Hawkes. *ad* Carmen Dillon. *m* John Cameron. *cast* Peter Cook, Denholm Elliott, Ronald Fraser, Vanessa Howard, Arthur Lowe, George A Cooper, Harold Pinter, Roland Culver, Dennis Price, John Cleese, Ronnie Corbett, Graham Chapman.

● Billington once described this political satire as a kind of British *Z*, but after the subtlety of his first feature, *Interlude*, it seemed blunt and a bit pointless. Written and performed by a host of satirical talent, it chronicles the rise of a self-appointed business efficiency expert (Cook), who becomes an autocratic dictator by submitting every issue to national referendum. Somehow the jokes fall a bit thin, and the script can't make up its mind whether to go out for narrative or a string of weak sketches. Despite Cleese's script credit (along with Cook, Chapman and Billington), the writing is miles below *Monty Python* standard. DP

Rise to Power of Louis XIV, The

see Prise de Pouvoir par Louis XIV, La

Rising Damp

(1980, GB, 98 min)
d Joe McGrath. *p* Roy Skeggs. *sc* Eric Chappell. *ph* Frank Watts. *ed* Peter Weatherley. *ad* Lewis Logan. *m* David Lindup. *cast* Leonard Rossiter, Frances de la Tour, Don Warrington, Christopher Strauli, Denholm Elliott, Carrie Jones, Glynn Edwards, John Cater.

● In which it is demonstrated that moderately droll TV boarding-house sitcoms ought not to be stretched to 98 minutes. Scriptwriter Eric Chappell (he also wrote the series) seems to have bundled together a few rejected TV scripts while in the grip of some sort of *Carry On* frenzy. At feature length, the characters – angular spinster, seedy landlord, young painter, smirking black medical student with public school accent – would have been better placed circa 1960. Their sentiments and prejudices (mostly about race and sex) are so overblown, archaic and unlikely that the sour, deft humour of the telly programmes has simply gone. JS

Rising Sun

(1993, US, 129 min)
d/p Philip Kaufman. *sc* Philip Kaufman, Michael Crichton, Michael Backes. *ph* Michael Chapman. *ed* Stephen A Rotter, William Scharf. *pd* Dean Tavoularis. *m* Toru Takemitsu, Richard Marriot. *cast* Sean Connery, Wesley Snipes, Harvey Keitel, Cary-Hiroyuki Tagawa, Kevin Anderson, Steve Buscemi.

● Striving to downplay the more racist elements of Michael Crichton's novel, Kaufman's PC adaptation falls awkwardly between the conventions of the Hollywood conspiracy thriller and something intended as more artily significant. When a good-time girl is found dead at a party given by a Japanese conglomerate, various cops – boorish lieutenant Keitel, liaison officer Snipes, and Connery's semi-retired expert on all things Japanese – move in to investigate. Connery lectures at length on his favourite subject, which wouldn't be so dull if the suspense was more adroitly handled, but Kaufman, regrettably, gets the pacing all wrong. *Blow-Up*-style video detection scenes provide a modicum of interest. GA

Risky Business

(1983, US, 99 min)
d Paul Brickman. *p* Jon Avnet, Steve Tisch. *sc* Paul Brickman. *ph* Reynaldo Villalobos, Bruce Surtees. *ed* Richard Chew. *pd* William J Cassidy. *m* Tangerine Dream. *cast* Tom Cruise, Rebecca De Mornay, Joe Pantoliano, Richard Masur, Bronson Pinchot, Curtis Armstrong, Nicholas Pryor, Janet Carroll.
●17-year-old Cruise suddenly finds himself in possession of the classic young man's dream: parents away for the weekend, empty house, his father's forbidden Porsche. He finds a girl, and she's a hooker, and they get on fine with all his friends ('Nice friends you have – clean, polite, quick'), and then the Porsche falls into Lake Michigan, and he gets pursued by Guido the Killer Pimp. So far, so glossy, a working comedy of embarrassment that hinges on the weird, and all as hip as a pair of Ray-Bans. What distinguishes it, however, is that it's hovering permanently on the brink of stark, staring disaster in a way that strangely recalls *The Graduate*. Good performances from Cruise and De Mornay. CPea

Rita Sue and Bob Too

(1986, GB, 93 min)
d Alan Clarke. *p* Sandy Lieberson. *sc* Andrea Dunbar. *ph* Ivan Strasburg. *ed* Stephen Singleton. *pd* Len Huntingford. *m* Michael Kamen. *cast* Siobhan Finneran, Michelle Holmes, George Costigan, Lesley Sharp, Willie Ross, Patti Nicholls, Kulvinder Ghir.
●Trading as ribald comedy, this film reflects a cruel and widespread reality, yet maintains an unnerving distance from its own implications. Neighbours on the rough side of a run-down Bradford estate, Rita and Sue (Finneran and Holmes, grittily authentic) are best buddies nearing school-leaving age. They babysit for nouveau riche sleazeball Bob (Costigan) and his wife Michelle (Sharp), whose disaffection with sex becomes her husband's justification for getting it any which way he can – one way being on the reclining front seat of his flash car, taking Rita and Sue, incredibly, in quick succession. It's all fun and games until Michelle finds out: Rita becomes pregnant, moves in with Bob, and has a miscarriage; and Sue opts for a haphazard shack-up with a bully of an Asian boy. Thereafter director Clarke's keenly observed 'naff' character nuances, never a comfortable laugh, really begin to stick in the throat, and his persistent rib-tickling in the face of the girls' desperation provokes a moral dilemma which the ludicrous 'Carry On Coupling' finale simply aggravates. Humour in the worst possible taste. EP

Rite, The (Riten)

(1969, Swe, 74 min, b/w)
d/sc Ingmar Bergman. *ph* Sven Nykvist. *ed* Siv Lundgren. *ad* Lennart Blomqvist. *cast* Ingrid Thulin, Anders Ek, Gunnar Björnstrand, Erik Hell.
●All Bergman's films around this time centre on isolated social groups (often the partners of a marriage) and show them under attack from both inside and out: Laingian fissures and cracks open up between the characters, and their precarious security is challenged by irruptions from the outside world. Bergman preserves and extends his private mythologies (witness the way that images and names recur from film to film), but in a broader (less precious, more honest) context: *The Rite*, with a trio of actors under examination by a judge on charges of obscenity, tries to expose the bonds that tie an artist to his audience, and pushes towards a theory of non-communication. A bold step forward in Bergman's analysis of human isolation. TR

Ritratto di Borghesia in Nero

see Nest of Vipers

Ritz, The

(1976, GB, 91 min)
d Richard Lester. *p* Denis O'Dell. *sc* Terrence McNally. *ph* Paul Wilson. *ed* John Bloom. *pd* Philip Harrison. *m* Ken Thorne. *cast* Jack Weston, Rita Moreno, Jerry Stiller, Kaye Ballard, F Murray Abraham, Paul B Price, Treat Williams, John Everson, Dave King, Bessie Love, George Coulouris.
●A camp farce, based with unrelenting obviousness on a Broadway play, this is one of those masochistic comedies that rely entirely on the (corpulent) vacillations of the leading man. Jack Weston proves that he is strictly a one-dimensional character actor, yet the action is constructed to provide as little relief from him as possible. It concerns his frenetic adventures as a straight forced to hide out in an all-gay New York bath-house of dream-like dimensions populated by cosmetic studs. After the single joke (Weston is nearly raped by a short, thin 'chubby-chaser'), Lester devotes himself with single-minded malevolence to repeating the same routine with weak variations for the entire length of the film. Despite the plot's superficial claims to be breaking new sexual ground, the resulting stale comedy is likely to be as boring to the gay community as to every other. DP

River, The

(1951, US/Ind, 99 min)
d Jean Renoir. *p* Kenneth McEldowney. *sc* Rumer Godden, Jean Renoir. *ph* Claude Renoir. *ed* George Gale. *ad* Eugène Lourié, Bansi Chandra Gupta. *m* MA Partha Sarathy. *cast* Patricia Walters, Radha, Adrienne Corri, Nora Swinburne, Esmond Knight, Thomas E Breen, Sahjan Singh, Arthur Shields, Richard Foster.
●Adapted from Rumer Godden's novel about an English family living in Bengal during the autumn years of the Raj, *The River* is cast as a nostalgic recollection of life as experienced by an adolescent girl undergoing the splendours and miseries of first love. Contemporary guru-worship may have overtaken Renoir's mystic view of India as an alien, unfathomable landscape which lends due proportion to the everyday sufferings and aspirations of humanity, but his tranquil vision of life as a river flowing on, barely disturbed by the ripples of being born, growing up, falling in love, and dying, remains enormously moving. The performances are sometimes amateurish, the exotic detail sometimes a little touristy (though captured in colour as exquisite as anything ever likely to grace the screen), but it hardly matters. The magisterial lyricism and the warmth of Renoir's humanity are the thing. TM

River, The

(1984, US, 124 min)
d Mark Rydell. *p* Edward Lewis, Robert Coates. *sc* Robert Dillon, Julian Barry. *ph* Vilmos Zsigmond. *ed* Sidney Levin. *pd* Charles Rosen. *m* John Williams. *cast* Mel Gibson, Sissy Spacek, Shane Bailey, Becky Jo Lynch, Scott Glenn, Don Hood, Billy Green Bush, James Tolkan.
●Another in a long line of films dealing with the hardships of smallholdings in the sort of rural America usually depicted as containing nothing but corn silos and bigotry. This time, Gibson and Spacek battle against odds much the same as far as nature goes (floods from the river, rather than the conventional tornado), but different on the human front. The villain here is less the Government than the local land baron, who has expansionist schemes, a ploy which vitiates the film's point since the villain is no more than the hero writ larger. Moreover, the message of continuous hardship is somewhat at odds with the same impulse towards idyllic lyricism that Rydell brought to *On Golden Pond*. Vilmos Zsigmond contributes his usual handsome photography, but this is one river that seems unlikely to run. CPea

River, The (Heliu)

(1997, Tai, 124 min)
d Tsai Ming-Liang. *p* Hsu Li-Kong, Chiu Shun-Ching. *sc* Tsai Ming-Liang, Yang Pi-Ying, Tsai Yi-Chun. *ph* Liao Pen-Jung. *ed* Chen Sheng-Chang, Lei Chen-Ching. *pd* Tony Lan. *cast* Lee Kang-Sheng, Miao Tien, Lu Hsiao-Ling, Chen Chaorong, Chen Shiang-Chyi.
●A top prize-winner in Berlin, this takes the absurd/poignant observation of urban isolation and loneliness found in Tsai's two earlier features one step further. A father, mother and son live together-but-apart in a nondescript Taipei apartment, each trapped in a private circle of hell. The taciturn father visits the city's gay saunas for anonymous hand-jobs; the deeply unhappy mother is stuck with an apathetic lover; and the sullen and resentful son finds himself with an agonising (and seemingly incurable) neck pain after an unwise dunking in the polluted Tanshui River. The film's narrative drive has two motors: the quest to alleviate the son's pain and the father's berserk attempts to shore up the ceiling of his room against a leak from the apartment above. Tsai brilliantly conflates the two problems in a climax which is in equal parts real, surreal, melodramatic and inexplicably mysterious. Looks like a future classic. TR

River of Grass

(1994, US, 75 min)
d Kelly Reichardt. *p/sc* Jesse Hartman, Kelly Reichardt. *ph* Jim Denault. *ed* Larry Fessenden. *ad* David Dorenberg. *cast* Lisa Bowman, Larry Fessenden, Dick Russel, Michael Buscemi.
●Born in the backwaters of Florida, the daughter of a homicide detective father and a narcotics agent mother, 31-year-old co-writer and director Reichardt clearly puts a lot of herself into this striking feature debut, which turns the roster of love-on-the-run B-picture clichés right on its head. An unprepossessing 30-year-old with a couple of children and an absent husband, Cozy (Bowman) lives out the dreariest of existences until one night she sneaks out of the house, hooks up with the extremely aimless Lee (Fessenden), and winds up on the lam after the pair think they've shot a local home-owner. With its cast of losers and never-weres, its catalogue of lives in apparent suspension, this down-home drama must be the slackest piece of slacker cinema yet to hit our screens, but the film's crisp framing and even crisper editing signals a sharp intelligence at work behind the camera. What emerges is a wry and telling account of the kind of folks most movies never reach. Watch out for a terrific climactic moment that out-guns *Thelma & Louise*, listen out for a top soundtrack that makes superb use of the Beach Boys' lulling 'Disney Girls'. TJ

River of No Return

(1954, US, 91 min)
d Otto Preminger. *p* Stanley Rubin. *sc* Frank Fenton. *ph* Joseph LaShelle. *ed* Louis Loeffler. *ad* Lyle Wheeler, Addison Hehr. *m* Cyril Mockridge. *cast* Robert Mitchum, Marilyn Monroe, Rory Calhoun, Tommy Rettig, Murvyn Vye, Douglas Spencer.
●Saloon singer Monroe, two-fisted farmer Mitchum, and the young son he hardly knows, may be drifting down-river by raft from both immediate dangers and their immediate pasts, but the thrust of Preminger's only Western consistently forces them to attempt the 'impossible' return: to restart their variously broken lives and reconstitute the 'ideal' family. While Mitchum's performance is excellent, the film holds most interest as an early appraisal of the Monroe enigma: in revealing analogy to the posthumous cult, Mitchum's ability to see beyond her sex symbol/whore facade extends only as far as her fitness for the role of Mother. There really is no return. PT

River Rat, The

(1984, US, 93 min)
d Tom Rickman. *p* Robert E Larson. *sc* Tom Rickman. *ph* Jan Kiesser. *ed* Dennis Virkler. *pd* John J Lloyd. *m* Mike Post. *cast* Tommy Lee Jones, Nancy Lea Owen, Brian Dennehy, Martha Plimpton.
●Tom Rickman was screenwriter on C&W biopic *Coal Miner's Daughter* in which Tommy Lee Jones played Loretta Lynn's husband. Here, in Rickman's directorial debut, the ever-reliable Jones is first rate as an ex-con visiting his family after an absence of many years and trying to make up for lost time with awkward teenager Martha Plimpton. Regrettably, the film doesn't find a great deal to do with their burgeoning relationship. TJ

River Runs Through It, A

(1992, US, 123 min)
d Robert Redford. *p* Robert Redford, Patrick Markey. *sc* Richard Friedenberg. *ph* Philippe Rousselot. *ed* Lynzee Klingman, Robert Estrin. *pd* Jon Hutman. *m* Mark Isham. *cast* Craig Sheffer, Brad Pitt, Tom Skerritt, Brenda Blethyn, Emily Lloyd, Edie McClurg, Stephen Shellen, Nicole Burdette.
●Montana, 1910. Norman and his younger brother Paul grow up under the watchful eye of their father (the ever-wonderful Skerritt), a Presbyterian minister of Scots descent. Mornings are spent studying, afternoons devoted to fly-fishing in the nearby river, a quasi-mystical pastime

which serves as the film's central metaphor: while they cast their lines and wait, the boys learn the importance of grace, harmony and patience. At home, however, the family's inability to express emotions hints at trouble to come; and so while nice-guy Norman (Sheffer) matures and dates good-girl Jessie (Lloyd), reckless Paul (Pitt) turns to gambling and liquor. Redford (who reads passages from Norman Maclean's source novella in voice-over) explores the brothers' changing relationship with intelligence and restraint; however, because events are filtered through the author's fictional persona, certain sequences involving Paul lack his much-needed perspective. Humour brings things back to earth, and saves the film from becoming over-earnest. Leave your preconceptions about fishing at the door: you'll be caught hook, line and sinker. CM

River's Edge, The

(1957, US, 87 min)
d Allan Dwan. *p* Benedict Bogeaus. *sc* Harold J Smith, James Leicester. *ph* Harold Lipstein. *ed* James Leicester. *ad* Van Nest Polglase. *m* Lou Forbes. *cast* Ray Milland, Anthony Quinn, Debra Paget, Harry Carey Jr, Byron Foulger.

●Made for spare change like the rest of his flurry of late, worthwhile B-pictures, this is yet another example of Dwan's enterprise under pressure. He gets a scathing performance out of Milland, for instance, as the crook with a wad of hot money he needs to smuggle into Mexico, proves characteristically at home with the expanses of CinemaScope, and blithely proceeds with a storyline that oh-so-conveniently marries off the villain's old flame to border guide Quinn. TJ

River's Edge

(1986, US, 100 min)
d Tim Hunter. *p* Sarah Pillsbury, Midge Sanford. *sc* Neal Jiminez. *ph* Frederick Elmes. *ed* Howard Smith, Sonya Sones. *pd* John Muto. *m* Jürgen Knieper. *cast* Crispin Glover, Keanu Reeves, Ione Skye Leitch, Daniel Roebuck, Dennis Hopper, Joshua Miller, Roxana Za

●Kicking off with an overweight and slobbish teenager (Roebuck) sitting dispassionately next to the naked corpse of the girl he's just murdered, this raw picture of the lost generation tackles thorny issues of responsibility and loyalty: will the psycho killer's peers remain true to their (lack of) ideals, or turn fink and risk retribution? In Hunter's smalltown hell, the dilemma is not easily dealt with: on the one hand, Roebuck's barely motivated act of violence escalates beyond fun into nightmare territory; on the other, society is truly fucked – why bother saving it? – with the kids gripped by the baleful influence of the dope-dealin', gun-totin', mannequin doll-lovin' Feck (Hopper, excessively indulged). For all its uncompromising toughness, the film, like the kids, gets out of hand, its bleak portrait of alienated, antisocial behaviour increasingly wrecked by hysterical performances (Glover especially), a sentimental teen-romance subplot, and melodramatic contrivance. There are some good, frightening scenes of volatile lunacy, but the whole thing badly lacks a controlling distance and perspective; much inferior to Hunter's script for Jonathan Kaplan's superficially similar *Over the Edge*, it continually teeters on the verge of self-parody. GA

River Wild, The

(1994, US, 111 min)
d Curtis Hanson. *p* David Foster, Lawrence Turman. *sc* Denis O'Neill. *ph* Robert Elswit. *ed* Joe Hutshing, David Brenner. *pd* Bill Kenney. *m* Jerry Goldsmith. *cast* Meryl Streep, Joseph Mazzello, David Strathairn, Kevin Bacon, John C Reilly, Elizabeth Hoffman, Victor H Galloway.

●This tense family-therapy thriller doesn't produce any surprises, but sometimes, perhaps, it's enough just to go along for the ride, knowing you'll arrive not too far from where you set off. Gail (Streep) whisks reluctant husband Tom (Strathairn) and troubled son Roarke (Mazzello) to Montana for a week's white-water rafting. The purpose of the trip is not only to commune with nature, but to heal the rift between husband and wife, father and son. Tom, though, is not unduly delighted to be at his wife's mercy, especially when the suspiciously charming Wade (Bacon) starts paddling in their wake, a line at the ready, a rod in his pocket. While it's true that the men rely on Streep's superior kayak skills and knowledge of the river, the movie is only interested in a kind of halfway feminism: much of it is concerned with young Roarke, and the contrasting father-figures of Wade and Tom. Bacon scores strongly, but it is Streep's beautifully natural, unshowy performance which keeps the film on course, even when the machinations of the plot become very rocky indeed. TCh

Rivières Pourpres, Les

see Crimson Rivers, The

Road, The

see Strada, La

Road, The (Jol)

(2001, Fr/Jap/Kazakhstan/Neth, 85 min)
d Darejan Omirbaev. *p* Elise Jalladeau, Joël Farges, Ueda Makoto. *sc* Darejan Omirbaev, Limara Jeksembaeva. *ph* Boris Troshev. *pd* Marina Trosheva. *cast* Djamshed Usmonov.

●A film-maker, so self-obsessed he has nightmares about film festival screenings going wrong, hears that his mother is ill, and takes the long drive to his remote native village, reappraising his life en route, but barely able to grasp or appreciate his wife's love for him. A road movie, then, with all the digressions and taciturn introspection you'd expect; there is, however, also a nice line in droll, deadpan, deprecatory humour. Patchy, but its quiet virtues reward patience. GA

Road Builder, The (aka The Night Digger)

(1971, GB, 102 min)
d Alastair Reid. *p* Alan D Courtney, Norman S Powell. *sc* Roald Dahl. *ph* Alex Thomson. [*ed* not credited.] *ad* Anthony Pratt. *m* Bernard Herrmann. *cast* Patricia Neal, Nicholas Clay, Pamela Brown, Jean Anderson, Graham Crowden, Brigit Forsyth.

●Brown rules the roost in her rambling old mansion, gossiping with cronies about the vicar's (entirely imaginary) sex-change operation and visiting casual cruelties on her aging adopted daughter (Neal). Her other mistake is to hire personable itinerant Clay to look after the garden, when someone called the Travelling Maniac is on the loose. Starting as an analogue of *Night Must Fall*, Dahl's script segues fascinatingly into areas explored contemporaneously in Chabrol's *Le Boucher*. The contributions of Thomson, Pratt and Herrmann are exemplary, but Reid is the sort of plodding director something of this sort absolutely doesn't need. From the novel *Nest in a Falling Tree* by Joy Cowley. BBa

Road Flower

(1993, US, 86 min)
d Deran Sarafian. *p* John Flock, Lance Hool. *sc* Tedi Sarafian. *cast* Christopher Lambert, Craig Sheffer, David Arquette, Adrienne Shelley, Noah Fleiss.

●A cautionary thriller which plays like a cross between *The Hitcher* and *Cape Fear*. It's the story of a middle-class family whose vacation turns into a nightmare when they get on the wrong side of a bunch of tearaways halfway across a Midwestern desert. Goaded into playing chicken with the youths, one adult ends up dead, and the others are taken prisoner while the mentally unstable leader (Sheffer) decides how to dispose of them. After a taut, provocative opening, the improbabilities soon mount up (a situation not helped by Sheffer's OTT performance). The film never really finds its feet, but settles down to a series of action clichés (note how Lambert's specs disappear once his gravitas has been established). It's ironic, given the emphasis on dysfunctional families of one kind or another, that the film is itself a family affair: written and produced by Tedi Sarafian, while sometime director Richard Sarafian appears in a cameo role. TCh

Roadgames

(1981, Aust, 100 min)
d/p Richard Franklin. *sc* Everett de Roche. *ph* Vince Monton. *ed* Edward McQueen-Mason. *pd* Jon Dowding. *m* Brian May. *cast* Stacy Keach, Jamie Lee Curtis, Marion Edward, Grant Page, Thaddeus Smith, Stephen Millichamp.

●It's precisely its pretensions which make this a surprisingly agreeable cross of angst-ridden '70s road movie with Hitchcockian thriller. In homage to *Rear Window*, the windshield of poetry-quoting truck driver Keach's lorry stands in as the blank sheet upon which he sketches fantasies about what he observes on the road. A string of grisly murders which follow him across Australia, and a lift given to hitchhiker Jamie Lee Curtis, who later disappears, fuel his already vivid imagination still further. Effective as a string of cinematic shocks, the movie manages a good number of coups, with its cargo of raw meat, use of Jamie Lee's association with endless knife-flicks, and the ever-so-slightly surreal placing of figures in a vast landscape, making for an endearing horror pic. RM

Road Home, The

(1987, GB/Pol, 95 min)
d Jerzy Kaszubowski. *p* Glenn Wilhide, Andrzej Kowalczyk. *sc* Jerry Kaszubowski. *ph* Wit Dabal. *ed* Marek Denys. *pd* Andrzej Kowalczyk. *m* Zygmunt Konieczny. *cast* Rafal Synowka, Jerzy Binczycki, Marzena Trybala, Slawa Kwasniewska, Boguslaw Linda, Jerzy Kaszubowski.

●In 1945, the Red Cross take Jerzy (Synowka) from Germany, where he has spent the war, back home to his mother and his paternal grandparents who occupy a large house somewhere near the Black Forest, then under the jurisdiction of the Red Army. The boy's father, a Polish cavalryman, disappeared in 1939 and a flame is kept burning at night to guide him home. Written and directed by the English-born Jerzy Kaszubowski, this Anglo-Polish production focuses tight on its historical moment, on a section of Poland sandwiched between its past (Germany) and its future (the Soviet Union). It's heavily symbolic, with an eagle and a grey horse making several appearances (and the director himself playing the father's ghost). At the end Jerzy and his stepfather Edward, a government placeman, wander through a forest after their truck has been ambushed by partisans. Jerzy has often imagined killing the now terrified usurper. The opportunity presents itself, but he declines to take it. Cue the grey horse. JPy

Road Home, The

see Lost Angels

Road Home, The (Wo de Fuqin Muqin)

(1999, China, 100 min)
d Zhang Yimou. *p* Zhang Weiping, Zhao Yu, Zhang Zhengyan, Hu Xiaofeng. *sc* Bao Shi. *ph* Hou Yong, Li Xiaoping. *ed* Zhai Ru. *ad* Cao Jiuping. *m* San Bao. *cast* Zhang Ziyi, Sun Honglei, Zheng Hao, Zhao Yuelin, Li Bin, Chang Guifa.

●Zhang's Berlin Special Jury Prize-winner sees the present in grey, dispiriting monochrome, but flashes back to the politically fraught 1950s in rapturous colour – questionably suggesting that the Chinese were tougher, truer and more sincere in the good old days of political persecution. Set in a remote northern village, it charts one pretty girl's dogged courtship of the young teacher at the local school – the first obstacle being social taboos against unchaperoned meetings, the second being his lengthy disappearance for questioning in connection with 1957's 'Anti-Rightist campaign'. Both subject and style recall Xie Jin's *The Herdsman* (1981), a prime example of the kind of cinema that the 'Fifth Generation' directors supposedly swept away. The ultra-sentimental ending spells out the point that the Chinese can be as good as they ever were if only they stay in touch with their traditions. TR

Road House

(1948, US, 95 min, b/w)
d Jean Negulesco. *p/sc* Edward Chodorov. *ph* Joseph LaShelle. *ed* James B Clark. *ad* Lyle R Wheeler, Maurice Ransford. *m* Cyril Mockridge. *cast* Ida Lupino, Cornel Wilde, Celeste Holm, Richard Widmark, OZ Whitehead, Robert Karnes.

●A bizarre, subdued weepie-cum-thriller, centered around Lupino's sultry presence as a nightclub chanteuse who inspires such feelings of love and hate in her blood-brother employers (Widmark and Wilde) that they turn on each other with a vengeance. Aided by strong performances, Negulesco smooths over the strange shifts in plot and characterisation, manages somehow to lend credibility to the melodramatic proceedings, and delivers one of the great drunkard scenes en route. Mad, perhaps, but memorable too. GA

Road House

(1989, US, 114 min)
d Rowdy Herrington. *p* Joel Silver. *sc* David Lee Henry, Hilary Henkin. *ph* Dean Cundey. *ed* Frank Urioste, John F Link. *m* Michael Kamen. *cast* Patrick Swayze, Kelly Lynch, Sam Elliott, Ben Gazzara, Marshall Teague, Julie Michaels, Red West, Sunshine Parker, Kevin Tighe, Kathleen Wilhoite.

●Swayze gives up 'Dirty Dancing' for dirty fighting in this violent, spectacular and immensely enjoyable study of Zen and the art of Barroom Bouncing. A former philosophy student now majoring in martial arts, he is hired to clean up the Double Deuce, a beleaguered Missouri nightclub where the band plays behind wire and the staff 'sweep up the eyeballs after closing'. Like a modern Western hero, Swayze cleans out the sadists, till-skimmers, drug dealers and loafers, but he's also up against a ruthless businessman (Gazzara) whose heavies extort money for a 'town improvement' scheme. When Swayze's employer refuses to cross Gazzara's palm with silver, heads roll, bones crack, blood flows, buildings explode, and plausibility flies right out the window along with the bodies. Swayze's drippy romance with the local Doc, a leggy blonde (Lynch) who tends his wounds and more besides, slows things down; but when his ageing mentor (Elliott) comes to town, they kick serious ass, while director Herrington and stuntman Charlie Picerni pile on the senseless mayhem as the two factions perform their Dance of Death. Mindless entertainment of the highest order. NF

Roadie

(1980, US, 105 min)
d Alan Rudolph. *p* Carolyn Pfeiffer. *sc* Big Boy Medlin, Michael Ventura. *ph* David Myers. *ed* Tom Walls. *pd* Paul Peters. *m* Craig Hundley. *cast* Meatloaf, Kaki Hunter, Art Carney, Gailard Sartain, Don Cornelius, Rhonda Bates, Joe Spano, Richard Marion.

●Meatloaf plays a Texas lunk called Travis W Redfish whose ability to fix electronics with manure and bits of potatoes gets him caught up in a highly sanitised, if surreal, version of the rock business. Hank Williams Jr, Roy Orbison, Alice Cooper and Blondie all show up, but the film's best quality is its combination of trash-culture gags and redneck humour: 'I just love these National Geographic Specials' cries Redfish as he watches *The Giant Spider Invasion* on TV. The good ole boy gags are keen enough to make *Roadie* a late night staple, but you can see why UA had cold feet about a wider audience for the film. DP

Roadkill

see Joy Ride

Roadmovie

(2002, SKor, 106 min)
d Kim In-Shik. *p* Tcha Sung-Jai, Choi Jae-Won, Kim Jae-Won. *sc* Kim In-Shik. *ph* Kim Jae-Ho. *ed* Lee Jae-Woong. *ad* Choi Ki-Ho. *m* Lee Han-Na. *cast* Hwang Jung-Min, Jung Chan, Seo Lin.

●Remarkable debut feature that takes Korean macho masculinity literally to the end of the road. Ruined stockbroker Suk-Won (Jung) becomes one more piece of social jetsam. Rejected by his wife, he discovers a community of sorts among the winos on the streets of Seoul, dominated by the ultra-macho Dae-Shik (Hwang), a one-time celebrity mountaineer. Dae-Shik helps rescue Suk-Won from himself and suggests a cross-country trip together; only after encounters with various damaged women and men (including strung-out waitress Il-Joo and Dae-Shik's abandoned wife and son) does Suk-Won realise that he's the focus of an all-male love story. There are several strange assumptions about love, pain and gay self-hatred running close to the surface here, but the fearless performances and arresting visuals (somewhere between Cassavetes and Koreeda) carry a high level of conviction. TR

Roadside Prophets

(1992, US, 96 min)
d Abbe Wool. *p* Peter McCarthy, David Swinson. *sc* Abbe Wool, David Swinson. *ph* Tom Richmond. *ed* Nancy Richardson. *pd* J Rae Fox. *m* Pray For Rain. *cast* John Doe, Adam Horovitz, John Cusack, Arlo Guthrie, David Carradine, Timothy Leary.

●Writer/director Wool has created a genuine weirdo with her part allegorical, part satirical road movie. Complete with cameos from Timothy Leary, Arlo Guthrie and David Carradine, it's a throwback to the vacuous philosophising and psychobabble of the late '60s. And maybe this is fitting. As Joe (Doe) quests for a contemporary El Dorado in Nevada – where he wants to bury a fellow biker who electrocuted himself on a video game – we're continually witness to the conflict between present-day values, as embodied by Sam (Horovitz), who may just be the dead man's ghost, and those of the Summer of Love, as represented by virtually everyone Sam and Joe meet. For deadhead druggies only. GA

Roads of Exile, The (Les Chemins de l'Exil)

(1978, Fr/Switz/GB, 165 min)
d Claude Goretta. *p* Etienne Laroche. *sc* George Haldas, Claude Goretta. *ph* Philippe Rousselot. *ed* Joële van Effenterre. *ad* Jacques Bufnoir, Enrique Sonois. *m* Arié Dzierlatka. *cast* François Simon, Dominique Labourier, Roland Bertin, Michel Berto, Gabriel Cattand, Martine Chevallier, Sylvain Clément, William Fox.

●Long, slow, and probably not to everybody's taste, but a fascinating study of the Swiss philosopher/novelist Jean-Jacques Rousseau, which attempts to elucidate certain aspects of his life and work left obscure in his supposedly completely honest *Confessions*. Covering the years from Rousseau's exile after the burning of *Emile* in 1762 to his death in 1778 (years marked by his progressive persecution mania), it also ranges back to privileged earlier moments as he attempts to alleviate his present misery by recapturing or exorcising his past. It's almost a pointilliste film, as quietly undemonstrative as *The Lacemaker*, alternating between gorgeously idyllic natural landscapes and stark, severe interiors that would not have shamed Vermeer. Rossellini was originally slated to direct, but Goretta has done the subject proud, very much in the master's manner. TM

Road to Corinth, The

see Route de Corinthe, La

Road to El Dorado, The

(2000, US, 90 min)
d Eric Bergeron, Don Paul. *p* Bonne Radford, Brooke Breton. *sc* Terry Rossio, Ted Elliott. *ed* (supervising) John Carnochan, Dan Molina. *pd* Christian Schellewald. *m* Elton John; (score) Hans Zimmer, John Powell. *lyrics* Tim Rice. *cast* voices: Kevin Kline, Kenneth Branagh, Rosie Perez, Armand Assante, Edward James Olmos. *narrator* Elton John.

●Hope and Crosby's *Road* series never made it to El Dorado, but their wisecracking, lighthearted spirit is the inspiration for this DreamWorks challenge to Disney's pre-eminence in the animated field. Spain, 1519: adventurers Tulio and Miguel have just won in a dice game a map pinpointing El Dorado, legendary city of gold. Stowing away on the ship carrying conquistador Cortes, they fortuitously hit the right spot on the other side of the Atlantic, whereupon the scenario switches to *Man Who Would Be King* territory. Acclaimed as gods by the tribespeople, the rapscallions are unsure how deities behave, but with canny native girl Chel in on the ruse, an arrangement may yet be struck to benefit everyone. The banter between the roguish duo provides amiable diversion, while intermittently impressive action sequences bring on a deadly whirlpool, a forerunner of basketball, and an imposingly scary demon. TJ

Road to Fort Alamo

see Strada per Forte Alamo, La

Road to Frisco, The

see They Drive By Night

Road to Glory, The

(1936, US, 95 min, b/w)
d Howard Hawks. *p* Darryl F Zanuck. *sc* Joel Sayre, William Faulkner. *ph* Gregg Toland. *ed* Edward Curtiss. *ad* Hans Peters. *m* Louis Silvers. *cast* Fredric March, Warner Baxter, Lionel Barrymore, June Lang, Gregory Ratoff, Victor Kilian, Paul Stanton, John Qualen.

●Hawks brings *The Dawn Patrol* down into the trenches, with Baxter as the (French) CO coming to the end of his tether as the death toll mounts, and March as the junior officer who takes over. There's a conventional love interest (Lang as a nurse), a sticky subplot involving Barrymore (he's Baxter's father, and though considerably over-age, joins up to do his bit alongside his son), and some swivelling between anti-war and jingoistic moods. The climax, a heroic twin death scene (with Barrymore redeeming his former cowardice by suicidally guiding the blinded Baxter to a crucial observation post) is embarrassingly OTT. But elsewhere Hawksian understatement keeps the lachrymose tendencies at bay (though William Faulkner co-scripted, it appears that Nunnally Johnson did a rewrite job), turning the film into another of his finely-tuned studies of comradeship under stress; and there is some superb battle footage, in fact borrowed from a French film of 1932, Raymond Bernard's *Les Croix de Bois*. TM

Road to Morocco

(1942, US, 83 min, b/w)
d David Butler. *p* Paul Jones. *sc* Frank Butler, Don Hartman. *ph* William C Mellor. *ed* Irene Morra. *ad* Hans Dreier, Robert Usher. *songs* Johnny Burke, James Van Heusen. *cast* Bing Crosby, Dorothy Lamour, Bob Hope, Dona Drake, Anthony Quinn, Vladimir Sokoloff, Monte Blue, Yvonne De Carlo.

●The third, and along with *Road to Utopia*, probably the best in a series which began in 1940 with *Road to Singapore*, continued with *Road to Zanzibar* (1941), *Road to Utopia* (1945), *Road to Rio* (1947), *Road to Bali* (1952), *The Road to Hong Kong* (1962). Like Webster's dictionary, Bob and Bing are Morocco bound and gagging as they vie, as ever, for Lamour's hand. The Hope persona is here at its most complete – the stud who baulks at the last fence, the sharp talker who always seems to be talking to himself, the complacent wit who depends on our recognition of references, situations, generalised feelings. At base, it's an unsympathetic character – asexual, craven, treacherous – but Hope's skill in timing, and his ability to work cold what is an extended cabaret act, carries him through. Frank Butler and Don Hartman, who also wrote the two earlier *Road* movies, know their man completely. Crosby is a pleasant foil, and croons 'Moonlight Becomes You' as his party piece. SG

Road to Nhill, The

(1995, Aust, 95 min)
d Sue Brooks. *p* Sue Maslin. *sc* Alison Tilson. *ph* Nicolette Freeman. *ed* Tony Stevens. *pd* Georgina Campbell. *m* Elizabeth Drake. *cast* Bill Young, Bill Hunter, Patricia Kennedy, Vikki Blanche, Monica Maughan, Terry Norris.

●One day in the sleepy outback community of Nhill, four elderly members of the ladies' bowls team have a car accident and find themselves hanging upside down by their seat belts. The wait begins for the emergency services, and an extended comedy of errors gets under way – not out-and-out farce, but a kind of amiable, plausible fumbling. Alison Tilson's screenplay tells us again and again that Australian men are crap, but the womenfolk have to put up with them, while Sue Brooks' direction backs it up with a lot of portentous aerial shots. If droll detachment was intended, such over-emphasis breaks the spell. TJ

Road to Salina (Sur la Route de Salina)

(1969, Fr/It, 103 min)
d Georges Lautner. *p* Robert Dorfmann, Yvon Guezel. *sc* Georges Lautner, Pascal Jardin, Jack Miller. *ph* Maurice Fellous. *ed* Michelle David, Elisabeth Guido. *ad* Jean d'Eaubonne. *m* Bernard Gérard, Christophe, Ian Anderson. *cast* Mimsy Farmer, Robert Walker, Rita Hayworth, Ed Begley, Bruce Pêcheur, Sophie Hardy, David Sachs.

●A complicated little epic, told in flashback, concerning a rather sinister case of mistaken identity being imposed by Rita Hayworth and her screen daughter (tubby, snub-nosed Farmer) on an itinerant stud (Walker). In explaining just why this should be, the film gets through incest, a very unconvincing murder or two, a few flashes of rather unattractive genitalia, and a fair bit of sexual grumbling and grunting. As an excuse for the odd flash of tit and prick, well, better skinflicks have been made for less than a sixth of what Joe Levine must have coughed up to produce this.

Road to the Racetrack (Kyongmachang Kanungil)

(1991, SKor, 138 min)
d Jang Sun-Woo. *p* Lee Taw-Won. *sc* Ha Il-Ji. *cast* Moon Sung-Kuen, Kang Soo-Yeon, Kim Bo-Yeon, Lee In-Ok.

●The film which shot Jang into the premier league nudges the sex-war into the 21st century. 'R' (Moon) comes back to Korea from several years of study in France, expecting to resume his affair with fellow student 'J' (Kang). But she is now a 'different' woman, adept at abandoning him in hotel rooms every time he tries to corner her and insistent that he should go back to his working-class wife and kids. Jang raises indirection to a fine art: he maintains the sense that the film could veer off in any direction at any time, and never fully explains the title metaphor. But anyone struggling through a screwed-up relationship will recognise this as the real thing. TR

Road to Utopia

(1945, US, 90 min, b/w)
d Hal Walker. *p* Paul Jones. *sc* Norman Panama, Melvin Frank. *ph* Lionel Lindon. *ed* Stuart Gilmore. *ad* Hans Dreier, Roland Anderson. *m* Leigh Harline. *songs* Johnny Burke, Jimmy Van Heusen. *cast* Bing Crosby, Bob Hope, Dorothy Lamour, Hillary Brooke, Douglass Dumbrille, Jack LaRue.

●A typical *Road* movie (Utopia being Alaska), this has Lamour oscillating between Bob and Bing for possession of both halves of the map to her goldmine. But kiss-kiss and moonlight serenading aside, it's always the quipping rivalry of the duo that rules (Bing: 'We've shared a couple of things that money can't buy' – Bob: 'Yeah, and I always got the ugly one'), where possession is the objective and *L'Amour* the object. But share they do, right down the middle. She loves Bing, marries Bob, but the offspring is a dead ringer for 'We adopted him' they chorus, to the tune of Family Entertainment, accompanied by a broad wink. FF

Road to Wellville, The

(1994, US, 120 min)
d Alan Parker. *p* Armyan Bernstein, Robert F Colesberry, Alan Parker. *sc* Alan Parker. *ph* Peter Biziou. *ed* Gerry Hambling. *pd* Brian Morris. *m* Rachel Portman. *cast* Anthony Hopkins, Bridget Fonda, Matthew Broderick, John Cusack, Dana Carvey, Michael Lerner, John Neville.

●If you're tickled by rectal complaints, this film of T Coraghessan Boyle's novel about Dr Kellogg and his turn-of-the-century sanitarium is the movie for you. It's an ensemble piece, but the real star is the re-creation of the Battle Creek Sanitarium, replete with sitz baths, a Fecal Analysis room, and enemas on the hour. Alan Parker has the true cartoonist's eye for the juxtapositioning of wobbly flesh and corrective machinery, and Hopkins' Kellogg does nothing to let him down. All bounce and buck teeth, this Cornflake King is a splendid comic creation, though his adopted son (Carvey) errs on the side of Fungus the Bogeyman. The stories are less interesting than the setting, with constipated Will (Broderick) and his sexually curious wife (Fonda) the victims of, respectively, colonic irrigation and a fraudulent clitoris expert. Battle Creek, Michigan, was like a gold-rush town in 1907, with rival cereal manufacturers battling to dominate the credulous market – clearly an appealing pathology to an old socialist like Parker, but sloppily rendered here. Still, an amusing farce. BC

Road Trip

(2000, US, 94 min)
d Todd Phillips. *p* Daniel Goldberg, Joe Medjuck. *sc* Todd Phillips, Scot Armstrong. *ph* Mark Irwin. *ed* Sheldon Kahn, Peter Teschner. *pd* Clark Hunter. *m* Mark Simpson. *cast* Breckin Meyer, Seann William Scott, Amy Smart, Paulo Costanzo, DJ Qualls, Rachel Blanchard, Anthony Rapp, Fred Wards, Tom Green.

●Josh (Meyer) has videoed himself singing love songs and whispering sweet nothings to his beloved on a far off campus. But the tape he's mailed actually features him having sex with another girl. There's only one solution – *road trip!* – which entails piling in a car with some mates and driving half across America to intercept the package. The ensuing frolics – the theft of a bus from a blind school, a visit to a sperm bank, an ill advised drop-in on an all-black fraternity, and some almost surreal business with a mouse – echo the-Farrelly brothers. But there's more on offer than outrageous action highlights. Although Meyer makes a colourless, if likeable lead, MTV comic Tom Green provides off the wall interludes as the narrator stringing the tale along, and best of all is DJ Qualls, the geek made good who finally rebels against his own timidity as the script's 'seize the day' ethos homes in on *Revenge of the Nerds*-style positivity. As in the inferior *American Pie*, the rutting males are rather sweetly befuddled creatures, which allows the good natured joshing to get away with parodically gratuitous nudity and some extremely non-judgmental, drug-related humour. TJ

Roald Dahl's Matilda

(1996, US, 98 min)
d Danny DeVito. *p* Danny DeVito, Michael Shamberg, Stacey Sher, Liccy Dahl. *sc* Nicholas Kazan, Robin Swicord. *ph* Stefan Czapsky. *ed* Lynzee Klingman, Brent White. *pd* Bill Brzeski. *m* David Newman. *cast* Mara Wilson, Danny DeVito, Rhea Perlman, Embeth Davidtz, Pam Ferris, Brian Levinson.

●This adaptation is paradoxical, a film celebrating the fruits of book-reading that's not as good as the original novel. DeVito can't resist the Hollywood touch – special effects, suspect stereotypes, crushing music – especially in the latter stages. Still, mainly he's stuck to the book, and anyway, there's scope enough in Dahl's slipstream for something worthwhile. Our heroine (Mara Wilson) is a precocious, bright, spunky young thing somehow born to mindless, amoral, stupid neanderthals. Dad (DeVito) is a crooked car dealer, Mum (Perlman) a bingo junkie; they both ignore her. When she's finally sent to school, it's as part-receipt for a used car Dad's sold to the headmistress, Miss Trunchbull (Ferris). Alas, the teaching methods of this Olympic hammer-throwing harridan are open to question – her idea of a perfect school is one with no children. DeVito's snappy, kinetic visual style fits the cartoon feel of the material, and the cast is great. It's a modern-day pantomime about childhood solidarity and self-empowerment: the real joy here is the view of generational war, the children's assumption of zero tolerance for injustices inflicted by absurd adults, and the recognition that the big meanies should be punished, by fair means or foul. NB

Roar

(1981, US, 101 min)
d Noel Marshall. *p* Noel Marshall, Tippi Hedren. *sc* Noel Marshall. *ph* Jan de Bont. *ed* Jerry Marshall, Jan de Bont. *pd* Joel Marshall. *m* Terence P Minogue. *cast* Noel Marshall, Tippi Hedren, John Marshall, Jerry Marshall, Melanie Griffith, Kyalo Mativo.

●Being savaged by delinquent gulls in Hitchcock's *The Birds* must have given Tippi Hedren a masochistic approach to wildlife. In *Roar*, the brainchild of husband Marshall, the hapless woman is pursued around an African jungle holiday home by 150 assorted Big Cats and a couple of jumbos. The narrative is a farcical melange of pseudo David Attenborough and Disneyspeak, married to equally fickle camerawork. The bizarre contradictions insist that the film be evaluated as a curiosity. Its value is as an ingenuous documentary portrait of the Marshalls as mega-eccentrics and misguided animal lovers (they have more than 100 lions and tigers as pets at their LA pad). Who can deny the grisly charm of Noel explaining what wonderful human beings leos are as a pride member playfully gnaws his leg? BPa

Roaring Twenties, The

(1939, US, 106 min, b/w)
d Raoul Walsh. *p* Hal B Wallis. *sc* Jerry Wald, Richard Macaulay, Robert Rossen. *ph* Ernest Haller. *ed* Jack Killifer. *ad* Max Parker. *m* Heinz Roemheld. *cast* James Cagney, Priscilla Lane, Humphrey Bogart, Gladys George, Jeffrey Lynn, Frank McHugh, Paul Kelly, Joe Sawyer.

●Marvellously mixing semi-documentary aspects with traditional genre motifs, Walsh's archetypal gangster thriller follows the fates of three WWI doughboys who return to an America plagued with unemployment: while Lynn goes straight, Cagney's the good guy reluctantly drawn into bootlegging and killing by a ruthless Bogart, and forever pining for good girl Lane while ignoring the attentions of George's tart-with-a-heart. Most impressive for its frantic pace and its suggestion that in times of Depression almost everyone is corruptible, it's also a perverse elegy to a decade of upheaval: that sense of sadness and waste is perfectly encapsulated by George's final line, laconically pronounced over Cagney's corpse, 'He used to be a big shot'. GA

Robbery

(1967, GB, 114 min)
d Peter Yates. *p* Michael Deeley, Stanley Baker. *sc* Edward Boyd, Peter Yates, George Markstein. *ph* Douglas Slocombe. *ed* Reginald Beck. *ad* Michael Seymour. *m* Johnny Keating. *cast* Stanley Baker, James Booth, Frank Finlay, Joanna Pettet, Barry Foster, William Marlowe, Clinton Greyn, George Sewell, Glynn Edwards.

●It was thanks to his brash handling of the chases in this thriller, loosely based on the Great Train Robbery, that Peter Yates was asked to go to America to make *Bullitt*. That said, there's more than a whiff of *The League of Gentlemen* (1959) about the script, but Yates makes efficient use of his locations, and the chase sequences are genuinely exciting. PH

Robbery Under Arms

(1985, Aust, 141 min)
d Ken Hannam, Donald Crombie. *p* Jock Blair. *sc* Tony Morphett, Graeme Koetsveld. *ph* Ernest Clark. *ed* Andrew Prowse. *pd* George Liddle. *m* Garry McDonald. *cast* Sam Neill, Steven Vidler, Christopher Cummins, Liz Newman, Ed Devereaux.

●A would-be Australian Western, based on Rolf Boldrewood's novel (previously filmed, equally tediously, in 1957). Raffish pommy crook Captain Starlight and his faithful abo lead a couple of brothers on a sequence of japes that includes bushwhacking, rustling, jail-breaking and bank-robbing. There is also skinny-dipping, elephants and fireworks, but the interest of these supposedly rumbustious antipodean antics is never more than vague. Without a trace of irony or parody, the emotional response of the characters is either a fist in the face or a knee in some cobber's cobblers. With 148 'actors', 2,000 extras (mainly cattle) and 120 crew members, it claims to be 'the most ambitious and expensive film ever made in Australia': a shame it only really deserves the title 'Wankabout'. MS

Robe, The

(1953, US, 135 min)
d Henry Koster. *p* Frank Ross. *sc* Philip Dunne. *ph* Leon Shamroy. *ed* Barbara McLean. *ad* Lyle Wheeler, George W Davis. *m* Alfred Newman. *cast* Richard Burton, Jean Simmons, Victor Mature, Michael Rennie, Richard Boone, Jay Robinson, Dawn Addams, Dean Jagger, Betta St John.

●Much touted on release as the first film made in CinemaScope (though it was also shot in Academy ratio, which is how it is seen on TV), *The Robe* has now receded into that lost genre, the religious epic. An uncomfortable Burton plays a Roman centurion whose love of a slave girl leads him to a more sympathetic view of the man his forces are about to crucify. Turgid direction, probably not helped by a necessarily cautious approach to framing, is married to creaky dialogue and stiff performances to render this of purely historical interest. DT

Roberta

(1935, US, 105 min, b/w)
d William A Seiter. *p* Pandro S Berman. *sc* Jane Murfin, Sam Mintz. *ph* Edward Cronjager. *ed* William Hamilton. *ad* Van Nest Polglase. *songs* Jerome Kern. *cast* Irene Dunne, Fred Astaire, Ginger Rogers, Randolph Scott, Helen Westley, Claire Dodd, Victor Varconi, Luis Alberni.

●Fred'n'Ginge fans won't need a nudge, but the uninitiated should start with almost any of their other movies. The star role here belongs to Irene Dunne, hard to warm to as a musical performer. She gets the classiest Jerome Kern numbers, 'Lovely to Look At' and the indestructible 'Smoke Gets in Your Eyes', both accompanied by staggeringly unimaginative camerawork. Other pills are Randolph 'Gee, that's swell' Scott, the fashion parade (this is what was called 'a woman's picture' before women became people), and the yukky plot revolving around Dunne's fluctuating fortunes as a Parisian fashion designer. Still, Fred – mind-bogglingly in a role Bob Hope played on stage – and Ginger do 'I Won't Dance'. And Ginger does her Polish accent. Remade in 1952 as *Lovely to Look At*. SG

Robert A. Heinlein's The Puppet Masters

see Puppet Masters, The

Robert Altman's Jazz '34: Remembrances of Kansas City Swing

(1996, US, 72 min)
d Robert Altman. *p* James McLindon, Matthew Seig, Brent Carpenter, Robert Altman. *ph* Oliver Stapleton. *ed* Brent Carpenter, Dylan Tichenor. *pd* Stephen Altman. *m* Hal Wilner. *with* Jesse David, David 'Fathead' Newman, Ron Carter, Christian McBride, Tyrone Clarke, Don Byron, Russell Malone, Mark Whitfield, Victor Lewis, Geri Allen, Cyrus Chestnut.

● An off-shoot from *Kansas City*, this keeps the focus entirely on KC's legendary all-night jam sessions where the likes of Lester Young plied their trade. The music is stonking, but the documentary aspects are disappointingly half-hearted (brief oral testimonies sound suspiciously phony), and even the jam re-creations feel contrived. Handsomely shot and immaculately recorded, so it should please the jazzers. TCh

Roberto Succo

(2001, Fr/Switz, 125 min)
d Cédric Kahn. *p* Gilles Sandoz, Patrick Sobelman. *sc* Cédric Kahn. *ph* Pascal Marti. *ed* Yann Dedet. *pd* François Abelanet. *m* Julien Civange. *cast* Stefano Cassetti, Isild Le Besco, Patrick Dell'Isola, Vincent Dénériaz, Aymeric Chauffert, Viviana Aliberti. Estelle Perron.

● Making his acting debut, Cassetti is frighteningly plausible as the real-life multiple killer of the title. He's first seen (years after the Italian cops discover of his parents' bodies) in a Toulon disco, where, he picks up a teenage girl who over the next few months shows remarkably little curiosity despite his strange and volatile behaviour. Indeed, his ability to continue killing, stealing and living out his strange fantasies is due partly to luck, partly to the shortcomings of others (including the cops), partly to his own extraordinarily uninhibited character. Kahn never opts for easy explanations but presents the facts coolly to subtly build up a portrait of the world where disorder rules, where notions of 'good' and 'evil' are finally so inadequate as to be meaningless, where even Succo's death can be seen as in some ways tragic. Tough, and very impressive indeed. GA

Robert Ryland's Last Journey

(1996, Sp/GB, 100 min)
d Gracia Querejeta. *p* Elias Querejeta. *sc* Gracia Querejeta, Elias Querejeta. *ph* Antonio Pueche. *ed* Nacho Ruiz-Capillas. *ad* Richard Field. *m* Angel Illarramendi. *cast* Ben Cross, William Franklyn, Cathy Underwood, Gary Piquer, Lalita Ahmed, Maurice Denham.

● 'Freely' adapted from Javier Marias' acclaimed novel, this mystery-cum-psychological drama, about the return of a veteran non-conformist professor (Franklyn) to Oxford after a decade away, and the effect of this on a don (Cross) and his sister (Underwood), is so stilted, clumsy and dramatically tedious as to be virtually unwatchable. Celluloid Oxbridge at its very worst. GA

Robin and Marian

(1976, US, 107 min)
d Richard Lester. *p* Denis O'Dell. *sc* James Goldman. *ph* David Watkin. *ed* John Victor Smith. *pd* Michael Stringer. *m* John Barry. *cast* Sean Connery, Audrey Hepburn, Robert Shaw, Richard Harris, Nicol Williamson, Denholm Elliott, Kenneth Haigh, Ronnie Barker, Ian Holm, Bill Maynard, Esmond Knight.

● Maybe it was because audiences expected another *Four Musketeers*-style romp that this flopped on its first release. There are quite a few typical Lester gags on the fringes of its tale of an elderly Robin returning to Sherwood from the Crusades and finding that Marian has become Abbess of a local priory; but the movie is conceived and executed in an elegaic key (not unlike Siegel's *The Shootist*), and played with an unfashionable depth of feeling (especially by Connery and Hepburn, both terrific). It's one of those rare movies, like King Hu's *Touch of Zen*, that handles its historical imagery so cleanly, and contains its pretensions so solidly within sure characterisation and plotting, that it is often sublimely expressive. TR

Robin and the 7 Hoods

(1964, US, 123 min)
d Gordon Douglas. *p* Frank Sinatra. *sc* David Schwartz. *ph* William H Daniels. *ed* Sam O'Steen. *ad* LeRoy Deane. *m* Nelson Riddle. *songs* Sammy Cahn, James Van Heusen. *cast* Frank Sinatra, Dean Martin, Bing Crosby, Sammy Davis Jr, Edward G Robinson, Barbara Rush, Peter Falk, Sig Ruman.

● The Rat Pack moves the 'robbing the rich...' routine from mouldy old Sherwood Forest to Prohibition-era Windy City, else the plot motivation for Sinatra belting out 'My Kinda Town, Chicago Is' might have seemed somewhat opaque. Otherwise, it's exactly as you'd expect. The gang do their stuff (for the last time on screen), and Sammy Cahn and Jimmy Van Heusen picked up an Oscar nomination for the songs. TJ

Robin Hood

(1922, US, 10,680 ft, b/w)
d Allan Dwan. *p/sc* Douglas Fairbanks. *ph* Arthur Edeson. *ed* William Nolan. *ad* Wilfred Buckland, Irvin J Martin. *m* Edward M Langley. *cast* Douglas Fairbanks, Wallace Beery, Enid Bennett, Sam De Grasse, Paul Dickey, William Lowery, Alan Hale, Willard Louis.

● Dwan's control of crowds and imaginative use of the sets give an effect of epic pageant that's better than many a later blockbuster. The extras do at least look as if they're in on the action, and not just there to fill up the screen. However, the acting of the central characters disarms criticism. Fairbanks possesses all the skill and enthusiasm of an 11-year-old in a school play, and behaves like one too, usually backslapping and tussling with the lads. His other characteristic expression, exaggerated surprise, reminds you of the Bisto Kids. In Sherwood, he skips everywhere, flapping his arms: merriness at all costs in the face of the darkest the Dark Ages can offer. The fact that Sam De Grasse turns in a very good performance as Prince John hardly matters.

Robin Hood

(1973, US, 83 min)
d/p Wolfgang Reitherman. *sc* Larry Clemmons. *ed* Tom Acosta, Jim Melton. *ad* Don Griffith. *m* George Burns. *cast* voices: Brian Bedford, Peter Ustinov, Terry-Thomas, Roger Miller, Phil Harris, Andy Devine, Monica Evans.

● Er, basically, no one makes cultural appropriation as much fun as Walt Disney. America is what he does best, so he does it to Robin Hood. Animated, Sherwood Forest becomes more like Nashville, Tennessee, with a slob of a sheriff humming 'Taxes are doo, doo de doo', and cute suburban kid byplay among the bunnies. While Prince John, 'a lion of diminished character', sucks his thumb, the furry faces of the poor are being relentlessly ground, the raccoons are on the chain gang, and Allan-a-Dale sings a Johnny Cash prison lament. Ustinov is the voice of the lion, flattered by Terry-Thomas as Sir Hiss, a courtly reptile: it is their domestic bickering and not the foxy schmaltz of Little John, Robin and Marian that jollies the film along. Good baddies, good poignant bits, and an archery contest that degenerates into all-action American football make up for the familiar, repetitive plot and the several lapses of taste and intelligence inevitable in medieval Nashville. RP

Robin Hood

(1991, GB, 104 min)
d John Irvin. *p* Sarah Radclyffe, Tim Bevan. *sc* Sam Resnick, John McGrath. *ph* Jason Lehel. *ed* Peter Tanner. *ad* Austen Spriggs. *m* Geoffrey Burgon. *cast* Patrick Bergin, Uma Thurman, Jürgen Prochnow, Jeroen Krabbé, Edward Fox, Jeff Nuttall.

● Judging by this swashbuckler, the genre has died and been teleported to outer space. Robin's outlawry, escape, encounters with Little John and Friar Tuck are routine, and the love story is limp. Not much pledging troth and sighing like furnaces about this Robin and Marian; he's phoning it in, she's truculent and dislikeable, and what varlet would not see through her (big Uma Thurman) disguise as a boy? Fatally, Bergin's Robin Hood lacks the snap for action, scrambling where bounding is required, good-eggish rather than noble in resolve, and mistaking lounging for blithe insouciance in the courtship. The main interest lies in the trio of villains: a death's-head Folcanet with extraordinary Norman consonants (Prochnow), a perplexingly ambiguous Baron Daguerre (Krabbé), and a brief, effective guest spot for Prince John (Fox). BC

Robin Hood – Men in Tights

(1993, US, 104 min)
d/p Mel Brooks. *sc* Mel Brooks, J David Shapiro, Evan Chandler. *ph* Michael O'Shea. *ed* Stephen Rivkin. *pd* Roy Forge Smith. *m* Hummie Mann. *cast* Cary Elwes, Richard Lewis, Roger Rees, Amy Yasbeck, Isaac Hayes, Tracey Ullman, Patrick Stewart, Mel Brooks, Clive Revill.

● What took the director so long to get around to Robin Hood? A standard, camp, unapologetic Mel Brooks parody, with digs at Kevin Costner's *Prince of Thieves* and its multi-racial Merry Men, and an arsenal of throw-away gags. An impressive cast – Stewart, Hayes, Ullman – cannot unfortunately save the day. NKe

Robin Hood of El Dorado, The

(1936, US, 86 min, b/w)
d William A Wellman. *p* John W Considine Jr. *sc* William A Wellman, Melvin Levy, Joseph Calleia. *ph* Chester Lyons. *ed* Robert J Kern. *ad* David Townsend, Gabriel Scognamillo. *m* Herbert Stothart. *cast* Warner Baxter, Ann Loring, Bruce Cabot, Margo, J Carrol Naish, Edgar Kennedy, Eric Linden.

● A Western of some reputation, largely undeserved. Based on the Walter Noble Burns biography of Joaquin Murrieta, set in California in 1848, it deals with the racial tensions in the newly-ceded territory, exacerbated by the discovery of gold at Sutter's Mill. Baxter (uncomfortably cast) plays Murrieta, a Mexican farmer who believes in peaceful co-existence until his wife (Margo) is raped and killed by riff-raff American prospectors; outlawed after exacting revenge, he continues to wage a guerrilla war for justice, realising too late that he has become little better than the villainous bandit Three-Fingered Jack (Naish) with whom he joins forces. Though fuelled by an admirable anger at racist barbarities, the film is sunk by poor performances (Naish excepted) and a below-par script which indulges endless montage sequences (gold rush, wanted posters, fiestas, etc) or sententious intertitles in the silent movie manner ('Where men and women lived for the moment's happiness – with danger and death ever the next day's promise'). Wellman and cameraman Chester Lyons at least contrive a pleasant, soberly muted visual sheen. TM

Robin Hood: Prince of Thieves

(1991, US, 143 min)
d Kevin Reynolds. *p* John Watson, Pen Densham, Richard B Lewis. *sc* Pen Densham, John Watson. *ph* Douglas Milsome. *ed* Peter Boyle. *pd* John Graysmark. *m* Michael Kamen. *cast* Kevin Costner, Morgan Freeman, Mary Elizabeth Mastrantonio, Christian Slater, Alan Rickman, Sean Connery, Geraldine McEwan, Michael McShane, Brian Blessed, Nick Brimble.

● After escaping his infidel captors with Indiana Jones-style panache, Robin of Locksley (Costner) returns from the Crusades with Moorish companion Azeem (Freeman), ready to avenge his father's murder. Azeem cracks jokes about the English weather while Robin gets to know Marian (Mastrantonio), but it isn't until they engage in open conflict with the Sheriff of Nottingham (a gloriously hammy Rickman) that the pace picks up and arrows start to fly. The mix of comedy, '90s sensibility, and swashbuckling action is more hit than miss, even if the overall effect is rather slapdash. Spirited, irreverent stuff, but not for those who like their myths kept sacred. CM

Robinson Crusoe (aka Adventures of Robinson Crusoe)

(1952, Mex/US, 89 min)
d Luis Buñuel. *p* Oscar Dancigers, Henry F Ehrlich. *sc* Luis Buñuel, Phillip Roll. *ph* Alex Phillips. *ed* Carlos Savage, Alberto Valenzuela. *ad* Edward Fitzgerald. *m* Anthony Collins. *cast* Dan O'Herlihy, Jaime Fernández, Felipe de Alba.

● A deceptively simple adaptation of Defoe's classic desert island novel. Few strikingly surrealist flourishes here: brief dreams of guilt, sexual frustration, and cruel power. Rather, Defoe's caustic analysis of mankind's foibles is translated into a moving account of one man's moral rebirth. The isolation and hardships that befall the bourgeois Crusoe, previously so dependent on servants for survival, leave him faithless, fearful for his sanity, and forced to become his own God, feeding insects and despairing of salvation. But with Friday's arrival, his ideas of religion and civilisation's hierarchy are really put to the test: trust, equality, and mercy replace the master-servant relationship as the necessary conditions of companionship and contentment. As in his other films, irony and a refusal to indulge in sentimentality are the hallmarks of Buñuel's vision; but the overwhelming impression here is one of surprising warmth, proof that, whatever humanity's faults, he remained forever interested in his own species and ultimately sympathetic to them. GA

Robinson Crusoe on Mars

(1964, US, 109 min)
d Byron Haskin. *p* Aubrey Schenck. *sc* Ib Melchior, John C Higgins. *ph* Winton C Hoch. *ed* Terry Morse. *ad* Hal Pereira, Arthur Lonergan. *m* Van Cleave. *cast* Paul Mantee, Vic Lundin, Adam West.

● Intelligently imaginative sci-fi version of the Defoe classic, in which an astronaut and his monkey are stranded on Mars, and later joined by the humanoid slave of an alien race. Haskin and producer George Pal provide the same excellent camerawork and special effects that marked their earlier *War of the Worlds* and *Naked Jungle* (the hostility of the Martian landscape is spectacularly evoked in California's Death Valley); but here, harnessed to a surprisingly faithful rendition of Defoe's conception, the result is an economical, subtle study both of Crusoe's will to survive, and of the hesitant growing friendship between the astronaut and his futuristic Friday. Most remarkably, Haskin avoids sentimentality even when dealing with the monkey, such is the assured sensitivity of the film. GA

Robinson in Space

(1997, GB, 82 min)
d Patrick Keiller. *p* Keith Griffiths. *sc/ph* Patrick Keiller. *ed* Larry Sider. *narrator* Paul Scofield.

● In *London*, the anonymous, unseen narrator (Paul Scofield) accompanied the art lecturer Robinson on a series of eccentric, quizzical journeys in and around the capital. Here, he's again invited by his friend, now an impoverished teacher, to help with a project initiated by an ad agency and designed to investigate 'the problem of England'. As the pair embark on their seven voyages, ranging from the Thames to the Channel ports, the Midlands to the far North, Robinson meditates in his inimitable way on geography, history, architecture, economy, politics and culture. Like its predecessor this is an offbeat, verbose, witty mix of documentary, fiction and essay: are we really a poor, terribly provincial nation plagued by industrial decline, or are our hardships and low morale the outcome of choices made by self-serving politicians? As before, references abound: Defoe, Wilde, Austen; the Tolpuddle Martyrs, Engels, Michael Portillo, Greenpeace; the Stones; the Cerne Abbas Giant, architect Buckminster Fuller, Dracula. All this erudition is balanced by the writer/director/cameraman's admirably dry, deeply ironic sense of humour, and by his immaculately framed images, which manage to make the familiar look strangely strange yet oddly normal. And if the satirical political asides don't have quite the bite of those in the earlier movie, this is still provocative, determinedly left-field film-making: bright, adventurous, engrossing and… well, very English. GA

RoboCop

(1987, US, 102 min)
d Paul Verhoeven. *p* Arne Schmidt. *sc* Edward Neumeier, Michael Miner. *ph* Jost Vacano. *ed* Frank J Urioste. *pd* William Sandell. *m* Basil Poledouris. *cast* Peter Weller, Nancy Allen, Daniel O'Herlihy, Ronny Cox, Kurtwood Smith, Miguel Ferrer.

● In a futuristic Old Detroit, the crime rates are soaring. Thirty-one cops have been wasted since Omni-Consumer Products took over responsibility for the police department; but, undaunted, Officer Murphy (Weller) and his cocky colleaguette Lewis (Allen) pursue a van-load of bank bandits into a derelict steel mill, where the sado-capitalists corner Murphy and use him for target practice. OCP's plans to construct Delta City can only go ahead if the designated area is safe enough for workers to go about their business unmolested. Their 'enforcement droid' ED 209, a galumphing giant cyborg, short-circuits at its unveiling, leaving the moribund Murphy, his insides wired into a computer-controlled titanium shell, to save the day. But RoboCop is not programmed to deal with corruption within the organisation. Verhoeven's blend of comic strip and snuff movie is vile, violent, and very funny. The pace is breakneck, and when the wit does run out, way-out weaponry and whole-scale destruction keep the appalled excitement burning. MS

RoboCop 2

(1990, US, 118 min)
d Irvin Kershner. *p* Jon Davison. *sc* Frank Miller, Walon Green. *ph* Mark Irwin. *ed* William Anderson. *pd* Peter Jamison. *m* Leonard Rosenman. *cast* Peter Weller, Nancy Allen, Belinda Bauer, Daniel O'Herlihy, Tom Noonan, Gabriel Damon, Willard Pugh, Felton Perry, Patricia Charbonneau.

● The title refers to both the sequel and the rival, a new megadeath killing machine built on the same lines as the original, but employing the spinal column and brain of the chief villain, demonic drug king-cum-seer Cain (Noonan). But while RoboCop 2, the model, is a mean mother with a positive state-of-the-art kitchen of murderous gadgets, *RoboCop 2* the movie is every bit as messy as a dog's breakfast. It still has all the old wit, the hellish vision of a Detroit plagued by everything from Little League robber gangs to bent or striking cops, and the dependable line-up of actors (Allen, O'Herlihy, Weller). What it doesn't have very much of is the original's energy, passion and remorseless narrative logic. Kershner's direction is never more than adequate, and the story seems full of unfulfilled promise and tangled threads. It's also deeply, disturbingly violent in a way which is more manipulative than gory; unlike the original, with its prophetic vision of the future, this sequel seems to spend too much time glorying in the very horrors it has outlined. SGr

RoboCop 3

(1992, US, 104 min)
d Fred Dekker. *p* Patrick Crowley. *sc* Fred Dekker, Frank Miller. *ph* Gary B Kibbe. *ed* Bert Lovitt. *pd* Hilda Stark. *m* Basil Poledouris. *cast* Robert Burke, Nancy Allen, Rip Torn, Remy Ryan, John Castle, Jill Hennessy, CCH Pounder, Mako.

● Dekker's third instalment also comes third in terms of merit. In tune with the times, the techno-violence here is tempered with appeal to 'family' values. Omni Consumer Product Corporation are now in uneasy alliance with the Japanese multi, Kanemitsu. Debts and permanent crisis have forced them into an ambitious city-building project, Delta, which requires the clearing of the remaining city-centre communities of Detroit. Meanwhile guerilla gangs make life hard for underground groups of determined hippie-like evictees. When RoboCop (Burke) finds himself in loco parentis to kid Nikko (Ryan), he also finds his loyalties and martial arts skills siding with the homeless. The familiarity of the high-armour shoot-outs and sfx-assisted set-pieces make most of this sequel feel surprisingly low-tech. Not bad entertainment, though. WH

Robot Monster

(1953, US, 63 min, b/w)
d/p Phil Tucker. *sc* Wyott Ordung. *ph* Jack Greenhalgh. *ed* Bruce W Schoengarth. *m* Elmer Bernstein. *cast* George Barrows, Gregory Moffett, George Nader, Claudia Barrett, Selena Royle, John Mylong.

● 'For the budget and for the time' said Tucker, 'I felt I had achieved greatness'. His 3-D cheapster in fact lifted all its special effects wholesale and without reconsideration from its 1940 predecessor, *One Million B.C.* Yet it's the winner of the Golden Turkey Award for Most Ridiculous Monster in Screen History (a plump, hirsute little robot). CR

Rob Roy

(1994, US, 130 min)
d Michael Caton-Jones. *p* Peter Broughan, Richard Jackson. *sc* Alan Sharp. *ph* Karl Walter Lindenlaub. *ed* Peter Honess. *pd* Assheton Gorton. *m* Carter Burwell. *cast* Liam Neeson, John Hurt, Tim Roth, Brian Cox, Jessica Lange, Eric Stoltz.

● The Scottish Highlands, 1713. Clan-leader Rob Roy MacGregor (Neeson) asks the Marquis of Montrose (Hurt) for a loan. The aloof Machiavellian hesitantly agrees; but Rob hasn't bargained for the laird's house-guest, the foppish wastrel Cunningham (Roth), who together with Montrose's scheming factor (Cox) steals the money, killing Rob's friend Alan (Stoltz) in the process. The scene is set for deadly enmity between Rob and Montrose. As scripted by Alan Sharp and directed by Caton-Jones, this stirring historical drama is less swashbuckler than transposed Western, with a feel for landscape, intrigue, romance and questions of honour reminiscent of Mann's *Last of the Mohicans*. Neeson makes a less dashing action hero than did Day-Lewis, but he brings enough gravitas to his role to endow his love for his wife Mary (Lange) and his conflict with Cunningham with real emotional punch. Still better are Lange, Hurt, Cox and, notably, Roth, whose final duel with Neeson is a tour de force. While the film's chief virtue is the mythic clarity, Sharp's script, which shifts easily between the fruity innuendo of the aristos and the more demotic colloquialisms of the clansmen, never soft-pedals the historical and political context. GA

Rocco and His Brothers (Rocco e i Suoi Fratelli)

(1960, It/Fr, 180 min)
d Luchino Visconti. *p* Goffredo Lombardo. *sc* Suso Cecchi D'Amico, Pasquale Festa Campanile, Massimo Franciosa, Enrico Medioli, Luchino Visconti. *ph* Giuseppe Rotunno. *ed* Mario Serandrei. *m* Nino Rota. *cast* Alain Delon, Renato Salvatori, Annie Girardot, Katina Paxinou, Roger Hanin, Paolo Stoppa, Suzy Delair, Claudia Cardinale, Spiros Focas.

● The last gasp of the neo-realist spirit in Visconti's work, *Rocco* chronicles at length the misfortunes that befall an Italian peasant family when they move to The Big City. There's a grey conviction about much of the scene-setting and the location shooting, but the film gathers interest as it escalates into melodrama; the tragic climax is pure opera. Delon is unconvincing as the saintly Rocco, but Renato Salvatori makes the thuggish elder brother who falls in with a gay boxing promoter his best part ever. TR

Rocinante

(1986, GB, 93 min)
d Ann Guedes, Eduardo Guedes. *p* Gustav Lamche. *sc* Ann Guedes, Eduardo Guedes. *ph* Thaddeus O'Sullivan. *ed* Eduardo Guedes, Richard Taylor. *ad* Caroline Amies. *m* Jürgen Knieper. *cast* John Hurt, Maureen Douglass, Ian Dury, Carol Gillies, Jimmy Jewel, Gillian Heasman.

● At the start of this portrait of England as 'a garden of secrets, full of tradition and myth, violence and cover-up', Hurt hides away from reality in a derelict cinema (geddit?), until a conversation about narrative with the ex-projectionist (Jewel) forces him to take to the road aboard a truck named Rocinante. The allusion to Quixote's horse (and thus, presumably, to Cervantes' wittily wayward storytelling) is misleading: during the ideologically unconscious Hurt's aimless odyssey to Dartmoor, his main encounter is with Jess (Douglass), a political activist scarred by the '84 miners' strike and intent on industrial sabotage. Meanwhile, 'jester' Dury pops up to spout poetry and make ironic comment. Despite the film's good intentions, it is, quite simply, appalling. Such bourgeois conventions as plausible, pacy narrative, realist characterisation, and the potential for an audience's emotional involvement, are jettisoned in favour of stilted, 'significant' dialogue, banal parallels with myth, and clumsily contrived symbolism. The result is a mess: dry, humourless, half-baked obscurantism that insults the viewer. GA

Rock, The

(1996, US, 136 min)
d Michael Bay. *p* Don Simpson, Jerry Bruckheimer. *sc* David Weisberg, Douglas S Cook, Mark Rosner. *ph* John Schwartzman. *ed* Richard Francis-Bruce. *pd* Michael White. *m* Nick Glennie-Smith, Hans Zimmer. *cast* Sean Connery, Nicolas Cage, Ed Harris, Michael Biehn, William Forsyth, David Morse, John Spencer, John C McGinley, Tony Todd, Bokeem Woodbine.

●The Rock, of course, is Alcatraz, prison-turned-tourist site, which is seized by disgruntled, decorated-to-hell General Harris with his elite corps (psycho captain, loyal colonel); they take 83 hostages and aim four VX-gas missiles at San Francisco; the rockets will be fired unless pensions are provided for the families of dead, 'deniable' Special Forces. The twist here is getting Navy SEALS *into* the rock to take the bastards *out*. Step forward as team-leaders reluctant heroes Cage, a Beatles-lovin' FBI boffin with chemical-weapons badges, and ex-SAS officer Sean Connery, the only man to escape from Alcatraz, and presently serving 30-odd years for obtaining US government secrets. Director Michael Bay (with only *Bad Boys* to his name) propels this brew of combat war-movie, *Die Hard*-style actioner and *Indiana Jones* adventure on enough octane to leave objections to the clichéd dialogue and implausible of the plot in the slipstream. Fake countdown and knowing reactionary tone, but the best SF car chase to date. WH

Rock-a-Bye Baby

(1958, US, 103 min)
d Frank Tashlin. *p* Jerry Lewis. *sc* Frank Tashlin. *ph* Haskell Boggs. *ed* Alma Macrorie. *ad* Hal Pereira, Tambi Larsen. *m* Walter Scharf. *songs* Harry Warren, Sammy Cahn. *cast* Jerry Lewis, Marilyn Maxwell, Connie Stevens, Salvatore Baccaloni, Reginald Gardiner, James Gleason, Hans Conried, Isobel Elsom.

●An often forgotten Lewis/Tashlin production (loosely based on Preston Sturges' script for *The Miracle of Morgan's Creek*) that contains some very good stuff indeed – all in the first half, unfortunately. Lewis is the lifelong fan of a movie star (Maxwell) who gives him her triplets to look after while she's in Africa making a film. The supporting cast is particularly good (Gardner, Conried, Connie Stevens), but the gear-change from manic slapstick (watch out for the berserk hosepipe) to cringing sentimentality about babies and nappies is hard to take. DMcG

Rock-a-Doodle

(1990, GB, 77 min)
d Don Bluth. *p* Don Bluth, Gary Goldman, John Pomeroy, Robert Enrietto. *sc* David N Weiss. *ph* Bob Paynter. *ed* Dan Molina, Bernard Caputo, Fiona Trayler, Lisa Dorney, Joe Gall. *pd* David Goetz. *m* Robert Folk, TJ Kuenster. *cast* voices: Phil Harris, Glen Campbell, Eddie Deezen, Christopher Plummer, Sandy Duncan, Sorrell Booke.

●With a gob-smacking opening zoom, Bluth grabs his audience and transports them from outer space to an earthbound farmyard. Here, Chanticleer the rocking rooster (voiced by velvet-larynxed Campbell) is humiliated in front of his animal chums when the sun rises one morning without his usual boisterous bidding. Dismissed as useless, Chanticleer trudges off to seek stardom in the big city, whence he is pursued by his erstwhile pals and by the evil emissaries of the fiendish Grand Duke Owl (Plummer), who now threatens to devour the rain-drenched farmyard. As with so much of Bluth's work, the narrative strengths necessary to support his fiesta of colourfully frenzied animated action are sadly absent. The film's dizzying pace leaves one longing for the plodding reliability of a sturdy Disney storyline. Bluth remains a rebellious visual talent to be reckoned with, but the overall effect is messy. MK

Rock All Night

(1957, US, 63 min, b/w)
d/p Roger Corman. *sc* Charles B Griffith. *ph* Floyd Crosby. *ed* Frank Sullivan. *ad* Robert Kinoshita. *cast* Dick Miller, Russell Johnson, Jonathan Haze, Abby Dalton, The Platters, Robin Morse.

●Fugitive killers Johnson and Haze stumble into hot-spot Cloud Nine, where Miller's aptly nicknamed Shorty has just reached the point where he's truly fed up with taller guys pushing him around. Pretty flimsy, but it's cheering to see much-loved character stalwart Miller play the lead. Stand by for some perfunctory and completely unrelated footage of The Platters in action at the start of the movie. TJ

Rock Around the World

see Tommy Steele Story, The

Rockers

(1979, US/Jam, 99 min)
d Theodoros Bafaloukos. *p* Patrick Hulsey. *sc* Theodoros Bafaloukos. *ph* Peter Sova. *ed* Susan Steinberg. *ad* Lilly Kilvert. *m* Kiddus-I, Jacob Miller and the Inner Circle, Burning Spear, Gregory Isaacs, Peter Tosh, Rockers All Stars. *cast* Leroy Wallace, Richard Hall, Monica Craig, Marjorie Norman, Jacob Miller, Gregory Isaacs.

●A Trenchtown variant on *Robin Hood*, with dreadlocked drummer Horsemouth (Wallace) up against the local minor-league mafia. An excellent soundtrack (Peter Tosh, Burning Spear, Bunny Wailer, etc), and an endearingly witty script which digresses through explanations of the Rasta faith and countless idiosyncratic solidarity rituals, make for a delightful piece of whimsy. Complete with subtitles transliterating the Rasta patois. FL

Rocketeer, The

(1991, US, 108 min)
d Joe Johnston. *p* Lawrence Gordon, Charles Gordon, Lloyd Levin. *sc* Danny Bilson, Paul DeMeo. *ph* Hiro Narita. *ed* Arthur Schmidt. *pd* James D Bissell. *m* James Horner. *cast* Bill Campbell, Jennifer Connelly, Alan Arkin, Timothy Dalton, Paul Sorvino, Terry O'Quinn, Ed Lauter, James Handy, Tiny Ron.

●In this comic book adaptation, chisel-faced pilot Cliff Secord (Campbell) discovers a rocket pack that enables him to zoom through the skies, only to find himself pursued by villains employed by film star Neville Sinclair (Dalton). Sinclair, a dastardly egomaniac, wants the rocket, but so do the Feds, since the Nazis are after it. Poor old Cliff can't tell the good guys from the bad. What's his actress girlfriend Jenny (Connelly) to do? Her man isn't earthbound long enough to finish a date. The late '30s are beautifully evoked, Hiro Narita's cinematography captures some lush images, and director Johnston has a freshness and lightness of touch. The rocket sequences are quite exhilarating, but the scenes in between are the problem; Cliff and Jenny make a bland couple, and the Fascist threat lacks real menace. Neat idea, peachy visuals, but there ain't much else to grip the imagination. CM

Rockets Galore (aka Mad Little Island)

(1958, GB, 94 min)
d Michael Relph. *p* Basil Dearden. *sc* Monja Danischewsky. *ph* Reginald Wyer. *ed* John D Guthridge. *ad* Jack Maxsted. *m* Cedric Thorpe Davie. *cast* Jeannie Carson, Donald Sinden, Roland Culver, Gordon Jackson, Noel Purcell, Duncan Macrae, Ian Hunter, Jean Cadell, Catherine Lacey.

●Rank's belated riposte to the 1948 Ealing hit *Whisky Galore!*, adapted from another Compton Mackenzie story by Monja Danischewsky who, from the position of associate producer, had fought Alexander Mackendrick over the first film's script. This time the Hebridean Todday islanders are up in arms over plans to site a missile base in their midst, and resort to such quaint defensive tactics as painting seagulls pink to mobilise the naturalist lobby. A rare attempt at whimsy by social drama stalwarts Relph and Dearden, it's amusing enough but somewhat faltering in tone. PT

Rock Hudson's Home Movies

(1993, US, 63 min)
d/p/sc Mark Rappaport. *ph* Mark Daniels. *with* Eric Farr.

●This humorous video lecture replays and freeze-frames the movies of model-male beefcake and former truck driver Hudson until his gayness stares you in the face. It's also a passionate, albeit critical, tribute to the man, an analysis of the screen parts, and a warning. Hudson's AIDS diagnosis and subsequent death in 1985 rocked a few preconceptions. Here are clips from the early Universal days, through the '50s adventure pics, the Oscar-nominated role in *Giant*, his melodramatic grand hour with Douglas Sirk, the suggestive pyjama games with Doris Day, right up to the late comedies and soaps. Eric Farr, a weed in white singlet, impersonates the Rock and presents the well-argued case for the offence, taking the liberty of having Hudson discuss himself from beyond the grave, wringing his screen hypochondria to dubious premonitory effect. When Rock explains his dislike of 'fish' to Paula Prentiss in *Man's Favorite Sport?*, Farr screams, 'What do you *think* they were talking about, dickhead?' Such hectoring palls, but all in all it's a healthy rant. WH

Rocking Horse Winner, The

(1949, GB, 90 min, b/w)
d Anthony Pélissier. *p* John Mills. *sc* Anthony Pélissier. *ph* Desmond Dickinson. *ed* John Seabourne. *ad* Carmen Dillon. *m* William Alwyn. *cast* John Howard Davies, Valerie Hobson, John Mills, Ronald Squire, Hugh Sinclair, Charles Goldner, Susan Richards.

●In introducing DH Lawrence to the screen, the Mills/Pelissier team made a strange choice with this brief, terse evocation of Oedipal love (a sensitive child, threatened by a rift between extravagant mother and jobless father, discovers an ability to predict racing winners while pretending to be a jockey, frenziedly astride his rocking horse). Though no one noticed at the time, the Lawrentian sexual undertones are clearly transposed to the film. The boy's masturbatory riding is given a frightening potency, and his attempt to win the love of his glitteringly powerful mother has little to do with filial affection. Pelissier's direction is occasionally overblown, but Mills (as the groom who feeds the boy's fantasies), obviously relishing the opportunity to use his native Suffolk accent, is admirably restrained, and a British film which explores the complex links between sex, money and power is rare indeed. RMy

Rock n'Roll Cop (Sheng-Gang Yihao Tongji Fan)

(1994, HK, 93 min)
d Kirk Wong. *sc* Winky Wong. *ph* Ko Tsiu-lam. *ed* Kam Ma. *ad* Eddie Ma. *m* Tsung Ding-yat. *cast* Anthony Wong, Carrie Ng, Wu Xingguo, Wu Wing-Kwong.

●The last of three Kirk Wong films drawn from the reminiscences of a real-life cop, this centres on an idiosyncratic Hong Kong detective (actually more a 'bring back vinyl' man than a rocker) who's sent across the border into China to help their police track down a vicious killer. It complicates matters that the villain's current squeeze was once seduced and abandoned by the China cop. The movie contrasts stolid Mainland procedures with laconic Hong Kong pragmatism (Anthony Wong contributes his usual 'Michel Piccoli plays Caliban' persona as the laid-back detective), but ends up bending over backwards to stress the joys of future co-operation. It sure delivers as an action thriller, though. TR

Rock'n'Roll High School

(1979, US, 93 min)
d Allan Arkush. *p* Michael Finnell. *sc* Richard Whitley, Russ Dvonch, Joseph McBride. *ph* Dean Cundey. *ed* Larry Bock, Gail Werbin. *ad* Marie Kordus. *m* The Ramones. *cast* PJ Soles, Vincent Van Patten, Clint Howard, Dey Young, Mary Woronov, Dick Miller, Paul Bartel, Don Steele, Grady Sutton, The Ramones.

●For all its throwaway humour, this is basically just a pleasant reworking of the kids versus adults rock'n'roll movie format of the '50s, with Paul Bartel in the traditional role of the adult kook who goes hip, and legendary DJ Don Steele as the radio commentator who brings the confrontation to the nation. Naturally the struggle between the generations goes a little further than before, with a high school burned to the ground and adults thrown out of windows, but it's basically kleenteen fun. If you're worried about the Ramones, rest assured; they make a very adequate chunka chunka chunka sound. DP

Rock Rock Rock!

(1956, US, 83 min)
d Will Price. *p* Max J Rosenberg, Milton Subotsky. *sc* Milton Subotsky. *ph* Morris Hartzband. *ed* Blandine Hafela. *ad* Daniel Van Blomberg. *cast* Tuesday Weld, Jacqueline Kerr, Ivy Schulman; *with* Alan Freed, Chuck Berry, Frankie Lymon and the Teenagers, LaVern Baker, Cirino and the Bowties.
●Pioneering DJ/impresario Alan Freed (later harassed by payola probes and mythologised by *American Hot Wax*) chaperones a customarily incongruous bunch of early rockers through this prototype rocksploitation quickie, in which 13-year-old Tuesday Weld (playing 18, and lyrically dubbed by Connie Francis) pines for a strapless dress for the school prom, until perked up by such authentic novelties as Lymon's kitsch classic 'I'm Not a Juvenile Delinquent'. Wonderfully grotesque. PT

Rockshow

(1979, US, 103 min)
d Uncredited. *ph* Jack Priestly. *ed* Robin Clark, Paul Stein. *with* Paul McCartney, Linda McCartney, Jimmy McCulloch, Joe English, Denny Laine.
●Not so much a movie as a scrapbook folly which captures Wings' last concert on their 1976 world tour. Held at the cavernous King Dome in Seattle, it's beer and skittles for affluent suburbia. Cheesy grins and dully-directed spectacle abound as the band zip through a selection of the greatest hits from the period – with an odd Beatle song thrown in to show who actually wrote it. Paul McCartney is the epitome of good-natured professionalism; Linda is gawky and excited; the late Jimmy McCulloch, pasty-faced and a mite nervous; Joe English, beefy and flailing; Denny Laine, laddish and competent. The show reinforces how erratic McCartney can be. While his voice, bass playing and songwriting can be genuinely adventurous ('Maybe I'm Amazed' is a rare high point), he still comes up with an inanity like 'Silly Love Songs' (surely a nadir in pop). And why does he persist in surrounding himself with musicians who flatter rather than provoke his talent? An interminable experience. IB

Rock Star

(2001, US, 105 min)
d Stephen Herek. *p* Robert Lawrence, Toby Jaffe. *sc* John Stockwell. *ph* Ueli Steiger. *ed* Trudy Ship. *pd* Mayne Berke. *m* Trevor Rabin. *cast* Mark Wahlberg, Jennifer Aniston, Jason Flemyng, Timothy Olyphant, Timothy Spall, Dominic West, Jason Bonham, Jeff Pilson, Zakk Wylde.
●Herek's fable of life in a heavy rock group spins on a promising enough axis: what would happen if you fronted a tribute band to your favourite rock act – only to end up joining the real thing when their lead singer leaves? Beneath all the hair extensions, this is a textbook loss of innocence movie – so, given his success in similar roles, it made sense to cast Wahlberg as copier-maintenance man Chris Coles, whose devotion to Steel Dragon is so intense that even the other guys in his tribute band sack him. 'Write your own stuff!' suggests girlfriend Emily (Aniston). Does he listen? Pah! Thereafter, it's *Boogie Nights* with hair and added misogyny. Herek might protest at that – after all, Aniston's character is there to see through the glitz of Wahlberg's newfound stardom. She keeps her distance from the other band wives, portrayed as broken gorgons resigned to their fate as muses to mollycoddled idiots. But Herek fails to recognise that a surrogate family can still be a family, no matter how dysfunctional. As a result, every character becomes a cipher for a strangely reactionary morality tale. PP

Rocky

(1976, US, 119 min)
d John G Avildsen. *p* Irwin Winkler, Robert Chartoff. *sc* Sylvester Stallone. *ph* James Crabe. *ed* Richard Halsey. *pd* William J Cassidy. *m* Bill Conti. *cast* Sylvester Stallone, Talia Shire, Burt Young, Carl Weathers, Burgess Meredith, Thayer David, Joe Spinell.
●'I coulda been a contender, Charlie': Brando's classic lament in *On the Waterfront* finds a new and vigorous echo in this low-budget film whose huge success, against all odds, mirrors its own theme. *Rocky* is an old-fashioned fairytale brilliantly revamped to chime in with the depressed mood of the '70s. Although its plot – nonentity gets to fight the heavyweight champ – is basically fantasy, the film deftly manages to suspend disbelief by drawing back at its more implausible moments. Despite a few clumsy early scenes, the dialogue hits some bull's-eyes ('I'm really a ham-and-egger' mumbles Stallone in disbelief when he hears he'll get a crack at the champ), and Burgess Meredith gives his best performance in years as a slobbering, aged trainer. But without its climax, *Rocky* would add up to very little: the big fight is cathartic, manipulative Hollywood at its best. In a word: emotion. DP

Rocky II

(1979, US, 119 min)
d Sylvester Stallone. *p* Irwin Winkler, Robert Chartoff. *sc* Sylvester Stallone. *ph* Bill Butler. *ed* Stanford C Allen, Janice Hampton, James R Symons. *ad* Richard Berger. *m* Bill Conti. *cast* Sylvester Stallone, Talia Shire, Burt Young, Carl Weathers, Burgess Meredith, Tony Burton, Joe Spinell.
●An old-fashioned sequel which plumbs depths and hits heights, in which the lovable Rocky Balboa gets another crack at the world heavyweight championship. On the way, the script really sweats to get your heart pumping: with a risk of blindness and doe-eyed wife Talia Shire's postnatal coma, Rocky's virtuoso dumbness (unable to read the idiot-cards on TV) gets close to the bone. Stallone's performance as a Philadelphia saint in a B movie physique leaves you undecided whether to gag or sob, but the final fight sequences make up for it; a full-blooded Hollywood finale reaching giddy heights of cathartic glee. As a comic strip story stretched to 119 minutes, it has few rivals. DMacp

Rocky III

(1982, US, 99 min)
d Sylvester Stallone. *p* Irwin Winkler, Robert Chartoff. *sc* Sylvester Stallone. *ph* Bill Butler. *ed* Don Zimmerman, Mark Warner. *pd* William J Cassidy. *m* Bill Conti. *cast* Sylvester Stallone, Talia Shire, Burt Young, Carl Weathers, Burgess Meredith, Tony Burton, Mr T, Hulk Hogan.
●Learning, especially from Scorsese, in his approach to action and performance, writer/director/star Stallone has somehow contrived to make each of his movies into a more magnificent spectacle than the last, eliminating much of the coy sentimentality that tainted the first film, and pacing the boxing scenes with an increasing fury that makes them less like a sport than the epic symbolic struggle of Ray Harryhausen monsters. 'The worst thing happened to you that could happen to any fighter' someone tells Rocky here, 'You got civilised'. And *Rocky III* depicts the fighter's struggle to come to terms with success, in a progression from danger and defeat to triumph which – as in all the best genre movies – is incredibly simple. As audience movie-making in its purest form, the film is a delight, but it's also so obviously based on Stallone's own personal struggle with success that the mind boggles as to what Rocky can possibly do next. Make movies, perhaps? DP

Rocky IV

(1985, US, 91 min)
d Sylvester Stallone. *p* Irwin Winkler, Robert Chartoff. *sc* Sylvester Stallone. *ph* Bill Butler. *ed* Don Zimmerman, John W Wheeler. *pd* Bill Kenney. *m* Vince DiCola. *cast* Sylvester Stallone, Talia Shire, Burt Young, Carl Weathers, Brigitte Nielsen, Tony Burton, Michael Pataki, Dolph Lundgren, James Brown.
●Film reduced to the barest of three acts. Act I: Russian bionic mauler Drago (Lundgren) clubs Rocky's chum (Weathers) to extinction. Act II: Spaniel Features drives around in the dark night of his soul, compiling memories of *Rockys I/II/III* into a flashy rock vid. Act III: He goes to Russia, trains in the snow, and takes revenge. Never mind that all other characters are reduced to shadows, that the dialogue is witless, that the political message is a heart-warming call for detente. This, as Fuller said, is film as battleground, love, hate, violence, action, death – in a word: emotion. Pity it's about Rocky. CPea

Rocky V

(1990, US, 104 min)
d John G Avildsen. *p* Robert Chartoff, Irwin Winkler. *sc* Sylvester Stallone. *ph* Steven Poster. *ed* John G Avildsen, Michael N Knue. *pd* William J Cassidy. *m* Bill Conti. *cast* Sylvester Stallone, Talia Shire, Burt Young, Sage Stallone, Burgess Meredith, Tommy Morrison, Richard Gant.
●The 15-year soap opera of Rocky Balboa comes full circle. Bankrupted by a crooked accountant, suffering from brain damage which prevents him from fighting again, Rocky sells his mansion and returns to the Philadelphia back streets of his youth. He trains up a young boxer (Morrison), but as his protégé falls prey to the manipulations of an impresario (Gant), Rocky almost loses sight of the most important thing in his life: his son. This is yooman drama, with Rocky as New Man and the fights taking place outside the ring. The back-to-basics approach, with original director Avildsen back at the helm, is sensible, since nothing could have topped the bone-crunching climax of *Rocky IV*. But whereas the first and far superior *Rocky* had real heart, this tries and fails to have brains. Sentiment is substituted for sorrow, shouting for anger, mumbling for self-doubt. The scenes between Sly and his real-life son Sage have a certain poignancy, but there are more perceptive insights into parent-child relationships in an Oxo ad. And Sage acts his dad off the screen. DW

Rocky Horror Picture Show, The

(1975, GB, 101 min)
d Jim Sharman. *p* Michael White. *sc* Richard O'Brien, Jim Sharman. *ph* Peter Suschitzky. *ed* Graeme Clifford. *ad* Terry Ackland-Snow. *m* Richard O'Brien. *cast* Tim Curry, Susan Sarandon, Barry Bostwick, Richard O'Brien, Jonathan Adams, Nell Campbell, Peter Hinwood, Meatloaf, Patricia Quinn, Christopher Biggins, Charles Gray.
●Why did the fans turn late-nite screenings of this cult favourite into an elaborate ritual of dressing-up, singing along, throwing rice and waving cigarette lighters? Well, for one thing, the material inspires affection, given its knowing pastiche of everything from Universal horrors to '50s grade-Z sci-fi, and a shamelessly hedonistic, fiercely independent sensibility that must have seemed a welcome relief from the mainstream bombast of other '70s musicals (not exactly *Jesus Christ Superstar*, is it?). However, dare we suggest that the whole participation angle evolved to boost a movie that is something of an enthusiastic shambles, and collapses altogether in the final reel? Fresh-faced Sarandon and Bostwick are the all-American honeymooners who wind up in the tender care of Tim Curry's camper-than-thou Transylvanian transvestite, O'Brien's hunchback butler and sundry kinky cronies. A string of hummable songs gives it momentum, Gray's admirably straight-faced narrator holds it together, and a run on black lingerie takes care of almost everything else. TJ

Rodents (Ratas, Ratones, Rateros)

(1999, Ecuador, 107 min)
d Sebastian Cordero. *p* Lisandra Rivera. *sc* Sebastian Cordero. *ph* Matthew Jensen. *ed* Sebastian Cordero, Mateo Herrera. *pd* Isabel Dávalos. *m* Sergio Sacoto-Arias. *cast* Simón Brauer, Marco Bustos, Cristina Dávila, Fabrizio Lalama, Irina López, José Antonio Negret, Carlos Valencia
●Grim street-level drama in the tradition of *Pixote*, following its young protagonists' rapid descent from social misdemeanours to capital crime. It's a narrative trajectory we've seen before, but perhaps not in this specific context. No tourist poster for Ecuador. TCh

Roger & Me

(1989, US, 90 min, b/w & col)
d/p/sc Michael Moore. *ph* Christopher Beaver, John Prusak, Kevin Rafferty, Bruce Schermer. *ed* Wendey Stanzler, Jennifer Beman. *with* Michael Moore, Roger Smith.
●Moore's hilarious, scathing film traces the decline of his home town of Flint, Michigan, after General Motors systematically closed down plants and laid off thousands of workers. The action spans three years as Moore (camera team in tow) tracks GM chairman Roger Smith in order to confront him with the human consequences of corporate policy. Interspersed are Moore's narrative, outlining the changes which beset the town, and on-camera interviews with assorted locals, celebrities and executives. Chronology has been jumbled, resulting in controversy over this

'documentary'. Moore terms it a 'docucomedy', a political sketch rather than a measured analysis, deploying humour and exaggeration to make its point. It's only right that Moore should be accountable to standards of journalistic 'truthfulness'; but ultimately, remaining constant at the heart of his film, is the way it tellingly and ruthlessly presents the cumulative effects of industrial ruthlessness. CM

Roger Corman: Hollywood's Wild Angel

(1978, US, 58 min)
d/p Christian Blackwood. *sc* Richard Koszarski. *ph* Christian Blackwood. *ed* Harvey Greenstein, Christian Blackwood. *with* Roger Corman, Allan Arkush, Paul Bartel, David Carradine, Joe Dante, Jonathan Demme, Peter Fonda, Ron Howard, Jonathan Kaplan, Martin Scorsese.
● It may have nothing particularly profound to say about its subject-hero, but this documentary is put together with the slam-bang panache of Corman's own movies as director. It also provides a welcome and entertaining update on Corman's own thoughts about his role at this time as head of his own immensely successful production company, New World Pictures. The mix of extracts, trailers, and anecdotal interviews with Corman and many of his protégés, past and present, makes it perfect late-night viewing. RM

Roger Corman's Frankenstein Unbound

(1990, US, 85 min)
d Roger Corman. *p* Thom Mount, Roger Corman, Kabi Jaeger. *sc* Roger Corman, FX Feeney. *ph* Armando Nannuzzi. *ed* Jay Cassidy, Mary Bauer. *pd* Enrico Tovaglieri. *m* Carl Davis. *cast* John Hurt, Raúl Julia, Bridget Fonda, Jason Patric, Michael Hutchence, Nick Brimble, Catherine Rabett, Bruce McGuire, Catherine Corman.
● Despite a starry cast, the daft plot premise (loosely derived from Brian W Aldiss' novel *Frankenstein Unbound*) scuppers any hope of intelligent entertainment from the outset. Aided by cheapo effects, scientist Buchanan (Hurt) is catapulted back from the future to a Gothic-style past. Worse still, Corman's directing style is stuck in a '60s time warp. Vacillating between all-out gore and tongue-in-cheek humour, Corman manages occasional flashes of wit (such as a scene in which Buchanan presents Mary Shelley with a photocopy of her unfinished novel *Frankenstein*). Mostly, it's too ludicrous even to aspire to campness. No explanation is offered as to why Mary Shelley's *fictional* Monster comes to be roaming the shores of Lake Geneva in a rubber suit, while the antics of Byron (Patric) and his poet pal Shelley (Hutchence) are as redundant as they are fey. Meanwhile, the painfully under-used Hurt, Julia (Baron Frankenstein) and Fonda (Mary Shelley) wander the Villa Diodati in search of a plot that seems to have slipped through a hole in the time continuum. NF

Rogue Cop

(1954, US, 92 min, b/w)
d Roy Rowland. *p* Nicholas Nayfack. *sc* Sydney Boehm. *ph* John F Seitz. *ed* James E Newcom. *ad* Cedric Gibbons, Hans Peter. *m* Jeff Alexander. *cast* Robert Taylor, Janet Leigh, George Raft, Anne Francis, Steve Forrest, Vince Edwards.
● The year after writing *The Big Heat*, the story of an upright detective avenging his murdered wife, William McGivern published *Rogue Cop*, a more interesting variation, in which a corrupt detective avenges his murdered brother. Auteur principles being what they are, Fritz Lang's movie of the former is a classic, while Rowland's adaptation of the latter is little known, though dramatically it's tougher, more complex, more unpredictable. It also has Anne Francis playing, as it were, Gloria Grahame, which many will find an improvement, and an iconic, if dull Janet Leigh. The fashion for location filming having just ended, we are returned, unfortunately, to MGM's standing city-street set, though it's atmospherically shot by John Seitz. BBa

Rogue Trader

(1998, GB/US, 101 min)
d James Dearden. *p* James Dearden, Paul Raphael, Janette Day. *sc* James Dearden. *ph* Jean-François Robin. *ed* Catherine Creed. *pd* Alan MacDonald. *m* Richard Hartley. *cast* Ewan McGregor, Anna Friel, Yves Beneyton, Betsy Brantley, Caroline Langrishe, Nigel Lindsay, Tim McInnerny, Irene Ng, John Standing, Pip Torrens.
● Ewan McGregor is Nick Leeson, the Watford chancer who single-handedly destroyed the oldest private bank in the world. How he did this is a source of fascination, yet the film's portrayal of futures trading on the Singapore International Money Exchange is a decidedly plodding assemblage of flashing computer displays, jostling traders in striped blazers, and cutaways to McGregor, bright-eyed or sunken-cheeked as the occasion demands. Rather than aiming for savage satire or ultrablack comedy, the film (based on Leeson's own book) simply plays it down the middle, taking the line that this child of Thatcherism was merely doing his employers' bidding, got in way too deep, and never had the proper management around him. Though his 'gor blimey' accent may grate, McGregor puts his all into the role; his sweating earnestness, however, isn't enough to break the overall inertia, and the rest of the cast are simply bystanders. Anna Friel gets the thankless task of bored housewife Lisa Leeson, while the likes of Tim McInnerny and John Standing compete for the upper-class twit-of-the-year honours as the flailing, plum-toned Barings Bank top brass. TJ

Roi de Coeur, Le

see King of Hearts

Roi de Paris, Le (The King of Paris)

(1993, Fr/GB, 102 min)
d Dominique Maillet. *p* Jean Gontier. *sc* Jacques Fieschi, Jérôme Tonnerre, Bernard Minoret, Dominique Maillet. *ph* Bernard Lutic. *ed* Marie Castro. *pd* Jacques Rouxel. *m* Quentin Damamme. *cast* Phillipe Noiret, Michael Aumont, Manuel Blanc, Veronika Varga, Ronny Coutteure, Franco Interlenghi, Paulette Dubost, Sacha Briquet, Corinne Cléry, Jacques Roman.
● Victor Derval (Noiret) rules the turn-of-the-century Parisian stage, and projects equal pomp off it. Walking home after a good night's work (audience enraptured, playwright enraged) he's approached by a young woman, Lisa Lanska (Varga), who wants him to know how he's inspired her. She's first patronised, then bullied, and finally charmed into his bed and employed as his secretary, sending the usual society tongues wagging. More vexing is the reaction of Derval Jr (Blanc), a dissolute poet languishing in his father's shadow, who also takes a shine to the girl. Lisa elopes with him, but harbours theatrical ambitions of her own. A showcase for the imposing talents of Noiret – it's directed and co-written by his biographer, Dominque Maillet – this grandstanding melodrama offers little else of remark. Characterisation is thin – and none of the other actors comes close to Noiret's standard – while the drama's distinctly long in the tooth (remember *All About Eve*). Grasping at straws, however, there's an intriguing hint of tension between stage and screen in a couple of scenes, which see the impresario sneering at the nascent rival art form while taking its money. NB

Roi des Aulnes, Le (The Ogre)

(1996, Fr/Ger/GB, 116 min)
d Volker Schlöndorff. *sc* Jean-Claude Carrière, Volker Schlöndorff. *ph* Bruno De Keyser. *ed* Nicolas Gaste. *ad* Ezio Frigerio. *m* Michael Nyman. *cast* John Malkovich, Marianne Sägebrecht, Armin Mueller-Stahl, Volker Spengler.
● Schlöndorff and Jean-Claude Carrière find in Michel Tournier's novel a companion piece to their earlier Günter Grass adaptation, *The Tin Drum*. The focus is again on a highly peculiar individual set on ignoring the onslaught of history, this time by remaining in a world of magical forests, loving animals, innocent children, despite accumulating evidence that life is providing something altogether opposite. Malkovich, wearing the creepiest pair of specs in movie history, is successively an unjustly convicted child molester, a PoW, a flunky at Goering's hunting lodge, and finally a hooded horseman combing the countryside for suitably Aryan youths to enroll in the SS academy: the catcher in the rye turned into the big bad wolf, or, from another viewpoint, Buñuel's Nazarin let loose in the Third Reich. As in *The Tin Drum*, the director shapes individual scenes so powerfully (cameraman Bruno De Keyser, composer Michael Nyman) that the abstractions we should presumably be inferring seem piffling alongside such muscularly rendered specifics: this snorting stag, that dead child. BBa

Roi et l'Oiseau, Le

see King and Mister Bird, The

Role, The (Bhumika)

(1977, Ind, 142 min)
d Shyam Benegal. *p* Lalit M Bulani, Freni M Variava. *sc* Girish Karnad, Satyadev Dubey, Shyam Benegal. *ph* Govind Nihalani. *ed* Bhanudas. *ad* Shama Zaidi. *songs* Vanraj Bhatia, Majrooh Sultanpuri. *cast* Smita Patil, Anant Nag, Amrish Puri, Naseeruddin Shah, Swabha Deshpande.
● Based on a book by one of Bombay's movie queens from the '40s, this sometimes looks like one of those riproaring melodramas through which Joan Crawford used to suffer so splendiferously. But put together with deceptive skill, it draws remarkable riches from its interlocking of past and present as the movie star heroine – saddled with a workshy husband, breadwinner for her entire family, but not allowed even a chequebook of her own – simultaneously tries to break out of her sexist cage and to understand how she came to be locked into it. The result is a complex exploration of female emancipation, making striking use of the Hindi cinema (wonderful parodies of the traditional *Madras Curry*, with its stoic, self-sacrificing heroines) as setting, symbol and catalyst. TM

Roller and Violin

see Katok i Skrypka

Rollerball

(1975, US, 129 min)
d/p Norman Jewison. *sc* William Harrison. *ph* Douglas Slocombe. *ed* Antony Gibbs. *pd* John Box. *m* André Previn. *cast* James Caan, John Houseman, Maud Adams, John Beck, Moses Gunn, Pamela Hensley, Barbara Trentham, Ralph Richardson, Shane Rimmer.
● Behind the vision of a future society, where the corporate world state controls the bloodlust of the populace through lethal games of rollerball, lies the familiar theme of individual struggle: Caan's champ takes on the grey eminence who wants to force his retirement. The script grapples with notions of freedom and privilege, but finally remains too oblique to throw much light either on our own society or on our possible future. Occasionally, though, insight triumphs, and Caan's struggle towards articulation remains one of the film's strong points. Otherwise, its main interest lies in the tensions generated by the gap between the script's intellectual aspirations and the gut reaction appeal of the games, which are highly physical and brutal. Hence, a group of drunken revellers deliberately and callously burning down some old fir trees makes more impression than all the destruction of human meat in the games. Ultimately, *Rollerball* gets by on its sheer monolithic quality – an abundance of quantity. Despite indifferent direction and dire humour, it is well mounted and photographed. CPe

Rollercoaster

(1977, US, 118 min)
d James Goldstone. *p* Jennings Lang. *sc* Richard Levinson, William Link. *ph* David M Walsh. *ed* Edward A Biery, Richard M Sprague. *pd* Henry Bumstead. *m* Lalo Schifrin. *cast* George Segal, Richard Widmark, Timothy Bottoms, Henry Fonda, Harry Guardino, Susan Strasberg, Helen Hunt, Dorothy Tristan.
● In 1952, when Cinerama was born, its makers placed a camera on the front of a Coney Island rollercoaster to magnificent effect. Universal here came up with the ingenious idea of incorporating the rollercoaster gimmick into a mad bomber thriller, and adding Sensurround for good measure. The results should have been sensational, not just because of the added sound effects, but because American rollercoasters were far bigger, faster and more chilling than they ever were in 1952. *Rollercoaster* does deliver its share of thrills, but ultimately the film-makers botched the job. Many of the best runs are interrupted by close-ups, and the filler plot is dumb in the extreme. DP

Roller Derby

see Derby

Rollicking Adventures of Eliza Fraser, The (aka A Faithful Narrative of the Capture, Sufferings and Miraculous Escape of Eliza Fraser)

(1976, Aust, 112 min)
d/p Tim Burstall. *sc* David Williamson. *ph* Robin Copping. *ed* Edward McQueen-Mason. *ad* Leslie Binns. *m* Bruce Smeaton. *cast* Susannah York, Noel Ferrier, John Waters, Trevor Howard, John Castle, Bill Hunter.
●Beware rollicking heroines, especially from the perpetrator of *Stork* and *Alvin Purple*. The factual history of Eliza Fraser (shipwrecked and conscripted as a member of an aboriginal tribe) is thrown away in a lumberingly burlesque period romp about a lady with a roving eye, and a pompously straitlaced husband, who becomes involved in a farce of lusty humiliations before ending up peddling a spicy account of her adventures in carnivals. Moments of bizarrerie escape the general heavy-handedness, but the more serious purpose evident in David Williamson's script – of confronting sexual attitudes and hypocrisies – doesn't get a look in. TM

Rollover

(1981, US, 115 min)
d Alan J Pakula. *p* Bruce Gilbert. *sc* David Shaber. *ph* Giuseppe Rotunno. *ed* Evan Lottman. *pd* George Jenkins. *m* Michael Small. *cast* Jane Fonda, Kris Kristofferson, Hume Cronyn, Josef Sommer, Bob Gunton, Macon McCalman.
●A generally underrated film, admittedly not always easy to follow in its voyage through the rarefied reaches of high finance and merchant banking, discovering conspiracy and murder along the way, with the fate of the entire Western economy hanging in the balance. Disconcerting in its kaleidoscopic shifts in tone, it's nevertheless too absorbing simply to dismiss. Matching gamesmanship with gamesmanship as his financiers elaborate on their abstruse gambits in incomprehensible computer-speak, what Pakula seems to be trying to demonstrate – with the final confrontation suggesting a standoff between two gunfighters, stalemated because the villain proves able to justify his villainy – is that the complex power plays of international finance constitute an entirely new genre with which the old ones arrayed here (*film noir*, romantic comedy, political exposé, Western) are ill-equipped to cope. It's a fascinating experiment, well worth seeing anyway as another of Pakula's marvellous evocations of urban paranoia. TM

Roma

see Fellini's Roma

Roma, Città Aperta (Open City/Rome, Open City)

(1945, It, 101 min, b/w)
d Roberto Rossellini. *sc* Sergio Amidei, Federico Fellini, Roberto Rossellini. *ph* Ubaldo Arata. *ed* Eraldo De Roma. *m* Renzo Rossellini. *cast* Anna Magnani, Aldo Fabrizi, Marcello Pagliero, Maria Michi, Harry Feist.
●Rossellini's film, one of the definitive works of the Italian neo-realist period, was shot under extremely difficult circumstances at the end of WWII. Its greatest achievement remains its study and placing of the Resistance movement – and on a wider level, the war itself – against a background of everyday events. The film evolved from a documentary about a priest serving in the Resistance, which perhaps accounts for its refusal to compromise or to entertain conventional notions of heroism. CPe

Romance

see Some Kinda Love

Romance

(1998, Fr, 95 min)
d Catherine Breillat. *p* Jean-François Lepetit. *sc* Catherine Breillat. *ph* Yorgos Arvanitis. *ed* Agnès Guillemot. *ad* Frédérique Belvaux. *m* DJ Valentin, Raphaël Tidas. *cast* Caroline Ducey, Sagamore Stévenin, François Berléand, Rocco Siffredi, Reza Habouhossein, Ashley Wanninger, Emma Colberti, Fabien de Jomaron.
●Serious films about sex are rare, but it's perhaps unsurprising that French writer/director Breillat should have produced such an extraordinarily focused study, as she's been making movies on the subject since 1976. This is her most ambitious and audacious work to date. The story itself is so simple, it has the clarity of a fable: bored, depressed and 'dishonoured' by her lover Paul's lack of physical interest in her, schoolteacher Marie (Ducey) embarks on a sexual odyssey. That's it for the plot. Breillat's interest is in her heroine's psychology, and in her steady growth through transgression, experiment and self-analysis, however painful or potentially self-destructive the consequences may be. Entailing a kind of sentimental education, the film is distinguished by its cool refusal to judge or applaud Marie's actions; Breillat simply observes and analyses. Not that her aesthetic is 'realist'. Marie's philosophical/poetic voice-over, the inexorable linear progress of her actions, and the stark, subtly stylised interiors situate the film in the realm of metaphor. At the same time, however, the very frank physicality roots it in a world recognisably our own, while the gaze at erotic activity results not in titillation but in a contemplation of sexual congress as an outward manifestation of deeper, more complex needs. Indeed, while this is clearly 'a woman's film' in its point of view, the cool, detached air of enquiry, the focus on paraphernalia and emotional sophistication recall Buñuel, Borowczyk and Oshima. GA

Romance and Rejection

(1997, GB, 92 min)
d Kevin W Smith. *p* Jonathan English, Bruce Sharman. *sc* Kevin W Smith. *ph* Ian Salvage. *ed* Mark Talbot-Butler. *pd* Lucy Reeves. *m* Howard J Davidson. *cast* Reece Dinsdale, John Hannah, Victoria Smurfit, Clara Bellar, Frank Finlay, Rowena King, Susannah York, Maryam D'Abo.
●Very Nick Hornby, but some way short of the real thing. Mike – 36, single, and unhappy about it – hasn't had much luck with the fairer sex since his mother abandoned him and dad back in the dark ages. His congenital jealousy is the problem, though it should be said neither of his current hot and cold girlfriends wins marks for consistency. Dinsdale lacks the charm to allow us to overlook Mike's failings, and the big emotional scenes with the parents are heavy handed. TCh

Romance of a Horse Thief

(1971, Yugo/US, 100 min)
d Abraham Polonsky. *p* Gene Gutowski. *sc* David Opatoshu. *ph* Piero Portalupi. *ed* Kevin Connor. *ad* Otto Pishinger, Vlastimir Gavrik. *m* Mort Shuman. *cast* Yul Brynner, Eli Wallach, Jane Birkin, Oliver Tobias, Lainie Kazan, David Opatoshu, Serge Gainsbourg.
●Blacklisted director Polonsky (best known for 1949's John Garfield boxing classic *Force of Evil*) made a comeback in the early '70s with Robert Redford's liberal Western *Tell Them Willie Boy Is Here* and this now rarely seen Yugoslavian-shot offering. In turn-of-the-century Poland, Jewish horse traders try to best Cossack soldiers seeking to commandeer their animals for the Russo-Japanese war, a scenario (by David Opatoshu) to which Polonsky brings both humour and equine action. TJ

Romance of Book & Sword, The (Shujian Enchou Lu)

(1987, HK, 181 min [2 parts])
d Ann Hui. *p* Leung Yam-wing, Fu Chi. *sc* Louis Cha, Ann Hui. *ph* Bill Wong. *ed* Chou Muk-liang. *pd* Ho Kwan, Woo Chun. *m* Lo Wing-fei, Gu Kun-yun, Chow Kit. *cast* Zhang Duofu, Da Shichang, Oyilore, Liu Gui.
●A two-part historical epic, filmed all over China, centred on conflict between the Manchu Emperor Qianlong and a resistance group who are fighting to restore Chinese rule. (Echoes of contemporary debates about the future of Hong Kong under Chinese sovereignty are not entirely coincidental.) This is the nearest thing in present-day Chinese cinema to the spectacles that King Hu made in the 1960s: prodigious use of locations, rousing action climaxes, shameless exoticism, and set pieces that flaunt it because they've got it. Part II gets rather bogged down in folksy frippery about a Muslim tribe in Xinjiang, but the breathtaking act of treachery at the end erases any doubts about Hui's vision and seriousness of purpose. TR

Romance on the High Seas (aka It's Magic)

(1948, US, 99 min)
d Michael Curtiz. *p* Alex Gottleib, George Amy. *sc* Julius J Epstein, Philip G Epstein, IAL Diamond. *ph* Elwood Bredell. *ed* Rudi Fehr. *ad* Anton Grot. *songs* Jule Styne, Sammy Cahn. *cast* Jack Carson, Janis Paige, Don DeFore, Doris Day, Oscar Levant, SZ Sakall, Fortunio Bonanova, Franklin Pangborn, Eric Blore.
●A bland but amiable musical marking Doris Day's debut. With vague jealousies in the air, millionaire DeFore hires a private eye (Carson) to check up on his wife (Paige) while she is on a cruise to Rio. But Paige, with her own checking up in mind, hires an aspiring singer (Day) with a yen for luxurious travel to take her place. Carson and Day promptly fall in love during the cruise, and much confusion ensues when Carson guiltily confesses in his report to her supposed husband, while Day can't resist a career-enhancing chance to sing under her assumed name at a society charity do in Rio. Likeable performances (backed by a sterling supporting cast), plus good Jule Styne-Sammy Cahn songs, make it all pleasantly painless. TM

Romance with a Double Bass

(1974, GB, 41 min)
d Robert Young. *p* Ian Gordon, David King. *sc* Bill Owen. *ph* Clive Tickner. *ed* Gregory Harris. *m* Leon Cohen. *cast* Connie Booth, John Cleese, Graham Crowden, Freddie Jones, John Moffatt, Denis Ramsden, June Whitfield.
●An adaptation of a Chekhov short story, set in Russia, with Cleese as a doleful double-bass player booked to perform for the forced engagement of Princess Constanza (Booth). To pass time before rehearsals, he strips off for a quick dip in a nearby river, whereupon someone steals his clothes. Meanwhile, downstream, the same fate has befallen the Princess. This leads to a very funny, innocent and tastefully filmed nudist romp in which the two of them (without peeking) try to work their way back to the huge mansion, the Princess squeezed into his double-bass case. One classic moment has Cleese running back and forth across the picturesque countryside, dropping the case and having to sprint back to pick up his double-bass. DA

Romancing the Stone

(1984, US, 106 min)
d Robert Zemeckis. *p* Michael Douglas. *sc* Diane Thomas. *ph* Dean Cundey. *ed* Donn Cambern, Frank Morriss. *pd* Lawrence G Paull. *m* Alan Silvestri. *cast* Michael Douglas, Kathleen Turner, Danny DeVito, Zack Norman, Alfonso Arau, Manuel Ojeda, Holland Taylor, Mary Ellen Trainor.
●Treasure maps, crocodiles, romantic novelists and psychotic Latins, this slings them all together, along with a hefty slug of wish-fulfilment, to engaging effect. Stuck with her miniatures and cat called Romeo in New York, Turner pines for schmaltz to turn into life as she churns out Mills and Boonies. Then sister Elaine (Trainor) gets kidnapped by the splendid Zack Norman and his cackling sidekick down in Columbia, and it's eyes down for galloping caper thrills. The script is sharp and funny, the direction sure-footed on both the comedy and action fronts, and the whole thing adds up to rather more concerted fun than Indiana Jones' flab-ridden escapade in the Temple of Doom. There's also the added bonus of Ms Turner, at the sight of whom this dispassionate arbiter of public taste came perilously close to self-combustion. JP

Roman de Renard, Le (The Tale of the Fox)

(1930, Fr, 65 min, b/w)
d Wladyslaw Starewicz. *p* Louis Nalpas, Roger Richebé. *sc* Wladyslaw Starewicz, Irène Starewicz, Roger Richéby, Jean Nohain, Antoinette Nordmann. *ed* Laura Séjourné. *pd* Wladyslaw Starewicz. *m* Vincent Scotto. *cast* voices: Claude Dauphin, Romain Bouquet, Sylvain Itkine.

●Adapted from Goethe's fable – about a fox whose carnivorous cunning, deplored and feared by the rest of the animal kingdom, brings him into legal conflict with the lion king – this vintage animated film impresses, first of all, by the sheer virtuosity of its stop-motion puppet work. Some sequences feature literally dozens of immaculate creatures on superbly detailed sets. Its creator, Wladyslaw Starewicz (1882–1965), was a Polish-Lithuanian who moved to France after the Soviet revolution, whose work today is known mostly by reputation. *The Tale of the Fox* is marked by a sardonic wit. Much of the frantic violence puts Tom and Jerry to shame, and much of the imagery – hares drunk on communion wine, tightrope walking mice, a castle filled with Heath Robinson battle contraptions – springs from a genuinely surreal imagination. GA

Roman d'un Tricheur, Le (The Story of a Cheat)

(1936, Fr, 85 min, b/w)
d Sacha Guitry. *p* Serge Sandberg. *sc* Sacha Guitry. *ph* Marcel Lucien. *ed* Myriam Borsoutzky. *ad* Maurice Guerbe, Henri Ménessier. *m* Adolphe Borchard. *cast* Sacha Guitry, Jacqueline Delubac, Rosine Deréan, Pauline Carton, Serge Grave, Pierre Assy.

●At age 12, our hero is sent to bed supper-less for stealing eight sous. When he wakes up his entire family is dead from food poisoning, leading him to conclude that dishonesty and survival are intimately linked. We follow his subsequent career as thief and card sharp (Guitry demonstrates a few tricks for us). The peculiarity of the narrative is that it forgoes dialogue in favour of a non-stop commentary by the author. This allows Guitry to pack the soundtrack with elegant witticisms, though rather leaving the actors stranded on occasion. But it's quite unique, with the hero's ruthlessness paralleled by Guitry's own in never letting anyone else get a look in. Borchard's tiresome score is the only really dated element. BBa

Roman Holiday

(1953, US, 119 min, b/w)
d/p William Wyler. *sc* Ian McLellan Hunter, John Dighton. *ph* Franz Planer, Henri Alekan. *ed* Robert Swink. *ad* Hal Pereira, Walter Tyler. *m* Georges Auric. *cast* Audrey Hepburn, Gregory Peck, Eddie Albert, Tullio Carminati, Harcourt Williams, Hartley Power.

●This has the hallmarks of a Billy Wilder picture – Americans abroad, masquerades leading to moral transformation – and Wilder would doubtless have turned it into a blazing masterpiece. Wyler's style was not particularly suited to comedy – the film is a little long, a little heavy at times, the spontaneity a little over-rehearsed – and he simply makes a wonderfully enjoyable movie. Hepburn is the Princess bored with protocol who goes AWOL in Rome; Peck (Holden would have been better, edgier) is the American journalist who has the scoop fall into his lap; and Albert (the best performance) is the photographer who has to snap all of Hepburn's un-royal escapades. This sort of thing was churned out by Lubitsch in the '30s, on the Paramount backlot; Wyler went on location, and in 1953 that was a real eye-opener, Hollywood's answer to neorealism. The movie remains a great tonic. ATu

Roman Scandals

(1933, US, 92 min, b/w)
d Frank Tuttle. *sc* William Anthony McGuire, George Oppenheimer, Arthur Sheekman, Nat Perrin. *ph* Gregg Toland, Ray June. *ed* Stuart Heisler. *ad* Richard Day. *songs* Al Dubin, Harry Warren. *cast* Eddie Cantor, Ruth Etting, Edward Arnold, Gloria Stuart, David Manners, Verree Teasdale, Alan Mowbray.

●A pleasantly entertaining pot-pourri of humour, song, and dance, structured around the goggle-eyed gaucheries of Cantor as the small-town boy, run out by the authorities because of his troublesome social conscience, who dreams that he is a slave in Ancient Rome (graduating to the perilous post of food-taster for Arnold's Emperor). Though the wit has dated somewhat, it's still worth seeing for its typically lavish Goldwyn production values: Richard Day's impressive set designs, Gregg Toland's camerawork, and Busby Berkeley's usual excesses in a slave-market scene, populated by masses of all but naked Goldwyn girls. GA

Roman Spring of Mrs Stone, The

(1961, US, 104 min)
d José Quintero. *p* Louise de Rochemont. *sc* Gavin Lambert. *ph* Harry Waxman. *ed* Ralph Kemplen. *pd* Roger Furse. *m* Richard Addinsell. *cast* Vivien Leigh, Warren Beatty, Lotte Lenya, Jill St John, Jeremy Spenser, Coral Browne, Ernest Thesiger.

●Typical Tennessee Williams seediness (it's an adaptation of his first novel), with Vivien Leigh doing her faded beauty bit as a widowed actress lolling around in Rome and trying to find final romance with gigolo Beatty. Florid and sordid simultaneously, and forever verging on the nonsensical, but saved by a charismatic performance from Lotte Lenya as a bitchy procuress. GA

Romantic Agony, The (Vaarwel)

(1973, Neth, 85 min)
d Guido Pieters. *p* Joseph Vliegen. *sc* Guido Pieters, Ton Ruys. *ph* Theo van de Sande. *ed* Ton Ruys. *m* Ennio Morricone. *cast* Pieke Dassen, Nettie Blanken, Rik Bravenboer, José Ruyter, Wim Hoogendam.

●An excursion into an area of Tolkien-type fantasy, centering on a seemingly immortal old man's wanderings through time, taking in episodes historical and modern. Its obvious low budget is compensated by some pleasantly autumnal photography, and by Morricone's score. But its myth-weaving trendiness at times becomes excessively cute, with embarrassing episodes (like a nocturnal rite around a phallic totem, detachedly observed by the old man) jarring against others handled with some delicacy (like those involving a ghost unable to frighten anyone any more, and a lady vampire now living on bottled plasma from the blood bank).

Romantic Englishwoman, The

(1975, GB/Fr, 116 min)
d Joseph Losey. *p* Daniel M Angel. *sc* Thomas Wiseman, Tom Stoppard. *ph* Gerry Fisher. *ed* Reginald Beck. *ad* Richard MacDonald. *m* Richard Hartley. *cast* Glenda Jackson, Michael Caine, Helmut Berger, Marcus Richardson, Kate Nelligan, Rene Kolldehoff, Michel Lonsdale, Béatrice Romand, Nathalie Delon.

●'Return to Losey Country' might be a more suitable title for *The Romantic Englishwoman,* in which Caine plays a prestigious novelist whose wife (Jackson) feeds his jealous fantasies by slipping off to Baden Baden for the weekend. The two play out their trapped games, prior to a highly romanticised intrusion from Helmut Berger, amid an opulence so mannered and preposterous that it verges on self-parody; in fact, the familiar icy excess of Richard MacDonald's set matches the pomposity of the characters. Most of the film is passably entertaining, and Tom Stoppard's dialogue has its moments, but the basic material contains less that is real or relevant about it than the flimsiest of romantic melodramas. DP

Romeo and Juliet

(1968, GB/It, 152 min)
d Franco Zeffirelli. *p* Anthony Havelock-Allan, John Brabourne. *sc* Franco Brusati, Masolino D'Amico. *ph* Pasqualino De Santis. *ed* Reginald Mills. *pd* Renzo Mongiardino. *m* Nino Rota. *cast* Leonard Whiting, Olivia Hussey, Milo O'Shea, Michael York, John McEnery, Pat Heywood, Natasha Parry, Paul Hardwick, Robert Stephens.

●Zeffirelli's mod adaptation of *Romeo and Juliet* isn't one of the very slim handful of masterfully filmed Shakespeare plays, but it's nowhere near as mawkish as the simple-minded pantheism on display in the later *Brother Sun, Sister Moon.* It is successful in one very important respect, the handling of the hot-headed youth of the feuding Verona families, and the street brawling scenes are admirable. The rot sets in with Zeffirelli's treatment of the 'stern' parents, the sentimentality of his Irish friar (O'Shea) and Cockney nurse (Heywood), and the tragic denouement. Mostly it remains enjoyable for its colour and visual flair. Danilo Donati's costumes are, as usual, breathtaking. RM

Romeo & Juliet

see William Shakespeare's Romeo & Juliet

Romeo in Pyjamas

see Parlor, Bedroom and Bath

Romeo Is Bleeding

(1992, US, 109 min)
d Peter Medak. *p* Hilary Henkin, Paul Webster. *sc* Hilary Henkin. *ph* Dariusz Wolski. *ed* Walter Murch. *pd* Stuart Wurtzel. *m* Mark Isham. *cast* Gary Oldman, Lena Olin, Annabella Sciorra, Juliette Lewis, Roy Scheider, Will Patton.

●Jack Grimaldi (Oldman) is a New York cop on the take and then some. He sells out witnesses to the Mob and buries the pay-offs in his backyard. He's got a wife (Sciorra) and a girlfriend (Lewis). He's keeping it together, he thinks. Then he meets Mona Demarkov (Olin). A glamorous Russian gangster, she's in bed with the Feds and at the head of the Mafia's death list – but Jack just could be her trump card. Director Medak goes off the rails in high style with this dementedly doleful exercise in pop *noir.* But the film plays out the battle of the sexes at such an unflinchingly amoral pitch it really isn't funny anymore. Like Oldman's deluded operator – playing both ends and getting caught in the middle – Hilary Henkin's script isn't as smart as it thinks it is, and only Olin's breathtakingly excessive femme fatale hits the right note of campy panache. TCh

Romeo Must Die

(2000, US, 114 min)
d Andrzej Bartkowiak. *p* Joel Silver, Jim Van Wyck. *sc* Eric Bernt, John Jarrell. *ph* Glen MacPherson. *ed* Derek G Brechin. *pd* Michael Bolton. *m* Stanley Clarke, Timbaland. *cast* Jet Li, Aaliyah, Isaiah Washington, Russell Wong, Henry O, DB Woodside, Edoardo Ballerini, Jon Kit Lee, Anthony Anderson, DMX, Delroy Lindo.

●Capitalising on his scene stealing role as the stonefaced Triad villain in *Lethal Weapon 4,* veteran HK martial artist Jet Li lands his first Hollywood lead in a slick, Joel Silver-produced action movie with a borderline straight to video feel. As a showcase for Li's fighting moves, the film works well, but only when Corey Yuen's inspired choreography, *Matrix*-style wire work and CGI-enhanced bonecrunching are centre screen. The uninvolving plot sees black gangster Isaak O'Day (Lindo) and crime lord Ch'u Sing (Henry O) held in uneasy balance by a shared interest in ousting small businesses from their respective waterfront patches, to make way for a semi-legit, Jewish backed syndicate's American football stadium. Not even the lynching of Ch'u Sing's wayward son can scupper this money laundering scheme by provoking gang war. Despite the trouble stirred up by the dead man's brother (Li), a disgraced ex-cop who escapes from a HK prison to avenge his brother's death, the real threat to the fragile peace seems to come from ambitious rogue elements within the black and Chinese gangs. NF

Rome, Open City

see Roma, Città Aperta

Romero

(1989, US, 105 min)
d John Duigan. *p* Ellwood Kieser. *sc* John Sacret Young. *ph* Geoff Burton. *ed* Frans Vandenburg. *ad* Francisco Magallon. *m* Gabriel Yared. *cast* Raúl Julia, Richard Jordan, Ana Alicia, Eddie Vélez, Alejandro Bracho, Tony Plana, Harold Gould, Claudio Brook, Martin Lasalle.

●Financed in part by Catholic organisations in the States, this was apparently made under Church auspices, nearly ten years after the death of the Salvadorean archbishop it commemorates. One wonders, however, whether the Vatican is quite as fond of these turbulent priests when they're alive. Certainly the screenplay dramatises the intolerable position of a passionate priest in El Salvador: mistrusted as an agent of the state by the guerillas, menaced by the army for his championship of human rights, Romero (Julia), initially selected as a soft, safe candidate for archbishop, surprised everyone by speaking out against violence on both sides. Certain scenes seem almost too heroic, but overall this treatment has a ring of truth; horrendous events occur, but there's no lewd lingering over the details of death. Though the slightly ponderous script jars in the early scenes (leaden exposition of political verities, characterisation by numbers), the bulk of the film works up a considerable emotional charge, with doe-eyed Julia attaining a mythic simplicity. SFe

Rommel – Desert Fox

see Desert Fox, The

Romper Stomper

(1992, NZ, 91 min)
d Geoffrey Wright. *p* Daniel Scharf, Ian Pringle. *sc* Geoffrey Wright. *ph* Ron Hagen. *ed* Bill Murphy. *pd* Steven Jones-Evans. *m* John Clifford White. *cast* Russell Crowe, Daniel Pollock, Jacqueline McKenzie, Alex Scott, Leigh Russell, Daniel Wyllie.

● If it's hard to fault Wright's stated anti-racist reasons for making this portrait of Melbourne's skinhead life, you can't help but doubt the wisdom of the stylistic choices he's made. A disaffected young girl, Gabe (McKenzie), who takes up with a gang led by neo-Nazi Hando (Crowe), is attracted by his brute sexuality, the power he wields over his less articulate minions, and the bloody violence they mete out to Vietnamese immigrants. But when the victims decide to fight back, the gang begins to fall apart, and Gabe's affections are transferred to Hando's right-hand man Davey (Pollock). The fact that Wright has opted for such a visceral style tends to vitiate what few insights he may provide into the racist mentality; the raw, semi-documentary narrative may make for plausibility, but the high-adrenaline, souped-up visuals ensure a lack of moral perspective. The cheap 'message' of the ending fails to salvage a film that at best is well-meant but misguided, at worst, flashy and garbled. GA

Romuald et Juliette (Romuald & Juliette)

(1989, Fr, 112 min)
d Coline Serreau. *p* Philippe Carcassonne, Jean-Louis Piel. *sc* Coline Serreau. *ph* Jean-Noël Ferragut. *ed* Catherine Renault. *ad* Jean-Marc Stehle. *cast* Daniel Auteuil, Firmine Richard, Pierre Vernier, Maxime Leroux, Gilles Privat, Muriel Combeau, Alain Fromager.

● Coline Serreau's last film inspired (if that is the word) *Three Men and a Baby*, and this one also looks a likely candidate for an American remake. Despite the title, there's little here Shakespeare would recognise, with the star-crossed romance a long time coming. Instead, Serreau builds up a complicated situation involving insider dealing at Romuald's yoghurt company. Ousted and cuckolded, Romuald (Auteuil) finds himself with only one friend in the world, the company's black cleaning-woman Juliette (Richard, splendid). Together, they plot to put him back at the top; in the meantime, he hides out in Juliette's cramped, broken-down apartment with her five children. Cross-cutting between the life-styles of rich and poor (or of whites and blacks), Serreau makes her points implicitly, but also fashions a surprisingly generous, romantic movie in which everyone has the right to follow his or her heart. Spirited performances and some fine blues on the soundtrack help to make this warm comedy a real pleasure. TCh

Romy and Michele's High School Reunion

(1997, US, 91 min)
d David Mirkin. *p* Laurence Mark. *sc* Robin Schiff. *ph* Reynaldo Villalobos. *ed* David Finfer. *pd* Mayne Berke. *m* Steve Bartek. *cast* Mira Sorvino, Lisa Kudrow, Alan Cumming, Julia Campbell, Janeane Garofalo, Vincent Ventresca.

● Longtime pals Sorvino and Kudrow have achieved, well, not very much since graduation day, but both film-makers and tuned-in performers contrive never to look down on their big hair, Valley Girl vowels and full set of vacant attitudes. The pair do comic-irrepressible to a tee, as gnawing curiosity draws them back to the old school, and old scores are just waiting to be settled. Flavourful character playing jazzes up the central riff on friendship surviving the scorn of the mainstream. Cumming has obliterated his Scots accent sufficiently to play the teenage übergeek in the flashbacks, but star of the show is undoubtedly Garofalo's hilariously abrasive turn as the adolescent outsider of yore, who's turned her chain-smoking habit to advantage by inventing a quick-drawing ciggie you can inhale with a single puff. She looks haggard, wears a lot of shit-brown, and, boy, do you miss her when she's off screen. First-time director Mirkin doesn't quite sustain the momentum, and the big 'Post-It' gag is laboriously over-extended, but by then Lisa and Mira have won you over. A chipper little comedy (exec producer Robin Schiff adapted her play *The Ladies Room*) with a hint of *Simpsons* bite. TJ

Ronde, La

(1950, Fr, 97 min, b/w)
d Max Ophüls. *p* Sacha Gordine. *sc* Jacques Natanson, Max Ophuls. *ph* Christian Matras. *ed* Léonide Azar. *ad* Jean d'Eaubonne. *m* Oscar Straus. *cast* Anton Walbrook, Simone Signoret, Serge Reggiani, Simone Simon, Daniel Gélin, Danielle Darrieux, Fernand Gravey, Odette Joyeux, Jean-Louis Barrault, Isa Miranda, Gérard Philipe.

● Not one of the director's very greatest films on desire (see *Letter from an Unknown Woman* and *Lola Montès* for those), Ophüls' circular chain of love and seduction in 19th century Vienna is still irresistible. Embellishing Arthur Schnitzler's text with metaphors that are entirely his own (a carousel; an omniscient/omnipotent narrator/MC, with Walbrook at times actually seen splicing the celluloid stories together; and that perfect expression of the Ophülsian circle, the waltz), Ophüls almost manages to make you forget that the performances in the first half (Signoret, Reggiani, Simon, Gélin, Darrieux, Gravey) are much better than those in the second. And there are more than enough moments of cinematic magic to excuse the occasional longueurs of talkiness. RM

Ronin

(1998, US, 121 min)
d John Frankenheimer. *p* Frank Mancuso Jr. *sc* JD Zeik, Richard Weitz [David Mamet]. *ph* Robert Fraisse. *ed* Tony Gibbs. *pd* Michael Z Hanan. *m* Elia Cmiral. *cast* Robert De Niro, Jean Réno, Natascha McElhone, Stellan Skarsgård, Sean Bean, Michael Lonsdale, Jonathan Pryce, Katarina Witt.

● Given Frankenheimer's claims in the press notes that his 'intelligent suspense thriller... questions our ethics', you might be forgiven for expecting a superior character study instead of the laughably hackneyed genre fluff it very soon shows itself to be. The French-set plot, about an international group of criminal experts hired by an unknown client to get their hands on a mysterious briefcase, is rambling and uninvolving; the characters are paper-thin stereotypes; the dialogue is clumsy and trite; the use of familiar landmarks an insult to audience intelligence – though not, perhaps, as insulting as the absurd pretensions to some sort of political relevance. As for the title, don't ask. Some critics have applauded the non-digitalised car chases, and yes, it's fun for a while to see them speed through narrow Nice streets and on the Parisian *périphérique*, though by the third time round, the novelty of old-fashioned set-pieces – which still consist of collisions, explosions and expendable extras – palls. So, too, does De Niro's lazy performance as an ex-CIA strategist, McElhone's rogue brogue, the ugly camerawork, fashionably explicit blood-letting, and everything. Dire. GA

Rooftops

(1989, US, 95 min)
d Robert Wise. *p* Howard W Koch Jr. *sc* Terence Brennan. *ph* Theo Van de Sande. *ed* William Reynolds. *pd* Jeannine C Oppewall. *m* Michael Kamen, David A Stewart. *cast* Jason Gedrick, Troy Beyer, Eddie Vélez, Tisha Campbell, Alexis Cruz, Allen Payne, Steve Love.

● With such a preposterously dewy-eyed premise, how could this have been anything but awful? Orphaned T (Gedrick) lives in an empty water-tower atop a deserted Lower East Side tenement in New York. In fact there's an entire community of kids up there, who hang out by night in a vacant lot named 'The Garden of Eden', peaceably sorting out their differences through 'combat dance' (a stylised descendant of the Afro-Brazilian martial arts discipline Capoeira, which involves no physical contact). Enter serpent-like trouble in the form of neighbourhood pusher Lobo (Vélez), aided and abetted by nubile young Elena (Beyer), with whom our hero is besotted. Time for teen-love torn apart once more by divided loyalties. Nearly 30 years after *West Side Story*, Wise's return to the 'street-sussed musical' is painfully disappointing: a parade of frantic, vacuous gestures which, like combat dancing itself, simply never delivers the punch as lithesome muscles sweat aimlessly under clingy vests, accompanied by Dave (Eurythmics) Stewart's blusterous soundtrack. By the time Lobo's henchmen start blowing up water-towers and chucking kids off rooftops, you can't help but sympathise. MK

Rookery Nook

(1930, GB, 76 min, b/w)
d Tom Walls, (supervisor) Byron Haskin. *p* Herbert Wilcox. *sc* Ben Travers, WP Lipscomb. *ph* Freddie Young. *ed* J Maclean Rogers *cast* Ralph Lynn, Tom Walls, Winifred Shotter, Mary Brough, Robertson Hare, Ethel Coleridge, Margot Grahame.

● Though Hitchcock's *Blackmail* is remembered as the first great British talkie, it was this filmed version of Ben Travers' Aldwych farce – distressed damsel embarrasses newly-wed chinless wonder in country cottage rest-cure setting – which scored at the box-office. According to producer Herbert Wilcox, it cost £14,000 to make and grossed £150,000 in Britain alone. Recorded on discs rather than film and directed by Walls with an arrogant unconcern for anything cinematic, the bizarre look and sound of the film give it the quality of a fascinating historical relic. RMy

Rookie, The

(1990, US, 121 min)
d Clint Eastwood. *p* Howard G Kazanjian, Steven Siebert, David Valdes. *sc* Boaz Yakin, Scott Spiegel. *ph* Jack N Green. *ed* Joel Cox. *ad* Judy Cammer. *m* Lennie Niehaus. *cast* Clint Eastwood, Charlie Sheen, Raúl Julia, Sonia Braga, Tom Skerritt, Lara Flynn Boyle, Pepe Serna.

● Having salved his artistic conscience with *White Hunter, Black Heart*, Eastwood returned to the action-adventure genre with this astonishingly inadequate piece of piffle. Promoted to the Grand Theft Auto Division of the LAPD, rookie cop David Ackerman (Sheen) teams up with Nick Pulovski (Eastwood), a cigar-smoking ex-racing driver hell-bent on avenging his former partner's murder. Naturally, Ackerman at first despises his new colleague's working methods – beating people up, using his badge as an AMEX card, etc –but when Pulovski is kidnapped by fiendish, mustachioed hun Eric Strom (Julia), the nappie-brained new boy realises it's time to get manly forthwith. Directed by Eastwood with the same stupefied lethargy that characterises his performance, this tedious rites of passage movie is full of caricatured cops and robbers, and punctuated with interminably dull car-chases. Only Sheen's hysterically inept handling of the godawful dialogue relieves the boredom. MK

Rookie of the Year

(1993, US, 103 min)
d Daniel Stern. *p* Robert Harper. *sc* Sam Harper. *ph* Jack N Green. *ed* Donn Cambern, Raja Gosnell. *pd* Steven Jordan. *m* Bill Conti. *cast* Thomas Ian Nicholas, Gary Busey, Albert Hall, Amy Morton, Bruce Altman, Eddie Bracken, Dan Hedaya, Daniel Stern.

● It was a magic bat in *The Natural*, and a magic park in *Field of Dreams*; now it's a magic arm. The 100 mph pitch which propels 12-year-old Henry Rowengartner (Nicholas) into major league baseball is not, however, manna from heaven, but the surprising result of a fall. For this is not an enchanting, mystical film, but an exhaustingly physical one. Surrounded by such stock characters as the single mum and her slimy boyfriend, the conniving pitcher and his has-been employer, Henry inspires the goodies, foils the baddies. First-time director Stern – Macaulay Culkin's punching bag in the *Home Alone* films – gives a broad performance as the pitching coach who knows nothing about baseball. Approach with aspirin. AO

Roomates

(1993, US, 90 min)
d Alan Metzger. *p* Tom Rowe. *sc* Robert W Lenski. *ph* Geoffrey Erb. *ed* Seth Flaum. *pd* Douglas Higgins. *m* Lee Holdridge. *cast* Randy Quaid, Eric Stoltz, Elizabeth Peña, Charles Durning, Frank Buxton, Jill Teed.

● An AIDS picture about an angry Irish-American roughneck (Quaid) and a saintly piano-playing WASP (Stoltz) thrown together in a Seattle apartment house for the terminally ill, in which the death of the latter teaches the former the virtues of tolerance and acceptance. It's hard to write ill of a film so obviously made from the heart, but sentimentality is, regrettably, the dominant mood of this sanitised and improbable story. JPy

Room at the Top

(1959, GB, 117 min, b/w)
d Jack Clayton. *p* John Woolf, James Woolf. *sc* Neil Paterson. *ph* Freddie Francis. *ed* Ralph Kemplen. *ad* Ralph Brinton. *m* Mario Nascimbene. *cast* Laurence Harvey, Simone Signoret, Heather Sears, Donald Wolfit, Donald Houston, Allan Cuthbertson, Hermione Baddeley, Raymond Huntley.

●Acclaimed as the first British film to treat sex seriously – i.e. to show it as enjoyable rather than sinful – and as one of the first to show the North of England as it 'really was'. In retrospect, this adaptation of John Braine's Bradford-set novel, with its moral melodramatics as Laurence Harvey cheats his way to success (a good marriage) via the death of his 'true love' and the bed of his mistress (Signoret), may not stand the test of time. But it remains intriguing as a sort of *Brief Encounter*, '50s-style. PH

Room for Romeo Brass, A

(1999, GB/Can, 90 min)
d Shane Meadows. *p* George Faber, Charles Pattinson. *sc* Paul Fraser, Shane Meadows. *ph* Ashley Rowe. *ed* Paul Tothill. *pd* Crispian Sallis. *m* Nick Hemming. *cast* Andrew Shim, Ben Marshall, Paddy Considine, Frank Harper, Julia Ford, James Higgins, Vicky McClure, Bob Hoskins.

●More shrewdly judged than *TwentyFourSeven*, this is a small picture with a deceptively big kick. In terms of scale, you can't get much more down-to-earth than a portrait of a couple of 12- to 13-year-old boys growing up on a Midlands estate. Romeo (Shim) is a jolly, well nourished lad, who lives next door to his best friend Knocks (Marshall). The boys are inseparable – until they meet Morrell (Considine), who takes Romeo under his wing. Knocks he despises: because of his limp, and because he plays a prank which humiliates Morrell in front of his sister Ladine (McClure). Meadows begins with the kind of honest attention to detail you find in Ken Loach, then, like Mike Leigh, builds up comic observation almost to the point of caricature, but with none of Leigh's latent contempt. He likes these boys for their foibles, their vulnerability and fecklessness as much as for their fundamentally good nature. But the joker in the pack is Morrell, and Considine's dangerous comic turn, which twists the film from affectionate larkiness to arrive at some genuinely shocking conclusions about what it may be that constitutes 'manhood'. Throw in a soundtrack featuring The Specials, Ian Brown, Beth Orton, Billy Bragg and Fairport Convention. This smashing movie is fresh, true and poignant as a song. TCh

Room Service

(1938, US, 78 min, b/w)
d William A Seiter. *p* Pandro S Berman. *sc* Morrie Ryskind. *ph* J Roy Hunt. *ed* George Crone. *ad* Van Nest Polglase, Al Herman. *m* Roy Webb. *cast* The Marx Brothers, Frank Albertson, Ann Miller, Lucille Ball, Donald MacBride, Cliff Dunstan.

●Under some sad whim, the Marx Brothers moved to RKO to appear in this limp version of a popular Broadway comedy, slightly adapted to fit their established characters. It's a loose fit indeed: Groucho plays a penniless theatrical manager trying to mount a socially-conscious play about miners (oh yes); Chico is the play's director, quotes Latin, and wears a check suit. Harpo at least is still unbridled, and does nice things chasing a turkey and eating food like an automaton. Apart from Harpo's bits, *Room Service* is to be seen once, and then forgotten. GB

Room to Rent

(2000, GB/Fr, 95 min)
d Khalid El Hagar. *p* Ildikó Kemény. *sc* Khalid El Hagar. *ph* Romain Winding. *ed* John Richards. *pd* Eli Bø. *m* Safy Boutella. *cast* Saïd Taghmaoui, Juliette Lewis, Rupert Graves, Anna Massey, Karim Belkhadra, Richard Lumsden, Clémentine Célarié, FlaminiaCinque.

●Unworldly, experience-hungry and penniless, Ali (Taghmaoui), a would-be writer, is let loose among the fleshpots and bizarre denizens of the emphatically evoked 'Arab quarter' of Edgware Road. It's not a world average Londoners would instantly recognise, meaning they have to view Ali's haunts, abodes and contacts from his perspective. The sexual gusto displayed by wealthy middle-aged French 'lover' Vivienne, the Monroe obsession of his friend Lina (Lewis), the streetwise cynicism of his pal Ahmed, who tries to fix him a fake bride for visa purposes, and the ridiculous formality of the traditional dress he's required to wear as a nightclub waiter are merely amusing examples of the mad, eccentric world that is London. If the oversimplified characters can be put down to directorial inexperience, less forgivable is the unrelenting tone of forced optimism and the seeming acceptance of Ali's degree of self-delusion. WH

Room With a View, A

(1985, GB, 117 min)
d James Ivory. *p* Ismail Merchant. *sc* Ruth Prawer Jhabvala. *ph* Tony Pierce-Roberts. *ed* Humphrey Dixon. *pd* Gianni Quaranta, Brian Ackland-Snow. *m* Richard Robbins. *cast* Maggie Smith, Helena Bonham Carter, Denholm Elliott, Julian Sands, Daniel Day Lewis, Simon Callow, Judi Dench.

●Hard on the heels of David Lean's grandiose, touristic version of EM Forster's *A Passage to India*, the Merchant/Ivory/Jhabvala team get the scale of Forster's vision down to its right size. The story of the awakening of young Lucy (Bonham Carter), thanks to the liberating effect of the Tuscan countryside and the Latin temperament, is translated with perfect judgment, with the only lapses occurring over Forster's wry sense of humour. His satiric judgments can too often become arch: the 'grotesquely' illustrated intertitles here are a miscalculation of this order. None the less, in line with Forster's dicta on 'fully rounded characters', there is a fine gallery here; and the 'tea tabling' effect of the Home Counties upon grand emotion, from an era when dynastic families could topple over a single kiss, is mapped out with perfect precision. Decent, honest, truthful and, dearest of all to Forster, it connects. CPea

Rooster Cogburn

(1975, US, 108 min)
d Stuart Millar. *p* Hal B Wallis. *sc* Martin Julien. *ph* Harry Stradling Jr. *ed* Robert Swink. *ad* Preston Ames. *m* Laurence Rosenthal. *cast* John Wayne, Katharine Hepburn, Anthony Zerbe, Richard Jordan, John McIntire, Strother Martin.

●Obviously meant to cash in on the success of *True Grit* – the Wayne vehicle that won him a sentimental Oscar – this pairing of two Hollywood veterans is forced to rely totally on their performances and personalities, in the absence of any other interesting features. Wayne repeats his role as the ornery ol' crittur of a marshal, teaming up with the Bible-pounding spinster Hepburn in an attempt to bring her father's killers to justice. Like *The African Queen* (to which it bears a strong resemblance), and to a lesser extent *On Golden Pond*, it's the sort of film whose *raison d'être* consists in manipulating an audience's familiar sympathies with its ageing stars. In this case, however, it fails dismally. GA

Roosters

(1993, US, 93 min)
d Robert M Young. *p* Susan Block-Reiner, Norman I Cohen, Kevin Reidy. *sc* Milcha Sanchez-Scott. *ph* Reynaldo Villalobos. *ed* Arthur Coburn. *ad* Helen Britten. *m* David Kilay. *cast* Edward J Olmos, Sonia Braga, Maria Conchita Alonso, Danny Nucci, Sarah Lassez.

●A broody melodrama, set on the US-Mexican border, with Olmos, the con released after eight years in stir, returning to his family and occasioning crisis. He's a cock-fighting man, a macho old-schooler. He dismisses his son's bird-fighting prowess as a Filipino-Mexican match looms. His disturbed daughter (Lassez, looking like a younger Julia Roberts) wears angel wings and builds elaborate graveyards for dead pets, and clearly misses paternal care. His sister, 'the encyclopaedia of love' (Alonso), has sex coming out of every pore. This plays like a melancholic Tennessee Williams piece – its dialogue betrays its theatrical roots – beautifully shot (by Villalobos Reynaldo) from dirt level under clear blue skies, accompanied by plaintive slide-guitar. Atmospheric, well-acted (especially by Olmos), but, as ever with middlebrow director Young, it ends disappointingly: all showing and no meaning. WH

Roots Rock Reggae

(1977, GB, 55 min)
d/p/sc Jeremy Marre. *ph* Chris Morphet, Jeff Baynes. *ed* Pat O'Dell. *cast* Bob Marley and the Wailers, Jimmy Cliff, The Heptones, Junior Murvin, The Gladiators, The Mighty Diamonds.

●Marre's documentary is not just about a form of music, but about its cultural source. Although it deliberately makes political points, it sensibly allows the people involved to explain themselves, and it's here that it is most successful. No amount of commentary could evoke the class barriers and poverty as poignantly as shots of kids 'auditioning' in the hills for a big Kingston producer; nor could commentary explain as effectively as film of Bob Marley's lifestyle why the kids choose music as their way out. But perhaps it all works so well because it captures some of the spontaneity that lies at the heart of the music – a spontaneity undoubtedly assisted by the biggest joints in the world, and by a sense of humour in the face of desperation. SM

Rope

(1948, US, 81 min)
d Alfred Hitchcock. *p* Sidney Bernstein, Alfred Hitchcock. *sc* Arthur Laurents, Hume Cronyn. *ph* Joseph Valentine, William V Skall. *ed* William Ziegler. *ad* Perry Ferguson. *m* Leo F Forbstein. *cast* James Stewart, John Dall, Farley Granger, Cedric Hardwicke, Joan Chandler, Constance Collier, Douglas Dick.

●One of Hitchcock's more experimental films, with the tale of two young gays, keen to prove their intellectual and spiritual superiority, killing a friend and hiding his body in a trunk in order to see whether dinner guests will suspect anything. Constructed entirely from uncut ten-minute takes, shot on a beautifully-constructed set, it's certainly a virtuoso piece of technique, but the lack of cutting inevitably slows things down, entailing the camera swooping from one character to another during dialogues. On a thematic level, however, the film is more successful: while the arguments about Nietzschean philosophy between the couple and their professor, Stewart (whose ideas have inadvertently prompted the murder), are hardly profound, what is interesting is the way Hitchcock's sly amorality forces us, through the suspense, to side with the killers. Add to that the black wit and strong performances from Dall, Granger and Stewart, and you have a perverse, provocative entertainment. GA

Rosa e Cornelia (Rosa and Cornelia)

(2000, It, 90 min)
d Giorgio Treves. *p* Grazia Volpi. *sc* Remo Binosi, François De Maulde, Giorgio Treves. *ph* Camillo Bazzoni. *ed* Carla Simoncelli. *pd* Lorenzo Baraldi. *m* Franco Piersanti. *cast* Stefania Rocca, Chiara Muti, Athina Cenci, Massimo Poggio, Daria Nicolodi, Massimo De Rossi.

●Becoming pregnant after an encounter at the Venice Carnival in 1748, the already engaged young Countess Cornelia is exiled by her shocked parents to their country house. Rosa, a servant there, is in the same situation. After initial antagonism, the women grow close. However, when the time comes for them to give birth, suppressed schemes and intentions come violently to the surface, with terrible consequences. This atmospheric and controlled chamber drama reveals its theatrical origins in a tight use of locations. At times the psychological intention of the mise-en-scène – the choice of colouring, the faded rooms, ascetic decor and few potent objects – suggest the charged importance of such details in Borowczyk's *Blanche*. And at their best the performances are equally precise, with the latent ambiguities of each woman's role effectively highlighted. It's about the shifts in power and authority, gender relations and betrayal. A human comedy then, in the Chekhovian mould, but stripped down to its lonely, humane skeleton. GE

Rosalie Goes Shopping

(1989, WGer, 94 min)
d Percy Adlon. *p* Percy Adlon, Eleonore Adlon. *sc* Percy Adlon, Eleonore Adlon, Christopher Doherty. *ph* Bernd Heinl. *ed* Jean-Claude Piroué. *ad* Stephen Lineweaver. *m* Bob Telson. *cast* Marianne Sägebrecht,

Brad Davies, Judge Reinhold, Erika Blumberger, Willy Harlander, John Hawkes, Patricia Zehentmayr, Alex Winter.
● Rosalie (Sägebrecht) would seem to have it made: her crop duster hubby (Davis) dotes on her, her countless kids dote on her, even her priest (Reinhold) is less than harsh in his condemnation of her penchant for cheque and credit card fraud. But Rosalie – a corpulent, ever-smiling *hausfrau* who has landed up in Stuttgart, Arkansas – is so infected by the material greed of the American Way that she can never own enough. Adlon's third film with Sägebrecht may have been conceived as an anarchic dig at Western capitalism, but it is so smugly conspiratorial that any such intentions have been transformed into a paean to avaricious cunning. Ethics aside, the film also suffers from having no plot to speak of; a good hour is spent dwelling on the loveable wackiness of Rosalie's brood, and the mix of sluggish sentiment and forced eccentricity is tiresomely reminiscent of Capra's oddball simple folk in *You Can't Take It With You*. Adlon does his usual stuff with bright-coloured decor, but the vaguely modernist veneer can't conceal the dearth of genuine feeling at the film's manipulative core. GA

Rosa Luxemburg

(1986, WGer, 124 min)
d Margarethe von Trotta. *p* Eberhard Junkersdorf. *sc* Magarethe von Trotta. *ph* Franz Rath. *ed* Dagmar Hirtz. *ad* Bernd Lepel, Karel Vacek. *m* Nicolas Economou. *cast* Barbara Sukowa, Daniel Olbrychski, Otto Sander, Adelheit Arndt, Jürgen Holtz, Doris Schade.
● Rosa Luxemburg has a lot going for her when it comes to the myth factory: female, lame, Polish, internationalist, pacifist, revolutionary, imprisoned on nine separate occasions, a leader of the Spartacists in their brief revolutionary success in postwar Germany, and cruelly murdered in 1919. This film won awards at Cannes and Berlin, two for Sukowa in the title role; and utterly splendid she is too, conveying a delicate mixture of strength and vulnerability. But though the film avoids many of the pitfalls of the *Hello Mozart, Hello Salieri* school of biopic, it still falls badly between the two stools of personal chronicle and politico-historical analysis, despite the intriguing use of archive newsreel footage, and the sterling contributions of Sander (as Karl Liebknecht) and Olbrychski (Leo Jogiches). SGr

Rosary Murders, The

(1987, US, 101 min)
d Fred Walton. *p* Robert G Laurel, Michael Mihalich. *sc* Elmore Leonard, Fred Walton. *ph* David Golia. *ed* Sam Vitale. *m* Bobby Laurel, Don Sebesky. *cast* Donald Sutherland, Charles Durning, Josef Sommer, Belinda Bauer, James Murtaugh.
● Although director Walton worked with Elmore Leonard, no less, in adapting William X Kienzle's novel for the screen, somewhere along the line someone must have seen Hitchcock's *I Confess*, to which this suspense thriller bears a distinct resemblence. Here it's Father Sutherland who hears the confession of Detroit's most wanted man, the killer who's targeted the city's priests, but instead of breaking his vow of secrecy, this man of the cloth takes to the streets to track down the perpetrator himself. Oddly enough, the more derivative first half works better than the lame detective work in the second. TJ

Rose, The

(1979, US, 134 min)
d Mark Rydell. *p* Marvin Worth. *sc* Bill Kerby, Bo Goldman. *ph* Vilmos Zsigmond. *ed* Robert L Wolfe. *pd* Richard MacDonald. *m* Paul A Rothchild. *cast* Bette Midler, Alan Bates, Frederic Forrest, Harry Dean Stanton, Barry Primus, David Keith, Sandra McCabe.
● The Rise to Fame; the Stab in the Back; the Tragic Demise… With its ageless conventions and stylish history, the musical biopic is Hollywood's haiku, and the last two years have seen two of its finest examples: *The Buddy Holly Story* and *Coal Miner's Daughter*. But *The Rose* mixes its models and pays the price, stumbling awkwardly between a historical portrait (of Janis Joplin and other shooting stars of '60s rock) and a concert movie showcase for Bette Midler. Even her fiery mix of raunch'n'tease, though, can't make up for a bubblegum plot and sentimentality on parade. Only Alan Bates, surprisingly well cast as the Rose's ruthless manager, and Harry Dean Stanton (confirming himself as the grittiest sourpuss actor in Hollywood) raise a frown or a smile. The rest of it will just have you yawning in the aisles. CA

Roseanna's Grave (aka For Roseanna)

(1996, US/GB, 98 min)
d Paul Weiland. *p* Paul Trijbits, Alison Owen, Dario Poloni. *sc* Saul Turtletaub. *ph* Henry Braham. *ed* Martin Walsh. *pd* Rod McLean. *m* Trevor Jones. *cast* Jean Réno, Mercedes Ruehl, Polly Walker, Mark Frankel, Luigi Diberti, Roberto Della Casa, Giovanni Pallavicino.
● Stereotypical Italian drama which hammers home the indomitable, colourful, roguish but romantic spirit of the simple rural life. Marcello (Réno) will do anything to ensure that his beloved, ailing wife Roseanna (Ruehl) gets one of the last three plots in the village cemetery. Trouble is, old age, illness and accidents throw up rivals for the remaining space. Meanwhile, Roseanna, worried that Marcello will be alone after her death, tries to fix him up with her younger sister Cecilia (Walker). She, however, already has an admirer in lawyer Antonio (Frankel), nephew of a wealthy local who refuses to sell the church the land it needs for burial purposes. While Saul Turteltaub's screenplay fleetingly suggests the film might turn into a mildly interesting black comedy, too often the broad acting, the sentimentality and the manipulation of our emotions give the impression that this is an inferior attempt to cash in on the success of *Il Postino*. GA

Roseaux Sauvages, Les (The Wild Reeds)

(1994, Fr, 113 min)
d André Téchiné. *p* Alain Sarde. *sc* André Téchiné, Gilles Taurand, Olivier Massart. *ph* Jeanne Lapoirie. *ed* Martine Giordano. *pd* Pierre Soula. *cast* Elodie Bouchez, Gaël Morel, Stéphane Rideau, Frédéric Gorny, Michèle Moretti.
● An intelligent, bitter-sweet account of teenage life in south-west France in 1962. The Algerian War still rages, forging alliances and creating divisions between a group of schoolchildren already confused by issues of class and sexuality: François anguished over his passion for the briefly responsive Serge, peasant brother of a would-be army deserter; Maïté, daughter of the boys' communist teacher, and François' best friend; and new-kid Henri, clever, stand-offish and, having been born in Algeria, virulently against the idea of independence. These four variously fall out, make up, and edge hesitantly towards adulthood. The film impresses for its authenticity, careful delineation of mood, and subtle balancing of the personal and political. Téchiné wins sterling support from his young cast, who give the kind of quiet, naturalistic performances the French are so good at. A delicacy to savour. GA

Rosebud

(1974, US, 126 min)
d/p Otto Preminger. *sc* Erik Lee Preminger. *ph* Denys Coop. *ed* Peter Thornton, Thom Noble. *pd* Michael Seymour. *m* Laurent Petitgirard. *cast* Peter O'Toole, Richard Attenborough, Cliff Gorman, Claude Dauphin, John V Lindsay, Peter Lawford, Raf Vallone, Adrienne Corri, Amidou, Isabelle Huppert, Kim Cattrall, Françoise Brion.
● Preminger's wordy, sprawling, but mostly involving, movie exploits Middle East tensions with a plot about the search for five rich girls kidnapped by the Palestinian Liberation Army in an effort to bring the Arab cause to international attention. But in a world of irreconcilable differences of opinion, governments too prove capable of using terrorist tactics to their own ends. Preminger handles the dramatic exposition with a curious mixture of panache and risible heavy-handedness, making it look increasingly like a Frederick Forsyth thriller, an imbalance that O'Toole's 'star' performance does little to correct. With the English O'Toole tracking down a fellow countryman, the eccentric mastermind Sloat (Attenborough) – and the former's government agent ethics perhaps more dubious than the latter's – the film engagingly if irrelevantly suggests that Perfidious Albion is still capable of pulling a few strings in world power games. Doubtless, like most Preminger, it'll improve with age. CPe

Roseland

(1977, US, 104 min)
d James Ivory. *p* Ismail Merchant. *sc* Ruth Prawer Jhabvala. *ph* Ernest Vincze. *ed* Humphrey Dixon, Richard Schmiechen. *m* Michael Gibson. *cast* Teresa Wright, Lou Jacobi, Geraldine Chaplin, Helen Gallagher, Joan Copeland, Christopher Walken, Lilia Skala, David Thomas.
● The far-flung projects of independent director/producer team Ivory and Merchant have resulted in films ranging from the staggeringly pretentious to the absorbingly informative. This trilogy of short stories set in the famed New York ballroom could easily have suffered from Ivory's most irritating characteristic as a director: an aloof condescension to the weaknesses of even his most sympathetic characters. Moreover, Ruth Prawer Jhabvala's script suffers from an obvious 'literariness', although its subtle, sharp and sympathetic qualities make the film surprisingly likeable. As do the patently sincere performances (which avoid mawkishness) and, most important, the themes rarely touched upon in commercial cinema: the loneliness, decay, and tenaciously held illusions of impending old age. RM

Roselyne and the Lions (Roselyne et les lions)

(1989, Fr, 137 min)
d/p Jean-Jaques Beineix. *sc* Jean-Jacques Beineix, Jacques Forgeas. *ph* Jean-François Robin. *ed* Dominique Mannequin, François Groult. *ad* Carlos Conti. *m* Reinhardt Wagner. *cast* Isabelle Pasco, Gérard Sandoz, Phillippe Clevenot, Gunter Meisner, Wolf Harnisch, Gabriel Monnet.
● Roselyne (Pasco), a teenage lion-tamer with a blonde mane of her own, befriends Thierry (Sandoz), who plays truant to hang around the Marseilles zoo where – under the demanding tutelage of a veteran (Monnet) – she cracks the whip to put the beasts through their paces. Fired by mutual passion, the pair fall in love both with the exhilaration of facing the big cats, and with each other. On the road with a circus, honing their skills, they graduate into professional artistes. Beineix says the film is a metaphor for the act of creation, 'the transformation of rough material into a piece of choreography, a moment of show, a performance'. However, like an underlying concern with the price of professionalism – as the pair become more skilled, innocence and love are lost – this theme remains implicit. Most viewers will remember only the dangerous exoticism of the caged beasts, and the lingering, sensuous shots of Roselyne's lithe, bespangled body. The dazzling finale, in which the elemental confrontation between female and feline aspires through baroque artifice to the level of myth, is a sensational moment. But two hours is a long time to wait for it. NF

Rosemary's Baby

(1968, US, 137 min)
d Roman Polanski. *p* William Castle. *sc* Roman Polanski. *ph* William A Fraker. *ed* Sam O'Steen, Robert Wyman. *pd* Richard Sylbert. *m* Krzysztof Komeda. *cast* Mia Farrow, John Cassavetes, Ruth Gordon, Sidney Blackmer, Maurice Evans, Ralph Bellamy, Angela Dorian, Patsy Kelly, Elisha Cook, Charles Grodin.
● A supremely intelligent and convincing adaptation of Ira Levin's Satanist thriller. About a woman who believes herself impregnated by the Devil (in the guise of her husband), its main strength comes from Polanski's refusal to simplify matters: ambiguity is constant, in that we are never sure whether Farrow's paranoia about a witches' coven is grounded in reality or a figment of her frustrated imagination. Sexual politics, urban alienation, and a deeply pessimistic view of human interaction permeate the film, directed with a slow, careful build-up of pace and a precise sense of visual composition. Although it manages to be frightening, there is little gore or explicit violence; instead, what disturbs is the blurring of reality and nightmare, and the way Farrow is slowly transformed from a healthy, happily-married wife to a haunted, desperately confused shadow of her former self. Great performances, too, and a marvellously melancholy score by Krzysztof Komeda. GA

Rosemary's Killer

see Prowler, The

Rosencrantz and Guildenstern Are Dead

(1990, US, 118 min)
d Tom Stoppard. *p* Michael Brandman, Emanuel Azenberg. *sc* Tom Stoppard. *ph* Peter Biziou. *ed* Nicolas Gaster. *pd* Vaughan Edwards. *m* Stanley Myers. *cast* Gary Oldman, Tim Roth, Richard Dreyfuss, Joanna Roth, Iain Glen, Donald Sumpter, Joanna Miles, Ian Richardson.

● Stoppard's 1967 play was a delicious and profound theatrical conceit, a pastiche which turned Shakespeare's famous flunkies from *Hamlet* into pathetic, confused victims. It seems odd that we should be treated to a cinematic version of what is essentially a very theatrical experience, while other more obviously filmable Stoppard works remain unadapted. Stoppard opens up the narrative, turning the pair from passive clowns into a restless duo, a costumed Butch Cassidy and Sundance Kid, constantly turning up in the wrong place at the wrong time. Every piece of stage business, from pirate siege to coin toss to verbal banter in a tennis court, is aimed at needlessly fleshing out the original; while, as Ros and Guildy, both Oldman and Roth turn in flat and uninspiring performances. Only Sumpter as a youthful Claudius, and Richardson's splendid Polonius give life to the *Hamlet* scenes. Disappointing. SGr

Rose of Washington Square

(1939, US, 86 min, b/w)
d Gregory Ratoff. *p/sc* Nunnally Johnson. *ph* Karl Freund. *ed* Louis Loeffler. *ad* Richard Day, Rudolph Sternad. *songs* BG De Sylva, Gus Kahn, Mack Gordon, Noble Sissle. *cast* Tyrone Power, Alice Faye, Al Jolson, William Frawley, Hobart Cavanaugh, Horace McMahon, Moroni Olsen.

● A fictionalised biopic of Fanny Brice, later celebrated in *Funny Girl* but unacknowledged here, which led to a law suit (settled out of court). Faye sings (nicely and nostalgically), Power is the nogoodnik she loves, and Jolson the 'Mammy'-singing buddy who advises her to pour her heart into a rendition of 'My Man', thus making Power see the error of his ways. Stock stuff but enjoyably done, with excellent camerawork from Karl Freund, and notable chiefly for the number of Jolson standards crammed in for him to sing. TM

Rosetta

(1999, Bel/Fr, 91 min)
d Luc Dardenne, Jean-Pierre Dardenne. *p* Luc Dardenne, Jean-Pierre Dardenne, Michèle Pétin, Laurent Pétin. *sc* Luc Dardenne, Jean-Pierre Dardenne. *ph* Alain Marcoen. *ed* Marie-Hélène Dozo. *ad* Igor Gabriel. *cast* Emilie Dequenne, Fabrizio Rongione, Anne Yernaux, Olivier Gourmet.

● A deserving Palme d'Or winner at Cannes '99, *Rosetta* is in the same, grim realist mould as the Dardennes' earlier *La Promesse*; it, too, offers a glimmer of hope through the prospect of friendship. Teenage Rosetta (Dequenne) has it tough: living in a trailer park with her promiscuous, alcoholic mother, she tries to hang on to whatever mundane jobs she can get, but for all her determination and hard work, bad luck and her surly, volatile disposition repeatedly tell against her. Is life really worth living? Using very little dialogue and long, hand-held tracking shots (the relentlessly restless visuals perfectly reflect Rosetta's unsettled life, the secret to which is provided only halfway through the movie – and even then, subtly), the Dardennes never sentimentalise their heroine but respect the mysteries of her soul; the result is a film almost Bressonian in its rigour and power to touch the heart. GA

Rosie

(1998, Bel, 97 min)
d Patrice Toye. *p* Antonino Lombardo. *sc* Patrice Toye. *ph* Richard Van Oosterhout. *ed* Ludo Troch. *m* John Parish. *cast* Aranka Coppens, Dirk Roofthooft, Frank Vercruyssen, Sara de Roo, Joost Wijnant.

● Coming hot on the heels of *Rosetta*, another Belgian film which takes a long hard look at the woes of a working class teenage girl. Rosie (Coppens) also lives alone with her mum – or her 'sister', as Irene (de Roo) prefers to pretend in front of her boyfriends. At 13, Rosie is a loner with a taste for the steamier sort of romantic fiction, making her easy prey for a handsome delinquent like Jimi (Joost Wijnant), who rocks her world with his petty thieving and joyriding. Out of a warped and wounded kindness, Rosie picks up a crying baby and carries it off, playing happy families with Jimi at the oil works in the old part of town. Call me 'Mummy', she instructs the poor infant, louder and louder. You want to give her a good shake, and then you want to hug her. Somewhere in translation, Patrice Toye's movie has lost its original subtitle, 'The Devil in My Head,' which gave a hint that this is not just social realism, but something closer in spirit to the tortured psychodramas of pulp crime novelist Jim Thompson (*The Killer Inside Me*; *The Grifters*). Toye seems unsure just how much of a melodrama he wants to make – an alert viewer will tease out the twists well before the end – but the discrepancy between the flat, mundane treatment and the heightened American narrative hovering in the background works quite effectively. Pain in this film is too all-encompassing to be expressed in short, sharp shocks; instead Rosie endures a dulled, mute suffering. If Ken Loach had made *Badlands* it might have looked something like this: depressing, claustrophobic, not romantic, but innocent. TCh

Rosie Dixon, Night Nurse

(1978, GB, 88 min)
d Justin Cartwright. *p* Davina Belling, Clive Parsons. *sc* Christopher Wood, Justin Cartwright. *ph* Alex Thomson. *ed* Geoffrey Foot. *pd* Albert Witherick. *m* Ed Welch. *cast* Debbie Ash, Caroline Argyle, Beryl Reid, John Le Mesurier, Arthur Askey, Liz Fraser, Lance Percival, John Junkin, Bob Todd.

● Christopher Wood's screenplay is stamped with the Gold Seal of the Ancient Order of Most-Elementary British Scriptwriters. This string of charmless high-jinks is naturally set in a hospital: Bob Todd malingers without his dentures; John Le Mesurier, an absent-minded consultant, dithers over the racing pages; Arthur Askey pinches bums; a quartet of bibulous junior doctors attempt to tumble our vacuous heroine. Come back, James Robertson Justice. JPy

Rothschild's Violin (Le Violon de Rothschild/ Rothschildin Viulu)

(1996, Fr/Switz/Fin/Hun, 98 min)
d Edgardo Cozarinsky. *p* Serge Lalou. *sc* Edgardo Cozarinsky. *ph* Jacques Bouquin. *ed* Martine Bouquin. *ad* Toomas Hörak, Tamás Vayer. *cast* Sergei Makovetsky, Dainius Kazlauskas, Miklós B Székely, Mari Töröcsik, Sándor Zsótér.

● Things are tense at the Leningrad Conservatoire in 1939. Shostakovich's *Lady Macbeth of the Mtensk District* has been berated in the press, and such criticism can have fatal results. In class, the discussion on Mussorgsky's *Boris Godunov* focuses on the character of the holy fool – but who now will speak the truth in music about today's Russia? This superb study of musical expression under totalitarian rule follows the efforts of Shostakovich's pupil Benjamin Fleischmann to answer this question. He was to die in the siege of Leningrad, but not before writing a one act opera, *Rothschild's Violin*, about the struggle for existence in a rural Jewish community. Here was a work drawing on traditional folk melodies and daring to suggest that all was not rosy in the Russian state. The authorities were not amused. Splicing footage of smiling Joe Stalin and May Day parades into a persuasive dramatic reconstruction, Cozarinsky also delivers where current TV arts documentaries usually fall down: he lets us hear a full performance of the opera (Gennady Rozhdestvensky conducting the Rotterdam orchestra). TJ

Rotten to the Core

(1965, GB, 88 min, b/w)
d John Boulting. *p* Roy Boulting. *sc* Jeffrey Dell, Roy Boulting, John Warren, Len Heath. *ph* Freddie Young. *ed* Teddy Darvas. *ad* Alex Vetchinsky. *m* Michael Dress. *cast* Anton Rodgers, Eric Sykes, Ian Bannen, Dudley Sutton, Kenneth Griffith, James Beckett, Charlotte Rampling, Victor Maddern, Thorley Walters, Avis Bunnage, Raymond Huntley.

● Two people are credited with the 'idea' elaborated by four other writers into the script for this movie; all of which seems rather excessive, given that everything in it has seen long and tedious service in British comedy over the years. Newly out of jail, three moronic crooks (Griffith, Sutton and Beckett) attach themselves to a big army payroll robbery set up by a mastermind (Rodgers). The plan involves establishing a phony nature cure clinic as a cover (comic business about old ladies swigging spa waters liberally laced with gin), is attended by many funny disguises (Eric Sykes's private eye sporting Indian garb, Rodgers as a German general), and ends in farcical disaster with crooks, army and police meeting face to face. Some mildly funny moments, but most of the jokes are laboriously set up and loudly telegraphed (like the comic highlight in which the most moronic crook has his IQ tested, and the computer collapses in a fit of grumbling despair). TM

Rouge (Yanzhi Kou)

(1987, HK, 93 min)
d Stanley Kwan. *p* Jackie Chan. *sc* Li Bihua, Qui-Dai Anping. *ph* Bill Wong. *ed* Peter Cheung. *ad* Piao Ruomu, Horace Ma. *m* Michael Lai. *cast* Anita Mui, Leslie Cheung, Emily Chu, Man Tsz-leung.

● Tale of a courtesan who died for love in the 1930s, roaming present-day Hong Kong as a wraith because she has failed to meet her lover in the after-life. A sharp, mildly satirical portrait of Hong Kong life in the '80s is shot through with flashbacks to the '30s, suffused with a heady, opium-hazed decadence worthy of Huysmans, yielding an elegant and deeply felt movie about the transience of things – especially love. Stunning visuals and sophisticated performances add up to a terrific, stylish movie. TR

Rouge Baiser

(1985, Fr/WGer, 112 min)
d/p Véra Belmont. *sc* Véra Belmont, Guy Konopnicki, David Milhaud. *ph* Ramón F Suarez. *ed* Martine Giordano. *ad* Bruno Held, Roland Fruytier, Laurent Barbat, Eric Saymard, Delphine Berroyer, Olivier Raoux, Christophe Liomax, Bernard Vasseur, Jacques-Henri Lourrieux, Laurent Jarriau. *m* Jean-Marie Sénia. *cast* Charlotte Valandrey, Lambert Wilson, Marthe Keller, Günter Lamprecht, Laurent Terzieff, Laurent Arnal.

● Belmont's endearing if daft reminiscences of a '50s Parisian adolescence. In the jazz clubs of St Germain, Bechet-soundalikes occupy the stand, and black rollneck sweaters proliferate in the audience, but despite the title (the name of a hit lipstick of the period), the film is more interested in the evanescence of ideologies. 15-year-old Nadia (Valandrey) is an ardent Stalinist, tirelessly selling the party paper and demonstrating against American imperialism, which doesn't stop her longing to be Rita Hayworth in *Gilda*. She is rescued from a police beating by cool, non-political Paris Match photographer Stéphane (Wilson), who soon erodes her beliefs and underwear. Her Polish-Jewish mother's old lover Moische (Terzieff) arrives in Paris from Siberia, and his revelations about the gulags compound the teenager's turnaround. The make-up department are over-enthusiastic on wounds and the pallors of pining, but the genuine memories of a rite of passage survive the shortcomings. BC

Rough Cut

(1980, US, 111 min)
d Donald Siegel. *p* David Merrick. *sc* Francis Burns [Larry Gelbart]. *ph* Freddie Young. *ed* Douglas Stewart. *pd* Ted Haworth. *m* Nelson Riddle. *cast* Burt Reynolds, Lesley-Anne Down, David Niven, Timothy West, Patrick Magee, Al Matthews, Susan Littler, Joss Ackland, Isobel Dean.

● There are a few extreme auteurists who claim that everything Siegel shoots is wonderful, but some of his more recent efforts have been frankly disappointing, few more so than this glossy, shallow comic heist movie. Down and Reynolds are rival jewel thieves, half prepared to help, half to betray each other, as Niven of the Yard tries to bag Reynolds by using the kleptomaniac Down as bait. The whole thing is incredibly anonymous, jokey without wit, and spattered with pointless movie references (to Hitchcock in particular). And to make matters worse, the Ellington tunes on the soundtrack have been turned into pure muzak by Nelson Riddle. GA

Rough Cut and Ready Dubbed

(1982, GB, 56 min)
d/p Hasan Shah, Dom Shaw. *ph* Hasan Shah, Dom Shaw, Neil Conrich. *ed* Alan Mackay. *with* Patrik Fitzgerald, Colin Peacock, Jake Burns, Stiff Little Fingers, UK Subs, Cockney Rejects.
●A slick editing job (courtesy of a BFI grant) applied to street-level *vérité* footage produces a virtual *Disappearing World* on the tribal poses and fragmented rock culture of 1980, replete with mutual slag-offs from bands and fans about skins, mods, police, fascists, and 'selling out', a laughable subtext of pop-press punditry, and much middling gig coverage. Something of a wake for punk's decline, it's full of self-parodic shock values, and best communicates a sense of musical recession, mapping a territory rife for the subsequent easy ascendancy of back-tracking trends. John Peel contributes his customary good sense in small doses; almost everyone else dissipates enthusiasm in antagonism. Primarily one for the sociologists and amnesiac nostalgists. PT

Rough Diamonds

(1994, Aust, 88 min)
d Donald Crombie. *p* Damien Parer. *sc* Donald Crombie, Christopher Lee. *ph* John Stokes. *ed* Wayne Le Clos. *pd* Georgina Greenhill. *m* Mark Moffatt, Wayne Goodwin. *cast* Jason Donovan, Angie Milliken, Peter Phelps, Max Cullen, Hayley Toomey, Joceyln Gabriel.
●Deep in the outback, a girl and her mother are distancing themselves from the adulterous man of the family, when grizzled cattle-rancher Mike (a single father, as it happens) puts their car in the garage and offers them lodgings while it's fixed. You can see where this is headed: comedy of manners, attraction of opposites, slow-burning romance. Indeed, that's about the size of it. Mike is the sort of role Burt Reynolds or Clint Eastwood might have taken in their redneck days, but Jason Donovan is hardly the type. Mundane and mediocre. TCh

Rough Magic (Miss Shumway jette un sort)

(1995, GB/Fr, 105 min)
d Clare Peploe. *p* Laurie Parker, Declan Baldwin. *sc* Paul Alexander, Clare Peploe, Robert Mundy, William Brookfield. *ph* John Campbell. *ed* Suzanne Fenn. *pd* Waldemar Kalinowski. *m* Richard Hartley. *cast* Bridget Fonda, Russell Crowe, Jim Broadbent, DW Moffet, Paul Rodriguez, Euva Anderson.
●A cack-handed venture into *Romancing the Stone* territory (from the James Hadley Chase novel *Miss Shumway Waves a Wand*), miscast, racist, old-fashioned, and all in all not much fun. Nice scenery, though. As a magician's assistant who takes off for Mexico to consult a shamen, Fonda lacks the charisma to hold this ramshackle lark together, while Peploe's duff special effects aren't exactly magical. The funniest sequence is also the most offensive: a comic-relief Mexican heavy is transformed into a fat sausage, and promptly eaten by a dog. Oh yes, and Bridget lays an egg. TCh

Rough Night in Jericho

(1967, US, 102 min)
d Arnold Laven. *p* Martin Rackin. *sc* Sydney Boehm, Marvin H Albert. *ph* Russell Metty. *ed* Ted J Kent. *ad* Alexander Golitzen, Frank Arrigo. *m* Don Costa. *cast* Dean Martin, George Peppard, Jean Simmons, John McIntire, Slim Pickens, Don Galloway, Brad Weston.
●It's a rough night anywhere with this dispiritingly routine Western. Dean Martin is the bad guy determined to become boss of his whole town, Simmons the victim of his evil machinations (she owns the stagecoach line), and Peppard the handsome stranger (ex-deputy marshal, now professional gambler) looking on. The only question is, how long will it take Peppard to make up his mind to intervene? The answer is, a long time. The characterisation is rudimentary, the direction sluggish, the action brutishly brutal. TM

Rough Shoot (aka Shoot First)

(1952, GB, 87 min, b/w)
d Robert Parrish. *p* Raymond Stross. *sc* Eric Ambler. *ph* Stan Pavey. *ed* Russell Lloyd. *ad* Ivan King. *m* Hans May. *cast* Joel McCrea, Evelyn Keyes, Herbert Lom, Marius Goring, Roland Culver, Karel Stepanek, Frank Lawton, Patricia Laffan, David Hurst, Megs Jenkins, Laurence Naismith.
●Scripted by Eric Ambler from Geoffrey Household's novel, this curiously pedestrian thriller, set during the Cold War, looks like a throwback to Hitchcock's British period on a very off day. An American army colonel (McCrea), having rented a cottage in Dorset for a spot of shooting on the moors, fires a deterrent charge of buckshot at an intruder he takes to be a poacher. Panicking when the man dies (though not at his hands), McCrea hides the body, and soon finds himself up to his neck in British secret service agents (led by Culver) and a Nazi spy ring (headed by Goring). With credibility already low as plot and characters bumble around like something out of a *Boy's Own Paper* serial, it sinks even lower as a German plane (landing on rough moorland at night!), brings in a specialist agent (Hurst) to collect information about atomic tests, his rendezvous with the traitor being scheduled (in a chase climax that goes off half-cocked) at Madame Tussaud's. Only Lom, as a perky Polish agent busily swashing an Errol Flynn buckle, brings any enlivening wit to the proceedings. TM

Rough Treatment (Bez Znieczulenia)

(1978, Pol, 114 min)
d Andrzej Wajda. *sc* Agnieszka Holland, Andrzej Wajda, Krzysztof Zaleski. *ph* Edward Klosinski. *ed* Halina Prugar. *ad* Allan Starski, Maria Lubelska-Chrolowska. *m* Jerzy Derfl. *cast* Zbigniew Zapasiewicz, Ewa Dalkowska, Andrzej Seweryn, Krystyna Janda, Emilia Krakowska, Roman Wilhelmi.
●*Rough Treatment* takes up where *Man of Marble* left off, with its exploration of the contemporary (1978) political situation in Poland and its pursuit of the relationship between the individual and society. The film follows the downfall of an urbane and well-known political correspondent (a phenomenal performance from Zapasiewicz), who steps out of line during a TV interview and simultaneously discovers that his wife is leaving him. The cold, grey society of which he's part is discovered in the grim attitudes of those around him; at the same time his own faults and inadequacies build with every scene. Working in the wake of the censorship problems which beset *Man of Marble*, Wajda had this to say on its release: 'I worked on this film in a blind rage…it has no flourishes. Its impact was to come solely from a logically constructed chain of events'. The end isn't entirely satisfactory, but that doesn't matter – the rest is fascinating, and he's already made his point. HM

Roujin Z (Rojin Z)

(1991, Jap, 84 min)
d Hiroyuki Kitakubo. *p* Yasuhito Nomura, Yasuku Kazama, Yoshiaki Motoya. *sc* Katsuhiro Otomo. *ph* Hideo Okazaki. *ed* Eiko Nishiide. *ad* Hiroshi Sasaki. *m* Fumi Itakura, Michio Ogawa. *cast* voices: Allan Wenger, Toni Barry, Barbara Barnes.
●Not exactly a parody of Katsuhiro Otomo's *Akira*, this Japanese animated feature (shorn of six minutes in its English version) does have a lot of fun challenging and sometimes reversing the psychedelic-punk precepts of the earlier film. Otomo's storyline and machinery designs are as imaginative as ever, but the sci-fi elements are subordinated to a celebration of old-time Japanese working-class humour, sexuality and values. It's set in the real world, where women are strong and make all the running, and men are bombastic, cowardly or weak – none weaker than the elderly widower Takazawa, who must have his every want attended to by student nurse Haruko. Takazawa is selected as guinea-pig for trials of a computer-controlled bed, which offers all the services of a geriatric ward in one ultra-tech package. The plot hinges on the moment when the machine's core bio-chip is taken over by the spirit of Takazawa's wife, who wants to resume a mature sexual relationship with her husband. TR

Rounders

(1998, US, 121 min)
d John Dahl. *p* Joel Stillerman, Ted Demme. *sc* David Levien, Brian Koppelman. *ph* Jean-Yves Escoffier. *ed* Scott Chestnut. *pd* Rob Pearson. *m* Christopher Young. *cast* Matt Damon, Edward Norton, John Turturro, Gretchen Mol, Famke Janssen, John Malkovich, Martin Landau, Josh Mostel.
●A 'rounder' is someone who earns a living from winning at the poker tables, and Dahl's thriller introduces us to a myriad of smoky backrooms, illicit gambling dens and glitzy casinos from New York to Atlantic City. Damon plays a law student with excellent job prospects and a stable relationship with classmate Mol. But there he is, sneaking out of their flat in the dead of night, pockets filled with cash he's about to lose to Malkovich's Russian heavy. It's not the gambling bug that has bitten Damon, but the sense that his developing skill at poker represents his true calling in life. The last thing he needs, however, is the release from jail of his old buddy Norton, whose urgent need to pay off debts racked up inside places both young men in more peril than they ever anticipated. Powerhouse casting is the film's strong suit. Damon captivates the attention by underplaying at every turn, Malkovich luxuriates in an overstated Russian accent, Norton is suitably weasel-like, and sterling support comes from Landau and Turturro. The alternative universe in which they move is dazzlingly photographed by Jean-Yves Escoffier and given a smokin' score by Christopher Young. For all that, the end result is still short of a winning hand, since the screenplay is so utterly predictable. TJ

Rounders, The

(1964, US, 85 min)
d Burt Kennedy. *p* Richard E Lyons. *sc* Burt Kennedy. *ph* Paul C Vogel. *ed* John McSweeney. *ad* George W Davis, Urie McCleary. *m* Jeff Alexander. *cast* Henry Fonda, Glenn Ford, Sue Ane Langdon, Hope Holiday, Chill Wills, Edgar Buchanan, Kathleen Freeman, Denver Pyle, Barton MacLane.
●A pleasantly lackadaisical comedy Western, about a pair of itinerant cowboys who are forever talking about settling down, but instead find themselves once more moving on to the next job. Their running battle with a cussed horse that perennially refuses to be broken is delightful; their run-in with two zany chorus girls (Langdon and Holiday) might have been equally so but for Holiday's over-playing. Ford and Fonda are excellent, but the contrived sentimentality involving the horse gets a little hard to take, and the gently quirkish humour misses out rather too often for comfort. TM

'Round Midnight (Autour de Minuit)

(1986, US/Fr, 131 min)
d Bertrand Tavernier. *p* Irwin Winkler. *sc* David Rayfiel. *ph* Bruno de Keyzer. *ed* Armand Psenny. *pd* Alexandre Trauner. *m* Herbie Hancock. *cast* Dexter Gordon, François Cluzet, Gabrielle Haker, Sandra Reaves-Phillips, Lonette McKee, Christine Pascal, Herbie Hancock, Victoria Gabrielle Platt, John Berry, Martin Scorsese, Philippe Noiret.
●Tavernier's offbeat love letter to bebop gets the best jazz film award since *Sven Klang's Combo.* Night after night in the pouring rain, a young Frenchman (Cluzet) squats outside a Parisian jazz club, listening to the sublime saxophone of one 'Dale Turner'. Since Turner, a shambling bear of a man, is troubled by the jazzman's classic demons of drink and drugs, it is not long before the young man has befriended him, rescued him from cheap flophouses, and installed him in his own flat, where kindness and devotion achieve some kind of advance over the depredations of the jazz life. The film reeks of the authentic stuff of jazz, smoky with atmosphere and all as blue as a Gauloise packet. Dale Turner, as played by Dexter Gordon, seems to be an amalgam of Bud Powell and Lester Young, but the private, rueful dignity that he brings to bear is all his own. CPea

Round-Up, The (Szegénylegények)

(1965, Hun, 94 min, b/w)
d Miklós Jancsó. *sc* Gyula Hernadi. *ph* Tamás Somlo. *ed* Zoltán Farkas. *ad* Tamás Banovich. *cast* János Görbe, Tibor Molnár, András Kozák, Gábor Agárdy, Zoltán Latinovits.
●A vast, burned-out plain; dwarfed in the middle of it two buildings, whitewashed walls blazing in the sun, against which black-cloaked

figures flit to and fro; silence, except for occasional curt words of command, as a man running for the horizon is coolly shot down, others are taken away never to return. As one watches, fascinated but mystified, a pattern begins to emerge, and one realises that a terrifying cat-and-mouse game is being played. The setting is the years following the collapse of the 1848 revolution against Hapsburg rule; the authorities, to crush the last traces of rebellion, must eliminate the legendary Sándor Rózsa's guerilla bandits; and the plan deploys a Kafkaesque mix of fear and uncertainty to winnow, slowly but inexorably, the guerrillas from the peasant populace which has been rounded up. Jancsó's formally choreographed camera movements later developed into a mannerism; but here the stylisation works perfectly in making an almost abstract statement of the relationship between oppressor and oppressed. There are effectively no characters, no heroes one can admire or villains to hate; simply the men who always win, those who always lose. TM

Route de Corinthe, La (The Road to Corinth)

(1967, Fr/It/Greece, 100 min)
d Claude Chabrol. *p* André Génovès. *sc* Claude Brûlé, Daniel Boulanger. *ph* Jean Rabier. *ed* Jacques Gaillard, Monique Fardoulis. *ad* Mariléna Aravantinou. *m* Pierre Jansen. *cast* Jean Seberg, Maurice Ronet, Christian Marquand, Michel Bouquet, Saro Urzi, Antonio Passalia, Claude Chabrol.
●One of the most outrageous films from Chabrol's first 'commercial' period, before *Les Biches* renewed critical interest in the wayward New Wave instigator. Released here cut, dubbed and lacking an essential prologue featuring a mad illusionist, lumbered with the title *Who's Got the Black Box?* in the States, it's a wonderfully maddening mix of clattering allusions (to Greek tragedy and Hitchcock), characteristic black humour, and stunning visual irrelevancies, all poured into the deliberately banal mould of the spy thriller. 'I do not ask you to believe it, but I suggest that you dream about it' runs the film's opening epigraph. 'The silliness was more important than the spying' runs Chabrol's own retrospective line. PT

Route enchantée, La

(1938, Fr, 88 min, b/w)
d Pierre Caron. *sc* Charles Trenet. *ph* Georges Benoit. *ed* André Gug. *ad* Jean Douarinou. *songs* Charles Trenet. *cast* Charles Trenet, Marguerite Moreno, Jacqueline Pacaud, Jeanne Fusier-Gir, Julien Carette, The Bluebell Girls.
●In his movie debut, star singer Trenet plays Le Fou Chantant (The Singing Loon) and proves to be a high-energy performer of breezy tunes (his standard 'Boum!' is featured) but no kind of actor. And no kind of scriptwriter either, offering what seems merely a digest of some movies he happened to have liked recently. Easily identifiable are Capra and the Marx Brothers, Trenet himself being a ringer for Harpo. Still, the Bluebell Girls of 1938 were an impressively Amazonian bunch, Pierre Caron – not a name in many reference books – achieves a surprisingly lively mise-en-scène and those intrigued by the convergences of cinema and popular music should find this worth a look. BBa

Route One/USA

(1989, US/Fr/GB/It, 255 min)
d/p Robert Kramer. *ph* Richard Copans. *ed* Guy Lecorne, Robert Kramer, Keja Kramer, Pierre Choukroun, Claire Laville. *m* Barre Philips. *with* Paul McIsaac, Robert Kramer.
●On the road again, two uneasy riders: Doc (McIsaac), back from ten years in Africa, and independent film maker Kramer, ageing liberals who decide to follow Route 1, from the Canadian border through New England to Miami. Much of what they find is depressing. Endemic paranoia, poverty and bigotry – be it religious or patriotic – induce a desperate, introspective mood. With Kramer behind the camera, Doc becomes the focal point of interest, conducting hesitant, respectful interviews, meeting old friends, missing others, and not finding much to reassure him en route. There are odd glimmers of light: the liberal tradition of Massachusetts, Thoreau and Whitman, and community care projects that battle on against the odds. Not for Doc or Kramer the cool irony of Errol Morris or the conscious wackiness of Michael Moore. Doc wants to 'do something useful in all this shit', and three-quarters into the movie he surprisingly drops out to do just that. The last 45 minutes or so become distinctly ramshackle, with shifting centres and over-lapping voices. The camerawork and cutting have a snapshot feel, and the overall effect is rather like a book of photographs, 'A day in the life of America', fascinating in its detail, overwhelming in its diversity. TCh

Roxanne

(1987, US, 107 min)
d Fred Schepisi. *p* Michael Rachmil, Daniel Melnick. *sc* Steve Martin. *ph* Ian Baker. *ed* John Scott. *pd* Jackson DeGovia. *m* Bruce Smeaton. *cast* Steve Martin, Daryl Hannah, Rick Rossovich, Shelley Duvall, John Kapelos, Fred Willard, Max Alexander, Michael J Pollard.
●Rostand's *Cyrano de Bergerac*, thanks to Martin's adaptation which translates the big-nosed duellist-philosopher-poet into the Fire Chief of a small American town, provides the perfect vehicle for his comic intelligence. His Chief Bales is a complex creation, falling in love with astronomer Roxanne (Hannah), a romantic beauty who craves communion with a fine mind, but automatically taking a back seat because of his appearance. Chivalrously, he supports the courtship of Roxanne by Chris (Rossovich), the dimmest of his firemen, winning her for him with his words, dictating the love letters and even hilariously stage-managing the wooing via radio-waves until the duffer repeats police messages. Chris, and the inept firemen in general, seem to have been cast in Martin's old role as the jerk, leaving the star free to parade subtler gifts. As a result, *Roxanne* is far and away his richest film to date, lyrical, sweet-natured, touching, and very, very funny. BC

Roxie Hart

(1942, US, 75 min, b/w)
d William Wellman. *p/sc* Nunnally Johnson. *ph* Leon Shamroy. *ed* James B Clark. *ad* Richard Day, Wiard Ihnen. *m* Alfred Newman. *cast* Ginger Rogers, Adolphe Menjou, George Montgomery, Lynne Overman, Nigel Bruce, Phil Silvers, William Frawley, Spring Byington, Iris Adrian.
●Rogers is Roxie Hart, a brash, perpetual gum-chewer, who admits to a murder that was obviously committed by her weak, rat-fink husband. Not, however, the story of a strong woman sacrificing herself on the altar of love and marital devotion, but that of a sly minx, banking on attracting invaluable publicity for her so far non-existent dancing career. This long shot in the name of ambition is based on the premise that 'a Chicago jury would never convict a pretty woman'; an over-riding vein of cynicism that filters down from the gaggle of fickle press scribblers, interested only in hot news, never the truth, to the posturing defence counsel, who never defend the innocent. The total lunacy culminates in a courtroom melodrama with a difference, where Roxie crosses and uncrosses her legs for the jury's benefit, faints, cries, but always manages a radiant smile for the courtroom photographers, and where justice ultimately depends on the wrinkling of a pert nose. Subversive, outrageous, but always very funny. FF

Royal Affairs at Versailles

see Si Versailles m'était conté…

Royal Flash

(1975, GB, 118 min)
d Richard Lester. *p* David V Picker, Denis O'Dell. *sc* George MacDonald Fraser. *ph* Geoffrey Unsworth. *ed* John Victor Smith. *pd* Terence Marsh. *m* Ken Thorne. *cast* Malcolm McDowell, Alan Bates, Florinda Bolkan, Britt Ekland, Oliver Reed, Lionel Jeffries, Tom Bell, Christopher Cazenove, Joss Ackland, Alastair Sim, Michael Hordern, Roy Kinnear.
●Lester long cherished an ambition to make a film out of George MacDonald Fraser's *Flashman* books, but once the swashbuckling gets under way, it begins to seem far too much like *The Four Musketeers* Part III. The director's visual style is as strong and witty as ever, and he does score one bull's-eye with Oliver Reed's Bismarck. But after an opening which promises some kind of riotous comic strip of Victorian England, and a particularly good scene involving a boxing-match, the plot begins to parody itself too overtly and too loosely, finally overreaching itself completely with an endless and unimaginative duel between Bates and McDowell. The film might perhaps get by on its superb visuals and the occasional good gag, but the casting sinks it: whatever Lester's intentions, McDowell and Bolkan are no match for Michael York and Faye Dunaway at this kind of thing. DP

Royal Hunt of the Sun, The

(1969, GB, 121 min)
d Irving Lerner. *p* Eugene Frenke, Philip Yordan. *sc* Philip Yordan. *ph* Roger Barlow. *ed* Peter Parasheles. *ad* Eugène Lourié. *m* Marc Wilkinson. *cast* Robert Shaw, Christopher Plummer, Nigel Davenport, Michael Craig, Leonard Whiting, Andrew Keir, James Donald, William Marlowe, Percy Herbert.
●Given that Peter Shaffer's play was ripe for screen adaptation, it's surprising that this is so resolutely stagey. Concentrating almost entirely on the intimate confrontation between the Spanish conquistador Pizarro and the Inca god-king Atahualpa, which takes in issues of immortality, religious belief, and the worth of gold (Pizarro is searching for El Dorado), it unwisely ignores the material's potential for the combined spectacle of landscape and material wealth. That said, it's still quite watchable, thanks largely to the intelligence of Shaffer's original, and to strong if idiosyncratic performances from Shaw and Plummer. GA

Royal Scandal, A (aka Czarina)

(1945, US, 94 min, b/w)
d Otto Preminger. *p* Ernst Lubitsch. *sc* Edwin Justus Mayer. *ph* Arthur Miller. *ed* Dorothy Spencer. *ad* Lyle R Wheeler, Mark-Lee Kirk. *m* Alfred Newman. *cast* Tallulah Bankhead, Charles Coburn, Anne Baxter, William Eythe, Vincent Price, Sig Ruman, Mischa Auer.
●This should have been an Ernst Lubitsch film: it's a remake of his 1924 movie *Forbidden Paradise*, and he had just started it when he succumbed to his fifth heart attack. (He still gets nominal producer credit.) Preminger stepped in, fresh from the triumph of *Laura*, and obviously had little success in getting Tallulah Bankhead to tone down the fruitiness of her performance as Catherine the Great, torn, as usual, between lust and sentimentality. There are hints of what might have been in the performances of Coburn and Price. TR

Royal Tenenbaums, The

(2001, US, 110 min)
d Wes Anderson. *p* Wes Anderson, Barry Mendel, Scott Rudin. *sc* Wes Anderson, Owen Wilson. *ph* Robert Yeoman. *ed* Dylan Tichenor. *pd* David Wasco. *m* Mark Mothersbaugh. *cast* Gene Hackman, Anjelica Huston, Ben Stiller, Gwyneth Paltrow, Luke Wilson, Owen Wilson, Bill Murray, Danny Glover, Seymour Cassel, Kumar Pallana, Larry Pine.
●Wittier, more enjoyable and infinitely richer than the year's major Oscar contenders, this is clearly a blood brother to Anderson's *Rushmore*. The Tenenbaums are New York high society gone to seed. Scandalous Royal (Hackman) separated from wife Etheline (Huston) two decades ago, and kept his distance as his once prodigious offspring slumped. Business whizz Chas (Stiller) has become a paranoid neurotic; Richie (Wilson) is a tennis star whose career went to love; adopted daughter Margot (Paltrow) is a closed book of a playwright. Financially embarrassed and claiming a dying man's last rights, Royal returns to put his house in order. The milieu is reminiscent of Preston Sturges' screwball fancies from the early 1940s – albeit scored to '70s rock. Anderson's unusually pronounced literary influences include Salinger, Edith Wharton and the *New Yorker* magazine, and the film sometimes resembles a cartoon from that august publication's glory days: an elegantly composed caricature topped by the immaculately turned one-liner. It exists in a bubble – Anderson's New York doesn't exist and never did – but the rarefied atmosphere is a bit of a blind; what sneaks up on you is how, in his deliciously roundabout way, Anderson wears irony on his sleeve to camouflage a deeper sincerity. At heart, this is a comedy of unrequited love, melancholy and disappointment. One to savour. TCh

Royal Wedding (aka Wedding Bells)

(1951, US, 93 min)
d Stanley Donen. *p* Arthur Freed. *sc* Alan Jay Lerner. *ph* Robert Planck. *ed* Albert Akst. *ad* Cedric Gibbons, Jack Martin Smith. *songs*

Alan Jay Lerner, Burton Lane. *cast* Fred Astaire, Jane Powell, Sarah Churchill, Peter Lawford, Keenan Wynn.
●Not, thankfully, a documentary about a couple with cotton wool in their mouths, but a lively Technicolor musical (produced by Arthur Freed), with Astaire and Powell as a brother-and-sister musical act who travel from America to London at the time of the Queen's wedding (then Princess Elizabeth, of course), and both find romance, he with a dancer, she with a lord. A pleasant enough score by Burton Lane and Alan Jay Lerner, helped out by Donen's stylish direction; best number is 'You're All the World to Me', with Astaire energetically dancing his way round the walls and ceiling of a hotel room. GA

Roy Cohn/Jack Smith

(1993, US, 90 min)
d Jill Godmilow. *p* Ted Hope, James Schamus, Marianne Weems. *ph* Ellen Kuras. *ed* Merril Stern. *m* Michael Sahl. *cast* Ron Vawter.
●Roy Cohn was Senator Joe McCarthy's right-hand attorney and a vociferous opponent of the loosening of gay rights; Jack Smith a wild performer and film-maker whose celebration of transvestite perversity, *Flaming Creatures*, became a notorious underground film of the '60s. Both men died of AIDS within a year or so of each other. As 'presented' by Jonathan Demme and filmed in New York, Vawter's one-man show places these two apparently dissimilar individuals side by side, focusing on the element of performance that seems to have enabled each to have survived in his particular stratum of society. Vawter is extraordinary in the way he switches roles: zeroing in on a toweringly homophobic speech Cohn gave to the American Society for the Preservation of the Family in 1978, then adorning himself in glitter for a distilled re-creation of one of Smith's languorous, fragmented monologues. Some jarring cross-cutting aside, the film's an absorbing, intelligent take on the compromises of gay identity and the masks people hide behind. It's also a testament to Vawter, who himself died of AIDS, shortly after this performance was recorded. TJ

Rub Love

(1998, SKor, 89 min)
d Lee Suh-Goon. *p* Park Chul-Soo, Hwang Kyoung-Sung. *sc* Lee Suh-Goon. *ph* Cho Yong-Kyu. *ed* LIM. *ad* Park Hwai-Min, Oh Jae-Won. *m* Gang-A-Ji Culture/Art. *cast* Ahn Jae-Wook, Lee Ji-Eun, Joshua Klausner.
●Rare to find a woman directing anything in Korea, let alone a 23-year-old directing a post-feminist sci-fi feature about her emotional disconnection from society and desire for escape – and so *Rub Love* is kind of special. We're in 2028. Nana is a sleek young hitwoman with three hits to her credit, who installs herself in Motel 99 to stake out the louche nightclub opposite, where she will carry out her final hit before retiring to China. Her neighbour in the motel is a nerdy cartoonist with an overactive fantasy life who throws himself at her feet and tries to make her stay by slipping her a drug to erase her memories. Uncompromisingly bloody, wittily designed, and remarkably well acted (not least by Klausner as a seedy black marketeer), this is a genuine original. Lee, who wrote the script for *301, 302*, clearly has great things in prospect. TR

Ruby

(1977, US, 85 min)
d Curtis Harrington. *p* George Edwards. *sc* George Edwards, Barry Schneider. *ph* William Mendelhall. *ed* Bill Magee. *ad* Tom Rasmussen. *m* Don Ellis. *cast* Piper Laurie, Stuart Whitman, Roger Davis, Janit Baldwin, Crystin Sinclaire, Paul Kent.
●This starts rather well: it's 1951, and a drive-in projectionist is attacked and strangled by the film he is projecting. Unfortunately it's the high-point of the film, for as the unseen force which animated the celluloid is revealed to be the spirit of Piper Laurie's murdered lover, Harrington strolls the gamut of contemporary horror influences in search of the completely predictable. He finds it: Ruby's daughter (Baldwin) is possessed and thrashes on a levitating bed. The cluttered art direction and the nostalgic flashbacks to the gangster '30s are stillborn mementoes of Harrington's own *What's the Matter with Helen?*, and the drive-in location never has its possibilities fully developed. Given that the film is always watchable, if never exciting, the drive-in isn't so much a location as the film's probable market. SM

Ruby

(1992, US, 110 min)
d John MacKenzie. *p* Sigurjon Sighvatsson, Steve Golin. *sc* Stephen Davis. *ph* Philip Meheux. *ed* Richard Trevor. *pd* David Brisbin. *m* John Scott. *cast* Danny Aiello, Sherilyn Fenn, David Duchovny, Arliss Howard, Marc Lawrence, Tobin Bell, Joe Cortese, Richard Sarafian, Joe Viterelli.
●Sadly, MacKenzie's film about Jack Ruby will probably be viewed as an appendix to Oliver Stone's *JFK*, though it has merits in its own right. Particularly well caught is the easy-going and long-standing venality between strip-joint owner Ruby and the Dallas police, the CIA and the Mafia. Ruby is a bafflingly multi-faceted character, and Aiello pulls out all the stops in portraying the whole ingratiating, generous, sentimental, homicidal, paranoid mess. Perhaps the most startling depiction of Ruby's volatility occurs in Cuba when, forced against his wishes to carry out a hit, he suddenly turns the gun on the hirer. His relationship with stripper Candy Cane (Fenn) seems oddly avuncular, but then he may have been a non-practising homosexual. Writer Stephen Davis drafts Candy into JFK's bed, and plasters her with blood from the President's assassination in Dealey Plaza – without straining credulity. Veteran Marc Lawrence, as Santos Alicante, makes a chillingly believable mobster. BC

Ruby Cairo

(1992, US, 100 min)
d Graeme Clifford. *p* Lloyd Phillips. *sc* Robert Dillon, Michael Thomas. *ph* Laszlo Kovacs. *ed* Caroline Biggerstaff. *pd* Richard Sylbert. *m* John Barry. *cast* Andie MacDowell, Liam Neeson, Viggo Mortensen, Jack Thompson.
●'What on earth was Johnny going to do with all that ink? And what did it have to do with his airplane salvage business?' What, indeed? Talking like a character out of a '40s thriller, Bessie Faro (MacDowell) follows a trail of baseball cards left by her deceased husband to a fortune stashed in various exotic locations: Mexico, Berlin, Athens. Neeson pops up briefly in Vera Cruz as a humanitarian 'Feed the World' worker, before reappearing as a romantic lead in sunny Cairo. Cue travelogue footage of pyramids, deserts, bustling markets. The script is packed with lines like 'Dead men do not write cheques' and 'Ink is the life-blood of civilisation', while Bessie must vocalise her every thought: 'Hmmm, this must be a code,' she declares, fingering a card covered in hieroglyphics that must, indeed, be a code. Add some unbelievably straggly plot ends, and you've got a good-looking package tour which can doubtless be written off against tax. MK

Ruby Gentry

(1952, US, 82 min, b/w)
d King Vidor. *p* Joseph Bernhard, King Vidor. *sc* Silvia Richards. *ph* Russell Harlan. *ed* Terry Morse. *ad* Daniel Hall. *m* Heinz Roemheld. *cast* Jennifer Jones, Charlton Heston, Karl Malden, Josephine Hutchinson, Tom Tully, Bernard Phillips.
●With *Duel in the Sun*, the most primitive and hysterical of Vidor's films, *Ruby Gentry* is a Southern family drama set in motion by the love of a girl from the wrong side of the tracks (Jones) for a member of the local gentry (Heston). An explicitly sensual film – notably in the ride along the beach and in the final sequences – it draws much of its force from Vidor's consistent identification of the viewer with Ruby as she struggles to come to terms with each situation her high-powered emotions place her in. Not entirely successful, but well worth seeing. PH

Ruby in Paradise

(1993, US, 114 min)
d/sc Victor Nuñez. *ph* Alex Vlacos. *ed* Victor Nuñez. *ad* John Lacovelli. *m* Charles Engstrom. *cast* Ashley Judd, Todd Field, Bentley Mitchum, Allison Dean, Dorothy Lyman.
●Ruby (Judd) is running from her mother's death and thankless chores in the family business in Tennessee. She arrives in Florida, the Sunshine State, at nightfall, seeking identity and love. Her first priority is work, however, and though it's off-season, perseverance pays off with a job in a tacky gift shop. She's warned not to mess with the owner's flashy son (Mitchum), but loneliness drives her to joyless sex. Then she meets Mike (Field), a sensitive intellectual, and it looks as though she might realise the 'dream of belonging'. You know there's truth in these drab small-town lives, but, regrettably, there's little drama or humour to sustain interest in Ruby's vague musings on her bleak search for paradise. CO'S

Rude Awakening

(1989, US, 100 min)
d Aaron Russo, David Greenwalt. *p* Aaron Russo. *sc* Neil Levy, Richard LaGravenese. *ph* Tim Sigel. *ed* Paul Fried. *ad* Dan Davis. *m* Jonathan Elias. *cast* Cheech Marin, Eric Roberts, Robert Carradine, Buck Henry, Louise Lasser, Cindy Williams, Andrea Martin, Cliff De Young, Julie Hagerty.
●After 20 years 'out to grass' in Central America, draft-dodgers Jesus (Marin) and Fred (Roberts) wake up to modern political reality when they find the body of a CIA agent whose suitcase contains secret plans for a full-scale American invasion of Managuador. Realising that when they dropped out they also copped out, they instantly resume radical politics and return to New York to spill the beans. To their horror, their far-out pals now pursue respectable careers while enjoying the consumerist benefits of post-Reagan capitalism. A string of unrelated skits masquerading as a plot, this is a feeble one-joke movie: idealistic hippies culture-shocked by yuppie lifestyles, nuclear power, the ozone layer, acid rain and, most heinous of all, the colorisation of black-and-white movies. Only Louise Lasser, as the vivacious owner of the Nouveau Woodstock vegetarian restaurant, gives any hint of what might have been achieved with a little imagination. NF

Rude Boy

(1980, GB, 133 min)
d/p Jack Hazan, David Mingay. *sc* David Mingay, Ray Gange, Jack Hazan. *ph* Jack Hazan. *ed* David Mingay, Peter Goddard. *cast* Ray Gange, The Clash, Johnny Green, Barry Baker, Terry McQuade, Caroline Coon.
●Scoring highly, if only for its excellent Clash concert footage, this blunt portrait of post-Jubilee Britain actually does much more: showing both left and right as cynical manipulators, and a Clash fan following his leftish band even though himself a potential National Front recruit, it has its finger (if not brains) on the pulse. Marred by some simplistic editing, it's another nail hammered into the coffin of rock and roll. See it and find out why The *Daily Mail* was disgusted and The Clash disowned it. DMacp

Rudy

(1993, US, 116 min)
d David Anspaugh. *p* Cary Woods, Rob Fried. *sc* Angelo Pizzo. *ph* Oliver Wood. *ed* David Rosenbloom. *pd* Robb Wilson. *m* Jerry Goldsmith. *cast* Sean Astin, Ned Beatty, Charles S Dutton, Jason Miller, Robert Prosky, Lili Taylor, Christopher Reed.
●Rudy (Astin) is an all-American dreamer: he wants to play football for Notre Dame, but, as everyone keeps telling him, 'Notre Dame is not for everyone.' The son of a steelworker, he has only a mediocre academic record, a slight build, and he's not a great natural athlete. At 22, after four years in the steel mill, the death of his best friend moves Rudy to re-evaluate his life. He goes East and enrolls in a junior college, determined to make the grade. Eventually, he does – but surely all the guts and determination in the world can't make him a varsity football star? Underdogs are the grist of sports movies; even so, it's unusual to find a hero so ill-equipped for the task at hand. Directed with composure, but no great fervour, the film's conspicuously uninterested in American football, and much concerned with testing the limits and the resilience of the American dream. TCh

Rudyard Kipling's The Jungle Book

see Jungle Book, The

Rue Cases Nègres

see Black Shack Alley

Rue Saint-Sulpice

see Favour, the Watch and the Very Big Fish, The

Ruggles of Red Gap

(1935, US, 91 min, b/w)
d Leo McCarey. *p* Arthur Hornblow Jr. *sc* Walter de Leon, Harlan Thompson, Humphrey Pearson. *ph* Alfred Gilks. *ed* Edward Dmytryk. *ad* Hans Dreier, Robert Odell. *m* Ralph Rainger. *cast* Charles Laughton, Mary Boland, Charlie Ruggles, ZaSu Pitts, Roland Young, Leila Hyams.
● Ruggles is a British butler (don't you know), Red Gap is the American shack of a town he comes to work in, having been won in a poker game. After initial incomprehension, he recites Lincoln's Gettysburg address and becomes the country's greatest fan. Sounds awful? Not so; this is the archetypal film they don't make any more, partly because comedy has now grown too raucous to favour the quiet drollery of players like Charlie Ruggles and Mary Boland, partly because after the '30s even McCarey himself had problems in separating sentiment from sentimentality. Laughton, as always, enjoys himself enormously; we can only follow. GB

Rugrats Movie, The

(1998, US, 80 min)
d Norton Virgien, Igor Kovalyov. *p* Arlene Klasky, Gabor Csupo. *sc* David N Weiss, J David Stem. *ed* John Bryant. *ad* Dima Malanitchev. *m* Mark Mothersbaugh. *cast* voices EG Daily, Christine Cavanaugh, Kath Soucie, Melanie Chartoff, Phil Proctor, Cree Summer, Tara Charendoff.
● In this 'movie-isation' of the justly top-rated Nickelodeon TV cartoon, the producers have left the formula intact, changing little beyond extending the running time, fleshing out the animation (unobtrusively), inserting an 'Indiana Jones' premovie sequence, and giving the Pickles family a new member (baby Dylan). Those unfamiliar with the series will have a chance to marvel at Klasky and Csupo's refreshing innovations: their affectionate play with traditional presentations of 'sweet' baby behaviour and 'pretty' toddler looks – these terrors are warring pug-ugly monsters with bad attitude and unteachable manners. Like the series, the movie is shot from carpet level with exploded perspectives. WH

Rugrats in Paris: The Movie

(2000, US/Ger, 79 min)
d Paul Demeyer, Stig Bergqvist. *p* Arlene Klasky, Gabor Csupo. *sc* David N Weiss, J David Stern, Jill Gorey, Barbara Herndon, Kate Boutilier. *ed* John Bryant. *pd* Dima Malanitchev. *m* Mark Mothersbaugh. *cast* voices: EG Daily, Tara Charendoff, Cheryl Chase, Christine Cavanaugh, Cree Summer Franck, Debbie Reynolds, Susan Sarandon, John Lithgow.
● It makes a change to see a TV-inspired kids' movie that's not only competently animated but whose storyline and level of dialogue don't induce drowsiness in accompanying adults. This merchandise tie-in begins at home in America. After seeing his cousins cuddling up to their respective family members, motherless rugrat Chuckie yearns to do the same. The rugrats cast accompany Tommy to Paris where his father must fix a theme park's malfunctioning dinosaur ride. The park's manageress has learned that her boss plans to retire and is looking for a suitable 'family-oriented' successor. If only she could persuade Chuckie's lonesome father to marry her. This is one kids' film that's actually quite charming.DA

Rules of Engagement

(2000, US/Ger, 127 min)
d William Friedkin. *p* Richard D Zanuck, Scott Rudin. *sc* Stephen Gaghan. *ph* Nicola Pecorini, William A Fraker. *ed* Augie Hess. *pd* Robert Laing. *m* Mark Isham. *cast* Tommy Lee Jones, Samuel L Jackson, Guy Pearce, Bruce Greenwood, Blair Underwood, Philip Baker Hall, Anne Archer, Mark Fuerstein, Ben Kingsley, Gordon Clapp.
● A potboiler in the vein of *Courage Under Fire*, Friedkin's movie convinces while staging visceral action in the combat zone, but quickly loses momentum in the courtroom scenes that follow. The script's view of military ethics echoes Jack Nicholson's famous speech in *A Few Good Men* ('You can't handle the truth!'), the implication being that decisions made in the heat of battle are beyond the ken of mere civilians. Indeed, their actions, under fire are above and beyond the petty expediencies of everyday morality and international politics. The evacuation of the ambassador from the US embassy in riot-torn Yemen ends in a massacre of men, women and children by Col Childers (Jackson) and his team of crack Marines. Jobbing lawyer Col Hodges (Jones) reluctantly agrees to defend the man who saved his life in Vietnam 28 years before. The proceedings are diplomatic window dressing, however, since a video containing key evidence has been destroyed by a two-dimensional black hat (Greenwood). Once any ambiguity has been erased, the verbose arguments of Hodges and the prosecuting lawyer (Pearce) become little more than windy generic wordplay. NF

Rules of the Game, The

see Règle du Jeu, La

Ruling Class, The

(1971, GB, 155 min)
d Peter Medak. *p* Jules Buck, Jack Hawkins. *sc* Peter Barnes. *ph* Ken Hodges. *ed* Ray Lovejoy. *pd* Peter Murton. *m* John Cameron. *cast* Peter O'Toole, Alastair Sim, Arthur Lowe, Harry Andrews, Coral Browne, Michael Bryant, Nigel Green, William Mervyn, James Villiers, Hugh Burden, Carolyn Seymour, Graham Crowden, Kay Walsh.
● Peter Barnes' adaptation of his own play takes as its targets British chauvinism, British institutions, the sadistic education system, and the sexual perversion and social misery it feeds off. Loosely the plot covers the death of the old Earl of Gurney (Andrews) during one of his masochistic evening rituals, and the accession to the title of his insane son (O'Toole), who believes he is God but eventually switches to Jack the Ripper. This is buried beneath a load of old jokes, song'n'dance routines, bad jokes, physical obsessions, random send-ups. A very long two and a half hours does throw up some good performances and a few memorable images; otherwise the latent and overt ideas are fleshed out all too obviously. VG

Rumba

(1935, US, 71 min, b/w)
d Marion Gering. *p* William Le Baron. *sc* Howard J Green. *ph* Ted Tetzlaff. ed Hugh Bennett. *ad* Hans Dreier, Robert Usher. *songs* Ralph Rainger, Leo Robin. *cast* George Raft, Carole Lombard, Lynne Overman, Margo, Gail Patrick, Akim Tamiroff, Iris Adrian.
● Criminal waste of the delectable Lombard, once more playing second fiddle to Raft at his most repellently lounge lizardish in this follow-up to their inexplicably successful *Bolero*. Even the dances (again performed mostly by doubles) are shoddy this time round, while the fatuous plot oozes sluggishly to a climax in which Raft defies a supposed death threat from gangsters to go on stage and perform a dreary rumba routine. TM

Rumble Fish

(1983, US, 94 min, b/w & col)
d Francis Ford Coppola. *p* Fred Roos, Doug Claybourne. *sc* SE Hinton, Francis Ford Coppola. *ph* Stephen H Burum. *ed* Barry Malkin. *pd* Dean Tavoularis. *m* Stewart Copeland. *cast* Matt Dillon, Mickey Rourke, Diane Lane, Dennis Hopper, Diana Scarwid, Vincent Spano, Nicolas Cage, Christopher Penn, Larry Fishburne, Tom Waits, SE Hinton.
● Shot back-to-back with *The Outsiders*, similarly based on a novel by SE Hinton, and signalled by Coppola as 'Camus for kids', *Rumble Fish* does indeed have a hero figure (Rourke) who belongs to a former age of existential 'outsiders', coasting through the world in an insulated state of deafness and colour blindness from too many rumbles. His kid brother (Dillon) idolises him, but is too stupid to see the damage done to all concerned by the continuous gang-fights of frightful violence but no importance. All of which is all very well; but Coppola's recent viewing seems to have been German silent films of the '20s, so he has decided to coat the whole enterprise in a startling Expressionist style, which is very arresting but hardly appropriate to the matter in hand. As with *The Outsiders'* it's very hard to picture the audience at which the film is aimed. CPea

Rumble in the Bronx (Hongfan Qu)

(1995, HK, 105 min)
d Stanley Tong. *p* Barbie Tung. *sc* Edward Tang, Fibe Ma. *ph* Jingle Ma. *ed* Peter Cheung. *pd* Oliver Wong. *m* Wong Chun-Yin. *cast* Jackie Chan, Anita Mui, Françoise Yip, Bill Tung, Marc Akerstream, Garvin Cross.
● Actually shot in Vancouver, this is the Jackie Chan movie which finally cracked the US market, grossing some $28m on first release. Chan plays a Hong Kong cop visiting NYC for an uncle's wedding; he tangles with a multi-ethnic street gang and then teams up with them to defeat ultra-vicious Mafia types bent on retrieving some stolen gems. Not the best of Chan's large-scale action comedies: the big set-pieces (the demolition of a city building, a hovercraft rampage through downtown streets) strain for effect. But Chan's insistence on his own fallibility and vulnerability, taken with virtuoso scenes like the fight involving 101 domestic appliances, shows why he means more to his countless fans than six US action stars put together. TR

Runaway

(1984, US, 100 min)
d Michael Crichton. *p* Michael Rachmil. *sc* Michael Crichton. *ph* John A Alonzo. *ed* Glenn Farr, James Coblentz. *pd* Douglas Higgins. *m* Jerry Goldsmith. *cast* Tom Selleck, Cynthia Rhodes, Gene Simmons, Kirstie Alley, Stan Shaw, GW Bailey, Joey Cramer, Chris Mulkey.
● This near-future tale, in which Selleck heads a police division tracking murderous machines, is technically quite as accomplished as Crichton's previous work, carrying a strong atmosphere of menace and some virtuoso effects (including a tracking shot behind a bullet that makes the Bond movies seem old-fashioned). But once it turns from the hardware and the action to people, you can hardly believe your eyes or your ears. 'That's no bullet, it's an exploding shell' Selleck announces to a colleague. 'God, you're right' the other replies, not even turning to look at it. With its villain straight out of *Batman*, Crichton is clearly intending to lighten the tone, but instead the thing congeals. DP

Runaway Bride

(1999, US, 116 min)
d Garry Marshall. *p* Ted Field, Tom Rosenberg, Scott Kroopf, Robert Cort. *sc* Josann McGibbon, Sara Parriott. *ph* Stuart Dryburgh. *ed* Bruce Green. *pd* Mark Friedberg. *m* James Newton Howard. *cast* Julia Roberts, Richard Gere, Joan Cusack, Hector Elizondo, Rita Wilson, Paul Dooley, Christopher Meloni, Donal Logue.
● It had to come: Roberts and Gere together again nine years after *Pretty Woman*. With director Marshall back on board too, one supposes the studio reckoned the rest of the movie would somehow take care of itself. Gere does grumpy and smug as Ike Graham, NY newspaper columnist, who turns a drunk's story about a small town gal with a penchant for leaving men at the altar into a typically combative think piece. It elicits a sharp letter from one Maggie Carpenter (Roberts), who has only left three guys high and dry thus far, and claims a host of other inaccuracies in the story. Chastened, Ike hastens off to write a feature on the so-called 'Runaway Bride'. The succession of contrived dilemmas on the way to an obviously unalterable destination does drag after a while – a shame, since Gere and Roberts are comfortable on screen, and Cusack brings a wealth of charm to her thankless part of the best girl pal. In the end, though, it surrenders to lame synthetic mush and the light goes out of its eyes. TJ

Runaway Train

(1985, US, 110 min)
d Andrei Konchalovsky. *p* Menahem Golan, Yoram Globus. *sc* Djordje Milicevic, Paul Zindel, Edward Bunker. *ph* Alan Hume. *ed* Henry Richardson. *pd* Stephen Marsh. *m* Trevor Jones. *cast* Jon Voight, Eric Roberts, Rebecca De Mornay, Kyle T Heffner, John P Ryan, TK Carter, Kenneth McMillan.
● So brutish a prisoner that the Warden (Ryan) had him welded into his cell for three years, Voight goes on the run through the Alaskan winter with only Eric Roberts to keep him warm. They sneak into the back of a four-engine work train, but the engineer has a heart attack, the brakes burn out, the track controller's computers can't cope, and the engineer's sleeping assistant turns out to be – a woman. So sit tight and watch four matt black shunters, looking like beasts from the pit of hell, go charging through the tundra, while Voight and Roberts slug it out over the girl, life, fate, and who's going to have to go outside. Then there is the problem of the Warden being winched down by chopper for one last showdown. The surprise is that

Konchalovsky has taken such an obviously pat formula (from an original screenplay by Kurosawa) and made it work remarkably well. Somehow one leaves aside the blatant implausibilities, the coincidences, even Eric Roberts, and takes great pleasure in a breakneck ride to the end of the line. And Voight has finally found his niche, abandoning all those wet-eyed liberal roles and playing to the hilt a hideous, raving beast, with scars. Great ending, too. CPea

Run for Cover

(1955, US, 93 min)
d Nicholas Ray. *p* William H Pine, William C Thomas. *sc* Winston Miller. *ph* Daniel L Fapp. *ed* Howard Smith. *ad* Hal Pereria, Henry Bumstead. *m* Howard Jackson. *cast* James Cagney, John Derek, Viveca Lindfors, Jean Hersholt, Grant Withers, Ernest Borgnine.

●Made between *Johnny Guitar* and *Rebel Without a Cause*, Ray's second Western lacks the baroque, bizarre excesses of his first, and the intensely troubled romanticism of the Dean film. Despite its superficially conventional plot, however, its theme is again the gulf between generations: Cagney rides into town with Derek, whom he has only just met, only to be mistaken for train-robbers. Before the error is recognised, the boy is crippled by a bullet, provoking his bitter slide into delinquency while his surrogate father accepts a job as sheriff. The situations may be the stock ones of deception, betrayal and revenge, but the film is rare in Ray's work in that it focuses not on the youth but on Cagney, who attempts to curb his own anger at the injustices he has suffered. Despite the violence of certain scenes, it's a strangely gentle, even poignant Western, and Ray's sensitive handling of actors and his exact compositional sense are as much in evidence as ever. GA

Run for Money (Kaç Para Kaç)

(1999, Tur, 100 min)
d Reha Erdem. *p* Ali Ömer Atay. *sc* Reha Erdem. *ph* Florent Hery, Jean-Louis Vialard. *ed* Nathalie Le Guay. *pd* Ali Ömer Atay. *m* Pressure Drop. *cast* Taner Birsel, Bennu Yildirimlar, Zuhal Gencer.

●Money, money, money … Selim's a straight kind of guy, unimpressed with the usual day to day temptations of graft and greed, whether at his shirt shop or at home. But when a flash encounter leaves him sitting on half a million dollars of stolen loot in the back of a taxi, he turns worm. Played with conviction, this is a standard issue *noir* thriller of spiralling self-entrapment and alienation limited by the very same secular condition it depicts. NB

Run for the Sun

(1956, US, 99 min)
d Roy Boulting. *p* Harry Tatelman. *sc* Dudley Nichols, Roy Boulting. *ph* Joseph LaShelle. *ed* Frederick Knudtson. *ad* Alfred Ybarra. *m* Fred Steiner. *cast* Richard Widmark, Jane Greer, Trevor Howard, Peter Van Eyck, Carlos Henning.

●An adaptation, by Boulting and Dudley Nichols, of Richard Connell's much filmed short story *The Most Dangerous Game*. Widmark is a novelist and Greer a journalist who crash-land in the jungle, are given hospitality by three Europeans who may be Nazis, and escape pursued by a pack of dogs. The film never really gets to grips with the grotesquerie of the original story, though Howard, as a dead ringer for Lord Haw-Haw, is excellent. It was filmed in SuperScope 235, one of the widest film processes available. ATu

Run for Your Money, A

(1949, GB, 85 min)
d Charles Frend. *p* Michael Balcon. *sc* Richard Hughes, Charles Frend, Leslie Norman. *ph* Douglas Slocombe. *ed* Michael Truman. *ad* William Kellner. *m* Ernest Irving. *cast* Donald Houston, Meredith Edwards, Moira Lister, Alec Guinness, Hugh Griffith, Julie Milton, Joyce Grenfell.

●Released in a vintage Ealing year (*Passport to Pimlico, Whisky Galore!, Kind Hearts and Coronets*), this comic effort, co-written by the novelist Richard Hughes, seems a bit winded. Edwards and Houston are the Welsh brothers who win a newspaper competition to see their countrymen take on the England rugby team at Twickenham; Guinness is the journo who tags along to do the story on them, and grows anxious as their misadventures take unexpected (but not that unexpected) turns. TJ

Run Lola Run (Lola Rennt)

(1998, Ger, 80 min)
d Tom Tykwer. *p* Stefan Arndt. *sc* Tom Tykwer. *ph* Frank Griebe. *ed* Mathilde Bonnefoy. *ad* Alexander Manasse. *m* Tom Tykwer, Johnny Klimek, Reinhold Heil. *cast* Franka Potente, Moritz Bleibtreu, Herbert Knaup, Nina Petri, Armin Rohde, Joachim Król, Ludger Pistor.

●Lola (Potente) has a problem: her boyfriend Manni (Bleibtreu) is in a state of terminal panic after losing a hefty slice of his gangster boss's fortune; unless Lola can somehow raise 100,000 marks and reach him in 20 minutes, he'll do something seriously stupid – rob a store, say – before the boss turns up. So off she runs; trouble is, with time tight, one slip might mean curtains for Manni. Tykwer's film has already taken a fortune in various territories, and it's not hard to see why. For one thing, the plotting, which posits three different scenarios for Lola's rescue mission, is both a familiar old warhorse and ingeniously modern. For another, Tykwer deploys various eye-catching visual techniques to transform what is essentially a very simple story into a slick, tricksy entertainment. Finally, with its techno score, super-fit punk heroine and cynical take on the adult establishment, it's cannily aimed at the youth market. That said, it's as shallow as a puddle. Not only is the story contrived and often implausible, and the sporadic romanticism superficial, but it's hard to feel real sympathetic concern for Manni; if it weren't for Potente's solid, spirited performance, Lola's desperate quest would be revealed as the high-concept narrative hook it really is. GA

Runner, The (Dawandeh)

(1984, Iran, 94 min)
d Amir Naderi. *sc* Amir Naderi, Behruz Gharibpur. *ph* Firuz Malekzadeh. *ed* Balram Beyzai. *pd* Gholam Reza Ramezani. *cast* Majid Nirumand, Musa Torkizadeh, A Gholamzadeh, Reza Ramezani.

●An astonishing piece of film-making in which Naderi's harsh account of modern poverty supports passages of extravagant but unsentimental lyricism. Amiro (Nirumand) is an illiterate ten-year-old orphan living in a rusting tanker hulk, beached in a Persian Gulf shantytown. Life is a struggle, and garbage-picking and peddling water just about pay for a watermelon diet. Bigger boys try to steal his empty bottles, a man snatches the block of ice he needs to cool the water he sells. Amiro learns to fight back. He's a runner, and he wants to run with the best of them. Young Nirumand gives a performance to make Rossellini weep, and the soundtrack is a joy. PHo

Runners

(1983, GB, 106 min)
d Charles Sturridge. *p* Barry Hanson. *sc* Stephen Poliakoff. *ph* Howard Atherton. *ed* Peter Coulson. *pd* Arnold Chapkis. *m* George Fenton. *cast* Kate Hardie, James Fox, Jane Asher, Eileen O'Brien, Robert Lang, Ruti Simon, Shay Gorman, Bernard Hill.

●How does it feel when your teenage daughter goes missing? *Runners* poses the question that even a heartless tabloid hack might hesitate over, but looks forward two years after Rachel's disappearance, when sympathy has waned. Her father (a role well suited to Fox's seedily neurotic screen manner), alone in his conviction that she is alive, and encouraged by a self-help group where he meets Asher, a woman who has similarly lost her son, goes to London to find her. The amazing thing is that he does – briefly – and what seems to be just a behind-the-headlines story of an obsessive odyssey becomes an impressively ambiguous thriller. The unfancy realism of Sturridge's direction emphasises that this is a small film; but unlike, say, a TV drama-doc, it doesn't just flesh out a contemporary social problem. Rather, *schadenfreude* gives way to shaggy dog as writer Stephen Poliakoff weaves a quirky tale out of the loose ends of the here and now. JS

Runner Stumbles, The

(1979, US, 110 min)
d/p Stanley Kramer. *sc* Milan Stitt. *ph* Laszlo Kovacs. *ed* Pembroke J Herring. *pd* Alfred Sweeney Jr. *m* Ernest Gold. *cast* Dick Van Dyke, Kathleen Quinlan, Maureen Stapleton, Ray Bolger, Tammy Grimes, Beau Bridges.

●The appeal of Kramer's consistent line in numbing worthiness (*Judgment at Nuremberg, Ship of Fools, Guess Who's Coming to Dinner?*) has always been to those who like their popcorn heavily salted. A veteran auteur-for-all-issues, he now comes up with this irrelevantly monumental crisis-of-faith movie, in which Father Dick Van Dyke (as close to Hamlet as he'll ever get) finds himself on trial for the murder of young nun Kathleen Quinlan, over whom he's been getting increasingly hot under the dog-collar. Deadly earnestness over Van Dyke's tortured celibacy becomes risible long before the Perry Mason conclusion and a final scene of indescribable bathos. Now perhaps if Sidney Poitier had played the role… PT

Running Brave

(1983, US, 106 min)
d DS Everett [Donald Shebib]. *p* Ira Englander. *sc* Henry Bean, Shirl Hendryx. *ph* François Protat. *ed* Tony Lower, Earle Herden. *pd* Carol Spier. *m* Mike Post. *cast* Robby Benson, Pat Hingle, Claudia Cron, August Schellenberg, Margo Kane, Jeff McCracken.

●This is the true story of soft-spoken Billy Mills, a Sioux who left the reservation on an athlete's scholarship to the University of Kansas. There he encounters a dictatorial coach, a selection of racist bigots, the WASP girl he eventually marries. The real story is Mills' internal struggles – grasping the 'killer' notion of winning, dealing with the attitude of whites, and with the contempt of the Sioux who think he's become white. The examination of Mills' motivation is sketchy, though Benson endows him with a thoroughgoing niceness (runs well, too), and the climax of Mills' athletic career – and of the film – concerns one of the great long distance finals (the 1964 Olympic 10,000 metres), ending in a final lap of unsurpassed drama. Sadly, the staged race does not recapture the excitement of the original. GB

Running Hot (aka Highway to Hell)

(1983, US, 95 min)
d Mark Griffiths. *p* David Colloway. *sc* Mark Griffiths. *ph* Tom Richmond. *ed* Andy Blumenthal. *pd* Katherine Vallin. *m* Al Capps. *cast* Monica Carrico, Eric Stoltz, Stuart Margolin, Richard Bradford, Joe George, Virgil Frye, Sorrells Pickard.

●Sentenced to death for the patricide actually committed by his sexually-abused sister, Stoltz escapes from his escort and reaches the fantasising romantic hooker (Carrico) who has been writing to him in prison. They take off on the run, with the humiliated and vengeful police escort (Margolin) on their heels. Griffiths (his debut as writer/director) knows how to use a camera and set up a scene, but he wrote this for Monica Carrico, and it shows. She's terrific, vibrant, sexy and compelling; but Stoltz, who has all the acting vices of the young Peter Fonda and then some, lacks the resources to overcome the inherent weaknesses of his role, and leaves a gaping hole in the heart of what is otherwise a rather good low-budget movie. An odd piece of miscasting, since everybody else, down to the smallest bits, is superb (especially Pickard as an ex-con). JCo

Running Man, The

(1963, GB, 103 min)
d/p Carol Reed. *sc* John Mortimer. *ph* Robert Krasker. *ed* Bert Bates. *ad* John Stoll. *m* William Alwyn. *cast* Laurence Harvey, Lee Remick, Alan Bates, Felix Aylmer, Eleanor Summerfield, Allan Cuthbertson, Fernando Rey, Fortunio Bonanova.

●Alas, this is no Panavision and colour version of *The Third Man*, despite the teaming of Reed and ace cameraman Robert Krasker. Scripted by John Mortimer (from a novel by Shelley Smith), it's an extremely routine thriller about an insurance swindle, with Harvey as the ne'er-do-well, Remick as his soon disenchanted wife, and Bates as the man from the Pru who smells a rat while on holiday in travel brochure Spain. The scenery takes first place, and you almost expect the dire Anne Gregg to pop up to show Harvey how to buy an orange in the market. ATu

Running Man, The

(1987, US, 101 min)
d Paul Michael Glaser. *p* Tim Zinnemann, George Linder. *sc* Steven E de Souza.

ph Thomas Del Ruth. *ed* Mark Warner, Edward A Warschilka, John Wright. *pd* Jack T Collis. *m* Harold Faltermeyer. *cast* Arnold Schwarzenegger, Maria Conchita Alonso, Yaphet Kotto, Jim Brown, Jesse Ventura, Erland Van Lidth, Marvin J McIntyre, Richard Dawson.

●Pretty warmed-over stuff, this future world of the terminal TV game shows, and director Glaser fails to muster much pace and punch. Lifer Schwarzenegger, framed for a massacre he didn't commit, hops the hutch with fellow con (Kotto), hooks up with love interest (Alonso), and briefly takes refuge with the underground revolutionaries before being betrayed and recaptured. Offered up to the bloodthirsty populace as a sacrificial contestant on TV's *Running Man* show, he is shot down a chute on to the wasteland killing floor to be hunted by big, grotesquely specialised assassins – Buzzsaw, Subzero, Dynamo, Fireball. None is unstoppable, and each is awarded the appropriate jokey payoff line. The film doesn't look good; it's as if the flat lighting and boring set of the TV show had infected everything else. And Big Arnie's quilted outfit makes him look like a duvet. (From the novel by Richard Bachman, i.e. Stephen King.) BC

Running on Empty

(1988, US, 116 min)
d Sidney Lumet. *p* Amy Robinson, Griffin Dunne. *sc* Naomi Foner. *ph* Gerry Fisher. *ed* Andrew Mondshein. *pd* Philip Rosenberg. *m* Tony Mottola. *cast* Christine Lahti, River Phoenix, Judd Hirsch, Jonas Abry, Martha Plimpton, Ed Crowley, LM Kit Carson, Steven Hill, Augusta Dabney.

●Growing up is hard, but the difficulties are compounded for 17-year-old Danny Pope (Phoenix) by the fact that Mom and Dad (Lahti and Hirsch) are still on the run years after their engagement in terrorist action against America's napalm bombing raids on Vietnam. Danny merely wants to come to terms with school, girls, and his talent as a musician, but the Popes' record forces them into a nomadic life spent in rented rooms in various towns. This is a rites of passage movie with a difference, in that it's politically intelligent and never crass. Danny's relationships, with family, girlfriend (Plimpton) and teachers are sensitively handled, while the film's attitude towards the value of radical commitment balanced against individual pain is gently probing. Both acting (particularly Phoenix) and characterisation are top-notch. A film about lives indelibly marked by the past, and by the lies we tell each other just to protect ourselves, it displays the narrative sophistication and ironic grasp of moral and emotional nuances characteristic of Lumet's best work. GA

Running Out of Time

see Dias Contados

Running Scared

(1972, GB, 98 min)
d David Hemmings. *p* Gareth Wigan. *sc* Clive Exton, David Hemmings. *ph* Ernest Day. *ed* Ralph Sheldon. *ad* Bill McCrow. *m* Michael J Lewis. *cast* Robert Powell, Gayle Hunnicutt, Barry Morse, Stephanie Bidmead, Edward Underdown, Maxine Audley, Georgia Brown.

●Hemmings' debut as a director, an odd, Antonioni-ish mood piece, adapted from a novel by Gregory Mcdonald, about a student (Powell) who leaves Cambridge under a cloud because he sat and looked on while his best friend bled to death after slashing his wrists in their rooms. He had no right to interfere, he insists; and the rest of the film is a sort of *crise de conscience* in which, under an assumed name, he seeks self-justification and/or forgiveness in an oblique confrontation with the dead friend's sister (Hunnicutt). Beautifully acted throughout, attractively shot (much of the action takes place around canals and barges), it emerges as a curious mixture of razor-sharp incisiveness (the tentative inquiry into the suicide; a tongue-tied dinner party) and soulfully introspective tedium. TM

Running Scared

(1986, US, 107 min)
d Peter Hyams. *p* David Foster, Lawrence Turman. *sc* Gary DeVore, Jimmy Huston. *ph* Peter Hyams. *ed* James Mitchell. *pd* Albert Brenner. *m* Rod Temperton. *cast* Gregory Hines, Billy Crystal, Steven Bauer, Darlanne Fluegel, Joe Pantoliano, Dan Hedaya, Jonathan Gries, Tracy Reed, Jimmy Smits.

●Following in Eddie Murphy's footsteps, Billy Crystal – another stand-up comedian from TV's *Saturday Night Live* – here patrols Chicago's mean streets in his first feature, teamed with Gregory Hines as a pair of streetwise cops who prefer firing wisecracks to bullets to get them through the day. With four weeks until retirement, all they have to do is stay alive. Unfortunately, evil dope pusher Julio Gonzales (Smits), along with what would appear to be Chicago's entire Hispanic community, is out to get them. With their sloppy slapstick and wet Menudo jokes, one only wonders why more people aren't out to kill them. But Crystal and Hines do flavour the film with genuine warmth, and despite some cheap gags, work well together to produce some truly funny moments. SGo

Run of the Arrow

(1957, US, 85 min)
d/p/sc Samuel Fuller. *ph* Joseph Biroc. *ed* Gene Fowler Jr. *ad* Albert S D'Agostino, Jack Okey. *m* Victor Young. *cast* Rod Steiger, Sarita Montiel, Brian Keith, Ralph Meeker, Jay C Flippen, Charles Bronson, Tim McCoy, Olive Carey.

●With an ostensibly similar narrative and theme to *Lawrence of Arabia*, Fuller's film exhibits all the genuine cinematic intelligence and forcefulness that Lean's so sadly lacks. Here Steiger is the 'victim' of a cultural identity crisis, turning his back on America after the Civil War and being accepted into a Sioux tribe, his sojourn equating in many ways with Lawrence's among the Arabs. A 'mere' genre movie, but its subject is the concept, the ideal and the imperfect reality of the United States; political and psychological reconciliation in the face of hate, prejudice and guilt, vigorously expressed. PT

Run of the Country, The

(1995, Ire, 109 min)
d Peter Yates. *p* Ruth Boswell, Peter Yates. *sc* Shane Connaughton. *ph* Mike Southon. *ed* Paul Hodgson. *pd* Mark Geraghty. *m* Cynthia Miller. *cast* Albert Finney, Matt Keeslar, Victoria Smurfit, Anthony Brophy, David Kelly, Dearbhla Molloy.

●If Gillies MacKinnon's *The Playboys* came closer to Shane Connaughton's portrait of County Cavan village life, it did not supply the star part that Albert Finney simply inhabits in Peter Yates' film of the same writer's novel *The Run of the Country*. They're both small but touching movies, though here Finney's policeman father is so psychologically layered that his magnetic field at times suggests Lear, the Mayor of Casterbridge and Liam O'Flaherty's anguished protagonists. Teenage Danny (Keeslar) finds it impossible to reconcile himself to life with father (Finney) after his mother dies, and moves out to shack up with Prunty (Brophy), the local wide-boy. Danny falls in love with Annagh (Smurfit), gets her pregnant, and falls foul of the local lynch mob. There's a cautious reconciliation with his father, and a realisation that they both suffer similar character deficiencies. Finney's village policeman dreams of the windfall of a murder in place of missing tail-lights, and bitterly resents what Ireland has become after its republican idealism. But the root cause of his frustration is sexual, and this gives great momentum to the clashes with his randy son. BC

Run on Gold, A

see Midas Run

Rupture, La

(1970, Fr/It/Bel, 125 min)
d Claude Chabrol. *p* André Génoves. *sc* Claude Chabrol. *ph* Jean Rabier. *ed* Jacques Gaillard. *ad* Guy Littaye. *m* Pierre Jansen. *cast* Jean-Pierre Cassel, Stéphane Audran, Annie Cordy, Michel Bouquet, Michel Duchaussoy, Marguerite Cassan, Jean-Claude Drouot, Mario David, Catherine Rouvel, Dominique Zardi, Margo Lion.

●Another characteristic Chabrol onslaught on the bourgeois family, which falls chronologically between the warmth of *Le Boucher* and the aridity of *Ten Days' Wonder*, and comprises the usual scrupulous mix of elements chosen to shock with the kind of cinematic references critics feel happy about only in quality movies. The plot comes from a Charlotte Armstrong thriller (*The Balloon Man*), and is loaded with the true stuff of pulp. Sex and dope, for instance, meet in a scene where a subnormal girl is drugged and forced to watch porn movies; earlier, Audran's husband, escalating to schizophrenia with help from interfering in-laws, tries to murder wife and child; while countering these, along with references to Balzac, is a wonderful echo of Murnau's *Sunrise*. What does it all add up to? Essentially, the Chabrol puppet threesome again, but in a different combination this time: a crazy construction that is magical and magnificent, although you may have to look twice to make sure it isn't just crazy.

Rush

(1991, US, 120 min)
d Lili Fini Zanuck. *p* Richard D Zanuck. *sc* Pete Dexter. *ph* Kenneth MacMillan. *ed* Mark Warner. *pd* Paul Sylbert. *m* Eric Clapton. *cast* Jason Patric, Jennifer Jason Leigh, Sam Elliott, Max Perlich, Gregg Allman, Tony Frank, William Sadler, Special K McCray.

●Despite a gritty screenplay by Pete Dexter from Kim Wozencraft's factual book, Zanuck's debut feature fails to keep its dramatic sightlines clear. Perhaps it would take an ironist like the Kurt Vonnegut of *Mother Night* to give us some perspective on the two undercover narcotics cops (Patric and Leigh) who begin to use the stuff heavily as a cover, and blur into the sort of mess they're pledged to eradicate. Set in the unlovely '70s, there's no shortage of going downhill in loons. If the film doesn't cheat, it doesn't stir one to pity either, perhaps because neither lead is sympathetic – both cops pose and mumble – and their love affair on the physical level borders on rape. Leigh simply isn't police material, particularly for Texas. Eric Clapton's music and the presence of a villainous Gregg Allman will be flashcards to those who like that sort of thing. A downer. BC

Rush Hour

(1998, US, 98 min)
d Brett Ratner. *p* Roger Birnbaum, Arthur Sarkissian, Jonathan Glickman. *sc* Jim Kouf, Ross LaManna. *ph* Adam Greenberg. *ed* Mark Helfrich. *pd* Robb Wilson King. *m* Lalo Schifrin. *cast* Jackie Chan, Chris Tucker, Tom Wilkinson, Philip Baker Hall, Mark Rolston, Tzi Ma, Chris Penn, Elizabeth Peña.

●When the daughter of the Chinese consul is kidnapped in America, the consul insists dutiful Hong Kong detective Lee (Chan) should play a part in the investigation. The FBI assume he'll be a nuisance and choose an LAPD cop, shrieky show-off Carter (Tucker), to 'baby-sit'. Lee and Carter see right through the plan. America is embodied by the rebellious, ambitious black man. Dope-smoking black gangsters are also shown to present a minimal threat to the establishment (they should be left in peace, is the implication). Much of the best dialogue, you suspect, was improvised by Tucker and Chan, who seem truly taken with each other and make a delightful, ordinary-extraordinary pair. CO'Su

Rush Hour 2

(2001, US, 90 min)
d Brett Ratner. *p* Arthur Sarkissian, Roger Birnbaum, Jay Stern, Jonathan Glickman. *sc* Jeff Nathanson. *ph* Matthew F Leonetti. *ed* Mark Helfrich. *pd* Terence Marsh. *m* Lalo Schifrin. *cast* Chris Tucker, Jackie Chan, John Lone, Alan King, Chris Penn, Roselyn Sanchez, Harris Yulin, Zhang Ziyi, Don Cheadle.

●Reversing the fish out water *Beverly Hills Cop* routine, helium-voiced Tucker is brought to Hong Kong, cue gags about Asians' lack of stature and the American's imperfect command of Cantonese. The plot involves counterfeit smuggling, with a sketchy revenge motive thrown in. Isn't there a knacker's yard for lame old scenarios like this? If things pick up for the Las Vegas climax, that's down to the stunt choreography being far more imaginative than anything the screenwriters came up with. Except, perhaps, for Tucker's brilliant philosophy of crime detection. 'Follow the rich white man,' he says, cutting to the chase. Certainly it's refreshing to see a Hollywood movie with no concern for white sensibilities. The movie also gets points for its sexy villains: John Lone and *Crouching Tiger*'s Zhang Ziyi, not quite making her English-speaking debut. But the laughs come louder and longer during the end credit out-takes than in the movie proper. TCh

Rushmore

(1998, US, 93 min)
d Wes Anderson. *p* Barry Mendel, Paul Schiff. *sc* Wes Anderson, Owen Wilson. *ph* Robert Yeoman. *ed* David Moritz. *pd* David Wasco. *m* Mark Mothersbaugh. *cast* Bill Murray, Olivia Williams, Jason Schwartzman, Seymour Cassel, Brian Cox, Mason Gamble, Sara Tanaka.

●His grades are so poor he risks being thrown out of school, but Max Fischer (Schwartzman) isn't about to let a academic performance cramp his career at Rushmore Academy. He's editor of the student paper, president of the chess, astronomy, German and French clubs, captain of the fencing and debate teams, and the creative force of the Max Fischer Players. Then there's his unreciprocated passion for Miss Cross (Williams), the new first grade teacher. With the help of his industrialist friend Mr Blume (Murray), Max reckons he can win her heart by constructing an aquarium on the school baseball field. This is a peculiar, poignant comedy, with an outstanding character turn from Murray, but what are we to make of this character, Max, in his beret, braces and blazer? He's part Ferris Bueller, part Jay Gatsby. His class affectations are just that (dad is actually a barber), yet his romantic yearning edges towards psychosis. Bemusing. TCh

Rush to Judgment

(1967, US, 110 min, b/w)
d Emile de Antonio. *p* Emile de Antonio, Mark Lane. *ed* Mark Lane. *with* Mark Lane.

●A documentary on the Kennedy assassination and the Warren Report. Mark Lane proffers the legal brief for the defence of Lee Harvey Oswald he could not give in court and was barred from presenting to the Warren Commission, and develops a compelling point-by-point refutation of the governmental and judicial conclusions on JFK's assassination. Meanwhile, de Antonio is simultaneously presenting a damning indictment of the media's role in shaping the public image of the events of November 1963. His insistence on underlining every cut or dissolve, and buffeting together network and amateur footage, belies the seamlessness of the 'authorised version', the hastily-erected TV consensus which soon had eyewitnesses disbelieving their own evidence, and which rapidly assumed the status of 'reality'. Lane may come to a worthy and credible conclusion, but de Antonio restores the dimension of healthy inconclusiveness; Lane fights selective facts, but more importantly in the long run, de Antonio exposes a selected myth. PT

Russia House, The

(1990, US, 123 min)
d Fred Schepisi. *p* Paul Maslansky, Fred Schepisi. *sc* Tom Stoppard. *ph* Ian Baker. *ed* Peter Honess. *ad* Roger Cain. *m* Jerry Goldsmith. *cast* Sean Connery, Michelle Pfeiffer, Roy Scheider, James Fox, John Mahoney, Michael Kitchen, JT Walsh, Ken Russell, David Threlfall, Klaus Maria Brandauer.

●John Le Carré's far-from-best novel gets the big-bucks treatment: Connery and Pfeiffer in unlikely amorous conjunction; script by the much-employed Tom Stoppard; a strong supporting cast; and ravishing location work in Moscow and Leningrad. Pfeiffer can act, but her assumption of a role for which her pouty glamour is inappropriate – a Russian office-worker seen rubbing shoulders in the bus queues – is a jarring note in a film which brings from Connery, as bluff, incorrigible, jazz-loving publisher Barley Blair, his finest performance in ages. And almost as an antidote to Pfeiffer's restrained Hollywoodness, there is Brandauer, oozing rugged charm and earnestness as the dissident scientist who sets this spy-versus-spy thriller moving. Overtaken by East-West events, and with an over-optimistic ending which sets personal against political loyalty, it's still highly enjoyable, wittily written, and beautiful to behold in places, at others somehow too glossy for its own good. SGr

Russian Ark

(2002, Rus, 96 min)
d Alexander Sokurov. *p* Jens Meuer, Karsten Stöter. *sc* Anatoly Nikiforov, Alexander Sokurov. *ph* Tilman Büttner. *pd* Alexander Sokurov. *m* Sergey Yevtushenko. *cast* Sergey Dreiden, Maria Kuznetsova, Leonid Mozgovoy, David Giorgobiani, Alexander Chaban, Maxim Sergeyev, Natalia Nikulenko, Yuliy Zhurin, Svetlana Svirko, Anna Aleksahina, Vladimir Baranov, Boris Smolkin.

●Despite the almost inevitable longueurs, not to mention mumbling melancholy offscreen comments that sometimes verge on the self-parodic, this is certainly a superior Sokurov feature, and not only for its extraordinarily virtuoso *mise-en-scène*. Digitally shot in a single continuous take, it wanders around St Petersburg's Hermitage, taking in the building, its furnishings and objets d'art, and a host of characters, historical and contemporary, both named (Peter the Great, Catherine the Great, Nicholas, Alexandra, Anastasia) and anonymous, while pondering the Russian soul and its ambivalent relationship with Europe. As the unseen filmmaker and a 19th century French diplomat guide us on our journey through space and time, it's hard not to be distracted by thoughts of how it was all choreographed, but a magnificent ball scene and the final poignant departure manage to work their magic. GA

Russian Roulette

(1975, US, 93 min)
d Lou Lombardo. *p* Jerry Bick. *sc* Tom Ardies, Stanley Mann, Arnold Margolin. *ph* Brian West. *ed* Richard Marden. *ad* Roy Walker. *m* Michael J Lewis. *cast* George Segal, Cristina Raines, Denholm Elliott, Gordon Jackson, Richard Romanus, Bo Brundin, Val Avery, Louise Fletcher, Nigel Stock, Peter Donat.

●With the producers, director, and a number of the cast associated with Robert Altman films, one might have expected something a little more idiosyncratic than this straightforward thriller. Set in Vancouver prior to a visit by Kosygin, the film follows the sudden upsurge of movement by the Russians, the CIA and the Canadian Secret Police around a suspected plot to assassinate the Russian premier. Lombardo handles it all quite comfortably, dealing best with the action set pieces, and getting solid performances from most of the cast, with Segal as reliable as ever as a reluctant recruit to the espionage game.

Russicum

(1987, It, 112 min)
d Pasquale Squitieri. *p* Mario Cecchi Gori, Vittorio Cecchi Gori. *sc* Valerio Riva, Robert Balchus. *ph* Giuseppe Tinelli. *ed* Mauro Bonanni. *ad* Emilio Baldelli. *m* Renato Serio. *cast* F Murray Abraham, Treat Williams, Danny Aiello, Rita Rusic, Luigi Montini, Robert Balchus, Nigel Court, Leopoldo Mastelloni, Rosanno Brazzi.

●An incompetently directed, incredibly tedious espionage thriller set in Rome. Williams is an American embassy official, Abraham a Jesuit priest, and Aiello the US consul: good actors wasted by the execrable process of dubbing. Although in sync, the line readings are all wrong; heavy pauses in mid-sentence, emphasis misplaced, the voices flat and unnatural. Trying to unravel the incomprehensible plot could be dangerous (despite several lengthy explanatory speeches at the end), but it revolves around a planned visit by the Pope to Russia; an unlikely cue for covert shenanigans from glamorous KGB agents, rough CIA men, worldly carabinieri, and Jesuit computer buffs. It's not nearly so much fun as it sounds, although the Gregorian chants are pleasant. TCh

Rust Never Sleeps

(1979, US, 108 min)
d Bernard Shakey [Neil Young]. *p* LA Johnson. *ph* Paul Goldsmith, Jon Else, Robby Greenberg, Hiro Narita, Richard Pearce, Daniel Pearl. *ed* Neil Young. *with* Neil Young and Crazy Horse.

●The film catches Neil Young and backing band Crazy Horse in fine form during the 1979 'Live Rust' tour, and showcases both sides of Young's music, lyrical and abrasive, very satisfyingly indeed for fans. It would be pointless to pretend it's of any interest to the unconverted, despite Young's attempt to inject some cinematic interest with stage props dwarfing the musicians and standing as part of Young's statement about his 'small' place in rock history. But those who consider that his place in the rock pantheon is well deserved will reject the false modesty on display here and simply enjoy. RM

Ruthless

(1948, US, 104 min, b/w)
d Edgar G Ulmer. *p* Arthur S Lyons. *sc* SK Lauren, Gordon Kahn. *ph* Bert Glennon. *ed* Francis D Lyon. *ad* Frank Sylos. *m* Werner Janssen. *cast* Zachary Scott, Louis Hayward, Diana Lynn, Sydney Greenstreet, Lucile Bremer, Martha Vickers, Raymond Burr.

●Often described as Ulmer's *Citizen Kane*, this is, alongside *The Black Cat*, *Bluebeard* and *Detour*, one of the Poverty Row king's very finest films. Given a far better cast and a slightly larger budget than usual, he follows Welles in choosing to view the rise to power of Horace Woodruff Vendig (an admirably cast Scott) through flashbacks which both stress his destructive use of others and refuse to explain his ambitions through clear-cut motivations (although, as with Kane, lost love is hinted at as a subconscious driving force). Indeed, like so many of Ulmer's unsympathetic protagonists, Vendig seems to be a puppet of Fate, a motif perhaps reinforced by the harsh precision of the stark, even *noir*-like visuals. Whether the film is a subversive critique of the American Dream, or merely adheres to the populist sop that wealth necessarily entails loneliness and anxiety, is ambiguous; there is no doubting, however, the effectiveness of Ulmer's pulp poetry, especially in the final scenes when Vendig drowns, choked by Greenstreet's vengeful, ruined Southern tycoon. GA

Ruthless People

(1986, US, 94 min)
d Jim Abrahams, David Zucker, Jerry Zucker. *p* Michael Peyser. *sc* Dale Launer. *ph* Jan DeBont. *ed* Arthur Schmidt. *ad* Don Woodruff. *m* Michael Colombier. *cast* Danny DeVito, Bette Midler, Judge Reinhold, Helen Slater, Anita Morris, Bill Pullman, William G Schilling.

●The *Airplane* team dusts off the old idea of kidnappers abducting someone so obnoxious that no one wants to know. Sleazy garment mogul DeVito is planning how to murder his wife Midler ('I had to live with that squealing, corpulent toad all these years'), when she is bundled away by two young innocents – Slater, designer of the Spandex miniskirt which DeVito stole, and Reinhold, a wimp who sells dodgy hi-fi. It is Midler who sets the tone of prurient sexual hatred, flaring her nostrils and threatening the couple with chainsaw enemas if they don't set her free. With everyone else also deep in sin and sexual blackmail, it's all going splendidly along its nasty route when, alas, the tone shifts three-quarters of the way in, and Midler acquires some of her captors' tedious niceness, conniving with them at the downfall of the baddies. A pity that the directors prove less ruthless than their own creations, but there is more than enough here for people who enjoy murder attempts on cute pet poodles. CPea

Ryaba My Chicken

see Riaba Ma Poule

Ryan's Daughter

(1970, GB, 206 min)
d David Lean. *p* Anthony Havelock-Allan. *sc* Robert Bolt. *ph* Freddie Young. *ed* Norman Savage. *pd* Stephen Grimes. *m* Maurice Jarre. *cast* Sarah Miles, Robert Mitchum, Trevor Howard, Christopher Jones, John Mills, Leo McKern, Barry Foster.

●An awe-inspiringly tedious lump of soggy romanticism, set in Ireland amid the Troubles of 1916, but with much of the action centring on clifftop and beach, where the characters tend to congregate either to have sex or to brood about not having it, and where the wind and waves have a pathetically fallacious time of it. Pert Rosy Ryan (Miles), as Trevor Howard's wise old Father Collins knows, isn't one to settle for just any old lad from the village. So she marries the kindly, prosaically middle-aged schoolteacher (Mitchum), but is soon prancing into the woods with a dashingly battle-scarred English officer (Jones), to dally while spiderwebs glisten, dandelion puffballs flutter away in the soughing winds, and so forth. Banal, utterly predictable, ludicrously overblown, it drags on interminably, with our heroine finally getting her comeuppance by being accused (falsely) of betraying the Nationalist cause and having her hair cut off by a flock of rhubarbing peasants. TM

S

Shrek

Saadia

(1953, US, 82 min)
d/p/sc Albert Lewin. *ph* Christopher Challis. *ed* Harold F Kress. *ad* John Hawkesworth. *m* Bronislau Kaper. *cast* Cornel Wilde, Mel Ferrer, Rita Gam, Michel Simon, Cyril Cusack, Wanda Rotha, Marne Maitland, Peter Bull.

●Lewin's weakest film, which he adapted from a French novel (*Echec au destin* by Francis D'Autheville), is set in Morocco and deals with the efforts of a Parisian doctor (Ferrer), abetted by the progressive, French-educated Caid (Wilde), to stamp out witch-doctoring in the villages. He begins with a successful field operation on lovely young Saadia (Gam), popularly believed to be possessed by devils, for acute appendicitis; whereupon the evil Fatima (Rotha) sharpens up her spells to conjure vengeful demons. You can see why Lewin wanted to make it, since the doctor's sceptical stance allows Lewin to pursue his own scholarly preoccupation with the rational foundations of myth and superstition. But the plot is a fine old farrago, choppily strung and drained of all credibility by the pot-pourri cast: Michel Simon as a bandit chief, Cusack as a wise old *mullah*, Wilde and Gam as Hollywood hero and heroine, Ferrer about as expressive as a block of wood. Some fascinating details, and good camerawork (Christopher Challis) where crude colour processing permits. TM

Sábado

see Saturday

Sabata (Ehi, Amico...C'è Sabata, hai chiuso!)

(1969, It, 106 min)
d Frank Kramer [Gianfranco Parolini]. *p* Alberto Grimaldi. *sc* Renato Izzo, Gianfranco Parolini. *ph* Sandro Mancori. *ed* Edmondo Lozzi. *ad* Carlo Simi. *m* Marcello Giombini. *cast* Lee Van Cleef, William Berger, Franco Ressel, Linda Veras, Pedro Sanchez, Gianni Rizzi.

●This flamboyant spaghetti Western comes with acrobats, bearded knife-wielding drunks, a strolling minstrel with a banjo which doubles as a gun, pantomime villains and standard virtuoso gunplay. Van Cleef, all in black, looks mean and surly, but this doesn't stop him from standing up for the Texas small folk whose livelihoods are threatened by rapacious railroad tycoons. The sound editing is ludicrous, the costumes are absurdly gaudy, performances come close to caricature and the dubbing is always noticeable, but that doesn't lessen the entertainment value one jot. GM

Sabotage

(1936, GB, 76 min, b/w)
d Alfred Hitchcock. *p* Michael Balcon, Ivor Montagu. *sc* Charles Bennett. *ph* Bernard Knowles. *ed* Charles Frend. *ad* Albert Jullion. *cast* Oscar Homolka, Sylvia Sidney, John Loder, Desmond Tester, Joyce Barbour, Martita Hunt, Peter Bull, Torin Thatcher.

●One of the most playful of Hitchcock's British thrillers, this was adapted by Charles Bennett from Joseph Conrad's novel *The Secret Agent*, which in fact had been the title of Hitch's previous film. The foreign saboteur at large in London is cinema-owner Homolka, and in part at least, his profession allows Hitchcock to indulge in the sort of movie-movie self-consciousness of which he would become the object some 40 years on. The film proceeds from the point where the lights go out (Battersea power station is the first sabotage target), and even includes a telling screen-within-a-screen homage to Disney and the *Silly Symphonies*. The narrative's a bit perfunctory, but is neatly overbalanced by the joyously rule-breaking sequence of a boy, a bus and a time bomb. PT

Saboteur

(1942, US, 109 min, b/w)
d Alfred Hitchcock. *p* Frank Lloyd. *sc* Peter Viertel, Joan Harrison, Dorothy Parker. *ph* Joseph Valentine. *ed* Otto Ludwig. *ad* Jack Otterson. *m* Frank Skinner. *cast* Robert Cummings, Priscilla Lane, Norman Lloyd, Otto Kruger, Alan Baxter, Alma Kruger.

●A trial run for *North by Northwest*, though lacking the thematic resonances, with the innocent hero (Cummings) on the run after being framed as a saboteur in the munitions factory where he works, and trying to get the Nazi agents before the police get him. A little on the bland side in its two leads, though suave Kruger and sweaty Lloyd compensate with their vivid villainies. Lots of echoes of earlier British Hitchcock, plus the charmingly bizarre encounter with the caravan-load of circus freaks, the charity ball from which there appears to be no exit, and the classic climax atop the Statue of Liberty. TM

Sabrina

(1995, US, 127 min)
d Sydney Pollack. *p* Scott Rudin, Sydney Pollack. *sc* Barbara Benedek, David Rayfiel. *ph* Giuseppe Rotunno. *ed* Frederick Steinkamp. *pd* Brian Morris. *m* John Williams. *cast* Harrison Ford, Julia Ormond, Greg Kinnear, Nancy Marchand, John Wood, Richard Crenna, Angie Dickinson, Fanny Ardant.

●There's the touch of a dead hand on this remake of Billy Wilder's romantic tale of a love between April bloom and late September, but it doesn't flatten it completely. Trouble is, disbelief is never suspended. In Pollack's film, one's always aware that Ford (workaholic mega-corporation boss Linus) is competing with Humphrey Bogart; and Ormond (his servant's gawky daughter Sabrina, moonstruck since her puppy days on his playboy brother David) has the inimitable Audrey Hepburn dogging her tracks. As a cure for her infatuation, Sabrina's despatched to Paris as an assistant on *Vogue* – a whirl through famous landmarks, berets and Piaf – and returns a damned Pretty Woman, sporting a makeover so complete that David doesn't recognise the chauffeur's daughter. When David, engaged to a rival billionaire's daughter, falls for this Cinderella, Linus must take action to secure the merger. Ormond's face is certainly not hard to gaze at, but she looks so often ill at ease that her 'confident' gay smiles suggest, inappropriately, some masked pyschological distress. Likewise, Ford's hard, impassive demeanour takes an age to warm up, almost past the patience point. WH

Sabrina (aka Sabrina Fair)

(1954, US, 114 min, b/w)
d/p Billy Wilder. *sc* Billy Wilder, Samuel Taylor, Ernest Lehman. *ph* Charles Lang Jr. *ed* Arthur P Schmidt. *ad* Hal Pereira, Walter Tyler. *m* Frederick Hollander. *cast* Humphrey Bogart, Audrey Hepburn, William Holden, John Williams, Walter Hampden, Martha Hyer, Marcel Dalio, Francis X Bushman.

●Bogart plays a cold-hearted tycoon whose sole companion in life is *The Wall Street Journal*. Holden is his wastrel brother, and Hepburn the chauffeur's daughter. Yes, you've guessed what happens. Holden fools around with her, she attempts suicide, is sent to France for a cookery course, returns to melt Bogart's heart, and Holden is left to chair the board. Getting to this characteristic Wilder reversal of roles is romantic, funny and astringent all at the same time. Bogart is the man of plastic – he doesn't burn, melt or scorch – and Wilder satirises him and his ideals ruthlessly. Bogart's age here is crucial: he looks like an undertaker who has sidestepped the youth which Hepburn will give him. The golden boy Holden is the other extreme and equally ridiculous, driving around in his snazzy cars, coerced into a marriage between corporations, and forced to sit on some champagne glasses, enabling Bogart to sort out the Hepburn problem. It's a Cinderella story that gets turned on its head, a satire about breaking down class and emotional barriers (neatly signified in the array of window and glass imagery), and a confrontation between New World callousness and Old World humanity. ATu

Sabrina Fair

see Sabrina

Sac de Billes, Un (A Bag of Marbles)

(1975, Fr, 99 min)
d Jacques Doillon, *sc* Jacques Doillon, Denis Ferraris. *ph* Yves Lafaye. *ed* Noëlle Boisson. *ad* Christian Lamarque. *m* Philippe Sarde. *cast* Richard Constantini, Paul-Eric Schulmann, Joseph Goldenberg, Reine Bartève, Michel Robin, Dieter Schidor.

●Doillon's facility for extracting astonishing, apparently spontaneous performances from child players presumably explains his involvement in this adaptation of Joseph Joffo's autobiographical best-seller, describing the experiences of a Jewish family during the Occupation. Always on the move, pretending to be Catholic, to be Algerian, splitting up and reuniting, never safe: the family's adventures are nothing if not affecting. But for Doillon, with his evident loathing of 'big scenes' and push-button responses, the film becomes an exercise in deflection, with all the obvious drama pushed into the background, the children's games and fantasies or a confusion over some orange juice taking precedence over Nazis, police raids and so on. The material may have been uncongenial, but Doillon does his honourable best by it. BBa

Sacred Flesh

(1999, GB, 75 min)
d Nigel Wingrove. *p* Louise Ross. *sc* Nigel Wingrove. ph Chris Herd, James MacDonald, Geoff Mills. *ed* Chris Shaw, Jake West. *ad* Nigel Wingrove. *m* Steve Pittis, Band of Pain. *cast* Sally Tremaine, Moyna Cope, Simon Hill, Kristina Bill, Rachel Taggart, Eileen Daly, Daisy Weston, Moses Rockman, Emily Booth, Willow.

●Nigel Wingrove's earlier short, *Visions of Ecstasy*, was banned in Britain as blasphemous. Mother Superior Elizabeth (Daly) lies in her convent tower. Amid her crucifixes, she tries to reconcile her sexual urges and her divine calling. Her vows are threatened by a crisis of faith, her yearnings are too much for her, and, in her hallucinations, she protests her virtue and virginity to Mary Magdalene, playing devil's advocate. Mother Superior's torment is intercut with her fantasies, cue dolled-up 'nuns' pleasuring themselves and each other with crucifixes. AL

Sacrifice

(1998, US, 50 min)
d Ellen Bruno, Hseng Noung Litner. *p/ph* Ellen Bruno.

●An unusual and impressive documentary on the plight of young girls from the Burmese hill tribes, seduced away from their villages in alarming numbers to the fleshpots of Thailand. Most have no conception of what awaits them. Bruno gets remarkably frank, moving interviews from the girls, and frames the film as a poetic, impressionistic essay – video images seldom look this evocative. TCh

Sacrifice, The (Offret)

(1986, Swe/Fr, 149 min, b/w & col)
d Andrei Tarkovsky. *p* Katinka Farago. *sc* Andrei Tarkovsky. *ph* Sven Nykvist. *ed* Andrei Tarkovsky, Michael Leszczylowski. *ad* Anna Asp. *m* JS Bach. *cast* Erland Josephson, Susan Fleetwood, Valérie Mairesse, Allan Edwall, Gudrún Gísladóttir.

●In a house on the south Swedish coast, a retired actor and critic (Josephson) holds court over an unfaithful wife (Fleetwood), a moody daughter, an unpleasant doctor (the wife's lover), and various other eccentrics. Midway through their peculiar meditations, the unthinkable happens — an announcement of doom from the TV, and the end of the world is nigh. The man then makes a pact with the Almighty that he will sacrifice himself, and all that he is, if only the world is restored to its former condition. In Tarkovsky's elliptical and visionary world, the outcome is indeterminate; but the opening condition of fear and the later weight of prayer are as palpable as a roll of distant thunder. No one else can approach his sense of the Apocalyptic. His death leaves a gaping hole in the cinema of spiritual quest. CPea

Sacrificed Youth (Qingchun Ji)

(1985, China, 96 min)
d Zhang Nuanxin. *p* Zhao Yamin. *sc* Zhang Nuanxin. *ph* Mu Deyuan, DengWei. *ed* Zhao Qihua. *ad* Li Yonxin, Wang Yanjin. *m* Liu Suola, Qu Xiaosong. *cast* Li Fengxu, Feng Yuanzheng, Song Tao, Guo Jianguo, Yu Da.

●A lyrical, elegiac tale about the generation of students banished to remote agricultural regions of China during the Cultural Revolution. 17-year-old Li Chun, a shy, even repressed Han girl from Beijing, is sent to work in a small village in the Dai countryside, down near Laos. At first disdainful of the natives' rural superstitions and poverty, only slowly does she overcome her outsider status and learn the value of the Dais' appreciation of beauty, nature and human warmth. An unsentimental celebration of tradition, exotic landscape and cultural independence, Zhang's film is both a loving portrait of Dai life and a sensitive, partly autobiographical study of one girl's hesitant awakening to sensuality. Infused with a discreet, gentle eroticism and a final, touching sense of loss, it charms through its narrative simplicity and visual elegance. GA

Saddle the Wind

(1958, US, 84 min)
d Robert Parrish. *p* Armand Deutsch. *sc* Rod Serling. *ph* George Folsey. *ed* John McSweeney. *ad* William A Horning, Malcolm Brown. *m* Jeff Alexander. *cast* Robert Taylor, Julie London, John Cassavetes, Donald Crisp, Charles McGraw, Royal Dano, Richard Erdman, Ray Teal.

● As contemporary reviewers mockingly noted, Cassavetes brings an inescapable tang of Method juvenile delinquency to the old West, which doesn't prevent this Western (scripted by Rod Serling) from being way above par. He plays a youth brought up since childhood by a much older brother (Taylor), now a rancher but hero-worshipped in the boy's memory as a once-feared gunslinger; Taylor changed under the influence of his own father-figure, a puritanically upright cattle baron (Crisp); and Cassavetes conceives it as his role to protect the protector he now sees as grown old and weak. He hones himself as a fast draw, but in so doing unleashes a mad dog killer instinct in himself... Parrish handles both action and relationships with great fluency and flair, bringing off moments of genuine inspiration: as Cassavetes obsessively practises his gun-slinging, for instance, he impulsively fires at his own reflection in a pool, gazing awe-struck as the human image abruptly shatters. Julie London is striking in an underdeveloped role as a saloon singer, shyly picked by Cassavetes as a bride, then standing helplessly by as Jekyll turns into Hyde; and there are stand-out cameos from McGraw, Dano and Erdman. TM

Sade

(2000, Fr, 100 min)
d Benoît Jacquot. *p* Patrick Godeau. *sc* Jacques Fieschi. *ph* Benoît Delhomme. *ed* Luc Barnier. *pd* Sylvain Chauvelot. *m* Francis Poulenc. *cast* Daniel Auteuil, Marianne Denicourt, Jeanne Balibar, Grégoire Colin, Isild Le Besco, Jean-Pierre Cassel, Philippe Duquesne, Vincent Branchet, Raymond Gérome.

● Although very different from Kaufman's *Quills*, Jacquot's film also focuses on an aging and incarcerated marquis, this time on the orders of Robespierre, in a country house run like a hotel for the enemies of the Republic. Here, however, the infamous libertine is portrayed as a free thinker and convivial, erudite intellectual. At the climax he deflowers a virgin of noble birth by proxy, and insists he's whipped for it, but that's the only remotely salacious sequence in a reasonably engrossing, well acted if underwhelming drama. TCh

Sadie Thompson

(1928, US, 97 min, b/w)
d Raoul Walsh. *p* Gloria Swanson. *sc* Raoul Walsh. *ph* Oliver T Marsh, George Barnes, Robert Kurrle. *ed* C Gardner Sullivan. *ad* William Cameron Menzies. *cast* Gloria Swanson, Lionel Barrymore, Raoul Walsh, Blanche Frederici, James Marcus, Charles Lane.

● The first of three adaptations of Somerset Maugham's novella (the others were Lewis Milestone's *Rain* and Curtis Bernhardt's *Miss Sadie Thompson*), Walsh's late silent movie profited from the absence of dialogue to avoid some of the inevitable censorship problems. Sadie, a prostitute escaping prosecution in San Francisco, lands up on a South Pacific island where she finds a sympathetic sailor lover (played by Walsh himself), but is threatened with deportation by a reformer – a priest in the novella – whose feelings towards her are not entirely spiritual. Walsh's version is high on atmosphere and vitality, though sadly the final reel has been lost, and a restoration has had to resort to stills to reach the conclusion. DT

Sadistic City (Ma-o Gai)

(1993, Jap, 88 min)
d Ryuichi Hiroki. *m* John Zorn. *cast* Tomoro Taguchi, Haku Ryu, Sakurako Akino, Rena Hirota, Rie Kondo.

● Another unheralded wonder from the bizarre sub-culture of Japanese sex movies. Kishi (Taguchi from the *Tetsuo* films) is a timid salaryman, married with one neglected daughter. His one-time classmate Daimon (Haku Ryu, looking more like Christopher Walken than ever) singles him out for what seems to be an experiment in psycho-sexual damage. Daimon transforms Kishi's life by offering kinky sexual encounters with his own girlfriend – but then wants disturbing reciprocal favours. Backed by a great John Zorn score, Hiroki's ultra-sheer visual style turns Tokyo into an elegant fantasy city, bursting with perversity and paranoia. Just the thing to erase unhappy memories of Polanski's *Bitter Moon*. TR

Safe

(1995, US, 118 min)
d Todd Haynes. *p* Christine Vachon, Lauren Zalaznick. *sc* Todd Haynes. *ph* Alex Nepomniaschy. *ed* James Lyons. *pd* David Bomba. *m* Ed Tomney. *cast* Julianne Moore, Xander Berkeley, Dean Norris, Julie Burgess, Peter Friedman, Susan Norman, James LeGros, Jessica Harper.

● A superbly ditzy Julianne Moore plays Carol White, a San Fernando Valley housewife whose closeted middle-class existence results in multiple allergies, a nervous breakdown and her eventual absorption into a 'New Age' retreat for the socially dysfunctional. Haynes' earlier films include a life of Karen Carpenter featuring animated Bardie Dolls and the stylistically splintered *Poison*. Here, he again beats his own path in terms of genre and tone, but his stance is so coolly detached that one's left at the end in a state of deliberate uncertainty about whether Carol quits or finds a 'safe' life. The ironic handling of decor and characterisation builds an eerie portrait of the blissed-out West Coast bourgeoisie at their most brainwashed. DT

Safe Men

(1998, US, 88 min)
d John Hamburg. *p* Andrew Hauptman, Ellen Bonfman, Jeffrey Clifford, Jonathan Cohen. *sc* John Hamburg. *ph* Michael Barrett. *ed* Suzanne Pillsbury, Scott Smith. *pd* Anthony Gasparro. *m* Theodore Shapiro. *cast* Sam Rockwell, Steve Zahn, Mark Ruffalo, Josh Pais, Paul Giamatti, Christina Kirk, Michael Lerner, Harvey Fierstein.

● Providence, RI. After yet another disappointing gig ('it is a Polish tradition to express appreciation through silence'), shambolic musicians Sam (Rockwell) and Eddie (Zahn) are feted at a bar by one Veal Chop (Giamatti), a fellow incompetent, who's recruiting safe crackers for his gangster boss Big Fat Bernie (Lerner). Pressed into service, the boys are happily surprised to be credited with the jobs they singularly failed to pull off. As it happens, Veal Chop's intended targets (Pais and Ruffalo) are busily and smoothly tidying up across town. Writer/director John Hamburg's first feature is a sympathetic study of bumbling underachievers, apparently aiming at low key comedy in the vein of *Palookaville*. In fact, it's so easy-going it barely stands up. Little attempt is made to hide the contrivances of the plot, and the film's sketchy narrative and an oddly unresolved finale undermine the better points, which include a relaxed, good-natured cast and several amusing conversational detours. NB

Safe Passage

(1994, US, 98 min)
d Robert Allan Ackerman. *p* Gale Anne Hurd. *sc* Deena Goldstone. *ph* Ralf Bode. *ed* Rick Shaine. *ad* Dan Bishop. *m* Mark Isham. *cast* Susan Sarandon, Sam Shepard, Nick Stahl, Marcia Gay Harden, Robert Sean Leonard, Sean Astin, Matt Keeslar.

● Though she's seen all but one of her seven sons grow up and leave home, Mag Singer (Sarandon) still has sufficiently strong maternal impulses to get in a blind funk every time she has a dream she thinks is a premonition of danger; she'll even ring her reluctantly estranged husband (Shepard) about her anxieties. However, just as she and 14-year-old Simon are about to move out of the family home, one of Mag's 'signs' proves true: Percival, who'd become so tired of life at home that he'd joined the Marines, is feared dead after a terrorist bomb at his Sinai barracks. Cue for the rest of the family to gather to work over old resentments, rivalries, loyalties and memories. Despite sturdy performances (the sons include Leonard and Astin), this film, from a novel by Ellyn Bache, is a tepid, dispiriting effort. A tidy, small-town world is on display. Irritations are minor and all, ultimately, forgivable. Everyone, however outcast they may sometimes feel, has a place and function in the grand familial scheme of things. The metaphors – notably Shepard's incipient blindness – are flagged, and the whole thing's a string of clichés. GA

Safe Place, A

(1971, US, 92 min)
d Henry Jaglom. *p* Bert Schneider. *sc* Henry Jaglom. *ph* Dick Kratina. *ed* Pieter Bergema. *cast* Tuesday Weld, Jack Nicholson, Orson Welles, Philip Proctor, Gwen Welles.

● Jaglom's first feature is a non-narrative fairy story of the emotional vulnerabilities of a young New York girl. Her yearning for past innocence reflects in her relations with a magician of uncertain powers, and in her interweaving fantasy around the two men who serve but can't fulfil her needs. Although a psychological reading is there for the taking, the film also offers a lament on the cinema's loss of magic. The nostalgic songs, the conspicuous presence of Orson Welles as the magician, show how much its roots lie in the past, while the film's experimental structure reveals the impossibility of trying to recapture that past. Despite the non-linear development, Jaglom's composition is sufficiently coherent, and Tuesday Weld's performance adds a real focus point. The result is sometimes indulgent, often fragile, and occasionally enchanting. With Welles as presiding spirit, it's also funnier than you might expect. CPe

Safety Last

(1923, US, 77 min, b/w)
d Fred Newmeyer, Sam Taylor. *p* Harold Lloyd. *sc* Harold Lloyd, Sam Taylor, Tim Whelan, Hal Roach. *ph* Walter Lundin. *ed* Thomas J Crizer. *ad* Fred Guiol. *cast* Harold Lloyd, Mildred Davis, Bill Strothers, Noah Young, Westcott B Clarke, Mickey Daniels.

● One of the best of Lloyd's thrill-comedies, developing the precarious perch-clinging scenes in earlier shorts like *High and Dizzy* and the stunning *Never Weaken*. If he steered clear of the cloying sentimentality that characterised Chaplin and Langdon, Lloyd nevertheless lacked the narrative and visual ambitions that made Keaton a truly great director/comedian. That said, the clock-hanging climax that caps this generally charming tale of a country boy out to make his fortune in the big city – having suggested a high-rise climb as a publicity stunt for the store where he is employed, he finds himself forced to substitute when the real 'human fly' proves otherwise engaged – is a superb example of his ability to mix suspense and slapstick. GA

Saga of Anatahan, The (Anatahan)

(1953, Jap, 90 min, b/w)
d Josef von Sternberg. *p* K Takimura. *sc/ph* Josef von Sternberg. *ed* Mitsuzo Miyata. *ad* Kono. *m* Akira Ifukube. *cast* Akemi Negishi, Tadashi Suganuma, Kisaburo Sawamura, Shoji Nakayama, Jun Fujikawa. *narrator* Josef von Sternberg.

● Sternberg's last film was made in a Japanese studio, and drawn from a factual incident: a dozen Japanese merchant seamen were shipwrecked on Anatahan in 1944, and found a man and woman living on the island; by the time they were persuaded that World War II was over, in 1951, five men had died in fights over the woman. If the material is fascinating, the treatment is just amazing. Sternberg respects what's known of the historical truth, but uses it as a point of entry to darker, more dangerous areas. Sequences of dream-like abstraction and images of staggering beauty are recognisably the work of the man who created the image of Marlene Dietrich, but here they go way beyond Hollywood evasions and compromises. The surface perfection seems a little remote at first sight, but the film works subversively by implicating its audience in the patterns of desire and violence, discipline and surrender. It's brilliant. When was the last time you felt stark naked after a movie? TR

Sahara

(1943, US, 97 min, b/w)
d Zoltan Korda. *p* Harry Joe Brown. *sc* John Howard Lawson, Zoltan Korda. *ph* Rudolph Maté. *ed* Charles Nelson. *ad* Lionel Banks, Eugène Lourié. *m* Miklós Rozsa. *cast* Humphrey Bogart, Bruce Bennett, Lloyd Bridges, Rex Ingram, Dan Duryea, J Carrol Naish, Kurt Kreuger.

● WWII actioner in which Bogart's tank corps sergeant, retreating from El Alamein, picks up a motley crew of stragglers and survivors of assorted creeds and colours, who band together to defend a desert well against 500 Germans. Watchable more for its strong cast than for its credibility or its pretensions: the script was adapted from a Russian movie called *The Thirteen* by John Howard Lawson (one of the Hollywood Ten), who saw the mixed ethnic group as an allegory of brotherhood. TM

Sahara

(1983, US, 111 min)
d Andrew V McLaglen. *p* Menahem Golan, Yoram Globus. *sc* James R Silke. *ph* David Garfinkel, Armando Nannuzzi. *ed* Michael J Duthie. *pd* Luciano Spadoni. *m* Ennio Morricone. *cast* Brooke Shields, Lambert Wilson, Horst Buchholz, John Rhys-Davies, Ronald Lacey, Cliff Potts, Perry Lang, John Mills, Steve Forrest.

● This isn't as bad as one might expect. Brooke Shields as Dale Gordon, a leggy little rich girl attempting to fulfil her dead daddy's dream by winning a trans-Sahara car race, is bound to attract some cheap jokes. Yet although an ugly crier and an indifferent actress, Shields throws herself into the part with gusto, doing many of her own stunts and suggesting that, given the right script, she would work real hard to be more than just a pretty face. But this isn't the right script, and everyone is just a pretty face, including Lambert Wilson as the dashing sheik who takes her in his strong arms. McLaglen marshals his desert scenery well, and the plot almost manages to hold one's attention much of the time. It really isn't as bad as one might expect; but then expectations raised by this sand-strewn romantic adventure, inspired by the Prime Minister's son driving a fast car into the middle of Africa and getting lost, barely reached ankle height. FD

Saigon

see Off Limits

Sailor Beware (aka Panic in the Parlor)

(1956, GB, 86 min, b/w)
d Gordon Parry. *p* Jack Clayton. *sc* Philip King, Falkland L Cary. *ph* Douglas Slocombe. *ed* Stanley Hawkes. *ad* Norman Arnold. *m* Peter Akister. *cast* Peggy Mount, Shirley Eaton, Ronald Lewis, Gordon Jackson, Cyril Smith, Thora Hird, Esma Cannon, Alfie Bass.

● Much-loved British character actress Peggy Mount got her film break when the stage farce (by Philip King and Falkland Cary) that she'd made a huge success transferred to the big screen. She dominates the proceedings as the potential mother-in-law from hell, who gives sailor Lewis a major attack of cold feet when he realises just what he's getting into with his plans to marry fiancée Eaton. This being a '50s British movie though, it turns out she's not as bad as all that, just misunderstood. Hits you right there, doesn't it? TJ

Sailor from Gibraltar, The

(1966, GB, 91 min, b/w)
d Tony Richardson. *p* Oscar Lewenstein, Neil Hartley. *sc* Christopher Isherwood, Don Magner, Tony Richardson. *ph* Raoul Coutard. *ed* Bill Blunden. *ad* Marilena Aravantinou. *m* Antoine Duhamel. *cast* Jeanne Moreau, Ian Bannen, Vanessa Redgrave, Orson Welles, Zia Mohyeddin, Hugh Griffith, Umberto Orsini, John Hurt.

● Highfalutin nonsense adapted (though not so you would notice) from a Marguerite Duras novel. Bannen plays an English registry office clerk on holiday in Italy, bored by his life and a mistress (Redgrave) who keeps shepherding him off to art museums. In search of he knows not what, he takes up with a mysterious Frenchwoman (Moreau) who sails the seas in her yacht searching for the lover – a sailor from Gibraltar – with whom she experienced perfect happiness until he disappeared. The sailor, it seems, is symbolic of something everyone needs but doesn't usually find; so when Moreau and Bannen decide they are madly in love after sailing about the world a bit, she stops worrying about the sailor. Encounters *en route* with assorted enigmatic characters bring more loony tunes, none more so than Orson Welles, grubbily impersonating one Louis from Mozambique, since you can't understand a word he says. The whole film, in fact, seems to be coming filtered through cotton-wool. In the circumstances, Raoul Coutard's camerawork isn't half bad. TM

Sailor's Return, The

(1978, GB, 112 min)
d Jack Gold. *p* Otto Plaschkes. *sc* James Saunders. *ph* Brian Trufano. *ed* Michael Taylor. *ad* Carmen Dillon. *m* Carl Davis. *cast* Tom Bell, Shope Shodeinde, Mick Ford, Paola Dionisotti, George Costigan, Clive Swift, Ray Smith, Ivor Roberts, Bernard Hill.

● Originally intended for cinema release, this independently-produced feature finally surfaced on TV. Every frame looks like a movie, with detail and composition in depth only possible in 35 mm. But that, Tom Bell's typically strong performance, and Mick Ford's exuberant support, are as much as there is to be enthusiastic about. As a tale from the mid-19th century, with an English master mariner bringing home a black princess as his wife, it's curiously devoid of any contemporary resonance. Scripted by James Saunders from David Garnett's 1924 novel, it seems confused and naive in its treatment of the racism the couple encounter in a sleepy Dorset village. Religion and an awareness of class are seen to form attitudes, but there's no real sense of a historical context. An awareness of the vital element of imperialism is entirely lacking, so the supposed plea for a multi-racial society seems, to be charitable, only muddle-headed. JW

Sailor Who Fell from Grace with the Sea, The

(1976, GB, 105 min)
d Lewis John Carlino. *p* Martin Poll. *sc* Lewis John Carlino. *ph* Douglas Slocombe. *ed* Antony Gibbs. *pd* Ted Haworth. *m* John Mandel. *cast* Sarah Miles, Kris Kristofferson, Jonathan Kahn, Margo Cunningham, Earl Rhodes, Paul Tropea.

● A farcically misconceived attempt to transplant Yukio Mishima's engagingly perverse novel to an English setting, and to make its peculiarly Japanese psychology and motivations work with a set of improbable Anglo-American characters. The two main strands of plot (genteel but sex-starved widow falls for sailor who's ready to quit the sea; teenage son gets hooked on the Dangerous Ideas of the school bully and his gang) remain obstinately unrelated, and both swing wildly between inept naturalism and half-assed melodrama; the whole thing is shot like a cross between a travelogue and a substandard '50s weepie. Writer-director Carlino first castrates the book by betraying both its tone and its meaning, but then tries to compensate by introducing bits of would-be nastiness (an exploding seagull!) and scenes of would-be daring (Miles and Kristofferson discreetly nude). The result is more depressing than amusing, an insult to any audience. TR

Saint, The

(1997, US, 116 min)
d Phillip Noyce. *p* David Brown, Robert Evans, William J MacDonald, Mace Neufeld. *sc* Jonathan Hensleigh, Wesley Strick, Terry Hayes. *ph* Philip Meheux. *ed* Terry Rawlings. *pd* Joseph C Nemec III. *m* Graeme Revell. *cast* Val Kilmer, Elisabeth Shue, Rade Serbedzija, Valery Nikolaev, Henry Goodman.

● This glossy action picture bears little resemblance to the '60s British TV series on which it's based. Simon Templar, multi-faceted thief turned rescue-hero, is suffering an identity crisis: you can tell by the frequency with which he changes persona. Thankfully, a tough upbringing has prepared him for a world full of megalomaniacs like Ivan Tretiak (Serbedzija), a corporate boss with an eye on the presidency of the new Russian Empire. Ivan needs something to get the public vote: the fusion formula discovered by British scientist Dr Emma Russell (Shue). Emma takes Templar to her bosom, where, conveniently, she keeps the equations to her theory. Cue more improbablities than *Mission Impossible.* Kilmer has the Templar face, but not the charm. Eminently forgettable. DA

St Ann's

(1969, GB, 47 min, b/w)
d Stephen Frears. *p* Ian Martin. *ph* Mike Fash. *ed* Beryl Wilkins. *m* Carl Davis.

● The St Ann's district of Nottingham has two cinematic associations. In 1899 it was the birthplace of Alma Reville, future writer and wife of Alfred Hitchcock; and almost a lifetime later, after the place had become a sodden, peeling slum and its narrow Toytown streets were being demolished brick by brick, Stephen Frears, leading-British-director-to-be, then the merest tyro, showed up to record an anomaly, as it seems in retrospect – the poverty-stricken '30s still persisting alongside the swinging '60s. Frears' directorial tone (lucid, unsentimental, unassertive) is displayed here already fully formed, ensuring that the piece has hardly dated at all, except for the style of deprivation being recorded. BBa

St Elmo's Fire

(1985, US, 108 min)
d Joel Schumacher. *p* Lauren Shuler Donner. *sc* Joel Schumacher, Carl Kurlander. *ph* Stephen H Burum. *ed* Richard Marks. *ad* William Sandell. *m* David Foster. *cast* Emilio Estevez, Rob Lowe, Andrew McCarthy, Demi Moore, Judd Nelson, Ally Sheedy, Mare Winningham, Martin Balsam, Joyce Van Patten.

● This definitive Brat Pack movie, a yuppie coming-of-age yarn, is co-written and directed by Joel Schumacher – all, perhaps, anyone really needs to know. But still, filling in the blanks, it's a portrait, drawn in crayon, of a group of friends in Washington, DC, recently graduated from college, but light years from maturity, struggling to cope with the fragilities of their relationships and the complexities of what MTV later termed The Real World. Estevez and Nelson are as unappealing here as in *The Breakfast Club*, though in fairness they're hampered by a script that seems to despise its characters. So, by the end, will you. WFJ

Saint-Ex

(1995, GB, 86 min)
d Anand Tucker. *p* David Johnson. *sc* Frank Cottrell-Boyce. *ph* David Johnson. *ed* Peter Webber. *m* Barrington Pheloung. *cast* Bruno Ganz, Miranda Richardson, Janet McTeer, Ken Scott, Katrin Cartlidge, Brid Brennan, Eleanor Bron.

● A biographical reverie on the life of Antoine de Saint-Exupéry (1900-44) that makes a virtue of a limited budget. The flying shots are clearly studio jobs, but lit so that they convey the romance of the air that utterly seduced Saint-Ex from childhood on. Mixing interviews with family, friends and fellow writers with imaginative re-enactments of key moments in his life – the death of his boyhood friend (to become the spectral Little Prince), the postal delivery runs over the stormy Atlas Mountains, the crash in the Libyan Desert, the courtship of the Argentinian Consuela (Richardson) and their turbulent marriage – the essay concludes that the writer/aviator (Ganz) never really grew up. The best scene has the imperious Consuela ('I'm bored. Astonish me') persuaded to kiss Saint-Ex during an engineless free fall. BC

Saint in New York, The

(1938, US, 71 min, b/w)
d Ben Holmes. *p* William Sistrom. *sc* Charles A Kaufman, Mortimer Offner. *ph* Joseph August, Frank Redman. *ed* Harry Marker. *ad* Van Nest Polglase. *cast* Louis Hayward, Kay Sutton, Sig Ruman, Jack Carson, Paul Guilfoyle, Jonathan Hale, Frederick Burton.

● A one-off for Louis Hayward, kicking off RKO's series featuring Leslie Charteris' latter-day Robin Hood, although he did in fact return to the role in 1953 for Hammer's attempt to revive the character, *The Saint's Return* (aka *The Saint's*

Girl Friday). Rakishly raffish rather than dashingly debonair, Hayward was less bland than his successor George Sanders, and *The Saint in New York* is accordingly much darker than subsequent films in the series as the Saint sets out to dispose of six New York gangsters, disguises himself as a nun, falls in love (happily for the series, it runs into a dead end), and ends up uncovering a seventh villain known as The Big Fellow. The plus here is Joe August's fine camerawork. Sanders took over for five films, starting with *The Saint Strikes Back* (1939, admirably directed by John Farrow), and continuing to formula, enjoyably but unexceptionally, with *The Saint in London* (1939, a British quota quickie), *The Saint's Double Trouble* (1940), *The Saint Takes Over* (1940), *The Saint in Palm Springs* (1941). Following a dispute with Leslie Charteris, RKO simply metamorphosed the character into *The Falcon*; RKO British tried Hugh Sinclair in two films (*The Saint's Vacation* and *The Saint Meets the Tiger* both 1941); and the character found a happy home on TV during the '60s in the person of Roger Moore. TM

St Ives

(1976, US, 94 min)
d J Lee Thompson. *p* Pancho Kohner, Stanley Canter. *sc* Barry Beckerman. *ph* Lucien Ballard. *ed* Michael F Anderson. *pd* Philip M Jefferies. *m* Lalo Schifrin. *cast* Charles Bronson, John Houseman, Jacqueline Bisset, Maximilian Schell, Elisha Cook, Burr De Benning, Harry Guardino, Harris Yulin, Robert Englund, Jeff Goldblum.

● Neither Houseman's presence as the criminal mastermind, nor Lucien Ballard's crisp photography can rescue this routine thriller from the implausibilities of script (from a novel by Ross Thomas, writing as Oliver Bleeck) and heavy-handed direction. Bronson seems tired from the start as the ex-crime reporter turned would-be novelist who gets involved in a simple theft that escalates into murder and large-scale robbery. Though the script is larded with post-Watergate cynicism – the caper is the stealing of an American electronics firm's huge bribe to an Arab oil sheik, and all the cops but one are corrupt – the film consistently skirts the issues it raises, however obliquely, preferring instead such time honoured clichés as the cutaway to Bisset looking glamorous/mysterious or Bronson looking muscular/brooding for its resolutions. PH

Saint Jack

(1979, US, 115 min)
d Peter Bogdanovich. *p* Roger Corman. *sc* Howard Sackler, Paul Theroux, Peter Bogdanovich. *ph* Robby Müller. *ed* William Carruth. *ad* David Ng. *cast* Ben Gazzara, Denholm Elliott, James Villiers, Joss Ackland, Rodney Bewes, Mark Kingston, Lisa Lu, Monika Subramaniam, Judy Lim, George Lazenby, Peter Bogdanovich.

● Gazzara simply plays himself, in this adaptation of Paul Theroux's novel, as a genial American pimp in Singapore who tangles first with the local Triads, and then with the CIA. Bogdanovich turns the character into a sentimental paragon of virtue, and softens the hard profile of America's Far Eastern imperialism, ending up with a movie that reeks of the hollow travelogue sincerity it purports to despise. The director's smugness effortlessly trumps Robby Müller's camera-work and the good performances (notably from Denholm Elliott). Hard to imagine how anyone could make less of such a promising subject.

Saint Joan

(1957, GB, 110 min, b/w)
d/p Otto Preminger. *sc* Graham Greene. *ph* Georges Périnal. *ed* Helga Cranston. *pd* Roger Furse. *m* Mischa Spoliansky. *cast* Jean Seberg, Richard Widmark, John Gielgud, Anton Walbrook, Richard Todd, Harry Andrews.

● Even hardcore Preminger fans number this stage adaptation among his lesser works. As usual ambiguity is the theme within the theme – no big surprise when a play by an agnostic (GB Shaw) is adapted by a Catholic (Graham Greene). The film inverts the Joan enigma, with a number of ironical insights. The very production seems equivocal: deliberately bare and skimped to enable us to concentrate on the text, and/or because Preminger was not about to splash out on such a dubious box office prospect. The subsequent troubled progress and self-murder of Jean Seberg adds a further layer of ambiguity, both as eerie distraction and poignant complement. BBa

St Louis Blues

(1958, US, 93 min, b/w)
d Allen Reisner. *p* Robert Smith. *sc* Robert Smith, Ted Sherdeman. *ph* Haskell Boggs. *ed* Eda Warren. *ad* Hal Pereira, Roland Anderson. *songs* William C Handy. *m* Nelson Riddle. *cast* Nat King Cole, Eartha Kitt, Juano Hernandez, Pearl Bailey, Cab Calloway, Mahalia Jackson, Ruby Dee, Ella Fitzgerald.

● The usual liberties are taken in this so-called biopic of WC Handy, which ends with the usual embarrassingly patronising attempt to dignify jazz by showing its triumphant arrival in the concert hall. Otherwise, despite some heady melodramatics (Handy suffering psychosomatic blindness because of his preacher father's stern disapproval) which are defused by sympathetic handling and excellent performances from Nat King Cole and Juano Hernandez, this is a pleasing film with a distinct feel for jazz. Above all, Nelson Riddle's arrangements provide an excellent account of Handy's marvellous blues, and the cast assembled to play and sing them is well worth listening to (with only Eartha Kitt remaining obstinately out of period). TM

St Martin's Lane (aka Sidewalks of London)

(1938, GB, 85 min, b/w)
d Tim Whelan. *p* Erich Pommer. *sc* Clemence Dane. *ph* Jules Kruger. *ed* Hugh Stewart, Robert Hamer. *ad* Tom Morahan. *m* Arthur Johnston. *cast* Charles Laughton, Vivien Leigh, Rex Harrison, Tyrone Guthrie, Larry Adler, Gus McNaughton.

● A ripe performance from Laughton as an ageing busker pouring heart and soul into stirring renditions of 'If'... and 'The Green Eye of the Little Yellow God' But despite location shooting among theatre queues and some convincingly shabby sets, verisimilitude is not high (not with Leigh's Cockney accent shading into Kensington), nor are the musical sequences particularly appealing. Though written by Clemence Dane for Laughton, the script as revised by producer Erich Pommer constantly seems to be edging into Emil Jannings territory, with much gloom and sentimentality as Laughton is seemingly spurned on the way to stardom by the waif he has helped. This was the second of three productions from the Pommer/ Laughton partnership, sandwiched between *Vessel of Wrath* and *Jamaica Inn*. TM

Saint of Fort Washington, The

(1993, US, 103 min)
d Tim Hunter. *p* David V Picker, Nessa Hyams. *sc* Lyle Kessler. *ph* Frederick Elmes. *ed* Howard Smith. *pd* Stuart Wurtzel. *m* James Newton Howard. *cast* Danny Glover, Matt Dillon, Rick Aviles, Nina Siemaszko, Ving Rhames, Joe Seneca.

● Matthew, a gentle homeless Brooklyn boy (Dillon), makes his way to the Fort Washington shelter, and is befriended and defended by the grouchy veteran Jerry (Glover). We learn, bit by bit, of his history of schizophrenia and abandonment. Jerry takes this holy fool under his wing, teaching him the lore of the road, the car-wash game, and introducing him to his homeless friends, the crack down at The Blarney Stone boozer, and big plans. Though something of a failure in its own terms, this social-conscience movie does produce a strong emotional tug, helped no end by the dignified performances of Dillon and Glover. Essentially, however, content and form work against each other. Fred Elmes' fine location camerawork imbues the movie with a warm but inappropriate air of nostalgia. Likewise, Lyle Kessler's honourable script and Hunter's leisurely direction drive for a sense of distance – which results, regrettably, in only a glaze of humanitarian compassion. WH

St Valentine's Day Massacre, The

(1967, US, 99 min)
d/p Roger Corman. *sc* Howard Browne. *ph* Milton Krasner. *ed* William B Murphy. *ad* Jack Martin Smith, Philip M Jefferies. *m* Fred Steiner. *cast* Jason Robards, George Segal, Ralph Meeker, Jean Hale, Clint Ritchie, Frank Silvera, Joseph Campanella, Bruce Dern, David Canary, Kurt Kreuger, John Agar, Jack Nicholson.

● One of Corman's best films, far superior to Richard Wilson's *Al Capone* as a study of Capone's Chicago. The film revels in the mythology of the genre, both paying homage to it and reinterpreting it. It was one of the few films up to that time, for example, to stress the purely Sicilian nature of the Mafia and its relations with non-Sicilians like Capone. The elaborate intrigue of the gang warfare is treated in a hard, almost documentary style, with newsreel-type commentary. It also remains unmarred by spurious moralising: morality, in fact, is suspended in favour of mythology. DP

Saison des Hommes, La

see Season of Men, The

Salaam Bombay!

(1988, Ind/Fr/GB, 114 min)
d/p Mira Nair. *sc* Sooni Taraporevala. *ph* Sandi Sissel. *ed* Barry Alexander Brown. *pd* Mitch Epstein. *m* L Subramaniam. *cast* Shafiq Syed, Raghubir Yadav, Aneeta Kanwar, Nana Patekar, Hansa Vithal.

● The streets of Bombay teem with children begging, dealing, sleeping rough, surviving. Working on a scale that would make Dickens envious, Nair draws together the seemingly disparate threads of life in a red-light district, centering around the experience of an 11-year-old boy who runs away from his village. At first frightened and alienated, he soon becomes part of a complex hierarchy of exploitation, abuse and affection as he befriends the prostitutes, drug-dealers and children of the streets. Far from being episodic or disjointed, the film brings the lives of all its characters into a common embrace, never pointing a finger of blame but constantly emphasising the difficulties and dangers that surround young and old alike. Shot entirely on location with its child actors recruited from the streets, *Salaam Bombay*! enters into its subjects' lives with rare authority and absolute compassion, the material generated largely from workshops that Nair and her team ran for a period of months prior to filming. A revelation for audiences of any background. RS

Saladin (An-Nasr Salah ad-Din)

(1963, Egypt, 183 min)
d Youssef Chahine. *sc* A Rahman Er Charcaoui, Youssef Chahine. *ph* Wadid Sirry. *ed* R Abdel Salam. *m* Francesco Lavagnino, A Saad El Dine. *cast* Ahmed Mazhar, Nadia Loutfi, Salah Zulfikar, Leila Fawzi, Hussein Riad.

● After enduring years of Anthony Quinn playing Arabs, the Egyptian film industry finally wreaks its dreadful revenge. With a nomadic cast of zillions, *Saladin* sets out to boil your brains with three hours of unrelieved apology for hanging on to Jerusalem. Caught up in endless exposition, Richard I is no *Coeur de Lion* but, like all the Europeans, a red-wigged mongoloid given to lines like 'We can take Acre by lunchtime.' Saladin smoulders. Any visual magnificence (massed gatherings in the desert) is blown by tacky action sequences. CPea

Salaire de la Peur, Le

see Wages of Fear, The

Salamandre, La (The Salamander)

(1971, Switz, 129 min)
d/p Alain Tanner. *sc* Alain Tanner, John Berger. *ph* Renato Berta, Sandro Bernardoni. *ed* Brigitte Sousselier, Marc Blavet. *m* Patrick Moraz. *cast* Bulle Ogier, Jean-Luc Bideau, Jacques Denis, Véronique Alain, Marblum Jéquier, Marcel Vidal.

● A journalist recruits a novelist friend to help him rustle up a quick TV script based on a news item in a local paper about a man who accused his niece of shooting and wounding him. She claimed the gun went off while he was cleaning it; eventually dropped for lack of evidence, the case was never resolved. The novelist (Denis) sets out to create the script from imagination, while the journalist (Bideau) goes after the facts.

But dedicated to a celebration of instinctive revolt, the film is less concerned with what happened than with the girl herself; and Bulle Ogier conveys volumes in the part as the film counterpoints her view of society with its varying view of her. There is, for instance, a scene where she has a job as sales-girl in a shoe shop, and without warning begins to caress the legs the customers present to her: it's a gesture that's at once funny, profoundly erotic, incongruous, and deeply shocking, and one that places both Rosemonde and the world she finds herself living in. A rare treat, infused with a rich and unforced vein of quiet humour. VG

Salem's Lot

(1979, US, 112 min)
d Tobe Hooper. *p* Richard Kobritz. *sc* Paul Monash. *ph* Jules Brenner. *ed* Carol Sax, Tom Pryor. *pd* Mort Rabinowitz. *m* Harry Sukman. *cast* David Soul, James Mason, Lance Kerwin, Bonnie Bedelia, Lew Ayres, Reggie Nalder, Ed Flanders, Elisha Cook, Marie Windsor, Kenneth McMillan.
● A surprisingly successful small screen adaptation of Stephen King's vampire novel. In the Maine town of Jerusalem's Lot, it slowly dawns on writer Soul that antique dealer Mason is a harbinger of blood-sucking evil. Edited down from the 190 minute, two-part TV movie, this cinema release version is slightly gorier and tighter than the original. Paring away the excessive plot exposition of Paul Monash's teleplay, it places the emphasis on Hooper's fluid camerawork, creepy atmospherics, and skilful handling of the gripping climax. NF

Sallah

(1964, Isr, 105 min, b/w)
d Ephraim Kishon. *p* Menahem Golan. *sc* Ephraim Kishon. *ph* Floyd Crosby. *ed* Roberto Cinquini, Danny Schick. *ad* Joseph Carl. *m* Yohanan Zarai. *cast* Haym Topol, Geula Noni, Gila Almogor, Arik Einstein, Shraga Friedman.
● An early Menahem Golan production, this is a sort of Yiddish Ealing comedy, with Topol as the eponymous hero, an Oriental Jew who arrives in Israel in 1948 with his wife and seven kids. He finds his family being housed in a ramshackle transit camp instead of the elegant flat they were led to expect; and the comedy, such as it is, revolves around the workshy patriarch's remorselessly cute and very repetitive efforts to avoid doing a hand's turn while battling bureaucracy and accumulating enough money for a flat. Strictly for fans of Topol's particular brand of folksy charm. TM

Sally of the Sawdust

(1925, US, 9,500 ft b/w)
d/p DW Griffith. *sc* Forrest Halsey. *ph* Harry Fischbeck, Hal Sintzenich. *ed* James Smith. *ad* Charles M Kirk. *cast* Carol Dempster, WC Fields, Alfred Lunt, Effie Shannon, Erville Alderson, Glenn Anders.
● A slightly heavy-handed, sentimental melodrama, from Griffith's years of decline when he lost full control of his projects. Its interest would be no more than historical were it not also the movie that launched WC Fields. His show-stopping performance as Eustace McGargle, conman and sideshow juggler, contains the seeds of all his later glories. Highlights are his 'find the lady' routines, and his struggles to get out of an overheating oven or to master a juggernaut Ford, the latter as it crosses a furrowed field. There's also Carol Dempster's best role in a Griffith film as the tomboy heroine; and Griffith himself clearly found some rapport with his own vaudeville childhood in the backstage circus scenes. TR

Salmonberries

(1991, Ger, 95 min)
d Percy Adlon. *p* Eleonore Adlon. *sc* Percy Adlon, Felix Adlon. *ph* Tom Sigel. *ed* Conrad Gonzalez. *ad* Amadeus Capra. *m* Bob Telson. *cast* kd lang, Rosel Zech, Chuck Connors, Jane Lind, Oscar Kawagley, Wolfgang Steinberg.
● Adlon wrote this slight, quirky but often moving film for singer-songwriter kd lang. Shot in English, set partly in the icy wastes of Alaska, partly in the wintry former no man's land of a newly reunified Berlin, it casts her as an orphaned Eskimo who hides his/her gender beneath layers of baggy clothes, and his/her emotional emptiness behind the scowling face of a Wild Child. Zech plays an exiled and widowed German librarian who befriends her and comes to terms, through their edgy relationship, with her own familial past. The fragmented early scenes fail to gel, but once lang lures Zech out of the warm interior of her cabin into the magical, frozen landscape, lang's haunting theme song ('Barefoot') helps to establish a more consistent, engaging tone. During a subsequent visit to Berlin, their ambiguous relationship trembles on the edge of lesbian love, but is complicated by Zech's coyness and lang's longing for maternal affection. A minor return to form for Adlon after *Rosalie Goes Shopping;* but the real praise goes to the two stars for breathing so much human warmth into some chilly scenes of winter. NF

Salome

(1922, US, 7,200 ft, b/w)
d Charles Bryant. *sc* Peter M Winters. *ph* Charles Van Enger. *ad* Natacha Rambova. *m* Ulderico Marcelli. *cast* Alla Nazimova, Mitchell Lewis, Nigel de Brulier.
● 1920s art, California style. Despite careful stylisation and exquisite photography, this adaptation of Oscar Wilde's play boasts a healthy streak of vulgarity of which Wilde, one suspects, would have secretly approved. Sets and costumes, designed by Valentino's wife Natacha Rambova, are fashioned after Beardsley's drawings, but the film's atmosphere comes less from the artist's effete preciousness than from the robust and strapping decadence of '20s Hollywood.

Salomé

(1985, Fr/It, 95 min)
d Claude d'Anna. *p* Henry Lange. *sc* Claude D'Anna, Aaron Barzman. *ph* Pasqualino de Santis. *ed* Roberto Perpignani. *pd* Giantito Burcheillaro. *m* Egisto Macchi. *cast* Tomas Milian, Pamela Salem, Tim Woodward, Jo Champa, Fabrizio Bentivoglio, Jean-François Stévenin.
● Despite putting us on 'contemporary relevance' alert by having a Roman centurion brandish a cigarette lighter, d'Anna interests himself more in the peculiarities and particularities of King Herod's power games than in any abiding relevance they might hold. It amounts to a not unenjoyable shambles, with a pick 'n' mix cast, layers of diverse source material (Oscar Wilde, Richard Strauss, the Bible), plus softcore trimmings. Champa's nymphet Salomé is eclipsed by the mature sexuality of Pamela Salem (Herodias) – though that, like everything else in the picture, will be a matter of taste and temperament. BBa

Salome's Last Dance

(1987, GB, 89 min)
d Ken Russell. *p* Penny Corke. *sc* Ken Russell. *ph* Harvey Harrison. *ed* Timothy Gee. *ad* Michael Buchanan. *cast* Glenda Jackson, Stratford Johns, Nickolas Grace, Douglas Hodge, Imogen Millais-Scott, Denis Ull, Russell Lee Nash, Ken Russell.
● Russell's worst film to date. Stagily constrained to a single set, it has Oscar Wilde (Grace) taking time off from enviable epigrams to suffer a private production of his banned play, put on by his friends, the staff and clients of a singularly decadent Victorian brothel. They're a motley crew: Johns made up like a pier-show performer as Herod, Jackson whining Mrs Cravatt-style as Herodias, and our Ken himself as a dementedly salacious photographer. The petulant nymph, as incarnated by Millais-Scott – seemingly a graduate of the Toyah Wilcox School of Over Emphatic Diction and Hyper-active Eyelids – is depressingly tiresome; as is Russell's spastic balancing act between reality and illusion, which tenuously ties the text to Wilde's tormented longings for handsome young Bosie (Hodge). The in-jokes are plain silly, Russell's customary irreverence a matter of flatulent, leering *Carry On*-style humour, the decor sub-Beardsley, the whole thing redolent of a retarded pornographer's revue. GA

Salonique, nid d'espions

see Mademoiselle Docteur

Salon Kitty

(1976, It/WGer/Fr, 129 min)
d Tinto Brass. *p* Giulio Sbarigia, Emanno Donati. *sc* Ennio de Concini, Maria Pia Fusco, Tinto Brass. *ph* Silvano Ippoliti. *ed* Tinto Brass. *pd* Ken Adam. *m* Fiorenzo Carpi, Derry Hall. *cast* Helmut Berger, Ingrid Thulin, Teresa Ann Savoy, Bekim Fehmiu, John Steiner, Stefano Satta Flores, John Ireland, Tina Aumont, Maria Michi.
● Masquerading as an essay on decadence and Fascism, this predictably speculative slice of Nazi sex is aimed squarely at the box-office. Brass says his film is about 'denuding power', a thesis which he pursues with cretinous earnestness: mostly Nazis spend time stripping off in a brothel bugged by the SS. Helmut Berger stalks through this 'Cabaret' playing the Snow Queen, hiding his glacial passions beneath increasingly outrageous haute couture Nazi uniforms. A dreary love story gives the film a supposedly decent core, but the camera's gaze is firmly fixed elsewhere at the climax: Helmut's final piece of upstaging is to have himself gunned down in the shower, naked saved for Swastika wristbands. CPe

Salón México

(1948, Mex, 95 min, b/w)
d Emilio Fernández. *p* Salvador Elizondo. *sc* Emilio Fernández, Mauricio Magdaleno. *ph* Gabriel Figueroa. *ed* Gloria Schoemann. *ad* Jesus Bracho. *m* Antonio Diaz Conde. *cast* Marga López, Miguel Inclán, Rodolfo Acosta, Roberto Cañedo.
● Inspired (like Aaron Copland's suite of the same name) by the eponymous Mexico City dance club, this engagingly exotic melodrama focuses on the trials and tribulations of a reluctant *cabaretera* (López), struggling to pay her sister's boarding school fees and determined to conceal her profession and her pimp lover. Tragedy will out, and not without a heap of escapist moralising (catch the sister's air force hero fiancé!); despite the hackneyed plotting, however, Gabriel Figueroa's *noir* photography and the splendidly glamorous seediness of the nightclub scenes make for passable entertainment. GA

Saló, o le Centoventi Giornate di Sodoma (Saló, or the 120 days of Sodom)

(1975, It/Fr, 117 min)
d Pier Paolo Pasolini. *p* Alberto Grimaldi. *sc* Pier Paolo Pasonlini. *ph* Tonino Delli Colli. *ed* Nino Baragli. *ad* Dante Ferretti. *m* Ennio Morricone. *cast* Paolo Bonicelli, Giorgio Cataldi, Umberto P Quintavalle.
● Pasolini's last movie before his being brutally murdered may now seem strangely prophetic of his death, but it is undeniably a thoroughly objectionable piece of work. Transporting De Sade's novel to Mussolini's Fascist republic of 1944, Pasolini observes with unflinching gaze the systematic humiliation and torture of beautiful young boys and girls, herded into a palatial villa by various jaded, sadistic members of the wealthy upper classes. According to the director, the story was meant to be a metaphor for Fascism, but the revolting excesses shown on screen (shit-eating and sexual violence included), coupled with the fact that the victims seem complaisant in, rather than resistant to, their ordeals, suggest murkier motives in making the movie. It's *very* hard to sit through and offers no insights whatsoever into power, politics, history or sexuality. Nasty stuff. GA

Salsa

(1988, US, 99 min)
d Boaz Davidson. *p* Menahem Golan, Yoram Globus. *sc* Boaz Davidson, Tomas Benitez, Stephen Goldman. *ph* David Gurfinkel. *ed* Alain Jakubowicz. *pd* Mark Andrew Haskins. *cast* Robby Rosa, Rodney Harvey, Magali Alvarado, Miranda Garrison, Moon Orona, Angela Alvarado, Loyda Ramos.
● Rico (Rosa) plans to be this year's 'King of Salsa' if he can sort out the complications of the threadbare plot. With father dead, he works as a motor-mechanic to support mother and sister, and he doesn't get down in grease all day just so Sis (Magali Alvarado) can jeopardise her schooling by dating his best friend. What's more he has women problems: will girlfriend and dance partner Vicki (Angela Alvarado) forgive him for flirting with Lola (Orona)? Will he sacrifice love for a better chance of winning the big prize with ex-Salsa Queen Luna (Garrison)? Will anyone care? Not with the cast delivering lines as if they're

reading off autocue, and Davidson treating the plot as a meddlesome device required to stretch out the dance sets. So it's up to salsa to save the movie, but there's nothing hot and spicy served up here. The finale has the feel of a junior *Come Dancing*. EP

Salsa

(2000, Fr, 100 min)
d Joyce Sherman Buñuel. *p* Aïssa Djabri, Farid Lahouassa, Manuel Munz. *sc* Joyce Sherman Buñuel, Jean-Claude Carrière. *ph* Javier Aguirresarobe. *ed* Nicole Saunier. *pd* Jean Bauer. *m* Sierra Maestra, Jean-Marie Sénia. *cast* Vincent Lecoeur, Christianne Gout, Catherine Samie, Michel Aumont, Roland Blanche, Alexis Valdés, Elisa Maillot, Aurore Basnuevo, Estéban Socrates Cobas Puente.

● Aspiring classical pianist Rémi (Lecoeur) abandons the *académie* to seek old friends at the Salsa-oriented Bamboo Club in Paris, but he can only join the band if he blacks up à la Cubana. He falls for bespectacled travel agent Nathalie (who's brought to his attention by her Latin-loving grandma) who turns out to be hot on the dance floor when she lets her hair down. But will she love him when he reveals his deceit and resorts to mere white boy? Buñuel's film, written with Jean-Claude Carrière, is a lively *Flashdance*-style entertainment – made to capitalise on the French craze for the sultry, sexy, *son*-derived dance music – whose generally clichéd storyline doesn't overly distract from what is a sunny, life-affirming celebration. Music is by 'Kings of Cuban *son*' Sierra Maestra, some of whose players appear. WH

Salt & Pepper

(1968, GB, 101 min)
d Richard Donner. *p* Milton Ebbins. *sc* Michael Pertwee. *ph* Ken Higgins. *ed* Jack Slade. *pd* William Constable. *m* John Dankworth. *cast* Sammy Davis Jr, Peter Lawford, Michael Bates, Ilona Rodgers, John Le Mesurier, Graham Stark, Robertson Hare.

● Salt (Davis) and Pepper (Lawford) are owners of a Soho (London) nightclub, where a Chinese girl is murdered and turns out to have been a British secret agent. Harried by suspicious police, hunted by murderous thugs, the pair eventually uncover and contrive to thwart a coup d'état by power-crazed Colonel Woodstock (Le Mesurier), who plans to hijack a Polaris submarine and threaten to destroy a major city unless the Government bows out. The action is threadbare sub-James Bond, the gags are invariably mistimed, and most of the jokes are repeated to make sure you got them the first time round. Jerry Lewis was roped in to direct a sequel, *One More Time*, but it was, if anything, even worse. TM

Salto al Vacio

see Jump into the Void

Salt of the Earth

(1953, US, 94 min, b/w)
d Herbert J Biberman. *p* Paul Jarrico. *sc* Michael Wilson. *ed* Ed Spiegel, Joan Laird. *pd* Sonja Dahl, Adolfo Bardela. *m* Sol Kaplan. *cast* Rosaura Revueltas, Juan Chacon, Will Geer, Mervin Williams, Frank Talavera, Clinton Jencks, Virginia Jencks.

● Director Biberman, producer Paul Jarrico, writer Michael Wilson, composer Sol Kaplan and actor Will Geer were all blacklisted at the time, and this extraordinary film was a unique act of defiance. Production was subject to constant FBI harassment, the leading actress was repatriated to Mexico (shots of her final scenes were done surreptitiously), and projectionists refused to screen the finished film, which *still* looks incredibly modern. Financed by the American mineworkers union, it deals with a strike in the New Mexico community of Zinc Town, formerly San Marcos. While the Anglo workers enjoy reasonable living conditions, the Mexicans live without adequate sanitation in a form of apartheid. At pains not to feature traditional romantic leads (like *Matewan* or *The Milagro Beanfield War*), it focuses on two decidedly unglamorous people, a Mexican worker (Chacon) and his pregnant wife (Revueltas), who are victims of an economic trap, and whom America's post-war boom – symbolised by the gleaming cars that drive through the picket line – has passed by. As the strike for better conditions progresses, the women play an increasing role, overcoming the traditional macho ethos by doing both picket duty and time in jail (while the men, fed up with washing dishes, go off hunting). The film's targets multiply – workers' rights, racism, feminism – and for 1953 this is pretty amazing. ATu

Salto nel Vuoto

see Leap into the Void

Saltwater

(1999, Ire/GB, 97 min)
d Conor McPherson. *p* Robert Walpole. *sc* Conor McPherson. *ph* Oliver Curtis. *ed* Emer Reynolds. *pd* Luana Hanson. *m* The Plague Monkeys. *cast* Peter McDonald, Brian Cox, Conor Mullen, Laurence Kinlan, Brendan Gleeson, Valerie Spelman.

● After the theatrical phenomenon of *The Weir* and his buzzing screenplay for *I Went Down*, Conor McPherson makes a promising directorial debut with this slow-burning comedy-drama (opened out from his play *This Lime Street Bower*) set at the Irish seaside. McDonald feels stuck serving in his widower dad's chippy, and frustrated by the old man being in iniquitous hock to a loan shark (Gleeson). While he ponders direct action, his older brother's romantic life proceeds shambolically apace, and just because he's a philosophy tutor doesn't mean he knows how to set things in order. Judged in the harshest light, the film suffers from a certain lack of tension, as McDonald half comically crosses the line of legality and lives to sidestep the consequence. It's also undermined by a niggling lack of resolution to a couple of minor plotpoints, and by its somewhat underdeveloped female characters. But McPherson's funny, lucid dialogue manages to take the strain, slipping questions of moral responsibility into the conversation, and provoking a steady flow of laughter. TJ

Salut Cousin! (Hey Cousin!)

(1996, Fr/Bel/Alg/Luxembourg, 102 min)
d Merzak Allouache. *p* Jacques Bidou. *sc* Merzak Allouache. *ph* Pierre Aïm. *ed* Denise de Casabianca. *ad* Olivier Raoux, Alexis McKenzie Main, Pascale Morin, Christophe Colomer, Laurent Jarriau, Stéphan Cavelier. *m* Safy Eddine Boutella. *cast* Gad Elmaleh, Mess Hattou, Magaly Berdy, Ann-Gisel Glass, Jean Benguigui, Xavier Maly.

● Alilo (Elmaleh) arrives in Paris from Algiers on an errand from his fashion wholesaler boss. He must collect a consignment of clothes, but he's lost the contact details. It's the weekend, so he's stranded on the streets until he remembers cousin Mok (Hattou). Mok seems to have it made, with his hipster clothes, his own flat and an upcoming gig as a rap artist. By his side, Alilo feels like a real country bumpkin, yet the more time he spends around this self-styled city slicker, the more he realises that the Parisian dream can easily turn hollow. This is no dogged social realist trudge through the immigrant nightmare. There's much sly comedy as we gradually see through Mok's motormouth bragging, a touch of tingly romance as Alilo starts making eye contact with Mok's West African neighbour Fatoumata (Berdy), and a sturdy narrative line that builds up tension the closer Alilo comes to delivery day. The performances never mistake insight for exaggeration, and the rich camerawork refuses to settle for off-hand grunge. Most memorable of all is the film's feeling for those Algerians who can never return to their ravaged homeland, but know they'll never truly be at home in France. TJ

Salute of the Jugger, The

(1989, Aust, 91 min)
d David Peoples. *p* Charles Roven. *sc* David Peoples. *ph* David Eggby. *ed* Richard Francis-Bruce. *pd* John Stoddart. *m* Todd Boekelheide. *cast* Rutger Hauer, Joan Chen, Anna Katarina, Vincent Philip D'Onofrio, Delroy Lindo, Gandhi McIntyre, Justin Monju.

● Or, Mad Max Beyond Rollerball. After the apocalypse, nomadic juggers roam the wastelands, challenging local teams to bouts of gladiatorial rugby. Seduced by this life of glamour, petite peasant Chen persuades rugged Hauer to sign her up. He resists, relents, and eventually sets up a showdown exhibition match with big subterranean city juggers. Scripted by Peoples himself, this thin, sloppy scenario hasn't an original idea to its name. Despite defiantly cool stars (Chen was Bertolucci's last empress and the *Twin Peaks* mill-owner; Hauer will always be Batty), there's little to look at and nothing worth hearing. Even the game itself is a drag. Footnote: Peoples shot the movie at Coober Pedy, in the Australian outback, because 'deserts in the US have been filmed a lot and have become well-known'. 'Coober Pedy' comes from the aboriginal words for 'white man's hole'. TCh

Salvador

(1986, US, 122 min)
d Oliver Stone. *p* Gerald Green, Oliver Stone. *sc* Oliver Stone, Richard Boyle. *ph* Robert Richardson. *ed* Claire Simpson. *pd* Bruno Rubeo. *m* Georges Delerue. *cast* James Woods, James Belushi, Michael Murphy, John Savage, Elpidia Carrillo, Tony Plana, Colby Chester, Cindy Gibb.

● In 1980, Richard Boyle, an American journalist on the skids, drove down to Salvador, believing the place would provide both a story and all those things he remembered so fondly from the late 1960s – booze, drugs, sexual freedom. What he found was civil war, with his own government supporting the right wing incumbents and their death squads. Boyle, as portrayed by the excellent Woods, is naïve, manic, and dangerous. He suffers terror and humiliation, risks death, and re-discovers his professional integrity. Stone's film (co-written by Boyle with the director) is about North American ignorance, Central American tragedy, and how the two are related. The polemic may seem obvious and at times laboured, but the action sequences are brilliant, and the film does achieve a brutal, often very moving, power. RR

Salvation! Have You Said Your Prayers Today? (aka Salvation!)

(1987, US, 85 min)
d Beth B. *p* Beth B, Michael Shamberg. *sc* Beth B, Tom Robinson. *ph* Francis Kenny. *ed* Elizabeth Kling. *pd* Lester Cohen. *cast* Stephen McHattie, Dominique Davalos, Exene Cervenka, Viggo Mortensen, Rockets Redglare, Billy Bastiani.

● Quite what Beth B – known best, if at all, for her Super-8 and pop promo work – is trying to do with this uneasy blend of camp melodrama and straight satire is unclear. The film starts promisingly with barely-sane TV evangelist Reverend Randall (McHattie) ranting direct to camera about atheism in the Big Apple. But things immediately slide downward into some sort of strident 'alternative' comedy when a sacked factory worker and his sister (Mortensen and Davalos) break into Randall's Fort Knox-like mansion and hold him hostage. Heavy Metal gets an airing, there is much post-punk posturing, and the depiction of both Randall and his devotee-abductors as universally corruptible is stale and unfunny. GA

Salvation Hunters, The

(1925, US, 7,650 ft, b/w)
d/p/sc Josef von Sternberg. *ph* Josef von Sternberg, Edward Gheller. *ed* Josef von Sternberg. *cast* Georgia Hale, George K Arthur, Bruce Guerin, Otto Matiesen, Nellie Bly Baker, Olaf Hytten, Stuart Holmes.

● It's hard now to appreciate the bomb-shell that Sternberg's first feature must have been in Hollywood at the time: its slow pace, its lyrical pessimism, and its strong emphasis on the psychological over the physical set it far apart from anything that the American cinema had produced. The angry-young-man plot (apathetic, cowardly boy loses girl to city slicker, who presses her into brothel service) verges on allegory, despite the wish-fulfilment ending, and looks more pretentious than committed at this remove. Yet there are lots of pointers towards Sternberg's future glories, and the sheer nagging intensity of mood is still extremely potent. TR

Salvatore Giuliano

(1961, It, 125 min, b/w)
d Francesco Rosi. *p* Franco Cristaldi. *sc* Francesco Rosi, Suso Checchi d'Amico, Enzo Provenzale, Franco Solinas. *ph* Gianni di Venanzo. *ed* Mario Serandrei. *ad* Sergio Canevari, Carlo Egidi. *m* Piero Piccioni. *cast* Frank Wolff, Salvo Randone, Federico Zardi, Pietro Cammarata, Fernando Cicero.

● The film that first brought Rosi international recognition: a masterly semi-documentary about – or rather around – the notorious Sicilian bandit, told in a series of flashbacks taking off from scenes recreating the discovery of his bullet-riddled body in July 1950, his laying-out and burial, and the trial of his associates. If Giuliano himself remains an enigma as the centrepiece of the jigsaw – deliberately so, since Rosi refuses to guess at mysteries – the complex lessons offered by his life and death in terms of Sicilian society and Mafia politics are laid out with exemplary clarity. Stunningly shot in stark black-and-white by Gianni Di Venanzo. TM

Samba Traore

(1992, Burkina Faso, 85 min)
d Idrissa Ouédraogo. *p* Sophie Salbot, Idrissa Ouédraogo, Silvia Voser. *sc* Idrissa Ouedraogo, Jacques Arhex, Santiago Amigoréna. *ph* Pierre-Laurent Chénieux, Mathieu Vadepied. *ed* Joelle Dufour. *ad* Yves Brover. *m* Wasis Diop, Falon Cahen, Lamine Konté. *cast* Bakary Sangare, Mariam Kaba, Abdoulaye Komboudri, Irene Tassembedo.

● On the face of it, Samba is a village boy who struck it rich in the city. He comes home, marries the single mother Saratou and opens a bar with his friend Salif. But then awkward questions start to arise about the source of his wealth. The hint of ethnography which hovered just off screen in Ouedraogo's *Yaaba* and *Tilai* is missing here. This tale of a criminal trying to go straight is almost generic, and could be set almost anywhere. Maybe this points the way out of African cinema's impasse? As usual the director picks a fine cast and directs them with great empathy. TR

Same Old Song (On connaît la chanson)

(1997, Fr/Switz/GB, 120 min)
d Alain Resnais. *p* Bruno Pesery. *sc* Jean-Pierre Bacri, Agnès Jaoui. *ph* Renato Berta. *ed* Hervé de Luze. *ad* Jacques Saulnier. *m* Bruno Fontaine. *cast* Pierre Arditi, Sabine Azéma, Jean-Pierre Bacri, André Dussollier, Lambert Wilson, Jane Birkin.

● Dedicated to Dennis Potter, this borrows his idea of having characters burst into lip synched song to express the feelings they cannot voice in ordinary conversation. This doesn't work quite the same way with French *chansons* as it did with Anglo-American standards (although there is a delicious moment when Jane Birkin, doing a cameo, 'sings' a snatch of one of her own songs), but the real problem is that Resnais remains fixated on the toothless bourgeois satire which has dominated his work since *Mélo*. The characters here – an unhappy salesman who writes radio plays on the side, a tourist guide, a ruthless property developer – are simply too banal for their romantic longings and mis-understandings to matter to most viewers. And that fatally weakens Resnais' point that clichéd passions simmer beneath the blandest exteriors. TR

Same Time, Next Year

(1978, US, 119 min)
d Robert Mulligan. *p* Walter Mirisch, Morton Gottlieb. *sc* Bernard Slade. *ph* Robert Surtees. *ed* Sheldon Kahn. *pd* Henry Bumstead. *m* Marvin Hamlisch. *cast* Ellen Burstyn, Alan Alda, Ivan Bonar, Bernie Kuby, Cosmo Sardo.

● A holiday romance begun in 1952 somehow stumbles over 25-plus years. Annually, the only-slightly odd couple desert their spouses and kids for a passionate weekend reunion. Every five years or so, we pick up on them and their inevitable changes, as the world spins in a montage of stills. OK, so with only two lead actors and a single location, the film wears its Broadway origins prominently on its chest, and sits somewhat anachronistically amid the movie-movie flow of New Hollywood. But for all that it's a surprisingly, refreshingly welcome throwback, with the sort of sparklingly literate dialogue it used to take an army of studio screenwriters to polish and which you rarely hear today; with two superbly versatile performances from Burstyn and Alda; and with direction from Mulligan that's the undemonstrative epitome of old-fashioned craftsmanship. And it is very funny. PT

Sammy and Rosie Get Laid

(1987, GB, 101 min)
d Stephen Frears. *p* Tim Bevan, Sarah Radclyffe. *sc* Hanif Kureishi. *ph* Oliver Stapleton. *ed* Mick Audsley. *pd* Hugo Luczyc-Wyhowski. *m* Stanley Myers. *cast* Shashi Kapoor, Frances Barber, Claire Bloom, Ayub Khan Dim, Roland Gift, Wendy Gazelle, Badi Uzzman.

● A genial, retired Indian political torturer (Kapoor) returns to England to visit son Sammy (Dim) and daughter-in-law Rosie (Barber) in war-torn Ladbroke Grove. Family explanations are conducted in the thick of riots, the first of many preposterous juxtapositions. Sammy accommodates his father because he wants his money; social worker (yawn) Rosie is less of a pushover, wanting political commitment and sexual freedom, ie. to have her cock and eat it. So does this film, tossed together from a Hanif Kureishi screenplay which labours so many right-on themes that none leave their mark. Black Danny (Gift) smiles enigmatically in a woman's hat ('Call me Victoria'), symbolising some seraphic quality or other; hectoring lesbians swap het-hating slogans; a peace commune beneath the Westway is bulldozed to the strains of patriotic music; and in one of the worst sequences in this oratorio of half-baked agitprop, the screen splits into three layers to show six people fucking at once, serenaded by close-harmony Rastas. Finally, in a last-ditch attempt at dramatic structure, the retired torturer, hounded by the grotty ghost of one of his victims, strings himself up. *My Beautiful Laundrette* it is not. MS

Sammy Going South (aka A Boy Ten Feet Tall)

(1963, GB, 128 min)
d Alexander Mackendrick. *p* Hal Mason. *sc* Denis Cannan. *ph* Erwin Hillier. *ed* Jack Harris. *ad* Ted Tester. *m* Tristram Cary. *cast* Fergus McClelland, Edward G Robinson, Constance Cummings, Harry H Corbett.

● While widely regarded as an example of Mackendrick's decline after the masterpiece that was *Sweet Smell of Success*, this is certainly not the mere 'family fodder' that disappointed Leslie Halliwell. Indeed, like *A High Wind in Jamaica* and *Mandy*, it is another of the director's dark, somewhat sour studies in child psychology: as the young McClelland, suddenly orphaned during an air-raid on Port Said, makes his long and lonely journey down through Africa in search of his aunt in Durban, he encounters all kinds of danger and criminality with barely a blink of an eye. If the pace is oddly flaccid in places and the photography sometimes verges on travelogue territory, there is no denying the vitality of the performances, Robinson being particularly affecting as the diamond mining outlaw who takes Sammy temporarily under his wing. Indeed, as in *High Wind*, it is the adults, rather than Sammy, who finally suffer the most, and the film stands alongside *The Man in the White Suit*, *Whisky Galore!* and *The Ladykillers* as a sceptical overturning of conventional ideas about innocence and experience. GA

Samourai, Le 100 (The Samurai)

(1967, Fr/It, 95 min)
d Jean-Pierre Melville. *p* Eugène Lepicier. *sc* Jean-Pierre Melville. *ph* Henri Decaë. *ed* Monique Bonnot, Yolande Maurette. *ad* François de Lamothe. *m* François de Roubaix. *cast* Alain Delon, Nathalie Delon, François Périer, Cathy Rosier, Jacques Leroy, Jean-Pierre Posier, Catherine Jourdan.

● Melville's hombres don't talk a lot, they just move in and out of the shadows, their trenchcoats lined with guilt and their hats hiding their eyes. This is a great movie, an austere masterpiece, with Delon as a cold, enigmatic contract killer who lives by a personal code of *bushido*. Essentially, the plot is about an alibi, yet Melville turns this into a mythical revenge story, with Cathy Rosier as Delon's black, piano-playing nemesis who might just as easily have stepped from the pages of Cocteau or Sophocles as *Vogue*. Similarly, if Delon is Death, Périer's cop is a date with Destiny. Melville's film had a major influence in Hollywood: Delon lying on his bed is echoed in *Taxi Driver*, and Paul Schrader might have remade *Le Samourai* as *American Gigolo*. Another remake is *The Driver*, despite Walter Hill's insistence that he'd never seen it: someone on that movie *had* to have seen it. ATu

Samsara

(2001, Ger/Ind, 138 min)
d Pan Nalin. *p* Karl Baumgartner, Christoph Friedel. *sc* Pan Nalin, Tim Baker. *ph* Rali Ralchev. *ed* Isabel Meier. *ad* Petra Barchi. *m* Cyril Morin, Dadon. *cast* Shawn Ku, Christy Chung, Neelesha BaVora, Sherab Sangey, Jamayang Jinpa.

● After a three-year meditative retreat (it looks more like hibernation), Buddhist monk Tashi (Ku) rejoins monastery life. But desire stirs in his loins when he espies the beautiful Pema (Chung) during harvest prayers. Next thing he's renounced his vows – not to mention his clothes – and the two of them are rutting like rabbits. After all, Tashi reflects, Buddha himself knew earthly delights before choosing the path of enlightenment. But after being unfaithful to his wife, Tashi feels guilt and decides to return to the ascetic life – only to be confronted by Pema, who has strong feelings about being abandoned to bring up the kids alone. Shot in remote Himalayan locations (actually Ladakh), this plays like a massively extended remake of Conrad Rooks' Siddhartha: phoney spirituality plus softcore sex in a scenic package. No surprise to learn that the Indian director cut his teeth on National Geographic travelogues. TR

Samson and Delilah

(1949, US, 128 min)
d/p Cecil B DeMille. *sc* Jesse L Lasky Jr, Fredric M Frank. *ph* George Barnes. *ed* Anne Bauchens. *ad* Hans Dreier, Walter Tyler. *m* Victor Young. *cast* Victor Mature, Hedy Lamarr, George Sanders, Angela Lansbury, Henry Wilcoxon, Olive Deering, Fay Holden, Russ Tamblyn.

● Wonderfully chintzy and hokey Bible epic once described as the only film in which the hero had bigger tits than the heroine. Mature looks as constipated as ever, and Lamarr is the Philistine's philistine, but great camp performances from Sanders and Lansbury, and glorious papier-maché sets. Fab.

Samurai, The

see Samourai, Le

Sam Whiskey

(1969, US, 97 min)
d Arnold Laven. *p* Jules Levy, Arthur Gardner, Arnold Laven. *sc* William Norton. *ph* Robert Moreno. *ed* John Woodcock. *ad* Loyd S Papez. *m* Herschel Burke Gilbert. *cast* Burt Reynolds, Clint Walker, Ossie Davis, Angie Dickinson, Rick Davis, William Schallert, Woodrow Parfrey.

● A dim script and flat direction counteract amiably lively performances in this comedy Western, which functions very much as a caper movie in reverse: Reynolds is the gambler leader of a trio of ne'er-do-wells employed by Dickinson to return a mass of gold to the Denver Mint, whence her now dead husband stole it. The plotting is laborious enough to ensure that the audience is always two steps ahead of the characters, but Reynolds – in his first serious attempt to be funny – just about keeps it watchable. GA

Sanctuary

(1961, US, 100 min, b/w)
d Tony Richardson. *p* Richard D Zanuck. *sc* James Poe. *ph* Ellsworth J Fredricks. *ed* Robert Simpson. *ad* Jack Martin Smith, Duncan Cramer. *m* Alex North. *cast* Lee Remick, Yves Montand, Bradford Dillman, Odetta, Reta Shaw, Howard St John, Strother Martin.

● Invited to Hollywood after *Look Back in Anger* and *The Entertainer*, Tony Richardson made only one film there before fleeing back to Britain. That film was *Sanctuary* a disastrous attempt to bring Faulkner to the screen: it forever fudges the issues, preferring the easy dramatics of a Tennessee Williams-like script to the mythic drama of the Faulkner novel. Richardson's diffidence in handling his story of rape and murder, eliciting nervous performances from Remick and Montand, points the way forward to the failure of nerve that characterises the majority of his subsequent films. PH

San Demetrio, London

(1943, GB, 105 min, b/w)
d Charles Frend. *p* Robert Hamer. *sc* Robert Hamer, Charles Frend. *ph* Ernest Palmer, Roy Kellino. *ed* Eily Boland. *m* John Greenwood.

cast Walter Fitzgerald, Mervyn Johns, Ralph Michael, Robert Beatty, Charles Victor, Frederick Piper, Gordon Jackson.
● A prototype docudrama, still inspiring in its fusion of entertainment and wartime propaganda, produced by Michael Balcon at Ealing Studios and co-directed by Robert Hamer after Frend fell ill. The San Demetrio is an oil tanker, critically damaged by German gunfire in mid-Atlantic and abandoned to the flames by its crew, then heroically salvaged and brought safely home by part of the same crew when they happen on it, still floating, after drifting for three days in a lifeboat. The ship, in fact, becomes a microcosm or a symbol of the war: the ship is Island Britain, almost sunk (Dunkirk), its salvage the Churchillian ethos in action, with all hands pulling together and without a pompous officer chappie ordering people around. There is even an American aboard (Beatty) to make it an Allied victory. A fascinating and rather neglected picture. ATu

Sandlot, The (aka The Sandlot Kids)

(1993, US, 101 min)
d David Mickey Evans. *p* William S Gilmore, Dale de la Torre. *sc* David Mickey Evans, Robert Gunter. *ph* Anthony Richmond. *ed* Michael A Stevenson. *pd* Chester Kaczenski. *m* David Newman. *cast* Tom Guiry, Mike Vitar, Patrick Renna, Chauncey Leopardi, Marty York, Brandon Adams.
●Ever since *Stand by Me*, it seems that every Boy's Own yarn is deemed incomplete without a nostalgic, pseudo-ironic voice-over waxing lyrical about the mythology of short pants and acne. There was too much of this baloney in director Evans' spec script for *Radio Flyer*, but he obviously hasn't got it out of his system yet. His directorial debut is chock-a-block with cute reminiscence – which is a shame, because if it weren't so knowing, this would be quite a likeable little comedy about nothing in particular. A spotty crew of dead-end kids throw a baseball around. The new kid in town, Scotty Smalls (Guiry), is accepted simply as a gofer, but the gang's leader, Rodriguez (Vitar), takes him under his wing. The boys are quirkily characterised and spiky dialogue mercifully keeps the sporting ardour in check, but the pumped-up climax ('the biggest pickle any of us had ever seen,' we're assured three times) turns out to be the biggest botch. TCh

Sandman, The (Der Sandmann)

(1995, Ger, 94 min)
d Nico Hofmann. *p* Norbert Sauer. *sc* Matthias Seelig. *ph* Tom Faehrmann, Becker Britta. *ed* Inge Behrens. *pd* Thomas Freudenthal. *m* Nick Glowna. *cast* Götz George, Karoline Eichhorn, Barbara Rudnik, Martin Armknecht, Jürgen Hentsch, Michael Brandner.
● An ambitious young TV researcher (Eichhorn) looks to boost her show's ratings by interviewing a controversial, arrogant author, Henry Kupfer, who killed a prostitute in his youth. As she gets to know Kupfer, she becomes convinced he's responsible for a number of brutal sex-murders committed in the locality and resolves to unmask him on air. Undecided as to whether it's a sinister (if fairly ingenious) thriller or a comment on media attitudes towards violence and morbid psychology, Hofmann's film is intriguing and frustrating in equal measure. George is charismatic as the suspected serial killer, but genre clichés, implausibilities, and a few gloating women-in-peril scenes make this less satisfying than it might have been. GA

Sand Pebbles, The

(1966, US, 193 min)
d/p Robert Wise. *sc* Robert Anderson. *ph* Joseph MacDonald. *ed* William H Reynolds. *pd* Boris Leven. *m* Jerry Goldsmith. *cast* Steve McQueen, Richard Attenborough, Richard Crenna, Candice Bergen, Marayat Andriane, Mako, Larry Gates, Simon Oakland, Joseph Turkel.
●Splendid camerawork by Joseph MacDonald, otherwise a three-hour plod through a bestseller by Richard McKenna. Set in China in 1926, it deals with the trials and tribulations of an American gunboat crew who learn to love the natives while trying to save them from their own follies and the depredations of everybody else. Behind its timid criticism of imperialist attitudes, lies a much louder and heartfelt American cry – with China 1926 standing in for Vietnam 1966 – of 'Why doesn't everybody love us when we do our best for you?' To leaven the message, McQueen and Attenborough, as the two most humanitarian members of the crew of a ship run by coolie labour, both get romances: McQueen with Bergen's American mission teacher (hair in tight bun), Attenborough with Andriane's half-caste girl (highly cultured). There are also some well-staged battles. TM

Sandpiper, The

(1965, US, 116 min)
d Vincente Minnelli. *p* Martin Ransohoff. *sc* Dalton Trumbo, Michael Wilson. *ph* Milton Krasner. *ed* David Bretherton. *ad* George W Davis,Urie McCleary. *m* Johnny Mandel. *cast* Elizabeth Taylor, Richard Burton, Eva Marie Saint, Charles Bronson, Robert Webber.
●Despite the behind-the-camera credits – not only Minnelli, but writers Dalton Trumbo and Michael Wilson – a truly dire romantic melodrama. Taylor is the free-lovin' atheist beatnik artist who lives in a Big Sur beach shack; Burton's the married Episcopal minister who falls in love after coming into conflict with her over her bastard son's lack of proper schooling. Meanwhile, a repressed and angst-ridden Eva Marie Saint hovers in the wings as his wife, and Bronson makes for an extremely unlikely sculptor. The film is quite simply so much soap: Burton's guilt is unreal, Taylor's redemptive boho is an embarrassingly clichéd travesty of '60s idealism, and the dialogue is both risible and turgid. Only the shots of the Californian coastline are at all classy, and they are totally superfluous to everything. GA

Sandra

see Vaghe Stelle dell'Orsa

Sands of Iwo Jima

(1949, US, 110 min, b/w)
d Allan Dwan. *p* Edmund Grainger. *sc* Harry Brown, James Edward Grant. *ph* Reggie Lanning. *ed* Richard L Van Enger. *ad* James W Sullivan. *m* Victor Young. *cast* John Wayne, John Agar, Adela Mara, Forrest Tucker, Arthur Franz, Julie Bishop, Richard Jaeckel.
●Hugely successful Republic flag-waver, recounting in heroic terms the World War II capture of a strategic Pacific island by US marines. Wayne is in his element as the tough sergeant sternly moulding a group of recruits, from training camp to beachhead, into an efficient fighting force. They hate him for it, but he only wants them to stay alive, as they eventually learn. Dwan's deft handling of the action counteracts the dramatic clichés of the conflict between Wayne and his rebellious substitute son, Agar. GA

Sandwich Man, The (Erzi de Da Wan'ou)

(1983, Tai, 102 min)
d Hou Xiaoxian, Zeng Zhuangxiang, Wan Ren. *p* Ming Ji. *sc* Wu Nianzhen *ph* Chen Kunhou. *ed* Liao Qingsong. *ad* Li Fuxiong. *m* Wen Longjun. *cast* Chen Bozheng, Yang Liyin, Jin Ding, Fang Dingtai, Zhuo Shengli, Jiang Xia.
●One of several portmanteau films made at Taiwan's CMPC in the early 1980s to give new directors a chance to flex creative muscles. Here, all three episodes (each a vignette of economic hardship in the 1960s) are based on stories by then fashionable 'nativist' writer Huang Chunming and consequently full of Taiwanese (rather than Mandarin) dialogue. Hou's near plotless episode goes for pathos: a young man desperate to feed his wife and baby takes a demeaning job as a walking billboard. The other two episodes hinge on irony. Zeng's is about two salesmen coming to grief as they try to flog unsafe Japanese pressure-cookers in rural towns; Wan's shows a squatter-hut family going from grief to jubilation as it realises that a road accident will produce a compensation payment windfall. Early ripples of Taiwan's new wave. TR

San Francisco

(1936, US, 115 min, b/w)
d WS Van Dyke. *p* John Emerson, Bernard H Hyman. *sc* Anita Loos. *ph* Oliver T Marsh. *ed* Tom Held. *ad* Cedric Gibbons. *m* Herbert Stothart. *cast* Clark Gable, Spencer Tracy, Jeanette MacDonald, Jack Holt, Jessie Ralph, Ted Healy, Shirley Ross, Al Shean, Harold Huber.
●MGM's old war-horse just about scrapes by on starpower – Gable's cynical saloon keeper, MacDonald's showgirl, and Tracy's Irish priest battle for each other's souls – until San Francisco gets clobbered by the earthquake of 1906. Then it's another matter entirely, for this is one of the greatest action sequences in the history of cinema, rivalling the chariot race in both *Ben-Hurs* as well as the Odessa Steps in *Battleship Potemkin*. It's a symphony of editing and special effects that more than makes up for the first 90 minutes or so. ATu

Sang des Autres, Le

see Blood of Others, The

Sang des Bêtes, Le

(1949, Fr, 22 min, b/w)
d/sc Georges Franju. *commentary* Jean Painlevé. *ph* Marcel Fradetal. *ed* André Joseph. *m* Joseph Kosma. *narrators* Georges Hubert, Nicole Ladmiral.
●Despite the grim content, this description of three abbatoirs (horses, cattle, sheep) is no vegetarian tract. What most fascinates Franju is the inflicting of violent death as a matter of banal 9-to-5 routine. We soon pick up the process: the pickaxe through the skull, the throatcutting, the steaming blood (it's winter) spilling across the stone floor, the hacking and dismembering. We become accustomed to the echoing sounds: the banging and clattering, someone off-camera singing 'La Mer'. The slaughterhouses are placed in geographical context, with Kosma's lilting waltz theme accompanying an evocation of the outskirts of post-war Paris: canals, junk markets, scrubby wasteland. It's a gift of a subject for a surrealist like Franju: an everyday nightmare, at once atrocious and outlandishly beautiful. BBa

Sang d'un Poète, Le (The Blood of a Poet)

(1930, Fr, 53 min, b/w)
d Jean Cocteau. *p* Vicomte de Noailles. *sc* Jean Cocteau. *ph* Georges Périnal. *ed* Jean Cocteau. *ad* YG D'Eaubonne. *m* Georges Auric. *cast* Lee Miller, Pauline Carton, Odette Thalazac, Enrique Rivero, Jean Desbordes, Fernand Dichamps. *narrator* Jean Cocteau.
●Cocteau described this first feature as the playing with one finger of a theme that he orchestrated in *Orphée* twenty years later. That puts it fairly enough: the movie has an avant-garde roughness and unpredictability in its construction and use of symbols, but it's fundamentally a very characteristic, neo-Romantic study of the joys and agonies of being an artist. It's in two distinct parts. The first presents the artist (Rivero) trapped by his own work, eventually opting for the rebirth of a romantic martyrdom; the second plunges back into autobiography (reworking the snowball fight from *Les Enfants Terribles*), and resolves itself into a 'cosmic' riddle. The honesty and robustness of the images prevents the movie from lapsing into pretension or preciousness; it remains extremely interesting as a source of Cocteau's later work. TR

Sangue vivo

see Living Blood

Sanjuro (Tsubaki Sanjuro)

(1962, Jap, 96 min, b/w)
d Akira Kurosawa. *p* Ryuzo Kikushima, Tomoyuki Tanaka. *sc* Ryuzo Kikushima, Hideo Oguni, Akira Kurosawa. *ph* Fukuzo Koizumi, Kozo Saito. *ed* Akira Kurosawa. *ad* Yoshiro Muraki. *m* Masaru Sato. *cast* Toshiro Mifune, Tatsuya Nakadai, Yuzo Kayama, Takashi Shimura, Takako Irie, Reiko Dan.
●Kurosawa was pressured by his producers into directing this sequel to *Yojimbo*, and rose to the occasion by making his funniest and least overtly didactic film. The plot has Sanjuro (Mifune) running lazy rings around nine would-be samurai and two genteel ladies while cleaning up a spot of corruption in local government. Kurosawa plays most of it for laughs by expertly parodying the conventions of Japanese period action movies, but the tone switches to a magnificent vehemence in the heart-stopping finale. TR

Sankofa

(1993, US/Ger/Ghana/Burkina Faso, 125 min)
d/p/sc Haile Gerima. *ph* Augustin Cubano. *m* David J White. *cast* Oyafunmike Ogunlano, Alexandra Duah, Kofi Ghanaba, Nick Medley, Mutabaruka.

● While Mona (Ogunlano), a black American fashion model, cavorts for a (white) photographer during a shoot at a fortress town on the Ghanaian coast, an old drummer, Sankofa (Ghanaba), warns that her actions are sacrilegious to the now-forgotten sufferings of what was once a slaving post, and orders her to return to the past. Miraculously, she is transported back through time to become Shola, house slave on an American sugar plantation, where she is repeatedly abused by her master and where she witnesses the different resistance strategies of her lover Shango and her African-born friend Nunu, who has a power verging on the magical. While there's no doubting the sincerity of writer/director Gerima's film, one can't help sensing more than a little déjà vu in his account of the manifest evils of slavery. GA

Sansho Dayu 100 (100) (Sansho the Bailiff)

(1954, Jap, 123 min, b/w)
d Kenji Mizoguchi. *p* Masaichi Nagata. *sc* Yoshikata Yoda, Yahiro Fuji. *ph* Kazuo Miyagawa. *ed* Mitsuzo Miyata. *ad* Kisaku Ito, Kozaburo Nakajima. *m* Fumio Hayasaka. *cast* Kinuyo Tanaka, Yoshiaki Hanayaki, Kyoko Kagawa, Eitaro Shindo, Akitake Kono, Masao Chimizu.

● A humane provincial governor in 11th century Japan is forced into exile by his political opponents, and the members of his family (wife, son and daughter) fall victim to all the cruelties of the period while on their way to join him. Mizoguchi views this deliberately simple story (in Japan it is known as a folk-tale) from two perspectives at once: from the inside, as an overwhelmingly moving account of a man (the son) facing up to his own capacity for barbarism; and from the outside, as an infinitely tender meditation on history and individual fate. The twin perspectives yield a film that is both impassioned and elegiac, dynamic in its sense of the social struggle and the moral options, and yet also achingly remote in its fragile beauty. The result is even more remarkable than it sounds. TR

Sans Pitié

see Sin Compasión

Sans Soleil (Sunless) 100

(1983, Fr, 100 min)
d Chris Marker. *p* Anatole Dauman. *sc* Chris Marker. *ph* Sana Na N'Hada, Danièle Tessier, Jean-Michel Humeau, Mario Marret, Eugenio Bentivoglio, Haroun Tazieff. *ed* Chris Marker. *m* Michel Krasna, Mussorgsky, Sibelius. *narrator* Alexandra Stewart.

● Imagine getting letters from a friend in Japan, letters full of images, sounds and ideas. Your friend is an inveterate globe-trotter, and his letters are full of memories of other trips. He has a wry and very engaging sense of humour, he's a movie fan, he used to be quite an activist (though he was never much into 'ideology'), and he's thoughtful and very well read. In his letters, he wants to share with you the faces that have caught his eye, the events that made him smile or weep, the places where he's felt at home. He wants to tell you stories, but he can't find a story big enough to deal with his sense of contrasts, his wish to grasp fleeting moments, his recurring memories. Above all he hopes to excite you, to share his secrets with you, to consolidate your friendship. Now stop imagining things and go to see *Sans Soleil*, in which Marker, the cinema's greatest essayist, sums up a lifetime's travels, speculations and passions. Among very many other things, his film is the most intimate portrait of Tokyo yet made: from neighbourhood festivals to robots, under the sign of the Owl and the Pussycat. TR

Sans Toit ni Loi

see Vagabonde

Santa Claus

(1985, GB, 108 min)
d Jeannot Szwarc. *p* Ilya Salkind, Pierre Spengler. *sc* David Newman. *ph* Arthur Ibbetson. *ed* Peter Hollywood. *pd* Anthony Pratt. *m* Henry Mancini. *cast* Dudley Moore, John Lithgow, David Huddleston, Burgess Meredith, Judy Cornwell, Jeffrey Kramer.

● Children are now facing the prospect of permanent brain-softening from 1985's *Superman* stand-in. High up in the glacial wastes, stunted people with names like Boog, Vout and Honka fight a losing battle to be noticed among a production line of toys in hideous primary colours. Moore is relieved of his elf duties, and so defects to sell trade secrets to the villainous toy manufacturer BZ (Lithgow). After the Christmas hostilities, when you are finally sick to death of the little beasts, get your revenge. Pack them off to this. CPea

Santa Claus Conquers the Martians

(1964, US, 82 min)
d Nicholas Webster. *p* Paul Jacobson. *sc* Glenville Mareth. *ph* David Quaid. *ed* Maurice Gordon. *m* Milton Delugg. *cast* John Call, Leonard Hicks, Vincent Back, Victor Stiles, Donna Conforth, Pia Zadora.

● Suitably tacky tale of how some depressed Martians kidnap Santa to brighten things up at home. A staple after-midnight cult movie, this hilariously bad stab at sci-fi naturally earned a high position in the book *The Fifty Worst Movies of All Time*. One of the Martian kids appropriately grew up to be Pia Zadora, the pouter pigeon of the equally awful *Butterfly* and *Lonely Lady*. CR

Santa Clause, The

(1994, US, 98 min)
d John Pasquin. *p* Brian Reilly, Jeffrey Silver, Robert Newmyer. *sc* Leo Benvenuti, Steve Rudnick. *ph* Walt Lloyd. *ed* Larry Bock. *pd* Carol Spier. *m* Michael Convertino. *cast* Tim Allen, Judge Reinhold, Wendy Crewson, Eric Lloyd, David Krumholtz, Larry Brandenburg, Peter Boyle.

● A vehicle for Tim Allen, star of TV's *Home Improvements*, this turns out to be an unexpected treat. Divorced businessman Scott Calvin rediscovers the love of son Charlie when he dons Santa's red mantle after an unfortunate accident on his roof. The sleigh, the elves, and the magic all seem to indicate a dream, but when, ten months later, Scott can't stop himself putting on the pounds and growing a fluffy white beard, he realises that perhaps he should have read the small print before signing the Santa clause. Perennial bug-bears like the absence of chimneys and the size of Santa's sack are readily explained by contemporary morphing effects, while the sarcastic Allen makes an admirably grumpy Father Christmas. The movie steers a shrewd course between bracing cynicism and old-fashioned make-believe. TCh

Santa Fe Trail

(1940, US, 110 min, b/w)
d Michael Curtiz. *p* Robert Fellows. *sc* Robert Buckner. *ph* Sol Polito. *ed* George Amy. *ad* John Hughes. *m* Max Steiner. *cast* Errol Flynn, Olivia de Havilland, Raymond Massey, Ronald Reagan, Alan Hale, Van Heflin, William Lundigan, Ward Bond, Guinn Williams.

● History is bunk, and politics pushed aside in favour of professionalism, as Flynn's Jeb Stuart – the future Rebel general – leads a bunch of West Point graduates against abolitionist John Brown, and finally gets involved in the battle at Harper's Ferry, thus beginning the Civil War. Far from liberal in attitude (Massey's John Brown is seen as a fanatic, ruthless and violent; the blacks are portrayed as barely willing to fight for their freedom), it's nevertheless fast and spectacular enough to warrant a look, if only to see Reagan playing Custer. Now that was inspired casting. GA

Santa Sangre

(1989, It, 123 min)
d Alejandro Jodorowsky. *p* Claudio Argento. *sc* Alejandro Jodorowsky, Roberto Leoni, Claudio Argento. *ph* Daniele Nannuzzi. *ed* Mauro Bonanni. *pd* Alejandrp Luna. *m* Simon Boswell. *cast* Axel Jodorowsky, Blanca Guerra, Guy Stockwell, Thelma Tixou, Sabrina Dennison.

● Like some Fellini-esque nightmare, this heady mix of circus freaks (a tattooed lady, an exotic midget, sad-faced clowns) and weird religious and hallucinatory imagery (an armless virgin saint, writhing snakes, zombie brides) is pregnant with disturbing psychological undercurrents. Traumatised at an early age by a violent argument between his knife-throwing father (Stockwell) and trapeze-artist mother (Guerra), former child magician Fenix (Axel Jodorowsky), now 20, escapes from an asylum into the outside world. Reunited with his jealous mother, Fenix becomes her 'arms' in a bizarre pantomime act, a role which spills dangerously over into real life. With a tapestry of cultural references that embraces the Venus de Milo, Marcel Marceau, Liberace and *Night of the Living Dead*, Jodorowsky's is a strange, violent, but ultimately liberating vision. NF

Santee

(1972, US, 93 min)
d Gary Nelson. *p* Deno Paoli, Edward Platt. *sc* Brand Bell. *ph* Donald M Morgan. *ed* George W Brooks. *ad* Mort Rabinowitz. *m* Don Randi. *cast* Glenn Ford, Michael Burns, Dana Wynter, Jay Silverheels, Harry Townes, John Larch, Robert Wilke.

● Soft-centred Western. Ford, close to pensionable age, plays a gnarled, misanthropic cowboy whose values have been warped by the murder of his son. All he wants out of life is to hunt down outlaws with high prices on their heads. After killing a renegade, he adopts the man's homeless teenage son. Gradually, his bitterness thaws and he forgets his grudge against the world. GM

Santiago (aka The Gun Runner)

(1956, US, 93 min)
d Gordon Douglas. *p* Martin Rackin. *sc* Martin Rackin, John Twist. *ph* John Seitz. *ed* Owen Marks. *ad* Edward Carrere. *m* David Buttolph. *cast* Alan Ladd, Rossana Podesta, Lloyd Nolan, Chill Wills, Paul Fix, LQ Jones.

● Formula adventure, with gun-running mercenary Ladd discovering conscience, cause and commonsense when righteously 'politicised' by the passion of Cuban patriot (1898 version) Rossana Podesta. Martin Rackin produced and co-scripted to protect his own novel from too much imaginative input, while director Douglas – fresh from the lunacies of the Liberace showcase *Sincerely Yours* – treated the whole thing as a cakewalk. PT

Santos Inocentes, Los

see Holy Innocents, The

São Paulo, SP

(1991, Neth, 94 min)
d/p Olivier Koning. *sc* Maarten de Kroon, Maria Lúcia Frores, Wim Romeijn. *ph* Adrian Cooper. *ed* Hanns Dunnewijk.

● 'It's astonishing and frightening,' says an engineer, dwelling on statistics which reveal that there's a building erected every hour in São Paulo, Brazil. Koning's absorbing documentary selects a cross-section of residents – from an architect to a street-sweeper – and alternates interviews in which they talk about their lives and ambitions. Packed with fascinating insights and, as in the case of a family who make their home under a viaduct, an often moving depiction of resilience. CM

Saphead, The

(1920, US, 81 min, b/w)
d Herbert Blaché. *p* John L Golden, Winchell Smith. *sc* June Mathis. *ph* Harold Wenstrom. *cast* Buster Keaton, William H Crane, Irving Cummings, Carol Holloway, Beulah Booker.

● Buster Keaton's first feature, though charming and lightly amusing, is something of a disappointment. Having picked up on his talent after the Fatty Arbuckle shorts, MGM clearly had no idea what to do with it, and settled for an old warhorse of a play (*The New Henrietta* by Winchell Smith and Victor Mapes) which had already served as a vehicle for Douglas Fairbanks. Playing the dim, pampered son of *The Wolf of Wall Street*, Keaton dumbfounds everyone by making an unexpected killing on the stock market, thereby winning the girl of his dreams. The character closely foreshadows Keaton's later persona, but is wedged in throughout by acres of creaky, conventional plotting, which only once opens out – a splendid scene of upheaval on the stock market floor – to allow him to do his own acrobatic thing. TM

Sapphire

(1959, GB, 92 min)
d Basil Dearden. *p* Michael Relph. *sc* Janet Green. *ph* Harry Waxman. *ed* John D Guthridge. *ad* Carmen Dillon. *m* Philip Green. *cast* Nigel Patrick, Michael Craig, Paul Massie, Yvonne Mitchell, Bernard Miles, Earl Cameron, Gordon Heath, Orlando Martins.

● Hot on the heels of the Notting Hill race riots came *Sapphire*. Children playing ball on Hampstead Heath stumble across a murdered girl. A nice, respectable white girl in prim tweeds. But, horror of horrors, she's three months pregnant and wearing scarlet taffeta undies! Poor Sapphire only looks white and, as the film sagely informs us, 'No matter what the colour of the skin, you can always tell when the bongo-drums start beating'. Actually, in spite of Horace Big Cigar and a host of no-good blacks, the real murderer is a fanatical white racist. Dearden's analysis of English prejudice is comprehensive and uncompromising, but the film's 'impartiality' leads it perilously close to condoning what it sets out to condemn. RMy

Saps at Sea

(1940, US, 57 min, b/w)
d Gordon Douglas. *p* Hal Roach. *sc* Charles Rogers, Felix Adler, Gilbert W Pratt, Harry Langdon. *ph* Art Lloyd. *ed* William Ziegler. *ad* Charles D Hall. *m* Marvin Hatley. *cast* Stan Laurel, Oliver Hardy, James Finlayson, Dick Cramer, Ben Turpin.

● The last film Laurel and Hardy made for Hal Roach, a scrappy but often very funny affair in which Dr Finlayson prescribes a sea cruise after Ollie goes crazy working in a honking horn factory (a sequence destructively elaborated from *Modern Times)*. Less inventive when, after Stan has inadvertently destroyed their apartment, they find themselves not only at sea (they meant to stay safely tied up in harbour) but slaving on behalf of an evil-tempered escaped convict (Cramer): the highlight here – they prepare a revolting meal for Cramer, but are forced to eat it themselves – is both drawn-out and unfunny. A comedy of much charm, nevertheless. TM

Saraband for Dead Lovers

(1948, GB, 96 min)
d Basil Dearden. *p* Michael Balcon. *sc* John Dighton, Alexander Mackendrick. *ph* Douglas Slocombe. *ed* Michael Truman. *pd* Michael Relph. *m* Alan Rawsthorne. *cast* Stewart Granger, Joan Greenwood, Flora Robson, Françoise Rosay, Peter Bull, Frederick Valk, Anthony Quayle, Michael Gough, Megs Jenkins.

● One of Ealing Studios' most lavish period pieces. A sombre, romantic drama about the arranged marriage between the young Sophie (Greenwood) and the gross George Louis of Hanover, later George I of Britain (Bull, superbly repulsive), and the unhappy lady's dalliance with the dashing Konigsmark (Granger). Warner Brothers would have made it as a swashbuckling epic, but the English approach to these things was always different: the emphasis here is on power politics and doomed love, with special weight given to an anarchic carnival presided over by the Lord of Misrule, and to Flora Robson's role as an ageing lady of the court. Relph's designs are magnificent; Dearden's direction veers towards the pretentious (rain on stained glass makes a Madonna 'weep') but is for the most part functionally emotional. TR

Sarafina!

(1992, SAf, 116 min)
d Darrell James Roodt. *p* Anant Singh. *sc* William Nicholson, Mbongeni Ngema. *ph* Mark Vicente. *ed* Peter Hollywood, Sarah Thomas. *ad* David Barkham. *m* Stanley Myers. *cast* Leleti Khumalo, Whoopi Goldberg, Miriam Makeba, John Kani, Dumisani Diamini, Mbongeni Ngama.

● A (Molotov) cocktail mixing scenes of appalling violence with song and dance, Mbongeni Ngema's 1987 Soweto-based musical makes an uneasy transition to the screen. After some awkward opening sequences, the film's agenda becomes more readily apparent. Reprising her lead role as an embattled, starstruck schoolgirl, Khumalo plays Sarafina, who dreams of staging a school musical about Nelson Mandela, while at the same time teaming up with young activists who seek mass action against apartheid. Their energies are guided by teacher Mary (Goldberg), who flouts the authorised syllabus in order to instil knowledge of people power. A low-key Goldberg serves as catalyst and the children's conscience, while the emotions are left to Khumalo in a striking, moving depiction of defiance. Even her charismatic character, however, fails to give a proper consistency to the narrative, and the structure goes badly adrift. CM

Saragossa Manuscript, The (Rekopis Znaleziony w Saragossie)

(1964, Pol, 175 min, b/w)
d Wojciech Has. *p* Ryszard Straszewski. *sc* Tadeusz Kwiatkowski. *ph* Mieczyslaw Jahoda. *ad* Jerzy Skarzynski, Tadeusz Myszorek. *m* Krzysztof Penderecki. *cast* Zbigniew Cybulski, Kazimierz Opalinski, Iga Cembrzynska, Joanna Jedryka, Franciszek Pieczka.

● Wojciech Has contrives a Chinese-box, Borgesian teaser from his story of a Belgian officer (Cybulski) who travels across Spain during the Peninsular War and becomes involved in a chain of narratives. But the film's real (and secret) subject is the Gothic imagery of the Tarot and Cabbalistic traditions: multiple storyline, trains of resemblance, mysterious icons of Fate and Death. It remains sadly unclear, though, from the British print (cut by a third of its length to 124 minutes) whether this elaborately literary film fails because it is now too short...or because it was always too long. CA

Saratoga Trunk

(1945, US, 135 min)
d Sam Wood. *p* Hal B Wallis. *sc* Casey Robinson. *ph* Ernest Haller. *ed* Ralph Dawson. *ad* Carl Jules Weyl. *m* Max Steiner. *cast* Gary Cooper, Ingrid Bergman, Flora Robson, Jerry Austin, John Warburton, Florence Bates, John Abbott, Ethel Griffies.

● A thoroughly bad, seriously miscast costume drama, with Bergman playing the illegitimate Creole beauty who upsets New Orleans society in the Gay Nineties when she sets out to avenge her mother by trashing the well-heeled family of her father. Cooper is a gambler called Clint Maroon whom she takes up with, while Robson, smeared with boot polish, plays Hattie McDaniel. Edna Ferber's doorstop novel should have become a delirious vehicle for Bette Davis or Tallulah Bankhead. Bergman is all wrong – she has the beauty but not the bravado – and Sam Wood hasn't a clue. ATu

Saroja

(1999, Sri Lanka, 110 min)
d Somaratne Dissanayake. *p* Renuka Balasooriya. *sc* Somaratne Dissanayake. *ph* Sumindra Weerasinghe. *ed* Stanley de Alwis. *pd* Heenetigala Premadasa. *m* Rohana Weerasinghe. *cast* Janaka Kumbukage, Neeta Fernando, Pramudi Karunarathne, Nithyavani Kandasamy, Mervin Maheshan.

● Dedicated to those who suffer the inhumanity of war, this protracted first feature follows former Tamil Tiger Sundaram (Maheshan) and his daughter Saroja, aged seven, on their flight to the jungle to escape the Sinhalese army. Wounded and fearing he'll die, Sundaram sends Saroja (Kandasamy) to a Sinhalese village in the hope that, despite her origins, she'll be given refuge. Varuni, a girl of the same age, discovers Saroja and persuades her teacher father and more resistant mother to help, with fateful repercussions for everyone. JFu

Sarraounia

(1986, Fr/Burkina Faso, 121 min)
d/p/sc Med Hondo. *ph* Guy Famechon. *ed* Marie Thérèse Boiche. *pd* Jacques d'Ovidio. *m* Pierre Akendenqué, Abdoulaye Cissé, Issouf Compaore. *cast* Aï Keïta, Jean-Roger Milo, Féodor Atkine, Didier Sauvegrain, Roger Mirmont, Luc-Antoine Diquero.

● Sarraounia is a young warrior queen of the Azna tribe, whose mastery of the ancient 'magic' skills of martial arts and pharmacology is first put to the test when she defends her people from attack by a neighbouring tribe. But the real trial of strength comes when the French army marches south to widen its colonial grip on the African continent. The second half of the film centres on the French, acidly but plausibly satirised as little tyrants whose megalomania swells in proportion with their failure to grasp the realities of the culture they are trying to crush. Everything here is grounded in careful but never pedantic historical research. The film is superbly crafted and expansive; the tone is celebratory, loud, assertive and spirited; but Hondo doesn't allow the visual and musical splendours to swamp his certainty that Africans need to learn to value and develop the identity that was theirs before the white man came. TR

Sasuke and His Comedians (Sanada Fu-unroku)

(1963, Jap, 100 min)
d Tai Kato. *sc* Yoshiyuki Fukuda, Ryunosuke Ono, Fumio Konami. *ph* Osamu Furuya. *ed* Shintaro Miyamoto. *ad* Norimichi Ikawa. *m* Hikaru Hayashi. *cast* Kinnosuke Nakamura, Misako Watanabe, Hitoshi Omae, Kei Sato, Fujio Tokita.

● This, er, unorthodox account of the 1615 siege of Osaka Castle is a batty mix of cartoon historiography (characters representing real life figures are captioned on first appearance), political satire (the whole thing is a commentary on the fate of the early 1960s student movement) and psychedelic visual effects (the laddish protagonists are guided by the ninja Sasuke, whose exposure as an infant to a glowing blue meteorite gave him supernatural powers). Toei almost fired Kato for making it, but it's become a minor cult favourite in Japan. Very much of its time, it holds up as a rueful, dreamlike account of the shortcomings of revolutionary idealism. TR

Satan Bug, The

(1964, US, 113 min)
d/p John Sturges. *sc* James Clavell, Edward Anhalt. *ph* Robert Surtees. *ed* Ferris Webster. *ad* Herman A Blumenthal. *m* Jerry Goldsmith. *cast* George Maharis, Richard Basehart, Anne Francis, Dana Andrews, Edward Asner, Frank Sutton, John Larkin.

● One of umpteen Alistair MacLean paperback thrillers (this one written under the pseudonym of Ian Stuart) definitively pulped in their transition to celluloid, this is the would-be *Dr Strangelove* of biological warfare, with rebel scientist Basehart legging it alone with a stolen vial of deadly virus, threatening global annihilation. Half-hearted and dull, despite the contributions of heavyweight adaptors James Clavell and Edward Anhalt, working at odds with an out-of-his element Sturges. PT

Satanic Rites of Dracula, The (aka Count Dracula and His Vampire Bride)

(1973, GB, 88 min)
d Alan Gibson. *p* Roy Skeggs. *sc* Don Houghton. *ph* Brian Probyn. *ed* Chris Barnes. *ad* Lionel Couch. *m* John Cacavas. *cast* Christopher Lee, Peter Cushing, Michael Coles, William Franklyn, Freddie Jones, Joanna Lumley, Richard Vernon, Patrick Barr.

● The beguiling message underlying Hammer's modern-dress Dracula movie is that the real vampires of modern London are property speculators. The legendary Count (Lee in fine form) has built a Centre Point-type construction on the site of his old crypt, and comes on like a cross between Howard Hughes and Harry Hyams as he plans to lay waste the city. The idea is amazing (after all, Dracula started as a subversive myth), but inevitably it tends to get lost in the usual mundane complexities of espionage melodrama and occult lore. A lot of weak action scenes and weaker lines, but still a vast improvement on *Dracula A.D.1972*. DP

Satan Met a Lady

(1936, US, 75 min, b/w)
d William Dieterle. *p* Henry Blanke. *sc* Brown Holmes. *ph* Arthur Edeson. *ed* Warren Low. *ad* Max Parker. *m* Leo F Forbstein. *cast* Warren William, Bette Davis, Alison Skipworth, Arthur Treacher, Marie Wilson, Winifred Shaw, Porter Hall.

● The second version of Hammett's *The Maltese Falcon*, somewhat disguised (doubtless because the novel had been filmed only five years earlier): the Fat Man becomes a dignified dowager, Joel Cairo is turned into a languid Englishman, and the falcon is replaced by Roland's fabled horn, stuffed with jewels by the Saracens to silence it after the hero's death. It doesn't bear comparison with the 1941 Huston version, mainly because Sam Spade (here 'Ted Shane'), as played by Warren William with an eye to the success of *The Thin Man*, is a cavalier, wisecracking ladies' man-about-town; the darker overtones of the Huston film are therefore elided, and his final unmasking of Bette Davis goes for nothing by comparison with the two-way Bogart-Astor 'betrayal'. Thanks to Dieterle's stylishly witty direction and excellent performances, it's nevertheless enjoyably and quirkily funny, at least until just before the end, when a whole wedge of undigested plot exposition suddenly catches up with the action. TM

Satan Never Sleeps (aka The Devil Never Sleeps)

(1962, US/GB, 126 min)
d/p Leo McCarey. *sc* Claude Binyon, Leo McCarey. *ph* Oswald Morris. *ed* Gordon Pilkington. *pd* Tom Morahan. *m* Richard Rodney Bennett. *cast* William Holden, Clifton Webb, France Nuyen, Weaver Lee, Athene Seyler, Martin Benson, Edith Sharpe.

●McCarey's last film is a dreadful, trashy yarn about two priests in China (Holden and Webb) sticking out for their beliefs against the onslaught of communism. The man had clearly gone feeble-minded. The film is propaganda designed to equate Communism with Satan. China is the Evil Empire here (though it was in fact filmed in England and Wales). As *Variety* noted, more occurs in the final 15 minutes than in the whole of the rest of the picture. Satan may not sleep, but you will. TCh

Satan's Brew (Satansbraten)

(1976, WGer, 112 min)
d Rainer Werner Fassbinder. *p* Michael Fengler. *sc* Rainer Werner Fassbinder. *ph* Michael Ballhaus, Jürgen Jürges, Peter Braumüller. *ed* Thea Eymesz, Gabi Eichel. *pd* Kurt Raab, Ulrike Bode. *m* Peer Raben. *cast* Kurt Raab, Margit Carstensen, Helen Vita, Volker Spengler, Ingrid Caven, Ulli Lommel, Armin Meier.

●The scurrilous movie that marked a turnaround in Fassbinder's film-making practice, following the disbandment of his 'stock company' of actors as a theatre troupe. The familiar faces are still around, this time distorted by pebble glasses, pustules or gross make-up, but there's a new sense of liberation from theatrical stylisation gusting through the proceedings. The plot is a benignly black celebration of the art of literary theft: Kurt Raab plays a clapped-out writer who regains his stride when he begins 'accidentally' reproducing the complete works of Stefan George. He is surrounded by freaks, perverts and grotesques, and so hardly anyone notices. It's no accident that this frolicsome tale reverses Fassbinder's standard 'victim' formula: it transpires that the tyrannical Raab is secretly a masochist, and one who actively enjoys being victimised. Bouncy. TR

Satan's Skin (aka Blood on Satan's Claw)

(1970, GB, 93 min)
d Piers Haggard. *p* Peter L Andrews, Malcolm B Heyworth. *sc* Robert Wynne-Simmons. *ph* Dick Bush. *ed* Richard Best. *ad* Arnold Chapkis. *m* Marc Wilkinson. *cast* Patrick Wymark, Linda Hayden, Barry Andrews, Avice Landon, Simon Williams, Tamara Ustinov, Howard Goorney, James Hayter, Michele Dotrice.

●Not nearly so atmospheric as Michael Reeves' *The Witchfinder General*, but for the first hour Piers Haggard keeps his theme and the blood flowing nicely. It begins in style, with a farmer in 17th century England digging up a skull with one eye still working, and then there is a disembodied furry arm and claw on the rampage. The only thing the cast of Olde Worlde actors can think of is human sacrifice, and there are a lot of nubile actresses to choose from. Sadly, Haggard lets things slip, and the make-up man takes over. ATu

Satan's Slave

(1976, GB, 86 min)
d Norman J Warren. *p* Les Young, Richard Crafter. *sc* David McGillivray. *ph* Les Young. *ad* Hayden Pearce. *m* John Scott. *cast* Michael Gough, Martin Potter, Candace Glendenning, Barbara Kellermann, Michael Craze, James Bree, David McGillivray.

●Another absolute stinker from the withered pen of David McGillivray, who this time permits himself a small but telling role – yes that's the author playing the priest who drags the naked witch to the tree ('filmed entirely on location in Surrey') in order to brand and then flog her. Elsewhere this home movie drags out the theme of possession, with the nutty-family-in-big-country-house striving to reincarnate the witch (imaginatively named Camilla) in Candace Glendenning's body. It also shows how bad experienced actors – Potter, Kellermann, Gough – can be when handed dialogue as matchless as 'It's at moments like this that I'm glad I'm a doctor'. AN

Satan's Tango

see Sátántangó

Sátántangó (Satan's Tango)

(1994, Hun/Ger/Switz, (Pt 1) 300 min/(Pt 2) 135 min, b/w)
d Béla Tarr. *p* György Fehér, Joachim von Vietinghoff, Ruth Waldburger. *sc* László Krasznahorkai, Béla Tarr. *ph* Gábor Medvigy. *ed* Agnes Hranitzky. *m* Mihály Vig. *cast* Mihály Vig, Miklos B Szekely, Putyi Horvath, János Derzsi, Erika Bók, Erzsébet Gaal, László Lugossy, Eva Almássy Albert.

●Tarr's most ambitious work is structured in 12 chapters – it's a b/w adaptation of László Krasznahorkai's novel – and the narrative movement follows the titular dance steps, moving back and forth around pivotal scenes, viewed from multiple perspectives. It opens with arguments and planned betrayals over the year's wages for a failing collective farm – with the tense interaction noted by an alcoholic doctor. It then shifts into a larger frame with the reappearance of a quasi-Messianic leader. Allegorical yet historically precise, it is an anti-authoritarian satire and metaphysical treatise. In addition, it might well be the great film of entropy. A soundscape of weary accordion and resounding bells balances the sacred and profane spheres. Formally in dynamic tension between the claustrophobic intimacy of Tarr's early influence, Cassavetes, and the rigorously choreographed grace of Tarkovsky and Jancsó, this startling, apocalyptic work is sometimes over-extended, but it builds to a powerful, rhythmic climax of breakdown and withdrawal. GE

Satin Spider

see Araignée de Satin, L'

Satisfaction

(1988, US, 92 min)
d Joan Freeman. *p* Aaron Spelling, Alan Greisman. *sc* Charles Purpura. *ph* Thomas Del Ruth. *ed* Joel Goodman. *m* Michel Colombier. *cast* Justine Bateman, Liam Neeson, Trini Alvarado, Britta Phillips, Julia Roberts, Scott Coffey, Deborah Harry.

●A tacky rock'n'roll drama which regurgitates clichés without any sense of shame. The script might have been written twenty-five years ago – like the rock standards the band specialise in – but it is meant to be taken seriously. Bateman, the daughter from TV's *Family Ties*, can't sing. Nor does Julia Roberts play the drums too convincingly; and as for Liam Neeson, moping around as a songwriter who's lost the muse, he ought to be ashamed of himself. TCh

Saturday (Sábado)

(2001, Arg, 72 min)
d Juan Villegas. *p* Nathalie Cabiron. *sc* Juan Villegas. *ph* Paola Rizzi. *ed* Martin Mainoli. *pd* Luciana Inda. *cast* Gastón Pauls, Daniel Hendler, Camila Toker, Mariana Anghileri, Leonardo Murúa, Eva Sola.

●For the first half-hour or so, with its Pinter-like conversational absurdities, non sequiturs and antagonisms, this wry study of three couples whose lives become intertwined one otherwise ordinary Saturday looks set to be a real winner. It's fresh, funny, fast and full of surprises. Then, suddenly, it all begins to fall a bit flat. Too many dialogues lead nowhere, the twists and switches in relationships are faintly predictable, and there's rather too much repetition. Its wit and pace pick up again by the end,confirming its opening promise. Gastón Pauls, as himself, is particularly to be commended for sending himself up as a womanising celebrity. Yet more proof that something's stirring in Argentina, filmwise. GA

Saturday Night and Sunday Morning

(1960, GB, 89 min, b/w)
d Karel Reisz. *p* Harry Saltzman, Tony Richardson. *sc* Alan Sillitoe. *ph* Freddie Francis. *ed* Seth Holt. *ad* Edward Marshall. *m* John Dankworth. *cast* Albert Finney, Rachel Roberts, Shirley Anne Field, Bryan Pringle, Hylda Baker, Norman Rossington, Colin Blakely.

●The big box-office success of the British New Wave in the early '60s, no doubt because its hero's defiant watchword of 'Don't let the bastards grind you down' struck a responsive chord before everybody started never having had it so good. Much of the freshness survives in Finney's abrasive performance as the young Nottingham factory worker lashing blindly out at the bleak working class horizons to which he has been bred by parents 'dead from the neck up'. Trying to grab what life can offer with both hands without regard for consequences or for anybody else, he ends up with nothing but the final gesture of defiance of hurling a stone at the housing estate where he is about to settle down and live unhappily for ever after. But it all seems terribly glib now, at worst sailing close to parody, at best suffused with the faintly patronising sincerity of the Angry Young Man/New Left era. TM

Saturday Night at the Baths

(1974, US, 90 min)
d David Buckley. *p* David Buckley, Steve Ostrow. *sc* Franklin Khedouri, David Buckley. *ph* Ralf D Bode. *ed* Jackie Raynal, Suzanne Fenn. *m* Ron Frangipane. *cast* Robert Aberdeen, Ellen Sheppard, Don Scotti, Steve Ostrow, Janie Olivor, Larry Smith.

●Unlike *Fox*, *Dog Day Afternoon* and *A Bigger Splash*, in which the central theme of homosexuality occurred within a larger framework, *Saturday Night at the Baths* approaches its subject on a more basic level. Against a semi-documentary background of New York's Continental Baths, the film traces a straight musician's progression from a heterosexual relationship to a homosexual one. It approaches the subject sympathetically and seriously, but finally becomes trapped by its own lack of resources: uneven acting and an indifferent script which does little more than put the characters through the motions. Good footage of the Baths, and the film's increasing confidence as it develops help it along. CPe

Saturday Night at the Palace

(1987, SAf, 90 min)
d/p Robert Davies. *sc* Paul Slabolepszy, Bill Flynn. *ph* Robert Davies. *ed* Lena Farugia, Carla Sandrock. *ad* Wayne Attrill, Sandy Attrill. *cast* Paul Slabolepszy, Bill Flynn, John Kani, Marius Weyers.

●Slabolepszy is a foul-mouthed unemployed white racist, Kani the manager of a Johannesburg diner and the victim whom he singles out for abuse. Slabolepszy created the role in his own play, which he adapted for the screen with co-star Flynn, and though time and politics have moved on, the film version stands as a concerned reminder of South Africa's bitter divisions. TJ

Saturday Night Fever

(1977, US, 119 min)
d John Badham. *p* Robert Stigwood. *sc* Norman Wexler. *ph* Ralf D Bode. *ed* David Rawlins. *pd* Charles Bailey. *m* Barry Gibb, Robin Gibb, Maurice Gibb. *cast* John Travolta, Karen Lynn Gorney, Barry Miller, Joseph Cali, Paul Pape, Donna Pescow, Julie Bovasso.

●A disco movie for people who don't go to discos, this is really about Growing Up – which the movie interprets as Growing Out of a Disco Mentality and into Personal Relationships. The relationship between Tony (Travolta) and Stephanie (Gorney) is at least as angst-ridden as anything in *Annie Hall*, but like almost everything else in the movie, it's played dead straight. This, of course, makes it extremely funny, up to a point, though in the end the real killer is the movie's abject sincerity. Pity, really, since there's certainly room for at least one decent movie about the actual appeal and experience of discos. The only true drug culture of the '70s, they deserve better than to be represented as watering-holes for arrested adolescents. TR

Saturday's Children

(1940, US, 101 min, b/w)
d Vincent Sherman. *p* Henry Blanke. *sc* Julius J Epstein, Philip G Epstein. *ph* James Wong Howe. *ed* Owen Marks. *ad* Hugh Reticker. *m* Adolph Deutsch. *cast* John Garfield, Anne Shirley, Claude Rains, Lee Patrick, George Tobias, Roscoe Karns, Dennis Moore.
● This third version of Maxwell Anderson's play in less than 12 years indicates how much producers and audiences were willing to buy its smug middlebrow social conscience. Adapted by the *Casablanca* brothers Julius and Philip Epstein, it follows the struggling young couple Garfield and Shirley as they try to cope with poverty and unemployment in the tough urban arena of New York City. Rains steals the movie as her dear old dad, who's willing to commit suicide so they can cash in on the insurance, but it's po-faced stuff.

Saturday the 14th

(1981, US, 77 min)
d Howard R Cohen. *p* Julie Corman. *sc* Howard Cohen. *ph* Daniel Lacambre. *ed* Joanne D'Antonio, Kent Beyda. *ad* Arlene Alen. *m* Parmer Fuller. *cast* Richard Benjamin, Paula Prentiss, Jeffrey Tambor, Severn Darden, Kari Michaelsen, Kevin Brando, Rosemary De Camp.
● Mr and Mrs Average inherit a creepy old mansion in which is hidden an ancient book that can summon up monsters, mostly from a cheap costume-rental shop, from the look of what turns up after Average Junior finds the manual. The book is also high on the wants list of Mr and Mrs Vampire, who in turn head the list of local exterminator Mr Van Helsing. Pretty soon the house is swamped with Things, the proceedings being played for (hard to find) laughs. It might be possible to extort money from Benjamin and Prentiss to forget you've seen this. DO

Saturn

(1999, US, 95 min)
d Rob Schmidt. *p* Palmer West. *sc* Rob Schmidt. *ph* Matthew Libatique. *ed* Gabriel Wrye, Michael Ross. *pd* James Chindlund. *m* Ryeland Allison. *cast* Scott Caan, Leo Burmester, Mia Kirshner, Anthony Ruivivar.
● Melancholy and gloomy, if not entirely cold, this minor American indie earns its title and points for promise if not quite achievement. Caan is eminently watchable as Drew, a capable but uninspired student and bit-time mechanic living out of a Brooklyn industrial loft and stuck with his dear, incapacitated father; but one of an increasingly recognisable breed of directionless twenty-somethings on film. There's little story – Drew tries to fit a drugs and sex binge with a 'weird but cute' junkie around panic attacks about his father. Instead, first time director Schmidt attempts an impressionistic montage of blue moments, the best of which are compellingly stylish, but the sum of which lacks focus. NB

Saturn 3

(1980, GB, 87 min)
d Stanley Donen. *p* Stanley Donen. *sc* Martin Amis. *ph* Billy Williams. *ed* Richard Marden. *ad* Stuart Craig. *m* Elmer Bernstein. *cast* Farrah Fawcett, Kirk Douglas, Harvey Keitel, Douglas Lambert, Ed Bishop.
● Some handy tips on how to enjoy *Saturn 3* One, you can play 'Spot the Rip-off', a game requiring only a cursory knowledge of successful sci-fi/horror movies. Watch for the *Star Wars* special effects, the claustrophobic chase scenes from *Alien*, the rampant robots of *Dark Star*. Or you can while away the credibility gaps by guessing how much Kirk Douglas got paid for not cracking up over lines like 'I guess I'm near aborttime', or how much Martin Amis got paid for writing them. Alternatively, try to figure out whether Harvey Keitel's baddie talks in such a clipped monotone because he's a baddie, or because he's gritting his teeth. And if all else fails, you can ponder the absurd central premise: could any biped – let alone the film's Meccano-built robot – be driven blood-lust crazy for Farrah Fawcett's fanny? Just another miserable muddle from the Lew Grade empire; there's more fun to be had cleaning out your cat litter tray. FL

Satyricon

see Fellini-Satyricon

Saudade do Futuro (Saudate for the Future)

(2000, Braz/Fr/Bel, 94 min)
d César Paes. *p/sc* César Paes, Marie-Clémence Blanc-Paes. *ph* Michel Berck, César Paes. *ed* Agnes Contensou. *m* Fábio Freire, Thomas Rohrer. *with* Luiza Eruindina, Fábio Freire, Ezequias Lira, Thomas Rohrer.
● Like New Orleans, Havana and Kingston, São Paulo has an infectious musical vibe. Every location visited by this competent documentary is buzzing with the city's unique blend of Spanish, Cuban and New Orleans-style Zydecko. Indeed, the whole thing is almost entirely narrated through song or poetry. Some of these musical poets might sing the praises of this poor, bustling city, but others bravely wax political about the 'corrupt politicians' running/ruining their country. There's a lot of joyous dancing – a little too much, in fact – and the whole could have been a bit more snappily edited. Hardly a Buena Vista Social Club, then, but insightful and warm none the less. DA

Sausalito (Yi Jian Zhongqing)

(2000, HK, 97 min)
d Andrew Lau. *p* Wong Jing, Jessinta Liu. *sc* Chan Sap-Saam. *ph* Andrew Lau. *ed* Danny Pang. *ad* Patrick Ludden. *m* Chen Kwong-Wing. *cast* Maggie Cheung, Leon Lai, Eric Kot, Scott Leong, Richard Ng, Snooky Kwan, Valerie Chow.
● Single parent Ellen (Cheung) struggles to make ends meet driving a taxi in San Francisco and dreams of retiring to Sausalito with her young son. Mike (Lai) is a brilliant software designer with limitless access to casual sex, but scared of committing to a relationship. Their on-off romance, which starts with a back-wrenching shag in the taxi, is designed to snare the *Comrades, Almost a Love Story* audience. But the pseudonymous script (vulgar incidentals suggest that producer Wong Jing had a hand in it) is an anthology of clichés and the underlying assumptions about material success and 'integrity' are fairly obnoxious. Cheung does her best with Ellen and Lau tries to add interest with visual shtick. But the material remains inert. TR

Saut de l'Ange, Le

see Cobra

Sauvage, Le

(1975, Fr/It, 107 min)
d Jean-Paul Rappeneau. *p* Raymond Danon. *sc* Jean-Paul Rappeneau, Elisabeth Rappeneau, Jean-Loup Dabadie. *ph* Pierre Lhomme. *ed* Marie-Josèphe Yoyotte. *ad* Max Douy. *m* Michel Legrand. *cast* Yves Montand, Catherine Deneuve, Luigi Vannucchi, Dana Wynter, Bobo Lewis, Tony Roberts.
● A commonplace *toujours l'amour* tragi-farce whose only justification lies in the decorative presence of its two stars. The urbane Montand as a self-sufficient *sauvage* on the run from the unacceptable face of his wife's cosmetic empire, growing vegetables on an island retreat, is a strain on the imagination. But for credibility he has the edge on Deneuve. Her divine sang-froid hardly lends itself to a role that requires her to be part Doris Day, part Claudia Cardinale. The runaway pace is maintained by operatic slapstick, tempestuousness verging on insanity, hysterical dialogue that occasionally lurches into Spanish and American, and a dazzling range of locations (Venezuela, New York, Provence). JS

Sauve Qui Peut – la Vie (Every Man for Himself/Slow Motion)

(1980, Switz/Fr, 89 min)
d Jean-Luc Godard. *p* Alain Sarde, Jean-Luc Godard. *sc* Anne-Marie Miéville, Jean-Claude Carrière, Jean-Luc Godard. *ph* William Lubtchansky, Renato Berta, Jean-Bernard Menoud. *ed* Anne-Marie Miéville, Jean-Luc Godard. *ad* Romain Goupil. *m* Gabriel Yared. *cast* Isabelle Huppert, Jacques Dutronc, Nathalie Baye, Roland Amstutz, Anna Baldaccini.
● Godard's return to celluloid after a decade of experiment in video is in one sense forced: the sources of finance for his projects were drying up, and he himself admits that the film was made as a passport back into the business. But in another, this is his most personal work in years, less important for its return to narrative (the story of two women and a man joined in almost arbitrary ways) than for its chilled sense of autobiography – Dutronc plays an egotistical, washed-out video film-maker called 'Godard'. In that light, the resurrection of earlier themes (especially prostitution) is no return at all, but a confessional fantasy about a generation of men now in middle age, alienated from their sexuality, dissatisfied with their 'commerce', and unwilling to cope with a new sexual/political order. It would be hard to imagine a more courageous project; harder still to find one executed with the kind of stylistic wit and haunting elegance that have made Godard leader of the pack for over twenty years. CA

Savage Bees, The

(1976, US, 99 min)
d/p Bruce Geller. *sc* Guerdon Trueblood. *ph* Richard C Glouner. *ed* George Hively, Bud Friedgen. *m* Don Kirshner. *cast* Ben Johnson, Michael Parks, Gretchen Corbett, Paul Hecht, Horst Buchholz, Bruce French, James Best.
● 'Somebody's poisoned mah dawg' wails Sheriff Ben Johnson, only to discover that the mutt's been stung to death by a swarm of killer bees up from South America (pause for lecture) for the New Orleans Mardi Gras. This made-for-TV movie, unwarrantedly exposed on the big screen, is so weakly plotted that efforts to generate suspense never appear more than mechanical. The bees look real enough, but attention wanders long before Horst Buchholz gets himself killed trying to capture the queen bee in a hot-dog stand. For the protracted finale, the bees obligingly settle on the heroine's VW, only to succumb without a murmur. CPe

Savage Capitalism

(1993, Braz, 86 min)
d Andre Kloetzel. *p* Flávio. *sc* Andre Klotzel, Djalma Limongi Batista. *ph* Pedro Farkas. *ed* Daniel Tadeu. *m* David Tygel. *cast* Fernanda Torres, Jose Mayer, Marisa Orth.
● Investigating a mining company which is encroaching on Indian lands, journalist Elisa (Torres) discovers that the company's handsome, schizophrenic chairman (Mayer) is actually of native descent. They embark on a passionate affair, until the man's 'dead' wife comes back to life. This eccentric ecological romance was apparently inspired by the films of Pedro Almodóvar – but it's hard to believe the director has ever seen one. For all the weirdness on display (notably an office that transforms into a jungle), this is a fundamentally banal picture, with embarrassingly naive hippie-mystic sentiments ('You aren't the man I met behind a desk, you are the Lord of the Forest…' etc). And is the title ironic? It is not. TC

Savage Honeymoon

(1998, NZ, 95 min)
d Mark Beesley. *p* Steve Sachs. *sc* Mark Beesley. *ph* Leon Narby. *ed* Margot Francis. *pd* Gary Mackay. *m* Dean Savage Band. *cast* Nicholas Eadie, Perry Piercy, Craig Hall, Elizabeth Hawthorne, Stephen Hall, Theresa Healey, Stephen Lovatt.
● A broad, largely predictable and mostly unamusing Kiwi comedy about a biker family beset by internal and external pressures and trying to preserve their sense of freedom and individuality in a conformist world. True, characters like the leather clad forty-something parents are seldom seen as central, and the film is fundamentally good natured, but the narrative is too thin to sustain interest at feature length. GA

Savage Innocents, The

(1960, It/Fr/GB, 110 min)
d Nicholas Ray. *p* Maleno Malenotti. *sc* Nicholas Ray, Hans Reusch, Franco Solinas. *ph* Aldo Tonti, Peter Hennessy. *ed* Ralph Kemplen. *ad* Don Ashton. *m* Angelo Francesco Lavagnino. *cast* Anthony Quinn, Yoko Tani, Peter O'Toole, Carlo Giustini, Marie Yang, Andy Ho, Lee Montague.

●Though scuppered by problems worse than those usually associated with international coproductions, this is nonetheless rather more than just another engaging oddity from Ray. Further evidence of his ethnological interest in 'outsider' societies, it charts the hardships suffered by Quinn the Eskimo as he struggles to survive not only against the harsh conditions of life in the Artic, but – more lethally – against the invasion of Western 'civilisation', embodied by Christianity, capitalism and rock'n'roll. Much of the story is episodic and semi-documentary in tone, illustrating Eskimo hunting habits, marital rituals, and so forth, while the misguidedly 'poetic' dialogue is stilted and unconvincing. But, as ever, Ray's deployment of the 'Scope frame throws up images of an often startling, even surreal beauty: polar bears diving from the ice-flows become a rhapsody in blinding whites and br illiant blues, and the sound of a juke box screaming out over the empty, snowy wastes is a withering, wicked symbol of man's destructive influence on nature. GA

Savage Islands (aka Nate and Hayes)

(1983, NZ, 99 min)
d Ferdinand Fairfax. *p* Lloyd Phillips, Rob Whitehouse. *sc* John Hughes, David Odell. *ph* Tony Imi. *ed* John Shirley. *pd* Maurice Cain. *m* Trevor Jones. *cast* Tommy Lee Jones, Michael O'Keefe, Max Phipps, Jenny Seagrove, Grant Tilly, Peter Rowley.

●More in the vein of *Raiders of the Lost Ark* thrills and spills than Fairbanks swash and buckle, the story is told in flashback with good old-fashioned cut-and-thrust. In the South Pacific islands in the 1880s, Captain Bully Hayes (Jones) saves maidens in distress, performs impossible feats of agility, does battle with a German count (Tilly) intent on nasty military annexations with the aid of an ironclad warship, in a plot that is as credible as Hitler's diaries. Which makes not a lot of difference, for the film is to be enjoyed on a tongue-in-cheek level: lots of stunts and not too much mushy lovey-dovey stuff. Originality never raises its head, but it'll keep the kids from clammering for a glimpse of those video nasties. FL

Savage Man...Savage Beast (Ultime Gride della Savana)

(1975, It, 100 min)
d/p/sc/ph/ed Antonio Climati, Mario Morra. *m* Carl Savina.

●A bloody, blatantly exploitative mess of a movie, cutting bewilderingly between North and South America, Australia, Europe and Africa, with flimsily related scenes of animals killing each other and men killing animals for survival, sport and profit. A woefully inadequate English commentary (the original was by Alberto Moravia) tries to make sense of all this slaughter. Finally, however, this patched-up documentary reveals its true colours: just another opportunity to gawp at raw scenes of sex and (more especially) violence. In the Burundi jungle, two soon-to-be-hanged brothers are seen squatting in the rain with the cannibalised remains of their father; a foolish tourist leaves his car and is eaten by lions; a van carrying a crew filming cheetahs overturns at sickening speed. Rock bottom is reached with the inclusion of 16 mm home movie footage of white mercenaries cheerfully mutilating and butchering Amazonian tribesmen. JPy

Savage Messiah

(1972, GB, 103 min)
d/p Ken Russell. *sc* Christopher Logue. *ph* Dick Bush. *ed* Michael Bradsell. *pd* Derek Jarman. *m* Michael Garrett. *cast* Dorothy Tutin, Scott Antony, Helen Mirren, Lindsay Kemp, Michael Gough, John Justin, Aubrey Richards, Peter Vaughan.

●Vorticist sculptor Henri Gaudier-Brzeska (Antony) becomes Russell's archetypal angry young man, scorching his way through a stereotyped collection of Edwardian culture figures, dashing off sculptures by candlelight. Henri's interesting relationship with the ageing authoress Sophie Brzeska (they decided to unite in name) is lost in the director's overriding credo that both art and films are a matter of how much energy you exert.

Savage Nights (Les Nuits Fauves)

(1992, Fr, 126 min)
d Cyril Collard. *p* Nella Banfi. *sc* Cyril Collard, Jacques Fieschi. *ph* Manuel Téran. *ed* Lise Beaulieu. *m* René-Marc Bini, Cyril Collard. *cast* Cyril Collard, Romane Bohringer, Carlos Lopez, Corine Blue, Claude Winter.

●Based on his partly autobiographical novel, the late Cyril Collard's film is an exception to most AIDS-issue movies. Returning from a trip to Morocco in 1986, Jean (Collard) finds he is HIV-positive. However, the 30-year-old bisexual film-maker/musician continues to live to the full – cruising strangers, taking up with Samy (Lopez), embarking on a relationship with Laura (Bohringer), with whom Jean has unsafe sex, initially omitting to warn her. But that's not what upsets the teenager, who believes her love is stronger than death. Only when she fears losing him to Samy does she crack up. Besides the raw vitality of its visuals, what distinguishes Collard's film is its unrepentant honesty. If none of the main characters is especially admirable, or likeable, they are all credible. The film has a few longueurs, but its refusal to simplify or soften the plight facing Jean, Laura and Samy guarantees a powerful provocative and relevant account of lives on the emotional edge. GA

Savages

(1972, US, 106 min, b/w & col)
d James Ivory. *p* Ismail Merchant. *sc* George Swift Trow, Michael O'Donoghue. *ph* Walter Lassally. *ed* Kent McKinney. *m* Joe Raposo. *cast* Louis Stadlen, Anne Francine, Thayer David, Susan Blakely, Russ Thacker, Salome Jens, Kathleen Widdoes, Sam Waterston.

●Strip away our veneer of civilisation, cast a dispassionate eye on our frantic attempts to gratify ourselves, and what do you find? You guessed. Ivory's earlier made-in-India movies got by on their 'delicacy' and 'sensitivity'; but this half-assed fable – about a bunch of jungle primitives turning, when a croquet ball mysteriously intrudes on their human sacrifice, into '30s socialites and then reverting back again – exposed the pseud beneath the aesthete. No wit, no thought, no surrealist flair, just vacuous decoration. It plays like a Ken Russell movie worked over by a taxidermist. TR

Savage Souls

see Ames Fortes, Les

Save the Last Dance

(2000, US, 113 min)
d Thomas Carter. *p* Robert W Cort, David Madden. *sc* Duane Adler, Cheryl Edwards. *ph* Robbie Greenberg. *ed* Peter E Berger. *pd* Paul Eads. *m* Mark Isham. *cast* Julia Stiles, Sean Patrick Thomas, Kerry Washington, Fredro Starr, Terry Kinney, Bianca Lawson, Vince Green, Garland Whitt.

●In *Footloose*, if memory serves, young Kevin Bacon was the cool city kid who got toes tapping and pulses racing in some small Midwestern burg by introducing the hicks to...Kenny Loggins. Flash forward 17 years and it's immediately apparent that time has stood still in Middle America. Model student Sara (Stiles) favours knitwear and braids, and dreams of being a ballerina. Then – and we're still stuck in a *Readers' Digest* opening credit sequence, I'm afraid – mom dies in her mad rush to get to her daughter's Julliard audition (which she flunks anyway) and a dejected Sara hangs up her ballet shoes. She moves into her estranged dad's fleapit Chicago apartment and adjusts to being the only white face in her new school. This race element is the most interesting aspect of the film. Urban hip has always condescended to provincial square but rarely has it been so overtly identified as black hip, white square. Sara comes under the protective tutelage of first Chenille (Washington), then Chenille's brother Derek (Thomas), who teaches her to dance for real. As teen melodrama, well, Carter's film is what it is; but for such a mainstream black-consciousness movie, at least it doesn't shy from addressing some touchy issues about masculinity, parenthood, and black attitudes to whites. TCh

Save the Tiger

(1972, US, 100 min)
d John G Avildsen. *p/sc* Steve Shagan. *ph* James Crabe. *ed* David Bretherton. *ad* Jack T Collis. *m* Marvin Hamlisch. *cast* Jack Lemmon, Jack Gilford, Laurie Heineman, Norman Burton, Patricia Smith, Thayer David.

●Lemmon's nervy performance as the garment manufacturer harassed by financial problems and moral compromises is the best thing in this well-meaning but very wordy look at the failure of the American Dream. Middle-aged, disillusioned, and nearing a nervous breakdown, he bewails the passing of his youth when things were simpler, while resorting to insurance fraud to revive his ailing fortunes. Cynical, occasionally hollow stuff (scripted by Steve Shagan), but thanks to Lemmon, sometimes quite moving. GA

Saving Grace

(1985, US, 111 min)
d Robert M Young. *p* Herbert F Solow. *sc* Joaquin Montana. *ph* Reynaldo Villalobos. *ed* Michael Kelly, Peter Zinner. *pd* Giovanni Natalucci. *m* William Goldstein. *cast* Tom Conti, Fernando Rey, Erland Josephson, Giancarlo Giannini, Donald Hewlett, Edward James Olmos, Patricia Mauceri, Guido Alberti.

●A troubled man, hemmed in by the protocol of his position, Pope Leo XIV (Conti) impulsively opts for a working holiday. Moved by a little girl's story of her village – stricken by an earthquake and without a priest – the undercover Holy Father hitchhikes deep into the (picture postcard) Italian south, and proceeds to preach the protestant work ethic to people whose major source of income is government aid derived from the odd staged epidemic. Through his arduous efforts – 'he's a Pope who smiles, a Pope who cries, a Pope who loves, hates, and learns to love again' – Leo sets the villagers in motion once more. Despite a plot veiled in about as much mystery as an uncracked soft-boiled egg, *Saving Grace* does retain a certain Disneyesque charm as an innocent modern fable. SGo

Saving Grace

(1999, GB, 93 min)
d Nigel Cole. *p* Mark Crowdy. *sc* Craig Ferguson, Mark Crowdy. *ph* John de Borman. *ed* Alan Strachan. *pd* Eve Stewart. *m* Mark Russell. *cast* Brenda Blethyn, Craig Ferguson, Martin Clunes, Tchéky Karyo, Jamie Foreman, Bill Bailey, Valerie Edmond, Tristan Sturrock, Clive Merrison, Leslie Phillips, Diana Quick, Phyllida Law.

●This turns on the comic incongruity of a prim and proper country lady (Blethyn) venturing into the high end dope-dealing business after finding her late husband has left her with something less than nothing. It's an evident confection, generous with provincial whimsy – and turns out to be very merry fun. What's different? In the first place, breadth of constituency: its populist inclusiveness encompasses diverse characters and audiences. After all, no one's going to set out specifically to ingratiate middle-aged housewives with a drug peddling romp, nor dope freaks with a story of a Cornish widow's belated liberation; compounding the two, however, results in refreshingly poignant silliness. The sensibility's very Ealing, which makes it a rose-tinted vision of England, but eminently lively and charming. NB

Saving Private Ryan

(1998, US, 170 min)
d Steven Spielberg. *p* Steven Spielberg, Ian Bruce, Mark Gordon, Gary Levinsohn. *sc* Robert Rodat. *ph* Janusz Kaminski. *ed* Michael Kahn. *pd* Tom Sanders. *m* John Williams. *cast* Tom Hanks, Tom Sizemore, Matt Damon, Edward Burns, Barry Pepper, Adam Goldberg, Ted Danson, Dennis Farina.

●D-Day: Capt John Miller (Hanks), a decent school teacher in another life, is among the unfortunates storming Omaha Beach. As men are mown down and blown apart, the visceral editing and urgent camerawork tug us into the heart of chaos. No viewer can doubt that war, however justified, is hell. Only after 30 minutes does the pace ease and the story begin, with Miller and his platoon assigned to find and bring back Private Ryan, the brother of three soldiers killed in the same week, who's missing behind enemy lines. Thereafter the movie becomes more conventional and, mercifully, less relentlessly gory, at least until Ryan (Damon) and a few other soldiers are finally found, and Miller and his surviving men join them in defending a bridge, at which point the nightmare begins again. Except for a redundant epilogue, sentimentality is mostly held at bay, but the film remains an utterly American take on WWII, with the lack of political, ethical and historical perspective which that implies. Why did Spielberg make it? He wants us to imagine we can feel the terror of being there, but does that make us any wiser about this or any other conflict? Probably not. GA

Saving Silverman (aka Evil Woman)

(2001, US, 96 min)
d Dennis Dugan. *p* Neal H Moritz. *sc* Greg DePaul, Hank Nelken. *ph* Arthur Albert. *ed* Debra Neil-Fisher, Patrick J Don Vito. *pd* Michael Bolton. *m* Mike Simpson. *cast* Jason Biggs, Steve Zahn, Jack Black, Amanda Peet, R Lee Ermey, Amanda Detmer, Neil Diamond.

● There comes a point in every young man's development when a woman threatens to come between him and his buddies, and to rectify matters his pals must kidnap the bitch. The two soon to be bereft friends are Wayne (Zahn) and JD (Black), rodent wrangler and unemployable, respectively, who determine to rescue their romantically credulous pal Darren Silverman (Biggs) from the clutches of Dr Judy Fessbeggler (Peet), a lithe but heartless succubus. Not only won't she reciprocate his sexual favours, she's intent on total domination. Gender semioticians will note that Judy's rival (in the boys' eyes) is a trainee nun. Well, Judy's no whore, either despite the film-makers predeliction for dressing her down to the barest fripperies wherever possible. Mainly she's a cartoon villain who likes to play rough, but gets her due in the end. Part tongue in cheek, part genuinely inane, this is tough to get a handle on. As cinema, Dugan's lowlife comedy is bunk, full of clumsy filler flashbacks and frenetic guitar-signalled forced humour, yet interspersed with moments of wit. NB

Savior

(1997, US, 103 min)
d Peter Antonijevic. *p* Oliver Stone, Janet Yang. *sc* Robert Orr. *ph* Ian Wilson. *ed* Ian Crafford, Gabriella Cristiani. *pd* Vladislav Lasic. *m* David Robbins. *cast* Dennis Quaid, Nastassja Kinski, Stellan Skarsgård, Natasa Ninkovic, Pascal Rollin, Catlin Foster.

● Two soldiers enter a bomb-shattered house. There are bodies on the floor. A baby has been hidden in the closet; the child's grandmother lies petrified on the bed. The soldiers – a Serb and a foreign mercenary – chop off the old woman's finger for sport. We are in Bosnia, 1993. The Serb's sister is returned to him in a prisoner swap. She is pregnant after being raped by her Muslim captors. Shamed and dishonoured, the man beats the baby out of her. Before he can finish the job, he is shot dead by the mercenary, who undertakes to transport the suicidal mother and newborn infant to safety. This is a relentlessly grim and harrowing movie. It's said that military recruitment tends to rise after even the best anti-war films. Only a psychopath would volunteer for the hell Quaid goes through here. This Oliver Stone production squares up to the war in Yugoslavia and never looks for the Hollywood cop-out, save, perhaps, for the first five minutes, a redundant, perfunctory prologue which attempts to explain Quaid's 'motivation', and dispatches with Kinski before the credits have rolled. It's unnecessary, because Quaid's dead eyes tell you all you need to know – this is a brave, concentrated, resolutely unsympathetic performance unlike anything he's done before. The politics are even-handed, the violence brutal and unflinching. It's hard to recommend a movie that resembles nothing so much as a good kick in the head, but Serbian director Antonijevic gives it a raw, ugly force that feels not only authentic, but legitimate. TCh

Sawdust and Tinsel

see Gycklarnas Afton

Say a Little Prayer

(1992, Aust, 97 min)
d Richard Lowenstein. *p* Carol Hughes. *sc* Richard Lowenstein. *ph* Graham Woods. *ed* Jill Babcock. *pd* Chris Kennedy. *m* Not Drowning, Waving. *cast* Sudi de Winter, Fiona Ruttelle, Lynn Murphy, Micky Camilleri, Rebecca Smart.

● Less audacious than Lowenstein's underrated *Dogs in Space*, this at first seems a rather tame tale of meeting-cute between a bored kid in his early teens – staying with a strict guardian for the summer holidays – and a spacy girl of around 20 who lives nearby. Gradually, however, it becomes noticeably tougher, as it fills in the reasons – without sermonising – for the girl's damaged innocence. But what finally impresses is the fluid elegance of the camera movements, the top-notch design, and the director's light touch with the boy's fantasy life, which even runs to a delicious interlude incorporating the Aretha Franklin classic of the title. Most engaging. GA

Say Anything

(1989, US, 100 min)
d Cameron Crowe. *p* Polly Platt. *sc* Cameron Crowe. *ph* Laszlo Kovacs. *ed* Richard Marks. *pd* Mark Mansbridge. *m* Richard Gibbs, Anne Dudley, Nancy Wilson. *cast* John Cusack, Ione Skye, John Mahoney, Joan Cusack, Lili Taylor, Amy Brooks, Pamela Segall, Eric Stoltz, Lois Chiles.

● This product of the factory of youth, written and directed by first-timer Cameron Crowe, sports the intelligence and humanity of producer James L Brooks (*Terms of Endearment, Broadcast News*) like a buttonhole on a blind date. It's a relief to find characters with dignity in this context: Mahoney, in particular, relishes the opportunity to play an adult with some depth to him. Essentially though, it is teen romance time. Ione Skye is a (very) straight 'A' student, and John Cusack an easygoing kid who thinks his future might be in kickboxing. They fall for each other. The love story is as old-fashioned as the jokes are old hat, but Crowe's amusing script and unforced direction allow the actors to develop reasonably authentic characters from stereotypical roles … and the Cusacks are something special. Joan, who in *Working Girl* and *Stars and Bars* wiped the floor with everyone in sight, gently underplays in a cameo to her brother John, whose quiet integrity and oddball personality tap the charm of a jive-talking Jimmy Stewart. We are always growing up with American teenagers at the movies; at least these two are coming of age. TCh

Say It Isn't So

(2001, US, 96 min)
d JB Rogers. *p* Bobby Farrelly, Bradley Thomas, Peter Farrelly. *sc* Peter Gaulke, Gerry Swallow. *ph* Mark Irwin. *ed* Larry Madaras. *pd* Sidney J Bartholomew Jr. *m* Mason Daring. *cast* Chris Klein, Heather Graham, Orlando Jones, Sally Field, Richard Jenkins, John Rothman, Jack Plotnick, Eddie Cibrian, Mark Pellegrino, Brent Hinkley.

● Produced by the Farrelly Brothers, this gross-out love story is their lamest comedy yet. The main characters – butter-fingered small town hairdresser Jo, amiable, dreamy Animal Control worker Gilly – are conceived as innocents, the first a breezy survivor, the latter a stoic fatalist. As played by Graham and Klein, they'd make a sufficiently interesting and sympathetic odd couple for a left-field romance, but prove unsuitable stock as recipients of bad taste satire's pratfalls and humiliations. As in *There's Something About Mary*, a detective provides the McGuffin. Having fallen in love and accustomed himself to Jo's hardly ideal family – Sally Field excelling with full-on white trash philistinism as mum Valdine; Jenkins more repetitive as the disabled grump of a father – orphan Gilly is told Valdine is his long lost mother, Jo his sister. Cue comedy of social stigmatisation. End of Act One. Act Two sees Jo disappear to Oregon to marry a millionaire and the film disappear up its own rear end. Poor timing and muffed set pieces are compounded by implausibility and inconsequence. WH

Sayonara

(1957, US, 147 min)
d Joshua Logan. *p* William Goetz. *sc* Paul Osborn. *ph* Ellsworth J Fredricks. *ed* Arthur P Schmidt, Philip W Anderson. *ad* Ted Haworth. *m* Franz Waxman. *cast* Marlon Brando, Red Buttons, Miiko Taka, Miyoshi Umeki, James Garner, Patricia Owens, Ricardo Montalban.

● This operatic picture from James A Michener's novel has worn remarkably well. An ace fighter pilot (Brando) is unwillingly pulled from combat in the Korean War and sent to Japan so that romance can blossom with a general's daughter. The affair falters and the pilot slowly falls for the distant charms of a Japanese actress (Miiko Taka). The big theme is the injustice of the US policy of the day discouraging but not forbidding American servicemen from taking Japanese brides. The cruelty of this policy, demonstrated in a powerful subplot which ends in a double suicide, cuts through the film's overlay of exoticism and romantic sentimentality. Brando, more matinee idol than method actor, and none the worse for that, is contained and always watchable; but Red Buttons, in his first major role, as a chipper, angry young flier, with no family in America but the possibility of a life in Japan, gives perhaps the more heartfelt performance. JPy

Sbarco di Anzio, Lo (Anzio/The Battle for Anzio)

(1968, It, 117 min)
d Edward Dmytryk. *p* Dino de Laurentiis. *sc* Harry AL Craig. *ph* Giuseppe Rotunno. *ed* Alberto Gallitti, Peter Taylor. *ad* Luidi Scaccianoce. *m* Riz Ortolani. *cast* Robert Mitchum, Peter Falk, Earl Holliman, Mark Damon, Reni Santoni, Arthur Kennedy, Patrick Magee, Robert Ryan.

● Timidity at the top is soundly but turgidly castigated in this otherwise run-of-the-mill account of World War II's Anzio landing, when the Allies might have marched straight on Rome, but instead dug in on the beaches and allowed the Germans to prepare emergency defences. Some superb camera-work by Giuseppe Rotunno, and nicely choreographed action sequences; but the whole thing is sunk by the pseudo-philosophical profundities spouted by a war correspondent (the hapless Mitchum). TM

Scalawag

(1973, US/It, 93 min)
d Kirk Douglas. *p* Anne Douglas. *sc* Albert Maltz, Sid Fleischman. *ph* Jack Cardiff. *ed* John C Howard. *ad* Zeljko Senecic. *m* John Cameron. *cast* Kirk Douglas, Mark Lester, Neville Brand, George Eastham, Don Stroud, Lesley Anne Down, Danny DeVito, Phil Brown.

● Well accustomed to losing bits of his anatomy for his art (an eye in *The Vikings*, an ear in *Lust for Life*, a finger in *The Big Sky*), Kirk Douglas quite naturally appears in his own directorial debut, a kids' treasure hunt yarn based on Robert Louis Stevenson, as a one-legged pirate. Having set up a potential stablemate to *A High Wind in Jamaica*, though, he blows it conclusively with an increasingly treacly performance and erratic direction. The involvement of veteran 'Hollywood Ten' screenwriter Albert Maltz seems as incongruous as the decision to have Yugoslavian locations doubling for Mexico and California. PT

Scalphunters, The

(1968, US, 103 min)
d Sydney Pollack. *p* Jules Levy, Arthur Gardner, Arnold Laven. *sc* William Norton. *ph* Duke Callaghan, Richard Moore. *ed* John Woodcock. *ad* Frank Arrigo. *m* Elmer Bernstein. *cast* Burt Lancaster, Ossie Davis, Telly Savalas, Shelley Winters, Armando Silvestre, Dan Vadis, Dabney Coleman, Nick Cravat.

● An amiable enough liberal comedy Western, with colour-coded cultural conflict worked through an ironic circular plot. Lancaster's trapper is forcibly traded an ex-slave (Davis) for his pelts by an Indian band, after which the pair set off in uneasy alliance and in pursuit as the pelts are in turn appropriated by a gang of scalphunters. William Norton's script glosses both the racial antagonism and interdependence with a thankfully light hand; Pollack gets in some backwoods practice for the later mythologisation of *Jeremiah Johnson*. PT

Scamp, The

(1957, GB, 89 min, b/w)
d Wolf Rilla. *p* James H Lawrie. *sc* Wolf Rilla. *ph* Freddie Francis. *ed* Bernard Gribble. *ad* Elven Webb. *m* Francis Chagrin. *cast* Richard Attenborough, Terence Morgan, Dorothy Alison, Jill Adams, Colin Petersen, Geoffrey Keen, Margaretta Scott.

● Attenborough gives a decent enough performance as a schoolmaster who befriends the winsome ten-year-old urchin of the title (Petersen), finds that he is being neglected by his drink-swilling father (Morgan), and contrives to take him home under his temporary care. Cue some soapy melodramatics, what with the father coming on like Bill Sikes, Attenborough's wife getting antsy (she's a career woman, so the boy seems to point a finger at their childless marriage), and Attenborough himself provoking the crisis when forced to thrash the boy for a minor theft by a snotty woman (Scott) who threatens otherwise to call in the police. In a lurid climax, the boy comes to believe he caused his father's death: 'All my life I'll know I killed my father,' he emotes woodenly (a scriptwriter's line, not a child's, if ever there was one), whereupon the wheels grind loudly into the happy ending. TM

Scandal

(1988, GB, 115 min)
d Michael Caton-Jones. *p* Stephen Woolley. *sc* Michael Thomas. *ph* Mike Molloy. *ed* Angus Newton. *pd* Simon Holland. *m* Carl Davis. *cast* John Hurt, Joanne Whalley-Kilmer, Bridget Fonda, Ian McKellen, Leslie Phillips, Britt Ekland, Daniel Massey, Roland Gift, Jean Alexander, Ronald Fraser, Jeroen Krabbe.
●Caton-Jones' first feature is a serious, almost low-key affair, strong on period detail and imbued with a sense of genuine outrage on behalf of both the ruined Stephen Ward (Hurt) and the deranged and derailed Christine Keeler (Whalley-Kilmer) which lifts it above the merely exploitative. Both main performances are strong at the core of a still compelling story (Hurt in particular, a riveting jumble of weakness, seediness, vanity and kindness). Less satisfying are McKellen's Profumo, who looks more like a samurai warrior than a war minister; Bridget Fonda's Mandy Rice-Davies, and Jean Alexander's Mrs Keeler, who seem to have succumbed to the cutting-room jitter machine. Others must decide on the propriety of this cinematic exhumation; for those who weren't around at the time of the scandal in the early '60s, and even for those who were, it certainly makes dismaying if illuminating viewing. SGr

Scandale, Le

see Champagne Murders, The

Scandal in Montmartre

see Môme Pigalle, La

Scandalous

(1983, GB, 92 min)
d Rob Cohen. *p* Arlene Sellers, Alex Winitsky. *sc* Rob Cohen, John Byrum. *ph* Jack Cardiff. *ed* Michael Bradsell. *pd* Peter Mullins. *m* David Grusin. *cast* Robert Hays, John Gielgud, Pamela Stephenson, M Emmet Walsh, Nancy Wood, Conover Kennard, Jim Dale.
●Feeble comic flummery, shot in London from a tourist's-eye view, as TV reporter Hays tangles with madcap blackmailers Stephenson and Gielgud while trying to extricate himself from suspicion that he murdered his wife. Passing '80s pop sensations Bow Wow Wow drop by for a number, while master-of-disguise Sir John does himself up as a traffic warden, a Japanese businessman, and a leather-clad punk, bringing a particular poignancy to his line 'Just give me the money, dear boy, and let's be done with this nonsense.' Many a true word spoken in jest. TJ

Scanners

(1980, Can, 103 min)
d David Cronenberg. *p* Claude Héroux. *sc* David Cronenberg. *ph* Mark Irwin. *ed* Ron Sanders. *ad* Carol Spier. *m* Howard Shore. *cast* Jennifer O'Neill, Stephen Lack, Patrick McGoohan, Lawrence Dane, Michael Ironside, Adam Ludwig, Robert Silverman.
●This looks less like Cronenberg's popular mid-'70s exploiters (*Rabid, Shivers*) than one of his early experimental films remade on a higher budget, with a small group of 'scanners' (warrior-telepaths) fighting off a sinister mind-war army that is backed, indirectly, by industry and the state. Part conspiracy thriller, part political tract, it is Cronenberg's most coherent movie to date, drawing a dark (but bland) world in which corporate executives engineer human conception to produce ever more powerful mental samurai. And he punctuates it with spectacular set piece confrontations which really do dramatise the abstract, ingenious premise. As always, there's a nagging feeling that the script is not quite perfectly realised on screen, but Patrick McGoohan's bizarre cameo performance, and the extraordinary moral and sexual ambiguity of the final scanning contest, more than make up for it. CA

Scanners II: The New Order

(1991, Can, 105 min)
d Christian Duguay. *p* René Malo. *sc* BJ Nelson. *ph* Rodney Gibbons. *ed* Yves Langlois. *pd* Richard Tassé. *m* Marty Simon. *cast* David Hewlett, Deborah Raffin, Yvan Ponton, Isabelle Mejias, Tom Butler, Raoul Trujillo, Vlasta Vrana.
●It is telling that this superfluous sequel to Cronenberg's mind-blowing 1980 movie opens, not with an exploding head, but with a psycho scanner using his telepathic powers to trash a video games arcade. The plot suggests a computer game called 'RoboCop meets the Scanners', while Duguay's visual style consists entirely of pop promo clichés. For years, Dr Morse (Butler) and ambitious police commander Forrester (Ponton) have been trying to harness the scanners' powers, frustrated by the addictive drugs needed to control their volatile guinea-pigs. Then they stumble upon 'clean' scanner David Kellum (Hewlett), a naive country boy whose latent powers they plan to use to fight crime and instigate a fascistic New Order. The cast is anonymous, the plot confused and sluggish; only Michael Smithson's cheap, inventive special effects warrant attention. NF

Scar, The

see Hollow Triumph

Scar, The (Blizna)

(1976, Pol, 104 min)
d Krzysztof Kieslowski. *p* Zbigniew Stanek. *sc* Romauld Karas. *ph* Slawomir Idziak. *ed* Krystyba Gornicka. *ad* Andrzej Plocki. *m* Stanislaw Radwan. *cast* Franciszek Pieczka, Mariusz Domochowski, Jerzy Stuhr, Jan Scotnicki, Stanislaw Igar, Stanislaw Michalski, Michal Tarkowski, Halina Winiarska, Agnieszka Holland.
●Kieslowski's first theatrical feature is a rather dour slice of social realism. Adapted from a journalist's report, it's set in 1970 and examines the ramifications surrounding the construction of a huge chemical plant near a relatively backward rural community. Pieczka's project director suffers an ongoing crisis of conscience when the locals complain about the disruption. Meanwhile Stuhr's sinister Party manager tries to keep the lid on negative reporting by a roving film crew. There's understanding for points of view on all sides, but the absence of dramatic impetus reveals the film-maker's difficulty in adapting from the documentary work which had comprised the bulk of his previous output. That's bespectacled Agnieszka Holland as the factory secretary. TJ

Scar, The (Prae Kaow)

(1978, Thai, 130 min)
d Cherd Songsri. *cast* Sarapong Chatri, Nantana Ngaokrachang.
●Made for local distribution but by a partly Western-trained director, this – the first feature from Thailand to be seen in Britain – is based on a true Romeo and Juliet story set in the medieval Thai society of fifty years ago. Reflecting the conventions of Indian popular film, a couple of songs are crucial to the courtship; but otherwise the considerable technical expertise is at the service of a vivid narrative style. BP

Scaramouche

(1952, US, 118 min)
d George Sidney. *p* Carey Wilson. *sc* Ronald Millar, George Froeschel. *ph* Charles Rosher. *ed* James E Newcom. *ad* Cedric Gibbons, Hans Peters. *m* Victor Young. *cast* Stewart Granger, Eleanor Parker, Janet Leigh, Mel Ferrer, Henry Wilcoxon, Lewis Stone, Nina Foch, Richard Anderson, Robert Coote.
●A near-classic swashbuckler, adapted from the Rafael Sabatini novel set in 18th century France, with Granger desperate to avenge his dead friend by killing Mel Ferrer. But since he's not quite deadly enough with the rapier, he has to get some tuition. While all this revenge stuff simmers away, he falls in love with Miss Leigh, who may be his sister; and so, drawing the line at incest, he goes moodily back to sharpening his blade, while the plot unravels everyone's ancestry. Granger shows he can swash a buckle with the best of them, but whereas Fairbanks and Flynn did it with a grin, Granger wields the dirk with a smirk. ATu

Scarecrow

(1973, US, 115 min)
d Jerry Schatzberg. *p* Robert M Sherman. *sc* Garry Michael White. *ph* Vilmos Zsigmond. *ed* Evan Lottman. *pd* Albert Brenner. *m* Fred Myrow. *cast* Gene Hackman, Al Pacino, Dorothy Tristan, Ann Wedgeworth, Richard Lynch, Eileen Brennan.
●A tale with a moral about two drifters who meet on a deserted highway, and find antagonism gradually replaced by curiosity, need, trust and love. Lion (Pacino) clasps a present he is taking to the kid he deserted all those years ago; Max (Hackman) is an ex-con moving a step closer towards his dream of a self-owned carwash. Their relationship is charted like a love affair, full of petty jealousies, little tricks to forestall bad moods, recriminations, regrets. Then Schatzberg throws away the more interesting implications in order to make emotional hay. The pair land in prison, their relationship is tested by the grim realities they find there, and we are off into an embarrassing last section which ends with Max mourning over Lion's catatonic body. A pity – there could have been a movie in there. As it is, *Scarecrow* owes a lot to Vilmos Zsigmond's photography and little to Garry Michael White's over-insistent and finally rather silly script.

Scarecrow, The

(1981, NZ, 88 min)
d Sam Pillsbury. *p* Rob Whitehouse. *sc* Michael Heath, Sam Pillsbury. *ph* James Bartle. *ed* Ian John. *pd* Neil Angwin. *m* Schtung. *cast* John Carradine, Tracy Mann, Jonathan Smith, Daniel McLaren, Denise O'Connell, Anne Flannery.
●Set in the Kiwi equivalent of Middle Wallop in the '50s (with an intrusive jazz soundtrack to date it), Pillsbury's adaptation of a local classic is a valiant but botched first effort. Related by a voice-over reminiscent of Clive James with dyspepsia, the story concerns Ned and Pru Poindexter's last summer of adolescence. Into their lives of chicken rustling, gangs, and skinny dips comes the embodiment of destructive sexual power in the guise of arthritic-fingered Carradine, looking more like Steptoe on a rough day than any crazed killer bogeyman. Better at evoking the grim horrors of small town life than the terrors of a murder mystery, the film suffers from a plot which takes a beard-growing age to get going, then hops, skips and jumps to the dénouement. Unsentimental character portrayals, the depiction of parochial decay, the sly humour, and the odd haunting, sinister image are in its favour, but add up to little more than wrapping around a dull present. FL

Scarecrows

(1988, US, 88 min)
d William Wesley. *cast* Ted Vernon, Michael Simms, Richard Vidan, Kristina Sanborn, Victoria Christian, David Campbell.
●Thieves who have hijacked a plane, its crew and the $3 million it was carrying, make a forced landing near a seemingly deserted farmhouse after a greedy member of the gang bails out with money. The cornfields around the house are dotted with scarecrows, whose spindly limbs and rag faces take on an eerie quality as the sun goes down. Tensions between captors and captives heighten as members of both groups mysteriously disappear, to turn up later as disembowelled corpses stuffed with straw. Although a little slow to get started, this better-than-average horror móvie makes excellent use of its creepily-lit monsters, is reasonably well put together, and features some stomach-turning grisliness. NF

Scarface

(1932, US, 90 min, b/w)
d/p Howard Hawks. *sc* Ben Hecht, Seton I Miller, John Lee Mahin, WR Burnett. *ph* Lee Garmes, L William O'Connell. *ed* Edward Curtiss. *m* Adolph Tandler, Gus Arnheim. *cast* Paul Muni, Ann Dvorak, Karen Morley, Osgood Perkins, Boris Karloff, C Henry Gordon, George Raft, Vince Barnett.
●Its seminal importance in the early gangster movie cycle outweighed only by its still exhilarating brilliance, this Howard Hughes production was the one unflawed classic the tycoon was involved with. Hawks and head screenwriter Ben Hecht were after an equation between Capone and the Borgias: they provided so much contentious

meat for the censors amid the violent crackle of Chicago gangland war that they managed to slip a subsidiary incest theme through unnoticed. Two years' haggling ended with the subtitle *Shame of a Nation* being appended, one cardboard denunciation scene being added, and a hanging finale being substituted for the shootout – happily restored – which closes proceedings with forceful poetry. Unmissable – if only as the first film in which George Raft flips a dime… PT

Scarface

(1983, US, 170 min)
d Brian De Palma. *p* Martin Bregman. *sc* Oliver Stone. *ph* John A Alonzo. *ed* Jerry Greenberg, David Ray. *ad* Ed Richardson. *m* Giorgio Moroder. *cast* Al Pacino, Steven Bauer, Michelle Pfeiffer, Mary Elizabeth Mastrantonio, Robert Loggia, Miriam Colon, F Murray Abraham, Paul Shenar, Harris Yulin, Angel Salazar.

●The first motel shootout bodes well, a set piece handled with panache and the right note of clammy terror, but the rest of this lengthy modern morality tale (updating Hawks' film to 1980) is downhill all the way. When Castro last threw out all his scum, most of them fetched up in Florida, including Tony Montana (Pacino), a man with only 'balls of steel and my word, and I don't break either for anyone'. He attaches to the right sort of godfather, and rises and rises through a world of conspicuous consumption which make the Borgias blanch. Filmed in the bright widescreen glare of a thousand white suits, the movie is still empty at its heart; where Coppola gave you a whole dynasty in *The Godfather*, with a world and all its moral confusions behind it, De Palma spends three hours sketching out another tetchy little fiend with no more than the ability to nose-dive into mountains of cocaine and come up to razor a few more rivals. Pacino gives a monstrous performance as the Cuban heel, clearly aiming for role of the year, but the abiding memory is of just another Method boy chewing the scenery in his quiet way. CPea

Scarlet Blade, The (aka The Crimson Blade)

(1963, GB, 82 min)
d John Gilling. *p* Anthony Nelson-Keys. *sc* John Gilling. *ph* Jack Asher. *ed* James Needs, John Dunsford. *pd* Bernard Robinson. *m* Gary Hughes. *cast* Lionel Jeffries, Oliver Reed, Jack Hedley, June Thorburn, Duncan Lamont, Suzan Farmer, Michael Ripper.

●A fairly presentable but sometimes tedious Hammer romp through Cromwell's England, with Hedley and Thorburn battling for the Royalist cause against Colonel Judd (Jeffries), while Reed hovers in between as a love-smitten, treacherous turncoat. Judd is prepared to use the torture chamber when it suits him, but – apart from the period – there is no analogy with *Witchfinder General*, since this film carried a 'U' certificate and lacks any real period atmosphere. Gilling went on to do much better things for Hammer like *The Reptile* and *Plague of the Zombies*. DP

Scarlet Buccaneer, The

see Swashbuckler

Scarlet Claw, The

(1944, US, 74 min, b/w)
d/p Roy William Neill. *sc* Edmund Hartmann, Roy William Neill. *ph* George Robinson. *ed* Paul Landres. *ad* John B Goodman, Ralph M DeLacey. *m* Paul Sawtell. *cast* Basil Rathbone, Nigel Bruce, Gerald Hamer, Arthur Hohl, Miles Mander, Ian Wolfe, Paul Cavanagh, Kay Harding.

●One of a run of three films in the Rathbone/Bruce Sherlock Holmes series – it came sandwiched between *Sherlock Holmes and the Spider Woman* and *The Pearl of Death* – which made effective use of elements more properly belonging to the horror genre. Here Holmes and Watson travel to remoter Quebec (cue for some of the World War II propaganda uplift deemed essential at the time) to solve the mystery of the marsh monster of La Morte Rouge. With the fog machine working overtime, Neill makes nicely atmospheric use of the old inn and the gloomy marshes where citizens are having their throats bloodily torn out and a revenge-crazed old actor lurks in assorted disguises. Highly enjoyable. TM

Scarlet Empress, The

(1934, US, 109 min, b/w)
d Josef von Sternberg. *p* Adolph Zukor. *sc* Josef von Sternberg. *ph* Bert Glennon. *ad* Hans Dreier, Peter Ballbusch, Richard Kollorsz. *m* John Leipold, W Franke Harling. *cast* Marlene Dietrich, John Lodge, Louise Dresser, Sam Jaffe, C Aubrey Smith, Gavin Gordon.

●Sternberg's penultimate film with Dietrich was the visual apotheosis of their work together: a chronicle of the rise of Catherine of Russia, with elements of burlesque and pastiche, conceived principally as a delirious, extravagant spectacle. (It could almost be read as Sternberg's homage to silent cinema, with its strong alliance of music and visuals, and its narrative relegated to intertitles; but it's also a prefiguration of *Ivan the Terrible*) Catherine begins as an ostensibly naive innocent, tucked up in bed to tales of the Tsars' atrocities, and winds up in male military drag, killing her halfwit husband, leading her cavalry into the palace, herself merging with icons of Christ. In other words, beneath the surface frivolities, it's tough stuff. The decor and costumes, and the *mise-en-scène* that deploys them, have never been equalled for expressionist intensity. TR

Scarlet Letter, The

(1926, US, 8,229 ft, b/w)
d Victor Sjöström. *sc* Frances Marion. *ph* Hendrick Sartov. *ed* Hugh Wynn. *ad* Cedric Gibbons, Sidney Ullman. *cast* Lillian Gish, Lars Hanson, Karl Dane, Henry B Walthall, William H Tooker.

●One of Gish's great performances as Hester Prynne, a woman branded an adulteress in 17th century Salem, and forced to wear a scarlet 'A' of shame. Necessarily truncated from Hawthorne's novel about the terrors of Puritan intolerance, the film itself stumbles over occasional loose ends and melodramatic coincidences, not least the inopportune reappearance of Hester's husband, presumed dead but brought in from the wilderness for ransom by Indians. More damagingly, the references to witchcraft have gone, and with them Hawthorne's implication that Hester's illigitimate child is something of a changeling, and that her seducer – the parson Dimmesdale (a fine performance from Hanson) – has become satanically tainted over the years by his guilt. Sjöström papers this over quite effectively by turning the errant husband into a sort of Wandering Jew, vengefully hounding the tormented parson into his eventual confession and expiation. But what holds the film together above all is Sjöström's extraordinary feeling for rural Americana (despite the theme, much of the action takes place in bright sunlight and idyllically pastoral settings), which was to achieve its fullest expression in *The Wind* the following year. TM

Scarlet Letter, The (Der scharlachrote Buchstabe)

(1972, WGer/Sp, 89 min)
d Wim Wenders. *p* Peter Genée, Primitivo Alvaro. *sc* Wim Wenders, Bernardo Fernandez. *ph* Robby Müller. *ed* Peter Przygodda. *ad* Manfred Lütz, Adolfo Cofiño. *m* Jürgen Knieper. *cast* Senta Berger, Hans Christian Blech, Lou Castel, Yelena Samarina, Yella Rottländer, William Layton.

●Hawthorne's novel offers, however improbable a project, themes that connect with the main lines of Wenders' work: the central figure of the adulteress is an outsider in her own society, and the community of European immigrants are strangers in a strange land. But the movie is as uncharacteristic as you'd expect. Wenders made it (just after *The Goalkeeper's Fear of the Penalty*) as a kind of exercise in fiction, and it definitely lacks the emotional conviction that usually distinguishes his work. But Wenders' admirers will find a lot to interest them. The only major weakness is Jürgen Knieper's excessive score. TR

Scarlet Letter, The

(1995, US, 135 min)
d Roland Joffé. *p* Roland Joffé, Andrew G Vajna. *sc* Douglas Day Stewart. *ph* Alex Thomson. *ed* Thom Noble. *pd* Roy Walker. *m* John Barry. *cast* Demi Moore, Gary Oldman, Robert Duvall, Lisa Jolliff-Andoh, Edward Hardwicke, Robert Prosky, Joan Plowright, Roy Dotrice, Tim Woodward.

●New England, the 17th century, when everyone spake in 'thees' and 'thous'. Independent Hester Prynne (Moore) arrives from England to begin a new life in a puritanical community entrenched on the beautiful coastline. Her husband (Duvall) is to follow her. If only he knew what lay ahead. For less than seven seconds elapse between Hester learning of her husband's alleged death at the hands of Indians, and her jumping into the grain with the estimable Rev Dimmesdale (Oldman). The result's a baby girl, followed by imprisonment and ostracism for Hester, who's eventually forced by her elders to wear a scarlet 'A' and divulge the name of 'the fornicator'. Those acquainted with Hawthorne's novel, from which Joffé's long, cumbersome, at times unintentionally Python-esque, period saga was 'freely adapted', may think they know the outcome. They'd be wrong, because the word 'freely' in the opening credits should have read 'ever so freely'. Not only does the film bear little resemblance to the source novel, but it's cluttered with ridiculous symbolism (a Dayglo bird signposts Hester's way, Duvall dances around with a dead deer on his head) and filtered through a horrid chocolate-ad score. DA

Scarlet Pimpernel, The

(1934, GB, 98 min, b/w)
d Harold Young. *p* Alexander Korda. *sc* Lajos Biro, Sam Bermann, Robert E Sherwood, Arthur Wimperis. *ph* Harold Rosson. *ed* William Hornbeck. *ad* Vincent Korda. *m* Arthur Benjamin. *cast* Leslie Howard, Merle Oberon, Raymond Massey, Joan Gardner, Nigel Bruce, Bramwell Fletcher, Anthony Bushell, Walter Rilla.

●Though it meant changing directors midstream (he initially took over himself when Rowland Brown was fired), Korda determinedly eschewed blood-and-thunder and structured the film around the dual personality of the Pimpernel. The low-key action scenes seem indeed to function as an alibi, assuring us that the outrageously effeminate Howard is a man's man really, cool and resourceful enough to defeat even the machinations of sneeringly sinister Chauvelin (Massey zestfully playing the villain). With an eye to the American market, Korda subtly caricatures the reactionary sentiments of Orczy's novel (America too had its revolution!); and with Oberon's opaque beauty making her an ideally iconic counterfoil to Howard's fey Pimpernel, the film seems to operate more as a meditation on heroism and romantic love than as a celebration of aristocratic ideals. RMy

Scarlet Street

(1945, US, 103 min, b/w)
d/p Fritz Lang. *sc* Dudley Nichols. *ph* Milton Krasner. *ed* Arthur Hilton. *ad* Alexander Golitzen. *m* Hans J Salter. *cast* Edward G Robinson, Joan Bennett, Dan Duryea, Jess Barker, Margaret Lindsay, Rosalind Ivan, Samuel S Hinds, Vladimir Sokoloff.

●A remake of Renoir's *La Chienne* of 1931, and a key psychological *film noir*, one of Holly wood's most tortuous and bleak visions of the delusive power of the imagination. Edward G Robinson's meek, middle-aged, middle class cashier/Sunday painter suffers with 'problems with perspective' when driven into an obsessive infatuation with Joan Bennett's sensual, scheming prostitute/actress; and a potent combination of Fate, an unusually incisive script, Lang's claustrophobic visuals, and a haunting score are enough to shape him into the essential portrait of tragic vulnerability. The film, taking representation and perception as its dominant themes, practically begs for close textual analysis while rushing headlong towards its subversive climax – offering further proof that the tight framework of American narrative genres provided the ideal context for Lang to work in. PT

Scarlet Tunic, The

(1997, GB, 92 min)
d Stuart St Paul. *p* Daniel Figuero, Zygi Kamasa. *sc* Mark Jenkins, Colin Clements, Stuart St Paul. *ph* Malcolm MacLean. *ed* Donald Fairservice. *pd* Richard Elton. *m* John Scott. *cast* Jean-Marc Barr, Emma Fielding, Simon Callow, Jack Shepherd, John Sessions, Lynda Bellingham.

●Former stuntman Stuart St Paul's first feature is an adaptation of Thomas Hardy's story *The Melancholy Hussar*. Though it cost only

£350,000, it has none of the self-conscious flashiness of a 'calling card' movie. Never balking at the melodramatic elements of Hardy's vision, this tale of doomed love is told with clarity, passion and a keen eye for the beauty of Dorset. Barr smoulders as the German hussar, whose love for solicitor's daughter Fielding leaves her torn between duty and desire, while Sessions is slyly convincing, too, as the weasel-like suitor favoured by Fielding's loving but misguided father. Only the eye rolling Callow, as the martinet captain whose hounding of Barr betrays his own homosexual desire, misjudges the emotionally overwrought tone – one expects him to start twirling his impressive moustaches at any moment. Disappointingly, St Paul also over-eggs the pudding with a conciliatory coda that softens the original tragic ending. A credit, however, to all those who lent their time and talent. NF

Scarred

(1983, US, 85 min)
d Rose-Marie Turko. *p* Rose-Marie Turko, Mark Borde. *sc* Rose-Marie Turko. *ph* Michael Miner. *ed* Rose-Marie Turko. *ad* Cecilia Rodarte. *cast* Jennifer Mayo, Jackie Berryman, David Dean, Rico L Richardson, Debbie Dion.

●Calling the film *Scarred* rather than 'Teenage Hollywood Hookers' indicates some level of serious intent, though it prowls the same sort of sidewalk. Originally a UCLA film course project with AFI support, shot on 16mm apparently with available light, it's realistic about the relationships between hookers, pimps and customers. At the same time it's not above tapping into a vein of sentimentality when the script opts to rescue a couple of girls from The Life to give them a chance of a Better Life at the end. First time director Turko appears to have opted for her own Better Life – little has been heard of her subsequently. DO

Scars of Dracula, The

(1970, GB, 96 min)
d Roy Ward Baker. *p* Aida Young. *sc* Anthony Hinds. *ph* Moray Grant. *ed* James Needs. *ad* Scott MacGregor. *m* James Bernard. *cast* Christopher Lee, Dennis Waterman, Jenny Hanley, Christopher Matthews, Patrick Troughton, Michael Gwynn, Anoushka Hempel.

●This was Hammer's last 'period' Dracula before they plunged the Count disastrously into Swinging London. The plot follows the usual ploy of bringing a young couple (Waterman and Hanley) to the vampire's doom-laden castle, in this instance with the twist that they are bent on revenge. Despite attempts to restore some elements from Stoker previously omitted in the Hammer cycle (the Count is seen scaling the castle walls), and despite Lee's dogged efforts to give the Count a truly aristocratic bearing, the strained plot simply lurches from one gory set piece to another with (literally) extra lashings of sadism and sex. DT

Scary Movie

(2000, US, 88 min)
d Keenen Ivory Wayans. *p* Eric L Gold, Lee R Mayes. *sc* Shawn Wayans, Marlon Wayans, Buddy Johnson, Phil Beauman, Jason Friedberg, Aaron Seltzer. *ph* Francis Kenny. *ed* Mark Helfrich. *pd* Robb Wilson King. *m* David Kitay. *cast* Jon Abrahams, Carmen Electra, Shannon Elizabeth, Anna Faris, Kurt Fuller, Regina Hall, Lochlyn Munro, Cheri Oteri, Dave Sheridan, Marlon Wayans, Shawn Wayans.

●In this hugely successful movie – a pastiche of *Scream* – the *Airplane!*-style comedy is scattershot and stupid, but with an extra cup of grossout humour thrown in for bad measure. While the zany *Airplane!* pictures at least made one ponder the absurd conventions of disaster movies, this lamebrain lampoon offers neither wit nor insight. Instead, it regurgitates a random stream of snot, fart and hairy bollock gags. After the phone taunting and pre-credits slaughter of *Baywatch* babe Carmen Electra, the ramshackle plot plunders not only the expected titles, but also *The Blair Witch Project, The Sixth Sense, The Matrix* and *Riverdance*. There are a few nice touches, otherwise, the interchangeable pretty boys, busty babes and virginal girls next door are simply sliced, diced and humiliated to order. Despite the tagline promise of the American poster – 'No mercy. No shame. No sequel' – *Scary Movie 2* is already in the works. NF

Scary Movie 2

(2001, US, 82 min)
d Keenen Ivory Wayans. *p* Eric L Gold. *sc* Shawn Wayans, Marlon Wayans, Alyson Fouse, Greg Grabiansky, Dave Polsky, Michael Anthony Snowden, Craig Wayans. *ph* Steven Bernstein. *ed* Peter Teschner, Richard Pearson. *pd* Cynthia Charette. *cast* Shawn Wayans, Marlon Wayans, Anna Faris, Regina Hall, Chris Masterson, Kathleen Robertson, James Woods, Tim Curry, Tori Spelling, Chris Elliott, Veronica Cartwright.

●When, after the unexpected success of the first *Scary Movie*, Miramax immediately demanded a sequel, director Wayans and his younger brothers and co-writers Shawn and Marlon were given less than half the time it took to write the first. The result is a hack job that picks over the still warm carcass of its predecessor, regurgitating jokes which barely warranted their first screen outing. If this movie were a foodstuff, it would be processed cheese spread. The likes of *House on Haunted Hill, The Haunting* and *Poltergeist* are given the Wayans treatment, and it says a lot that any one of the original movies spoofed here contains more genuine laughs than this lacklustre effort. It shows no understanding of or insight into the genre it's attempting to parody, nor indeed of cinema in general. Many of the original cast who died at the end of the first film are mysteriously reanimated for the second. We can only hope that this time they stay dead. WI

Scavengers, The

see Recuperanti, I

Sceicco Bianco, Lo

see White Sheik, The

Scene at the Sea, A (Ano Natsu, Ichiban Shizukana Umi)

(1991, Jap, 101 min)
d Takeshi Kitano. *p* Masayuki Mori. *sc* Takeshi Kitano. *ph* Katsumi Yanagishima. *ed* Takeshi Kitano. *pd* Shinji Komiya. *m* Jo Hisaishi. *cast* Kuroko Maki, Hiroko Oshima.

●A U-turn in the blood-spattered career of actor-director Takeshi Kitano, still fondly remembered as the sentimental sadist Sergeant Hara in *Merry Christmas, Mr Lawrence*. This time he stays behind the camera and does without his usual recourse to violence. A boy working on a garbage truck in a seaside town (we realise only gradually that he and his girlfriend are profoundly deaf) finds a broken surf-board, tries to repair it, and teaches himself to surf. That's pretty much the whole plot, but it encompasses a truly rapturous love story, a lot of humour, and some piercing truths about human nature. It's also superbly acted, and has the best-judged editing since Bresson's last movie. TR

Scene of the Crime, The (Le Lieu du Crime)

(1986, Fr, 90 min)
d André Téchiné. *p* André Téchiné, Pascal Bonitzer, Olivier Assayas. *ph* Pascal Marti. *ed* Martine Giordano. *ad* Jean-Pierre Kohut-Svelko. *m* Philippe Sarde. *cast* Catherine Deneuve, Victor Lanoux, Danielle Darrieux, Wadeck Stanckzak, Nicolas Giraudi.

●The scene is the rustic vicinity of a small provincial town, the crime what happens to a small boy disaffected by his parents' divorce and by troubled loyalties when an escaped convict commits murder to save him from harm. His mother (Deneuve) promptly falls ass-over-tit for the convict (Stanckzak), his father (Lanoux) huffs around stockbroker-style, and his grandparents (including the imperishable Darrieux, alas) seem to have wandered in from a yokel movie. As vacuously pretentious as Téchiné's earlier *Rendez-vous*. TM

Scènes de Crimes

(2000, Fr, 100 min)
d Frédéric Schoendoerffer. *sc* Yann Brion, Olivier Douyère, Frédéric Schoendoerffer. *ph* Jean-Pierre Sauvaire. *ed* Dominique Mazzoleni. *pd* Jean-Baptiste Poirot. *m* Bruno Coulais. *cast* Charles Berling, André Dussollier, Ludovic Schoendoerffer, Pierre Mottet, Eva Darlan, Djemel Barek, Camille Japy.

●Despite the presence of art-house favourites Dussollier and Berling as the cops on the trail of a serial killer with a dismemberment fetish, this grim thriller turns out to be a mostly routine assignment, about on a par with TV's *Cracker* or *Prime Suspect*. Downbeat and determinedly unpleasant, the film is at least reasonably credible in the police procedural stakes. TCh

Scènes de lit (Bed Scenes)

(1997, Fr, 26 min)
d François Ozon. *cast* Margot Abascal, François Delaive, Camille Japy, Bruno Slagmulder.

●Seven vignettes with different couples on the point of soiling the sheets, as it were. In one tale, we learn the secret of a whore's speciality (giving head while singing 'La Marseillaise'), in another, a woman balks when her partner refuses to leave the light on ('Do you mind if I masturbate?' he asks politely). Sharp, funny stuff; Ozon respects no sexual boundaries, but unlike the disappointing *Sitcom* these provocations aren't scoring points at the expense of bourgeois stereotypes; any transgressions are ultimately liberating. TCh

Scenes from a Mall

(1990, US, 88 min)
d/p Paul Mazursky. *sc* Paul Mazursky, Roger L Simon. *ph* Fred Murphy. *ed* Stuart H Pappé. *pd* Pato Guzman. *m* Marc Shaiman. *cast* Woody Allen, Bette Midler, Bill Irwin, Paul Mazursky, Daren Firestone, Rebecca Nickels.

●In this irksome comedy, set mostly in the Beverly shopping mall in LA, Allen – his first dramatic outing since *The Front* – plays a neurotic, pony-tailed sports lawyer, married 16 years (she says 17) to successful shrink and writer Midler. They pack off the kids, have their anniversary fuck, then proceed to discuss the secret of their success. The discussions go on all movie. We move down to the mall and all the lies come out – infidelity, hypocrisy, yawn, yawn, yawn. Ugly amounts of bucks were spent on rebuilding the mall so that cameras could swoop up and down every inch of it, ogling merchandise and fetishising every commodity as 2,000 extras pass by, trying not to gaze at the camera. Woody and Bette eat sushi, clothe themselves, waltz in the piano bar, followed around by a mime, a rap group, and a Victorian-style barber-shop quartet harmonising – it's Christmastime – 'Walking in a Winter Wonderland'. Allen's admittedly funny lines get lost in the mess, and Midler, in relatively restrained mode, fades away altogether. Thematically, the film comes over as a piss-take of Mazursky by Mazursky. WH

Scenes from a Marriage (Scener ur ett äktenskap)

(1973, Swe, 168 min)
d/p/sc Ingmar Bergman. *ph* Sven Nykvist. *ed* Siv Lundgren. *ad* Björn Thulin. *cast* Liv Ullmann, Erland Josephson, Bibi Andersson, Jan Malmsjö, Anita Wall, Gunnel Lindblom.

●Though edited down (under Bergman's supervision) from a six-part series originally made for TV, this remains an exhaustive study of the doubt, despair, confusion and loneliness experienced by a woman (Ullmann) when she learns that her fickle husband (Josephson) is having an affair. Bergman, as in *Face to Face*, is here at his most stylistically stark: very little actually happens (much of the film consists of conversations in rooms), so that it's left to the performers (all superb, and mostly framed by Sven Nykvist in revealing close-ups) to bring the litany of pain to life. And they do, with the result that the film is an uncompromisingly harrowing and honest account of male-female relationships. (The TV version runs 300 minutes.) GA

Scenes from the Class Struggle in Beverly Hills

(1989, US, 103 min)
d Paul Bartel. *p* James C Katz. *sc* Bruce Wagner. *ph* Steven Fierberg. *ed* Alan Toomayan. *pd* Alex Tavoularis. *m* Stanley Myers. *cast* Jacqueline Bisset, Ray Sharkey, Mary Woronov, Robert Beltran, Ed Begley Jr, Wallace Shawn, Arnetia Walker, Paul Bartel, Paul Mazursky, Edith Diaz.

●Less the poor versus the rich than the poor struggling to emulate the rich. 'Anyone who spends $3,000 on a bathrobe deserves to die' says one of the scheming manservants who form the pivot of this cheerful sex comedy, but Bartel takes pains to show both flunkeys lolling in said garment. The sexual oneupmanship (a mild satire on decadence) revolves around widowed ex-soap star Clare (Bisset), keeping house with resident 'thinologist' (a camp cameo by Bartel) and dishy Hispanic houseboy (Beltran). Next door lives neurotic Lisabeth (Woronov), who's having her mansion de-infested in an unconscious attempt to rid it of her ex-husband's noxious influence. As this involves pumping it full of poison gas, she and her withdrawn teenage son, her playwright brother, his new black bride, and the houseboy (Sharkey) all take refuge with Clare. The servants each vow to bed the other's employer, and the sumptuous stage is set for frantic upstairs-downstairs bed-swapping, performed with charm and gusto. SFe

Scenes of the Crime

(2001, Ger/US, 95 min)
d Dominique Forma. *p* Marc Frydman, Rod Lurie, Willie Baer, Deborah Lee. *sc* Dominique Forma, Daniel Golka, Amit Mehta. *ph* James R Bagdonas. *ed* Sidney Levin. *ad* Jeff Knipp. m Gernot Wolfgang, Christopher Young. *cast* Jon Abrahams, Mädchen Amick, Jeff Bridges, Lloyd Catlett, Morris Chestnut, Whitney Dylan, Chase Ellison, Nicholas Gonzalez, Henry Rollins, Noah Wyle.

●The excellent debut feature of expat French director Forma is a thriller self-consciously in the vein of Peckinpah, Scorsese and Jean-Pierre Melville. It opens with the kidnapping of a high-powered Mafia type, Jimmy (Bridges), who ends up stranded in the back of a van on a street corner with a gun at his head. What happens next? That's all down to negotiation between the various self-interested parties. They're professionals, used to making momentous decisions in the flicker of an eye. Emotion plays no part in their decisions. Loyalty only matters as long as it pays. Inadvertently caught in the middle of the cat and mouse negotiations is Lenny (Abrahams), an ingenuous young mechanic who's been making extra money by driving for the Mob. Reportedly based on a true story, this is a claustrophobic but nifty yarn, largely set in a single location. Forma's influences are easy to spot – the nods in the direction of *Bullitt* and Steve McQueen become a little grating – but this is still riveting entertainment. GM

Scenic Route, The

(1978, US, 76 min)
d/p/sc Mark Rappaport. *ph* Fred Murphy. *ed* Mark Rappaport. *ad* Lilly Kilvert. *cast* Randy Danson, Marilyn Jones, Kevin Wade, Grant Stewart, Arthur Ginsberg.

●Rappaport contrives a strikingly seductive fusion of wit with seriousness, a New York tale of two sisters – Estelle (Danson) and Lena (Jones) – both working through a sort of love for Paul (Wade): male, fake-macho, hilariously silent. Though its baroque 'landscape' of interiors and tableaux, opera and soap opera, is held together by an unerring sense of visual style and persistently wry humour, the film ultimately suffers from an overweening sense of ironical self-esteem. Estelle, neurotic fantasist, diarist, reader of the voice-over that comments the action, is constantly undercut by the stylish visual gags, and confessions like 'I must have made it happen' make her an object of laughter: woman under a yoke of Christian (or Freudian) guilt. Here women are tyrants or martyrs (or both), and the token male in the film is irrelevant because we're busy endorsing the male behind the film. Estelle finally burns her diaries: castration. It's a strange example of sophisticated chauvinism; how much you laugh will depend on just how witty, intelligent and cultured you feel. CA

Scent of Deceit

see Nez au Vent, Le

Scent of a Woman

(1992, US, 156 min)
d/p Martin Brest. *sc* Bo Goldman. *ph* Donald Thorin. *ed* William Steinkamp. *pd* Angelo Graham. *m* Thomas Newman. *cast* Al Pacino, Chris O'Donnell, James Rebhorn, Gabrielle Anwar, Philip S Hoffman, Richard Venture, Bradley Whitford.

●This takes its inspiration from an Italian film of 1974, *Profumo di donna*, and concerns the relationship between Frank Slade (Pacino), a blind and very bitter ex-Vietnam army officer, and a 17-year-old boy (O'Donnell) hired to look after him over a weekend. The film splices two plots together, more ambitiously than successfully: O'Donnell's Charlie Simms is a bright young scholarship kid whose academic hopes face the chop when he becomes embroiled in a schoolboy prank played by some well-off classmates. Charlie has the weekend to decide whether to tell or not; Slade plans to enjoy himself on a spree to New York before ending his life in a military-style suicide. The outcome is as predictable as it is wholesomely traditional, but Pacino pulls out all the stops as the blind warrior, dancing a mean impromptu tango, taking a car for a suicidal spin, barking orders, charming ladies with his super-hearing, and finally coming good on Charlie's behalf. Corny and heart-warming, with O'Donnell proving almost a match for the master. SGr

Scent of Green Papaya, The (L'Odeur de la Papaye Verte/ Mui Du Du Xanh)

(1993, Fr, 104 min)
d Tran Anh Hung. *p* Christophe Rossignon. *sc* Tran Anh Hung. *ph* Benoît Delhomme. *ed* Nicole Dedieu, Jean-Pierre Roques. *ad* Alain Negre. *m* Ton That Tiết. *cast* Yen-Khe Tran Nu, Man San Lu, Thi Loc Truong, Anh Hoa Nguyen, Hoa Hoi Vuong.

●The story of Mui, a peasant girl who comes to Saigon to serve in the house of a bourgeois family: grandmother, parents, three sons and a maid. It's 1951, the influence of the West is beginning to make itself felt, but already the old conventions are beginning to crack. Tran's first feature – shot, remarkably, in France – is sensuous, evocative and politically ambivalent. It focuses particularly on the servitude of women. We watch in close-up as Mui learns her duties: cleaning up after the youngsters, running errands, cooking rice and papaya for the family. At first these are mere chores, but later, as she grows into a woman, they take on a more fulfilling purpose. The movie's poetic-realist design meshes detailed, patient observation and delectable, poignant travelling shots; it grounds us in the quotidian duties of service and dissects contemporary Vietnamese social hierarchies, yet adds up to something much more subtle and enticing: a lyrical portrait of the human spirit in work and in love. Exquisitely controlled. TCh

Schatten (Warning Shadows)

(1922, Ger, 80 min approx, b/w)
d Arthur Robison. *sc* Rudolf Schneider, Arthur Robison, Albin Grau. *ph* Fritz Arno Wagner. *ed* Arthur Robison. *ad* Albin Grau. *cast* Fritz Kortner, Ruth Weyher, Alexander Granach, Gustav von Wangenheim, Fritz Rasp.

●Well, yes, a whole world of shadows, this being a classic of silent German cinema. It begins as a dream of jealousy. An angst ridden husband seethes as his flimsily clad wife is pursued around the house by four admirers – three comic, one serious. A travelling mesmerist arrives and puts them all in a trance (a hallucination within a reverie) where they see a preview of bloody things to come. Day breaks, the admirers leave the couple in peace, the mesmerist rides off on a pig. Rich pickings for thesis writers (Freud, Expressionism, German Romanticism), but it's the look of the thing that will count for most viewers, especially the costumes, flamboyant parodies of 18th century dress.The film dispenses almost entirely with inter-titles. BBa

Schaukel, Die

see Swing, The

Schiele in Prison

(1980, GB, 48 min)
d Mick Gold. *cast* Grant Cathro, David Suchet, Nicholas Selby.

●Sex, boredom and suicide in crumbling World War I Vienna. An Arts Council documentary by former rock photographer Gold on Egon Schiele (with readings from his prison diary): a paranoiac narcissist, jailbird, and friend of Klimt, his tortured, spindly self-portraits once heavily influenced David Bowie. Oddly dull, considering its subject, it errs on the side of politeness. DMacp

Schindler's List 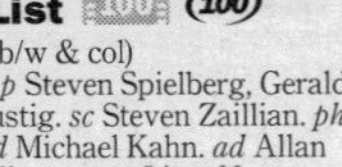

(1993, US, 195 min, b/w & col)
d Steven Spielberg. *p* Steven Spielberg, Gerald R Molen, Branko Lustig. *sc* Steven Zaillian. *ph* Janusz Kaminski. *ed* Michael Kahn. *ad* Allan Starski. *m* John Williams. *cast* Liam Neeson, Ben Kingsley, Ralph Fiennes, Caroline Goodall, Jonathan Sagalle, Embeth Davidtz.

●The film of Thomas Keneally's novel is Spielberg's finest since *Jaws*. The elastic editing and grainy camerawork lend an immediacy as surprising as the shockingly matter-of-fact depiction of violence and casual killing. And Spielberg can handle actors – Neeson as Schindler, the German profiteer whose use of cheap labour in his Cracow factory saved 1,100 Jews from death; Kingsley as Stern, the canny accountant; Fiennes as Goeth, bloodless commandant of Plaszow camp. Wisely, the director rarely seeks to simplify the mysterious complexity of Schindler, an opportunist whose deeds became giddily selfless. As in his earlier work, there's a sense of wonder at the inexplicable, but it's no longer childlike. At times the film becomes a scream of horror at the inhumanity it recalls and recreates, and the b/w images never become aesthetically sanitised. True, the Jews are huddled, victimised masses. True, too, that Spielberg finally relents and tries to 'explain' Schindler so that the last hour becomes steadily more simplistic and sentimental. Otherwise, however, it's a noble achievement, and essential viewing. GA

Schizo

(1976, GB, 109 min)
d/p Pete Walker. *sc* David McGillivray. *ph* Peter Jessop. *ed* Alan Brett. *ad* Chris Burke. *m* Stanley Myers. *cast* Lynne Frederick, John Leyton, Stephanie Beacham, John Fraser, Jack Watson, Queenie Watts, Trisha Mortimer, John McEnery.

●Walker and writer David McGillivray's most ambitious project to date attempts to shake off the low-budget horror/exploitation tag with a move into more up-market psychological suspense. If the formula is threadworn – a trail of victimisation, sexual paranoia, and murder in the wake of the heroine's wedding – at least some effort is made to locate it (rich middle class London). But things collapse disastrously in the second half. Caught between sending itself up and taking itself seriously, the film ends closer to the silliness of Francis Durbridge than to the menace of Alfred Hitchcock. CPe

Schizophrenia (aka Angst)

(1983, WGer, 82 min)
d/p Gerald Kargl. *sc* Gerald Kargl, Zbigniew Rybczynski. *ph* Zbigniew Rybczynski. *m* Klaus Schulze. *cast* Erwin Leder, Silvia Rabenreither, Edith Rosset, Rudolf Götz, Renate Kastelik.

●Released after serving a prison sentence for the shooting of an old lady he had never met, a psychopath (Leder) breaks into a house, terrorising and ultimately murdering an old lady, her wheelchair-bound husband and their daughter. Savage, stylistically brilliant and at times virtually unwatchable, this film bears comparison with *Henry: Portrait of a Serial Killer*. But where *Henry* employed a cold objectivity, Kargl achieves a curious pull-push effect, the camera-work rubbing our noses in the as-it-happens atrocity while the director's disturbingly intimate voice-over gives a cool, dislocated account of events. Moments of black humour, as when the family dachshund picks up the old lady's false teeth, only serve to emphasise the quotidian nature of the horror. Stunning. NF

Schizopolis

(1996, US, 96 min)
d Steven Soderbergh. *p* John Hardy. *sc/ph* Steven Soderbergh. *ed* Sarah Flack. *cast* Steven Soderbergh, Betsey Brantley, David Jensen.

●Soderbergh's 1996 guerilla movie is perhaps the strangest film from the American indie scene to date. A surreal, eccentric comedy, its triptych narrative is so fragmented that it's almost impossible to provide an accurate synopsis. Suffice to say it's about sexual and professional intrigues in suburbia, with the main character (Soderbergh) becoming so paranoid about industrial espionage that he fails to notice his wife is having an affair with a dentist who's his exact double. At first, the endless succession of wacky vignettes suggests there's no plot whatsoever. Eventually, however, it becomes clear that, while satirical swipes are taken at male paranoia, corporate business politics, New Age philosophies, soap operatics and the American obsession with dental hygiene, this is really 'about' verbal and filmic language. Basically off-the-cuff, off-the-wall nonsense – and frequently very funny. GA

Schloss, Das

see Castle, The

Schöne Tag, Der

see Fine Day, A

School (La Scuola)

(1995, It, 102 min)
d Daniele Luchetti. *p* Vittorio Cecchi Gori. *sc* Domenico Starnone, Stefano Rulli, Daniele Luchetti, Sandro Petraglia. *ph* Alessio Gelsini Torresi. *ed* Mirco Garrone. *pd* Giancarlo Basili. *m* Bill Frisell. *cast* Silvio Orlando, Anna Galiena, Fabrizio Bentivoglio.

● A critical and commercial hit in Italy, this portrait of a hard-pressed Roman secondary school is a witty, well-observed exposé of the foibles of institutional life, while at the same time hinting at the moral funk and the economic strictures affecting the wider national psyche. Instead of the usual *Blackboard Jungle* melodramatics, the tone here is affectionate and faintly absurdist, and the focus is as much on the clashing personalities of the staff – fumbling likeable history teacher Orlando has the hots for Galiena's maths mistress, but she seems taken by Bentivoglio's disciplinarian deputy head – as it is on the ever-boisterous students. A hugely enjoyable movie which barely wastes a scene. TJ

School Daze

(1988, US, 120 min)
d/p/sc Spike Lee. *ph* Ernest Dickerson. *ed* Barry Alexander Brown. *pd* Wynn Thomas. *m* Bill Lee. *cast* Larry Fishburne, Giancarlo Esposito, Tisha Campbell, Spike Lee, Kyme, Joe Seneca, Ossie Davis.

● Swiftian satires on popular taste can backfire badly, and Spike Lee's attempt at black consciousness-raising through the armature of *Animal House* movies almost dies of the contusion it is trying to lance. One glance at Julian (Esposito) leading the Gamma Phi Gamma fraternity, who crawl along barking in unison in gladiatorial togas, is enough to topple satire into farce. Half-Pint (Lee) finally passes his initiation test and loses his virginity in the frat Bone Room. The football coach (Davis) delivers a locker-room pep talk straight out of Sanctified Church, and the Dean is in bed with the college's white benefactress. The musical numbers are uniformly uninventive. Here and there the sociology is clear, but much of the film may seem incomprehensible to English audiences. On the evidence of *She's Gotta Have It*, Lee has a small, intimate talent; here he goes for the big podium and blows it. BC

School for Postmen

see Ecole des Facteurs, L'

School for Scoundrels

(1959, GB, 94 min, b/w)
d Robert Hamer. *p* Hal E Chester. *sc* Patricia Moyes, Hal E Chester. *ph* Erwin Hillier. *ed* Richard Best. *ad* Terence Verity. *m* John Addison. *cast* Ian Carmichael, Alastair Sim, Terry-Thomas, Janette Scott, Dennis Price, Peter Jones, Edward Chapman, John Le Mesurier.

● Hamer's last film before losing out to alcohol is, ironically, about taking short cuts to success. Based around the sneeringly facile concept of 'one-upmanship' (how to tread on people and make them thank you for it), the film follows the fortunes of upper class twit Carmichael as he struggles for supremacy with waiters, women and Terry-Thomas. The first half, in particular a sequence where used-car salesmen Dudley and Dunstan Dorchester 'the Winsome Welshmen' (Price and Jones) perpetrate a con even Richard Nixon would have been proud of, has its moments of cruel humour; but when, with the benefit of a course in 'lifemanship', Carmichael is reborn as a winner, things become tediously silly. RMy

School for Vandals

(1986, GB, 80 min)
d Colin Finbow. *p* Joanie Blaikie. *sc* Colin Finbow, Children's Film Unit. *ph* Titus Bucknell, Orlando Wells, Will Grove-White, Leigh Melrose. *ed* Colin Finbow. *m* David Hewson. *cast* Anne Dyson, Charles Kay, Tamara Hinchco, Peter Bayliss, Jeremy Coster, Samantha McMillan.

● A mixture of 'Famous Five' antics and kidnapping from the Children's Film Unit. The parents of youngsters Rupert and Tiger Lily (so named because of their mother's obsession with Rupert Bear) have invested a pools win in a rundown former reform school in Sussex, which they plan to reopen as a school. The winnings have dwindled, so chancing upon the elderly Miss Duff (Dyson) wandering around her former school, the kids and three friends plan her kidnapping with the intention of squeezing some money out of the locals. No such luck. However, they soon strike up a friendship with the old dear, who isn't quite what she seems... Cosier than some of the unit's earlier productions, but with youngsters on both sides of the camera, what we are seeing here is hopefully the future of the British film industry; and it's looking good. DA

School of Flesh, The

see Ecole de la Chair, L'

School Ties

(1992, US, 107 min)
d Robert Mandel. *p* Sherry Lansing, Stanley R Jaffe. *sc* Darryl Ponicsan, Dick Wolf. *ph* Freddie Francis. *ed* Jerry Greenberg, Jacqueline Cambas. *ad* Jeannine Claudia Oppewall. *m* Maurice Jarre. *cast* Brendan Fraser, Matt Damon, Randall Batinkoff, Chris O'Donnell, Cole Hauser, Anthony Rapp, Ben Affleck, Amy Loncane.

● More notable perhaps for a roster of future stars and Oscar winners than for its unexceptional plot, this well executed film nevertheless has its charms. The setting is 1950s America: David (Fraser) is the son of a Jewish miner who wins a football scholarship to a privileged (but anti-semitic) school. Initially he conceals his religion until he's exposed by a jealous friend (Damon). The script effectively dramatises the school's competitive, hothouse atmosphere and is sensitive to the situations of all the pupils, as well as to the pressure of expectation and tradition. However, David's stereotypically pure and hardworking blue collar origins muddy the moral, making it unclear whether the film's main target is anti-semitism or the corruption of the privileged. The cop-out Hollywood ending further gums up an otherwise polished and thoughtful work. TCo

Schramm

(1992, Ger, 75 min)
d/p/sc Jörg Buttgereit. *ph* Manfred Jelinski. *ed* Manfred Jelinski, Jörg Buttgereit. *m* Max Mueller, Gundula Schmitz. *cast* Florian Koerner von Gustorf, Monika M.

● This cinematic excuse for extremity – from the director of *Nekromantic* – is based on the true story of 'The Lipstick Killer', murderer and necrophile Lothar Schramm (von Gustorf), and his relationship with prostitute Marianne (Monika M). As well as his taste for having sex with the dead, Schramm's unusual style of DIY includes nailing his own penis to the table. NF

Schreckliche Mädchen, Das

see Nasty Girl, The

Schtonk!

(1992, Ger, 111 min)
d Helmut Dietl. *p* Gunter Rohrbach, Helmut Dietl. *sc* Helmut Dietl, Ulrich Limmer. *ph* Zaver Schwarzenberger. *ed* Tanja Schmidbauer. *ad* Götz Weidner, Benedikt Herforth. *m* Konstantin Wecker. *cast* Götz George, Uwe Ochsenknecht, Christiane Hörbiger, Rolf Hoppe, Dagmar Manzel, Veronica Ferres.

● This *could* have been funny – after all, the 1983 scandal of the forged Hitler diaries should be fertile ground for satire – but Dietl and producer Ulrich Limmer's script is so leadenly obvious that the film is almost wholly bereft of laughs. Focused on the swindling partnership of 'Professor' Fritz Knobel (Ochsenknecht) – a past master of forgery in the art and antiques field – and scoop-hungry hack Hermann Willié (George), the story seems intended to highlight the hypocrisy, corruption, and enduring Nazi sympathies rampant in certain sectors of modern German society. Fair enough; but hysterical scenes of nostalgia for the Führer, witless innuendoes, and repeated readings of ludicrously banal diary entries about flatulence don't exactly make for a light touch. Indeed, the whole movie is woefully heavy-handed, with grotesquely OTT performances, most of it looks ugly, and it never gets beyond that one-joke premise about hypocrisy, corruption, etc. GA

Scissors

(1991, US, 105 min)
d Frank De Felitta. *p* Mel Pearl, Hal W Polaire. *sc* Frank De Felitta. *ph* Anthony B Richmond. *ed* John Schreyer. *pd* Craig Stearns. *cast* Sharon Stone, Steve Railsback, Ronny Cox, Michelle Phillips.

● An identikit psycho thriller sadly in need of a bit of sex, gore or something to liven up a plot that employs every predictable twist, cliché and red herring in the book. Stone is a woman haunted by a repressed childhood trauma involving – you guessed it – scissors. Cox is her sympathetic but sexually frustrated shrink, and Railsback her smitten neighbour. Railsback's embittered, wheelchair-bound brother and his spurned ex-lover (Phillips) are the obvious bad guys, which means that it's someone else trying to drive her mad. Pretty daft, but perversely enjoyable in a ludicrously overheated kind of way. NF

Scorchers

(1991, US, 82 min)
d David Beaird. *p* David Beaird, Morrie Eisenman, Richard Hellman. *sc* David Beaird. *ph* Peter Deming. *ed* David Garfield. *pd* Bill Eigenbrodt. *m* Carter Burwell. *cast* Faye Dunaway, Denholm Elliott, James Earl Jones, Emily Lloyd, Jennifer Tilly, James Wilder, Anthony Geary, Leland Crooke.

● Beaird's adaptation of his own play begins with a folksy five-minute monologue exhorting us to believe what we feel, not what we are told. It is set in Bayou country, where accents are thick as molasses and the nights fair palpitate with desire. Lloyd is Splendid, a Louisiana belle terrified by the prospect of losing her virginity. It's her wedding night. As the groom reaches the end of his tether, it falls to Jumper (Crooke) to philosophise his daughter out from under the bed. Meanwhile, at the town bar, alcoholic has-been actor Howler (Elliott) debates sex and the classics with barkeep Bear (Jones) and prostitute Thais (Dunaway), until irate bridesmaid Talbot (Tilly) storms the joint with a bellyful of sexual resentment and a revolver. Saddled with a derivative script that apes Tennessee Williams none too successfully – a perilous mixture of ribald humour and high-flown poeticism – the cast revert to type: Jones growls, Elliott snivels, Dunaway smokes, and Lloyd tries ever so hard, bless her. A hopelessly theatrical film from what must have been a poor play. TCh

Score, The

(2001, US/Ger, 124 min)
d Frank Oz. *p* Gary Foster, Lee Rich. *sc* Kario Salem, Lem Dobbs, Scott Marshall Smith. *ph* Rob Hahn. *ed* Richard Pearson. *pd* Jackson De Govia. *m* Howard Shore. *cast* Robert De Niro, Edward Norton, Angela Bassett, Marlon Brando, Gary Farmer, Jamie Harrold, Paul Soles, Martin Drainville, Serge Houde, Jean René Ouellet.

● Apparently Edward Norton says he did this movie for the poster – to see his name up there alongside Marlon Brando and Robert De Niro. And who could blame him? But it's a safe bet that Brando and De Niro did it for the money. Here's the thing: De Niro and Brando built their greatness on terrific performances in demanding roles in powerful films. They took their profession to the limit. Evidently they burnt out. And then they sold out – settling for the lucrative complacency of movie stardom. This is a laborious piece of genre mechanics, a heist movie so standard some have persuaded themselves it's a welcome throwback to old-fashioned entertainment. De Niro is the master cracksman seduced into one last job by jackpot booty and the finagling of mentor Brando. Norton is the Young Turk manipulating everybody with his already overfamiliar schizo act. Bassett is the love interest. Everything here is predictable, lazy and old hat. Brando? De Niro? Norton? Boring, boring, boring. TCh

Scorpio

(1972, US, 114 min)
d Michael Winner. *p* Walter Mirisch. *sc* David W Rintels, Gerald Wilson. *ph* Robert Paynter. *ed* Frederick Wilson. *ad* Herbert Westbrook. *m* Jerry Fielding. *cast* Burt Lancaster, Alain Delon, Paul Scofield, John Colicos, Gayle Hunnicutt, JD Cannon, Joanne Linville, James B Sikking.

●Conventional and convoluted tale of betrayal and death among spies, with Lancaster's CIA agent coming under suspicion, being marked for extermination by the reluctant but seemingly persuadable freelance killer he trained (Delon), and turning in his disillusionment to his equally disillusioned Russian opposite number (Scofield) for aid. Winner directs with typically crass abandon, wasting a solid performance from Lancaster and a story that a director like Jean-Pierre Melville might have made something of. GA

Scorpion, The (De Schorpioen)

(1984, Neth, 98 min)
d Ben Verbong. *p* Chris Brouwer, Haig Balian. *sc* Ben Verbong, Peter de Vos. *ph* Theo van de Sande. *ed* Ton de Graaff. *ad* Dorus van der Linden. *m* Nicola Piovani. *cast* Peter Tuinman, Monique Van De Ven, Rima Melati, Senne Rouffaer, Walter Kous, Adrian Brine.

●When Lew Wolff (Tuinman), burdened with a criminal past and a bleak future, arrives in an out-of-season coastal resort on his way to a new life in America, he's hardly prepared for the danger and confusion that arise after he exchanges his own papers for a false passport: he reads reports of his death, is warned off, finds his room ransacked. For all the potential thrills thrown up by this premise, Verbong's film resembles his earlier *The Girl with the Red Hair* in emphasising theme, character and atmosphere rather than suspense. Set in Holland in 1956, the film examines the mysterious legacy of that country's colonial involvement in Indonesia during the '40s; and in asking where Sukarno's rebels obtained their arms in order to repel the Dutch, proposes some pretty unconvincing answers in some pretty awkward flashbacks. The main body of the film, however, is sensitive and engaging, and in moments of *noir*-flecked seediness comes truly alive. GA

Scorpion King, The (Jie zi zhan shi/aka Operation Scorpio)

(1992, HK, 96 min)
d David Lai. *p* Pui Wah Chan, Leonard Ho, Sammo Hung. *sc* Che Wei Chan, Sau Pung Lui, Barry Wong. *ph* Che Chung Tsang, Bo Man Wong. *pd* Che Wei Chan, Kim Man Ho. *cast* Chin Gar Lok, Yuan Jeung, Liu Chia Liang, May Law.

●Much more stylishly produced than earlier kung-fu movies, even if the story itself is little more than cartoon melodrama. Yuk Su (Chin) is a schoolboy weakling, an aspiring artist, who beefs up and indeed learns beef noodle kung-fu in one inventive sequence to defend his egalitarian ideals from slave traders and bully boys. He wins an MBE for his troubles. The movie is dominated by its exotic villains, and especially by the Korean Yuan Jeung who made his debut here, sporting a Phil Oakey haircut with pigtail accessory, dressed in purple silk, scuttling along floors and up walls and kicking like Nijinsky in his eye-popping scorpion kung-fu style. TCh

Scorpion King, The

(2002, US/Ger, 91 min)
d Chuck Russell. *p* Stephen Sommers, Sean Daniel, James Jacks, Kevin Misher. *sc* Stephen Sommers, William Osborne, David Hayter. *ph* John R Leonetti. *ed* Michael Tronick, Greg Parsons. *pd* Ed Verreaux. *m* John Debney. *cast* The Rock [Dwayne Johnson], Steven Brand, Kelly Hu, Bernard Hill, Grant Heslov, Peter Facinelli, Ralph Moeller, Michael Clark Duncan, Branscombe Richmond, Roger Rees, Sherri Howard.

●In terms of milking a cash cow, this spin-off, inspired by the appearance of WWF wrestling star The Rock in Stephen Sommers' *The Mummy Returns*, is hard to beat. But it's mindlessly entertaining, all the same. It's produced and co-scripted by Sommers, ensuring it looks good and doesn't take itself seriously. Five thousand years ago, and evil ruler Memnon (Brand), aided by the accurate premonitions of his beautiful Sorceress (Hu), is on a roll, his vast armies annihilating all before them. What he hasn't banked on is Mathayus (The Rock), one of the last remaining members of the extinct Akkadians tribe and a dab hand with a bow and arrow. In true WWF fashion, the action here is relentless. Just as well, because The Rock isn't the most eloquent of talkers. Director Russell, meanwhile, keeps matters rollicking, but it's wall to wall hokum nevertheless. Move over, Arnie, there's a new barbarian in town. DA

Scorpio Rising

see Anger Magick Lantern, Cycle

Scorta, La (The Escort)

(1993, It, 92 min)
d Ricky Tognazzi. *p* Claudio Bonivento. *sc* Simona Izzo, Graziano Diana. *ph* Alessio Gelsini. *ed* Carla Simoncelli. *ad* Mariangela Capuano. *m* Ennio Morricone. *cast* Claudio Amendola, Enrico Lo Verso, Carlo Cecchi, Ricky Memphis, Leo Gullotta, Tony Sperandeo.

●An old man upsets his drink in panic at a loud explosion outside. Racing to investigate, his fears are confirmed…a judge has been assassinated, and the old man's son along with him. This is bold, emotional film-making, torn from the headlines, and from here on director Tognazzi never leaves the side of his four protagonists. *La scorta* – the escort – are the ordinary young policemen assigned to protect magistrates investigating the Mafia in Italy. The film focuses on the bodyguards of a particularly determined Sicilian judge. Andrea (Lo Verso) is the supervising officer. Married with kids, he's an obvious target for blackmail. Angelo (Amendola) is a tougher customer: a friend of the murdered escort, he's out to bring the killers to justice. Police work is just a job for Raffaele and Fabio (Sperandeo and Memphis), but they too become inspired by the integrity of their charge (Checchi) and the camaraderie of the group. An effective thriller, closer to Hollywood's muckraisers than any of Francesco Rosi's political gangster movies. Not subtle, exactly, but pointed. TCh

Scotch on the Rocks

see Laxdale Hall

Scott of the Antarctic

(1948, GB, 111 min)
d Charles Frend. *p* Michael Balcon. *sc* Walter Meade, Ivor Montagu, Mary Hayley Bell. *ph* Jack Cardiff, Osmond Borradaile, Geoffrey Unsworth. *ed* Peter Tanner. *ad* Arne Åkermark. *m* Ralph Vaughan Williams. *cast* John Mills, Derek Bond, James Robertson Justice, Kenneth More, John Gregson, Harold Warrender, Reginald Beckwith, Diana Churchill, Christopher Lee.

●Respectable account of Scott's doomed expedition to the South Pole. With so many frozen upper lips, the performances are rather buried behind balaclavas (at the end it's hard to tell who's who), and the studio colour backdrops are sometimes intrusive. However, Vaughan Williams' score effectively upstages the dialogue; and the early scenes, when Mills scratches around for financing and assembles his crew, are a fair evocation of Edwardian England, even if the failure of the mission, and the reverberations that failure had for Imperial Britain, are beyond the scope of the movie. The movie says, with characteristic aplomb, well done chaps, at least you tried. ATu

Scoumoune, La (Hit Man/Scoundrel)

(1972, Fr/It, 105 min)
d José Giovanni. *p* Raymond Danon. *sc* José Giovanni. *ph* Andréas Winding. *ed* Françoise Javet. *ad* Jean-Jacques Caziot. *m* François de Roubaix. *cast* Jean-Paul Belmondo, Claudia Cardinale, Michel Constantin, Michel Pereylon, Aldo Bufi Landi.

●Giovanni, a *Série Noire* writer, here adapted and directed his own novel about the Marseille underworld, previously filmed in 1961 (also with Belmondo) by Jean Becker as *Un Nommé la Rocca*. Ineptitude in both departments makes a hash of the theme of underworld loyalties so beautifully handled in Melville's *Le Deuxième Souffle* (also based on a Giovanni novel). Even the original title (meaning 'the jinx') becomes pointless, because Belmondo's crude tough guy performance makes the persistent failure of his gallant efforts on behalf of a friend look more like bad scripting than the consequence of changing underworld ways. TM

Scoundrel

see Scoumoune, La

Scoundrel in White

see Docteur Popaul

Scratch

(2001, US, 87 min)
d Doug Pray, Bonner Bellew. *p* Brad Blondheim, Ernest Meza. *sc* Doug Pray. *ph* Robert Bennett. *ed* Ken Glickstein, Doug Pray, (contributing) Joan Zapata. *ad* Chris Meyer. *with* Afrika Bambaataa, Yoga Frog, Mix Master Mike, DJ Q-Bert, DJ Shadow, DJ Swamp, DJ Krush, DJ Jazzy Jay, DJ Shortee, Grand Wizard Theodore, Grand Master Flash, Grand Master DST.

●A competent, fairly comprehensive history of scratching records, this works through the history and methodology of what's now – judging by equipment sales – a more popular musical pastime than playing guitar. The film's a bit muffled when it comes to explaining the insider slang (beat-boxing?); nor is it particularly strong visually, being heavily dominated by talking heads and stuttering turntables, although the editing is often razor-sharp. Rather, the film's strength is in its cast of characters: everyone from Afrika Bambaataa and Grand Master Flash, DJs Shadow, Krush, Jazzy Jay and Shortee to the Invisibl Skratch Piklz pop up to disseminate their ideas, experience and techniques (cue home demos a go-go). Grand Master DST – of Herbie Hancock's 'Rocket' fame – and DJ Q-Bert win most of the acclaim for influence past and present; both Q-Bert and Mix Master Mike, it transpires, talk to aliens. NB

Scream

(1996, US, 111 min)
d Wes Craven. *p* Cary Woods, Cathy Konrad. *sc* Kevin Williamson. *ph* Mark Irwin. *ed* Patrick Lussier. *pd* Bruce Miller. *m* Marco Beltrami. *cast* Drew Barrymore, Neve Campbell, David Arquette, Courteney Cox, Rose McGowan, Skeet Ulrich.

●Wes Craven draws on a shared pop cultural heritage in horror flicks to fashion this bloody brand of post-modern comedy. 'So you like scary movies? Name the killer in *Friday the 13th*?' demands the anonymous caller of Barrymore's lone teen in the prologue. 'Hang up again and I'll gut you like a fish!' The killer describes his apparently irrational vendetta against the high school population of Woodsboro as a game, and in this he's surely speaking for screenwriter Kevin Williamson and director Craven, who kill off the clichés and all the wrong characters with panache. At times, it's too clever, but it's sure scary, with the jokes notching up the general level of hysteria. As a bonus, Craven throws in half a dozen of Hollywood's brightest hopefuls: Campbell in the central role of the teenager haunted by the murder of her mother; Arquette as a naive local deputy; Cox as a TV star; McGowan as the doomed best friend; and Ulrich as the evocatively named Billy Loomis. Intelligence, wit and sophistication – at last, a horror movie to shout about! TCh

Scream 2

(1997, US, 120 min)
d Wes Craven. *p* Cathy Konrad, Marianne Maddalena. *sc* Kevin Williamson. *ph* Peter Deming. *ed* Patrick Lussier. *pd* Bob Ziembicki. *m* Marco Beltrami. *cast* Neve Campbell, Courteney Cox, David Arquette, Liev Schreiber, Sarah Michelle Gellar, Jamie Kennedy, Laurie Metcalf, Elise Neal, Jerry O'Connell, Timothy Olyphant, Jada Pinkett, Wes Craven.

●This being the sequel, scriptwriter Kevin Williamson includes a scene in which film students discuss the fact that such movies never match the inventiveness of the original. Quite so. To be fair, by changing the location and concentrating on the haunted victims rather than the demonic killer(s), No 2 avoids a couple of obvious pitfalls. Two years after the Woodsboro murders, Sidney Prescott (Campbell) is a college student, piecing her life together with a new boyfriend, her old friend Randy (Kennedy) and a sympathetic roommate. But when a spectator is slashed to death during the local premiere of horror movie *Stab* – from a book on the Woodsboro incident by cynical TV reporter Gail Weathers (Cox) – the nightmare begins anew. Although returning characters such as ex-deputy Dewey (Arquette) have moved on, the film itself is stuck in a cycle of repetition, with slight variations. Compared to most contemporary horror fare, this is intelligent and frightening; compared to the original, it just doesn't cut it. NF

Scream 3

(2000, US, 118 min)
d Wes Craven. *p* Cathy Konrad, Kevin Williamson, Marianne Maddalena. *sc* Ehren Kruger. *ph* Peter Deming. *ed* Patrick Lussier. *pd* Bruce Alan Miller. *m* Marco Beltrami. *cast* David Arquette, Neve Campbell, Courteney Cox Arquette, Patrick Dempsey, Scott Foley, Lance Henriksen, Matt Keeslar, Jenny McCarthy, Emily Mortimer, Parker Posey.
●About a third of the way through this tiresomely over-plotted sequel, dead movie geek Randy delivers a video message from beyond the grave, reminding us that this is not a sequel but the concluding part of a trilogy. So does this mean tortured heroine Sidney Prescott (Campbell), TV anchorwoman Gale Weathers (Cox Arquette) and ex-deputy sheriff Dewey Riley (David Arquette) are in just as much peril as the actors playing them in the film-within-the-film, 'Stab 3, Return to Woodsboro'? One suspects not, since Miramax may want to extend the franchise. So there's no real jeopardy or suspense, just a lot of complicated, self-referential plotting punctuated by mechanical jolts. Even so, Campbell has grown into the central role, imbuing Sidney with a deep melancholy. Indie queen Parker Posey is very watchable, too, as the self-absorbed actress typecast as Gale Weathers in 'Stab 3'. But one knows all along that the new characters are merely 'body doubles' for the bankable stars. Hamstrung by this, director Craven has produced a poor carbon copy of his own *New Nightmare*. NF

Scream and Scream Again

(1969, GB, 95 min)
d Gordon Hessler. *p* Max J Rosenberg, Milton Subotsky. *sc* Christopher Wicking. *ph* John Coquillon. *ed* Peter Elliot. *pd* William Constable. *m* David Whitaker. *cast* Vincent Price, Christopher Lee, Peter Cushing, Alfred Marks, Anthony Newlands, Peter Sallis, Michael Gothard.
●An impressive if somewhat fragmented horror film in which mad scientist Price uses surgery and organ transplants to create a super race of emotionless creatures, one of which (Gothard) attracts the attentions of the police by going berserk and committing a number of grisly vampiric murders. The underlying narrative thread about the creatures taking over positions of authority is not sufficiently well developed to have any real impact, but individual scenes are conceived to gory and striking effect. NF

Screamers

(1995, Can/US/Jap, 109 min)
d Christian Duguay. *p* Tom Berry , Franco Battista. *sc* Dan O'Bannon, Miguel Tejada-Flores. *ph* Rodney Gibbons. *ed* Yves Langlois. *pd* Perri Gorrara. *m* Normand Corbeil. *cast* Peter Weller, Andy Lauer, Jennifer Rubin, Roy Dupuis, Charles Powell, Ron White, Michael Caloz.
●Based on a Philip K Dick story, scripted by Dan O'Bannon and Miguel Tejada-Flores, and directed by the maker of *Scanners II*, this Canadian sci-fi movie lacks the intelligence to follow through its grim premise. That said, and a worrying resemblance to Charles Band's cheapo, quarry-bound sci-fi pics aside, it does offer many of the guilty pleasures of unachieving B-pictures. The mining planet of Sirius 6B, in 2078: a handful of Alliance soldiers led by Col Hendricksson (Weller) and including rookie hotshot Ace Jefferson (Lauer) resolves to negotiate peace with their similarly depleted New Economic Block enemies. But the post-nuclear wasteland they must cross is guarded by self-replicating 'Screamers', anti-personnel devices with flying blades that slice and dice. The sporadic and increasingly sophisticated Screamer attacks lend suspense to an unexceptional plot, the least intriguing aspect of which is a telegraphed flip-over finale. Weller's fine and Lauer has a nice line in gung-ho naiveté, but Rubin's wasted as a permanently pissed-off black-marketeer. Despite limited resources, the design and effects teams have lent scale and impact to the futuristic locations and sets. If only Duguay's flashy, aimless direction had succeeded in filling these barren wastes and antiseptic interiors with something resembling human life. NF

Scream for Help

(1984, US, 90 min)
d/p Michael Winner. *sc* Tom Holland. *ph* Bob Paynter, Dick Kratina. *ed* Christopher Barnes. *ad* Tony Reading. *cast* Rachael Kelly, David Brooks, Marie Masters, Rocco Sisto, Lolita Lorre, Corey Parker.
●Where most Winner films go straight from offensive to forgotten, this teenager-in-peril movie went from forgotten to such deep obscurity that it's often missing even from Winner filmographies. Snoopy teen Christie finds out that cheating on her mother is the least sinister thing her stepfather is up to. He's planning to dispose of Mom and doesn't mind including Christie in the deal. She tells the police. They all laughed, and you will too. Expect gory exits for almost-famous indifferent actors and a haphazard sense of plot logic and camera placement. DO

Scream from Silence, A

see Mourir à Tue-Tête

Screaming Mimi

(1958, US, 79 min, b/w)
d Gerd Oswald. *p* Harry Joe Brown, Robert Fellows. *sc* Robert Blees. *ph* Burnett Guffey. *ed* Gene Havlick, Jerome Thoms. *ad* Cary Odell. *m* Mischa Bakaleinikoff. *cast* Anita Ekberg, Phil Carey, Harry Townes, Gypsy Rose Lee, Romney Brent, Red Norvo.
●Curious cod Freudian potboiler from a novel by Fredric Brown with Ekberg playing a woman who topples into a nervous breakdown after being sexually assaulted, takes a job as a stripper, and ends up on the couch of a dubious shrink. If only Oswald had injected such a provocative scenario with the same eerie imagination that fuelled his version of *A Kiss Before Dying* then this might have been truly something to shout about. LF

Screamin' Jay Hawkins: I Put a Spell on Me

(2001, Greece, 102 min)
d/sc Nicholas Triandafyllidis. *ph* Christos Karamanis. *ed* Yannis Sakarides. *with* Screamin' Jay Hawkins, Jim Jarmusch, Bo Diddley, Eric Burdon, Diamanda Galas, Arthur Brown.
●The late R&B shouter Screamin' Jay Hawkins was a character made for documentary. Fascinating to listen to, and with a face that totally belies his then 70 years, Hawkins was a fresh alternative to BB King and his ilk, yet never attained their level of status or success. The ex-WWII sergeant (described here as the Bela Lugosi of music) was best known for his intense voodoo-style performances, and was clearly loved and admired by such fellow artists as director Jim Jarmusch and Animals frontman Eric Burdon. DA

Scream of Fear

see Taste of Fear

Screwballs

(1983, Can, 80 min)
d Rafal Zielinski. *p* Maurice Smith. *sc* Linda Shayne, Jim Wynorski. *ph* Miklos Lente. *ed* Brian Ravok. *ad* Sandra Kybartas. *m* Tim McCauley. *cast* Peter Keleghan, Kent Deuters, Lynda Speciale, Alan Deveau, Linda Shayne.
●Few hopes of good cinema survive the title; none the opening scenes, where two big-breasted cheerleaders and an outsize sausage set the tawdry tone. What relentlessly follows concerns the students of Taft and Adams High School, remarkable only for their average age (around thirty) and their avid interest in tits. Now, however one rates the bosom as an erogenous zone, it takes the talents of a Russ Meyer to make it interesting for eighty minutes. Watching the unflagging, unfunny efforts of five callow youths to see the homecoming queen's breasts, one only wonders if ever in the field of endeavour so much has been done by so many for just two. FD

Screwballs II – Loose Screws

(1985, Can, 92 min)
d Rafal Zielinski. *p* Maurice Smith. *sc* Michael Cory. *ph* Robin Miller. *ed* Stephan Fanfara. *ad* Judith Lee. *m* Fred Mollin. *cast* Bryan Genesse, Lance Van Der Kolk, Alan Deveau, Jason Warren, Annie McAuley, Karen Wood, Liz Green, Mike McDonald, Cyd Belliveau.
●A sequel to *Screwballs* (idiot schoolboys rising to the challenge of the school's last virgin, Purity Busch) in which another wave of moronic adolescents drool over bigger and yet bigger breasts. No very serious intent is involved though – the boys, like Steve Hardman and Hugh G Rection, only want to watch the girls in the changing room, or at most cop a feel with any unoccupied hand. Were Zielinski, his cast and crew as crass and pathetic as their characters for making these movies for us to watch? Well, which of us was getting paid? DO

Scrooge

(1951, GB, 86 min, b/w)
d/p Brian Desmond Hurst. *sc* Noel Langley. *ph* CM Pennington-Richards. *ed* Clive Donner. *ad* Ralph Brinton. *m* Richard Addinsell. *cast* Alastair Sim, Kathleen Harrison, Jack Warner, Michael Hordern, Mervyn Johns, Hermione Baddeley, Glyn Dearman, George Cole, Miles Malleson, Ernest Thesiger.
●Surprisingly, there isn't a film version of the Dickens novella which merits the imprimatur 'classic'. The Muppets had a good stab at it, and Bill Murray was well cast in the otherwise scattershot *Scrooged*. On the plus side, this version is cast like an engraved illustration: Thesiger, Johns, Hordern, Harrison, Malleson, Baddeley and, above all, the splendidly aloof Sim, who feasts on Dickens' best lines ('I expect you want the whole day off tomorrow?'), greets each new ghost with a weary shiver, and handles his giddy rebirth with aplomb. A jobbing director who knew how to point a camera, Hurst never betrayed much facility for cutting or movement. He stages the action competently, but the transitions between scenes are so choppy you wonder where the ads are. Add to this a prosaic adaptation by Noel Langley which gets bogged down in the backstory (the relatively dull visitation from the ghost of Christmas Past which explains how nice Ebenezer – a bashful Cole – fell from the path of righteousness), some rather depressed-looking spirits, and the cringeworthy sentimentality of the Tiny Tim scenes, and you have what Scrooge himself might call 'Ho-hum-bug'. TCh

Scrooge

(1970, GB, 118 min)
d Ronald Neame. *p* Robert H Solo. *sc* Leslie Bricusse. *ph* Oswald Morris. *ed* Peter Weatherly. *pd* Terence Marsh. *m* Leslie Bricusse. *cast* Albert Finney, Alec Guinness, Edith Evans, Kenneth More, Michael Medwin, Laurence Naismith, David Collings, Anton Rodgers, Suzanne Neve.
●A misbegotten musical adaptation of Dickens' much too perennial tale, featuring songs by Leslie Bricusse that are not only anaemic but piffling in their up-front relevance ('I Hate People', 'I Like Life', 'I'll Begin Again'). Even Dickens would surely have blenched when Tiny Tim, hugging a manifestly unnecessary crutch, hobbles up to simper blessings on us every one, and to brighten the Cratchit Christmas by singing of 'The Beautiful Day' he hopes is just around the corner. Finney, in a balding wig, mugs abominably as Scrooge; the dances are full of energy but not noticeably choreographed; and the colour (musty brownish for the Scrooge-and-poverty scenes, garishly tinselled for the Christmas fantasy visions) is variable to say the least. Some slight relief is afforded by cameos from Guinness (looking like a camp pixie as Marley's

Ghost), Edith Evans (regally quavering in scarlet robe as the Ghost of Christmas Past), and Kenneth More (vastly bearded and militantly jolly as the Ghost of Christmas Present). TM

Scrooged

(1988, US, 101 min)
d Richard Donner. *p* Richard Donner, Art Linson. *sc* Mitch Glazer, Michael O'Donoghue. *ph* Michael Chapman. *ed* Fredric Steinkamp, William Steinkamp. *pd* J Michael Riva. *m* Danny Elfman. *cast* Bill Murray, Karen Allen, John Forsythe, John Glover, Bobcat Goldthwait, David Johansen, Carol Kane, Robert Mitchum, Michael J Pollard, Alfre Woodard, John Murray, Robert Goulet, John Houseman, Buddy Hackett, Lee Majors.

● In update on the Dickens classic, with Murray as a miserly TV network president who rejoins the human race following spectral visitations. The tone is set by a machine-gun assault on Santa's North Pole toy workshop and the timely arrival of the first of a series of guest star drop-ins. Miles Davis and David Sanborn busk in the wintry streets beside a needy musicians' sign, the usually elegant Forsythe turns up as a disintegrating ghoul, a golf ball embedded in his skull. *Scrooged* is not subtle stuff, and since Murray's comic persona is uniquely hands-off in terms of emotion, his final impassioned speech about the true meaning of Christmas is as embarrassing as Chaplin's at the end of *The Great Dictator*. Rowdy stuff for the light in head. BC

Scrubbers

(1982, GB, 93 min)
d Mai Zetterling. *p* Don Boyd. *sc* Roy Minton, Jeremy Watt, Mai Zetterling. *ph* Ernest Vincze. *ed* Rodney Holland. *ad* Celia Barnett. *m* Michael Hurd. *cast* Amanda York, Chrissie Cotterill, Elizabeth Edmonds, Kate Ingram, Amanda Symonds.

● Part-written by Roy (*Scum*) Minton, this follows the career of two Borstal girls: a lesbian orphan who busts herself back inside to rejoin her faithless lover, and a single mother who, separated from her child, puts an ever-increasing gap between them by her escalating violence. But blatant audience manipulation backfires: the more the mother bashes her way through the film, the less your sympathies are engaged. A script which bridles with a grim wit more akin to *Porridge* than *Scum*-in-a-skirt, and a filtered use of colour so dense it appears to be shot in black-and-white, are both points in favour. But no amount of effing and blinding, unconvincing slow-motion violence, scatological inventiveness, and buckets of flying excreta, can hide the fact that *Scrubbers* is a very noisy film that manages to say nothing novel. An entertaining washout. FL

Scum

(1979, GB, 97 min)
d Alan Clarke. *p* Clive Parsons, Davina Belling. *sc* Roy Minton. *ph* Philip Meheux. *ed* Michael Brasell. *ad* Mike Porter. *cast* Ray Winstone, Mick Ford, Julian Firth, John Blundell, Phil Daniels, John Fowler.

● Roy Minton's teleplay about Borstal life and its vicious circle of violence, remade as a movie after being banned by the BBC: a toughened docudrama (schools of BBC/old Warners/Corman) that carries the same force as the improvised weapons Ray Winstone uses to bludgeon his way through the Borstal power structure. A far-from-blunt instrument itself (and containing some necessary leavening humour), this is potentially knife-edge film-making: will audiences buy the reformist liberalism and stomach the violence, or in fact buy the violence and racism and miss the message? The careful calculations show, but you're still likely to leave at the end feeling righteously angry. PT

Scuola, La

see School

Sea, The

see Mar, El

Sea Chase, The

(1955, US, 117 min)
d/p John Farrow. *sc* James Warner Bellah, John Twist. *ph* William Clothier. *ed* William Ziegler. *ad* Franz Bachelin. *m* Roy Webb. *cast* John Wayne, Lana Turner, David Farrar, Tab Hunter, Lyle Bettger, James Arness, Claude Akins, John Qualen.

● WWII yarn with The Duke as a German, though not of course a card-carrying Nazi. That's Lana Turner as a sultry spy who goes all gooey. The Duke is captain of a freighter leaving Sydney Harbour en route for the Mudderland as the war begins. If he makes it across the Pacific and the Atlantic, he'll be arrested for *not* card-carrying; and if he doesn't – then blame the British Navy, who have him in their gunsights. Lyle Bettger makes a strutting SS psycho, and Tab Hunter is a very Aryan-looking cadet. ATu

Seacoal

(1985, GB, 82 min)
d Murray Martin. *sc* Tom Hadaway. *ph* Peter Roberts. *ed* Ellin Hare. *ad* Sirkka-Liisa Konttinen. *m* Alasdair Robertson. *cast* Amber Styles, Ray Stubbs, Corrina Stubbs, Benny Graham, Tom Hadaway, Murray Martin.

● Mixing fiction with documentary, this looks at the lives of the sea-coal collectors working the beaches of the Northumberland coast, and at the economic and political realities permeating their hard, rude existence. Gritty Loach-style realism, leavened by lyrical camerawork and a strong – even romantic – sense of community, as seen through the eyes of a woman newly introduced to the unrelenting labour of hardship by her chauvinist lover. Intelligent and sensitive, but be warned: the dialect and accents are sometimes impenetrable. GA

Seafood (Haixian)

(2001, China/HK, 86 min)
d/p/sc Zhu Wen. *ph* Liu Yonghong. *ed* Zhu Wen. *ad* Gao Jianxin. *cast* Jinzi, Cheng Taisheng, Ma Daming, Jin Hairui, Cheng Dongping, Su Ming.

● Novelist/scriptwriter Zhu Wen (he wrote *Rainclouds over Wushan* and worked on *Seventeen Years*) turns underground director with a movie sure to induce apoplexy in the Film Bureau if they ever see it. A young woman who calls herself Zhang Xiaomei (she has other IDs, other names) visits Beidaihe in mid-winter, clearly intending to kill herself. (The resort is where China's upper-echelon communists take their summer vacations.) But the suicide of a taciturn poet in her hotel makes her hesitate, and the investigating cop pounces on her hesitation. Much – not all – of the film explores the edgy, violent relationship between the cop (a strange, excitable man who thinks women are like seafood) and the woman (a hooker from Beijing, it turns out). But Zhu springs a huge narrative surprise around an hour in, upending the dramatic structure and refocusing the theme to contemplate the space between the real and the fake. Daring, provocative, highly original. TR

Sea Gull, The

(1968, GB, 141 min)
d/p Sidney Lumet. *sc* Moura Budberg. *ph* Gerry Fisher. *ed* Alan Heim. *pd* Tony Walton. *cast* James Mason, Vanessa Redgrave, Simone Signoret, David Warner, Harry Andrews, Ronald Radd, Eileen Herlie, Kathleen Widdoes, Denholm Elliott, Alfred Lynch.

● Basically an actors' film, for which Lumet has assembled a distinguished cast, found a marvellous lakeside location in Sweden, and vaselined the lens to give an air of autumn melancholy. That the result is sometimes dull and almost always unsatisfactory, despite excellent performances, is thanks partly to the traditional English-speaking failure to play Chekhov for comedy and let his tragedy take care of itself (hence the miscasting of Mason as a darkly brooding Trigorin, the over-intensity of Warner's Konstantin); and partly because the prerequisite of any Chekhov cast is a sense of familiarity bred of a lifetime together (so how come Signoret's Arkadina, with an accent you could cut with a knife, has the impeccably English Harry Andrews as a brother?). TM

Sea Gypsies, The (aka Shipwreck!)

(1978, US, 101 min)
d Stewart Raffill. *p* Joseph C Raffill. *sc* Stewart Raffill. *ph* Thomas McHugh. *ed* Dan Greer, R Hansel Brown. *m* Fred Steiner. *cast* Robert Logan, Mikki Jamison-Olsen, Heather Rattray, Cjon Damitri Patterson, Shannon Saylor.

● A fairly formulary kid's adventure out of the Wilderness-Family-Robinson mould, this makes a half-hearted attempt to break away from the triteness of the Disney stereotype, before succumbing to a catalogue of the beauties and savageries of nature and the blissful benefits of family life. Peopled with such representatives of the 'New Consciousness' as a widowed father ready to sail his young daughters round the world to show them 'what kind of man' he is, an independent female photojournalist, and a 12-year old street-smart black stowaway, the film spends a short time promising interesting tensions between them, before dumping them on the Alaskan coastline to fend for themselves in exemplary Baden-Powell fashion (though the women do turn out to be the better providers) while awaiting rescue/attempting escape. *Déja vu* for all but the youngest viewer. PT

Sea Hawk, The

(1940, US, 127 min, b/w)
d Michael Curtiz. *p* Hal B Wallis, Henry Blanke. *sc* Howard Koch, Seton I Miller. *ph* Sol Polito. *ed* George Amy. *ad* Anton Grot. *m* Erich Wolfgang Korngold. *cast* Errol Flynn, Flora Robson, Brenda Marshall, Claude Rains, Henry Daniell, Donald Crisp, Alan Hale, Gilbert Roland, Una O'Connor.

● A hugely enjoyable swashbuckler from the days when 'packaging' wasn't such a dirty word and Jack Warner was a master of the art. Flynn plays novelist Rafael Sabatini's privateer, royally encouraged into deeds of derring-do against the wicked Spanish, as an amalgam of *Captain Blood* (also Sabatini-based) and *Robin Hood*. Robson repeats her Good Queen Bess from *Fire Over England*. House action specialist Curtiz directs what is in total a remake of a 1924 Frank Lloyd silent. Practice, as they say, makes perfect. PT

Seance (Korei)

(2000, Jap, 95 min)
d Kiyoshi Kurosawa. *p* Takehiko Tanaka, Yasuyuki Uemura. *sc* Tetsuya Onishi, Kiyoshi Kurosawa. *ph* Takahide Shibanushi. *ed* Junichi Kikuchi. *m* Gary Ashiya. *cast* Koji Yakusho, Jun Fukubi, Tsuyoshi Kusanagi, Ittoku Kishibe.

● Perhaps because it's inspired by a novel (Mark McShane's *Seance on a Wet Afternoon*, previously filmed in Britain), this is one Kurosawa film which doesn't fall apart before the end. But the gain in coherence is balanced by distinct shortfalls in excitement and energy. This is a routine B-movie with a better cast than it has any right to expect. Koji (Yakusho) is a sound recordist working on location who improbably fails to notice that one of his equipment boxes doubles in weight – a young girl has escaped from kidnappers and hidden herself inside. By the time he finds her, she's unconscious. His wife Junko (Fukubi), a screwed-up psychic who sometimes works with the police, suggests a scam: she will boost her career and her morale by 'seeing' clues that will eventually lead to the recovery of the girl. But the film feels clunky well before the scam starts to go seriously wrong. TR

Seance on a Wet Afternoon

(1964, GB, 116 min, b/w)
d Bryan Forbes. *p* Richard Attenborough, Bryan Forbes. *sc* Bryan Forbes. *ph* Gerry Turpin. *ed* Derek York. *ad* Ray Simm. *m* John Barry. *cast* Kim Stanley, Richard Attenborough, Mark Eden, Nanette Newman, Judith Donner, Patrick Magee, Gerald Sim.

● Kim Stanley can hardly be known to most of today's cinema audiences: she appears in only four films, and her fame rests on her stage work (even that is pretty sparse). She plays degenerating women, yet her technique is not the Mad Medusa writ large, such as Swanson in *Sunset Blvd.* or Davis in *What Ever Happened to Baby Jane?* She's creepier than that, and more believable. In the movie, she is married to a meek and mild Attenborough – a childless marriage in a gloomy Victorian house. She concocts a scheme to kidnap a child, and then gain notoriety by discovering the child's whereabouts through psychomancy. Her performance is utterly superb, and so too is Attenborough's: with his leather crash helmet, goggles and clapped-out motorbike, he looks like a reject Hell's Angel from *Orphée*. ATu

Sea of Love

(1989, US, 113 min)
d Harold Becker. *p* Martin Bregman, Louis A Stroller. *sc* Richard Price. *ph* Ronnie Taylor. *ed* David Bretherton. *pd* John Jay Moore. *m* Trevor Jones. *cast* Al Pacino, Ellen Barkin, John Goodman, Michael Rooker, William Hickey, Richard Jenkins, Paul Calderon, Gene Canfield.
●Efficient enough as a thriller, but what makes this mandatory viewing is the return of Pacino. There are isolated scenes as good as anything he's done, and if the role is less demanding than Sonny in *Dog Day Afternoon* or Michael in *The Godfather*, his presence lifts the production in the way De Niro lifted *Midnight Run*. Lonely, middle-aged, divorced, Frank Keller (Pacino) breaks a major cop rule by falling for a suspect while investigating a series of Lonely Hearts murders. Someone has been answering ads in a singles' magazine and bumping off the guys; and Helen (Barkin), sexually predatory in spades, could be the one. Following a night of passion – the standard frisk for weapons takes on tropical dimensions here – Frank scratches her from the list. The conclusion is pretty guessable, and you wonder whether the trust theme wouldn't play outside the genre. Goodman brings warmth and wit to Keller's sidekick, and Barkin is just fine. BC

Sea of Sand

(1958, GB, 97 min, b/w)
d Guy Green. *p* Robert Baker, Monty Berman. *sc* Robert Westerby. *ph* Wilkie Cooper. *ed* Gordon Pilkington. *ad* Maurice Pelling. *m* Clifton Parker. *cast* Richard Attenborough, John Gregson, Michael Craig, Vincent Ball, Barry Foster, Andrew Faulds, Ray McAnally.
●Just before the Battle of El Alamein, in 1943, the Eighth Army's Long Range Desert Group launches an attack on one of Rommel's key petrol dumps. Object: knock out the Afrika Korps. Standard heroics, partially redeemed by trenchant visuals, courtesy of former cameraman Green, and a typically sweaty performance by Attenborough. TJ

Search, The

(1948, US, 105 min, b/w)
d Fred Zinnemann. *p* Lazar Wechsler. *sc* Richard Schweizer, David Wechsler. *ph* Emil Berna. *ed* Hermann Haller. *m* Robert Blum. *cast* Montgomery Clift, Aline MacMahon, Wendell Corey, Ivan Jandl, Jarmila Novotna.
●As the first Hollywood movie to be shot in post-WWII Germany, the authenticity of Zinnemann's film cannot be faulted. Recounting the wartime experiences of a ten-year-old Czech boy (Jandl), separated from his mother and cared for by an American soldier (Clift), it seems snatched from the pages of a newspaper. Although there's a slight suspicion that (as in Rossellini's work from this period) the plight of children is being used as a sort of emotional shorthand, the integrity and moving effect of this piece is never really in doubt. TJ

Searchers, The 100 (100)

(1956, US, 119 min)
d John Ford. *p* Merian C Cooper. *sc* Frank S Nugent. *ph* Winton C Hoch. *ed* Jack Murray. *ad* Frank Hotaling, James Basevi. *m* Max Steiner. *cast* John Wayne, Jeffrey Hunter, Vera Miles, Ward Bond, Natalie Wood, Hank Worden, Henry Brandon, Harry Carey Jr, Olive Carey, John Qualen, Antonio Moreno.
●A marvellous Western which turns Monument Valley into an interior landscape as Wayne pursues his five-year odyssey, a grim quest – to kill both the Indian who abducted his niece and the tainted girl herself – which is miraculously purified of its racist furies in a final moment of epiphany. There is perhaps some discrepancy in the play between Wayne's heroic image and the pathological outsider he plays here (forever excluded from home, as the doorway shots at beginning and end suggest), but it hardly matters, given the film's visual splendour and muscular poetry in its celebration of the spirit that vanished with the taming of the American wilderness. TM

Searching for Bobby Fischer (aka Innocent Moves)

(1993, US, 110 min)
d Steven Zaillian. *p* Scott Rudin, William Horberg. *sc* Steven Zaillian. *ph* Conrad Hall. *ed* Wayne Wahrman. *pd* David Gropman. *m* James Horner. *cast* Max Pomeranc, Joe Mantegna, Joan Allen, Ben Kingsley, Laurence Fishburne, Michael Nirenberg.
●An absorbing, fact-based study – a first feature from the writer of *Schindler's List* – of the trials and triumphs of a young chess prodigy. Max Pomeranc (a top 100 player himself) is Josh Waitzkin, seven-year-old son of New York sports reporter Fred (Mantegna), a child whose fascination with chess is initially spurred on by park hustler Vinnie (Fishburne, remarkably convincing) before pushy dad signs him up with tutor Bruce Pandolfini (Kingsley). As Josh battles through increasingly daunting tournament matchplay, his progress reflects his mentors' unfulfilled aspirations as much as the his own developing strategic maturity. Ranking performances, and evocative camerawork from veteran Conrad Hall. True, James Horner's score seems to have strayed in from a fists-in-the-air crowd-pleaser, but it's the one weak link in an accomplished, unexpectedly winning movie. TJ

Searching Wind, The

(1946, US, 108 min, b/w)
d William Dieterle. *p* Hal B Wallis. *sc* Lillian Hellman. *ph* Lee Garmes. *ed* Warren Low. *ad* Hans Dreier, Franz Bachelin. *m* Victor Young. *cast* Robert Young, Sylvia Sidney, Ann Richards, Dudley Digges, Albert Basserman, Norma Varden, Douglas Dick.
●A smooth and surprisingly sharp-tongued version of Lillian Hellman's play berating America for its persistently blinkered isolationism during the years preceding World War II. The weakness it never quite overcomes is the taint of soap opera apparent in the way every major political crisis, from Mussolini's March on Rome in 1922 to the Munich Pact by way of the Spanish Civil War, is trotted out as yet another stage in the diplomat hero's domestic troubles between wife (Richards, who keeps hobnobbing with well-placed Fascists) and Other Woman (Sidney, a journalist who tries to arouse his political awareness). Heady stuff, but given credibility by fine performances and excellent packaging. TM

Seashell and the Clergyman, The (La Coquille et le Clergyman)

(1928, Fr, 44 min, b/w)
d Germaine Dulac. *sc* Antonin Artaud. *ph* Paul Guichard. *cast* Alex Allin, Lucien Bataille, Gênica Athanasiou.
●One of the most celebrated of French avant-garde movies of the '20s, partly because Antonin Artaud wrote the script, partly because the British censor of the time banned it with the legendary words 'If this film has a meaning, it is doubtless objectionable'. Artaud was reputedly unhappy with Dulac's realisation of his scenario, and it's true that the story's anti-clericalism (a priest develops a lustful passion that plunges him into bizarre fantasies) is somewhat undermined by the director's determined visual lyricism. But the fragmentation of the narrative and the innovative imagery remain provocative, and the film is of course fascinating testimony to the currents of its time. TR

Season Five (Fassloh Padjom/Cinquième saison)

(1997, Iran/Fr, 80 min)
d Rafi Pitts. *p* Sophie Goupil. *sc* Behram Beyzai. *ph* Nemat Haghighi. *ed* Hassan Hassandoost. *ad* Malak Khazai. *m* Jamshid Poratai, Jalal Zolonoon, Bigan Kamkar. *cast* Roya Nonahali, Ali Sarkhani, Parviz Poorhosseni, Ghorban Nadjafi, Golab Adineh.
●Based on an unfilmed screenplay by Bahram Beyzai (a thorn in the side of the Shah's censors during an earlier flowering of Iranian cinema), this is a first feature from an Anglo-Iranian director working out of France. On the day of his intended wedding to Mehrbanou, villager Kamarat deliberately rekindles the ancient feud between their clans, which the marriage was supposed to heal. He goes on to lease a dilapidated bus to provide the first mechanised transport to the nearest town. The jilted bride, implacably set on revenge, pushes her hapless brother into launching a rival service – and the internecine struggle soon starts to threaten lives. The vision of the village as a mullah-free zone tips you the wink that there are elements of social satire in play here, which will inevitably by-pass non-Iranians, but there is plenty to enjoy in the performances and the working out of the underlying morality play. TR

Season of Dreams (aka Stacking)

(1987, US, 109 min)
d/p Martin Rosen. *sc* Victoria Jenkins. *ph* Richard S Bowen. *ed* Patrick Dodd. *pd* Linda Bass. *m* Patrick Gleason. *cast* Christine Lahti, Frederic Forrest, Megan Follows, Jason Gedrick, Ray Baker, Peter Coyote, James Gammon, Kaiulani Lee.
●Director Rosen made animated features in Britain (*Watership Down* and *The Plague Dogs*) before moving to the US for this unenlightening rites-of-passage tale set in 1954 Montana. Megan Follows is the teenager trying to hold off the romantic advances of older youth Gedrick while rebuilding her own relationship with hard-pressed waitress mum Lahti, left to cope on her own when her husband is hospitalised. A solid cast make it all easily watchable, but there's not quite enough in the material to make it really distinctive (the similar *Desert Bloom*, for instance, has an A-bomb angle that gives its story a significant lift). TJ

Season of Men, The (La Saison des Hommes)

(1999, Fr, 122 min)
d Moufida Tlatli. *p* Margaret Ménégoz, Mohamed Tlatli. *sc* Moufida Tlatli, (adaptation/dialogue) Nouri Bouzid. *ph* Youseff Ben Youssef. *ed* Isabelle Devinck. *ad* Khaled Joulak. *m* Anouar Braham. *cast* Rabiaa Ben Abdallah, Sabah Bouzouita, Ghalia Ben Ali, Hend Sabri, Ezzedine Guennoun, Mouna Noureddine.
●Tlatli's long-awaited follow-up to *The Silences of the Palace* plies similar territory: a family of women returns to the island where they used to live, cloistered away by absent working menfolk, to take stock. Cue flashbacks. The director's themes are sisterhood and sacrifice, eternal growing pains, inequity and inhibition, the weight of the past, the yielding of tradition to modernity. It's less ornate, the focus broader, the treatment open- and a little loose-ended; the tone more deftly ambivalent but gently hopeful. NB

Season of the Witch

see Jack's Wife

Season's Beatings

see Bûche, La

Seawife

(1957, GB, 81 min)
d Bob McNaught. *p* André Hakim. *sc* George K Burke. *ph* Ted Scaife. *ed* Peter Taylor. *ad* Arthur Lawson. *m* Kenneth V Jones, Leonard Salzedo. *cast* Richard Burton, Joan Collins, Basil Sydney, Cy Grant, Ronald Squire.
●Ludicrously portentous adaptation of JM Scott's novel (originally published as *Sea-Wyf and Biscuit*) elucidating the real-life mystery of the small ads in which one 'Biscuit' agonised after the whereabouts of a certain 'Seawife'. Flashback to World War II unfolds a heady mash of romance, religion and racism, so silly that it's almost disarming, as four survivors from a ship torpedoed during the fall of Singapore make it by life raft to a desert island. There broody Burton falls for Collins, but gets no joy because she (though wearing no wimple) is actually a nun, and God seems to have answered her with a miracle to pull them through; meanwhile the token racist (Sydney) succumbs to devilish impulses to get rid of the token black (Grant), and starts suffering guilts… Rossellini was the original director but copped out, sensible fellow. TM

Sea Wolf, The

(1941, US, 90 min, b/w)
d Michael Curtiz. *p* Henry Blanke. *sc* Robert Rossen. *ph* Sol Polito. *ed* George Amy. *ad* Anton F Grot. *m* Erich Wolfgang Korngold. *cast* Edward G Robinson, John Garfield, Ida Lupino, Alexander Knox, Gene Lockhart, Barry Fitzgerald, Stanley Ridges, Howard da Silva.
●A superbly malevolent adaptation of Jack London's story about two fugitives (Garfield and Lupino) who come together on a ship, only to find

themselves trapped as witnesses to a demonic battle of wits between Robinson's psychopathic captain (a Bligh in sadism, an Ahab in driven obsession) and an altruistic writer (Knox) attempting to assert intellectual dominion with no other weapon but his understanding. Given Robert Rossen's strikingly literate script, Sol Polito's wonderfully eerie camerawork, and Robinson's terrific performance – all pulling together to elaborate the Luciferian motto borrowed from Milton by which the captain lives, 'Better to reign in hell than to serve in heaven' – this is one of Curtiz's best movies. TM

Sea Wolves, The

(1980, GB/US/Switz, 122 min)
d Andrew V McLaglen. *p* Euan Lloyd. *sc* Reginald Rose. *ph* Tony Imi. *ed* John Glen. *ad* Syd Cain. *m* Roy Budd. *cast* Gregory Peck, Roger Moore, David Niven, Trevor Howard, Barbara Kellerman, Patrick Macnee, Patrick Allen, Bernard Archard, Faith Brook, Kenneth Griffith, Donald Houston.

● *The Sea Wolves* answers the pressing problem of how to repay the debt we owe to all those superannuated English stiff-upper-lippers now that all the major war campaigns have been filmed. Solution: dredge up some creaking piece of now-it-can-be-told war marginalia about a retired Territorial regiment of polo-playing boozers (The Calcutta Light Horse!) who bid goodbye to the memsahib for a fortnight and blow up some Jerry ships in Goa harbour. McLaglen previously demonstrated a certain competence with physical action in *The Wild Geese*, but here it's a very pedestrian hour-and-three-quarters before the final crunch – a risible affair with geriatric schoolboys wheezing about, getting hernias. Peck and Niven shamble amiably through the dross as if it were a Navaronian old boys reunion (class of '44), and Roger Moore finds new ways of smirking in a dinner jacket. As a genre – the arterio-sclerotic war movie – it'll never catch on. CPea

Sebastian

(1995, Nor/Swe, 84 min)
d Svend Wam. *p* Petter Vennerod, Hansi Mandoki, Lars Kolvig. *sc* Svend Wam, Per Källberg. *ph* Per Källberg. *ed* Einar Ageland. *ad* Crispin Gurholt. *cast* Hampus Björck, Nicolai Cleve Broch, Ewa Fröling, Helge Jordal.

●Sixteen going on 17, Sebastian is in the back-bedroom casualty stage, spending hours cloistered away when he's not dawdling around his rural Norwegian home town with the pals he's known for years. Mum and dad sense there's something eating at him, but only in the course of this rudimentary youth drama does Sebby himself come to terms with what it is – he thinks he's gay, and he's sure he's in love with best mate Ulf. Plodding and obvious. TJ

Sebastiane

(1976, GB, 86 min)
d Derek Jarman, Paul Humfress. *p* James Whaley, Howard Malin. *sc* Derek Jarman, James Whaley. *ph* Peter Middleton. *ed* Paul Humfress. *pd* Derek Jarman. *m* Brain Eno. *cast* Leonardo Treviglio, Barney James, Neil Kennedy, Richard Warwick, Donald Dunham, Ken Hicks, Lindsay Kemp.

●Not exactly typical of the British independent cinema, this not only tackles an avowedly 'difficult' subject (the relationship between sex and power, and the destructive force of unrequited passion), but does so within two equally 'difficult' frameworks: that of exclusively male sexuality, and that of the Catholic legend of the martyred saint, set nearly 1,700 years ago. Writer/director Jarman sees Sebastian as a common Roman soldier, exiled to the back of beyond with a small platoon of bored colleagues, who gets selfishly absorbed in his own mysticism and then picked on by his emotionally crippled captain. It's filmed naturalistically, to the extent that the dialogue is in barracks-room Latin, and carries an extraordinary charge of conviction in the staging and acting; it falters only in the slightly awkward elements of parody and pastiche. One of a kind, it's compulsively interesting on many levels. TR

Seclusion Near a Forest (Na samote u lesa)

(1976, Czech, 97 min)
d Jirí Menzel. *sc* Zdenek Sverák, Ladislav Smoljak. *ph* Jaromir Sofr. *ad* Zbynek Hloch. *m* Jiri Sust. *cast* Josef Kemr, Zdenek Sverák, Dana Kolárová, Ladislav Smoljak.

●Menzel was still treading very warily after five years in the political doghouse. Skilfully avoiding any sort of dangerous involvements or interpretations, this is a featherweight comedy about the rural hazards encountered by a city family when they rent a summer cottage with a view to permanence. Not least of their problems, especially since they want to start renovations in a hurry, is the obstinate presence of the ancient peasant owner, who has changed his mind about selling up and going to live with his family. There's not a lot to it, but with exquisite camerawork casting a shimmering summery haze over his characteristically delicate blend of tenderness and humour in observing human foibles, Menzel transforms the film into a magical invocation of a lost, simpler and more leisurely world. TM

Seconda Volta, La

see Second Time, The

Second Awakening of Christa Klages, The (Das zweite Erwachen der Christa Klages)

(1977, WGer, 93 min)
d Margarethe von Trotta. *p* Gunther Witte. *sc* Margarethe von Trotta, Luisa Francia. *ph* Franz Rath, Thomas Schwan. *ed* Annette Dorn, Marie-Louise Beutner. *pd* Thomas Lüdi. *m* Klaus Doldinger. *cast* Tina Engel, Sylvia Reize, Katharina Thalbach, Marius Müller-Westernhagen, Peter Schneider.

●Few film-makers wear their hearts as openly on their sleeves as Margarethe von Trotta, and her fascination with women (their relationships with each other and their definition – often redefinition – of themselves) is as apparent in this, her first solo feature, as it was in the later *The German Sisters* or *Friends and Husbands*. Christa Klages (Engel) is a young mother who turns terrorist and bank robber to prevent the closure of a crêche which she helps to run and her daughter attends. On the run with her friend and sometime lover, Christa is pursued by the police, and more mysteriously by a young woman (Thalbach) who was her hostage in the bank raid. What von Trotta has to say about her women is compelling, and she remains one of the few film-makers to portray terrorists convincingly. But the enigma of the hostage runs through the film as elusively as a character in a dream – vitally important at any given moment, but irritatingly meaningless when taken as a whole – and undermines the conviction of this feminist thriller which is otherwise so gloriously rooted in West Germany's present. FD

Second Best

(1993, US, 101 min)
d Chris Menges. *p* Sarah Radclyffe. *sc* David Cook. *ph* Ashley Rowe. *ed* George Akers. *pd* Michael Howells. *m* Simon Boswell. *cast* William Hurt, Chris Cleary Miles, Jane Horrocks, Keith Allen.

●William Hurt, who works in a sub-Post Office in rural Wales, is the son of self-absorbed parents. He decides to adopt a child and is finally allocated the disturbed son of Keith Allen's wild survivalist con. The movie starts in a threatening register with the boy being 'abducted' from school and taken to a woodland foxhole where he is forced to promise to love only his father, and then settles down to a 'Play for Today'-like examination of the difficult path towards trust and acceptance between boy and adopted father. Hurt excels in these buttoned-down roles and his performance here is something of an exemplar, full of intelligence and feeling. Allen's character and performance are misguided, but they don't scupper the film. WH

Second Breath

see Deuxième Souffle, Le

Second Century (Segundo Siglo)

(1999, Mex, 110 min, b/w & col)
d Jorgé Bolado. *p* Juan E Garcia, Simon Bross, Jorgé Bolado. *sc* Jorgé Bolado. *ph* Jon Walker. *ed* Eddie Hamilton, Jorgé Bolado. *pd* Lorenzo Hagerman. *m* Ignacio Maldonaldo. *with* Martin Lassalle, Robert Frank, Philippe de Saint Phallé, Tania Negrete, Alai González, Eugenia Souza, Miguel de Luna, Lorenzo Hagerman.

●Surely a candidate for one of the most bizarre movies you are ever likely to see. Young Mexican film-maker Bolado came up with the notion of taking Martin Lasalle (yes, the star of Bresson's *Pickpocket*) and walking across Scotland with him and a small film crew. So we see this icon of world cinema, now grey with age, wandering through Moffat and Melrose as he tackles the Southern Upland Way. Having paused beforehand on a New York stopover seeking inspiration from legendary photographer Robert Frank, Bolado captures the rolling scenery and the variable weather in 35mm, Super-8 and still photographs. The money did not extend to sound recording however, so three different unseen Spanish women of different generations comment on the story, adding Beatles lyrics and TS Eliot at will. Oh yes, and the noise of passing cars is dubbed in by someone going 'broom! broom!' in the background. In truth, the film goes on way too long, but it leaves you with spirits high in the knowledge that the cinema has not run out of new ideas and wild combinations. TJ

Second Chance

(1953, US, 82 min)
d Rudolph Maté. *p* Edmund Grainger. *sc* Oscar Millard, Sydney Boehm. *ph* William Snyder. *ed* Robert Ford. *ad* Albert S D'Agostino, Carroll Clark. *m* Roy Webb. *cast* Robert Mitchum, Linda Darnell, Jack Palance, Reginald Sheffield, Roy Roberts.

●Originally made in 3-D, this unpretentious and very enjoyable RKO thriller has Mitchum as a prizefighter helping out ex-gangster's moll Darnell in Mexico, where she is being stalked by hired killer Palance. Far from *noir*, given the simplicity of the plot and the lack of romantic pessimism, it nevertheless works very well thanks to the assured performances (the luscious Darnell makes a lovely companion for the similarly statuesque Mitchum), and to a genuinely exciting climax aboard a broken-down cable car. GA

Second Chance (Si c'était à refaire)

(1976, Fr, 99 min)
d/p/sc Claude Lelouch. *ph* Jacques Lefrançois. *ed* Georges Klotz. *ad* Eric Moulard. *m* Francis Lai. *cast* Catherine Deneuve, Anouk Aimée, Charles Denner, Francis Huster, Niels Arestrup, Colette Baudot, Jean-Pierre Kalfon.

●'The whole idea is mad!' screams lawyer Denner when the newly imprisoned heroine (Deneuve) suggests that they conceive a child in her cell to give her something to live for. But this is a film by Claude Lelouch, the master of eccentric kitsch, and everything is mad – not least the finale, when yet another man and another woman find total happiness on the heights of Mont Blanc. But for once the madness isn't full-blooded enough to be satisfying: instead of juggling four storylines in the air, Lelouch is content with one and a half. And time hangs increasingly heavy as the plot ambles along portentously, following the heroine's adjustment to the pangs of life and love after sixteen years in a swish prison. Not exactly a cruel disappointment, but a disappointment none the less. GB

Second Generation

(1999, GB, 80 min)
d Shane O'Sullivan. *p* Jack Kellett, Shane O'Sullivan. *sc* Shane O'Sullivan. *ph* Mark Duffield. *ed* Kavi Pujara, Brian Saunderson. *ad* Kanako Hiramoto. *m* (additional) Masaki Hiramoto. *cast* Hanayo, Shigetomo Yutani, Nitin Chandra Ganatra, Adrian Pang, Kriss Dosanjh, Saeed Jaffrey.

●Shane O'Sullivan shot this first feature on DigiBeta for £20,000. Then he persuaded Barco, one of a handful of companies manufacturing digital projectors, that he could showcase their equipment if they'd lend him a projector and hire London's ABC Piccadilly for a week. Regrettably, his ingenuity didn't stretch to arranging a press preview, so we can't comment on the system, only how the film looks on VHS tape. It's like a soap opera with a fetish for fluorescent filters – a bohemian fable, set in and around Brick Lane, in the hipster manner of *Stranger Than Paradise* or *Mystery Train*. Lili (Hanayo), a free spirit in pigtails and mini skirts, has fled an arranged HK marriage to be with 'Bobby'. She bumps into Go (Shigetomo), a young Japanese detective living in a spare warehouse flat in E1. He lets her sleep on the couch and they go their separate ways, then he gets his first case – to find a runaway Chinese girl. O'Sullivan has made a thoroughly 'London' film, yet there isn't an Anglo-Saxon in the cast. It's well scored and marked by nice touches, but it's unevenly acted and too flimsy to generate anything approaching suspense.TCh

Seconds

(1966, US, 105 min, b/w)
d John Frankenheimer. *p* Edward Lewis. *sc* Lewis John Carlino. *ph* James Wong Howe. *ed* Ferris Webster, David Webster. *ad* Ted Haworth. *m* Jerry Goldsmith. *cast* Rock Hudson, Salome Jens, John Randolph, Will Geer, Jeff Corey, Richard Anderson, Murray Hamilton, Karl Swenson, Khigh Diegh, Wesley Addy, Frances Reid, Robert Brubaker.

● Hemmed in by an arid marriage, paunchy middle-aged banker Randolph grasps another chance at life when a secret organisation transforms him into hunky Hudson and gives him a new start as an artist in Californian beach-front bohemia. Freedom, however, turns out to be a rather daunting prospect, and the struggle to fill the blank canvas comes to typify Hudson's unease with his new existence. Saul Bass' unsettling title sequence sets the scene for the concise articulation of fifty-something bourgeois despair, as visualised by James Wong Howe's distorting camerawork and the edgy discord of Jerry Goldsmith's excoriating score. After that, the film's uptight view of the hang-loose West Coast feels like a slightly forced argument, until Frankenheimer regroups and the jaws of the narrative shut tight on one of the most chilling endings in all American cinema. Little wonder it flopped at the time, only to be cherished by a later generation, notably film-makers Siegel and McGehee who drew extensively on its themes and visuals in their debut *Suture*. (This downbeat sci-fi thriller completed Frankenheimer's loose 'paranoid' trilogy – earlier instalments being *The Manchurian Candidate* and *Seven Days in May*.) TJ

Second Skin (Segunda Piel)

(1999, Sp, 104 min)
d Gerardo Vera. *p* Andrés Vicente Gómez. *sc* Angeles González-Sinde. *ph* Julio Madurga. *ed* Nicholas Wentworth. *ad* Ana Alvargonzález. *m* Roque Baños. *cast* Javier Bardem, Jordi Mollá, Adriana Gil, Cecilia Roth, Javier Albalá, Adrián Sac, Mercedes Sampietro, Cristina Espinosa.

● How different this could have been if the spirit of the opening titles (big music and a Bond riff, but with a male torso doing the twist) had been maintained. Instead we get a cod psychological drama about a perfect couple going off the rails because he's having an affair – with a man (Bardem, as a young surgeon). A lesser addition to Spanish cinema's recent forays into gay affairs, the film sports a reasonable absence of sheets in the bed scenes, counterbalanced by lack in almost all other departments. There's no sense of place or the play of time, and with the psychological focus on this stressed triangle passing from one to another faster than a plate of dodgy tapas, would-be character 'complexity' comes over simply as structural confusion. Husband Alberto's fluctuations of denial and excess are woefully played. GE

Second Time, The (La Seconda Volta)

(1996, It/Fr, 80 min)
d Mimmo Calopresti. *cast* Nanni Moretti, Valeria Bruni Tedeschi, Valeria Milillo, Roberto de Francesco.

● Calopresti's feature debut is a modest but intriguing study of the psychological legacy of the terrorism that beset Italy in the '70s. Set in a hauntingly gloomy Turin, the film follows the actions and emotions of Moretti, a lecturer and ex-Fiat executive, after he recognises in the street a woman sentenced to 30 years in prison for having shot him in the head some 12 years earlier. As he sets about getting to know her – she, not having recognised him, thinks he's merely trying to chat her up, and pretends she's just a normal working woman – Calopresti leaves us in the dark as to Moretti's exact intentions, so that his cool, intelligent drama also achieves a welcome level of unsettling suspense. GA

Secret, The (Le Secret)

(1974, Fr/It, 103 min)
d Robert Enrico. *p* Jacques-Eric Strauss. *sc* Pascal Jardin, Robert Enrico. *ph* Eitenne Becker. *ed* Eva Zora. *ad* Jean Saussac. *m* Ennio Morricone. *cast* Jean-Louis Trintignant, Marlène Jobert, Philippe Noiret, Jean-François Adam, Solange Pradel.

● Best known for his short film *Incident at Owl Creek*, Enrico here deals once more with a man at the end of his rope. Trintignant plays a fugitive from an institute who is befriended by an artistic couple (Noiret, Jobert), refugees from Paris now living a slightly dull life in the country. Suspense is generated somewhat needlessly through teasing the audience about Trintignant's sanity: is he a maniac on the loose, or as he claims, the victim of a government conspiracy? The film shamelessly litters red herrings along the way. More promisingly, it elsewhere displays (but does not explore) the philosophical anxieties that the French have so often found in American movies, leading to an increasing fatalism as events move towards a bleak conclusion. But too much remains withheld from the audience by the film's sleights of hand, although Trintignant's worried performance counters one's graver doubts. CPe

Secret, Le

(2000, Fr, 109 min)
d Virginie Wagon. *p* François Marquis. *sc* Virginie Wagon, Erick Zonca. *ph* Jean-Marc Fabre. *ed* Yannick Kergoat. *ad* Brigitte Brassart. *cast* Anne Coësens, Michel Bompoil, Tony Todd, Quentin Rossi, Jacqueline Jehanneuf, Aladin Reibel, Valérie Vogt, Frédéric Sauzay, Natalya Ermilova.

● An involving look into the most private recesses of the female psyche. Marie (Coësens) is an ordinary set of statistics: she's 35, married for 12 years to François (Bompoil), with a two-year-old son. Her husband would like another child, but she's not sure and doesn't know why. Her job doesn't quite provide satisfaction, though she's a very practised door to door rep for an encyclopedia company. Still, her latest lead is somewhat bewildering, since Bill (Todd), a black American, hardly needs a set of books in French. It turns out he's house-sitting, By now Marie is fascinated by his imposing confidence, which somehow frees her to be herself when she's with him. Such liberation swiftly leads to his bedroom, and her marriage will never be the same. This doesn't push at cinema's sexual boundaries like *Romance* or *Intimacy*. It's an ostensibly lighter piece, but without the distraction of such explicitness, its very lucidity gives the viewer room to reflect. Does a marriage stifle our individual sexual selves? Is self-expression different from infidelity? It's a film of sincere, troubling transparency. TJ

Secret, The (Fengjie)

(1979, HK, 89 min)
d Ann Hui. *p* Audrey Li. *sc* Joyce Chan. *ph* Chung Chi-man. *ed* Hamilton Yu. *m* Violet Lam. *cast* Sylvia Chang, Teresa Chiu, Tsui Siu-Keung, Alex Man, George Lam.

● Aside from fleeting glimpses of a hospital and a disco, Hui's first feature shows nothing of modern Hong Kong – which is fitting, since the theme is the hold of the past over the present and the focus is on the power of superstition in the characters' lives. Based on a then recent real-life murder mystery, the film takes an inconclusive autopsy, a supposedly dangerous madman and a suspected haunting in its stride as it moves to a truly hysterical climax. Gory, suspenseful, impressive. TR

Secret Admirer

(1985, US, 98 min)
d David Greenwalt. *p* Steve Roth. *sc* Jim Kouf, David Greenwalt. *ph* Victor J Kemper. *ed* Dennis Virkler. *pd* William J Cassidy. *m* Jan Hammer. *cast* C Thomas Howell, Lori Laughlin, Kelly Preston, Dee Wallace Stone, Cliff De Young, Leigh Taylor-Young, Fred Ward.

● An unsigned billet doux slipped between the pages of 'The Pageant of World History' triggers an escalating comedy of errors as it passes round a group of college kids and their equally gullible parents, massaging each reader's *amour propre* with wild fantasies of a secret admirer. Here is the stuff of classic French farce – Marivaux rewritten Neil Simon-style – were it not that this game of love and chance offers no notable insights into the lust, gluttony, and other deadly boring sins of Middle America. Howell, the young star of *The Outsiders* and *Red Dawn*, evinces a certain ingenuous comedic flair. For the rest, the characters are rather less memorable than the Pepsi cans, Fruit Loops and other brand name junk foods looming large in the foreground of almost every frame. And how could anyone endorse an ending wherein the girl-next-door gives up a world cruise to stay at home with the boy-next-door? SJo

Secret Adventures of Tom Thumb, The

(1993, GB, 60 min)
d Dave Borthwick. *p* Richard Hutchison. *sc* Dave Borthwick. *ph* Frank Passingham, Dave Borthwick. *ed* David Borthwick. *m* Startled Insects, John Paul Jones. *cast* Nick Upton, Deborah Collard, Frank Passingham, John Schofield, Mike Gifford.

● This animated film from Bristol's bolexbrothers studio impresses for its interwoven techniques (mainly claymation and pixilated live action) and its nightmare vision. Born to a poor, boorish couple after an accident at an artificial insemination plant, little Tom is soon abducted by government heavies and subjected to torturous experiments. With the help of a mutant, he escapes from the lab into a cruel, filthy world where desperate little people wage an unending war of survival against the ordinary 'giants'. Borthwick, the writer, editor and director, has the knack of making everyday things seem peculiarly strange and sinister. GA

Secret Agent, The

(1936, GB, 85 min, b/w)
d Alfred Hitchcock. *p* Michael Balcon, Ivor Montagu. *sc* Charles Bennett, Ian Hay, Jessy Lasky. *ph* Bernard Knowles. *ed* Charles Frend. *ad* OF Wendorff. *m* Louis Levy. *cast* Madeleine Carroll, John Gielgud, Peter Lorre, Robert Young, Percy Marmont, Lilli Palmer, Charles Carson, Michael Redgrave.

● Based loosely on a couple of Somerset Maugham's *Ashenden* stories, this thriller may not be one of Hitchcock's best English films, but it is full of startling set pieces and quirky characterisation. About a British spy (Gielgud) who travels to Switzerland to kill an enemy agent, but murders the wrong man, it delights in the rivalry for Madeleine Carroll's affections between Gielgud, Lorre and Young, and in the numerous opportunities for unusual thriller ingredients that the (studio-concocted) Swiss settings afford: a chase through a chocolate factory, murder atop a mountain, death in a quaint church. And there is a more serious side, with Gielgud doubting his profession and patriotism after killing the wrong man. GA

Secret Agent, The (aka Joseph Conrad's The Secret Agent)

(1996, US/GB, 95 min)
d Christopher Hampton. *p* Norma Heyman, Gérard Depardieu. *sc* Christopher Hampton. *ph* Denis Lenoir. *ed* George Akers. *pd* Caroline Amies. *m* Philip Glass. *cast* Bob Hoskins, Patricia Arquette, Gérard Depardieu, Jim Broadbent, Christian Bale, Eddie Izzard, Elizabeth Spriggs, Peter Vaughan, Robin Williams.

● In 1936, Alfred Hitchcock took the bones of Joseph Conrad's 1907 novel and sculpted the contemporary thriller *Sabotage*, with Oscar Homolka as a cinema owner waging a terrorist campaign on London with the unwitting assistance of his wife and her brother. Hampton's version restores the tale to the 1880s, and is more respectful of Conrad's narrative, characters and tone, yet it's this new adaptation which travesties the novel. At least, the Hitchcock – minor, by his standards – catches an authentic whiff of terror. On the plus side, Hoskins is well cast as the 'corpulent anarchist', Verloc, who is in fact a double agent working for the Russian embassy and Scotland Yard. With his bowler hat, umbrella and squat rotund frame, Hoskins makes an appropriately sorry spy, but Hampton squanders the performance. After an atmospheric opening, he loses his grip on the material and shuffles awkwardly between a handful of variable cameos. Most disastrous is Arquette's phonetically precarious Mrs Verloc, Cockney by way of Timbuktu. TCh

Secret Agent Club, The

(1996, US, 90 min)
d John Murlowski. *p* Brian Shuster, Jimmy Lifton. *sc* Rory Johnston. *ph* Stephen Douglas-Smith. *ed* Leslie Rosenthal. *pd* James Scanlon. *m* Jan Hammer. *cast* Hulk Hogan, Richard Moll, Lesley-Anne Down, Matthew McCurley, Edward Albert, Lyman Ward, Barry Bostwick.
●Raymond Chase (Hogan) seems to be a 'dweeb', a klutzy single-parent who can't catch a ball to save his life. In fact he's a member of the secret government agency, Shadow. Ray's pre-teen son Jeremy (McCurley) discovers this the hard way when father turns superhuman in a failed effort to elude the henchmen of terror-queen Eve (Down). Chase has Eve's billion-dollar laser gun, and she wants it back. An inane farce, dreadfully acted, with echoes of *Crocodile Dundee II* and several Bond films. DA

Secret Ballot (Raye Makhfi)

(2001, Iran/It, 100 min)
d Babak Payami. *p* Marco Müller, Babak Payami. *sc* Babak Payami. *ph* Farzad Jodat. *ed* Babak Karimi. *m* Michael Galasso. *cast* Nassim Abdi, Cyrus Abidi, Youssef Habashi, Farokh Shojail, Gholbahar Janghali.
●That this was financed in Europe is a sign of just how celebrated Iranian cinema has become around the world. The result – while by no means a travesty – does smack of 'Kiarostami-lite'. Like *The Wind Will Carry Us*, its setting is so remote Sam Beckett would feel right at home. Two soldiers take turns standing guard on a deserted beach. Then, out of the blue, a ballot box drops from the sky, soon followed by an electoral official. Today is election day, and the soldier on day shift must accompany her around the island as she collects everyone's vote. As an absurdist satire on the inviolate ideal of Western democracy, well, it's actually pretty lugubrious. Rather more subtle is the touching respect the soldier develops for the single-minded registrar. TCh

Secret Beyond the Door...

(1948, US, 98 min, b/w)
d/p Fritz Lang. *sc* Silvia Richards. *ph* Stanley Cortez. *ed* Arthur Hilton. *ad* Max Parker. *m* Miklós Rozsa. *cast* Joan Bennett, Michael Redgrave, Anne Revere, Barbara O'Neil, Natalie Schaefer, Paul Cavanagh.
●An example of Hollywood's mooncalf affair with Freud during the '40s, ending in an absurd instant cure for psychopathy. But the premise is fascinating, and fraught with Gothic overtones as Bennett's heroine ('This is not the time to think of danger', she murmurs at the outset, shaking off premonition, 'this is my wedding day') gradually realises that, married to an architect (Redgrave) who literally and obsessively 'collects' rooms in which murders have occurred, she must uncover the secret of the one room always kept locked. Lang himself didn't think much of the film, but nevertheless set it under his usual sign of destiny ('This is not the time to think of danger...') and invested it with roots in older myths of the magic power of love. His direction is masterly, imposing meanings and tensions through images that are spare, resonant and astonishingly beautiful. A remarkable film. TM

Secret Ceremony

(1968, GB, 109 min)
d Joseph Losey. *p* John Heyman, Norman Priggen. *sc* George Tabori. *ph* Gerry Fisher. *ed* Reginald Beck. *pd* Richard MacDonald. *m* Richard Rodney Bennett. *cast* Elizabeth Taylor, Mia Farrow, Robert Mitchum, Pamela Brown, Peggy Ashcroft.
●It's difficult to know why Mitchum, slouching through a few scenes in the ill-fitting disguise of an ageing, bearded academic with little girls on his mind, should have accepted this part. Taylor, however, is very fine as a tacky madonna: a devout prostitute who's offered a respite from the streets when a regressive child-woman called Cenci (Farrow in long wig and Pollyanna tights) adopts her as substitute mother and moves her into a mansion of art-déco splendour. No wonder then that Taylor/Laura should fervently pray 'Oh Lord, let no one snatch me from this heaven'; and as the strange 'secret ceremonies' begin, her treatment of Cenci displays the same mix of greed and generosity. Losey's mannered direction, somehow entirely appropriate, makes for a memorable film. JCl

Secret Cinema, The

(1965, US, 28 min)
d Paul Bartel. *p* Paul Bartel, Bob Schulenberg. *sc* Paul Bartel. *ph* Fred Wellington. *pd* Bob Schulenberg. *cast* Amy Vane, Gordon Felio, Philip Carlson.
●An early film by Bartel, putty-faced schoolmaster (and comic) of the Roger Corman stable (he made *Death Race 2000*), which exudes an amiable naïveté. A mad secret society, of uncertain membership and dubious morality, runs a 'secret cinema' in which they screen *ciné-vérité* films of the characters in this film losing their marbles. Some of it is hilarious; all of it is fresh enough; but none of it is avant-garde: the camp sensibility of the New York underground now increasingly looks like irony updated. Remade by Bartel in 1985 as an episode of TV series *Amazing Stories*. CA

Secret Défense

(1997, Fr/Switz/It, 173 min)
d Jacques Rivette. *p* Martine Marignac, Christian Lambert. *sc* Pascal Bonitzer, Emmanuelle Cuau, Jacques Rivette. *ph* William Lubtchansky. *ed* Nicole Lubtchansky. *ad* Manu de Chauvigny. *cast* Sandrine Bonnaire, Jerzy Radziwilowicz, Laure Marsac, Grégoire Colin, Bernadette Giraud, Françoise Fabian.
●Working late one night, Sylvie (Bonnaire) discovers her brother Paul (Colin) searching her desk for a handgun. He says he's found out that their father's death five years past was murder – he has evidence implicating Walser (Radziwilowicz), their father's closest colleague. Sceptical and instinctively cautious, Sylvie is compelled to follow up the investigation to save her brother from himself, or so she thinks. Rivette doesn't exactly cut to the chase. The most memorable sequence follows Sylvie as she goes into the Métro. She boards the train, deep in thought, and Rivette stays with her in real time right through to the next stop, where she alights, crosses to the next platform, and waits again. A decision has been reached. The scene is by no means atypical. Rivette seems intent on probing that which must remain unspoken, on photographing the unconscious – hence the title, which translates as 'Top Secret'. Sternly ascetic and unerringly contemplative, this 170-minute film is, nevertheless, a thriller – and something of a potboiler at that. It's a problem, because for all its mysteries, the movie thoroughly repudiates suspense.What the film does have in its favour is a performance of concerted, gaunt integrity from Bonnaire. TCh

Secret de Mayerling, Le

(1948, Fr, 96 min, b/w)
d Jean Delannoy. *p* Claude Dolbert. *sc* Jacques Rémy. *ph* Robert Le Febvre. *m* Louis Beydts. *sc* Jacques Rémy, Jean Delannoy, Philippe Hériat. *ph* Robert Lefebvre. *ed* James Cuenet. *ad* Raymond Druart. *m* Louis Beydts. *cast* Jean Marais, Dominique Blanchar, Jean Debucourt, Silvia Monfort.
●Time was, circles were, you were liable to be treated like the scum of the earth for even *seeing* a Jean Delannoy movie, let alone finding things to admire in it. Yet this seizes the attention from the start: midnight, the Archduke in his carriage, his body propped up by boards, the head rolling back and forth, Marie Vetsera marched away between two strong shoulders, feet dragging in the snow, her shattered forehead glimpsed through reflected light. This is narrative cinema at its most vigorous, and the whole piece manifests an intelligence unfazed by a subject apparently squeezed dry already by Litvak and Ophuls. Marais' regal authority is to the fore, even as another Marais quality – he is sometimes referred to by the euphemism 'feline' – undermines his suitability for the role of a Habsburg stud. BBa

Secret Face, The (Gizli Yuz)

(1991, Ger, 115 min)
d Omer Kavur. *sc* Orhan Pamuk. *ph* Erdal Kahraman. *cast* Zuhal Olcay, Fikret Kushan, Utkay Aziz.
●This esoteric movie starts with a quote from Ferriduddin Attar and gets more obscure by the moment. A young man having defied his father by refusing to study, takes to photographing faces in late night Istanbul cafés. These he shows to a mysterious woman. She sends him off to locate one of the faces, a clockmaker in a provincial town. The woman subsequently disappears and he embarks on a year-long quest (through the City of the Sad and the City of the Hearts) to find her. The movie is hard to categorise. If the faces seen against the walls and the shots of strange lone trees remind one of Tarkovsky, the woman's Maria Casarès-like face receding into the shadows evokes the poetry of Cocteau; and the unexplained histories and motivations of the characters suggest Kafka. Director Omer Kavur is nevertheless determinedly his own man. It's a disconcerting, captivating, spiritual journey, perfectly accompanied by atmospheric oscillating, one-note music reminiscent of Popul Vuh. WH

Secret Friends

(1991, GB, 97 min)
d Dennis Potter. *p* Rosemarie Whitman. *sc* Dennis Potter. *ph* Sue Gibson. *ed* Clare Douglas. *pd* Gary Williamson. *m* Nick Russell-Pavier. *cast* Alan Bates, Gina Bellman, Frances Barber, Tony Doyle, Joanna David, Colin Jeavons, Rowena Cooper, Ian McNeice, Davyd Harries.
●Beset by fantasies careering out of control, John (Bates) is driven towards madness and a total obliteration of self. As a child, he conjured up an imaginary 'secret friend' rebellious enough to withstand his father's Victorian discipline. Years later, the friend is still on hand, feeding the anger and guilt which find a compliant victim in John's wife Helen (Bellman). In this adaptation of his own novel *Ticket to Ride*, Potter's complex linking of sexual fantasy and destructive forces is unwieldy and embittered. Nothing is what it seems. John appears to have committed a murder, and as the film intercuts between past and present to reveal clues, he struggles with amnesia and impending insanity. Did he, will he kill his wife? Is she, was she a prostitute? Sex exacts penalties ('We all pay for it'), bleak humour recompenses ('Sex is funny, a bloody hoot'), and women, tiresomely, are by turns dependent and predatory. CM

Secret Game, The

see Jeux Interdits

Secret Garden, The

(1949, US, 92 min, b/w & col)
d Fred M Wilcox. *p* Clarence Brown. *sc* Robert Ardrey. *ph* Ray June. *ed* Robert J Kern. *ad* Cedric Gibbons, Urie McCleary. *m* Bronislau Kaper. *cast* Margaret O'Brien, Herbert Marshall, Dean Stockwell, Gladys Cooper, Brian Roper, Elsa Lanchester.
●The first screen version of the Frances Hodgson Burnett story has O'Brien (in her last film role before she retired, aged 12) as the orphan who transforms the lives of embittered uncle Marshall and his bed-ridden son Stockwell when she starts tending an off-limits garden in the grounds of their country mansion. All is gothic doom and gloom to begin with, Ray June's b/w camerawork streaking the imposing mansion sets with dark shadow, but more and more light intrudes, brightening with master Stockwell's psychological regeneration (disarmingly insightful from a child performer), and culminating in a climactic *coup de cinéma* when Technicolor proves the very essence of Life itself. MGM's production recalls *The Wizard of Oz*, but there's some stiffness here and Garland is not eclipsed. TJ

Secret Garden, The

(1993, GB, 100 min)
d Agnieszka Holland. *p* Fred Roos, Tom Luddy, Fredric S Fuchs. *sc* Caroline Thompson. *ph* Roger Deakins. *ed* Isabelle Lorente. *pd* Stuart Craig. *m* Zbigniew Preisner. *cast* Maggie Smith, John Lynch, Kate Maberly, Heydon Prowse, Andrew Knott, Laura Crossley.
●Frances Hodgson Burnett's much-loved children's novel could all too easily come across on screen as the last word in period fustian, but the unforced approach of Holland and scriptwriter Caroline Thompson pierces to the emotional core of a still potent tale. Shipped back from colonial India to the inhospitable Yorkshire manor of her reclusive hunchback uncle (Lynch), orphan Mary Lennox (newcomer Maberly) tangles petulantly with the no-nonsense housekeeper (Smith). Even so, the spoilt girl's rebelliousness soon distils into a recuperative influence over her bedridden cousin Colin (Prowse) when she begins to tend the

long-neglected walled garden tucked away in the grounds. With well-judged performances played straight, and topical subtexts (Green consciousness, the dysfunctional family), this 'children's' film sets no age limit on its potential audience. TJ

Secret Honor

(1984, US, 90 min)
d/p Robert Altman. *sc* Donald Freed, Arnold M Stone. *ph* Pierre Mignot. *ed* Juliet Weber. *ad* Stephen Altman. *m* George Burt. *cast* Philip Baker Hall.

● Alone in his study late at night, Richard Milhouse Nixon ponders the pardon he's been offered for the Watergate scandal, and contrasts his secret honour with his public shame. Cue for raving resentment galore and perceptive insights into the politics of power and money. Made with a student crew at the University of Michigan, Altman's one-man theatrical adaptation, for all its dense verbosity, is resolutely cinematic, employing a prowling camera to illuminate the dark areas of its melancholy, megalomaniac hero's soul. While Baker Hall, ranting with drunken fervour at presidential portraits and a bank of security videos, suggests nothing less than a sometimes lucid, sometimes lunatic incarnation of mediocrity, irredeemably tainted by fame and failure. Fascinating stuff. GA

Secret Invasion, The

(1964, US, 95 min)
d Roger Corman. *p* Gene Corman. *sc* R Wright Campbell. *ph* Arthur E Arling. *ed* Ronald Sinclair. *ad* John Murray. *m* Hugo Friedhofer. *cast* Stewart Granger, Raf Vallone, Henry Silva, Mickey Rooney, Edd Byrnes, William Campbell, Mia Massini.

● This *Dirty Dozen* predates Aldrich's by three years, with Granger leading five convicts, against the promise of free pardons, in a suicidal World War II bid to kidnap an influential Italian general from a Nazi fortress in Dubrovnik. Corman delivers the action all right, making particularly suspenseful use of a device – lacking watches, each member of the team keeps time by rhythmically snapping his fingers so that stages of the kidnap plan can be coordinated – which springs several ingenious surprises on both Nazis and audience. But the real fascination of the film is the extent to which it is cloaked in characteristic Corman/Gothic motifs: Silva's role as the killer with 'dead eyes', inevitably fated to kill his own love; the disguise as hooded monks adopted for the final showdown; Granger's death in an idyllic forest glade after using his own blood to lead a pack of tracker dogs astray. Unexpectedly, the overall tone is strangely elegiac. TM

Secret Laughter of Women, The

(1998, GB/Can, 99 min)
d Peter Schwabach. *p* OO Sagay, Jon Slan. *sc* OO Sagay. *ph* Martin Fuhrer. *ed* Michael David. *pd* Christopher J Bradshaw. *m* Yves Laferrière. *cast* Colin Firth, Nia Long, Dan Lett, Joke Silva, Ariyon Bakare, Joy Elias Rilwan, Hakeem Kae-Kazim, Bella Enaharo, Oluwafisayo Roberts.

● Single mother and landscape gardener Nimi (Long) likes life among the close knit Nigerian community of a coastal town in southern France, but finds herself subjected to a tussle between the traditionally minded womenfolk and her fanciful 7-year-old Sammy (Roberts). While the former eye up the eligible new preacher (Bakare) as a potential husband, Sammy hatches similar ambitions for his new friend Matthew (Firth), a successful English fantasy comicbook author who summers from his 'open' modern marriage in a nearby villa. Though not short on good intentions, as a would-be romantic comedy the film's unguarded naivety doesn't pay off, and attempts to keep the drama light, sunny and sensitive often lapse into rose tinted whimsy or quixotism. It's more romantic than comic, and more rambling than romantic; and while on the whole the acting is a plus, there are times when the performers sound like they're reading from the page. NB

Secret Life of an American Wife, The

(1968, US, 92 min)
d/p/sc George Axelrod. *ph* Leon Shamroy. *ed* Harry Gerstad. *ad* Ed Graves, Jack Martin Smith. *m* Billy May. *cast* Walter Matthau, Anne Jackson, Patrick O'Neal, Edy Williams, Richard Bull, Paul Napier.

● Basically, as Axelrod has pointed out, the feminine angle on *The Seven Year Itch* (which he also scripted, from his own play): a charmingly immoral little morality play about a suburban housewife, apprehensive about her declining desirability, who nervously hires herself out for the afternoon as a callgirl in order to test the response. Jackson's excellent performance is matched by Matthau's as her client, an ageing Hollywood star sagging in all directions, and too riddled with hangover, sinus and self-pity to maintain his image as a sex symbol. The 25-minute bedroom sequence in which the pair gradually strip away their protective shells and pretences is funnier and more touching than anything Neil Simon ever dreamed up. Axelrod makes his mistakes here and there, but never resorts to the snide sniggers with which Wilder disfigured *The Seven Year Itch*. TM

Secret Life of Walter Mitty, The

(1947, US, 105 min)
d Norman Z McLeod. *p* Samuel Goldwyn. *sc* Ken Englund, Everett Freeman. *ph* Lee Garmes. *ed* Monica Collingwood. *ad* George Jenkins, Perry Ferguson. *m* David Raksin. *cast* Danny Kaye, Virginia Mayo, Boris Karloff, Fay Bainter, Ann Rutherford, Florence Bates, Thurston Hall, Robert Altman.

● A buoyant adaptation from James Thurber (who in turn offered Sam Goldwyn $10,000 to leave the book well alone), following the vibrant fantasy life of a timid publishing worker whose escape into daydream makes up for a humdrum existence, until, that is, genuine adventure falls into his lap in the shape of distressed heiress Virginia Mayo. It degenerates into slapstick at the end, but Danny Kaye makes pathological shyness seem charismatic.

Secret Nation, The (La Nación clandestina)

(1989, Bol, 120 min)
d Jorge Sanjinés. *p* Beatriz Palacios. *sc* Jorge Sanjinés. *ph* César Perez. *ed* Jorge Sanjinés. *m* Cergio Prudencio. *cast* Reynaldo Yujra, Delfina Mamani, Orlanda Huanca, Roque Salgado.

● Eight years in the making, with a cast of hundreds of Aymara Indians – assisted, the credits tell us, 'by the powerful didactic gods of the altiplano' – Sanjinés' film explores the multiplicity of nations composing his native Bolivia. The 'secret nation' is the indigenous culture that continues alongside the urban-based and westernised political structures. It is also the 'society within society' of a nation divided into soldiers and spies on the one hand, and those labelled and hunted down as 'subversives' on the other. The conflicts and contradictions are explored through the person of Don Sebastián, a coffinmaker living on the city outskirts, who returns to his native village to die in the dance of expiation and death that opens and closes the film. Wearing a mask of both angel and devil, his propitiation is to the extraordinary high and misty mountains, wild skies and haunting music that are the true 'gods' – or inspiration – of this powerful film. AH

Secret of Convict Lake, The

(1951, US, 82 min, b/w)
d Michael Gordon. *p* Frank P Rosenberg. *sc* Oscar Saul. *ph* Leo Tover. *ed* James B Clark. *ad* Lyle Wheeler, Richard Irvine. *m* Sol Kaplan. *cast* Glenn Ford, Gene Tierney, Ethel Barrymore, Zachary Scott, Ann Dvorak, Barbara Bates, Cyril Cusack, Richard Hylton, Helen Westcott, Jeanette Nolan, Ruth Donnelly.

● Somewhat ponderous revenge-morality tale (allegedly true), set in the California mountains in 1871, about five escaped convicts who seek refuge in a hamlet where the women have been left to hold the fort while their menfolk are off prospecting. Ford, it turns out, is intent on killing Tierney's absent fiancé who in another life framed him for murder and vamoosed with some loot. Moves along quite nicely, with one of the convicts, a disturbed teenage rapist, pitchforked to death by the women, but as soon as Ford shaves off his wicked whiskers it becomes pretty obvious how things are going to turn out. JPy

Secret of My Success, The

(1987, US, 111 min)
d/p Herbert Ross. *sc* Jim Cash, Jack Epps Jr, AJ Carothers. *ph* Carlo Di Palma. *ed* Paul Hirsch. *pd* Edward Pisoni, Peter Larkin. *m* David Foster. *cast* Michael J Fox, Helen Slater, Richard Jordan, Margaret Whitton, John Pankow, Christopher Murney, Fred Gwynne.

● In this, the ultimate yuppie wish-fulfilment movie, Fox plays an enterprising post-room boy who, simply by reading the mail which passes through his hands, devises a brilliant scheme for streamlining his rich uncle's multinational corporation. On his way up the ladder of success, Fox catches the eye of attractive fellow-executive Helen Slater, but also suffers the unwelcome amorous advances of his boss' wife – whose husband is in turn involved in a clandestine office affair with the capable Ms Slater. So far, so neat. But as the action shifts from boardroom to bedroom, the film degenerates into a silly bed-hopping farce, and the corporate back-stabbing gets filed away until the final reel, when the whole thing is resolved by a wave of the wicked wife's magic wand. The same old capitalist fairytale, in other words. NF

Secret of NIMH, The

(1982, US, 82 min)
d Don Bluth. *p* Don Bluth, John Pomeroy, Gary Goldman. *sc* Don Bluth, John Pomeroy, Will Finn, Gary Goldman. *ed* Jeffrey Patch. *m* Jerry Goldsmith. *cast* voices: Derek Jacobi, Elizabeth Hartman, Arthur Malet, Dom DeLuise, Hermione Baddeley, John Carradine, Aldo Ray.

● Two years earlier, several Walt Disney animators (including Bluth) left the company to set up on their own, complaining that Disney was lowering its animation standards and heading for the dreadful cut-price techniques that are pumped out daily on children's television. This is their first animation feature, and visually they make their point well. It's a spectacular return to the shimmering, mesmerising deep-focus animation associated with Disney's classic period: a marvellous use of lighting to create atmosphere, dewdrops glisten from every tree, and the villains are as primally terrifying as cartoon villains should be. The choice of material (Robert O'Brien's novel *Mrs Frisby and the Rats of NIMH*) is less fortunate, since it lacks the wonder of early Disney, and the mouse heroine is far too insipid and twee. It's still a pretty effective family film, though. DP

Secret of Roan Inish, The

(1993, US, 103 min)
d John Sayles. *p* Sarah Green, Maggie Renzi. *sc* John Sayles. *ph* Haskell Wexler. *ed* John Sayles. *pd* Adrian Smith. *m* Mason Daring. *cast* Mick Lally, John Lynch, Jeni Courtney, Eileen Colgan, Richard Sheridan.

● This Irish fable, from a novel by Rosalie K Fry, may be pretty atypical of John Sayles' work, but it's still a lovely movie. Set in a remote Irish fishing community in the '40s, it charts the experiences of a young girl who comes to stay with her grandparents and is intrigued by the mysterious, seemingly fantastic stories of an infant relative's death. Tales within tales, a subtle sense of economic and social realities, fine landscape photography and strong performances make for an engrossing, unusual fantasy. GA

Secret of Santa Vittoria, The

(1969, US, 140 min)
d/p Stanley Kramer. *sc* William Rose, Ben Maddow. *ph* Giuseppe Rotunno. *ed* William A Lyon, Earle Herdan. *pd* Robert Clatworthy. *m* Ernest Gold. *cast* Anthony Quinn, Anna Magnani, Virna Lisi, Hardy Krüger, Sergio Franchi, Renato Rascel, Giancarlo Giannini, Valentina Cortese, Eduardo Ciannelli.

● Lost without a message to sledgehammer home, Kramer turned to bombastic comedy with this World War II yarn of an Italian village's attempts to hide a million bottles of wine from the occupying Germans. Just to keep the irritation factor of his movies constant, though, he hand-picked a full-throttle cast more than adequate to the task of previewing the effect of Sensurround. PT

Secret of the Sword, The

(1985, US, 91 min)
d Ed Friedman, Lou Kachivas, Marsh Lamore, Bill Reed, Gwen Wetzler. *p* Arthur H Nadel. *sc* Larry Ditillo, Bob Forward. *ed* George

Mahana. *m* Shuki Levy, Haim Saban, Erika Levy. *cast* voices: John Erwin, Melendy Britt, Alan Oppenheimer.
● It is a dark and stormy night in this animated feature. Prince Adam of Eternia (alias He-Man) is summoned to Castle Grayskull and magicked to Etheria to quest the meaning of the secret of the sword, a secret worthy of Dynasty. In the Whispering Woods, our Aryan hero teams up with swish Bo and villeins against the evil Hordak, leader of the Horde, whose villains include Shadow Weaver and other Mattel characters from the TV series *He-Man and Masters of the Universe*. Magna-Beam Transporters are no defence against Good Manners. There is the usual gamut of silly voices and gang of goody-goody creatures, including a gluttonous green tiger, but the cuteness is kept to a minimum. The amalgam of fairytale, sci-fi and Greek mythology is exciting, the backgrounds dynamic, the music catchy, the pace furious: kids will love it. MS

Secretos del corazón

see Secrets of the Heart

Secret People

(1951, GB, 96 min, b/w)
d Thorold Dickinson. *p* Sidney Cole. *sc* Thorold Dickinson, Wolfgang Wilhelm, Christianna Brand. *ph* Gordon Dines. *ed* Peter Tanner. *ad* William Kellner. *m* Roberto Gerhard. *cast* Valentina Cortese, Serge Reggiani, Audrey Hepburn, Charles Goldner, Irene Worth, Megs Jenkins, Reginald Tate, Athene Seyler, Michael Shepley.
● A striking thriller inspired by a newspaper item about a woman working for the IRA who suffered a change of heart, informed on her husband, and was forced to assume a new identity under police protection. Set in London in 1937, the film generalises the issue by turning the heroine into a refugee from the dictatorship that killed her father (Fascist Italy by any other name), and who is persuaded by her lover to join a terrorist plot to kill the dictator, which goes horribly wrong. Although slipping into convention here and there (stereotyping of minor characters, the facile melodrama of the final scene), the script manages to avoid offering easy answers to its questions as to whether violence corrupts and whether it can ever be justified, at least until the scene of the bomb outrage at a society reception, almost Hitchcockian in its suspense as the wrong people come and go and a waitress finally becomes the victim. Superbly staged by Dickinson (directing with fluid subtlety throughout), this sequence brings the film unequivocally out on the side of its motto borrowed from Auden: 'We must love one another or die'. But the complex abysses that lie between private feelings and political beliefs are nevertheless plumbed with remarkable thoroughness in the relationship between Cortese and Reggiani (both giving superb performances). TM

Secret Places

(1984, GB, 98 min)
d Zelda Barron. *p* Simon Relph, Ann Skinner. *sc* Zelda Barron. *ph* Peter MacDonald. *ed* Laurence Méry-Clark. *pd* Eileen Diss. *m* Michel Legrand. *cast* Marie-Therèse Relin, Tara MacGowran, Claudine Auger, Jenny Agutter, Cassie Stuart, Ann-Marie Gwatkin, Pippa Hinchley, Adam Richardson.
● Zelda Barron's first feature as director is a sympathetically observed story of how a group of English schoolgirls react when an exotic German refugee arrives in their midst early in World War II. The film's main quality lies in a luminous performance from Tara MacGowran as Patience, who befriends the refugee and experiences with her the early rites of sexual passage. Its weakness is its lack of ambition: little is made of the wartime setting, and the central relationship is shut off just at the point when it becomes fascinating. As such, stifled by its own good manners, *Secret Places* cries out to be shown on the small rather than the large screen. RR

Secret Policeman's Ball, The

(1979, GB, 94 min)
d Roger Graef. *p* Roger Graef, Thomas Schwalm. *ph* Ernest Vincze, Clive Tickner, Pasco MacFarlane. *ed* Thomas Schwalm, Andy Attenburrow. *cast* John Cleese, Peter Cook, Clive James, Eleanor Bron, Pete Townshend, Rowan Atkinson, John Williams, Billy Connolly, Tom Robinson, Michael Palin.
● Second of the ragbag stage revues in which satirists and musicians did their thing on behalf of Amnesty International (the first was *Pleasure at Her Majesty's*). With Cleese and Cook sticking to their party pieces, much of the material seemed pretty *déjà vu* even at the time. But there were highlights like Rowan Atkinson's malevolent roll-call of a class of imaginary pupils, and Billy Connolly's ruminations on the mysteries of life ('How come, every time you're sick, there's always diced carrots in it?') in a disquisition on drunken Scotsmen. TM

Secret Policeman's Other Ball, The

(1982, GB, 99 min)
d Julien Temple. *p* Martin Lewis, Peter Walker. *sc* Marty Feldman, Michael Palin, Martin Lewis. *ph* Oliver Stapleton. *ed* Geoffrey Hogg. *cast* Rowan Atkinson, Alan Bennett, John Cleese, Billy Connolly, Sting, Bob Geldof, Phil Collins, John Fortune, Michael Palin, John Wells.
● Technically smoother than its predecessors, this is otherwise the mixture as before: comics and musicians, sometimes in unfamiliar permutations, doing their party pieces on behalf of Amnesty. The musical punctuations are often outstanding: Sting soaring on a contemplative 'Message in a Bottle', Jeff Beck and Eric Clapton reunited for a loose-limbed blues. Among the bright moments: a perfectly controlled dialogue for John Fortune and Alan Bennett, a Billy Connolly ramble, and John Wells in his Denis Thatcher role. JC

Secret Policeman's Third Ball, The

(1987, GB, 96 min)
d Ken O'Neill. *p* Neville Bolt, Tony Hollingsworth. *sc* Michael Frayn, Chris Langham, Jonathan Lynn, Johnny Speight. *ph* Stephen Foster. *ed* John Hackney. *ad* Dennis De Groot. *cast* Joan Armatrading, John Cleese, Robbie Coltrane, Phil Cool, Duran Duran, Stephen Fry, Hugh Laurie, Ben Elton, Lenny Henry, Lou Reed, Ruby Wax.
● Real music is provided by Joan Armatrading, Lou Reed, Mark Knopfler with Chet Atkins, and Peter Gabriel, whose Biko lament closes the film. There is also a tribute to Los Campañeros of El Salvador by Paul Brady, but otherwise – apart from a few swipes at Reagan and Thatcher courtesy of Spitting Image – politics are out. All the comedians are on top form: Fry & Laurie cocking up 'The Hedge Sketch' to perfection; Phil Cool impersonating the XR4i'd rep on the jammed M25; Lenny Henry as an ancient bluester; and Ben Elton on liberation sexuality (i.e. DIY). O'Neill's direction makes for more than just a run-of-the-mill variety bill. MS

Secret Rapture, The

(1993, GB, 95 min)
d Howard Davies. *p* Simon Relph. *sc* David Hare. *ph* Ian Wilson. *ed* George Akers. *pd* Barbara Gosnold. *m* Richard Hartley. *cast* Juliet Stevenson, Joanne Whalley-Kilmer, Penelope Wilton, Neil Pearson, Alan Howard, Robert Stephens, Milton McRae.
● Whiffle, whiffle, whiffle. There's a dead old man in the bed and Stevenson is balled on the floor, weeping, moisture pouring from every facial orifice. Enter Wilton, surreptitiously. Giving her father's corpse a scant glance, not even noticing her grieving sister, she rummages through the jewellery on the dressing table and purloins a ring. Caught out, she's shamed, then furious. It's a response Stevenson's Isobel Coleridge seems to provoke, an illustration of writer David Hare's central question: why do good people make everyone around them behave badly? Everyone wants to dump or defuse the alcoholic widow (Whalley-Kilmer). Long-suffering Isobel takes her on, only to discover too late she sucks up everything in her path. The film is something of an '80s morality play, with characters behaving like Lust, Greed and Ambition instead of real people, but thanks to first-time director Davies' luminous moods, accelerating menace and chiaroscuro images, it packs a considerable emotional punch – while holding the mirror implacably up to the audience. SFe

Secrets

(1933, US, 85 min, b/w)
d Frank Borzage. *p* Mary Pickford. *sc* Salisbury Field, Leonard Praskins. *ph* Ray June. *ed* Hugh Bennett. *ad* Richard Day. *m* Alfred Newman. *cast* Mary Pickford, Leslie Howard, C Aubrey Smith, Blanche Frederici, Doris Lloyd, Ned Sparks.
● The last picture Mary Pickford acted in, a fairly nutty tale of pioneer homesteaders heading across America in covered wagons. Leslie Howard makes the most unlikely Westerner in movie history (but there must have been some wimps out West), and Pickford suffers all the privations of the journey and the Indian attacks just the way she always did – Victorian picture-book style. First time around, Little Mary wrote off $300,000 on the film in 1930. She started over in 1932, hiring sentimental story specialist Borzage (who had made the silent version with Norma Talmadge in 1924) to direct. It flopped, arguably because it didn't feel like a real Western. Today it's an engaging curiosity. MA

Secrets

(1971, GB, 107 min)
d Philip Saville. *p* John Hanson. *sc* Rosemary Davies. *ph* Harry Hart, Nic Knowland. *ed* Tony Woollard. *ad* Brian Eatwell. *m* Mike Gibbs. *cast* Jacqueline Bisset, Robert Powell, Per Oscarsson, Shirley Knight, Martin C Thurley.
● Drearily familiar stuff as a young married couple (Powell and Bisset), still in love but bored with each other, each enjoy a brief encounter (with Knight and Oscarsson, respectively), and then return – surprise, surprise – renewed and refreshed to their marriage. The acting is fair, but script and direction are dismayingly obvious. This was the first feature shot in Super-16mm, a process designed to reduce costs and (not that you would guess from this sample of pure predictability) 'liberate' film-makers from conventional pressures. TM

Secrets

(1992, Aust, 90 min)
d/p Michael Pattinson. *sc* Jan Sardi. *ph* David Connell. *ed* Peter Carrodus. *pd* Kevin Leonard-Jones. *m* Dave Dobbyn. *cast* Beth Champion, Malcolm Kennard, Dannii Minogue, Noah Taylor.
● On the day the Beatles arrive in Melbourne, the accompanying scrum at the hotel sees five teenagers accidentally locked in the basement, where confined surroundings force them to reveal the innermost longings behind their fandom, or indeed hatred of the Fab Four. This antipodean cross between 'I Wanna Hold Your Hand' and *The Breakfast Club* is intriguing for its opening archive footage, but screenwriter Jan Sardi (*Shine*) makes the characters and their revelations all too cut-and-dried. Taylor, though, is engaging as a self-proclaimed man of the world, complete with fake Scouse accent. TJ

Secrets & Lies

(1995, GB, 141 min)
d Mike Leigh. *p* Simon Channing-Williams. *sc* Mike Leigh. *ph* Dick Pope. *ed* Jon Gregory. *pd* Alison Chitty. *m* Andrew Dickson. *cast* Timothy Spall, Brenda Blethyn, Marianne Jean-Baptiste, Phyllis Logan, Claire Rushbrook, Elizabeth Berrington, Michele Austin, Lee Ross, Lesley Manville.
● Her adoptive parents now dead, Hortense (Jean-Baptiste), a young middle-class optometrist, decides to find her natural mother. What she doesn't anticipate is that her search will lead to Cynthia (Blethyn), a sad, boozy woman saddled with an argumentative, determinedly morose road-sweeper daughter, Roxanne (Rushbrook), and lent spasmodic moral and financial support by her brother Maurice (Spall), a successful wedding-and-portrait photographer whose prissy suburban house is the obsessive delight of his wife Monica (Logan). When Hortense first phones Cynthia, she knows nothing of the family or the tensions that divide it – and is she really her daughter anyway? After all, she's black, and Cynthia's white. Even as Leigh derives gentle comedy from the plight, aspirations and often pathetic attempts at communication of Cynthia and her tribe, an immense, unforced sympathy is extended to all involved, a generosity of spirit thoroughly in keeping with the performances. Everyone's superb, Blethyn and Spall in particular. Yes, it's long, visually a

little static, and rather narrowly concerned with the everyday experiences of one family, but that depth, focus and intensity of concentration result in a film of extraordinary emotional riches. Spellbinding. GA

Secrets of a Soul (Geheimnisse einer Seele)

(1926, Ger, 7,265 ft, b/w)
d GW Pabst. *p* Hans Neumann. *sc* Colin Ross, Hans Neumann, GW Pabst. *ph* Guido Seeber, Curt Oertel, Robert Lach. *ad* Ernö Metzner. *cast* Werner Krauss, Ruth Weyher, Jack Trevor, Pavel Pavlov, Ilka Grüning.
●Fascinating as the first 'serious' attempt to deal with Freudian psychoanalysis on the screen, Pabst's film is also notable for bringing a solid intellectual perspective to the 'expressionist' idiom of contemporary German movies. It's essentially a bourgeois melodrama, about a chemistry professor whose frustrated desire to father a child meshes with his jealousy of his wife's childhood sweetheart. The professor's fantasies are, of course, generously illustrated in the remarkable dream sequences, awash with sexual symbols. The deciphering of these dreams as he consults a psychoanalyst is necessarily too pat, but Pabst's aims still look as bold and daring as they must have done in 1926. TR

Secrets of the Heart (Secretos del corazón)

(1997, Sp, 105 min)
d Montxo Armendáriz. *p* Andres Santana, Imanol Uribe. *sc* Montxo Armendáriz. *ph* Javier Aguirresarobe. *ed* Rori Sainz de Rozas. *pd* Félix Murcia. *m* Bingen Mendizabal. *cast* Andoni Erburu, Carmelo Gómez, Charo López, Vicky Peña, Silvia Munt, Alvaroo Nagore.
●A nine-year-old gradually discovers the skeletons in the family closet when he and his elder brother, who live with their aunts in Pamplona during the 1960s, pay a visit to their widowed mother in a Pyrenean village. The portrait of lives partly defined by repression and superstition is sensitive, the re-creation of the rituals of rural Basque life fascinating, and the characterisations mostly subtly detailed. Unlike such comparable films as *The Spirit of the Beehive* and *Cria Cuervos*, however, this one never really pulls away from the curious young protagonist to tell us much about the wider political realities of the period. GA

Secrets of the Phantom Caverns

(1984, GB, 90 min)
d Don Sharp. *p* Sandy Howard, Robert D Bailey. *sc* Christy Marx, Robert Vincent O'Neil. *ph* Virgil Harper. *ed* John R Bowey. *ad* Stephen Marsh. *m* Michael Rubini, Denny Jaeger. *cast* Robert Powell, Lisa Blount, Richard Johnson, Timothy Bottoms, Anne Heywood, AC Weary.
●Lacklustre British adventure in which Powell's mission to install a radio transmitter in a Spanish mountainside is stymied by archeologists' shock discovery of a malign presence deep within the caverns. It's one of those occasions when you wait a long time for something to happen, only to sigh with disappointment when the great whatever-it-is is finally unveiled. TJ

Secret Tears (Bimil)

(2000, SKor, 105 min)
d Park Ki-Hyung. *p* Lee Yu-Jin. *sc* Park Ki-Hyung. *ph* Moon Yong-Sik. *ed* Ham Sung-Won. *pd* Shin Bo-Kyung. *m* Kim Kyu-Yang. *cast* Kim Seung-Woo, Yoon Mi-Jo, Chung Hyun-Woo, Park Eun-Sook, Chon Sun-Hwa.
●Park's follow-up to the surprise hit *Whispering Corridors* is an ethereal not-quite-romance between recently divorced insurance investigator Ku-Ho (Kim) and a young girl he knocks down while driving home drunk in the small hours: the silent, amnesiac Mi-Jo (Yoon), who turns out to have supernatural powers. While Ku-Ho's colleagues fret over his apparent 'Lolita complex' and investigate Mi-Jo's shadowy background, Ku-Ho himself forms a tight, telepathic bond with the girl and resolves to protect her, even when male corpses start showing up in her vicinity. The investigation of Mi-Jo's secrets gives the film its structure and denouement, but the film is at least as much a study of Ku-Ho's middle-aged frustrations and anomie as it is a supernatural thriller. The two aspects don't fully mesh, resulting in slow patches, but much of it is engrossing, intriguing and finally rather moving. TR

Secret Wedding (Boda secreta)

(1989, Arg/Neth/Can, 95 min)
d Alejandro Agresti. *p* Lujan Pflaum. *sc* Alejandro Agresti. *ph* Ricardo Rodriguez. *ed* Rene Wiegmans. *pd* Juan Collini. *m* Paul Michael Van Brugge. *cast* Tito Haas, Mirtha Busnelli, Sergio Poves Campos, Nathan Pinzon, Floria Bloise, Elio Marchi.
●A naked man emerges at dawn on the deserted streets of Buenos Aires. Arrested and questioned, he protests total ignorance of his identity or past; but files lead the police to assume he is one Fermin Garcia, a bus driver and political activist reported to have been executed 13 years before. He travels to a remote village to find his girlfriend; she, like the other villagers, doesn't recognise him… Agresti's third feature, part love story, part political drama, returns to a theme from his earlier *Love Is a Fat Woman*: the spectre of the *desaparecidos*, the thousands who 'vanished' in Argentina's unfunny dirty little war. Again he employs parable to investigate the hypocrisy at work in the 'new democratic' Argentina, his target the unholy trinity of church, business and state. This, a calmer, more mature and subtle film, has beautiful colour compositions which lend dignified repose to the rural landscape; the performances (Haas' Fermin is excellent) are restrained and expressive. Fired by a feeling of intense, hidden anger and disappointment, the film has all the persuasive force of a nightmare giving way to reality. WH

Sect, The (La Setta)

(1991, It, 120 min)
d Michele Soavi. *p* Mario Cecchi Gori, Vittorio Cecchi Gori. *sc* Giovanni Romoli, Michele Soavi, Dario Argento. *ph* Raffaele Mertes. *ed* Franco Fraticelli. *pd* M Antonello Geleng. *m* Pino Donaggio. *cast* Kelly Leigh Curtis, Herbert Lom, Mariangela Giordano.
●This third film by Italian horror maestro Dario Argento's most gifted acolyte (Soave previously directed *Stagefright* and *The Church)* establishes him as a horror stylist in his own right. Relying more on suspense and scares than graphic gore, it's an atmospheric chiller about a young German schoolteacher (Curtis) who becomes involved with the Manson-like devil-worshipping sect headed by Lom. The *Alice in Wonderland* references, subterranean secrets, and general dreamlike ambience echo Argento's *Inferno;* but the stylish visuals and bravura set pieces achieve a subtle terror that is all Soave's own. NF

Section Spéciale (Special Section)

(1975, Fr/It/WGer, 118 min)
d Costa-Gavras. *p* Jacques Perrin, Giorgio Silvagni. *sc* Jorge Semprun, Costa-Gavras. *ph* Andréas Winding. *ed* Françoise Bonnot. *ad* Max Douy. *m* Eric de Marsan. *cast* Louis Seigner, Michel Lonsdale, Jacques Perrin, Ivo Garrani, Bruno Crémer, François Maistre, Roland Bertin, Henri Serre, Pierre Dux.
●One of Costa-Gavras' glossy political melodramas, set in Occupied France and dealing with one of the Vichy government's shabbier episodes: the drafting of retroactive anti-terrorist laws which allowed the French judiciary to re-sentence a number of pathetically harmless prisoners in order to appease the Germans. At first the glossy production provides a rather effective counterpoint to the political intrigue. But issues here become clear-cut – over-simplified, even – and the visual elegance looks increasingly hollow. The script becomes bogged down in wordy repetitions on the corruption of power and the power of corruption. The final third – the show trials – is pure playing to the gallery, in much the same way as *Z*. By way of compensation, some of the performances – Louis Seigner, especially, as the Minister of Justice – stand against the film's tendency towards caricature. CPe

Seduction of Joe Tynan, The

(1979, US, 107 min)
d Jerry Schatzberg. *p* Martin Bregman. *sc* Alan Alda. *ph* Adam Holender. *ed* Evan Lottman. *ad* David Chapman. *m* Bill Conti. *cast* Alan Alda, Barbara Harris, Meryl Streep, Rip Torn, Melvyn Douglas, Charles Kimbrough, Carrie Nye.
●A film using familiar themes – the personal pressures of success, power as an aphrodisiac – to recount its Kennedy-style success story of the young, dynamic, but blandly selfish Senator Tynan (Alda), who jeopardises family and friends in pursuit of power, and succumbs with understandable swiftness to Meryl Streep. Though it shows political and personal distinctions blurred by ambition and by the inevitable erosion of honesty, the film still seems to want the system to work. Perhaps Schatzberg deferred too much to Alda, who stars and wrote the script; a pity, because he seems less sympathetic to Tynan than Alda is. Once again Schatzberg proves himself a strong director of actors, but keeps the film within the safe confines of semi-sophisticated Adult Entertainment. CPe

Seedling, The

see Ankur

See Here My Love

see Ecoute Voir…

See How They Fall

see Regarde les hommes tomber

Seems Like Old Times

(1980, US, 121 min)
d Jay Sandrich. *p* Ray Stark. *sc* Neil Simon. *ph* David M Walsh. *ed* Michael A Stevenson. *pd* Gene Callahan. *m* Marvin Hamlisch. *cast* Goldie Hawn, Chevy Chase, Charles Grodin, Robert Guillaume, Harold Gould, George Grizzard, Yvonne Wilder.
●After such hits as *The Goodbye Girl, Murder by Death* and *California Suite*, screenwriter/playwright Neil Simon has cornered the market in Broadway-inspired snappy comedies for, or about, the suave and sophisticated: all in all, 'the kind of movies they used to make'. In this madcap comic farce, the homage to '30s screwball is explicit in the title, unflagging pace, and plot: a liberal lawyer (Hawn), married to an uptight DA (Grodin), gets messed up by a rogue ex-husband (Chase), their ex-convict servants, and her six dogs. A little of *Adam's Rib* or *The Philadelphia Story* creeps in as you drift into wondering how Cary Grant or Katharine Hepburn would have mastered the roles of slightly cracked, snobbish professionals. But after an hour, you begin to realise the irony of Neil Simon winning awards for Outstanding Writing: it doesn't mean it's funny, just that it stands out like a sore thumb. Once you realise that, the whole exercise gets to be an expertly crafted drag. DMacp

See No Evil, Hear No Evil

(1989, US, 102 min)
d Arthur Hiller. *p* Marvin Worth. *sc* Earl Barret, Arne Sultan, Eliot Wald, Andrew Kurtzman, Gene Wilder. *ph* Victor J Kemper. *ed* Robert C Jones. *pd* Robert Gundlach. *m* Stewart Copeland. *cast* Richard Pryor, Gene Wilder, Joan Severance, Kevin Spacey, Alan North, Anthony Zerbe, Louis Giambalvo, Kirsten Childs.
●Pryor is blind, Wilder is deaf. Together they witness a murder, become principal suspects, and are threatened by the real killers: you can probably work out the rest for yourself. Given it's a comedy, you might imagine a scene in which the blind man drives a car, and you'd be right. You might imagine a fight in which the blind man does the punching, following instructions from his sighted pal; right again. Pryor is his usual loudmouth self; Wilder is in shy, sensitive mode. There's a resolutely untouching scene in which the pair discuss their relative philosophies for dealing with disability, but otherwise it's a long, painfully unfunny series of things being smashed up and fallen over. Worst of all, the male villain has the most embarrassing 'English' accent heard in many a long year, old chap, don't you know. JMo

See Spot Run

(2001, US/Aust, 97 min)
d John Whitesell. *p* Robert Simonds, Tracey Trench, Andrew Deane. *sc* George Gallo, Gregory Poirier, Danny Baron, Chris Faber. *ph* John Bartley. *ed* Cara Silverman. *pd* Mark Freeborn. *m* John Debney. *cast* David Arquette, Michael Clarke Duncan, Leslie Bibb, Joe Viterelli, Angus T Jones, Anthony Anderson, Paul Sorvino.

●Goofball Gordon (Arquette) is a US mailman who can deal with any man-hating canine. It's women and small children he can't handle. So when his uptight neighbour Stephanie is looking for a babysitter for son James, Gordon's offer is rash indeed. Things take a downturn when FBI über-dog Agent 11 escapes from a witness protection programme and winds up in Gordon's truck. James (Jones) isn't the only one who wants the cute dawg. On his trail are a couple of goons hired by mobster, Sonny Talia, to 'put the whack' on the drug-detecting pooch; Agent 11's emotionally distraught partner, Agent Murdoch (Duncan) is close behind. James adopts the dog and calls him 'Spot'. Let the chaos commence. Crude and lewd, and the dog's the smartest act in the movie – the kids will love it. JFu

See the Sea

see Regarde la Mer

See You in Hell, Darling

see American Dream, An

See You in the Morning

(1988, US, 119 min)
d Alan J Pakula. *p* Alan J Pakula, Susan Solt. *sc* Alan J Pakula. *ph* Donald McAlpine. *ed* Evan Lottman. *pd* George Jenkins. *m* Michael Small. *cast* Jeff Bridges, Alice Krige, Farrah Fawcett, Drew Barrymore, Lukas Haas, David Dukes, Frances Sternhagen, Linda Lavin, Theodore Bikel.
●This risible divorce drama opens strikingly. Successful psychiatrist Larry Livingston and wife Jo (Bridges and Fawcett) with a couple of cute infants gambolling in the countryside; cut to another happy couple (Krige and Dukes) with two kids moving into their New York dream home; cut to Bridges and Krige *in flagrante*. Turns out her concert pianist husband died, while his vapid wife left him to continue a modelling career. It's about starting over, with Krige's kids forced to come to terms with a (somewhat ingratiating) new dad. The story of their new life is reasonably told, but the Farrah Fawcett subplot is a major drawback as Bridges skips over to remonstrate with his ex-wife, visit his small children, and swap philosophies with a sickeningly spiritual mother-in-law (Sternhagen). There's a lengthy scene with Bridges (who rises engagingly above the tosh) reading a retch-inducing bedtime story about a dolphin called Caring, and spook-eyed, sinister Krige is less than ideally cast as a sweet young mother. SFe

Segunda Piel

see Second Skin

Sehnsucht der Veronika Voss, Die

see Veronika Voss

Seins de glace, Les (Someone Is Bleeding)

(1974, Fr, 97 min)
d Georges Lautner. *p* Jacques Dorfmann, Ralph Baum. *sc* Georges Lautner. *ph* Maurice Fellous. *ed* Michèle David. *ad* Jean André. *m* Philippe Sarde. *cast* Alain Delon, Mireille Darc, Claude Brasseur, Nicoletta Machiavelli.
●Brasseur as a hack TV writer who meets the beautiful Darc on a beach, and finds that she is being kept more or less a prisoner by the mysterious Delon in a villa. What he doesn't know (yet) is that she is a psychopath… and Delon is pretty mixed up too. A routine but watchable, well-acted thriller adapted from Richard Matheson's first novel (*Someone Is Bleeding*), which manages to screw up, not least by being altogether too glossy. TM

Seize the Day

(1986, US, 93 min)
d Fielder Cook. *p* Chiz Schultz. *sc* Ronald Ribman. *ph* Eric Van Haren Norman. *ed* Sidney Katz, Rachel Igel. *pd* John Robert Lloyd. *m* Elizabeth Swados. *cast* Robin Williams, Joseph Wiseman, Jerry Stiller, Glenne Headly, Tony Roberts, Richard Shull, Jo Van Fleet, Eileen Heckart.
●A Robin Williams film for people who don't really like Robin Williams, this edgy adaptation of Saul Bellow's novel sees the star for once submerging his overpowering comic persona inside the demands of the role – and the result is certainly the least mannered, arguably the most effective performance of his screen career to date. Williams is Tommy Wilhelm, a failed actor hitting 40 and still scraping a buck selling children's furniture, who vainly looks to his successful doctor father (Wiseman) and a commodities broker pal (Stiller) to help him out of the mess his life's become. As a grim, compelling trudge through familiar Bellow neuroses, it makes for surprisingly uncompromising viewing. TJ

Sélect Hotel

(1996, Fr, 85 min)
d Laurent Bouhnik. *p* Francisco Guiterrez. *sc* Laurent Bouhnik. *ph* Gilles Henry. *ed* Jacqueline Mariani, Clémence Bielov. *ad* Isabelle Millet. *m* Jérôme Coullet. *cast* Julie Gayet, Jean-Michel Fête, Serge Blumental, Marc Andreoni, Sabine Bail, Eric Aubrahn.
●Volatile, alienated but still hanging together, Tof (Fête) is loyal to his drugged out sister Nathalie (Gayet), but frustrated by her inability to dispense with the insistent services of her smarmy pimp (Andreoni). Their problems escalate as Tof turns to robbery, and, carried away with contempt and a sudden sense of power, sexually humiliates a shopkeeper and his wife. Tragedy beckons. Set in and around a seedy hotel in Place Clichy, the movie (from a first-time writer/director) clearly isn't out to paint a pretty picture. Though rough at the edges, it features fine photography and an impressive use of music. There may be misjudgments: using Blumental's wronged shopkeeper as a kind of audience identification figure, for example, or the misleading faux documentary opening; but overall the film has conviction, honesty and the smack of truth. WH

Self-Made Hero, A

see Héros très discret, Un

Sellout, The

(1975, GB/It, 102 min)
d Peter Collinson. *p* Josef Shaftel. *sc* Judson Kinberg, Murray Smith. *ph* Arthur Ibbetson. *ed* Raymond Poulton. *ad* Anthony Pratt. *m* Mike Green, Colin Frechter. *cast* Richard Widmark, Oliver Reed, Gayle Hunnicutt, Sam Wanamaker, Vladek Sheybal, Ori Levy, Assaf Dayan.
●Routine espionage thriller in which the CIA and KGB play silly buggers in Israel, much to the chagrin of the local secret service. Meanwhile a more personal triangle works itself out between former colleagues Reed and Widmark, and Hunnicutt, ex-lover of the former now living with the latter. But all this confusion adds up to very little. The script relates everything, with increasing tedium, to the games that people and nations play. Everything else about the film helps make it a journeyman's outing – from the boring references to old Bogart movies to the uncomfortable acting, tourist locations, and succession of unnecessary camera angles. CPe

Selon Mathieu

(2000, Fr, 100 min)
d Xavier Beauvois. *p* Pascal Caucheteux, Alain Sarde. *sc* Xavier Beauvois, Cédric Anger, Catherine Breillat. *ph* Caroline Champetier. *ed* Christophe Nowak. *pd* Denis Barber. *cast* Benoît Magimel, Nathalie Baye, Antoine Chappey, Fred Ulysse, Jean-Marie Winling, Françoise Bette, Mélanie Leray, Virginie Dessèvre.
●This modern day parable marries the edgy naturalistic style of Beauvois' first two films (*Nord* and *Don't Forget You're Going to Die*) to a more overt narrative framework. Set in a vividly rendered Normandy community, the story focuses on Magimel's anguish when his father is sacked from the factory. The workforce is too cowed to respond to the young man's agitation, so he plots a more intimate revenge, seducing the factory owner's wife (Baye). Inevitably, things get messy. Beauvois seems unsure how far he wants to pitch into melodrama – or tragedy: he opts for Bach on the soundtrack. And if the film doesn't really hold any surprises, it nevertheless creates a compelling aura of political and emotional estrangement. TCh

Semaine de Vacances, Une (A Week's Holiday)

(1980, Fr, 103 min)
d Bertrand Tavernier. *p* Alain Sarde, Bertrand Tavernier. *sc* Bertrand Tavernier, Marie-Françoise Hans, Colo Tavernier. *ph* Pierre-William Glenn. *ed* Armand Psenny. *ad* Jean-Baptiste Poirot. *cast* Nathalie Baye, Michel Galabru, Philippe Noiret, Flore Fitzgerald, Gérard Lanvin, Jean Dasté, Philippe Léotard.
●Twelve years on from 1968, and the children of Marx and Coca-Cola are hitting their first mid-life crises' – in this case forcing a Lyonnaise teacher (Baye) to take *une semaine de vacances* and reassess her life. Tavernier avoids the reactionary ploys of 'unmarried women' stories, and his combination of solidly-crafted European finesse and fluid transatlantic shooting style effectively staves off intimations of the film's middlebrow nature. At the same time, the tentative celebrations of life's minor felicities – food, friendship, a community of good, nameless people – provide genuine warmth, and the final mood of cautious optimism is justified surprisingly well. CPea

Semi-Tough

(1977, US, 107 min)
d Michael Ritchie. *p* David Merrick. *sc* Walter Bernstein. *ph* Charles Rosher Jr. *ed* Richard A Harris. *pd* Walter Scott Herndon. *m* Jerry Fielding. *cast* Burt Reynolds, Kris Kristofferson, Jill Clayburgh, Robert Preston, Bert Convy, Roger E Mosley, Lotte Lenya, Richard Masur, Carl Weathers, Brian Dennehy.
●Though not as sharp or as unusual as Ritchie's earlier *Smile*, this is still a delightful, gentle satire on the American ideal of winning, which also takes broad but often hilarious swipes at fashionable health fads. Concerning the cracks that appear in the strange *ménage à trois* between pro-footballers Reynolds and Kristofferson, and multi-divorcee Clayburgh, when the guru of a weird EST-style therapy cult finds a disciple in Kristofferson, the film succeeds because the comedy derives less from smart one-liners than from character. Although some of Ritchie's targets are a little obvious, what makes the film so appealing is the immense generosity extended toward the protagonists. Beautifully performed, subtly scripted, it accentuates the sadness of Ritchie's later descent into more conventional material. GA

Senator Was Indiscreet, The

(1947, US, 74 min, b/w)
d George S Kaufman. *p* Nunnally Johnson. *sc* Charles MacArthur. *ph* William Mellor. *ed* Sherman A Rose. *ad* Bernard Herzbrun, Boris Leven. *m* Daniele Amfitheatrof. *cast* William Powell, Ella Raines, Peter Lind Hayes, Arleen Whelan, Hans Conried, Allen Jenkins, Myrna Loy.
●Playwright George S Kaufman had a somewhat arm's length relationship with Hollywood (although he was famously well paid for his work on *A Night at the Opera*) and this jaunty political satire, scripted by Charles MacArthur, proved to be his only film as director. The lost diary of presidential candidate Powell, and the incriminating detail contained within it, provide the impetus for some mild, somewhat unfocused fun. Powell's *Thin Man* partner Myrna Loy pops up unbilled. TJ

Sender, The

(1982, GB, 91 min)
d Roger Christian. *p* Edward S Feldman. *sc* Thomas Baum. *ph* Roger Pratt. *ed* Alan Strachan. *pd* Malcolm Middleton. *m* Trevor Jones. *cast* Kathryn Harrold, Zeljko Ivanek, Shirley Knight, Paul Freeman, Sean Hewitt, Marsha Hunt.
●Having attempted suicide, 'John Doe 83' is taken to the state mental hospital. Involuntarily, he transmits his nightmares into the world where others witness them. In trying to build a relationship with the young amnesiac (Ivanek) and save him from electroshock therapy, Dr Farmer (Harrold) makes herself vulnerable to his night terrors. Not half as vulnerable as us, though: mirrors that bleed, a room full of rats, a head that comes off – and these are child's play compared to Shirley Knight's terrifying performance as John Doe's mother. Ivanek went on to put together a string of appearances throughout the next two decades, including roles in *Hannibal* and

TV's *24*, while director Christian would eventually fail the good taste and judgment test by adapting Scientology boss L Ron Hubbard's *Battlefield Earth*. NRo

Send Me No Flowers

(1964, US, 100 min)
d Norman Jewison. *p* Harry Keller. *sc* Julius Epstein. *ph* Daniel L Fapp. *ed* J Terry Williams. *ad* Alexander Golitzen, Robert Clatworthy. *m* Frank DeVol. *cast* Rock Hudson, Doris Day, Tony Randall, Paul Lynde, Edward Andrews, Clint Walker.
●Probably the best of the Doris Day/Rock Hudson vehicles, extracting a surprising amount of black (though sugar-coated) comedy out of the situation in which hypochondriac Rock, mistakenly believing he is dying, thoughtfully tries to arrange a remarriage for his widow-to-be with an old flame (Walker); whereupon she, sniffing out self-interest, suspects an attempt to cover up an affair of his own. Nicely set in a pastel-coloured suburban dreamworld, but the ineradicable blandness gets you down in the end. TM

S'en fout la mort (No Fear, No Die)

(1990, Fr, 91 min)
d Claire Denis. *p* Francis Boespflug, Philippe Carcassonne. *sc* Claire Denis, Jean-Pol Fargeau. *ph* Pascal Marti. *ed* Dominique Auvray. *m* Abdullah Ibrahim. *cast* Isaach de Bankolé, Alex Descas, Jean-Claude Brialy, Solveig Dommartin.
●From the director of the acclaimed *Chocolat*, this is something else entirely: rough-edged almost to the point of being documentary, it's a look at the world of cockfighting in the Paris suburbs, with de Bankolé as an African lovingly guiding his feathered charges through a casual daily bloodletting. An extremely uncomfortable film to watch – although it was apparently filmed without violence to the birds – it has a seedy, claustrophobic power that says as much about human as about animal exploitation. Wenders protégée Dommartin lends a largely decorative presence, but New Wave veteran Brialy stands out as a slimeball entrepreneur. Abdullah Ibrahim again provides broody, pacy music. JRo

Seniors, The (aka The Senior)

(1978, US, 87 min)
d Rod Amateau. *p* Stanley Shapiro, Carter de Haven. *sc* Stanley Shapiro. *ph* Robert Jessup. *ed* Guy Scarpitta. *m* Pat Williams. *cast* Jeffrey Byron, Gary Imhof, Dennis Quaid, Lou Richards, Priscilla Barnes.
●US college seniors open a bogus sex clinic for reasons that soon become obvious, yet unwittingly find themselves at the centre of a million-dollar business. A lot of foolish plotting is wrapped around not very much in the way of excitement – with a young, very geeky Dennis Quaid. A satire of sorts. TJ

Sensations

(1993, Ecuador, 110 min)
d/sc/ed Juan Esteban, Viviana Cordero. *m* Juan Esteban. *cast* Juan Esteban, Viviana Cordero, Ricardo Contag, Luis Miguel Campos.
●A newly formed band, sequestered in the high Andes, get together musically and emotionally. Zac, the leader, is the arrogant one, recently returned from a successful few years in New York, who tries to discipline the disparate musicians: a gay schizo hedonist, Zac's footloose brother, a guy in touch with his Ecuadorian roots, a sexy singer known as 'the fake'. Lines like, 'Let's make Inca blues!' and 'Art is flying, not making money!' sum up the philosophical debate. It's beautifully shot and contains extensive sequences of the group jamming, rehearsing and playing . The music is mostly composed by the film's writing/directing/producing team of Esteban and Cordero. WH

Sensations of 1945 (aka Sensations)

(1944, US, 85 min, b/w)
d/p Andrew Stone. *sc* Dorothy Bennett. *ph* Peverell Marley, John Mescall. *ed* James E Smith. *ad* Charles Odds. *songs* Al Sherman, Harry Tobias. *cast* Eleanor Powell, Dennis O'Keefe, C Aubrey Smith, Eugene Pallette, WC Fields, Sophie Tucker, Cab Calloway, Woody Herman.
●*Sensations of 1945*... no, not Hiroshima, the Labour landslide or Hitler's suicide. These sensations include a dancing horse, some roller-skating bears and Cab Calloway singing 'Hepster's Dictionary'. Powell and O'Keefe play feuding press agents, a framework which permits a succession of variety acts and song-and-dance routines. Amid acres of tedium there are some curiosities, including WC Fields' final appearance, the ravages of the bottle so evident that in half his footage his back is to the camera (and in the other half you wish it were). Powell tap dances her way around a pinball machine set: she is sensational, but the set's chronic. BBa

Sense and Sensibility

(1995, US, 136 min)
d Ang Lee. *p* Lindsay Doran. *sc* Emma Thompson. *ph* Michael Coulter. *ed* Tim Squyres. *pd* Luciana Arrighi. *m* Patrick Doyle. *cast* Emma Thompson, Hugh Grant, Kate Winslet, Alan Rickman, Greg Wise, Elizabeth Spriggs, Robert Hardy, Hugh Laurie, Harriet Walter, Imelda Staunton, Imogen Stubbs, Jemma Jones.
●Rendered homeless and relatively poor by the patrilineal laws that dictated their father's will, Elinor and Marianne Dashwood (Thompson and Winslet) are not exactly the most marriageable young women in a world where desirability is usually conferred by property and birth. Shy, kindly Edward Ferrars (Grant) – favoured by the pragmatic Elinor – is likely to be disinherited should he marry 'low', while solid Col Brandon (Rickman) is forgotten by the headstrong Marianne as soon as popular, dashing John Willoughby (Wise) appears on the scene. First impressions, however, aren't always reliable. While this is hardly adventurous or original cinema, it's most enjoyable. Thompson's screenplay stays true both to Austen's themes (the gulf between romanticism and materialism, the difference between hearsay, opinion and empirical knowledge) and to her delightfully ironic wit. Grant is just Grant (albeit with old togs and deeper stammer), and Rickman sometimes looks a little creepy, but Thompson and Winslet give fine performances ably supported by the rest of the ensemble. GA

Sense of Loss, A

(1972, US/Switz, 132 min)
d/p Marcel Ophüls. *ph* Simon Edelstein. *ed* Marion Kraft. *with* Ian Paisley, Bernadette Devlin, Michael Farrell, Rita O'Hare, Gerry O'Hare, Sam Dowling.
●Though the BBC's rejection of Ophüls' documentary in 1972 added fuel to the arguments of those who maintained that a conspiracy of silence operated regarding reportage of events in Northern Ireland, the fact is that his film is not particularly enlightening. Ophüls' partisanship is undisguised from very early on, but it's still difficult to forgive the way he loads the evidence (Bernadette Devlin interviewed on a deserted beach, Paisley fulminating from his pulpit); and the long funeral sequence at the end is shot and edited as all-stops-out melodrama. When left to speak for themselves, the spokesmen for the British presence and some of the more bigoted Protestants are sufficiently eloquent in condemning themselves without interference from Ophüls' self-satisfied liberal smugness. Still, in the absence of anything better... RM

Senso (The Wanton Countess)

(1954, It, 115 min)
d Luchino Visconti. *p* Domenico Forges Davanzati. *sc* Luchino Visconti, Suso Cecchi D'Amico, Carlo Alianello, Giorgio Bassani, Paul Bowles, Tennessee Williams. *ph* GR Aldo, Robert Krasker. *ed* Mario Serandrei. *ad* Ottavio Scotti. *m* Anton Bruckner. *cast* Alida Valli, Farley Granger, Massimo Girotti, Heinz Moog, Rina Morelli, Marcella Mariani, Christian Marquand.
●Like other Visconti melodramas, sumptuous in its Technicolor expressionism, *Senso* sees heterosexual love through homosexual eyes: Farley Granger (in the Helmut Berger role) plays the young Austrian officer in the force occupying Venice in the 1860s, and Alida Valli (in the Burt Lancaster role) the older, married woman who falls insanely in love with him, betraying her husband, her principles, and finally Italy itself in the headlong folly of her passion. The man sadistically exploits his own beauty and willingly prostitutes himself; the woman submits to one humiliation after another, her masochism finally indistinguishable from madness. Fassbinder's version of this story was called *The Bitter Tears of Petra von Kant*. Visconti, using English dialogue by Tennessee Williams and Paul Bowles, generates emotions so violent that even his operatic vision can barely contain them. TR

Sensual Paradise

see Together

Sentimental Journey

(1946, US, 94 min, b/w)
d Walter Lang. *p* Walter Morosco. *sc* Samuel Hoffenstein, Elizabeth Reinhardt. *ph* Norbert Brodine. *ed* J Watson Webb. *ad* Lyle Wheeler, Albert Hogsett. *m* Cyril Mockridge. *cast* Maureen O'Hara, John Payne, William Bendix, Cedric Hardwicke, Mischa Auer, Connie Marshall.
●A domestic drama in which a Broadway actress (O'Hara) succumbs to a heart complaint of which her doting producer husband (Payne) is miraculously unaware, yet in the meantime she's adopted orphan Connie Marshall and trained the child to care for the old boy after she's gone. The film is more or less the epitome of '40s slush. Depending on temperament, it's either vastly enjoyable as camp spectacle, or steadfastly resistible as cheesiest hokum. TJ

Sentinel, The

see Sentinelle, La

Sentinel, The

(1976, US, 92 min)
d Michael Winner. *p/sc* Michael Winner, Jeffrey Konvitz. *ph* Dick Kratina. *ed* Bernard Gribble, Terry Rawlings. *pd* Philip Rosenberg. *m* Gil Mellé. *cast* Chris Sarandon, Cristina Raines, Martin Balsam, John Carradine, José Ferrer, Ava Gardner, Arthur Kennedy, Burgess Meredith, Sylvia Miles, Deborah Raffin, Eli Wallach, Christopher Walken, Beverly D'Angelo, Tom Berenger, Jeff Goldblum.
●A film which plagiarises so brazenly – and so badly – that it seems like little more than a pile of out-takes from recent supernatural successes. Take a Catholic heroine and her treacherous lover in a spooky apartment block (*Rosemary's Baby*). Add the nutty priest and the ominous prophecy from *The Omen*, not to mention a touch of demonic masturbation from *The Exorcist*. And what do you have? In Winner's hands, just a mass of frequently incomprehensible footage, acted so badly that even the most blatant shocks go for little. Out of sheer desperation, given the thinnest basis imaginable for a horror movie (fashion model finds her apartment is over the gateway to hell), some genuinely deformed people are brought in for the climax. The only frightening thing about *The Sentinel* is its director's mind. DP

Sentinelle, La (The Sentinel)

(1992, Fr, 145 min)
d Arnaud Desplechin. *p* Pascal Caucheteux. *sc* Arnaud Desplechin. *ph* Caroline Champetier. *ed* François Gédigier. *cast* Emmanuel Salinger, Thibault de Montalembert, Jean-Louis Richard, Valerie Dreville, Marianne Denicourt, Jean-Luc Boutte, Fabrice Desplechin.
●Uneven but fascinating movie in which a medical student from a diplomatic family suddenly finds himself the unexpected owner of a severed head, following which he's plunged into the dark confusing world of espionage. Too long for its own good, but packed with intriguing, beautifully observed details. GA

Senyora, La

(1987, Sp, 103 min)
d Jordi Cadena. *p* Jonni Bassiner. *sc* Jordi Cadena, Silvia Tortosa. *ph* José Garcia Galisteo. *ed* Amat Carreras. *pd* José Maria Espada. *m* José Pagan. *cast* Silvia Tortosa, Hermann Bonnin, Luis Merlo, Fernando Guillén-Cuervo.
●Lorca and the Buñuel of *El* contribute to the deep Catalan atmosphere of this study of stifled sexuality and its misshapen fruit. Teresa (Tortosa) is married off to old Nicolau (Bonnin),

who wears gloves in bed, fears dirt on the Howard Hughes model, and in place of sexual congress offers her a golden thimble of semen. She masturbates with fans, he watches. He wants an heir, she rinses his thimbles down the sink, the marriage drags on until he dies, when she contemptuously makes free with his corpse. Teresa inherits everything, but the nephew she wishes to settle upon – in both senses – dies of shock diving into her pool to wash prior to consummating their passion. Hard cheese on Teresa, and she has to make do with her gardener (Merlo). Eventually the story comes full circle, with her terms as inhuman as Nicolau's. Pathological, indeed, but not remotely leering, the history certainly puts a damper on the hope centres. BC

Separate Lives

(1994, US, 98 min)
d David Madden. *p* Mark Amin, Diane Nabatoff, Guy Reidel. *sc* Steven Pressfield. *ph* Kees Van Oostrum. *ed* Janice Hampton. *ad* Bernt Capra. *m* William Olvis. *cast* Linda Hamilton, James Belushi, Vera Miles.

●As a result of childhood trauma, an uptight psychotherapist splits personality at night to become a sexually rapacious club-goer. But is she also responsible for a spate of murders? You can see why Hamilton signed on for this one: a dual role is always a good showcase. But though she tries hard, as does Belushi as the ex-cop who falls for her (but which one of her?), neither can rise above the collection of clichés that passes for a script. DW

Separate Rooms

see Notre Histoire

Séparation, La

(1994, Fr, 88 min)
d Christian Vincent. *p* Claude Berri. *sc* Dan Franck, Christian Vincent. *ph* Denis Lenoir. *ed* Françoise Ceppi. *ad* Christian Vallerin. *cast* Daniel Auteuil, Isabelle Huppert, Jérôme Deschamps, Karin Viard, Laurence Lerel, Louis Vincent.

●'We have to change our way of living.' So says Ingrid Bergman in the Rossellini film Pierre (Auteuil) and Anne (Huppert) go to see shortly before she feels moved to tell him she's fallen in love with another man. And Ingrid's right: Pierre and Anne may have been comfortable together for years – they're well-off, they have a smart apartment, a two-year-old son, supportive friends – but while Anne's admission seems at first barely to impinge on Pierre's consciousness, pretty soon he's suffering wild swings of emotion. Could they stay together? Will she leave? Should he throw her out? Whatever, the entire edifice of the relationship they've built up over the years looks set to crumble. Plotwise, that's about it in this study of a disintegrating partnership, but no matter: the film (a subtle, intelligent adaptation of Dan Franck's perceptive but rather indulgent novel) is about the minute shifts in power that occur as Anne tries to make up her mind about her future and Pierre attempts to keep up with or even forestall her changing behaviour. Happily, Vincent is beautifully served by the performers, with Huppert and Auteuil equally superb as the couple striving, against all odds, to emerge intact from a nightmare scenario. GA

September

(1987, US, 83 min)
d Woody Allen. *p* Robert Greenhut. *sc* Woody Allen. *ph* Carlo Di Palma. *ed* Susan E Morse. *pd* Santo Loquasto. *cast* Denholm Elliott, Dianne Wiest, Mia Farrow, Elaine Stritch, Sam Waterston, Jack Warden.

●Like *Interiors*, a Serious Drama: a Chekhovian chamber piece investigating the twisted bonds that tether a handful of lonely, arty, upper-crust Americans gathered, as fall approaches, at a Vermont country retreat. Unlike *Interiors*, however, this is no misguided tribute to Bergman: Allen's style is now so self-assured that the film simply looks like *Hannah and Her Sisters* without the laughs. Admittedly it's all rather familiar and schematic: disillusioned writer (Waterston) torn in his affections between Farrow and her best friend Wiest; Farrow's former film star mother (Stritch) turning up with latest lover (Warden), threatening to deprive Farrow of her home and to embarrass all with a volume of lurid memoirs; neighbour (Elliott) whose forlorn eyes betray unrequited love for Farrow. There are moments in Allen's script that smack of self-conscious contrivance, and Farrow's miserable victim is so wimpy as to be genuinely irritating. But the other performances – most notably those of Wiest and Warden – are superb, while Allen's direction shows admirable economy both in establishing and sustaining mood, and in clearly delineating the claustrophobic parameters of his characters' emotional lives. GA

September Songs: The Music of Kurt Weill

(1994, Can, 89 min)
d Larry Weinstein. *p* Niv Fichman, Larry Weinstein. *sc* Larry Weinstein, David Morton. *ph* Horst Zeilder. *ed* David New. *pd* Michael Levine. *m* Kurt Weill. *with* Lou Reed, PJ Harvey, Elvis Costello, William S Burroughs, Betty Carter, Teresa Stratas.

●A career trajectory that includes collaboration with Bertolt Brecht, and takes in both the Hollywood screen and the Broadway stage makes Kurt Weill among the most fascinating 20th century composers, but this is a sketchy tribute. Serving chiefly as a showcase for sundry stars to deliver their own versions of Weill's tunes, it relegates the strictly biographical information to odd moments between the numbers. More frustrating is the lack of contextualising information around the performances, and the often wayward choice of artists (Lou Reed murders the normally swoonsome 'September Song'). Chief highlights are Elvis Costello and the Brodsky String Quartet with an impassioned 'Lost in the Stars' and PJ Harvey's superbly controlled 'Ballad of a Soldier's Wife'. A very mixed bag. TJ

SER

see Freedom Is Paradise

Sérail

(1976, Fr, 87 min)
d Eduardo de Gregorio. *p* Hubert Niogret, Hugo Santiago, Jacques Zajdermann. *sc* Eduardo de Gregorio, Michael Graham. *ph* Ricardo Aronovich. *ed* Alberto Yaccelini. *ad* Eric Simon. *m* Michel Portal. *cast* Leslie Caron, Bulle Ogier, Marie-France Pisier, Corin Redgrave, Marilyn Jones, Pierre Baudry.

●As a scriptwriter (mainly for Rivette and Bertolucci), de Gregorio repeatedly subverted narrative expectations, and here – his first feature as writer/director – he indulges in the perilous but pleasing game of developing the characters played by Ogier and Pisier in the film-within-the-film of *Céline and Julie*. An English novelist (Redgrave) is lured, with disconcerting and disorienting results, into purchasing a crumbling mansion by what he imagines are the deliberately 'literary' ploys of its housekeeper (Caron) and two mysterious, lurking women. Richly photographed, what starts as a slightly self-conscious exercise develops, after many deceptive twists, into an intriguing and gratifying sensual entertainment. JPy

Será Posible el Sur

(1985, WGer, 75 min)
d Stefan Paul. *p* Chris Sievernich. *sc* Stefan Paul. *ph* Hans Scalk, Hans Warth, Jorge Casal. *ed* Hildegard Schröder. *with* Mercedes Sosa.

●Paul's documentary about Argentinian singer Mercedes Sosa's return to her native country, after a three-year exile caused by the Junta's censorship of her politically oriented songs, is something of a fiasco. Sloppily put together, it substitutes banal propaganda and sycophantic hagiography for an analysis either of the political problems facing the Argentinian people, or of Sosa's own elevated position as a celebrated national heroine. GA

Serbian Girl, The (Das serbische Mädchen)

(1990, Ger, 96 min)
d/sc Peter Sehr. *ph* Dietrich Lohmann. *ed* Dagmar Hirtz. *ad* Uta Reichardt. *m* Goran Bregovic. *cast* Mirjana Jokovic, Ben Becker, Iva Bekjarew.

●A Yugoslav girl (Jokovic) sneaks across the border and sets off to meet her German boyfriend (Becker) in Hamburg. Her journey starts out promisingly enough, but evading the authorities proves easier than forging a relationship with her lover. Sehr's road movie (his debut feature) is consistently absorbing: it throws up all manner of hazards – from near-rape to robbery – yet remains ultimately optimistic, and Jokovic's performance is fresh and defiant. CM

Serena

(1962, GB, 62 min, b/w)
d Peter Maxwell. *p* John I Phillips. *sc* Reginald Hearne, Edward Abraham. *ph* Stephen Dade. *ed* Allan Morrison. *ad* George Provis. *m* John Gregory. *cast* Patrick Holt, Emrys Jones, Honor Blackman, Bruce Beeby, John Horsley, Vi Stevens, Wally Patch.

●Stagy detective picture in which an artist (Jones) devises a switched-identity scam to get hold of an inheritance, by having his girlfriend (Blackman) call at a rose-covered cottage and blast his wife in the face with a shotgun (off screen, naturally). The sort of British B-picture in which artists wear cravats and oil paintings of nude women appear to have no nipples. Not a very taxing mystery, though Scotland Yard (Holt) is slow on the uptake. JPy

Serendipity

(2001, US, 91 min)
d Peter Chelsom. *p* Peter Abrams, Robert L Levy, Simon Fields. *sc* Marc Klein. *ph* John de Borman. *ed* Christopher Greenbury. *pd* Caroline Hanania. *m* Alan Silvestri. *cast* John Cusack, Kate Beckinsale, Molly Shannon, Jeremy Piven, John Corbett, Bridget Moynahan, Eugene Levy, Lucy Gordon, Kate Blumberg.

●English rose Sara (Beckinsale) and seasoned New Yorker Jonathan (Cusack) meet by accident over a cashmere glove in Bloomingdale's. She believes in fate, yet the signs are against them. Years later, when each is unhappily betrothed to another, they both grab their best mates for an identical last fling: a quest to find the mysterious stranger who stole their heart in NY's famous store. Cusack usually makes good film choices, but not this time. Despite borrowing two of its supporting cast from TV's *Sex and the City*, the film has no bite and too few jokes; its unabashed romanticism is just plain flimsy when a vapid Beckinsale is supposedly The One. CF

Sergeant Madden

(1939, US, 82 min, b/w)
d Josef von Sternberg. *p* J Walter Ruben. *sc* Wells Root. *ph* John Seitz. *ed* Conrad A Nervig. *ad* Cedric Gibbons, Randall Duell. *m* William Axt. *cast* Wallace Beery, Tom Brown, Alan Curtis, Laraine Day, Fay Holden, Marc Lawrence, David Gorcey, Horace McMahon.

●A Sternberg rarity these days, but little cause for excitement since it's one of MGM's insufferably smug family entertainments. Beery (his usual mugging toned down somewhat) plays a roguish New York cop, much given to adopting strays on his beat, but let down when his natural son (Curtis) follows him into the force, gives way to his overweening ambition, and drifts into crime. Stoically, Beery sets out to take him in; but never mind, his ploddingly honest adopted son (Brown) is there to take over dad's mantle. Sternberg, abetted by John Seitz's fine camerawork, lends the film vestiges of his UFA look, but can do nothing about the gross mawkishness. TM

Sergeant Rutledge

(1960, US, 118 min)
d John Ford. *p* Willis Goldbeck, Patrick Ford. *sc* James Warner Bellah, Willis Goldbeck. *ph* Bert Glennon. *ed* Jack Murray. *ad* Eddie Imazu. *m* Howard Jackson. *cast* Jeffrey Hunter, Woody Strode, Constance Towers, Billie Burke, Carleton Young, Juano Hernandez, Willis Bouchey, Mae Marsh.

●Though often pigeonholed as one of Ford's late trio of guiltily amends-making movies (to blacks here; to Indians in *Cheyenne Autumn*; to women in *Seven Women*), *Sergeant Rutledge* is both more complex and infinitely more confused than that simplistic formula would suggest. Possessing in broad outline an integrationist perspective (at a time when the Civil Rights movement was gaining strength), it's riddled with liberal compromises and evasions with its portrait of Strode's dignified black cavalry sergeant on trial for alleged miscegenatory rape. Ford can show us an innocent victim of

American racism, and stress in courtroom flashbacks his heroic credentials in white man's uniform, but he can never make the leap to offering us a black who actually rejects the role of honorary white. He can make the cinepolitical connection back to *The Birth of a Nation* (by the bit-casting of Mae Marsh, the rape victim in Griffith's film) and consider his film compensatory, but he can't confront the cultural fear of miscegenation that mechanises both movies, only its distorted expression. PT.

Sergeant York

(1941, US, 134 min, b/w)
d Howard Hawks. *p* Jesse L Lasky, Hal B Wallis. *sc* Abem Finkel, Harry Chandlee, Howard Koch, John Huston. *ph* Sol Polito, Arthur Edeson. *ed* William Holmes. *ad* John Hughes. *m* Max Steiner. *cast* Gary Cooper, Walter Brennan, Joan Leslie, George Tobias, Stanley Ridges, Margaret Wycherley, Ward Bond, Noah Beery Jr.

●Based on the true story of a deeply religious pacifist who became a much-decorated WWI hero, this is simultaneously Hawks' most 'respectable' and most artistically conventional major film. Oscar-winning Cooper is in engagingly relaxed form as the country boy who goes to war, in a fit of pique, after feeling cheated out of some farmland he wanted to buy, and Hawks manages to chart his transformation from pacifist to soldier with disarming ease. But, with serious issues and moral pieties at its heart, it lacks the subversive wit and depth of feeling for individuals that typifies his best work; too often it is picturesque (although the battle scenes, with the exception of the famous 'turkey-shoot' in which Germans are bumped off like birds, are shot with a strong feel for the pain and squalor of war) and poorly paced. GA

Serial Lover

(1998, Fr, 83 min)
d James Huth. *p* Philippe Rousselet. *sc* James Huth, Romain Berthomieu, Hugo Jacomet. *ph* Jean-Claude Thibaut. *ed* Scott Stevenson. *pd* Pierre-Emmanuel Chatilliez. *m* Bruno Coulais. *cast* Michèle Laroque, Albert Dupontel, Elise Tielrooy, Michel Vuillermoz, Zinedine Soualem, Antoine Basler, Gilles Privat.

●Claire invites her three suitors, and her supposedly gay 'Teddy Bear', to dinner on her 35th birthday, with the intention of choosing her lucky fiancé – despite the fact she hasn't had sex for three months. Unfortunately, beau number one accidentally ends up with a knife in his chest and his hand in the food mixer. She panics and stashes the corpse in the freezer, only for beau number two to meet with equally grisly misfortune (though not before obliviously munching on number one's mashed fingers). And so on. Huth shoots this in zany wide-angles and a surfeit of pop trash style, with hyper comic cuts and big, loud performances. Against the odds, he also keeps it going for 83 more or less hilarious minutes. It's a bit like *Basic Instinct*. Only, you know, more basic. TCh

Serial Mom

(1994, US, 93 min)
d John Waters. *p* John Fiedler, Mark Tarlov. *sc* John Waters. *ph* Robert Stevens. *ed* Janice Hampton, Erica Huggins. *pd* Vincent Peranio. *m* Basil Poledouris. *cast* Kathleen Turner, Sam Waterston, Ricki Lake, Matthew Lillard, Scott Wesley Morgan, Justin Whalin.

●Housewife Beverly Sutphin (Turner) seems to enjoy a life of domestic bliss. She has a loving husband (Waterston), two fine teenage kids, and a beautiful Baltimore home. Hell, she even gives the birds in her backyard Christian names. Admittedly, she's a little highly strung. A comedy, persuasively illustrating how suburban conformity hides its own latent psychopathic tendencies. When Beverly goes on the rampage with a knife, chasing a scruffy teenager through the streets in her Sunday best, it's in defence of all she holds most dear: family values, impeccable manners, road safety. Although this is John Waters' most approachable effort yet (a sign, perhaps, of how inextricably linked camp and mainstream cultures have become), the film loses focus in a poorly scripted courtroom anti-climax. A killer comedy all the same, with an uproariously funny, marvellously malicious performance from Turner. TCh

Series 7: The Contenders

(2000, US, 87 min)
d Daniel Minahan. *p* Jason Kliot, Joana Vicente, Christine Vachon, Katie Roumel, ('Series 7' Promo) Jason Bowers. *sc* Daniel Minahan. *ph* Randy Drummond. *ed* Malcolm Jamieson. *pd* Gideon Ponte. *m* Girls Against Boys. *cast* Brooke Smith, Glenn Fitzgerald, Marylouise Burke, Richard Venture, Michael Kaycheck, Merritt Wever, Angelina Phillips

●On a US reality TV show, 'The Contenders', six press-ganged individuals must kill or be killed. Surly mother-to-be Dawn (Smith) is reigning champion, but can she survive the latest round? One new contestant is her gentle high school sweetheart Jeff (Fitzgerald), now dying of testicular cancer. Writer/director Minahan has all the elements in place for tragedy, but he's sidetracked by farce. The latest in a long line of fake media creations (*Drop Dead Gorgeous*, *Best In Show*), the film endlessly lampoons the tricks of the TV trade and the idiot hopefuls so willing to join in the contrived fun. As satire, too, the movie cops out: the only really shocking killing is committed by the one individual we know barely anything about. By comparison, Dawn's crimes appear victimless, which means we don't have to question where our sympathies lie. How convenient. We get the point that 'The Contenders' audience is as dumb as it is savage, but we never have to face that truth about ourselves. Nevertheless, the film is affecting, especially towards the end. Smith (so good as the kidnapped victim in *The Silence of the Lambs*) is astonishingly vital; Fitzgerald is a brittle dream. The snippets we see of a goth pop-video Dawn and Jeff made at school are a tad glossy, but also haunting. More than anything, the grim rapture the teenagers enjoy while posing to Joy Division's 'Love Will Tear Us Apart' makes the message hit home: we're doomed. CO'Su

Serpent, The (Le Serpent)

(1973, Fr/It/WGer, 121 min)
d/p Henri Verneuil. *sc* Henri Verneuil, Gilles Perrault. *ph* Claude Renoir. *ed* Pierre Gillette. *ad* Jacques Saulnier. *m* Ennio Morricone. *cast* Yul Brynner, Henry Fonda, Dirk Bogarde, Philippe Noiret, Michel Bouquet, Martin Held, Farley Granger, Virna Lisi, Marie Dubois, Robert Alda.

●A very traditional spy fable based on 'true events' in which a top-ranking KGB colonel (Brynner) defects and delivers a list of traitors who are in positions of great power in each major Western country. There is the usual glib characterisation, and the usual wall of disillusionment descending at the end. In fact, the only thing that sets this film apart is the totally consistent layer of impenetrable gloss with which Verneuil covers it, and his general directorial tricksiness, which runs the gamut from the irrelevant to the pretentious and back. He has a capable starry cast on hand; why he never uses it is a mystery. VG

Serpent and the Rainbow, The

(1987, US, 97 min)
d Wes Craven. *p* David Ladd, Doug Claybourne. *sc* Richard Maxwell, AR Simoun. *ph* John Lindley. *ed* Glenn Farr. *pd* David Nichols. *m* Brad Fiedel. *cast* Bill Pullman, Cathy Tyson, Zakes Mokae, Paul Winfield.

●Craven's tale of voodoo and revolution on the island of Haiti is like a bad Graham Greene adaptation seen under the influence of hallucinogenic substances. A Harvard anthropologist (Pullman), searching for the toxic drug used by voodoo priests to zombify their victims, spends a lot of time hanging around graveyards, checking out charlatan goat-revivers, and experiencing weird dreams. He is much taken with psychiatrist Cathy Tyson, less keen on the attentions of Baby Doc Duvalier's Ton Ton Macoute, especially when head honcho Winfield acquaints him with a blowtorch and threatens to drive a nail through his dick. Making effective use of snakes, tarantulas, scorpions and zombie brides, Craven piles on the nightmare sequences and nerve-jangling sounds. Unfortunately, the political parallel between the ideological repression of Baby Doc's regime and the stultifying effects of the zombifying fluid is only sketchily developed, leaving us with a series of striking but isolated set pieces. NF

Serpent's Egg, The (Das Schlangenei)

(1977, WGer/US, 119 min)
d Ingmar Bergman. *p* Dion de Laurentiis. *sc* Ingmar Bergman. *ph* Sven Nykvist. *ed* Jutta Hering, Petra von Oelffen. *pd* Rolf Zehetbauer. *m* Rolf Wilhelm. *cast* Liv Ullmann, David Carradine, Gert Fröbe, Heinz Bennent, James Whitmore, Glynn Turman.

●Whether stimulated by his brush with the Swedish tax-man or his brief self-imposed exile in West Germany, Bergman's paranoia runs dementedly and tediously out of control in this Grand Guignol recreation of 1923 Berlin as studio set for close encounters of the most portentous kind. Carradine is improbably cast in the central role of a Jewish trapeze artist called Abel Rosenberg, wandering innocently through a night-town world of bottles, brothels, and (inevitably) cabarets, and trying to ignore the violence, depravity and anti-semitism screeching at him from every street corner. The torments he endures, with a sadly miscast Ullmann (who's further afflicted with throwaway lines like 'I can't stand the guilt'), have indeed been devised by a foresighted mad scientist straight out of *Dr Strangelove.* This last-reel revelation comes too late to restore audience disbelief to its proper state of suspension. JD

Serpent's Kiss, The

(1997, GB, 110 min)
d Philippe Rousselot. *p* Tim Rose Price, Robert Jones, John Battsek. *sc* Tim Rose Price. *ph* Jean-François Robin. *ed* Mick Audsley. *pd* Charles Garrad. *cast* Ewan McGregor, Greta Scacchi, Pete Postlethwaite, Richard E Grant, Carmen Chaplin.

●A misbegotten attempt to ring changes on the British costume drama, former cameraman Rousselot's directorial debut tells of a landscape gardener (McGregor) tumbling into a snake's pit of deceit and deadly intrigue when he agrees to create a new estate for wealthy landowner Postlethwaite and his wife Scacchi. The film founders on stilted performances (Grant's death throes are spectacularly risible), conspicuously artificial set design, and dialogue – half 'literary', half colloquially contemporary (including inappropriate modern profanities) – that makes much of supposedly sophisticated metaphor but barely makes sense. And there's another problem: it's all too clearly derivative of *The Draughtsman's Contract*, comparison with which only makes Tim Rose Price's screenplay seem even worse. GA

Serpico

(1973, US, 130 min)
d Sidney Lumet. *p* Martin Bregman. *sc* Waldo Salt, Norman Wexler. *ph* Arthur J Ornitz. *ed* Dede Allen, Richard Marks. *pd* Charles Bailey. *m* Mikis Theodorakis. *cast* Al Pacino, John Randolph, Jack Kehoe, Biff McGuire, Barbara Eda-Young, Cornelia Sharpe, Tony Roberts.

●Like a practice run for Lumet's *Prince of the City*, this deals with police corruption in New York: Pacino's idealism and odd-style dress alienate him from his fellow cops, who take bribes left, right and centre. But whereas the later film built up an impressively complex series of narrative strands and psychological motivations, this is far more one-dimensional, and is so laxly structured that its rambling story seems to last longer than the (almost) three-hour *Prince of the City*. Another problem, these days, is Pacino's characterisation; he seems at times more like a misplaced hippy than a plainclothes cop. GA

Servant, The

(1963, GB, 115 min, b/w)
d Joseph Losey. *p* Joseph Losey, Norman Priggen. *sc* Harold Pinter. *ph* Douglas Slocombe. *ed* Reginald Mills. *pd* Richard MacDonald. *m* John Dankworth. *cast* Dirk Bogarde, James Fox, Wendy Craig, Sarah Miles, Catherine Lacey, Richard Vernon, Ann Firbank, Patrick Magee, Harold Pinter.

●Losey's first bid for success as a 'prestige' director now looks embarrassingly contrived: an allegory on class conflict (derived from Robin Maugham's novel) in which Bogarde's crafty manservant achieves a sinister, game-playing role-reversal in the home of his wealthy, decadent, upper class master (Fox). Neither Pinter's pregnant dialogue nor the generally svelte performances can disguise the fact that there's less here than meets the eye and ear. TR

Servante et Maîtresse
(1976, Fr, 90 min)
d Bruno Gantillon. *p* Gilbert de Goldschmidt. *sc* Dominique Fabre. *ph* Etienne Szabo. *ed* Georges Klotz. *pd* Michel François. *m* Jean-Marie Benjamin. *cast* Victor Lanoux, Andrea Ferreol, Evelyne Buyle, Gabriel Cattand, David Pontremoli, Jean Rougerie.
● Tediously artistic game-playing in a luxurious mansion. An old man dies, the maid (Ferreol) gets all the money and becomes mistress, forcing the expected beneficiary, a no-good nephew (Lanoux), to assume the servant's role. And so the film plods it's weary way, offering nothing that couldn't be said in half-an-hour. However, it would be far wearier with less accomplished performers. GB

Servicer, The (Cream – Schwabing-Report)
(1970, WGer/US, 85 min)
d Leon Capetanos. *p* Ernst von Theumer, Harry L Ross. *sc* Leon Capetanos, Ernst von Theumer. *ph* Klaus König. *ed* Peter Przygodda. *m* Can. *cast* Sabi Dor, Astrid Bonin, Rolf Zacher, Hartmut Solinger, Ula Kopa.
● Age and disillusionment catch up with the speed generation of the '60s (Schwabing being Munich's Chelsea or Greenwich Village). Everyone succumbs: Franco, a gigolo suffering his share of ennui, marries the girl with her hair in plaits, who steals (a revolutionary and purifying act) but only in order to surround herself with the trappings of bourgeois comfort; his friend George wants to open a huge Disneyland for sex where you can make it with Mickey Mouse. Well-made and surprisingly ambitious for what is ostensibly a sex film, the result is a curious but not unlikeable mixture. The more pretentious overtones are deliberately spiked by the hack American commentary, which ends with 'the names, of course, have been changed to protect the innocent'. Such a confusion of styles emphasises the film's uncertainty about what it has to say, but the humour and general readiness to try something slightly different make it a cut above its type.

Se Sei Vivo, Spara
see Django Kill

Set It Off
(1996, US, 122 min)
d F Gary Gray. *p* Dale Pollock, Oren Koules. *sc* Takashi Bufford, Kate Lanier. *ph* Marc Reshovsky. *ed* John Carter. *pd* Robb Wilson-King. *m* Christopher Young. *cast* Jada Pinkett, Queen Latifah, Vivica A Fox, John C McGinley, Kimberly Elise, Blair Underwood.
● Frankie (Fox) has a bank job – until someone she knows from South Central LA holds her at gun-point, the attempted robbery turns into a blood-bath, and the boss sends her packing. Life gets much harder. Her homegirls (Pinkett, Latifah, Elise) fix her up with the office-cleaning firm where they work nights, but it's not long before they hatch a plan to capitalise on Frankie's qualifications, in particular her inside knowledge of bank security procedures. In the wake of all those gun-toting white women and black men, black women are due their own loaded action adventure. This noir *Thelma and Louise* rekindles some of the subversive fire of Jonathan Demme's '70s exploitation flicks, although it's far too polished to have come from the Corman stable. The intense heist sequences show a command of thriller dynamics that's right up there with the best of them, but director Gray is equally convincing on the character front, eliciting funny, grounded performances from the four women (Latifah notably refuses to caricature her lesbian role). On the down side, Blair Underwood is too good to be true as the man who comes into Pinkett's life, while the police procedural stuff is strictly routine. Minor misdemeanours, though, given such an energising spree for the Girlz n the hood. TCh

Setta, La
see Sect, The

Set-Up, The
(1948, US, 72 min, b/w)
d Robert Wise. *p* Richard Goldstone. *sc* Art Cohn. *ph* Milton Krasner. *ed* Roland Gross. *ad* Albert S D'Agostino, Jack Okey, C Bakaleinikoff. *cast* Robert Ryan, Audrey Totter, George Tobias, Alan Baxter, Wallace Ford, Percy Helton, Darryl Hickman, James Edwards.
● One for the Ten Best lists. This is the boxing movie to lick all others, with Ryan impeccable as the ageing fighter gearing up for a bout he's expected to lose; Audrey Totter leaving him because she can't stand the mental and physical battering of the fight business, wandering the streets amid snatches of ringside radio commentary; and an invading sense of desolation the result. Great blue moments in black-and-white from a director whose early work is still outstanding: the film burns with the humanity that *Raging Bull* never quite achieves, an expression of masochism mixed with futile pride that is the essence of boxing as a movie myth. CA

Set Up, The
(1995, US, 90 min)
d Strathford Hamilton. *p* Julia Verdin. *ph* David Lewis. *ed* Marcy Hamilton. *pd* Richard Reynolds. *m* Conrad Pope. *cast* Billy Zane, James Coburn, Mia Sara, James Russo.
● Not to be confused with the '40s boxing classic, this is a double-crossing latter-day caper, with security expert Zane working for banker Coburn, and in the process falling for his daughter Sara. His old buddy Russo then becomes the fly in the ointment, holding her hostage to force Zane into breaking into the bank for him. And there are further complications on the way, in a movie that's more plot than characterisation, and is already doomed from the moment they cast the synthetic male lead. Based on James Hadley Chase's *My Laugh Comes Last*. TJ

Seul, avec Claude
see Being at Home With Claude

Seul contre tous
see I Stand Alone

Seven
(1979, US, 101 min)
d/p Andy Sidaris. *sc* Bill Driskill, Robert Baird. *ph* Quito. *ed* Alan E Ferguson. *ad* Sal Grasso, William Pryor. *cast* William Smith, Guich Koock, Barbara Leigh, Art Metrano, Martin Kove, Ed Parker, Richard LePore, Reggie Nalder.
● Called on to perform a 'no-news wipeout' on seven Hawaiian mafiosi, Drew Sevano (Smith) assembles his own charmless bunch of seven heavies, and then spends his time driving around brooding on new methods of homicide. It's the sort of film where you keep seeing the microphone boom; in other words a tawdry mess, unrelieved by acts of crazed eccentricity (skateboarding crossbowmen, a hang-gliding bomber), and epitomised by its grossly insulting attitude to women, their sole function being to climb in and out of bikinis. Strictly for the brain-damaged. CPea

Seven (aka Se7en) (100)
(1995, US, 127 min)
d David Fincher. *p* Arnold Kopelson, Phyllis Carlyle. *sc* Andrew Kevin Walker. *ph* Darius Khondji. *ed* Richard Francis-Bruce. *pd* Arthur Max. *m* Howard Shore. *cast* Brad Pitt, Morgan Freeman, Gwyneth Paltrow, Richard Roundtree, R Lee Ermey, Kevin Spacey.
● Serial killers and mismatched cops overcoming antagonism are seldom fresh, fruitful subjects for movies, but this exceptionally (and impressively) nasty thriller blends genres to grim and gripping effect. Somerset (Freeman) and Mills (Pitt) are the detectives brought together when an obese corpse is discovered in a dismal apartment. Mills, who with his wife (Paltrow) has recently moved to the city from upstate, resents what he perceives as Somerset's patronising attitude; still, the older cop, about to retire and weary of crime and moral apathy, is unusually educated, as becomes clear when they find a second mutilated body and he insists his young partner start reading the likes of Milton, Chaucer and Dante. Somerset's theory? That a messianic murderer is perpetrating crimes to punish the Seven Deadly Sins – in which case there are five more to go. The film's world is so shadowy, decaying and intentionally dated that one often wonders whether anyone involved has heard of electricity; at the same time, however, Somerset and Mills' slow voyage from claustrophobic murk into blinding light makes for a vivid dramatic metaphor. Moreover, Fincher handles the violence with sensitivity, announcing its obscenity in spoken analyses and briefly glimpsed post mortem shots, but never showing the murderous acts themselves. GA

Seven Beauties (Pasqualino Settebellezze)
(1975, It, 115 min)
d Lina Wertmüller. *p* Lina Wertmüller, Giancarlo Giannini, Giancarlo Giannini. *sc* Lina Wertmüller. *ph* Tonino Delli Colli. *ed* Franco Fraticelli. *ad* Enrico Job. *m* Enzo Jannacci. *cast* Giancarlo Giannini, Fernando Rey, Shirley Stoler, Elena Fiore, Piero Di Iorio.
● American art house success led to Wertmller being compared to Bergman and Fellini, but as *Seven Beauties* confirms, it is her taste for a vaguely intellectualised sado-masochism which aroused middle class American enthusiasm. The film recounts the picaresque adventures of a pop-eyed Italian shark (Giannini) who lives off women, is institutionalised for killing in defence of his honour, 'rehabilitated' by army service after committing rape in the asylum, and ends up facing the problem of survival in a Nazi concentration camp. Much of it is fifth-rate slapstick, decked out in gaudy sub-Ken Russell style with the occasional interpolation of gruesome or violent images, plus some nudgingly insistent music. There is a lingering climax in which he steels himself to seduce the pig-like woman Commandant of the concentration camp (awesomely played by Shirley Stoler of *The Honeymoon Killers*); his subsequent sexual debasement is memorable, but in such an uninspiring context it reeks of artifice. DP

Seven Brides for Seven Brothers
(1954, US, 103 min)
d Stanley Donen. *p* Jack Cummings. *sc* Albert Hackett, Frances Goodrich, Dorothy Kingsley. *ph* George Folsey. *ed* Ralph E Winters. *ad* Cedric Gibbons, Urie McCleary. *m* Gene De Paul. *cast* Howard Keel, Jane Powell, Jeff Richards, Russ Tamblyn, Tommy Rall, Marc Platt, Matt Mattox, Jacques d'Amboise, Virginia Gibson, Julie Newmar.
● Circuitously derived from the tale of the rape of the Sabine women, this rather archly symmetrical movie musical is best seen as a dance-fest, with Michael Kidd's acrobatic, *pas d'action* choreography well complemented by ex-choreographer Donen's camera. Gene De Paul and Johnny Mercer's score is cosy ('Spring, Spring, Spring' and all that), and Keel, avoiding even the odd faked toe-step, is at his least expressive, but it's vigorous and colourful if you can watch the Anscocolor process which also marred *Brigadoon*. The bearded Matt Mattox went on to become something of a legend for his jazz classes at London's Dance Centre. SG

Seven Chances
(1925, US, 6,210 ft, b/w)
d Buster Keaton. *p* Joseph M Schenck. *sc* Clyde Bruckman, Jean C Havez, Joseph A Mitchell. *ph* Elgin Lessley, Bryon Houck. *cast* Buster Keaton, Ruth Dwyer, Ray Barnes, Snitz Edwards.
● Less ambitious and less concerned with plastic values than the best of Keaton, this is nevertheless a dazzlingly balletic comedy in which Buster has a matter of hours to acquire the wife on which a seven million dollar inheritance depends. Having insulted his sweetheart by explaining the necessity of marriage, been turned down by seven possible candidates at the country club, and (in a series of innocently inept gags) found his path beset by uglies, blacks or female impersonators, he advertises – only to find a horde of applicants besieging the church. From this leisurely start, the film takes off into a fantastically elaborate, gloriously inventive chase sequence, in which Buster escapes the mob of pursuing harridans only to find an escalating avalanche of rocks taking over at his heels as he hurtles downhill. Added only after an initial preview, the rocks make for one of the great Keaton action gags. TM

Seven Days in May
(1964, US, 118 min, b/w)
d John Frankenheimer. *p* Edward Lewis. *sc* Rod Serling. *ph* Ellsworth Fredricks. *ed* Ferris Webster. *ad* Cary Odell. *m* Jerry Goldsmith. *cast* Burt Lancaster, Kirk Douglas, Fredric

March, Ava Gardner, Edmond O'Brien, Martin Balsam, George Macready, Whit Bissell, Hugh Marlowe, John Houseman.
●Political thriller in which the military Chiefs of Staff (led by Lancaster) plot to overthrow the US president (March) after he concludes what they consider to be a disastrous nuclear treaty with Russia. Conspiracy movies may have become more darkly complex in these post-Watergate days of Pakula and paranoia, but Frankenheimer's fascination with gadgetry (in his compositions, the ubiquitous helicopters, TV screens, hidden cameras and electronic devices literally edge the human characters into insignificance) is used to create a striking visual metaphor for control by the military machine. Highly enjoyable. TM

Seven Days to Noon

(1950, GB, 94 min, b/w)
d John Boulting. *p* Roy Boulting, John Boulting. *sc* Frank Harvey, Roy Boulting. *ph* Gilbert Taylor. *ed* Roy Boulting, John Boulting. *ad* John Elphick. *m* John Addison. *cast* Barry Jones, Olive Sloane, Andre Morell, Joan Hickson, Sheila Manahan, Marie Ney.
●When an atomic scientist (Jones) entertains serious doubts about his work and promises to blow up London unless the government rids Britain of nuclear weapons, rumours of war spread, panic grows, and the suspense is killing. Still relevant and surprisingly powerful, *Seven Days to Noon* impresses by its ambiguity: while we sympathise with the ordinary Londoners menaced by the professor's drastic policy, and are told by politicians and boffins that he is mad from overwork, what we see is an intelligent, sane man of intense, apolitical commitment. London, both in the grip of evacuation and deserted, is beautifully evoked by the *noir*-ish camerawork, and John Addison's Herrmannesque score helps to keep the atmosphere nervy. Only the cosy Cockney cameos (all pluck and chatter) deflate the otherwise carefully sustained paranoia. GA

7 Faces of Dr Lao

(1963, US, 100 min)
d George Pal. *sc* Charles G Finney. *ph* Robert Bronner. *ed* George Tomasini. *ad* George W Davis, Gabriel Scognamillo. *m* Leigh Harline. *cast* Tony Randall, Barbara Eden, Arthur O'Connell, John Ericson, Kevin Tate, Lee Patrick, Argentina Brunetti, Noah Beery Jr, John Qualen.
●Randall gets to show off as the old, bald Chinese illusionist who arrives in a Western town and whose multifarious circus show soon begins to cast a spell over local events (newspaperman Ericson is leading a fight against expansionist magnate O'Connell). A pleasingly inventive diversion from top movie fantasist George Pal, here coming up with an original story (script by Charles Beaumont from Charles G Finney's novel *The Circus of Dr Lao*), rather than adapting a fairytale (*Tom Thumb*) or a myth (*Atlantis, The Lost Continent*). Make-up artist William Tuttle won an Oscar for his endeavours. TJ

Seven Men from Now

(1956, US, 78 min)
d Budd Boetticher. *p* Andrew V McLaglen, Robert E Morrison. *sc* Burt Kennedy. *ph* William H Clothier. *ed* Everett Sutherland. *ad* Leslie Thomas. *m* Henry Vars. *cast* Randolph Scott, Gail Russell, Lee Marvin, Walter Reed, John Larch, Donald Barry.
●Neither as bleak nor as concise as the greatest collaborations between Scott and Boetticher (*The Tall T, Ride Lonesome, Comanche Station*), their first outing together nevertheless remains a terrific B Western. Scott is beautifully assured as Ben Stride, vengefully hunting down the men who killed his wife during a robbery, while Larch and (most especially) Marvin are memorable as the outlaws he encounters out in the desert, keen to get their hands on a gold shipment secretly being carried by a couple from back east. Burt Kennedy's script is characteristically terse and witty, William Clothier's camerawork sharp and direct, and Boetticher's direction a model of inventive economy. GA

Seven Minutes (Georg Elser)

(1989, US/WGer, 90 min)
d Klaus Maria Brandauer. *p* Moritz Borman, Rainer Söhnlein. *sc* Stephen Sheppard. *ph* Lajos Koltai. *ed* Dagmar Hirtz. *pd* Wolfgang Hundhammer. *m* Georges Delerue. *cast* Klaus Maria Brandauer, Rebecca Miller, Brian Dennehy, Nigel Le Vaillant.
●Brandauer, an arresting screen actor, notably in Szabo's *Mephisto* and *Colonel Redl*, turns plodding director for this functional fact-based thriller, adapted by Stephen Sheppard from his novel *The Artisan*. Brandauer stars as the Munich clockmaker Georg Elser who intends to assassinate Hitler when he visits a nearby beer hall. But the waitress Elser's in love with is scheduled to be on duty in the hall at the time set for the killing. Dennehy gets on with the job as the Gestapo security chief. TJ

Seven Minutes, The

(1971, US, 115 min)
d/p Russ Meyer. *sc* Richard Warren Lewis. *ph* Fred Mandl. *ed* Dick Wormell. *ad* Rodger Maus. *m* Stu Phillips. *cast* Wayne Maunder, Marianne McAndrew, Yvonne De Carlo, Philip Carey, Jay C Flippen, Edy Williams, Lyle Bettger, Ron Randell, John Carradine, Tom Selleck.
●Based on Irving Wallace's novel about a pornography trial, with much ado around a politically-motivated attempt to link a murder to the supposedly corrupting influence of a book condemned as obscene on its publication thirty years earlier. This is Russ Meyer's dullest film, because it abandons his usually salacious tone to attempt a 'serious' attack on the American version of the Mary Whitehouse brigade. Curious only for its unwitting fag-end-of-the-'60s proof that moralists and pornographers are equally appalled by the prospect of sexual liberation.

Seven Nights in Japan

(1976, GB/Fr, 104 min)
d/p Lewis Gilbert. *sc* Christopher Wood. *ph* Henri Decaë. *ed* John Glen. *pd* John Stoll. *m* David Hentschel. *cast* Michael York, Hidemi Aoki, James Villiers, Peter Jones, Charles Gray, Lionel Murton, Yolande Donlan.
●A loose update of *Roman Holiday*, with Michael York in the Audrey Hepburn role and without Wyler's witty handling. It's the hoariest of escapist fantasies, mixing royalty (in disguise as a common chap, no less), romance and foreign parts in equal measure as our Prince – obviously Charles, though called George – absconds from convincingly boring duties to savour love on the loose with a Japanese tour guide. The first two nights slip by painlessly enough, but after that it's minutes one counts, not nights. There's an alarmingly silly assassination plot, and only very tentative gags (like the familiar voice on the telephone, backed by yelping corgis). VG

Seven-Per-Cent Solution, The

(1976, US, 114 min)
d/p Herbert Ross. *sc* Nicholas Meyer. *ph* Oswald Morris. *ed* Chris Barnes. *pd* Ken Adam. *m* John Addison. *cast* Alan Arkin, Vanessa Redgrave, Robert Duvall, Nicol Williamson, Laurence Olivier, Joel Grey, Samantha Eggar, Jeremy Kemp, Charles Gray, Georgia Brown.
●Conan Doyle's description of Holmes' ultimate struggle with Moriarty, *The Final Problem*, was written with such a quasi-religious intensity that it was a sacred text of popular fiction until 1974, when Nicholas Meyer conceived that the story had been written to disguise both Holmes' cocaine dependency and his encounter with Freud in Vienna. As a book, *The Seven-Per-Cent Solution* was a pertinent pastiche. As a film, it is an almost unrelievedly insipid costume drama. Once the basic coup of teaming Holmes (Williamson) and Freud (Arkin) has been achieved, the 'mystery' simply degenerates into a spectacularly silly chase across Europe, blandly staged and staggeringly boring. The whole cast appear to be struggling, and ultimately it's camp whodunit. DP

Seven Samurai 100 (100) (Shichinin no Samurai)

(1954, Jap, 200 min, b/w)
d Akira Kurosawa. *p* Shojiro Motoki. *sc* Akira Kurosawa, Shinobu Hashimoto, Hideo Oguni. *ph* Asaichi Nakai. *ad* So Matsuyama. *m* Fumio Hayasaka. *cast* Takashi Shimura, Toshiro Mifune, Yoshio Inaba, Seiji Miyaguchi, Minoru Chiaki, Daisuke Kato, Ko Kimura.
●Kurosawa's masterpiece, testifying to his admiration for John Ford and translated effortlessly back into the form of a Western as *The Magnificent Seven*, has six masterless samurai – plus Mifune, the crazy farmer's boy not qualified to join the elect group, who nevertheless follows like a dog and fights like a lion – agreeing for no pay, just food and the joy of fulfilling their duty as fighters, to protect a helpless village against a ferocious gang of bandits. Despite the caricatured acting forms of Noh and Kabuki which Kurosawa adopted in his period films, the individual characterisations are precise and memorable, none more so than that by Takashi Shimura, one of the director's favourite actors, playing the sage, ageing, and oddly charismatic samurai leader. The epic action scenes involving cavalry and samurai are still without peer. RM

Seven Sinners (aka Doomed Cargo)

(1936, GB, 70 min, b/w)
d Albert de Courville. *p* Michael Balcon. *sc* Sidney Gilliat, Frank Launder. *ph* Max Greene. *ed* Michael S Gordon. *ad* Ernö Metzner. *m* Bretton Byrd. *cast* Edmund Lowe, Constance Cummings, Thomy Bourdelle, Henry Oscar, Felix Aylmer, Allan Jeayes, OB Clarence.
●Crisply scripted by Frank Launder and Sidney Gilliat, this set out as a remake of *The Wrecker*, a 1929 melodrama about sabotage on the railways, but – evidently under their influence – metamorphosed into something rather different: a fast-moving, serio-comic thriller which kicks off with an American detective (Lowe) investigating a murder when a corpse turns up in his hotel room in Nice, then mysteriously vanishes, only to reappear subsequently amid the debris of a wrecked train (the plot allows for several crashes, using spectacular footage from *The Wrecker*, as it moves back and forth across the Channel). Clearly intending to ape Hitchcock in both plot and manner, the film creaks here and there, but is brisk, occasionally gripping, and often amusing. Lowe (well backed up by Constance Cummings as a sidekick Nora to his Nick Charles) proves surprisingly adept at the throwaway touch and the nonchalant wisecracks. TM

Seven Sinners

(1940, US, 87 min, b/w)
d Tay Garnett. *p* Joe Pasternak. *sc* John Meehan, Harry Tugend. *ph* Rudolph Maté. *ed* Ted J Kent. *ad* Jack Otterson. *m* Frank Skinner, Hans J Salter. *cast* Marlene Dietrich, John Wayne, Albert Dekker, Broderick Crawford, Anna Lee, Billy Gilbert, Mischa Auer, Oscar Homolka.
●A return to the territory (if not quite the spirit or the style) of Dietrich's great films with von Sternberg in the early '30s. Here she plays Bijou, another member of that 'foreign legion of women' introduced in *Morocco*: a singer who shuttles around the islands of South-East Asia on a string of deportation orders, a trail of wrecked nightclubs and local riots in her wake. This time, her hopeless affair is with Wayne's staunch US Navy lieutenant (fortunately they both love the navy as much as each other), but she winds up sharing a tipple with the alcoholic doctor of a tramp steamer. True to form, Garnett directs it with panache but without finesse. His lighting and his use of Dietrich as an icon both reflect a viewing of the Sternberg films, but he doesn't seriously attempt the cruelty or the emotional pain of his models. Dietrich, as the woman 'not quite ready for the word derelict', is wonderful. TR

17 rue Bleue

(2001, Fr, 95 min)
d Chad Chenouga. *p* Jérôme Vidal. *sc* Chad Chenouga, Philippe Donzelot. *ph* Eric Guichard. *ed* Marie-France Cuenot. *m* Ahmet Gülbay, Chad Chenouga. *cast* Lysiane Meis, Abdel Halis, Aimen Ben Hamed, Nassim Sakhoui, Sofiane Abramowitz.
●What starts out as a lively if seemingly somewhat bland account of an Algerian woman coming with her kids to live in France at the end of the Algerian War pretty soon takes an interesting turn into far darker territory when her married lover – who has always supported her – dies unexpectedly. Adda decides to fight for his fortune in court, but his wife has other ideas, and Adda, her two boys and her sisters fall on hard times. If there's nothing especially remarkable about the

film, it does at least boast a muscular storyline that never flinches from dealing with real pain, a clutch of vivid naturalistic performances, and an aura of authenticity born of the fact that the film is autobiographical. Strong stuff. GA

1776

(1972, US, 141 min)
d Peter H Hunt. *p* Jack L Warner. *sc* Peter Stone. *ph* Harry Stradling Jr. *ed* Florence Williamson. *ad* George Jenkins. *m* Sherman Edwards. *cast* William Daniels, Howard da Silva, Ken Howard, Donald Madden, Blythe Danner, John Cullum, David Ford.
●Straightforward transfer of the Broadway musical by Sherman Edwards and Peter Stone about the conception and passing of the American Declaration of Independence. Suspense mounts as the nays change to yeas, and Benjamin Franklin and Thomas Jefferson do a one-two-three-kick routine. They also sing. Everybody sings. Amazingly plastic film-making. The mind boggled, gave up, and enjoyed it. They've even included the slavery cop-out. Very long at 141 minutes.

Seventeen Years (Guonian Hui Jia)

(1999, China/It, 99 min)
d Zhang Yuan. *p* Zhang Yuan, Willy Tsao, Zhang Peimin. *sc* Yu Hua, Ning Dai, Zhu Wen. *ph* Zhang Xigui. *ed* Jacopo Quadri, Zhang Yuan. *pd* Zhao Xiaoyu. *m* Zhao Jiping. *cast* Liu Lin, Li Bingbing, Le Yeping, Liang Song, Li Jun.
●Seventeen years after accidentally murdering her stepsister in a fight, Tao Xiaolan (Liu) is given a new year furlough from prison. Since no one shows up to collect her, young prison guard Chen (Li Bingbing) offers to escort her home. But the family house in Tianjin has been demolished. In the course of finding where Tao's parents now live (and steering the nervous woman into a reunion with them), Tao and Chen form an unexpected bond. Zhang's first fiction feature since his rapprochement with the Film Bureau is a solid art movie: sensitive, understated, psychologically acute and quietly emotive. In other words, less interesting than the risky, provocative and often revelatory work he did as an 'illegal' underground film-maker. TR

7/25 (Nana/Ni-Go)

(1999, Jap, 67 min)
d Wataru Hayakawa. *p* Yukari Hatano. *sc* Maho Arakida. *ph* Tadanori Kunimatsu. *ed* Wataru Hayakawa. *m* Takashi Watanabe. *cast* Isamu Hyuga, Mihoko Umetsu, Junya Nakano, Risa Miyanaga.
●Only connect… This mildly intriguing indie feature has two seemingly disparate storylines which may or may not have hidden links and parallels. The rural one centres on a tree doctor guarding the last surviving pair of starline maples against a woman who apparently wants to make a cello from their wood. The urban one, set in Sapporo, is about a would-be gumshoe hired to catch a girl who shoplifts on the 25th of each month. Having set up its characters and their problems, the film fast-forwards to the title date for some climactic revelations involving a graffiti-covered room, an undelivered cello and the pollination problems of the maple tree. Not exactly Borgesian in its metaphysical implications, but it does offer an interesting spot sample of young adult concerns in present-day Japan. TR

7th Cavalry

(1956, US, 75 min)
d Joseph H Lewis. *p* Harry Joe Brown. *sc* Peter Packer. *ph* Ray Rennahan. *ed* Gene Havlick. *ad* George Brooks. *m* Mischa Bakaleinikoff. *cast* Randolph Scott, Barbara Hale, Jay C Flippen, Jeanette Nolan, Frank Faylen, Leo Gordon, Harry Carey Jr, Denver Pyle.
●One of Lewis' two colour films, a weird and occasionally wonderful little Western focusing on the enmity between white and red man as Scott, accused of deserting Custer out of cowardice during the fiasco of Little Big Horn, sets out to discover the truth of the massacre. Beautifully shot and briskly paced, it's most interesting for a surprising anti-Custer stance, and for its surreal, almost supernatural finale, which sees Custer's horse appearing like a ghost from the wilderness to bring peace between enemies. GA

7th Continent, The (Siebente Kontinent)

(1989, Aus, 111 min)
d Michael Haneke. *p* Veit Heiduschka. *sc* Michael Haneke. *ph* Toni Peschke. *ed* Marie Homolkova. *pd* Rudi Czettel. *cast* Birgit Doll, Dieter Berner, Leni Tanzer, Udo Samel, Sylvia Fenz, Robert Dietl.
●The first part of Haneke's trilogy dealing with the 'emotional glaciation' of contemporary Austria, this deploys a pared, matter of fact, almost Bressonian visual and narrative style to chart the preparations made by a youngish, well-to-do couple who decide, quite coolly, to take their own lives and that of their uncomprehending young daughter. Though no explicit explanation is given for their decision, Haneke's attention to detail is such that the malaise affecting them and the frustrations of conformity soon become apparent. Moreover, the stark, calm visuals, the understated performances, and the measured but inexorable pace of the film gradually build to a terrifying emotional intensity. Hugely chastening, strangely beautiful, and extremely impressive. GA

Seventh Cross, The

(1944, US, 110 min, b/w)
d Fred Zinnemann. *p* Pandro S Berman. *sc* Helen Deutsch. *ph* Karl Freund. *ed* Thomas Richards. *ad* Cedric Gibbons, Leonid Vasian. *m* Roy Webb. *cast* Spencer Tracy, Signe Hasso, Hume Cronyn, Jessica Tandy, Agnes Moorehead, George Macready, Ray Collins, Felix Bressart, Steve Geray, George Zucco, Karen Verne.
●With Tracy heading the cast and a host of great character actors in support, it's hardly surprising that the performances are the most memorable aspect of Zinnemann's first major feature. Tracy pulls all the stops out as one of seven anti-Nazi Germans escaping from a concentration camp in 1936, and heading (with the Gestapo in pursuit) for Holland and freedom; en route, his bitterness dissipates and his faith in human nature is restored. Polished professionalism all round, in fact, with the odyssey tensely evoked in the studio by ace cameraman Karl Freund. GA

7th Dawn, The

(1964, US/GB, 123 min)
d Lewis Gilbert. *p* Charles K Feldman. *sc* Karl Tunberg. *ph* Freddie Young. *ed* John Shirley. *pd* John Stoll. *m* Riz Ortolani. *cast* William Holden, Susannah York, Capucine, Tetsuro Tamba, Michael Goodliffe, Allan Cuthbertson, Maurice Denham, Sidney Tafler.
●A very pale shadow of *The Ugly American*, attempting to sort out tangled loyalties during the terrorist troubles in Malaya but only succeeding in reducing them to a mess of pottage. Clichés blossom in the wilderness and love, of course, becomes a many-splendoured thing as the cardboard characters react to assorted atrocities and slog through endless jungle, with poor Holden as the planter trying to sort out his politics while getting into sentimental difficulties between an Eurasian (Capucine) and an English rose (York). TM

7th Heaven

(1927, US, 8,500 ft, b/w)
d/p Frank Borzage. *sc* Benjamin F Glazer. *ph* Ernest Palmer, Joseph Valentine. *ed* Barney Wolf. *ad* Harry Oliver. *cast* Janet Gaynor, Charles Farrell, Ben Bard, David Butler, Albert Gran, Marie Mosquini, Gladys Brockwell, Emile Chautard, George Stone.
●Borzage's films – or at least the coherent collection made between the mid-twenties and World War II – are sublime demonstrations of a system of sensual spirituality; products of their director's uncompromising romanticism and fluent sense of cinemotion. *7th Heaven* tracks the transformational love of Farrell and Gaynor from the sewers to the stars, across time and space, and beyond death itself, affirming triumphantly that melodrama can mean much more than just an excuse for a good weep. PT

Seventh Heaven

(1937, US, 102 min, b/w)
d Henry King. *p* Raymond Griffith. *sc* Melville Baker. *ph* Merritt B Gerstad. *ed* Barbara McLean. *ad* William Darling. *m* Louis Silvers. *cast* Simone Simon, James Stewart, Jean Hersholt, Gregory Ratoff, Gale Sondergaard, J Edward Bromberg, John Qualen.
●Henry King's remake of Borzage's incandescent romance is a film of some sensitivity but little conviction. The setting is again a Paris slum, but Borzage's eternal anywhere becomes both too specific and too vague, tying the action to a time and place that is a never-never land of novelettish convention, while the dark shadow cast by World War I seems more a dramatic convenience than a haunting memory. But the real problem is James Stewart's ineradicably American persona: the ebullient optimism with which his Chico shows Simone's Diane the way to the stars, teaching her to shed her fear of life and to have faith in love, makes him sound like a gung ho boy scout. An affecting little tale, all the same. TM

Seventh Seal, The (Det Sjunde Inseglet) 100

(1956, Swe, 95 min, b/w)
d Ingmar Bergman. *p* Allan Ekelund. *sc* Ingmar Bergman. *ph* Gunnar Fischer. *ed* Lennart Wallén. *ad* PA Lundgren. *m* Erik Nordgren. *cast* Max von Sydow, Gunnar Björnstrand, Bengt Ekerot, Nils Poppe, Bibi Andersson, Ake Fridell, Maud Hansson, Gunnel Lindblom.
●Bergman's portentous medieval allegory takes its title from the Book of Revelations – 'And when he (the Lamb) opened the seventh seal, there was a silence in heaven about the space of half an hour'. In the opening scene, a knight returning from the Crusades is challenged to a game of chess by the cloaked figure of Death (Ekerot), and from this point onwards an air of doom hangs over the action, like the hawk which hovers in the air above them. The time of Death and Judgement prophesied in the Bible has arrived, and a plague is sweeping the land. Bergman fills the screen with striking images: the knight and Death playing chess for the former's life, a band of flagellants swinging smoking censers, a young witch manacled to a stake. Probably the most parodied film of all time, this nevertheless contains some of the most extraordinary images ever committed to celluloid. Whether they are able to carry the metaphysical and allegorical weight with which they have been loaded is open to question. NF

Seventh Sign, The

(1988, US, 97 min)
d Carl Schultz. *p* Ted Field, Robert Cort. *sc* WW Wicket, George Kaplan. *ph* Juan Ruiz-Anchia. *ed* Caroline Biggerstaff. *pd* Stephen Marsh. *m* Jack Nitzsche. *cast* Demi Moore, Michael Biehn, Jürgen Prochnow, Peter Friedman, Manny Jacobs, John Taylor.
●An apocalyptic thriller which focuses on an intimate familial dilemma, this should find favour among those who prefer supernatural disquiet to visceral shocks. A young mother-to-be (Moore) suffers recurring nightmares. Disturbed by these fragmentary premonitions, she begins to imagine that the fate of her child is somehow bound up with a series of strange natural phenomena which, some say, herald the end of the world: the sea around a Haitian island boils, an Israeli desert village freezes over, the sun is eclipsed, the moon glows red. Her nightmares also seem to be linked to a mysterious stranger (Prochnow), who moves into an adjoining apartment, and whose silent brooding and unnatural interest in the unborn child she interprets as a diabolical threat. Schultz's stylish visuals and sympathetic handling of the actors creates an unsettling atmosphere of understated menace; and the unfolding mystery (drawing upon both the Book of Revelations and ancient Jewish mythology) generates a tremendous cumulative tension, the climactic scene working all the better for being staged on a human scale. NF

Seventh Veil, The

(1945, GB, 94 min, b/w)
d Compton Bennett. *p* Sydney Box. *sc* Sydney Box, Muriel Box. *ph* Reginald Wyer. *ed* George Hales. *ad* Jim Carter. *m* Benjamin Frankel. *cast* James Mason, Ann Todd, Herbert Lom, Hugh McDermott, Albert Lieven.
●Ineffable tripe which mixes a heady stew of kitsch, culture and Freud as a concert pianist obsessed with the idea that she can never play again (people will keep rapping her over the

knuckles) is cured by a psychiatrist (Lom) who guides her through her past in quest of the man she really loves. With Mason providing the catchpenny dream of (masochistic) romance – lame, dark and sardonically brooding, he's the guardian who relentlessly drives her towards success and away from frivolous affairs of the heart – you know that McDermott's cheery bandleader and Lieven's society portrait painter don't stand a chance. Enjoyable, sort of. TM

Seventh Victim, The

(1943, US, 71 min, b/w)
d Mark Robson. *p* Val Lewton. *sc* Charles O'Neal, DeWitt Bodeen. *ph* Nicholas Musuraca. *ed* John Lockert. *ad* Albert S D'Agostino, Walter Keller. *m* Roy Webb. *cast* Tom Conway, Jean Brooks, Isabel Jewell, Kim Hunter, Evelyn Brent, Elizabeth Russell, Erford Gage, Ben Bard, Hugh Beaumont.

●What other movie opens with Satanism in Greenwich Village, twists into urban paranoia, and climaxes with a suicide? Val Lewton, Russian emigré workaholic, fantasist, was one of the mavericks of Forties' Hollywood, a man who produced (never directed) a group of intelligent and offbeat chillers for next-to-nothing at RKO. All bear his personal stamp: dime-store cinema transformed by 'literary' scripts, ingenious design, shadowy visuals, brooding melancholy, and a tight rein over the direction. *The Seventh Victim* is his masterpiece, a brooding melodrama built around a group of Satanists. The bizarre plot involves an orphan (Hunter) searching for her death-crazy sister (Brooks), but also carries a strong lesbian theme, and survives some uneven cameos; the whole thing is held together by a remarkably effective mix of menace and metaphysics – half *noir*, half Gothic. CA

Seventh Voyage of Sinbad, The

(1958, US, 87 min)
d Nathan Juran. *p* Charles Schneer. *sc* Kenneth Kolb. *ph* Wilkie Cooper. *ed* Edwin Bryant, Jerome Thoms. *ad* Gil Parrondo. *m* Bernard Herrmann. *cast* Kerwin Mathews, Kathryn Grant, Richard Eyer, Torin Thatcher, Alec Mango, Danny Green.

●Ray Harryhausen's first Dynamation effort in Arabian Nights territory. His knockout special effects include a cyclops, dragon, and duelling skeleton (forerunner of the battling skeletons sequence in *Jason and the Argonauts*), all expertly and realistically manipulated, employing techniques learned and developed from his mentor, the late, great Willis H *King Kong* O'Brien. Torin Thatcher's evil magician (a part he repeated for the less enthralling *Jack the Giant Killer*, also for Juran, three years later) more than compensates for Kerwin Mathews' rather wet Sinbad, while Bernard Herrmann's typically effective score tops off the whole adventure. PM

71 Fragments of a Chronology of Chance (71 Fragmente einer Chronologie des Zufalls)

(1994, Aus/Ger, 95 min)
d Michael Haneke. *p* Veit Heiduschka. *sc* Michael Haneke. *ph* Christian Berger. *ed* Mariae Homolkova. *cast* G Cosmin Urdes, Lukas Miko, Otto Grühandl, Anne Rennent.

●As cool, cerebral and painstaking as Haneke's earlier *Benny's Video*, this fragmented account of numerous events leading up to or loosely linked with a seemingly motiveless murder never really gets very far beyond images of alienation, anxiety and frustration, but thanks to its awareness of how time's very passing affects us, the film weaves a persuasively hypnotic spell. Oddly, the structure, which unexpectedly makes for considerable suspense, suggests not chance but destiny, while the final news collage is a corrosive statement on how even the most extraordinary events are packaged and trivialised by the media. GA

Seven-Ups, The

(1973, US, 103 min)
d/p Philip D'Antoni. *sc* Albert Ruben, Alexander Jacobs. *ph* Urs Furrer. *ed* Stephen A Rotter, John C Horger, Jerry Greenberg. *pd* Ed Wittstein. *m* Don Ellis. *cast* Roy Scheider, Victor Arnold, Jerry Leon, Ken Kercheval, Tony Lo Bianco, Larry Haines, Richard Lynch, Bill Hickman.

●D'Antoni, who produced *The French Connection*, here turned director and came up with a flawed mirror image of the earlier film. Led by Scheider in the Gene Hackman-type role, the Seven-Ups, a crack squad of New York detectives, pit their wits against a gang of heavies whose hit-man is played by the film's stunt coordinator, Bill Hickman. Most of the excitement is well handled, usually as a result of Hickman's amazing skill at setting up car chases and spectacular bits of action. But even the best sequences can't redeem an unremarkable and rather confused script, or D'Antoni's unimpressive handling of actors. DP

Seven Women

(1965, US, 87 min)
d John Ford. *p* Bernard Smith. *sc* John McCormick, Janet Green. *ph* Joseph LaShelle. *ed* Otho Lovering. *ad* George W Davis, Eddie Imazu. *m* Elmer Bernstein. *cast* Anne Bancroft, Margaret Leighton, Sue Lyon, Flora Robson, Mildred Dunnock, Betty Field, Anna Lee, Eddie Albert, Mike Mazurki, Woody Strode.

●Easy to disparage Ford's last feature, a bizarre transposition of a classic Western situation into war-torn China of the '30s, with a group of WASP women trapped at a mission besieged by brutal Mongols. The plot is almost formulaic, the fear of miscegenation outdated, a made-up Mazurki as the Mongol leader faintly ludicrous. But in many ways this does qualify as the director's mature masterpiece of his twilight years, partly because he is for once treating women as more than just (h)earth mothers, partly because his sympathies lie so completely with Bancroft, who manages to face a fate worse than death with admirable stoicism. The sense of menacing claustrophobia and sexual repression is beautifully conveyed by the studio setting; the shifting relationships between the women are handled with lucid economy; and the film is totally devoid of the sentimentality that mars so much of Ford's work. GA

Seven Women for Satan (Les Weekends Maléfiques du Comte Zaroff)

(1974, Fr, 80 min)
d Michel Lemoine. *ph* Philippe Theaudiere. *ed* Bob Wade. *m* Guy Bonnet. *cast* Michel Lemoine, Nathalie Zeiger, Joél Coeur, Martine Azencot, Howard Vernon.

●Essentially an offshoot from the fashion for sex and sadism that blanketed the nether reaches of the French cinema during the '70s, this spices its de Sadeian theme with tenuous horror connections (the excuse for the protagonist's strange sexual tastes being his descent from Count Zaroff). The trouble with the film is that Lemoine seems unwilling to relinquish either the bounds of bourgeois good taste or an undernourished, 'Vogue'-ish style of camera-work. The result, with sanitised sadism inserted among the blameless pleasures of the good life, is a dauntingly pretentious exercise. VG

Seven Year Itch, The

(1955, US, 105 min)
d Billy Wilder. *p* Charles K Feldman, Billy Wilder. *sc* Billy Wilder, George Axelrod. *ph* Milton Krasner. *ed* Hugh S Fowler. *ad* Lyle Wheeler, George W Davis. *m* Alfred Newman. *cast* Marilyn Monroe, Tom Ewell, Evelyn Keyes, Sonny Tufts, Victor Moore, Oscar Homolka, Carolyn Jones, Robert Strauss.

●Fondly remembered as the film in which Marilyn has problems with her skirt on a New York subway grating, this isn't quite the smasheroo that *Some Like It Hot* is: Monroe flaunts her attributes too blatantly, and seems less human because of it, while George Axelrod's play, fresh and risqué in the '50s, now appears a little obvious and over-plotted. Writer Tom Ewell's wife goes on a summer vacation, and the timid hubby becomes a flaming ball of sex, but – as with most Axelrod heroes (Roddy McDowall in *Lord Love a Duck*, Jack Lemmon in *How to Murder Your Wife*) – it's all in the mind. GB

Seven Years in Tibet

(1997, US/GB, 136 min)
d Jean-Jacques Annaud. *p* Jean-Jacques Annaud, John H Williams, Iain Smith, Catherine Moulin. *sc* Becky Johnston. *ph* Robert Fraisse, Allen Smith. *ed* Noëlle Boisson. *pd* At Hoang. *m* JohnWilliams. *cast* Brad Pitt, David Thewlis, BD Wong, Mako, Danny Denzongpa, Victor Wong, Ingeborga Dapkunaite, Lhakpa Tsamchoe.

●Ace mountaineer Heinrich Harrer (Pitt, inert) leaves wife, unborn child and Austria to take a crack at the unconquered Himalayan peak of Nanga Parbat. The expedition ends prematurely in India, however, when Harrer and the nominal leader, Peter Aufshnaiter (Thewlis), are interned at the start of WWII. Escape to Tibet brings the men closer to the nub of the drama as Harrer is unexpectedly taken on by the country's youthful figurehead to provide a potted education in Western culture. Though French director Annaud's camerawork persuades us that Tibet is a special place, the dramatic structure seems to imply that it's all a mere backdrop to one man's path from self-absorbed arrogance to enlightened humanity. (Harrer neglected to mention his Nazi associations in the memoir on which the film is based.) TJ

Severed Arm, The

(1973, US, 92 min)
d Thomas S Alderman. *p* Gary Adelman. *sc* Darrel Presnell, Thomas S Alderman. *ph* Robert Maxwell. *ed* Sonny Klein, Joe Ravetz. *cast* Deborah Walley, Paul Carr, David G Cannon, Vincent Martorano, Roy Dennis, Marvin Kaplan.

●Dismal hokum about a group of geologists who find themselves trapped in a cave by a rockfall. One of them has the bright idea of surviving by eating one anothers' limbs. Of course, no sooner have they amputated the first limb than they are rescued. Years later, the guy goes on the rampage… or does he? The trouble is that the film is directed with a total lack of conviction that has to be seen to be believed, and the script is riddled with lines indicative of desperation ('Gee, he has to show himself soon', or 'What do we do now?'). Someone has evidently added a professionally-shot final sequence in an attempt to save the day. They needn't have bothered. VG

Sevillanas

(1992, Sp, 55 min)
d Carlos Saura. *p* Juan Manuel Lebron. *sc* Carlos Saura. *ph* José Luis Alcaine. *ed* Pablo Del Amo. *ad* Rafael Palmero. *m* Manuel Sanlucar. *cast* Paco De Lucia, Manolo Sanlúcar, Rocio Jurado, Lola Flores.

●Yet another Saura excursion into flamenco (though this time without a story), this simply works its way through various dance and musical forms, using solos, duets and ensemble pieces performed in stark rooms, to paint a picture of a popular culture that appeals to all ages and types. It's all elegantly shot, of course, and there's a certain fascination in seeing OAP's strutting their stuff; but after a while, the accent on variety actually becomes tedious, so that one finally feels exhausted by the endless parade of dancers proudly tossing their heads, waving their arms, twisting their wrists, and flashing their eyes. GA

Sex and Lucía (Lucía y el sexo)

(2001, Sp/Fr, 128 min)
d Julio Medem. *p* Fernando Bovaira, Enrique López Lavigne. *sc* Julio Medem. *ph* Kiko de la Rica. *ed* Iván Aledo, El Igloo PC LS. *pc* Montse Sanz. *m* Alberto Iglesias. *cast* Paz Vega, Tristán Ulloa, Najwa Nimri, Daniel Freire, Javier Cámara, Elena Anaya, Silvia Llanos, Diana Suárez.

●Lorenzo (Ulloa) is blocked. His book editor suggests he write about a sexual tryst his friend has told him about, an anonymous one-night stand of some years previously. 'Put lots of sex in it,' the editor urges him. Their meeting is interrupted by a beautiful young woman, Lucía (Vega), who confesses she has been watching him for some time, since she fell in love with his first novel. Maybe if they spent some time together, he could grow to love her too? 'I think I just did,' he tells her. Sex and love are the dual starting points for the entwined plot strands of another Medem walk in the woods, though the movie itself begins later, fanning outwards and backwards, teasing with its secrets. Medem likes to disorient; his characters like to challenge each other too. Conversation is playful and exploratory: in a word, flirtatious. There's lots of sex here – exuberant, ecstatic, exhibitionist, giving way to a more damaging hedonism, a guilty quasi-incestuous betrayal which almost chokes the movie halfway through – yet this mysterious, surprising and ravishingly beautiful film rights itself triumphantly in an intoxicatingly romantic last act of redemption and resurrection. TCh

Sex and the Single Girl

(1964, US, 110 min)
d Richard Quine. *p* William T Orr. *sc* Joseph Heller, David R Schwartz. *ph* Charles Lang Jr. *ed* David Wages. *ad* Cary Odell. *m* Neal Hefti. *cast* Natalie Wood, Tony Curtis, Lauren Bacall, Henry Fonda, Mel Ferrer, Fran Jeffries, Leslie Parrish, Edward Everett Horton, Otto Kruger, Howard St John, Stubby Kaye.

● A coyly leering comedy, with Wood as Helen Gurley Brown (real-life author of a bestseller on marital relations), and Curtis as the smut-magazine writer out to demonstrate her lack of personal experience in sexual matters. But... oh, you guessed? That's right, they fall in love. Graceless stuff, criminally wasting Bacall and Fonda as a couple with marital problems (they're in love, but constantly quarrelling), and with Quine's moderate flair for comedy nowhere in evidence. TM

Sex and the Vampire

see Frisson des Vampires, Le

Sex Crime of the Century

see Last House on the Left, The

Sex Is...

(1992, US, 80 min)
d Marc Huestis. *p* Peter Gowdy, Cheryl Swannack. *ph* Fawn Yakker. *ed* Lara Mac, Hrabba Gunnarsdottir.

● Such candour! Years in the making, Huestis' documentary on hot sex in the time of HIV eclipses all those sensitive coming-out testimonies that were so important in the early years of Gay Lib. The opening dump on the noxious Jesse Helms sets the tone for an extremely raunchy collage of memories, life stories, object lessons and fantasies that gets to grips with the challenge of keeping desire alive and in focus. TR

sex, lies and videotape

(1989, US, 100 min)
d Steven Soderbergh. *p* Robert Newmyer, John Hardy. *sc* Steven Soderbergh. *ph* Walt Lloyd. *ed* Steven Soderbergh. *ad* Joanne Schmidt. *m* Cliff Martinez. *cast* James Spader, Andie MacDowell, Peter Gallagher, Laura San Giacomo, Ron Vawter, Steven Brill.

● Ann (MacDowell) is not happy: her husband John (Gallagher) is a lawyer who, unbeknownst to her, is having an affair with her virtually estranged sister (San Giacomo). The deception only comes to light with the arrival of John's old friend Graham (Spader), a shy, impotent eccentric who gets his kicks from watching interviews he has taped with women about their sexual experiences... Soderbergh's first feature is impressively mature, less concerned with actions *per se* than with the gulf between deed and motivation, between what we feel and what we say we feel. Despite the title, there is almost no explicit nudity or sexual activity; by avoiding sensationalism, Soderbergh leaves himself free to focus unblinkingly on moral and psychological complexities. No character is entirely without dishonesty or hang-ups; all initially shrink from taking full responsibility for their actions. The actors are superb; working from Soderbergh's funny, perceptive, immaculately wrought dialogue, they ensure that the film stimulates both intellectually and emotionally. GA

Sex Life in a Convent (Klosterschülerinnen)

(1971, WGer, 92 min)
d Eberhard Schroeder. *sc* Werner P Zibaso. *ph* Helmut W Mewes. *ed* Ingeborg Taschner. *cast* Doris Arden, Ulrich Beiger, Astrid Bohner, Felix Francky, Ellen Frank.

● A confused semi-documentary effort in which a Voice of America-style commentator tries to wring some titillation from the much-repeated fact that the daughters of the nasty rich are abandoned in convents through lack of parental concern, and hence exposed to unnatural temptations (by which the film seems to mean lesbianism and the odd jaunt into town for a quickie with a local lad). One great scene in which the whole dorm leaps into bed, each girl clutching her own candle – but such moments are few. VG

Sex Life in L.A.

(1998, Ger, 90 min)
d/ph Jochen Hick. *ed* Ingrid Molnar. *m* David Harrow. *with* Matt Bradshaw, Tony Ward, Cole Tucker, Kevin Kramer, Patrick Morgan, David Kendall, John Garwood, Rick Castro, Ron Athey.

● This talking head documentary throws a more sobering light than the work of Bruce LaBruce on the lives of the hustlers, porn stars, models and entertainers working off Santa Monica Bvd, Los Angeles. Besides interviewing film-maker Rick Castro, studs Tony Ward and Kevin Kramer, and extremist body artist Ron Athey, the director includes portraits of less celebrated locals, such as homeless, disillusioned Patrick, porn reject John and aspirant underwear model David. The interviewees are revealing rather than self-analytical, and none is particularly articulate, amusing or sparky – but maybe that's the point. WH

Sex Mission, The (Seksmisja)

(1984, Pol, 121 min)
d Juliusz Machulski. *sc* Juliusz Machulski, Jolanta Hartwig, Pavel Hajny. *ph* Jerzy Lukaszewicz. *ed* Miroslawa Garlicka. *ad* Janusz Sosnowski. *m* Henryk Kuzniak. *cast* Olgierd Lukaszewicz, Jerzy Stuhr, Bozena Stryjkwna, Boguslawa Pawelec, Beata Tyszkiewicz.

● Two men volunteer as guinea-pigs for an experiment in human hibernation, but instead of waking up in three years, they regain consciousness fifty years behind schedule in a totalitarian post-nuclear world populated entirely by women. Machulski's comic strip fantasy may be intended as a withering satire on any form of authoritarianism, but quite frankly it fails, partly due to a stance that may easily be interpreted as extremely misogynistic (all that these futuristic femmes need is a good hetero fuck, etc), partly because it simply isn't funny. GA

Sexo, pudor y lágrimas

see Sex, Shame and Tears

Sexorcist, The (L'Ossessa)

(1974, It, 87 min)
d Mario Gariazzo. *p* Riccardo Romano, Paulo Azzoni. *sc* Ambrogio Molteni. *ph* Carlo Carlini. *ed* Roberto Colangeli. *ad* Ovidio Taito. *m* Marcello Giombini. *cast* Stella Carnacina, Chris Avram, Lucretia Love, Luigi Pistilli, Gianrico Tondinelli, Umberto Raho, Ivan Rassimov.

● Blatant Italian rip-off which ages the possessed heroine of *The Exorcist* by a few years to get its sexploitation angle. What is intermittently interesting (but only just) is the director's preoccupation with the disintegration of the affluent Italian family, and with Ken Russell (he actually contrives to have the heroine transferred to a convent hospital to enable elaborate cross-cutting with the nuns during the exorcism scenes). But an excessively noisy soundtrack hardly compensates for the visual poverty of this quickie. RM

Sex Play (aka The Bunny Caper)

(1974, GB, 90 min)
d Jack Arnold. *sc* Peter J Oppenheimer, Jameson Brewer. *ph* Alan Hume. *ed* Don Deacon. *ad* Bill Alexander. *m* John Cameron. *cast* Christina Hart, Ed Bishop, Murray Kash, Eric Young, Steve Plytas, David Beale.

● Yes, Jack Arnold – the incredible shrinking sci-fi film director, who since the early '60s has been providing various varieties of pap, mainly for TV. As sex movies go, this is particularly well crafted, and at one or two points even manages to be (intentionally) funny. The heroine is the daughter of a bigwig American who comes to London and causes havoc among visiting diplomats (including a crude caricature of Henry Kissinger). But it's not really interesting – Arnold fans would be better off dreaming of creatures from the black lagoon and incredible shrinking men. GB

Sex, Shame and Tears (Sexo, pudor y lágrimas)

(1999, Mex, 109 min)
d Antonio Serrano. *p* Matthias Ehrenberg. *sc* Antonio Serrano. *ph* Xavier Pérez Grobót. *ed* Samuel Larson. *pd* Brigitte Broch. *m* Aleks Syntek. *cast* Demián Bichir, Susana Zabaleta, Mónica Dionne, Jorge Salinas, Cecilia Suárez, Victor Huggo Martin, Angélica Aragón.

● While the title's similarity to Soderbergh's hit suggests a certain derivative unoriginality (and the film does concern problems in modern marital relationships), Serrano's coarse, overly schematic farce has none of the dramatic or psychological subtlety of the American film. Rather, the loud wackiness, the insistent modishness, the pseudo-sophisticated take on sexual mores and the heavy-handed stereotypes (cynical advertising photographer, neurotic, impotent would-be writer, feisty wives) suggest a forlorn, chaotic attempt to replicate Almodóvar. The sexual politics are dubious, the world on view movie-inspired rather than realistic, the whole tiresome in the extreme. GA

Sex Shop

(1972, Fr/It/WGer, 105 min)
d Claude Berri. *sc* Claude Berri. *ph* Pierre Lhomme. *ed* Sophie Coussein. *ad* Jacques Dugied. *m* Serge Gainsbourg. *cast* Juliet Berto, Claude Berri, Nathalie Delon, Jean-Pierre Marielle, Francesca Romana, Catherine Allégret, Batrice Romand, Claude Piéplu, Grégoire Aslan.

● To call this an adult comedy would be generous, it's really no more than smug titillation. Happily-married bookshop owner (Berri) can't make ends meet, so opens sex shop instead; makes ends meet, but isn't happy; returns to his loving wife (Berto), having learned the error of his ways and after failing to make Nathalie Delon. Conventional happy ending: all else wilts in the face of *L'Amour Vrai*. The husband's errant ways provide an excuse for the usual round of female torsos, plus the odd snatch of pubic hair as a concession to these liberal times, but it's all pretty synthetic. Limp voyeurism that provides a few laughs along the way, but not enough to justify anything. CPe

Sex Symbol, The

(1974, US, 110 min)
d David Lowell Rich. *p* Douglas S Cramer. *sc* Alvah Bessie. *ph* JJ Jones. *ed* Byron 'Buzz' Brandt. *ad* Ross Bellah. *m* Jeff Williams. *cast* Connie Stevens, Shelley Winters, Jack Carter, William Castle, Don Murray, James Olson, Nehemiah Persoff, Madlyn Rhue.

● The biopic at its most seedy and vulgarly full-blown, scripted by 'Hollywood Ten' blacklist victim Alvah Bessie from his own novel *The Symbol*. Dripping with clichés, it's based, perhaps too closely for some, on the life of Marilyn Monroe. Connie Stevens acts as far as the title and the camera's preoccupation with her cleavage will allow, displaying at least a talent for tantrums. The film's value, if any under the leering censoriousness and tatty analysis, lies in its stripping of illusions to reveal the pathetic vulnerabilities underneath. A callous, if unintentional, exposé of a myth, and another instance of Hollywood's insensitivity towards itself. This version, prepared for cinema release, is half-an-hour longer than the original shown on American TV under threat of libel action.

Sex – The Annabel Chong Story

(1998, US, 89 min)
d Gough Lewis. *p* Hugh F Curry, David Whitten, Gough Lewis. *ph* Jim Michaels, Kelly Morris, Gough Lewis, Tony Morrone. *ed* Kelly Morris. *m* Peter Mundinger. *with* Grace Quek [Annabel Chong], John Bowen, Ed Powers, Dr Walter Williams, Charles Conn, Dick James, Monica Moran, Ron Jeremy, Jack Hammer.

● Charlatan, victim or post-modern sex goddess? The three faces of student turned gangbang queen Annabel Chong (aka Grace Quek) dreamily overlap in this disquieting documentary. Grace herself seems keen to look on the bright side and is all the more irritating for it. But as we trawl through the various dishevelled porn producers surrounding her, something shifts. She's clearly detested by her colleagues, and the fans are just as scary – one shows us a photo of her dressed all in white: 'She looks so innocent,' he pants, 'I really like that one.' As the film delves deeper, following Grace to her parents' home in Singapore and then to the scene of a gang rape in London, things become even more distressing – and chronologically disjointed. It's almost as though the past is trying to head off the present; the seemingly endless 251-man gangbang Grace endures with the most terrifying of smiles. And for what? A year later, her record gets broken by Jasmin St Claire (Grace there to watch, gimlet-eyed). Snatches of conversation, meanwhile, alert us to the health risks. It's not pity that makes us love Grace. She's a willing freak, buttressed between notoriety and failure; but her indifference to the mainstream commands respect. CO'Su

Sexual Life of the Belgians 1950–1978, The (La Vie Sexuelle des Belges 1950–1978)

(1995, Bel, 80 min)
d/p Jan Bucquoy. *sc* Jan Bucquoy, Valérie Weyer. *ph* Michael Baudour. *ed* Matyas Veress. *pd* Nathalie André, Nicole Lenoir. *m* Francis de Smet. *cast* Jean-Henri Compère, Sophie Schneider, Noé Franq, Isabelle Legros, Pascale Binneri, Michele Shor.

● Belgian writer/director Jan Bucquoy can hardly be accused of vanity in his choice for the central role in this autobiographical portrait of the artist as a young slob. Hair by Mazola, complexion by Blue Circle, Compère only puts away one bag of chips and mayo during the course of the film, but looks as though he subsists on nothing else. The first thing we see in his mouth, however, is his mother's breast; and it's her money-saving motto ('Life is so expensive') that dominates the first half of the film and, like her equally stingy affection for her son, rings throughout his subsequent progress. From awkward, greasy small-town boy to awkward, greasy big-city nearman: such is the making of this would-be revolutionary, aspirant novelist and ever-hopeful lover, the anti-Gump with whom we spend the rest of the picture. Episodic and conversational, this is no lurid exposé of salacious goings-on in the realm of beer and mussels; instead, it's a shambling, rather disarming survey of the amorous mishaps and potentially numbing provincialism that make post-'68 model Jan ready to change the world, and downright desperate to get his leg over in the interim. Not that the point is pushed home too hard in a film that ambles along through a welter of endearing emphemera (from tacky caravan parks and errant homing pigeons, to jibes at Godard's 'political' period and a striking tribute to *Johnny Guitar*), plays sleight-of-hand with fantasy and reality, and half by accident, half by design, ends up matching its abundant slow-burn humour with an unexpected degree of genuine poignancy. TJ

Sexy Beast

(2000, GB/Sp/US, 88 min)
d Jonathan Glazer. *p* Jeremy Thomas. *sc* Louis Mellis, David Scinto. *ph* Ivan Biurd. *ed* John Scott, Sam Sneade. *pd* Jan Houllevigue. *m* Roque Baños. *cast* Ray Winstone, Ben Kingsley, Ian McShane, Amanda Redman, Cavan Kendall, Julianne White, Alvaro Monje, James Fox.

● From the off it's clear at once that Jonathan Glazer will be a ballsy, switched-on film-maker: Winstone's belly burns in the Spanish sun, an ice-cold flannel slyly folded over his privates – and then an a boulder bumps down the hill and bounces over the oblivious ex-villain's head to splashland in the swimming pool. The verve isn't so surprising, but Glazer goes on to prove that he's got much more than flash in his arsenal. A macabre comedy played out in deadly earnest, this has dramatic heft and tension. Kingsley's bald and beady-eyed Don Logan is so tightly wrapped in his neuroses, he's an alien in any social context, a monster in a man's skin. Easy to believe Winstone's scared to death of this maggot. The first two thirds of this superbly acted film is dynamite, even as nothing happens, really. Gal (Winstone) and wife Deedee (Redman) play reluctant hosts to Don, who's intent on bringing Gal back to London for a big score. Gal refuses. Don insists. The tension racks up until something has to give, but you'll be hard pressed to guess how and where the break will come. TCh

S.F.W.

(1994, US, 96 min)
d Jefery Levy. *p* Dale Pollock. *sc* Danny Rubin, Jefery Levy. *ph* Peter Deming. *ed* Lauren Zuckerman. *pd* Eve Cauley. *m* Graeme Revell. *cast* Stephen Dorff, Reese Witherspoon, Jake Busey, Joey Lauren Adams, Pamela Gidley, David Barry Gray, Jack Noseworthy.

● An aggressive satire on consumerism, violence and the media, this mind-numbingly profane film apes the shrill, in-your-face teenage disaffection which makes its protagonist, Cliff Spab (Dorff), a TV phenomenon and a colossal bore. Spab is one of the customers held hostage for weeks at a supermarket by what appears to be an armed group of radical documentary film-makers, who insist their acuality footage is broadcast to the nation – and that's just the first five minutes. Very alienating. TCh

Sgt Bilko

(1996, US, 94 min)
d Jonathan Lynn. *p* Brian Grazer. *sc* Andy Breckman. *ph* Peter Sova. *ed* Tony Lombardo. *pd* Lawrence G Paull. *m* Alan Silvestri. *cast* Steve Martin, Dan Aykroyd, Glenne Headly, Phil Hartman, Daryl Mitchell, Max Casella, Eric Edwards, Austin Pendleton, Catherine Silvers.

● For anyone who loves the classic '50s TV army base sit-com, the notion of doing Bilko without Phil Silvers suggests a travesty. Bilko was the ultimate finagler, but Martin hasn't the required calculation, though he's proved capable of inspired lunacy in the past, and has an ironic cool that might have seen him through. Director Lynn did a good job with *My Cousin Vinny* (not forgetting his *Yes, Minister* days) and Silvers' daughter Catherine pops up in the supporting cast, along with Aykroyd (Col Hall) and Headly (Bilko's girl). You might be forgiven for hoping against hope that these people couldt produce the goods just this once. You'd be wrong. This is a travesty all right, but a travesty with perhaps four laughs, tops. There's a good sight gag involving a horse early on, and one chuckles indulgently when Martin updates one of Bilko's classic routines (mistaking the Colonel's wife for Sharon Stone), but it's apparent within minutes not only that this isn't going to work, but that no one much cares. This is shoddy hackwork, replaying classic scenarios (the honest new recruit, audits by Pentagon bigwigs and manoeuvres in Nevada) with such disregard for narrative structure the reels might be in the wrong order. TCh

Sgt. Pepper's Lonely Hearts Club Band

(1978, US/WGer, 111 min)
d Michael Schultz. *p* Robert Stigwood. *sc* Henry Edwards. *ph* Owen Roizman. *ed* Christopher Holmes. *pd* Brian Eatwell. *m* John Lennon, Paul McCartney. *cast* Peter Frampton, The Bee Gees, Frankie Howerd, Paul Nicholas, Donald Pleasence, Sandy Farina, Steve Martin, Aerosmith, Alice Cooper, George Burns.

● The Stigwood Organisation did the '70s (*Saturday Night Fever*), the '50s (*Grease*), and here tackle a prolonged dramatisation of the Beatles' lyrics and images. The songs themselves were so archly attuned to the highs and lows of the '60s that any sustained literal approximation (Strawberry Fields as the girl-next-door?) is risky. This crass moral pantomime is plain embarrassing. The story, an allegory of big business versus simple music and love is centred around 'Heartland', home town of the Lonely Hearts Club Band, which depressingly combines the ethics and appearances of Toytown and Peyton Place, picked out in nursery colours. The Bee Gees (who do all the numbers impeccably) and little Peter Frampton fight off evil, which materialises as punks, litter, and a sadly unfunny Frankie Howerd. But somehow Bee Gees Against Capitalism doesn't quite ring true. It's almost 'guaranteed to raise a smile'. JS

Shackleton's Antarctic Adventure

(2001, US, 40 min, b/w & col)
d George Butler. *p* George Butler, Susanne Simpson, Scott Swofford. *sc* Mose Richards, Crystal V Spijer. *ph* Reed Smoot, (addit ph) David Douglas. *ed* Stephen L Johnson. *pd* Roger Crandall. *m* Sam Cardon. *with* Conrad Anker, Reinhold Messner, Stephen Venables. *narrator* Kevin Spacey.

● The extraordinary story of Ernest Shackleton's doomed expedition to the Antarctic in 1914 really doesn't need the grandiose verbosity of Kevin Spacey's voice-over narration, nor the bland, schools programming-style dramatic reconstruction it gets here. Imagine what James Cameron, say, could do with this material, but a straight documentary would also be fascinating. This mediocre halfway house benefits more from the archive photography and film shot at the time (familiar from the film *South*) than from the IMAX format. TCh

Shadey

(1985, GB, 106 min)
d Philip Saville. *p* Otto Plaschkes. *sc* Snoo Wilson. *ph* Roger Deakins. *ed* Chris Kelly. *pd* Norman Garwood. *m* Colin Towns. *cast* Antony Sher, Billie Whitelaw, Patrick Macnee, Katherine Helmond, Leslie Ash, Bernard Hepton.

● Preposterous piffle in which hopelessly miscast stage actor Sher makes a ludicrous plot worse by parading a veritable text-book of camp and wildly inappropriate theatrical gestures as the eponymous hero, a bankrupt garage owner who tries to cash in on his precognitive powers in order to raise funds for a sex-change operation. Desperate for cash, Shadey approaches an eminent businessman (Macnee), who sells him to a military research establishment, where his pacifist leanings conflict with their hawkish aspirations. Thrown in for bad measure is a voyeuristic subplot concerning Macnee's incestuous desire for his daughter (Ash). The only enjoyable moment is when Macnee's mad wife (Helmond) stabs Shadey in the balls with a fork, his exquisite agony matched by our gratifying sense of revenge. NF

Shadow, The

(1994, US, 107 min)
d Russell Mulcahy. *p* Martin Bregman, Willi Baer, Michael S Bregman. *sc* David Koepp. *ph* Stephen H Burum. *ed* Peter Honess. *pd* Joseph C Nemec III. *m* Jerry Goldsmith. *cast* Alec Baldwin, John Lone, Ian McKellen, Penelope Ann Miller, Peter Boyle, Tim Curry, Jonathan Winters, André Gregory.

● Can the original haunted superhero of the '30s and '40s connect with a modern audience? Probably not. Despite classy production values, Mulcahy's attempt to emulate the sombre appeal of Tim Burton's *Batman* movies is too episodic, sketchy and uneven. Hiding his true identity beneath a cloak of invisibility, the Shadow (Baldwin) is a self-appointed crime fighter haunted by a murky past as a drug-dealer in the East. Now redeemed, he uses his supernatural powers to thwart the plans of Oriental villain Shiwan Khan (Lone), who through mind-control has forced Professor Lane (McKellen) to create a pseudo-atomic bomb. The Shadow's suave alter ego, playboy Lamont Cranston, finds time to romance Lane's daughter Margot (Miller). Baldwin's low-key performance lacks charisma, Lone alternates between lip-smacking villainy and camp humour, and Miller is chiefly a clothes-horse for a series of slinky '30s frocks. NF

Shadow Conspiracy

(1996, US, 103 min)
d George P Cosmatos. *p* Terry Collis. *sc* Adi Hasak, Ric Gibbs. *ph* Buzz Feitshans IV. *ed* Robert A Ferretti. *pd* Joe Alves. *m* Bruce Broughton. *cast* Charlie Sheen, Donald Sutherland, Linda Hamilton, Stephen Lang, Ben Gazzara, Nicholas Turturro, Theodore Bikel, Sam Waterston, Gore Vidal.

● An action movie for the wannabe liberal '90s, this tracks the political awakening of slick but decent presidential aide Bobby Bishop (Sheen). Right-wing traitors are at work in the White House – when Bobby starts to investigate, all hell breaks loose. His only allies are an ex-girlfriend (Hamilton) and the paternal Chief of Staff (Sutherland), but can they be trusted? Shadows are a bit of a theme here, and Washington, DC, provides plenty. Unfortunately, the movie has no such murky depths. Instead of an atmosphere of corruption, we have repeated shots of a cinema showing *Touch of Evil*. Similarly, there's no deep dialogue, just lots of deep faces: Sutherland, with his bulging, psychotically innocent eyes; Hamilton, with her rawhide skin and generous, manly mouth. Meatiest of all is Vidal, who pops up as a Southern politician. Sadly, Sheen doesn't even look profound. Like a zombie who's spent too much time in the gym, he blunders heavily from one stunt to the next, his pursed lips conveying nothing more than pique. CO'Su

Shadowlands

(1993, GB, 131 min)
d Richard Attenborough. *p* Richard Attenborough, Brian Eastman. *sc* William Nicholson. *ph* Roger Pratt. *ed* Lesley Walker. *pd*

Stuart Craig. *m* George Fenton. *cast* Anthony Hopkins, Debra Winger, Joseph Mazzello, Peter Firth, John Wood, Michael Denison.

● 1952. Theologian and essayist, CS 'Jack' Lewis (Hopkins) conducts a life of faintly mildewed bachelorhood at Magdalen College, Oxford. If there's any hint of desperation in his quietude, it's not to be found in his philosophical discourse, but in his children's books about Narnia, the magical land that lies behind the wardrobe. These strange and wonderful tales bring American poet Joy Gresham (Winger) and her son Douglas (Mazzello) into Lewis's small circle, an unlikely meeting which is to affect them all. Biting down on his pipe, his shirt collar permanently askew, Hopkins assays another concerted study in English repression – a condition unexpectedly relieved by Winger's brash intelligence and brittle wit. Attenborough does a good job with the musty hallowed halls and condescending donnish banter without letting the mise-en-scène clog up the works. Taken from the play by William Nicholson, this is the director's least sanctimonious, least verbose picture. It's just a shame that, given the emphasis on the primacy of emotional experience, it feels like such a self-contained, studious exercise. TCh

Shadow Makers

see Fat Man and Little Boy

Shadowman

see Street of Shadows

Shadowman

see Nuits Rouges

Shadow of a Doubt

(1943, US, 108 min, b/w)
d Alfred Hitchcock. *p* Jack H Skirball. *sc* Thornton Wilder, Sally Benson, Alma Reville. *ph* Joseph Valentine. *ed* Milton Carruth. *ad* John Goodman. *m* Dimitri Tiomkin. *cast* Joseph Cotten, Teresa Wright, Macdonald Carey, Patricia Collinge, Henry Travers, Hume Cronyn, Wallace Ford.

● One of Hitchcock's finest films of the '40s, with Cotten as the infamous 'Merry Widow' murderer, who takes refuge with the small-town family of his sister (Collinge). Focusing on adoring niece Wright's dawning realisation that her kind, generous and handsome uncle is in fact a cold and cynical killer, the film is not only psychologically intriguing (both niece and uncle are called Charlie, and he arrives in town as if in answer to her prayers for excitement), but a sharp dissection of middle American life, in its own quiet way an ancestor of *Blue Velvet.* Is Uncle Charlie all these gentle folk deserve, when adolescent girls dream of the romantic life, and middle-aged men (papa Travers and neighbour Cronyn) endlessly discuss gruesome murder? Funny, gripping, and expertly shot by Joe Valentine, it's a small but memorable gem. GA

Shadow of Doubt, A

see Ombre du Doute, L'

Shadow of the Hawk

(1976, Can, 92 min)
d George McCowan. *p* John Kemeny. *sc* Norman Thaddeus Vane, Herbert J Wright. *ph* John Holbrook, Reginald Morris. *ed* O Nicholas Brown. *ad* Keith Pepper. *m* Robert McMullin. *cast* Jan-Michael Vincent, Marilyn Hassett, Chief Dan George, Pia Shandel, Marianne Jones, Jacques Hubert.

● A tired, TV-style chase movie, which has 200-year-old evil spirits hounding a young man of Red Indian descent over 300 miles of assault course: snakes, bears, evil winds and the like. The only points of interest are Chief Dan George as the hero's medicine-man grandfather, and McCowan, whose previous directorial credits include the excellent natural pest/exploitation movie, *Frogs.* RG

Shadow of the Vampire

(2000, GB/US, 93 min)
d E Elias Merhige. *p* Nicolas Cage, Jeff Levine. *sc* Steven Katz. *ph* Lou Bogue. *ed* Chris Wyatt. *ad* Chris Bradley. *cast* John Malkovich, Willem Dafoe, Cary Elwes, John Aden Gillet, Eddie Izzard, Udo Kier, Catherine McCormack, Ronan Vibert.

● Intriguing, eccentric, sporadically entertaining tosh (but tosh all the same), this fictionalised account of the shooting of Murnau's *Nosferatu* rests heavily on the engagingly loopy but finally limiting conceit that the director's mysterious star, Max Schreck, was indeed a vampire, and had to be fed and flattered accordingly. Malkovich, typically, enters into the crazed spirit of the piece with a vengeance, Dafoe is witty and affecting as Schreck, and there are, intentionally or otherwise, some very funny moments. But the whole is far too uneven and unfocused to make proper sense (the use of 'clips' is mind-bogglingly misjudged), whether as comedy, suspense or serious study of the ontological intersection between reality, myth and movie-making. Indeed, the opening credits, interminably padded out and featuring slow zooms into bizarre pictures that have nothing to do with the rest of the film, hint at the scattershot nonsense to follow. GA

Shadows

(1959, US, 87 min)
d John Cassavetes. *p* Maurice McEndree. *ph* Erich Kollmar. *ed* Len Appelson, Maurice McEndree. *m* Charles Mingus. *cast* Lelia Goldoni, Ben Carruthers, Hugh Hurd, Anthony Ray, Rupert Crosse.

● Admirers of *Mean Streets* may have wondered how Scorsese came by his dizzy vision of nervy New York neurotics: Cassavetes' first film may well have been a strong influence. As in the later film, what matters is less the story – two brothers and a sister working out various tensions between themselves and other friends and lovers – than the electric atmosphere and edgy performances. The trio trudge through their seedy city lives (smoky nightclubs, pretentious parties, disastrous sexual encounters, brawls, and beery beatnik conversations) suffering from heady hypertension, although what is now so surprising about this milestone of improvisational cinema is that it is often very funny. The jumpy editing, free-focus camerawork, and naturalistic dialogue (made the same year as Godard's *Breathless,* it centres around many of the same impulses towards a new form of film-making) may no longer shock, but back in '59 must have been a revelation. With a blue and moody Mingus soundtrack and steel-grey photography, it's still a delight. GA

Shadows and Fog

(1991, US, 86 min)
d Woody Allen. *p* Robert Greenhut. *sc* Woody Allen. *ph* Carlo Di Palma. *ed* Susan E Morse. *pd* Santo Loquasto. *m* Kurt Weill. *cast* Woody Allen, Kathy Bates, John Cusack, Mia Farrow, Jodie Foster, Fred Gwynne, Julie Kavner, Madonna, John Malkovich, Kenneth Mars, Kate Nelligan, Donald Pleasence, Lily Tomlin, Philip Bosco, Wallace Shawn, Josef Sommer, David Ogden Stiers.

● An inconclusive charade for celebrity guests, Allen's film – made before *Husbands and Wives* – will add to the general sifting through the *oeuvre* for relevances to his personal predicament, without registering as a work on its own. This is Woody as Bergman, Woody as Punchinello, both over-familiar. He plays Kleinman, a *nebbich,* hopelessly besotted with a sword-swallower from the circus (Farrow). She has run away from her husband (Malkovich), an egotistical womanising clown who is cheating with the trapeze artiste (Madonna). There's a desultory subplot about The Ripper, but most of the action features Woody and Mia wandering nighttown, he witteringly supportive, she kvetching. The shadows of German Expressionist cinema have been superbly revived, but to little purpose. BC

Shadows in the Night

(1944, US, 67 min, b/w)
d Eugene Forde. *p* Rudolph C Flothow. *sc* Eric Taylor. *ph* James S Brown Jr. *ed* Dwight Caldwell. *ad* John Datu Arensma. *cast* Warner Baxter, Nina Foch, George Zucco, Minor Watson, Edward Norris, Charles Halton.

● The third in the *Crime Doctor* series of whodunits (ten films, 1943-49), by which time the character's peculiarly unconvincing history had been safely got out of the way (a criminal suffering from amnesia, he studied psychiatry and turned to doctoring crime). Fairly tacky stuff, with Foch being driven mad in rehearsal for *My Name Is Julia Ross.* But the Gothic elements, headed by Zucco as a suavely sinister uncle and a ghostly apparition dripping wet from the sea, are done with great relish, and even some flair until the wrap-up explanations come. TM

Shadows of Our Forgotten Ancestors (Teni Zabytykh Predkov)

(1964, USSR, 95 min, b/w & col)
d Sergo Paradjanov. *sc* Ivan Chendey, Sergo Paradjanov. *ph* Viktor Ilienko. *ed* M Ponomarenko. *ad* I Lakovsky, B Yakutovic. *m* Y Shorik. *cast* Ivan Nikolaichuk, Larissa Kadochnikova, Tatiana Bestaeva, Spartak Bagashvili.

● Paradjanov was considered a safe director of Ukrainian 'quota' features until he seized a unique moment of freedom to make this Carpathian rhapsody, which spoke loud his own closet dissidence and ushered in a flood of non-conformist movies from the other regional Soviets, including Tarkovsky's *Andrei Rublev* and Abuladze's *The Wishing Tree.* The 'forgotten ancestors' are mid-19th century villagers, who frolic naked in their youth and grow up into adulterers, lovelorn misfits, and feuding murderers. Their 'shadows' are not exactly sombre either: Paradjanov stops at nothing in his quest for startling images. The athletic camerawork and the bizarre visual effects take their tone from the folk ballads that recur on the soundtrack, sometimes touching an authentically barbaric or tragic poetry. The film is as chaotic as *The Colour of Pomegranates* is formalised, but it confirms that Paradjanov was 'dangerous' because he was committed to artifice – and imagination. TR

Shaft

(1971, US, 100 min)
d Gordon Parks. *p* Joel Freeman. *sc* Ernest Tidyman, John DF Black. *ph* Urs Furrer. *ed* Hugh A Robertson. *ad* Emanuel Gerard. *m* Isaac Hayes. *cast* Richard Roundtree, Moses Gunn, Charles Cioffi, Christopher St John, Gwenn Mitchell, Lawrence Pressman, Victor Arnold.

● Renowned for its Isaac Hayes score, and as the first mainstream, commercially successful film about a black private eye, Parks' film is a hip, cool, entertaining thriller that in fact never really says very much at all about the Black experience in America; rather, it merely takes the traditional crime-fighting hero, paints him black, and sets him down in a world populated by more blacks than Hollywood movies were used to. Roundtree turns in a strong performance, investigating a racketeer's criminal activities, while at the same time trying to find the man's kidnapped daughter. GA

Shaft

(2000, US/Ger, 99 min)
d John Singleton. *p* Scott Rudin, John Singleton. *sc* Richard Price, John Singleton, Shane Salerno. *ph* Donald E Thorin. *ed* John Bloom, Antonia Van Drimmelen. *pd* Patrizia von Brandenstein. *m* David Arnold, Isaac Hayes. *cast* Samuel L Jackson, Vanessa Williams, Jeffrey Wright, Christian Bale, Busta Rhymes, Dan Hedaya, Toni Collette, Richard Roundtree, Ruben Santiago-Hudson, Josef Sommer, Lynne Thigpen, Philip Bosco, Pat Hingle.

● A credit sequence commingles succulent skin and glistening weaponry, set to a beefed up version of Isaac Hayes' theme tune, but this turns out to be the cinematic equivalent of sticking a gherkin down your pants. Shaft's a new man – John Shaft Mk II, nephew of the original private eye, and working within, if not for, the system as a representative of the NYPD. As embodied by Jackson, he's slick and street savvy, but a little ground down. Some geriatric honky judge has let loose his recent catch, racist yuppie brat Walter Wade Jr (Bale), charged with a wanton race murder. When the villain returns from a two-year bail-hop to cock a snook, Shaft throws in his badge and races Walter to find waitress Collette, the sole witness to the killing. With this humdrum plot, there's plenty of scope for Wright to try hijacking the proceedings with a near unintelligible turn as a Latino drug dealer; also for a bunch of shoot-outs, car chases and other surprises. In short, anonymous and business-like. NB

Shaft in Africa

(1973, US, 112 min)
d John Guillermin. *p* Roger Lewis. *sc* Stirling Silliphant. *ph* Marcel Grignon. *ed* Max Benedict. *pd* John Stoll. *m* Johnny Pate. *cast* Richard Roundtree, Frank Finlay, Vonetta McGee, Neda Arneric, Debebe Eshetu, Spiros Focas, Glynn Edwards, Cy Grant.

●Third of the *Shaft* films (followed by a TV series), this one spreading itself pretty thinly over three continents, with Shaft versus slave-trader Frank Finlay. The uptown private eye of the first film makes it into the big league caper and goes international, probably at the demand of the producers. The wisecracks are still dutifully tripped out, and Shaft himself is obliged to fill the gaps between the action by furnishing the myth of black potency. It's surprising that Roundtree, like Connery in the Bond films (and the similarities between the two series don't end there, in spite of Shaft's protests that he's no James Bond), manages to conduct himself with some dignity through all the surrounding debris. CPe

Shaft's Big Score!

(1972, US, 105 min)
d Gordon Parks. *p* Roger Lewis, Ernest Tidyman. *sc* Ernest Tidyman. *ph* Urs Furrer. *ed* Harry Howard. *ad* Emanuel Gerard. *m* Gordon Parks. *cast* Richard Roundtree, Moses Gunn, Drew Bundini Brown, Joseph Mascolo, Kathy Imrie, Wally Taylor, Julius W Harris, Joe Santos.

●Disappointing sequel to the likeable *Shaft*, with Roundtree's black private eye – here up against rival takeover bidders for an illegal numbers racket – now operating from a lavish love nest instead of his fly-blown office. The film, in other words, has developed an 007 complex, and instead of being Chandler in Harlem, threading its way through a maze of quirky characters and dark mysteries, it makes a dreary beeline for its prolonged climax: a duel between superman Shaft and a hovering helicopter. TM

Shag

(1987, US, 98 min)
d Zelda Barron. *p* Stephen Woolley, Julia Chasman. *sc* Robin Swicord, Lanier Laney, Terry Sweeney. *ph* Peter MacDonald. *ed* Laurence Méry-Clark. *pd* Buddy Cone. *cast* Phoebe Cates, Scott Coffey, Bridget Fonda, Annabeth Gish, Page Hannah, Robert Rusler, Tyrone Power Jr, Shirley Anne Field.

●Lest you snigger, the title refers to a dance indigenous to South Carolina. Set in 1963, this teen movie with a well-connected cast has Gish (no relation), Fonda (daughter of Peter), Hannah (sister of Daryl) and Cates set off on a pre-college romp to Myrtle Beach, 'where the boys are'. Their aim is to dissuade the morally self-righteous Cates from marrying deadly dull Tyrone Power Jr; she resists, but soon hunky Buzz (Rusler), an advocate of free love, is tapping her primal instincts. Meanwhile, the other three pursue their aim of 'getting engaged by 20'. Kenny Ortega (*Dirty Dancing, Salsa*) choreographs, but has little to do; the dance sets are minimalised, and too often shot inappropriately at shoulder height. The adolescent antics may be familiar, but Barron directs with affection both for her characters and for back-combing and boned underskirts; her young professionals turn in appropriately corny performances; and the soundtrack is a corker. EP

Shaggy D.A., The

(1976, US, 92 min)
d Robert Stevenson. *p* Bill Anderson. *sc* Don Tait. *ph* Frank Phillips. *ed* Bob Bring, Norman Palmer. *ad* John B Mansbridge, Perry Ferguson. *m* Buddy Baker. *cast* Dean Jones, Tim Conway, Suzanne Pleshette, Jo Anne Worley, Vic Tayback, Dick Bakalyan, Keenan Wynn, Dick Van Patten, Warren Berlinger, Hans Conreid.

●Some of Stevenson's Disney entertainments have been very polished and respectable, but not this mess. The sieve-like script tries to mix together Dean Jones' would-be district attorney turning into a lolloping dog (not once but repeatedly), some satire of electioneering and crooked politics, a slap-up pie fight, jokes about Dean Martin and Sarah Bernhardt, satire of ladies' clubs and other small-town Americana, police cars skidding on ice-cream fillings, dogs who talk with Bogart and Cagney voices. Nothing jells at all – least of all the central conceit of the hero becoming shaggy (sometimes the dog's a dog, sometimes a man with fur). It's also not much fun seeing Jones, Pleshette and Wynn getting older and older, staler and staler, playing the parts they've been stuck with for years. GB

Shakedown (aka Blue Jean Cop)

(1988, US, 96 min)
d James Glickenhaus. *p* J Boyce Harman Jr. *sc* James Glickenhaus. *ph* John Lindley. *ed* Paul Fried. *pd* Charles Bennett. *m* Jonathan Elias. *cast* Peter Weller, Sam Elliott, Patricia Charbonneau, Antonio Fargas, Blanche Baker, Richard Brooks, Jude Ciccolella.

●'Hey, Boesky, you wanna condom?' No, but the heavy black mutha sharing his cage does; such is the humour going down in NY penitentiaries, according to the man who brought you *The Exterminator*. Glickenhaus' state-of-the-art thriller on cracked-up, seamy New York stars the familiar unlikely duo as a legal attorney (Weller) and a renegade detective (Elliott) attempt to solve a fatal shooting between a drugs dealer and a corrupt cop. No celluloid cliché that could possibly fit into *Escape from New York* or *Dirty Harry* is left unstitched. Plenty of blood, tension, and complex stunt sequences leave precious little time to ruminate on the popcorn. This heady mix of sleaze and comic book heroes smacks of big box office bucks and a long life on the video shelf. There ain't many better accolades than that. JCh

Shaker Run

(1985, NZ, 90 min)
d Bruce Morrison. *p* Larry Parr, Igo Kantor. *sc* Jim Kouf, Henry Fownes, Bruce Morrison. *ph* Kevin Hayward. *ed* Ken Zemke, Bob Richardson. *pd* Ron Highfield. *m* Stephen McCurdy. *cast* Cliff Robertson, Leif Garrett, Lisa Harrow, Shane Briant, Peter Hayden, Peter Rowell.

●Ex-racing ace Robertson and his mechanic sidekick (Garrett), a couple of down-on-their-luck Yanks touring New Zealand with a stunt team, are enlisted by a concerned scientist (Harrow) to race a deadly virus to a remote rendezvous, safe from unscrupulous clutches. Director Morrison straps a camera to their souped-up Trans Am, hurtling along the highways of South Island, pursued by a grisly assortment of baddies, CIA agents, and military. The whole thing is really an excuse for a series of finely executed daredevil stunts, but what holds it together is the tongue-in-cheek direction and humorous ensemble playing. No masterpiece, but we's only out for some fun, ain't we? WH

Shakespeare in Love

(1998, US, 123 min)
d John Madden. *p* David Parfitt, Donna Gigliotti, Harvey Weinstein, Edward Zwick, Marc Norman. *sc* Marc Norman, Tom Stoppard. *ph* Richard Greatrex. *ed* David Gamble. *pd* Martin Childs. *m* Stephen Warbeck. *cast* Joseph Fiennes, Gwyneth Paltrow, Judi Dench, Ben Affleck, Colin Firth, Simon Callow, Geoffrey Rush, Tom Wilkinson, Antony Sher, Imelda Staunton, Jim Carter.

●London,1593. Will Shakespeare (Fiennes) has lost his muse, and the prospects for his latest commission, 'Romeo and Ethel, the Pirate's Daughter,' look troubled. Enter Viola Lesseps (Paltrow), who auditions for the still unwritten play and captures both the lead role and its author. John Madden's remarkably busy film – which took seven Oscars – is a far shout from the drawing-room period drama of old. It combines an interest in British regal heritage and a swift, populist, plainspoken perspective free of traditional deference. Again, too, it's at least as informed by present-day British theatre and TV as by classical literature, as a cast ranging from Dame Judi to two members of *The Fast Show* indicates. The film sports its superficiality with good humour, and the cast deserve much of the credit: Fiennes is at last truly convincing; Paltrow and Ben Affleck (as the company's star player) hold their own; and the rest of the ensemble gel seamlessly. Finally, though, it's Tom Stoppard's witty, intelligent script which proves so satisfying, effortlessly combining and recasting period comedy, creative biopic, *Romeo and Juliet* adaptation, and his own brand of clever pun and play. NB

Shakespeare-Wallah

(1965, Ind, 125 min, b/w)
d James Ivory. *p* Ismail Merchant. *sc* Ruth Prawer Jhabvala, James Ivory. *ph* Subrata Mitra. *ed* Amit Bose. *m* Satyajit Ray. *cast* Felicity Kendal, Shashi Kapoor, Geoffrey Kendal, Laura Liddell, Madhur Jaffrey, Utpal Dutt.

●The second film from the Merchant-Ivory-Jhabvala collaboration: despite occasional longueurs, a hauntingly funny, rather Chekhovian piece about a group of English-led travelling players stoutly striving to keep Shakespeare alive in India long after the Raj has gone. Loosely inspired by the experiences of the Kendal family, who here recreate parts of their Shakespearean repertory, it was shot by Ray's cameraman Subrata Mitra, has a fine score by Ray himself, and at its best has much of Ray's quizzical charm. Dialogue and performances, though, tend towards the stilted; and although Felicity Kendal and Shashi Kapoor aren't bad as the young lovers parted not so much by the racial divide as by character and circumstance, Madhur Jaffrey runs away with all prizes as an outrageously arrogant Indian movie queen further spurred by jealousy. TM

Shaking the Tree

(1990, US, 107 min)
d Duane Clark. *p* Robert J Wilson. *sc* Duane Clark, Steven Wilde. *ph* Ron Schmidt. *ed* Martin L Bernstein. *m* David E Russo. *cast* Arye Gross, Gale Hansen, Doug Savant, Steven Wilde, Courteney Cox, Christina Haag.

●Four old high school buddies now face the '90s with mounting dread. The marital and extra-marital agonies, late adolescent angst attacks, flirtations with low life: Clark's film could almost be 'Diner: The Next Generation'. Michael (Savant) is wondering whether his wife will produce a baby before he produces his novel; nerdish power broker Barry (Gross) can't stop kvetching about his wife's sexual history; amiable ex-boxer Duke (Wilde) is having trouble Relating to Daddy; and Sully (Hansen), a rich kid, likes to live seedy. For the first half-hour, the film just about overcomes its limitations by fielding sound acting, promising characterisations, and a winning sense of place (this is a Chicago movie and proud of it). But having told their menfolk 'We need to talk' once too often, the women vanish into the background, while the guys embark on a dreary, mechanical round of griping, barroom buddying, and nick-of-time problem solving. JRo

Shalako

(1968, GB, 113 min)
d Edward Dmytryk. *p* Euan Lloyd. *sc* JJ Griffith, Hal Hopper, Scot Finch. *ph* Ted Moore. *ed* Bill Blunden. *ad* Herbert Smith. *m* Robert Farnon. *cast* Sean Connery, Brigitte Bardot, Stephen Boyd, Jack Hawkins, Peter Van Eyck, Honor Blackman, Woody Strode, Eric Sykes, Alexander Knox.

●There's an engaging premise to this British Western shot in Spain, with a group of European aristocrats on safari in the wild west (complete with chilled wine and sterling silver), looking for big game but finding warlike Apaches. But its notions of humour (Eric Sykes as an imperturbable butler) don't go too well with Dmytryk's attempts to ape the spaghetti Western style, and it very quickly goes downhill. TM

Shallow Grave

(1994, GB, 92 min)
d Danny Boyle. *p* Andrew Macdonald. *sc* John Hodge. *ph* Brian Tufano. *ed* Masahiro Hirakubo. *ad* Kave Quinn. *m* Simon Boswell. *cast* Kerry Fox, Christopher Eccleston, Ewan McGregor, Ken Stott, Keith Allen, Colin McCredie.

●When their mysterious new flatmate suffers a fatal overdose, David, Alex and Juliet (Eccleston, McGregor and Fox) find a fortune in bank notes stashed in his room. They quickly resolve to keep the money, but nothing comes for free, and the price here involves not only dismemberment and burial, but the trio's trust, sanity and friendship. This impressively assured, highly accomplished British feature doesn't dwell on moral niceties, but goes straight for the gut. John Hodge's screenplay has the kind of unrelenting forward momentum and close-to-the bone sense of purpose which sees you safely through a good many logical minefields, even if nagging question marks occur in retrospect. Given that most of the action takes place in the flat, it's remarkable how agile and invigorating Boyle's direction is. As the friends fall out, the movie loses some of its black comic edge, perhaps, but only to gain in sheer, backstabbing, bloody-minded mayhem. TCh

Shallow Hal

(2001, US/Ger, 113 min)
d Bobby Farrelly, Peter Farrelly. *p* Bradley Thomas, Charles B Wessler, Bobby Farrelly, Peter Farrelly. *sc* Sean Moynihan, Peter Farrelly, Bobby Farrelly. *ph* Russell Carpenter. *ed* Christopher Greenbury. *pd* Sidney J Bartholomew Jr. *m* Ivy. *cast* Gwyneth Paltrow, Jack Black, Jason Alexander, Joe Viterelli, Rene Kirby, Bruce McGill, Tony Robbins, Susan Ward, Zen Gesner, Brooke Burns.
●The Farrelly brothers put a more sentimental spin on their trademark gross-out/arrested adolescent schtick, wresting the issue of fatness from the feminists and kicking it into the comedy arena with mixed results. The film is not as funny as their best, but fascinates in the discomforting way it foregrounds the brothers' normally buried, facile moral dialectic. Black brings a bravely unattractive self-satisfaction to the leading character, Hal, an uncool, semi-orphaned jerk, unaware of how his relationships with women have been distorted by the shocking deathbed testament of his clergyman father. Disappointing his equally sad sidekick Mauricio (Alexander), a sexual perfectionist, he is converted into the very paradigm of PC following an encounter with a TV guru (Robbins) who hypnotises him. Now seeing people only for their 'inner beauty', he falls for incredulous 300lb millionaire's daughter Rosemary – Paltrow alternately svelte (and breast-enhanced) and wading around in a body suit. Most of the gags cater magnificently to the lowest common denominator – the Farrellys impress with their sheer audacity, if nothing else. Few mainstream filmmakers scratch so violently at the scabs on the modern psyche. The optimism they display in poking fun at the hypocrisy of modern social behaviour is both moving and funny. WH

Shall We Dance?

(1937, US, 116 min, b/w)
d Mark Sandrich. *p* Pandro S Berman. *sc* Allan Scott, Ernest Pagano. *ph* David Abel. *ed* William Hamilton. *ad* Van Nest Polglase. *songs* George Gershwin, Ira Gershwin. *cast* Fred Astaire, Ginger Rogers, Edward Everett Horton, Eric Blore, Jerome Cowan, Ketti Gallian, Harriet Hoctor.
●RKO temporarily parted Fred and Ginger after this musical, which didn't have the flow of earlier efforts. Taking off from an ocean-going romance, in which the outrageous assumption is made that Astaire has got Rogers pregnant, it stops adumbrating Leo McCarey's great *Love Affair* by getting into a silly will-they-won't-they round, saved only by the Gershwin numbers. These include 'Let's Call the Whole Thing Off', which has a rather strained and cumbersome roller-skating sequence with sticky moments on Ginger's part, and the outright winner, 'They Can't Take That Away from Me'. SG

Shall We Dance?

(1995, Jap, 136 min)
d Masayuki Suo. *p* Yasuyoshi Tokuma. *sc* Masayuki Suo. *ph* Naoki Kayano. *ed* Junichi Kikuchi. *pd* Kyoko Heya. *m* Yoshikazu Suo. *cast* Koji Yakusho, Tamiyo Kusakari, Naoto Takenaka, Eriko Watanabe, Akira Emoto.
●This entertaining Japanese comedy opens with a dreamy shot of Blackpool's Tower Ballroom, but it's back in suburban Tokyo that Masayuki Suo's film really begins. A salaryman (Yakusho) is locked in routine until curiosity gets the better of him: each evening, from the train, he sees a beautiful woman gazing out of the window of a ballroom dancing class, and one night he plucks up the courage to go in. As lessons progress, his secret cannot remain hidden for long – dancing has entered his bloodstream and he'll never be the same again. All he needs now is the girl. While the film's balancing act, between the love interest in fragile beauty Tamiyo Kusakari and the call of the protagonist's domestic ties, is ultimately contrived, unlike Hollywood tosh, it never feels blatantly manipulative. The salaryman's reserve carries a significant charm, and although the overly careful pacing at times threatens to dull our involvement, director Suo still knows when to throw in the comic fizz. The real star of the show is Naoto Takenaka as the office colleague transformed into a rumba tornado. TJ

Shame

(1987, Aust, 94 min)
d Steve Jodrell. *p* Damien Parer, Paul Barron. *sc* Beverly Blankenship, Michael Brindley. *ph* Joseph Pickering. *ed* Kerry Regan. *pd* Phil Peters. *m* Mario Millo. *cast* Deborra-Lee Furness, Tony Barry, Simone Buchanan, Gillian Jones, Peter Aanensen, Margaret Ford, David Franklin.
●From the shadow of the controversial *The Accused* comes Jodrell's first feature, also dealing with gang rape. Furness (excellent) plays Asta, a self-reliant barrister and biker who breaks down while travelling alone through the outback. The garage mechanic's daughter Lizzie (Buchanan) has been gang-raped by a group of local hoods, and is trapped in a 'she asked for it' conspiracy of silence. Asta takes on Lizzie's case, finding herself in a vicious battle with the sheriff and the rest of the male community. Furness handles her role with calm strength and obvious skill; and where *The Accused* manipulated sensation, this avoids the gratuitous voyeurism of including the rape scene. Working by allusion, it succeeds in striking exactly the right note, responsibly, movingly, and yet rivetingly. IA

Shame, The (Skammen)

(1968, Swe, 103 min, b/w)
d Ingmar Bergman. *p* Lars-Owe Carlberg. *sc* Ingmar Bergman. *ph* Sven Nykvist. *ed* Ulla Ryghe. *ad* PA Lundgren. *cast* Liv Ullmann, Max von Sydow, Gunnar Björnstrand, Sigge Fürst, Birgitta Valberg.
●Bergman's magisterial confrontation with war, set in a characteristically ambivalent decor, either a peaceful farm somewhere in Sweden or a landscape from Goya secreting intimations of disaster. Here live a man and wife, indifferent to the war until it arrives on their doorstep to strip their lives to the bone. Presenting war with shattering power as a blindly destructive force, Bergman uses it brilliantly as a background to the real pain: the way the couple are forced to look at each other, and to realise that the only honest feeling they have about their relationship is shame. It ends with one of the cinema's most awesomely apocalyptic visions: not the cheeriest of films, but a masterpiece. TM

Shameless Old Lady, The

see Vieille Dame indigne, La

Shampoo

(1975, US, 110 min)
d Hal Ashby. *p* Warren Beatty. *sc* Robert Towne, Warren Beatty. *ph* Laszlo Kovacs. *ed* Robert C Jones. *pd* Richard Sylbert. *m* Paul Simon. *cast* Warren Beatty, Julie Christie, Goldie Hawn, Lee Grant, Jack Warden, Tony Bill, Carrie Fisher, Jay Robinson, Luana Anders, Brad Dexter.
●Made with all the awareness of hindsight, *Shampoo* offers a sharp sexual satire and a mature statement on both America and Hollywood in 1968, *The Graduate* as it should have been, perhaps. Everyone is shown to act out of the same fatal expediency, as the country elects Nixon for President while Beatty's chic Hollywood hairdresser tries to sort out an increasingly dishevelled sex life, a campaign against the Establishment via its wives and mistresses that's subversive only by default. Ostensibly a farce about fucking for fun and its repercussions, but the laughs are tempered by bleakness and the film ends up saddened by its characters' waywardness. CPe

Shampoo and Set (Waschen und Legen)

(1999, Ger, 90 min)
d/sc Alice Agneskirchner. *ph* Marcus Winterbauer. *ed* Matthias Spranger.
●As near as you can get to Berlin life without actually living it, this is a comic and touching record of what goes on in four hairdressing salons: Turkish, posh, cool and cornershop. A lot of the fun is in the non-stop conversation, especially in the posh salon where showbiz clients exchange a stream of gags with the urbane boss. But there's a melancholy streak. The young man in charge of the 'cool' salon is arrogantly uninterested in his customers as people, whereas the middle-aged owner of the cornershop takes a personal interest in hers, who often come in as a relief from loneliness. Pointed but uncondescending. SB

Shamus

(1972, US, 106 min)
d Buzz Kulik. *p* Robert M Weitman. *sc* Barry Beckerman. *ph* Victor J Kemper. *ed* Walter Thompson. *ad* Philip Rosenberg. *m* Jerry Goldsmith. *cast* Burt Reynolds, Dyan Cannon, John Ryan, Joe Santos, Giorgio Tozzi, Ron Weyland.
●No-nonsense title for a no-nonsense ex-pool player turned private eye. Hired by a shady rich man to find out who killed a diamond thief, Reynolds stumbles on something bigger: gunrunning and the illicit sale of surplus US military equipment. He is also stumbled upon (metaphor intended) by Dyan Cannon, as the voluptuous sister of an ex-football star, who thinks her brother's somehow involved and enlists the shamus' professional help. It's a stereotyped, amoral tale; the film doesn't bother to tell us who is running guns, where and why. Kulik is more concerned with careful social and dramatic realism; the shamus is no Bond-fantasy hero, just a tough guy who hits first and asks questions later, and is frankly a stud. Little details (like the way he mouths 'Shit!', and when the window sticks), the unsentimental but real moments of male comradeship between him and a cop, him and his underworld contacts, the downbeat ending, make the film worth watching. MV

Shane

(1953, US, 118 min)
d/p George Stevens. *sc* AB Guthrie Jr. *ph* Loyal Griggs. *ed* William Hornbeck, Tom McAdoo. *ad* Hal Pereira, Walter Tyler. *m* Victor Young. *cast* Alan Ladd, Jean Arthur, Van Heflin, Jack Palance, Brandon de Wilde, Ben Johnson, Edgar Buchanan, Elisha Cook Jr, Emile Meyer, John Dierkes.
●Stevens' classic Western, with its inflated reputation, now looks as if it were self-consciously intended as a landmark film right from the start. Certainly its story, of a lone, laconic stranger riding out of the desert to lend aid to a pioneer farming family in their battle against a gang of dark-hearted villains, has been much imitated since (notably in Clint Eastwood's *Pale Rider*), while its deliberately epic landscape photography is now a *sine qua non* of the genre. But the slow pace and persistent solemnity reduce tension, prefiguring the portentous nature of Stevens' later work. That said, the cast is splendid, and both the emotional tensions between Ladd and Arthur, and the final confrontation with Palance, are well handled. GA

Shanghai Blues (Shanghai zhi Ye)

(1984, HK, 108 min)
d Tsui Hark. *p* Anna Law. *sc* Chan Gun-chung, Do Gok-wai, Seto Cheuk-hon. *ph* Ngor Chi-kwan. *ed* Chou Siu-sum. *pd* Au-yeung Hing-yee. *m* James Wong, Wong Ching-yu. *cast* Sylvia Chang, Sally Yip, Kenny Bee, Loretta Li.
●Shanghai before and after the Japanese occupation, but gleefully anachronistic in every way. The plot (boy meets girl; boy loses girl; boy and girl wind up as feuding neighbours without recognising each other) is collaged together from classic Shanghai movies like *Street Angel Crossroads* and *8000 Li Under the Clouds and Moon*. The cast is pretty, but it looks and sounds like a 90-minute commercial. It will certainly boost sales of paracetamol. TR

Shanghai Express

(1932, US, 80 min, b/w)
d Josef von Sternberg. *sc* Jules Furthman. *ph* Lee Garmes. *ad* Hans Dreier. *m* W Franke Harling. *cast* Marlene Dietrich, Clive Brook, Warner Oland, Anna May Wong, Eugene Pallette, Lawrence Grant, Gustav von Seyffertitz, Louise Closser Hale.
●Von Sternberg, who was forever looking for new kinds of stylisation, said that he intended everything in *Shanghai Express* to have the rhythm of a train. He clearly meant it: the bizarre stop-go cadences of the dialogue delivery are the most blatantly non-naturalistic element, but the

overall design and dramatic pacing are equally extraordinary. The plot concerns an evacuation from Peking to Shanghai, but it's in every sense a vehicle for something else: a parade of deceptive appearances and identities, centering on the *Boule de Suif* notion of a prostitute with more honour than those around her. Dietrich's Shanghai Lily hasn't aged a day, but Clive Brook's stiff-upper-lip British officer (her former lover) now looks like a virtual caricature of the type. None the less, the sincerity and emotional depth with which Sternberg invests their relationship is quite enough to transcend mere style or fashion. TR

Shanghai Gesture, The

(1941, US, 106 min, b/w)
d Josef von Sternberg. *p* Arnold Pressburger. *sc* Karl Vollmoeller, Geza Herczeg, Jules Furthman, Josef von Sternberg. *ph* Paul Ivano. *ed* Sam Winston. *ad* Boris Leven. *m* Richard Hageman. *cast* Gene Tierney, Walter Huston, Victor Mature, Ona Munson, Maria Ouspenskaya, Phyllis Brooks, Albert Basserman, Eric Blore, Mike Mazurki.

●Sternberg's last Hollywood masterpiece, a delirious melodrama of decadence and sexual guilt that uses its Oriental motifs as a cypher for all that is unknown or unknowable. The battle is waged between a Western hypocrite (Huston) and an Eastern pleasure queen (Munson); the erotic skirmishes occur between the self-willed but helpless heroine (Tierney) and the apathetic object of her passion (Mature, amazing, 'Doctor of nothing, poet of Shanghai... and Gomorrah'); the chief arena is a casino built like a circle of hell, where nothing is left to 'chance'. Subversive cinema at its most sublime. TR

Shanghai Lil (Hao Ke/aka The Champion)

(1973, HK, 91 min)
d Zhuge Qingyun, Yang Jingchen. *p* Yen Wu Tung. *sc* Yang Ching Chen, Chang Hsin I. *ph* Chuang Yin Chien. *ed* Kuo Tinh-Hung. *cast* Shih Szu, Chin Han, I Yuan, Lung Fei, Chang Feng.

●A fair example of mid-period Shaw Brothers martial arts film, enlivened by some fairly lethal-looking stunt work around a mine face, and an attractive performance from female martial artist Shih Szu. Chin Han's hero, released from prison after serving a term in place of his half-brother, returns to find the latter working the family mine in cahoots with the Russians. Inevitably, rejecting an underhand offer of Japanese aid, he goes on (with the aid of Shih Szu) to win the mine back – quite explicitly sidestepping a situation with revolutionary potential. The Chin Han character, while physically resembling the heroes of mainland Chinese films very closely, fails to carry the kind of populist charge so crucial to the martial arts hero, and without this he comes off decidedly palely compared to the trenchant Japanese contingent, despite the statutory Chinese triumph at the end. VG

Shanghai Noon

(2000, US/HK, 110 min)
d Tom Dey. *p* Roger Birnbaum, Gary Barber, Jonathan Glickman. *sc* Alfred Gough, Miles Millar. *ph* Dan Mindel. *ed* Richard Chew. *pd* Peter J Hampton. *m* Randy Edelman. *cast* Jackie Chan, Owen Wilson, Lucy Liu, Roger Yuan, Walton Goggins, Xander Berkeley, Jason Connery, Brandon Merrill, Rafael Baez.

●Jackie Chan (b 1954; work it out) doesn't do high risk stunts any more, and so Hollywood needs to find other ways to showcase his athletic slapstick talents. No doubt there was much brainstorming before they hit on this idea for a rerun of *Rush Hour* in period drag. This is a comedy Western in which Jackie again comes to the US to rescue yet another girl kidnapped for ransom by yet another Chinese renegade. Since Hollywood doesn't yet trust Jackie to carry a picture, it's still necessary to give him an adversary/foil, someone to help him 'become American'. This time the role goes not to a black stand-up comic, but to white actor Wilson. Surprisingly, the result is rather good: funnier than *Rush Hour* and better staged and cut than Jackie's recent HK pictures. Much of its strength comes from the central clash between Jackie's indomitable energy and Wilson's knowingly anachronistic cool, while lots of visual and verbal gags keep things whistling. The plot is suitably negligible, but first-time director Dey knows from his years making commercials how to block and pace scenes. TR

Shanghai Panic (Women hai Pa)

(2001, China/Aust, 87 min)
d/p/sc/ph/ed Andrew YS Cheng. *m* Zhao Ke. *cast* Mian Mian, Li Zhinan, Yang Yuting, He Weiyan, Zhou Zhijie, Zhou Liang, Wang Shiyuan.

●If 'broken-backed' can be a term of praise, Cheng's extraordinary DV feature earns it. Inspired by a banned novel by Mian Mian (who here plays Kika, a character not a million miles from herself), it offers a discontinuous panorama of the various panics that grip Shanghai's *jeunesse dorée* – the pampered, solipsistic kids produced by the communist government's one-child policy. The first half centres on HIV panic: disco boy Bei has a fever that won't subside, but won't go for an AIDS test because he's heard that China ships HIV+ people off to a prison island. He and his friends Kika, Fifi and Casper deal with the problem by clubbing even harder and taking even more 'E's and ketamine. The second half veers off into panic about sexual identity: Bei shacks up with his friend Jie in a borrowed apartment and tries to persuade him to have sex – although Bei denies being gay, and anyway has a thing for paedophile websites. Although it's fiction, every frame feels intrusively real: the benefit of asking a non-pro cast to act out their real lives and shooting it as a one-man crew. Very possibly the start of a new chapter in Chinese cinema. TR

Shanghai Surprise

(1986, GB, 97 min)
d Jim Goddard. *p* John Kohn. *sc* John Kohn, Bob Bentley. *ph* Ernest Vincze. *ed* Ralph Sheldon. *pd* Peter Mullins. *m* George Harrison, Michael Kamen. *cast* Sean Penn, Madonna, Paul Freeman, Richard Griffiths, Philip Sayer, Clyde Kusatsu, Kay Tong Lim, Michael Aldridge.

●A water-coloured, watered-down romantic comedy set in Shanghai in 1937, with the helplessly miscast Madonna (would you buy a used Bible from this woman?) trading on her ironic stage name to play an American missionary. She, with the aid of Penn's gaudy tie salesman, is desperately seeking 'Faraday's Flowers', a hidden opium stockpile which will help relieve the suffering of soldiers wounded in the war with Japan. The action is simply an implausible chain of events sensationally strung together, a Saturday morning serial formula which worked for *Raiders of the Lost Ark*; here, the heavy-handed manipulation of genre ingredients simply results in vulgar, often embarrassing, kitsch. SGo

Shanghai Triad (Yao a Yao Yao dao Waipo Qiao)

(1995, HK/China/Fr, 108 min)
d Zhang Yimou. *p* Jean-Louis Piel. *sc* Bi Fei Yu. *ph* Lu Yue, Olivier Chiavassa, Bruno Patin. *ed* Du Yuan. *pd* Cao Juiping. *m* Zhang Guangtian. *cast* Gong Li, Wang Xiaoxiao, Li Baotian, Li Xuejian, Sun Chun, Fu Biao, Chen Shu, Liu Jiang.

●To '30s Shanghai comes 14-year-old yokel Shuisheng (Wang Xiaoxiao), whose uncle finds him work with the triad gang headed by ruthlessly manipulative Tang (Li Baotian). His job is to wait on fiery-tempered Bijou (Gong Li), the boss's mistress whose routines have made her 'Queen' of the Shanghai music halls. Dealing with her demands is difficult enough, but when Tang's rival Fat Yu seeks revenge for a murder by Tang and his right-hand man Song (who, it transpires, is Bijou's secret lover), Bijou and the boy flee to a remote island, Shuisheng little knows what treachery he will witness. Despite being related through the eyes of the naive Shuisheng, this sumptuous gangster drama centres on the experience of Bijou, a woman who initially believes she's able to exploit her position as the mistress of an ageing crime boss, but who comes, belatedly, to realise she's simply a pawn in a man's world and, thereby, to regain some of her lost innocence. Unfortunately, with its faintly uneven pacing and straggling structure, the film lacks depth or narrative economy. That said, Zhang's use of colour is as vivid as ever, his stylised depiction of violence is mostly effective, and Gong Li is gloriously watchable. GA

Shanks

(1974, US, 93 min)
d William Castle. *p* Steven North. *sc* Ranald Graham. *ph* Joseph Biroc. *ed* David Berlatsky. *pd* Boris Leven. *m* Alex North. *cast* Marcel Marceau, Tsilla Chelton, Philippe Clay, Cindy Eilbacher, Helena Kallianiotes, Larry Bishop.

●The old gimmick-master's last film, a genuine weirdie with the mime Marceau in a dual role (one speaking, one not) as a scientist working on the galvanic reanimation of dead animals, and as a downtrodden puppeteer brought in to assist with his experiments. When the old scientist dies, the puppeteer gleefully discovers that he can re-animate human corpses: some extraordinary stuff here, making macabre use of mimic talents (Clay and Chelton in addition to Marceau) to suggest the nightmarishly jerky, tortured movements of the living dead as the puppeteer deals with his immediate enemies. It gravitates into more routine territory – revenge against a gang of brutish Hell's Angels who rape and kill a sweet young girl (Eilbacher) who had become the puppeteer's only friend – but nevertheless remains a strikingly effective experiment. TM

Shaolin Soccer (Shaolin Zuqiu/aka Kung-fu Soccer)

(2001, HK/China, 112 min)
d Stephen Chow, Lee Lik-Chee. *p* Yeung Kwok-Fai. *sc* Stephen Chow, Tsang Kam-Cheong. *ph* Kwong Ting-Wo, Kwan Pak-Huen. *ed* Kai Kit-Wai. *ad* Ho Kim-Hung. *m* Raymond Wong. *cast* Stephen Chow, Vicky Zhao [Zhao Wei], Ng Man-Tat, Patrick Tse, Li Hui, Karen Mok, Cecilia Cheung, Vincent Kok.

●Ever since Chow (formerly 'Chiau') stopped making four films a year and launched his (unsuccessful) bid for Canadian citizenship, he's been reaching for a blockbuster hit – and this live-action cartoon is it. He plays garbage scavenger Steel Leg, a former Shaolin monk with magical martial art skills, recruited by Fung (Ng, Chow's regular stooge) to rustle up a team of other ex-monks to play in a national soccer tournament. Fung's target is the evil Hung (Tse), who runs a team of macho bullies and cheats. Hard to see why Chow hired Ching Siu-Tung to choreograph the action when so much of it is created digitally, but the mix of slapstick comedy, primitive melodrama, born-again heroism and zappy visual effects gels into a passable entertainment. It's been Miramaxed for US release under the title *Kung-fu Soccer*. Chow shot it in Shanghai in a bid to crack the vast China market, but the Film Bureau banned it for 'presenting a disrespectful image of soccer'. TR

Shape of Things to Come, The

(1979, Can, 98 min)
d George McCowan. *p* William Davison. *sc* Martin Lager. *ph* Reginald Morris. *ed* Stan Cole. *ad* Gerry Holmes. *m* Paul Hoffert. *cast* Jack Palance, Carol Lynley, Barry Morse, John Ireland, Nicholas Campbell, Eddie Benton.

●Somewhere deep in hype-space, the crew of the spaceship Starstreak ponder over the fact that once they were almost stars, and continue the seemingly never-ending search for their script, lost in the black hole of the *Star Wars* boom. 'Man's future is limited only by his imagination', the scientist says; and films only by his greed, the audience sighs. HG Wells' novel was filmed in 1936 as *Things to Come*, with brilliant set designs by William Cameron Menzies and a script in part by Wells himself, full of (admittedly often half-digested) ideas. Masquerading under the original title, but set 50 years later and providing its own risibly inept plot, this is the unacceptable face of exploitation. SM

Shark

(1969, US/Mex, 92 min)
d Samuel Fuller. *p* Skip Steloff, Mark Cooper, José Luis Calderon. *sc* Samuel Fuller, John Kingsbridge. *ph* Raúl Martinez Solares. *ad* Mañuel Fontanals. *m* Rafael Moroyoqui. *cast* Burt Reynolds, Barry Sullivan, Arthur Kennedy, Silvia Pinal, Enrique Lucero.

●Although Fuller disowns this because it was cut against his wishes, it still remains worth seeing for what's left. The search for sunken treasure by four totally amoral protagonists, all intent on double-crossing each other, is capably handled; but the lasting impression is of how well Fuller conveys the atmosphere of hot and dusty small towns in the middle of nowhere.

Shark Callers of Kontu, The

(1986, Aust, 52 min)
d Dennis O'Rourke.
● In Papua New Guinea, in the coastal village of Kontu, there are men who are able to kill sharks with their bare hands. First mentioned by Abel Tasman back in 1643, the fishermen attribute their power to catch the creatures – which they believe carry the spirits of their ancestors – to magic. But as 'civilisation' gains its hold upon the village, that magic is inevitably disappearing, together with the village's community spirit. Though superbly detailed in its observation of the rituals and daily rounds of Kontu life, O'Rourke's marvellous documentary is no mere anthropological record. Refusing to indulge in paternalistic notions of the noble savage, he offers a persuasive analysis of how and why this culture is being destroyed by the outside world. Closer to, say, Lévi-Strauss than to romantics like JG Frazer or Werner Herzog, O'Rourke's sympathies are deeply political, although *Shark Callers* is no dry manifesto. Rather, by allowing the villagers to speak for themselves and the camera simply to reveal the remarkable nature of the men's work, he relates the spiritual world of 'magic' to more comprehensible forces with admirable lucidity. GA

Sharks' Cave, The (Bermude: La Fossa Maledetta)

(1978, It/Sp, 90 min)
d Anthony Richmond [Teodoro Ricci]. *p* Nino Segurini. *sc* Fernando Galiana, Manrico Melchiorre, Teodoro Ricci. *ph* Juan Jurado. *ed* Angelo Curi. *m* Stelvio Cipriani. *cast* Andrés Garcia, Janet Agren, Arthur Kennedy, Pino Colizzi, Maximo Valverde.
● The pulse of any trash addict must pound over the idea behind this fin film (molto cheapo), where the mysteries of the Bermuda Triangle are explained in terms of killer sharks controlled by tiny Toltec aquanauts. Hapless, scantily-outfitted divers keep running across their underwater city (made out of fish-bowl decorations), Arthur Kennedy plays a threatening Mafioso much as Truman Capote might, and the planes and ships which founder in the Triangle are obviously toys. The powers of the Toltecs ('ultimately inexplicable', thanks to the low budget) are symbolised by orgasmic moans. There is one great totally unexplained scene, with a cruiser full of hippies, looking like a floating detoxification project, who commit mass suicide by jumping over the side. CR

Shark-skin Man and Peach-hip Girl (Samehada Otoko to Momojiri Onna)

(1998, Jap, 108 min)
d Katsuhito Ishii. *p* Kazuto Takida. *sc* Katsuhito Ishii. *ph* Hiroshi Machida. *ed* Yumiko Doi. *pd* Tomoyuki Maruo. *m* Dr Strangelove. *cast* Tadanobu Asano, Sie Kohinata, Ittoku Kishibe, Susumu Terajima.
● First time director Katsuhito Ishii took Minetaro Mochizuki's cult manga about a fashion-conscious hitman on the run from the mob teaming up with a spunky girl on the run from her incestuous uncle, twice storyboarded the film he wanted to make from it, twice shot the storyboards on video as 'conceptual rehearsals' and finally shot the film. Somewhere in the process, he added in lengthy homages to his favourite movies: *Twin Peaks*, *Silence of the Lambs* and other neglected titles urgently needing his endorsement. Thanks to his ad agency background, he secured a first rank cast headed by Asano and Kitano movie veteran Terajima. Only one thing was missing: talent. TR

Shark's Son (Le Fils du Requin)

(1993, Fr, 90 min)
d Agnès Merlet. *p* François Fries. *sc* Agnès Merlet. *ph* Gérard Simon. *ed* Guy Lecorne, Pierre Choukron. *ad* Laurent Allaire. *m* Bruno Coulais. *cast* Sandrine Blancke, Ludovic Van Den Daele, Erick Da Silva.
● Though apparently based on a real-life story, this study of two uncontrollable delinquent brothers – it comes on like *Les Valseuses* for ten-year-olds – often seems far-fetched. The children are convincing, but the narrative is not, alternating as it does between scenes of outrageous anti-social behaviour, implausible escapes from authority, and poetic interludes of dreamy meditation. Aren't these knowing boys *ever* just boys? Despite Merlet's admirably unsentimental handling of her amoral script, the two-note tone soon becomes wearisome. GA

Sharks' Treasure

(1974, US, 95 min)
d/p/sc Cornel Wilde. *ph* Jack Atcheler. *ed* Byron Brandt. *ad* ME Wilkinson. *m* Robert O Ragland. *cast* Cornel Wilde, Yaphet Kotto, John Neilson, David Canary, Cliff Osmond, David Gilliam, Caesar Cordova.
● Always primitive, Wilde's films seem to operate increasingly in a strange limbo, with no points of reference outside their own simple view of the world. The astonishing naïveté of Wilde's script can scarcely cope with the different strands of the plot queueing up and waiting to be dealt with: fights against sharks (well handled), underwater searches for treasure (*Look at Life*-like), confrontations with desperadoes (risible). Rather more unified is Wilde's homespun philosophising: the perils of nicotine and drink, and the virtues of keeping fit, with the spry 60-year-old Wilde doing one-handed press-ups on deck. But most curious are the closeted emotions of the all-male group, which threaten to run riot without writer/producer/director/star Wilde in the least aware of them. A real oddity.

Sharky's Machine

(1981, US, 120 min)
d Burt Reynolds. *p* Hank Moonjean. *sc* Gerald DiPego. *ph* William A Fraker. *ed* William Gordean, Dennis Virkler. *pd* Walter Scott Herndon. *m* Al Capps. *cast* Burt Reynolds, Vittorio Gassman, Brian Keith, Charles Durning, Earl Holliman, Bernie Casey, Henry Silva, Darryl Hickman, Rachel Ward, Joseph Mascolo.
● Demoted to the vice squad after a bungled drugs bust, Reynolds puts together a team of 'loser' cops to investigate links between high class hookers and possible political corruption. Unfortunately, Reynolds the director is as uncertain about the tone of the picture as Reynolds the star is about his screen *persona*. So while the action veers from lightweight action to extreme violence, Reynolds' character vacillates between macho tough guy and sensitive, vulnerable leading man. One minute he's busting heads and uttering expletives, the next he's talking to emotionally scarred tart-with-a-heart Ward about his passion for wood-carving. Still, William A Fraker's first-rate location photography invests the seedy locations with an authentic feel, while the relish with which the unhinged assassin (Silva) and Oriental torturers go about their business enliven the routine plot about a mysterious Mr Big. NF

Shattered (Les Passagers)

(1976, Fr/It, 103 min)
d Serge Leroy. *p* Léo L Fuchs. *sc* Christopher Frank, Serge Leroy. *ph* Walter Wottitz. *ed* Françoise Ceppi. *m* Claude Bolling. *cast* Jean-Louis Trintignant, Mireille Darc, Bernard Fresson, Adolfo Celi, Richard Constantini.
● Trintignant escorts his 11-year-old stepson from school in Italy to their new home in Paris, where wife (Darc) awaits. They're pursued, *Duel* style, by a psychopathic killer (Fresson) who terrorises them with his Ford Panel van. Along the way, Leroy handles a host of proven topical elements capably enough – urban paranoia, misogynistic killer, precocious kid, bigoted cop (Celi); and the rip-off of the basic plot mechanism from Spielberg's movie (by way of Dean Koontz's novel *Shattered*, published under the pseudonym K.R. Dwyer) is effective enough. But casting and payoff are both too predictable to make what emerges anything more than an efficient, glossy thriller delivered without any particular conviction. RM

Shattered

(1991, US, 98 min)
d Wolfgang Petersen. *p* Wolfgang Petersen, John Davis, David Korda. *sc* Wolfgang Petersen. *ph* Laszlo Kovacs. *ed* Hannes Nikel, Glenn Farr. *pd* Gregg Fonseca. *m* Angelo Badalamenti. *cast* Tom Berenger, Bob Hoskins, Greta Scacchi, Joanne Whalley-Kilmer, Corbin Bernsen, Scott Getlin, Theodore Bikel.
● Based on Richard Neely's novel *The Plastic Nightmare*, Petersen's first American feature is a credible and gripping thriller, using ambiguous clues and a complex flashback structure to draw us into the dark heart of an amnesiac maze. Berenger plays a wealthy architect whose life is shattered when he and his wife (Scacchi) plunge over a cliff in their car. Emerging from a coma, he has his face reconstructed, but his memory of the crash has been erased. When he tries to reassemble his life with the help of his wife, who was thrown clear, some pieces of the jigsaw just won't fit. Photos of Scacchi with another man lead him to private eye Hoskins, whom he had hired before the accident to spy on her infidelities with a mystery lover. Meanwhile, his partner's wife (Whalley-Kilmer) is insisting that she and Berenger had been having a torrid affair. Knowing only what Berenger knows, we share his sense of disorientation and vulnerability, while Petersen's sure-footed script and controlled direction eschew self-conscious *hommage* for good old-fashioned adult entertainment. NF

Shattered Dreams: Picking Up the Pieces

(1987, GB, 173 min)
d Victor Schonfeld. *p/sc* Victor Schonfeld, Jenifer Millstone. *ph* Peter Greenhalgh, Amnon Salomon, Dani Schneur, Jimmy Dibling, Zachariah Raz, Yossi Wein, Yaacov Saporta, Eytan Harris. *ed* Jenifer Millstone. *m* Shalom Hanouch, Shlomo Barr. *narrator* Jack Klass.
● A documentary chronicle of what Schonfeld sees as the present-day betrayal of Israel's original democratic and cooperative ideals, this traces the contradictions within Zionism back to an unresolved conflict between religious and secular law, and to an ongoing critis of racial and national identity. He emphasises the wide range of responses to the so-called 'Holy War in Galilee' (the invasion of Lebanon), the expropriation of Palestinian land on the West bank, and the racist views of Rabbi Kahane. Contrasting the idealistic newsreels of the late '40s with contemporary footage and interviews, he suggests that such chauvinist notions are not endemic to Zionism but a corruption of it. The film's left-of-centre liberalism isn't always as clearly focused as it might be, but for the most part it eschews partisan rhetoric in favour of opening up new and vital areas of debate. NF

Shattered Image

(1998, US, 103 min)
d Raul Ruiz. *p* Barbet Schroeder, Susan Hoffman, Lloyd A Silverman. *sc* Duane Poole. *ph* Robby Müller. *ed* Michael Duthie. *pd* Robert DeVico. *m* Jorge Arriagada. *cast* Anne Parillaud, William Baldwin, Lisanne Falk, Graham Greene, Bulle Ogier, Billy Wilmott, O'Neil Peart, Leonie Forbes.
● With his first American film, eccentric exiled Chilean Ruiz may be making a foray into the kind of sex 'n' thrills normally associated with straight-to-video schlock, but it's as ambitious, weird and intriguing as one would expect. Basically this is a lurid psycho-thriller in which Parillaud lives two lives: one as a rich heiress who suspects her new husband (Baldwin) is planning to kill her, the other as a femme fatale hit woman. Which is real, which the dream? She, for one, has no idea, and nor probably will you. Not that it matters, since this is Ruiz at his most playful, messing about irreverently with generic clichés and tropes, eliciting some dazzlingly exotic trompe l'oeil images from the amazing Robby Müller, and revelling not only in his two leads' robotic performances but (not once but twice) in a passing Chinaman who wanders very obviously into shot at a key moment. Absurd nonsense but great fun. GA

Shawshank (100) Redemption, The

(1994, US, 142 min)
d Frank Darabont. *p* Niki Marvin. *sc* Frank Darabont. *ph* Roger Deakins. *ed* Richard Francis-Bruce. *pd* Terence Marsh. *m* Thomas Newman. *cast* Tim Robbins, Morgan Freeman, Bob Gunton, William Sadler, Clancy Brown, Gil Bellows, Mark Rolston.
● In 1946 a young New England banker, Andy Dufresne (Robbins), is convicted of murdering his wife and her lover and sentenced to life at the Shawshank State Prison – twice over. Quiet and

introspective, he gradually strikes up a friendship with the prison 'fixer', Red (Freeman), and over the next two decades wins the trust of the governor and guards, but in his heart, he still yearns for freedom. Darabont's adaptation of a Stephen King novella is a throwback to the kind of serious, literate drama Hollywood used to make (*Birdman of Alcatraz*, say) though the big spiritual resolution takes some swallowing – ditto the colour-blind relationships within the prison and the violent disavowal of any homosexual implications. Against this weighs the pleasure of discovering a first-time director with evident respect for the intelligence of his audience, brave enough to let character details accumulate without recourse to the fast-forward button. Darabont plays the long game and wins: this is an engrossing, superbly acted yarn, while the Shawshank itself is a truly formidable mausoleum. TCh

She

(1935, US, 95 min, b/w)
d Irving Pichel, Lansing C Holden. *p* Merian C Cooper. *sc* Ruth Rose, Dudley Nichols. *ph* J Roy Hunt. *ed* Ted Cheesman. *ad* Van Nest Polglase. *m* Max Steiner. *cast* Helen Gahagan, Randolph Scott, Helen Mack, Nigel Bruce, Gustav von Seyffertitz, Noble Johnson.
●The first talkie version of Rider Haggard's much (and unsatisfactorily) filmed yarn. Though produced by Merian C Cooper, who was very much at home in the jungles of King Kong and Count Zaroff, the action was for some ineffable reason shifted in locale from Africa to the Arctic, so that the fantastic underground kingdom of She (who bathed in the mysterious Flame of Life centuries ago and tries to entice Scott away from his mortal love) nestles picturesquely among the snowscapes. Frequent recourse to backdrops rather undercuts the spectacular effect (though the furnishings and costumes prevailing in She's domain have a certain tacky splendour); the dialogue is routine Hollywood period adventurespeak; and it's difficult to decide, between Gahagan and Scott as the two leads, who gives the more inexpressive, uncharismatic performance. TM

She

(1965, GB, 165 min)
d Robert Day. *p* Michael Carreras. *sc* David Chantler. *ph* Harry Waxman. *ed* James Needs, Eric Boyd-Perkins. *ad* Robert Jones, Don Mingaye. *m* James Bernard. *cast* Ursula Andress, John Richardson, Peter Cushing, Bernard Cribbins, Christopher Lee, Andre Morell, Rosenda Monteros.
●Rider Haggard's *She Who Must Be Obeyed* (now you know where Rumpole of the Bailey got his tag line from) emerges predictably in this low-rent exotica from Hammer as she who must be ogled, and the old hunt-for-the-lost-city formula doesn't even cut it as camp. At least the setting returned to warmer climes from the Arctic setting of the 1935 version, no doubt to explain Andress' undress. PT

Sheba Baby

(1975, US, 89 min)
d William Girdler. *p* David Sheldon. *sc* William Girdler. *ph* William Asman. *ed* Harry Asman, Jack Davies. *pd* J Patrick Kelly III. *m* Monk Higgins, Alex Brown. *cast* Pam Grier, Austin Stoker, D'Urville Martin, Rudy Challenger, Dick Merrifield.
●Private eye Sheba Shayne plays a lone hand against a gang of racketeers trying to take over her father's business. Any 'generic significance' claimed for Pam Grier's movies clearly dissipated long before this travesty, where jive-talkin', posturing blacks conform so closely to stereotype that they are not merely uninteresting but offensive. Not only do all the characters behave as the epitome of the urban 'street nigger', they have all assimilated the American Dream without question: a dream of patronising liberalism, non-confrontation and self-fulfilment, here clearly used to keep everyone in their places. Pap, made with contempt. SM

She Creature, The

(1956, US, 77 min, b/w)
d Edward L Cahn. *p* Alex Gordon. *sc* Lou Rusoff. *ph* Frederick E West. *ed* Ronald Sinclair. *ad* Don Ament. *m* Ronald Stein. *cast* Chester Morris, Tom Conway, Cathy Downs, Lance Fuller, Ron Randell, Marla English, Frieda Inescort.
●Cheerful grade-Z monster mayhem as the assistant of a carnival hypnotist is sent into a trance only to reveal her true self, swiftly transforming into a rampaging prehistoric sea beast. In time-honoured showbiz tradition, the mesmerist and his associates soon try to make a fast buck by 'predicting' the creature's killings. Quite a convincing monster. TJ

She Demons

(1958, US, 80 min, b/w)
d Richard E Cunha. *p* Arthur A Jacobs. *sc* Richard R Cunha, HE Barrie. *ph* Meredith M Nicholson. *ed* William Shea. *m* Nicholas Carras. *cast* Irish McCalla, Tod Griffin, Victor Sen Yung, Rudolph Anders, Leni Tana.
●If you're curious about the more baroque sensations usually untapped by the normal film-making brain, this is your tacky dream drama. A vicious hurricane shipwrecks our heroes on a suspicious island, where the beached debutante combs her peroxide locks and complains, 'Where's my powder blue cashmere shortie?' Attention is soon distracted by Native Drums, then by radio news that they're sitting on a Navy bomb target (promptly forgotten for the next hour by the cast), and the discovery of a bevy of jungle babes in bikinis engaged in a hoochie-coo hula around a fire. Festivities are interrupted by a whip-wielding Nazi who holds the franchise on this Iggy Pop School of Dance... and from there the action proceeds along paths explicable only in terms of heavy hallucinogenic use among the script team. CR

She-Devil

(1989, US, 99 min)
d Susan Seidelman. *p* Jonathan Brett, Susan Seidelman. *sc* Barry Strugatz, Mark R Burns. *ph* Oliver Stapleton. *ed* Craig McKay. *pd* Santo Loquasto. *m* Howard Shore. *cast* Meryl Streep, Roseanne Barr, Ed Begley Jr, Sylvia Miles, Linda Hunt, Elisebeth Peters, Bryan Larkin, A Martinez.
●Cinematic adaptations of novels are under no obligation to remain rigorously faithful to the original, but even with that in mind, this version of Fay Weldon's *The Life and Loves of a She-Devil* is misjudged. The story is relocated across the Atlantic, its tone altered to leave audiences on an upbeat note. Fat, frumpy housewife Ruth (Barr) is deserted by her husband (Begley), who goes to live with glamorous romantic novelist Mary Fisher (Streep) in her high tower by the sea. With demonic conviction, Ruth sets about depriving the lovers of their new-found happiness. She makes a list of her husband's assets – Home, Family, Career and Freedom – and destroys each in turn. Thus circumscribed, the film plods to its conclusion. Streep's tentative foray into comedy is deliberately mannered, but the breathy delivery and constant fluttering of hands are nevertheless excessive. And in her film debut, Barr just isn't imposing enough to inspire notions of devilish vengeance. The film-makers have opted for frothy satire, but as comedies go this is lamentably short on laughs. CM

She Done Him Wrong

(1933, US, 66 min, b/w)
d Lowell Sherman. *p* William Le Baron. *sc* Harvey Thew, John Bright. *ph* Charles Lang Jr. *ed* Alexander Hall. *ad* Robert Usher. *songs* Ralph Rainger, Leo Robin. *cast* Mae West, Cary Grant, Owen Moore, Gilbert Roland, Noah Beery, Rochelle Hudson, Rafaela Ottiano, Louise Beavers.
●West's first starring vehicle, and one of her best (i.e. least diluted) movies. Adapted from her stage success *Diamond Lil*, it features her as Diamond Lou (a change occasioned by the original's notoriety), mistress of a Naughty Nineties saloon, setting her sights on the righteous young man (Grant) investigating the place for signs of corruption. West, making her way through ditties like 'I Like a Man What Takes His Time' and 'Frankie and Johnny', keeps most of her double-meanings single. Marvellous stuff. GA

Sheena (aka Sheena – Queen of the Jungle)

(1984, US, 117 min)
d John Guillermin. *p* Paul Aratow. *sc* David Newman, Lorenzo Semple Jr. *ph* Pasqualino De Santis. *ed* Ray Lovejoy. *pd* Peter Murton. *m* Richard Hartley. *cast* Tanya Roberts, Ted Wass, Donovan Scott, Elizabeth of Toro, France Zobda, Trevor Thomas, Clifton Jones.
●Inane jungle adventure with Roberts as a sort of Tarzanette, an all-American girl raised from childhood in the jungle by a shaman after her parents died in a rockfall. Thus she learns to talk to the animals, swing through the greenery, stitch together a suede bikini and shave her armpits. Her greatest challenge will come, however, when tribal prince Thomas, back from an American football career, threatens the harmony of this untouched enclave by aiming to exploit its lucrative titanium deposits; so it's fortunate TV sports reporter Wass is around to help thwart his plans. Oh, and since this is the first white man she's come across, Sheens falls sappily in love. Is this family movie just an excuse for the star to romp around wearing not an awful lot? Very probably. TJ

Sheepman, The

(1958, US, 91 min)
d George Marshall. *p* Edmund Grainger. *sc* William Bowers, James Edward Grant. *ph* Robert Bronner. *ed* Ralph E Winters. *ad* William A Horning, Malcolm Brown. *m* Jeff Alexander. *cast* Glenn Ford, Shirley MacLaine, Leslie Nielsen, Mickey Shaughnessy, Edgar Buchanan, Pernell Roberts, Slim Pickens.
●A minor but irresistibly amiable semi-comic Western that looks both backwards to Marshall's own glorious *Destry Rides Again* and forwards to the Burt Kennedy films of the late '60s. The plot is archetypal – sheep farmer Ford arrives in town, only to incur the wrath of cattle baron Nielsen, whose girl MacLaine he eventually steals – and the comedy lies in the twists of characterisation. The tone is set as soon as Ford mildly asks for a cigar instead of setting up the usual whisky in the saloon: a symbol not of weakness (as the town bully reads it) but of his uncompromising independence (he immediately proceeds to beat up said thug). Sturdy performances all round, so that even the action sequences deliver a punch. GA

She Gods of Shark Reef

(1957, US, 63 min)
d Roger Corman. *p* Ludwig Gerber. *sc* Robert Hill, Victor Stoloff. *ph* Floyd Crosby. *ed* Frank Sullivan. *m* Ronald Stein. *cast* Don Durant, Bill Cord, Lisa Montell, Jeanne Gerson, Carol Lindsay.
●Strictly zero-budget exotica, less Corman's *South Pacific* than, one suspects, an excuse for the film unit to take a Hawaiian holiday. Despite the flimsiest of scripts and not much evidence of more than a long day's shooting, Corman at least honours the implications of the title and offers two chunky beefcake Tab Hunter/Pat Boone lookalikes, prowling around somewhat hilariously in loincloths, as brothers (one good, one bad) stranded on an island inhabited only by women. A film that invites running commentary from the stalls. CPe

She Lives to Ride

(1994, US, 76 min)
d/p/ed Alice Stone. *sc* Diane Hendrik. *ph* Maryse Alberti. *m* Mason Daring.
●This debut documentary looks behind the lust'n'leather, 'Girl of a Motorcycle' clichés to portray the everyday women who decide that riding pillion is no longer enough. Constructed round a series of interviews, including one with the leader of the lesbian pack who form the vanguard of New York's Gay Pride marchers, and another with the redoubtable owner of a shocking pink Harley, still biking in her 82nd year, this entertaining and informative film reveals the camaraderie and sense of freedom these women gain from hitting the road together – without waiting for the man to decide where to stop for a pee. TJ

She'll Be Wearing Pink Pyjamas

(1984, GB, 90 min)
d John Goldschmidt. *p* Tara Prem, Adrian Hughes. *sc* Eva Hardy. *ph* Clive Tickner. *ed* Richard Key. *pd* Colin Pocock. *m* John Du Prez. *cast* Julie Walters, Anthony Higgins, Jane Evers, Janet Henfrey, Paula Jacobs, Penelope Nice.
●Eight women on an Outward Bound course in the Lake District. Cross-reference: *The Way Ahead*, minus the saluting, with the characters grousing at the hardships and chafing at the

discipline, yet all the time being prepared by their instructors to go out and kill or be killed in the big campaign of life. Apparently scriptwriter Eva Hardy is recycling her own experiences, though it seems improbable that her real-life companions were as entirely lacking in the unexpected as this lot. Not bad, just very conventional. BBa

Sheltering Sky, The

(1990, GB/It, 138 min)
d Bernardo Bertolucci. *p* Jeremy Thomas. *sc* Mark Peploe, Bernardo Bertolucci. *ph* Vittorio Storaro. *ed* Gabriella Cristiani. *ad* Gianni Silvestri. *m* Ryuichi Sakamoto. *cast* Debra Winger, John Malkovich, Campbell Scott, Jill Bennett, Timothy Spall, Eric Vu-An, Amina Annabi.

● Paul Bowles' novel presents the problem of interiorisation, and a presiding morbidity that would clear most movie-houses. Bertolucci has wisely elected to open things out and to humanise his characters, relenting a little in favour of romance. The American travellers in North Africa, Kit and Port Moresby, still go down the drain, but in this version you care. Remote husband Port (Malkovich) unwisely samples Arab prostitutes, neurotic Kit (Winger) has a fling with their travelling companion Tunner (Scott); but where the story really hooks in is their realisation, after an abortive attempt at sex, that reconciliation is impossible. Port contracts typhoid, and the couple's frantic search for help in increasingly primitive terrain makes for horrifyingly powerful cinema. After Port's death, Kit loses both identity and compass bearings, wanders into the desert, and enters into a sexual delirium with the Tuareg Belqassim (Vu-An). As you'd expect, it's a big, handsome film, rich and strange in psychological depths and eroticism. Malkovich and Winger play woundingly well. BC

Shelter of the Wings (Charachar)

(1993, Ind, 97 min)
d Buddhadeb Dasgupta. *p* Shankar Gope, Gita Gope. *sc* Buddhadeb Dasgupta. *ph* Soumendu Roy. *ed* Ujjal Nandi. *pd* Shatadal Mitra. *m* Biswadeb Dasgupta. *cast* Rajit Kapoor, Laboni Sarkar, Sadhu Mehar, Shankar Chakraborty.

● Dull if well-meaning fable, written and directed by the Bengali poet Buddhadeb Dasgupta, about an impoverished bird-catcher whose preference for freeing birds causes trouble with his more practical, less poetically inclined wife. Slow, slight and (speaking as a die-hard ornithologist/conservationist) excessively sentimental. GA

She Must Be Seeing Things

(1987, US, 91 min)
d/p/sc Sheila McLaughlin. *ph* Mark Daniels. *ed* Ila von Hasperg. *ad* Leigh Kyle. *m* John Zorn. *cast* Sheila Dabney, Lois Weaver, Kyle DiCamp, John Erdman, Ed Bowes, Uzi Parnes.

● Vivacious blonde Jo (Weaver) is making a film about Catalina, a 17th century woman forced to live her life as a man. Jo's lover Agatha (Dabney), suffering a crisis when she reads Jo's diary detailing previous affairs with men, takes to spying on Jo and imagining her in compromising situations with male members of the film crew. Meanwhile, Catalina's experiences in Jo's film mirror Agatha's inner turmoil. The vague cross-cutting between what Agatha sees and what she imagines becomes intriguing, as does Catalina's tragic story, but there's a disconcerting subtext. Agatha's insecurity manifests itself as penis envy – a too simplistic response to a complex situation which, coupled with McLaughlin's disruptive technique of having her characters speak to camera whenever they're alone, sets a slightly patronising tone. On the other hand, the sex scenes are refreshingly frank and often funny. EP

Sheriff, Le (Le Juge Fayard dit le Sheriff)

(1976, Fr, 112 min)
d Yves Boisset. *p* Yves Gasser. *sc* Yves Boisset, Claude Veillot. *ph* Jacques Loiseleux. *ed* Albert Jurgenson, Lawrence Leininger. *ad* Serge Sommier. *m* Philippe Sarde. *cast* Patrick Dewaere, Aurore Clément, Philippe Léotard, Michel Auclair, Jean Bouise, Jean-Marc Thibault, Daniel Ivernel, Jacques Spiesser.

● Judge Fayard (Dewaere) is a bright-eyed amalgam of Errol Flynn and Uomo Vogue, whose cowboy nickname is the result of his tendency to come on like *The Sweeney*. A petty crime leads him to uncover a major one, its multi-million franc haul partly ending up as a Gaullist candidate's campaign bankroll. Unfortunately the film skates to a familiar denouement, content to offer the occasional crumb of irony amid an odd blend of plodding realism and tough guy staples.

Sheriff of Fractured Jaw, The

(1958, GB, 110 min)
d Raoul Walsh. *p* Daniel M Angel. *sc* Howard Dimsdale. *ph* Otto Heller. *ed* John Shirley. *ad* Bernard Robinson. *m* Robert Farnon. *cast* Kenneth More, Jayne Mansfield, Bruce Cabot, Henry Hull, William Campbell, Robert Morley, Ronald Squire.

● An oddball comic Western, shot by Walsh on Spanish locations (and British studio interiors), with Kenneth More as the unsuccessful English inventor, turned gun salesman in the American West, who is mistaken for a gunman and eventually tames the town with the aid of some amiable Indians. Chiefly memorable for the strange vision of buxom Jayne Mansfield and wimpish sheriff More grappling with the incompatibility of their bodies, providing an occasional hoot and many an exercise in single entendre. DMacp

Sherlock Holmes

see Adventures of Sherlock Holmes, The

Sherlock Holmes and the Spider Woman

(1944, US, 62 min, b/w)
d/p Roy William Neill. *sc* Bertram Millhauser. *ph* Charles Van Enger. *ed* William Austin. *ad* John B Goodman, Martin Obzina. *m* Hans Salter. *cast* Basil Rathbone, Nigel Bruce, Gale Sondergaard, Denis Hoey, Vernon Downing, Alec Craig.

● With Gale Sondergaard providing a superbly malevolent adversary, this is one of the most striking entries in the Rathbone/Bruce Sherlock Holmes series. Making her social calls accompanied by an unnervingly unsmiling mute child who catches flies on the wing, she is secretly masterminding a devilish insurance racket, preying on the wealthiest men in London by using a dwarf to gain entrance to their homes and leave venomous spiders to do their bit. She also (hopefully) reserves a fiendish fate for Holmes at the carnival which serves as her HQ: Dr Watson proudly demonstrates his skill at the shooting gallery, unaware that behind the effigy of Hitler serving as his patriotic target, Holmes waits helplessly bound and gagged. Started by 20th Century-Fox (*The Hound of the Baskervilles* and The *Adventures of Sherlock Holmes*, both 1939), the series was revived by Universal with *Sherlock Holmes and the Voice of Terror* (1942), the new regime signalled by a switch to modern dress (neatly pointed by having Holmes select, then discard, his deerstalker as inappropriately old-fashioned). Although saddled with a tag-line or two of World War II propaganda uplift, and sometimes direct confrontation with evil Nazi agents, the watchword was Holmesian business as usual; and thanks to a gift for sinister atmospherics displayed by Roy William Neill (who directed the last eleven films in a series of fourteen, ended with his death in 1946), a remarkably high standard was maintained throughout this B movie series. TM

Sherlock Holmes' Smarter Brother

see Adventures of Sherlock Holmes' Younger Brother

Sherlock Junior

(1924, US, 4,065 ft, b/w)
d Buster Keaton. *p* Joseph M Schenck. *sc* Jean Havez, Joseph Mitchell, Clyde Bruckman. *ph* Elgin Lessley, Byron Houck. *ed* Buster Keaton. *ad* Fred Gabourie. *cast* Buster Keaton, Kathryn McGuire, Joe Keaton, Ward Crane, Jane Connelly.

● Keaton's third feature under his own steam is an incredible technical accomplishment, but also an almost Pirandellian exploration of the nature of cinematic reality. Buster plays a cinema projectionist, framed for theft by a jealous rival for his girl's hand, who daydreams himself into life as a daring detective. In an unforgettable sequence, Buster (actually fallen asleep beside the projector) forces his way onto the screen and into the movie he is projecting, only to find himself beset by perils and predicaments as the action around him changes in rapid montage. The sequence is not just a gag, but an astonishingly acute perception of the interaction between movie reality and audience fantasy, and the role of editing in juggling both. The timing here is incredible (a technical marvel, in fact); even more so in the great chase sequence, an veritable cascade of unbelievably complex gags (like the moment when Buster, on the handlebars of a riderless, runaway motor-bike passing some ditch-digging roadworks, receives a spadeful of earth in the face from each oblivious navvy in turn). It leaves Chaplin standing. TM

Sherman's March

(1985, US, 160 min)
d/p/sc/ph/ed Ross McElwee. *narrators* Ross McElwee, Richard Leacock.

● General Sherman's march through the South in the American Civil War was unrivalled up to that time for its ferocity towards a civilian population. McElwee's march through identical terrain was little more than a *cinema verité* girl hunt, though the alternative ethos is closer to the era of Richard Brautigan's *A Confederate General from Big Sur* than *The Confessions of a Window Cleaner*. It is extremely long, inconsequential and low-budget, but if you surrender to it, it is not devoid of delights and resources. Honours are divided between the director's sister, with her reluctant explanation of her 'fanny tuck', and the buxom and biting Charleen, who tries to bully him into falling for one of her stable of eligible girls. McElwee's voice-over commentary is another of the movie's little pleasures. BC

She's All That

(1999, US, 95 min)
d Robert Iscove. *p* Peter Abrams, Robert L Levy, Richard N Gladstein. *sc* R Lee Fleming Jr. *ph* Francis Kenny. *ed* Casey O Rohrs. *pd* Charles Breen. *m* Stewart Copeland. *cast* Freddie Prinze Jr, Rachael Leigh Cook, Matthew Lillard, Paul Walker, Jodi Lyn O'Keefe, Kevin Pollak, Kieran Culkin, Elden Henson, Usher Raymond.

● High school golden boy Zak (Prinze) has been dumped by his glamorous, bitchy girlfriend. Determined to reassert his cool, he bets he can turn any girl into a prom queen. The chosen one is an arty, impoverished goth, 'scary' Laney Boggs (Cook). Says Zak to his friend, 'Fat I can handle, even weird boobs, but not scary.' Yeah, right. A formula flick like this couldn't handle fat or weird boobs in a million years (name one current female teen dream over 140lb). But 'scary' – that just translates as 'hard to get'. Of course, Laney's angry facade takes little to crack. She wears glasses because, as she explains to Zak, she doesn't like contact lenses. Yet, without explanation, those unflattering specs disappear and soon she's magazine pretty. Her anti-social integrity also proves a neat way to keep her virginal for Zak. Once Laney finds out about the bet, the 'tension' revolves around whether she'll forgive him or let his best friend Dean go where no man has gone before. Guess which way she jumps, folks. CO'Su

She's Been Away

(1989, GB, 103 min)
d Peter Hall. *p* Kenith Trodd. *sc* Stephen Poliakoff. *ph* Philip Bonham-Carter. *ed* Ardan Fisher. *pd* Gary Williamson. *m* Stephen Edwards. *cast* Peggy Ashcroft, Geraldine James, James Fox, Rachel Kempson, Rebecca Pidgeon.

● Scripted by Stephen Poliakoff, the first 35mm movie wholly financed by the BBC, this has the incomparable Ashcroft as an elderly woman, put into institutional care when still a young woman, released in her twilight years by the agency of her liberal nephew (Fox). Ashcroft's problem is not mental illness but a surfeit of stubborness and independence, the former communicated by her weapon of silence against repressiveness, the latter by flashbacks which show her as a young, vaguely libertarian and feminist black sheep. But the impetus of the film is the relationship between Ashcroft and Fox's contented but stifled wife (splendidly played by Geraldine James). The grudging but gradual bond between the two women leads, almost inevitably with Poliakoff, into a spot of picaresque delinquency in the family Daimler and the realisation that all is not well with this seemingly ideal marriage. Good stuff, slightly pat, but as with most of Poliakoff's writing, always engaging and often amusingly sly. SGr

She's Gotta Have It

(1986, US, 85 min, b/w & col)
d Spike Lee. *p* Shelton J Lee. *sc* Spike Lee. *ph* Ernest Dickerson. *ed* Spike Lee. *pd* Wynn Thomas. *m* Bill Lee. *cast* Tracy Camila Johns, Tommy Redmond Hicks, John Canada Terrell, Spike Lee, Ray Dowell, Joie Lee.

● Lee's first feature focuses around the attempts of Nola Darling (Johns), aware but not ashamed of her reputation as a good-time girl, to sort out the three steady men in her life with a view (maybe) to marriage: the sincere and caring Jamie (Hicks), the self-obsessed model Greer (Terrell), and the outrageous bicycle messenger Mars (Lee). Each lover, convinced that he is the solution to Nola's problem, makes his prospective pitch (to the girl and audience alike) in a series of painfully funny character vignettes. The action centres on Nola's spacious Brooklyn studio, where the men take it in turns to assassinate each other's characters, before gathering round Nola's Thanksgiving table to do it face-to-face. Structurally, it could be compared to Kurosawa's *Rashomon* for its subjective cross-examination of Nola's loves; but this delightful low-budget comedy, with its all black cast and black humour, is 100 per cent Lee. SGo

She's Having a Baby

(1988, US, 106 min)
d/p/sc John Hughes. *ph* Don Peterman. *ed* Alan Heim. *ad* John W Corso. *m* Stewart Copeland, Nicky Holland. *cast* Kevin Bacon, Elizabeth McGovern, Alec Baldwin, Isabel Lorca, William Windom, Cathryn Damon, Dennis Dugan, Edie McClurg, Dan Aykroyd.

● Taking his erstwhile teen lovers into young adulthood, marriage and parenthood, John Hughes fashions a curiously disaffected portrait of the artist as a frustrated chauvinist. Bacon – an aspiring writer who lands a job in advertising, just as Hughes did – narrates the film. We are privy to his daydreams about freedom and his resentment towards his bride (McGovern in a terrible role), and then we watch his change of heart in a thoroughly unconvincing last reel. This is bitter-sweet compartmentalised, with the saccharine spooned on at the end. Even then it lacks flavour. TCh

She's Out of Control

(1989, US, 95 min)
d Stan Dragoti. *p* Stephen Deutsch, John G Wilson. *sc* Seth Winston, Michael J Nathanson. *ph* Donald Peterman. *ed* Dov Hoenig. *pd* David L Snyder. *m* Alan Silvestri. *cast* Tony Danza, Catherine Hicks, Wallace Shawn, Dick O'Neill, Ami Dolenz, Laura Mooney, Derek McGrath, Dana Ashbrook.

● What Katie (Dolenz), daughter of single parent Doug (Danza), has out of control is her sexuality. She's sweet 15, never been kissed (teeth brace and glasses don't help), and Dad can't hear the prologue of 'The Rites of Spring' playing for her. Then he returns from a convention connected with his failing '60s-sounds radio station to find his ugly duckling descending the stairs (slo-mo, to Frankie Avalon's 'Venus') in swan-white mini, cascading hair and contacts. Suitors follow in numbers: every dope-head, biker and cast-eyed no-hoper in Southern California queues outside the door, while precocious little sister mans the telephone dating system. It's desperation time for dad, his only hope being loopy Middle-European child psychiatrist Dr Fishbinder (another Wallace Shawn caricature). Dragoti's dire, dishonest, seldom humorous social comedy has all the nauseating hallmarks of a big-budget sitcom. Can't wait for the John Waters remake. WH

She's So Lovely

(1997, US, 112 min)
d Nick Cassavetes. *p* René Cleitman. *sc* John Cassavetes. *ph* Thierry Arbogast. *ed* Petra von Oelffen. *pd* David Wasco. *m* Joseph Vitarelli. *cast* Sean Penn, Robin Wright Penn, John Travolta, Harry Dean Stanton, Debi Mazar, Gena Rowlands, James Gandolfini.

● Based on what looks like an unfinished script written by his late father, Nick Cassavetes' film – about the troubled, on-off relationship between lowlife boozers Eddie and Maureen (the two Penns), the latter taking up with a steadier type (Travolta) while Eddie serves time – merely shows the gulf between the sloppily 'naturalistic' mannerisms on view here and the kind of authentic psychological and emotional epiphanies John Cassavetes used to give us. Harry Dean Stanton provides some much needed humour, but the film's celebratory attitude towards a dangerously wild love that defies logic and convention lacks depth and genuine insights. GA

She's the One

(1996, US, 96 min)
d Edward Burns. *p* Ted Hope, James Schamus, Edward Burns. *sc* Edward Burns. *ph* Frank Prinzi. *ed* Susan Graef. *pd* William Barclay. *m* Tom Petty. *cast* Jennifer Aniston, Maxine Bahns, Edward Burns, Cameron Diaz, Mike McGlone, John Mahoney, Anita Gillette.

● Burns' follow-up to *The Brothers McMullen* is a disappointment. It's basically the same film, only longer, more expensive, and a whole lot more tiresome. This time, Burns plays Mickey, 'the only English-speaking white guy driving a cab in New York.' He's still hung up on Heather, a blonde dream who long ago turned into a nightmare. That is, until he picks up a fare, Hope (Bahns), and she picks up him. Meanwhile, McGlone (the religious McMullen) gets to be the philandering brother this time, Francis, an obnoxious yuppie who's cheating on wife Renee (Aniston) with – you guessed it – Heather. Confused? You won't be, as the film spells out every relationship in detail. The brothers Fitzpatrick lay the blame squarely on pop (Mahoney), but the writer/director is much too easy on them. His characters' blank incomprehension when it comes to the female of the species looks less like comic observation, more unalloyed chauvinism. This movie reeks of it like aftershave. Diaz's Heather is one of the most misogynistic femmes fatales this side of *film noir*. A bland, so-so romantic comedy without the charm to see it through. TCh

She Wore a Yellow Ribbon

(1949, US, 103 min)
d John Ford. *p* John Ford, Merian C Cooper. *sc* Laurence Stallings, Frank S Nugent. *ph* Winton Hoch. *ed* Jack Murray. *ad* James Basevi. *m* Richard Hageman. *cast* John Wayne, Joanne Dru, John Agar, Ben Johnson, Harry Carey Jr, Victor McLaglen, Mildred Natwick, George O'Brien, Arthur Shields.

● The centrepieee of Ford's cavalry trilogy (flanked by *Fort Apache* and *Rio Grande)* and a film of both elegiac sentiment and occasionally over-eloquent sentimentality, structured around a series of ritual incidents rather than narrative conflicts. Wayne's captain and McLaglen's sergeant face up to impending retirement from a force whose role and self-awareness is changing in the wake of Custer's defeat; America, however, still has to be willed into existence and unity. Winton Hoch's Technicolor cinematography of Monument Valley (modelled at Ford's insistence on Remington pictorialism) won him an Oscar. PT

Shikoku

(1999, Jap, 101 min)
d Shunichi Nagasaki. *p* Masato Hara. *sc* Kunimi Manda, Takenori Sento. *ph* Noboru Shinoda. *ed* Yoshiyuki Okuhara. *pd* Yohei Taneda. *m* Satoshi Kadokura. *cast* Yui Natsukawa, Michitaka Tsutsui, Chiaki Kuriyama, Kie Negishi, Ren Osugi.

● Contributing to the current Japanese cycle of ghost chillers wasn't the most obvious career move for Nagasaki, better known for deviant *noir* thrillers, but *Shikoku* is a qualified success. The title puns on the name of Japan's most laid-back prefecture (depending how you write it, Shikoku can mean 'Four Counties' or 'Land of the Dead') and the plot exploits the island's traditions of esoteric Buddhism and shamanism. Hinako (Natsukawa) revisits her childhood home to find that her best friend Sayori has drowned – and that Sayori's mother is making the *o-henro* pilgrimage around Shikoku's 88 coastal temples in reverse order, hoping to open a gateway to the netherworlds and bring back her daughter. The supernatural stuff is mostly routine, but Nagasaki pulls off several psychological frissons. TR

Shine

(1996, Aust/GB, 106 min)
d Scott Hicks. *p* Jane Scott. *sc* Jan Sardi. *ph* Geoffrey Simpson. *ed* Pip Karmel. *pd* Vicki Niehus. *m* David Hirschfelder. *cast* Armin Mueller-Stahl, Noah Taylor, Geoffrey Rush, Lynn Redgrave, John Gielgud, Googie Withers, Sonia Todd, Nicholas Bell.

● Teenage pianist David (Taylor) has all the usual problems and then some. His father, a Polish-Jewish immigrant in working-class Perth, Australia, places such a burden of hope on his son that he won't let him leave the family nest, and insists on his working towards 'The Rach 3' – Rachmaninov's bone-crunching 3rd Piano Concerto – whether he's ready for such a super-virtuoso piece or not. With a scholarship to London's Royal College of Music there for the taking, the future has some tough questions to ask, answered by a nervous collapse of cataclysmic proportions, years of psychological damage, and a painful recovery sprung from the most unlikely surroundings – requests for the popular classics in a Perth wine bar. Scott Hicks' film, where the rites-of-passage pic meets high-falutin' backstage melodrama, is based on the true story of the prodigy David Helfgott, whose flashing finger work we hear on the soundtrack. Stage actor Geoffrey Rush has total command of the mature artist's chattering eccentricities and with striking on-screen keyboard skills creates a characterisation so minutely observed you expect him to stride naked off the screen. Helfgott's turbulent personal history fits few preconceived patterns. Entirely attuned, Hicks' switchback time-scheme reserves a canny facility for surprise as it guides us round a fine supporting cast – Gielgud (ripe old piano tutor), Mueller-Stahl (a stage papa to reckon with), Lynn Redgrave (warmly supportive spouse) – while the music comes over as if life itself depended on it. Compassionate, deft, unsentimental, inspirational. TJ

Shiner

(2000, GB, 99 min)
d John Irvin. *p* Geoffrey Reeve, Jim Reeve. *sc* Scott Cherry. *ph* Mike Molloy. *ed* Ian Crafford. *pd* Austen Spriggs. *m* Paul Grabowsky. *cast* Michael Caine, Martin Landau, Frances Barber, Frank Harper, Andy Serkis, Claire Rushbrook, Danny Webb, Matthew Marsden, Kenneth Cranham.

● Caine plays the East End boxing promoter of the title whose family finances depend, precariously, on his gibbering wreck of a son defeating the relaxed-looking champ of his American counterpart Frank Spedding (Landau). No chance. It's all over hours before the fight, and when the knockout's followed by a shooting, Shiner is frantic, determined to root out the people who got to his boy. Irvin's thriller ambles along for 30 minutes following preparations for the event. Then the mood shifts, the banter between Shiner and his entourage turning tense as his best ever day goes rapidly wrong. If the diffuse plotting initially feels scrappy, it gels after the fight. It's unfair to bracket this within the recent British gangster cycle, as the lowlifes and violence are endemic to the boxing world Shiner inhabits. What's at stake here is a deluded Cockney small fry, living on borrowed time and cheap glitz, whose relationships have gone sour. It makes sense, too, that there's nothing flash in the film's technique. The back to basics approach is refreshing: a great story, classy ensemble, and a director confident enough to take his time. SS

Shin Heike Monogatari (New Tales of the Taira Clan)

(1955, Jap, 107 min)
d Kenji Mizoguchi. *p* Masaichi Nagata. *sc* Yoshikata Yoda, Masashige Narusawa, Kyuichi Tsuji. *ph* Kazuo Miyagawa. *ad* Hiroshi Mizutani. *m* Fumio Hayasaka, Masaru Sato. *cast* Raizo Ichikawa, Ichijiro Oya, Michiyo Kogure, Eijiro Yanagi, Tatsuya Ishiguro, Yoshiko Kuga.

● One of Mizoguchi's two late films in colour, this describes a conflict between three power groups in feudal Japan: the priests, the court, and a clan of samurai. The samurai embody ideals of individual integrity, just service, and male prowess; the court, ideals of rightful authority, but equally, the faults of ministerial corruption; the clerics, the degeneration of institutionalised religion into factional Fascism (gang-like violence in support of political ends). Characteristically, the tale of the conflict is hinged round a courtesan figure's relations with the three groups ('mother' for the samurai, 'mistress' for the court, 'whore' for the priests). Needless to say, the 'personal' virtues of the samurai win out, the hero becomes superman. Shot with all the sensitivity and stylish trappings to be expected from Mizoguchi; also, some sharp observation of social relations, and some acute insights into the vagaries of the power boys' shit-games. JDuC

Shining, The 100

(1980, GB, 146 min)
d/p Stanley Kubrick. *sc* Stanley Kubrick, Diane Johnson. *ph* John Alcott. *ed* Ray Lovejoy. *pd* Roy Walker. *m* Wendy Carlos. *cast* Jack Nicholson, Shelley Duvall, Danny Lloyd, Scatman Crothers, Barry Nelson, Philip Stone, Joseph Turkel, Anne Jackson.

●If you go to this adaptation of Stephen King's novel expecting to see a horror movie, you'll be disappointed. From the start, Kubrick undercuts potential tension builders by a process of anti-climax; eerie aerial shots accompanied by ponderous music prove to be nothing more than that; the setting is promising enough – an empty, isolated hotel in dead-of-winter Colorado – but Kubrick makes it warm, well-lit and devoid of threat. Granted, John Alcott's cinematography is impressive, and occasionally produces a 'look behind you' panic; but to hang the movie's psychological tension on the leers and grimaces of Nicholson's face (suited though it is to demoniacal expressions), while refusing to develop any sense of the man, is asking for trouble. Similarly, the narrative is too often disregarded in favour of crude and confusing visual shocks. Kubrick's unbalanced approach (over-emphasis on production values) results in soulless cardboard cutouts who can do little to generate audience empathy. FF

Shining Hour, The

(1938, US, 80 min, b/w)
d Frank Borzage. *p* Joseph L Mankiewicz. *sc* Ogden Nash, Jane Murfin. *ph* George Folsey. *ed* Frank E Hull. *ad* Cedric Gibbons, Paul Groesse. *m* Franz Waxman. *cast* Joan Crawford, Margaret Sullavan, Robert Young, Melvyn Douglas, Fay Bainter, Allyn Joslyn, Hattie McDaniel, Frank Albertson.

●Produced by Joseph L Mankiewicz, this is a stylish soap with Crawford as a night-club dancer, of some notoriety but yearning for respectability, who lets herself be persuaded to marry a gentleman farmer from Wisconsin (Douglas). But at the home farm – a stately mansion – she is met with implacable hostility from the groom's matriarchal older sister (Bainter), and similar hostility that turns to desire from his younger brother (Young); only Young's devoted wife (Sullavan) welcomes her unreservedly. Uneasily aware that she is tempted by Young, Crawford begs Douglas to take her away, only to be stymied by Sullavan's willingness to sacrifice herself if her husband can find happiness in his new love. So far, so good, with a sharpish script (Ogden Nash contributed) that makes good use of the casting (Crawford's disillusioned cynicism versus Sullavan's naive romanticism) to make incisive points about the many-splendoured aspects of love. Latterly, alas, the film nosedives into silly melodrama, with Bainter running mad to commit arson, Crawford saving the self-immolating Sullavan, and all the problems coming out Persil-white in the wash. Recognisable, with all faults, as a Borzage film. TM

Shining Through

(1992, US, 132 min)
d David Seltzer. *p* Carol Baum, Howard Rosenman. *sc* David Seltzer. *ph* Jan de Bont. *ed* Craig McKay. *pd* Anthony Pratt. *m* Michael Kamen. *cast* Michael Douglas, Melanie Griffith, Liam Neeson, Joely Richardson, John Gielgud, Francis Guinan, Sheila Allen, Sylvia Syms, Mathieu Carrière.

●A lavish, ludicrous WWII melodrama in which Griffith plays a plucky, half-Jewish secretary from New York who, through her job with lawyer and secret spymaster Douglas, becomes involved in romance, mystery and adventure. Hired for her German-speaking skills, Griffith is on hand when a key Berlin spy is murdered, and volunteers to replace him. Taken on as a cook by a prominent Nazi, she plans to microfilm documents and pass them on to US Intelligence. In no other respect does intelligence, or plausibility, come into it. As Griffith tries to save the Free World from prototype 'doodlebug' rockets, the contrived plot and manufactured suspense spiral into absurdity ('Mein Gott, you've got guts'). Griffith provides an earthy counterpoint to Douglas' stern father-figure, but everyone else is just plain embarrassing. NF

Shining Victory

(1941, US, 80 min, b/w)
d Irving Rapper. *p* Robert Lord. *sc* Howard Koch, Anne Froelick. *ph* James Wong Howe. *ed* Warren Low. *ad* Carl Jules Weyl. *m* Max Steiner. *cast* James Stephenson, Geraldine Fitzgerald, Donald Crisp, Barbara O'Neil, Montagu Love, Sig Ruman.

●Perfunctory medical drama, adapted from an AJ Cronin play (*Jupiter Laughs*), in which Stephenson is a gifted scientist who takes a posting at a private Scottish mental hospital after his earlier reasearch results have been commandeered by an unscrupulous Budapest department head. In the new environment, he at first fails to register nurse Fitzgerald's affection for him, but the jealousy of co-worker O'Neil soon snaps the plot into predictable shape. TJ

Shinjuku Triad Society (Shinjuku Kuro Shakai: China Mafia Senso)

(1995, Jap, 102 min)
d Takashi Miike. *cast* Kippei Shina, Takeshi Caesar, Sabu, Tomoro Taguchi, Eri Yu, Shinsuke Izutsu.

●Even viewers hardened to the perversities which tend to crop up in Japanese exploitation genres may find themselves rubbing their eyes at some of the images and incidents in Miike's extremist thriller about a Taiwanese triad gang muscling in on traditional yakuza territory in Tokyo. A near-psychotic 'lone wolf' from Shinjuku police station sets out to bust the Dragon's Claw gang for its involvement in drugs, body-parts trading, extortion racketeering and male prostitution; one obstacle is that his own (sexually ambivalent) younger brother is a legal adviser to the gang, which is fronted by a deranged gay sadist (Taguchi, from the *Tetsuo* films). Just when you think that a scene of sodomy – used as an aid to police interrogation – can't be topped, along comes an eye-gouging or another coke-fuelled blow job to keep things moving. Miike's stylish, gleeful direction establishes him as the most distinctive new 'voice' in the genre since Rokuro Mochizuki. TR

Ship of Fools

(1965, US, 149 min, b/w)
d/p Stanley Kramer. *sc* Abby Mann. *ph* Ernest Laszlo. *ed* Robert C Jones. *pd* Robert Clatworthy. *m* Ernest Gold. *cast* Simone Signoret, Oskar Werner, Vivien Leigh, José Ferrer, Lee Marvin, Michael Dunn, Heinz Rühmann, George Segal, Elizabeth Ashley, José Greco, Lilia Skala, Charles Korvin.

●Don't look now, but as you might expect with message-mad Kramer at the helm of this adaptation of Katherine Anne Porter's novel, there's a heavy allegory aboard: it's 1933, the ship is German, and there's a Jew among the mixed bag of passengers. Yards and yards of liberal cliché are relentlessly unfolded, but the superb cast – struggling valiantly with the sort of problems more at home in disaster movies – make it almost watchable. Among them are Signoret as a drug-addicted countess mournfully loving the ship's doctor (Werner), Vivien Leigh as a divorcee looking for a last fling before middle-age sets in, and Michael Dunn as a marvellously sharp-tongued dwarf who finds himself in a minority group of two with the Jew (Rhümann). TM

Shipping News, The

(2001, US, 117 min)
d Lasse Hallström. *p* Irwin Winkler, Linda Goldstein Knowlton, Leslie Holleran. *sc* Robert Nelson Jacobs. *ph* Oliver Stapleton. *ed* Andrew Mondshein. *pd* David Gropman. *m* Christopher Young. *cast* Kevin Spacey, Julianne Moore, Judi Dench, Scott Glenn, Rhys Ifans, Pete Postlethwaite, Cate Blanchett, Gordon Pinsent, Jason Behr, Larry Pine.

●There's a significant scene in Hallström's adaptation of E Annie Proulx's bestseller. Friends of an eccentric English adventurer (Ifans) gather on the rugged Newfoundland shore for an all night party to mark his imminent departure, and boozily destroy his boat while he looks stoically on. Tough love. This is the close, windswept ancestral home – full of cruel ironies, ghostly secrets, inherited superstitions and harsh realities – to which the timorous Quoyle (Spacey) returns, child in tow, formidable aunt (Dench) in support, after the traumatising death of his wild, selfish wife (Blanchett). The task facing Hallström is credibly to chart the course Quoyle takes from mouse to man, under the hardening inclemency of this environment. The movie has its frontiersman pleasures. It's fun to see the gradual refurbishment of the Quoyles' exposed 'salt-box' family house, as its ghouls and harboured secrets are whitewashed with the industry of new life. But Quoyle's early moral victories are hard to take unless you forget the docile no-hoper Spacey presents in his New York incarnation. Holding his head sideways like a little boy as he's kissed by fellow outsider Wavey (Moore), he takes 'low key' close to the edge of self-consciousness. Still, he generally succeeds. So does the director, but it's a pretty, shallow victory. WH

Ship That Died of Shame, The (aka PT Raiders)

(1955, GB, 95 min, b/w)
d Basil Dearden. *p* Michel Relph. *sc* John Whiting, Michael Relph, Basil Dearden. *ph* Gordon Dines. *ed* Peter Bezencenet. *ad* Bernard Robinson. *m* William Alwyn. *cast* Richard Attenborough, George Baker, Bill Owen, Virginia McKenna, Roland Culver, Bernard Lee.

●A valuable record of bewildered British masculinity in the post-war years. Some old mates discover their trusty former gunboat decommissioned and languishing in the knacker's yard. They vow to make her seaworthy again, but betray the faithful sloop by using her for smuggling. Take away the absurd nautical anthropomorphism and the tortuous stuff about how hard it is for WWII veterans to adapt to civvy street, and you're left with a pretty threadbare thriller (from a Nicholas Monsarrat novel). The story is told in such a brisk, understated fashion that it's easy to overlook quite how odd it is. Memorable finale seemingly filmed in the producer's bath. GM

Ship Was Loaded, The

see Carry On Admiral

Shipwreck!

see Sea Gypsies, The

Shipwrecked

see Naufragos, Los

Shipyard Sally

(1939, GB, 80 min, b/w)
d Monty Banks. *p* Edward Black. *sc* Karl Tunberg, Don Ettlinger. *ph* Otto Kanturek. *ed* ER Dearing, Alfred Roome. *ad* Alex Vetchinsky. *m* Louis Levy. *cast* Gracie Fields, Sydney Howard, Morton Selten, Norma Varden, Tucker McGuire, Oliver Wakefield, Monty Banks.

●Shoddily mounted populist pap, with our Gracie as a singing barmaid taking the plight of the Clydeside shipyard workers to heart, masquerading farcically as an American star to bulldoze her way to the Minister concerned, and making such an impassioned plea that their jobs are saved. Her last British film before her departure for America, it ends glutinously with her rendition of 'Land of Hope and Glory' as royalty launches a new liner. TM

Shiri (Swiri)

(1999, SKor, 124 min)
d/p/sc Kang Je-Gyu. *ph* Kim Sung-Bok. *ed* Park Gok-Ji. *ad* Park Il-Hyun. *m* Lee Dong-Jun. *cast* Han Suk-Kyu, Kim Yu-Jin, Choi Min-Sik, Song Kang-Ho.

●Special agents Ryu (Han) and Lee (Song) work to track down North Korean spies who have infiltrated South Korean society; their prime target is a woman (Kim), a crack sniper known to be somewhere in Seoul. Meanwhile a team of ruthless Northern renegades hijack supplies of a volatile new explosive and plant bombs in Seoul, timed to explode on the day a soccer 'friendly' between the two Koreas is due to inaugurate a thaw in diplomatic relations. Kang's film is the all-time box office champion in Korea, thanks in part to an ad campaign which told audiences it was their 'patriotic duty' to see it. What they got for their money was a crudely plotted thriller with sub-par action scenes and a set-piece climax filched from *The Manchurian Candidate* and *Black Sunday* crossed with old-fashioned Korean melodrama. The cheesiest twist is the revelation that the woman sniper is living with Ryu as his girlfriend. TR

Shirin's Wedding (Shirins Hochzeit)

(1976, WGer, 116 min, b/w)
d Helma Sanders-Brahms. *p* Volker Canaris. *sc* Helma Sanders-Brahms. *ph* Thomas Mauch, Jürgen Pietzner. *ed* Margot Löhlein, Gabriele Unverdross. *ad* Manfred Lütz. *m* Zülfü Livaneli. *cast* Ayten Erten, Aras Oren, Jürgen Prochnow, Peter Franke.

● What John Berger's book *A Seventh Man* did for the male migrant worker, this unrelenting and delicate film attempts for his female counterpart. Shirin, a peasant girl from Anatolia, follows her betrothed Mahmud to Cologne, taking her hand-made trousseau. Inevitably she is drawn into the downward spiral of female immigrant labour, and even the support and affection of other women cannot mitigate the tragic ironies of the circumstances in which she finally meets Mahmud. Sanders-Brahms' understanding of the unorganised impotence of both migrant and German workers is enacted not only through the storyline, as Shirin is made into a Western woman, but through a projective narration which both conveys information and – by suggesting indictment rather than despair – hints at the possibility of a solidarity more political than that shown in the film itself. Very moving. MV

Shirley Valentine

(1989, US, 108 min)
d/p Lewis Gilbert. *sc* Willy Russell. *ph* Alan Hume. *ed* Lesley Walker. *pd* John Stoll. *m* Willy Russell, George Hatzinassios. *cast* Pauline Collins, Tom Conti, Julia McKenzie, Alison Steadman, Joanna Lumley, Sylvia Syms, Bernard Hill, George Costigan.

● Willy Russell transforms his one-hander into a superior kitchenette adventure which roams from Liverpool to Mykonos, finding room for all the characters who in the more satisfying theatre version were figments of Shirl's imagination. 42-year-old Shirley (Collins) is so raddled by life that she talks to the wall of her strip-pine kitchen, and wonders 'Why, if they give us so much life, aren't we allowed to make use of it?' Hence an improbable plot device by which her feminist friend wins a holiday for two in Greece, and Shirley, after much guilt, doubt and abuse from her plankish husband (Hill), decides to go. But the virtue of Russell's writing is that, for all the cracks, occasional duff lines, and tendency to simplify and stereotype, few can match his ability to make us laugh, cry and ultimately care. Loneliness creeps with Shirley to the Med, and only after a brief dalliance with a Greek local (Conti) does she start to live for real: self-respect and self-reliance beat sex on a boat anyday. Collins is magnificent, and though the film's sexual politics may not be to all tastes, it deserves to be seen for its glowing belief in the worth of personal rediscovery. SGr

Shivers

see Parasite Murders, The

Shoah

(1985, Fr, 566 min)
d Claude Lanzmann. *ph* Dominique Chapuis, Jimmy Glasberg, William Lubtchansky. *ed* Ziva Postec, Anna Ruiz.

● Lanzmann's 9 hour documentary meditation on the Holocaust is a distillation of 350 hours of interviews with living 'witnesses' to what happened at the extermination camps of Treblinka, Auschwitz, Sobibor, Chelmno and Belzec. Feeling that the familiar newsreel images have lost their power to shock, Lanzmann concentrates instead on the testimony of those survivors who are 'not reliving' but 'still living' what happened, and on 'the bureaucracy of death'. One of the two Jews to survive the murder of 400,000 men, women and children at the Chelmno death camp describes his feelings on revisiting Poland for the first time. A train driver who ferried victims to the concentration camps is seen making that same journey to 'the end of the line' again and again; a retired Polish barber who cut the hair of those about to enter the gas chambers describes his former work; an SS officer talks about the 'processing' of those on their way to the concentration camps; a railway official discusses the difficulties associated with transporting so many Jews to their deaths. The same questions are repeated like an insistent refrain, the effect is relentless and cumulative. One word of caution as you watch the witnesses giving testimony; bear in mind Schiller's observation that 'individual testimony has a specific place in history but doesn't, alone, add up to it'. NF

Shock Corridor

(1963, US, 101 min, b/w & col)
d/p/sc Samuel Fuller. *ph* Stanley Cortez. *ed* Jerome Thoms. *ad* Eugène Lourié. *m* Paul Dunlap. *cast* Peter Breck, Constance Towers, Gene Evans, James Best, Hari Rhodes, Larry Tucker, William Zuckert, Philip Ahn.

● You may have to swallow a morsel of disbelief over the wonderfully Fullerian premise that a reputable newspaper editor and a psychiatrist would connive at the crazy scheme whereby the reporter hero (Breck) has himself committed to an asylum so that he can win the Pulitzer Prize by solving the murder of an inmate. Once done, you're in for a gripping ride. The journalist's latent paranoia is beautifully observed in his relationship with his stripper girlfriend (Towers), as well as in the relish with which he notes the success of his simulation of madness; and the gradual descent into real madness, as he frustratedly waits and watches for flashes of lucidity in the three inmates who witnessed the murder, is riveting story-telling. The camera-work (Stanley Cortez), tracking and constantly adumbrating the descent into darkness, is amazing. TM

Shocker

(1989, US, 110 min)
d Wes Craven. *p* Marianne Maddalena, Barin Kumar. *sc* Wes Craven. *ph* Jacques Haitkin. *ed* Andy Blumenthal. *pd* Randy Moore. *m* William Goldstein. *cast* Mitch Pileggi, Peter Berg, Michael Murphy, Cami Cooper, John Tesh, Heather Langenkamp, Jessica Craven.

● Wholesome college boy Jonathan (Berg) is beset by nightmares, visions of mayhem which are subsequently enacted in real life by serial killer Horace Pinker (Pileggi). When his foster family and girlfriend come under the knife, the teenager uses his 'psychic bond' to facilitate Pinker's arrest and electrocution. The massive shock turns Pinker into a vengeful entity who can travel through bodies, televisions and household wiring with ease…After the uncertain cross-generic wanderings of *The Serpent and the Rainbow*, this finds Craven returning to his low budget origins, delivering straightforward kinetic horror with unapologetic brashness, his usual preoccupations to the fore: psychic dream states, parental guilt revisited upon children, the intrusion of a chaotic, alternative world into comfy suburbia. Problems arise from an uncharacteristically loose structure, which frequently brings the movie to the brink of narrative collapse; Craven's visual flair and enthusiastic pacing nevertheless deliver ample (if sometimes frustrating) rewards. MK

Shockproof

(1949, US, 79 min, b/w)
d Douglas Sirk. *p* S Sylvan Simon. *sc* Helen Deutsch, Samuel Fuller. *ph* Charles Lawton Jr. *ed* Gene Havlick. *ad* Carl Anderson. *m* George Duning. *cast* Cornel Wilde, Patricia Knight, John Baragrey, Esther Minciotti, Howard St John.

● Written by none other than the great Sam Fuller, this superior blend of love-on-the-run thriller and social comment, filtered through *film noir*, follows the fraught, doomed relationship between a parole officer and the female ex-con with whom he falls in love. The depiction of the ways in which society refuses to forgive criminals for their past misdemeanours is none too sophisticated, but Fuller's punchy, tabloid-like script, Sirk's stylishly economical direction, and the unsentimental characterisations lend it power. A pity about the contrived ending, imposed on Sirk by Columbia, but the film still looked good enough for Richard Hamilton to base a series of paintings on its shots of Knight. NF

Shock to the System, A

(1990, US, 88 min)
d Jan Egleson. *p* Patrick McCormick. *sc* Andrew Klavan. *ph* Paul Goldsmith. *ed* Peter C Frank, William A Anderson. *pd* Howard Cummmings. *m* Gary Chang. *cast* Michael Caine, Elizabeth McGovern, Peter Riegert, Swoosie Kurtz, Will Patton, Jenny Wright, John McMartin, Barbara Baxley, Philip Moon.

● Alec Guinness played almost all the parts in the homicidal black comedy *Kind Hearts and Coronets*. Michael Caine, with a smaller repertoire, once pointed out that he could play both Woody Allen and Clint Eastwood, and in the not dissimilar *A Shock to the System*, proves it. Ageing advertising executive Graham Marshall (Caine) starts out as *schlemiel*, henpecked at home and passed over for promotion at work. The worm's turning point occurs on the subway, when Marshall shoves a panhandler under a train and gets away with it, after which murder becomes a shot in his locker. He hooks up his wife (Kurtz) to the National Grid, and consoles his bereavement with Stella at work (McGovern). Interestingly, murder puts lead in his pencil, confirming Mailer's thesis in *The American Dream*. The corporate world's dedication to ruthless efficiency meets its apotheosis in Marshall, and his obnoxious new boss (Riegert) wins the battles but loses the war. Seldom have Caine's cobra eyes been used to better effect; it's a chilling tale, cleanly directed. BC

Shock Treatment

see Traitement de Choc

Shock Treatment

(1981, GB, 94 min)
d Jim Sharman. *p* John Goldstone. *sc* Richard O'Brien, Jim Sharman. *ph* Mike Molloy. *ed* Richard Bedford. *pd* Brian Thomson. *m* Richard Hartley, Richard O'Brien. *cast* Cliff De Young, Jessica Harper, Patricia Quinn, Richard O'Brien, Charles Gray, Nell Campbell, Ruby Wax, Barry Humphries, Rik Mayall.

● *The Rocky Horror Picture Show* again, thinly disguised. The same writers (Richard O'Brien and Richard Hartley), the same director, virtually the same songs. As an exercise in nostalgia, it might work, but who wants to remember the '70s? Harper proves she can sing, O'Brien proves he can't act, and Sharman films inventively, but fringe theatre material does not a big screen musical make. *Rocky Horror* succeeded in its spot-on sense of style, but here the style, like the whole concept of rock musicals, seems a decade out of date, bypassed by films like *Quadrophenia* which integrate music and story in a different way. MB

Shoemaker

(1996, Can, 82 min)
d Colleen Murphy. *p* Elizabeth Yake. *sc* Jaan Kolk. *ph* Christophe Bonnière. *ed* Wiebke von Carolsfeld. *pd* Ray Lorenz. *m* Bill Thompson. *cast* Randy Hughson, Alberta Watson, Hardee T Lineham, Carl Marotte, Ellen Ray Hennessy.

● The Mr Happy Face shoe repair shop becomes an unexpected hotbed of romantic intrigue in this gentle, though ultimately unsatisfying Canadian independent. Hughson is the shy unprepossessing cobbler who strikes up a hesitant relationship with travel agent Alberta Watson (of *Spanking the Monkey* fame), despite the alternating concern and scorn he meets from his embittered boss. While Watson makes believable her character's need for a sincere and uncalculating partner, Hughson's contribution overplays the ungainliness and naivety of a role that never really lifts off the printed page. TJ

Shoes of the Fisherman, The

(1968, US, 157 min)
d Michael Anderson. *p* George Englund. *sc* John Patrick, James Kennaway. *ph* Erwin Hillier. *ed* Ernest Walter. *ad* Edward C Carfagno, George W Davis. *m* Alex North. *cast* Anthony Quinn, Oskar Werner, Laurence Olivier, David Janssen, Barbara Jefford, Leo McKern, Vittorio De Sica, John Gielgud, Clive Revill, Paul Rogers, Niall MacGinnis.

● A dour and thoroughly unconvincing film of Morris West's novel about a Russian bishop who survives twenty years in Siberia to become Pope Zorba, and who undertakes to spend the Church's wealth to stave off nuclear war. At which point you might expect the Vatican to have him quietly bumped off, but there's no such realism here, just weighty performances, rich settings, and David Janssen as a US journalist with domestic troubles. TCh

Shogun

(1980, US, 151 min)
d Jerry London. *p/sc* Eric Bercovici. *ph* Andrew Laszlo. *ed* Jack Tucker, Bill Luciano, Donald R Rode. *pd* Joseph R Jennings. *m* Maurice Jarre. *cast* Richard Chamberlain, Toshiro Mifune, Yoko Shimada, Frankie Sakai, Alan Badel, Michael Hordern, Damien Thomas.

●Startled blue eyes above silky beard, Richard Chamberlain in a kimono looks more like an actor on his way to the bathroom than a grizzled English seafarer, cast ashore in 17th century Japan, where he turns samurai and becomes romantically and actively involved in a violent political intrigue. Based on James Clavell's huge novel, *Shogun* was originally a 10-hour TV mini-series. Shamefully hacked down to 151 minutes (still a yawning long haul), the plot has been rendered action-packed but utterly incomprehensible. Though production credits and cast point to a lively synthesis of oriental/occidental interests, the end result reduces the complex moral codes of feudal Japan to an inexplicable death wish. The threat of harakiri follows Chamberlain's illicit hanky-panky with the Lady Mariko (Shimada) as surely as day follows night, and yet again that rising sun blobs onto the screen like a pulpy tangerine. JS

Shogun Assassin

(1980, Jap/US, 86 min)
d Kenji Misumi (US version Robert Houston). *p* Shintaro Katsu, Hisaharu Matsubara, (US version) Robert Houston, David Weisman. *sc* Kazuo Koike, (US version) Robert Houston, David Weisman. *ph* Chishi Makiura. *ed* Toshio Taniguchi, (US version) Lee Percy. *ad* Akira Naito. *m* Hideakira Sakurai, (US version) W Michael Lewis, Mark Lindsay.

●This started screen life in Japan in 1972 as a Kenji Misumi samurai sword actioner with the wonderful export title of *Baby Cart at the River Styx*; it was then thoroughly overhauled by Roger Corman's New World (gaining a credit for 'psycho-acoustics', and the dubbed voice of Lamont Johnson for the hero) as a quickie cash-in on the popular TV mini-series *Shogun*. Any sense of *déja vu* is down to the fact that the simultaneously-shot sequel to *Baby Cart*, featuring the same pram-pushing avenger and son, has been doing the rounds here for years as *Lightning Swords of Death*. Clear as mud, innit? The exotic cheap thrills are, anyway, with the self-parodying laughs and gory comic-strip savagery making it a snappy little mongrel all round. PT

Shonen

see Boy

Shooter, The

(1994, US, 104 min)
d Ted Kotcheff. *p* Paul Pompian, Silvio Muraglia. *sc* Yves Andre Martin, Mag Thayer, Billy Ray. *ph* Fernando Arguelles. *ed* Ralph Brunjes. *pd* Brian Eatwell. *m* Stefano Mainetti. *cast* Dolph Lundgren, Maruschka Detmers, John Ashton, Assumpta Serna, Gavan O'Herlihy, Simon Andreu.

●While Jean-Claude Van Damme, his erstwhile rival in the Euro Action Hero stakes, ploughs on in A-picture productions, Dolph Lundgren, who showed greater acting range when they were paired in *Universal Soldier*, gets stuck in dreck like this. In a nod to thawing East-West relations, this action adventure is set in Prague on the dawn of a US-Cuban summit, where feelings are running high after the murder of Castro's ambassador to New York. Enter Lundgren's Czech-born CIA man, teamed with his former agency mentor (Ashton) and given the task of tracking down the alleged assassin, Detmers' Gallic femme fatale. Very dull. TJ

Shooters

(2000, Neth/US/GB, 95 min)
d Colin Teague, Glenn Durfort. *p* Margery Bone. *sc* Gary Young, Andrew Howard, Louis Dempsey. *ph* Tom Erisman. *ed* Kevin Whelan. *pd* Robin Tarsnane. *m* Kemal Ultanur. *cast* Adrian Dunbar, Andrew Howard, Louis Dempsey, Gerard Butler, Jason Hughes, Matthew Rhys, Ioan Gruffydd, Jamie Sweeney, Melanie Lynskey, Emma Fielding.

●It's that old 'one last job' scenario, set in London's East End, with a dash of friendship going sour. Gilly (Dempsey) gets out of jail after doing time for a killing actually committed by his mate J (Howard), only to find that the cash he's owed is tied up in a gun-selling deal with Glaswegian hardcase Jackie Junior (Butler). What our two boys don't know is that J's boss (Dunbar) is on to their little scheme, and sooner or later something will have to give. Here's plot spinning for its own sake, routine gunplay, low rent locations by the yard, and no very compelling reason for any of it. TJ

Shoot First

see Rough Shoot

Shooting, The

(1966, US, 81 min)
d Monte Hellman. *p* Jack Nicholson, Monte Hellman. *sc* Adrien Joyce [Carole Eastman]. *ph* Gregory Sandor. *ad* Wally Moon. *m* Richard Markowitz. *cast* Warren Oates, Will Hutchins, Millie Perkins, Jack Nicholson, BJ Merholz, Guy El Tsosie, Charles Eastman.

●Probably the first Western which really deserves to be called existential. Bounty hunter Gashade (Oates) and his young sidekick Coley (Hutchins) are persuaded by an unknown woman (Perkins) to lead her into the desert. On the skyline appears a spectral figure who later turns out to be Billy Spear (Nicholson), a sadistic gunman whose relationship to the woman remains obscure. The prevailing atmosphere of fear and despair intensifies as Gashade and Coley realise they are involved in the hunting of an unidentified man, and as strange suggestions about the nature of the hunt multiply. On the way they encounter a dying man, and Coley, in an absurdist gesture typical of the film, offers him coloured candy. There is talk of 'a little person, maybe a child', who was killed back in the town they left, but this is never clarified; instead Hellman builds remorselessly on the atmosphere and implications of the 'quest' until it assumes a terrifying importance in itself. 'It's just a feeling I've got to see through' says the bounty hunter, and Gregory Sandor's excellent photography manages to create the feeling visually, with dialogue kept to a bare minimum. What Hellman has done is to take the basic tools of the Western, and use them, without in anyway diluting or destroying their power, as the basis for a Kafkaesque drama. DP

Shooting Fish

(1997, GB, 112 min)
d Stefan Schwartz. *p* Richard Holmes, Glynis Murray. *sc* Stefan Schwartz, Richard Holmes. *ph* Henry Braham. *ed* Alan Strachan. *pd* Max Gottlieb. *m* Stanislas Syrewicz. *cast* Dan Futterman, Stuart Townsend, Kate Beckinsale, Nickolas Grace, Claire Cox, Peter Capaldi, Annette Crosbie, Jane Lapotaire, Phyllis Logan.

●The slang title refers to the ease with which mugs are found for scams. Dylan (Futterman) is a brash American tethered by friendship and history to Jez (Townsend), a gifted but unsophisticated inventor. The film begins with an attempt at the big time – a con involving voice-recognition computers and City investors – before introducing us to Jez and Dylan's home, an Aladdin's cave inside a large gasometer in the London suburbs. Cash-strapped trainee doctor Georgie (Beckinsale) is lured to work for the boys. Though she soon susses their game, she stays on board for a complicated mixture of motives involving her Down's Syndrome brother and her growing affection for the lads. The straggly plot – they're saving to buy a country house – has an Ealing-esque energy, but the portrayal of Englishness seems ersatz and overly accommodating to the international audience. A succession of cameos provides light relief, and the film's saved by the amiable performances of Futterman, Beckinsale and, especially, Townsend. WH

Shooting Party, The

(1984, GB, 96 min)
d Alan Bridges. *p* Geoffrey Reeve. *sc* Julian Bond. *ph* Fred Tammes. *ed* Peter Davies. *pd* Morley Smith. *m* John Scott. *cast* James Mason, Edward Fox, Dorothy Tutin, John Gielgud, Gordon Jackson, Cheryl Campbell, Robert Hardy, Aharon Ipal, Rebecca Saire, Sarah Badel, Rupert Frazer, Judi Bowker.

●Infidelity, class exploitation, and mindless male competitiveness pepper this adaptation of Isabel Colegate's novel, set just before the First World War, when an assortment of toffs gather for pheasant shooting and post-prandial charades. The producer obviously spent a small fortune acquiring the excellent cast, and the film evokes the period admirably, especially through a series of cut-ins anticipating the coming European carnage. But the attack on the values of the time is ultimately far too glossy and toothless. CS

Shooting Stars (Le Ciel est à nous)

(1996, Fr, 87 min)
d Graham Guit. *p* Frederic Robbes, Eric Névé. *sc* Graham Guit, Eric Névé. *ph* Olivier Cariou. *ed* Jean-Guy Monpetit. *pd* Gilles Chapat. *cast* Romane Bohringer, Melvil Poupaud, Elodie Bouchez, Jean-Philippe Ecoffey, Jean-Claude Flamand, Patrick Lizana.

●This very flash, very knowing, vastly entertaining French thriller is so ironic it almost ends back at innocence. Poupaud is a naive small time con artist who gets in way over his head when he puts together a drugs deal with the reptilian Ecoffey and his independent-minded protégée, Bohringer. Graham Guit, director and co-writer, has fun and games with a Tarantino-esque chronology, a joyous kitsch soundtrack, and a novice's delight in the mechanics of the genre: he tears it apart, reassembles it, then hides the spare parts behind a ready wit. Bright stuff. TCh

Shootist, The

(1976, US, 100 min)
d Don Siegel. *p* MJ Frankovich, William Self. *sc* Miles Hood Swarthout, Scott Hale. *ph* Bruce Surtees. *ed* Douglas Stewart. *pd* Robert Boyle. *m* Elmer Bernstein. *cast* John Wayne, Lauren Bacall, Ron Howard, James Stewart, Richard Boone, Hugh O'Brian, Bill McKinney, Harry Morgan, John Carradine, Sheree North, Scatman Crothers.

●From the opening montage of clips from Wayne's earlier films to the final superb shootout in a cavernous saloon, Siegel's film is a subtle, touching valedictory tribute to both Wayne and the Western in general. With none of the indulgence that permeated *True Grit*, Wayne is perfect as the dying gunfighter attempting to live out his last days in peace and obscurity, but prevented from doing so by various younger gunmen out for revenge or to prove their worth against him. The performances are uniformly excellent, Bruce Surtees' photography is infused with an appropriately wintry feel, and Siegel handles both pace and tone beautifully; the admitted sentimentality is thoroughly in keeping with the elegiac tale of old-timers reconsidering their lives. If you're one of those who still feel that Wayne couldn't act, watch this and change your mind. GA

Shoot the Moon

(1981, US, 123 min)
d Alan Parker. *p* Alan Marshall. *sc* Bo Goldman. *ph* Michael Seresin. *ed* Gerry Hambling. *pd* Geoffrey Kirkland. *cast* Albert Finney, Diane Keaton, Karen Allen, Peter Weller, Dana Hill, Viveka Davis, Tracey Gold, Tina Yothers, Leora Dana.

●There is a sentimental optimism in both Parker's films and Bo Goldman's scripts. So it's no surprise that together they made this Californian coming-to-terms-with-a-relationship movie. Finney plays a successful writer who first picks up a literary award, and then throws up his marriage (to Keaton), four believable daughters, and a large country house. It's a superior film of its kind, for much as one may kick against Finney and Keaton's much-exploited mannerisms (rage and winsomeness respectively), they, like the script, have impressive moments, balancing hilarity and tragedy. But even Parker's direction, with its unerring sense of pace, cannot disguise an awkwardly episodic narrative which just cannot find a sense of an ending. JS

Shoot the Pianist

see Tirez sur le Pianiste

Shoot to Kill

see Disparen a Matar

Shoot to Kill (aka Deadly Pursuit)

(1988, US, 110 min)
d Roger Spottiswoode. *p* Ron Silverman, Daniel Petrie Jr. *sc* Harv Zimmel, Michael Burton, Daniel Petrie Jr. *ph* Michael Chapman. *ed* Garth Craven, George Bowers. *pd* Richard Sylbert. *m* John Scott. *cast* Sidney Poitier, Tom Berenger, Kirstie Alley, Clancy Brown, Richard Masur, Andrew Robinson.

●Nice to see Poitier back and full of pep, albeit in a routine thriller. It begins promisingly with the owner of a jewellery store helping himself to the gems, getting busted, and breaking down to explain that he needs them because his wife is being held hostage by a homicidal maniac. Presiding FBI agent Stantin (Poitier) is outsmarted at every turn, and the hostage is killed. Vengefully, Poitier follows the trail up into the remote mountains on the Canadian border, a city cop comically out of water. The killer hijacks a fishing party, and makes off with the good scout girlfriend (Alley) of the trail guide Knox (Berenger). Knox and Stantin reluctantly team up, and earn each other's respect over daunting terrain in the usual way. All the clichés clock in, characterisation is cardboard, but the locations are stunning. BC

Shop Around the Corner, The

(1940, US, 97 min, b/w)
d/p Ernst Lubitsch. *sc* Samson Raphaelson. *ph* William H Daniels. *ed* Gene Ruggiero. *ad* Cedric Gibbons. *m* Werner R Heymann. *cast* James Stewart, Margaret Sullavan, Frank Morgan, Joseph Schildkraut, Felix Bressart, Sara Haden, William Tracy.

●Teaming Stewart, Sullavan and Morgan, just as in Borzage's *The Mortal Storm* (made the same year), this also deals with troubled romance in Central Europe, though here the threat is not Nazism but pride and the interference of others, as Stewart and Sullavan, shop staff at loggerheads in Morgan's gossip-ridden emporium in Budapest, only slowly realise that they have been carrying on an anonymous romance by letter. It's a marvellously delicate romantic comedy, finally very moving, with the twisted intrigues among the staff also carrying narrative weight, Morgan's cuckolded proprietor being especially affecting. Thoroughly different from *To Be or Not To Be* but just as exhilarating, it's one of the few films truly justifying Lubitsch's reputation for a 'touch'. It was later turned into a musical as *In the Good Old Summertime*. GA

Shop on the High Street, A (Obchod na Korze)

(1964, Czech, 128 min)
d Ján Kadár, Elmar Klos. *sc* Ladislav Grosman, Ján Kadár, Elmar Klos. *ph* Vladimir Novotny. *ad* Karel Skvor. *m* Zdenek Liska. *cast* Ida Kaminská, Jozef Króner, Hana Slivková, Frantisek Zvarik, Helena Zvariková, Martin Holly, Martin Gregor.

●Kadar and Klos deal with the horror of the Holocaust by detailing the moral plight of an Everyman: In 1942, thanks to his brother-in-law, an official of the Nazi occupation, a small town Slovak carpenter, Anton Brtko (Króner), is made Aryan controller of the little shop of Mrs Lautmann (Kaminská), a deaf elderly Jewish widow. The directors and co-writers play the story just like a provincial comedy of the time – dialectically countered by Zdenek Liska's minatory string score – as they trace the tragicomic relationship that develops between the widow and the controller in the brief period before the cattle trains are mustered for the transports. It shades darker and darker as 'Tono' finds himself getting more and more deeply involved in the secret Jewish support sytem, only to burst into the finale's remarkable dream sequence, where the couple wander free as lovers under the town's sun-dappled limes. WH

Shopping

(1993, GB, 107 min)
d Paul Anderson. *p* Jeremy Bolt. *sc* Paul Anderson. *ph* Tony Imi. *ed* David Stiven. *pd* Max Gottlieb. *m* Barrington Pheloung. *cast* Sadie Frost, Jude Law, Sean Pertwee, Fraser James, Sean Bean, Marianne Faithfull, Jonathan Pryce, Danny Newman.

●Poised precariously between raw, 'realist' social comment and neon-lit, American-influenced genre-riffing, Anderson's directorial debut is praiseworthy for its high-octane, unsentimental look at the contemporary phenomena of joyriding and ram-raiding. Billy (Law, photogenic but expressively limited) is a 19-year-old nihilist who finally cares only for the speedy glee of stealing a car – usually in company with Jo (Frost), a feisty but marginally more cautious Irish girl in her early 20s – racing down empty streets with cops in pursuit, and crashing through any suitable shopfront that presents itself. The film is impressively energetic and for the most part appropriately amoral, although motivation rarely rises above 'There must be more than this' or 'I want to be somebody' variety. GA

Shores of Twilight

(1998, Greece, 101 min)
d Efthimios Hatzis. *sc* Efthimios Hatzis, Dimitris Nollas. *ph/ed* Panayiotis Kliaras. *pd* Nikos Politis. *m* Dimitris Katakouzinos. *cast* Mirto Alikaki, Stefanos Iatridis, Anna-Maria Papaharalambous, Marie Shoula.

●Based on a story by Alexandros Papadiamantis, this tells of a mature man disturbed by the vision of a young woman glimpsed at a window, who is compelled to make a journey by sea. Disconsolate, wistful and near-suicidal, he's found by a cave-dwelling recluse and introduced to the troglodyte's two equally individualistic friends whose stories bring him greater emotional peace. The director's fascination with primitive methods of storytelling has resulted in a movie of poetic kitsch, but, possibly, there are references here that may intrigue the informed. WH

Short Circuit

(1986, US, 98 min)
d John Badham. *p* David Foster, Lawrence Turman. *sc* Steven S Wilson, Brent Maddock. *ph* Nick McLean. *ed* Frank Morriss, Jeff Jones, Dallas Puett. *ad* Dianne Wager. *m* David Shire. *cast* Ally Sheedy, Steve Guttenberg, Fisher Stevens, Austin Pendleton, GW Bailey, Brian McNamara.

●A message film to please all ages. Goofy Guttenberg plays a brilliant but totally reclusive inventor who has constructed robots with the power to nuke whole cities. At a military demonstration, the fifth of the series is struck by lightning, and receives the intelligence that it is alive. Eager to escape those who wish to terminate it, Number Five – a multi-purpose kitchen implement on wheels – takes refuge with fanatical animal lover Sheedy, and the chase is on. Cuteness is never far off, though Badham has enough sense of pace, and the robotics are sufficiently inventive, to keep the laughs coming. Only Guttenberg's tongue-twisted Asian sidekick (Stevens) is off-key. DT

Short Circuit 2

(1988, US, 110 min)
d Kenneth Johnson. *p* David Foster, Lawrence Turman, Gary Foster. *sc* Steven S Wilson, Brent Maddock. *ph* John McPherson. *ed* Conrad Buff. *pd* Bill Brodie. *m* Charles Fox. *cast* Fisher Stevens, Michael McKean, Cynthia Gibb, Jack Weston, Dee McCafferty, David Hemblen.

●If the original *Short Circuit* brought us a mechanised version of *E.T*, this sequel is more a chromium *Crocodile Dundee*. Number Five, a military robot which received the spark of life, turned peacenik, and renamed himself Johnny Five, answers a distress call from his co-creator (Stevens) to join him in the Big City. His naive candour and sociological observations provide simple humour (of punks: 'Whoah! Human porcupines!'), as does his unwitting involvement in a bank robbery; and a terrific set piece is his attempt to prompt love-struck Stevens from afar by way of the '50s manual *Dating Dos and Don'ts for Modern Teens*. Though the direction by TV veteran Johnson is a little sparing of the big screen, and though the saccharine monitor keeps lurching dangerously into the red, this is that rare thing – a moderately intelligent kids' film, and a sequel that is better than the original. But why, when the theme is the prejudice encountered in Johnny Five's quest for acceptance among humans, is his Indian friend an absurd stereotype played by a blacked-up white actor? DW

Short Cuts

(1993, US, 188 min)
d Robert Altman. *p* Cary Brokaw. *sc* Robert Altman, Frank Barhydt. *ph* Walt Lloyd. *ed* Geraldine Peroni. *pd* Stephem Altman. *m* Mark Isham. *cast* Tim Robbins, Lily Tomlin, Tom Waits, Matthew Modine, Frances McDormand, Andie MacDowell, Annie Ross, Jack Lemmon.

●From the exhilarating opening, you know Altman's epic 'adaptation' of eight stories and a poem by Raymond Carver is going to be special. Like *Nashville*, it's a tragicomic kaleidoscope of numerous barely interlinked stories (plus a similarly portentous ending). Here, the focus is on couples whose relationships are, at one point or another, subjected to small, seismic shudders of doubt, disappointment or, in a few cases, disaster. A surgeon suspects his wife's fidelity; a pool-cleaner worries over his partner's phone-sex job; a waitress is racked by guilt after running down a child; a baker makes sinister phone calls to the injured boy's parents; the discovery of a corpse threatens a fishing-trip…and a marriage. The marvellous performances bear witness to Altman's iconoclastic good sense, with Tomlin, Waits, Modine, Robbins, MacDowell and the rest lending the film's mostly white, middle-class milieu an authenticity seldom found in American cinema. But the real star is Altman, whose fluid, clean camera style, free-and-easy editing, and effortless organisation of a complex narrative are quite simply the mark of a master. GA

Shortcut to Paradise

see Desvio al Paraiso

Short Film About Killing, A (Krótki Film o Zabijaniu)

(1987, Pol, 85 min)
d Krzysztof Kieslowski. *p* Ryszard Chutkowski. *sc* Krzysztof Piesiewicz, Krzysztof Kieslowski. *ph* Slawomir Idziak. *ed* Ewa Small. *ad* Halina Dobrowolska. *m* Zbigniew Preisner. *cast* Miroslaw Baka, Krzysztof Globisz, Jan Tesarz.

●Kieslowski's title is accurate: a hideous murder is directly followed by a hideous execution; both illegal and legal acts are detailed and protracted. The film does not set out to explain the punkish young killer's motivation, but restricts the viewer to his tunnel vision from the start, with the edges of the picture sludged over and a lowering yellow light at the centre. The depiction of violence is far removed from the usual camera choreography, and is, in consequence, truly appalling. The killing of the taxi driver is achieved in amateurish instalments, and takes even longer than the famous killing in Hitchcock's *Torn Curtain*. Not for the squeamish. See also the original TV version *Dekalog 5: 'Thou shalt not kill'*. BC

Short Film About Love, A (Krótki film o milosci)

(1988, Pol, 87 min)
d Krzysztof Kieslowski. *p* Ryszard Chutkowski. *sc* Krzysztof Piesiewicz, Krzysztof Kieslowski. *ph* Witold Adamek. *ed* Ewa Smal. *pd* Halina Dobrowolska. *m* Zbigniew Preisner. *cast* Grazyna Szapolowska, Olaf Lubaszenko, Stefania Iwinska, Piotr Machalica.

●Like *A Short Film About Killing*, this is a movie spin-off from Kieslowski's ten-part TV series *The Decalogue*, each segment of which sardonically re-examines one of the Ten Commandments. It's about a 19-year-old postal clerk who covets the slightly older woman in the flat opposite, to the extent that he keeps his astronomical telescope fixed on her windows and spends his every free minute glued to its sys-piece. Without fathoming the depths of his passion, the woman learns of his obsession and starts responding to his surveillance – with potentially disastrous results. Well aware that Hitchcock and Michael Powell have been down these streets before him, Kieslowski turns in an absolutely masterly movie that yields equal parts of humour and wry emotional truth. As an account of love in the late 20th century, it's in a league of its own. See also *Dekalog 6: 'Thou shalt not commit adultery'*. TR

Short Time

(1987, US, 102 min)
d Gregg Champion. *p* Todd Black. *sc* John Blumenthal, Michael Berry. *ph* John Connor. *ed* Frank Morriss. *pd* Michael Bolton. *m* Ira

Newborn. *cast* Dabney Coleman, Matt Frewer, Teri Garr, Barry Corbin, Joe Pantoliano, Xander Berkeley, Rob Roy.
●Dabney Coleman has a problem. He's a cop just eight days short of retirement, but his doctors also give him only two weeks to live. With admirable pragmatism, he resolves to die in the line of duty, thereby bequeathing a fortune in insurance money to pay his ten-year-old son's Harvard fees. Naturally, dying turns out to be a pain in the neck, and he becomes an inadvertent supercop. Directed by former second unit man Gregg Champion, *Short Time* boasts some well-staged action sequences; in particular a hilarious car chase with Coleman in kamikaze pursuit of Uzi-toting hoods, yelling his war cry, 'This one's for you, little guy'. Matters get bogged down when the film-makers feel the need to redress the hero's death wish with schmaltzy life-affirming sentiments. Still, when did you last see a movie where the hero dived *towards* an exploding grenade? TCh

Shot Down

(1987, SAf, 90 min)
d Andrew Worsdale. *p* Jeremy Nathan. *sc* Rick Shaw. *ph* Matthys Mocke, Giulio Biccari. *pd* David Barkham. *m* Lloyd Ross, James Phillips. *cast* Robert Colman, Megan Kruskal, Mavuso, Irene Stephano.
●Made by the Johannesburg group Weekend Theatre, this follows the moral and political confusion of one Paul Gilliat, hired by the State Bureau to investigate a subversive township performance group and track down its leader, enigmatic Black artist Rasechaba. He hitches up with a bunch of white bohemians who perform satirical cabaret, and sees for himself the systematic intimidation by security forces and assorted right wing bully-boys. Turning his back on his employers, he wanders off into the wilderness to find himself, and ends up battered and bewildered, despised by Rasechaba and his cabaret friends. The film is at its strongest when it relies on the performance skills of the actors: the cabaret scenes are heady and dangerous, garishly lit and with a real sense of illegality enhanced by some (deliberately?) shaky camerawork. Sadly, too much time is spent following Gilliat on his interior journey, and interest flags after one too many moral crises. As a slice of South African cultural resistance, however, *Shot Down* is extraordinary, full of self-mocking humour, and – in bursts – exhilarating. RS

Shot in the Dark, A

(1964, GB, 101 min)
d/p Blake Edwards. *sc* Blake Edwards, William Peter Blatty. *ph* Christopher Challis. *ed* Ralph E Winters, Bert Bates. *pd* Michael Stringer. *m* Henry Mancini. *cast* Peter Sellers, Elke Sommer, George Sanders, Herbert Lom, Tracy Reed, Graham Stark, Burt Kwouk.
●First of the *Pink Panther* sequels, establishing Sellers' incompetent Inspector Clouseau as a viable series character, and prompting Blake Edwards into an unchallenging downhill coast for far too long. Sellers, smitten by Elke Sommer's pretty parlourmaid and determined to prove her innocent of the charge of shooting her lover, is given plenty of opportunity for knockabout. PT

Shot Through the Heart

(1998, GB, 106 min)
d David Attwood. *p* Su Armstrong. *sc* Guy Hibbert. *ph* Gábor Szabó. *ed* Tim Wellburn. *pd* Barbara Dunphy. *m* Edward Shearmur. *cast* Linus Roache, Vincent Perez, Lothaire Bluteau, Lia Williams, Adam Kotz, Soo Garay, Viktória Bajza, Balázs Farkas.
●BBC Films' stab at the Sarajevo drama of conscience tries to sidestep Western guilt trips by casting international actors as Bosnians speaking English in a variety of swarthy accents. (Not very ingenious, admittedly.) Roache and Perez are sharp-shooting buddies who end up sniping on opposite sides of the fence – Linus is Muslim, Vincent's a Serb. The locations look real, but not much else does in this well-meaning, but leadenly predictable effort. TCh

Shout

(1991, US, 89 min)
d Jeffrey Hornaday. *p* Robert Simonds. *sc* Joe Gayton. *ph* Robert Brinkmann. *ed* Seth Flaum. *pd* William F Matthews. *m* Randy Edelman. *cast* John Travolta, James Walters, Heather Graham, Richard Jordan, Linda Fiorentino, Scott Coffey, Glenn Quinn, Gwyneth Paltrow.
●Rural Texas in the '50s finds rebellious teen Walters landed high and dry at the Benedict Home for Boys, until new teacher Travolta arrives and starts getting the kids hip to the sounds of rock'n'roll. You'll count the clichés in this affectionate but unpersuasive romp. From Travolta's pre-Tarantino doldrum days. TJ

Shout, The

(1978, GB, 86 min)
d Jerzy Skolimowski. *p* Jeremy Thomas. *sc* Michael Austin, Jerzy Skolimowski. *ph* Mike Molloy. *ed* Barrie Vince. *ad* Simon Holland. *m* Rupert Hine, Anthony Banks, Mike Rutherford. *cast* Alan Bates, Susannah York, John Hurt, Robert Stephens, Tim Curry, Julian Hough.
●'Every word I'm telling you is true,' adds Crossley (Bates), beginning his terrible story which makes up the substance of *The Shout*: a means of whiling away time at the village *versus* asylum cricket match where he and Robert Graves (author of the source story, played by Curry) are designated scorers. And fascinatingly, it is the boundaries between truth and falsehood that merge, rather than those between madness and insanity. For Crossley is undoubtedly mad, mendacious and cunning, viciously manipulating his chosen victims – a musician (Hurt) and his wife (York) – appealing sometimes across omniscient peaks of rationality and sometimes by scornful superiority. But what seems like his biggest whopper – his claim to kill with his shout – is proven. Skolimowski's second feature made in Britain is something of a triumph for independent production, with an impressively streamlined screenplay and faultless performances. JS

Shout at the Devil

(1976, GB, 147 min)
d Peter Hunt. *p* Michael Klinger. *sc* Wilbur Smith, Stanley Price, Alastair Reid. *ph* Mike Reed. *ed* Michael Duthrie. *pd* Syd Cain. *m* Maurice Jarre. *cast* Lee Marvin, Roger Moore, Barbara Parkins, Ian Holm, Rene Kolldehoff, Gernot Endemann, Karl Michael Vogler, Jean Kent, George Coulouris, Murray Melvin.
●Set in East Africa in 1913 in the days of German and English brinkmanship, this ostentatiously displays its large budget, but makes a mostly unsuccessful return to the world of colonial intrigues. Combining a slim plot about ivory poaching with some *African Queen* malarkey (involving blowing up a battleship), the film offers a comedy adventure that Ford or Hawks could have directed standing on their heads. But Peter Hunt seems incapable of controlling his leading men. Marvin behaves increasingly like a caricature of himself, turning to leer at the camera at the end of each take, while Moore, displaying officer qualities with all the conviction of Biggles, shows little aptitude for comedy. Barbara Parkins provides the only emotional complexity on display. Otherwise it's a Big Man's Adventure – Big locations, Big hearted, full of Manly Sentiments. CPe

Show Boat

(1936, US, 112 min, b/w)
d James Whale. *p* Carl Laemmle Jr. *sc* Oscar Hammerstein II. *ph* John Mescall. *ed* Ted Kent, Bernard W Burton. *ad* Charles D Hall. *m* Jerome Kern. *cast* Irene Dunne, Allan Jones, Helen Morgan, Paul Robeson, Charles Winninger, Hattie McDaniel, Donald Cook.
●No one ever made more than a singing dummy of Allan Jones, and no one could possibly carry off the last-minute flurry of plot preparing for a ludicrously mushy happy ending (made even worse by a risibly 'aged' Jones). Otherwise Whale does superbly by this much-loved Kern-Hammerstein musical, abetted by modestly handsome sets and lustrous camerawork from John Mescall. Dunne and Jones may look and act a little pallid, but they do well by Jerome Kern's lovely melodies, while Paul Robeson (in magnificent voice for 'Ol' Man River' and 'I Still Suits Me') and Helen Morgan ('Can't Help Lovin' That Man' and 'Bill') are as near perfection as makes no odds. Morgan, through her phrasing of the heart-rending 'Bill', almost makes a tragic figure out of the tragic Julie – no mean achievement. TM

Show Boat

(1951, US, 108 min)
d George Sidney. *p* Arhur Freed. *sc* John Lee Mahin. *ph* Charles Rosher. *ed* John Dunning. *ad* Cedric Gibbons, Jack Martin Smith. *cast* Kathryn Grayson, Ava Gardner, Howard Keel, Joe E Brown, Marge and Gower Champion, Agnes Moorehead, William Warfield, Robert Sterling.
●Not surprisingly, Arthur Freed's production values put this ahead of Whale's 1936 version as sheer spectacle, but the earlier version had two big plusses in Robeson (Warfield here is secure, but lacks the mystique), and Helen Morgan (here Ava Gardner's voice is dubbed, and try as she might she can't shake off the big star bit). Keel and Grayson are as colourless as ever, but no less so than Jones and Dunne were in 1936. As a film musical it survives on sheer class and some of Jerome Kern's richest melodies. As an anti-racist tract, though, it must have looked a lot less ingenuous when it first opened than it does now. Instead, enjoy the unashamed sentiment of the tale, and the spirited hoofing of Marge and Gower Champion. SG

Shower (Xizao)

(1999, China, 93 min)
d Zhang Yang. *p* Peter Loehr. *sc* Zhang Yang, Liu Fendou, Huo Xin, Diao Yinan, Cai Xiangjun. *ph* Zhang Jian. *ed* Yang Hongyu. *ad* Tian Meng. *m* Ye Xiaogang. *cast* Zhu Xu, Pu Cunxin, Jiang Wu, Li Ding, Dui Shun, Du Peng.
●It's a bit disconcerting that it starts with its most amusing scene – a daydream vision of the bath-house of the future as a kind of carwash for humans – but Zhang's wry lament for the public baths of yesteryear is fresh, funny and sad enough to survive playing its trump cards too early. The elderly Mr Liu (Zhu) runs the dilapidated Qingshui Bath-house in Beijing, offering baths, showers, body scrubs, aria practice and a sense of community to men of all ages. His retarded son Erming (Jiang, brother of the great Jiang Wen) is a loyal helper; his elder son Daming, embarrassed by the family business, has gone off to get rich in the Special Economic Zones down south. The characters, twists and sub-plots are all straight out of soap opera, but Zhang marshalls them with enough skill to make the whole a credible reflection of modernisation and loss in present-day China. TR

Showgirls

(1995, US, 131 min)
d Paul Verhoeven. *p* Alan Marshall, Charles Evans. *sc* Douglas Day Stewart, Joe Eszterhas. *ph* Jost Vacano. *ed* Mark Goldblatt, Mark Helfrich. *pd* Allan Cameron. *m* David A Stewart. *cast* Elizabeth Berkley, Kyle MacLachlan, Gina Gershon, Glenn Plummer, Robert Davi, Alan Rachins, Gina Ravera, Lin Tucci.
●Joe Eszterhas' by-numbers script recycles the baggy, Faustian 'ingénue comes to the big bad city' tale and stuffs it into a skimpy, lamé-bedecked version of the 'let's put on a show' musical. Plus topless. Alarm bells sound in the gauche opening sequence where hot-panted Nomi (Berkley) hitches her way into Las Vegas in the car of a predatory 'slick'. Thereafter, it's red lights all the way. You couldn't call the film misogynist; director Verhoeven's targets are too wide-ranging for it to be anything less than purely misanthropic. WH

Show Me Love (Fucking Åmål)

(1998, Swe/Den, 89 min)
d Lukas Moodysson. *p* Lars Jönsson. *sc* Lukas Moodysson. *ph* Ulf Brantås. *ed* Michael Leszczylowski, Bernhard Winkler. *ad* Lina Strand, Heidi Saikkonen. *cast* Alexandra Dahlström, Rebecca Liljeberg, Mathias Rust, Erica Carlson, Stefan Hörberg, Ralph Carlsson, Maria Heborg.
●Fourteen is still old enough to know there has to be something better than this. Firecracker blonde Dahlström rankles at being stuck in small town Åmål, but salvation comes from an unlikely corner when her path crosses with Liljeberg, the class swot, who just happens to be in love with her. A massive hit and multiple award winner in its native Sweden, this first feature adds an entertaining all-girl twist to the high school romance genre, neatly encapsulating the teenage frustration of waiting for your life to begin. While

the storyline has few surprises, the central performances create a touching relationship, despite the suspicion that the male writer/director's interest in the subject is slightly dubious, or at least tokenistic. TJ

Show of Force, A

(1990, US, 93 min)
d Bruno Barreto. *p* John Strong. *sc* John Strong, Evan Jones. *ph* James Glennon. *ed* Henry Richardson, Sonya Polansky. *pd* William J Cassidy. *m* Georges Delerue. *cast* Amy Irving, Robert Duvall, Andy Garcia, Lou Diamond Phillips, Kevin Spacey, Joe Campanella.

● Amid turbulent events in Puerto Rico, in 1978, TV reporter Irving uncovers the hand of the FBI in killings intended to influence the local elections. There might be a sound documentary to be made from this material, but between the fact and the drama Barreto's film falls oddly flat. Watch out for Phillips cast against type as an eccentric heavy, but blink a couple of times and you'll miss Duvall and Garcia – strongly billed, barely featured. TJ

Show People

(1928, US, 97 min, b/w)
d King Vidor. *p* Marion Davies, King Vidor. *sc* Agnes Christine Johnson, Laurence Stallings, Wanda Tuchock. *ph* John Arnold. *ed* Hugh Wynn. *ad* Cedric Gibbons. *m* William Axt, David Mendoza. *cast* Marion Davies, William Haines, Dell Henderson, Paul Ralli, Polly Moran, Albert Conti.

● Although perhaps not the hilarious comic masterpiece of repute, nevertheless a delightful look at silent Hollywood, in which Marion Davies (the mistress of William Randolph Hearst and thus the model for Susan Alexander in *Citizen Kane*) reveals her talents as a likeable parodist, playing a young hopeful who graduates from custard-pie target in slapstick comedies to Gloria Swanson-style grande dame. All twitchy lips and histrionic gestures, she manages to make credible the character's rise to fame, despite minimal talent, through her combination of glamour, seduction and acute ambition. A fine example of Hollywood gently satirising itself, with cameo appearances from many luminaries (including Fairbanks, Chaplin, William S Hart, John Gilbert and Elinor Glyn), plus Vidor himself during the final romantic reunion with her long-forgotten fiancé GA

Showtime

(2002, US/Aust, 95 min)
d Tom Dey. *p* Jorge Saralegui, Jane Rosenthal. *sc* Keith Sharon, Alfred Gough, Miles Millar. *ph* Thomas Kloss. *ed* Billy Weber. *pd* Jeff Mann. *m* Alan Silvestri. *cast* Robert De Niro, Eddie Murphy, Rene Russo, Frankie R Faison, William Shatner, Rachel Harris, Zaid Farid, Alex Borstein, Holly Mandel, Marshall Manesh.

● Potato-faced LAPD detective Mitch Preston (De Niro) takes cop movies to task – and expectations raise for this comic thriller. Mitch is teamed with patrol officer and buffoonish thespian Trey Sellars (Murphy) for a reality TV show produced by Chase Renzi (Russo), who needs a hit after faking a flammable baby pyjamas exposé. The casting is an extended in-joke (the three leads have all served time in buddy movies), but the film, far from being a knowing send-up of the genre, plays out the old routines with a disheartening lack of new tricks. A Johnnie Cochran walk-on and a riff on the dual meanings of the word 'shoot' are among the indications that director Dey aspires to satire. Then he stages another car chase or fawns over the villain's arsenal of Really Big Guns, and his true agenda is exposed. Even the out-takes, that last refuge of the desperate director, are abysmal. Alan Silvestri's zany score, which over-eggs every one-liner, deserves special derision. RGi

Shrek (100)

(2001, US, 90 min)
d Andrew Adamson, Vicky Jenson. *p* Aron Warner, John H Williams, Jeffrey Katzenberg. *sc* Ted Elliott, Terry Rossio, Joe Stillman, Roger SH Schulman. *ed* Sim Evan-Jones. *pd* James Hegedus. *m* Harry Gregson-Williams, John Powell. *cast* voices: Mike Myers, Eddie Murphy, Cameron Diaz, John Lithgow, Vincent Cassel, Michael Galasso.

● Shrek is the sort of 'new' ogre the world's been waiting for – he's house-proud, a keen chef, mild-mannered (unless provoked), and a heart beats under his thick green skin, if only someone could break through his gruff isolation. Princess Fiona reckons she's the one; but the trouble with princesses who've spent too long cooped up in castles is that they tend to have a shaky grasp of reality. When Shrek comes a-rescuin' her from the dragon that's been gobbling her suitors, she takes a while to comprehend that her real claimant is Lord Farquaad, a tyrant of limited personal stature, who has contracted out her deliverance in return for ridding Shrek of the various pesky fairytale characters milling around his manor. DreamWorks is clearly picking up the pace with its animated features. Technically, the film's a triumph. Gag by gag – and there's a stream – it's merrily irreverent, visually and vocally. The bigger picture, though, is rather more conventional. The play with fairytale clichés merely freshens them up for re-use; and the moral comes served with earnest sentimentality. Not sure about the 'hip' soundtrack playlist, either. NB

Shtetl

(1996, US, 180 min)
d Marian Marzynski.

● Narrated by the Polish-born film-maker, Marzynski, this engrossing, sober, deeply moving documentary reconstructs, through visits, photographs and memories the Shtetl of Bransk, a town 160 km east of Warsaw with a Jewish population of 2,500 in 1939, now with none. Most perished in the Holocaust, the rest scattered throughout the world. Marzynski, who survived the Holocaust by hiding with Christians, acts as translator for, first, a 70-year-old Chicago Jew, Nathan Kaplan, whom he takes to Bransk to visit the home of his family, and later another American, Jack Ruby, a concentration camp survivor who revisits his childhood home. In the middle section, Marzynski takes a Gentile historian of Bransk Jewish history, Zbyszek Romaniuk, to America to meet Kaplan, thus raising questions of Romaniuk's objectivity and the Polish people's responsibility for the fate of the Jews. Marzynski is an intent interviewer, but he adopts a leisurely, slightly meandering approach to structure, which nevertheless pays off in moments of extraordinary passion. WH

Shuroo

(1991, Isr, 83 min)
d Savi Gabizon. *p* Jonathan Aroch, Johanan Raviv. *sc* Savi Gavizon, Jonathan Aroch, Johanan Raviv. *ph* Yoav Kosh. *ed* Tali Halter. *ad* Shmuel Maoz. *m* Lior Tevet. *cast* Moshe Ivgi, Sharon Hacoen, Sinai Peter.

● This comedy about life among Tel Aviv's 30-something bourgeoisie is nothing if not proof that self-absorbed, would-be hipsters are the same the world over. The central character is Asher, an unbecoming depressive amd all-round *schlemiel* who publishes a book on 'How to Be an Idiot', and finds himself becoming the guru of a self-help circle. A liberal sprinkling of sight gags and non-sequiturs – and even a slight flavour of Almodóvar in the sexual absurdities – keeps things lively. But unless a lot has got lost in the subtitling, the all-pervading psychobabble is nothing like as funny as it's clearly meant to be. JRo

Shut Down

(1978, GB, 41 min)
d Curtis Clark. *cast* Brian Godber, Lydia Lisle, Tim Cook.

● A glossy companion-piece to Clark's earlier essay on the same subject, *Cruisin'* – all chrome, custom-jobs and bubblegum rock – this focuses on British drag racers and street rodders, in another celebration of adopted US culture. Information for non-initiates is in short supply, restricted to the Santa Pod Raceway tannoy commentary and a few mechanics' rhubarbs, while the whole enterprise is cripplingly sabotaged by the intrusion of a cliché scripted encounter between two would-be James Deans. Very much the colour supplement movie, complete with compilation soundtrack album. PT

Shvitz, The

(1993, US, 47 min)
d Jonathan Berman.

● An enjoyable look at New York's vanishing steambath culture, which provides warm, wet gathering places for Jews of every profession, class and moral hue (including gangsters). The rub-downs, massages and hose-downs are only part of the appeal. Here, senior citizens meet to escape the family, swap intimate secrets and gags, play cards and indulge in a nostalgia taken up by this sweet, funny film. An engaging slice of oral history. GA

Shy People

(1987, US, 119 min)
d Andrei Konchalovsky. *p* Menahem Golan, Yoram Globus. *sc* Gérard Brach, Andrei Konchalovsky, Marjorie David. *ph* Chris Menges. *ed* Alain Jakubowicz. *pd* Stephen Marsh. *m* Tangerine Dream. *cast* Jill Clayburgh, Barbara Hershey, Martha Plimpton, Merritt Butrick, John Philbin, Don Swayze, Pruitt Taylor Vince.

● Worried by the precocious habits of her teenage daughter Grace (Plimpton), Cosmo journo Diana (Clayburgh) visits distant relations living a spartan existence down in the Louisiana bayou. At first, Konchalovsky's depiction of the culture clash is merely clichéd: while Diana and Grace worry about things like make-up, matriarch Ruth (Hershey) still sets a place at table for her long-lost outlaw husband and exercises an iron will over her own cretinous brood. Pretty soon, however, it's a case of loony tunes with a vengeance: an attack on her son by poachers provokes Ruth to take a rare trip to town, gun in hand; Grace's druggy seduction of a cousin under lock and key results in violence and panicky flight; Diana's excursion into the misty swamps in search of the girl courts alligators and ghosts. Proceeding from hackneyed *Cold Comfort Farm* territory to a grotesque Gothic nightmare, Konchalovsky's fatuous fable misfires on all counts: it remains melodramatic hokum, pure and simple-minded, the luminous photography and Hershey's sterling performance notwithstanding. GA

Siam Sunset

(1999, Aust/GB, 92 min)
d John Polson. *p* Al Clark. *sc* Max Dann, Andrew Knight. *ph* Brian Breheny. *ed* Nicholas Beauman. *pd* Steven Jones-Evans. *m* Paul Grabowsky. *cast* Linus Roache, Danielle Cormack, Ian Bliss, Roy Billing, Alan Brough, Rebecca Hobbs, Terry Kenwrick.

● This memorably quirky first feature by actor Polson both benefits and suffers from wild shifts in tone. It embraces everything, from dry humour through surreal weirdness to slapstick violence and warm romance. Widowed by a freak accident involving a skyborne fridge freezer, industrial chemist Roache takes a break from paint mixing to enjoy a bingo prize trip to the outback. Grieving, vulnerable and accident prone, he finds himself on a jalopy with a rude owner-driver and a bunch of crazies. Stranded by a breakdown at a remote roadhouse, his one consolation is sparky optimist Cormack, who's on the run from an unhinged, drug-dealing boyfriend with a wad of his ill-gotten gains. Throughout the film, the chemist experiments with paint mixes, searching for the 'Siam Sunset' which reminds him of his dead wife's hair colour. Polson's approach has a similarly experimental feel, as he flings together diverse genres. More consistent in their tonal range are the ravishing desert compositions and the ambitious orchestral score from respected Oz composer Paul Grabowski. NF

Siao Yu (Shaonü Xiao Yu)

(1995, Tai, 104 min)
d Sylvia Chang. *p* Ang Lee, Hsu Li-Kong, Dolly Hall. *sc* Sylvia Chang, Yan Geling. *ph* Joe DeSalvo. *ed* Mei Feng. *pd* Wing Lee. *m* Bobbi Dar. *cast* Joyin Liu, Daniel J Travanti, Tou Chung-Hua, Marj Dusay.

● Why are Chinese women directors so drawn to illegal immigrant/Green Card movies set in New York? After Mabel Cheung and Clara Law comes Sylvia Chang with this modest adaptation of a novel by Geling Yan, reciting the familiar litany of dead-end jobs and marriages of convenience. Siao Yu (newcomer Liu, promising) has to cohabit with her paid-for Italian-American husband (Travanti, impressive) to convince the Immigration Department that the marriage isn't phoney. The predictable complications include her growing to like him, her long-term boyfriend Jiang getting ratty and the husband having a guilty secret in his closet. Sensitive, decent, fatally dull. TR

Siberia

(1998, Neth/Fr, 87 min)
d Robert Jan Westdijk. *p* Clea de Koning. *sc* Robert Jan Westdijk, Jos Driessen. *ph* Bert Pot. *ed* Herman P Koerts. *ad* Anouk Damoiseaux. *m* Junkie XL. *cast* Hugo Metsers, Roeland Fernhout, Vlatka Simac, Nicole Eggert, Johnny Lion, Jessica Stockmann.

●Summer in Amsterdam. Oddly matched buddies Hugo and Goof seduce female travellers and steal their possessions. Hugo (Metsers) is confident, cunning and romantically bitter, while Goof (Fernhout) is slow, sweet and apparently innocent. Despite their differences, these larky lads agree that their takings should be pooled. That is until they cross paths with Lara (Simac), an inscrutable, unscrupulous Russian. Goof falls for her, Hugo certainly doesn't, and suddenly the games turn personal. Dicing together motley film stocks and video with an agitated camera style, bursts of techno, and a narrative of fits and starts, needless to say Westdijk's second feature is all too mixed up. The aim is surely to reflect the vibrant urban cosmopolitanism already conveyed by the racial and linguistic mix, but the result is intrusive and hackneyed. The deeper problem, beneath the overbearing style, is the woolly characterisation, making it hard to feel the problems of these three add up to a tin of beans. NB

Siberian Lady Macbeth (Sibirska Ledi Magbet)

(1961, Yugo, 95 min, b/w)
d Andrzej Wajda. *sc* Sveta Lukic. *ph* Aleksander Sekulovic. *cast* Olivera Markovic, Ljuba Tadic, Kapitalina Eric, Bojan Stupica, Mile Lazarevic.

●Shakespeare at substantially more than a mere geographical remove: Wajda's Yugoslav production is based on Russian novelist Nikolai Leskov's imaginative transposition of the tragedy, while the catalogue of *crimes passionnels* at its heart suggests nothing so much as Eastern bloc Cain: 'The Swineherd Always Rings Twice' perhaps. Katerina, brooding mistress of the village mill, coolly despatches father-in-law and long-absent husband to instal hired hand Sergei at her side; shading motivation and psychology away from *femme fatale* typing, only to be betrayed by her own emotional investment. Wajda, carefully composing in 'Scope, tops his functional naturalism with a bleakly symbolic retributive coda, in the first of several 'exile' parentheses in his more fruitful interaction with postwar Polish history. PT

Sibling Rivalry

(1990, US, 88 min)
d Carl Reiner. *p* David V Lester, Don Miller, Liz Glotzer. *sc* Martha Goldhirsh. *ph* Reynaldo Villalobos. *ed* Bud Molin. *ad* Jeannine Claudia Oppewall. *m* Jack Elliott. *cast* Kirstie Alley, Bill Pullman, Carrie Fisher, Jami Gertz, Scott Bakula, Frances Sternhagen, John Randolph, Sam Elliott, Ed O'Neill.

●From the moment Alley – a doctor's frustrated wife urged by her sister to indulge in an affair – screws charming, grey-haired stranger Sam Elliott to death, you know this is going to be a stiff. Pullman mugs his way through the part of a bungling window-blind salesman who agrees to help Alley make it look like suicide. Gertz is the randy sister who falls for the investigating cop (O'Neill), while Fisher heads Alley's medically-obsessed in-laws. The sitcom contrivance of Martha Goldhirsh's script is exacerbated by farcically overwrought performances. Chief among these is from Alley herself, all 'big hair', neurotic snivelling and shrieking hysteria. And the scene where she has to remove a condom from the corpse's rigor mortised dick… Laugh? I almost changed my method of contraception. NF

Si c'était à refaire

see Second Chance

Sicilian, The

(1987, US, 146 min)
d Michael Cimino. *p* Michael Cimino, Joann Carelli. *sc* Steve Shagan. *ph* Alex Thomson. *ed* Françoise Bonnot. *pd* Wolf Kroeger. *m* David Mansfield. *cast* Christopher Lambert, Terence Stamp, Joss Ackland, John Turturro, Richard Bauer, Barbara Sukowa, Giulia Boschi, Ray McAnally, Barry Miller, Aldo Ray.

●In adapting Mario Puzo's novel, eschewing the political complexity of Francesco Rosi's classic *Salvatore Giuliano*, Cimino opts for silly and mendacious mythologising. Here the Sicilian bandit Giuliano (Lambert) becomes a heroic Christ figure, his acts of theft and murder prompted by sympathy for the peasantry, his death the result of a Judas-like betrayal manipulated by sinister and dishonorable figures of State, Church and Underworld; incredibly, he is even exonerated from responsibility for the notorious massacre of innocent Communists. Bathos abounds: American Duchess Sukowa falls head over heels for the noble savage; even Mafia capo Ackland sheds a tear for the brave son he never had. The dialogue is ponderously poetic, stilted and overemphatic, characters are convenient cyphers, and both cutting and photography tend towards the bombastic. Folly, then, but gloriously inept and overblown. GA

Sicilian Clan, The (Le Clan des Siciliens)

(1968, Fr, 120 min)
d Henri Verneuil. *p* Jacques-Eric Strauss. *sc* Henri Verneuil, José Giovanni, Pierre Pélégri. *ph* Henri Decaë. *ed* Albert Jurgenson, Pierre Gillette, Jean-Michel Gautier. *ad* Jacques Saulnier. *m* Ennio Morricone. *cast* Jean Gabin, Alain Delon, Lino Ventura, Irina Demick, Amedeo Nazzari, Sydney Chaplin, Karen Blanguernon.

●Cast as the patriarch of a spaghetti-eating Sicilian family who are crooks to a man, the once formidable Gabin – stout, white-haired and now a bit past it – mostly sits back and glowers while the younger members of the cast squabble, lust and plot a caper involving the hijack of a planeload of jewels. He finally rouses himself from his lethargy to defend his honour by executing Delon, a Corsican who had the temerity to play around with his daughter-in-law. Verneuil, not for the first time, tries to direct like Jean-Pierre Melville and fails to make it, though the action scenes are passable, and Henri Decaë's moody photography is rather more than that. TM

Sicilian Cross (Gli Esecutori)

(1976, It, 102 min)
d Maurizio Lucidi. *p* Manolo Bolognini, Luigi Borghese. *sc* Ernest Tidyman, Randal Kleiser, Gianfranco Bucceri, Roberto Leoni, Nicola Badalucco, Maurizio Lucidi. *ph* Aiace Parolin. *ed* Renzo Lucidi. *ad* Gastone Carsetti. *m* Luis Enriquez Bacalov. *cast* Roger Moore, Stacy Keach, Ivo Garrani, Fausto Tozzi, Ennio Balbo, Ettore Manni, Rosemarie Lindt.

●A run-of-the-mill Mafia potboiler which leaps between San Francisco and Sicily in a tediously bloody search for a stolen heroin consignment, and asks us to accept Roger Moore as an Italo-American lawyer. A committee of six came up with the derivative mess of a script, surprisingly including *Grease* director Randal Kleiser and *Shaft* author/*French Connection* scriptwriter Ernest Tidyman. Surprises, however, stop there. PT

Sicily! (Sicilia!)

(1999, Fr/It, 66 min, b/w)
d Jean-Marie Straub, Danièle Huillet. *p* Martine Marignac. *sc* Jean-Marie Straub, Danièle Huillet. *ph* William Lubtchansky. *cast* Gianni Buscarino, Angela Nugara, Vittorio Vigneri, Carmelo Maddio, Gianini Interlandi, Simone Nucatola.

●Veteran experimentalists Straub and Huillet offer a compact adaptation of *Conversation in Sicily*, Elio Vittorini's anti-fascist novel of 1939 which was banned outright by the Italian authorities in 1942. Buscarino plays the author's alter ego, and the narrative charts his return from the north to visit old haunts and family after some 15 years in exile. Shot in high contrast b/w, which somehow only emphasises the luminescence of the Sicilian sunshine, it takes the form of static images and exchanges of dialogue. The centrepiece is a lengthy scene with the protagonist's mother whose revelations reshape the family's emotional and political history, and who naturally directs the discussion towards simple but wonderful food. The starkness of the project may alienate many viewers, but there's no doubting the film-makers' committed investment in their subject matter. TJ

Sick: The Life & Death of Bob Flanagan, Supermasochist

(1997, US, 90 min)
d/p Kirby Dick. *ph* Jonathan Dayton, Kirby Dick, Geza Sinkovics. *ed* Kirby Dick, Dody Jane. *m* Blake Leyh. *cast* Bob Flanagan, Sheree Rose, Cathy Flanagan, Bob Flanagan Sr, Tim Flanagan, Sara Douchette.

●Bob Flanagan was a sick man. Born with cystic fibrosis in 1952, the doctors gave him a life expectancy of six or seven years – but rather than conform, he survived to 1995, hammering nails into his penis, and the like, and turning the results into art. This documentary, shocking and enlightening, succeeds in contextualising, and thus humanising, misunderstood sexual 'deviancy'. You get some insight into Bob's troubled relationship with his body, watching him create a clear plastic, self-modelled 'Invisible Man' that produces a flow of brown, white and green goo from three orifices. He met his perfect dominatrix partner in Sheree Rose, and married her in 1982, while she hung him upside down from the celing. Documenting Bob's domestic life, masochism, art, illness and more masochism for good measure, it's a tough watch – certain scenes especially – but warm and witty, too. And the moral? 'You always hurt the one you love.' NB

Sid and Nancy

(1986, GB, 114 min)
d Alex Cox. *p* Eric Fellner. *sc* Alex Cox, Abbe Wool. *ph* Roger Deakins. *ed* David Martin. *pd* Andrew McAlpine. *m* Joe Strummer, Pogues, Pray for Rain. *cast* Gary Oldman, Chloe Webb, David Hayman, Debby Bishop, Andrew Schofield, Xander Berkeley, Perry Benson, Courtney Love.

●As Cox has been at pains to point out, this is not the story of the Sex Pistols but a love story pure and simple. And since love is never simple and rarely pure, Cox follows his emetic pair, Sid Vicious and Nancy Spungen, on their long downhill slide. From the coarse idiocies of the punk movement, through the permanent scrabble for any mind-frying drug, through the screeching knock-down rows to the final abandonment far from home in the Chelsea Hotel, New York, it's a long hard ride down a tunnel filthy with every kind of degradation. Why then should anyone of sane disposition wish to see the film? Because it is still a love story, and a very touching one at that; whether waiting for her in the rain, or ripping her stockings so he can suck on her toes, or simply kissing in an alley with garbage falling all around them, there never seems to be any doubt that Sid loves Nancy OK. Quite why is hard to explain; but the movie (like Sid, as portrayed by Oldman, not without a sense of humour) is shot through with an oblique feeling for the blacker absurdities of life. Not the least of which is that, nowadays, love is not stronger than death. CPea

Siddhartha

(1972, US, 94 min)
d/p/sc Conrad Rooks. *ph* Sven Nykvist. *ed* Willy Kemplen. *ad* Malcolm Golding. *m* Hemanta Kumar. *cast* Shashi Kapoor, Simi Garewal, Romesh Sharma, Pincho Kapoor, Zul Vellani.

●A glossy feature-length ad whose genesis is Hesse's slight novel about a beautiful Brahmin who hits the road in search of truth. Accompanied by his baby-faced friend, he freaks out with the Sadhus in the wild, listens to Buddha in his grove (exit friend as monk), fucks in silhouette with a rich courtesan, and makes a lot of money as a merchant. He drops out again to find ultimate and absolute contentment ferrying folks across a river. The familiar Hesse dialectic between profligacy and asceticism is followed faithfully enough, and there's small chance of anyone leaving without receiving the message that there is no path to truth, that to search is not to find, and that 'everything returns' on the wheel of life. Unfortunately the film is made with such lack of imagination that it's impossible to get the true feel of the states of mind our Bombay ad-star goes through. Everything becomes a soft, vaguely symbolic spectacle, a love story in a chocolate-box landscape. JDuC

Side by Side

(1975, GB, 84 min)
d Bruce Beresford. *p* Drummond Challis. *sc* Garry Chambers, Ron Inkpen, Peter James, Bruce Beresford. *ph* Harvey Harrison. *ed* Ray

Lovejoy. *ad* Terry Gough. *m* Hello, Mac & Katie Kissoon, Bob Kerr's Whoopee Band, Desmond Dekker and the Israelites. *cast* Terry-Thomas, Barry Humphries, Stephanie De Sykes, Billy Boyle, Frank Thornton, Dave Mount.
●This unbelievably dreadful piece of '70s kitsch has rival club owners Boyle and Terry-Thomas battling to evade closure by searching out new pop talent, with the latter's right-hand man Humphries and his recording agency contact De Sykes off to a head start. The acts include Mud, the Rubettes and Second Generation, the big finale has the wall between the two establishments falling down to make one big party, and, yes, the director is *that* Bruce Beresford – the one who made *Tender Mercies* and *Driving Miss Daisy*. TJ

Side Streets

(1998, US, 131 min)
d Tony Gerber. *p* Bruce Weiss. *sc* Lynn Nottage, Tony Gerber. *ph* Russell Lee Fine. *ed* Kate Williams. *pd* Stephen McCabe. *m* Evan Lurie. *cast* Valeria Golina, Shashi Kapoor, Leon, Art Malik, Shabana Azmi, Mirjana Jokovic, Marc Tissot, John Ortiz, David Vadim.
●The New York melting pot gets another stir in this uncharacteristic, lighthearted Merchant Ivory production. Gerber's kaleidoscopic first feature presents five tangentially connecting stories, one for each borough. In Queens, a heart throb Romanian butcher boy steals from his wife to feed his compulsion for gambling; in Manhattan, an air-head aspirant designer fails to persuade a buyer from Italy; a food-obsessed, fading Indian screen idol comes between his Staten Island taxi-driver brother and his wife; a Cadillac nut West Indian finds love is better than gleaming metal; and a promiscuous Puerto Rican tries to raise cash for a designer frock for his sexy girlfriend. Dreams and aspirations get a light going over, diversity is celebrated, but there are no searing insights or real admissions of difficulties. Still, it's a fine enough calling card, with an agreeable comic feel. WH

Sidewalks of London

see St Martin's Lane

Sidewalks of New York

(2000, US, 108 min)
d Edward Burns. *p* Margot Bridger, Edward Burns, Cathy Schulman, Rick Yorn. *sc* Edward Burns. *ph* Frank Prinzi. *ed* David Greenwald. *cast* Edward Burns, Rosario Dawson, Dennis Farina, Heather Graham, David Krumholtz, Brittany Murphy, Stanley Tucci, Michael Leydon Campbell, Nadia Dajani, Callie Thorne, Aida Turturro.
●In this roundelay of Manhattan lives and loves, all-rounder Burns moves upmarket from the down home Irish-American milieu of his 1995 breakthrough *The Brothers McMullen*. Working in Woody Allen territory, however, leaves his solid mid-table talents slightly exposed; he and his cast graft away honestly enough for results which are far from inspired but just about agreeable. He takes the most attractive male role himself, playing the media type who gets chucked by his girlfriend because he wants kids. The other men fall into the categories of geek or scumbag. Dawson shines brightest, though, pulling the plot together as Burns' potential object of affection and Krumholtz's ex-wife (not that we buy those two as a couple for a minute). Such miscalculations reveal the joins in Burns' grand design, which deploys shaky handheld camera and fake vox pop interviews with the cast in order to appear grittier and more inventive than it actually is. TJ

Sidewalk Stories

(1989, US, 97 min, b/w)
d/p/sc Charles Lane. *ph* Bill Dill. *ed* Anee Stein, Charles Lane. *pd* Lyn Pinezich. *m* Marc Marder. *cast* Charles Lane, Nicole Alysia, Sandye Wilson, Darnell Williams, Trula Hoosier.
●An ambitious but sadly misguided attempt to make a contemporary silent comedy which opts for simplistic plotting, sentimentality and mime as it tells of a homeless, black New York street artist's attempts to trace the mother of a baby girl whose father's murder he has witnessed. The black-and-white photography is of some appeal, but Lane's own central performance is so winsome that the plot's (unintentional?) borrowings from Chaplin's maudlin *The Kid* become irritating in the extreme. Only the last minute is memorable, but it comes far too late to endow the film with anything but novelty value. GA

Sidney Sheldon's Bloodline

see Bloodline

Siebente Kontinent

see 7th Continent, The

Siebtelbauern, Die

see Inheritors, The

Siege

(1982, Can, 81 min)
d Paul Donovan, Maura O'Connell. *p* Michael Donovan, John Walsch, Maura O'Connell, Paul Donovan. *sc* Paul Donovan. *ph* Les Krizsan. *ed* Ian McBride. *pd* Malachi Salter. *m* Peter Jermyn, Drew King. *cast* Doug Lennox, Tom Nardini, Brenda Bazinet, Darel Haeny, Terry-David Despres, Jack Blum.
●Such a blatant low-budget steal of the *Assault on Precinct 13* idea that one could almost praise it for bare-faced cheek. On the first night of an official police strike, a gay club is invaded by some vile recruits of the 'New Order', a local variant on the National Front, who sport a nasty line in queer-bashing (shooting them in the back of the head). One gay runs free, takes refuge in a large house peopled by resourceful outdoor types of that particularly Canadian sort, and the siege begins. Many scenes are badly in need of tightening, but there is some pleasure to be had from the ingenuity of the besieged in contriving makeshift weaponry (a drainpipe bazooka, the old James Bond flaming aerosol trick). There's the Hawksian standby of the last cigarette, and there's even the dead-villain-who-won't-lie-down. Not quite there, but not a bad try. CPea

Siege, The

(1998, US, 116 min)
d Edward Zwick. *p* Lynda Obst, Edward Zwick. *sc* Lawrence Wright, Menno Meyjes, Edward Zwick. *ph* Roger Deakins. *ed* Steven Rosenblum. *pd* Lilly Kilvert. *m* Graeme Revell. *cast* Bruce Willis, Denzel Washington, Annette Bening, Tony Shalhoub, Sami Bouajila, David Proval, Lance Reddick.
●This earnest thriller confronts urban terrorism head-on; however, its frightening depiction of bombings and repressive martial law in NY is undercut by muddled political thinking and a conventional storyline. Moslem fanatics are pitted against three conflicting forces of 'good': Washington's FBI anti-terrorism task force, Bening's National Security Agency operation, and rogue army general Willis. Reinforcing a self-conscious sense of fair play, Edward Zwick includes reams of special pleading on behalf of law-abiding Arab-Americans. Brilliantly captured by Roger Deakins' bleached-out camerawork and Steve Rosenblum's urgent editing, the best scenes are those depicting Washington's impotence in the face of a ruthless bombing campaign that culminates in a suicide attack on FBI HQ. Utterly absurd is Willis's slide from gung-ho patriot to 'might is right' megalomaniac, while not even Washington can lend credibility to lines like, 'If we torture this man, we've already lost.' NF

Siege of Sidney Street, The

(1960, GB, 94 min, b/w)
d/p Robert S Baker, Monty Berman. *sc* Jimmy Sangster, Alexander Baron. *ph* Monty Berman. *ed* Peter Bezencenet. *pd* William Kellner. *m* Stanley Black. *cast* Donald Sinden, Nicole Berger, Peter Wyngarde, Kieron Moore, Leonard Sachs, TP McKenna, Tutte Lemkow.
●Baker-Berman hardly rival Powell-Pressburger in the creative collaboration stakes. But their exploitations of various lurid bits of British history – see *The Flesh and the Fiends*, *The Hellfire Club* – aren't entirely negligible. This one's about the gang of anarchists led by the enigmatic Peter the Painter who peppered the East End with gunfire in 1910–11. The shoot-ups aren't bad, but apart from Wyngarde – why didn't he become a film star? – cops and robbers alike are a dull lot. Where the film scores is in its unexpected sympathy for the gang's agenda and in its thoughtful picture of a Victorian world of barrel organs and horse dung giving way to one of phones, cars and automatics. That's Jimmy Sangster as Winston Churchill in the climactic siege sequence. BBa

Siegfried

see Nibelungen, Die

Sierra

(1950, US, 83 min)
d Alfred E Green. *p* Michael Kraike. *sc* Edna Anhalt. *ph* Russell Metty. *ed* Ted J Kent. *ad* Bernard Herzbrun, Robert Boyle. *m* Walter Scharf. *cast* Audie Murphy, Wanda Hendrix, Dean Jagger, Burl Ives, Elliott Reid, Tony Curtis, Sara Allgood.
●It's safe to say that Audie Murphy was the only film star to have killed 240 men, and here we catch him just a few years after his wartime tribulations, trying his luck in Hollywood. He marches into the frame like a good soldier and duly recites his lines; but he's nowhere near an actor and, despite the baby faced looks, a slightly disturbing presence. This is a characteristic example of the sort of juvenile-oriented Western in which he made his name. Burl Ives, as Lonesome the Hermit, sings 'The Ballad of Suzie the Whale' and such, while Tony Curtis, being groomed for stardom, looks cool in a black hat. The location scouts have assembled a choice assortment of geography for Russell Metty's camera to celebrate. BBa

Siesta

(1987, US, 97 min)
d Mary Lambert. *p* Gary Kurfist. *sc* Patricia Louisiana Knop. *ph* Bryan Loftus, Michael Lund. *ed* Glenn A Morgan. *pd* John Beard. *m* Marcus Miller. *cast* Ellen Barkin, Jodie Foster, Gabriel Byrne, Martin Sheen, Julian Sands, Isabella Rossellini, Alexei Sayle, Grace Jones.
●Barkin, coming to on an airfield, dress around her ears and blood all over the place, utters the first of many crass expositions: 'This isn't my blood, so it must be somebody else's!' In a crazed panic, she sets off to solve the mystery, along the way falling into the clutches of a lecherous taxi-driver and a group of young ingrates (Sands and Foster among them) emulating Fellini party scenes. Flashbacks reveal that Barkin is Claire, a brassy American stunt-woman, whose fear of dying in a dare has driven her away from her rail-roading husband (Sheen) for one last night of spunky passion in Spain with her former lover and trapeze instructor (Byrne), whose new wife (Rossellini) stalks them with a knife. Lambert's debut fields farcical menace, wildly theatrical performances, a confusing plot and a corny resolution, while the script is a hilariously overblown gem. Miles Davis' soundtrack is the sole subtlety. EP

Si Gentille Petite Fille, Une

see Cathy's Curse

Sight Behind the Bandaged Eye, The (Ishiki Saizuri)

(1997, Jap, 23 min)
d Koji Shirakawa. *collaborators/cast* Hiroshi Shirakawa, Toshiko Shirakawa, Teru Shirakawa, Yoko Okusawa , Ishida.
●Arresting attempt to summon up a kind of diseased, blighted vision. A hardcore thrash movie comprising a pixel blitz of strobes and distorted, rythmic mantras. Extraordinary, but not for the faint-hearted (or epileptics). TCh

Sigmund Freud's Dora

(1979, US, 35 min)
d/p/sc Anthony McCall, Claire Pajaczkowska, Andrew Tyndall, Jane Weinstock. *ph* Babette Mangolte. *cast* Suzanne Fletcher, Joel Kovel, Silvia Kolbowski, Anne Hegira.
●Feminine desire, displacement, obsessive housewifery, the image of the Madonna, smoke… fire. No wonder Freud's fragmented analysis of his rebellious teenage patient has become a feminist touchstone. This witty and ambitious film bends the rules of classic couch cinema, while inserts of telly ads and porno films interrogate woman's status as the object of desire. MM

Signal Left, Turn Right (Da Zuo Deng, Xiang You Zhuan)

(1996, China/HK, 110 min)
d Huang Jianxin. *p* Bao Wen Xiong. *sc* Ye Guang Qin, Huang Jianxin. *ph* Ma De Lin. *ed* Lei Qin. *cast* Niu Zhenhua, Ding Jiali, Ju Hao, Qi Qiao, Wang Gang.

●As its title makes plain, the final part of Huang's 'urban attitude' trilogy is about a driving school. Any connection with larger questions about China's current direction is, of course, purely coincidental. Driving schools are run on military lines. The film focuses on one group of three adult pupils (there should be four, but one has married a foreigner and emigrated) and dissects their dubious reasons for wanting to learn to drive. Niu, the trilogy's chubby mascot, plays a wily photo-journalist with a yen for prestige; he is the first to cotton on to the various scams operated by their instructor. Less a plot-driven film than a series of vignettes and gags, it's often riotously funny and certainly says a lot about Chi…er, Chinese driving schools in the 1990s. TR

Signal 7

(1983, US, 92 min)
d Bob Nilsson. *sc* Signal 7 Group [Victoria Bennett, Hildy Burns, Steve Burns, Roy Kissin, Sara Morris, Rob Nilsson, David Schickele]. *ph* Geoff Schaaf, Tomas Tucker. *ed* Richard Harkness. *ad* Hildy Burns, Steve Burns. *m* Andy Narell. *cast* Bill Ackridge, Dan Leegant, Bob Eldross, Herb Mills, Hagit Farber, John Tidwell.
●Shot over six nights on videotape and partially funded by the film-maker's own credit cards, this portrait of life amid the San Francisco cabbing community unfolds in semi-improvised fashion, focusing on failed actors Ackridge and Leegant, who can't quite leave their former aspirations behind. Nothing new really, but the performers look comfortable with the rambling dialogue, and the dedication to John Cassavetes is not entirely unwarranted. TJ

Signed: Lino Brocka

(1987, US/GB/WGer, 83 min)
d/p/sc/ph Christian Blackwood. *ed* Monika Abspacher, Michael Riesman. *with* Lino Brocka, JayIlagan.
●Documentaries about film-makers are generally a major snooze, but Lino Brocka (arch-foe of Imelda Marcos, best known for his *Manila: In the Claws of Darkness*) tells tales that could cure deafness. Blackwood has the good sense to simply let him rip, and he ranges freely over his extraordinary life story, his attachment to the city's slum-dwellers, his struggle to make movies of adult interest, and his troubles with successive Filipino governments. Most movingly, Brocka comes out as gay, presents clips from his first gay-themed film (the long-lost *Gold-Plated),* and shows rehearsals for his upcoming film about a rent boy, *Macho Dancer*. The combustible mixture of sex, radicalism and soap generates more heat than many a fiction film. TR

Signe du Lion, Le (The Sign of Leo)

(1959, Fr, 102 min, b/w)
d Eric Rohmer. *p* Roland Nonin, Claude Chabrol. *sc* Eric Rohmer, Paul Gégauff. *ph* Nicolas Hayer. *ed* Anne-Marie Cotret, Marie-Josèphe Yoyotte. *m* Louis Saguer. *cast* Jess Hahn, Van Doude, Michèle Girardon, Jean Le Poulain, Stéphane Audran, Franoise Prévost, Jean-Luc Godard, Macha Méril.
●Rohmer's first feature, not so much a moral tale as a cautionary anecdote (loosely modelled on Murnau's *The Last Laugh*) in which an impoverished American musician living in Paris (Hahn) runs himself into debt on the strength of an inheritance he doesn't inherit. Very much of its *nouvelle vague* day in its amused anatomy of the Latin Quarter fauna as the hero desperately does the rounds in quest of a loan, having no luck because it is summer and everyone's on holiday, and gradually slipping without realising it into becoming a *clochard*. But also a precise, poetic documentary on Paris, with the city turning into a stone prison that gradually crushes resistance until the musician suffers total moral and physical disintegration. TM

Sign of the Cross, The

(1932, US, 124 min, b/w)
d Cecil B DeMille. *sc* Waldemar Young, Sidney Buckman. *ph* Karl Struss. *ed* Anne Bauchens. *ad* Mitchell Leisen. *m* Rudolph Kopp. *cast* Fredric March, Elissa Landi, Charles Laughton, Claudette Colbert, Ian Keith, Vivian Tobin, Nat Pendleton.
●A prologue tacked on in 1944 ludicrously attempts to link the Allies' advance over Italy to the dreadful happenings in Nero's time. But history was always a plaything to DeMille, useful only as a surefire way of offering up sex, violence and visual spectacle under the guise of cultural and moral enlightenment. And this slice of 'history' has it all: Laughton's implicitly gay Nero fiddling away while an impressive miniature set burns, Colbert bathing up to her nipples in asses' milk, Christians and other unfortunates thrown to a fearsome menagerie, much suggestive slinking about in Mitchell Leisen's costumes, much general debauchery teetering between the sadistic and the erotic. Not for people with scruples. GB

Sign of the Gladiator (Nel segno di Roma)

(1958, It/Fr/WGer, 100 min)
d Guido Brignone. *p* Rino Merolle. *sc* Antonio Thellung, Francesco de Feo, Sergio Leone, Giuseppe Mangione, Guido Brignone. *ph* Luciano Trasatti. *ed* Nino Baragli. *ad* Ottavio Scotti. *m* Angelo Francesco Lavagnino. *cast* Anita Ekberg, Georges Marchal, Jacques Sernas, Folco Lulli, Lorella De Luca, Gino Cervi, Chelo Alonso.
●Syrian queen Zenobia (Ekberg) takes time out from rebellion against the Roman Empire to fall for enslaved general Marco Valerio (Marchal). He remains faithful to Rome, however, and in the climactic battle receives a javelin in the chest from Zenobia. The general recovers from his wound in time to plead successfully for Zenobia – who's by now up before the Senate in an off-the-shoulder evening dress. Lavishly mounted and splendidly preposterous. Sergio Leone – then Roberti Sergio Leone – was one of the five scriptwriters. Cut by 15 minutes on its first British release. TJ

Sign of the Pagan

(1954, US, 92 min)
d Douglas Sirk. *p* Albert J Cohen. *sc* Oscar Brodney, Barré Lyndon. *ph* Russell Metty. *ed* Al Clark, Milton Carruth. *ad* Alexander Golitzen, Emrich Nicholson. *m* Frank Skinner, Hans J Salter. *cast* Jeff Chandler, Jack Palance, Ludmilla Tcherina, Rita Gam, Jeff Morrow, George Dolenz, Eduard Franz, Alexander Scourby.
●An immensely interesting though finally unsuccessful film. Sirk's hopes of transforming the project into a version of Marlowe's *Tamburlaine the Great* were thwarted by Universal. However, the film's historical dimension – Attila the Hun's attempt to destroy the Roman Empire, with Palance as Attila, and Chandler as Rome's would-be Christian defender – together with Sirk's unusually hysterical conception of the central character, throw a suggestive light on the seemingly slight reverberations of his better-known domestic melodramas. PH

Signora di Tutti, La

(1934, It, 97 min, b/w)
d Max Ophuls. *p* Emilio Rizzoli. *sc* Max Ophuls, Hans Wilhelm, Curt Alexander. *ph* Ubaldo Arata. *ed* Ferdinando Maria Poggioli. *ad* Giuseppe Capponi. *m* Daniele Amfitheatrof. *cast* Isa Miranda, Memo Benassi, Tatiana Pavlova, Nelly Corradi, Federico Benfer, Franco Coop.
●Ophuls' only Italian film, in which once again his subject is female sexuality – as a 'danger' or threat, as a source of beauty, as a marketable commodity. The film star Gaby Doriot (Miranda) attempts suicide, and under anaesthetic she recalls the events that shaped her life. Commerce, industry and high finance are viewed with sharp irony throughout, but the melodrama centres on a seductive ambiguity: is Gaby a victim of those around her, or their willing accomplice? As ever, Ophuls' highly mobile camera shows rather than tells, emotionally sensitising all it lights upon. TR

Signora senza camelie, La (Camille without Camellias/ The Lady without Camellias)

(1953, It, 105 min, b/w)
d Michelangelo Antonioni. *p* Domenico Forges Davanzati. *sc* Michelangelo Antonioni, Suso Cecchi D'Amico, Francesco Maselli, PM Pasinetti. *ph* Enzo Serafin. *ed* Eraldo Da Roma. *ad* Giani Polidori. *m* Giovanni Fusco. *cast* Lucia Bosè, Andrea Cecchi, Gino Cervi, Ivan Desny, Alain Cuny.
●An early Antonioni drama that looks at the sad fate of a manipulated woman, as well as taking a satirical swipe at the commercial end of the Italian film industry. Bosè plays a shopgirl, recently elevated to movie stardom, whose idolising producer husband (Cecchi) puts her into a disastrous production of *Joan of Arc* and sends her career into a downward spiral. Characteristically, Antonioni is less concerned with plot than with creating fluid set pieces and eloquent framings of his beautiful actress and the surrounding decor. The resulting cocktail is slight on psychology, but invariably stunning to behold. DT

Signs of Life (Lebenszeichen)

(1968, WGer, 90 min, b/w)
d/p/sc Werner Herzog. *ph* Thomas Mauch. *ed* Beate Mainka-Jellinghaus, Maximiliane Mainka. *m* Stavros Xarchakos. *cast* Peter Brogle, Wolfgang Reichmann, Julio Pinheiro, Athina Zacharopoulou, Wolfgang von Ungern-Sternberg.
●Herzog's first feature is his most conventional: three bored German soldiers spend the last months of the World War II occupation 'guarding' a useless munitions dump on the Greek island of Cos, killing time as best they can until one of them – inevitably – flips out. It's the one occasion that Herzog has tried to draw characters in any psychological depth, and (predictably) the going is sometimes heavy, but the film is still loaded with idiosyncratic, remarkable details… like the devastating moment that sparks the soldier's madness. TR

Si Jolie Petite Plage, Une (Such a Pretty Little Beach)

(1948, Fr, 90 min, b/w)
d Yves Allégret. *p* Emile Darbon. *sc* Jacques Sigurd. *ph* Henri Alekan. *ed* Léonide Azar. *ad* Maurice Colasson. *m* Maurice Thiriet. *cast* Gérard Philipe, Madeleine Robinson, Jane Marken, Jean Servais, Julien Carette.
●A late bloom for the Carné-Prévert brand of poetic realism, set in a wintry beach resort in Normandy where a young man (Philipe), returns to the scene of his childhood after involvement in a crime of passion in Paris (he has just killed the singer he was seduced by and ran away with to escape his orphanage background). Undergoing much soul-searching torment, focused by the presence of a sinister stranger (Servais) as well as by speculation and gossip about the crime centering on the nosy hotel proprietress (Marken), he finds some temporary warmth in the love of the bedraggled chambermaid (Robinson). An exercise in unrelieved gloom, much admired at the time, it now looks much too studied; despite sound performances and Henri Alekan's impressively moody evocation of the deserted, permanently rain-swept landscape, it emerges as rather a bore. TM

Silas Marner

(1985, GB, 92 min)
d Giles Foster. *p* Louis Marks. *sc* Louis Marks, Giles Foster. *ph* Nat Crosby. *ed* Robin Sales. *pd* Gerry Scott. *m* Carl Davis. *cast* Ben Kingsley, Jenny Agutter, Patrick Ryecart, Freddie Jones, Rosemary Martin, Patsy Kensit, Jim Broadbent, Frederick Treves, Angela Pleasence.
●For sheer prettiness, this is the apotheosis of BBC tea-time classicism. Real locations (carefully muddied roads, immaculately authentic masonry) look more artificial than any studio mock-up. Foster's ambling treatment of George Eliot's novel – embittered outcast rediscovering humanity – generates the urgency of a waxworks show in its picturesque rollcall of accomplished players, Kingsley's self-consciously actorish miser included. MHoy

Silence, The (Tystnaden)

(1963, Swe, 96 min, b/w)
d/p/sc Ingmar Bergman. *ph* Sven Nykvist. *ed* Ulla Ryghe. *ad* PA Lundgren. *cast* Ingrid Thulin, Gunnel Lindblom, Jörgen Lindström, Hakan Jahnberg, Birger Malmsten.
●The final part of Bergman's trilogy (after *Through a Glass Darkly* and *Winter Light*) is a bleak and disturbing study of loneliness, love and obsessive desire. Sisters Ester (Thulin) and Anna (Lindblom), together with the latter's young son, book into a vast but virtually empty hotel – the only other guests are a troupe of dwarf

entertainers – in a country seemingly occupied or threatened by war. Once again exploring the conflicts between physicality and spirituality, Bergman candidly portrays Ester's latent lesbian desire for her sister, as well as Anna's own compulsive sexuality (she picks up a waiter and brings him back to the hotel). Despite the overt eroticism, the sisters' craving for emotional warmth is filmed in a cold, objective style; in this way, Bergman's severe symbolism emphasises both the seeming impossibility of, and the absolute necessity for, human tenderness in a Godless world. NF

Silence, The

(1998, Iran, 77 min)
d/p/sc Mohsen Makhmalbaf. *ph* Ebrahim Ghafori. *ed* Mohsen Makhmalbaf. *cast* Tahmineh Normatova, Nadereh Abdeelahyeva, Golbibi Ziadolahyeva, Hakem Ghassem.

●This esoteric art movie from Makhmalbaf senior is visually arresting, I suppose, in the self-consciously poetic manner of Paradjanov, but only if you can look past the stultifyingly whimsical nature of its allegory. Korshid is a young blind boy who works tuning musical instruments. Although his mother is in arrears with the rent, the lad allows himself to be led astray en route to work by an irresistible impulse to follow the sound of music. It is, one appreciates, a film directed from the inner eye – just what the world's been waiting for, a structuralist neo-realist art musical for blind kids. TCh

Silence and Cry (Csend és Káiltás)

(1967, Hun, 79 min, b/w)
d Miklós Jancsó. *sc* Gyula Hernadi, Miklós Jancsó. *ph* János Kende. *ed* Zoltán Farkas. *ad* Tamás Banovich. *cast* András Kozák, Zoltán Latinovits, Jószef Madaras, Mari Törocsik, Andrea Drahota.

● *The Round-Up* and *The Red and the White* both dealt with key moments in the Hungarian suppression of Communism, and introduced Jancsó's method as an ultra-stylised manipulation of politically symbolic figures in harsh, unyielding landscapes. *Silence and Cry* resumes the discussion at a newly intimate, domestic level, and introduces the psychological questions that dominate some of Jancsó's later movies. It centres on a refugee from the 'Red' army, hiding out from the police in the farmhouse of some politically dubious peasants, and focuses on his horror at his hosts' bland acceptance of their situation, which eventually provokes a 'meaningless' tragedy. Jancsó's characteristic sequence-shots turn the chamber drama into a political thriller pregnant with wider connotations, including veiled comments on the contemporary state of Hungary. TR

Silence de la mer, Le

(1947, Fr, 95 min, b/w)
d/p/sc Jean-Pierre Melville. *ph* Henri Decaë. *ed* Jean-Pierre Melville. *m* Edgar Bischoff. *cast* Howard Vernon, Nicole Stéphane, Jean-Marie Robain, Ami Aroe, Denis Sadier.

●Melville's extraordinary first feature, an adaptation of Vercors' classic novella about the French Resistance, is in effect a triangular drama in which two people don't speak. A German officer (Vernon), convalescing from a wound, is billeted on an elderly Frenchman (Robain) and his niece (Stéphane). Respecting their obstinate refusal to address the hated invader, he meets their silence with a series of monologues, apparently ignored, in which he recalls his life before the war and all the things he values; but what he reveals about himself causes the girl to fall in love, without being able to declare her feelings. Filmed in the most daring way imaginable, using a new cinematic language of transient expressions and glances, the film was a root influence on Bresson and the whole French New Wave. CPea

Silence est d'Or, Le (Man About Town)

(1947, Fr, 100 min, b/w)
d/p/sc René Clair. *ph* Armand Thirard. *ed* Louisette Hautecoeur, Henri Taverna. *ad* Léon Barsacq. *m* Georges Van Parys. *cast* Maurice Chevalier, François Périer, Marcelle Derrien, Dany Robin, Robert Pizani, Raymond Cordy, Paul Olivier, Gaston Modot.

●Even in 1947, Clair's belated Valentine to the silent period, one of his few memorable postwar films, was so deliciously *passé* in style as almost to pass for an example of the work to which it pays wistful tribute. With Chevalier (whose heavily accented delivery sounds decidedly odd in French) as an ageing boulevardier, Périer as his youthful nemesis, and Dany Robin as the *midinette* who comes between them, the plot is pure convention, but the gentle humour and wealth of period detail (from both the turn of the century and the '40s) have an enduring charm. GAd

Silence of the Hams, The (Il silenzio dei prosciutti)

(1993, It/US, 81 min)
d Ezio Greggio. *p* Ezio Greggio, Julie Corman. *sc* Ezio Greggio. *ph* Jacques Haitkin. *ed* Robert Barrere, Andy Horvitch. *pd* Jim Newport. *m* Parmer Fuller. *cast* Billy Zane, Ezio Greggio, Dom DeLuise, Charlene Tilton, Joanna Pacula, Martin Balsam, Phyllis Diller, Shelley Winters.

●The US debut of Italy's favourite television comedian, Ezio Greggio, in which trainee FBI agent Jo Dee Fostar (Zane) encounters characters called Sharon Bone, Dr Animal Cannibal Pizza (an incarcerated psychiatrist who ate his patients in a pizzeria after closing time), and Inspector Putrid, is a wholly redundant exercise. The vogue for this flimflam is to forget pointed satire and instead recycle old plots in knowingly cack-handed fashion, along with some blunt physical comedy. NB

Silence of the Lambs, The (100)

(1990, US, 118 min)
d Jonathan Demme. *p* Edward Saxon, Kenneth Utt, Ron Bozman. *sc* Ted Tally. *ph* Tak Fujimoto. *ed* Craig McKay. *pd* Kristi Zea. *m* Howard Shore. *cast* Jodie Foster, Anthony Hopkins, Scott Glenn, Ted Levine, Anthony Heald, Diane Baker, Brooke Smith, Kasi Lemmons, Tracey Walter, Roger Corman.

●In its own old-fashioned way, this is as satisfying as that other, more modernist Thomas Harris adaptation, *Manhunter*. When FBI trainee Clarice Starling (Foster) is sent to conduct an interview with serial killer shrink Dr Hannibal Lecter (Hopkins) in his high-security cell, she little knows what she is in for. The Feds want Lecter to help them in their search for homicidal maniac 'Buffalo Bill'; but in exchange for clues about Bill's behaviour, Lecter demands that Clarice answer questions about herself, so that he can penetrate the darkest recesses of her mind. It's in their confrontations that both film and heroine come electrically alive. Although Demme does reveal the results of the killer's violence, he for the most part refrains from showing the acts themselves; the film could never be accused of pandering to voyeuristic impulses. Under-standably, much has been made of Hopkins' hypnotic Lecter, but the laurels must go to Levine's killer, admirably devoid of camp overstatement, and to Foster, who evokes a vulnerable but pragmatic intelligence bent on achieving independence through sheer strength of will. GA

Silences of the Palace, The (Saimt el Qusur/Les Silences du Palais)

(1994, Fr/Tun, 127 min)
d Moufida Tlatli. *p* Ahmed Attia, Richard Magnien. *sc* Moufida Tlatli. *ph* Youssef Ben Youssef. *ed* Moufida Tlatli. *ad* Claude Bennys, Mondher Dhrif. *m* Anouar Brahem. *cast* Ahmel Hedhili, Hend Sabri, Najia Ouerghi, Ghalia Lacroix, Sami Bouajila, Kamel Fazaa.

●Moufida Tlatli's remarkable debut describes the days of slavery in her native Tunisia. At 25, Alia, a singer and lute-player, who is pregnant by her boyfriend, learns of the death of Prince Sidi Ali. This prompts a visit to his palace, giving rise to memories of her own and her mother's days of service there years ago. The film captures the texture of life in the palace – its gardens, its fading opulence, the kitchens, corridors and ante-rooms, all lit crystal clear. There are scenes of group activity (dyeing, washing, dancing, singing), but the dominating mood is of the monotony and soul-threatening burden of servitude. The prince exercised his *droit du seigneur*: an indignity which would drive Alia's mother to near-frenzy – had not her life been so focused on the interests of her 15-year-old daughter. A most memorable account of the complex relationship between mothers and daughters suffering the distortions of injustice. WH

Silencieux, Le (The Man Who Died Twice/The Silent One)

(1973, Fr/It, 118 min)
d Claude Pinoteau. *sc* Jean-Loup Dabadie, Claude Pinoteau. *ph* Jean Collomb. *ed* Marie-Josèphe Yoyotte. *ad* Claude Pignot. *m* Jacques Datin, Alain Goraguer. *cast* Lino Ventura, Leo Genn, Robert Hardy, Lea Massari, Suzanne Flon, Bernard Dhéran, Pierre Zimmer.

●Lino Ventura, like Robert Mitchum, has held together more than one movie by his presence alone, and almost does so here. He plays a French nuclear scientist, kidnapped by the Russians some 16 years earlier, forced to defect back by the British, who offer him 'freedom' in exchange for names. With the KGB after his blood, the film develops into a watchable chase thriller, best when reminiscent of Hitchcock: escapes from hotels, a killing on a train, and a climax involving a Russian orchestral conductor, the key to Ventura's real freedom. A bit too glossy, and the English dubbed version is appalling.

Silent Cry, The

(1977, GB/WGer/Fr, 98 min, b/w & col)
d/p Stephen Dwoskin. *sc* Stephen Dwoskin, Bobby Gill. *ph* Stephen Dwoskin. *ed* Stephen Dwoskin, Mary Dickinson. *m* Ben Mason. *cast* Ernst Brightmore, Bobby Gill, Harry Waistnage, Mary Rose, Beatrice Cordua.

●The title recalls Münch, but the film could almost be a radicalised Resnais project. Dwoskin traces the history of a woman dominated from childhood by male definition of her 'place'. She's trapped within a series of reflections of her image, which the film explores in an obsessive forward-and-backward movement that ranges over memory, fantasy, and 'the presentation of self in everyday life'. Although highly fragmented, this constructs a fuller narrative than any of Dwoskin's earlier features; but the narrative line is constantly disorganised by the disturbance of childhood memory and speech. An impressive renewal of the concerns that had been preoccupying Dwoskin for nearly a decade. IC

Silent Fall

(1994, US, 101 min)
d Bruce Beresford. *p* James Robinson. *sc* Akiva Goldsman. *ph* Peter James. *ed* Ian Crafford. *pd* John Stoddart. *m* Stewart Copeland. *cast* Richard Dreyfuss, Linda Hamilton, JT Walsh, John Lithgow, Ben Faulkner, Liv Tyler, Zahn McClarnon.

●When their parents are brutally murdered, Sylvie (Tyler) names her autistic younger brother Tim (Faulkner), aged nine, as the culprit. However, sheriff Mitch Rivers (Walsh) has his doubts, and calls in reluctant, haunted shrink Jake Rainer (Dreyfuss) to break down the boy's wall of silence. Although this device is a variation on that old thriller stand-by, 'selective amnesia', interest in the unravelling mystery is sustained not by a need to discover the killer's identity (obvious early on), but by involvement with the damaged characters and the need to establish a motive. Initially avoiding clever plot-twists in favour of intense character study, Beresford draws the best from a fine cast. Only when he tries to up the thrill quotient near the end are the contrivances of Akiva Goldsman's debut script revealed, like cracks in the smooth surface of a frozen lake. NF

Silent Flute, The (aka Circle of Iron)

(1978, US, 95 min)
d Richard Moore. *p* Sandy Howard, Paul Maslansky. *sc* Stirling Silliphant, Stanley Mann. *ph* Ronnie Taylor. *ed* Ernest Walter. *pd* Tambi Larsen. *m* Bruce Smeaton. *cast* David Carradine, Jeff Cooper, Roddy McDowall, Eli Wallach, Christopher Lee, Erica Creer, Earl Maynard.

●Made in Israel with predominantly Israeli money and technicians, this is a berserk attempt at a martial arts fantasy, somewhat in the vein of *Conan the Barbarian*. Cooper plays the monosyllabic Cord, who wins a martial arts contest by what are considered foul means, and is disqualified from participating in a quest for a book of knowledge. He goes anyway, and meets a variety of bizarre challenges on the road, as well as a variety of foes, all played by David Carradine except for the man who is dissolving his penis in a barrel of oil, who is played by Eli Wallach.

Eventually, having learned that man cannot live by brawn alone, he reaches the cloistered isle where a cowled Christopher Lee guards the book… It may sound, well, different, but Richard Moore's cumbersome direction reduces everything to the pedestrian or the banal. The storyline is credited to Bruce Lee and James Coburn (it was actually no more than the ghost of an idea dreamed up during Lee's days as a martial arts instructor in Los Angeles), but it's more significant that the script is credited to Stirling Silliphant, the 'versatile' writer lately responsible for the script of *The Swarm*. TR

Silent Movie

(1976, US, 87 min)
d Mel Brooks. *p* Michael Hertzberg. *sc* Mel Brooks, Ron Clark, Rudy de Luca, Barry Levinson. *ph* Paul Lohmann. *ed* John C Howard, Stanford C Allen. *pd* Albert Brenner. *m* John Morris. *cast* Mel Brooks, Marty Feldman, Dom DeLuise, Bernadette Peters, Sid Caesar, Harold Gould, Ron Carey, Fritz Feld.
●Right from the opening seconds, when the single word 'Hello' appears on the screen, we all know that *Silent Movie* is going to be very silly indeed, even for Mel Brooks. And so it is – a silent movie about the attempts of Mel Funn (Brooks), a has-been director dragged down by drink, to film a contemporary all-star silent movie, complete with raucous musical effects and explanatory titles. The trouble is, it's the kind of silliness that's too strained and self-indulgent to be enjoyable. James Caan, Liza Minnelli, Burt Reynolds and others contribute grating guest appearances. Only Brooks himself combines frenzy with grace, and there are occasional moments of barmy splendour. GB

Silent One, The

see Silencieux, Le

Silent Partner, The

(1978, Can, 105 min)
d Daryl Duke. *p* Joel B Michaels, Stephen Young. *sc* Curtis Hanson. *ph* Billy Williams. *ed* George Appleby. *pd* Trevor Williams. *m* Oscar Peterson. *cast* Elliott Gould, Christopher Plummer, Susannah York, Celine Lomez, Michael Kirby, Sean Sullivan, John Candy.
●Tarting up a flagging project has rarely been taken quite so literally as here, with the climactic revelation that the misogynistic, sadistic villain (Plummer) has a predilection for drag. If it weren't for the gimmicks (and the sadism is so gratuitous it could be nothing else), then the film could easily pass for a minor caper thriller of the '60s, all convoluted plot and calculated kookiness. But cyphers (both female leads) and question-marks (who'll get the money, who'll survive – who cares?) dominate the script as every labyrinthine twist becomes more plodding. SM

Silent Rage

(1982, US, 105 min)
d Michael Miller. *p* Anthony B Unger. *sc* Joseph Fraley. *ph* Robert Jessup, Neil Roach. *ed* Richard C Meyer. *m* Peter Bernstein, Mark Goldenberg. *cast* Chuck Norris, Ron Silver, Steven Keats, Toni Kalem, William Finley, Brian Libby, Stephen Furst.
●The idea of pitting karate champion Norris against a virtually indestructible psychopath is intriguing, but the resulting confusion of clichés proves disappointingly incompetent. Itching to try out his new drug, one of a trio of Frankenstein doctors fastens upon a mad axeman who has been shot to pieces (Libby), and revives him with startling effectiveness. Norris, as a small-town sheriff lumbered with a comic teddy-bear of a deputy and a posse of suspiciously well-scrubbed Hell's Angels, has to take time off to deal with the problem. The doctors bumble through their moral dilemmas, the biologically reinforced monster expresses his silent rage, and a bemused Norris wanders through the *Halloween*-ish landscape unsure whether he's playing Clint Eastwood or Hopalong Cassidy. Still, his *jodan mawashi geri* (a swivelling kick to the head) is a joy to behold. RMy

Silent Running

(1971, US, 89 min)
d Douglas Trumbull. *p* Michael Gruskoff. *sc* Deric Washburn, Michael Cimino, Steve Bochco. *ph* Charles F Wheeler. *ed* Aaron Stell. *m* Peter Schickele. *cast* Bruce Dern, Cliff Potts, Ron Rifkin, Jesse Vint.
●A wonderful film. The message of *2001: A Space Odyssey* (for which Trumbull did the special effects) was that man needed guidance from beyond; the message of *Silent Running*, symbolically set in the year 2001, is that man (and his creations: the film's robots) must, even at the risk of madness, be his own saviour. Adrift in space in a literal Garden of Eden that was intended to refurbish an Earth devastated by nuclear war, Bruce Dern refuses to destroy his private world when ordered to. Instead, with the help of his drones (robots), he tends his garden, and then sends it out into deep space to seek a possible second chance for mankind. Full of stunning visuals, the ideas in the film more than compensate for the awkward scene-setting of the beginning. PH

Silent Scream

(1989, GB, 85 min)
d David Hayman. *p* Patrick Higson. *sc* Bill Beech, Jane Beech. *ph* Denis Crossan. *ed* Justin Krish. *pd* Andy Harris. *m* Callum McNair. *cast* Iain Glen, Paul Samson, Anne Kristen, Alexander Morton, Andrew Barr, John Murtagh.
●After shooting a barman in a Soho pub in 1963, Larry Winters was sentenced to life imprisonment. In 1973, a violent prisoner addicted to the drugs prescribed to control his depressions, he became one of the first inmates at the Barlinnie Special Unit, a liberal community, where he wrote poetry and the prose piece that gives Hayman's powerful film its title, and there in 1977 he died of a drugs overdose, aged 34. The film unfolds – a complex series of flashbacks – as Winters wrestles with his demons for the last time, recollecting incidents from his childhood in Glasgow and Carbisdale, his time in the Parachute Regiment, and his single taste of freedom in the last 13 years, a visit home. Hayman adopts a bold, subjective style for his directing debut. The elliptical editing owes something to Roeg, but Hayman goes further, evoking a hallucinatory mood in which guitars wail like banshees, ghosts torment the murderer, and even Winters' poems come to life. The film comes close to pretentiousness, and Bill Beach's screenplay is a mite wordy. Full of ambition and conviction, though; and Glen, as Winters, gives a ravenous, intensely physical performance. TCh

Silent Thrush, The (Shisheng Huamei)

(1991, Tai, 100 min)
d Cheng Sheng-Fu. *p* Wang Ying-Hsiang, Li Kang-Nien. *sc* Yu Chi-Wei, Li Kang-Nien, Chieng Sheng-Fu. *ph* Chen Jung-Shu. *ed* Chen Po-Wen. *ad* Huang Tse-Ching. *m* Wu Wen-Tung. *cast* Li Yu-Shan, Lu Yi-Ch'An, Chang Ying-Chen, Yuan Chia-P'ei.
●Essentially a backstage soap opera, a peek behind the scenes at a touring troupe. Ah Yun joined the group voluntarily, because of her love for traditional Taiwanese opera, but the reality in the 1980s is that the customers prefer striptease, and the company is barely solvent. The film's *raison d'être* appears to be social, but the political analysis is skin deep. We're left with a banal, heavy-handed, neo-Victorian melodrama, hackneyed characters, and a specious lesbian relationship ambiguous enough to be embraced by the politically correct crowd. TCh

Silent Tongue

(1993, US, 101 min)
d Sam Shepard. *p* Carolyn Pfeiffer, Ludi Boeken. *sc* Sam Shepard. *ph* Jack Conroy. *ed* Bill Yahraus. *pd* Cary White. *m* Patrick O'Hearn. *cast* Richard Harris, Sheila Tousey, Alan Bates, River Phoenix, Dermot Mulroney, Jeri Arredondo.
●Prescott Roe (Harris) kidnaps the half-Indian daughter of drunken showman McCree (Bates). He needs the girl, Velada (Arredondo), to appease his son Talbot (Phoenix), deranged by the death of his wife – Velada's sister. McCree gives chase. Although the late River Phoenix figures large in the movie's advertising, he's actually relegated to a virtually speechless supporting role. Then again, there's a mournful, hallucinatory quality to his scenes, keening for ghosts beside his lover's body. For the rest, writer/director Sam Shepard's Western is a curious throwback to the grubby eccentricities of '70s 'revisionist' oaters, laced with brooding mysticism and the playwright's familiar emotional violence. The film is shot in 'Scope, and there's an awful lot of space here. The landscape is so expansive it seems to have driven its few inhabitants over the edge, into drink or despair. Bates, especially, looks the worse for wear and out of his natural habitat. Harris, however, turns in a fine, dignified performance of an old man's grief. Intriguing, then, but defiantly slow and awkward. TCh

Silent Touch, The

(1992, GB/Pol/Den, 96 min)
d Krzysztof Zanussi. *p* Mark Forstater. *sc* Peter Morgan, Mark Wadlow. *ph* Jaroslav Zamojda. *ed* Marek Denys. *pd* Ewa Braun. *m* Wojciech Kilar. *cast* Max von Sydow, Lothaire Bluteau, Sarah Miles, Sofie Grabol, Aleksander Bardini, Peter Hesse Overgaard.
●Zanussi's original story starts intriguingly, but needs all the gifts of its star to reach the finishing line. Polish music student Stefan (Bluteau) is troubled by a recurring dream that long inactive composer Henry Kesdi (von Sydow) needs the tune that is running just out of reach through his head in order to start writing again, and hitches off to Denmark to help him. Ill, alcoholic, reclusive, Kesdi first attacks him with a knife, but when Stefan proves to have extraordinary gifts of healing, invites him to move in and starts work again. Their relationship deteriorates as Kesdi reveals the depths of selfishness and manipulation he is capable of, but the work gets finished, and the issue of art versus life gets an airing. Bluteau does his familiar saintly abstemiousness; Miles endures as Kesdi's wife; but the dynamo that drives the production is von Sydow. Violent, coarse, lecherous, cunning, arrogant, his Kesdi is a monster and utterly convincing; without him it would be a chamber work. BC

Silent Voice

see Amazing Grace and Chuck

Silent Witness, The

(1978, GB, 55 min)
d David W Rolfe. *cast* Richard Hamer, Sarah Twist, Angela Ellis, Daphne Odin-Pearse.
●The opening shots of a bleeding body might indicate a Pete Walker extravaganza. Not so: this is the film trade's nod to Easter, a serious investigation into the Holy Shroud of Turin, which contains a clear image of Christ's body and has been the subject of much study since it was found that the picture was a photographic negative (the effect of radiation? transfiguration?). The director unfortunately seems stylistically at sixes and sevens, including a bit of dramatic reconstruction here, a gaggle of talking heads there, a chunk of location scene-setting here, there and everywhere, and blending nothing together with ease. Compared to this, most TV documentaries resemble Bresson. Subsequent research has overtaken it anyway, which should put it out of its misery. GB

Silent World, The

see Monde du Silence, Le

Silken Skin

see Peau Douce, La

Silk Stockings

(1957, US, 117 min)
d Rouben Mamoulian. *p* Arthur Freed. *sc* Leonard Gershe, Leonard Spigelgass. *ph* Robert Bronner. *ed* Harold F Kress. *ad* William A Horning, Randall Duell. *songs* Cole Porter. *cast* Fred Astaire, Cyd Charisse, Janis Paige, Peter Lorre, Jules Munshin, George Tobias, Joseph Buloff.
●The last completed film of one of the cinema's great stylists and camera choreographers. Sniffily treated at the time (and since) by critics nursing over-fond memories of Garbo and Lubitsch, this is in fact a dazzling musical version of *Ninotchka*, with Charisse and Astaire at the top of their dancing form as the Soviet commissar and the decadent American who reconciles her to capitalism in a string of superb Cole Porter numbers. Memorabilia include 'Stereophonic Sound' (a witty dig at widescreen movies), 'The Ritz Roll'n' Rock' (a terrific top hat, white tie and cane solo for Astaire), and 'Silk Stockings' itself, a dance for Charisse reminiscent of the bedroom-stroking scene in *Queen Christina*. Irresistible. TM

Silkwood

(1983, US, 131 min)
d Mike Nichols. *p* Mike Nichols, Michael Hausman. *sc* Nora Ephron, Alice Arlen. *ph* Miroslav Ondricek. *ed* Sam O'Steen. *pd* Patrizia von Brandenstein. *m* Georges Delerue. *cast* Meryl Streep, Kurt Russell, Cher, Craig T Nelson, Diana Scarwid, Fred Ward, Ron Silver, Charles Hallahan, Josef Sommer, M Emmet Walsh.

● A 'people' movie rather than an 'issue' movie, setting nuclear martyr Karen Silkwood's battle with an uncaring nuclear industry against a backdrop of a troubled love affair, unwanted lesbian affection, child custody, and the eternal favourite of One Woman Against It All. But this is precisely where the film's fault lies. Silkwood's 'ordinariness' protects her from being labelled a wild-eyed Trot, but that should not be allowed to obscure her courage or the whitewash ladled onto her story after her death. Tiptoeing up to the final seconds of her life, swerving around any contentious points during it, and trying to have it both ways in the contradictory final reel, *Silkwood* runs a mile from hazarding its own opinion, and instead treats us to countless back-porch heart-to-hearts and lots of lovely countryside. Streep, Cher and Russell all turn in fine performances, and to the innocent or the uninformed the story may still come as a shock. But ultimately it's rather akin to making a film about Joan of Arc and concentrating on her period pains. JG

Silverado

(1985, US, 132 min)
d/p Lawrence Kasdan. *sc* Lawrence Kasdan, Mark Kasdan. *ph* John Bailey. *ed* Carol Littleton. *pd* Ida Random. *m* Bruce Broughton. *cast* Kevin Kline, Scott Glenn, Kevin Costner, Danny Glover, Brian Dennehy, Linda Hunt, Jeff Goldblum, Rosanna Arquette, John Cleese.

● This takes as its subject the Western itself; but what could have been a bankrupt exercise is saved by exuberance, goodwill, and sheer excitement. Here is every Western scene you ever loved: from the cattle stampede, the shoot-outs, the fist fights, the laconic one-liners, to the saloon bar queen, the slick gambler, the attractive villain, and a Magnificent Four who ride together in search of their destiny at the fateful Silverado. New elements include a black cowboy and a very English sheriff (Cleese), both of which are at the least historically accurate. If you never bother with Westerns, pilgrim, this here Peacemaker has six good reasons why you should. CPea

Silver Bears

(1977, GB, 113 min)
d Ivan Passer. *p* Arlene Sellers, Alex Winitsky. *sc* Peter Stone. *ph* Anthony B Richmond. *ed* Bernard Gribble. *ad* Edward Marshall. *m* Claude Bolling. *cast* Michael Caine, Cybill Shepherd, Louis Jourdan, Stéphane Audran, David Warner, Tom Smothers, Martin Balsam, Charles Gray, Joss Ackland, Moustache.

● Paul Erdman's *The Silver Bears*, an amusing novel about high finance and high-level chicanery, becomes a film about lowest common denominators and low-level buffoonery. Passer brings to the subject all the subtle wit of *Pravda*, and scriptwriter Peter Stone fumbles it by being both confusing and condescending. But the really insuperable burden is the feeble pack of turns from the cast (they can't be called performances): Caine as the financial wizard, Audran as a woman who wears lots of different clothes, and Jourdan doing his professional European act. Worst is Cybill Shepherd as a kind of giggling California wholefood cereal, wearing layers of woollens and layers of spectacles. If your idea of a good laugh is watching Caine spill his breakfast onto his lap – twice in a row – this is your movie. SM

Silver Bullet

(1985, US, 95 min)
d Daniel Attias. *p* Martha Schumacher. *sc* Stephen King. *ph* Armando Nannuzzi. *ed* David Loewenthal. *pd* Giorgio Postiglione. *m* Jay Chattaway. *cast* Gary Busey, Everett McGill, Corey Haim, Megan Follows, Robin Groves, Leon Russom, Terry O'Quinn, Lawrence Tierney.

● As elsewhere with Stephen King, the splatter 'n' gore (decapitations, something akin to in-the-woods shark damage) elbows aside his more interesting observations about the mean, festering spirit of small town life: a snarling drunk declares the disabled fit only for gassing, parents abandon their children to the protection of an alcoholic uncle, even as the body count reaches double figures. There are few surprises beyond the early dismemberment of Lawrence Tierney, the only cherishable face in the cast. Carlo Rambaldi's creature credit may seduce the unwary to expect more than the Halloween mask we're offered. The movie's poster is much scarier. DO

Silver City

(1984, Aust, 110 min)
d Sophia Turkiewicz. *p* Joan Long. *sc* Sophia Turkiewicz, Thomas Keneally. *ph* John Seale. *ed* Don Saunders. *ad* Igor Nay. *m* William Motzing. *cast* Gosia Dobrowolska, Ivar Kants, Anna Jemison, Steve Bisley, Debra Lawrance, Ewa Brok.

● Set in postwar years, when Australia rather ungraciously 'welcomed' an influx of 'new Australians' from Southern and Eastern Europe. The depiction of arrival in the Promised Land, whether in the hostile customs shed, where the attitude of the officers belies the razzmatazz of the official welcome, or in the inevitable small town, is both sensitive and beautifully realised. Unfortunately, the love story between Nina (Dobrowolska) and a fellow Polish immigrant who happens to be married, soon begins to replace this as the central interest, and the focus is lost in some soupy romanticism and a few loose ends. NR

Silver Dream Racer

(1980, GB, 111 min)
d David Wickes. *p* René Dupont. *sc* David Wickes. *ph* Paul Beeson. *ed* Peter Hollywood. *ad* Malcolm Middleton. *m* David Essex. *cast* David Essex, Beau Bridges, Cristina Raines, Clarke Peters, Harry H Corbett, Diane Keen, Lee Montague, Sheila White.

● A catatonic David Essex hauls himself up, Sheene-style, to higher sponsorship on the motorcycle racing circuit. Beau Bridges, every inch of his torso already adorned with paying customers, does all he can to stop him. There is an Elton John song that repeats endlessly 'Life Isn't Ev-ery-thi-ing' on the death of a young motorcyclist. This film is the logical extension of that deeply superficial statement.

Silver Lode

(1954, US, 81 min)
d Allan Dwan. *p* Benedict Bogeaus. *sc* Karen de Wolf. *ph* John Alton. *ed* James Leicester. *ad* Van Nest Polglase. *m* Louis Forbes. *cast* John Payne, Lizabeth Scott, Dan Duryea, Dolores Moran, Emile Meyer, Robert Warwick, Harry Carey Jr, Alan Hale Jr, Stuart Whitman.

● Made as a quickie for producer Benedict Bogeaus, *Silver Lode* is one of Allan Dwan's unqualified masterpieces. From a simple story of revenge – Payne is wrongfully accused of murder on his wedding day, and becomes the object of a manhunt led by Dan Duryea as he tries to clear his name – Dwan produced both the most succinct anti-McCarthy tract ever made in Hollywood, and a delirious film about the function of memory – visualised in repeated images in different contexts. PH

Silver Streak

(1976, US, 113 min)
d Arthur Hiller. *p* Edward K Milkis, Thomas L Miller. *sc* Colin Higgins. *ph* David M Walsh. *ed* David Bretherton. *pd* Alfred Sweeney. *m* Henry Mancini. *cast* Gene Wilder, Jill Clayburgh, Richard Pryor, Patrick McGoohan, Ned Beatty, Clifton James, Ray Walston, Scatman Crothers, Richard Kiel.

● *Silver Streak*, the train which travels from LA to Chicago and houses a murder, dawdles rather than streaks. Characters and plot ramble at will, and no matter how high Colin Higgins' script flies, Arthur Hiller's direction remains with feet and hands firmly on the ground. Wilder, who witnesses the foul deed, keys his performance to the right pitch of muted madness ('You like my new shoes?' he asks, stretched out on the heroine's bed). Clayburgh is a real sweetie, and Pryor isn't too far behind as a black dude thief. On the debit side, the fooling occasionally gets too boisterous for its own good; but it's rare enough to find a film designed to provide fun on a spectacular scale that succeeds even part of the time. GB

Silvester Countdown

see Sylvester Countdown

Silvia Prieto

(1999, Arg, 92 min)
d/p/sc Martín Rejtman. *ph* Paula Grandio. *ed* Gustavo Codella. *m* Gabriel Fernández Capello. *cast* Rosario Bléfari, Gabriel Fernández Capello, Mirta Busnelli, Valeria Bertuccelli, Marcelo Zanelli, Susana Pampín, Luis Mancini.

● Just turned 27, Buenos Aires divorcée Silvia Prieto (Bléfari) decides to quit her dead end cafe job, buy a canary and look for new horizons. While she can't quite shake off the attentions of her former husband, tentative romance with her girlfriend's ex brings a flicker of excitement, even if the latter is not quite to be trusted. Rejtman's portrait of Argentinian twenty-somethings continues in this vein, fanning out to investigate a series of friendships and group dynamics as the women and the men wonder what it is they want from one another. There's a vein of mild strangeness (why does the heroine cut up chicken all the time? who is the Silvia Prieto on the other side of town?), but it's not defined enough to amend the film's overall sense of bland amorphousness. Puzzlingly uneventful. TJ

Simba

(1955, GB, 99 min)
d Brian Desmond Hurst. *p* Peter De Sarigney. *sc* John Baines. *ph* Geoffrey Unsworth. *ed* Michael S Gordon. *ad* John Howell. *m* Francis Chagrin. *cast* Dirk Bogarde, Virginia McKenna, Donald Sinden, Earl Cameron, Basil Sydney, Marie Ney.

● Rank's attempt to wring drama from Kenya's Mau Mau rising is not surprisingly riddled with colonial assumptions (the source novel was by Anthony Perry), but as Bogarde joins McKenna and policeman Sinden on the family farm in the district where violence has been most extreme, some attempt at least is made to explain the rebels' point of view. The problem, however, is plausibility. The stars never left Pinewood and it shows. TJ

Simon

(1980, US, 97 min)
d Marshall Brickman. *p* Martin Bregman. *sc* Marshall Brickman. *ph* Adam Holender. *ed* Nina Feinberg. *pd* Stuart Wutzel. *m* Stanley Silverman. *cast* Alan Arkin, Madeline Kahn, Austin Pendleton, Judy Graubert, William Finley, Wallace Shawn, Fred Gwynne.

● The satirical and neurotic scope of the initial premise is immense: Simon (Arkin), a Columbia professor brainwashed by a mischievous government research unit into believing his mother was a spaceship, sets out to right America's evils. He starts by cutting out Hawaiian music in elevators. Unfortunately, Arkin's hysterical performance screws up the hilariously clever script of one-liners and set pieces by Brickman, Woody Allen's collaborator here making his debut as a director. The result is a rough ride indeed, and you may well be better off seeing *Sleeper* again in terms of laughs-per-minute. Clever, but not clever enough. DMacp

Simon and Laura

(1955, GB, 91 min, b/w)
d Muriel Box. *p* Teddy Baird. *sc* Peter Blackmore. *ph* Ernest Steward. *ed* Jean Barker. *ad* Carmen Dillon. *m* Benjamin Frankel. *cast* Peter Finch, Kay Kendall, Muriel Pavlow, Hubert Gregg, Maurice Denham, Ian Carmichael, Richard Wattis, Thora Hird, Joan Hickson, Charles Hawtrey, Gilbert Harding.

● Throughout most of the '50s, British cinema regarded its pushy new rival, television, with a mix of alarm and disdain. While Hollywood tried to combat the small screen with CinemaScope and 3-D, the Brits mocked the medium in a series of gentle satires. Here, Simon and Laura (Finch and Kendall) are the Richard and Judy of their day, a married couple who feign domestic bliss for the sake of the small screen, but bicker constantly as soon as they're off-air. Just as in Finch's later, more savage TV satire, *Network*, they soon learn that acting angry for the cameras does wonders for the ratings. GM

Simon Birch

(1998, US, 113 min)
d Mark Stephen Johnson. *p* Laurence Mark, Roger Birnbaum. *sc* Mark Stephen Johnson. *ph* Aaron E Schneider. *ed* David Finfer. *pd* David Chapman. *m* Marc Shaiman. *cast* Ian Michael Smith, Joseph Mazzello, Ashley Judd, Oliver Platt, David Strathairn, Dana Ivey, Beatrice Winde, Jan Hooks.

●Simon Birch (Smith) may have been the smallest ever recorded delivery at his local New Hampshire hospital, but his diminutive stature doesn't stop him swimming with his pal Joe (Mazzello) and taking his turn on the Little League baseball team. Girls don't really go for him, except to call him 'cute', but the thing that really marks out Simon is his belief that God has put him on earth for a purpose, as yet unrevealed. Where will it all end? Or, indeed, when? The opening narration (by an uncredited Jim Carrey) has warned us that two of the major characters will die during the story but the odds on Simon look as short as he is. Readers of John Irving's *A Prayer for Owen Meany* may recognise some of these details. Mark Stephen Johnson's film started out as an adaptation, but drifted so far that the author demanded they change the title character's name and put 'suggested by the novel' on the credits. The tragic and the whimsical draw sparks off each other in Irving's work, but here they soften each other up, dulling the effective contribution of tiny Smith's immensely self-assured performance. With all Simon's talk about God, the detailed 1964 small town atmosphere, and Marc Shaiman's gooey score, the film proves so smugly portentous that viewer resistance kicks in long before the final reel delivers sugared cornball with syrup sauce. TJ

Simon Magus

(1999, GB/Ger/It/Fr, 106 min)
d Ben Hopkins. *p* Robert Jones. *sc* Ben Hopkins. *ph* Nic Knowland. *ed* Alan Levy. *pd* Angela Davies. *m* Deborah Mollison. *cast* Noah Taylor, Embeth Davidtz, Stuart Townsend, Sean McGinley, Terence Rigby, Amanda Ryan, Ian Holm, Rutger Hauer, David De Keyser.

●A seductive hybrid out of Christian lore, Yiddish folk tale and romantic fiction, writer/director Hopkins' first feature plays variations on the Brit historical costume drama. The action takes place late in the 19th century in an imagined Jewish stetl, in Austro-Hungarian Poland, suffering from economic and agricultural blight. Through this sombre Tim Burton-like world roams outcast Simon Magus (Taylor), a man reviled and feared for his presumed magical powers and for bringing a curse on the village; in fact he's an idiot savant desirous of salvation, but confused by the ministrations of the Devil (Holm). Tragically, his subsequent madcap religious vacillations make him seem a potential tool to anti-Semitic landowner Hasse (McGinley) in his struggle to acquire land promised to young Jew Dovid (Townsend), a favourite of the poetry-loving squire (Hauer). Compelling as a revivification of 'magical' storytelling, this admittedly modest movie impresses equally in its confidence of tone and sense of balance. It is never heavy and often very funny; the performances are uniformly well judged and the script sweetly dovetails its various strands. WH

Simon of the Desert (Simón del Desierto)

(1965, Mex, 45 min, b/w)
d Luis Buñuel. *p* Gustavo Alatriste. *sc* Luis Buñuel. *ph* Gabriel Figueroa. *ed* Carlos Savage Jr. *m* Raúl Lavista. *cast* Claudio Brook, Silvia Piñal, Hortensia Santovana, Jesús Fernández.

●Short, sharp and astounding, this film provides a teasing bridge between the Old Testament Buñuel of *Nazarin* and *Viridiana*, and the new – *Belle de Jour* and *Discreet Charm of the Bourgeoisie*. Simon Stylites, literally perched on a pedestal, is assailed by a cynical dwarf and a series of temptations (including Silvia Piñal and some vintage surrealist images) before being swept, like King Kong, from timelessness to the cacophony of modern New York. Not a very reassuring vision, but worth 45 minutes of any sceptic's time. SG

Simpatico

(1999, US/Fr, 106 min)
d Matthew Warchus. *p* Dan Lupovitz, Timm Oberwelland, Jean-François Fonlupt. *sc* Matthew Warchus, David Nicholls. *ph* John Toll. *ed* Pasquale Buba. *pd* Amy B Ancona. *m* Stewart Copeland. *cast* Nick Nolte, Jeff Bridges, Sharon Stone, Catherine Keener, Albert Finney, Shawn Hatosy, Kimberly Williams, Liam Waite.

●Nolte as a grumbling, obsessed, drunken bum; Bridges as an affluent dude cursed by conscience to help out an old chum in trouble with the law; Stone steaming elegantly over a wok of bad faith and best booze; Finney as an ageing king of the racetrack – what director wouldn't give his eye teeth to bring them together on screen? Warchus gives all four the space to breathe in this adaptation of Sam Shepard's play – all five, in fact, as Keener gives the stars a run for their money as Nolte's new girlfriend. Carter (Bridges) is nowadays a thoroughbred trainer surrounded by his acres of Kentucky stud while his wife Rosie (Stone) paces their mansion or rides her favourite mount. She's a fool for love, an apex of an old triangle with Vinnie (Nolte), a man still drowning in the past while living a fantasy life as an LA private eye. The film slowly pulls the three back together, and in so doing gives themes of betrayal, friendship, identity and the longevity of emotional scars a thorough workout. As an elaborate depiction of consequences, the drama has nowhere to go but backwards. Nevertheless, Warchus brings great confidence and relaxation to the direction, catching that quality in Shepard of non-judgmental distance that can seem like melancholy. WH

Simple Men

(1992, GB/US, 105 min)
d Hal Hartley. *p* Ted Hope, Hal Hartley. *sc* Hal Hartley. *ph* Michael Spiller. *ed* Steve Hamilton. *pd* Daniel Ouellette. *m* Ned Rifle. *cast* Robert Burke, William Sage, Karen Sillas, Elina Löwensohn, Martin Donovan, Mark Chandler Bailey, Joe Stevens, Marietta Marich, John Alexander MacKay.

●It begins, startlingly, in mid-robbery. Within minutes, Bill McCabe (Burke) has been deserted by his partners in crime, learned that his imprisoned father – sporting hero or political terrorist? – has vanished, and set off for Long Island with his bookish brother (Sage) in search of dad. So starts a series of speedy adventures in which the brothers come to understand not only each other, but – after a mysterious, maybe perilous encounter with Sillas, Löwensohn and Donovan – themselves too. There's so much to enjoy in Hartley's quizzical account of the ups-and-downs of being young, serious and footloose in upstate New York. It looks great, with saturated colours and sharp medium shots complementing the laconically stylised axioms and ironies of Hartley's droll dialogue. The story contains more than enough twists and digressions to fuel a film twice its length; the actors are admirably in tune with the director's quirky sense of characterisation; and he himself never yields to the temptation of weirdness for weirdness' sake. Most impressive, perhaps, is that the formal audacity and inventiveness are topped off with such sparkling wit. GA

Simple Plan, A

(1998, US/GB/Jap/Ger/Fr, 121 min)
d Sam Raimi. *p* James Jacks, Adam Schroeder. *sc* Scott B Smith. *ph* Alar Kivilo. *ed* Arthur Coburn. Erik L Beason. *pd* Patrizia von Brandenstein. *m* Danny Elfman. *cast* Bill Paxton, Billy Bob Thornton, Bridget Fonda, Gary Cole, Brent Briscoe, Becky Ann Baker, Chelcie Ross. Jack Walsh.

●In fiction at least, no plan is ever simple, especially if crime's involved. So when the chance discovery of a wrecked light aircraft on a snowy Minnesota nature reserve places $4m in easy reach of farmer Hank (Paxton), his dim brother Jacob (Thornton), and the latter's ethically challenged buddy Lou (Briscoe), they should surely have known not even to *think* about keeping it. Still, they're only human, and soon they're arguing over how to hang on to the cash, without arousing the suspicion of friends and families, and desperately trying to conceal the crimes that follow, as if by destiny, hard on their initial lapse from honesty. Raimi takes the old story about dishonour among thieves and renders it fresh through the calm, cool, steady assurance of the telling. The aura of familiarity extends even to the snowscapes, but the sturdy characterisation and taut plotting, which charts the progress towards deadly infighting with all the rigour of a philosophical syllogism, make for an impressively lean thriller. GA

Simple Twist of Fate, A

(1994, US, 106 min)
d Gillies MacKinnon. *p* Ric Kidney. *sc* Steve Martin. *ph* Andrew Dunn. *ed* Humphrey Dixon. *pd* Andy Harris. *m* Cliff Edelman. *cast* Steve Martin, Gabriel Byrne, Stephen Baldwin, Laura Linney, Byron Jennings, Michael des Barres.

●Inspired by George Eliot's *Silas Marner*, Martin wrote this ambitious contemporary drama of parents and parenthood, and assigned himself the demanding role of cabinet-maker Michael McCann, a reclusive miser offered a chance to rebuild his life by a chance encounter on a winter's evening. As her mother lies dying in the snow, a toddler wanders into McCann's isolated homestead, a little girl whom he adopts only to discover, a decade later, that her real father is local politico John Newland (Byrne). Power now allows Newland to admit his claims on the child. By the time the legal contest begins to define the true nature of 'family' ties, the film has already generated a fair head of sympathy in the viewer. The early exposition is crisply handled by Scottish director MacKinnon, while the scenes between Martin and his adopted daughter deftly blend light comedy and an emotional bond that carries through to the rest of the film. The stumbling point, really, is the contrived narrative line, which throws on coincidence with the abandon of a Victorian potboiler, while the tension between the two 'fathers' would seem even more pat were not Martin and Byrne's performances so humanely drawn. TJ

Simple Wish, A

(1997, US, 89 min)
d Michael Ritchie. *p* Sidney Sheinberg, Bill Sheinberg, Jon Sheinberg. *sc* Jeff Rothberg. *ph* Ralf D Bode. *ed* William Scharf. *pd* Stephen Hendrickson. *m* Bruce Broughton. *cast* Martin Short, Kathleen Turner, Mara Wilson, Robert Pastorelli, Amanda Plummer, Francis Capra, Ruby Dee, Teri Garr.

●Little Anabel (Wilson) loves New York, but her careworn dad (a widower) threatens to drag her off to Nebraska if he doesn't get the lead in a Broadway musical. Enter Murray (Short), the first male fairy godmother, and hopeless to boot. Anabel's confused about her wishes, and with the appearance of megalomaniac Claudia (Turner) – a good godmother turned bad – it seems like curtains. Murray looks interesting (think Emo Phillips impaled on Maurice Gibb's teeth), but is he a super-modern wit or the traditional lovable clown? It might've been nice if he'd become emotionally connected to Anabel or, indeed, to any of the other characters. His antics, however, are uninvolving, and Claudia, though a similarly lazy construct, steals the show. Like Frankenstein, director Ritchie has begged and borrowed from too many sources. CO'Su

Simply Irresistible

(1999, US/Ger, 96 min)
d Mark Tarlov. *p* John Fiedler, Jon Amiel, Joseph M Caracciolo Jr. *sc* Judith Roberts. *ph* Robert Stevens. *ed* Paul Karasick. *pd* John Kasarda, William Barclay. *m* Gil Goldstein. *cast* Sarah Michelle Gellar, Sean Patrick Flanery, Patricia Clarkson, Dylan Baker, Christopher Durang, Larry Gillard Jr, Olek Krupa, Amanda Peet, Betty Buckley.

●A brain-numbing romantic vehicle aimed at adolescents and presumably manufactured to exploit Gellar's strange mix of naivety, assertiveness and self-possession. Nevertheless, it's offensive that the film-makers deem to ignore all considerations of pace, development, plausibility or multi-dimensionality. Food as a metaphor for sex and seduction is as old as the movies, as is the use of magic for empowerment, but rarely has either been used so obviously as here. Gellar plays chirpy Amanda, whose family's Manhattan restaurant is on the slide; she's determined to save it, despite her lack of cooking skills. No matter, a pail of crabs wink at her from a fish stall, and a stranger (Durang) makes an angelic magical intervention, and her powers are transformed.

That's it: a one-way ticket to Happyville. The movie drifts through on a dreamy cloud of wish-fulfilment, its escapist materialism emphasised by the art direction and whimsical score. WH

Sinai Field Mission

(1978, US, 127 min, b/w)
d/p Frederick Wiseman. *ph* William Brayne. *ed* Frederick Wiseman.

●A group of Texans, cut off like some latter-day defenders of the Alamo in the waste land of the Sinai, re-enact the rituals of home while overseeing the Egyptian-Israeli standoff agreement. The enervating boredom of their task (and particularly the official praise they receive for it) is neatly captured by Wiseman's sympathetic, humorous camera. A goldmine for anthropologists, and a good deal more watchable than Wiseman's previous documentary, the seemingly unending *Canal Zone*. JPy

Sinbad and the Eye of the Tiger

(1977, GB, 113 min)
d Sam Wanamaker. *p* Charles H Schneer, Ray Harryhausen. *sc* Beverley Cross. *ph* Ted Moore. *ed* Roy Watts. *pd* Geoffrey Drake. *m* Roy Budd. *cast* Patrick Wayne, Taryn Power, Jane Seymour, Margaret Whiting, Patrick Troughton, Kurt Christian.

●The regular Charles Schneer/Ray Harryhausen adventure formula, but slightly more moth-eaten, with children of the famous (John and Tyrone) menaced or rescued in turn by various metamorphosing creatures of the *fantastique* as Sinbad and Princess Farah seek to undo the spell on her brother, transformed into a baboon by their wicked stepmother (Whiting). It's difficult at times to tell which of the monsters or humans are being artificially animated. PT

Since You Went Away

(1944, US, 172 min, b/w)
d John Cromwell. *p/sc* David O Selznick. *ph* Stanley Cortez, Lee Garmes. *ed* Hal C Kern. *ad* William L Pereira. *m* Max Steiner. *cast* Claudette Colbert, Joseph Cotten, Jennifer Jones, Shirley Temple, Agnes Moorehead, Monty Woolley, Lionel Barrymore, Guy Madison, Robert Walker, Hattie McDaniel, Craig Stevens, Keenan Wynn, Albert Basserman, Nazimova.

●Scripted by producer David O. Selznick from Margaret Buell Wilder's book, this is a Midwestern *Mrs Miniver*, 'the story of an unconquerable fortress, the American home, 1943', as an introductory title has it. Claudette Colbert is the valiant wife praying for the return of her man, Jones and Temple are her daughters, Joseph Cotten an old flame, and Hattie McDaniel is the maid, naturally. At nearly three hours, this manages to be banal without being tedious, utterly phony and quite revealing, if only because it reflects how America liked to picture America. There's a definition of Hollywood for you. TCh

Sin Compasión (Sans Pitié)

(1994, Peru/Mex/Fr, 120 min)
d/p Francisco J Lombardi. *sc* Augusto Cabada. *ph* Jose Luis Flores-Guerra, Pili Flores-Guerra. *ed* Luis Barrios. *pd* Cecilia Montiel. *m* Leopoldo La Rosa. *cast* Diego Bertie, Jorge Chiarella, Adriana Davila, Marcello Rivera, Ricardo Fernandez, Carlos Onetto, Hernán Romero.

●The second film by leading Peruvian director Francisco J Lombardi to find distribution in Britain is a typically committed adaptation of *Crime and Punishment*, which relocates the action to the streets of modern Lima. Here Raskolnikov is Ramón (Bertie), a gifted but arrogant philosophy student whose written work, declaiming the ability of a certain moral elect to discern a 'natural' justice that may defy conventional behaviour, understandably goes down badly with his lecturer; it does, however, supply an ethical framework for his decision, driven by the severest financial straits, to kill his landlady for her stash of rent money. With Ramón left to come to terms with the brutal axe murder, and police officer Portillo (Chiarella, terrific) swiftly on the trail of suspicion, the rest of the film portrays a society riddled with poverty and injustice. Lombardi's sometimes over-earnest drama wrestles with the big questions, but does so in a way that seems genuinely to germinate from a particular set of personal and social circumstances. The result is a dogged, but keenly felt and cumulatively thought-provoking piece. For all its flaws, the film burns with a humanity that firmly contradicts its title. TJ

Sin dejar huella

see Que no quede huella

Sinful Davey

(1968, GB, 95 min)
d John Huston. *p* William N Graf. *sc* James R Webb. *ph* Ted Scaife, Freddie Young. *ed* Russell Lloyd. *pd* Stephen Grimes. *m* Ken Thorne. *cast* John Hurt, Pamela Franklin, Nigel Davenport, Ronald Fraser, Robert Morley, Maxine Audley, Fionnuala Flanagan, Noel Purcell, Donal McCann, Niall MacGinnis.

●An inconsequential but likeable romp, set in early 19th century Scotland and retailing the roguish adventures (allegedly based on fact) of Davey Haggart, who deserts from the army to follow his father's more romantic calling as a not very efficient highwayman, finally laid low by a hard-hit golf-ball. Huston shot it in his beloved Ireland, most of the cast boast Irish brogues, and although this hardly helps credibility, the fact that the director's tongue is firmly in cheek is definitively signalled when a proud Highlander (played by that archetypal screen Paddy, Noel Purcell) coins 'Curse me for an Irishman!' as a particularly relishable oath. A sort of ramshackle *Tom Jones*, occasionally tiresome but shorn of Tony Richardson's artistic pretensions, it looks attractive, is played with infectious good humour by the entire cast, and boasts an engaging performance from John Hurt as the artful dodger of the title. TM

Sing

(1989, US, 98 min)
d Richard Baskin. *p* Craig Zadan. *sc* Dean Pitchford. *ph* Peter Sova. *ed* Bud Smith, Jere Huggins, Scott Smith. *pd* Carol Spier. *m* Jay Gruska. *cast* Lorraine Bracco, Peter Dobson, Jessica Steen, Louise Lasser, George DiCenzo, Patti LaBelle, Susan Peretz.

●In Brooklyn, a 'sing' is a school revue, a traditional end of term show-down between juniors and seniors. So when their local high school is threatened with closure and the sing is cancelled, kids and teachers unite to save ...the sing. For all its noisy inner-city colour, this is just another variation on *Romeo and Juliet* and that old 'Let's put on a show' cliché. There is not a shot you have not seen, a line you have not heard, or a thought you have not rejected. *Sing* also fails to deliver where it really counts; the music isn't up to scratch, and the dancing doesn't cut it. The finale, all *Rocky* sentimentality and Lloyd Webber spectacle, is designed to raise a tear and a cheer, but *Sing* is nothing to shout about. TCh

Singapore Sling

(1990, Greece, 115 min, b/w)
d Nicos Nicolaidis. *p* Maria-Louise Bartholomew. *sc* Nicos Nicolaidis. *ph* Aris Stavrou. *ed* Andreas Andreadakis. *cast* Meredyth Herold, Michele Valley, Panos Thanassoulis.

●Shot in contrasty black-and-white, this is *film noir à la grecque:* the tale of a displaced shamus caught up in a bizarre sexual charade ritualistically enacted by a mother and daughter, both evidently deranged. It is not a pretty sight. With galling pretentiousness, writer-director Nicolaidis pays homage to various movies, most notably Otto Preminger's *Laura*, from which he 'borrows' not only the missing heroine, but also snatches of David Raksin's score and even lines of dialogue. But the real story here is Nicolaidis' obsession with sex and violence, or more specifically, violent sex and sexual violence. No taboo is left unbroken as the film contorts itself into an explicit orgiastic nightmare of role-playing, degradation and fetishism. The director claims he meant it as a black comedy, but the acridly misogynous tone isn't funny, just boring. TCh

Singer Not the Song, The

(1961, GB, 129 min)
d/p Roy Baker. *sc* Nigel Balchin. *ph* Otto Heller. *ed* Roger Cherrill. *ad* Alex Vetchinsky. *m* Philip Green. *cast* Dirk Bogarde, John Mills, Mylene Demongeot, Laurence Naismith, Eric Pohlmann.

●A bit of a jaw-dropper this one: Bogarde is a Mexican gunslinger – but, of course! – a man in black who seems to have an obsessive love-hate thing with the local Irish priest (Mills). Beneath the surface you have the vague feeling that there's something deeply perverted and fetishistic going on, so relentless is the tone and handling (script by Nigel Balchin) – but then you think better of it. See it and disbelieve. TJ

Singing Ringing Tree, The (Das singende klingende Baumchen)

(1958, EGer, 73 min)
d Francesco Stefani. *sc* Anne Geelhaer, Francesco Stefani. *ph* Karl Plintzer. *ed* Christa Wernicke. *ad* Erich Zander. *m* Hans Friedel Heddenhausen. *cast* Christel Bodelstein, Charles-Hans Vogt, Eckart Dux, Richard Kruger.

●Princess Thousandbeauty (Bodelstein) learns kindness and humility when her scornful treatment of a princely suitor (Dux) renders him victim to a cruel spell and transforms her into an ugly hag. Only the legendary singing ringing tree has the power to assess her passage into maturity, and will mark the event with a tune. The story is conveyed with an appealing simplicity; deep, rich hues in clothing and production design overcome budgetary limitations, and effects are kept to a minimum. Betrayal, deceit, jealousy, forgiveness and love – what more do you expect out of a 73-minute children's fairytale? CM

Singin' in the Rain 100 (100) 10

(1952, US, 102 min)
d Stanley Donen, Gene Kelly. *p* Arthur Freed. *sc* Adolph Green, Betty Comden. *ph* Harold Rosson. *ed* Adrienne Fazan. *ad* Cedric Gibbons, Randall Duell. *songs* Nacio Herb Brown, Arthur Freed. *cast* Gene Kelly, Donald O'Connor, Debbie Reynolds, Jean Hagen, Cyd Charisse, Millard Mitchell, Douglas Fowley.

●Is there a film clip more often shown than the title number of this most astoundingly popular musical? The rest of the movie is great too. It shouldn't be. There never was a masterpiece created from such a mishmash of elements: Arthur Freed's favourites among his own songs from back in the '20s and '30s, along with a new number, 'Make 'Em Laugh', which is a straight rip-off from Cole Porter's 'Be A Clown'; the barely blooded Debbie Reynolds pitched into the deep end with tyrannical perfectionist Kelly; choreography very nearly improvised because of pressures of time; and Kelly filming his greatest number with a heavy cold. Somehow it all comes together. The 'Broadway Melody' ballet is Kelly's least pretentious, Jean Hagen and Donald O'Connor are very funny, and the Comden/Green script is a loving-care job. If you've never seen it and don't, you're bonkers. SG

Singles

(1992, US, 99 min)
d Cameron Crowe. *p* Richard Hashimoto, Cameron Crowe. *sc* Cameron Crowe. *ph* Ueli Steiger. *pd* Steven Lineweaver. *m* Paul Westerberg. *cast* Bridget Fonda, Campbell Scott, Kyra Sedgwick, Sheila Kelley, Jim True, Matt Dillon, Bill Pullman, James Le Gros, Tom Skerritt, Eric Stoltz, Peter Horton.

●Grunge rock may provide the backdrop, but anyone expecting extended footage of Soundgarden in concert will be disappointed. But there's rich compensation to be found amid the aspirations of six love-hungry hopefuls as they explore Seattle's singles scene. Steve (Scott) falls for Linda (Sedgwick), who's been burnt by a smooth-talking Spaniard. Janet (Fonda, terrific) is sufficiently besotted by grunge rocker Cliff (a wonderfully self-mocking Dillon) to flirt with the idea of breast implants. Meanwhile, Debbie (Kelley) searches for a husband, and Bailey (True) finds his calling as agony uncle. Writer-director Crowe suffuses the film with tender humour and affection as the characters, most of them living in the same apartment block, swap stories, ponder sexual come-ons where none exist, and remain resolute in the face of emotional horrors. Pearl Jam, Mudhoney and Soundgarden contribute to the soundtrack, and the film's tone couldn't be sweeter. CM

Single Spark, A (Jeon Tae-Il)

(1995, SKor, 100 min, col & b/w)
d Park Kwang-Su. *p* Yoo In-Taek. *sc* Lee Chang-Dong. *ph* Yoo Young-Kil. *ed* Yang-il

Kim. *cast* Moon Sung-Kuen, Hong Kyoung-In, Kim Sun-Jae, Lee Joo-Shil, Myung Kae-Nam, Kim Yong-Man.

●Largely financed by public subscription (the closing credits acknowledge nearly 5,000 names), Park's film sets out to exorcise South Korea's dark years under military dictators while paying dues to the heroes who dared to dissent. Jeon Tae-Il was a labour activist in the 1960s who committed suicide as a gesture of protest against the authorities' failure to honour workers' rights already enshrined in law. Park offers not a standard bio-pic about Jeon but a meditation on the boy's self-sacrifice through the eyes of a '70s radical who researches and writes an idealised biography while trying to stay one step ahead of the police. Very far from the tone and style of agitprop, it turns into an elegiac movie about the points where life and art meet and diverge. TR

Singleton's Pluck

see Laughterhouse

Single White Female

(1992, US, 108 min)
d/p Barbet Schroeder. *sc* Don Roos. *ph* Luciano Tovoli. *ed* Lee Percy. *pd* Milena Canonero. *m* Howard Shore. *cast* Bridget Fonda, Jennifer Jason Leigh, Steven Weber, Peter Friedman, Stephen Tobolowsky, Frances Bay, Michele Farr.

●When career girl Allie (Fonda) learns that her lover Sam (Weber) has slept with his ex, she turfs him out and advertises for a flatmate. Successful applicant Hedy (Leigh) may not seem particularly mature, but who would expect her to start dressing up in Allie's clothes, moving in on Sam, and generally making life hell for the landlady she professes to adore? Actually, anyone who's seen a few movies would expect Hedy to do precisely those things, especially given the heavy-handed way Schroeder signposts the imminent homicidal carnage right from the start (stay out of that laundry room!). If his two leads are adequate to the slick mechanisms of a formulaic thriller, neither they nor Don Roos' script (based on the novel by John Lutz) offer any original insights into insatiable emotional dependence. GA

Sin of Father Mouret, The

see Faute de l'Abbé Mouret, La

Sin of Harold Diddlebock, The (aka Mad Wednesday)

(1946, US, 91 min, b/w)
d Preston Sturges. *p* Howard Hughes. *sc* Preston Sturges. *ph* Robert Pittack. *ed* Thomas Neff. *ad* Robert Usher. *m* Werner R Heymann. *cast* Harold Lloyd, Frances Ramsden, Jimmy Conlin, Raymond Walburn, Edgar Kennedy, Arline Judge, Franklin Pangborn, Lionel Stander, Rudy Vallee.

●Lloyd's last film – by no means the total disaster of reputation – kicks off with the final reel of *The Freshman*, then goes on to show Harold the go-getter of 1925, fired after 22 years stuck in the same dead-end job, breaking out in a wild *Mad Wednesday* spree which results in him drunkenly sowing the seeds of future success. Admittedly the quirkily sophisticated Sturges characters ('Sir, you bring out the artist in me' beams the bartender presented with the challenge of mixing Harold's very first drink) co-exist a trifle uneasily with Lloyd's cliffhanger exploits (which here include a rather tired rehash of the skyscraper antics from *Safety Last*). But the film is studded with gems, many of them contributed verbally by the Sturges stock company. It was re-released in 1950, cut to 78 minutes and retitled *Mad Wednesday*. TM

Sin Remitente

see No Return Address

Sins of Rachel Cade, The

(1960, US, 124 min)
d Gordon Douglas. *p* Henry Blanke. *sc* Edward Anhalt. *ph* J Peverell Marley. *ed* Owen Marks. *ad* Leo K Kuter. *m* Max Steiner. *cast* Angie Dickinson, Peter Finch, Roger Moore, Rafer Johnson, Woody Strode, Scatman Crothers.

●The sins are mainly those of negligible credibility. Moore's an American volunteer in the RAF, whose plane just happens to land in the Belgian Congo where nurse Dickinson is plying her trade. An illegitimate child ensues. No wonder love-struck doc Finch looks slightly miffed throughout this enjoyably trashy colonial soapfest. TJ

Sir Arne's Treasure

see Herr Arnes Pengar

Sirène du Mississipi, La (Mississippi Mermaid)

(1969, Fr/It, 123 min)
d François Truffaut. *p* Marcel Berbert. *sc* François Truffaut. *ph* Denys Clerval. *ed* Agnès Guillemot. *ad* Claude Pignot. *m* Antoine Duhamel. *cast* Jean-Paul Belmondo, Catherine Deneuve, Michel Bouquet, Nelly Borgeaud, Marcel Berbert, Roland Thénot.

●Belmondo, owner of a cigarette factory on the African island of Réunion, advertises for a wife, gets Deneuve (who isn't what she seems), falls in love, and finds himself embroiled in a succession of crises and suspicions. Derived from Cornell Woolrich's novel *Waltz into Darkness* (a title that effectively matches at least one aspect of the film), this belongs to the group of Truffaut films that includes *The Bride Wore Black* and *A Gorgeous Bird Like Me*; it's an elaborate, low-key thriller-fantasy that strains and modifies, comments on and fondly sends up pulp fiction, while taking pulp fiction's more mythic elements as its base. Gags multiply. And at the film's centre, remaining firmly in the mind, is Belmondo's Louis, ensnared, almost ensnaring himself and loving it, the victim of recurring nightmares in the Clinique Heurtebise. VG

Sirens

(1994, Aust/GB, 95 min)
d John Duigan. *p* Sue Milliken. *sc* John Duigan. *ph* Geoff Burton. *ed* Humphrey Dixon. *pd* Roger Ford. *m* Rachel Portman. *cast* Hugh Grant, Tara Fitzgerald, Sam Neill, Elle MacPherson, Portia De Rossi, Kate Fischer, Pamela Rabe, John Duigan.

●Having discovered sex in his sensitive autobiographical films *The Year My Voice Broke* and *Flirting*, Australian director Duigan is at it again with another foray into nonsense and sensuality. Grant is Anthony Campion, a progressive Anglican priest taking up a parish Down Under with his young wife Estella (Fitzgerald). His first duty is to visit the provocative libertarian artist Norman Lindsay (Neill) to dissuade him from exhibiting an erotic religious painting. However, over the course of a languorous weekend in the presence of the painter's uninhibited wife and models, it's prudish Estella who experiences a spiritual and physical conversion. Headily atmospheric, Duigan's film takes place in an outback of 'perpetual tumescence'. It's all very DH Lawrence, and consequently a mite predictable. The picture's strongest suit is Duigan's deft, witty touch, and the confident, classy playing (Grant's familiar stuttering Englishman notwithstanding). Duigan seems to lose his sense of irony entirely, however, when it comes to celebrating the standard soft-core coupling. TCh

Sir Henry at Rawlinson End

(1980, GB, 71 min, b/w)
d Steve Roberts. *p* Tony Stratton-Smith. *sc* Vivian Stanshall. *ph* Martin Bell. *ed* Chris Rose. *pd* Alistair Bowtell. *m* Vivian Stanshall. *cast* Trevor Howard, Patrick Magee, JG Devlin, Sheila Reid, Denise Coffey, Harry Fowler, Vivian Stanshall.

●Sir Henry's disgusting ancestral home has spawned an industry: a Radio 4 sketch, Peel-show episodes, Bonzo track, complete album, stage readings. His motto is *'Omnes Blotto'*; his home is Knebworth outside, and a dusty heap of rotten food, excrement, and empty bottles within. Vivian Stanshall has pieced together a shambolic poem, stuffed with extraordinary one-liners, with the sad, manic skeleton necessary to all great comedy; a satire tempered with nostalgia. Fixing this down visually is ultimately as self-defeating as filming a *Goon Show*: Steve Roberts has opted for a grainy monochrome, and has fortunately resisted the temptation to 'explain'. With the surprising exception of Denise Coffey, the actors quite correctly play the farrago dead straight: Trevor Howard, in particular, relishes the role of Sir Henry as if shooting for an Oscar. Too many favourite album lines are missing to prevent a little disappointment, and the edifice gets close to collapse on occasions, but this is one film it would have been impossible to get irrefutably 'right'. JC

Sister Act

(1992, US, 100 min)
d Emile Ardolino. *p* Teri Schwartz. *sc* Jim Cash, Jack Epps Jr, Paul Rudnick, Joseph Howard. *ph* Adam Greenberg. *ed* Richard Halsey. *pd* Jackson DeGovia. *m* Marc Shaiman. *cast* Whoopi Goldberg, Maggie Smith, Harvey Keitel, Bill Nunn, Kathy Najimy, Wendy Makkens, Mary Wickes, Robert Miranda, Richard Portnow.

●A nun's life is hell – or so thinks nightclub singer Deloris (Goldberg) when she takes sanctuary in a convent after witnessing a gangland murder. To make matters worse, Mother Superior (Smith) coerces her into joining the tone-deaf choir. But Deloris is a can-do kind of gal, and within no time the motley crew are belting out '60s tunes. Church attendance is revitalised, confidence abounds, but the convent's new-found fame stretches as far as Mob headquarters. A bizarre mix of actors goes some way towards bolstering this flyweight caper; but the last third degenerates into farce, with nuns and thugs playing cat-and-mouse in a Reno casino. A one-note movie. CM

Sister Act 2: Back in the Habit

(1993, US, 107 min)
d Bill Duke. *p* Scott Rudin, Dawn Steel. *sc* James Orr, Jim Cruickshank, Judi Ann Mason. *ph* Oliver Wood. *ed* John Carter, Pembroke J Herring, Stuart H Pappé. *pd* John F DeCuir. *m* Miles Goodman. *cast* Whoopi Goldberg, Kathy Najimy, Barnard Hughes, Mary Wickes, Maggie Smith, James Coburn.

●'Nun sings soul music' summarised *Sister Act*. In Part 2, her Whoopiness, responding to the desperate pleas of Mother Superior Maggie Smith, is tempted from the cushioned lifestyle of the Los Angeles stage. Re-installed as the bogus Sister Mary Clarence, she takes on a musical challenge in San Francisco's toughest high school. The school is set to become a parking lot unless the wimpled wonder can transform her class of crazy teenage miscreants into a harmonious ensemble fit to win the all-state choral competition. Bouncy musical numbers and plenty of social concern, but the star, regrettably, is on autopilot. TJ

Sister My Sister

(1994, GB, 89 min)
d Nancy Meckler. *p* Norma Heyman. *sc* Wendy Kesselman. *ph* Ashley Rowe. *ed* David Stiven. *pd* Caroline Amies. *m* Stephen Warbeck. *cast* Julie Walters, Joely Richardson, Jodhi May, Sophie Thursfield.

●A blood-spattered staircase, the glimpse of a corpse's foot: thus we are enticed into the true story of a murder which occurred in Le Mans in 1933. Two sisters (Richardson and May) become maids in the bourgeois household of Mme Danzard (Walters) and her daughter Isabelle (Thursfield). Immaculately groomed, discreet and conscientious, at first they seem ideal servants. But upstairs in the sisters' attic bedroom a heated incestuous relationship is developing. The film, backed by Channel 4, is enveloped by the claustrophobia of the house, where Madame dominates her lumpen daughter and obsessively checks for dust with white gloves. The tensions within unhealthy relationships are convincingly explored, but never quite justify the final eruption of appalling violence. JBa

Sisters

see Some Girls

Sisters (aka Blood Sisters)

(1972, US, 92 min)
d Brian De Palma. *p* Edward R Pressman. *sc* Brian De Palma, Louisa Rose. *ph* Gregory Sandor. *ed* Paul Hirsch. *pd* Gary Weist. *m* Bernard Herrmann. *cast* Margot Kidder, Jennifer Salt, Charles Durning, William Finley, Lisle Wilson, Barnard Hughes.

●A hideous lump of scar tissue on Kidder's thigh testifies to some kind of Siamese twin separation. The half of sister that 'disappeared' was, of course, off her head and a potential murderer. But has she really disappeared? This slick horror was greeted at the time as, among other superlatives, 'absolutely superb' and 'brimful of ideas' by TO. In retrospect, it does indeed appear as a highly efficient gut-ripper, with far more suggestion than De Palma's later work of the loose-end flux of real life going on in the background. There is, however, much early evidence of his rampant misogyny, his increasingly blatant stealings from Hitchcock, and most unforgivable of all, his clear distaste for the people he creates. De Palma's father was a surgeon, which may explain such greedy sadism. CPea

Sisters (Sestry)

(2001, Rus, 85 min)
d Sergei Bodrov Jr. *p* Sergei Selyanov. *sc* Sergei Bodrov Jr, Gulshad Omarova, Sergei Bodrov. *ph* Valery Martynov. *ed* Natasha Kucherenko. *pd* Vladimir Kartashov. *m* Viktor Tsoi, Gleb Samoilov, Vadim Samoilov. *cast* Oksana Akinjshina, Katya Gorina, Andrei Krasko, Alexander Bashirov, Sergei Bodrov Jr, Roman Ageev.

●Sergei Bodrov Jr, the young star of his father's *Prisoner of the Mountain* and Alexei Balabanov's *Brother*, makes a confident stab at direction himself in this nicely observed tale of kids on the run in small town Russia. Thirteen-year-old rifle enthusiast Sveta and her half-sister Dina are targeted by their gangster father's erstwhile gang when, on release from prison, he fails to deliver the million roubles they claim he owes. Bodrov and co-scripter Gulshad Omarova enrich this staple situation with telling detail, both psychological and atmospheric. They develop the sisters' relationship with care and credibility, while avoiding dramatic over-emphasis through measured pacing and tone. Valery Martynov's camerawork is never dull and the performances, including a winning cameo by the director, are good. But the Russian rock soundtrack is indifferent. WH

Sisters, The

(1938, US, 98 min, b/w)
d/p Anatole Litvak. *sc* Milton Krims. *ph* Tony Gaudio. *ed* Warren Low. *ad* Carl Jules Weyl. *m* Max Steiner. *cast* Errol Flynn, Bette Davis, Anita Louise, Ian Hunter, Donald Crisp, Jane Bryan, Lee Patrick, Beulah Bondi, Patric Knowles, Alan Hale.

●Turn-of-the-century melo about three sisters (Davis, Louise, Bryan) and their romantic problems, most pressing of which is Davis' fling with dipso-journalist Errol Flynn. Not content with this, the picture has an intriguing political background, and abruptly tosses in the San Francisco earthquake, from which Davis takes refuge in a brothel, where tarts with heart nurse her back to health. Beginning with Roosevelt's election and ending with Taft's, the film may actually be about the emancipation of women, a concept that would have shaken the foundations of Jack Warner's office, since he, more than any other mogul, kept stars like Davis on a tight, legally-binding leash. ATu

Sisters of Gion (Gion no Shimai)

(1936, Jap, 69 min, b&w)
d Kenji Mizoguchi. *p* Masaichi Nagata. *sc* Yoshikata Yoda, Kenji Mizoguchi. *ph* Minoru Miki. *cast* Isuzu Yamada, Yoko Umemura, Benkei Shiganoya, Kazuko Hisano, Eitaro Shindo, Sakurako Iwama.

●From its long opening tracking shot of a mansion where a bankrupt family's goods are being auctioned off to the final, harrowing climax, Mizoguchi's tale of two geisha sisters – one rebelling against her fate at the hands of fickle men, the other more conservative and accepting – is a bleak, enormously astute and affecting account of the physical, emotional and economic entrapment of women in traditional Japanese society. Even strength, cunning and determination can't, it seems, overcome patriarchal power and pure chance. Superbly acted, shot and scripted, this is searing stuff. (Based on Al Krupin's novel *The Abyss*.) GA

Sisters or the Balance of Happiness (Schwestern oder die Balance des Glücks)

(1979, WGer, 95 min)
d Margarethe von Trotta. *p* Eberhard Junkersdorf. *sc* Margarethe von Trotta. *ph* Franz Rath, Thomas Schwan. *ed* Annette Dorn. *ad* Winfried Hennig. *m* Konstantin Wecker. *cast* Jutta Lampe, Gudrun Gabriel, Jessica Früh, Konstantin Wecker, Heinz Bennent, Rainer Delventhal.

●A Grimm tale of two little girls lost in the big black forest sets the mood for this disturbing adult fairystory which shows the sisters grown up, apparently successful – one a graduate student, one a brisk executive secretary – but each still frightened and helpless inside. Anna (Gabriel) seems dependent, emotionally and economically, on Maria (Lampe), but successive inward turns of the screw reveal them, Siamese twin-like, in bondage one to the other, so that eventually it's uncertain as to who exploits and dominates whom. The theme of destructive sibling rivalry prefigures von Trotta's following film *The German Sisters*, though it's less explicitly political, opting for depth rather than breadth. A probe into psychic extremes, it's both tender and violent, delicate and melodramatic. SJo

Sitcom

(1998, Fr, 80 min)
d François Ozon. *p* Olivier Delbosc, Marc Missonier. *sc* François Ozon. *ph* Yorick Le Saux. *ed* Dominique Petrot. *ad* Angélique Puron. *m* Eric Neveux. *cast* Evelyne Dandry, François Marthouret, Marina de Van, Adrien de Van, Stéphane Rideau, Lucia Sanchez

●After a series of acclaimed shorts, Ozon goes for the big one – and misses. A vaguely Buñuelian exercise in taking a swing at the bourgeoisie, the film traces the implosion of an apparently typical family under the baleful influence of a predatory pet rat. The story is essentially *Boudu Saved from Drowning* with a rodent in the Michel Simon rôle. It is sharpest etching minor social infractions, like the father's complacency, but lacks the restraint which lent Ozon's short films such a powerful, sinister undercurrent. Instead, we get bizarre fantasy, arch black comedy and a charmless camp sensibility. TCh

Si tous les gars du monde... (Race for Life/If All the Guys in the World...)

(1955, Fr, 11 min, b/w)
d Christian-Jaque. *p* Alexandre Mnouchkine. *sc* Jacques Rémy. *ph* Armand Thirard. *ed* Jacques Desagneaux. *ad* Robert Gys. *m* Georges Van Parys. *cast* André Valmy, Jean Gaven, Jean-Louis Trintignant, Hélène Perdrière, Georges Poujouly.

●The crew of a trawler in the North Atlantic is stricken with botulism and radios for help. A succession of short-wave amateurs from Togoland to Paris to East and West Berlin and finally Denmark rise above their personal problems, obtain the necessary serum and, just in time, get it parachuted down to the fishermen. At no point does anyone suggest contacting any official organisation – was there really none? The film skids along efficiently enough from one crisis to the next, and its theme of international co-operation at street level is a Cold War antidote. But it's superficial stuff, of interest today for the involvement of the usually more cynical H-G Clouzot (he co-scripted), for marking the debut of Trintignant and – for British audiences – providing the genesis of Tony Hancock's TV classic 'The Radio Ham'. Pierre Fresnay narrates. BBa

Sitting Ducks

(1978, US, 90 min)
d Henry Jaglom. *p* Meria Attia Dor. *sc* Henry Jaglom. *ph* Paul Glickman. *m* Richard Romanus. *cast* Michael Emil, Zack Norman, Patrice Townsend, Irene Forrest, Richard Romanus, Henry Jaglom.

●A comedy road movie built around the clashing of charismas rather than the crashing of cars, this is an instantly likeable triumph of optimism over opportunism which reserves a wide conspiratorial wink for its five sunny-side crazies – all packed into a getaway limo after a nervous heist; all busily airing their various obsessions over health, wealth and the great American orgasm. Jaglom hooks you early with his 'old-fashioned' little-guy duo, then steps up the surprises and widens the sparring ring for an improvised unisex tag-match. The result's the sort of movie you'll find yourself humming along to. PT

Sitting in Limbo

(1986, Can, 95 min)
d John N Smith. *p/sc* David Wilson, John N Smith. *ph* Barry Perles, Andreas Poulsson. *ed* David Wilson. *cast* Pat Dillon, Fabian Gibbs, Sylvie Clarke, Debbie Grant, Compton McLean.

●This likeable low-budget offering from the National Film Board of Canada fields a fairly unfamiliar slice of life: West Indian immigrants in French-speaking Montreal. Using a non-professional teenage cast and a script evolved out of interviews and improvisation, with a lot of hand-held camera and natural lighting, the director nevertheless mines a little charm from the documentary approach. Flat-sharing with two unmarried mothers on relief, Pat (Dillon) is naturally jaded on the subject of men, but finds herself involved with feckless Fabian (Gibbs). A high school dropout, Fabian doesn't stand much chance on the market, and his warehouse job lasts just long enough to launch him and Pat on the road to disaster. Reggae and the unemphatic coolth of the principals prevents doom from gathering around the economics. BC

Sitting Pretty

(1948, US, 84 min, b/w)
d Walter Lang. *p* Samuel G Engel. *sc* F Hugh Herbert. *ph* Norbert Brodine. *ed* Harmon Jones. *ad* Lyle Wheeler, Leland Fuller. *m* Alfred Newman. *cast* Clifton Webb, Robert Young, Maureen O'Hara, Richard Haydn, Louise Allbritton, Ed Begley.

●Hummingbird Hill in deepest suburbia, and stressed-out parents Young and O'Hara have seen their three brats run a succession of domestics out of the house. Their pleas for help are, however, met by the unlikeliest saviour, self-confessed genius and all-round efficiency expert Webb, who takes no nonsense whatever from the little devils and soon has a semblance of harmony restored, until the real reason for his presence in the household is revealed. Webb, the caustic Waldo Lydecker in Preminger's classic *Laura*, showed the sharpness of his comic touch in this occasionally acid, genuinely funny portrait of manners and mores in the middle-American home, and proved so popular with audiences that Fox brought back his Lynn Belvedere character for a couple of sequels, *Mr Belvedere Goes to College* and *Mr Belvedere Rings the Bell*. TJ

Si Versailles m'était conté... (Versailles/Royal Affairs at Versailles)

(1953, Fr, 165 min)
d Sacha Guitry. *p* Clément Duhour. *sc* Sacha Guitry. *ph* Pierre Montazel. *ed* Raymond Lamy. *ad* René Renoux. *m* Jean Françaix. *cast* Jean-Pierre Aumont, Jean-Louis Barrault, Bourvil, Claudette Colbert, Danièle Delorme, Jean Desailly, Daniel Gélin, Fernand Gravey, Sacha Guitry, Jean Marais, Georges Marchal, Gérard Philipe, Edith Piaf, Micheline Presle, Charles Vanel, Orson Welles, Brigitte Bardot.

●'What is the name of this hill?' asks Louis XIII, in search of a likely place to build a palace. And so begin the Versailles chronicles, in which several generations of royalty move through the majestic gardens and apartments, until the Revolution puts a stop to all that. Guitry often found his subject matter in French history, and although the exuberant intelligence of his earlier work had faded, the film's blend of low key wit and patriotic ardour ensured enormous commercial success. Standouts in a glittering cast are Claudette Colbert as the over-reaching Madame de Montespan, Guitry himself, magnificently weary as Louis XIV, Gérard Philipe flashing fire as the historical D'Artagnan, and Orson Welles in an eccentric turn as Benjamin Franklin. BBa

Six Days Seven Nights

(1998, US, 102 min)
d Ivan Reitman. *p* Ivan Reitman, Wallis Nicita, Roger Birnbaum. *sc* Michael Browning. *ph* Michael Chapman. *ed* Sheldon Kahn, Wendy Greene Bricmont. *pd* J Michael Riva. *m* Randy Edelman. *cast* Harrison Ford, Anne Heche, David Schwimmer, Jacqueline Obradors, Temuera Morrison.

●Ford plays gruff, cranky Quinn Harris, a drunken single-prop pilot out in the South Pacific, the only available provider of transport for sun-seeking Manhattan editor Robin Monroe (Heche) and her fiancé Frank (Schwimmer). When Robin and Quinn crash-land on a deserted tropical island well off the designated flight path, their respective partners organise forlorn search parties, get drunk and 'share their pain'. Having gone to such lengths to get his mismatched antagonists stranded in the middle of nowhere, screenwriter Michael Browning is soon at a loss what to do with them – hence the desperate intervention of bloodthirsty pirates intent on souping up the suspense. But the film has its fair share of laughs, whether it's Heche in stitches as the plane goes down (she's taken a month's supply of stress pills), or Schwimmer backing into bed with Ford's voluptuous island squeeze (Obradors). Despite the playfully acknowledged age difference, Ford and Heche make a fun, sexy couple – his comic talents have always been undervalued, and she's all out to impress, so you'll probably forgive the movie its banality and somewhat old-fashioned sexual politics. TCh

Six Degrees of Separation

(1994, US, 111 min)
d Fred Schepisi. *p* Fred Schepisi, Arnon Milchan. *sc* John Guare. *ph* Ian Baker. *ed* Peter Honess. *pd* Patrizia von Brandenstein. *m* Jerry Goldsmith. *cast* Will Smith, Donald Sutherland, Stockard Channing, Ian McKellen, Mary Beth Hurt, Bruce Davison, Richard Masur, Kitty Carlise Hart, Osgood Perkins.

●John Guare's adaptation of his stage hit has Smith's young pretender talking his way into the Central Park household of 'liberal' art dealer Sutherland. In preppy clothes and purportedly a friend of his host's student son, Smith assuages the suspicions of Sutherland and wife Channing, and also of their prospective client, millionaire South African McKellen, to such an extent that he's soon cooking them a gourmet meal and letting on that he's the son of actor Sidney Poitier. Too safe to work as satire, Schepisi's film comes over more as bourgeois farce, beginning at a frenetic pitch as Ian Baker's camera darts madly around the apartment when a painting is discovered to be missing, and flashing back repeatedly to the ruse. Smith's fine as the impostor, but scenes of his Travis Bickle-style preparations stretch credulity (this guy's clearly too gifted an actor not to find work), and although he manages to retain the requisite mystery as to his identity, it's hard to accept him as a mirror to hypocrisy or as a catalyst to responsibility. In the end only Channing, reprising her award-winning stage role, manages to inject some authentic feeling into this somewhat mechanical enterprise. WH

6.5 Special (aka Calling All Cats)

(1958, GB, 85 min, b/w)
d Alfred Shaugnessy. *p* Herbert Smith. *sc* Norman Hudis. *ph* Leo Rogers. *ed* Jocelyn Jackson. *ad* George Provis. *m* Geoff Love. *cast* Avril Leslie, Diane Todd, Pete Murray, Jo Douglas, Finlay Currie, Josephine Douglas, Lonnie Donnegan, Dickie Valentine, Jim Dale, Petula Clark, Russ Hamilton, Joan Regan, Johnny Dankworth, Cleo Laine, Mike and Bernie Winters.

●BBC TV's hit pop series of the '50s transferred to the cinema with the minimum of plot and the maximum of music: showbiz wannabes Leslie and Todd hop on the 6.05 Glasgow to London train; a host of stars, not surprisingly, are rehearsing on board. The line-up includes Petula Clark, Dankworth and Laine, Jim Dale (and youthful comic duo Mike and Bernie Winters), but when we finally reach the studio, it's Lonnie Donegan who closes the show. TJ

Six Inches Tall

see Attack of the Puppet People

Six in Paris

see Paris vu par…

Sixteen Candles

(1984, US, 93 min)
d John Hughes. *p* Hilton A Green. *sc* John Hughes. *ph* Bobby Byrne. *ed* Edward A Warschilka. *pd* John W Corso. *m* Ira Newborn. *cast* Molly Ringwald, Anthony Michael Hall, Michael Schoeffling, Paul Dooley, Gedde Watanabe, John Cusack, Joan Cusack.

●In which writer/director Hughes reinvented the teen movie by introducing real emotions and anxieties behind the usual run of dating decisions, wild parties and adolescent pranks. Ringwald's star-making turn plunges her into the trauma of turning 16, when her crush on the class hunk fails to work out and she finds unlikely solace in the shape of Hall's Ted the Geek. Sly humour and an appreciative ear for the demotic improv of teenage chat completes an attractive package. TCh

6th Day, The

(2000, US, 123 min)
d Roger Spottiswoode. *p* Mike Medavoy, Arnold Schwarzenegger, Jon Davison. *sc* Cormac Wibberley, Marianne Wibberley. *ph* Pierre Mignot. *ed* Mark Conte, Dominique Fortin, Michel Arcand. *pd* James Bissell, John Willett. *m* Trevor Rabin. *cast* Arnold Schwarzenegger, Tony Goldwyn, Michael Rapaport, Michael Rooker, Sarah Wynter, Wendy Crewson, Rod Rowland, Terry Crews, Robert Duvall.

●Scientific advances have eradicated world hunger, medical labs are replete with cloned human organs for transplants, cloned family 're-pets' mean never having to tell your child the pet bunny has died, and if you're fed up with your girlfriend you can get a virtual one instead. For some, birth-life-death is still the natural order. For others, including power broker Michael Drucker (Goldwyn), the prospect of immortality is too tempting to ignore. Disregarding the 'Sixth Day Law' (respecting the belief that God created man on the sixth day) that forbids human cloning, Drucker, helped by scientist Dr Weir (Duvall), is secretly doing just that. But when the wrong man – Adam Gibson (Schwarzenegger) – is accidentally cloned and comes home to discover another version of himself, Drucker is in danger of being exposed. This is slick and involving, if over-long, and manages to point (albeit unsubtly) to significant ethical issues. Any class, though, derives solely from the always impressive Duvall. KW

Sixth Happiness, The

(1997, GB/Ind, 97 min)
d Waris Hussein. *p* Tatiana Kennedy. *sc* Firdaus Kanga. *ph* James Welland. *ed* Laurence Méry-Clark. *pd* Lynne Whiteread. *cast* Firdaus Kanga, Souad Faress, Khodus Wadia, Nina Wadia, Ahsen Bhatti.

●Firdaus Kanga, born in Bombay, was different three times over: gay, disabled and a Parsee. His fictionalised autobiography, *Trying to Grow*, was a hilarious account of a kid with bones as brittle as clay pots, but a spirit stronger than steel. This adaptation conveys the book's joie de vivre and most particularly its gloriously non-PC take on the subject. Kanga wrote the screenplay, plays the lead and also does pieces to camera commenting on the action. Astonishingly, he pulls off all three with aplomb, assisted by a strong cast – notably Souad Faress as his mother. Waris Hussein's direction uses some interesting tricks without being tricksy. A witty film: perspicacious and generous in its gaze. AJ

Sixth Sense, The (100)

(1999, US, 107 min)
d M Night Shyamalan. *p* Frank Marshall, Kathleen Kennedy, Barry Mendel. *sc* M Night Shyamalan. *ph* Tak Fujimoto. *ed* Andrew Mondshein. *pd* Larry Fulton. *m* James Newton Howard. *cast* Bruce Willis, Toni Collette, Olivia Williams, Haley Joel Osment, Donnie Wahlberg, Glenn Fitzgerald, Mischa Barton, Trevor Morgan, Bruce Norris.

●Writer/director Shyamalan's sombre shocker was a massive sleeper hit in the US, proving that jaded mainstream audiences have an untapped appetite for disturbing, grown-up horror. Reminiscent of Polanski's *Repulsion* or *Rosemary's Baby*, it generates an insidious, incremental horror. Also, its scares grow out of carefully delineated human relationships, their immediate impact matched by a deep emotional undertow. Eight-year-old Cole (Osment) whispers his secret to shrink Malcolm Crowe (Willis): 'I see dead people.' But why have these purgatorial souls made contact with this bright, ultra-sensitive boy? Osment's extraordinary, moving portrayal of the brave but bewildered Cole might have unbalanced the film had not Willis, as the obsessive shrink, given his most subtle, sympathetic performance to date. Haunted by his failure to help a former patient, Crowe is oblivious to his estranged wife's emotional needs and desperate to redeem himself by saving the boy. Tak Fujimoto's muted colour photography imbues the everyday interiors and evocative Philadelphia locations with a gloomy but never depressing atmosphere. Similarly, the tone of the understated direction is melancholy rather than maudlin. A poignant study of the searing pain caused by loss, this all-too-human horror film provokes tears as well as fears. NF

'68

(1988, US, 98 min)
d Steven Kovacs. *p* Dale Djerassi, Isabel Maxwell, Steven Kovacs. *sc* Steven Kovacs. *ph* Daniel Lacambre. *ed* Cari Coughlin. *ad* Joshua Koral. *m* John Cippolina, Shony Alex Braun. *cast* Eric Larson, Robert Locke, Sandor Tecsi, Anna Dukasz, Mirlan Kwun, Terra Vandergaw, Neil Young.

●Kovacs' episodic attempt to evoke the trippy, dippy and momentous days of '68 centres on San Francisco, where Hungarian exile Zoltan Szabo (Tecsi) and family are putting the final touches to their newly acquired ethnic restaurant. Throughout, radio bulletins, television broadcasts and posters conveniently announce that this is the year of the Tet offensive, the Chicago Convention, etc, but that's as deep as it goes. Zoltan puts his faith in his two sons, but law student Peter (Larson) is soon dropping out, turning on, wising up and getting laid, and his brother (Locke) comes out as gay to beat the draft. Shot like a pastiche of '60s soap opera, it finally peters out in a bathetic happy resolution of sorts. WH

6ixty-nin9 (Ruang Talok 69)

(1999, Thai, 114 min)
d Pen-ek Ratanaruang. *p* Charoen Iamphungporn, Pen-ek Ratanaruang. *sc* Pen-ek Ratanaruang. *ph* Chankit Chamnivikaiping. *ed* Patamanadda Yukol. *ad* Saksiri Chantarangsri. *cast* Lalita Panyopas, Tasanawalai Ongartittichai, Black Phomtong, Sritao, Arun Wannarbodeewong.

●Right after losing her job in banking because of the economic crisis, Tum finds a cardboard box stuffed with banknotes on her doorstep. Partly by accident, the burly men who come looking for it meet untimely ends in her apartment; so do several others in the following days, including the cop who lives downstairs. Meanwhile Tum equips herself with a fake passport and an air ticket to London. Will piled-up corpses, nosey neighbours, suicidal friends, her crooked former boss or, worst of all, her conscience foil her getaway plan? Cheekily titled (less in reference to oral sex than to a door-number '6' which drops to become a '9'), shot with grungy flair and acted with great aplomb, Pen-ek's black comedy-thriller is a post-Hitchcockian delight, replete with references to *Psycho* but with a strong Thai accent. Minced penis salad, anyone? TR

67 Days (Uziska Republika)

(1974, Yugo, 175 min)
d Zika Mitrovic. *p* Stevo Petrovic. *sc* Ana Marija Car, Arsen Diklic, Zika Mitrovic. *ph* Pega Popovic. *ed* Katarina Stojanovic. *ad* Mirodrag Nikolic. *m* Zoran Hristic. *cast* Boris Buzancic, Bozidarka Frajt, Neda Arneric, Rade Serbedzija.

●Given that the socialist-realism school of Eastern European film-making – 'the aesthetic of the short-sighted camera' – tends to concentrate on historical reconstructions for home-market consumption/inspiration, it is surprising to find this turning up in London (even cut to 118 minutes). It's perhaps not so surprising that the film itself is a truly dire partisan epic, of minor interest only as a didactic lesson on the 'Uzice Republic', which survived as a springboard for Yugoslav communist resistance for a couple of months in 1941, in the face of a combined assault by the Germans and royalist Chetniks. A predictable script outlines the fate of a workers' battalion led by a Tito surrogate (while the great man himself is portrayed in mock actuality footage), and runs its tedious course through a series of logistically-confusing battle scenes and a few sentimental vignettes. PT

Six Weeks

(1982, US, 108 min)
d Tony Bill. *p* Peter Guber, Jon Peters. *sc* David Seltzer. *ph* Michael D Margulies. *ed* Stu Linder. *ad* Hilyard Brown. *m* Dudley Moore,

Richard Hazard. *cast* Dudley Moore, Mary Tyler Moore, Shannon Wilcox, Bill Calvert, John Harkins, Joe Regalbuto, Katherine Healy.
●Signs of desperation here: like the aptly titled *Lovesick* (made later, though shown in Britain first), this Dudley Moore vehicle uses every trick in the Hollywood book to tug at the heartstrings – not to mention the pursestrings – of whatever bankable generation lapped up the lachrymose *Love Story* a decade ago. *Six Weeks* might have worked in 1932, but looks decidedly dodgy in the tense present. Who'd believe a congressional candidate would take time off to enrich the last weeks of the fatherless, leukemia-doomed child of a perfume heiress? And if that heiress happens to be the still glam Mary Tyler Moore (her throat's not what it was, but then neither is Dud's), who'd believe the relationship would remain platonic? The Moral Majority will lap up every tear-jerking minute; if you're lucky, you may just be able to keep your lunch. GD

Sizzlers

see Delinquent School Girls

Skateboard

(1977, US, 97 min)
d George Gage. *p* Harry N Blum, Richard A Wolf. *sc* Richard A Wolf, George Gage. *ph* Ross Kelsay. *ed* Robert Angus. *m* Mark Snow. *cast* Allen Garfield, Kathleen Lloyd, Leif Garrett, Richard Van Der Wyk, Tony Alva, Anthony Carbone.
●This would seem to promise a rip-off *Bad News Bears* on wheels, and visions of yet another exploitative US sub-culture package hardly whet the appetite. Yet anticipations of doom are happily dashed: the familiar ingredients of cynical but loveable coach (Garfield), bronzed, blond-curled Southern Californian kids, the absurdist razzmatazz of American competitive sport, and a rock soundtrack, here actually mesh into a rather endearing entertainment. The film neatly explores the psychology (and the economics) of hype and 'pressure', and its many skateboard action sequences are well shot and edited. A good, lightweight, upbeat family film. PT

Ski Bum, The

(1971, US, 136 min)
d Bruce Clark. *p* David R Dawdy. *sc* Bruce Clark, Marc Siegler. *ph* Vilmos Zsigmond. *ed* Bruce Clark, Mischa Norland. *m* Joseph Byrd. *cast* Zalman King, Charlotte Rampling, Joseph Mell, Dimitra Arliss, Tedd King, Anna Karen.
●This adaptation of Romain Gary's novel emerges as a nebulous something about a naïve young man caught up with a moneyed bunch of schemers who are after his body, not only to seduce but to run errands and to stumble after on the slopes. Clark doesn't make things easy by having the characters babble, sometimes all at once; if, despite this ploy, you manage to catch what's going on, you're faced with characters so utterly unbelievable that you begin to doubt what little you thought you knew. How can one believe the hero to be the darling of the jet set when he has a nose capable of casting half the skiable piste into shadow? As for the jet setters, they simply haven't got the Right Stuff. If you're just greedy for a glimpse of any skiing, don't bother; you'd see more icy action staring at your refrigerator. FD

Skin & Bone

(1995, US, 110 min, b/w & col)
d Everett Lewis. *p* Claudia Hoover, Gardner Monks. *sc* Everett Lewis. *ph* Fernando Arguelles. *ed* Everett Lewis. *m* Geoff Harper, Mark Jan Wlodarkiewicz. *cast* B Wyatt, Alan Boyce, Garret Scullin, Nicole Dillenberg, Chad Kula, Susannah Melvoin.
●A couple of cops pull over a car and beat up its occupant, an army general. Turns out he's paying for their services. An episodic portrait of hustlers making ends meet by acting out sexual fantasies for the '12 Noon' male escort agency, this low-budget indie reveals just how demeaning it is to be an out-of-work actor in LA – or even an in-work actor, if you're reduced to crud like this. Are there no restaurant jobs anymore? The movie's pretensions (flash-frame editing, b/w and colour visuals) are particularly galling given the lame dialogue and hackneyed dramatics, not to mention a cast with across the board learning difficulties (the soundtrack is so appalling it merits special mention; it's not aided by Lewis's inexplicable propensity for staging scenes beside the LA freeway). Presumably this is getting a UK release on the strength of its (bisexual) prurience quota, which is really nothing to get excited about. TCh

Skin Deep

(1989, US, 101 min)
d Blake Edwards. *p* Tony Adams. *sc* Blake Edwards. *ph* Isidore Mankofsky. *ed* Robert Pergament. *pd* Rodger Maus. *cast* John Ritter, Vincent Gardenia, Alyson Reed, Joel Brooks, Julianne Phillips, Chelsea Field, Peter Donat, Don Gordon, Nina Foch, Michael Kidd.
●It's voyage around my fodder time again in another of Blake Edwards' cautionary comedies. All the staples clock in, with Ritter going through the motions as alcoholic, blocked Pulitzer Prizewinner and compulsive womaniser Zach, who we see dumped in scene three by pissed-off wife Alex (Reed), and watch crawl his pathetic way to forgiveness by the end credits. Be impressed by the ritzy Pacific Palisades locations; enjoy the kitschy decor and designer threads of the rich and famous; be instructed, between tears of laughter, by the serious undertow about self-delusion and the possibility of discovery. The film's difficulty is the total obnoxiousness of the central character. Set pieces include a funny nighttime encounter involving fluorescent penises, and Zach being attacked by a strangely out-of-time Brit-punk musician. After much maudlin mooning over the piano in Barney's Bar, Zach has a midnight revelation on the beach: 'God's a gag writer!' Must be. WH

Skin Flick

(1999, Ger/GB/Can/Jap, 67 min)
d/sc Bruce LaBruce. *ph* James Carman. *ed* Manfred Mancini, Joerg Andreas. *ad* Peter Armstrong. *m* Gavin Brown. *cast* Steve Master, Eden Miller, Tom International [Yaroslav Mogutin], Ralph Steel, Tim Vincent, Jens Hammer, Nikki Richardson [Nikki Uberti].
●*No Skin Off My Ass* goes *Romper Stomper*. LaBruce's dilettantish rough-trade porn jape proves horribly misguided. Meet cheeky chappies Dirk, Dieter, Wolfgang, Reinhold and Manfred, a dissolute skinhead troupe whose butch bonding adventures around London – queer-bashing and buggering, all in a day's play – are the film's singular interest. LaBruce introduces them separately, in the crudest of broad strokes. Dirk and Dieter administer a kicking in Abney Park Cemetry, intercut with the Changing of the Guard. Wolfgang raids old ladies' handbags, before a cottaging opportunity distracts. Reinhold, a plumber, is servicing a client's pipes. Manfred however, still a virgin, gets to perform pratfalls and come over a copy of *Mein Kampf*. NB

Skinflicker

(1972, GB, 41 min, b/w & col)
d Tony Bicat. *p* Christopher Phillips. *sc* Howard Brenton. *ph* Christopher Phillips. *ed* Peter Harvey. *cast* Hilary Charlton, Will Knightley, Henry Woolf, William Hoyland, Brendan Barry, Elizabeth Choice.
●*Skinflicker* is about the kidnapping and assassination of a government minister (Barry), intended as a symbolic revolutionary act by three dissidents. The entire event is filmed by the kidnappers themselves on 8mm colour stock, and (by arrangement with them, to secure a more objective record) by a blue movie cameraman on 16mm black-and-white sound stock; and the whole is presented as part of a secret government training film. Howard Brenton's script is thus masterly in deploying the low-budget at his disposal, with the silent colour footage used to underline the extremity of the violence, and the dialogue in the black-and-white footage revealing the near-insane elation of the protagonists (brilliantly edgy, unnerving performances from Knightley and Woolf). Bicat's sure direction fails only in the rather heavy-handed opening sequence, and in the capture of the minister (it's too cleanly shot amid the confusion, and you sometimes wonder who is supposed to be holding the camera, which erodes the documentary reality). A fascinating experiment nevertheless, even if what it's trying to say remains obscure. JF

Skinless Night

(1991, Jap, 105 min)
d Rokuro Mochizuki. *p/m* Akira Kobayashi. *sc* Shink Saito, Rokuro Mochizuki. *ph* Mashashi Endo. *ed* Junichi Kikuchi. *ad* Hishao Kato. *cast* Kin Ishikawa, Yasuko Yagami, Aya Katsuragi.
●Kayama, pushing middle-age, makes video porn for a living. His average day might include a shopping trip to a rubberware boutique, a child-minding stint at the office, and an evening shoot spent struggling with the special effects for a 'golden shower' scene. One day he gets it into his head that he needs to make a 'serious' feature film, and meets steadfast opposition from his financier, his staff and his wife. *Skinless Night* (the title is swiped from Japan's best-selling brand of condoms) offers a wry portrait of Kayama as a man belatedly in search of 'integrity', and an authentic and riotously funny account of the sex industry. It takes on added piquancy when you know that its obviously talented director Mochizuki *is* a prolific maker of porno tapes. TR

Skin of Man, Heart of Beast (Peau d'homme coeur de bête)

(1999, Fr, 96 min)
d/sc Hélène Angel. *ph* Isabelle Razavet. *ed* Laurent Rouan, Eric Renault. *ad* Mathieu Menut. *m* Philippe Miller. *cast* Serge Riaboukine, Bernard Blancan, Pascal Cervo, Maaïke Jansen, Cathy Hinderchied, Virginie Guinand, Jean-Louis Richard.
●Aurélie, five, and Christelle, 13, go to stay with their gran and uncle Alex after mum walks out. When their dad Francky, a womanising, hard-drinking Marseilles cop, is told to take some leave and calm down, he follows them to the family farm in the Provençal Alps. Also just back, as it happens, is Coco, a third brother unheard of for 15 years – away with the Foreign Legion, or so he says. Cue boozing, brawling and hanging out at a friend's disco-cum-brothel where Alex does odd jobs. Quiet Coco, though, never looks at ease with all the machismo. Other French accounts of dysfunctional families and violent masculinity spring to mind, but this is better than most. That's due partly to the marvellous casting and acting, to the telling but unsentimental placing of the kids within the narrative, and to a mood of tragic inexorability established from the start; but also, crucially, to the detached yet compassionate truth of its depiction of everyday horrors. GA

Ski Patrol

(1989, US, 92 min)
d Richard Correll. *p* Phillip B Goldfine, Don West. *sc* Steven Long Mitchell, Craig W Van Sickle. *ph* John M Stephens. *ed* Scott Wallace. *pd* Fred Weiler. *m* Bruce Miller. *cast* Roger Rose, Yvette Nipar, TK Carter, Leslie Jordan, Ray Walston, Martin Mull, Corby Timbrook.
●'The idea', explains executive producer Paul *Police Academy* Maslansky, 'is to make the first mainstream ski film in about six years, which will appeal to skiing enthusiasts, and to put it in comedic form with gorgeous actresses and interesting, panoramic scenic backgrounds, and then combine it with high action skiing and a hot music track'. First-time director Correll faithfully relays his boss' vision of a world populated entirely by haircuts with legs, playmates, second-rate clowns, and the Machiavellian rich. The plot, obviously not a high priority, has baddies scheming to oust nice old Pop by ensuring that his ski lodge fails a safety inspection; but wait…our wacky heroes in the Ski Patrol get wise to the saboteurs in the nick of time. 'I think you're an immature, wisecracking ski bum,' gorgeous Ellen tells hunky Jerry, 'actually I think you're pretty irresistible'. Actually, she was right the first time. Why do these 'zany' comedies fall back on the corniest situations and the most predictable stereotypes? TCh

Skip Tracer

(1977, Can, 94 min)
d Zale R Dalen. *p* Laara Dalen. *sc* Zale R Dalen. *ph* Ron Orieux. *ed* Zale R Dalen. *ad* Elinor Barg. *m* J Douglas Dodd. *cast* David Peterson, John Lazarus, Rudy Szabo, Mike Grigg, A Rose, Sue Astley.
●Operating at the extremer edges of capitalism's unacceptable face, a skip tracer is a man who pulls your legs off if you don't repay his company's

loan. What might have been another action flick of routine Sweeneyish nastiness is lent a worthwhile extra dimension by the psychological tensions that the job clearly entails – all that externalised aggro is seen as just another sign of internal fear and loathing. David Peterson carries the film single-handed, playing the tracer as mean as a wired ferret, until the pressure tells and he hits the slide. Some scenes and most of the supporting cast are best excused by Vancouver's general lack of a glorious cinematic heritage; but there's still enough low-budget energy and lurking menace to mark it up as a genuine curio. CPea

Skull, The

(1965, GB, 83 min)
d Freddie Francis. *p* Milton Subotsky, Max J Rosenberg. *sc* Milton Subotsky. *ph* John Wilcox. *ed* Oswald Hafenrichter. *ad* William Constable. *m* Elisabeth Lutyens. *cast* Peter Cushing, Patrick Wymark, Christopher Lee, Jill Bennett, Nigel Green, Michael Gough, George Coulouris, Patrick Magee.

●Originally *The Skull of the Marquis de Sade*, but the title had to be changed when De Sade's descendants in France complained. It's about a collector of occult objects (Cushing) who is offered the skull of the 'divine Marquis', and the vicious murders that subsequently take place. The script from Robert Bloch's short story hasn't been worked out very well, but there is one extraordinary dream sequence, and the whole film is directed by Freddie Francis with much technical panache. DP

Skullduggery

(1969, US, 105 min)
d Gordon Douglas. *p* Saul David. *sc* Nelson Gidding. *ph* Robert Moreno. *ed* John Woodcock. *pd* Hilyard Brown. *m* Oliver Nelson. *cast* Burt Reynolds, Susan Clark, Roger C Carmel, Paul Hubschmid, Chips Rafferty, Alexander Knox, Edward Fox, Wilfrid Hyde-White.

●An engagingly ramshackle adventure that gradually takes on a burden of messages as Reynolds and Carmel latch on to Susan Clark's archaeological expedition, which has permission to explore the New Guinea interior. The pair are secretly prospecting for phosphorus (highly profitable since the advent of colour TV), but instead find a tribe of ape-like, intelligent creatures (played by diminutive University of Djakarta students in gingery, hairy suits) who may be 'the missing link'. Dropouts one and all, they certainly believe in flower-power, which turns Reynolds all radical when the Establishment – in the shape of the archaeological expedition's financial backer – proposes to breed them like animals for cheap labour. Cue for a rousingly melodramatic courtroom finale, engineered in desperation by Reynolds, in which the definition of 'humanity' comes under hot debate from all sides (Black Panthers, apartheid apologists, et al). Naïve, uncertain in tone, but despite all faults, an appealing curiosity. TM

Skulls, The

(2000, US, 107 min)
d Rob Cohen. *p* Neal H Moritz, John Pogue. *sc* John Pogue. *ph* Shane Hurlbut. *ed* Peter Amundson. *pd* Bob Ziembicki. *m* Randy Edelman. *cast* Joshua Jackson, Paul Walker, Hill Harper, Leslie Bibb, Christopher McDonald, Steve Harris, William Petersen, Craig T Nelson, David Asman.

●Members of Yale's real-life secret society, the Skull and Bones, have included business magnates, CIA men and (purportedly) both Presidents Bush. This nugget is more thought provoking than anything else in Rob Cohen's pulpy thriller, which is a blend of po-faced seriousness and knuckle-headed miscalculation. Jackson, from TV's *Dawson's Creek*, is the rowing star from a humble background who gets the call from 'The Skulls', where most of his fellow inductees are the scions of old money. Having passed the scary initiation rites, Jackson is presented with a wad of money and a new sports car, which helps ease the hot iron branding on his wrist. The Skulls are so very secret that even though they have their own building on campus with catacombs, spires and a logo on top, nobody ever seems to notice it. Will Jackson blow the whistle? The mysterious suicide of college reporter Harper helps make up his mind, priming us for a thriller finale, even though the movie's unintentionally played like a comedy all the way. TJ

Skyjacked

(1972, US, 101 min)
d John Guillermin. *p* Walter Seltzer. *sc* Stanley R Greenberg. *ph* Harry Stradling Jr. *ed* Robert Swink. *ad* Edward C Carfagno. *m* Perry Botkin Jr. *cast* Charlton Heston, Yvette Mimieux, James Brolin, Claude Akins, Jeanne Crain, Roosevelt Grier, Walter Pidgeon, Leslie Uggams, Mariette Hartley, Mike Henry.

●A routine *Airport*-style thriller, with Heston as the pilot whose nerves are battered when the 707 he's flying from LA to Minneapolis is discovered to have a bomb on board, ready to explode unless he agrees to head for Moscow. The skyjacker is a disgruntled Vietnam veteran (Brolin), but the film is much too busy with its disaster movie routine (pregnant lady giving birth, and so forth) to make anything of this. Only a highly professional cast alleviates the general predictability and tedium. GA

Skyline (La Linea del Cielo)

(1983, Sp, 86 min)
d Fernando Colomo. *sc* Fernando Colomo. *ph* Angel Luis Fernandez. *ed* Miguel Angel Santamaria. *m* Manzanita. *cast* Antonio Resines, Beatriz Pérez-Porro, Patricia Cisarano, Jaime Nos, Roy Hoffman, Irene Stillman, Whit Stillman.

●This charming Spanish feature, about a photographer (Resines) who travels to New York with the intention of finding work and learning English, is based on the director's own experiences while trying to set up a film. Shot on a low budget, it gently pokes fun at various Big Apple pretensions and rituals – the dinner party, how to handle a telephone call – while making a few serious observations en route about innocents and foreigners abroad. GA

Sky Pirates

(1985, Aust, 86 min)
d Colin Eggleston. *p* John Lamond, Michael Hirsh. *sc* John Lamond. *ph* Garry Wapshott. *ed* John Lamond, Michael Hirsh. *pd* Kristian Fredrickson. *m* Brian May. *cast* John Hargreaves, Meredith Phillips, Max Phipps, Bill Hunter, Simon Chilvers, Alex Scott.

●Third-rate cash-in on *Raiders of the Lost Ark*: Dakota pilot Bomber Harris (bet they thought hard on that one) meets up with a scatty brunette, and both go off in search of some ancient stone tablet that is supposed to provide amazing power to whoever possesses it. 'Bomber' is played by Hargreaves, a hammy sort of bloke who tries ever so hard to be the macho Indiana Jones, but fails dismally. In fact, nearly everything about this movie is pretty awful, and that includes the most appalling editing you're ever likely to see. DA

Sky Riders

(1976, US, 93 min)
d Douglas Hickox. *p* Terry Morse Jr. *sc* Jack DeWitt, Stanley Mann, Garry Michael White. *ph* Ousama Rawi. *ed* Malcolm Cooke. *ad* Terry Ackland-Snow. *m* Lalo Schifrin. *cast* James Coburn, Susannah York, Robert Culp, Charles Aznavour, Werner Pochath, Zou Zou, Kenneth Griffith, Harry Andrews, JohnBeck.

●Pure slop. 'Hang-Gliders versus Left Wing Political Extremists' sounds like a bad kung-fu film, and it has about the same depth of characterisation. Laconic Coburn rescues ex-wife (braless Susannah) and brood from clutches of 'World Activists Revolutionary Army' (sic), who pack even bazookas in their mountain retreat somewhere in Greece. How to get at them, there's the prob. Hey! A nearby group of hang-gliding freaks! Sure enough, the Pepsi generation outwit the former Paris rioters. Hickox directs in his usual cold-blooded style, and the last twenty minutes is sheer violence and destruction (like the end of a Godzilla picture, only more mindless). AN

Sky's the Limit, The

(1943, US, 89 min, b/w)
d Edward H Griffith. *p* David Hempstead. *sc* Frank Fenton, Lynn Root. *ph* Russell Metty. *ed* Roland Gross. *ad* Albert S D'Agostino, Carroll Clark. *songs* Harold Arlen, Johnny Mercer. *cast* Fred Astaire, Joan Leslie, Robert Benchley, Robert Ryan, Elizabeth Patterson.

●Astaire returned to RKO with the chance to dance to his own choreography, and amid some primitive airman-on-leave musical plotting, took it with both feet in one memorable nocturnal solo ('One for My Baby') in a deserted bar. Leslie is a magazine snapper who unwittingly scoops the incognito war hero; Benchley contributes a characteristically cockeyed oration; and the score is by Harold Arlen and Johnny Mercer. PT

Slacker

(1991, US, 97 min)
d/p/sc Richard Linklater. *ph* Lee Daniel. *ed* Scott Rhodes. *ad* Deborah Pastor. *cast* Richard Linklater, Rudy Basquez, Jean Caffeine, Jan Hockey, Stephen Hockey, Mark James, Bob Boyd.

●A little like David Byrne's *True Stories*, minus the music and plot, this is a freewheeling, documentary-style celebration of the bizarrely normal, charmingly oddball, and terminally hip residents of Austin, Texas. It starts with a guy boring a taxi driver to death with talk about parallel realities, shifts gear when the backseat philosopher sees a woman hit by a car, then swerves into comic absurdity when the victim's son is arrested for her murder. And that's just the first five minutes. After this, one character from each scene provides the link to the next, as we encounter a string of bar-room philosophers, New Agers, old anarchists, and other weirdly entertaining specimens – one of whom is hawking what she claims is Madonna's cervical smear. At times, it's like watching someone else's home movies, but there's something oddly compelling about such studied eccentricity. NF

Slackers

(2002, US, 87 min)
d Dewey Nicks. *p* Neal H Moritz, Erik Feig. *sc* David H Steinberg. *ph* James Bagdonas. *ed* Tara Timpone. *pd* William Arnold. *m* Joey Altruda, Venus Brown, Printz Board, Justin Stanley. *cast* Devon Sawa, Jason Schwartzman, James King, Jason Segel, Michael Maronna, Mamie Van Doren, Joe Flaherty, Leigh Taylor Young.

●With this first feature, Nicks may have cracked the 'slacker' genre with a tightly scripted, eccentric and at times insane tale of the exploits of Dave, Sam and Jeff: a high-school trio whose increasingly complex methods of avoiding work (while still making the grades) are eventually uncovered by creepy geek Ethan (Schwartzman). His prize for not squealing? The guys must bag him Angela (King), brightest, most beautiful girl on campus. But in his pursuit of duty, Dave (Sawa) falls for Angela himself. The movies given the nod here include *Mrs Doubtfire*, *There's Something About Mary*, *The Graduate* and *William Shakespeare's Romeo & Juliet*. It's undoubtedly a lads' film (the implausible romantic stuff feels like an afterthought), though the laughs are almost entirely at their expense. If it's unlikely to stimulate the brain cells, it will almost certainly make you laugh out loud. JFu

Slade in Flame

see Flame

Slam

(1998, US, 103 min)
d Marc Levin. *p* Henri M Kessler, Richard Stratton, Marc Levin. *sc* Sonja Sohn, Marc Levin, Bonz Malone, Saul Williams, Richard Stratton. *ph* Mark Benjamin. *ed* Emir Lewis. *m* DJ Spooky. *cast* Saul Williams, Sonja Sohn, Beau Sia, Bonz Malone, Lawrence Wilson, Rhozier Brown, Mayor Marion Barry Jr.

●This eschews the clichés of gangsta rap to find a new slant on African-American experience. In the wrong place at the wrong time, Ray Joshua (Williams) is picked up for drug dealing and held in a Washington, DC, penitentiary. There, in a startling scene just on the right side of absurd, he disarms the prison yard muscle with a burst of impromptu verse. Paroled into the eager care of the prison writing tutor (Sohn), Ray is introduced to a new cosmopolitan society where his gifts could flourish, given half a chance. But in the real world, that court date looms. Shot on actual locations in just nine days by Levin, a former documentarist, and improvised within a detailed scene-by-scene outline, this is a perplexing mix of truth and falsity, spontaneity and cliché. Inspired by the slam poetry scene in which Williams has found some fame (a slam is a competitive reading akin to a jazz cutting contest), at its best the movie achieves some of the piercing subjective insight of live performance. Williams is a lucid and passionate witness. Yet Ray is too good to be true, the softest drug pusher in town, and Levin can't resist the lure of shimmering sunsets and the like. TCh

Slam Dance

(1987, US, 101 min)
d Wayne Wang. *p* Rupert Harvey, Barry Opper. *sc* Don Opper. *ph* Amir Mokri. *ed* Lee Percy, Sandy Nervig. *pd* Eugenio Zanetti. *m* Mitchell Froom. *cast* Tom Hulce, Mary Elizabeth Mastrantonio, Don Opper, Harry Dean Stanton, Adam Ant, Robert Beltran, Virginia Madsen, Millie Perkins.

● Cynical cartoonist CC Drood (Hulce) has problems: his wife (Mastrantonio) has left him, his landlady opens his mail, and a mysterious girl he had a brief affair with (Madsen) has been found dead. Suspected of murder by Detective Smiley (Stanton), he is also the victim of brutal interrogations carried out by a hood named Buddy (Opper). Combining state-of-the-art stylishness with comedy and suspense, Wang turns an otherwise straightforward conspiracy thriller into a pacy, racy fable with distinctly oddball dimensions. The deft, dark humour (notably a supremely funny scene set in a police station seemingly populated by psychos) reinforces the shock value of its sudden incursions of crunching violence; while Drood's descent into danger involves a drastic reassessment of his shallow, self-regarding attitudes. Tautly scripted (by Don 'Android' Opper, who also turns in a bizarrely touching performance as Buddy), stunningly shot and designed, the movie may not display the emotional honesty and complexity of Wang's earlier *Dim Sum*, but as polished adult entertainment it sparkles. GA

Slanted Vision

(1995, US, 50 min)
d/p/sc/ph/ed Ming-Yuen S Ma.

● An ambitious, perceptive but finally rather chaotic exploration (taped on video) of attitudes towards the sexuality of Asian (gay) men. Part one examines their representation in porn and martial arts cinema; part two their responses to AIDS and safe sex; part three is a not very funny, sexually oriented parody of a TV cooking show. GA

Slap Shot

(1977, US, 124 min)
d George Roy Hill. *p* Robert J Wunsch, Stephen J Friedman. *sc* Nancy Dowd. *ph* Victor J Kemper. *ed* Dede Allen. *ad* Henry Bumstead. *m* Elmer Bernstein. *cast* Paul Newman, Michael Ontkean, Lindsay Crouse, Jennifer Warren, Jerry Houser, Strother Martin, Andrew Duncan, Melinda Dillon.

● While Newman's ice hockey manager struggles to revive his ailing team's fortunes with a trio of recruits who specialise most successfully in foul tactics, the movie tries, sadly, to have its cake and eat it: ostensibly deploring the commercialisation and violence that has increasingly taken over the arena, it simultaneously revels in the bone-crunching dirty play on display. Similarly, it's really just an old-fashioned piece of wish fulfilment, rather duplicitously dressed up in foul language and sexual references in a cynical attempt to look modern. That said, there are still some nice touches of absurdist satirical wit hanging out along the sidelines, given extra bite by Dede Allen's superbly pacy editing. GA

Slasher, The

see Cosh Boy

Slate, Wyn & Me

(1987, Aust, 91 min)
d Don McLennan. *p* Tom Burstall. *sc* Don McLennan. *ph* David Connell. *ed* Peter Friedrich. *pd* Paddy Reardon. *m* Bluey & Curly Productions. *cast* Sigrid Thornton, Simon Burke, Martin Sacks, Tommy Lewis, Lesley Baker, Harold Baigent.

● Recipe for Road Movie Rehash, Australian-style. Take basic stock of bungled bank robbery, panic shooting of cop, and flight of two Chevy-driving teenage delinquents with young female hostage. Throw in leftovers from *Bonnie and Clyde, Badlands, Thieves Like Us* or *The Grissom Gang*. Add slices of indigenous wild life and a pinch of James Dean posturing, then spice with three-way sexual power games. A smidgen of rock'n'roll and the vaguest hint of early '60s iconography will impart the requisite period flavour. Half-bake under a hot sun for approximately 90 minutes, checking from time to time for signs of originality. Garnish generously with widescreen sunsets and shots of attractive young men and women in figure-hugging jeans. This is a useful recipe for making something out of nothing; it is reasonably filling, and if presented properly can make an impression on the eye. Consume immediately, as the contents tend to evaporate rapidly. NF

Slaughter

(1972, US, 92 min)
d Jack Starrett. *p* Monroe Sachson. *sc* Mark Hanna, Don Williams. *ph* Rosalio Solano. *ed* Renn Reynolds. *m* Luchi de Jesus. *cast* Jim Brown, Stella Stevens, Rip Torn, Don Gordon, Cameron Mitchell, Marlene Clark.

● Opening with Billy Preston singing about 'bold, beautiful and black… ', this is the familiar mixture of mafia machismo (laced with a little camp) and black avenger theme, as Jim Brown's Slaughter, Vietnam vet, takes out after the syndicate responsible for the death of his parents. Best things about the film are its outrageous set-ups (for once, visual distortion is used to genuinely amazing effect), and Rip Torn's mean-arsed slob of a mafioso. Otherwise it tends to the mechanical: a broad beaten up here, a car chase there… Not in the *Superfly* class.

Slaughter's Big Rip-Off

(1973, US, 93 min)
d Gordon Douglas. *p* Monroe Sachson. *sc* Charles Johnson. *ph* Charles F Wheeler. *ed* Christopher Holmes. *ad* Alfeo Bocchicchio. *m* James Brown, Fred Wesley. *cast* Jim Brown, Ed McMahon, Brock Peters, Don Stroud, Gloria Hendry, Art Metrano.

● If nothing else, Gordon Douglas keeps the action moving in this sequel to *Slaughter*. Jim Brown's eponymous hero (the rest is equally subtle) tracks down the organisation that's after him for what he did to them in the earlier film. As he moves through the coke-sniffing city jungle, he encounters the usual police/syndicate tie-ups and the list in a safe that names names. Apart from some scenes and casting of total miscalculation, there are things to enjoy: a miserable hit-man who has missed his target is introduced to his own assassin at a poolside party; a man sniggers while trying to pick a safe and listen to the love-making couple in the next room. And for collectors of punko dialogue there are such gems as 'I should have known you ten years ago. We'd have ripped off the whole world in a week.' CPe

Slaughterhouse-Five

(1972, US, 103 min)
d George Roy Hill. *p* Paul Monash. *sc* Stephen Geller. *ph* Miroslav Ondricek. *ed* Dede Allen. *pd* Henry Bumstead. *m* Johann Sebastian Bach, Glenn Gould. *cast* Michael Sacks, Ron Leibman, Eugene Roche, Sharon Gans, Valerie Perrine, Roberts Blossom, Sorrell Booke, John Dehner, Perry King, Friedrich Ledebur.

● A curiosity, really. A slight and conservative adaptation of Kurt Vonnegut's tale about a man whose time sense is dislocated: his wartime past, which includes being bombed in Dresden, his American bourgeois present as an optometrist, and his sci-fi fantasy future on the planet Tralfamadore, develop as three concurrent narratives. Occasionally Hill comes up with some nice touches of the unexpected: a few moments of black humour, the suggestion of a deliberate pastiche here and there, but on the whole he's too resolutely fashionable a director to really get behind Vonnegut's idea of time-tripping. It ends up the wrong side of unadventurous. CPe

Slave of Love, A (Raba Lubvi)

(1976, USSR, 94 min)
d Nikita Mikhalkov. *sc* Friedrich Gorenstein, Andrei Konchalovsky. *ph* Pavel Lebeshev. *ad* Alexander Adabashian, Aleksandr Samulekin. *m* Eduard Artemiev. *cast* Elena Solovei, Rodion Nakhapetov, Alexander Kalyagin, Oleg Basilashvili.

● Crimea, 1917: a film crew shooting a silent melodrama while away a long summer in sub-Chekhovian languor. Gradually, intimations of distant revolution become intrusive. In true social-realist style, the idyll gives way to grainy realism, but the film is fatally undecided on whether to celebrate the glamour of a world with which it is more than half in love yet feels obliged to condemn. CPea

Slave of the Cannibal God

see Montagna del Dio Cannibale, La

Slavers

(1977, WGer, 102 min)
d/p Jürgen Goslar. *sc* Henry Morrisson, Nathaniel Kohn, Marcia McDonald. *ph* Igor Luther. *ed* Fred Srp. *ad* John Rosewarne, Peter Röhrig. *m* Eberhard Schöner. *cast* Trevor Howard, Ron Ely, Britt Ekland, Jürgen Goslar, Ray Milland, Ken Gampu, Cameron Mitchell.

● Darkest Africa, 1884: cynical, grizzled trader (Howard), beautiful white woman (Ekland), self-aggrandising husband (Goslar), illicit lover (Ely), plus an endless supply of disposable natives and evil, foul-mouthed whites. The incoherent narrative sometimes tries to rectify itself with lumpen expository dialogue, and – no doubt in the name of historical accuracy – it's nasty to watch, unless you relish brandings, rape, cruelty to animals, spurting arteries, vultures working over dead natives, baby trampling, assorted deaths, and repeated shots of ankles chafed to the bone by iron anklets during the great slave trek. Black exploitation at its worst. JS

Slaves

see Blacksnake

Slaves of New York

(1989, US, 125 min)
d James Ivory. *p* Ismail Merchant, Gary Hendler. *sc* Tama Janowitz. *ph* Tony Pierce-Roberts. *ed* Katherine Wenning. *pd* David Gropman. *m* Richard Robbins. *cast* Bernadette Peters, Madeleine Potter, Adam Coleman Howard, Nick Corri, Charles McCaughan, Jonas Abry, Steve Buscemi, Betty Comden, Tammy Grimes, Mary Beth Hurt, Mercedes Ruehl, Chris Sarandon, Tama Janowitz.

● Tama Janowitz' collection of stories – some of which she adapted for this film – focuses on the middlebrow, middle class thirty-somethings who colonised Manhattan's East Village. Dizzy hat-designer Eleanor (perfectly played by Peters) lives with a shit called Stash (Howard) who paints cans of spinach. The decline of their doomed relationship is the pretext for a saunter through an airless world of galleries, parties and clubs, where everyone is on the make and no one except Eleanor has redeeming features. This doesn't matter so much, given that New York itself is the leading character; it's in the short scenes capturing the atmosphere of the city – skyscrapers at sunrise, sidewalks at sunset, rain reflected neon, a raccoon truffling through trash, gleaming limos parked beside burnt-out wrecks – that Ivory is at his best. He works hard to find a visual equivalent of Janowitz's jaunty prose, but the result, despite an eclectic rock score, bold colours, and nifty optical tricks, is more cooked-up than kooky. Relentlessly good-looking, the movie is all surface; the few moments of wit and comic tenderness hint at what might have been. MS

Slayground

(1983, GB, 89 min)
d Terry Bedford. *p* John Dark, Gower Frost. *sc* Trevor Preston. *ph* Stephen Smith, Herb Wagreich. *ed* Nick Gaster. *pd* Keith Wilson. *m* Colin Towns. *cast* Peter Coyote, Mel Smith, Billie Whitelaw, Philip Sayer, Bill Luhrs, Marie Masters.

● An adaptation of a Richard Stark novel which, like *Point Blank* pits a small-time crook against an implacable, all-powerful enemy. When their driver falls victim to a marauding sex kitten, nice guy hold-up man Coyote and his chicken-farmer buddy (Luhrs) recruit a crazy punk car thief to help out, with disastrous consequences: a rich and unscrupulous promoter's little daughter is accidentally killed, and nemesis in the form of the sadistic Shadowman stalks Coyote (his partner already gunned down in his chicken house) from New York to London and a sinister finale in a Southport funfair. Unfortunately, in making the transition from cameraman to director, Terry Bedford seems to have neglected to learn about old-fashioned virtues like pace and plausibility, suspense and characterisation. Despite some eerily atmospheric photography, it's about as exciting as a rainy night in Rotherham. RMy

SLC Punk!

(1999, US/Aust, 98 min)
d James Merendino. *p* Sam Maydew, Peter Ward. *sc* James Merendino. *ph* Greg Littlewood. *ed* Esther P Russell. *pd* Charlotte Malmlof. *cast* Matthew Lillard, Michael Goorjian, Annabeth Gish, Jennifer Lien, Chris McDonald, Devon Sawa, Jason Segal, James Duval, Summer Phoenix.

●Salt Lake City, 1985: a good place to get the hell out of. Or, if not, at least to dye your hair blue, beat up on rednecks, and proclaim your punkiness. 'America – well fuck America!' rails Stevo (Lillard) at the outset of this junior rebellion 'story'. Given that he's talking to the camera, and continues to do so for the bulk of this meandering nostalgia trip, it's curious how the movie feels as though it's hiding its intentions. It's a good hour in before we're done making introductions: Stevo describes his uptight buddy-in-arms Bob (Goorjian), and acid casualty Sean (Sawa), and dissertates on the hypocrises of parents, poseurs and American advocates of English punk, before moving to a party where we're asked to meet countless further friends and peers. The flavour of autobiography permeates the proceedings, and it becomes clear at least five minutes from the end that this is a rites of passage movie, small and sweetly inconsequential. Merendino, a SLC native, films this all with a jumped-up, excitable and slightly amateurish style presumably aiming to represent the energised punk aesthetic. There's sufficient evidence of talent and intelligence, however, to promise brighter things to come. NB

Sleeper

(1973, US, 88 min)
d Woody Allen. *p* Jack Grossberg. *sc* Woody Allen, Marshall Brickman. *ph* David M Walsh. *ed* O Nicholas Brown, Trudy Ship. *pd* Dale Hennesy. *m* Woody Allen. *cast* Woody Allen, Diane Keaton, John Beck, Mary Gregory, Don Keefer, Don McLiam.

●She: 'You haven't had sex in 200 years!?!?' He: '204, if you count my marriage'. Woody Allen's Rip Van Winkle movie, in which his Greenwich Village jazz musician/health food faddist awakes from an accidental cryogenic immersion to find that he's in 2174, cast reluctantly in the role of Little Man against the Fascist State. Plenty of one-liners, and it has the best banana-skin joke in film history. TR

Sleepers

see Little Nikita

Sleepers

(1996, US, 147 min)
d Barry Levinson. *p* Barry Levinson, Steve Golin. *sc* Barry Levinson. *ph* Michael Ballhaus. *ed* Stu Linder. *pd* Kristi Zea. *m* John Williams. *cast* Robert De Niro, Dustin Hoffman, Brad Pitt, Kevin Bacon, Jason Patric, Vittorio Gassman, Billy Crudup, Ron Eldard.

●According to Lorenzo Carcaterra's best-seller, in the summer of 1967, four friends from New York were sent to reform school after a fatal, misjudged prank. There, they were mentally and physically abused by the guards. In 1981, two of the boys – now gangsters – came face to face with one of their old tormentors, and murdered him. The district attorney who volunteered to prosecute the case was, in fact, another of the original four friends, and he secretly conspired with the defence to ensure a not-guilty verdict, while finally exposing the heinous activities of the guards. And this is a true story? The novel is badly written but queasily compelling – indeed the clumsy prose is one of the more authentic aspects of an illogical, highly improbable revenge fantasy. In his flat-footed, exorbitant adaptation, writer/director Levinson has done nothing to sift the half-truths from the melodrama, and the baroque handling of the reform school sequence even undermines the material's strongest claim on our attention, the revelation of child abuse. In the first half – with De Niro as a basketball-playing priest – Levinson never distills whatever it is that makes these kids stick together, while the second is strictly sub-Lumet courtroom histrionics. It's indicative of the all-round lack of focus that Hoffman (as an alcoholic lawyer) and Bacon (as the terrifying chief guard) are able to steal the movie with extravagant supporting turns, while the ostensible leads – Patric as the narrator Lorenzo, Pitt as the DA, Billy Crudup and Ron Eldard as the defendants – make such meagre impressions. TCh

Sleeping Beauty

(1959, US, 75 min)
d Clyde Geronimi. *p* Ken Peterson. *sc* Erdman Penner. *ed* Roy M Brewer Jr, Donald Halliday. *pd* Don de Gradi, Ken Anderson. *songs* George Bruns, Tom Adair, Winston Hibler, Erdman Penner, Sammy Fain, Jack Lawrence, Ted Sears. *cast* voices: Mary Costa, Bill Shirley, Eleanor Audley.

●Although this rarely achieves the heights of classics like *Snow White* and *Dumbo*, it still has its moments. Typical Disney elements abound: polished if sometimes stodgy animation; sugary soundtrack based on Tchaikovsky; a delicate, vapid princess, square-jawed prince, and cutesy creatures of the forest. The early scenes of domestic bliss with the matronly good fairies, interspersed with interludes of romance and regal pomp, are frequently overlong and uninspired. But in the final thundering confrontation with the wicked witch, set in the decaying Gothic splendours of the Forbidden Mountain, the magic works once more. An epic brilliance conjures up impossible monumental castles, shadows and monstrosities, with exciting action marvellously orchestrated across the CinemaScope frame. GA

Sleeping Car Murder, The (Compartiment Tueurs)

(1965, Fr, 95 min, b/w)
d Costa-Gavras. *p* Julien Derode. *sc* Costa-Gavras. *ph* Jean Tournier. *ed* Christian Gaudin. *ad* Rino Mondellini. *m* Michel Magne. *cast* Yves Montand, Simone Signoret, Pierre Mondy, Catherine Allégret, Jacques Perrin, Jean-Louis Trintignant, Michel Piccoli, Claude Mann, Charles Denner.

●Straightforward detective thriller (adapted from a whodunit by Sébastien Japrisot), made by Costa-Gavras – his first film – before he climbed on his political bandwagon. The plot is pure Agatha Christie as the witnesses to a murder on a train are picked off one by one, but at least the characters inhabit the 20th century and are beautifully played (especially Signoret as the obligatory ageing actress, and Piccoli as a furtive lecher). The ending is one of those ingenious absurdities that haunt the genre, but the lively pace and attention to detail make up for the implausibility. TM

Sleeping Dogs

(1977, NZ, 101 min)
d/p Roger Donaldson. *sc* Ian Mune, Arthur Baysting. *ph* Michael Seresin. *ed* Ian John. *m* Murray Grindlay, David Calder, Matthew Brown. *cast* Sam Neill, Warren Oates, Bernard Kearns, Nevan Rowe, Ian Mune.

●Noteworthy mainly for its rarity (at the time) as a New Zealand feature, and for a brief cameo as a US military 'adviser' by Warren Oates, this formulary political action-thriller rests on a less than intriguing paradox: to emphasise the realism and spectacle of his tale of a totalitarian government beefing up its power through anti-terrorist legislation (and devoting most of its energies to hunting a back-to-nature innocent), Donaldson enlists and prominently displays the cooperation of no less than the NZ Air Force. Subversive, eh? PT

Sleeping Man (Nemuru Otoko)

(1995, Jap, 103 min)
d Kohei Oguri. *p* Munashi Masuzawa, Hiroshi Fujikura. *sc* Kohei Oguri, Kiyoshi Kenmochi. *ph* Osamu Maruike. *ed* Nobuo Ogawa. *pd* Yoshinga Yokoo. *m* Toshio Hosokawa. *cast* Sung-Ki Ahn, Christine Hakim, Koji Yakusho, Masao Imafuku, Akiko Nomura, Masako Yagi.

●Gunma Prefecture in rural Japan conceived an unusual way to celebrate its population passing the two million mark, commissioning Kohei Oguri to take this reflective look at life in the region. Injured in a climbing accident, a young man lies in a coma, much to the consternation of family and friends, but the film's focus is more on the community as a whole, and life must go on. It's an ensemble piece which seems to pick up and drop plot strands and incident as it goes along, reflecting on both the influence of immigration and the call of escape. Oguri's determination to leave things tantalisingly unresolved may frustrate the viewer's expectations, but his pacing and composition have an other-worldly resonance. TJ

Sleeping Tiger, The

(1954, GB, 89 min, b/w)
d Joseph Losey. *p* Victor Hanbury. *sc* Derek Frye [Harold Buchman, uncredited]. *ph* Harry Waxman. *ed* Reginald Mills. *ad* John Stoll. *m* Malcolm Arnold. *cast* Dirk Bogarde, Alexis Smith, Alexander Knox, Hugh Griffith, Patricia McCarron, Maxine Audley, Glyn Houston, Harry Towb, Billie Whitelaw.

●Forget the plot, which errs on the wild side as a psychoanalyst (Knox) experimentally instals a handsome young gunman (Bogarde) in his home, only to discover – to no one's surprise but his own – that the sleeping tiger of his wife's id easily outbids his patient's. Enjoy the high-wire tension of Losey's direction, the lurking paranoia that charges his images with electricity. Losey's first British feature, made under a pseudonym in the shadow of the blacklist, it sheds the classic modulations of *The Prowler*. Instead, you see the birth pangs of what came to be known as Losey baroque, erupting grandiosely in the closing sequence, with the lovers' car crashing through a hoarding to founder beneath the rampant paws of the Esso tiger. TM

Sleeping with the Enemy

(1990, US, 99 min)
d Joseph Ruben. *p* Leonard Goldberg. *sc* Ronald Bass. *ph* John Lindley. *ed* George Bowers. *pd* Doug Kraner. *m* Jerry Goldsmith. *cast* Julia Roberts, Patrick Bergin, Kevin Anderson, Elizabeth Lawrence, Kyle Secor, Claudette Nevins.

●This is in the 'never trust appearances' mould popularised by *Fatal Attraction* and *Pacific Heights*. Julia Roberts is Laura, whose particularly smooth but psychotic hubby (Bergin) demands gourmet dinners and sex on tap, and is prone to duffing her up if she fails to hang towels in the prescribed manner. Roberts is so driven by such mistreatment that she fakes her own death, reappearing as a free-at-last nobody, and is courted by a yukkily wholesome drama teacher (Anderson) in the film's risible middle section. Cue return of Bergin's unreconstituted psycho, madder and nastier than ever, for the usual climactic punch-out and final, audience-cheering pay-off. A tacky footnote to the battered wife issue. SGr

Sleepless (Nonhosonno/ aka Non ho sonno)

(2000, It, 117 min)
d/p Dario Argento. *sc* Dario Argento, Carlo Lucarelli, Franco Ferrini. *ph* Ronnie Taylor. *ed* Anna Rosa Napoli. *pd* Massimo Antonello Geleng. *m* Goblin (Agostino Marangolo, Massimo Morante, Fabio Pignatelli, Claudio Simonetti). *cast* Max von Sydow, Stefano Dionisi, Chiara Caselli, Gabriele Lavia, Rosella Falk, Paolo Maria Scalandro, Roberto Zibetti, Roberto Accornero.

●A disappointing *giallo* shocker from Dario Argento. Two bravura sequences aside – one a snaking, knee-level pan through a theatre during a ballet performance – the film confirms that the Italian horror maestro's best work is way behind him. Retired cop Max von Sydow is drawn back into a murder mystery he investigated years before, when a killer with the same MO surfaces. The key lies in a children's nursery rhyme, but the convoluted plot is ludicrous and the supporting performances wildly erratic. Despite faint echoes of *Deep Red* and *Opera*, this is silly, soporific stuff. NF

Sleepless in Seattle

(1993, US, 105 min)
d Nora Ephron. *p* Gary Foster. *sc* Nora Ephron, David S Ward, Jeff Arch. *ph* Sven Nykvist. *ed* Robert Reitano. *pd* Jeffrey Townsend. *m* Marc Shaiman. *cast* Tom Hanks, Meg Ryan, Ross Malinger, Rita Wilson, Rosie O'Donnell, Rob Reiner, Bill Pullman.

●A comedy for the AIDS era, Ephron's movie puts a continent between the lovebirds. Sex doesn't come much safer than this. Mourning his beloved wife, widower Sam Baldwin (Hanks) moves to Seattle with his young son. When the boy arranges for dad to discuss his pain on air with a radio shrink, journalist Annie Reed (Ryan) is just one of thousands of women to fall in love at first sob with 'Sleepless in Seattle'. Unfortunately, she's 3,000 miles away and otherwise engaged to dull, dependable Walter (Pullman). This variation of the 'him and hers' schtick Ephron first tapped in her screenplay for *When Harry Met Sally* comes complete with another of Ryan's ditzy romantics and a fine cameo from *Harry* director Rob Reiner. The picture is both old fashioned and very knowing, and occasionally tart. As Annie's friend Becky (O'Donnell) recognises, it's about 'movie love' – the love that will not be denied. The schmaltzy soundtrack is overdone, but cameraman Sven Nykvist wraps it all up in an appropriately warm glow. TCh

Sleepless Town (Fuya Jyo)

(1998, Jap, 122 min)
d Lee Chi-Ngai. *p* Tsuguhiko Kadokawa, Masato Hara. *sc* Lee Chi-Ngai, Hisashi Nozawa. *ph* Arthur Wong. *pd* Yohei Taneda. *m* Shigeru Umebayashi. *cast* Takeshi Kaneshiro, Mirai Yamamoto, Eric Tsang, Seijun Suzuki, Lang Sihung, Tomoro Taguchi, Kippei Shiina.

● Gang war melodrama (adapted from a pulp novel and directed by a Hong Kong émigré), designed to capitalise on Taiwanese-Japanese actor Kaneshiro's sudden rise to megastardom in Japan. He plays Liu Kenichi, a mixed-race fence for stolen goods in Kabuki-cho, the red light area of Shinjuku. With only a seriously untrustworthy femme fatale on his back, he finds himself given three days to track down a psychotic loner wanted by the city's Shanghai triads. This had the potential to be a Chinese riposte to *Shinjuku Triad Society*, albeit without the ultraviolence and gay sex, but it fails for two reasons. One, it's ridiculously complicated: too many factions and betrayals, an absurd quadruple-cross climax. Two, it's too goddam tame: all sleek *noir* style and no bad-attitude grit. Seijun Suzuki (present in a cameo) did it all much, much better 25 years earlier. TR

Sleep, My Love

(1948, US, 97 min, b/w)
d Douglas Sirk. *p* Charles Rogers, Ralph Cohn. *sc* St Clair McKelway, Decla Dunning. *ph* Joseph Valentine. *ed* Lynn Harrison. *ad* William Ferrari. *m* Rudy Schrager. *cast* Claudette Colbert, Robert Cummings, Don Ameche, Rita Johnson, George Coulouris, Hazel Brooks, Queenie Smith, Keye Luke, Raymond Burr, Ralph Morgan.

● Though dismissed by Sirk himself, and far from equal to his superb work of the mid to late '50s, this is a fine thriller in the *Gaslight* mould, with Colbert's demise being planned by her apparently loving husband Ameche. From the opening moments aboard a train rushing through the night, the tension is kept up by taut pacing and Joseph Valentine's expressionist photography, giving rise to a suitably nightmarish evocation of insanity and shifting appearances; while the acting is strong throughout, nowhere more so than a sinister Coulouris as a bogus psychiatrist. GA

Sleepwalkers

(1992, US, 91 min)
d Mick Garris. *p* Mark Victor, Michael Grais, Nabeel Zahid. *sc* Stephen King. *ph* Rodney Charters. *ed* O Nicholas Brown. *pd* John DeCuir Jr. *m* Nicholas Pike. *cast* Brian Krause, Madchen Amick, Alice Krige, Jim Haynie, Cindy Pickett, Ron Perlman, Lyman Ward, Dan Martin, John Landis, Joe Dante, Stephen King, Clive Barker, Tobe Hooper.

● Teen hunk Krause and his incestuous mother Krige are the last of a line of creatures who feed on the virtue and suffering of small-town virgins like Amick. So when Amick takes Krause to a graveyard to make out, he transforms into the date-rapist from Hell. The creature and transformation effects are impressive, but undermined by wild swings of tone: here, for example, explicit physical horror gives way to misjudged jokey taunts, until ended by the truly laughable intervention of a fearsome kitty cat. The slide into implausibility gathers pace as the scratched and wounded Krause is nursed by his fading mother in a house surrounded by a growing horde of vengeful pussies. It's never explained why they're afraid of domestic cats, why they're the last of their line, or why they're called Sleepwalkers. Garris is left by Stephen King's typically threadbare script to extract what few frights he can with tricksy camerawork, shock effects, and flesh-ripping gore. NF

Sleep With Me

(1994, US, 94 min)
d Rory Kelly. *p* Michael Steinberg, Roger Hedden, Eric Stoltz. *sc* Duane Dell'Amico, Roger Hedden, Neal Jiminez, Joe Keenan, Rory Kelly, Michael Steinberg. *ph* Andrzej Sekula. *ed* David Moritz. *pd* Randy Eriksen. *m* David Lawrence. *cast* Eric Stoltz, Meg Tilly, Craig Sheffer, Todd Field, Susan Traylor, Dean Cameron, Thomas Gibson, Quentin Tarantino.

● Dreamed up over drinks by Eric Stoltz, Rory Kelly and their writing buddies, this contemporary relationships comedy might be described as a kind of Californian *Four Weddings and a Funeral* – just forget any religious aspect! Instead we have half a dozen party scenes (each by a different screenwriter), spanning the period between Stoltz's wedding to Tilly and the near breakdown of their relationship a few months later. The twenty-something central drama is not desperately engaging, but the ensemble scenes around it are well observed and often acutely funny, with each party plumbing new depths of social embarrassment. TCh

Sleepy Eyes of Death: The Chinese Jade

see Nemuri Kyoshiro: The Book of Killing-Rules

Sleepy Hollow

(1999, US/Ger, 105 min)
d Tim Burton. *p* Scott Rudin, Adam Schroeder. *sc* Andrew Kevin Walker. *ph* Emmanuel Lubezki. *ed* Chris Lebenzon. *pd* Rick Heinrichs. *cast* Johnny Depp, Christina Ricci, Miranda Richardson, Michael Gambon, Caspar Van Dien, Jeffrey Jones, Richard Griffiths, Ian McDiarmid, Michael Gough, Christopher Walken, Claire Skinner, Christopher Lee, Alun Armstrong, Martin Landau.

● 1799: New York police inspector Ichabod Crane (Depp) is sent to investigate a murder case in the provinces, in the hope it will purge him of his newfangled scientific theories. But there's little mystery about the crimes at Sleepy Hollow. Everyone knows the guilty party is the legendary 'headless horseman', a Prussian hussar who used to terrorise the countryside. Much taken by the enigmatic Katrina Van Tassel (Ricci), Crane chooses to confront his fear and dig a little deeper, even as everyone who's anyone in the town begins to lose his head. Burton's free interpretation of Washington Irving's classic bogey tale has a lustrous, black velvet look that draws on fairy tale traditions, Disney, Gothic and Dutch Colonial styles – with a pinch of Hammer Horror thrown in. Depp affects a vaguely English accent and a prissy, slightly effeminate demeanour as Crane. It's a witty but fatally caricatured performance which precludes much in the way of emotional investment, and generates negligible chemistry with a pallid Ricci. This is more plot-driven than Burton's norm, and it moves at a fair lick, but even so, its attractions are all atmospheric, while narrative convolutions tend to come in undigested gobbets of explanation. For about an hour it's a fine, ghoulish carnival sideshow, and that has its charms, but there's a thin desperation about the climax. TCh

Sleepy Time Gal, The

(2001, US, 94 min)
d Christopher Münch. *p* Ruth Charny, Christopher Münch. *sc* Christopher Münch. *ph* Rob Sweeney. *ed* Annette Davey, Dody Dorn. *pd* Melissa Frankel, Jody Asnes, Bryan Hodge. *cast* Jacqueline Bisset, Martha Plimpton, Nick Stahl, Amy Madigan, Frankie R Faison, Peggy Gormley, Seymour Cassel, Carmen Zapata.

● 'What if life's nothing but a shitload of missed chances?' wonders Frances (Bisset), a middle-aged woman trying to make sense of a rich, successful, tragic life after she's diagnosed with cancer. 'Hopes realised. People loving people,' counters the man she should have married (Cassel). 'A recognition of shared destiny. A willingness to move with things.' Münch's film is full of elegant conversations like this. It feels more like a literary novel than a movie. The subplot involving Plimpton as a lawyer trying to track down her natural mother – who put her up for adoption – also feels like a literary device. That said, Munch's rather awkward cerebral style is infinitely preferable to the tear-sodden melodrama Hollywood specialises in, and he gets a complex, beautifully honest performance out of Bisset. TCh

Slender Smile, A (Oru Cheru Punchiri)

(2000, Ind, 95 min)
d MT Vasudevan Nair. *p* Jisha John. *sc* MT Vasudevan Nair. *ph* Sunny Joseph. *ed* Beena Paul. *pd* Radhakrishnan Mangalath. *m* Johnson. *cast* Oduvil Unnikrishnan, Nirmal Srinivasan, Vignesh, PK Venukuttan Nair, Aliyar.

● The fecund landscape of Kerala is the backdrop to this gently paced yet accute celebration of marriage, place and human priorities. It's a warm, simple tale of an elderly couple in the ebb and flow of their days, resisting pressures to move them off their beloved farm to the city. Larger forces of urbanisation might be at work, but here they don't corrode the spirit. The gentle resistance of the pair is believably played and succeeds – sometimes poignantly – in conjuring an uncluttered way of life with much to recommend to anyone looking in from such a complex distance. GE

Sleuth

(1972, GB, 139 min)
d Joseph L Mankiewicz. *p* Morton Gottlieb. *sc* Anthony Shaffer. *ph* Oswald Morris. *ed* Richard Marden. *pd* Ken Adam. *m* John Addison. *cast* Laurence Olivier, Michael Caine.

● Although a previous TO reviewer's claim that this is closer to Borges than Agatha Christie is perhaps overstating the case, it must be said that Mankiewicz films Anthony Shaffer's two-hander play – about a thriller writer's attempts to play lethal games with his wife's lover – with admirable style and intelligence. Less a whodunit than a howdunit, Shaffer's plot is labyrinthine enough to grip from start to finish, and the performances are superb; and while he never tries to open the action out, Mankiewicz explores his set with an amazing attention to detail and atmosphere, emphasising the twists and turns of the perverse power play at work. Thoroughly entertaining. GA

Sliding Doors

(1997, US/GB, 99 min)
d Peter Howitt. *p* Sydney Pollack, Philippa Braithwaite, William Horberg. *sc* Peter Howitt. *ph* Remi Adfarasin. *ed* John Smith. *pd* Maria Djurokovic. *m* David Hirschfelder. *cast* Gwyneth Paltrow, John Hannah, John Lynch, Jeanne Tripplehorn, Zara Turner, Douglas McFerran, Virginia McKenna.

● Helen (Paltrow) loses her high-powered PR job and returns unexpectedly to her London flat to find boyfriend Gerry (Lynch) in bed with his ex Lydia (Tripplehorn). Or she doesn't. In some alternate reality, Helen is delayed, arrives home a few minutes after Lydia has left, and remains in the dark about the affair. Meanwhile, the other Helen – the one who walked out – finds a new life and a new admirer, a real charmer, James (Hannah). While touching on such perennials as the nature of destiny, fate and self-determination, this is essentially a romantic comedy with a nifty gimmick. As such, it's entertaining and smart. Although writer/director Howitt botches the dramatic fulcrum – the point where Helen's twin fates diverge – he pulls off the more difficult task of keeping both scenarios in the air with ease. The actors are crucial, none more so than the wonderful Paltrow, whose impeccable English accent is so precise it's disconcerting. Howitt might have pushed her harder to distinguish between the two Helens (she lets her hairdo do the work), but then this isn't meant to change your life – that's just a happy side effect. TCh

Slight Case of Murder, A

(1938, US, 85 min, b/w)
d Lloyd Bacon. *sc* Earl Baldwin, Joseph Schrank. *ph* Sid Hickox. *ed* James Gibbon. *ad* Max Parker. *m* MK Jerome, Jack Scholl. *cast* Edward G Robinson, Jane Bryan, Allen Jenkins, Willard Parker, Ruth Donnelly, John Litel, Edward Brophy, Harold Huber, Bobby Jordan.

●This broad, acidic black comedy allows Edward G Robinson the opportunity to spoof his tough guy persona, as a beer baron who goes straight when Prohibition ends, only to find his fortune rapidly dwindling because his ale is unpalatable. Both accomplices and rivals naturally take a dim view of things, especially when his daughter (Bryan) starts dating a state trooper (Parker); and dastardly schemes are hatched to frame or fix him for good (notably by way of a stash of dead bodies, which have to be carefully redistributed, then re-collected when they prove to have a reward on their heads). The pace rises with the body count in this amusing version of a Damon Runyon/Howard Lindsay farce. Remade with Broderick Crawford in 1952 as *Stop, You're Killing Me*. TCh

Slight Case of Murder, A

(1999, US, 90 min)
d Steven Schachter. *p* Mitch Engel. *sc* William H Macy, Steven Schachter. *ph* André Pienaar. *ed* Paul Dixon. *pd* Dan Davis. *m* Mader. *cast* William H Macy, Adam Arkin, James Cromwell, Julia Campbell, Paul Mazursky, Felicity Huffman.

●'He Hitchcocks me, I'll Spielberg him,' confides Macy, Oliver Hardy-ing us with a sidelong look to camera. He plays a film critic (speciality: '40s *noir*) who accidentally kills a girlfriend and tries to cover it up.The cop on the case turns out to be an aspiring scriptwriter, with a wife bent on Lana Turner-ing every male on the scene. A blackmailing private eye (Cromwell) shows no sign of going to the movies much. It's moderately amusing, but while Macy and Schachter never stoop to gags, they gleefully Wes Craven us with this illustration/exploitation of the truism that 'everyone's a film buff now'. The most significant cross-reference is implicit, with Macy reprising his *Fargo* persona, brooding with schoolboy resentment as his misdeeds catch up with him. Made for cable TV, from Donald E Westlake's novel *A Travesty*. BBa

Slightly Pregnant Man, The (L'Evénement le plus Important depuis que l'Homme a Marché sur la Lune)

(1973, Fr/It, 95 min)
d Jacques Demy. *p* Raymond Danon. *sc* Jacques Demy. *ph* Andréas Winding. *ed* Anne-Marie Cotret. *ad* Bernard Evein. *m* Michel Legrand. *cast* Catherine Deneuve, Marcello Mastroianni, Micheline Presle, Marisa Pavan, Claude Melki, Michéle Moretti, Mireille Mathieu.

●Demy's usually feather-light touch deserts him with this clodhopping farce that hectically proceeds nowhere from a motive idea/image that only someone like Marco Ferreri should really have had: a pregnant Mastroianni, getting over morning sickness and into modelling 'paternity' clothes, before an inevitable anticlimax. A few limp forays into a philosophy of societal imbalance are belied by the overall stultifying air of comic convention. PT

Slightly Scarlet

(1956, US, 99 min)
d Allan Dwan. *p* Benedict Bogeaus. *sc* Robert Blees. *ph* John Alton. *ed* James Leicester. *ad* Van Nest Polglase. *m* Louis Forbes. *cast* John Payne, Rhonda Fleming, Arlene Dahl, Kent Taylor, Ted de Corsia, Lance Fuller.

●Based on a novel by James M Cain, this big-city corruption chronicle is a smart example of Dwan's '50s output, a *film noir* that just happens to be in colour and SuperScope. Gang leader Payne meeting his comeuppance when he tangles with sisters Fleming and Dahl, the former the mayor's innocent secretary, the latter a dangerous kleptomaniac. (Martin Scorsese, incidentally, has tipped his cap to Dwan and acknowledged him as an influence.) TJ

Sling Blade

(1996, US, 126 min)
d Billy Bob Thornton. *p* Brandon Rosser, David L Bushell. *sc* Billy Bob Thornton. *ph* Barry Markowitz. *ed* Hughes Winborne. *pd* Clark Hunter. *m* Daniel Lanois. *cast* Billy Bob Thornton, Dwight Yoakum, JT Walsh, John Ritter, Lucas Black, Natalie Canerday, Robert Duvall, James Hampton, Jim Jarmusch.

●Thornton made his mark as writer and actor in *One False Move*, and his directorial debut (from his own Oscar-winning script) is similarly impressive. He gives a magnificent, hugely credible performance as a retarded man who returns to his hometown in the Deep South after spending years in a psychiatric hospital for having murdered his mother as a child. When he befriends a young boy, his life takes a dramatic new turn. Tender but rarely sentimental, beautifully acted, and shot through with dark humour, this sensitive, insightful drama avoids the usual stereotypes to powerful effect. (And catch the lovely Jim Jarmusch cameo.) GA

Slingshot, The (Kådisbellan)

(1993, Swe, 102 min)
d Åke Sandgren. *p* Waldemar Bergendahl, Miro Vostiar. *sc* Åke Sandgren. *ph* Göran Nilsson. *ed* Grete Moldrup. *pd* Lasse Westfelt. *m* Björn Isfält. *cast* Jesper Salén, Stellan Skarsgård, Basia Frydman, Niclas Olund, Ernst-Hugo Järegård.

●It doesn't take long to realise that Jesper Salén's 12-year-old Roland is going to have a hard time in '20s Stockholm: daddy's a rampant socialist with a dodgy back; mum's an expatriate Russian (and Jewish); his schoolmaster is stern and handy with the cane. With suffering duly dispatched, it's time for the dash of eccentricity – to the lad's rescue comes a handy box of prophylactics, banned by the authorities but actively distributed by the welfare-conscious Red underground. A condom catapult earns Roland social acceptability – but also, eventually, a place in reform school. Given assured performances and a convincing, unshowy production job, these events proceed convincingly enough. It's just that the director plods through it all with the flattening style of a TV movie. TJ

Slipper and the Rose, The

(1976, GB, 146 min)
d Bryan Forbes. *p* Stuart Lyons. *sc* Bryan Forbes, Robert B Sherman, Richard M Sherman. *ph* Tony Imi. *ed* Timothy Gee. *pd* Ray Simm. *m* Richard M Sherman, Robert B Sherman. *cast* Richard Chamberlain, Gemma Craven, Annette Crosbie, Edith Evans, Christopher Gable, Michael Hordern, Margaret Lockwood, Kenneth More, Julian Orchard.

●A musical version of *Cinderella* that looked redundant before even leaving the starting-blocks. Despite all the critical plaudits (a misplaced patriotism?), it's top heavy, over-lavishly mounted, full of unmemorable songs in the Disney vein by Richard and Robert Sherman, and moves at a snail's pace. In a coasting cast, only Annette Crosbie as the harassed Fairy Godmother manages to alleviate the gloom.

Slipstream

(1989, GB, 102 min)
d Steven M Lisberger. *p* Gary Kurtz. *sc* Tony Kayden. *ph* Frank Tidy. *ed* Terry Rawlings. *pd* Andrew McAlpine. *m* Elmer Bernstein. *cast* Mark Hamill, Bob Peck, Bill Paxton, Kitty Aldridge, Eleanor David, Ben Kingsley, F Murray Abraham, Robbie Coltrane.

●Much of the exceptional aerial footage for this futuristic fantasy was shot, appropriately, in Turkey. The incomprehensible storyline concerns a purifying wind which swept the polluted planet clean, leaving a detritus of nomadic pilots and wind-worshippers. Star warrior Hamill is surprisingly hard-edged as the lawman trying to bring renegade robot Peck to justice. Perhaps hoping to compensate for the atrocious dialogue, Paxton overacts wildly as a bounty hunter with an eye on the reward. For some reason, they all end up in an isolated community of wind-worshipping hippies, whose watchword seems to be 'Go fly a kite', by which time you'll wish you had. Religious leader Kingsley dies under a millstone, and F Murray Abraham pops up as the leader of a bunch of decadent aristos holed up in an abandoned museum. Sentiment runs rampant near the end, when Peck's android falls for the film's only credible character (David). NF

Slither

(1973, US, 96 min)
d Howard Zieff. *p* Jack Sher. *sc* WD Richter. *ph* Laszlo Kovacs. *ed* David Bretherton. *ad* Dale Hennessy. *m* Tom McIntosh. *cast* James Caan, Peter Boyle, Sally Kellerman, Louise Lasser, Allen Garfield, Richard B Shull, Alex Rocco.

●The movie that virtually defines the term 'off-beat', in the very best sense of the word. Part thriller, part road movie, part heist caper, and part parody (most notably of *Duel*) Zieff's first and (along with *Hollywood Cowboy*) best film sees ex-con car thief Caan joining up with *recvee* (recreation vehicle, ie. caravan) fanatic Boyle and his wife Lasser in a search for an embezzled fortune, and getting into pretty nasty trouble en route. What makes the film so disarmingly enjoyable is its cool, dry sense of absurdity, and its unsentimental affection for the eccentric but definitely not wacky characters. It's a tale of ordinary people with extraordinary dreams and delusions, the sort of film that can conjure magical mayhem out of a caravan park bingo tournament. GA

Sliver

(1993, US, 108 min)
d Phillip Noyce. *p* Robert Evans. *sc* Joe Eszterhas. *ph* Vilmos Zsigmond. *ed* Richard Francis-Bruce, William Hoy. *pd* Paul Sylbert. *m* Howard Shore. *cast* Sharon Stone, William Baldwin, Tom Berenger, Polly Walker, Colleen Camp, Martin Landau, CCH Pounder.

●Stone looks distinctly ordinary in this glossy, glassy sex-thriller. She's an uptight book editor who moves into a fancy Manhattan high-rise (the sliver of the title). Neighbours include blocked crime novelist Berenger and smirking Baldwin. Both pursue her, but which is the blonde-fixated serial killer? If *Basic Instinct* played off *Vertigo*, Noyce's film would like to be a sort of sexed-up *Rear Window*. Here, however, voyeurism is not so much subtext as designer-look apparel trimmed with chic post-feminist accessories. Though based on an Ira Levin novel, the movie is essentially just another variation on Joe Eszterhas's rudimentary 'psychotic fuck' scenarios. TCh

Slogans

(2001, Albania/Fr, 90 min)
d Gjergj Xhuvani. *p* Pascal Judelewicz, Anne-Dominique Toussaint. *sc* Ylljet Aliçka, Yves Hanchar. *ph* Gerald Thiaville. *ed* Didier Ranz. *m* Denis Barbier. *cast* Artur Gorishti, Birce Hasko, Niko Kanxheri, Robert Ndrenika, Agim Qirjaqi, Luiza Xhuvani.

●'American Imperialism Is Only a Paper Tiger.' As slogans go, it's neither very catchy, nor very true. Worst of all, it's 36 letters long, which means hours of labour for Diana's class of kids, who have to spell out this Party propaganda in white stones across a hillside overlooking the village. We're in Albania, just a little over 20 years ago – it might feel like a different century, but those kids are still under 30 and apparently this was common practice. Comrade Andre, the new biology teacher, puts his pupils to work on 'Up with the Revolutionary Spirit', and is surprised they're impressed by its brevity. Andre has a lot to learn about the way slogans influence life in this rural backwater. Xhuvani's film of Ylljet Aliçka's novel *The Stones Slogans* is vaguely reminiscent of recent Loach-lite proletarian comedies (*Brassed Off*, *The Full Monty*) and, more specifically, of those wry Eastern European satires which occasionally slipped through the Iron Curtain in the late '60s. Dry and rueful rather than bitter and angry, the film still adds up to a devastating critique of the Enver Hoxha regime. Local Party apparatchiks exploit their position to blackmail citizens for sexual favours and punish personal enemies with public humiliation. Meanwhile, the kids accept their lot with impassive resignation. Remember: 'The Worst Enemy Is the Forgotten One.' TCh

Slow Attack (Endstation Freiheit)

(1980, WGer, 112 min)
d Reinhard Hauff. *p* Eberhardt Junkersdorf, Dieter Schidor. *sc* Burkhard Driest. *ph* Frank Bruhne. *ed* Peter Pryzgodda, Barbara von Weitershausen. *m* Irm Schmidt. *cast* Burkhard Driest, Rolf Zacher, Katja Rupé, Carla Egerer, Kurt Raab.

●In which art (violent criminal fresh out of jail writes a book about a kidnapping) mirrors crime (his doomed partner carries out the job for real). The irony inherent in the plot's development is horribly overstated in the climax, but more disturbing is the lack of distance established by Hauff from the protagonist's macho problems.

Gays and women versus leather jacket and cratered face results in a thriller with possibly 'limited appeal'. SJ

Slow Dancing in the Big City

(1978, US, 110 min)
d John G Avildsen. *p* Michael Levee, John G Avildsen. *sc* Barra Grant. *ph* Ralf D Bode. *ed* John G Avildsen. *ad* Henry M Shrady. *m* Bill Conti. *cast* Paul Sorvino, Anne Ditchburn, Nicolas Coster, Anita Dangler, Hector Jaime Mercado.

●'New York is a people place… and ultimately, *Slow Dancing in the Big City* is a people movie'. The mawkishness of this snippet from the movie's PR belies a curiously offbeat film, in which sentimentality for once seems more deliberate than accidental, with Sorvino playing a chubby New York news columnist who, while simultaneously trying to rescue an eight-year-old Puerto Rican drug addict, falls in lurv with divine (but actually rather wooden) ballet dancer Anne Ditchburn, who is struggling against a physical affliction that will eventually put an end to her dancing. Avildsen's career has a certain wavering integrity to it (from *Save the Tiger* to *Rocky*) which mixes gently left-of-Hollywood-centre politics with an unfortunate degree of righteousness. Which is why this one is, in the end, a failure, with its socially conscientious plot too episodic, and its kids (as always) too cute by half. Audiences will simply go to town on the finale: the journalist's street waif hits a heroin overdose, and his beloved collapses, crippled for life, after a triumphant final performance. CA

Slow Motion

see Sauve Qui Peut – la Vie

Slow Moves

(1983, US, 93 min)
d Jon Jost. *cast* Roxanne Rogers, Marshall Gaddis, Debbie Krant, Barbara Hammes, Geoffrey Rotwein.

●Jost has supplied his audience with plenty of reasons for avoiding this film. He freely admits that its characters make a pair of Mike Leigh marrieds look like *Fun with Dick and Jane*, and that the usual narrative trappings – backgrounds, personalities, events, causality – are obscured, that the film parts with its secrets only grudgingly. But with that established, it becomes a fascinating, oddly gripping, and often visually stunning film. It's not unlike a Peter Greenaway mystery translated to the dry, dusty heartland of Malick's *Badlands*, although here the emphasis is on spiritual paralysis rather than Greenaway's elegant intellectual conceits. It does have a similar wit – sly games with camera angles, image, dialogue and cliché – but unravelling them yourself is half what the movie is about. Jost's story of two charmless no-hopers, drifting through life without reason or direction, might sound like pure valium, but the gradual seepage of narrative turns it into all manner of movies. JG

Slumber Party '57

(1976, US, 88 min)
d William A Levey. *p* John Ireland Jr. *sc* Frank Farmer. *ph* Bob Caramico. *ed* Bill Casper. *ad* Ed Bash. *m* Miles Goodman. *cast* Janet Wood, Debra Winger, Rainbeaux Smith, Noelle North, Bridget Holloman, Mary Ann Appleseth, Rafael Campos, Will Hutchins.

●A film for those for whom the spoken bits of Shangri-La's tracks strike a special chord. Six high school girls decide to have a slumber party, and clad in baby-doll shorty pyjamas they swap stories about their romances ('Did you really go all the way?'). The characters of the girls are nicely contrasted, and signs of the times are inserted into the dialogue like neon billboards ('Hey, give me back my hula hoop!'). As an exercise in nostalgia it never attempts the solidity of *American Graffiti*, but its lack of pretension and soundtrack backing of key tracks from the period (Paul and Paula, Big Bopper, Jerry Lee Lewis) make it rather winning entertainment. VG

Slumber Party Massacre, The

(1982, US, 84 min)
d/p Amy Jones. *sc* Rita Mae Brown. *ph* Steve Posey. *ed* Sean Foley. *ad* Francesca Bartoccini. *m* Ralph Jones. *cast* Michele Michaels, Robin Stille, Michael Villela, Debra DeLiso, Andree Honore, Gina Mari.

●Amy Jones, an editor without much of a track record, talked her way on to the picture by providing Roger Corman with a sample reel at her own expense, a very Corman-like strategy. Despite the unlikely script credit for Rita Mae Brown, Jones's debut feature is little more than a *Halloween* clone, reliant on buckets of blood and sudden surprise rather than suspense. As the title subtly hints, sleep-over cuties fall victim to malicious prankster boyfriends and the usual psycho with a power tool. The movie is in and out in less than 90 minutes, made a stack of money, spawned rip-offs of its own, and Jones was rewarded with *Love Letters* the following year. DO

Slums of Beverly Hills

(1998, US, 91 min)
d Tamara Jenkins. *p* Michael Nozik, Stan Wlodkowski. *sc* Tamara Jenkins. *ph* Tom Richmond. *ed* Pamela Martin. *pd* Dena Roth. *m* Rolfe Kent. *cast* Alan Arkin, Natasha Lyonne, Kevin Corrigan, Jessica Walter, Rita Moreno, David Krumholtz, Carl Reiner, Marisa Tomei.

●A small film with plenty of incidental pleasures, writer/director Jenkins' debut feature puts a winning new spin on the adolescent comedy-drama. Told from the point of view of gawky, pubescent Vivian (Lyonne), it follows the peripatetic Abramowitch family as they motor around the low-rent quarters of Beverly Hills in their car salesman father's gas guzzler, often having packed in a mad rush before the landlord descends. Everybody has their problems: for Dad (Arkin), time and money are clearly running out fast; his wise cracking son Ben (Krumholtz) is finding it hard gaining his first start as an actor; younger son Rickey can't get a word in; and Vivian is finding puberty a matter of consternation. When wacky neighbour Eliot (Corrigan) starts making overtures, and ditzy rehabilitating druggie Rita (Tomei), intent on a new career as a nurse, joins the family and starts proffering Vivian her vibrator, you wonder what could happen next. Jenkins does well in toning down the usual schtick and schmaltz associated with the bitter-sweet Jewish family comedy, and re-invigorating the dialogue with a winning forthrightness. Furthermore, the ambling road movie atmosphere allows space for the film to explore, with affectionate detail, life from the lower end of the social scale. WH

Small Back Room, The

(1948, GB, 108 min, b/w)
d/p/sc Michael Powell, Emeric Pressburger. *ph* Christopher Challis. *ed* Clifford Turner. *pd* Hein Heckroth. *m* Brian Easdale. *cast* David Farrar, Kathleen Byron, Jack Hawkins, Leslie Banks, Michael Gough, Cyril Cusack, Milton Rosmer, Walter Fitzgerald, Renée Asherson, Robert Morley.

●Powell made *The Small Back Room* just after *The Red Shoes*, and was clearly looking for a 'homely', manageable subject after the lavish ambitions of the earlier film. He found it in Nigel Balchin's novel about a military bomb-disposal wizard, and turned in a thriller that would look like a masterpiece in the filmographies of most British directors. But it rests on a not-very-interesting dramatic idea: a man whose private life is in ruins (he's lost a foot in a bomb blast, is having trouble with his girlfriend, and is becoming alcoholic) gets new drive from the challenge of mastering a new kind of German bomb. And Powell's characteristic desire to ornament leads to the inclusion of some bizarre fantasy footage (when the hero suffers DTs) which simply doesn't belong in this context. It remains extremely tense in a workmanlike way, and full of good visual and syntactic ideas… but it's a fair way short of Powell's best. TR

Small Change

see Argent de Poche, L'

Smallest Show on Earth, The

(1957, GB, 81 min, b/w)
d Basil Dearden. *p* Michael Relph. *sc* William Rose, John Eldridge. *ph* Douglas Slocombe. *ed* Oswald Hafenrichter. *ad* Alan Harris. *m* William Alwyn. *cast* Bill Travers, Virginia McKenna, Peter Sellers, Margaret Rutherford, Bernard Miles, Leslie Phillips, Sidney James.

●A delightfully eccentric comedy, with Travers and McKenna inheriting a fleapit cinema called The Bijou, and fighting a takeover by the owners of The Grand, which 'conveniently' burns down. An Ealing-style allegory of English resolve, scripted by William Rose and John Eldridge, it's memorable chiefly for Sellers' drunken old projectionist, clinging to his machines whenever a train goes by, and Rutherford's belligerent cashier. ATu

Small Faces

(1995, GB, 108 min)
d Gillies MacKinnon. *p* Bill MacKinnon, Steve Clark-Hall. *sc* Gillies MacKinnon, Bill MacKinnon. *ph* John de Borman. *ed* Scott Thomas. *pd* Zoë MacLeod. *m* John Keane. *cast* Ian Robertson, JS Duffy, Joseph McFadden, Clare Higgins, Laura Fraser, Kevin McKidd, Mark McConnochie.

●Glasgow, 1968: time for the Maclean brothers to decide where their loyalties and ambitions lie. The eldest, Bobby (Duffy), misses his dead dad, suffers nightmares, and hangs out with a local gang; Alan (McFadden) devotes his time to painting and Joanne (Fraser), an uncommonly self-assured lass, known to have attracted the jealous attentions of various neighborhood hardnuts; while Lex (Robertson), a feisty 13-year-old, is not only torn between the lifestyles of his brothers, but is facing pressure from the hoodlum tribes who engage in battle in and around the estates. Small wonder the boys' mother (Higgins) is often at her wits' end. It's hard to pin down exactly why Gilles MacKinnon's quasi-autobiographical rites-of-passage movie, co-written with his producer brother Billy, is so satisfying. As ever there's an unflashy visual intelligence at work, and again MacKinnon proves an expert director of actors. But what perhaps best distinguishes the film is its unsentimental honesty: everything – from the bloody rumbles between rival gangs to the mysteries of courtship, from anxieties over the precise intentions of a visiting uncle to Alan's anti-Americanism and Lex's first alcoholic binge – seems somehow absolutely right. A gem. GA

Small Soldiers

(1998, US, 110 min)
d Joe Dante. *p* Michael Finnell, Colin Wilson. *sc* Gavin Scott, Adam Rifkin, Ted Elliott, Terry Rossio. *ph* Jamie Anderson. *ed* Marshall Harvey, Michael Thau. *pd* William Sandell. *m* Jerry Goldsmith. *cast* Kirsten Dunst, Gregory Smith, Jay Mohr, Phil Hartman, Kevin Dunn, Denis Leary, Frank Langella.

●This gung-ho kids' flick blends live action with computer-generated imagery to arrive at *Toy Story* with a body count – a marketing coup so callous the film has to perform comic somersaults to accommodate it. Hence, we have your friendly, old-fashioned toy manufacturer taken over by a ruthless corporate speculator (Leary), whose big idea is GI Joe with killer computer chips and an enemy alien species pre-programmed to lose. When prototypes for the Commando Elite cut loose in a small suburban town, the only thing standing between the passive Gorgonites and premature extinction is new boy in school Alan (Smith) and his admirably feisty neighbour Christy (Dunst). Dante set the template for this kind of story with *Gremlins*. This is much scrappier and more juvenile, though it's sometimes hard to tell if the target audience is under ten or over 30, given the plethora of cinephile in-jokes and satiric sideswipes. TCh

Smalltime

(1996, GB, 61 min)
d/p/sc Shane Meadows. *ph* Helene Whitehall. John Arnold. *ed* David Wilson. *m* Gavin Clarke. *cast* Mat Hand, Dena Smiles, Shane Meadows, Gena Kawecka, Jimmy Hynd.

●Sneinton, a suburb of Nottingham: Should Malc (Hand) carry on a dud life of petty crime with his boozing pals, or clean up his act, as his wife Kate (Smiles) insists? It's a tough choice, influenced not only by questions of cash and camaraderie, but by the fact that Jumbo (writer/director Meadows in memorably terrible wig) seems bent on wrecking any relationship Malc tries to establish outside their gang. Shot on video for a pittance, *Smalltime* may be rough and ready, but the title belies its big heart and acute perceptions. Though often very funny, this proudly parochial fable never opts for knowing caricature: the authenticity of these lives, defined by a shell-suited, Lambrusco-glugging lack of sophistication and unthinking laddishness, still allows for unsentimental affection and the odd serious insight. GA

Small Time

(1990, US, 90 min)
d/p/sc Norman Loftis. *ph* Michael C Miller. *ed* Marc Cohen. *pd* Nancy Evangelista. *m* Arnold Bieber. *cast* Richard Barbozo, Carolyn Kinebrew, Scott Ferguson.
● An impressive low-budgeter, dealing with the hard life and times of Vince, an ineffectual young New York hood, Loftis' film uses a mix of dramatic vignettes, location vérité, and staged vox-pop 'witness' interviews to create a picture of a two-time loser dwarfed by circumstances he can't begin to comprehend. Occasionally, the film reveals a street theatre staginess, letting its dramatic flow get swamped under a slightly antiseptic, at times teacherly, tone. But as a sympathetic portrait of a thoroughly unsympathetic protagonist, *Small Time* is impressively tough, capturing the pulse of the small-time life, without for a minute glamorising it. JRo

Small Time Crooks

(2000, US, 95 min)
d Woody Allen. *p* Jean Doumanian. *sc* Woody Allen. *ph* Zhao Fei. *ed* Alisa Lepselter. *pd* Santo Loquasto. *cast* Woody Allen, Tony Darrow, Hugh Grant, George Grizzard, Jon Lovitz, Elaine May, Michael Rapaport, Elaine Stritch, Tracey Ullman.
● Unusually broad but often very amusing, Allen comedy in which he plays against type as a none too bright petty thief, who leads a gang of dim lowlifes in a plot to tunnel into a jeweller's from a neighbouring property disguised as his wife's cookie store. Inevitably, the heist fails, but the cookies take off, bringing belated fame and fortune to Allen, wife Ullman and the rest of the team. So far, so funny, but once Ullman, keen to (im)prove herself as a culture vulture, begins neglecting unambitious spouse in favour of art collector Grant, the plot becomes rather more predictable and, regrettably, moralistic. Even this late, however, Elaine May's performance as a near moronic cousin continues to delight. GA

Small Time Obsession

(2000, GB, 119 min)
d/p/sc Piotr Szkopiak. *ph* Niels Reedtz Johansen. *ed* Piotr Szkopiak. *pd* Vince Raj. *m* Martin Bell. *cast* Alex King, Juliette Caton, Jason Merrells, Oliver Young, Richard Banks, Kirsten Parker, Geoff Lawson, Giles Ward.
● Set within the expatriate Polish community of S London, Szkopiak's first feature was made with determination, if little else. Childhood friends fall out when petty crimes go awry. Michael (King, sullen and brooding) is obsessed with his greyhound Bullitt and his best friend's girl (Caton). The girl's other half Chris (Merrells) is a wideboy with ambitions to move up the criminal food chain. But Michael has other ideas, alienating not only Chris but, it seems, half the capital's gangster fraternity. WI

Smalltime Thief (Le Petit Voleur)

(1999, Fr, 65 min)
d Erick Zonca. *p* Gilles Sandoz. *sc* Erick Zonca, Virginie Wagon. *ph* Pierre Milon. *ed* Jean-Robert Thomann. *pd* Kristina Zonca. *cast* Nicolas Duvauchelle, Yann Trégouet, Jean-Jérôme Esposito, Martial Bezot, Jean-Armand Dalomba, Joe Prestia, Ingrid Preynat, Véronique Balme.
● Made for TV, Zonca's follow-up to *Dream Life of Angels* is a taut and insightful account of the steady, self-destructive slide into crime of a bakery assistant who, once fired, swears revenge on society. Pacy, grainy realism is the order of the day. Until the final 20 minutes, the film lacks the depth of its predecessor, but there's no denying the power of the acting (Duvauchelle's near-wordless lead turn is particularly impressive) or the authenticity of its observations. At first, it may seem as if Zonca is overly indulgent of the macho posturings of the hoodlums the protagonist falls in with, but with time it's clear there's no sentimentality here about 'thieves' honour' and the like. Bracingly tough. GA

Small Wonders

(1995, US, 77 min)
d Allan Miller. *p* Susan Kaplan. *ph* Kramer Morgenthau. *ed* Alan Miller, Donald George Klocek. *with* Roberta Guaspari-Tzavaras, Itzhak Perlman, Isaac Stern, Midori, Arnold Steinhardt, Mark O'Connor.
● The East Harlem Violin Program and its moving force, tutor Roberta Guaspari-Tzavaras, are the subject of this rousing musical documentary which shows the forging of perspiration and inspiration in her multi-ethnic primary school charges. The junior violinists make their way from the elementary exercises to the annual parents' night – and a Carnegie Hall all-star fundraiser. TJ

Smash Palace

(1981, NZ, 108 min)
d/p/sc Roger Donaldson. *ph* Graeme Cowley. *ed* Michael Horton. *ad* Reston Griffiths. *m* Sharon O'Neill. *cast* Bruno Lawrence, Anna Jemison, Keith Aberdein, Greer Robson, Desmond Kelly, Lynne Robson.
● This turkey treads similar ground to Mike Newell's *Bad Blood* (middle-aged New Zealander cracks up and is forced into the role of outlaw). But while Newell constructed a web of social, communal and familial tensions, Donaldson wallows in male menopausal *angst* via dumbly overstated symbols. Thus the hero runs a wrecked car dump (his marriage is failing), but is building a racing car (he clings to a relationship with his daughter, whom he eventually kidnaps). Get the connections? Instantly forgettable. SJ

Smash-Up, The Story of a Woman

(1946, US, 103 min, b/w)
d Stuart Heisler. *p* Walter Wanger. *sc* John Howard Lawson. *ph* Stanley Cortez. *ed* Milton Carruth. *ad* Alexander Golitzen. *m* Daniele Amfitheatrof. *cast* Susan Hayward, Lee Bowman, Eddie Albert, Marsha Hunt, Carl Esmond.
● Hayward hits the skids with a flourish in the kind of showy role Bette Davis or Joan Crawford might have made even more of. As husband Bowman's crooning career hits the big time, her liquor bill makes it big too, before a burning orphanage takes a bow in the finale and schematic redemption is the order of the day. It makes you smile to think that the alcoholic misanthrope Dorothy Parker had a hand in the script. TJ

Smell of Camphor, Fragrance of Jasmine (Booye Kafoor, Atre Yas)

(2000, Iran, 93 min)
d Bahman Farmanara. *p* Morteza Shayeste. *sc* Bahman Farmanara. *ph* Mahmoud Kalari. *ed* Abbas Ganjavi. *pd* Zhila Mehrjoui. *m* Ahmed Pezhman. *cast* Bahman Farmanara, Roya Nonahali, Reza Kianian, Valiyallah Shirandami, Parivash Nazarieh, Hossein Kasbian, Mahtaj Nojoomi.
● This semi-autobiographical examination of mortality, political pressure and social ritual offers further evidence if Iranian cinema's refelxivity. Writer/director Farmanara takes the lead as a hangdog depressive director banned from shooting for two decades. Deciding to film his own funeral – his heart's not too reliable – he soon gets caught in a web of fiction/reality narratives involving assassinated intellectuals, dead babies on car seats and talking birds. Some striking images of isolation and abandonment, a clear love of nature and an elegiac sense of lost time all help. It's drily humorous too – Nanni Moretti-style – and clearly sincere, but the three-act structure sometimes drags and the tone is uneven. GE

Smile

(1974, US, 113 min)
d/p Michael Ritchie. *sc* Jerry Belson. *ph* Conrad Hall. *ed* Richard A Harris. *m* Daniel Osborn. *cast* Bruce Dern, Barbara Feldon, Michael Kidd, Geoffrey Lewis, Nicholas Pryor, Colleen Camp, Annette O'Toole, Melanie Griffith.
● A gentle, sometimes sharp look at small-town American life via the build-up to Santa Rosa's *Young American Miss* competition, a meat market underlining the community's obsession with appearances, its self-deception and complacency. At its centre, the film is concerned with the lack of intercourse, both social and private, between men and women, and how institutions like the *Young American Miss* reinforce the sexes' suspicions of each other. Perhaps a more caustic picture was intended, but the film grows to like its characters, and the final result is amusingly indulgent and generous in a way few current American films are: one has to look to East Europe (especially the work of Milos Forman) for a similar quality of ironic compassion. CPe

Smile Orange

(1974, Jam, 88 min)
d Trevor D Rhone. *p* Eddie Knight. *sc* Trevor D Rhone, David Ogden. *ph* David McDonald. *ed* Joseph Staton. *m* Melba Liston, Trevor D Rhone. *cast* Carl Bradshaw, Glen Morrison, Vaughan Crosskill, Robin Sweeney, Stanley Irons.
● Where Trevor Rhone's script for *The Harder They Come* relocated Hollywood B movie conventions in a specifically Jamaican context, his first film as director does much the same with the stock material of British comedy. From this he's crafted a genuinely hilarious politicised farce; a satire on tourism that centres on hotel waiter Ringo Smith's efforts to exploit the exploiters. One long, two-handed scene exemplifies the balance Rhone achieves, when Ringo (Bradshaw) takes a raw busboy in hand, informs him that 'any black man that can't play a part's gonna starve to death', and proceeds first to teach him waiting etiquette, then how to screw white tourists, literally and figuratively. The Mocho Beach Hotel, main locale of this anarchic entertainment, has inevitably been characterised as a Jamaican *Fawlty Towers*, but it's hard to imagine even Basil rigging a crab race! Black joy indeed, from which a few technical rough ends detract nothing. PT

Smiles of a Summer Night (Sommarnattens Leende)

(1955, Swe, 110 min, b/w)
d/sc Ingmar Bergman. *ph* Gunnar Fischer. *ed* Oscar Rosander. *ad* PA Lundgren. *m* Erik Nordgren. *cast* Eva Dahlbeck, Ulla Jacobsson, Harriet Andersson, Margit Carlqvist, Gunnar Björnstrand, Jarl Kulle, Ake Fridell, Björn Bjelvenstam, Naima Wifstrand, Bibi Andersson.
● Bergman's first major success, inspiration for both Stephen Sondheim's *A Little Night Music* and Woody Allen's *A Midsummer Night's Sex Comedy*, this enchanting comedy of manners assembles a team of couples, ex-couples and would-be couples, and puts them through their paces in a game of love at a country house party during one heady midsummer weekend in 1900. Ruthless towards its characters' amorous pretensions, but extending a kind of ironic tenderness when they get hoist with their own petards, it is a wonderfully funny, genuinely erotic, and quite superbly acted *rondo* of love. Dig too deeply and it disintegrates, but its facade – decked out in elegant turn-of-the-century settings and costumes – has a magical, shimmering beauty. TM

Smiling Ghost, The

(1941, US, 71 min, b/w)
d Lewis Seiler. *sc* Kenneth Gamet, Stuart Palmer. *ph* Arthur Todd. *ed* Jack Killifer. *ad* Hugh Reticker. *cast* Wayne Morris, Brenda Marshall, Alexis Smith, Alan Hale, Lee Patrick, David Bruce, Willie Best, Richard Ainley.
● Very much the *Cat and the Canary* formula, set in an old dark house with the wisecracks flying and the secret panels flapping, while Willie Best provides his usual study in knock-kneed terror. Cheaply made but moderately amusing/exciting, thanks largely to the accomplished cast, with Smith as the heiress whose three previous fiancés have come to grisly grief, Morris as the young man hired for bait, Hale as the bumbling detective, and Marshall as the intrepid girl reporter determined to fathom the mystery. TM

Smiling Madame Beudet, The

see Souriante Madame Beudet, La

Smilla's Feeling for Snow (Fräulein Smillas Gespür für Schnee/aka Smilla's Sense of Snow)

(1996, Ger/Den/Swe, 122 min)
d Bille August. *p* Bernd Eichinger, Martin Moszkowicz. *sc* Ann Biderman. *ph* Jörgen Persson. *ed* Janus Billeskov-Jansen. *pd* Anna Asp. *m* Harry Gregson-Williams, Hans Zimmer. *cast* Julia Ormond, Gabriel Byrne, Richard Harris, Robert Loggia, Mario Adorf, Bob Peck, Jim Broadbent, Tom Wilkinson, Vanessa Redgrave.

●This intellectual thriller, adapted from Peter Høeg's best-seller, is dominated by Ormond's frosty heroine, half-American, half-Greenlander, who tries tenaciously to unravel the mysterious death of six-year-old Isaiah, son of an alcoholic Greenlander neighbour. Helped only by another neighbour, the enigmatic Engineer (Byrne), Smilla pursues cryptic clues and interrogates frightened witnesses. Could there be a link between Isaiah's rooftop fall and the death of the boy's father some years earlier in a hushed-up mining accident? The ensuing quest takes Smilla from Copenhagen to Greenland, where her Inuit skills come into their own. The strength of the novel lay chiefly in the Copenhagen scenes, where an interplay of skilfully drawn characters established a narrative enigma and an authentic sense of pinched, alienated lives. The same is true of the film, by Høeg's Danish compatriot Bille August: the first half benefits from the foursquare contributions of Redgrave, Broadbent and Wilkinson, but thereafter it ploughs like an ice-breaker on a suicide mission. Our involvement, however, melts once Smilla and the others board the rusting Russian ship 'Kronos' and set sail for the preposterous anti-climax. NF

Smithereens

(1982, US, 93 min)
d/p Susan Seidelman. *sc* Ron Nyswaner, Peter Askin. *ph* Chirine El Khadem. *ed* Susan Seidelman. *pd* Franz Harland. *m* Glenn Mercer, Bill Million. *cast* Susan Berman, Brad Rinn, Richard Hell, Nada Despotovich, Roger Jett, Kitty Summerall.

●Wren (Berman) is a working class girl from the wrong side of the Hudson River, come to Manhattan to take her peck at the big, bad apple. Equipped with little more than a talent for self-promotion, she plays the peacock in her bright punk plumage, chasing a dream of rock'n'roll fame and fortune amid the lotus eaters of the Lower East Side. This debut feature from Seidelman (ex-New York Film School) may be small and unambitious, but its old tale of the little girl lost in the city is told with energy and verve. Seidelman's sure feeling for the squalor and glamour of urban decay, and her speedy, stylish editing, combine with a pulsating soundtrack from The Feelies to create a febrile sense of Lower Manhattan street life: fast living on a permanent adrenalin high. SJo

Smoke

(1995, US, 108 min)
d Wayne Wang. *p* Greg Johnson, Peter Newman, Hisami Kuriowa, Kenzo Hurikoshi. *sc* Paul Auster. *ph* Adam Holender. *ed* Maysie Hoy. *pd* Kalina Ivanov. *m* Rachel Portman. *cast* Harvey Keitel, William Hurt, Forest Whitaker, Stockard Channing, Harold Perrineau, Clarice Taylor, Jared Harris.

●Wang's full atonement for the melodramatic excesses of *The Joy Luck Club* is a collaboration with the novelist Paul Auster, who contributes his first original screenplay. Five main characters, each with his or her own quirk or problem, find their lives criss-crossing over a few days in 1990 in and around Brooklyn, in ways that leave all of them changed for the better. Keitel's tobacco-store manager, serving as the neighbourhood sage and grieving over a stash of Cuban cigars ruined in a plumbing accident, is the most colourful; Whitaker's failed father and husband, presiding over a run-down garage, the most touching. The precision of the plotting and execution sometimes seems a shade over-calculated, but the sheer warmth of the performances (and the spirit behind them) carries the film through to its extremely cheering finale. TR

Smoke Signal

(1955, US, 88 min)
d Jerry Hopper. *p* Howard Christie. *sc* George F Slavin, George W George. *ph* Clifford Stine. *ed* Milton Carruth. *ad* Alexander Golitzen, Richard Riedel. *m* Joseph Gershenson. *cast* Dana Andrews, Piper Laurie, William Talman, Rex Reason, Douglas Spencer, Milburn Stone, Robert J Wilke.

●This is an interesting one for any student delving into Hollywood's iconography of the Indian nations. The heavies are the Utes – we don't often come across Utes – while the Apaches, for a change, are characterised as peacemakers. The movie is a pre-make, so to speak, of the better-known *The Last Wagon*, with a despised 'Indian lover' prisoner again proving the deliverance of a mixed band of whites. This journey to safety is by water: locations were shot on the Grand Canyon stretch of the Colorado River, so the film is appealing to look at even when it flags dramatically. Casting is conventional, but Douglas Spencer (the gangling reporter in Hawks' *The Thing*) has a good part as a friendly trapper. BBa

Smoke Signals

(1998, US, 89 min)
d Chris Eyre. *p* Scott Rosenfelt, Larry Estes. *sc* Sherman Alexie. *ph* Brian Capener. *ed* Brian Berdan. *pd* Charles Armstrong. *m* BC Smith.*cast* Adam Beach, Evan Adams, Irene Bedard, Gary Farmer, Tantoo Cardinal, Cody Lightning, Simon Baker, Monica Mojica, John Trudell.

●The first feature made wholly by native Americans isn't quite what you'd expect. About two argumentative friends who leave their Idaho reservation to go check out the pathetic trailer park estate left by the late, estranged father of one of them, the film deals with history, social injustice, crisis of identity, poverty and other pertinent issues. But it does so in a delightfully witty, offbeat way that simultaneously sends up and celebrates supposedly typical aspects of Indian culture. The gags, visual and verbal, generally hit the spot, including a nice dig at *Dances with Wolves*. The film looks terrific, the 'mythic/mystical storytelling' bit is handled with just the right amount of tongue in cheek, and the performances are very engaging. Original, audacious, entertaining, and an all-round impressive debut. GA

Smokey and the Bandit

(1977, US, 97 min)
d Hal Needham. *p* Mort Engelberg. *sc* James Lee Barrett, Charles Shyer, Alan Mandel. *ph* Bobby Byrne. *ed* Walter Hannemann, Angelo Ross. *ad* Mark Mansbridge. *m* Bill Justis, Jerry Reed, Dick Feller. *cast* Burt Reynolds, Sally Field, Jerry Reed, Jackie Gleason, Mike Henry, Pat McCormick, Paul Williams.

●The first of the 'Citizens Band' movies to reach Britain. Despite a thin premise for an action-comedy road chase, the film's enthusiasm makes up for its lack of ideas. Reynolds and Reed accept a bet to ship an illegal lorry-load of beer back to Georgia, getting involved with Field (a chorine running from marriage to the sheriff's dim son) along the way. The direction, by a former stuntman, concentrates on the action and happily leaves everyone to their own devices, with almost nothing to do. Field shows what natural acting is all about, and Reynolds' send-ups of himself are, despite repetition, becoming more likeable. Here his kidding around is exactly in tune with this fast-moving but essentially lazy vehicle. CPe

Smokey and the Bandit II (aka Smokey and the Bandit Ride Again)

(1980, US, 104 min)
d Hal Needham. *p* Hank Moonjean. *sc* Jerry Belson, Brock Yates. *ph* Michael Butler. *ed* Donn Cambern, William Gordean. *pd* Henry Bumstead. *m* Snuff Garrett. *cast* Burt Reynolds, Jackie Gleason, Jerry Reed, Dom DeLuise, Sally Field, Paul Williams, Pat McCormick, David Huddleston, Mike Henry.

●Three years after *Smokey and the Bandit* took the hard-drinking, fast-driving, trickster ethos of the American redneck into the big box-office league, Reynolds has proved he 'just does what he does best: show off'. This reunites the hit team round Reynolds as the self-mocking, loveable sonofabitch who, this time, goes on the road with a cargo of an elephant, hotly pursued by overweight cop Gleason and his dumb son. Alternating exquisitely timed gags with stunts, and going for broke with a massive demolition derby, means there's little to grouse about. From the start, when Reynolds surfaces from behind a mountain of empty beer cans, you know what's in store – a lightweight chase caper that Reynolds must truly be sick of by now, but which he has elevated into something impossible to dislike. DMacp

Smoking/No Smoking

(1993, Fr, [*Smoking*] 146 min/[*No Smoking*] 147 min)
d Alain Resnais. *sc* Alan Ayckbourn. *ph* Renato Berta. *ed* Albert Jurgenson. *pd* Jacques Saulnier. *m* John Pattison. *cast* Sabine Azéma, Pierre Arditi.

●Resnais's double-barrelled screen version of Alan Ayckbourn's expansive stage cycle *Intimate Exchanges* immediately hits the stumbling block of language. Here are the emotionally stunted denizens of the English middle class; yet what we hear is the vernacular French of Azéma and Arditi grandstanding in five roles apiece. In short, if you're expecting a BBC-style adaptation, almost everything about these films will seem fake – which is precisely what makes them so captivating. Once you get used to dialogue in translation and the cartoonish view of Little England, what's on offer is a disarming, impish delight in storytelling. Each piece proceeds to travesty dysfunctional marriages and illusory dreams of escape before fanning out in a series of alternative destinies for its variably articulate protagonists. When the films are seen singly, the overriding concept is clear enough. Viewed in tandem, their criss-crossing content provides all sorts of contextual pay-offs. There are miscalculations in some of the broader comedy, and *No Smoking* is probably the more entertaining of the two, but this is Ayckbourn gone Cubist, and that you have to see. TJ

Smoky

(1946, US, 87 min)
d Louis King. *p* Robert Bassler. *sc* Dwight Cummings, Lillie Hayward, Dorothy Yost. *ph* Charles Clarke. *ed* Nick De Maggio. *ad* Lyle Wheeler, Chester Gore. *m* David Raksin. *cast* Fred MacMurray, Anne Baxter, Burl Ives, Bruce Cabot, Esther Dale, Roy Roberts.

●Technicolor Fox Western from a novel by Will James: MacMurray's the cowboy, Baxter the Nebraska ranch owner he works for, but the real star's Smoky, one of those Western wonder horses who seems considerably more intelligent than any of its riders. GM

Smooth Talk

(1985, US, 91 min)
d Joyce Chopra. *p* Martin Rosen. *sc* Tom Cole. *ph* James Glennon. *ed* Patrick Dodd. *pd* David Wasco. *m* Billy Payne, Russ Kunkel, George Massenburg. *cast* Treat Williams, Laura Dern, Mary Kay Place, Margaret Welch, Sarah Inglis, Levon Helm.

●Chopra's sympathetically observed study of a teenage girl trembling on the brink of womanhood is adapted from a short story by Joyce Carol Oates, and sometimes it shows. It begins, deceptively, like a standard 'coming of age' picture, with Laura Dern's gawky girlishness and tough relationship with her perplexed parents deftly sketched in. But Dern is left alone in the house, and the older, enigmatic Treat Williams drives up in his flashy convertible, his powerful physicality and cajoling seductiveness conjuring a more dangerously appealing sexuality. This central confrontation is a mesmerising set piece, but the allegorical subtleties (is this episode real, or merely a product of Dern's wishful imagining?) work better in a literary context. Here, as elsewhere, one senses that the images are being asked to carry rather more metaphorical weight than they are able to bear. NF

Smugglers

see Kung-Fu Gangbusters

Snake Eyes (aka Dangerous Game)

(1993, US, 107 min)
d Abel Ferrara. *p* Mary Kane. *sc* Nicholas St John. *ph* Ken Kelsch. *ed* Anthony Redman. *pd* Alex Tavoularis. *m* Joe Delia. *cast* Harvey Keitel, Madonna, James Russo, Nancy Ferrara.

●When he's in the mood no one digs deeper into the emotional gut than Abel Ferrara – like *Bad Lieutenant*, this is a gruelling experience. Many will find it alienating. Keitel is a director (his wife is Nancy Ferrara) making a movie about a couple breaking up – Madonna and Russo are the stars. There's inevitable confusion between reality and illusion, but the real subject here is the battle (or rather massacre) of the sexes. TCh

Snake Eyes

(1998, US, 98 min)
d/p Brian De Palma. *sc* David Koepp. *ph* Stephen H Burum. *ed* Bill Pankow. *pd* Anne Pritchard. *m* Ryuichi Sakamoto. *cast* Nicolas Cage, Gary Sinise, John Heard, Carla Gugino, Stan Shaw, Kevin Dunn, Michael Rispoli.

●De Palma's coldly executed techno-thriller opens with a signature sequence: a continuous Steadicam shot starts outside an Atlantic City sports arena, then snakes its way along corridors, up stairs and down an escalator, to reveal the packed crowd awaiting the start of a heavyweight boxing match. We're following flamboyant Rick Santoro (Cage), a corrupt cop who revels in the fact that he sees every angle. Inside, his old pal, Navy commander Kevin Dunne (Sinise), is keeping an eye on Secretary of Defence Kirkland, who has a ringside seat courtesy of arena owner and munitions tycoon Gilbert Powell (Heard). Minutes later, the odds-on favourite hits the canvas, a shot rings out, and Kirkland is fatally wounded. Santoro immediately seals the crowd inside the arena and, using TV and surveillance camera playback, scans the screens for clues as to the killer's identity. As Santoro interviews key witnesses, the film turns into *Rashomon* with action replays, as we see flashbacks from multiple points of view. The film echoes the technical wizardry and complex plotting of De Palma's best film, *Blow Out*. Edgy suspense and powerful kinetic energy are generated by the intriguing revelations and razor-sharp editing, while the truth behind its convoluted conspiracy has a surprisingly serious political and emotional undertow. NF

Snake Fang (Dandane Mar)

(1990, Iran, 105 min)
d Masud Kimiai. *p* Majid Modaresi, MM Dadgoo. *sc* Masud Kimiai. *ph* Iraj Sadeghpour. *ed* Mehdi Rajaiyan. *ad* Masud Kimiai. *m* Mehdi Rajaiyan. *cast* Faramarz Sedighi, Ahmad Najafi, Golchehreh Sajjadieh.

●Since Khomeini's death, Iranian cinema has regained a lot of its former energy and unpredictability, producing movies like this bizarre mixture of frontier western and neo-realist drama. A middle-aged intellectual, poleaxed by the deaths of his mother and brother (the latter in the Iran-Iraq war), takes up residence in a seedy hotel room that he shares with a swaggering black marketeer, and gets a crash course in low-life realities. The mood of post-war anomie and desolation is caught strongly, and the director (who has twelve other features to his credit) has a keen eye for the details of crime and violence. The climactic plot twists made very little sense to me, but maybe you had to be there to understand. TR

Snake Pit, The

(1948, US, 108 min, b/w)
d Anatole Litvak. *p* Anatole Litvak, Robert Bassler. *sc* Frank Partos, Millen Brand. *ph* Leo Tover. *ed* Dorothy Spencer. *ad* Lyle R Wheeler, Joseph C Wright. *m* Alfred Newman. *cast* Olivia de Havilland, Mark Stevens, Leo Genn, Celeste Holm, Leif Erickson, Glenn Langan, Beulah Bondi, Lee Patrick, Isabel Jewell, Ruth Donnelly, Betsy Blair.

●Overrated at the time as a piece of mature and realistic cinema with a strong social conscience, this now works best as lurid melodrama. De Havilland pulls out the stops as the woman committed to a mental hospital; pronounced fit to leave before her consultant thinks she's ready, she soon returns in an even worse state, and enters the ward for the very seriously disturbed. The plea for better treatment might now seem rather muddled, given the film's advocacy of shock treatment; and the documentary-style footage inside the asylum merges poorly with the strong narrative. But it's entertaining enough in a hysterical sort of way, even if it never matches up to the excesses of Fuller's later *Shock Corridor*. GA

Snakes and Ladders

see Jeu de l'oie, Le

Snapper, The

(1993, GB, 90 min)
d Stephen Frears. *p* Lynda Myles. *sc* Roddy Doyle. *ph* Oliver Stapleton. *ed* Mick Audsley. *cast* Tina Kellegher, Colm Meaney, Ruth McCabe, Eanna MacLiam, Peter Rowen, Joanne Gerrard.

●This adaptation of Roddy Doyle's novel may not display the glitz and relentless energy of *The Commitments*, but it has wit, feeling and authenticity. The story is tougher and potentially more downbeat – a Dublin family, the Curleys, face a crisis when 20-year-old Sharon (Kellegher) finds herself pregnant but refuses to name the father – nevertheless, there's still enough laconic humour to lift it above dour urban realism. In particular, Colm Meaney shines as the warm, well-meaning dad torn by shame, anger, guilt and pride. Indeed, that tangle of emotions indicates the film's unpretentious complexity as Doyle's script charts the subtle changes in the relationships between family, friends and neighbours. While the film is less obviously feel-good than *The Commitments*, its final resolution is more thoroughly earned – and, as a result, deeply affecting. GA

Snares

see Pièges

Snatch

(2000, US/GB, 103 min)
d Guy Ritchie. *p* Matthew Vaughn. *sc* Guy Ritchie. *ph* Tim Maurice-Jones. *ed* Jon Harris. *pd* Hugo Luczyc-Wyhowski. *m* John Murphy. *cast* Benicio Del Toro, Dennis Farina, Vinnie Jones, Brad Pitt, Rade Sherbedgia, Jason Statham, Alan Ford, Mike Reid, Robbie Gee, Lennie James, Ewen Bremner, Jason Flemyng.

●Ritchie's follow-up to *Lock, Stock* is an even more craftily concocted underworld entertainment, helped no end by the casting of Pitt as the bare-knuckle boxer Mickey, hellraising kingpin of a caricatured Irish Romany encampment, who get messily involved with psychopathic promoter Bricktop (Ford). The comic tone is more risqué, confident and richly enjoyed than in the earlier film. The knowing macho heroics, pubwise patter, tongue in cheek ethnic comparisons, locations and designer violence are balanced with a showman's bravado, fending off offensiveness with neat reversals, little ironies and hyperbolic buffoonery. Creating a thread through the cross-weave of plot strands – involving a diamond theft, a vengeful Russian hitman and three hopeless black trainee thieves – are the antics of Tommy (Graham) and narrator Turkish (Statham). The latter is a find. His reserve, straightfaced demeanour and spot-on delivery typify Ritchie's ability to find the actors and faces that put the manners of London on screen. WH

Snatched (aka Little Girl...Big Tease)

(1975, US, 83 min)
d/p/sc Roberto Mitrotti. *ph* Joao Fernandes. *ed* Mick Benderoth. *ad* Adam Tihany. *m* David Spangler. *cast* Jody Ray, Rebecca Brooks, Robert Furey, Phil Bendone, Joey Mancini, Joey Adinaro.

●'You've been fucked, and you've been fucked good, by one of the best' says kidnapper to kidnapped in this depressing piece of gym-slip rubbish. Heiress naturally falls in love with captors – the woman among them being her domestic science teacher – and proceeds to have it away with all three. That's about it, apart from mild stabs at a fetish or two, and the usual business of blowjob and rapes being performed with the trousers firmly fastened. Guarantees a high walk-out rate even on a wet afternoon. AN

Sneakers

(1992, US, 125 min)
d Phil Alden Robinson. *p* Walter F Parkes, Lawrence Lasker. *sc* Phil Alden Robinson, Walter F Parkes, Lawrence Lasker. *ph* John Lindley. *ed* Tom Rolf. *pd* Patrizia von Brandenstein. *m* James Horner. *cast* Robert Redford, Dan Aykroyd, Ben Kingsley, Mary McDonnell, River Phoenix, Sidney Poitier, David Strathairn, James Earl Jones, Timothy Busfield, George Hearn, Stephen Tobolowsky.

●This is a bizarre hybrid, a hi-tech caper movie with lo-tech charm; an action pic with incongruously mellow Californian pacing; a post-Cold War thriller with sassy wit. Redford heads a team of 'sneakers' – freelance tech-heads who execute computer heists to test corporate security systems. It's basically an old folks' operation, with crusty CIA vet Poitier, wild card conspiracy nut Aykroyd, blind genius Strathairn, and McDonnell as a mature femme fatale; only Phoenix guarantees the teen market. When Redford's radical past catches up with him, so do the intelligence goons, who want him to procure a black box, the ultimate hackers' McGuffin. The plot gets twistier than a Mandelbrot curve, leading to Kingsley as a slimy master criminal. A '60s-radical alternative to the 'flying glass' action pic prevalent in Hollywood, the film is sustained by a personable ensemble who generously trade off each other rather than grandstand. Right up to an ending designed to crack the sternest critical poker-face, this is gourmet popcorn of the highest order. JRo

Sniper

(1992, US, 97 min)
d Luis Llosa. *p* Robert L Rosen. *sc* Michael Frost Beckner, Crash Leyland. *ph* Bill Butler. *ed* Scott Smith. *pd* Herbert Pinter. *m* Gary Chang. *cast* Tom Berenger, Billy Zane, Aden Young, Ken Radley, JT Walsh, Reinaldo Arenas.

●As action films go, Llosa's debut is more mindful than mindless. Berenger is Marine sniper Tom Beckett, a military hit-man with 74 kills under his belt and a troubled conscience squirming in his head. In partnership with greenhorn government agent Richard Miller (Zane), a training school grad with top brass plans but no field experience, his latest mission is to penetrate the jungles of post-Noriega Panama and take out a would-be right wing dictator. The smooth running of the operation is swiftly jeopardised by growing personal tensions… A virtual two-hander, the narrative proceeds by contrasting Berenger's edgy pragmatism with Zane's unwilling induction to the art of murder, though the director's inventive bullets' eye-view shots still fail to dispel the suspicion that the film has little new to say. TJ

Sniper, The

(1952, US, 87 min, b/w)
d Edward Dmytryk. *p* Edna Anhalt, Edward Anhalt. *sc* Harry Brown. *ph* Burnett Guffey. *ed* Aaron Stell. *pd* Rudolph Sternad. *m* George Antheil. *cast* Adolphe Menjou, Arthur Franz, Gerald Mohr, Richard Kiley, Marie Windsor, Mabel Paige.

●After a couple of years under the Hollywood blacklist cloud, Dmytryk returned to the fray with this low-budget offering for producer Stanley Kramer, shot on location in the self-consciously realist *Naked City* style then making waves. Franz doesn't quite convince as the psycho obsessively drawn to taking fatal potshots at passing brunettes, but Menjou, one of the movies' great professionals, registers his involvement as the cop on his tail. Good use of the streets of San Francisco, and you can see the film's influence on Peter Bogdanovich's rather artsier 1967 offering *Targets*. TJ

Snobs

(1961, Fr/Switz, 90 min, b/w)
d Jean-Pierre Mocky. *p* Bernard Davidson. *sc* Jean-Pierre Mocky. *ph* Marcel Weiss. *ed* Marguerite Renoir. *ad* D Cardwell. *m* Joseph Kosma. *cast* Gérard Hoffmann, Véronique Nordey, Francis Blanche, Michel Lonsdale, Claude Mansard, Henri Poirier, Elina Labourdette, Noël Roquevert, Jacques Dufilho.

●An outrageous satire on the in-fighting which ensues among four possible successors when the chairman of a milk cooperative disappears down the drain of a vat. Undeniably funny, intermittently at least, as it flails wildly at every conceivable target from church and army to sex and snobbery, in the hope of offending everybody. With all the characters despicable in one way or another, the aim is evidently Swiftian. But since much of the direction is dismayingly crude ('Your life…' one character starts to say – sound of family squabble starting up – 'is filled with love'), and since most of the cast tart up their caricatures with grotesquely unfunny accents, the effect as often as not is of a Gallic *Carry On*. TM

Snow Day

(2000, US/Ger, 89 min)
d Chris Koch. *p* Albie Hecht, Julia Pistor. *sc* Will McRobb, Chris Viscardi. *ph* Robbie Greenberg. *ed* David Finfer. *pd* Leslie McDonald. *m* Steve Bartek. *cast* Chris Elliot, Mark Weber, Jean Smart, Schuyler Fisk, Iggy Pop, Pam Grier, John Schneider, Chevy Chase, Emmanuelle Chriqui.

●Spring may be in the air, but the kids at an upstate New York high school have their prayers answered when deep snowdrifts mean a day off. Ice skating and snowboarding beckon; just the moment for young Hal (Weber) to impress his charms on Claire (Chriqui), and for his dad (Chase) to stake his claim as the area's top TV weathercaster. While father and son battle against the odds, on the streets Snowplowman (Elliot) is doing his worst to ensure that the roads are cleared for school to start again, and the kids are doing their best to make sure he doesn't succeed. Chase brings intermitent jollity to the generally uninspired proceedings. TJ

Snow Days

see Let It Snow

Snow Falling on Cedars

(1999, US, 127 min)
d Scott Hicks. *p* Harry J Ufland, Ron Bass, Kathleen Kennedy, Frank Marshall. *sc* Ron Bass, Scott Hicks. *ph* Robert Richardson. *ed* Frank Corwin. *pd* Jeannine Oppewall. *m* James Newton Howard. *cast* Ethan Hawke, James Cromwell, Richard Jenkins, James Rebhorn, Sam Shepard, Max von Sydow, Youki Kudoh, Rick Yune.

●The setting is a North Pacific island, nine years after the attack on Pearl Harbor and the subsequent internment of the island's Japanese-American inhabitants. Restored to an uneasy harmony after the war, the Anglo/Japanese community is polarised once again when a fisherman dies mysteriously and his Japanese childhood friend is charged with murder. The narrative of David Guterson's bestseller is propelled by the characters' memories. While this works well on the page, it doesn't immediately lend itself to cinema, with numerous flashbacks filling in the backstory. The trial is the framework on which the film is hung, inextricably linking the lives of each participant. Local reporter Ishmael Chambers (Hawke) watches from the press gallery, his impartiality threatened by his obsession with the defendant's wife, childhood sweetheart Hatsue (Youki). Meanwhile, anti-Japanese sentiment is rife in some sectors of the population, a rather clumsily drawn bunch of pantomime baddies. As the case progresses it seems to be not the man but his nationality that's on trial. The film may be visually powerful, but no amount of evocative shots can redeem this turgid courtroom drama. WI

Snow Queen, The (Snezhnaya Koroleva)

(1966, USSR, 83 min)
d Gennadi Kazanski. *sc* Eugeni Schwartz. *ph* S Ivanov. *ed* I Novojilova. *ad* B Buristrov. *m* N Simonian. *cast* Natalya Klimova, V Nikitieako, L Proklova, S Tsiupa, E Melzhnikova.

●The Snow Queen (Klimova) withers the red roses given to Kay and his sister Gerda by their teacher. She then freezes the boy's heart and abducts him to her palace in the north. Gerda to the rescue. In the original, peculiarly eerie Hans Andersen story, childish innocence and Christian love overcome evil; in this less fanciful Lenfilm adaptation (part live action, part animation), human love and an adult capacity to overcome fear do the job. Nothing is made of Andersen's significant anthropomorphism, and some tiresome knockabout dilutes the powerful storyline. JPy

Snows of Kilimanjaro, The

(1952, US, 117 min)
d Henry King. *p* Darryl F Zanuck. *sc* Casey Robinson. *ph* Leon Shamroy. *ed* Barbara McLean. *ad* Lyle Wheeler, John F DeCuir. *m* Bernard Herrmann. *cast* Gregory Peck, Susan Hayward, Ava Gardner, Hildegard Knef, Leo G Carroll, Torin Thatcher, Marcel Dalio.

●Hemingway's portrait of the artist as a romantic hero provides Twentieth Century-Fox with ample scope to meander from Africa to Paris, Spain and back again, sampling the attractions of Hayward, Gardner and Knef en route. Although Henry King shows some sympathy for these suppliant females, veteran screenwriter Casey Robinson's intelligent, talky adaption finally endorses the great white writer's bullish philosophy: 'Real writing is like a hunt... a life-long safari; and the prey is truth'. Framed as a deathbed reminiscence, the film does tend to ramble, and seems particularly uneven in its mixture of back-projected wildlife footage, studio and location work, while Peck's weighty Harry Street remains resolutely aloof, to the point where he will not deign to expire. TCh

Snow Was Black, The

see Neige était sale, La

Snow White and the Seven Dwarfs

(1937, US, 83 min)
d David Hand. *p* Walt Disney. *sc* Ted Sears, Otto Englander, Earl Hund, Dorothy Ann Blank, Richard Creedon, Dick Richard, Merrill de Maris, Webb Smith. *m* Frank Churchill, Leigh Harline, Paul Smith. *cast* voices: Adriana Caselotti, Harry Stockwell, Lucile La Verne, Moroni Olsen.

●Disney's first animated feature takes the Grimms' fairy-tale and turns it into a generally cute fantasy for American kids: Snow White herself might be felt to be almost unbearably winsome, and the anthropomorphic characterisation of the forest creatures soon becomes tiresome. But the animation itself is top-notch, and in a number of darker sequences (Snow White's terrified entry into the forest, for example), Disney's adoption of Expressionist visual devices makes for genuinely powerful drama. Ideologically, however, what remains most intersting, as one writer has noted, is the way Walt's obvious desire to promote the American Way (off to work we go, indeed!) is married – presumably unthinkingly – to a virtual celebration of polygamy in which, moreover, it is a woman, not a man, who lives with seven members of the opposite sex! GA.

Snow White: A Tale of Terror

(1996, GB/US, 100 min)
d Michael Cohn. *p* Tom Engelman. *sc* Thomas Szollosi, Deborah Serra. *ph* Mike Southon. *ed* Ian Crafford. *pd* Gemma Jackson. *m* John Ottman. *cast* Sigourney Weaver, Sam Neill, Gil Bellows, Taryn Davis, David Conrad, Brian Glover, Monica Keena, Bryan Pringle.

●Stripped of Grand Guignol theatricality and the usual sentimentality, Weaver's 'straight' wicked stepmother and Neill's caring, if ineffectual father stress the sheer unattractiveness of the roles in this adult fairytale. Putting the Grimm back in the story is not necessarily a bad thing, but here the makers provide insufficient atmosphere or developed characterisation to satisfy grown-ups. The film plays like light Hammer horror with inappropriate period finery and design. The script goes the cod Freudian route, with Weaver's actions explained by postnatal depression and grief (accompanied by lots of menstrual imagery), her narcissistic fear of ageing, her unhealthy relationship with her mute brother, and the baggage she brings with her, notably the armoire with its gigantic looking glass. Monica Keena's Lilli/Snow White is a problem. A lightweight, pretty actress, she seems too insignificant to raise her stepmother's vengeful jealousy, and you couldn't care less about her rites of passage. WH

Soapdish

(1991, US, 97 min)
d Michael Hoffman. *p* Aaron Spelling, Alan Greisman. *sc* Robert Harling, Andrew Bergman. *ph* Ueli Steiger. *ed* Garth Craven. *pd* Eugenio Zanetti. *m* Alan Silvestri. *cast* Sally Field, Kevin Kline, Robert Downey Jr, Whoopi Goldberg, Carrie Fisher, Cathy Moriarty, Teri Hatcher, Paul Johansson, Elizabeth Shue, Garry Marshall.

●Celeste (Field) is getting all the awards for her performance in a tacky daytime soap, 'The Sun Also Sets', and the rest of the cast naturally despise her. Meanwhile, co-star Montana (Moriarty) teases the producer (Downey) with seductive talk; and in a bid to sabotage Celeste's character in the soap, these two scheme to bring back Celeste's real-life ex-lover (Kline), last seen in the series minus his head. His arrival leaves the star teetering between rage and insanity; and when his charm snares Celeste's actress niece (Shue), the trio start to enact genuine dramas live on the air. Nothing succeeds like excess, this comedy would have us believe. But the thwarted egos, rampant libidos, and starry cast – while wonderful at first – begin to look frayed around halfway through. CM

S.O.B.

(1981, US,121 min)
d Blake Edwards. *p* Blake Edwards, Tony Adams. *sc* Blake Edwards. *ph* Harry Stradling Jr. *ed* Ralph E Winters. *pd* Rodger Maus. *m* Henry Mancini. *cast* Julie Andrews, William Holden, Richard Mulligan, Robert Vaughn, Robert Webber, Robert Preston, Larry Hagman, Shelley Winters, Marisa Berenson, Loretta Swit, Stuart Margolin, Rosanna Arquette, Craig Stevens, Robert Loggia, Larry Storch.

●Though, like many of Edwards' films, it lurches uncertainly from slapstick farce to mordant humour in an extremely hit-or-miss fashion, this surprisingly bitter satire on Tinseltown – in which a producer (Mulligan) beefs up his latest turkey of a movie by introducing some pornographic sex scenes and having his wife/star (Andrews) bare her breasts on screen – does hit the mark once or twice. That said, it seems more like an expectorant for Edwards' bile than an entertainment aimed at an audience. NF

Sobreviviré

see I Will Survive

Society

(1989, US, 99 min)
d Brian Yuzna. *p* Keith Walley. *sc* Woody Keith, Rick Fry. *ph* Rick Fichter. *ed* Peter Teschner. *pd* Mathew C Jacobs. *m* Mark Ryder, Phil Davies. *cast* Bill Warlock, Devin DeVasquez, Evan Richards, Ben Meyerson, Charles Lucia, Connie Danese, Patrice Jennings, Heidi Kozak, Ben Slack, Tim Bartell.

●A bizarre fable that starts like a TV soap but soon darkens into a disturbing thriller about an idyllic Beverly Hills community where something is subtly skewed. Handsome teenager Bill (Warlock) feels uncomfortable with his affluent peers. But the usual teen insecurities take on a more sinister aspect when his sister's ex-boyfriend Blanchard plays him a clandestine recording of her 'coming out' party which suggests perverse, incestuous sexual initiation; but when Bill's shrink later plays the tape back to him, he hears only innocuous conversation. How does this connect with rich kid Ted's exclusive teen clique, or Blanchard's death in a road accident? Is there a dark conspiracy, or is Bill losing his marbles? First-time director Yuzna is happier with the sly humour and clever plot shifts than with the appropriately iconic but sometimes dramatically unconvincing cast. He nevertheless generates a compelling sense of paranoid unease, and shifts into F/X overdrive for an unforgettable horror finale. Suffice it to say that the 'surrealistic make-up designs' by Screaming Mad George (who did the cockroach sequence in *Nightmare on Elm Street 4*) will stretch even the most inelastic mind. NF

So Close to Paradise (Yuenan Guniang)

(1998, China, 93 min)
d Wang Xiaoshuai. *p* Han Sanping, Tian Zhuangzhuang, Li Buo. *sc* Wang Xiaoshuai, Pang Ming. *ed* Liu Fang, Yang Hongyu. *ad* Cheng Guangming. *m* Liu Lin. *cast* Wang Tong, Shi Yu, Guo Tao, Wu Tao.

●Shot in 1995 but shelved by its producers until it could pass the censors, this was Wang's first 'legal' film after two underground features, *The Days* and the pseudonymous *Frozen*. Two country hicks in Wuhan, the notoriously sleazy city on the Yangtze, get tangled up with karaoke bar hostess Ruan (Wang), advertised as being 'from Vietnam' (that is, sexually available), but actually the mistress of a local triad boss. The elder guy, Gao Ping (Guo), becomes her lover while trying to use her to get to a triad thug who has tricked him. Their doomed relationship is seen through the eyes of the other guy Dongzi (Shi), a 'shoulder pole' labourer in the docks, who delivers a typical Wang Xiaoshuai voice-over wryly looking back on these events from some point in the future. An accomplished piece of neo-urban realism with *noir* inflections, but it doesn't have the resonances of Wang's earlier films. TR

So Dark the Night

(1946, US, 70 min, b/w)
d Joseph H Lewis. *p* Ted Richmond. *sc* Aubrey Wisberg, Martin Berkeley, Dwight Babcock. *ph* Burnett Guffey. *ed* Jerome Thoms. *ad* Carl Anderson. *m* Hugo Friedhofer. *cast* Steven Geray, Micheline Cheirel, Eugene Borden, Ann Codee, Egon Brecher, Helen Freeman.

●This is what Joseph H Lewis is all about. The script is a perfunctory and frequently silly murder mystery, with an ending that's equal parts cod-Freud and O Henry. Furthermore, it is set in a ludicrous evocation of France, most embarrassing in the opening scenes in Paris, but still irritating when the plot takes the police inspector hero (Geray) into the country to romance with an innkeeper's daughter (Cheirel) who yearns for the Big City. However, none of this matters. The film is directed like a million bucks. Visually, it compares with *The Big Combo* as one of Lewis' purest *noir* achievements; beyond that, it has more cinematic ideas and effects per square foot of screen than any number of contemporary A features. In other words, it's a 'typical' Lewis movie: low on thinks, but with enough style to send lovers of cinema reeling. TR

Sodom and Gomorrah (Sodoma e Gomorra)

(1962, It/Fr, 153 min)
d Robert Aldrich. *p* Goffredo Lombardo. *sc* Hugo Butler, Giorgio Prosperi. *ph* Silvano Ippoliti, Mario Montuori, Cyril Knowles. *ed* Peter Tanner. *ad* Ken Adam. *m* Miklós Rozsa. *cast* Stewart Granger, Anouk Aimée, Stanley Baker, Pier Angeli, Rossana Podesta, Claudia Mori, Daniele Vargas, Rik Battaglia.
●A low point in Aldrich's erratic career, this tale of Lot's dealings with the treacherous inhabitants of the twin cities of evil never lives up to its first line of dialogue, in which a beautiful spy is warned to 'Beware of the Sodomites', who come up and capture her from behind. Sin is suggested by languid groups of people, nattily dressed in '60s evening gowns, lolling around on the floor, while the virtuous Hebrews look more like a bunch of self-sufficient drongos droning on about making the land fertile. Granger's Lot wields a mighty staff, Anouk is as charmingly beautiful as ever as the evil Queen of Sodom, and Baker gets by on leering at every woman who comes near. Watchable for Ken Adam's sets, though God's final destruction of the cities is very tacky. They don't make 'em like this any more. GA

So Evil My Love

(1948, GB, 109 min, b/w)
d Lewis Allen. *p* Hal B Wallis. *sc* Leonard Spigelgass, Ronald Millar. *ph* Max Greene. *ed* Vera Campbell. *ad* Tom Morahan. *m* Victor Young, William Alwyn. *cast* Ray Milland, Ann Todd, Geraldine Fitzgerald, Raymond Huntley, Martita Hunt, Leo G Carroll, Raymond Lovell, Moira Lister, Finlay Currie, Hugh Griffith.
●A not uninteresting offshoot from the *noir* cycle, made by Paramount in Britain and derived from a factually-based novel by Joseph Shearing, who specialised in Victorian Gothic (*Moss Rose, Blanche Fury*). Lots of loving period frills as Milland, a caddish charmer taking over the *femme fatale* role, lures a missionary's staid widow into (literally) letting her hair down, then wantonly sets her on the path to blackmail and murder. Allen's bleakly measured direction (he made the wonderfully atmospheric *The Uninvited*) is unfortunately tipped towards dullness by somewhat bland characterisations from Todd and Milland. TM

Sofie

(1992, Den, 146 min)
d Liv Ullmann. *p* Bo Christensen, Lars Kolvig. *sc* Liv Ullman, Peter Poulsen. *ph* Jörgen Persson. *ed* Grete Moldrup. *pd* Peter Hoimark. *cast* Karen-Lise Mynster, Ghita Norby, Erland Josephson.
●Denmark, 1886. 29-year-old Sofie lives with her affluent, extended Jewish family, but her happiness is marred by parental fears that she will become a spinster. Despite her love for a gentile painter, she is manoeuvred into marriage with a respectable Jewish cousin... Ullmann's directorial debut is marked by an attention to fussy period detail and rigorous, symmetrical framing, which convey a sense of repression; but combined with a running-time of nearly two-and-a-half hours, this leaves the film somewhat airless. Most impressive are the sensitive performances she elicits from her cast, especially Mynster (as Sofie) and Josephson (as her father). CM

So Fine

(1981, US, 91 min)
d Andrew Bergman. *p* Mike Lobell. *sc* Andrew Bergman. *ph* James A Contner. *ed* Alan Heim. *pd* Santo Loquasto. *m* Ennio Morricone. *cast* Ryan O'Neal, Jack Warden, Mariangela Melato, Richard Kiel, Fred Gwynne.
●On the long list of comedy ideas screenwriters should never have had, this film must rank high. O'Neal reprises his performance from *What's Up, Doc?*, here cast as a *klutz* of a college professor co-opted to revive his father's ailing rag-trade business when he accidentally hits upon a craze in denims. The gimmick is jeans with see-through derrière, and most of the humour on display in this would-be screwball comedy has an inanity which follows suit with this central conceit. Directing his own script, Bergman executes his knowing movie references – O'Neal as Cary Grant, embarrassed in improvised drag; a nod toward the lustful satire of Tashlin's *The Girl Can't Help It*; a Marx Brothers-inspired night at the opera finale – with a kind of vulgar energy that does little to decorate his otherwise threadbare sitcom material. RM

Soft Beds, Hard Battles

(1973, GB, 107 min)
d Roy Boulting. *p* John Boulting. *sc* Leo Marks, Roy Boulting. *ph* Gilbert Taylor. *ed* Martin Charles. *ad* John Howell. *m* Neil Rhoden. *cast* Peter Sellers, Lila Kedrova, Curt Jürgens, Béatrice Romand, Jenny Hanley, Françoise Pascal, Gabriella Licudi, Rula Lenska, Timothy West, Thorley Walters.
●A wretchedly titled offering in the Boulting Brothers' compulsively satirical vein, largely set in a brothel in occupied Paris, with Kedrova and Jürgens typecast as the sentimental madame and a friendly German officer, and the gorgeous Béatrice Romand wasted as Madame's innocent niece. But its raison d'être is Peter Sellers, back in brilliant form as six variations on blinkered authority, including Hitler and a De Gaulle-ish French general, but particularly as the Gestapo chief Schroeder, limping-cum-strutting from disaster to disaster, an extraordinary amalgam of Dr Strangelove and Fred Kite. Worth a visit for Sellers and one classic joke about a PoW. SG

Soft on the Inside

(1990, GB, 46 min)
d Katy Radford. *with* Andy Sheppard.
●A nicely done concert film featuring the 15-piece band British saxophonist Andy Sheppard put together for a short tour of France and Britain. The band, composed of soloists from all over the world (nutter drummer Hans Bennink, Gary Valente's superb trombone, the inspired Peruvian guitarist Manc Ventura among them), perform four songs for Sheppard's eponymous new album. Intercut is the usual on-the-road commentary, of the 'So-and-so's a wild and crazy guy and I've always wanted to play with him' kind, here done with a minimum of pretentiousness. Sheppard says he prefers 'inside' players. He certainly gets them cooking. WH

Soft Skin, The

see Peau Douce, La

Soft Top, Hard Shoulder

(1992, GB, 95 min)
d Stefan Schwartz. *p* Richard Holmes. *sc* Peter Capaldi. *ph* Henry Braham. *ed* Derek Trigg. *pd* Sonja Klaus. *m* Chris Rea. *cast* Peter Capaldi, Elaine Collins, Richard Wilson, Frances Barber, Phyllis Logan, Simon Callow, Catherine Russell, Jeremy Northam.
●Having failed to make it in London as a comic-book artist, Gavin Bellini (Capaldi) – an Italian-Glaswegian from an ice-cream dynasty – reluctantly yields to his uncle's demands that he return home for his dad's sixtieth birthday party; if he makes it, the uncle (Wilson) may give him a share of the family fortune. But as he heads north in his worn-out Triumph convertible, Gavin meets countless obstacles. When the car breaks down, hitcher Yvonne (Collins) helps to get it going, but Gavin soon tires of her company. Worse, he loses his wallet, and their progress becomes ever slower. Will Gavin reach the party on time? Can he and his feisty passenger put aside their differences? The echoes of *It Happened One Night* and Bill Forsyth's comedies are rather too strong, but Capaldi's script has its fair share of engagingly offbeat one-liners, and the characters are deftly sketched. The ending doesn't convince, and Schwartz's direction is erratic, but overall this is a modestly enjoyable comedy. GA

Soigne ta Droite

(1986, Fr/Switz, 81 min)
d/sc Jean-Luc Godard. *ph* Caroline Champetier. *m* Rita Mitsouko. *cast* Jean-Luc Godard, Jacques Villeret, François Périer, Jane Birkin, Dominique Lavanant, Michel Galabru, Rufus, Eva Darlan, Isabelle Sadoyan, Les Rita Mitsouko.
●The relationship between Godard and his audience has for ages been that of teacher and pupil, with Godard the invariably foul-tempered prof, and his audience the recalcitrant C stream, regarded as bringing nothing to the encounter except their own shortcomings. This is modified in those films where Godard is an on-screen participant: teacher starring in the school play. Here his role is a film director, referred to as 'The Idiot', who'll make any rubbish assigned him, and who Godard renders via a rather good imitation of Harry Langdon (or possibly Pee-Wee Herman). The film comprises a series of charades (as opposed to 'scenes') which never achieve a middle ground between the over-obvious and the over-obscure. (Air travel as a metaphor for – what? Life?) As in *One Plus One* much time is spent with a bunch of musicians trying to get their sound right. But the hail of allusions, quotes and gnomic declarations seldom coalesce into more than a groan of schoolmasterly dissatisfaction over things in general. BBa

So I Married an Axe Murderer

(1993, US, 92 min)
d Thomas Schlamme. *p* Jonathan Sanger, Rob Fried, Cary Woods. *sc* Robbie Fox. *ph* Julio Macat. *ed* Richard Halsey, Colleen Halsey. *pd* John Graysmark. *m* Bruce Broughton. *cast* Mike Myers, Nancy Travis, Anthony LaPaglia, Brenda Fricker, Charles Grodin, Alan Arkin.
●Myers (half of the *Wayne's World* duo) takes a giant step for nerdkind in this less than subtle Hitchcock spoof, which aims a blunderbuss at serial killers, multi-lingual lounge singers, and the Queen Mother. While buying haggis for his bizarre Scottish family, Myers meets butcher's assistant Travis. Despite an aversion to long-term relationships, he falls for her hook, line and sinker – until he begins to suspect that she may be a deadly serial marrier who has already claimed three victims. The crass Scots jokes are irresistible; Alan Arkin's cameo as a mild-mannered police chief is sheer perfection; and the cultish references to Beat poetry should please slumming hipsters. Like an exploding haggis, funny but extremely messy. NF

Soir, un Train, Un

(1968, Bel/Fr, 86 min)
d André Delvaux. *p* Mag Bodard. *sc* André Delvaux. *ph* Ghislain Cloquet. *ed* Suzanne Baron. *ad* Claude Pignot. *m* Frédéric Devreese. *cast* Yves Montand, Anouk Aimée, Adriana Bogdan, Hector Camerlynck, François Beukelaers, Michael Gough, Patrick Conrad.
●In a chill, wintry Flanders, university lecturer Mathias (Montand) and partner Anne (Aimée) embark on a train journey. Mathias wakes from a doze to see Anne gone and his other fellow passengers all fast asleep. When the train stops in the middle of nowhere, Mathias and two other men, one younger, one older, get off. The train sets off without them and they are reduced to picking their way across inhospitable terrain in search of civilisation. In the dead of night they come to a village where no one understands a word they say. Their vain efforts to make themselves understood create an atmosphere of vague menace and growing unease. The problems of communication may be read as a reflection of the linguistic and cultural schisms in Belgium, although Delvaux has tried harder than most film-makers to both work with and appeal to members of the Flemish and Francophone communities. The pace may seem slow to begin with, but the steady build is shrewdly balanced by the gradual slide into fantasy in the second half of the picture. Look out for a finely judged cameo by Michael Gough in a flashback set in London's Rotherhithe. NRo

Solarbabies (aka Solarwarriors)

(1986, US, 94 min)
d Alan Johnson. *p* Irene Walzer, Jack Frost Sanders. *sc* Walon Green, Douglas Anthony Metrov. *ph* Peter MacDonald. *ed* Conrad Buff. *pd* Anthony Pratt. *m* Maurice Jarre. *cast* Richard Jordan, Jami Gertz, Jason Patric, Lukas Haas, Charles Durning.
●All-purpose sci-fi rip-off, set on a planet where evil Jordan lords it over a cadre of roller-skating minor brat-packers who call on ancient mystical force – 'Bodhi' – to escape his sway. A misbegotten Brooksfilm which sank without trace in the US. Director Johnson remains best known for staging the 'Springtime for Hitler' routine in *The Producers*.

Solaris

(1972, USSR, 165 min)
d Andrei Tarkovsky. *sc* Andrei Tarkovsky, Friedrich Gorenstein. *ph* Vadim Iusov. *ad* Mikhail Romadin. *m* Eduard Artemiev. *cast* Donatas Banionis, Natalya Bondarchuk, Yuri Jarvet, Anatoli Solonitsin, Vladislav Dvorjetzki.
●Apparently conceived as a socialist response to *2001: A Space Odyssey*, Tarkovsky's film in fact offers only the flabbiest kind of sentimental humanism by way of a riposte to Kubrick. It starts out promising both poetry (of the Dovzhenko Ukrainian school) and dialectics (of the Marxist school?), and proceeds to squander both on kindergarten psychology and inane melodrama. Its hero journeys into space only as a metaphor for a journey inward; after 2 hours, he's got no further than the lap of his father, which he rejected ten years earlier. Watching Tarkovsky render the sci-fi mechanics of his own movie redundant as he goes along is a genuinely brain-freezing experience. TR

Solarwarriors

see Solarbabies

Solas

(1999, Sp, 98 min)
d Benito Zambrano. *p* Antonio P Pérez. *sc* Benito Zambrano. *ph* Tote Trenas. *ed* Fernando Pardo. *ad* Lala Obrero. *m* Antonio Meliveo. *cast* María Galiana, Ana Fernández, Carlos Alvarez, Antonio Dechent, Paco de Osca, Juan Fernández, Miguel Alcíbar.
●Much lauded in Spain last year, Zambrano's film is a let-down. Fernández plays Maria, a hardboiled forty-nothing struggling to keep it all together: she smokes too much, stretches her tab at the neighbourhood bar, and fucks an unsympathetic trucker when he's in town. Forced to stay in the city while her sick husband is laid up in hospital, Maria's elderly mother (Galiana) finds her lifestyle distressing – but she bites her tongue, as always, quietly cleans the place up, and surprises herself by falling into a discreet courtship with the gallant old gentleman in the flat downstairs (Alvarez). Their Platonic romance is handled with delicacy, and at first our emotions are evenly pulled between kindly mother and angry daughter. On some level, Zambrano means to criticise patriarchal oppression by making the sick father a hateful figure. But as the film goes on, it becomes clear the director has other fish to fry. For a start, he has designs on our tear ducts, as the increasingly maudlin score signals. He's a closet conservative, too: the movie implicitly indicts the big bad city and its irreligious modern ways – especially the sexually liberated single working woman, packed off to the country with a baby and an asexual surrogate husband/father in the deadly last reel. Your granny might like it. TCh

Sol del Membrillo, El

see Quince Tree Sun, The

Soldier, The (aka Codename: The Soldier)

(1983, US, 96 min)
d/p/sc James Glickenhaus. *ph* Robert M Baldwin Jr. *ed* Paul Fried. *pd* William De Seta. *m* Tangerine Dream. *cast* Ken Wahl, Alberta Watson, Klaus Kinski, William Prince, Jeremiah Sullivan.
●The credits signal 'world politics' to Tangerine Dream, the opening carnage disposes of a KGB hit squad by judicious use of the posed square jaw and helicopters. The Soldier is a secret, extra-legal square jaw, with what the Russians (the bald ones chewing toothpicks) term an 'unusually broad charter'. Glickenhaus' *The Exterminator* at least gave us a witty and reluctant killer with an understandable grudge and modest ambitions. Here nothing less than global salvation will do: kidnapped nuclear stuff, oilfields threatened, Middle East crisis, Mossad sex interest, Moscow implicated – the kind of nonsense best left to real puppets in *Thunderbirds*. RP

Soldier and the Lady, The

see Adventures of Michael Strogoff, The

Soldier Blue

(1970, US, 114 min)
d Ralph Nelson. *p* Gabriel Katzka, Harold Loeb. *sc* John Gay. *ph* Robert B Hauser. *ed* Alex Beaton. *ad* Frank Arrigo. *m* Roy Budd. *cast* Candice Bergen, Peter Strauss, Donald Pleasence, Bob Carraway, Jorge Rivero, Dana Elcar, John Anderson.
●A grimly embarrassing anti-racist Western about the US Cavalry's notorious Sand Creek Indian massacre in 1864. In the interests of propaganda, one might just about stomach the way the massacre itself is turned into a gleefully exploitative gore-fest of blood and amputated limbs; but not when it's associated with a desert romance that's shot like an ad-man's wet dream, all soft focus and sweet nothings. To complete the rout, the script has an unerring instinct for cliché. 'Why, why, why?' yells the appalled hero. Box-office, is the curt answer. TM

Soldier Girls

(1980, US, 87 min)
d Nicholas Broomfield, Joan Churchill. *p/ph* Joan Churchill. *ed* Nicholas Broomfield.
●For their second American documentary, British film-makers Broomfield and Churchill took on the US Army, following three women recruits through induction and basic training. They learn the marching chant 'Kill, maim, rape, pillage', how to bite the head off a chicken, and how to accept/subvert the repressive machine of the military that still believes it was cheated of victory in Vietnam and is guaranteed to win the next war. An object lesson in the mechanisms of patriarchal power-play that is by turns appalling, amusing and amazing. MA

Soldier of Orange (Soldaat van Orange)

(1977, Neth, 149 min)
d Paul Verhoeven. *p* Rob Houwer. *sc* Gerard Soeteman, Kees Holierhoek, Paul Verhoeven. *ph* Jost Vacano. *ed* Jane Sperr. *pd* Roland de Groot. *m* Rogier Van Otterloo. *cast* Rutger Hauer, Jeroen Krabbé, Susan Penhaligon, Edward Fox, Derek De Lint, Rijk De Gooyer, Peter Faber.
●This brilliantly made war film helped alert Hollywyood to Verhoeven's talents. Loosely based on war hero Erik Hazelhoff Roelfzema's memoir, it follows six college friends, showing the different ways in which they coped with the Nazi occupation. Some collaborated, some joined the resistance. Verhoeven is helped immeasurably by charismatic performances from two of the biggest stars of recent Dutch cinema, Hauer and Krabbé. They're old college pals who escape to England, share a girlfriend (the rosy-cheeked Penhaligon) and return to Holland on a mission doomed from the outset. Just occasionally, the film-making becomes self-conscious (certain sequences seem directly inspired by Bertolucci's *The Conformist*). Verhoeven can't resist throwing in some voyeuristic moments in which couples are spied love-making or cracking crass jokes at the expense of the eccentric Queen Wilhelmina, but he steers clear of jingoism and pomposity. His real coup is in combining the epic with the intimate. Despite a portentous score and often flashy visuals, the characterisation remains subtle and closely focused. GM

Soldier's Daughter Never Cries, A

(1998, GB, 127 min)
d James Ivory. *p* Ismail Merchant. *sc* James Ivory, Ruth Prawer Jhabvala. *ph* Jean-Marc Fabre. *ed* Noëlle Boisson. *pd* Jacques Bufnoir, Pat Garner. *m* Richard Robbins. *cast* Kris Kristofferson, Barbara Hershey, LeeLee Sobieski, Jesse Bradford, Anthony Roth Costanzo, Jane Birkin, Macha Méril.
●Adapted from an autobiographical novel by Kaylie Jones, daughter of James Jones, Merchant Ivory's film offers a leisurely, episodic account of the experiences of a well-off American family seemingly fated always to be outsiders. It's not just that writer Bill (Kristofferson) and wife Marcella (Hershey) are a touch bohemian; they also live in '60s Paris, so that daughter Channe (Sobieski) and adopted son Benoît/Billy never quite fit in or make friends easily at school. Eventually, dad takes them back to New England, but things hardly improve: he's ailing, Channe, now in mid-teens, is having boy problems, and poor Billy's screwed up about his origins. Some rate this meandering film, probably for the solid performances and Ivory's 'sensitive' direction. Others, like myself, find it pretty pointless. The main problem is not the usual dull tastefulness, but Ivory and Ruth Prawer Jhabvala's script, which never establishes any clear perspective, let alone who or what it's actually about: by the end, for example, we're clearly meant to admire and feel strongly about Bill's achievements as a husband and father – impossible given his earlier marginal role. Regrettably, the second best thing in the film – Channe's eccentric friend Francis (Costanzo) – is scuppered when he suddenly disappears from the narrative, while the best of all – a brief scene from a mind-bogglingly pretentious, coke-sniffing, crotch-rubbing production of *Salome* he and Channe go to see – is so funny and, well, different that one would far rather watch the whole opera than the film that frames it. GA

Soldier's Story, A

(1984, US, 101 min)
d Norman Jewison. *p* Norman Jewison, Ronald L Schwary, Patrick Palmer. *sc* Charles Fuller. *ph* Russell Boyd. *ed* Mark Warner, Caroline Biggerstaff. *pd* Walter Scott Herndon. *m* Herbie Hancock. *cast* Howard E Rollins Jr, Adolph Caesar, Art Evans, David Alan Grier, David Harris, Dennis Lipscomb, Denzel Washington.
●From the man who brought you *In the Heat of the Night*, another spotlessly liberal look at racial problems, again in the Deep South. This time it's a question of murder as, back in 1944, Rollins' Poitier-style army captain is called in to investigate the killing of a black sergeant (Caesar) on a military base. Here the subject is less racial hatred between whites and blacks than problems with racial identity: what it means to be black in a white man's world. Nothing very original, to be sure, and the film's theatrical origins are clear from both the wordy script and the intense performances. But Rollins' charisma works wonders, and Jewison reveals enough solid professionalism in the deft handling of flashbacks to make it gripping entertainment. GA

Sole anche di notte, Il

see Night Sun

Soleil des Hyénes

see Hyenas' Sun

Soleil trompeur

see Burnt by the Sun

Solid Gold Cadillac, The

(1956, US, 99 min, b/w)
d Richard Quine. *p* Fred Kohlmar. *sc* Abe Burrows. *ph* Charles Lang Jr. *ed* Charles Nelson. *ad* Ross Bellah. *m* Cyril J Mockridge. *cast* Judy Holliday, Paul Douglas, Fred Clark, John Williams, Arthur O'Connell, Neva Patterson, Ray Collins.
●Several classic Hollywood notions combine here: that capitalism is tickety-boo as long as businessmen aren't corrupt, that one dumb broad can defeat the wiliest crooks in the business, that a male and a female goody will inevitably fall in love. With the rallying cry of 'Somebody's got to keep an eye on these big businesses', Judy Holliday, in a variation on the part that made her in *Born Yesterday*, takes on the wicked businessmen and rallies Middle America behind her. It's pernicious, but fun. SG

Solitaire for 2

(1994, GB, 106 min)
d Gary Sinyor. *p* Gary Sinyor, Richard Holmes. *sc* Gary Sinyor. *ph* Henry Braham. *ed* Ewa J Lind. *pd* Carmel Collins. *m* David A Hughes, John Murphy. *cast* Mark Frankel, Amanda Pays, Roshan Seth, Jason Isaacs, Maryam D'Abo, Helen Lederer, Annette Crosbie.
● Daniel Becker (Frankel) knows all the right moves. A management consultant on body language and behavioural science, and the author of a self-help manual, he's a dab hand at manipulating people. Especially women. Then he meets beautiful palaeontologist Katie Burrill (Pays), and suddenly he can't put a foot right. She sees through his every ploy, beats him to every punchline, almost as if she can read his mind. In fact, that's exactly what she's doing. The question is: can Daniel make it up? It's a fantastic idea for a screwball comedy, but writer/director Sinyor's first solo effort after the *Leon the Pig Farmer* collaboration doesn't entirely come off. The fault is less with the script – which is packed with sharp observations and promising comic set-ups – than with the hit-or-miss direction. Some subtle scenes prove unduly tentative, while more physical sequences veer towards the inflated buffoonery of sit-com land. For all that, it's a convivial entertainment, with enough wit and imagination to bode well for Sinyor's future. TCh

Soliti Ignoti, I (Big Deal on Madonna Street/Persons Unknown)

(1958, It, 105 min, b/w)
d Mario Monicelli. *p* Franco Cristaldi. *sc* Age, Scarpelli, Suso Cecchi D'Amico, Mario Monicelli. *ph* Gianni De Venanzo. *ed* Adriana Novelli. *ad* Piero Gherardi. *m* Piero Umiliani. *cast* Vittorio Gassman, Renato Salvatori, Marcello Mastroianni, Toto, Memmo Carotenuto, Claudia Cardinale.
● A charming comedy, perhaps a little *déjà vu* after countless imitations and variations culminating in Louis Malle's distinctly iffy 1983 remake as *Crackers.* Countering the famous sequence in *Rififi* which observed in meticulous detail the perfect execution of a robbery, Monicelli offers a robbery equally meticulously planned (by a sad sack mix of desperate unemployed and washed-up pros) in which everything goes hilariously wrong. It may not sound much, but Monicelli's timing (giving the series of disasters an almost malevolent inevitability) is brilliant, the ensemble playing couldn't be bettered, and the deliberate cartoon-style stereotyping of the characters is neatly offset by a neo-realist emphasis on real locations in the dank slums of Rome. TM

So Little Time

(1952, GB, 88 min, b/w)
d Compton Bennett. *p* Aubrey Baring, Maxwell Setton. *sc* John Cresswell. *ph* Oswald Morris. *ed* V Sagovsky. *ad* Edward Carrick. *m* Robert Gill. *cast* Maria Schell, Marius Goring Gabrielle Dorziat, Barbara Mullen, John Bailey, Lucie Mannheim Harold Lang.
● A World War II movie set in Occupied Belgium which has a marginally unusual plot. It's about a good German officer, Colonel von Hohensee (Goring), who is appointed military governor of Brussels, and falls in love with a Belgian girl, Nicole (Schell). After a time, Nicole is approached by the gangster-type Resistance movement and told to steal some documents, but she finds Hohensee considerably more sympathetic... There were protests when the movie first came out, and it's certainly refreshing to find this kind of inversion (Nazi humanitarian versus cruel 'freedom fighters') in a British film, even though it remains on a naive level. DP

Solomon and Gaenor (Solomon a Gaenor)

(1998, GB, 104 min)
d Paul Morrison. *p* Sheryl Crown. *sc* Paul Morrison. *ph* Nina Kellgren. *ed* Kant Pan. *pd* Hayden Pearce. *m* Ilona Sekacz. *cast* Ioan Gruffudd, Nia Roberts, Sue Jones Davies, William Thomas, Mark Lewis Jones, Maureen Lipman, David Horovitch, Bethan Ellis Owen.
● The Welsh valleys, 1911. Solomon (Gruffudd) is the son of a Jewish family which sells drapery and glazing. Times are hard for the pit community, not least in the household where Solomon strikes up a conversation with Gaenor (Roberts), whose father may soon be on strike with the rest of the miners. Knowing she's from chapel stock, Solomon poses as 'Sam Livingston', son of an English engineer, and the pair soon find themselves spending afternoons together in a hayloft. Eventually the strain of the pretence tells. A familiar theme, but the film's modest accomplishment is to place it in unfamiliar terrain. It all starts to go awry, however, when Gaenor's pregnancy is discovered, and soon melodramatic tribulation is being piled on hackneyed adversity. TJ

Solomon and Sheba

(1959, US, 142 min)
d King Vidor. *p* Ted Richmond. *sc* Anthony Veiller, Paul Dudley, George Bruce. *ph* Freddie Young. *ed* Otto Ludwig. *ad* Richard Day, Alfred Sweeney, Luis Perez Espinosa. *m* Mario Nascimbene. *cast* Yul Brynner, Gina Lollobrigida, George Sanders, Marisa Pavan, David Farrar, John Crawford, Laurence Naismith, Alejandro Rey, Harry Andrews.
● The Bible's sultriest couple, bar Samson and Delilah, deserve better than this empty Super Technirama epic. There's so much visual padding (feathers, armour, redundant crowd scenes) it's hard to focus on the romance. Lollobrigida does her pouting best, but she's no Gloria Swanson. Tyrone Power, the original Solomon, died halfway through production; Brynner, his replacement, is decidedly ill at ease. More fun to tuck up with the Old Testament. GM

So Long at the Fair

(1950, GB, 86 min, b/w)
d Terence Fisher, Anthony Darnborough. *p* Betty E Box. *sc* Hugh Mills, Anthony Thorne. *ph* Reginald Wyer. *ed* Gordon Hales. *ad* Cedric Dawe. *m* Benjamin Frankel. *cast* Jean Simmons, Dirk Bogarde, David Tomlinson, Honor Blackman, Cathleen Nesbitt, Felix Aylmer, Marcel Poncin, Eugene Deckers, Austin Trevor.
● A visitor to the Paris World Fair of 1889 vanishes overnight, along with his hotel room and all traces of his existence. An appropriate training ground for Fisher's later ventures into horror, but his opportunities for exploring the macabre are restricted here by the demands of an insipid romance between Simmons, as the disappearing man's distraught sister, and Bogarde as the English artist who believes her story. Simmons is too sweet and self-assured to inspire more than mild concern for her predicament, and Bogarde's potential for debonair caddishness remains sadly unfulfilled in the face of his partner's redoubtable innocence. Enthusiasm has to be reserved for the period trappings, a clever Offenbach-ish score, and the fine support playing of Nesbitt, Blackman and Poncin. RMy

Sombre

(1998, Fr, 112 min)
d Philippe Grandrieux. *p* Catherine Jacques. *sc* Philippe Grandrieux, Pierre Hodgson, Sophie Fillières. *ph* Sabine Lancelin, Philippe Grandrieux. *ed* Françoise Tourmen. *pd* Gerbaux. *m* Alan Vega. *cast* Marc Barbé, Elina Löwensohn, Geraldine Voillat.
● A distinctly arty variation on the serial killer genre, with sparse dialogue, lingering shots of landscape and sexual/murderous encounters, and an elliptical, impressionistic narrative in which solitary, joyless killer Barbé simply travels around France from (uncharacterised) victim to victim until he slips into a strange, fragile, clearly perilous relationship with the haunted, seemingly virginal Löwensohn and her flightier sister. Certainly the film mostly avoids thriller clichés, but for all its evident seriousness of purpose, there's far too much picturesque but uninformative out-of-focus imagery, often on the brink of abstraction, for it to be particularly enlightening about murderers or their victims. That said, Barbé is convincing, and Löwensohn, playing far from Hartley, is extraordinary. GA

Somebody Killed Her Husband

(1978, US, 97 min)
d Lamont Johnson. *p* Martin H Poll. *sc* Reginald Rose. *ph* Andrew Laszlo, Ralf D Bode. *ed* Barry Malkin. *pd* Ted Haworth. *m* Alex North. *cast* Farrah Fawcett-Majors, Jeff Bridges, John Wood, Tammy Grimes, John Glover, Patricia Elliott.
● Good comic acting might have pumped some life into this leaden comedy-thriller scripted by Reginald Rose, a tale of cutesy lovers secreting hubby's corpse in the fridge while tracking the killer who's framed them. But Jeff Bridges is given a nigh-impossible brief (he responds by breathing heavily to convey panic), while Farrah Fawcett-Majors, in her big screen debut, proves predictably inadequate to the task of impersonating Goldie Hawn (let alone Myrna Loy), and simply flashes her teeth at regular intervals. Charmless and dispiriting, the film incidentally elevates word (Bridges sidelines as a writer) over image (cinemas are places to go to annoy other patrons) to confirm its own redundancy. PT

Somebody to Love

(1994, US, 102 min)
d Alexandre Rockwell. *p* Lila Cazes. *sc* Sergei Bodrov, Alexandre Rockwell. *ph* Robert Yeoman. *ed* Elena Maganini. *pd* J Rae Fox. *m* Mader. *cast* Rosie Perez, Harvey Keitel, Anthony Quinn, Michael DeLorenzo, Steve Buscemi, Stanley Tucci, Sam Fuller, Quentin Tarantino.
● Rockwell's shambolic follow-up to *In the Soup* fails to confirm whatever promise the earlier film suggested. Mercedes, an LA taxi dancer, steps on a few toes in her determination to make it big in pictures. She has a thing going with a one-time bit-part actor (Keitel), but can't entirely resist the innocent courtship of a Mexican immigrant labourer (DeLorenzo). When it falls to a benevolent old gangster (Quinn) to play cupid, it's pretty clear we're back 'In the Soup'. Rockwell favours long takes and authentic locations, but his movie stumbles from one actory moment to the next: Keitel in a gorilla suit, Buscemi in drag. At times the film feels like a throwback to the '60s New Wave, with its Sam Fuller cameo and nods to Fellini, at others it resembles one long Rosie Perez audition tape (she sings! she dances! she does improv!). It's a credit to Perez that the story holds together at all (she can practise elocution brushing her teeth with a book on her head, and make it seem natural), but the film's occasional virtues don't survive a prevailing sense of self-indulgence. TCh

Somebody Up There Likes Me

(1956, US, 113 min, b/w)
d Robert Wise. *p* Charles Schnee. *sc* Ernest Lehman. *ph* Joseph Ruttenberg. *ed* Albert Akst. *ad* Cedric Gibbons, Malcolm Brown. *m* Bronislau Kaper. *cast* Paul Newman, Pier Angeli, Everett Sloane, Sal Mineo, Eileen Heckart, Robert Loggia, Harold J Stone, Steve McQueen.
● A disappointing biopic of Rocky Graziano, East Side delinquent turned World Middleweight Champion. The trouble is that Wise forsakes the terse economy and unpretentious naturalism of *The Set-Up* for a rather straggling narrative which spends far too long throwing up mildly socially-conscious observations about poverty, and trying to turn the whole thing into a movie with a message about hope and determination. It's still not that bad a film, however. Newman's performance, though inflected by Method mannerisms, is powerful, and Joseph Ruttenberg's photography keeps the atmosphere sleazy and strong. Perhaps the main problem is the fact that it is a biopic, thus demanding an uplifting ending which seems to go against the grain of the romantic pessimism that governs the boxing genre. GA

Some Call It Loving

(1973, US, 103 min)
d/p/sc James B Harris. *ph* Mario Tosi. *ed* Paul Jasiukonis. *ad* Rodger Maus, Ray Storey. *m* Richard Hazard. *cast* Zalman King, Carol White, Tisa Farrow, Richard Pryor, Veronica Anderson, Logan Ramsey.
● Wonderfully bizarre fantasy, based on a John Collier short story, about a world-weary jazz musician (King) obsessed with the dream of innocence incarnated by a carnival sleeping beauty (Farrow) whom he buys, takes back to his baroque Californian mansion (already inhabited by two ambivalently voluptuous women), and awakens for a haunting game of death and love betrayed. Conceived by Harris after working with Kubrick on the script of *Lolita*, it works as a kind

of free jazz improvisation (there is a marvellous score by Richard Hazard), and might be described as a further exploration of what Nabokov's Humbert Humbert called his 'petrified paroxysm of desire'. Unmissable for anyone with an open mind and a sense of cinematic adventure. TM

Some Came Running

(1958, US, 136 min)
d Vincente Minnelli. *p* Sol C Siegel. *sc* John Patrick, Arthur Sheekman. *ph* William H Daniels. *ed* Adrienne Fazan. *ad* William A Horning, Urie McCleary. *m* Elmer Bernstein. *cast* Frank Sinatra, Dean Martin, Shirley MacLaine, Martha Hyer, Arthur Kennedy, Nancy Gates, Leora Dana.

● A marvellous, garish drama about a writer (Sinatra) returning from the war to the small town he grew up in, *Some Came Running* is probably best remembered for the reference in Godard's *Le Mépris*. Like Godard's, it's a contrived film, populated by types rather than characters: Martha Hyer = conformity, Shirley MacLaine = freedom, Dean Martin = conformity. Minnelli's great achievement is the superbly orchestrated intensity of feelings the central characters generate in their various clashes. As a result, the dramatic curve of Sinatra's agonising voyage of self-discovery through the cheap neon-lit bars and cold houses, which ends in the clam of self-acceptance, is given an intensified realism which precisely reflects the neurotic 'writerly' view of life that he must overcome before he can write again. PH

Some Girls (aka Sisters)

(1988, US, 93 min)
d Michael Hoffman. *p* Rick Stevenson. *sc* Rupert Walters. *ph* Ueli Steiger. *ed* David Spiers. *pd* Eugenio Zanetti. *m* James Newton Howard. *cast* Patrick Dempsey, Jennifer Connelly, Sheila Kelley, Lance Edwards, Lila Kedrova, Florinda Bolkan, André Gregory, Ashley Greenfield.

● Michael (Dempsey) arrives in Quebec to spend Christmas with his girlfriend (Connelly), but no sooner has he stepped through the imposing door of the family mansion than she tells him she no longer loves him. Thus a chain of peculiar incidents is set in motion, with Michael an innocent among eccentrics. Dad (Gregory) is an intellectual who wanders the house naked, Mum (Bolkan) is a strict Catholic, Granny (Kedrova) mistakes Michael for her dead husband, and the sisters (Kelly, Greenfield) share a strange bond which translates into a common desire for their confused visitor. A number of interesting ideas are thrown up but never fully developed. Instead, we get teen comedy laden with plenty of Adult Atmosphere. To its credit, the film is well cast and boasts imaginative production design, but is neither particularly funny nor emotionally credible. CM

Some Kinda Love (Romance)

(1995, Jap, 94 min)
d Shunichi Nagasaki. *p* Shiro Sasaki, Hidekazu Uehara. *sc* Shunichi Nagasaki. *ph* Shigeru Honda. *ed* Ryuji Miyajima. *ad* Yohei Taneda. *m* Koji Tamaki. *cast* Koji Tamaki, LaSalle Ishii, Kaori Mizushima, Shinya Tsukamoto, Takeshi Naito, Chikako Aoyama.

● Two former classmates (one a town hall planner, the other a less than high minded property developer) have their lives turned upside down by close encounters with Kiriko (Mizushima), a charming flake whose obsession with UFOs somehow matches her inability to stay in one place for long. Probably too light to be a real *Jules et Jim* for the 1990s; it needs more of the darker colourings Nagasaki brings to most of his films. But it has many pleasures, including cameos from *Tetsuo* director Shinya Tsukamoto as a corruptible bureaucrat and Nagasaki veteran Takeshi Naito as Kiriko's hapless husband, a forlorn but stoic dentist. TR

Some Kind of Hero

(1981, US, 97 min)
d Michael Pressman. *p* Howard W Koch. *sc* James Kirkwood, Robert Boris. *ph* King Baggot. *ed* Christopher Greenbury. *ad* James Schoppe. *m* Patrick Williams. *cast* Richard Pryor, Margot Kidder, Ray Sharkey, Ronny Cox, Lynne Moody, Olivia Cole, Paul Benjamin.

● A minor but infinitely more appealing comedy vehicle for Pryor than the earlier *Stir Crazy*. He plays a hapless PoW returning from Vietnam to find he can't draw his army pay, his wife has fallen for someone else, his business is bankrupt, and a stroke has left his mother with only one word in her vocabulary: 'Shit!' What follows could easily have been mawkish drivel, but Pryor is one of the great exponents of comic masochism, and is able to make even such ancient set pieces as the timid bank robber passably funny. Kidder pitches into the comparatively feeble role of a high-class hooker with her usual exuberance, and the result is an amiable but hardly memorable two-against-the-world farce that can't quite persuade you Pryor's talents are being properly used. DP

Some Kind of Life

(1995, GB, 102 min)
d Julian Jarrold. *p* Bill Boyes. *sc* Kay Mellor. *ph* David Odd. *ed* Edward Mansell. *pd* Michael Young. *m* David Ferguson. *cast* Jane Horrocks, Ray Stevenson, Gwen Taylor, Andrew Tiernan.

● A low-key tale, funded by Granada TV, of a woman's struggle to rebuild her life after husband Steve, a mechanic, is brain-damaged in a motorcycle accident. Alison (Horrocks) has to fight for compensation and fend off over-protective parents, but she also has to stop Steve (Stevenson) initiating food fights with the young son whose mental age he now shares. Before long, she's considering what she wants. Not without clichés, but the performances are unfussy and a Kay Mellor's screenplay avoids 'issue drama' dreariness. JO'C

Some Kind of Love

see Some Kinda Love

Some Kind of Wonderful

(1987, US, 93 min)
d Howard Deutch. *p/sc* John Hughes. *ph* Jan Kiesser. *ed* Bud Smith, Scott Smith. *pd* Josan Russo. *m* Stephen Hague, John Musser. *cast* Eric Stoltz, Mary Stuart Masterson, Lea Thompson, Craig Sheffer, John Ashton, Elias Koteas, Molly Hagan.

● Who said John Hughes doesn't have artistic integrity? When preview audiences threw out his misfit romance in favour of preppie love at the end of *Pretty in Pink* (which Deutch also directed), Hughes sat right down and wrote the story again – this time with Stoltz in the Molly Ringwald role, Masterson as Jon Cryer, and Thompson as Andrew McCarthy. And this time it ends with the underdogs together. Oddly enough, it's this conclusion that feels phony, seeing as Stoltz has spent the last 80 minutes arranging his dream date with Lea. Watch the opening title sequence for a handy summation of the teen movie's staple ingredients: class, sex, music. TCh

Some Like It Hot 100 (100)

(1959, US, 121 min, b/w)
d/p Billy Wilder. *sc* Billy Wilder, IAL Diamond. *ph* Charles Lang Jr. *ed* Arthur P Schmidt. *ad* Ted Haworth. *m* Adolph Deutsch. *cast* Tony Curtis, Jack Lemmon, Marilyn Monroe, Joe E Brown, George Raft, Pat O'Brien, Nehemiah Persoff, Joan Shawlee.

● Still one of Wilder's funniest satires, its pace flagging only once for a short time. Curtis and Lemmon play jazz musicians on the run after witnessing the St Valentine's Day massacre, masquerading in drag as members of an all-girl band (with resulting gender confusions involving Marilyn) to escape the clutches of Chicago mobster George Raft (bespatted and dime-flipping, of course). Deliberately shot in black-and-white to avoid the pitfalls of camp or transvestism, though the best sequences are the gangland ones anyhow. Highlights include Curtis' playboy parody of Cary Grant, and what is surely one of the great curtain lines of all time: Joe E Brown's bland 'Nobody's perfect' when his fiancée (Lemmon) finally confesses that she's a he. RM

Some Mother's Son

(1996, Ire/US, 111 min)
d Terry George. *p* Jim Sheridan, Arthur Lappin, Edwin Burke. *sc* Terry George, Jim Sheridan. *ph* Geoffrey Simpson. *ed* Craig McKay. *pd* David Wilson. *m* Bill Whelan. *cast* Helen Mirren, Fionnula Flanagan, Aidan Gillen, John Lynch, David O'Hara, Tom Hollander, Tim Woodward, Ciaran Hinds, Gerard McSorley.

● As the title suggests, this film about the 1981 Republican Hunger Strikes, by Belfast-born writer/director Terry George, is more interested in human emotions than political manoeuvring. Ten men starved themselves to death when the IRA prisoners' strategic request for 'political' status came up against the Thatcher administration's determined 'criminalisation' of the terrorists. Into that grinding head-to-head, we follow two very different mothers whose boys are part of the protest. Mirren's Kathleen Quigley is a quiet middle-class widow, shocked by the conviction of her eldest son Gerard (Gillen) for murdering a British soldier, while Flanagan's Annie Higgins, from staunch Republican stock, takes pride in her son Frank (O'Hara), when he's arrested after the same incident. Detailing their contrasting responses to a traumatic situation allows the film to tap unpartisan sympathy while keeping its own counsel on the terminal machinations of the ideologues on both sides. Performances scar the screen, while George shows keen organisational instinct and delivers the urgent immediacy of news footage throughout. IRA propaganda it is not. Instead, it's a plea for simple humanity over ideological point-scoring, an urgent message even yet, no matter that the film seems to expose old wounds. Of all the films to have come out of the Troubles, this one offers the most complex analysis and cuts the deepest. TJ

Someone at the Door

(1936, GB, 74 min, b/w)
d Herbert Brenon. *p* Walter C Mycroft. *sc* Jack Davies, Marjorie Deans. *ph* Bryan Langley. *ad* Cedric Dawe. *cast* Billy Milton, Aileen Marson, Noah Beery, Edward Chapman, John Irwin, Hermione Gingold.

● Brenon was a leading Hollywood director in the '20s, working with the likes of Theda Bara and Ronald Colman. But his career fizzled with the coming of sound. He couldn't see it lasting. By the time he pulled his head out of the sand, there was no work left, so he returned to his native England and made a series of lively but forgettable comedies. This is a prime example of British Brenon, a creaky but well-crafted comic thriller (from a play by Dorothy and Campbell Christie) about a mischievous journalist who fabricates a murder mystery to further his career. GM

Someone Else's America (L'Amérique des autres)

(1995, Fr/GB/Ger, 96 min)
d Goran Paskaljevic. *p* Antoine de Clermont-Tonnerre, Gordan Mihic, David Rose, Helga Bähr. *sc* Gordan Mihic. *ph* Yorgos Arvanitis. *ed* William Diver. *ad* Wolf Seeselberg, Milenko Jeremic, Caty Maxey. *m* Andrew Dickson. *cast* Tom Conti, Miki Manojlovic, Maria Casarès, Zorka Manojlovic, Sergej Trifunovic.

● This Euro pudding film, made by a Belgrade-born director, finds a corner of low-rent New York that is forever the Old Country. In the backyard of Brooklyn's Paradiso bar, the blind mother of the Spanish owner, Alonso, draws water each morning from a well and milks the goat. When the family of Montenegran odd-job man Bayo eventually gains illegal entry to the US, his mum isn't so immediately at home, but ne'er-do-well eldest boy Luka gets right into the enterprise spirit and starts creating a future everyone can build on. This sentimental, deeply unpersuasive look at the immigrant's lot, dies virtually the minute Conti ambles on as Alonso, reprising his caricature Greek fisherman from *Shirley Valentine*. Almost as bad is the Brooklyn backdrop rigged up in a Hamburg studio, which resembles nothing so much as a set for *Sesame Street*. TJ

Someone Is Bleeding

see Seins de glace, Les

Someone Like You... (aka Animal Attraction)

(2001, US, 97 min)
d Tony Goldwyn. *p* Lynda Obst. *sc* Elizabeth Chandler. *ph* Anthony B Richmond. *ed* Dana Congdon. *pd* Dan Leigh. *m* Rolfe Kent. *cast* Ashley Judd, Greg Kinnear, Hugh Jackman, Marisa Tomei, Ellen Barkin, Laura Regan, Catherine Dent.

● Jane Goodale (Judd) is a talent-booker, her job to 'get the ungettable' guest for demanding daytime talk-show host Diane (Barkin). Charming exec producer Ray (Kinnear) is coming on strong to Jane, but just as they're about to sign on a spectacular love nest, he cools, inexplicably. Heartbroken and homeless, she moves in with womanising workmate Eddie (Jackman), who provides an unusually sympathetic shoulder as well as an excellent case study for her ensuing analysis of male amatory patterns. When best friend and serial dater Liz (Tomei), editor of a men's magazine, persuades Jane to write a pseudonymous column expounding her ideas, before long she's become that 'ungettable' guest for Diane's show. Recalling *Bridget Jones* and TV's *Sex and the City*, the protagonist's emotional crises provide the plotline, and there's even a voice-over. Unlike its models, however, it's neither clever nor that funny, the starry cast is underused, and the potential for a much wittier script never fulfilled. JFu

Someone to Love

(1987, US, 105 min)
d Henry Jaglom. *p* MH Simonsons. *sc* Henry Jaglom. *ph* Hanania Baer. *ed* Henry Jaglom. *cast* Orson Welles, Henry Jaglom, Andrea Marcovicci, Michael Emil, Sally Kellerman, Oja Kodar, Stephen Bishop, Dave Frishberg.
●Having re-lived, in *Always*, the dissolution of his own marriage, Jaglom here confronts the dilemma of post-marital solitude: try again, or opt for autonomy? Film-maker Danny (Jaglom) wants to settle down, but girlfriend Helen (Marcovicci, Jaglom's real-life girlfriend) is reluctant to surrender her independence. Curious why so many of his peers live alone, Danny hosts a party in an abandoned theatre, and invites his guests to open up for the camera. Only Jaglom/Danny's friend and mentor Orson Welles – his last performance – injects some objectivity into the proceedings. Orson's observations on film, feminism ('the great revolution of our times'), marriage etc. are as wittily perceptive as one might expect; but our Henry lacks any proper perspective on his own reactionary mores, and seems as ill-equipped as Danny to divorce life from the movies. As an exercise in creative editing and a sociological document, the film is occasionally fascinating; but its endless romantic confessions and airhead philosophising make you want to scream. GA

Someone to Watch Over Me

(1987, US, 106 min)
d Ridley Scott. *p* Thierry de Ganay. *sc* Howard Franklin. *ph* Steven Poster. *ed* Claire Simpson. *pd* James D Bissell. *m* Michael Kamen. *cast* Tom Berenger, Mimi Rogers, Lorraine Bracco, Jerry Orbach, John Rubinstein, Andreas Katsulas.
●Most of New York, indoors and out, looks about as good as the Chrysler Building in Scott's gleaming fusion of eternal triangle and killer-on-the-loose. Happily married cop Berenger is assigned to protect a key witness to a murder, wealthy Upper East Side socialite Rogers, and they fall in love. She has class, he has none. Would a slob and a snob go for each other? Well, possibly, since his professionally protective side is involved, and her poise is replaced by fear for her life. It is beautifully played, and the restaurant scene in which the honest cop finds himself unable to lie to his wife (Bracco) shudders with shame, dread, pain and helplessness. You feel for all three of them. There are splendid economies, too: Rogers' mirrored dressing-room registers first as a social humiliation for the cop, who can't find the exit, but later his intimacy with her surroundings gives him an edge over a killer. There's little waste, though the thriller element could have been tuned up a bit. BC

Somersault in a Coffin (Tabutta Rövasata)

(1996, Tur, 76 min)
d Dervis Zaim. *p* Ezel Akay, Dervis Zaim. *sc* Dervis Zaim. *ph* Mustafa Kuscu. *ed* Mustafa Freseva. *cast* Ahmet Ugurlu, Tuncel Kurtiz, Aysen Aydemir, Serif Erol, Fuat Onan.
●This no-budget first feature from a Cyprus-born director is very likely the best Turkish movie of the 1990s. Mahsun (Ugurlu, a distinguished stage actor) is an alcoholic and a street sleeper, known to the Istanbul cops as an expert car thief. Essentially a picaresque account of this human wreck's exploits, which include a turbulent relationship with a junkie prostitute and the theft of a peacock from a national park, the film uses Mahsun as an index of the currents of fear and loathing which it sees permeating life in 'modern' Turkey. Zaim says the character is based on a real-life prototype, but the film has none of the limitations of docu-drama: vigorous hand-held camerawork complements a sophisticated grasp of pacing and structure. TR

Something Big

(1971, US, 108 min)
d/p Andrew V McLaglen. *sc* James Lee Barrett. *ph* Harry Stradling Jr. *ed* Robert Simpson. *ad* Alfred Sweeney. *m* Marvin Hamlisch. *cast* Dean Martin, Brian Keith, Honor Blackman, Carol White, Ben Johnson, Albert Salmi, Paul Fix, Denver Pyle, Harry Carey Jr.
●One gruesome symptom of the Death of the Western was the 'comedy Western', a messy, confused genre that flourished briefly in the late '60s and early '70s. Occasionally, the genre produced the odd bizarre gem – notably *Cat Ballou* and *There Was a Crooked Man* – but this was one of the less honourable efforts. Martin plays a baddie in town to give his retiring adversary, cavalry colonel Keith, a last, leadenly parodic run for his money. Typically for the genre, a few Brits are around to add incongruity – here, Blackman and then-trendy starlet White. TCh

Something for Everyone (aka Black Flowers for the Bride)

(1970, US, 113 min)
d Harold Prince. *p* John P Flaxman. *sc* Hugh Wheeler. *ph* Walter Lassally. *ed* Ralph Rosenblum. *pd* Herta Pischinger. *m* John Kander. *cast* Angela Lansbury, Michael York, Anthony Corlan, Heidelinde Weis, Eva-Marie Meineke, John Gill.
●Black comedy from stage director Prince, based on Harry Kressing's novel *The Cook*, fatally flawed by the casting of York as the mastermind behind various 'disappearances' and so forth as he schemes his way to ownership of Ornstein Castle. Shot on location in Bavaria, and full of downhill-going nobility with shrinking purses and growing pretensions. If you can take stray eyefuls of *Sound of Music*, you'll be rewarded by a beautiful performance from Angela Lansbury.

Something Happened

(1987, Swe, 24 min)
d/p/sc Roy Andersson. *ph* István Borbás. *ed* Roy Andersson.
●Andersson reckons the health authorities wouldn't let him finish the AIDS-awareness film they'd commissioned because he'd discovered the virus was probably the product of medical research. Maybe, but perhaps they weren't expecting anything as bizarre or as occasionally hilarious as this startling precursor to the aesthetic strategies of *Songs from the Second Floor*. That's not to say there aren't scenes here as harrowing as a nightmare; but the merciless satirising of the medical establishment's absurd scapegoating of minorities and hapless inadequacy in the face of disaster is scathingly brilliant. GA

Something of Value

(1957, US, 113 min, b/w)
d Richard Brooks. *p* Pandro S Berman. *sc* Richard Brooks. *ph* Russell Harlan. *ed* Ferris Webster. *ad* William A Horning, Edward C Carfagno. *m* Miklós Rozsa. *cast* Rock Hudson, Sidney Poitier, Dana Wynter, Wendy Hiller, Robert Beatty, Michael Pate.
●The best-seller status of Robert Ruark's novel, and Brooks' affinity with liberal issues generally, explains why MGM rather improbably found itself tackling the ramifications of the Mau Mau campaign against white settlers of the early 1950s. With Kenya represented by the leafier bits of the studio backlot plus sore-thumb location inserts, with the blacks speaking in variously Puerto Rican and Jamaican accents, and with Hudson and Hiller supposed to be brother and sister, this never really stood a chance. Brooks' chief insight – good and bad on both sides, tolerance the answer – hardly seizes the imagination, and the contentious climax, with Hudson carrying a wounded Poitier on his back, has every indication of being intended symbolically. A brief prologue written and spoken on-camera by Winston Churchill was deleted pre-release, having bored a preview audience. BBa

Something to Believe In

(1997, GB/Ger, 113 min)
d/p John Hough. *sc* John Goldsmith, John Hough. *ph* Tony Pierce Roberts. *ed* Peter Tanner. *pd* Nello Giorgetti. *m* Lalo Schifrin. *cast* William McNamara, Maria Pitillo, Tom Conti, Maria Schneider, Ian Bannen, Robert Wagner, Jill St John, Roddy McDowall.
●A jaw-dropping amalgam of syrupy romance, terminal illness, divine intervention and classical music. McNamara plays an American pianist whose improvisatory flair shocks the Paris Conservatoire, but who may still secure a concert career if he wins the Barbarina competition in Naples. Pitillo is a Las Vegas croupier forced to quit her job after diagnosis of fatal disease. Her sole hope lies in travelling to an Italian village church where a weeping Madonna has prompted talk of miracle cures. Guess who she bumps into? This sets up a finale that works in the redemptive power of love over mortality, Lalo Schifrin's Piano Concerto performed on live TV watched by the entire world, and the hand of the Almighty Himself. TJ

Something to Hide

(1971, GB, 99 min)
d Alastair Reid. *p* Michael Klinger. *sc* Alastair Reid. *ph* Wolfgang Suschitzky. *ed* Reginald Beck. *ad* Anthony Pratt. *m* Roy Budd, Jack Fishman. *cast* Peter Finch, Shelley Winters, Colin Blakely, John Stride, Linda Hayden, Harold Goldblatt.
●Winters and Finch, sparring out a last drunken evening together, make a sufficiently unlikely married couple for one to regret her exit after ten minutes. What might have happened between them is a more interesting conjecture than what actually develops in this adaptation of Nicholas Monsarrat's novel, with Finch acting reluctant midwife to an unmarried teenage hitchhiker (Hayden) under very implausible circumstances. He goes through his alcoholic male menopause looking as if he wished Burton had got the part. What really sinks the thing is the impossible mixture of symbolism – striving for universal significance and stopping little short of lionesses whelping in the streets – and heavy-handed observation, where (for example) mental crack-up is primarily indicated by wearing odd-coloured socks. Melodrama runs amok on the Isle of Wight, and the nodding references to Chabrol make it all the more uncomfortable. CPe

Something to Talk About

(1995, US, 105 min)
d Lasse Hallström. *p* Anthea Sylbert, Paula Weinstein. *sc* Callie Khouri. *ph* Sven Nykvist. *ed* Mia Goldman. *pd* Mel Bourne. *m* Hans Zimmer, Graham Preskett. *cast* Julia Roberts, Dennis Quaid, Robert Duvall, Gena Rowlands, Kyra Sedgwick, Brett Cullen, Haley Aull.
●After a couple of false starts, Lasse Hallström appears to have found a niche for himself in Hollywood as a purveyor of eccentric character pieces; mellow-dramas with class. Working here from a choice script by Callie Khouri (*Thelma & Louise*), he's fashioned a gently caustic soap about adultery, parenthood and independence. Roberts is Grace Bichon, wife, mother, daughter and manager at the family's award-winning stables – not necessarily in that order. Grace has allowed herself to drift into the absent-minded inertia expected of a respectable Southern woman. She's shocked to find out that husband Eddie (Quaid) has been fooling around, but disappointed when the folks (Duvall and Rowlands) try to talk her back into the fold. Only her sister (Sedgwick, very plausible) understands, planting her knee firmly in Eddie's groin. Although the film-makers ill-advisedly saddle themselves with a brattish kid with a speech impediment and a corny-as-Kelloggs show jumping finale, for the most part this is a pleasing, polished affair, honest enough to steer a compassionate middle course without succumbing to caricature or conservative sentimentality. TCh

Something Wicked This Way Comes

(1982, US, 95 min)
d Jack Clayton. *p* Peter Douglas. *sc* Ray Bradbury. *ph* Stephen H Burum. *ed* Argyle Nelson, Barry Mark Gordon. *pd* Richard MacDonald. *m* James Horner. *cast* Jason Robards, Jonathan Pryce, Diane Ladd, Pam Grier, Royal Dano, Vidal Peterson, Shawn Carson, James Stacy.

● No wonder Disney executives went wild when they saw what Clayton had done to Ray Bradbury's novel, turning the tone several shades blacker and dampening down the sentimentality. With the arrival of Dark's Pandemonium Carnival in a small midwestern town, all hell breaks loose. Soon the locals are queueing up outside the Temple of Temptation where, for a quick moral sacrifice, everything your heart desires pops up in glorious array; children start to despise their parents, who in turn hanker after their children's youth. Clayton takes a distinctly unwholesome relish in stirring up this puritan nightmare, piling a heap of torments on the heads of his two boy heroes, and finally restoring cosy order with thoroughly forced conviction. Ultimately, though, it's an uneasy blend of horror and whimsy, with the allegory being hammered a little too hard for comfort. It's also marred by some dreadfully tacky special effects and set designs. JP

Something Wild

(1986, US, 114 min)
d Jonathan Demme. *p* Jonathan Demme, Kenneth Utt. *sc* E Max Frye. *ph* Tak Fujimoto. *ed* Craig McKay. *pd* Norma Moriceau. *m* John Cale, Laurie Anderson. *cast* Jeff Daniels, Melanie Griffith, Ray Liotta, Margaret Colin, Tracey Walter, Dana Preu, Jack Gilpin, John Waters, John Sayles.

● When squeaky-clean Big Apple businessman Charlie Driggs (Daniels) walks away from a diner without paying the bill, his brief excursion into crime attracts the attention of Louise Brooks lookalike Lulu (Griffith). This distinctly downmarket *femme fatale* hijacks the lad with the offer of a lift that soon develops into a lunatic weekend of stealing booze and bondage sex. More alarmingly, Charlie's confusion at the woman's wobbly, protean personality is soon aggravated by the arrival of her ex-con ex (Liotta), who abducts the odd couple for his own violently vengeful purposes. A truly original cocktail, mixing *Bringing Up Baby*-style comedy with the lethal paranoia of *film noir*, Demme's gem distinguishes itself from other 'yuppie nightmare' movies (*Blue Velvet, After Hours*) by its very real sympathy for its oddball characters. Demme observes the human eccentricity that underlies the corner-store banalities of Middle America with warmth and loving detail; while a magnificent rock soundtrack and faultless performances from Daniels, Griffith and Liotta ensure pleasures galore. GA

Sometimes a Great Notion (aka Never Give an Inch)

(1971, US, 114 min)
d Paul Newman. *p* John Foreman. *sc* John Gay. *ph* Richard Moore. *ed* Robert Wyman. *ad* Philip M Jefferies. *m* Henry Mancini. *cast* Paul Newman, Henry Fonda, Lee Remick, Michael Sarrazin, Richard Jaeckel, Linda Lawson, Cliff Potts.

● Taken on by Newman half way through (the film was started by Richard A Colla), the surprising thing about this adaptation of Ken Kesey's novel is that it holds together at all: a drama about a family of independent lumberjacks, ruled over by Henry Fonda's biblical father, whose unity is shattered by the arrival of a wayward son (Sarrazin) in the midst of a dispute with other (striking) loggers. If the struggle within the family too quickly degenerates into hand-me-down Tennessee Williams dramatics, Newman's handling of the outdoor scenes, especially those involving work, is – like his own acting – restrained but powerfully evocative. PH

Sometimes I Look at My Life (A Veces Miro Mi Vida)

(1982, Cuba, 79 min)
d Orlando Rojas. *p* Jesús Diaz de la Cerda. *sc* Rafael Hernandez, Orlando Rojas, Ana Rodriguez. *ph* Adriano Moreno, Julio Simoneau. *ed* Gladys Cambre, Roberto Bravo. *cast* Harry Belafonte, Letta Mbulu, Falumi Prince.

● It's rare to see any movie which manages to get everything so conclusively wrong as this does. From its random use of film clips (often in the wrong format, and in black-and-white from colour films) to its central uninspired interview with Belafonte, this 'Cuban view of an American entertainer' (who visited Cuba for a concert in 1980) takes a potentially interesting subject and squanders it. If you like Belafonte, you'd be better off with an album; if you don't, then rest assured that this would do nothing to kindle your enthusiasm. SM

Sometime, Somewhere (Oridathu)

(1987, Ind, 112 min)
d/sc/pd/m G Aravindan. *ph* Shaji. *ed* KR Bose. *cast* Nedumudi Venu, Sreenivasan, Thilakan, Vineeth, MS Trippunithura.

● Aravindan's incandescent film is a dream come true: a perfectly plotless movie that is paradoxically crammed with incident, much of it at least notionally dramatic. It offers a richly detailed picture of life in a Kerala village in the 1950s, at the moment of transition prompted by the arrival of electricity. The tyranny of a storyline is kept at bay by spreading the focus around a huge cast; what binds it all together is the unique poetry of the film language, full of unorthodox editing patterns and compositions. Aravindan looks more and more like India's answer to Ozu, but his poetry is less rigorous, more intuitive, and possibly even more beautiful. TR

Some Voices

(2000, GB, 101 min)
d Simon Cellan Jones. *p* Damian Jones, Graham Broadbent. *sc* Joe Penhall. *ph* David Odd. *ed* Elen Pierce Lewis. *pd* Zoë MacLeod. *m* Adrian Johnston. *cast* Daniel Craig, David Morrissey, Kelly MacDonald, Julie Graham, Peter McDonald, Nicholas Palliser, Edward Tudor Pole.

● Released after years of mental healthcare, Ray (Craig) is put on medication and placed in the care of brother Pete (Morrissey), the owner of a café. Walking again through Shepherd's Bush, W London, is uncomfortable, but badgering Pete for a job in the kitchen should give Ray stability, while an encounter with Laura (MacDonald) may open new possibilities. Laura's attracted to Dave because he's direct to the point of foolhardiness, spontaneous and fun to be with. She senses, however, that he's not quite like anyone she's met before. Penhall's adaptation of his play remains an actors' showcase. Morrissey skilfully registers abiding filial love tested by simmering exasperation; MacDonald's adept at lippy on top, vulnerable underneath; and Craig's vibrant yet haunted expressiveness tells us everything needful about this doomed sweetheart. It's thus overegging it somewhat when the whirling camera effects and freaky sound mix overstates the point that our man really is not well. TJ

Somewhere in Berlin... (Irgendwo in Berlin...)

(1946, EGer, 83 min, b/w)
d/sc Gerhard Lamprecht. *ph* Werner Krien. *ed* Lena Neumann. *ad* Otto Erdmann. *m* Erich Einegg. *cast* Charles Knetschke, Hans Trinkaus, Harry Hindemith, Hedda Sarnow, Fritz Rasp.

● Children playing war games among the rubble, soldiers returning home listless and traumatised, a boy tumbling to his death from the shard of a bombed building. It's the same world as Rossellini's *Germany Year Zero* – but viewed so oppositely that each film seems like a ghastly parody of the other. Lamprecht made the '30s kids' classic *Emil and the Detectives*, and here his ragamuffins set about putting food on the table and motivating despondent adults with the same vim and resourcefulness that Emil's lot applied to catching a gang of crooks. It's optimistic and inspirational to the same degree that Rossellini's film is bleak and despairing. No one could fail to be irritated by one or the other. BBa

Somewhere in the Night

(1946, US, 110 min, b/w)
d Joseph L Mankiewicz. *p* Anderson Lawler. *sc* Howard Dimsdale, Joseph L Mankiewicz, Lee Strasberg. *ph* Norbert Brodine. *ed* James B Clark. *ad* James Basevi, Maurice Ransford. *m* David Buttolph. *cast* John Hodiak, Nancy Guild, Lloyd Nolan, Richard Conte, Josephine Hutchinson, Fritz Kortner, Margo Woode, Sheldon Leonard, John Russell, Houseley Stevenson.

● Hodiak as a marine blown up at Okinawa who returns to Los Angeles armed only with a name that means nothing to him and a letter from a girl, now dead, who hated him. Out of this familiar premise, Mankiewicz has fashioned a classic *film noir* account of the amnesiac who suspects he isn't going to like rediscovering the man he once was. His odyssey in quest of himself leads through a long dark night with murder and a missing $2 million dollars at the end of it, peopled along the way by the lost and the lonely, the suave and the sinister (wonderful supporting performances) and taking in a series of suitably clammy settings (waterfront fortune-telling parlour, mission hall, sanatorium for the insane). Mankiewicz's superb control of a complex plot (as both writer and director) takes him into at least one outstanding set piece: an elaborate nightclub sequence in which Hodiak questions a bartender, the latter casually tips off two hoods, a bowl of pretzels is slipped down the bar to identify the target, and just as something is about to explode, the lights dim as the band strikes up a new number... TM

Somewhere in Time

(1980, US, 104 min)
d Jeannot Szwarc. *p* Stephen Deutsch. *sc* Richard Matheson. *ph* Isidore Mankofsky. *ed* Jeff Gourson. *pd* Seymour Klate. *m* John Barry. *cast* Christopher Reeve, Christopher Plummer, Jane Seymour, Teresa Wright, Bill Erwin, George Voskovec.

● Adapting his own novel *Bid Time Return*, and with characteristic indifference to current film taste, Richard Matheson has here provided one of the most idiosyncratic scripts of 1980, about a writer who wills himself back in time to the early 1900s in order to fall in love with a distinguished actress. In its unashamed romanticism, this is the kind of thing David O Selznick was producing in the 1940s; but scripts cannot make themselves, and *Somewhere in Time* is cursed with truly atrocious staging, plus Christopher Reeve looking awkwardly man-of-steelish as the hero. A few emotional echoes remain, and one climactic coup in which the hero is dragged forward in time; otherwise this must go down as a missed opportunity. DP

Sommaren med Monika (Monika/Summer with Monika)

(1952, Swe, 97 min, b/w)
d Ingmar Bergman. *p* Allan Ekelund. *sc* Ingmar Bergman, Per Anders Fogelström. *ph* Gunnar Fischer. *ed* Tage Holmberg, Gösta Lewin. *ad* PA Lundgren, Nils Svenwall. *m* Erik Nordgren. *cast* Harriet Andersson, Lars Ekborg, John Harryson, Georg Skarstedt, Dagmar Ebbeson, Ake Fridell.

● A tender yet unsentimental account of a love affair that turns sour. Harriet Andersson gives a precociously assured performance as a wild, feckless girl from Stockholm's poorer quarter who falls in love with a 19-year-old youth. During an idyllic motor-boat holiday among the islands of the Stockholm archipelago, the girl becomes pregnant and the couple, forced to marry, set up home in a tiny, cramped flat. Very soon, love gives way to distrust and hostility, and they agree to part. Bergman's sympathetic eye and Gunnar Fischer's atmospheric photography invest the locations with a poetic significance, the light and open spaces of the holiday islands contrasted tellingly with the dark claustrophobia of the city, where the flame of the couple's love is slowly extinguished by the lack of air. NF

Sommarlek (Illicit Interlude/ Summer Interlude)

(1950, Swe, 96 min, b/w)
d Ingmar Bergman. *sc* Herbert Grevenius, Ingmar Bergman. *ph* Gunnar Fischer. *ed* Oscar Rosander. *ad* Nils Svenwall. *m* Erik Nordgren. *cast* Maj-Britt Nilsson, Birger Malmsten, Alf Kjellin, Georg Funkquist, Renée Björling, Mimi Pollak.

● Told in flashback as the memories of a ballerina approaching the end of her career, this sensitively observed story traces a teenage love affair which took place one idyllic summer on the archipelago near Stockholm. Bergman's preoccupation with the transition from youthful innocence to adult experience is already clearly marked here, as is the double movement of a journey backward into one's own past which nevertheless marks a spiritual progression. For it is through her reliving of her past that the heroine comes to embrace the tentative possibilities for her future. The translation of the title, incidentally, is incorrect and misleading. *Sommarlek* means *Summer Games*, and Bergman's concern is with the transience of playful youth. NF

Sommersby

(1993, US/Fr, 113 min)
d Jon Amiel. *p* Arnon Milchan, Steven Reuther. *sc* Nicholas Meyer, Sarah Kernochan. *ph* Philippe Rousellot. *ed* Peter Boyle. *pd* Bruno Rubeo. *m* Danny Elfman. *cast* Richard Gere, Jodie Foster, Bill Pullman, James Earl Jones, Lanny Flaherty, William Windom.
●Seven years after leaving to fight in the Civil War, Jack Sommersby (Gere) returns to his wife (Foster), son and Tennessee home a changed man. Formerly a brute and none-too-successful plantation owner, he credits his much-improved personality to what he learned from a fellow PoW, now dead. But is he Jack? The doubt, strongest in his wife's mind but also entertained by the community, is swept aside, thanks to the happiness and prosperity he brings. But accusations of murder are less easily ignored... This sumptuous Hollywood remake of *The Return of Martin Guerre* is better than one might expect (though Jack comes over as far too much the modern New Man: sensitive hubby, visionary businessman, committed to racial equality, etc). The solid script makes the most of the dilemmas and paradoxes of the couple's predicament; Philippe Rousselot's photography manages to be lyrical without becoming too cloyingly picturesque; and surprisingly (the *only* surprise in this craftsmanlike but unremarkable movie), it doesn't cop out at the end. GA

Son, The (Le Fils)

(2002, Bel, 103 min)
d Jean-Pierre Dardenne, Luc Dardenne. *p* Jean-Pierre Dardenne, Luc Dardenne, Denis Freyd. *sc* Jean-Pierre Dardenne, Luc Dardenne. *ph* Alain Marcoen. *ed* Marie-Hélène Dozo. *pd* Igor Gabriel. *cast* Olivier Gourmet, Morgan Marinne, Isabella Soupart, Rémy Renaud, Nassim Hassaïni, Kevin Leroy, Félicien Pitsaer.
●Olivier (Gourmet) is a good teacher of carpentry, but a touch gruff; even so, when he refuses to accept young Francis into his workshop, that doesn't explain why he takes to following the boy, as if he were spying on him. Might it have something to do with his own dead son, as his estranged wife insists? One strength of the Dardennes' follow-up to *Rosetta*, winner of the Cannes Palme d'Or, is that, once again, they ask us to discover certain crucial facts for ourselves: by the time we're faced with questions of ethical and spiritual import, we've done enough groundwork to assess the evidence properly. Wisely, the camera stays close to Gourmet, with the result that, notwithstanding his subtle understatement and a relatively taciturn script, we're privy to his every fleeting thought and nagging emotion. Never manipulative or sensationalist, the film is none the less deeply moving. GA

Sonatine

(1993, Jap, 94 min)
d Takeshi Kitano. *p* Masayuki Mori, Hisao Nabeshima, Takio Yoshida. *sc* Takeshi Kitano. *ph* Katsumi Yanagishima. *ed* Takeshi Kitano. *ad* Osamu Sasaki. *m* Joe Hisaishi. *cast* Takeshi Kitano, Aya Kokumai, Tetsu Watanabe, Masanobu Katsumura, Susumu Terashima.
●The terrific thing about *Sonatine* is its freshness, its ability to surprise. Basically, it's a slightly offbeat variation on the traditional yakuza thriller, with Kitano as Murakawa, the taciturn, influential hit-man who, pushed by his boss to involve himself in an Okinawa gang war, comes to realise that he wants out. But what's truly arresting is the star/director's attitude towards the film's formal qualities. Structurally, the movie – like a sonata – is tripartite. It starts fortissimo with tempestuous scenes of gangland machinations and warfare. Then when Murakawa and his men take refuge in a coastal hideaway, their surreal, jokey seaside antics have all the light playfulness of a scherzo. While the final lyrical focus on death is virtually an adagio of moody introspection. Challenging, witty, adventurous and utterly singular. GA

Söndags Barn (Sunday's Children)

(1992, Swe/Den, 121 min)
d Daniel Bergman. *p* Katinka Faragó. *sc* Ingmar Bergman. *ph* Tony Forsberg. *ed* Darek Hodor. *pd* Sven Wichman. *cast* Thommy Berggren, Henrik Linnros, Lena Endre, Jakob Leygrat, Anna Linnros, Per Myrberg.
●1926: the Bergman family spends a summer holiday in the lush Swedish countryside, with eight-year-old Ingmar troubled by glimpses of sexuality and death and by his relationship with his father, Pastor Bergman, who is variously friendly, forbidding, nurturing, violent. 1968: middle-aged Ingmar Bergman, cold and unforgiving, pays a visit to his father, who's confused, and fearful about his approaching death. Advancing on these twin fronts via some beautifully timed cuts, the picture proceeds towards two moments of reconciliation over 40 years apart. Immensely sympathetic, viewed either as a self-contained work or as part of the Bergman canon, it is written by Ingmar and directed by his son Daniel. BBa

Song for Beko, A (Ein Lied für Beko/ Klamek ji bo Beko)

(1992, Ger/Arm, 99 min)
d Nizamettin Ariç. *p* Margarita Woskanjan. *sc* Nizamettin Ariç, Christine Kernich. *ph* Thomas Mauch. *m* Nizamettin Ariç. *cast* Nizamettin Ariç, Bêzara Arsen, Lusika Hesen, Cemalê Jora.
●This elegy for the persecuted Kurdish peoples of Turkey, Iraq and Iran is simple, unforced, and extremely moving. It may lack the epic grandeur of *Yol*, but it has the same telling eye for figures in a harsh landscape, and is infused with the same heartfelt compassion. After his brother Cemal flees the village to avoid conscription into the Turkish army, Beko is arrested in his place, but soon escapes. Peshmerga freedom fighters take him to the mountain hideout in the Iraqi highlands where their wives, and orphans from a nearby village, have taken refuge. While waiting for news of his brother, Beko befriends the children, including the painfully withdrawn Ziné. A more obvious film would have focused on Cemal's brave flight; Beko, we learn, served his two-year military service without complaint. The exiled Ariç's vision, though, is a broader one, dealing with how an ordinary man, the strong women and the orphaned children cling to their tenuous Kurdish identity. The first film to be made in the suppressed Kurdish language, this gives eloquent voice to the plight of a displaced people. NF

Song for Tibet

(1991, Can, 57 min)
d Anne Henderson.
●A moving documentary which conveys rare sympathy for a family exiled to Canada in the aftermath of the Chinese invasion of Tibet, as they affirm their determination to stay in touch with Tibetan people and tradition, and their unshakeable faith in the future. The sober account of Chinese atrocities, and the evident dignity and compassion of the Dalai Lama (who was ignored by the government when he visited Ottawa), paint a shameful picture of western foreign policy and China's restored Most Favoured Nation trading status. TCh

Song Is Born, A

(1948, US, 113 min)
d Howard Hawks. *p* Samuel Goldwyn. *sc* Harry Tugend. *ph* Gregg Toland. *ed* Daniel Mandell. *ad* George Jenkins, Perry Ferguson. *songs* Don Raye, Gene de Paul. *cast* Danny Kaye, Virginia Mayo, Steve Cochran, Hugh Herbert, Felix Bressart, J Edward Bromberg, Ludwig Stossel.
●A curiously lifeless musical remake of Hawks' own comedy classic *Ball of Fire*, with Kaye taking the Gary Cooper role and transformed into a shy musicologist, whose quiet existence is disturbed by the arrival of Mayo's nightclub singer, who not only brings the attention of the Mob down on Kaye and his elderly colleagues, but also teaches them the joy of jazz. Mainly wrecked by the performances, although there are some fine musical spots for the likes of Louis Armstrong, Benny Goodman, Lionel Hampton and Tommy Dorsey. GA

Song of Bernadette, The

(1943, US, 156 min, b/w)
d Henry King. *p* William Perlberg. *sc* George Seaton. *ph* Arthur Miller. *ed* Barbara McLean *ad* James Basevi, William Darling. *m* Alfred Newman. *cast* Jennifer Jones, William Eythe, Charles Bickford, Vincent Price, Lee J Cobb, Gladys Cooper, Anne Revere, Roman Bohnen, Patricia Morison, Linda Darnell.
●A two-and-a-half hour wallow, adapted by George Seaton from the Franz Werfel novel, with Jennifer Jones becoming a star as the peasant girl who had a vision of the Virgin Mary (that's Linda Darnell, uncredited) and thereby gave birth to the tourist industry at Lourdes. Some of the political and religious shenanigans momentarily conceal the mush at the heart of the picture, which begins with a glorious prologue that says if you believe it you're okay, and if not, shove off. ATu

Song of Ceylon, The

(1934, GB, 40 min, b/w)
d Basil Wright. *p* John Grierson. *ph/ed* Basil Wright. *m* Walter Leigh. *narrator* Lionel Wendt.
●Stigmatised by leftist critics as a hymn to imperialism, Wright's complex documentary essay is much, much more ambiguous. The lyrical, evocative imagery is pushed and prodded into functional service by a subtle multi-layered soundtrack. Overt criticism was hardly possible in a film sponsored by the Ceylon Tea Board, but Wright radically declines either to romanticise Ceylon's pre-colonial past or to celebrate the 'progress' brought by British imperialism. RMy

Song of Chao-Phrya, The (Nong Mia)

(1990, Thai, 100 min)
d Chatri-Chalerm Yukol. *cast* Chatchai Plengpanich, Passorn Boonyakiat, Pattamawan Khaomoonkhadee, Komsom Pongsutham.
●Named after the river which flows through Bangkok, Prince Chatri's film is an updated remake of another written and shot by his father, Prince Anusorn Mongkalkarn. It plays like a tropical variation on *L'Atalante*. A family (husband, wife, baby, sister-in-law) scrapes a living ferrying goods up and down the river; the wife runs away in search of urban glamour and excitement, and her husband has to comb the city's brothels and girlie bars to look for her. It's not shy of the odd glimpse of cruelty and violence, but too stylish to get trapped in grimy social realism. One of its many pleasures is a cameo by film director Komson Pongsutham as a taxi driver who gets plastered at the husband's expense. TR

Song of Norway

(1970, US, 141 min)
d Andrew L Stone. *p* Andrew L Stone, Virginia Stone. *sc* Andrew L Stone. *ph* Davis Boulton. *ed* Virginia Stone. *ad* William Albert Havemeyer. *m* Robert Wright, George Forrest. *cast* Toralv Maurstad, Florence Henderson, Christina Schollin, Frank Poretta, Harry Secombe, Robert Morley, Edward G Robinson, Oscar Homolka.
●A saccharine fantasy biopic of Grieg, with 45 musical numbers, 25 songs, international uvulas, and production line fjords. Grieg lived a life of exemplary dullness, and Stone has tried to ginger it up with white-knuckle cliff-hangers like whether the composer will be able to create an indigenous national music for Norway or not. Edvard, hold the phone. Edward G Robinson plays a piano salesman, Harry Secombe does not play Neddy Seagoon, Little Eyolf fails to show. *Life* magazine raved: 'Godawful'. *The New Yorker* wondered whether it had been made by trolls. The Medved Brothers dubbed Florence Henderson, who plays Grieg's wife, 'the female Peter Frampton for the Geritol generation'. BC

Song of Scheherazade

(1947, US, 106 min)
d Walter Reisch. *p* Edward Kaufmnan. *sc* Walter Reisch. *ph* Hal Mohr, William V Skall. *ed* Frank Gross. *ad* Jack Otterson. *m* Rimsky-Korsakov (adapt Miklós Rózsa). *cast* Yvonne De Carlo, Jean-Pierre Aumont, Brian Donlevy, Eve Arden, Philip Reed, Charles Kullman, John Qualen.
●Colourful campery with Donlevy baring his manly torso as a martinet Russian naval captain striking terror into his fledgling crew. Among the musical comedy sailors is Rimsky-Korsakov (Aumont), soon to unearth his muse (De Carlo) dancing in a Moroccan dive, transport her (disguised as a cadet) to the St Petersburg opera, and write his immortal melodies for her. Typical Hollywood tripe, presumably tongue-in-cheek but done with more verve than wit. TM

Song of Songs

(1933, US, 89 min, b/w)
d/p Rouben Mamoulian. *sc* Leo Birinski, Samuel Hoffenstein. *ph* Victor Milner. *pd* Hans Dreier. *m* Karl Hajos, Milan Rodern. *cast* Marlene Dietrich, Brian Aherne, Lionel Atwill, Alison Skipworth, Hardie Albright.

● A delightful mix of Sternbergian splendour and Mamoulian send-up, this hits exactly the right note of knowingness as Dietrich puts in her first appearance, an innocent peasant maid complete with demure braids and Bible (her favourite reading being the erotic ecstasies of the *Song of Solomon*). She quickly finds 'him whom my soul loveth' in a sculptor (Aherne) whom she inspires to his masterwork; but financial stringencies being what they are, she is passed on to the eagerly lecherous baron (Atwill) who had commissioned the sculpture; and it only remains for her to achieve a woman's revenge, then find her natural habitat as a sultry chanteuse in a nightclub (where she embarks on the sexy 'Johnny' with all she's got: 'I need a kiss or two, or maybe more...'). Needless to say, Dietrich positively glows with demure innocence or malice aforethought as the need arises – posing shyly in the nude for the handsome sculptuor, or swooping into the arms of an abashed but responsive riding-master – and the whole thing has a glitteringly opulent beauty, sparked with an irresistible sense of the absurd. TM

Song of the Exile (Ketu Qiu Hen)

(1989, Tai, 98 min)
d Ann Hui. *p* Jessinta Liu, We Nien-jen. *sc* Wu Nien-jen. *ph* David Chung. *ed* Wong Yee-shun. *pd* Yee Chung-man. *m* Ch'en Yang. *cast* Chang Shwu-Fen, Maggie Cheung.

● Ann Hui's semi-autobiographical film about a troubled mother-daughter relationship opens shakily with scenes set in the London of the late 1960s, but finds its feet as soon as it reaches Hong Kong and sets off for other points East. Hui uses an intricate web of flashbacks to explore the roots of the problem between the two women: the mother turns out to be Japanese, and she had a very hard time when she married into a Chinese family just after the war; the daughter has always considered herself wholly Chinese, and was taught by her grandparents to despise her mother. The complications are explored (and ultimately exorcised) in moving and intelligent scenes that throw light on areas long dark. Very well acted, too, especially by Maggie Cheung as the daughter. TR

Song of the Road

(1937, GB, 71 min, b/w)
d John Baxter. *sc* Gerald Elliott, HF Maltby, Geoffrey Orme. *ph* Jack Parker. *ed* Sidney J Stone. *ad* John Bryan. *m* Kennedy Russell. *cast* Bransby Williams, Muriel George, Tod Slaughter, Percy Parsons, Peggy Novak, Fred Schwartz.

● Artless and soft-centred it may be, but Baxter's movie has great symptomatic interest, and its celebration of decency and kindness seems unusually heartfelt. Williams plays a redundant council worker who takes to the road with his beloved cart-horse Polly. His adventures with a travelling fair and then as a farmworker suggest a middle-aged Cockney Shane, sorting out people's problems, giving the villain a pasting, then moving on. Some irksome comic business betrays Baxter's music hall origins, but you don't expect such extensive location work in a British film of this vintage, nor to encounter the matter-of-course assumption that war is just around the corner. BBa

Song of the Shirt, The

(1979, GB, 135 min, b/w)
d/sc Susan Clayton, Jonathan Curling. *ph* Jonathan Collinson, Anne Cottringer, Ieuan Morris, Andy Murrow. *ed* Fran McLean. *ad* Marion Schapiro. *m* Lindsay Cooper. *cast* Martha Gibson, Geraldine Pilgrim, Anna McNiff, Liz Myers, Jill Greenhalgh.

● A remarkably ambitious, multi-faceted project that uses the condition of the sweated seamstresses of 19th century London as a starting point from which to examine such varied subjects as the establishment of a sexual division of labour under capitalism, the nature of the Welfare State as a prop of male dominance, History as a disparate series of representations, and film itself. What should be stressed is the pleasure afforded by its strategic variation of image quality (video, etchings, stills) and by a witty score (by members of the Feminist Improvisation Group) which challenges the conventions of film music. MM

Song of the Siren, The (Shirat Ha'Sirena)

(1995, Isr, 91 min)
d Eytan Fox. *cast* Dalit Kahn, Boaz Gur-Lavi, Yair Lapid, Avital Diker, Orly Zilberschatz-Banai, Yaffa Yarkoni.

● This slightly sour, not particularly funny romantic comedy, set in Tel Aviv at the outbreak of the Gulf War, centres on Talila, a young advertising executive who vacillates between the lover who ditched her for a 22-year-old, her boss, and a seemingly sweet hick named Noah with whom, against her own expectations, she falls in love. The precautions widely adopted against Saddam's SCUDs and the marital problems of the heroine's sister contextualise and counterpoint Talila's own reckless rush towards marriage, though she's too moody, possessive and self-obsessed, even selfish, to elicit wholehearted sympathy. GA

Song of the South

(1946, US, 94 min)
d Wilfred Jackson (cartoon director), Harve Foster (photoplay director). *p* Perce Pearce. *sc* Dalton Raymond, Morton Grant, Maurice Rapf. *ph* Gregg Toland. *ed* William H Morgan. ad Perry Ferguson. *m* Daniele Amfitheatrof (photoplay score), Paul J Smith (cartoon score), Charles Wolcott (conductor). *cast* Ruth Warrick, James Baskett, Bobby Driscoll, Luana Patten, Hattie McDaniel.

● A plantation in the Old South: young Bobby Driscoll learns of life through the stories of former slave Uncle Remus (James Baskett). This rather mushy combination of animation and live-action remains one of Disney's most controversial efforts. It contains magical graphic work – notably the standout 'Zip-a-Dee-Do-Dah' number – but racial stereotyping drew furious protests from the National Association for the Advancement of Colored People. Hollywood's response? An honorary Oscar for Baskett. TJ

Song Remains the Same, The

(1976, GB, 136 min)
d Peter Clifton, Joe Massot. *p* Peter Grant. *ph* Ernest Day. *ed* Peter Clifton, Humphrey Dixon. *m* Led Zeppelin. *with* John Bonham, John Paul Jones, Jimmy Page, Robert Plant, Peter Grant.

● This could trouble even the devout in the Led Zeppelin coven. Essentially a chord by chord documentation of their '73 Madison Square concert, the heavy metal onslaught is intercut with lavish psychedelic effects, New York by night, seedy backstage wrangles, and five fantasy sequences. Here the band and manager Peter Grant indulge in some awesomely heavy-handed wish fulfilment. It ranges from the laboured (Grant as overblown Chicago gangster) to the dire (vocalist Robert Plant interprets his Viking saga like a TV ad for hairspray) and neurotic (guitarist Jimmy Page supernaturally experiences the seven ages of man). It's gruellingly long, the four-track stereo relentless, and the music a mechanical recreation of Zeppelin standards (eg. 'Whole Lotta Love', 'Stairway to Heaven). IB

Songs from the Second Floor (Sånger från Andra Våningen)

(2000, Swe, 100 min)
d Roy Andersson. *p* Lisa Alwert. *sc* Roy Andersson. *ph* István Borbás, Jesper Klevenås. *m* Benny Andersson. *cast* Lars Nordh, Stefan Larsson, Hanna Eriksson, Peter Roth, Klas Gösta Olsson, Lucio Vucino.

● For the first 20 minutes or so this slice of Nordic surrealism – a blend of millennial metaphorical allegory and bizarre black comedy – looks set to become some sort of hilarious masterpiece, before the novelty begins to wear off and the lack of a strong narrative thread takes its toll. That said, its very loosely connected vignettes – largely centred on elderly office, workers and their families coping with redundancy, inept magicians, bad hospitals and unending traffic jams – are visually striking, frequently fertile in their dark, deadpan inventiveness, and now and then truly evocative of apocalyptic insanity. A genuinely fascinating oddity, though its echoes of late Buñuel and Aki Kaurismäki provoke comparisons from which Andersson's film inevitably suffers. GA

Song to Remember, A

(1944, US, 113 min)
d Charles Vidor. *p* Louis Edelman. *sc* Sidney Buchman. *ph* Tony Gaudio, Allen Davey. *ed* Charles Nelson. *ad* Lionel Banks, Van Nest Polglase. *m* Chopin. *cast* Cornel Wilde, Paul Muni, Merle Oberon, Stephen Bekassy, Nina Foch, George Coulouris, Sig Arno, George Macready.

● Hilariously inept even by Hollywood biopic standards, this preposterous farrago has Wilde's Chopin, a Polish freedom fighter against the Czarist oppressor, forgetting his patriotic principles in the heady wine of Paris, success and Georges Sand's possessive arms, but coming to himself in time to cough out his life's blood on a grand concert tour for the cause. Amazingly stilted kitsch, packed with unspeakable dialogue. TM

Song Without End

(1960, US, 142 min)
d Charles Vidor. *p* William Goetz. *sc* Oscar Millard. *ph* James Wong Howe. *ed* William A Lyon. *ad* Walter Holscher. *m* Morris W Stoloff. *cast* Dirk Bogarde, Capucine, Genevieve Page, Patricia Morison, Martita Hunt, Ivan Desny, Lyndon Brook, Alex Davion, Lou Jacobi.

● Outstandingly silly biopic of Liszt, and a return to the floridly romantic style of Vidor's earlier film about Chopin, *A Song to Remember*. History is bunk, and the conception of creative genius as half-baked as, say, a Ken Russell film, in that it's purely love that makes the music flow. But at least James Wong Howe's photography of the elegant sets is suitably impressive. Cukor finished the film after Vidor's death – but it doesn't show. GA

Songwriter

(1984, US, 94 min)
d Alan Rudolph. *p* Sydney Pollack. *sc* Bud Schrake. *ph* Matthew F Leonetti. *ed* Stuart H Pappé, Stephen Lovejoy, George A Martin. *pd* Joel Schiller. *m* Kris Kristofferson. *cast* Kris Kristofferson, Willie Nelson, Melinda Dillon, Rip Torn, Lesley Ann Warren, Richard C Sarafian.

● Unexpectedly, at three days' notice, Rudolph was asked by producer Sydney Pollack to take the helm on this carefree comedy set in the world of Country & Western music. The result was Rudolph's fastest paced and most uninhibited film to date: a quirky, rambling tale of two star performers on the road. Incorporating songs specially written by Nelson and Kristofferson, the film indulges their male-bonding, hard-drinking, womanising life style, as well as giving Lesley Ann Warren her own shot at performing (not bad). A likeable shaggy dog of a movie, assuming the music's to your taste. DT

Sonic Outlaws

(1995, US, 88 min)
d/p Craig Baldwin. *ph/ed* Bill Daniel.

● The subject matter of this film/video documentary – copyright infringement and (some of) the consequences – is interesting enough. What isn't so interesting is the manner in which director Baldwin and cameraman/editor Bill Daniel have presented it. It runs like an early '80s 'scratch' video: masses of found footage (most of it unrelated to the accompanying sound-bites) is cut, tossed, turned and generally fiddled with to produce either a slant on the original or a different interpretation. And it's fine when taken in small doses. At the film's centre is a group of American 'Media Hackers' called Negativland who incurred the wrath of Irish rockers U2 for infringement of copyright. Questions are asked, few are answered (the interviews create the impression of an empty bread bin). Indeed, it's a relief when we get introduced to some of the other forms of artistic plagiarism (or parody, as some hackers call it) including billboard 'vandalism' (some of it amusing) and a hilarious item on the work of the 'Barbie Liberation Organisation'. DA

Son in Law

(1993, US, 95 min)
d Steve Rash. *p* Michael Rotenberg, Peter M Lenkov. *sc* Fax Bahr, Adam Small, Shawn Schepps. *ph* Peter Deming. *ed* Dennis M Hill. *pd* Joseph T Garrity. *m* Richard Gibbs. *cast* Pauly Shore, Carla Gugino, Lane Smith, Cindy Pickett, Mason Adams, Patrick Renna.
●This teen comedy is the second vehicle for Pauly Shore, a purveyor of spacey West Coast dude-talk. His character is a reprise of his post-adolescent wisecracker in *California Man*. He plays a geek called Crawl, a student advisor at a California co-ed college. When print-frocked Rebecca (Gugino) finds the crazy partying at Halloween all too much, Crawl steps in and persuades her into a Valley-girl make-over and butterfly tattoo. Within days she's down on the beach, eyeing up 'the guys with the big stones'. By Thanksgiving they're firm enough friends for her to invite him home to South Dakota to meet the folks. When Crawl poses as Rebecca's fiancé, to save her from her old beau, and declares an interest in their farmin' ways he's subject to a series of humiliations. But you know he's a-startin' to win their hearts. Mind-boggling stuff of moronic banality, but most appealing. Anybody cool or sane should think twice. WH

Sonnenallee

see Sun Alley

Son of Blob

see Beware! the Blob

Son of Dracula

(1943, US, 79 min, b/w)
d Robert Siodmak. *p* Ford Beebe. *sc* Eric Taylor. *ph* George Robinson. *ed* Saul Goodkind. *ad* John B Goodman, Martin Obzina. *m* Hans Salter. *cast* Lon Chaney Jr, J Edward Bromberg, Robert Paige, Louise Albritton, Evelyn Ankers, Frank Craven.
●A characteristically stylish piece from Siodmak, who nevertheless looks somewhat constrained by budget and genre. Chaney is fine as the Count (not, note, his son, despite the title), masquerading as one Alucard when he turns up in American Deep South society, and woos Louise Albritton over to the vampiric cause. But the script is far from wonderful, and offers Siodmak little to get his teeth into, notwithstanding a beautifully atmospheric first entry for the Count (Chaney and coffin rising from the misty depths of a lake) and an effective finale. GA

Son of Frankenstein

(1939, US, 99 min, b/w)
d/p Rowland V Lee. *sc* Willis Cooper. *ph* George Robinson. *ed* Ted J Kent. *ad* Jack Otterson. *m* Frank Skinner. *cast* Basil Rathbone, Boris Karloff, Bela Lugosi, Lionel Atwill, Josephine Hutchinson, Edgar Norton, Donnie Dunagan.
●Predictably, with four of the horror genre's most sinister presences in the cast, this is highly entertaining; but Rowland Lee (who made the wonderful *Zoo in Budapest)* creates a sumptuous, atmospheric tale worthy of following Whale's originals. The set, shot in a style reminiscent of the German Expressionist classics, is superb – a labyrinthine castle of gloomy shadows – and there are enough strong moments, as when the monster (Karloff, far less sympathetic than in his previous incarnations) tears off policeman Atwill's artificial arm, to make the film memorable in its own right. GA

Son of Godzilla (Gojira no Musuko)

(1967, Jap, 86 min)
d Jun Fukuda. *sc* Shinichi Sekizawa, Kazue Shiba. *ph* Kazuo Yamada. *ed* Ryohei Fujii. *ad* Takeo Kita. *m* Masaru Sato. *cast* Tadao Takashima, Akira Kubo, Beverly Maeda, Akihiko Hirata, Yoshio Tsuchiya.
●A scientific experiment on a Pacific atoll goes wrong, causing flowers to grow into triffids and mangoes to swell like footballs. Praying mantises become mechanical diggers, and an unearthed egg hatches out the son of you know who. Big Daddy is snorkelling out on the reef, but soon runs back for a bit of the usual murder and mayhem (though a giant spider is the real anti-mankind villain). The energy level is high, the technology ridiculous, and the subtext bang up to date. This one's about global warming. ATu

Son of Paleface

(1952, US, 95 min)
d Frank Tashlin. *p* Robert L Welch. *sc* Frank Tashlin, Robert L Welch, Joseph Quillan. *ph* Harry J Wild. *ed* Eda Warren. *ad* Hal Pereira, Roland Anderson. *m* Lyn Murray. *cast* Bob Hope, Jane Russell, Roy Rogers, Douglass Dumbrille, Bill Williams, Lloyd Corrigan, Harry Von Zell.
●A superior sequel to the original Hope/Russell vehicle, *The Paleface*, which Tashlin co-wrote. Again it's the tale of a timid braggart who falls in with a far more able woman (here an outlaw on the run from Rogers' federal marshal), and it's tailor-made for Hope's cowardly bluster and Russell's sassy sensuality. What's more, the verbal gags are nicely complemented by Tashlin's brashly wacky visual slapstick, which – like his later work – takes great pleasure in spoofing/deconstructing the genre to which the film subscribes. GA

Sons

(1989, US, 90 min)
d Alexandre Rockwell. *p* Marc Toberoff. *sc* Alexandre Rockwell, Brandon Cole. *ph* Stefan Czapsky. *ed* Jay Freund. *pd* Virginia Fields. *m* Mader. *cast* William Forsythe, DB Sweeney, Robert Miranda, Samuel Fuller, Jennifer Beals.
●Erratic talent Alexandre Rockwell, perpetrator of one of the *Four Rooms*, made his breakthrough with the Steve Buscemi movie-movie *In the Soup*. This is one of three earlier efforts, a comedy drama that played the festival circuit before vanishing without trace. Forsythe, Sweeney and Miranda are the trio of stepbrothers accompanying paralysed father Fuller on a jaunt to Normandy, where the old boy saw combat and romantic action during the war. (Jennifer Beals, a regular in husband Rockwell's movies, plays a transvestite.) TJ

Sons (Erzi)

(1996, China, 95 min)
d/p Zhang Yuan. *sc* Ning Dai. *ph* Zhang Jian. *ed* Feng Shungyuan. *cast* Li Maojie, Fu Rongde, Li Ji, Li Wei.
●A shatteringly intense docu-drama chronicling episodes in the breakdown of the Li family in present-day Beijing. The central problem is the father, Li Maojie, a former dancer who's declined into alcoholism and violence since stiffening joints forced him to retire. Both his sons hate him, partly because they're afraid they'll take after him; they're slackers, on the fringes of the city's underground rock scene. Seeing something universal in their problems – especially the mutual withholding of love – Zhang has the family re-enact its own domestic strife for the camera. Made with palpable warmth and affection for its characters, the film provides the most credible account of street-level realities in China's cities yet seen. TR

Sons and Lovers

(1960, GB, 103 min, b/w)
d Jack Cardiff. *p* Jerry Wald. *sc* Gavin Lambert, TEB Clarke. *ph* Freddie Francis. *ed* Gordon Pilkington. *ad* Tom Morahan, Lionel Couch. *m* Lambert Williamson. *cast* Dean Stockwell, Trevor Howard, Wendy Hiller, Mary Ure, Heather Sears, Donald Pleasence, Ernest Thesiger.
●A slack and superficial adaptation of Lawrence's novel. Laudably avoiding the temptation to sensationalise Paul Morel's amorous adventures, the film finds little else to stress, since these affairs take up an awful lot of screen time, while the character's inner conflicts (with his background, his mother etc) are left ill-defined and inconclusive. Great care has been taken with the period atmosphere (splendid camerawork by Freddie Francis), but the rather stiffly literary dialogue makes it all look like a series of animated Edwardian tableaux. TM

Sons of the Desert (aka Fraternally Yours)

(1933, US, 69 min, b/w)
d William A Seiter. *p* Hal Roach. *sc* Frank Craven, Byron Morgan. *ph* Kenneth Peach. *ed* Bert Jordan. *cast* Stan Laurel, Oliver Hardy, Charley Chase, Mae Busch, Dorothy Christie, Lucien Littlefield.
●One of the very finest Laurel and Hardy features, and certainly the most typical in terms of plot and characterisation, this sees the pair as henpecked husbands who manage to fulfil their dream of attending an absurdly infantile, riotous convention (held by the eponymous fraternity) only by lying to their wives; the trouble inevitably is that the girls discover their deceit, thus turning L & H's return into a nightmare of flattery, feigned innocence, and farcical intrigue. Despite Ollie's inimitable slow burn whenever confronted by Stanley's whimpering idiocy. the film is far faster than most of their features, while the duo's essentially childish amiability is beautifully contrasted both with the down-to-earth if somewhat aggressive maturity of their spouses, and with the ghastly mischief wrought by Chase's ever-effervescent convention regular. GA

Son's Room, The (La Stanza del Figlio)

(2001, It/Fr, 99 min)
d Nanni Moretti. *p* Angelo Barbagallo, Nanni Moretti. *sc* Linda Ferri, Nanni Moretti, Heidrun Schleef. *ph* Giuseppe Lanci. *ed* Esmeralda Calabria. *ad* Giancarlo Basili. *m* Nicola Piovani. *cast* Nanni Moretti, Laura Morante, Jasmine Trinca, Giuseppe Sanfelice, Silvio Orlando, Claudia Della Seta, Stefano Accorsi, Sofia Vigliar.
●The first half-hour or so of Moretti's Palme d'Or winner deftly paints an unsentimental portrait of an ordinary, almost complacently happy family in a small Italian coastal town. Then the unthinkable occurs. The teenage son dies in a diving accident, and his parents and sister find themselves so distracted by guilt, anger and confusion that they start drifting apart. Then an unexpected letter arrives for the boy from a girlfriend they never even knew existed. Subtle, psychologically astute and engagingly unassertive in tone, the film builds gently but surely to an emotionally powerful climax in which the family – especially the psychiatrist father (Moretti) – are forced to reassess everything they ever put their faith in. Wisely, Moretti steers clear of sentimentality (though Piovani's overly sweet music provides the film's only miscalculation), allowing the deceptively simple narrative speak for itself. A gem. GA

Sophie's Choice

(1982, US, 158 min)
d Alan J Pakula. *p* Alan J Pakula, Keith Barish. *sc* Alan J Pakula. *ph* Nestor Almendros. *ed* Evan Lottman. *pd* George Jenkins. *m* Marvin Hamlisch. *cast* Meryl Streep, Kevin Kline, Peter MacNicol, Rita Karin, Stephen D Newman, Greta Turken, Josh Mostel.
●A summer in Brooklyn in 1947, and an infatuated boy (MacNicol) tries to learn the dreadful secret of Sophie's awful Choice. It's Pakula's first film as his own screenwriter, and his scrupulous adherence to the dense details of William Styron's novel seems to have slowed down the deft visual sense so marked in *Klute*. A more serious problem occurs in long flashback scenes as Sophie describes her ordeal in Auschwitz. The information (for on one level, this is a tantalising Gothic romance) comes thrillingly, in fits and starts, with revelations following on the heels of half-truths. But one watches uneasily as the obscenity of the Holocaust is served up for our entertainment yet again, and another actress with perfect cheekbones and a crew cut loses a few pounds to lend credibility to a death camp scene. By the end, the accumulated weight and lethargy of the production fails to invest Sophie's fate with the significance Styron achieves. JS

Sopyonje (Seo-Pyon-Jae)

(1993, SKor, 112 min)
d Im Kwon-Taek. *p* Lee Taw-Won. *sc* Kim Myung-Gon. *ph* Jung Il-sung. *ed* Park Sun-Deok. *m* Kim Soo-Chul. *cast* Kim Myung-Gon, Oh Jung-Hae, Kim Kyu-Chul.
●This heart-rending and accessible melodrama concerns the relationship between two children and their adoptive 'father'/master, a travelling – necessarily poor – *pansori* musician. The *pansori*, a traditional music of aching love laments or upbeat festive songs, performed to the accompaniment of a lone drum, gives the movie its elegiac tone. Flashing back to the early '50s, it follows the three

on their journeys through the loving photographed by Korean landscapes, in all seasons, as they fight for a living, while their music is literally drowned out by the emerging fashion for Western sounds. It's a film of looks, rhythms, intimations and feelings, expressed in pure cinematic terms, and it's almost impossible not to be moved by it. The *sopyonje* is a song described as sorrowful and tender – there are few films more tender, if not more sorrowful than this. Unmissable. WH

Sorcerer (aka Wages of Fear)

(1977, US, 121 min)
d/p William Friedkin. *sc* Walon Green. *ph* John M Stephens, Dick Bush. *ed* Bud Smith, Robert K Lambert. *pd* John Box. *m* Tangerine Dream. *cast* Roy Scheider, Bruno Crémer, Francisco Rabal, Amidou, Ramon Bieri, Peter Capell.

● Friedkin's remake of Clouzot's 1953 thriller, *The Wages of Fear*, at a cost of more than twenty million dollars, bombed spectacularly in the States. Even cut by almost thirty minutes for British release, the film's narrative of four desperate men trucking nitroglycerin through 300 miles of South American jungle advances at far too slow a pace to aspire to the suspense value of the original. Friedkin hints at political themes, but the film suffers most from condescendingly over-emphatic direction, and a generally tedious, relentless grimy realism in the opening half hour. One simply wonders what, say, Peckinpah might have made of it. RM

Sorcerers, The

(1967, GB, 104 min)
d Michael Reeves. *p* Patrick Curtis, Tony Tenser. *sc* Michael Reeves, Tom Baker. *ph* Stanley Long. *ed* David Woodward. *ad* Tony Curtis. *m* Paul Ferris. *cast* Boris Karloff, Catherine Lacey, Ian Ogilvy, Elizabeth Ercy, Susan George, Victor Henry.

● Perhaps the much-touted multiplex generation of movie-brat directors who purport to care so much about British genre cinema should take a look at this picture some time. Reeves directed his first feature when he was only 23, already displaying the virtuosity which would make its most astonishing manifestation in *Witchfinder General*. The story, adapted from John Burke's novel, follows an ageing couple, the Monserrats (Karloff and Lacey), who have devised a contraption that allows them to control the minds of others and vicariously experience the world through them. This has a particular kick when they find young prey in the form of Ogilvy to experiment on. As the Monserrats play audience to their victims' living scenarios, which the couple write to their own perverse specifications, this psychedelic horror film deals with the apparatus of cinema, and it still puts the mind in a spin. LF

Sordid Affair, A

see Maledetto Imbroglio, Un

Sorority Girl (aka The Bad One)

(1957, US, 61 min, b/w)
d/p Roger Corman. *sc* Ed Waters. *ph* Monroe P Askins. *ed* Charles Gross Jr. *m* Ronald Stein. *cast* Susan Cabot, Dick Miller, Barboura O'Neill, Barbara Crane, Fay Baker, June Kenney.

● A delightfully over-the-top campus drama, which Corman has said he originally intended as a microcosmic portrait of the ills of modern society, but which actually works best as a gleeful comic celebration of emotional sadism. Cabot is utterly entrancing as the twisted bad girl who has no truck with notions of sisterhood, preferring to get her kicks from blackmailing fellow students into abject submission and exposing unwanted pregnancies. She gets her comeuppance, naturally, but it's clear where Corman's sympathies lie. Deliriously cheap and nasty. GA

Sorrow and the Pity, The

see Chagrin et la Pitié, Le

Sorry, Wrong Number

(1948, US, 89 min, b/w)
d Anatole Litvak. *p* Hal B Wallis, Anatole Litvak. *sc* Lucille Fletcher. *ph* Sol Polito. *ed* Warren Low. *ad* Hans Dreier, Earl Hendrick. *m* Franz Waxman. *cast* Barbara Stanwyck, Burt Lancaster, Ann Richards, Wendell Corey, Ed Begley, William Conrad, Leif Erickson.

● Stanwyck in one of her most famous roles, as an invalid who overhears a telephone conversation between conspiring murderers, and slowly realises that she is their intended victim. Based on Lucille Fletcher's celebrated 22-minute radio play, the film is none the less well sustained. Litvak's camera paces the confines of Stanwyck's lacy bedroom like an accused man in his cell; and although she is for the most part restricted to acting from the head up, Stanwyck's metamorphosis from indolence to hysteria is brilliantly executed. TCh

Sorted

(2000, GB, 102 min)
d Alex Jovy. *p* Fabrizio Chiesa, Mark Crowdy. *sc* Nick Villiers. *ph* Mike Southon. *ed* Justin Krish. *pd* Eve Stewart. *m* Guy Farley. *cast* Matthew Rhys, Sienna Guillory, Fay Masterson, Jason Donovan, Tim Curry, Ben Moor, Claire Harman.

● The bereaved brother of a well-heeled raver who plunged to death in a clubbing accident, Carl (Rhys) metamorphoses from a Scunthorpe beer drinker to pill-munching club kid in a textbook example of London-centric condescension. Accompanying Carl on this odyssey are a transvestite (Donovan) and his brother's former girlfriend (Guillory). In the infrequent moments when he can think straight, Carl realises that his brother's death may have been linked to impresario and drug wholesaler Damian (Curry in standard flamboyant form). Not to be taken too seriously, but entertaining in an overblown, high camp fashion. WI

Sorum

(2001, SKor, 109 min)
d Yoon Jong-Chan. *p* Baek Jong-Hak. *sc* Yoon Jong-Chan. *ph* Hwang Seo-Sik. *ed* Kyung Min-Ho. *pd* Jung Eun-Young. *m* Park Jung-Ho, Yoon Min-Hwa. *cast* Kim Myung-Min, Jang Jin-Young.

● Classy Korean frightener in which taxi driver Kim moves into a desolate, ramshackle apartment block, only to find himself set upon by all manner of undesirable neighbours, each with a tale to tell about the would-be novelist who died in the very room he rents. It's more subtle and enigmatic than that thumbnail suggests, although writer/ director Yoon knows how to twist the screws when it counts. Strikingly photographed, it's a haunting torture chamber of a movie. TCh

S.O.S. Titanic

(1979, GB, 105 min)
d William Hale. *p* Lou Morheim. *sc* James Costigan. *ph* Christopher Challis. *ed* Rusty Coppleman. *pd* Herbert Westbrook. *m* Howard Blake. *cast* David Janssen, Cloris Leachman, Susan Saint James, David Warner, Ian Holm, Helen Mirren, Harry Andrews, John Moffatt.

● Historical and disaster should be a lucrative combination: this succeeds elegantly with its plush settings, but it hams the spectacle dreadfully. 'The Titanic' never seems more than a model, especially when the unsinkable happens in mid-Atlantic, and director Hale seems a little confused about the weather conditions, which change from shot to shot. The film drops all too soon and too snugly into the standard disaster formula, though there are a couple of good observations; the rich ladies adjusting their life jackets in front of the mirror, for instance, and the illuminating depiction of the ship's rigid three-tier class system (first class: first saved). MPl

So That You Can Live

(1981, GB, 83 min)
d Cinema Action. *cast* Shirley Butts, Roy Butts, Royston Butts, Diane Butts.

● This is a spiky and uncompromising non-fiction feature: part-biography, part-documentary, part-history, and part elegy to a dying landscape. It's structured around five years in the life of Shirley Butts, a union convener who, as the film opens, loses first her job, and consequently her union card. The effect that this has on her life is then used as an opportunity to study the political and social history of the Cardiff working class area where she lives. Made by the independent Cinema Action collective, *So That You Can Live* avoids nudging its audience towards any facile political conclusion, however. Instead, the technical presentation of the film is used to destroy the illusion that this is a 'story' with a 'message', and to force the audience to make up its own mind. RR

So there, (Alors voilà,)

(1997, Fr, 93 min)
d Michel Piccoli. *p* Paulo Branco. *sc* Michel Piccoli, Thomas Cheysson. *ph* Laurent Machuel. *ed* Emmanuelle Castro. *m* Arno. *cast* Maurice Garrel, Dominique Blanc, Arno, Roland Amstutz, Bernard Bloch.

● A wretched first feature from the 72-year-old Piccoli, which aims for the space between Raoul Ruiz and Mike Leigh, but winds up stewing in its own misanthropy, misogyny and latent sadism. A grizzled patriarch with gangster connections (Garrel) presides over his three sons and their families, who live in identical apartments in the same block. One son is suicidal, and spends more time in hospital than out; another runs a trucking company but goes into sudden psychotic rages. Presumably intended as grunge surrealism, the view of dysfunctional working class families is actually redolent of the most patronising middle class attitudes. Less a French answer to *Nil by Mouth* than an hysterically brutalised soap, as tedious in its way as *Neighbours*. TR

Souffle au Coeur, Le (Dearest Love/Murmur of the Heart)

(1971, Fr/It/WGer, 118 min)
d Louis Malle. *p* Vincent Malle, Claude Nedjar. *sc* Louis Malle. *ph* Ricardo Aronovich. *ed* Suzanne Baron. *ad* Jean-Jacques Caziot, Philippe Turlure. *m* Charlie Parker, Sidney Bechet, Gaston Frèche, Henri Renaud. *cast* Lea Massari, Daniel Gélin, Benoît Ferreux, Michel Lonsdale, Fabien Ferreux, Marc Winocourt.

● Although it stirred up a double vein of controversy – from those outraged, and those disappointed – Malle's film is less about incest and its implications than about the frustrations of bourgeois convention. The year is 1954, and the period is effortlessly caught in the opening sequence as two schoolboys swing down a street in Dijon, rattling collecting-boxes for the wounded of Dien-Bien-Phu in the intervals of rhapsodising over Charlie Parker, whose latest record they airily steal while making the shop-owner fork out a donation, 'pour la France, Monsieur'. More than anything else, the film reminds one of Truffaut and the joyous spontaneity of *Les Quatre Cents Coups* as 14-year-old Laurent (a stunningly natural performance by Benoît Ferreux) agonises over the problem of how to lose his virginity in the face of a tight family circle which cramps his style while ignoring his needs. He finally makes it when convalescing at a spa from a heart murmur brought on by scarlet fever, and his mother – who has hitherto treated him as a baby, while seeking escape from her own unhappiness in an extra-marital affair – obliges (after a quaintly old-fashioned courtship) in a moment of pure, liberating joy. Tender and funny rather than daring or provocative, it's a film as gracefully and elegantly teasing as the best of Eric Rohmer. TM

Soufrière, La

(1977, W Ger, 30 min)
d/p/sc Werner Herzog. *ph* Jörg Schmidt-Reitwein, Ed Lachman. *ed* Beate Mainka-Jellinghaus. *narrator* Werner Herzog.

● As 75,000 people were being evacuated from the island of Guadeloupe in 1976, Herzog characteristically flew in to film the predicted eruption of 'La Soufrière' volcano and find the one peasant reported to have remained behind. Manic adventure had its reward. The holocaust didn't occur, the one peasant turned out to be a handful of calmly resigned natives; and the film metamorphosed into an essay on a deserted civilisation, like a surreal fourth chapter to *Fata Morgana*, or a sci-fi documentary on a city of starving dogs and blinking traffic lights. PT

Soul Food

(1997, US, 115 min)
d George Tillman Jr. *p* Tracey E Edmonds, Robert Teitel. *sc* George Tillman. *ph* Paul Elliott. *ed* John Carter. *pd* Maxine Shepard. *m* Wendy Melvoin, Lisa Coleman. *cast* Vanessa L

Williams, Vivica A Fox, Nia Long, Michael Beach, Mekhi Phifer, Jeffrey D Sams, Irma P Hall, Gina Ravera, Brandon Hammond.
●Sunday lunches are the gist of the movie: communal nourishment prepared the traditional way, back home under the aegis of Mother Joe (Hall). We're in modern-day Chicago, among Mother Joe's three daughters, their spouses and offspring. The eldest, Teri (Williams), a professional success, but hard and embittered, rubs against her sisters and even her husband Miles (Beach); Maxine (Fox) lives more easily with Kenny (Sams) and their two young children; and newly-wed Bird (Long) finds life with Lem (Phifer) is loving but uncertain. It's Maxine's eldest, Ahmad (Hammond), who assumes Mother Joe's burden when she's hospitalised, and narrates the story which, as he says, is about the things that brought the family together and the things that tried to pull it apart. This is the limit of the film's ambitions, but if there are no surprises, it nevertheless makes sense: the dilemmas have emotional grounding, thanks to sure, steady direction and, especially, the ensemble cast. A hearty, old fashioned meal of a film. NB

Soul in the Hole

(1995, US, 99 min)
d Danielle Gardner. *p* Lilibet Foster. *ph* Paul Gibson. *ed* Melissa Neidich. *with* Kenny Jones, Ed 'Booger' Smith, Gary Sims, Javone 'Bam' Moore, Braheen 'Beez' Cotton, Charles 'CJ' Jones, Dennis Miller.
●The annual street basketball championships mark the beginning of another long hot summer in Brooklyn, and Kenny's Kings, with their young star 'Booger', are the team on everybody's lips. It's impossible not to think of the cross-over documentary hit *Hoop Dreams*, and it isn't just the basketball which rings bells, for Booger is the pride of the streets and destined for college, if he can just survive them. This differs, however, in its pulse and attitude: it remains raw and unsanitised, and refuses to clean up its subjects or its soundtrack. The result is a compelling (if sometimes incoherent) piece which is intelligent enough to recognise that the real star here is coach Kenny Jones, who beneath the swagger is one of those genuine local heroes who rarely receive the glory. FM

Soul Investigator, The

(1994, Can, 82 min)
d/p/sc Kal Ng. *ph* Derek Rogers. *ed* Adrienne Amato. *m* Mark Lam, Kal Ng. *cast* Patrick Cho, Edwin Cheung, Alice Ng, Edmond Chu, Kal Ng.
●At last: an émigré Chinese movie which goes beyond the templates Wayne Wang designed all those years ago in *Chan Is Missing* and *Dim Sum*. Kal Ng's dark psychodrama, shot mostly in steely, psychedelic shades of grey but with spasms of luscious colour, sends a downcast man on a spiritual quest to discover why he has a perpetually bleeding wound which no one else can see. Guidance comes from the title character Chide the Wind (played by Ng himself), who tells him three anti-Confucian parables designed to help him out of his personal prison. Wonderfully idiosyncratic, it plays rather like *Doctor Strange* stories directed by Bresson. TR

Soul Man

(1986, US, 105 min)
d Steve Miner. *p* Steve Tisch. *sc* Carol Black. *ph* Jeff Jur. *ed* David Finfer. *pd* Gregg Fonseca. *m* Tom Scott. *cast* C Thomas Howell, Arye Gross, Rae Dawn Chong, James Earl Jones, Melora Hardin, Leslie Nielsen, James B Sikking.
●The plot of' *Soul Man* – white middle class boy takes an overdose of suntan pills to enable him to qualify fraudulently for a black law students' scholarship – is sufficient to leave the meekest ideologue screeching with rage. But it's hard to be angry with a film which at least is an honest attempt to make a responsible (if lightweight) comedy encompassing aspects of racism in America. It's often extremely funny, but the problem is that Miner undermines his good intentions by allowing too many jokes about racial stereotypes. *Soul Man* is at its most incisive when questioning everyday racist assumptions, and is helped to that end by fine performances from Howell (as the fraud), Chong and Jones. In the end, however, it's let down by one easy laugh too many. DPe

Soul Survivors

(2001, US, 85 min)
d Stephen Carpenter. *p* Neal H Moritz, Stokely Chaffin. *sc* Steve Carpenter. *ph* Fred Murphy. *ed* Janice Hampton, Todd Ramsay. *pd* Larry Fulton. *m* Daniel Licht. *cast* Casey Affleck, Wes Bentley, Eliza Dushku, Angela Featherstone, Melissa Sagemiller, Luke Wilson, Allen Hamilton, Ken Moreno, Carl Paoli.
●That this comes from the producers of *I Know What You Did Last Summer* is probably all you need to know. If you're a fan, start chewing your hair in anticipation. If you're not, choose life, because you won't find it in this dodo of suspense. When student Cassandra (Sagemiller) unintentionally kills boyfriend Sean (Affleck) in a road accident, she enters a world of pain, where reality proves unstable and only Sean's spectral reappearance and counsel might save her from the suspicious behaviour of friends and a clutch of church-based, fetish club Goths. GE

Soultaker

(1990, US, 94 min)
d Michael Rissi. *p* Eric Parkinson, Connie Kingrey. *sc* Vivian Schilling. *ph* James A Rosenthal. *ed* Jason Coleman. *ad* Thad Carr. *m* Jon McCallum. *cast* Vivian Schilling, Gregg Thomsen, David Shark, Joe Estevez, Jean Reiner, David Fawcett, Chuck Williams, Robert Z'Dar.
●This micro-budget variation on *Ghost* starts with a 'fatal' car crash, following which Natalia (Schilling), her old flame Zach (Thomsen), and bad boy Brad (Shark) are caught in limbo between life and death. Invisible to others and unable to influence events around them, they are pursued by 'Soultaker' (Estevez), racing against time to reunite their displaced souls with their barely living bodies. Rissi's uneven direction and cheapo special effects are no match for actor/writer Vivian Schilling's neatly turned script, but the film as a whole pays off nicely. NF

Soul to Soul

(1971, US, 96 min)
d Denis Sanders. *p* Richard Bock, Tom Mosk. *sc* Denis Sanders. *ph* Erik Daarstad, Harmon Lougher, David Myers, Jeri Sopanen, Vilmos Zsigmond, Leslie Blank, Robert Grant, Jor Longo, Robert Thomas. *ed* Denis Sanders. *m* Richard Bock. *cast* Wilson Pickett, Ike and Tina Turner, Santana, Willie Bobo, Roberta Flack, Les McCann, Eddie Harris.
●The *Soul to Soul* Festival was staged in Ghana to mark the 14th anniversary of the country's independence. It was basically a 'roots' idea: getting black American musicians and singers to perform alongside native artists. It doesn't look as if it worked, and the film certainly doesn't have any tricks up its sleeves to make it work. Some of the performances are great (notably Flack and Pickett), but the filming is hopelessly dull; and the spliced-in travelogue interludes don't help at all. TR

Sound Barrier, The (aka Breaking the Sound Barrier)

(1952, GB, 118 min, b/w)
d/p David Lean. *sc* Terence Rattigan. *ph* Jack Hildyard. *ed* Geoffrey Foot. *ad* Joseph Bato, John Hawkesworth. *m* Malcolm Arnold. *cast* Ralph Richardson, Ann Todd, Nigel Patrick, Denholm Elliott, Dinah Sheridan, John Justin, Joseph Tomelty.
●In his third and final film with his erstwhile wife Ann Todd, Lean strove to chart the human cost of scientific progress; unfortunately, Terence Rattigan's script, while solidly structured, never probes beyond the basic conceit that an obsession which works towards the glory of mankind in general may wreak havoc on private lives. Certainly Richardson impresses as the De Havilland-like aircraft manufacturer whose passion brings suffering, even death, to his own family, while Nigel Patrick, as his test pilot son-in-law, is solid. But Todd herself typifies the awfully upper-crust restraint of the whole movie, and for all the intimate drama on view, it is the stirring aerial footage, accompanied by Malcolm Arnold's score, that remains most firmly fixed in the memory. GA

Sounder

(1972, US, 105 min)
d Martin Ritt. *p* Robert B Radnitz. *sc* Lonne Elder III. *ph* John A Alonzo. *ed* Sidney Levin. *ad* Walter Scott Herndon. *m* Taj Mahal. *cast* Cicely Tyson, Paul Winfield, Kevin Hooks, Carmen Mathews, Taj Mahal, James Best, Yvonne Jarrell.
●Conscientiously made, with a script by a well-known black playwright and small parts filled in by locals, this attempts to go some way beyond the merely nostalgic in its recreation of the life of a black sharecropper's family during the Depression. Beneath the apparent resignation of the characters, there lurks a determination to beat the life they've been forced into. It even points, through the boys' discovery of an all-black school which teaches black history and black pride, to a militant future. But if you compare Ritt's film to Third World movies about oppressed people living in startlingly similar conditions, you notice what's missing: the feeling of bone-edge existence and incipient anger. Those films serve an immediate function, to change the lives of the people they're made about and for; Ritt's film must respond to the needs of an entertainment industry, and in its desire to be uplifting, leaves its characters one-dimensional without ensuring that the one dimension is heroic. VG

Sound of Brazil (Moro no Brasil)

(Ger/Bra/Fin, 2002, 105 min)
d Mika Kaurismäki. *p* Phoebe Clarke. *sc* Mika Kaurismäki, George Moura. *ph* Jacques Cheuiche. *ed* Karen Harley. *with* Jacinto Silva, Antonio Nobrega, Gabriel Nobrega, Darui Malungo, Walter Alfaiate, Mika Kaurismäki, Margareth Menezes, Velha Guarda da Mangueira.
●The lugubrious Finnish director Mika Kaurismäki is not an obvious choice to make a documentary about Brazilian music. He deliberately avoids the usual suspects – Astrid Gilberto, the bossa nova – concentrating instead on musicians, singers and dancers he met on his travels, most of them unknown outside their own communities. In his gruff, deadpan way, he offers an authoritative enough survey of all the different influences – Portuguese, African, Indian – behind the country's music and he unearths some spectacularly gifted performers. But the documentary is very slackly structured and his narrational style is glum and monotone. GM

Sound of Fury, The (aka Try and Get Me)

(1951, US, 92 min, b/w)
d Cyril Endfield. *p* Robert Stillman. *sc* Jo Pagano. *ph* Guy Roe. *ed* George Amy. *ad* Perry Ferguson. *m* Hugo Friedhofer. *cast* Frank Lovejoy, Lloyd Bridges, Richard Carlson, Kathleen Ryan, Katherine Locke, Adele Jergens, Irene Vernon, Art Smith, Renzo Cesana.
●A flawed but strikingly dark thriller about a World War II veteran (Lovejoy), unable to provide for his family, who drifts into petty crime, is inveigled by an unbalanced acquaintance (Bridges) into a kidnapping that goes wrong, and ends on the wrong side of a lynch mob. Although based on a factual case from the '30s, it is designed as an anti-McCarthyist plea (Endfield was blacklisted soon after), and its weakness lies in the elements of message: the journalist who whips up mob hysteria against the criminals, and the Italian professor who provides a civilised commentary deploring what is going on. But the background is sharply observed, the first half is rivetingly done, and the tension reasserts itself for the lynching finale. TM

Sound of Music, The

(1965, US, 174 min)
d/p Robert Wise. *sc* Ernest Lehman. *ph* Ted McCord. *ed* William H Reynolds. *pd* Boris Leven. *m* Irwin Kostal. *songs* Richard Rodgers, Oscar Hammerstein II. *cast* Julie Andrews, Christopher Plummer, Eleanor Parker, Richard Haydn, Peggy Wood, Charmian Carr, Heather Menzies.
●Call me a drongo, but this really is quite watchable (yes, I've seen it more than once). Of course it's reactionary shit, about how a woman's true vocation is to look after kids (even if they're not her own), turn curtains into clothes, and stand by her man. But the threat of Nazism is better evoked than in *Cabaret*, it's remarkably well edited, and it's cleverly scripted by Ernest Lehman (of *North by Northwest* and *Sweet Smell of Success* fame). Get smashed first, and you'll be singing along with the inescapably memorable tunes. GA

Sound of Trumpets, The

see Posto, Il

Soupirant, Le (The Suitor)

(1962, Fr, 85 min, b/w)
d Pierre Etaix. *p* Paul Claudon. *sc* Jean-Claude Carrière, Pierre Etaix. *ph* Pierre Levant. *ed* Pierre Gillette. *m* Jean Paillaud. *cast* Pierre Etaix, Laurence Lignères, France Arnell, Claude Massot.

●Etaix's first feature after serving as assistant to Jacques Tati. Though his penchant for obtrusive sound effects (mostly creaks and squeaks) at the expense of dialogue makes this uncomfortably reminiscent of a silent classic revamped by Robert Youngson, and though his approach to humour can on occasion be as laboured as his protagonist's endeavours to acquire a wife, the comic temperament is real enough, and the gags are often brilliant. GAd

Sour Grapes

(1998, US, 92 min)
d Larry David. *p* Laurie Lennard. *sc* Larry David. *ph* Victor Hammer. *ed* Priscilla Nedd-Friendly. *pd* Charles Rosen. *cast* Craig Bierko, Steven Weber, Robyn Peterman, Karen Sillas, Viola Harris, Matt Keeslar, Orlando Jones.

●Richie (Bierko) wins a bundle on a fruit machine in Atlantic City during a weekend excursion with his cousin Evan (Weber) and their respective girlfriends Roberta (Peterman) and Joan (Sillas). Since Evan lent Richie two of the three quarters that produced the jackpot, he naturally sees a half share as his due, a claim Richie fails to recognise. Typically, the argument between these urban petty sophisticates – Evan's a brain surgeon, Richie designs trainer soles – is less over the value of the booty than over protocol, and their responses are driven not by greed but by stubborn, petulant attitudinising which leads to Richie contracting a mercy hit on his doting mother (Harris) and Evan being vengefully stalked by a TV soap star (Keeslar). Though the film has its moments, these ideas look better on paper. Its traits and themes will be familiar to fans of TV's *Seinfeld*, which was co-created by first time writer/director Larry David, and the script attempts to replicate both the show's manic cross-plotting of coincidences and incongruities, and its inimitable synthesis of funny peculiar and funny ha-ha. NB

Souriante Madame Beudet, La (The Smiling Madame Beudet)

(1922, Fr, 32 min, b/w)
d Germaine Dulac. *sc* André Obey. *ph* A Morrin. *cast* Germaine Dermoz, Alexandre C Arquillière, Madeleine Guitty, Jean d'Yd.

●Now celebrated as the first explicitly feminist film, *Madame Beudet* is a rare and outstanding example of Dulac's pioneering work (hard to categorise, the director is best known as a theorist and a leading member of the avant-garde). It marked a major advance towards psychological development in film, with its symbolism and experimental use of camera, lighting, superimposition and slow motion techniques to evoke the shifting mental and emotional state of an unsmiling woman (Germaine Dermoz) crushed by an oppressive marriage and finding momentary liberation in fantasy. LH

Soursweet

(1988, GB, 111 min)
d Mike Newell. *p* Roger Randall-Cutler. *sc* Ian McEwan. *ph* Mike Garfath. *ed* Mick Audsley. *pd* Adrian Smith. *m* Richard Hartley. *cast* Sylvia Chang, Danny An-Ning Dun, Jodi Long, Speedy Choo, Han Tan, Soon-Teck Oh, William Chow.

●Timothy Mo's novel, via Ian McEwan and Mike Newell, reaches the screen as something of a mess: so many narrative points fail to register, so many scenes are misjudged, that the viewer is left dangling, and the ending doesn't help. Chen (Dun, rotten) marries Lily (Chang) in Hong Kong, and the pair start a new life in London. He works as a waiter until he falls foul of the Soho Triad societies through a gambling debt. Rather than be roped in as a drug runner, Chen hightails it for the wastelands of the East End and opens a takeaway. A family idyll ensues, with instant examples of culture shock for each generation. Meanwhile rival Chinatown gangs work through some old-style feuding (bloody stuff with cleavers and shotguns) but they haven't given up the search for Chen. Chinese ways are shown as being chipmunk cute, and the symbolism is thumpingly obvious. The biggest mistake is to raise expectations of Lily's lethal fists as the daughter of a martial arts expert, and then give her nothing to do when push comes to shove. BC

Sous le sable

see Under the Sand

Sous le Soleil de Satan (Under Satan's Sun)

(1987, Fr, 103 min)
d Maurice Pialat. *p* Daniel Toscan du Plantier. *sc* Sylvie Danton. *ph* Willy Kurant. *ed* Yann Dedet. *ad* Katia Vischkof. *m* Henri Dutilleux. *cast* Gérard Depardieu, Sandrine Bonnaire, Maurice Pialat, Alain Artur, Yann Dedet, Brigitte Legendre, Jean-Claude Bourlat, Jean-Christophe Bouvet.

●Adapted from Georges Bernanos' novel, Pialat's ascetic meditation on faith, sainthood, and the nature of evil is a film of shattering intensity. Depardieu plays troubled Father Donissan, whose chance meeting with an insinuating horse-dealer (the Devil?) and confrontation with pregnant teenage murderess Mouchette (Bonnaire) convince him that human actions are governed not by God but by a manipulative Satan. The worries of Donissan's concerned superior (Pialat) about the priest's excessive physical and psychological self-flagellation are tempered by intimations of an unorthodox saintliness. Is Donissan motivated by a divine calling or merely by mortal pride? Through the coldly-lit images and restrained flesh-and-blood performances, self-confessed atheist Pialat insists on the absolute reality of events, an approach which allows something intangible (spiritual?) to seep in at the edges of the frame. Despite the confusing cutting from scene to scene, the narrative's rigorous logic, the performances, and the stark visual beauty yield profound pleasures. NF

Sous les Toits de Paris

(1930, Fr, 92 min, b/w)
d René Clair. *p* Frank Clifford. *sc* René Clair. *ph* Georges Périnal. *ed* René Le Hénaff. *pd* Lazare Meerson. *m* Armand Bernard. *cast* Albert Préjean, Pola Illéry, Gaston Modot, Edmond Gréville, Paul Olivier.

●From its graceful opening pan across the (studio recreated) rooftops of the title to the multiple variations on its naggingly memorable theme song, the enchantment of Clair's first talkie has remained intact. Even the slight awkwardness of the semi-synchronised soundtrack, as scratchy as if played on a wind-up phonograph, complements its nostalgic, almost anachronistic visuals. That, plus Lazare Meerson's elegantly spare sets, George van Parys' jingly score, and the naïve if still affecting performances, make for a miniaturist masterpiece. GAd

South

(1919, GB, 81 min, b/w)
ph Frank Hurley. *with* Sir Ernest Shackleton, Captain Worsley, Lt Stenhouse, Captain Hussey.

●This record of Shackleton's 1914–17 Antarctic expedition concedes that the venture was a cock-up from the start. His ship, *Endurance*, got itself frozen in pack-ice without making landfall. Even the penguins were unsociable, and when the ship began to break up, the men had to leg it across the floes. They were rescued, ignominiously, by a Chilean tugboat, with nothing achieved but pain and suffering. Hurley, with time on his hands, seems to have explored all possible ways to photograph a barren waste, while big, bluff Shackleton demonstrates the first requirement of leadership: looking the part. The BFI has done a handsome restoring and re-tinting job, adding a discreet piano accompaniment. BBa

South, The (El Sur)

(1983, Sp/Fr, 94 min)
d Victor Erice. *sc* José Luis Lopez Linares. *ph* José Luis Alcaine. *ed* Pablo G del Amo. *ad* Antonio Belizon. *cast* Omero Antonutti, Lola Cardona, Sonsoles Aranguren, Iciar Bollàn, Rafaela Aparicio, Germaine Montero, Aurore Clément.

●The sublime *Spirit of the Beehive* was a daunting act to follow, but ten years on Erice produced a film to equal that earlier masterpiece. The setting is northern Spain in the late '50s. We look again through the eyes of a child, ever watchful and all-seeing, winkling out the secrets of this world apart, where there is neither Good nor Evil; no heroes, no escape; and life is lived in spluttering bursts of poetic intensity. Erice creates his film as a canvas, conjuring painterly images of slow dissolves and shafts of light that match Caravaggio in their power to animate a scene of stillness, or freeze one of mad movement. The dramatic impact of gorgeous image and tantalising message is enormous. FD

South Africa Belongs to Us

(1980, WGer/SAf, 55 min)
d Chris Austen.

●Shot covertly and smuggled out of South Africa, this portrait of five ordinary black women experiments with a non-conceptual form of documentary – minimal voice-over, direct address to camera, narrative-style establishing shots. This creates a powerful, almost textural feel for the day-to-day existences of women kept permanently separated from their families by the oppressive economy of apartheid and its system of migrant workers, tribal trustlands, and single-sex hostels. But it's also a tribute to the resilience and growing militancy, a source of great strength for the women activists who broke banning orders to participate in the film. MPo

South Central

(1992, US, 99 min)
d Steve Anderson. *p* Janet Yang, William Steakley. *sc* Steve Anderson. *ph* Charlie Lieberman. *ed* Steve Nevius. *pd* David Brian Miller, Marina Kieser. *m* Tim Truman. *cast* Glenn Plummer, Carl Lumbly, Byron Keith Minns, LaRita Shelby, Christian Coleman.

●Writer/director Anderson's debut feature is a parable – punching its message home – about the enormous effort required from within the poor black community to break the cycle of violence in South Central Los Angeles. When Bobby (Plummer) is released from jail, he finds things have changed in the 'hood: friend Ray (Minns) has turned their gang into a drug ring, while his 'bitch' Carole (Shelby) is neglecting the baby born while he was inside. Torn between paternal instinct and peer pressure, Bobby is cajoled into murder; back behind bars, he undergoes a miraculous conversion. Low on directorial inspiration, but more relevant and resonant than much of the big-budget white trash churned out by Hollywood. CO'S

South Dock (Dársena Sur)

(1997, Arg, 77 min)
d Pablo Reyero. *p* Lita Stantic. *sc* Pablo Reyero. *ph* Marcelo Iaccarino. *ed* Oscar Parajón. *m* Gaby Kerpel. *cast* Juan Carlos Enriques, Liliana Raquel Cáceres, Eliseo Kurytow.

●The difficulties faced by three families living in Buenos Aires' polluted shanty towns are presented in a touching, yet non-judgmental way. Made for TV – but with a subsequent cinematic release – the film is an often moving portrayal of dignity in poverty, the continued importance of machismo, and the sheer pain of merely trying to survive. Restrained in tone and form – at times too much so – this profile may not lack heart, but remains more interesting as anthropology than cinema. FM

Southern Comfort

(1981, US, 106 min)
d Walter Hill. *p* David Giler. *sc* Michael Kane, Walter Hill, David Giler. *ph* Andrew Laszlo. *ed* Freeman Davies. *pd* John Vallone. *m* Ry Cooder. *cast* Keith Carradine, Powers Boothe, Fred Ward, Franklyn Seales, TK Carter, Lewis Smith, Peter Coyote, Les Lannom.

●Transposing *The Warriors* from Brooklyn to the bayous of Louisiana, this reactivates the old genre of the platoon movie, echoes to the distant trumpets of Vietnam, unconcernedly risks pigeonholing as *Deliverance II*, and generally sets up more reverberations from its pared-down premise than do any number of scattershot epics. Nine part-time National Guardsmen embark on weekend training manoeuvres in the southern swamplands, expecting only a long, wet walk towards a whorehouse – until the gunplay abruptly stops being kids' stuff, and eight virgin soldiers suddenly face long odds on survival, lost and leaderless in a guerrilla war of attrition against the native Cajuns. Hill's characters exercise their own deadly group dynamics in the firing line, while Ry Cooder's score, an eerily-shot alien landscape, and a lifestyle familiar mainly from Les Blank documentaries point up the internal cultural divide. Straight-line conflicts, low-light visuals: the film's basics, its strengths, and its critical Achilles' heel are all those of the classic American male action movie. PT

Southern Cross (aka The Highest Honor – A True Story)

(1982, Aust, 143 min)
d Peter Maxwell. *p/sc* Lee Robinson. *ph* John McLean. *ed* David Stiven. *pd* Bernard Hides. *m* Eric Jupp. *cast* John Howard, Atsuo Nakamura, Stuart Wilson, Steve Bisley, Michael Aitkins, George Mallaby.

● Adding the subtitle *A True Story* for British release doesn't make this any the more convincing. Even though the World War II friendship it resurrects between an earnest young Australian captain, survivor of an abortive raid on Singapore, and one of his Japanese captors, comes to an improbable head by Western standards, it's the inadequate, *Boy's Own* serial treatment that wrecks the film's credibility. A rambling first half tries to map out the two main characters, but they're swathed in loose ends. While the characters sweat and frown, all efforts to underline the inherent pathos end up as mawkish melodrama, and the film's ironies – the parallels between Eastern and Western notions of heroism and honour – get only a nod in passing. HH

Southerner, The

(1945, US, 91 min, b/w)
d Jean Renoir. *p* David L Loew, Robert Hakim. *sc* Jean Renoir, Hugo Butler. *ed* Gregg Tallas. *pd* Eugène Lourié. *m* Werner Janssen. *cast* Zachary Scott, Betty Field, J Carrol Naish, Beulah Bondi, Percy Kilbride, Blanche Yurka, Charles Kemper, Norman Lloyd.

● A harsh yet human antidote to traditional Hollywood attitudes about 'real people', this is (with *Diary of a Chambermaid*) Renoir's most successful American film, loose, free-flowing, honest. A year-in-the-life of Zachary Scott, Betty Field and family, poor sharecroppers turned self-employed, both romantic and realistic in its investigation of courage and freedom, both accurate and impressionistic in its view of 'nature', so that you can smell the river and the dead rain after the flood that almost ends their struggle. (From the novel *Hold Autumn in Your Hand* by George Sessions Perry.) CW

Southern Yankee, A (aka My Hero)

(1948, US, 90 min, b/w)
d Edward Sedgwick. *p* Paul Jones. *sc* Harry Tugend. *ph* Ray June. *ed* Ben Lewis. *ad* Cedric Gibbons, Randall Duell. *m* David Snell. *cast* Red Skelton, Brian Donlevy, Arlene Dahl, George Coulouris, John Ireland.

● A Yankee ninny causes comic turmoil during the Civil War in this poor reworking of Keaton's *The General*. Skelton is no match for Buster in any department and the script is clearly beyond salvation, even after Keaton himself had been hired for the gag sequences and his old director Sedgwick dragged from retirement to supervise the proceedings.

South of a Passion, The (El Sur de una Pasion/aka From South to South)

(2000, Arg, 87 min)
d/sc Cristina Fasulino. *ph* Paula Grandio. *ed* José del Peon. *pd* Pepe Uria. *m* Marcelo Ferreyra. *cast* Analia Couceyro, Isis Krüger, Gabriel Molinelli, Ingrid Pelicori, Ruben Szuchmacher.

● Perennial dreams of escape meet the equally persistent realities of social and emotional stasis, as a young woman passes first through failed and shallow encounters with men, and then into financial entrapment to reduce the debts of her drunken musician father to a second-rate club owner. A potent atmosphere of sterility, blankness and shutdown pervades the locales – boarding hotels, tango bars and destitute apartments. The closing intimations of success, albeit at a cost, might acknowledge that we all prostitute ourselves in the market to a degree just to get by, but it's a late victory, even if it's not an entirely convincing one, wrestled from a brooding tale of tawdry hopes knocked back. GE

South of St Louis

(1948, US, 88 min)
d Ray Enright. *p* Milton Sperling. *sc* Zachary Gold, James R Webb. *ph* Karl Freund. *ed* Clarence Kolster. *ad* Leo K Kuter. *m* Max Steiner. *cast* Joel McCrea, Alexis Smith, Zachary Scott, Dorothy Malone, Douglas Kennedy, Alan Hale, Victor Jory, Bob Steele, Art Smith.

● McCrea, Scott and Kennedy are partners in a Texan ranch burned out by 'Cottrell's Raiders' (a snarling Jory standing in for Quantrill) during the Civil War. Kennedy joins the Confederate army, while McCrea and Scott – balking at army discipline – are recruited by a saloon girl (Smith) for a profitable venture running munitions from Mexico through the Union blockades. Disillusioned by Scott's increasingly murderous lust for money, McCrea opts out and turns to drink after his girl (Malone) falls for Kennedy. When the war ends, Scott decides to consolidate his position by eliminating Kennedy, now a Texas Ranger; and McCrea is persuaded by Smith, who loves him, to retrieve his self-respect by helping Kennedy. Plenty of action, plus personable performances (McCrea especially); but the characters are so thin, the situations so contrived, and the dialogue so unfocused that one couldn't care less who does what to whom. TM

South Pacific

(1958, US, 170 min)
d Joshua Logan. *p* Buddy Adler. *sc* Paul Osborn. *ph* Leon Shamroy. *ed* Robert Simpson. *ad* Lyle Wheeler, John F DeCuir. *songs* Richard Rodgers, Oscar Hammerstein II. *cast* Rossano Brazzi, Mitzi Gaynor, John Kerr, Ray Walston, Juanita Hall, France Nuyen.

● Plodding screen version of Rodgers and Hammerstein's stage musical in which an American Navy nurse on a South Pacific island falls in love with a middle-aged French planter, who later becomes a war hero. The lush visuals make the most of the exotic locations, but Logan's excessive use of colour filters is more distracting than effective. Some of the songs, at least, survived the transition: 'There Is Nothing Like a Dame', 'I'm Gonna Wash That Man Right Outa My Hair', and, of course, 'Bali Ha'i'. NF

South Park: Bigger, Longer & Uncut

(1999, US, 81 min)
d Trey Parker. *p* Trey Parker, Matt Stone, (anim) Frank C Agnone III. *sc* Trey Parker, Matt Stone, Pam Brady. *ed* John Venzon. *ad* JC Wegman. *m* Trey Parker. *cast* voices: Trey Parker, Matt Stone, Mary Kay Bergman, Isaac Hayes, Minnie Driver, Eric Idle.

● The opening credit sequence artfully mimics the reassuring tone of Disney does Rodgers and Hammerstein and introduces the diminutive heroes, third-graders Stan, Cartman, Kenny and Kyle. Their first port of call, however, is a movie house, where they bribe a bum to walk them into the R-rated comedy 'Asses of Fire', starring the scatological Canadian clowns Terrance and Philip. The boys emerge with a new vocabulary they can't wait to show off, and pressing questions about the nature of the clitoris. The first half hour aims low and rarely misses. A below-the-(Bible-)belt satiric assault on the pieties of the censorship brigade, this feature spinoff from the animated TV series takes no prisoners, and blows gratuitous raspberries at the Baldwin brothers, Saddam Hussein and Winona Ryder among others. Genuinely outrageous and sometimes hilarious – but size does eventually matter, and all-rounder Trey Parker just can't keep it up for the full 81 minutes. TCh

Southpaw

(1998, Ire/GB, 80 min)
d Liam McGrath. *p* Robert Walpole, Paddy Breathnach. *ph* Cian De Buitléar. *ed* James E Dalton. *m* Dario Marianelli. *with* Francis Barrett, Chick Gillen, Tom Humphries, Colum Flynn, Nicolas Cruz Hernandez.

● Training on waste ground surrounded by the flotsam of a travellers' caravan site hardly seems the first step to Olympic boxing glory, but such is the real-life *Rocky* story uncovered by this engaging Irish documentary. Director McGrath followed the progress of 19-year-old amateur light welterweight Francis Barrett for more than two years, and the sunny good nature of this quietly spoken pocket destroyer has you rooting for him in no time. TJ

South Riding

(1937, GB, 91 min, b/w)
d Victor Saville. *p* Alexander Korda, Victor Saville. *sc* Ian Dalrymple, Donald Bull. *ph* Harry Stradling. *ed* Hugh Stewart. *ad* Lazare Meerson. *m* Richard Addinsell. *cast* Ralph Richardson, Edna Best, Ann Todd, John Clements, Edmund Gwenn, Marie Lohr, Glynis Johns, Milton Rosmer, Edward Lexy.

● 'Take a look at the baby, Liz,' a slum-dweller tells his big, tough, poetry-spouting daughter, 'he's frothing like a bottle of beer'. And not surprising, too, born into this hot-bed of passion and corruption. Saville carries Winifred Holtby's tart, witty exposé of Yorkshire power politics to the screen with breathtaking, and totally unexpected, panache. A film which makes a hero of the local squire (Richardson) and a dupe of the idealistic socialist councillor (Clements) must be ideologically suspect; but as rivalries are resolved in midnight calfing sessions and school cloakroom brawls, all reservations are swept aside. The sort of consensus politics which has the gentry converting stately homes into schools and building council houses in the grounds is, after all, irresistible. RMy

South West Nine

(2001, GB/Ire, 99 min)
d Richard Parry. *p* Allan Niblo. *sc* Richard Parry. *ph* Graham Fowler. *ed* Christine Pancott. *pd* Rob Lunn. *m* David Bradnum. *cast* Wil Johnson, Stuart Laing, Mark Letheren, Amelia Curtis, Orlessa Edwards, Nicola Stapleton, Frank Harper, Zebida Gardener-Sharper, Robbie Gee, Roshan Seth.

● Writer/director Parry paints an anxious picture of London as a melting-pot society. Freddy (Johnson), the Brixton-bred narrator, is a bedroom musician and a runner for creepy dealer Jel (Gee). But, while Freddy is likeably pensive, his omniscience seems less convincing. In his account of 24 spiralling hours, set to heady dub/trance/HipHop rhythms, he links numerous characters, including middle-class crusty Kat, wideboy club entrepreneur Jake, unwitting acid casualty Mitch and aloof city slicker Helen, whose lost briefcase contains corporation-toppling information. Parry was a documentarist, and it shows in the resonant camerawork. The tightly edited film is also makes great use of urban locations. Those familiar with the area may appreciate the insidious cameos from locals, and the telling use of archive footage. Unfortunately, as the plot wobbles between volatile drama and pure pantomime, it's evident that this is Parry's first full length writing venture. AHa

Southwest to Sonora

see Appaloosa, The

Souvenir

(1987, GB, 93 min)
d Geoffrey Reeve. *p* Tom Reeve, James Reeve. *sc* Paul Wheeler. *ph* Fred Tammes. *ed* Bob Morgan. *pd* Morley Smith. *m* Tony Kinsey. *cast* Christopher Plummer, Catherine Hicks, Michel Lonsdale, Christopher Cazenove, Lisa Daniely, Jean Badin, Patrick Bailey, Amelia Pick.

● Based on David Hughes' novel *The Pork Butcher*, this is the tale of ageing German expatriate Kestner (Plummer), who heads for France to see daughter Tina (Hicks), rescues her from a loveless marriage, and whisks her off to the small town of Lascaud where, as a Nazi soldier in the Occupation, he had a torrid affair with a French girl. Befriended by a British journalist (Cazenove), they discover that Lascaud was the scene of a Nazi massacre in 1944, and that Kestner's erstwhile girlfriend was among the victims. The bulk of the film concentrates on questioning the extent of Kestner's guilt, interspersed with flashbacks of the young lovers romping in haylofts. Sadly, a potentially absorbing moral conundrum is rendered pedestrian by a banal script, and superficial performances from Hicks and Cazenove. Plummer is convincing, and the recreation of occupied Lascaud reasonably schmaltz-free, but complexities of character, ethics and politics are too often reduced to lowest-common-denominator thrillerama. RS

Souvenir

(1998, GB, 78 min)
d/p/sc Michael H Shamberg. *ph* James Herbert. *ed* Michael Shamberg. *m* Simon Fisher Turner and others. *cast* Stanton Miranda, Melvil Poupaud, Kristin Scott Thomas, Hugues Quester; voices: Christina Ricci, Adam Hann-Byrd.

●A haunting debut from Shamberg, hitherto a producer of music videos for the likes of New Order. Shot in Paris, it chronicles a couple of distracted days in the life of Orlando (Miranda), an American sports journalist, during which her near-incestuous obsession with her late brother finally prompts her French lover to pack his bags and split. Little else happens: she misses a deadline (Scott Thomas cameos as her editor), meets a basketball team in their locker room and replays some of her brother's old smell-o-vision software (designed by Chris Marker). But Shamberg uses digital editing to seamlessly integrate her memories/fantasies and larger reflections on the film's themes into the minimal narrative, generating images of uncommon density and beauty and turning the film into a kind of nervous rhapsody. The ending consolidates the various levels of paradox, bringing us back to earth with an elegiac bump. TR

Soy Cuba

see I Am Cuba

Soylent Green

(1973, US, 97 min)
d Richard Fleischer. *p* Walter Seltzer, Russell Thatcher. *sc* Stanley R Greenberg. *ph* Richard H Kline. *ed* Samuel E Beetley. *ad* Edward C Carfagno. *m* Fred Myrow. *cast* Charlton Heston, Leigh Taylor-Young, Edward G Robinson, Chuck Connors, Joseph Cotten, Brock Peters, Paula Kelly, Mike Henry, Whit Bissell.

●Fleischer's dystopian sci-fi – adapted from Harry Harrison's *Make Room! Make Room!* – may have its flaws (it gets a bit messagey and sentimental at times, and the ending is not as surprising as it could be), but it certainly knocks the silly juvenilia epitomised and inspired by *Star Wars* and *ET* for six. In some respects not unlike the (admittedly more complex) *Blade Runner*, it envisages the year 2022 as so ravaged by overpopulation, pollution and climate change that New York has become a teeming Babel of 40 million. Heston is the cop investigating the murder of an executive of the company that produces the titular synthetic food on which everyone now depends for survival; Robinson, wonderful in his final role, is his pal, savouring memories of earlier, better times as he nears death. Good, solid stuff, assembled efficiently enough to be pretty persuasive. GA

Spaceballs

(1987, US, 96 min)
d Mel Brooks. *p* Mel Brooks, Ezra Swerdlow. *sc* Mel Brooks, Thomas Meehan, Ronny Graham. *ph* Nick McLean. *ed* Conrad Buff. *pd* Terence Marsh. *m* John Morris. *cast* Mel Brooks, John Candy, Rick Moranis, Bill Pullman, Daphne Zuniga, Dick Van Patten, George Wyner, John Hurt.

●Brooks' *Star Wars* spoof employs the familiar scattergun approach, featuring gags old and new, something borrowed and something blue. Typically, the best conceits end in pratfalls, and non-Brooks fans may find that the gravitational pull towards the thumpingly obvious outweighs the wit. The story is a chip off the old Lucas block, with Darth Vader translated into the pipsqueak Dark Helmet (Moranis), The Force into The Schwartz, and Luke Skywalker becomes the slobbish space bum Lone Starr (Pullman), accompanied by his trusty dog Barf (Candy). The director's 2000-year-old man turns up, as well as a Druish princess (Zuniga) threatened with the return of her old nose. A flying Winnebago, a giant vacuum cleaner, and controls marked Light Speed and Ludicrous Speed get plenty of play, and there's a protracted rib-nudge as Brooks lets us in on the mystery of filming before proceeding to advertise Spaceball merchandise. In short, it is all exactly as you would imagine. BC

SpaceCamp

(1986, US, 108 min)
d Harry Winer. *p* Patrick Bailey, Walter Coblenz. *sc* WW Wicket [Ellen Green, Clifford Green], Casey T Mitchell. *ph* William A Fraker. *ed* John W Wheeler, Timothy Board. *pd* Richard MacDonald. *m* John Williams. *cast* Kate Capshaw, Lea Thompson, Kelly Preston, Larry B Scott, Leaf Phoenix, Tate Donovan, Tom Skerritt, Barry Primus.

●'We're going to train you just like real astronauts', says SpaceCamp instructor Capshaw, 'We're here to provide you with hands-on hardware'. In real life, SpaceCamp is like a NASA-sponsored playgroup, a cross between summer camp and Colditz, where teenagers who believe in the American space dream can learn how it feels to be an astronaut. In the movie, it's more of a device to explore the usual hang-ups and foibles of the five teenage participants, none of whom carry much conviction. The action starts to heat up as the young astros get a chance to put what they've learned into practice. Up until then, *Space Camp* plods along like any other half-baked teenage flick; but once in space, it gathers momentum for a gripping hands-on hardware climax. CB

Space Cowboys

(2000, US/Aust, 130 min)
d Clint Eastwood. *p* Clint Eastwood, Andrew Lazar. *sc* Ken Kaufman, Howard Klausner. *ph* Jack N Green. *ed* Joel Cox. *pd* Henry Bumstead. *m* Lennie Niehaus. *cast* Clint Eastwood, Tommy Lee Jones, Donald Sutherland, James Garner, James Cromwell, Marcia Gay Harden, William Devane, Loren Dean, Courtney B Vance, Rade Sherbedgia, Barbara Babcock, Blair Brown.

●The set-up is obliviously hilarious: the opening ten minutes are a monochrome rip-off/reprise of *The Right Stuff*, with 1950s fighter-plane test pilots hurtling to the outer limits of the atmosphere, before being leapfrogged into space by a monkey. Fast forward 40-odd years. The Cold War is over and NASA is enlisted to repair an obsolete Soviet satellite before it falls to earth. But the design is so archaic, none of today's computer nerds can figure it out. Hence a call-up for the old coots. By any sane criteria this would be considered an insult to audience intelligence, but in the context of contemporary blockbusters, you'd have to say it's all in fun. And it *is* fun: tongue in cheek but straightfaced enough to have you pulling for them. Messrs Garner and Sutherland don't have much to do but make the most of every scrap they get, while Clint generously cedes the lion's share of the big emotional scenes to Tommy Lee, who ropes them and rides them home. They puff around the running track, cheat on the physicals, override the automatic pilot – override pretty much everyone and everything that gets in their way, in fact – and show the new pups some old tricks. If the purpose of the exercise was to prove that the codgers can still get it up, then Mission Accomplished. TCh

Spaced Invaders

(1989, US, 102 min)
d Patrick Read Johnson. *p* Luigi Cingolani. *sc* Patrick Read Johnson, Scott Alexander. *ph* James L Carter. *ed* Seth Gaven, Daniel Bross. *pd* Tony Tremblay. *m* David Russo. *cast* Douglas Barr, Royal Dano, Ariana Richards, JJ Anderson, Gregg Berger, Fred Applegate, Patrika Darbo, Tonya Lee Williams.

●A half-hearted, plagiaristic kids' sci-fi comedy, featuring one amusing idea which woefully fails to sustain an entire movie. After receiving a pasting from the neighbouring Arcturians, a disoriented Martian warship mistakenly intercepts a Halloween-night radio broadcast of *War of the Worlds* from Earth. Believing their comrades to be industriously trashing the humans, Captain Bipto and his crew – little green men with antennae – proceed swiftly to Earth to join the invading forces, only to be met with derision by the locals who, mistaking them for children in fancy dress, enlist them for a trick-or-treat party. Despite the neat comic inversion of its central premise (this time it's the spacemen who are taken in by Welles' classic hoax), the film soon comes a cropper as the chaotic script descends into a mêlée of limp and disjointed knockabout gags. MK

Space Firebird

(1983, Jap, 116 min)
d Osamu Tezuka.

●Tesuka's animated vision of Earth in the future: babies are born in test tubes, evaluated at an early age, and raised by robots to be trained in requisite skills. There is a stringent social hierarchy, with dissenters sent to labour camps, and the planet is slowly being destroyed as its mineral resources are consumed. Not exactly the stuff of light-hearted children's science fantasy, yet that's what it's meant to be. There are some conventional kiddies' bits, like the odd nauseating musical interlude, and a Jiminy Cricket-like whingeing dice-bird (or something), but these are the weakest points in the film. The animation is uniformly excellent, with some very effective sequences, especially in outer space, where the occasional quite violent moment is assisted by a glorious splash of colour. The whole thing is a very odd mix of cataclysmic religious hysteria, the worst imaginable Orwellian vision, and a Weetabix commercial. Loopy. And interesting. But hardly for kids. DPe

Spacehunter: Adventures in the Forbidden Zone

(1983, US, 90 min)
d Lamont Johnson. *p* Don Carmody, André Link, John Dunning. *sc* David Preston, Edith Rey, Dan Goldbert, Len Blum. *ph* Frank Tidy. *ed* Scott Conrad. *pd* Jackson De Govia. *m* Elmer Bernstein. *cast* Peter Strauss, Molly Ringwald, Ernie Hudson, Andrea Marcovicci, Michael Ironside, Beeson Carroll.

●*True Grit* gets mugged by *Mad Max 2* along an outer-space backstreet in this 3-D extravaganza for kids. Galactic adventurer Strauss matches the resoluteness of the late Duke Wayne with Mel Gibson's leather-glam, and teaming up with a teenage waif (Ringwald), boldly goes into the plague-infested technological wasteland of the Forbidden Zone. Their mission is to rescue three stranded Earth girls captured by the wonderfully villainous tyrant Overdog (Ironside), whose mechanical appendages make the dark side of The Force look positively pedestrian. Thankfully, Johnson uses the 3-D with restraint and doesn't bombard the audience with unnecessary projectiles, the copious action sequences being all the more effective as a result. The film suffers, however, from having to keep to a PG certificate: some fantastically eerie moments (brushes with barracuda women in the indoor swamp, and with humanoid blobs that appear out of nowhere) are not exploited to their full potential. What could have been a sci-fi horror classic is instead just a better-than-average children's adventure story. DPe

Space Jam

(1996, US, 87 min)
d Joe Pytka. *p* Ivan Reitman, Joe Medjuck, Daniel Goldberg. *sc* Leo Benvenuti, Steve Rudnick, Timothy Harris, Herschel Weingrod. *ph* Michael Chapman. *ed* Sheldon Kahn. *pd* Geoffrey Kirkland. *m* James Newton Howard. *cast* Michael Jordan, Wayne Knight, Theresa Randle, Manner 'Mooky' Washington, Larry Bird, Bill Murray, Charles Barkley.

●As a cynical exercise in franchise exploitation this live-action/animated feature takes some beating; as a film, its target audience appears to be child fans of the cartoon characters' live-action co-star, basketball player Michael Jordan. Realising he doesn't get a penny from the spin-off toys owned by Jordan's kids, Bugs Bunny considers getting a better agent. To revive his ailing Moron Mountain theme park, Swackhammer dispatches his minions, the Nerdlucks, to Looney Tunes Land, to kidnap Bugs, Daffy Duck, Wile E Coyote, et al. To save their skins, the Looney Tunes challenge their would-be abductors to a game of basketball, whereupon the Nerdlucks transform themselves into their fearsome alter egos, the Monstars, before siphoning off the ball-playing skills from a bunch of NBA stars. To even up the odds, Bugs and Co kidnap Jordan and beg him to lick them into shape for the big game. The set plays are transparently simple, the execution sloppy and the ending signposted days in advance. Visually, it's a mess: the attempts to blend 2- and 3-D animation with live-action and computer-generated images produce scenes that are fuzzier than the storyline. NF

Spaceman and King Arthur, The

see Unidentified Flying Oddball, The

Space Truckers

(1996, US/Ire, 96 min)
d Stuart Gordon. *p* Peter Newman, Greg Johnson, Ted Mann, Stuart Gordon, Mary Breen-Farrelly. *sc* Ted Mann. *ph* Mac Ahlberg. *ed* John Victor Smith. *pd* Simon Murton. *m* Colin Towns. *cast* Dennis Hopper, Stephen Dorff, Debi Mazar, George Wendt, Vernon Wells, Barbara Crampton, Shane Rimmer, Charles Dance.

●Stuck in a dead-end job trucking square pigs across the galaxy for Interpork, John Canyon (Hopper) is happy enough to agree to ferry a one-off cargo of 'sex dolls' to Earth for a black market contractor. For one thing, it'll mean he can give his girlfriend Cindy (Mazar) a lift back to the home planet in time for her mum's operation; for another, if he can meet his delivery deadline, he's promised five times his standard wages – not bad, given that the company doesn't pay him anyway. But Canyon doesn't realise that he'll actually be ferrying a cargo of new-fangled killer Bio-Mechanical Warriors to kick-start corporate head EJ Saggs' plans for universal conquest. Director Gordon's sci-fi comedy, a dystopian spoof, comes across as a toytown *Alien*-cum-*Total Recall* pastiche. Bright, brash and occasionally almost amusing, perhaps, but also a waste of space. NB

Spaceways

(1953, GB, 76 min, b/w)
d Terence Fisher. *p* Michael Carreras. *sc* Paul Tabori, Richard Landau. *ph* Reginald Wyer. *ed* Maurice Rootes. *ad* J Elder Wills. *m* Ivor Slaney. *cast* Howard Duff, Eva Bartok, Andrew Osborn, Michael Medwin, Alan Wheatley, Philip Leaver, Cecile Chevreau.

●Before *Dracula* and *Curse of Frankenstein* made his name and put Hammer Films on the map, Fisher turned out this U-certificate adaptation of a radio play by Charles Eric Maine for the studio. Howard Duff is the US scientist accused of stashing his wife's corpse in a rocket, but the budget didn't stretch to much in the way of effects work. A decided oddity. TJ

Spagnola, La

(2001, Aust, 90 min)
d Steve Jacobs. *p/sc* Anna-Maria Monticelli. *ph* Steve Arnold. *ed* Alexandre de Franchesci. *pd* Dee Molineaux. *m* Cezary Skubiszewski. *cast* Lola Marceli, Alice Ansara, Lourdes Bartolome, Alex Dimitriades, Simon Palomare, Helen Thomson.

●An oddball heightened realist comedy, *La Spagnola* is set in the pastel '60s and centres on volatile Spanish immigrant Lola, her inconstant Italian husband and their late-teenage daughter living in industrial New South Wales. Daughter Lucia keeps family photographs lightly buried in the garden, next to her pigeon loft; perhaps she senses her daddy, whom she adores, is about to leave home with the family savings and mum will soon bake the pigeons in a pie. Lusciously shot by Steve Arnold, this is a piece of social observation disguised as farce, given a wash of post-Campion Australian surrealism. As sexually rumbustious ethnic drama, it gallops through the clichés, but doesn't run deep. WH

Spanish Fly

(1975, GB, 86 min)
d Bob Kellett. *p* Peter James, Gerald Flint-Shipman. *sc* Robert Ryerson. *ph* Jack Atcheler. *ed* Al Gell. *ad* Jacquemine Charrot-Lodwidge. *m* Ron Goodwin. *cast* Leslie Phillips, Terry-Thomas, Graham Armitage, Nadiuska, Frank Thornton, Ramiro Oliveros, Sue Lloyd.

●Dire comedy which doubles as a series of plugs for an underwear company. It's clearly intended as entertainment for the businessman – all the jokes are about impotence and gins-and-tonics – and it's shot mainly in close-up, like a TV show. Here's the plot: desperate for some dough to preserve his lavish life-style in sun-kissed Minorca, Sir Percy de Courcy (Terry-Thomas) buys up all the local plonk, having discovered that mixing it with ground-up flies produces a powerful aphrodisiac. So when fashion photographer Mike Scott (Phillips) descends on the island with a bevy of beautiful models, the fun comes fast and furious. But what's this? An unpleasant side-effect whereby everyone drinking the wine starts barking like a dog? Whoops… AN

Spanish Gardener, The

(1956, GB, 97 min)
d Philip Leacock. *p* John Bryan. *sc* Lesley Storm, John Bryan. *ph* Christopher Challis. *ed* Reginald Mills. *pd* Maurice Carter. *m* John Veale. *cast* Dirk Bogarde, Jon Whiteley, Michael Hordern, Cyril Cusack, Maureen Swanson, Bernard Lee, Rosalie Crutchley, Geoffrey Keen.

●Minor diplomat Hordern, separated from his wife and repeatedly passed over for promotion, becomes jealous of the developing friendship between his small son Whiteley and Bogarde's locally hired gardener. Based on AJ Cronin's novel, this is the kind of small scale, low-key character study that British film-makers can sometimes do rather well, and one of the earliest suggestions that then matinee idol Bogarde might be turning into a fine screen actor. At this stage, though, he can't compete with Hordern, who's growing sense of desperation is affectingly detailed. TJ

Spanish Main, The

(1945, US, 101 min)
d Frank Borzage. *p* Robert Fellows. *sc* George Worthing Yates, Herman J Mankiewicz. *ph* George Barnes. *ed* Ralph Dawson. *ad* Albert S D'Agostino, Carroll Clark. *m* Hanns Eisler. *cast* Paul Henreid, Maureen O'Hara, Walter Slezak, Binnie Barnes, John Emery, Barton MacLane, JM Kerrigan, Nancy Gates, Fritz Leiber.

●No scope for Borzage's gorgeously swooning, religiose romanticism in this swashbuckler, one of his most conventional movies. But it's also very enjoyable, most notably for Slezak, revelling as the villainous Spanish viceroy whose intended (O'Hara in fine fiery mood) is abducted by honest pirate Henreid, and for George Barnes' lavish Technicolor photography, which makes the most of the glorious sets, costumes and locations. If the script (co-written by Herman J Mankiewicz and George Worthing Yates) is hackneyed, Borzage films it with just the right amount of tongue in cheek. Wittier than Polanski's *Pirates* by a long way. GA

Spanish Prisoner, The

(1997, US, 110 min)
d David Mamet. *p* Jean Doumanian. *sc* David Mamet. *ph* Gabriel Beristain. *ed* Barbara Tulliver. *pd* Tim Galvin. *m* Carter Burwell. *cast* Ben Gazzara, Felicity Huffman, Ricky Jay, Steve Martin, Rebecca Pidgeon, Campbell Scott.

●On a Caribbean trip to discuss his as yet secret, invaluable new 'process' with his boss Klein (Gazzara), whizz kid Joe Ross (Scott) has a strange, faintly aggressive encounter with rich sophisticate Jimmy Dell (Martin), who apologises by inviting Joe to dine with him and his sister back in New York. Though Susan (Pidgeon), a new, evidently adoring secretary at the company, tells Joe of her suspicions about the invite, he goes along and ends up agreeing to meet a lawyer Dell recommends in an effort to allay his fears about Klein ripping him off (suspicions which, ironically, Susan also entertains). Is she jealous? Just cautious? Or should Joe share her paranoia? You bet. Far from being the answer to Joe's dreams of fame and fortune, that Caribbean trip was the start of a nightmare. David Mamet's most consistently enjoyable film to date is a cool, typically clever con-trick drama packed with deliciously inventive twists that get ever more convoluted and unnerving as the plot proceeds. Where this particular scam saga succeeds over Mamet's earlier efforts is in the acting: Scott's stiff, slightly nerdy but just about sympathetic turn as Joe is characteristically subtle, Martin's oddly still, reptilian creepiness has never been used so well, and Pidgeon, Gazzara and Jay (as Joe's pal George) all lend impressive support. GA

Spanking the Monkey

(1994, US, 100 min)
d David O Russell. *p* Dean Silvers. *sc* David O Russell. *ph* Michael Mayers. *ed* Pamela Martin. *pd* Susan Block. *m* David Carbonara. *cast* Jeremy Davies, Alberta Watson, Benjamin Hendrickson, Carla Gallo.

●A nicely matter-of-fact, sensitively performed US indie debut about a white middle-class pre-medical student lumbered by his dad, a travelling video salesman, with the task of caring for his attractive invalid mum during the summer holidays. Much confusion and anxiety result, mainly because the boy suddenly begins to feel longings for his mother. Russell's script and direction hit just the right note: the film being at once wittily satirical and poignant, erotic and uncomfortable, as it refuses either to romanticise or to make a mountain out of an admittedly troubling molehill. Watson and Davies, as mother and son, are especially watchable. GA

Spare Time

(1939, GB, 15 min, b/w)
d/sc Humphrey Jennings. *commentary* Laurie Lee. *ph* H Fowle. *with* The Steel, Peech & Tozer Phoenix Works Band, The Victorians Carnival Band, The Handel Male Voice Choir.

●An impression of working class leisure activities in Sheffield, Bolton, Manchester and Pontypridd, this was produced by the GPO Film Unit under Cavalcanti but was heavily influenced by the Mass Observation movement. The material is mundane: the greyhounds, the bike club, the Palais, and so on. But Jennings' eye for rich, resonant images and the fluency with which it's all stitched together, in harmony or counterpoint with some pre-existing piece of music, impressively foreshadows his wartime pictures. Centrepiece is a kazoo band, The Victorians, desperately cold on a winter's day, performing a grotesque version of *Rule Britannia* on a misty, forlorn playing field. A touching, troubling encapsulation of 1930s Britain. BBa

Sparklehorse

(1999, Can, 9 min)
d/p/ph/ed Gariné Torossian. *m* Mark Linkous.

●A three-part short animation 'inspired by' the (excellent) Neil Young-tinged junked out strummings of the rock band Sparklehorse. All three pure experimental collage pieces investigate visual analogies for the music. Minimally interesting. NB

Sparrow (Storia di una Capinera)

(1993, It, 106 min)
d Franco Zeffirelli. *p* Mario Cecchi Gori, Vittorio Cecchi Gori. *sc* Allan Baker, Franco Zeffirelli. *ph* Ennio Guarnieri. *ed* Richard Marden. *m* Claudio Cappani, Alessio Vlad. *cast* Angela Bettis, Jonathan Schaech, Sara-Jane Alexander, John Castle, Valentina Cortese, Sinead Cusack, Frank Finlay, Dennis Quilley, Vanessa Redgrave.

●It's 1854, and Maria (Bettis), soon to become a nun, is evacuated from plague-ridden Catania in Sicily to the opulent villa near Mt Etna shared by her loving father (Castle) and manipulative stepmother (Cusack). Here Maria meets Nino (Schaech), a family friend whose passionate love prompts a conflict between her instincts and her vocation. Finlay plays a nasty priest, and Redgrave a crazed nun. A full-blown very unpersuasive Zeffirelli melodrama, lamentably performed, with so many poorly framed wide-angles and zooms that no two shots seem capable of being edited together smoothly. AO

Sparrow of Pigalle, The

see Piaf

Sparrows Can't Sing

(1962, GB, 94 min, b/w)
d Joan Littlewood. *p* Donald Taylor. *sc* Stephen Lewis, Joan Littlewood. *ph* Max Greene, Desmond Dickinson. *ed* Oswald Hafenrichter. *ad* Bernard Sarron. *m* James Stevens. *cast* James Booth, Barbara Windsor, Roy Kinnear, Avis Bunnage, Brian Murphy, George Sewell, Barbara Ferris, Murray Melvin.

●Pity Joan Littlewood left no filmed record of her major Theatre Workshop productions, which shook semi-moribund classics such as *Arden of Faversham* and *Edward II* into dazzling life, and bore witness to the most excitingly inventive imagination in the British theatre of the '50s. This one was distinctly minor, a Cockney chortle about a merchant seaman (Booth) who comes back to his native Stepney to find his wife (Windsor) living with another man. Much bouncy good humour, but no real pace or incisiveness, as he tangles with perky local characters in trying to persuade her to come back, while the real locations simply point up the sitcom phoniness. TM

Spartacus

(1960, US, 196 min)
d Stanley Kubrick. *p* Edward Lewis. *sc* Dalton Trumbo. *ph* Russell Metty. *ed* Robert Lawrence. *pd* Alexander Golitzen. *m* Alex North. *cast* Kirk Douglas, Laurence Olivier, Jean Simmons, Tony Curtis, Charles Laughton, Peter Ustinov, John Gavin, Nina Foch, Woody Strode, John Ireland, John Dall, Herbert Lom, Charles McGraw.
●Although not a Kubrick project (he took over direction from Anthony Mann, and had no hand in Dalton Trumbo's script), this epic account of the abortive slave revolt in Ancient Rome emerges as a surprisingly apt companion piece to *Paths of Glory* in its consideration of the mechanisms of power. The first half, up to the superbly staged revolt and escape, is brilliant as it details the purchase and selection of slaves, the harsh discipline and routine of the gladiators' school, the new comradeship balked by the realisation that a gladiator must kill or be killed, the point of no return when the black slave (Strode) unexpectedly refuses to break the bond of brotherhood by killing Spartacus (Douglas). Thereafter some excellent performances come into play (Laughton, Olivier, Ustinov) as vested interests spark an involved struggle for power in the senate, but tension is simultaneously dissipated by the protracted battle sequences, and by a fulsome account of joyous fraternisation amid the slave army (sing-songs, swimming in the nude, having babies, etc). The sentimentality, rampant in the finale (Spartacus dying on the cross, his wife holding up his baby son before they walk free into the sunset) seems alien to Kubrick. TM

Spawn

(1997, US, 96 min)
d Mark AZ Dippé. *p* Clint Goldman. *sc* Alan McElroy, Mark AZ Dippé. *ph* Guillermo Navarro. *ed* Michael N Knue. *pd* Philip Harrison. *m* Graeme Revell. *cast* John Leguizamo, Michael Jai White, Martin Sheen, Theresa Randle, Melinda Clarke, Miko Huges, Nicol Williamson, DB Sweeney.
●Live-action cartoon about a cape. It's a big cape, smooth, crimson and graceful, and it belongs to Spawn (White) who, having died, has unwittingly sold his soul to the Devil, who reckons the ex-assassin will lead his army to the Gates of Heaven. In return, Spawn gets a metallic body armour-cum-armoury, with matching cape. Now he can fly, form an impenetrable cocoon or disappear. He can even provide fancy cuts between scenes. Admittedly, that's a simplified analysis: you could argue the subject's a hunchbacked clown (Leguizamo), Satan's henchman, who, having tired of spewing out grim jokes, morphs into a monstrous dog-beast. In future, Dippé, an old SFX hand, needs to think about how to tell a story, rather than merely throw together elements of *Batman*, *Blade Runner*, *Star Wars* and James Bond. NB

Speakers of the Truth

see Diseurs de Vérité, Les

Speaking Parts

(1989, Can, 92 min)
d/sc Atom Egoyan. *ph* Paul Sarossy. *ed* Bruce McDonald. *ad* Linda Del Rosario. *m* Mychael Danna. *cast* Michael McManus, Arsinée Khanjian, Gabrielle Rose, Tony Nardi, David Hemblen, Patricia Collins, Gerard Parkes.
●Pursuing the obsession with sex, death and videotape evident in *Family Viewing*, Egoyan here addresses the dangers of 'living in a situation in which everything depends upon one's attachment to, or rejection of, certain images'. For Clara (Rose), the danger lies in her desire to turn her dead brother's life into a TV movie, a project from which she is progressively erased. For shy hotel chambermaid Lisa (Khanjian), who watches videos of the man she loves as an extra in movies, it's her naïve ignorance of the medium's potential for manipulation. Handsome gigolo Lance (McManus) has a role in both their lives; as the object of Lisa's unrequited, strangely ritualised love; as Clara's lover and the actor playing her brother in the film. In striking contrast to the flat, degraded video images of *Family Viewing*, the visuals here are lush and beautifully designed; still, a sensation of unreality persists. Machines like the video telephone link used by Lance and Clara as a sex aid seem to hinder rather than aid communication. Nevertheless, far from condemning recording media out of hand, Egoyan scrutinises our ambiguous relationship with them; and as the characters grope towards less alienated (self) images, the film achieves a remarkable synthesis of intellectual analysis and deeply felt emotion. NF

Speak Like a Child

(1998, GB, 77 min)
d John Akomfrah. *p* Fiona Morham, Lazell Daly. *sc* Danny Padmore. *ph* Jonathan Collinson. *ed* Annabel Ware. *pd* Paul Cheetham. *m* Adrian Thomas. *cast* Cal MacAninch, Richard Mylan, Rachel Fielding, Fraser Stuart Ayres.
●After some years apart, Billy reunites with pregnant girlfriend Ruby and their old school ally Sammy, and drives them to their now abandoned school, a children's home on the Northumberland coast. Here, Billy hopes to resurrect the unconventional family unit he presided over as a boy (cue interminable flashback). A thin script gets strained, pretentious treatment from a director who's evidently more interested in emblems than characters. Ropey performances, self-consciously arty compositions and undistinguished camerawork. TCh

Special Day, A (Una Giornata Particolare)

(1977, It/Can, 105 min)
d Ettore Scola. *sc* Ruggero Maccari, Ettore Scola. *ph* Pasqualino De Santis. *ed* Raimondo Crociani. *ad* Luciano Ricceri. *m* Armando Trovaioli. *cast* Sophia Loren, Marcello Mastroianni, John Vernon, Françoise Berd, Nicole Magny, Patrizia Basso.
●If American audiences could buy the films of Lina Wertmüller wholesale, it's hardly surprising that *A Special Day*, a more restrained but equally spurious piece of Italo-attitudinising on sex and politics, pulled two Oscar nominations. It looks 'serious': newsreels set the scene as the day of Hitler's visit to Rome in May 1938; the colour is bleached to an approximation of sepia; Loren eschews make-up. It sounds 'meaningful': Mastroianni mouths philosophy down the phone; the radio blares Fascist agit-prop. It boils down, however, to the worst kind of sentimental tosh, as Loren's dowdy housewife sets aside her dreams of the *Duce* for a day and embarks on a brief encounter with Mastroianni's hounded homosexual from across the courtyard. And its supposed 'achievement' is to present this unlikely coupling as a revolt against their mutual oppression, itself 'explained' by Fascism. QED: rubbish. PT

Special Effects

(1984, US, 103 min)
d Larry Cohen. *p* Paul Kurta. *sc* Larry Cohen. *ph* Paul Glickman. *ed* Armond Lebowitz. *pd* Teri Kane. *m* Michael Minard. *cast* Zoe Tamerlis, Eric Bogosian, Brad Rijn, Kevin O'Connor, Bill Oland, Richard Greene.
●A ditzy blonde (Tamerlis) hits NYC hoping to make it in movies, but her first gig is a death scene – her own. A failing director secretly films himself and the actress in the sack, then murders her and sets about making a movie based on the killing, with the dead girl's husband as the likely murderer. This brass-necked approach includes inviting the investigating cop (O'Connor) to advise on procedure. Bogosian plays the director, Chris Neville, as a suave monster, avoiding any psychological or moral dimension (although we're told the reason he likes flowers is because they're so beautiful and they die so quickly). After a shaky start, the twists of the plot begin to take hold, and there's even a serious angle. This is the age of the non-entity, the glorification of the nobody, as long as they're victims, says Neville. Consider the virtually non-existent careers of a Dorothy Stratton or a Frances Farmer. What makes them worthy of a $10m eulogy on film? Murder, madness, suicide – that's what stars are made of today. NRo

Specialist, The

(1994, US, 110 min)
d Luis Llosa. *p* Jerry Weintraub. *sc* Alexandra Seros. *ph* Jeffrey Kimball. *ed* Jack Hofstra. *pd* Walter P Martishius. *m* John Barry. *cast* Sylvester Stallone, Sharon Stone, James Woods, Rod Steiger, Eric Roberts, Mario Ernesto Sanchez.
●Stallone is Ray Quick, a bomb-disposal expert with a difference: it's people he disposes of. Not indiscriminately, mind you. He can 'control his explosions, shape his charges' – which must be why May Munro (Stone) decides he's just the man to execute her revenge on half a dozen Cuban sleazeballs (played by the likes of Roberts and Steiger). Cast as a security expert hired by the sleazeballs, Woods clearly knows trash when he's in it: conjuring up a spellbinding sequence out of a gram of Semtex and a ballpoint pen, or hilariously scandalising a funeral congregation, he has a bite and gusto at odds with the vacuity of almost everything else going on around him. TCh

Specialist, The (Ein Spezialist/Un spécialiste, portrait d'un criminel moderne)

(1999, Fr/Ger/Bel/Aus/Isr, 128 min, b/w)
d Eyal Sivan. *p* Eyal Sivan, Armelle Laborie. *sc* Eyal Sivan, Rony Brauman. *ph* Leo T Hurwitz. *ed* Audrey Maurion. *m* Béatrice Thiriet, Yves Robert, Krishna Levy, Jean-Michel Levy, Tom Waits. *with* Adolf Eichmann, Robert Servatius, Moshe Landau, Benjamin Halevy, Yitzak Raveh, Gideon Hausner.
●Sivan takes archive footage of the 1961 Jerusalem trial of the Nazi bureaucrat Adolf Eichmann for organising the transport of racial deportees to the death camps, and edits it into narrative shape with the help of Hannah Arendt's *Eichmann in Jerusalem: A Report on the Banality of Evil*. A slow, detailed haul, but it builds a compelling portrait. NB

Special Section

see Section Spéciale

Special Treatment (Poseban Tretman)

(1980, Yugo, 93 min)
d Goran Paskaljevic. *p* Milan Zmukic, Dan Tana. *sc* Dusan Kovacevic, Filip David, Goran Paskaljevic. *ph* Aleksandar Petkovic. *ed* Olga Skrigin. *ad* Dragoljub Ivkov. *m* Vojislav Kostic. *cast* Ljuba Tadic, Dusica Zegarac, Milena Dravic, Danilo Stojkovic, Petar Kralj.
●*Special Treatment* is what the inmates of an alcoholic ward receive from their doctor/director – a dour regimen of psychodrama, physical jerks and Nietzschean will-to-power, dished out with the usual righteous sadism. A 'therapeutic' trip to a beer factory confronts authoritarianism with the more human desire for a little happy excess: the old joke of a piss-up in a brewery is crossed with some high-key political power-plays. If Paskaljevic's relentless focus on the nature of Fascism is a shade extended, it's tempered by some great moments of outrageous hilarity, playful echoes of Pirandellian illusion, an electric enactment of sexual politics from the wonderful Milena Dravic (the sex-warrior in *W.R.– Mysteries of the Organism*), and a conclusion of joyous anarchy. If Fassbinder's persistent cruelty gets you down, then see a film just as tough on the vanity of totalitarianism, but which genuinely likes people. CPea

Species

(1995, US, 108 min)
d Roger Donaldson. *p* Frank Mancuso Jr, Dennis Feldman. *sc* Dennis Feldman. *ph* Andrzej Bartkowiak. *ed* Conrad Buff. *ad* John Muto. *m* Christopher Young. *cast* Ben Kingsley, Michael Madsen, Alfred Molina, Forest Whitaker, Natasha Henstridge, Marg Helgenberger.
●A hybrid created from human and alien DNA escapes from the top-secret laboratory of Dr Xavier Fitch (Kingsley); with her accelerated growth and insatiable desire to procreate, Sil (Henstridge, 'conceived and designed' by HR Giger) is a primed mobile sex-bomb. Fitch assembles a team of experts and weirdos to track down and destroy the broody alien babe. Madsen's

heartless killing machine, Helgenburger's token female scientist, and Molina's dorky anthropologist join the hunt. But Whitaker's wigged-out 'empath' feels more deeply, and alone can tell the wood from the trees: standing in a wrecked train carriage, he looks down at a dead guard on the floor, then at the slime-oozing cocoon clinging to the wall, before declaring in a hushed voice, 'Something bad happened here.' Like some state-of-the-art remake of *Lifeforce*, this is every bit as bad as Tobe Hooper's film, but nothing like as enjoyable. Worst is the transition in the final scenes from snatched glimpses of a woman in a rubber suit to some oddly alienating motion-control effects. Floating like the ghosting on a poorly tuned TV, these are far too clean and artificial to be believable or remotely scary. Deserves extinction. NF

Species II

(1998, US, 93 min)
d Peter Medak. *p* Frank Mancuso Jr. *sc* Chris Brancato. *ph* Matthew F Leonetti. *ed* Richard Nord. *pd* Miljen Kreka Kljakovic. *m* Edward Shearmur. *cast* Michael Madsen, Natasha Henstridge, Marg Helgenberger, George Dzundza, James Cromwell, Austin Lazard, Peter Boyle.

● The one group likely to find this amusing are, in theory, too young to be allowed near it. Moving briskly from one Grand Guignol number to the next, Medak hardly pretends to tell a story, let alone a plausible one. Again, sex and horror are associated in scenes where copulating bodies are rent asunder and turned into an arrangement of what look like pulsating worms and turds, plus spurting blood and sticky stuff generally. The routine obscenities in the dialogue are interrupted only by some deliberately dumb one-liners, to provoke the audience. BBa

Specter of the Rose

(1946, US, 90 min, b/w)
d Ben Hecht. *p* Ben Hecht, Lee Garmes. *sc* Ben Hecht. *ph* Lee Garmes. *ed* Harry Keller. *pd* Ernst Fegté. *m* Georges Antheil. *cast* Judith Anderson, Michael Chekhov, Ivan Kirov, Viola Essen, Lionel Stander.

● A ballet melodrama with a score by George Antheil, this is one of eight pictures directed by the legendary screenwriter Ben Hecht, one of Hollywood's most grizzled cynics. The storyline centres on a schizophrenic male ballet star (an American with a 'continental' pseudonym) who starts murdering his partners during performances of the title ballet. Hecht's plotting fulfils every hope it may conjure up, but the real delight is his dialogue, which is among the most ineffably pretentious ever heard on screen. 'Press yourself against me so hard that you're tattooed on to me' whispers our hero (Kirov) as he chats up his ballerina wife-to-be (Essen) in a seedy hotel foyer. It has a curious and quite moving integrity at heart…but it's also the *Beyond the Valley of the Dolls* of its day. TR

Spectre of Edgar Allan Poe, The

(1972, US, 86 min)
d/p/sc Mohy Quandour. *ph* Robert Birchall. *ed* Abbas Amin. *ad* Michael Milgrom. *m* Allen D Allen. *cast* Robert Walker, Mary Grover, Cesar Romero, Tom Drake, Carol Ohmart.

● A rather endearing slice of hokum in which Edgar Allan Poe becomes a horror film hero battling to save his cataleptic love Lenore (Grover) from the clutches of an old-fashioned mad scientist (Romero), whose private asylum comes complete with basement snake-pit and furtive man-beast experiments. Robert Walker looks right for Poe, but the overall tone of the production is finally no more interesting than the average TV series. DP

Spectres of the Spectrum

(2000, US, 88 min, b/w & col)
d/sc Craig Baldwin. *ph/ed* Bill Daniel. *ad* Matt Day, Thad Povey, Chris Santeramo, Molli Simon. *cast* Sean Kilkoyne, Caroline Koebel, Beth Lisick.

● A rogue transmission from the underground, Baldwin's ethereal essay in science fact takes a futuristic vantage point – 2007 – to look back over the history (and shadow history) of electricity. Baldwin posits a dissident rear-guard action against the 'New Electro-magnetic Order', but this dramatic concept is really just a hook for analytical channel surfing through time and space. Clearly indebted to Chris Marker (*La Jetée*) and Godard (*Alphaville*), this is densely textured and tangential, touching on cosmology, spiritualism, capitalism and *King Kong*. It takes a while to adjust your (mind-)set, but Baldwin warms to his argument as he reaches the age of telecommunications, and the monopolistic commodification of information through corporate control of radio, television, and latterly the Internet. *The Terminator* for Chomsky fans. TCh

Speechless

(1995, US, 98 min)
d Ron Underwood. *p* Renny Harlin, Geena Davis. *sc* Robert King. *ph* Don Peterman. *ed* Richard Francis-Bruce. *pd* J Dennis Washington. *m* Marc Shaiman. *cast* Michael Keaton, Geena Davis, Christopher Reeve, Bonnie Bedelia, Ernie Hudson, Charles Martin Smith, Gailard Sartain, Mitchell Ryan.

● The premise is promising – a couple 'meet cute', each unaware that the other is a speechwriter for opposing candidates in an Arizona senate race – but the treatment sinks it. Unlike say, *Dave*, which wove a well-chosen cast into a nicely topical scenario to produce a Capra-esque comedy of populist ideology, this relegates the fertile ground of American politics to mere backdrop for a misconceived *Adam's Rib*-style screwball romance. Mugging to an unfunny script, Keaton and Davis are no Tracy and Hepburn, and the funereal pace doesn't help. AO

Speed

(1994, US, 116 min)
d Jan De Bont. *p* Mark Gordon. *sc* Graham Yost. *ph* Andrzej Bartkowiak. *ed* John Wright. *pd* Jackson de Govia. *m* Mark Mancina. *cast* Keanu Reeves, Dennis Hopper, Sandra Bullock, Joe Morton, Jeff Daniels, Alan Ruck.

● Reeves is a Los Angeles SWAT cop, Hopper the regulation bomber-with-a-grudge who wires first a lift, then a public bus. If the bus's speed drops below 50 mph, boom! Keanu hops on board to map-read, and, when the driver retires hurt, feisty passenger Bullock takes the wheel – and effectively steals the movie. It's mindless, but ingenious. Graham Yost's script dispenses with excess baggage: a handful of characters face certain – well, near-certain – death. First-time director De Bont (cameraman of *Die Hard* and *Basic Instinct*) makes good use of a hand-held camera and conveys a real sense of volition: you'll believe a bus can fly! He seems to identify so thoroughly with the characters that the pace never flags. Eventually, inevitably, he goes too far, too fast, and ends up off the rails. TCh

Speed 2: Cruise Control

(1997, US, 125 min)
d Jan De Bont. *p* Jan De Bont, Steve Perry, Michael Peyser. *sc* Randall McCormick, Jeff Nathanson. *ph* Jack N Green. *ed* Alan Cody. *pd* Joseph C Nemec III, Bill Kenney. *m* Mark Mancina. *cast* Sandra Bullock, Jason Patric, Willem Dafoe, Temuera Morrison, Brian McCardie, Christine Firkins, Lois Chiles.

● Further evidence, after the computer-generated vapidity of *Twister*, that De Bont's directorial career has expended the promise of his debut *Speed*. Making the sequel without Keanu Reeves was a desperate move, and this proceeds to throw overboard every other component of the first film's success: familiar settings, fleet pacing, a witty plot and irreverent characterisation. Here the characters are cut-outs, the settings alien (who outside Hollywood can picture themselves trapped on a luxury cruiser?), and the action interminable. 'Relationships based on extreme circumstances never work out,' Bullock's character repeats incessantly to explain (and remind us of) Keanu's absence. She thinks her new beau's a beach guard – only to discover he's actually another daredevil cop. To make up, they take a Caribbean holiday, alongside Dafoe, recently sacked, feeling under-appreciated and planning revenge. Dafoe's take on Dennis Hopper's Hopper impersonation is plain pointless; Bullock too is wasted in a ditzy half-role; and Patric is unsmiling and resolutely uncharismatic. NB

Speedtrap

(1977, US, 101 min)
d Earl Bellamy. *p* Howard Pine. *sc* Walter M Spear, Stuart A Segal. *ph* Dennis Dalzell. *ed* Mike Vejar. *ad* Fred Hope. *m* Anthony Harris. *cast* Joe Don Baker, Tyne Daly, Richard Jaeckel, Robert Loggia, Morgan Woodward, Dianne Marchal, Timothy Carey.

● 'The only trouble with this business is that it's one wild goose chase after another', says pudgy 'all-American-saint' Joe Don Baker of his assignment to catch the notorious Roadrunner, purloiner of flash fast cars. That's an accurate summation of *Speedtrap*, a tedious little number which trades heavily on burning rubber, squealing tires, and a police force hell-bent on crashing into each other at every available opportunity. FF

Speedy

(1928, US, 86 min)
d Ted Wilde. *p* Howard Lloyd. *sc* John Grey, Lex Neal, Howard Emmett Rogers, Jay Howe. *ph* Walter Lundin. *cast* Harold Lloyd, Ann Christy, Bert Woodruff, Brooks Benedict, George Herman Ruth.

● Lloyd's last silent picture is a lazy affair, of interest chiefly, now at the end of the century, for its affectionate and detailed portrait of New York City in the 1920s. The story concerns an old timer who drives the city's last horse drawn tram along a certain route which he won't give up to satisfy some ruffianly railroad developers. Harold 'Speedy' Swift (Lloyd), who works as a soda jerk and is baseball mad (cue Babe Ruth cameo), is in love with the old man's daughter, and shows her a good time (interminably) on Coney Island. There are one or two elegant sight gags (a dollar bill attached to a piece of cotton obtains the love birds a seat on a trolley), but the climactic rescue of the clanky hijacked tram lacks the adrenalin rush of an authentic Lloyd chase sequence. JPy

Speedy Boys

(1999, US, 75 min)
d/p/ph James Herbert. *ed* Mark Jordan. *cast* Andy Piedilato, Carter Davis, Aline Nari, Alessandra Palma, Kari Malievich, Sylvia Picchi.

● Professor of Art at the University of Georgia, James Herbert is an established painter, occasional director of pop promos (for local heroes REM and The B52s), and a film-maker with a particular interest in the human form. This second feature is difficult to judge in conventional movie terms since its interest is not really in narrative and characterisation, but in exploring the aesthetic possibilities of the male and female nude. Luckily, Herbert is also a brilliant cinematographer, so this series of tableaux, of two young American men carousing their way through Tuscany, mainly without clothes on, is consistently a pleasure to behold. These are non-actors, choreographed into various positions of display which achieve a sense of intimacy and blur the lines between performance and their own sexual arousal. While the interlinking dialogue sometimes seems impossibly precious, the sense of erotic reverie, reminiscent of Derek Jarman and *The Angelic Conversation*, proves cumulatively captivating. Not to be mistaken for soft porn, this is an arresting experiment in bringing fine art photography to life. And Brownie points for putting the soaring vocals of Lisa Gerrard on the soundtrack before Michael Mann got there with *The Insider*. TJ

Spell, The (Telesm)

(1988, Iran, 90 min)
d/sc Dariush Farhang. *ph* Ali Reza Zarrindast. *ed* Roohollah Emami. *ad* Amir Esbati. *m* Babak Bayat. *cast* Jamshid Mashayekhi, Soosan Tasslimi, Parviz Poorhosseini, Attila Pessyani.

● A stirring mish-mash of cultural allusion, sledgehammer symbolism, and something approaching camp humour, if such a thing exists in modern Iran. It's an Old Dark House movie, in which a newly-wed peasant couple take shelter from the storm in a sinister palace. The young bride finds herself imprisoned with the master's wife, a pallid ghost who plots revenge on her tormentor, the hollow-cheeked servant who engineered her disappearance. The protracted agonies of revenge and reconciliation look exactly like late Strindberg; the high seriousness invites and allows laughs aplenty. Altogether surprising, and unexpectedly moving. RS

Spellbound

(1945, US, 111 min, b/w)
d Alfred Hitchcock. *p* David O Selznick. *sc* Ben Hecht. *ph* George Barnes, Salvador Dalí. *ed* William Ziegler. *ad* James Basevi. *m* Miklós

Rozsa. *cast* Ingrid Bergman, Gregory Peck, Leo G Carroll, John Emery, Michael Chekhov, Wallace Ford, Rhonda Fleming.
● In 1945, Freud & Co were beginning to have a profound influence on American thinking, so armed with a script by Ben Hecht and the services of a consultant, Hitchcock decided to 'turn out the first picture on psychoanalysis'. The story is simple enough: Bergman is a psychoanalyst who falls in love with her new boss Peck, and when it's discovered that he has a Problem (an amnesiac, he may also be a killer), goes to work on his memory. The characterisation is also straightforward, with a maternal Bergman fascinated by father figures (a delightful cameo from Michael Chekhov) and young boys (Peck, suitably artless). But *Spellbound* is also a tale of suspense, and Hitchcock embellishes it with characteristically brilliant twists, like the infinite variety of parallel lines which etch their way through Peck's mind. The imagery is sometimes overblown (doors open magically down a corridor when Peck and Bergman kiss), and the dream sequences designed by Dali are exactly what you'd expect; but there are moments, especially towards the end, when the images and ideas really work together. HM

Speriamo che sia Femmina

see Let's Hope It's a Girl

Spetters

(1980, Neth, 115 min)
d Paul Verhoeven. *p* Joop van den Ende. *sc* Gerard Soeteman. *ph* Jöst Vacano. *ed* Ine Schenkkan. *ad* Dick Schillemans, Peter Jasnai. *m* Ton Scherpenzeel. *cast* Hans Van Tongeren, Renee Soutendijk, Toon Agterberg, Maarten Spanjer, Marianne Boyer, Rutger Hauer, Jeroen Krabbé.
● The friendships and loyalties of three motorcross riders are tested by the eruption into their lives of Fientje (Soutendijk), a scarlet woman with an Olivia Newton-John fixation who peddles dogfood croquettes from her Hook of Holland chip van. Rien (Van Tongeren) forms the initial attachment to Fientje by protecting her from a biker gang, but when an accident dumps him in a wheelchair, Fientje's affections are swiftly transferred to his friends Eef (Agterberg) and Hans (Spanjer). Imagine a Mike Leigh film set in Holland with motorbike stunts, packed with authentic action sequences and sexual frankness, including an eye-popping cock-measuring contest. Great locations, from the docks and shipping lanes, to a municipal dump, via the gay cruising haunts of Rotterdam, and a soundtrack that catches such sounds of the times as Blondie, M and Abba. Hauer, as world motorcross champ, doesn't have much to do apart from swopping his white suit and tie for biker's leather, and then making way for his stunt double. NRo

Sphere

(1998, US, 134 min)
d Barry Levinson. *p* Michael Crichton, Andrew Waid, Barry Levinson. *sc* Stephen Hauser, Paul Attanasio. *ph* Adam Greenberg. *ed* Stu Linder. *pd* Norman Reynolds. *m* Elliot Goldenthal. *cast* Dustin Hoffman. Sharon Stone, Samuel L Jackson, Peter Coyote, Queen Latifa, Liev Schreiber.
● Author Michael Crichton is to science fiction what Stephen King is to horror: although his work lacks originality, his ability to write page turning pulp novels allows him to pass off recycled ideas as something apparently more profound. For *Sphere*, he lifted the premise of Tarkovsky's *Solaris*, in which a physical object – here a mysterious shimmering sphere discovered in a submerged spaceship at the bottom of the ocean – causes those who enter it to give physical form to their inner thoughts. Drawn to the sci-fi genre by a scenario that relied less on hardware than the relationships between a group of investigating scientists trapped inside a claustrophobic submarine pod, director Levinson has made a *Solaris*-meets-*The Abyss* with dramatic knobs on. Hoffman's idealistic psychologist, Stone's emotionally unstable biochemist and Jackson's sceptical mathematician all apply specialist knowledge to the conundrum, watched over by enigmatic team leader Coyote. Three major stars being involved, it all wraps up happily but implausibly. NF

Sphinx

(1980, US, 118 min)
d Franklin J Schaffner. *p* Stanley O'Toole. *sc* John Byrum. *ph* Ernest Day. *ed* Robert E Swink, Michael F Anderson. *pd* Terence Marsh. *m* Michael J Lewis. *cast* Lesley-Anne Down, Frank Langella, Maurice Ronet, John Gielgud, Vic Tablian, Martin Benson, John Rhys-Davies.
● Scripted by John Byrum from a Robin Cook novel, this is basically *Coma*-goes-to-Egypt, with smuggling statuettes replacing smuggling live organs. Striking use of locations, but lousy script, uneasy heroine, and weak material. A clear case of a lame project that only a 'best selling' (ie. heavily pre-sold) novel could have financed. Avoid. MA

Spice World

(1997, GB, 93 min)
d Bob Spiers. *p* Uri Fruchtmann, Barnaby Thompson. *sc* Kim Fuller. *ph* Clive Tickner. *ed* Andrea McArthur. *pd* Grenville Horner. *m* Paul Hardcastle. *cast* The Spice Girls, Richard E Grant, Barry Humphries, Alan Cumming, Claire Rushbrook, Naoki Mori, Meatloaf. Stephen Fry, Elvis Costello, Richard Briers, Roger Moore, Bob Geldhof, Bob Hoskins, Bill Paterson, Jennifer Saunders.
● The Spice Girls (not quite the Beatles) try to make their Albert Hall gig in the face of mounting pressure from the press, their manager (Grant) and, in a literal sense, their best friend Nicola (Mori). Spiers' pseudo-documentary bubble-and-squeak allows the girls to dress up, dress down, change identities, ride around in a Union Jack bus, rub shoulders with a large cameo cast, and indulge in vacuous banter. Help! DA

Spicy Rice (Drachenfutter)

(1987, WGer/Switz, 72 min, b/w)
d Jan Schütte. *sc* Jan Schütte, Thomas Strittmatter. *ph* Lutz Konermann. *ed* Renate Merck. *pd* Katharina Mayer-Wöppermann. *m* Claus Bantzer. *cast* Bhasker, Ric Young, Buddy Uzzaman, Wolf-Dieter Sprenger.
● Shot in high-contrast b/w, documentarist Schütte's first fiction feature is a disarmingly low-key look at the lives of immigrant workers in Hamburg. One such is Shezad, a Pakistani seeking political asylum from the less-than-sympathetic West German authorities; another is Xiao, waiter at the Chinese eatery where Shezad works, who dreams of opening his own restaurant. With wry humour and an admirable lack of sentimentality, Schütte charts the hesitant progress of the pair's friendship. While the realist tone and understated performances sustain interest in themselves, still more affecting is the assured control of mood, with a lovingly shot, wintry Hamburg constituting a major character. A modest, deceptively simple film, its brevity is a distinct bonus. You're left wishing it had continued for another 30 minutes. GA

Spider

(2002, Can, 98 min)
d David Cronenberg. *p* Catherine Bailey. *sc* Patrick McGrath. *ph* Peter Suschitzky. *ed* Ron Sanders. *pd* Andrew Sanders. *m* Howard Shore. *cast* Ralph Fiennes, Miranda Richardson, Gabriel Byrne, Lynn Redgrave, John Neville, Bradley Hall.
● Working from Patrick McGrath's adaptation of his own novel, Cronenberg creates his most meticulously controlled and, perhaps, his finest film to date. Fiennes is extraordinarily persuasive as the closed-off Spider, released into the community – or at least a dismal halfway-house in London's East End – after years in a mental hospital. Revisiting his childhood haunts, he begins to disinter and relive his experiences as a child, particularly his painfully strong feelings towards his mother (Richardson) and plumber father (Byrne). It's primarily the precision – of performance, pacing, writing, camerawork and especially design – that make this Freudian drama so involving, though Cronenberg's ability to establish and sustain a relentlessly grim mood while simultaneously accumulating a wealth of telling details also deserves mention. Byrne gives one of his best performances yet, while Richardson's richly nuanced work in several 'roles' is hugely impressive. GA

Spider, The

see Earth vs the Spider

Spider and Rose

(1994, Aust, 94 min)
d Bill Bennett. *p* Lyn McCarthy, Graeme Tubbenhauer. *sc* Bill Bennett. *ph* Andrew Lesnie. *ed* Henry Dangar. *pd* Ross Major. *cast* Ruth Cracknell, Simon Bosell, Max Cullen.
● Writer/director Bennett's road comedy pits an irresponsible young ambulance driver (on his last day at work) against a grouchy old widow, still reeling from her husband's death in a car accident a year earlier. During a long, eventful journey together, the pair predictably come to terms with each other, but thanks to an occasionally tart script and Ruth Cracknell's unsentimental, convincingly vigorous performance, the movie manages to avoid the worst pitfalls of the genre. Minor but – at least after a hesitant start – surprisingly engaging. GA

Spider and the Fly, The

(1949, GB, 95 min, b/w)
d Robert Hamer. *p* Aubrey Baring. *sc* Robert Westerby. *ph* Geoffrey Unsworth. *ed* Seth Holt. *ad* Edward Carrick. *m* Georges Auric. *cast* Eric Portman, Guy Rolfe, Nadia Gray, Edward Chapman, Harold Lang, George Cole, Maurice Denham, Sebastian Cabot, Jeremy Spenser, Arthur Lowe.
● Undervalued at the time, more mood piece than thriller, this is a fascinating attempt to express the uncertain moral climate of a period of change (eve of WWI) through a cat-and-mouse game between a gentleman cracksman (Rolfe) and a Parisian police inspector (Portman) who knows very well who the thief is, but is unable to discover how he covers his tracks. A sort of friendship springs up between them, foundering only on ethical and legal barriers; but their curious kinship is further defined by the lovely provincial innocent (Gray) used as a decoy by Rolfe, then abandoned to her fate when she is arrested by Portman in an attempt to force a gentlemanly confession. Struck by her dignity and integrity under duress, both men begin to fall in love with her… Instead of fully exploring the moral and psychological implications, the script opts for a lightly ironic (but still pleasingly apt) coda in which both men find themselves hoist by their own prejudices and petards. But the look of the film, bleak and penumbral, with sets, camerawork and beautifully chosen locations conspiring to recapture the poetic quality of Feuillade's Paris, makes it rank with Hamer's best work. TM

Spider-Man

(1977, US, 94 min)
d EW Swackhamer. *p* Edward J Montagne. *sc* Alvin Boretz. *ph* Fred Jackman Jr. *ed* Aaron Stell. *ad* James Hulsey. *m* Johnnie Spence. *cast* Nicholas Hammond, Lisa Eilbacher, Michael Pataki, David White, Thayer David, Ivor Francis, Jeff Donnell.
● In translating comic strips to the screen (in this case, as pilot for a TV series), film-makers generally seem either to remove all the guts, or to adopt such a derisive tone that they come out looking a whole lot dumber than their source. Some attempt is made to avoid these traps here: Stan Lee worked on the script, and most of Marvel Comics' larger-than-life characters are retained, while the plot just about takes itself seriously enough to generate a certain momentum. But the film falls down largely because its lack of resources necessitates so much repetition. The video special effects of Spider-Man crawling up walls work a whole lot better than the way it was done on *Batman*; but as *Star Wars* so decisively showed, comic strips demand budgets as lavish as their conception. DP

Spider-Man

(2002, US, 121 min)
d Sam Raimi. *p* Laura Ziskin, Ian Bryce. *sc* David Koepp. *ph* Don Burgess. *ed* Bob Murawski, Arthur Coburn. *pd* Neil Spisak. *m* Danny Elfman. *cast* Tobey Maguire, Willem Dafoe, Kirsten Dunst, James Franco, Cliff Robertson, Rosemary Harris, JK Simmons, Gerry Becker, Bill Nunn, Jack Betts, Stanley Anderson, Stan Lee.
● With the stir and crash of Elfman's opening theme, the vertiginous weave of the credit crawl and the hardbitten *noir* voice-over ('Who am I? Are you *sure* you want to know?'), this accomplished blockbuster announces itself as a stylish piece of pop myth-spinning. Director and writer

afford the old *Marvel* comic strip the reverence film-makers used to reserve for the Scriptures – which is not to suggest that they miss the fun of it. Every inch the nerd's nerd, Maguire is adroitly cast as Peter Parker, a brainy orphan with a suppressed wild streak and a lot of growing up to do. When the worm turns (courtesy of a GM spider bite), his elation is palpable, a testosterone rush which sends him sky-high. The first thing is to score some greenbacks to impress the red-head next door (Dunst). Meanwhile. Dafoe's arms inventor, Norman Osborn, is the fly in the ointment, trying on his own altered ego – the Green Goblin – to test Spider-boy's moral mettle. Despite the movie's solid storytelling virtues, it must be admitted that the action spectacular scenes are a somewhat disappointing, and that Dunst is little more than an old-style scream queen. TCh

Spider-Man Strikes Back

(1978, US, 93 min)
d Ron Satlof. *p* Ron Satlof, Robert Janes. *sc* Robert Janes. *ph* Jack Whitman. *ed* David Newhouse, Erwin Dumbrille. *ad* William McAllister. *m* Stu Phillips. *cast* Nicholas Hammond, Robert F Simon, Michael Pataki, Chip Fields, JoAnna Cameron, Robert Alda, Randy Powell.

● The insubstantiality of this low-rent product is pleasantly refreshing – we learn that Spider-Man is a lot smaller than most of the villains, sensitive to slurs about his 'little blue tights', and chronically short of cash. For a change, the script is riddled with trashy jokes, silly set-ups, and a lack of excessive special effects. CR

Spider Man – The Dragon's Challenge

(1979, US, 96 min)
d Don McDougall. *p/sc* Lionel E Siegel. *ph* Vince Martinelli. *ed* Erwin Dumbrille, Fred Roth. *ad* Julian Sacks. *m* Dana Kaproff. *cast* Nicholas Hammond, Robert F Simon, Ellen Bry, Chip Fields, Myron Healey, Rosalind Chao, Richard Erdman, Benson Fong, Ted Danson.

● Min Lo Chan (Fong), Minister for Industry and Development in the People's Republic of China, visits New York editor Jonah Jameson (Simon) for help in clearing himself of the charge that he sold secrets about Mao's advancing army to US Marines during World War II. And Jameson enlists Peter Parker (Hammond), in reality superhero Spider-Man. Kung-fu and an acupuncture cure (when Spider-Man gets wounded) are both mooted, but when the moment arrives to deliver, the camera weasels out. And sad to say, there's a complete lack of the slight but delightful political savvy that redeemed *Spider-Man Strikes Back*. CR

Spiders, The

see Spinnen, Die

Spider's Stratagem, The (Strategia del Ragno)

(1970, It, 97 min)
d Bernardo Bertolucci. *p* Giovanni Bertolucci. *sc* Bernardo Bertolucci, Eduardo de Gregorio, Marilù Parolini. *ph* Vittorio Storaro, Franco Di Giacomo. *ed* Roberto Perpignani. *ad* Maria Paola Maino. *cast* Giulio Brogi, Alida Valli, Tino Scotti, Pippo Campanini, Franco Giovanelli, Allen Midgett.

● Bertolucci's precipitous decline into political and aesthetic misjudgments (signalled by parts of *Last Tango* and confirmed by long stretches of *1900)* shouldn't make anyone forget that his intelligence, erotic sensibility, and wit once made him the only Italian director comparable to Pasolini. Made after *The Conformist* and showing Bertolucci at the height of his powers, *The Spider's Stratagem* transposes a Borges short story to the Po Valley in Italy, introduces a dazzling density of cultural references, and remains thrilling and extraordinary. Athos Magnani (Brogi) returns to his home town, where the defacement of the memorial to his father (a hero of '36) sets him on the trail of the truth about his parent; the world he explores is full of mysteries, omens, ambiguities, and signs of incipient madness, and it resolves itself into a riddle that is the cinema's richest homage to all that's remarkable in Borges. TR

Spiegel, Der

see Mirror, The

Spies

see Spione

Spies Like Us

(1985, US, 109 min)
d John Landis. *p* Brian Grazer, George Folsey Jr. *sc* Dan Aykroyd, Lowell Ganz, Babaloo Mandel. *ph* Bob Paynter. *ed* Malcolm Campbell. *pd* Peter Murton. *m* Elmer Bernstein. *cast* Dan Aykroyd, Chevy Chase, Steve Forrest, Charles McKeown, Donna Dixon, Derek Meddings, Bruce Davison, William Prince, Bernie Casey.

● A double act with Chase and Aykroyd playing US State Department misfits whose gross bad behaviour during an informal exam leads them into hurried training for a deadly mission in Soviet-controlled Pakistan and Afghanistan. Sadly, the script is so patchy that most of the genuine laughs are squeezed into the first half; the rest is a rather tacky and confused extended joke about the nuclear arms race, which is tasteless only because it fails to be funny. There are token guest slots for the likes of Bob Hope, BB King, and a whole string of film-makers from Ray Harryhausen and Larry Cohen to Costa-Gavras and Michael Apted. SGr

Spikes Gang, The

(1974, US, 96 min)
d Richard Fleischer. *p* Walter Mirisch. *sc* Irving Ravetch, Harriet Frank Jr. *ph* Brian West. *ed* Ralph E Winters, Frank J Urioste. *ad* Julio Molino. *m* Fred Karlin. *cast* Lee Marvin, Gary Grimes, Ron Howard, Charlie Martin Smith, Arthur Hunnicutt, Noah Beery.

● An engaging Western, based on Giles Tippette's novel *The Bank Robber* but designed more or less as a sequel to Robert Benton's *Bad Company*, with Marvin as a wounded gunman helped by three boys, and later (after they run away from home in search of the excitement and easy living conjured by his reminiscences) tutoring them on the downward path. Familiar territory (ageing outlaw hemmed in by shrinking frontiers and cruel options), but beautifully acted, sharply scripted, and often very funny en route to the bitter final lessons in disillusionment. One of Fleischer's best movies from the '70s. TM

Spin

(1994/5, US, 76 min)
d Brian Springer. *with* George Bush, Bill Clinton, Ross Perot, Larry King, Pat Robertson.

● Satellite interviews are part of the furniture of news and current affairs programmes. If you've ever felt concern about the degree of collusion between the politicos and the media, this documentary will set your jaw dropping. In a brief intro, Springer describes how he used an ordinary satellite tuner to record some 100 hours of TV satellite link time, capturing the studio-to-interviewee feeds in their entirety, rather than just the familiar on-air Q&A routines we see every day. What follows, distilled to 76 minutes, is a catalogue of off-hand revelations, unwitting gaffes, blind prejudice and unalloyed hucksterism: the off-guard moments of Bush, Clinton and Perot during 1992's presidential election campaign. Some of this stuff is amazing. CNN talk-show host Larry King boasts how he's changed the world, between talking about sleeping pills with Bush; Perot mentions the time he took Michael Jackson out on his speed boat; moral majority hatemonger Pat Robertson is a smiling mound of brazen homophobia. Springer avoids authorial comment. He doesn't need it: most of these guys have just hanged themselves thrice over before our very eyes. Unreservedly recommended. TJ

Spinnen, Die (The Spiders)

(1919/20, Ger, (Pt I) 6,240 ft/(Pt II) 7,281 ft, b/w)
d/sc Fritz Lang. *ph* (Pt I) Emil Schünemann, (Pt II) Karl Freund. *ad* Hermann Warm, Otto Hunte, Carl Ludwig Kirmse, Heinrich Umlauff. *cast* Carl de Vogt, Ressel Orla, Lil Dagover, Paul Morgan, Georg John, Bruno Lettinger.

● Lang's third venture as a director, which he also scripted. Often reminiscent of Feuillade in its delirious invention and tongue-in-cheek humour, it's a wild and woolly serial about a secret society of arch-criminals who plan (of course) to dominate the world, and make a start by initiating a quest for the fabulous lost treasure of the Incas. Fiendish cruelties, fluttering heroines, and Oriental villains are all welded together in some wonderfully exotic settings by Lang's superb architectural sense. Two projected further instalments were never filmed, although Lang had already prepared the scripts. TM

Spione (Spies/The Spy)

(1928, Ger, 14,318 ft, b/w)
d/p Fritz Lang. *sc* Fritz Lang, Thea von Harbou. *ph* Fritz Arno Wagner. *ad* Otto Hunte, Karl Vollbrecht. *m* Werner R Heymann. *cast* Rudolf Klein-Rogge, Gerda Maurus, Willy Fritsch, Lupu Pick, Fritz Rasp, Lien Deyers, Craighall Sherry.

● In its very idiosyncratic way, *Spione* beats Lang's three Mabuse pictures as his definitive vision of a criminal mastermind. The reason is probably that this film entirely lacks the socio-political overtones of the Mabuse trilogy: the exploits of the evil genius Haghi (Klein-Rogge) here represent criminality almost in the abstract, and plunge the movie into a delirium of disguises, deaths, double-motives, and labyrinthine tricks. The tone is somewhere between true pulp fiction and pure expressionism, and the result remains wholly thrilling. TR

Spiral Staircase, The

(1946, US, 83 min, b/w)
d Robert Siodmak. *p* Dore Schary. *sc* Mel Dinelli. *ph* Nick Musuraca. *ed* Harry Marker, Harry Gerstad. *ad* Albert S D'Agostino, Jack Okey. *m* Roy Webb. *cast* Dorothy McGuire, George Brent, Ethel Barrymore, Kent Smith, Rhonda Fleming, Elsa Lanchester, Gordon Oliver, Rhys Williams.

● Superb thriller about a manic killer dedicating himself to beauty by ridding the world of maimed or disfigured women. Hitchcock couldn't have bettered the casual mastery with which the opening defines not just time and place (small town, turn of the century) but the themes of voyeurism and entrapment as a carriage draws up outside a hotel, the townsfolk assemble inside for a silent picture show, and the camera lifts to a room above where a crippled girl is being watched by a malevolently glaring hidden eye as she undresses. This first murder, discreetly executed as the girl pulls her dress over her head and we see her arms convulsively cross in agony, introduces a note of expressionism which Siodmak uses sparingly but with unfailing elegance throughout as the shadows close in on McGuire's mute, terrified heroine. It's one of the undoubted masterpieces of the Gothic mode, even if the happy ending comes more than a shade too pat. TM

Spiral Staircase, The

(1975, GB, 89 min)
d Peter Collinson. *p* Peter Shaw. *sc* Andrew Meredith [Allan Scott, Chris Bryant]. *ph* Ken Hodges. *ed* Raymond Poulton. *ad* Disley Jones. *m* David Lindup. *cast* Jacqueline Bisset, Christopher Plummer, Sam Wanamaker, Mildred Dunnock, Gayle Hunnicutt, Sheila Brennan, Elaine Stritch, John Ronane, Ronald Radd, John Phillip Law.

● Who has been killing off young girls with physical defects, and obviously has an eye on Jacqueline Bisset, rendered speechless by a shock (doubtless on finding herself in a movie like this)? There's a lush in the kitchen, a bedridden grandmother, a secretary on the make, an ex-Vietnam vet, a kindly uncle, an even more kindly doctor, a trigger-happy cop, and a storm outside. Any interest soon gets lost in the rambling rooms of the huge house that serves as the base for the plot. The moral of the tale would seem to be that if you want your voice back, have someone try to strangle you. Whatever happened to the chilling Gothic tale made by Robert Siodmak in 1946? CPe

Spirited Away (Sen to Chihiro no Kamikakushi)

(2001, Jap, 122 min)
d Hayao Miyazaki. *p* Toshio Suzuki. *sc* Hayao Miyazaki. *animation d* Masashi Ando. *ad* Yoji Takeshige. *m* Joe Hisaishi. *cast* voices: Rumi Hiragi, Miyu Irino, Mari Natsuki, Takashi Naito, Bunta Sugawara.

● Miyazaki's first digitally animated feature (the highest-grossing Japanese film ever) initially seems like a *Through the Looking-Glass* fantasy, but rapidly picks up a resonance, weight and complexity that make it all but Shakespearean. Chihiro, a sullen and resentful 10-year-old, is moving house with her parents when they stumble into the world of the Japanese gods – where the greedy parents are soon turned into pigs. Chihiro bluffs her way into a job in the resort spa run by the sorceress Yubaba, but at the cost of her human name and identity; she becomes Sen. With her links to her own past slipping away, she finds an ally in Yubaba's factotum Haku, a mysteriously powerful boy who also has a lost identity behind him. Never remotely didactic, the film is ultimately a self-fulfilment drama that touches on religious, ethical, ecological and psychological issues. (There's also an undercurrent of satire: Miyazaki admits that Yubaba's bathhouse is a parody of his own Studio Ghibli.) No other word for it: a masterpiece. TR

Spirit of Mopti, The (L'Esprit de Mopti)

(1999, Fr/Mali, 54 min)
d Moussa Ouane. *p* Philip Brooks, L Bocahut. *concept* Pascal Letellier, Moussa Ouane. *ph* Jacques Besse. *ed* Carol Equer-Hamy.

●Mopti, Mali's port town on the river Niger, is known as 'the Venice of Africa'. This engaging, documentary-style Franco-Malian drama follows a number of local traders and farmers to examine how long established traditions have knitted together a cohesive society. We see dried fish coming in for barter from upriver, a cattle herder on his way to better pastures, a Mopti porter kept busy by the to and fro of the thronging marketplace; and although conditions are rudimentary by Western standards, it's easy to sense the ingrained resilience with which these people get on with their lives. The film-makers never force the point, leaving the weathered faces and uproarious laughter to do the talking. TJ

Spirit of St. Louis, The

(1957, US,135 min)
d Billy Wilder. *p* Leland Hayward. *sc* Billy Wilder, Wendell Mayes, Charles Lederer. *ph* Robert Burks, J Peverell Marley. *ed* Arthur P Schmidt. *ad* Art Loel. *m* Franz Waxman. *cast* James Stewart, Murray Hamilton, Patricia Smith, Bartlett Robinson, Marc Connelly, Robert Burton.

●Charles Lindbergh, 'Lucky Lindy', made the world's first solo transatlantic flight in 1927. Either this is Wilder's most cynical picture or his most purely affirmative one, as he takes the notoriously aloof, pro-Nazi aviator and magics him into the person of good ol' Jimmy Stewart, just plain folks, bumbling along against all odds, triumphing almost by accident, or perhaps with a little help from the Lord. The narrative is non-chronological but very simple: raising the cash, building the plane, flying the flight. It's quite engrossing, with the period trappings lovingly presented. Perhaps that was the project's real attraction for Wilder: the 1920s, an era he seems drawn to above all others. BBa

Spirit of the Beehive, The (El Espíritu de la Colmena) 100

(1973, Sp, 98 min)
d Victor Erice. *p* Elias Querejeta. *sc* Victor Erice, Angel Fernandéz Santos. *ph* Luis Cuadrado. *ed* Pablo G del Amo. *ad* Adolfo Cofiño. *m* Luis de Pablo. *cast* Fernando Fernan Gómez, Terésa Gimpera, Ana Torrent, Isabel Telleria, Laly Soldevilla, José Villasante.

●Erice's remarkable one-off (he has made only one film since, the generally less well regarded *El Sur*) sees rural Spain soon after Franco's victory as a wasteland of inactivity, thrown into relief by the doomed industriousness of bees in their hives. The single, fragile spark of 'liberation' exists in the mind of little Ana, who dreams of meeting the gentle monster from James Whale's *Frankenstein*, and befriends a fugitive soldier just before he is caught and shot. A haunting mood-piece that dispenses with plot and works its spells through intricate patterns of sound and image. TR

Spirit of the Eagle

(1991, US, 90 min)
d Boon Collins. *cast* Dan Haggerty, William Smith, Trevor Yarrish.

●Fans of the *National Geographic* will enjoy this lumbering saga about an anguished father (Haggerty) roaming mountains, forests and prairies in search of his son, who's been sold to the Indians. The script borrows from *The Searchers*, but the landscapes are what really matter. GM

Spirit of the Wild

see Adventures of Frontier Fremont, The

Spirits of the Dead

see Histoires Extraordinaires

Spite Marriage

(1929, US, 9 reels, b/w)
d Edward Sedgwick. *p* Lawrence Weingarten. *sc* Richard Schayer, Ernest Pagano. *ph* Reggie Lanning. *ed* Frank Sullivan. *ad* Fredric Hope. *cast* Buster Keaton, Dorothy Sebastian, Edward Earle, Leila Hyams, Will Bechtel, Hank Mann.

●Keaton's last silent feature takes the classic Keaton form: an incompetent discovers a growing sense of confidence and physical ingenuity, overcomes the villains, and wins the girl. Part of the plot harks back to *The Navigator*, but three of the sequences (a play ruined by Buster's gaucheness, getting a drunk bride to bed, and an extraordinary shipboard fight) put the film up in Division One, crowning a decade of unparalleled creativity which was then stifled by studio inflexibility. JC

Spitfire

see The First of the Few

Spitfire

(1934, US, 88 min, b/w)
d John Cromwell. *p* Pandro S Berman. *sc* Jane Murfin. *ph* Edward Cronjager. *ed* William M Morgan, Van Nest Polglase, Carroll Clark. *m* Max Steiner, Lula Vollmer. *cast* Katharine Hepburn, Robert Young, Ralph Bellamy, Martha Sleeper, Sara Haden, Sidney Toler.

●Cromwell, who played the doddery priest in Altman's *A Wedding*, had a lengthy career as a director particularly adept with women leads; and certainly the entirely wonderful Katharine Hepburn constitutes the main interest in this otherwise plain sentimental comedy of backwoods superstition confronting civilisation in the form of a dam construction company. Not remotely dismayed by the role of hillbilly, nor by having to mouth down-home Christian cracker mottoes, she cuts an acidic path through the general coyness, and runs counter to the formulary script by suggesting that finally she remains a shrew. CPea

Spitfire Grill, The (aka Care of the Spitfire Grill)

(1996, US, 116 min)
d Lee David Zlotoff. *p* Forrest Murray. *sc* Lee David Zlotoff. *ph* Robert Draper. *ed* Margaret Goodspeed. *pd* Howard Cummings. *m* James Horner. *cast* Alison Elliott, Ellen Burstyn, Marcia Gay Harden, Will Patton, Louise De Cormier, Ida Griesemer.

●Elliott's released from prison into a waitressing job at Burstyn's cafe, under the watchful eyes of the entire town. This would-be inspirational, Capra-esque melodrama wears its heart on its sleeve. It's not a bad heart, just very soft. James Horner supplies a bathetic scorer, the Maine locations (actually Vermont) are made much of, and the wistful vision of small town America is too cute for words. On the plus side, newcomer Elliott stands up to heavily accented performances from Burstyn and Harden. TCh

Splash

(1984, US, 110 min)
d Ron Howard. *p* Brian Grazer. *sc* Lowell Ganz, Babaloo Mandel, Bruce Jay Friedman. *ph* Don Peterman. *ed* Daniel Hanley, Michael Hill. *pd* Jack T Collis. *m* Lee Holdridge. *cast* Tom Hanks, Daryl Hannah, Eugene Levy, John Candy, Dody Goodman, Shecky Greene, Richard B Shull, Bobby DiCicco.

●The beauty here is that the love is purely innocent. Not quite sexually innocent, although the carnal problems of falling for a mermaid are handled very well by the movie, which simply ignores them; rather, it is a love which has nothing to do with getting to know him, or his friends, or whether you like his apartment, or his job. It is love without conditions, much as in *E.T.*, except that here, one half of the match (Hanks) is adult, and the other half (Hannah) considerably more attractive than the waddling mud pie. Howard demonstrates exactly the correct soft touch, skirting the myriad problems of taste; and Hannah, who was the punkish replicant in *Blade Runner*, is somehow, very much, right there. CPea

Splendor

(1988, It/Fr, 99 min, b/w & col)
d Ettore Scola. *p* Mario Cecchi Gori, Vittorio Cecchi Gori, Ettore Scola. *sc* Ettore Scola. *ph* Luciano Tovoli. *ed* Francesco Malvestito. *ad* Luciano Ricceri. *m* Armando Trovaioli. *cast* Marcello Mastroianni, Massimo Troisi. Marina Vlady, Paolo Panelli, Pamela Villoresi, Giacomo Piperno.

●To the priest in a small Italian town, the Splendor cinema (now sold for redevelopment) is a 'dark grotto of sin'; to owner Jordan (Mastroianni), it's a shrine. But writer/director Scola is more concerned with the grey areas between such views: the patrons who desert cinema in droves when TV offers cheap, undemanding entertainment. Using flashback and clips, he conveys something of the medium's superiority over the box, at the same time beautifully unravelling a tale of life-long devotion and hard graft from Jordan, his long-term lover/usherette (Vlady), and the projectionist (Troisi). Their temperamental relationships over two decades are conveyed with great affection by the accomplished cast; and the film is full of wonderful moments – such as the homage to Capra at the climax – which manage to be both magical *and* unsentimental. CM

Splendor in the Grass

(1961, US, 124 min)
d/p Elia Kazan. *sc* William Inge. *ph* Boris Kaufman. *ed* Gene Milford. *ad* Richard Sylbert. *m* David Amram. *cast* Natalie Wood, Warren Beatty, Pat Hingle, Barbara Loden, Sandy Dennis, Audrey Christie, Gary Lockwood, Zohra Lampert, Phyllis Diller.

●With Beatty (his debut) and Wood star-crossed by parental opposition to their adolescent romance, William Inge's script is a sort of *Romeo and Juliet* translated to Depression Kansas. Attacked by many as being a hysterical account of sexual neurosis, praised by others for the acting (especially of Wood, as the daughter who goes mad) and for its occasional moments of great beauty, this is probably Kazan's most fought-over movie. A complicated film that never really successfully yokes together the themes of money-making and sexuality, it reveals both Kazan's operatic sensibility and his inability to follow an argument rigorously through. PH

Split, The

(1968, US, 91 min)
d Gordon Flemyng. *p* Robert Chartoff, Irwin Winkler. *sc* Robert Sabaroff. *ph* Burnett Guffey. *ed* Rita Roland. *ad* Urie McCleary, George W Davis. *m* Quincy Jones. *cast* Jim Brown, Diahann Carroll, Julie Harris, Gene Hackman, Ernest Borgnine, Warren Oates, Donald Sutherland, James Whitmore, Jack Klugman.

●Based (like *Point Blank* and *The Outfit*) on a novel by Richard Stark (Donald E Westlake), this often impressively bleak caper-thriller benefits enormously from its strong cast. Brown is the gang-leader who recruits a number of criminal experts to rob the LA Coliseum after a sold-out football game; Hackman is the cop who hunts him down after the chance murder of Brown's wife links him with the immaculately executed heist. Flemyng's direction is efficient if lacking in real flair, but Burnett Guffey's crisp camera-work, the taut plotting, and the generally high standard of the performances make for a pleasing, if undemanding modern *noir* thriller in the tradition of *The Killing* and *The Asphalt Jungle*. GA.

Split Second

(1991, GB, 90 min)
d Tony Maylam. *p* Laura Gregory. *sc* Gary Scott Thompson. *ph* Clive Tickner. *ed* Dan Rae. *pd* Chris Edwards. *m* Stephen Parsons, Francis Haines. *cast* Rutger Hauer, Kim Cattrall, Neil Duncan, Michael J Pollard, Alun Armstrong, Pete Postlethwaite, Ian Dury, Roberta Eaton, Tony Steedman.

●Set in the flooded and polluted London of 2008, this low-budget sci-fi movie has renegade cop Harley Stone (Hauer) and his rookie partner Durkin (Duncan) on the trail of a monstrous serial killer who rips out his victims' hearts.

Splashing about the waterlogged city, Stone senses some telepathic connection with the killer, who leaves cryptic occult messages written in blood. Neither the instinctive Stone nor his eccentric boffin partner can figure it out, so they do what all good macho cops do when confronted with an evil force they don't understand: they strap on some major firepower and blast everything in sight. This derivative eco-horror movie recycles dozens of disposable plots, flinging together all-purpose action man Hauer, a futuristic setting, and a reptilian alien. Hauer could do this stuff in his sleep, and the film looks as though Maylam did. NF

Splitting Heirs

(1993, GB, 87 min)
d Robert Young. *p* Simon Bosanquet, Redmond Morris. *sc* Eric Idle. *ph* Tony Pierce-Roberts. *ed* John Jympson. *pd* John Beard. *m* Michael Kamen. *cast* Eric Idle, Rick Moranis, Barbara Hershey, Catherine Zeta Jones, John Cleese, Sadie Frost, Stratford Johns, Brenda Bruce, Eric Sykes.
●Eric Idle's script may pack in any amount of would-be comedic standbys – big bosoms, naked men hiding in wardrobes, national and ethnic stereotypes, bungled murder attempts, more big bosoms – but its cynical contrivance and lumbering execution fail to raise a laugh from beginning to end. The basic plot is *Kind Hearts and Coronets* rewritten for the mall-rat generation. Tommy Patel (Idle), a humble city broker, discovers that he's the lost Duke of Bournemouth, heir to a fortune currently hogged by American imposter Henry Maitland (Moranis). With the sinister complicity of legal vulture Shadgrind (Cleese, self-parodic), our aspirant aristo decides to bump off the Yank pretender; but before he can claim the title, there's a near-incestuous entanglement with the man-hungry widowed Duchess (Hershey) to be negotiated. Hershey's embarrassed presence, and the flailing efforts of the former Pythons, make this tedious cavalcade of thumping obviousness even more cringe-worthy than it already is. TJ

Split William to Chrysis: Portrait of a Drag Queen

(1992, US, 58 min)
d Andrew Weeks, Ellen Fisher Turk.
●Told through a combination of interviews, archive and home movie footage, this story of a boy who wanted to be more than just William has the makings of a modern parable. Rejected by his family, driven to accentuating his natural assets with dangerously high doses of hormones, the poor boy from Brooklyn created Chrysis, the woman he grew up to be. In her relatively short life, Chrysis turned herself from a downtown hooker into an international attraction, wowing audiences, winning the affections of Warhol (among others) and becoming muse to Salvador Dali, before finally succumbing to the cancer which started in her artifical breasts. Interviewed shortly before and after her death, friends testify to her courage, generosity, and ability to make the best of any situation. But the only proof we need is Chrysis herself. Already in advanced stages of illness by the time filming started, she's a performer to the end, refuting suggestions that she's taken the tough route with the dismissive 'Somebody's got to do it'. It's a dizzying story, and a moving one. PBur

Spoiled Children

see Des Enfants Gâtés

Spooky Bunch, The (Zhuang Dao Zheng)

(1980, HK, 97 min)
d Ann Hui. *cast* Josephine Siao, Kenny Bee, Kwan Chung, Tina Lau, Lau Hark-Sun.
●Quick and quirky, this follow-up to Ann Hui's debut feature, *The Secret*, juggles broad farce with guignol in an oddball yarn about a second-rate Cantonese Opera troupe bedevilled by an army of revenge-seeking ghosts. Exotic theatricals and their backstage rivalries, eccentric characterisations (which include a playfully vengeful spirit named 'Cat Shit'), and an energetic camera style jostle for attention a little too clamorously at times, but the deceptive aura of greasepaint tackiness and the slapstick horror are all of a uniquely entertaining piece. PT

Spoor (aka Guns Across the Veldt)

(1975, SAf, 81 min)
d Howard Rennie. *p* John D Merriman, Dawie van Heerden. *ph* Andre Liebenberg. *ed* Peter Thornton. *m* Michael Hankinson. *cast* Giles Ridley, George Jackson, Ivor Kissin, Victor Melleney, Ian Yule.
●A monumentally hamfisted movie set in 1901 South Africa, when the British under Kitchener were fighting the insurgent Boers. A neurotic, Sandhurst-starched captain (Ridley) obsessively tries to hunt down an elusive guerilla general. With him go a brooding Afrikaaner scout, the *Observer* correspondent who shudders at the notion of 'participation', and two gin-swilling, recalcitrant privates. In addition to their hysterically wooden performances, an insulting script, misuse of location, and extremely laborious pace make this a must to avoid. IB

Spoorloos

see Vanishing, The

Spot

see Dogpound Shuffle

Spotswood

(1991, Aust, 95 min)
d Mark Joffe. *p* Timothy White, Richard Brennan. *sc* Max Dann, Andrew Knight. *ph* Ellery Ryan. *ed* Nicholas Beauman. *pd* Chris S Kennedy. *m* Ricky Fataar. *cast* Anthony Hopkins, Ben Mendelsohn, Toni Collette, Alwyn Kurts, Dan Wyllie, Bruno Lawrence, Rebecca Rigg, Russell Crowe.
●Errol Wallace (Hopkins) is all that one could ask of a time-and-motion expert. But when he moves from recommending redundancies at a Melbourne car factory to figuring out the financial problems of Ball's Moccasin Factory – a small family affair in the backwater suburb of Spotswood – he slowly realises that he lacks one essential virtue: the warming, common touch of humanity. Joffe's gentle comedy-drama, set in the mid-'60s, is as old-fashioned as the Ealing-esque community that is its main setting; a faintly hackneyed romantic subplot and the quietly sentimental tone of moral uplift only underline the film's overall caution. That said, it is genuinely funny, thanks to deft characterisations, a wry eye for the absurdities of working life, and a nice line in throwaway visual gags and verbal non-sequiturs. Hopkins' taciturn performance, meanwhile, injects a welcome, credible note of pain into the light-hearted proceedings. Small, slight, but surprisingly affecting. GA

Spriggan

(1998, Jap, 90 min)
d Hirotsugu Kawasaki. *p* Ayao Ueda, Kazuhiko Ikeguchi, Kazuya Hamana, Haruo Sai, Eiko Tanaka. *sc* Katsuhiro Otomo. *ph* Hisao Shirai. *ed* Takeshi Seyama. *pd* Mutuo Koseki. *m* Yota Tsuruoka. *cast* voices: Shotaro Morikubo, Tatsushi Aigase, Ken Shiroyama, Takehito Koyasu.
●Supervised by Katsuhiro Otomo (*Akira*), Kawasaki's typically spectacular manga animation begins in James Bond/Indiana Jones territory, with 17-year-old Ominai Yu – premier agent of the Spriggan, highly-trained warriors working for Arcam, a covert international association dedicated to sealing off the world's ancient ruins and their secrets – jetting to Turkey where Arcam's guardianship of Noah's Ark is under threat from two freaky villains and an army of cyborgs apparently trained by the Pentagon. Things take a turn for the improbable when Arcam's senior scientist and a viciously prodigious little boy calculate that the Ark is in fact a superior atmosphere control system which caused the original Biblical flood. Shortly, the kid is playing God with the planet's thermostat. Quite what the Turkish authorities make of these apocalyptic goings-on remains unclear, but they're certainly left with heaps of bodies to dispose of. Characterisation is regulation thin, plotting largely nonsensical, 'camerawork' and effects increasingly pyrotechnical until an amazing final light show inside the Ark. NB

Spring and Port Wine

(1969, GB, 101 min)
d Peter Hammond. *p* Michael Medwin. *sc* Bill Naughton. *ph* Norman Warwick. *ed* Fergus McDonell. *pd* Reece Pemberton. *m* Douglas Gamley. *cast* James Mason, Diana Coupland, Susan George, Rodney Bewes, Hannah Gordon, Adrienne Posta, Arthur Lowe, Frank Windsor, Bernard Bresslaw.
●Obdurate Rafe Crompton (Mason), an engineer at a Bolton, Lancashire, cotton mill, finds his authority challenged when Hilda (George), the younger of his two daughters, refuses to eat a plate of herring, which he then serves up to her day after day, forcing the battle of wills to breaking point. Bill Naughton's play may have worked on stage, but on screen (in the playwright's own adaptation) it's as inconsequential as an expanded sitcom, and Mason's much too big a star for the material. TJ

Spring in a Small Town (Xiao Cheng zhi Chun)

(1948, China, 85 min)
d Fei Mu. *cast* Wei Wei, Shi Yu, Li Wei, Zhang Hongmei, Cui Chaoming.
●The crowning achievement of one of China's finest directors, this unique film both reflects and dissects the mood of helpless impotence which afflicted many Chinese in the years after the war. After a 10-year absence, a doctor visits a married couple living in a bomb-scarred country town. The husband is a broken man, close to suicide; the wife was once his lover and they start to drift back into an affair under the nose of her husband. The sense of frustration and enervation is palpable, underlined by Fei's brilliant idea to use dissolves within scenes, but the counter-current of renascent desire (sparked by Wei Wei's phenomenal performance as the wife) makes this also a very sensual movie. TR

Spring in My Hometown (Areumdaun Sijeol)

(1998, SKor, 110 min)
d Lee Kwang-Mo. *cast* Ahn Sung-Ki, Bae Yoo-Jung, Song Ok-Sook, Yoo Seon-Hoi, Lee In.
●Lee, a UCLA graduate who is now Korea's leading art-film distributor, excavates two histories (one domestic, one national) from the time of the Korean War. The story unfolds in discrete episodes, shot in wide angle, each prefaced with a caption counterpointing events in one village with off-screen affairs of state. Sung-Min's father (Ahn, excellent as ever) is the first villager to find lucrative work at a nearby US Army base, because his daughter Young-Sook is the first local to date a GI. But Sung-Min and his best friend Chang-Hee discover that dad's services to the Americans include pimping for local women – including Chang-Hee's mother. The parallels between the ensuing tragedies and the fate of South Korea in the early 1950s remain tantalisingly elusive, but Lee directs both kids and adults with real insight and captures the flavour of distant childhood memories with some precision. TR

Spring into Summer (Pleure Pas la Bouche Pleine)

(1973, Fr, 117 min)
d Pascal Thomas. *p* Claude Berri. *sc* Pascal Thomas, Roland Duval. *ph* Colin Mounier. *ed* Hélène Plemiannikov. *ad* Jean-Pierre Kohut-Svelko. *m* Vladimir Kosma. *cast* Annie Colé, Frédéric Duru, Jean Carmet, Christiane Chamaret, Bernard Menez.
●The sap rises, the blood flows, lush verdant hues and a robust fecundity abounds: little girls have their first periods, while the heroine and elder sister loses her virginity, not to the bumbling boy she'll perhaps marry but to some oaf who's been around and drives a white sports car. Get the picture? Pascal Thomas' loving picture of the cycle of life in a French village has both humour and an obvious charm; at its best when dealing with the heroine's relationship seen through the eyes of her elders and youngers, or with the banality of her seduction (it's he who undresses behind the screen). But with every shot set up with the same loving care, from the old venerables in the café to our heroine painting her nails, the final impression, for all the warm-heartedness and sensitivity, is of Thomas slowly loving his film to death.

Spring River Flows East, The (Yijiang Chunshui Xiang Dong Liu)

(1947, China, 189 min, b/w)
d Zheng Junli, Cai Chusheng. *p* Xia Yunhu, Tao Boxun. *sc* Cai Chusheng, Zheng Junli. *ph*

Zhu Jinming. *ed* Wu Tiangfang, Chen Zhaoxi, Fu Zhengyi. *pd* Han Shangyi. *m* Zhang Zhengfan. *cast* Bai Yang, Tao Jin, Wu Yin, Yan Gongshang, Shangguan Yunzhu, Shu Xiuwen, Qin Xiaolong.
●The second Peak Film Industries production (after *8,000 Li*) was this epic melodrama released in two parts: *Eight Years of Turmoil* and *Before and After Dawn*. Idealistic night school teacher Zhang (Tao Jin, terrific) marries factory worker Sufen (Bai Yang, too glamorous!) in Shanghai in 1931. When the Japanese invasion begins, he goes off to the front lines with the Red Cross – but winds up in Chungking, where he subsides into drink and self-pity. Gradually he reinvents himself as a businessman and marries a society hostess, while his real family, evicted by the Japanese, starves in a squatter camp. This was political dynamite at the time, and it stands up remarkably well as a Dickensian saga rhyming one family's tragedy with the nation's fate. The staginess of the dialogue scenes is offset by the visual eloquence of the rest. The director credit properly belongs to Zheng Junli; co-author Cai Chusheng was reportedly too scared of the KMT censors to show up on the set. TR

Spring Shower

see Tavaszi Zápor

Spring Symphony (Frühlingssinfonie)

(1983, WGer, 103 min)
d/p Peter Schamoni. *sc* Peter Schamoni. *ph* Gerard Vandenberg. *ed* Elfi Tillack. *pd* Alfred Hirschmeier. *m* Schumann. *cast* Nastassja Kinski, Herbert Grünemeyer, Rolf Hoppe, André Heller, Bernhard Wicki.
●A serious, if ponderous, biopic that traces a tumultuous ten years in the life of composer Robert Schumann. Schumann's life lurches queasily between the prosaic and the paradisaical (as he turns from the piano to drink, and from his engagement to the titled Ernestine to sex with a serving wench), driven by a dual passion for Clara Wieck (the daughter of his tutor) and music, which seems to be no more than a by-product of a monumental and masochistic selfishness. Schamoni's film is impeccably cast, with Hoppe as Wieck, his damp eyes suggesting incest here as chillingly as they did evil in his portrayal of Goering in *Mephisto;* Grünemeyer pale and intense as the boy-genius; and Kinski irritatingly placid as Clara. And the director captures perfectly the spirit of a Germany founded equally upon the tenets of stuffy burghers and high-minded student drinking associations, while cinematically echoing the Romantic style of Schumann's music. FD

Spy, The

see Spione

Spy Game

(2001, Ger/US/Jap/Fr, 126 min)
d Tony Scott. *p* Douglas Wick, Marc Abraham. *sc* Michael Frost Beckner, David Arata. *ph* Dan Mindel. *pd* Norris Spencer, (Morocco) Chris Seagers, (Vancouver) Nina Ruscio. *m* Harry Gregson-Williams. *cast* Robert Redford, Brad Pitt, Catherine McCormack, Stephen Dillane, Larry Bryggman, Marianne Jean-Baptiste, Ken Leung, David Hemmings, Matthew Marsh.
●Changing times at CIA headquarters. It's 1991, a week before the US president is due in China to renegotiate trade relations, and former operative Bishop (Pitt) has been captured during a rogue raid on a Shanghai prison. The agency has 24 hours to formulate a response before the Chinese authorities execute him, so a high level 'psychological profiling' session brings in veteran officer Muir (Redford), Bishop's mentor since their first encounter in Vietnam in 1975. Thus the flashbacks reel through the years, taking in bumps and scrapes in divided Berlin and wartorn mid-'80s Beirut, all handily arranged into a series of suspense set pieces, car chases and explosions. Best not taken too seriously, as the shaping factor seems to be the fading liberal star power of Redford as a rebel within the system, shored up by Pitt's low key contribution as an assassin discovering scruples. But the film's pared characterisation leaves these ideas unrealised, while Brad's supposedly significant romance with committed aid worker McCormack is a clumsy plot catalyst. Scott directs the military hardware with characteristic efficiency, even as the movie falls down around him. TJ

Spy Hard

(1996, US, 81 min)
d Rick Friedberg. *p* Rick Friedberg, Doug Draizin, Jeffrey Konvitz. *sc* Rick Friedberg, Dick Chudnow, Jason Friedberg, Aaron Seltzer. *ph* John Leonetti. *ed* Eric Sears. *pd* William Creber. *m* Bill Conti. *cast* Leslie Nielsen, Nicollette Sheridan, Andy Griffith, Charles Durning, Marcia Gay Harden, Barry Bostwick, John Ales, Stephanie Romanov.
●Nielsen is the Agency's star operatve Dick Steele (codename: WD-40). Intrepid, debonair, yet surprisingly accident-prone, Steele leaves a trail of destruction in his wake. When his beloved fellow agent Victoria Dahl falls to her death from a cliff as Steele puts paid to the ambitions of his nemesis General Rancor (Griffith), WD-40 feels it's time to hang up his badge. Fifteen years on, and Rancor's back, unarmed limb-wise, though he does have a very large rocket and he's threatening to use it unless he gets the final microchip that'll bring him world domination. Bond may be the main target, but *Spy Hard* is hardly frugal with its references. After the *Naked Guns*, and *Wayne's Worlds*, this Hollywood spoofery is becoming almost a genre in itself. Like *Hot Shots!* there's the same mistaken belief that simply tagging other films will be intrinsically funny: Nielsen running into a convent dressed as a nun and conducting the sisters through 'Raindrops Keep Falling on My Head' does not a great *Sister Act* parody make. NB

Spy in Black, The

(1939, GB, 82 min, b/w)
d Michael Powell. *p* Irving Asher. *sc* Emeric Pressburger. *ph* Bernard Browne. *ed* William Hornbeck, Hugh Stewart. *ad* Vincent Korda. *m* Miklós Rozsa. *cast* Conrad Veidt, Valerie Hobson, Sebastian Shaw, Marius Goring, June Duprez, Athole Stewart.
●Darkness, foreboding and regret, rather than any sense of propaganda, dominate this extraordinarily atmospheric World War I spy story made on the eve of World War II. It signals the end of a peacetime era even more clearly than *The Lady Vanishes*. Daringly, the audience is asked to sympathise with the 'enemy' as the magnificent, shadowy Veidt moves through remarkable Scottish sets on a mission to Scapa Flow to destroy the British fleet. Intrigue, uncertainty and confused loyalties build to a bitter, ironic climax, and along the way Powell effortlessly produces more memorable shots and scenes than can be found in a dozen contemporary films. CPe

Spy Kids

(2001, US, 88 min)
d Robert Rodriguez. *p* Robert Rodriguez, Elizabeth Avellan. *sc* Robert Rodriguez. *ph* Guillermo Navarro. *ed* Robert Rodriguez. *pd* Cary White. *m* Danny Elfman, Gavin Greenaway, Heitor Pereira, John Debney, Robert Rodrigues, Los Lobos. *cast* Antonio Banderas, Carla Gugino, Alan Cumming, Teri Hatcher, Cheech Marin, Danny Trejo, Robert Patrick, Tony Shalhoub, Alexa Vega, Daryl Sabara, George Clooney.
●Ingrid (Gugino) and Gregorio Cortez (Banderas), semi-retired government spies, are called back to the ranks following the demise of their erstwhile colleagues at the hands of kids' puppet-show host and techno wizard Feban Floop (Cumming) and his assorted army. Ingrid and Gregorio disappear and the Cortez children (Vega and Sabara) have to don the jet-packs, slide on the computer specs and save the world. One-time rebel director Robert (*El Mariarchi*) Rodriguez treads a neat line, reversing a common (and mistaken) emphasis in kids' movies. He plays the danger/adventure lightly, and treats the garish design, environments, effects and various gadgets with the gravitas demanded by the young connoisseur. In terms of its family ethos, this makes an interesting comparison with the Addams Family films. Refreshingly, both portray a sexualised parental relationship and view family as a specialised enclave, within which audacity and independence are accepted. The plot deviations are endless and confusing, but children can handle that, no prob. WH

SPYS

(1974, GB, 100 min)
d Irvin Kershner. *p* Irwin Winkler, Robert Chartoff. *sc* Mel Mormenstein, Lawrence J Cohen, Fred Freeman. *ph* Gerry Fisher. *ed* Keith Palmer. *pd* Michael Seymour. *m* Jerry Goldsmith. *cast* Donald Sutherland, Elliott Gould, Zouzou, Joss Ackland, Kenneth Griffith, Vladek Sheybal, Kenneth J Warren, Nigel Hawthorne.
●Finely written espionage spoofery, with the finesse of a classic Hollywood comedy. Very classy, very assured, with exactly the right degree of underlying blackness: international relations come down to an openly acknowledged credo of a corpse for a corpse, a Russian defects for the promise of a Thunderbird, CIA torturers take time out to join in a chorus of 'America, America' with the tortured. *SPYS* takes post-Watergate disillusionment as read, and goes on to outdo *M*A*S*H*, the humour moving with ease from the verbal to the visual to the situational and back. Sutherland and Gould counterpoint each other superbly (Sutherland in particular performing excellently, like a zanier Cary Grant). Kershner directs with utter skill, enabling even the most notoriously cameo-ridden actor to rise to unexpected heights. VG

Spy Story

(1976, GB, 102 min)
d/p Lindsay Shonteff. *ph* Les Young. *ed* John Gibson. *m* Roger Wootton, Andrew Hellaby. *cast* Michael Petrovitch, Philip Latham, Don Fellows, Michael Gwynne, Nicholas Parsons, Tessa Wyatt, Derren Nesbitt.
●Len Deighton's cold and vivid view of cynical power-mongering, his existential anti-heroes coopted forcibly into a labyrinthine and rigid power structure, translated an American idiom into a specifically British context. It is an acerbic distillation that should have fuelled a far richer strand of cinema than it has. Shonteff's film catches Deighton's nuances of power and corruption, but sequences that do for starters hardly work as a continuing ploy; and soon characters are locked in limp confrontation, exchanging increasingly cryptic chunks of information while the plot works towards total incomprehensibility. VG

Spy Who Came In From the Cold, The

(1965, GB, 112 min, b/w)
d/p Martin Ritt. *sc* Paul Dehn, Guy Trosper. *ph* Oswald Morris. *ed* Anthony Harvey. *pd* Tambi Larsen. *m* Sol Kaplan. *cast* Richard Burton, Claire Bloom, Oskar Werner, Peter Van Eyck, Sam Wanamaker, George Voskovec, Rupert Davies, Cyril Cusack, Michael Hordern, Robert Hardy, Bernard Lee, Beatrix Lehmann, Esmond Knight.
●Without his customary good liberal message to hang on to, Ritt is forced to rely on pure professionalism, and as a result turns out one of his better films. John Le Carré's novel about betrayal and disillusionment in the world of East/West espionage is treated with intelligence and a disarming lack of sentimentality or moralising, while Burton gives one of his best screen performances as the spy out to get even with an East German counterpart. What finally impresses, however, is the sheer seediness of so much of the film, with characters, buildings, and landscapes lent convincingly grubby life by Oswald Morris' excellent monochrome camera-work. GA

Spy Who Loved Me, The

(1977, GB, 125 min)
d Lewis Gilbert. *p* Albert R Broccoli. *sc* Christopher Wood, Richard Maibaum. *ph* Claude Renoir. *ed* John Glen. *pd* Ken Adam. *m* Marvin Hamlisch. *cast* Roger Moore, Barbara Bach, Curd Jürgens, Richard Kiel, Caroline Munro, Walter Gotell, Geoffrey Keen, Bernard Lee, George Baker.
●Bond for Britain: 007's spectacular ski jump is aided by an ostentatious Union Jack parachute; caught in bed by his superiors, Bond smirks that he's keeping the British end up. Something of a straggler from the campy late '60s, this one mainly pushes the myth of British technological wizardry. Patriotic schoolboy flagwaving is accompanied by pre-pubescent sexuality and puerile innuendoes. Britain, Russia, and Martini-style locations conspire to thwart Curd Jürgens from destroying the world. The film has its moments – Kiel's indestructible heavy racks up a good score – but the rest is desperately weak. Interesting that a film which seems so often on the verge of impotence should boast so many phallic substitutes. CPe

Squale, La

(2000, Fr, 99 min)
d Fabrice Genestal. *p* Pierre Forette, Thierry Wong. *sc* Fabrice Genestal, Nathalie Valloud. *ph* Eric Guichard. *ed* Christophe Pinel. *pd* Yann Mercier. *m* Cut Killer. *cast* Esse Lawson, Tony Mpoudja, Khereddine Ennasri, Stéphanie Jaubert, Denis Lavant, Foued Nassah, François Delaive.

● Opening to a gang rape and branding (in the name of Suleiman, a legendary gang leader gone AWOL), this sets out its stall straight off. Cousin to *La Haine*, but exchanging Kassovitz's hyperactive camera for a more studied framing against which the endemic violence of French immigrant ghetto life beats like harsh weather, the film boasts an undeniable street-level authenticity. The *squale*, or rebellious adolescent, of the title is Desirée, a wired and angry new kid on the block who, not knowing her father's identity, claims she's the absent Suleiman's daughter. Soon she's heading up the neighbourhood girl gang while bedding down with genetically unreliable and vicious local hood Toussaint. Add familial breakdown to the mix and the main goal is trying to stay human amid such alienation and despair. Efficiently paced with sudden sharp jolts of real aggression, it's no joyride but, seeded with small daily hopes, the film finds a truthful balance in refusing to let environmental frustration entirely smother the delayed aspirations of Desirée and her like for a simple stability. GE

Square, The (Guangchang)

(1994, China, 100 min)
d Zhang Yuan, Duan Jinchuan. *p* Zhang Yuan, Chang Yi. *ph* Zhang Yuan. *ed* Yang Hongyu.

● Zhang Yuan's defiant response to finding his name on a government blacklist was to shoot this 'illegal' documentary in and about Tiananmen Square – not only the most public space in Beijing, but also the symbolic heart of Communist China. Observing without comment, the film sees the activities in the square as a microcosm of the state. It builds up a convincing analysis of China's political and social economy simply by watching the way the square is policed, patrolled and used by both the authorities and the public; it also poses some trenchant questions about China's future by showing the 'Little Emperors' who are the product of the country's single-child policy. No politics, of course, but the absence of references to 1989 speaks loudly enough. TR

Square Circle, The (Daayraa)

(1996, Ind, 98 min)
d Amol Palekar. *p* Pravesh Sippy. *sc* Timeri N Murari. *ph* Debu Deodhar. *ed* Waman Bhonsle. *pd* Prem Pillai. *m* Anand-Milind. *cast* Nirmal Pandey, Sonali Kulkarni, Faiyyaz, Rekha Sahay.

● An unnamed woman (Kulkarni) is kidnapped into prostitution by a madam and her henchmen, then gang raped by a three louts when she's plucky enough to escape. Salvation is at hand, however, in Pandey, a wandering entertainer. Having found his own identity through dressing as a woman, he puts the girl in men's clothes so they can pass as a 'straight' couple and travel in relative safety back to her home village. The direction is restrained for Bollywood (the dance number has been cut for the UK print), but pretty rough and ready to Western eyes, though once you adjust, it's easy to get swept up in the way every emotion is played to the hilt. The film's thematic daring is exceptional: the exploration of the tension between sexual identity and social circumstane in a staunchly traditional society. TJ

Square Dance

(1986, US, 112 min)
d/p Daniel Petrie. *sc* Alan Hines. *ph* Jacek Laskus. *ed* Bruce Green. *pd* Jan Scott. *m* Bruce Broughton. *cast* Jason Robards, Jane Alexander, Winona Ryder, Rob Lowe, Deborah Richter, Guich Koock, Elbert Lewis.

● Petrie's handling of this odd, faintly moralistic tale is at best sickly, at worst sick. Teenage Bible-basher Gemma (Ryder) abandons her crotchety grandfather (Robards) to join her loose-living mother (Alexander). Horrified to discover that Mom likes to get poked by the local cowpokes, Gemma strikes up a loving, innocent bond with hunky, mentally deficient Rory (Lowe), until an enthusiastic floozie introduces him to more stimulating games and Gemma catches them in the act. Rory, in vague remorse, viciously attacks his offending member (yeuch!), while Gemma hightails it back to Dullsville. Alexander and Ryder's intelligent performances are upstaged by Lowe, who comes across like rampant beefcake on valium. Ultimately, though, Petrie's twee vision of Midwest life kills the film – it's so cotton-pickin' clichéd. *The Waltons* with willies. EP

Squeaker, The

(1937, GB, 77 min, b/w)
d William K Howard. *p* Alexander Korda. *sc* Edward O Berkman, Bryan Edgar Wallace. *ph* Georges Perinal. *ed* Russell Lloyd. *ad* Vincent Korda. *m* Miklós Rozsa. *cast* Edmund Lowe, Ann Todd, Sebastian Shaw, Alastair Sim, Tamara Desni, Robert Newton, Stewart Rome.

● Clumsy casting and sloppy direction from the once-promising alcoholic Howard drain the vitality from Edgar Wallace's story of the unmasking of a master criminal who holds the underworld in thrall and uses Scotland Yard for his own advantage. Vincent Korda's elegant sets and Georges Périnal's subtle, inventive lighting are memorable, but the attempt to substitute atmosphere for suspense fails, despite a flamboyantly melodramatic climax. Fading American star Lowe seems out of his element in English crime, and Tamara Desni struggles in vain to bring exoticism to the British cinema. Fortunately there is compensation in young Alastair Sim, and in Robert Newton's passionate jewel thief, desperately trying to 'give up crime and live like a human being'. RMy

Squeeze, The

(1977, GB, 107 min)
d Michael Apted. *p* Stanley O'Toole. *sc* Leon Griffiths. *ph* Denis Lewiston. *ed* John Shirley. *ad* Bill McCrow. *m* David Hentschel. *cast* Stacy Keach, David Hemmings, Edward Fox, Stephen Boyd, Carol White, Freddie Starr, Hilary Gasson.

● Booze-sodden ex-cop (Keach) has to dry out when ex-wife and daughter are kidnapped. For the most part, this flashy, hard-edged film sells itself to a TV audience by providing more nudity, sexual innuendo, strong language, and thumping violence than the small screen. Under the surface brashness, Apted's direction does attempt to think the film through, although his handling of certain episodes suggests too much sensitivity for the job in hand. Good performances. CPe

Squeeze, The

(1987, US, 102 min)
d Roger Young. *p* Rupert Hitzig, Michael Tannen. *sc* Daniel Taplitz. *ph* Arthur Albert. *ed* Harry Keramidas. *pd* Simon Waters. *m* Miles Goodman. *cast* Michael Keaton, Rae Dawn Chong, Joe Pantoliano, Danny Aiello III, Leslie Bevis, Lou Criscoulo, Meatloaf.

● Keaton is a snake on the make who cheats at cards and whose life's ambition is to win the great American lotto. He spends most of his time building a room-size neon-lit lizard, and generally fooling around like he never left high school. Then into his life steps the alluring Chong, a private dick carrying a court summons from Keaton's ex-wife over non-payment of alimony. The couple haven't seen each other for three years, but she turns up wanting a favour: can he pick up a black box from her apartment? It sounds simple enough, but the box is also wanted by a couple of hoods working for a French dealer in shrunken heads, who has hired the unwitting Chong to track it down. This attempt at comedy is a disaster, laboriously plotted and inanely scripted; the enthusiasm of the cast can do nothing to redeem its sheer lack of wit and invention. CB

Squibs

(1935, GB, 77 min, b/w)
d Henry Edwards. *p* Julius Hagen. *sc* Michael Hogan, H Fowler Mear. *ph* Sydney Blythe. *ed* Jack Harris. *pd* James Carter. *songs* Maurice Sigler, Geoffrey Goodhart. *cast* Betty Balfour, Gordon Harker, Stanley Holloway, Margaret Yarde, Morris Harvey, Michael Shepley, Ronald Shiner.

● A Cockney flower girl (Balfour) falls in love with a policeman (Holloway) after he saves her from an oncoming car. But her inveterate gambler of a dad (Harker) is in trouble with the law. A cheerful enough British comedy with surprisingly high production values, this none the less seems like a film out of time. Its star is reprising a role she first performed in 1921 in a play by Clifford Seyler and George Pearson. Inevitably, the years tell. Judging by all the singalongs, the film-makers are trying to pass her off as London's answer to Gracie Fields. Unfortunately Britain's one time 'Queen of Happiness' has long since passed her sell by date. GM

Squirm

(1976, US, 92 min)
d Jeff Lieberman. *p* George Manasse. *sc* Jeff Lieberman. *ph* Joe Mangine. *ed* Brian Smedley-Aston. *ad* Henry Shrady. *m* Robert Prince. *cast* John Scardino, Patricia Pearcy, RA Dow, Jean Sullivan, Peter MacLean, Fran Higgins.

● Far better and more interesting than the obvious schlock appeal its plot would suggest: a small town is terrorised by a plague of lethal worms. In his debut, Lieberman reveals a genuine talent and ambitiousness (subsequently confirmed by *Blue Sunshine*), turning the film into a variation on the sexual paranoia theme, distinguished by his tendency to present his characters – especially the mother of the two wittily-observed girls who are central to the story – as keyed-up to an unexplained pitch of barely-controlled hysteria. The whole thing resembles a black Famous Five adventure. The atmosphere of the Georgia swampland locations is convincing, and the excellent special effects deliver the requisite shocks. Slyly entertaining stuff. VG

Srebrenica: A Cry from the Grave

(1999, GB/US, 104 min)
d/p/sc Leslie Woodhead. *ph* Gerry Pinches. *ed* Tony Meering. *with* Naser Oric, Louise Arbour, Sandy Vershbow, Yasushi Akashi, Jean-René Ruez. *narrator* Bill Moyers.

● This detailed account of the massacre of an estimated 7,000 Muslim men in July 1995, at the Bosnian 'safe enclave' of Srebrenica, relies not only on eye witness testimony, but on some astonishing telltale footage. Video recordings from a variety of sources, including a British reporter, the Dutch army and even Serb camera crews, are offset against each other to form a lacerating record. The testimonies of those who are dealing with survival take the film to a place of personal horror most of us will struggle to recognise. FM

Sssssss (aka Ssssnake)

(1973, US, 99 min)
d Bernard L Kowalski. *p* Dan Striepeke. *sc* Hal Dresner. *ph* Gerald Perry Finnerman. *ed* Robert Watts. *ad* John T McCormack. *m* Patrick Williams. *cast* Strother Martin, Dirk Benedict, Heather Menzies, Richard B Shull, Tim O'Connor, Jack Ging.

● Often so bad that you have to laugh. Reckoning that snakes will be among the creatures to survive the imminent ecological holocaust, Dr Carl Stoner attempts to turn his unsuspecting assistant David into a King Cobra. Complications arise when the boy falls for Stoner's daughter, but by the time she's twigged that the snake man in a circus sideshow is a former assistant to her father, David's no more than a cobra being chewed up by a mongoose. A complete mess, with biblical references (for some reason the central love story parallels the Fall), hallucinatory sequences, laboured borrowings, and moronic direction, yet quite enjoyable in its rubbishy way. Nice performance from Strother Martin as the doctor, plus some good special effects. CPe

S.T.A.B. (aka Thong)

(1975, Thai, 91 min)
d Chalong Pakdivijt. *cast* Greg Morris, Sombat Metanee, Krung Srivilai, Tham Thuy Hang.

● An oriental potboiler, of tangential interest as a rabid anti-Communist tract, with bounty hunter Morris mowing down Vietcong hordes during a behind-the-lines operation to recover skyjacked gold earmarked for an opium deal. Early on, one of his help-mates, a large girl in hotpants, strips down in a jungle monsoon to divert two enemy guards, and the film is littered with similar scenes of classic improbability. No one, incidentally, makes any reference to the Strategic Tactical Airborne Brigade of the opportunistic title. JPy

Stacking

see Season of Dreams

Stacy's Knights

(1983, US, 95 min)
d Jim Wilson. *p* Joann Locktov, Freddy Sweet. *sc* Michael Blake. *ph* Raoul Lomas. *ed* Bonnie Koehler. *ad* Florence Fellman. *m* Norton Buffalo. *cast* Andra Millian, Kevin Costner, Eve Lilith, Mike Reynolds, Garth Howard, Ed Semenza.

●Costner met up with writer Michael Blake and director Wilson, the team with whom he'd later make *Dances with Wolves*, on this early effort, the first time he'd played a leading part on film. The central role in this pretty duff thriller though goes to Millian as a shy young woman whose gambling fever leads her to get together a gang of card-sharps to take on the blackjack tables at a Mafia-owned casino. TJ

Stade de Wimbledon, Le

see Wimbledon Stage, The

Stagecoach

(1939, US, 96 min, b/w)
d John Ford. *p* Walter Wanger. *sc* Dudley Nichols. *ph* Bert Glennon. *ed* Otho Lovering, Dorothy Spencer, Walter Reynolds. *ad* Alexander Toluboff. *m* Boris Morros. *cast* John Wayne, Claire Trevor, Thomas Mitchell, George Bancroft, John Carradine, Andy Devine, Louise Platt, Donald Meek, Berton Churchill, Tim Holt.

●Impossible to overstate the influence of Ford's magnificent film, generally considered to be the first modern Western. Shot in the Monument Valley which Ford was later to make his own, it also initiated Wayne's extraordinarily fertile partnership with the director, and established in embryo much of the mythology explored and developed in Ford's subsequent Westerns. Wayne plays the Ringo Kid, an outlaw seeking revenge for the murder of his father and brother, first seen 'holding up' the stagecoach containing banished prostitute Trevor, dipso doctor Mitchell, cynical gambler Carradine, timid salesman Meek, and a pair of ostensibly respectable characters: pregnant 'lady' Platt, and crooked banker Churchill. The contrast between the innocence of the wilderness and the ambiguous 'blessings of civilisation' are brilliantly stitched into a smoothly developed narrative, which climaxes with the famous Indian attack on the stagecoach. NF

Stagecoach

(1966, US, 114 min)
d Gordon Douglas. *p* Martin Rackin. *sc* Joseph Landon. *ph* William H Clothier. *ed* Hugh S Fowler. *ad* Jack Martin Smith, Herman A Blumenthal. *m* Jerry Goldsmith. *cast* Alex Cord, Van Heflin, Bing Crosby, Red Buttons, Ann-Margret, Michael Connors, Robert Cummings, Stefanie Powers, Slim Pickens, Keenan Wynn.

●Look again at the credits before you're tempted: this is the witless remake of Ford's classic, with neither colour nor Cord anything like adequate recompense for Bert Glennon's dusty monochrome or Wayne's early strut as the Ringo Kid. PT

Stage Door

(1937, US, 92 min, b/w)
d Gregory La Cava. *p* Pandro S Berman. *sc* Morrie Ryskind, Anthony Veiller. *ph* Robert De Grasse. *ed* William Hamilton. *ad* Van Nest Polglase, Carroll Clark. *m* Roy Webb. *cast* Katharine Hepburn, Ginger Rogers, Adolphe Menjou, Andrea Leeds, Gail Patrick, Constance Collier, Lucille Ball, Eve Arden, Ann Miller, Franklin Pangborn, Jack Carson.

●Alongside *The Women* and *Dance, Girl, Dance*, one of the great sassy-women comedy-dramas of the '30s. Taken from the stage success by Kaufman and Ferber, it's a bitchy, pacy slice of sociology that throws together a bunch of aspiring actresses in a theatrical boarding house, and watches them interact with lecherous producers (Menjou, marvellous), boyfriends, and most of all each other. The casting is perfect: Hepburn as the Bryn Mawr upper crust type determinedly slumming it, Rogers (in her first bid as a serious actress) as the no-nonsense girl-next-door, and Leeds as the frail, hypersensitive thesp with real talent who introduces a touch of melodrama into the proceedings. Individuals and darker moments apart, however, it's the crackling ensemble pieces that remain in the memory, expertly timed by La Cava's civilised, generous direction, and located in lovingly authentic sets beautifully shot by Robert de Grasse. GA

Stage Door

see Hu-Du-Men

Stage Fright

(1950, GB, 110 min, b/w)
d/p Alfred Hitchcock. *sc* Whitfield Cook, Ranald MacDougall. *ph* Wilkie Cooper. *ed* EB Jarvis. *ad* Terence Verity. *m* Leighton Lucas. *cast* Marlene Dietrich, Jane Wyman, Michael Wilding, Richard Todd, Alastair Sim, Sybil Thorndike, Kay Walsh, Joyce Grenfell.

●A fairly routine thriller, noted chiefly for its cheating flashback, though with much more to enjoy than its detractors – including Hitchcock – make out. The plot involves a young RADA student (Wyman) trying to clear a boyfriend (Todd), who claims he's been framed for the murder of his mistress' husband. Along the way, the heroine disguises herself as a maid, falls in love with the investigating detective (Wilding), and discovers that her friend is actually guilty. The proceedings are enlivened mainly by two good comic performances, from Dietrich at her most blatantly vulgar as the musical comedy star/mistress, and Sim as the heroine's droll father. There are also some good set pieces towards the climax, notably the garden party and the theatrical dénouement in a theatre. RM

Staggered

(1993, GB, 95 min)
d Martin Clunes. *p* Philippa Braithwaite. *sc* Simon Braithwaite, Paul Alexander. *ph* Simon Kossoff. *ed* Peter Delfgou. *pd* Iain Andrews. *m* Peter Brewis. *cast* Martin Clunes, Michael Praed, John Forgeham, Anna Chancellor, Sylvia Syms, Griff Rhys Jones, David Kossoff, Virginia McKenna.

●Toy-demonstrator Neil (Clunes) wakes up in the all-together, stranded on the empty beach of a remote Scottish island hundreds of miles from the previous night's stag party. It seems his best man Gary (Praed) has pulled off quite a prank – but perhaps it's not so funny: the wedding's fast approaching, and Gary's using the groom's absence to put the moves on his intended. This low-budget farce has a frustrating tendency to set up promising situations only to squander them. The script is both too devious for its own good and insufficiently thought through, while Clunes' debut as a director is decidedly hit or miss. Amusing and eventful, none the less. TCh

Stain, The (Laka)

(1987, USSR, 90 min)
d/sc Aleko Tsabadze. *ph* Nodar Namagaladze. *ad* Gogi Tatishvili. *cast* Kishward Glunchadze, Rusudan Kvlividze, Z Begalishvili, O Bazgadze.

●Made in Georgia on the sly with filmstock earmarked for another production, Tsabadze's first feature, a grungy yet darkly comic portrait of the bohemian underworld, was greeted with dismay by the Soviet authorities, who were nevertheless chuffed when it came away with a prize at the 1987 Locarno TV Festival. The story of a free-wheeling student who bets a million cigars on the toss of a coin and subsequently finds himself on the run from the local Mafia, it's often rough at the edges technically, but presents a compelling picture of a society in the midst of falling apart. The Soviet broadcasting chief condemned the film for looking at 'a certain stratum of society with a cold pernicious, venomous atmosphere which cannot but provoke disgust, resentment and disapprobation.' Bloody students, eh? TJ

Stain on the Snow, The

see Neige était sale, La

Staircase

(1969, US, 101 min)
d/p Stanley Donen. *sc* Charles Dyer. *ph* Christopher Challis. *ed* Richard Marden. *ad* Willy Holt. *m* Dudley Moore. *cast* Richard Burton, Rex Harrison, Cathleen Nesbitt, Beatrix Lehmann, Stephen Lewis.

●A drab, sincere homosexual drama, essentially a stage two-hander stupidly glossied up and opened out, but still emerging as dreadfully verbose. Burton and Harrison – the latter in the Liz Taylor part – do their best as two Brixton hairdressers whose 30-year relationship is beginning to fray, further taxed by worries about Burton's ailing mum (Nesbitt) and Harrison's impending court appearance on a charge of transvestism. On this evidence, they've already lasted better than Charles Dyer's play. Dudley Moore wrote the musical score, and if you don't recognise Brixton, that's because it was filmed in Paris. TCh

Stairway to Heaven

see Matter of Life and Death, A

Stakeout

(1987, US, 117 min)
d John Badham. *p* Jim Kouf, Cathleen Summers. *sc* Jim Kouf. *ph* John Seale. *ed* Tom Rolf, Michael Ripps. *pd* Philip Harrison. *m* Arthur B Rubinstein. *cast* Richard Dreyfuss, Emilio Estevez, Madeleine Stowe, Aidan Quinn, Dan Lauria, Forest Whitaker.

●Quinn is surprisingly thrilling in the role of a crazed murderer, and the bone-crushing brutality of the opening sequence (he pummels a prison doctor's head to pulp with a truncheon) gives this bad guy an unpredictable edge. It's a deceptive ploy on Badham's part, as the film soon pitches into familiar car chase territory, where a couple of cops are establishing a prickly love/hate relationship. Dreyfuss is cuddly, cheeky and caring (when is he not?) as Chris Lecce, an experienced detective who should know better than to fall in love with the girlfriend of an escaped convict while staking out her apartment. Young Bill Reimers (Estevez, poor) is keen and conscientious, and resents covering for his partner's philandering. Between Lecce's illicit courtship and Reimers' consternation, there are some hearty laughs of a juvenile nature. Meanwhile, the raging Quinn approaches… It's all tied up in a slick, empty package by Badham's direction. EP

Stakeout (Harikomi)

(2000, Jap, 79 min, b/w & col)
d Tetsuo Shinohara. *p* Kosaburo Sasaoka, Susumu Nakajima, Reiko Arakawa. *sc* Keisuke Toyoshima. *ph* Shogo Ueno. *ed* Yasushi Nakamura. *ad* Hisao Inagaki, Toshiharu Aida. *m* Tatsuya Murayama. *cast* Shiho Wakabayashi, Mantaro Koichi, Masato Sakai.

●Yoshioka (Koichi), a man who says he's a cop, persuades Sumire (Wakabayashi) to let him into her high-rise apartment; he says he needs to use her balcony to stakeout a suspected criminal in the block opposite. For security, she claims to have a husband, due back soon from a business trip. But Yoshioka behaves oddly from the start: makes himself too much at home, intrudes into her privacy, keeps talking about sex. And then he refuses to leave. Shot on DV in b/w, with flashbacks in colour, this exceptionally tense thriller is by far the best thing Shinohara has done since his indie featurette *Work on the Grass*. It's essentially a two-hander, superbly played by both leads, and it's their interaction that ignites the series of narrative and psychological twists. TR

Stalag 17

(1953, US, 120 min, b/w)
d/p Billy Wilder. *sc* Billy Wilder, Edwin Blum. *ph* Ernest Laszlo. *ed* George Tomasini. *ad* Hal Pereira, Franz Bachelin. *m* Franz Waxman. *cast* William Holden, Don Taylor, Robert Strauss, Harvey Lembeck, Neville Brand, Richard Erdman, Otto Preminger, Peter Graves, Sig Ruman.

●Wilder's PoW movie is a mass of contradictions, perhaps explained by the fact that it was based on a successful Broadway play which partly resisted his characteristic attempt to have his black squalor and eat his airy comedy. On the one hand, uproariously and buffoonishly funny, it can be seen simply as the natural sire of such TV sitcoms as *Hogan's Heroes* and *Sergeant Bilko*. On the other, anticipating *King Rat* through the character of the cynical PoW capitalist played by Holden, it satirically notes that the free enterprise ethic, extended into PoW circumstances, can no longer command Horatio Alger approval; and goes on from there to ask what price democracy when a traitor is suspected, and the PoWs gang up like Fascists to assign arbitrary blame and punishment. The problem is that the two moods aren't properly cross-fertilised, with the resolute bleakness of the settings and Wilder's direction positing a reality that is constantly undercut by the comic opera crew of Germans headed by Preminger. A fascinating film, nevertheless. TM

Stalingrad

(1992, Ger, 138 min)
d Joseph Vilsmaier. *p* Joseph Vilsmaier, Hanno Huth, Günther Rohrbach. *sc* Johannes Heide, Jürgen Büsche, Joseph Vilsmaier. *ph* Joseph Vilsmaier. *ed* Hannes Nikel. *pd* Wolfgang Hundhammer, Jindrich Goetz. *m* Norbert J Schneider. *cast* Dominique Horwitz, Thomas Kretschmann, Jochen Nickel, Sebastian Rudolph, Dana Vavrova, Martin Benrath.
●Director/cinematographer Vilsmaier's WWII chronicle is a convincingly hard-edged movie, contextualising subtitles to the fore, detailing the most fateful hours of the European conflict. But, impressive as a monument of reconstruction, the film lacks the extra emotive dimension which would fulfil its humanist aspirations. Instead, surrounded by production values which suggest the Russian city has been demolished anew, the sentiments are very much of the war-is-hell and all-officers-are-bastards school, as a group of German soldiers is whittled away one by one during the ill-fated 1942 Siege of Stalingrad. With efficient performances that leave the big statements to the action set-pieces and a screenplay which merely hints at exorcising Nazi culpability in a single evasive exchange, the film's enveloping veracity is its most striking aspect. You'll certainly feel you've been to the Russian front – a fact which, ironically perhaps, may endear the film more to genre buffs and Sven Hassel readers than the youthful generation for whom the monolithic display of carnage is obviously intended as a bitter warning. TJ

Stalker (100)

(1979, USSR, 161 min, b/w & col)
d Andrei Tarkovsky. *sc* Arkady Strugatsky, Boris Strugatsky. *ph* Aleksandr Knyazhinsky. *ed* Lyudmila Feiginova. *pd* Andrei Tarkovsky. *m* Edmund Artemiev. *cast* Aleksandr Kaidanovsky, Anatoly Solonitsin, Nikolai Grinko, Alisa Freindlikh.
●Against the fractured density of *Mirror*, *Stalker* sets a form of absolute linear simplicity. The Stalker leads two men, the Writer and the Professor, across the Zone – a forbidden territory deep inside a police state – towards the Room, which can lay bare the devices and desires of your heart. However, let no one persuade you that this is sci-fi or common allegory. The ragged, shaven-headed men are familiar from Solzenitzyn, and the zone may be a sentient landscape of hallucinatory power, but its deadly litter of industrial detritus is all too recognisable. The wettest, grimmest trek ever seen on film leads to nihilistic impasse - huddled in dirt, the discovery of faith seems impossible; and without faith, life outside the Zone, impossible. But hang on in to the ending, where a plain declaration of love and a vision of pure magic at least point the way to redemption. As always, Tarkovsky conjures images like you've never seen before; and as a journey to the heart of darkness, it's a good deal more persuasive than Coppola's. Cpea

Stamboul Quest

(1934, US, 88 min, b/w)
d Sam Wood. *p* Walter Wanger. *sc* Herman J Mankiewicz. *ph* James Wong Howe. *ed* Hugh Wynn. *ad* Cedric Gibbons, Stan Rogers. *m* Herbert Stothart. *cast* Myrna Loy, George Brent, Lionel Atwill, C Henry Gordon, Douglas Dumbrille, Mischa Auer.
●Good credits for this hokey slice of MGM exotica. Written by Herman J Mankiewicz (*Citizen Kane*), photographed by James Wong Howe, and directed by the reliable Sam Wood, the only thing wrong is that it's nothing special. Loy's a top German agent during WWI, Brent's the American student vacationing in Turkey, the rest (romance, espionage, the studio backlot) you can probably figure out for yourself. TJ

Stammheim

(1985, WGer, 107 min)
d Reinhard Hauff. *sc* Stefan Aust. *ph* Frank Brühne. *ed* Heidi Handorf. *ad* Dieter Flimm. *m* Marcel Wangler. *cast* Ulrich Pleitgen, Ulrich Tukur, Therese Affolter, Sabine Wegner, Hans Kremer.
●Hauff's reconstruction of the Baader-Meinhof trial is the most honourable shot at tackling the terrorism conundrum since Fassbinder's *The Third Generation*. Cast with lookalikes and using the trial transcripts as the basis for its script, it ploughs through the issues with almost hysterical intensity, comparing the fanaticism of the defendants with the unthinking brutality of the court. More controversially, it also imagines ideological arguments between Baader, Meinhof, Ensslin and Raspe in the 'privacy' of their cells, citing 'letters and prison reports' as its sources. The film ultimately fails, because its scrupulously liberal stance prevents it from developing any coherent point of view of its own. But as a microcosm of West German society tearing itself apart at the seams, it's one hell of a lot tougher than the kind of earnest socio-political dramas that the BBC and C4 tend to produce. ATu

Stamping Ground (aka Love and Music)

(1971, WGer, 101 min)
d Hansjürgen Pohland. *p* Wolf Schmidt, Sam Waynberg. *ph* Harry Hart, Nic Knowland, Barry Male, Jan De Bont, Theo van de Sande, Mat van Hensbergen, Paul van de Bos, Fred van Kuyk, Hans Menke. *with* Jefferson Airplane, Santana, Country Joe MacDonald, Pink Floyd, Dr John, Family, Soft Machine.
●Was the 1970 Rotterdam Pop Festival as dull as this? It probably was, but that's no excuse for the scrappiness of the filming and editing, or for the sheer incompetence of the linking interviews (conducted in English). TR

Stan and George's New Life

(1990, Aust, 102 min)
d Brian McKenzie. *p* Margot McDonald. *sc* Brian McKenzie, Deborah Cox. *ph* Ray Argall. *ed* Edward McQueen-Mason, Daryl Mills. *m* Michael Atkinson. *cast* Paul Chubb, John Bluthal, Julie Forsyth, Margaret Ford.
●Stan is a shy, none too quick-witted 40-year-old who abandons the tedium of the family barber's shop for the relative excitement of a clerical job in a backwater meteorological office; George – perhaps the only sane person to work there – is the dumpy but determined girl of his dreams. McKenzie's oddball romantic comedy has a tendency towards lethargic pacing, but Chubb and Forsyth are credible and engaging as the misfit lovers; and if you ignore the contrived conspiracy subplot, the quirky account of office politics offers some sharp insights. Though not nearly as good as Jane Campion's work, its similar eye for absurdity is far from negligible. GA

Stand and Deliver

(1988, US, 103 min)
d Ramon Menendez. *p* Tom Musca. *sc* Ramon Menendez, Tom Musca. *ph* Tom Richmond. *ed* Nancy Richardson. *ad* Milo. *m* Craig Safan. *cast* Edward James Olmos, Lou Diamond Phillips, Rosana De Soto, Andy Garcia, Virginia Paris, Carmen Argenziano.
●Jaime Escalante (Olmos) gives up a lucrative job in electronics to teach math at an East LA barrio school notorious for drugs and gang-related violence. Many students have difficulty writing their own names, but Escalante, oozing oddball charm, transmogrifies his 18 airheads into an educational élite, making them sign a contract promising they will do no less than 30 hours homework a week, attend pre-school classes, and extra lessons on Saturdays and holidays. Sums hardly come into it; emotional blackmail ensures there are no failures, and everybody receives a college credit. However, the Educational Testing Service, amazed at the results, cries 'Foul!', and the celebrating swots are compelled to stand and deliver, ie resit the exam. It's hard to believe this really happened, but Escalante is apparently still performing the same miracle. The ensemble acting is excellent. Remember, kids, it all comes down to Self Respect. MS

Stand by Me

(1986, US, 89 min)
d Rob Reiner. *p* Andrew Scheinman, Bruce Evans, Raynold Gideon. *sc* Raynold Gideon, Bruce Evans. *ph* Thomas Del Ruth. *ed* Robert Leighton. *pd* Dennis Washington. *m* Jack Nitzsche. *cast* Wil Wheaton, River Phoenix, Corey Feldman, Jerry O'Connell, Kiefer Sutherland, Casey Siemaszko, Richard Dreyfuss.
●In Reiner's superior slice of teen nostalgia, Dreyfuss is the now middle-aged writer, looking back at the dear dead days beyond recall when he and a group of young friends ventured into the local woods where they believed a corpse was buried. Based on an (apparently) semi-autobiographical story by Stephen King, the film covers similar territory to countless other rites-of-passage dramas. The Ben E King theme song and all the imagery of tousled adolescents preening themselves like miniature James Deans rekindle memories of old jeans commercials, but the film is so well-observed and so energetically acted by its young cast that mawkishness is kept at bay. GM

Stand-In

(1937, US, 90 min, b/w)
d Tay Garnett. *p* Walter Wanger. *sc* Gene Towne, Graham Baker. *ph* Charles G Clarke. *ed* Otho Lovering, Dorothy Spencer. *ad* Alexander Toluboff. *m* Heinz Roemheld. *cast* Leslie Howard, Joan Blondell, Humphrey Bogart, Alan Mowbray, Marla Shelton, C Henry Gordon, Jack Carson.
●With a few scabrous exceptions (*The Big Knife*, *The Bad and the Beautiful*, *The Last Command*, possibly *Sunset Boulevard*), Hollywood movies on Hollywood tend to end up endorsing the body politic of the studio system after indulging in gentle satirical sideswipes at the warts along the way. *Stand-In* is an example of this peculiar form of incest. Howard plays a mathematical whizzkid (very reminiscent of Cary Grant's professor in the later *Bringing Up Baby*) sent West to save an ailing independent studio almost crippled by its temperamental female superstar and its last-gasp epic, *Sex and Satan*. Howard displays few of the lapses into sanctimonious drivel he was later party to, while Blondell (as down-at-heel stand-in) and Bogart (dipsomaniac producer) lend admirable support. But what's most interesting is the Capra-style populism which informs the script's cockeyed notion of grassroots capitalism, and lifts the film well above the level of lightweight screwball comedy. RM

Stand Up, Don't Grovel! (Zhanzhiluo, Bie Paxia!)

(1993, China, 115 min)
d Huang Jianxin. *sc* Huang Xin. *ph* Zhang Xiaoguang. *ed* Zhang Xiaodong. *m* Zhang Dalong. *cast* Niu Zhenhua, Feng Gong, Da Shichang, Zhang Lu, Fu Lili, Liu Xiaohua, Ma Shuanqing.
●Looking for peace, quiet and privacy, a writer (Feng) and his wife move into a new apartment, only to find themselves sandwiched between conservative communist-party cadre Liu (Da) on one side and bolshie entrepreneur Zhang (Niu) on the other. Simmering tensions erupt when Zhang turns his apartment into a fish farm and strange moulds start appearing on the walls. Huang's delicious comedy (inaugurating his 'urban attitude' trilogy) is also a pitiless satire. It gets as much mileage out of the rise of get-rich-quick freelancers and the endemic spinelessness of China's intellectuals as it does out of the communists' waning sense of their own correctness and authority. TR

Stand Up Virgin Soldiers

(1977, GB, 90 min)
d Norman Cohen. *p* Greg Smith. *sc* Leslie Thomas. *ph* Ken Hodges. *ed* Geoffrey Foot, Bryan Tilling. *pd* Harry Pottle. *m* Ed Welch. *cast* Robin Askwith, Nigel Davenport, George Layton, John Le Mesurier, Warren Mitchell, Robin Nedwell, Edward Woodward, Irene Handl, Pamela Stephenson.
●Though the original *Virgin Soldiers* was no masterpiece, it certainly never deserved the retrospective slur of association with this appalling sequel, upping the nudge-nudge quotient with Leslie Thomas' apparent complicity, and all too easily characterised as *Confessions of a National Serviceman*. One for old Singapore sweats and lovers of jokes about parading privates. PT

Stanley & Iris

(1989, US, 105 min)
d Martin Ritt. *p* Alex Winitsky, Arlene Sellers. *sc* Harriet Frank Jr, Irving Ravetch. *ph* Donald McAlpine. *ed* Sidney Levin. *pd* Joel Schiller. *m* John Williams. *cast* Jane Fonda, Robert De Niro, Swoosie Kurtz, Martha Plimpton, Feodor Chaliapin, Zohra Lampert.

●Written by Harriet Frank Jr and Irving Ravetch, this free adaptation of Pat Barker's *Union Street* is relocated from Teeside to the industrial landscape of New England and turned into a worthy vehicle for two mature stars. All that remains from Barker's original seems to be the survival instinct of the average home-maker. Iris King is a cake factory veteran, recently widowed, who takes on the task of teaching illiterate Stanley to read when she inadvertently causes his dismissal from said confectionery establishment. We're talking quality here, Ritt being the man who directed *Hud, Sounder* and *Norma Rae*, the leads being De Niro and fellow double Oscar winner Jane Fonda, and the overriding theme of literal word blindness being handled with charm and dignity. The problem is that, given Fonda and De Niro's established images, one can't help thinking what is their *problem*; and the ending, despite good intentions, is American cinema at its tackiest and most hollow. SGr

Stanno tutti bene

see Everybody's Fine

Stanza del Figlio, La

see Son's Room, The

Star!

(1968, US, 174 min)
d Robert Wise. *p* Saul Chaplin. *sc* William Fairchild. *ph* Ernest Laszlo. *ed* William H Reynolds. *pd* Boris Leven. *m* Lennie Hayton. *cast* Julie Andrews, Richard Crenna, Michael Craig, Daniel Massey, Robert Reed, Bruce Forsyth, Beryl Reid, Jenny Agutter.

●Julie Andrews has been compared to everything from a mechanically charming air hostess to a knitted coverlet for a toilet roll, but one comparison she has escaped – especially since *Star!* – is to Gertrude Lawrence. Nevertheless, Wise's biopic hardly deserved the rough treatment it received from most critics and audiences, who had been led by the studio's advertising to expect another *Sound of Music*. This was a far more ambitious project; it backfired, but it backfired with a certain amount of honour. Daniel Massey's mincing portrayal of his godfather Noël Coward wins hands down over all the other impersonations. GB

Star, The

(1952, US, 89 min, b/w)
d Stuart Heisler. *p* Bert E Friedlob. *sc* Katherine Albert, Dale Eunson. *ph* Ernest Lazslo. *ed* Otto Ludwig. *ad* Boris Leven. *m* Victor Young. *cast* Bette Davis, Sterling Hayden, Natalie Wood, Warner Anderson, Minor Watson, June Travis.

●A couple of years on from *All About Eve*, Bette Davis plays an Oscar-winning actress coming to the realisation that her fading career is at an end. Hayden's the ordinary Joe who tries to get her a new start outside the movie industry in this intriguing, though small-scale drama dominated by a ripe star presence. Davis sometimes overdoes the drink-fuelled self-pity, but at least she got another Oscar nomination out of it. TJ

Star Chamber, The

(1983, US, 109 min)
d Peter Hyams. *p* Frank Yablans. *sc* Roderick Taylor, Peter Hyams. *ph* Richard Hannah. *ed* Jim Mitchell. *pd* Bill Malley. *m* Michael Small. *cast* Michael Douglas, Hal Holbrook, Yaphet Kotto, Sharon Gless, James B Sikking, Joe Regalbuto, Don Calfa.

●Where is the justice, High Court Judge Hardin (Douglas) wonders, when the innocent suffer and the clearly guilty go free on a technicality. In books? In the judicial system he has sworn to uphold? Or is he the law? Reluctantly, he joins The Star Chamber, a clandestine society of judges who re-try and pass sentence on certain 'messy' cases. From the opening sequence – a pell-mell chase through a confusion of colour, movement and sound – Hyams constructs a tense and absorbing thriller; but as in previous filmic efforts to confront this elusive moral issue (...*And Justice for All*, for example), the subtleties escape faster than the criminals. Just as Douglas discovers that he can go only so far along the extra-judicial path, so the film's line of reasoning twists part-way, falters, then ties itself into tangled and inconclusive knots. FD

Starchaser: The Legend of Orin

(1985, US, 100 min)
d/p Steven Hahn. *sc* Jeffrey Scott. *ed* Donald W Ernst. *m* Andrew Belling. *cast* voices: Joe Colligan, Carmen Argenziano, Noelle North, Anthony Delongis, Les Tremayne.

●In this animated feature, the obsession with technology only serves to hurtle the kids' space-fantasy genre along the cosmic cul-de-sac it has already entered. The plot is the usual hotchpotch of quasi-heroics and mock-mythical exploits, transposed to a futuristic world realised with all the eclectic imagery (embellished with 3-D) one has come to expect. Orin, our svelte young hero, takes the predictable step from oppressed toiler in megabaddie Zygon's mines to nascent superhero with ne'er a doubting moment. Teaming up with cigar-chewing crystal smuggler Dagg, and armed with the obligatory magic sword, he sets out to foil Zygon's plans to subjugate the universe. Along the way, we are treated to some pretty spectacular landscapes and a whole range of repulsively animalistic robots. The otherwise fine vocal characterisations are spoiled by overemphasis on sexual innuendo, and the length will probably have kids screaming for ice-creams long before the finish. WH

Starcrash

(1979, US, 91 min)
d Lewis Coates [Luigi Cozzi]. *p* Nat Wachsberger, Patrick Wachsberger. *sc* Luigi Cozzi, Nat Wachsberger. *ph* Paul Beeson, Roberto D'Ettorre Piazzoli. *ed* Sergio Montanari. *pd* Aurelio Crugnola. *m* John Barry. *cast* Marjoe Gortner, Caroline Munro, Christopher Plummer, David Hasselhoff, Robert Tessier, Joe Spinell.

●A trash-addict sci-fi spectacular from AIP in which Stella Star (Munro) and sundry buddies leap millions of light years around the universe, with enviable nonchalance and a distinct lack of consideration for the laws of nature. Their mission: to save Imperialism from Something Far Worse, and along the way to provide for Stella's future by convincing Plummer's heir apparent that, despite her bizarre style of dress, she'd make a neat Empress one day. FF

Stardom

(2000, Can/Fr, 102 min)
d Denys Arcand. *p* Robert Lantos, Denise Robert. *sc* Denys Arcand, J Jacob Potashnik. *ph* Guy Dufaux. *ed* Isabelle Dedieu. *pd* Zoë Sakellaropoulo. *m* Egberto Gismonti. *cast* Jessica Paré, Dan Aykroyd, Charles Berling, Robert Lepage, Thomas Gibson, Frank Langella.

●Some who lasted the course reported that there were a few funny moments in the latter half of this satire on the media and its obsession with fashion, beauty and celebrity, but I gave up after 40 minutes, worn down by the heavy-handed obviousness of it all. A pity, given the intelligence of Arcand's past efforts, but this story of a hockey playing student, who finds fame and fortune in the designer capitals is let down by dismal performances, predictable satire and narrative clumsiness. GA

Stardust

(1974, GB, 111 min)
d Michael Apted. *p* David Puttnam, Sandy Lieberson. *sc* Ray Connolly. *ph* Anthony B Richmond. *ed* Michael Bradsell. *ad* Brian Morris. *m* Dave Edmonds. *cast* David Essex, Adam Faith, Larry Hagman, Ines Des Longchamps, Rosalind Ayres, Marty Wilde, Ed Byrnes, Keith Moon.

●Enjoyable attempt at the impossible task of reflecting the whole sprawl of '60s British pop through the rise and fall of one rock star. Ray Connolly's script for this sequel to *That'll Be the Day* functions on numerous levels: as a piece of nostalgia for over 25s; as wish fulfilment for Essex's teenage fans, in which he becomes the greatest rock'n'roll singer in the world; and, God help us, as a would-be art movie, with its central relationship between Essex's singer and roadie Adam Faith more than reminiscent of *The Servant*. The script is at its best when knocking the stuffing out of the music industry and its myths, less successful when asking us to believe in the fictional achievements of its central character (3,000,000 fans and a *Time* magazine cover). Best are Adam Faith, Keith Moon's anarchic performance, and Dave Edmunds' music. CPe

Stardust Memories

(1980, US, 88 min, b/w)
d Woody Allen. *p* Robert Greenhut. *sc* Woody Allen. *ph* Gordon Willis. *ed* Susan E Morse. *pd* Mel Bourne. *m* Dick Hyman. *cast* Woody Allen, Charlotte Rampling, Jessica Harper, Marie-Christine Barrault, Tony Roberts, Helen Hanft, John Rothman.

●The schlemiel strikes back: at critics, at sycophants, at pigeons ('rats with wings'), and at a universe that can contain both Charlotte Rampling's face and human-skin lampshades. Tactically adopting his most autobiographical persona yet, Allen finally lets his anger loose, and it dumps on everything with unaccustomed savagery. Crossed with the strain of vengeance are his own attempts to make a film (which looks like Art), and also his snagged-up relations with three different ladies. A movie of great moments rather than the coherence of *Manhattan*, as if acknowledging that Memory works best in fragments. But, having stolen Fellini's 8 ½ structure, Allen stands in danger of likewise painting himself into a corner of solipsism. His 'early, funny' films, that everyone complains he no longer makes, were good exactly because they contained sufficient sadness and pain to make the comic triumph well-earned. One long cry of anguish about the price of fame comes perilously close to self-pity. And self-abuse. CPea

Star 80

(1983, US, 103 min)
d Bob Fosse. *p* Wolfgang Glattes, Kenneth Utt. *sc* Bob Fosse. *ph* Sven Nykvist. *ed* Alan Heim. *ad* Jack G Taylor Jr, Michael Bolton. *m* Ralph Burns. *cast* Mariel Hemingway, Eric Roberts, Cliff Robertson, Carroll Baker, Roger Rees, David Clennon, Josh Mostel, Lisa Gordon.

●The all singin'n'dancin' Fosse turns his hand to straight tragedy with the true story of Dorothy Stratten's pathetically short career as *Playboy* pin-up and film starlet (her only starring role was in Peter Bogdanovich's *They All Laughed*), before being cruelly, senselessly murdered by her jealous husband. Hemingway has reinforced not only her breasts but her promise of becoming a sensitive and accomplished actress in her portrayal of the ill-fated Dorothy. The rest, however, is a disappointingly shallow display of images cut together in an apparently haphazard fashion; flashes back and forward are liberally sprinkled with meaningless vistas of naked flesh. This superficial view extends to the characters; in particular, Dorothy's ambitious, hustling husband (Roberts), and her quiet film director/lover (Rees), never really step outside their cardboard cut-outs, making the whole thing feel more like a naughty snapshot than any artistic achievement. HR

Starflight: The Plane That Couldn't Land (aka Starflight One)

(1982, US, 155 min)
d Jerry Jameson. *p* Peter Nelson, Arnold Orgolini. *sc* Robert M Young. *ph* Hector Figueroa. *ed* John F Link II. *pd* David L Snyder. *m* Lalo Schifrin. *cast* Lee Majors, Hal Linden, Lauren Hutton, Ray Milland, Gail Strickland, Tess Harper, Michael Sacks, Robert Webber.

●Like a souped-up *Airport* episode, made for TV and cut by 40 minutes for cinema release, this populates the world's first hypersonic jet on its maiden flight with the usual selection of stereotypes, and – thanks to the dastardly designs of several greedy opportunists – plunges them out of the atmosphere into orbit. Then the problems really begin as the cast struggle hopelessly with trite script and flaccid direction. Through a totally unconvincing series of manoeuvres – like an advert for NASA – most of these cardboard characters make it back to Earth; that an audience might survive unscathed is far less likely. GA

Stargate

(1994, US, 121 min)
d Roland Emmerich. *p* Joel B Michaels, Oliver Eberle, Dean Devlin. *sc* Dean Devlin, Roland Emmerich. *ph* Walter Lindenlaub. *ed* Michael J Duthie, Derek Brechin. *pd* Holger Gross. *m*

David Arnold. *cast* Kurt Russell, James Spader, Jaye Davidson, Viveca Lindfors, Alexis Cruz, Mili Avital, Leon Rippy.
●Approached with a generous spirit and a vacant mind, this bombastic sci-fi epic is hugely enjoyable. Having deciphered the symbols on an ancient stone, eccentric Egyptologist Dr Jackson (Spader), accompanied by hardass Colonel O'Neil (Russell) and a crack marine patrol, walks through the stone portal to an alternate world where a raggle-taggle band of desert-dwellers are ruled by despotic King Ra (Davidson). O'Neil has secretly brought with him an atomic device, his suicide mission to close the Stargate for ever. The unwitting Jackson, however, has eyes only for the lovely Skaara (Cruz), whose downtrodden people rise up against their oppressors. At this point, it's best to surrender to the bombardment of glossy images and spectacular fx, a (manu)script from which many pages appear to be missing, and a stirring score that drives all before it. Futuristic tosh, certainly, but fun all the same. NF

Star Is Born, A

(1937, US, 111 min)
d William Wellman. *p* David O Selznick. *sc* Dorothy Parker, Alan Campbell, Robert Carson. *ph* W Howard Greene. *ed* Hal C Kern, Anson Stevenson. *ad* Lyle Wheeler. *m* Max Steiner. *cast* Fredric March, Janet Gaynor, Adolphe Menjou, May Robson, Andy Devine, Lionel Stander, Franklin Pangborn.
●Despite the tragic ending, Cukor's remake of *A Star Is Born* is primarily a glowingly nostalgic evocation of Hollywood knowhow and razzmatazz, with Garland's musical numbers blending effortlessly with the gala premieres, Oscar ceremonies, and privileged moments on set. Wellman's non-musical version (attractively shot in the early Technicolor process), though starting more sentimentally with Gaynor as a wide-eyed innocent dreaming every girl's dream of stardom in her small-town home, develops a much more caustic edge, maintaining a bitterly critical distance from the dream factory. This is no doubt because in 1937 the real-life tragedies that fuelled the script were so much closer in time (Esther Blodgett and Norman Maine were inspired by the story of Colleen Moore and her husband/producer John McCormick, though March's Maine, here an actor, draws variously on the fates of John Gilbert, John Barrymore and John Bowers). The two films make fascinating comparison. TM

Star Is Born, A

(1954, US, 175 min)
d George Cukor. *p* Sidney Luft. *sc* Moss Hart. *ph* Sam Leavitt. *ed* Folmar Blangsted. *pd* Gene Allen. *m* Harold Arlen. *cast* Judy Garland, James Mason, Jack Carson, Charles Bickford, Tommy Noonan, Lucy Marlow.
●Of all Hollywood's heartbreakers, this must be one of the saddest. Made at a time when Garland was fast approaching final crack-up, the story of the rise of a young singing star at the expense of the actor she loves and yearns to keep intact (Mason) seemed to touch exactly the right raw nerves in its performers to make it a major discomfort to watch. Garland's tremulous emotionalism, which so often left her unwatchable, is here decently harnessed to a story which makes good sense of it and to a man worth yearning for. But the acting honours belong to Mason: whether idly cruising the LA dance-halls for a new woman, sliding into alcoholism, or embarrassing everyone at an Oscar ceremony, he gives a performance which is as good as any actor is ever allowed. Previewed at 182 minutes, the film was promptly trimmed by Warners and released at 152 minutes. The version reissued in 1983 features much of the excised footage, rediscovered in archives. Many scenes admirably fill gaps in the original, a few are redundant, but it's a major work of movie archaeology, and a very good wallow. CPea

Star Is Born, A

(1976, US, 140 min)
d Frank Pierson. *p* Jon Peters. *sc* John Gregory Dunne, Joan Didion, Frank R Pierson. *ph* Robert Surtees. *ed* Peter Zinner. *pd* Polly Platt. *m* Paul Williams. *cast* Barbra Streisand, Kris Kristofferson, Paul Mazursky, Gary Busey, Oliver Clark, Marta Heflin.
●70mm screens have been filled with some vacuous stuff in their time, but this monstrous remake takes the biscuit. It's set in the rock world, but the kind of rock these people peddle is the softest thing next to jelly. And the embarrassment when Streisand gets to shake her loins in rhythm…Kristofferson is much better as the fading drunkard who promotes and marries the rising star. Apart from the flash new environment, this version vaunts its modernity by vulgarising everything in sight, making the characters mouthpieces for foul language and equally foul sentimentality. Maybe Brian De Palma in his *Phantom of the Paradise* days could have wrested a film from all this, but Pierson (replacing Jerry Schatzberg, Streisand's hairdresser Jon Peters, and probably a million others) just lets it hang out, uncoordinated and ridiculous. GB

Starke Ferdinand, Der (Strong-Man Ferdinand)

(1976, WGer, 97 min)
d/p/sc Alexander Kluge. *ph* Thomas Mauch. *ed* Heidi Genée. *m* Emil Waldteufel. *cast* Heinz Schubert, Verena Rudolph, Joachim Hackethal, Heinz Schimmelpfennig, Gert Günther Hoffmann.
●Kluge's marvellously deadpan parable about society and its official guardians is irresistible. Ferdinand the Strong (Schubert) is an ex-policeman turned factory security expert who carries out his duties with surrealistic fervour, finally becoming so obsessed with possible security leaks that he turns terrorist to prove his own case. Unlike some of Kluge's more cerebral works, a highly accessible film, bitingly funny in its satire of the perils of power syndromes. TM

Star Kid

(1997, US, 101 min)
d Manny Coto. *p* Jennie Lew Tugend. *sc* Manny Coto. *ph* Ronn Schmidt. *ed* Bob Ducsay. *pd* CJ Strawn. *m* Nicholas Pike. *cast* Joseph Mazello, Ashlee Levitch, Joey Simmrin, Lauren Eckstrom, Corinne Bohrer.
●The peaceable Trelkins are defending their planet against the Broodwarriors. Closer to home, young Spencer (Mazello) is also down on his luck: dad lives for work, big sis (Levitch) calls him 'fungus', school bully Turbo Bruntley (Simmrin) has singled him out. Worse yet, classmate Michelle (Eckstrom) is too good to be true – she's pretty, she likes the 'Midknight Warrior' comics behind which Spencer hides. She's even tried speaking to him. His nice teacher (Bohrer) explains how running away from scary things just makes it worse. At this point a Phase One Cyber Assault Suit lands behind his house, requiring a biotic host to test its combat enhancement abilities. Climbing inside, Spencer finds himself piloting an intelligent eight-foot robot, with bionic powers and very friendly to boot. Writer/director Coto's film may be taken tongue in cheek, but it's immensely enjoyable both as straightforward kids' entertainment and, perhaps, as a subtle, fanciful induction in matters pubescent. NB

Starlight Hotel

(1987, NZ, 94 min)
d Sam Pillsbury. *p* Finola Dwyer, Larry Parr. *sc* Grant Hinden-Miller. *ph* Warrick Attewell. *ed* Michael Horton. *pd* Michael Becroft. *m* Andrew Hagen, Morton Wilson. *cast* Greer Robson, Peter Phelps, Marshall Napier, Ian Brackenbury Channell, Alice Fraser.
●This tale of a 12-year-old girl's cross-country trek to find her father seems like a New Zealand version of *The Journey of Natty Gann*, lacking the winsome dog and mercifully much else in the winsome line. During the Depression, Kate (Robson) is parked with relatives so that her father can seek work in the big city. Unhappy, she runs away, hooking up with a young war veteran (Phelps), himself on the run. They ride the rails, pilfer from farms, queue up at soup kitchens, and sleep under the stars. He doesn't notice a substantial young bosom under her boy's disguise until he throws her into a creek – 'Christ! A bloody sheila!' – a myopia which perhaps explains the lack of compass bearing in his life. It's a thin, underwritten film, with muffled emotional climaxes, and with neither of the main players equipped to bring much to their parts. A walk on the mild side. BC

Starmaker, The

see Uomo delle stelle, L'

Starman

(1984, US, 115 min)
d John Carpenter. *p* Larry Franco. *sc* Bruce Evans, Raynold Gideon. *ph* Donald M Morgan. *ed* Marion Rothman. *pd* Dan Lomino. *m* Jack Nitzsche. *cast* Jeff Bridges, Karen Allen, Charles Martin Smith, Richard Jaeckel, Robert Phalen, Tony Edwards.
●Carpenter forsakes action and horror, and delivers a rather lame sci-fi love story. Alien Bridges journeys to Earth on what he imagines will be a straightforward mission of friendship. He imagines wrong, of course, as all the pesky earthlings prove to be nasty, brutish and violent. All, that is, except for widowed, childless Karen Allen, who is first kidnapped by Bridges, then falls in love, and finally has to save him. This lacks the drive, energy and surprise which one associates with Carpenter. The best special effects are in the first five minutes. Thereafter, it's all rather predictable. The normally excellent Bridges shuffles his way through a robotic performance as though he's just been unplugged, and the film's (very) basic gag – his naïve response to what he experiences – wears thin pretty quick. RR

Stars and Bars

(1988, US, 94 min)
d Pat O'Connor. *p* Sandy Lieberson. *sc* William Boyd. *ph* Jerzy Zielinski. *ed* Michael Bradsell. *pd* Leslie Dilley, Stuart Craig. *m* Stanley Myers. *cast* Daniel Day Lewis, Harry Dean Stanton, Kent Broadhurst, Maury Chaykin, Matthew Cowles, Joan Cusack, Keith David, Glenne Headly, Laurie Metcalf.
●William Boyd's novel may be set in the States, but it isn't a million miles away from the comical crew of *Cold Comfort Farm*. O'Connor's version is fortunate in its cast. Day Lewis in particular, as silly ass Henderson Dores, a diffident Britisher who relocates in New York, doodles a hilarious bumbler, one of nature's natural de-bagees. Despatched by art auctioneers to acquire a legendary Renoir in an unlikely Georgia Dogpatch household, he is promptly overwhelmed by grotesques. Patriarch Stanton is willing to sell, but his eldest son (Elvis-lookalike Chaykin) has sold it already on the sly, and threatens death. One brother believes himself to be a damaged Vietvet, but is just damaged, and another is a time-warp hippy. A horny fundamentalist preacher is added to the mix, along with a pregnant alcoholic runaway, no phones, no car, and no trousers. No trousers befalls our empty-handed hero again back in New York, placing the proceedings unashamedly in the farce bag. I laughed a lot. BC

Starship Troopers

(1997, US, 129 min)
d Paul Verhoeven. *p* Alan Marshall, Jon Davison. *sc* Edward Neumeier. *ph* Jost Vacano. *ed* Mark Goldblatt, Caroline Ross. *pd* Allan Cameron. *m* Basil Poledouris. *cast* Casper Van Dien, Dina Meyer, Denise Richards, Jake Busey, Neil Patrick Harris, Clancy Brown, Michael Ironside.
●High school graduates Johnny Rico, Dizzy, Carmen and Carl enlist in the armed forces of the Federation. Training takes its toll, and Johnny is on the point of throwing in the towel when space insects wipe out his home town Buenos Aires. The infantry are despatched to the outer limits of the galaxy to give 'em what for, but…you guessed it. An adaptation of a Robert A Heinlein novel, this replays World War II as sci-fi spectacular – and this time we're rooting for the fascists. Presumably director Verhoeven meant it as a sour, ironic joke. If so, he's kept an admirably straight face. His totalitarian utopia looks like a daytime soap: bright, clean, empty. And his lead players might be caricatures of Aryan perfection. It falls to Ironside's motivational teacher/commander, Rasczak, to whip them into shape ('If you don't do your job, I shoot you!'). It says a lot about the director that the movie only kicks into life when the carnage starts. The bugs make up in numbers what they lack in charm, the scale of the battle scenes takes the breath away, and the violence is unremittingly gruesome. On the surface, this is grotesque, reactionary trash, yet by the end, when Verhoeven turns a giant brain-sucking maggot into an object of pity, it's hard not to be impressed by the sheer perversity of the enterprise. TCh

Stars Look Down, The

(1939, GB, 110 min, b/w)
d Carol Reed. *p* Isadore Goldschmidt. *sc* JB Williams. *ph* Max Greene. *ed* Reginald Beck. *ad* James Carter. *m* Hans May. *cast* Michael Redgrave, Margaret Lockwood, Emlyn Williams, Edward Rigby, Nancy Price, Allan Jeayes, Cecil Parker, Linden Travers.
●Some two decades before the Kitchen Sink cinema of the British New Wave, Carol Reed made this serious, committed film about life in a northern mining community, co-scripted by AJ Cronin from his own novel. The central romance, though by no means all roses, dates the picture (Redgrave, an idealistic miner's son, goes to university, and temporarily forgets his political resolve when he marries Margaret Lockwood); but the mining sequences have a degree of authenticity (above-ground sequences were shot at Workington, in Northumberland), and the film ends with a rousing call for nationalisation of the industry, to 'purge the old greeds'. TCh

Star! Star!

(1999, US/Ger, 76 min)
d Jette Müller, Andreas Schimmelbusch. *p* Allison Silver, Vladimir Anani Yavachev. *sc* Jette Müller, Andreas Schimmelbusch. *ph* Radoslav Spassov. *cast* Nick Moran, Sienna Guillory, Dominic Chianese Jr, Barbara Sukowa.
●Nick Moran is Anatol, an Andy Warhol-like artist with a coterie of bohemian hangers-on, in this grotesquely pretentious study of grotesque pretension. The gimmicky direction (direct to camera address; freeze-frames; intertitles) vies for attention with over the top peformances, unspeakable dialogue, and low budget production values. Guy Ritchie looks like Orson Welles in comparison. TCh

Starstruck

(1982, Aust, 102 min)
d Gillian Armstrong. *p* David Elfick, Richard Brennan. *sc* Stephen MacLean. *ph* Russell Boyd. *ed* Nicholas Beauman. *pd* Brian Thomson. *m* Swingers, Tim Finn, Jo Kennedy. *cast* Jo Kennedy, Ross O'Donovan, Margo Lee, Max Cullen, Pat Evison.
●An unlikely follow-up to *My Brilliant Career*, this comic rock opera in which two weirdo kids from downtown Sydney stare hungrily across the bay to where the talons of the Opera House beckon, promising fame and fortune in a talent contest. Jackie (Kennedy) can sing but no one will listen, until her cousin Angus (O'Donovan), a dwarfish Svengali, persuades her to don a bird costume and tightrope walk high above a busy street. From that angle her star quality, like her false plastic tits, sticks out a mile (opportune knockers, as the TV show almost had it). Although at times a little ragged around the edges, the whole is so persistently bizarre, and the two leads so consistently excellent, that the plusses (her voice, his legs, their spit-and-sawdust family) quickly outweigh the minuses (some dire set pieces and some ugly, ugly people). Alternately cudgelled and cajoled, one cannot help but have a good time. FD

Starting Over

(1979, US, 106 min)
d Alan J Pakula. *p* James L Brooks, Alan J Pakula. *sc* James L Brooks. *ph* Sven Nykvist. *ed* Marion Rothman. *pd* George Jenkins. *m* Marvin Hamlisch. *cast* Burt Reynolds, Jill Clayburgh, Candice Bergen, Charles Durning, Frances Sternhagen, Austin Pendleton, Mary Kay Place.
●What to do if you are male, American, no spring chicken, and abandoned by your wife on the ground that you get in the way of her career? One answer is to wedge the tongue firmly in cheek, join a Divorced Men's Workshop, get yourself a new girl, and regard your ex-wife with the careful patience usually reserved for the demented. The irrepressible ebullience of Burt Reynolds, which has been known to buoy up less fragile craft than this, is here in danger of swamping not only Jill Clayburgh's rather mousy rendition of Marilyn-the-nursery-school-teacher, but the movie as a whole. Moments of little-boy-lost helplessness, thrown in to indicate his 'earnestness', merely make you wonder if he's schizoid or just a complete philanderer. It's as if Pakula had got on a fairground horse that has gone out of control, and is undecided whether to go with it or try to stop it. FD

Star Trek – The Motion Picture

(1979, US, 132 min)
d Robert Wise. *p* Gene Roddenberry. *sc* Harold Livingstone. *ph* Richard H Kline, Richard Yuricich. *ed* Todd Ramsey. *pd* Harold Michelson. *m* Jerry Goldsmith. *cast* William Shatner, Leonard Nimoy, DeForest Kelley, James Doohan, George Takei, Majel Barrett, Walter Koenig, Nichelle Nichols, Stephen Collins.
●Before embarking on *Star Trek II*, Paramount engaged in market research to see whether fans would tolerate the demise of Mr Spock. In the event he was indeed killed off (though not permanently). Here the Vulcan is very much alive, aiding his buddies from the old starship Enterprise in their sluggish fight against a malignant force field headed Earthwards. For non-addicts, the smart plot and effects go some way towards compensating for the plastic characters and costumes. DP

Star Trek II: The Wrath of Khan

(1982, US, 114 min)
d Nicholas Meyer. *p* Robert Sallin. *sc* Jack B Sowards. *ph* Gayne Rescher. *ed* William P Dornisch. *pd* Joseph R Jennings. *m* James Horner. *cast* William Shatner, Leonard Nimoy, DeForest Kelley, James Doohan, Walter Koenig, George Takei, Nichelle Nichols, Ricardo Montalban, Paul Winfield, Kirstie Alley.
●Not only a movie sequel, but a follow-up to the 1967 TV series episode *Space Seed*, in which Captain (now Admiral) Kirk exiled cosmic renegade Khan to the outer limits, where he's been hatching revenge ever since. Foregoing the special effects bonanza of its predecessor, it settles for low camp humanoid melodrama. The ageing Shatner and his equally self-amused Enterprise cohorts now 'boldly go' wreathed in soft focus, smiling down on a shipful of apprentice Trekkies until summoned to urgent comic strip action when Khan threatens to reverse creation with a destructively-wielded Genesis device. The net effect, between embarrassed guffaws, is incredulity: a movie at once post-TV and pre-DW Griffith. PT

Star Trek III: The Search for Spock

(1984, US, 105 min)
d Leonard Nimoy. *p/sc* Harve Bennett. *ph* Charles Correll. *ed* Robert F Shugrue. *ad* John E Chilberg II. *m* James Horner. *cast* William Shatner, Leonard Nimoy, DeForest Kelley, James Doohan, Walter Koenig, George Takei, Nichelle Nichols, Judith Anderson, James B Sikking, Christopher Lloyd, Robert Hooks.
●An all-time low for the Enterprise and her crew, with Spock dead, the ship condemned, and everyone else looking about 104. But hold! Why is Bones behaving so oddly? Could it be that he contains part of Spock's essence? A sluggish start gives way to quite a fun romp, as the crew's valiant efforts to find Spock are impeded by a bunch of malign Klingons (all with a distinct resemblance to Lemmy of Motorhead), and reaching one surprising anti-climax when the lilywhite Kirk actually starts spluttering and swearing! Decent SFX, but a little more action wouldn't have gone amiss. GD

Star Trek IV

see Voyage Home: Star Trek IV, The

Star Trek V: The Final Frontier

(1989, US, 107 min)
d William Shatner. *p* Harve Bennett. *sc* David Loughery. *ph* Andrew Laszlo. *ed* Peter E Berger. *pd* Herman Zimmerman. *m* Jerry Goldsmith. *cast* William Shatner, Leonard Nimoy, DeForest Kelley, James Doohan, Walter Koenig, Nichelle Nichols, George Takei, David Warner, Laurence Luckinbill, Charles Cooper.
●A portentous *Dune*-like prologue is followed by an aerial shot of an awesome cliff-face; the camera swirls, picks out a fearless lone climber, zooms in, then cuts to a close up of…you guessed it, ageing paunch-features Kirk himself. Thereafter the plot, about a quest for the Ultimate Answer, resembles something Douglas Adams would have thrown in the bin, complete with triple-breasted whores decorating the journey to God's front door. 'Nobody ever went *through the barrier*!' scream the cast. One sub-*2001* light show later, Kirk is boldly splitting infinitives in heaven itself, unscarred and (naturally) unimpressed by God, who after all isn't any good with girls. Polarities are duly reversed while Uhura does the dance of the seven veils and smooches with Scotty (warped factor 5!), whose dilithium crystals clearly canna take it any more. Beam me up this instant. MK

Star Trek VI: The Undiscovered Country

(1991, US, 110 min)
d Nicholas Meyer. *p* Ralph Winter, Steven-Charles Jaffe. *sc* Denny Martin Flinn, Nicholas Meyer. *ph* Hiro Narita. *ed* Ronald Roose. *pd* Herman Zimmerman. *m* Cliff Eidelman. *cast* William Shatner, Leonard Nimoy, DeForest Kelley, James Doohan, Walter Koenig, Nichelle Nichols, George Takei, Kim Cattrall, Christopher Plummer, David Warner, Mark Lenard, Grace Lee Whitney, Brock Peters, John Schuck, Kurtwood Smith, Iman, Christian Slater.
●A quarter of a century after the Enterprise first went where no TV programme had gone before, it's Zimmer frames ho! as the crew finally shuffle off to the Dunbeamin' Twilight Home for Bewildered Space Travellers. The film is full of in-jokes about their age, but with a serious point: in a none-too-subtle parallel with the fall of the Soviet Union, the ailing Klingon Empire is on the verge of making peace with the Federation, and Kirk feels too old to adjust. When he is charged with the assassination of the Klingon ambassador, and exiled to a grim prison planet with only Bones and an alien shape-changer (supermodel Iman) for company, he has time to reflect on the evils of prejudice. Though patchy, this is a lot more fun than the disastrous *Star Trek V*. DW

Star Trek: Generations

(1994, US, 118 min)
d David Carson. *p* Rick Berman. *sc* Ronald D Moore, Brannon Braga. *ph* John A Alonzo. *ed* Peter E Berger. *pd* Herman Zimmerman. *m* Dennis McCarthy. *cast* Patrick Stewart, Malcolm McDowell, William Shatner, Walter Koenig, Levar Burton, Michael Dorn, Gates McFadden, Marina Sirtis, Whoopi Goldberg.
●Kirk, Scottie and Chekov join the inaugural voyage of a newly commissioned Starship, but when Kirk (Shatner) is 'killed' while facing evil immortality-seeker Dr Soran (McDowell), he gets lost in the mists of time, while the plot jumps forward 78 years and goes on without him. Then, the Next Generation commanded by Picard (Stewart) takes over, confronting the ageless Soran and his Klingon cohorts as Soran tries to re-enter the Utopian time continuum of the Nexus, where past, present and future are one. The series' dullest instalment. NF

Star Trek: First Contact

(1996, US, 111 min)
d Jonathan Frakes. *p* Rick Berman. *sc* Brannon Braga, Ronald D Moore. *ph* Matthew F Leonetti. *ed* John W Wheeler. *pd* Herman Zimmerman. *m* Jerry Goldsmith. *cast* Patrick Stewart, Jonathan Frakes, Alice Krige, Brent Spiner, LeVar Burton, Michael Dorn, Gates McFadden, Marina Sirtis, Alfre Woodard.
●This makes little concession to non-initiates. The Borg, a species of cyborg linked in a hive-consciousness and dedicated to the 'absorption' of all other life-forms, build on their reputation as the TV series' best baddies to invade the Federation: only Picard (Stewart) stands between them and conquest of the Earth. But just when we think we're in for 'Independence Day 2', the routed Borg go back in time to win the war before it began, and we're hurled along with the Enterprise into much darker territory. The Borg's infiltration of the starship recalls some of the tension of *Alien*, while the attempts of the Borg Queen (Krige) to convert the android Data (Spiner) to the pleasures of the New Flesh are positively transgressive. Certainly Spiner convinces you that androids do dream of electric sheep, and electric ladylands; while Stewart, confronting his conscience, draws a sci-fi blockbuster audience into the intimacy of a fringe play. DW

Star Trek: Insurrection

(1998, US, 103 min)
d Jonathan Frakes. *p* Rick Berman. *sc* Michael Piller. *ph* Matthew F Leonetti. *ed* Peter E Berger. *pd* Herman Zimmerman. *m* Jerry Goldsmith. *cast* Patrick Stewart, Jonathan Frakes, F Murray Abraham, Brent Spiner, Michael Dorn, Anthony Zerbe, LeVar Burton.
●This recaptures something of the appeal of the original TV series. In fact, it feels like an extended small screen episode, with one strong idea and a simple, linear storyline.When the android Data (Spiner) runs amok during a Federation sponsored observation, Capt Picard (Stewart) and his crew uncover a conspiracy to deprive the pacifist Ba'ku people of their idyllic, technology free existence. The incentive is the planet's unique atmosphere, which gradually reverses the ageing process. With the Federation's blessing, political opportunist Admiral Dougherty (Zerbe) and So'na leader Ru'afo (Abraham) plan to beam the inhabitants off the planet and relocate them elsewhere. Forced to defy the Federation in order to preserve the integrity of its first principle – non-interference in the separate cultural development of indigenous peoples – Picard and his crew help the Ba'ku to fight back against their would-be dispossessors. Despite the usual strained stabs at topical social significance, Frakes maintains a brisk pace, staging the battle scenes with panache and undercutting the absurd techno gibberish with crass but leavening humour. NF

Startup.com

(2001, US, 108 min)
d Jehane Noujaim, Chris Hegedus. *p* DA Pennebaker. *ph* Jehane Noujaim. *ed* Chris Hegedus, Erez Laufer, Jehane Noujaim. *with* Kaleil Isaza Tuzman, Tom Herman, Kenneth Austin, Tricia Burke, Roy Burston, David Camp, Bill Clinton, Maynard Jackson.
●Tom Herman and Kaleil Isaza Tuzman are best buddies, so once they graduate from Amherst High it's only a matter of time before they set up in business together, Tom inviting the whizzkid investment banker to become CEO of an internet outfit designed to ease communication and understanding between government and public. Soon the ambitious and apparently very able twenty-somethings are raising millions in investment, hiring extra staff, making the magazine covers and even meeting Bill Clinton. The rise of govWorks.com is a dream come true – except for a tricky third partner, corporate espionage, cash flow problems and the realisation that every relationship has its price. A surprise hit in the US, this fly on the wall doc might serve as a cautionary tale for dotcom entrepreneurs and wannabe tycoons everywhere; for many, most of the fascination will derive from the base, but probably universal impulse of Schadenfreude. Comeuppance is just what the doctor ordered. If the film is a little predictable, Kaleil is so watchable that it's easy to hang in there and relish the grisly details. GA

Star Wars (100)

(1977, US, 121 min)
d George Lucas. *p* Gary Kurtz. *sc* George Lucas. *ph* Gilbert Taylor. *ed* Paul Hirsch, Marcia Lucas, Richard Chew. *pd* John Barry, Elliot Scott. *m* John Williams. *cast* Mark Hamill, Harrison Ford, Carrie Fisher, Peter Cushing, Alec Guinness, Peter Mayhew, David Prowse.
●Hollywood began in an amusement arcade, so it's appropriate that its most profitable film should be as formally enchanting and psychologically sterile as a Gottlieb pinball machine. *Star Wars* is at least 40 years out of date as science fiction, but objections pale beside the film's major achievement: nearly 50 years after it was conceived, pulp space fiction is here for the first time presented as a truly viable movie genre. Discounting *2001*, which isn't a genre movie, it's like watching the first Western to use real exteriors. And audiences rightly feel that this is something they've been owed for some time. *Star Wars* itself has distinct limitations, but the current return to a cinema of spectacle and wonder is wholly encouraging. Or would you prefer *The Sound of Music*? DP

Star Wars, Episode IV, A New Hope

(1977/1997, US, 125 min)
d George Lucas. *p* Gary Kurtz. *sc* George Lucas. *ph* Gilbert Taylor. *ed* Paul Hirsch, Marcia Lucas, Richard Chew. *pd* John Barry, Elliot Scott. *m* John Williams. *cast* Mark Hamill, Harrison Ford, Carrie Fisher, Peter Cushing, Alec Guinness, Peter Mayhew, David Prowse.
●Don't expect radical revisions in this 20th anniversary reissue of George Lucas's spellbinding space opera. The sfx may now be unimpeachable, but none of the much heralded extra sequences fashioned from out-takes – the confrontation between Han Solo and Jabba the Hutt; Luke and his childhood friend, Biggs, bantering about the good old days – actually contributes anything meaningful in narrative terms. It's the minor tweaks which most impress. The computer-generated beasties scurrying around Mos Eisley's spaceport are triumphs of animation, and the dogfight scenes benefit immensely from more convincingly nuclear-looking explosions and the removal of unsightly matte lines. For the most part, you'd never guess the film was 20 years old. Only the innocence of its universe testifies to the sea change in film-making it provoked. The jaw-dropping wetness of Mark Hamill's Luke continues to astound, while Harrison Ford's amphetamine enema of a turn, which shifts the film into top gear after its rather too leisurely first act, merely confirms what we've always known: stars will out. JO'C

Star Wars Episode I The Phantom Menace

(1999, US, 132 min)
d George Lucas. *p* Rick McCallum. *sc* George Lucas. *ph* David Tattersall. *ed* Paul Martin Smith, Ben Burtt. *pd* Gavin Bocquet. *m* John Williams. *cast* Liam Neeson, Ewan McGregor, Natalie Portman, Jake Lloyd, Pernilla August, Franz Oz, Ian McDiarmid, Oliver Ford Davies, Hugh Quarshie, Anthony Daniels, Ahmed Best, Kenny Baker, Terence Stamp, Brian Blessed, Celia Imrie, Samuel L Jackson.
●If Lucas's brief '70s directorial career saw him regress further into immaturity at each step, it's hardly surprising that after a 22-year gestation his return to the fray should prove both so inanely childish and so thoroughly unskilled, however saturated with state-of-the-art special effects. What you don't expect is just how dramatically drab and impenetrable it proves: right from the opening title scroll, the film grinds its way from nonsensical plot exposition to anti-climactic finale through vast stretches of intergalactic tedium. The space-set pastichess of old-time childhood favourites – war films, underwater adventures, swashbucklers, Harryhausen-modelled Greek myths (McGregor's performance is straight out of a Gerry Anderson cartoon) – are familiar from the earlier films (as is the spiritual mumbo-jumbo), but the absolute dearth of human reference in Lucas's entirely imaginary universe must be almost unprecedented. With much of the action and most of the intrigue taking place off-screen (where are the baddies?), the menace's phantom nature at least seems clear: this is just a crude curtain-raiser of Episode II. Charmless, sexless, passionless and robot-humoured, it's preposterously uninvolving. NB

Star Wars Episode II Attack of the Clones

(2002, US, 142 min)
d George Lucas. *p* Rick McCallum. *sc* George Lucas, Jonathan Hales. *ph* David Tattersall. *ed* Ben Burtt. *pd* Gavin Bocquet. *m* John Williams. *cast* Ewan McGregor, Natalie Portman, Hayden Christensen, Frank Oz, Ian McDiarmid, Pernilla August, Ahmed Best, Oliver Ford Davies, Temuera Morrison, Anthony Daniels, Silas Carson, Kenny Baker, Samuel L Jackson, Christopher Lee, Jimmy Smits.
●After the longueurs of *The Phantom Menace*, George Lucas was taking no chances: ten minutes in, Obi-Wan Kenobi is diving through an 800th-floor window on a thrilling aerial chase after an assassin. Sub-*Dune* galactic politics take a back seat to torrid tales of teen lust (with dialogue to match), as trainee Jedi Anakin Skywalker (later to succumb to the Dark Side of the Force and become Darth Vader – keep up at the back there) develops a forbidden pash for Senator Amidala (Portman). Christensen is a winning mix of sultry and sulky as the now older Anakin, while McGregor is finally beginning to relax as the mentor who understandably refuses to treat his moody pupil like a grown-up. On the debit side, the film is designed to bridge episodes 1 and 3, and to foreshadow the original trilogy, and is thus pregnant with exposition – but without many twists or insights. Until the last half-hour, that is. Then here comes Christopher Lee, in enlivening Saruman mode, as chief goodie gone bad. After an astonishing *Gladiator* scene, Samuel Jackson finally gets to kick some ass – 'This party is *over*!' – and old Yoda moseys into the kind of showdown likely to get the faithful leaping from their seats. DW

Star Without Light

see Etoile sans Lumière

State and Main

(2000, US, 106 min)
d David Mamet. *p* Sarah Green. *sc* David Mamet. *ph* Oliver Stapleton. *ed* Barbara Tulliver. *pd* Gemma Jackson. *m* Theodore Shapiro. *cast* Alec Baldwin, Charles Durning, Clark Gregg, Philip Seymour Hoffman, Patti LuPone, William H Macy, Sarah Jessica Parker, David Paymer, Rebecca Pidgeon, Julia Stiles, Michael Higgins.
●A 19th century romance about integrity, courage and fire fighting, 'The Old Mill' may not be a sure thing at the box office, but it does star the very hot Bob Barrenger (Baldwin) and sizzling siren Claire Wellesley (Parker). Now all director Walt Price (Macy) has to do is convince neophyte screenwriter Joe White (Hoffman) that they really can't afford to build another mill to replace the one that burned down; persuade Claire she must honour her contractual obligation to disrobe on camera; and ensure that Bob keeps his pecker out of the under-age denizens of Waterford, Vermont. *State and Main* is a lovely title: smalltown USA to a tee, and subtly suggestive of the intersection between provincialism and the world at large. Too bad Mamet's movie is such a toss-off. We've seen this story before in*Sweet Liberty, After the Fox*, and it's no great twist that the condescending movie types are no more sussed than the not so guileless townsfolk. But the problem here isn't with the dialogue or the smoothly professional comic playing (the opening 20 minutes are a masterly exhibition of apparently effortless badinage), but with the grinding, mechanical plot. TCh

State Fair (aka It Happened One Summer)

(1945, US, 100 min)
d Walter Lang. *p* William Perlberg. *sc* Oscar Hammerstein II. *ph* Leon Shamroy. *ed* J Watson Webb Jr. *ad* Lyle Wheeler, Lewis H Creber. *songs* Richard Rodgers, Oscar Hammerstein II. *cast* Charles Winninger, Jeanne Crain, Dana Andrews, Vivian Blaine, Dick Haymes, Fay Bainter, Frank McHugh, Percy Kilbride, Donald Meek.
●Odious Rodgers and Hammerstein musical, as fey and insipid as they come, too obviously modelled on *Meet Me in St Louis* (1944). The story's about the (non-) adventures of the Frake family at the Iowa State Fair. If you're a fan of the music, you may be able to overlook the general mawkishness, but it'll take an effort. Songs include 'Isn't It Kinda Fun' and the Oscar-winning 'It Might As Well Be Spring'. Henry King made an earlier version with Will Rogers and Janet Gaynor in 1933. GM

State of Grace

(1990, US, 134 min)
d Phil Joanou. *p* Ned Dowd, Randy Ostrow, Ron Rotholz. *sc* Dennis McIntyre. *ph* Jordan Cronenweth. *ed* Claire Simpson. *pd* Patrizia von Brandenstein. *m* Ennio Morricone. *cast* Sean Penn, Ed Harris, Gary Oldman, Robin Wright, John Turturro, John C Reilly, RD Call, Joe Vitorelli, Burgess Meredith.
●While not in the same class as *GoodFellas*, this saga about Irish-American hoods in Hell's Kitchen during the 1970s is out of the same stable; and though sometimes monstrously violent, it's a hugely impressive piece of work for a young director previously known for his documentary *U2 Rattle and Hum*. The plot is familiar: youthful loyalty compromised, betrayal, kinship, ethnic rivalry, protection of territory, return to roots, revenge. More important is the visual impact of the film, which begins in a blur of motion and ends with a bloody St Patrick's Day shoot-out. But most impactful are the per-

formances: the much underrated Penn as a prodigal returnee, Wright as the ghetto woman who moved up and away, Harris as the bossman, and – most astonishingly – Oldman showing the ferocity of a Joe Pesci, the aimlessness of a *Mean Streets* De Niro, and the sex-appeal of a pre-fight Mickey Rourke. SGr

State of Siege (Etat de Siège)

(1973, Fr/It/WGer, 120 min)
d Costa-Gavras. *p* Jacques Perrin. *sc* Franco Solinas, Costa-Gavras. *ph* Pierre-William Glenn. *ed* Françoise Bonnot. *ad* Jacques d'Ovidio. *m* Mikis Theodorakis. *cast* Yves Montand, Renato Salvatori, OE Hasse, Jacques Weber, Jean-Luc Bideau, Evangeline Peterson, Maurice Teynac.

●How easily should one dismiss political potboilers? *Z* caused a lot of stir, with its topical subject and excellent performance from Trintignant; its audience was large, its message clear. *State of Siege* betrays its later date in the laboured difficulty of its subject: Tupamaro guerillas vs the CIA. It's the more courageous film, but far less 'successful', simply unable to contain the subject of terrorism within a basically thriller format. Both films sacrifice analysis and integrity in favour of popular polemic and an exploitative format, but then both films told the truth before it became 'true'; well worth seeing, if only to wonder what similar films could be made on Ulster or any of the other 'forgotten' aspects of British democracy in action. CA

State of the Union (aka The World and His Wife)

(1948, US, 124 min, b/w)
d/p Frank Capra. *sc* Anthony Veiller, Myles Connolly. *ph* George Folsey. *ed* William Hornbeck. *ad* Cedric Gibbons, Urie McCleary. *m* Victor Young. *cast* Spencer Tracy, Katharine Hepburn, Van Johnson, Angela Lansbury, Adolphe Menjou, Lewis Stone, Raymond Walburn, Charles Dingle.

●An over-long and over-emphatic political satire, in which Tracy's presidential candidate enlists the help of his estranged wife (Hepburn) in order to present a happy, respectable front to the voters (as always with Capra, seen as gullible little people, here in danger of being duped by corrupt industrialists). It's the usual Capra recipe of homespun sentiment and mindless optimism, enlivened a little by the performances (though one can only dream of what Cukor might have done with Hepburn and Tracy), but turned unusually bitter by Cold War cracks. Horribly dated, too. GA

State of Things, The

(1982, US/Port, 121 min, b/w)
d Wim Wenders. *p* Chris Sievernich. *sc* Robert Kramer, Wim Wenders. *ph* Henri Alekan, Fred Murphy. *ed* Barbara von Weitershausen. *ad* Ze Branco. *m* Jürgen Knieper. *cast* Patrick Bauchau, Allen Garfield, Isabelle Weingarten, Samuel Fuller, Roger Corman, Geoffrey Carey.

●Shooting a remake of an old Hollywood sci-fi film on the furthest westerly point in Portugal, the cast and crew suddenly find themselves high and dry on the beach, looking across the water to the US where the producer has vanished with the money. The motley crew begin killing time, relaxing into those day-to-day 'things' which somehow become privileged under Wenders' gaze; the need for narrative vanishes along with the old Hollywood pressures. When the director finally pursues the producer to LA and finds him fleeing the Mob, he encounters a different kind of killing time. Literally made on the run, during a hiatus in the troubled shooting of *Hammett*, the film is far more than Wenders' slap in the face to Hollywood. Supremely assured of itself and its method, it becomes a grave and beautiful meditation on the state of the art: the creative impasse of European film, the narcotic temptations of the last resort, the impossibility of telling stories any more, death. Wenders calls it the last of the B movies, but it may be cinema at its very limits. CPea

State Secret (aka The Great Manhunt)

(1950, GB, 104 min, b/w)
d Sidney Gilliat. *p* Frank Launder, Sidney Gilliat. *sc* Sidney Gilliat. *ph* Robert Krasker. *ed* Thelma Myers. *ad* Wilfrid Shingleton. *m* William Alwyn. *cast* Douglas Fairbanks Jr, Jack Hawkins, Glynis Johns, Herbert Lom, Walter Rilla, Karel Stepanek, Carl Jaffe, Anton Diffring.

●Launder (co-producer) and Gilliat (writer/co-producer/director) drew on the lessons they'd learned when working for Hitchcock in the '30s to turn out this nifty little thriller (from a novel by Roy Huggins) with a welcome sprinkling of humour. Fairbanks is the American surgeon called into the authoritarian Mittel-European state of Vosnia to receive honours from the country's medical fraternity, but he's embroiled in the local political turmoil when asked to operate on the ailing military premier, becoming one of the privileged few who know the secret of the general's fading health. TJ

Static

(1985, US, 93 min)
d Mark Romanek. *p* Amy Ness. *sc* Keith Gordon, Mark Romanek. *ph* Jeff Jur. *ed* Emily Paine. *pd* Cynthia Sowder. *cast* Keith Gordon, Amanda Plummer, Bob Gunton, Lily Knight, Barton Heyman.

●Ernie Blick (Gordon) whiles away his time in a crucifix factory collecting the assembly line cock-ups. His mind, however, is far away, on the invention he is perfecting in his motel room, which he hopes will give people a vision of heaven. All very weird and amiable in a Capraesque way, until frustration sets in, and Ernie hijacks a bus and demands local air-time in order to publicise his invention. If the film is about the different ways in which people seek to believe, then it is not held down by any preaching or heavy-weight message; it's all far too open-ended, optimistic and humorous for that. Its very unclassifiability is its strength. CPea

Stationmaster's Wife, The

see Bolwieser

Station Six – Sahara

(1962, GB/WGer, 101 min, b/w)
d Seth Holt. *p* Victor Lyndon. *sc* Bryan Forbes, Brian Clemens. *ph* Gerald Gibbs. *ed* Alastair McIntyre. *ad* Jack Stephens. *m* Ron Grainer. *cast* Carroll Baker, Peter Van Eyck, Ian Bannen, Denholm Elliott, Jörg Felmy, Mario Adorf, Biff McGuire.

●On an isolated oil pipeline station in the desert, five men bicker and squabble in the appalling heat and boredom. Then the incredible happens: a large American car crashes in their midst, one of its two occupants a beautiful blonde siren (Baker). Her presence drives the men crazy with lust for her, and with increasing antagonism towards each other. From a script by Bryan Forbes and Brian Clemens, the underrated Holt directs with a tight grip, and clearly delights in such moments as the frisson created by Baker's bra-strap falling casually from her shoulder. It's an unexpected black sheep of British cinema, not least for its unrepressed sense of anger and strident eroticism. DT

Stavisky...

(1974, Fr/It, 117 min)
d Alain Resnais. *p* Alain Belmondo. *sc* Jorge Semprun. *ph* Sacha Vierny. *ed* Albert Jurgenson. *ad* Jacques Saulnier. *m* Stephen Sondheim. *cast* Jean-Paul Belmondo, François Périer, Anny Duperey, Michel Lonsdale, Robert Bisacco, Claude Rich, Charles Boyer, Jacques Spiesser, Gérard Depardieu.

●Resnais' film about political destiny in France in the '30s is always thoroughly chilling, never merely elegant. The chill stems not simply from the cold precision of the images, but from the unshakeable implications of what he allows us to witness. On the one hand, and occupying centre stage, is Stavisky (Belmondo), swindler and entrepreneur; on the other, in the wings, is Trotsky, arriving in France, working, and finally exiled. Around them, *sotto voce* political machinations in which gradually and unmistakeably a grand design becomes visible – the breaking of the Left and the drift to Fascism. Stavisky's fall reveals him to be a pawn in a swindle of vaster dimensions than even he dreamed of, the fall itself a screen behind which other forces operate. Resnais conveys the atmosphere of moral degeneracy with a tact which makes it all the more insidious, through a film that is superbly paced. VG

Stay Alive

see Bemani

Stay Hungry

(1976, US, 102 min)
d Bob Rafelson. *p* Harold Schneider, Bob Rafelson. *sc* Bob Rafelson, Charles Gaines. *ph* Victor J Kemper. *ed* John F Link II. *pd* Toby Carr Rafelson. *m* Bruce Langhorne, Byron Berline. *cast* Jeff Bridges, Sally Field, Arnold Schwarzenegger, RG Armstrong, Robert Englund, Helena Kallianiotes, Roger E Mosley, Woodrow Parfrey, Scatman Crothers.

●After the sombre melancholy of *Five Easy Pieces* and *The King of Marvin Gardens*, Rafelson pursued his interest in social dropouts and marginal life-styles with this offbeat comedy drama. Bridges oozes carefree charm as a young Alabama heir caught up in a property speculation involving a gym, but instead investing his interest in Arnie and his muscle-building pals. His relationship with gutsy working gal Field helps fill out the picture, although the preponderance of loose narrative threads tends to leave one with an impression of individual scenes rather than any sense of coherent plot. The scene in which Bridges slips though a hole in the social hedge to join a bunch of fiddle players in a country hoedown epitomises the gentle, quirky feel of the film. Based on a Charles Gaines novel about the rootlessness of the so-called 'New South', it has its slack spells, but Rafelson's sure feel for the inexpressible subtleties of emotional relationships is evident throughout. NF

Staying Alive

(1983, US, 96 min)
d Sylvester Stallone. *p* Robert Stigwood, Sylvester Stallone. *sc* Sylvester Stallone, Norman Wexler. *ph* Nick McLean. *ed* Don Zimmerman, Mark Warner. *pd* Robert Boyle. *m* Johnny Mandel, Robin Garb. *cast* John Travolta, Cynthia Rhodes, Finola Hughes, Steve Inwood, Julie Bovasso, Charles Ward.

●Six years on from *Saturday Night Fever*, Travolta's Tony Manero is very much the same: one dimensional, bovine, manipulating, self-obsessed, as he fights his way from dancing obscurity to a starring role in some God-awful Broadway parody of a multi-million-pound Zanussi ad. On the way, he falls in and out with the ice-cool English star (Hughes), before opting for faithful old stablemate Jackie (Rhodes). The dance sequences seem poor beer when set against the vibrant amateurism of *Saturday Night Fever*, mostly rudimentary Martha Graham, with lots of close-ups to hide Travolta's obvious failings in that department. All could be forgiven if it weren't for the soulless overall slickness. SGr

Staying Together

(1989, US, 91 min)
d Lee Grant. *p* Joseph Feury. *sc* Monte Merrick. *ph* Dick Bush. *ed* Katherine Wenning. *pd* Stuart Wurtzel. *m* Miles Goodman. *cast* Sean Astin, Stockard Channing, Melinda Dillon, Jim Haynie, Levon Helm, Dinah Manoff, Dermot Mulroney, Tim Quill, Keith Szarabajka, Daphne Zuniga.

●This genial family drama is formulaic without being entirely predictable. There's a symmetry to the story of three sons going through that troublesome teen phase: the smooth flow of their emotional lives is disturbed as each in turn has problems relating to Mom and Pop, and to the opposite sex. Gradually they come to realise – aaah! – that their greatest strength is each other. Everyone gets a Big Problem to wrestle with. How's Brian (Quill) ever gonna get reconciled with Pop? He's breaking his Mom's heart. How's Kit (Mulroney) gonna rescue his girl, due to be married to the town rich creep? How's Duncan (Astin) ever gonna lose his irksome virginity? When will any of them twig that Mom (Dillon) is more than just a service unit? There's an admirable lack of wish-fulfilment plotting, plus a casual, bollocks-scratching realism in the depiction of the teenage boys. The three leads all strain a bit after sensitivity, but overall it's amiable enough. SFe

Stay Tuned

(1992, US, 88 min)
d Peter Hyams. *p* James G Robinson. *sc* Tom S Parker, Jim Jennewein. *ph* Peter Hyams. *ed* Peter E Berger. *pd* Philip Harrison. *m* Bruce

Broughton. *cast* John Ritter, Pam Dawber, Jeffrey Jones, David Tom, Heather McComb, Bob Dishy, Joyce Gordon.

● A pointless 'satire' which attempts to ridicule American television by revelling in the conventions of game shows, commercials and mini-series. Roy (Ritter) is your average TV junkie: he watches over seven hours a day and is blind to the needs of his wife (Dawber) and two children (Tom and McComb). Enter devilish Spike (Jones), the supremo of an other-worldly entertainment channel who sells Roy a 600-channel satellite system, thereby luring him into a Faustian pact that will test his devotion to the box. The question is: does this human sponge possess a soul? The film boasts the emotional depth of a 30-second soap commercial, and Hyams' direction fails to sustain humour or tension. A dismal affair which goes down the tube. CM

Stazione Termini

see Terminal Station

Steal, The

(1994, GB, 91 min)
d John Hay. *p* Gary Kurtz, Barbara Stone. *sc* John Hay. *ph* Ronnie Taylor. *ed* David Martin. *pd* Phil Robertson. *m* Barry Kirsch. *cast* Heathcote Williams, Alfred Molina, Helen Slater, Patricia Hayes, Stephen Fry, Jack Dee, Peter Bowles, Dinsdale Landen, Bryan Pringle, Patricia Hayes.

● Williams is the mysterious lawyer who acts as commissioning officer for a PC scam to liberate funds from an evil merchant bank whose investment portfolios have devastated the Asian demi-paradise of Golanda. To this end, he enlists brash computer hacker Slater and old pal Molina, a reserved council traffic-planner. Pretty much a non-starter as a Brit caper-comedy, writer/director Hay's barely adequate picture is nevertheless sweet in the way it fails. It's like the kind of keen, bad school essay which shows all the heart-breaking evidence of a pupil having heard, but not learned, from teacher's advice. In their efforts to make an economic modern Ealing comedy the producers have thrown everything into the pudding: American star, impersonations, car chases, rural interludes – all executed in delightfully mid-scale, lightweight, familiar and mildly diverting style. The rest is spot the TV actor. Undemanding, old-fashioned and old hat. WH

Steal Big, Steal Little

(1995, US, 134 min)
d Andrew Davis. *p* Andrew Davis, Fred Caruso. *sc* Andrew Davis, Lee Blessing, Jeanne Blake, Teresa Tucker-Davies. *ph* Frank Tidy. *ed* Don Brochu, Tina Hirsch. *pd* Michael Haller. *m* William Olvis. *cast* Andy Garcia, Alan Arkin, Rachel Ticotin, Joe Pantoliano, Holland Taylor, Ally Walker, David Ogden Stiers, Kevin McCarthy.

● Double trouble, take two. Garcia is Reuben, who runs an organic farm as a collective for South American immigrants; and Garcia is Robert, who's trying to steal the land out from under their feet, to convert it into a holiday ranch for businessmen. Reuben wears natty collarless shirts and a Boho leather waistcoat, while Robert sports garish cowboy suits and a ten-gallon hat. Director Davis paid his dues making disreputable action films with Steven Seagal and Chuck Norris, before graduating to reputable action films with Harrison Ford. But while this reveals a hitherto latent Marxist tendency, it lacks any of the distinctive qualities the director brought to his genre work: the powerhouse narrative drive, unsentimental intelligence and brusque humour. Sincerely philanthropic, predictably dismal. TCh

Stealing Beauty (lo ballo da sola/Beauté Volée)

(1995, It/GB/Fr, 118 min)
d Bernardo Bertolucci. *p* Jeremy Thomas. *sc* Susan Minot. *ph* Darius Khondji. *ed* Pietro Scalia. *pd* Gianni Silvestri. *m* Richard Hartley. *cast* Sinead Cusack, Jeremy Irons, Jean Marais, Liv Tyler, Donal McCann, Carlo Cecchi, DW Moffett, Rachel Weisz, Steffania Sandrelli, Joseph Fiennes, Jason Flemyng.

● When Lucy (Tyler), a 19-year-old American, whose poet mother has recently died, visits friends in a Tuscan villa, her plans involve more than a simple holiday. For one thing, she cherishes memories of a first kiss, four years earlier, from young Niccolò to whom she'd now like to lose her virginity; for another, she's puzzled by a note in her mother's diary hinting that the man she's considered her father isn't her real parent. At the same time, she soon becomes the focus of interest for the villa's inhabitants, notably the jaded menfolk who are revitalised by her innocence and burgeoning womanhood.The self-obsessed complacency of the arty, Chiantishire expats tries the patience, and the camera's relentless ogling of Tyler's limbs opens the film to charges of voyeurism. And yet, after the deliberate, over-blown portentousness of his recent epics, the looseness, leisurely pacing and the intimacy of mood are a welcome reminder of Bertolucci's directorial assurance. He brings a light touch to small details: the expats' isolation from the 'real world' being revealed through deft short scenes depicting, say, their reaction to the building of a nearby television mast or their encounter with an army officer. But there's also a real sensuousness, less in the emphasis on Tyler herself than in the evocation of the colours, aromas, temperatures and sounds of a particular time and place. GA

Stealing Heaven

(1988, GB/Yugo, 115 min)
d Clive Donner. *p* Simon MacCorkindale, Andros Epaminondas. *sc* Chris Bryant. *ph* Mikael Salomon. *ed* Michael Ellis. *pd* Voytek Roman. *m* Nick Bicat. *cast* Derek de Lint, Kim Thomson, Denholm Elliott, Bernard Hepton, Kenneth Cranham, Rachel Kempson, Angela Pleasence, Patsy Byrne, Cassie Stuart, Philip Locke.

● Abelard and Heloise retold with more than a touch of *Emmanuelle*, and no sense of the medieval anywhere. All in all, the tale comes across like a Mills & Boon bodice-ripper. Theirs is a forbidden passion since his vocation as a teacher enjoins chastity, but boarding in her uncle's house and giving her private tuition saps his resolve. Tolerant Bishop Martin (Hepton) would probably have let him off lightly, but Uncle Fulbert (Elliott), a vain, power-hungry prelate who sells bogus holy relics on the side, sends a gang to castrate him. After that, Abelard and Heloise take holy orders, but bump into each other a bit around the cloisters and get to play house as the century wears on. Fairly feeble except for Denholm Elliott, who tops up his role with such a convincing character study that you regret every minute he's off screen. BC

Stealing Home

(1988, US, 98 min)
d Steven Kampmann, Will Aldiss. *p* Thom Mount, Hank Moonjean. *sc* Steven Kampmann, Will Aldis. *ph* Bobby Byrne. *ed* Antony Gibbs. *ad* Vaughan Edwards. *m* David Foster. *cast* Mark Harmon, Jodie Foster, Blair Brown, William McNamara, Harold Ramis, Jonathan Silverman, Richard Jenkins, John Shea.

● Down-at-heel baseball pro Harmon returns home when he learns that his childhood sweetheart Foster has killed herself. It's up to him to dispose of her ashes. Lame melodrama, pitched firmly at the emotions, which comes complete with syrupy music and excruciating flashback sequences. The baseball references are hardly an integral part of the story, but seem to have been tagged on to ensure a punchy title. Foster's intense, heartfelt, and entirely humourless performance as the young rebel with the death wish just about takes the movie to first base. GM

Steamboat Bill, Jr

(1928, US, 6,400 ft, b/w)
d Charles F Reisner. *p* Joseph M Schenck. *sc* Carl Harbaugh. *ph* J Devereux Jennings, Bert Haines. *ed* J Sherman Kell. *ad* Fred Gabourie. *cast* Buster Keaton, Ernest Torrence, Marion Byron, Tom McGuire, Tom Lewis, Joe Keaton.

● A marvellous comedy set in a lazy riverside town in the Deep South, with Buster as the fop-pish, city-educated boy who returns home to prove a grave disappointment to his father, a burly steamboat captain looking for stout filial support, and reluctantly joins him in his efforts to fight off a wealthy rival threatening to take over the river. Hilarious, of course, with both delicately observed jokes and energetically athletic stuntwork coursing through the movie. But what really delights is the detailed depiction of small town life, plus Keaton's comic awareness of his own persona; a sequence in which he and his father are buying a hat to replace his wimpy beret is a model of film comedy, played, remarkably, direct to camera. And the final masterstroke is the cyclone sequence, in which the entire town is destroyed but Buster remains miraculously untouched. GA

Steaming

(1984, GB, 95 min)
d Joseph Losey. *p* Paul Mills. *sc* Patricia Losey. *ph* Christopher Challis. *ed* Reginald Beck. *pd* Maurice Fowler. *m* Richard Harvey. *cast* Vanessa Redgrave, Sarah Miles, Diana Dors, Patti Love, Brenda Bruce, Felicity Dean, Sally Sagoe, Anna Tzelniker.

● Losey was 73 and dying of cancer when he returned from France to make this modest adaptation of Nell Dunn's stage success about the Ladies' Night regulars at a London Turkish baths. Here middle-class Miles and Redgrave rub shoulders with the likes of working-class Love to unfold secrets and reveal their true feelings about their varied relationships, while the threat of demolition creates a new-found sense of solidarity. Virtually confined to a single location, it's claustrophobic, talky and rather too full of stereotypes, magnifying all the faults usually encountered when unsuitable theatrical material has been given the big screen treatment. The cast, however, retain their dignity while measuring up to the screenplay's dramatic demands in various stages of undress. Dors' final film, and Losey himself didn't live to see it released. TJ

Steamroller and the Violin, The

see Katok i Skrypka

Steel

(1979, US, 101 min)
d Steve Carver. *p* Peter S Davis, William N Panzer. *sc* Leigh Chapman. *ph* Roger Shearman. *ed* David Blewitt. *pd* Ward Preston. *m* Michel Colombier. *cast* Lee Majors, Jennifer O'Neill, Art Carney, George Kennedy, Harris Yulin, Redmond Gleason, Terry Kiser, Richard Lynch, Roger Mosley, Albert Salmi, RG Armstrong.

● Uninspired piece of high-rise melodrama. O'Neill is the svelte daughter of a hard-hat steel construction boss (Kennedy) who steps into daddy's shoes when he falls to a tragic death. The jokes and the sexual sparring are predictable, sexist, and too lame to redeem themselves with even a minimum of irony. And the cracks at trade union safety regulations look particularly ugly when you think that one of the stuntmen on the crew really did fall to his death during shooting. CA

Steel Bayonet, The

(1957, GB, 85 min, b/w)
d/p Michael Carreras. *sc* Howard Clewes. *ph* Jack Asher. *ed* Bill Lenny. *ad* Edward Marshall. *m* Leonard Salzedo. *cast* Leo Genn, Kieron Moore, Michael Medwin, Robert Brown, Michael Ripper.

● No-budget British war movie (avoid confusion with Sam Fuller's *The Steel Helmet* or *Fixed Bayonets*) directed by Michael Carreras, a Hammer studios' mainstay. Salisbury Plain stands in for Tunis, 1943, as a group of infantrymen hold a farmhouse dangerously close to enemy lines. Despite an honourable effort in the direction of psychological grittiness, the picture never really exerts much grip. TJ

Steel Helmet, The

(1950, US, 84 min, b/w)
d/p/sc Samuel Fuller. *ph* Ernest Miller. *ed* Philip Cahn. *ad* Theobold Holsopple. *m* Paul Dunlap. *cast* Gene Evans, Robert Hutton, Richard Loo, Steve Brodie, James Edwards, Sid Melton, Richard Monahan.

● A characteristically hard-hitting war movie from Fuller, charting the fortunes of Gene Evans' Sergeant Zack, sole survivor of a PoW massacre in Korea. Saved by a Korean orphan and joining up with other GIs cut off from their units, Evans' cynical veteran embodies the writer-director's abiding thesis that, to survive the madness of war, a ruthless individualism is necessary. Fuller glamorises neither his loner protagonist nor the war itself: if he clearly supports the US presence in Korea, battle is still a chaotic, deadly affair, and nobody has much idea of why they fight. The action scenes are terrific, belying the movie's very low budget. GA

Steel Highway

see Other Men's Women

Steel Magnolias

(1989, US, 117 min)
d Herbert Ross. *p* Ray Stark. *sc* Robert Harling. *ph* John A Alonzo. *ed* Paul Hirsch. *pd* Gene Callahan, Edward Pisoni. *m* Georges Delerue. *cast* Sally Field, Dolly Parton, Shirley MacLaine, Daryl Hannah, Olympia Dukakis, Julia Roberts, Tom Skerritt, Sam Shepard, Kevin J O'Connor.

● The loves, lives and losses of six Southern women of different ages, fortunes and temperaments, united by a feisty self-confidence, irrepressible humour, and steely fortitude in the face of life's setbacks. It takes place over several years – much of it set in the beauty parlour run by Dolly Parton – from the wedding of beautiful Shelby Eatenton (Roberts), through the birth of her first child and her untimely death. The plot's main thrust deals with diabetic Shelby's determination, against the wishes of her mom (Field) to have a child despite the risks. Thanks to Field's no-nonsense performance, this potentially maudlin scenario is briskly handled. Set against flower-like Shelby (a strong, sensitive characterisation by Roberts) are two raddled fairy godmothers: MacLaine and Dukakis, revelling in some wonderful one-liners. With all the male characters kept strictly functional, it makes a shameless bid for your heart, aiming to have you smiling one moment, sniffling the next. SFe

Steelyard Blues

(1972, US, 93 min)
d Alan Myerson. *p* Tony Bill, Michael Phillips, Julia Phillips. *sc* David S Ward. *ph* Laszlo Kovacs, Stevan Larner. *ed* Robert Grovenor. *ad* Vince Cresciman. *m* Nicholas Gravenites. *cast* Jane Fonda, Donald Sutherland, Peter Boyle, Garry Goodrow, Howard Hesseman, John Savage.

● Perhaps the best American comedy since *The President's Analyst*, mainly because its humour is never imposed, but allowed to develop from the situations in which the characters find themselves. Demolition derby fanatic Sutherland teams up with a gang of junkyard misfits, including Boyle as a nut who dresses up and takes off movie actors, plus Fonda as the inevitable hooker, and they set about resurrecting an old seaplane with the idea of flying away from it all. Humour and paranoia go hand in hand, before the film spirals off into fantasy. There's enough to suggest that it considers itself an allegory on dark America, but this remains sufficiently deadpan to take or leave. Otherwise it's just very funny, full of moments of irrelevant humour. Good soundtrack too, from Nick Gravenites and Paul Butterfield. An impressive first film. CPe

Stella

(1990, US, 109 min)
d John Erman. *p* Samuel Goldwyn Jr, David V Picker. *sc* Robert Getchell. *ph* Billy Williams. *ed* Jerrold L Ludwig. *pd* James Hulsey. *m* John Morris. *cast* Bette Midler, John Goodman, Trini Alvarado, Stephen Collins, Marsha Mason, Eileen Brennan, Linda Hart, Ben Stiller, William McNamara.

● This second remake of *Stella Dallas* updates the story, with Stella (Midler) a single parent struggling through the '70s who still makes the ultimate sacrifice, giving up her daughter in the interest of the latter's social advancement. Handsome doctor Stephen Dallas (Collins) first notices bartender Stella when she leaps on the bar to do a mock striptease routine. Becoming pregnant, she fiercely rejects his offers of marriage or financial support. Years later, their teenage daughter Jenny (Alvarado) grows weary of mother's bad dress sense, and the ultimate humiliation comes when Stella is arrested outside a local bar. Off she goes to Dad and prospective stepmother (Mason) for blueberry pancakes and cocktails. Whatever challenge existed in rendering the class conflict credible has been missed: Robert Getchell's script milks the story for maximum tears, but wrestles unsuccessfully with the inherent absurdity of Stella's predicament, delivering clichéd situations and dialogue. And Midler's larger-than-life performance is daunting against the subtler approaches of Alvarado and Mason. CM

Stella Dallas

(1937, US, 105 min, b/w)
d King Vidor. *p* Samuel Goldwyn. *sc* Victor Heerman, Sarah Y Mason. *ph* Rudolph Maté. *ed* Sherman Todd. *ad* Richard Day. *m* Alfred Newman. *cast* Barbara Stanwyck, John Boles, Anne Shirley, Alan Hale, Barbara O'Neil, Tim Holt, Marjorie Main.

● A pretty millworker with her mind on upward mobility via a suet-faced, sexless millionaire's son (Boles), Stella (Stanwyck, wonderful) turns from radiant grisette into a restless wife who sublimates frustration into maternal martyrdom and ever more outrageous dress. Meanwhile husband Stephen flees to a wealthy and conveniently widowed old flame who epitomises pedigree breeding and impeccable (but mean-spirited) good taste. The film stays tantalisingly undecided whether Stella's vulgarity and wild narcissism are a fatal flaw or a snook knowingly cocked at country-club dullness and decorum; and Stanwyck's extraordinary performance keeps open the cleft between weepy pathos and mocking defiance to the very end when, alone outside in the rain, she spies on her daughter's high society wedding through a window, then turns from the puppet-show, striding, smiling enigmatically, towards the camera. SJo

Stella Does Tricks

(1996, GB, 99 min)
d Coky Giedroyc. *p* Adam Barker. *sc* Alison Kennedy. *ph* Barry Ackroyd. *ed* Budge Tremlett. *pd* Lynne Whiteread. *m* Nick Bicat. *cast* Kelly Macdonald, Hans Matheson, James Bolam, Ewan Stewart, Lindsay Henderson, Andy Serkis.

● It may not be explicit on the physical front, but this kitchen-sink study of teenage prostitution is dubious: yes, we should know that such exploitation exists, but what's this first feature actually saying? Kelly Macdonald (from *Trainspotting*) is impressive in the lead, oppressed by deceptively helpful pimp Bolam and prepared to make a new start with junkie Mathieson, but she's not helped by AL Kennedy's obvious script, clumsy flashbacks, and, despite the project's liberal stance, an overall prurience (a gang-rape scene is particularly nasty). GA

Stepfather (Beau-père)

(1981, Fr, 120 min)
d/sc Bertrand Blier. *ph* Sacha Vierny. *ed* Claudine Merlin. *ad* Théo Meurisse. *m* Philippe Sarde. *cast* Patrick Dewaere, Ariel Besse, Maurice Ronet, Nicole Garcia, Nathalie Baye, Maurice Risch.

● What is a man to do when the accidental death of his wife leaves him alone with a 14-year-old stepdaughter who keeps crawling into his bed with the dewy-eyed persistence of Humbert Humbert's Lolita? The answer, wrapped up in yards of dreary solemnity before ultimately blowing up into absurdity, provides some polite porn designed for bourgeois coffee tables. Not one of Blier's more successful provocations. TM

Stepfather, The

(1986, US, 98 min)
d Joseph Ruben. *p* Jay Benson. *sc* Donald E Westlake. *ph* John Lindley. *ed* George Bowers. *pd* James William Newport. *m* Patrick Moraz. *cast* Terry O'Quinn, Jill Schoelen, Shelley Hack, Charles Lanyer, Stephen Shellen, Stephen E Miller.

● This above-average domestic slasher derives a modicum of interest from the script's discreet, if unoriginal, reworking of Hitchcockian motifs and situations. Teenage Stephanie happily shares her Seattle home with her young widowed mother until Jerry Blake (O'Quinn) appears out of the blue to court and marry mom. Steph's natural jealousy soon turns into outright suspicion when she is led to believe that he is in fact a psychokiller with a history of changed identities and previous slaughtered families who had failed him somehow. An over-emphatic score, heavy symbolism, and the inevitable Steadicam stuff are thankfully countered by an admirable lack of gore. But while O'Quinn is effectively scary, one is left longing for Hitchcock's dark, daring wit and disturbingly amoral insights. GA

Stepfather II, The

(1989, US, 86 min)
d Jeff Burr. *p* William Burr, Darin Scott. *sc* John Auerbach. *ph* Jacek Laskus. *ed* Pasquale A Buba. *pd* Byrnadette Disanto. *m* Jim Manzie, Pat Regan. *cast* Terry O'Quinn, Meg Foster, Jonathan Brandis, Caroline Williams, Mitchell Laurance, Henry Brown, Renata Scott.

● A welcome return for O'Quinn's sinister psycho. Picking up where the previous slasher left off, this has him in a psychiatric hospital for the criminally insane, where a caring shrink ponders the question as to what drove a seemingly charming gentleman to move in with a series of fatherless families, assuming happy paternal roles, only to leave them gurgling on their own claret. Explaining in simple terms before driving home his primitive blade, the psycho then strolls out of the hospital, throws on a new, somewhat inadequate-looking disguise, and ventures forth in search of his next kill. Forget the supporting cast (most of them are dispensed with anyway): this is essentially O'Quinn's film, his glassy-eyed killer moving from relaxed father-figure to enraged psychotic in less time than it takes for one's heart to skip a beat, while his effective delivery of such murderous connotations as 'You go ahead while I just crack open this bottle' adds a spattering of humour to the grisly proceedings. DA

Stepfather III

(1992, US, 105 min)
d Guy Magar. *p* Guy Magar, Paul Moen. *sc* Guy Magar, Marc B Ray. *ed* Patrick Gregston. *cast* Rob Wightman, Priscilla Barnes, David Tom, John Ingle, Season Hubley.

● This second sequel is far better than one might expect from the end of *Stepfather II*, when the titular psycho was being butchered and battered by various members of his latest family. Miraculously surviving, he opens proceedings here in a particularly gruesome bout of plastic surgery, without anaesthetic and performed by a drunken surgeon. He then fixes himself up with another widow and child in no time, and is on his beastly traditional-values way again. The reason for the plastic surgery, of course, is that the excellent Terry O'Quinn has been replaced. Wightman, with that prissy, scary, whiny voice makes a good fist of it, and seems more barmy than ever. The violence is genuinely gory, and climaxes with a death in a garden threshing-machine that surely defies all efforts at restorative surgery. SGr

Stepford Wives, The

(1974, US, 115 min)
d Bryan Forbes. *p* Edgar J Scherick. *sc* William Goldman. *ph* Owen Roizman. *ed* Timothy Gee. *pd* Gene Callahan. *m* Michael Small. *cast* Katharine Ross, Paula Prentiss, Peter Masterson, Nanette Newman, Patrick O'Neal, Tina Louise, Carol Rossen, William Prince.

● William Goldman's leisurely script and Forbes' dull direction never quite capture the subtleties of Ira Levin's novel about an idyllic Connecticut commuter village where the housewives are a bunch of domesticated dummies. Ross and Prentiss play a pair of newly-arrived wives who are puzzled by the excessive clubbishness of the men and the unquestioning docility of their wives. The final revelation is marred by a melodramatic, sub-Hitchcockian showdown that dispels the more subtly unnerving atmosphere of polite menace. That said, the final supermarket scene does at least have the courage to see the original premise through to its logical conclusion. NF

Stephen King's Thinner

(1996, US, 92 min)
d Tom Holland. *p* Richard P Rubinstein, Mitchell Galin. *sc* Michael McDowell, Tom Holland. *ph* Kees Van Oostrum. *ed* Marc Laub. *pd* Laurence Bennett. *m* Daniel Licht. *cast* Robert John Burke, Joe Mantegna, Lucinda Jenney, Michael Constantine, Kari Wuhrer, Joy Lenz, Stephen King.

● Billy Halleck (Burke, unrecognisable as the Hal Hartley actor) is a well connected attorney in Fairview, Maine, whose body is ballooning as his arrogance grows. His attention distracted while driving (by a congratulatory blow-job from his wife), Billy knocks down an ageing gypsy woman. His cronies cover up the crime, but gypsy elder Tadzu Lempke (Constantine) utters a curse which sets Greg Cannom's make-up effects department into reverse, with Halleck wasting away into a cadaverous skeleton. Even as the psychological tension is wound up – as the ghost-cheeked attorney suffers tormented nightmares, fantasises infidelities, and falls deeper into the compromising grip of mobster Ginelli (Mantegna) – second league horror director Holland seems unable to invest the film with anything resembling conviction. Having reached the crossroads signposted 'Spoof' and 'Delirious Nightmare', he sits down and goes nowhere. Light fun can be had either from watching ethnic minorities and women take their revenge (albeit, intriguingly, through the agency of supernatural spells), or from idly scrutinising Burke's wobbling bodysuits. But this is basically best left as fodder for a media studies thesis entitled 'Anxiety in American Cinema in the age of PC'. WH

Stepkids

see Big Girls Don't Cry...They Get Even

Stepmom

(1998, US/Ger, 125 min)
d Chris Columbus. *p* Wendy Finerman, Chris Columbus, Mark Radcliffe, Michael Barnathan. *sc* Gigi Levangie, Jessie Nelson, Steven Rogers, Karen Leigh Hopkins, Ron Bass. *ph* Donald M McAlpine. *ed* Neil Travis. *pd* Stuart Wurtzel. *m* John Williams. *cast* Julia Roberts, Susan Sarandon, Ed Harris, Jena Malone, Liam Aitken, Lynn Whitfield, Darrell Larson.

● Businessman Luke (Harris) has a new girlfriend, gorgeous trendy Isabel (Roberts). His children prefer their mom, reliable protective Jackie (Sarandon). She isn't too keen on her replacement either, but she's dying from cancer. It's hard not to feel like a puppet while watching this – at every moment there's a cold hand prodding you into laughter or tears. Director Chris Columbus has been doing this for years, and as conservative propaganda goes (the message is good mums sacrifice all for their kids) it's as smooth as butter. The cast are more than adequate. Sarandon ennobles the dumbest of lines – contorting that intelligently clownish face into a million expressions of hurt – and Roberts does her urban-girl schtick to perfection. CO'Su

Stepmother, The

(1972, US, 94 min)
d/p/sc Hikmet Avedis. *ph* Jack Beckett. *ed* Ralph Hall, Tony de Zarraga. *ad* Roger Franks. *cast* Alejandro Rey, John Anderson, Katherine Justice, Larry Linville, Marlene Schmidt, Duncan MacLeod, Rudy Herrera Jr, John D Garfield.

● A building contractor (Rey) strangles his wife Margo's lover and while burying the body sees a man beating up a Mexican girl who's later murdered. A cop (Anderson) fits the jigsaw together. Producer/director Avedis (who later answered to the first name Howard) scripted this overheated Southern California thriller: punctuated by ugly freeze shots, the plot trudges in a straight line, while striving to give the impression of twisting in the Chandler manner, and comes to a bloodstained conclusion when Margo (Justice) is discovered in bed (in almost forgotten justification of the come-on title) with her college stepson. JPy

Steppenwolf

(1974, US, 106 min)
d Fred Haines. *p* Melvin Fishman, Richard Herland. *sc* Fred Haines. *ph* Tomislav Pinter. *ed* Irving Lerner. *ad* Leo Karen. *m* George Gruntz. *cast* Max von Sydow, Dominique Sanda, Pierre Clémenti, Carla Romanelli, Roy Bosier, Alfred Baillou.

● Faced with Hesse's intensely introspective text about the intellectual and emotional crisis of a middle-aged man, Haines opts for a '60s-ish semi-psychedelic approach, with some fetching animated interpolations, an amusing appearance by Clémenti, and a marginal, simplistic 'let's all get stoned' moral. The latter aspect now looks distinctly corny, and some might regard it as a gross misreading of the original. But even the staunchest Hesse devotee will find compensations in Sydow's characterisation and the comparative fidelity of the film's first half. DP

Stepping Out

(1991, US, 110 min)
d/p Lewis Gilbert. *sc* Richard Harris. *ph* Alan Hume. *ed* Humphrey Dixon. *pd* Peter Mullins. *m* Peter Matz. *cast* Liza Minnelli, Shelley Winters, Robyn Stevan, Jane Krakowski, Bill Irwin, Ellen Greene, Sheila McCarthy, Andrea Martin, Julie Walters, Carol Woods, Luke Reilly, Nora Dunn.

● Schlepping out, more like. Another feel-good movie to follow *Shirley Valentine*, this is set in a New York dance class run by feisty coulda-been Mavis (Minnelli), who had her week of glory understudying on Broadway. Now, her career hampered by her boyfriend's ego, fulfilment lies in teaching a lovable bunch of stereotypes and social inadequates under the steely eye of cantankerous pianist Winters. Asked to stage a routine for a charity show, Mavis has to whip these no-hopers into a crack *corps de tap*. This isn't a Willy Russell job, but the rules are the same: plain folk overcome problems in one life-affirming moment, braving the disapproval of society and/or him at home. There's little room for a strong cast to manoeuvre. Minnelli plies her gamine act likeably, although when it comes to her big 'what good is it sitting alone in your room' closer, tacked on as a cynical box-office sop, she's the same old Liza with a Zzzz. Gilbert opens up Richard Harris' church-hall bound stage play with all the visual flair of a sitcom episode. JRo

Stepping Razor – Red X

(1992, Can, 104 min)
d Nicholas Campbell. *p* Edgar Egger. *sc* Nicholas Campbell. *ph* Edgar Egger. *ed* Trevor Ambrose. *cast* Peter Tosh, Lloyd 'Rocky' Allen, Edward 'Bigs' Allen, Andrea Davis, Rab Leon, Ron Headley.

● 'I learned to multiply zero with zero and get one,' mutters the recorded voice of reggae star Peter Tosh in this thunderous documentary of his life and times, at once defying logic and hitting the spot, as was his wont throughout an iconoclastic career as Wailer, ex-Wailer, political agitator and spiritual rhetorician. Tosh was murdered in ambiguous circumstances in 1987 and this long, dense film rumbles across the infernal landscape of his world with the dispassion of an apocalyptic war report. A harsh, angry, frightened description of a harsh, angry, frightened life. NC

Sterile Cuckoo, The (aka Pookie)

(1969, US, 107 min)
d/p Alan J Pakula. *sc* Alvin Sargent. *ph* Milton Krasner. *ed* Sam O'Steen, John W Wheeler. *ad* Roland Anderson. *m* Fred Karlin. *cast* Liza Minnelli, Wendell Burton, Tim McIntire, Elizabeth Harrower, Austin Green.

● Pakula's debut as a director, two years before making *Klute*, is one of those rare American films which manage to be gently observational without succumbing to the Europeanism of Mazursky or Cassavetes. Liza Minnelli, improbably, is the kook of the title, a college girl who tumbles through an autumn romance with a bashful student (Burton). Not a lot happens: the camera watches, winter comes, the kids split up, Pookie drops out...but the sympathy of the direction for once makes ...romantic realism likeable. CA

Stevie

(1978, US/GB, 102 min)
d/p Robert Enders. *sc* Hugh Whitemore. *ph* Freddie Young. *ed* Peter Tanner. *ad* Robert Jones. *m* Patrick Gowers. *cast* Glenda Jackson, Mona Washbourne, Alec McCowen, Trevor Howard, Emma Louise Fox.

● This at least captures two fine performances, both from the original stage production of Hugh Whitemore's play about the late poet Stevie Smith, the Emily Dickinson of Palmers Green: Glenda Jackson as Stevie, Mona Washbourne as her maiden aunt. But the screen adaptation is fairly calamitous. Instead of sucking us into Stevie Smith's claustrophobic world, it jolts us about with sepia flashbacks, mood shots of trains entering tunnels and of Highgate Ponds in winter. Perhaps such tricks were needed, though, to obscure the play's lack of direct action: it's almost entirely reminiscences and confidences. GB

Stick

(1985, US, 109 min)
d Burt Reynolds. *p* Jennings Lang. *sc* Elmore Leonard, Joseph C Stinson. *ph* Nick McLean. *ed* William Gordean. *pd* James Shanahan. *m* Barry DeVorzon, Joseph Conlan. *cast* Burt Reynolds, Candice Bergen, George Segal, Charles Durning, José Perez, Richard Lawson, Alex Rocco.

● Poor old Elmore Leonard, always getting dud movies made of his books. In this case, he's partly responsible, since he co-wrote the script, which sees Reynolds as an ex-con bent on avenging the death of a buddy and getting involved with the drug-dealing low-lifers of Miami. It's deeply flawed by Reynolds' less than lustrous but screen-hogging performance, by a tortuous but dull plot, and by leaden direction. One for completists only. NF

Stick, The

(1988, SAf, 90 min)
d Darrell Roodt. *p* Anant Singh. *sc* Darrell Roodt, Carole Shore. *ph* Paul Witte. *ed* David Heitner. *ad* Dave Barkham. *m* Dana Kaproff. *cast* Nicky Rebelo, James Whyle, Frank Opperman, Winston Nishana, Sean Taylor.

● A 'stick' is a small infantry detachment, and this one is used to browbeat the audience into realising that war is futile. No marks for originality of thought, then, nor for that matter for the director, who seems to be paying homage to *Platoon*. A bunch of Boer brutes (including, of course, a drug-crazed maniac) is sent on a search-and-destroy mission 'across the border'. When they encounter a zebra's head in a tree, their black tracker goes all funny, and when a witch doctor is shot all hell breaks loose. The naive voice-over is corny, but the veldt is stunningly photographed, and the action is full of nasty moments. Crude but effective. MS

Sticky Fingers

(1997, US, 97 min)
d Catlin Adams. *p* Catlin Adams, Melanie Mayron. *sc* Catlin Adams, Melanie Mayron. *ph* Gary Thieltges. *ed* Robert Reitano. *pd* Jessica Scott-Justice. *m* Gary Chang. *cast* Helen Slater, Melanie Mayron, Eileen Brennan, Loretta Devine, Christopher Guest, Carol Kane, Stephen McHattie, Danitra Vance, Shirley Stoller, Gwen Welles.

● Red-haired Lolly (Mayron, who co-wrote with Adams) and bleached-blonde Mattie (Slater) dress loudly and needle each other's neuroses. They busk for rent money, but squander it on hash delivered by streetwise dudette Diane (Devine), who leaves a mysterious green bag containing $1 million in their Manhattan pad. Threatened with eviction and then burgled, they're soon dipping into the stashed cash – and for less pressing purposes, like therapeutic shopping. Trouble starts when Diane returns, ruthless hoods on her heels. For the most part, Adams' debut is a lot of fun; she directs with a feel for the state of suspended adolescence induced by flat-sharing, and with an irreverent but affectionate eye for bohemian Manhattan that's supported by some intriguingly eccentric peripheral characters, notably the sublime Brennan's brassy landlady. EP

Sticky Fingers of Time, The

(1996, US, 81 min. col & b/w)
d Hilary Brougher. *p* Isen Robbins, Susan Stover. *sc* Hilary Brougher. *ph* Ethan Mass. *ed* Sabine Hoffmann, Hilary Brougher. *pd* Teresa Mastropierro. *m* Miki Navazio. *cast* Nicole Zaray, Terumi Matthews, Belinda Becker, James Urbaniak, Leo Marks, Samantha Buck.

● This adventurous, amusing no-budget picture uses the prism of time travel to afford a fresh perspective on that tired old standby, the New York relationships drama. It pays off in spades. The witty script bounces '50s attitudes off '90s knowingness (about the Bomb, sexuality, commitment), but the talented cast of unknowns make sure we care about the characters as well as the ideas. Imagine *Walking and Talking* remade by Troma – only it's a lot better than you'd think. TCh

Stiff Upper Lips

(1997, GB, 90 min)
d Gary Sinyor. *p* Jeremy Bolt, Gary Sinyor. *sc* Paul Simpkin, Gary Sinyor. *ph* Simon Archer. *ed* Peter Hollywood. *pd* Mike Grant. *m* David Hughes, John Murphy. *cast* Peter Ustinov, Prunella Scales, Georgina Cates, Samuel West, Sean Pertwee, Brian Glover, Frank Finlay, Kate Harper.

● Sinyor revels in the snooty aristos, the wrinkled retainers, the corseted beauties, the bons mots and buttoned-up passions of BritLit cinema at its most risibly predictable. The story, set in

1908 and divided into 'chapters' introduced by curlicued intertitles, is a nonsensical romance that follows the sentimental education ('I want my sexual awakening and I want it now!') of young Emily (Cates), torn between Lawrentian, well-hung scum-of-the-earth George (Pertwee) and the upper crust suitors favoured by her aunt Agnes (Scales) and halfwit brother Edward (West). As the characters leave Ivory Hall for a rather less than Grand Tour of Tuscany and India, the heat and lust, linens and (portable) lawns, fillies and facial hair take their toll. Frequently silly, consistently spot on, and beautifully acted, this may be obvious, but it's a delight. While the gags, visual and verbal, are precise enough to lampoon the excesses of individual movies, the tone remains affectionate, from the opening salvo against *Chariots of Fire* bombast to Glover's ludicrously servile underling and Ustinov's dotty colonial plantation owner. Spiffing! GA

Stigmata

(1999, US, 102 min)
d Rupert Wainwright. *p* Frank Mancuso Jr. *sc* Tom Lazarus, Rick Ramage. *ph* Jeffrey J Kimball. *ed* Michael R Miller, Michael J Duthie. *pd* Waldemar Kalinowski. *m* Billy Corgan, Elia Cmiral. *cast* Patricia Arquette, Gabriel Byrne, Jonathan Pryce, Nia Long, Enrico Colantoni, Dick Latessa, Thomas Kopache, Ann Cusack, Portia de Rossi.

● Though a self-professed non-believer, Philadelphia hairdresser Frankie (Arquette) suffers visions and stigmata that include bleeding wrists and the illusion of being lashed with a whip. Confronted by this young woman, Vatican investigator Father Andrew Kiernan (Byrne) abandons his scepticism and risks all to protect her – especially after he discovers a tangential link to a secret gospel, possibly a contemporary record of Jesus' own words, that would undermine the worldly authority so jealously guarded by his boss, the devout but devious Cardinal Houseman (Pryce). In a subtler context, the fate of Arquette's confused, frightened victim might have invested the conflict between individual belief and institutional power with a human quality. But her affecting vulnerability is drowned out by a head-banging visual and aural assault that tries to batter us into submission. A full-blooded horror film, perhaps, but a cold-blooded one, too. NF

Still Crazy

(1998, US/GB, 95 min)
d Brian Gibson. *p* Amanda Marmot. *sc* Dick Clement, Ian La Frenais. *ph* Ashley Rowe. *ed* Peter Boyle. *pd* Max Gottlieb. *m* Clive Langer. *cast* Stephen Rea, Billy Connolly, Jimmy Nail, Timothy Spall, Bill Nighy, Juliet Aubrey, Phil Daniels, Frances Barber, Phil Davis.

● It's difficult to convey the deranged insanities of the rock experience: Rob Reiner managed it in *This Is Spinal Tap* and made us laugh. It's even harder to encapsulate that brief time when the crap falls away and group harmony prevails, as Alan Parker did in *The Commitments*. To do both is nearly a miracle; in Brian Gibson's film, with screenplay by comedy survivors Clement and La Frenais (who also scripted Parker's film), a first-rate cast and an assortment of musical talents pull off this race with the amplified devil. Strange Fruit are a late '70s middle league rock outfit seeking to re-form in the nervous late '90s; Robin Hood meets TV's *Auf Wiedersehen Pet* as Nighy's struggling solo artist reunites with Spall's tax-dodging drummer and Nail's bass-playing roofer. Through thin, thin, thin and a bit of thick, the lads try to rekindle the flame, propped up by Juliet Aubrey's long suffering manager and Connolly's Zappa-esque roadie. The jokes are good, the music loud, but what makes the film so special is that it tells you why you ever bought an album or queued for ten hours in the rain to see Alice Cooper. SGr

Stille nach dem Schuss, Die

see Legends of Rita, The

Still Love You After All (Nian Ni Hao Xi)

(1997, HK/Tai, 43 min)
d Stanley Kwan.

● A personal memoir on the state of Hong Kong made during the last months of British rule. While Ann Hui's companion piece (*As Time Goes By*) puts together half a dozen friends around a table, Kwan takes a more idiosyncratic approach, dwelling on his sense of place as an openly gay director, his relationship with his mother, and a recent theatre work (*Journey to the East*). TCh

Still of the Night

(1982, US, 91 min)
d Robert Benton. *p* Arlene Donovan. *sc* Robert Benton. *ph* Nestor Almendros. *ed* Jerry Greenberg, Bill Pankow. *pd* Mel Bourne. *m* John Kander. *cast* Roy Scheider, Meryl Streep, Jessica Tandy, Joe Grifasi, Sara Botsford, Josef Sommer, Rikki Borge.

● A welcome attempt to redevelop the Hitchcock-style thriller form minus violence or supernatural bogeymen. Scheider plays a psychiatrist who falls in love with a woman (Streep) who may have brutally murdered one of his patients. The film is classy enough to be enjoyable, with a few set pieces deliberately resembling such classics as *North by Northwest*, Tourneur's *Cat People*, and others. But Benton's movie is eventually suffocated, perhaps by the gloss of the Manhattan auction world in which it is set. The plotting becomes rushed and implausible, while Streep falls into the breathless clichés of screen neuroses. Worst of all, a narrative which might have broken new ground by adding a feminine dimension, reverts to that most familiar of B feature formats: the psychological sleuth. Indeed, the hero's faith in dream interpretation would have seemed touching even in the '40s. DP

Sting, The

(1973, US, 129 min)
d George Roy Hill. *p* Tony Bill, Michael Phillips, Julia Phillips. *sc* David S Ward. *ph* Robert Surtees. *ed* William H Reynolds. *ad* Henry Bumstead. *m* Scott Joplin. *cast* Paul Newman, Robert Redford, Robert Shaw, Charles Durning, Ray Walston, Eileen Brennan, Harold Gould, John Heffernan, Dana Elcar.

● Hill's follow-up to *Butch Cassidy and the Sundance Kid*, teaming Newman and Redford again, sticks to the same proven box-office formula. The story takes place in 1936 Chicago this time, but the two protagonists remain the same, outlaws who ply their trade as conmen. The film ends up relying on different chapter headings to explain what's going on, but it's all very professional, with fine attention to period detail. All a bit soulless, but at least there's no equivalent of the 'Raindrops Keep Falling on My Head' sequence. All those who liked the earlier film should enjoy this as much. CPe

Sting II, The

(1983, US, 102 min)
d Jeremy Paul Kagan. *p* Jennings Lang. *sc* David S Ward. *ph* Bill Butler. *ed* David Garfield. *pd* Edward C Carfagno. *m* Lalo Schifrin. *cast* Jackie Gleason, Mac Davis, Teri Garr, Karl Malden, Oliver Reed, Bert Remsen.

● Laborious sequel set in 1940 New York, with the victim of the original elaborate con (Robert Shaw, now played by Reed), out for revenge against Paul Newman and Robert Redford (now played by Gleason and Davis), but getting taken all over again. First time round, if you got bored with the endlessly twisting convolutions of the scam, there were compensations in the fancifully nostalgic settings and the host of quirky minor characters. This time you stay bored. TM

Sting of Death, The (Shi no Toge)

(1990, Jap, 115 min)
d Kohei Oguri. *p* Toru Okuyama. *sc* Kohei Oguri. *ph* Shohei Ando. *ed* Nobuo Ogawa. *ad* Yoshinaga Yokoo. *m* Toshio Hosokawa. *cast* Keiki Matsuzaka, Ittoku Kishibe, Takenori Matsumura.

● This lugubrious auteur-piece won a top prize at Cannes (from the same jury that gave its Grand Prix to *Wild at Heart*) – a decision not greeted with universal enthusiasm. It's a weird adaptation of an 'I-novel' by Toshio Shimao about the near break-up of a marriage in the 1950s. Oguri's answer to the problem of dramatising the novel's committed subjectivity is to adopt an oppressive degree of stylisation: lingering static compositions and performances that come from some deeply sedated fog of the mind. Some Japanese critics took it as black comedy, but Oguri's earlier movies (*Muddy River, For Kayako*) don't suggest a very developed sense of humour. TR

Stir

(1980, Aust, 100 min)
d Stephen Wallace. p Richard Brennan. *sc* Bob Jewson. *ph* Geoff Burton. *ed* Henry Dangar. *ad* Lee Whitmore. *m* Cameron Allan. *cast* Bryan Brown, Max Phipps, Dennis Miller, Michael Gow, Phil Motherwell, Gary Waddell.

● The title has it: indicating just what Wallace has done (rather well) with the choicest ingredients of prison-pic precursors from *Riot in Cell Block 11* to *Scum*. Within the common angry blend of casual sadism and communal solidarity, though, the individualised confrontation of reluctant opponents neatly re-emphasises the mutually brutalising effect of a repressive penal system. PT

Stir Crazy

(1980, US, 111 min)
d Sidney Poitier. *p* Hannah Weinstein. *sc* Bruce Jay Friedman. *ph* Fred Schuler. *ed* Harry Keller. *pd* Alfred Sweeney. *m* Tom Scott. *cast* Gene Wilder, Richard Pryor, Georg Stanford Brown, JoBeth Williams, Miguel Angel Suarez, Craig T Nelson.

● Repeating the teaming first aired in *Silver Streak*, Pryor plays a street-sussed cynic, the perfect foil to Wilder's (by now tedious) ingenuous naif. In the first and funniest half, these no-hopers, disenchanted with the Broadway melody, head for Hollywood in seach of…well, it doesn't matter. Halfway there, they get framed for a bank robbery and end up in clink serving a 125-year sentence, where the golden moment occurs (Pryor doing a chicken impersonation in an attempt to 'look ba-a-a-a-d, look mean'). Maybe the disruption caused by Pryor's accident taxed their imaginations, or maybe the slapstick's just too wild; mildly amusing, at best. FL

Stir of Echoes

(1999, US, 99 min)
d David Koepp. *p* Gavin Polone, Judy Hofflund. *sc* David Koepp. *ph* Fred Murphy. *ed* Jill Savitt. *pd* Nelson Coates. *m* James Newton Howard. *cast* Kevin Bacon, Kathryn Erbe, Illeana Douglas, Liza Weil, Kevin Dunn, Conor O'Farrell, Jenny Morrison, Zachary David Cope, Luisa Strus.

● A classy, chilling adaptation of Richard Matheson's 1958 novel which shifts the setting from late '50s California to Chicago in the late '90s. A boy, Jake Witzky (Cope), talks to people who aren't there. But attention soon shifts to his father, Tom (Bacon), who – following an impromptu hypnosis session with his trainee hypno-therapist sister-in-law (Douglas) – is assailed by hallucinations. This fragmentary barrage of supernatural images and sounds includes encounters with a pale young woman – an apparition linked, in Tom's mind at least, to the disappearance, six months before, of a slow-witted neighbourhood girl. Tom withdraws into himself, never leaving the house and obsessing about the mystery that threatens to overwhelm him. His wife Maggie (Erbe) finally loses patience when he digs up the entire garden in the hope of finding the missing girl's body. Grounding the events in tangible blue collar reality, writer/director Koepp contrasts the Witzkys' mundane family life with the terrifying flashes of horror that erupt into it. The skillful shock cuts will make you jump out of your skin, but it's the digital visualisation of the ghostly Samantha which really makes the flesh crawl. NF

Stockade

see Count a Lonely Cadence

Stolen Children, The (Il Ladro di bambini)

(1992, It, 110 min)
d Gianni Amelio. *p* Angelo Rizzoli, Stefano Munaf. *sc* Gianni Amelio, Sandro Petraglia, Stefano Rulli. *ph* Tonino Nardi, Renato Tafuri. *ed* Simona Paggi. *ad* Andrea Crisanti. *m* Franco Piersanti. *cast* Enrico Lo Verso, Valentina Scalici, Giuseppe Iaercitano.

● What is it about Italian neo-realists, even in this day and age, which drives them to film their view of the corruptions of society through the eyes of a child? Sentimentality, perhaps. Amelio's film, at any rate, soon falls foul of maudlin worthiness as it recounts the tale of two kids – the 11-year old girl (Scalici) a prostitute – taken away from their mother and entrusted to a cop (Lo

Verso). As he escorts them from Milan to Sicily after an orphanage in Rome refuses to accept the girl, the pair gradually come to love and be loved by their reluctant guardian. Decently acted, but alarmingly bereft of originality or analytical insights, it's a well-meaning dirge of a movie. GA

Stolen Hearts

see Two if by Sea

Stolen Hours

(1963, GB, 97 min)
d Daniel Petrie. *p* Denis Holt. *sc* Jessamyn West. *ph* Harry Waxman. *ed* Geoffrey Foote. *pd* Wilfred Shingleton. *m* Mort Lindsey. *cast* Susan Hayward, Michael Craig, Diane Baker, Edward Judd, Paul Rogers, Jerry Desmonde, Victor Spinetti, Chet Baker.

● Chet Baker, behind blackest shades, blows his horn in a Home Counties mansion, where Susan Hayward jives with old super-stooge Jerry Desmonde. Other memorable incongruities include a full-blown Hayward tirade in the middle of Portobello Road and her epiphany in a Cornish village, following victory in the egg-and-spoon race. This is the pre-war Bette Davis weepie *Dark Victory*, altered round the edges but with the same hook: a year to live, snatched happiness, all that. Petrie tries sternly to keep campiness at bay, but the whole enterprise is as doomed as its heroine. Slightly cherishable, though, thanks to Hayward's lightning flashes of temperament and her touchingly unconvincing simulation of vulnerability. BBa

Stolen Kisses

see Baisers Volés

Stolen Life, A

(1946, US, 107 min, b/w)
d Curtis Bernhardt. *p* Bette Davis. *sc* Catherine Turney, Margaret Buell Wilder. *ph* Sol Polito, Ernest Haller. *ed* Rudi Fehr. *ad* Robert M Haas. *m* Max Steiner. *cast* Bette Davis, Glenn Ford, Dane Clark, Walter Brennan, Charles Ruggles, Bruce Bennett.

● Bette Davis' first film as producer for Warners, a remake of a 1938 British vehicle for Elisabeth Bergner, also offered her the first chance to play the double role of identical twins she was to repeat in 1964 in Paul Henreid's *Dead Ringer*. Here her split-screen performance lasts only until good sister Kate falls victim to bad sister Pat's murderous jealousy over Glenn Ford, but Bernhardt encourages her to glorious melodramatic excess as she subsequently plays wolf in sheep's clothing, stealing Kate's identity. The cod psychology of doubling and splitting had by now infiltrated the Hollywood public domain with a vengeance: Bernhardt's next film saw him directing Joan Crawford as a schizophrenic in *Possessed*. PT

Stone

(1974, Aust, 103 min)
d Sandy Harbutt. *p* Sandy Harbutt. *sc* Sandy Harbutt, Michael Robinson. *ph* Graham Lind. *ed* Ian Barry. *pd* Sandy Harbutt. *m* Billy Green. *cast* Ken Shorter, Sandy Harbutt, Helen Morse, Hugh Keays-Byrne, Vincent Gil, Bindi Williams.

● Eight years after its Australian debut, *Stone* was wheeled onto the British circuits by distributors clearly chasing the audience that made the *Mad Max* cycle so successful. But any comparison with those films – or its true American ancestor *Wild Angels* – reveals that this is strictly a moped of a movie. To be fair, L plates are on display: it's a first feature for director Harbutt, who also produced, co-stars, and co-scripted. Stone himself (Shorter) is an undercover cop who infiltrates a gang of bikers known as The Undertakers (they bury their dead standing up 'so they won't have to take anything lying down'). His cover eloquently blown – 'This cat's a pig, man' – Stone ingratiates himself by riding a mean machine. Much footage of bikers abusing less than picturesque locals – cadging ciggies, stealing sauce-bottles, and so on – follows until suddenly it's all over. Like its hero's 'Levi originals', *Stone* badly needs the piss taken out of it. PK

Stone Boy, The

(1984, US, 93 min)
d Christopher Cain. *p* Joe Roth, Ivan Bloch. *sc* Gina Berriault. *ph* Juan Ruiz-Anchia. *ed* Paul Rubell. *pd* Joseph G Pacelli. *m* James Horner. *cast* Robert Duvall, Jason Presson, Glenn Close, Frederic Forrest, Wilford Brimley, Cindy Fisher.

● Another quietly good film from Robert Duvall, sharing a similar emotional appeal to *Tender Mercies*. A young boy is killed in a shooting accident, and his nine-year-old brother is traumatised by the feeling of guilt and lack of emotional response from his family, who are cracking up all around him. The sense of stoicism from these Midwestern farm people is very well conveyed; as are some magic scenes between the boy and his grandfather, played by Wilford Brimley. CPea

Stone Cold

(1991, US, 92 min)
d Craig R Baxley. *p* Yoram Ben-Ami. *sc* Walter Doniger. *ph* Alexander Gruszynski. *ed* Mark Helfrich, Larry Bock, Edward A Warschilka Jr. *pd* John Mansbridge. *m* Sylvester LeVay. *cast* Brian Bosworth, Lance Henriksen, William Forsythe, Arabella Holzbog, Sam McMurray, Richard Gant, David Tress.

● Way down in Mississippi, a group of outlaw bikers is all revved up, performing William Tell acts with cans of beer while one bald, mean dare-devil blasts priests from their pulpits. Uncovering the Brotherhood's plans to join forces with the Mafia, the FBI recruits suspended cop Joe Huff (ex-American football star Bosworth in his debut); a maverick with anti-social tendencies and a sterling record in 'biker-related arrests', he goes undercover to infiltrate the Brotherhood. The first ten minutes offer rampaging bikers and Bosworth laying waste to armed thugs, with the remaining running-time spent on variations of the same. Stuntman turned director Baxley piles on the corpses, punch-ups and exploding cars with the passion of a pro in this formulaic action fodder. Henriksen, as the maniacal lead biker, steals the movie from under Bosworth's nose. CM

Stone Killer, The

(1973, US, 96 min)
d/p Michael Winner. *sc* Gerald Wilson. *ph* Richard Moore. *ed* Frederick Wilson. *ad* Ward Preston. *m* Roy Budd. *cast* Charles Bronson, Martin Balsam, Ralph Waite, David Sheiner, Norman Fell, Eddie Firestone, Paul Koslo.

● Do we need yet another lone cop movie? This time it's Bronson uncovering an underworld plot to take over part of the Mafia. Winner manages to make Bronson look dull even by his standards (which is some feat), and resorts to formula car chases (which he handles with more flair than he does actors). There's a picture of America that occasionally phases into near fantasy, and one or two nice moments: like the ex-Vietnam soldiers brought in to execute the coup, and the ending where the Mafia leader, with a lot of blood on his hands, confesses a string of venial sins to his priest. A serviceable thriller, but a few weeks later you won't be able to remember a thing about it.

Stoner (Tiejin Gang Da Po Zi Yang Guan)

(1974, HK, 105 min)
d Huang Feng. *p* Raymond Chow. *sc* I Kuang, Huang Feng. *ph* Li Yu-Tang. *ed* Chang Yao-Chung, Michael Kaye. *ad* Chin Chin-Shan. *m* Tony Orchez, Li Shao-Hua. *cast* George Lazenby, Angela Mao, Betty Ting Pei, Wong In-Sik, Joji Takagi.

● Dreadful martial arts potboiler in which an Australian cop goes after a Hong Kong drugs ring when his girlfriend dies from an overdose in Sydney. Charming policewoman Angela Mao does her best to make one forget the inanities of this cobbled-together revenge plot by pounding the opposition in her best athletic form. George ('Deadlier than Bond') Lazenby is the poker-faced Aussie cop who gets driven sex-mad by a new drug being pushed by the ring. JPy

Stonewall

(1995, GB, 99 min)
d Nigel Finch. *p* Christine Vachon. *sc* Rikki Beadle Blair. *ph* Chris Seager. *ed* John Richards. *pd* Thérèse DePrez. *m* Michael Kamen. *cast* Guillermo Diaz, Frederick Weller, Brendan Corbalis, Duane Boutté, Bruce MacVittie, Peter Ratray, Dwight Ewell.

● Director Nigel Finch of BBC TV's 'Arena' series (who died of AIDS during editing) and New York independent producer Christine Vachon (*Swoon, Go Fish*) only partly succeeded in constructing a dramatic narrative around a legendary moment in the history of gay liberation, the 1969 riot outside the Stonewall Inn, Greenwich Village. The intersecting lives of drag queen LaMiranda, peachy-keen new boy Matty Dean, cross-dressing bartender Bostonia, and repressed bar-owner Skinny Vinnie were intended to cohere into an emotionally compelling whole. That this never quite happens is partly down to the ensemble (only MacVittie's Vinnie really makes us feel for him), partly a by-product of a tight budget and zero access to key locations (notably the Stonewall Inn itself). More significant, however, is the unresolved tension between the flashy, trashy side of the movie, which flaunts its all-conquering drag artistes to effect, and the documentary side which turns up all manner of uncomfortable details about the conditions gay men and women had to endure not that long ago. TJ

Stone Years (Petrina Chronia)

(1985, Greece, 142 min)
d/p/sc Pantelis Voulgaris. *ph* Yorgos Arvanitis. *ed* Andreas Andreadakis. *ad* Julia Stavridou. *m* Stamatis Spanoudakis. *cast* Themis Bazaka, Dimitris Katalifos, Maria Martika, Irene Iglesi, Nikos Birbilis. Ilias Katevas, Thanos Grammenos.

● One of the originators of the New Greek Cinema, Voulgaris tackles the post-civil war 'Stone Years' (1954 to '74), of the right wing Karamanlis and Colonels' junta, by elaborating the torn relationship of provincial leftists Babis (Bazaka) and Eleni (Martika). The former is imprisoned for pamphleteering, the latter is an aspirant doctor forced into hiding while, ridiculously, her reputation is developed as a notorious Mata Hari. For the normally objective and subtly ironic Voulgaris, this comes close to an angry and condemnatory work. At pains to emphasise the couple's dignity, stoicism and romantic commitment, which survives being together only 40 hours in 15 years, he nevertheless ends the film with a plaintive, accusatory stare at camera. WH

Stoolie, The

(1972, US, 88 min)
d John G Avildsen. *p* Chase Mellen III. *sc* Eugene Price, Larry Alexander, Marc B Ray. *ph* Ralf D Bode. *ed* Jerry Greenberg, Stanley Rochner. *ad* Charles Bailey. *m* William Goldstein. *cast* Jackie Mason, Marcia Jean Kurtz, Dan Frazer, Richard Carballo, Lee Steele, William McCutcheon, Anne Marie.

● Financed by nightclub comedian Mason, completed by George Silano (it was shot in sequence) when Avildsen left to start *Save the Tiger*, this wry look at society's margins and its realities is quite a charmer in its modest way. Mason plays a small-time drug-pusher and police informer who absconds to Miami with police funds after coming face-to-face with the bleak future that awaits him. Frazer is the police officer blamed for the loss, who hounds him but (a little predictably) comes to view life from the other side of the fence, and Kurtz the lonely secretary who brings a fumbling hint of romance to his life. A touch of *Marty* here (although the film is really more like *Midnight Cowboy* without the pretensions), but whenever sentimentality threatens to raise its head, it is kept firmly at bay by the quirkish characters, the marvellously offbeat locations, and the gently mocking humour that reigns throughout. TM

Stop Making Sense

(1984, US, 88 min)
d Jonathan Demme. *p* Gary Goetzman. *ph* Jordan Cronenweth. *ed* Lisa Day. *pd* Jeffrey Beecroft. *with* Talking Heads.

● A documentary record of Talking Heads in concert, using material from three shows in Hollywood, December '83. Apart from what artifice the Heads themselves allow on stage, Demme restricts himself to a cool, almost classic style, with the camera subservient to the action. Building from David Byrne performing a solo acoustic 'Psycho Killer', to the full nine-piece leaping through 'Take Me to the Water', its distinction is more what it omits than what it includes. Tacky rock theatre razzle is stripped down to humorously 'minimal' conceits of staging, lighting and presentation. Apart from a few moments of incongruous boogieing, the allegedly over-intellectual Heads are revealed to be human, warm-hearted, and possessed of a sizeable humour. A quietly large achievement. JG

Stop! or My Mom Will Shoot

(1992, US, 95 min)
d Roger Spottiswoode. *p* Ivan Reitman, Joe Wizan, Michael C Gross, Todd Black, Joe Medjuck. *sc* William Davies, Blake Snyder, William Osborne. *ph* Frank Tidy. *ed* Mark Conte. *pd* Charles Rosen. *m* Alan Silvestri. *cast* Sylvester Stallone, Estelle Getty, JoBeth Williams, Roger Rees, Martin Ferrero, Gailard Sartain, Dennis Burkley, John Wesley.
●Stallone plays LA cop Joe Bomowski, confirmed slob, who finds his life disrupted when his bossy mom Tutti (Getty) comes to visit: she regales strangers with baby stories, does housework at 3am, and interferes in his romance (with JoBeth Williams). After witnessing a murder, Tutti becomes embroiled in the subsequent investigation, dispensing wisecracks and threatening the villain (Rees) with a good spanking. Most of the blame for this unimaginative effort can be attributed to the script, but Spottiswoode's flat direction doesn't help. He seems to have given up on his actors: Stallone merely goes through the motions, while Getty suffers when deprived of the ensemble playing and sharper writing offered on TV's *The Golden Girls*. CM

Storia di una Capinera

see Sparrow

Stories from a Flying Trunk

(1979, GB, 88 min)
d Christine Edzard. *p* John Brabourne, Richard Goodwin. *sc* Christine Edzard. *ph* Robin Browne, Brian West. *ed* Rex Pyke, MJ Knatchbull, Irene Groudinsky. *m* Gioacchino Rossini. *cast* Murray Melvin, Ann Firbank, Tasneem Maqsood, John Tordoff, John Dalby, Johanna Sonnex.
●Why does the idea persist that Hans Andersen's stories should still be enjoyed by children? These three tales are preciously middlebrow in appeal: a combination of choreography, live-action and stop-frame animation, contemporary in setting but frankly Victorian in spirit. A fey and sinister Andersen (Melvin) introduces sickly little episodes in which death and gloom are never far away. For example, in the middle episode, a poor Asian girl from Dickensian East End slums meets a crazed tramp who sends her up West, where she dies after imagining that she has seen the Queen (!). CPe

Stories of the Kronen (Historias del Kronen)

(1995, Sp, 95 min)
d Montxo Armendariz. *p* Elias Querejeta. *sc* Montxo Armendariz. *ph* Alfredo Mayo. *ad* Julio Esteban. *cast* Juan Diego Botto, Jordi Molla, Nuria Prims, Aitor Merino.
●The Kronen being the club where 21-year-old Carlos (Botto) and his cronies go, night after night, to dance, get blasted, find a partner and generally do what bored, hedonistic middle-class kids do. Only Carlos is a little more hedonistic, bored, selfish, vain and irresponsible than the rest, so – this being a movie – a comeuppance is in the offing. Hackneyed, obvious and strangely dated, Armendariz' hyper-agitated film tells us nothing about flaming youth that we haven't heard many times before, and does so in such a relentless, repetitive way that its characters soon become irritating rather than figures we'd like to try and understand. Charmless stuff. GA

Stork

(1971, Aust, 90 min)
d/p Tim Burstall. *sc* David Williamson. *ph* Robin Copping. *ed* Edward McQueen-Mason. *ad* Leslie Binns. *m* Hans Poulsen. *cast* Bruce Spence, Graham Blundell, Sean McEuan, Helmut Bakaitis, Jacki Weaver, Peter Green.
●Stork is the nickname of a 6 foot 7 inch Walter Mitty with revolutionary leanings, who quits his secure job with General Motors to opt out in a flat full of frowning, culturally-aspiring colleagues. At the heart of Stork's freak behaviour, sick practical jokes, and constant fantasising, a vast timidity with women unfortunately lies. *Stork* is in fact more *Adventures of Barry McKenzie*; and if you were able to wheeze and giggle your way through that, you'll probably do the same with this totally appalling mess of dismal Aussie gags about beer and chundering.

Storm Center

(1956, US, 85 min, b/w)
d Daniel Taradash. *p* Julian Blaustein. *sc* Daniel Taradash, Elick Moll. *ph* Burnett Guffey. *ed* William A Lyon. *ad* Cary Odell. *m* George Duning. *cast* Bette Davis, Brian Keith, Kim Hunter, Paul Kelly, Joe Mantell.
●The first explicitly anti-McCarthyite Hollywood movie, *Storm Center* took five years to reach the screen. Davis plays a small-town librarian who refuses, on principle, to remove a book called 'The Communist Dream' from the shelves when the local council deems it subversive. Her stand is undermined by a political opportunist (Keith) who plays on the citizens' intrinsic suspicion of intellectuals and anything remotely pinko. The only film directed by Taradash (who scripted *From Here to Eternity* and *Rancho Notorious*), it is, sadly, a didactic, laborious piece, making far too much play with a confused small boy driven from an eager exploration of books into angry arson on the library. Played with some conviction by Davis, though. TCh

Storm Over Asia (Potomok Chingis-Khan)

(1928, USSR, 102 min, b/w)
d Vsevolod Pudovkin. *sc* Osip Brik. *ph* AN Golovnya. *ad* Sergei Kozlovsky, N Aaronson. *cast* Valeri Inkishinov, I Inkishinov, A Chistyakov, A Dedintsev, Anna Sudakevich, K Gurnyak, Boris Barnet, V Tzoppi, V Ivanov, Vladimir Pro, Paulina Belinskaya.
●Made immediately after the completion of *The End of St Petersburg*, Pudovkin's semi-ethnographic, semi-polemical epic about a Mongol uprising against British occupiers during the post-revolutionary civil war makes a striking, but for all that slightly naive fable. Adapted from a Novokshenov novel, the story has a young Mongol herdsman falling out with a scurrilous colonial fur trader and falling in with partisan fighters. When he's captured by the Brits, they take him for a descendant of Genghis Khan and mistakenly install him as a puppet ruler. Pudovkin's satire is notably subtler than Eisenstein's – he extracts some lovely comedy from the imperial elite and Buddhist religious authorities exchanging ritual pleasantries in front of a new-born Lama – and the storytelling and low key characterisation are certainly engaging. It's just that Pudovkin's strict, building block editing, proficient as it is, tends to cramp the film's flow and suggestive space. NB

Stormriders, The (Feng Yun Xiongba Tianxia)

(1998, HK, 127 min)
d Andrew Lau. *p* Lee Chuk-On, Manfred Wong. *sc* Manfred Wong. *ph* Andrew Lau. *ed* Mak Chi-Sin, Pang Fat. *pd* Cyrus Ho. *m* Comfort Chan. *cast* Ekin Cheng, Aaron Kwok, Shinichi 'Sonny' Chiba, Kirsty Yeung, Shu Qi, Michael Tse, Lai Yiu-Cheung.
●The team behind the *Young and Dangerous* series adapt another bestselling comic (the *Fengyun* storyline from Ma Wing-Shing's *Tianxia*) with the aid of some variable digital effects. Lord Conquer, advised by the Mud Buddha that he will achieve global dominion only with two disciples at his side, murders the fathers of Wind (Cheng) and Cloud (Kwok, with a fetching blue-tint hairdo) to bring the boys into his clan. After ten years of routine martial-arts-fiction exploits, our heroes learn the awful truth and turn against their master. Glad to be generic, the film is vastly indebted to Tsui Hark for everything from the swordsmithy opening (*The Blade*) to the protracted aerial swordfights and cod-mythic trappings (*Zu*). TR

Storm Within, The

see Parents Terribles, Les

Stormy Monday

(1987, GB, 93 min)
d Mike Figgis. *p* Nigel Stafford-Clark. *sc* Mike Figgis. *ph* Roger Deakins. *ed* David Martin. *pd* Andrew McAlpine. *m* Mike Figgis. *cast* Melanie Griffith, Tommy Lee Jones, Sting, Sean Bean, James Cosmo, Mark Long, Brian Lewis.
●Mix American gangsters, molls and majorettes with Polish avant-garde jazz musicians against a Newcastle background – and what you've got is a curious homage to B movie Hollywood and the rain-washed neon of the pulps. The plot stammers a bit trying to sustain these exotic transplants in Geordieland – it's America week – and generally sacrifices believability for the flourish, but it's an endearingly personal enterprise. At its oddest, the Cracow Jazz Ensemble plays a whinnyingly discordant 'Star Spangled Banner' to Newcastle councillors; at its most violent, enforcers descend upon jazz club owner Sting with a blowtorch, but find they've bitten off more than they can chew. Night-town drifter (Bean) falls in love with American waitress (Griffith), who is struggling to ditch her old life as a hostess in the employ of a vicious businessman (Jones) with plans to muscle in on the city. All these strands are brought together in a fireball conclusion that owes everything to life learned from the screen, tilts at tragedy, but racks up merely moody bad luck. On the credit side, Roger Deakins' camerawork is ravishing, Don Weller takes a solo, and Sting shows he hasn't forgotten his old accent or instrument. BC

Stormy Waters

see Remorques

Stormy Weather

(1943, US, 77 min, b/w)
d Andrew L Stone. *p* William LeBaron. *sc* Fred Jackson, Ted Koehler. *ph* Leon Shamroy. *ed* James B Clark. *ad* James Basevi, Joseph C Wright. *m* Emil Newman. *cast* Lena Horne, Bill Bojangles Robinson, Cab Calloway, Fats Waller, Dooley Wilson, Ada Brown, Katherine Dunham.
●Fox's all-black musical answer to MGM's *Cabin in the Sky*. No Minnelli this time, so no contest, especially as the wispy plot – one of those up-down romances that span 25 years – serves chiefly to string together a revue collection of items matching the various periods. With those stars let loose on classic songs, and the Nicholas Brothers providing a stunning tap dancing finale, who's complaining? Often quite imaginatively staged, the numbers are strikingly well shot by Leon Shamroy. TM

Story of a Cheat, The

see Roman d'un Tricheur, Le

Story of Adèle H., The (L'Histoire d'Adèle H.)

(1975, Fr, 98 min)
d François Truffaut. *p* Marcel Berbert, Claude Miller. *sc* François Truffaut, Jean Gruault, Suzanne Schiffman. *ph* Nestor Almendros. *ed* Yann Dedet. *ad* Jean-Pierre Kohut-Svelko. *m* Maurice Jaubert. *cast* Isabelle Adjani, Bruce Robinson, Sylvia Marriott, Joseph Blatchley, Reubin Dorey, François Truffaut.
●Truffaut's film follows the course of Adèle Hugo (Adjani), the daughter of Victor Hugo, as she travels from Guernsey to Nova Scotia, and finally to Barbados, in search of a man who clearly doesn't love her. The film is a disaster because, in place of the self-conscious reflection of her predicament conveyed by Adèle's journal (on which the film is based), Truffaut opts for the Hollywood formula of hapless unrequited love. The result is a movie that centres on a woman's weakness, rather than on the strength necessary to put into practice her considered decisions. PH

Story of GI Joe, The

(1945, US, 109 min, b/w)
d William Wellman. *p* Lester Cowan. *sc* Leopold Atlas, Guy Endore, Philip Stevenson. *ph* Russell Metty. *ed* Otto Lovering, Albrecht Joseph. *ad* James Sullivan, David Hall. *m* Ann Ronell, Louis Applebaum. *cast* Burgess Meredith, Robert Mitchum, Freddie Steele, Wally Cassell, Jimmy Lloyd, Jack Reilly.
●Not so very different in mood from *The Big Red One*, Wellman's film about the WWII Italian campaign not surprisingly won Sam Fuller's nod of approval for 'its feeling of death and mass murder'. Based on the front-line dispatches of war correspondent Ernie Pyle, this is not a film about flag-waving or heroism. Shot almost documentary style, with deliberately sketchy characterisation of individual soldiers (though Mitchum

makes a powerful impression), it presents what is very much an infantryman's view of war as a meaningless vista of mud, muddle and fatigue, ending very probably in a wooden cross. Its masterstroke is to use Pyle himself (beautifully played by Meredith) as the omnipresent eyes and ears of the film, stuggling to fathom the mystery of the ordinary soldier ('This was their baptism of fire; it was chaos… each boy facing the worst moment of his life, alone') and to find the words to explain it to the folks back home. His homely dispatches may fringe sentimentality at times, but Wellman's images magnificently capture their compassion for the GI 'who lives so miserably, dies so miserably'. TM

Story of Gilbert and Sullivan, The (aka The Great Gilbert and Sullivan)

(1953, GB, 109 min)
d Sidney Gilliat. *p* Frank Launder, Sidney Gilliat. *sc* Sidney Gilliat, Leslie Baily. *ph* Christopher Challis. *ed* Gerald Turney-Smith. *pd* Hein Heckroth. *m* Arthur Sullivan. *cast* Robert Morley, Maurice Evans, Peter Finch, Eileen Herlie, Martyn Green, Dinah Sheridan, Isabel Dean, Wilfrid Hyde-White.

● Despite the importance of Gilbert and Sullivan as an English institution, the lives of two such solidly respectable Victorians offer little in the way of dramatic excitement. Fortunately Launder and Gilliat are able to burrow deep into their scriptwriting past, coming up with a whole galaxy of tricks and devices to fill out the flimsy narrative and overcome the obstacle of obligatory slabs of operetta, producing a chocolate-box extravaganza where less hardy professionals would have made a celebratory mess. They're helped by some splendid performances, particularly from Morley, amazingly effective as Gilbert once he's able to channel his exuberant eccentricity into pathos rather than caricature. RMy

Story of O, The (Histoire d'O/ Geschichte der O)

(1975, Fr/Ger, 95 min)
d Just Jaeckin. *p* Gérard Lorin, Eric Rochat. *sc* Sébastien Japrisot. *ph* Robert Fraisse. *ed* Francine Pierre. *ad* Baptiste Poirot. *m* Pierre Bachelet. *cast* Corinne Cléry, Udo Kier, Anthony Steel, Jean Gaven, Christiane Minazzoli, Martine Kelly, Jean-Pierre Andréani.

● For those who enjoy kitsch, Just (*Emmanuelle*) Jaeckin's adaptation of Pauline Réage's S&M novel is a must. There's puffy, blank-faced O (Cléry) with cruel lover René, (Kier), the one with the husky eyes and 'I'm an arsehole' hairdo. So far, so risible. But then the film gets a story. It's Sir Stephen (Steel) who does it, the older man who brands O's bottom with his own initials. She suddenly seems madder, but not in a photogenic, wild child way; what she comes to resemble most is a raging bourgeois housewife, a role she's been prepared for from childhood. Having lived the modern life, complete with her own apartment and *Vogue* photoshoots, O gravitates towards a house with servants and lacy tablecloths and realises her taste for them. Thus, when she finally turns the tables on Sir Stephen it doesn't feel like a coda tacked on to appease feminists: she's just discovered what it means to be adult, and her attendant sensations rush over us too. As anyone who's seen *Romance* will know, the film has obviously been influential – but not enough so. Stanley Kubrick borrowed the visuals – the ornate face masks and the cloaks – but his orgy slaves were pure Barbara Cartland. *The Story of O* disturbs precisely because it takes us through the dumb mask, to the damaged, unpredictable human brain beneath. CO'Su

Story of Qiu Ju, The (Qiu Ju da Guansi)

(1992, China/HK, 100 min)
d Zhang Yimou. *p* Feng Yitang. *sc* Liu Heng. *ph* Chi Xiaoning, Yu Xiaoqun, Lu Hongyi. *ed* Du Yuan. *ad* Cao Jiuping. *m* Zhao Jiping. *cast* Gong Li, Lei Laosheng, Ge Zhijun, Liu Peiqi, Yang Liuchun.

● Zhang and his constant muse Gong Li reinvent themselves (and Chinese social-realist cinema in the process) with this docu-drama about a peasant woman's dogged fight for what she thinks is justice. Qiu Ju is furious when the chief of her village refuses to apologise for kicking her husband in the balls during a fight, and takes the matter to court to demand compensation; the film charts her stubborn climb up the legal hierarchy. The plot seems expressly designed to placate the bureaucrats who banned Zhang's two previous films in China, but the quasi-documentary approach (involving scores of non-professional actors, hidden cameras and radio mikes) is brilliantly finessed. TR

Story of Sin, The (Dzieje Grzechu)

(1975, Pol, 128 min)
d/sc Walerian Borowczyk. *ph* Zygmuny Samosiuk. *ed* Lidia Pacewicz. *ad* Teresa Barska. *m* Felix Mendelssohn. *cast* Grazyna Dlugolecka, Jerzy Zelnik, Olgierd Lukaszewicz, Roman Wilhelmi.

● Like Borowczyk's earlier *Blanche*, this traces the misfortunes that befall an erotic innocent when she tries for love in a world dedicated to repressing or exploiting it. The source here is a turn-of-the-century Polish novel, and Borowczyk films it (with absolute period fidelity) as a full-blooded melodrama, carrying his audience off on swings of emotion, alternately rapturous and harrowing. At the same time, though, he invests it with countless reminders of his own background as the most idiosyncratic of contemporary surrealists: by bringing décor and design to the same prominence throughout as the physical action (incidentally 'eroticising' many of the objects that appear), and by framing the story of Eva's *amour fou* with precise descriptions of the religious, moral and economic factors that conspire to thwart it. His control of everything from his attractive cast to his speed-of-thought editing is unassailable. The result is passionately intense, and extremely entertaining. TR

Story of the Late Chrysanthemums, The (Zangiku Monogatari)

(1939, Jap, 143 min, b/w)
d Kenji Mizoguchi. *p* Nobutaro Shirai. *sc* Yoshikata Yoda. *ph* Minoru Miki, Yozo Fuji. *ed* Koshi Kawahigashi. *ad* Hiroshi Mizutani. *m* Senji Ito, Shiro Fukai. *cast* Shotaro Hanayagi, Kakuko Mori, Kokichi Takada, Gonjuro Kawarazaki, Yoko Umemura.

● Bristling with passion, Mizoguchi's film is a true find: a heartbreaker to end them all. Tokyo, 1885: a Kabuki actor of little self-awareness offends his famous father and transgresses tradition by insisting on his love for his brother's nurse. Trapped by the father's refusal to countenance the affair, dragged together into ignominy, she realises that only through her self-sacrifice can her love reclaim his familial glory. As the plot twists inexorably round their doomed affair, it says much more by showing less: an eloquently long tracking shot can follow remarkably understated scenes of intense emotion so that tears flow as if by magic. Unashamed sentimentality and anger controlled by extreme formal precision justify its reputation as the peak of Mizoguchi's film-making. DMacp

Story of Us, The

(1999, US, 96 min)
d Rob Reiner. *p* Rob Reiner, Jessie Nelson, Alan Zweibel. *sc* Alan Zweibel, Jessie Nelson. *ph* Michael Chapman. *ed* Robert Leighton, Alan Edward Bell. *pd* Lilly Kilvert. *m* Eric Clapton. *cast* Michelle Pfeiffer, Bruce Willis, Rita Wilson, Julie Hagerty, Paul Reiser, Tim Matheson, Red Buttons, Rob Reiner.

● Reiner's sour romantic comedy offers little interest, fun or insight as it anatomises a failing marriage. Katie (Pfeiffer) and Ben (Willis) have been married for 15 years, warring for the last five, and reduced to playacting the perfect couple at the breakfast table for the benefit of their offspring, Erin and Josh. Ben, a comedy writer, is the dreamer, the funster; Katie is the 'designated driver' of their relationship. Tired of endless slanging matches and unimpressed with the counsel of distracting or distracted marriage advisors, they opt for separation while their kids go off to summer camp. Beware of movies with straight-to-camera confessions. Time has steadily coarsened Reiner's once sure touch for frantic comedy, and although he neutralises the more sentimental elements of Alan Zweibel and Jessie Nelson's banal screenplay, his failure to flesh out or evoke sympathy for either character reduces the movie to an unedifying slanging match. WH

Story of Vernon and Irene Castle, The

(1939, US, 90 min, b/w)
d HC Potter. *p* George Haight, Pandro S Berman. *sc* Richard Sherman, Oscar Hammerstein II, Dorothy Yost. *ph* Robert de Grasse. *ed* William Hamilton. *ad* Van Nest Polglase. *songs* Con Conrad, Bert Kalmar, Harry Ruby, others. *cast* Fred Astaire, Ginger Rogers, Edna May Oliver, Walter Brennan, Lew Fields, Etienne Girardot, Donald MacBride.

● Fred and Ginger's last partnership (until their reunion in 1949 with *The Barkleys of Broadway*) was a nostalgic biopic about a famous ballroom couple from World War I days whose career was cut short by an air accident. Ably welding dance numbers and plot, courtesy of light comedy director Potter, it overcomes its lack of '30s snap and crackle with lavish doses of elegance and charm to a tango or foxtrot rhythm. DMacp

Story of Women, A (San ge Nüren)

(1988, China, 90 min)
d Peng Xiaolian. *sc* Xiao Mao. *ph* Liu Lihua. *ed* Shen Zhuanti. *pd* Zhou Xinren. *m* Yang Mao. *cast* Zhang Wen Rong, Zhang Min, Shong Ru Hui.

● A road movie from one of the few women directors of China's 'Fifth Generation' (Peng's subsequent film was halted in mid-production, and she moved to New York). Three peasant women from a village near the Great Wall decide to earn some money by taking their spun and dyed yarn to the free markets in the cities; they travel first to Beijing, and then much further south to Chongqing. Their journey embodies a panorama of women's lives in present-day China, taking in everything from the weight of patriarchal traditions to the issue of enforced abortions. Peng achieves a convincing level of naturalism and keeps melodrama at bay. TR

Story of Woo Viet, The (Hu Yue de Gushi)

(1981, HK, 92 min)
d Ann Hui. *cast* Chow Yun-Fat, Cora Miao, Cherie Chung, Lo Lieh.

● Rooted in Hui's research into real-life 'boat people' refugees from Vietnam, her third feature is essentially a doomed *noir* romance which incorporates – as Hong Kong movies do – everything from action thriller shoot-outs to a transvestite hooker and a dwarf cabaret troupe. The charismatic Chow Yun-Fat plays a Vietnamese-Chinese refugee who's trying to smuggle himself from Hong Kong to the US when he gets stuck in Manila and enmeshed in its vice; Lo Lieh (fondly remembered as the hero of kung-fu movies like *King Boxer*) is memorable as an ageing Chinese roué who's been marooned there for years. TR

Storytelling

(2001, US, 87 min)
d Todd Solondz. *p* Ted Hope, Christine Vachon. *sc* Todd Solondz. *ph* Frederick Elmes. *ed* Alan Oxman. *pd* James Chinlund. *m* Belle & Sebastian, Nathan Larson. *cast* ('Fiction') Selma Blair, Robert Wisdom; ('Nonfiction') Paul Giamatti, John Goodman, Lupe Ontiveros, Jonathan Osser, Mark Webber.

● Two typically dystopian tales (rumour has it a third was dropped): the shorter 'Fiction' concerns college kids in a creative writing class taught by a black Pulitzer Prize-winner who holds back neither from trashing their efforts, nor from seducing his students; 'Nonfiction' sees a nerdy loser attempt to get ahead by making a documentary about his former high school, focusing on the dim, TV- obsessed, terminal slacker son of a risibly straitlaced family. Cruelty, misery, stupidity and loneliness are the common currency, but the impression of déjà vu is compounded by the fact that the film's seldom as funny, moving or insightful as Solondz's earlier work, while hints of self-justification add to the air of misanthropic self-pity. Audacious, intriguing, peppered with good moments, but disappointing. GA

Storyville

(1992, US, 113 min)
d Mark Frost. *p* David Roe, Edward R Pressman. *sc* Mark Frost, Lee Reynolds. *ph* Ron Garcia. *ed* BJ Sears. *pd* Richard Hoover. *m* Carter Burwell. *cast* James Spader, Joanne Whalley-Kilmer, Jason Robards, Charlotte Lewis, Woody Strode, Piper Laurie.
●Mark Frost's ambitious directorial debut is an oedipal thriller – Greek tragedy by way of *Chinatown* – in which the sins of the father have political, social and environmental ramifications. Even so, this flat transposition of an Australian novel (*Juryman* by Frank Galbally and Robert Macklin) will disappoint admirers of Frost's scripts for *Twin Peaks* and *Hill Street Blues*. Cray Fowler (Spader), scion of a Louisiana dynasty, is expected to assume the family seat in Congress. Unaware that one should never dally with cocktail waitresses during an election campaign, he lays himself open to blackmail and a murder charge, at which point the skeletons start to emerge from the family closet. Whalley-Kilmer wraps a Cajun accent around lines of numbing banality. TCh

Stowaway Girl

see Manuela

Strada, La (The Road)

(1954, It, 104 min, b/w)
d Federico Fellini. *p* Carlo Ponti, DinoDe Laurentiis. *sc* Federico Fellini, Ennio Flaiano, Tullio Pinelli. *ph* Otello Martelli.*ed* Leo Cattozzo. *ad* Mario Ravasco. *m* Nino Rota. *cast* Giulietta Masina, AnthonyQuinn, Richard Basehart, Aldo Silvani, Marcella Rovena.
●For all its sentimentality, this overshadows virtually everything Fellini has made since *La Dolce Vita*. As ever for *il maestro*, life is both cyclic odyssey and circus, a teeming, tragicomic arena of pain, cruelty and solitude. Masina plays Gelsomina, a naïve waif whose simpleton innocence provides a direct line to life's eternal mysteries; when she is sold into virtual slavery to play clown to itinerant strongman Zampano (Quinn), the boorish brute simply exploits his new assistant's desire for affection at every opportunity. It's basically a road movie: she vainly tries to escape, they join a circus, and her friendship with the tightrope-walking Fool (Basehart) brings its own problems. Despite the pessimism of much of the story, memorably embodied in the grey, desolate towns the pair visit, Fellini has already moved far from his roots in neo-realism; symbols, metaphors, and larger-than-life performances hold sway, and moments of bizarre if inconsequential charm abound. GA

Strada per Forte Alamo, La (Arizona Bill/The Road to Fort Alamo)

(1964, It/Fr, 80 min)
d John Old [Mario Bava]. *p* Pier Luigi Torri. *sc* Vincent Thomas [Enzio Gicca Palli], Charles Price [Franco Prosperi], Jane Brisbane [Livia Contardi]. *ph* Bud Third [Ubaldo Terzano]. *ed* Wilson Dexter [Mario Serandrei]. *ad* Demos Philos [Demofilo Fidani]. *m* Piero Umiliani. *cast* Ken Clark, Jany Clair, Michel Lemoine, Andreina Paul, Kirk Bert.
●Deploying his slender resources across what looks like about two acres of some Italian quarry, Bava shifts his plastic cactus about from shot to shot and stirs up furious dust clouds in a touching attempt to evoke the rolling Western plains. This was a very early spaghetti, and the director can't quite hit off the right tone, as he ploughs through a narrative encompassing two buddies (Beel and Sleem), an outlaw gang, the cavalry, Indians, imposture, rape, massacre, the colonel's lady and Rosie O'Grady, a bank hold-up and the Civil War. The bright reds and yellows flashing through the dust are pretty, but otherwise this is strictly for collectors of cinematic waifs and strays, its level exemplified by those 'Indian' extras trying to fathom, on camera, how to work their bows and arrows. BBa

Straight Out of Brooklyn

(1991, US, 91 min)
d/p/sc Matty Rich. *ph* John Rosnell. *ed* Jack Haigis. *pd* Walter Meade. *m* Harold Wheeler. *cast* George T Odom, Ann D Sanders, Lawrence Gilliard Jr, Barbara Sanon, Reana E Drummond, Matty Rich, Mark Malone.
●From its powerhouse opening, in which young, gifted and black New Yorker Dennis (Gilliard) is woken by his father's ferocious attack on his mother, it's immediately evident that Rich's low-budget debut as writer-director will be a no-holds-barred affair. Dennis has had it with his dad's drunkenly despairing rages, even though they're fired by poverty and racism; so, despite his plans to go to college and his girlfriend's vows that she'll leave him if he does anything illegal, his desire to make fast money for his family impels him to coax a couple of friends into joining him in armed robbery. If this harrowing melodrama is raw and occasionally a mite predictable in terms of plot, its emotional maturity, honesty and assurance are suggestive of a talent far older than the film-maker's 19 years. GA

Straight Story, The

(1999, US/Fr, 111 min)
d David Lynch. *p* Alain Sarde, Mary Sweeney, Neal Edelstein. *sc* John Roach, Mary Sweeney. *ph* Freddie Francis. *ed* Mary Sweeney. *pd* Jack Fisk. *m* Angelo Badalamenti. *cast* Richard Farnsworth, Sissy Spacek, Everett McGill, John Farley, Harry Dean Stanton.
●Lynch gets humanist – and produces a gem. The title has multiple resonance: based on fact, it charts the journey through the empty Midwestern plains embarked on by elderly Iowan Alvin Straight (Farnsworth), who to see his ailing brother attempts to cover 350 miles on a motorised lawnmower. Atypically for the director, it's also told straight, in naturalistic, linear fashion, but for all that the elegant, faintly formal compositions and camera movements (courtesy Freddie Francis), the expert and subtle use of sound and music, and the wry, gently humorous take on the absurdities of smalltown life make the film recognisably Lynchian. Farnsworth's easy, twinkle eyed charm is a winner all the way, but it's finally the film's deceptive simplicity and unabashed warmth that make it one of Lynch's most artistically and emotionally satisfying movies. GA

Straight Talk

(1992, US, 91 min)
d Barnet Kellman. *p* Robert Chartoff, Fred Berner. *sc* Craig Bolotin, Patricia Resnick. *ph* Peter Sova. *ed* Michael Tronick. *pd* Jeffrey Townsend. *m* Brad Fiedel. *cast* Dolly Parton, James Woods, Griffin Dunne, Michael Madsen, Deirdre O'Connell, John Sayles, Teri Hatcher, Spalding Gray, Jerry Orbach, Philip Bosco.
●Scuzzy Chicago news-hound Jack Russell (Woods) is ordered to sniff out the truth about radio agony aunt Doctor Shirlee Kenyon (Parton). Shirlee isn't really a doctor, merely a simple country girl with a blouse full of straight-talkin', homespun advice. Russell's editor wants Shirlee nailed, and soon Russell's penis shares a similar goal. Sharply written by Craig Bolotin and Patricia Resnick, this sassy comedy has musical aspirations, with diphthong-clanging Dolly numbers offering a running (if unnecessary) commentary. But the film's success rests squarely upon the efficacy of the Woods-Parton double act, an amiable partnership of mismatched, seasoned troupers. Only in the third act, with its 'on-air confession' denouement, do things take a gushing, sentimental nosedive. Otherwise it's a tongue-in-cheek romp with far less hog-washing than you'd expect. MK

Straight Time

(1977, US, 114 min)
d Ulu Grosbard. *p* Stanley Beck, Tim Zinnemann. *sc* Alvin Sargent, Edward Bunker, Jeffrey Boam. *ph* Own Roizman. *ed* Sam O'Steen, Randy Roberts. *pd* Stephen Grimes. *m* David Shire. *cast* Dustin Hoffman, Theresa Russell, Gary Busey, Harry Dean Stanton, M Emmet Walsh, Rita Taggart.
●Hoffman, spivvy and moustached for maximum seediness, is an ex-con on parole who can't go straight, adrift like a midnight bellboy in lowlife LA. One yearns for a routine cops and robbers story, but Grosbard lingers with illusory impartiality over the technical details of the parole system, the problems of finding accommodation and work, and the nastiness of the backyard pool-and-barbecue life-style of *riche* America. Not for a moment are you allowed to suspect that hoodlums might be smart or attractive, or that crime pays. It's such a relief when Hoffman finally drives off into his bleak future, and this fiction of fact reaches its non-conclusion. JS

Straight to Hell

(1986, GB, 86 min)
d Alex Cox. *p* Eric Fellner. *sc* Dick Rude, Alex Cox. *ph* Tom Richmond. *ed* David Martin. *pd* Andrew McAlpine. *m* Pogues, Pray for Rain. *cast* Dick Rude, Sy Richardson, Joe Strummer, Courtney Love, Biff Yeager, Shane MacGowan, Spider Stacy, Frank Murray.
●Cox's Spanish quickie comes on like a snorter's rag revue and resembles the result of roadies bouncing ideas off each other after the gig. With the exception of Richardson, the cast are every bit as tall in the saddle as Arthur Askey in *Ramsbottom Rides Again*. As a parody of the spaghetti Western, it is as witless and one-note as The Young Ones' *A Fistful of Travellers Cheques*, and longer, by Christ. Students of end-of-tether desperation will find a sexpot in hot pants shampooing the exhaust pipe of a motorbike, a Spanish fly which settles on various noses, and no shortage of bandidos with Lancashire accents and tartan thermos flasks. The trio of gringos wear Warren Oates grifter suits, and there are many pans around Mexicans laughing. The penultimate line in this yawping indulgence says it all: 'Who's paying for all this?' BC

Strait-Jacket

(1963, US, 93 min, b/w)
d/p William Castle. *sc* Robert Bloch. *ph* Arthur E Arling. *ed* Edwin Bryant. *ad* Boris Leven. *m* Van Alexander. *cast* Joan Crawford, Diane Baker, Leif Erickson, Howard St John, John Anthony Hayes, Rochelle Hudson, George Kennedy.
●Robert Bloch (*Psycho*) scripted this *What Ever Happened to Baby Jane?* rip-off which unleashes Crawford for another bout of unrestrained self-parody. She's an axemurderer, who's released after 20 years in an asylum and returns to daughter Baker, whereupon the old girl's hallucinations recur and (surprise!) the slayings begin again. Basically terrible, and there's another mask-ripping scene at the end, but Joan's fans will not be disappointed. No patented gimmicks from director William Castle this time though, because cinema managers had gotten sick of his cheap tricks. TJ

Strange Affair, The

(1968, GB, 106 min)
d David Greene. *p* Howard Harrison, Stanley Mann. *sc* Stanley Mann. *ph* Alex Thomson. *ed* Brian Smedley-Aston. *pd* Brian Eatwell. *m* Basil Kirchin. *cast* Michael York, Jeremy Kemp, Susan George, Jack Watson, George A Cooper, Artro Morris, Barry Fantoni, Nigel Davenport, Madge Ryan.
●York plays a solemn young constable new to the Metropolitan Police who is convinced that right is right, but gradually discovers that life just isn't like that; caught in a squeeze, he takes one hapless step after another, until the bitterly cynical ending has him languishing in jail while the particularly vicious gang of crooks go free. Essentially it's a well-written anecdote about police manners and methods, straight out of some TV cop series, but as viewed by Greene's wilfully wayward camera, it becomes a bizarre, quirkishly funny thriller which laces its documentary surface with a fine grain of fantasy. Much of Greene's later work disappointed, but here he displays a visual flair (gang violence in an echoing warehouse, murder among the wrecked cars in a scrapheap, seduction in a fantastically opulent boudoir) that would not entirely have shamed Welles in his *Lady from Shanghai* mood. TM

Strange Affair of Uncle Harry, The (Uncle Harry)

(1945, US, 80 min, b/w)
d Robert Siodmak. *p* Joan Harrison. *sc* Stephen Longstreet, Keith Winter. *ph* Paul Ivano. *ed* Arthur Hilton. *ad* John Goodman, Eugène Lourié. *m* Hans J Salter. *cast* George Sanders, Geraldine Fitzgerald, Ella Raines, Sara Allgood, Moyna McGill, Samuel S Hinds.
●Though less deliriously *noir* than Siodmak's best work (*Phantom Lady, The Killers, Cry of the City*) this rather Hitchcockian smalltown thriller, produced by the Englishman's former associate Joan Harrison, is a typically impressive psychological study in various forms of obsession. Sanders is both superb and unusually touching as the shy, naive designer who falls for Raines,

newly arrived from the city; Allgood and Fitzgerald are the sisters he lives with, the latter a scheming hypochondriac so possessive of her brother that she'll do anything to wreck his budding romance. A relatively conventional story is lent depth and originality by Siodmak's sense of detail and mood; Raines literally introduces colour into Sanders' life by daubing paint on his pedantically minaturist floral illustrations, while his repressed romanticism is evoked through his obsession with astrology. Sadly. Siodmak was saddled with an ending that undercuts the dark emotions preceeding it, but the overall effect is still gripping, intelligent, and oddly critical of staid petit bourgeois aspirations. GA

Strange Brew

(1983, US, 90 min)
d Dave Thomas, Rick Moranis. *p* Louis M Silverstein. *sc* Rick Moranis, Dave Thomas, Steven de Jarnatt. *ph* Steven Poster. *ed* Patrick McMahon. *pd* David L Snyder. *m* Charles Fox. *cast* Dave Thomas, Rick Moranis, Max Von Sydow, Paul Dooley, Lynne Griffin, Angus MacInnes, Tom Harvey, Douglas Campbell.

● Stars, directors and co-writers Dave Thomas and Rick Moranis originated Bob and Doug McKenzie, their beer-making, beer-swilling sibling act in a series of TV sketches. Here Von Sydow's a rival beer manufacturer hoping to take over the world by drugging his brew, but the plotline (derived from *Hamlet*) soon goes flat. TJ

Strange Cargo

(1940, US, 113 min, b/w)
d Frank Borzage. *p* Joseph L Mankiewicz. *sc* Lawrence Hazard. *ph* Robert Planck. *ed* Robert J Kern. *ad* Cedric Gibbons. *m* Franz Waxman. *cast* Clark Gable, Joan Crawford, Ian Hunter, Peter Lorre, Paul Lukas, Albert Dekker, Eduardo Ciannelli.

● Ace melodramatist Borzage always injected his tales of romance and hardship with more than a touch of spiritual redemption, and this is one of his most explicit statements about the uplifting power of love. Gable is one of a group of convicts who escapes from the prison on Devil's Island; through his relationship with Crawford, which develops from basic sexual attraction to intense emotional commitment, and through his hardships as they trek through the jungle, he finds not only physical but also spiritual liberation. Most remarkable, however, is the Ian Hunter character, who helps lead them to salvation: omniscient and at one with nature, he becomes almost a Christ-figure endowed with strange powers and the gift of mercy. Borzage lends the tale quite extraordinary conviction. GA

Strange Case of Dr Rx, The

(1942, US, 66 min, b/w)
d William Nigh. *sc* Clarence Upson Young. *ph* Elwood Bredell. *ed* Bernard W Burton. *ad* Jack Otterson, Martin Obzina. *m* Hans J Salter. *cast* Patric Knowles, Lionel Atwill, Anne Gwynne, Samuel S Hinds, Mona Barrie, Paul Cavanagh, Ray Corrigan, Mantan Moreland, Shemp Howard.

● A routine but fast-moving whodunit with horror-comedy overtones as private eye Knowles, pursuing a masked killer, is threatened with a gorilla brain transplant. This is merely bluff, alas, designed to scare him out of his wits while the killer pursues his purpose: eliminating a series of shady businessmen whom justice has failed to deal with. Atwill is great fun in a red herring role as the sinister, aptly-named Dr Fish, and the underrated Woody Bredell contributes some nicely creepy camerawork. TM

Strange Days

(1995, US, 145 min)
d Kathryn Bigelow. *p* James Cameron, Steven-Charles Jaffe. *sc* James Cameron, Jay Cocks. *ph* Matthew F Leonetti. *ed* Howard Smith. *pd* Lilly Kilvert. *m* Graeme Revell. *cast* Ralph Fiennes, Angela Bassett, Juliette Lewis, Tom Sizemore, Michael Wincott, Vincent D'Onofrio, Glenn Plummer, Josef Sommer.

● LA, Year Zero: 30 December 1999. Riot police are on the streets. The angry, poor, disenfranchised – the blacks – are ready to tear down the walls of the city. Yet Lenny Nero fiddles while LA burns. A sleazeball in an Armani suit, Lenny's dealing illicit 'playback clips', raw human experience recorded direct from the cerebral cortex. Bigelow's spectacular millennial maelstrom has divided critics, and apparently repelled audiences. Written by James Cameron and Jay Cocks, this is tech-*noir*, action movie and love story rolled into one. It also pursues a sophisticated treatise on the nature of voyeurism, the psychic dangers of vicarious entertainment and cinema itself. A sequence in which Nero watches a snuff clip of rape and murder has excited accusations of exploitation and hypocrisy. It's certainly hard to stomach, but then shouldn't it be? The impeccable moral centre is to be found in Bassett's karate-chopping single mother 'Mace', who rescues Lenny from his own faithless stupor. Nero isn't irredeemable, either: Fiennes makes him a persuasively seedy knight errant. In fact, despite its own barely suppressed despair, the film exhibits markedly progressive leanings. Flawed, but often brilliant, provocative film-making. TCh

Strange Door, The

(1951, US, 81 min, b/w)
d Joseph Pevney. *p* Ted Richmond. *sc* Jerry Sackheim. *ph* Irving Glassberg. *ed* Edward Curtiss. *ad* Bernard Herzbrun, Eric Orbom. *m* Hans Salter. *cast* Charles Laughton, Boris Karloff, Sally Forrest, Richard Stapley, Michael Pate, Alan Napier.

● Very much a B movie, luridly adapted from Stevenson's story *The Sire de Malétroit's Door*, but solidly implanted in the old *Frankenstein* sets and looking like a rough prototype for Corman's Poe series. Laughton goes enjoyably over the top as a love-crazed madman prowling a Gothic castle where the rightful owner (his elder brother) lies rotting in a dungeon and a room with clashing walls awaits the unwary intruder. Karloff balances him beautifully as the baleful but sympathetic servant who bides his time, eventually contriving a rather splendid comeuppance involving a remorselessly grinding water-wheel. It's surprisingly imaginatively put together in its thick-ear way. TM

Strange Incident

see Ox-Bow Incident, The

Strange Invaders

(1983, US, 93 min)
d Michael Laughlin. *p* Walter Coblenz. *sc* Bill Condon, Michael Laughlin. *ph* Louis Horvath. *ed* John W Wheeler. *pd* Susanna Moore. *m* John Addison. *cast* Paul LeMat, Nancy Allen, Diana Scarwid, Michael Lerner, Louise Fletcher, Wallace Shawn, Fiona Lewis, Kenneth Tobey, June Lockhart.

● 'I've got you, under mah skeeen-ah!'. Loss of face gets a whole new twist in this unexpectedly well-developed pastiche: a welcome surprise, as it initially looks like a Disneyish soft-pedal over the familiar territory of *Invasion of the Body Snatchers*. The twist is that when the aliens colonised a small town in the '50s – doing the usual trick of covering their own unsightly physogs with plastic replicas of several hundred decent Americans –it all happened with full governmental approval. Hassled hero LeMat has to confront opposition from both the official and the alien fronts before getting to the bottom of the mystery. The necessarily upbeat ending is all but made up for by some brilliant SFX and stabs of humour in the midnight vein of the great Gahan (*National Lampoon*, *Playboy*, etc) Wilson. Hugely entertaining and refreshingly gore-free. GD

Strange Love of Martha Ivers, The

(1946, US, 117 min, b/w)
d Lewis Milestone. *p* Hal B Wallis. *sc* Robert Rossen. *ph* Victor Milner. *ed* Archie Marshek. *ad* Hans Dreier, John Meehan. *m* Miklòs Rozsa. *cast* Barbara Stanwyck, Van Heflin, Kirk Douglas, Lisabeth Scott, Judith Anderson, Roman Bohnen, Frank Orth.

● Superb performance by Stanwyck (as coldly calculating as she was in *Double Indemnity*) as the apex of a traumatic triangle comprising the two men who (maybe) saw her club her wealthy aunt to death when they were children. Now a tycoon in her own right, bonded to one of the witnesses (Douglas) in a guilt-ridden marriage, she finds the other (Heflin) resurfacing in her life as both promise of escape and threat to security – and the stagnant waters begin to stir again with murderous crosscurrents of fear and desire. A gripping *film noir*, all the more effective for being staged by Milestone as a steamy romantic melodrama. TM

Strange One, The (aka End as a Man)

(1957, US, 100 min, b/w)
d Jack Garfein. *p* Sam Spiegel. *sc* Calder Willingham. *ph* Burnett Guffey. *ed* Sidney Katz. *ad* Joseph C Wright. *m* Kenyon Hopkins. *cast* Ben Gazzara, George Peppard, Pat Hingle, Mark Richman, Geoffrey Horne, James Olson.

● Advertised as 'the first picture filmed entirely by a cast and technicians from The Actors' Studio, New York': in 1957, this was quite a selling point, because the screen was under invasion by young, brilliant Method actors, and Elia Kazan, co-founder of the Studio, was *the* prestigious movie and play director. Calder Willingham's novel (*End As a Man*), about a sadistic cadet in a Southern military academy, certainly went against the Hollywood grain. Most movie versions of military life – Ford's *The Long Gray Line* is a fair example – endorsed the system, but Willingham, who had suffered under a similar regime, dissented: discipline and honour were dehumanising, and bred only bullying. Garfein, Kazan's assistant, wasn't much of a director, and some of the actors appear almost incapacitated with mannerisms. Gazzara, however, is sensational, playing the malevolent Jocko De Paris with a subtlety honed by Studio stage performances. Reptilian, glowering with banked-down hatred – even his outfit of military cap, Hawaiian shirt, shorts and sock suspenders, cigarette holder and swagger stick, communicates a sardonic androgyny that couldn't have done much for the military peace of mind. He is, in short, Iago. Fellow cadets Peppard and Hingle don't stand a chance against his cunning. BC

Strange Ones, The

see Enfants Terribles, Les

Strange Place to Meet, A (Drôle d'Endroit pour une rencontre)

(1988, Fr, 98 min)
d François Dupeyron. *p* Patrick Bordier. *sc* François Dupeyron, Dominique Faysse. *ph* Charlie van Damme. *ed* Françoise Collin. *ad* Carlos Conti. *cast* Catherine Deneuve, Gérard Depardieu, André Wilms, Nathalie Cardone, Jean-Pierre Sentier, Alain Rimoux.

● Talk about minimal: Dupeyron's feature debut is a road movie where they only travel 10 kilometres. Deneuve, booted out of her husband's car after a row, ends up in a lay-by with Depardieu, who's mending his motor (metaphor for mending his life). They get a lift to the service station, and spend the next two days alternately chasing and repulsing each other. Deneuve's in the throes of a very heavy, possibly masochistic relationship with the man who dumped her; Depardieu is a lonely, romantic doctor who's doggedly hopeless with the opposite sex. Nothing is entirely resolved, tempting hints about the characters' lives aren't elaborated upon (*is* she married, mad, or a high class hooker?), and the film retains the haunting inconsequentiality of a chance encounter. The romantic protestations, set against the grim background of a plastic café, are poignant and dreamlike, the characters are drifters seeking refuge or escape, and the whole film is comic and bitter-sweet. SFe

Strange Planet

(1999, Aust, 96 min)
d Emma-Kate Croghan. *p* Stavros Kazantzidis, Anastasia Sideris. *sc* Stavros Kazantzidis, Emma-Kate Croghan. *ph* Justin Brickle. *ed* Ken Sallows. *pd* Annie Beauchamp. *cast* Claudia Karvan, Naomi Watts, Alice Garner, Tom Long, Aaron Jeffery, Felix Williamson, Hugo Weaving, Rebecca Frith.

● It's New Year, and time is running out for Judy and her pals Alice and Sally, and Ewan and his mates Joel and Neil. A couple of steps out of college, they're still learning about the world and their own place in it. Judy (Karvan), for example, is a hard-boiled careerist who wants to get over her thing for married men, while Ewan (Long) feels 'emotionally numb' and drops out of his law firm job to write. Following this six-pack over the course of a year, we begin to get a sense of who's meant for whom; the only real surprise is how long it takes them to find each other. Australian writer/director Croghan made her first film, *Love and Other Catastrophes*, when she was only 24. Her second is another ensemble romantic comedy, a little older, and on a slightly more expansive scale; smart, bitty, but never more than half-achieved. This has plenty of energy, but at the expense of focus – indeed, it bears the hallmarks of an editing fix-up. Woody Allen makes this stuff look very easy. Croghan proves it isn't. TCh

Stranger, The

(1946, US, 95 min, b/w)
d Orson Welles. *p* Sam Spiegel. *sc* Anthony Veiller. *ph* Russell Metty. *ed* Ernest Nims. *ad* Perry Ferguson. *m* Bronislau Kaper. *cast* Orson Welles, Loretta Young, Edward G Robinson, Richard Long, Konstantin Shayne, Philip Merivale, Billy House.

● Welles' third film, often described as his worst, but still a hugely enjoyable thriller as Robinson's man from the Allied War Crimes Commission patiently stalks Welles' former top Nazi, now ensconced as a prep school teacher in a small Connecticut town and newly married to the innocent Young. Admittedly some wobbles develop (not least in Orson's own overpitched performance), and the script has its naïve moments (as when the Nazi gives himself away in a dinner-table gambit: 'Marx wasn't a German, he was a Jew'). But it is studded with great scenes like the stranger's furtive flight through the dockyards at the beginning, the murder in the woods with boys streaming by on a paperchase, or the Nazi's death high on the clock tower, impaled by the sword wielded by a mechanical figure as the hour begins to strike. Terrific camerawork from Russell Metty throughout. TM

Stranger, The

see Intruder, The

Stranger, The (Agantuk)

(1991, Ind/Fr, 105 min)
d/p/sc Satyajit Ray. *ph* Barun Raha. *ed* Dulal Dutt. *m* Satyajit Ray. *ad* Ashoke Bose. *cast* Deepankar Dey, Mamata Shankar, Bikram Bhattacharya, Utpal Dutt, Dhritiman Chatterjee.

● Out of the blue, Anila receives a letter from her uncle Manmohan. After 35 years abroad, he wants to stay a few days with his only living relative. While Anila prepares for his arrival, her husband Sudhindra remains suspicious: what is the nature of this man who invites himself to their home? How can they even know he is who he claims to be? Manmohan's arrival hardly clarifies matters. Cultured and intellectually superior to his perplexed hosts and their friends, he is prepared to play devil's advocate when they quiz him about his past and his motives. Like much of his late work, Ray's final film has a rigidly functional visual style and a rather old-fashioned trust in dialogue ('It's a Bengali invention, discussion,' says Manmohan). For all that, it's a pleasingly graceful last testament, both engrossing and emotionally revealing. Manmohan is clearly Ray himself – a traditionalist yet a stranger in his own land, an anthropologist 'with Shakespeare, Tagore, Marx and Freud in my bloodstream'. The film, which is beautifully played, reflects Ray's ambivalence about the nature of civilisation. It works as a mystery, and as a satire on bourgeois mores – the perpetual struggle between faith and good form. It ends on a subtle, touching, grace note. TCh

Stranger (Yoru no Stranger – Kyofu!)

(1991, Jap, 90 min)
d Shunichi Nagasaki. *cast* Yuko Natori, Kentaro Shimizu, Takeshi Naito.

● A model for all directors given the chance to make a low-budget genre quickie, *Stranger* offers Nagasaki's most charged vision of fear and loathing on the streets of Tokyo. Kiriko was a bank teller until she went to jail for fraud. Now she works as a taxi driver, lives alone and does her best to be 'one of the guys'. Her problems begin the night a passenger gives her a big note and leaves without waiting for change. Next time he gets in her cab, he tries to kill her – in what turns out to be the start of a sustained assault on her life at work and at home. Like the truck in *Duel*, this stranger just keeps on coming and Kiriko has no choice but to gear herself up to fight back. Powerhouse stuff. TR

Stranger and the Gunfighter, The

see Blood Money

Stranger in Between, The

see Hunted

Stranger Inside

(2000, US, 97 min)
d Cheryl Dunye. *p* Jim McKay, Michael Stipe, Effie T Brown. *sc* Cheryl Dunye, Catherine Crouch. *ph* Nancy Schreiber. *ed* Cecily Rhett. *pd* Candi Guterres. *m* Mychael Danna, (addit) Andrew Lockington. *cast* Yolonda Ross, Davenia McFadden, LaTonya 'T' Hagans, Mary Mara, Rain Phoenix, Marc Vann, Medusa.

● Impressive HBO drama set in a women's prison. Treasure makes sure she's transferred from juve, intent on meeting the mother she has never known, a lifer who goes by the name of 'Brownie'. It turns out Brownie is a hardcase who controls the flow of contraband among the black prisoners – a 'mother' to all her 'daughters', as long as they don't fuck with her. It's a compelling set-up, with cracking performances from Ross and McFadden, and a refreshingly hardboiled, unexploitative view of prison life, which is only slightly undercut by a latent Group Therapy sensibility. TCh

Stranger on the Run

(1967, US, 96 min)
d Donald Siegel. *p* Richard E Lyons. *sc* Dean Riesner. *ph* Bud Thackery. *ed* Richard G Wray. *ad* William D DeCinces. *m* Leonard Rosenman. *cast* Henry Fonda, Anne Baxter, Michael Parks, Dan Duryea, Sal Mineo, Tom Reese, Bernie Hamilton, Zalman King, Rodolfo Acosta.

● Fonda, a drunk in search of redemption, shows up in a dusty railhead town whose population includes an unstable sheriff, several homo-erotically fixated gunslingers and an assortment of ready-mades, like the comely widow whose teenage son is ripe for a few life lessons. This early telefeature (Siegel's third) is based on a story by Reginald Rose and its blend of popular Freud and social consciousness includes some unexpected themes, e.g. the depiction of the railroad not as an emblem of progress but as a bringer of violence and corruption. Siegel barrels energetically through a tangle of sub-plots: the film was his ticket back to big-screen projects. Michael Parks as the sheriff looks splendid but sounds as though he's speaking Bulgarian. BBa

Stranger on the Third Floor, The

(1940, US, 64 min, b/w)
d Boris Ingster. *p* Lee Marcus. *sc* Frank Partos. *ph* Nick Musuraca. *ed* Harry Marker. *ad* Van Nest Polglase. *m* Roy Webb. *cast* Peter Lorre, John McGuire, Margaret Tallichet, Charles Waldron, Elisha Cook Jr.

● A weird expressionist investigation of personal guilt that takes its jaunty, banal hero (McGuire) from the bright lights of a cafeteria into a strange interior odyssey. The plot revolves around the reporter hero's unwitting conviction, through his evidence, of an innocent man (Cook) at a murder trial. He returns to his apartment to rest, and the brittle, unremarkable surface of the film begins to break up in a kind of guilt-whirlpool of humiliation and sexual repression. The court, jury and whole legal system are exposed in the hero's dreams as little more than vampiric; and when he wakes up, even reality begins to take on the dimensions of nightmare (with a special spot reserved for Lorre, terrific). Finally the film returns its audience to the banal starting-point of its investigation, but the happy ending just can't look the same in the light of everything that has preceded it. A remarkable movie. DP

Strangers

see Viaggio in Italia

Strangers

(1991, GB, 67 min)
d Danny Cannon. *p* Andrea M Franden. *sc* Danny Cannon. *ph* Gavin Finney. *ed* Alex Mackie. *pd* Tom Conroy. *m* David Arnold. *cast* Michael Ceveris, Al Sapienza, Michele Palermo.

● Two brothers are reunited under terrifying circumstances in this impressive offering from the British National Film and Television School. John Reece (Ceveris) has made a precarious living by selling cocaine to actors and bands, but now he owes his violent associates in the Los Angeles underworld $30,000 – and they don't care how they get it. His upstanding brother (Sapienza) tries to rescue him, in turn exposing his wife and young son to danger. Polished direction, an intelligent use of music, and atmospheric visuals from cinematographer Gavin Finney combine to make this a menacing, highly accomplished thriller. CM

Strangers in Love

see In Love

Strangers Kiss

(1983, US, 94 min, b/w & col)
d Matthew Chapman. *p* Douglas Dilge. *sc* Blaine Novak, Matthew Chapman. *ph* Mikhail Suslov. *ed* William Carruth. *ad* Ginny Randolph. *m* Gato Barbieri. *cast* Peter Coyote, Victoria Tennant, Blaine Novak, Dan Shor, Richard Romanus, Carlos Palomino, Linda Kerridge.

● Fascinating film structured a little like a series of Chinese boxes. First comes the fiction of a young director in Hollywood (Coyote) trying to set up an independent B movie about a young boxer's *noir*-ish efforts to save a taxi dancer from her villainous protector. This, given the date 1955 and a marked resemblance between the two plots, merges into a speculative 'history' of the circumstances surrounding the making of Kubrick's *Killer's Kiss*. Then life begins to imitate art as the villainous realtor backing Coyote's movie, in which his girl is playing the lead, realises that she is falling for the actor playing the boxer; and art begins to give life a stage direction or two as Coyote encourages this perilous triangle in the hope of lending emotional conviction to his film. Marvellously shot and finely acted, it grips simultaneously as a critical extension of Kubrick's film, as a comment on movie-making mania, and as a dark thriller in its own right. TM

Strangers on a Train

(1951, US, 101 min, b/w)
d/p Alfred Hitchcock. *sc* Raymond Chandler, Czenzi Ormonde. *ph* Robert Burks. *ed* William Ziegler. *ad* Ted Haworth. *m* Dimitri Tiomkin. *cast* Farley Granger, Robert Walker, Ruth Roman, Leo G Carroll, Patricia Hitchcock, Laura Elliott, Marion Lorne, Howard St John.

● Adapted from Patricia Highsmith's novel, *Strangers on a Train* takes as its central proposition the meeting and ensuing guilty association of two complete strangers, Granger and Walker. Walker buttonholes Granger, a star tennis player anxious to remarry but with a clinging wife, and initiates a hypnotic discussion of exchange murders. Walker then does 'his' murder (the wife), and threatens to incriminate Granger if he doesn't fulfil his half of the 'bargain' (Walker's father). Significantly, Hitchcock didn't use much of Raymond Chandler's original script, because Chandler was too concerned with the characters' motivation. In place of that, Hitchcock erects a web of guilt around Granger, who 'agreed' to his wife's murder, a murder that suits him very well, and structures his film around a series of set pieces, ending with a paroxysm of violence on a circus carousel, when the circle Granger is trapped within is literally blown to pieces, leaving Walker dead beneath it and Granger a free man again. PH

Strangers When We Meet

(1960, US, 117 min)
d/p Richard Quine. *sc* Evan Hunter. *ph* Charles Lang Jr. *ed* Charles Nelson. *ad* Ross Bellah. *m* George Duning. *cast* Kirk Douglas, Kim Novak, Ernie Kovacs, Barbara Rush, Walter Matthau, Virginia Bruce.

● Evan Hunter adapted his novel of suburban infidelities for this glossy but unsatisfying and very dated 'Scope melodrama, in which unhappily wed architect Douglas carries on with restless housewife Novak, until neighbour Matthau happens on one of their trysts and and makes a play for Novak himself. Ends tamely with Douglas and wife Rush reconciled and setting off for a new life in Hawaii. TJ

Stranger Than Paradise

(1984, US/WGer, 89 min, b/w)
d Jim Jarmusch. *p* Sara Driver. *sc* Jim Jarmusch. *ph* Tom DiCillo. *ed* Jim Jarmusch, Melody London. *m* John Lurie. *cast* John Lurie, Eszter Balint, Richard Edson, Cecillia Stark, Danny Rosen.

●A beautiful little independent film that paved the way for the more accessible (but perhaps less exhilarating) delights of *Down by Law*, this three-part road-movie-with-a-difference is shot in long, static black-and-white takes, and features an excellent score that straddles both Screaming Jay Hawkins and Bartok. The story is slight: cool, laconic New Yorker Lurie (of Lounge Lizards fame) reluctantly plays host when his young female cousin arrives on a visit from Hungary. When the girl finally disappears to Ohio to stay with an eccentric old aunt, Lurie suddenly finds himself feeling lonely, and he and his buddy Edson slope off westwards in search of…whatever. It's an ironic fable about exile, peopled by carefully, economically observed kooks who, at least after the first half-hour, are drawn with considerable warmth and generosity. Not a lot to it, certainly, but the acting and performances combine to produce an obliquely effective study of the effect of landscape upon emotion, and the wry, dry humour is often quite delicious. GA

Strangler, The

(1964, US, 89 min, b/w)
d Burt Topper. *p* Samuel Bischoff, David Diamond. *sc* Bill S Ballinger. *ph* Jacques R Marquette. *ed* Robert S Eisen. *ad* Hal Pereira, Eugène Lourié. *m* Marlin Skiles. *cast* Victor Buono, David McLean, Ellen Corby, Jeanne Bates, Wally Campo, James Sikking.

●Having played a chubby mother's boy in Robert Aldrich's *What Ever Happened to Baby Jane?*, Victor Buono brought a certain class to this compelling tawdry exploiter as an obese mother-fixated lab technician who murders nurses. Predating *The Boston Strangler* by a few years, this is a very different take from that offered by Tony Curtis in Richard Fleischer's 1968 movie. NF

Stranglers Morgue

see Curse of the Wraydons, The

Stranglers of Bombay, The

(1959, GB, 80 min, b/w)
d Terence Fisher. *p* Anthony Hinds. *sc* David Zelag Goodman. *ph* Arthur Grant. *ed* James Needs, Alfred Cox. *ad* Bernard Robinson, Don Mingaye. *m* James Bernard. *cast* Guy Rolfe, Allan Cuthbertson, Andrew Cruickshank, George Pastell, Marne Maitland, Marie Devereux.

●One of Hammer and Terence Fisher's most notorious and Sadean horror movies, about the thuggee atrocities in India in the 1820s. Guy Rolfe battles against a fatal sect of Kali worshippers whose mascot is a sexy teenager called Karim (Devereux). As men have their tongues pulled out or are castrated, Karim drools and wriggles so much that the film became a cult sensation on the continent and was cut in England. Actually, it isn't at all bad, even on a straight adventure level, and the Karim figure remains one of the purest incarnations of evil in all of Fisher's work. Be prepared for a few laughs, though, as rural Bucks is substituted for the sweltering plains of India. DP

Strapless

(1988, GB, 100 min)
d David Hare. *p* Rick McCallum. *sc* David Hare. *ph* Andrew Dunn. *ed* Edward Marnier. *pd* Roger Hall. *m* Nick Bicat. *cast* Blair Brown, Bruno Ganz, Bridget Fonda, Alan Howard, Michael Gough, Hugh Laurie, Suzanna Burden.

●Romance is explored here with logical exactitude; an uneasy, not altogether satisfying combination of impulses. Lillian (Brown) is an overworked American doctor, single and approaching 40. Against the life-and-death extremities of her work, she has established a controlled routine. But she is disturbed by two influences: the attentions of mysterious millionaire Raymond (Ganz), and the freewheeling lifestyle of her pregnant, husbandless sister Amy (Fonda). Will Lillian scurry back into her corner, or mellow and adopt a more spontaneous approach to her professional and private lives? 'They shouldn't stay up but they do', murmurs Fonda in reference to her strapless gowns, by implication a testament to female independence. A forced comparison, it's a mite condescending. Ganz's catalytic character embodies an ideal, but is so exaggerated in depiction that the relationship with Lillian fails to ring true. An interesting conception has suffered in execution. CM

Strapped

(1993, US, 102 min)
d Forest Whitaker. *p* Nellie Nugiel. *sc* Dena Kleiman. *ph* Larry Banks. *ed* Glenn T Morgan. *m* Joe Romano. *cast* Bokeem Woodbine, Kia Joy Goodwin, Fredro, Michael Biehn.

●This first feature strains a little hard (it's another in-your-face Scorsese), but the handling becomes more assured and the final result is impressive. Set on the streets of New York, it's the tale of Diquan, a youth who turns to selling guns *and* information as a way of raising his pregnant girlfriend's bail. A burning indictment of the inner-city circle of strife. TCh

Strasse, Die (The Street)

(1923, Ger, 75 min, b/w)
d Karl Grune. *sc* Karl Grune, Julius Urgiss. *ph* Karl Hasselmann. *ad* Karl George, Ludwig Meidner. *cast* Eugen Klöpfer, Aud Egede-Nissen, Lucie Höflich, Max Schreck.

●Rebellious middle-aged bourgeois ventures out from his parlour to sample the fleshpots of *The Street*, only – inevitably – to skulk home chastened to the cosy security of spouse and soup tureen. Variations on this artless moral fable formed the basis for a whole cycle of 1920s 'street films', of which Murnau's first American movie, *Sunrise*, was perhaps the most memorable. Ex-theatre director and Max Reinhardt disciple, Grune tells the story with minimal intertitles and some visual panache in suggesting the iridescent but deadly seductiveness of the street. This is his most famous film, but it doesn't rank with the very best of German silent cinema: poor characterisation (Klöpfer contrives to be both dull and dislikeable as the ill-fated philistine, though Egede-Nissen, the dancer in *Dr Mabuse the Gambler*, is more lively as the vamp), flaccid sentimentality, and an often flagging pace make it seem more like a deserving revival than an exciting rediscovery. SJo

Strategia del Ragno, La

see Spider's Stratagem, The

Strategy of the Snail, The (La Estratagia del Caracol)

(1993, Col, 116 min)
d/p Sergio Cabrera. *sc* Humberto Dorado. *ph* Carlos Congote. *ed* Manuel Navia, Nicholas Wentworth. *m* German Arrieta. *cast* Frank Ramirez, Humberto Dorado, Florina Lemaitre, Gustavo Angarito, Vicky Hernandez.

●An oddly likeable movie about the tenants of an old tenement ('the Casa Uribe') in central Bogotá who decide to resist eviction. The story proceeds a bit like an Ealing comedy. The fight for the right strategy is between the legal delaying tactics of Dr Romero ('The Fox') and the more inventive ideas of an old Spanish Civil War veteran. Politically a little sentimental, but made with gusto and a fine feel for eccentricity. WH

Strawberry and Chocolate (Fresa y Chocolate)

(1993, Cuba, 111 min)
d Tomás Gutiérrez Alea, Juan Carlos Tabío. *sc* Senel Paz. *ph* Mario Garcia Joya. *ed* Miriam Talavera, Osvaldo Donatien, Rolando Martinez. *pd* Fernando O'Reilly. *m* José Maria Vitier. *cast* Jorge Perugorría, Vladimir Cruz, Mirta Ibarra, Francisco Gattorno.

●The core problem with Cuba's first gay-themed movie is that it's so…Cuban. It's about everybody's favourite party topics, but it's so busy worrying about machismo and homophobia that it forgets to let its hair down. In Cuban terms, it must seem tremendously daring to put acid social criticisms into the mouth of a raging queen. To the rest of us, the result feels more like Stanley Kramer than Lily Savage. The film replays the central gestalt of *Kiss of the Spiderwoman* (stolid communist meets and is subverted by florid queen) with a simple twist: here the queen is the smart one. Sociology student David, a true child of Castro's revolution and an inner minefield of misogyny and prejudice, runs into long-suffering queer Diego, whose cluttered apartment is a cross between a library, a dodgy art gallery and a junk shop. The encounter changes both of them. Dull, obvious and bafflingly timid. TR

Straw Dogs

(1971, GB, 118 min)
d Sam Peckinpah. *p* Daniel Melnick. *sc* David Zelag Goodman, Sam Peckinpah. *ph* John Coquillon. *ed* Paul Davies, Roger Spottiswoode, Tony Lawson. *pd* Ray Simm. *m* Jerry Fielding. *cast* Dustin Hoffman, Susan George, David Warner, Peter Vaughan, TP McKenna, Del Henney, Sally Thomsett, Colin Welland, Peter Arne.

●Taking elements of both the Western and the British horror film, Peckinpah's masterstroke was to shoot *Straw Dogs* absolutely straight, without the reassuring signposts of either type of film. Hoffman's American mathematician settles with his wife in the village where she grew up, encountering first hostility, then violence from the remote, backward (inbred?) Cornish community. 'Civilised' man's confrontation with irrational violence is handled with impeccable logic. Indeed, looking back, it's hard to see what the charges of gratuitous violence were all about. More intriguing and questionable is Peckinpah's total annihilation of Hoffman's marriage. The violence that befalls it can be interpreted partly as an externalisation of the couple's latent incompatibility (stressed again and again). But the ensuing mixture of fantasy wish fulfilment and pure terror seems more informed by a general misogyny than specific doubts about that particular relationship. CPe

Stray Dog (Nora Inu)

(1949, Jap, 122 min, b/w)
d Akira Kurosawa. *p* Sojiro Motogi. *sc* Ryuzo Kikushima, Akira Kurosawa. *ph* Asakazu Nakai. *ad* So Matsuyama. *m* Fumio Hayasaka. *cast* Toshiro Mifune, Takashi Shimura, Ko Kimura, Keiko Awaji, Reisaburo Yamamoto.

●An early encounter between Kurosawa and two of his favourite actors, Mifune and Shimura, both playing detectives in Japan's uneasy post-war period under US imperialism. When Mifune's pistol is stolen, he is overwhelmed by a feeling of dishonour rather than failure, and sets out on a descent into the lower depths of Tokyo's underworld, which gradually reveals Dostoievskian parallels between himself and his quarry. A sweltering summer is at its height, and Kurosawa's strenuous location shooting transforms the city into a sensuous collage of fluttering fans and delicate, sweating limbs. A fine blend of US thriller material with Japanese conventions, it's a small classic. CPea

Streamers

(1983, US, 118 min)
d Robert Altman. *p* Robert Altman, Nick J Mileti. *sc* David Rabe. *ph* Pierre Mignot. *ed* Norman Smith. *pd* Wolf Kroeger. *m* Stephen Foster. *cast* Matthew Modine, Michael Wright, Mitchell Lichtenstein, David Alan Grier, Guy Boyd, George Dzundza, Albert Macklin.

●Another of Altman's gripping demonstrations of how to transform theatre by means of composition and close-up. As in *Come Back to the 5 & Dime*, he restricts his material to a single set, this time an army barracks dormitory, where a group of young US recruits live, laugh and lay into each other while waiting to be sent off to action in Vietnam. Sex, class, race and war are the main topics under discussion, brought to boiling point by the arrival of the ranting Carlyle (Wright), an argumentative black whose abrupt changes in articulacy and temper reveal a madman's insights into reality. Confusion and confinement are the keynotes here: freedom of thought and action has been removed from these boys, with the result that finally they turn with inexorable anguish upon one another. Altman's direction keeps the atmosphere admirably taut and claustrophobic, while allowing the cast plenty of opportunity to excel with spontaneous, vivid performances, subtly explored by a hesitantly prowling camera. GA

Street, The

see Strasse, Die

Street Angel

(1928, US, 9,221 ft, b/w)
d Frank Borzage. *p* William Fox. *sc* HH Caldwell, Philip Klein, Henry Robert Symonds. *ph* Ernest Palmer, Paul Ivano. *ed* Barney Wolf. *ad* Harry Oliver. *cast* Janet Gaynor, Charles Farrell, Alberto Rabagliati, Gino Conti, Guido Trento, Henry Armetta.

● 'Everywhere... in every town... in every street ... we pass, unknowing, souls made great by adversity.' Not, perhaps, the most modish sentiment for the '80s, but nevertheless the cornerstone of a wholly modern movie: one in the coherent collection made between the mid-'20s and World War II, sublime demonstrations of a system of sensual spirituality, the products of their director's uncompromising romanticism and fluent sense of cinemotion. Testing the same screen lovers almost as stringently as he had in *Seventh Heaven*, Borzage here damns 'morality' and opts for the pure passion of a sacred *amour fou*. Both films affirm, triumphantly, that melodrama can mean much more than just an excuse for a good weep. Both just have to be seen to be believed. (From the play by Marion Orth.) PT

Street Angel (Malu Tianshi)

(1937, China, 100 min, b/w)
d/sc Yuan Muzhi. *ph* Wu Yinxian. *ed* Qian Xiaozhang. *ad* Ma Yuhong. *m* He Luting. *cast* Zhao Dan, Wei Heling, Qian Qianli, Zhou Xuan.

● This glimpse of the Chinese left wing cinema of the '30s is a true revelation. Maturely assimilating various lessons from Hollywood, it sketches the street life of the poorest quarter of Shanghai just before the city's fall to the Japanese; the main characters are a street musician, a hooker, a newsvendor, and a 'sing-song' girl. Its conclusions are inevitably pessimistic, but both script and performances are warmly humorous; and the attitude to issues like prostitution makes Western cinema of the '60s seem antiquated by comparison. TR

Streetcar Named Desire, A

(1951, US, 122 min, b/w)
d Elia Kazan. *p* Charles K Feldman. *sc* Tennessee Williams. *ph* Harry Stradling. *ed* David Weisbart. *ad* Richard Day. *m* Alex North. *cast* Vivien Leigh, Marlon Brando, Kim Hunter, Karl Malden, Randy Bond.

● The film in which the Marlon mumble and scratch gave the Method a bad name and Tennessee Williams a yellow paper reputation as the playwright of steamy sex. Actually pretty mild (Stanley's 'liberating' rape of Blanche is coyly elided while we watch a hose washing away garbage with portentous symbolism), it remains impressive largely because of Brando's superbly detailed performance (which rather wipes the floor with Leigh's showy but superficial bundle of mannerisms). Directing with his camera sticking as close to the characters as if they were grouped on a stage, Kazan achieves a sort of theatrical intensity in which the sweaty realism sometimes clashes awkwardly with the stylisation that heightens the dialogue into a kind of poetry. What the film lacks, in fact, is some sort of perspective – and perhaps a dash of the dark humour that made *Baby Doll* both Kazan's best film and the screen's best Williams adaptation. TM

Street Fighter

(1994, US, 102 min)
d Steven E de Souza. *p* Edward R Pressman, Kenzo Tsujimoto. *sc* Steven E de Souza. *ph* William A Fraker. *ed* Dov Hoenig, Anthony Redman, Robert F Shugrue. *pd* William J Creber. *m* Graeme Revell. *cast* Jean-Claude Van Damme, Raul Julia, Ming-Na Wen, Damian Chapa, Kylie Minogue, Simon Callow, Roshan Seth, Wes Studi.

● As a scriptwriter, Steven E de Souza made his name with *Die Hard* and its sequel; on the strength of this directorial debut, the day-job option would seem the better bet. Like many before him, director de Souza falls foul of transferring a necessarily repetitive computer game to the big screen: instead of a fluid narrative, we have a stop-start plot with too many heroes, multiple plot threads, and virtually no suspense or excitement. Having taken 63 hostages, renegade warlord General M Bison (Julia) demands a hefty ransom. Colonel Guile (Van Damme) and more than a dozen multi-ethnic heroes then try to penetrate the defences of Bison's impregnable hi-tech fortress. Julia (in his final role) hams it up shamelessly as the camp commandant, but not even his suave presence and throwaway quips can save this noisy, brainless mess. NF

Streetfighter, The

see Hard Times

Street Fleet

see D.C.Cab

Street Girls

(1974, US, 84 min)
d Michael Miller. *p* Paul Pompian, Jeff Begun. *sc* Michael Miller, Barry Levinson. *ph* Bob Wilson. *m* Terry Smith. *cast* Carol Case, Paul Pompian, Art Burke, Chris Souder, Jimmy Smith, Michael Albert Weber.

● Street life in cheerless Eugene, Oregon, focusing on a topless bar where the owner boosts his income by having his dancers turn tricks on the side, and where coke-head Angel is coerced into degradation by her dealer boyfriend Mario. Meanwhile, Angel's brutish father is out to track her down. A youthful collaboration by soon-to-be big names Miller and Levinson, accommodating some thoughtful asides on race and gender in between the statutory strippings and whippings, thumpings and humpings. DO

Streetlife

(1995, GB, 98 min)
d Karl Francis. *p* Ruth Caleb. *sc* Karl Francis. *ph* Nigel Walters. *ed* Roy Sharman. *pd* Ray Price. *m* Annie Lennox, John Hardy. *cast* Helen McCrory, Rhys Ifans, Christine Tuckett, Donna Edwards.

● Tough, uncompromising and very bleak story of a woman on a Caerphilly housing estate, so unlucky in life and love that she ends up killing her baby, born in secret and alone in her mother's caravan, and then sending it down a rural stream like Moses in his basket. This is a telling indictment of the '90s 'dustbin' society in which dysfunctional people seem abandoned and prey to council worker and drug dealer alike. Clumsy in parts and laid on a mite too thick, the film is nevertheless a cry of anguish that Ken Loach would have recognised. McCrory gives a vibrant performance in her first big film role. SGr

Street Music

(1981, US, 93 min)
d Jenny Bowen. *p/ph* Richard Bowen. *ed* Lisa Fruchtman, Diane Pelligrini. *ad* Don De Fina. *m* Eric Bogas, Judy Munson. *cast* Elizabeth Daily, Larry Breeding, Ned Glass, Marjorie Eaton, WF Walker.

● In the Tenderloin district of San Francisco, an old residential hotel (ironically named 'The Victory') is scheduled for demolition. Will the residents (most of them elderly) accept their fate or become politicised in the struggle to defend their collective home? You guessed it. If only Bowen, writer/director of this independent feature (her first), had risked making the old folk the protagonists, instead of focusing on a dumb street singer and her boorish bus driver boyfriend, she might have overcome the cuteness that undercuts the movie's humanist pleading. MA

Street of Shadows (aka Shadowman)

(1953, GB, 84 min)
d Richard Vernon. *p* WH Williams. *sc* Richard Vernon. *ph* Phil Grindrod. *ed* Geoffrey Muller. *ad* George Haslam. *m* Eric Spear. *cast* Cesar Romero, Kay Kendall, Edward Underdown, Victor Maddern, Simone Silva, Bill Travers.

● Part matron, part vamp, Kendall manages to combine the dowdy appeal of a '50s housewife who's just bought her first washing machine with Hollywood-style glamour. Romero is Luigi, the Soho nightclub owner who falls for her, Bogart to her Bacall. An excellent harmonica-based score and a half sympathetic villain in Maddern's scorned, deformed Limpy make for a dark atmospheric frame-up thriller, more Graham Greene than Edgar Wallace. GM

Street of Shame (Akasen Chitai)

(1956, Jap, 96 min, b/w)
d Kenji Mizoguchi. *p* Masaichi Nagata. *sc* Masashige Narusawa. *ph* Kazuo Miyagawa. *ed* Kanji Sugawara. *ad* Hiroshi Mizutani. *m* Toshiro Mayuzumi. *cast* Machiko Kyo, Ayako Wakao, Aiko Mimasu, Michiyo Kogure.

● Mizoguchi's final film is a grim but profoundly moving study of a group of prostitutes in Tokyo's red light district. While they go about their daily business, there are constant references to the anti-prostitution legislation which Parliament is debating. As is made clear, merely passing a law won't save the women. For whatever reasons they became prostitutes (money-related in every case), they can never escape the judgment passed on them by the repressive, patriarchal society which shunned them in the first place. The settings are a far removed from the medieval landscapes of *Ugetsu* or *The Life of Oharu*, but Mizoguchi's focus on the plight of his women characters is as intent and heart-rending as ever. GM

Streets of Fire

(1984, US, 94 min)
d Walter Hill. *p* Lawrence Gordon, Joel Silver. *sc* Walter Hill, Larry Gross. *ph* Andrew Laszlo. *ed* Freeman Davies, Michael Ripps, James Coblentz, Michael Tronick. *pd* John Vallone. *m* Ry Cooder. *cast* Michael Paré, Diane Lane, Rick Moranis, Amy Madigan, Willem Dafoe, Deborah van Valkenburgh, Richard Lawson, Rick Rossovich, Elizabeth Daily, Marine Jahan.

● Continuing his love affair with movies that go bang in the night, Hill here gives us a futuristic rock fantasy which is, at heart, a Western. An itinerant soldier (Paré) returns to his home to discover that his former girlfriend, the local girl who's made it big in the rockbiz (Lane), has been kidnapped by a villainous street-gang. Cue for fisticuffs and fireworks as Paré, aided by a tough-talking female sidekick (Madigan), hikes over to the bad part of town and unlocks Ms Lane from the bed to which she's been handcuffed. Result? Showdown. *Streets of Fire* is fast and loud, with music from Ry Cooder and, perhaps misguidedly, Jim Steinman; it is also violent, though its violence lies not in the depiction of blood and entrails, but in the sheer energy and speed with which the dark and brooding images rush after one another. The message is that there is no message; if this isn't action cinema in its purest form, then it's pretty close. RR

Streets of Gold

(1986, US, 94 min)
d Joe Roth. *p* Joe Roth, Harry J Ufland. *sc* Heywood Gould, Richard Price, Tom Cole. *ph* Arthur Albert. *ed* Richard Chew. *pd* Marcos Flaksman. *m* Jack Nitzsche. *cast* Klaus Maria Brandauer, Adrian Pasdar, Wesley Snipes, Angela Molina, Elya Baskin, Rainbow Harvest, Daniel O'Shea, John Mahoney.

● Brandauer plays an exiled Soviet boxing champ, now a self-pitying drunk and washer-up in a New York Russian restaurant. Banned from fighting in the Soviet Union for using his anti-Semitic coach as a punch-bag, he takes on a couple of local prospects, training them up for a grudge match against a visiting Soviet team. You can guess the rest, right down to the *Rocky*-style finale. Director Roth never uses a short jab when he can take a wild swing, usually at the cold inhumanity of Soviet society. NF

Streetwalker, The

see Marge, La

Streetwalkin'

(1984, US, 85 min)
d Joan Freeman. *p* Robert Alden. *sc* Joan Freeman, Robert Alden. *ph* Steven Fierberg. *ed* John K Adams, Patrick Rand. *ad* Jeffery Robbins. *m* Matthew Ender, Doug Timm. *cast* Melissa Leo, Randall Batinkoff, Dale Midkiff, Deborah Offner, Julie Newmar, Julie Cohen, Greg Germann, Kirk Taylor, Antonio Fargas.

● In flight from a wretched family life, naive Cookie (Leo) arrives in New York with only her tears, pocket money, and dumb younger brother (Batinkoff) for company. Quick to comfort her is charming, handsome Duke (Midkiff); trouble is, he's a psychopathically violent pimp, and soon she's selling her body on the seedy streets. Blinded by love, it's only after he's transformed her room-mate's face into steak tartare that she turns to another pimp for protection, and Duke sets out in search of his errant breadwinner, murder on his mind. Given that, like Penelope Spheeris and Amy Jones, Joan Freeman made this, her first feature, under the aegis of producer Roger Corman, high hopes seemed in order. No such luck. Starting off as lurid, documentary-style melodrama before it settles into an over-extended and often risible cat-and-mouse chase, this witless pile of prurient sleaze is poorly paced and saddled with a predictable script, stereotype characterisations, and distastefully voyeuristic direction. GA

Streetwise

(1984, US, 91 min)
d Martin Bell. *p* Cheryl McCall. *ph* Martin Bell. *ed* Nancy Baker. *m* Tom Waits.

● A grimly fascinating *cinéma-vérité* documentary about a bunch of kids (aged between 13 and 19) living rough on Pike Street, Seattle. Unable or unwilling to live with their parents, the kids hustle a living by begging, diving into garbage dumpsters for thrown-out pizzas, and selling their bodies. Seen through the unblinking eye of Bell's sharply focused camera, the kids flirt with, fight, support and sometimes exploit one another. Police, social workers and parents drift in and out, but their concern for the kids' long-term future seems irrelevant in the face of their immediate struggle to survive until the next meal or meal-ticket. Saddest of all, given the raw deal they've had from the system, is the kids' unquestioning conservatism. All they want from life is a nice house, a colour TV, and a life-style that conforms to their soap opera ideals. The inevitable reservations aside (56 hours of footage reduced to 91 minutes; the occasionally voyeuristic camerawork), this is an impressive achievement. Bell and his team clearly gained the confidence of their subjects, and despite their depressing lives, the kids reveal themselves in all their naive vitality. NF

Street with No Name, The

(1948, US, 91 min, b/w)
d William Keighley. *p* Samuel G Engel. *sc* Harry Kleiner. *ph* Joseph MacDonald. *ed* William H Reynolds. *pd* Lyle Wheeler, Chester Gore. *m* Lionel Newman. *cast* Mark Stevens, Richard Widmark, Lloyd Nolan, Barbara Lawrence, Ed Begley, Donald Buka, Joseph Pevney, John McIntire.

● Fresh from giggling his sadistic way through *Kiss of Death*, Widmark steals a march on this follow-up to the documentary approach of *House on 92nd Street* with his brilliantly quirky characterisation of a gangster in the throes of hypochondria (terrified of germs and draughts, he draws his nasal inhaler more often than his gun) and misogyny (in between bouts of wife-beating, he flirts coyly with Stevens, the young FBI agent who has infiltrated his gang). Inspired by the FBI's concern over the re-emergence of organised crime, and saddled with a narrator boasting what a great job the Bureau is doing, the film slips quietly into the *noir* genre with its shadowy camerawork, its ambiguous relationships, and its subversive delight in the personable Widmark's city of corruption. It was later reworked by Fuller as *House of Bamboo*. TM

Strictly Ballroom

(1992, Aust, 94 min)
d Baz Luhrmann. *p* Tristram Miall, Ted Albert. *sc* Baz Luhrmann, Craig Pearce. *ph* Steve Mason. *ed* Jill Bilcock. *pd* Catherine Martin. *m* David Hirschfelder. *cast* Paul Mercurio, Tara Morice, Bill Hunter, Pat Thomson, Gia Carides, Peter Whitford, Barry Otto, John Hannan, Sonia Kruger, Antonio Vargas.

● Right from the glorious opening, it's obvious that Baz Luhrmann knows *exactly* what he's doing. The story recounts the struggles of talented dancer Scott (Mercurio) to make it to the Pan-Pacific Grand Prix, despite setbacks resulting from his refusal to stick to the steps approved by his team: his dance-tutor mum (Thomson) has screaming fits, the Dance Federation director (Hunter) threatens disbarment, and the only club member prepared to partner him is shy, clumsy novice Fran (Morice). Partly a hilarious satire of the bizarre rituals of the ballroom world, partly a contemporary fairytale romance, Luhrmann's exhilarating debut transcends its shamelessly familiar plot through endlessly inventive details, through an expertly balanced blend of stylish cinematic technique and camp theatricality, and through the care and affection it devotes to the characters, dancing and music. Crucially, the film's enormous charm is never rammed down the throat, but acknowledged for the calculating ploy it is, with a winning, ironic wink. GA

Strictly Confidential

see Broadway Bill

Strictly Sinatra

(2000, GB, 97 min)
d Peter Capaldi. *p* Ruth Kenley-Letts. *sc* Peter Capaldi. *ph* Stephen Blackman. *ed* Martin Walsh. *pd* Martin John. *m* Stanislas Syrewicz. *cast* Ian Hart, Kelly Macdonald, Brian Cox, Alun Armstrong, Tommy Flanagan, Iain Cuthbertson, Una McLean, Jimmy Chisolm, Jimmy Yuill.

● You can see what writer/director Capaldi is trying to do, as he plays the self-deluding ambitions of Glaswegian cabaret singer Tony Cocozza (Hart) against the glitzy Vegas associations of the Sinatra repertoire he performs each night, while shading in a dark underworld threat from the gangland figures whose patronage may come at an ugly price. A sensible lass (Macdonald) offers another escape, if only Tony weren't so fixated by the bright lights. But much as we may admire Hart's application as the bighearted nobody barking up the wrong tree, the humiliation heaped upon him by a hideous perm and sad wardrobe rather hinders his ability to carry the picture. It's a tougher crime movie than, say, *Comfort and Joy*, but Bill Forsyth's whimsical ear for dialogue always made his characters that bit special. Here, the dialogue leaves strong actors like Brian Cox, scarred Tommy Flanagan (the errant dad in *Ratcatcher*) and old-timer Ian Cuthbertson struggling to make the heavies distinctive.Capaldi's highly attentive way with the camera shows promise, as does cinematographer Stephen Blackman's rich-hued take on the grim urban surroundings, but the final cut feels several rewrites short of a finished article. TJ

Strike (Stachka)

(1924, USSR, 6,460 ft, b/w)
d Sergei Eisenstein. *sc* The Proletcult Collective (Sergei Eisenstein, Valeri Pletniov, I Kravchinovski). *ph* Eduard Tissé. *ed* Sergei M Eisenstein. *ad* Vasili Rakhals. *cast* Maxim Straukh, Grigori Alexandrov, Mikhail Gomorov, I Ivanov, I Klukvin.

● Eisenstein's first feature also remains his most watchable; if his theories of montage and typage were already much in evidence, at least they had not yet turned into the over-emphatic academic tropes that marred so much of his later work. The story itself is simple: workers clash violently with employers and police during a drawn-out factory strike provoked by the sacking and subsequent suicide of one of their number. But Eisenstein's methods are both complex and extraordinary: his decision to make the masses rather than any single individual his hero lends the film a truly epic sweep; the vicious caricatures of the bourgeois capitalists make for wit and effectively powerful emotional manipulation; and the editing, rapid, fluid and razor-sharp, provides not only pace but a myriad of metaphorical meanings that extend way beyond mere propaganda. The harshly beautiful imagery – most memorably, shots of a slaughterhouse intercut with the massacre of the strikers – roots the movie effortlessly in down-to-earth reality, but its relentless energy and invention transform the whole thing into a raucous, rousing hymn to human dignity and courage. GA

Strikebound

(1983, Aust, 100 min)
d Richard Lowenstein. *p* Miranda Bain, Timothy White. *sc* Richard Lowenstein. *ph* Andrew De Groot. *ed* Jill Bilcock. *pd* Tracy Watt. *m* Declan Affley. *cast* Chris Haywood, Carol Burns, Hugh Keays-Byrne, Rob Steele, Nik Forster, David Kendall.

● Appalling conditions at Australia's Sunbeam Colliery in the '30s led to a miners' strike, and Agnes Doig, a dour Salvation Army schoolmistress, to a lifelong commitment to the labour movement. Although filmed with visual flair and authenticity, this reconstruction never works up steam. Perhaps the fact that Agnes and her miner husband Wattie appear in person, recalling the strike and affirming their continuing pride in being of the working-class, explains the rather deferential handling. In the flashback sequences, Haywood's Wattie has a puckish charm, and Burns works hard to establish Agnes's compassion and grit, but they rarely engage the emotions. The events of the strike likewise unfold with a terse cheeriness that rarely gains a truly threatening accent or a compelling momentum; and, before you know it, the action has petered out. HH

Strike Up the Band

(1940, US, 120 min, b/w)
d Busby Berkeley. *p* Arthur Freed. *sc* John Monks Jr, Fred Finklehoffe. *ph* Ray June. ed Ben Lewis. *ad* Cedric Gibbons, John S Detlie. *songs* George Gershwin, Ira Gershwin, Arthur Freed. *cast* Mickey Rooney, Judy Garland, Paul Whiteman, June Preisser, William Tracy, Larry Nunn.

● Don't be misled by the Berkeley credit – this is no girlie extravaganza. Rather, it's the second of those musical concoctions designed for the strident, irrepressible Rooney to dominate with Garland tagging along. Whiteman is once again offered as everybody's favourite uncle. High school big band theme, with Rooney determinedly whipping the school orchestra into a sensational swing band, and a rather sticky plot about raising funds for an operation. But the Roger Edens-Arthur Freed songs are just so-so, and Berkeley keeps a low profile except in the dizzily shot 'Do The La Conga' number. Title song is Gershwin. SG

Striking Distance

(1993, US, 101 min)
d Rowdy Herrington. *p* Arnon Milchan, Tony Thomopoulos, Hunt Lowry. *sc* Rowdy Herrington, Martin Kaplan. *ph* Mac Ahlberg. *ed* Pasquale Buba, Mark Helfrich. *pd* Greg Fonseca. *m* Brad Fiedel. *cast* Bruce Willis, Dennis Farina, Sarah Jessica Parker, Tom Sizemore, Brion James.

● After the shooting of his police-captain father, Pittsburgh cop Tom Hardy (Willis) accuses the force of hushing up the murder and finds himself demoted to the river patrol. Two years later, with his uncle Nick (Farina) in charge and an unlikely assailant convicted of the crime, Hardy is sure that a new spate of killings is the work of the same hand. His unauthorised investigation, with partner Jo Christman (Parker), is a routine affair, the film's familial and professional tensions sunk by a script that's all development and no pay-off. The supporting cast supplies some basic viewer-comfort, but this and the stock video ingredients are hardly enough to captivate the audience. TCh

Stripes

(1981, US, 106 min)
d Ivan Reitman. *p* Ivan Reitman, Daniel Goldberg. *sc* Len Blum, Daniel Goldberg, Harold Ramis. *ph* Bill Butler. *ed* Eva Ruggiero, Michael Luciano, Harry Keller. *pd* James H Spencer. *m* Elmer Bernstein. *cast* Bill Murray, Harold Ramis, Warren Oates, PJ Soles, John Larroquette, Sean Young, John Diehl, Lance LeGault, John Candy.

● Purposeless slob Murray loses car (repossessed), apartment and girlfriend (thrown out) all in the same day, and on a whim joins the US Army; a decision he spends most of the film regretting. Though the overall tone is as unquestioning of the virtues of the military life – discipline, duty, honour, etc – as was *Private Benjamin*, at least at its centre Murray is a genuine couldn't-give-a-shit character for the early '80s. Reitman, who also originated *Animal House* and *Meatballs*, manages a reasonable success rate at pulling off the numerous verbal and sight gags with which the script is peppered. RM

Strip Jack Naked: Nighthawks II

(1991, GB, 91 min, b/w & col)
d Ron Peck. *p/sc* Ron Peck, Paul Hallam. *ph* Ron Peck, Christopher Hughes. *ed* Ron Peck, Adrian James Carbutt. *m* Adrian James Carbutt. *cast* John Brown, John Diamon, Nick Bolton.

●When *Nighthawks* was released, its sincere but self-pitying study of a gay London teacher searching for Mr Right while struggling to emerge from the closet already looked dated. A dozen years on, Peck attempts to put his feelings at that time into some sort of context, mixing personal and political histories with a selection of out-takes from the original movie. Though it doesn't really work – the dreamy connecting shots of naked men fiddling with an editing machine are far too self-consciously arty – there are moments which, due to Peck's readiness to reveal his own discomfort, achieve a genuine if somewhat naive poignancy. His story begins with an unrequited schoolboy crush, proceeds through years of guilt and repression, and ends on a note of hope, with Peck arguing that the gay community's reaction to AIDS has made it both more conspicuous and more united. As autobiographical documentary, the film is ambitious, earnest, heartfelt; as a history of the British gay experience, it suffers from excessive subjectivity. GA

Striptease

(1995, US, 117 min)
d Andrew Bergman. *p* Mike Lobell. *sc* Andrew Bergman. *ph* Stephen Goldblatt. *ed* Anne V Coates. *pd* Mel Bourne. *m* Howard Shore. *cast* Demi Moore, Burt Reynolds, Rumer Willis, Ving Rhames, Armand Assante, Robert Patrick, Paul Guilfoyle.

●The first of Carl Hiaasen's hilarious thrillers to reach the screen, this faithfully reproduces the novel's anti-Republicanism. Reynolds plays right-wing Congressman David Dilbeck as a bewigged buffoon with a penchant for vaseline, and a fatal obsession with stripper Erin Grant (Moore). Writer/director Bergman contrasts Dilbeck's hypocritical advocacy of traditional family values with the sustaining alternative-family group at the Eager Beaver club – in which single mom Erin brings up her daughter (Rumer Willis) – comprising a bunch of strippers and bouncer Shad (Rhames). Unfortunately, the movie's so dire you wonder if it isn't an elaborate double-bluff designed to reveal the ineptitude of liberals. The kind of comedy thriller which cancels itself out, this is pitched too close to caricature to engender suspense, but lacks the crisp, acerbic wit which distinguishes Hiaasen's prose. There's a no-nonsense approach to nudity in general, but everything gets very self-conscious whenever Demi is called on to strut her stuff – which is often. TCh

Striptease Lady

see Lady of Burlesque

Strokes of Fire

see Chihwaseon

Stroller in the Attic, The (Yaneura no Sanposha)

(1976, Jap, 76 min)
d Noboru Tanaka. *p* Yoshiteru Yuuki, Hiroshi Ichiji. *sc* Akio Ido. *ph* Masaru Mori. *ed* Osamu Inoue. *ad* Yoshie Kikukawa. *cast* Junko Miyashita, Renji Ishibashi, Hiroshi Cho, Tokuko Watanabe, Yasuji Yashiro.

●Exceptionally pervy sexploitation movie from the first flowering of the Nikkatsu company's 'roman-porno' (romantic-pornographic) genre. A merely decadent exposition (landlord spies on bizarre erotic activities of his tenants in 1920s Tokyo) leads into a seriously pathological drama (landlord and aristo tenant team up for a series of thrill kills), climaxing with a vision of the 1923 Kanto earthquake (which wiped out the city) as the ultimate fusion of Eros and Thanatos. The perversity derives in part from the source story by Edogawa Ranpo (the Japanese 'Edgar Allan Poe'), but Tanaka was the right director for the job: less a skin merchant than a connoisseur of the extremist frisson. TR

Stromboli, Terra di Dio (Stromboli)

(1949, It, 107 min, b/w)
d/p Roberto Rossellini. *sc* Sergio Amidei, Gian Paolo Callegari, Roberto Rossellini. *ph* Otello Martelli. *ed* Jolanda Benvenuti. *m* Renzo Rossellini. *cast* Ingrid Bergman, Mario Vitale, Renzo Cesana, Mario Sponza.

●In Rossellini's first film with Bergman, the overpowering symbol of the volcanic island almost overwhelms its delicate story: a World War II refugee (Bergman) marries a young fisherman to escape from an internment camp. Brutalised by war, but coming to loathe the terrifying savagery of the island, her drama is a conflict between self-pity and acceptance of Something Greater. Praised as an example of cinema devoid of the excesses of formal artifice, a 'lesson in humility', its achievement is less modest: a sequence of tunny-fishing remains one of the most amazing ever filmed. (The English-language version distributed by RKO was cut to 82 minutes.) DMacP

Stronger Than Fear

see Edge of Doom

Strong Language

(1998, GB, 76 min, col & b/w)
d Simon Rumley. *p* Simon Rumley, Alex Tate. *sc* Simon Rumley. *ph* Armando Smit. *ed* Sasha Austen, Rick Moore, Simon Rumley. *pd* Joanna Cross. *m* David Conway, Laurence Elliot-Potter. *cast* Ricci Harnett, Kelly Marcel, Tania Emery, Julie Rice, Thomas Dyton, Robyn Lewis, Stuart Laing, Shireen Abdel-Moneim, Al Nedjari, Paul Tonkinson, Ruth Purser, Charlie De'Ath, Elaine Britten, Chris Pavlo, Kate Allenby, Colin Warren, David Groves.

●Talk is cheap, they say, and that's just as well for this British indie, a cheeky, amusing and intriguing faux vox-pop which very cleverly laces together some 16 interviews to camera from a varied range of London twenty-somethings. Matching various film and video stocks paced by an increasingly urgent electronic dance beat score, this deceptively natural earful of opinion is proof positive that ideas and energy can more than fill the holes that scant resources leave gaping. As the roll call of lift operators, the unemployed, video directors, fetish models, astrologers and the like offer their passionate views on indebtedness, cynicism, Oasis or clubbing, you initially wonder who's interviewing them and are they for real? But soon you are pulled in by the pure variety, humour and frankness of what they have to say. It is a tribute to director Rumley's writing that something real and recognisable comes across. It also teases that old conundrum about how fiction and documentary sometimes complete each other's work. WH

Strong Man, The

(1926, US, 6,882 ft, b/w)
d Frank Capra. *sc* Frank Capra, Hal Conklin, Robert Eddy. *ph* Elgin Lessley, Glenn Kershner. *ed* Harold Young. *ad* Lloyd Brierly. *cast* Harry Langdon, Priscilla Bonner, Gertrude Astor, William V Mong, Robert McKim, Arthur Thalassa.

●Second of the three features on the strength of which Langdon was briefly hailed as another Chaplin, here playing a Belgian soldier happily resorting to his catapult instead of a machine-gun in the World War I trenches, then heading for America after the armistice (as assiastant to a brutish strong man) in quest of the pen pal he has fallen for, unaware that she is blind. Pathos aside, there are some really very funny gags, and – if you can stand Langdon's somewhat obscene persona as an overgrown, pudding-faced baby – a beautifully constructed sequence in which he is subjected to ferociously close pursuit by a vamp, hungering not for his body as he assumes but for the loot hidden in his pocket. Capra's first feature, incidentally. TM

Strong-Man Ferdinand

see Starke Ferdinand, Der

Stroszek

(1977, WGer, 108 min)
d/p/sc Werner Herzog. *ph* Ed Lachman, Thomas Mauch. *ed* Beate Mainka-Jellinghaus. *m* Chet Atkins, Sonny Terry. *cast* Bruno S, Eva Mattes, Clemens Scheitz, Burkhard Driest, Pitt Bedewitz, Wilhelm von Homburg.

●Herzog seems to have run for cover after *Heart of Glass*, a supposedly 'difficult' film beneath whose seemingly impenetrable surface lay a simple reconstruction of key elements from horror films. And *Stroszek* has been labelled unfairly as a travelogue comedy featuring Bruno S from *The Enigma of Kaspar Hauser*. Bruno (S for Superstar? He struts like some remedial cousin of Jack Nicholson) and oddball entourage – including the excellent Eva Mattes as prostitute girlfriend – leave modern Berlin for the golden opportunities of America; in reality, the despair of Railroad Flats, Wisconsin. Although relatively indulgent for Herzog, the film's comedy works well enough, because Herzog's idiosyncratic imagination finds an ideal counterpoint in the bleak flatlands of poor white America. His view of that country is the most askance since the films of Monte Hellman. For all the supposed lightness, it is the film's core of despair which in the end devours everything. CPe

Struggle, The

(1931, US, 87 min, b/w)
d/p DW Griffith. *sc* Anita Loos, John Emerson, DW Griffith. *ph* Joseph Ruttenberg. *ed* Barney Rogan. *m* Philip A Chieb, DW Griffith. *cast* Hal Skelly, Zita Johann, Charlotte Wynters, Jackson Halliday, Evelyn Baldwin, Edna Hagan.

●Griffith's last movie looks like a naturalistic 'human' story struggling to emerge from a stern moral tract on the evils of demon alcohol, a tension that's fascinating at this remove. Despite a robust DTs nightmare climax, it gets nowhere near the intended attack on Prohibition and the perils of 'bad' liquor; but it does have a good eye for the vulnerability of its miserable hero (Skelly, excellent), and a surprisingly sharp way with its pre-Depression satire (catch the Jewish insurance salesman with a sideline in home-made wine). No question, much of the humour springs from Anita Loos' swing-time script ('Get hot, Bozos!'), but it incidentally proves that Griffith mastered the innovations of talkies better than any of his contemporaries believed. TR

Stuart Little

(1999, US, 84 min)
d Rob Minkoff. *p* Douglas Wick. *sc* M Night Shyamalan, Greg Brooker. *ph* Guillermo Navarro. *ed* Tom Finan, Julie Rogers. *pd* Bill Brzeski. *m* Alan Silvestri. *cast* Geena Davis, Hugh Laurie, Jonathan Lipnicki, Jeffrey Jones, Connie Ray, Allyce Beasley, Brian Doyle-Murray, Estelle Getty; voices: Michael J Fox, Nathan Lane, Chazz Palminteri, Steve Zahn.

●An adaptation of EB White's classic 1950s story of an orphanage mouse with red sneakers and his adopted (human) family. Mr and Mrs Little (Laurie and Davis) and nine-year-old George (Lipnicki) live in a brownstone sandwiched between skyscrapers on Fifth Avenue, NY, and are given to such pleasantries as 'This meatloaf is delicious, dear.' As voiced by Fox, Stuart is a bookish, self-deprecating sort, who appeals through the thousand gradations of hurt he registers, rather than the expected play made of his stature. Essentially, the plot goes, 'paradise lost then paradise regained,' with miffed cat Snowbell co-opting some alley mogs to abduct the little fella. In other words, peril stands in for character development. Director Rob (*The Lion King*) Minkoff's animation experience ensures that the digital/live action matches are faultless, showing off his skill in a bravura episode on the Central Park pond with Stuart taking the helm of a kids' sailing boat. Otherwise, the film is strangely uninvolving. WH

Stuart Saves His Family

(1995, US, 95 min)
d Harold Ramis. *p* Lorne Michaels. *sc* Al Franken. *ph* Lauro Escorel. *ed* Pembroke J Herring, Craig Herring. *pd* Joseph T Garrity. *m* Marc Shaiman. *cast* Al Franken, Laura San Giacomo, Vincent D'Onofrio, Shirley Knight, Harris Yulin, Lesley Boone, John Link Graney.

●Stuart Smalley's beloved self-help Chicago cable show is cancelled, whereupon he discovers that, what with depression, alcoholism, unemployment and obesity, his dysfunctional family back in Minnesota is far worse off than he is. Writer/performer Al Franken created Smalley for TV's *Saturday Night Live*, but his catchphrase – 'I'm good enough, I'm smart enough, and doggone it, people like me' – here in an expanded context proves somewhat wide of the mark. Franken squeezes a few chuckles out of the moon-faced, cardigan-wearing, therapy-dependent Stuart, and those familiar with Alcoholics Anonymous' 12-step recovery programme may bond in sympathy. The sentimentality, however, doesn't play. AO

Stubby (Fimpen)

(1974, Swe, 89 min)
d/p/sc Bo Widerberg. *ph* John Olssonm, Hanno Fuchs, Roland Sterner, Åke Åstrand. *ad* Lotta Melanton. *m* Sergei Prokofiev. *cast* Johan Bergman, Magnus Hörenstan, Inger Bergman, Arne Bergman.

●Six-year-old kid gets to play for the local league team, moves on to the Swedish side one game later, and scores a string of Roy of the Rovers goals in the World Cup qualifying games, usually after the opposition has gone ahead, culminating in the defeat of the USSR at Dynamo Stadium. But he gives it all up to learn how to read and write. As a fantasy, *Stubby* is reasonably engaging, if somewhat unimaginative; but as a satire on fame and exploitation, it's barely even sketchy. Writer/director Widerberg doesn't develop his ideas much beyond the comic strip stage. The film was shot on the fringes of the World Cup, and offers the novelty of various national sides taking on a six-year-old, except that it looks like action replay, because they have to slow down to make him look fast. CPe

Stud, The

(1978, GB, 90 min)
d Quentin Masters. *p* Ronald S Kass. *sc* Jackie Collins. *ph* Peter Hannan. *ed* David Campling. *ad* Michael Bastow. *m* Biddu. *cast* Joan Collins, Oliver Tobias, Sue Lloyd, Mark Burns, Doug Fisher, Walter Gotell.

●Like Dickens, Joan and Jackie Collins (the former starring in this adaptation of the latter's novel) offer a panoramic exposition of contemporary urban life, tracing the decline of stud Tony Blake (Tobias), from promising young disco manager and darling of lonely, beautiful women who treat him as a sex object, back to his East End origins, where he suddenly displays a three-day growth of beard and a new moral awareness. Joking and comparisons apart, this is a dreadful film. The dreary, awkward narrative seems largely dependent on the locations they could get – disco, swimming pool, lift. The script (by Jackie herself), permeated with an appalling and deep-rooted snobbery, contrives to be completely inaccurate and therefore offensive to every facet of the social structure, in a London that swings like a corpse at the end of a rope. JS

Student Days (Xuesheng zhi Ai)

(1981, Tai, 85 min)
d Lin Ch'ing-chieh. *p* Li Lien-mao. *sc* Lin Ch'ing-chieh, Li Lien-Mao. *ph* Lin Hung-chung. *m* Lin Lin, T'ang Lin. *cast* Li Mu-ch'en, Lin Nan-shih, Ch'in Ch'ang-ming, Wang Hsing.

●Director Lin, himself an ex-teacher, has made four low-budget independent features about the lives of high school kids in provincial Taiwan, with more or less the same cast each time. This one is the most polished, although not the most imaginative. By Taiwanese standards, it has a likeable taste of reality in its character sketches, and depiction of delinquency and emotional problems. However, it also suffers from both major vices of Taiwanese cinema: careless photography and scenes of outrageously excessive sentiment. TR

Student Teachers, The

(1973, US, 79 min)
d Jonathan Kaplan. *p* Julie Corman. *sc* Danny Opatoshu. *ph* Steven Katz. *ed* George Van Noy. *m* David Nichtern. *cast* Susan Damante, Brooke Mills, Bob Harris, John Cramer, Dick Miller, Don Steele, Robert Phillips, Chuck Norris.

●Foremost among Kaplan's virtues as a film-maker are economic characterisation and a fast, taut sense of pacing, learned no doubt during his apprenticeship with the Roger Corman exploitation factory. Demonstrating that he always showed promise, this movie from those cheapo, cheerful days takes the typical tale of its heroines' extra-curricular activities and turns it against all expectations. While paying lip-duty to traditional audience titillation techniques by frequently baring the upper regions of the nubile educationalists, Kaplan prefers to concentrate on issues of sexual politics, crime and racism, at the same time revelling in an often hilarious sense of absurd parody (Sandra Dee as a source of syphilis in a sex-education film). No great movie, but great fun. GA

Study in Terror, A

(1965, GB, 95 min)
d James Hill. *p* Henry E Lester. *sc* Donald Ford, Derek Ford. *ph* Desmond Dickinson. *ed* Henry Richardson. *ad* Alex Vetchinsky. *m* John Scott. *cast* John Neville, Donald Houston, John Fraser, Anthony Quayle, Barbara Windsor, Adrienne Corri, Frank Finlay, Judi Dench, Peter Carsten, Robert Morley, Cecil Parker, Georgia Brown, Barry Jones, Kay Walsh.

●A careful but curiously ineffective piece of Sherlockiana in which Holmes (Neville) and Watson (Houston) tangle with Jack the Ripper in circumstances much less ingenious than those imagined for *Murder by Decree*. Donald and Derek Ford's script goes for the Conan Doyle flavour, but gets caught between the devil and the deep blue sea, since the producers (Compton, raised above their station, willy-nilly, by Polanski and *Repulsion*) were exploitation merchants at heart. All the pedantically pastiched dialogue, reverently played straight by a distinguished cast, therefore sits very uncomfortably with the crudely and gleefully shock-cut murders. The colour is nice, so are Alex Vetchinsky's sets, which include a delightfully smoky Whitechapel pub for Georgia Brown to belt out a couple of period numbers in. TM

Stuff, The

(1985, US, 87 min)
d Larry Cohen. *p* Paul Kurta. *sc* Larry Cohen. *ph* Paul Glickman. *ed* Armond Lebowitz. *ad* Marlene Marta, George Stoll. *m* Anthony Guefen. *cast* Michael Moriarty, Andrea Marcovicci, Garrett Morris, Paul Sorvino, Scott Bloom, Danny Aiello, Patrick O'Neal, Alexander Scourby, Brooke Adams, Tammy Grimes.

●Larry Cohen's demons have never been your average little devils: Q the Winged Serpent lived atop the Chrysler Building, his anti-Christ lived in a Brooklyn basement, and J Edgar Hoover wasn't exactly human. This one is a white glop which comes bubbling out of the ground, tastes nice, and is immediately mined and marketed by a fast food chain under the logo 'Enough is never enough'. In other words, the monster doesn't come after you, you have to go out and consume it. Once eaten, it does strange things to people. Leading the anti-Stuff campaign for the forces of good is Michael Moriarty, in his customary persona as the laid back bozo who isn't as stupid as he looks ('Nobody is as stupid as I look'). As usual, Cohen's humour is chaotic (importing a right wing private army for the finale), surreal, and very, very subversive. If the drive-in crowd took its message to heart, they'd never eat again. *Invasion of the Body Snatchers* for our time. CPea

Stunde Null (Zero Hour)

(1977, WGer, 112 min, b/w)
d Edgar Reitz. *sc* Peter Steinbach, Karsten Witte, Petra Kiene, Edgar Reitz. *ph* Gernot Roll. *ed* Ingrid Broszat. *ad* Max Panitz. *m* Nicos Mamangakis. *cast* Kai Taschner, Herbert Weissbach, Anette Jünger, Klaus Dierig, Erika Wackernagel.

●War's end, a village outside Leipzig. A bunch of representative German types learn that they are not, after all, in the American zone: they have been traded for a piece of Berlin. Edgily they await the Russians who on arrival prove to be as loutish and dangerous as feared. Teenage hero and heroine escape, but the first jeep-load of Americans they meet brutally disabuse them of any idea of a safe haven. *Ende*. There's a bit of a McGuffin involving buried Nazi treasure, but mainly this is Reitz looking back in anger – though how sympathetic non-Germans will feel towards his characters' plight is an interesting question. Stylistically, pre-*Heimat* Reitz veers uncertainly between relaxed naturalism and Wajda-like expressionism. BBa

Stunt Man, The

(1979, US, 130 min)
d/p Richard Rush. *sc* Lawrence B Marcus. *ph* Mario Tosi. *ed* Jack Hofstra, Caroline Ferriol. *ad* James Schoppe. *m* Dominic Frontière. *cast* Peter O'Toole, Barbara Hershey, Steve Railsback, Sharon Farrell, John Garwood, Allen Garfield, Alex Rocco, Adam Roarke, Chuck Bail.

●Lacking the innocence of Rush's previous work, this is also short on the really sardonic wit that its storyline (based on Paul Brodeur's novel) demands. A young Vietvet on the run (Railsback) tumbles onto the location of an all-action World War I epic, and falls into uneasy partnership with the movie's imperious, soliloquising director, O'Toole. That piece of casting is driven home with a sledgehammer insistence, while Railsback's engagingly twitchy performance – as the new stuntman filling in for a dead predecessor – is passed over in favour of more 'serious' themes. The result is a movie filled with gags and excellent stunts which remains curiously humourless at heart. Stunted, not stunning.

Stunts

(1977, US, 89 min)
d Mark L Lester. *p* Raymond Lofaro, William Panzer. *sc* Dennis Johnson, Barney Cohen. *ph* Bruce Logan. *ed* Corky Ehlers. *m* Michael Kamen. *cast* Robert Forster, Fiona Lewis, Joanna Cassidy, Darrell Fetty, Bruce Glover, James Luisi, Richard Lynch, Candice Rialson.

●From the director of *Truck Stop Women* comes a respectful showcase for the stunt trade with a cool regard for the fast buck. Lester twins the investigations by an outsider woman journalist (Lewis) and insider stunt hero (Forster) into the 'accidental' deaths of stunt people on the location for some clapped-out all-action pic. The result is a rehash of Hollywood's pathetic dedication to the cult of the gambler, which sacrifices visual opportunism in order to sit awestruck at the risks it boasts as 'truth' ('You can't bullshit a stunt – it either works or it doesn't'). Without the courage to trust fully in the action set pieces or the suspense plot, it still gives a sense of the stupefying, routine greed of movie production…and almost makes us believe that this highly-paid freedom to smash things is the last hope of mankind. Less than cunning. RP

Stuntwoman, The

see Ah Kam

Stupids, The

(1995, US, 94 min)
d John Landis. *p* Leslie Belzberg. *sc* Brent Forrester. *ph* Manfred Guthe. *ed* Dale Beldin. *pd* Phil Dagort. *m* Christopher Stone. *cast* Tom Arnold, Jessica Lundy, Bug Hall, Alex McKenna, Mark Metcalf, Matt Keeslar, Christopher Lee, David Cronenberg, Costa-Gavras, Gillo Pontecorvo.

●The Stupids are a weird family, but entirely lacking the intriguingly dysfunctional nature of, say, the Simpsons (which Tom Arnold used to write). Ex-mailman Stanley (Arnold), Joan (Lundy), and kids Buster (Hall) and sweet Petunia (McKenna) inhabit a '50s world of candy-stripe colours, gingham bows, puff skirts and alien-movie speech patterns. Their true provenance, however, is American children's television and its dim never-never land of permutational studio sitcoms. The dumb surreal – Stanley taking the goldfish for a walk, the expostulations on the weekly theft of their garbage – one can accept. But the rambling, episodic narrative, laden with naff sight gags, dissipates attention in minutes. WH

Subject Was Roses, The

(1968, US, 107 min)
d Ulu Grosbard. *p* Edgar Lansbury. *sc* Frank D Gilroy. *ph* Jack Priestley. *ed* Jerry Greenberg. *ad* George Jenkins. *m* Lee Pockriss. *cast* Patricia Neal, Jack Albertson, Martin Sheen, Don Saxon, Elaine Williams, Grant Gordon.

●Having done Frank D Gilroy's Pulitzer Prize-winner on Broadway, Albertson and Sheen reprised their roles for this respectable film version, stage director Grosbard made his feature debut, and Neal came back from a serious stroke to complete the team. Sheen's the WWII veteran whose return to a less-than-happy home ignites long-standing animosities between mom and pop (Neal and Albertson), a set-up which may have had some residual resonance during the Vietnam era, but which is mainly a platform for three detailed, honest performances. TJ

Subjective Factor, The (Der subjektive Faktor)

(1981, WGer, 144 min)
d Helke Sander. *p* Marianne Gassner. *sc* Helke Sander. *ph* Martin Schäfer. *ed* Ursula Höf. *ad* Jürgen Rieger. *m* Heiner Goebbels. *cast*

Angelika Rommel, Nikolaus Dutsch, Lutz Weidlich, Dominik Bender, Johanna Sophia.
● Anni, the 'heroine' and thinly fictionalised director-surrogate, is a single mother who joins a Berlin commune, gets turned on to the utopian militancy of '68, then quickly converted to a figurehead of the emergent Women's Movement by the discovery that her male comrades are chauvinistic *Schweine* who affect macho trenchcoats and keep their socks on during sex. As the title implies, it's a defiantly and meanderingly personal film that often drags, then ends up by jumping abruptly from the first stirrings of feminism to 1980s sell-out (erstwhile anti-Nam demonstrators dining out at a chic Vietnamese eatery). Sander's modish theme is a suppressed woman's history, but with the heady radicalism under consideration now evaporated into the mists of history, the film emerges (presumably unintentionally) almost as a piece of period nostalgia. SJo

Submarine Patrol

(1938, US, 95 min, b/w)
d John Ford. *p* Darryl F Zanuck. *sc* Rian James, Darrell Ware, Jack Yellen. *ph* Arthur Miller. *ed* Robert Simpson. *ad* William Darling, Hans Peters. *m* Charles Maxwell. *cast* Richard Greene, Nancy Kelly, Preston Foster, George Bancroft, Slim Summerville, John Carradine, J Farrell McDonald, Elisha Cook Jr, Maxie Rosenbloom, Jack Pennick, Ward Bond, George E Stone.
● A claustrophobic and mannered flagwaver (adapted by several hands from Ray Milholland's novel *The Splinter Fleet of the Otranto Barrage*) in which an arrogant playboy, Perry Townsend III (Greene), signs up with the US Navy in WWI and is put aboard a rickety old boat to chase submarines. A strict but decent disciplinarian shapes up an unruly crew. Greene has the conceit knocked out of him and wins the affections of all-American girl Nancy Kelly. Ford keeps the narrative and action buzzing, but this is a pale example of the Master's work. The following year he made *Stagecoach* and *Young Mr Lincoln*. GM

Submarine X-1

(1967, GB, 90 min)
d William Graham. *p* John C Champion. *sc* Donald S Sanford, Guy Elmes. *ph* Paul Beeson. *ed* John S Smith. *ad* Bill Andrews. *cast* James Caan, Norman Bowler, David Sumner, Brian Grellis, William Dysart.
● Standard WWII drama in which Lt Commander Caan and his three midget subs mount a revenge attack on the German battleship 'Lidendorf' in a Norwegian fjord. Writer/producer John Champion churned out another very similar picture, Paul Wendkos' *Attack on the Iron Coast*, in 1967, also for the Mirisch company. Caan's career had not quite turned the corner, and he found little to get his teeth into in this attenuated story. TJ

Substitute, The

(1996, US, 114 min)
d Robert Mandel. *p* Morrie Eisenman, Jim Steele. *sc* Roy Frumkes, Rocco Simonelli, Alan Ormsby. *ph* Bruce Surtees. *ed* Alan MacKie. *pd* Ron Foreman. *m* Gary Chang. *cast* Tom Berenger, Ernie Hudson, Diane Venora, Glenn Plummer, Marc Anthony, Cliff De Young, Richard Brooks, Rodney A Grant.
● Most pupils at George Washington High, the Miami hellhole where Jane Hetzko (Venora) struggles to stay alive, let alone teach, may be marginally younger than the seeming thirty-somethings in *The Lords of Flatbush*, but they're far more heavily armed. Typical is the sneering class nasty, Juan (Anthony), who has Hetzko's legs baseball-batted for a slight. At hand, luckily, kicking his heels after a covert operation in Miami, is a facially scarred, wish-fulfilling avenger, Hetzko's Special Forces boyfriend Shale (Berenger), who takes over the class, posing as a Harvard man named 'Mr Smith'. It's not long before he discovers a drug ring, implicating the politically aspirant head Mr Rollé (Hudson), but first, to wage successful war, the class's respect has to be won. In director Mandel's unsophisticated hands, this all comes over like an amusingly preposterous mix of *Kindergarten Cop* and *Dangerous Minds*. But the script, by at least three writers, doesn't have the dialogue, characterisations, plotting, or plain interest to sustain a school-based drama. You can sense Mandel's sigh of relief when he's finally able to launch into an Uzi-blazing actioner, second grade. WH

Subterraneans, The

(1960, US, 89 min)
d Ranald MacDougall. *p* Arthur Freed. *sc* Robert Thom. *ph* Joseph Ruttenberg. *ed* Ben Lewis. *ad* George W Davis, Urie McCleary. *m* André Previn. *cast* George Peppard, Leslie Caron, Janice Rule, Roddy McDowall, Anne Seymour, Jim Hutton, Scott Marlowe, Art Pepper, Art Farmer, Gerry Mulligan, Carmen McRae.
● Jack Kerouac's Beat odyssey is well and truly beaten to a pulp in this sanitised Hollywood claptrap. Groovester Peppard falls not for the black girl featured in the original novel but for decidedly French waif Caron. Jazz musos passing through on their way to their connection include saxman Art Pepper and flugelhorn virtuoso Art Farmer. McDowall's words of youthful wisdom: 'Hey, life is a party and everyone else is a party-crasher!' Like profoundsville, daddy-o, and in 'Scope to boot. Hypnotically abominable. TJ

Suburban Commando

(1991, US, 90 min)
d Burt Kennedy. *p* Howard Gottfried. *sc* Frank Cappello. *ph* Patrick J Swovelin. *ed* Terry Stokes. *pd* Ivo Cristante, SJ Strawn. *m* David Michael Frank. *cast* Hulk Hogan, Christopher Lloyd, Shelley Duvall, William Ball, Laura Mooney, Michael Faustino, Larry Miller, Tony Longo, JoAnn Dearing, Roy Dotrice, Dennis Burkley, Jack Elam.
● In this likeable kids' action-adventure, Hulk Hogan, the blond-maned, 6'7" World Wrestling Federation superstar, plays an intergalactic warrior, first seen traversing the universe in silver-plastic armour (the production design is self-consciously tacky), single-handedly saving planets from arch-villain Suitor (Ball). Dropped into 'stressed-out' suburban California when the crystals on his space-pod need recharging, he finds board and lodging – posing as a Frenchman – with a downtrodden wimp (Lloyd), his loopy wife (Duvall) and their kids. Most of the laughs come from watching the gentle giant learning to skateboard with the kids, taking video games 'for real', and the like. His intergalactic bounty-hunting enemies arrive, and Lloyd, his help enlisted, turns from wimp to hero. Directed with glee, from a fine tongue-in-cheek script, it should amuse boys and child psychologists of all ages. WH

Suburbia

see Wild Side, The

SubUrbia

(1996, US, 121 min)
d Richard Linklater. *p* Anne Walker-McBay. *sc* Eric Bogosian. *ph* Lee Daniel. *ed* Sandra Adair. *pd* Catherine Hardwicke. *m* Sonic Youth. *cast* Jayce Bartok, Amie Carey, Nicky Katt, Ajay Naidu, Parker Posey, Giovanni Ribisi, Samia Shoaib, Steve Zahn.
● Linklater's film covers much the same territory as *Slackers* and *Dazed and Confused*. It charts one long momentous night in the lives of a group of suburban 20-year-olds, for whom entertainment consists mainly of booze, banter and arguments with the Pakistani proprietors of the convenience store where they habitually hang out, and examines the friends' reactions to the visit of a former schoolmate-turned-rock star. Allegiances shift, animosities erupt, violence rears its head, tragedy looms. While it's true that playwright Eric Bogosian's screenplay fails to avoid the kind of tidy twists and contrivances favoured by theatre, and that the reluctance to leave the street corner setting makes for a certain staginess, Linklater keeps matters engrossing, partly through the strong performances he elicits, partly through his firm grasp of the rhythms, colours and moods of suburban existence. Crucially, no character is quite as he or she first appears, nor is the film's attitude towards the kids simplistically sympathetic or condemnatory. GA

Subway

(1985, Fr, 102 min)
d Luc Besson. *p* Luc Besson, François Ruggieri. *sc* Luc Besson, Pierre Jolivet, Alain Le Henry, Marc Perrier, Sophie Schmit. *ph* Carlo Varini. *ed* Sophie Schmit. *ad* Alexandre Trauner. *m* Eric Serra, "Lucky Guy" Rickie Lee Jones. *cast* Isabelle Adjani, Christopher Lambert, Richard Bohringer, Michel Galabru, Jean-Hugues Anglade, Jean-Pierre Bacri.
● Safecracker Lambert hides in the Parisian Métro from a wealthy businessman's wife (Adjani), with whom he has fallen in love; from her husband's thugs; and from the Métro police. He becomes part of a strange netherworld of eccentric social misfits, all living outside the law. Setting the movie in this unfamiliar but realistic world is intriguing enough, and Besson handles the action with consummate mastery. But the punk-chic style only accentuates the film's emptiness. That said, Adjani once again proves herself not only one of the most versatile actresses in European cinema, but also the most beautiful. GA

Subway Riders

(1981, US, 118 min)
d/p/sc Amos Poe. *ph* Johanna Heer. *ed* Orlando Gallini, Johanna Heer, Amos Poe. *cast* Robbie Coltrane, Charlene Kaleina, Cookie Mueller, John Lurie, Amos Poe, Susan Tyrrell, Bill Rice.
● Not so much subway riders as underground poseurs, Poe's Manhattan melodramatists – psychotic saxophonist, sweaty cop, junkie *femme fatale*, assorted night people – do little more than stand still for Johanna Heer's stylishly *noir*-conscious camera. Every shot might come ready to be framed, but it's a frustratingly long walk through the post-Pop gallery when Poe shows no inclination to cut, and even less to encourage his cast to get on with the off-handedly minimal 'plot'. Irksome narcissism. PT

Subway Stories
Tales from the Underground

(1997, US, 85 min)
d Jonathan Demme, Craig McKay, Bob Balaban, Patricia Benoit, Seth Rosenberg, Lucas Platt, Alison Maclean, Julie Dash, Abel Ferrara, Ted Demme. *p* Richard Guay, Valerie Thomas. *sc* Adam Brooks, John Guare, Lynn Grossman, Angela Todd, Seth Rosenberg, Albert Innaurato, Danny Hoch, Julie Dash, Marla Hanson, Joe Viola. *ph* Anthony Janelli, Tom Hurwitz, Ken Kelsch, Adam Kimmel. *ed* Andy Keir, Colleen Sharp, Angelo Correro, Elizabeth Kling, Donna Stern, Jeffrey Wolf. pd Edward Check. *m* Mecca Bodega. *cast* Bill Irwin; Dennis Leary, Christine Lahti; Steve Zahn, Jay Stiller; Bonnie Hunt; Lili Taylor, Michael Rapoport; Mercedes Ruehl, Zachary Taylor; Sarita Chaudhury; Taral Hicks; Rosie Perez, Mike McGlone; Gregory Hines, Ann Heche.
● This is the HBO production later reprised in London as *Tube Tales*. Ten sketches set on the far side of the ticket barrier, that place of late-night perils and unexpected comedy, of random encounters that are strange or dangerous, and where abrasiveness and generosity contend. The most successful episodes preserve the mystery of glimpsed fragments of other people's lives: McKay's 'The Red Shoes', Ted Demme's 'Miracle in Manhattan'. Jonathan Demme offers a slight shaggy dog story, 'Subway Car from Hell,' and Ferrara an uncharacteristically mellow anecdote, 'Love on the A Train.' Unlike the London version there are no outright duds, although the balance between the distressing and the uplifting is not quite so well struck. BBa

Success

see American Success Company, The

Success Is the Best Revenge

(1984, GB/Fr, 91 min)
d/p Jerzy Skolimowski. *sc* Jerzy Skolimowski, Michael Lyndon. *ph* Mike Fash. *ed* Barrie Vince. *pd* Voytek. *m* Stanley Myers, Hans Zimmer. *cast* Michael York, Joanna Szczerbic, Michael Lyndon, Jerry Skol, Michel Piccoli, Anouk Aimée, John Hurt, Jane Asher.
● Like *Moonlighting*, this was shot very quickly, using the director's Kensington home as a major location. Once again the Polish crisis is central: Alex Rodak (York) is a theatrical director exiled with his family (actually the Skolimowskis) and planning an ambitious theatrical 'happening' to establish himself. While his self- preoccupation leads everyone to despair, his 15-year-old son Adam mulls over his own comparative lack of identity and plans to fly to Warsaw. Adam is played by Skolimowski's son (credited as Michael Lyndon); the film's basic idea was his, and clear-

ly a lot of subsequent dabbling with the script is to blame for the way the various strands shoot off in all directions. The result is very disjointed and discursive (with time for a hilarious Thatcherite bank manager cameo from Jane Asher); but reservations aside, Skolimowski creates something which is genuinely cinematic. Spritely, humorous, dazzlingly filmed, the intense energy easily compensates for the often bewildered acting. DT

Succubus (Necronomicon – Geträumte Sünden)

(1967, WGer, 82 min)
d Jesús Franco. *p* Adrian Hoven. *sc* Pier A Caminneci. *ph* Franz X Lederle, Georg Herrero. *ed* Fritzi Schmidt. *ad* H Peter Krause, Carlos Viudes. *m* Friedrich Gulda. *cast* Janine Reynaud, Jack Taylor, Howard Vernon, Nathalie Nort, Michel Lemoine, Adrian Hoven.
●Franco, the prolific Spanish director, decks out a glossy Freudian sex movie with a mass of undigested cultural reference, and an endless series of studiously sub-surrealist dream sequences. But despite a promisingly erotic opening, he can't hide the grinding banality of the plot, which has absolutely nothing to do with the title or even 'bizarre sexual rites' (as the ads claimed). In fact, it's a standard 'girl commits murder in a trance' situation which will have you sunk in boredom within a very few minutes. DP

Such a Gorgeous Kid Like Me

see Belle Fille comme moi, Une

Such a Long Journey

(1998, Can/GB, 113 min)
d Sturla Gunnarsson. *p* Paul Stephens, Simon MacCorkindale. *sc* Sooni Taraporevala. *ph* Jan Kiesser. *ed* Jeff Warren. *pd* Nitin Desai. *m* Jonathan Goldsmith. *cast* Roshan Seth, Om Puri, Soni Razdan, Naseeruddin Shah, Sam Dastor, Vrajesh Hirjee, Kurush Deboo.
●1971: India is on the brink of war with Pakistan, but the timid Parsi bank clerk Gustad Noble (Seth) has his own problems. Forced to live in an unhygienic Bombay apartment, he's tortured by a rebellious son and the mysterious disappearance of his friend Jimmy. When Jimmy gets in touch, however, things only get worse. Adapted by Sooni Taraporevala (*Salaam Bombay!*) from the novel by Rohinton Mistry, the film takes some time to loosen up and shed its hobnail boots. Seth is astonishing. Those bags under his eyes suggest Gustad is a man who does all his dreaming in the daytime, forever retreating into a gilded past. Also excellent is Shah as the doomed Jimmy, who morphs from a political spider into a fly. Visually, the film becomes curious, then curiouser. The first hint comes with Gustad's dreams, which swish along to overwrought music. Gradually, Canadian director Gunnarsson allows a surreal sense of urgency to seep into the present, creating sights for our sore eyes that are both woozy and crazily colourful, both magical and real. As journeys go, this one's entirely confounding. CO'Su

Such a Pretty Little Beach

see Si Jolie Petite Plage, Une

Such Good Friends

(1971, US, 102 min)
d/p Otto Preminger. *sc* Elaine May. *ph* Gayne Rescher. *ed* Harry Howard. *pd* Rouben Ter-Arutunian. *m* Thomas Shepard. *cast* Dyan Cannon, James Coco, Jennifer O'Neill, Ken Howard, Nina Foch, Lawrence Luckinbill, Louise Lasser, Burgess Meredith, Sam Levene, Rita Gam, Nancy Guild.
●Made in the same year as *The Hospital*, but the script by Esther Dale (Elaine May) is less of a medical exposé than Chayevsky's for the Arthur Hiller film, more of a brittle comedy about the rich at play while one of their number (Luckinbill) slowly dies in hospital after a simple operation – to remove a mole on his neck – goes disastrously wrong. Sadly, Preminger seems unsure whether to take May's characters at face value or to 'feel' for them. As a result, the cardboard emotions of Cannon (the wife seeking revenge for her dying husband's newly-discovered infidelities) and Coco (the family doctor who is losing his patient) are too often taken for real, and the script's brilliantly witty cameos are shunted too quickly out of sight. PH

Such Is Life (Asi es la Vida)

(1999, Mex/Sp. 98 min)
d Arturo Ripstein. *p* Laura Imperiale, Jorge Sánchez, Alvaro Garnica. *sc* Paz Alicia Garcíadiego. *ph* Guillermo Granillo. *ed* Carlos Puente. *pd* Claudio Contreras. *m* David Mansfield, Leoncio Lara. *cast* Arcelia Ramírez, Luis Felipe Tovar, Patricia Reyes Spindola, Ernesto Yañez, Francesca Guillén, Martha Aura, Daniela Carvajal.
●After the disaster that was the near impenetrable *Divine*, Ripstein returns to melodramatic form with this digitally shot, contemporary version of *Medea*, based not on Euripides' play, but on Seneca's more declamatory version of the myth. Lured to the city by the fickle Nicolás, only to be forced to work as an abortionist/witch when he leaves her for the younger, more moneyed daughter of a crime boss, country girl Julie plots her terrible revenge in long takes and lachrymose monologues. Meanwhile, Ripstein gets Brechtian here and there with a ranchero quartet serving as chorus, performing ballads on and, bizarrely, off the TV. The measured pacing occasionally makes for great emotional intensity, though the regular irruptions of irony and absurdism prevent it ever accumulating tragic force. GA

Sud

(1999, Fr/Bel, 70 min)
d/sc Chantal Akerman. *p* Xavier Carniaux. *ph* Raymond Fromont. *ed* Claire Atherton.
●Context can change everything. The first 15 minutes or so of Akerman's documentary offer a series of everyday shots of a town in the Deep South. Someone mows the lawn in front of a church, people go about their business. There's no narration until the reminiscences of the black population begin to reveal the details of the 1998 James Byrd murder, when a group of white supremacists dragged a black man to his death behind their truck. Pieces of his body were found along the three-mile route. Suddenly, the film's banal images of Jasper, Texas, acquire a whole different resonance of horror and racial tension. Extraordinary footage of Byrd's memorial service at the modest local church ups the emotional ante, while Akerman's final, long-held shot takes us right along the death road, almost every inch of the way. An image which would normally seem so ordinary becomes something else again, with every second of the journey screaming out in pain. TJ

Sudden Death

(1995, US, 110 min)
d Peter Hyams. *p* Moshe Diamant, Howard Baldwin. *sc* Gene Quintano. *ph* Peter Hyams. *ed* Steven Kemper. *pd* Philip Harrison. *m* John Debney. *cast* Jean-Claude Van Damme, Powers Boothe, Raymond J Barry, Whittni Wright, Ross Malinger, Dorian Harewood.
●Reuniting Hyams and Van Damme, director and star of *Timecop*, this spectacular nail-biter exploits their combined, if limited, abilities to the full. As 17,000 fans cheer on their ice hockey teams in Pittsburgh's magnificent Civic Arena, ruthless smoothie Joshua Foss (Boothe) and *his* team infiltrate the owner's box and kidnap the US Vice President. Foss's demands include the electronic transfer of frozen foreign-government funds, allowing hi-tech thief Boothe to siphon off a cool $500 million. Unless these fiscal transactions are completed before the game ends, bombs planted all over the stadium will explode. Foss however, has not reckoned with Darren McCord (Van Damme), a haunted ex-fireman turned security guard whose young son and daughter are in the crowd. Fortunately, McCord has seen *Die Hard* and *Under Siege*, so he's able to use his hand-me-down Bruce Willis-like quips and Steven Seagal-style booby traps to frustrate Foss's plans. As always, Van Damme's at his best when cracking heads; his overplaying of the caring, sensitive father role, on the other hand, is irksome in the extreme. NF

Sudden Fear

(1952, US, 110 min, b/w)
d David Miller. *p* Joseph Kaufman. *sc* Lenore J Coffee, Robert Smith. *ph* Charles Lang Jr. *ed* Leon Barsha. *ad* Boris Leven. *m* Elmer Bernstein. *cast* Joan Crawford, Jack Palance, Gloria Grahame, Bruce Bennett, Virginia Huston, Mike Connors.
●Definitely a walk on the wild side, this has Crawford as a well-heeled playwright sacking hatchet-faced Palance from her latest production as lacking the right romantic personality, then falling for him in a whirlwind courtship when they 'happen' to meet on a train. Cue for a deadly cat-and-mouse game as Palance, aided by sulky Grahame, sets out to kill Crawford for her money and she uses her playwright's wiles to devise a counterplot. With suspense screwed way beyond the sticking point, superb camerawork from Charles Lang, and Crawford in nerve-janglingly extravagant form, it's hugely enjoyable. TM

Sudden Fortune of the Good People of Kombach, The (Der plötzliche Reichtum der armen Leute von Kombach)

(1970, WGer, 102 min)
d Volker Schlöndorff. *sc* Volker Schlöndorff, Margarethe von Trotta. *ph* Franz Rath. *ed* Klaus von Boro. *m* Klaus Doldinge. *cast* Georg Lehn, Reinhard Hauff, Karl-Josef Kramer.
●In 1819, a desperate band of Hessian peasants hold up a tax-wagon, only to find their sudden wealth even more dangerous than the threat of starvation that provoked them; they have brought the full legal, intellectual and moral weight of the ruling class down upon themselves, and they have no defences. Schlöndorff chronicles the situation rather than the individual characters, and uses elements like an anachronistic score to undercut a merely emotional involvement. His analysis of the events as a chapter in an ongoing class struggle tends to the obvious; the movie functions best as a kick in the teeth to the romantic notion of jolly rustics. Bonus for collectors: Fassbinder appears in a tiny bit part. TR

Sudden Impact

(1983, US, 117 min)
d/p Clint Eastwood. *sc* Joseph C Stinson. *ph* Bruce Surtees. *ed* Joel Cox. *pd* Edward C Carfagno. *m* Lalo Schifrin. *cast* Clint Eastwood, Sondra Locke, Pat Hingle, Bradford Dillman, Paul Drake, Audrie J Neenan, Jack Thibeau.
●It's the man again; back with a flatulent dog and his brand new .44 Magnum Automatic, investigating the trail of a corpse with 'a .38 calibre vasectomy' and a woman on a rape revenge crusade. This, the fourth of the *Dirty Harry* cycle, finds Clint as the usual pillar of troubled infuriation, his brows creased even more deeply by the usual dilemmas of inadmissible evidence and consequent vigilante justice; the villains are the standard Hollywood collection of unshaven lowlife, lesbians and giggling psychos bent upon the familiar course of distressing the more gentle citizenry ('One false move and the retard's brains get spread across the wall'). It seems rather pointless to cry Fascist once more in the looming face of Inspector Harry Callahan. The real problem here is technical; Eastwood the director is far less sure-footed than he was with the likes of *Play Misty for Me* or *The Outlaw Josey Wales*. Eastwood the star needed a hit to bolster his flagging ratings; now that he's got it, maybe Harry will be put out to stud, with his Magnum. CPea

Suddenly

(1954, US, 77 min, b/w)
d Lewis Allen. *p* Robert Bassler. *sc* Richard Sale. *ph* Charles G Clarke. *ed* John F Schreyer. *ad* F Paul Sylos. *m* David Raksin. *cast* Frank Sinatra, Sterling Hayden, James Gleason, Nancy Gates, Willis Bouchey, Kim Charney, Paul Frees.
●The title refers to a small town in California, upon which a trio of assassins descends, taking over a house with a fine parallax view of the railroad station, and making prisoners of the occupants, an upstanding suburban family (Gleason and Gates). The movie is lifted from the routine – it was made as a four-week quickie – by Sinatra's performance. When he was interested he could be terrific (*Some Came Running*, *Pal Joey*, *The Detective*). As John Baron, the nobody who became a somebody when WWII put a rifle in his hands and taught him to be a sniper, he's a strutting, sneering psycho. Even better he wears his hat indoors. He won a Silver Star for wiping out Germans. Now he's hauling down $500,000 to hit the President and nobody's gonna get in his way, including town sheriff Sterling Hayden. BC

Suddenly Last Summer

(1959, US, 114 min, b/w)
d Joseph L Mankiewicz. *p* Sam Spiegel. *sc* Gore Vidal, Tennessee Williams. *ph* Jack Hildyard. *ed* William Hornbeck, Thomas Stanford. *pd* Oliver Messel. *m* Buxton Orr, Malcolm Arnold. *cast* Elizabeth Taylor, Katharine Hepburn, Montgomery Clift, Mercedes McCambridge, Albert Dekker, Gary Raymond.
●From a Tennessee Williams play, an outrageous, melodramatic shocker touching on madness, homosexual prostitution, incest, disease and cannibalism, replete with enough imagery to sustain an American Lit seminar for months. On film, with Taylor as the woman who saw something nasty and Clift as the psychiatrist trying to probe her trauma, the one-act material is stretched perilously thin; but it works for Hepburn as the incarnation of civilised depravity, the matriarch trying to keep the lid on things by persuading Clift to lobotomise her niece (Taylor, whose performance suggests that surgery has already taken place). JS

Sudden Terror

see Eyewitness

Suez

(1938, US, 104 min, b/w)
d Allan Dwan. *p* Gene Markey. *sc* Philip Dunne, Julien Josephson. *ph* J Peverell Marley. *ed* Barbara McLean. *ad* Bernard Herzbrun, Rudolph Sternad. *m* Louis Silvers. *cast* Tyrone Power, Loretta Young, Annabella, Henry Stephenson, Joseph Schildkraut, J Edward Bromberg, George Zucco, Nigel Bruce, Sig Ruman.
●The story of the building of the Suez canal, this highlights both Dwan's virtues and his flaws. The action/catastrophe sequences are marvellously assured without ever going over the top, as is the handling of the human drama. However, in contrast to directors like Walsh, Vidor and Anthony Mann, who use dramatic action to exteriorise the inner tensions of their characters, Dwan – who is concerned with the modest virtues of honesty and fairness – is unable, indeed unwilling, to so combine both strands of his story. Accordingly, *Suez* is a series of incidents unconnected by dramatic urgency; Dwan, quite simply, is unconcerned with the building of the canal. PH

Sugarbaby (Zuckerbaby)

(1985, WGer, 86 min)
d Percy Adlon. *p* Eleonore Adlon. *sc* Percy Adlon. *ph* Johanna Heer. *ed* Jean-Claude Piroué. *ad* Matthias Heller. *m* Dreieier, Franz Erlmeier, Fritz Köstler, Paul-Würges-Combo. *cast* Marianne Sägebrecht, Eisi Gulp, Toni Berger, Manuela Denz, Will Spindler.
●A sweet romantic comedy, with chubby Sägebrecht playing a lonely undertaker's assistant who falls for a young knight on a shiny yellow subway train and stalks him in, one initially supposes, forlorn pursuit – the punchline being that her U-Bahn inamorato (Gulp) is married to a black-clad harpy and highly susceptible to a little old-fashioned seduction. Adlon paints working class Munich like Pabst on speed, in acid-drop colour and expressionistic camera angles – a kaleidoscopic visual gloss on the characters' repressed and unspoken emotions. He ponders on the feminist and fatness and the folly of cultural stereotypes in the most diverting and persuasive of ways, providing food for thought as well as a feast for the eye. SJo

Sugar Cane Alley

see Black Shack Alley

Sugar Hill

(1993, US, 123 min)
d Leon Ichaso. *p* Rudy Langlais, Gregory Brown. *sc* Barry Michael Cooper. *ph* Bojan Bazelli. *ed* Gary Karr. *pd* Michael Helmy. *m* Terence Blanchard. *cast* Wesley Snipes, Michael Wright, Theresa Randle, Clarence Williams III, Abe Vigoda, Larry Joshua.
●Roemello and Raynathan Skuggs may be partners in drug-dealing, but temperamentally they're so different that only their mutual love holds them together. Roe (Snipes) wants out of the dangerous game they play with the Family men who resent and challenge their control of the streets, while Ray can't bear the thought of little brother leaving him to fend for himself. Something's gotta give – especially after Roe meets Melissa (Randle), a nice middle-class girl who abhors the life he's always promising to abandon. There's much to commend in Ichaso's not unambitious movie. The generally strong performances do justice to scriptwriter Barry Michael Cooper's evident desire to avoid the New Jack stereotyping of many contemporary black crime movies; the fluid camera and lush jazz score ensure that it looks and sounds classy; and much of the time the director's understatement and attention to detail are a distinct advantage. However, matters are not helped by an actorly tone, some plot-stopping big speeches, and an often sluggish pace. GA

Sugarland Express, The

(1974, US, 110 min)
d Steven Spielberg. *p* David Brown, Richard D Zanuck. *sc* Hal Barwood, Matthew Robbins. *ph* Vilmos Zsigmond. *ed* Edward Abroms, Verna Fields. *ad* Joseph Alves Jr. *m* John Williams. *cast* Goldie Hawn, Ben Johnson, Michael Sacks, William Atherton, Gregory Walcott, Steve Kanaly, Louise Latham.
●Fugitive couple (Hawn, Atherton) plus kidnapped cop (Sacks) and patrol car take on police chief Ben Johnson and an ever-growing caravan of assorted cars, newsmen, sightseers and wideboys out for a shoot-up in an across-Texas chase caper that has its protagonists overtaken by events beyond their control and comprehension. Despite the obvious similarity to the Roadrunner cartoon that appears at one point – both as a comedy and in the casually destructive violence employed – Spielberg's first feature for the big screen also touches on many aspects of American life and cinema: the role of the media, the matriarchal society, consumer possession, the decline of the American hero, and the increasing depersonalisation of everything. A beautifully put together, assured film. CPe

Sugartime

(US, 1995, 110 min)
d John N Smith. *p* David Coatsworth. *sc* Martyn Burke. *ph* Pierre Letarte. *ed* Ralph Brunjes. *pd* Barbara Dunphy. *m* Sidney James. *cast* John Turturro, Mary-Louise Parker, Maury Chakin, Elias Koteas, Louis Del Grande, Deborah Duchene.
●Passable if routine biopic (for TV) about onetime Chicago Mafia king, Sam Giancana, the original Teflon Don, against whom nothing would stick. But this is less a gangster film than a love story about Giancana's long-time affair with minister's daughter and singing sister Phyllis McGuire (Parker). It's hard to make someone like Giancana loveable, especially when his lavish courting technique is intercut with images of associates being clubbed to death with baseball bats. Giancana's more fascinating links through lust with the Kennedys are hardly explored, and while Turturro is always watchable as the Worm Giancana, one is hardly moved at the conclusion, which posits that the Mob had him killed because he wouldn't give up the excessively popular entertainer. SGr

Suicide Club (Jisatsu Circle)

(2002, Jap, 99 min)
d Shion Sono. *p* Toshikazu Tomita, Masaya Kawamata, Seiji Yoshida. *sc* Shion Sono. *ph* Kazuto Sato. *ed* Akihiro Onaga. *ad* Yoshihiro Nishimura. *m* Tomoki Hasegawa. *cast* Ryo Ishibashi, Masatoshi Nagase, Tamao Sato, Mai Hosho, Akaji Maro.
●Just as teen Japan goes wild for an idol band called Desert, who have secret messages in their visuals and lyrics, 54 schoolgirls join hands on the Yamanote Line platform in Shinjuku Station and jump in front of an oncoming train. The resulting tsunami of blood heralds hundreds more mass and individual suicides. Three shopworn cops (Ishibashi, Nagase, Maro) investigate and discover any number of potential triggers, even as their own lives collapse around them. Is it all caused by a dangerous website? By a deranged glam rocker? Or just by living in contemporary Japan? Sono has been making weird, formalist indie films for more than a decade, but this represents a shift into weird, free-form exploitation. None of it makes any real sense, but it sure does keep you watching. TR

Suite 16

(1995, GB/Bel, 110 min)
d Dominique Deruddere. *p* Paul Breuls. *sc* Charles Higson, Lise Mayer. *ph* Jean-François Robin. *ed* Kant Pan. *m* Walter Hus. *cast* Pete Postlethwaite, Antonie Kamerling, Geraldine Pailhas, Tom Jansen, Bart Slegers, Suzanne Colin.
●A young hustler, Chris, hides from the police in a hotel room. He threatens the resident, a rich invalid called Glover (Postlethwaite): he has killed once, he says, and will do so again. Glover is entirely accommodating; in fact, he persuades Chris (Kamerling) to stay on after the storm has passed. He will provide for the youth's every need in return for the vicarious pleasure this will afford him. At first, Chris can't believe his luck... but soon Glover's jaundiced palette demands more violent stimulation. Deruddere's third film is a sleazy, degenerate and thoroughly compelling yarn, a wayward thriller which calls equally on the extremes of continental exploitation and art movies. Despite a colourless performance from Kamerling, Deruddere mines the maximum impact from the psychological power games, and the film kicks into a higher gear with the introduction of the talented Pailhas as Helen, the third side of a climactic SM triangle. It runs hot and cold – like blood. TCh

Suitor, The

see Soupirant, Le

Sukiyaki

(1995, Jap, 94 min)
d Junichi Suzuki. *p* Shohei Motomani. *sc* Junichi Suzuki, Tetsutomo Kosugi. *ph* Kazuhiko Nara. *ed* Hiroshi Matsuo. *pd* Kazutsuga Shisido. m Masamichi Shigeno. *cast* Rica Sekiya, Yuka Sekiya, Sachiko Hidari, Tamio Kawachi, Kai Shishido.
●The average Godzilla pic is closer to believable human values than this fatuous blend of soap and sitcom, which plays like the omnibus edition of a daytime TV series. The inept cook running the Boston Grill in Yokohama has twin daughters, both with romance problems: one is epileptic and sure no man will marry her, the other unsure of her love for her fiancé. A couple of oddball merchant-marine cooks come along to take over the kitchen and set the girls' hearts aflutter. Even worse than it sounds. TR

Sullivan's Travels

(1941, US, 91 min, b/w)
d Preston Sturges. *p* Paul Jones. *sc* Preston Sturges. *ph* John F Seitz. *ed* Stuart Gilmore. *ad* Hans Dreier, Earl Hedrick. *m* Leo Shuken, Charles Bradshaw. *cast* Joel McCrea, Veronica Lake, Robert Warwick, William Demarest, Franklin Pangborn, Porter Hall, Robert Greig, Eric Blore.
●Irresistible tale of a Hollywood director, tired of making comedies and bent on branching out with an arthouse epic called *Brother, Where Art Thou?*, who sets out to research the meaning of poverty. Suitably costumed as a hobo and starting down the road, discreetly dogged by a studio caravan ready to record the great man's thoughts and serve his needs, he angrily sends this absurd prop packing; only to realise much later, while sweating out a sentence on a chaingang, that severing the lifeline has left him to all intents and purposes a stateless person. He emerges a wiser and more sober man, having seen his fellow-convicts forget their misery in watching a Disney cartoon. The film has sometimes been read as a defence of Hollywood escapism, but what Sturges is really doing is putting down the awful liberal solemnities of problem pictures and movies with a message. Whatever, *Sullivan's Travels* is a gem, an almost serious comedy not taken entirely seriously, with wonderful dialogue, eccentric characterisations, and superlative performances throughout. TM

Summer Affair, A

see Moment d'Egarement, Un

Summer and Smoke

(1961, US, 118 min)
d Peter Glenville. *p* Hal B Wallis. *sc* James Poe, Meade Roberts. *ph* Charles Lang Jr. *ed* Warren Low. *ad* Walter Tyler. *m* Elmer Bernstein. *cast* Geraldine Page, Laurence Harvey, Una Merkel, John McIntire, Pamela Tiffin, Rita Moreno, Thomas Gomez.

●Faltering, prissy adaptation of Tennessee Williams play set in 1916. Geraldine Page (Oscar-nominated) an ageing small-town Mississippi spinster gets the hots for medical student Harvey, who in turn is more interested in Hispanic firebrand Moreno. Much overwrought dialogue, but the whole thing's treated like bone china by British theatre type Glenville, and even Page is curiously studied. One for students of the thick-stirred Southern accent. TJ

Summer at Grandpa's, A (Dongdong de Jiaqi)

(1984, Tai, 98 min)
d Hou Xiaoxian. *p* Zhang Huakun. *sc* Zhu Tianwen, Hou Xiaoxian. *ph* Chen Kunhou. *ed* Liao Qingsong. *m* Edward Yang, Du Duzhi. *cast* Wang Qiguang, Gu Jun, Mei Fang. Lin Xiuling.

●Young Tung-Tung and his little sister spend the vacation with their grandparents while mother lies sick in hospital. It's an eventful stay, but Hou never opts for melodrama, and at first his quietly amused observation of events seems to border on the inconsequential. Not so, however. What makes the film so affecting is its unflinching honesty. As boy and girl take time off from playing games to become barely comprehending witnesses to the adult world, the film examines, with precision and wit, both the innocence and the unthinking cruelty of childhood. But life among the grown-ups is no better, and the children are confronted with violence, crime, sexual passion, and the presence of death. It's a clear-eyed movie, never sentimental, always intelligent and revealing. GA

Summerfield

(1977, Aust, 93 min)
d Ken Hannam. *p* Patricia Lovell. *sc* Cliff Green. *ph* Mike Molloy. *ed* Sara Bennett. *ad* Graham 'Grace' Walker. *m* Bruce Smeaton. *cast* Nick Tate, Elizabeth Alexander, John Waters, Michelle Jarman, Geraldine Turner, Charles Tingwell.

●Hannam remains best known here for *Sunday Too Far Away*, an intelligent outback variant on Howard Hawks' poignant Hollywood classics of male camaraderie and competitive professionalism. This follow-up also invokes an honoured movie heritage, but only insofar as it toys inventively with audience expectations of the genre patterns of the mystery-thriller. A new schoolteacher arrives in a small coastal community, to be immediately assailed by portents of unease: off-centre welcomes from adults and children alike, casual news that his predecessor has inexplicably disappeared, a violently accidental introduction to the enigmatic family at isolated Summerfield. 'You've come the wrong way' is the first line in the film, and all the subsequent atmospherics revolve around the teacher's inevitable attempt to make things add up: only to find the equation both more tragically complex and infinitely simpler than suspected. Neither as accomplished nor as affecting as Hannam's debut, but a neatly manipulative entertainment. PT

Summer Holiday

(1962, GB, 107 min)
d Peter Yates. *p* Kenneth Harper. *sc* Peter Myers, Ronnie Cass. *ph* John Wilcox. *ed* Jack Slade. *ad* Syd Cain. *m* Stanley Black. *cast* Cliff Richard, Lauri Peters, Melvyn Hayes, Una Stubbs, Ron Moody, David Kossoff.

●As guys'n'gals commandeer a red London bus and head Europe-wards for sun, it's easy to mock the put-on jollity of it all, yet somehow the high spirits are infectious. And doesn't Cliff have a much lighter touch on the screen than the dread Elvis? TJ

Summer Interlude

see Sommarlek

Summer in La Goulette, A (Un été à La Goulette)

(1996, Fr/Tun, 100 min)
d/sc Férid Boughedir. *ph* Robert Alazraki. *ed* Catherine Poitevin, Andrée Davanture, Isabelle Devinck. *pd* Claude Bennys. *m* Jean-Marie Sénia. *cast* Gamil Ratib, Mustapha Adouani, Gay Nataf, Ivo Salerno, Claudia Cardinale.

●Tunis, 1967: Three teenage girlfriends, neighbours in a cheap apartment building, seem to embody hope for the future: one is Jewish, another Muslim, and the third Catholic. When they make a pact to lose their virginity, however, their fathers' friendship breaks down, as each blames the others for instilling loose morals in the children. Shot in a warm, amber light, this is a modest but quietly affecting re-creation of a moment of optimism in Mid-East relations. TCh

Summer in the City

(1970, WGer, 143 min, b/w)
d/p/sc Wim Wenders. *ph* Robby Müller. *ed* Peter Przygodda. *cast* Hanns Zischler, Edda Köchl, Libgart Schwartz, Marie Bardischewski, Gerd Stein, Helmut Farber, Wim Wenders.

●Titled in English, made on a shoestring provided by the Munich film school, Wenders' first feature – 'My longest short', as he wryly put it – has a plot about an ex-jailbird drifting through Germany until he escapes, not to the America of his dreams but to Holland. Essentially, though, it's a documentary about the time and the place, and as such it's a fascinating source book for Wenders' later work. The aimless odyssey with ubiquitous rock songs; the endless shots (by Robby Müller) of landscapes and nocturnal streets seen speeding by from the windows of cars and trains; the tangential encounters with strange friends or friendly strangers; the laments for lost movie palaces; above all, the celebration of obsessive enthusiasms, including a delightfully tangled attempt by someone never seen again to articulate the solemnity of John Wayne's association with the Three Wise Men in Ford's *Three Godfathers*. TM

Summer Love (O Da Beni Seviyor)

(2001, Tur, 100 min)
d Baris Pirhasan. *sc* Baris Pirhasan, Gül Dirican. *ph* Jürgen Jürges. *ed* Adnan Elial. *pd* Mustafa Ziya Ülkenciler. *m* Mare Nostrum, Ulas Özdemir. *cast* Lale Mansur, Luk Piyes, Hale Akinli, Ayla Algan, Cezmi Baskin, Taner Birsel, Ece Eksi, Kemel Inci, Esme Madra, Ali Ökçelik, Ugur Polat, Ayse Nil Samlioglu, Serra Yilmaz.

●A record of a girl's first summer crush (based on a story by co-writer Gül Dirican), it begins with Esma being carted off to country relatives for the holiday as some sort of remedy for her poor grades in religion at school. The village is rife with prune-faced crones nattering about land politics and trading disapproval of the girl's beautiful aunt Saliha's abandonment of her fiancé; it's also full of possibilities, and Esma swivels between tomboyish scrapes and new-found feminine fancies, in particularl handsome tractor boy Hüseyin. If it's never very clear, at a more detailed level, what's going on or why, it must be said that Pirhasan conjures a sweet sense of place and personality. NB

Summer Lovers

(1982, US, 98 min)
d Randal Kleiser. *p* Mike Moder. *sc* Randal Kleiser. *ph* Timothy Galfas. *ed* Robert Gordon. *pd* Bruce Weintraub. *m* Basil Poledouris. *cast* Peter Gallagher, Daryl Hannah, Valerie Quennessen, Barbara Rush, Carole Cook.

●Improbably bland sweethearts Michael and Cathy (Gallagher, Hannah) rent a holiday villa on a Greek island teeming with wanton youths sporting colourful nylon rucksacks and all-over tans. The couple's fragile happiness is shattered when Michael has an affair with another woman (Quennessen), then restored when she moves into their villa and bed. For us to believe in these liberated living arrangements, Kleiser brings the women into unusually sharp relief (for this type of film), knocking Michael from the film's and *ménage*'s centre. However, by so revealing the two women, Kleiser makes us wonder why they would turn to the resoundingly dull Michael for anything. But the film plays safe, presumably a concession (like the pounding disco soundtrack) to the conservative taste of the American public, which was polled throughout the making of the film. But all this cannot entirely remove the piquant sensuality that will titillate more subtle palates. FD

Summer Madness

see Summertime

Summer Magic

(1962, US, 104 min)
d James Neilson. *p* Ron Miller. *sc* Sally Benson. *ph* William Snyder. *ed* Robert Stafford. *ad* Robert Clatworthy, Carroll Clark. *m* Buddy Baker. *cast* Hayley Mills, Burl Ives, Dorothy McGuire, Deborah Walley, Una Merkel, Michael J Pollard.

●Widow McGuire does up a dilapidated house in Maine as a home for her three kids. Hayley Mills, Disney's top live-action draw of the time, spreads sweetness, light and a queasy feeling in the pit of the stomach in this adaptation of Kate Douglas' novel *Mother Carey's Chickens*, but it's singing postman Osh Popham (Ives) who delivers the most memorable moment, the hit song 'The Ugly Bug Ball'. Rowland V Lee filmed an earlier version in 1938. TJ

Summer Manoeuvres

see Grandes Manoeuvres, Les

Summer of Aviya, The (Hakayitz shel Aviya)

(1988, Isr, 95 min)
d Eli Cohen. *p* Eitan Even, Gila Almagor. *sc* Eli Cohen, Gila Almagor, Haim Bouzaglo. *ph* David Gurfinkel. *ed* Tova Neeman. *ad* Yoram Shayer. *m* Shem-Tov Levi. *cast* Gila Almagor, Kaipo Cohen, Eli Cohen, Marina Rossetti, Avital Dicker, Dina Avrech.

●A beautifully modulated, affecting film (based on an autobiographical book by Gila Almagor) dealing with the aftermath of the Holocaust. Set in a small settlement in the harsh early years of the Israeli state (1951), it depicts the summer 'holidays' unexpectedly spent by nine-year-old Aviya (Kaipo Cohen) with her mother Henya (Almagor), an institutionalised survivor of the camps who turns up on graduation day at Aviya's boarding-school. The delineation of the mother-daughter relationship is accomplished with remarkable sensitivity and restraint. That the bonding may not be easy is shown when Henya, convinced that Aviya has lice, ruthlessly shaves her hair until she resembles a camp inmate; but equally well conveyed are their tentative moves toward an expression of mutual love, despite the mother's severe emotional lurches and outbursts. Cohen never indulges in the pain and suffering of his characters, but anchors the film in significant detail, gently recalling the pressures and realities of their situation. Rich, insightful, and healing. WH

Summer of '42

(1971, US, 104 min)
d Robert Mulligan. *p* Richard A Roth. *sc* Herman Raucher. *ph* Robert Surtees. *ed* Folmar Blangsted. *ad* Albert Brenner. *m* Michel Legrand. *cast* Jennifer O'Neill, Gary Grimes, Jerry Houser, Oliver Conant, Lou Frizell, Christopher Norris, Katherine Allentuck.

●Zeroing in (with much of Mulligan's usual quiet sympathy) on adolescence and the moment of sexual awakening with the added weight of *The Way We Were* type of nostalgia, this is a mess of contradictions. A surprising commercial success with its tale of the teenager and the unhappy war widow – as a sort of cry tough version of *Love Story*? – it forever misses, unlike *American Graffiti*, the heady sexual climate of adolescence to concentrate on the circumstances of the sex act itself. PH

Summer of Sam

(1999, US, 142 min)
d Spike Lee. *p* Jon Kilik, Spike Lee. *sc* Victor Colicchio, Michael Imperioli, Spike Lee. *ph* Ellen Kuras. *ed* Barry Alexander Brown. *pd* Thérèse DePrez. *m* Terence Blanchard. *cast* John Leguizamo, Mira Sorvino, Adrien Brody, Jennifer Esposito, Anthony LaPaglia, Ben Gazzara, John Savage, Spike Lee.

●This is less about the 1977 exploits of serial killer 'Son of Sam' and more about the tensions that concurrently arise in an Italian-American New York neighbourhood: not only does a local Capo's decision to rid the 'hood of the murderous scourge through vigilante methods foster paranoia, suspicion and violence, but the culture clash between macho wiseguys and gays, disco straights and a punk just back from England results in a scenario not so very different from *Do the Right Thing*. Trouble is, the overlong narrative, however entertaining from minute to minute, is a mess: Sam's (sometimes comically depicted) reign of terror sheds no light on the dynamics of society at large, the characterisation is uneven, and there are a few too many stereotypes on view for comfort – Italian-Americans, especially, may not applaud the almost blanket depiction of them as violently homophobic, misogynist boors. GA

Summer Paradise (Paradistorg)

(1976, Swe, 113 min)
d Gunnel Lindblom. *p* Ingmar Bergman. *sc* Ulla Isaksson, Gunnel Lindblom. *ph* Tony Forsberg. *ed* Siv Lundgren. *pd* Anna Asp. *m* Georg Riedel. *cast* Birgitta Valberg, Sif Ruud, Margaretha Byström, Agneta Ekmanner, Solveig Ternström, Holger Löwenadler.

●Produced by Bergman and dealing with tensions between a family and friends gathered in the country to celebrate midsummer's eve, Gunnel Lindblom's debut as a director seemed all too likely to fall foul of terminal Swedish gloom. But she is clearly too talented and sensitive to be heavy-handed about her ideas, and the film carries an affecting sense of its characters' continuing existence outside the film's time/space. From reactionary father and middle-aged doctor daughter to disturbed adolescent, Lindblom displays a serious commitment to portraying complex human behaviour and emotions. There are no facile answers here; there is as fine a depiction of family life, friendship, and especially middle-age, as one is likely to see on film. Any occasional unsureness of tone is easily overcome by superb central performances from Valberg and Ruud. SM

Summer School

(1987, US, 98 min)
d Carl Reiner. *p* George Shapiro, Howard West. *sc* Jeff Franklin, Stuart Birnbaum, David Dashev. *ph* David M Walsh. *ed* Bud Molin. *pd* David L Snyder. *m* Danny Elfman. *cast* Mark Harmon, Kirstie Alley, Robin Thomas, Dean Cameron, Gary Riley, Shawnee Smith, Courtney Thorne-Smith, Carl Reiner.

●Genial teen comedy about a high school teacher (Harmon) on vacation in Hawaii who's inveigled into looking after an anarchic class of delinquents at a remedial school. A bit bland compared to Reiner's Steve Martin comedies, but engagingly played. GM

Summer Snow (Nüren Sishi)

(1994, HK, 100 min)
d Ann Hui. *p* Raymond Chow. *sc* Chan Man-Keung. *ph* Li Ping-Bin. *ed* Wong Yee-Shun. *pd* Wong Yan-kwai. *m* Otomo Yoshihida. *cast* Josephine Siao, Roy Chiao, Law Kar Ying, Allen Ting.

●This is Hui's most wholly satisfying movie since *The Spooky Bunch* (1981) – which also, perhaps not coincidentally, starred HK cinema's greatest comedienne, Josephine Siao. Her role here isn't written as comedy (she plays a woman beset with problems at work and at home who finds herself stuck looking after her senile father-in-law, a man she's always hated), but her expertly judged playing is irresistibly comic: deadpan reaction shots, little surges of pride and self-esteem to help her through her worst moments, strategic eruptions of exasperation. TR

Summer Soldiers

(1971, Jap, 103 min)
d Hiroshi Teshigahara. *p* Yukio Tomizawa. *sc* John Nathan. *ph* Hiroshi Teshigahara. *ed* Fusako Shuzui. *ad* Kiyoshi Awazu. *m* Toru Takemitsu. *cast* Keith Sykes, Lee Reisen, Kazuo Kitamura, Toshiro Kobayashi, Barry Cotton.

●Using mostly non-professional actors, Teshigahara's movie deals with the plight of US Forces deserters from Vietnam on the run in Japan, centering on the culture clash between various fugitives and the Japanese who try to help them. Its weaknesses are slightly misplaced emphases in the English dialogue scenes, and a certain over-schematisation in John Nathan's script, which flanks the uncommitted central character with a racist slob on one side and a firebrand radical on the other. Its strengths, which are considerable, include a rigorous honesty about the psychology of desertion, a complete absence of sentimentality, and a meticulous naturalism in the settings and incidental details. TR

Summer Stock (aka If You Feel Like Singing)

(1950, US, 109 min)
d Charles Walters. *p* Joe Pasternak. *sc* George Wells, Sy Gomberg. *ph* Robert Planck. *ed* Albert Akst. *ad* Cedric Gibbons, Jack Martin Smith. *songs* Harry Warren, Mack Gordon, Saul Chaplin, Jack Brooks, Harold Arlen, Ted Koehler. *cast* Judy Garland, Gene Kelly, Eddie Bracken, Gloria De Haven, Phil Silvers, Marjorie Main, Carleton Carpenter.

●The British release title was a cruel irony, since Judy Garland did not feel like singing. Indeed, after the six months of shooting were completed, she was fired by MGM and slashed her own throat with a broken glass. The picture added to her depression: it's just a rehash of all those juvenile Garland-Rooney affairs, with farm girl Judy outraged that her barn has been loaned to a theatre troupe to put on a show, falling in love with Kelly, and becoming a star. The undisputed highlight is Garland's great number 'Get Happy', filmed three months after principal photography and when she had lost a considerable amount of excess weight. ATu

Summer Storm

(1944, US, 106 min, b/w)
d Douglas Sirk. *p* Seymour Nebenzal. *sc* Rowland Leigh. *ph* Archie J Stout, Eugen Schüfftan. *ed* Gregg Tallas. *ad* Rudi Feld. *m* Karl Hajos. *cast* George Sanders, Linda Darnell, Edward Everett Horton, Anna Lee, Sig Ruman, Hugo Haas, Frank Orth.

●Not even Sirk's intelligence and stylish visuals can save this adaptation of Chekhov's short story *The Shooting Party* from collapsing into compromised mainstream ordinariness. The action takes place in Russia in 1912, and Darnell turns in an excellent performance as the peasant girl whose passionate affair with a provincial judge (Sanders) escalates into tragedy. The black-and-white photography by Archie Stout lends an eye-pleasing gloss to the proceedings, and the flashback device reinforces the sense of the inexorability of the characters' fates. Ultimately, though, the mismatch between European culture and Hollywood screen romanticism is just too incongruous. NF

Summer's Tale, A

see Conte d'été

Summer Story, A

(1987, GB, 96 min)
d Piers Haggard. *p* Danton Rissner. *sc* Penelope Mortimer. *ph* Kenneth MacMillan. *ed* Ralph Sheldon. *pd* Leo Austin. *m* Georges Delerue. *cast* Imogen Stubbs, James Wilby, Ken Colley, Sophie Ward, Susannah York, Jerome Flynn.

●Frank Ashton (Wilby), a sensitive, poetic type of chappie, and Balliol man to boot, espies rosy-lipped-and-cheeked Megan (Stubbs) a-gathering flowers on the blooming Dartmoor heather. She's a poor orphan. He's twisted his ankle. He lodges at the humble 19-roomed cottage lovingly polished by Megan's adopted aunt Mrs Narracombe (York), and love blooms, much to the dismay of Mrs Narracombe and son Joe (he of the cloth cap). Piers Haggard adapts John Galsworthy's Edwardian Wessex-set novella in suitably tasteful scenes: a dappled shot of Megan hanging out washing, framed in leaves; much wistful glancing out of windows; a lamp-lit scene of merry country dancing with the yokel peasants, where they first touch; a warm and glowing love-tryst in a cowshed loft. Sadly, Frank is called away, but promises to return and marry, for be damned their class differences. The film is framed as a remembrance, in *Go-Between* fashion, of an older, sadder, and wiser Frank. Old-fashioned and avoidable. WH

Summertime (aka Summer Madness)

(1955, US, 99 min)
d David Lean. *p* Ilya Lopert. *sc* David Lean, HE Bates. *ph* Jack Hildyard. *ed* Peter Taylor. *pd* Vincent Korda. *m* Alessandro Cicognini. *cast* Katharine Hepburn, Rossano Brazzi, Isa Miranda, Darren McGavin, Mari Aldon, Andre Morell.

●Hepburn is a spinster from Ohio making a lone trip to Venice, desperately in search of a 'miracle'. She gets more than she bargained for, though, when she falls for the distinctly continental charms of antique dealer Rossano Brazzi. *Shirley Valentine* later shamelessly milked all the exotic romance clichés, but this (based on Arthur Laurents' play *The Time of the Cuckoo*) is an infinitely more subtle, poignant piece, with a lovely performance from Hepburn at its centre. David Lean may well have identified with this 'fancy secretary', her ciné camera always primed, for the film marks a turning point in his career: this was his first movie shot on location abroad, an experience he obviously enjoyed. ATu

Summer Vacation 1999 (Sen-Kyuhayaku-Kyuju-Kyu-Nen no Natsu Yasumi)

(1988, Jap, 90 min)
d Shusuke Kaneko. *p* Naoya Narita, Mitsuhisa Hida. *sc* Rio Kishida. *ph* Kenji Takama. *ed* Isao Tomita. *ad* Shu Yamaguchi. *m* Yuriko Nakamura. *cast* Eri Miyajima, Tomoko Otakara, Miyuki Nakano, Rie Mizuhara.

●This is every imagined childhood summer, and it focuses on those fleeting months when you had a crush on your most beautiful and unapproachable classmate. Three boys are whiling away their vacation in a deserted boarding school; a fourth has just killed himself because one of the others rejected his love. Then a newcomer arrives early for next term, and turns out to be a dead ringer for the boy who died. Is he a ghost? Or has the boy feigned his death and come back to work things out differently? Laying siege to the heart of the beautiful loner, the newcomer finally gets him to admit that he doesn't know how to accept affection; but this step forward unleashes jealous passions in the other two boys…Brilliantly original, Kaneko's sci-fi approach uses a lush visual style to evoke pre-pubescent feelings with great poignancy, but it also uses a precise, coiled-spring structure to snap everything into place. The result plays like a secret, stoned collaboration between Oscar Wilde and Alain Robbe-Grillet. But what makes the film truly remarkable is the casting: the boys are played by teenage girls. TR

Summer Wishes, Winter Dreams

(1973, US, 93 min)
d Gilbert Cates. *p* Jack Brodsky. *sc* Stewart Stern. *ph* Gerald Hirschfeld. *ed* Sidney Katz. *pd* Peter Dohanos. *m* Johnny Mandel. *cast* Joanne Woodward, Martin Balsam, Sylvia Sidney, Dori Brenner, Win Forman, Tresa Hughes.

●Sensitive study of an ordinary, well-off woman's fast-cracking facade, or just a superior piece of schmaltz about a selfish woman with two ungrateful grown-up kids, a difficult mother, and a boring husband? The best thing is Joanne Woodward in a not particularly sympathetic role, constantly finding fault in others while her own weaknesses are suppressed to the level of hallucinations and dreams. But she too often gets lost in the development of the plot, which pulls out quite a few stops on the way to its ray-of-hope ending, and unwisely strays from America to Tourist London and the Continent. For those who can get over that, plus that it tries too hard to be an 'art' movie with its references to Bergman, there should be enough to appreciate. CPe

Summer with Monika

see Sommaren med Monika

Sumo Bruno

(2000, Ger, 100 min)
d Lenard Fritz Krawinkel. *p* Dirk Beinhold, Friedrich-Carl Wachs. *sc* Marius del Mestre, Jan Berger, Lenard Fritz Krawinkel. *ph* Piotr Lenar. *ed* Adam Boome. *pd* Claus-Jürgen Pfeiffer. *m* Biber Gullatz, Eckes Malz. *cast* Hakan Orbeyi, Oliver Korittke, Julia Richter, Martin Seifert, Thomas Drechsel, Martin Semmelrogge, Uwe Steimle.

●Germany's answer to *The Full Monty* and *Strictly Ballroom*. The small town of Riesa realises it has a potential world-class Sumo wrestler in jobless 400lb hulk Bruno (Orbeyi) after his impromptu session at a party. The owner of a sushi restaurant is hired as trainer and the gentle Bruno ends up, somewhat predicably, at the German round of the World Sumo Wrestling Amateur Championships. End of story. Krawinkel's feelgood debut has its share of comic moments – usually of the muted slapstick variety – but he rarely follows through, leaving several scenes just to peter out. Still, the wrestling sequences are impressively shot in slo-mo, and Orbeyi's huge cartoon-like character is almost huggable. DA

Sumo Do, Sumo Don't (Shiko Funjatta)

(1992, Jap, 105 min)
d Masayuki Suo. *p* Shoji Masui. *sc* Masayuki Suo. *ph* Naoki Kashiwano. *ed* Junichi Kikuchi. *ad* Kyoko Hotani. *m* Yoshikazu Suo. *cast* Masahiro Motoki, Misa Shimizu, Naoto Takenaka, Akira Emoto, Kaori Mizushima, Hiromasa Taguchi.

● A funnier re-run of *Fancy Dance* (with sumo wrestling replacing Zen Buddhism) and an even more self-confident trial run for *Shall We Dance?* Got-it-made student Akihei (Motoki) is told that his poor grades will oblige him to repeat his senior year – unless he agrees to join and help revive the university's dying sumo club. Various other no-hopers are recruited, including an American student who's shy about baring his legs. Only one of them has anything like the requisite weight and girth. But slowly, inexorably, they get into the spirit of sumo and by the time the college championships come around. Lots of jockstrap jokes, gay innuendo, farting and humiliation jokes, plus the odd Cocteau quotation. It gained piquancy at the time from the fact that pretty boy star Motoki had just posed for an album of nude photos by Kishin Shinoyama. TR

Sumurun (One Arabian Night)

(1920, Ger, 90 min approx, b/w)
d Ernst Lubitsch. *sc* Hans Kräly, Ernst Lubitsch. *ph* Theodor Sparkhul. *ad* Kurt Richter, Ernö Metzner. *cast* Pola Negri, Ernst Lubitsch, Paul Wegener, Jenny Hasselquist, Paul Graetz, Jacobb Tiedtke.

● 'Based on a pantomime by Friedrich Freksa,' say the credits. Evidently 'pantomime' in German signified 'anything goes' since the plot, set in no certain time or place, accommodates knockabout for the kids, Feydeau-like farce with characters hiding in trunks, a couple of love stories and a climax of corpse-strewn melodrama. Original audiences seem to have responded to the crowds and the big sets, but what's striking now is the florid acting, notably Negri's extraordinary contortions to indicate voluptuousness, Lubitsch's own Harpo-esque grimacing and Tiedtke's turn as the keeper of the harem – or Über-Eunuch, as the titles designate him. BBa

Sun Alley (Sonnenallee)

(1999, Ger, 90 min)
d Leander Haussmann. *p* Claus Boje, Detlev Buck. *sc* Thomas Brussig, Leander Haussmann. *ph* Peter J Krause. *ed* Sandy Saffeels. *m* Stephen Keusch, Paul Lemp, Einstürzende Neubauten. *cast* Alexander Scheer, Alexander Beyer, Katharina Thalbach, Detlev Buck, Henry Hübchen.

● A teen pic set in the '70s following the lives of a gang of 17-year-old boys in East Berlin: falling in love, trying to buy rock'n'roll records and avoiding national service. The sinister absurdities of the regime provide ample opportunities for jokes – good, bad and indifferent – but it's a lightweight offering, buoyed chiefly by a great music track. SB

Sun Also Rises, The

(1957, US, 129 min)
d Henry King. *p* Darryl F Zanuck. *sc* Peter Viertel. *ph* Leo Tover. *ed* William Mace. *ad* Lyle Wheeler, Mark-Lee Kirk. *m* Hugo Friedhofer. *cast* Tyrone Power, Ava Gardner, Errol Flynn, Mel Ferrer, Juliet Greco, Marcel Dalio, Henry Daniell.

● Lavish but lifeless adaptation of Hemingway's novel about the 'lost generation' of expatriates who hung out in Paris after WWI. King's plodding direction and the miscasting of Power as the impotent, thrill-seeking hero are major handicaps. Singer/actress Greco's sympathetic prostitute is a scene-stealer, Gardner is stunning as the lubricious aristo whom Power falls for, and Flynn – in his penultimate screen role – is delightfully self-mocking. Even so, only the occasional sequence, such as the running of the bulls at Pamplona, achieves any real excitement. NF

Sun and Rain (Taiyang Yu/ aka Sunshine and Showers)

(1988, China, 90 min)
d Zhang Zeming. p Dai Dawei. *sc* Lui Xihong, Shang Zeming. *ph* Yao Lin, Pang Lei. *ed* Hu Jianwei. *pd* Peng Jun, Zhang Song. *m* Zhou Xiaoyuan. *cast* Yan Xiaopin, Sun Chun, Yi Xinxin.

● This second movie from the director of *Swan Song* gives the most eye-opening picture yet of modern Chinese city life. A quiet young woman drifts away from her brash boyfriend and, despite her inhibitions, develops a crush on a blowsy teenage girl. Elegantly shot and persuasively acted, it is set in the libraries, boutiques and high-rise apartments of Shenzhen, just across the border from Hong Kong… but it could equally well be Paris or Notting Hill. TR.

Sunburn

(1979, GB/US, 98 min)
d Richard C Sarafian. *p* John Daly, Gerald Green. *sc* John Daly, Stephen Oliver, James Booth. *ph* Alex Phillips. *ed* Geoffrey Foot. *pd* Ted Tester. *m* John Cameron. *cast* Farrah Fawcett-Majors, Charles Grodin, Art Carney, Joan Collins, William Daniels, John Hillerman, Eleanor Parker, Keenan Wynn.

● Lumpy-but-loveable Charles Grodin is the insurance investigator, sniffing out a swindle among Acapulco's lotus-eaters; Fawcett-Majors (comely but coy) is posing as his wife, while emphasising that a quick bunk-up is out of the question. Together they're in a routine comedy-thriller, which looks good but is neither funny nor thrilling, and carelessly wastes its supporting cast, with Art Carney reduced to caricature and Joan Collins on automatic pilot in a hilarious replay of her rich-bitch nympho persona. AC

Sunchaser, The

(1996, US, 122 min)
d Michael Cimino. *p* Arnon Milchan, Michael Cimino, Larry Spiegel, Judy Goldstein, Joe Vecchio. *sc* Charles Leavitt. *ph* Douglas Milsome. *ed* Joe D'Augustine. *pd* Victoria Paul. *m* Maurice Jarre. *cast* Woody Harrelson, Jon Seda, Anne Bancroft, Alexandra Tydings, Matt Mulhern, Talisa Soto, Richard Bauer, Harry Carey Jr.

● When high-flying but psychically unsatisfied doctor Michael Roberts (Harrelson), on the verge of a major promotion, examines Blue (Seda), a dangerous half-Navajo prisoner, his diagnosis – Blue's sarcoma means he has weeks to live – is overheard by his patient. Roberts agrees with senior staff to transfer Blue to a neighbouring hospital, but en route Blue overpowers him and a police officer, and forces Roberts to drive him to a sacred Navajo mountain site in Colorado. As the long journey progresses – with attempted escapes, fights with redneck bikers, near-death rattles, etc – a relationship painfully develops, so that WASP achiever and ghetto no-hoper slowly come to recognise their common humanity and spiritual connectedness. But with death beckoning, where to place one's faith? In the mountain's magic or your fellow man? Cimino's film takes him back to the bonding movies that started his career, but is shot with the technical overkill and dramatic over-emphasis of his post-*Heaven's Gate* action pictures. Doug Milsome's often superb landscape photography, the generally languid pace, the pseudo-Western themes and soundtrack may give a hint of the film's would-be epic ambition, but the kindergarten psychology of Charles Leavitt's script, the implausible dramatic development and contrived emotions render it hollow. WH

Sunday

(1997, US, 92 min)
d Jonathan Nossiter. *p* Alix Madigan, Jonathan Nossiter. *sc* James Lasdun, Jonathan Nossiter. *ph* Michael Barrow, John Foster, Daniel Lerner. *ed* Madeleine Gavin. *pd* Kathryn Nixon. *m* David Ellinwood. *cast* David Suchet, Lisa Harrow, Jared Harris, Larry Pine, Joe Grifasi, Arnold Barkus.

● A man leaves a flophouse in Queens, New York. He's greeted by an actress who recognises him as one of her old directors. He's monosyllabic, bewildered, and quite possibly not who she says he is. She takes him home. He tells her a story, about being mistaken for a film director by a woman on the street. They make love. The masquerade continues (if it is a masquerade). This beguiling first feature won the grand prize at the 1997 Sundance festival, gathered great reviews, then disappeared in the States. It's a small picture, little more than an anecdote on the surface, but immensely tantalising. TCh

Sunday, Bloody Sunday

(1971, GB, 110 min)
d John Schlesinger. *p* Joseph Janni. *sc* Penelope Gilliatt. *ph* Billy Williams. *ed* Richard Marden. *pd* Luciana Arrighi. *m* Ron Geesin. *cast* Glenda Jackson, Peter Finch, Murray Head, Peggy Ashcroft, Maurice Denham, Vivian Pickles, Frank Windsor, Thomas Baptiste, Tony Britton.

● In effect, if not intention, a reworking of *Brief Encounter* given a gloss of modernism. In its plot (Murray Head is the detached lover of both Peter Finch and Glenda Jackson), acting (threshing limbs and facial twitching), and direction (stridency alternating with 'cool' observation), *Sunday, Bloody Sunday* is a classic example of a film running out of control at every moment, while its creators, director Schlesinger and screenwriter Penelope Gilliatt, strive for 'meaning' with little regard for the simple matters of shot-by-shot consistency, let alone formal unity. Finch tries hard as the Jewish homosexual doctor, but Jackson (like Julie Christie in *Darling*) is given little opportunity to be anything other than a cypher by Schlesinger's exploitative camera. PH

Sunday Daughters (Vasárnapi Szlüok)

(1979, Hun, 100 min)
d János Rózsa. *p* Lajos Ovari. *sc* István Kardos. *ph* Elemér Ragalyi. *ed* Zsuzsa Csakany. *ad* Vilmos Nagy. *m* Levente Szörényi. *cast* Julianna Nyakó, Julianna Balogh, Andrea Blizik, Melinda Szakács, Erszi Pásztor.

● Rózsa's reputation in Hungary is founded on a series of Ken Loach-like problem pictures of which *Sunday Daughters*, a story of delinquent girls in a remand home who are fostered out on Sundays to long-suffering guardians, is easily the strongest. Performances are passionate, and while Rózsa's direction is at times over-dramatic, there's a keen sense of social criticism on show here, which will surprise those who subscribe to the view that movies in Eastern Europe can only attack the system through allusion or allegorical comedy. MA

Sunday in Hell, A (En Forådsdag i Helvede)

(1977, Den, 105 min, col & b/w)
d Jørgen Leth. *with* Eddie Merckx, Roger de Vlaeminck, Freddy Maertens, Francesco Moser.

● Although not quite as prominent a cycle race as the Tour de France, the Paris-Roubaix is, nevertheless, no less gruelling. The final stage is especially arduous: a narrow, cobbled roadway more suited to mountain bikes than highly tuned racers. Not for nothing has this section been dubbed 'L'Enfer du Nord' (Hell of the North). This documentary on the 1976 event is especially fascinating as it focuses on the tussle between three of the greatest road racers of the period: Eddie Merckx, the Miguel Indurain of his day; his chief rival and three-times winner, Roger de Vlaeminck; and Freddy Maertens, the predominant rider at that time. There's no comfort zone here: in the wet, it's muddy and miserable; in the dry, as in this particularly drought-ridden year, the bikes and support vehicles kick up huge clouds of lung-filling dust. Despite a few lagging moments, the film is most notable for its honest, home-movie structure and its informative, old-fashioned commentary. DA

Sunday in the Country

(1974, Can, 92 min)
d John Trent. *p* David Perlmutter. *sc* Robert Maxwell, John Trent. *ph* Marc Champion. *ed* Tony Lower. *ad* James Milton Parcher. *m* Paul Hoffert, William McCauley. *cast* Ernest Borgnine, Michael J Pollard, Hollis McLaren, Louis Zorich, Cec Linder, Vladimir Valenta.

● Three killer hoodlums on the run get more than they bargained for when they come up against churchgoing country farmer Borgnine, a man with his own brand of rough justice. A film that revolves around little more than a clash between the acting styles of Pollard and Borgnine. The flyweight against the heavyweight in a battle to define the meaning of psychopath: the one snivelling, giggling and spastic, the other granite-like and pop-eyed. Elsewhere it's messy and violent, but quite competently handled. CPe

Sunday in the Country (Un Dimanche à la Campagne)

(1984, Fr, 94 min)
d Bertrand Tavernier. *p* Alain Sarde. *sc* Bertrand Tavernier, Colo Tavernier. *ph* Bruno de Keyser. *ed* Armand Psenny. *ad* Patrice Mercier. *m* Gabriel Fauré. *cast* Louis Ducreux, Sabine Azéma, Michel Aumont, Geneviève Mnich, Monique Chaumette, Claude Winter.
●1910, a French country house in high summer. A well-honoured painter is at the end of his working life. As usual, he invites his son, son's family, and his single daughter to visit him, and in the span of one hot day, Tavernier encompasses not only the happiness and sorrows of family life, but also subtler side-comments on life, art and the relation of one to the other. For the painter has lived through the Impressionist revolution, but preferred to hoe his own quiet furrow, away from what he admired but could not connect with. The statement is brave, for it aligns with Tavernier's own position as the leader of the mainstream in France. A mention of Renoir is no accident: the film once more returns to the solid decency and the hedonism of both Renoir *père* (painter) and *fils* (film-maker). Tavernier still shoots in a fluid transatlantic/classic style, but his forte is those fleeting moments that are happy until destroyed by reflection. CPea

Sunday's Children

see Söndags Barn

Sunday Too Far Away

(1974, Aust, 95 min)
d Ken Hannam. *p* Gil Brealey, Matt Carroll. *sc* John Dingwall. *ph* Geoff Burton. *ed* Rod Adamson. *ad* David Copping. *m* Patrick Flynn. *cast* Jack Thompson, Phyllis Ophel, Reg Lyle, John Charman, Gregory Apps, Max Cullen.
●Easily one of the best of the 'new' Australian films: an outback variant on the Hawksian Hollywood formula of male camaraderie and competitive professionalism, set on an isolated sheep station where the shearing sheds become both a personal and a political testing ground for notions of individualism and collectivism. Marked by an unemphatic but affecting poignancy that owes nothing to nostalgia (though it's set in 1955) or spurious romanticism, the film trades of a resonant matter-of-fact engagement with character against any temptation to strain the material towards 'epic' statement or national myth. PT

Sundown

(1989, US, 90 min)
d Anthony Hickox. *cast* David Carradine, Bruce Campbell, Jim Metzler, John Ireland, Morgan Brittany, Maxwell Caulfield, M Emmet Walsh.
●An engaging modern-day Vampire Western, about a community of bloodsuckers that has settled down in the remote desert town of Purgatory, where – with the help of a visiting scientist (Metzler) – they are trying to perfect an artificial blood-making machine that will free them from their anti-social appetites. But the rebellious Ireland and his degenerate cohorts hanker for the delicious pleasures of the Old Ways. Despite the tacky bat effects and an over-busy plot, Hickox makes good use of existing vampire lore, while introducing some new twists: sun-block cream (factor 200) and wooden bullets instead of stakes. Carradine is excellent as the vampires' imposing leader, Count Mardulak, and there are good cameos by Campbell (as vampire-hunter Van Helsing's grandson) and Walsh (as an old-timer with a taste for the red stuff). The ending, too, is bold and surprising, which after 70 years of vampire movies is no small achievement. NF

Sundowners, The

(1960, GB, 124 min)
d Fred Zinnemann. *p* Gerry Blattner. *sc* Isobel Lennart. *ph* Jack Hildyard. *ed* Jack Harris. *ad* Michael Stringer. *m* Dimitri Tiomkin. *cast* Deborah Kerr, Robert Mitchum, Peter Ustinov, Glynis Johns, Chips Rafferty, Dina Merrill, John Meillon, Ronald Fraser, Mervyn Johns.
●Sprawling family saga set in the Australian wilderness of the '20s finds Kerr, Mitchum and his old shipmate Ustinov hoping to make a new life for themselves from the proceeds of a lengthy cross-country sheep-drive. Zinnemann's customary care for detail pays occasional dividends, but the film goes on rather too long. Sturdy performances and location work. Isobel Lennart wrote the script from a novel by Jon Cleary. TJ

Sunflower (I Girasoli)

(1969, It/Fr, 107 min)
d Vittorio De Sica. *p* Carlo Ponti, Arthur Cohn. *sc* Tonino Guerra, Cesare Zavattini. *ph* Giuseppe Rotunno. *ed* Adriana Novelli. *ad* Piero Poletto. *m* Henry Mancini. *cast* Sophia Loren, Marcello Mastroianni, Ludmila Savelyeva, Galina Andreeva, Germano Longo.
●Excruciating tosh in which Loren plays a bereft Italian spouse wandering over what feels like the whole of Russia looking for hubby Mastroianni, who never returned after serving on the Russian front in World War II. Much picturesque scenery and soul-searching later, she finds him with a Russian wife, a child, and amnesia. Off she slogs back to Italy to forget, marry, have a child. At which point guess who turns up, having remembered? It's much worse than it sounds. TM

Sunless

see Sans Soleil

Sunless Days (Meiyou Taiyang de Rizi)

(1990, HK/Jap, 90 min)
d Shu Kei. *p* Masami Ogahara. *sc* Wu Nien-jen. *cast* Duo Duo, Hou Xioxian, Cheung Kin-Ting.
●Shu Kei's documentary takes as its starting point the fact of the Tiananmen Square massacre; then, just when you expect the film to start the usual trawl through personal testimonies and political protests, it takes off in a different direction entirely. The director's first person narration (spoken in English) explains: Shu Kei wanted to express his feelings of outrage and helplessness, but didn't want to make another journalistic documentary like the ones shown on TV every night that summer. so he turned to his family and friends for their thoughts, embarking on a journey that took him to Australia and Canada, London and Venice, tracing the ways in which the Beijing crackdown affected all who think of themselves as Chinese. It's a Chinese tradition to keep intimate family matters to yourself; when Shu Kei discusses his brother's decision to emigrate and his own quandary over the future of his mother, his words have the force of a full-scale transgression. The willingness to confront personal feelings with great honesty makes the film exceptionally moving, and takes it into the area previously associated with mavericks like Chris Marker, far above the grind of mere reportage. TR

Sunlight on Cold Water

see Peu de Soleil dans l'Eau Froide, Un

Sun Ra: A Joyful Noise

(1980, US, 60 min)
d Robert Mugge. *with* Sun Ra and his Arkestra, John Gilmore, Marshall Allen, June Tyson, James Jacson.
●A wholly apt description of this film on the eccentric visionary Sun Ra. His noise spans and includes styles from post-bop big band jazz to the outer limits of contemporary improvisation. The joy is the totally natural, celebratory, and always danceable way Ra and Arkestra play that noise. Open ears will wallow in his amniotic funk – even those shocking solos – and rock fans will cower at his invention. There's a sly irony about his cosmic/Egyptian theories, and the interviews with his band, their involvement in Philadelphia's black community, and final, blessedly noisy live proof will leave you wondering – what if he's right? JG

Sunrise 100 10

(1927, US, 8,729 ft, b/w)
d FW Murnau. *p* William Fox. *sc* Carl Mayer. *ph* Charles Rosher, Karl Struss. *ed* Harold Schuster. *ad* Rochus Gliese. *m* Hugo Riesenfeld. *cast* George O'Brien, Janet Gaynor, Margaret Livingston, Bodil Rosing, J Farrell MacDonald.
●Apart from its sheer poignancy, the main achievement of Murnau's classic silent weepie is how it puts pep into pap. Its folksy fable is distinctly unusual: a love triangle dissolving into an attempted murder is only the start; two thirds of the movie is actually about a couple making up. The tension is allowed to drop in a glorious jazz-age city sequence, and then twisted into breaking-point as a journey of murderous rage is repeated. But its dreamlike realism is also to be enjoyed: when lovers appear to walk across a crowded city street, into (superimposed) fields, and back to kiss in a traffic jam, you have an example of True Love styled to cinema perfection. Simple, and intense images of unequalled beauty. DMacp

Sunset

(1988, US, 107 min)
d Blake Edwards. *p* Tony Adams. *sc* Blake Edwards. *ph* Anthony B Richmond. *ed* Robert Pergament. *pd* Rodger Maus. *m* Henry Mancini. *cast* Bruce Willis, James Garner, Malcolm McDowell, Mariel Hemingway, Kathleen Quinlan, Jennifer Edwards, Patricia Hodge, Richard Bradford, M Emmet Walsh, Joe Dallesandro.
●Willis gets to wear the rhinestone suits and the made-to-measure role of self-regarding actor Tom Mix, legendary big-hat cowboy of silent screen oaters. It's 1929, and Mix is saddled with living-legend gunslinging marshal Wyatt Earp (Garner, a delight throughout), who is drafted in as Technical Advisor by the sadistic, manipulative studio boss (McDowell) to help Mix cope with the threat of the new talkies. From here on in, we're into a Tinseltown detective romp involving the murdered proprietress of the famous Candy Store, an array of vintage cars, in-jokes, and arcane and Kenneth Anger-ry allusions to the Golden Days of Hollywood. All complete nonsense, of course, with Willis grinning, prancing and tango-dancing himself into ridiculousness, while Garner upstages him with wit, mastery, drapes and ribbon tie. For a comedy, it rarely raises a laugh and soon runs out of steam; but for an hour, it's great entertainment. WH

Sunset Blvd. 100 (100)

(1950, US, 111 min, b/w)
d Billy Wilder. *p* Charles Brackett. *sc* Charles Brackett, Billy Wilder, DM Marshman Jr. *ph* John F Seitz. *ed* Arthur P Schmidt. *ad* Hans Dreier, John Meehan. *m* Franz Waxman. *cast* Gloria Swanson, William Holden, Erich von Stroheim, Nancy Olsen, Fred Clark, Jack Webb, Cecil B DeMille, Buster Keaton, Hedda Hopper.
●One of Wilder's finest, and certainly the blackest of all Hollywood's scab-scratching accounts of itself, this establishes its relentless acidity in the opening scene by having the story related by a corpse floating face-down in a Hollywood swimming-pool. What follows in flashback is a tale of humiliation, exploitation, and dashed dreams, as a feckless, bankrupt screenwriter (Holden) pulls into a crumbling mansion in search of refuge from his creditors, and becomes inextricably entangled in the possessive web woven by a faded star of the silents (Swanson), who is high on hopes of a comeback and heading for outright insanity. The performances are suitably sordid, the direction precise, the camerawork appropriately *noir*, and the memorably sour script sounds bitter-sweet echoes of the Golden Age of Tinseltown (with has-beens Keaton, HB Warner and Anna Q Nilsson appearing in a brief card-game scene). It's all deliriously dark and nightmarish, its only shortcoming being its cynical lack of faith in humanity: only von Stroheim, superb as Swanson's devotedly watchful butler Max, manages to make us feel the tragedy on view. GA

Sunsets

(1997, US, 98 min, b/w)
d/sc Michael Idemoto, Eric Nakamura. *ph* Eric Nakamura. *ed* Michael Idemoto, Eric Nakamura. *m* Ken Kawamura. *cast* Josh Brand, Nicholas Constant, Michael Idemoto.
●Co-directed by the editor of *Giant Robot* magazine, this account of three young men growing up bored and drunk in Watsonville, California, fits into the long line of male rite-of-passage movies which stretches back to Fellini's *I Vitelloni*. The three friends have varied racial origins: Gary is white trash, constantly in and out of jail on assault charges; Dave is Hispanic,

damaged by a bad love affair and stuck working in a comic-book store; and Mark is Japanese-American, the brainy one who'll leave for college in San Francisco after the summer. Shot in extended takes (16mm, b/w) which throw a lot of weight on the actors, the film's stylistic purity makes it unexpectedly compelling. And as a sketch of the mediocrity of the California backwoods, it's smarter and more credible than anything Gregg Araki has come up with. TR

Sunshine

(1973, US, 103 min)
d Joseph Sargent. *p* George Eckstein. *sc* Carol Sobieski. *ph* Bill Butler. *ed* Budd Small, Richard M Sprague. *ad* George Webb. *m* Hal Taylor. *cast* Cristina Raines, Cliff De Young, Meg Foster, Brenda Vaccaro, Billy Mumy, Corey Fischer.

●Based on a true story and originally made for TV (where it ran 130 minutes), this contains some redeeming features behind its blandness. At worst it's the *Love Story* of the Woodstock generation, with its couple and their alternative society patronisingly depicted for a mass audience (John Denver's songs being entirely consistent with this vision). Its plot – young, beautiful mother, dying from a malignant tumour – for the most part places the film firmly in the realms of Hollywood's Terminal Casebook. However, Carol Sobieski's script manages to hint at deeper things. Kate, the heroine (Raines), appears sympathetic and misguided in turns, and the tensions that her illness cause are treated with some integrity. Equally, the sustained and irritating zaniness of her husband (De Young) in the face of something he can't and doesn't want to comprehend is absolutely right. She is left recording her thoughts into a tape recorder while he has an affair with the neighbour. That she dies a human being, rather than in the angelic limbo usually reserved for such occasions, remains some sort of achievement. But the valid confusions of the script become dissipated by the direction. Thus, in the context of Sargent's pedestrian direction, Kate's 'Life was just so incredibly beautiful' takes on an unintended irony. CPe

Sunshine Part II (aka My Sweet Lady)

(1973/75, US, 94 min)
d Daniel Haller, John Badham, Leon Benson, Robert Day, Joseph Sargent. *p* George Eckstein. *sc* Carol Sobieski, M Charles Cohen, William Froug, Milt Rosen. *ph* Harry Wolf, Leonard South, Bill Butler. *ed* Budd Small, Lee Burch, Jerrold Ludwig, Larry Strong, Douglas Steward, Richard M Sprague. *ad* Ira Diamond, Arch Bacon, George Webb. *m* Lee Holdridge. *cast* Cliff De Young, Elizabeth Cheshire, Bill Mumy, Meg Foster, Corey Fischer, Cristina Raines.

●After Kate's death, husband Sam (De Young) struggles without success to bring up his stepdaughter Jill; they decamp to a dilapidated houseboat somewhere in the Canadian West; the boat breaks its moorings and Sam contracts pneumonia swimming ashore; girlfriend Nora (Foster), a free spirit, repeatedly turns down Sam's offers of marriage; at the close, Jill tells her dad she doesn't need a new mother – like him, she's sustained by the memory of Kate. A mawkish compilation of flashbacks to Part I and clips from the TV soap which sprang from it: Jill will doubtless grow into an '80s high-achiever, while the witless Sam will probably continue to strum his guitar into old age and beyond. JPy

Sunshine (A napfény íze/Ein Hauch von Sonnenschein)

(1999, Hun/Ger/Can/Aus/GB, 180 min)
d István Szabó. *p* Robert Lantos, András Hámori. *sc* István Szabó, Israel Horovitz. *ph* Lajos Koltai. *ed* Michel Arcand, Dominique Fortin. *pd* Attila F Kovács. *m* Maurice Jarre. *cast* Ralph Fiennes, Rosemary Harris, Rachel Weisz, Jennifer Ehle, Deborah Kara Unger, Molly Parker, James Frain, David de Keyser, John Neville, Miriam Margolyes, Rüdiger Vogler, Bill Paterson, William Hurt.

●Szabó's personal history of modern Hungary spans 150 years and has Fiennes incarnate three generations of the Sonnenschein family. Jews of peasant stock who make their fortune with a family recipe for herbal tonic, the Sonnenscheins achieve respectability in the early 20th century with the meteoric career of Ignatz (Fiennes), a lawyer and judge who changes his surname to Sors ('Destiny') and pledges allegiance to the Hapsburg Empire. Adam (Fiennes) inherits his father's assimilationist zeal, converts to Catholicism, and wins a gold medal in fencing at the 1936 Berlin Olympics; in the film's most powerful scene, he's stripped, beaten and murdered in a Nazi labour camp. Consumed by his father's death, Ivan (Fiennes again) becomes a scourge of the fascists in post-war Communist Hungary, but is forced to re-evaluate as the regime falls back on the same totalitarian instincts that have plagued the country through the century. Szabó has an awful lot to cram into the three hours he's allowed himself to do the saga justice. That the Sors men are inveterate ladykillers thickens the stew, entailing romantic complications with Ehle, Weisz, Unger and Parker. Szabó's characteristically dense, ambitious film is a little dry, conservative and (understandably) humourless. Yet it's an absorbing, weighty picture, which worries at still important ideas about duty and inheritance, and at how we may define ourselves against the tide of history. TCh

Sunshine and Showers

see Sun and Rain

Sunshine Boys, The

(1975, US, 111 min)
d Herbert Ross. *p* Ray Stark. *sc* Neil Simon. *ph* David M Walsh. *ed* John F Burnett. *pd* Albert Brenner. *m* Harry V Lojewski. *cast* Walter Matthau, George Burns, Richard Benjamin, Carol Arthur, Lee Meredith, F Murray Abraham, Howard Hesseman, Fritz Feld.

●Relatively young actors playing old men is usually an excuse for some indulgent theatricals, and Matthau's 70-year-old is unfortunately no exception. George Burns was tempted out of retirement (when Jack Benny died) to appear alongside him in this Neil Simon comedy about two old boys reviving their vaudeville act – despite a mutual loathing – for the sake of posterity and a TV spectacular; a winning enough formula for a hit and a couple of Oscar nominations, but the film still disappoints. The ponderous direction is a good deal less spritely than the 80-year-old Burns, and though it correctly ignores the script's fumbling attempts to confront old age, it places far too much emphasis on the performances. Matthau overplays his grouchiness dreadfully. At least Burns is an old man, but more than that, his glint-eyed, deadpan performance is the only natural element in an otherwise contrived and over-theatrical picture. CPe

Sunshine for the Scoundrels

see Du Soleil pour les Gueux

Sun Shines Bright, The

(1953, US, 92 min)
d John Ford. *p* John Ford, Merian C Cooper. *sc* Laurence Stallings. *ph* Archie J Stout. *ed* Jack Murray. *ad* Frank Hotaling. *m* Victor Young. *cast* Charles Winninger, Arleen Whelan, John Russell, Stepin Fetchit, Jane Darwell, Grant Withers, Russell Simpson.

●Usually cited as Ford's personal favourite among his own films, this picks up the story of *Judge Priest*, his 1934 Will Rogers vehicle, and follows the picaresque experiences of the old judge of Fairfield, Kentucky, some 15 years on, as the twentieth century exerts a pull forward equal to the retrograde magnetism of the Civil War. Winninger's judge casts benevolent paternalism over an American community idealised almost to the extent of the Irish village in *The Quiet Man*, but still riven with vestiges of racism, religious prudery, and the scars of the North/South divide, and now facing an electoral tussle between the Old and the New. A mosaic of Americana both sentimental and self-consciously critical, with the emphatic past tense its safety valve. PT

Sunshine State

(2002, US, 141 min)
d John Sayles. *p* Maggie Renzi. *sc* John Sayles. *ph* Patrick Cady. *ed* John Sayles. *pd* Mark Ricker. *m* Mason Daring. *cast* Edie Falco, Jane Alexander, Ralph Waite, Angela Bassett, James McDaniel, Mary Alice, Bill Cobbs, Gordon Clapp, Mary Steenburgen, Timothy Hutton.

●Like *City of Hope* and the early scenes in *Limbo*, this is one of Sayles' multi-character social tapestries investigating a community in transition, striving to come to terms with its past and to sort out a future. This being a Florida beach resort, complete with a once segregated, once thriving black enclave, the real estate people have almost taken over (with a little help from local politicians), the wilderness is virtually extinct, and new histories have to be invented. Revolving around a couple of women – failed actress Bassett revisiting her mom after years away, motel proprietor Falco looking to escape the doomed family business – the film weaves together a typically vivid array of characters, relationships and stories over one difficult holiday weekend, its observations as politically astute, its dialogue as witty, and its performances as top-notch as we've come to expect from Sayles. GA

Sun Valley (Riguang Xiagu)

(1996, China/HK, 100 min)
d He Ping. *p* Ma Fung Kwok. *sc* Zhang Rui. *ph* Yang Lun. *ed* Yuan Hong. *cast* Yang Kuei-Mei, Zhang Fengyi, Wang Xueqi, Ku Feng, Chan Yuen.

●He Ping invented the 'Chinese Western' in *The Swordsman in Double-Flag Town*, and the Freudian psycho-drama with Chinese characteristics in *Red Firecracker, Green Firecracker*. This sets out to combine the two in the self-consciously mythic tale of a widow, her lover and the taciturn hitman who turns up to kill the lover. If the result is less than terrific, it's because He has to strain so hard to avoid repeating himself; only the extraordinary PoV shots in which all colours except red are bleached to monochrome (expressing the killer's pathological fear of blood) are genuine visual and dramatic coups. But the actors are fine and the Gansu locations help, anchoring the psycho-sexual problems in credible physical details: scorching days, cold nights, hot baths, encrustations of mud. TR

Sun Valley Serenade

(1941, US, 86 min, b/w)
d H Bruce Humberstone. *p* Milton Sperling. *sc* Robert Ellis, Helen Logan. *ph* Edward Cronjager. *ed* James B Clark. *ad* Richard Day, Lewis Creber. *m* Emil Newman. *songs* Mack Gordon, Harry Warren. *cast* Sonja Henie, John Payne, Glenn Miller, Milton Berle, Lynn Bari, Joan Davis, Dorothy Dandridge, Nicholas Brothers.

●Forget the slim storyline which has Payne, on tour as band manager with the Glenn Miller Orchestra, signing up as a publicity stunt to adopt a war orphan. What he gets is the sickeningly cute Sonja Henie, irrepressibly throwing herself at his head until she wins him away (an unlikely story) from Lynn Bari. Tune in instead for the band playing 'Chattanooga Choo-Choo' (beautifully danced to by the Nicholas Brothers), 'In the Mood' and other evergreens, and a marvellous bit of Hermes Pan choreography performed by skater Henie on black ice. GA

Suor omicidio

see Killer Nun

Superargo (Superargo e i Giganti Senza Volto)

(1968, It/Sp, 95 min)
d Paul Maxwell [Paolo Bianchini]. *p* Luigi Annibaldi. *sc* Julio Buchs. *ph* Godofredo Pacheco. *ed* Juan Maria Pison. *ad* Jaime Pérez Cubero. *m* Berto Pisano. *cast* Guy Madison, Ken Wood ie.Giovanni Cianfriglia, Luisa Baratto, Diana Loris, Aldo Sambrell.

●A diabolically soporific effort, too dull to be funny, and so lacking in imagination as to be utterly unable to wring any mileage from its promisingly ridiculous plot about a Batman-like ex-wrestler (Cianfriglia) called in by the Secret Service to track down the man behind the disappearance of hordes of athletes. Madison makes a singularly colourless villain, and it becomes hard to tell the automata our hero confronts apart from the equally robot-like characters who make up the rest of the cast. VG

Superbeast

(1972, US, 93 min)
d/p/sc George Schenck. *ph* Nonong Rasca. *ed* Tony DiMarco. *ad* Henrando Balon. *m*

Richard La Salle. *cast* Antoinette Bower, Craig Littler, Harry Lauter, Vic Diaz, Jos Romulo, John Garwood.
●Shot back-to-back in the Philippines with the dreadful *Daughters of Satan*, this is a surprisingly imaginative and topical revamping of *The Hounds of Zaroff*. In this version, the Zaroff character becomes a well-intentioned medical researcher (Littler), who is forced to use a big game hunter (Lauter) in order to track and kill the human animals that result from his experiments on incurable psychopaths. The direction is stylish and ambitious, and Schenck doesn't altogether skate over the issues raised by the plot. In particular, he reserves a memorable coup for the climax, in which the scientist/hero mistakenly swallows his own serum, is transformed into an apeman, and then abandoned by the heroine to roam through the jungle in solitary splendour. DP

Super Citizen Ko (Chaoji Da Guomin)

(1995, Tai, 104 min)
d Wan Jen. *sc* Liao Ching-song, Wan Jen. *ph* Shen Jui-yuan. *ed* Liao Ching-song. *cast* Lin Yang, Su Ming-ming, Ke Yizheng.
●This is what the Germans call a *Trauerarbeit*: a labour born of unassuageable sadness. Ko (Lin Yang) was one of many victims of the fanatical anti-communist White Terror of the 1950s; imprisoned for his membership of a political study group, he was wrecked physically by prison tortures and destroyed mentally by a mixture of guilt, fear and incomprehension. In old age he stumbles through a Taipei he no longer recognises, trying to make sense of the past and to patch things up with his near-estranged daughter. The story is in essence a political melodrama, but Wan turns it into a dignified elegy for dead ideals and hushed-up crimes against the heart and mind. TR

Super Cops, The

(1973, US, 94 min)
d Gordon Parks Jr. *p* William Belasco. *sc* Lorenzo Semple Jr. *ph* Dick Kratina. *ed* Harry Howard. *ad* Stephen Hendrickson. *m* Jerry Fielding. *cast* Ron Leibman, David Selby, Sheila E Frazier, Pat Hingle, Dan Frazer, Joseph Sirola.
●After tributes to real-life cops Popeye Doyle (*The French Connection*) and Frank Serpico, comes this rather directionless homage to two New York rookie cops who spent their off-duty time busting the Bedford-Stuyvesant drug trade. Instead of analysing the motives of the duo, the film opts for investing them with a semi-mythical standing (constant comparisons with Batman and Robin) that avoids the need to probe why they do what they do (perhaps wisely, given the implausibility of the very similar *Serpico*). As such, a comedy adventure that occasionally cranks into life, especially in its amusing look at the totally baffling and conflicting investigations made by various departments (The Knapp Commission, the Police Department's Division, the CLU, the DA's office, etc.) into corruption within the force. As for the two cops, one looks like Phil Everly, the other like something from a Cheech and Chong album come to life. CPe

Superdad

(1974, US, 95 min)
d Vincent McEveety. *p* Bill Anderson. *sc* Joseph L McEveety. *ph* Andrew Jackson. *ed* Ray de Leuw. *ad* John B Mansbridge. *m* Buddy Baker. *cast* Bob Crane, Barbara Rush, Kurt Russell, Joe Flynn, Kathleen Cody, Dick Van Patten.
●Disney film devoted to that timeless source of gags and nervous breakdowns, the relationship between father (Crane) and teenage daughter (Cody) just out of bobbysox into 36C cups. With its all-American storyline and cast, it recalls happier times when Eisenhower was in the White House and Hollywood had been given the Joe McCarthy seal of approval. There are signs, however, that subversion is reaching even such havens of security. Part of the plot turns around a strike, and one scene is actually shot on a picket line. NJ

Super Dick

see Cry Uncle

Super 8½

(1994, Can/Ger, 100 min)
d Bruce LaBruce. *sc* Bruce LaBruce. *ph* Donna Mobbs. *ed* James Manse, Robert Kennedy. *cast* Bruce LaBruce, Liza Lamonica, Christeen Martin.
●Circumstantially low-down and committedly dirty, LaBruce is a white-collar faggot's nightmare: an unrepentant queer who amuses himself by fictionalising episodes from his own sordid life and bringing them to the screen in the name of art. *No Skin Off My Ass* was bad enough, but *Super 8½* is much worse. For one thing, it's made with four times the technical skill and ten times the wit of the earlier movie, which makes it, to say the least, dangerously provocative. For another, as the indefensible title suggests, this time he casts himself as a major cine-auteur and gives himself the full Fellini 'blocked artist' treatment. To be specific, LaBruce appears as a burnt-out porno star, an alcoholic wreck supported by his ex-boyfriend (that punk skinhead again), who works as a hustler. Our man gets new hope for his career when avant-dyke film-maker Googie proposes to shoot a portrait-documentary of him, little suspecting that she's using her Canadian Film Board grant to finance her own pet project Submit to My Finger. In short, it's closer to scumbags like George Kuchar, John Waters and Andy Warhol than Fellini. Still, it's sexier than *Forrest Gump* and funnier than *Priest*. Me, I gurgled like a drain. TR

Superfly

(1972, US, 98 min)
d Gordon Parks Jr. *p* Sig Shore. *sc* Philip Fenty. *ph* James Signorelli. *ed* Bob Brady. *m* Curtis Mayfield. *cast* Ron O'Neal, Carl Lee, Sheila Frazier, Julius W Harris, Charles McGregor, Nate Adams, Polly Niles.
●One of the most successful of the early '70s blaxploitation cycle. Coke-dealing Priest (O'Neal), so-called because he carries his samples in a crucifix, sinks his capital into purchase of thirty keys of the stuff – the final deal that will get him out of 'the life', so the legend goes. Dancing along from tacky prologue to no-shit ending, it strips the old dream down to its last threads and then sends it up. Notable as having been picketed by blacks on the grounds of its 'glorification of drug-pushers'. VG

Supergirl

(1984, GB, 124 min)
d Jeannot Szwarc. *p* Timothy Burrill. *sc* David Odell. *ph* Alan Hume. *ed* Malcolm Cooke. *pd* Richard MacDonald. *m* Jerry Goldsmith. *cast* Faye Dunaway, Helen Slater, Peter O'Toole, Mia Farrow, Brenda Vaccaro, Peter Cook, Simon Ward, Mart McClure, Hart Bochner.
●Most delightful of the Super-series for its good-natured disregard of narrative considerations. How does Kara transform into Supergirl? Where did her costume come from? What are the Omega Hedron and the Burundi Wand? You won't ask because you won't care, and the Salkinds knew that before they started – just as they knew that Szwarc was TV-fast and presumably TV-cheap, that teeny girls would want to be Helen Slater and teeny boys would stick around hoping the Phantom Zone vortex would waft her skirt up. The Midwest landscape is patently Pinewood, the swirly paint effects sub-AIP and the sinister magician (and high school maths teacher!) is Peter Cook. Dunaway and O'Toole, resplendent in floppy knitwear, give more than the film demands. DO

Supergrass, The

(1985, GB, 107 min)
d Peter Richardson. *p* Elaine Taylor. *sc* Peter Richardson, Pete Richens. *ph* John Metcalfe. *ed* Geoffrey Hogg. *ad* Niki Wateridge. *m* Keith Tippett, Working Week Big Band. *cast* Adrian Edmondson, Jennifer Saunders, Peter Richardson, Dawn French, Keith Allen, Nigel Planer, Robbie Coltrane, Alexei Sayle, Michael Elphick.
●Pretending to be a drugs-smuggler in order to impress a girlfriend, naive and boorish young Dennis (Edmondson) finds himself in a pickle when eavesdropping cops refuse to believe in his innocence. Agreeing to inform on non-existent villains, he is carted off to the West Country by surly sergeant (Richardson) and WPC (Saunders), themselves troubled lovers in a state of perpetual jealousy. This first feature by the talented Comic Strip mines much the same vein as their TV work, gently parodying genre while revelling in absurdly petty characters indulging daft dreams of self-importance. The thriller context barely thrills, and at times the material seems stretched perilously thin, but there are some wonderful characters and glorious moments. GA

Superman

(1978, GB, 143 min)
d Richard Donner. *p* Pierre Spengler. *sc* Mario Puzo, David Newman, Leslie Newman, Robert Benton. *ph* Geoffrey Unsworth. *ed* Stuart Baird. *pd* John Barry. *m* John Williams. *cast* Christopher Reeve, Margot Kidder, Gene Hackman, Marlon Brando, Valerie Perrine, Ned Beatty, Jackie Cooper, Marc McClure, Glenn Ford, Phyllis Thaxter, Trevor Howard, Susannah York, Jeff East, Harry Andrews, Maria Schell, Terence Stamp, Larry Hagman.
●Given the publicity hoop-la, it is easy to overlook how effectively Richard Donner visualised this revamping of the Depression-born defender of the weak and righter of wrongs. Without really plumping for any particular interpretation of the myth (or any one visual style for that matter), Donner and his screenwriters Mario Puzo, Robert Benton and David Newman (plus Leslie Newman) flip through various genre possibilities, and allow that we might see Superman as either a Big Joke or the Son of God. By keeping the spectacular possibilities open, through the opening scenes of the destruction of Krypton, and the subsequent growth to manhood of the planet's only son on the plains of the Midwest, the film allows naiveté and knowingness to coexist. Only when it goes all out for cold Batmanesque villainy in the second half does it narrow its focus and lose its way. MA

Superman II

(1980, GB, 127 min)
d Richard Lester. *p* Pierre Spengler. *sc* Mario Puzo, David Newman, Leslie Newman. *ph* Geoffrey Unsworth, Bob Paynter. *ed* John Victor Smith. *pd* John Barry. *m* Ken Thorne. *cast* Christopher Reeve, Margot Kidder, Gene Hackman, Ned Beatty, Jackie Cooper, Valerie Perrine, Susannah York, Clifton James, EG Marshall, Marc McClure, Terence Stamp, Sarah Douglas, Jean-Pierre Cassel, Jack O'Halloran.
●This is movie-making on a less grandiose scale than before, but the combination of Richard Donner's superb original casting and visual attack with Lester's wit and his ear for sound proves a pretty formidable alliance. The basic plot (Supervillains enslave Earth) is potentially far more interesting than before, and though you occasionally miss the essential seriousness Donner brought to the subject, Lester generally replaces it with an intelligent satirical edge and some good gags. Purists may find certain things hard to take, but audiences have little cause for complaint. DP

Superman III

(1983, GB, 125 min)
d Richard Lester. *p* Pierre Spengler. *sc* David Newman, Leslie Newman. *ph* Bob Paynter. *ed* John Victor Smith. *pd* Peter Murton. *m* Ken Thorne. *cast* Christopher Reeve, Richard Pryor, Jackie Cooper, Marc McClure, Annette O'Toole, Annie Ross, Pamela Stephenson, Robert Vaughn, Margot Kidder.
●A splendid opening during the credits, with Lester displaying his dazzling skills in perfectly timed slapstick, sets the tone for the most satirical of the series so far. Here our superhero undergoes a psychotic reversal and turns into a real sleazo as he comes up against a megalomaniac tycoon (Vaughn in fine form) who is using computer wizard Pryor as an accomplice in his attempts to take over the world and destroy Superman. Unfortunately the pacy humour of the first half soon dwindles to a weak climax, and Pryor hams shamelessly, yet again proving that he's best in serious parts or as a stand-up man. Enjoyable, nevertheless. GA

Superman IV: The Quest for Peace

(1987, US, 93 min)
d Sidney J Furie. *p* Menahem Golan, Yoram Globus. *sc* Lawrence Konner, Mark Rosenthal. *ph* Ernest Day. *ed* John Shirley. *pd* John

Graysmark. *m* John Williams. *cast* Christopher Reeve, Gene Hackman, Jackie Cooper, Marc McClure, Jon Cryer, Sam Wanamaker, Mariel Hemingway, Margot Kidder, Mark Pillow.
● About as dreary as a summit conference in Belgium. Moved by a schoolboy's letter requesting him to intervene in the nuclear arms race, Superman whizzes about the ionosphere bagging up missiles unilaterally. Once again Lex Luthor (Hackman) is his implacable enemy, and clones Nuclear Man (Pillow) from a single strand of the Caped Crusader's hair, stolen from a museum. Unfortunately, since both titans are subject to energy crises, the clash in outer space resembles a push-fight between sea cucumbers. The flight sequences seem more shuddery around the edges than usual, and special effects in general are half-hearted. Worst of all, the story lacks momentum to a degree. There's a weedy subplot in which Warfield's daughter (Hemingway) falls for Clark to beef up the flagging yearnings of Lois Lane (Kidder) for Superman, but the comic possibilities of a double date soon ground in tiresome quick costume changes. BC

Super Mario Bros.

(1993, US, 104 min)
d Rocky Morton, Annabel Jankel. *p* Roland Joffé, Jake Eberts. *sc* Tom S Parker, Jim Jennewein, Parker Bennett, Terry Runte, Ed Solomon. *ph* Dean Semler. *ed* Mark Goldblatt, Caroline Ross. *pd* David L Snyder. *m* Alan Silvestri. *cast* Bob Hoskins, John Leguizamo, Dennis Hopper, Samantha Mathis, Fiona Shaw, Fisher Stevens.
● The Mario industry is the biggest outpouring of the computer age – and all from the ramblings of two Brooklyn plumbers of Italian extraction, who spend their time leaping and bouncing, dodging turtles and dinosaurs. What do punters reap for 48 million bucks? Hoskins mugging in a romper-suit; Hopper mugging as a Lizard King villain; Shaw ditching her cred as villainess Lena; and a garbled storyline about Dinohattan, where a parallel reptilian world exists some 65 million years after a meteorite supposedly wiped out all the big lizards. Yes, designer David L Snyder has done wonders with the set; yes, there's decent photography and effects; yes, the giant Goombas are splendid. But the whole is not a dinosaur, it's a dog. It will baffle kids, bore adolescents, and depress adults. SGr

Supernatural

(1933, US, 60 min, b/w)
d Victor Halperin. *p* Edward Halperin. *sc* Harvey Thew, Brian Marlow. *ph* Arthur Martinelli. *cast* Carole Lombard, Randolph Scott, Vivienne Osborne, HB Warner, Beryl Mercer, William Farnum.
● A rip-along Paramount weirdie that gaily yokes primitive psychobabble with spiritualist charlatanism, yet concedes to the afterlife all the important plot interventions, *Supernatural* was the only big studio outing for the unsung Halperin brothers (Victor Hugo directing, Edward producing), whose low-budget toils had paid off the previous year with the poetic horror classic *White Zombie*. Here a mourning Lombard falls prey to a fake medium, while her doctor's dabblings lead to her possession by the evil soul of an executed murderess – seeking, wouldn't you know it, revenge on the same medium. Looney stuff, of course, but enlivened by a superb opening montage sequence (school of Vorkapich); by Halperin's toying comparisons of the trickster's art with his own accomplished illusionism; and by Lombard's half-incredulous presence in such surroundings. PT

Supernova

(1999, US, 90 min)
d Thomas Lee [Walter Hill]. *p* Ash R Shah, Daniel Chuba, Jamie Dixon. *sc* David Campbell Wilson. *ph* Lloyd Ahern II. *ed* Michael Schweitzer, Melissa Kent. *pd* Marek Dobrowolski. *m* David Williams. *cast* James Spader, Angela Bassett, Robert Fosrster, Lou Diamond Phillips, Peter Facinelli, Robin Tunney, Wilson Cruz.
● Based on a 10-year-old story and a much rewritten script, this production claimed two directors as casualties. the Australian Geoffrey Wright quit early; Hill then shot the film, but left before editing began. Coppola is rumoured to have helped with the cutting. The film looks good and moves at a clip, but it doesn't make sense. Answering a distress call, a 22nd century medical rescue vessel jumps dimensions and is pulled towards a star about to implode. During frantic repairs, Phillips and paramedic Tunney enjoy weightless sex, while laidback co-pilot Spader and spiky chief MO Bassett face off. But with the arrival of Facinelli, sole survivor of an illegal ice mining disaster, things turn ugly. Spader, Bassett and Tunney struggle to invest their underwritten characters with some kind of emotional substance. Hill's direction of the large scale action scenes is never less than efficient and the SFX are more than adequate. In the end, however, this still feels like a $60m B-movie. NF

Supersonic Man

(1979, Sp, 88 min)
d Juan Piquer. *p* Dick Randall, Faruk Alatan, Tonino Moi. *sc* Tonino Moi, Juan Piquer Simon. *ph* Juan Mariné. *ed* Pedro del Rey, George Akers. *ad* Francisco Prosper, Emilio Ruiz. *m* Gino Peguri, Juan Luis Izaguirre, Carlos Attias. *cast* Michael Coby, Cameron Mitchell, Diana Polakow, Richard Yesteran, José Maria Caffarel.
● This *Superman* spin-off doesn't just fall flat; it's right down there with the most incoherent movies ever made. It features cod science, cod dialogue, Supersonic Man's codpiece, and an understandable air of resignation which permeates every scene. Just as Biblical B-fodder lets you know that Our Redeemer shaved his armpits, so this tortuous D-flick surprises you with the information that 'Shakespeare said death can be expensive, painful and ugly'. Bombastic Cameron Mitchell plays the heavy, endlessly misquoting history's megalomaniacs so you'll know that he's one too, and Supersonic Man looks like Ted Kennedy in tights. Send back the cornflakes; this one isn't even fit for Saturday morning TV. CR

Superstar: The Karen Carpenter Story

(1987, US, 43 min)
d Todd Haynes.
● Haynes examines the Carpenter phenomenon without succumbing to the sensationalism which surrounded Karen's death at the age of 32. But in using Barbie dolls and minatures, his film pays less heed to the individual and more to the singer's status as a symbol for wholesome America. On the more intimate level, it links impossibly overbearing parents to Karen's anorexia nervosa, cutting between family rows, images of food, and on-screen text to outline the psychological basis and physical symptoms of the illness. But our emotional grasp on the subject is somewhat compromised by Haynes' methods. The use of dolls is inventive, and successfully conveys the idiocy of objectifying women's bodies, but it's also unintentionally funny to see them bobbing around on screen with voice-overs spouting deliberately clichéd dialogue. The effect is curiously distancing, and one is left with an uncomfortable sense that a real-life death is being trivialised. CM

Superstition (aka The Witch)

(1982, US, 85 min)
d James W Roberson. *p* Ed Carlin. *sc* Donald G Thompson. *ph* Leon Blank. *ed* Al Rabinowitz. *ad* Penny Hadfield. *m* David Gibney. *cast* James Houghton, Albert Salmi, Larry Pennell, Lynn Carlin, Maylo McCaslin.
● Crude catch-penny Grand Guignol involving the spirit of a long-executed witch still loitering with intent, despatching various authority figures (cops, priests), plus an entire family that's unwise enough to move into her ancient pad. On the scene, like the rest of the cast, simply to register trepidation, dismay and then be rent asunder is the usually admirable Lynn Carlin (*Faces, Taking Off*), her presence explained, presumably, by the surname of the producer. BBa

Supervixens

(1975, US, 105 min)
d/p/sc/ph/ed Russ Meyer. *ad* Michel Levesque. *m* William Loose. *cast* Shari Eubank, Charles Pitts, Charles Napier, Uschi Digard, Henry Rowland, Christy Hartburg, Sharon Kelly.
● Not Chapter 2 of *Beyond the Valley of the Dolls*, but it does find that old sexist reprobate Russ Meyer in agreeably rumbustious form. It returns to the format of Meyer's early independent successes, following its long-suffering hero as he flees across country from a trumped-up charge of murdering his wife, trying to keep his trousers and his hands clean. Things begin spectacularly with some racy cross-cutting, then get bogged down in repetitions, but eventually rally with a hilarious race-against-time finale that outdoes a dozen vintage serials. Meyer's ideas are consistently good, and the dexterity of his editing makes contemporary mainstream Hollywood look all but geriatric; applied to more substantial material, his talents could obviously have produced something really remarkable. But his gift for caricature still makes him a wittier comedy director than, say, Mel Brooks. TR

Support Your Local Gunfighter

(1971, US, 92 min)
d Burt Kennedy. *p* Bill Finnegan. *sc* James Edward Grant. *ph* Harry Stradling. *ed* Bill Gulick. *ad* Phil Barber. *m* Jack Elliot, Allyn Ferguson. *cast* James Garner, Suzanne Pleshette, Jack Elam, Joan Blondell, Harry Morgan, Marie Windsor, Henry Jones, John Dehner, Chuck Connors, Dub Taylor.
● An amiable but rather disappointing sort-of-sequel to *Support Your Local Sheriff*, sharing the same director but different scriptwriters (here it's James Edward Grant). Conman Garner is the link, though not the same character, alighting from a train in the town of Purgatory to be mistaken for an infamous gunslinger. Unabashed, Garner adopts bumbling oaf Elam as his sidekick, with the latter delightedly playing up until the missing gunfighter he's impersonating turns up bent on settling scores ('I'm slow,' Garner assures the uneasy Elam, 'but you're slower'), and Garner meanwhile playing both ends against the middle in order to profit from a local mining dispute. Garner's laid-back charm helps to fill the gaps between funny scenes. GA

Support Your Local Sheriff

(1968, US, 93 min)
d Burt Kennedy. *p/sc* William Bowers. *ph* Harry Stradling. *ed* George W Brooks. *ad* Leroy Coleman. *m* Jeff Alexander. *cast* James Garner, Joan Hackett, Walter Brennan, Harry Morgan, Jack Elam, Bruce Dern, Henry Jones, Walter Burke, Gene Evans.
● Kennedy's best film, an irresistibly irreverent Western parody which starts with a streak of yellow (actual, not metaphorical) spotted in the late sheriff's newly-dug grave and starting a wild gold rush. Soon after, stranger Garner rides into the badass town, proves himself the fastest draw by shooting a hole through a rubber washer ('The bullet went through the centre'), and gets himself the sheriff's job. Beautifully played by Garner with deadpan wit, he tames the town less by his gunfighting than by his Lewis Carroll logic. A sequence in which, not at all put out by the fact that the brand-new jail has no bars yet, he brainteases the villainous Dern into mesmerised captivity – with some chalk, a little red paint, and the limitless power of suggestion – is high comedy of the first order. One by one, all the Western clichés are turned upside down and reinvented, with William Bowers' fine script proliferating enough invention and wonderful gags to make one forgive the occasional sag. TM

Sur

(1988, Arg/Fr, 127 min)
d Fernando E Solnas. *p* (Argentina) Envar El Kadri, Fernando E Solnas, (France) Patricia Novat, Pierre Novat. *sc* Fernando E Solnas. *ph* Felix Monti. *ed* Juan Carlos Macias, Pablo Mari. *pd* Fernando Solanos. *m* Astor Piazzolla. *cast* Miguel Angel Sola, Susu Pecoraro, Phillippe Léotard, Lito Cruz, Ulises Dumont, Roberto Goyeneche.
● The exiled Solanas marked his return to post-dictatorship Argentina with this melancholy and enthrallingly cinematic love letter – to home, liberty and love itself. It takes the form of a long night's wandering through a city by political prisoner Floreal (Sola); freed after five years in jail, he finds he needs time for reflection before returning to wife Rosi (Pecoraro). It begins and ends with a tango, whose impassioned, poetic impact it shares: the main set is a sad café, suffused in misty greys and blues through which flashes a red neon sign ('Sur' – 'South'). An old musician sings as figures from Floreal's past pass by: the

dead, the disappeared, stopping to share memories and stories, bringing Floreal up to date. He discovers Rosi has taken up with his best friend Roberto the Corsican (Léotard), and flashbacks show how these two lonely people came painfully together. How can Floreal reunite with his wife, with his life? Solanas excitingly fuses theatrical forms, song, poetry, operatic choreography, the personal and the political. The chronology may be broken, but the emotional flow is sustained, making it almost unbearably moving when morning comes and the long-separated husband and wife prepare to come together. WH

Sur, El

see South, The

Sur de una Pasion, El

see South of a Passion, The

Sure Fire

(1990, US, 83 min)
d Jon Jost. *p* Henry S Rosenthal. *sc/ph/ed* Jon Jost. *m* Erling Wold. *cast* Tom Blair, Kristi Hager, Robert Ernst, Kate Dezina.

●Wes (Blair) is a boomer. 'Boom,' he'll say. 'There are two sides to every coin: win and lose.' And 'Boom!' again, to ram home the point. These verbal eruptions echo the explosion of gunpowder – Wes's only true rapport is with his rifle. Wes lords it over family and 'friends' in Circleville, Utah – the Mormon Dixie. A successful entrepreneur and a driven man, he'll pay off a neighbour's bank loan without so much as a by-your-leave, but can't accept rejection from any quarter, least of all from his teenage son during their annual hunting trip. Blair plays Wes as if he had walked off the pages of a Jim Thompson novel, but for the rest the pickings are relatively slim. There are persuasive performances, three long (baffling) Mormon texts and a leisurely sense of pace, but Jost's curious, avant-garde naturalism doesn't find much purchase on this terrain. TCh

Sure Thing, The

(1985, US, 94 min)
d Rob Reiner. *p* Roger Birnbaum. *sc* Steven L Bloom, Jonathan Roberts. *ph* Robert Elswit. *ed* Robert Leighton. *pd* Lilly Kilvert. *m* Tom Scott. *cast* John Cusack, Daphne Zuniga, Anthony Edwards, Boyd Gaines, Tim Robbins, Lisa Jane Persky, Viveca Lindfors, Nicollette Sheridan.

●Reiner's splendidly confident, witty teenage variation on *It Happened One Night* focuses on two students hitching across the States through rainstorms, starvation and show tunes. He's a libidinous layabout who inadvertently dropped in to college. She's an uptight goody-goody who believes spontaneity has its time and its place. There's plenty of mileage in this pairing, even if the movie isn't going anywhere unexpected. It now looks like a dry run for *When Harry Met Sally*..., and some of the dialogue is every bit as sharp: 'Have you ever considered a sexual encounter so intense it could conceivably change your political views?' TCh

Surf Nazis Must Die

(1986, US, 83 min)
d Peter George. *p* Robert Tinnell. *sc* Jon Ayre. *ph* Rolf Kestermann. *ed* Craig Colton. *ad* Bernadette Disanto. *m* Jon McCallum. *cast* Barry Brenner, Gail Neely, Dawn Wildsmith, Michael Sonya, Joel Hile, Dawne Ellison, Bobbie Bresee.

●Nadir of the 'great title, shame about the movie' genre. Abysmally uninteresting scenes of rival youth gangs hanging around on a pseudo-post-apocalyptic beach, intercut with apparently unconnected (and uninteresting) surfing footage, and occasional soft-core fumblings. Neither the 'female vengeance' nor the racial tension motifs succeed in raising even a glimmer of interest. Utter horse-shit. MK

Sur la Route de Salina

see Road to Salina

Surrender

(1987, US, 95 min)
d Jerry Belson. *p* Aaron Spelling, Alan Greisman. *sc* Jerry Belson. *ph* Juan Ruiz Anchia. *ed* Wendy Greene Bricmont. *pd* Lilly Kilvert. *m* Michel Colombier. *cast* Sally Field, Michael Caine, Steve Guttenberg, Peter Boyle, Jackie Cooper, Iman, Julie Kavner, Louise Lasser.

●In his Beverly Hills dream home, successful pulp novelist Sean Stein (Caine) broods over the wrong done him by women in the alimony courts. Elsewhere in LA, dreamy painter Daisy (Field) works in a commercial art studio and wonders when she will meet the man she wants to have babies with. Then a strange quirk of fate finds them face-to-face, victims of a stick-up, naked and in bondage, at which point Stein appears to fall in love...What could so easily have turned into a sickly parable of the unimportance of money compared to Real Human Virtues in fact comes over as an exhilaratingly cynical comic view of the love market, completely undermining the banalities that usually come with the territory. Misogynistic, misanthropic, nasty-minded, *Surrender* is great comedy. RS

Surrender Dorothy

(1998, US, 90 min, b/w)
d Kevin DiNovis. *p* Richard Goldberg. *sc* Kevin DiNovis. *ph* Jonathan Kovel. *ed* Kevin DiNovis. *pd* Michael Doyle. *m* Christopher Matarazzo. *cast* Peter Pryor, Kevin DiNovis, Jason Centeno, Elizabeth Casey, Marcos Muniz, Keri Merboth, Richard Goldberg, Marion Wrenn.

●Trevor, 27, is so afraid of women that he masturbates over fantasies of forks they've used in restaurants, until his lonely life is transformed when a junkie comes to stay. Allegedly a black comedy about psychological and sexual SM, this grungy US indie is short on laughs, narrative structure, insights and appeal. GA

Surrogate Mother (Sibaji)

(1987, SKor, 85 min)
d Im Kwon-Taek. *p* Jung-Do-hwan. *sc* Song-Gil-han. *ph* Gu Jeung-mo. *ed* Bak Sun-duk. *pd* Weong Gi-su, Shin Byung-ha. *cast* Kang Soo-Yeon, Lee Goo-Soon, Han Eun-Jin, Bang Hee, Yoon Yang-Ha.

●Im's first international prize-winner (best actress for Kang at Venice) is a more-in-sorrow-than-in-anger attack on the principles of male lineage and ancestor worship in the traditional Korean family. It's set in the late Yi Dynasty (late 19th century) to stress how deep rooted these things are, but its resonances are squarely contemporary. The well-born Shin and his wife are happy but lack an heir; behind his back, the family conspires with his wife to bring in a surrogate to bear him a son. Their choice is Ok-Nyo (Kang), a free-spirited girl who endures various physiological and sexual indignities (intended to ensure that she produces a boy) because she comes to like Shin and enjoy the relatively pampered life – forgetting she is there only as a servant. The emphasis on female suffering has come in for some critical stick, but Im's analysis of Confucian blockages in the Korean psyche seems all too cogent. And his mastery of image, tone and rhythm is unassailable. TR

Surveillance (Maifu)

(1997, China, 105 min)
d Huang Jianxin. *p* Kang Jianmin. *sc* Sun Yuan. *ph* Yang Wei. *ed* Lei Qin. *ad* Teng Jie. *m* Zhang Dalong. *cast* Feng Gong, Jiang Shan, Niu Zhenhua, Teng Rujun, Zhang Xiaotong, Shi Xiaohong.

●This is a sort-of thriller, but as in Huang's 'urban attitude' trilogy the emphasis is on humour, human foibles and the fallibility of 'the system'. Ye is a hard-working security guard who has a good sexual relationship with his girlfriend. At just the moment that he's assigned to a round-the-clock stake-out, a rival for the girl's affections turns up in the shape of her handsome former boyfriend. There's plenty of incident (Ye nearly starves to death before we find out whether or not he'll get the girl), but Huang sensibly leaves some mysteries unsolved. The best thing here is seeing what he makes of a 'mystical' relationship born from a misdialled phone number. TR

Survive! (Supervivientes de los Andes)

(1976, Mex, 86 min)
d/p/sc René Cardona Sr. *ph* Luis Medina. *ed* Marshall M Borden. *ad* AL de Guevara. *m* Gerald Fried. *cast* Hugo Stiglitz, Norma Lazareno, Luz Maria Aguilar, Fernando Larranga, Lorenzo De Rodas.

●Based on the air disaster of 1972, when a plane taking a Uruguayan college rugby team across the Andes crashed into the mountains, and the revelations of cannibalism that followed the rescue, *Survive!* has all the ingredients for the ultimate in disaster movies. More's the pity, then, that it is relentlessly cheapskate, woodenly performed, and appallingly dubbed. VG

Surviving Desire

(1991, US, 53 min)
d Hal Hartley. *p* Ted Hope. *sc* Hal Hartley. *ph* Michael Spiller. *ed* Hal Hartley. *pd* Steve Rosenzweig. *m* Hal Hartley. *cast* Martin Donovan, Mary Ward, Merritt Nelson, Matt Malloy.

●Seen by Hartley partly as a workshop experiment providing an opportunity to tell an unresolved story, film a rock band, and choreograph a dance number, this made-for-TV featurette nevertheless bears a strong resemblance to his feature work proper. About a lecturer in literature (Donovan) whose obsession with Dostoievsky is replaced by an infatuation with one of his students (Ward), it's packed with literary allusions, ironic wit, sparkling non-naturalistic banter, and moments of playful formal experimentation (most notably a deliciously absurd street dance performed without music). The cast of Hartley regulars makes the most of the droll, discursive dialogue, the saturated primary colours are a joy to behold, and there's the usual concentration on themes relating to trust, ambition, and the solaces and dangers of living too cerebrally. Great fun. GA

Surviving Picasso

(1996, US/GB, 125 min)
d James Ivory. *p* Ismail Merchant, David L Wolper. *sc* Ruth Prawer Jhabvala. *ph* Tony Pierce-Roberts. *ed* Andrew Marcus. *pd* Luciana Arrighi. *m* Richard Robbins. *cast* Anthony Hopkins, Natascha McElhone, Jane Lapotaire, Julianne Moore, Susannah Harker, Peter Eyre, Joss Ackland, Joseph Maher, Bob Peck, Joan Plowright, Vernon Dobtcheff.

●For Merchant Ivory to choose the man who is arguably the 20th century's greatest artist for a film portrait might suggest a departure from their recent studies of (usually English) repression. Nobody could accuse Pablo of being a wallflower, and his at times arrogant, selfish and sexually voracious zest gives Anthony Hopkins a field day, enabling him to avoid the restraint, for instance, of his portrayal of the buttoned-up Stevens in *The Remains of the Day*. This film, loosely adapted from Arianna Stassinopoulos' tome *Picasso Creator and Destroyer*, focuses on the years 1943 to 1953, tracing the ups and downs in the stormy relationship he struck up with an artist almost 40 years his junior, Françoise Gilot (McElhone, a serene, Sphinx-like presence). For all the (episodic) scenes of furious artistic and domestic activity, the movie turns out to be about suffering, fortitude and dignity at a price – the price of living with or near this Spanish force of nature. Merchant Ivory's ability to make a still-life from a tempest doesn't fail them here. There's much to admire, not least sterling support from an accomplished cast (Lapotaire, Moore and Harker's trio of mistresses, Eyre superb as the agent Sabartes, Ackland's keenly judged Matisse), Tony Pierce-Roberts' diverting cinematography of the Paris cafés and the aquamarine skies of the South of France, and the reconstructions of the studios by Luciana Arrighi. But as the movie progresses, its lack of dramatic heart becomes more apparent; this is spectacle without a committed moral view. Watching Hopkins' Picasso is like watching a beautiful animal: a magnificent bull left to head-butt and impale with impunity the sensibilities and psyches of all who venture into his arena. WH

Surviving the Game

(1994, US, 96 min)
d Ernest Dickerson. *p* David Permut. *sc* Eric Bernt. *ph* Bojan Bazelli. *ed* Sam Pollard. *pd* Christiaan Wagener. *m* Stewart Copeland. *cast* Rutger Hauer, Ice-T, Gary Busey, F Murray Abraham, Charles S Dutton, John C McGinley, Jeff Corey.

●A mysterious businessman (Hauer) takes a tough, homeless man (Ice-T) from the city to the wilderness to act as prey in a deadly manhunt for a group of wealthy thrill-seekers – among them

Abraham's powerful Wall Street exec and Busey's unstable CIA psychiatrist. Technically adept and capably performed, this is above average for its type (you've seen it before in *The Most Dangerous Game*), and though the downside is some excessive cruelty without much governing morality, that's a given in action pictures these days. AO

Survivor, The

(1980, Aust, 93 min)
d David Hemmings. *p* Antony I Ginnane. *sc* David Ambrose. *ph* John Seale. *ed* Tony Paterson. *m* Brian May. *cast* Robert Powell, Jenny Agutter, Angela Punch-McGregor, Peter Sumner, Joseph Cotten.

● An airliner crashes, killing everyone on board except the pilot (Powell), who walks out of the carnage in a daze. Eye witness Agutter makes contact and tries to help him find out what happened. It turns out there's a lot more going on than the aircrash investigators are ever likely to discover, because Ambrose's script is based on a supernatural novel by English schlockmeister James Herbert. Hemmings handles the set-pieces well enough, wisely filming the crash scene at night and using darkness as his ally. We build up a complete picture from brief, panicky impressions. He also delivers on the shocks front – notably when a dead little girl's hand takes hold of Powell's in a soft-focus cemetery scene. Brian May's creepy soundtrack cranks up the tension, but despite the (non-specific) Australian setting, the atmosphere remains chilly. May, Powell, producer Ginnane and Hemmings (as actor rather than director) worked around the same time on *Harlequin*, another internationally package that didn't gel quite so effectively. NRo

Survivors, The

(1983, US, 102 min)
d Michael Ritchie. *p* William Sackheim. *sc* Michael Leeson. *ph* Billy Williams. *ed* Richard A Harris. *pd* Gene Callahan. *m* Paul Chihara. *cast* Walter Matthau, Robin Williams, Jerry Reed, James Wainwright, Kristen Vigard, Annie McEnroe.

● When executive Robin Williams is fired by a parrot because his boss cannot cope with confrontations, one has high hopes. And even when Matthau's garage blows up, the movie is still amusing. But shortly afterwards, when the two stars meet on the dole queue, witness a hold-up and become targets for a hit-man, the ideas evaporate. Matthau and Williams look good on the marquees, but actually they fail to play well together, mainly because the script has not been tailor-made to their requirements. Produced by Ray Stark, it's a bland piece of merchandise. ATu

Survivors, The Blues Today

(1984, US, 87 min)
d Robert Schwartz, Cork Marcheschi. *p* Cork Marcheschi. *ph* Eric Young, Nicola Pecorini, Kathleen Laughlin, Ed Pincus. *ed* Tom De Biaso. *cast* John Lee Hooker, Dr John, Gravenites-Cipollina Band, Willie Murphy & the Bees, Minnesota Barking Ducks, Lady Bianca.

● A 'celebration' of contemporary American blues of various hues shot at a weekend festival in St Paul, Minnesota. Live performances are interspersed with chats with some of the dozen or so featured artists. Sadly, those one would expect to excel in this context – notably Dr John and John Lee Hooker – merely go through the motions. The film leans heavily on white boys playing de blooz, such as the Nick Gravenites/John Cipollina Band, who approach their music with the subtlety of Status Quo. Others of the bar band ilk – Willie Murphy & the Bees, the Minnesota Barking Ducks – are defter, while Lady Bianca, a merry black woman, injects the ribaldry which is the life blood of fifty percent of blues. As to the interviews, several of the performers are less than responsive (some of them clearly not on this planet at the time). The most effusive speaker, Gravenites, tells how a few young men (he in particular, one infers) 're-invented' blues in Chicago at the end of the '60s. His claim to be a saviour is not reflected in the cumbersome playing of his plodding bar band. GBr

Susan Slept Here

(1954, US, 98 min)
d Frank Tashlin. *p* Harriet Parsons. *sc* Alex Gottlieb. *ph* Nick Musuraca. *ed* Harry Marker. *ad* Albert S D'Agostino, Carroll Clark. *m* Leigh Harline. *songs* Jack Lawrence, Richard Myers. *cast* Dick Powell, Debbie Reynolds, Anne Francis, Glenda Farrell, Alvy Moore, Red Skelton.

● Powell plays a Hollywood writer (author of 'The Gob and the Geisha'), Reynolds a 17-year-old reform school girl who's supposed to be 'research' for his script on juvenile delinquency. Talk about meeting cute. This started life as a Broadway comedy and remains very theatrical, despite Tashlin's efforts to goose it into life, notably with Susan's dream sequence, a pink and blue affair featuring a sexy spider, a birdcage and a big gold key. Leading *noir* cameraman Nicholas Musuraca unobtrusively colour codes the characters, the set of Powell's apartment is a cornucopia of early-'50s chic; and Debbie is adept at delivering such lines as her hopeful 'Great additional dialogue, huh?' as she checks out one of her intended's early credits. Incidentally at least 20 seconds go by before Tashlin ventures the first breast joke, something involving an actress with an Oscar clutched to her cleavage. BBa

Suspect

(1987, US, 121 min)
d Peter Yates. *p* Daniel A Sherkow. *sc* Eric Roth. *ph* Billy Williams. *ed* Ray Lovejoy. *pd* Stuart Wurtzel. *m* Michael Kamen. *cast* Cher, Dennis Quaid, Liam Neeson, John Mahoney, Joe Mantegna, Philip Bosco.

● Morality seems to be the issue in Yates' courtroom thriller, but issues remain at the level of character traits, and there is no serious investigation of the alliances necessary to achieve simple justice. *Suspect* remains a routine *Jagged Edge* follow-up. Tired but tireless public defender (Cher) is stuck with a violent deaf-and-dumb derelict defendant (Neeson) in a murder trial. Prosecution (Mantegna) is nasty, the judge (Mahoney) partial, and the case apparently unwinnable, when on to the jury is drafted Sanger (Quaid), a Washington lobbyist. Used to greasing the wheels and bending the rules, Sanger starts sleuthing on his own, and progresses from being an embarrassment to being indispensable. Far from the open-and-shut case of a vagrant killing for a few bucks, the trail leads dangerously upwards, and there are close shaves among the filing cabinets after hours, and a red herring. Cher is workmanlike, Quaid excellent before he settles for loveable, Neeson unexpected, and the killer wildly improbable. BC

Suspect, The

(1944, US, 85 min, b/w)
d Robert Siodmak. *p* Islin Auster. *sc* Bertram Millhauser. *ph* Paul Ivano. *ed* Arthur Hilton. *ad* John B Goodman, Martin Obzina. *m* Frank Skinner. *cast* Charles Laughton, Ella Raines, Henry Daniell, Rosalind Ivan, Stanley Ridges, Dean Harens.

● Oppression, guilt, blackmail and murder in turn-of-the-century London's quiet Laburnum Terrace – the plot specifics of *The Suspect* inevitably evoke Hitchcock's world, even if the studio choice of *noir* specialist Siodmak as director suggests a more darkly labyrinthine atmosphere. As it turns out, the generic common denominator of psychological suspense proves stronger than the auteurist imprint, and if any individual has a right to 'sign' the film, it is Laughton in one of his most engaged and engaging roles, as a sympathetic wife-killer and victim of blackmail, whose fatal flaw is eventually revealed to be his sense of simple decency. Between the characters of Laughton, his shrewish wife (Ivan), innocent *femme fatale* (Raines), a suspicious detective (Ridges), and a wife-beating good-for-nothing neighbour (Daniell), are etched some intricate moral shadings; and some teasing reflections on manipulation emerge from within the narrative, echoing the virtuoso audience manipulation. PT

Suspicion

(1941, US, 99 min, b/w)
d/p Alfred Hitchcock. *sc* Samson Raphaelson, Joan Harrison, Alma Reville. *ph* Harry Stradling. *ed* William Hamilton. *ad* Van Nest Polglase. *m* Franz Waxman. *cast* Cary Grant, Joan Fontaine, Nigel Bruce, Cedric Hardwicke, May Whitty, Leo G Carroll, Isabel Jeans, Heather Angel.

● Despite a silly cop-out ending (imposed by RKO), a gripping domestic thriller with Fontaine suitably nervy as the prim young woman who marries Grant, only to come increasingly to suspect that he intends to murder her. Marred by a blatantly artificial English countryside and by a somewhat clichéd story, it's nevertheless a supreme example of Grant's ability to be simultaneously charming and sinister, and of the director's skill with neat expressionistic touches (most notably, the glass of milk). GA

Suspicious River

(2000, Can, 93 min)
d Lynne Stopkewich. *p* Michael Okulitch, Raymond Massey. *sc* Lynne Stopkewich. *ph* Gregory Middleton. *ed* Allan Lee. *pd* Don MacAulay. *m* Don MacDonald. *cast* Molly Parker, Callum Keith Rennie, Mary Kate Welsh, Joel Bissonette, Deanna Milligan, Sarah Jane Redmond, Norman Armour, Byron Lucas.

● Stopkewich won plaudits for her necrophile *Kissed*, but this second outing, based on a novel by Laura Kasischke, plays more like softcore titillation masquerading as arty psycho-drama. Working at a motel in the middle of nowhere, Leila takes to selling herself to the business travellers who make up the clientele. This seems to be more out of boredom than anything else, although she takes a particular shine to the guy who beats her up. We're asked to suffer a grimly predictable chain of events, a numb non-performance from Parker, and an offensively pat psychological explanation for all this trash. TCh

Suspiria

(1976, It, 97 min)
d Dario Argento. *p* Claudio Argento. *sc* Dario Nicoladi. *ph* Luciano Tovoli. *ed* Franco Fraticelli. *pd* Giuseppe Bassan. *m* Dario Argento. *cast* Jessica Harper, Stefania Casini, Flavio Bucci, Miguel Bosé, Udo Kier, Rudolf Schöndler, Alida Valli, Joan Bennett.

● From his stylish, atmosphere-laden opening – young American ballet student arriving in Europe during a storm – Argento relentlessly assaults his audience: his own rock score (all dissonance and heavy-breathing) blasts out in stereo, while Jessica Harper gets threatened by location, cast, weather and camera. Thunderstorms and extraordinarily grotesque murders pile up as Argento happily abandons plot mechanics to provide a bravura display of his technical skill. With his sharp eye for the bizarre and for vulgar over-decoration, it's always fascinating to watch; the thrills and spills are so classy and fast that the movie becomes in effect what horror movies seemed like when you were too young to get in to see them. Don't think, just panic. SM

Suture

(1993, US, 96 min, b/w)
d/p/sc Scott McGehee, David Siegel. *ph* Greg Gardiner. *ed* Lauren Zuckerman. *pd* Kelly McGehee. *m* Cary Berger. *cast* Dennis Haysbert, Mel Harris, Sab Shimono, Dina Merrill, Michael Harris, David Graf, Fran Ryan.

● Vincent (Michael Harris), a wealthy sophisticate, and Clay (Haysbert), a construction worker, have met only once, at their father's funeral. So when Vincent asks his half-brother to visit him in Phoenix, Arizona, then disappears on a business trip, Clay is perplexed. But that's only the start of his worries. After dropping Vincent at the airport, the car Clay is driving explodes, leaving him burnt beyond recognition and with amnesia. Then, when psychoanalyst Shinoda (Shimono) and plastic surgeon Renée Descartes (Mel Harris) start piecing his mind and body together, as if they were (the now missing) Vincent's, Clay's enjoyment of his newly acquired riches is tempered by the fact that, as Vincent, he's suspected of murder. This first feature is a witty, imaginative *noir* thriller exploring questions of identity, memory, and the duality of mind and body. In this last respect, the seemingly perverse decision to have Vincent and Clay played, respectively, by a white and a black actor makes perfect sense, complementing the balanced ironies and structural antitheses of the narrative. Most impressive. GA

Suzaku (Moe no Shuzaku)

(1997, Jap, 95 min)
d Naomi Kawase. *p* Takenori Sento, Koji Kobayahi. *sc* Naomi Kawase. *ph* Masaki Tamura. *ed* Shuichi Kakesu. *cast* Jun Kunimura, Machiko Ono, Sachiko Izumi, Kotaro Shibata, Yasuyo Kamimura.

●Impressionistic portrait of a dying family in a dying mountain village in Nara Prefecture: a 'nothing happens' film which ratherly cleverly camouflages its own lack of grip and focus by hinting at hidden themes (incest, ghosts) and using people from the real-life village as actors. It opens in 1971: recession is already thinning the population but Kozo Tahara (Kunimura, the only professional actor) believes that a rail link will bring new prosperity and eagerly helps dig the tunnel through the mountain. Fifteen years later the railroad is a forgotten dream, the tunnel seems haunted and the Taharas are fading fast. According to Kawase, the obscure title refers to a local bird deity; she wants to see the Tahara family as if through this creature's eyes. Somebody must buy this stuff, because the film won the 1997 *Caméra d'Or* at Cannes. TR

Suzanne Simonin, La Religieuse de Denis Diderot

see Religieuse, La

Suzanne's Profession

see Carrière de Suzanne, La

Suzhou (Suzhou He/ aka Suzhou River)

(2000, China/Ger, 83 min)
d Lou Ye. *p* Nai An, Philippe Bober. *sc* Lou Ye. *ph* Wang Yu. *ed* Karl Riedl. *ad* Li Zhuoyi. *m* Jörg Lemberg. *cast* Zhou Xun, Jia Hongsheng, Yao Anlian, Nai An.

●In the absence of Lou's previous features *Weekend Lover* and *Don't Be Young*, this serves to introduce one of the smartest talents in current Chinese cinema. Mardar (Jia) is a motorcycle courier hired by a black marketeer to keep his daughter Moudan (Zhou) out of the way for several hours each day. The boy starts to fall for the flirtatious girl, but agrees regardless to join a plot to kidnap and hold her to ransom. Moudan is so upset by his betrayal that she throws herself into Suzhou Creek and apparently drowns. Several years in jail later, Mardar returns to the mean streets of Shanghai and encounters Meimei (also played by Zhou), a dead ringer for Moudan, who does a mermaid act in a nightclub. This riff on themes and motifs from *Vertigo*, underpinned by a score which half-echoes Bernard Herrmann, is recounted by an unseen narrator – Lou himself? – who claims to be Meimei's ex-lover. Terrific. TR

Sven Klang's Combo (Sven Klangs Kvintett)

(1976, Swe, 100 min, b/w)
d Stellan Olsson. *p* Per Berglund. *sc* Ninne Olsson, Henric Holmberg, Stellan Olsson. *ph* Kent Person, Bengt Franzén. *ed* Roger Sellberg. *ad* Elisabeth Carlström. *m* Christer Boustedt. *cast* Anders Granström, Henric Holmberg, Eva Remaeus, Jan Liddell, Christer Boustedt.

●Thought by many to be one of the best ever films about the jazz environment, this follows the travails of the members of an amateur dance band that for a moment becomes a jazz group when a real jazzman, saxophonist Lars Nilsson (Boustedt) joins them, bringing with him (the year is 1958) the tang of Charlie Parker. Slowly, however, the group retreats from the inspiring but fearful world Lars has introduced them to – here, for once, the clichéd association of drugs and jazz works well – leaving Lars listening to the music in his head but stumbling through life. Ultimately, the film holds to the romantic view of creativity, but its virtues lie in director Olsson's careful (often very funny) observation of its characters and their worlds. PH

Swallows and Amazons

(1974, GB, 92 min)
d Claude Whatham. *p* Richard Pilbrow. *sc* David Wood. *ph* Denis Lewiston. *ed* Michael Bradsell. *ad* Simon Holland. *m* Wilfred Josephs. *cast* Virginia McKenna, Ronald Fraser, Simon West, Sophie Neville, Zanna Hamilton, Stephen Grendon.

●Claude Whatham continues his love affair with the past, moving back from working class youth of the '50s in *That'll Be the Day* to middle class children of the '20s in this adaptation of Arthur Ransome's story, which used to be required reading for all well brought up kids. Dealing with the adventures of six children one suitably idyllic summer holiday spent messing about in boats in the Lake District, it comes over as a labour of love rather than a commercial proposition. Period detail is strong, and the children gain in confidence as the story develops, but it's probably too slight to hold the attention of either children or accompanying adults, though individual scenes work, like the meeting with the charcoal-burners, and Sophie Neville is very good as one of the kids. It's pleasant/innocuous, depending on your frame of mind. CPe

Swallowtail Butterfly

(1996, Jap, 149 min)
d Shunji Iwai.

●Is this meant to be self-parody? If so, it backfires; if not, it's horribly shallow and pretentious. A vaguely futuristic 'fairytale', at times reminiscent of Kurosawa's *Dodes'ka-den*, about a bunch of outsiders trying to make a go of it in 'Yentown' (i.e. Tokyo), the film opts for an alarming plethora of clichés, including the old warhorse of puttin' on a show (here a punk nightclub – cue naff musical numbers) against the wishes of gangsters and establishment alike. GA

Swamp, The

see Ciénaga, La

Swamp Bait

see 'Gator Bait

Swamp Thing

(1982, US, 91 min)
d Wes Craven. *p* Benjamin Melniker, Michael Uslan. *sc* Wes Craven. *ph* Robin Goodwin. *ed* Richard Bracken. *ad* David Nichols, Robb Wilson-King. *m* Harry Manfredini. *cast* Louis Jourdan, Adrienne Barbeau, Ray Wise, Davis Hess, Nicholas Worth, Dick Durock.

●A research scientist (Wise), contaminated while working on a government project in Louisiana bayou country, mutates into the peaceable and amorous 'swamp thing' (played by Durock). Craven tries to do this 'veggie-man' horror in a suitable DC Comics style; and with Louis Jourdan as arch-villain 'Arcane', not to mention Adrienne Barbeau (Mrs John Carpenter) as the Thing's object of desire, he's definitely on the right track. At other times, the picture is right off its trolley. The budget limitations are pretty obvious, though the money did stretch to oodles of gunk and goo. TCh

Swamp Water

(1941, US, 92 min, b/w)
d Jean Renoir. *p* Irving Pichel. *sc* Dudley Nichols. *ph* J Peverell Marley. *ed* Walter Thompson. *ad* Richard Day, Joseph C Wright. *m* David Buttolph. *cast* Dana Andrews, Walter Brennan, Anne Baxter, Walter Huston, Virginia Gilmore, John Carradine, Ward Bond, Guinn Williams, Eugene Pallette.

●Renoir's first job in America for Fox: a rather sullen affair set in a Georgia swamp which harbours snakes, alligators, mud, and Walter Brennan, a fugitive criminal with whom the hero (Andrews) becomes strangely and melodramatically involved. As Raymond Durgnat points out in his Renoir book, it's a film with strong John Ford overtones in the casting, the regional subject-matter (post *Tobacco Road* and *Grapes of Wrath*), its music, and its script by the worthy but wordy Dudley Nichols. But Ford would undoubtedly have punched the story out with more action, more obvious emotion; Renoir is content to let the scenes lie there moodily, looking a bit drab and unbelievable for all the location shooting (quite a rare occurrence for this kind of Hollywood product at the time). GB

Swamy

(1987, Ind, 100 min)
d Shankar Nag. *p* TS Narashimi. *sc* Mariam Jetpurwala. *ph* S Ramachandra. *ed* Swesh Urs. *ad* John Devraj. *m* Sharang Dev. *cast* Manjunath, Rohit, Raghuram, Girish Karnad, Vaishali Kasaravalli.

●Less than enticing tale of childhood in a small Indian town at the time of coming independence, taken from the Malgudi (town) tales of RK Narayan. It focuses on a 9-year-old boy, Swamy, son of a Hindi lawyer, who finds his Eurocentric school lessons (Lisbon is the capital of Spain, he's told) and the sadistic religious-affairs teacher to his distaste. New pal Rajam, son of the local police superintendent, sparks arguments in the playground with assertive Mani, but all is partly resolved over a game of cricket. Episodic and poorly paced, the film is rumoured to have been compiled from a kiddies' TV series, and the politics look like street theatre. Best scenes are of the kids chucking stones by the riverside. WH

Swan Lake – The Zone (Lebedinoie ozero – Zona)

(1990, USSR/Can/US/Swe, 96 min, b/w)
d Yuri Illienko. *p* Virko Baley, Yuri Illienko. *sc* Yuri Illienko, Sergo Paradjanov. *cast* Victor Solovyov, Ludmila Yefimenko, Pylyp Illienko, Maya Bulgakova, Victor Demertash.

●Written by the Georgian director Sergo Paradjanov while imprisoned by the Soviet authorities between 1974 and 1977 – and filmed by his former cameraman Illienko – this bleak, sometimes elusive parable bears some resemblance to Paradjanov's renowned works in terms of its elliptical development, startling imagery and lack of dialogue. Shot in high-contrast b/w, however, the film adopts a more realist visual approach than the painterly tableaux of *The Colour of Pomegranates*, and the narrative has more flow. It starts with Solovyov on the run, taking refuge inside a metal hammer and sickle monument. The mother of a boy who plays there comes to his aid – and falls in love – until the son betrays him to the authorities. Back in prison he attempts suicide, only to be rescued from the dead at the morgue because of a crude blood transfusion from his accompanying prison guard, and is thus indebted... Despite its enigmatic nature, the film has a real and direct power thanks to Solovyov's haunting, cadaverous performance. Some searing images, too – not least that of swans, lured by the gleam of water to land on a washed down prison yard amid the baying inmates. NB

Swann

(1996, Can/GB, 96 min)
d Anna Benson Gyles. *p* Ann Scott, Christina Jennings. *sc* David Young. *ph* Gerald Packer. *ed* Robin Sales. *pd* John Dondertman. *m* Richard Rodney Bennett. *cast* Miranda Richardson, Brenda Fricker, Michael Ontkean, David Cubitt, Sean Hewitt, John Neville.

●Low-key drama set in rural Ontario, from a novel by Carol Shields, with Fricker as the spinster librarian guarding the memorabilia and reputation of a local 'primitive' poet murdered by her husband. When celebrity author Richardson turns up to research a book on the dead woman, desperate to beat the ruthless academics who want a monopoly on the subject, Fricker finds her hitherto tranquil lifestyle threatened. Thanks to a firm grasp of detail and the sturdy lead performances, the film works rather better as a character study than a feminist drama about the varieties of violence inflicted on women by men. GA

Swann in Love (Un Amour de Swann)

(1983, Fr, 111 min)
d Volker Schlöndorff. *p* Margaret Ménégoz. *sc* Peter Brook, Jean-Claude Carrière, Marie Hélène Estienne. *ph* Sven Nykvist. *ed* Françoise Bonnot. *ad* Jacques Saulnier. *m* Hans Werner Henze. *cast* Jeremy Irons, Ornella Muti, Alain Delon, Fanny Ardant, Marie-Christine Barrault, Anne Bennent, Nathalie Juvet.

●The filming of Proust's massif central had been looming on the horizon for eighteen years, surely the longest gestation period of any movie ever. Proustians had been hiding under the bed ever since this latest stab was announced, directed by a German, part-scripted by an Englishman (Peter Brook), starring an Englishman as Swann (Irons), and with an Italian (Muti) as Odette. In spite of the multi-national packaging, however, it is pulled off with a good grace and considerable emphasis on the humour and sexiness of the original – two factors that people seem to forget. Schlndorff shows an uncharacteristic visual organisation; and the clever notion of collapsing the thing into just one day in the life of Swann is vindicated by an elegiac coda which casts a suitable Proustian net over the whole enterprise. Piquant; if only for the fact that the subject matter – consuming jealousy – is rare in modern cinema. CPea

Swan Princess, The

(1994, US, 89 min)
d Richard Rich. *p* Richard Rich, Jared F Brown. *sc* Richard Rich, Brian Nissen. *ed* Jim Koford, Armetta Jackson. *ad* Mike Hodgson, James Coleman. *m* Lex de Azevedo. *cast* voices: John Cleese, Jack Palance, Steven Wright, Michelle Nicastro, Sandy Duncan.

● This likeable animated fairytale takes the story of *Swan Lake* and ruffles up its feathers for '90s PC audiences. Prince Derek is about to marry his childhood sweetheart Princess Odette when he goes and spoils it all by making a chauvinistic remark regarding his bride-to-be's gorgeous looks. Miffed, Odette sulks back to her own kingdom only to be abducted by Rothbart (voice by Palance), a morphing megalomaniac desperate for her hand in marriage so that he may become ruler of her father's kingdom. When she proves unwilling, Rothbart seethes, then rages, then turns her into a swan for the hours from dawn to dusk. Derek, in the meantime, enlists the help of the cute forest creatures – a frog called Jean-Bob, a turtle called Speed, and a puffin called Puffin – to investigate her disappearance. Youngsters will find much to enjoy in the jokey dialogue, lush landscapes and comical action sequences, though not, one suspects, in the naff theatrical songs. DA

Swan Song (Juexiang)

(1985, China, 100 min)
d/sc Zhang Zeming. *ph* Zheng Kangzhen, Zhao Xiaoshi. *ed* Yan Xiuying. *ad* Zhang Jingwen, Peng Jun. *m* Zhou Xiaoyuan. *cast* Kong Xianzhu, Chen Rui, Mo Shaoying, Liang Yujin, Lui Qianyi.

● Zhang Zeming's beautiful debut feature opens in the early 1960s, just before the nightmare of the Cultural Revolution, and focuses on a Cantonese composer unable to get his music published or performed. His troubles with the authorities are lifelong; he entered 'New China' with an opium habit, a black mark that cost him his job, broke up his marriage, and pushed him into the shadows, where the only people who will play his stuff are a street orchestra of blind musicians. All his hopes are invested in his son, a promising musician, who runs off as a 'Red Guard' and returns ten years later a street-smart delinquent. Tracing an elaborate pattern of betrayals and disappointments, the films avoids all taint of miserabilism. The spirit running through it is that of the music itself: haunting and elegiac, but also strong and proudly rooted in traditional Cantonese culture. TR

Swarm, The

(1978, US, 116 min)
d/p Irwin Allen. *sc* Stirling Silliphant. *ph* Fred J Koenekamp. *ed* Harold F Kress. *pd* Stan Jolley. *m* Jerry Goldsmith. *cast* Michael Caine, Katharine Ross, Richard Widmark, Richard Chamberlain, Olivia de Havilland, Henry Fonda, Ben Johnson, Lee Grant, José Ferrer, Patty Duke Astin, Slim Pickens, Bradford Dillman, Fred MacMurray, Cameron Mitchell.

● Swarms of African killer bees infiltrate a Texan Air Force base, stinging a number of missile button-pushers to death. But relax; in their wake strolls Caine, an able entomologist who has in his wallet the phone number of leading immunologist Dr Krim (Fonda). He also has the ear of a presidential advisor, and was passing through with a truckload of miracle sting-relief called Cardio-pep. 'Cardio-pep?' breathes the doctor (Ross), strangely excited. Their eyes meet. Meanwhile, the bees have brought down a couple of helicopters, sharply curtailed a family picnic, and…At this point a number of journalists, rolling in the aisles with laughter, were ejected from the press screening. All they missed was the slow death of a risibly inadequate disaster movie. JS

Swarm in May, A

(1983, GB, 82 min)
d/sc Colin Finbow. *ph* Andrew Fleury. *m* Colin Myles. *cast* Oliver Hicks, Milo Twomey, Frank Middlemass, Jack May, Charles Lewsen, Hugh Hastings, Douglas Storm, Petra Davies.

● The Children's Film Unit's third feature, this is surprisingly adult in its nostalgia for childhood (pre 'Grange Hill', prime Billy Bunter). Returning to Cathedral Choral School from his broken home, an unpopular 'wet' (Hicks) learns to his greater misery that he is to be 'bee-keeper', a symbolic role merely requiring plenty of singing. Mix the occasional melodious 'Nunc Dimittis' with some investigation into the mystery of the first bee-keeper's secrets, and you come up with a moral that tradition is a Good Thing when you know what it's all about. Finbow avoids the amateur raucousness of the earlier *Captain Stirrick*; and his youthful production team has evoked a fine sense of the close-up familiarity of boys (strictly no girls), summer warmth, and the lingering flow of time. LU

Swashbuckler (The Scarlet Buccaneer)

(1976, US, 101 min)
d James Goldstone. *p* Jennings Lang. *sc* Jeffrey Bloom. *ph* Philip H Lathrop. *ed* Edward A Biery. *pd* John J Lloyd. *m* John Addison. *cast* Robert Shaw, James Earl Jones, Peter Boyle, Genevieve Bujold, Beau Bridges, Avery Schreiber, Geoffrey Holder, Anjelica Huston, Dorothy Tristan.

● The success of *Jaws* sent Hollywood scurrying for movie adventure styles to refurbish; hence this multi-million dollar pirate swashbuckler. Although Jeffrey Bloom's arch and relatively uninspired script lacks the more evocative components of a Robert Louis Stevenson story, it still manages to combine all the staples of the genre with a certain gusto: treasure, duelling, knife-throwing, ambushes, dungeon escapes, sea fights, disguise, and hints of exotic sado-masochism are all here in grandiose style, plus the usual sexual hostility between hero (Shaw) and heroine (Bujold). Shaw and Boyle (the villain) camp it up too much, but at least the pirate ship and tropical sea beaches are spectacularly real, not the tanks and crude sets that the genre has almost invariably suffered in the past. DP

Swastika

(1973, GB, 113 min, b/w & col)
d Philippe Mora. *p* Sandy Lieberson, David Puttnam. *sc* Philippe Mora, Lutz Becker. *ed* Andrew Patterson. *m* Richard Wagner, Ludwig van Beethoven, Noël Coward, Jay Gorney.

● Philippe Mora's study of Nazism (using documentary material, including 16mm colour footage shot by Eva Braun) works best as a testament to the lost hopes of a duped generation, charting the slow slide from apparent peaceful prosperity to the takeover of more sinister elements; by which time the process of seduction was well under way. You realise what an insidiously high standard of propaganda the Nazis developed. The portrait of Hitler, mainly through Eva Braun's home movies, although fascinating, is less successful. It attempts to give the man a human face, but the strange washed-out colours, the repetition of footage to a point where it assumes a hallucinatory quality, and the credit sequence of a huge gold swastika revolving in space, do little to make the myth more accessible. Rather, they reinforce it. A fascinating document, none the less, that spares us a commentary, letting the material speak for itself. CPe

Swedish Massage Parlour (Blutjunge Masseusen)

(1972, Switz, 82 min)
d/p/sc Manfred Gregor [Erwin C Dietrich]. *ph* Peter Baumgartner. *ed* MC Bushke. *m* Walter Baumgartner. *cast* Rena Bergen, Nadine de Rangot, Chitta Coray, Claudia Fielers, Antje Schlärf.

● Purported sex comedy which raises not a single snigger and from which all traces of the sex act have been censor-trimmed. A world tour of massage parlour brothels via Copenhagen, Bangkok, Zurich, Paris, Granada and Rome, it contrives to set all its interiors in the same orange-and-blue painted office block. Producer/director Dietrich hides behind a pseudonym but will be laughing all the way to the bank: he must have had change from a fiver on his production budget. PT

Sweeney!

(1976, GB, 89 min)
d David Wickes. *p* Ted Childs. *sc* Ranald Graham. *ph* Dusty Miller. *ed* Chris Burt. *ad* Bill Alexander. *m* Denis King. *cast* John Thaw, Dennis Waterman, Barry Foster, Ian Bannen, Colin Welland, Diane Keen, Michael Coles, Joe Melia, Brian Glover.

● For a piece of shitty incompetence, this spin-off from the seventies' TV cop series would be hard to outdo. Shot with a contemptuous disregard for focus, colour and composition, it tells a ridiculous tale of oil sheiks, callgirls and Big Deals, dressed up in everyone's favourite London locations. Ranald Graham's script is mainly to blame – how come one of the regular TV writers didn't get to do it? – with the Regan/Carter (Thaw/Waterman) relationship consisting of 'You sod!', 'You bastard!' etc.; the fictitious names – 'Media Ltd', 'The Dunchester Club', 'New Democrat' magazine – give further clues as to what the whole is like. The Bad-Acting honours are shared by Barry Foster (American) and Ian Bannen (pissed). AN

Sweeney 2

(1978, GB, 108 min)
d Tom Clegg. *p* Ted Childs. *sc* Troy Kennedy Martin. *ph* Dusty Miller. *ed* Chris Burt. *ad* William Alexander. *m* Tony Hatch. *cast* John Thaw, Dennis Waterman, Denholm Elliott, Barry Stanton, John Flanagan, Georgina Hale.

● On TV, *The Sweeney* usually got its story under way with minimum fuss, and allowed Regan and Carter to carry the show. But here Regan (Thaw) is at his most avuncular and long-suffering as he tackles a bunch of violent bank robbers, a would-be League of Gentlemen operating out of Malta. Unfortunately the film-makers (many of the TV team) can bring little pictorial or thematic depth to the big screen, opting for easy laughs, slick action, and large filler sections which develop neither plot nor character. CPe

Sweeney Todd

(1997, US, 91 min)
d John Schlesinger. *p* Ted Swanson. *sc* Peter Buckman. *ph* Martin Fuhrer. *ed* Mark Day. *pd* Malcolm Thornton. *m* Richard Rodney Bennett. *cast* Ben Kingsley, Joanna Lumley, Campbell Scott, Katharine Schlesinger, David Wilmot, Peter Woodthorpe, Peter Jeffrey.

● For some reason, Hammer omitted Sweeney Todd from their Grand Guignol repertoire, but this cable version catches the flavour of the old firm, even down to the fiery climax. In opposition to Tod Slaughter's pre-war hiss-me-I'm-a-villain rendition, Ben Kingsley offers a rather gentle monster. In fact apart from the odd severed windpipe, the horror is limited to the camera's examination of Mrs Lovett's equivocal meat pies. Most successful is the design, especially the slimy passages and shadowy horror chambers beneath Fleet St. Joanna Lumley appears with blackened teeth and grimy drawers, but despite an itinerary which includes flagellation and cannibalism, that familiar mist of refinement obstinately refuses to disperse. BBa

Sweet and Lowdown

(1999, US, 95 min)
d Woody Allen. *p* Jean Doumanian. *sc* Woody Allen. *ph* Zhao Fei. *ed* Alisa Lepselter. *pd* Santo Loquasto. *m* Dick Hyman. *cast* Antony LaPaglia, Brian Markinson, Gretchen Mol, Samantha Morton, Sean Penn, Uma Thurman, James Urbaniak, John Waters.

● The title of Woody Allen's film just about sums it up in three respects. First, it evokes the '30s jazz scene setting. Second, it pinpoints the two lead characters: waifish laundress Hattie (Morton), a mute, passive, generous-spirited halfwit; and Emmett Ray (Penn), the philandering, hard-living, self-obsessed guitar virtuoso who, having been lumbered with her on a double date, remains far too busy talking about himself ever to finish with her properly once and for all. Third, 'lowdown' might be one's initial impression of this potentially poor-taste conceit, but 'sweet' is spot-on for the film's tender warmth, which lingers in the memory long after it's over. The story is simple, charting the ups and downs in the relationship between Ray (whose idea of showing a girl a good time is to take her rat-shooting, and whose main concern in life is that he'll never measure up to his hero Django Reinhardt) and the devoted Hattie, and their various encounters with slumming sophisticates (Thurman as a writer who lures Ray away from Hattie), mobsters (the dependable LaPaglia), Hollywooders, musos and so on. Meanwhile, 'interviews' with jazz fans – Woody included – commenting on Ray's life and art interrupt and reflect on what is finally a fable of pride, prejudice, self-obsession and redemption.Like many of Allen's best films, this is a deceptively modest affair, funny and charming but seemingly slight and inconsequential – until the killer coda. The sense of period and place is assured, the music delicious, the performances terrific. Penn, particularly, is a joy to behold, never ingratiating or maudlin, wholly credible even in the musical scenes, effortlessly expressing both the latent insecurity and artistic determination that fuel Ray's energies. Bittersweet indeed. GA

Sweet Angel Mine

(1996, GB/Can, 88 min)
d Curtis Radclyffe. *p* Sam Taylor, Christopher Zimmer. *sc* Sue Maheu, Tim Willocks. *ph* Witold Stok. *ed* Anne Sopel. *pd* Maria Djurkovic. *m* John McCarthy. *cast* Oliver Milburn, Margaret Langrick, Anna Massey, Alberta Watson, John Dunsworth, Mike Crimp.
● Nova Scotia, the present day: Paul (Milburne), a young Englishman on a motorbike, goes out to the woods where his dad once disappeared, and gets a jolly surprise. In an isolated farmhouse on the edge of the water, he comes across a lone family of women – daughter, mother, grandmother – silently stewing in their juices. He takes a shine to the young one (Langrick) – and maybe her mum (Watson) – and won't go away when they tell him to. Big mistake. Obviously we wouldn't be out in this social wasteland if there weren't female repression and latent hysteria waiting to explode, and Paul waits for it; the film only once follows him away from women's cove, for a bit of far-fetched macho business in the local town. Clear as it is that something is to be revealed, the passage towards it is both wearisomely convoluted with hallucinatory intimations of gore and empty of any sensible character detail; moreover, the punch, when it comes, is hyperbolically ugly. NB

Sweet Bird of Youth

(1961, US, 120 min)
d Richard Brooks. *p* Pandro S Berman. *sc* Richard Brooks. *ph* Milton Krasner. *ed* Henry Berman. *ad* George W Davis, Urie McCleary. *m* Harold Gelman. *cast* Paul Newman, Geraldine Page, Ed Begley, Rip Torn, Shirley Knight, Mildred Dunnock, Madeleine Sherwood.
● Brooks' second involvement with Tennessee Williams has Newman repeating his Broadway role as the no longer quite pristine gigolo who returns to his home town with fading movie queen (Page) in tow, scheming to establish himself as someone in the eyes of the corrupt political boss (Begley) who once ran him out of town for aspiring to marry his daughter (Knight). Like *Cat on a Hot Tin Roof*, the play gets the glossy clean-up treatment, so that Newman's comeuppance (what he hadn't realised in leaving town was that he also left Knight pregnant) no longer comes through castration, but simply by having his pretty face messed up a bit. It might still have worked, except that Brooks' direction seems a little too stolid for all the sleazy, flaming passions. These are, however, given full measure by an excellent cast. Geraldine Page, in particular (like Newman, repeating her Broadway role) is stunningly and wittily outsized in her rendition of the ageing movie queen seeking refuge in a haze of drink, drugs and sex. TM

Sweet Bird of Youth

(1989, US, 100 min)
d Nicolas Roeg. *p* Fred Whitehead. *sc* Gavin Lambert. *ph* Francis Kenny. *ed* Pamela Malouf-Cundy. *pd* Penny Hadfield. *m* Ralph Burns. *cast* Elizabeth Taylor, Mark Harmon, Rip Torn, Valerie Perrine, Ruta Lee, Kevin Geer.
● Liz Taylor takes the role Genevieve Page made her own, on stage and in Richard Brooks' 1961 movie version, as the fading Hollywood idol seeking solace in booze, pills, and the arms of masseur Harmon. Retreating to his small home town, she exploits his dreams of glamour, but the threatening ghosts of his past aren't far away. For all the cast's earnest efforts, passion fails to rise, and the stature of the Tennessee Williams source material seems diminished this time round (for TV), even if modern frankness allows more of the playwright's savage vision to come through than three decades previously. TJ

Sweet Charity

(1968, US, 149 min)
d Bob Fosse. *p* Robert Arthur. *sc* Peter Stone. *ph* Robert Surtees. *ed* Stuart Gilmore. *ad* Alexander Golitzen, George Webb. *m* Cy Coleman. *cast* Shirley MacLaine, Sammy Davis Jr, Ricardo Montalban, John McMartin, Chita Rivera, Paula Kelly, Stubby Kaye, Barbara Bouchet.
● Making his debut as a director on this adaptation of the Broadway musical derived from Fellini's *Notte di Cabiria*, Fosse starts on the wrong foot by showing off with an irritating flurry of zooms, dissolves and jump-cuts. Luckily his own choreography intervenes, settling the film down and offering at least two classic anthology pieces: the superbly weary, sleazy erotica of 'Hey, Big Spender', in which a row of disillusioned taxi-dancers laconically display their wares, and the trio of bizarre fantasies ('The Rich Man's Frug') performed by a vampiric night-club dancer. For the rest, the film belongs to Shirley MacLaine, splendidly funny as the 'extremely open, honest and stupid broad' who earns a dubious living as a taxi-dancer at the Fandango Ballroom, meanwhile overflowing with innocent love for everybody and everything and being left short of the altar by a succession of men. No masterpiece, but a generally underrated musical all the same. TM

Sweet Degeneration (Fang Lang)

(1997, Tai/Jap, 118 min)
d Lin Cheng-Sheng. *p* Hsu Li-Kong. *sc* Lin Cheng-Sheng. *ph* Tsai Cheng-Hui. *ed* Chen Po-Wen. *pd* An Che-Yi. *m* Chang Hong-Yi. *cast* Lee Kang-Sheng, Chen Xiangqi, Chen Shihuang, Zhang Penyu, Lin Zhilong.
● A plaintive sax solo blows through Lin's third feature, evoking both the romantic fecklessness of Chuen-Sheng (Lee), a young man fresh out of military service with dreams of making it as a musician, and the forlorn longing of his sister Ah Fen, unhappily married, who nurses a secret incestuous passion for him. While Chuen-Sheng steals money from his father and squanders it on roach-infested hotel rooms and cheap hookers, Ah Fen decides she can't face her life any more and runs away. In other words, there's no plot: just scenes from unfulfilled lives, acutely framed and sharply observed, which work to dissect all the ways that people can fool themselves emotionally. Lin has said that Chuen-Sheng is essentially a candid self-portrait, based on the years when he was a petty criminal and jailbird; maybe that, as much as Lee's excellent performance, explains why it all rings so true. TR

Sweet Dreams

(1985, US, 115 min)
d Karel Reisz. *p* Bernard Schwartz. *sc* Robert Getchell. *ph* Robbie Greenberg. *ed* Malcolm Cooke. *pd* Albert Brenner. *m* Charles Gross. *cast* Jessica Lange, Ed Harris, Ann Wedgeworth, David Clennon, James Staley, Gary Basaraba, John Goodman, PJ Soles.
● Reisz's film concentrates almost exclusively on the ups and downs of Patsy Cline's painful marriage to the aptly named Charlie Dick (Harris). In outline, this is the stuff of soap opera – rags to celebrity plane crash via grievous bodily harm – but of a superior kind. The two main performances are excellent: Lange plays the singer without a hint of condescension to her dreams of 'a big house with yellow roses', while Harris is persuasively menacing, with an inventively foul mouth. And Reisz studiously avoids any of those crashingly neat life/lyric juxtapositions until the very end, by which time even the most hardened palenecks should be sobbing into their beer. KJ

Sweet Emma, Dear Böbe (Edes Emma, Drága Böbe)

(1992, Hun, 81 min)
d István Szabó. *p* Lajos Ovari, Gabriella Grosz. *sc* István Szabo. *ph* Lajos Koltai. *ed* Eszter Kovacs. *pd* Attila Kovacs. *m* Tibor Bornai, Mihaly Moricz, Fero Nagy, Robert Schumann. *cast* Johanna Ter Steege, Enikö Börcsök, Péter Andoral, Eva Kerekes, Erszi Gaal, Zoltan Mucsi.
● Szabó's return to Hungary after *Meeting Venus* resulted in this almost heart-breaking account of a country in transition; an intimate portrait which may lack the production values of lavish period dramas like *Mephisto* and *Colonel Redl*, but which exerts a subtle pressure and exposes raw wounds. The story revolves around two women, Budapest-based teachers of Russian who find their skills useless in a post-Communist society and adopt English as their speciality, practising consonants and staying only one step ahead of their students. Emma (Ter Steege in a striking performance) is unhappy about her married, vacillating lover, while Böbe picks up rich foreign men. As they share a room in a hostel, their friendship withstands disturbing revelations and differences which remain unfathomable. Portraying a society where anger and exploitation have replaced mediocrity, Szabó's sensitive handling of the material culminates in a meditative passage in which Emma stands in church, musing on the 'passion for love' which masks lack of purpose. 'Collective sin' may be dead, according to Böbe, but this movingly delineates the private pain of atonement. CM

Sweet Grass (Huang Sha, Qing Cao, Hong Taiyang)

(1995, China, 87 min)
d Zhou Youchao. *p* Cindy Jin Zhang. *sc* Yang Zhengguang. *ph* Zhao Fei, Li Ziaoping. *ed* Hong Yuan. *m* Zhao Jiping. *cast* Zheng Tianwei, Sun Haiying, Wang Gang.
● Another Chinese 'Western', set on the grasslands of Gansu in the 1920s, scripted by the writer of *The Swordsman in Double-Flag Town* and directed by a former assistant of Zhang Yimou. Nothing startlingly new in the plot (young widow has to choose between two surrogate fathers for her son – one a feckless gambler and knife-thrower, the other a klutzy itinerant pedlar – and she makes the mistake of choosing the sexy one), but plenty of pleasure in the performances, the score, the widescreen cinematography, and in baroque details like a game of mahjong played with tiles the size of tombstones. TR

Sweetheart of the Campus (aka Broadway Ahead)

(1941, US, 69 min, b/w)
d Edward Dmytryk. *p* Jack Fier. *sc* Robert D Andrews, Edmund Hartmann. *ph* Franz Planer. *ed* William Lyon. *ad* Lionel Banks. *songs* Eddie Cherkose, Jacques Press, Walter G Samuels, Jacques Krakeur. *cast* Ruby Keeler, Ozzie Nelson, Harriet Hilliard, Gordon Oliver, Don Beddoe, Kathleen Howard
● 'Zig me baby with a gentle zag.' This amiable relic from the Swing era has the usual pompous authority figures trying and failing to stop the music – though the absence, despite the college setting, of any character much under 30 marks the picture off from later rock/pop equivalents. Dmytryk, clearly bursting to get off the B-picture treadmill, makes rapid work of the idiotic plot and concentrates on the numbers, which he stages as inventively as a meagre budget and schedule allow. European exile Planer (cameraman for Murnau, Ophuls) gives it a classier look than the material merits. BBa

Sweethearts

(1996, US, 83 min)
d/p/sc Aleks Horvat. *ph* John Peters. *ed* Terry Kelley. *pd* Mimi Gramatky. *m* Carl Schultz, Chris Anderson. *cast* Janeane Garofalo, Mitch Rouse, Bobcat Goldthwait, Margaret Cho, Van Quattro.
● Janeane Garofalo may have no more than a cult following here, but it's growing fast. She's the best reason to check out this near-miss, a black sex war comedy about a blind date which proves that love isn't (blind, that is). Waiting for his dream girl to walk in, Arliss (Rouse) is buttonholed by the unfashionably forthright Jasmine (Garofalo). He's looking for slender and attractive; she's up for stimulating conversation – as long as he's doing the listening. This rather static piece, written, directed and produced by Aleks Horvat, is pretty funny for a while, but loses credibility when it tries for something wilder. It's refreshing to see a woman on screen who can string whole paragraphs together; a pity she has to be a bipolar manic depressive. TCh

Sweet Hearts Dance

(1988, US, 101 min)
d Robert Greenwald. *p* Jeffrey Lurie. *sc* Ernest Thompson. *ph* Tak Fujimoto. *ed* Robert Florio, Janet Bartells. *pd* James Allen. *m* Richard Gibbs. *cast* Don Johnson, Susan Sarandon, Jeff Daniels, Elizabeth Perkins, Kate Reid, Justin Henry.
● After 15 years together, Wiley and Sandy Boon (Johnson and Sarandon) seem to have lost their desire for each other; Wiley moves out, prompting

good buddy and neighbour Sam (Daniels) – himself struggling to establish an on-going romance with fellow teacher Adie (Perkins) – to try and get the family together again. After a meandering start, the scene is set for an ensemble piece which strives to show that staying in love is a question of continuous hard work. The acting (especially Sarandon) is fine, the Vermont small-town setting picturesquely photographed, and much of the dialogue successfully suggests the awkwardness of people unable to speak openly about their emotions. Yet potentially riveting rows are abbreviated before they get properly under way, continually deflecting the pain and confusion of separation into scenes of near inconsequentiality, worsened by a dire revamped rock'n'roll soundtrack, and rounded off with the usual mawkish ending. Not so much bad as frustrating. GA

Sweet Hereafter, The

(1997, Can, 110 min)
d Atom Egoyan. *p* Camelia Frieberg, Atom Egoyan. *sc* Atom Egoyan. *ph* Paul Sarossy. *ed* Susan Shipton. *pd* Phillip Barker. *m* Mychael Danna. *cast* Ian Holm, Sarah Polley, Bruce Greenwood, Tom McCamus, Arsinée Khanjian, Alberta Watson.

● Adapted from the Russell Banks novel, this is Egoyan's warmest and, despite the sophisticated time structure of the fragmented narrative, his most conventional film to date. Holm is the big-city lawyer – with family problems of his own – who starts investigations into a tragic school bus accident that has robbed a remote rural community of all but one of its children, in the hope of persuading the parents to sue for compensation; inevitably, they react in different ways to his solicitude. Beautifully performed, edited and shot (the crash itself is extraordinarily effective), the film is certainly sensitive in its treatment of grief, guilt and anger, and strong on atmosphere. Whether it finally offers any fresh insights into how a community is changed by such a tragedy is less certain. GA

Sweet Hunters

(1969, Pan, 100 min)
d Ruy Guerra. *p* Claude Giroux. *sc* Ruy Guerra, Philippe DuMarçay. *ph* Ricardo Aronovich. *ed* Kénout Peltier. *ad* Bernard Evein. *m* David Whitaker. *cast* Sterling Hayden, Maureen McNally, Susan Strasberg, Stuart Whitman, Andrew Hayden.

● An ornithologist (Hayden) goes on a field trip to a deserted island near the mainland with his wife (McNally) and small son, and is joined by the wife's sister (Strasberg), who is getting over an abortion; later, an escaped convict (Whitman) is discovered. A situation which may seem naturalistic enough, but the form never is: incidents are isolated, cross-relations are oblique, emotions are unexplained. And as the narrative gradually coheres, Guerra daringly undercuts it with a series of disturbing emphases. As haunting and ambiguous as anything of Herzog's. TR

Sweetie

(1989, Aust, 100 min)
d Jane Campion. *p* John Maynard. *sc* Jame Campion, Gerard Lee. *ph* Sally Bongers. *ed* Veronika Haussler. *ad* Peter Harris. *m* Martin Armiger. *cast* Genevieve Lemon, Karen Colston, Tom Lycos, Jon Darling, Dorothy Barry, Michael Lake.

● Kay (Colston) fears darkness and the secret, stifling power of plants; her teenage sister Dawn (Lemon) is crazy, throwing tantrums at all and sundry, and dreaming, unrealistically, of stardom. When the latter and her bombed-out boyfriend (Lake) arrive unannounced at the suburban home Kay shares with her equally loopy lover Lou (Lycos), all hell breaks loose. Tragedy looms. And all the aforementioned is played, partly, as comedy. Campion's first theatrical feature is a remarkable, risky exploration of the weird and wonderfully surreal undercurrents that can lie just beneath the surface of everyday suburban life, ordinary folk harbour dark, unfathomable obsessions, phobias and desires, and a familiar world is unsettlingly distorted by grotesque close-ups, harsh overhead angles and narrative ellipses. Amazingly, as she veers without warning from black comedy to bleak melodrama and back again, she manages to make us laugh at *and* like her confused, barely articulate characters, so that her *dénouement* is simultaneously ludicrous and deeply affecting. *Sweetie* confirms Campion as a highly original movie talent. GA

Sweet Kill (aka The Arousers)

(1971, US, 87 min)
d Curtis Hanson. *p* Tamara Asseyev. *sc* Curtis Hanson. *ph* Daniel Lacambre. *ed* Gretel Ehrlich. *ad* James Kenney. *m* Charles Bernstein. *cast* Tab Hunter, Cherie Latimer, Nadyne Turney, Isabel Jewell, Linda Leider, Roberta Collins, Kate McKeown.

● Something smells very peculiar here, and it's not just the body of his first victim which Tab Hunter has hidden in the pigeon loft. The aged beach boy, interestingly enough, plays an impotent PE instructor surrounded by predatory women. He picks them off one by one, and is gradually revealed as a pantie-collector, foot fetishist, and the type who wanks by the bedside of a call-girl dressed up as his dead mom. With his stark titles and moodily shot interiors, writer/director Hanson no doubt wanted it all to add up to a classy case history; but there's too much that's hackneyed and explicit, and too little clarification of Tab's psychosis. AN

Sweet Liberty

(1985, US, 107 min)
d Alan Alda. *p* Martin Bregman. *sc* Alan Alda. *ph* Frank Tidy. *ed* Michael Economou. *pd* Ben Edwards. *m* Bruce Broughton. *cast* Alan Alda, Michael Caine, Michelle Pfeiffer, Bob Hoskins, Lise Hilboldt, Lillian Gish, Saul Rubinek, Lois Chiles, Linda Thorson.

● Alda casts himself as a liberal college professor whose *Reader's Digest*-style book on the War of Independence is being made into a gross-out movie by the manic film crew who take over his somnolent home town for the summer. His struggles to drag the production back to the path of middlebrow virtue are impeded by the film's pathologically vulgar screenwriter (Hoskins), by his dotty old mother (Gish), and by his growing fascination with the leading lady (Pfeiffer). Surprisingly, all this is nearly as dull as it sounds, intermittently enlivened only by Hoskins and Caine, the latter effortlessly amusing as the production's leading man. KJ

Sweet Movie

(1974, Fr/Can/WGer, 99 min)
d/sc Dusan Makavejev. *p* Vincent Malle. *ph* Pierre Lhomme. *ed* Yenn Dedet. *ad* Jocelyn Joly, Christian Lamarque. *m* Manos Hadjidakis. *cast* Carole Laure, Pierre Clémenti, Anna Prucnal, Sami Frey, Jane Mallet, Marpessa Dawn, Roy Callender, John Vernon.

● Potentially one of the most scandalous films ever made – except that it has been little seen outside France and has not aged well. Seemingly completely episodic, the 'plot' follows the adventures of a beauty queen (Laure), a certified virgin who escapes a disastrous honeymoon with the richest man in the world to join a group of carefree sensualists. The latter are the once-notorious Otto Muehl troupe, who delight in pissing and shitting as a public spectacle. This is cross-cut with the journey of the good ship SS Survival (which sports Karl Marx for a masthead) on the Seine. Laure herself sought legal suppression of certain shots which, in their blanked out form, ironically suggest even more sexual activity on her part. Sadly, this highly idiosyncratic melange of sex and politics, for all its liberating pretensions, only served to put Makavejev's career back a good few steps. DT

Sweet November

(1968, US, 113 min)
d Robert Ellis Miller. *p* Jerry Gershwin, Elliot Kastner. *sc* Herman Rauchner. *ph* Daniel L Fapp. *ed* James Heckert. *ad* John J Lloyd. *m* Michel Legrand. *cast* Sandy Dennis, Anthony Newley, Theodore Bikel, Burr DeBenning, Sandy Baron, Marj Dusay.

● Not written by Neil Simon, though you might be forgiven for so guessing, this is a comedy with heart. Sandy Dennis, positively twitching with charm, plays a kooky girl – beloved by everybody in a neighbourhood seemingly peopled exclusively by oddballs – who shares her apartment with a new man every month (she favours the insecure, sending them on their way with new confidence). After she and November's patient (Newley) fall madly in love, it transpires that she is suffering, Marguerite Gautier style, from an incurable disease. It all ends in a flood of insufferably gooey tears. TM

Sweet November

(2001, US, 120 min)
d Pat O'Connor. *p* Erwin Stoff, Deborah Aal, Steven Reuther, Elliot Kastner. *sc* Kurt Voelker. *ph* Edward Lachman. *ed* Anne V Coates. *pd* Naomi Shohan. *m* Christopher Young. *cast* Keanu Reeves, Charlize Theron, Jason Isaacs, Greg Germann. Liam Aiken, Robert Joy, Lauren Graham, Michael Rosenbaum.

● Master of the blank expression, Reeves is still blessed with those dumb good looks. Which means he's well suited to playing Nelson Moss, a successful ad exec with the emotional range of a cyborg. Before long the high flyer has an improbable encounter with Sara Deever (Theron), a hippy savant who embraces life and instinctively knows that Nelson, bless his Armani socks, must have a heart. Nelson strides manfully about barking into his mobile and obsessed by work. Sara cajoles and harangues him, and after the most perfunctory of rebuffs, Nelson is set to spend one month at Sara's home. That's all the time she believes she needs 'to help'. Opposites attract and the thirty-day sentence becomes – surprise! – 'Sweet November'. Wooden Reeves doesn't cut it as a romantic lead, while Theron's giant cardigans, whooping laugh and 'my giddy aunt' glee only cunderline her aptitude for a career in kids' TV. Both are hampered by the endless clichés: having fun is always free (playing kiss-chase, walking cute dogs, turning cartwheels); gay men are a troubled woman's best friend (Isaacs' cross-dressing housemate Chas/Cheri); and, of course, the *Love Story* biggie – wasting diseases leave the sufferer wan but never less than beautiful. CF

Sweet Revenge

see Dandy, the All-American Girl

Sweet Scent of Death, A (Un Dulce Olor a Muerte)

(1998, Mex/Sp/Arg, 98 min)
d Gabriel Retes. *sc* Guillermo Arriaga. *ph* Claudio Rocha. *ed* Carlos Salcés. *m* Iván Wyszogrod. *cast* Karra Elejalde, Ana Alvarez, Diego Luna, Héctor Alterio, Laila Saab, Ignacio Retes.

● This is a slick and pacy, but – in both senses of the word – terribly Americanised thriller. The murder of a teenage nymphet in a Mexican village leads to widespread paranoia, machismo, cover-up and the threat of imprisonment of execution for the innocent teenager who fancied her. It's a tale of sex, violence, corruption and clichés, complete with bluesy guitar track, backlit lighting, hammy acting and a not very interesting denouement. But Alterio is dependable as ever as the ambiguous, ageing sheriff, and it all passes by innocuously and amiably enough. GA

Sweet Sixteen

(2002, GB, 106 min)
d Ken Loach. *p* Rebecca O'Brien. *sc* Paul Laverty. *ph* Barry Ackroyd. *ed* Jonathan Morris. *pd* Martin Johnson. *m* George Fenton. *cast* Martin Compston, Annmarie Fulton, William Ruane, Michelle Coulter, Gary McCormack, Tommy McKee.

● With his junkie mum in jail and struggling to get clean, and her violent lover requiring his help in self-serving dirty deeds, 15-year-old Liam dreams of a better life. So he takes to dealing drugs with his chaotic mate Pinball, hoping he'll have enough put away to buy a caravan before mum gets out, and finds himself up against a local Mr Big. Loach and scriptwriter Laverty's look at young Scottish lives stifled by crime, family strife, poverty and lack of opportunity is one of their best efforts, with the message mercifully never drowning out the drama. The naturalistic performances help no end, of course, particularly the very likeable lead turn from Compston, and the dialogue has enough dry Scottish wit to counterbalance the prevailing downbeat mood. Only the predictable (but perhaps necessary) final few minutes manage to disappoint. GA

Sweet Smell of Success 100

(1957, US, 96 min, b/w)
d Alexander Mackendrick. *p* James Hill. *sc* Clifford Odets, Ernest Lehman. *ph* James Wong Howe. *ed* Alan Crosland Jr. *ad* Edward Carrere. *m* Elmer Bernstein. *cast* Burt Lancaster, Tony Curtis, Susan Harrison, Martin Milner, Sam Levene, Barbara Nichols, Emile Meyer.

●A *film noir* from the Ealing funny man? But Mackendrick's involvement with cosy British humour was always less innocent than it looked: remember the anti-social wit of *The Man in the White Suit*, or the cruel cynicism of *The Ladykillers*? *Sweet Smell of Success* was the director's American debut, a rat trap of a film in which a vicious NY gossip hustler (Curtis) grovels for his 'Mr Big' (Lancaster), a monster newspaper columnist who is incestuously obsessed with destroying his kid sister's romance... and a figure as evil and memorable as Orson Welles in *The Third Man* or Mitchum in *The Night of the Hunter*. The dark streets gleam with the sweat of fear; Elmer Bernstein's limpid jazz score (courtesy of Chico Hamilton) whispers corruption in the Big City. The screen was rarely so dark or cruel. CA

Sweet Sweetback's Baadasssss Song

(1971, US, 97 min)
d/p/sc Melvin Van Peebles. *ph* Robert Maxwell, Jose Garcia. *ed/m* Melvin Van Peebles. *ad* Kert Lundell. *cast* Melvin Van Peebles, Rhetta Hughes, John Amos, Simon Chuckster.

●Arguably the most important black American film of its age, yet it's remained virtually unseen in Britain. In part that's because it *is* truly independent, shot on a shoestring and determinedly flouting Hollywood conventions of self-censorship. A 'Yeah Production', 'starring The Black Community', and dedicated to 'all the Brothers and Sisters who had enough of the Man', it's not what you'd call 'bourgeois art'. The story, such as it is, concerns a stud, Sweetback (Van Peebles), who's moved to fight back when two white cops casually beat up a political activist in front of him. He's on the run for the rest of the movie, with occasional stops for sex and/or further police brutality. Totally uncompromising and grindingly repetitive, the film nevertheless accumulates a kind of hallucinatory groove, with unexpected shafts of bizarre humour and vigorous, experimental new wave direction (psychedelic negative images, split screen and so forth). Written, composed, produced, directed and edited by Van Peebles, it remains one of a kind. TCh

Sweet William

(1979, GB, 90 min)
d Claude Whatham. *p* Jeremy Watt. *sc* Beryl Bainbridge. *ph* Les Young. *ed* Peter Coulson. *pd* Eileen Diss. *m* Marcus Dods. *cast* Sam Waterston, Jenny Agutter, Anna Massey, Daphne Oxenford, Geraldine James, Arthur Lowe, Peter Dean.

●Taken from a Beryl Bainbridge novel, this is basically the education of the English Rose by an American *Sweet William*. She wears bras, uses the term 'queers', and screws on the floors of taxis; he uses lines like 'This is an idyll... They're episodic'. Basically he (Waterston) is supposed to be a loveable, irresistible shit; unfortunately he comes across as neither of the first two, only 100% the last, and herein lies the collapse of the movie. For instead of feeling any sense of identification with the lovers in this 'contemporary romance', the sheer implausibility of their relationship leads to an intense sense of frustration and confusion as to which of the two – him, for being such a self-obsessed bastard, or her (Agutter), for being such a self-destructive ninny – one would most like to strangle. FF

Swept Away...by an Unusual Destiny in the Blue Sea of August (Travolti da un Insolito Destino nell'Azzurro Mare d'Agosto)

(1975, It, 120 min)
d Lina Wertmüller. *p* Romano Cardarelli. *sc* Lina Wertmüller. *ph* Ennio Guarnieri. *ed* Franco Fraticelli. *pd* Enrico Job. *m* Piero Piccioni. *cast* Giancarlo Giannini, Mariangela Melato, Riccardo Salvino, Aldo Puglisi.

●The film that started the Wertmüller vogue in the States. Beautiful, blonde Raffaella of the jet-set loses her yacht while with beautiful, dark Gennarino of the working class. Their dinghy founders on a sun-soaked island. A banal political polarisation, fostered by North-South Italian antagonism, keeps them at each other's throats for a while; but it's no surprise when proximity resolves itself in a blissful, sado-masochistic orgy. Raffaella's shrill invective turns to self-abasing adoration; Gennarino gets his freshly caught fish cooked, and flower arrangements in his pudenda. Though seemingly a prettily made, pretty erotic exploitation movie, one suspects that there is value in Wertmüller's observation of the potency of sexual chauvinism. The film fails, however, through the absence of credibility and objectivity, and its refusal to move into the realms of fantasy, allegory, or even irony. JS

Swept from the Sea – The Story of Amy Foster

see Amy Foster

Swimmer, The

(1968, US, 95 min)
d Frank Perry. *p* Frank Perry, Roger Lewis. *sc* Eleanor Perry. *ph* David Quaid. *ed* Sidney Katz, Carl Lerner, Pat Somerset. *ad* Peter Dohanos. *m* Marvin Hamlisch. *cast* Burt Lancaster, Janet Landgard, Janice Rule, Tony Bickley, Marge Champion, Nancy Cushman, Bill Fiore, Kim Hunter.

●A largely loony but oddly compulsive allegory, taken from a John Cheever story, in which Lancaster, clad only in swimming trunks, makes his slow way home by swimming through various people's pools. Partly an obscure satire on the idle rich, partly an eccentric commentary on disillusionment and dreams, it is almost – but, importantly, not quite – nonsense. That said, it is totally engrossing, thanks to its very strangeness, and to the superb performances and the vivid location photography. GA

Swimming Prohibited (Yuei Kinshi)

(1989, Jap, 89 min)
d Hiroyuki Oki. *cast* Hiroyuki Oki.

●The first major film from Oki, the pioneer of Japanese queer cinema, is an extraordinary experiment in first-person film-making, related to the Japanese tradition of the *shi-sosetsu* ('I-novel'). The off-screen protagonist (played, of course, by Oki himself) journeys from the mountain resort Tsumeta, where he has a job in a youth hostel, to the Osaka suburb Suita and on to the sea. He's present visually only when his hands, feet or penis enter the frame, but editorially all the time, since his moods affect what he looks at and his tastes dictate where he goes and what he does. His behaviour is sometimes frisky, as when he approaches schoolboys in the street and asks them whether or not they masturbate yet. But his voiced thoughts are often dark, despite the hints that he's a Buddhist. A movie unique in form, tone and content. TR

Swimming to Cambodia

(1978, US, 85 min)
d Jonathan Demme. *p* RA Shafransky. *sc* Spalding Gray. *ph* John Bailey. *ed* Carol Littleton. *pd* Sandy McLeod. *m* Laurie Anderson. *cast* Spalding Gray.

●In filming Spalding Gray's mesmerising monologue 'about' his experiences acting in Roland Joffé's *The Killing Fields*, Demme simply shoots the raconteur seated behind a table and lets him rant. Equipped only with a glass of water, two maps, and a pointing-stick, Gray takes us on a meandering magical mystery tour that encompasses poetry, humour, political education and the confessional. Linking it all is a lucid personal history of US military aggression and Cambodia Year Zero. And it is here that Gray is most powerful: tossing out outrageous analogies, images, conceits and connections for our quick consideration, he paints a portrait of genocide as perceptive as it is original, as scary as it is scathingly funny. Remarkably, Demme does the man justice, utilising only lighting, Laurie Anderson's sound images, and eminently sensible editing to bring the love, pain and the whole damn thing gloriously to life. GA

Swimming with Sharks

(1994, US, 93 min)
d George Huang. *p* Steve Alexander, Joanne Moore. *sc* George Huang. *ph* Steven Finestone. *ed* Ed Marx. *pd* Veronika Merlin, Cecil Gentry. *m* Tom Heil. *cast* Kevin Spacey, Frank Whaley, Michelle Forbes, Benicio del Toro, TE Russell, Roy Dotrice, Matthew Flynt.

●Nobody hates Hollywood like the people who live and work there. Most movie-movies concentrate on the creative talent: ego-maniacal stars, hard-pressed directors, and abused screenwriters. Unusually, this film sticks to business. Buddy Ackerman (Spacey) is senior VP in charge of production at Keystone Pictures. When he says 'Jump', the ground shakes. His new assistant Guy (Whaley) is the latest in a prestigious line of dogsbodies: as Guy discovers, a year with Buddy and you're ready for anything. Even murder. Given that first-time writer/director Huang spent six years in menial jobs at Lucasfilm and Columbia, this is not so much a calling card as a poison-pen letter to the system. Ackerman is the boss from hell, a megalomaniac who wields his authority like a machete. It's biting stuff, but despite fashionably tricky flashbacks and a sour punchline, it feels a little flimsy, even naive. It's hard to believe Buddy would go for a project called 'Real Life' by one Foster Kane. Still, the picture's raison d'être has to be Spacey's 'loud and nasty' performance: he's the sort of actor who grabs you by the throat and beats you about the head without ever lifting his feet from the desk. And when he's off screen, you miss him. TCh

Swimming with Tears (Afureru Atsui Namida)

(1992, Jap, 104 min)
d Hirotaka Tashiro. *p* Syuijiro Kawakami. *sc* Hirotaka Tashiro. *ph* Koichi Sakuma. *ed* Masahiro Matsumara. *ad* Masayuka Minami, Toshiya Hirai. *m* Hitoshi Hashimoto. *cast* Ruby Moleno, Shiro Sano, Jun Togawa.

●Tashiro's debut feature is a weird mix of breast-beating, social concern, museum-piece melodramatics and coolly detached style. It's one of the many contemporary movies to focus on Asian immigrants to Japan: in this case, a Filipina mail-order bride who gives up on her Japanese peasant husband and flees to Tokyo in search of her Japanese father. There are a couple of interesting plot strands (the best concerns a kindly but odd Japanese couple with a guilty secret in their closet), but the film founders on the sheer sentimentality of its view of Asians in Japan. Pity: if it had an ounce of cynicism to it, comparisons with Fassbinder might have been in order. TR

Swindlers, The

see Bidone, Il

Swing

(1998, US, 97 min)
d Nick Mead. *p* Su Lim, Louise Rosner. *sc* Nick Mead. *ph* Ian Wilson. *ed* Norman Buckley. *pd* Richard Bridgland. *m* Ian Devaney. *cast* Hugo Speer, Lisa Stansfield, Rita Tushingham, Tom Bell, Alexei Sayle, Paul Usher, Danny McCall, Clarence Clemons, Tom Georgeson, Scot Williams, James Hicks, Nerys Hughes.

●Feckless loser Martin Luxford (Speer) emerges from prison in Liverpool with only a saxophone to his name (which he has now changed by deed poll to Martin Jean Baptiste Dechamps). His girl Joan (Stansfield) has wed the cop who nicked him (McCall), and his parents (Bell and Tushingham) barely give him the time of day. There's only one thing for it – with the wise words of his ex-cellmate and sax coach Jack (Bruce Springsteen's saxophonist Clarence Clemons) ringing in his ears, Martin assembles a swing band composed of a Man Utd wannabe, an ex-National Front roadie and a group of mercenary brass-playing Orangemen. An upbeat, nonchalantly mediocre Britcom which cheaply and cheerfully knocks off such successes as *The Commitments* and *The Full Monty*. NB

Swing, The (Die Schaukel)

(1983, WGer, 133 min)
d Percy Adlon. *p* Eleonore Adlon. *sc* Percy Adlon. *ph* Jürgen Martin. *ed* Clara Fabry, Margit Quabus, Ilona Demuth. *ad* Heidi Lüdi. *m* Peer Raben. *cast* Anja Jaenicke, Lena Stolze, Joachim Bernhard, Susanne Herlet, Rolf Illig, Christine Kaufmann.

●This could hardly be more different from Adlon's earlier *Celeste*; where that sombre duologue crept at a stately (not to say sluggish) pace, *The Swing* fairly races along as it traces the changing fortunes of a French/German family in Munich towards the end of the 19th century. It's not merely the colourful sequence of events –

parties, theatre visits, hesitant romantic trysts, country outings – that hold the interest, but also the generally playful tone and the energetic, even eccentric direction, which manages to invest the most mundane of domestic occurrences with a bright, breathless vitality. The film effortlessly avoids the dull conventions of TV costume drama by means of its breezy way with narrative and its eye-catching style. GA

Swingers

(1996, US, 96 min)
d Doug Liman. *p* Victor Simpkins. *sc* Jon Favreau. *ph* Doug Liman. *ed* Steve Mirrione. *pd* Brad Halvorson. *m* Justin Reinhardt. *cast* Jon Favreau, Vince Vaughn, Ron Livingston, Patrick Van Horn, Alex Desert, Heather Graham, Deena Martin.

●This first feature follows Mike (Favreau) as he gets back into the dating game after the abrupt and unwelcome termination of a six-year relationship. An out-of-work New York actor looking for a break in LA, he's dragged out of his mope by pals Rob (Livingston), Charles (Desert), Sue (Van Horn) and, especially, the irrepressible Trent (Vaughn), who insists they chase down some honeys in Vegas. Wiser, and poorer, they return to trawl the Angelino hotspots. Love it and loathe it, this film wants it both ways. We're supposed to be appalled at the callous chauvinism of the predatory male, but also to get off on his jive, sharp suits and cool car. We do, too. It's a bit smug, a bit smarmy, but you should still see this movie, and here are ten reasons why: (i) Vince Vaughn – a louche, lanky ego salesman, he's the definitive '90s lounge lizard. (ii) Jon Favreau – a subtler actor than Vaughn, he spends the entire picture sulking, and still has you pulling for him. Plus, he wrote the script, and (iii) this is the most quotable movie since *Clueless*. (iv) It boasts the best answerphone gag in the history of the movies. Bar none. (v–x) Ninety minutes spent learning how not to pick up girls. This is what the movies were made for, isn't it? TCh

Swingin' Summer, A

(1965, US, 80 min)
d Robert Sparr. *p* Reno Carell. *sc* Leigh Chapman. *ph* Ray Fernstrom. *ed* James T Heckert. *m* Harry Betts. *cast* William Wellman Jr, Quinn O'Hara, James Stacy, Martin West, Raquel Welch, Mary Mitchell, Allan Jones.

●By the '60s, we'd evidently got past the syndrome of 'putting on a show right here'; but promoting one was a different matter. So the rocky road to getting the Righteous Brothers, the Rip Chords, and Gary & the Playboys on stage at Lake Arrowhead is duly traversed in this early dim-witted script from the prosaic pen of Leigh Chapman (*Steel, Boardwalk* etc.). On the way a certain morbid fascination hinges on the wait for Raquel Welch to shed glasses, head-band and psycho-jargon in order to swing, but you've also got to put up with a chicken-run on water-skis, and the obligatory appearance of the crooked killjoys. Given the director's obsession with bikini bottoms, this really is the arse-end of the beach movie cycle. PT

Swing Kids

(1993, US, 114 min)
d Thomas Carter. *p* Mark Gordon, John Bard Manulis. *sc* Jonathan Feldman. *ph* Jerzy Zielinski. *ed* Michael R Miller. *pd* Allan Cameron. *m* James Horner. *cast* Robert Sean Leonard, Christian Bale, Frank Whaley, Barbara Hershey, Kenneth Branagh, Martin Clunes, Tushka Bergen, Noah Wyle.

●Germany in the '30s: Peter (Leonard) and Thomas (Bale) are devoted to Swing, record collecting and wild dancing. They aren't oblivious to the activities of the Hitler Jugend, though it takes time for the *pfennig* to drop. The dice are fatally loaded when it comes to fellow swingster Erwin. Bespectacled, wise, humane and crippled, he takes an inevitable early bath, leaving the two friends to choose between conformity or an increasingly risky rebellion. The dance-hall scenes have a wonderful febrility, as have the counterpointed HJ rituals. This appears to be a youth movie, but even the dumbest teen will gather there was more to Nazism than sending kids with long hair into the army. The use of token Jews turns the stomach, and it's hard not to conclude that the Swing Kids' idealisation of America is the real message. SFe

Swing Shift

(1984, US, 100 min)
d Jonathan Demme. *p* Jerry Bick. *sc* Rob Morton, Ron Nyswaner, Bo Goldman, Nancy Dowd. *ph* Tak Fujimoto. *ed* Craig McKay. *pd* Peter Jamison. *m* Patrick Williams. *cast* Goldie Hawn, Kurt Russell, Christine Lahti, Ed Harris, Fred Ward, Sudie Bond, Holly Hunter, Roger Corman.

●A gentle romantic comedy set during World War II, which sees housewife Hawn finding her feet when hubby Ed Harris goes off to fight. First, against his wishes, she takes a job in an aircraft factory, then – after a lengthy courtship – she takes a lover in the form of hunky, helpful, hot trumpeter Kurt Russell. Hawn, atypically cast and supported by all-round excellent performances, proves that she can act. But still this bitter-sweet concoction is very much Demme's: not only in the warming celebration of friendship and community values (the unsentimental generosity extended towards the characters positively glows), but also in the assured handling of period, place, music and mood. GA

Swing Time

(1936, US, 103 min, b/w)
d George Stevens. *p* Pandro S Berman. *sc* Howard Lindsay, Allan Scott. *ph* David Abel. *ed* Henry Berman. *ad* Van Nest Polglase, Carroll Clark. *m* Nathaniel Shilkret. *songs* Jerome Kern, Dorothy Fields. *cast* Fred Astaire, Ginger Rogers, Victor Moore, Helen Broderick, Eric Blore, George Metaxa, Betty Furness.

●The slow burn of misunderstanding brings Fred and Ginger together at last in the second of Stevens' three musicals for RKO, long before he got into the serious business of *Shane* and *Giant* and *The Diary of Anne Frank*. 'No one could teach you to dance in a million years' is typical of the irony's light touch. However, if plot, script and supporters are below par, the score by Jerome Kern and Dorothy Fields is peerless – 'A Fine Romance', 'The Way You Look Tonight', 'Pick Yourself Up', and Fred's turn with Berkeley-esque trimmings, 'Bojangles of Harlem'. And nothing Fred and Ginger did together surpasses their lengthy, climactic duet, taking off from 'Never Gonna Dance', which reminds you that dance is the most perfect sexual metaphor of them all. SG

Swiss Conspiracy, The

(1975, US/WGer, 89 min)
d Jack Arnold. *p* Red Silverstein, Helmut Jedele. *sc* Norman Kleinman, Philip Saltzman, Michael Stanley. *ph* WP Hassenstein. *ed* Murray Jordan. *pd* Rolf Zehetbauer. *m* Klaus Doldinger. *cast* David Janssen, Senta Berger, John Ireland, John Saxon, Ray Milland, Anton Diffring, Elke Sommer, Arthur Brauss.

●A monotonous, glossily vacuous co-production thriller that sends Janssen skidding through the scenic snow in the midst of an incomprehensible blackmail-and-murder plot involving five shadowy Zurich account-holders. Such farragos, along with stabs at softcore comedy and blaxploitation, were the dispiriting lot of veteran sci-fi/mutant movie auteur Arnold after the studio system fell apart. From the German side of the package, incidentally, comes Arthur Brauss, Wenders' hangdog 'Goalkeeper', as a heavy. PT

Swissmakers, The (Die Schweizermacher)

(1978, Switz, 108 min)
d Rolf Lyssy. *p* Marcel Hoehn. *sc* Rolf Lyssy, Christa Maerker. *ph* Fritz E Maeder. *ed* Georg Janett. *ad* Edith Peier, Bernhard Sauter. *m* Jonas C Haefeli. *cast* Walo Lüönd, Emil Steinberger, Beatrice Kessler, Wolfgang Stendar, Hilde Ziegler.

●Lyssy's essentially fond, humane parody of cuckoo-clock Switzerland, in which an amiable young bureaucrat has to snoop on immigrants to see if they are 'suitable' for Swiss citizenship. British political parallels immediately spring to mind, but the humour here is more slapstick than documentary, so Love and Liberalism carry the day with little difficulty. Not exactly sophisticated (and the camerawork leaves something to be desired), but infinitely preferable to the forced, jangling misanthropy of the Italian *Bread and Chocolate* in dealing with the same subject. CA

Switch

(1991, US, 114 min)
d Blake Edwards. *p* Tony Adams. *sc* Blake Edwards. *ph* Dick Bush. *ed* Robert Pergament. *pd* Rodger Maus. *m* Henry Mancini. *cast* Ellen Barkin, Jimmy Smits, JoBeth Williams, Lorraine Bracco, Tony Roberts, Perry King, Bruce Martyn Payne, Lysette Anthony, Victoria Mahoney.

●Blake Edwards playing with questions of sexual identity again. King and Barkin share the role of a man who has his sex switched in a pact between God and the Devil. Steve Brooks (King), a sexist pig, is murdered by three of the women he has mistreated. Instead of going straight to hell, Brooks' soul ends up in purgatory; God decides that Brooks must return to earth and find one woman who actually likes him before he can pass through the pearly gates. To spice things up, the Devil insists that he must perform this feat while inhabiting a woman's body. Much simple comedy ensues as Brooks, waking up as Barkin, has to cope with breasts, heels and long hair, then returns to his/her career in advertising to face discrimination. There are some funny moments, and though she hams it up at times, Barkin is very good in her first comic role. But Edwards milks the comedy, keeps the sexual comment to a minimum, and brings the film to a silly, cop-out resolution. CO'S

Switchblade Sisters (aka Playgirl Gang/The Jezebels)

(1975, US, 86 min)
d Jack Hill. *p* John Prizer. *sc* FX Maier. *ph* Stephen Katz. *ed* Mort Tubor. *pd* Robinson Royce, BB Neel. *m* Medusa. *cast* Robbie Lee, Joanne Nail, Monica Gayle, Asher Brauner, Chase Newhart, Marlene Clark, Kate Murtaugh.

●This girl gang exploitation flick plays like an episode of TV's *Happy Days* hijacked by roller-skating revolutionaries. Maggie (Nail) is inducted into the Jezebels after proving herself in a face-off with Patch (Gayle). She befriends the girls' leader, Lace (Lee), but has an enemy for life in Patch, a one-eyed Iago who sees that Lace's boyfriend has the hots for her rival. It ends in a turf war in which the Jezebels side with black Maoist femme guerillas. Maggie's a reasonable feminist role model, but the movie couples radical rhetoric with exploitation requirements quite shamelessly. The appeal here is to kitsch (anyone who gets off on bad acting, risible contrivance, cheapjack production work) and to academics (anyone sniffing a theory of gender in genre). Either way, there's only limited value in such cinephiliac slumming. TCh

Switchboard Operator, The (Ljubavni Slucaj)

(1967, Yugo, 69 min, b/w)
d/sc Dusan Makavejev. *ph* Aleksandar Petkovic. *ed* Katarina Stojanovic. *ad* Vladislav Lazic. *m* Dusan Aleksic. *cast* Eva Ras, Slobodan Aligrudic, Ruzica Sokic, Dr Aleksander Kostic, Dr Zivojin Aleksic.

●Given that four of Makavejev's first five features are essentially the same film, it seems increasingly unlikely that he'll ever improve on this, his second movie, the most interesting and concentrated treatment of his recurrent themes. A tragi-comic love affair between a switchboard operator and a corporation rat-catcher starts out idyllic, but turns sour under external pressures; Makavejev breaks up the time sequence of his story with constant flashes forward, and brings in a lot of apparently extraneous material, from lectures on sex in art to a poem about rats. The disjunctions and contradictions yield a lot of ideas about personal freedom and oppression (especially within a 'socialist' state), and the profusion of images is well enough organised to make the movie continuously provocative and suggestive. The use of historical newsreels is finally as glib as in *W.R.*, but the emphasis on the banalities of day-to-day living is trenchant, and more than compensates. TR

Switching Channels

(1987, US, 105 min)
d Ted Kotcheff. *p* Martin Ransohoff. *sc* Jonathan Reynolds. *ph* François Protat. *ed* Thom Noble. *pd* Anne Pritchard. *m* Michel Legrand. *cast* Kathleen Turner, Burt Reynolds, Christopher Reeve, Ned Beatty, Henry Gibson, George Newbern, Al Waxman.

●This fourth cinema version of Hecht and MacArthur's *The Front Page* warrants only a brief mention in the obituary column. Kotcheff's workmanlike update shifts the action to the newsroom of a satellite TV station, where Reynolds' workaholic newshound is trying to lure ex-wife and fellow hotshot journo Turner away from tanned tycoon Reeve with talk of a once-in-a-lifetime scoop. The human interest angle is Gibson, a doomed convict who killed the man who supplied his son with the drugs on which he OD'd. But the supplier happened to be an undercover policeman, hence the tabloid moniker 'Cop Killer Dad' and the imminent appointment with the electric chair. Ned Beatty gets the best comic lines as the slimy DA who's also trying to manipulate the situation to his best advantage. Neither Jonathan Reynolds' enervated script nor the lacklustre performances do anything to dispel the feeling of *déjà vu*. NF

Swoon

(1991, US, 94 min, b/w)
d Tom Kalin. *p* Tom Kalin, Christine Vachon. *sc* Tom Kalin, Hilton Als. *ph* Ellen Kuras. *ed* Tom Kalin. *pd* Therese Deprez. *m* James Bennett. *cast* Daniel Schlachet, Craig Chester, Ron Vawter, Michael Kirby, Michael Stumm, Valda Z Drabla, Robert Read.

●The story of Leopold and Loeb – two young intellectual aesthetes, from wealthy Jewish families, who murdered a 14-year-old boy for kicks in Chicago in 1924 – has been filmed twice before. *Rope* located the roots of fascism in Nietzschean discourse. *Compulsion* was a more muddled 'true crime' saga. Kalin's film is the least naturalistic and most factual. It is also the first to expand on Clarence Darrow's argument for the defence, that the pair's homosexuality was a sign of pathological deviance; *ergo* they were not accountable for their actions. The film's second half sticks to court transcripts, to diagnose a repressive, racist, homophobic pathology on a wider social scale, endemic to patriarchy itself. Sketched in deft, sharp strokes, this is no more than a postscript to the earlier exploration of the lovers' sadomasochistic relationship: how Loeb bartered crime for sex, and how their transgressive games escalated to the point of no return. With its sinuous monochrome finish, *Swoon* is decadent and economical, subjective and detached, fascinating and appalling – conjunctions Sacher Masoch himself might have recognised. TCh

Sword and the Flute, The

(1959, US, 24 min)
d/p/sc James Ivory. *ph* Mindaugis Bagdon. *m* Ali Akbar Khan, Ravi Shankar, T Visvanathan, Chatur Lal, DR Parvatikar.

●A documentary composed entirely of shots of Indian miniature paintings illustrating the history of the Mogul and Rajput schools. James Ivory, who became his own photographer when his original cameraman was conscripted, was later to return directly to the subject in *Hullabaloo Over Georgie and Bonnie's Pictures*, and indirectly in a number of his theatrical feature films, in which the appreciation of fine art is regarded, in a sense, as an index of civilisation (and also of greed and vanity). JPy

Sword and the Sorcerer, The

(1982, US, 99 min)
d Albert Pyun. *p* Brandon Chase, Marianne Chase. *sc* Thomas F Karnowski, John Stuckmeyer, Albert Pyun. *ph* Joe Mangine. *ed* Marshall Harvey. *ad* George Costello. *m* David Whitaker. *cast* Lee Horsley, Kathleen Beller, Simon MacCorkindale, George Maharis, Richard Lynch, Richard Moll, Barry Chase, Nina Van Pallandt, Jeff Corey.

●Having raised (and disposed of) an ancient sorcerer to capture a kingdom, medieval tyrant Cromwell (Lynch) naturally finds himself plagued by revolts. Director Pyun apparently trained under Kurosawa, and one might have expected some of the Master's empathy with myth and legend to have rubbed off; but there's only a clumsy amalgam of sci-fi special effects and old-style blood and thunder, with a mind-numbing thickie of a hero and a scrawny underage heroine. There are compensations, though: the real baddie, born-again sorcerer Xusia (Moll), makes a splendidly bad-tempered villain, and there are nice cameos from a bald-headed torturer, a Rastafarian pirate, and a sex-mad python; and editor Marshall Harvey stitches the messy pieces together with considerable panache. RMy

Swordfish

(2001, US/Aust, 99 min)
d Dominic Sena. *p* Joel Silver, Jonathan D Krane. *sc* Skip Woods. *ph* Paul Cameron. *ed* Stephen Rivkin. *pd* Jeff Mann. *m* Christopher Young, Paul Oakenfold. *cast* John Travolta, Hugh Jackman, Halle Berry, Don Cheadle, Vinnie Jones, Sam Shepard, Drea De Matteo, Rudolf Martin, Zach Grenier, Camryn Grimes.

●Carnage is fixed in mid-air as the camera exacts an oh so elegant 180 degree arc around exploded bodies in suspended animation, and we're still only three minutes into the movie! More of a stylist than a director, Dominic Sena (*Kalifornia*, *Gone in 60 Seconds*) photographs everything like a fashion shoot. Sporting a natty goatee and slicked-back hair, Travolta looks every inch the criminal mastermind. Jackman is an improbably muscular computer nerd, roped in reluctantly to hack for billions – and as for Berry, there ought to be a law (in some cultures there surely is). You don't care about these characters, but their clothes are out of sight. Especially Halle's. Forget *Intimacy*, if it's porn you're after, how about the scene where Travolta holds a gun to Jackman's head, giving him 60 seconds to break a top secret government code, while a hooker sucks him off at the same time? Cyber porn. Money porn. Gore porn. Even the film's reactionary politics are obscene (not just a criminal, Travolta is also a true patriot, a terrorist vigilante). Slick, amoral and not half as clever as it thinks it is, it's the perfect lads' movie. I confess: I enjoyed it – so shoot me. TCh

Sword in the Stone, The

(1963, US, 80 min)
d Wolfgang Reitherman. *p* Walt Disney. *sc* Bill Peet. *ed* Donald Halliday. *ad* Ken Anderson. *m* George Bruns. *cast* voices: Ricky Sorenson, Sebastian Cabot, Karl Swenson, Junius Matthews.

●A beautifully animated Disney feature, adapted from TH White's tale of the young (soon to be King) Arthur and his mad adventures with Merlin the Magician. Together with snooty sidekick Archimedes the owl, Merlin educates the boy in some of the basic facts of life. With his magic wand, he can change both himself and his pupil into anything he wishes, which results in one of the best episodes: a duel between Merlin and the evil witch Madam Mim, where they both try to gain the upper hand by transforming themselves into some of the nastiest creatures possible. It was produced by Walt himself, with tuneful music supplied by the Sherman brothers. DA

Sword of Doom, The (Daibosatu Toge)

(1966, Jap, 119 min)
d Kihachi Okamoto. *p* Sanezumi Fujimoto, Masayuki Sato. *sc* Shinobu Hashimoto. *ph* Hiroshi Murai. *ad* Shu Matsuyama. *m* Masara Sato. *cast* Tatsuya Nakadai, Toshiro Mifune, Yoko Naito, Michiyo Aratama, Kei Sato, Yuzo Kayama.

●Nakadai is memorably psychotic as Tsukue, a samurai gone to the bad, a hired assassin whose cruelty is only exceeded by his swordsmanship. Mifune has little more than a supporting role as a fencing master – Shimada – who proves Tsukue's spiritual nemesis. ('The sword is the soul,' Shimada says. 'Study the sword to study the soul.') The script goes to some trouble to contextualise the action (the early 1860s, when brigands were threatening anarchy) and to introduce a wide array of characters, but the numerous strands never cohere and some are left hanging, as if the production ran short of money and cut back on plot development. The film stands up due to the dynamic 'Scope camerawork and half-a-dozen set pieces, including duels choreographed with chess-like solemnity and an astonishing climax in which the whole world seems to turn against the haunted Tsukue. Based on the novel by Kaizan Nakazato. TCh

Sword of the Valiant – The Legend of Gawain and the Green Knight, The

(1983, GB, 102 min)
d Stephen Weeks. *p* Menahem Golan, Yoram Globus. *sc* Stephen Weeks, Howard C Pen, Philip M Breen. *ph* Freddie Young, Peter Hurst. *ed* Richard Marden, Barry Peters. *pd* Maurice Fowler, Derek Nice. *m* Ron Geesin. *cast* Miles O'Keefe, Trevor Howard, Sean Connery, Peter Cushing, Ronald Lacey, Cyrielle Claire, Emma Sutton, Douglas Wilmer, Lila Kedrova, Leigh Lawson, John Rhys-Davies.

●Writer/director Weeks made the low-budget medieval saga *Gawain and the Green Knight* in 1973 and not many people noticed, so somehow he persuaded Cannon to let him do it again, with perhaps predictably underwhelming results. Connery is, naturally, imposing as the legendary Green Knight, but O'Keefe's Gawain is hardly a worthy opponent. His heavy-rocker's blonde wig elicits more laughter than the script's painful attempts at wit, as he crosses the land for solutions to the Green Knight's riddling, facing the axe if he comes up blank. Dreary jousting, production values that make *Monty Python and the Holy Grail* look lavish, and an excruciating synthesiser score make this a real trial. No wonder grim-faced Trevor Howard's the most miserable King Arthur you'll ever see. TJ

Swordsman (Xiao'ao Jianghu)

(1990, HK, 120 min)
d King Hu, Tsui Hark, Ching Siu-Tung. *p* Tsui Hark. *sc* Kwan Man-leung, Wong Ying, Lam Kei-tou, Lau Tai-muk, Leung Fi-ming, Tai Fu-ho. *ph* Peter Pao, Lam Kwok-wa. *ed* David Wu, Mak Chi-seen. *pd* Leung Wa-sang. *m* James Wong, Romeo Diaz. *cast* Samuel Hui, Jacky Cheung, Cecilia Yip, Fennie Yuen, Cheung Mun.

●Rather tendentiously credited to the veteran King Hu (it was supposed to be a 'comeback' film for the director of *A Touch of Zen*, but he left the production very early on and none of his footage remains), this actually plays like a vulgar and resolutely modern-spirited pastiche of the kind of movie he used to make. As such, it's a lot of fun: a roller-coaster ride through memories of the great Chinese swordplay movies of the '60s. It plays out the joke about an explosion in a dye-factory, and then romps through a series of gravity-defying fight scenes in which the antagonists not only clash in mid-air and slice each other in half, but also unleash darts, poisons and swarms of deadly insects at each other. TR

Swordsman II (Xiao'ao Jianghu zhi Dongfang Bu Bai)

(1991, HK, 111 min)
d Ching Siu-Tung. *p* Tsui Hark. *sc* Tsui Hark, Peter Chan, Tang Pik Yin. *ph* Lau Moon Tong. *ed* Mak Chi Sin. *m* Richard Yuen. *cast* Jet Li, Lin Ching Hsia, Rosamund Kwan, Fannie Yuen, Michelle Li.

●A further collaboration between the director of *A Chinese Ghost Story* and producer Tsui Hark, *Swordsman II* resembles a super-hero comic book brought to life. Set in a mythical past at a time of internecine power struggles within competing clans and sects, the film finds Ling and his siblings taking a stand against the ruthless 'Master Asia', who has sacrificed his manhood to attain magical powers, and who anonymously flirts with Ling as a woman. A playful attitude to sexuality permeates the movie; more to the point, however, are countless spectacularly realised supernatural confrontations which would have Albert Einstein's head spinning. Camp it may be, and messy, but mundane it ain't. TCh

Swordsman in Double-Flag Town, The (Shuang Qi Zhen Dao Ke)

(1991, China, 95 min)
d He Ping. *p* Zhao Wanmin. *sc* Yang Zhengguang, He Ping. *ph* Ma De Lin. *ed* Yuan Hong. *ad* Qian Yunxuan. *m* Tao Long. *cast* Giao Wei, Zhao Ma Lin, Chang Jiang, Sun Hai Ying.

●Parched with thirst and jumpy from encounters on the trail, young Hai Ge rides into town (actually a walled village in the desert) to find and marry the girl he was engaged to in the cradle. He finds the place cowering with fear of two bandit brothers and their gang, and more by accident than design, kills one of the brothers. Facing up to swordplay skills he never knew he had, he waits nervously for the inevitable showdown with the dead man's vengeful brother… Whether you take He Ping's film as a sardonic commentary on American Westerns or as a new approach (in the vein of *Red Sorghum)* to Chinese folk-myth, it's a show-stopper. Leone himself would have cheered. TR

Sybil

(1977, US, 132 min)
d Daniel Petrie. *p* Jacqueline Babbin. *sc* Stewart Stern. *ph* Mario Tosi. *ed* Michael S McLean, Rita Roland, Robert Pickarts. *pd* Tom H John. *m* Leonard Rosenman. *cast* Joanne Woodward, Sally Field, Brad Davis, Martine Bartlett, Jane Hoffman, Charles Lane, William Prince.

● This began life as a two-part TV movie (here edited down from 198 minutes) based on the true story of the eleven-year treatment by psychiatrist Cornelia Wilbur of Sybil Dorsett and her sixteen warring personalities. As Dr Wilbur, Joanne Woodward (who had herself essayed a schizophrenic role in *The Three Faces of Eve* back in 1957) is fascinating, because she employs a theatrical stillness around which all Sally Field's agonised personalities flutter like trapped birds. Field herself resists the temptation to let go and ham. The result is essentially a classic two-hander: moving despite the surrounding schlock. DSi

Sylvester Countdown (aka In With the New/ Silvester Countdown)

(1997, Ger, 83 min)
d Oskar Roehler. *p* Rolf Peter Kahl, Oskar Roehler. *sc* Oskar Roehler. *ph* Lorenz Haarmann. *ed* Christine Boock. *ad* Denise Dashel, Katia Fouquet. *m* Dieter Webel, George Brasch. *cast* Rolf Peter Kahl, Marie Zielcke, Robert Victor Minich, Laura Tonke, Doreen Jacobi.

● The film begins with the hero doing a frantic lone dance wearing nothing but a Native American headdress, and ends with him masturbating in front of his girlfriend's photo. This concise image of his insecure and obsessively sexual character also depicts the isolating quality of the couple's life together, consisting solely of sex and quarrels. On a New Year's Eve trip to Warsaw, they close in ever more destructively on each other. Roehler skilfully plays up the bleak pathos of these egotists' self-made hell by showing them getting lost in a city which is itself hostile: a grey, icy place where taxi drivers cheat them or get lost, and a strip joint offers a frightening parody of their relationship. Restless camerawork heightens the sense that even when partying or travelling, they're going nowhere. SB

Sylvia

(1984, NZ, 98 min)
d Michael Firth. *p* Don Reynolds, Michael Firth. *sc* Michael Quill, Ferdinand Fairfax, Michael Firth. *ph* Ian Paul. *ed* Michael Horton. *pd* Gary Hansen. *m* Leonard Rosenman. *cast* Eleanor David, Nigel Terry, Tom Wilkinson, Mary Regan, Martyn Sanderson, Terence Cooper.

● Sylvia Ashton-Warner develops her own teaching methods based on the emotional, personal life of the children in her classroom. She achieves wondrous results but is more than just a teacher, and in a remarkably sensitive portrayal, Eleanor David depicts her artistry, nervousness, gift for friendship, cultural isolation, and courage. Unfortunately, Firth concentrates on her passing romance with a sympathetic schools' inspector (Terry). With tantalising glimpses of the uneasy coexistence of white man and Maori, but with little individualisation of the children or understanding of their background, this is a sympathetic biopic when it could have been something altogether more inspirational and fascinating. JE

Sylvia Scarlett

(1936, US, 90 min, b/w)
d George Cukor. *p* Pandro S Berman. *sc* Gladys Unger, John Collier, Mortimer Offner. *ph* Joseph August. *ed* Jane Loring. *ad* Van Nest Polglase, Sturges Carne. *m* Roy Webb. *cast* Katharine Hepburn, Cary Grant, Edmund Gwenn, Brian Aherne, Dennie Moore, Natalie Paley.

● A small and intriguingly bizarre gem, its picaresque story once again revealing Cukor's abiding interest in the joys and pains, deceptions and truths associated with the art of acting. The performer here is young Sylvia (Hepburn), forced to dress as a boy when her embezzler father (Gwenn) returns to England from France in dire straits. The pair fall in with troublesome landladies, a touring theatrical company, a roguish con-man (Grant), and a romantic painter (Aherne); and the film comes to centre on the way Hepburn's life of pretence affects not only her own emotional development but those around her. Just as the sexual nuances of her various encounters remain ambiguous, so the film seems unable to decide whether to opt for comedy, romantic adventure, or tragedy; Gwenn, for example, gradually loses his sanity, a darkening backdrop to the scenes of light, breezy banter between the leads. Odd, then, but entirely civilised and engaging, and Hepburn was rarely more radiant or moving. GA

Sympathy for the Devil

see One Plus One

Symphonie Pastorale, La

(1946, Fr, 105 min, b/w)
d Jean Delannoy. *sc* Jean Aurenche, Pierre Best, Jean Delannoy. *ph* Armand Thirand. *ed* Suzanne Fauvel. *ad* René Renoux. *m* Georges Auric. *ed* Suzanne Fauvel. *cast* Michèle Morgan, Pierre Blanchar, Line Noro, Louvigny, Jean Desailly, Andrée Clément.

● A French Protestant pastor (Blanchar) falls in love with his blind ward (Morgan, the '40s Faye Dunaway). Delannoy's version of Gide's then still scandalous novel is correct, melancholy, icy. That's his auteurial tone. André Bazin admired the movie, and speculated that its emphasis on snow was a true filmic equivalent of Gide's use of tenses. It oddly mixes hot drama, cold style, and an accusatory stance; and the weathering of age may have sharpened its Sirkian effect. RD

Symphony of Love

see Extase

Symptoms (aka The Blood Virgin)

(1974, GB/Bel, 91 min)
d Joseph Larraz. *p* Jean Dupuis. *sc* Joseph Larraz, Stanley Miller. *ph* Trevor Wren. *ed* Brian Smedley-Aston. *ad* Ken Bridgeman. *m* John Scott. *cast* Angela Pleasence, Peter Vaughan, Lorna Heilbron, Nancy Nevinson, Ronald O'Neil, Marie-Paul Mailleux.

● Made by a Spanish director working for an English company, with Angela Pleasence running mad in an old dark house and giving murderous vent to her sexist grievances, this is the finest British horror movie from a foreigner since Polanski's *Repulsion*. The comparison is inevitable, because thematically the films have a good deal in common, charting the gradual mental dissolution of their spectral heroines. *Symptoms* imitates, but also improves on its original in a multiplicity of ways. The muted love affair between Pleasence and Lorna Heilbron is etched with enormous suggestiveness, and Larraz's eye for visual detail is mesmerising.

t

This Is Spinal Tap

Täällä Pohjantähden alla (Here Beneath the North Star/Akseli and Elina)

(1968/70, Fin, 279 min)
d Edvin Laine. *p* Mauno Mäkelä. *sc* Väino Linna, Juha Nevalainen, Edvin Laine, Matti Kassila. *ph* Olavi Tuomi. *ed* Juho Gartz. *pd* Mauri Jaakkola. *m* Heikki Aaltoila. *cast* Afarno Sulkanen, Risto Taulo, Titta Karakorpi, Ulla Eklund, Anja Pohjola.
●If the action seems a trifle hectic early on, it's probably because an hour was trimmed for British release. But only a masochist would demand the full version of this lumbering Finnish family chronicle derived from a famous trilogy by Väinö Linna, detailing the break-up of feudal society early in the century and the farmers' fight for socialism. This dinosaur of a film played in Finland as a television serial, as well as being carved up into two features for cinema release; and the television influence shows in the relentless artificial lighting, the cramped compositions which hinder Laine's attempt to achieve an epic sweep. Occasional scenes are pretty in a picture postcard way (workers marching through snow shouting the national anthem), but it's all laboriously unreal and unimaginative. GB

Table for Five

(1983, US, 124 min)
d Robert Lieberman. *p* Robert Schaffel. *sc* David Seltzer. *ph* Vilmos Zsigmond. *ed* Michael Kahn. *pd* Robert Boyle. *m* John Morris. *cast* Jon Voight, Richard Crenna, Marie-Christine Barrault, Millie Perkins, Roxana Zal, Robby Kiger, Son Hoang Bui, Kevin Costner.
●Prodigal parent Voight comes to reclaim his kids from their mother and her new husband, and scoops them off on a plush Mediterranean cruise. Yes, it's another of New Hollywood's hymns to the Joys of Fatherhood, though this time potential custody tussles are forestalled by conveniently dispatching the wife in a car crash. Voight's shipboard romance is kept safely marginal too, and the final happy family – three kids, two fathers – looks decidedly bizarre. Lieberman pads out thin material with a welter of reaction shots and sequences of Voight mooning around looking very, very sad. What's worse, he seems to have scant confidence in the potency of his characters' emotions, attempting to make them into something monumental by having Voight's life crumble amid the more spectacular ruins of Western civilisation. This is essentially soap opera with fancy production values and grandiose pretensions: the result is the purest kitsch. SJo

Taboo (Gohatto)

(1999, Jap, 101 min)
d Nagisa Oshima. *p* Eiko Oshima, Shigehiro Nakagawa, Kazuo Shimizu. *sc* Nagisa Oshima. *ph* Toyomichi Kurita. *ed* Tomoyo Oshima. *pd* Yoshinobu Nishioka. *m* Ryuichi Sakamoto. *cast* 'Beat' Takeshi Kitano, Ryuhei Matsuda, Shinji Takeda, Tadanobu Asano, Yoichi Sai, Tomoro Taguchi. *narrator* Kei Sato.
●Oshima's first feature in 14 years (and the first since the 1995 stroke which left him part-paralysed) adapts two short stories by Ryotaro Shiba about the Shinsen-gumi, a Shogunate militia of the 1860s notorious for both ruthless violence and homosexuality. Inducted into the force for his cool head and expert swordsmanship, the exquisite teenager Kano (Matsuda, son of the late Yusaku Matsuda) sets many hearts aflutter; the plot details the lust and sexual jealousies surrounding him in the barracks and the callous machinations of his superiors (directors Kitano and Sai) to put an end to the 'trouble'. Oshima conjures an odd mix of realistic elements (the settings, the kendo practice) and stylisation (Emi Wada's costumes, Sakamoto's excellent score) to produce one of his most bitter accounts of passion and individuality snuffed out. TR

Tabu

(1931, US, 90 min, b/w)
d/p/sc FW Murnau. *ph* Floyd Crosby, Robert Flaherty. *m* Hugo Riesenfeld. *cast* Anna Chevalier, Matahi, Hitu, Kong Ah.
●Murnau's last film (after three years of mixed fortunes in Hollywood) was begun as a collaboration with the documentarist Robert Flaherty, but resolved itself into Murnau's purest and least inhibited celebration of physical sensuality and love. Its plot is a simple Pacific islands folk tale: a young man and woman fall in love, thereby violating a local taboo, and their romance ends in inevitable tragedy. The film is a rhapsody of textures and an exceptionally sensuous play of light, rhythm and composition. Its narrative pretext is (necessarily) heterosexual, but Murnau's homosexual sensibility was never clearer: the central image (and texture) of the film is the flesh of its young hero, and it is his virility that sets the tragedy in motion. Fetishistic to a degree, the film is none the less never patronising to its subject or its actors. It plays as a pre-colonial anachronism, rather like one of Melville's South Seas novels. It's extremely beautiful. TR

Tacones lejanos

see High Heels

Tadpole and the Whale (La Grenouille et la baleine)

(1988, Can, 92 min)
d Jean-Claude Lord. *p* Rock Demers. *sc* Jacques Bobet, André Melançon. *ph* Tom Burstyn. *ed* Hélène Girard. *ad* Dominique Ricard. *m* Guy Trepanier, Norman Dubé. *cast* Fanny Lauzier, Denis Forest, Marina Orsini, Félix-Antoine Leroux, Jean Lajeunesse.
●Winsome, winning adventure tale from producer Rock Demers, about a young girl, gifted with exceptional hearing, who forms a close relationship with a dolphin named Elvar. The film has a strong educational element: lots of footage of hump-backed whales spouting off the East Canadian coast (and elsewhere), and a marine biologist at hand to explain the science. The adventure seems to consist of characters rushing about everywhere and much falling out of speedboats, followed by lots of affirmative hugging and smiles. An eco-sound kids' movie, with a liberal pinch of sea-salt. WH

Taebaek Mountains, The (Taebaek Sanmaek)

(1994, SKor, 168 min)
d Im Kwon-Taek. *cast* Ahn Song-Gi, Kim Gap-Soo, Kim Myung-Kon, Oh Jung-Hae, Shin Hyun-Joon.
●Im's masterly epic opens up the shadowiest period in Korea's modern history: the months in 1948/9 when a region in the deep south went communist and the state fought dirty to bring it back under control in what was effectively a dress rehearsal for the coming Korean War. The core issues are ideological, of course, but Im carefully relates them to family rivalries and other down-to-earth factors: the fascistic leader of the anti-communist guerillas, for instance, is the brother of the idealist who tries to promote communist values. The whole thing is seen through the neutral eyes of a local schoolteacher (Ahn, working with Im for the first time in ten years), who finally seeks solace in the rituals of a shaman. Kim Soo-Chul contributes a truly memorable score. TR

Taffin

(1987, GB/US, 96 min)
d Francis Megahy. *p* Peter Shaw. *sc* David Ambrose. *ph* Paul Beeson. *ed* Rodney Holland. *pd* William Alexander. *m* Stanley Myers, Hans Zimmer. *cast* Pierce Brosnan, Ray McAnally, Alison Doody, Jeremy Child, Dearbhla Molloy, Jim Bartley, Alan Stanford.
●A confused and unexciting thriller set in a small Irish coastal town, where the hero Taffin (Brosnan) earns his keep as a debt collector who's handier with his fists than with the legal paperwork. When it is revealed that a newly built access road will serve a proposed chemical plant, Taffin at first refuses to help the action committee set up by his former teacher (McAnally). But when the crooked businessmen behind the scheme, who have the local councillors in their pockets, start roughing up OAPs, he agrees to act as the protesters' paid heavy. The character of Taffin is too complex for Brosnan's limited acting talents, though he's good in the action scenes and displays his coarse good looks to some advantage. Also unconvincing are Taffin's passionate affair with an independent and worldly-wise barmaid (Doody), and his father-son conflict with former mentor McAnally. Struggling hard against the script's stock elements, Megahy delivers some effective bursts of action without ever generating any real tension or involvement. NF

Tagebuch einer Verlorenen, Das

see Diary of a Lost Girl

TAG, The Assassination Game

(1982, US, 92 min)
d Nick Castle. *p* Peter Rosten, Dan Rosenthal. *sc* Nick Castle. *ph* Willy Kurant. *ed* Tom Walls. *ad* Randy Moore, Craig Stearns. *cast* Robert Carradine, Linda Hamilton, Kristine DeBell, Perry Lang, Frazer Smith, John Mengatti, Bruce Abbott.
●This first film by ex-John Carpenter collaborator Castle may wear its references too visibly on its sleeve, but at least they're to a disparate group, ranging from Ida Lupino to *The Man from UNCLE*. Its unusual amalgam of comedy (a battery of amusing supporting characters and absurd situations) and thrills (De Niro lookalike Abbott as a killer who aspires to stylish assassination) blends with a sexy '40s-style romance to produce a pleasingly human thriller. Particularly strong performances make it a perfect entertainment for late-night viewing. SM

Tailor of Panama, The

(2001, US/Ire,110 min)
d/p John Boorman. *sc* Andrew Davies, John le Carré. *ph* Philippe Rousselot. *ed* Ron Davis. *pd* Derek Wallace. *m* Shaun Davey. *cast* Pierce Brosnan, Geoffrey Rush, Jamie Lee Curtis, Brendan Gleeson, Catherine McCormack, Leonor Varela, Martin Ferrero, David Hayman, John Fortune, Harold Pinter.
●Smuggling, larceny, character assassination and subversion: John le Carré and his collaborator John Boorman get away with murder here. Under the guise of turning out an exotic spy thriller starring 007 himself – Pierce Brosnan – Boorman has instead fashioned a deft, dapper, quintessentially English comedy playing on our aggrandised post-colonial self-image. As Harry Pendel (Geoffrey Rush) puts it: 'We each of us have a dream of ourselves to be more than we are.' That goes double for MI6 man Andy Osnard (Brosnan), an unscrupulous scoundrel prepared to incite an international incident if he smells money in it. Exiled to Panama in disgrace, Osnard immediately insinuates himself into high society, using gentleman's tailor Harry as his conduit. Blackmailed and flattered, bullied and bribed, Harry dreams up an entire rebel movement – 'the Silent Opposition' – to boost Osnard's spending allowance. When that begins to flag, the pair concoct a mind-boggling intrigue in which Panama plans to sell the Canal to the Chinese. It's the biggest thing to hit British Intelligence since Suez. Le Carré's 1996 novel acknowledged a debt to *Our Man in Havana*, and Geoffrey Rush's performance might have been modelled on Alec Guinness: he makes Harry an endearingly decent mediocrity, a romantic whose sincerity far exceeds his honesty – making him easy prey for Brosnan's venal opportunist, casually suave to his very soul. (Brosnan so clearly relishes this chance to make mischief with Bond's credibility, it's hard to see how he can be trusted with the franchise again.) Working in a lighter register, Boorman has crafted a witty, classy and richly enjoyable morality play, which skewers the mercenary self-interest behind Anglo-American imperialism almost as an afterthought. TCh

Taipei Story (Qingmei Zhuma)

(1984, Tai/China, 115 min)
d Edward Yang. *p* T'an Yi-hua. *sc* Edward Yang, Chu T'ien-wen, Hou Hsiao-hsien. *ph* Yang Wei-han. *ed* Wang Chi-yang, Sung Fan-chen. *pd* T'sai Cheng-pin. *cast* Ts'ai Ch'in, Hou Hsiao-hsien, Wu Nien-chen, Lin Hsiu-ling.
●The film that introduced Yang's prodigious talent to the West is a quietly stunning drama which sees the various problems facing a rapidly modernised city reflected in the lives of a dozen or so subtly observed characters. At the centre are a troubled upper middle-class couple: a failed businessman lost in dreams of the past (Hou), and a budding executive whose reaction to redundancy is more in tune with the future. Though there's little in the way of story, Yang's insights and honesty about emotions ensure interest throughout; and it looks absolutely superb. TCh

Take, The

(1974, US, 92 min)
d Robert Hartford-Davis. *p* Howard Brandy. *sc* Del Reisman, Franklin Coen. *ph* Duke Callaghan. *ed* Aaron Stell. *ad* Kirk Axtell. *m* Fred Karlin. *cast* Billy Dee Williams, Eddie Albert, Frankie Avalon, Vic Morrow, Sorrell Booke, Tracy Reed, Albert Salmi.
●Super-tough, super-cynical product of the Nixon era in which it is futile to worry overmuch about such hair-splitters as whether our hero is a bent cop playing good or vice versa. Hartford-Davis' direction is all flash, laced with a couple of this'll knock 'em dead-type shock cuts and an introductory countdown to the shootout that threatens to be never-ending. Lovers of bizarre relics from the great age of pop will relish Frankie Avalon in a small part as a punk gangster screaming 'Don't hurt me! Don't hurt me!' to our hero in a police cell. As the cop, Billy Dee Williams, who may be remembered for a soulful performance in *Lady Sings the Blues*, is plainly misused. VG

Take a Hard Ride

(1975, US/It, 109 min)
d Anthony M Dawson [Antonio Margheriti]. *p* Harry Bernsen. *sc* Eric Bercovici, Jerry Ludwig. *ph* Riccardo Pallottini. *ed* Stanford C Allen. *ad* Julio Molina. *m* Jerry Goldsmith. *cast* Jim Brown, Lee Van Cleef, Fred Williamson, Catherine Spaak, Jim Kelly, Barry Sullivan, Harry Carey Jr, Dana Andrews.
●A rather crude attempt to expand the Italian Western, cashing in on the blaxploitation and kung-fu markets. Two black dudes (Brown, Williamson), in uneasy alliance and carrying a heap of money, pick up a couple of waifs and strays, including a kung-fu fighting Indian, while a vast army of bounty hunters headed by Lee Van Cleef chase after the loot. All an excuse for some undemanding thrills, listlessly put together. The film only rouses itself to kill people off: they don't just die, they fall from heights, slam into railings, and throw themselves into puddles just in front of the camera. Ironic that it's only in their dying seconds that most of the cast come alive. CPe

Take Care of My Cat (Goyang Yirul Butakhae)

(2001, SKor, 112 min)
d Jung Jae-Eun. *p* Oh Ki-Min. *sc* Jung Jae-Eun. *ph* Choi Young-Hwan. *ed* Lee Hyun-Mee. *ad* Kim Jin-Chul. *m* M&F. *cast* Bae Doo-Na, Lee Yoo-Won, Ok Ji-Young, Lee Eun-Shik, Lee Eun-Joo.
●Five young women who met and bonded as classmates in an Incheon high school face adulthood. When the upwardly mobile Hae-Joo (Lee Yoo-Won) ups sticks and heads for Seoul, making clear that she feels a need to distance herself from her socially inferior past – and friends – the other four are left to take stock. A new bond forms between the romantic dreamer Tae-Hee (Bae) and the arty Ji-Young (Ok), and both start to think about going abroad to study. Jung's debut feature (her short films have won prizes at the Korean festivals) is kaleidoscopic in structure and deliberately light on plot, and it offers a likeably informal group portrait of its 20-year-old protagonists. But little here is as 'realist' or credible as it first appears (least of all the virtual absence of sexual feelings and impulses), and the film ultimately seems no less far-fetched than the male fantasies about women (the abominable *Girls' Night Out*, written and directed by Im Sang-Soo, comes to mind) that it implicitly criticises. Snazzy title-design, though. TR

Take Care of Your Scarf, Tatjana (Pida Huivista Kinni, Tatjana)

(1994, Fin, 65 min)
d/p Aki Kaurismäki.*sc* Aki Kaurismäki, Sakke Järvenpää. *ph* Timo Salminen. *ed* Aki Kaurismäki. *ad* Kari Laine, Markku Pätilä, Jukko Salmi. *cast* Kati Outinen, Matti Pellonpaa, Kirsi Tykkylainen, Mato Valtonen.
●A gem from the variable Kaurismäki, this beautifully economic anti-romantic road comedy is both hilarious and strangely touching. The slim story charts the encounter between two morose Finns (one devoted to vodka, the other to coffee) and two Russian women who hitch a lift on their way back to Estonia. The men suffer much discomfiture at the proximity of two talkative members of the opposite sex. Marvellously observed and understated, the film exudes a delicious sense of the absurd. This is deadpan as good as it gets. GA

Take It Easy

(1986, US, 101 min)
d Albert Magnoli. *p* Robert Schaffel, Doug Chapin. *sc* Evan Archerd, Jeff Benjamin, Susan Williams. *ph* Donald Thorin. *ed* James Oliver. *pd* Ward Preston. *m* Alan Silvestri. *cast* Mitch Gaylord, Janet Jones, Michelle Phillips, John Aprea, Michael Pataki, Stacy Maloney.
●Steve's father is a little upset that his son, one time high school football and gymnast star, is going to seed; Steve (Gaylord) is a little miffed that father doesn't seem to care any more – 'We were a team!' – and runs from the house into the arms of new girl in town Julie (Jones). She's a gymnast too, and he joins her in training under the stern gaze of Coach Soranhoff (Pataki), who is busy drumming discipline into his class before they take a crack at getting into the national team. The film offers a full schedule of gratuitous muscle-stretching, in which the fact that Jones and ex-Olympic champ Gaylord do their own flip-flops would have been more impressive had it also come up with anything resembling a proper plot. The 'boy from the wrong side of the track makes good theme', already used in Magnoli's awful *Purple Rain*, simply doesn't wash, while the tedious disco soundtrack serves only to thud home the pointlessness of it all. CB

Take It Like a Man, Ma'am (Ta' det som en Mand, Frue!)

(1975, Den, 96 min)
d Elisabeth Rygård, Mette Knudsen, Li Vilstrup. *p* Ilse M Haugård, Annelise Hovmand, Trine Hedmann. *sc* Mette Knudsen, Li Vilstrup, Elisabeth Rygård. *ph* Katia Forbert Petersen, Judy Irola, Lene Fog-Møller, Leni Schou. *ed* Ann-Lis Lund. *pd* Malene Ravn. *m* Fuzzy, Nina Larsen, Gudrun Steen-Andersen, Maria Marcus. *cast* Tove Maës, Alf Lassen, Berthe Quistgård, Hans Kragh Jacobsen.
●An entertaining commercial feature arising from certain preoccupations within the women's movement, this represents a reasonably successful attempt to popularise aspects of feminist theory and film-making practice: respectively, the potential relationship between the movement and the older woman, and the realisation of an all-female production. The film traces the gradual coming-to-consciousness of a 50-year-old housewife, diagnosed as menopausal and prescribed tranquillisers and a little dog to look after. But the basis of its broad appeal is a long dream sequence which is a devastatingly accurate and hilarious depiction of role reversal. It's the seemingly simple strategy of this section which proves to be the film's real strength. PT

Take It or Leave It

(1981, GB, 87 min, b/w & col)
d/p Dave Robinson. *sc* Madness, Philip McDonald, Dave Robinson. *ph* Nic Knowland. *ed* Michael Ellis. *ad* Bert Davey. *m* Madness. *with* Graham McPherson, Mark Bedford, Lee Thompson, Carl Smith, Dan Woodgate, Christopher Foreman, Mike Barson, John Hasler.
●This purports to be the 'true story' of the formative years of the north London bluebeat-inspired band Madness. By conveniently ending just before the onset of the band's unbroken spell of singles charts successes, the film sidesteps the usual rock movie concerns: the pressures of the music biz, the personal toll of overnight success, etc. Instead, it delivers an enjoyable enough picture of what it's like to be young, broke, working class, and trying to put a band together. The problems, according to Madness, are personnel changes, in-fighting, sheer idleness and selfishness, and – not least – lack of musical competence. But given the band's succession of fine hit singles, this last claim, and the fact that it fudges the issue of Madness' relationship with its early skinhead following, are the two things it's most difficult to swallow about the film. Otherwise, it's an adequately mythologising promo job. RM

Take Me Out to the Ball Game (aka Everybody's Cheering)

(1949, US, 93 min)
d Busby Berkeley. *p* Arthur Freed. *sc* Harry Tugend, George Wells. *ph* George Folsey. *ed* Blanche Sewell. *ad* Cedric Gibbons, Daniel B Cathcart. *songs* Betty Comden, Adolph Green, Roger Edens. *cast* Gene Kelly, Frank Sinatra, Esther Williams, Jules Munshin, Betty Garrett, Edward Arnold.
●More like a Donen/Kelly musical than a Busby Berkeley (not a chorine in sight), which is hardly surprising since they staged and filmed the numbers, while Berkeley left after doing the dialogue scenes. With Kelly, Sinatra and Munshin teaming up for the brilliant vaudeville-baseball routine of a number like 'O'Brien to Ryan to Goldberg', it often looks like a run-in for *On the Town*. Less 'integrated', perhaps, but enormously enjoyable. The plot is an airy something with a non-swimming Esther Williams becoming the new owner of a turn-of-the-century baseball team, and charming the boys out of their chauvinist scowls. But what matters is the stylish ebullience, and the excellent score by Roger Edens, Adolph Green and Betty Comden. TM

Take Me to Town

(1952, US, 81 min)
d Douglas Sirk. *p* Ross Hunter. *sc* Richard Morris. *ph* Russell Metty. *ed* Milton Carruth. *ad* Alexander Golitzen, Hilyard Brown. *m* Joseph Gershenson. *cast* Ann Sheridan, Sterling Hayden, Philip Reed, Lee Patrick, Phyllis Stanley, Lane Chandler.
●A charming slice of backwoods Americana (with music) about three boys who decide that saloon gal Sheridan, no better than she ought to be and keeping a wary eye out for the law, is just the thing to make a wife for their widowed preacher father (Hayden), in preference to the more 'suitable' widow lady (Stanley) he has in mind. All the traditional stops are pulled out as Sheridan proves herself a born housewife, at the end even graduating to conducting a Bible class. But glowingly shot by Sirk without any of the subversive malice that marked his view of bourgeois America, it has real tenderness and warmth. Lovely performances from Sheridan and Hayden, too. TM

Take Out, The

(1994, GB, 15 min)
d Jamie Thraves. *p* Rob Small. *sc* Jamie Thraves. *ph* Seamus McGarvey. *ed* Tobias Zaldva, Jamie Thraves. *cast* Joe Tucker, Louise Delamere, Peter Kenny, Audrey Tom.
●Third of Thraves' six shorts, made for the BFI's 1994 New Directors' package: a ticky, tricksy account of a double-date going to the dogs. With elements of both the nervous obsessiveness of his previous *Scratch* and the listless languor of his subsequent *The Hackney Downs*, it's not quite the equal of either, but it's still an enticingly off-centre inspection of (dis)trust, diffidence, and the little perversities folk trade in. NB

Take the Money and Run

(1969, US, 85 min)
d Woody Allen. *p* Charles H Joffe. *sc* Woody Allen, Mickey Rose. *ph* Lester Shorr. *ed* Paul Jordan, Ron Kalish. *ad* Fred Harpman. *m* Marvin Hamlisch. *cast* Woody Allen, Janet Margolin, Marcel Hillaire, Jacquelyn Hyde, Lonny Chapman, Jan Merlin.
●Discounting the abortive *What's Up, Tiger Lily?*, this was Woody Allen's debut as his own director, and it marked the beginnings of his idiosyncratic 'one shot – one gag' technique. Its tale of the eagerly criminal career of Virgil Starkwell is as unpredictably structured as *Annie Hall*, if not yet anything like as sustained in tone and mood. But it has plenty of hilarious jokes and concepts, like the ventriloquists' dummies at prison visiting time, and the return home from a chain-gang break with five shackled cons in tow. TR

Taking Care of Business (aka Filofax)

(1990, US, 108 min)
d Arthur Hiller. *p* Geoffrey Taylor. *sc* Jill Mazursky, Jeffrey Abrams. *ph* David M Walsh. *ed* William Reynolds. *pd* Jon Hutman.

m Stewart Copeland. *cast* James Belushi, Charles Grodin, Anne DeSalvo, Veronica Hamel, Mako, Hector Elizondo.

● Take a con and a yuppy: the con (Belushi) is a good-natured slob, popular with the guys, into baseball and chicks; the yuppy (Grodin) is wound a little tight, basically okay, but ambitious and a tad prissy. Now give the con a break, teach the yuppy a lesson. Put them in neutral territory – the no man's land of LA – and give Belushi Grodin's credit cards, ID and contacts. Give him his filofax. And Grodin gets zilch. There's a good comic idea somewhere here, and it's called *Trading Places*. Through crass over-emphasis and sloppy continuity errors, Hiller fumbles most of the jokes away. The roles fit Belushi/Grodin like rubber, but the rest is second-rate. TCh

Taking Off

(1971, US, 92 min)
d Milos Forman. *p* Alfred W Crown. *sc* Milos Forman, John Guare, Jean-Claude Carriere, John Klein. *ph* Miroslav Ondricek. *ed* John Carter. *ad* Robert Wightman. *cast* Lynn Carlin, Buck Henry, Linnea Heacock, Georgia Engel, Tony Harvey, Audra Lindley, Allen Garfield.

● A delightfully touching comedy, Forman's first in America and far better than his later *One Flew Over the Cuckoo's Nest* or *Ragtime*, this deals with the attempts of a middle-aged, middle class American couple to trace and lure back their runaway daughter. Scenes of their search are intercut with sequences at a musical audition for disillusioned youth, and Forman's wry but sympathetic humour derives largely from the incongruities he observes in both situations: deserted parents, concerned and conservative, getting stoned in an effort to understand why kids smoke dope; a rosy, virginal young girl singing a quiet folk song in praise of fucking. Never taking sides, but allowing both factions engaged in the generation gap war plenty of space and generosity, its gentle wit has aged far more gracefully than the hectoring sermons of most youth movies churned out in the late '60s and early '70s. GA

Taking of Pelham One Two Three, The

(1974, US, 104 min)
d Joseph Sargent. *p* Gabriel Katzka, Edgar J Scherick. *sc* Peter Stone. *ph* Owen Roizman. *ed* Jerry Greenberg, Robert Q Lovett. *ad* Gene Rudolf. *m* David Shire. *cast* Walter Matthau, Robert Shaw, Martin Balsam, Hector Elizondo, Earl Hindman, James Broderick, Dick O'Neill, Lee Wallace, Tom Pedi, Kenneth McMillan.

● Four hijackers, got up like Groucho Marx and led by Robert Shaw with the voice of a Dalek, kidnap a New York subway train and hold the city to ransom. Saviour of the system is Transit Authority Inspector Matthau, harking back to his early acting days as a grim heavy, and with a Bronx accent as thick and fancy as a piece of angel cake. It's a slice of Urban Crisis life, you see, and to prove it the occupants of the train 'represent a cross-section of New York: a pimp, a Puerto Rican pregnant girl, a hippie, a hooker, a WASP, a wino and a homosexual'. This movie's so up-to-date even the mayor's a laughing-stock. Yet, despite the caricature, the facile screenplay by Peter Stone, and the desperate direction from Sargent ('who has directed some of television's finest hours'), the film retains a fascination – the way *Juggernaut* did; and needless to say, it's been a monster hit in cities with an underground system. AN

Talented Mr Ripley, The

(1999, US, 139 min)
d Anthony Minghella. *p* William Horberg, Tom Sternberg. *sc* Anthony Minghella. *ph* John Seale. *ed* Walter Murch. *pd* Roy Walker. *m* Gabriel Yared. *cast* Matt Damon, Gwyneth Paltrow, Jude Law, Cate Blanchett, Philip Seymour Hoffman, Jack Davenport, James Rebhorn, Sergio Rubini, Philip Baker Hall, Celia Weston, Lisa Eichhorn.

● The late '50s. New York lavatory attendant Tom Ripley (Damon) may not be conventionally talented, but he's very able when it comes to reacting on the spot, especially with little white lies. When shipbuilder Herbert Greenleaf assumes he's an old college pal of his son Dickie (Law), Ripley's quick to snap up the opportunity to visit Europe, purportedly to lure the playboy home, but actually to sample la dolce vita for himself. But, having wormed his way into the affections of Dickie and his girlfriend Marge (Paltrow), he can't face losing his new-found life of leisure. Minghella's imaginative but mostly faithful adaptation of Patricia Highsmith's classic study of a sociopathic killer is a class act, in every sense. Not only is it an elegantly polished affair, with top notch performances all round, and magnificent camerawork and editing, it's also acutely aware of how class, money and sex shape desire and resentment, and of the distinctions between presenting a facade to the world, outright pretence and the more radical practice of reinventing oneself. It's into these registers that Minghella weaves the most intriguing and ironic undertones. GA

Tale of a Vampire

(1992, GB, 102 min)
d Shimako Sato. *p* Simon Johnson. *sc* Shimako Sato. *ph* Zubin Mistry. *ed* Chris Wright. *pd* Alice Normington. *m* Julian Joseph. *cast* Julian Sands, Kenneth Cranham, Suzanna Hamilton, Marian Diamond, Michael Kenton.

● Shot on inventive locations around London, this modern-day vampire pic takes its thematic inspiration from Edgar Allan Poe's sombre poem 'Annabel Lee'. Sands plays Alex, an ageless bloodsucker haunted by the loss of his true love, Virginia. Trailing Alex is a mysterious stranger (Cranham) hell-bent on revenge; and when Alex becomes obsessed with Virginia-lookalike Anne (Hamilton, gratingly winsome), the stranger uses her to lure his prey. Although director Sato is Japanese, her visual style owes more to Tony Scott than to any oriental tradition; smoke swathes the screen and light blasts elegantly through half-drawn blinds at every opportunity. For such a low-budget film, it looks terrific, and comparison with *The Hunger* does it an injustice, in that understated dialogue is used here to evoke a genuine sense of loss entirely lacking from most mainstream fodder. Although Sato's script unravels far too slowly, strong performances by Cranham and Sands keep the life-blood flowing in this flawed but impressive debut. MK

Tale of Springtime, A

see Conte de printemps

Tale of the Fox, The

see Roman de Renard, Le

Tale of the Three Jewels (Conte des trois diamants)

(1995, Bel/GB/Palestine, 112 min)
d Michel Khleifi. *p* Michel Khleifi, Moar Al-Qattan. *sc* Michel Khleifi. *ph* Raymond Fromont. *ed* Ludo Troch, Marie Castro. *ad* Bashir Abu Rabia, Françoise Rabu, Noelle Shawwa, Ahmad Masri, Mohammad Masharawi, Hafez Daoud, Mohammad Khalifa. *m* Abed Azariah. *cast* Makram Khouri, Bushra Qaraman, Mohammad Bakri, Hana Ne'meh.

● A frontline portrait of Palestinian life on the Gaza Strip (in a period between the Hebron events and the withdrawal and new peace initiatives), told from the viewpoint of a 12-year-old boy who becomes involved with a 'gypsy' girl. The raids by Israeli special forces are powerfully filmed and cleanly integrated into the narrative – as unexceptional to the boy as the activities of the young Palestinian fighters. Michel Khleifi (writer, director, producer) adds an elevating metaphysical/religious dimension that embraces elements of orthodox Middle Eastern mysticism, the boy's dream-founded intuition and the girl's nature-oriented world view. WH

Tales from a Hard City

(1994, GB, 80 min)
d Kim Flitcroft. *p* Alex Usborne, Jacques Bidou. *ph* Paul Otter, Richard Ranken. *ed* David Hill, Yann Dedet. *m* Don Carey.

● Lively documentary about a handful of dreamers in Sheffield: a petty thief into dope, karaoke, awful mates and sponging off his mum; a boxer turned would-be actor hustling for sponsored advertising gigs; a single mum hoping to become a pop star; and a well-off nightclub owner with massive entrepreneurial ambitions. All are naive and fuelled by a need for a sense of self-importance (though none approaches the vacuity and arrogance of the self-appointed 'image consultant' working on the boxer). A saddening film, leavened by humour and flashes of hope. GA

Tales from the Crypt Presents Demon Knight

(1995, US, 92 min)
d Ernest Dickerson. *p* Gilbert Adler. *sc* Ethan Reiff, Cyrus Voris, Mark Bishop. *ph* Rick Bota. *ed* Stephen Lovejoy. *pd* Christiaan Wagener. *m* Ed Shearmur. *cast* John Kassir, Billy Zane, William Sadler, Jada Pinkett, Brenda Bakke, CCH Pounder, Thomas Hayden Church, John Schuck, Dick Miller.

● Dickerson, who shot most of Spike Lee's films before directing the feature *Juice*, knows his way round a horror picture, but in the end this spin-off from the HBO cable TV series (derived from the 1950s EC comic books of William Gaines) feels pedestrian and moribund. Mysterious fugitive Brayker (Sadler) takes refuge from demonic, stetson-hatted smoothie the Collector (Zane) in a small-town flophouse that's immediately besieged by flesh-eating, green-eyed demons. Matters get bogged down as Brayker seals the building's doors with holy blood in order to protect the stereotyped characters trapped within. Not to be thwarted, the Collector uses telepathy to exploit their vulnerabilities, offering mock affection to love-starved tart Cordelia (Bakke), super-model stardom to delinquent Jeryline (Pinkett) and a topless bar awash with hooch to pickled old-timer Uncle Willy (Miller). The action is set-bound, the gory sfx no more than adequate, and the fright quotient far too low. Nor is any depth lent to the proceedings by repeated flashbacks to an MTV video of the Crucifixion. The first in a series, but standards will need to impove if it's to survive. NF

Tales from the Darkside: The Movie

(1991, US, 93 min)
d John Harrison. *p* Richard P Rubinstein, Mitchell Galin. *sc* Michael McDowell, George A Romero. *ph* Robert Draper. *ed* Harry B Miller III. *pd* Ruth Ammon. *m* Donald A Rubinstein, Pat Regan, Chaz Jankel, John Harrison. *cast* Deborah Harry, Matthew Lawrence, Christian Slater, Robert Sedgwick, Steve Buscemi, Julianne Moore, David Johansen, William Hickey, James Remar, Rae Dawn Chong, Robert Klein.

● An anthology featuring stories adapted by George Romero and Michael McDowell. The latter also wrote the neat 'wraparound story', in which a housewife (Harry) is distracted from roasting and eating a young boy (Lawrence) by his reading of stories from a favourite anthology. In the '40s-style 'Lot 249', a boffin (Buscemi) tricked out of a scholarship revives a 3,000-year-old mummy to exact his revenge. Hickey takes the honours for 'Cat from Hell' – in which cat's eye view shots add suspense – as a mad millionaire who hires a killer (Johansen) to rid him of a homicidal puss. Though it relies on the same flip irony and black humour, 'Lover's Vow' comes closest to succeeding in its own right. After seeing a winged monster tear off a man's head, a struggling New York artist (Remar) is spared on condition that he never reveals the creature's hideous appearance. Fame, fortune and romance (with Chong) ensue, but can he keep a secret forever? Definitely an improvement on the lamentable *Creepshow* or *Cat's Eye*, but Harrison never quite transcends the inherently limited format. NF

Tales from the Gimli Hospital

(1988, Can, 77 min, b/w)
d Guy Maddin. *p* Greg Klymkiw. *sc/ph/ed* Guy Maddin. *ad* Jeff Solyo. *cast* Kyle McCulloch, Michael Gottli, Angela Heck, Margaret-Anne MacLeod.

● There's a thin line between weird and strange, and Maddin's debut falls just the wrong side. For all that, it's hugely enjoyable, a shaggy-dog story set in Manitoba in a bygone age of bucolic gambolling, innocent erotic idylls, and dark, dark shadows. Lonely Einar succumbs to an epidemic that leaves cracks across its victims' faces, and ends up in the local hospital, where he whiles away the hours carving bark fishes and envying the narrative skills of his voluminous neighbour. The two spin tales of love, loss and necrophilia, and mortal combat ensues, to the sound of ghostly bagpipes. A nearly wordless '20s pastiche, the film obeys no logic except the impulse to fling in as many campy, incongruous images as possible. There are moments of jaw-dropping inspiration, and many that are just impenetrably odd. But this is immensely winning for the rawness alone. JRo

Tales from the Vienna Woods (Geschichten aus dem Wiener Wald)

(1979, WGer/Aus, 96 min)
d/p Maximilian Schell. *sc* Christopher Hampton, Maximilian Schell. *ph* Klaus König. *ed* Dagmar Hirtz. *ad* Ernst Wurzer. *m* Toni Stricker. *cast* Birgit Doll, Hanno Pöschl, Helmut Qualtinger, Jane Tilden, Adrienne Gessner, Lil Dagover.

● You'd never guess it from this film version, but Odin von Horvath's play, premiered in Germany in 1931 and successfully staged by Schell at the National Theatre in 1977, has been held up for favourable comparison with Brecht. Set in the Vienna of Hitler's day but ironically drenched in Strauss waltzes, it chronicles the tragi-comic tribulations of an honest middle class shopkeeper whose rebellious daughter runs away from an approved marriage, gets herself pregnant, and ends up face-to-face with daddy in the nightclub to which she has sinfully gravitated. The film is so lumpishly stagebound that its satire of the bourgeoisie and conventional values emerges as painfully crude caricature. TM

Tales of Beatrix Potter (aka Peter Rabbit and Tales of Beatrix Potter)

(1971, GB, 90 min)
d Reginald Mills. *p* Richard Goodwin. *sc* Richard Goodwin, Christine Edzard. *ph* Austin Dempster. *ed* John Rushton. *pd* Christine Edzard. *m* John Lanchbery. *cast* Dancers from the Royal Ballet company.

● Largely unimaginative interpretation of a number of Beatrix Potter's stories, which accumulates a lot of top-line dancers and totally obscures them from view under piles of rigid costumes (Michael Coleman's Jeremy Fisher is a rare exception). There was, perhaps, a virtue in the ballet being set in a natural (as opposed to theatrical) landscape, and the muted photography evokes the original Potter drawings. Inserts show Potter as a young girl drawing animals in the nursery of a forbidding Victorian household, taking her solitary joy in the Lakeland countryside. Otherwise, perhaps the chief interest lies in choreographer Frederick Ashton's performance as Mrs Tiggy-Winkle, and in the fact that the film was co-written and designed by one Christine Edzard, who went on to direct *Little Dorrit*, *The Fool*, etc. WH

Tales of Hoffmann, The

(1951, GB, 127 min).
d/p/sc Michael Powell, Emeric Pressburger. *ph* Christopher Challis. *ed* Reginald Mills. *pd* Hein Heckroth. *m* Jacques Offenbach. *cast* Moira Shearer, Robert Helpmann, Leonid Massine, Ludmilla Tcherina, Pamela Brown, Frederick Aston.

● Made at the instigation of Sir Thomas Beecham – who conducts the Offenbach operetta – Powell and Pressburger's follow-up to *The Red Shoes* lacks the earlier film's coherence and emotional pull, but is equally lavish in its attempts to combine dance, music and film. Basically a trio of stories (plus prologue and epilogue) in which unrequited love figures strongly, the movie is inevitably uneven, and some have pointed to a rather kitschy element in its equation of Cinema and Great Art. But Powell's eye – aided by Hein Heckroth's designs and Chris Challis's camera – is as sharp and distinctive as ever, revelling in rich colours, fantastic compositions, and swooning movements (most notably in the lavish episode featuring a Venetian courtesan). Sumptuous spectacle. GA.

Tales of Kish (Ghessé Hayé Kish)

1999, Iran, 72 min)
d Nasser Taghvaï, Abolfazl Jalili, Mohsen Makhmalbaf. *p* Mohsen Gharib. *sc* Nasser Taghvaï, Abolfazl Jalili, Mohsen Makhmalbaf. *ph* Azim Javanrouh, Massoud Karani, Mohamad Ahmadi. *ed* Abbas Ganjavi, Abolfazl Jalili, Meysam Makhmalbaf. *m* Traditional Iranian music. *cast* Hossein Panahi, Atefeh Razavi, Hafez Pakdel, Mohamad A Babhan, Norieh Mahigiran.

● Three short tales set on the island of Kish. Taghvaï's 'The Greek Ship' tells how the lives of a shopkeeper and his wife are transformed by crates swept onshore from a wrecked cargo ship; Jalili's 'The Ring' concerns a student paying his way by working in a shack in the middle of nowhere; Makhmalbaf's 'The Door' (which intriguingly echoes Polanski's *Two Men and a Wardrobe* while anticipating Makhmalbaf's script for his daughter Samira's later *Blackboards*) concerns a postman trying to deliver a letter to a man who wanders the desert carrying a door on his back. All the episodes are visually stunning, making magnificent use of colour and landscape; all are at once fairytale-like in their simplicity, yet somewhat oblique as to their precise meaning; and all are perfectly paced and structured as shorts, never outstaying their welcome. GA

Tales of Mystery

see Histoires Extraordinaires

Tales of Ordinary Madness (Storie di Ordinaria Follia)

(1981, It/Fr, 108 min)
d Marco Ferreri. *p* Jacqueline Ferreri. *sc* Sergio Amidei, Marco Ferreri, Anthony Foutz. *ph* Tonino Delli Colli. *ed* Ruggero Mastroianni. *ad* Dante Ferretti. *m* Philippe Sarde. *cast* Ben Gazzara, Ornella Muti, Susan Tyrrell, Tanya Lopert, Roy Brocksmith, Katia Berger.

● 'When Hemingway put his brains on the wall, that was style...' drones the gutbucket poet (Gazzara) to a dozing audience in New York, before retreating home to LA among the 'defeated, demented and damned' to stagger through his quotidien tales of ordinary madness. A groan from the lower depths, this is adapted from the autobiography of leftover-beat poet Charles Bukowski. The problem is that Ferreri's grip on the English language seems too infirm to inject the necessary irony into a phrase like the one above. Gazzara is fine as the grizzled soak of a poet, his snake eyes forever gloating on some distant private joke, but his portentous pronouncements would look better in subtitles. And among the various madonna/whores that people his circle of purgatory is a sloe-eyed seraph (Muti) given to such acts as closing up her vagina with a safety-pin (presumably the corollary to Depardieu carving off his own prick in The Last Woman). For all that, there is a final scene on a beach which proves that Ferreri is the equal of Antonioni when it comes to spatial beauty. CPea

Tales of Terror

(1961, US, 90 min)
d/p Roger Corman. *sc* Richard Matheson. *ph* Floyd Crosby. *ed* Anthony Carras. *pd* Daniel Haller. *m* Les Baxter. *cast* Vincent Price, Peter Lorre, Basil Rathbone, Debra Paget, Joyce Jameson.

● For the fourth of his Poe films, Corman adopted a portmanteau front and introduced, into the second of his three stories, a vein of grisly black comedy that would reappear more successfully in the later *The Raven*. The first tale, *Morella*, has Price as a typically necrophile introvert mourning the death in childbirth of his mummified wife until his long banished daughter returns to the fold; in *The Black Cat*, Lorre dominates as the drunkard who reacts to Price's adulterous liaison with his wife by walling the couple up in his wine cellar; and in *The Case of M Valdemar*, a dead Price exacts revenge on the hypnotist who sent his soul to eternal limbo with a view to stealing his wife. Stylish and fun, but the short story format denies Corman the stately, melancholy pace that distinguished his best work in the cycle. GA.

Talking History

(1983, GB, 60 min)
d HO Nazareth. *with* CLR James, EP Thompson.

● The two most famous radical historians of our day – EP Thompson and CLR James – talk to each other about Paris 1968, Nelson Mandela, Solidarity, 'Atlanticism in crisis', and the nature and purpose of their kind of history. The predominant image is of two grey-haired, one-time *enfants terribles* slipping easily into the roles of charismatic prophets. They share a devotion to history, not as a frozen catalogue of isolated events, but as signposts to future developments – what Thompson calls 'history as process'. They both discern the coming end of political parties – in the East and the West – and the growth of large 'people's movements'. The film-makers have sought to enliven the proceedings with headlines and film clips that illustrate the topics of conversation; but despite the assiduousness of their picture research, the end effect is simply distracting. James and Thompson talking are excitement enough for the attentive viewer. MH

Talk of the Town, The

(1942, US, 118 min, b/w)
d/p George Stevens. *sc* Irwin Shaw, Sidney Buchman. *ph* Ted Tetzlaff. *ed* Otto Mayer. *ad* Lionel Banks. *m* Frederick Hollander. *cast* Cary Grant, Jean Arthur, Ronald Colman, Edgar Buchanan, Glenda Farrell, Charles Dingle, Rex Ingram, Lloyd Bridges.

● An attractive serio-comic tale of civic corruption, with Grant as a factory worker on the run from a trumped-up charge of arson and murder, Arthur as the childhood friend with whom he seeks shelter, and Colman as the stuffy professor already ensconced as her lodger (and whose presence requires that Grant be passed off as the gardener when he tires of seclusion in the attic). The comedy of social proprieties as the inevitable triangle raises its head is nicely played against discussions in which the two men bring each other to a new understanding of the law and its application. Beautifully written by Irwin Shaw and Sidney Buchman, it's equally well directed and acted, even if the situations (including a lynch mob that comes complete with laughs) are not a little contrived. TM

Talk Radio

(1988, US, 109 min)
d Oliver Stone. *p* Edward R Pressman, A Kitman Ho. *sc* Eric Bogosian, Oliver Stone. *ph* Robert Richardson. *ed* David Brenner. *pd* Bruno Rubeo. *m* Stewart Copeland. *cast* Eric Bogosian, Alec Baldwin, Ellen Greene, Leslie Hope, John C McGinley, John Pankow, Michael Wincott.

● Bogosian co-scripts and stars in this adaptation of his play about 'shock broadcasting' (the provocation of extremist attitudes), here expanded to incorporate details from Stephen Singular's book *Talked to Death: The Life and Murder of Alan Berg*. Barry Champlain (Bogosian) is a late-night radio host based in Dallas. He indulges in a perversely abusive relationship with callers. It's a formula that works, and Champlain is offered a chance for national syndication. But his tendency towards self-destruction gets into full swing, and he brings his ex-wife (Greene) to Dallas for what amounts to a distressing, seemingly pointless stroll down memory lane. Much too long, these flashbacks are decidedly less effective than the studio-bound sequences which focus on Champlain's mania and rapid-fire exchange with his lonely, lunatic fans, one of whom finally gets out of hand. At these moments, Champlain's distorted perspective is compelling, despite Stone's sometimes flashy direction as he attempts to wrest cinematic qualities out of the essentially stagey material. CM

Tall Guy, The

(1989, GB, 92 min)
d Mel Smith. *p* Paul Webster. *sc* Richard Curtis. *ph* Adrian Biddle. *ed* Dan Rae. *pd* Grant Hicks. *m* Peter Brewis. *cast* Jeff Goldblum, Emma Thompson, Rowan Atkinson, Geraldine James, Emil Wolk, Kim Thomson, Harold Innocent, Anna Massey.

● This tall tale concerns Dexter (the excellent Goldblum), an actor unlucky in love, life, hay fever, and job as fall guy to obnoxious, egocentric comedian Ron Anderson (Atkinson). Falling for nurse Kate Lemon (Thompson), he subjects himself to a course of injections, ostensibly to cure his sneezing. Close encounters with the needle pay off in an unbridled close encounter with Kate, but also get him the push for missing a show. Richard (*Blackadder*) Curtis' script then leads Dexter through a series of failed auditions (including a fine Berkoff take-off) before he lands the title role in the musical of *The Elephant Man* (which features the memorable lyrics of 'I'm Packing My Trunk') and settles accounts with Ron. Mel Smith's directorial debut is uninhibited by finesse, but it has its laughs. JGl

Tall Men, The

(1955, US, 122 min)
d Raoul Walsh. *p* William A Bacher, William Hawks. *sc* Sydney Boehm, Frank S Nugent. *ph* Leo Tover. *ed* Louis Loeffler. *ad* Lyle Wheeler, Mark-Lee Kirk. *m* Victor Young. *cast* Clark

Gable, Jane Russell, Robert Ryan, Cameron Mitchell, Juan Garcia, Harry Shannon, Emile Meyer.

● An unpretentious but masterly trail-drive epic, one of the purest and simplest examples of the effortless professionalism of Walsh and his collaborators (including co-writer Frank Nugent, John Ford's son-in-law and writer-in-chief), and almost incidentally a sustained exploration of the Western landscape and the place of the stock characters within it. Gable pushes the herd and his own horizons westward through disaster and peril; though the film is probably best remembered by some for Jane Russell's bath scene, frontier-style. PT

Tall T, The

(1957, US, 77 min)
d Budd Boetticher. *p* Harry Joe Brown. *sc* Burt Kennedy. *ph* Charles Lawton Jr. *ed* Al Clark. *ad* George Brooks. *m* Heinz Roemheld. *cast* Randolph Scott, Richard Boone, Maureen O'Sullivan, Skip Homeier, Henry Silva, John Hubbard, Arthur Hunnicutt.

● Admirably scripted by Burt Kennedy from a story by Elmore Leonard, this is the best and bleakest of the Boetticher/Scott Westerns. A marvellous mechanism is set in motion by the stagecoach hold-up at the beginning where a solid citizen cravenly bargains for his life by suggesting that his wife be held for ransom. Boone's bluffly amiable villain promptly guns him down in contempt, but fulfils his elective role by taking up the suggestion. Thereafter, conceptions of justice and social justification are slyly questioned as Boone is hounded by Scott, bodies pile up, and the two men, gradually emerging as opposite sides of the same coin, face the inevitable showdown that neither of them wants but which society demands. Wonderful, with a full roster of fine performances. TM

Tall Target, The

(1951, US, 77 min, b/w)
d Anthony Mann. *p* Richard Goldstone. *sc* George Worthing Yates, Art Cohn. *ph* Paul C Vogel. *ed* Newell P Kimlin. *ad* Cedric Gibbons, Eddie Imazu. *cast* Dick Powell, Paula Raymond, Adolphe Menjou, Marshall Thompson, Ruby Dee, Richard Rober, Leif Erickson, Will Geer, Florence Bates.

● A cheapo gem of a thriller: a *noir*-influenced costume drama set largely aboard a train carrying Abe Lincoln (the date is 1861) to Baltimore to make a pre-inauguration speech. Hitching a ride is Powell, a New York cop who has wind of an assassination attempt, has resigned from the force because of the scepticism of his superiors, and finds that playing a lone wolf hand with no official backing has its hazards as he does everything in his power to avert disaster. Ingeniously and inventively plotted, taut and unpretentious, the film dashes along at a furious pace, with a strong period feel and nicely understated performances, well served by Mann's straightforward direction. GA

Talmage Farlow

(1981, US, 58 min)
d/p Lorenzo DeStefano. *ph* Thomas Ackerman. *ed* Lorenzo DeStefano. *with* Talmage Farlow, Tommy Flanagan, Red Mitchell, George Benson, Lenny Breau, Red Norvo.

● A gentle and intimate portrait of the lauded jazz guitarist Tal Farlow. The dinner-plate-handed virtuoso was discovered by pianist Jimmy Lyons, but 'disappeared' in the late '50s, cloistering himself in the New England port of Sea Brake, fishing and resuming his first job of sign-painting. His preference for this quiet idyll away from the numbing club round is obvious, and enviable, but as vibist Red Norvo and other friends point out in the film, the gentle giant is far from retired. DeStefano's film proves as much with a sensitivity that never slips into sycophancy. JG

Tamarind Seed, The

(1974, GB, 125 min)
d Blake Edwards. *p* Ken Wales. *sc* Blake Edwards. *ph* Freddie Young. *ed* Ernest Walter. *ad* Harry Pottle. *m* John Barry. *cast* Julie Andrews, Omar Sharif, Anthony Quayle, Dan O'Herlihy, Sylvia Syms, Oscar Homolka, Bryan Marshall.

● Blake Edwards sometimes has an amazing way with plastic people and plastic situations, but he can't do much with the weighty, wordy romance that blooms as Julie Andrews and Omar Sharif spar leadenly, and at length, and fend off the final clinch until an appropriate *Sound of Music*-style landscape descends around their ears. Nor can he do much with the spy story that develops out of this holiday affair in Barbados, because she happens to be a Home Office secretary, and he a KGB official. Much more satisfying is the round of Embassy parties captured in all their ritualistic bitchness of acrid marriages and double-faced relationships. As usual, too, Edwards invests the film with a great spatial feeling, but the good things remain strictly marginal. VG

Tampopo

(1986, Jap, 114 min)
d Juzo Itami. *p* Juzo Itami, Yasushi Tamaoki, Seigo Hosogoe. *sc* Juzo Itami. *ph* Masaki Tamura. *ed* Akira Suzuki. *ad* Takeo Kimura. *m* Kunihiko Murai. *cast* Tsutomu Yamazaki, Nobuko Miyamoto, Koji Yakusho, Ken Watanabe, Rikiya Yasuoka.

● Into Tampopo's ramen-bar trundles trucker Goro who, Shane-like, offers to make her the finest noodle-chef in Tokyo. This involves a *Seven Samurai*-style gathering of talents, military regimentation, and industrial espionage. On to this loose structure, Itami grafts a plethora of comic vignettes whose sole link is their focus on food: a Zen lesson in the proper way to contemplate, caress, and devour pork noodles; how to enhance your love life with salt, lemon and cream; how to let dreams of yam sausages ease the onset of death. Itami's episodic satire bulges with invention, ranging from a continuing concern with Japanese concepts of correct behaviour to numerous quirky movie parodies (from Western, gangster and sex films to *Seven Samurai* and *Death in Venice*). It is often very amusing, although the ragged, free-wheeling structure tends to blunt Itami's somewhat obvious thesis, that eating is more closely connected to sex than we would normally admit. Spasmodically effective rather than bitingly funny. GA

Tango

(1993, Fr, 90 min)
d Patrice Leconte. *p* Philippe Carcassonne, René Cleitman. *sc* Patrice Leconte. *ph* Eduardo Serra. *ed* Geneviève Winding. *pd* Ivan Maussion. *m* Angélique Nachon, Jean-Claude Nachon. *cast* Philippe Noiret, Richard Bohringer, Thierry Lhermitte, Carole Bouquet, Jean Rochefort, Miou-Miou.

● This comic-strip caper sees Leconte taking a truculent detour from his previous wacky explorations of sexual obsession, *Monsieur Hire* and *The Hairdresser's Husband*. For this road movie, he bonds together a trio of despicable males: the judge (Noiret), a self-satisfied epicurean; the aviator, Vincent (Bohringer), grounded by guilt for the unpunished murder of his unfaithful wife and her lover; and the pathetic cuckold Paul (Lhermitte), who wishes to kill his wife ('So I can forget her!'). The judge, having fixed Vincent's trial, now blackmails him into killing Paul's wife. They set off south to Valence to do the deed. An absurd Gallic leg-pull, the movie takes sly swipes at psycho-sexual politics – though unlike Buñuel and Blier, Leconte tries less to *épate le bourgeoisie* than simultaneously to flabbergast and titillate the politically correct. Shot in 'Scope and primary colours, the film delights in attention-grabbing wide-angles, isolating long shots, airplane swoops and car chases. The melancholic undertow is echoed by Leconte's ever idiosyncratic choice of music: here 'sensuous and fateful' tango-rock. WH

Tango

(1998, Sp/Arg, 115 min)
d Carlos Saura. *p* Juan Carlos Codazzi, Luis Alberto Scalella, Carlos Luis Mentasti. *sc* Carlos Saura. *ph* Vittorio Storaro. *ed* Julia Juaniz. *pd* Emilio Basaldua. *m* Lalo Schifrin. *cast* Miguel Angel Solá, Cecilia Narova, Mia Maestro, Juan Carlos Copes, Carlos Rivarola, Julio Bocca, Juan Luis Gagliardo.

● A tired, clumsy, imaginatively arthritic tribute to the expressive and romantic power of tango, this integrates well-performed but uninspired dance sequences into a flaccid, studio-bound narrative about a brilliant, uncompromising, ageing director (a self-portrait?) putting on a tango extravaganza and having problems with philistine producers, his grief over the loss of his wife to another man, and his feelings for a beautiful young dancer. True, the film tries to explore many different facets of tango, but it fails throughout; even Storaro's uninspired camerawork can't save an appallingly misguided ballet recreating the fate of Argentina's 'disappeared'. Banal musings on creativity, reactionary crap about sexual politics, tricksy gimmicks with mirrors and silhouettes, the narcissistic portrait of the artist – all this would be bad enough, but Saura doesn't even shoot the dance sequences with any feeling for framing, movement or rhythm. GA

Tango & Cash

(1989, US, 102 min)
d Andrei Konchalovsky. *p* Jon Peters, Peter Guber. *sc* Randy Feldman. *ph* Donald E Thorin. *ed* Hubert de La Bouillerie, Robert Ferretti. *pd* J Michael Riva. *m* Harold Faltermeyer. *cast* Sylvester Stallone, Kurt Russell, Jack Palance, Teri Hatcher, Michael J Pollard, Brion James, Geoffrey Lewis.

● 'I heard you were the second best cop in LA', quips sartorially sleek Tango (Stallone). 'That's funny', retorts T-shirted slob Cash (Russell), 'I heard the same thing about you', The buddy-buddy banter is a set-up; so is the doped and 'wired' stiff they find on their first 'joint' operation. Result: a one-way ticket to the slammer on a trumped-up charge, leaving big-shot gun-runner Jack Palance free to take delivery of his biggest-ever shipment. All that remains is for our mismatched duo to go through the motions. So, after taking the obligatory beating from their fellow prisoners, they escape, tool up, and set about clearing their names while plotting Palance's comeuppance. Konchalovsky handles the slam-bang action with robust efficiency, but what makes this shoot-'em-up nonsense surprisingly watchable is Randy Feldman's rapid-fire dialogue, which constantly undercuts the macho posturings while parodying Stallone's screen image…even though the spectacularly empty finale eschews character-based comedy in favour of Bond-style megabuck explosions and gadgetry. NF

Tango Lesson, The

(1997, GB/Fr/Arg/Jap/Ger, 102 min, b/w & col)
d Sally Potter. *p* Christopher Sheppard. *sc* Sally Potter. *ph* Robby Müller. *ed* Hervé Schneid. *pd* Carlos Conti. *m* Sally Potter. *cast* Sally Potter, Pablo Verón, Gustavo Naveira, Fabian Salas, David Toole, Peter Eyre, Heathcote Williams.

● While working on a thriller, British film-maker Sally Potter attends a Parisian dance recital by Pablo Verón, and is so entranced that she asks him to give her tango lessons. As time passes, her obsession with the music, the dance and her teacher becomes all consuming. She abandons her script to improve her skills as a dancer, and to prepare a movie about tango featuring herself and Verón. On one level, it's simply a terrific dance movie. On another, it offers a canny analysis of male-female relationships, with tango functioning as a model for the interrogation of power, passion, independence and cultural difference. And, inspired by writer/directer Potter's real life experiences, Potter, Verón and most of the cast play 'versions' of themselves, allowing the movie to explore the fertile no man's land between reality and fiction. Though some may find Potter's cinematic presence a little 'cool' in terms of charisma and dramatic range, there's no denying that her partnering of Verón and others on the dance floor is both skilful and exhilarating. GA

Tank

(1984, US, 113 min)
d Marvin Chomsky. *p* Irwin Yablans. *sc* Dan Gordon. *ph* Don Birnkrant. *ed* Donald R Rode. *pd* Bill Kenney. *m* Lalo Schifrin. *cast* James Garner, Shirley Jones, C Thomas Howell, Mark Herrier, Jenilee Harrison, GD Spradlin.

● An Army sergeant due for retirement, Zack Carey (Garner) is the proud owner of a World War II Sherman tank, which he has been patiently restoring; and which he uses to flatten a small-town Georgia jail when the redneck local sheriff (Spradlin), irritated by Zack's intervention in a matter involving police brutality, trumps up a drug charge against his teenage son (Howell). The tank then carries the pair, plus Harrison as the cheery tart who was being slapped around when Zack intervened, across the state line (with the aid of some good guy Hell's Angels) and into folk-hero status (in imitation of *The Sugarland Express*). Part vigilante movie, part sitcom, part tearjerker, part cracker melodrama, it's redeemed by yet another of Garner's graceful, effortless performances.

Tank Girl

(1995, US, 104 min)
d Rachel Talalay. *p* Richard B Lewis, Pen Densham, John Watson. *sc* Tedi Sarafian. *ph* Gale Tattersall. *ed* James R Symons. *ad* Catherine Hardwicke. *m* Graeme Revell. *cast* Lori Petty, Malcolm McDowell, Naomi Watts, Ice T, Don Harvey, Jeff Kober, Reg E Cathey, Iggy Pop.

●Generous souls may try to blame this travesty of the Deadline comic-strip on the studio execs who forced director Talalay to tone down and re-edit her cut. But what remains of Petty's anodyne sexless heroine and the dull, episodic live-action sequences suggests we may have been spared something worse even than this movie. At least the dynamic, vibrantly coloured (and clearly inserted) animation sequences allow us to imagine a tougher, ballsier film. In 2033, our post-apocalyptic planet is a desert where water is jealously guarded by megalomaniac Kesslee (McDowell). Fighting a rearguard action is Tank Girl – here pathetically renamed Rebecca – a crop-headed punkette who guzzles beer, sucks on ciggies, tries to swear properly and, yes, drives a tank. Providing back-up are the fearsome Rippers, a gang of rubber-faced, mutant kangaroos led by an embarrassed-looking Ice T. The damage-control editing aside, the most chaotic element is a soundtrack that throws together Richard Hell's punk anthem 'Blank Generation', the theme from *Shaft*, Hole's 'Drown Soda', and a jaw-dropping song-and-dance number based on Cole Porter's 'Let's Do It'. NF

Tank Malling

(1988, GB, 109 min, b/w & col)
d James Marcus. *p* Glen Murphy, Jamie Foreman. *sc* James Marcus, Mick Southworth. *ph* Jason Lehel. *ed* Brian Peachey. *pd* Geoffrey Sharpe. *m* Rick Fenn, Nick Mason. *cast* Ray Winstone, Jason Connery, Amanda Donohoe, Glen Murphy, Marsha Hunt, Peter Wyngarde, John Conteh, Terry Marsh.

●'I wonder if he's still wearing his rubber underpants', ponders high-class prostitute Helen (Donohoe). She knows the Met's Assistant Commisioner of old, but now she's in hiding with investigative reporter Tank Malling (Winstone), spilling the beans on high-level involvement with prostitutes and drug abuse. Police, judiciary, politicians – none averse to a spot of S&M – are manipulated by Sir Robert Knights (Wyngarde), who oversees the depravity under the auspices of the Moral Revival Campaign. The last time Tank took on Sir Robert and his shady lawyer (Connery), he ended up framed for perjury; but this time the dogged newshound intends to write the definitive exposé. *Tank Malling* doesn't believe in subtlety where a sledgehammer will do. Characters don't talk, they shout; scenes don't merely evolve, they're telegraphed. The actors do their best (Donohoe in particular), but they're left struggling with impossible stereotypes and hackneyed dialogue. CM

Tano da Morire (To Die for Tano)

(1997, It, 80 min)
d Roberta Torre. *p* Leos Kamsteeg, Donatella Palermo. *sc* Roberta Torre. *ph* Daniele Cipri, Giuseppe Schifani. *ed* Giorgio Franchini. *pd* Fabrizio Lupo. *m* Nino D'Angelo. *cast* Ciccio Guarino, Mimma de Rosalia, Enzo Paglino, Maria Aliotta, Anna M Confalone, Adele Aliotta, Vincenzo di Lorenzo, Lorenzo LaRosa.

●Tano Guarrassi, Mafia enforcer, died in a hail of bullets in 1988, rubbed out by a hitman from the real-life Corleone family. A decade on and the story reaches the screen, but this is no dynastic crime saga in the grand Coppola manner. Instead, first time director Torre has turned it into a brightly coloured slice of musical kitsch, shot on location in Palermo and using local residents and tradespeople in the cast. Song and dance numbers performed karaoke-style unfurl the sorry tale, but as musical parody it's just not accurate enough to hit home, and the result is a one-joke movie that wears thin after about ten minutes. TJ

Tant qu'on a la Santé (As Long as You're Healthy)

(1965, Fr, 78 min, b/w)
d Pierre Etaix. *p* Paul Claudon. *sc* Pierre Etaix, Jean-Claude Carriere. *ph* Jean Boffety. *ed* Henri Lanoe. *ad* Jacques d'Ovidio. *m* Jean Paillaud, Luce Klein. *cast* Pierre Etaix, Denise Peronne, Simone Fonder, Sabine Sun, Véra Valmont.

●Etaix's last worthwhile feature in a relatively short career shows him emulating his master Jacques Tati (Etaix was assistant on the execrable *Mon Oncle)* as a young man at odds with his modern urban environment, especially building sites. There's nothing here you haven't seen in Buster Keaton or in Chaplin's *Modern Times*. Watching Etaix and Tati in action suggests that the French must be profoundly worried by the apparatus or trappings of the modern world if they find this sort of caper funny. MA

Tao of Steve, The

(2000, US, 87 min)
d Jenniphr Goodman. *p* Anthony Bregman. *sc* Duncan North, Greer Goodman, Jenniphr Goodman. *ph* Teodoro Maniaci. *ed* Sarah Gartner. *pd* Rosario Provenza. *m* Joe Delia. *cast* Donal Logue, Greer Goodman, Kimo Wills, Ayelet Kaznelson, David Aaron Baker, Nina Jaroslaw, John Hines.

●Dex doesn't look like a lady's man – he looks like a darts player. He wears Hawaiian shirts, works in a kindergarten, and boasts questionable facial hair. So what's his secret? How is it that women find him well nigh irresistible? With his scorecard, Dex can afford to be magnanimous. And so it is that he admits an eager young convert into the mysteries of 'the Tao of Steve', a philosophy inspired by Steve McQueen, Buddha, Steve (*Hawaii Five-O*) McGarrett and other icons of Zen. Jenniphr Goodman's US indie is a wry romantic comedy which ambles by pleasantly without summoning up much energy. A big, genial slob of an actor, Logue easily makes you believe he could charm the pants off anyone he set his sights on – at least until he meets his match in Syd (the director's sister Greer), an astute New Yorker. The comedy is about as cutting and subversive as the last Nora Ephron Tom 'n' Meg love-in, when you get down to it, but the witty, sophisticated dialogue and the unusual New Mexico locale set the mood all right. TCh

Tap

(1988, US, 111 min)
d Nick Castle. *p* Gary Adelson, Richard Vane. *sc* Nick Castle. *ph* David Gribble. *ed* Patrick Kennedy. *pd* Patricia Norris. *m* James Newton Howard. *cast* Gregory Hines, Suzzanne Douglas, Sammy Davis Jr, Savion Glover, Joe Morton, Dick Anthony Williams, Sandman Sims, Bunny Briggs.

●An undemanding backstage romantic melodrama set in contemporary New York, *Tap* is also a homage to the great black dancers who liberated tap with their exuberant, inventive and personal interpretations pre rock'n'roll. The plot concerns Max (Hines) and his redemption from Ye Traditional Life of Crime through his paternal heritage as a tapper. The twists and turns are entirely predictable, but at least it's better plotted and acted than *Dirty Dancing*, doesn't attempt to rewrite black cultural history like *The Cotton Club*, and isn't cluttered with too many subplots as was *Fame*. Most enjoyment comes from the dance set pieces, notably a 'challenge' in which old-timers like Bunny Briggs, Sammy Davis Jr and the wonderfully grouchy Sandman Sims trade licks with each other and with Max, newly freed from Sing Sing. GBr

Tapdancin'

(1980, US, 75 min)
d/p Christian Blackwood. *ph* Christian Blackwood, Mead Hunt, Mark Trottenberg. ed Jill Godmilow. *cast* John Bubbles, Nicholas Brothers, Chuck Green, Tommy Tune, Jerry Ames, Honi Coles, Jazz Tap Percussion Ensemble.

●Blackwood (director of the slick and snappy *Roger Corman: Hollywood's Wild Angel*) has rather irritatingly tailored his fascinating documentary on the dying art of tap dancing for sale to American television. Again and again, his (unlabelled) clips of tap veterans in action are cut short. But the film at least displays an intriguing sense of cultural ironies: the skill's black origins and its appropriation by whiteys. RM

Tapeheads

(1988, US, 97 min)
d Bill Fishman. *p* Peter McCarthy. *sc* Bill Fishman, Peter McCarthy. *ph* Bojan Bazelli. *ed* Mondo Jenkins. *ad* Catherine Hardwicke. *m* Fishbone, David Kahnp. *cast* John Cusack, Tim Robbins, Katy Boyer, Mary Crosby, Clu Gulager, Doug McClure, Connie Stevens, Lyle Alzado, Jessica Walter, Susan Tyrell, Junior Walker, Sam Moore.

●Cusack and Robbins are a couple of bored security guards who get their kicks by playing around with the closed circuit television. This leads them first to unemployment, then to a new career as music promo auteurs. It's all good fun: likeable performances, unpretentious, larky direction, and a haphazard story encompassing political shenanigans, an ageing hip soul duo called The Swanky Modes (Walker and Moore), deep fried chicken, and Jello Biafra of the Dead Kennedys as an FBI agent! If *Repo Man* bounced politics off a B movie sensibility, this does the same with MTV. TCh

Taps

(1981, US, 126 min)
d Harold Becker. *p* Stanley R Jaffe, Howard B Jaffe. *sc* Darryl Ponicsan, Robert Mark Kamen. *ph* Owen Roizman. *ed* Maury Winetrobe. *ad* Stan Jolley, Alfred Sweeney. *m* Maurice Jarre. *cast* George C Scott, Timothy Hutton, Ronny Cox, Sean Penn, Tom Cruise, Brendan Ward.

●About a group of American cadets who take over their military college by force when they learn it is to be sold as real estate, this proved to be a freak success in America. Written off from scratch by industry insiders, including 'Variety', with even Fox itself evidently holding out no hopes, it nevertheless became a top box-office grosser, offering an intriguing reflection of America's military anxieties at the time. Hutton is highly effective as the senior boy who is so inspired by his school's head (Scott doing a *Patton* replay) that he mounts a full-scale military operation to repel the police; ultimately, though, a fascinating first hour is drowned in the clichés of siege cinema. DP

Tarantula

(1955, US, 80 min, b/w)
d Jack Arnold. *p* William Alland. *sc* Robert M Fresco, Martin Berkeley. *ph* George Robinson. *ed* William M Morgan. *ad* Alexander Golitzen, Alfred Sweeney. *m* Henry Mancini. *cast* John Agar, Mara Corday, Leo G Carroll, Nestor Paiva, Ross Elliott, Eddie Parker, Ed Rand, Clint Eastwood.

●An uneven but largely effective merging of mad scientist and mutant monster movie from one of the best sci-fi directors of the '50s. Though it's far more routine than, say, *Creature from the Black Lagoon*, not to mention *The Incredible Shrinking Man*, there is a pulp poetry to the desert scenes through which the giant arachnid, created by Carroll's careless experiments, stalks murdering all and sundry. The cast is as wooden as ever, though sharp eyes might catch a glimpse of a young Clint Eastwood in a minute role as a fighter pilot during the climactic napalming of the creature. GA

Tarea, La

see Homework

Target

(1995, Ind, 104 min)
d/p Sandip Ray. *sc* Satyajit Ray. *ph* Barun Raha. *ed* Dulal Dutt. *ad* Ashoke Bose. *m* Sandip Ray. *cast* Om Puri, Mohan Agashe, Anjan Srivastava.

●Hired as the *shikari* (huntsman) for an overbearing landowner, untouchable Rambharosa (Puri) can't believe his luck. He's housed, fed and clothed – but on the day of the hunt, he learns that there is something more important than money: respect. Directed by Sandip Ray from a script by his late father Satyajit Ray, *Target* takes aim at the entire caste system, but proves such an melodramatic blunderbuss one half expects the heroine to be tied to the rail tracks for the climax. TCh

Target

(1985, US, 118 min)
d Arthur Penn. *p* Richard D Zanuck, David Brown. *sc* Howard Berk, Don Petersen. *ph* Jean Tournier, Robert Jessup. *ed* Stephen A Rotter. *pd* Willy Holt. *m* Michael Small. *cast* Gene Hackman, Matt Dillon, Gayle Hunnicutt, Victoria Fyodorova, Ilona Grubel, Herbert Berghof, Josef Sommer.

●The Lloyds are a typical middle class American family, beset by dullness and young Chris' feelings that his Dad is a staid, materialist cop-out. Typical, that is, until Mom (Hunnicutt) suddenly disappears during a trip to Paris: when father (Hackman) and son (Dillon) follow in search and are welcomed by hails of bullets, all kinds of mysteries erupt, not the least of which concerns Dad's secret past as a CIA agent. Penn's film might seem an altogether ordinary foray into the world of international espionage were it not for his teasing examination of various concepts of 'family', a word much abused throughout to denote not only the Lloyds, but also the several murderous organisations out to destroy them. An uneven film, to be sure, but far more ambitious and intelligent than most spy thrillers. GA

Targets

(1967, US, 90 min)
d/p/sc Peter Bogdanovich. *ph* Laszlo Kovacs. *ed* Peter Bogdanovich. *pd* Polly Platt. *cast* Boris Karloff, Tim O'Kelly, Nancy Hsueh, James Brown, Sandy Baron, Arthur Peterson, Peter Bogdanovich.

●Karloff in effect plays himself as Byron Orlok, a horror star on the point of retiring, who suddenly confronts the reality of contemporary American horror in the form of a psychopathic sniper (O'Kelly) picking off anyone he can see with a vast artillery of weapons. Bogdanovich was given the money to make the film by Roger Corman, who also allowed him to use extensive footage from Corman's Poe movie *The Terror* in the sequences at the drive-in cinema where the confrontation takes place. The result is a fascinatingly complex commentary on American mythology, exploring the relationship between the inner world of the imagination and the outer world of violence and paranoia, both of which were relevant to contemporary American traumas. It was Bogdanovich's first film, and despite his subsequent success, he has yet to come up with anything half as remarkable. DP

Target Shoots First, The

(1999, US, 70 min)
d/p/sc/ph Christopher Wilcha. *ed* Bill Yoelim. *m* Sasha Frere-Jones, Adam S Goldman. *with* Christopher Wilcha, Rick Hunt, John S Wilcha, Steven Tyler, David Hasselhoff.

●Needing cash to pay the rent, 22-year-old Wilcha, an assistant product manager (music marketing), took his camcorder (a graduation present) into Columbia House, the biggest music mail-order firm in the US, and emerged with the raw materials – footage and experience – for this home video essay on corporate office culture and the mainstream assimilation of rebel culture. The wayward trajectory of Nirvana and Kurt Cobain's time in the public eye provide a backbone to the diary story – it was Nirvana's appeal to the alienated that Wilcha was brought in to harness. There's little here that comes as a surprise, and more analytical depth would have helped the film, but as personal testimony, it's sympathetic and honest. NB

Tarka the Otter

(1978, GB, 91 min)
d/p David Cobham. *sc* Gerald Durrell, David Cobham. *ph* John McCallum. *ed* Charles Davies. *m* David Fanshawe. *cast* Peter Bennett, Edward Underdown, Brenda Cavendish, John Leeson.

●This episodic adaptation of Henry Williamson's novel seems determined to include stock shots of all British flora and fauna, whether relevant or not. It's a tale of love, tears, adventure, and close shaves, in which the animal stars act well; but only at the end, in the final confrontation between Tarka and his nemesis, Deadlock the otter-hound, does the film really jell. The rest suffers, as does the book, from a mixture of feyness and anthropomorphism, perhaps endearing in the 1920s but emerging as weakness in this more cynical age. SP

Tarnished Angels, The

(1957, US, 91 min, b/w)
d Douglas Sirk. *p* Albert Zugsmith. *sc* George Zuckerman. *ph* Irving Glassberg. *ed* Russell Schoengarth. *ad* Alexander Golitzen, Alfred Sweeney. *m* Frank Skinner. *cast* Rock Hudson, Robert Stack, Dorothy Malone, Jack Carson, Robert Middleton, Troy Donahue.

●Arguably Sirk's bleakest film – perhaps because it was shot in greyish monochrome rather than luridly stylised colour – and one of his finest, this adaptation of Faulkner's *Pylon* reassembles the three principles from *Written on the Wind* for a probing but sympathetic study in failure and despair. In the South during the Depression, Hudson's down-at-heel reporter becomes fascinated by a group of stunt fliers, led by Stack's disillusioned WWI veteran pilot and Malone's parachute jumper. In terms of plot very little really happens; characters deceive each other and themselves, try in vain to communicate more fully, and repeatedly sell themselves short. Inevitably, it all culminates in death, which ironically provides some sort of half-hearted liberation, but Sirl's sombre, tender awareness of the illusions that fuel his no-hopers' lives allows no respite. A film totally at odds with the bland optimism of postwar America, it might be depressing were it not for the consummate artistry on view. And Hudson, Stack, Malone and Carson were never better. GA

Tartuffe, Le

(1984, Fr, 138 min)
d Gérard Depardieu. *p* Margaret Ménégoz. *ph* Pascal Marti. *ed* Hélène Viard. *ad* Yannis Kokkos. *cast* Gérard Depardieu, François Périer, Elisabeth Depardieu, Hélène Laptower.

●Depardieu's directorial debut is difficult to assess, since it is little more than a long, sombre and stately record of the Molière play. The sets are minimal, and since the camera doesn't move much, the film exists for the performances. Happily, these are excellent. As the grasping, lecherous cleric who takes over a gullible man's household, Depardieu is arrestingly different from the comically robust reading embodied in Anthony Sher's stage performance. This false devout is a loathsome creation, his cunning as bloodless as his white face make-up. His evil is beyond explanation, like something vampirical from German Expressionist cinema; and the closing shot of him lying powerless on the floor, staring into the camera, is deeply unsettling. The hapless householder Orgon (Périer) is persuaded to surrender his daughter – a stunning moment from Laptower as she screams soundlessly – and his property to the intruder, and only comes to his senses when his wife (Elisabeth Depardieu) exposes Tartuffe as a lecher. One either surrenders to the slow drip of Molière's mesmerism or one doesn't. BC

Tarzan

(1999, US, 88 min)
d Kevin Lima, Chris Buck. *p* Bonnie Arnold. *sc* Tab Murphy, Bob Tzudiker, Noni White. *ed* Gregory Perler. *ad* Daniel St Pierre. *songs* Phil Collins. *m* Mark Mancina. *cast* voices: Brian Blessed, Glenn Close, Minnie Driver, Tony Goldwyn, Nigel Hawthorne, Lance Henriksen, Rosie O'Donnell.

●Consolidating the computer-aided advances in 'deep focus' cel animation made in *Beauty and the Beast* and elsewhere, the directors of this animated Disney version of the Tarzan novels have produced a remarkably fluid, dynamic visual style, climaxing in the prehensile Tarzan's joyous flights through the jungle. Though the greater muscular definition of Tarzan has the effect of sexualising his image, the film otherwise makes little or no play with any erotic subtext, while stepping back also from postmodern wordplay and parody. Storywise, it's a far cry from Edgar Rice Burroughs. Tarzan's aristo background is ignored. Jane is thoroughly modern, arriving with personifications of colonial good and evil: her sympathetic naturalist father and the dastardly Clayton, who blackmails Tarzan into betraying his adopted family to save Jane. What makes the mind boggle is the application of PC to inter-species relationships. Gorilla Kala insists on saving the shipwrecked orphan against the wishes of her husband, and the early scenes of Tarzan growing up thus become an extended (and intriguingly absurd) examination of prejudice, difference and belonging. Bucking the trend, also, is the use of Phil Collins' songs as accompaniment rather than as sung musical set-pieces. No classic, but very enjoyable. WH

Tarzan and the Mermaids

(1948, US, 68 min, b/w)
d Robert Florey. *p* Sol Lesser. *sc* Carroll Young. *ph* Jack Draper, Gabriel Figueroa, Raul Martinez Solares. *ed* Merrill Pye, John Sheets. *ad* McClure Capps. *m* Dimitri Tiomkin. *cast* Johnny Weissmuller, Brenda Joyce, Linda Christian, George Zucco, Andrea Palmer, Edward Ashley.

●Tarzan's all puffy and gone to seed (it was Weissmuller's last appearance in the role), Africa looks weird (the movie was shot in Mexico) and the African tribe looks weirdest of all, what with George Zucco in his campy witch doctor outfit, Linda Christian – toast of Acapulco – as the jungle princess, and a bunch of tribesmen who might be extras from *Viva Zapata!* There's a strange-looking, virgin-demanding deity who must have frightened the kids' audience out of their wits, and a spatchcocked visual 'style' ranging from florid (Figueroa, presumably) to primitive. Despite much to-ing and fro-ing, there's no sense of time or distance, and the disjointed, dreamlike state which the film embodies is more usually achieved by the ingestion of not necessarily legal substances. As to the mermaids, but they stay below the surface, out of sight. BBa

Tarzan, the Ape Man

(1981, US, 112 min)
d John Derek. *p* Bo Derek. *sc* Tom Rowe, Gary Goddard. *ph* John Derek. *ed* James B Ling. *ad* Alan Roderick-Jones. *m* Perry Botkin. *cast* Bo Derek, Richard Harris, John Phillip Law, Miles O'Keeffe, Akushula Selaya, Steven Strong.

●Judging by the amount of time everybody spends swimming, the African jungle resembles Hornsey Baths filled with oversized pot plants. When not actually in the water, Bo Derek is having water poured over her, giving her mammary glands the Playboy Wet Look. Asked to act, the Wet Look invades her face and she whimpers, giggles, and sticks a finger in her mouth while reciting such blatant lies as 'I'm still a virgin'. Harris, as dad, takes the opposite approach and shouts all his lines at the top of his lungs. But O'Keeffe, as Tarzan, has the best part: he never says a word, unless you count 'Aaa-awaa-awaa'. His visual presence is striking enough: Bjorn Borg's head bolted on to Arnold Schwarzenegger's body. The plot, such as it is, climaxes when Bo is kidnapped by a bunch of sex-mad darkies, ruthlessly washed, and then painted white. A classic closing credits sequence finds Bo, Tarzan and an orang-utan – all officially still virgins – struggling to invent the Missionary Position. MB

Task Force (Rexue Zuiqiang)

(1997, HK, 100 min)
d Patrick Leung. *p* Raymond Chow Man-Wai. *sc* Chan Ping-Ka. *ph* Lee Ping-pan. *ed* Ka-fai Cheung. *cast* Leo Ku, Charlie Young, Eric Tsang, Karen Mok, Waise Lee, Orlando To, John Woo.

●Vaulting over the wreckage of a film industry in deep recession, Patrick Leung's witty policier does nothing very new but still registers as one of the best Hong Kong movies of its year. Virginal cop Rod Lin (Ku, cute) first meets hooker Fanny Chan (Young, terrific) during an operation to entrap illegal immigrants working in the sex trade. She becomes the bane of his life, alternately a tormentor and a flirt; but she's really in love with a jailed boyfriend who has promised to take her to Paris for the World Cup. Their non-affair (which comes with quizzical voice-overs in the *Chungking Express* vein) is interspersed with non-stop subplots, digressions and flashbacks, not to mention homages to various Chinese and Japanese action classics. But as Danny Wong's unusual piano score suggests, it's finally less a thriller than a study of emotional reckonings: how to cope with a dying parent, how to handle an uncommitted lover. John Woo and other directors put in cameo appearances. TR

Taste of Cherry, A (Ta'ame-Gilas)

(1997, Iran, 99 min)
d/p/sc Abbas Kiarostami. *ph* Homayoon Payvar. *ed* Abbas Kiarostami. *ad* Hassan Yekta Panah. *cast* Homayoon Irshadi, Abdol Hossain Bagheri, Afshin Khorshid Bakhtiari, Safar Ali Moradi.

●A man drives around villages and the desert hills offering a series of carefully selected men a lift and unusually well paid work; he's not looking for a pick-up but, as we discover after a while, someone to help in his planned suicide. Characteristically, Kiarostami's *Palme d'Or* winner is low on narrative drive, slowly but steadily revealing more and more information, visual and verbal, until we are totally caught up in his protagonist's psychological and ethical dilemma. (Suicide is forbidden to Muslims.) As ever, the subtle, deceptively simple *mise-en-scène* speaks volumes, notably a nightmare of noisy industrialism in the desert, and the remarkable penultimate scene, which goes even further in its minimalist ambiguity than the final shots of the last two movies of Kiarostami's trilogy. GA

Taste of Fear (aka Scream of Fear)

(1960, GB, 81 min, b/w)
d Seth Holt. *p/sc* Jimmy Sangster. *ph* Douglas Slocombe. *ed* James Needs, Eric Boyd-Perkins. *ad* Tom Goswell. *m* Clifton Parker. *cast* Susan Strasberg, Ann Todd, Ronald Lewis, Christopher Lee, Leonard Sachs.

●An above-par Hammer thriller, scripted by Jimmy Sangster and brazenly plagiarising Clouzot's *Les Diaboliques* as wheelchair-bound Strasberg arrives to visit her father on the Riviera, believes she sees his corpse (more than once), but is told that he's away on a trip. The plotting is very contrived indeed, but thanks partly to Douglas Slocombe's camerawork and to taut, shock-cut editing, Holt manages a *tour de force* of brooding, genuinely unsettling atmosphere. GA

Taste of Honey, A

(1961, GB, 100 min, b/w)
d/p Tony Richardson. *sc* Shelagh Delaney, Tony Richardson. *ph* Walter Lassally. *ed* Antony Gibbs. *ad* Ralph Brinton. *m* John Addison. *cast* Rita Tushingham, Dora Bryan, Robert Stephens, Murray Melvin, Paul Danquah.

●A perfect example of how the 'New British Cinema' of the late '50s and early '60s has dated and become almost unwatchable. Richardson's version of Shelagh Delaney's play about a Salford girl getting pregnant after leaving home highlights the style's many faults: kitchen sink realism, when pursued as an end in itself, can be as tedious and unrevealing as an uninspired episode of *Coronation Street*. It's all very well dwelling on grimy streets, factory chimneys, sluttish individuals, and so on, but with no real attempt to place characters in an explicit social or political context, the story becomes reduced to a drab, voyeuristic celebration of ordinariness and poverty. There's no anger, no joy, and ultimately no insight in this film; its shallow reliance on clichés reeks of complacency. GA

Taste of the Black Earth, The (Sól Ziemi Czarnej)

(1969, Pol, 103 min)
d/sc Kazimierz Kutz. *ph* Wieslaw Zdort. *ed* Irina Chorynska. *ad* Boleslaw Kamykowski. *m* Wojciech Kilar. *cast* Olgierd Lukaszewicz, Jerzy Binczycki, Jerzy Cnota, Wieslaw Dymny, Daniel Olbrychski.

●A film about the 1920 Silesian uprising, when bands of insurgents rebelled against the German occupation troops. The story is told through the eyes of a 16-year-old boy, youngest of a family of seven sons who join the uprising; and in approach the film owes more to Hollywood than to a Communist propaganda tradition, though without the simplification of issues or the false heroics of the Western attitude to immediate history. Visually it's a small masterpiece, stunningly shot in the beautiful browns and greens of the 'land' for which the men are fighting.

Taste the Blood of Dracula

(1969, GB, 95 min)
d Peter Sasdy. *p* Aida Young. *sc* Anthony Hinds. *ph* Arthur Grant. *ed* Chris Barnes. *ad* Scott Macgregor. *m* James Bernard. *cast* Christopher Lee, Geoffrey Keen, Gwen Watford, Linda Hayden, Peter Sallis, Ralph Bates, John Carson, Anthony Corlan, Isla Blair, Roy Kinnear.

●Depraved Lord Courtley (Bates) involves three other rich Victorian thrill-seekers in the resurrection of the blood-sucking Count (Lee), by means of an elaborate ritual performed in a derelict church. Imaginatively realised and shot with flamboyant style, the ritual ends with Courtley's death and the flight of the three others, setting the scene for a lurid tale in which Dracula wreaks revenge on the fugitives by seducing and corrupting their daughters. Though the film never quite lives up to its brilliantly staged opening scenes, its variation on the idea of the decadent, aristocratic Dracula's threat to the sanctity of the Victorian middle class family highlights an intriguing aspect of Hammer's vampire mythology. NF

Tatie Danielle

(1990, Fr, 112 min)
d Etienne Chatiliez. *p* Charles Gassot. *sc* Florence Quentin. *ph* Philippe Welt. *ed* Catherine Renault. *pd* Geoffroy Larcher. *m* Gabriel Yared. *cast* Tsilla Chelton, Catherine Jacob, Isabelle Nanty, Neige Dolsky, Eric Prat, Laurence Février.

● After *Life Is a Long Quiet River*, Chatiliez' second film is again a black comedy, a scabrous assault on middle class mores. Tatie Danielle (Chelton) is an ailing, respectable widow – or so she appears. As her relatives the Billards soon discover, behind her feeble demeanour lurks an indomitable will and a malicious mind. If only for sheer bloody-mindedness, the movie earns a few chuckles in the beginning, but once Tatie's true nature is established, it goes nowhere fast. Chatiliez seems to share Tatie's contempt for this stereotyped middle class family; but on the evidence presented, it is hard not to conclude that the bourgeoisie are in pretty good shape, their restraint and kindness lasting well beyond the call of duty. After this satiric backfire, there's the inevitable back-down as the old lady meets her match in the shape of a no-shit young house-sitter (Nanty). For an encore, Chatiliez stages an ending that is at once anticlimactic, predictable and illogical: an apt conclusion for a clumsy, tiresome, unendearing film. TCh

Tattoo

(1980, US, 103 min)
d Bob Brooks. *p* Joseph E Levine, Richard P Levine. *sc* Joyce Bunuel. *ph* Arthur J Ornitz. *ed* Thom Noble. *pd* Stuart Wurtzel. *m* Barry DeVorzon. *cast* Bruce Dern, Maud Adams, Leonard Frey, Rikke Borge, John Getz, Peter Iachangelo.

●Made by a British-based commercials and TV director, working from a script by Buñuel's daughter-in-law, this emerges as a reworking of John Fowles' *The Collector*. Only the kinks have been changed to excite the prurient. Loner tattooist (played by Hollywood's favourite nutter, Dern) stalks, abducts, and tattoos his beautiful model (Adams) before he fucks her. Despite vague attempts to give tattoos global significance, the result is a peepshow of psychopathology, devoid of insight or even context. See the mad artist kidnap the hysterical girl! See him make her masturbate while he watches through a hole in the door! Roll over Sigmund Freud and tell Bill Reich the bad news. MB

Tattooed Tears

(1978, US, 85 min)
d/p/ph/ed Nick Broomfield, Joan Churchill.

●Broomfield and Churchill's 'sequel' to their controversial *Juvenile Liaison* raises urgent structural and institutional problems for the investigative form. The workings of a purportedly liberal Youth Training School for delinquents in California are examined, and condemned through an intensely dramatic concentration on four of its victims, ostensibly there for rehabilitation, but actually undergoing repetitive and vindictive punishment. In the process, the film raises the spectre of individual suffering exploited: one inmate dramatising his resistance specifically for the camera receives humiliating treatment which the camera duly observes but cannot forestall. Though the film's purpose may be agitational in the immediate US context, the result as received here tends, unfortunately, to the disturbingly voyeuristic. PT

Taurus

(2000, Rus, 90 min)
d Alexander Sokurov. *p* Victor Sergeyev. *sc* Yuri Arabov. *ph* Alexander Sokurov. *ed* Leda Semyonova. *pd* Natalia Kochergina. *m* Andrei Sigle. *cast* Leonid Mozgovoi, Maria Kuznetsova, Sergei Razhuk, Natalia Nikulenko, Lev Yeliseyev, Nikolai Ustinov.

●Even more hermetic and impenetrable (albeit less offensive) than *Moloch*, the second film in Sokurov's tetralogy about influential 20th century men finds Lenin dying in a confiscated dacha, surrounded by his wife and sister, officials, servants, doctors and nurses, and visited at one point by Stalin. Of course, it's a meditation on power – its tendency to corrupt and destroy, its inevitable evanescence in terms of the individual – but it sheds little or no light on the topic, since Sokurov can't be bothered to contextualise for those less well versed than himself in the details of his subject's last few hours. Dramatically, it tends towards the inert, while the director's own camerawork – all long, woozy takes and pea-green tints – is merely an irritating distraction. GA

Tausend Augen des Dr Mabuse, Die

see 1000 Eyes of Dr Mabuse, The

Tavaszi Zápor (Marie – a Hungarian Legend/Marie, légende hongroise/Spring Shower)

(1932, Hun/Fr, 68 min, b/w)
d Paul Fejos [Pál Fejös]. *sc* Fülöp Ilona. *ph* Eiben Istvan, J Peverell Marley. *ad* Keleti Marton. *m* Angyal Laszlo, Vincent Scotto. *cast* Annabella, István Gyergyai, Ilona Dajbukát, Karola Zala, Germaine Aussey.

●The 'legend' itself is sanctimonious drivel: Marie (Annabella), dismissed from her job as a maid for getting pregnant, wanders lonely and rejected, weeping for her namesake the Blessed Virgin, until she's taken in by the fallen women of a brothel; her soul fetches up in a heavenly replica of the kitchen where she started out, safeguarding the virtue of her illegitimate daughter back on earth. Censorship of the time gave her an 'invisible' pregnancy, and left the depiction of the brothel and its dykey madame bafflingly opaque. The large redeeming features are Fejös' visual style, and László Angyal's more or less continuous score. TR

Tawny Pipit

(1944, GB, 85 min)
d Bernard Miles, Charles Saunders. *p* Bernard Miles. *sc* Bernard Miles, Charles Saunders. *ph* Eric Cross. *ed* Douglas Myers. *ad* Alex Vetchinsky. *m* Noel Mewton-Wood. *cast* Bernard Miles, Rosamund John, Niall MacGinnis, Jean Gillie, George Carney, Christopher Steele, Joan Sterndale Bennett, Katie Johnson.

●English whimsy at its mildest follows the fuss and consternation when convalescent airman MacGinnis and his nurse John discover a pair of tawny pipits nesting in the meadow near their Cotswold village. It's a rare event, since the birds have only once been sighted in England before, so the whole local community ends up guarding the spot day and night to ward off prospective egg-snatchers. Scripted by the directors and printed in sepia. TJ

Taxandria

(1994, Fr/Bel/Ger, 80 min)
d Raoul Servais. *sc* Alain Robbe-Grillet, Frank Daniel, Raoul Servais. *ph* Walther van den Ende, Gilberto Azevedo. *ed* Chantal Hymans. *pd* Yvan Buyere, Hubert Pouillé (live action), François Schuiten (animation). *m* Kim Bullard. *cast* Armin Mueller-Stahl, Daniel Emilfork, Andrew Sachs.

●This technically innovative blending of actors with, for much of the movie, animated settings is a surreal, allegorical fantasy about a young prince who, with the help of a lighthouse-keeper, witnesses a strange world where progress, clocks, modern machinery and sexual equality have been banned. Alain Robbe-Grillet had a hand in the screenplay, but it's still something of a dog's dinner, initially intriguing but delivering a tale far too unfocused to be anything more than a visual curiosity. GA

Taxi

(1996, Sp, 113 min)
d Carlos Saura. *p* Concha Diaz, Javier Castro. *sc* Santiago Tabernero. *ph* Vittorio Storaro. *ed* Julia Juaniz. *pd* Juan Botella. *m* Manu Chao. *cast* Ingrid Rubio, Carlos Fuentes, Agata Lys, Angel de Andres Lopez, Eusebio Lazaro.

●Saura's first film scripted by another hand is a crude, uneven exposé of vigilante taxi drivers who spend their nights ridding Madrid of undesirables – blacks, gays and drug addicts. While it concentrates on the middle-aged cabbies' murderous conspiracy, the flesh-and-blood performances by Lys and Lopez fuse with Vittorio Storraro's crisp, almost futuristic cinematography, drawing us into their nocturnal world. However, once Santiago Tabernero's script shifts to the drippy teen romance between idealistic teenager Paz (Rubio) and her reluctantly racist/homophobic boyfriend Dani, matters go fuzzy at the edges. Only the instinctive power of 19-year-old newcomer Ingrid Rubio relieves the tedium of watching liberal sentiments fall into place. NF

Taxi

(1998, Fr, 90 min)
d Gérard Pirès. *p* Michèle Pétin, Laurent Pétin. *sc* Luc Besson. *ph* Jean-Pierre Sauvaire. *ed* Véronique Lange. *ad* Jean-Jacques Gernolle. *m* IAM. *cast* Samy Nacéri, Frédéric Diefenthal, Marion Cotillard, Emma Sjöberg, Manuela Gourary, Bernard Farcy.
●Written and produced by Luc Besson, this car chase caper would like to think of itself as a race-tuned Formula One machine. In fact, it's more like a customised Ford Mondeo with a go-faster stripe and alloy wheels. The B movie plot, flimsy characters and cursory dialogue straddle the white line between computer games and cartoons, and have precious little relationship to reality. The emphasis throughout is on the skilful stunts, the best of which are saved for the final, '70s-style car chase through the streets of Marseilles. Caught red-handed doing 120 mph in a 30 mph limit, taxi driver Daniel (Nacéri) reluctantly teams up with bungling cop Emilien (Diefenthal). The ill-matched buddies try to capture a gang of international bank robbers who always make their getaway in a distinctive red Mercedes. The female characters, meanwhile, just hang around being decorative: sexy police inspector Pétra (Sjöberg) is the object of Emilien's unrequited love; Daniel's girlfriend Lilly (Cotillard) suffers from unrequited lust; and Emilien's mother Camille (Gourary) literally makes the sandwiches. NF

Taxi 2

(2000, Fr, 82 min)
d Gérard Krawczyk. *p* Luc Besson, Michèle Pétin, Laurent Pétin. *sc* Luc Besson. *ph* Gérard Sterin. *ed* Thierry Hoss. *ad* Jean-Jacques Gernolle. *m* Al Khemya. *cast* Samy Nacéri, Frédéric Diefenthal, Marion Cotillard, Emma Sjöberg, Bernard Farcy, Jean-Christophe Bouvet, Frédérique Tirmont, Marc Faure.
●This sequel to the French car chase caper is a little more streamlined, the jerky comic-book pacing of the original replaced by a smoother narrative ride. That said, scriptwriter Besson and director Krawczyk have tweaked rather than redesigned the plot engine, so it's essentially just the same model with a new paint job. Instead of German car thieves, we get a yakuza gang attempting to kidnap the Japanese Secretary of State for Defence during a visit to Marseilles. Their action plays havoc with Chief Insp Gilbert's 'Operation Ninja', intended to land a lucrative longterm contract for guarding the visiting dignitary. But the custom made 'stealth' limo proves no match for the yakuza, leaving taxi driver Daniel (Nacéri) and bumbling cop Emilien (Diefenthal) to clear up the mess again. As before the car chases are the film's raison d'être. If the non-PC racial slurs are at least even handed, the women fair no better than last time. At 82 minutes, it's too short to get really boring, but it doesn't help to know that a cameraman was killed while filming one of the stunts. NF

Taxi!

(1931, US, 68 min, b/w)
d Roy Del Ruth. *sc* Kubec Glasmon, John Bright. *ph* James Van Trees. *ed* James Gibbon. *ad* Esdras Hartley. *cast* James Cagney, Loretta Young, David Landau, Guy Kibbee, George E Stone, Leila Bennett, Matt McHugh.
●Cagney gets to bawl a lot, talk to a customer in Yiddish and even enter a dance competition in this busy little entertainment set in New York's cab community. He's an independent taxi company boss who defends his drivers against the tactics of organised syndicate head honcho Landau, who wants all the best spots for his men. The action spirals into violence and revenge, but it's much less of a hard-hitting exposé than the general run of '30s Warners crime pictures, and pleasingly compact with it. TJ

Taxi Blues

(1990, USSR/Fr, 110 min)
d Pavel Lounguine. *p* Marin Karmitz. *sc* Pavel Lounguine. *ph* Denis Evstigneev. *ed* Elisabeth Guido. *pd* Valery Yourkevich. *m* Vladimir Chekessine. *cast* Piotr Mamonov, Piotr Zaitchenko, Vladimir Kachpour.
●There's something basically phony about Lounguine's flashy debut feature, which is forever congratulating itself on being so 'daring' in showing the wrong side of Moscow's tracks. It centres on an 'odd couple' relationship between a stolid, seen-it-all cab driver (Zaitchenko) and a wayward, alcoholic Jewish jazz musician (Mamonov), thrown together by one's demand that the other meet his debts (after the musician skips out on paying his cab fare). The director apparently sees this as a paradigm of worker-intellectual relations, but he's too interested in exposing scuzzy life-styles, and wallowing in vodka, crime and sex, to get too tied up in politics. Trouble is, he has no idea at all how to end it. Skip the last 15 minutes, and you might come out with a wry smile. TR

Taxi Driver 100 (100)

(1976, US, 114 min)
d Martin Scorsese. *p* Michael Phillips, Julia Phillips. *sc* Paul Schrader. *ph* Michael Chapman. *ed* Marcia Lucas, Tom Rolf, Melvin Shapiro. *ad* Charles Rosen. *m* Bernard Herrmann. *cast* Robert De Niro, Cybill Shepherd, Jodie Foster, Harvey Keitel, Peter Boyle, Leonard Harris, Martin Scorsese, Steven Prince, Diahnne Abbot, Albert Brooks.
● *Taxi Driver* makes you realise just how many directors, from Schlesinger to Friedkin and Winner, have piddled around on the surface of New York in their films. Utilising, especially, Bernard Herrmann's most menacing score since *Psycho*, Scorsese has set about recreating the landscape of the city in a way that constitutes a truly original and terrifying Gothic canvas. But, much more than that: *Taxi Driver* is also, thanks partly to De Niro's extreme implosive performance, the first film since *Alphaville* to set about a really intelligent appraisal of the fundamental ingredients of contemporary insanity. Its final upsurge of violence doesn't seem to be cathartic in the now predictable fashion of the 'new' American movie, but lavatorial: the nauseating effluence of the giant flesh emporium that the film has so single-mindedly depicted. DP

Taxi Mauve, Le

see Purple Taxi, The

Taxing Woman, A (Marusa no Onna)

(1987, Jap, 127 min)
d Juzo Itami. *p* Yashushi Tamaoki, Seigo Hosogoe. *sc* Juzo Itami. *ph* Yonezo Maeda. *ed* Akira Suzuki. *ad* Shuji Nakamura. *m* Toshiyuki Honda. *cast* Nobuko Miyamoto, Tsutomu Yamazaki, Masahiko Tsugawa, Yasuo Daichi, Eitaro Ozawa.
●In this, his third helter-skelter satire on modern Japanese mores, Itami turns his witty attention to the subject of Money, with tighter construction and deeper characterisation making it his most entertaining yet. Miyamoto plays divorcée Ryoko, an Inspector for the Japanese National Tax Agency whose considerable energies are channelled into the collaring of tax evaders. Her tenacious, seemingly heartless exposure of the scams, perks and false expenses of small-time gambling arcade proprietors, corner-shop owners and the like, trades beautifully on the guilty pleasures to be had in seeing the other guy get his deserts. But success gives her the chance to go for the big fish: Rachmanesque hoodlum and 'entertainment' hotel boss Gondo (Yamazaki). As the movie gears up for the final bust, Itami exploits and inverts every known cliché of the detective thriller with a breathless style, and a sexual excitement in criminal minutiae reminiscent of Bresson's *Pickpocket*. WH

Taxi zum Klo

(1980, WGer, 94 min)
d Frank Ripploh. *p* Laurens Straub, Frank Ripploh. *sc* Frank Ripploh. *ph* Horst Schier. *ed* Marina Runne, Matthias von Gunten. *m* Hans Wittstatt. *cast* Frank Ripploh, Bernd Broaderup, Orpha Termin, Peter Fahrni, Dieter Gîdde.
●Ill-matched gay lovers: Bernd prefers to stay at home cooking supper and scrubbing pans, while Frank (engagingly played by director Ripploh) scours Berlin's Klos (public lavatories) and leather-bars for cheap thrills and one-night stands. With an impressive sureness of touch, the schoolteacher/cruiser double life-style is shown in explicit though never exploitative detail, as undoubtedly 'different' yet in no way perverse (contrast the sexpol prudery of *Nighthawks* or *Looking for Mr Goodbar*). Shot on a very thin shoestring (ú25,000; no State grant) and, like many good – and not so good – first films, openly autobiographical, it succeeds on the strength of a surprising irony and wit, and a tacky exuberance (the title says it all) that can't fail to disarm, entertain, and maybe even dispel a few myths along the way. SJo

Tchao Pantin

(1983, Fr, 93 min)
d Claude Berri. *p* Pierre Grunstein. *sc* Claude Berri, Alain Page. *ph* Bruno Nuytten. *ed* Hervé de Luze. *ad* Alexandre Trauner. *m* Charlélie Couture. *cast* Coluche, Richard Anconina, Agnès Soral, Philippe Léotard, Mahmoud Zemmouri.
●Devastated by the drugs death of his son, ex-cop Coluche is a boozy recluse in a grisly Paris suburb, working the night shift at a petrol station. Grudgingly and grumpily he begins to thaw out via the friendship of hang-dog drugs courier Anconina. When the latter is murdered by his employers, Coluche grabs his gun and goes looking for his own death as much as for revenge. Anconina's girlfriend (Soral) may change the picture; or not. This is Berri's stab at neo-*noir*, but his optimistic, rather sentimental heart isn't really in it. Still, Coluche – all tattoos, greasy sideburns and alcoholic slow motion – is effective in the 'less is more' mode, and Nuytten's rain-and-neon cityscapes have the right ambience. Alain Page wrote the source novel. BBa

T. Dan Smith

(1987, GB, 86 min)
d/p/sc Amber Films. *m* Ray Stubbs. *cast* T Dan Smith, Jack Johnston, Ken Sketheway, Dennis Skinner, George Vickers.
●Resembling Evelyn Waugh facially and perhaps Huey 'Kingfish' Long historically, T Dan Smith proves a mesmerising speaker in this documentary by the Amber Films collective. Was he the fall-guy for the Establishment in the Poulson Affair, imprisoned to save Home Secretary Reginald Maudling's neck, or was he a Trot idealist who dreamed of transforming Newcastle into the Milan of the North, infiltrated the system, but surrendered his soul in the process? That face doesn't give much clue, and the linking investigatory journalists confess themselves no wiser by the end. A compilation of newsreel, interview and dramatic reconstruction, the film is sometimes clumsy, but the facts are strong enough to tether the viewer. Unfair immunity at the top seems to be the commercial. BC

Tea and Sympathy

(1956, US, 122 min)
d Vincente Minnelli. *p* Pandro S Berman. *sc* Robert Anderson. *ph* John Alton. *ed* Ferris Webster. *ad* William A Horning, Edward C Carfagno. *m* Adolph Deutsch. *cast* Deborah Kerr, John Kerr, Leif Erickson, Edward Andrews, Darryl Hickman, Dean Jones, Norma Crane.
●Filming *The Servant* with Harold Pinter, Losey could treat the homosexual relationship between master and manservant with both visual élan and verbal acuity. Minnelli was less lucky. Robert Anderson's sensitive if fancifully written play, about a housemaster's wife coaxing a pupil out of latent tendencies, was weakened to such a degree through the combined forces of censorship and CinemaScope that the tendencies threatened to disappear completely. Which can hardly be said for the students' garish shirts and pullovers, the phony exterior sets, or the gleaming '50s automobiles – all on constant parade. Yet the film's details – indeed, its very timidity – still ensure fascinating viewing. GB

Teacher, The (El Brigadista)

(1977, Cuba, 119 min)
d Octavio Cortazar. *p* Sergio San Pedro. *sc* Luis Rogelio Nogueras, Octavio Cortazar. *ph* Pablo Martinez. *ed* Roberto Bravo, Rolando Pérez. *ad* Carlos Arditti. *m* Sergio Vittier. *cast* Salvador Wood, Patricio Wood, René de la Cruz, Luis Alberto Ramirez, Mario Balmaseda, Luis Rielo, Elien Amat.
●Replace rhinos with 'gators and you have *Hatari!*'s hunting set-pieces inserted into an otherwise worthy account of the struggle to eradicate widespread illiteracy in early '60s Cuba. The Hawks reference can be taken further, since this accomplished tale of a young city student newly arrived to teach peasants in an impoverished swamp region concerns professionalism, self-respect, integration into the community and other motifs beloved by Hawksians. GA

Teachers

(1984, US, 106 min)
d Arthur Hiller. *p* Aaron Russo. *sc* Wr McKinney. *ph* David M Walsh. *ed* Don Zimmerman. *pd* Richard MacDonald. *m* Sandy Gibson. *cast* Nick Nolte, JoBeth Williams, Judd Hirsch, Ralph Macchio, Allen Garfield, Lee Grant, Richard Mulligan, Royal Dano, William Schallert, Art Metrano, Laura Dern, Zohra Lampert.
●This is about wastage in the field of education. But the film manages to waste: Nolte, playing a disillusioned teacher with all the fire of a tranquillised tiger; fine character actors like Royal Dano and Allen Garfield; and, finally, a potentially dynamic subject. Hiller's sledgehammer direction turns the problems common in education into an endless parade of clichés, feebly propped up by wacky humour, inarticulacy, ham and corn. Avoid. GA

Teahouse of the August Moon, The

(1956, US, 123 min)
d Daniel Mann. *p* Jack Cummings. *sc* John Patrick. *ph* John Alton. *ed* Harold F Kress. *ad* William A Horning, Eddie Imazu. *m* Saul Chaplin. *cast* Marlon Brando, Glenn Ford, Eddie Albert, Machiko Kyo, Paul Ford, Henry Morgan.
●A likeable, if overlong and distinctly verbose adaptation of John Patrick's Broadway play, which wrings some mild amusement out of a clash between cultural stereotypes (American efficiency gives way to Oriental lethargy as the occupying force on Okinawa is beguiled into building a teahouse rather than a schoolhouse). The very stuff that sitcoms are made of, it's kept alive by genial contributions from Glenn Ford, Eddie Albert, and especially Paul Ford as the mulishly obtuse Colonel (who later resurfaced as a fixture in TV's *Sergeant Bilko* series). As all too often in Brando movies, his performance as the crafty Okinawan interpreter is streets ahead of the dialogue and direction he gets. TM

Tears of the Black Tiger (Fa Talai Jone)

(2000, Thai, 110 min)
d Wisit Sasanatieng. *p* Nonzee Nimibutr, Bunbhot Ngamkhum. *sc* Wisit Sasanatieng. *ph* Nattawut Kittikhun. *ed* Dusanee Puinongpho. *pd* Ek Iemchuen. *m* Amornbhong Methakunavudh. *cast* Chartchai Ngamsan, Stella Malucchi, Supakorn Kitsuwon, Arawat Ruangvuth, Sombati Medhanee.
●The screenwriter of *Dang Bireley's* and *Nang Nak* turns director to make a gleefully excessive homage to Thai movies of the '60s, framed as a Thai Western. Most of the references are generic enough to work for non-Thai viewers, and some of the gags (an action replay in slow-mo of a ricocheting bullet) are killers. Innocent country boy Dum and city girl Rumpoey meet as children and fall in love as students, but he turns bandit to avenge his murdered father while she finds herself forced to marry the uptight Captain Kumjorn, who pledges to rid Supanburi of bandits. Earnest performances, bold artifice and ripe melodrama maintain a state of continuous combustion. With its over-saturated, clashing colours (it was retouched shot by shot in post-production) Wisit's amazing film goes so far beyond kitsch that it enters Powell and Pressburger territory. The 'export version' has been cut by some 13 minutes, not by the director. TR

Tea with Mussolini (Te con Il Duce)

(1998, It/GB, 116 min)
d Franco Zeffirelli. *p* Riccardo Tozzi, Giovannella Zannoni, Clive Parsons. *sc* John Mortimer, Franco Zeffirelli. *ph* David Watkin. *ed* Tariq Anwar. *ad* Carlo Centolavignia, Gioria Fiorella Mariani. *m* Alessio Vlad, Stefano Arnaldi. *cast* Cher, Judy Dench, Joan Plowright, Maggie Smith, Lily Tomlin, Charlie Lucas, Baird Wallace, Massimo Ghini, Michael Williams.
●Franco Zeffirelli's autobiographical WWII Tuscan drama is edged with (uncharacteristic) irony and artistic reserve, turning what is essentially an old-fashioned, faintly twee exercise in nostalgia into an amusing historical entertainment. The master of Chianti-shire manners, John Mortimer has co-scripted, and it feels as much his film as Zeffirelli's. Mortimer details the pretensions, rivalries and snobberies of the so-called Florentine *scorpione* among whom the film's young hero, the bastard Luca, is fostered; and it's this colony of dotty, politically inert, artistically bent British ex-pats, either taking tea in the Uffizi or talking art in Doney's café, and variously oblivious, contemptuous or supportive of the fascists, which holds centre stage. They're played with ease by a roll call of theatrical dames. The rest is a gently teasing tribute to wartime British pluck (read: muddling through) and American 'can-do', lit like a lost summer by David Watkin. WH

Teckman Mystery, The

(1954, GB, 90 min, b/w)
d Wendy Toye. *p* Josef Somlo. *sc* Francis Durbridge, James Matthews. *ph* Jack Hildyard. *ed* Bert Rule. *ad* William Kellner. *m* Clifton Parker. *cast* Margaret Leighton, John Justin, Michael Medwin, Roland Culver, George Colouris, Raymond Huntley.
●Commissioned to write the biography of a dead test pilot, John Justin walks into more than a tight deadline. He's knocked unconscious, his flat's turned upside down and he's offered lots of dosh by a very shady character. A mindlessly diverting British thriller, neatly adapted from a Francis Durbridge TV serial, but essentially unremarkable. TJ

Teenage Caveman

(1958, US, 66 min, b/w)
d/p Roger Corman. *sc* R Wight Campbell. *ph* Floyd Crosby. *ed* Irene Morra. *m* Albert Glasser. *cast* Robert Vaughn, Leslie Bradley, Darrah Marshall, Frank De Kova.
●You'll chuckle the first time you see fresh-faced Vaughn in his off-the-shoulder loincloth, but Corman's no-budget prehistoric epic is endearing in the way it refuses to cheapen an admittedly fairly tacky sub-genre. In fact, as the youthful protagonist ignores the warnings of his tribe and crosses the river to face the much-feared monster that lives on the other side, the picture gathers imaginative momentum and conjures up at least one satisfying plot reversal. No wonder the star called it 'one of the best-worst films of all time'. TJ

Teenage Hooker Became Killing Machine in Daehakroh (Daehakno-yeseo maechoon-hadaka tomaksalhae danghan yeogosaeng ajik Daehakno-ye Issda)

(2000, SKor, 60 min)
d Nam Gee-Woong. *p* Woon Ki-Jin. *sc/ph* Nam Gee-Woong. *ed* Lee Chang-Man, Nam Gee-Woong. *m* Nam Gee-Woong. *cast* Lee So-Yun, Kim Dae-Tong, Bae Soo-Baek, Kim Ho-Kyum, Yank Hyuk-Joon, Yoo Joon-Za.
●Salacious, sarcastic and totally swinging, this gleefully depraved acid exploitation musical makes whoopee with a bunch of revenge thriller clichés and a risible attitude to human life. The plot's all there in the title – just 60 minutes long, it's streamlined and single-minded – but that doesn't convey the leering line-up of febrile degenerates who populate its urban pigsty world: the rampant high-school whore ('Honey? Or Dad?'), her club-fisted pick-ups, the ghoulish lipsticked teacher whose grandmother's peace she disturbs, the trio of giggling saw murderers he duly sets on her. Shot through neon flared, fish eye lenses and set to a preposterous medley of rock, opera, trip-hop and Spanish guitar, it's deliriously rabid ham. You can but snigger. NB

Teenage Kicks – The Undertones

(2001, GB, 72 min)
d Tom Collins. *p* Vinny Cunningham. *ph* Mark McCauley, Vinny Cunningham. *ed* David Fox. *with* The Undertones, John Peel, Seymour Stein.
●Whether or not you like John Peel's favourite post-punk Derry group The Undertones is a matter of personal taste. But there's no denying the instant accessibility of their most popular single, 'Teenage Kicks'; or the appeal of lead singer Feargal Sharkey's distinctively warbly voice. The rest of their material, though, is pretty turgid. This overlong documentary covers those early years when Peel first discovered them, their acrimonious split and unwise reformation, without Sharkey, who followed his solo career with a stint as a record company executive. Only their most devoted fans will be braving the cold to sit this one out. DA

Teenage Mutant Ninja Turtles

(1990, US, 93 min)
d Steve Barron. *p* Kim Dawson, Simon Fields, David Chan. *sc* Todd W Langen, Bobby Herbeck. *ph* John Fenner. *ed* William Gordean, Sally Menke, James Symons. *pd* Roy Forge Smith. *m* John Du Prez. *cast* Judith Hoag, Elias Koteas, Josh Pais, Michelan Sisti, Leif Tilden, David Forman.
●This live action feature pits the crime-fighting, man-sized turtles against Shredder, their arch enemy, who is recruiting hordes of teens to his evil ways. Reporter April O'Neil (Hoag) has been investigating a sudden increase in New York crime, and becomes embroiled in their mission after the pizza freaks save her from a mugging. Jim Henson's Creature Shop has created splendid animatronic characters (including a four-foot talking rat), though extra distinguishing marks between the turtles would be appreciated. Between the dubbed dialogue and the dark visuals, the cumulative effect is curiously dislocating. The big plus for fans, of course, is the boisterous interplay between the four heroes and some engaging slapstick humour; both redeem more functional elements like the love-hate relationship between April and martial arts enthusiast Casey (Koteas). CM

Teenage Mutant Ninja Turtles II: The Secret of the Ooze

(1991, US, 87 min)
d Michael Pressman. *p* David Chan, Kim Dawson, Thomas K Gray. *sc* Todd W Langen. *ph* Shelly Johnson. *ed* John Wright, Steve Mirkovich. *pd* Roy Forge Smith. *m* John Du Prez. *cast* Paige Turco, David Warner, Michelan Sisti, Leif Tilden, Ernie Reyes Jr, Kenn Troum, Mark Caso, Kevin Clash.
●The first 'Turtles' film aroused a ridiculous controversy over how, because they ate pizza and grew big and strong from radioactive ooze, the Turtles were not healthy role-models. Perhaps in response, this sequel's 'plot' centres on saving the city from that self-same ooze. The original fell between two age groups: the late teens and gonzo students at whom the 1984 comic book was aimed, and the tiny tots who enjoyed the subsequent TV cartoons. The sequel drags the target audience back towards the latter, with toned-down violence, a terrifically funny cameo from two retarded mutant Muppets, and a terrifically crass cameo from the similarly retarded Vanilla Ice. It does, however, retain the essential elements that first turned the world Turtle – the affectionate squabbling between the four, the pantomime villains, the cracking one-liners – and the bigger budget is a blessing. DW

Teenage Mutant Ninja Turtles III

(1992, US, 96 min)
d Stuart Gillard. *p* Tom Gray, David Chan, Kim Dawson. *sc* Stuart Gillard. *ph* David Gurfinkel. *ed* William Gordean, James R

Symons. *pd* Roy Forge Smith. *m* John Du Prez. *cast* Elias Koteas, Paige Turco, Stuart Wilson, Sab Shimono, Vivian Wu, Mark Caso.
● The first *Teenage Mutant Ninja Turtles* was, for all its faults, a minor miracle. Here, for small children, were heroes who were streetwise, anti-authority, and loved to fight. It couldn't last. In their third film, which is shorn of nearly all the elements which made the Ninjas popular, one turtle pontificates: 'Fighting's for grown-ups, and only if they've got no other choice.' One of the most enjoyable things about the Turtles was their interaction with a modern city. Here, however, writer/director Gillard misguidedly sends them back to medieval Japan. The wisecracks have been cut back, and where once the Ninjas' dude-speak was original (influencing, for example, *Wayne's World*) it's now merely imitative. DW

Teen Agent

(1991, US, 88 min)
d William Dear. *p* Craig Zadan, Neil Meron. *sc* Darren Star. *ph* Doug Milsome. *pd* Guy J Comtois. *m* David Foster. *cast* Richard Grieco, Linda Hunt, Roger Rees, Robin Bartlett, Gabrielle Anwar, Geraldine James, Michael Siberry, Carole Davis, Roger Daltrey.
● This marriage made in TV heaven boasts a script by *Beverly Hills 90210* writer Darren Star, while the nice teeth and hair are modelled by *21 Jump Street* star Grieco, playing Michael Corben, a high school dunce who must get a pass grade in French in order to graduate. While travelling to Paris with his teacher and classmates, he is mistaken for a secret agent and briefed by British Intelligence. Off he zooms in his specially-equipped sportscar, ready to rid the world of whip-wielding Ilsa Grunt (Hunt) and maniacal Augustus Steranko (Rees). Aside from Michael's curious penchant for dark eyeliner, it's hard to find anything of interest in this mediocre offering. Even the hi-tech gadgetry is boring. CM

Teenage Psycho Meets Bloody Mary

see Incredibly Strange Creatures Who Stopped Living and Became Mixed-Up Zombies, The

Teenagers from Outer Space (aka The Gargon Terror)

(1959, US, 87 min, b/w)
d/p/sc/ed/m Tom Graeff. *cast* David Love, Dawn Anderson, Harvey B Dunn, Bryan Grant, Tom Lockyear.
● An epic attempting to cash in on the teenpic boom with its tale of two alien teens sent to Earth. One is 'good', and falls in love with a local high school honey; one is 'bad', and rampages with a ray gun. A major period feature is the theme of teen martyrdom: the 'good' alien commits suicide in a bid to save Earth from an army of spaceships (never seen on the screen) and the giant lobster (watch for the hand holding what you can see of it) which has accompanied them. CR

Teen Kanya (Two Daughters)

(1961, Ind, 171 [114] min, b/w)
d/p/sc Satyajit Ray. *ph* Soumendu Roy. *ed* Dulal Dutta. *ad* Bansi Chandragupta. *m* Satyajit Ray. *cast* Soumitra Chatterjee, Aparna Das Gupta, Anil Chatterjee, Chandana Banerjee, Kanika Mazumdar.
● The title should translate as *Three Daughters*, since the film originally comprised a trio of Tagore stories, all touching on the problems of emancipation through women of contrasting classes. In the export version, one episode was cut for reasons of length: a ghost story about a woman obsessed by her jewellery, this is comparatively weak (though extremely striking visually). But the other two are Ray at his best, particularly the tale of a young university graduate who rejects the bride his mother has selected for him, but offers to marry the village tomboy (who has caught his eye but piqued his pride by her mockery of his pretensions). A marriage is duly arranged, despite the tomboy's furious protests, and what follows is a variation on *The Taming of the Shrew*, wonderfully funny and tender, and played to perfection by Soumitra Chatterjee and Aparna Das Gupta. But a bitterly ironic undertone lingers despite the happy end (love prevails): too emancipated to agree to a marriage with a girl he does not love, the hero never for a moment realises that he is denying the same privilege to the girl of his choice. TM

Teen Wolf

(1985, US, 92 min)
d Rod Daniel. *p* Mark Levinson, Scott Rosenfeld. *sc* Joseph Loeb III, Matthew Weisman. *ph* Tim Suhrstedt. *ed* Lois Freeman-Fox. *m* Miles Goodman. *cast* Michael J Fox, James Hampton, Susan Ursitti, Jerry Levine, Matt Adler, Lorie Griffin.
● Clean-cut teenagers, a small town hardware store, a dark secret. But *Blue Velvet* this is not. Being a member of a perpetually outclassed basketball team isn't all Michael J Fox has to contend with: full moon turns him into a werewolf just like his dad. This amiable entry in the rarely popular wolfman genre wears its horror lightly, preferring the comic possibilities of the high school sporting 'n' dating movie. Apart from one not very ambitious transformation, the budget requires other boy-wolf-boy switches to happen off-screen. Popular enough for a sequel and an animated TV series, but the mostly unknown cast and crew stayed that way. DO

Teen Wolf Too

(1987, US, 94 min)
d Christopher Leitch. *p* Kent Bateman. *sc* R Timothy Kring. *ph* Jules Brenner. *ed* Steven Polivka, Kim Secrist, Harvey Rosenstock, Raja Gosnell. *ad* Peg McClellan. *m* Mark Goldenberg. *cast* Jason Bateman, Kim Darby, John Astin, Paul Sand, James Hampton, Mark Holton, Estee Chandler.
● While *Teen Wolf* didn't exactly provoke howls of laughter, its innocuous humour did benefit greatly from the light comic touch of its diminutive star, Michael J Fox. This tedious sequel casts the producer's uncharismatic son (Bateman) as Fox's similarly afflicted cousin Todd, but offers only a faint echo of its predecessor. Having come to terms with his lupine lineage, relished the ensuing *Teen Wolf* mania, and ditched studious virgin Nicki (Chandler) in favour of fast times in a Porsche with a pair of big-breasted bimbettes, Todd suffers the same crisis of identity. Do his fickle fans love him or the wolf? Parents forced to suffer alongside their kids may salvage some amusement from the antics of Todd's gluttonous chum Chubby (Holton), who steals the show throughout. NF

Teeth (Denti)

(2000, It, 98 min)
d Gabriele Salvatores. *p* Vittorio Cecchi Gori, Maurizio Totti. *sc* Gabriele Salvatores. *ph* Italo Petriccione. *ed* Massimo Fiocchi. *pd* Rita Rabassini. *m* Federico De Robertis, Teho Teardo, Eraldo Bernocchi. *cast* Sergio Rubini, Anouk Grinberg, Tom Novembre, Anita Caprioli, Fabrizio Bentivoglio, Paolo Villaggio, Claudio Amendola.
● A complete change of style for the director of *Mediterraneo*. Antonio (Rubini) has Bugs Bunny teeth, so large that as a kid he tries chomping on rocks to whittle them down, which only makes things worse. When he's middle-aged, divorced, but to all intents and purposes settled with a nice girl, his teeth start bothering him again. Dentists all over Rome are awed by the scale of his problem – but as Salvatores makes clear, hysterical fear of *vagina dentata* may be the root of Antonio's unhappiness. Luridly styled as a comic nightmare, this tests the patience more than the magazines in a dentist's waiting room. TCh

Tel-Club (Natsu ni Umareru)

(1998, Jap, 76 min)
d/p/sc/ph Kenji Murakami. *ed* Kazuhiro Shirao. *m* Satoshi Yajima. *cast* Kenji Murakami, Rie Uematsu, Yukiyasu Shimada, Shinobu Kuribayashi, Tel-Club girls in Takasaki.
● All diary films are ego-driven, but Murakami's very funny contribution to the genre is much more self-deprecatory and self-mocking than most. Returning to his family home in Takasaki (= sticksville) for the birth of his sister-in-law's first child, he goes a bit stir crazy waiting for the baby to arrive. He chances on the Penguin Telephone Dating Club, pays and sits waiting for girls to call. Four in a row stand him up; then the fifth shows up and agrees to go out with him but won't let him shoot her face. Your guess is as good as mine where documentary slides into fiction, but Murakami wittily puts his finger on a problem central to all documentary film-making: some subjects just don't want to be filmed. TR

Telefon

(1977, US, 103 min)
d Don Siegel. *p* James B Harris. *sc* Peter Hyams, Stirling Silliphant. *ph* Michael Butler. *ed* Douglas Stewart. *pd* Ted Haworth. *m* Lalo Schifrin. *cast* Charles Bronson, Lee Remick, Donald Pleasence, Tyne Daly, Alan Badel, Patrick Magee, Sheree North, John Mitchum.
● At least the Cold War fired Hollywood's imagination, which is more than can be said for the first East-West détente picture (from the producer of *Dr Strangelove*). Russian agents planted as ordinary US citizens years earlier are suddenly activated via *Telefon* by a crazy unreconstructed Stalinist (Pleasence), and perform sundry kamikaze sabotage missions. Moscow is embarrassed, and sends in Bronson to team up with Remick, in fact a double agent. Not unlike the 'sleeper' agents, Bronson gives a strong impression of deep-hypnosis throughout, thereby suggesting possible plot twists infinitely more interesting than those provided in the dull script by Peter Hyams and Stirling Silliphant. Most disappointing is Siegel's contribution: he, of all directors, should have been able to inject some life into the proceedings, but this is his most nondescript outing in years. CPe

Telephone Book, The

(1971, US, 88 min)
d Nelson Lyon. *p* Merwin A Bloch. *sc* Nelson Lyon. *ph* Leon Perer. *ed* Len Saltzberg. *ad* Jim Taylor. *m* Nate Sassover. *cast* Sarah Kennedy, Norman Rose, James Harder, Jill Clayburgh, Ondine, Barry Morse, Ultra Violet, Roger C Carmel.
● Any humour in the original idea – an obscene phone-caller of such seductive skill that his victims long for aural molestation – is soon sabotaged by the director's blind intent on demonstrating that, although it may be a comedy, he sure knows how to make a film, and an arty one at that. The brief presence of three ex-Warhol personalities merely emphasises that, where the Warhol movies were funny and interesting (and boring) because the people in them were recognisable human beings, the characters teetering through this tired script are actors pretending to be kooky people. Having misunderstood the connection between sex and '60s avant-garde, Lyon – in a desperate bid to save a failed project – tarts things up at the end with a bit of explicit animation. SM

Tell England

(1931, GB, 88 min, b/w)
d Anthony Asquith, Geoffrey Barkas. *p* H Bruce Woolfe. *sc* Anthony Asquith, AP Herbert. *ph* Jack Parker, Stanley Rodwell, James E Rogers. *ed* Mary Field. *ad* Arthur Woods. *cast* Fay Compton, Tony Bruce, Carl Harbord, Dennis Hoey, CM Hallard, Wally Patch.
● Few enough films deal with the traumatic experience of the First World War, and Asquith deserves some credit for tackling the disastrous Gallipoli campaign. His gilded youth protagonists now look unbearably priggish: 'Just fetch my bath-water in the morning and brush my clothes and see that my buttons are clean and polish my boots and my belt', an 18-year-old officer tells the middle-aged soldier detailed to look after him. And the action sequences, handled by veteran director Barkas, endorse the public-school heroism. Asquith, with his staunch liberal insistence on the futility of war, puts up a brave fight, but overwhelmed by the 8,000 extras and the flotillas of troop-carriers, he ends up celebrating patriotism rather than pacifism. RMy

Telling Lies in America

(1997, US, 101 min)
d Guy Ferland. *p* Ben Myron, Fran Rubel Kuzui. *sc* Joe Eszterhas. *ph* Reynaldo Villalobos. *ed* Jill Savitt. *pd* James Gelarden. *m* Nicholas Pike. *cast* Kevin Bacon, Brad Renfro, Maximilian Schell, Calista Flockhart, Paul Dooley, Jonathan Rhys Meyers.
● It's 1960 and Renfro's Hungarian immigrant teen determines to get into the pants of winsome co-worker Flockhart by having his name mentioned on the 'High School Hall of Fame' by Cleveland's top DJ, Billy Magic (Bacon). Whizz-kid Billy is so impressed by Renfro's denial that he sent in several hundred nomination cards himself

that he makes the lad his assistant. These are the days of payola, but young Master Sheltered Life is unaware of the significance of the envelopes he passes to his boss from sundry shady types. And since he and his dad (Schell) are applying for US citizenship, trouble with the police is the last thing he wants. Bacon revels in the greased back hair, flip on-air patter and ersatz R&B stylings on the soundtrack, but it's absolutely no surprise that his icon of cool turns out to be a dud. Director Ferland can only move the elements of the hackneyed plot (by Joe Eszterhas) into place and hope we like Bacon enough not to notice. TJ

Telling Tales

(1978, GB, 93 min)
d/sc Richard Woolley. *ph* Russel Murray. *ed* Richard Woolley. *cast* Bridget Ashburn, Stephen Trafford, Patricia Donovan, James Woolley, Ian Masters.

● Woolley's reference points here are British TV soap serials like *Coronation Street* and *Crossroads*, contemporary British politics of class, and the school of 'deconstructed' narrative film-making in which Woolley has situated himself. Dealing with the life of two typical households, one middle and the other working class, *Telling Tales* attempts a breakdown of the inventory of clichés of which much of filmic language consists. It's often very funny and revealing, as in the use of sound effects early on in the film, and in the use of deliberately banal dialogue foregrounded by Woolley's deadpan use of actors moving in and out of the camera frame. Sometimes it's less effective: where the actors are required to be more emotional, for instance. But there is no escaping the film's value as an implicit criticism of the humourlessness of most current work in this area. RM

Tell Me a Riddle

(1981, US, 90 min)
d Lee Grant. *p* Mindy Affrime, Rachel Lyon, Susan O'Connell. *sc* Joyce Eliason, Alev Lytle. *ph* Fred Murphy. *ed* Suzanne Pettit. *pd* Patrizia von Brandenstein. *m* Sheldon Shkolnik. *cast* Melvyn Douglas, Lila Kedrova, Brooke Adams, Lili Valenty, Dolores Dorn, Ron Harris, Zalman King.

● An elderly Midwestern couple take off across America for a last visit to their children (and aghast confrontation with dropout San Francisco). They are Russian-Jewish, which naturally means that every other image conjures a pogrom-haunted memory. And just to open the taps on the already gushing sentimentality, she (Kedrova at her most winsome) is dying of cancer. Douglas, thank God, is at least agreeably tart. TM

Tell Me Something

(1999, SKor, 117 min)
d Chang Youn-Hyun. *p* Koo Bon-Han. *sc* Kong Su-Chang, In Eun-Ha, Shim Hye-Won, Kim Eun-Jung, Chang Youn-Hyun. *ph* Kim Seong-Bok. *ed* Kim Sang-Beom. *pd* Chung Koo-Ho. *m* Cho Young-Wook. *cast* Han Suk-Kyu, Shim Eun-Ha, Chang Han-Sun, Yum Jung-A, Ahn Suk-Hwan.

● Rash to promote this as 'a hard-gore thriller' when its lurid Grand Guignol effects (torrents of blood, sackfuls of severed limbs and heads) are so unconvincing. Suspected of accepting bribes, Detective Cho (Han, colourless) is given a chance to redeem himself by solving a string of gruesome murders: three male corpses with their limbs exchanged. It quickly emerges that they were ex-lovers of Chae (Shim), an introvert screwed up by childhood abuse at the hands of her father, a famous painter. Cho is targeted by the killer as he follows up obvious red herrings; his slob assistant Oh (Chang) becomes another victim. Garbled plotting, derivative imagery (*Se7en*'s rain falls throughout) and absurdly arty cinematography make for joyless viewing. And both climactic twists are depressingly misogynistic. TR

Tell Me That You Love Me, Junie Moon

(1969, US, 113 min)
d/p Otto Preminger. *sc* Marjorie Kellogg. *ph* Boris Kaufman. *ed* Henry Berman, Dean O Ball. *ad* Lyle Wheeler. *m* Philip Springer. *cast* Liza Minnelli, Ken Howard, Robert Moore, James Coco, Kay Thompson, Fred Williamson, Ben Piazza, Leonard Frey, Anne Revere.

● Another in the great series of disasters with which Preminger seemed intent on finishing his career, this is the tale of three mentally and physically handicapped social outcasts (facially disfigured girl, homosexual paraplegic, introverted epileptic) who set up home together. For all its SAS-like attacks on its audience's desire for charmingly handicapped people – Preminger refuses to favour the 'good' profile of Liza Minnelli's scarred Junie Moon – the script is little but a series of smart aleck exchanges/platitudes. PH

Tell Them Willie Boy Is Here

(1969, US, 98 min)
d Abraham Polonsky. *p* Philip A Waxman. *sc* Abraham Polonsky. *ph* Conrad Hall. *ed* Melvin Shapiro. *ad* Alexander Golitzen, Henry Bumstead. *m* Dave Grusin. *cast* Robert Redford, Katharine Ross, Robert Blake, Susan Clark, Barry Sullivan, Charles McGraw, John Vernon, Shelly Novack.

● Polonsky's return to direction after 21 blacklist years since *Force of Evil*, with a contemporary Western about a manhunt for a Piute Indian (Blake, excellent) presumed guilty of a crime defined by circumstance rather than by fact. The allegory about witch-hunting is there for the asking, taken a stage further than usual in the bitter irony whereby the hitherto Americanised Willie, accused in effect of being an Indian, gradually reverts to being an Indian in the archetypally savage sense. A powerful film, even though the script wears its liberal conscience on its sleeve (and further hedges its bets by casting nice Robert Redford as the sheriff), directed with austere authority in desert landcapes marvellously shot by Conrad Hall. TM

Temenos

(1998, GB, 75 min)
d Nina Danino.*p* James Mackay, Nino Danino. *sc* Nino Danino. *ph* David Scott, Nick Gordon Smith. *ed* Nino Danino *cast* Catherine Bott, Sainkho Namtchylak, Shelley Hirsch.

● Brooding b/w landscapes make up much of the running time in this evocation of the lingering sense of history in a number of sacred geographical sites. The testimonies of various Marian visionaries are spoken in voice-over as the camera prowls through deep forest and across rugged mountain, while vocal performances at the extreme end of female expressiveness, from guttural howling to soaring soprano, provide an aural complement. It's all very vivid for a while, but not easy to discern just what director Danino is getting at. Encouraging to see the tradition of the artist's film still alive in Britain, but many will find this a tad impenetrable, despite its undeniably haunting quality. TJ

Tempest

(1982, US, 142 min)
d/p Paul Mazursky. *sc* Paul Mazursky, Leon Capetanos. *ph* Donald McAlpine. *ed* Donn Cambern. *pd* Pato Guzman. *m* Stomu Yamashta. *cast* John Cassavetes, Gena Rowlands, Susan Sarandon, Vittorio Gassman, Raúl Julia, Molly Ringwald, Sam Robards, Paul Stewart.

● Just what we need, another Mazursky film where bright women wear the whitest of knickers, and where New Yorkers hide insecurities of seismic scale beneath that wonderfully direct way they have of talking at each other. Shakespeare's story is just another Manhattan mid-life crisis, and frankly, who cares? Mr Success (Cassavetes) ditches everything for a simple life in remotest Greece with his daughter Miranda. Yet Cassavetes, sporting the fanciest haircut since Frederic Forrest in *Hammett*, performs with such crusty conviction that one does start to care about what happens. That old Shakespearean magic survives even this loosest of adaptations, and by the end one is wallowing in the length and indulgence of it all (thinking as much about a summer holiday as about the film). Only later does one realise with the greatest relief what has been missing all along from the picture: Woody Allen. CPe

Tempest, The

(1979, GB, 95 min)
d Derek Jarman. *p* Guy Ford, Mordecai Schreiber. *sc* Derek Jarman. *ph* Peter Middleton. *ed* Lesley Walker. *pd* Yolanda Sonnabend. *m* Wavemaker. *cast* Heathcote Williams, Karl Johnson, Toyah Wilcox, Peter Bull, Richard Warwick, Elizabeth Welch, Jack Birkett.

● Jarman's rendering of the Bard's last act is his best picture to date, superbly shot in crumbling abbeys and mansions that look like Piranesi's Gothic drawings of fallen Rome, and turning the triteness of camp into absurdist comedy. The ending is pure Python and a major mistake – a cabaret with Elizabeth Welch singing 'Stormy Weather' – but until then Jarman's gleeful re-imagining of the play and his serious debate with it works wondrously well. Ages and influences crash together – Caliban as an Edwardian butler, Ariel a sight for gay eyes, Prospero a character out of Blake – but it's all of a piece, directed like a magic show. ATu

Temps pour l'ivresse des chevaux, Un

see Time for Drunken Horses, A

Temps retrouvé, Le

see Time Regained

Temptation (Pokuszenie)

(1995, Pol, 101 min)
d Barbara Sass. *sc* Barbara Sass, Wladyslaw Bielski. *ph* Wieslaw Zdort. *ed* Maria Orlowska. *pd* Wladyslaw Bielski. *m* Michal Lorenc. *cast* Magdalena Cielecka, Olgierd Lukaszewicz, Krzysztof Pieczynski, Maria Ciunelis, Edward Zentara.

● Post-war Poland in the tightening grip of the Communist authorities is the setting for this sombre drama of faith from a contemporary of Agnieszka Holland. Cielecka is the young nun moved to a rural detention centre, where she re-encounters an interned cardinal for whom she's long had a secretive burning passion. As their military overseers try to play both sides off against each other, the notion of confession takes on both spiritual and political meanings as personal, theological and ideological imperatives vie for supremacy. Although the performances milk every nuance from Sass's careful screenplay, the avoidance of overt melodramatics and the predominant tones of grey are a constant reminder of the worthiness of the material. TJ

Temptation Harbour

(1947, GB, 104 min, b/w)
d Lance Comfort. *p* Victor Skutezky. *sc* Victor Skutezky, Frederic Gotfurt, Rodney Ackland. *ph* Otto Heller. *ed* Lito Carruthers. *ad* Cedric Dawe. *m* Mischa Spoliansky. *cast* Robert Newton, Simone Simon, William Hartnell, Margaret Barton, Marcel Dalio, Edward Rigby, Charles Victor.

● Reviewers contrasted this unfavourably with Renoir's *La Bête Humaine*, but Simenon's story, with the fates leading a well-intentioned hero to his destruction in the docks of Dieppe (here Newhaven), now looks like an interesting bridge between the gloomy French melodramas of the '30s and American *film noir*. Newton is the harbour signalman who retrieves a suitcase full of money after witnessing a murder, fails to report it to the police, and finds himself the object of murderous and mercenary interest. He gives a wonderfully tension-ridden performance, fleetingly caressing Simone Simon's slip, erupting into exasperated anger with the nervy Hartnell, but never allowing full expression to the lust and violence clearly visible beneath the kindly surface. The ending may appear disappointingly conformist, and Simone's bored *femme fatale* fails to fulfil her potential (despite having 'enough atomic energy in the lobes of her ears to flatten London'); but this is the price one has to pay for Comfort's dogged refusal to simplify, to sacrifice realism to melodrama, which is in itself interesting. RMy

Tempter, The (Il Sorriso del Grande Tentatore)

(1973, It/GB, 106 min)
d Damiano Damiani. *p* Anis Nohra, Martin C Chute. *sc* Damiano Damiani, Fabrizio Onofre, Edna O'Brien, Audrey Nohra. *ph* Mario Vulpiani. *ad* Umberto Turco. *m* Ennio Morricone. *cast* Glenda Jackson, Claudio Casinelli, Lisa Harrow, Adolfo Celi, Arnoldo Foà, Francisco Rabal.

● A diabolical piece of work which pointlessly indulges the Italian obsession with convents, nuns, and – ever so discreetly – mortification of the flesh. Just who tempts whom and why remains a mystery: possibly the clues were lost in translation. It is never really sorted out why the film's medley of tormented characters – an incestuously-inclined minor prince; a woman remorseful after betraying her secret police torturer husband to her revolutionary lover; a worker priest who has been provoking strikes; a radical Bishop – remain within the decidedly photogenic but otherwise uninteresting confines of this particular convent hostelry. Nor is it at all obvious who the devil in the woodpile is – Glenda Jackson's Mother Superior or Claudio Casinelli's intruder. As Damiani protractedly works and reworks his material, the whole thing – especially with our heroine offering herself to the most ghoulish TV repairman ever to have graced the screen – looks more and more like a reworking of *Theorem* on a more pedestrian level. VG

Tempter, The

see Anticristo, L'

Temptress Moon (Fengyue)

(1996, HK/China, 132 min)
d Chen Kaige. *p* Tong Cunlin, Hsu Feng. *sc* Shu Kei, Wang Anyi, Chen Kaige. *ph* Christopher Doyle. *ed* Pei Xiaonan. *ad* Huang Qiagui. *m* Zhao Jiping. *cast* Leslie Cheung, Gong Li, Kevin Lin, He Saifei, David Wu.

● Opium addiction, incestuous desire, thwarted dreams, blackmail, secrets and lies: Chen's lavish, tortuous film has all this and more. Set mainly in the '20s, it concerns the wealthy but dysfunctional Pang family and the unrequited passions afflicting gigolo Cheung, clan head Gong Li and her poor but devoted cousin Lin. After a confusing start, it's an enthralling melodrama, sumptuously and imaginatively shot by Chris Doyle, which deals tangentially with the clash between the new and the old China, and shows, for probably the first time in Chen's work, a very real interest in sexual passion. GA

'10'

(1979, US, 122 min)
d Blake Edwards. *p* Blake Edwards, Tony Adams. *sc* Blake Edwards. *ph* Frank Stanley. *ed* Ralph E Winters. *pd* Rodger Maus. *m* Henry Mancini. *cast* Dudley Moore, Julie Andrews, Bo Derek, Robert Webber, Dee Wallace, Sam Jones, Brian Dennehy, Max Showalter.

● Before *'10'* was released in America, its producers were so certain it was a clinker that they tore up contracts for two other Blake Edwards pictures. The miscalculation was understandable. Much of the film comes on like a Jill Clayburgh picture someone rewrote for Bob Hope, with Moore playing an ageing Unmarried Man who pursues lubricious women (rating them out of an ideal ten) to stave off menopause. Technically it's atrocious, trading on absurd coincidence, lame slapstick, and some peculiarly ugly photography. But the studio failed to see that Edwards had hit on a subject (male sexual insecurity) which was bound to strike a chord with the post-Clayburgh audience. The climactic love scene – in which Moore proves utterly unable to perform when he gets his emancipated dream woman (Derek) to bed – is very funny and represents a real catharsis in the history of Hollywood romance: Dudley Moore became the first actor to turn screen impotence into superstardom. DP

10

(2002, Iran/Fr, 94 min)
d Abbas Kiarostami. *crew/cast* Mania Akbari, Roya Arabshahi, Katayoun Taleidzadeh, Mandana Sharbaf, Amene Moradi, Amin Maher, Kamran Adl, Morteza Tabatabaii, Bahman Kiarostami, Mastaneh Mohajer, Mazdak Sepanlu, Reza Yadzdani, Vahid Ghazi.

● Shot entirely from the dashboard of a car and using (with one brief exception) just two camera angles – one trained towards the driver's seat, the other towards the passenger's – Kiarostami's digital film looks like fly-on-the-windscreen documentary, but isn't. Rather, it explores the predicament of six women and one child in today's Tehran, as they argue, joke, cajole and comfort each other during ten brief journeys; this being Kiarostami, of course, it also explores the knotty relationship between reality, fiction and truth, and between actors, audience and filmmaker. Ostensibly, as the discussions cover love, sex, marriage, divorce, sex, parenthood, prostitution, independence and identity, the film's about the position of women in Iranian society, but it's also far more than that. Funny, surprising, illuminating, ambiguous and at times extremely moving, the film is a quietly audacious experiment in which its (primary) creator's determination to remove all visible traces of 'direction' from the equation makes for unusually forthright viewing. *Pace* Godard, Nick Ray is no longer alone in having been desirous – or indeed capable – of reinventing the cinema. GA

Tenant, The (Le Locataire)

(1976, Fr, 126 min)
d Roman Polanski. *p* Andrew Braunsberg. *sc* Gérard Brach, Roman Polanski. *ph* Sven Nykvist. *ed* Françoise Bonnot. *pd* Pierre Guffroy. *m* Philippe Sarde. *cast* Roman Polanski, Isabelle Adjani, Shelley Winters, Melvyn Douglas, Jo Van Fleet, Bernard Fresson, Lila Kedrova, Claude Dauphin, Claude Piéplu.

● With Polanski becoming a naturalised Frenchman, it was logical that he should start tackling specifically French subjects, and this small-scale return to the territory of *Repulsion* seemed a promising beginning. But it's precisely because Polanski and urban paranoia were made for each other that *The Tenant* is so disappointing. The tenant (Polanski himself) takes over the lease of a gloomy Parisian apartment from a suicide victim, and soon finds himself at the centre of a real or imagined conspiracy that pushes him into assuming the identity of his predecessor. The twist is that the last tenant was a girl, and our nervous, virginal hero's exploration of his latent bisexuality hits the one new note in an otherwise formulary catalogue of bizarre coincidences, inexplicable appearances, and hints of the supernatural. Everything except the dubbing of the French supporting cast is a model of craftsmanship, but as the plot escalates into increasingly arbitrary excesses of fantasy and heads for the predictable pay-off, the movie looks more and more like a potboiler. TR

Ten Commandments, The

(1956, US, 220 min)
d/p Cecil B DeMille. *sc* Aeneas MacKenzie, Jesse L Lasky Jr, Jack Gariss, Fredric M Frank. *ph* Loyal Griggs. *ed* Anne Bauchens. *ad* Hal Pereira, Walter Tyler, Albert Nozaki. *m* Elmer Bernstein. *cast* Charlton Heston, Yul Brynner, Anne Baxter, Edward G Robinson, John Derek, Yvonne De Carlo, Vincent Price, Cedric Hardwicke, Debra Paget, HB Warner, Nina Foch, Martha Scott, Judith Anderson, Henry Wilcoxon, John Carradine.

● According to Jesse L Lasky Jr, he and his fellow-writers 'felt so inoculated with significance that we hardly dared write at all, certainly not with such profane tools as pencils and typewriters'. *The Ten Commandments* sure isn't remembered as literature – the script is a sort of prose doggerel Biblespeak of unerring shallowness; or for its acting, with only Edward G Robinson and Hardwicke emerging as more than pawns in DeMille's vast game. Rather it's the gigantic vulgarity, the obsessive righteousness of the director himself, which keeps the show on the road and suffuses the movie with its daft power. There are two wondrous scenes. The exodus itself, gigantic aerial shots of the DeMillions underpinned by meticulous detail, is a genuine mover. The other goodie, surprisingly, is a dialogue scene in which Hardwicke, confronted by an enchained Heston, hands the succession (and Anne Baxter as a smouldering bonus) to Brynner. Most of the rest is arid nonsense a mile high. But you have to admire DeMille's seriousness of purpose. He took three weeks on the orgy scene alone. SG

Ten Days That Shook the World

see Oktyabr

Ten Days Without Love (El Cielo Abierto)

(2000, Sp, 107 min)
d Miguel Albaladejo. *p* Francisco Ramos, Fernando de Garcillan. *sc* Miguel Albaladejo, Elvira Lindo. *ph* Alfonso Sanz Alduan. *ed* Angel Hernandez Zoido, Ascen Marcha. *pd* Eduardo Hidalgo II. *m* Lucio Godoy. *cast* Sergi López, Mariola Fuentes, Maria Jose Alfonso, Emilio Gutierrez Caba, Geli Albaladejo, Marcela Wallerstein, Javier Dorado.

● Another likeable and thoughtful turn from Sergi López anchors this low key, grown-up urban love story. He's a psychiatrist in a funk brought on by his wife's elopement to Tokyo, followed by the arrival on his doorstep of her mother who's yet to hear the news, and reinforced by the procession of troublesome headcases who circulate through his office, particularly when one steals his wallet. Retrieving the wallet, however, brings him into contact with the thief's elder sister Jasmina, a sparky working-class beautician saddled with her own family burdens. Albaladejo's warm, wry, remedial comedy is principapally a study of the transfer of affections, albeit it one broad enough to bring several other characters into its engaging fold.

Ten Days' Wonder (La Décade Prodigieuse)

(1971, Fr, 108 min)
d Claude Chabrol. *p* André Génoves. *sc* Claude Chabrol, Paul Gégauff. *ph* Jean Rabier. *ed* Jacques Gaillard. *ad* Guy Littaye. *m* Pierre Jansen. *cast* Orson Welles, Marlène Jobert, Anthony Perkins, Michel Piccoli, Guido Alberti, Tsilla Chelton.

● Here Chabrol inaugurates a new genre, the theological thriller. Charles (Perkins at his most charismatically unstable) wakes from a dream of Creation to find himself with blood on his hands. He turns for help to his erstwhile professor of philosophy (Piccoli), and persuades him back to the Van Horn country estate to use his 'Logic of Science' in sorting out the family mess. The estate is a 1925 dream engineered by Charles' adoptive father Theo Van Horn (Welles), who is worshipped by his child-bride (Jobert), and sculpted as Jupiter by the awed Charles. Chabrol's movies, echoing Fritz Lang's, have long been edging towards a confrontation with the theme of Fate. This is it. Theo Van Horn chooses to play God, creating his own world, dictating the behaviour of those he places in it, taking care to add flaws to his creation to keep it breathing. But God hasn't reckoned with his own capacity for imperfection, for such shining qualities as jealousy, hatred, revenge; so he comes to his own grief, faced with the lonely fact that his creation is a nine-day wonder… Chabrol's movies grow less and less like anyone else's; this is one worth seeing again and again. TR

Tender Comrade

(1943, US, 102 min, b/w)
d Edward Dmytryk. *p* David Hempstead. *sc* Dalton Trumbo. *ph* Russell Metty. *ed* Roland Gross. *ad* Albert S D'Agostino, Carroll Clark. *m* Leigh Harline. *cast* Ginger Rogers, Robert Ryan, Ruth Hussey, Patricia Collinge, Mady Christians, Kim Hunter, Jane Darwell.

● A remarkable curiosity, if nothing else, this sentimental tale of World War II has Rogers, 'widowed' while her husband is away fighting, turning first to work as a welder in an aircraft factory, and then to a communal household arrangement with other women in the same circumstances. It was later denounced during the HUAC witch-hunts as Commie propaganda. Hard to see how the domestic economies practised by working girls (even phrased as 'Share and share alike, that's democracy') could cause so much trouble for Dmytryk and writer Dalton Trumbo (two of the 'Hollywood Ten'); especially when there is so much American patriotism on view, not least the glutinously stirring speech Rogers makes to her baby when she finally gets word that her husband has been killed. GA

Tender Hours (Dulces Horas)

(1981, Sp, 103 min)
d Carlos Saura. *p* Elias Querejeta. *sc* Carlos Saura. *ph* Teodoro Escamillo Serrano, Alfredo Fernandez Mayo. *ed* Pablo G del Amo. *ad* Antonio Belizón Jurado. *m* George Stoll. *cast* Assumpta Serna, Iñaki Aierra, Alvaro de Luna, Jacques Lalande, Luisa Rodrigo.

● A playwright rehearses his latest work, a melodrama that delves into his own childhood incest fantasies and his adult obsession with understanding his mother's character and suicide. As in *Cria Cuervos,* Saura has his actors take double, even triple roles, and moves deftly between past and present, dream, fiction and memory, putting on a bravura display of technique which dazzles by its skill, but which – despite the title (surely ironic) – has an emotional chilliness that is ultimately faintly unpleasant. SJo

Tender Mercies

(1982, US, 92 min)
d Bruce Beresford. *p* Philip S Hobel. *sc* Horton Foote. *ph* Russell Boyd. *ed* William Anderson. *ad* Jeannine C Oppewall. *m* George Dreyfus. *cast* Robert Duvall, Tess Harper, Betty Buckley, Wilford Brimley, Ellen Barkin, Allan Hubbard.
●A real gem. As it tells of Duvall's drunken, down-on-his-luck country singer's slow road to redemption by way of an unromantic marriage to a Texan widow, Beresford's film (scripted by the admirable Horton Foote) offers an attractive if unassuming alternative to the Hollywood mainstream. Refusing to get into heavy plotting – the story's most dramatic event occurs off-screen – it relies on mood, gesture and observation to offer the unfashionable thesis that life, however hard or disappointing, is always worth living. Stunningly shot and performed (not least by Duvall, singing his own songs with conviction, as well as producing), it bears more resemblance to, say, the films of Wenders (or even, at a stretch, Ozu) than to commercial Hollywood, though it grips from start to finish. Beautiful. GA

Tenderness of the Wolves (Zärtlichkeit der Wölfe)

(1973, WGer, 83 min)
d Ulli Lommel. *p* Rainer Werner Fassbinder. *sc* Kurt Raab. *ph* Jürgen Jürges. *ed* Thea Eymèsz. *ad* Kurt Raab. *m* Bach. *cast* Kurt Raab, Jeff Roden, Margit Carstensen, Hannelore Tiefenbrunner, Wolfgang Schenck, Rainer Hauer, Rainer Werner Fassbinder, Brigitte Mira, Ingrid Caven, Jürgen Prochnow.
●Fritz Haarmann, con-man, black marketeer and police informer, got through the depression years in Germany in an enterprising way: he picked up runaway boys, seduced them, vampirised them, and then sold their remains as meat. His crimes inspired Fritz Lang's *M*, made six years after his execution. In Lommel's remarkable film, the character gets the Fassbinder treatment: he's the resourceful but ultimately helpless loser at the centre of a black social comedy of manners. Lommel and his writer/star Kurt Raab (both veterans of numerous Fassbinder movies) tell Haarmann's story through a patchwork of broadly comic vignettes – from nosy neighbours and complicit cops to lovers' tiffs and expert con-tricks – and finally draw their plot threads together in a pastiche of the Hollywood crime thriller. The comedy doesn't blunt the horror of Haarmann's murders, but it does enable Lommel to implicate the 'tender wolves' – the society that makes such crimes possible – without resorting to didacticism or moralising. TR

Tender Place, A (Yawaraka na Hoo)

(2000, Jap, 201 min)
d Shunichi Nagasaki. *p* Takayuki Suzuki, Shirou Sasaki, Miyuki Sato. *sc* Shunichi Nagasaki. *ph* Shigeru Honda. *ed* Shunichi Nagasaki, Utan Nagasaki. *pd* Katsumi Kaneda. *cast* Yuki Amami, Tomokazu Miura, Shunsuke Matsuoka, Ikkei Watanabe, Kumi Nakamura.
●Nagasaki's gem centres on Kasumi (the superb Amami), whose life is transformed by the mysterious disappearance of five-year-old daughter Yuka while she and her husband are at a Hokkaido holiday park with another couple. Based on a novel by Natsuo Kirino, the film investigates how Kasumi came to be sleeping late when Yuka vanished, and its subsequent impact on her life. Of course, it also seeks an explanation for the disappearance. Guilt, grief, trust, doubt and recrimination come into play. The unfolding narrative produces subtle, even surprising twists, uncovering further levels of rich, relevant nuance, through which the film achieves a psychological and philosophical depth and complexity seldom found outside seriously good long novels. That's partly because the writer/director allows himself 201 minutes to explore the web of cause and effect that spreads backwards, forwards, even sideways from a life changing moment. Shooting on high definition video, Nagasaki keeps the story – flashbacks, fantasies, speculation – lucid and perfectly paced; from its riveting start to profoundly satisfying end, it grips like a vice. GA

Tendre Ennemie, La

(1936, Fr, 69 min, b/w)
d Max Ophuls. *sc* Curt Alexander, Max Ophuls, André-Paul Antoine. *ph* Eugen Schuftan. *ed* Pierre de Hérain. *ad* Jacques Gotko. *m* Albert Wolff. *cast* Simone Berriau, Georges Vittray, Marc Valbel, Jacqueline Daix, Lucien Nat.
●Antoine's source play was called *The Enemy*, but the tenderness is all Ophuls'. Three ghosts who were put in their graves by their 'enemy' (Berriau) foregather at the wedding of her daughter – to reminisce and to see that history doesn't repeat itself. This is quintessential Ophuls: catastrophes of the affections viewed warmly, ironically and non-judgmentally; the preoccupation with time; the speed and fluency of the storytelling. Small-scale (by Ophuls' standards) perfection. BBa

Tendres Cousines

see Cousins in Love

Tendresse Ordinaire, La (Ordinary Tenderness)

(1973, Can, 82 min)
d Jacques Leduc. *p* Paul Larose. *sc* Robert Tremblay. *ph* Alain Dostie. *ed* Pierre Bernier. *m* Jocelyn Berude, Don Douglas. *cast* Esther Auger, Jocelyn Bérubé, Luce Guilbeault, Jean-René Ouellet.
●The sort of plotless film (about a young Quebec couple, she waiting for him to return home on the train) which gives the word 'charm' a bad name. The tedium of waiting is almost perfectly transferred to the spectator. You'd be much better off visiting a friend and catching him/her peel vegetables. RM

Tenebrae (Sotto gli Occhi dell'Assassino)

(1982, It, 110 min)
d Dario Argento. *p* Claudio Argento. *sc* Dario Argento, Geoge Kemp. *ph* Luciano Tovoli. *ed* Franco Fraticelli. *ad* Giuseppe Bassan. *m* Pignatelli, Claudio Simonetti, Elsa Morante. *cast* Anthony Franciosa, John Saxon, Giuliano Gemma, Daria Nicolodi, Christian Borromeo, John Steiner.
●A hybrid horror, both thriller and slasher, not to mention chopper and shocker, this confirms what *Suspiria* and *Inferno* led one to suspect. When it comes to plotting, Argento is one hell of a basket weaver: with holes in his story big enough to sink credibility, he cheats and double-crosses like mad to conceal the killer's identity. Successful crime writer (Franciosa) arrives in Rome to promote his new book 'Tenebrae', an event which triggers off a trail of bloody murders in the manner described in his book. By the end, the entire cast save one has undergone savage cutting, something which would have benefited the film itself, which is unpleasant even by contemporary horror standards. It does confirm Argento's dedication to the technicalities of constructing images – Grand Guignol for L'Uomo Vogue, perhaps – but you'll still end up feeling you've left some vital digestive organs back in the seat. FL

Ten Fingers of Steel (Tangren Biao Ke)

(1973, Tai, 96 min)
d Jian Long. *p* Chan Wein Chien, Che Tsao Shin. *sc* Wang Pi Jen. *m* Chow Liang. *cast* Wang Yu, Chang Chin Chin, Kan Tai, Tze Lan.
●Poverty row kung-fu entertainment. With one clue, a perfume sachet, Tai Yuang (an interestingly unheroic, almost diffident performance from Wang Yu) comes to Japan to seek the villain who murdered his family. It isn't giving anything away to say he gets his man, with the help of a female pickpocket who turns out to be a Chinese martial arts champion. The film is so fragmented, so concerned to ring the changes on the fights (on a moving train and in a river) that any suspense involved in the tale is dissipated. The fact that nothing of interest is made of some promising scenes – a fight on a beach with a background of towering waves, the appearance of a character playing a flute and wearing a basket on his head – suggest that the film may have been tampered with. VG

Ten Little Indians

see And Then There Were None

Ten Little Indians

(1965, GB, 91 min, b/w)
d George Pollock. *p* Harry Alan Towers. *sc* Peter Yeldham, Harry Alan Towers. *ph* Ernest Steward. *ed* Peter Boita. *ad* Frank White. *m* Malcolm Lockyer. *cast* Hugh O'Brian, Shirley Eaton, Fabian, Leo Genn, Stanley Holloway, Wilfrid Hyde-White, Daliah Lavi, Dennis Price.
●Excruciatingly boring version of the Agatha Christie play filmed as *And Then There Were None* in 1945 and 1974. This time the setting is a remote house in the Austrian Alps, with cardboard characters hovering around mouthing chunks of exposition while waiting to get murdered. Tedium is not helped by a 'whodunit break' (for audiences to play detective) attended by instant replays of the murders. TM

Ten Little Niggers

see And Then There Were None

Ten Minutes Older – The Trumpet

(2002, GB/Ger, 92 min, b/w & col)
d Aki Kaurismäki, Victor Erice, Werner Herzog, Jim Jarmusch, Wim Wenders, Spike Lee, Chen Kaige. *p* Ulrich Felsberg, Nicolas McClintock, Nigel Thomas. *ed* Peter Christelis. *m* Paul Englishby.
●Despite an inevitable unevenness (with Chen's final 'comedy' the standout disappointment), this portmanteau of ten-minute shorts loosely linked by the theme of time has a higher strike rate than most such compilations. Lee and Herzog's documentaries (on the Bush election fiasco and an Amazonian Indian tribe, respectively) are slight but illuminating, the Wenders a silly thriller improved by its landscape photography, and the Kaurismäki an engagingly droll romantic fable. Better, Jarmusch has fun exploring the notion of 'dead time' in a wry, elegant tale of an actress's trailer-break, while Erice steals the show with a beautiful monochrome vignette poetically juxtaposing Spain in 1940 with a newborn child in mortal danger. Quite masterly, it only makes you wish he worked more frequently. GA

Tennessee's Partner

(1955, US, 87 min)
d Allan Dwan. *p* Benedict Bogeaus. *sc* Milton Krims, DD Beauchamp, Graham Baker, Teddi Sherman. *ph* John Alton. *ed* James Leicester. *ad* Van Nest Polglase. *m* Louis Forbes. *cast* John Payne, Ronald Reagan, Rhonda Fleming, Coleen Gray, Angie Dickinson, Leo Gordon, Morris Ankrum.
●While nowhere near as strong as *Silver Lode*, this is still an impressive little Western, adapted from a story by Bret Harte: a complex tale of loyalty, deceit and betrayal, with Payne as the smooth gambler in a mining township, Reagan as the cowpoke who saves his life, Fleming as the former's saloon-owner girlfriend, and Gray as the girl who becomes an object of contention. Like most of the Westerns Dwan made for producer Benedict Bogeaus, the film features typically impressive colour camerawork by John Alton (the red-headed Fleming seldom seemed riper!) and typically muscular, no-nonsense direction. GA

10 Rillington Place

(1970, GB, 111 min)
d Richard Fleischer. *p* Martin Ransohoff, Leslie Linder. *sc* Clive Exton. *ph* Denys Coop. *ed* Ernest Walter. *ad* Maurice Carter. *m* John Dankworth. *cast* Richard Attenborough, Judy Geeson, John Hurt, Pat Heywood, Isobel Black, Phyllis MacMahon, Geoffrey Chater, Robert Hardy, Andre Morell.
●For a director whose work reveals a fascination with the reconstruction of actual events, especially famous murder cases (*The Girl in the Red Velvet Swing*, *Compulsion*, *The Boston Strangler*), Fleischer seems oddly at sea with the Christie/Evans cause célèbre. Although all the '40s period details are (presumably) correct – Clive Exton's script is based on Ludovic Kennedy's book – none of the ambience of post-war Britain is caught on the screen. Also, by concentrating closely on Christie (Attenborough) and the hysterical Evans (Hurt), Fleischer leaves himself open to the excesses of British character acting. The result is a melodrama rather than an examination of criminal pathology. PH

Ten Seconds to Hell

(1958, GB/US, 94 min, b/w)
d Robert Aldrich. *p* Michael Carreras. *sc* Robert Aldrich, Teddi Sherman. *ph* Ernest Laszlo. *ed* James Needs, Henry Richardson. *ad*

Ken Adam. *m* Kenneth Jones. *cast* Jack Palance, Jeff Chandler, Martine Carol, Robert Cornthwaite, Dave Willock, Richard Wattis.
●Fair to middling Aldrich, which would pack more punch if the characterisation had a little more oomph. The storyline certainly grabs at the nerve ends: six German bomb disposal experts return from a British PoW camp to post-war Berlin, where they agree to pool their monthly pay packets in a kitty to be offered to the last survivor from their number. Palance and Chandler are left to sweat it out over unexploded devices and the similarly potent presence of love interest Carol. Ernest Laszlo's crisp monochrome camerawork makes the German capital look grim indeed. TJ

Tension at Table Rock

(1956, US, 93 min)
d Charles Marquis Warren. *p* Sam Wiesenthal. *sc* Winston Miller. *ph* Joseph Biroc. *ed* Harry Marker, Dean Harrison. *ad* Albert S D'Agostino, John B Mansbridge. *m* Dimitri Tiomkin. *cast* Richard Egan, Dorothy Malone, Cameron Mitchell, Billy Chapin, Angie Dickinson, DeForest Kelley.
●Agreeably taut minor Western has outlaw Egan riding into town and saving nervy lawman Mitchell's bacon by seeing off a gang of gung-ho desperadoes. The down side is that he falls for sheriff's wife Malone. An above-average RKO programmer that works well within its own rather derivative limits, it's buoyed by lots of familiar faces in the supporting cast. Look out, in particular, for young DeForest Kelley, a good decade before he picked up his galactic stethoscope as *Star Trek*'s Bones.

Tentacles (Tentacoli)

(1976, It, 102 min)
d Oliver Hellman [Sonia Assonitis]. *p* Enzo Doria. *sc* Jerome Max, Tito Carpi, Steven Carabatsos, Sonia Molteni [Sonia Assonitis]. *ph* Roberto D'Ettorre Piazzoli. *ed* Angelo Curi. *ad* M Spring. *m* Stelvio Cipriani. *cast* John Huston, Shelley Winters, Bo Hopkins, Henry Fonda, Delia Boccardo, Cesare Danova, Claude Akins.
●Having ripped off *The Exorcist* with *Devil Within Her*, Oliver Hellman here does a follow-up Italian job on *Jaws*. Taking *Tentacles* to the lab for analysis would reveal many similarities to its finny predecessor, with the following exceptions: wit, imagination, storytelling skill. Huston is grotesque as the type of grizzled investigative journalist who wears his nightdress on the porch. Winters is worse in yet another of her fat flustered parts, and Fonda must have needed the few days' work as 'Mr Whitehead', whose drilling company sends the octopus mad with its vibrations. One scene *Jaws* doesn't have, thankfully, is ichthyologist Bo Hopkins addressing his killer whales as though they were long-lost buddies from 'the streets' whence he came. They duly dispatch the monster, which incidentally seems of quite normal size, as in *Grizzly*. AN

10 Things I Hate About You

(1999, US, 98 min)
d Gil Junger. *p* Andrew Lazar. *sc* Karen McCullah Lutz, Kirsten Smith. *ph* Mark Irwin. *ed* O Nicholas Brown. *pd* Carol Winstead Wood. *m* Richard Gibbs. *cast* Julia Stiles, Heath Ledger, Joseph Gordon-Levitt, Larisa Oleynik, Larry Miller, Andrew Keegan, Daryl 'Chill' Mitchell, Allison Janney.
● *The Taming of the Shrew* set in American teendom ('Padua', a suburb of Seattle) may not sound a great idea. A snooty riot grrrl (Stiles) as Kate/Katharina? An impoverished Jim Morrison clone (Ledger) as Patrick/Petruchio? Another loud-mouthed, narcissistic rich boy as the baddie (Keegan)? Junger's film is a quiet revelation, a study in female distemper that makes the original look mean-minded. For starters, the script draws out the character of Kate's father, here a divorced doctor, who insists sister Bianca (Oleynik) can't go on a date until Kate does because he assumes the latter's not interested in boys. His scenes with girls sizzle with Oedipal anxiety; at one bizarre moment, he has a pre-date Bianca parade around in a prosthetic vision of pregnancy. In the play, Bianca's a bitch in sheep's clothing; here, she's a sly take on *Clueless*'s Cher, a mixed-up kid whose desire to fit in has simply dragged her away from the deep end. Her friendship with Kate develops sweetly and plausibly, with the latter's secret about the wicked Joey providing a real twist. Stiles grows into her character and Ledger is effortlessly charming. Baz Luhrmann's *Romeo & Juliet* was a more spectacular, hungry make-over, but for gentle, cheeky wit this has the edge. CO'Su

10:30 P.M. Summer

(1966, US/Sp, 85 min)
d Jules Dassin. *p* Jules Dassin, Anatole Litvak. *sc* Jules Dassin, Marguerite Duras. *ph* Gabor Pogany. *ed* Roger Dwyre. *ad* Enrique Alarcon. *m* Cristóbal Halffter. *cast* Melina Mercouri, Romy Schneider, Peter Finch, Julián Mateos, Beatriz Savón.
●Nobody had a good word to say for this adaptation of Marguerite Duras' novel which, though a potentially good script (by Duras and Dassin), is treated so heavily that it becomes risible. Finch and Schneider play a couple deciding whether to or not, while Finch's alcoholic wife (Mercouri) goes bananas to the point of being obsessed by a local *crime passionel*. Much of the blame can be attributed directly to Mercouri's barnstorming performance, though the inappropriately tarted-up Spanish postcard settings don't help either. Strange that a director like Dassin, who spearheaded the neo-realist movement in Hollywood after World War II, should look so completely out of touch with any level of reality in later years. CPe

10 to Midnight

(1983, US, 102 min)
d J Lee Thompson. *p* Pancho Kohner, Lance Hool. *sc* William Roberts. *ph* Adam Greenberg. *ed* Peter Lee-Thompson. *ad* Jim Freiburger. *m* Robert O Ragland. *cast* Charles Bronson, Lisa Eilbacher, Andrew Stevens, Gene Davis, Geoffrey Lewis, Robert Lyons, Wilford Brimley.
●'I remember when legal meant lawful' mutters cop Bronson, 'Now it means some kind of loophole'. Bronson's had a case thrown out of court after he's forced to admit that he planted evidence on a psychopathic murderer (Davis) too smart to leave any of his own. The psycho's release puts Bronson back in his *Death Wish* shoes. The producers have made it clear that the movie isn't intended to be a mere vigilante thriller, but rather a film that questions the law as regards insanity pleas. Smokescreen. For all its emotional blackmail, it's nothing more than a brutal reiteration of the most basic macho values, and one that leaves a nasty aftertaste. GD

Tenue de Soirée (Evening Dress)

(1986, Fr, 85 min)
d Bertrand Blier. *p* Philippe Dussart. *sc* Bertrand Blier. *ph* Jean Penzer. *ed* Claudine Merlin. *ad* Théo Meurisse. *m* Serge Gainsbourg. *cast* Gérard Depardieu, Michel Blanc, Miou-Miou, Michel Creton, Jean-François Stévenin, Mylène Demongeot, Bruno Crémer.
●Blier's scabrous comedy is, for most of its length, achingly funny. The opening is misanthropically arresting. At a dance, Monique (Miou-Miou) tears into her meekly devoted spouse Antoine (Blanc), itemising his shortcomings while ever closer looms the enormous, eavesdropping Bob (Depardieu). With shocking suddenness, Bob knocks her to the floor and contemptuously pelts her with banknotes – 'Here's a grand – now shut up!' – before outlining his blueprint for solvency and spiritual emancipation, and sweeping the stunned pair along on a night of burglary. Noise doesn't seem to be a consideration: wealthy awakened householders are so bored that they happily collaborate with the intruders. A *ménage-à-trois* develops, but with a twist: Big Bob is desperately smitten with mousy Antoine, and egged on by the pimping Monique, who doesn't want to lose the meal ticket, pursues the scuttling hetero around the breakfast bar. The physical casting is preposterously inspired; if the coda is less than satisfying, blame Blier's anarchistic spirit and reluctance to finish a film. BC

Teorema

see Theorem

Tequila Sunrise

(1988, US, 115 min)
d Robert Towne. *p* Thom Mount. *sc* Robert Towne. *ph* Conrad Hall. *ed* Claire Simpson. *pd* Richard Sylbert. *m* David Grusin. *cast* Mel Gibson, Michelle Pfeiffer, Kurt Russell, Raúl Julia, JT Walsh, Arliss Howard, Budd Boetticher.
●A romantic thriller which confirms Towne's outstanding talent as a screenwriter, but like *Personal Best*, leaves doubts about his skill as a director. Gibson is an ex-drugs dealer looking for a way out, Russell is the relentless cop who's out to nail his old high school pal, and Pfeiffer is a beautiful restaurant owner suspected of fronting for Gibson's drugs business. Gibson is in the clear until another old friend, dealer Julia, calls in one last favour involving several million dollars worth of drug money. The set-up has the precision of fine needlepoint, picking out the plot outline before embroidering it with a complex pattern of interwoven relationships. Pfeiffer is perfect as the immaculately dressed and icily controlled restaurateur caught between Gibson's honest (ex-)criminal and Russell's ambiguously motivated cop. For while Gibson is totally upfront about both his shady past and his emotions, Russell's romantic advances are overlaid by professional interest in his rival's criminal activities. Sadly, when Julia finally shows up, this fascinating exploration of the limits of friendship, loyalty and trust gives way to explosive action and empty pyrotechnics. NF

Terence Davies Trilogy, The

(1974–83, GB, 85 min)
d/p/sc Terence Davies. *ph* William Diver. *ed* Digby Rumsey, Sarah Ellis, William Diver, Mick Audsley. *ad* Miki can Zwanenberg. *cast* Phillip Maudesley, Terry O'Sullivan, Wilfrid Brambell, Sheila Raynor.
●Not so much an 'I had it tough' catalogue of economic and physical hardships as a strangely stirring account of human dignity triumphing over emotional and spiritual confusion. And indeed, the form reflects this, transforming Liverpudlian Robert Tucker's development – from victimised schoolboy, through a Catholic closet-gay middle-age, to death in a hospital – into a rich, resonant tapestry of impressionistic detail. There is plenty to enjoy: a bleak, wry wit and an imaginative use of music undercutting the grim but beautiful imagery; flashes of surrealism; and superb performances throughout (none more so than Brambell as the 80-year-old Tucker, wordlessly struggling the last few steps to meet his Maker). But what really elevates the films into their own timeless realm is the luminous attention to faces in close-up: a stylish strategy that turns an otherwise chastening look at a lonely man's life into an uplifting experience. (The film is in three parts: *Children*, 1974; *Madonna and Child*, 1980; *Death and Transfiguration*, 1983.) GA

Terminal Man, The

(1974, US, 107 min)
d/p/sc Mike Hodges. *ph* Richard H Kline. *ed* Robert L Wolfe. *ad* Fred Harpman. *cast* George Segal, Joan Hackett, Richard A Dysart, Jill Clayburgh, Donald Moffat, Matt Clark, James B Sikking.
●A thoughtful and unusually pessimistic sci-fi pic based on Michael Crichton's novel about a psychotic (Segal) who has a tiny computer planted in his brain to control his violent impulses. Unfortunately, the plan backfires: Segal enjoys the sensation of being calmed down so much that he goes on a murder spree in order to enjoy further mental restraint. Opening with a brilliant sequence in which Segal is reborn on the operating table, and building towards a finale in which the scientists realise that they can do nothing to control this hi-tech monster of their own making, the film's bleak futuristic vision also benefits greatly from some extraordinary sets, and from writer/producer/director Hodges' confident direction. NF

Terminal Station (Stazione Termini/Indiscretion of an American Wife)

(1952, It/US, 97 min, b/w)
d/p Vittorio De Sica. *sc* Cesare Zavattini, Luigi Chiarini, Giorgio Prosperi, Truman Capote. *ph* GR Aldo, Oswald Morris. *ed* Eraldo Da Roma, Jean Barker. *ad* Virgilio Marchio. *m* Alessandro Cicognini. *cast* Jennifer Jones, Montgomery Clift, Gino Cervi, Richard Beymer.

●De Sica started out wanting to film a small scale love story, but the casting of Jennifer Jones brought with it the attentions of her producer husband David Selznick. He insisted on shooting in Rome's grand new central railway station and drafted in Truman Capote to polish up Zavattini's screenplay about an ill-fated romance between a visiting American and an Italian with an American mother (Clift, who gives a tender performance). In the end, though, Selznick reckoned the finished picture too arty and cut it to 63 minutes for US distribution (as *Indiscretion of an American Wife*). TJ

Terminal Velocity

(1994, US, 102 min)
d Deran Sarafian. *p* Scott Kroopf, Tom Engelman. *sc* David N Twohy. *ph* Oliver Wood. *ed* Frank J Urioste, Peck Prior. *pd* David L Snyder. *m* Joel McNeely. *cast* Charlie Sheen, Nastassja Kinski, James Gandolfini, Christopher McDonald, Gary Bullock, Melvin Van Peebles, Hans R Howes.

●Sheen is a dumb, daredevil sky-diving instructor mixed up with the Russian Mafia and $600m of stolen Soviet gold. Things get off to an attention-grabbing start when, soon after her flatmate is murdered by Russkie thugs, blonde babe Chris (Kinski) persuades 'Ditch' Brodie (Sheen) to take her up for her first jump. She then redefines the meaning of drop-dead beautiful – she jumps, she drops, she's dead. Or is she? Is that unidentifiable body really hers? To cut a long story short, Ditch stumbles about looking for clues to Chris's nose-dive, which lead him to members of the KG-used-to-B, who plan to fund an anti-democratic coup with the stolen gold. While Kinski unwisely takes the whole thing seriously, Sheen simply grins inanely and makes flip remarks. If you can wait long enough, the extended airborne finale is one of the most extraordinary stunts you're ever likely to see; but like the soundtrack, it's too big for the picture. Most people will have bailed out long before then. NF

Terminator, The (100)

(1984, US, 107 min)
d James Cameron. *p* Gale Anne Hurd. *sc* James Cameron, Gale Anne Hurd. *ph* Adam Greenberg. *ed* Mark Goldblatt. *ad* George Costello. *m* Brad Fiedel. *cast* Arnold Schwarzenegger, Michael Biehn, Linda Hamilton, Paul Winfield, Lance Henriksen, Rick Rossovich, Bess Motta, Earl Boen, Dick Miller.

●Back from the future in which the machines rule comes a rippling robot (Schwarzenegger) who terminates opponents with extreme prejudice (like ripping their hearts out). His goal is to kill a woman (Hamilton) destined to bear the child who will become the great freedom fighter of the future. Fortunately she has a champion in the shape of another time traveller, Arnold's all-too-human opponent (Biehn). The gladiatorial arena is set, with vulnerable flesh and cunning versus a leviathan who totes around massive weapons like so many chic accessories and can rebuild his organs as they get shot away. The pacing and the action are terrific, revelling in the feral relentlessness which characterised *Assault on Precinct 13* and *Mad Max 2*; even the future visions of a wasted LA are well mounted. More than enough violence to make it a profoundly moral film; and Arnold's a whizz. CPea

Terminator 2: Judgment Day

(1991, US, 135 min)
d/p James Cameron. *sc* James Cameron, William Wisher. *ph* Adam Greenberg. *ed* Richard A Harris, Mark Goldblatt, Conrad Buff. *pd* Joseph Nemec III. *m* Brad Fiedel. *cast* Arnold Schwarzenegger, Linda Hamilton, Edward Furlong, Robert Patrick, Earl Boen, Joe Morton, S Epatha Merkerson, Xander Berkeley, Jenette Goldstein.

●Having failed, in Cameron's impressive original, to prevent the birth of future resistance leader John Connor, the machines running the world in 2029 again send a cyborg to our era to kill him off as an unruly LA teenager (Furlong). Again, too, the resistance responds by sending the boy a protector: a T800 cyborg (Schwarzenegger) physically identical to the one which formerly laid siege to John's mom Sarah (Hamilton). That Arnie is now a good guy is one twist; the other is that he's the underdog, since the T1000 (Patrick) despatched by the machines is far more sophisticated, constructed from liquid steel so that it can adopt the appearance of anyone or anything it chooses. The film is much the same as its predecessor, except that the effects are more spectacular, there's a lumbering anti-nuke subtext, and the script's good-natured wit is undercut by the sentimentality of Arnie's becoming a caring cyborg. Structured as a simple chase, the story sags midway, but the first hour and last 30 minutes display an enjoyably relentless bravura. GA

Terminus

(1986, Fr/WGer, 110 min)
d Pierre-William Glenn. *p* Anne François. *sc* Pierre-William Glenn, Patrice Duvic. *ph* Jean-Claude Vicquery. *ed* Thierry Derocles. *ad* Alain Challier. *m* David Cunningham. *cast* Johnny Hallyday, Karen Allen, Jürgen Prochnow, Gabriel Damon, Julie Glenn, Dieter Schidor.

●It had to happen: the film of the video game. The plot, with 27 minutes cut in this dubbed release print, is utterly incomprehensible. The Monster, a hi-tech camper-van driven by gutsy heroine Gus (Allen), is trying to reach the Terminus, evading Government Forces and an evil Doctor's camouflaged pursuit vehicle en route. A little later Max Max clone Stump (Hallyday) takes over The Monster. The game seems to have something to do with the stowaway Princess he finds on board, and some experiments in genetic mutation being conducted by the evil Doctor. It's hard to tell, but only a masochist would wish this snail-paced kiddies sci-fi pic – with its second-hand images, appalling dialogue, and cardboard sets – to last a moment longer. Terminal boredom sets in long before the end of the journey, its purpose still obscure. NF

Term of Trial

(1962, GB, 130 min, b/w)
d Peter Glenville. *p* James Woolf. *sc* Peter Glenville. *ph* Oswald Morris. *ed* Jim Clark. *pd* Wilfrid Shingleton. *m* Jean-Michel Damase. *cast* Laurence Olivier, Simone Signoret, Sarah Miles, Hugh Griffith, Terence Stamp, Roland Culver, Thora Hird, Frank Pettingell, Dudley Foster.

●Olivier as a boozing schoolteacher, trapped in a fearful marriage to Signoret, and trapped also by nympho student Sarah Miles, who has a crush on him and, crikey, offers herself during a school outing to Paris. Instead of laying her or giving her a good slippering, he simply tells her to go home and do her homework. So she accuses him of rape, which leads to some real acting, especially when Olivier, after being cleared of misconduct by the enquiry, has to lie to his wife to earn her respect as a man with a spine. Terence Stamp as the school bully deservedly gets a good thrashing for non-acting, and this trip through the blackboard jungle is about as convincing as the jungle in Kew Gardens. ATu

Terms of Endearment

(1983, US, 132 min)
d/p/sc James L Brooks. *ph* Andrzej Bartkowiak. *ed* Richard Marks. *pd* Polly Platt. *m* Michael Gore. *cast* Shirley MacLaine, Debra Winger, Jack Nicholson, John Lithgow, Danny DeVito, Jeff Daniels, Lisa Hart Carroll.

●Until Debra Winger finds she has The Illness, this ambles along quite amusingly but unremarkably as a sharp-eyed family comedy: Winger leaves her neurotic mother (MacLaine) for an unfaithful husband, while MacLaine consoles herself with astronaut-next-door Nicholson. It is Nicholson who dominates this section, attacking the role and usefully distracting attention from the blatant unreality and sentimentality of the MacLaine character. Then The Illness strikes, and the film changes gear completely, pulling out all the stops and almost incidentally delivering one of the best-acted, most moving death-bed scenes in recent memory. The emotional wipe-out is impressive, confirming Winger as one of the major stars of the '80s. But it also unbalances the film, and makes you wonder if director Brooks is as good at construction as he obviously is at emotion. DP

Terra-Cotta Warrior, A (Qin Yong)

(1990, HK/Can, 120 min)
d Ching Siu-Tung. *p* Hon Pou-Chu, Kam Kwok-Leung, Zhang Yimou, Ng Tin Ming. *sc* Lee Bik Wah. *ph* Peter Pau. *ed* Mak Chi Shin. *pd* Yee Chung Man. *m* Joseph Koo. *cast* Zhang Yimou, Gong Li, Yu Yung Kang.

●A misfired attempt at a sweeping adventure-comedy in the *Indiana Jones* style. Back in the Qin Dynasty, an imperial guardsman is turned into a terra-cotta soldier as punishment for seducing a virgin – but she passes him a Pill of Immortality when she gives him One Last Kiss. Two thousand-odd years later, in the 1930s, he wakes to defend the Qin Emperor's tomb from robbers, and finds his long-lost love reincarnated as a pin-brained Shanghai starlet filming on location in Xi'an. Slack scripting and pacing conspire with the overall shortage of laughs and thrills to make this less than exhilarating, despite the plethora of talents on both sides of the camera. TR

Terra Nova

(1998, Aust, 87 min)
d Paul Middleditch. *p* Peter Masterson. *sc* Martin Edmond. *ph* Steve Arnold. *ed* Heidi Kenessey. *pd* Catherine Mansill. *m* Graeme Tardiff. *cast* Jeanette Cronin, Paul Kelman, Trent Atkinson, Angela Punch McGregor, Eloise Atkinson, Teo Gebert, Ritchie Singer, Gillian Jones, Vincent Gil.

●What with a mad skinhead downstairs, a landlady who accepts sexual favours in lieu of rent, and the boy next door having a family crisis of his own, the Terra Nova apartment block is not the first place you would chose to bring up your child. Just right for Cronin's Ruth, however, since it's also the last place anyone might think to look for her and her daughter, snatched illicitly from grandma and grandpa. They want to see the young mum back in psychiatric care: all she wants is a chance to run her own life for a change. In the event, this is easier imagined than done, as the film pitches its vulnerable protagonist between the frightening demands of personal freedom and the suffocating arena of misplaced parental concern. Familiar material perhaps, but Cronin's performance is refreshingly free of empty exaggeration, and the director is attuned to the sudden rush of everyday anxiety. TJ

Terres Froides, Les (Cold Lands)

(1999, Fr, 63 min)
d Sébastien Lifshitz. *sc* Sébastien Lifshitz, Stéphane Bouquet. *ph* Pascal Poucet. *ed* Yann Dedet. *pd* Laurent Gantes. *m* Arvo Pärt. *cast* Yasmine Belmadi, Bernard Verley, Valérie Donzelli, Sébastien Charles, Sébastien Lifshitz.

●A stark, powerful political fable about haves and have-nots, the film tracks a young outsider's relentless pursuit of a factory boss. Narrower in scope than *Ressources Humaines*, it still packs a hefty punch, and Belmadi's bruised determination is eloquence itself. TCh

Terrible Beauty, A (aka Night Fighters)

(1960, GB, 90 min, b/w)
d Tay Garnett. *p* Raymond Stross. *sc* Robert Wright Campbell. *ph* Stephen Dade. *ed* Peter Tanner. *ad* John Stoll. *m* Cedric Thorpe Davie. *cast* Robert Mitchum, Anne Heywood, Dan O'Herlihy, Richard Harris, Cyril Cusack, Hilton Edwards.

●A provocative theme – the dilemma in WWII of an IRA volunteer when he finds the organisation making common cause with the Nazis – becomes merely background noise in a stock melodrama that might as well be set anywhere. Technically British but co-produced by Mitchum's own company, it feels more American than anything else. Certainly the English didn't relish being cast in the Redskin role, skittled over in numbers by the film's heroes, any more, perhaps, than the Irish welcomed a reminder of this period of history. And Garnett's old fashioned, unimaginative handling killed it for audiences everywhere else. But as a Mitchum movie it's interesting for the way it re-examines (after *The Wonderful Country*) matters of nationality and loyalty. BBa

Terror, The

(1963, US, 81 min)
d/p Roger Corman. *sc* Leo Gordon, Jack Hill. *ph* John Nickolaus Jr. *ed* Stuart O'Brien. *ad* Daniel Haller. *m* Ronald Stein. *cast* Boris Karloff, Jack Nicholson, Sandra Knight, Dick Miller, Jonathon Haze.

●Notable mainly for being the film that was screened at the drive-in in Bogdanovich's *Targets*, this is the real dud of Corman's Poe cycle, largely because he said, 'I had the weekend off before the last week of shooting *The Raven*; I was going to play tennis and it rained'. Not wanting to waste the set he'd had built, he embarked upon an almost incomprehensible tale of an officer in Napoleon's army (Nicholson) who falls for a woman who keeps disappearing; it turns out she's the long dead wife of Mad Baron Karloff. The film, despite its elements of necrophilia, has nothing whatsoever to do with Poe, and the fact that it was directed by about five different people (including Coppola, Monte Hellman and Nicholson himself) hardly makes for coherence. There are, however, a few strikingly moody images that make effective use of the California coastline, and the general air of chaotic improvisation is not altogether without its own special charm. GA.

Terror

(1978, GB, 87 min)
d Norman J Warren. *p* Richard Crafter. *sc* David McGillivray. *ph* Les Young. *ed* Jim Elderton. *ad* Hayden Pearce. *m* Ivor Slaney. *cast* John Nolan, Carolyn Courage, James Aubrey, Sarah Keller, Tricia Walsh, Glynis Barber.

●Atmospheric camerawork and some bright dialogue provide momentary relief in what is otherwise stock schlock about a film-maker (Nolan) who inadvertently conjured a malevolent ancestral witch while making a movie about his own family history. Nasty things start happening when he previews it at a party; but echoes of *The Exorcist* tend to hang increasingly heavy over the proceedings, while Warren's direction administers the coup de grâce by persistently cutting to lip-licking close-ups of slashed or garrotted throats. TM

Terror at the Opera

see Opera

Terror by Night

(1946, US, 60 min, b/w)
d Roy William Neill. *p* Howard Benedict. *sc* Frank Gruber. *ph* Maury Gertsman. *ed* Saul A Goodkind. *ad* John B Goodman, Abraham Grossman. *m* Hans Salter. *cast* Basil Rathbone, Nigel Bruce, Alan Mowbray, Dennis Hoey, Renee Godfrey, Mary Forbes, Billy Bevan.

●Holmes, Watson, a suspiciously eccentric passenger list, and the Star of Rhodesia diamond are all aboard the London to Edinburgh express (which, if the wonderfully inconsistent exterior stock footage is to be believed, changes engines several times *en route*), and the ensuing mayhem ranges from a corpse in a carriage to a false-bottomed coffin in the guard's van. Despite the train-movie format, there are distinct signs that Universal's Rathbone-Bruce series was running out of steam (only one more film was to come, in fact). An early screenplay from Frank Gruber, who merrily titled his autobiography *The Pulp Jungle*. PT

Terror House

see Night Has Eyes, The

Terror in a Texas Town

(1958, US, 80 min, b/w)
d Joseph H Lewis. *p* Frank N Seltzer. *sc* Ben L Perry. *ph* Ray Rennahan. *ed* Frank Sullivan, Stefan Arnsten. *ad* William Ferrari. *m* Gerald Fried. *cast* Sterling Hayden, Sebastian Cabot, Carol Kelly, Ned Young, Eugene Martin, Victor Millan.

●Take a hired gun with a steel fist and an almost tragic awareness of his failing nerve (Young). Pit against him a stolid Scandinavian armed only with a whaling harpoon (Hayden), and the film does at least achieve the kind of bizarre climax appropriate to its low-budget format. The rest is a triumph of expression over economy: Lewis makes a virtue of the frame's emptiness (the budget, it seems, didn't run to extras), and disguises the excessive talk with unobtrusive camera movements that show a craftsmanship and pureness lacking in many more expensive films. Something of an exemplar of its type. CPe

Terror in the Aisles

(1984, US, 85 min, b/w & col)
d Andrew J Kuehn. *p* Stephen J Netburn, Andrew J Kuehn. *sc* Margery Doppelt. *ph* John A Alonzo. *ed* Gregory McClatchy. *m* John Beal. *with* Donald Pleasence, Nancy Allen.

●Comprising a cascade of clips (61 movies are plundered) that's supposed to illustrate different sorts of suspense-creation, this compilation seems more interested in the pay-offs (when the axe descends, the head explodes). With Allen and Pleasence as hosts, you can be sure nothing very original is going to get said; and the organisation of the extracts is never especially meaningful. But it's undeniable that these Jack Horner movies – stick in your thumb, pull out a plum – do collar the attention, no matter how bland the presentation. BBa

Terroriser, The (Kongbufenzi)

(1986, Tai/HK, 109 min)
d Edward Yang. *p* Xiao Ye. *sc* Xiao Ye, Edward Yang. *ph* Zhang Zhan. *ed* Liao Qingsong. *ad* Lai Mingtang. *m* Weng Xiaoliang. *cast* Cora Miao, Li Liqun, Jin Shijie, Gu Baoming, Wang An.

●Yang's masterly film keeps numerous plot strands going in parallel, finds a high level of interest and suspense in all of them, and dovetails them together into a composite picture plausible enough to make you cry and shocking enough to leave you gasping. The characters span the full urban spectrum: a research scientist jockeying for promotion, a bike-gang hoodlum on the run from the cops, a woman novelist looking for a painless way to end her marriage. Yang sees each of them clearly and with consummate honesty, and notes how their taste in clothes and decor serve to underline their personalities and betray their histories. Neither sociological essay nor soap opera, it's an intensely cinematic movie, finding mystery, pity and fear in every life it scans. The title character is a girl delinquent whose prank phone calls spark off crises in the lives of other characters. But the film suggests that we all have our ways of 'terrorising' each other, and that we'd all like our lives to be as coherent and resolved as fiction. Yang reaches high, and his aim is true. TR

Terrorist, The

(1997, Ind, 95 min)
d Santosh Sivan. *p* A Sriram, Abhijeeth. *sc* Santosh Sivan, Ravi Deshpande, Vijay Deveshwar. *ph* Santosh Sivan. *ed* Sreekar Prasad. *pd* Shyam Sunder. *m* Sonu Sisupal, Rajamani. *cast* Ayesha Dharkar, Vishnu Vardhan, Bhanu Prakash, K Krishna, Sonu Sisupal, Vishwas, Parmeshwaran.

●A standard, though reasonably engrossing drama about a 19-year-old Tamil Tigress sent on a kamikaze mission to assassinate a VIP. As Malli (Dhakar) travels up river, rooms with a mad teacher and trains up for the big day, her mind casting back to her father's own martyrdom and an encounter with a wounded fellow soldier, the pace is just a little slow, and the soundtrack oddly filled with Malli's amplified heavy breathing. NB

Terrorists in Retirement (Des Terroristes à la retraite)

(1983, Fr, 84 min, b/w & col)
d Mosco Boucault. *ph* Jean Orjollet, Philippe Rousselot. *ed* Christiane Lehérissey. *m* Jean Schwarz. *with* Jean-Paul Bonnaire. *narrators* Simone Signoret, Gérard Desarthe.

●In 1943 the Nazis executed 24 Resistance 'terrorists'. The victims were Jews, mainly from Eastern Europe, mainly communists. Boucault interviews the survivors of the group – septuagenarians re-enacting the heroism of youth – and suggests de Gaulle and the leaders of the French Underground 'sacrificed' their comrades. That the film was suppressed in France for years suggests he may be right. TCh

Terror of Dr Chaney, The

see Mansion of the Doomed

Terror Train

(1979, Can, 97 min)
d Roger Spottiswoode. *p* Harold Greenberg. *sc* TY Drake. *ph* John Alcott. *ed* Anne Henderson. *pd* Glenn Bydwell. *m* John Mills-Cockle, Larry Cohen. *cast* Ben Johnson, Jamie Lee Curtis, Hart Bochner, David Copperfield, Derek MacKinnon, Sandee Currie, Timothy Webber.

●This effectively exploits all the inherent violence and abandon of a riotous student party aboard a hired steam train. The horror elements are accounted for 'naturally': party masks provide grotesque images and a disguise for the killer; darkness alternating with the mottled lights of a disco give an uneasy visual feel, heightened by the swaying of the train; and the feats of a performing magician arouse expectations of a supernatural dimension. Instead, there is a psychological angle: the students, the killer's victims, are fairly callous themselves, given to gruesome medical school 'pranks' and fundamentally self-centred. Jamie Lee Curtis plays the only one of the gang with a conscience – and the only one to survive. But although the film's terror mileage is fuelled by her outwitting the killer, being a woman she must – as usual – finally be saved by the fatherly guard. Still, better than most of its kind. JWi

Terror 2000

(1992, Ger, 80 min)
d Christophe Schlingensief. *p* Christian Fürst. *sc* Oskar Roehler, Christoph Schlingensief. *ph* Reinhard Köcher. *cast* Margit Carstensen, Peter Kern, Susanne Bredehöft, Alfred Edel, Udo Kier.

●A shrill, chaotic and confused exposé of the racism allegedly inherent in German culture, in which ex-gangster Edel and sidekick Kern open a furniture store in a small town, and then set about harassing immigrant families and campaigning against a local home for them. The last part of the trilogy that began with *100 Years of Adolf Hitler* and continued with *The German Chainsaw Massacre*. NF

TerrorVision

(1986, US, 85 min)
d Ted Nicolaou. *p* Albert Band. *sc* Ted Nicolaou. *ph* Romano Albani. *ed* Thomas Meshelski. *pd* Giovanni Natalucci. *m* Richard Band. *cast* Diane Franklin, Mary Woronov, Gerrit Graham, Chad Allen, Jonathan Gries, Bert Remsen, Alejandro Rey, Randi Brooks.

●From Planet Pluton (apparent surface area: three feet by five) a horribly mutated domestic pet is tele-ported into the tacky, fallout-bunkered suburban home of the swinging Puttermans. It would be a cold heart that didn't sing as the Puttermans become lunch for their uninvited guest. Contact-mag swingers and assorted freaks turn up at the door like guest stars in a sit-com and rapidly become pools of slime on the tiled floor of the 'pleasure den'. Apart from Grampa's enthusiasm for self-regenerating lizard tails as a food source, very little of this is as funny as intended. Yet the monster, a huge, wobbling regurgitated meal with several rotating eyes, is genuinely likeable, and the sight of Mary Woronov poured into skin-tight sky-blue leather seems destined to linger in the mind's eye. DO

Terry Fox Story, The

(1983, Can, 97 min)
d Ralph L Thomas. *p* Robert Cooper. *sc* Edward Hume. *ph* Richard Ciupka. *ed* Ron Wisman. *ad* Gavin Mitchell. *m* Bill Conti. *cast* Robert Duvall, Eric Fryer, Christopher Makepeace, Rosalind Chao, Michael Zelniker.

●Cancer survivor and amputee Terry Fox embarks on a cross-country run to raise money for cancer research. Public awareness is haphazard until a professional promoter climbs on board, and Terry becomes a national hero despite having to abandon the run. Kinder viewers will find the picture inspirational; others will see it as a worthy but dull tract, barely brought to life as a cheap TV movie. Briefly enlivened by Robert Duvall, the film relies heavily on Eric Fryer, his status as an amputee over-riding his limited acting ability. DO

Terry on the Fence

(1985, GB, 70 min)
d Frank Godwin. *p* Harold Orton, Frank Godwin. *sc* Frank Godwin. *ph* Ronnie Maasz. *ed* Gordon Grimward. *ad* Maurice Fowler. *m* Harry Robertson. *cast* Jack McNicholl, Neville Watson, Tracey Ann Morris, Jeff Ward, Matthew Barker.

●Though distinctly tame and old-fashioned compared with, say, *Grange Hill*, this low-budget Children's Film Foundation feature does succeed in its stated intention of 'getting away from the black and white of goodies and baddies'. Innocent victim Terry is forced by skinhead Les and his gang to join them in a raid on his own school, from which they steal a cassette radio each. When the police arrive at his school the next day, Terry confesses, but insists that he was coerced. However, crucial evidence given by the caretaker tends to undermine Terry's position, as does his continuing refusal to implicate Les. In addition to the relationship between victimiser and victim, the film's clear narrative delves into the fuzzy area between right and wrong. NF

Tesis

see Thesis

Tess

(1979, Fr/GB, 180 min)
d Roman Polanski. *p* Claude Berri. *sc* Gérard Brach, Roman Polanski, John Brownjohn. *ph* Geoffrey Unsworth, Ghislain Cloquet. *ed* Alastair McIntyre, Tom Priestley. *pd* Pierre Guffroy. *m* Philippe Sarde. *cast* Nastassja Kinski, Leigh Lawson, Peter Firth, John Collin, Richard Pearson, John Bett.

● Having all the strengths and excesses of a middlebrow film (visual beauty, lush soundtrack, arty direction), this adaptation's appeal to the senses leaves them cloyed. Although true enough to Thomas Hardy's novel to become a useful aid to 'O' and 'A' levels, Polanski omits small but vital details (such as the initial cause of Tess' guilt, which does much to explain her ensuing acquiescence), and misuses those he includes (the landscape, in Hardy both a part of and a mirror to the protagonists, is relegated to a pastoral backcloth, and was furthermore filmed in Brittany and Normandy instead of Dorset), thus removing substance from this hollow film. Finally, *Tess* tells one rather more about its director's much publicised preoccupations than about Hardy's themes. FD

Tess of the Storm Country

(1960, US, 84 min)
d Paul Guilfoyle. *p* Everett Chambers. *sc* Charles Lang. *ph* James Wong Howe. *ed* John Bushelman. *ad* John Mansbridge. *m* Paul Sawtell, Bert Shefter. *cast* Diane Baker, Jack Ging, Lee Philips, Wallace Ford, Robert F Simon, Bert Remsen, Archie Duncan, Nancy Valentine.

● This umpteenth version of Grace White's overwrought novel, scripted by Charles Lang, follows Scots lass Tess MacLean (Baker) who comes to Pennsylvania only to find that her fiancé has been fatally poisoned by the pollution from a chemical plant. Before matters are sorted out, Tess's new love, a young Mennonite named Peter (Ging), whose family sold the polluters their land, is wrongfully imprisoned for burning down the despised plant. Highly contrived; CinemaScope photography by James Wong Howe. JPy

Testament

(1983, US, 90 min)
d Lynne Littman. *p* Jonathan Bernstein, Lynne Littman. *sc* John Sacret Young. *ph* Steven Poster. *ed* Suzanne Pettit. *pd* David Nichols. *m* James Horner. *cast* Jane Alexander, William Devane, Ross Harris, Roxana Zal, Lukas Haas, Philip Anglim, Lilia Skala, Leon Ames, Lurene Tuttle, Kevin Costner.

● In a momentary flash, an American suburb (carefully established) is pitched into nightmare: clearly the end has come, but apart from a power failure, the town's position in a mountain bowl has saved it from the worst effects of nuclear blast. With Dad (Devane) missing, Mother (Alexander) and her three kids have to struggle on as radioactive dust appears on their cereal bowls, friends and neighbours begin to succumb to radiation sickness, everything begins to fall apart, and finally the first of the family has to be sewn into a shroud for burial in the garden. The subject of a family and community falling victim to a silent, invisible massacre is hardly usual cinema fare, but Littman keeps sentimentality at bay, refuses to court sensationalism, and coaxes some superb performances from her cast. A gentle, loving, noble, angry and heartrending film. JG

Testament

(1988, GB, 80 min)
d John Akomfrah. *p* Avril Johnson, Lina Gopaul. *sc* John Akomfrah. *ph* David Scott. *ed* Brand Thumin. *m* Trevor Mathison. *cast* Tania Rogers, Evans Hunter, Emma Francis Wilson, Frank Parkes, Errol Shaker.

● A subtitle, 'The War Zone of Memories', gives a better indication of this film's fragmentary, poetic style, in which a plot about a television journalist's quest for an interview is interspersed with recurrent images of conflict and renewed faith. The setting is Ghana, and Abena (Rogers) has returned to her native land from Britain in order to interview Werner Herzog on location with *Cobra Verde*. But Herzog proves elusive, leaving Abena with time to ponder her hasty departure from Ghana following the collapse of the Nkrumah regime and her subsequent arrest by the military. Akomfrah and the Black Audio Film Collective offer the complex ethical and emotional issues in telling flashes and seemingly inconclusive discussions. Abena's dilemma and her political past are revealed only gradually, and the process of exposition, while sometimes bewildering, is always fascinating. Ambitious and visually inventive, this acutely personal tale of discovery is marred only by Rogers' rather lifeless performance. CM

Testament d'Orphée, Le (Testament of Orpheus)

(1959, Fr, 83 min, b/w)
d Jean Cocteau. *p* Jean Thuillier. *sc* Jean Cocteau. *ph* Roland Pontoizeau. *ed* Marie-Josèphe Yoyotte. *ad* Pierre Guffroy, Janine Janet. *m* Georges Auric, Martial Solal, Jacques Météhen. *cast* Jean Cocteau, Edouard Dermithe, Henri Crémieux, Jean-Pierre Léaud, Maria Casarès, François Périer, Jean Marais, Yul Brynner, Pablo Picasso, Lucia Bosè, Charles Aznavour, Françoise Sagan, Roger Vadim, Daniel Gélin.

● Cocteau's last film is as personal and private as its title suggests, and it makes little sense for viewers unfamiliar with his other work. It's a wry, self-conscious re-examination of a lifetime's obsessions, with Cocteau playing himself at the centre of the mythology that he created in countless books, plays, films and paintings. This mythology yields a torrent of familiar characters, situations, effects and images, all of them quoted in a spirit of bewilderment and growing disillusionment: Cocteau finally disappears into his fictional world, leaving the real world to a noisy new generation. Nothing about the film is in the least seductive except for its fundamental openness; the tone veers between gentle irony and low-key pessimism. Cocteau admirers will probably find it very moving. TR

Testament du Docteur Cordelier, Le (Experiment in Evil)

(1959, Fr, 95 min, b/w)
d/p/sc Jean Renoir. *ph* Georges Leclerc. *ed* Renée Lichtig. *ad* Marcel-Louis Dieulot. *m* Joseph Kosma. *cast* Jean-Louis Barrault, Teddy Bilis, Michel Vitold, Jean Topart, Gaston Modot, Jean Renoir.

● This is minor Renoir, 'Jekyll and Hyde' transposed to contemporary Paris. An early example of the TV/cinema hybrid, it was sufficiently a curiosity at the time to justify an irrelevant opening about Renoir arriving at the RTF studios to record a prologue. Shot fast using TV techniques (lots of cameras and mikes covering a single long take), it consequently looks flat and unatmospheric, while some of the performances are mysterious (Why is Vitold so manic? Is Bilis meant to be such a prig?). But the redeeming asset, indeed the film's entire justification, is Barrault in his Opale (i.e. Hyde) manifestation. Shambling, twitching, cocky and looking for trouble, turning ferociously on anyone weak who crosses his path, he is the epitome of aggression and the absence of pity. Forget March and Malkovich, Barrymore and Beswick: none comes within a mile of this chilling creation. BBa

Testament of Dr Mabuse, The (Das Testament des Dr Mabuse)

(1933, Ger, 122 min, b/w)
d Fritz Lang. *p* Seymour Nebenzal. *sc* Thea von Harbou, Fritz Lang. *ph* Fritz Arno Wagner. *pd* Karl Vollbrecht, Emil Hasler. *m* Hans Erdmann. *cast* Rudolf Klein-Rogge, Otto Wernicke, Oscar Beregi, Gustav Diessl, Vera Liessem, Karl Meixner.

● In 1922, Fritz Lang conceived Mabuse as a cypher for Weimar Germany's corruption and decadence: the two-part *Dr Mabuse, the Gambler/Inferno* shows him as a criminal mastermind, casinos and stock exchange equally in hand, enmeshed in a web of dope, killing, fake seances and madness. By 1932, the character had become rather more than just king villain of the serials: *Testament* finds him mouthing undisguised Nazi slogans from his asylum prison, and using hypnotism to maintain control over his criminal empire outside; he's opposed by the same cop who hunted Peter Lorre in Lang's *M* the year before. Goebbels banned the movie but offered leadership of the German film industry to Lang, who left the country overnight. TR

Testigos Ocultos

see Hidden Witnesses

Testimony

(1987, GB, 157 min, b/w & col)
d/p Tony Palmer. *sc* David Rudkin, Tony Palmer. *ph* Nic Knowland. *ed/pd* Tony Palmer. *m* Dmitri Shostakovich. *cast* Ben Kingsley, Terence Rigby, Ronald Pickup, Sherry Baines, Magdalen Asquith, John Shrapnel, Robert Stephens.

● Palmer's epic biopic of the Soviet composer Dmitri Shostakovich (Kingsley), adapted from memoirs he 'related' shortly before his death in 1975, concentrates primarily on the period (early '30s to '50s) of his deeply ambivalent relationship with Stalin (Rigby). Long, daringly shot in 'Scope and glorious black-and-white, it's a fascinating, ambitious work, but finally overwrought and unrevealing. Despite some stunning individual scenes, featuring expressionist imagery, montage techniques, and historical reconstructions, (and inventive use of our dour Victorian industrial landscape to suggest the Leningrad and Moscow locations), the cumulative effect is bewildering and lacking in intellectual rigour; the array of 'hello Meyerhold, goodbye Khachaturyan' cameos distract (Pickup's betrayed Marshal Tukhachevsky excepted), and Kingsley, scribbling away, is left as little more than a pile of soulless period clothing. The music (the Violin Concerto No 1, the late symphonies, the Michelangelo sonnet) is magnificent. WH

Test Tube Babies (aka The Pill)

(1953, US, 70 min, b/w)
d Merle Connell. *cast* John Maitland, Monica Davis.

● George and Kathy talk about babies, but get distracted by protracted peekaboo necking parties, California early '50s-style, which lead to anything but consummation. More talk about babies before it's discovered that George is 'sterel'. A very odd doctor performs the necessary op upon Kathy (after a long lecture on the benefits of artificial insemination) wearing *leather* gloves, a detail typical of the effortless surrealism this film unintentionally achieves. Classical stuff in that everyone acts like statues. Is there life on Mars? CPe

Teta y la luna, La

see Tit and the Moon, The

Tête contre les Murs, La (The Keepers)

(1958, Fr, 98 min, b/w)
d Georges Franju. *sc* Jean-Pierre Mocky. *ph* Eugen Schüfftan. *ed* Suzanne Sandberg. *ad* Louis Le Barbenchon. *m* Maurice Jarre. *cast* Jean-Pierre Mocky, Pierre Brasseur, Paul Meurisse, Anouk Aimée, Charles Aznavour, Jean Galland, Edith Scob.

● Franju's first feature (after a notably idiosyncratic career as a director of shorts) confirmed his stature as a poet of the darker regions of the human psyche, and his vision as that of one of the cinema's least blinkered social moralists. It deals with an upper middle class dropout (played by Mocky, who scripts and intended to direct it himself) who finds himself in an insane asylum after committing 'irrational' acts of vandalism aimed against his father; he breaks out with an epileptic friend (Aznavour, in his first screen role), and lands in deeper water than ever… It's part psychological thriller, part subversive bourgeois drama, and all *film noir* of the most devastating sort. TR

Tête de Normande St-Onge, La

(1975, Can, 116 min)
d Gilles Carle. *p* Pierre Lamy. *sc* Gilles Carle, Ben Barzman. *ph* François Protat. *ed* Gilles Carle, Avde Chiraieff. *pd* Jocelyn Joly. *m* Lewis Furey. *cast* Carole Laure, Raymond Cloutier, Renée Girard, Reynald Bouchard, Carmen Giroux.

●Quite where the lady's head is at, as they used to say, is a question better left to clinical enquiry than the speculations of one unconvinced by the film's anti-psychiatric contortions. It's the sort of film where fantasies (erotic and otherwise) proliferate, and the lines between sanity and madness are purposefully blurred; as, in passing, are the lines between exploitation, voyeurism, and (?) art. The erratic Normande (an outsider like the heroine of Carle's *The True Nature of Bernadette*) she 'rescues' her mother from a mental home to set up a counter-culture family) is framed and reflected in a compatibly fragmented, flashy style, so it's all of a piece. Either you buy it or you don't – in which case it's intensely irritating. PT

Tête d'un Homme, La (A Man's Neck)

(1932, Fr, 97 min, b/w)
d Julien Duvivier. *sc* Julien Duvivier, Louis Delaprée, Pierre Calmann. *ph* Armand Thirard. *ed* Marthe Bassi. *ad* Georges Wakhévitch. *m* Jacques Dallin. *cast* Harry Baur, Valéry Inkijinoff, Alexandre Rignault, Gina Manès, Gaston Jacquet.

●'Night envelops me,' wails the chanteuse, keying the mood of lethargy and doom, as the movie follows consumptive killer Inkijinoff in pursuit of his death wish. The erratic Duvivier could be quite a sharp director on occasion: the opening survey of feet trudging a greasy pavement, the sound of dice in a cup overriding the bar-side hubbub, the single shot of a cop interviewing a series of back-projected witnesses. But this early Simenon adaptation (Baur as Maigret) has far too much time for the tiresome Inkijinoff, and the film will appeal most to extreme romantics and to those investigating the origins of *noir*. BBa

Tetsuo (Tetsuo: The Iron Man)

(1991, Jap, 67 min, b/w)
d/p/sc Shinya Tsukamoto. *ph* Shinya Tsukamoto, Kei Fujiwara. *ed/ad* Shinya Tsukamoto. *m* Chu Ishikawa. *cast* Tomoroh Taguchi, Kei Fujiwara, Nobu Kanaoku, Shinya Tsukamoto.

●This is a movie that springs from all the fantasy entertainment Japanese kids grow up with: Godzilla movies, sci-fi animation, manga comic strips and 'hardcore' rock music. In Tsukamoto's hands, these childhood influences mature into fantasies with a more adult shading: dark sexual fantasies, fantasies of brutal violence, fantasies of molecular mutation, apocalyptic fantasies. Not for nothing have Tokyo critics referred to Tsukamoto as 'Japan's answer to Sam Raimi, David Cronenberg *and* David Lynch'. TR

Tetsuo II: Bodyhammer

(1991, Jap, 81 min)
d Shinya Tsukamoto. *p* Fuminori Shishido, Fumio Kurokawa. *sc/ph/ed* Shinya Tsukamoto. *m* Chu Ishikawa. *cast* Tomoroh Taguchi, Nobu Kanaoka, Shinya Tsukamoto, Keinosuke Tomioka, Sujin Kim.

●Significantly more accessible than Tsukamoto's first, black-and-white, 16mm foray into new-flesh-horror (*Tetsuo: The Iron Man*), this colour, hi-tech reworking of the original is a relentlessly inventive sci-fi cinepoem, whose story – again about a man suffering strange and deadly anatomical changes, which this time result partly from the rage he feels at his son being abducted – is largely an excuse for a series of virtuoso sequences based around the motif of physical/psychological mutation. *Manga* merges with Cronenbergian grotesquerie in a violent, frantic, technically audacious epic full of images that are alternately homoerotic and heart-stopping in their cruel brilliance. GA

Texas, Addio (aka The Avenger)

(1966, It/Sp, 92 min)
d Ferdinando Baldi. *p* Manolo Bolognini. *sc* Franco Rossetti, Ferdinando Baldi. *ph* Enzo Barboni. *ed* Sergio Montanari. *ad* Luigi Scaccianoce, Eduardo Terre de la Fuente. *m* Antón Garcia Abril. *cast* Franco Nero, Cole Kitosch, José Suarez, Elisa Montes, Livio Lorenzon, José Guardiola.

●Ultrascope spaghetti Western in which Texas sheriff Burt Sullivan (Nero, standard issue laconic) crosses the border with kid brother Jim (Kitosch) to square matters with Cisco Delgado (Suarez), the outlaw who murdered their father. The twist? Jim turns out to be Cisco's abandoned son. Workmanlike and unpretentious, but not a patch on Leone or even the Django series. TJ

Texas Chain Saw Massacre, The

(1974, US, 83 min)
d/p Tobe Hooper. *sc* Kim Henkel, Tobe Hooper. *ph* Daniel Pearl. *ed* Sallye Richardson, J Larry Carroll. *ad* Robert A Burns. *m* Tobe Hooper, Wayne Bell. *cast* Marilyn Burns, Gunnar Hansen, Allen Danziger, Edwin Neal, Paul A Partain, William Vail.

●A band of charmless youngsters ignore all the warnings and stumble across a psychopathic family (closer to Charles Addams than *Psycho*) in remote farmland. This abattoir of a movie boasts sledgehammers, meathooks and chainsaws, and the result, though not especially visceral, is noisy, relentless, and about as subtle as having your leg sawed off without anaesthetic. It's notable only for taking woman-in-jeopardy about as far as she can go. The three men are despatched unceremoniously, and the women (bra-less and hotpants respectively), their screams rising into orgasms of fear, are toyed with endlessly while the camera often assumes a pointedly aggressive stance. Pernicious stuff and not even true, like the ads suggested – the Ed Gein case, on which this is supposedly based, bears little relation. CPe

Texas Chainsaw Massacre 2, The

(1986, US, 100 min)
d Tobe Hooper. *p* Menahem Golan, Yoram Globus. *sc* LM Kit Carson. *ph* Richard Kooris. *ed* Alain Jakubowicz. *ad* Cary White. *m* Tobe Hooper, Jerry Lambert. *cast* Dennis Hopper, Caroline Williams, Bill Johnson, Jim Siedow, Bill Moseley.

●After the claustrophobic horrors of the original, Hooper's messy stab at outré black humour comes as something of a relief. Deep in the bowels of Texas, the mutant family display their annoyance at a local DJ's blatherings in typically visceral style. Hopper hams it up massively as a psychotic ex-Texas Ranger, hell-bent upon bringing the cannibals to justice, while Williams provides a feisty female lead who (once again) gives the inbred mental cases a run for their money. Despite the BBFC's perfunctory refusal to certificate the movie for public showing in Britain, it contains little to offend anyone with the slightest sense of irony. Gaudy highlights include: a driver having his head chainsawed in half to lively effect; Hopper picking out the biggest bastard chainsawer in a hardware store; Williams taunting Leatherface about his inability to 'get it up' as he impotently waggles an unstartable chainsaw between her legs. The only truly yucky moment comes when Williams is forced to don facial skin freshly peeled from a corpse's face, but in these post-*Silence of the Lambs* days even that seems a tad tame. Not a patch on the original (or indeed Jeff Burr's Part III), but amusing enough none the less. Isn't it about time the censors developed a sense of humour? MK

Texas Chainsaw Massacre III

see Leatherface: The Texas Chainsaw Massacre III

Texas Rangers, The

(1936, US, 97 min, b/w)
d/p King Vidor. *sc* Louis Stevens. *ph* Edward Cronjager. *ed* Doane Harrison. *ad* Hans Dreier, Bernard Herzbrun. *cast* Fred MacMurray, Jack Oakie, Jean Parker, Lloyd Nolan, Edward Ellis, George Hayes.

●Riding silently in column, past towering cliffs and beneath ornate cloudscapes, the Rangers proceed on their implacable way, to showdowns featuring such declarations as 'Ain't no more room for your kind of Texan' and would-be amusing dialogue equating dead Indians with rotten apples. Redskin beware! Outlaw beware! (Though the latter merits the post-mortem valediction, 'Hope you'll let him in up there. He just got on the wrong trail, that's all.') The dilemma arising from this movie is whether to emphasise the correspondences between it and contemporary Nazi cinema or whether to focus on the distinctions. Vidor was himself a Texan and unembarrassed, it seems, by the concept of Texas as (after the elimination of undesirable elements) a paradise situated in the south of Utopia. It's mildly amusing, therefore, that the archetypal scenery framing all those stereotypical characters should actually be situated near Gallup, New Mexico. Nothing else is amusing though. BBa

Texasville

(1990, US, 125 min)
d Peter Bogdanovich. *p* Barry Spikings, Peter Bogdanovich. *sc* Peter Bogdanovich. *ph* Nicholas von Sternberg. *ed* Richard Fields. *pd* Phedon Papamichael. *cast* Jeff Bridges, Cybill Shepherd, Annie Potts, Cloris Leachman, Timothy Bottoms, Eileen Brennan, Randy Quaid.

●Bogdanovich's sequel to *The Last Picture Show*, set in 1984, finds the small Texan town of Anarene afflicted by moral, economic and social breakdown. Duane Jackson (Bridges), now an oil mogul, faces bankruptcy, his kids are virtually delinquent, and his marriage to Karla (Potts) is on the rocks. Duane's old flame, homecoming B movie queen Jacy (Shepherd) looks set to seduce his family away from him; and the mayor, Duane's lifelong buddy Sonny (Bottoms), with whom he is organising Anarene's centennial pageant, is mentally and emotionally unstable. In other words, life is a mess. So is the film's narrative, adapted by Bogdanovich himself from Larry McMurtry's sprawling novel. The first half comes over as deliriously cynical satire, suggesting nothing less than a Paul Bartel pastiche of *Dallas*. Then sentimentality intrudes as Bogdanovich, determined to introduce a hymn to the healing power of friendship, loses the courage of his comic convictions. It all looks good, though, and the actors – epecially Bridges and Potts – are clearly having a ball. GA

TGV

(1998, Sen/ Fr, 90 min)
d Moussa Touré. *p* Jean-François Lepetit. *sc* Moussa Touré, Alain Choquart. *ph* Alain Choquart. *ed* Josie Miljevic. *m* Wasis Diop. *cast* Makéna Diop, Bernard Giraudeau, Philippine Leroy-Beaulieu, Al Hamdou Traore, Joséphine M'Boup, Joséphine Zambo.

●A polished, eventful and very engaging road movie in which two friends, running a bus service from Dakar to Guinea, take an assortment of passengers through dangerous territory where tribal guerillas are fighting in order to get back a tribal totem currently in a French museum. The clientele – young and old, rich and poor, Muslim and Christian, black and white – bring their own problems and tensions, of course, so that the film becomes a kind of latter-day Senegalese *Stagecoach*, marked by fine droll humour, energetic performances and fluid, elegant camerawork. GA

Thank God It's Friday

(1978, US, 89 min)
d Robert Klane. *p* Rob Cohen. *sc* Barry Armyn Bernstein. *ph* James Crabe. *ed* Richard Halsey. *pd* Tom H John. *cast* Valerie Landsburg, Terri Nunn, Chick Vennera, Donna Summer, Ray Vitte, Jeff Goldblum, Debra Winger, The Commodores.

●Like several other movies that have trodden in the wake of *American Graffiti*, this evening-in-the-life-of-a-disco uses a largely unknown cast and keeps eight or nine lines of narrative going at once. It also crams in countless plugs for its sponsors, Motown and Casablanca. It's at least as formulary and dumb as it sounds – but it's also very, very funny. The jokes are strictly mainstream, of course, but the fact that most of them are anti-sexist and anti-racist distinctly helps, as does the freshness of the cast. Most commendable of all is the fact that no one feels the need to moralise or get serious in the closing scenes: the running gags keep right on running, and they're strong enough to send you out with a fixed grin. TR

Thank You, Aunt
see Grazie Zia

Thank You, Jeeves!
(1936, US, 57 min, b/w)
d Arthur Greville Collins. *p* Sol M Wurtzel. *sc* Joseph Hoffman, Stephen Gross. *ph* Barney McGill. *ed* Nick DeMaggio. *m* Samuel Kaylin. *cast* Arthur Treacher, Virginia Field, David Niven, Lester Matthews, Colin Tapley.
●Niven was a support player for Sam Goldwyn when Fox borrowed him for third-billing in this charming B-picture scripted by Joseph Hoffman and Stephen Gross from the novel by PG Wodehouse. Bertie Wooster gets entirely the wrong idea when mystery woman Field asks for help in fending off pursuing gangsters. Treacher steals the show as Jeeves, but Niven makes a very passable Bertie. Relatively minor, but, unlike a lot of bigger movies, it knows not to demand too much of your time. TJ

Thank You, Life
see Merci la vie

Thank Your Lucky Stars
(1943, US, 127 min)
d David Butler. *p* Mark Hellinger. *sc* Norman Panama, James V Kern, Melvin Frank. *ph* Arthur Edeson. *ed* Irene Morra. *ad* Anton F Grot. *songs* Frank Loesser, Arthur Schwartz. *cast* Eddie Cantor, Dennis Morgan, Joan Leslie, Bette Davis, Humphrey Bogart, Errol Flynn, John Garfield, Ida Lupino, Olivia de Havilland.
●During WWII, Hollywood came up with the notion that all-star revues would be just the thing to revive the audience's flagging spirits, and soon these extravaganzas started rolling out of the backlot like dreadnoughts down a slipway. Paramount turned out *Star Spangled Rhythm*, followed a year later by this Warners offering, which gave the studio's contract players a rare opportunity to strut their stuff in a musical context. The plot's the usual puttin'-on-a-show concoction, but the excessive length is worth it for Bette Davis' showstopping 'They're Either Too Young or Too Old' and Errol Flynn (that's right, all-singing all-dancing) offering the worst Cockernee accent this side of Dick Van Dyke in his party piece, 'That's What You Jolly Well Get'. TJ

That Championship Season
(1982, US, 109 min)
d Jason Miller. *p* Menahem Golan, Yoram Globus. *sc* Jason Miller. *ph* John Bailey. *ed* Richard Halsey. *pd* Ward Preston. *m* Bill Conti. *cast* Bruce Dern, Stacy Keach, Robert Mitchum, Martin Sheen, Paul Sorvino.
●Backslapping, whooping, and blubbering abound when four college buddies foregather to relive the moment twenty years earlier when coach (Mitchum) led them to glory in the state basketball league. Jollity soon gives way to maudlin nostalgia, and as the liquor flows, the inner men begin to peek through in a depressingly familiar succession of outbursts, breakdowns, and confessions of inadequacy. Locker-room camaraderie is held up as the US apotheosis of brotherly love, and the old 'winning is everything' ethic gets trotted out with suspiciously few ironic sideswipes. Excellent performances, but writer/director Miller obviously couldn't bear to discard one finely crafted chestnut of his Pulitzer prizewinning play, and makes his distinguished cast wade through one of the most torrential masses of verbiage ever to hit the screen. JP

That Cold Day in the Park
(1969, Can, 112 min)
d Robert Altman. *p* Donald Factor, Leon Mirell. *sc* Gillian Freeman. *ph* Laszlo Kovacs. *ed* Danford B Greene. *ad* Leon Ericksen. *m* Johnny Mandel. *cast* Sandy Dennis, Michael Burns, Susanne Benton, Luana Anders, Michael Murphy, John Garfield Jr.
●Made immediately before *M*A*S*H*, this has Sandy Dennis, in her characteristic role as a frustrated spinster, picking up a dropout (Burns) on a Vancouver park bench and inviting him home for food, care and shelter. The results are distressingly predictable (though, to be fair to Altman, this area of modern Gothic hadn't been quite so overworked in 1969). With signs of the visual daring evident in Altman's later work, however, there is sufficient interest in his treatment of yet another woman character going bananas to repay committed admirers. RM

That Darn Cat
(1965, US, 116 min)
d Robert Stevenson. *p* Walt Disney. *sc* Mildred Gordon, Gordon Gordon, Bill Walsh. *ph* Edward Colman. *ed* Cotton Warburton. *ad* Carroll Clark, William H Tuntke. *m* Bob Brunner. *cast* Hayley Mills, Dean Jones, Dorothy Provine, Roddy McDowall, Neville Brand, Elsa Lanchester, William Demarest, Ed Wynn.
●This typical – not unentertaining – mid-'60s Disney live-actioner has Hayley's Siamese following a trail of juicy salmon and unwittingly uncovering a kidnap plot. Federal agent Jones and neighbour McDowall are in personable form, but the two legged cast play second string to the marvellous moggie. TJ

That Eye, the Sky
(1994, Aust, 105 min)
d John Ruane. *p* Peter Beilby, Grainne Marmion. *sc* Jim Barton, John Ruane. *ph* Ellery Ryan. *ed* Ken Sallows. *pd* Chris Kennedy. *m* David Bridie. *cast* Lisa Harrow, Peter Coyote, Jamie Croft, Amanda Dogue, Mark Fairall.
●Australian writer/director Ruane followed his first film, the sparkling black comedy *Death in Brunswick*, with this very different, mystical rites-of-passage chronicle. When his father is returned home in a coma after a car accident, 12-year-old Ort (Croft) places his faith in a charismatic stranger (Coyote) to effect a cure. But what role in the healing process has the weird light which the boy spots in the sky above the house? The emotional knots of a problem family are played against an unfussily supernatural background affecting all their lives. Hard to categorise, but ultimately haunting. TJ

That Gang of Mine
(1940, US, 62 min, b/w)
d Joseph H Lewis. *p* Sam Katzman. *sc* William Lively. *ph* Robert Cline, Harvey Gould. *ed* Carl Pierson. *pd* Fred Preble. *cast* Bobby Jordan, Leo Gorcey, Clarence Muse, Dave O'Brien, Joyce Bryant, David Gorcey.
●A salutary reminder of the poverty row milieu in which Lewis had to toil for years before producing the belatedly recognised masterpieces of his maturity, made on budgets only marginally more luxurious. A Monogram series movie featuring the East Side Kids in an absurd horse race comedy that induces as many groans (not least for racist stereotyping) as laughs, it's none the less distinguished (and lifted) by the energetic visual style and wit with which Lewis invests it. PT

That Hamilton Woman (aka Lady Hamilton)
(1941, US, 128 min, b/w)
d/p Alexander Korda. *sc* RC Sherriff, Walter Reisch. *ph* Rudolph Maté. *ed* William Hornbeck. *ad* Vincent Korda. *m* Miklos Rozsa. *cast* Vivien Leigh, Laurence Olivier, Alan Mowbray, Gladys Cooper, Sara Allgood, Henry Wilcoxon, Heather Angel.
●Being Churchill's favourite film may not be much of a recommendation, but it's easy to see why he welcomed this wartime offering from the English community in Hollywood. Olivier may be outrageously hammy, but his Lord Nelson is an icon of eccentric English heroism. Patriotism is only half the story, though. Olivier and the splendidly coquettish Leigh distil the essence of their stormy off-screen romance so effectively that the Americans insisted on a ridiculously prurient prologue showing its unfortunate consequences for the lady. RMy

That Lady
(1955, GB, 100 min)
d Terence Young. *p* Sy Bartlett. *sc* Anthony Veiller, Sy Bartlett. *ph* Robert Krasker. *ed* Raymond Poulton. *ad* Frank White. *m* John Addison. *cast* Olivia de Havilland, Gilbert Roland, Paul Scofield, Françoise Rosay, Dennis Price, Anthony Dawson, Christopher Lee.
●Soporific yarn from a novel by Kate O'Brien set in 16th century Madrid. Olivia de Havilland is Ana de Medoza, a widow with a Moshe Dayan eyepatch, who stirs up unholy feelings at court. Scofield's King Philip II has a crush on her and is furious when she starts an affair with one of his ministers. The film falls victim to spectacularly fussy production design and Robert Krasker's 'Scope photography. Everybody's decked out in best medieval finery and we're treated to endless picture postcard shots of historic Spain, but there isn't a hint of any sexual tension between de Havilland and Scofield. GM

That'll Be the Day
(1973, GB, 91 min)
d Claude Whatham. *p* David Puttnam, Sandy Lieberson. *sc* Ray Connolly. *ph* Peter Suschitzky. *ed* Michael Bradsell. *ad* Brian Morris. *cast* David Essex, Ringo Starr, Rosemary Leach, James Booth, Billy Fury, Keith Moon, Rosalind Ayres, Robert Lindsay, Brenda Bruce.
●An intriguing hybrid, this yarn about a young, John Lennon-like West Country lad (Essex) who abandons his A-levels ('I've had enough of sodding school!') and heads off to find his fortune in a shabby, seaside town is made in the same downbeat, naturalistic way as the so-called kitchen sink films of a decade before, but boasts a very upbeat rock-'n'roll soundtrack. Director Whatham (better known for his TV work than for anything he did on the big screen) elicits suprisingly strong performances from Essex and from Ringo Starr as his teddy boy guru. Look out, too, for Billy Fury as the aptly named rocker, Stormy Tempest. The film marked an important staging post in the career of its relentlessly ambitious producer, David Puttnam, and spawned an excellent sequel, *Stardust*. GM

That Lucky Touch
(1975, GB, 93 min)
d Christopher Miles. *p* Dimitri de Grunwald. *sc* John Briley. *ph* Douglas Slocombe. *ed* Tom Priestley. *pd* Tony Masters. *m* John Scott. *cast* Roger Moore, Susannah York, Shelley Winters, Lee J Cobb, Jean-Pierre Cassel, Raf Vallone, Sydne Rome, Donald Sinden.
●After the success of *Gold*, Moore and York team again, smoothiechops as an arms merchant to her independent journalist with principles, a divorce, and a young son. Out to scupper Moore's weapons deal with NATO, while trying not to fall in love with him, York's real nature is revealed through a remark her son and the scriptwriter let slip: 'Mother makes news happen where she wants to be'. The film itself is just as calculating – a romantic comedy bogged down by some desperately protracted humour, tourist Brussels locations, and the manner in which British, American, and Continental sales are all glaringly kept in mind. The result is, as one character says apropos of something else, like getting a troop of horses to piss at the same time. CPe

That Man Bolt
(1973, US, 103 min)
d Henry Levin, David Lowell Rich. *p* Bernard Schwartz. *sc* Quentin Werty [Ranald MacDougall], Charles Johnson. *ph* Gerald Perry Finnerman. *ed* Carl Pingitore, Robert F Shugrue. *ad* Alexander Golitzen. *m* Charles Bernstein. *cast* Fred Williamson, Byron Webster, Miko Mayama, Teresa Graves, Satoshi Nakamura, Jack Ging, Paul Mantee.
●Packaged consumer product, with a black hero (albeit somewhat like Uncle Tom's answer to Desperate Dan – all chin and about as subtle), and a plot that escalates from straightforward thriller (he's an international 'courier') into a fantasy of Bond-like proportions, which ends with Bolt coming on like a one-man army. It's given something of a lift by the now almost obligatory kung-fu influence: Bolt lands up in Hong Kong, taking on the local syndicate villain and a score of oriental pugilists, the highlight being a fight in a firework factory (preceded by a bit of torture by acupuncture) which ends with a large firework display. CPe

That Man from Rio
see Homme de Rio, L'

That Man George
see Homme de Marrakesh, L'

That Night
(1992, US, 89 min)
d Craig Bolotin. *p* Arnon Milchan, Steven Reuther. *sc* Craig Bolotin. *ph* Bruce Surtees. *ed*

Priscilla Nedd-Friendly. *pd* Maher Ahmad. *m* David Newman. *cast* C Thomas Howell, Juliette Lewis, Helen Shaver, Eliza Dushku, John Dossett, J Smith-Cameron.

●Although whisked out with no great fanfare, this familiar tale of growing up in the early '60s is actually pretty good. It's 1961, Sputnik is circling the skies, and JFK's in the White House. Kicked around by her slightly older friends and largely ignored by her father, Alice (Dushku) becomes besotted with 17-year-old Sheryl (Lewis) across the street. She's everything Alice wants to be: confident, attractive and a little wild. The two become firm friends when the youngster paves the way for Sheryl's liaison with Brooklyn bad boy Rick (Howell). Writer/director Bolotin's sensitive, nuanced adaptation of Alice McDermott's novel surpasses expectations by keeping nostalgia at arm's length, adopting a comparatively restrained voice-over narration, and adhering closely to the ten-year-old's perspective. Lewis acts her bobby sox off as the teenager in heat, but she's hardly the princess Alice describes, while Howell is an unprepossessing object for her affections. Thankfully, young Dushku is very good, and Bruce Surtees' photography lifts the film to an altogether higher plane. TCh

That Night in Rio

(1941, US, 90 min)
d Irving Cummings. *p* Fred Kohlmar. *sc* George Seaton, Bess Meredyth, Hal Long. *ph* Leon Shamroy, Ray Rennahan. *ed* Walter Thompson. *ad* Richard Day, Joseph C Wright. *songs* Mack Gordon, Harry Warren. *cast* Don Ameche, Alice Faye, Carmen Miranda, SZ Sakall, J Carrol Naish, Curt Bois, Leonid Kinsky, Maria Montez.

●Rudolph Lothar and Hans Adler's play *The Red Cat* was first adapted for the cinema as *Folies Bergère de Paris* (Roy Del Ruth, 1935), with Maurice Chevalier, and later metamorphosed into *On the Riviera* (Walter Lang, 1951), with Danny Kaye. Between times it served in this Fox frolic. Dapper count Ameche lands in bother when spouse Faye unwittingly hires a showbiz entertainer (his own secret sideline) to impersonate him as part of a business deal, a situation that requires nifty footwork when, as the nightclub impressionist rather than the married aristo, he falls for Faye all over again. Miranda strutts her stuff to a little ditty titled, 'Chica, Chica Boom Chic'. TJ

That Night in Varennes (La Nuit de Varennes)

(1982, Fr/It, 165 min)
d Ettore Scola. *p* Renzo Rossellini. *sc* Sergio Amidei, Ettore Scola. *ph* Armando Nannuzzi. *ed* Raimondo Crociani. *pd* Dante Ferretti. *m* Armando Trovaioli. *cast* Jean-Louis Barrault, Marcello Mastroianni, Hanna Schygulla, Harvey Keitel, Jean-Claude Brialy, Daniel Gélin, Andrea Ferreol, Michel Vitold, Laura Betti, Jean-Louis Trintignant.

●Featuring such notables as Tom Paine (Keitel), the ageing Casanova (Mastroianni), the randy writer Restif de la Bretonne (Barrault), and an Austrian countess (Schygulla), this is a picaresque story of the coach and party that followed hard on the one which tried to transport Louis XVI and Marie Antoinette to safety in 1791. Thus is history viewed not through the eyes of its main participants, but through the appetites, passions and prejudices of its commentators and bit players. The result is like *Tom Jones* crossed with *Stagecoach*, with the addition of Sergio Amidei and Scola's wise and witty dialogue, some sumptuous painterly landscapes, and a subtle feeling for the period far removed from the clichés of British imagining. There's a real sense both of history in the making and of life in the living: a warm, bravura work of lasting majesty. SGr

That Night's Wife (Sono yo no tsuma)

(1930, Jap, 65 min, b/w)
d Yasujiro Ozu. *sc* Kogo Noda. *ph/ed* Hideo Mohara. *ad* Yoneichi Wakita. *cast* Tokihiko Okada, Emiko Yagumo, Mitsuko Ichimura, Togo Yamamoto, Tatsuo Saito, Chishu Ryu.

●One of seven films Ozu made in 1930, this seems at first to be a prime example of his 'atypical' early silent period, when he experimented with numerous Hollywood-influenced genres and techniques before gradually refining the minimalist style and thematic focus of his mature career. The film opens as an effective heist drama pastiche, with Okada trussing up bank clerks and dodging the long shadows of a police dragnet, fox-like; we follow him home to his wife and their critically ill baby daughter, as does a wily police chief. As captor and prey sit out the night, waiting for the child's recovery, the scene is set for a claustrophobic battle of nerves. But see how Ozu – and his characters – constantly forgo the opportunities for conventional melodramatic conflict. The antagonists accepting with remarkable equanimity both their roles and their fate on opposing sides of the law. Seeds of Ozu's conservatism are well in evidence, then, but so too is his sedate pace and his even-handed sympathy and contemplativeness. NB

That Obscure Object of Desire (Cet Obscur Objet du Désir)

(1977, Fr/Sp, 103 min)
d Luis Buñuel. *p* Serge Silberman. *sc* Luis Buñuel, Jean-Claude Carrière. *ph* Edmond Richard. *ed* Hélène Plemiannikov. *ad* Pierre Guffroy. *m* Richard Wagner. *cast* Fernando Rey, Carole Bouquet, Angela Molina, Julien Bertheau, André Weber, Piéral, Milena Vukotic.

●Buñuel's last film, adapted from the Pierre Louys novel (about a woman who drives a man to distractions of frustrated desire) which also served as a basis for Sternberg's *The Devil Is a Woman*. Full of echoes from Buñuel's earlier work, it might almost be seen as a summation of his preoccupation with the connection between sex and violence, first annotated in *L'Age d'or*. His great coup here is to have the object of the hero's lusts played by two different actresses, with the alternation of svelte coolness and steamy voluptuousness lending teasing credibility to the way in which his ardour is cruelly cooled and heated by turns. These sexual games are brilliantly and tantalisingly funny, but the film is meanwhile secretly pursuing another obscure object of desire: the terrorism which surfaces in various forms (moral, social, cultural, economic, psychological, and even political), ranging from the bomb outrages that accompany the hero in his sexual odyssey down to the financial pressures he exerts in order to have his way. And just as *L'Age d'or* ended with an equation between the sexual and revolutionary acts, so does *That Obscure Object of Desire*, though in a deliberately coded, mystificatory form. TM

That Old Feeling

(1997, US, 105 min)
d Carl Reiner. *p* Leslie Dixon, Bonnie Bruckheimer. *sc* Leslie Dixon. *ph* Steve Mason. *ed* Richard Halsey. *pd* Sandy Veneziano. *m* Patrick Williams. *cast* Bette Midler, Dennis Farina, Paula Marshall, Gail O'Grady, David Rasche, Jamie Denton, Danny Nucci.

●Movie star Lilly (Midler) and journalist Dan (Farina) have always bickered like Punch and Judy. Now, as ex-partners, they're about to be flung together for their daughter Molly's prim-and-proper wedding. Though both have new mates, their genitals engage in a fit of nostalgia. Let the chaos begin. As ever, Midler – a queasy cross between Dolly Parton and Anna Magnani – is a sight to behold, the cruel lighting transforming her skin into a substance worthy of *Star Trek*. Farina, too, has rarely looked worse. Both, however, have enough pure showbiz talent, flinty and vulgar, to hook you. Grim, nevertheless. CO'Su

That Riviera Touch

(1966, GB, 98 min)
d Cliff Owen. *p* Hugh Stewart. *sc* SC Green, RM Hills, Peter Blackmore. *ph* Otto Heller. *ed* Gerry Hambling. *ad* John Blezard. *m* Ron Goodwin. *cast* Eric Morecambe, Ernie Wise, Suzanne Lloyd, Paul Stassino, Armand Mestral, Peter Jeffrey.

●When British TV comics become firmly established as household favourites, some klutz will always suggest that they make a feature film (even Cannon and Ball made one,*The Boys in Blue*). This was Morecambe and Wise's second cinema job (after *The Intelligence Men*): a routine caper with jewel thieves, gangsters, and speedboats – and plenty of padding shots of the Côte d'Azur. It was unworthy of their talents then; it looks even worse now. MA

That's Carry On

(1977, GB, 95 min, b/w & col)
d Gerald Thomas. *p* Peter Rogers. *sc* Tony Church. *ph* Tony Imi. *ed* Jack Gardner. *m* Eric Rogers. *cast* Barbara Windsor, Kenneth Williams.

●Kenneth Williams and Barbara Windsor are trapped in a projection box with cans containing prints of the 28 *Carry On* films: they enthusiastically reminisce in that inimitable fashion which has become part of our national heritage, and with the help of clips lead us in a rather desultory way through the history of the series. Strictly for addicts, who will doubtless chortle, as they have done for twenty years, at the changeless sexual innuendoes. JPy

That's Dancing!

(1985, US, 104 min, b/w & col)
d Jack Haley Jr. *p* David Niven Jr, Jack Haley Jr. *sc* Jack Haley Jr. *ph* Andrew Laszlo, Paul Lohmann. *ed* Bud Friedgen, Michael J Sheridan. *m* Henry Mancini. *narrators* Gene Kelly, Sammy Davis Jr, Mikhail Baryshnikov, Ray Bolger, Liza Minnelli.

●This is the way to see Hollywood dance sequences: no flimsy plot or vacuous dialogue, just the dancers doing their stuff. The only problem is that the pleasure of seeing the clips themselves is compromised by the sycophantic narration (Liza Minnelli's contribution in particular) and the random chronology of the arbitrary selection. So, while we may be mesmerised by the extraordinary silent Charleston sequence from *So This Is Paris* or the kaleidoscopic patterns of Busby Berkeley's *42nd Street*, the compilation itself is a formless mess. An extraneous ballet sequence featuring Mikhail Baryshnikov sticks out like a sore toe amid the furious tap dancing of the Nicholas Brothers, the sinuous sexiness of Cyd Charisse, and a charming ad-lib routine featuring Shirley Temple and 'Mr Bojangles'. And when the suave smoothness of Fred and Ginger in *Swing Time* gives way to the tight-trousered posturing of John Travolta and the gymnastic gracelessness of flashdancer Marine Jahan, the nostalgia bubble bursts. NF

That's Entertainment!

(1974, US, 137 min, b/w & col)
d/p/sc Jack Haley Jr. *ph* Gene Polito, Ernest Laszlo, Russell Metty, Ennio Guarnieri, Allan Green. *ed* Bud Friedgen, David E Blewitt. *m* Henry Mancini. *narrators* Fred Astaire, Bing Crosby, Gene Kelly, Peter Lawford, Liza Minnelli, Donald O'Connor, Debbie Reynolds, Mickey Rooney, Frank Sinatra, James Stewart, Elizabeth Taylor.

●On with the motley. Hollywood begins to package its feasts, and *That's Entertainment!* has all the flavour of the Vesta dehydrated line. The wondrous progeny of producers Arthur Freed and – to a lesser extent – Jack Cummings made MGM the home of the film musical. Jack Haley Jr has selected his fave raves, chopped them into skimpy segments, and thrown them together with little rhyme and less reason. Ageing superstars stroll on to recite his deliberately agog script. Little info, no view, no shape, no explanations emerge. The rarity of some items makes a trip worthwhile, but to seek out showings of *The Broadway Melody of 1938, Babes in Arms, Meet Me in St Louis, On the Town, The Band Wagon* and *Gigi* would be to learn much more about how Metro and Freed together developed the genre. SG

That's Entertainment Part II

(1976, US, 126 min, b/w & col)
d Gene Kelly. *p* Saul Chaplin, Daniel Melnick. *sc* Leonard Gershe. *ph* George Folsey. *ed* Bud Friedgen, David Blewitt, David Bretherton, Peter C Johnson. *m* Nelson Riddle. *narrators* Fred Astaire, Gene Kelly.

●With the most obvious plums already picked and the less obvious plums still ignored, this concoction is boosted with some non-musical items. It would be a hard-hearted person who couldn't find odd morsels of pleasure, but the compilation still enshrines the mediocre: Gene Kelly's ungainly stabs at Art, Doris Day, and scenes from thudders like *Till the Clouds Roll By*. The juxtaposition of clips is mindless; and between the indigestible chunks come newly-filmed scenes with Kelly and Astaire, which manage to be even worse than some of the clips. And their asinine commentary damagingly intrudes into the numbers. Who wants to hear Kelly reminisce when Garland's singing the sublime 'Have Yourself a Merry Little Christmas'? That's not entertainment. GB

That's Entertainment! III

(1994, US, 113 min, b/w & col)
d/p/sc Bud Friedgen, Michael J Sheridan. *ph* Howard A Anderson III. *ed* Bud Friedgen, Michael J Sheridan. *m* Marc Shaiman. *narrators* June Allyson, Cyd Charisse, Lena Horne, Howard Keel, Gene Kelly, Ann Miller, Debbie Reynolds, Mickey Rooney, Esther Williams.

● An MGM 70th anniversary 'docutainment' directed by the editors of the two previous clipfests. Since many of the famous sequences have been bagged already, this trawl through the archives is padded with out-takes, screen tests and off-screen footage. The period covered is bookended by *Hollywood Revue of 1929* and *Gigi* (1958). Some stuff we can do without, and did: Joan Crawford dancing like a donkey as she mimes 'Two Faced Woman' for *Torch Song*. On the other hand, Ava Gardner's 'Can't Help Loving Dat Man', unused in *Showboat*, is sweet indeed. Prints have been restored and soundtracks digitally enhanced, though there's some rough editing and aspect ratios are not always respected. Minor buff's stuff, but fun. WH

That Sinking Feeling

(1979, GB, 92 min)
d/p/sc Bill Forsyth. *ph* Michael Coulter. *ed* John Gow. *ad* Adrienne Atkinson. *m* Sydney Devine. *cast* Robert Buchanan, John Hughes, Janette Rankin, Derek Millar, Danny Benson, Eddie Burt.

● The image of the Scots in British films had largely been confined in the past to the wayward eccentrics of *Whisky Galore!* or to Glaswegian thugs. Refreshingly, in his first feature (independently produced on a risibly small budget), Bill Forsyth successfully captured the subversively ironic optimism of the Glasgow streets and somehow managed to combine it with the good-humoured charm of the best Ealing comedies. It's a street-smart fairytale about a group of unemployed teenagers embarking, enthusiastically but incompetently, on a big heist, and is played with such relish by members of the Glasgow Youth Theatre that it's guaranteed to win any audience over to its side within minutes: the British dispossessed's version of *Rockers*. SM

'That's Life'

(1986, US, 102 min)
d Blake Edwards. *p* Tony Adams. *sc* Milton Wexler, Blake Edwards. *ph* Anthony B Richmond. *ed* Lee Rhoads. *m* Henry Mancini. *cast* Jack Lemmon, Julie Andrews, Sally Kellerman, Robert Loggia, Jennifer Edwards, Rob Knepper, Chris Lemmon, Felicia Farr.

● A none-too-edifying examination of middle-life crisis, much in the autobiographical vein of *S.O.B* and set in Edwards' own home in Malibu, where he has gathered around him a veritable plethora of real-life friends and family. Lemmon plays a hypochondriacal architect, panicked at the thought of his impending 60th birthday, who is too obsessed with his fear of failing sexual and creative powers to notice the real anxieties of his family. While his singer wife (Andrews) busies herself organising a family get-together in his honour (while awaiting, unbeknownst to him, the results of a biopsy for suspected throat cancer), he is off indulging himself in a little extra-marital shenanigan with a seductive client, dabbling with a return to the church, or finding solace with a sexy fortune-teller's therapeutic line in massage. Lemmon, though presented with funny lines and set pieces, is irritating rather than sympathetic, and allowed to coast in a hackneyed retread of the neurotic he has been playing for too many years. The rest is a thinly veiled tribute to Edwards' wife Andrews, which shows him at his most embarrassing. WH

That Summer!

(1979, GB, 93 min)
d Harley Cokliss. *p* Davina Belling, Clive Parsons. *sc* Janey Preger. *ph* David Watkin. *ed* Michael Bradsell. *ad* Tim Hutchinson. *m* Ray Russell. *cast* Ray Winstone, Tony London, Emily Moore, Julie Shipley, Jon Morrison, Andrew Byatt, Ewan Stewart, John Junkin.

● Unfairly treated in the rock press, because the excellent soundtrack album led everyone into believing they were getting a hard-nosed film about the summer of punk. In fact this is a polished, if rather traditional, summerfuntime feature about a group of kids hanging out in Torquay. The storyline is necessarily slim, and to win an 'AA' certificate the film had to go easy on sex, drugs and rock'n'roll, but within his limited format Cokliss has performed small wonders: the acting is good (notably Byatt as a stomping Glasgow heavy), the script is funny, and the photography has some of the shimmering surface energy of *American Graffiti*. The pity is that the superb music has largely been thrown away, and the ending degenerates into Boy's Own Paper twaddle. DP

That Summer of White Roses

(1989, GB/Yugo, 103 min)
d Rajko Grlic. *p* Simon MacCorkindale, Zdravko Mihalic. *sc* Borislav Pekic, Rajko Grlic, Simon MacCorkindale. *ph* Tomislav Pinter. *ed* Damir F German. *pd* Dinka Jericevic. *m* Brane Zivkovic, Junior Campbell, Mike O'Donnell. *cast* Tom Conti, Susan George, Rod Steiger, Nitzan Sharron, Alun Armstrong, John Gill, John Sharp, Geoffrey Whitehead, Miljenko Brlecic, Vanja Drach.

● Although the riverside bathing beach proves popular with the Nazis (this being Yugoslavia in 1945), the token lifeguard – simple-minded Andrija (Conti) – hardly has his work cut out, and can therefore spend his days gazing at the water and mummering on about the 'river demon'. Considering the proximity to the Nazi base, it seems perverse that fugitive Ana (George) should pick this spot as a hideout; even stranger that she thinks a rush marriage to the village idiot will deflect suspicion. The gentle rhythms of life continue until Andrija dramatically saves a fat old gent from drowning. Is he partisan or Nazi? Whatever, good-hearted Andrija seems fated to attract unwelcome attention… Conti invests the character with cheerful dignity, but remains some way short of the noble and tragic dimensions hopefully indicated. The elegiac riverside scenes, set against crashing portrayals of Nazi swinishness, work rather better than the romantic or action stuff. SFe

That Thing You Do!

(1996, US, 108 min)
d Tom Hanks. *p* Gary Goetzman, Jonathan Demme, Edward Saxon. *sc* Tom Hanks. *ph* Tak Fujimoto. *ed* Richard Chew. *pd* Victor Kempster. *m* Howard Shore. *cast* Tom Hanks, Tom Everett Scott, Liv Tyler, Johnathon Schaech, Steve Zahn, Ethan Embry, Rita Wilson.

● The year's 1964, and young Guy (Hanks-lookalike Scott) is drafted in to play drums with a rock'n'roll high school band. One catchy tune transforms the One-ders into local heroes, and brings them to the attention of first regional, then national talent scouts, until 'The Wonders' find themselves with a Top Ten hit and a record contract. Their progress is uncomplicated, if not exactly quick. Hanks is such a nice guy, he can't bring himself to imagine anyone who isn't, which tends to preclude anything so base as dramatic conflict. Episodes of *Happy Days* have more narrative tension. The nearest we get to a bad guy is Schaech as the group's career-driven singer-songwriter: the artist. Love-interest Tyler gets to mouth lyrics in the wings; when things hot up, she catches a cold. As writer/director, Hanks recreates the period with nostalgic affection, in pastel shades and design straight from a retro catalogue, but his film shows no interest in the musical process, and the title track is reprised ad nauseam (eight times!). Sweet nothing, then, but what would you expect of a rock movie devoted to the drummer? TCh

That Was Then... This Is Now

(1985, US, 101 min)
d Christopher Cain. *p* Gary R Lindberg, John M Ondov. *sc* Emilio Estevez. *ph* Juan Ruiz-Anchia. *ed* Ken Johnson. *ad* Chester Kaczenski. *m* Keith Olsen, Bill Cuomo. *cast* Emilio Estevez, Craig Sheffer, Kim Delaney, Jill Schoelen, Barbara Babcock, Morgan Freeman, Frank Howard.

● If that was then and this is now, now certainly bears one uncanny resemblance to then: the joyrides, the high school dance, the midnight parking-lot punch-ups which send cowardly punks running as that venomous taunt of taunts hangs in the still night air – 'Get a haircut!'. Get a haircut? The fact is that SE Hinton's novel, published in 1971 and set in the late '60s, has been updated, complete with contemporary rock score, for the '80s. The story is classic – a pair of childhood friends go their separate ways as adolescence gives way to manhood – the treatment pure Hollywood. Mark (Estevez) and Bryon (Sheffer) are the dynamic duo of suburban St Paul, Minnesota, laying down the law in whatever batmobile they can get their hands on. There's a girl who comes between them, and a death that brings an understanding of their own mortalities. Estevez is the rebel without a cause, newcomer Sheffer is cast as the romantic lead, and both are heading at breakneck pace towards an inescapable loss of innocence. SGo

That Woman, That Man (Ke Yeoja, Ke Namja)

(1993, SKor, 109 min)
d Kim Ui-Seok. *p* Park Sang-in. *sc* Park Hun-soo. *ph* Koo Joong-mo. *ed* Park Sun-Deok. *cast* Kang Soo-Yeon, Lee Kyung-Young, Ha Yu-Mi, Kim Sung-Su, Cho Sun-Mook.

● Kim's follow-up to *Marriage Story* redefines everything that can go wrong in 1990s relationships. Eun (Kang) and Chang (Lee) are neighbours in Peace Apartments; both are on the rebound from failed affairs. She's a maternity nurse who hates babies; he's a TV journalist who compiles obit material for the not-yet-dead. They hate each other on sight, and the stormy non-romance which develops between them is as much scary as funny, not least because it's so frank about the sex. Kim has the wit to frame this front-line bulletin from the sex war as an oblique homage to the late Audrey Hepburn. TR

Théâtre de Monsieur et Madame Kabal

(1967, Fr, 72 min)
d Walerian Borowczyk. *p* Jacques Forgeot. *sc* Walerian Borowczyk. *ph* Guy Durban, Francis Pronier. *ed* Claude Blondel. *pd* Walerian Borowczyk. *m* Avenir de Monfred.

● Borowczyk's first feature (and his longest animation) is a domestic allegory of change and decay that emphasises the transformative essence of the Surrealist position. Extending the concerns of his previous shorts, the titular couple – crude but evocative in their drawn outlines – choose a range of heads, wander the dunes and run a foundry to stockpile armaments. Images of freedom repeat in wing motifs, which pitch in against totalitarian excess. The drawing itself drives the work as much as anything in the narrative: objects are alive and constantly mutate; live action inserts underscore the dysfunction. Relentlessly inventive, Borowczyk's is a singular vision, and his imagination is genuinely fecund, responsive to the century at both its creative and nihilistic edges. Sudden cuts (or rather clashing encounters), attention to textures and the latent violence of the whole enterprise all command attention. GE

Theatre Girls

(1978, GB, 82 min, b/w)
d Kim Longinotto, Claire Pollak.

● Down in Soho's Greek Street is the Theatre Girls Club, a dilapidated hostel for homeless single women. This stark documentary picture of some of its occupants by National Film School students allows the women (many were in the theatre, and are delightfully, painfully extroverted) to tell their own story; humour and self-deprecating irony are punctuated by moments of aggression, tenderness, and sheer, terrifying isolation. There's not enough analysis: of the reasons the women are there; of why their 'open door' refuge is so pitifully under-subsidised; or, ultimately, of the film's own motives. But it does present a shocking vision of largely middle-aged, frustrated losers, their minds often addled by drink or drugs, their fantasies injected with the harshest self-knowledge. Not a film recommended if you're already depressed, but one which ought to make you think. HM

Theatre of Blood

(1973, GB, 102 min)
d Douglas Hickox. *p* John Kohn, Stanley Mann. *sc* Anthony Greville-Bell. *ph* Wolfgang Suschitzky. *ed* Malcolm Cooke. *pd* Michael Seymour. *m* Michael J Lewis. *cast* Vincent

Price, Diana Rigg, Ian Hendry, Harry Andrews, Coral Browne, Robert Coote, Jack Hawkins, Michael Hordern, Arthur Lowe, Robert Morley, Dennis Price, Diana Dors.
●Comedy horror that really does give Vincent Price a chance to do his stuff, with deliciously absurd results. He plays a vilified classical actor driven to mount a series of elaborate Shakespearean charades in which eight drama critics will die: one is decapitated in his bed, another is forced to give a pound of flesh, yet another is drowned in a barrel of wine, and all are subjected beforehand to the manic posturing and rambling of the mad actor romping through a succession of tragic characters with grotesque brilliance. Price's Richard III is enough on its own to make the film worthwhile (as he snakes his way through a cobwebbed corridor in full royal gear, hissing 'Now is the Winter of our discontent...'); but unfortunately the overlong script eventually runs out of steam, and the ending is feeble. DP

Theft Under the Sun (Haoqing Gai Tian)

(1997, HK, 110 min)
d Cha Chuen-Yee. *cast* Michael Fitzgerald Wong, Cheung Chi-Lam, Gigi Lai, Francis Ng, So Chi-Wai, Timmy Ho.
●Act One of Cha's workmanlike thriller centres on a large scale robbery foiled by the involvement of Ka-Ho (Cheung), an undercover cop who has spent three years posing as a triad footsoldier; the standard shoot outs and explosions are executed with some panache. But Act Two never really catches fire as Ka-Ho tags along with American-Chinese mercenary Dan Peterson (Wong) on a trip to Mongolia to buy black market missiles and then drive them back to Hong Kong in a truck; the edgy progress of their relationship is cross cut with extended debates about Ka-Ho's trustworthiness between a no nonsense officer and a bullshitting psychologist back in police HQ. Act Three, in which the truck reaches Hong Kong and all hell breaks loose in a docklands warehouse, is fairly spiffy. But it looks as if Cha is one of those directors who is most interesting when he's stuck with tight schedules and limited budgets. TR

Thelma & Louise

(1991, US, 129 min)
d Ridley Scott. *p* Ridley Scott, Mimi Polk. *sc* Callie Khouri. *ph* Adrian Biddle. *ed* Thom Noble. *pd* Norris Spencer. *m* Hans Zimmer. *cast* Susan Sarandon, Geena Davis, Harvey Keitel, Michael Madsen, Christopher McDonald, Stephen Tobolowsky, Brad Pitt.
●Leaving her husband a meal in the microwave, Thelma (Davis) sets off with her friend Louise (Sarandon) for a weekend holiday. But at their first stop, Thelma is nearly raped outside a bar; Louise shoots and kills the man. Gone is the carefree mood, and their destination is now Mexico. Along the way, the pistol-packing fugitives become ever bolder, robbing a convenience store, shooting up a leering driver's truck, and locking a cop in his car boot. Directing with blistering energy, Scott delivers the goods, while Sarandon and Davis, together with sympathetic cop Keitel, are acutely convincing throughout the deepening chaos. Callie Khouri's script is nevertheless simplistic in the way it reduces many of the men to stereotypes, while the women gain strength less through self-knowledge than through the American gun laws. Ultimately, this road movie calls on too many knee-jerk reactions: its shocking and funny scenes rely squarely on role reversals within a traditionally male genre. CM

Thelonious Monk: Straight No Chaser

(1988, US, 90 min, b/w & col)
d Charlotte Zwerin. *p* Bruce Ricker, Charlotte Zwerin. *ph* Christian Blackwood. *ed* Nöelle Penraat. *with* Thelonious Monk, Nelly Monk, Johnny Griffin, Thelonious Monk Jr.
●The image that sticks is Monk rotating slowly like a great black top, impregnable, unknowable, and sadly knowing. Produced for Clint Eastwood's Malpaso company, this is a jazz film in the old sense, which means that it is dignified and museumly. It comprises documentary footage from 1967 of the great pianist in transit, in the studio and playing live, intercut with interviews with relevant dudes; a downbeat, often dull, but unfailingly honest imprint of a singular mystique. Yes, the guy was weird; no, you can't see the stitching; certainly, we shall never see his like again. He wrote ugly-beautiful tunes, and improvised on them in entropic frenzy. In bamboo spectaculars and halibut hat, he addressed the keyboard like a man pats an alligator. Ultimately, this is a portrait of a man who dared, which means, by cosmic law, that the picture sells the subject way short. There is nothing here that really adds to what we know. We might be moved by Monk's childlike dependency on his wife, baffled by his esoteric humour, honoured simply by his presence, but all we really need now are the records. NC

Them!

(1954, US, 94 min, b/w)
d Gordon Douglas. *p* David Weisbart. *sc* Ted Sherdeman. *ph* Sid Hickox. *ed* Thomas Reilly. *ad* Stanley Fleischer. *m* Bronislau Kaper. *cast* James Whitmore, Edmund Gwenn, Joan Weldon, James Arness, Onslow Stevens, Chris Drake, Leonard Nimoy, Dub Taylor, Fess Parker.
●By far the best of the '50s cycle of 'creature features', *Them!* and its story of a nest of giant radioactive ants (the result of an atomic test in the New Mexico desert) retains a good part of its power today. All the prime ingredients of the total mobilisation movie are here: massed darkened troops move through the eerie storm drains of Los Angeles, biblical prophecy is intermixed with gloomy speculation about the effect of radioactivity. Almost semi-documentary in approach, the formula is handled with more subtlety than usual, and the special effects are frequently superb. DP

Theme, The (Tema)

(1979, USSR, 100 min)
d Gleb Panfilov. *sc* Gleb Panfilov, Aleksander Cervinski. *ph* Leonid Kalashnikov. *m* Vadim Bibergan. *cast* Inna Churkova, Stanislav Lubshin, Natalya Seleznyova, Mikhail Oulianov, Evguenia Netchaieva.
●A key movie in *glasnost* cinema, Panfilov's film was refused a release by the Soviet authorities until 1987, when it promptly won the Golden Bear at Berlin. Oulianov is a mediocre writer who makes a good living toeing the Party line, but he knows he's a fake and that his success has little to do with genuine talent. By siding with the real artists rejected by the system, Panfilov makes a courageous statement against the conformity suffocating cultural life under the Brezhnev regime. A dour, very Russian piece, but a substantial one. TJ

Themroc

(1972, Fr, 110 min)
d Claude Faraldo. *p* Jean-Claude Bourlat. *sc* Claude Faraldo. *ph* Jean-Marc Ripert. *ed* Noun Serra. *ad* C Lamarque. *cast* Michel Piccoli, Béatrice Romand, Marilú Tolo, Francesca R Coluzzi, Coluche.
●A quirky, anarchic satire that sees factory worker Piccoli cracking up, turning his bedroom into an urban cave, enjoying incest with his sister, and preying on cops for dinner. Some hilarious moments depicting the absurdity of routine life, but the predictable, episodic plot, and the gimmick of using grunts rather than dialogue, wear too thin to sustain more than one viewing. Joyfully tasteless, nevertheless. GA

Theodora Goes Wild

(1936, US, 94 min, b/w)
d Richard Boleslawski. *p* Everett Riskin. *sc* Sidney Buchman. *ph* Joseph Walker. *ed* Otto Meyer. *ad* Stephen Goosson. *m* Morris Stoloff. *cast* Irene Dunne, Melvyn Douglas, Thomas Mitchell, Thurston Hall, Spring Byington, Rosalind Keith.
●A forerunner of much '30s craziness: literary editor Douglas discovers that the author of several racy best-sellers is, in fact, small-town girl Irene Dunne, who nobody would suspect of such a thing. Regrettably, the movie dips in the second half, when attention shifts from Douglas's attempts to persuade Dunne to go public, to her efforts to make him stand up to his corrupt politician father. TJ

Theorem (Teorema)

(1968, It, 98 min)
d Pier Paolo Pasolini. *p* Franco Rossellini, Manolo Bolognini. *sc* Pier Paolo Pasolini. *ph* Giuseppe Ruzzolini. *ed* Nino Baragli. *m* Ennio Morricone. *cast* Terence Stamp, Silvana Mangano, Massimo Girotti, Anne Wiazemsky, Laura Betti, Andrés José Cruz, Ninetto Davoli.
●In *Theorem*, Pasolini achieved his most perfect fusion of Marxism and religion with a film that is both political allegory and mystical fable. Terence Stamp plays the mysterious Christ or Devil figure who stays briefly with a wealthy Italian family, seducing them one by one. He then goes as quickly as he had come, leaving their whole life-pattern in ruins. What would be pretentious and strained in the hands of most directors, with Pasolini takes on an intense air of magical revelation. In fact, the superficially improbable plot retains all the logic and certainty of a detective story. With bizarre appropriateness, it was one of the last films made by Stamp before he virtually disappeared from the international film scene for some years. DP

Theory of Flight, The

(1998, SAf/GB, 101 min)
d Paul Greengrass. *p* David M Thompson, Ruth Caleb, Anant Singh, Helena Spring. *sc* Richard Hawkins. *ph* Ivan Strasburg. *ed* Mark Day. *pd* Melanie Allen. *m* Rolfe Kent. *cast* Helena Bonham Carter, Kenneth Branagh, Gemma Jones, Holly Aird, Ray Stevenson, Sue Jones Davies, Gwenyth Petty.
●Bonham Carter is in a wheelchair with Motor Neurone Disease. Branagh is the quirky artist who keeps her company while building his own flying machine. The combination of luvvies, disability, whimsy and feelgood sentiment hardly makes for an enticing set-up, so the merest suggestion that this is not quite as bad as it sounds is actually modest praise. The heart does sink when we first see Branagh plunging off the Royal Exchange with his man-made wings, but the more we get to know him the more likeable this screwed-up grim bastard seems. The court sentences him to community service in the countryside, which means pushing Bonham Carter's wheelchair around after her testy temperament has driven off a host of other would-be carers. Her terminal condition destroys the muscles but leaves the mind intact, pissed off with life, swearing like a trooper and more than ready for a shag. These qualities make her and Branagh well-matched, but even he initially baulks when she asks for his help in returning to London and hiring a gigolo to take her virginity. Richard Hawkins' screenplay is all the more effective for its surprising lack of slushiness – yet there does come a point when the film simply loses its bottle and becomes dismayingly gooey for the final reel. TJ

There's a Girl in My Soup

(1970, GB, 96 min)
d Roy Boulting. *p* MJ Frankovich, John Boulting. *sc* Terence Frisby. *ph* Harry Waxman. *ed* Martin Charles. *ad* John Howell. *m* Mike D'Abo. *cast* Peter Sellers, Goldie Hawn, Tony Britton, Nicky Henson, John Comer, Diana Dors, Gabrielle Drake.
●In this adaptation of Terence Frisby's stage play – a traditional romantic comedy, despite its cynical trappings – Peter Sellers is badly miscast as the suave TV personality and professional wolf who meets his match in an innocently depraved girl. Looking more like a moonlighting comedian than a ladykiller (he plays with a fixed smirk evidently meant to suggest irresistible charm), Sellers makes it a very long haul to the point where he finally makes up his mind, too late, that marriage might be preferable to a life of one-night stands. Goldie Hawn is delightful as the fey charmer who, for reasons of her own, disconcertingly counters his seduction techniques by jumping the gun. But even she cannot turn suet pudding into soufflé. TM

There's Always Tomorrow

(1956, US, 84 min, b/w)
d Douglas Sirk. *p* Ross Hunter. *sc* Bernard C Schoenfeld. *ph* Russell Metty. *ed* William M Morgan. *ad* Alexander Golitzen, Eric Orbom. *m* Herman Stein, Heinz Roemheld. *cast* Barbara Stanwyck, Fred MacMurray, Joan Bennett, Pat Crowley, William Reynolds, Jane Darwell.
●Sirk's second ostensible triangle drama with Stanwyck is, like the earlier *All I Desire*, a brilliant example of his mastery of lacerating irony. In demolishing the social fantasy of the 'happy home', the embodiment of the complacent surface values of '50s America, Sirk simultaneously exposes its tragic pervasiveness. Toy manufacturer MacMurray's alienation and isolation from his savagely conformist household is marked immediately by his blatant identification with his

invention, Rex the Walkie-Talkie Robot. Yet when Stanwyck returns from his past, conventionally cast as the 'designing woman' (and at one point wearing a triangle-patterned dress!), it eventually transpires that all she has to offer him is a twenty-year-old romantic fantasy of (re-)establishing that same conformist model. Her generically-correct fairytale 'sacrifice' of self to the sanctity of the family, and the sanctioned role of the independent woman, merely intensifies the romantic agony of both dreamer-victims. Tomorrow never comes. PT

Thérèse

(1986, Fr, 91 min)
d Alain Cavalier. *p* Maurice Bernart. *sc* Alain Cavalier. *ph* Philippe Rousselot. *ed* Isabelle Dedieu. *ad* Bernard Evein. *m* Offenbach, Fauré. *cast* Catherine Mouchet, Aurore Prieto, Sylvie Habault, Hélène Alexandridis, Jean Pelegri, Clémence Massart.

● Thérèse Martin achieved sainthood by doing very little. Along with her three sisters, she entered the Carmel convent in Lisieux at the end of the 19th century, and after contending with the appalling privations of the order, the death of her father, and a bout of tuberculosis for which she was allowed no medical attention, she died in her early twenties. Goodness which is not active does not sound like the most promising of cinematic subjects, but in the scrupulous hands of Alain Cavalier, one is virtually forced to reassess just what is meant by cinematic. Filmed against the barest of grey walls, convent life is mapped out in a series of tableaux in which drama resides in the minute shifts of the human face and the odd telling gesture. Catherine Mouchet as Thérèse achieves that most difficult task of embodying goodness without being dull; her face glows with the innocent beauty of a medieval icon. Bresson is always a dangerous name to invoke for comparison; but while *Thérèse* lacks the master's taste for complexity and the paradoxes of the Catholic faith, the film's purity and simplicity nevertheless qualify it as another great enquiry into the operation of divine grace in our daily lives. CPea

There's No Business Like Show Business

(1954, US, 117 min)
d Walter Lang. *p* Sol C Siegel. *sc* Phoebe Ephron, Henry Ephron. *ph* Leon Shamroy. *ed* Robert Simpson. *ad* Lyle Wheeler, John F DeCuir. *songs* Irving Berlin. *cast* Ethel Merman, Dan Dailey, Donald O'Connor, Marilyn Monroe, Johnnie Ray, Mitzi Gaynor, Hugh O'Brian, Frank McHugh.

● In this archetypal Fox musical, such details as plot, cast, and character development are swept aside by the mindless but fairly irresistible anthem to razzmatazz embodied in its title. For the record (and with a dozen Irving Berlin standards enshrined in decors of surpassing garishness, one might be better off buying it), the plot involves two generations of a vaudevillian family; the cast includes Merman at her loudest, Dailey at his crassest, and Monroe, thank heaven, at her 20th Century Foxiest; while character development is mostly confined to crooner Johnnie Ray's anguished decision to enter the priesthood (in scenes that are not merely mawkish but downright mawk). GAd

There's No Sex Like Snow Sex (Beim jodeln juckt die Lederhose)

(1974, WGer, 85 min)
d/sc Alois Brummer. *ph* Hubertus Hagen. *m* Fred Strittmater. *cast* Judith Fritsch, Franz Muxeneder, Rosl Mayr, Peter Wacker.

● The English title says it all: an ineffable example of the writer/director Alois Brummer's broad Bavarian humour. A bouncing couple swish down a snowy mountain on top of a mobile hayrick observed by two impassive oldsters in leather breeches. Brummer churned out a string of similar films in the '70s. They found an audience in West Germany, but somehow failed to catch on in Britain. JPy

There's Only One Jimmy Grimble

(2000, GB/Fr, 106 min)
d John Hay. *p* Sarah Radclyffe, Jeremy Bolt, Alison Jackson. *sc* Simon Mayle, John Hay, Rik Carmichael. *ph* John de Borman. *ed* Oral Norrie Ottey. *pd* Michael Carlin. *m* Simon Boswell, Alex James. *cast* Robert Carlyle, Ray Winstone, Gina McKee, Lewis McKenzie, Jane Lapotaire, Ben Miller, Wayne Galtrey, Ciaran Griffiths, Bobby Power.

● It's hard being a small, shy, sensitive, lone Mancunian with unrealised dreams of footballing glory, and though Jimmy Grimble's mum (McKee) gives him her best, her penchant for dodgy boyfriends raises another obstacle between him and the world. Confidence doesn't come easy, but when it does, it seems to be in the form of an old pair of magic boots. What follows is unashamed wish-fulfilment – a Maine Road final beckons if Greenock High's unlikely lads can mount a run in the schools' championship – grounded, to a degree, by its breadth of human interest. Jimmy's are far from the only insecurities on show. Indeed, if anything the film's over-generous, with its range of characters and therapeutic wisdom. Winstone is improbably wholesome as the exiled ex of Jimmy's mum; Carlyle, on the other hand, gives a consummately restrained performance as sulky football coach Wirral; McKee is typically good value; and newcomer McKenzie is most watchable as Jimmy. NB

There's Something About Mary

(1998, US, 119 min)
d Peter Farrelly, Bobby Farrelly. *p* Frank Beddor, Michael Steinberg, Charles B Wessler, Bradley Thomas. *sc* Ed Decter, John J Strauss, Peter Farrelly, Bobby Farrelly. *ph* Mark Irvin. *ed* Christopher Greenbury. *ad* Arlan Jay Vetter. *m* Jonathan Richman. *cast* Cameron Diaz, Matt Dillon, Ben Stiller, Lee Evans, Chris Elliott, Lin Shaye.

● Critics are supposed to be immune to bad taste, but this film from the Farrelly brothers is as bad as it gets. Stiller stars as the geeky Ted, still hooked on his high school dream girl ten years after their prom date ended in humiliation and hospitalisation. Prompted by a wandering romantic troubadour, Ted sets seedy private investigator Healy (Dillon) on the case. He tracks down Mary (Diaz) in Miami, but falling for her himself, he tries to throw Ted off the scent. The ploy doesn't work, and the two men vie for her affections, with Evans' crippled Tucker also sticking his crutch in. You wouldn't expect discretion, subtlety or anything politically correct from the makers of *Dumb & Dumber*, and you don't get it. The gross out humour here includes Stiller getting caught in his zip; Dillon giving mouth-to-mouth to Diaz's long-suffering dog; Stiller masturbating prior to his big date (and losing the evidence); and all sorts of jokes at the expense of the halt and the lame. Funnily enough, the one thing the Farrellys don't find funny is Mary – hair gel apart, Diaz is gamely reduced to playing straight gal throughout. So there you are: crude, offensive, sexist – and embarrassingly hilarious. TCh

There Was a Crooked Man...

(1970, US, 126 min)
d/p Joseph L Mankiewicz. *sc* David Newman, Robert Benton. *ph* Harry Stradling Jr. *ed* Gene Milford. *ad* Edward Carrere. *m* Charles Strouse. *cast* Kirk Douglas, Henry Fonda, Hume Cronyn, Warren Oates, Burgess Meredith, John Randolph, Arthur O'Connell, Martin Gabel, Lee Grant.

● A sharply and literately witty Western comedy of manners, scripted by Benton and Newman (of *Bonnie and Clyde*) and set largely in an Arizona prison, 1883 vintage, peopled by a wonderful collection of rogues including a homicidal Chinaman, a dimwitted gunslinger (Oates), a pair of old-maidish conmen (Cronyn, Randolph), and – most memorably – the Missouri Kid (Meredith), once a great train robber but now a rheumy-eyed old man dreaming of the past and of the idyllic little farm he will never own. King of this community is new arrival Douglas, a cold-blooded outlaw smiling amiably behind steel-rimmed glasses, biding his time (he has loot stashed outside) but seen as a potential leader of men by the new warden (Fonda), a staunch believer in the milk of human kindness who enlists his aid in turning the place into a model prison. The resolution, cynically demonstrating the relativity of good and evil, comes a little too pat; but the performances, the set pieces, and the overall tone are irresistible. TM

These Are Not My Images (neither there nor here)

(2000, US/Fr/Ger/GB, 80 min, b/w & col)
d/sc/ph/ed Irit Batsry. *m* Stuart Jones.

● Irit Batsry is commissioned by a priest in India to shoot a film through the eyes of a half-blind guide, giving up any rights to the film in exchange for the privilege of making it. Slow and languorous, the heavily altered and treated images (blurred, overlapping, repeated, moving from b/w to colour and back again) intensify a viewing experience created through the juxtaposition of a visually impaired guide and visually selective film-maker. The syncopated backing of myriad sounds, such as wind, water, music and silence, complements the images perfectly, and the random use of the protagonists' narrative underscores the nature of their awkward relationship: are they accomplices or rivals, adversaries or mirrors? JFu

These Foolish Things (Daddy Nostalgie)

(1990, Fr, 107 min)
d Bertrand Tavernier. *p* Adolphe Viezzi. *sc* Colo Tavernier O'Hagan. *ph* Denis Lenoir. *ed* Ariane Boeglin. *ad* Jean-Louis Poveda. *m* Antoine Duhamel. *cast* Dirk Bogarde, Jane Birkin, Odette Laure, Emmanuelle Bataille.

● Tetchy, selfish, plagued by the pains of old age, retired Brit Tony (Bogarde) lives on the Côte d'Azur with his distant, taciturn French wife (Laure). He's never been very close, either, to their screenwriter daughter (Birkin), who arrives from Paris when he's suddenly taken into intensive care. A virtual three-hander, largely set in and around a small villa, Tavernier's film – about the problems of communication that often infect family life – might seem a most unappealing concoction were it not for the talent involved both before and behind the camera. With Bogarde (lent strong support by Birkin and Laure) giving one of his best performances ever, and Tavernier demonstrating his usual quietly assured professionalism, it impresses in the way it avoids all the usual pitfalls (with a welcome absence of maudlin, moralising sentiment). But what finally lifts this touching, consistently intelligent chamber piece is Tavernier's absolute control of mood, with Denis Lenoir's exquisite 'Scope compositions and stealthy camera movements illuminating every nook and cranny of the trio's troubled relationships. GA

These Three

(1936, US, 93 min, b/w)
d William Wyler. *p* Samuel Goldwyn. *sc* Lillian Hellman. *ph* Gregg Toland. *ed* Daniel Mandell. *ad* Richard Day. *m* Alfred Newman. *cast* Miriam Hopkins, Merle Oberon, Joel McCrea, Bonita Granville, Marcia Mae Jones, Catherine Doucet, Alma Kruger, Margaret Hamilton, Walter Brennan.

● The original talking point about Wyler's film was that Lillian Hellman's play *The Children's Hour* had been shamefully bowdlerised, with the lesbian theme masked behind a plot which has the two teachers victimised because gossip says one has slept with the other's fiancé. The film tries to hint at the original theme, not very satisfactorily, by shooting certain scenes so that it remains momentarily ambiguous as to who loves who. Paradoxically, though, as Wyler's more outspoken 1962 remake *The Loudest Whisper* demonstrated, this expurgation proves to be the film's strength. No longer having to worry about attitudes to lesbianism, and no longer adrift in areas of special pleading, it can simply expose the social mechanism whereby (as in the McCarthy witch hunts) idle malice can wreck innocent lives. It's still a stagey piece, but its closed world of lies and hysteria suits Wyler's rat-trap style to perfection, and the performances couldn't be bettered. TM

Thesis (Tesis)

(1995, Sp, 125 min)
d Alejandro Amenábar. *p* José Luis Cuerda. *sc* Alejandro Amenabar. *ph* Hans Burman. *ad* Wolfgang Burman. *m* Alejandro Amenabar. *cast* Ana Torrent, Rafael Martínez, Eduardo Noriega, Nieves Herranz, Rosa Campillo.

● Torrent, a student researching violence in audiovisual media, gets more than she bargained for after asking a porno/gorefest freak to show her some of his heaviest videos. It's not his sick fascination that's so disturbing as the fact that her professor dies after watching what turns out to be a snuff movie, perhaps shot by someone in the university. A slick thriller muddled by its attempt to give its basic woman-in-peril theme a serious spin: it condemns our morbid interest in producing and watching violent images, then proceeds to satisfy it. Dubious and derivative, but delivered with some élan. GA

They All Laughed

(1981, US, 121 min)
d Peter Bogdanovich. *p* George Morfogen, Blaine Novak. *sc* Peter Bogdanovich. *ph* Robby Müller. *ed* Scott Vickrey, William Carruth, Robert Barrere. *ad* Kert Lundell. *cast* Ben Gazzara, Audrey Hepburn, John Ritter, Colleen Camp, Patti Hansen, Dorothy Stratten, Blaine Novak.

● The temptation to respond 'No, they didn't' is overwhelming, and unfortunately it's also accurate. Bogdanovich's romantic comedy (involving three operatives from a detective agency and the women they have been assigned to watch) crucially lacks wit, and gauche clumsiness proves no substitute. Ritter's totally graceless performance punctures more laughs than it raises, and Gazzara is still in his expressionless period. There are occasional glimmers of what might have been in the fresh performances of the actresses. But it plods where it should sparkle, like a celebration where the champagne's gone flat. SM

They Call Him Marcado (Los Marcados)

(1972, Mex, 82 min)
d Alberto Mariscal. *p* Antonio Aguilar. *sc* Mario Hernandez, Antonio Aguilar. *ph* Rosalio Garibay. *ed* Carlos Savage, David Bretherton, Elyane Vuillarmoz. *ad* Salvador Lozano Mena, Fernando Ramirez. *m* Bert Shefter, Paul Sawtell. *cast* Antonio Aguilar, Flor Silvestre, Eric Del Castillo, Javier Ruan, José Carlos Ruiz.

● In spite of looking a mess (as though it had been subjected to some sort of butchery), this remains a weirdie of the first order: a perverse religious allegory in the form of a Western. The Kid (Ruan) is a vicious psychopath given to laughing a lot, an actor manqué (anyone who doesn't like his 'performance' is shot) who leads a gang of looters and rapists, and is incestuous with his father (Del Castillo) to boot. The town's resident Mater Dolorosa (Silvestre), madam of the brothel, hires her lover Marcado (meaning scarred: 'We all have scars, and the ones inside never heal'), a tight-lipped killer in the Eastwood mould (Aguilar), to kill the Kid, who is of course her son. The characters are all Western stereotypes, but given a strained and exaggerated twist – as, for example, when the Kid is given a snake tattoo, while the tattooist ridicules him for the softness of his skin and the design begins to run with blood. Unsurprisingly, the shadow of Nicholas Ray never seems all that far away. VG

They Call Me Bruce

(1982, US, 88 min)
d/p Elliott Hong. *sc* David Randolph, Johnny Yune, Elliott Hong, Tim Clawson. *ph* Robert Roth. *ed* Lee Edward Percy, Helwyn Spears London. *pd* Ivo Cristante. *m* Tommy Vig. *cast* Johnny Yune, Ralph Mauro, Pam Huntington, Margaux Hemingway, John Louie, Bill Capizzi.

● Korean comedian Johnny Yune plays a Los Angeles cook and Bruce Lee fan assigned by his Mafia employers to unwittingly courier drugs across country, thus becoming embroiled in various predictable scrapes. This amiable kung-fu/Mob comedy runs out of fizz well before the end but succeeded in begetting a No 2, *They Still Call Me Bruce*. We continue to await 'Bruce 3: You Never Call Me Anymore'. DO

They Call Me MISTER Tibbs!

(1970, US, 108 min)
d Gordon Douglas. *p* Herbert Hirschman. *sc* Alan R Trustman, James R Webb. *ph* Gerald Perry Finnerman. *ed* Bud Molin. *ad* Addison F Hehr. *m* Quincy Jones. *cast* Sidney Poitier, Martin Landau, Barbara McNair, Anthony Zerbe, Jeff Corey, David Sheiner, Juano Hernandez, Edward Asner.

● Further adventures of Lieutenant Virgil Tibbs, the black cop who took on an entire Southern town in *In the Heat of the Night*. Poitier plays the role again, but this time his beat is San Francisco, the script studiously avoids racial issues, and the film goes the way of most sequels. Poitier duly solves his murder mystery and survives some domestic problems, but neither he nor director Gordon Douglas can turn this into anything more than a routine thriller. TM

They Call Me Trinity (Lo Chiamavano Trinità)

(1970, It, 100 min)
d EB Clucher [Enzo Barboni]. *p* Italo Zingarelli. *sc* Enzo Barboni. *ph* Aldo Giordani. *ed* Giampiero Giunti. *ad* Enzo Bulgarelli. *m* Franco Micalizzi. *cast* Terence Hill [Mario Girotti], Bud Spencer [Carlo Pedersoli], Farley Granger, Steffen Zacharias, Dan Sturkie, Gisela Hahn.

● The first and best in the 'Trinity' series of spaghetti Westerns, rare in that it is successful in combining laughter and some degree of interest in the action. It's carried off with considerable panache, thanks largely to the inspired Laurel & Hardy teaming of 'Hill', the sloppiest fast draw in the West, with the large, laconic 'Spencer' as his straight-man brother. Here they find themselves in conflict with an insane band of Mexicans manipulated by Farley Granger as the effete Major Harriman, who is bent on driving a settlement of Mormons from their fertile land. As usual it's horribly dubbed into English, but the nonchalant and expertly calculated ham that decorates the easy, breezy action makes you drop any reservations you might have in that direction.

They Call That an Accident (Ils Appellent ça un Accident)

(1981, Fr, 90 min)
d Nathalie Delon. *p* Stéphane Sperry. *sc* Nathalie Delon. *ph* Dominique Chapuis. *ed* Yves Deschamps. *ad* Claude Maury, Jérôme Fourquin, Philippe Grunebaum. *m* Steve Winwood, Wally Badarou. *cast* Nathalie Delon, Patrick Norbert, Gilles Ségal, Jean-Pierre Bagot, Robert Benoît.

● A woman's only son is killed through the negligence of his doctor. Her husband, in practice at the same clinic, colludes in the cover-up. *They Call That an Accident* has interesting credentials: it's the first directorial effort of its star, Nathalie Delon (who also scripted); it was produced by Island, and features music by their artists Steve Winwood and Marianne Faithfull, including her splendidly sour song 'Guilt'; and it's a revenge thriller, a sort of *Death Wish* with a female protagonist. A clue to the film's main problem is in fact in the title of that Faithfull song: the tightrope between self-destructiveness and revenge proves a difficult one to negotiate generically in a way that leaves the heroine with her – and our – convictions intact. Obsession is on occasion frittered away into mere whimsy, or even modishness, despite some unfaultably bleak locations. VG

They Came from Within

see Parasite Murders, The

They Came to Rob Las Vegas (Las Vegas 500 Millones)

(1968, Sp/Fr/WGer/It, 129 min)
d Antonio Isasi. *sc* Antonio Isasi, Jo Eisinger, Luis José Comeron, Jorge Illa, Giovanni Simonelli. *ph* Juan Gelpi. *ed* Elena Jaumandreu, Emilio Rodriguez Oses. *ad* Antonio Cortés, Juan Alberto Soler. *m* George Garvarentz. *cast* Gary Lockwood, Elke Sommer, Lee J Cobb, Jack Palance, Georges Géret, Jean Servais, Roger Hanin.

● An EEC production and an audacious thriller, mainly due to the consistency of Isasi's direction (overriding the usual hybrid problems) and to the casting of Cobb and Palance. The opening is tremendous: Jean Servais breaks out of jail, fails to persuade brother Lockwood to help out on a robbery of Cobb's security business, and is gunned down. Then Lockwood goes out for revenge, insinuating his way inside Cobb's mistress (Sommer) and his IBM systems. Palance is the T-Man who smells a rat. Shot mainly in Almeria, it's a thriller equivalent to Leone's Westerns, reworking old formulas and paying tribute to them at the same time. But the parallel with Leone goes only so far: Isasi, rather than swirl his camera about, adopts the static, Zen-like posture of Ozu. Not flawless by any means, but well worth a look. ATu

They Died With Their Boots On

(1941, US, 140 min, b/w)
d Raoul Walsh. *p* Robert Fellows. *sc* Wally Kline, Aeneas MacKenzie. *ph* Bert Glennon. *ed* William Holmes. *ad* John Hughes. *m* Max Steiner. *cast* Errol Flynn, Olivia de Havilland, Arthur Kennedy, Gene Lockhart, Sydney Greenstreet, Anthony Quinn, Charley Grapewin, Stanley Ridges.

● Never did Walsh's reputation as an action director and master of period flavour fit more comfortably. Cheerfully agreeing that history is bunk and printing the legend, he turns what is essentially a biopic of George Armstrong Custer (Flynn at his most dashing) from West Point to Little Big Horn into a glorious Western. Few facts here, but what matter when the fiction of Custer as tempestuous cavalier and Indian sympathiser, chivalrously dying to save his army colleagues and simultaneously acknowledge the validity of Crazy Horse's cause, has the breathless sweep and dash of the last romantic gesture. Absolutely irresistible. TM

They Drive By Night

(1938, GB, 84 min, b/w)
d Arthur Woods. *p* Jerome Jackson. *sc* Derek Twist, Paul Dongelin, James Curtis. *ph* Basil Emmott. *ed* Leslie Norman. *ad* Peter Proud, Michael Relph. *m* Bretton Byrd. *cast* Emlyn Williams, Ernest Thesiger, Allan Jeayes, Anna Konstam, Ronald Shiner.

● Warner Brothers churned out hundreds of 'quota quickies' from their small British studio in Teddington, most of which are no doubt best left in the dustbin of history. Occasionally, though, the fusion of quirky British realism and slick Hollywood melodramatics produced a real gem. Here the revelation of '30s British society as a world of spivs and cardsharps, lecherous lorry drivers and sybaritic sex maniacs, is worth discovering in itself. But director Woods, soon to die in the war, takes the workmanlike story of a petty criminal (Williams) hunted for a murder he didn't do, and invests it with an atmosphere of unrelenting wind, rain and gloom which makes the average American *film noir* look bright and breezy by comparison. RMy

They Drive By Night (aka The Road to Frisco)

(1940, US, 93 min, b/w)
d Raoul Walsh. *p* Mark Hellinger. *sc* Jerry Wald, Richard Macaulay. *ph* Arthur Edeson. *ed* Thomas Richards. *ad* John Hughes. *m* Adolph Deutsch. *cast* George Raft, Ann Sheridan, Ida Lupino, Humphrey Bogart, Alan Hale, Gale Page, Roscoe Karns.

● A good example of Warner Brothers' social 'realism', adapted from AI Bezzerides' novel *Long Haul*: Raft and Bogart as truck-driving brothers trying to set up their own business, directed in typically gutsy style by Walsh. It degenerates into a courtroom murder melodrama about halfway through, with Ida Lupino (bored wife of their boss, trying to involve Raft in a little *Postman Always Rings Twice* malarkey) losing her marbles in the witness box in what Hollywood likes to think of as an acting *tour de force*. Still, the first half has pace, and the wisecracking wit is often laid on thick and fast by Jerry Wald and Richard Macaulay's script, particularly in a scene with Ann Sheridan as a roadside café waitress. All the performances are good. RM

They Knew What They Wanted

(1940, US, 96 min, b/w)
d Garson Kanin. *p* Erich Pommer. *sc* Robert Ardrey. *ph* Harry Stradling. *ed* John Sturges. *ad* Van Nest Polglase. *m* Alfred Newman. *cast* Charles Laughton, Carole Lombard, William Gargan, Harry Carey, Frank Fay, Karl Malden.

● More concerned with selfless charity than the title might suggest, this astringent social comedy (the third screen adaptation of Sidney Howard's play) sets an Italian grape-farmer to woo his San Franciscan mail-order bride, and embodies its implicit racial tensions in the opposed acting styles of the central characters: ugly Laughton, unabashedly running the gamut of racial stereotypes (virility-conscious, volatile, forgiving), against the effortless acting of WASP pin-up Carole Lombard. His tolerance eventually conquers her more venal qualities, but the ending is left peculiarly open – presumably by a studio wary of the star system and anxious about the implications of miscegenation. CPea

They Live

(1988, US, 94 min, b/w & col)
d John Carpenter. *p* Larry Franco. *sc* Frank Armitage. *ph* Gary B Kibbe. *ed* Gib Jaffe, Frank E Jiminez. *ad* William Durrell Jr, Dan Lomino. *m* John Carpenter, Alan Howarth. *cast* Roddy Piper, Keith David, Meg Foster, George 'Buck' Flower, Peter Jason, Raymond St Jacques, Jason Robards III.

●John Nada (Piper) is grouchy because ever since he arrived in Los Angeles from Colorado, there's been nothing but trouble. People are rude, he lives on a campsite, and then the place is demolished by the cops. Things get worse when he happens across a hidden stash of special sunglasses. Donning a pair, his vision is literally reduced to black-and-white, revealing a terrible plot being perpetrated on the underclass. Skeletal aliens have invaded earth, taking on human guise, hogging the best jobs, and placing subliminal messages on hoardings and magazines which instruct the man on the street to 'Obey', 'Submit', 'Marry and Reproduce'. It's sunglasses for all as Nada and his pal Frank (David) attempt to infiltrate the media and expose the conspiracy. The black-and-white visuals disturb for only so long, and while themes of indoctrination and conspiracy prove initially intriguing, the film quickly descends into fistfights and gunfire. Still, there's little about the comic strip action to suggest that we should be taking this too seriously. CM

They Live By Night

(1948, US, 95 min, b/w)
d Nicholas Ray. *p* Dore Schary, John Houseman. *sc* Charles Schnee. *ph* George E Diskant. *ed* Sherman Todd. *ad* Albert S D'Agostino, Al Herman. *m* Leigh Harline. *cast* Farley Granger, Cathy O'Donnell, Howard da Silva, Jay C Flippen, Helen Craig, Will Wright.

●Where Altman's later adaptation of Edward Anderson's novel (as *Thieves Like Us*) opted for the detachment of hindsight, Ray offers us the poetry of doomed romanticism, introducing his outcast lovers with the caption, 'This boy and this girl were never properly introduced to the world we live in'. Though Ray never shirks from action and violence (indeed, Howard da Silva's crushing of Christmas baubles as he warns Granger against going straight is extremely menacing), he turns the film to focus upon his misfit innocents, continually contrasting their basically honourable ideals with the corrupt compromises of 'respectable society'. Passionate, lyrical, and imaginative, it's a remarkably assured debut, from the astonishing opening helicopter shot that follows the escaped convicts' car to freedom, to the final, inexorably tragic climax. GA

They Might Be Giants

(1971, US, 98 min)
d Anthony Harvey. *p* Paul Newman, John Foreman. *sc* James Goldman. *ph* Victor J Kemper. *ed* Barry Malkin. *pd* John J Lloyd. *m* John Barry. *cast* Joanne Woodward, George C Scott, Jack Gilford, Lester Rawlins, Rue McClanahan, Ron Weyand, Kitty Winn, Sudie Bond, M Emmet Walsh, F Murray Abraham.

●A delightfully quirky movie about a New York lawyer (Scott) who imagines he is Sherlock Holmes, adopting the deerstalking garb and savouring four-pipe problems. The pressures of modern life and the death of his wife have, of course, turned him into a textbook case of paranoid delusion. His somewhat sinister brother sends him to a shrink, Dr Mildred Watson (Woodward), whose Freudian analysis of him is rather overshadowed by his Holmesian analysis of her. Watson's other case is a man who refuses to speak – he thinks he's silent screen star Valentino. Meanwhile, Scott refuses to get better; indeed, he lures everyone into his fantasy, gathering a bunch of Bleeker Street Irregulars who go into snowbound Central Park for a final showdown with the Napoleon of crime, Moriarty. Produced by Paul Newman, it was a box-office disaster (shorn of ten minutes on its original release) that now seems years ahead of its time. ATu

They Passed This Way (aka Four Faces West)

(1948, US, 90 min, b/w)
d Alfred E Green. *p* Harry Sherman. *sc* Graham Baker, William Brent, Milarde Brent. *ph* Russell Harlan. *ed* Edward Mann. *ad* Duncan Cramer. *m* Paul Sawtell. *cast* Joel McCrea, Frances Dee, Charles Bickford, Joseph Calleia.

●Excellent minor Western, beautifully shot by Russell Harlan (*Red River*). Joel McCrea is the reluctant outlaw who robs the bank when it won't lend him the money he needs to help his father – and to show he's no ordinary thief he leaves an IOU. Charles Bickford, always a commanding screen presence, is the town's new marshal, Pat Garrett, who pursues him across the desert. GM

They're a Weird Mob

(1966, Aust/GB, 112 min)
d/p Michael Powell. *sc* Richard Imrie [Emeric Pressburger]. *ph* Arthur Grant. *ed* Gerald Turney-Smith. *ad* Dennis Gentle. *m* Lawrence Leonard, Alan Boustead. *cast* Walter Chiari, Claire Dunne, Chips Rafferty, Alida Chelli, Ed Devereaux, John Meillon.

●The first of Michael Powell's Australian ventures, a very bizarre comedy about the prejudicial problems that face a young Italian who emigrates to Sydney. There are many delightful moments of almost Hitchcockian humour centred around social embarrassment (how to eat a meringue without making a mess), and pleasing parodies of movie styles (epic Eisensteinian expressionism at a building site). Hardly a great film, but an exhilarating and playful demolition of nationalist stereotypes. GA

They're Playing with Fire

(1984, US, 96 min)
d Howard Avedis. *p* Howard Avedis, Marlene Schmidt. *sc* Howard Avedis, Marlene Schmidt. *ph* Gary Graver. *ed* Jack Tucker. *m* John Cacavas. *cast* Sybil Danning, Andrew Prine, Eric Brown, Paul Clemens, KT Stevens.

●Sleazy slasher pic with the statuesque Danning cast as a greedy English professor (?!) who seduces a young male student, then embroils him in the murder of her mother. Meanwhile, a psycho killer in a ski-mask is bumping off all and sundry with an axe. Punctuated by gruesome slayings and shots of the ex-'Playboy' pin-up's naked body. NF

They Shoot Horses, Don't They?

(1969, US, 129 min)
d Sydney Pollack. *p* Irwin Winkler, Robert Chartoff. *sc* James Poe, Robert E Thompson. *ph* Philip H Lathrop. *ed* Fredric Steinkamp. *pd* Harry Horner. *m* Johnny Green. *cast* Jane Fonda, Michael Sarrazin, Susannah York, Gig Young, Red Buttons, Bonnie Bedelia, Michael Conrad, Bruce Dern, Severn Darden, Allyn Ann McLerie.

●Pollack's adaptation of Horace McCoy's novel about the competitive dance marathons of the Depression years was enthusiastically received when first released, and had a string of Academy Award nominations, several of them for its performances. The acting is strident and overblown, the narrative technique gimmicky and obvious, and the implication that the competitors' situation is a microcosm of a wider-reaching American malaise (though safely distanced by the period and the flash-back-and-forth narrative technique) rather pretentious.

They Were Expendable

(1945, US, 135 min, b/w)
d/p John Ford. *sc* Frank Wead. *ph* Joseph H August. *ed* Frank E Hull, Douglas Biggs. *ad* Cedric Gibbons, Malcolm Brown. *m* Herbert Stothart. *cast* Robert Montgomery, John Wayne, Donna Reed, Ward Bond, Jack Holt, Marshall Thompson, Louis Jean Heydt, Russell Simpson, Leon Ames, Cameron Mitchell, Robert Barrat.

●Ford and Montgomery were both under Navy orders when returning from active service to MGM to make this tribute to World War II hero John Bulkeley (Brickley in the film) and his squadron of motor torpedo boats which had covered the Pacific retreat of US forces in the wake of Pearl Harbor. The tugs of docudrama, emotionalism and sheer timing produced a major work of surprisingly downbeat romanticism. Commitments to cause and career are raised as genuine conflicts as Wayne's second-in-command questions notions of teamwork and sacrifice; and even at the end, when Ford has ennobled his warriors in a succession of classic images, the narrative has to acknowledge that the ranking pair's heroism consists in knowingly leaving their men to a near-certain doom. A curious movie, whose premises Ford would obsessively rework in his subsequent cavalry pictures, with the luxury of historical distance. PT

They Were Not Divided

(1950, GB, 102 min, b/w)
d Terence Young. *p* Earl St John. *sc* Terence Young. *ph* Harry Waxman. *ed* Ralph Kemplen, Vera Campbell. *m* Lambert Williamson. *cast* Edward Underdown, Michael Brennan, Ralph Clanton, Helen Cherry, Stella Andrews.

●Writer/director Young went on to helm the first James Bond offering *Dr No*, but in this wartime slice-of-life he's on somewhat different terrain. Englisher Underdown, Welshman Brennan and Yank Clanton all join the Welsh Guards during WWII, and the narrative charts their experiences as it swings between propaganda and quasi-documentary and back again. In its day a sound success at the home box office. TJ

They Were Sisters

(1945, GB, 115 min, b/w)
d Arthur Crabtree. *p* Harold Huth. *sc* Ronald Pertwee. *ph* Jack Cox. *ed* Charles Knott. *ad* David Rawnsley. *m* Hubert Bath. Louis Levy. *cast* James Mason, Phyllis Calvert, Hugh Sinclair, Anne Crawford, Peter Murray Hill, Dulcie Gray, Thorley Walters.

●Over-ripe but enjoyable Gainsborough Studios melodrama set in the sleepy Home Counties and charting the marital problems of three middle class sisters. Cads don't come any worse than James Mason's sneering, scowling, sadistic alcoholic, who is equally cruel to animals and children (he tries to kill his son's pet dog), and who gradually drives his long-suffering wife (Dulcie Gray) to the brink. Also unhappy in her marriage is headstrong Vera (Anne Crawford), who's hitched to a decent but dull chap and yearns for some extramarital excitement. Only Phyllis Calvert is content, but she and her husband have their own trials to endure – they can't have children. The plotting may be schematic, the performances overwrought, but that's true of all the best soap operas. ('From the famous novel by Dorothy Whipple.') GM

They Won't Believe Me

(1947, US, 95 min, b/w)
d Irving Pichel. *p* Joan Harrison. *sc* Jonathan Latimer. *ph* Harry J Wild. *ed* Elmo Williams. *ad* Albert S D'Agostino, Robert Boyle. *m* Roy Webb. *cast* Robert Young, Susan Hayward, Jane Greer, Rita Johnson, Tom Powers, George Tyne, Don Beddoe, Frank Ferguson.

●A man (Young) comes round after a car accident, and realises that a perfect crime is now possible: any movie with this scene can't fail. From this halfway point, the anxious mood of this rare *noir* thriller thickens fast, with specialities in its whiff of a James M Cain world in which women literally explode: 'She was a special kind of dynamite neatly wrapped in nylon and silk… But I was powder shy' says Robert Young. Jane Greer and Susan Hayward in turn tempt Young (a spineless louse) from his rich wife (Johnson). We know he's wretched, but is he guilty of murder? No prizes for guessing the pulpy symbolism of a palomino stallion 'with a weakness for sugar'. DMacp

They Won't Forget

(1937, US, 95 min, b/w)
d/p Mervyn LeRoy. *sc* Aben Kandel, Robert Rossen. *ph* Arthur Edeson. *ed* Thomas Richards. *ad* Robert M Haas. *m* Adolph Deutsch. *cast* Claude Rains, Gloria Dickson, Otto Kruger, Allyn Joslyn, Elisha Cook Jr, Edward Norris, Clinton Rosemond, Lana Turner.

●Certainly the bleakest of Hollywood's social conscience cycle of the '30s. At its most impressive in the elaborate opening sequence which rhymes the Memorial Day parade in a Southern town (Civil War veterans waxing nostalgic about the heroic past as they watch) with the murder of a white girl in the school-house (a tightly sweatered Lana Turner making her debut). The subsequent machinations seem a little contrived now as the ambitious DA deliberately selects the most inflammatory of three suspects (not the black janitor but a Northern teacher), planning to railroad him to the death cell and himself to the governor's chair on a wave of Southern pride. And although the script (by Robert Rossen and Aben Kandel) steamrollers through the resulting lynching without having to worry about a happy ending like *Fury*, Lang's remains the better film because he is more honestly involved with the characters than with the logistics of the plot. One of LeRoy's best films, even so, and the performances (especially Rains as the DA and Joslyn as a greedy journalist) are terrific. TM

Thief (aka Violent Streets)

(1981, US, 123 min)
d Michael Mann. *p* Jerry Bruckheimer, Ronnie Caan. *sc* Michael Mann. *ph* Donald Thorin. *ed* Dov Hoenig. *pd* Mel Bourne. *m* Tangerine Dream. *cast* James Caan, Tuesday Weld, Willie Nelson, James Belushi, Robert Prosky, Tom Signorelli.

●A silently professional night-time jewel robbery, reduced to near-abstract essentials and paced by a Tangerine Dream score, sets the electric tone for Mann's fine follow-up to *The Jericho Mile*: a philosophical thriller filled with modernist cool. Caan's the thief, contradictorily building and risking a future mapped out as meticulously as any of his lucrative hi-tech jobs; testing his emotional and criminal independence to the limits; eventually recognising that he's either exercising or exorcising a death wish. PT

Thief, The

(1952, US, 85 min, b/w)
d Russell Rouse. *p* Clarence Greene. *sc* Clarence Greene, Russell Rouse. *ph* Sam Leavitt. *ed* Chester W Schaeffer. *pd* Joseph St Amand. *m* Herschel Burke Gilbert. *cast* Ray Milland, Martin Gabel, Rita Gam, Harry Bronson, Rita Vale, Rex O'Malley.

●A phone shrills, two bursts of three rings; the man on the bed (Milland) leaves his room; out in the night a waiting man (Gabel) lights a cigarette, throws down the empty packet, and vanishes. Milland picks up the packet, reads the message in his room, resignedly gets out a micro-camera; a shot of an award for his services to nuclear physics; and Rouse's movie is embarked on its challenge to tell the story of a spy without dialogue. There's an element of gimmickry here (even passers-by never say a word), but it's far outweighed by the tangible sense of a man isolated by his sense of fear (you never learn his motives), by the anonymity of his associates (all contact is by prearranged signal and at second remove), by the caution which edges into paranoia as things suddenly go wrong. Rouse's dispassionate, evenly-paced direction, abetted by Sam Leavitt's superb noir camerawork, strands Milland in a shadowy world of fellow-humans, any one of whom might spell disaster. The moment at the end, as Milland waits despairingly for word of his escape, and the teasingly sexy girl across the hall (Gam) closes her door in his face as she realises he is watching her, is one Bresson might have been proud of. TM

Thief, The (Vor)

(1997, Rus/Fr, 97 min)
d Pavel Chukhrai. *p* Igor Tolstunov. *sc* Pavel Chukhrai. *ph* Vladimir Klimov. *ed* Marina Dobrianskaia, Natalia Kucherenko. *pd* Victor Petrov. *m* Vladimir Dashkevich. *cast* Vladimir Mashkov, Ekaterina Rednikova, Misha Filipchuk, Dima Chigarev, Amaliia Mordvinova.

●Sania was six in 1952. His memories of Russia in the years after WWII are dominated by his mother's fleeting relationship with a soldier, Tolian – the only father the boy ever knew. They meet on a train, disembark as a family, and take a room in a boarding house. The landlady accepts Tolian's uniform as sufficient character reference, and though Sania is resentful at being displaced in mama's affections, they settle down reasonably happily. And Tolian teaches his new charge about being a man: intimidation, fear and theft. When Tolian confides to the boy that he's Stalin's son, we see it's another con – but, metaphorically speaking, that's exactly who he is. Chukhrai's previous film was *The Hawk*, a documentary about the Russian nationalist Zhirinovsky, and *The Thief* is apparently intended as some kind of prequel, a film about the sons of the sons of Stalin. The pained love-hate relationship between Tolian and Sania gives the film welcome emotional grit, and Mashkov brings the requisite dash of cavalier charm to the brutal surrogate father. The least that can be said is that this is a moving, decent and worthy film. Even so, it's also deeply conventional. TCh

Thief of Bagdad, The

(1924, US, 11,812 ft, b/w)
d Raoul Walsh. *p* Douglas Fairbanks. *sc* Lotta Woods, Douglas Fairbanks. *ph* Arthur Edeson. *ed* William Nolan. *pd* William Cameron Menzies, Irvin J Martin. *m* Lee Erwin. *cast* Douglas Fairbanks, Julanne Johnston, Anna May Wong, Snitz Edwards, Charles Belcher, Brandon Hurst, Sojin.

●Fairbanks' Arabian Nights spectacle presents American silent cinema at its most flamboyant. The collection of sets were said to extend over six-and-a-half acres; the designs, partly by William Cameron Menzies, are a dizzy conglomeration of Manhattan chic, Art Deco, and rampant Chinoiserie, guaranteed to amaze the eyes. Fairbanks leaps and grins through them all, the personification of American 'pep'. Korda's version of 1940 has the quirks and the luscious colour, but this one has the electric energy. GB

Thief of Bagdad, The

(1940, GB, 106 min)
d Michael Powell, Ludwig Berger, Tim Whelan. *p* Alexander Korda, Zoltan Korda. *sc* Miles Malleson, Lajos Biro. *ph* Georges Périnal, Osmond Borradaile. *ed* William Hornbeck, Charles Crichton. *ad* Vincent Korda. *m* Miklos Rozsa. *cast* Conrad Veidt, Sabu, June Duprez, Rex Ingram, John Justin, Miles Malleson, Mary Morris, Morton Selten.

●A delightful hocus-pocus of colour, dashing adventure, and special effects, this Korda-produced epic for grown-up kids is basically *Star Wars* meets *The Arabian Nights* with its plot of an all-seeing eye stolen from a Tibetan temple. The highlight has to be the genie (Ingram) who escapes from the bottle, though Sabu the elephant boy lends just that dash of imperialist sentiment to lift it into camp. Magical, classically entertaining, and now revalued by Hollywood moguls Lucas and Coppola, it was made fitfully in Britain during the World War II Blitz (but completed in Hollywood) by a team of directors spearheaded by the remarkable Powell. DMacp

Thief of Baghdad, The

(1978, GB/Fr, 102 min)
d Clive Donner. *p* Aida Young. *sc* AJ Carothers. *ph* Denis Lewiston. *ed* Peter Tanner. *ad* Edward Marshall. *m* John Cameron. *cast* Roddy McDowall, Peter Ustinov, Terence Stamp, Kabir Bedi, Frank Finlay, Marina Vlady, Pavla Ustinov, Daniel Emilfork, Ian Holm.

●It's a faltering hand stoking the high camp fire here. Behind the ornate theatricality and sumptuous effects of this remake there lurks a total lack of conviction. Hyperactive McDowall (the thief) is upstaged by old pro Ustinov as the Caliph; Kabir Bedi, once India's 'highest paid male model', is a joke as the prince, meant to symbolise the alliance of magic and muscle; and Terence Stamp, as a lethargic representative of Supreme Evil, simply waits around for henchmen or flying carpets to do the dirty work. CR

Thief of Saint Lubin, The (La Voleuse de Saint-Lubin)

(1999, Fr, 72 min)
d Claire Devers. *p* Gilles Sandoz. *sc* Claire Devers, Jean-Louis Benoît. *ph* Hélène Louvart. *ed* Marie Castro, Monica Coleman. *pd* Jean Castelnau. *m* Béatrice Thiriet. *cast* Dominique Blanc, Denis Podalydès, Michèle Goddet, Chantal Neuwirth, Serpentine Teyssier, Yves Verhoeven, Gérard Giroudon.

●A powerful, unshowy account of a single mother who finds that her job no longer puts food on the table for the kids, and ends in court charged with shoplifting. Her case becomes a political cause célèbre for the far right (she considers welfare to be charity), but the film exposes the opportunism of her supporters, and digs out a complex understanding of cause and effect. If it starts in Ken Loach territory, this admirable work ends closer to the world of Abbas Kiarostami. TCh

Thieves' Highway

(1949, US, 94 min, b/w)
d Jules Dassin. *p* Robert Bassler. *sc* AI Bezzerides. *ph* Norbert Brodine. *ed* Nick De Maggio. *ad* Lyle Wheeler, Chester Gore. *m* Alfred Newman. *cast* Richard Conte, Valentina Cortese, Lee J Cobb, Barbara Lawrence, Jack Oakie, Millard Mitchell, Joseph Pevney, Morris Carnovsky.

●Jules Dassin's trendy reputation (and an awful lot of money) was made with *Rififi*, *Never on Sunday* and *Topkapi* – triumphant European success for a blacklisted Hollywood talent. But cultists groaned, for the 'real' Dassin was surely to be found in the baroque and electrifying *Brute Force*, the grotesquely Dickensian *Night and the City*, and – a personal favourite – *Thieves' Highway*. AI Bezzerides' script (from his own novel *Thieves' Market*) and the performances of Conte, Cobb, and Cortese (in her American debut) help restrain Dassin's feverish artistic ambitions in this tale of racketeering in the California fruit markets. The result slots sleazy eroticism and rigorous action seamlessly together into a high-grade trucking melo. Nothing more, but nothing less, which in the '40s was the most triumphant kind of American success. CW

Thieves Like Us

(1973, US, 123 min)
d Robert Altman. *p* Jerry Bick. *sc* Calder Willingham, Joan Tewkesbury, Robert Altman. *ph* Jean Boffety. *ed* Lou Lombardo. *cast* Keith Carradine, Shelley Duvall, John Schuck, Bert Remsen, Louise Fletcher, Ann Latham, Tom Skerritt.

●Perhaps Altman's most persistently charming film, a remake of Nicholas Ray's *They Live By Night* (or rather, second adaptation of Edward Anderson's novel), in which a trio of semi-competent bank robbers attempt to emulate the big-time gangsters publicised by the media, comics, and radio serials, and finally get their come-uppance after a brief respite from prison and poverty. Altman adheres to Ray's conception of the youngest criminal (Carradine) and his plain-Jane lover (Duvall) as innocents all at sea in an uncaring world, although the tone here is one of bitter-sweet irony rather than romantic pessimism. And while casting a critical eye on Depression America, with a New Deal being promised that would keep democracy safe, there is none of the cynicism that has occasionally flawed some of Altman's fascinating genre parodies/tributes. Never portentous, never a mere spoof, this is a touching, intelligent, and – in its own small way – rather wonderful movie. GA

Thin Air

see Body Stealers, The

Thin Blue Line, The

(1988, US, 101 min)
d Errol Morris. *p* Mark Lipson. *ph* Stefan Czapsky, Robert Chappell. *ed* Paul Barnes, Elizabeth Kling. *pd* Ted Bafaloukos. *m* Philip Glass. *with* Randall Adams, David Harris, Edith James, Dennis White, Don Metcalfe.

●Documentarist-extraordinary Morris' original and delightfully bizarre slice of investigative film-journalism attempts, successfully, to set the record straight about one Randall Adams, imprisoned in 1976 for the murder of a Dallas cop. It is also a philosophical thesis on problems of knowledge and truth, which uses highly stylised dramatic reconstructions of the crime to offer a multitude of perspectives on what really happened, and a darkly comic, nightmarish study in self-delusion and deception. The legal figures and witnesses Morris interviews are transparently weird, shifty, obsessive and unreliable. Indeed, the movie – immaculately structured, beautifully shot, sensitively scored by Philip Glass – is a poignant and hilarious essay on oddball America. Morris' skill in suggesting that Adams' original trial involved at best a miscarriage of justice, at worst corruption, ensures that the audience becomes a surrogate jury. The film provokes sadness, anger, relief, admiration, and wonder; enjoy it, and worry. GA

Thing, The

(1982, US, 109 min)
d John Carpenter. *p* David Foster, Lawrence Turman. *sc* Bill Lancaster. *ph* Dean Cundey. *ed* Tom Ramsay. *pd* John J Lloyd. *m* Ennio Morricone. *cast* Kurt Russell, Wilford Brimley, TK Carter, David Clennon, Richard Dysart, Richard Masur, Donald Moffat.

●In re-adapting the John W Campbell story (*Who Goes There?*) already filmed so superbly in 1951 as *The Thing from Another World*, Carpenter provides a punchy enough action thriller as the men of a lonely Antarctic research team are menaced by a shape-changing alien from outer space. But there comes a time when spectacular special effects – even by the estimable Rob Bottin – are just not enough. Carpenter avoids the subtle suspense of the earlier version – all the guessing and paranoia and wonder – in favour of a mindlessly macho monster mash which looks and feels just like an ineptly plotted remake of *Alien*, right down to the chest-bursting scene. Russell's sub-Eastwood heroics hardly compensate for the absence of all characterisation, while Bill Lancaster's script boasts the most illogical climax any monster movie ever had. It's only fair to add that, had this been made by anybody else, one might be recommending it for its special effects; but that's the price Carpenter pays for having made so much better movies. DP

Thing Called Love, The

(1993, US, 116 min)
d Peter Bogdanovich. *p* John Davis. *sc* Carol Heikkinen. *ph* Peter James. *ed* Terry Stokes. *pd* Michael Seymour. *cast* River Phoenix, Samantha Mathis, Dermot Mulroney, Sandra Bullock, KT Oslin.

●Would-be country singer Miranda Presley (Mathis) arrives in Music City – Nashville, Tennessee – and is soon waitressing, failing auditions and watching other people get the breaks. Her friends include like-minded young hopefuls: Phoenix (in his last completed film), the talented, driven one; Mulroney, sensitive and sweet; and Bullock, nervous and lost. Not a lot happens. But a thoughtful script (by Carol Heikkinen) reminds us that there's more to growing up than fast cars and Tom Cruise: that experience brings sacrifice as well as rewards. Bogdanovich's modest staging is occasionally awkward – his kids still watch John Wayne movies at the drive-in – but there's a convincing sense of what Nashville's like and how country music works. As for the stars, Phoenix is fine in an odd, transitional role, but Mathis (who looks more like his sister than his girlfriend) really steals the show with a bright, sassy performance. TCh

Thing from Another World, The

(1951, US, 87 min, b/w)
d Christian Nyby. *p* Howard Hawks. *sc* Charles Lederer. *ph* Russell Harlan. *ed* Roland Gross. *ad* Albert S D'Agostino, John Hughes. *m* Dimitri Tiomkin. *cast* Kenneth Tobey, Margaret Sheridan, Robert Cornthwaite, James Arness, Douglas Spencer, Dewey Martin.

●One of the great sci-fi classics, a Hawks film in all but director credit (he produced, planned the film, supervised the shooting). The gradual build-up of tension, as a lonely group of scientists in the Antarctic discover a flying saucer and its deadly occupant, is quite superb; while The Thing itself (played by Arness) is shown sufficiently little to create real menace. As in most of Hawks' work, the emphasis is on professionalism in a tiny, isolated community, on a love relationship evolving semi-flippant fashion into something important, and on group solidarity. Also characteristic is the contrast with a film like Robert Wise's *The Day the Earth Stood Still* (made the same year), which took a liberal stand in exposing the stupidity of men when confronted with an alien. Hawks rejects out of hand the idea that the alien might be worth trying to understand or communicate with; in fact, the scientist who tries to do this is made to seem feeble and even inhuman, so that the overall message of *The Thing* emerges as distinctly hawkish. Reactionary or not, though, it's still a masterpiece. DP

Things Behind the Sun

(2000, US, 118 min)
d Allison Anders. *p* Dan Hassid, Doug Mankoff, Robin Alper. *sc* Allison Anders, Kurt Voss. *ph* Terry Stacey. *ed* Chris Figler. *pd* Jeffrey Scott Taylor. *m* Sonic Youth. *cast* Kim Dickens, Gabriel Mann, Don Cheadle, Eric Stoltz, Elizabeth Peña, Patsy Kensit.

●Clearly a personal movie for Anders, this goes horribly awry. Kim Dickens is okay as the hard-living rock chick Sherry McGrale whose career might just be about to take off – if only she can stop getting arrested for drunken misdemeanours, and finally lay the ghosts of that teenage gang rape that still haunt her. Anders' courageous treatment of abused sexuality is not what you might expect, but the narrative framework is cheap and tinny. Mann gets the worst of the flea-bitten script as the world's limpest rock journalist, Owen, sent down to Florida to interview Sherry, and at the same time get something off his chest. TCh

Things Change

(1988, US, 100 min)
d David Mamet. *p* Michael Hausman. *sc* David Mamet, Shel Silverstein. *ph* Juan Ruiz-Anchia. *ed* Trudy Ship. *pd* Michael Merritt. *m* Alaric Jans. *cast* Don Ameche, Joe Mantegna, Robert Prosky, JJ Johnston, Ricky Jay, Mike Nussbaum, Jack Wallace.

●Mamet's second film is not intellectually fast, nasty, and dazzling like *House of Games*, but more like a leisurely variant on *The Last Detail* (and indeed, some Preston Sturges and Capra capers). It chronicles a masquerade whereby an insignificant shoeshine man, Gino (Ameche), is paid to become a fall guy for the Mob. His boastful minder Jerry (Mantegna), assigned to keep Gino on ice until his reluctant court confession, takes pity on him and resolves to give him an outing at the Lake Tahoe gambling resort. 'They always like you when you're someone else' is Jerry's one observation in life, and he is soon hoist by it, floundering in the wake of the folk-wisdom-spouting oldster as he finds himself at the high table with the Dons. It's a film of enormous charm and beguiling sentimentality, and it's played to the hilt by Ameche and Mantegna, the veteran blithely dignified, his captor sweatily alive to every danger, and right to fear the worst. Together, they cast quite a spell. BC

Things I Never Told You

(1995, Sp/US, 93 min)
d Isabel Coixet. *p* Javier Carbo, Dora Medrano. *sc* Isabel Coixet. *ph* Teresa Medina. *ed* Kathryn Himoff. *pd* Charles Armstrong. *m* Alfonso Villalonga. *cast* Lili Taylor, Andrew McCarthy, Alexis Arquette, Richard Edson, Debi Mazar, Leslie Mann, Seymour Cassel.

●Engagingly offbeat take on the meeting-cute movie in which camera shop assistant Taylor, grieving over the boyfriend who left her, encounters McCarthy, a despairing real-estate salesman who comforts the lonely and depressed over a Samaritan-style phone line. Strong performances, quirky characterisations, and a seemingly wayward narrative with a capacity to surprise. GA

Things of Life, The

see Choses de la Vie, Les

Things To Come

(1936, GB, 113 min, b/w)
d William Cameron Menzies. *p* Alexander Korda. *sc* HG Wells. *ph* Georges Périnal. *ed* Charles Crichton, Francis D Lyon. *ad* Vincent Korda. *m* Arthur Bliss. *cast* Raymond Massey, Ralph Richardson, Edward Chapman, Margaretta Scott, Cedric Hardwicke, Sophie Stewart, Ann Todd, Derrick de Marney.

●HG Wells thought *Metropolis* to be 'quite the silliest film', but a decade later Alexander Korda gave him enormous creative freedom to write a movie version of *The Shape of Things to Come*, which turned out to be just as silly. However, like *Metropolis*, it isn't just silly. It is a spectacular production wherein Wells takes his 'science versus art' preoccupations into the future (as seen from the '30s); and to make it work, only lacks the kind of pure cinematic form which a Powell/Pressburger would have given it, for its scale and love of 'ideas' pre-figure their films and make it just as unique in British cinema history. In the realm of 'prophetic science fiction', it is a genre landmark. CW

Things to Do in Denver When You're Dead

(1995, US, 115 min)
d Gary Fleder. *p* Cary Woods, Cathy Konrad. *sc* Scott Rosenberg. *ph* Elliot Davis. *ed* Richard Marks. *pd* Nelson Coates. *m* Michael Convertino. *cast* Andy Garcia, Christopher Walken, Gabrielle Anwar, William Forsythe, Treat Williams, Christopher Lloyd, Bill Nunn, Jack Warden, Steve Buscemi.

●Former gangster Jimmy the Saint (Garcia) has got himself a legit business (video-recording advice from the dying to their families), so he's reluctant to do one more job for the Man (Walken), who wants the frighteners put on the creep dating his slow-witted son's dream girl. Besides, after meeting Dagney (Anwar), Jimmy's in love himself. Still, the Man wants no real violence done, and lets Jimmy pick his own team: Franchise (Forsythe), Pieces (Lloyd), Easy (Nunn), and Critical Bill (Williams), a deranged morgue attendant and boxer who works out by using corpses as punch-bags. Thanks, however, to Bill's volatile temper, the job goes horribly wrong, with the result that the Man deems Jimmy's crew 'buckwheats', human prey for hitman Mr Shhh (Buscemi) to kill in the most painful way possible. Much of the fun to be had from Fleder's stylish, engrossing first feature derives from Scott Rosenberg's lively, literate and engagingly offbeat script. The witty dialogue, its slangy, profane poetry is even more delightful than the plot's tight twists and turns, while the colourful characterisations, sufficiently rock solid to have attracted and inspired a marvellous cast, simultaneously play fast and loose with the conventions of crime fiction. GA

Things You Can Tell Just by Looking at Her

(2000, US, 80 min)
d Rodrigo Garcia. *p* Jon Avnet, Lisa Lindstrom, Marsha Oglesby. *sc* Rodrigo Garcia. *ph* Emmanuel Lubezki. *ed* Amy E Duddleston. *pd* Jerry Fleming. *m* Edward Shearmur. *cast* Glenn Close, Calista Flockhart, Holly Hunter, Kathy Baker, Valeria Golino, Cameron Diaz, Amy Brenneman, Noah Fleiss, Gregory Hines, Danny Woodburn.

●Garcia's debut as writer/director comprises five vignettes touching on the lives of various women – a doctor, a tarot card reader and her girlfriend, a bank manager, a single mother, a police detective and her blind sister – living in the San Fernando Valley. Unusually and impressively for a former cameraman, Garcia excels at eliciting strong performances throughout and maintaining a consistent mood (despite the inevitably variable quality of the slight stories) poised delicately between wry comedy and more serious contemplation of contemporary American female lives. GA

Thing with Two Heads, The

(1972, US, 93 min)
d Lee Frost. *p* Wes Bishop. *sc* Lee Frost, Wes Bishop, James Gordon White. *ph* Jack Steely. *ed* Ed Forsyth. *m* Robert O Ragland. *cast* Ray Milland, Roosevelt Grier, Don Marshall, Roger Perry, Chelsea Brown.

●One of AIP's carefully cultivated jokes-in-bad-taste, in which the head of a terminally ill, racist brain surgeon (Milland) is grafted onto the body of a death row black (Grier) intent on clearing his name. This outrageous notion is milked for all it's worth as the two heads wisecrack away, tussle for control of 'the body', and charge around pursued by some inept cops. Special effects are in keeping with the general tone of the film (the difference between Milland's florid face in close-up and the ashen colour of the wax model used for long shot is hilariously obvious), and there are sufficient laughs along the way to sustain interest. Don't expect too much, though. CPe

Thin Ice

(1994, GB, 92 min)
d/p Fiona Cunningham Reid. *sc* Geraldine Sherman, Fiona Cunningham Reid. *ph* Belinda Parsons. *ed* Rodney Sims. *pd* Patricia Boulter. *m* Claire Van Kampen, Richard Allen, Pete Baikie. *cast* Charlotte Avery, Clare Higgins, Sabra Williams, James Dreyfus, Cathryn Harrison, Gwyneth Strong, Suzanne Bertish, Guy Williams, Ian McKellen.

●Black lesbian Steffi needs a partner for the skating pairs in the Gay Games, and the only gal good enough in the time available is shy Natalie

(Avery). Straight, white, middle-class, she's Steffi's polar opposite (though Steffi's strangely free from family, or indeed black culture). Natalie's own family suffers from a strange premature-ageing disease. Mum looks like her gran, her sister (Higgins, camping it) seems old enough to be her mum, and Nat herself will clearly never see 21 again. The predictable playing out of the plot (will Nat fall for Steffi and her schemes?) is underlined by naff dialogue. It's not all disaster, though. Williams' Steffi and Dreyfus as her gay photographer friend find an emotional balance that anchors the film, and it would take a harder heart than mine not to be charmed by the women's blithe performance in the Gay Games. SFe

Thin Ice (aka Lovely to Look at)

(1937, US, 78 min, b/w)
d Sidney Lanfield. *p* Raymond Griffith. *sc* Boris Ingster, Milton Sperling. *ph* Robert Planck, Edward Cronjager. *ed* Robert Simpson. *ad* Mark-Lee Kirk. *m* Louis Silvers. *songs* Mack Gordon, Harry Revel, Lew Pollack. *cast* Sonja Henie, Tyrone Power, Arthur Treacher, Raymond Walburn, Joan Davis, Sig Rumann, Alan Hale.

●A three-power Ruritanian summit convenes at an Alpine hotel and Prince Rudolph (Power) falls for skating instructor Lilly Heiser (Henie). Joan Davis, a daffy, slip-sliding orchestra singer ('My Swiss Hilly Billy', 'Olga from the Volga'), and Arthur Treacher, the Prince's camp butler Nottingham, take one's mind off the romantic cottonwool, while Sonja Henie still skates with the captivating elegance which made her a star at Fox for a brief period before the war. JPy

Thin Line Between Love and Hate, A

(1995, US, 120 min)
d Martin Lawrence. *p* Doug McHenry, George Jackson. *sc* Martin Lawrence, Bentley Kyle Evans, Kenny Buford, Kim Bass. *ph* Francis Kenny. *ed* John Carter. *pd* Simon Dobbin. *m* Roger Troutman. *cast* Martin Lawrence, Lynn Whitfield, Della Reese, Regina King, Bobby Brown, Malinda Williams.

●This *faux* thriller kicks off with a nod to Sunset Boulevard: smooth womaniser and club manager Darnell Wright (star TV comedian Lawrence) face down in a Beverly Hills pool with blood pouring from his head. Flash back to Chocolate City, Darnell's night-spot, where Brandi (Whitfield), a classy 'honey', is passing by outside – or so she thinks. This fatal attraction takes a lot of chatting up, but Darnell's soon in the back of her stretch limo, having rejected the advice of his wiseacre Ma (Reese, excellent) and the evidently more suitable attractions of childhood pal Mia (King), who's recently returned to the neighbourhood. When Darnell begins to dither, Brandi unleashes the psychosis of the woman scorned. This self-consciously upbeat enterprise trades on Lawrence's pooky persona and a soundtrack of modern hip R&B. There are some fun 'hangin'' scenes, with the boys in the back chewing the cud and cracking jokes, and Lawrence's ejaculations prove him an able physical comedian. But the script lacks wit and depth, while Lawrence's direction is meandering and undramatic, full of showy, over-elaborate camera movements. WH

Thin Man, The

(1934, US, 93 min, b/w)
d WS Van Dyke. *p* Hunt Stromberg. *sc* Albert Hackett, Frances Goodrich. *ph* James Wong Howe. *ed* Robert J Kern. *ad* Cedric Gibbons. *m* William Axt. *cast* William Powell, Myrna Loy, Maureen O'Sullivan, Nat Pendleton, Minna Gombell, Cesar Romero, Edward Brophy.

●Dashiell Hammett's fifth and last novel was something of a departure in that it was less a hard-boiled thriller than a spray of sophisticated banter in which nobody – least of all detective Nick Charles and his delightful Nora – took the tough guy ethos very seriously. With Powell and Loy fitting the roles to perfection, the film draws happy doodles around the mystery of the missing scientist (lingering, for instance, over an irresistibly irrelevant sequence in which Nick, given an air-gun as a present by the understanding Nora, spends a contented hour potting baubles on the Christmas tree). What enchants, really, is the relationship between Nick and Nora as they live an eternal cocktail hour, bewailing hangovers that only another little drink will cure, in a marvellous blend of marital familiarity and constant courtship, pixillated fantasy and childlike wonder. None of the five sequels that followed (1936–47) recaptured quite the same flavour. TM

Thinner

see Stephen King's Thinner

Thin Red Line, The

(1998, US, 170 min)
d Terrence Malick. *p* Robert Michael Geisler, John Roberdeau, Grant Hill. *sc* Terrence Malick. *ph* John Toll. *ed* Billy Weber, Leslie Jones, Saar Klein. *pd* Jack Fisk. *m* Hans Zimmer. *cast* Sean Penn, Adrien Brody, James Caviezel, Ben Chaplin, Nick Nolte, Elias Koteas, John Cusack, Woody Harrelson, George Clooney, John Savage, John Travolta.

●We're unlikely to see a more extraordinary Hollywood movie in 1999 than Malick's masterpiece, a stunning piece of work from one of cinema's true visionaries. Typically for Malick, the story, adapted from James Jones' novel, is simple and straightforward, charting the fortunes of a US army platoon as they attempt, against all odds, to wrest control of Guadalcanal from the Japanese. Nothing very unusual happens: soldiers get killed, go crazy with fear, fall out with superiors, and try to find ways of surviving with body and mind intact. But while Malick is not overly preoccupied with plot, the film's three hours are far from empty: thematically, philosophically and spiritually, no war movie has been so profoundly rich. For it's not just an essay on the hellish madness of war or a tribute to courage under fire, but a mythic, almost pantheist meditation on the role of conflict, violence and death in nature. With its multiple voice-overs representing the thoughts and feelings of men facing death, its imagery of flora and fauna, its philosophical, religious and literary allusions, and its cogent central metaphor of paradise lost, it's a genuinely epic ciné-poem that essentially sidesteps history, politics and conventional ethics to deal with war as an absolute, inevitable and eternal facet of existence. GA

Third

see Boy Called Third, A

Third Generation, The (Die Dritte Generation)

(1979, WGer, 111 min)
d/p/sc Rainer Werner Fassbinder. *ph* Rainer Werner Fassbinder, Hans-Günther Bücking. *ed* Juliane Lorenz. *ad* Raul Gimenez. *m* Peer Raben. *cast* Volker Spengler, Bulle Ogier, Hanna Schygulla, Harry Baer, Vitus Zeplichal, Udo Kier, Margit Carstensen, Eddie Constantine.

●Just what we always wanted: the every-day angsts of a terrorist cell as *Life with the Lyons*. Fassbinder's basic proposition is simple: the West German state is already so repressive that it might well have invented its terrorists as scapegoats for its own growing totalitarianism. Hence this 'comedy in six acts, just like the fairy stories we tell our children, to make their short lives more bearable'. It's a return to the grotesquely overplayed melodrama of *Satan's Brew*, acted by the entire RWF stock company, plus Bulle Ogier and Eddie Constantine, with a gaggle of haute couture 'subversives' going through the *film noir* motions of paranoia and anti-capitalist rhetoric. And it's formulated as an affront to all conceivable audiences: if the concept doesn't make you ill, then the interpolations of lavatory graffiti and the constant barrage of background noise from TV and radio will certainly give you headaches. Essential viewing. TR

Third Key, The

see Long Arm, The

Third Man, The 100 (100)

(1949, GB, 104 min, b/w)
d/p Carol Reed. *sc* Graham Greene. *ph* Robert Krasker. *ed* Oswald Hafenrichter. *pd* Vincent Korda. *m* Anton Karas. *cast* Joseph Cotten, Orson Welles, Alida Valli, Trevor Howard, Bernard Lee, Paul Hörbiger, Ernst Deutsch, Wilfrid Hyde-White.

●Justly celebrated British *noir*, charting post-war disease in Vienna as Cotten's naïve American pulp writer chases the shadows of Welles' quintessential underground man Harry Lime, an old friend now involved in black market drug-dealing and hiding out in the foreign sector of the rubble-strewn city. Robert Krasker's camerawork matches the baroque conception of Graham Greene's characters, Welles' contributions (script rewrites included) add intriguing internal tension, and even the 'gimmick' of Anton Karas' solo zither score works perfectly. A tender/tough classic. PT

Third Page, The (Üğüznuc Sayfa)

(1999, Tur, 94 min)
d/sc Zeki Demirkubuz. *ph* Ali Utku. *ed* Nevzat Disiacik. *cast* Ruhi Sari, Basak Köklükaya, Cengiz Sezici, Serdar Orcin, Erol Babaoglu, Emrah Elciboga, Naci Tasdoven.

●Dedicated to 'the defeated, the forgotten', this grim anti-thriller offers a problematic but provocatively obverse, inward outlook on life. The title means 'a new start', which is what seems to be offered to the film's protagonist Isa after he takes a gun to his mounting debts, threats and loneliness, only to wake up apparently absolved, with no blood on his hands. In turn, he tries to help the abused mother of two who lives opposite him, offering to do anything for her. The last act strikes a slight note of *noir* misogyny; like the opening, it's rather too curt to engage. Indeed, the writer/director seems to be working through some distinctly interior anxieties here. He doesn't fully communicate them, but his downbeat distillation of still, silent, luckless lives certainly makes some impression. NB

Third Part of the Night, The (Trzecia Czesc Nocy)

(1971, Pol, 106 min)
d Andrzej Zulawski. *sc* Miroslaw Zulawski, Andrzej Zulawski. *ph* Witold Sobocinski. *ed* H Pruger. *ad* Teresa Barska. *m* Andrzej Korzynski. *cast* Malgorzata Braunek, Leszek Teleszynski, Jerzy Golinski, Jan Nowicki.

●World War II Poland: a man gets a second chance. Michal's wife and child are killed by German soldiers, but in a nearby town he discovers and stays with a woman in labour who looks just like his dead wife. A complex and surreal work, the film is obsessed with the distinctions between love as self-preservation and self-sacrifice. But it's just as much the hallucinations of a dying man. Images of death are everywhere: endless corridors, figures framed in doorways (and later in coffins), a couple gunned down in bed. Not an easy film to come to terms with because of its cerebral nature and its self-consciousness; a haunting first feature, all the same.

Third World Cop

(1999, Jam, 98 min)
d Chris Browne. *p* Carolyn Pfeiffer Bradshaw. *sc* Suzanne Fenn, Chris Browne, Chris Salewicz. *ph* Richard Lannaman. *ed* Suzanne Fenn. *pd* Richard Lannaman. *m* Wally Badarou, Sly & Robbie. *cast* Paul Campbell, Mark Danvers, Carl Bradshaw, Winston Bell, Audrey Reid, Lenford Salmon, Desmond 'Ninja Man' Ballentine, O'Neil 'Elephant Man' Bryan, Andrew 'Night Kutchie' Reid, Devon 'Angel Doolas' Douglas.

●This Jamaican rehash of *Dirty Harry* follows maverick crime fighter Capone (Campbell) on a gun-running case in his old Kingston 'hood. He has to rethink his no-nonsense attitude to community policing, however, when it seems his long-time ghetto friend Ratty (Danvers) may be financing his record producing with more than the occasional block party. Low budget and shot on digital video, this first feature is a peppy morality tale which casts a cynical eye over Kingston's ambivalent attachment to the gun. If you can penetrate the patois, ignore the dodgy sexual politics and let the thumping reggae soundtrack do its work, there's an enjoyably rude energy here. MHi

Thirteen

(1998, US, 87 min)
d/p/sc/ph/ed David Williams. *m* Cecil Hooker, Shep Williams, Carlos Garza. *cast* Wilhamenia Dickens, Lillian Foley, Don Semmens, Michael Aytes, Michael Jeffrey, Dawn Tinsley, David Scales.

●A modest but finally very engaging low-budget indie about a year in the life of a taciturn, rather serious black teenager whose increasingly obsessive ambition to buy herself a car leads first to a sudden, unexplained disappearance from home, then to a series of odd jobs which encourage her to lighten up. Set in rural suburbs, this is worlds away from the sex, drugs, rock-'n'roll and violence of most US teen dramas, and rings refreshingly true as a result. Thanks to fine performances, mostly from non-professionals, dry humour, and sensitive, compassionate direction, it's a gentle, surprisingly affecting study of everyday aspirations, private dreams, and quiet dignity. GA

Thirteen Days

(2000, US, 145 min)
d Roger Donaldson. *p* Armyan Bernstein, Peter O Almond, Kevin Costner. *sc* David Self. *ph* Andrzej Bartkowiak. *ed* Conrad Buff. *pd* Dennis Washington. *m* Trevor Jones. *cast* Kevin Costner, Bruce Greenwood, Steven Culp, Dylan Baker, Michael Fairman, Henry Strozier, Frank Wood, Kevin Conway, Tim Kelleher, Len Cariou, Ed Lauter.

● Donaldson's film of the Cuban Missile Crisis sticks entirely to the view from Washington, DC – or more accurately, to the perspective of Kenny O'Donnell, special assistant to President Kennedy. His approach pays legitimate dramatic dividends: Because we have no idea what strategic advisors are thinking in Moscow or Havana, we're fully immersed in Kennedy's dilemma. He's faced with blanket assurances from his military chiefs of staff that only a pre-emptive strike can avert disaster, despite his own natural disinclination to kickstart World War III. The film recounts a blind poker game played for the very highest stakes. It's also a kind of American Civil War movie fought between the reactionary right and conscience-stricken liberals within the confines of the Oval Office. Donaldson and screenwriter David Self sift the debates judiciously. It's easy to forget that we know how it's going to come out, and Greenwood makes a credible job of JFK. Against that, domestic scenes with Costner's nasal O'Donnell and his family are sentimental and redundant, arbitrary switches from monochrome to colour are a distracting flourish, and the score is altogether too rhapsodic. It's engrossing all the same to watch how we bluffed our way to the brink. (From the book *The Kennedy Tapes*, edited by Ernest R May, Philip D Zelikow.) TCh

Thirteen Ghosts (aka Thir13en Ghosts)

(2001, US, 91 min)
d Steve Beck. *p* Gilbert Adler, Joel Silver, Robert Zemeckis. *sc* Neal Marshall Stevens, Richard D'Ovidio. *ph* Gale Tattersall. *ed* Derek G Brechin, Edward A Warschilka. *pd* Sean Hargreaves. *m* John Frizzell. *cast* Tony Shalhoub, Matthew Lillard, Shannon Elizabeth, Alec Roberts, JR Bourne, Rah Digga, F Murray Abraham, Embeth Davidtz, Matthew Harrison.

● William Castle – on whose original this horror film is based – was something of a downmarket Hitchcock and master of extravagant promotion. When his *Thirteen Ghosts* (1960) came out, the audience were handed 3D-style glasses to see the on-screen spectres – no such gimmick this time, regrettably. Single father Arthur (Shalhoub) inherits a house from creepy uncle Cyrus (Abraham, camping), the basement of which is full of ghosts, each representing a sign of the dark zodiac. Cue mayhem. The house is the best thing in the film, a fantastic entanglement of glass, steel and Latin script. Passable SFX provide some distraction from all the frenzy and screaming. PW

13th Warrior, The

(1999, US, 103 min)
d John McTiernan. *p* Ned Dowd, John McTiernan, Michael Crichton. *sc* William Wisher, Warren Lewis. *ph* Peter Menzies Jr. *ed* John Wright. *pd* Wolf Kroeger. *m* Jerry Goldsmith. *cast* Antonio Banderas, Diane Venora, Dennis Storhøi, Vladimir Kulich, Omar Sharif, Anders T Andersen.

● Adapted from Michael Crichton's *Eaters of the Dead* (1976), and originally shot under that title by *Die Hard* director McTiernan, this bloody 10th century epic completed filming in 1997. However, expensive re-shoots supervised by writer/co-producer Crichton pushed back the release date and upped the budget from $60m to $100m. What's been salvaged? A surpisingly grim but painfully truncated action picture, featuring three extraordinary battle sequences separated by yards of sword and sorcery tosh, some dodgy dialogue and a lot of ill-judged humour. A soothsayer declares that 12 Norsemen must return home to tackle a monstrous evil that's consuming everything in its path. But they must take with them a 13th warrior, one who's not from the North. Intrigued by tales of a 'fire snake', exiled Arab emissary Ahmed Ibn Fahdlan (Banderas), a cultured scholar, reluctantly throws in his lot with these hairy-arsed, hard-drinking Nordic types. They face huge, bear-like creatures that emerge from the night to slash and maul and carry off their victims' remains. Some breathtaking wide screen images linger in the mind. At its best, this achieves the beauty and grandeur of a Kurosawa epic – at its worst, however, it feels like a Python remake of *The Vikings*. NF

39 Steps, The

(1935, GB, 86 min, b/w)
d Alfred Hitchcock. *p* Michael Balcon. *sc* Charles Bennett, Ian Hay, Alma Reville. *ph* Bernard Knowles. *ed* Derek Twist. *ad* OF Werndorff. *m* Hubert Bath, Jack Beaver, Charles Williams. *cast* Robert Donat, Madeleine Carroll, Godfrey Tearle, Lucie Mannheim, Peggy Ashcroft, John Laurie, Wylie Watson, Helen Haye.

● Other English Hitchcocks may be more provocative, but few offer such a ripping good yarn. Donat's smooth and upright Richard Hannay flees from London in pursuit of a spy ring, responsible for leaving a murdered woman in his flat; the police inevitably take him for the murderer, and the spies are after him too. His itinerary includes an overnight stop in John Laurie's crofter's cottage, a political meeting where he improvises a speech without knowing who or what he's supporting, and a period when he's handcuffed to the resentful heroine. It ends, suitably, in a music hall. The inspiration came from John Buchan's novel, though Hitchcock followed it at some distance, concocting with scriptwriter Charles Bennett what really amounts to a little anthology of Hitchcock stories and motifs. Great fun. GB

39 Steps, The

(1959, GB, 93 min)
d Ralph Thomas. *p* Betty E Box. *sc* Frank Harvey. *ph* Ernest Steward. *ed* Alfred Roome. *ad* Maurice Carter. *m* Clifton Parker. *cast* Kenneth More, Taina Elg, Barry Jones, Brenda de Banzie, Faith Brook, James Hayter, Michael Goodliffe, Sidney James.

● More an attempt to copy Hitchcock than to re-film Buchan, and it suffers by the comparison. The few changes are not for the better (Peggy Ashcroft's wistfully frustrated crofter's wife, for instance, becomes a man-hungry spiritualist, played by Brenda de Banzie), since they broaden the characterisations into caricature. For the rest, the tension is dismally slack, the comedy overdone, and the Scottish scenery ladled out in travelogue dollops.

Thirty-Nine Steps, The

(1978, GB, 102 min)
d Don Sharp. *p* Greg Smith. *sc* Michael Robson. *ph* John Coquillon. *ed* Eric Boyd-Perkins. *pd* Harry Pottle. *m* Ed Welch. *cast* Robert Powell, David Warner, Eric Porter, Karen Dotrice, John Mills, George Baker, Ronald Pickup, Timothy West.

● Though boasting a greater period fidelity to John Buchan's novel than either the Hitchcock entertainment or its dire Ralph Thomas remake, and blessed with the resonant image of Powell hanging from the face of Big Ben in an attempt to make time stand still, this blows its coherence as a thriller by a ramshackle construction of gimmicky set pieces and a nostalgic sheen of BBC costume drama proportions. Strangely enough, archetypal British hero Richard Hannay had been better served, placed and analysed on TV in Mark Shivas' almost contemporaneous adaptation of *The Three Hostages*: here he merely rushes from pillar to post to avert the inevitable outbreak of World War I (and the 20th century) by a matter of days. PT

37°2 le Matin

see Betty Blue

36 Chowringhee Lane

(1981, Ind, 122 min)
d Aparna Sen. *p* Shashi Kapoor. *sc* Aparna Sen. *ph* Ashok Mehta. *ed* Bhanudas Divkar. *ad* Bansi Chandragupta. *m* Vanraj Bhatia. *cast* Jennifer Kendal, Dhritiman Chatterjee, Debashree Roy, Geoffrey Kendal, Soni Razdan.

● Being the tatty Calcutta apartment where a sixty-ish Anglo-Indian schoolteacher stagnates in austere spinsterhood. The companionship temporarily promised by a young couple who use her flat as a secret trysting-place tempts her out of self-imposed purdah, but her disillusionment is swift and terrible. In fact her life is portrayed as a succession of downbeat events – from the early loss of a sweetheart, fallen in the war, to her brother's death and the final indignity of demotion – and the material doesn't mesh with debut director Aparna Sen's predilection for extravagant effects (arty editing, a surreal dream sequence, clumsily signalled climaxes). However, the film is miraculously rescued from shallow melancholia by Jennifer Kendal's performance, which invests the 'repressed old maid' stereotype with surprising subtlety and tenderness. SJo

36 Hours

(1964, US, 115 min, b/w)
d George Seaton. *p* William Perlberg. *sc* George Seaton. *ph* Philip H Lathrop. *ed* Adrienne Fazan. *ad* George W Davis, Edward C Carfagno. *m* Dimitri Tiomkin. *cast* James Garner, Eva Marie Saint, Rod Taylor, Werner Peters, John Banner, Russell Thorson, Celia Lovsky, Alan Napier, Martin Kosleck.

● A spiffing WWII adventure in which a US intelligence officer (Garner) is kidnapped by Nazis, and subjected to an elaborate plot to make him hink that D-Day happened five years ago, so that he will give away vital invasion secrets. It might have been even more spiffing had the audience been kept hoodwinked for as long as Garner. But Seaton's inventive script keeps it going beautifully as a sort of cat-and-mouse game in which Garner tells the Nazis (Taylor and Peters) all they need to know, is horrified to discover the deception (through an ingenious, carefully planted detail), but realises that they don't quite believe him... Highly enjoyable. TM

36th Chamber of Shaolin, The (Shaolin Sanshiliu Fang)

(1978, HK, 105 min)
d Lau Kar-Leung [Liu Jialiang]. *cast* Gordon Liu, Lo Lieh, Qiang Han, Lau Kar-Wing, Tsui Siu-Keung.

● The first half hour is standard Shaw Bros melodrama: vignettes from the Manchu army's subjugation of Canton in the early Qing Dynasty, following the usual script, staged on the usual sets with all the usual 'guest stars' and extras. But once the wounded hero (Liu) reaches the Shaolin Temple and – one year of sweeping floors later – starts learning the monks' secret knowledge of martial arts, the movie becomes extraordinary. The temple has 35 training rooms, each one dedicated to the perfection of a physical skill, a mental reflex or a spiritual insight. Once our boy graduates *cum laude* the abbot pragmatically expels him for insubordination, freeing him to rally anti-Manchu resistance in the province and turn the whole of Guangdong into a 36th 'chamber' of Shaolin. Fine myth making, anchored in a heroic central performance. The UK video release is panned-and-scanned, dubbed and cut: a travesty. TR

'36 to '77

(1978, GB, 97 min)
d/p/sc/ph Marc Karlin, Jon Sanders, James Scott, Humphrey Trevelyan. *with* Myrtle Wardally, Alan Nielsson.

● This curious movie began life as *Nightcleaners 2* by the Berwick Street Collective, and ended up as a kind of portrait of a Grenadan woman called Myrtle Wardally (born in 1936 – hence the title), credited to four members of the former Collective. Ms Wardally was a leader of the Cleaners' Action Group strike in Fulham in 1972, and she here reminisces about the limited success of that campaign, but also describes her childhood in Grenada and speaks about her present life. There is rigorous separation of sound and image throughout, to the extent that the film is less about social politics than about the politics of film-form. There are visual recollections from *Nightcleaners,* but most of the image-track comprises shots of Ms Wardally's face, frames frozen and then slowly animated, out of synch with her words. Curious. TR

32 août sur terre, Un

see August 32nd on Earth

Thirty Two Short Films About Glenn Gould

(1993, Can, 93 min)
d François Girard. *p* Niv Fichman. *sc* François Girard, Don McKellar. *ph* Alain Dostie. *ed* Gaétan Huot. *ad* John Rubino. *m* Bach, Beethoven. *cast* Colm Feore, Derek Keurvorst, Katya Ladan, Devon Anderson, Joshua Greenblatt, Sean Ryan.

●Some films are so good that they remind us of cinema's capabilities, by, in a sense, reinventing, the medium's customary form. This is one of those films. It's true that director Girard and his co-writer Don McKellar started out with an extraordinary subject – the great, eccentric Canadian pianist Glenn Gould (who died, aged 50, in 1982) – but Girard's masterstroke was to take his cue from Gould's most famous piece, his interpretation(s) of Bach's Goldberg Variations, and to structure the film as 32 fragments, each revealing a different perspective. This approach pays off handsomely. We see Gould at various junctures, but while they're loosely in chronological order, these sequences are not really biographical, but tasters of a strangely distant, always compelling personality. Beyond this, Girard gives us interviews with those who knew Gould, excerpts from radio broadcasts, brief excursions into abstraction, even a segment of Norman McLaren's animation *Spheres*. Despite such formal dexterity, however, what's most impressive is the simplicity and clarity of the enterprise – and, of course, the music. TCh

This Above All

(1942, US, 110 min, b/w)
d Anatole Litvak. *p* Darryl F Zanuck. *sc* RC Sherriff. *ph* Arthur Miller. *ed* Walter Thompson. *ad* Richard Day, Joseph Wright. *m* Alfred Newman. *cast* Tyrone Power, Joan Fontaine, Thomas Mitchell, Nigel Bruce, Alexander Knox, Henry Stephenson, Gladys Cooper, Melville Cooper.

●Companion piece to *Mrs Miniver* which contrives to take all the edge off Eric Knight's novel (a surprising bestseller for 1941) about a working class soldier who deserts because he feels the ruling classes are conspiring to preserve the status quo. Played by Power (as much like a Yorkshire tyke as a Borzoi), carefully established as heroic before he deserts, he suffers more of a spiritual crisis than a political revelation. Not that it matters, since he meets a WAAF (Fontaine) who is true blue (and proves it with one of the stickiest speeches of uplift to grace the World War II movie scene), is swept up into fulsome romance, and realises what he should be fighting for. Lushly directed crap. TM

This Boy's Life

(1993, US, 115 min)
d Michael Caton-Jones. *p* Art Linson. *sc* Robert Getchell. *ph* David Watkin. *ed* Jim Clark. *pd* Stephen J Lineweaver. *m* Carter Burwell. *cast* Robert De Niro, Leonardo DiCaprio, Ellen Barkin, Jonah Blechman, Eliza Dushku.

●Michael Caton-Jones's second US outing is an able adaptation of Tobias Wolff's autobiographical novel about growing up in backwoods Washington state. It's a rites-of-passage drama with the kind of period small-town setting that the director is making his own. Teenage Toby (DiCaprio, fine throughout) and mom (Barkin) leave dad and big bro' back East and motor West with high hopes of a new life. First stop Utah offers evidence of mom's unerring eye for male suitors, which is confirmed when they hightail to Washington, where she accepts some old-fashioned courting from Dwight (De Niro). She marries only to discover, too late for escape, that Dwight is a tyrant. De Niro unfolds Dwight's character by stages, and resists toppling into *Cape Fear*-style psychosis, but he's clearly driving in cruise gear. WH

This Boy's Story

(1992, GB, 50 min)
d John Roberts. *p* Michele Camarda. *sc* John Roberts, Andrew Simister. *ph* Gavin Finney. *ed* David Freeman. *m* Julian Wastall. *cast* Simon Adams, Steven Arnold, Kevin Arnold, Jennifer Calvert, Thomas Craig, Daryl Fishwick, Carl Chase, Arturo Venegas, George Best.

●Writer/director Roberts, who went on to make the children's film *War of the Buttons* for producer David Puttnam, shot this affecting, well-acted '60s slice-of-life as his graduation project from the National Film and TV School. Navy man Adams recalls his childhood and the time he and his young brother (the Arnold siblings) set out from a broken home in search of their soccer idol, the great George Best. Catching the train to Liverpool with money stolen from ma's purse, they hope to make it to Anfield where Manchester United are the visitors, but fate places more than a few obstacles between them and their hero. TJ

This Day and Age

(1933, US, 85 min, b/w)
d/p Cecil B DeMille. *sc* Bartlett Cormack. *ph* Peverell Marley. *ed* Anne Bauchens. *m* Howard Jackson, LW Gilbert, Abel Baer. *cast* Charles Bickford, Judith Allen, Richard Cromwell, Harry Green, Eddie Nugent, Ben Alexander.

●A crude but efficient vigilante melodrama from the early sound days, and quite unlike the epics that came to be associated with DeMille, except in its reactionary nature. Bickford gives a powerful performance as a wealthy gangster who kills an old shopkeeper the local kids looked on as a friend; corrupt city officials do nothing, so a group of high school boys torture him into a confession (they hold him over a pit full of rats). Dismayingly fascistic, all the more so in that the action takes place during 'youth week', when the school kids temporarily assume positions of civic authority in the interests of learning how government works, and as such subject the gangster to 'trial'. TCh

This Filthy Earth

(2001, GB, 111 min)
d Andrew Kötting. *p* Ben Woolford. *sc* Andrew Kötting, Sean Lock. *ph* NG Smith. *ed* Cliff West. *pd* Judith Stanley-Smith. *m* David Burnand. *cast* Rebecca Palmer, Shane Attwooll, Demelza Randall, Xavier Tchili, Dudley Sutton, Ina Clough, Peter-Hugo Daly.

●The follow-up to Kötting's road movie/autobiographical essay *Gallivant* recounts a fictional tale of familial and social strife inspired by Zola's *La Terre*. Sisters Francine (Palmer) and Kath (Randall) work the rundown farm left them by their parents. Though neighbour Buto (Attwooll) sired Kath's Emma, he pays mother and child no mind till he realises marriage might pay property dividends, even as he openly lusts after Francine. Meanwhile, she has her eyes on farmhand Lek, an Eastern European viewed with suspicion and contempt by the superstitious locals. As the squabbles over land, bodies and blood spiral towards stormy conflict, Kötting uses cutting, variegated digital visuals and art direction to plunge us into a stagnant, oddly timeless world of earthy physicality. Wit there certainly is, alongside an insistent poeticism that highlights the carnal and primeval. Paradoxically, the decay feels as if it's been there forever or, if you're feeling ungenerous, as if it's just a dramatic device run amok. Uneven, even a little dotty perhaps, but it's robust, unrestrained and mercifully worlds away from the slicker British fare of recent years. GA

This Gun for Hire

(1942, US, 80 min, b/w)
d Frank Tuttle. *p* Richard Blumenthal. *sc* Albert Maltz, WR Burnett. *ph* John F Seitz. *ed* Archie Marshek. *ad* Hans Dreier, Robert Usher. *m* David Buttolph. *cast* Alan Ladd, Veronica Lake, Robert Preston, Laird Cregar, Tully Marshall, Marc Lawrence, Mikhail Rasumny.

●A definitive opening: Alan Ladd's hired gun wakes in a seedy hotel, then, with the distracted air of a schizophrenic, pays visit to his victims, first gunning down the man, then the woman as she tries to hide behind the door. Ladd's unsmiling performance – the prototype of the killer as angel of death – employs a repertory of classic gestures: no wonder Melville and Delon lifted so much of this film for *Le Samouraï*. The film's amorphous conspiracy plot (this in 1942) lacks the conviction of the terse introduction, but director Tuttle wisely concentrates on the set pieces and performances rather than the script's loose adaptation of Graham Greene's novel. The dialogue, however, remains admirably laconic – 'How do you feel when you're doing it?' 'I feel fine' – faltering only at the end with Freudian motivation. Laird Cregar's urbane heavy and Veronica Lake's slinky undercover agent offer fine support. Ladd smiles in the end. He shouldn't have. CPe

This Happy Breed

(1944, GB, 114 min)
d David Lean. *p* Noël Coward, Anthony Havelock-Allan. *sc* Noël Coward. *ph* Ronald Neame. *ed* Jack Harris. *ad* CP Norman. *m* Muir Matheson. *cast* Robert Newton, Celia Johnson, John Mills, Kay Walsh, Stanley Holloway, John Blythe, Amy Veness, Alison Leggatt.

●One of a number of British films in the '40s attempting to depict the lives of 'ordinary people', adapted by Noël Coward from his own play. Coward's homage to his roots daringly spans the whole of the inter-war period through the lives of Frank Gibbons (Newton) and his bickering, feuding, lower middle class family. Ronald Neame's camera rarely strays outside the family home of the decidedly un-funky Gibbonses, but there is a constant in-rush of public events – from wars to Wembley festivals – to leaven the domestic squabbling, and the evocation of the recent past proved enormously successful in war-torn Britain. Though Lean and Coward are less happy here than in the brittle, refined atmosphere of *Brief Encounter*, their adventurous excursion into suburban Clapham remains endlessly fascinating. RMy

This Is Elvis

(1981, US, 101 min, b/w & col)
d/p/sc Malcolm Leo, Andrew Solt. *ph* Gil Hubbs. *ed* Bud Friedgen. *pd* Charles Hughes. *m* Walter Scharf. *cast* David Scott, Paul Boensch, Johnny Harra, Lawrence Koller.

●Documentary footage intercut with dramatic reconstructions. Easy to overlook the risible 'dramatised' inserts: a substantial proportion of the footage is for real, and it includes numerous gems. Shadow kinescopes of early TV appearances point an almost obscene contrast with the close-up coverage of Presley at the end, mumbling through the ironies of 'My Way'; while in between, such socialising agents as Sullivan, Sinatra, the US Army, and MGM are seen contributing to the taming of a legend. PT

This Island Earth

(1955, US, 86 min)
d Joseph Newman. *p* William Alland. *sc* Franklin Coen, Edward G O'Callaghan. *ph* Clifford Stine. *ed* Virgil W Vogel. *ad* Alexander Golitzen, Richard H Riedel. *m* Joseph Gershenson. *cast* Jeff Morrow, Faith Domergue, Rex Reason, Lance Fuller, Russell Johnson, Douglas Spencer.

●Let down by variable acting and less evocative in theme than *Forbidden Planet* (the plot has aliens shanghai-ing two human scientists – male and female by happy coincidence – to help save their doomed planet), but still done with a grandiose solemnity that makes it worthy of the name of space opera. The settings, in particular, are brilliantly imaginative, with superb use of colour in conjuring the almost surrealistic landscape of Metaluna, a cratered wasteland concealing the labyrinthine underground city soon to be overrun by a hideous race of insect-like mutants with exposed brains and dead eyes, originally bred by the Metalunians for menial work. TM

This Is My Affair (aka His Affair)

(1936, US, 101 min, b/w)
d William A Seiter. *p* Kenneth MacGowan. *sc* Allen Rivkin, Lamar Trotti. *ph* Robert Planck. *ed* Allen McNeil. *ad* Rudolph Sternad. *m* Arthur Lange. *cast* Robert Taylor, Barbara Stanwyck, Victor McLaglen, Brian Donlevy, Sidney Blackmer, John Carradine, Alan Dinehart.

●In 1901, a young naval lieutenant (Taylor) is entrusted by President McKinlay with a mission to infiltrate a gang responsible for a string of bank robberies; since crucial information is evidently being leaked to the gang from high places, no one else is to be privy to the assignment. This promising premise is rather let down when the gang turns out to be the usual B movie unit: smooth-talking Donlevy, McLaglen as his brutish henchman, Stanwyck as the reluctant moll who falls for the handsome lieutenant. Routine shenanigans end with mission accomplished. But the President has been assassinated, so unless Taylor can prove it *was* a mission, he faces the electric chair. Sterling lead performances (plus a delightful cameo from Blackmer as Teddy Roosevelt), and elegant camerawork from Robert Planck; but it never quite makes the grade on credibility. TM

This Is My Life

(1992, US, 105 min)
d Nora Ephron. *p* Lynda Obst. *sc* Nora Ephron, Delia Ephron. *ph* Bobby Byrne. *ed* Robert Reitano. *pd* David Chapman. *m* Carly Simon. *cast* Julie Kavner, Samantha Mathis, Gaby Hoffmann, Carrie Fisher, Dan Aykroyd, Bob Nelson, Marita Geraghty.

●As her script for *When Harry Met Sally* proved, Nora Ephron is a gifted, extremely funny writer; on the evidence of her directorial debut, however, she should not give up her day job. Despite the formidable comic presence of Kavner, as a single mother from Queens who gives up selling cosmetics to become a full-time stand-up comedienne, the film suffers from too much syrup and not enough schtick. When she gets her first club date, her daughters (Mathis and Hoffmann) are thrilled to bits; but when she graduates to big-time Vegas shows, they begin to resent her maternal neglect. They also resent her tendency to incorporate these familial tensions into her act. Most disappointingly, it is the script more than the images that lacks focus; by dividing the voice-over narration between mother and daughters, Ephron and her sister/co-writer Delia multiply the points of view and introduce unnecessary confusion. Like her character, Kavner struggles valiantly to reconcile the demands of comedy and domestic drama, but ultimately succumbs to a surfeit of schmaltz and Carly Simon songs. NF

This Is Not a Love Song

(2002, GB, 94 min)
d Bille Eltringham. *p* Mark Blaney, Kate Ogborn. *sc* Simon Beaufoy. *ph* Robbie Ryan. *ed* Ewa J Lind. *ad* Jon Henson. *m* Adrian Johnston, Mark Rutherford. *cast* Michael Colgan, Kenny Glenaan, David Bradley, John Henshaw, Adam Pepper.

●Impressively shot on digital to make sinister use of the northern moors, and with effective lead performances, this is chiefly engrossing as a rural-menace thriller in the *Straw Dogs* tradition, just as long as you forget some of its more implausible elements. Colgan and Glenaan are the familiarly contradictory buddies – one childishly irresponsible, the other more mature – whose relationship is sorely tested when one of them accidentally kills someone on a remote farm and the pair are pursued by a posse of countryfolk determined to take the law into their own hands. Beaufoy's script occasionally labours its points about trust and loyalty, but the director keeps things moving quickly enough for the film to survive closer perusal. GA

This Is Spinal Tap

(1983, US, 82 min)
d Rob Reiner. *p* Karen Murphy. *sc* Christopher Guest, Michael McKean, Harry Shearer, Rob Reiner. *ph* Peter Smokler. *ed* Robert Leighton, Kent Beyda, Kim Secrist. *pd* Bryan Jones. *m* Christopher Guest, Michael McKean, Harry Shearer, Rob Reiner. *cast* Christopher Guest, Michael McKean, Harry Shearer, RJ Parnell, David Kaff, Rob Reiner, June Chadwick, Ed Begley Jr.

●Since the antics of so many heavy metal bands already teeter on the edge of self-parody, it would have been no surprise if this spoof 'rockumentary' about a comeback tour by a has-been English rock group had turned out to be a one-joke movie. In the event, Reiner's brilliantly inventive script and smart visuals avoid all the obvious pitfalls, making this one of the funniest ever films about the music business. Filmed in *cinéma vérité* style, it follows the group from venue to venue, observing the trials and tribulations of life on the road, personal tensions within the group, and problems with expanding egos. Interviews with the group fill in the details of their chequered musical career: they have trouble keeping their drummers, one of whom choked on vomit (somebody else's), while another spontaneously combusted on stage. Most importantly of all, the musical numbers acutely mimic the crashing drums, thudding bass lines, whining lead guitar solos, and juvenile, sexist lyrics of heavy rock. NF

This Is the Garden (Questo è il giardino)

(1999, It, 90 min)
d Giovanni Davide Maderne. *p* Andrea Occhipinti. *sc* Carolina Freschi, Giovanni Davide Maderne. *ph* Luca Bigazzi. *ed* Jacopo Quadri. *pd* Marco Beolchini. *cast* Carolina Freschi, Denis Fasolo, Alessandro Quattri, Emanuela Macchniz, Delia Boccardo, Tiziana Bergamaschi, Ashley Cancian.

●A deeply Catholic youth movie, this has a very straight cello student moving in with her boyfriend, a gifted pianist, forgoing mass, and ending up pregnant. Meanwhile her fella neglects his studies, takes a demeaning job and starts drinking heavily. That's just for starters: the wages of sin are abortion and a stolen grand piano – and I'll surely be damned straight to Hell for daring to venture this competently observed movie plays like a set text. TCh

This Is the Sea

(1996, Ire/US/GB, 104 min)
d Mary McGuckian. *p* Michael Garland. *sc* Mary McGuckian. *ph* Des Whelan. *ed* Kant Pan. *pd* Claire Kenny. *m* Mike Scott, The Waterboys, Brian Kennedy. *cast* Richard Harris, Gabriel Byrne, John Lynch, Dearbhla Molloy, Samantha Morton, Ross McDade, Stella McCusker.

●Northern Ireland during the IRA ceasefire of 1995: a Romeo and Juliet story of two youngsters (McDade and Morton) trying to make a go of it despite distrust and enmity between Catholics and Plymouth Brethren. The film's heart is in the right place, but dramatically it alternates between clumsy, contrived and predictable, while the performances are generally disappointing, given the impressive cast. Waterboys fans might enjoy the soundtrack, but this, like *Resurrection Man*, offers further evidence that there's only so much cinematic mileage in returning to the Troubles for inspiration. GA

This Land Is Mine

(1943, US, 103 min)
d Jean Renoir. *p/sc* Jean Renoir, Dudley Nichols. *ph* Frank Redman. *ed* Frederic Knudtson. *ad* Eugène Lourié. *m* Lothar Perl. *cast* Charles Laughton, Maureen O'Hara, George Sanders, Walter Slezak, Kent Smith, Una O'Connor, Philip Merivale, George Coulouris.

●Renoir's second American film, made in the same brutal year as Stalingrad and El Alamein, is one of his quietest and least startling, featuring Laughton as a timid village schoolteacher 'somewhere in occupied Europe' who muddles his way to martyrdom. Both Laughton – happier in this role than many – and O'Hara are fine, but the film's main attractions remain the elegant Renoir set-ups (some recalling *La Bête Humaine*) and the script's unusual ethical stance: not that Nazism was wrong because it denied free enterprise, but that it was wrong because it stood against the possibility of Socialism, human dignity, and political emancipation. CA

This Love of Mine (Wo de Ai)

(1986, Tai, 107 min)
d Chang Yi. *p* Ling Teng-fei. *sc* Hsiao Sa, Chang Yi. *ph* Yang Wei-han. *ed* Wang Chin-ch'en. *pd* Wang Hsia-chun. *m* Chang Hung-yi. *cast* Yang Hui-shan, Wang Hsia-chun, Ch'en Yen-yen, Yang Li-ching.

●An impressive study of a wealthy Taipei woman – already neurotically obsessed with hygiene and health – driven to total distraction by the discovery that her husband is having an affair with another, younger woman. Hardly innovatory, the film nevertheless benefits from strong, understated performances (none more so than Yang Hui-shan as the wife), and brilliant, precisely framed images reminiscent of Bergman's more claustrophobic work. GA

This Other Eden

(1959, GB, 80 min, b/w)
d Muriel Box. *p* Alec C Snowden. *sc* Patrick Kirwan, Blanaid Irvine. *ph* Gerald Gibbs. *ed* Henry Richardson. *ad* Tony Inglis. *m* Lambert Williamson. *cast* Audrey Dalton, Leslie Phillips, Niall MacGinnis, Geoffrey Golden, Norman Rodway, Milo O'Shea, Harry Brogan.

●Lame comedy, from a play by Louis d'Alton, in which Phillips plays a hothead who reacts explosively to the news that his dad was an IRA boss. Of interest to feminist film students, as a Muriel Box film, and to anyone composing a thesis on Ireland and the British cinema. GM

This Property Is Condemned

(1966, US, 112 min)
d Sydney Pollack. *p* John Houseman. *sc* Francis Ford Coppola, Fred Coe, Edith Sommer. *ph* James Wong Howe. *ed* Adrienne Fazan. *ad* Hal Pereira, Stephen Grimes, Phil Jeffries. *m* Kenyon Hopkins. *cast* Natalie Wood, Robert Redford, Mary Badham, Kate Reid, Charles Bronson, Jon Provost, Alan Baxter, Robert Blake.

●Considering the wealth of talent that participated in this Tennessee Williams adaptation, the results are disappointing in the extreme. It was co-scripted by Francis Coppola, produced by John Houseman, photographed by James Wong Howe, and features a more than acceptable cast. But despite the array of talent, it's a very banal reworking of Williams' one-act play about a tragic Southern belle longing for a handsome gentleman caller to whisk her away from the family boarding-house to glamorous New Orleans, but who dies disillusioned of a lung complaint. Originally a two-hander, the play told her tawdry story entirely through the eyes of her younger sister, magically transformed through romantic adolescent reminiscence. On screen, inevitably and disastrously opened out, it is constructed as a series of long, unmemorable flashbacks. DP

This Sporting Life

(1963, GB, 134 min, b/w)
d Lindsay Anderson. *p* Karel Reisz. *sc* David Storey. *ph* Denys Coop. *ed* Peter Taylor. *ad* Alan Withy. *m* Roberto Gerhard. *cast* Richard Harris, Rachel Roberts, Alan Badel, William Hartnell, Colin Blakely, Vanda Godsell, Arthur Lowe.

●A reminder that something really was stirring in those days of the British New Wave before it frittered itself away. There's a touch of the cloth-cap poseur about the way this adaptation of David Storey's novel flaunts pubs, tenements and North Country accents, but also real intelligence in its use of rugby league football as a sidelong metaphor for the rat race, and real passion behind its tormented affair between Harris' inarticulately demanding miner/footballer and his dowdily uncomprehending landlady (Roberts), which ultimately acquires the authentic ring of *amour fou*. Anderson films here with a rare power, compared to which most of his later work is mere petulance. TM

This Sweet Sickness (Dites-lui que Je l'aime)

(1977, Fr, 106 min)
d Claude Miller. *p* Hubert Niogret, Maurice Bernard. *sc* Claude Miller, Luc Béraud. *ph* Pierre Lhomme. *ed* Jean-Bernard Bonis. *ad* Hilton Mac Connico, Diego Blanco. *m* Alain Jomy. *cast* Gérard Depardieu, Miou-Miou, Claude Piéplu, Dominique Laffin, Jacques Denis, Christian Clavier.

●Miller's second film, an adaptation of Patricia Highsmith's novel about a young man (Depardieu) who secretly builds a house for his childhood sweetheart (Laffin), then busily sets about getting her to live there with him, oblivious not only to the fact that she is already married and can't stand him anyway, but to the other girl (Miou-Miou, terrific) meanwhile pursuing him with a love just as hopeless. Often a little self-conscious in its nods to Hitchcock and one rather forced echo of Cocteau, it perhaps errs in departing from Highsmith's original (to favour the psychology over the *policier*), but is often dazzlingly effective. Particularly striking is the dreamy, semi-subjective camera work (it's beautifully shot by Pierre Lhomme throughout) which turns the snowbound roadways leading to the house of fantasy into a mental landscape. TM

This Whole Life of Mine (Wo zhei Yibeizi/aka The Life of a Peking Policeman)

(1950, China, 108 min, b/w)
d Shi Hui. *p* Xu Jin. *sc* Yang Liuqing. *ph* Ge Weiqing. *ed* Fu Jiqiu. *pd* Wang Yuebai. *m* Huang Yijun. *cast* Shi Hui, Li Wei, Wei Heling, Jiang Xiu, Cheng Zhi, Xiao Hao.

●Shi Hui, driven to suicide in Mao's 'Anti-Rightist Purge' of the late 1950s, was one of the greatest screen actors ever and a very fine director; this adaptation of a short story by Lao She was probably his best work. An old man (Shi, 22 at the time) dying on the winter streets of Beijing looks back over a lifetime of defeats, betrayals and humiliations, from his enlistment in the city's police force in 1910 to his arrest and imprisonment in 1946 for trying to denounce an official who collaborated with the invading Japanese. Rich in Beijing argot, the film is superbly acted and observed. Communist censors forced Shi to add a 'positive' coda (the policeman's son is seen as a soldier in the communist army), but the underlying idea that ordinary Chinese have suffered abysmal government all century comes through loud and clear. TR

This Window Is Yours (Kono Mado wa Kimi no Mono)

(1993, Jap, 95 min)
d Tomoyuki Furumaya. *p* Takenori Sento, Tamotsu Kanamori. *sc* Tomoyuki Furumaya. *ph* Kazushiro Suzuki. *ed* Mari Kishi. *pd* Toshihiro Isomi. *m* Isao Yamada. *cast* Yukako Shimizu, Hideo Sakai, Toshio Kamiaki, Yoshiyuki Kubota, Hiromi Kurose, Ayako Noma.

●The long summer holiday begins in a rural town, and Yoko (Shimizu) is taking reluctant leave of her friends while her family finalise plans to move to Hokkaido. It's clear she'd rather stay with her friend Taro (Sakai), who's laid up with a broken leg. A delicately observed, warm, languorous rear-window romance, strong on mood, group dynamics and the hestitations of teenage relationships. A highly accomplished first feature.

This World, Then the Fireworks

(1996, US, 100 min)
d Michael Oblowitz. *p* Chris Hanley, Brad Wyman, Larry Gross. *sc* Larry Gross. *ph* Tom Priestley. *ed* Emma Hickox. *pd* Maia Javan. *m* Pete Rugolo. *cast* Billy Zane, Gina Gershon, Sheryl Lee, Rue McClanahan, Seymour Cassel, William Hootkins, Will Patton.

●The most perverse and most powerful of pulp *noir* writers, Jim Thompson worked on the scripts of Kubrick's *The Killing* and *Paths of Glory*, but it wasn't until censorship broke down in the 1970s that his novels started reaching the screen: *The Getaway* and *The Kill-Off*, among others. It's a pity that his belated popularity with film-makers coincides with the fashion for retro-*noir* chic and all things ironic. That said, this Thompson adaptation begins with a bang: Fourth of July fireworks, adultery, murder and incest, all in the first two minutes. It doesn't leave the film anywhere to go. Twins Marty and Carol grow up despising everyone but each other. She's a hooker, he's a con-man. Such harmless diversions turn nasty as their incestuous love gets out of hand. Director Oblowitz tries to keep faith with the material with a distorting wide-angle lens, lurid, theatrical lighting and a chopped, staccato rhythm. The movie is the spit of a '50s dime store paperback cover, not brought to life, but preserved in amber. Even the actors resemble old B-movie icons. Throw screenwriter Larry Gross's voice-over into the mix, simmer with cod-blues sax and banjo, and the stylisation is complete. Too bad they forgot to put over the story.TCh

This Year's Love

(1999, GB, 109 min)
d David Kane. *p* Michele Camarda. *sc* David Kane. *ph* Robert Alazraki. *ed* Sean Barton. *pd* Sarah Greenwood. *m* Simon Boswell. *cast* Ian Hart, Kathy Burke, Dougray Scott, Douglas Henshall, Catherine McCormack, Jennifer Ehle, Emily Woof, Bronagh Gallagher.

●Camden Town, North London: star-crossed lovers, 1990s-style. The marriage of Danny (Henshall) and Hannah (McCormack) fails to survive the reception, shattered by a revelation of prenuptial infidelity. Pub band singer Marey (Burke) lands Danny on the rebound, but soon tires of her role as a comforting 'fat bird' whose own emotional needs are ignored. Rich single mother Sophie (Ehle) is too selfish to let anyone into her life for long, not even womaniser Cameron (Scott), a handsome serial seducer who combs the lonely hearts ads for potential conquests. Most troubled of all is the inept Liam (Hart), whose volatile neediness is at once comical and desperate. Writer/ director Kane's deftly understated dialogue suggests rather than insists, and the result is an engaging comic portrait of flesh-and-blood people just getting by, in a world where little is as permanent as the 'Celtic Forever' insignia which a drunken Danny tattoos on to the similarly squiffy Marey's bum. NF

Thomas and the Magic Railroad

(2000, US/GB, 86 min)
d Britt Allcroft. *p* Britt Allcroft, Phil Fehrle. *sc* Britt Allcroft. *ph* Paul Ryan. *ed* Ron Wisman. *pd* Oleg M Savytski. *m/songs* Hummie Mann; ('Thomas') JNR Campbell, Mike O'Donnell. *lyrics* Don Black, Sue Ennis. *cast* Peter Fonda, Mara Wilson, Alec Baldwin, Didi Conn, Michael E Rodgers, Cody McMains; voices: Eddie Glen, Neil Crone, Colm Feore.

●The Rev W Awdry's classic, early-reading railway stories inspired the quaintly agreeable '80s TV series *Thomas the Tank Engine*, with its catchy signature tune and Ringo Starr narration. Thomas has, however, suffered a regrettable makeover. Some of the engines, most of the cast and even the narrator have American accents. And that theme tune's gone. Now embellished with Lewis Carroll-style surrealism, the story takes up the series' much exploited theme of the new vs the old. Thomas' elevated position on the magical island of Sodor is again under threat from Diesel, who wants him shuffled off to the sidings once for all. Meanwhile, Mr Conductor (Baldwin) has lost his magic sparkle and, back in the real world, a miscast Fonda is having trouble starting a female engine with the power to put Sodor back on track. If all this sounds convoluted, well, it's a toddlers' film and anything goes. DA

Thomas Crown Affair, The

(1968, US, 102 min)
d/p Norman Jewison. *sc* Alan R Trustman. *ph* Haskell Wexler. *ed* Ralph E Winters, Byron Brandt. *ad* Robert Boyle. *m* Michel Legrand. *cast* Steve McQueen, Faye Dunaway, Paul Burke, Jack Weston, Yaphet Kotto, Todd Martin, Biff McGuire.

●Slick, silly romantic thriller, with Dunaway as an insurance investigator falling for McQueen, the property developer led to commit a bank robbery through boredom. Much obvious 'significance' (the pair playing chess; symbolic, see?), much glossy imagery (courtesy of Haskell Wexler) fashionably fragmented into interminable split-screen nonsense, and little of any real interest. The whole thing is as irritatingly meaningless as its Oscar-winning song, 'Windmills of My Mind'; a sad product of its times. GA

Thomas Crown Affair, The

(1999, US, 113 min)
d John McTiernan. *p* Pierce Brosnan, Beau St Clair. *sc* Leslie Dixon, Kurt Wimmer. *ph* Tom Priestley. *ed* John Wright. *pd* Bruno Rubeo. *m* Bill Conti. *cast* Pierce Brosnan, Rene Russo, Denis Leary, Ben Gazzara, Frankie Faison, Fritz Weaver, Charles Keating, Mark Margolis.

●Forget McQueen, Dunaway and sexy chess, the remake's much much better. First, Brosnan is more believable in a suit than McQueen; beneath his usual suave restraint, the Irishman capably suggests the inner turmoil of a self-made billionaire who has everything – and nothing. Yes, he can allow himself a certain smile after snaffling a priceless Monet from a New York museum, but what really perks up his attention is Russo as the insurance company's maverick investigator, who intuitively pegs him as the likely perp. Their relationship starts out cagily, before it becomes apparent that they make an exquisite match. But can they really trust one another enough not to let a stolen Monet come between them? Along the way, there's a deft robbery sequence, a sexy awayday in Martinique, and, that rarity in big budget thrillers, a plot pushed along by the conflicting emotions of the characters. Brosnan and Russo positively leap on the chance to behave like grown-ups, excited by and wary of each other's intelligence. Plaudits too for Leary (heroic as the NY detective), Tom Priestley's luscious camerawork, effective ethnic percussion on the soundtrack, and direction by McTiernan which combines precision technique with unexpected lyricism. First rate popular entertainment. TJ

Thomas l'Imposteur (Thomas the Imposter)

(1964, Fr, 93 min, b/w)
d Georges Franju. *p* Eugène Lépicier. *sc* Jean Cocteau, Michel Worms, Georges Franju. *ph* Marcel Fradetal. *ed* Gilbert Natot. *ad* Claude Pignot. *m* Georges Auric. *cast* Emmanuèle Riva, Fabrice Rouleau, Jean Servais, Sophie Darès, Michel Vitold, Rosy Varte, Edith Scob, André Méliès. *narrator* Jean Marais.

●On the face of it, it's hard to imagine two artists with less in common than Jean Cocteau and Georges Franju, but Cocteau himself chose Franju to film his early novel. Cocteau's Thomas is a magically charming innocent who poses as the nephew of a general in order to serve in a civil (aristocratic!) ambulance corps during World War I; the war is the circus of his dreams, and his fantasies connect with fact only at the moment of his death. Tougher, more materialistic in his view of fantasy, and with a broader sense of philosophical and social contexts, Franju reformulates the book with surprising fidelity, but disengages his audience from Thomas' subjective experience. The war is seen as an 'absurd' unreal backdrop, a network of extraordinary images and moods, but Franju has made a film about fantasy, not a fantasy film. It is compulsive, and utterly absorbing. TR

Thong

see S.T.A.B.

Thoroughly Modern Millie

(1967, US, 138 min)
d George Roy Hill. *p* Ross Hunter. *sc* Richard Morris. *ph* Russell Metty. *ed* Stuart Gilmore. *ad* Alexander Golitzen, George Webb. *m* Elmer Bernstein. *songs* Sammy Cahn, James Van Heusen, others. *cast* Julie Andrews, Mary Tyler Moore, Beatrice Lillie, James Fox, John Gavin, Carol Channing, Jack Soo, Philip Ahn.

●Patchy but lively musical following in the wake of Sandy Wilson's *The Boy Friend* (though more movie-oriented in its terms of reference) and gently guying the era of the flapper, the Charleston, and the raccoon coat as Julie Andrews sallies forth from Kansas to the Big Apple in search of spouse, success and sophistication *à la mode*. Nicely acted by a reliable cast (Bea Lillie's white-slave-trading landlady is a delight), while the selection of standards and new songs is listenable enough, but the film is far too long for its own good. GA

Those Glory, Glory Days

(1983, GB, 90 min)
d Philip Saville. *p* Chris Griffin. *sc* Julie Welch. *ph* Philip Meheux. *ed* Max Lemon. *ad* Maurice Cain. *m* Trevor Jones. *cast* Zoe Nathenson, Sara Sugarman, Cathy Murphy, Liz Campion, Julia McKenzie, Bryan Pringle, Danny Blanchflower.

●Julie Welch, football writer on *The Observer*, has written a charming – perhaps too charming – tale of schoolgirl enthusiasm based on her own youthful adulation of Tottenham Hotspur's '60s captain Danny Blanchflower. Only flashes of the acerbic wit and gift for satirical characterisation that graced her teleplay *Singles* are evident in this drawn-out and cloying contribution to David Puttnam's *First Love* series for C4 (unwisely given a cinema release after being seen on TV). 14-year-old Zoe Nathenson acts her heart out as the football-mad Julia, but the film itself, though likeable enough, never catches fire. MH

Those Who Love Me Will Take the Train (Ceux qui m'aiment prendront le train)

(1998, Fr, 120 min)
d Patrice Chéreau. *p* Charles Gassot. *sc* Danièle Thompson, Patrice Chéreau, Pierre Trividic. *ph* Eric Gautier. *ed* François Gedigier. *ad* Richard Peduzzi, Sylvain Chauvelot.

cast Pascal Greggory, Valéria Bruni-Tedeschi, Charles Berling, Jean-Louis Trintignant, Vincent Perez, Roschdy Zem.

● A group of family, friends, hangers-on and assorted others travel by train from Paris to Limoges for the funeral of a seemingly misanthropic, promiscuous painter; on arrival, they encounter the artist's nearest (but not, necessarily, his dearest), and a host of revelations and resentments. There's not much substance to this drama of all round dysfunctionality, but the well chosen cast are excellent, the script is intriguingly naturalistic (and at times inconsequential), and the direction often virtuoso: not merely in the use of music and the skilled exploration of the characters on the confined train, but in a stunning final shot swooping over a huge cemetery. GA

Those Wonderful Movie Cranks (Bájecni Muzi s Klikou)

(1978, Czech, 88 min)
d Jirí Menzel. *p* Jan Suster. *sc* Oldrich Vlcek, Jirí Menzel. *ph* Jaromír Sofr. *ed* Jiri Brozek. *pd* Zbynek Hloch. *m* Jirí Sust. *cast* Rudolf Hrusinsky, Vlasta Fabiánová, Blazena Holisová, Vladimir Mensik, Jirí Menzel.

● The cranks in question are pioneers of the Czech silent cinema – an opportunist travelling showman and his female entourage, a dopey documentarist, and a faded stage actress – vacillating over whether or not posterity deserves a record of the latter's histrionics. They are not wonderful. And the film, in its *faux-naïf* flatness, is not 'charming': it's leaden, slushy and slapdash, and ill serves the memory of silent cinema. Saddening, tedious, and intermittently annoying. PT

Thousand Acres, A

(1997, US, 105 min)
d Jocelyn Moorhouse. *p* Marc Abraham, Steve Golin, Lynn Arost, Kate Guinzburg, Sigurjon Sighvatsson. *sc* Laura Jones. *ph* Tak Fujimoto. *ed* Maryann Brandon. *pd* Dan Davis. *m* Richard Hartley. *cast* Michelle Pfeiffer, Jessica Lange, Jennifer Jason Leigh, Colin Firth, Keith Carradine, Kevin Anderson, Pat Hingle, Jason Robards.

● A patriarch (Robards) announces that he means to divide his land between his three daughters, but when one of them, the most beloved (Leigh), tries to dissuade him, he sends her packing. Jane Smiley's novel earned points for chutzpah, but Jocelyn Moorhouse's adaptation makes heavy weather of this latter-day *King Lear*. Despite the leisurely *Waltons*-style voice-over, Larry Cook and his kin don't convince as a Midwestern farming dynasty, while the film itself has only a picturesque sense of the land. It makes for rocky terrain on which to base the ensuing melodramatics. Breast cancer, infertility, adultery, wife beating – it seems as if someone's ticking off a list of female 'issues'. If only Laura Jones' screenplay had allowed the characters more respite, a time to draw breath between calamities, the fine performances from Pfeiffer and Lange (as the older daughters) might just have made it stick. Robards' senile paterfamilias is, regrettably, a grave embarrassment. TCh

1000 Eyes of Dr Mabuse, The (Die Tausend Augen des Dr Mabuse)

(1960, WGer/It/Fr, 103 min, b/w)
d/p Fritz Lang. *sc* Fritz Lang, Heinz Oskar Wuttig. *ph* Karl Löb. *ed* Walter Wischniewski, Waltraud Wischniewski. *ad* Erich Kettelhut, Johannes Ott. *m* Bert Grund, Gerhard Becker. *cast* Dawn Addams, Peter Van Eyck, Gert Fröbe, Wolfgang Preiss, Werner Peters, Andrea Checchi, Reinhard Kolldehoff, Howard Vernon.

● Lang's last film. Resisting the producer's requests for a remake, sequel or *Son of*... Lang instead updated the setting to postwar Germany, and invented a new Mabuse-type character (Preiss). Set in a large hotel where the characters' every move is monitored by the mastermind's TV screens, *1000 Eyes* is none the less distinctly and wilfully old-fashioned in a way that is all Lang's own. Lines like 'Don't leave town', exploding telephones, blind prophets, gadgets more quaint than modern, and a supremely elaborate thriller plot where no one and nothing are what they seem, give it an anti-realist ambience more reminiscent of the Hollywood serial than of contemporary film-making. And, of course, Lang's anti-Fascist sentiments are unmistakably as up-to-date as they were in the '20s. Great stuff. RM

Thousand Pieces of Gold, A

(1990, US, 105 min)
d Nancy Kelly. *p* Nancy Kelly, Kenji Yamamoto. *sc* Anne Makepeace. *ph* Bobby Bukowski. *ed* Kenji Yamamoto. *pd* Dan Bishop. *m* Gary Malkin. *cast* Rosalind Chao, Dennis Dunn, Michael Paul Chan, Chris Cooper.

● The misadventures and sufferings of a mail-order Chinese bride in the 19th century California gold-rush, based on fact. Given that her Manchurian father sells her off to a 'marriage broker' without telling her what he's doing, Lalu has an understandably deep distrust of men in general; but the proto-feminist dimension of her struggle seems imposed from a modern perspective, not something that grows from the material. Still, it's decently written and directed, and features very assured performances from Chao as the heroine and Dunn (a regular in John Carpenter movies) as the kindly man she ought to have trusted. TR

Three (Tatlo...magkasalo)

(1998, Phil, 86 min)
d Carlos Siguion-Reyna. *p* Armida Siguion-Reyna. *sc* Bibeth Orteza. *ph* Romulo Araojo. *ad* Manet A Dayrit. *m* Ryan Cayabyab. *cast* Ara Mina, Tonton Gutierrez, Rita Avila, Gina Alajar.

● In this account of several complicated love triangles, Elsie (Mina) struggles to accept her sexuality while trapped in a loveless marriage to the heartless Tito (Gutierrez). Alice (Avila), the love of Elsie's life, waits for her, but her days are numbered. With no context except the characters' apartments, and an underwritten homophobe as the villain, the film offers only the most superficial examination of attitudes to lesbianism. TH

Three Ages

(1923, US, 6 reels, b/w)
d Buster Keaton, Eddie Cline. *p* Joseph M Schenck. *sc* Clyde Bruckman, Jean Havez, Joseph Mitchell. *ph* William McGann, Elgin Lessley. *ad* Fred Gabowie. *cast* Buster Keaton, Wallace Beery, Margaret Leahy, Joe Roberts, Lillian Lawrence.

● Keaton's first feature – a parody, to some extent, of films like Griffith's *Intolerance* – revels in the same anachronistic view of history as did his earlier short *The Frozen North*: the basic story common to all three intercut episodes, charting Buster and Beery's rivalry over their beloved Leahy, allows him to construct a delicious series of gags spoofing the clichés of film through their very absurdity and incongruity. In the Stone Age, Buster arrives to court Leahy sitting astride a dinosaur, and plays golf with real clubs; in ancient Rome, black slaves start up a crap game upon seeing a soothsayer's dice, and Buster, forced into a chariot race (neatly guying *Ben Hur*) during a blizzard, enters the arena on a sled-cum-chariot drawn by huskies. The modern-day story is least successful, though even here his eye for sheer idiocy of many contemporary fashions is admirably sharp. Widely underrated, the film may lack the sheer brilliance of, say *Our Hospitality* and *The General*, but its sense of detail and pace, its originality and invention remain undimmed. GA.

¡Three Amigos!

(1986, US, 104 min)
d John Landis. *p* Lorne Michaels, George Folsey Jr. *sc* Steve Martin, Lorne Michaels, Randy Newman. *ph* Ronald W Browne. *ed* Malcolm Campbell. *pd* Richard Sawyer. *m* Elmer Bernstein. *cast* Chevy Chase, Steve Martin, Martin Short, Alfonso Arau, Tony Plana, Patrice Martinez, Joe Mantegna.

● Already Hollywood has-beens by 1916, a trio of Western serial stars (Martin, Chase and Short) receive a cable offering them muchos pesos to strut their stuff in a Mexican village. Little do they know that they are expected to take on the forces of a vicious bandit (Arau) terrorising the village. Western spoofs are never notable for original plots, and this is no exception. Nevertheless, it revels in the cornball clichés of the low-budget oater, and benefits from amiably innocent performances. The characterisation is paper thin, and Landis' timing as sloppy as ever; but if you enjoy brainless slapstick that allows space for irrelvant absurdities like a singing bush and an invisible swordsman, it's entertaining enough. GA

Three Brothers (Tre Fratelli)

(1980, It/Fr, 111 min)
d Francesco Rosi. *p* Georgio Nocella, Antonio Macri. *sc* Francesco Rosi. *ph* Pasqualino De Santis. *ed* Ruggero Mastroianni. *ad* Andrea Crisanti. *m* Piero Piccioni. *cast* Philippe Noiret, Charles Vanel, Michele Placido, Vittorio Mezzogiorno, Andrea Ferreol, Maddalena Crippa.

● For too much of its length, Rosi's film threatens to disappear into the mist of its quest for Big Themes. Its story of three men – a Rome magistrate, a reform school teacher, and a trade union activist – summoned by their aged father to assemble in the southern Italian village of their upbringing for their mother's funeral, provides Rosi with the dynamic for investigations into various Burning Questions affecting Italy today – the issue of terrorism and political justification of terrorist violence; the division of the country into two distinct economic regions, one privileged, the other deprived, and what to do about it. So far, so relevant. Unfortunately, Rosi also sees fit to grapple with such eternal themes of the human condition as the symbolic contrasts offered between Life and Death, Youth and Age, Innocence and Experience, often leaving you wishing for the simpler but much more compelling attractions of investigative gangster and thriller genre pieces like *Lucky Luciano* and *The Mattei Affair*. It's only in the realisation of the various characters' dreams, reveries and memories that this really ever becomes seductive. RM

Three Bullets for a Long Gun

(1970, SAf, 84 min)
d Peter Henkel. *p* Ramsay Joynt. *sc* Keith van der Wat. *ph* Felix Meyburgh. *ed* Christina Jameson. *cast* Beau Brummell, Keith Van der Wat, Patrick Mynhardt, Tulio Moneta, Brian Kiley.

● Jokey, South African-financed spaghetti Western, concocted by its star Beau Brummell, in which the nameless 'Major' (who drops not a manly cigar stub but a faintly ludicrous peanut husk) makes common cause with a fast-talking bandit, Lucky, to find the hidden gold of Lucky's murdered father. Okay gunfights, but very ragged subplot. JPy

Three Came Home

(1950, US, 106 min, b/w)
d Jean Negulesco. *p/sc* Nunnally Johnson. *ph* Milton Krasner. *ed* Dorothy Spencer. *ad* Lyle Wheeler, Leland Fuller. *m* Hugo Friedhofer. *cast* Claudette Colbert, Patric Knowles, Sessue Hayakawa, Florence Desmond, Sylvia Andrew.

● Taken prisoner with husband Patric Knowles and their young son during the 1941 invasion of North Borneo, Claudette Colbert suffers courageously in a Japanese internment camp, in Nunnally Johnson's adaptation of the true-life testimony of writer Agnes Newton Keith. Hayakawa's impressive, too, as the humane commanding officer, thus holding xenophobia somewhat at bay. TJ

Three Coins in the Fountain

(1954, US, 102 min)
d Jean Negulesco. *p* Sol C Siegel. *sc* John Patrick. *ph* Milton Krasner. *ed* William H Reynolds. *ad* Lyle Wheeler, John F DeCuir. *m* Victor Young. *cast* Clifton Webb, Dorothy McGuire, Jean Peters, Louis Jourdan, Maggie McNamara, Rossano Brazzi, Howard St John, Cathleen Nesbitt.

● This touristy romance was an unexpected hit in its day, but you'd hardly think it to look at it now. Three American gals in Rome chuck their currency into the Trevi fountain to see if dreams really do come true – and guess what? McGuire ends up with Clifton Webb's charmer of a boss, while Peters and McNamara go for something a little more European (Jourdan, Brazzi). Meanwhile, Sinatra croons the title choon, and CinemaScope cameraman Milton Krasner made The Eternal City look so scrummy he got an Oscar for it. Remade by Negulesco in 1964 as *The Pleasure Seekers*, with Madrid taking over from Rome. TJ

Three Colours: Blue (100) (Trois Couleurs: Bleu)

(1993, Fr, 98 min)
d Krzysztof Kieslowski. *p* Marin Karmitz. *sc* Krzysztof Piesiewicz, Krzysztof Kieslowski. *ph* Slawomir Idziak. *ed* Jacques Witta. *ad* Claude Lenoir. *m* Zbigniew Preisner. *cast* Juliette Binoche, Benoît Régent, Hélène Vincent, Florence Pernel, Emmanuelle Riva.

●Failing to find the courage to commit suicide after her husband and infant daughter die in a car crash, Julie (Binoche) decides to build a new, anonymous and wholly independent life. Leaving her country mansion for a Paris apartment, she soon finds that freedom is not as easy to achieve as she hoped. Neighbours seek help and friendship, and doubts about her husband's fidelity inflame jealousy. Most troubling there's the music: Julia can't escape the sounds in her head. Kieslowski's film – the first of three inspired by the ideals of the French Revolution – is an arresting study of notions of individual freedom in the modern world. There's no facile moralising, simply a lucid examination of a woman's state of mind. Binoche responds with her best work to date: quiet, strong, stubborn, and deeply aware that the heart holds mysteries neither we nor those close to us will ever understand. GA

Three Colours: Red 100 (100) (Trois Couleurs: Rouge)

(1994, Fr/Switz/Pol, 99 min)
d Krzysztof Kieslowski. *p* Marin Karmitz. *sc* Krzysztof Kieslowski, Krzysztof Piesiewicz. *ph* Piotr Sobocinski. *ed* Jacques Witta. *ad* Claude Lenoir. *m* Zbigniew Preisner. *cast* Irène Jacob, Jean-Louis Trintignant, Frédérique Feder, Jean-Pierre Lorit, Samuel Lebihan, Juliette Binoche, Julie Delpy, Benoît Régent, Zbigniew Zamachowski.

●The conclusion to the 'Three Colours' trilogy is set in Geneva and focuses on Valentine (Jacob), a young model with an absent but possessive boyfriend. After running over a dog, Valentine tracks down its owner, a reclusive, retired judge (Trintignant) who eavesdrops on phone calls, including those between a law student and his lover, a weather reporter. While Kieslowski dips into various interconnecting lives, the central drama is the electrifying encounter between Valentine – caring, troubled – and the judge, whose tendency to play God fails to match, initially, the girl's compassion. It's a film about destiny and chance, solitude and communication, cynicism and faith, doubt and desire; about lives affected by forces beyond rationalisation. The assured direction avoids woolly mysticism by using material resources – actors, colour, movement, composition, sound – to illuminate abstract concepts. Stunningly beautiful, powerfully scored and immaculately performed, the film is virtually flawless, and one of the very greatest cinematic achievements of the last few decades. A masterpiece. GA

Three Colours: White (Trois Couleurs: Blanc)

(1993, Fr/Pol, 92 min)
d Krzysztof Kieslowski. *p* Marin Karmitz. *sc* Krzysztof Piesiewicz, Krzysztof Kieslowski. *ph* Edward Klosinski. *ed* Ursula Lesiak. *ad* Halina Dobrowolska, Claude Lenoir. *m* Zbigniew Preisner. *cast* Zbigniew Zamachowski, Julie Delpy, Janusz Gajos, Jerzy Stuhr, Juliette Binoche.

●After the visual sheen and spiritual uplift of *Blue*, part two of Kieslowski's trilogy may at first seem raw, even slight. The story, hung loosely round notions of political and personal equality, concerns the despair and desire for revenge felt by Polish hairdresser Karol (Zamachowski) when his French wife Dominique (Delpy) divorces him after six months of unconsummated marriage in Paris. Initially, having lost everything, he has no idea what to do with his life. But, after a macabre transaction with fellow expatriate Mikolaj (Gajos) enables him to return to Poland, Karol starts afresh and directs his newly developed cunning to re-igniting Dominique's love. A droll black comedy that takes a scalpel to the impoverished ethics of the new money-obsessed Poland, and to the selfish impulses tied up with our desires for a balanced sexual relationship, *White* is at times reminiscent of the satire of the last episode of the *Dekalog*. It's often cruel, of course, and cool as an ice-pick, but it's still endowed with enough unsentimental humanity to end with a touching, lyrical admission of the power of love. Essential viewing. GA

Three Comrades

(1938, US, 98 min, b/w)
d Frank Borzage. *p* Joseph L Mankiewicz. *sc* F Scott Fitzgerald, Edward Paramore. *ph* Joseph Ruttenberg. *ed* Frank Sullivan. *ad* Cedric Gibbons. *m* Franz Waxman. *cast* Robert Taylor, Margaret Sullavan, Franchot Tone, Robert Young, Lionel Atwill, Guy Kibbee, Monty Woolley, Henry Hull.

●Notable as the only film on which Scott Fitzgerald received a script credit, although his conception was softened by some pussyfooting around the crucial Atwill character. So what begins as a 'lost generation' tale as the three comrades (Taylor, Tone and Young) return home to Germany after the 1918 armistice, flaunting the familiar mixture of cynicism and idealism as they pursue fun and fast cars while trying to set about the task of rebuilding their lives, soon becomes sidetracked as Fitzgerald's pessimism runs into Borzage's romanticism. No question here that Sullavan's ethereal heroine, though penniless, jobless, and suffering from malnutrition which turns into terminal TB, will have any seriously sordid truck with the proto-Nazi sugar-daddy played by Atwill. Instead, the film exercises a little sleight-of-hand and, still trailing wisps of Fitzgerald's conception, takes off with Sullavan and Taylor into one of those incandescent Borzage romances where time is simply non-existent: impossibly pure, absurdly naïve, yet magically tender. TM

Three Crowns of the Sailor (Les Trois Couronnes du Matelot)

(1983, Fr, 122 min, b/w & col)
d Raúl Ruiz. *p* Jean Lefaux, Maya Feuillette, José Luís Vasconcelos. *sc* Raúl Ruiz. *ph* Sacha Vierny. *ed* Janine Verneau, Valeria Sarmiento, Jacqueline Simoni-Adamus, Pascale Sueur. *pd* Bruno Beauge, Pierre Pitrou. *m* Jorge Arriagada. *cast* Jean-Bernard Guillard, Philippe Deplanche, Nadége Clair, Lisa Lyon, Jean Badin, Claude Dereppe.

●Students commit mad and meaningless acts, sailors tell the tallest stories. When one of the former, having murdered his tutor, meets one of the latter at the start of Ruiz's film, the images are in muddy green sepia; but as the sailor begins his extraordinary life story – listening is his price for granting the youth safe passage on a departing ship – the movie becomes literally and figuratively more colourful. Story piles upon story, scenes grow vivid and dissolve, characters come and go as in a dream. No one speaks or behaves as they would in 'real life', for that is neither the territory nor the objective of Ruiz's cinema; his is a hypothetical world, governed by the reversal of narrative expectations. The sailor's tale begins in Valparaiso, and revisits in flashback the various ports of call in a lifetime's voyaging, each of which yields its own strange story. The elements of the sailor's yarn are timeless and universal: family ties, journeying away from home, sex, violence, and death. Ruiz conjures them into a poetic parable on the theme of debts long unpaid and finally called in… A vigorous imagination is at work here in the tradition of Cocteau, Fellini, Tarkovsky; open your eyes and your mind to it. A dream of a picture, in every sense. MA

Three Days of the Condor

(1975, US, 118 min)
d Sydney Pollack. *p* Stanley Schneider. *sc* Lorenzo Semple Jr, David Rayfiel. *ph* Owen Roizman. *ed* Don Guidice. *pd* Stephen Grimes. *m* David Grusin. *cast* Robert Redford, Faye Dunaway, Cliff Robertson, Max von Sydow, John Houseman, Addison Powell.

●Set in the world of CIA power games and scientific hardware, but dominated by an intriguing Borges-like riddle: why should a mystery thriller that didn't sell be translated into obscure languages? And why should the American Literary Historical Society in New York be massacred while one of their readers (Redford) is out getting lunch? With the telephone his only method of contact with Olympian and untrustworthy superiors, Redford becomes lost, unpredictable, even sentimental. He holes up in Dunaway's apartment and starts making mistakes. Thanks to an intelligent script, partly by Lorenzo Semple Jr (*Pretty Poison, The Parallax View*), the action rarely falters, and at its best the film offers an intriguing slice of neo-Hitchcock. A certain gloss irritates, but enough scenes compensate for the chic portrayal of the Redford/Dunaway relationship: Redford's sudden intrusion into civilisation when he visits a dead man's apartment, and finds the wife preparing her husband's dinner; the postman whose pen won't work; Redford in the strange, darkened house of his quarry, taking the initiative by blaring soul music from the hi-fi. CPe

Three Faces of Eve, The

(1957, US, 91 min, b/w)
d/p/sc Nunnally Johnson. *ph* Stanley Cortez. *ed* Marjorie Fowler. *ad* Lyle Wheeler, Herman A Blumenthal. *m* Robert Emmett Dolan. *cast* Joanne Woodward, David Wayne, Lee J Cobb, Nancy Kulp, Edwin Jerome, Vince Edwards.

●Based on a true case history of a schizophrenic – here a woman with three personalities: a slatternly housewife, a seductive flirt, and a smart, articulate woman – this is worthy but somewhat turgid and facile, a typically Hollywoodian account of mental illness. Despite fine monochrome camerawork by Stanley Cortez, Johnson's direction remains remarkably mundane in visual terms (one need only compare it to, say, *Psycho* or *Lilith* to realise its shortcomings), so that it's left to the cast to bring the film to life. And that Woodward certainly does, responding with what can only be described as a *tour de force*, for which she won the Best Actress Oscar. GA

Three for All

(1974, GB, 90 min)
d Martin Campbell. *p* Harold Shampan, Tudor Gates. *sc* Tudor Gates. *ph* Ian Wilson. *ed* Peter Musgrave. *ad* Frank White. *m* Graham Bonnet. *cast* Adrienne Posta, Lesley North, Cheryl Hall, Graham Bonnet, Robert Lindsay, Paul Nicholas, Christopher Neil, Richard Beckinsale, Diana Dors.

●Clap hands, another British movie. This one emanates from the Tudor Gates 9-5 Scriptwriting Factory (which brought you vampire horrors such as *Carmilla, Mircalla, Caramello* etc). Now the Great Pen has turned out a musical, built for TV stars and aimed at the C-D Benidorm market. *Billy Beethoven*, a group managed by Richard Beckinsale, tour Spain and are pursued by their three girlfriends (the fourth member has a fixation for Diana Dors, his mum). In order of appearance, the girls bump into Arthur Mullard, David Kossoff, Hattie Jacques, John Le Mesurier, Ian Lavender… What makes the film less than terrible is the professionalism of the players, who could all have used a much better story and dialogue. Adrienne Posta is great as usual; Graham Bonnet acts well and his songs are okay. AN

Three for the Road

(1987, US, 88 min)
d Bill WL Norton. *p* Herb Jaffe, Mort Engelberg. *sc* Richard Martini, Tim Metcalfe, Miguel Tejada-Flores. *ph* Stephen L Posey. *ed* Christopher Greenbury. *pd* Linda Allen. *m* Barry Goldberg. *cast* Charlie Sheen, Kerri Green, Alan Ruck, Sally Kellerman, Blaire Tefkin, Raymond J Barry.

●Wannabe political aide Sheen and college pal Ruck ferry misbehavin' senator's daughter Kerri Green to boarding school in this redundant youth-oriented road movie. TJ

Three Friends (Sechinku)

(1996, SKor, 92 min)
d Yim Soon-Rye. *cast* Kim Hyun-Sung, Lee Jang-Won, Jung Hee-Suk.

●This terrific first feature by one of Korea's very few women directors is focused entirely on young men: three kids from screwed-up families, failures at school and with no real social prospects, looking ahead with dismay at two years of compulsory military service. Yim's story (parts of which are a deliberate challenge to Korean censorship) faithfully reflects social realities at the bottom of the economic scale, but her approach to character and situation is far from grungy social realism. She never forgets that real people laugh, even when there's not much to laugh about, and she roots her underlying anger in her wry awareness that people tend to blame society when they've fucked up their own lives. TR

Three Fugitives

(1989, US, 96 min)
d Francis Veber. *p* Lauren Shuler Donner. *sc* Francis Veber. *ph* Haskell Wexler. *ed* Bruce Green. *pd* Rick Carter. *m* David McHugh. *cast* Nick Nolte, Martin Short, Sarah Rowland, Doroff, James Earl Jones, Alan Ruck, Kenneth McMillan, Bruce McGill.

● Adapted by Weber from his own French movie (*Les Fugitifs*, 1986), this robust, often very funny farce casts Nolte and Short as chalk-and-cheese bank robbers thrown together by ludicrous coincidence. Released after five years in the slammer for armed robbery, Nolte is greeted by the cop (Jones) who put him away, and who promises to do so again. Caught up in an inept hold-up attempt by Short, Nolte is taken hostage, then mistakenly presumed to be the perpetrator of the crime. Forced to assume that role in order to escape, hard man Nolte reveals a softer side when he learns that Short only pulled the job in order to pay for special schooling for his mute six-year-old daughter (Doroff). Some sentimentality creeps in around the angelic child; but making excellent use of Nolte's controlled toughness and Short's hysterical freneticism, Weber plays the comic action hard and fast, grounding the humour in believable reality that has spiralled out of control (one hilarious scene sees Nolte having a gunshot wound treated by a senile veterinarian who thinks he's a dog). NF

Three Godfathers

(1948, US, 105 min)
d/p John Ford. *sc* Laurence Stallings, Frank S Nugent. *ph* Winton C Hoch. *ed* Jack Murray. *ad* James Basevi. *m* Richard Hageman. *cast* John Wayne, Pedro Armendariz, Harry Carey Jr, Ward Bond, Mae Marsh, Jane Darwell, Ben Johnson, Mildred Natwick.

● Dedicated to the memory of Harry Carey Sr ('Bright star of the early western sky'), who had starred in Ford's first version of this much-filmed story (*Marked Men*, 1919), *Three Godfathers* is much better than is usually allowed. The bulk of the film, loosely paralleling the story of the Magi as three bank robbers on the run reluctantly give up their freedom to save a baby found in the desert, and are faced with a parched and desperate journey during which two of them die, is filmed with harsh and hallucinating splendour in Death Valley. Alas, with Wayne's arrival in New Jerusalem, to lay the baby on the saloon bar on what just happens to be Christmas Day ('Set 'em up, Mister, milk for the infant and a cold beer for me…'), the distressing Ford penchant for symbols of religiosity which had marred *The Fugitive* does the same disservice here. The last reel, with Wayne explicitly identified as the Prodigal Son and a general collapse into mawkishness, might almost have strayed in from another movie. TM

Three Hours to Kill

(1954, US, 77 min)
d Alfred L Werker. *p* Harry Joe Brown. *sc* Richard Alan Simmons, Roy Huggins. *ph* Charles Lawton Jr. *ed* Gene Havlick. *ad* George Brooks. *m* Paul Sawtell. *cast* Dana Andrews, Donna Reed, Dianne Foster, Stephen Elliott, Richard Coogan, Lawrence Hugo.

● A superior B-picture from the last years of Werker's 30-plus years in the business, a catalogue of routine assignments broken by highlights including *The Adventures of Sherlock Holmes* (1939), *He Walked by Night* (1949), the prototype serial-killer *film noir*, and a string of interesting minor Westerns from the '50s. Andrews plays a gunslinger accused of murdering his fiancée's brother and all but pulled to pieces by a small town lynch mob including many of his so-called friends. He's back in town now and wants to track down the real killer. The film neatly slots together the dual time frames and generates a strong sense of bitterness at the speed with which Andrews feels himself betrayed. TJ

301–302

(1995, SKor, 100 min)
d/p Park Chul-Soo. *sc* Lee Suh-Goon. *ph* Lee Eun-Gil. *ed* Park Gok-Ji. *pd* Jung-Wuo Choi. *m* Byun Sung-Ryong. *cast* Bang Eun-Jin, Hwang Sin-Hye, Kim Chu-Ryun, Park Chul-Ho.

● In this splendidly lurid thriller a detective checks out the disappearance of a single woman in Room 302 of the New Hope Apartments, Seoul, a haven for the upwardly mobile. His chief informant (and soon his prime suspect) is the woman's pushy neighbour in 301, another single woman in many ways the exact opposite of the absentee. What unfolds is a hair-raising history of marital discord, sexual abuse, anorexia and bulimia… and the truth about the Korean penchant for dog-meat. TR

Three Into Two Won't Go

(1969, GB, 94 min)
d Peter Hall. *p* Julian Blaustein. *sc* Edna O'Brien. *ph* Walter Lassally. *ed* Alan Osbiston. *ad* Peter Murton. *m* Francis Lai. *cast* Rod Steiger, Claire Bloom, Judy Geeson, Peggy Ashcroft, Paul Rogers, Lynn Farleigh, Elizabeth Spriggs, Sheila Allen.

● Irredeemably awful permissive melodrama from the Swinging Sixties, scripted by Edna O'Brien from Andrea Newman's novel about a middle-aged businessman's adulterous flirtations with a young hitchhiker, leading to the breakdown of his marriage. Overheated codswallop, given a ludicrous veneer of respectability by the distinguished cast, it already looked dated when it was made. And it has a score by Francis Lai. GA

Three Kings

(1999, US/Aust, 115 min)
d David O Russell. *p* Charles Roven, Paul Junger Witt, Edward L McDonnell. *sc* David O Russell. *ph* Newton Thomas Sigel. *ed* Robert K Lambert. *pd* Catherine Hardwicke. *m* Carter Burwell. *cast* George Clooney, Mark Wahlberg, Ice Cube, Nora Dunn, Jamie Kennedy, Mykelti Williamson, Cliff Curtis, Saïd Taghmaoui, Spike Jonze.

● Having lanced the boil of 'family values' in *Spanking the Monkey* and *Flirting with Disater*, former indie director Russell turns his attention to a bigger ill, 'international relations' (the setting is the aftermath of the Gulf War), without sacrificing any of his subversive sensibility. He throws himself gleefully under the blanket of official war coverage, introducing his ragbag of US infantrymen (Clooney, Wahlberg, Ice Cube, Jonze) casually shooting 'towelheads' (hostilities have just ended), fucking and fucking over reporters (the only American women about, interestingly), and describing bullet wound sepsis in visceral surgical detail. Strip-searching an Iraqi PoW, they find a map of secret loot, and take off in pursuit. It's an unashamedly hoary plot device, notwithstanding that it aptly summarises the mercenary motivations at the oil-black heart of Desert Storm. Russell constantly threatens to shoot himself in the foot with his charged but ramshackle deployment of dramatic clichés, grand standing action and basic political exposition (the tone's a little shaky, too, veering across merry black humour, denunciatory polemic and high octane thrills). That said, some searingly strong visions of the human impact of realpolitik are radical for a Hollywood film. Taghmaoui offers the most vivid performance as a bitter, angry torturer. The last reel descends into a muddle of trade-offs, heroic about-turns and romanticised rebels, but this is defiant, provocative cinema; Russell may yet prove a film-maker to treasure. NB

Three Lives and Only One Death

see Trois Vies et une Seule Mort

Three Men and a Baby

(1987, US, 102 min)
d Leonard Nimoy. *p* Ted Field, Robert W Cort. *sc* James Orr, Jim Cruickshank. *ph* Adam Greenberg. *ed* Michael A Stevenson. *pd* Peter Larkin. *m* Marvin Hamlisch. *cast* Tom Selleck, Steve Guttenberg, Ted Danson, Nancy Travis, Margaret Colin, Celeste Holm, Philip Bosco, Paul Guilfoyle.

● The American remake of *3 Men and a Cradle* is sleeker, costlier than the French original: the three swinging bachelors are still all thumbs around the infant which unexpectedly turns up on their doorstep, but shout less than the Frenchmen, and in the main eschew the klutzy walks. Inconvenient wee wees, poo poos, and nocturnal crying remain the same. As much of the action is confined to the bachelor pad, Nimoy was smart to fork out on the design. Even smarter, he pixillates little moments of life with Baby Mary, since it is much of a muchness. Guttenberg plays in the register hysterical, wearing a snorkel to entertain the six-month-old tot, Selleck features a roving dimple, and Danson changes from self-regarding sybarite to responsible parent, or nearest offer. It is shamelessly sentimental, and could well send the hardboiled home to kick the cat. BC

3 Men and a Cradle (3 Hommes et un Couffin)

(1985, Fr, 106 min)
d Coline Serreau. *p* Jean-François Lepetit. *sc* Coline Serreau. *ph* Jean-Yves Escoffier, Jean-Jacques Bouhon. *ed* Catherine Renault. *ad* Yvan Maussion. *cast* Roland Giraud, Michel Boujenah, André Dussollier, Philippine Leroy Beaulieu, Dominique Lavanant, Marthe Villalonga.

● In this comedy, three Parisian swingers find their bachelor pad invaded by the fruit of a night of forgotten passion. Horizons narrow to three-hourly feeds and nappy changes, during which the gesticulation rate rises into the paint cards. The father (Dussollier) gets off light, being on vacation in the Orient, but the other two not only learn to cope with parenthood, but also have to contend with a subplot dealing with drugs, drug-dealers and the police, in which the nappy features as a stash. When the mother reclaims the baby, the trio discover that their old ways no longer appeal, and begin to question the meaning of life itself. Only itchy-koo will do. Noisy, and not short of unison waddling walks. BC

Three Men and a Little Lady

(1990, US, 104 min)
d Emile Ardolino. *p* Ted Field, Robert W Cort. *sc* Charlie Peters, Josann McGibbon, Sarah Pariott. *ph* Adam Greenberg. *ed* Michael A Stevenson. *pd* Stuart Wurtzel. *m* James Newton Howard. *cast* Tom Selleck, Steve Guttenberg, Ted Danson, Nancy Travis, Robin Weisman, Christopher Cazenove, Sheila Hancock, Fiona Shaw, Jonathan Lynn.

● In this good-natured sequel to *Three Men and a Baby*, English actress Sylvia (Travis) and her daughter Mary have been living with our bachelor heroes for five years, but now Sylvia is hankering after a husband. Forget Michael (Guttenberg) and Jack (Danson), the obvious choice is upright architect Peter (Selleck). But both parties are scared to declare their feelings, so she accepts a proposal of marriage from smoothie English director Edward (Cazenove). Once it's understood that there's nothing even vaguely credible about the storyline, there's some harmless fun to be had as Michael and Peter go to England in pursuit, with their rescue mission taking on the proportions of a jailbreak when they discover that Mary is being primed for boarding school. Highlights stem chiefly from the performances: Fiona Shaw is funny as a frustrated headmistress, while Danson's variation on his *Cheers* persona keeps the mood light. CM

Three Men in a Boat

(1956, GB, 94 min)
d Ken Annakin. *p* Jack Clayton. *sc* Hubert Gregg, Vernon Harris. *ph* Eric Cross. *ed* Ralph Kemplen. *ad* John Howell. *m* John Addison. *cast* David Tomlinson, Jimmy Edwards, Laurence Harvey, Shirley Eaton, Jill Ireland, Martita Hunt, Lisa Gastoni, Robertson Hare, Miles Malleson.

● When they weren't making such prestigious Anglo-American affairs as *The African Queen* and *Moulin Rouge*, producers John and James Woolf often turned their hand to small-scale British comedy. This mannered, eccentric adaptation of Jerome K Jerome's equally mannered, eccentric novel, wasn't one of their great successes. Shooting was dogged by bad weather. Then, when the film was complete, it all but sank at the box office. (For some reason, it did extremely well in Paris, even as it failed elsewhere.) Still, it's entertaining stuff, enlivened by rum performances from Tomlinson, Edwards and Harvey as the three Edwardian duffers cruising down the Thames. GM

Three Musketeers, The

(1993, US, 106 min)
d Stephen Herek. *p* Joe Roth, Roger Birnbaum. *sc* David Loughery. *ph* Dean Semler. *ed* John F Link. *pd* Wolf Kroeger. *m* Michael Kamen. *cast* Kiefer Sutherland, Charlie Sheen, Chris O'Donnell, Rebecca De Mornay, Tim Curry, Oliver Platt, Gabrielle Anwar, Julie Delpy.

●The disbanded musketeers re-muster when they discover Richelieu's plans to assassinate boy-king Louis, who is showing foolish signs of wishing to grasp the reins of state power. The ageing brat-packers – Sutherland (Athos), Sheen (Aramis) – are under orders to play straight, which they do. Satisfying, old-fashioned family romp, but hardly a modern classic. WH.

Three Musketeers: The Queen's Diamonds, The

(1973, Pan, 107 min)
d Richard Lester. *p* Alexander Salkind. *sc* George MacDonald Fraser. *ph* David Watkin. *ed* John Victor Smith. *pd* Brian Eatwell. *m* Michel Legrand. *cast* Michael York, Oliver Reed, Raquel Welch, Richard Chamberlain, Frank Finlay, Charlton Heston, Faye Dunaway, Christopher Lee, Geraldine Chaplin, Jean-Pierre Cassel, Spike Milligan, Roy Kinnear, Sybil Danning.

●Lester romps through Dumas' novel, coming up with an indulgent and enjoyable excuse to revive and send up the swashbuckling film. The plot is perfunctory, and centres round Cardinal Richelieu's attempts to embarrass the Queen of France, and the efforts of the loyal D'Artagnan and the Three Musketeers to retrieve her diamonds which, of course, the King insists she must wear to the ball. No expense has been spared, and Lester obliges with a visually extravagant piece, a cross between the low-life realism of Pasolini and the lavishness of Zeffirelli. The cast is good (though it remains very much Lester's film), the fights appropriately energetic, and it all moves along at a fair pace, sprinkled with a number of good gags. The second half of the story was issued separately as *The Four Musketeers.* CPe

3 Ninjas (aka 3 Ninja Kids)

(1992, US, 87 min)
d Jon Turteltaub. *p* Martha Chang. *sc* Edward Emanuel. *ph* Richard Michalak, Chris Faloona. *ed* David Rennie. *pd* Kirk Petruccelli. *m* Rick Marvin. *cast* Victor Wong, Michael Treanor, Max Elliott Slade, Chad Power, Rand Kingsley.

●Wise old Japanese granddad (Wong) instructs three boys in the deadly ninja arts. Their dad, an FBI agent on the trail of gun-runner Kingsley, is dead against their training – at least until the latter kidnaps them to get the Feds off his back. Can the trio use their ninja secrets to escape? Will granddad defeat the gun-runner in hand-to-hand combat? If you can't guess the answers to these questions you are under 11 and will absolutely love this film, with its amazing fight scenes, bungling *Home Alone* kidnappers and thoroughly nasty bad guys. Send mum and dad shopping. NKe

Three O'Clock High

(1987, US, 101 min)
d Phil Joanou. *p* David E Vogel. *sc* Richard Christian Matheson, Thomas Szollosi. *ph* Barry Sonnenfeld. *ed* Joe Ann Fogle. *pd* William F Matthews. *m* Tangerine Dream, Sylvester Levay. *cast* Casey Siemaszko, Anne Ryan, Richard Tyson, Jeffrey Tambor, Philip Baker Hall, John P Ryan, Stacey Glick, Jonathan Wise.

●High-school shenanigans as Siemaszko is asked by Wise, editor of the student newspaper, to write a profile of the new kid in class without actually knowing that the subject is the meanest badass ever to stalk a lunch-hour corridor. Joanou, later to find greater exposure with the concert picture *U2 Rattle and Hum* and the Oldman/Penn crime movie *State of Grace*, directs with a lot of energy, but the material just isn't there. TJ

Three of Hearts

(1992, US, 110 min)
d Yurek Bogayevicz. *p* Joel B Michaels, Matthew Irmas. *sc* Adam Greenman, Mitch Glazer. *ph* Andrzej Sekula. *ed* Dennis M Hill, Suzanne Hines. *pd* Nelson Coates. *m* Richard Gibbs. *cast* William Baldwin, Kelly Lynch, Sherilyn Fenn, Joe Pantoliano, Gail Strickland.

●Shallow and virtually compromised out of existence, this film claims to examine the complex dynamics of a hetero-lesbian triangle, but does nothing of the kind. Jilted lesbian Connie (Lynch) hires outwardly macho, inwardly sensitive male escort Joe (Baldwin) to seduce her ex-lover Ellen (Fenn), break her heart and send her running back. The film settles for the obvious: half-hearted lesbian Ellen falls for Joe. Everything here is disingenuous, starting with the fact that the only lesbian relationship depicted is over before the film begins. Ironically, the one friendship which persuades is Joe and Connie's. NF

Three of Us, The

see Noi tre

Three Palm Trees

see Três Palmeiras

Threepenny Opera, The

see Dreigroschenoper, Die

3pm Paradise

see Oksutan

Three Resurrected Drunkards (Kaettekita Yopparai)

(1968, Jap, 80 min)
d Nagisa Oshima. *sc* Tsutomu Tamwa, Mamoru Sasaki, Masao Adachi, Nagisa Oshima. *ph* Yasuhiro Yoshioka. *ad* Jusho Toda. *m* Hikaru Hayash. *cast* Kazuhiko Kato, Osamu Kitayama, Norihiko Hashida, Kei Sato, Fumio Watanabe, Mako Midori.

●Oshima took to the spirit of '68 like a needle to a vein. This riotous comedy (in colour and Scope) is a cocktail of dumb cops, desperate Koreans, and Japanese students who don't know what's hit them. It starts with the students taking a swim, and finding their clothes stolen from the beach; the thieves are illegal immigrants from Korea, who soon want the identities that went with the clothes. It proceeds through a series of chases, misunderstandings, and riddles, which in turn evolve into conceptual games with the structure of the film itself. If anyone imagines that Oshima broke new ground when he cast Bowie and Sakamoto in *Merry Christmas, Mr Lawrence*, they should note that the lead here is Kazuhiko Kato, founder/leader of the Sadistic Mika Band, who also contributes an impeccable pop theme song. TR

3 Ring Circus

(1954, US, 103 min)
d Joseph Pevney. *p* Hal B Wallis. *sc* Don McGuire. *ph* Loyal Griggs. *ed* Warren Low. *ad* Hal Pereira, Tambi Larsen. *m* Walter Scharf. *cast* Dean Martin, Jerry Lewis, Joanna Dru, Zsa Zsa Gabor, Wallace Ford, Sig Ruman, Elsa Lanchester.

●Discharged soldiers Lewis and Martin run away and join the circus. Not one of the duo's most inspired vehicles, but there's a certain pleasure to be had watching Lewis pull faces at the lions. While the buck-toothed comedian gets up to his usual histrionics, Martin, the most laid-back actor since the late Robert Mitchum, tries in his own desultory way to fend off the advances of the equally predatory Zsa Zsa Gabor. GM

Three Seasons

(1998, US/Vietnam, 113 min)
d Tony Bui. *p* Jason Kivot, Joana Vicente, Tony Bui, Harvey Keitel. *sc* Tony Bui. *ph* Lisa Rinzler. *ed* Keith Reamer. *pd* Wing Lee. *m* Richard Horowitz. *cast* Don Duong, Nguyen Ngoc Hiep, Tran Manh Cuong, Harvey Keitel, Zoe Bui.

●Written and directed by a 26-year-old Vietnamese American, helped into production by Harvey Keitel (who gives a startlingly lazy performance as a returning GI) and shot on location in Saigon, this love letter to 'the new Vietnam' plays like a sanitised rehash of Tran Anh Hung's *Cyclo* for the simple-minded. It has three interwoven storylines, each of them a paragon of subtlety and taste: a lotus-picker bonds with a leper recluse because she warbles songs from his childhood, a cyclo driver falls for a hard-hearted hooker because he senses her inner innocence…you get the idea. The Sundance Festival audience, of course, loved it. TR

Three Seats for the 26th

see Trois Places pour le 26

Three Sisters

(1970, GB, 165 min)
d Laurence Olivier. *p* John Goldstone. *ph* Geoffrey Unsworth. *ed* Jack Harris. *pd* Josef Svoboda. *m* William Walton. *cast* Jeanne Watts, Joan Plowright, Louise Purnell, Derek Jacobi, Alan Bates, Kenneth Mackintosh, Sheila Reid, Laurence Olivier, Ronald Pickup, Frank Wylie.

●Olivier's painfully stagebound record of the 1967 National Theatre production of Chekhov's play, in which he himself took a comparative back seat as Chebutikin. Two fantasy sequences are added as a sop to cinema (one of them a redundant visualisation of Irina's wish-fulfilment dream of Moscow as a paradise of glittering ballrooms and theatres). Moments of passion survive from Joan Plowright's Masha; otherwise it's a catalogue of pregnant pauses from which all Chekhovian intent has long since ebbed away. TM

Three Sisters (Paura e amore)

(1990, It/Fr/Ger, 112 min)
d Margarethe von Trotta. *p* Angelo Rizzoli. *sc* Dacia Maraini, Margarethe von Trotta. *ph* Giuseppe Lanci. *ed* Enzo Meniconi. *ad* Giantito Burchiellaro. *m* Franco Piersanti. *cast* Fanny Ardant, Greta Scacchi, Valeria Golino, Peter Simonischek, Sergio Castellito, Agnès Soral, Paolo Hendel.

●Von Trotta uses Chekhov's sorority tale as a springboard, transposing the scene from Russia to a chilly and autumnal Italy. It opens with a funereal party following the death of the sisters' adored father. A guest, oleaginous lecturer Massimo (Simonischek) is the catalyst in their lives. The eldest, Velia (Ardant), also an academic, embarks on a shrewd and, she thinks, open-eyed affair; Massimo swiftly passes on to younger, sillier Maria (Scacchi). The thinly sketched youngest, Sandra (Golino), is bent on a medical career. It's a Euro production: multi-lingual cast puréed in a blender and poured out like glop. Every landscape is swathed in mist, buildings are clad in crumbling stucco, interiors dusty-creamy, and the actresses wear wool. There's a creditable ease and willingness just to let the women's story unroll, to let their beautiful, characterful faces tell the tale as negative gently turns to positive. Whiffs of testosterone, in the form of Simonischek and Castellito (hauntingly desperate as cuckolded brother Roberto), however loathsome/interesting, are seen strictly through female eyes. A muffled subplot concerns nuclear fears and student unrest, but you'd hardly notice. SFe

Threesome

(1994, US, 93 min)
d Andrew Fleming. *p* Brad Krevoy, Steve Stabler. *sc* Andrew Fleming. *ph* Alexander Gruszynski. *ed* William C Carruth. *pd* Ivo Cristant. *m* Thomas Newman. *cast* Lara Flynn Boyle, Stephen Baldwin, Josh Charles, Alexis Arquette, Martha Gehman, Mark Arnold, Michele Matheson.

●When Alex (Boyle) turns up at college, she's dismayed to find herself in adjoining rooms with two males: studious, uptight Eddy (Charles) and obnoxious, neanderthal Stuart (Baldwin). Stuart puts the moves on her, but it's intellectual Eddy she hankers after. Eddy, unfortunately, is more interested in Stuart. They become inseparable. Fleming's risqué comedy has a rather supercilious, hipper-than-thou attitude which makes it difficult to warm to, while sequences in which the threesome freeze out interlopers leave a somewhat sour aftertaste. And then, of course, in opening up this particular can of worms, the film courts suspicion from all sides of the sexual divide. (For my money, though, it doesn't have the courage to see through its bisexual convictions. The film is, however, notably more relaxed about the shifting sands of sexual identity than most, and at the very least it does dare to eroticise a male friendship.) Simply as a comedy, it's witty and assured enough to mark Fleming out as someone to watch. TCh

3.10 to Yuma

(1957, US, 92 min, b/w)
d Delmer Daves. *p* David Heilweil. *sc* Halsted Welles. *ph* Charles Lawton Jr. *ed* Al Clark. *ad* Frank Hotaling. *m* George Duning. *cast* Glenn Ford, Van Heflin, Felicia Farr, Leora Dana, Henry Jones, Richard Jaeckel, Robert Emhardt.

●A classic Western scenario, adapted from a short story by Elmore Leonard. For $200, the sum he desperately needs to save his land from drought, a small-time farmer (Heflin) agrees to escort a notorious outlaw (Ford) to the state penitentiary in Yuma; holed up in a hotel to await the train, with the outlaw's gang gathering in force outside, the escort finds himself in effect the prisoner; nevertheless, although the financial inducement evaporates (he's offered more to let matters slide by both the outlaw and the town's alarmed mayor), he insists on fulfilling his contract. It's of necessity a talkative film, with Ford working on Heflin's nerves in a stream of Machiavellian banter, but one held in perfect balance by Daves, who keeps the tension strung taut (especially in the gauntlet-running final walk to the station) while at the same time elaborating a subtle psychological conflict. The nerve centre is exposed in an early scene where Heflin, the dour family man careworn by responsibilities, watches as his wife and sons come under the spell of Ford's carefree charm: the conflict, ultimately, stems from each man's envy of what the other has. TM

Three the Hard Way

(1974, US, 92 min)
d Gordon Parks Jr. *p* Harry Bernsen. *sc* Eric Bercovici, Jerry Ludwig. *ph* Lucien Ballard. *ed* Robert Swink. *m* Richard Tufo. *cast* Jim Brown, Fred Williamson, Jim Kelly, Sheila Frazier, Jay Robinson, Charles McGregor, Howard Platt, Alex Rocco.

●This is the way the cycle ends, as in the days of the monster rallies. A Fascist millionaire (Robinson) is assuring his place in history through subsidy of a mad doctor's serum, a Tizer-ish liquid which, when dumped into the reservoir, will kill off all the black folks within hours (it doesn't work on whites). Why settle for one blaxploitation star? Not good enough. Why not make that three reservoirs, then we can have three of Shaft's grandchildren, three times the action, and turn a *Man from UNCLE* rewrite into a movie! Dully predictable, thoroughly gratuitous after the first few minutes as the possibilities for genuine suspense are forsaken in favour of a three-figure body count and several automobile demolition clichés. GD

Three to Tango

(1999, US, 98 min)
d Damon Santostefano. *p* Bobby Newmyer, Jeffrey Silver, Bettina Sofia Viviano. *sc* Rodney Vacarro, Aline Brosh McKenna. *ph* Walt Lloyd. *ed* Stephen Semel. *pd* David Nichols. *m* Graeme Revell. *cast* Matthew Perry, Neve Campbell, Dylan McDermott, Oliver Platt, Cylk Cozart, John C McGinley, Bob Balaban, Deborah Rush, Kelly Rowan.

●Oscar (Perry) and Peter (Platt) are architectural partners competing to design a new cultural centre for Chicago. Peter is gay, Oscar straight. Funding the project is tycoon McDermott. He mistakes Oscar for gay and asks him to keep an eye on his mistress Amy (Campbell), a sculptor, in case she gets too much male attention at her gallery opening. Needless to say, Perry and Campbell fall in love, because that's what they're there for, but of course Perry has to keep pretending to be gay. Judging by the mock '50s title sequence, this is masquerading as a revamped Doris Day frolic. Perry does befuddled, Campbell dazzles with a parade of low-cut dresses – nevertheless you only feel embarrassed for them. The final reel treats the gay community with unbelievable crassness, but such is the knuckle gnawing torment of the would-be clever resolution, this passes almost unnoticed. TJ

Three Wishes

(1995, US, 120 min)
d Martha Coolidge. *p* Clifford Green, Ellen Green, Gary Lucchesi. *sc* Elizabeth Anderson. *ph* Johnny Jensen. *ed* Stephen Cohen. *pd* John Vallone. *m* Cynthia Millar. *cast* Patrick Swayze, Mary Elizabeth Mastrantonio, Joseph Mazzello, Seth Mumy, David Marshall Grant, Jay O Sanders.

●In this torpid fantasy, proto-hippie Jack (Swayze) and his mangy mutt are taken in by Korean War widow Jeanne Holman (Mastrantonio) and her two sons, a decision that affects all their lives. This, after all, is America in the '50s, where an unattached woman taking a single man into her home is tantamount to shagging him on the front porch. Mastrantonio is admirably down-to-earth as a resourceful single parent struggling to raise troubled 11-year-old Tom (Mazzello) and five-year-old Gunny (Mumy) on her own; the elder is worried about not fitting in with his pals on the Little League baseball team, the younger terrified of everything from dogs to imaginary closet monsters. As the visionary vagabond, Swayze is even more metaphysical here than in *Point Break*, but going one better is his cosmic canine Betty Jane, who causes Gunny's irrational fears to manifest themselves as computer-generated special effects. Reasonably diverting family drama about kids coming of age in Edendale, California, in an era of stifling conformity, but too often spilling over into cod-Zen nonsense. NF

3 Women

(1977, US, 124 min)
d/p/sc Robert Altman. *ph* Charles Rosher Jr. *ed* Dennis M Hill. *ad* James D Vance. *m* Gerald Busby. *cast* Shelley Duvall, Sissy Spacek, Janice Rule, Robert Fortier, Ruth Nelson, John Cromwell.

●One of Altman's most enigmatic and personal films, this study of three women who exchange personalities (based on a dream of Altman's) combines comedy, suspense, social comment, and Bergmanesque reverie to weird but often wonderful effect. What really holds the film together is Shelley Duvall's breathtaking performance as the vacuous, gossipy therapist who becomes mentor to the naïve Spacek after the latter moves in as her flatmate. The third woman is a mute painter (Rule), fashioning her fears and fantasies into mythic murals of male aggression and female victimisation. Although any feminist content is undercut by the advent of insanity halfway through, and the plot construction is not entirely cohesive, the film succeeds through its perky, acute portrait of ordinary people living stunted lives against a backdrop of consumer-orientated glamour fuelled by films and advertising. Often very funny, always stylish, it's a fascinating film for all its faults. GA

3 Women in Love (Der Philosoph)

(1988, WGer, 83 min)
d/p/sc Rudolf Thome. *ph* Reinhold Vorschneider. *ed* Dörte Völz-Mammarell. *ad* Eve Schaenen. *m* Hanno Rinné. *cast* Johannes Herrschmann, Adriana Altaras, Friederike Tiefenbacher, Claudia Matschulla.

●A young, cropped-haired and other-worldly philosopher (Herrschmann) celebrates the publication of his book – on a snippet of the work of Heraclitus – by visiting an up-market clothes shop for a new suit, and there attracts the attention of three shop girls. One of the girls, Franziska (Altaras) seduces him, then persuades him to go and live in the apartment which the three girls share…Thome's film is an amusing comedy of sexual manners, not so much Rohmer-esque as fitting with that new breed of German satire (from such directors as Doris Dörrie and Percy Adlon) which employs a faux naïf stance the better to probe gently into people's motives, inhibitions and aspirations. Not for the hard-boiled. WH

Three Worlds of Gulliver, The

(1959, GB, 97 min)
d Jack Sher. *p* Charles H Schneer. *sc* Arthur A Ross, Jack Sher. *ph* Wilkie Cooper. *ed* Raymond Poulton. *ad* Gil Parrondo, Derek Barrington. *m* Bernard Herrmann. *cast* Kerwin Mathews, Jo Morrow, June Thorburn, Lee Patterson, Basil Sydney, Grégoire Aslan.

●This all-action – if bland – kids' version of *Gulliver's Travels* marks an early collaboration between producer Charles Schneer and special effects wizard Ray Harryhausen. By the standards of present-day technical expertise, it's pretty creaky, and Swift admirers are not advised to seek it out; but otherwise it is old-style adventure of a reasonable kind, with the distinct advantage of a Bernard Herrmann score. DP

Thrill of It All, The

(1963, US, 108 min)
d Norman Jewison. *p* Ross Hunter, Martin Melcher. *sc* Carl Reiner. *ph* Russell Metty. *ed* Milton Carruth. *ad* Alexander Golitzen, Robert Boyle. *m* Frank De Vol. *cast* Doris Day, James Garner, Arlene Francis, Edward Andrews, Reginald Owen, ZaSu Pitts, Elliott Reid.

●Frothy romantic comedy with Garner taking over from Rock Hudson as Day's foil. The script, by Carl Reiner, takes a mildly satiric look at the world of TV advertising. Day is a squeaky clean housewife who's snapped up to appear in soap-powder commercials. This enrages her husband who thinks she should stay at home and do the dishes.

Throne of Blood (Kumonosu-jo)

(1957, Jap, 110 min, b/w)
d Akira Kurosawa. *p* Akira Kurosawa, Sojiro Motoki. *sc* Hideo Oguni, Shinobu Hashimoto, Ryuzo Kikushima, Akira Kurosawa. *ph* Asaichi Nakai. *ad* Yoshiro Murai. *m* Masaru Sato. *cast* Toshiro Mifune, Isuzu Yamada, Minoru Chiaki, Akira Kubo, Takamaru Sasaki, Takashi Shimura.

●Kurosawa's adaptation of *Macbeth* is reckoned by many, Peter Brook among them, to be one of the very few successful efforts at filming Shakespeare. Translating the familiar story to medieval Japan, with Macbeth as the samurai Washizu (Mifune), the adaptation deletes most of the minor characters, transforms the witches' scenes into a magical encounter with an old woman spinning in a forest glade, perches 'Cobweb Castle' high in the hilly moorland where the clouds roll by like ground-fog, and conceives a stunningly graphic fate for the usurper, clinging stubbornly to his promise of glory even as he is being turned into a human pin-cushion by volleys of arrows. It's visually ravishing, as you would expect, employing compositional tableaux from the Noh drama, high contrast photography, and extraordinary images of rain, galloping horses, the birds fleeing from the forest; all of which contribute to the expression of a doom-laden universe whose only way out for its tragic hero is auto-destruction. RM

Through a Glass Darkly (Sasom i en Spegel)

(1961, Swe, 91 min, b/w)
d/sc Ingmar Bergman. *ph* Sven Nykvist. *ed* Ulla Ryghe. *ad* PA Lundgren. *m* Johann Sebastian Bach. *cast* Harriet Andersson, Gunnar Björnstrand, Max von Sydow, Lars Passgard.

●Preserving a strict unity of time and place, this stark tale of a young woman's decline into insanity is set in a summer home on a holiday island. It is the first part of the trilogy that comprises *Winter Light* and *The Silence*, films which are generally seen as addressing Bergman's increasing disillusionment with the emotional coldness of his inherited Lutheran religion. In particular here, Bergman focuses on the absence of familial love which might perhaps have pulled Karin (Andersson) back from the brink; while Karin's mental disintegration manifests itself in the belief that God is a spider. As she slips inexorably into madness, she is observed with terrifying objectivity by her emotionally paralysed father (Björnstrand) and seemingly helpless husband (von Sydow). NF

Through the Looking Glass

(1976, US, 91 min)
d/p Jonas Middleton. *sc* Ron Wertheim, David Maryla, Jonas Middleton. *ph* Harry Flecks. *ed* Maurizio Zaubmann, James MacReading. *ad* Tyrone Browne. *m* Arlon Ober, Harry Manfredini. *cast* Catharine Burgess, Douglas Wood, Jamie Gillis, Laura Nicholson, Marie Taylor.

●All we get on both sides of this particular looking glass, situated in the dark room at the top of the stairs, is a repetitive series of masturbatory fantasies as a poor man's Catherine Deneuve (Burgess) is beckoned into the hereafter, or at least the elsewhere, by her dead father. The film tricks some interest out of its echoes of countless Gothic woman-in-jeopardy pics, but abandons all in an absolutely risible Danté-esque pastiche at the end. Full of half-thought-out elements like a pair of incestuous servants, pubertal traumas, and a dose of good old Oedipus, this shallow movie hardly rates the 's' in sexploitation. PT

Through the Olive Trees (Zir-e darakhtan-e zeyton/ aka Under the Olive Trees)

(1994, Iran, 103 min)
d/p Abbas Kiarostami. *sc* Abbas Kiarostami. *ph* Hossein Djafarian, Farhad Saba. *ed* Abbas

Kiarostami. *cast* Mohammad Ali Keshavarz, Farhad Kheradmand, Hossein Rezai, Zarifeh Shiva,Tahereh Ladanian.
● In *And Life Goes On…* (1992), the 'director' of Kiarostami's earlier *Where Is My Friend's House?* (played by Farhad Kheradmand) returned to the mountain village of Koker. He wished to discover if the locals who'd acted in *Where Is My Friend's House?* had survived a devastating earthquake. In this third instalment, we see the (fictionalised) behind-the-scenes events that occurred during the shooting of *And Life Goes On…* If this Chinese Boxes format sounds confusing, fear not, for the storyline is simplicity itself; virtually all that happens is that the director of *Life…* (played by Mohammad Ali Keshavarz) talks to quake survivors about their lives, deals with non-professionals unable to remember their lines, and witnesses the romantic complications that arise when Hossein, an extra, decides to use his one and only scene to pursue his troubled courtship of Tahereh, the girl he loves in real life. Get used to the long takes and what at first appears to be an inconsequential narrative, and pretty soon the many levels of intellectual and emotional meaning will work their magic: it's a witty, poignant, illuminating film about the problems that affect movie-makers faced with intractable reality, about cinema's potential as a unifying force, and about the determination and the ability of people to survive tragedy, poverty, injustice and the vicissitudes of love. Sheer brilliance. GA

Throw Away Your Books, Let's Go into the Streets (Sho o Suteyo, Machi e Deyo)

(1971, Jap, 159 min)
d Shuji Terayama. *p* Eiko Kujo. *sc* Shuji Terayama. *ph* Masayoshi Sukita. *ed* Keiichi Uaoka. *ad* Seiichi Hayashi, Ryoichi Enomoto, Jiro Takamatsu. *cast* Hideaki Sasaki, Masaharu Saito, Yukiko Kobayashi, Fudeko Tanaka, Sei Hiraizumi.
● Japanese independent Terayama has a handful of recurrent obsessions, like monstrously tyrannical mothers, flying (as an image of freedom), and the difficulty of losing one's virginity. They're at the heart of this, his first feature, which tells the happy/sad story of an unemployed working class kid struggling towards adulthood. Terayama's extensive experience in Tokyo fringe theatre has led him to distrust 'realism': the movie is framed as a riotous collage of fantasies, digressions, and surrealist shocks, laced with moments of extraordinary pathos and outbursts of quite desirable rock. It's as entertaining and provocative as Ken Russell was in his BBC days. TR

Throwing Down

(1995, US, 90 min)
d Lawrence O'Neil. *p* David Schaye. *sc* Lawrence O'Neil. *ph* Tim McCann. *ed* Marisa Benedetto. *pd* Blue Kraning. *cast* Colleen Werthmann, Kevin Pinassi, Jeffrey Donovan, Timothy Wheeler, Scott Shepherd.
● A quirky genre piece, from a first-time director, about a couple of New York hoods – Scorsese exiles – bickering their way through a drugs scam which takes them to a West Virginia ratshack. The handheld, improvisational feel inspires loose, funny performances from Pinassi and Donovan, but the crummy soundtrack, lazy violence and inconsistent tone are major drawbacks, and it wasn't a great idea to pin the climax on a (late) mail delivery. TCh

Throw Momma from the Train

(1987, US, 88 min)
d Danny DeVito. *p* Larry Brezner. *sc* Stu Silver. *ph* Barry Sonnenfeld. *ed* Michael Jablow. *pd* Ida Random. *m* David Newman. *cast* Danny DeVito, Billy Crystal, Kim Greist, Anne Ramsey, Kate Mulgrew, Branford Marsalis, Rob Reiner, Bruce Kirby, Annie Ross, Oprah Winfrey.
● When creative-writing teacher Larry (Crystal) suggests that Owen (DeVito), dimmest of many dim students, see a Hitchcock movie to learn about motivation and alibi in murder thrillers, he little realises what he's letting himself in for. Owen, whose interpretation of *Strangers on a Train* leads him to believe that Larry would like him to kill his wife in return for the prof's disposal of Owen's obscenely senile, tyrannical mother, turns Larry's life (already a mess: ever since his wife stole his first novel, he's suffered from writer's block) into an absolute nightmare. A lively black comedy, surprisingly stylishly directed by DeVito (his début), it thankfully softpedals on the hysteria front to concentrate on verbal non-sequiturs and quirky characterisation. If it all gets a little soft-centred towards the end, there's more than enough vitality and invention to be going on with. GA

Thumbelina

(1994, US/Ire, 87 min)
d Don Bluth, Gary Goldman. *p* Don Bluth, Gary Goldman, John Pomeroy. *sc* Don Bluth. *ed* Thomas V Moss. *pd* Rowland B Wilson. *songs* Barry Manilow, Jack Feldman, Bruce Sussman. *cast* voices: Jodi Benson, Gino Conforti, Barbara Cook, Will Ryan, Joe Lynch, Carol Channing, John Hurt.
● An animated version of Hans Christian Andersen's story about a tot who wants to pick on someone her own size. The doe-eyed dame is whisked away from her dream prince, and suffers the predations of villainous low-life offering marriage and more: ugly Berkeley Beetle, an immature runt toad, an entirely unsuitable bachelor mole. Twittering in and out as Thumbelina's helpmeet is an annoying cartoon Frenchie, Jacquimo, whose rendition of Barry Manilow's 'Follow Your Heart' keeps her pure and true. Broad-line animation with little facial expression and poor lip-synching. For girls under 12 only. WH

Thunder Alley

(1984, US, 111 min)
d JS Cardone. *p* William R Ewing. *sc* JS Cardone. *ph* Karen Grossman. *ed* Daniel Wetherbee. *pd* Joseph T Garrity. *m* Robert Folk. *cast* Roger Wilson, Jill Schoelen, Scott McGinnis, Cynthia Eilbacher, Clancy Brown, Leif Garrett.
● Another glob of teen-scene fantasy from the Cannon duo of Golan and Globus. Hunks, chicks and rock'n'roll combine in a modern morality tale about a band who hit the little big time in Tucson, Arizona. The torrential expletives cannot disguise the naivety of the script nor the prudish attitude to sex – sadly, most of the meat on show is ham. MS

Thunder and Lightning

(1977, US, 93 min)
d Corey Allen. *p* Roger Corman. *sc* William Hjortsberg. *ph* James Pergola. *ed* Anthony Redman. *m* Andrew Stein. *cast* David Carradine, Kate Jackson, Roger C Carmel, Sterling Holloway, Ed Barth, Ron Feinberg, George Murdock.
● Basically a 90mph sleepwalk for David Carradine, the Corman factory's answer to Burt Reynolds, this formulary automotive action-comedy features an engaging line in absurd Southern-folksy dialogue and a frenzied attempt to ring the changes on the staples of the hot-car genre. A hovercraft duel across the Florida Everglades nevertheless soon gives way to the usual protracted car chase, interesting only for its blatant copying of stunts from numerous precursors, including the Bond movies. The script is a lame excuse for the invariably non-fatal, cartoon-style pyrotechnics, with moonshiner Carradine distinguished from Mob-backed gutrot-runner Carmel only by his stated independence (perhaps as close as you'll get to a policy statement on producer Corman's relationship to the Hollywood majors). PT

Thunderball

(1965, GB, 130 min)
d Terence Young. *p* Kevin McClory. *sc* Richard Maibaum, John Hopkins. *ph* Ted Moore. *ed* Peter Hunt. *pd* Ken Adam. *m* John Barry. *cast* Sean Connery, Claudine Auger, Adolfo Celi, Luciana Paluzzi, Rik Van Nutter, Bernard Lee, Martine Beswick, Roland Culver.
● The fourth Bond, marking the point at which spectacular hardware began to dominate the series. Sleek and quite fun all the same, with SPECTRE holding the world to ransom after stealing a couple of nuclear bombs, Bond almost getting his in the villain's shark-infested swimming pool, and a cleverly choreographed underwater battle to provide the icing on the mix.

Thunderbolt

(1929, US, 95 min, b/w)
d Josef Von Sternberg. *sc* Charles Furthman, Jules Furthman, Herman J Mankewicz. *ph* Henry Gerrard. *ed* Helen Lewis. *ad* Hans Dreier. *cast* George Bancroft, Richard Arlen, Fay Wray, Tully Marshall, Eugenie Besserer.
● Very much an inferior gangster picture designed to trade on the success of his earlier *Underworld*. Sternberg's first talkie suffers from painfully slow pacing, poor performances, and gobbets of excruciating sentimentality. It starts efficiently enough with Bancroft's eponymous hoodlum making plans to murder honest Arlen, old flame of his fur-loving mistress Wray, but after both men end up facing each other on Death Row (Arlen framed, of course, by Bancroft's mob), it grinds to a virtual standstill: endless threats, broken only by uneasy moments of misplaced comedy and much maudlin ado with a mutt (the chink in Bancrofts armour, natch). A museum piece, then, for Sternberg completists only. GA.

Thunderbolt and Lightfoot

(1974, US, 115 min)
d Michael Cimino. *p* Robert Daley. *sc* Michael Cimino. *ph* Frank Stanley. *ed* Ferris Webster. *ad* Tambi Larsen. *m* Dee Barton. *cast* Clint Eastwood, Jeff Bridges, George Kennedy, Geoffrey Lewis, Catherine Bach, Gary Busey, Jack Dodson, Vic Tayback, Dub Taylor.
● This was Cimino's only preparation as director for the epic undertakings of *The Deer Hunter* and *Heaven's Gate,* and is separated from them both in time (four years until *The Deer Hunter*) and in subject (a buddy love/honour among thieves caper). The male bonding of *The Deer Hunter* is one connection, but *Thunderbolt and Lightfoot* still more or less merges with its production circumstances. Having written the script, Cimino was given his first chance to direct by Eastwood (for whom he had previously collaborated with John Milius on *Magnum Force).* The likeable result, made for and with the personnel of Eastwood's Malpaso Company, looks like a throwaway Eastwood vehicle, through which he drifts as the 'older' partner, allowing Jeff Bridges to strike most of the sparks and steal the movie as his good-natured sidekick. MA

Thundercloud

see Colt .45

Thundercrack!

(1975, US, 158 min, b/w & col)
d Curt McDowell. *p* John Thomas, Charles Thomas. *sc* George Kuchar. *ph/ed* Curt McDowell. *m* Mark Ellinger. *cast* Marion Eaton, George Kuchar, Melinda McDowell, Mookie Blodgett, Moira Benson, Rick Johnson.
● The cult classic of weirdo hardcore, an irresistibly infuriating bad taste whip of raunch and skewed melodrama, like a very horny *Soap*, that quite literally leaves you unsure of whether you're coming or going. Often seen cut, but in the full-length version there's more of George Kuchar's parodically overripe dialogue, tracking the convergence of storm-tossed travellers (a gorilla included) on cackling Gertie's Old Dark masturbatorium, and giving a slower fuse to the series of casual libidinous explosions there. But there's also more of Kuchar's truly brilliant trash-*noir* lighting through which to peer at the pickles, the puke, and the polymorphs. PT

Thunderhead, Son of Flicka

(1945, US, 78 min)
d Louis King. *p* Robert Bassler. *sc* Dwight Cummins, Dorothy Yost. *ph* Charles Clarke. *ed* Nick De Maggio. *ad* Lyle R Wheeler. *m* Cyril Mockridge. *cast* Roddy McDowall, Preston Foster, Rita Johnson, James Bell, Diana Hale, Carleton Young.
● Young master McDowall enters his new young colt Thunderhead in the county handicap and helps pop Foster to track down the wild albino stallion that's been tempting the rancher's mares away. Equine entertainment by numbers. TJ

Thunderheart

(1992, US, 119 min)
d Michael Apted. *p* Robert DeNiro, Jane Rosenthal, John Fusco. *sc* John Fusco. *ph* Roger Deakins. *ed* Ian Crafford. *pd* Dan Bishop. *m* James Horner. *cast* Val Kilmer, Sam

Shepard, Graham Greene, Fred Ward, Fred Dalton Thompson, Sheila Tousey, Chief Ted Thin Elk, John Trudell.
●Ray Levoi (Kilmer), an FBI agent of Indian blood, is sent to a South Dakota reservation when an Oglala Sioux is found face down in the dust. While his cynical superior (Shepard) leads the hunt for the killer, Levoi – complete with gum, gun and shades – clings to power and the trappings of white privilege. Predictably enough, professional conflicts lead to personal growth and cultural reawakening: as Levoi uncovers evidence of conspiracy and environmental abuse, his sense of betrayal reflects on larger outrages perpetrated against Native Americans. Apted and cinematographer Roger Deakins focus unblinkingly on the poverty endemic to the reservation. This directness, however, contrasts with an overcomplicated script by John Fusco, who sets the action in the aftermath of the 1975 battle at Wounded Knee and the controversial arrest of American Indian Movement leader Leonard Peltier, accused of killing two FBI agents. But while appreciation may be enhanced by previous knowledge of these events, the story boasts integrity and serves as a forceful indictment of on-going injustice. CM

Thunder Road

(1958, US, 92 min, b/w)
d Arthur Ripley. *p* Robert Mitchum. *sc* James Atlee Phillips, Walter Wise. *ph* Alan Stensvold, David Ettenson. *ed* Harry Marker. *m* Jack Marshall. *cast* Robert Mitchum, Gene Barry, Jacques Aubuchon, Keely Smith, Trevor Bardette, Sandra Knight, Jim Mitchum.
●Very much a personal project for Mitchum – he produced, took the lead (his son also appears, as his younger brother), wrote the story, even composed the theme song – with a subject very dear to his heart, since it depicts the activities of an Appalachian community of moonshiners up against the feds (and more organised rivals) as they race the highways with tanks full of illegally-brewed whisky. Cheaply made, disreputable, and blatantly anti-authority, it's a winner all the way, what with a stunningly laconic performance from Mitchum, white-hot night-time road scenes, and an affectionate but unsentimental vision of backwoods America rarely seen in cinema to this day. GA

Thunder Rock

(1942, GB, 112 min, b/w)
d Roy Boulting. *p* John Boulting. *sc* Jeffrey Dell, Bernard Miles. *ph* Max Greene. *ed* Roy Boulting. *ad* Duncan Sutherland. *m* Hans May. *cast* Michael Redgrave, Barbara Mullen, James Mason, Lilli Palmer, Finlay Currie, Frederick Valk.
●Best known for their limp late '50s comedies, the Boulting Brothers are often far more interesting for their more serious earlier work, like this propagandist drama adapted from Robert Ardrey's anti-isolationist play. Redgrave plays the surly, cynical keeper of the eponymous Lake Michigan lighthouse; a former British war correspondent disillusioned by his compatriots' complacency towards the rise of Fascism in Europe, he now peoples his ivory tower with the ghosts of immigrants drowned in a shipwreck almost a century before. As his conscience – in the form of the boat's dead captain – forces him to rethink his romantic ideas about the simplicity and optimism of times past, and thus to regain his sense of political commitment, the film effortlessly transcends its theatrical origins, merging dream and reality, past and present, propaganda and psychological insight, to complex and intelligent effect. Beautifully performed, closer in tone and style to Powell and Pressburger than to the British mainstream, it's weird and unusually gripping. GA

Thursday

(1998, US, 87 min)
d Skip Woods. *p* Alan Poul. *sc* Skip Woods. *ph* Denis Lenoir. *ed* Paul Trejo, Peter Schink. *pd* Chris Anthony Miller. *m* Luna. *cast* Thomas Jane, Aaron Eckhart, Paula Marshall, Pauline Porizkova, Mickey Rourke, James LeGros.
●Nick (Eckhart) drops a case of drugs at the door of reformed Casey, his one time partner in crime – thus leaving Casey to 24 hours of getting stoned, tied up, raped and assaulted by Nick's acquaintances, who include the chainsaw-wielding Billy (LeGros), and rubber-clad superbitch Dallas (Porizkova). The question here is whether a woman can rape a man, as Dallas does Casey with a photo of his loving wife looking on, but the past is a watchful beast and Casey is soon seduced by his former ways. The presence of Neil LaBute acolyte Eckhart ensures a certain quirky quality which first time director Woods backs up with his clever script, dark shades of humour, and staccato pace. MD

THX 1138

(1970, US, 95 min)
d George Lucas. *p* Lawrence Sturhahn. *sc* George Lucas, Walter Murch. *ph* Dave Meyers, Albert Kihn. *ed* George Lucas. *ad* Michael Haller. *m* Lalo Schifrin. *cast* Robert Duvall, Donald Pleasence, Don Pedro Colley, Maggie McOmie, Ian Wolfe, Marshall Efron.
●Lucas' first film, a reworking of *1984* set in a computer-controlled future world where THX 1138 (Duvall) becomes an outlaw hounded by android police after rediscovering love, long banned in this drug-soothed Garden of Eden where children are created by test-tube. Overall the film is a little hazy, and inclined to fall back on familiar messages about humanity and inhumanity after what one presumes was the nuclear fall. But visually it is often extraordinary, with Lucas playing on perspectives and dislocations throughout, nowhere more brilliantly than in the 'prison' represented by a limbo of whiteness that seems to stretch as far as the eye can see. White-clad against this whiteness, human figures disappear except for their hands and faces, others mysteriously appear out of the blinding glare of nothingness, and one can readily believe in this infinity through which THX 1138 must journey endlessly if he is to escape. Some nice touches of humour, too. TM

Tiara Tahiti

(1962, GB, 100 min)
d William T Kotcheff. *p* Ivan Foxwell. *sc* Geoffrey Cotterell, Ivan Foxwell. *ph* Otto Heller. *ed* Anthony Gibbs. *ad* Alex Vetchinsky. *m* Philip Green. *cast* James Mason, John Mills, Rosenda Monteros, Herbert Lom, Claude Dauphin, Madge Ryan, Peter Barkworth, Roy Kinnear.
●Wartime tensions between working class Lt-Col Mills and aristocratic Capt Mason rumble on into peacetime and the South Seas, bringing further clashes between go-getting upstart and dissolute old money in this uneven mix of character study and situation comedy. Good roles for both the stars (Mills gets the tougher assignment, Mason the usual), but even co-writer Geoffrey Cotterell seemed at a loss in transferring the flavour of his original novel to the big screen. Lots of effort, but it doesn't really come off. First feature (for Rank) of the Canadian-born TV director Ted Kotcheff. TJ

Tibet: A Buddhist Trilogy

(1978, GB, 54/125/52 min)
d Graham Coleman.
●This three-part 'documentary on Tibetan Buddhist culture and politics' was four years in the making, and contains some footage of rituals and daily life rarely seen by outsiders (it was shot in Southern India, where the Dalai Lama and his followers fled in 1959 after the Maoist Revolution). But its framework is a sluggish mixture of *National Geographic* photography and liberal reverence; the voice-over is so awe-filled it sounds completely somnolent. Particularly amusing are some of the more bizarre juxtapositions ('His Holiness the Dalai Lama is looked upon by his people as the supreme embodiment of insight and compassion' intones the voice-over, as a title reading 'The Carpet Co-operative' pops up on the screen). There is much debate about 'the form and formlessness of the illumined mind', which sounds pretty woolly. But the narrator assures us that 'These contemplative gestures are very deep'. Deeply Tibetan, certainly. CR

Tibetan New Year, A

(1986, GB, 43 min)
d Jon Jerstad.
●A beautifully shot and fascinating documentary about the Tibetan New Year celebrations carried out by the monks at the Bonpo monastery, founded high in the mountains of Northern India in 1966, a few years after the Bonpos had fled the Chinese Red Army. Wisely, Jerstad never attempts to probe the complexities of the Bonpos' religious beliefs, although the significance of the monks' ritualised actions is briefly explained at every turn. What most impresses is the way Jerstad allows the music, dance, chants, costumes and masks to speak for themselves, using landscape, movement, colour and sound to convey a feeling of liberation and rejuvenation. And the Bonpos' Abbot – articulate, open, and evidently a man of great compassion ('Not all the monks have to take the ceremony that seriously') – is great. GA

Tichborne Claimant, The

(1998, GB, 98 min)
d David Yates. *p* Tom McCabe. *sc* Joe Fisher. *ph* Peter Thwaites. *ed* Jamie Trevill. *pd* Brian Sykes. *m* Nicholas Hooper. *cast* John Kani, Robert Pugh, Stephen Fry, Robert Hardy, John Gielgud, Rachael Dowling, Paola Dionisotti, Charles Gray, James Villiers, Anita Dobson, Dudley Sutton, Iain Cuthbertson.
●Yates instils mischief and artifice in a staid genre. It helps that fraud and legitimacy are at the heart of this tall, true tale. Kani plays Bogle, manservant to one of the richest families in England. Dispatched with a lesser son to investigate reports that the missing heir – Sir Roger – is living in Australia, Bogle is stranded when Tichborne minor perishes en route. Discerning that he'll never return to Britain unless it's in the company of his former master, Bogle interviews a series of unlikely prospects, and reaches an understanding with one Thomas Castro (Pugh), an inebriate butcher who nevertheless has a certain bearing. Bogle schools him so well that by the time they reach home, even Castro believes he's the real Lord Tich. Exquisitely urbane, the film teases out the enigma which still hangs over the claimant, and leaves you wondering if he wasn't for real after all. In so doing, it makes a mockery of the hereditary principle, and the snobbery and hypocrisy which sustains the establishment. Pugh's performance is appropriately larger than life: funny, vulgar and ridiculous, but also passionate and pathetic in the true sense of the word. TCh

Ticket

(1986, SKor, 100 min)
d Im Kwon-Taek. *p* Jin Sung-Man. *sc* Song Kil-Han. *ph* Fu Jung-Mo. *cast* Kim Ji-Mi, Jun Se-Young, Lee Hye-Young, Myoung Hee, Park Kun-Hyoung.
●Comparable with Mizoguchi's *Street of Shame*, this account of four prostitutes working from a snack bar in an unnamed port generated huge controversy in Korea on first release. The 'ticket' is a bar fine which the women must pay to their employer whenever they go out to 'deliver an order'. Madam Min (veteran star Kim at her career best) tries to run her 'teahouse' with an iron fist, but she's as doomed to disappointment as any of her girls: she discovers that the man she's waiting for (a political prisoner) has left jail and married someone more respectable. Each of the women suffers abuse or emotional setbacks in the course of her work, but Im's stance is notably matter of fact and unsentimental. Seen now, the film works less as an exposé than as an intimate and poignant portrait of a group of women. TR

Tickets for the Zoo

(1991, GB, 90 min)
d Brian Crumlish. *p/sc* Christeen Winford. *ph* Martin Singleton. *ed* Fiona Macdonald. *ad* Annette Gillies. *m* Wendy Weatherby. *cast* Alice Bree, Tom Smith, Micky MacPherson.
●On this evidence, Cormorant Films should have stuck to documentaries. Dramatising teenage homelessness in Edinburgh, Crumlish shoots for Little Nell. Orphan siblings Carol and George think positive, but lose their flat when she refuses to do a little bondage on the side for the landlord – clearly no man to mess with, since we later see his heavies hurling an old lady's Zimmer frame out the door. *Pixote* underdone. BC

Ticket to Heaven

(1981, Can, 108 min)
d Ralph L Thomas. *p* Vivienne Leebosh. *sc* Ralph L Thomas, BA Cameron. *ph* Richard Leiterman. *ed* Ron Wisman. *pd* Susan Longmire. *m* Micky Erbe, Maribeth Solomon. *cast* Nick Mancuso, Saul Rubinek, Meg Foster, Kim Cattrall, RH Thomson, Jennifer Dale.

●Unremarkable but fairly solid story of a young man, thrown into despair by the departure of his girlfriend, who joins up with the Heavenly Children, a Moonie-like group. When he comes increasingly to reject the outside world, his family is driven to kidnap and 'deprogramme' him back to some sense of normality. All fairly predictable stuff, but delivered without too much sensationalism, strong on showing how the apparently harmless cult insidiously undermines the man's confidence and independence. Notable for performances of unusual conviction. GA

Ticket to Tomahawk, A

(1950, US, 90 min)
d Richard Sale. *p* Robert Bassler. *sc* Mary Loos, Richard Sale. *ph* Harry Jackson. *ed* Harmon Jones. *ad* Lyle Wheeler, George W Davis. *m* Cyril J Mockridge. *cast* Dan Dailey, Anne Baxter, Rory Calhoun, Walter Brennan, Charles Kemper, Connie Gilchrist, Arthur Hunnicutt, Chief Yowlachie, Victor Sen Yung, Marilyn Monroe.

●Jolly comedy Western along *Paleface* lines. Dan Dailey's the greenhorn travelling salesman on an eventful train journey across the wilderness to the Colorado Rockies. The rival stagecoach company is determined to stop the train arriving on time and places all sorts of obstacles in its path. Dailey encounters trigger-happy gunslingers and a doe-eyed chorus girl (Marilyn Monroe). TJ

Tickle in the Heart, A

(1996, Ger, 87 min, b/w)
d Stefan Schwietert. *p* Thomas Kufus, Martin Hagemann, Edward Rosenstein. *ph* Robert Richman. *ed* Arpad Bondy. *with* Max Epstein, Willie Epstein, Julie Epstein.

●Max, Willie and Julie Epstein could have jumped from the pages of a Carl Hiaasen novel: three elderly Brooklyn brothers who've settled in the spick-and-span, horribly neat and conservative retirement community that is Florida. They're suitably colourful characters, too, whether reminiscing about their lives or achieving unexpected success performing on stage at home and abroad. For what makes them special is the Yiddish Klezmer music they play on clarinet, trumpet and drums, surprisingly coming back into fashion. And while this solid, amiable documentary is, cinematically speaking, nothing remarkable, the trio's music is for the most part terrific. GA

Ticks

(1993, US, 82 min)
d Tony Randel. *p* Jack F Murphy. *sc* Brent V Friedman. *ph* Steve Grass. *ed* Leslie Rosenthal. pd Anthony Tremblay. *m* Christopher L Stone. *cast* Rosalind Allen, Ami Dolenz, Seth Green, Virginia Keehne.

●An ecologically sound update of the classic '50s bug movie, efficiently directed by Tony (*Hellbound*) Randel and featuring 'the vampires of the insect world'. Two social workers take a party of misfit city kids to the woods for some therapeutic communing with nature. Instead, they're attacked by ticks affected by the steroid fertilisers sprayed on a secret marijuana crop. Cue scenes of scuttling blood-suckers burrowing into their victims and, in one case, growing giant-sized inside a body-builder's steroid-saturated body. Unusually for a low-budget horror film, Randel takes the trouble to establish his characters before the ticks start bugging them, which means we care a little more when they're confronted with pulsing egg sacs and fearsome claws. The suspenseful, crowd-pleasing 'bug hunt' finale rounds things off nicely. NF

Tic Tac

(1997, Swe, 96 min, col & b/w)
d Daniel Alfredson. *p* Katinka Farargó. *sc* Hans Renhäil. *ph* Peter Mokrosinski. *ed* Håkan Karlsson. *pd* Ernst Billgren. *m* Flaskkvartetten (Flesh Quartet). *cast* Thomas Hanzon, Jacob Nordenson, Tuv Novotny, Tintin Anderzon, Oliver Loftéen, Jacob Nordenson, Emil Forselius.

●Like Tarantino's *Pulp Fiction*, Alfredson's first feature plays around with time structure. We know the various stories in his film are unfolding over a single night, but it is for the viewer to work out the actual order in which events occur, because the film darts back and forth in time pretty much unannounced. Among the cast of characters are a pair of very sensitive skinheads who only beat people up on request, a manic husband obsessed with moving to Canberra, a dodgy cop working up a flat-swap scam, and a teenage arsonist who falls in love instead of setting the school alight. Individual scenes are diverting enough, but the entertainment value is more in assembling the jigsaw puzzle than in admiring the slightly banal end result. And since subtitles inevitably iron out the humour in the dialogue, it is less fun than it probably was for the home audience. TJ

Tidikawa and Friends

(1972, Aust, 83 min)
d/p/sc Jef Doring, Su Doring. *ph* Michael Edols, Jack Bellamy. *ed* Rod Adamson.

●A documentary about the Bedamini people in Papua, New Guinea. Aggressive and cannibalistic by reputation, they've led a comparatively secluded existence, farming in the jungle. With little commentary, the film-makers present the principal daily activities of the village, plus more unusual events like a child's funeral and the initiation ceremony of seven young males. The life appears friendly and unhurried, with no signs of the usual boss-slave structures. The photography is lush and uninspired, perhaps something to do with trying not to aggress on the subjects; the result is often a discreetness which can make concentration difficult. It remains interesting, though, for its presentation of such an obviously non-authoritarian society. JDuC

Tie Me Up! Tie Me Down! (Atame!)

(1989, Sp, 102 min)
d Pedro Almodóvar. *p* Agustin Almodóvar. *sc* Pedro Almodóvar. *ph* José Luis Alcaine. *ed* Jose Salcedo. *m* Ennio Morricone. *cast* Victoria Abril, Antonio Banderas, Loles Leon, Francisco Rabal, Julieta Serrano.

●After the kitschy melodrama of *Women on the Verge of a Nervous Breakdown*, Almodóvar returns to the darker terrain of *Law of Desire*, concentrating on the relationship between soft-porn actress Marina (Abril) and the two men who try to control her. The more benign is her director in the movie-within-the-movie (Rabal), a genial, wheelchair-bound obsessive who leaves romantic messages on her answering machine and beguiles his lonely hours watching her masturbate on video. Less kindly are the attentions of Ricky (Banderas), recently released from a psychiatric hostel and determined to father Marina's children. He kidnaps her in her apartment, beats her up, and ties her to the bed while he goes out to score drugs for her. Almodóvar turns a standard hostage thriller into a grim examination of the power games implicit in marriage; Marina, addictive in all things, soon becomes a willing accomplice in Ricky's fantasy. Almodóvar withholds all comment, and many will hate his refusal to moralise; others will relish the opportunity to think for themselves. A very black comedy in the vein of Buñuel's *Belle de Jour*, and worthy of the comparison. RS

Tierische Liebe (Animal Love)

(1995, Aus, 110 min)
d Ulrich Seidl. *p* Winfried Natter, Erich Lackner, Hans Selikovsky. *sc* Ulrich Seidl. *ph* Michael Glawogger, Peter Zeitlinger. *ed* Christof Schertenleib.

●Voyeuristic documentary about people using pets as substitute love (sex) objects. Various sad loners nuzzle, jerk off, frolic and sleep with their animals. Why does nobody here have a normal owner-pet relationship? Why are so very many of the human subjects grotesque low-lifes? Just how much of this is staged for the benefit of the camera, and why? Any film in which the most sympathetic character is a ferret has got to be doing something wrong. Horrible. GA

Tierra (Earth)

(1995, Sp, 125)
d Julio Medem. *p* Lola Pérez. *sc* Julio Medem. *ph* Javier Aguirresarobe. *ed* Ivan Aledo. *ad* Satur Idarreta. *m* Alberto Iglesias. *cast* Carmelo Gómez, Emma Suárez, Silke Klein, Karra Elejalde, Nancho Novo.

●Gómez is Angel, a bug fumigator with schizophrenic tendencies, called in to clear up the woodlice infecting a wine-growing district. The first thing he sees is an electrified sheep smouldering by the roadside after being struck by lightning. This is the kind of movie where lightning always strikes twice, a metaphysical melodrama which mixes everything up: absurdism, symbolism, romanticism, surrealism, and any other -ism you can think of. An acquired taste, perhaps, but distinctive. TCh

Tieta of Agreste (Tieta do Agreste)

(1996, Braz/GB, 120 min)
d Carlos Diegues. *p* Bruno Stroppiana, Don Ranvaud. *sc* Antonio Calmon. *ph* Edgar Moura. *ed* Mair Tavares. *ad* Lia Renha. *m* Caerano Veloso. *cast* Sonia Braga, Marilia Pera, Esteves Chico Anisio, Cláudia Abreu, Zezé Motta.

●Adapted from a popular Brazilian novel, *Homônimo* by Jorge Amado, that also spawned a TV soap opera, this shambolic, incident-packed melodrama, from the veteran director Diegues, is held together by a powerhouse performance from Braga. Her earthy, big-hearted and filthy rich Tieta returns in triumph from São Paolo to the village from which she was banished as a teenager. Although the source of her fortune's a mystery, she makes peace with her greedy family, wins the people's hearts, and stirs the loins of every man in town. But the spectre of pollution from a planned titanium processing plant threatens her idyllic homecoming. Unforgivably baggy, but so full of life it almost succeeds despite itself. NF

Tie That Binds, The

(1995, US, 98 min)
d Wesley Strick. *p* David Madden, Patrick Markey, John Morrissey, Susan Zachary. *sc* Michael Auerback. *ph* Bobby Bukowski. *ed* Michael N Knue. *ad* Marcia Hinds-Johnson. *m* Graeme Revell. *cast* Daryl Hannah, Keith Carradine, Vincent Spano, Julia Devin, Moira Kelly, Ray Reinhardt, Barbara Tarbuck.

●Six-year-old Janie (Devin) is abandoned by criminal couple Leann (Hannah) and John (Carradine), and later adopted by perfectly adjusted Russell (Spano) and Dana (Kelly). This second pair, who chose not to have a child of their own, deal with the traumatised Janie with love and care. Until, that is, Leann and John decide to reclaim their child. Domestic horror movies like this (technically efficient, emotionally exploitative) drive a pile into the heart. The odds are stacked in the yuppies' favour. The Pavlovian use of 'pure cinema' works – the rhythm and dart of the camera movements, Graeme Revell's score, Marcia Hinds-Johnson's production design – and the audience waits for sweet closure. Performances are secondary: Carradine, for instance, looking so bored you expect him to yawn, has only to incarnate threat; Hannah models perverted motherhood; Kelly and Spano enact the semblance of a functional couple, caught by the camera in poses of heartening 'normality'. The climax is a would-be tour de force in a half-built new house, reminiscent of the church in *Witness*. First-time director Strick, to be fair, does more than justice to Michael Auerbach's hyperbolic script. WH

Tiffany Jones

(1973, GB, 90 min)
d/p Peter Walker. *sc* Alfred Shaughnessy. *ph* Peter Jessop. *ed* Alan Brett. *m* Cyril Ornadel. *cast* Anouska Hempel, Ray Brooks, Susan Sheers, Damien Thomas, Eric Pohlmann, Richard Marner.

●Based on the *Daily Mail* comic strip, a British comedy of the worst type, full of banalities so trite that they don't even masquerade as clichés. Fascist president (Pohlmann) falls for reluctant dolly English model (a performance of laboured effervescence from Hempel), so providing an apology for a plot involving Marxist revolutionaries (all buffoons), denim-clad prince, and a score of nudes. Even Anouska Hempel's Health and Efficiency nudity palls after a while, and terminal boredom sets in long before the bread for the big pay-off turns up as several vanloads of Wonderloaf. CPe

Tiger of Eschnapur, The (Der Tiger von Eschnapur) [Part I]/ The Indian Tomb (Das Indische Grabmal) [Part II]

(1958, WGer/It/Fr, (Pt I) 101 min/(Pt II) 95 min)
d Fritz Lang. *p* Eberhard Meichsner, Louis de Masure. *sc* Werner Jörg Lüddecke, Fritz Lang.

ph Richard Angst. *ed* Walter Wischniewski. *ad* Willi Schatz, Helmut Netwig. *m* (Pt I) Michel Michelet, (Pt II) Gerhard Becker. *cast* Debra Paget, Walter Reyer, Paul Hubschmid, Claus Holm, Sabine Bethmann, Valery Inkijinoff, Victor Francen, Luciana Paluzzi.

● A two-part escapist adventure in exotic locations: a despot, a European architect who becomes involved with a temple dancer… It would be easy to fall into the trap that many did over Lang's American films, saying the subjects were unworthy of the director. But here the spectacle permits one of Lang's most formal achievements. Above all, here are two films to be *looked* at. In this respect, it's not surprising that the project started as a silent movie, which Lang co-scripted in 1920 with Thea von Harbou, and was preparing to direct until Joe May decided to make it himself. Nor is it coincidence that a central character is an architect: these two movies are like cathedrals of cinema. Eroticism, another perennial theme in Lang's work, is given its most tangible form in Debra Paget's temple dancer. Some may find the films irritating, but there's no denying their formal achievement. CPe

Tiger Bay

(1959, GB, 105 , b/w)
d J Lee Thompson. *p* John Hawkesworth. *sc* John Hawkesworth, Shelley Smith. *ph* Eric Cross. *ed* Sidney Hayers. *ad* Edward Carrick. *m* Laurie Johnson. *cast* Hayley Mills, John Mills, Horst Buchholz, Megs Jenkins, Anthony Dawson, Yvonne Mitchell, Kenneth Griffith.

● Young Hayley Mills made her screen bow as the Cardiff dockland stray, Gillie, who spots Polish sailor Buchholz killing his faithless girlfriend, then protects him from the law, in the mackintoshed person of Mills *père*. The storyline may be synthetic (co-scripted by producer John Hawkesworth from Noel Calef's novel *Rodolphe et le Revolver*), but the players are strong and affecting, and director Thompson makes the most of the grungy locale. TJ

Tiger by the Tail (aka Crossup)

(1955, GB, 85 min)
d John Gilling. *p* Robert S Baker, Monty Berman. *sc* John Gilling, Willis Goldbeck. *ph* Eric Cross. *ed* Jack Slade. *ad* Wilfred Arnold. *m* Stanley Black. *cast* Larry Parks, Constance Smith, Lisa Daniely, Cyril Chamberlain, Donald Stewart, Thora Hird.

● It was once a sure sign that a career was in decline when a Hollywood actor was reduced to accepting a part in a British movie. That was the fate that befell Larry Parks, who'd so memorably played Al Jolson a few years before. As a former communist, he was hounded by the House Un-American Activities Committee. It would be nice to think that the Brits found him a vehicle worthy of his talents, but this soporific thriller adapted from John Mair's novel *Never Come Back* is nothing of the sort. He plays an American journalist kidnapped by a gang of hoodlums when he gets wind of their plans. GM

Tigerland

(2000, US/Ger, 101 min)
d Joel Schumacher. *p* Arnon Milchan, Steven Haft, Beau Flynn. *sc* Ross Klavan, Michael McGruther. *ph* Matthew Libatique. *ed* Mark Stevens. *pd* Andrew Laws. *m* Nathan Larson. *cast* Colin Farrell, Matthew Davis, Clifton Collins Jr, Thomas Guiry, Shea Whigham, Russell Richardson, Nick Searcy, Afemo Omilami, Keith Ewell, Cole Hauser.

● Stylistically this is more interesting and more affected than Schumacher's *Flawless*. Either way, it's a big improvement on his past tendentious nonsense. A biographical record of a company of men training for Vietnam at a military academy, it's not unlike the first half of *Full Metal Jacket*, though less of a theorem than Kubrick's vision. Schumacher uses a gritty handheld style – standard but unobtrusive – and gets a testy lead performance from Farrell as the charismatic rebel. Involving but inconsequential. NB

Tigers Don't Cry

(1976, SAf, 102 min)
d Peter Collinson. *p* Alan Girney. *sc* Scot Finch. *ph* Brian Probyn. *ed* Harry Hughes. *ad* John Margetts. *m* Hennie Bekker. *cast* Anthony Quinn, John Phillip Law, Simon Sabela, Marius Weyers, Sandra Prinsloo, Joe Stewardson, Ken Gampu.

● Quinn, a beat-up ex-sailor suffering from a terminal illness, conceives a plan to kidnap the President of an emergent African nation who has flown to South Africa, would you believe, to undergo medical tests. Quinn becomes fast friends with the President (Sabela), and finally redeems himself by stopping an assassin's bullet intended for the latter. Collinson screws up the pace of this singularly distasteful cut-price thriller in a vain attempt to disguise the script's efforts to ignore, trivialise, and misrepresent the realities of social and political life in South Africa. JPy

Tiger Shark

(1932, US, 80 min, b/w)
d Howard Hawks. *sc* Wells Root. *ph* Tony Gaudio. *ed* Thomas Pratt. *ad* Jack Okey. *m* Leo F Forbstein. *cast* Edward G Robinson, Zita Johann, J Carrol Naish, Richard Arlen, Leila Bennett, Vince Barnett.

● A minor but highly enjoyable Hawks adventure, with Robinson in expansive form as the Portuguese tuna fisherman who marries a friend's daughter, only to find that she has lost her heart to his younger buddy. Warners revamped the love-triangle story countless times, and Hawks himself reworked it for *Barbary Coast*; but the film's virtues lie less in its plot (which, with its protagonist mutilated by a shark, occasionally drifts rather waywardly into *Moby Dick* territory) than in its jaunty mood and in the evocative tuna-fishing sequences, shot on location on the Monterey coast. GA

Tiger's Tale, A

(1987, US, 97 min)
d/p/sc Peter Douglas. *ph* Tony Pierce-Roberts. *ed* David Campling. *pd* Shay Austin. *m* Lee Holdridge. *cast* Ann-Margret, C Thomas Howell, Charles Durning, Kelly Preston, Ann Wedgeworth, William Zabka, Tim Thomerson.

● Between wrestling his pet tiger and pumping gas, Texas high school senior Bubber (Howell) finds time to seduce middle-aged lush Rose Butts (Ann-Margret). Her daughter Shirley – Bubber's ex-girlfriend – is real pissed off, and when the pair decide to live together for the summer, she joins her estranged father and his girlfriend. But not before getting her own back on the little prick by making a little prick of her own, in her mother's diaphragm. Before long, a kid is on the way, and the couple's idyll turns sour. Will Rose keep the baby? Will she and Bubber separate at the end of the summer as agreed? Will Bubber release the film's only sympathetic character, the pet tiger who steals the whole show by snaffling a customer's Pekinese? Will they ever stop making this sort of coy sex comedy? NF

Tiger Walks, A

(1963, US, 91 min)
d Norman Tokar. *p* Ron Miller. *sc* Lowell S Hawley. *ph* William Snyder. *ed* Grant K Smith. *ad* Carroll Clark, Marvin Aubrey Davis. *m* Buddy Baker. *cast* Brian Keith, Vera Miles, Pamela Franklin, Sabu, Kevin Corcoran, Edward Andrews, Una Merkel, Arthur Hunnicutt.

● Formulary Disney yarn about a tiger which escapes from a circus and prowls around a terrified community, hunted by all and sundry until the children start a nationwide Save the Tiger campaign. Ninety minutes seems an unnecessarily long time to take to prove that a tiger is an American citizen like anybody else. It doesn't even get to eat one of the little beasts. TM

Tiger Warsaw

(1987, US, 93 min)
d/p Amin Q Chaudhri. *sc* Roy London. *ph* Robert Draper. *ed* Brian Smedley-Aston. *pd* Tom Targownik. *m* Ernest V Troost. *cast* Patrick Swayze, Piper Laurie, Lee Richardson, Mary McDonnell, Barbara Williams, Bobby DiCicco.

● Chuck 'Tiger' Warsaw (Swayze), a reformed drug addict with hangover paranoia, returns to his home town 15 years after a violent family row that involved a shooting and left his father (Richardson) mentally unhinged. The cause of the fight is never made clear: was Tiger having an incestuous affair with sister Paula (McDonnell), or was he just peeking when she was undressing? Was he ransacking the house for drugs money? Only Tiger's mum (Laurie) and ex-girlfriend (Williams) are prepared to give him a second chance. It's a fraught movie that lurches between trauma and tearjerker towards a predictable conclusion, carrying the dubious message that matrimonial bliss and domestic harmony is the ultimate aspiration. Swayze gives the part knitted-brow intensity; he almost succeeds in shrugging off his heart-throb image by looking more pathetic than sympathetic. EP

Tigger Movie, The

(2000, US, 77 min)
d Jun Falkenstein. *p* Cheryl Abood. *sc* Jun Falkenstein. *ed* Makoto Arai, (Japan) Yasunori Hayama. *ad* Toby Bluth. *m* Harry Gregson-Williams. *songs* Richard M Sherman, Robert B Sherman. *cast* voices: Jim Cummings, Nikita Hopkins, Ken Sansom, John Fiedler, Peter Cullen, Andre Stojka, Kath Soucie, Tom Attenborough. *narrator* John Hurt.

● Tigger's suffering a bit of an identity crisis. Convinced there are other 'Tiggers' beyond the wood, Christopher Robin's disillusioned toy tiger is seriously considering quitting the place and heading over yonder in search of his non-existent relatives. His wiser playmates (including Pooh) sense a nervous breakdown on the horizon and, in an effort to placate him, pen a fictitious letter, allegedly from his estranged cousins. But things go terribly wrong. Disney's stop gap between its larger, more commercial offerings sticks fairly rigidly to the look of AA Milne's original cartoons and books, with a style of animation which is at best purposeful. What this simple, moralistic tale really lacks, though, is some get up and go. Needless to say, tiny tots will be enthralled. DA

Tight Little Island

see Whisky Galore

Tightrope

(1984, US, 114 min)
d Richard Tuggle. *p* Clint Eastwood, Fritz Manes. *sc* Richard Tuggle. *ph* Bruce Surtees. *ed* Joel Cox. *pd* Edward C Carfagno. *m* Lennie Niehaus. *cast* Clint Eastwood, Genevieve Bujold, Dan Hedaya, Alison Eastwood, Jennifer Beck, Marco St John.

● This features as nasty a piece of wacko-scum-on-the-loose as Clint has ever faced. Unlike the last three *Dirty Harry* thrillers, however, in which Eastwood's pillar of the law has been unequivocal, his new creation, New Orleans detective Wes Block, is more steeped in the mire than any major US star has ever dared play. His quarry is only one step ahead of Wes himself in frequenting the jacuzzis, massage parlours, and S/M dives of the red light district; and while the cop/killer *doppelgänger* game is nothing new, Wes' taste for using the handcuffs in bed as well as out would have choked Philip Marlowe. A film about desire and its control is hardly what one might expect, but then Eastwood has always been Hollywood's most experimental star. And he's still one of the best. CPea

Tigrero – A Film That Was Never Made

(1994, Fin, 75 min)
d/p/sc Mika Kaurismäki. *ph* Jacques Cheuiche. *ed* Mika Kaurismäki. *m* Nana Vasconcelos, Chuck Jonkey. *cast* Sam Fuller, Jim Jarmusch.

● Grizzled, cigar-chomping director Fuller returns to an Indian village in the Amazon forest – accompanied by Jarmusch, who watches over and interviews his pal and mentor – where 40 years previously he shot 16mm footage (seen briefly in *Shock Corridor*) in preparation for a Fox adventure drama that fell foul of insurance problems. A somewhat lackadaisical blend of anthropology, movie archaeology and character profile, held together by Jarmusch's laconic good sense and Fuller charismatic (and mercifully none too gaga) sense of fun and wonder. GA

Tilaï

(1990, Burkina Faso/Switz/Fr, 81 min)
d/p/sc Idrissa Ouedraogo. *ph* Jean Monsigny, Pierre Laurent Chenieux. *ed* Luc Barnier, Michel Klochendler. *m* Abdullah Ibrahim. *cast* Rasmane Ouedraogo, Ina Cissé, Roukietou Barry, Assane Ouedraogo, Mariam Ouedraogo.

● Saga (Rasmane Ouedraogo), the wayfarer returned, learns that in his absence his beloved Nogma (Cissé), the girl he has waited so long to marry, has been taken to wife by his father. When a rendezvous is arranged between Saga and Nogma, they realise at once that their destinies are sealed. Committing incest, they know that according to traditional law ('tilai') Saga's life will be called for. Explosive problems are unleashed. Who will be asked to kill Saga? Will he and Nogma be able to flee and avoid tragedy? Emphatically African, despite Ouedraogo's clear intention to universalise his themes, the story is mythic and simple. What is the role of law in society? To what does one owe one's greatest loyalty? If there are rules in social and moral conduct, are they fixed? The film is shot – with an emphasis on landscape – with a rare beauty, using a spare, ritualised style, aided by a bare and expressive score by Abdullah Ibrahim. Unflinching, almost to the degree of cynicism, Ouedraogo presents a fascinating, brave look at the contradictions at work in his impoverished homeland. WH

Till Death Us Do Part

(1969, GB, 100 min)
d Norman Cohen. *p* Jon Pennington. *sc* Johnny Speight. *ph* Harry Waxman. *ed* Tony Lenny. *pd* Terence Knight. *m* Wilfred Burns. *cast* Warren Mitchell, Dandy Nichols, Anthony Booth, Una Stubbs, Liam Redmond, Bill Maynard, Brian Blessed, Sam Kydd, Frank Thornton, Cleo Sylvestre.

● This big screen spin-off from the then current TV series (both written by Johnny Speight) traces the Garnett family saga right back to 1939 to figure out just how Alf (Mitchell) became such an opinionated old so-and-so in the first place. In its favour, it preserves the original characterisations at something like full strength and doesn't attempt to stitch three weekly episodes together and pass it off as a feature. TJ

Till Sex Us Do Part (Troll)

(1972, Swe, 99 min)
d/p Vilgot Sjöman. *sc* Vilgot Sjöman, Solveig Ternström, Börje Ahlstedt, Margaretha Byström, Frej Lindqvist. *ph* Rune Ericson, Uulf Björck. *ed* Carl-Olov Skeppstedt. *m* Verdi. *cast* Solveig Ternstöm, Börje Ahlstedt, Margaretha Byström, Frej Lindqvist, Jan-Olof Strandberg.

● Vilgot (*I Am Curious*) Sjöman here ventures into the awkward territory of parodying the sex film. Though happily married for five years, a young couple believe (and almost make you believe) that if they consummate their marriage they'll die. Ninety unsuccessful minutes later they decide on a suicide pact, taking the predictable way out. It's often leaden (he's particularly oafish), sometimes funny (an operatic sequence at an orgy), and occasionally touching; but the constant flashes of knickers do tend to obscure the film's basic point, which argues that there's more to sex than meets the eye.

Till There Was You

(1990, Aust, 95 min)
d John Seale. *p* Jim McElroy. *sc* Michael Thomas. *ph* Geoffrey Simpson, Robert Primes. *ed* Jill Bilcock. *pd* George Liddle, Susan Emshwiller. *m* Graeme Revell. *cast* Mark Harmon, Deborah Unger, Jeroen Krabbe, Shane Briant, Ivan Kesa.

● New Yorker Frank Flynn (Harmon) packs his saxophone and travels to the South Pacific island of Vanuatu, adopted home of his brother Charlie. On arrival, he learns of Charlie's murder, and encounters sultry blonde Anna (Unger). Regretting her marriage to raving villain Big Viv (Krabbe), she joins Frank in his investigation, which leads to the jungle where the Bunlap tribe reside. Seale (cameraman on *Dead Poets Society, Gorillas in the Mist*) makes an unremarkable debut as director on this laboured hokum, which involves sunken treasure and an uneasy mix of violence and humour. One notably silly scene has Frank execute a bungy jump, a sacred Bunlap ceremony rounded off when – complete with funny sound effects – tribal members line up to squeeze his balls. CM

Till We Meet Again

(1944, US, 88 min, b/w)
d/p Frank Borzage. *sc* Lenore Coffee. *ph* Theodor Sparkhul. *ed* Elmo Veron. ad Hans Dreier, Robert Usher. *m* David Buttolph. *cast* Ray Milland, Barbara Britton, Walter Slezak, Lucile Watson, Mona Freeman, Vladimir Sokoloff.

● Borzage's admirers – and who'll not claim at least associate membership of that circle? – will find this movie to be in a familiar case. The writing suggests melodrama at its most mechanical and life cheapening, yet the director infuses individual scenes with such warmth and spontaneity as to ensure that the affections are celebrated even as they're being betrayed. This time the love affair is explicitly non-sexual, since the plot is to do with shot down flyer Milland and virginal nun Britton pretending to be husband and wife while on the run in occupied France – a situation requiring fancy footwork from all concerned to keep the censors at bay. It's salutary to watch the usually tight-lipped Milland transformed into a model Borzage hero, enthusiastic and brimming with tenderness. BBa

Tilt

(1978, US, 111 min)
d Rudy Durand. *sc* Rudy Durand, Donald Cammell. *ph* Richard H Kline. *ed* Robert Wyman. *pd* Ned Parsons. *m* Lee Holdridge. *cast* Brooke Shields, Ken Marshall, Charles Durning, Harvey Lewis, Robert Brian Berger, John Crawford, Geoffrey Lewis, Gregory Walcott.

● Tilt (Shields) is a pinball wizard. She is also a precocious little squirt whose 14-year-old heart is touched by an aspiring singer (Marshall) who can't take the bad breaks, but can and does take her for a ride as they hustle pinball games from Santa Cruz to Texas. She thinks she's using her talent for 'art' (funding a demo record for him), but all he wants is easy money for more Elvis outfits. Don't be fooled, this is not about pinball, though there's much incidental footage of flashing lights, ricocheting balls, scores clicking over, and the gyrations of the players' hips. It is in fact a thoroughly objectionable movie which subscribes to the theory that behind every weak male is a strong woman – be she only fourteen – and then connives at her exploitation. Outrage subsides into apathy, however, with the wearisome smart-ass attitude and lack of appeal of the two leads; you feel they deserve all they get. FF

Tim

(1979, Aust, 108 min)
d/p/sc Michael Pate. *ph* Paul Onorato. *ed* David Stiven. *ad* John Carroll. *m* Eric Jupp. *cast* Piper Laurie, Mel Gibson, Alwyn Kurts, Pat Evison, Deborah Kennedy, Peter Gwynne.

● An older woman (Laurie) falls in love with her handsome, slightly retarded gardener (Gibson). A downer? Not really, it's triumph over adversity/love conquers all, and not a dry eye in the house at the fadeout. Gibson acquits himself well in this tricky early role, but Pate's adaptation of Colleen McCullough's first novel doesn't break any ground. TCh

Tim Burton's The Nightmare Before Christmas

see Nightmare Before Christmas, The

Time After Time

(1979, US, 112 min)
d Nicholas Meyer. *p* Herb Jaffe. *sc* Nicholas Meyer. *ph* Paul Lohmann. *ed* Donn Cambern. *pd* Edward C Carfagno. *m* Mikós Rozsa. *cast* Malcolm McDowell, David Warner, Mary Steenburgen, Charles Cioffi, Kent Williams, Patti D'Arbanville.

● An idealistic HG Wells (McDowell) chases the villainous Jack the Ripper (Warner) when he escapes into the 20th century – specifically, San Francisco in 1979 – by courtesy of the Time Machine. Once there, they respectively try to protect and destroy a cutesy women's libber (Steenburgen), discovering en route that violence is more at home in our times than gentleness. It's a bookish joke which comes unstuck: after nearly two hours the tension has evaporated, and all that's left is a curdle of jokes and brutality.

Time and Judgement

(1988, GB, 80 min)
d Menelik Shabazz. *p* Glenn Ujebe Masokoane. *sc* Menelik Shabazz. *ph* Roy Cornwall, Vusi Challenger, Sebastian Shah. *ed* Keith Lakhan. *ad* Shakka Dedi, Kenneth McCalla. *m* Cosmo Ben-Imhotep. *cast* Doris Harper-Wills, Thomas Pinnock, Anita Breveld, Prince Albert Morgan.

● Shabazz's first feature since his 1981 debut with *Burning an Illusion* eschews narrative for the more direct, didactic methods of narrated documentary. A rich collage of archive footage presents a picture of riots, assassinations, wars, famines and invasions, in Africa, the Caribbean, the US and Britain, the saddening year-by-year analysis punctuated by secondary gains like the sporting success of Carl Lewis or the election of black MPs in Britain. Although its anger and urgency may well offend liberal sensibilities, it is undoubtedly one of the most fascinating and substantial documents to come out of the independent black film-making community in recent years. A cogent, if non-consensual, political/religious agenda presented from the militant 'African' or Rastafarian standpoint, it is also something of a celebration of the range and creative abilities of British black poets (Zephaniah, Iyapo, Williams), painters and musicians. WH

Time and Tide (Shunliu Niliu)

(2000, HK, 116 min)
d Tsui Hark. *p* Tsui Hark, Nansun Shi. *sc* Koan Hui, Tsui Hark. *ph* Ko Chiu-Lam, Herman Yau. *ed* Marco Mak. *ad* Stanley Cheung, Chow Sai-Heung, Robert Lok. *m* Tommy Wai. *cast* Nicholas Tse, Wu Bai, Anthony Wong, Cathy Chui, Candy Lo, Couto Remotigue Jr.

● Financed (like *Crouching Tiger*) by Columbia Asia, this represents yet another attempt at self-renewal by Tsui Hark, lately reduced to doing Jean-Claude Van Damme movies. The two protagonists, both with nine-months-pregnant women on their backs, are small-time chancers who become friends and then find themselves in opposite camps. Tyler (Tse) works for Ji (Wong) and is assigned to guard a triad boss under threat of assassination by a Brazilian gang. Jack (Wu) is married to the threatened man's daughter, but his chequered past leaves him vulnerable to pressure from the Brazilians. The maternity-in-peril stuff has been done before by John Woo and Cha Chuen-Yee, and the set-piece climax (a full scale gun battle which rages from Hung Hom railway station to the Coliseum, hosting a rock concert at the time) is tediously over-extended and repetitive. But the earlier shoot-out in a crumbling resettlement estate is inventive, well-paced and superbly choreographed. TR

Time Bandits

(1981, GB, 113 min)
d/p Terry Gilliam. *sc* Michael Palin, Terry Gilliam. *ph* Peter Biziou. *ed* Julian Doyle. *pd* Millie Burns. *m* Mike Moran. *cast* John Cleese, Sean Connery, Shelley Duvall, Katherine Helmond, Ian Holm, Michael Palin, Ralph Richardson, Peter Vaughan, David Warner, David Rappaport, Craig Warnock.

● An extraordinarily inventive fantasy in which schoolboy Warnock is rescued from a dull suburban existence by a band of renegade dwarfs, who emerge from his wardrobe and whisk him off on an incredible journey through time and space. Guided by a 'Time Hole Map of the Universe', Warnock and his diminutive pals gatecrash history, meeting up with Robin Hood and Napoleon, and turning up uninvited in Ancient Rome and on the deck of the ill-fated Titanic. Sometime *Monty Python* animator Gilliam fills the screen with bizarre images, and directs with a breathless ingenuity. NF

Timecode

(2000, US, 97 min)
d Mike Figgis. *p* Mike Figgis, Annie Stewart. *sc* Mike Figgis. *ph* Patrick Alexander Stewart. *pd* Charlotte Malmlöf. *m* Mike Figgis, Anthony Marinelli. *cast* Holly Hunter, Salma Hayek, Jeanne Tripplehorn, Julian Sands, Saffron Burrows, Stellan Skarsgård, Xander Berkeley, Glenne Headly, Danny Huston, Kyle MacLachlan.

● Depending on how you look at it, Figgis' fascinating film is the story of an alcoholic movie producer on the verge of a nervous breakdown; or it's about a two-timing lesbian starlet who gets her first big break; or it's a critical day in the life of a fledgling film production company; or it's a portrait of spurned wives, lovers and actresses on the LA scene. Four movies in one, *Timecode* splits the screen on a horizontal and a vertical axis to showcase simultaneously four unbroken shots, each 93 minutes long. The initial dizzying sensory overload doesn't last. An ingenious sound mix and the familiar faces of Skarsgård, Hayek, Tripplehorn, Sands, Hunter and Burrows invite you to conspire order from the chaos. Characters from the top left screen bump into their neighbours from bottom right, while at two o'clock they're bitching about those assholes screwing them at eight. Like a riff on Altman's *Short Cuts* and *The Player*, it adds up to a properly jaundiced satire of Hollywood on the rocks. The movie is a stunt, a conceptual in-joke; or it's a portent of cinema to come; or it's a brilliant but hollow technical exercise; or it's a dynamic if erratic ensemble improv. Make of it what you will, it's certainly something to see. TCh

Timecop

(1994, US, 98 min)
d Peter Hyams. *p* Moshe Diamant, Robert Tapert, Sam Raimi. *sc* Mark Verheiden. *ph* Peter Hyams. *ed* Steven Kemper. *pd* Philip Harrison. *m* Mark Isham. *cast* Jean-Claude Van Damme, Mia Sara, Ron Silver, Bruce McGill, Gloria Reuben, Scott Bellis.

● Van Damme returns to the sci-fi genre as a human future-cop charged with policing Time itself. In the year 2004, the dream of time travel has become a nightmarish reality, with criminals and corrupt businessmen trying to alter the course of history. Together with his ballsy black partner Agent Fielding (Reuben), Timecop Max Walker (Van Damme) zips back to 1994 to unravel the mystery surrounding the meteoric rise of Senator McComb (Silver). Walker also has a private agenda of his own. Haunted by the death of his wife Melissa (Sara), he wants to discover the truth about her murder. Hyams is no stranger to large-scale sci-fi, so his management of the massive sets and slightly mechanical fx is more than adequate. His handling of the time-shift narrative and emotional undertow, on the other hand, is thoroughly pedestrian. NF

Time for Drunken Horses, A (Zamani Barayé Masti Asbha/Un Temps pour l'ivresse des chevaux)

(2000, Fr/Iran, 79 min)
d/p/sc Bahman Ghobadi. *ph* Saed Nikzat. *ed* Samad Tavazoi. *m* Hossein Alizadeh. *cast* Nezhad Ekhtiar-Dini, Amaneh Ekhtiar-Dini, Madi Ekhtiar-Dini, Ayoub Ahmadi, Jouvin Younessi.

● Ghobadi (who was Kiarostami's assistant on *The Wind Will Carry Us* and played a teacher in *Blackboards*) was born in Iranian Kurdistan; his debut film is a shattering docu-drama set on the region's mountainous Iran-Iraq border. Young teenager Ayoub, one of five orphaned siblings, tries to support the others by taking an adult job smuggling vehicle tyres into Iraq. In particular, he wants to earn money to pay for an operation which will briefly prolong the life of his retarded brother Madi. His eldest sister tries to help by agreeing to marry an Iraqi Kurd, but the groom's family fail to pay the dowry. As per the title, both men and pack mules swig local moonshine liquor to help them withstand the appalling winter conditions. Unstintingly physical, this must have been as hard to make as it is to be a cross-border smuggler. Completely unsentimental, and so intensely moving. TR

Time for Dying, A

(1969, US, 75 min)
d Budd Boetticher. *p* Audie Murphy. *sc* Budd Boetticher. *ph* Lucien Ballard. *ed* Harry Knapp. *ad* Les Thomas. *m* Harry Betts. *cast* Richard Lapp, Anne Randall, Bob Randon, Victor Jory, Audie Murphy.

● Boetticher's last Western (after a long gap filled with his work on a bullfighting project) is a sad affair, far removed from the precision and resonance of the Randolph Scott films. Produced by Audie Murphy, who takes a bit part as Jesse James, the film looks at the life of an aspiring gunfighter (Lapp), who meets his end through foolish bravado. Not much bravado is visible on-screen, however, as the production values are strictly TV (flat lighting, crummy sets), and the actors fail to give their characters any credibility. DT

Time for Loving

(1971, GB, 104 min)
d Christopher Miles. *p* Mel Ferrer. *sc* Jean Anouilh. *ph* Andréas Winding. *ed* Henri Lanoe. *pd* Théo Meurisse. *m* Michel Legrand. *cast* Joanna Shimkus, Mel Ferrer, Britt Ekland, Philippe Noiret, Susan Hampshire, Mark Burns, Lila Kedrova, Robert Dhéry, Michel Legrand.

● With the possible exception of Grémillon's *Pattes Blanches*, Anouilh's work as a scriptwriter has always proved dispiritingly leaden by comparison with his plays, nowhere more so than in his rewrite of Arthur Schnitzler for Vadim's horrible remake of *La Ronde*. Displaying much the same sort of predictable playfulness, this trilogy of bitter-sweet romantic anecdotes (the last with a touch of farce), set in Paris between 1937 and 1945, is not helped by direction which drenches it in an ooh-la-la atmosphere of Eiffel Tower, accordion music and toujours l'amour. TM

Time Is on Our Side

see Let's Spend the Night Together

Timeless Bottomless Bad Movie (Napun Younghwa)

(1997, SKor, 144 min)
d Jang Sun-Woo. *p* Yeo Hanku, Kim Soojin. *sc* Jang Sun-Woo, Kim Soohyun. *ph* Choi Jung-Woo. *ed* Kim Yong-Soo. *pd* Choi Jung-Wa. *m* Kang Kee-Yung.

● This dizzying collage of scenes from the lives of street kids and elderly winos in Seoul is in many ways the movie Larry Clark tried to make in *Kids*: a kaleidoscope of broken hopes, blow jobs, dope, petty crime, video games, liquor and rapes. Jang does everything possible to abdicate from the director's conventional role and responsibilities, using *ciné-vérité* to shoot the winos and turning over the scripting of the rest to the street kids themselves. He also shot everything with three cameras simultaneously (one 35mm, one 16mm, one digital 8) and cuts freely between the resulting rushes to minimise any sense of an orderly *mise en scène*. His own moral perspective on the characters is never stated but continuously implied by the juxtaposition of the two generations. Many of the episodes are shocking or disturbing; the film was released in Korea minus 30 minutes of sex and anti-social behaviour, but it can be seen uncut abroad. TR

Timeless Melody

(1999, Jap, 95 min)
d Hiroshi Okuhara. *p* Hiroshi Yanai, Maki Kai, Masaki Hayashi, Mayumi Amano. *sc* Hiroshi Okuhara. *ph* Jun Fukumoto. *ed* Hiroshi Okuhara, Takenori Sento. *ad* China Hayashi. *m* Takuji Aoyagi. *cast* Takuji Aoyagi, Mikao Ichikawa, Taro Kondo, Yo Kimiko, Takeshi Wakamatsu.

● Looking almost like a parody of a film by Koreeda or Hou Hsiao-Hsien, this slow, static study of a number of directionless individuals hanging out at a pool hall, sleeping a great deal and occasionally playing some none too inspiring music is beautifully shot and, for a while at least, fairly intriguing as to the precise nature of the relationships on view. However, the lack of information and narrative drive eventually becomes frustrating, and the terminally disaffected youth who are the film's main 'characters' risk losing the viewer's patience. GA

Time Machine, The

(1960, US, 103 min)
d/p George Pal. *sc* David Duncan. *ph* Paul C Vogel. *ed* George Tomasini. *ad* George W Davis, William Ferrari. *m* Russell Garcia. *cast* Rod Taylor, Alan Young, Yvette Mimieux, Sebastian Cabot, Tom Helmore, Whit Bissell, Doris Lloyd.

● Retaining the period setting but stripping away the attack on the British class system, George Pal (who made a much better job of *War of the Worlds*) reduces HG Wells' sci-fi novel to its bare bones. Taylor is the scientist flung forward in time to the year 802,701, where he encourages the peace-loving Elois to rise up against their subterranean enemies, the Morlocks. The quaint time machine and Oscar-winning special effects hold one's interest initially, but the overall effect is one of glossy emptiness. NF

Time of Destiny, A

(1988, US, 118 min)
d Gregory Nava. *p* Anna Thomas. *sc* Gregory Nava, Anna Thomas. *ph* James Glennon. *ed* Betsy Blankett. *pd* Henry Bumstead. *m* Ennio Morricone. *cast* William Hurt, Timothy Hutton, Melissa Leo, Francisco Rabal, Concha Hidalgo, Stockard Channing, Megan Follows.

● Sadly, though this sweeping World War II melodrama reunites Gregory Nava and producer/co-writer Anna Thomas from *El Norte*, the emotions here are not so much exquisitely overwrought as wildly over-pitched. Prevented from marrying her soldier lover (Hutton) by her domineering father (Rabal), Melissa Leo elopes on the eve of his departure. Her father pursues her, the car runs off the road into a river, and he drowns. Enter Hurt, black sheep of the Californian immigrant Basque family, who swears revenge for his father's death. Since Hutton has never met him, he transfers to Hutton's frontline regiment in Italy, scheming to kill him under cover of battle. From this point on, implausibility begins to stretch suspension of disbelief to breaking point. After each in turn saves the other's life, they become best pals, and the scene is set for confrontation when the war ends. The showdown turns out to be a reworking of the climax of Hitchcock's *Vertigo*. NF

Time of the Gypsies (Dom za Vesanje)

(1989, Yugo, 142 min)
d Emir Kusturica. *p* Mirza Pasic. *sc* Emir Kusturica, Gordan Mihac. *ph* Vilko Filac. *ed* Andrija Zafranovic. *pd* Miljen Kljakovic. *m* Goran Bregovic. *cast* Davor Dujmovic, Bora Todorovic, Ljubica Adzovic, Husnija Hasmovic.

● This remarkable tragic-comic drama, set in a Yugoslavian gypsy community, is hard to take seriously at first. Perhan, the bastard boy hero, seems a clichéd victim figure – patched spectacles, gormless face – wandering the noisy shantytown like a holy fool. His grandmother has healing powers; Perhan is telekinetic, and spends his time moving spoons up walls. Too poor to marry his beloved Azra, Perhan is taken to Italy by the 'Sheik', ostensibly to obtain a leg operation for his crippled sister, but in fact as part of the child-selling Sheik's business, to learn 'traditional' skills – pimping, begging, stealing – on the streets of Milan. His sad getting-of-wisdom is a long haul, but executed at breakneck pace, trilling with music, drama, tears and wry humour. The film has an eclectic look: an off-the-hip semi-documentary style, punctuated with Paradjanov-style miraculous imagery. Anchoring it to reality are the stunning performances by a cast of mostly illiterate Romany non-professionals, its precise observation of gypsy life, and its immense humanity. Astonishing and deeply moving. WH

Time Out (L'Emploi du temps)

(2001, Fr, 134 min)
d Laurent Cantet. *p* Caroline Benjo. *sc* Robin Campillo, Laurent Cantet. *ph* Pierre Milon. *ed* Robin Campillo, Stéphanie Léger. *pd* Romain Denis. *m* Jocelyn Pook. *cast* Aurélien Recoing, Karin Viard, Serge Livrozet, Jean-Pierre Mangeot, Monique Mangeot, Nicolas Kalsch, Marie Cantet, Félix Cantet, Olivier Le Joubioux.

● Like Cantet's first film, *Human Resources*, this sober, measured and terribly sad movie explores that most subtle of distinctions: what it is that separates who we are from what we do. Middle-aged executive Vincent (Recoing) has been 'let go', although his redundancy seems self-inflicted, an existential torpor he does everything to conceal from his family. He's transferred his expertise to the UN, he claims, working as a business consultant and persuading old friends to invest in a hush-hush get rich quick scheme. It's insane, yet Vincent's pretence is virtually sufficient to his needs, his assumption of propriety and well-being as good as the real thing. Or put another way, a proper job is scarcely more meaningful than this hollow charade. In Cantet's own words, 'Vincent is the sincerest of liars, an actor of his own life.' It's a profound, measured portrait of a man driven – and driving – with no end in sight. TCh

Time Regained (Le Temps retrouvé)

(1999, Fr/It/Port, 162 min)
d Raoul Ruiz. *p* Paulo Branco. *sc* Gilles Taurand, Raoul Ruiz. *ph* Ricardo Aronovich. *ed* Denise de Casabianca. *ad* Bruno Beaugé. *m* Jorge Arriagada. *cast* Catherine Deneuve, Emmanuelle Béart, Vincent Perez, Pascal Greggory, Marie-France Pisier, Chiara Mastroianni, Arielle Dombasle, Edith Scob, Elsa Zylberstein, John Malkovich, Marcello Mazzarella, Alain Robbe-Grillet, Ingrid Caven.
●An extraordinary conflation of avant garde art film and deluxe literary period drama, this ambitious assault on Proust's 15th volume in *Remembrance of Things Past* constitutes a peculiar triumph. Numerous film-makers have been defeated in the attempt, but exiled Chilean Ruiz never hesitates. His version is a bold, dazzling time trip which nevertheless honours the complexity of the original, and indeed will likely play best to those already familiar with it. The first scene serves notice that this is no ordinary adaptation: as Marcel (Mazzarella) dictates from his deathbed, and the camera pans across mementoes from a life among the French aristocracy at the turn of the last century, the furnishings loom ever larger, as if mocking the author with his own mortality. Ruiz goes on to use the full panoply of surrealist camera tricks. We're plunged into the very thick of French high society, as Marcel remembers his love for Gilberte (Béart), her equally ravishing mother Odette (Deneuve), the controversial Baron de Charlus (Malkovich), and his affair with the composer Morel (Perez). Now, it must be said, it's a toss-up which is more bewildering: the extremely entangled social relations which form the chief topic of everyone's conversation, or Ruiz's elegant, avant garde party tricks. Yet the starry cast helps us keep track (Malkovich is outstanding, even in French), and sustained over a mighty 155 minutes, the film casts quite a spell. Proust watches on, a smile on his face and a tear in his eye; the director's 'happy confusion' sums it up very well. TCh

Timescape (aka Grand Tour: Disaster in Time)

(1991, US, 90 min)
d David N Twohy. *p* John O'Connor. *sc* David N Twohy. *ph* Harry Mathias. *ed* Glenn Morgan. *ad* Michael Novotny. *m* Gerald Gouriet. *cast* Jeff Daniels, Adriana Richards, Emilia Crow, George Murdock.
●Small-town widower Ben Wilson (Daniels) is trying to function after the death of his wife and his ostracism by her socially powerful family. His life, shared with a small daughter in a large, rundown house, is suddenly overturned by the arrival of visitors who are suspiciously keen to rent his spare rooms. At first he thinks they're just eccentric out-of-towners, but when he sees one having difficulty tying his shoelaces – indeed, acting as if he's never worn shoes before – it becomes clear that the truth is stranger than that. They don't seem to belong to this century, shun overtures of friendship, are eagerly waiting for something to happen… To avert the doom facing the town, Ben, with the help of a lovely alien, has to tamper with the fabric of time itself. It's an intriguing premise, well teased out, and with enough mind-boggling twists to keep going. A telefeature, adapted from the story *Vintage Season* by Henry Kuttner and CL Moore. SFe

Timeslip (aka The Atomic Man)

(1955, GB, 93 min, b/w)
d Ken Hughes. *p* Alec C Snowden. *sc* Charles Eric Maine. *ph* AT Dinsdale. *ed* Geoffrey Muller. *ad* George Haslam. *cast* Gene Nelson, Faith Domergue, Peter Arne, Joseph Tomelty, Donald Gray.
●A typically tacky thriller from Merton Park Studios, latter-day home of the British B movie. But the script by sci-fi novelist Charles Eric Maine (later published as *The Isotope Man)* is quite ingenious, hingeing on a nuclear physicist (Arne) working on a secret project who suffers seven seconds of clinical death when attacked by saboteurs, and thereafter lives seven vital seconds ahead of the plot. Briskly competent direction helps it along nicely, even though the time-slip notion gets rather muffled by routine spy larks involving the inevitable impersonation by a double. TM

Times of Harvey Milk, The

(1984, US, 86 min)
d Robert Epstein. *p* Richard Schmiechen. *sc* Judith Coburn, Carter Wilson. *ph* Frances Reid. *ed* Deborah Hoffman, Robert Epstein. *m* Mark Isham. *cast* narrator: Harvey Fierstein.
●Harvey Milk, a gay activist elected to San Francisco's Board of Supervisors (or city council) in 1977, was assassinated in 1978 alongside mayor George Moscone by fellow-supervisor Dan White, who had recently lost his appointment and had targeted on the pinko left for his revenge. The murders inspired a 45,000-strong candlelit vigil, and the scandalously lenient sentence given White caused riots the like of which the city had never seen. Epstein and producer Richard Schmiechen expanded a projected film on anti-gay legislation into a feature-length documentary about America's first 'out' gay politician. Charismatic and outspoken, Milk was headed for the job of mayor, and deserves a place in the pantheon of specifically American radicalism. This documentary about his career and the repercussions of his assassination deservedly won an Oscar. JG

Times Square

(1980, US, 113 min)
d Allan Moyle. *p* Robert Stigwood, Jacob Brackman. *sc* Jacob Brackman. *ph* James A Contner. *ed* Tom Priestley. *pd* Stuart Wurtzel. *m* Blue Weaver. *cast* Tim Curry, Trini Alvarado, Robin Johnson, Peter Coffield, Herbert Berghof, David Margulies.
●Nail your TV to the floor and lock up your daughters: the message here – run away from home, live in a derelict warehouse, and you too can become a cult heroine – is an appealingly romantic one, and there's a fair sprinkling of magic dust to help the fairytale along. Streetwise Nicky (Johnson), elder of two runaways, metamorphoses from scruffy, disturbed urchin to punk-chic Jagger clone, venting her anger as lead singer of the Blondells. Sheltered Pamela (Alvarado), rich and introverted, breaks out and forces an overbearing parent to see her as she is, not as he wants her to be. It's a world where a black plastic bag is a fashion garment, where a TV-smashing campaign is a serious social statement, where teenage runaways in New York do not fall prey to pushers and pimps, where a jaded disc jockey (Curry) promotes their cause. Socially irresponsible and refreshingly optimistic: a *Wizard of Oz* for the '80s. FF

Time Stands Still (Megáll az Idó)

(1981, Hun, 99 min)
d Péter Gothár. *sc* Géza Bereményi, Péter Gothar. *ph* Lajos Koltai. *ed* Maria Nagy. *m* György Selmeczi. *cast* Istvàn Znamenàk, Henrik Pauer, Sàndor Söth, Péter Gálfy, Anikó Iván.
●An impressive period film which portrays the life of college kids in late '50s Hungary. Dubbed by some *Hungarian Graffiti,* this is always much more than a movie about students getting high on Coke (the capitalist drink) and screwing around. Gothár uses historical footage, even patches of pathos and bathos and snatches of rock'n'roll, to probe the painful memories of a generation (his own) that grew up under the shadow of the 1956 'National Tragedy'. Awkward and elusive in parts, it's still a rewarding experience from a director to watch out for. MA

Time to Die (Tiempo de Morir)

(1985, Col/Cuba, 98 min)
d Jorge Alí Triana. *p/sc* Gabriel García Márquez. *ph* Mario Garcia Joya. *ed* Nelson Rodriguez. *pd* Patricia Bonilla. *m* Leo Brower, Nafer Duran. *cast* Gustavo Angarita, Sebastiàn Ospina, Jorge Emilio Salazar, Maria Eugenia Davila, Lina Botero.
●After 18 years in jail, Juan Sáyago returns to his small Colombian home town. The proud sons of the man he had killed thirst for his blood, but Juan won't run, nor will he take up the gun again. Gabriel Garcia Márquez's first original screenplay, though set in contemporary Colombia, is first and foremost a Western. Besides the many pleasures to be had from the reworking of the genre's classical conventions, Márquez and Triana also construct a bleak, caustic critique of machismo and its absurd codes of honour. Vengeance is vain, bloodlust psychosis; amid superstition and self-sacrificing ritual, every man of violence is a loser. While occasionally brutal and prone to overstatement, the film retains a raw, unsentimental power, at once formally elegant and intelligent, thanks partly to Angarita's Juan, a morose Donald Sutherland lookalike exuding taciturn dignity. Simple, but oddly effective and very watchable. GA

Time to Kill

(1942, US, 61 min, b/w)
d Herbert I Leeds. *p* Sol M Wurtzel. *sc* Clarence Upson Young. *ph* Charles G Clarke. *ed* Alfred Day. *ad* Richard Day, Chester Gore. *m* Emil Newman. *cast* Lloyd Nolan, Heather Angel, Doris Merrick, Ralph Byrd, Richard Lane, Sheila Bromley, Morris Ankrum, Ethel Griffies.
●The seventh in Fox's B series starring Lloyd Nolan as Brett Halliday's private eye Mike Shayne. Tough, wisecracking and down-at-heel (the opening shot displays large holes in his shoes as he answers the phone with his feet on the desk), Shayne is hired by a venomous old battleaxe (Griffies) to retrieve a stolen doubloon (and a matching shot shows he's collected his advance: the shoes have been soled). Three murders later, the plot has become distinctly *déjà vu;* that's because it's borrowed intact from Chandler's *The Brasher Doubloon.* Cheap and cheerful, this lacks the fine Gothic atmospherics John Brahm brought to his version four years later, but it does have pace, wit, and an excellent performance from Nolan (he'd have made a fine Philip Marlowe). TM

Time to Kill, A

(1996, US, 149 min)
d Joel Schumacher. *p* Arnon Milchan, Michael Nathanson, Hunt Lowry, John Grisham. *sc* Akiva Goldsman. *ph* Peter Menzies Jr. *ed* William Steinkamp. *pd* Larry Fulton. *m* Elliot Goldenthal. *cast* Matthew McConaughey, Samuel L Jackson, Sandra Bullock, Donald Sutherland, Oliver Platt, Kevin Spacey, Brenda Fricker, Charles Dutton, Kiefer Sutherland, Patrick McGoohan.
●Justice may be blind, but rarely have courtroom dramas presumed quite so heavily on cultural myopia as this heinous version of John Grisham's first novel. An apologia for vigilantism masquerading as a liberal race-movie, it has McConaughey as small town Southern lawyer Jake Brigance, defending Jackson's Carl Lee after he shoots down the white trash who raped his daughter. The defendant's black, the crime was committed on the courthouse steps, and the judge is called Noose. No wonder Jake's reduced to tears – an unusual legal manoeuvre, but on this evidence, effective. An insulting travesty of Faulkner and Harper Lee, riven with such politically correct confusion that it implicitly equates the KKK with the NAACP, this would be more insidious if it weren't altogether botched. Jake's allies are idealistic student Bullock, boozy old mentor Donald Sutherland and sleazy divorce specialist Platt; that they have nothing to contribute to the plot but phoney histrionics is indicative of the fact that they don't have a case, legally speaking – everything is designed to disguise that void. TCh

Time to Love and a Time to Die, A

(1957, US, 133 min)
d Douglas Sirk. *p* Robert Arthur. *sc* Orin Jannings. *ph* Russell Metty. *ed* Ted J Kent. *ad* Alexander Golitzen, Alfred Sweeney. *m* Miklós Rozsa. *cast* John Gavin, Lilo Pulver, Jock Mahoney, Don DeFore, Keenan Wynn, Erich Maria Remarque, Dieter Borsche, Barbara Rutting, Thayer David, Dorothea Wieck, Klaus Kinski.
●Under the opening credits of Sirk's penultimate masterpiece, set during World War II and filmed on location in Germany, the camera rests on the branches of a tree, its blossom forced early by the heat of a nearby bomb blast. It is the perfect symbol for the love between John Gavin's German soldier on leave and a barely remembered childhood friend, Lilo Pulver: a love forced by the everyday facts of war. This superb adaptation of Erich Maria Remarque's novel rests on a painful symmetry between the scenes at the Russian front and the central section in the

half-ruined home town, and on a typically tough-minded acknowledgment of the irony that the doomed romance exists not in spite of the war, but because of it. PT

Time to Live and a Time to Die, A

see Feu Follet, Le

Time to Live and the Time to Die, The (Tongnian Wangshi)

(1985, Tai, 137 min)
d Hou Hsiao-hsien [Hou Xiaoxian]. *p* Zhang Huakun, Yue Wanli. *sc* Zhu Tianwen, Hou Hsiao-Hsien. *ph* Li Ping-Bin. *ed* Wang Qiyang. *ad* Lin Chongwen. *m* Wu Chuchu. *cast* You Anshun, Tian Feng, Mei Fang, Tang Ruyun, Xiao Ai.

● A subtle, deeply moving picture of Taiwanese history seen through the eyes of a boy whose family has recently emigrated from the Mainland. As a child in the '50s, Ah Xiao's life seems one long summer of playing marbles, chasing friends, and listening to grandma's plans to return home. But family illness provides his first taste of death, and years later he has grown into a loutish teenager, torn between filial duty and the need to prove himself on the streets. Hou's autobiographically-based film is as beautifully performed, shot and scored as his earlier *Summer at Grandpa's*, but there is a distinct progress in the depiction of the wider dynamics of society. It is the unflinching, unsentimental honesty that supplies the elegiac intelligence: Hou's quiet style bursts forth, here and there, into sudden, superlative scenes of untrammelled emotional power. It's a brilliantly simple but multi-faceted portrait of loss and the complacency of childhood: quite literally, we can't go home again. GA

Time Travellers, The

(1964, US, 84 min)
d Ib Melchior. *p* William Redlin. *sc* Ib Melchior. *ph* Vilmos Zsigmond. *ed* Hal Dennis. *ad* Ray Storey. *m* Richard La Salle. *cast* Preston Foster, Philip Carey, Merry Anders, John Hoyt, Steve Franken.

● In spite of some feeble romantic comedy (notably in the android factory sequence) and an occasionally trite musical score, this is an accomplished and enjoyable sci-fi film which contains more ideas than many movies made on far higher budgets. It's about a team of scientists who construct a mirror to the future. The mirror becomes a door, and they get stranded on the wrong side. The middle part has some relatively standard sub-Wellsian plot material involving two future civilisations; but the ending, in which they get caught in a time-trap, is utterly amazing and completely original; it even compares favourably to the trip sequence in *2001: A Space Odyssey*. The cameraman, incidentally, was Vilmos Zsigmond. DP

Time Will Tell

(1991, GB, 89 min, b/w & col)
d Declan Lowney.

● 'We don't have education, we have inspiration. If I was educated, I'd be a damn fool.' Just one thought-provoking statement from reggae superstar Bob Marley, and this documentary offers many more. It's a cut-and-paste montage of interviews, live and in-rehearsal footage, which follows Marley's life from the Trenchtown ghetto to superstardom, capturing simply and succinctly his spiritual and political beliefs, and the brilliance of his music. On-stage footage of the earnest, dreadlocked singer predominates, and there's many a passionate rendering of hits, as well as acoustic versions of less well-known numbers. Marley is the film's only narrator, and in heavy *patois* he expounds on Rastafarianism, human rights and the Herb, with forthright candour. It's a moving portrait, and the coverage of Marley's death is especially poignant. This will certainly make those who never saw him live wish they had. LC

Time Without Pity

(1957, GB, 88 min, b/w)
d Joseph Losey. *p* John Arnold, Anthony Simmons, Leon Clore. *sc* Ben Barzman. *ph* Freddie Francis. *ed* Alan Osbiston. *ad* Bernard Sarron. *m* Tristram Cary. *cast* Michael Redgrave, Ann Todd, Leo McKern, Peter Cushing, Alec McCowen, Renee Houston, Paul Daneman, Lois Maxwell, Richard Wordsworth, George Devine, Joan Plowright.

● An adaptation of Emlyn Williams' potboiling play *Someone Waiting*, about a young man wrongly convicted of murder (McCowen), and the last-minute hunt for the real killer by his dipsomaniac father (Redgrave). This was the first time Losey had filmed under his own name since the trauma of the blacklist, and it shows in the overstatement: the persistent play with clocks, for instance, indicating not just that Redgrave is racing against a 24-hour deadline to uncover the truth, but that his alcoholism was a way of making time stand still by shutting out his responsibilities (to his son, to society). By shifting the emphasis from thriller to anti-capital punishment pleading, Losey also strains the structure almost to breaking point. An undeniably powerful film, all the same, superbly shot by Freddie Francis and conceived with a raw-edged brilliance, right from the brutal opening murder, that accommodates even the symbolism of a Goya bull, with the real killer (McKern) finally cornered and goaded into a murderous/suicidal charge. TM

Tina: What's Love Got to Do With It (aka What's Love Got to Do With It)

(1993, US, 118 min)
d Brian Gibson. *p* Doug Chapin, Barry Krost. *sc* Kate Lanier. *ph* Jamie Anderson. *ed* Stuart H Pappé. *m* Stanley Clarke. *cast* Angela Bassett, Laurence Fishburne, Vanessa Bell Calloway, Phyllis Yvonne Stickney, Khandi Alexander.

● Tina Turner's story is like the song: river deep, mountain high – a tale of ambition, talent, desire; drugs, violence and despair. In other words, it's the usual showbiz tattle. This is very much the authorised biopic. It's based on the autobiography, *I, Tina*, and the singer was on hand throughout the production. Not surprising, then, that along with the usual streamlining of history, we get a good deal of first-hand emotion and little critical perspective. It's hard not to feel a twinge of cynicism, for example, when Tina turns her life round with a spot of Buddhist chanting. On the other hand, the movie is surprisingly hard-edged: it doesn't go easy on husband Ike's brutality, while Tina's resilience, her strutting sex appeal and performing heat all come through loud and clear. Angela Bassett shakes her tail feather with aplomb and pins down the singer's gestures with amazing precision. Top honours, however, belong to Fishburne's swaggering, savage portrayal of Ike. TCh

Tin Cup

(1996, US, 135 min)
d Ron Shelton. *p* Gary Foster, David V Lester. *sc* John Norville, Ron Shelton. *ph* Russell Boyd. *ed* Paul Seydor, Kimberly Ray. *pd* James D Bissell. *m* William Ross. *cast* Kevin Costner, Rene Russo, Cheech Marin, Don Johnson, Linda Hart, Dennis Burkley, Rex Linn.

● Roy 'Tin Cup' McAvoy (Costner) is a natural born swinger. Such a natural, in fact, that his golf sense by-passes his brain altogether. That's why he's marooned in Salome, West Texas, living out of a trailer, picking up chump change teaching follow-through to golf virgins like psychologist Molly Griswold (Russo). Molly makes Roy want to get his act together, especially when he sees she's with PGA star David Simms (Johnson). Thus, Tin Cup embarks on a quixotic tilt at the American Open and a belated date with destiny. After the perceived failure of the ambitious *Cobb*, Ron Shelton has come up with a light, relaxed return to the popular romanticism of his *Bull Durham*. The sexual sparring is a bit lop-sided, Molly is too much of an onlooker, especially during the prolonged final tournament, but Shelton never indulges Roy's own delusions of tragic grandeur: there's a kind of poetry in his bullshit. This is a wish-fulfilment movie about failure, and Roy's triumph is bitter-sweet indeed. Costner hasn't been this charming and spontaneous for years. TCh

Tin Drum, The (Die Blechtrommel)

(1979, WGer/Fr, 142 min)
d Volker Schlöndorff. *p* Franz Seitz. *sc* Jean-Claude Carrière, Franz Seitz, Volker Schlöndorff. *ph* Igor Luther. *ed* Suzanne Baron. *ad* Nicos Perakis. *m* Maurice Jarre. *cast* David Bennent, Mario Adorf, Angela Winkler, Daniel Olbrychski, Charles Aznavour, Heinz Bennent, Andrea Ferréol.

● Sumptuously shot and designed, Schlöndorff's respectful film of Günter Grass's epic novel is nevertheless inevitably inferior to the original. The problem perhaps is that it is all too literal an adaptation of the book, which looked at the realities of German history from the fantastic, subjective viewpoint of a child who, by sheer will-power, refuses ever to grow up; the result is that, as the kid witnesses the rise of the Nazis, what we see is rarely convincing in itself, while the complexities of Grass's book are largely sacrificed for eye-catching scenes of the grotesque and the bizarre. Still, the performances are strong and the film just about works as middlebrow entertainment for those put off by the length of the novel. GA

Tingler, The

(1959, US, 82 min, b/w & col)
d/p William Castle. *sc* Robb White. *ph* Wilfred M Cline. *ed* Chester W Scharffer. *ad* Phil Bennett. *m* Von Dexter. *cast* Vincent Price, Judith Evelyn, Darryl Hickman, Philip Coolidge, Patricia Cutts.

● A cultish chiller that acquired some fame on its original US release when Castle wired up the cinema seats with electrical buzzers to give his audiences a little extra shock value. The plot is ingeniously ludicrous: a doctor (Price) discovers that fear breeds a centipede-like organism in the base of the spine. The organism can kill if its grip is not released, and only a scream can do that. So the good doctor experiments on a deaf-mute, the wife of a cinema-owner who only shows silent movies. Castle was a real Hollywood showman, a downmarket Hitchcock whose work shows considerable flair. The scenes in the movie theatre are very striking, and the way the doctor torments his victim – by providing her with visual shocks (a kind of acid trip) and by causing running water from a tap to turn into blood (black-and-white gave way to colour here) – is clearly the work of a sick mind. Castle recalled, 'I was asked by somebody at Yale whether *The Tingler* was my statement against the establishment and whether it was my plea against war and poverty. I said, Who knows?' ATu

Tin Men

(1987, US, 112 min)
d Barry Levinson. *p* Mark Johnson. *sc* Barry Levinson. *ph* Peter Sova. *ed* Stu Linder. *pd* Peter Jamison. *m* David Steele, Andy Cox, Fine Young Cannibals. *cast* Richard Dreyfuss, Danny DeVito, Barbara Hershey, John Mahoney, Jackie Gayle, Stanley Brock, Seymour Cassel, Bruno Kirby.

● Levinson's Tin Men are aluminium siding salesmen not averse to posing as *Life* magazine photographers to get the foot in the door to offload their wares on the unwary householder. Among themselves, their vision is Jonsonian, and their respect is reserved for the fittest alone. A feud develops between two of them, BB (Dreyfuss) and Tilley (De Vito), over a bumped Cadillac fender, and escalates beyond knock-for-knock reprisals to the cruel seduction of Tilley's wife (Hershey) by BB as revenge. But BB finds himself hoist by his own petard when he falls in love, a depleting experience which has not previously figured in his game plan. Happily, the film does not turn squashy, and allows its salesmen to preserve their duplicity. It's a confident return to form and to Baltimore for the *Diner* man. A terrific cast grabs the naturalistic speech patterns, and Hershey manages movingly to register her reality as the sole bearer of human values. BC

Tin Star, The

(1957, US, 93 min, b/w)
d Anthony Mann. *p* William Perlberg, George Seaton. *sc* Dudley Nichols. *ph* Loyal Griggs. *ed* Alma Macrorie. *ad* Hal Pereira, Joseph McMillan Johnson. *m* Elmer Bernstein. *cast* Henry Fonda, Anthony Perkins, Betsy Palmer, Neville Brand, John McIntire, Lee Van Cleef, Michel Ray.

● Scripted by Dudley Nichols, a Western in the traditional mould, much more predictable than Mann's marvellous series with James Stewart, and a little too overtly didactic in detailing the relationship between a disillusioned sheriff turned bounty-hunter (Fonda) and the young greenhorn (Perkins) to whom he becomes a father-figure, teaching him the hard facts of a lawman's life and regaining his self-respect in the process. But Mann directs with an impressive classical elegance, and the performances are fine, even if (as David Thomson remarked) 'Fonda and Perkins look like business executives dressed up in cowboy togs'. TM

Tintorera

(1977, GB/Mex, 91 min)
d René Cardona Jr. *p* Gerald Green. *sc* Ramon Bravo, René Cardona Jr. *ph* Leon Sanchez. *ed* Peter Zinner, Earle Herdan. *m* Basil Poledouris. *cast* Susan George, Hugo Stiglitz, Andres Garciá, Fiona Lewis, Jennifer Ashley, Robert Guzman.

● *La Dolce Vita* on an exclusive island resort off Mexico is disrupted by a heavy-breathing shark. The standard of this *Jaws* rip-off is lamentable, as the press handout lets slip: 'The crazed shark attacks the hunter furiously – in a scene that is among the most appalling ever filmed'. Everyone and everything competes for last prize in this no-no: Susan George beds down with two shark-hunting dilettantes for one of the most listless three-way relationships ever; the script flounders even more than the shark. 'I am worried about how this is going to end' confides one character in a moment of rare candour. 'But I know it must end one of these days' he concludes hopefully – an act of faith beyond the grasp of the languishing audience. CPe

Tiré à Part

(1997, Fr, 90 min)
d Bernard Rapp. *p* Joël Foulon. *sc* Richard Morgieve, Bernard Rapp. *ph* Romain Winding. *ed* Anna Basurco. *pd* François Comtet. *m* Jean-Philippe Goude. *cast* Terence Stamp, Daniel Mesguich, Maria de Medeiros, Jean-Claude Dreyfuss, Hannah Gordon, Amira Casar, Frank Finlay.

● When Edward (Stamp), an established London publisher, receives a manuscript from Nicholas (Mesguich), a French friend and trashy novelist, he's shocked to discover that inspiration for this Tunisian romance came from events surrounding the suicide of his past beloved – in which, he believes, Nicholas was inextricably involved. Once the book is published to acclaim, and Nicholas is enjoying the trimmings of success, Edward seeks revenge by orchestrating a scam to accuse his friend of plagiarism. Despite Mesguich's convincing performance and stunning photography (London has rarely looked so stylish), Rapp's theatrical directing and limp script turns this into an insipid exercise, devoid of suspense and emotional tension. Most torturous is Stamp's rendition of the repressed English 'gentleman'. Stilted and corpse-stiff, you get a niggling suspicion he may just be playing it for laughs. HK

Tirez sur le Pianiste (Shoot the Pianist/ Shoot the Piano Player)

(1960, Fr, 80 min, b/w)
d François Truffaut. *p* Pierre Braunberger. *sc* Marcel Moussy, François Truffaut. *ph* Raoul Coutard. *ed* Cécile Decugis. *m* Georges Delerue. *cast* Charles Aznavour, Marie Dubois, Nicole Berger, Albert Rémy, Claude Mansard, Daniel Boulanger, Michèle Mercier, Richard Kanayan.

● Truffaut's second feature is now recognised as one of the key films of the French *nouvelle vague*. Based (not too loosely, except in mood) on David Goodis' novel *Down There*, it's a strange pastiche of gangster movie, love story, and cabaret film, with a totally and calculatedly unpredictable plot about a lonely pianist with a past. The story is by turns comic and pathetic, often flashing midstream from one mood to the other, and Aznavour's performance as the wounded hero is a masterstroke of casting. In many ways fantastic, the film is paradoxically much more realistic than most in the way it uses both character and environment. Which is, after all, what the New Wave was about. RM

'Tis Pity She's a Whore (Addio, Fratello Crudele)

(1971, It, 109 min)
d Giuseppe Patroni Griffi. *p* Silvio Clementelli. *sc* Giuseppe Patroni Griffi, Alfio Valdarnini, Carlo Carunchio. *ph* Vittorio Storaro. *ed* Franco Arcalli. *ad* Mario Ceroli. *m* Ennio Morricone. *cast* Charlotte Rampling, Oliver Tobias, Fabio Testi, Antonio Falsi, Rik Battaglia.

● What Patroni Griffi has done here is simply to lift the doom-laden incest theme out of the centre of Ford's Jacobean tragedy, carefully re-tailoring it into a loweringly measured mood piece exactly matching his own extraordinary first film *Il Mare*. A setting of brooding, obsessive melancholy; three characters locked in a personal hell of no exit (brother, sister, the importunate husband to whom she is hurriedly married when incest bears fruit); and a carnivorous battle escalating, not as in *Il Mare* into the despair of solitude, but into a fine bout of Jacobean blood-letting. Directing with breathtaking control over his images (the camerawork is by the remarkable Vittorio Storaro), Patroni Griffi has in effect turned the play into sonorous opera. The voices, given that this is an Italian film 'shot in English', admittedly leave something to be desired, but it hardly matters. TM

Tit and the Moon, The (La teta y la luna/La teta i la lluna/La Lune et le téton)

(1994, Sp/Fr, 91 min)
d Bigas Luna. *p* Andrés Vicente Gomez. *sc* Cuca Canals, Bigas Luna. *ph* José Luis Alcaine. *ed* Carmen Frias, Maria Luisa Hernandez. *ad* Aimé Deudé. *m* Nicola Piovani. *cast* Mathilda May, Gérard Darmon, Miguel Poveda, Biel Duran, Abel Folk, Genis Sanchez.

● After the satiric machismo of *Jamón, Jamón* and *Golden Balls*, Bigas Luna here adopts a more reflective approach. Nine-year-old Tete (Duran) has a problem any older brother can relate to, for the family's new arrival has replaced him at his mother's breast. He must invoke the moon for a new tit to call his own – which is where the imposing May comes in as Gallic cabaret performer Estrellita. However, adolescent Miquel (Poveda) already has his eyes on Estrellita, while the lady herself seems sweet on her *pétomane* stage partner, Maurice (Darmon), never mind his impotence. The director sets up symbolic oppositions between the relative youth and sexual experience of the various males, and even the French, Spanish and Catalan speaking participants in the drama – the whole affair being unified by the image of the breast suckling one and all. A paean to a Mediterranean culture, perhaps? That's as may be, but the movie's fundamental problem is its failure to generate the sort of narrative drive that would forge its metaphorical patterns into compelling drama. It's a gentler, more likeable piece than its immediate predecessors, however, and Darmon's anguished romantic is genuinely touching, but somehow it's the shock value of dream-sequence lactation that still succours the strongest impression. TJ

Titan A.E.

(2000, US, 95 min)
d Don Bluth, Gary Goldman. *p* David Kirschner, Gary Goldman, Don Bluth. *sc* Ben Edlund, John August, Joss Whedon. *ed* Fiona Trayler, Bob Bender. *pd* Philip A Cruden. *m* Graeme Revell. *cast* voices: Matt Damon, Bill Pullman, John Leguizamo, Nathan Lane, Janeane Garofalo, Drew Barrymore, Ron Perlman.

● An animated space adventure set in 3028 with lantern-jawed antagonists and a far from novel plot. Mankind's foe is a spindly alien breed, the Drej, which has devastated Earth. Humans are intergalactic outcasts, whose salvation lies with petulant Cale. He holds the key to the Titan, a ship constructed by his father, which could restore civilisation; he teams with strappingly cynical Han Solo-type Captain Korso, enigmatic beauty Akima and an alien crew. Blending blood and romance, the film has a bouncy soundtrack and impressive FX. Visually, it's engrossing, but it'll have cross-generational sci-fi fans hankering for *Star Wars* rather than hailing an animated revolution. AHa

Titan Find, The (aka Creature)

(1984, US, 97 min)
d William Malone. *p* William G Dunn Jr, William Malone. *sc* William Malone, Alan Reed. *ph* Harry Mathias. *ed* Bette Cohen. *ad* Michael Novotny. *m* Thomas Chase, Steve Rucker. *cast* Stan Ivar, Wendy Schaal, Lyman Ward, Robert Jaffe, Diane Salinger, Annette McCarthy, Klaus Kinski.

● On Saturn's moon Titan a long-dormant creature is hatched and proceeds to mistake US mineral prospectors for breakfast. Unlike the scriptwriters, the miners haven't seen *Alien* and therefore make themselves available for squishing and scrunching in the traditional one-at-a-time manner. The sole survivor of a rival German crew is none other than Klaus Kinski who, though, confers his presence only briefly. But it would be unfair to dismiss this as an *Alien* rip-off because after an hour of being just that, one of the remaining uneaten dinners remembers seeing *The Thing from Another World* so they recycle that plot instead. Much of the picture is played in close-up and dimly lit, to distract us from the cheap sets and electronic hardware scavanged, by the look of it, from an industrial dumpster. DO

Titanic

(1943, Ger, 85 min, b/w)
d Herbert Selpin, Werner Klingler. *sc* Walter Zerlett-Olfenius. *ph* Friedl Behn-Grund. *ed* Friedel Buckow. *ad* Fritz Maurischat, RA Dietrich, Fritz Lück, August Hermann. *m* Werner Eisbrenner, Hubert Patacky. *cast* Hans Nielsen, Sybille Schmitz, EF Fürbringer, Kirsten Heiberg, Otto Wernicke, Karl Schönbock.

● This Nazi account of the disaster looks like it filmed the collision in Hermann Goering's bathtub. It's also notable for acquainting us with a character previously unknown to history, a German first officer, a paragon of seamanship, who's forever issuing unheeded warnings to Lord Archibald of Canterbury and similarly named irresponsible Brits. As a tirade against capitalism, the National Socialist line proves indistinguishable from the Soviet one, being a matter of champagne-swilling profiteers who all turn into panic-stricken snivellers when the chips are down. A real curiosity, by now richly comic in a gruesome sort of way. BBa

Titanic

(1953, US, 98 min, b/w)
d Jean Negulesco. *p* Charles Brackett. *sc* Charles Brackett, Walter Reisch, Richard L Breen. *ph* Joseph MacDonald. *ed* Louis Loeffler. *ad* Lyle Wheeler, Maurice Ransford. *m* Sol Kaplan. *cast* Clifton Webb, Barbara Stanwyck, Robert Wagner, Thelma Ritter, Richard Basehart, Brian Aherne.

● An Oscar-winning screenplay by Charles Brackett and Walter Reisch foregrounds domestic drama for most of the ill-fated Atlantic crossing, yet proves that there's nothing like a major disaster to bring the most fractious family back together again. Webb and Stanwyck are the husband and wife not getting on, but both are outflanked by the model work in the final reel. Overall, not quite as sobering as the British take on the same events, 1958's *A Night to Remember*. TJ

Titanic (100)

(1997, US, 195 min)
d James Cameron. *p* James Cameron, Jon Landau. *sc* James Cameron. *ph* Russell Carpenter. *ed* Conrad Buff, James Cameron, Richard A Harris. *pd* Peter Lamont. *m* James Horner. *cast* Leonardo DiCaprio, Kate Winslet, Billy Zane, Kathy Bates, Frances Fisher, Jonathan Hyde, Danny Nucci, David Warner, Bill Paxton.

● Cost: well over $200m. Disregarding the ethics of such expenditure on a film, this unprecedented extravagance has not resulted in sophisticated or even very satisfying storytelling (11 Oscars notwithstanding). The main problem concerns characterisation and structure. A framing device in which contemporary fortune hunters question a now ancient survivor, followed by a romance between upper-crust but frustrated Rose (Winslet) and a poor but plucky artist (DiCaprio), entails not only a needlessly protracted build-up to the collision, but primitive plotting and performances. Moreover, the sudden, skimpy, soggy love story leads to a conclusion that's perversely uplifting: if your love's strong, you never really lose each other. (Piffle!) That said, the effects mostly ensure pretty gripping spectacle once the boat begins breaking up. Even then, however, most of the best scenes – excepting a memorably macabre floating necropolis – are so reminiscent of Rank's superior 1958 movie *A Night to Remember* that Eric Ambler's name would not look amiss on the new film's credits. (Bizarrely, however, Cameron neglects the poignant fact that a nearby ship failed to respond to the *Titanic*'s SOS, thus upping the body count considerably.) Unlike its namesake, this glossy, bombastic juggernaut will not sink. Everyone will see it anyway, and so they should, if only to ponder the future of mainstream cinema. GA

Titanic Town

(1998, GB/Ger/Fr, 101 min)
d Roger Michell. *p* George Faber, Charles Pattinson. *sc* Anne Devlin. *ph* John Daly. *ed* Kate Evans. *pd* Pat Campbell. *m* Trevor Jones. *cast* Julie Walters, Ciaran Hinds, Ciaran McMenamin, Nuala O'Neill, Jaz Pollock, James Loughran, Barry Loughran.

● The Catholic McPhelimy family move into Andersonstown, Belfast, in 1972 just as the estate descends into a battle zone, with the Brits and IRA fighting it out across the front lawns. Stunned into action by the death of an old friend in crossfire, born fighter Bernie (Walters, making a fine fist of her role), the mother of the brood, is emboldened to champion the cause of peace in an attempt to halt the pointless loss of life. This entails not only making demands on the Stormont representatives and challenging the IRA leadership, but overcoming the violent scorn and anger of local Catholic neighbours. Loosely adapted from Mary Costello's semi-autobiographical novel, the story is told from the point of view of the daughter Annie (O'Neill), with the certain partiality that entails. A little dramatically unsophisticated, and heir inevitably to some political simplification, it's none the less an arresting and timely drama. WH

Titfield Thunderbolt, The

(1952, GB, 84 min)
d Charles Crichton. *p* Michael Truman. *sc* TEB Clarke. *ph* Douglas Slocombe. *ed* Seth Holt. *ad* CP Norman. *m* Georges Auric. *cast* Stanley Holloway, John Gregson, George Relph, Naunton Wayne, Godfrey Tearle, Gabrielle Brune, Hugh Griffith, Sidney James.

● The film that marked the beginning of Ealing's decline into whimsy and toothless eccentricity. A confederation of local clergy and gentry band together to save their local branch-line from British Rail cuts by taking it over themselves (with an engine resurrected from the local museum). An unfunny hymn to British parochial values, bathed in a cosy, romantic glow by Douglas Slocombe's photography. TR

Titus

(2000, US/GB, 162 min)
d Julie Taymor. *p* Jody Patton, Conchita Airoldi, Julie Taymor. *sc* Julie Taymor. *ph* Luciano Tovoli. *ed* Françoise Bonnot. *pd* Dante Ferretti. *m* Elliot Goldenthal. *cast* Anthony Hopkins, Jessica Lange, Alan Cumming, Colm Feore, James Frain, Laura Fraser, Harry Lennix, Angus Macfadyen, Matthew Rhys, Jonathan Rhys Meyers, Geraldine McEwan.

● Riven with strife – war and political intrigue, lust, revenge, cannibalism, you name it – *Titus Andronicus* has always scared off film-makers. You suspect the play's twisted illogic and ignominious reputation have been a more significant disincentive than the violence. Best known for her fantastic staging of Disney's *The Lion King*, Taymor has bitten the bullet. Her *Titus* shirks nothing, rather it bombards us with great gobs of conceit – like the time travelling child who witnesses the infamy unfold. Then there's the production design which places pinball games and classic convertibles in Ancient Rome; and when Lavinia is raped and dismembered, Taymor gives her twigs for hands like a refugee from a nightmare fairytale. It's tasteless, maybe, but very much alive. Even when the film feels silly or embarrassing, sheer creative brio carries it through. Hopkins is a magnificent Titus, his pride humbled more devastatingly than Lear's. He gets gutsy support from Lange's Goth queen Tamora, and Lennix, as her manservant Aaron, a scheming manipulator on a par with Iago and Richard III. Boldly imagined and brimming with passion, this is a striking addition to the Shakespeare filmography. TCh

T-Men

(1947, US, 96 min, b/w)
d Anthony Mann. *p* Aubrey Schenck. *sc* John C Higgins. *ph* John Alton. *ed* Fred Allen. *ad* Edward C Jewell. *m* Paul Sawtell. *cast* Dennis O'Keefe, Alfred Ryder, Mary Meade, Wallace Ford, June Lockhart, Charles McGraw, Jane Randolph, Art Smith.

● The best of early Mann. A cracking little thriller about a pair of Treasury agents (O'Keefe and Ryder) required to infiltrate a Detroit counterfeiting gang, it effortlessly transcends its semi-documentary brief (with blandly 'official' commentary) to land deep in *noir* territory, concerned less with the heroic exploits of its T-Men than with personality perversities involved in undercover work (the wrenching imperative to deny friends, wives, feelings, even to the point of standing by while a partner is cold-bloodedly executed). John Alton's superlative camerawork counterpoints tensions and perspectives with almost geometrical precision. TM

To an Unknown God (A un Dios Desconocido)

(1977, Sp, 100 min)
d Jaime Chavarri. *sc* Elias Querejeta, Jaime Chavarri. *ph* Teo Escamilla. *ed* Pablo G del Amo. *ad* Rafael Palmero. *cast* Héctor Alterio, Angela Molina, Maria Rosa Salgado.

● A loose chain of affectionate encounters between a gay magician and his family, acquaintances, and lover, held together by the magnetic central presence of Alterio. Praised for its 'political' treatment and theme, it's actually less a crusading attack on sexual repression than an oblique meditation, inlaid with Lorca's lyrical if equally enigmatic verse, on (homo)eroticism, growing old, 'trying not to be afraid', relinquishing lost illusions and childhood dreams; and a muted but sympathetic portrait of the ageing prestidigitator, as gently elegiac as his own final words: 'Sleep well, for nothing abides'. SJo

Toast of New Orleans, The

(1950, US, 97 min)
d Norman Taurog. *p* Joe Pasternak. *sc* Sy Gomberg, George Wells. *ph* William Snyder. *ed* Gene Ruggiero. *ad* Cedric Gibbons, Daniel B Cathcart. *songs* Nicholas Brodszky, Sammy Cahn. *cast* Kathryn Grayson, Mario Lanza, David Niven, J Carrol Naish, Rita Moreno.

● Mario Lanza belts out 'Be My Love' and that's almost all you need to know about this rudimentary vehicle, retaining the romantic partnership from the previous year's star-making extravaganza *That Midnight Kiss*. This time Lanza's a humble Louisiana fisherman who becomes the tenor at the turn-of-the-century New Orleans opera house, where he quickly sets his sights on Grayson, the diva in *Madam Butterfly*. Niven, the show's director, looks as though he'd rather be elsewhere. TJ

Tobacco Road

(1941, US, 84, b/w)
d John Ford. *p* Darryl F Zanuck. *sc* Nunnally Johnson. *ph* Arthur Miller. *ed* Barbara McLean. *ad* Richard Day, James Basevi. *m* David Buttolph. *cast* Charley Grapewin, Marjorie Rambeau, Gene Tierney, William Tracy, Elizabeth Patterson, Dana Andrews, Ward Bond, Zeffie Tilbury, Russell Simpson.

● Ford's next film but one after *The Grapes of Wrath*, obviously intended by Fox as a follow-up in the Oscar-winning social conscience stakes, was generally castigated as a crude, stagy mockery, derived at one or two censorship removes from the play based on Erskine Caldwell's bawdily earthy novel. In retrospect, however, it emerges as a fascinatingly subversive piece, undermining the starry-eyed humanism of the earlier film's 'We are the people' view. Instead of Steinbeck's Joads of Oklahoma, stubbornly maintaining their faith in the American Dream even in the depths of misery, we get the Lesters of Georgia, poor white trash perfectly content to wallow fecklessly in their mire of animal sexuality (when young) or tranquil sloth (when old age takes over). Beautifully realised by Ford, not unlike Kazan's *Baby Doll* in its blackly comic blend of dark sexuality and overheated melodrama, *Tobacco Road* is often very funny, sometimes deeply moving, and always provocative in its acknowledgment of an alternative to 'the American way of life'. TM

To Begin Again (Volver a Empezar)

(1981, Sp, 92 min)
d/p José Luis Garci. *sc* José Luis Garci, Angel Llorente. *ph* Manuel Roja. *ed* Miguel Gonzalez Sinde. *ad* Gil Parrondo. *cast* Antonio Ferràndis, Encarna Paso, José Bódalo, Agustin González, Pablo Hoyos.

● A slow miniature about an expatriate author who, after collecting a Nobel Prize, returns to his home town and rekindles an old romance, this is nothing if not international in its theme of 'one only gets old when one doesn't love' (the film won an Oscar for Best Foreign Language film). Some deft performances do not really compensate for a painless academicism in the direction, and a truly numbing over-use of that baroque pop, Pachelbel's 'Canon', on the soundtrack. And the revelation that the author is suffering from a terminal disease only adds to the sentimental obviousness of the message. DT

To Be or Not To Be

(1942, US, 99 min, b/w)
d/p Ernst Lubitsch. *sc* Edwin Justus Mayer. *ph* Rudolph Maté. *ed* Dorothy Spencer. *pd* Vincent Korda. *m* Werner R Heymann. *cast* Jack Benny, Carole Lombard, Robert Stack, Felix Bressart, Lionel Atwill, Stanley Ridges, Sig Ruman, Tom Dugan.

● Like *Ninotchka*, Lubitsch's comedy was developed from an idea by Melchior Lengyel: an anti-Nazi satire set in World War II occupied Warsaw, centering on the resistance of a Polish theatre company and the ham antics of its narcissistic husband-and-wife stars (Benny and Lombard). It was criticised at the time for its alleged bad taste, but Benny, Lombard and script are all hilarious; while Lubitsch gets much mileage from the idea of role-playing, and his particular directorial tic of timing every conceivable gag around entrances and exits through doorways. It's certainly one of the finest comedies ever to come out of Paramount, the allegations of dubious taste missing the point of Lubitsch's satire – not so much the general nastiness of the Nazis as their unforgiveable bad manners. RM

To Be or Not To Be

(1983, US, 107 min)
d Alan Johnson. *p* Mel Brooks. *sc* Thomas Meehan, Ronny Graham. *ph* Gerald Hirschfeld. *ed* Alan Balsam. *pd* Terence Marsh. *m* John Morris. *cast* Mel Brooks, Anne Bancroft, Tim Matheson, Charles Durning, José Ferrer, George Gaynes, Christopher Lloyd, George Wyner.

● From the opening moment when Brooks and Bancroft belt out an impassioned and apparently faultless version of 'Sweet Georgia Brown' in Polish, it's clear that this is going to be nothing if not slick. In the event, Johnson has thankfully refrained from monkeying about with either the plot or the tone of the original, and opted for a reverent but nevertheless sprightly remake. For Lubitsch's film is, after all, one of the most perfectly structured and audacious of screen comedies as a troupe of Polish actors try to outwit the occuping Nazi forces in World War II Warsaw; the wit is constantly underlaced with danger, the absurd expedients prompted by mounting desperation. Johnson may not quite have Lubitsch's lightness of touch, but he puts an excellent cast through their paces with great verve, and the charm is as potent as ever. The only weak link is Durning as the Nazi commander, who hams it up rotten and thus dampens down the essential menace, without which the film is in danger of basking in the glow of its own good nature. JP

To Catch a Spy

see Catch Me a Spy

To Catch a Thief

(1955, US, 107 min)
d/p Alfred Hitchcock. *sc* John Michael Hayes. *ph* Robert Burks. *ed* George Tomasini. *ad* Hal Pereira, Joseph McMillan Johnson. *m* Lyn Murray. *cast* Cary Grant, Grace Kelly, Charles Vanel, Jessie Royce Landis, John Williams, Brigitte Auber.

● One of the most lightweight (and not even particularly deceptively so) of Hitchcock's comedy-thrillers; a retreat from the implications of *Rear Window* into the realm of private jokes and sunny innuendo, with a Côte d'Azur romance that hinges on Kelly's testing of retired high-line thief Grant, to find whether 'The Cat' has indeed been neutered or is still able to prowl the Riviera rooftops. Even determined analysts Rohmer and Chabrol had to take comfort in celebrating Hitch's 'flowers of rhetoric': the famous image of the cigarette stubbed out in an egg, and the cheeky cliché of cross-cutting foreplay and fireworks. PT

Today It's Me...Tomorrow You! (Oggi a me...domani a te!)

(1968, It, 95 min)
d Tonino Cervi. *p* Franco Cuccu. *sc* Dario Argento, Tonino Cervi. *ph* Sergio D'Offizi. *ed* Sergio Montanari. *ad* Carlo Gervasi. *m* Angelo Francesco Lavagnino. *cast* Brett Halsey, Bud Spencer, William Berger, Tatsuya Nakadai, Wayde Preston, Stanley Gordon, Diana Madigan.
●Kurosawa regular Tatsuya Nakadai is the ruthless villain who murders the Indian wife of Bill Kiowa (Halsey) then ensures that the grieving widower is framed for the killing. A five-man revenge posse is soon on the agenda in this worthwhile Italian Western. Some deft touches in a script co-written by horror specialist Dario Argento. The well-sustained climax takes place against a memorable autumnal landscape. TJ

Todd Killings, The

(1970, US, 93 min)
d/p Barry Shear. *sc* Dennis Murphy, Joel Oliansky. *ph* Harold Stine. *ed* Walter Thompson. *ad* Arthur Lonergan. *m* Leonard Rosenman. *cast* Robert F Lyons, Richard Thomas, Belinda Montgomery, Barbara Bel Geddes, Sherry Miles, Joyce Ames, Holly Near, James Broderick, Gloria Grahame, Fay Spain, Edward Asner, Michael Conrad.
● *The Todd Killings* establishes a microcosm of American matriarchal society, and then tosses in a suitably bourgeois Manson figure to stir it up. Good-looking dropout Skipper Todd (Lyons) hates old age (though the pensioners in his mother's hostel indirectly provide his allowance), hates girls (and screws them to prove what trash they are), and hates his father-substitute teacher (whose liberal homilies are very wide of the mark). Bored with dope of all kinds, he starts to live more dangerously: falling in love with a butch lad (Thomas) just out of remand home, and destroying the girls in a series of thrill-killings. Shear's astounding film goes beyond the alienation, bikini beaches, and campus revolt of earlier 'youth pics' to a hard-core nihilism, and it spells out the message underlying the long Hollywood heritage of misogynistic, latent homosexual heroes. Mounted like true tabloid journalism, as sensational as anything of Sam Fuller's, it's a genuinely provocative account of the souring of the American Dream. TR

To Die For

(1994, GB, 101 min)
d Peter Mackenzie Litten. *p* Gary Fitzpatrick. *sc* Johnny Byrne. *ph* John Ward. *ed* Jeffrey Arsenault. *pd* Geoff Sharp. *m* Roger Bolton. *cast* Thomas Arklie, Ian Williams, Tony Slattery, Dilly Keane, Jean Boht, John Altman, Caroline Munro, Ian McKellen.
●When drag queen Mark (Williams) died of AIDS, hunky, HIV-negative boyfriend Simon (Arklie) throws his belongings into the back of the closet and goes on the prowl. You can't keep a good drag queen down, however, and it isn't long before Mark comes back to haunt his faithless lover. The film doesn't live up to its billing as 'the first British gay mainstream movie'. But it is the first to handle the subject of AIDS with a comic touch. The script is patchy, making for more laughs than were intended, but the director draws impressive performances from newcomers Williams and Arklie. PBur

To Die For

(1995, US, 107 min)
d Gus Van Sant. *p* Laura Ziskin. *sc* Buck Henry. *ph* Eric Alan Edwards. *ed* Curtiss Clayton. *pd* Missy Stewart. *m* Danny Elfman. *cast* Nicole Kidman, Matt Dillon, Joaquin Phoenix, Casey Affleck, Illeana Douglas, Alison Folland, Dan Hedaya, Buck Henry, David Cronenberg.
●For New Hampshire girl Suzanne Stone (Kidman), you're nobody in America unless you're on TV; indeed, she'd die to achieve small-screen celebrity. Fortunately for her, she's both determined and attractive enough to work her seductive wiles on the local cable-station boss, who appoints her weather presenter – and then allows her to work on a documentary with and about high school kids. Against all odds, she befriends three awesomely inarticulate no-hopers – but there's method to her madness: her husband Larry (Dillon) wants to have kids, so she exerts her influence over the trio to defend her endangered career. If you've hitherto failed to respond to the laid-back oddball appeal of Van Sant's movies, fear not: this is a sharp, consistently funny blend of black comedy and satire on the deleterious effects of television. GA

Tödliche Maria, Die (Deadly Maria)

(1994, Ger, 80 min)
d Tom Tykwer. *p* Stefan Arndt, Tom Tykwer. *sc* Tom Tykwer, Christiane Voss. *ph* Frank Griebe. *ed* Katja Dringenberg. *pd* Sybille Kelber, Attila Saygel. *m* Tom Tykwer. *cast* Nina Petri, Josef Bierbichler, Peter Franke, Joachim Krol.
●Young German director Tykwer embraces a panoply of cinematic possibilities. In this story of a wife and daughter's drudgery-filled existence, he finds much light and shade, for, as Petri's put-upon heroine sacrifices her own liberty to the demands of her husband and father, you'll find a Fassbinder-like vision of domestic dystopia, Hitchcockian suspense, the tenderness of a Truffaut, and a whole lot more besides. A compassionate, sometimes shocking, very substantial achievement – with one truly gobsmacking sequence (you'll know when you get there). TJ

Todo Sobre Mi Madre

see All About My Mother

Todos Somos Estrellas (We're All Stars)

(1994, Peru, 86 min)
d Luis Felipe Degregori. *p* Felipe Degregori. *sc* Ronnie Tenoche. *ph* Eduardo Davila. *ed* Luis Barrios. *m* Miky Gonzalez. *cast* Milena Alva, Mariella Balbi, Elida Brere, Katia Condos.
●The Huanbachano family from Lima's tenements all watch the popular TV show *We're All Stars*; aspiring actress Rita is, however, the one who submits the forms applying for an appearance. A mix-up at the TV office sends two-faced presenter Mery and her cameraman along to the house, but student Tabo blows the show when he reveals that his absent real father is to be covertly replaced by his mum's naff suitor Nicolas. Degregori's engaging if facile satire has a sit-com plot and surface texture, but its moments of pathos are genuinely felt. The awesome music (dramatic moments signalled by bassoon farts, etc) shows how seriously the director stays true to the story's TV-saturated milieu. It's a surprisingly non-patronising film, which simultaneously exposes and dignifies the family's aspirations and conflicts, ending in a spirit of gentle celebration of their collective indviduality. WH

To Find a Man

(1971, US, 93 min)
d Buzz Kulik. *p* Irving Pincus. *sc* Arnold Shulman. *ph* Andrew Laszlo. *ed* Rita Roland. *pd* Peter Dohanos. *m* David Shire. *cast* Pamela Martin, Darren O'Connor, Lloyd Bridges, Phyllis Newman, Tom Ewell, Tom Bosley, Miles Chapin.
●The man in question is not what you might think: he's a doctor, needed to perform an abortion on a spoiled, rich, sex-obsessed New York schoolgirl who gets pregnant after being seduced by the gigolo who lives with the mother of one of her spoiled, rich, sex-obsessed schoolfriends. The film chronicles the attempt of an intellectual schoolboy admirer to solve 'her' problem for her: a lesson in life for the children of the idle rich. It's fairly trivial, but what is interesting about it – in spite of the often corny camerawork and post Simon and Garfunkel music – is the way, without hysteria or moralising – we become inextricably involved with the quest, even going through the abortion with the girl in the surgery. It's a rare thing for most people to have to spend 90 minutes contemplating abortion. MV

To Forget Venice

see Dimenticare Venezia

Together (aka Sensual Paradise)

(1971, US, 72 min)
d/p/sc Sean S Cunningham. *ph* Roger Murphy. *ed* Roger Murphy, Wes Craven. *m* Manny Vardi. *cast* Marilyn Chambers, Maureen Cousins, Sally Cross, Jade Hagen, Vic Mohica.
●The usual homage to permissiveness (what's left of it after the removal of 11 minutes by the British censor), wrapped up in the usual semi-sociological interviews with sexual pundits and some *vox pop*. The message urges the reciprocity of sexual response, the importance of doing away with competitiveness, and the reawakening of a genuine enjoyment of sensual experience. Not without its own brand of wish fulfilment, the film lets us watch the young and lean and privileged disport themselves at Dr Curry's sexual health farm, hear them comment gee whiz style on their new insights, and regale ourselves with a sequence of naked diving involving porno queen Marilyn Chambers. VG

Together (Tillsammans)

(2000, Swe/Den/It, 107 min)
d Lukas Moodysson. *p* Lars Jönsson. *sc* Lukas Moodysson. *ph* Ulf Brantås. *ed* Michael Leszczylowski, Fredrik Abrahamsen. *pd* Carl Johan de Geer. *cast* Lisa Lindgren, Gustav Hammarsten, Mikael Nyqvist, Emma Samuelsson, Sam Kessel, Anja Lundqvist, Jessica Liedberg, Ola Norell, Shanti Roney.
●If '70s radicalism seems a soft target – and ABBA's 'SOS' on the soundtrack makes the point – yet this movie accomplishes the more difficult task of sending up human foibles while remaining sympathetic to the ideals espoused by these Swedish communards. Moodysson's masterstroke is to capture the point of view of two children, dumped in this curious environment of free love, no TV, pot smoking and washing up rotas when their mum walks out on her abusive husband. An especially cherishable moment is when they take turns playing 'Pinochet'. Funny, affectionate and beautifully judged. TCh

To Have and Have Not

(1945, US, 100 min, b/w)
d/p Howard Hawks. *sc* Jules Furthman, William Faulkner. *ph* Sid Hickox. *ed* Christian I Nyby. *ad* Charles Novi. *songs* Hoagy Carmichael, Johnny Mercer. *cast* Humphrey Bogart, Lauren Bacall, Walter Brennan, Hoagy Carmichael, Dan Seymour, Marcel Dalio, Walter Molnar, Dolores Moran.
●An unassuming masterpiece, nominally based on Hemingway's novel and set in Martinique during World War II, this is Hawks' toughest statement of the necessity of accepting responsibility for others or forfeiting one's self-respect – the sum total of morality for Hawks – and the perfect bridge from the free and open world of *Only Angels Have Wings* to the claustrophobic one of *Rio Bravo*. Bogart is the doubting fishing-boat privateer who finally throws in his hand with the Free French because he loves a girl (Bacall, electric in one of filmdom's most startling debuts), and Walter 'stung by a dead bee' Brennan is his partner. Bogie and Bacall fell in love while making the film, and their scenes reflect this, giving *To Have and Have Not* a degree of emotional presence that is unusual in the 'bite on the bullet' world of Hawks. PH

To Have & to Hold

(1996, Aust, 100 min)
d John Hillcoat. *p* Denise Patience. *sc* Gene Conkie. *ph* Andrew De Groot. *ed* Stewart Young. *pd* Chris Kennedy. *m* Blixa Bargeld, Nick Cave, Mick Harvey. *cast* Tchéky Karyo, Rachel Griffiths, Steve Jacobs, Anni Finsterer, David Field, Robert Kunsa.
●Hillcoat's belated follow up to his ferocious prison drama, *Ghosts...of the Civil Dead*, addresses similar themes of isolation and entrapment, but in a more intimate, emotional context. Jack (Karyo) and Kate (Griffiths) are ill-fated lovers in a jungle town in Papua, New Guinea, obsessed not with one another but with a projected image of a lost/perfect partner. When the beams cross, fantasy and reality collide, and the picture gets very messy indeed. Two years ago, Jack's wife Rose drowned under suspicious circumstances. Now he's back with his new Australian girlfriend, novelist Kate, whose naive romantic fantasy finds expression in her book, 'Jungle of Love: A

Tropical Romance'. But Jack is soon sucked down into the whirlpool of memory, repeatedly viewing old home videos of Rose, and persuading Kate to wear his late wife's red dress. A cycle of drinking, victimisation and violent jealousy repeats itself, as Kate's dream turns into a sanity- and life-threatening nightmare. Thematically consistent and visually arresting, this ambitious modern melodrama works best when Karyo and Griffiths' performances infuse the slightly schematic screenplay with a raw emotional intensity. And yet for all its relentless fatalism, visual richness and lush, enveloping score (the soundtrack also features Scott Walker covering Dylan) it never quite reaches fever pitch. NF

To Kill a Mockingbird

(1962, US, 129 min, b/w)
d Robert Mulligan. *p* Alan J Pakula. *sc* Horton Foote. *ph* Russell Harlan. *ed* Aaron Stell. *ad* Alexander Golitzen, Henry Bumstead. *m* Elmer Bernstein. *cast* Gregory Peck, Mary Badham, Philip Alford, John Megna, Frank Overton, Rosemary Murphy, Brock Peters, Robert Duvall.

●Tackling Harper Lee's novel, Stanley Kramer would have hit us over the head with a hammer, so perhaps we can be grateful that Mulligan merely suffocates with righteousness. The film sits somewhere between the bogus virtue of Kramer's *The Defiant Ones* and the poetry of Laughton's *Night of the Hunter,* combining racial intolerance with the nightmares of childhood, born out of Kennedy's stand on civil rights and Martin Luther King's marching. In Alabama in the early '30s, Peck is a Lincoln-like lawyer who defends a black (Peters) against a charge of rape, while loony-tune Duvall scares the shit out of Peck's kids. It looks like a storybook of the Old South, with dappled sunlight and woodwormy porches, and Peck is everyone's favourite uncle. But screenwriter Horton Foote does less well by Harper Lee's novel than Lillian Hellman did by Foote's *The Chase* for Arthur Penn. That movie really was a pressure-cooker; this one is always just off the boil. ATu

To Kill a Priest

(1988, US/Fr, 117 min)
d Agnieszka Holland. *p* Jean-Pierre Alessandri. *sc* Agnieszka Holland, Jean-Yves Pitoun. *ph* Adam Holender. *ed* Hervé de Luze. *pd* Emile Ghigo. *cast* Christopher Lambert, Ed Harris, Joss Ackland, Tim Roth, Timothy Spall, Peter Postlethwaite, Cherie Lunghi, Joanne Whalley, David Suchet.

●Solidarity seen through a Cold War lens, i.e. plucky nationalist Catholics vs the club-wielding forces of darkness. *The Solidarnosc* we get here is against Communism (or, as translated here, Socialism), for religion, and barely aware of trade unionism. Instead, Father Alek (Lambert), a fictionalised version of the cleric Jerzy Popieluszko, enjoys a frustrated flirtation with Whalley while making the odd speech about the aspirations of the Poles. Alek then runs into a whole heap of trouble with gritty local Militia chief Harris, who bludgeons the priest and dumps him in the river before being dumped on himself by his superiors. The script (an international co-production number) sounds like a Lada service manual; Poland looks like the North Peckham Estate; The Zomo (secret police) behave like Keystone Cops; and the attempts to turn Father Al symbolically into JC himself offended even this card-carrying atheist. JMo

Tokyo Chorus (Tokyo no gassho)

(1931, Jap, 90 min, b/w)
d Yasujiro Ozu. *sc* Kogo Noda. *ph/ed* Hideo Mohara. *ad* Yoneichi Wakita. *cast* Tokihiko Okada, Emiko Yagumo, Hideo Sugawara, Hideko Takamine, Tatsuo Saito, Choko Iida, Takeshi Sakamoto.

●Ozu's social conscience family comedy is concerned with the financial and social pressures on insurance company man Okada and his wife and kids after he loses his job for protesting an elderly colleague's dismissal. Ozu plays the story partly for laughs and partly straight: an interesting enterprise in itself, and one that provides a rare glimpse in his work of both social perspective (Okada's travails on the Depression-era Tokyo job market) and comedy, centring on various battles between Okada and his wilful son (Sugawara, one of the brothers in *I Was Born, But...*, and a star here already). Typically, though, Ozu's chief emphasis is the (mis)fortunes of a family of individuals. NB

Tokyo Decadence (Topazu/aka Topaz)

(1992, Jap, 135 min)
d Ryu Murakami. *p* Chosei Funahara, Tadanobu Hiaro, Yousuke Nagata, Akiuh Suzuki. *sc* Ryu Murakami, (English version) Peter Fernandez. *ph* Tadash Aoki. *ed* Kazuki Katashima. *m* Ryuichi Sakamoto. *cast* Miho Nikaido, Sayoko Amano, Tenmei Kano, Kan Mikami, Masahiko Shimada, Yayoi Kusama, Chie Seman, Sayoko Maekawa, Hiroshi Mikami.

●Given that, strictly speaking, 'decadence' refers less to hanky-panky pure and unfettered, than to some kind of decline or dearth of moral fibre, it's fair to say that this 1994 film from ageing enfant terrible writer and media personality Ryu Murakami displays as much decadence as do its subjects. Lacking the intellectual, emotional and philosophical rigours of, say, a film by Oshima, this brazenly voyeuristic nonsense is finally as incoherent and unilluminating as it's hackneyed. Docile, a shade timid, and learning the sign language of the deaf, 22-year-old call-girl Ai readily caters to the S/M fantasies of various rich businessmen. She's naive and superstitious, it seems, optimistic and too trusting. Maybe that's why she's taking so long to get over an affair with a married TV celebrity, which may in turn explain why she submits to sadistic demands that put her at risk. To glean even this little from this attenuated 90-minute narrative is to milk it dry. So concerned is the film with leering at Ai's semi-naked body, that plot detail and depth of characterisation are soon forgotten. GA

Tokyo Drifter (Tokyo Nagaremono)

(1966, Jap, 83 min)
d Seijun Suzuki. *p* Tetsuro Nakagawa. *sc* Yasunori Kawauchi. *ph* Shigeyoshi Mine. *ed* Shinya Inoue. *m* So Kaburagi. *cast* Tetsuya Watari, Chieko Matsubara, Hideaki Natani, Ryuji Kita.

●Deliriously playful yakuza pic, in which Suzuki lets logic hang. Basically just another tale of gang warfare, it's kitted out with plot ellipses, bizarre sets and colour effects, inappropriate songs, absurd irrelevancies (nice hair-drier gags!), action scenes that verge on the abstract, and some visual jokes tottering precariously between slapstick and surrealism. Somehow, it still just about works as a thriller, with (very, very faint) echoes of Melville and Leone. Inspired lunacy. GA

Tokyo Fist

(1995, Jap, 87 min)
d/p/sc/ph/ed/ad Shinya Tsukamoto. *m* Chu Ishikawa. *cast* Shinya Tsukamoto, Koji Tsukamoto, Kaori Fujii, Naoto Takenaka, Naomasa Musaka, Koichi Wajima.

●Tsukamoto's follow-up to the *Tetsuo* diptych punches (and I do mean punches) into a new combat zone, beyond mere body horror. The director himself plays an insurance salesman whose life with his fiancée is turned upside down by an encounter with a former classmate, now a pro boxer with problems. A love triangle of the '90s: the 'new man' gets body conscious, the macho meathead gets nightmares, and the hip young woman flexes her options and gets her nipples pierced. Psycho-kinetic film-making in the patented Tsukamoto manner: bloody, convulsive, tender and blackly comic. TR

Tokyo-Ga

(1985, WGer/US, 92 min, b/w & col)
d Wim Wenders. *p* Chris Sievernich. *sc* Wim Wenders. *ph* Ed Lachman. *ed* Jon Neuberger. *m* Dick Tracy. *with* Chishu Ryu, Yuharu Atsuta, Werner Herzog.

●In this 'diary', Wenders tried to relate his impressions of Tokyo to those he had gleaned from the work of the late, great Yasujiro Ozu. No mere travelogue, the film is like a less complex version of Chris Marker's *Sans Soleil,* with Wenders' ideas fewer and less fruitful than his images. His eye for the bizarre, as sharp as it is selective, revels in long, engrossing sequences shot at a pachinko arcade, a golf stadium, a wax-food factory, and a rockabilly gathering; though his narration never admits to finding them absurd, he is clearly fascinated by the obsessive nature of his subjects' recreational activities. More rewarding (if less funny) are interviews with Chishu Ryu (lead actor in countless Ozu films) and cameraman Yuharu Atsuta, who worked almost exclusively with Ozu for decades. Both are modest, intelligent and very likeable, but Atsuta steals the show, shedding valuable light on Ozu's unique, contemplative camera style, and offering a profoundly moving personal valediction to the man himself. GA

Tokyo Kyodai

(1994, Jap, 92 min)
d Jun Ichikawa. *p* Takio Yoshida. *sc* Masahiro Fujita, Tashiro Inomata, Hideyuki Suzuki. *ph* Koichi Kawakami. *ed* Shizuo Arakawa. *pd* Norihiro Isoda. *m* Yuki Kajiura. *cast* Naoto Ogata, Urara Awata, Toru Tezuka.

●The Ozu-esque title (it means 'Tokyo Siblings') is supposed to alert you to the fact that this picture about the end of a brother-sister relationship is yet another 'homage' to the old master. What it lacks, of course, is the least hint of Ozu's wry and playful humour, along with anything to match his formal skills and worldly wisdom. The characters are young people who have lost their parents. Yoko waits hand and foot on her older brother Kenichi, who sells second-hand books, the deeply repressed erotic bond between them is shattered when Yoko finds a man she wants to marry. Most viewers will want to give the selfish and complacent Kenichi a good kicking long before this lugubrious movie grinds to its close. TR

Tokyo Olympiad 1964

(1965, Jap, 130 min)
d Kon Ichikawa. *p* Suketaru Taguchi. *sc* Natto Wada, Yoshio Shirasaka, Shuntaro Taninkawa. *ph* Shigeo Hayashida, Kazuo Miyagawa, Juichi Nagano, Kinji Nakamura, Tadashi Tanaka. *ed* Kon Ichikawa. *ad* Yusaku Kamekura. *m* Toshiro Mayuzumi.

●The director of *Fires on the Plain* and *An Actor's Revenge* didn't seem the obvious choice to mastermind a record of the 1964 Olympics, and in the event Ichikawa's film didn't please all the people all the time. Most riled were probably the bona fide sports fans, because Ichikawa's attitude to the games and participants seems quizzical rather than committed, sensual rather than gutsy. Least riled were probably Ichikawa fans, because the unpredictable humour, the 'bold delicacy' of the visuals, and the occasional real intensity, are all quite consistent with his fiction films. The only sustained 'performance' is Abebe Bikila's triumph in the marathon, but the rest is funny, sexy, beautiful, or atmospheric enough to give a lot of pleasure to the open-eyed. TR

Tokyo Pop

(1988, US, 99 min)
d Fran Rubel Kazui. *p* Kaz Kuzui, Joel Tuber. *sc* Fran Rubel Kuzui, Lynn Grossman. *ph* Jim Heyman. *ed* Camilla Toniolo. *pd* Terumi Hosoishi. *m* Alan Brewer. *cast* Carrie Hamilton, Yutaka Tadokoro, Taiji Tonoyama, Tetsuro Tamba, Daisuke Oyama, Hiroshi Kabayashi, Hirsohi Sugita.

●Rock'n'roll proves an international language in this amiable but naff musical travelogue. Hamilton's an aspiring artiste whose career's going nowhere in New York, so she accepts a friend's invite to join her in the Japanese capital, where local muso Tadokoro reckons she's the perfect frontwoman for his new beat combo. Tokyo itself comes over rather better than the songs devised by this cross-cultural supergroup. TJ

Tokyo Raiders (Dongjing Gonglüe)

(2000, HK, 101 min)
d Jingle Ma. *p* David Chan, Patricia Cheng. *sc* Susan Chan, Felix Chong. *ph* Jingle Ma, Chan Chi-Ying. *ed* Kwong Chi-Leung. *pd* Kenneth Mak. *m* Peter Kam. *cast* Tony Leung [Leung Chiu-Wai], Ekin Cheng, Kelly Chen, Cecilia Cheung, Toru Nakamura, Hiroshi Abe.

●Made to order for Chinese New Year release, this charmless action-comedy would like to be *Charade* but hasn't a clue how to handle plot structure, characterisation or secret-identity twists. Hong Kong heiress Macy (Chen) flies to Tokyo to track down the Japanese fiancé who jilted her on wedding day; interior decorator Yung (Cheng) tags along to get a bill settled. They immediately run into Lin (Leung), a Chinese private eye with a gaggle of *Charlie's Angels*-type assistants, and find themselves in one dangerous situation after another until it emerges that no one is who they say they are. The McGuffin is a microchip file containing details of a plot to devalue the yen by flooding the market with forged notes. Feeble, gimmicky action choreography, routine stunt work and utterly witless dialogue leave it stuck in first gear. Sad that Tony Leung has to do this stuff to pay the bills. TR

Tokyo Story 100 (100) 10 (Tokyo Monogatari)

(1953, Jap, 135 min, b/w)
d Yasujiro Ozu. *p* Takeshi Yamamoto. *sc* Kogo Noda, Yasujiro Ozu. *ph* Yuharu Atsuta. *ed* Yoshiyasu Hamamura. *ad* Tatsuo Hamada. *m* Takanori Saito. *cast* Chishu Ryu, Chiyeko Higashiyama, Setsuko Hara, So Yamamura, Kyoko Kagawa.

●Ozu's best known (because most widely distributed) movie is a very characteristic study of the emotional strains within a middle class Japanese family that has come to Tokyo from the country and dispersed itself. All that happens in dramatic terms is that the family grandparents arrive in Tokyo to visit their various offspring, and grow painfully aware of the chasms that exist between them and their children; only their daughter-in-law, widowed in the war, is pleased to see them. Ozu's vision, almost entirely un-inflected by tics and tropes of 'style' by this stage in his career, is emotionally overwhelming, and arguably profound for any engaged viewer; it is also formally unmatched in Western popular cinema. TR

Tolerance (Tolerância)

(2000, Braz, 108 min)
d Carlos Gerbase. *p* Nora Goulart, Luciana Tomasi. *sc* Giba Assis Brasil, Jorge Furtado, Carlos Gerbase, Alvaro Teixeira. *ph* Alex Sernambi. *ed* Giba Assis Brasil. *pd* Fiapo Barth. *m* Marcelo Fornazier, Flavio Santos. *cast* Maitê Proença, Roberto Bomtempo, Maria Riberio, Ana Maria Mainieri, Nélson Diniz, Werner Schünemann, Márcio Kieling.

●This begins as a thriller about a land dispute that ends in death. It then goes on to pursue the marital life of the lawyer in the case – both she and her husband have been adulterous. Particularly arresting is the scene in which the husband, who doctors images for porn photographers, is cornered by the thoroughness of his own trickery. Standard themes of illusion and their distortion are handled with subtle vindictiveness. LRo

To Live

see Ikiru

To Live (Huozhe)

(1994, HK, 125 min)
d Zhang Yimou. *p* Chiu Fu-Sheng. *sc* Yu Hua, Lu Wei. *ph* Lu Yue. *ed* Du Yuan. *ad* Cao Jiuping. *m* Zhao Jiping. *cast* Ge You, Gong Li, Niu Ben, Guo Tao, Jiang Wu, Ni Dahong, Liu Tianchi, Zhang Lu.

●China in the mid-'40s: relatively well off until his gambling results in the loss of the family house, Xu Fugui (Ge You) is temporarily abandoned by his pregnant wife Jiazhen (Gong Li) and their deaf-mute daughter Fengxia. Poverty, however, brings him to his senses, and when, working as a travelling shadow-puppeteer, he finds himself embroiled in the Civil War. But as Mao's regime tightens its grip with ever sterner strictures, it becomes harder and harder merely to survive. A straight synopsis may make Zhang Yimou's film sound similar to *The Blue Kite*, or even, perhaps, *Farewell My Concubine*. Certainly it shares with these films both a mix of the personal and the political, and a panoramic view of Chinese life. There, however, the similarities stop. For Zhang's purpose is less to show the oppressive iniquities of Mao's era than to evoke the optimistic spirit that allowed people to survive it. Accordingly, the film is lighter in tone, less provocative, complex and tough, even leavening scenes of misfortune with surprising incursions of black comedy. GA

To Live and Die in L.A.

(1985, US, 116 min)
d William Friedkin. *p* Irving H Levin. *sc* William Friedkin, Gerald Petievich. *ph* Robby Müller. *ed* Bud Smith. *pd* Lilly Kilvert. *m* Wang Chung. *cast* William L Petersen, Willem Dafoe, John Pankow, Debra Feuer, John Turturro, Darlanne Fluegel, Dean Stockwell, Steve James, Robert Downey.

●Dafoe is an LA supercrook, forging dollar bills for a city whose sole form of social intercourse resides in the getting, counting, and spending of large sums of money. This is a city (photographed by Robby Müller with the same luminosity he brought to *Paris, Texas*) where everyone is on the take, and that includes the two FBI agents (Petersen and Pankow) who are out to break Dafoe by any means. It all goes horribly wrong when they decide to pull their own heist in order to secure the necessary funds to stay in hot pursuit. Friedkin plays it as brutal and cynical as he ever did with *The French Connection*; and this time the car chase takes place on a six-lane freeway at the height of the rush hour, going against the traffic. Today, the play-dirty antics of Popeye Doyle probably look rather dated; God knows what state we will have to get into before all this looks tame. CPea

To Live in Freedom

(1974, GB, 54 min)
d Simon Louvish.

●A progressive rather than militant film on the Israel-Palestine problem. It does not claim to know the solution, nor does it take a dogmatic stance in presenting the issues. It sees Israel as a permanent State, but calls into question the values that maintain the State under the present conditions. The film-makers argue for a real class-oriented revolution, a revolution which must necessarily involve both Israelis and Palestinians. Where Golda Meir and her generation naturally have to justify their presence in Israel, these young film-makers go much further by questioning and analysing the very quality of life, as well as the official line the establishment clings to. The myth of Israel is exploded. JPi

Tom and Jerry: The Movie

(1992, US, 84 min)
d/p Phil Roman. *sc* Dennis Marks. *ed* Sam Horta, Julie Ann Gustafson. *m* Henry Mancini, Leslie Bricusse. *cast* voices: Richard Kind, Dana Hill, Anndi McAfee, Henry Gibson.

●A severely dull animated feature. After a brief reprise of the duo's antics, they *talk*...then become *chums*! The cutie-pie script has them leave the white-frame house to unite orphan Robyn Starling with her long-lost dad. Spot the sources: Robyn's aunt has traces of Cruella de Vil and Snow White's stepmum; lawyer Lickboot could be a George Sanders pastiche; Dr Applecheek behaves uncannily like the doctor from Altman's *The Long Goodbye* (and, surprise, the voice is Henry Gibson's). Very poor. WH

Tomándote

see Two for Tea

Tom & Viv

(1994, GB, 125 min)
d Brian Gilbert. *p* Peter Samuelson, Marc Samuelson, Harvey Kass. *sc* Michael Hastings, Adrian Hodges. *ph* Martin Fuhrer. *ed* Tony Lawson. *pd* Jamie Leonard. *m* Debbie Wiseman. *cast* Willem Dafoe, Miranda Richardson, Rosemary Harris, Tim Dutton, Nickolas Grace, Geoffrey Bayldon, Clare Holman, Philip Locke, John Savident,Joanna McCallum.

●Having eloped with eccentric aristo Vivienne Haigh-Wood, TS Eliot soon discovers that not only is his wife mentally unstable, but that she's afflicted with a hormonal imbalance causing her to menstruate almost continuously. This is tough on the shy, painfully repressed poet, but so, too, is Viv's increasingly bizarre behaviour, which culminates in a knife attack on the novelist Virginia Woolf. This is hardly the most flattering portrait of the author of 'The Waste Land', yet the emphasis on Viv's extreme behaviour often feels like special pleading, and Tom's precise role in her committal is fudged. Expanded from Michael Hastings' play, the film is too spacially and emotionally constricted to achieve its ends, a problem compounded by flat direction and stilted dialogue. Dafoe concentrates on reproducing Eliot's absurd diction, while the usually faultless Richardson overacts, making Viv's antics appear ridiculous rather than pitiable. NF

Tombés du Ciel (Lost in Transit)

(1993, Fr, 91 min)
d Philippe Lioret. *p* Enrique Posner, Michel Ganz. *sc* Philippe Lioret, Michel Ganz. *ph* Thierry Arbogast. *ed* Laurent Quaglio. *m* Jeff Cohen. *cast* Jean Rochefort, Michel Ganz, Marisa Paredes, Ticky Holgado, Laura del Sol.

●A socially concerned comedy tailor-made for the hangdog persona of Jean Rochefort. A well-to-do iconographer (Rochefort) is trapped in the transit zone of Charles de Gaulle airport, Paris, where he meets and gets to like a wacky band of displaced persons. Making their households in the corridors, engine rooms and back exits of the airport are a kid from Guinea, an ex-mercenary, an Ethiopian who speaks only an ancient lost language, a political refugee, and more. First-time director Lioret tackles the clichés head on, and thanks to fine performances creates a likeable if lightweight romantic drama. WH

Tomb of Ligeia, The

(1964, GB, 81 min)
d Roger Corman. *p* Pat Green, Roger Corman. *sc* Robert Towne. *ph* Arthur Grant. *ed* Alfred Cox. *ad* Colin Southcott. *m* Kenneth Jones. *cast* Vincent Price, Elizabeth Shepherd, John Westbrook, Oliver Johnston, Derek Francis, Richard Vernon, Ronald Adam.

●After his long sequence of Poe movies filmed in various studio interiors, Corman decided that *The Tomb of Ligeia* demanded a change of style and emphasis. Consequently he shot it on a number of highly effective English locations, having commissioned Robert Towne (who subsequently wrote *Chinatown*) to script it. The result is one of the best in the whole series, an ambiguous, open-ended film which features one of Vincent Price's most decisive performances. There is a long early sequence involving a long monologue by Verden Fell (Price), juxtaposed against Rowena (Shepherd) climbing a gothic tower, which has a syntactic originality that has rarely been equalled in horror movies. But even more importantly, Corman – like Michael Reeves in *Witchfinder General* – utilised the English landscape in a way that Hammer had often neglected. DP

Tom Brown's Schooldays

(1951, GB, 96 min, b/w)
d Gordon Parry. *p* Brian Desmond Hurst. *sc* Noel Langley. *ph* C Pennington-Richards. *ed* Kenneth Heeley-Ray. *ad* Fred Pusey. *m* Richard Addinsell. *cast* John Howard Davies, Robert Newton, Diana Wynyard, Hermione Baddeley, Kathleen Byron, James Hayter, John Forrest, John Charlesworth, Michael Hordern, Max Bygraves, Rachel Gurney.

●Master Howard Davies (later a successful BBC producer who worked on the early Monty Python series) may be a precursor of the Mark Lester school of terribly English moppetry, but he doesn't detract too much from this soldily carpentered third screen version of Thomas Hughes' famous Rugby story – atmospherically shot on location in the old school itself. Newton restrains himself admirably as the ultimately good-hearted headmaster, but it's Forrest's show as the caddish bully Flashman, dispensing ignominy with a curl of the lip and a dash of hauteur before his eventual and not unexpected comeuppance. TJ

Tombstone

(1993, US, 129 min)
d George P Cosmatos. *p* Andrew Vajna, Bob Misiorowski, Sean Daniel, Jim Jacks. *sc* Kevin Jarre. *ph* William A Fraker. *ed* Peter Davies, Frank J Urioste, Roberto Silvi, Harvey Rosenstock. *pd* Catherine Hardwicke. *m* Bruce Broughton. *cast* Kurt Russell, Val Kilmer, Sam Elliott, Bill Paxton, Powers Boothe, Michael Biehn, Joanna Pacula.

●The old story of how Wyatt Earp and Doc Holliday took on the Clanton mob and brought law and order to the town of Tombstone. This version fields an impressive supporting cast (in addition to the above, Michael Rooker, Stephen Lang, Charlton Heston, Harry Carey Jr, Billy Zane and Jason Priestley), a screenplay by Kevin Jarre which is at least on speaking terms with history, and decidedly no-frills direction by George (*Rambo*) Cosmatos. Kilmer makes a surprisingly effective and effete Holliday, but Russell lacks the stature for Earp – Sam Elliott as his older brother Virgil suggests a better movie. There's a misguided romantic subplot and the ending rather sprawls, but mostly this is rootin', tootin' entertainment with lots of authentic facial hair. TCh

Tom Horn

(1980, US, 97 min)
d William Wiard. *p* Fred Weintraub. *sc* Thomas McGuane, Bud Shrake. *ph* John A Alonzo. *ed* George Grenville. *ad* Ron Hobbs. *m* Ernest Gold. *cast* Steve McQueen, Linda Evans, Richard Farnsworth, Billy Green Bush, Slim Pickens, Peter Canon, Elisha Cook, Geoffrey Lewis.

● A severely beautiful Western based on the life of a semi-legendary cowboy who served as a cavalry scout, was then hired to wage secret war on Wyoming rustlers, and was eventually hanged by a society which had outgrown his maverick values. McQueen's performance is all the more affecting (his penultimate film) now that we know he was suffering from an incurable cancer. But the film's glaring production problems – rewrites to Thomas McGuane's script, change of director (it was started by James William Guercio), extensive re-editing – ruin what might otherwise have been an extraordinarily eloquent political fable. CPe

Tom Jones

(1963, GB, 128 min)
d/p Tony Richardson. *sc* John Osborne. *ph* Walter Lassally. *ed* Antony Gibbs. *pd* Ralph Brinton. *m* John Addison. *cast* Albert Finney, Susannah York, Hugh Griffith, Edith Evans, Joan Greenwood, Diane Cilento, George Devine, Joyce Redman, David Warner, David Tomlinson, John Moffatt, Wilfrid Lawson, Freda Jackson.

● Too risky for penny-pinching British financiers, *Tom Jones* was rescued by United Artists, and its massive success released a flood of American money into the British film industry. Richardson's England is full of 18th century atmospherics, but its big attraction was the bawdy licence it allowed '60s permissiveness. Osborne's courageous hatchet job on Fielding's 1,000 page classic novel and Finney's gutsy performance add up to produce an enjoyable piece of irreverent entertainment. RMy

Tommy

(1975, GB, 108 min)
d Ken Russell. *p* Robert Stigwood, Ken Russell. *sc* Ken Russell. *ph* Duck Bush, Ronnie Taylor. *ed* Stuart Baird. *ad* John Clark. *m* Pete Townsend, The Who. *cast* Ann-Margret, Oliver Reed, Roger Daltrey, Elton John, Eric Clapton, Keith Moon, Jack Nicholson, Robert Powell, Tina Turner.

● Although in criticising Russell's lack of discipline people tend to forget that he was virtually the first film-maker to escape the strictures of realism and telestyle that have dogged British cinema since the heyday of Powell and Pressburger, it must nevertheless be admitted that watching his more excessive movies tends to be a wearisome experience. The Who's ludicrous rock opera was in fact tailor-made for the baroque, overblown images and simplistic symbolism of Russell's style, which only means that this is both the movie in which he is most faithful to the ideas and tone of his material, and one of his very worst films. GA

Tommy Boy

(1995, US, 97 min)
d Peter Segal. *p* Lorne Michaels. *sc* Terry Turner, Bonnie Turner. *ph* Victor J Kemper. *ed* William Kerr. *pd* Stephen Lineweaver. *m* David Newman. *cast* Chris Farley, David Spade, Bo Derek, Dan Aykroyd, Brian Dennehy, Julie Warner, Sean McCann.

● When auto magnate Tommy Snr (Dennehy) dies in the arms of his scheming new bride (Derek), she persuades the board to put the factory up for sale – jeopardising the livelihood of the entire town. Only Tommy Boy (Farley) can save them, if he and Richard (Spade) can drum up enough business on a last desperate road trip. But Tommy takes to sales like a duck to soup, and the town looks to be dead in the water. This cinematic folly from the *Saturday Night Live* stable is enough to make you yearn for the golden days of John Belushi and Dan Aykroyd. Farley is the physical pratfaller, a clumsy oaf with the brawn of a bison and a brain to match; Spade the slimline sidekick with a long line in snide. It's some indication of the wit involved that Farley is reduced to cracking fat jokes at his own expense. TCh

Tommy Steele Story, The (aka Rock Around the World)

(1957, GB, 82 min, b/w)
d Gerard Bryant. *p* Herbert Smith. *sc* Norman Hudis. *ph* Peter Hennessy. *ed* Ann Chegwidden. *ad* Eric Saw. *songs* Lionel Bart, Tommy Steele. *cast* Tommy Steele, Lisa Daniely, Patrick Westwood, Hilda Fenemore, Dennis Price.

● This is one of the few biographical movies in which the subject has the gall to play himself. From humble beginnings in Bermondsey, young Thomas discovers his seemingly limitless talent, joins the Merchant Navy (his only sensible move), then finds fame and fortune in the coffee bars of Soho. All complete hokum, of course, but often unintentionally hilarious. Steele is so cute and wholesome you can't help fantasising that something horrible and sordid was going on behind the scenes. Worth seeing for purely kitsch reasons. RS

Tommy Tricker and the Stamp Traveller

(1988, Can, 105 min)
d Michael Rubbo. *p* Rock Demers, Ann Burke. *sc* Michael Rubbo, Andreas Poulsson. *ph* Andreas Poulsson. *ed* André Corriveau. *ad* Vianney Gauthier. *m* Kate McGarrigle, Anna McGarrigle, Jane McGarrigle. *cast* Lucas Evans, Anthony Rogers, Jill Stanley, Andrew Whitehead.

● Rubbo's made-for-kids philatelic tale starts with young sting-merchant Tommy Tricker smooth-talking his wimpish pal Ralph out of his father's most treasured stamp. In the doghouse, Ralph and his sister Nancy spot the rarity in the local stamp shop. No chance, $ 600 price tag, but the dealer offers the pair a dusty old album as solace. Lo and behold, out pops a hand-written letter dated 1928, stating the whereabouts and means of recovering several old and extremely valuable stamps. Ralph is reduced to pinhead size (by way of some fairly clever animation), planted firmly on a current 1st class stamp, and popped in a letter-box. En route to his final destination, the film gets bogged down in various worldwide locations: the whole thing could quite easily be condensed into a 45-minute TV short. DA

Tomorrow Never Comes

(1977, Can/GB, 109 min)
d Peter Collinson. *p* Julian Melzack, Michael Klinger. *sc* David Pursall, Jack Seddon, Sydney Banks. *ph* François Protat. *ed* John Shirley. *ad* Michel Proulx. *m* Roy Budd. *cast* Oliver Reed, Susan George, Raymond Burr, John Ireland, Stephen McHattie, Donald Pleasence, Paul Koslo, John Osborne.

● Young Frank (McHattie) returns from out-of-town to learn that his girl Janie (George) has given herself to a local big-shot (Osborne) in return for a teak-veneered cabana in the grounds of his luxury hotel. A nasty blow on the head in a bar fight has the effect of a lobotomy, and mild-mannered Frank is transformed into a twitchy psychopath. He holds Janie hostage in the cabana, and demands that her white-suited seducer make an appearance. Ollie Reed lumbers into the picture as a cheerless policeman who looks for the non-violent solution in the face of small-town political corruption. A drab, lightweight film with an extremely overweight cast from whom Collinson has extracted embarrassingly eccentric performances, notably Raymond Burr as a police chief who plays with clockwork toys. But what else can you do with such a crass script? JS

Tomorrow Never Dies

(1997, GB/US, 119 min)
d Roger Spottiswoode. *p* Michael Wilson, Barbara Broccoli. *sc* Bruce Feirstein. *ph* Robert Elswit. *ed* Dominique Fortin, Michel Arcand. *pd* Allan Cameron. *m* David Arnold. *cast* Pierce Brosnan, Jonathan Pryce, Michelle Yeoh, Teri Hatcher, Joe Don Baker, Desmond Llewelyn, Geoffrey Palmer, Judi Dench, Samantha Bond, Terence Rigby.

● Brosnan's second outing as agent 007. Media mogul Elliot Carver wants to start a war to ensure exclusive broadcast rights. He must be stopped (that's about it, for plot). The first half builds promisingly, adding depth to Bond's character, along with the usual mix of violence, humour and gadgetry, but after the amazing carpark car-chase, things start to go awry, as 007 resorts to standard tactics, waving weaponry about without bothering to dodge the bullets. All very entertaining, but not really Bond. This is a pity, because by then girl A (Hatcher, lacklustre) has been replaced by girl B, Wai Lin (Yeoh, who's such a great foil for the hero that she's worth a franchise of her own). Sadly, if her role is badly underwritten, the script problems are most evident in Pryce's Carver, who peaks too early and doesn't get nasty enough lines to elicit boos and hisses. Luckily, Brosnan, whose Bond is easily the best since Connery's, is more than strong enough to paper over the cracks. Flawed, but fantastic fun all the same. NK

Tomorrow's Warrior (Avrianos Polemistis)

(1981, Cyp, 95 min)
d/p/sc Michael Papas. *ph* John McCallum. *ed* Michael Papas. *ad* Stephan Athienites, Angelos Angeli. *m* Nicos Mamangakis. *cast* Christos Zannides, Aristodemos Fessas, Dimitri Andreas, Jenny Lipman, Joanna Shafkali.

● Set in Cyprus at the time of the 1974 Turkish invasion, this forms an impassioned and unashamedly partisan sequel to Michael Papas' previous saga of that country's troubled history, *The Private Right*. But 'tomorrow's warrior' unfortunately turns out to be a tousle-haired, insufferably winsome Greek Cypriot boy who imposes a confused, child's-eye perspective on events, not helped by hectic cutting and interminable reaction shots of his innocent, bewildered little face. What's worse, Papas opts for easy emotionalism in the future hero's heart-tugging devotion to his old grandpa, naïve painter of peasant lore, who exudes quiet dignity and will, of course, be killed off by wicked Turks. Sticky-sweet as a slice of baklava, this is highly resistible fare. SJo

Tom Sawyer

(1973, US, 103 min)
d Don Taylor. *p* Arthur P Jacobs. *sc* Richard M Sherman, Robert B Sherman. *ph* Frank Stanley. *ed* Marion Rothman. *pd* Philip M Jefferies. *m* Richard M Sherman, Robert B Sherman. *cast* Johnny Whitaker, Celeste Holm, Warren Oates, Jeff East, Jodie Foster, Henry Jones, Dub Taylor.

● A *Reader's Digest* production, with songs by the Sherman brothers of Disney fame, and surprisingly enjoyable. Highly professional old-style movie-making which has the wit to ditch its set piece white-picket-fenced Southern town, its inhabitants, and even Tom himself, to fill the screen with dazzling helicopter shots of the Mississippi River (complete with Howard Keel-style ballads) whenever it can. Of course there are the statutory moments of schmaltz, the Indian bogeyman, and a marked absence of blacks (in a Southern town?). Nice, if over-detailed, performance from Warren Oates as Muff Potter.

Tom Simpson: Something to Aim At

(1997, GB, 75 min)
d Ray Pascoe.

● Few have ever heard of the late Tom Simpson, but among the cycle racing fraternity (especially that of the late '60s), he was a hugely popular World Champion. What makes this lengthy documentary tribute especially moving is the circumstances surrounding Simpson's untimely death, which occurred as he was tackling a mountain stage in the 1967 Tour de France. Never one to give up, he literally rode himself to death. The first half-hour is perhaps a little too weighed down with reminiscences; crucially, there's hardly any archive material of Simpson during his early push to the top, so what we get is a stream of vaguely interesting vox-pops. Thankfully, it takes a turn for the better as soon as we reach the mid-'60s, when Simpson began making an impact in such prestigious races as the Tour of Flanders and the World Championship itself. DA

Tom's Midnight Garden

(1999, US/GB/Jap, 107 min)
d Willard Carroll. *p* Adam Shapiro, Charles Salmon, Tom Wilhite. *sc* Willard Carroll. *ph* Gavin Finney. *ed* Les Healey. *pd* James

Merifield. *m* Debbie Wiseman. *cast* Greta Scacchi, James Wilby, Joan Plowright, Anthony Way, David Bradley, Penelope Wilton, Nigel Le Vaillant, Liz Smith, Caroline Carver, Serena Gordon.
● The clock struck thirteen. Tom (Way) snuck a slipper in the doorway of his uncle and aunt's apartment, scampered down the great wooden staircase of the old house and opened the back-door which, he'd been told, led nowhere special. Gilded paintings materialise around the hallway, as he steps into the brilliant daylight of a vast Victorian country garden. Back inside next morning, Tom challenges his aunt and uncle: 'What if someone were lying to you about something they thought you shouldn't know about?' So the twerp thinks they're trying to hoodwink him. It's a thin line between magical and ridiculous, and though this rose-tinted adaptation of Philippa Pearce's timeless fantasy has its heart in the right place, it plainly hasn't much of a head for this stuff. It's no crime that the protagonist is slightly dim, but the film shows no more aptitude than the kid for making sense of the midnight timetrap. NB

Tom Thumb
(1958, US, 98 min)
d/p George Pal. *sc* Ladislas Fodor. *ph* Georges Périnal. *ed* Frank Clarke. *ad* Elliot Scott. *songs* Peggy Lee, Fred Spielman, Janice Torre, Kermit Goell. *cast* Russ Tamblyn, June Thorburn, Peter Sellers, Terry-Thomas, Alan Young, Jessie Matthews, Bernard Miles, Ian Wallace.
● A lively predecessor to *Honey, I Shrunk the Kids*, loosely based on the Brothers Grimm tale, but bearing a remarkable resemblance to *Pinocchio*. Tamblyn is the five-inch child bestowed on a peasant couple (Miles and Matthews) by the Forest Queen. All too soon, Tom falls in with bad company: Terry-Thomas and Sellers, relishing their own villainy. Pal, an architecture student whose first films were self-styled 'Puppetoons', put his training to good use here, cleverly meshing miniatures, giant props and animation techniques to create an impression of the world as Tom sees it. With a good deal of unforced humour, acrobatic dancing, and some likeable songs (a couple sung by Peggy Lee), it makes for pleasant entertainment. TCh

Tongpan
(1977, Thai, 65 min, b/w)
d Euthana Mukdasanit, Surachai Janthimathorn. *sc* Khamsing Srinork, Paijong Laisagoon, Mike Morrow. *ph* Frank Green. *ed* Isan Film Group. *m* Surachai Janthimathorn.
● The first serious movie from Thailand is a dramatised reconstruction of events in 1973-74, the one time when Thai peasants had been invited to participate in discussions about planning issues affecting them. It's a low-key, sombre film, spelling out the inadequacies of the consultation mechanisms as clearly as it reveals the staggering poverty of the peasants themselves. The film was completed outside Thailand after the military coup of 1976, and it stands as a chastening primer on the disgraceful state of Thai politics. TR

Tongue of the Butterfly, The
see Butterfly's Tongue

Tongues Untied
(1989, US, 55 min)
d/p Marlon T Riggs. *sc* Reginald Jackson, Steve Langley, Alan Miller, Donald Woods, Joseph Bream, Craig Harris, Marlon Riggs, Essex Hemphill. *cast* Kerrigan Black, Blackberri, Bernard Brannier, Gerald Davis.
● A polemical, avowedly personal video documentary on the American black gay experience. It's a bit of an ordeal: a barrage of images, newsreel, stories narrated to camera, poetry readings, 'Vogue' dance performance, voices and rap, which examines, with savage but poetic candour, those questions of identity, culture, history and self-expression that are most pertinent to black gays and lesbians. Are they gay first, or black first? Why have they little or no voice in the American gay movement? Riggs takes great risks: he challenges and threatens to offend all sensibilities here, gay or straight, black or white, but does so with remarkable composure, humour and positive attitude. At heart, it's a celebratory film which buzzes with intelligence, unashamed emotion, adrenalin, and that strange tenderness forged in suffering. As a character says in the film: 'If in America a black is the lowest of the low, what is a gay black?' Riggs says to black gays: stand up, speak out, tell your story; to others: listen. WH

Toni
(1935, Fr, 95 min, b/w)
d Jean Renoir. *p* Pierre Gault. *sc* Jean Renoir, Carl Einstein. *ph* Claude Renoir. *ed* Marguerite Renoir, Suzanne de Troeye. *pd* Léon Bourelly, Marius Brouquier. *m* Paul Bozzi. *cast* Charles Blavette, Célia Montalvan, Jenny Hélia, Max Dalban, Edouard Delmont, Andrex.
● A melodrama about love and sex, jealousy and murder – the sort of staples that have kept the cinema going for ninety years or so – but Renoir invests it with a sense of character and place that gives it an unusually blunt and sensual impact. Neither romanticising his workers nor turning them into rallying-points, he accepts them as they are and follows them where they go. The plot is based on a real crime that occurred during the '20s in Martigues, a small town in the South of France where the film was shot. Jacques Mortier, an old friend of Renoir's who was the local police chief, assembled the facts, and Renoir wrote the script with another friend, art critic Carl Einstein. The results are both stark and gentle, as well as sexy: Toni sucking wasp poison from Josefa's lissome neck is a particularly fine moment. JR

Tonight Let's All Make Love in London
see Tonite Let's All Make Love in London

Tonight's the Night
see Happy Ever After

Tonite Let's All Make Love in London
(1968, GB, 70 min)
d/p/sc/ph/ed Peter Whitehead. *with* Mick Jagger, Andrew Loog Oldham, Julie Christie, Michael Caine, David Hockney, Edna O'Brien, Vanessa Redgrave, Lee Marvin, Eric Burdon and The Animals.
● Whitehead's focus-pulling, dolly-bird-at-Biba documentary on Swinging London scores low on technique but fields fascinating interviews with the trend-setters of the era – Jagger (thick), Oldham (crunching), Christie (shy), Caine and Hockney (funny). BC

Tontaine et Tonton
(1999, Fr, 55 min)
d Tonie Marshall. *ph* Gérard de Battista. *ed* Jacques Comets. *pd* Emmanuel de Chauvigny. *m* Vincent Malone. *cast* Patrick Pineau, Emmanuelle Devos, Eric Petitjean, Hélène Fillières.
● Two friends meet and bemoan the state of their sex lives, yet the very same day they pick up Justine, a beautiful, single, apparently available young woman. Trouble is she's besotted with François Mitterrand and is wont to interrupt lovemaking with long quotations from the Great Man. Marshall's droll filmette has only the one joke and probably loses in translation. TCh

Tony Rome
(1967, US, 110 min)
d Gordon Douglas. *p* Aaron Rosenberg. *sc* Richard L Breen. *ph* Joseph Biroc. *ed* Robert Simpson. *ad* Jack Martin Smith, James Roth. *m* Billy May. *cast* Frank Sinatra, Jill St John, Richard Conte, Gena Rowlands, Simon Oakland, Jeffrey Lynn, Lloyd Bochner, Joan Shawlee, Sue Lyon, Rocky Graziano.
● Rather slow-moving, but otherwise a witty and thoroughly enjoyable attempt to revive the cynical, corpse-laden, bafflingly plotted Chandler thrillers of the '40s. Here the quest for a diamond pin lost by a rich but unhappy girl (Lyon) leads through some exotic Miami locations and a fine assortment of blackmailers and sleazy undesirables, including a striptease dancer and her lesbian protectress, a venal doctor and his moronically muscle-bound son, a raffish dope peddler, and a drink-sodden mamma kept shut away in a derelict house. Most of them come to a bad end while Sinatra, standing in ably for Bogart as the tough private eye, times his deadpan cracks perfectly, takes his beatings like a man, and batters his way to some sort of solution. TM

Too Beautiful for You
see Trop belle pour toi!

Too Hot to Handle
(1938, US, 105 min, b/w)
d Jack Conway. *p* Lawrence Weingarten. *sc* Laurence Stallings, John Lee Mahin. *ph* Harold Rosson. *ed* Frank Sullivan. *ad* Cedric Gibbons. *m* Franz Waxman. *cast* Clark Gable, Myrna Loy, Walter Pidgeon, Walter Connolly, Leo Carrillo, Johnny Hines, Virginia Weidler.
● An action-packed drama, with news cameramen Gable and Pidgeon fighting for footage and the girl, a famous aviatrix, in locations as diverse as China and the Amazon jungle. Taken at face value, the picture seems dated and even objectionable, but there's a lively black comic edge to it that suggests appearances may be deceptive. The first sequence might have come from TV's *Drop the Dead Donkey*, with Gable unscrupulously shooting at Japanese planes to provoke an air raid on-camera. TCh

Too Hot to Handle
see Marrying Man, The

Too Late (Trop Tard)
(1996, Fr/Romania, 104 min)
d Lucian Pintilié. *p* Marin Karmitz. *sc* Rasvan Popescu, Lucian Pintilie. *ph* Calin Ghibu. *ed* Victorira Nae. *pd* Calin Papura. *cast* Razvan Vasilescu, Cécilia Barbora, Victor Rebengiuc, Dorel Visan.
● A distinct disappointment after Pintilié's earlier *An Unforgettable Summer*, this clumsy blend of conspiracy thriller, comedy and political allegory centres on a public prosecutor sent to investigate a series of suspicious deaths in a mining town in contemporary Romania. Inevitably, there seems to be a cover-up, mainly on the part of the mine's management, who fear political unrest among their employees; equally inevitably, Pintilié implies (heavy-handedly) that old Commie habits die hard. The film's various mismatched components are held together only by the thesis that no one, save the investigator, wants to reveal or know the truth, while the 'romance' that develops between the hero and a surveyor seems sexist, hopelessly dated, and somewhat gratuitous. In short, a mess. GA

Too Late Blues
(1961, US, 103 min, b/w)
d/p John Cassavetes. *sc* John Cassavetes, Richard Carr. *ph* Lionel Lindon. *ed* Frank Bracht. *ad* Tambi Larsen. *m* David Raksin. *cast* Bobby Darin, Stella Stevens, Everett Chambers, Rupert Crosse, Vince Edwards, Seymour Cassel.
● Though regarded almost universally (and that includes Cassavetes) as a failure, this attempt to recapture the spontaneous energy and 'realism' of his much-acclaimed, independently-made *Shadows* in a rather more plot-bound film for Paramount remains one of the more impressive Hollywood movies set in the hip, flip jazz world. Admittedly, Darin and Stevens (as an uncompromising pianist wary of selling out, and the neurotically scarred would-be singer he loves but cannot trust) seem uncomfortable with Cassavetes' semi-improvisational methods, and at times the emotional scab-picking threatens to bring what story there is to a halt. But the music, scored by David Raksin and played by the likes of Benny Carter, Red Mitchell and Shelley Manne, is mostly terrific, and the mood convincingly edgy in the scenes of conflict between Darin and the band he finally abandons for the more lucrative cocktail circuit. GA

Too Late the Hero
(1969, US, 144 min)
d/p Robert Aldrich. *sc* Robert Aldrich, Lukas Heller. *ph* Joseph Biroc. *ed* Michael Luciano. *ad* James D Vance. *m* Gerald Fried. *cast* Michael Caine, Cliff Robertson, Ian Bannen, Harry Andrews, Denholm Elliott, Ronald Fraser, Lance Percival, Ken Takakura, Henry Fonda.
● Aldrich tries the *Dirty Dozen* formula again. This time the setting is the Pacific sector in World War II, and the premise has a band of reluctant

heroes required to get from one end of a Jap-infested island to the other in order to transmit a decoy message (hopefully to distract attention from the US fleet). Along with some wry reflections on class and officer-like qualities, fairly predictable anti-war sentiments are aired by Caine and Robertson as the two main protagonists, rubbing national hostilities off each other and chiefly concerned with saving their own skins. The usual collection of cowards, bullies and wimps go along for the trip, but there are some excellent character sketches (Denholm Elliott and Ian Bannen, in particular), the action has its moments (with the patrol's paranoia fed by taunting messages from Japanese loudspeakers hidden in the jungle), and the bantering dialogue is often very funny. TM

Toolbox Murders, The

(1977, US, 95 min)
d Dennis Donnelly. *p* Tony DiDio. *sc* Neva Friedenn, Robert Easter, Ann Kindberg. *ph* Gary Graver. *ed* Nunzio Darpino. *pd* DJ Bruno. *m* George Deaton. *cast* Cameron Mitchell, Pamelyn Ferdin, Wesley Eure, Nicolas Beauvy, Tim Donnelly.

● The gory, censor-hacked murders (all of women) and the revelation of the nut's identity (he's gone on to kidnap a virgin as substitute for his dead daughter) are all out of the way inside half-an-hour, leaving a lot of dead time to establish this awful movie's single original gimmick: the novelty encounter of two psychos, who end up at each other's throats. Orson Welles' cameraman Gary Graver (*The Other Side of the Wind*) makes it all look better than it deserves. PT

Too Many Chefs

see Who Is Killing the Great Chefs of Europe?

Too Much Happiness

see Trop de Bonheur

Tootsie

(1982, US, 116 min)
d Sydney Pollack. *p* Sydney Pollack, Dick Richards. *sc* Larry Gelbart, Murray Schisgal. *ph* Owen Roizman. *ed* Fredric Steinkamp, William Steinkamp. *pd* Peter Larkin. *m* David Grusin. *cast* Dustin Hoffman, Jessica Lange, Teri Garr, Dabney Coleman, Charles Durning, Bill Murray, Sydney Pollack, George Gaynes.

● Hoffman plays an actor, quite as temperamental and impossible as Hoffman himself evidently is in real life, who pretends to be a woman just to get a part in a daytime TV soap opera. Numerous writers came and went in production conditions that were apparently agonising, but for once little of this is apparent on the screen. The tone is quick-witted and appealing, with some of the smartest dialogue this side of Billy Wilder, and a wonderfully sure-footed performance from Jessica Lange (as her/his girlfriend). But the film never comes within a thousand miles of confronting its own implications: Hoffman's female impersonation is strictly on the level of Dame Edna Everage, and the script's assumption that 'she' would wow female audiences is at best ridiculous, at worst crassly insulting to women. Provided you ignore this central idiocy, *Tootsie* is certainly one of the most polished situation comedies in recent years. But then the field has hardly been over-crowded. DP

To Our Loves (A Nos Amours)

(1983, Fr, 102 min)
d Maurice Pialat. *p* Micheline Pialat. *sc* Arlette Langmann, Maurice Pialat. *ph* Jacques Loiseleux. *ed* Yann Dedet. *ad* Jean-Paul Camail, Arlette Langmann. *cast* Sandrine Bonnaire, Dominique Besnehard, Maurice Pialat, Evelyne Ker, Anne-Sophie Maillé, Christophe Odent, Cyr Boitard.

● 15-year-old Suzanne (Bonnaire) seems unable to progress beyond a rather doleful promiscuity in her relations with boys. Alone of her family, her father (played by Pialat himself) understands her, but when he leaves home for another woman, family life erupts into a round of appalling, casual violence, until Suzanne escapes into a fast marriage, and finally to America. Pialat's methods of close, intimate filming may place him close in many ways to our own Ken Loach, but his interests are rooted in a very cinematic approach to personal inner life, rather than any schematic political theory. The message may be that happiness is as rare as a sunny day, and sorrow is forever, but a counterbalancing warmth is provided by Pialat's enormous care for his creations. The rapport between father and daughter is especially moving. Pialat once acted in a Chabrol film, and one French critic's verdict on his performance can stand equally well for this film: 'Massive, abrupt, and incredibly gentle'. CPea

Too White for Me

(1992, GB, 81 min)
d/p Nick Broomfield. *ph* Barry Ackroyd. *ed* Richard Vick, Michael McCrea. *songs* Sello 'Chicco' Twala. *with* Sello 'Chicco' Twala, Nick Broomfield, Winnie Mandela.

● S Africa, just before the end of apartheid. Sello 'Chicco' Twala is a black pop star/promoter, a millionaire who can't vote. His planned Tracy Chapman concert is falling through and he's quarrelling with his white partner over differences in black and white singers' fees. He shuttles between several sets of wives and children, while arranging for the funeral of his brother, shot by 'gangsters'. (Chicco himself always goes armed.) Plus, he's got Nick Broomfield, festooned with recording devices, on his case. The result feels like only half a film, all loose ends and enigmas, with Chicco coming over as a mix of the sinister and the sympathetic: a snapshot of a complicated man living a strange life in troubled times. BBa

Too Young (Ye Maque)

(1997, Tai, 40 min)
d Huang Min-Chen. *p* Huang Min-Chen, Zheng Zewen, Zeng Wenzhen. *sc* Yang Yazhe, Huang Min-Chen. *ph* Zhang Zhiyuan. *ed* Lei Zhenqing. *m* Jemmy Chen, Nat 'King' Cole. *cast* Jia Xiaoguo, Mo Ziyi, Priest Qingshun, Lin Zhensheng, Yang Weiling.

● Huang's prize-winning debut deals with the stresses of adolescence: sexual stirrings, mental doubts, physical insecurities and the fear of death. A quiet schoolboy in the middle of the transition from dumbbells to New Age meditation tapes goes out of his way to befriend the new boy in class: a strong, pensive guy rumoured to have attempted suicide at his previous school. The nearest they ever get to making love is taking a nude swim together during a school air-raid drill, but they do penetrate each other's shells. Huang compares their hesitations with the absolute faith of a Buddhist monk, as if to suggest that they, too, are on a spiritual path. Thanks to remarkably believable performances from both boys, it has the aura of a small classic. TR

Too Young to Die (Jukeodo Jo A)

(2002, SKor, 67 min)
d Park Jin-Pyo. *p* Kim Hong-Baek. *sc* Lee Soo-Mee. *ph* Jung Yong-Woo. *ed* Moon In-Dae. *m* Park Ki-Heon. *cast* Park Chi-Gyu, Lee Sun-Ye.

● A simple (but not simple-minded) docu-drama, in which a real-life couple re-enact their first meeting, their current lives together and the high and low points of their relationship. What makes this interesting is that both of them are elderly – and that the film includes their splendidly vigorous sex-life. Park Chi-Gyu, 73, has lived on a state pension and odd jobs since he was invalided out of the Korean War 50 years ago. Lee Sun-Ye, 72, is a prize-winning folk singer and drummer. They met at a centre for the elderly in Seoul early in 2001 and began living together soon after. Park Jin-Pyo deliberately avoids going into their personal histories and backgrounds (both have outlived their spouses and both have adult children), the better to focus on their intense commitment to each other, their fears of being apart and their remarkably youthful love-making. TR

Topaz

see Tokyo Decadence

Topaz

(1969, US, 125 min)
d/p Alfred Hitchcock. *sc* Samuel A Taylor. *ph* Jack Hildyard. *ed* William Ziegler. *pd* Henry Bumstead. *m* Maurice Jarre. *cast* Frederick Stafford, Dany Robin, John Vernon, Karin Dor, Michel Piccoli, Philippe Noiret, John Forsythe, Roscoe Lee Browne, Claude Jade, Michel Subor.

● Despite the odd critical effort to salvage the film's reputation, it has to be said that Hitchcock's lumbering adaptation of Leon Uris' novel, about international espionage at the time of the Cuban missile crisis, has not aged well. The near-incomprehensible plot (something about French and American agents trying to find out more about a Russian undercover group, directly involved with Cuba and working within the French security network) might appeal to devotees of Le Carré et al, but it certainly doesn't make for dramatically exciting cinema, especially given Hitchcock's flat, seemingly uninterested direction. The bland performances don't help much, either. GA

Topaze

(1950, Fr, 141 min, b/w)
d/p/sc Marcel Pagnol. *ph* Philippe Agostini. *ed* Monique Lacombe. *ad* Hugues Laurent, Robert Giordani. *m* Raymond Legrand. *cast* Fernandel, Hélène Perdrière, Pierre Larquey, Jacques Morel, Jacqueline Pagnol.

● This was Pagnol's second go at putting on the screen his 1928 stage hit. Schoolmaster Topaze clings to his sense of right and wrong, despite being exploited at work and then tricked into becoming the front for a crooked businessman. Finally seeing himself as others do – a dupe and a dope – he changes character, seizes control and takes revenge on bullies past and present. Besides Pagnol's own adaptations, there are at least five other films of *Topaze*; this is the definitive text, of interest to students but way too long for ordinary purposes. However, stars love to play him, audiences enjoy watching him, so it's unlikely, even now, that we've seen the last of old Topaze. BBa

Top Dog (Wodzirej)

(1978, Pol, 115 min)
d/sc Feliks Falk. *cast* Jerzy Stuhr, Slawa Kwasniewska, Wiktor Sadecki, Michael Tarkowski.

● This enshrines a brilliantly loathsome characterisation by Stuhr as the provincial entertainer driven by the sweet smell of success as he wheels and deals to achieve his pathetic goal of becoming MC for a gala inaugurating a new hotel. The political parable is neat enough as his power plays are scrutinised in vivid detail, but also pretty facile. Satires digging at the state through representations in microcosm became a dime a dozen in Eastern European films around this time. TM

Top Gun

(1986, US, 110 min)
d Tony Scott. *p* Don Simpson, Jerry Bruckheimer. *sc* Jim Cash, Jack Epps Jr. *ph* Jeffrey Kimball. *ed* Billy Weber, Chris Lebenzon. *pd* John F DeCuir Jr. *m* Harold Faltermeyer. *cast* Tom Cruise, Kelly McGillis, Val Kilmer, Anthony Edwards, Tom Skerritt, Michael Ironside, Rick Rossovich.

● The story is risible, the direction routine, the underlying ethic highly questionable; but the flying stirs the blood like speed. This concerns the exploits of one 'Maverick' (Cruise), who aspires to be top gun at the Top Gun, the US Navy Fighter Weapons School at San Diego. In what looks suspiciously like a retread of the *An Officer and a Gentleman* storyline, Maverick, an arrogant piece of Officer Material, climbs the ladder of fly-boy success, falls in love with his aeronautics instructor (an unlikely McGillis), and has his best friend and navigator (Edwards) fall off the ladder and into a concrete cloud. However, the traditional mainstays of love and death are here supplemented by lengthy and highly realistic dog-fight sequences, in which the pupils and instructors tail-chase each other all over the desert sky, and then do it for real with an unnamed enemy over the Indian Ocean. A great ride to hell and back; kick the tyres, light the fires, and you're away. CPea

Top Hat

(1935, US, 101 min, b/w)
d Mark Sandrich. *p* Pandro S Berman. *sc* Dwight Taylor, Allan Scott. *ph* David Abel. *ed* William Hamilton. *ad* Van Nest Polglase, Carroll Clark. *songs* Irving Berlin. *cast* Fred Astaire, Ginger Rogers, Edward Everett Horton, Helen Broderick, Erik Rhodes, Eric Blore.

● The third Astaire-Rogers movie (not counting *Flying Down to Rio*) and one of the best, with a superlative Irving Berlin score (it includes 'No Strings', 'Isn't This a Lovely Day?', 'Top Hat, White Tie and Tails' and 'Cheek to Cheek'), and equally superlative Hermes Pan routines which spark a distinct sexual electricity between the pair. Oddly enough, the film is almost slavishly patterned on *The Gay Divorcee*, with the scene again shifting from London to a resort (Venice in this case), the plot again turning on mistaken identity, and the comedy again reliant on Horton, Blore and Rhodes. The reason you don't really notice this – with *Top Hat* readily springing to mind as the archetypal Fred'n'Ginger movie – is the booster given by Van Nest Polglase's stunning white Art Deco designs, which were to set the tone for the series. TM

Topkapi

(1964, US, 120 min)
d/p Jules Dassin. *sc* Monja Danischewsky. *ph* Henri Alekan. *ed* Roger Dwyre. *ad* Max Douy. *m* Manos Hadjidakis. *cast* Melina Mercouri, Peter Ustinov, Maximilian Schell, Robert Morley, Akim Tamiroff, Gilles Segal, Jess Hahn.

● An attempt by Dassin to top his own hit *Rififi*: a glossy international heist movie, using a hammy multi-cultural cast and a screenplay by ex-Ealing stalwart Monja Danischewsky (based on Eric Ambler's novel *The Light of Day*) to chart a hit on an Istanbul museum. As a caper, its convolutions of comedy and suspense are par for the course, and at least it's free of the pretensions that usually scuttle Dassin's efforts in Europe (especially in tandem with his wife Mercouri); but it's a far cry from his classic American thrillers or his brilliant British *noir*, *Night and the City*. PT

Topless Women Talk About Their Lives

(1997, NZ, 89 min)
d Harry Sinclair. *p* Fiona Copland, Harry Sinclair. *sc* Harry Sinclair. *ph* Dale McCready. *ed* David Coulson. *cast* Danielle Cormack, Joel Tobeck, Ian Hughes, Willa O'Neill, Andrew Binns, Shimpal Lelisi.

● This low budget first feature is somewhat in the vein of Emma-Kate Croghan's *Love and Other Catastrophes* (catchy title, freewheeling tone, and the romantic entanglements of a circle of pre-professional 20-year-olds). The title's a bit of a cheat: it's the name of the film-within-the-film, whose director proceeds to a nervous breadown after discovering his friends think the film's crap. Meanwhile, currently between boyfriends, Liz (Cormack) is pregnant after missing an abortion appointment. While the characters are more credibly real and messy than Croghan's cute packages, most of them lose out to the writer/director's rambling storytelling. Cormack, however, just about holds the picture together; and Sinclair does throw in a handful of memorably eccentric scenes – like have you ever seen a rabbit swimming lengths. NB

Topo, El (The Mole)

(1971, Mex, 124 min)
d Alexandro Jodorowsky. *p* Roberto Viskin. *sc* Alejandro Jodorowsky. *ph* Rafael Corkidi. *ed* Lilia Lupercio. *ad/m* Alejandro Jodorowsky. *cast* Alexandro Jodorowsky, Brontis Jodorowsky, Mara Lorenzio, David Silva, Paula Romo.

● A religious allegory in the framework of a Western, lavish, violent, and wildly eclectic, including Fellini and farce among its influences, with the first half following a leather-clad gunman (Jodorowsky) through a desert scattered with biblical references in a highly ritualised search for fulfilment through feats of physical prowess. Death, rebirth and the New Testament follow his failure, with Jodorowsky now cropped and clownish, playing Servant of Man to a bunch of cripples and freaks, while the film opens out into an indictment of Western society. For all the film's aspirations, the juxtapositions made often appear obvious, lacking the repercussions of true surrealism, while the symbolism is so oblique that it never rises above its own security. With style constantly contradicting content, and the prevailing mood redolent of egotism and misogyny, it leaves one the feeling of having waded through a full-blown fantasy where even the self-degradation emerges as just another form of narcissism. CPe

Top of the World

(1955, US, 90 min, b/w)
d Lewis R Foster. *p* Michael Baird, Lewis R Foster. *sc* John D Klorer, N Richard Nash. *ph* Harry J Wild. *ed* Robert Ford. *ad* Wiard Ihnen. *m* Albert Glasser. *cast* Dale Robertson, Evelyn Keyes, Frank Lovejoy, Nancy Gates, Paul Fix.

● The off-the-mark geography of the title is symptomatic of a military love story too tepid to melt the Alaskan snow: a routine set of meaningful glances between grounded USAF Major Robertson, his ex-wife (Keyes) and her latest ranking inamorato (Lovejoy). The unambitious Foster had just turned freelance after an eleven-film stint with Paramount's B units, only to follow his Reagan/Fleming/Payne vehicles with more of the same. PT

Topper

(1937, US, 97 min, b/w)
d Norman Z McLeod. *p* Hal Roach. *sc* Jack Jevne, Eric Hatch, Eddie Moran. *ph* Norbert Brodine. *ed* William Terhune. *ad* Arthur I Royce. *m* Hoagy Carmichael. *cast* Constance Bennett, Cary Grant, Roland Young, Billie Burke, Alan Mowbray, Eugene Pallette, Hedda Hopper.

● Thorne Smith's novel about a dull banker (Young) haunted by dashing ghosts (Bennett and Grant) proved popular enough as a film to spawn two sequels and a TV series. Now it seems an archetypal piece of cinematic fluff from the '30s – too gentle and leisurely to survive as a solid classic, though there's pleasure to be found in the cast's graceful way with comedy and their smooth ensemble playing. GB

Top Secret!

(1984, US, 90 min)
d Jim Abrahams, David Zucker, Jerry Zucker. *p* Jon Davison, Hunt Lowry. *sc* Jim Abrahams, David Zucker, Jerry Zucker, Martyn Burke. *ph* Christopher Challis. *ed* Bernard Gribble. *pd* Peter Lamont. *m* Maurice Jarre. *cast* Val Kilmer, Lucy Gutteridge, Peter Cushing, Christopher Villiers, Jeremy Kemp, Warren Clarke, Michael Gough, Omar Sharif.

● Having spoofed one genre with considerable success, the *Airplane* team cast their net wider to send up a host of venerable movie chestnuts. Set in a peculiar national and temporal limbo, it has US teen rock idol Nick Rivers (Kilmer) travelling to Nazified East Germany to entertain culturally deprived Iron Curtain bobby-soxers. The gags come thick, fast and arbitrary – surfing gags, Pacman gags, Steve McQueen *Great Escape* gags – all aimed at the belly or lower, with a variable strike rate. The first half chugs along quite happily, but whereas in *Airplane* the jokes could simply be strung on a hand-me-down storyline, here the demands of the plot start to play havoc with the levity. Signs of desperation have begun to creep in some time before the end. JP

Topsy-Turvy

(1999, GB/US, 160 min)
d Mike Leigh. *p* Simon Channing-Williams. *sc* Mike Leigh. *ph* Dick Pope. *ed* Robin Sales. *pd* Eve Stewart. *m* Carl Davis. *cast* Jim Broadbent, Allan Corduner, Timothy Spall, Lesley Manville, Ron Cook, Wendy Nottingham, Kevin McKidd, Shirley Henderson, Dorothy Atkinson, Martin Savage, Eleanor David, Alison Steadman, Dexter Fletcher, Katrin Cartlidge.

● 1884: the most successful partnership on the English stage is in trouble. An unkind review of *Princess Ida* has dubbed librettist WS Gilbert (Broadbent) 'the king of Topsy-Turvydom', while composer Sir Arthur Sullivan (Corduner) has decided to devote himself to more serious classical pieces rather than fulfil his contract with impresario D'Oyly Carte (Cook). The stalemate is broken when Gilbert visits an exhibition of Japanese arts and crafts, finds inspiration to pen *The Mikado*, engaging Sullivan's creativity once more. Leigh's first foray into period costume seems a radical departure from his usual provocative contemporary style, but, rustling frocks and painstaking enunciation aside, the concerns are familiar: tensions between inner lives and public faces, between men and women, work and pleasure. Over 159 minutes, we become immersed in these pressurised lives, sensing the satisfactions of the footlights and the emotional price paid by damaged individuals. As the fascinating rehearsals gather pace, *The Mikado* stumbles into life before our eyes, and Truffaut's *Day for Night* comes to mind. That said, Leigh's cast are beyond compare, and the whole bighearted, splendidly droll celebration of the entertainer's lot surely stands among British cinema's one-of-a-kind treasures. TJ

Tora no O o Fumu Otokotachi (The Men Who Tread on the Tiger's Tail/Walkers on the Tiger's Tail)

(1945, Jap, 58 min, b/w)
d Akira Kurosawa. *p* Motohiko Ito. *sc* Akira Kurosawa. *ph* Takeo Ito. *ed* Toshio Goto. *ad* Kazuo Kubo. *m* Tadashi Hattori. *cast* Denjiro Okochi, Susumu Fujita, Masayuki Mori, Takashi Shimura, Aritake Kono.

● Very early Kurosawa (although it wasn't released in Japan until 1952 because of the US censor's sensitivity about 'feudal' subjects) and in no sense a major work. Based on a traditional story that exists in both Noh and Kabuki stage versions, and Kurosawa makes use of elements from both. A young nobleman has to cross a checkpoint in his flight from a vengeful brother, and impersonates a porter to do so; one of his juniors has to beat him to make the deception more convincing, but thereby violates one of the prime tenets of the feudal code… Kurosawa's chief contribution to the project was to add a second, comic porter to the plot. TR

Tora! Tora! Tora!

(1970, US/Jap, 144 min)
d Richard Fleischer. *p* Elmo Williams. *sc* Larry Forrester, Hideo Oguni, Ryuzo Kikushima. *ph* Charles F Wheeler. *ed* James E Newcom, Pembroke J Herring, Inoue Chikaya. *ad* Jack Martin Smith, Yoshiro Muraki, Richard Day, Taizoh Kawashima. *m* Jerry Goldsmith. *cast* Martin Balsam, Soh Yamamura, Jason Robards, Joseph Cotten, Tatsuya Mihashi, EG Marshall, James Whitmore, Neville Brand, George Macready.

● A prototype disaster movie, reconstructing the attack on Pearl Harbor, which cost somewhere in the region of 25 million dollars, making it one of the most expensive American films to date. A distinguished cast gets a bit lost in the welter of special effects; and with the sequences giving the Japanese viewpoint directed by Japanese film-makers (Toshio Masuda and Kinji Fukasaku), there's something of a soft shoe shuffle to avoid treading on national sensibilities. But the climax, in particular, manages to be more than just a shoot-out, with Fleischer's intelligent direction generating a real feeling of chaos and apocalypse. DP

Torchlight

(1984, US, 90 min)
d Tom Wright. *p* Joel Douglas, Michael Schroeder. *sc* Pamela Sue Martin, Eliza Moorman. *ph* Alex Phillips. *ad* Craig Stearns. *m* Michael Cannon. *cast* Pamela Sue Martin, Steve Railsback, Ian McShane, Al Corley, Rita Taggart.

● Horrendously inept romance-cum-problem pic, with Ms Martin – reputed to be rampantly anti-drugs – falling for a loutish construction engineer (Railsback, who once played Charlie Manson) in the first five minutes, and then, in between dabbling in a little bit of painting, watching in horror as hubby gets hooked on assorted evil substances. The root of all evil is McShane, a hammy hustler who signals his debauched ways by wearing dressing-gowns, sporting a tacky tan, and grinning a lot. Ultra-conservative in tone, directed with little care for continuity or conviction, it might just send you into hysterics with its unintentional hilarity; or it could easily turn you into a valium addict. GA

Torch Song

(1953, US, 90 min)
d Charles Walters. *p* Sidney Franklin Jr, Henry Berman. *sc* John Michael Hayes, Jan Lustig. *ph* Robert Planck. *ed* Albert Akst. *ad* Cedric Gibbons, Preston Ames. *m* Adolph Deutsch. *cast* Joan Crawford, Michael Wilding, Marjorie Rambeau, Gig Young, Henry Morgan, Dorothy Patrick.

● All-singing, all-dancing Joan is a Broadway musical star whose tantrums cause her accompanist to walk out, only to be replaced by blind pianist Wilding, whose criticism of her professional standards tempers her growing romantic attachment to him. All's resolved, however, in a plot development of such gob-smacking trashiness that it needs Crawford at full tilt to put it over. With MGM welcoming the star back with full honours after a 10-year absence, this toweringly nutty melodrama should prove irresistible to fans of the bigger-than-life star. TJ

Torch Song Trilogy

(1988, US, 119 min)
d Paul Bogart. *p* Howard Gottfried. *sc* Harvey Fierstein. *ph* Mikael Salomon. *ed* Nicholas C Smith. *pd* Richard Hoover. *m* Peter Matz. *cast* Harvey Fierstein, Anne Bancroft, Matthew Broderick, Brian Kerwin, Karen Young, Eddie Castrodad, Ken Page.

●It's New York in 1971. Virginia Hamm wants a child, but the odds are stacked against her. She's single, given to emotionally masochistic relationships with immature men…and she's a Jewish professional female impersonator named Arnold Beckoff. But forget the drag, this is not another *La Cage aux Folles*; it's a straightforward, very funny love story which glows with fulfilment and promise. Beckoff (Fierstein) picks up Ed, a bi who's not happy about being so (Kerwin), and they embark on some sort of affair. It falls apart. Alan (Broderick), the big romantic interest, pursues the reluctant and disbelieving dragster, they set up home, they fight, they come through it and get ready to adopt. The second half of the movie – featuring a marvellous performance from Bancroft as Arnold's Ma, the epitome of Jewish Mommishness – is a rollercoaster of politics, parenthood (Arnold's and Ma's), death, independence, reconciliation, and more romance. It's a solid, old-fashioned, soppy movie – Arnold has been described as 'Doris Day with a dick' – and a great retro-romance. TC

Torment

see Enfer, L'

Torment

see Hets

Torn Between Two Lovers

(1979, US, 100 min)
d Delbert Mann. *p* Linda Otto, Joan Barnett. *sc* Doris Silverton. *ph* Ronald M Lautore. *ed* Gene Milford, Lloyd Nelson. *ad* David Jaquest. *m* Ian Fraser. *cast* Lee Remick, Joseph Bologna, George Peppard, Giorgio Tozzi, Murphy Cross, Jess Osuna.

●We must have done something awful bad to deserve first the song and now the film. Wherever possible, stereotypes are substituted for three-dimensional characters, and clichés for dialogue. It's the story of a middle-aged woman married to an Italian-American family (a macho 'all I gave up when I got married was my motor-bike' husband, a father-in-law who gives out pieces of advice as if they were sweeties, and a mother-in-law who makes you feel guilty by cooking). She falls in love with an architect who has only caviar and yoghurt in his fridge. The blossoming of their illicit love (indicated by blazing log fires being superimposed when they kiss) and her inability to choose between her lovers threatens to destroy her marriage. Made for TV, the film's elevation to the big screen only heightens its inadequacies. It's not that it's bad, merely insipid, like a Martini on the rocks. FD

Torn Curtain

(1966, US, 128 min)
d/p Alfred Hitchcock. *sc* Brian Moore. *ph* John F Warren. *ed* Bud Hoffman. *pd* Hein Heckroth. *m* John Addison. *cast* Paul Newman, Julie Andrews, Lila Kedrova, Hansjürg Felmy, Tamara Toumanova, Wolfgang Kieling, Ludwig Donath.

●Spy thriller in which Newman's defecting scientist is followed to East Berlin by his troubled fiancée/assistant (Andrews), unaware that he is playing a double agent game. Hitchcock, seemingly too dour or too uninterested to turn in the title's promise of a Cold War ripping yarn, settles instead for a dissection of the limits of domestic trust, as Andrews' doubts about Newman's fidelity (to her, to the American Way) hinder his undercover mission in pursuit of an Eastern bloc MacGuffin. An above-average quota of glaringly shaky process work; but at least one classic sequence of protracted violence in a farmhouse kitchen. PT

Torpedo Run

(1958, US, 98 min)
d Joseph Pevney. *p* Edmund Grainger. *sc* Richard Sale, William Wister Haines. *ph* George Folsey. *ed* Gene Ruggiero. *ad* William A Horning, Malcolm Brown. *cast* Glenn Ford, Ernest Borgnine, Diane Brewster, Dean Jones.

●Submarine commander Glenn Ford pursues the ship that led the attack on Pearl Harbor back to Tokyo, where he plans to sink the bastard. But there's a freighter in the way, and gee whiz, on board are his wife and children, who are prisoners of the Japs and whom we have grown to love in flashbacks. To hell with it, he thinks, his country comes first, and he blows the freighter out of the water. That's heroism for you. ATu

Torre de los Siete Jorobados, La

see Tower of the Seven Hunchbacks, The

Torrente, the Dumb Arm of the Law (Torrente, el brazo tonto de la ley)

(1997, Sp, 97 min)
d Santiago Segura. *p* Andrès Vicente Gómez. *sc* Santiago Segura. *ph* Carles Gusi. *ed* Fidel Collados. *pd* Arri, Biaffra and Los Zombis de Sahuayo. *m* Roque Baños. *cast* Santiago Segura, Javier Camara, Neus Arseni, Tony Leblanc, Chus Lampreave.

●It may have been a huge hit in Spain, but this black parodic comedy about an irredeemably sexist, racist, braggart, ex-cop slob and his 'investigations', made with a gullible neighbour, into the behind-the-scenes criminal operations of a Chinese restaurant is dismally broad, obvious, crude and visually ugly. Its anti-PC outrageousness notwithstanding, you can still see it heading for an upbeat sentimental ending; worse, because Segura's protagonist finally turns out to be some kind of hero, there no discernible distance between the character's odious attitudes and those of the film. Crass. GA

Torrents of Spring (Acque di primavera)

(1989, It/Fr, 101 min)
d Jerzy Skolimowski. *p* Angelo Rizzoli. *sc* Jerzy Skolimowski, Arcangelo Bonaccorso. *ph* Dante Spinotti, Witold Sobocinski. *ed* Cesare D'Amico. *pd* Francesco Bronzi. *m* Stanley Myers. *cast* Timothy Hutton, Nastassja Kinski, Valeria Golino, William Forsythe, Urbano Barberini, Christopher Janczar, Jerzy Skolimowski

●Russian landowner (Hutton) falls in love with German shopkeeper's daughter (Golino), is seduced by formidable aristocrat (Kinski), and loses both of them. So much for story. Even so, motives and desires remain confusingly ambiguous in Skolimowski's lightweight adaptation of Turgenev's novel. This aspires to be a prestigious international production, which means the ill-assembled cast speak in thick, dubbed accents, the photography is ravishing, the sun is always setting, and even the peasant extras are beautifully turned out. If chocolate boxes could move, this is how they'd look. Odd touches of bizarre humour apart, nothing spells the signature of the director of *The Shout* and *Moonlighting*, and when the man himself appears at the bewilderingly abrupt finale, ascribing to Hutton 'a life empty of all meaning', one wonders if that wasn't the problem all along. TCh

Torrid Zone

(1940, US, 88 min, b/w)
d William Keighley. *p* Mark Hellinger. *sc* Richard Macaulay, Jerry Wald. *ph* James Wong Howe. *ed* Jack Killifer. *ad* Ted Smith. *m* Adoph Deutsch. *cast* James Cagney, Pat O'Brien, Ann Sheridan, Andy Devine, Helen Vinson, Jerome Cowan, George Tobias.

●Rip-roaring Warners melodrama set in a South American banana plantation but with the same larger-than-life performances and coruscating dialogue found in the studio's best gangster movies. Cagney is the plantation foreman. He's sick of the job and wants to up sticks and head home to the States. But wily owner Pat O'Brien is determined to keep him where he is. Nightclub singer Ann Sheridan ('The Oomph Girl') is an added distraction. GM

Torso Murder Mystery, The

see Traitor Spy

Tortue sur le Dos, La

see Turtle on Its Back

Torture Garden

(1967, GB, 93 min)
d Freddie Francis. *p* Max J Rosenberg, Milton Subotsky. *sc* Robert Bloch. *ph* Norman Warwick. *ed* Peter Elliott. *ad* Don Mingaye, Scott Slimon. *m* Don Banks, James Bernard. *cast* Jack Palance, Burgess Meredith, Beverly Adams, Michael Bryant, John Standing, Peter Cushing, Maurice Denham, Robert Hutton.

●The second Amicus horror omnibus and one of the best, with a clever framing device involving Burgess Meredith as a Mephistophelean fairground charlatan who offers clients grisly glimpses of the future, in four Robert Bloch stories which get progressively better until the splendid climax of *The Man Who Collected Poe*. Terrific performances from Palance as the manic Poe collector who achieves apotheosis by turning himself into a character straight out of one of Poe's more apocalyptic stories, and from Standing as a concert pianist saddled with a murderously possessive grand piano. TM

Tosca

(2001, Fr/GB/Ger/It, 125 min)
d Benoît Jacquot. *p* Daniel Toscan du Plantier. *sc* Benoît Jacquot. *ph* Romain Winding. *ed* Luc Barnier. *ad* Sylvain Chauvelot. *m* Puccini. *cast* Angela Gheorghiu, Roberto Alagna, Ruggero Raimondi, David Cangelosi, Sorin Coliban, Enrico Fissore, Maurizio Muraro, Gwynne Howell.

●Opera singers aren't necessarily the greatest actors, and don't look their best straining for high notes in revealing close-up. Jacquot's version of the Puccini warhorse riskily pretends this isn't an issue; he gambles that we'll be won over by the emotional and physical commitment of the big name, real life couple Angela Gheorghiu and Roberto Alagna. Besides, since the plot is the hoariest melodrama (actress tries to save painter boyfriend by seducing the police chief about to have him executed), we'll hardly be expecting subtlety of characterisation, right? Regrettably, the gamble doesn't quite come off. There's some fine singing from tenor Alagna and soprano Gheorghiu, but the silent movie mugging does no one any favours. That said, the piece itself is to some degree indestructible, and first-timers may still find themselves swept along by wave upon wave of Puccini's glorious melody. TJ

To Sir, With Love

(1966, GB, 105 min)
d/p/sc James Clavell. *ph* Paul Beeson. *ed* Peter Thornton. *ad* Tony Woollard. *m* Ron Grainer. *cast* Sidney Poitier, Christian Roberts, Judy Geeson, Suzy Kendall, Lulu, Faith Brook, Geoffrey Bayldon.

●A British *Blackboard Jungle* that bears no resemblance to school life as we know it. The kids try hard, but apart from Lulu (an impressive feature debut) are very unconvincing, and the hoodlums' miraculous reformation a week before the end of term (thanks to teacher Sidney Poitier) is laughable. Incessant Cockney street market vignettes and shots of London buses seem to suggest that it was all primarily intended for American consumption anyway. DP

To Sleep, So As to Dream

(1986, Jap, 81 min, b/w)
d Kaizo Hayashi. *p* Kaizo Hayashi, Takashige Ichise. *sc* Kaizo Hayashi. *cast* Kamura Moe, Sano Shiro, Otake Koji, Oizumi Akira.

●A red herring-strewn mystery, shot in black-and-white and *almost* silent, Hayashi's debut is something like a Japanese *Tintin* adventure made by Alain Resnais. It concerns a silent swashbuckler film that combusts before its finale, a trio of magicians, and the venerable Madame Cherry-Blossom, whose daughter has been abducted by the shady consortium 'M Pathé and Co'. *To Sleep, So As to Dream* prospects the borders between film and reality, dream and wakefulness, but it's also a larky pastiche of the '20s sleuth genre, with detective heroes Uotsuka (Shiro) and Kobayashi (Koji) as intrepid stout-hearts in the Sexton Blake and Tinker tradition. Hayashi lays on surreal humour with flair, but the movie is above all a disquisition on film conventions, Japanese and Western, antique and modern. Most audaciously, Hayashi punctures the silence with ringing phones and the spoken interventions of a *benshi*, the traditional commentator of silent cinema. Although it doesn't quite approach the magic of *Circus Boys*, it's a wonderfully inventive, genuinely eerie narrative experiment. JRo

To Sleep with Anger

(1990, US, 102 min)
d Charles Burnett. *p* Caldecot Chubb, Darin Scott, Thomas S Byrnes. *sc* Charles Burnett. *ph* Walt Lloyd. *ed* Nancy Richardson. *pd* Penny Barrett. *m* Stephen James Taylor. *cast* Danny Glover, Paul Butler, Mary Alice, Carl Lumbly, Vonetta McGee, Richard Brooks, Sheryl Lee Ralph.

●Burnett's ambitious blend of folklore and family feuding opens startlingly: Gideon, an elderly black paterfamilias, sits unflinching as a conflagration slowly engulfs first his feet, then his body, to the soulful gospel strains of 'Precious Memories'. The scene, at once baffling, poignant and absurd, is a fine indication of the hybrid vision that follows. Emerging from his hallucination to a waking nightmare, Gideon (Butler) finds his family threatened with destruction. Catalysing the domestic turmoil is Harry Mention (Glover), a brooding, malevolent charmer whose mystique stems from a professed allegiance to the ancient forces of darkness, and whose arrival sows dissent between Gideon's sons, threatening his patriarchal role and even, perhaps, his life. Poised between mystical fantasy and humdrum melodrama, the film muses on the complex relationship between present and past, while remaining firmly grounded in a linear (yet ghostly) narrative. Despite uncertain pacing, Burnett's evocation of a thriving cultural milieu that embraces both superstition and mysterious wisdom is almost flawless. Laughs, too, are frequent and full-blooded. For those who fall under the film's spell, the rewards are magical. MK

To Speak the Unspeakable: The Message of Elie Wiesel (Mondani a mondhatatlant: Elie Wiesel uzenete)

(1996, Hun/Fr, 105 min, b/w & col)
d Judit Elek. *p* Sándor Simo. *sc* Judit Elek. *ph* Gábor Balog. *ed* Judit Elek. *m* László Melis. *with* Elie Wiesel.

●Framed between Wiesel's address at the American Holocaust Museum and his acceptance of the Nobel Peace Prize in 1986, this assembly of archive material recalls what appears to have been the lost pre-war paradise of schtetl, family and shul in the Carpathians. The b/w footage has the beauty of Roman Vishniac's work, and William Hurt's unassertive narration is deceptively powerful: 'If I explain, it's not so you'll understand, it's so you'll never understand.' Wiesel's journey back to find his roots is blocked by the discovery that there are no Jews in his part of Romania any more, and their houses have gone, giving rise to an urge to warn the world that there are people hungry for blood. 'We were naive. We didn't expect that our neighbours were mad dogs.' He revisits Auschwitz and Buchenwald where he lost his family – 'If we are separated, we'll meet back at the house after the war,' were his mother's parting words – and views again the 'unspeakable' set against the roar of the furnaces. BC

Total Balalaika Show

(1994, Fin, 55 min)
d/p Aki Kaurismäki. *ph* Heikki Ortand. *ed* Timo Linnasalo. *with* The Leningrad Cowboys Band, The Alexandrov Red Army Chorus and Dance Ensemble.

●From 'Finlandia' through 'Volga Boatman' to 'Knockin' on Heaven's Door' and 'Those Were the Days', this is a delightful record of a huge Helsinki concert bringing together the Leningrad Cowboys, the band that used to pride itself on being the worst in the world (they've improved no end) and the massed voices of the Red Army Chorus. The combination of outrageously long quiffs and winkle-pickers, with medals strewn across middle-aged military chests makes for a pleasing absurdity, especially when the Cowboys start Cossack dancing to 'Kalinka' – and it's clear that all but a few of the soldiers were having a ball too. Highlight: a magical version of the Turtles' 'Happy Together'. One helluva noise, and you won't stop smiling. GA

Total Eclipse

(1995, Fr/GB/Bel, 111 min)
d Agnieszka Holland. *p* Jean-Pierre Ramsay Levi. *sc* Christopher Hampton. *ph* Yorgos Arvanitis. *ed* Isabelle Lorente. *pd* Dan Weil. *m* Jan AP Kaczmarek. *cast* Leonardo DiCaprio, David Thewlis, Romane Bohringer, Dominique Blanc, Felicie Pasotti Carbarbaye, Nita Klein, Christopher Hampton.

●September, 1871: Arthur Rimbaud arrives in post-revolutionary Paris from Charleville at the invitation of Paul Verlaine. Verlaine, an accomplished poet with a growing reputation and a pregnant young trophy wife to match, is as instantly entranced by the precocious, anarchic, contemptuous 16-year-old as by the unprecedented talent evinced in the boy's poetry. Drinking their way through the city's literary salons, the pair strike out on a passionate, illicit affair. But it's a woefully imbalanced relationship, with Rimbaud compulsively abusing his elder, and the weak-willed Verlaine resorting ever more to the bottle. Christopher Hampton's screenplay presents a thoroughly researched reading whose historical authenticity only skims the surface of any emotional truths. Whether you take to this at all probably depends on your reaction to the affair on show. It's abusive, sordid, violent – but then this was hardly a coupling made in heaven. DiCaprio (Rimbaud) and Thewlis (Verlaine) provide dynamic if mismatched performances, though there's no excusing Hampton's own laughable cameo, nor the protracted coda with DiCaprio doing a Peter O'Toole in the desert. NB

Totally F***ed Up

(1993, US, 80 min)
d Gregg Araki. *p* Andrea Sperling, Gregg Araki. *sc* Gregg Araki. *ph* Todd Verow, Pryor Traczukowski, Gregg Araki. *ed* Gregg Araki. *cast* James Duval, Roko Belic, Susan Behshid, Jenee Gill, Gilbert Luna, Lance May, Alan Boyce.

●Turning aside from the in-your-face sloganeering of *The Living End*, Gregg Araki returns here to the slangy, intimate, domestic domain of his earlier work. Crashing ennui and tortured love-lives are again the keynote, as an assortment of young gay Angelinos laze around each other's apartments, get bored with cruising the local scene, mess up their relationships and major in teenage angst. Between times, Araki – who directed, co-produced, wrote, photographed and edited the picture – weighs in with an intermittent flutter of suicide statistics, found footage and pointed intertitles. It's all very self-consciously cool, of course, but from this side of the Atlantic, you can forgive the film's endless posturing and tune in to its honest, sympathetic portrayal of late adolescence. Araki covers any number of bases, revolving around two-timing would-be movie-maker Steven (Luna) and melancholy existential hipster Andy (Duval, a real find). Indeed, for all its rather obvious attitude, the film's conventional at heart: a soap for the slack generation, that'll strike a chord way outside the confines of the New Queer Cinema. TJ

Total Recall

(1990, US, 113 min)
d Paul Verhoeven. *p* Buzz Feitshans, Ronald Shusett. *sc* Ronald Shusett, Dan O'Bannon, Gary Goldman. *ph* Jost Vacano. *pd* William Sandell. *m* Jerry Goldsmith. *cast* Arnold Schwarzenegger, Rachel Ticotin, Sharon Stone, Ronny Cox, Michael Ironside, Marshall Bell.

●Picking up from where he left off in *RoboCop*, Verhoeven pictures a lean, mean future controlled by conglomerates via a hands-on designer technology. Doug Quaid (Schwarzenegger) is a working stiff who dreams of living on Mars. What quicker, cheaper, safer way of making his dreams come true than purchasing memory implants: a two-week trip to Mars, first class, with a personal ego-trip as an optional extra. But something goes wrong (or does it?). Quaid has already been to Mars (hence those dreams?), and his memories have been erased (hence those dreams?). Now They want him dead. 'The best mind-fuck yet!' says Quaid, as the plot takes another Z-bend at warp factor ten. Inevitably there are contrivances, but Verhoeven's gusto, ingenuity and guts know no bounds…especially the guts: the comic-edged violence is shockingly brutal. The inspiration, as with *Blade Runner*, comes from Philip K Dick (his short story *We Can Remember It For You Wholesale)*, and many of his themes recur: identity, self-determination, perception, and yes, we're talking about memories here, alongside a revolutionary parable, two great female characters, and some colossal effects. The future doesn't come any better. TCh

To the Devil a Daughter

(1976, GB/WGer, 93 min)
d Peter Sykes. *p* Roy Skeggs. *sc* Christopher Wicking. *ph* David Watkin. *ed* John Trumper. *ad* Don Picton. *m* Paul Glass. *cast* Richard Widmark, Christopher Lee, Honor Blackman, Denholm Elliott, Michael Goodliffe, Nastassja Kinski, Anthony Valentine.

●Hammer's second attempt at a Dennis Wheatley black magic thriller bears little comparison with the earlier *The Devil Rides Out*. It is very much a contemporary post-*Exorcist* movie, full of rampaging foetuses, obscene pregnancy rituals, and stray sexual suggestions as Lee's excommunicated priest and his satanist followers hound young Nastassja Kinski with malevolent intent. The film's unlikely trump card is Richard Widmark as a credibly sceptical supernatural investigator, who romps through the proceedings with a disarming stoicism, but regrettably faces his devilish opponent Lee only in the closing sequence. It's a good deal more interesting than the rest of the possession cycle, but still a disappointment. DP

To the Heart (Al Corazón)

(1995, Arg, 92 min)
d Mario Sábato. *p* Alberto Gonzalez. *sc* Mario Sabato, Irene Amuchastegui. *ph* Ever Latour, Ricardo Cosenza, Hector Collodoro. *ed* Norberto Rapado, Daniel Zottola. *cast* Sergio Renán, Adriana Varela, Ernesto Sábato, Enrique Cadicamo, Mónica Cadicamo and Trio, Sexteto Mayor, Cárlos Gardel.

●If you like tango – the music, the dance, the sensibility – you'll love this, since it trawls through a host of clips from the Argentinian cinema's golden age, featuring numerous greats including the legendary Cárlos Gardel. The explanatory interruptions from Enrique Cadicamo and Ernesto Sábato (seen wandering around rooms, streets and staircases) are regrettably rather a drag. GA

To the Last Drop (Até a Ultima Gota)

(1980, Braz, 52 min)
d Sergio Rezende. *p* Marisa Leao. *sc* Sergio Rezende. *ph* José Joffily. *ed* Vera Freire, Marisa Leao. *with* Hugo Carvana, José Dumont.

●In Latin America there are ten thousand commercial blood banks, where the forty million who are unable to sell their labour sell their blood, often in such large quantities that they die of anaemia. The blood and its by-products are resold at enormous profit, mostly to wealthier countries, via multi-national corporations. This blood traffic is both the documentary subject of the film, and a metaphor for the bleeding dry of Third World countries by the West, of the poor by the rich: a metaphor worked through in the commentary, with a passion often lacking from 'committed' documentaries. The wider resonances of the commentary are anchored by precise, pointed images; the uninhibited use of camera and editing to draw attention to things is refreshing rather than heavy-handed, and looks positively subtle by comparison with the crude and exploitative view of the world which sanctions profiteering in human blood. JWi

To the Starry Island (Gesom e Kako Shipta)

(1993, SKor, 102 min)
d Park Kwang-Su. *p* Park Kwang-Su, Park Ki-Yong. *sc* Im Chulwoo, Lee Chang-Dong, Park Kwang-Su. *ph* Yoo Young-Kil. *ed* Kim Hyun. *m* Song Hong-Sup. *cast* Ahn Song-Gi, Moon Sung-Kuen, Shim Hae-Jin.

●Like Park's earlier films, this provides an intimate close-up vision of a handful of characters, then pulls back to expose the political framework in which they are forced to exist. Unlike the other films, this takes place in a rural peasant community, and involves the supernatural as well as lengthy flashbacks to the Korean War of the 1950s. It's about the ramifications of that war on a lonely off-shore island – how a traditional people were swept up by events they barely understood, and how the bitterness of the experience still persists. A fascinating movie, with a bold, shocking climax. TCh

To the Victor

see Owd Bob

Toto the Hero (Toto le héros)

(1991, Bel/Fr/Ger, 91 min)
d Jaco Van Dormael. *sc* Jaco van Dormael, Laurette Vankeerberghen, Pascal Lonhay, Didier de Neck. *ph* Walther van den Ende. *ed* Susana Rossberg. *ad* Herbert Pouille. *m* Pierre van Dormael. *cast* Michel Bouquet, Jo De Backer, Gisela Uhlen, Mireille Perrier, Sandrine Blancke, Peter Böhlke, Didier Ferney.

● This deliciously offbeat film tells of the now elderly Thomas (Bouquet), who has harboured dreams of murderous revenge ever since it first occurred to him that, as a baby during a maternity ward fire, he was exchanged with Alfred, the kid next door. As Thomas sifts through his memories, revelling in his jealous hatred of Alfred, and wistfully recalling his love for his sister Alice and her adult lookalike Evelyne (Perrier), Van Dormael takes us on a twisting trip through his melancholy protagonist's mind: a trip jam-packed with the simple, surprising joys of existence. That Thomas' life, as we see it, is the product of his imagination is made clear not only by the presence of his comic-strip *alter ego* (the avenging detective of the title), but by the dreamily surreal story and visuals. But if the film's outlandish elements allow Van Dormael (in his feature debut) to exercise an engagingly witty eye for the absurd, he has rooted it in *emotional* reality, so that Thomas' life, loves, desires and anxieties take on great poignancy. An immensely vibrant, inventive, compassionate movie. GA

Totò Who Lived Twice (Totò che visse due volte)

(1998, It, 93 min, b/w)
d Daniele Ciprì, Franco Maresco. *p* Rean Mazzone. *sc* Daniele Ciprì, Lillo Iacolino, Franco Maresco. *ph* Luca Bigazzi. *ed* Daniele Ciprì, Franco Maresco, Cesar Augusto Meneghetti. *ad* Fabio Sciortino. *cast* Salvatore Gattuso, Marcello Miranda, Carlo Giordano, Pietro Arciadiacono, Camillo Conti, Angelo Prollo, Antonino Carollo.

● This typically scatological, bizarre and grotesque tale from Ciprì and Maresco bears a distinct if distant and blasphemous resemblance to the life of Christ – and more specifically to Pasolini's *Gospel According to Matthew*. The protagonist is a boss-eyed wanker who drools ecstatically at the mere idea of harlots and donkeys. The story takes in miracles, resurrection and crucifixion, not to mention trouble with the Mafia, and the film-makers paint a memorably vivid portrait of Sicilian manhood, at once parodic and poetic. GA

Totschweigen (A Wall of Silence)

(1990, Aus, 88 min)
d Margareta Heinrich, Eduard Erne. *p* Lukas Stepanik. *sc* Eduard Erne, Margareta Heinrich. *ph* Hermann Dunzendorfer. *ed* Paul M Sedlacek. *m* Peter Ponger.

● 'The Jews have their Wailing Wall and we have our wall of silence.' So says one of the occupants of Totschweigen Reichnitz, a village on the Austro-Hungarian border where, in 1945, 180 Jews were shot by the retreating Nazis and buried in a still unlocated mass grave. The locals' stonewalling frustrates all efforts to give them a proper burial. It's a compelling subject, and some pertinent links are made to wider issues. A pity, then, that the film's construction ties it down so: after the first half hour of exposition, there's nowhere to go, and it ends up tracing its footsteps as unproductively as the search it observes. NB

Touch

(1996, US/Fr, 97 min)
d Paul Schrader. *p* Lila Cazès, Fida Attieh. *sc* Paul Schrader. *ph* Ed Lachman. *ed* Cara Silverman. *pd* David Wasco. *m* David Grohl. *cast* Bridget Fonda, Christopher Walken, Skeet Ulrich, Tom Arnold, Gina Gershon, Lolita Davidovich, Paul Mazursky, Janeane Garofalo, Anthony Zerbe.

● Reputedly faithful to an atypical Elmore Leonard novel, Paul Schrader's film is an uneasy excursion into comedy, albeit of the spiritual kind. No blame attaches to Depp-alike Skeet Ulrich's performance as the saintly ex-Franciscan Juvenal – his 'cool' charisma itself serves to query Juvenal's genuineness – nor to Walken's high-octane, attention-grabbing turn as 'religionist without a cause' Bill Hill, a failed evangelist mad keen to milk a buck by selling the unwilling young faith healer to the air waves. But eyes start widening when tubby Tom Arnold's fundamentalist Catholic – Hill's potential rival – wanders in, seemingly from another movie. He cuts a ridiculous figure as the most clairvoyant self-seeker in a competitive field. This talky would-be satire can find neither an appropriate tone nor a realised human drama to communicate the ideas. But there are some sharp lines and good scenes, notably those with Bridget Fonda as Hill's accomplice (all dope-head languor), sent to help ensnare Juvenal: her expressed personal – sexual – response to meeting this embodiment of 'goodness' makes cartoons of the other characters. WH

Touch, The

(1970, US/Swe, 113 min)
d/p/sc Ingmar Bergman. *ph* Sven Nykvist. *ed* Siv Lundgren. *ad* PA Lundgren. *m* Jan Johansson. *cast* Elliott Gould, Bibi Andersson, Max von Sydow, Sheila Reid, Barbro Hiort af Ornäs.

● Bergman's first English language movie looks more accessible than most of his work at this period, a 'love story' (as he has called it) telling how middle class Swedish housewife Anna (Andersson) meets Anglo-Jewish archaeologist David (Gould), has an intermittent and rocky affair with him, and ends up losing both lover and husband, the penalty of compromise. 'It is possible to live two lives' says Anna hopefully to David, 'and slowly combine them in one good, wise life'. But the film demonstrates conclusively that it isn't: not only does the double life involve deceit, but it is always threatened by the incalculable factors in human nature. David's love for Anna alternates with spells of motiveless violence and morose indifference; Anna's seemingly kindly and myopic husband (von Sydow) does discover the affair and does give Anna an ultimatum. Anna thus keeps finding, to her dismay, that she cannot predict how either man will act next. Conversely, David's violence and the husband's growing coldness are their reactions to Anna's unpredictability. Bergman may have temporarily shelved his metaphysical concerns – no religious questionings, no fantasy, no artist-in- society debate – but his analysis of human relationships is as complex as ever. NAn

Touch and Go

(1986, US, 101 min)
d Robert Mandel. *p* Stephen Friedman. *sc* Alan Ormsby, Bob Sand, Harry Colomby. *ph* Richard H Kline. *ed* Walt Mulconery. *ad* Charles Rosen. *m* Sylvester Levay. *cast* Michael Keaton, Maria Conchita Alonso, Ajay Naidou, Maria Tucci, Max Wright, Jere Burns, Lara Jill Miller.

● An enjoyable, undemanding comedy-drama, with Michael Keaton as famous Chicago ice hockey player Bobby Barbato, a man with humour as dry as his ice and a constant look of hilarious vacancy. One evening Bobby is mugged by an incompetent gang of schoolkids, fronted by obnoxious 11-year-old Louis (Naidou). Grabbing the little toerag by the collar, he drags him home to confront his fiery Latin mum Denise (Alonso). They don't exactly hit it off at first, but soon the odd couple find their lives unavoidably interwoven when Denise is beaten up while Bobby is puck-whacking for the championship. Although a little more ice action wouldn't have gone amiss, the pace rarely slackens and Keaton is in fine form. DA

Touched by Love

(1980, US, 94 min)
d Gus Trikonis. *p* Michael Viner. *sc* Hesper Anderson. *ph* Richard H Kline. *ed* Fred Chulack. *ad* Claudio Guzman. *m* John Barry. *cast* Deborah Raffin, Diane Lane, Michael Learned, John Amos, Cristina Raines, Mary Wickes, Clu Gulager.

● Dreadful pap about a young nurse (Raffin) starting work at a home for handicapped children, finally managing to break the communication barrier with a girl obsessed by Elvis Presley (a pen-pal letter from Elvis figures in the therapy) and dying from cerebral palsy. Based on a true story, but sanitised throughout; only Raines, as Raffin's cynical room-mate, adds a touch of reality. GA

Touche pas à la femme blanche (Don't Touch the White Woman)

(1973, Fr/It, 109 min)
d Marco Ferreri. *p* Jean Yanne, Jean-Pierre Rassam. *sc* Marco Ferreri, Rafael Azcona. *ph* Etienne Becker. *ed* Ruggero Mastroianni. *m* Philippe Sarde. *cast* Catherine Deneuve, Marcello Mastroianni, Michel Piccoli, Philippe Noiret, Ugo Tognazzi, Alain Cuny, Serge Reggiani, Darry Cowl, Marco Ferreri.

● Righteous indignation about the Vietnam war was no guarantee of artistic merit, as this fiasco demonstrates. Conflating Then and Now, the film has the 7th Cavalry clattering through the streets of modern Paris, while the Sioux roam Les Halles (a vast building site at the time). On orders from President Nixon, General Custer (Mastroianni) sets about extirpating the savages ('Cheyennes, Algerians…'), with assists from Buffalo Bill (Piccoli) and General Terry (Noiret). But Sitting Bull (Cuny) turns the tables, the sinister figures in CIA sweatshirts slink off, and Bull delivers the message: 'We still have other Custers to kill.' Despite that cast, the film's pervasive shallowness and silliness render it unendurable. BBa

Touchez pas au Grisbi (Grisbi/Honour Among Thieves)

(1953, Fr/It, 94 min, b/w)
d Jacques Becker. *sc* Jacques Becker, Maurice Griffe, Albert Simonin. *ph* Pierre Montazel. *ed* Marguerite Renoir. *ad* Jean d'Eaubonne. *m* Jean Wiener. *cast* Jean Gabin, René Dary, Paul Frankeur, Paul Oettly, Lino Ventura, Jeanne Moreau, Dora Doll, Daniel Cauchy.

● This model French gangster picture set the rules for the great sequence of underworld movies from Jean-Pierre Melville that followed. An ageing and weary Gabin attempts to retire after one last robbery. Instead he finds himself in a world of moody double-crosses. Becker's film, full of neat angles and delightful little bits of business, is laconic and admirably methodical. If its code of honour and its world of safe houses (and the absence of any police) make it seem like a wartime resistance film, it does also show what other gangster movies often ignore: that the reason for earning money dishonestly is to be able to live in style. And this film takes as much pleasure in watching Gabin open a bottle of wine as it does observing him in action. A fine supporting cast includes a young Lino Ventura and an even younger Jeanne Moreau. CPe

Touch of Class, A

(1972, GB, 106 min)
d/p Melvin Frank. *sc* Melvin Frank, Jack Rose. *ph* Austin Dempster. *ed* Bill Butler. *pd* Terence Marsh. *m* John Cameron. *cast* George Segal, Glenda Jackson, Paul Sorvino, Hildegard Neil, Cec Linder, K Callan, Mary Barclay.

● For the most part, this romantic comedy (married American businessman *versus* divorcee English designer) successfully fights off the implications of its title and appalling theme song, thanks to some sharp dialogue and an excellent performance from Segal at his edgy, harassed best. Melvin Frank has put in his share of years as a comedy scriptwriter, which probably accounts for the distinctly old-fashioned air. Sharp at the edges but soft in the centre, the film starts well with Segal's middle class stud fantasies being ripped to shreds by Glenda Jackson in full flight. Barbs fly, but too soon she degenerates into devoted clock-watching mistress, and the film into routine formula. Often enjoyable, though, if mainly for Segal holding the seeping sentimentality at bay. CPe

Touch of Evil 100 *(100)*

(1958, US, 108 min, b/w)
d Orson Welles. *p* Albert Zugsmith. *sc* Orson Welles. *ph* Russell Metty. *ed* Virgil W Vogel,

Aaron Stell. *ad* Alexander Golitzen, Robert Clatworthy. *m* Henry Mancini. *cast* Charlton Heston, Janet Leigh, Orson Welles, Joseph Calleia, Akim Tamiroff, Marlene Dietrich, Dennis Weaver, Ray Collins, Mercedes McCambridge, Lalo Rios, Zsa Zsa Gabor, Joseph Cotten.
●A wonderfully offhand genesis (Welles adopting and adapting a shelved Paul Monash script for B-king Albert Zugsmith without ever reading the novel by Whit Masterson it was based on) marked this brief and unexpected return to Hollywood film-making for Welles. And the result more than justified the arrogance of the gesture. A sweaty thriller conundrum on character and corruption, justice and the law, worship and betrayal, it plays havoc with moral ambiguities as self-righteous Mexican cop Heston goes up against Welles' monumental Hank Quinlan, the old-time detective of vast and wearied experience who goes by instinct, gets it right, but fabricates evidence to make his case. Set in the backwater border hell-hole of Los Robles, inhabited almost solely by patented Wellesian grotesques, it's shot to resemble a nightscape from Kafka. PT

Touch of the Sun
see No Secrets!

Touch of Zen, A (Xia Nü)
(1969, Tai, 175 min)
d King Hu. *p* Sha Jung-Feng. *sc* King Hu. *ph* Hua Hui-Ying, Chou Yeh-Hsing. *ed* King Hu. *ad* Chen Shang-Liang. *m* Wu Ta-Chiang. *cast* Shih Chun, Hsu Feng, Pai Ying, Tian Feng, Roy Chiao, Han Yingjie.
●King Hu's remarkable Ming Dynasty epic deliberately makes itself impossible to define, beginning as a ghost story, then turning into a political thriller, and finally becoming a metaphysical battle as the role of the monk Hui-Yuan (Chiao) comes to the fore. Structured like a set of Chinese boxes, twice forcing you to expand your frame of reference and reassess the meaning of what you've seen, it begins with a realistic portrait of life in a sleepy town outside Peking, and ends with extended fantasies of Zen Buddhism in action – and in between has a core of action scenes that transform Peking Opera stagecraft into sheer flights of imagination. Delights include a heroine who holds her own with men without being 'masculine', and transcendent moments like the stabbing of the monk, who bleeds gold… And the visual style will set your eyes on fire. TR

Tough Guy
see Kung Fu – The Headcrusher

Tough Guys
(1986, US, 103 min)
d Jeff Kanew. *p* Joe Wizan. *sc* James Orr, Jim Cruickshank. *ph* King Baggot. *ed* Kaja Fehr. *pd* Todd Hallowell. *m* James Newton Howard. *cast* Burt Lancaster, Kirk Douglas, Charles Durning, Alexis Smith, Dana Carvey, Darlanne Fluegel, Eli Wallach, Monty Ash, Billy Barty.
●This excessively nostalgic caper comedy has Lancaster and Douglas as ex-cons of pensionable age attempting to fit in with the modern world following a 30-year jail stretch for a train robbery. Douglas, pushy and petulant, flexes his physique with aerobics teacher Fluegel, while Lancaster, more dignified and regretful of time lost, is relegated, jobless, to an old folks home. The observation that 'old is a dirty word' is swiftly shoved aside as the pair strut their stuff, fend off muggers, and indulge in amiably rebellious antics before making one last bid for fame and freedom by hijacking, once again, the Gold Coast Flier. So self-consciously elegiac that its too-good-to-be-true heroes are imprisoned in a slim storyline of implausible fantasy, the movie would have been more effective had Burt and Kirk simply been allowed to be themselves. Of course, it's fun to watch old pros, and Wallach, as a mad, myopic hit-man, is genuinely funny; but one can't help feeling that a rare gathering of Golden Age talent has been criminally wasted. GA

Tough Guys Don't Dance
(1987, US, 109 min)
d Norman Mailer. *p* Menahem Golan, Yoram Globus. *sc* Norman Mailer. *ph* Michael Moyer. *ed* Debra McDermott. *pd* Armin Ganz. *m* Angelo Badalamenti. *cast* Ryan O'Neal, Isabella Rossellini, Debra Sandlund, Wings Hauser, John Bedford Lloyd, Lawrence Tierney, Penn Jillette.
●Deserted husband and ex-drug dealer Tim Madden (O'Neal) wakes from a hangover to find gore all over his car, a new tattoo on his arm, and a severed head in his drug stash. The only person he can turn to is his old dad (Tierney), who has his work cut out deep-sixing heads and corpses in the ocean. Police Chief Regency (Hauser), involved with Madden's chippie wife and married to Madden's old flame (Rossellini), is out to fit him up for the murders, but has an epileptic fit in his Green Beret uniform instead. Norman Mailer's novel, *Tough Guys Don't Dance*, wasn't so hot, but his potboiler on screen is a disgrace. No scene generates a complex reaction, and his attempts at turning his Manichean material and existential dread into a chortle-fest is as unsuccessful as is the high camp, for the film forfeits sympathy from the start. Neither thrilling nor horrific, the camera, plotting, dialogue and atmosphere are uniformly unconvincing: a conservatoire of false notes. BC

Tough Life
see Monde sans pitié, Un

Tour Abroad (Auslandstournee)
(1999, Ger, 91 min)
d Ayse Polat. *p* Elke Peters. *sc* Ayse Polat, Basri Polat. *ph* Martin Gressmann. *ed* Margot Neubert-Marie. *cast* Hilmi Sözer, Özlem Blume, Özay Fecht, Birol Ünel, Martin Glade, Karen Friesicke, Siir Eloglu.
●If this road movie recalls Wenders' *Alice in the Cities*, it's not just because it features a grown-up man (here, gay Turkish singer Zeki) accompanying a girl (a recently orphaned 11-year-old foisted on him when he attends the funeral in Germany of his old friend, the motherless girl's father). It also echoes Wenders in the quiet, ever so slightly melancholy way it brings in such themes as geographical and cultural dislocation, abandonment, trust, family and identity. Writer/director Polat revels in road movie conventions – who doesn't love the rhythmic roll of reflected neon over the windscreen? He never overpacks or hurries his scenes, cuts well to the folk ballad soundtrack, and teases a nice performance from Blume, as the initially suspicious and frightened girl, and a fine, surprisingly understated one from Sözer. The director's sober liberalism makes the film a thoughtful index of prevailing prejudice and moral assumptions affecting the Turkish diaspora and its cinema. WH

Tournoi, Le (The Tournament)
(1928, Fr, 6,562 ft, b/w)
d Jean Renoir. *p* Henri Dupuy-Mazuel. *sc* Jean Renoir. *ph* Marcel Lucien, Maurice Des Fassiaux. *ed* André Cerf. *ad* Robert Mallet-Stevens. *cast* Aldo Nadi, Jackie Monnier, Enrique Rivero, Blanche Bernis, Manuel Raabi.
●This epic medieval drama, detailing the conflict between Catholics and Protestants in Carcassonne, would have little in common with Renoir's later, more personal and mature work, were it not for the decidedly human perspective from which he views the story. Not only is this a question of his clearly having felt rather more at home with the intimate scenes than with the action-packed spectacle; it's also a matter of his characters being far more recognisably prone to ordinary human shortcomings than are the larger-than-life heroes of more stilted epics. Indeed, his eye for telling detail was already sharp, while both the sparsely decorated interiors and the naturalistic performances lend his vision of the past a rare feeling of lived-in authenticity. GA

Tous les matins du monde
(1992, Fr, 115 min)
d Alain Corneau. *p* Jean-Louis Livi. *sc* Pascal Quignard, Alain Corneau. *ph* Yves Angelo. *ed* Marie-Josephe Yoyotte. *ad* Bernard Vezat. *m* Jordi Savall. *cast* Jean-Pierre Marielle, Gérard Depardieu, Anne Brochet, Guillaume Depardieu, Caroline Sihol, Carole Richert, Michel Bouquet.
●For all his success as court composer at Versailles, the aged Marin Marais (Gérard Depardieu) acknowledges the spiritual emptiness of his music. Lost in memories, he recalls another master of the *viola da gamba*, Monsieur de Sainte Colombe (Marielle), whose magnificent, melancholy compositions and hermetic life style, away from the tempting glamours of Paris, were inspired by undying love for his late wife. Not a warm man, Sainte Colombe had consented to tutor Marin Marais in his prodigious youth (Guillaume Depardieu), a favour which the pupil repaid by seducing one of Sainte Colombe's daughters (Brochet). Only years later had he taken to heart the real lesson his master had to offer… From its lengthy, opening close-up of Depardieu's face, it's clear that Corneau's 17th century fable will be no ordinary costume drama. The story is slow, stately, and told with minimal dialogue, with Corneau trusting to Yves Angelo's painterly camerawork – and even more importantly, to the lovely baroque music – to give his admirably restrained tale of passion, betrayal and creativity its emotional power. The cast, too, play beautifully. GA

Tout ça...pour ça!!! (All That...For This?!)
(1993, Fr, 120 min)
d/p/sc Claude Lelouch. *ph* Claude Lelouch, Philippe Pavans de Cecatty. *ed* Hélène de Luze. *ad* Laurent Tesseyre. *m* Francis Lai, Philippe Servain. *cast* Vincent Lindon, Gérard Darmon, Jacques Gamblin, Marie-Sophie L, Francis Huster, Fabrice Luchini, Alessandra Martinès, Charles Gérard, Salomé Lelouch, Evelyne Bouix.
●A judge (m), his lawyer lover (f) and their respective spouses take an uneasy holiday together on Mont Blanc. Meanwhile a taxi driver, a waiter and a hairdresser, in despair at the state of their love lives, join forces and embark on a petty crime spree. All ends in the courtroom, with a shift into fantasy and a fireworks-accompanied celebration of release and reconciliation. The director's geniality to characters and audience alike is displayed here at optimum force, and even dissenters should admire the skill with which he sends five separate stories hurtling around the film like dodgem cars, reversing into and out of flashback, and maintaining perfect clarity throughout. Again, we find a taste for contrasting a flamboyant visual style with understated performances, the agitated Luchini excepted. BBa

Toute une Nuit (All Night Long)
(1982, Fr/Bel, 89 min)
d/sc Chantal Akerman. *ph* Caroline Champetier. *ed* Luc Barnier. *pd* Michele Blondeel. *cast* Aurore Clément, Jan Decorte, Angelo Abazoglou, Frank Aendenboom.
●Akerman, the mistress of minimalism, has made her own midsummer night's sex comedy, with a superabundance of stories and a cast of (almost) thousands. The film shows an endless series of brief encounters that take place in Brussels in the course of one delirious, torrid June night, with the twist that each relationship is condensed into a single moment of high melodrama – the *coup de foudre*, the climax of passion, the end of an affair – with the spectator left to fill in the fictional spaces between scenes. Each couple compulsively plays through the same gestures, each mating rite is a variation on the same theme: repetitions which Akerman uses both as a rich source of comedy and as a device to show erotic desire as a pattern of codes and conventions. Marrying the pleasure of narrative to the purism of the avant-garde, this is her most accessible film to date. SJ

Toute une Vie
see And Now My Love

Tout Va Bien
(1972, Fr/It, 95 min)
d Jean-Luc Godard, Jean-Pierre Gorin. *p* JP Rassan. *sc* Jean-Pierre Gorin, Jean-Luc Godard. *ph* Armand Marco. *ed* Kénout Peltier. *ad* Jacques Dugied. *cast* Yves Montand, Jane Fonda, Vittorio Caprioli, Jean Pagnol, Pierre Oudry, Anne Wiazemsky.
●Godard's return to mainstream film-making after his self-imposed four-year Marxist-nihilist exile is a sort of auto-critique, craftily type-casting Fonda and Montand as media intellectuals (she an American journalist, he a former New Wave film-maker now working in commercials) who eagerly committed themselves to the revolutionary struggle in 1968, but are now led to revise that commitment (and their personal

relationship) through their involvement in a factory strike in 1972. A little simplistic at times but acidly funny, with Godard's genius for the arresting image once more well to the fore. TM

Tovarich

(1937, US, 98 min, b/w)
d Anatole Litvak. *p* Hal B Wallis. *sc* Casey Robinson. *ph* Charles Lang Jr. *ed* Henri Rust. *ad* Anton F Grot. *m* Max Steiner. *cast* Claudette Colbert, Charles Boyer, Basil Rathbone, Anita Louise, Isabel Jeans, Morris Carnovsky, Melville Cooper.

●Boyer, one of Hollywood's most exotic male leads, specialised in playing suave, displaced European aristocrats. He's at his most irrepressibly smooth here as a White Russian refugee who's reduced to working as a butler for a French banker. (His equally haughty wife Colbert is taken on as the maid.) There is no hiding the snobbery behind this upstairs/downstairs comedy. You never doubt for a moment that class will out and that the two unlikely domestics will be restored to their previous, lofty social positions. Director Litvak, himself a Russian émigré in Hollywood, acquits himself well enough, but this is a film which surely would have been better suited to the talents of Lubitsch. (From the play by Jacques Deval, adapted into English by Robert Sherwood.) GM

To Walk with Lions

(1999, Can/GB/Kenya, 110 min)
d Carl Schultz. *p* Pieter Kroonenburg, Julie Allan, Jamie Brown. *sc* Sharon Buckingham, Keith Ross Leckie. *ph* Jean Lépine. *ed* Angelo Corrao. *pd* Michael Devine. *m* Alan Reeves. *cast* Richard Harris, John Michie, Kerry Fox, Ian Bannen, Hugh Quarshie, Honor Blackman, Geraldine Chaplin, David Kakuta Mulwa, Steenie Njoroge.

●Made 32 years after *Born Free*, this is more 'labour of love' than a cash cow sequel. Not surprisingly, in view of the marriage breakdown and murders of the Kenyan wildlife conservationists Joy and George Adamson, Schultz's biopic, spanning George's 18-year struggle to hold on to his Kora reserve, tells a very different story. Reality bites. The lions, too – as wild 'n' broke Englishman Tony Fitzjohn (Michie) discovers when he takes a job at Kora and is promptly pounced on. The movie paints a convincing picture of perfection exhausted; as an action adventure and character study, however, it grips only in bursts. The dramatised account of the substitute father/son relationship between Adamson (Harris) and Fitzjohn is underripe and lacking any sense of development. Adamson's 'sublime communion' with his lions feels a bit like the macho flipside of the babying ways of his wife in the earlier film. SS

Toward the Unknown (aka Brink of Hell)

(1956, US, 115 min)
d/p Mervyn LeRoy. *sc* Beirne Lay Jr. *ph* Harold Rosson. *ed* William Ziegler. *ad* John Beckman. *m* Paul Baron. *cast* William Holden, Lloyd Nolan, Virginia Leith, Charles McGraw, Murray Hamilton, LQ Jones, James Garner, Paul Fix, Karen Steele.

●In this routine commingling of both mental and metal fatigue, Holden is a Korean veteran pilot (he broke under brainwashing) who's expected to grin and bear a desk jockey posting to Edwards Air Base, but itches to test the new X-2 rocket plane (which will retrieve his self-respect and his girl). Stolidly directed by former Warners contractee LeRoy in his men-in-uniform period, between the naval comedy *Mr Roberts* and the army farce *No Time for Sergeants*, and before the plainclothes hymn *The FBI Story*. James Garner makes his screen debut here, only a year before the first *Maverick*. PT

Towering Inferno, The

(1974, US, 165 min)
d John Guillermin. *p* Irwin Allen. *sc* Stirling Silliphant. *ph* Fred J Koenekamp, Joseph Biroc. *ed* Harold F Kress, Carl Kress. *pd* William J Creber. *m* John Williams. *cast* Steve McQueen, Paul Newman, William Holden, Faye Dunaway, Fred Astaire, Susan Blakely, Richard Chamberlain, Jennifer Jones, OJ Simpson, Robert Vaughn, Robert Wagner.

●Although producer Irwin Allen's *The Poseidon Adventure* actually led the way a couple of years before, this is the disaster film which set the style for the genre in the decade to come (the trailer for *The Towering Inferno* declared such skyscraper conflagrations to be nothing less than 'the new art form of the twentieth century'). A starry cast share out roles that are less like characters than places in a lifeboat, either as victims (Chamberlain, Wagner, Jones) or firefighters (McQueen and Newman). Director Guillermin deserved to be made an honorary fire chief, though he is driven to some desperate measures to cap each mounting disaster with ever more outlandish rescues. MA

Tower of the Seven Hunchbacks, The (La Torre de los Siete Jorobados)

(1944, Sp, 90 min, b/w)
d Edgar Neville. *cast* Antonio Casal, Isabel de Pomés, Julia Lajos, Manolita Moran, Julia Pachelo, Guillermo Marin.

●A real oddity: young Basilio is visited by the ghost of a dead, one-eyed archaeologist, who asks him to protect his niece from imminent danger. After introducing himself to the lovely girl, our intrepid hero discovers that the threat emanates from a huge underground city populated entirely by hunchbacks… Neville's film is not exactly *good*, but it certainly is fascinating. In many ways it's like a rather corny Universal horror movie of the '30s (featuring a few performances that would show even Lugosi in an impressive light); but no Hollywood film-maker – with the possible exception of Whale or Browning – would pepper a plot with such delightful nonsense (the ghost of Napoleon turns up at one point) and grotesquerie. The Spanish taste for the fantastic, the bizarre and the surreal is much in evidence, and one is left breathless by the sheer audacity of the ludicrous plot. It can, of course, be seen as an allegory on the state of the nation after the Civil War, but is best viewed as weird but wonderful wackiness. GA

Town & Country

(2001, US, 104 min)
d Peter Chelsom. *p* Andrew Karsch, Fred Roos, Simon Fields. *sc* Michael Laughlin, Buck Henry. *ph* William A Fraker. *ed* David Moritz, Claire Simpson. *pd* Caroline Hanania. *m* Rolfe Kent. *cast* Warren Beatty, Diane Keaton, Andie MacDowell, Garry Shandling, Jenna Elfman, Nastassja Kinski, Goldie Hawn, Charlton Heston, Marian Seldes, Josh Hartnett.

●It's hard not to muse on this film's notorious $90m backstory when it's so much more interesting than the tired, trite onscreen shenanigans. And then, how are we to account for the abrupt shifts in tone, from 'sophisticated' comedy of manners to shrill slapstick, or for a meandering plotline which shuttles Beatty's philandering husband across time zones and bed partners (Kinski, Hawn, MacDowell) with more desperation than sense – if not by noting that filming stretched from two months to two years of handwringing, re-edits and reshoots? Flat and tirelessly unfunny, the film boasts a conspicuous haute society setting which makes it all the more insulting and complacent. This is how *Shampoo* might have turned out if Beatty had played the Jack Warden character: Lee Grant's clueless super-rich husband. Beatty's patented passive adultery was already looking thin ten years ago. Here it's just self-serving and sad. TCh

Town Bloody Hall

(1979, US, 85 min)
d DA Pennebaker, Chris Hegedus. *p* DA Pennebaker. *ph* Jim Desmond, DA Pennebaker, Mark Woodcock. *ed* Chris Hegedus. *with* Jacqueline Ceballos, Germaine Greer, Jill Johnston, Norman Mailer, Diana Trilling, Susan Sontag.

●A hilarious documentary record of Norman Mailer chairing a debate on 'the feminist question' in New York's City Hall on April 30, 1971. Great cinema, with chauvinist Mailer shaking his fist at feminist hecklers and being ripped apart by Greer and Sontag: the camera patiently hears out one of its 'stars', then flashes across the crowd to catch a face in full flight of uncontrolled expression. The battle of ideas in the debate is fascinating, the effects of the gap between 1971 and 1979 bizarre (so little has changed). But above all this is a demonstration of how the apparent one-dimensionality of film can become intensely dramatic: sounds disproportionate to images, voices erupting off-screen, dreams and convictions at their purest because caught in the moment of conflict. CA

Town Called Bastard, A

(1971, GB/Sp, 97 min)
d Robert Parrish. *p* S Benjamin Fisz. *sc* Richard Aubrey. *ph* Manuel Berenguer. *ed* Bert Bates. *ad* Julio Molina. *m* Waldo de los Rios. *cast* Robert Shaw, Stella Stevens, Martin Landau, Telly Savalas, Michael Craig, Fernando Rey, Dudley Sutton, Al Lettieri.

●Shot in Spain with a motley cast and crew, starting with the striking image of Stella Stevens, beatifically asleep in a coffin and being driven in a hearse across the desert by a deaf-mute gunman (Sutton) to the little Mexican village where she intends to claim a corpse after killing the man who murdered her husband, this suffers from the worst excesses of the spaghetti Western. On the other hand, behind the leering violence and allied crudities, both a purpose and a director are clearly evident. Involving a whisky priest (Shaw), a sadistic bandit (Savalas), a puckish traitor to the Revolution (Craig), and a military catalyst (Landau), the complex plot hinges on illusion, arguing obliquely and hauntingly that there is no comfort in loyalty, friendship, heroism, or even in doing the right thing. Scripted by Richard Aubrey, it's a strange, disturbing film, despite being plain bloody awful for much of the time. TM

Town Like Alice, A (aka The Rape of Malaya)

(1956, GB, 117 min, b/w)
d Jack Lee. *p* Joseph Janni. *sc* WP Lipscomb, Richard Mason. *ph* Geoffrey Unsworth. *ed* Sidney Hayers. *ad* Alex Vetchinsky. *m* Matyas Seiber. *cast* Virginia McKenna, Peter Finch, Takagi, Marie Lohr, Maureen Swanson, Jean Anderson, Renee Houston, Nora Nicholson, Geoffrey Keen.

●This adaptation of Nevil Shute's best-seller looks dated now that the cinema is rather less reticent in depicting wartime brutalities. Needless to say, it's stiff upper-lips and Japanese stereotypes all round as a group of female PoWs suffer at the hands of their captors. The US release title, *The Rape of Malaya*, was more explicit than the movie itself, and the bogus sets don't help much either. BBC TV's long-running series *Tenko* capitalised on the same formula. TJ

Town of Love and Hope, A (Ai to Kibo no Machi)

(1959, Jap, 63 min, b/w)
d Nagisa Oshima. *p* Tomio Ikeda. *sc* Nagisa Oshima. *ph* Hiroyuki Kusuda. *ed* Yoshi Sugihara. *ad* Koji Uno. *m* Riichiro Manabe. *cast* Hiroshi Fujikawa, Yoko Mochizuki, Fumio Watanabe, Kakuko Chino, Yuki Tominaga.

●Early Oshima is forever being compared with early Godard, but this debut feature (exactly contemporary with *Breathless*) shows that Oshima's political acumen was a great deal stronger than Godard's at this time. A schoolboy lives in a slum with his widowed mother and infant sister; his sole income derives from selling (and reselling) his sister's pigeons, which invariably escape from their buyers and fly home. This 'fraud' is eventually discovered, and the boy angrily accepts society's verdict that he is a 'criminal'. Oshima defines poverty in explicit terms of class oppression, and celebrates the boy's anger and pride. Along the way, he demolishes various liberal stances, and gives Japan's ruling class several short, sharp shocks. The film is rather schematic, not much flesh on its bones, but none the less powerful for that. TR

To Wong Foo, Thanks For Everything! Julie Newmar

(1995, US, 108 min)
d Beeban Kidron. *p* G MacBrown. *sc* Douglas Carter Beane. *ph* Steve Mason. *ed* Andrew Mondshein. *pd* Wynn Thomas. *m* Rachel Portman. *cast* Patrick Swayze, Wesley Snipes, John Leguizamo, Chris Penn, Stockard Channing, Blythe Danner, Melinda Dillon.

●Three drag queens on a cross-country journey get bogged down in a one-horse town. Sounds familiar? Though the journey is from New York to LA, and the mode of transport a 1967 Cadillac convertible, this is a rip-off of *Priscilla, Queen of the Desert*. Made for Spielberg's Amblin Entertainment, it's low camp for narrow-minded Middle Americans who can't cope with the idea of a cock in a frock. Leguizamo's Chi Chi is the only one who looks anything like a drag queen, let alone a woman; yet we are asked to believe that it's Swayze's breathy Vida and Snipes' squealing Noxeema who've got their stocking seams straight. The queens' gayness is simply never addressed. These are not rope-suckers, these here are big, blowsy women with attitude. And for all their hip-wiggling, hand-flapping and eye-rolling, they still manage to liberate the town's battered wives, closet gays and lovestruck teenagers, while dealing in a more manly way with its shit-kicking good ol' boys and beer-swillin' wife-beaters. The script is as subversive as *Are You Being Served?*, and the cross-dressing on a par with *Mrs Doubtfire*. NF

Toxic Avenger, The

(1984, US, 100 min)
d Michael Herz, Samuel Weil. *p* Lloyd Kaufman, Michael Herz. *sc* Joe Ritter. *ph* Lloyd Kaufman. *ed* Richard W Haines. *ad* Barry Shapiro, Alexandra Mazur. *cast* Andree Maranda, Mitchell Cohen, Jennifer Baptist, Cindy Manion, Robert Prichard, Gary Schneider, Mark Torgi.

●Melvin, weedy gofer at the Tromaville Health Club, is bullied by the clientele until he hurls himself into a handy drum of toxic waste and emerges as a disfigured seven-foot, mop-wielding superhero. Despite 'borrowing' from sources as diverse as *Frankenstein* and *The Producer*, it all falls apart after an hour, chunks of the preceding entertainment reappearing as random montages, while for the climax the whole of some New Jersey town turns out to grin at the camera as toxic Melvin eviscerates the 300lb mayor. DO

Toxic Avenger Part II, The

(1988, US, 96 min)
d/p Michael Herz, Lloyd Kaufman. *sc* Gay Partington Terry. *ph* James London. *ed* Michael Schweitzer. *ad* Alexis Grey. *m* Barrie Guard. *cast* Ron Fazio, John Altamura, Phoebe Legere, Rick Collins, Rikiya Yasuoka, Tsutomo Sekine, Lisa Gaye.

●Having rid Tromaville of all evil, Toxie hangs out at the blind home with his visually-impaired bimbo girlfriend Claire – until the vengeful chairman of Apocalypse Inc, purveyors of toxic waste, trashes the home and lures our hero to Japan, to be reunited with his long-lost 'father'. Discovering that dad is a loathsome drug dealer, Toxie suffers an Oedipal crisis. Meanwhile, the toxic revengers terrorise the Tromavillians and turn their town back into a radioactive dump. An unimaginative re-run of Part I, minus the high school nerd comedy and chronic bad taste, plus some irrelevant Japanese footage. Puerile garbage with a memory half-life of about ten seconds. NF

Toy, The

(1982, US, 102 min)
d Richard Donner. *p* Phil Feldman. *sc* Carol Sobieski. *ph* Laszlo Kovacs. *ed* Richard A Harris, Michael A Stevenson. *pd* Charles Rosen. *m* Patrick Williams. *cast* Richard Pryor, Jackie Gleason, Ned Beatty, Scott Schwartz, Teresa Ganzel, Wilfrid Hyde-White.

●In this far from fair world, the larger a man's native talent, the higher the standard we set him, and so one's disappointment with successive Richard Pryor comedies has dragged the emotions from dismay to anger, forgiveness to apathy. While it's hard to be angered by this particular vehicle, *The Toy* (based on a 1976 French film, *Le Jouet*) is undeniably another wasted opportunity. The plot is fairly implausible: unemployed man (Pryor) is hired as a bauble for billionaire store-owner Gleason's nine-year-old son (welcome again to the New Depression). After virtually every imaginable stock comic situation, Pryor humanises both spoiled son and money/power fixated pop in a moral, weepy ending. Played straight, this could make some quite serious points about the predicament of the unemployed (Pryor as prostitute), but the film finds it easier to opt for cheap laughs. GB

To You, From Me (Neo-ege Narul Bonenda)

(1994, SKor, 107 min)
d Jang Sun-Woo. *p* Yoo In-Taek. *sc* Jang Sun-Woo, Koo Sung-Joo. *ph* Yoo Young-Kil. *ed* Kim Hyun. *m* Kang San-ae. *cast* Moon Sueng-Kuen, Chung Sun-Kyung, Yeo Kyun-Dong.

●One of the most gleefully offensive films ever made anywhere, Jang's excoriation of trash culture is directed specifically at Korean society in the go-getting '90s, but there's nothing parochial about its satire. Three main characters (a blocked writer/plagiarist, an impotent bank clerk with a thing about *Bonnie and Clyde*, and a factory girl/ex-jailbird) wrestle with each other and with weighty issues like pornography, fraud, drug use, civic corruption, prostitution, phoney activism, gay fascism – you name it. Relentlessly vulgar and committedly sexy, the film shows up American trash-culture celebrants like John Waters for the kindergarten figures they are. TR

Toys

(1992, US, 121 min)
d Barry Levinson. *p* Mark Johnson, Barry Levinson. *sc* Barry Levinson, Valerie Curtin. *ph* Adam Greenberg. *ed* Stu Linder. *pd* Ferdinando Scarfiotti. *m* Hans Zimmer. *cast* Robin Williams, Michael Gambon, Joan Cusack, Robin Wright, LL Cool J, Donald O'Connor, Arthur Malet, Jack Warden.

●Levinson's film not only establishes a daunting benchmark for the year's worst, its dire whimsicality will impel many viewers to rush home and kick the hamster. Following the death of toy manufacturer Zevo (O'Connor) whose beanie has ceased to spin, Zevo Toys is inherited by villainous Uncle Leland (Gambon), who plans to pervert the innocent business into the production of lethal military weapons. For most of the film, nephew Leslie (Williams) is too wimpish to oppose him, and his sister Alsatia (Cusack) is clearly one step ahead of the butterfly nets. It's all finally resolved by a war between the toys, with teddy bears dropping like ninepins before the computerised tanks. Some marks for Scarfiotti's sets, but the concept – 'Open the doors to your imagination' goes the injunction – is so sub-Tim Burton that those doors fly shut. The script is haphazard, and our Gambon gets a scene to explain why, as an American general, he sounds so English. Williams has been playing nauseatingly cute for ages, but achieves a new squashiness here as a chatterbox Andy Pandy. Unbelievably rotten. BC

Toy Soldiers

(1991, US, 112 min)
d Daniel Petrie Jr. *p* Jack E Freedman, Wayne S Williams, Patricia Herskovic. *sc* Daniel Petrie Jr, David Koepp. *ph* Thomas Burstyn. *ed* Michael Kahn. *pd* Chester Kaczenski. *m* Robert Folk. *cast* Sean Astin, Wil Wheaton, Keith Coogan, Andrew Divoff, Denholm Elliott, Louis Gossett Jr, R Lee Ermey, Mason Adams.

●When a notorious Colombian drug dealer is extradited to the US for trial, his son (Divoff) invades a school for problem students with his crack terrorist squad, planning to kidnap the judge's son. The boy has been removed, but there are enough errant offspring of famous fathers to provide the necessary leverage. As police and army surround the booby-trapped school, five tough young under-achievers (led by Astin) and two wimps play their part in keeping America safe for democracy. The kids' attainment of self-respect and adulthood through sabotage and risky business is achieved at considerable cost, with Petrie pulling no punches in his depiction of violence. The exciting action set pieces, likewise, are staged with a verve and skill above and beyond the call of duty. NF

Toy Story

(1995, US, 80 min)
d John Lasseter. *p* Ralph Guggenheim, Bonnie Arnold. *sc* Joss Whedon, Andrew Stanton, Joel Cohen, Alec Sokolow. *ed* Robert Gordon, Lee Unkrich. *ad* Ralph Eggleston. *m* Randy Newman. *cast* voices: Tom Hanks, Tim Allen, Don Rickles, Jim Varney, Wallace Shawn, John Ratzenberger, R Lee Ermey.

●Thanks to Lasseter's sure sense of characterisation (and his technical wizardry), the first wholly computer-generated animation feature is a gem. From a familiar premise (toys come alive whenever humans leave the room) the ingenious, witty script proceeds to work marvels. Hitherto, the likes of Mr Potato Head, Slinky the dog, Rex the dinosaur, Bo Peep and Hamm the piggy bank have accepted as their benevolent lawgiver Woody, a pullstring cowboy and Andy's favourite toy. Come the kid's birthday, however, their world is thrown into disarray by new arrival Buzz Lightyear, a Powers Boothe lookalike in hi-tech spacesuit who not only usurps Woody's place in Andy's affections, but doesn't know he's a toy. While kids will get off on the bewitching colours, the slapstick and the action-packed (and expertly paced) story, the film will probably be more fully appreciated by adults, who'll love the snappy, knowing verbal gags, the vivid, deftly defined characters, and the overall conceptual sophistication. After all, Randy Newman songs, mutant toys reminiscent of Bosch or Svankmajer, and a surprisingly affecting foray into existential crisis are hardly conventional Disney fare. GA

Toy Story 2

(1999, US, 95 min)
d John Lasseter. *p* Helene Plotkin, Karen Robert Jackson. *sc* Andrew Stanton, Rita Hsiao, Doug Chamberlin, Chris Webb. *ph* Sharon Calahan. *ed* Edie Bleiman, David Ian Salter, Lee Unkrich. *pd* William Cone, Jim Pearson. *m* Randy Newman. *cast* voices: Tom Hanks, Tim Allen, Joan Cusack, Kelsey Grammer, Don Rickles, Jim Varney, Wallace Shawn, John Ratzenberger, Annie Potts, R Lee Ermey.

●It's rare that sequels improve on their predecessors, especially when the original is as thoroughly inventive, intelligent and enjoyable as Lasseter's seminal computer-animated feature. Nevertheless, this second foray into the world of Woody, Buzz Lightyear, et al, is a work of still greater wit and imagination than the first. Crucially, the film-makers haven't taken the usual 'more is better' route (though there are marvellous new characters), nor have they simply relied on technical developments. Rather, what distinguishes the film is that, in addition to great gags, dazzling action and deft dialogue, it can touch the heart without a hint of bogus sentimentality. That's due to the fact that by the time Woody is swiped from Andy's yard for repair and export by ruthless, antique-collecting Al, it's hard to remember that none of the characters is a 'real' living being. Hence we can become wholly involved not only in Woody's predicament, as he finds himself imprisoned with other Western puppets from a vintage TV series, but in the epic crosstown rescue mission undertaken by his pals. The list of highlights is endless. Kids will love it; adults may react more deeply. Just wonderful. GA

Traces of Red

(1992, US, 105 min)
d Andy Wolk. *p* Mark Gordon. *sc* Jim Piddock. *ph* Tim Suhrstedt. *ed* Trudy Ship. *pd* Dan Bishop, Dianna Freas. *m* Graeme Revell. *cast* James Belushi, Lorraine Bracco, Tony Goldwyn, William Russ, Faye Grant, Michelle Joyner, Joe Lisi.

●Billed as 'an erotic thriller', but devoid of thrills or frills. As Belushi and his clean-cut partner (Goldwyn) trail a serial killer, the womanising Palm Beach detective narrates the events in flashback while lying face-down in a swimming pool, à la *Sunset Boulevard*. The murderer sends Belushi cryptic, taunting letters, written on a conveniently damaged daisy-wheel typewriter, à la *Jagged Edge*. The partner suspects Belushi's jealous lover (Bracco), who gets the Kathleen Turner *Body Heat* role of ex-stewardess turned gold-digger. But there's no shortage of suspects, and soon everyone's dirty linen is being washed in public. The problem is, you don't really *care* what any of them has to hide; and when you do find out, it's so laughable that you wish you hadn't. The upbeat, double-twist ending makes no sense, the visuals are tawdry rather than glossy, and the tepid sex scenes involving Bracco's body double are more ludicrous than lubricious. NF

Trackdown

(1976, US, 98 min)
d Richard T Heffron. *p* Bernard Schwartz. *sc* Paul Edwards. *ph* Gene Polito. *ed* Anthony De Marco. *ad* Vince Cresciman. *m* Charles Bernstein. *cast* Jim Mitchum, Karen Lamm, Anne Archer, Erik Estrada, Cathy Lee Crosby, Vince Cannon.

●After vaguely promising a low-grade version of *Coogan's Bluff* ('straight' Montana cowboy goes to 'hip' LA in pursuit of runaway sister, who has drifted into prostitution), this settles into a run-of-the-mill vigilante movie. As the film-makers run out of ideas, they resort to mayhem as the solution to all their problems, and Jim Mitchum obliges by becoming increasingly bull-like. He tries hard to emulate the deadpan acting of his father Robert, for whom he could almost double, but – somewhat hilariously – gets it all wrong.

Track of the Cat

(1954, US, 102 min)
d William A Wellman. *p* Robert Fellows. *sc* AI Bezzerides. *ph* William H Clothier. *ed* Fred MacDowell. *ad* Alfred Ybarra. *m* Roy Webb. *cast* Robert Mitchum, Teresa Wright, Diana Lynn, Tab Hunter, Beulah Bondi, Philip Tonge, William Hopper, Carl 'Alfalfa' Switzer.

●A magnificently dark, brooding Western – Wellman's second adaptation of a Walter Van Tilburg Clark novel (he also wrote *The Ox-Bow Incident)* – set during the 1880s on a small, isolated ranch in the Californian mountains, where the depredations of a mountain lion bring simmering family resentments to a head. The god-fearing puritanism of the matriarch (Bondi) has turned sour in her favourite son (Mitchum), brought up to ignore feelings and simply grab what he wants; another son (Hopper), a gentle soul, is mystically in tune with nature; the rest of the family have retreated into a variety of repressions and resentments. Scorning the idea that the marauding beast might be the 'black painter' of legend (spirit of the agelessly old, dispossessed Indian kept about the place as a handyman, Hopper suggests), Mitchum sets out to hunt and kill it. A little perfunctory compared to the novel, where the hunt turns into a dark night of the soul as the hunter gradually realises he has become the hunted, these scenes nevertheless have an extraordinary charge (and weird beauty, with the snowy landscapes shot by William H Clothier in black-and-white on colour stock), reinforcing the subtextual theme that the virgin land is at last exacting revenge on the pioneer who raped it. TM

Tracks

see Voyages

Tracks

(1976, US, 92 min)
d Henry Jaglom. *p* Howard Zuker. *sc* Henry Jaglom. *ph* Paul Glickman. *ed* George Folsey. *ad* Bryan Ryman. *cast* Dennis Hopper, Taryn Power, Dean Stockwell, Topo Swope, Michael Emil, Zack Norman, James Frawley.

●'He doesn't seem like he's connected' says a girl of Dennis Hopper's distraught Vietnam veteran. Connected? The man's a virtual zombie! In *Tracks*, as in *Taxi Driver*, the neuroses of the war come home to roost. In contrast to the latter's muddle of Catholic and Calvinist sensibilities, Jaglom opts for a more explicitly Freudian approach. Set on a train, with Hopper escorting the coffin of a dead buddy and encountering sundry American archetypes, the film becomes an increasingly specific psychological journey. But the deeper it delves into symbolism, the more incoherent and hallucinatory it becomes, fragmenting faster even than Hopper. Nevertheless, Hopper's sweaty paranoia, a sustained and terminal piece of Method acting, keeps the film on the rails. Perhaps Jaglom would be more incisive if he tried less hard to make 'art'. CPe

Track 29

(1987, GB, 90 min)
d Nicolas Roeg. *p* Rick McCallum. *sc* Dennis Potter. *ph* Alex Thomson. *ed* Tony Lawson. *pd* David Brockhurst. *m* Stanley Myers. *cast* Theresa Russell, Gary Oldman, Christopher Lloyd, Colleen Camp, Sandra Bernhard, Seymour Cassel, Leon Rippy.

●So obsessed with his model train set is North Carolina geriatrician Lloyd that he neglects the complaints of wife Russell about their sexless, childless union. Her suicide is averted only by the sudden arrival of English oddball Oldman, who claims to be her long-absent illegitimate son. Cue fiery rows and frantic role-playing. Roeg and screenplay-writer Dennis Potter's brash, overemphatic psychodrama tosses out enough tricky ambiguities (is Oldman merely a child of Russell's frustrated imagination?), musical and cinematic references, and verbal and visual puns, to suggest that there's far more here than meets the eye. Finally, however, it's merely an inflated Oedipal riddle, and an exploration of guilt, desire and impotence that ends up as a curiously unilluminating and predictable vision of the world as funny-farm. Lloyd performs with a certain verve, but Russell and Oldman seem to have confused range with wobbly histrionics. GA

Trade Off

(2000, US, 95 min)
d Shaya Mercer. *p* Thomas Lee Wright, Shaya Mercer, Tammy Strange. *sc* Thomas Lee Wright. *ph* Chris Towey. *ed* Charlotte Stobbs. *m* Laura Love. *with* Charlene Barshefsky, Jello Biafra, Bill Clinton, Mike Dolan, Michael Franti, Tom Hayden, Jerry Mander, Michael Moore, Vandana Shiva.

●A necessary corrective to the partial, misleading reporting of the Seattle World Trade Organisation talks of November 1999, which tarred 50,000 protesters as 'violent anarchists', this street-level doc charts the week from the demonstators' perspective. A loose coalition of trade unionists, environmentalists, students and concerned citizens makes the case for fair trade over free trade, and holds the WTO to account for abusing the Third World, natural resources, and our tastebuds. Their wit, imagination and determination are an inspiring example of participatory democracy. TCh

Trading Places

(1983, US, 116 min)
d John Landis. *p* Aaron Russo. *sc* Timothy Harris, Herschel Weingrod. *ph* Bob Paynter. *ed* Malcolm Campbell. *pd* Gene Rudolf. *m* Elmer Bernstein. *cast* Dan Aykroyd, Eddie Murphy, Ralph Bellamy, Don Ameche, Denholm Elliott, Jamie Lee Curtis, Kristin Holby, James Belushi.

●When two bastardly billionaire brothers, Duke and Duke of Duke & Duke Commodities Brokers (Bellamy, Ameche), have a one dollar wager about the respective merits of breeding or environment on a man's character, they engineer the 'trading places' of one of their young financial wizards (Aykroyd, in fine smug form) with a black low-life hustler (Murphy), and sit back to watch Murphy rise and Aykroyd fall. This absurdly wayward premise may be a re-run of the *Prince and the Pauper* theme, but its snowy Christmas setting in Philadelphia provides the film with more than a hint of *Christmas Carol* fairytale warmth; it's also a great vehicle for the talents of Murphy, who fulfils with outrageous confidence all that he promised in *48 HRS.* As a satire on the internecine savagery of fiscal doings under late Reaganite capitalism, the movie is not as biting as it thinks it is; but it's still the best hoot since *Arthur*. CPea

Traffic (Trafic)

(1970, Fr/It, 96 min)
d Jacques Tati. *p* Robert Dorfmann. *sc* Jacques Tati, Jacques Lagrange. *ph* Eduard van der Enden, Marcel Weiss. *ed* Maurice Laumain, Sophie Taischeff. *ad* Adriaan de Rooy. *m* Charles Dumont. *cast* Jacques Tati, Maria Kimberly, Marcel Fraval, Honoré Bostel, Tony Kneppers.

●Admirers of *Playtime* won't be too disappointed, but for the Tati heretic it's a long, slow haul between the occasional brilliant gag. With all the wonder of someone just back from Crusoe's island, Tati here discovers the joys of traffic problems. Jammed drivers, not just one but several, pick their noses as they wait, so that Tati can milk all the behavioural possibilities out of furtiveness, relish, pretending I'm doing something else, and so forth. Then there's the crash, a ballet of yawning boots and bonnets as cars pile up from nowhere and detached parts take on a life of their own as they spin off on unpredictable joyrides. Or there's the rainy bit, with windscreen wipers sweeping rhythmically, chattily, pompously or excitedly, depending on the personality of the owner. All very clever, but done with the sort of calculated precision that has one chalking up points rather than laughing. TM

Traffic

(2000, US, 147 min)
d Steven Soderbergh. *p* Edward Zwick, Marshall Herskovitz, Laura Bickford. *sc* Stephen Gaghan. *ph* Peter Andrews [Steven Soderbergh]. *ed* Stephen Mirrione. *pd* Philip Messina. *m* Cliff Martinez. *cast* Michael Douglas, Don Cheadle, Benicio Del Toro, Luis Guzmán, Dennis Quaid, Catherine Zeta-Jones, Steven Bauer, Erika Christensen, Amy Irving, Tomas Milian.

●Just as supreme court judge Douglas is made US drug tsar, his teenage daughter (Christensen) is sliding deeper into drug abuse. Douglas's Mexican counterpart (Milian) says he'll pool resources, but Tijuana cop Del Toro finds his efforts to prevent smuggling under pressure from cartels and corrupt authorities. In San Diego, meanwhile, dismayed to find hubby Bauer is indeed a drug baron, Zeta-Jones discovers she'll do anything to defend her kids and comfortable existence from threats posed on both sides of the law and both sides of the border. There's so much going for this movie. The performances are all topnotch, while director Soderbergh's seemingly effortless mastery of his medium goes from strength to strength. Steering us through a densely detailed script with a clear-eyed sense of purpose and balance, he contributes gritty reportage-style camerawork to enhance an aura of authenticity. It's wise about different kinds of addiction and concepts of family, about the folly, futility and hypocrisy of anti-drug 'wars', and about the awful human cost of it all. And it grips like a vice from start to end. GA

Trafico

(1998, Port/Fr/Den, 112 min)
d João Botelho. *p* Paulo Branco. *sc* João Botelho. *ph* Olivier Guéneau. *ed* Rodolfo Wedeles. *pd* Fernanda Morais, João Botelho. *cast* Rita Blanco, Adriano Luz, Canto e Castro, Suzana Borges, Paulo Bragança.

●Even by his own often eccentric standards, this absurdist comedy finds Botelho (*Hard Times, Three Palms*) in high spirits, merrily resurrecting the spirit of Buñuel with a series of very loosely linked surreal episodes. Anti-clericalism is rife, but there's also a good deal of fun at the expense of the nouveaux riches, and the old rich too. It's shot in saturated Day-Glo reds and blues, and that's just the wigs. Genuinely bizzare. TCh

Tragedy of a Ridiculous Man, The (La Tragedia di un Uomo Ridicolo)

(1981, It, 116 min)
d Bernardo Bertolucci. *p* Giovanni Bertolucci. *sc* Bernardo Bertolucci. *ph* Carlo Di Palma. *ed* Gabriella Cristiani. *pd* Gianni Silvestri. *m* Ennio Morricone. *cast* Ugo Tognazzi, Anouk Aimée, Laura Morante, Victor Cavallo, Olympia Carlisi, Riccardo Tognazzi, Vittorio Caprioli, Renato Salvatori.

●Tognazzi plays a rich Parma dairy farmer forced to sell up his greatest love – his material possessions – to meet the ransom demanded by a gang of terrorists who have kidnapped his son. In an attempt to fathom the siege mentality induced in an Italian society which had by then accepted terrorist violence as a commonplace, Bertolucci inverts the son-in-search-of-the-father theme of his most widely admired film, *The Spider's Stratagem*, and his small ensemble of lead characters begin to spin webs of deception – on each other, on us. The result is a mordantly witty tragi-comedy which matches the sombre tones of Carlo Di Palma's cinematography, but the style is no less flamboyant and seductive than that of Bertolucci's earlier films. RM

Tragedy of Carmen, The (La Tragédie de Carmen)

(1983, Fr, 85 min)
d Peter Brook. *p* Micheline Rozan. *sc* Marius Constant, Jean-Claude Carrière, Peter Brook. *ph* Sven Nykvist. *ed* Marina Michaka. *ad* Georges Wakhevitch. *m* Bizet. *cast* Hélène Delavault, Howard Hensel, Agnès Host, Jake Gardner, Jean-Paul Denizon, Alain Maratrat.

●Brook's interpretation of the evergreen myth (luminously photographed by Sven Nykvist) cuts incisively through the lush romanticism of Bizet's opera (although retaining all his best tunes) to the tighter fantasy of Mérimée's original story, leaving only a sinewy passion to bind together this tale of a gypsy, a soldier, and their love. Delavault is inspired as Carmen, displaying a malignity that is as motiveless as that of Shakespeare's Iago, but as resigned to the inexorable workings of fate as Lear. The rest of the excellent cast work at a fever pitch, keeping events within Brook's earthy arena at a rolling boil, while Brook's choice of title leaves no room to doubt that it will, as ever, end in tears. (Two other versions were filmed, one starring Eva Saurova, the other Zehava Gal Halet.) FD

Tragedy of the Street

see Dirnentragödie

Trail of the Pink Panther

(1982, GB, 96 min)
d Blake Edwards. *p* Blake Edwards, Tony Adams. *sc* Frank Waldman, Tom Waldman, Blake Edwards, Geoffrey Edwards. *ph* Dick Bush. *ed* Alan Jones. *pd* Peter Mullins. *m* Henry Mancini. *cast* Peter Sellers, David Niven, Herbert Lom, Richard Mulligan, Joanna Lumley, Capucine, Robert Loggia, Harvey Korman, Burt Kwouk.

●The presence of Blake Edwards and most of the original *Pink Panther* team shouldn't fool you into thinking that this is an entirely new adventure. Instead, there are some out-takes of Sellers from the previous movies, tacked together with an anorexic plotline. After that, we suffer Lumley's Fronch aksonted TV reporter, whose task is to track down 'the essential Clouseau', linking a lot of 'flashback' clips, interviews with the 'Panther' stars in character, and some embarrassingly unfunny reconstructions of the detective's early life. Made two years after Sellers' death, possibly motivated as a tribute, this garbled piece of incestuous myth-massaging forfeits any sympathy through its shamefully mismanaged construction. FL

Train, The

(1964, US/Fr/It, 140 min, b/w)
d John Frankenheimer. *p* Jules Bricken. *sc* Franklin Coen, Frank Davis, Walter Bernstein. *ph* Jean Tournier, Walter Wottitz. *ed* David Bretherton, Gabriel Rongier. *pd* Willy Holt. *m* Maurice Jarre. *cast* Burt Lancaster, Paul Scofield, Jeanne Moreau, Michel Simon, Suzanne Flon, Charles Millot, Albert Rémy, Wolfgang Preiss, Howard Vernon.

●Discount some self-conscious talk about Art as a national heritage, as well as clumsy dubbing of the supporting cast, and you have a rattling good thriller about a World War II German general (Scofield) determined to flee Paris just before the liberation with a trainload of Impressionist paintings. One obsession runs headlong into another as a French railway inspector (Lancaster), once unwillingly started out in opposition, finds he cannot stop, and must go on finding new ways and means of delaying the train for an hour here, a day there. In Frankenheimer's hands, the whole paraphernalia of trains, tracks and shunting yards acquires an almost hypnotic fascination as the screen becomes a giant chessboard on which huge metallic pawns are manoeuvred, probing for some fatal weakness but seemingly engaged in some deadly primeval struggle. TM

Training Day

(2001, US/Aust, 122 min)
d Antoine Fuqua. *p* Jeffrey Silver, Bobby Newmyer. *sc* David Ayer. *ph* Mauro Fiore. *ed* Conrad Buff. *pd* Naomi Shohan. *m* Mark Mancina. *cast* Denzel Washington, Ethan Hawke, Scott Glenn, Tom Berenger, Harris Yulin, Raymond J Barry, Cliff Curtis, Dr Dré, Snoop Dogg, Macy Gray, Charlotte Ayanna.

●For eager young detective Jake Hoyt (Hawke), today is his first day in the field under the tutelage of Washington's jaundiced narc, Alonzo Harris. Shades of *Seven* immediately evaporate when Harris compels his partner to sample the illegal substances they've just seized from some unlucky daytrippers. That's just for starters because Harris has plans. He shows Hoyt round the 'hood, then sets about blooding him big time. There's a nifty little B-movie lurking somewhere underneath this glossy cop thriller. Not that many punters will complain about the excess, or the slumming A list actors. Alonzo isn't exactly undercover, rather he operates in plain sight, playing both sides of the law against each other to his own ends. Washington certainly doesn't hold back: he's the best bad cop since Richard Gere in *Internal Affairs*. Suffering remorseless verbal and physical humiliation, Hawke doesn't get much time for goatee-scratching, which is just as well, given how the script is more propulsive than credible. Director Fuqua keeps it slick and sleazy and stokes up the race some, but this only accelerates the movie's deafening rush toward the top and ever over. TCh

Train of Events

(1949, GB, 88 min, b/w)
d Basil Dearden, Charles Crichton, Sidney Cole. *p* Michael Relph. *sc* Basil Dearden, TEB Clarke, Ronald Millar, Angus MacPhail. *ph* Lionel Banes, Gordon Dines. *ed* Bernard Gribble. *ad* Malcolm Baker-Smith, Jim Morahan. *m* Leslie Bridgewater. *cast* Valerie Hobson, John Clements, Jack Warner, Gladys Henson, Susan Shaw, Joan Dowling, Laurence Payne, Peter Finch.

●Trying to repeat the formula of *Dead of Night*, Ealing came a horrible cropper with this portmanteau telling, in flashback from a train crash, the stories which brought three groups of people aboard the Euston-Liverpool express. Shorn of the talents of Cavalcanti and Hamer, the direction is flat. The trilogy of shoddy yarns (melodramatic, comic, tragic) sprout clichés by the yard, and arbitrarily resort to the crash as a resolution. Worst of all is the linking device involving scenes from the life of a Cockney engine-driver and his wife, soon – as played by Jack Warner and Gladys Henson – to achieve cosy apotheosis as Mr and Mrs Dixon of Dock Green in *The Blue Lamp*. TM

Train of Shadows (Tren de Sombras)

(1996, Sp, 80 min)
d José Luis Guerin. *p* Hector Faver, Pedro Portabella. *sc* José Luis Guerin. *ph* Tomás Pladevall. *ed* Manuel Aliminana. *ad* Rosa Ros, Albert Bover. *cast* Juliette Gaultier, Ivon Orvain, Anne Céline Auché, Céline Laurent, Simone Mercier, Carlos Romagosa.

●Though slow, determinedly poetic, and in places rather abstract, this casts a spell. It begins with home movies shot at the family chateau in the '30s by Parisian lawyer Gérard Fleury, who disappeared mysteriously while off looking for a special quality of light. The film then visits the now empty Normandy chateau, the images suggesting the presence of ghosts. Finally, the archive footage is returned to, though this time treated, reversed and repeated, and new suggestions of relationships between the people begin to emerge. It's a strange exercise, haunting, even at times erotic (writer/director Guerin seems – quite understandably – obsessed by Fleury's stunningly beautiful daughter). GA

Train Robbers, The

(1973, US, 92 min)
d Burt Kennedy. *p* Michael Wayne. *sc* Burt Kennedy. *ph* William H Clothier. *ed* Frank Santillo. *ad* Alfred Sweeney. *m* Dominic Frontière. *cast* John Wayne, Ann-Margret, Rod Taylor, Ben Johnson, Bobby Vinton, Christopher George, Ricardo Montalban, Jerry Gatlin.

●Inoffensive Western with Wayne, rheumy-eyed and overweight, called upon to reminisce about old times with Ben Johnson at every available moment, leading a gang that rides like a U Certificate version of Peckinpah's *Wild Bunch*. Wayne, as self-appointed guardian of the law, injects his boys (including Bobby Vinton, singer from the early '60s) with his particular brand of benevolent fascism. In return for every fist-whipping, they learn to respect him all the more and to call him 'Sir'. The band ride after half a million's worth of stolen gold so they can turn it in for the 50,000 dollars reward; it's that sort of film. Loads of male camaraderie and big country theme music, plus Ann-Margret riding along as a box-office concession and to get the rest of the cast horny in a U Certificate sort of way.

Trainspotting (100)

(1995, GB, 93 min)
d Danny Boyle. *p* Andrew MacDonald. *sc* John Hodge. *ph* Brian Tufano. *ed* Masahiro Hirakubo. *pd* Kave Quinn. *cast* Ewan McGregor, Jonny Lee Miller, Ewen Bremner, Robert Carlyle, Kevin McKidd, Kelly Macdonald, Pauline Lynch, Irvine Welsh.

●A shocking, painfully subjective trawl through the Edinburgh heroin culture of the 1980s, Irvine Welsh's cult novel is hardly an obvious choice for the team who made *Shallow Grave*. Yet the film's a triumph. Audaciously punching up the pitch-black comedy, juggling parallel character strands and juxtaposing image, music and voice-over with a virtuosity worthy of Scorsese on peak form, *Trainspotting* the movie captures precisely Welsh's insolent, amoral intelligence. Amoral, but not unthinking, and certainly not unfeeling. Nihilism runs deep in this movie, emotion cannot be countenanced, only blocked off by another hit, another gag, but the anarchic, exhilarating rush of the highs can't drown out the subsequent, devastating lows – these are two sides of the same desperation. Danny Boyle's intuitive, vital, empathetic direction pushes so far, the movie flies on sheer momentum – that and bravura performances from Bremner's gormless Spud, Carlyle's terrifying Begbie and, especially, McGregor's Renton, who supplies a low-key, charismatic centre. This may not have the weight of 'Great Art', but it crystallises youthful disaffection with the verve of the best and brightest pop culture. A sensation. TCh

Traitement de Choc (The Doctor in the Nude/ Shock Treatment)

(1972, Fr/It, 91 min)
d Alain Jessua. *p* Raymond Danon, Jacques Dorfmann. *sc* Alain Jessua. *ph* Jacques Robin. *ed* Hélène Plemiannikov. *ad* Yannis Kokkos. *m* René Koering, Alain Jessua. *cast* Alain Delon, Annie Girardot, Michel Duchaussoy, Robert Hirsch, Jean-François Calvé, Guy Saint-Jean.

●Jessua's first two films, *Life Upside Down* and *Comic Strip Hero*, attracted little more than good notices over here, so his third was distributed as an exploitation picture retitled in honour of Delon's cock-flashing sequence. Don't be misled, since the film is actually a political allegory fashioned as a horror story. Girardot, visiting Dr Devilers' clifftop clinic for rejuvenation treatment, discovers behind the futuristic settings a nightmare world of primeval instincts and ruthless logic that holds no place for the weak. Jessua handles his mixture of suspense and satire with assurance, drawing fine performances from Girardot, confused and finally uncertain of her sanity, and Delon as the diabolic yet half-sympathetic doctor in whose arms she finds herself. A neat cautionary tale on human vanity cum fable about hypocrisy.

Traitor Spy (aka The Torso Murder Mystery)

(1939, GB, 75 min, b/w)
d Walter Summers. *p* John Argyle. *sc* Walter Summers, Jay Van Lusic, Ralph Bettinson. *ph* Robert Lapresle. *ed* E Richards. *ad* Ian White. *cast* Bruce Cabot, Marta Labarr, Tamara Desni, Romilly Lunge, Percy Walsh, Edward Lexy, Frederick Valk.

●If transposing Marie Stopes' *Married Love* to the screen didn't win undying fame for Summers, this – his last picture for an ungrateful world – surely should have done. Cabot plays a British armaments worker and freelance spy who is forced to go on the run after killing (and dismembering) a disgruntled German agent who makes an attempt on his life. As the film moves from toy-town Devon to a very seedy London, it rapidly takes off from the cardboard conventions of the British thriller. In its creation of authentic atmosphere – an Italian dentist/tattooist's parlour in the Waterloo Road, a sleazy night-club populated by spivs, whores and multi-national gangsters – the film offers a fascinating glimpse into the underworld of the '30s, and presages the realism of the following decade. Summers skilfully exploits the paranoia of the phony war to create satisfyingly red-blooded villains, and the melodramatic conflagration of an ending is remarkably, and effectively, uncompromising. RMy

Tramp, Tramp, Tramp

(1926, US, 5,625 ft, b/w)
d Harry Edwards, [Frank Capra]. *p* Harry Langdon. *sc* Frank Capra, Tim Whelan, Hal Conklin, J Frank Holliday, Gerald Duffy, Murray Roth. *ph* Elgin Lessley. *cast* Harry Langdon, Joan Crawford, Edwards Davis, Carlton Griffin, Alec B Francis.

●Langdon's first venture into features has echoes of Harold Lloyd (when our hero is dangling helplessly over the edge of a cliff), and concludes with a raging typhoon reminiscent of Keaton's natural disasters, but the bulk of the gags are wholly individual. Langdon enters a cross-continent walk to boost the local brand of footwear; Joan Crawford is the girl he can hug only if he crosses the finishing line first. After many strange convolutions, he does so. GB

Trancers (aka Future Cop)

(1984, US, 85 min)
d/p Charles Band. *sc* Danny Bilson, Paul DeMeo. *ph* Mac Ahlberg. *ed* Ted Nicolaou. *pd* Jeff Staggs. *m* Mark Ryder, Phil Davies. *cast* Tim Thomerson, Helen Hunt, Michael Stefani, Art Le Fleur, Telma Hopkins, Richard Erdman.

● This fizzing cheapo sci-fi actioner from no-frills genre specialist Band is a shameless amalgam of *Blade Runner* and *The Terminator*. So shameless, unpretentious and fast-paced, in fact, it's actually a lot of fun. Thomerson is Jack Deth, 23rd century cop in the battle against the human zombies (or Trancers) in thrall to Stefani's evil mastermind. The latter has skipped back in time and must be stopped before he wipes out the ancestors of Angel City's ruling Counsellors. With Hunt's 1985 heroine a plucky foil, and Thomerson an amiably modest superhero, the film offers breezy thrills and an amusing line in future speak ('Dry hair is for squids,' apparently), without ever taking on more than its budget will allow. TJ

Trances (El Hal)

(1981, Mor/Fr, 87 min)
d Ahmed El Maanouni. *with* Nass El Ghiwane, Taieb Seddiki.

● A documentary on the music group Nass El Ghiwane. We eavesdrop on the group, whose troubadour style has won them a large and rapturous following in their home country of Morocco. The debt owed to the musical traditions of their faith and land is freely acknowledged, and vividly brought to mind by the trance-like state their compelling, percussive music induces in their fans. Amid nostalgic and folkloric anecdotes, they bicker over recording contracts. Nothing new here, but interesting. FD

Tranchée, La

see Trench, The

Transatlantic Tunnel

see Tunnel, The

Trans-Europ-Express

(1966, Fr, 90 min, b/w)
d Alain Robbe-Grillet. *p* Samy Halfon. *sc* Alain Robbe-Grillet. *ph* Willy Kurant. *ed* Bob Wade. *m* Giuseppe Verdi. *songs* Clo Vanesco. *cast* Jean-Louis Trintignant, Marie-France Pisier, Nadine Verdier, Christian Barbier, Charles Millot, Daniel Emilfork, Alain Robbe-Grillet.

● Written and directed by the high priest of the French *nouveau roman*, this now looks considerably more literary than cinematic. Robbe-Grillet himself plays the focal character, the author-within-the-film, dreaming up a surreal melodrama involving a man (Trintignant) who boards the same train, during a journey through Europe: dope-pushing, gangsterism, bondage fantasies. Trintignant's cool is as unshakeable as ever, but the vague 'modernism' of the project can't conceal an underlying pomposity. CA

Transformers – The Movie, The

(1986, US, 85 min)
d Nelson Shin. *p* Joe Bacal, Tom Griffin. *sc* Ron Friedman. *ed* David Hankins. *m* Vince DiCola. *cast* voices: Eric Idle, Judd Nelson, Leonard Nimoy, Robert Stack, Lionel Stander, Orson Welles.

● Following on the bad scent of feature-length commercials for *The Care Bears* and *My Little Pony*, comes this animated sci-fi tinbot battle between the forces of good and evil. The good guys are a bunch of heavy metallurgists called Autobots who, involved in an age-old conflict, are once again waging war on the equally powerful Decepticons, led by the mega-nasty Megatron. You'd be amazed at what these characters, collectively known as *Transformers*, are capable of. With the flick of a hinge… Is it a bird? Is it a plane? No, it's… In fact, they all look rather similar, all talk with synthesised voices, and all race around the Galaxy to the thump of a diabolical but appropriate heavy metal score. Still, the animation is extremely well done, with plenty of action in the fight sequences as the heroic Autobots, with the help of the Matrix of Leaders (a sort of all-powerful crystal ball), restore peace to the Universe. Hopefully, for the last time. DA

Trapped

(1949, US, 82 min, b/w)
d Richard Fleischer. *p* Bryan Foy. *sc* Earl Felton, George Zuckerman. *ph* Guy Roe. *ed* Alfred De Gaetano. *ad* Frank Durlauf. *m* Sol Kaplan. *cast* Lloyd Bridges, Barbara Payton, John Hoyt, James Todd, Russ Conway.

● The familiar stern scoutmaster of a commentator asserts the omnipotence of the US Treasury Dept then, having got that out of the way, the movie proceeds to cases. Bridges, aggressively seedy, busts out of jail aiming to retrieve his counterfeiting plates, unaware that the T-men are watching his every move. The ensuing series of table-turnings and reversals of fortune is agreeably unpredictable, with a full measure of prevailing visual motifs: plots hatched in dimly lit apartments, guys in trilbies ascending ominous stairways, and violence in picturesque settings, notably the climactic shoot-out in a tramcar garage. For perhaps the only time in his career John Hoyt, usually a minor henchman, got to play the hero. BBa

Trapped in Paradise

(1994, US, 111 min)
d George Gallo. *p* Jon Davison, George Gallo. *sc* George Gallo. *ph* Jack N Green. *ed* Terry Rawlings. *pd* Bob Ziembicki. *m* Robert Folk. *cast* Nicolas Cage, Richard B Shull, Jon Lovitz, Mädchen Amick, Dana Carvey, Jack Heller, Vic Manni.

● This gormless Christmas comedy drama has a New York restaurant manager Bill Firpo (Cage), and his two con brothers, Dave (Lovitz) and Alvin (Carvey), plying their dumb klutz criminal ways. Alvin is the klepto who steals the toys from cereal packets; Dave the conniving one, masquerading as a Catskill comic; and Bill, the sensible one of these three latter-day Stooges, is suffering and exasperated. They go to Paradise, Pennsylvania, to succour the daughter of hard con Vic Mazzucci (Manni), but find the bank where she works irresistible to rob. It's an odd plot-potty, frenetic movie, shot at some snow-blown Canadian location with irrelevant panache. Cage looks cold most of the time, and has retractable stubble. The rest of the cast look like they're waiting for summer. WH

Trash

(1970, US, 103 min)
d Paul Morrissey. *p* Andy Warhol. *sc/ph* Paul Morrissey. *ed* Jed Johnson. *cast* Joe Dallesandro, Holly Woodlawn, Jane Forth, Michael Sklar, Geri Miller, Andrea Feldman.

● A companion piece to *Flesh*, with Dallesandro as a down-and-out junkie living on New York's Lower East Side whose heroin addiction has rendered him impotent; just as Joe's desirable virility formed the (nominal) subject of *Flesh*, so his undesirable impotence is at the centre of *Trash*. The surprise value of Morrissey's films (the 'liberating nudity', the frankness about sexuality, the playful reversals of sex-roles) camouflaged a number of crucial failings. *Flesh* and *Trash* are both eulogies to Dallesandro's body, but are also both moralistic to the point of being puritan about sex in general, and the female sex in particular. TR

Trauma

(1993, It, 105 min)
d/p Dario Argento. *sc* Dario Argento, TED Klein. *ph* Raffaele Mertes. *ed* Conrad Gonzalez. *m* Pino Donaggio. *cast* Asia Argento, Christopher Rydell, Frederic Forrest, James Russo, Laura Johnson, Piper Laurie, Brad Dourif, Hope Alexander-Willis.

● This rarely seen gorefest from Italian horror director Dario Argento failed to get a UK cinema release, despite containing all the best and worst elements of his uncompromising style. David Parsons (Rydell) is a journalist who takes young anorexic Aura Petrescu (Argento) under his wing after her parents are apparently murdered by a serial killer wielding a decapitating machine. As the unstable Aura and David become closer, a pattern to the killings emerges. Argento's first American backed film pays homage to *Psycho*, yet he conspicuously lacks Hitchcock's ability to direct actors – there isn't a half decent performance to be found here, and his own daughter in the female lead is particularly awful. Also, a barely credible plot and uneven pacing don't help. Yet Argento's occasionally brilliant camerawork and the evident glee with which he sets about the decapitation scenes make this just about worthwhile. TH

Traveling Executioner, The

(1970, US, 94 min)
d/p Jack Smight. *sc* Garrie Bateson. *ph* Philip H Lathrop. *ed* Neil Travis. *ad* George W Davis, Edward C Carfagno. *m* Jerry Goldsmith. *cast* Stacy Keach, Marianna Hill, Bud Cort, Graham Jarvis, James J Sloyan, M Emmet Walsh, John Bottoms, Ford Rainey.

● More a grotesque theatrical farce than a black comedy: Jonas Candide (Keach) travels the American South of 1918, hiring out his electric chair at 100 bucks a throw, but loses his omnipotence when he falls for his first lady 'victim' (Hill), and starts conniving to save her. It works best as – and is worth seeing for – an extravagant, outsize performance from Keach, a mixture of trash rhetoric, sinister dedication, and fairground showmanship. But what it desperately needs is a director capable of anchoring the fantasy in recognisable human realities. TR

Traveller

(1981, GB, 80 min)
d/p Joe Comerford. *sc* Neil Jordan. *ph* Thaddeus O'Sullivan. *ed* Joe Comerford. *cast* Judy Donovan, Davy Spillane, Alan Devlin, Johnny Choil Mhaidhc, Paddy Donovan, Joe Pilkington.

● Scripted by Neil Jordan, this has something of the same bizarre thriller quality as *Angel*, with a young couple – reluctantly submitting to an arranged marriage, and sent on a smuggling mission from Limerick to Strabane – running from a mysterious encounter into robbery and murder while crossing the border from Southern Ireland. Instead of the strange wonderland of *Angel*, a strikingly desolate picture of rural poverty, but the film never quite manages to clinch its supposedly thematic connection between politics and violence. TM

Traveller

(1997, US, 100 min)
d Jack Green. *p* Bill Paxton, Brian Swardstrom, Mickey Liddell, David Blocker. *sc* Jim McGlynn. *ph* Jack Green. *ed* Michael Ruscio. *pd* Michael Helmy. *m* Andy Paley. *cast* Bill Paxton, Mark Wahlberg, Julianna Marguilies, James Gammon, Luke Askew, Nikki Deloach.

● Intriguing set-up: gypsy initiation drama plus grifter thriller. The Travellers are an insular gypsy group with Oirish roots and smart suits, who congregate in the backwoods of the Deep South for a spot of traditional dancing before hiving off in their 4x4s to hoodwink local gullibles. Bokky (Paxton) likes selling them stitched-up trailers and water-based 'sealant' for their driveways. Enter Pat O'Hara (Wahlberg) who wants into the Family. He has the blood (and 'the blood don't lie'), but not the breeding – his father was cast out when he married a gentile. Could it be Bokky's turn to fall for one of his victims (Marguilies)? Though competently directed by Clint Eastwood's cameraman Jack Green, matters unravel when the film ratchets up the tension and become entirely implausible at the close. NB

Traveller, The (Mossafer)

(1974, Iran, 73 min, b/w)
d/sc Abbas Kiarostami. *ph* Firooz Malekzadeh. *ed* Amir Hassan Hami. *m* Kambiz Roshanravan. *cast* Masoud Zanbegleh, Hassan Darabi.

● Gassem is a soccer-mad 12-year-old who is determined to get to Teheran to see the international match. This was Kiarostami's first feature and his first disquisition on the theme of persistence – whether it is admirable, and ought to be rewarded. Cheeky-faced Gassem is an early example of all the lively, somewhat perplexed children who figure in the director's work. It's rough and ready technically, but Kiarostami's eye for the telling detail, unassumingly presented, is already evident. BBa

Travelling Light: a Portrait of Lindsay Kemp

(1991, It, 57 min)
d Theo Eshetu.
● Style over content has always been a hallmark of Lindsay Kemp, but in this case, Kemp's own outrageously marvellous sense of theatre is subverted by Eshetu's self-serving, self-congratulatory camera techniques. He leaves viewers with the impression that Kemp's visions, awash with a tacky, extravagant glamour all their own, need electronic manipulation. Eshetu's approach is jagged and uneven. Yes, there are clips from many of Kemp's most important works, but they leave you feeling dissatisfied and deprived of anything more substantial than soundbites. The clips, including some early footage of David Bowie, are interwoven with interviews, both backstage and at home. It all adds up to a frustrating hour-long trailer. AR

Travelling North

(1986, Aust, 97 min)
d Carl Schultz. *p* Ben Gannon. *sc* David Williamson. *ph* Julian Penney. *ed* Henry Dangar. *pd* Owen Paterson. *m* Alan John. *cast* Leo McKern, Julia Blake, Graham Kennedy, Henri Szeps, Michele Fawdon, Diane Craig.
● David Williamson's filmed play is a bit like an Australian *On Golden Pond*. Frank (McKern) retires to his Queensland dream home overlooking a lake with his middle-aged girlfriend Frances (Blake), but heart trouble erodes the idyll. A bossy old bully, Frank soon offends their boring but helpful neighbour Freddie (Kennedy), overrides the local doctor (Szeps) in the matter of prognosis and prescription, and drives even patient Frances back to her daughters in Melbourne with his increasing cantankerousness. This slight, unsensational history depends almost entirely upon our sympathy for the central character, a shoo-in thanks to the McKern outline in shorts, eye-patch and paunch. The actor would serve as a definition of the word curmudgeon. 'The autumn of our days?' he mocks the registrar, having asked Frances to return and marry him, 'Get on with it before we slide into winter'. BC

Travelling Players, The (O Thiassos)

(1975, Greece, 230 min)
d Theodor Angelopoulos. *p* Georges Samiotis. *sc* Theodor Angelopoulos. *ph* Yorgos Arvanitis. *ed* Takis Davlopoulos, Georges Trianthaphilou. *ad* Mikes Karapiperis. *m* Loukianos Kilaidonis. *cast* Eva Kotamanidou, Aliki Georgoulis, Statos Pachis, Maris Vassiliou, Petros Zarkadis.
● Made, incredibly, under the noses of the military police during the Colonels' regime, Angelopoulos' film examines, with a passionate radicalism, the labyrinth of Greek politics around that country's agonising civil war. This is done through the eyes of a troupe of actors, whose pastoral folk drama *Golfo the Shepherdess* is continually interrupted as they become unwitting spectators of the political events that ultimately polarise them. This slow, complex, four-hour film will obviously provide problems for people raised on machine-gun cutting techniques. Editing is very restrained, and some takes last up to five minutes, but the stately pace of the film soon becomes compulsive; and the shabby provincial Greece of rusting railway tracks and flaking facades which the slow camera examines is visually beguiling. The closing passage, when one of the actors is buried after being executed, and his colleagues spontaneously raise their hands above their heads to applaud not a performance but a life, is an incredibly moving moment. DPer

Traversée de Paris, La (Pig Across Paris/Four Bags Full)

(1956, Fr/It, 83 min, b/w)
d Claude Autant-Lara. *sc* Jean Aurenche, Pierre Bost. *ph* Jacques Natteau. *ed* Madeleine Gug. *ad* Max Douy. *m* René Cloërec. *cast* Jean Gabin, Bourvil, Louis de Funès, Jeanette Batti, Jacques Marin, Anouk Ferjac, Harald Wolff.
● Paris, 1943. Martin (Bourvil), a slow-witted spiv, persuades a stranger, Grandgil (Gabin), to help him shift four suitcases of pork from butcher to buyer during the blackout. As they dodge patrols, hungry dogs and air raids, Grandgil proves resourceful but explosively and abusively unpredictable. He turns out to be a celebrated painter out slumming, scolding the less fortunate from a position of absolute security – demonstrated when the pair are arrested by the Germans, Grandgil to be fawned on, Martin to be deposited with the rest of the hostages. A post-war postscript shows Grandgil striding along a station platform while Martin, now a porter and still lugging suitcases, trails unrecognised behind him. This sardonic anecdote (a novel by Marcel Aymé) is characteristic of its director, both in its sour disposition and its storytelling gusto. BBa

Traviata, La

(1982, Neth, 109 min)
d Franco Zeffirelli. *p* Tarak Ben Ammar. *sc* Francesco Maria Piave, Franco Zeffirelli. *ph* Ennio Guarnieri. *ed* Peter Taylor, Franca Silvi. *pd* Franco Zeffirelli. *m* Giuseppe Verdi. *cast* Teresa Stratas, Placido Domingo, Cornell MacNeil, Allan Monk, Axell Gall.
● Zeffirelli's talents are well-matched to *La Traviata*. Based on Dumas' novel *The Lady of the Camellias*, with an original soundtrack by Verdi, this is grand opera at its most pathetic, in which Romantic heroines suffer and expire amid the fluttering demi-monde of 19th century Paris. Teresa Stratas, as that most famous of TB cases, has a suitably angelic face, though her voice is a touch less seraphic in the higher registers; the masterful Placido Domingo brings an ingenuous charm to the role of Alfredo; Zeffirelli directs as he has always done, in a style high on gloss and bravura, with occasional nods to film realism via exteriors and voice-overs. The sumptuousness comes close to overkill, but fine musical moments help some magic to survive. LU

Treasure Island (Ostrov Sokrovishch)

(1971, USSR, 87 min)
d Eugen Fridman. *sc* Edgar Dubrovski, Eugen Fridman. *ph* Valeri Bazylev. *ed* G Sadonvikova. *ad* Constantin Zagorski. *m* A Rybnikoy. *songs* A Massulis, I Mikailov. *cast* Boris Andreiev, Aare Laanemets, L Noreika, A Massulis, L Urmonavichus, L Chagolova, A Pikialis, P Klass.
● This Gorky Studio production of Stevenson's romance is played chiefly for derring-do, and judging from the battle in the Admiral Benbow director/co-writer Fridman has seen a few spaghetti Westerns. Creditable re-creation of 18th century English life, plus plausible West Country dubbing for the British release print; but the attractive voyage out is too long for a pirate tale, and Jim's account of how none of his companions gained lasting happiness from his doubloons makes for a flat finish (as well as leaving us in no doubt about where the movie came from). JPy

Treasure Island

(1990, US, 132 min)
d/p/sc Fraser C Heston. *ph* Robert Steadman. *ed* Eric Boyd-Perkins, Bill Parnell, Gregory Gontz. *pd* Tony Woollard. *m* Paddy Maloney. *cast* Charlton Heston, Christian Bale, Richard Johnson, Julian Glover, Clive Wood, Oliver Reed, Christopher Lee.
● Ah-aaarh, Jim lad! Where would we be without Robert Louis Stevenson? With Heston *père et fils* attempting some kind of comeback for the great old piratical fable, this has coral-blue location cinematography somewhere off the Spanish Main, one of those solid True Brit casts, and Charlton Heston, plus parrot, making what is not even a really interestingly bad job of old Long John himself. An over-familiar (and over-*familial*) version of Stevenson's novel, made for TV, it has a few fine moments, an excellent eccentric Squire Trelawny from Richard Johnson, and some sweet seaside shots of late Georgian Bristol. Apart from that, it's even longer than Ben Gunn's whiskers, and deeply tedious, shiver me aching timbers. SGr

Treasure Island

see Ile au trésor, L'

Treasure of Matecumbe

(1976, US, 117 min)
d Vincent McEveety. *p* Bill Anderson. *sc* Don Tait. *ph* Frank Phillips. *ed* Cotton Warburton. *pd* Robert Clatworthy. *m* Buddy Baker. *cast* Robert Foxworth, Joan Hackett, Peter Ustinov, Vic Morrow, Johnny Doran, Billy Attmore, Jane Wyatt.
● Not a great deal more than a standard Disney yarn, to be sure: a chase down the Mississippi; two fearlessly resourceful schoolboys; man-eating mosquitoes, a spectacular hurricane; no sex, no serious injuries, and only one fatality. McEveety, having the measure of his duties, delivers the action with the minimum of fuss; and the plot, drawn from a novel by Pulitzer prizewinner Robert Lewis Taylor, bashes along at a cracking pace. Hackett, radiant and wet-lipped, offers an energetic character study of a sturdy Southern belle fleeing from a devilish Yankee suitor (the action takes place just after the Civil War); show-stealing honours, however, go to Ustinov as a loquacious quack pedlar whose foul medicine doubles, when the need arises, as the ingredients for Molotov cocktails. First-rate escapist nonsense. JPy

Treasure of the Four Crowns

(1982, US/Sp, 100 min)
d Ferdinando Baldi. *p* Tony Anthony, Gene Quintano. *sc* Lloyd Battista, Jim Bryce, Jerry Lazaus. *ph* Marcello Masciocchi, Giuseppe Ruzzolini. *ed* Franco Fraticelli. *ad* Luciano Spadoni. *m* Ennio Morricone. *cast* Tony Anthony, Ana Obregón, Gene Quintano, Jerry Lazarus, Francisco Rabal.
● A marked improvement on *Comin' at Ya!*, the previous miserable effort from the team of Tony Anthony, Gene Quintano and Baldi. Which isn't to say much for this nonsense about ancient prophecies and modern mettle, bloated with the cruder possibilities of 3-D, plus sound effects and scenes shamelessly stolen from other films. One sorry borrowing, where the hero is chased by a flaming ball of fire, doesn't even compare to the similarly plagiarised TV chocolate commercial, let alone their source in *Raiders of the Lost Ark*. Burning balls are the least of the hero's problems: when you're up to your neck in Visigoth legends, pitted against a multi-million dollar messianic sect with only a few unlikely friends for help, and a cheap rally jacket for cool-customer credibility, such physical imperfections hardly seem important. FD

Treasure of the Sierra Madre, The 100

(1948, US, 126 min, b/w)
d John Huston. *p* Henry Blanke. *sc* Robert Rossen, John Huston. *ph* Ted McCord. *ed* Owen Marks. *ad* John Hughes. *m* Max Steiner. *cast* Humphrey Bogart, Walter Huston, Tim Holt, Bruce Bennett, Barton MacLane, Alfonso Bedoya, John Huston.
● For once, Bogart plays a really vicious bastard, Fred C Dobbs, in this, the first of two movies he made in 1948 with Huston. It's a sort of lifeboat drama for three, with Holt the young innocent and director's dad Walter as the wise old buzzard, flanking Bogart's bravura paranoia. Director Huston tries to yank the basic elements – gold lust in a Mexican wilderness – into the spare eloquence of a fable, and tends to look pretentious rather than profound. In any case, outrageously Oscar-seeking performances like actor Huston's, coupled with director Huston's comparative conviction with action sequences, work against any yearning for significance. There's a quite enjoyable yarn buried under the hollow laughter. SG

Tree of Hands

(1988, GB, 89 min)
d Giles Foster. *p* Anne Scott. *sc* Gordon Williams. *ph* Kenneth MacMillan. *ed* David Martin. *pd* Adrian Smith. *m* Richard Hartley. *cast* Helen Shaver, Lauren Bacall, Malcolm Stoddard, Peter Firth, Paul McGann, Kate Hardie, Tony Haygarth, Phyllida Law.
● This unimaginative adaptation of Ruth Rendell's dark-edged psychological thriller, set in and around London, straightens out most of her subtle twists and kinks, dissipating tension and interest apace. Bacall, loony mom of Shaver (an American writer resident in Hampstead), steals a council estate kid to replace the divorced Shaver's recently deceased child. Shaver, initially horrified, is soon on the horns of a dilemma as the catatonic boy (his back a railway map of weals and lacerations) reawakens her maternal instincts. The abduction is soon broadcast news; a crazy chauffeur (Firth) and enamoured doctor friend (Stoddard) pitch in with their respective versions

of sweet-and-sour emotional blackmail. The result is on the whole pleasureless, uninvolving, and visually dull; it reflects little of Rendell's delicious and implicating sense of (a)moral relativism and distaste. Paul McGann, as the stolen child's contemptuous working class father, makes a stab at a performance, but is hauled away into implausibility and gun-toting mania. WH

Tree of Wooden Clogs, The (L'Albero degli Zoccoli)

(1978, It, 186 min)
d/sc/ph/ed Ermanno Olmi. *ad* Enrico Tovaglieri. *m* JS Bach. *cast* Luigi Ornaghi, Francesca Moriggi, Omar Brignoli, Antonio Ferrari Teresa Brescianini, Giuseppe Brignoli, Carlo Rota, Pasqualina Brolis, Massimo Fratus, Francesca Villa.

●Olmi's uncompromising reconstruction of peasant life in turn-of-the-century Lombardy marks a return to his origins in neo-realism and non-professional casts. Choreographed as an ensemble work that admits no star performers, his film takes its unhurried pace from the lives of the dirt farmers it observes – lives of repetitive drudgery punctuated by cautious moments of felicity. Its gently muted colour camerawork succeeds in covering the exquisite landscape with a thin patina of mud, while for two of its three hours the changing of the seasons is the closest the film comes to a dramatic event. By showing peasant exploitation as neither triumphant Calvary nor action-packed drama, Olmi refutes both *1900* and *Padre Padrone*, and creates a near-perfect hermetic universe, punctured only in those rare moments when, as tautologous as the film's English title, he dots the 'i's on the amply demonstrated Marxist message. Still, a near faultless and major film. JD

Trees Lounge

(1996, US, 95 min)
d Steve Buscemi. *p* Brad Wyman, Chris Hanley. *sc* Steve Buscemi. *ph* Lisa Rinzler. *ed* Kate Williams, Jane Pia Abramowitz. *pd* Steve Rosenzweig. *m* Evan Lurie. *cast* Steve Buscemi, Chloe Sevigny, Anthony LaPaglia, Elizabeth Bracco, Daniel Baldwin, Mark Boone Jr, Seymour Cassel, Carol Kane, Debi Mazar, Brooke Smith, Michael Imperioli, Mimi Rogers.

●Tommy Basilio (Buscemi), a no-hoper living in suburban Long Island, is not exactly happy. He's been sacked for 'borrowing' money from the garage owned by his buddy Rob (LaPaglia), with whom Tommy's girl Theresa (Bracco) has now taken up. His family tend to regard him as a black sheep, while Jerry (Baldwin), Theresa's volatile brother-in-law, is anxious about Tommy hanging around his teenage daughter Debbie (Sevigny). Small wonder Tommy takes to getting legless with troubled family man Mike (Boone), trying to pick up anyone in a skirt, and generally making a nuisance of himself in the unprepossessing Trees Lounge bar. Buscemi's semi-autobiographical first feature as writer/director is a beautifully low-key, disarmingly perceptive blue-collar character-study, reminiscent of vintage Cassavetes in its sociological and emotional authenticity. If nothing here is quite as risky or inspirational as the late indie king's nerviest masterpieces, there's still much to savour: a cherishably naturalistic, extremely witty script packed with tasty trivialities and non sequiturs; top-notch performances from a superb cast; a smattering of subtle sight-gags; and sufficient drama to ensure that the overall understatement never outstays its welcome. Crucially, despite the loose narrative structure and amiable air of inconsequentiality, it's all held together, and lent poignancy, by Buscemi's Tommy: irresponsible, selfish even, but endowed with enough scrawny charm to allow us to care about his need, and capacity, for some kind of redemption. GA

Tree, the Mayor and the Leisure Centre or The Seven Fortuities, The

see Arbre, le Maire et la Médiathèque ou Les Sept Hasards, L'

Tre Fratelli

see Three Brothers

Tregua, La

see Truce, The

Tremors

(1989, US, 96 min)
d Ron Underwood. *p/sc* Steven S Wilson, Brent Maddock. *ph* Alexander Gruszynski. *ed* O Nicholas Brown. *pd* Ivo Cristante. *m* Ernest Troost. *cast* Kevin Bacon, Fred Ward, Finn Carter, Michael Gross, Reba McEntire.

●'The phones are dead, the roads are out...we're on our own!' All is not well in Perfection, Nevada, a remote desert town. Itinerant cowpokes Val (Bacon) and Earl (Ward) are all set to up sticks when they happen across a corpse perched incongruously atop a telegraph pole...and then another, apparently swallowed up by the earth. Huge, carnivorous, worm-like creatures, capable of tunnelling at incredible speeds in response to seismic vibrations, are literally undermining Perfection. With a tip of the hat towards its '50s forefathers, this canny genre entry exploits its novel subterranean threat to the max, the ingenious situations being orchestrated with considerable skill by first-time director Underwood. Bacon and Ward project a wonderful low-key rapport, based initially on jokey ignorance before giving way to terse apprehension. It's great to hear authentic B movie talk again, especially when the cast takes it upon itself to name the monsters, only to come up with 'graboids' by default, and to debate their probable origin: 'One thing's for sure...them ain't local boys'. This is what a monster movie is supposed to be like, and it's terrific. TCh

Trench, The (La Tranchée)

(1999, GB/Fr, 99 min)
d William Boyd. *p* Steve Clark-Hall. *sc* William Boyd. *ph* Tony Pierce-Roberts. *ed* Jim Clark, Laurence Méry-Clark. *pd* Jim Clay. *m* Evelyn Glennie, Greg Malcangi. *cast* Paul Nicholls, Daniel Craig, Julian Rhind-Tutt, Danny Dyer, James D'Arcy, Tam Williams, Antony Strachan, Michael Moreland.

●The Somme valley, 1916: while a major offensive is being planned against the Germans, a reduced British force holds the front line, just 400 yds from the enemy. They're the usual mixed bunch: middle class officer (Rhind-Tutt), plagued by self-doubt; career soldier Sgt Winter (Craig); and the ordinary volunteers – some of them blustery braggarts, some gently sensitive, some cynical, like Daventry (D'Arcy), about the top brass's handling of the war, and others, like young Billy (Nicholls), simply determined to do their best for king and country. What few suspect and none know is that in two days' time, they'll be taking part in the most disastrous battle in the history of the British army. In some respects, novelist/screenwriter Boyd's directing debut doesn't have a lot going for it. First, it covers much the same hallowed ground as Great War dramas like *Journey's End* and *Paths of Glory*; secondly, with its modest budget and Boyd's slightly stolid approach to the visualisation of his story, we're never able to forget it's set throughout in a studio trench. That said, the claustrophobia contributes to an effective build-up of tension, and the film is actually very engrossing, partly due to the clarity, wit and assurance of Boyd's writing, partly to an excellent cast. Not original, then, but in its own old-fashioned, unpretentious way, impressive and affecting. GA

Trenchcoat

(1983, US, 91 min)
d Michael Tuchner. *p* Jerry Leider. *sc* Jeffrey Price, Peter S Seaman. *ph* Tonino Delli Colli. *ed* Frank J Urioste. *pd* Rodger Maus. *m* Charles Fox. *cast* Margot Kidder, Robert Hays, Daniel Faraldo, David Suchet, Ronald Lacey.

●It's a Maltese teaser for would-be thriller author Kidder when she finds herself involved in genuine murder and intrigue during a Mediterranean holiday. *Airplane!* pilot Hays is on hand as an undercover agent to explain the plot. A very minor offering from the Disney company at a time when it was tentatively trying to alter its image. TJ

Tren de Sombras

see Train of Shadows

32 août sur terre, Un

see August 32nd on Earth

37°2 le Matin

see Betty Blue

36 Fillette

see Virgin

Três Palmeiras (Three Palm Trees)

(1994, Port, 68 min)
d João Botelho. *p* Paulo Branco. *sc* Joao Botelho. *ph* Olivier Gueneau. *ed* Carla Bogalheiro. *pd* Fernanda Morais. *m* Antonio Vittorino de Almeida. *cast* Teresa Roby, Pedro Hestnes, Isabel de Castro, Rita Lopes Alves.

●Botelho's typically exquisite feature is a bizarre compendium of seemingly unrelated stories, told (mostly) by a man to his heavily pregnant wife, and taking place in Lisbon over a period of eight hours. Some of it is very sombre, though there are lovely irruptions of comedy and surreal fantasy. Tying it all together is the writer/director's assured control of mood, sensitive use of music, and the superbly elegant images. It's too experimental a narrative exercise to be to everyone's taste, but recommended to fans of *Hard Times* and *A Portuguese Goodbye*. GA

Trespass

(1992, US, 101 min)
d Walter Hill. *p* Neil Canton. *sc* Robert Zemeckis, Bob Gale. *ph* Lloyd Ahern. *ed* Freeman Davies. *pd* Jon Hutman. *m* Ry Cooder. *cast* Bill Paxton, Ice T, William Sadler, Ice Cube, Art Evans, De'Voreaux White, Bruce A Young.

●Starting from an implausible conceit – Arkansas firemen Paxton and Sadler lay their mitts on a map to stolen gold possibly hidden in a derelict East St Louis factory – this concerns the greedy pair's attempts to escape, alive and much the richer, from a black drugs gang who use the building for making deals and dumping corpses. Cue stereotyped characters, lashings of violence, fallings-out in the rival camps (with crack-king Ice T facing challenges from would-be usurper Ice Cube), and a tortuous plot that spirals inexorably from the ingenious to the ludicrously overblown. Everything subscribes to the modish: the moral cynicism, the superfluous use of video, the rap soundtrack, the flip aftermath to the fiery carnage of the finale. Perhaps that's the result of an uneasy meeting of disparate talents: scriptwriters Bob Gale and Robert Zemeckis are known for frantic action and slick twists, Hill (at least in his early, better films) for laconic, mythic heroes, pared-down plotting and sudden bursts of violence. For the undemanding, it may seem a fair stand-off; but compared to Hill's best work, it's merely a jerk-off. GA

Tre Volti della Paura, I

see Black Sabbath

Trial, The (Le Procès)

(1962, Fr/It/WGer, 120 min, b/w)
d Orson Welles. *p* Alexander Salkind. *sc* Orson Welles. *ph* Edmond Richard. *ed* Fritz Mueller. *ad* Jean Mandaroux. *m* Jean Ledrut. *cast* Anthony Perkins, Orson Welles, Jeanne Moreau, Elsa Martinelli, Romy Schneider, Akim Tamiroff, Suzanne Flon, Madeleine Robinson, Arnoldo Foà, Fernand Ledoux, Michel Lonsdale.

●The blackest of Welles' comedies, an apocalyptic version of Kafka that renders the grisly farce of K's labyrinthine entrapment in the mechanisms of guilt and responsibility as the most fragmented of expressionist *films noirs*. Perkins' twitchy 'defendant' shifts haplessly through the discrete dark spaces of Welles' ad hoc locations (Zagreb and Paris, including the deserted Gare d'Orsay), taking no comfort from Welles' fable-spinning Advocate, before contriving the most damning of all responses to the chaos around him. The remarkable prologue was commissioned from pioneer pinscreen animators Alexandre Alexeieff and Claire Parker. PT

Trial, The

(1992, GB, 120 min)
d David Jones. *p* Louis Marks. *sc* Harold Pinter. *ph* Philip Meheux. *ed* John Stothart. *pd* Don Taylor. *m* Carl Davis. *cast* Kyle MacLachlan, Anthony Hopkins, Jason Robards, Juliet Stevenson, Polly Walker, Alfred Molina, David Thewlis, Tony Haygarth.

●The effect of nightmare is muted in this Pinter-scripted version of Kafka's classic. MacLachlan would seem appropriately cast as the much put-upon minor bank official, but as soon as he's arrested problems arise. His variable English accent and declamatory style militate against audience identification essential to this dystopian chronicle, creating a hollowness at the film's core from which it never really recovers. A cavalcade of top British thesps do, however, come up with the goods (Hopkins' oppressive priest, Stevenson as K's enigmatic neighbour). The film pits an incredulous, almost self-righteous individual against the absurdist machinations of an institutionalised (in)justice system gone mad, and grounds events in authentic Prague locations and 1912 period detail, yet the result boxes in the parameters of Kafka's imagination. Unlike Welles' dizzying city of the imagination, Jones' faithful run-through doesn't quite conjure up the keynote of pervasive unease. TJ

Trial and Error

(1997, US, 98 min)
d Jonathan Lynn. *p* Gary Ross, Jonathan Lynn. *sc* Sara Bernstein, Gregory Bernstein. *ph* Gabriel Beristain. *ed* Tony Lombardo. *pd* Victoria Paul. *m* Phil Marshall. *cast* Michael Richards, Jeff Daniels, Charlize Theron, Jessica Steen, Austin Pendleton, Alexandra Wentworth, Rip Torn.

●Charles Tuttle (Daniels) is living in the fast track. Newly promoted to partnership in his LA law firm, he's also about to marry the boss's pampered daughter. But privilege entails corporate responsibility, and when he's despatched to a desert town to request a continuance on a fraud case, it looks like there'll be no stag party. That's reckoning without the perseverance of chronically accident-prone best man Richard Rietti (Richards), an out-of-work fringe actor who springs a surprise in Charles' hotel room; come the next morning, Charles is seeing Indians. Whoops! To help out, Rick dons a suit, goes to court and screws up the request. Double whoops! It's trial time, and the judge has Rick pegged as Counsellor Tuttle, to Charles' mounting horror. 'The Second Most Outrageous Trial of the Century,' this bills itself. That's a little harsh. Sure, I'd rather not have had to sit through the film – it's flaccid and substantially unfunny – but there's little to offend. The one highlight is Torn's preposterously blithe, perky defendant. NB

Trial by Combat (aka A Choice of Weapons/ Dirty Knight's Work)

(1976, GB, 90 min)
d Kevin Connor. *p* Fred Weintraub, Paul Heller. *sc* Julian Bond, Steven Rossen, Mitchell Smith. *ph* Alan Hume. *ed* Willy Kemplen. *pd* Edward Marshall. *m* Frank Cordell. *cast* John Mills, Donald Pleasence, Barbara Hershey, David Birney, Margaret Leighton, Peter Cushing, Brian Glover.

●An awkward line-up of stars adds little lustre to this tediously derivative, vaguely black comedy. The plot, cobbled together by several writers who seem to have been set to produce an *Avengers* spin-off, revolves creakingly around the attempts of an eccentric, unflappable ex-policeman (Mills) to link a series of underworld killings to an upper-crust fancy-dress society of knights (led by Pleasence), originally dedicated to the ideals of medieval chivalry. The action sequences – on which all attention is presumably meant to focus in compensation for the numbing silliness of the rest of the movie – consist of knights on horseback, brandishing lances, chasing a car across country in hopes of impaling an East End villain (Glover), plus interminable clanking sword fights, the last of which ends with Pleasence impaled on his own portcullis. JPy

Trial by Jury

(1994, US, 107 min)
d Heywood Gould. *p* James G Robinson, Christopher Meledandri, Mark Gordon. *sc* Jordan Katz, Heywood Gould. *ph* Frederick Elmes. *ed* Joel Goodman. *pd* David Chapman. *m* Terence Blanchard. *cast* Joanne Whalley-Kilmer, Armand Assante, Gabriel Byrne, William Hurt, Kathleen Quinlan, Ed Lauter.

●This New York courtroom drama crowds its narrative to such a degree that the small matter of characterisation doesn't really stand a chance. Valerie Aston (Whalley-Kilmer) is a single mother and proprietor of an antique clothes shop who finds herself under heavy pressure from mob boss Rusty Pirone (Assante) to stick with a 'not guilty' verdict when the said low-life faces a major murder trial. Prosecutor Graham (Byrne) is hoping to nail his man but unaware of the blackmail going on behind the scenes, while ex-cop Tommy Vesey (Hurt) is the mob gofer trying to ease the young woman into the shakedown, and falling in love in the process. Writer/director Gould never quite finds a way of grounding these people's dilemmas in convincing emotions. Not terrible, just ordinary. TJ

Trial of Joan of Arc

see Procès de Jeanne d'Arc

Trial on the Road (Proverka na Dorogakh)

(1971, USSR, 98, b/w)
d Alexei Gherman. *sc* Eduard Volodarsky. *ph* L Kolganov, B Aleksandrovsky, V Mironov. *ed* A Babushkina. *pd* V Yurkevich. *m* I Shvarts. *cast* Rolan Bykov, Anatoly Solonitsin, Vladimir Zamansky, Oleg Borisov, Fyodor Odinokov.

●Controversy hovered around Gherman's first film (shelved for fifteen years), largely because the main character is a Red Army officer who defected to the Nazis in the early stages of World War II. The film centres on his attempt to redeem himself after being captured by a Russian platoon, which is plotting to derail a German supply train. The ex-turncoat becomes a focus of conflict between two of the platoon's officers, a gruff, trusting lieutenant and an immature, over-zealous major, and his professed contriteness is put to the test in a series of skirmishes in the snows of Karnaukhovo. There are plentiful signs here of the Gherman films to come: seemingly oblique and offhand plotting, a strong preference for mobile camerawork, and an emphasis on human values at the expense of the usual ideological pedantry. It adds up to the most interesting debut film in Soviet cinema since Tarkovsky's *Ivan's Childhood*, which it sometimes resembles in its glittering black-and-white cinematography, its moments of stasis punctuated by violence, and its sense of larger, off-screen perspectives. TR

Trial Run

(1984, NZ, 89 min)
d Melanie Read. *p* Don Reynolds. *sc* Melanie Read. *ph* Allen Guilford. *ed* Finola Dwyer. *pd* Judith Crozier. *m* Jan Preston. *cast* Annie Whittle, Judith Gibson, Christopher Broun, Philippa Mayne, Stephen Tozer, Martyn Sanderson.

●Isolated woman (she's studying penguins) is stalked and terrorised by an unknown presence. Reminiscent of all those variations on *Les Diaboliques* that Hammer produced in the '60s, this mildly diverting chiller is notable for its derisory (to slasher fans) body count, its unfashionably mature heroine and for the disclosure of the culprit's preposterous motivation. BBa

Trials of Alger Hiss, The

(1979, US, 166 min, b/w & col)
d/p/sc John Lowenthal. *ph* Steven L Alexander, Charles A Bangert, Adam Giffard, Edward Gray, Vic Losick, William G Markle, Mark Obenhaus. *ed* Marion Kraft. *with* Alger Hiss, John Lowenthal, Gussie Feinstein, Robert E Stripling, Richard M Nixon, Whittaker Chambers.

●Hiss was a Roosevelt aide who served on the US delegation at the Yalta Conference; he was charged with being a Communist in 1949 by Whittaker Chambers, a former spy and guilty homosexual who had found religion and become a senior editor of *Time*. Lowenthal's long, intricate study of the case, using archive footage and interviews with many of the principals, clarifies the national hysteria of the early Cold War years and the opportunism of prosecutor Richard Nixon. It rationally argues the case for a re-examination of Hiss' conviction, proving that film and investigative journalism were made for each other. TR

Trials of Oscar Wilde, The (aka The Man With the Green Carnation)

(1960, GB, 123 min)
d Ken Hughes. *p* Harold Huth. *sc* Ken Hughes. *ph* Ted Moore. *ed* Geoffrey Foot. *pd* Ken Adam. *m* Ron Goodwin. *cast* Peter Finch, Yvonne Mitchell, James Mason, Nigel Patrick, Lionel Jeffries, John Fraser.

●One of two Oscar Wilde biopics produced in 1960, Ken Hughes' widescreen offering had the advantage of a charismatic and finally moving central performance by Finch as the great ill-fated writer, delivering the epigrammatic dialogue as the judicial noose tightens. A pity that Mason is so uncharacteristically bland in the final-reel courtroom conflict. TJ

Tribulation 99: Alien Anomalies Under America

(1991, US, 50 min)
d/sc Craig Baldwin. *ph* Bill Daniel. *ed* Craig Baldwin. *m* Dana Hoover.

●A scattershot onslaught of montaged found-footage, Baldwin's film starts off in strident '50s sci-fi fashion as an apocalyptic 'TRUE STORY!!'. Crazed energy-sucking vampires from the planet Quetzalcoatl arrive on Earth, mutant zombies stalk America, and Godzilla looms in all his rubbery glory over Manhattan. As the pace hots up, subliminal snippets of political information flash up on screen, and incongruous elements emerge from the sprawling paranoid narrative. JFK, UFOs, the Bay of Pigs and the Bermuda Triangle all take their place in a relentlessly incoherent babble about the alien menace that conspires to eat away at the very fabric of reality – reality Pentagon-style, that is. Using the language of '50s Cold War paranoia to account for the United States' murky intervention in world events, this brilliantly ironic ideological deconstruction invites us to imagine a world-view in which Third World politicians are fiends from hell, and in which Kissinger, Pinochet, Klaus Barbie and Contra goons are fearless vampire-fighters. This is dazzling, audacious political graffiti, like an unimaginable collaboration between Noam Chomsky and Edward D Wood Jr. JRo

Tribute

(1980, Can/US, 125 min)
d Bob Clark. *p* Joel B Michaels, Garth H Drabinsky. *sc* Bernard Slade. *ph* Reginald Morris. *ed* Richard Halsey, Ian McBride, Stan Cole. *pd* Trevor Williams. *m* Ken Wannberg. *cast* Jack Lemmon, Robby Benson, Lee Remick, Colleen Dewhurst, John Marley, Kim Cattrall, Gale Garnett.

●In a role designed to flatter his talents, Lemmon (who had starred in Bernard Slade's play on Broadway) is unwisely allowed to let rip as a wisecracking, rascally Broadway press agent who discovers – on the eve of his ex-wife (Remick) and grown son (Benson) arriving in New York for the summer vacation – that he has a critical illness. By a series of pitiful gags, he tries to win back the affection of his son, who only hates him the more. Shamelessly geared to theatrical applause, the movie is a truly grotesque mix: part soppy father/son love story, part new morality of how vulnerable men can be through fear of Failure and Meaningful Relationships. Addicts of filmed theatre and knighthood-aspiring performances will revel in it; all others are advised to carry smelling salts. DMacp

Tribute to a Bad Man

(1956, US, 95 min)
d Robert Wise. *p* Sam Zimbalist. *sc* Michael Blankfort. *ph* Robert Surtees. *ed* Ralph E Winters. *ad* Cedric Gibbons, Paul Groesse. *m* Miklós Rozsa. *cast* James Cagney, Irene Papas, Vic Morrow, Don Dubbins, Stephen McNally, Royal Dano, Lee Van Cleef.

●Cagney dominates the Wyoming range in this absorbing Western. Jack Schaefer's story focuses on a cattle baron's ruthless hold on his vast territory and the tension that arises when his Greek mistress Papas attracts the wrong kind of attention from farmhand Dubbins. Good stuff, with a worthwhile concentration on the way the West actually worked for a living, and Cagney making an impressive replacement for Spencer Tracy, who walked off the picture after quarrelling with director Wise. 'Scope photography by Robert Surtees; music by Miklos Rozsa. TJ

Trick

(1998, USA, 87 min)
d Jim Fall. *p* Eric d'Arbeloff, Jim Fall, Ross Katz. *sc* Jason Schafer. *ph* Terry Stacey. *ed* Brian A Kates. *pd* Jody Asnes. *m* David Friedman. *cast*

Christian Campbell, John Paul Pitoc, Tori Spelling, Lorri Bagley, Clinton Leupp.
●Slight but very likeable urban fairytale about the joys and limitations of wish-fulfilment fantasies. A mildly sappy composer (he aspires to write a Broadway hit) is cruised on the subway by the man of his dreams (a go-go boy with intellectual credentials), but can't find any place to take him to bed. The all-night quest takes them through the usual gallery of *After Hours* types, headed by a malicious drag queen, and a series of sitcom-style misunderstandings; it's no surprise that first time director Fall has a background in off-off-Broadway theatre. But the casting is spot-on (especially Pitoc as the brainy, charming sex object) and much of the dialogue is real funny. TR

Trick or Treat

(1986, US, 97 min)
d Charles Martin Smith. *p* Michael S Murphey, Joel Soisson. *sc* Michael S Murphey, Joel Soisson, Rhet Topham. *ph* Robert Elswit. *ed* Jane Schwartz Jaffe. *pd* Curtus Schnell. *m* Christopher Young. *cast* Marc Price, Tony Fields, Lisa Orgolini, Doug Savant, Elaine Joyce, Gene Simmons, Ozzy Osbourne.
●A high school romp pitched somewhere between *Carrie* and *Animal House*. Eddie (Price), a fanatical heavy metal fan desolated by the death in a fire of his idol, the hideous Sammi 'Ragman' Gurr (Fields), is somewhat consoled when a DJ friend gives him the only copy of Ragman's last album, having first taped it to broadcast (as per Ragman's instructions) at midnight on Halloween. Victimised by the school jocks, Eddie swears revenge, and receives unexpected occult help – via the album – when the deceased Ragman materialises. Soon Eddie's tormentors get their nasty deserts. But Ragman's destructiveness gets out of hand, and realising what it will mean if the record is played on Halloween, Eddie turns hero to stop the wave of terror. All utter rubbish but fun, benefiting greatly from outrageous SFX à la *Videodrome*, and from two neat cameos by real life HM stars Ozzy Osbourne and Gene Simmons. DPe

Trigger Happy

see Mad Dog Time

Trikal: Past Present and Future (Trikal)

(1985, Ind, 137 min)
d Shyam Benegal. *p* Freni M Variava, Lalit M Biljani. *sc* Shyam Benegal. *ph* Ashok Mehta. *ed* Bhanudas Divakar. *ad* Nitish Roy. *m* Vanraj Bhatia. *cast* Naseeruddin Shah, Kulbhushan Kharbanda, Leela Naidu, Neena Gupta, Anita Kanwar, Soni Razdan, Dalip Tahil.
●A potentially intriguing return for Shyam Benegal to the last days of colonialism in India, this time involving not the Raj but the Portuguese colony of Goa. Politically critical but elegiacally cast as a sort of latter-day *Cherry Orchard* (the setting is a fading mansion with the Indian army lurking at the off-screen gates), it is disappointingly pedestrian, with few of the subtle reverberations and sharp perceptions that marked Benegal's earlier *Junoon*. TM

Trio

(1950, GB, 91 min, b/w)
d Ken Annakin, Harold French. *p* Antony Darnborough. *sc* W Somerset Maugham, RC Sherriff, Noel Langley. *ph* Reginald Wyer, Geoffrey Unsworth. *ed* Alfred Roome. *ad* Maurice Carter. *m* John Greenwood. *cast* James Hayter, Kathleen Harrison, Michael Hordern, Nigel Patrick, Anne Crawford, Jean Simmons, Michael Rennie.
●One story less, otherwise much the same Somerset Maugham portmanteau mixture as *Quartet*, similarly introduced by Maugham himself, and with the cast similarly making up for indifferent staging. The first and last stories (*The Verger* and *The Sanatorium*) are diffuse, facile, and pretty predictable; but *Mr Knowall* – with a clever performance from Nigel Patrick as the insufferable bore whose veneer of crashing insensitivity, inflicted on his fellow passengers on a cruise ship, momentarily cracks to reveal a surprising delicacy – is a neatly judged anecdote. TM

Trio Infernal, Le

see Infernal Trio, The

Trip, The

(1967, US, 85 min)
d/p Roger Corman. *sc* Jack Nicholson. *ph* Arch R Dalzell. *ed* Ronald Sinclair. *m* Electric Flag. *cast* Peter Fonda, Susan Strasberg, Bruce Dern, Dennis Hopper, Salli Sachse, Katherine Walsh, Barboura Morris, Dick Miller, Luana Anders.
●An earlier Corman picture, *The Man with the X-Ray Eyes*, had uncannily predicted the rise and fall of a Timothy Leary-type hero, whose desire to see beyond human limits was punished by humiliation as a sideshow freak and by self-inflicted blindness. *The Trip*, a definitive commercial for acid scripted by Jack Nicholson, is in contrast boundlessly optimistic. Its advertising director hero, Fonda, takes a trip with no retribution at all: no death, no disillusionment, but much bikinied girls on sea shores, swirling psychedelia, and mumbling of 'Wow!' by the obligatory Dennis Hopper in the land of a thousand visual clichés. Despite the hedonistic panache, its lack of a comeuppance means it now lacks credence (as it once lacked a censor's certificate). Rich pickings for the pathologist of '60s life-styles, but it took Coppola to work out that the best movies were about bad trips, not good ones. DMacp

Triple Bogey on a Par Five Hole

(1991, US, 88 min, b/w & col)
d/p/sc Amos Poe. *ph* Joe DeSalvo. *ed* Dana Congdon. *pd* Jocelyne Beaudoin. *m* Anna Domino, Michel Delory, Mader, Chic Streetman. *cast* Eric Mitchell, Daisy Hall, Angela Goethals, Jesse McBride, Alba Clemente, Robbie Coltrane, Olga Bagnasco.
●The Levys, a glamorous couple, used to make their living robbing golfers, until they met their fatal handicap. Years later, scriptwriter Remy Gravelle (Mitchell), investigating their death, decides to observe the Levy progeny as they sail endlessly round Manhattan in their luxury yacht. It's a hothouse atmosphere, brat-generation neurosis taken to its limits: Satch (McBride) is a macho punk; dreadlocked kid sister (Goethals) is precociously insightful; and ice queen Amanda (Hall) walks like Madonna and talks like Truman Capote. Remy isn't likely to get the answers from them, their lawyer (Coltrane), or his niece (Clemente). Here is a Manhattan you won't have seen before, viewed strictly from the outside in sweeping vistas shot in glacial black-and-white, and starkly contrasting with the claustrophobic stillness below deck, as the Levys' cat-and-mouse dialogues with Remy are interspersed with Poe's own home-movie footage of family memories. A detective story with no real mystery and no solution, this is a stimulating, occasionally magical exercise in stylistic and intellectual tail-chasing, and that rare thing these days – a film that dares to go nowhere. JRo

Triple Cross, The (Itsuka giragirasuruhi/ aka Double Cross)

(1992, Jap, 108 min)
d Kinji Fukasaku. *sc* Shoichi Maruyama. *cast* Kenichi Hagiwara, Kazuya Kimura, Keiko Oginome, Sonny Chiba, Yoshio Harada, Renji Ishibashi.
●Also known as *Double Cross* (equally validly), this exciting heist movie is an arresting example of cultural cross-pollination, pitting a punk rock nihilist (and his crazy kook of a girl) against old school gangsters who seem to have taken style tips from Jean-Pierre Melville's *Le Samourai* (among them, the legendary Sonny Chiba). If Fukasaku's sympathies seem to lie with the older generation (this is the director who went on to make *Battle Royale* with such relish), well, there's nothing old or tired about his action scenes, which come on fast and furious. There are also a couple of surprisingly poignant quieter scenes when the young couple drop their defences. It's superior genre cinema, a hyperbolic action thriller with plenty of pulp punch. TCh

Triple Echo, The

(1972, GB, 94 min)
d Michael Apted. *p* Graham Cottle. *sc* Robin Chapman. *ph* John Coquillon. *ed* Barrie Vince. *ad* Edward Marshall. *m* Marc Wilkinson. *cast* Glenda Jackson, Oliver Reed, Brian Deacon, Anthony May, Gavin Richards.
●An adaptation of an HE Bates story, set in an isolated Wiltshire farm in 1942. With her husband a prisoner-of-war, lonely wife (Jackson) strikes up an intimate relationship with a young soldier (Deacon), a farmer's boy who hates the army. When he impulsively deserts, she hides him, disguised in drag as her sister. The inevitable tensions of their life are increased when two soldiers from the nearby camp discover 'the girls', and the lecherous sergeant (Reed) takes a fancy to the one in drag. The relationship between the wife and the deserter is built carefully and convincingly, but in going for laughs as the bullish sergeant, Oliver Reed lets some of the potential tension slip away. As with many of Bates' stories, the plot is in any case resolved suddenly and melodramatically. JC

Trip to Bountiful, The

(1985, US, 107 min)
d Peter Masterson. *p* Sterling Van Wagenen, Horton Foote. *sc* Horton Foote. *ph* Fred Murphy. *ed* Jay Freund. *pd* Neil Spisak. *m* JAC Redford. *cast* Geraldine Page, John Heard, Carlin Glynn, Richard Bradford, Rebecca De Mornay, Kevin Cooney.
●Jessie Mae (Glynn) refuses her mother-in-law (Page) her one pleasure in life: singing hymns. The doughty old lady lights out for a sentimental journey to her birthplace and her past, meeting all kinds of decent friendly folks along the way. Scripted by Horton Foote from his own play, this is a fragile blend of moods and memories with one solid showcase role for a skilled actress. Geraldine Page seizes her chance, though she is too generous to swamp the supporting players. Masterson's images of small-town America are imbued with a luminous and melancholy nostalgia, but otherwise the film is not mounted with any special imagination, and its fusty, old-fashioned (not to say reactionary) lauding of home-spun values sticks in the craw. SJo

Trip to My Country, A (Vacances au Pays)

(2000, Cameroon/Fr, 75 min)
d/p/sc Jean-Marie Teno. *ph* Jean-Marie Teno, Moussa Diakite. *ed* Christiane Badgley. *m* Ben's Belinga, Marianne Entat.
●A movie diary-cum-essay, this follows Jean-Marie Teno, as he travels from Yaoundé, capital of Cameroon, where he received a very European high school education, back to the village he lived in until the age of eleven. As he retraces past journeys, interviewing old acquaintances and strangers, Teno muses on how things have changed (or not), noting broken promises and interrogating notions of tropical 'modernity'. He recalls how the colonial system encouraged his generation to reject their elders' values. The strategy was so successful that a special festival was established to get townsfolk back to the villages – and, in time, it was inevitably transformed into something more commercial. Witty, tender, insightful, illuminating and deeply engaged (and engaging) film-making. GA

Tristana

(1970, Sp/It/Fr, 105 min)
d Luis Buñuel. *p* Juan Estelrich. *sc* Luis Buñuel, Julio Alejandro. *ph* José F Aguayo. *ed* Pedro del Rey. *ad* Enrique Alarcón. *cast* Catherine Deneuve, Fernando Rey, Franco Nero, Lola Gaos, Antonio Casas, Jesús Fernández.
●This is late Buñuel, mockingly sensible black comedy, set in Toledo in the early 1930s, in which an old guardian (Rey) seduces/rapes his young ward Tristana (Deneuve) but is unable to possess her, betrayed by Surrealist lurches in time and reality, and by Tristana's changing 'nature' (the amputation of a tumorous leg). Rey is brilliant as the mephistophelean, anti-clerical Socialist, dandy and outmoded master of social graces: father, lover and husband all in one. His passion ruins and softens him, but (caught as she is in the chauvinist paradox of woman as cause and eternal object of male aggression) it hardens Tristana from innocent virginity to icy revenge. CA

Triumph of the Spirit

(1989, US, 120 min)
d Robert M Young. *p* Arnold Kopelson, Shimon Arama. *sc* Andrzej Krakowski, Laurence Heath. *ph* Curtis Clark. *ed* Arthur Coburn, Norman Buckley. *pd* Jerzy Maslowska. *m* Cliff Eidelman. *cast* Willem

Dafoe, Edward James Olmos, Robert Loggia, Wendy Gazelle, Kelly Wolf, Costas Mandylor, Kario Salem.
●There's no doubting the sense of commitment which touches every aspect of this grimly detailed Holocaust drama. But the impulse to provide an authentic reconstruction of conditions in Auschwitz finds distractions (most glaringly from an intrusive score and Young's gimmicky direction) which swamp the stark brutalities. The plot is based on the real-life experience of Greek boxer Salamo Arouch (Dafoe), who survived the camp only after fighting endless bouts for the entertainment of his captors. The defeated, too weak to work, were sent to their deaths, while Arouch was awarded extra rations which he divided among his family. Arouch's fiancée and her sister are similarly incarcerated, and a subplot traces the back-breaking labour and physical indignities they suffer. Dafoe gives a charged, compelling performance, while Olmos provides convincingly understated support; but the attempt to convey the terrible magnitude of the atrocities has overwhelmed the film-makers and left them resorting to over-familiar tactics. CM

Triumph of the Will (Triumph des Willens)

(1935, Ger, 120 min, b/w)
d Leni Riefenstahl. *ph* Sepp Allgeier. *ed* Leni Riefenstahl. *m* Herbert Windt.
●Riefenstahl's record of the sixth Nazi congress at Nuremberg in 1934, a massive documentary tribute to the German concept of the Aryan superrace. Technically brilliant, and still one of the most disturbing pieces of propaganda around. Interesting to note that at the same time the British were also indulging in mass demonstrations of physical prowess – women were putting on large PT displays in Wembley Stadium. CPe

Triumphs of a Man Called Horse (El Triunfo de un Hombre Llamado Caballo)

(1982, Sp, 89 min)
d John Hough. *p* Derek Gibson. *sc* Ken Blackwell, Carlos Aured. *ph* John Alcott, John Cabrera. *ed* Roy Watts. *pd* Alan Roderick-Jones. *m* Georges Garvarentz. *cast* Richard Harris, Michael Beck, Ana De Sade, Vaughn Armstrong, Buck Taylor, Sebastian Ligarde, Anne Seymour.
●The Triumphs of a Man Called Horse are few in this second sequel, and those right puny. The man himself, who you will recall was an English aristo who obeyed the call of the wild and enlisted in the Sioux, returns only briefly in the now battered shape of Harris. He has only the barest time available for a quick flashback to his finest hour, when he was strung up by his pectorals, before being despatched by greedy prospectors looking for the gold on his land. The gauntlet is taken up for the rest of the film by his son, the aptly named Koda (Beck), who – in company with his faithful Crow girlfriend – rides like the wind, dynamites prospectors, and runs rings around the cavalry. What *Variety* used to call 'a routine oater'. CPea

Trois Couleurs: Blanc

see Three Colours: White

Trois Couleurs: Bleu

see Three Colours: Blue

Trois Couleurs: Rouge

see Three Colours: Red

Trois Couronnes du Matelot, Les

see Three Crowns of the Sailor

3 Hommes et un Couffin

see 3 Men and a Cradle

Trois Huit

see Nightshift

Trois Places pour le 26 (Three Seats for the 26th)

(1988, Fr, 103 min)
d Jacques Demy. *p* Claude Berri. *sc/lyrics* Jacques Demy. *ph* Jean Penzer. *ed* Sabine Mamou. *ad* Bernard Evein. *m* Michel Legrand. *cast* Yves Montand, Mathilda May, Françoise Fabian, Catriona MacColl, Paul Guers, Antoine Bourseiller.
●A wistful song, an iris-in on a train station, and another bittersweet Demy-Legrand musical is under way. Montand stars as Yves Montand, in Marseilles for a show based on his life. Between rehearsals, he revisits his old dockside haunts and thinks about lost love Mylène, left pregnant years before. And he meets a stage-struck girl who, inevitably, is handed her big chance when the show's female lead drops out. Unbeknownst, of course, she's the daughter of long-lost Mylène, and the film teasingly pirouettes around an impending act of incest. Demy indulges his penchant for corny choreography, mother-daughter relationships and structural complications (the fictionalised Montand on screen appearing as an unfictionalised Montand on stage). Quirky, appealing and, in effect, Demy's farewell to cinema. BBa

Trois Vies et une Seule Mort (Three Lives and Only One Death)

(1996, Fr, 123 min)
d Raúl Ruiz. *sc* Raúl Ruiz, Pascal Bonitzer. *ph* Laurent Machuel. *ed* Rodolfo Wedeles. *pd* Luc Chalon. *m* Jorge Arriagada. *cast* Marcello Mastroianni, Anna Galiena, Marisa Paredes, Melvil Poupard, Chiara Mastroianni, Arielle Dombasle, Féodor Atkine.
●Shock horror! Raul Ruiz makes an accessible, intelligible, entertaining film! An intriguing comedy in which Mastroianni plays four roles – a travelling salesman, an anthropologist-turned-tramp involved with a somewhat unusual hooker, a strangely laconic butler, and a wealthy industrialist – in (in)consequential stories which finally begin to overlap. What it all adds up to is a mystery (though the title may provide a hint), but the playfulness, the first-rate cast, the charm of Mastroianni's performance, and the discreet elegance of the whole make for very civilised entertainment. GA

Trojan Eddie

(1995, GB/Ire, 105 min)
d Gillies MacKinnon. *p* Emma Burge. *sc* Billy Roche. *ph* John de Borman. *ed* Scott Thomas. *pd* Frank Conway. *m* John Keane. *cast* Richard Harris, Stephen Rea, Brendan Gleeson, Sean McGinley, Angeline Ball, Brid Brennan.
●A predominantly downbeat tale of the relationship between Rea's down-at-heel chancer – a real loser despite his gab – and his boss (Harris, in convincingly nasty form), the big man of the local underworld, who puts Rea in a perilous middle-man position when he takes a shine to a young gypsy girl. Despite plenty of wit and pleasing twists in the story, this is essentially an unusually sombre character study, played to perfection by a strong cast and enormously assured in its vivid but decidedly untouristy depiction of Irish landscape and society. GA

Troll

(1985, US, 86 min)
d John Carl Buechler. *p* Albert Band. *sc* Ed Naha. *ph* Romano Albani. *ed* Lee Percy. *pd* Giovanni Natalucci. *m* Richard Band. *cast* Michael Moriarty, Shelley Hack, Noah Hathaway, Jenny Beck, Sonny Bono, Phil Fondacaro, Brad Hall, June Lockhart.
●An amiable and humorous fantasy-cum-Faery tale in the *Gremlins* mould. When the Potter family – Mom, Dad, little Wendy Ann and Harry Jr – move into their new apartment house, they have more than their kooky neighbours to contend with. Wendy is the first to go, possessed by the gruesome little meanies, and then it's cue special effects sequences as, flat by flat, the trolls transform the house into a burgeoning forest of ferns and all manner of repulsive creations. The whole thing is jogged along nicely by the cast (especially the excellent Moriarty, jigging around manically to his '60s records), and has exactly the right balance between child-like wonder and gentle self-parody. WH

Troma's War

see War

Tromeo & Juliet

(1996, US, 107 min)
d Lloyd Kaufman. *p* Michael Herz, Lloyd Kaufman. *sc* James Gunn, Lloyd Kaufman. *ph* Brendan Flynt. *ed* Frank Reynolds. *pd* Roshelle Berliner. *m* Willie Wisely. *cast* Jane Jensen, Will Keenan, Valentine Miele, Maximillian Shaun, Steve Gibbons, Sean Gunn, Lemmy.
●Motorhead's Lemmy is the narrator and stumbles through the verse in this schlock Shakespeare rewrite as lumpenly as the other cast members. Between times, sundry inadequates serve up a menu of body-piercing, decapitation, dismemberment, mutilation, soft-core nudity and lots of coloured goo. Strange that a film with so much carnage should prove so tedious, but that's the magic of Troma (*Toxic Avenger*) productions. TJ

Tron

(1982, US, 96 min)
d Steven Lisberger. *p* Donald Kushner. *sc* Steven Lisberger. *ph* Bruce Logan. *ed* Jeff Gourson. *pd* Dean Edward Mitzner. *m* Wendy Carlos. *cast* Jeff Bridges, Bruce Boxleitner, David Warner, Cindy Morgan, Barnard Hughes, Dan Shor.
●Disney's twenty million dollar bid to break into the booming fantasy market is a sympathetic but slightly clumsy rewrite of *The Wizard of Oz*, with a whizkid programmer (Bridges) trapped inside a computer world. The film boasts some impressive computer-generated animation, but for all its inventiveness, *Tron* never reaches a level of excitement commensurate with its effects budget. Indeed, in what might have proved to be a dire precedent for the cinema, *Tron* the video game is probably better than *Tron* the movie. DP

Troopship

see Farewell Again

Trop belle pour toi! (Too Beautiful for You)

(1989, Fr, 91 min)
d Bertrand Blier. *p* Bernard Marescot. *sc* Bertrand Blier. *ph* Philippe Rousselot. *ed* Claudine Merlin. *ad* Theobald Meurisse. *m* Schubert. *cast* Gérard Depardieu, Josiane Balasko, Carole Bouquet, Roland Blanche, François Cluzet.
●Bernard (Depardieu) is a wealthy businessman, happily married to beautiful, elegant Florence (Bouquet). Much to his astonishment, he falls in love with his comparatively dowdy secretary, Colette (Balasko). It's no office fling but the real thing, and – to Bernard – completely incomprehensible. Once again charting the outrageous repercussions of an obsessive love, Blier proceeds to explore the situation from every conceivable angle, merrily constructing and deconstructing alternative stories for all he's worth. Although the film fails to sustain itself over 90 minutes, much of the first half is very funny and occasionally sharp; Buñuelian motifs are mischievously resurrected, and Blier's parodies and fantasy sequences are brilliantly dovetailed in a series of waltzing, switchback camera movements that are a joy to behold. Blier is a classy, amusing film maker, but one suspects he is too fundamentally bourgeois to truly shock or surprise; and this movie ends dispiritingly with the most banal of all its potential options. TCh

Trop de Bonheur (Too Much Happiness)

(1994, Fr, 85 min)
d Cédric Kahn. *p* François Guglielmi, Elizabeth Deviosse. *sc* Cédric Kahn, Ismael Ferroukhi. *ph* Antoine Roch. *ed* Yann Dedet, Nathalie Hubert. *pd* Philippe Combastel. *cast* Estelle Perron, Caroline Trousselard, Malek Bechar, Didier Borga.
●An excellent feature, from a series in which various French directors treated a theme from their adolescence, set in a none-too-picturesque town in the Midi. It simply charts the shifts in relationships, over a day or so, between a bunch of kids around school-leaving age. Most of the last hour takes place at an impromptu drunken 'party', where the director's imaginative use of gesture, glances, dance and group composition to portray attraction and repulsion, lust and jealousy really comes into its own. Superbly evocative of teenage desire (with a few substantial asides on racial tension thrown in), this beautifully acted film takes an everyday situation and, thanks to acute observation, makes it both horribly familiar and totally compulsive. GA

Tropical Fish

(1994, GB, 27 min)
d Chris Rodley. *cast* Michael Harris, O-Lan Jones.
●This adaptation of Raymond Carver's story *Neighbors* is an exemplary short. While the neighbours are on vacation, a vaguely bored suburban couple agree to tend their fishtank, and find their lives subtly transformed by their insights into and impressions of other people's private lives. Stylishly shot, wittily scripted and beautifully performed. GA

Tropical Fish (Redai Yu)

(1995, Tai, 107 min)
d Chen Yu-Hsun. *p* Hsu Li-Kong. *sc* Chen Yu-Hsun. *ph* Liao Pen-Jung. *ed* Chen Sheng-Chang, Lei Chen-Chang. *m* Yu Kuang-Yen. *cast* Wen Yin, Lien Pi-Dong, Lin Cheng-Sheng, Shi Ching-Luen, Lin Chia-Hong.
●Quirky character-based comedy about a kidnapping which goes wrong when the prime mover is killed in a car crash; two kidnapped boys wind up being held for ransom by a none-too-smart peasant family in a fishing village. For one of the boys, an inveterate dreamer, this is a wonderful excuse not to swot for exams. Serious themes hover in the background (ecological disaster, the dumbing of the media, exam hell), but the film is more sweet than sour. The first-time director (an unreconstructed rock guitarist) makes it a paean to daydreaming. TR

Tropic of Cancer

(1969, US, 88 min)
d/p Joseph Strick. *sc* Joseph Strick, Betty Botley. *ph* Alain Derobe. *ed* Sidney Meyers, Sylvia Sarner. *m* Stanley Myers. *cast* Rip Torn, James Callahan, Ellen Burstyn, David Bauer, Laurence Lignères, Phil Brown, Dominique Delpierre.
●An incredibly tedious adaptation of Henry Miller's incredibly tedious novel. With the action transposed to contemporary Paris, America's famous lost generation of the '30s are stranded like fish out of water, scrabbling ludicrously for sexual satisfaction from prostitutes when all they need to do is ask any nice, permissive girl passing by. Bereft of its context, Miller's overheated prose – intoned, voice-off, by Rip Torn as Miller in the intervals between his breathless sexual encounters – is revealed as a mixture of bad poetry and bad travelogue. Four-letter words and female pubic hair have themselves a field day. TM

Trop Tard

see Too Late

Trou, Le (The Hole/ The Night Watch)

(1959, Fr/It, 83 min, b/w)
d Jacques Becker. *p* Serge Silberman. *sc* Jacques Becker, José Giovanni, Jean Aurel. *ph* Ghislain Cloquet. *ed* Marguerite Renoir, Geneviève Vaury. *ad* Rino Mondellini. *cast* Philippe Leroy, Marc Michel, Jean Kéraudy, Raymond Meunier, Michel Constantin, André Bervil.
●A secular response to Bresson's *A Man Escaped*. No question of grace here, simply of grind and grime as four prisoners – joined and eventually betrayed by a fifth – laboriously tunnel their way to a derisory glimpse of freedom. Telling a true story, Becker maintains a low-key approach, courting reality, avoiding music in favour of natural sound, constantly stressing the sheer physicality (warders' hands laconically slicing foodstuffs in search of hidden files, prisoners' hands feverishly hacking at the unrelenting stone). Yet there is more than a touch of Bresson (even more, however, of Becker's mentor Renoir) to the close-ups which punctuate the evolving relationship between the escapees and their final discovery of a sort of forgiveness for their betrayer. Classical in its intense simplicity, this is certainly Becker's most perfectly crafted film. TM

Trouble Every Day

(2001, Fr, 100 min)
d Claire Denis. *sc* Claire Denis, Jean-Pol Fargeau. *ph* Agnès Godard. *ed* Claire Denis. *pd* Arnaud de Moléron. *cast* Vincent Gallo, Tricia Vessey, Béatrice Dalle, Alex Descas, Florence Loiret-Caille, Nicolas Duvauchelle, Raphaël Neal, José Garcia.
●Shot and edited with Denis' customary expertise, but disappointing for both its (admittedly ambitious) script and its performances, this is rather too elliptical and enigmatic for its own good. It tells of two individuals consumed by cannibalistic bloodlust, but cared for by loved ones: Dalle, who keeps breaking out of the house in which disenchanted boffin Descas keeps her locked up; and Gallo, honeymooning with Vessey in Paris in the hope that he may make contact with Descas (or should that be Dalle?). Do the killers thirst for blood because they're victims of medical experiments, or are the experiments carried out to cure such impulses? Who knows or even, given Gallo and Dalle's hollow performances, cares. The murders are nasty, the play with genre tradition uneasy, and certain scenes (Descas wandering cool as a cucumber into a blazing house) laughably implausible. GA

Trouble in Mind

(1985, US, 112 min)
d Alan Rudolph. *p* Carolyn Pfeifer, David Blocker. *sc* Alan Rudolph. *ph* Toyomichi Kurita. *ed* Tom Walls, Sally Coryn Allen. *pd* Steven Legler. *m* Mark Isham. *cast* Kris Kristofferson, Keith Carradine, Lori Singer, Genevieve Bujold, Joe Morton, Divine, George Kirby, John Considine.
●After the witty, emotional roundelay of *Choose Me*, Rudolph here plunges even further into his own imaginative world, and the result is wonderful. Located in a mythic, dangerous 'Rain City', his tenderly observed characters pick their way through the battlefield of love, all in search of their peculiar fulfilment. Former cop Hawk (Kristofferson) completes his prison sentence for killing a mobster and returns to his favourite haunt, a café run by old flame Wanda (Bujold). There he falls for a blonde princess (Singer), while she loses touch with her recklessly ambitious hubby (ebulliently played by Carradine, sporting increasingly wacky hairdos as he falls deeper into criminal ways). Forever in the background lurks mean fat cat Hilly, a local Sydney Greenstreet (unexpectedly incarnated by a poised Divine). Rudolph's script is both playful and precise, his images fantastic yet real, the music elegiac but ecstatically sung by an impassioned Marianne Faithfull. Part thriller, part comic fantasy, part love story, *Trouble in Mind* even offers an ambiguous, high-flown ending that suggests this really is the stuff that dreams are made of. DT

Trouble in Paradise

(1932, US, 83 min, b/w)
d/p Ernst Lubitsch. *sc* Samson Raphaelson, Grover Jones. *ph* Victor Milner. *ad* Hans Dreier. *m* W Franke Harling. *cast* Herbert Marshall, Miriam Hopkins, Kay Francis, Edward Everett Horton, Charles Ruggles, C Aubrey Smith, Robert Greig.
●Right from its opening joke – a Venetian romantically serenading a gondola full of garbage – *Trouble in Paradise* spins a wonderful, sophisticated tale in praise of immorality, money and sex, with two aristocratic impostors (Marshall and Hopkins) battling over their plans to rob a rich widow (the languorous Kay Francis). Lubitsch's regular script collaborator Samson Raphaelson never bettered the lethal irony of his dialogue here, as the thieves pass insinuations to and fro with the same lightning grace they give to pickpocketing. And the director's famed 'touch', which can on occasion seem like a thump, remains featherweight and incisive throughout, matching the performances of his charmingly bogus lead players. If ever a film slipped down a treat, this one does. GB

Trouble in Store

(1953, GB, 85 min, b/w)
d John Paddy Carstairs. *p* Maurice Cowan. *sc* John Paddy Carstairs, Maurice Cowan, Ted Willis. *ph* Ernest Steward. *ed* Peter Seabourne, Geoffrey Foot. *ad* Alex Vetchinsky, John Gow. *m* Mischa Spoliansky. *cast* Norman Wisdom, Margaret Rutherford, Lana Morris, Moira Lister, Derek Bond, Jerry Desmonde, Joan Sims, Megs Jenkins.
●First of the Norman Wisdom comedies that provided Rank with a once-a-year commercial lifeline well into the 1960s, and established Wisdom as the natural heir to George Formby. His persona – shy, ever eager, haplessly uncoordinated, inevitably both misunderstood and prone to embarrassing accidents – not only transcended the context of a given film, but usually ended up demolishing it as well, as here where his window-dressing ambitions bring chaos to a department store run by eternal stooge Jerry Desmonde and plagued by shoplifters of Margaret Rutherford's class. PT

Troubles We've Seen, The

see Veillées d'Armes

Trouble with Harry, The

(1955, US, 99 min)
d/p Alfred Hitchcock. *sc* John Michael Hayes. *ph* Robert Burks. *ed* Alma Macrorie. *ad* Hal Pereira, John Goodman. *m* Bernard Herrmann. *cast* Edmund Gwenn, John Forsythe, Shirley MacLaine, Mildred Natwick, Mildred Dunnock, Jerry Mathers, Royal Dano.
●The trouble with Harry is that he's dead, won't stay buried, and won't give the inhabitants of a small Vermont village any peace: an elderly sea captain, an old maid, an artist, and the deceased's young widow get involved in the problem of disposing of him, because they all feel guilty about his demise. But Hitchcock loved the project's potential for macabre understatement, so he has the group reacting with cool, callous detachment toward death. There are delights to savour here: Robert Burks' location photography, all russet reds and golds, underlining the theme of death; Bernard Herrmann's spritely score, ironically counterpointing the dark deeds on screen; finely modulated performances from Natwick and (making her film debut) MacLaine. But Hitchcock is reluctant to follow the subversive premises of the story through to their outrageous logical conclusion; the dialogue's sexual innuendoes now seem coy and awkward; the male leads are wooden; the ending too complacent; and the discreet style stranded by that dreaded British restraint so dear to the director. Now, if Buñuel had made it… GA

Trou Normand, Le (Crazy for Love)

(1952, Fr, 98 min, b/w)
d Jean Boyer. *p* Jacques Bar. *sc* Arlette de Pitray, Jean Boyer. *ph* Charles Suin. *ed* Fanchette Mazin. *ad* Robert Giordani. *m* Paul Misraki. *cast* Bourvil, Brigitte Bardot, Jane Marken, Nadine Basile, Noël Roquevert, Pierre Larquey, Jacques Deray.
●This featherweight farce would have been long forgotten if it didn't mark Bardot's debut (introducing her posed in front of a mirror, buttoning her dress). Seventeen years old, not yet made-over by Vadim, with puppy fat still clinging to her cheeks, she's entirely captivating. Her co-heroine (Basile) takes one look and rushes off to sob into her pillow ('Papa, am I ugly?'), not appreciating that BB's aphrodisiac presence might have made Aphrodite herself feel inadequate. The film is a vehicle for Bourvil's good-natured simpleton character, a slightly less innocent George Formby (he even gets to sing a novelty number). The plot is similarly Formby-like: before he can inherit Le Trou Normand inn, our hero must return to the classroom and pass his school certificate. The humour, however, derives more from behaviour than gags, and is utterly conventional BBa

Trout, The (La Truite)

(1982, Fr, 103 min)
d Joseph Losey. *p* Yves Rousset-Rouard. *sc* Monique Lange, Joseph Losey. *ph* Henri Alekan. *ed* Marie Castro Vazquez. *pd* Alexandre Trauner. *m* Richard Hartley. *cast* Isabelle Huppert, Jean-Pierre Cassel, Jeanne Moreau, Daniel Olbrychski, Jacques Spiesser, Alexis Smith, Craig Stevens.
●Huppert is the trout, a cold fish who swims by herself, not needing much from anyone, tending to attract predators but equipped with very sharp teeth. She wears a T-shirt which has 'Maybe' on the front, but has 'Never' on the back, and 'It's all the same to me' is her key (indeed her exit) line. The film recounts the fate of several mostly disagreeable characters who fail to read the warning signs. Losey's penultimate film is one of his most assured, depicting with unusual objectivity the impact of a type of personality met with in life from time to time, but not often in the movies. From the novel by Roger Vailland. BBa

Truce, The (La Tregua)

(1996, It/Fr/Ger, 125 min)
d Francesco Rosi. *p* Leonardo Pescarolo, Guido De Laurentiis. *sc* Francesco Rosi, Sandro Petraglia, Stefano Rulli, Tonino Guerra, Véra Belmont. *ph* Pasqualino De Santis. *ed* Ruggero Mastroianni. *pd* Andrea Crisanti. *m* Luis Bacalov. *cast* John Turturro, Massimo Ghini, Rade Serbedziha, Stefano Dionisi.
● While there's no denying the integrity and general accuracy of Rosi's adaptation of Primo Levi's book about his post-war odyssey back to Italy from Auschwitz, heartfelt concern for the plight of the future author and other survivors of the Nazi camps doesn't guarantee a dramatically compelling movie. To be sure, the film is sensitive enough to the psychological dilemmas and doubts facing the liberated prisoners, and never underplays the obstacles strewn along the route to spiritual rebirth; the problem, rather, stems from the fact that Turturro's Levi is essentially a loner and an observer, and therefore too passive to function as the 'hero' proposed and required by the all too conventional narrative. As a result, the film never really comes alive emotionally, and remains a rather staidly cerebral, worthy exercise. GA

Truck Stop Women

(1974, US, 87 min)
d/p Mark L Lester. *sc* Mark L Lester, Paul Deason. *ph* John Morrill. *ed* Marvin Wallowitz. *ad* Tom Hassen. *m* Big Mack and The Truckstoppers. *cast* Lieux Dressler, Claudia Jennings, Gene Drew, Dolores Dorn, Dennis Fimple, Jennifer Burton, Paul Carr.
● A cult movie – about the Organisation's efforts to move in on the truck hijacking operation run by Anna and her girls – that drew lavish praise as Greek tragedy transposed to New Mexico and the funniest film since Lubitsch's *To Be or Not To Be*. How this relates to a juicy pulp movie with its (to quote the ad) 'double-clutchin'… gear-jammin' mamas who like a lot of hijackin' by day… a lot of heavy truckin' by night', you'll have to work out for yourself. The manic glee that Lester elicits from his performers, and his eye for incongruities, make for a true eccentricity. And the sight of his matriarchy consistently undermining male morale should shake staider patrons by the scruff of the neck. Complete with sub-Johnny Cash soundtrack and virtually incomprehensible plot. VG

True Believer (aka Fighting Justice)

(1988, US, 103 min)
d Joseph Ruben. *p* Walter F Parkes, Lawrence Lasker. *sc* Wesley Strick. *ph* John W Lindley. *ed* George Bowers. *pd* Lawrence Miller. *m* Brad Fiedel. *cast* James Woods, Robert Downey Jr, Yuji Okumoto, Margaret Colin, Kurtwood Smith, Tom Bower, Charles Hallahan.
● A riveting legal drama which casts James Woods as a jaded, ex-radical lawyer, once dubbed 'The bastard son of Mother Teresa' but now reduced to defending scumbag drug dealers. His '60s idealism rekindled by a new, wide-eyed assistant (Downey), he takes on the case of a young Korean serving '25 to life' for murdering a Chinatown gang leader. Things get nasty when the DA starts pressuring Woods to drop the case; but convinced of his client's innocence and determined to salvage his self-respect, he presses on with a desperate, almost evangelical zeal. Ruben's smart direction keeps one guessing throughout, with an investigation that takes in a paranoid Vietnam veteran, white racist vigilantes, a retired detective with a guilty secret, and plumbing supplies. A taut, intelligent and engrossing thriller, featuring yet another manic performance by Woods, the undisputed King of Misdirected Energy. NF

True Blue

(1996, GB, 117 min)
d Ferdinand Fairfax. *p* Clive Parsons, Davina Belling. *sc* Rupert Walters. *ph* Brian Tufano. *ed* Leslie Healey. *pd* Alison Riva. *m* Stanislas Syrewicz. *cast* Johan Leysen, Dominic West, Dylan Baker, Geraldine Somerville, Josh Lucas, Brian McGovern, Ryan Bollman.
● Would-be *Chariots of Fire*-style sports movie centred on the preparations for the celebrated 1987 Oxford vs Cambridge Boat Race. Many news stories focused on controversy about imported American pros up against traditionally trained Brit oarsmen, prompting Oxford coach Daniel Topolski to unravel the serpentine rivalries, machinations and mutinies that preceded the race in a successful book co-authored with Patrick Robinson. Rupert Walters' script straightens out the book's episodic ins and outs, but it still retains a dozen or so main oarsmen, resulting in a loss of focus and the niggling problem that the movie's half-over before the viewer can identify who's who. Thematically muffled and boring. WH

True Confession

(1937, US, 85 min, b/w)
d Wesley Ruggles. *p* Albert Lewin. *sc* Claude Binyon. *ph* Ted Tetzlaff. *ed* Paul Weatherwax. *ad* Hans Dreier, Robert Usher. *m* Frederick Hollander. *cast* Carole Lombard, Fred MacMurray, John Barrymore, Una Merkel, Porter Hall, Edgar Kennedy, Lynne Overman, Fritz Feld.
● Delightful screwball comedy, with the delectable Lombard as a compulsive liar who causes hubby MacMurray no end of embarrassment with her inventions (a lawyer with boy scout principles, he doesn't take kindly to being described to neighbours as insane, dead or a drug addict). Duly contrite, she confesses to a murder in the hope of furthering his career, on the blithe assumption that with hubby on hand to defend her – only he proves not so hot as a criminal lawyer – she is sure to get off. Invention flags latterly, with a particularly weak ending, but the performances are wonderful, not least Barrymore as the ghoulishly bizarre killer. TM

True Confessions

(1981, US, 108 min)
d Ulu Grosbard. *p* Irwin Winkler, Robert Chartoff. *sc* John Gregory Dunne, Joan Didion. *ph* Owen Roizman. *ed* Lynzee Klingman. *pd* Stephen Grimes. *m* Georges Delerue. *cast* Robert De Niro, Robert Duvall, Charles Durning, Kenneth McMillan, Ed Flanders, Cyril Cusack, Burgess Meredith, Rose Gregorio, Dan Hedaya.
● This adaptation of John Gregory Dunne's novel uses its plot base – who cut Lois Fazenda in two? – to explore and draw together the worlds of Tom Spellacy, cynical homicide cop, and his brother Des, priest on the make in the upper reaches of Los Angeles Catholicism in the '40s. Unfortunately, Grosbard's direction is full of overstated cross-cutting and nudging, empty 'references' (to *Kiss Me Deadly, Chinatown, The Godfather* among others), but never satisfactorily summons up the moral demons haunting his characters. In fact, scriptwriter Dunne (adapting his own novel with wife Joan Didion) is equally guilty, with a tragically schematic reduction of his own excellent novel. Numerous vital characters are dropped and the case-solving stripped of its complexity, with the resulting film overlinear and one-dimensional. The two Roberts (Duvall as cop, De Niro as priest) turn in potentially great performances, but are given precious little to work with. SJ

True Crime

(1999, US, 127 min)
d Clint Eastwood. *p* Clint Eastwood, Richard D Zanuck, Lili Fini Zanuck. *sc* Larry Gross, Paul Brickman, Stephen Schiff. *ph* Jack N Green. *ed* Joel Cox. *pd* Henry Bumstead. *m* Lennie Niehaus. *cast* Clint Eastwood, Isaiah Washington, Denis Leary, Lisa Gay Hamilton, Bernard Hill, James Woods, Diane Venora, Michael McKean.
● When a colleague dies in a car crash, Steve Everett (Eastwood) of the *Oakland Tribune* inherits a human interest story on the upcoming final few hours of Frank Beechum (Washington), a convicted killer on Death Row. Trouble is, Steve's an investigative reporter by trade, tradition and temperament and, when he begins researching the case, starts to suspect the remorseless Beechum may be innocent. Moreover, his life is such a mess that he hardly has time to meet Beechum for a last exclusive interview, let alone to search for clues and win a stay of execution. Though the closing quarter of an hour is inevitably flawed by the kind of contrivance parodied in *The Player* and repeated in numerous race-against-time stories, for the most part this is another typically intelligent Eastwood film, a thriller that's unusually and movingly perceptive about human emotions. Though a couple of plot developments are clumsily scripted, as a character study it's performed, written and directed with wit, sensitivity and insight, ranging from the engagingly non-PC comic exchanges between Everett and his boss (Woods) to the affecting scenes between Beechum and his family. GA

True Glory, The

(1945, GB/US, 85 min, b/w)
d Carol Reed, Garson Kanin. *sc* Eric Maschwitz, Arthur MacRae, Gerald Kersh, Guy Trosper, Jenny Nicholson. *ed* Robert Verrell. *m* William Alwyn.
● This expertly assembled WWII documentary, about the last year of the war in Europe, was financed by the American Office of War Information and the British MOI. It occupies a middle ground between the conventional propaganda films churned out in their hundreds and the poetic realism of Humphrey Jennings. Some of the footage is astonishing (unfortunately, William Alwyn's music is an often redundant dramatic enhancement), and parts of the commentary have a macabre humour. A British tommy, for instance, tells of his encounter in a bombed-out German village with a woman complaining that if the British had given up in 1940 she would still have a home to live in. ATu

True Grit

(1969, US, 128 min)
d Henry Hathaway. *p* Hal Wallis. *sc* Marguerite Roberts. *ph* Lucien Ballard. *ed* Warren Low. *pd* Walter Tyler. *m* Elmer Bernstein. *cast* John Wayne, Glen Campbell, Kim Darby, Jeremy Slate, Jeff Corey, Robert Duvall, Dennis Hopper, Strother Martin.
● It was in *El Dorado* that Wayne ruefully admitted his reflexes weren't quite what they were. Here, amiably sending up his own image, he plays a way-worn, one-eyed, drink-hardened marshal who would rather stay at home with his cat and the aged Chinaman who looks after him and lets him cheat at cards, but who is shamed out on to the trail by a teenage girl bent on avenging her murdered father, even if she has to do it herself. He gets his man in the end, of course, but only at the expense of a series of humiliations climaxed when, instead of hurling herself into his arms as a grateful heroine should, the tenderfoot girl (beautifully played by Kim Darby) sweetly tells him that when he dies she will make sure he is buried alongside her own dear father. Lazily directed by Hathaway, it's pleasant enough, if rather too self-consciously coy. Peckinpah did it so much better in *Ride the High Country*. TM

True Identity

(1991, US, 93 min)
d Charles Lane. *p* Carol Baum, Teri Schwartz. *sc* Andy Breckman. *ph* Thomas Ackerman. *ed* Kent Beyda. *pd* John DeCuir. *m* Marc Mardef. *cast* Lenny Henry, Frank Langella, Charles Lane, JT Walsh, Anne-Marie Johnson, Andreas Katsulas, Michael McKean, James Earl Jones, Melvin Van Peebles.
● Struggling black actor Miles Pope (Henry) is fed up with being offered parts in movies like 'Uptown Harlem Pimps on Crack'. Instead, he longs for the lead in *Othello*, but the closest he can get to stardom is as an understudy. Life is about to get worse: during the flight to an acting job, he learns that a fellow passenger is one-time mob boss Frank Luchino (Langella). Miles is now a marked man whose survival rests on the skills of special effects artist Duane (Lane). What better disguise, reasons Duane, than to change his pal into a white man? There are only so many jokes to be milked out of this scenario, and this frantic comedy milks them all. The transformation in Henry's appearance is truly amazing, but once the novelty has passed, the film proceeds to lumber from one signposted comic blunder to another. Henry's skills are tested by the poor script, but he does a spectacular job with a variety of American accents and guises. CM

True Lies

(1994, US, 141 min)
d James Cameron. *p* James Cameron, Stephanie Austin. *sc* James Cameron. *ph* Russell Carpenter. *ed* Mark Goldblatt, Conrad Buff, Richard A Harris. *pd* Peter Lamont. *m* Brad

Fiedel. *cast* Arnold Schwarzenegger, Jamie Lee Curtis, Tom Arnold, Bill Paxton, Tia Carrere, Art Malik, Eliza Dushku.
●Half the time, this hi-tech action movie delivers, in a mindless kind of way: it's fast, crude and has enough explosions and cartoon-style violence to satisfy our baser instincts. Harry Tasker (Schwarzenegger) is a special agent up against a terrorist group (led by wild-eyed Malik) out to show the world it means business by stealing a nuclear warhead. So far, so traditional. But what's meant to give the film its emotional edge is that Harry hasn't told his wife Helen (Curtis) what he does. The crunch comes when a predatory used-car salesman (Paxton) looks like worming his way into her pants by pretending to be an international spy. When Harry finds out, colleagues and agency gizmos are all pressed into service. The film's entire middle section is devoted to this marital 'crisis' which, thanks to Curtis' enthusiastic if barely plausible turn, is quite amusing, despite the offensive take on male-female relationships. Happily, the last 40 minutes pick up with a feast of neck-breaking, torso-blasting violence. GA

True Love

(1989, US, 104 min)
d Nancy Savoca. *p* Richard Guay, Shelley Houis. *sc* Nancy Savoca, Richard Guay. *ph* Lisa Rinzler. *ed* John Tintori. *pd* Lester W Cohen. *cast* Annabella Sciorra, Ron Eldard, Aida Turturro, Roger Rignack, Star Jasper, Michael J Wolfe, Kelly Cinnante.
●A bad-tempered, foul-mouthed, hilarious Bronx love story, this tells of Michael (Eldard) and Donna (Sciorra), young Italian-Americans about to get hitched. Savoca guides them twixt the Scylla and Charybdis of their respective families' expectations, only to have them founder on the rocks of their own selfishness. Michael and Donna have hard lessons to learn, and major humble pie to eat before they can even make it to the altar; and their strident battles are fought out against a backdrop of colourful, crude characters. Wise moms, sassy girlfriends and boozing mates, all chip in with advice on the debate: what do men and women seek from marriage, and can they ever be compatible? It's told in a belligerent, noisy, da-fucksa-matter-wit-you urban growl; a sour belch in the face of marriage, and very funny, too. SFe

True Nature of Bernadette, The (La Vraie Nature de Bernadette)

(1971, Can, 97 min)
d Gilles Carle. *p* Pierre Lamy. *sc* Gilles Carle. *ph* René Verzier. *ad* Jocelyn Joly. *m* Pierre Brault. *cast* Micheline Lanctôt, Donald Pilon, Reynald Bouchard, Maurice Beaupré, Ernest Guimond.
●A subversively light-hearted movie in which Bernadette, a Montreal housewife, leaves her lawyer husband to practice vegetarianism and free love on a dilapidated Quebec farm, while her disapproving and less romantic neighbour, Thomas, gets on with the harder task of earning a living from the land, and trying to form an agricultural union to combat the indifference of the federal government. Carle's script finally brings his heroine (an engaging debut performance from Lanctôt) down on Thomas' side; but the interest of this quirky movie lies less in the director's avowedly political moral than in his eclectic and often ironic method. Religion, factory farming, the sexual liberation of a group of old men, the disposal problem of a removal van full of 'possessions', all become loosely but satisfyingly involved, with Bernadette – revolutionary mother, saintly whore – radiating an infectious optimism and a joyful, open-hearted sexuality. JPy

True Romance (100)

(1993, US, 119 min)
d Tony Scott. *p* Bill Unger, Steve Perry, Samuel Hadida. *sc* Quentin Tarantino. *ph* Jeffrey Kimball. *ed* Michael Tronick, Christian Wagner. *pd* Benjamin Fernandez. *m* Hans Zimmer. *cast* Christian Slater, Patricia Arquette, Christopher Walken, Dennis Hopper, Val Kilmer, Gary Oldman.
●When Detroit comic-store assistant Clarence (Slater) and novice whore Alabama (Arquette) meet, not only do they immediately fall in love, but the tone of her voice-over lets us know that we're in for a *Badlands*-style rerun. Having killed her monstrous pimp (Oldman, OTT) and accidentally stolen his coke haul, the pair head for Hollywood, pausing only to bid farewell to his drunkard dad Clifford (Hopper). But the couple's get-rich-quick plans go awry when suave mob boss Coccotti (Walken) tries to 'persuade' Clifford to divulge his son's whereabouts. If the romance seldom seems 'true', the spiralling violence (script, Quentin Tarantino) does succeed, in a brutish, cod-Jacobean kind of way. GA

True Stories

(1986, US, 89 min)
d David Byrne. *p* Gary Kurfirst. *sc* Stephen Tobolowsky, Beth Henley, David Byrne. *ph* Ed Lachman. *ed* Caroline Biggerstaff. *pd* Barbara Ling. *m* David Byrne. *cast* David Byrne, John Goodman, Annie McEnroe, Jo Harvey Allen, Spalding Gray, Alix Elias, Swoosie Kurtz.
●Byrne gleaned the inhabitants for his hypothetical small town (Virgil, Texas) from mad American tabloids like the *Weekly World News*, which trades in stories about Mexicans who can read your nose, illegal immigrants from outer space, and suchlike. As the film's on-screen narrator, he wanders through the streets, homes and shopping malls of Virgil during its sesquicentennial 'celebration of specialness' with an air of quizzical, bemused wonder, and meets as rich and strange a bunch of characters as we've seen since Altman's *Nashville*. Like Altman's film, *True Stories* has a handful of brilliant musical set pieces, each in a different musical idiom, from gospel to C & W. It's also heir to *Nashville* in its multiple, interweaving plots and its plethora of vivid performances, notably from Jo Harvey Allen as the Lying Woman, and (best of all) John Goodman as Louis Fyne, the lonely bachelor with a consistent panda bear shape. And that's not the half of it. *True Stories* is an unprecedented cross-breed: a rock film with a brain, an 'art' movie with belly laughs, a state of the nation address without boredom. KJ

True Story of Eskimo Nell, The (aka Dick Down Under)

(1975, Aust, 104 min)
d Richard Franklin. *p* Richard Franklin, Ron Baneth. *sc* Richard Franklin, Alan Hopgood. *ph* Vincent Monton. *ed* Andrew London. *ad* Josephine Ford. *m* Brian May. *cast* Max Gillies, Serge Lazareff, Paul Vachon, Abigail, Kris McQuade, Elli Maclure.
●Entertainment from every orifice in this visceral demonstration of just what Australia stands for in the world today: boozing, screwing, pissing, spewing, farting, swearing, etc. It purports to be a version of the ballad in which legendary Eskimo Nell is sought by Deadeye Dick and Mexico Pete – now owner of 'the most famous prick in the southern hemisphere'. Ninety percent of the film is atrocious; but there are enough striking moments in the remainder – overtones of impotence and voyeurism, the odd sunset and bit of music, sepia tinting – to give it the occasional balladic feel and look. These moments are a long time coming, though, and as everything else is in such a different gear the overall effect is a pretty shithouse…or is that a strine compliment? AN

True Story of Jesse James, The (aka The James Brothers)

(1957, US, 92 min)
d Nicholas Ray. *p* Herbert B Swope Jr. *sc* Walter Newman. *ph* Joseph MacDonald. *ed* Robert Simpson. *ad* Lyle Wheeler, Addison Hehr. *m* Leigh Harline. *cast* Robert Wagner, Jeffrey Hunter, Hope Lange, Agnes Moorehead, Alan Hale, John Carradine, Alan Baxter, Frank Gorshin.
●Nick Ray takes the Jesse James legend and turns it around his own feelings of disenchantment. Freely adapting the original (1939) Nunnally Johnson script (which initiated the long line of motifs still recognisable in *The Long Riders*), he transmutes Jesse into one of his familiar outsiders ('the spokesman for everyone whose life is quietly desperate'): an adolescent who turns to outlawry from a disaffection with adult values, rather than Civil War rivalries. This outlaw, like James Dean in *Rebel Without a Cause*, entertains dreams of the good life (along the lines of teen-dream romance), but it's never more than a gesture of hope in a surrounding gone rotten. A fine Western, the only regret being Robert Wagner. Imagining Dean in the central role makes it one of the great might-have-beens. CPea

Truite, La

see Trout, The

Truly Human (Et Rigtigt Menneske)

(2001, Den, 90 min, b/w & col)
d Åke Sandgren. *p* Ib Tardini. sc Åke Sandgren. *ph* Dirk Brüel. *ed* Kasper Leick. *cast* Nikolaj Lie Kaas, Peter Mygind, Susan Olsen, Søren Hauch-Fausbøll, Clara Nepper Winther, Oliver Zahle.
●A bizarre liberal homily about a Kaspar Hauser-type innocent born out of a wall. Originally a phantom known only to his putative kid sister Lisa (b/w PoV shots from inside her bedroom wall confirm the presence of a spirit), he swaps places when she's killed in a car crash and the building is demolished. Emerging from the rubble with a bruised smile, a yen for his parents, and an innocent impressionability, he's clearly socially delinquent, though he's variously mistaken for an accident victim, a new immigrant and a paedophile. His own actions stack up little better than folks' reactions to him; but, thanks mainly to Lie Kaas' performance, the film manages moments of pathos within the parameters of its absurdity. Dogme-certified, for what it's worth. NB

Truly, Madly, Deeply

(1990, GB, 106 min)
d Anthony Minghella. *p* Robert Cooper. *sc* Anthony Minghella. *ph* Remi Adefarasin. *ed* John Stothart. *pd* Barbara Gosnold. *m* Barrington Pheloung. *cast* Juliet Stevenson, Alan Rickman, Bill Paterson, Michael Maloney, Jenny Howe, Carolyn Choa, Christopher Rozycki, Keith Bartlett, Stella Maris.
●The BBC's sweet, feminine answer to *Ghost* concentrates on the emotions (and the ratty flat) of Juliet Stevenson, so desperately unhappy after her lover's death that he comes back from the grave to be with her. As a metaphor for the experience of bereavement, the conceit is over-extended, though Stevenson almost makes it work. Minghella has an irritating sub-Forsythian tendency to cloy, most nauseatingly over Michael Maloney's New Man, who gradually comes to fill the gap in Stevenson's life. Much more fun is Alan Rickman's chauvinistic apparition, inviting his deathly mates round to watch Woody Allen videos at all hours of the night. TCh

Truman Show, The

(1998, US, 102 min)
d Peter Weir. *p* Scott Rudin, Andrew Niccol, Edward S Feldman. *sc* Andrew Niccol. *ph* Peter Biziou. *ed* William Anderson. *pd* Dennis Gassner. *m* Burkhard Dallwitz, Philip Glass. *cast* Jim Carrey, Ed Harris, Laura Linney, Noah Emmerich, Natascha McElhone.
●Truman Burbank is beginning to wise up. People seem to listen to him, but they never really connect; he feels trapped in a job he doesn't care about, a marriage he doesn't believe in, and a small island community he's never been able to leave. It's as if his life has been pre-programmed from the start: as indeed it has, for Truman is the unwitting subject of television's most audacious experiment, a real-life soap following one man from birth to death. When Truman (Carrey) appeals to a higher power, he's actually addressing the show's omniscient creator/director, Christof (Harris). The best comedy since *Groundhog Day* – better, even, than that – this is more than just a savvy and ingenious satire on media saturation, it's a moving metaphysical fable. One movie you can pronounce a modern classic with absolute confidence. TCh

Trust

(1990, GB/US, 106 min)
d Hal Hartley. *p* Bruce Weiss. *sc* Hal Hartley. *ph* Michael Spiller. *ed* Nick Gomez. *pd* Dan Ouellette. *cast* Adrienne Shelly, Martin Donovan, Merritt Nelson, John MacKay, Edie Falco, Gary Sauer, Matt Malloy, Suzanne Costellos.
●To some extent, Hartley's second feature may be seen as a reprise of the small-town situations of *The Unbelievable Truth*. Again it stars Shelly

as a disillusioned teenage brat, the slatternly Maria, whose admission that she is pregnant by her football jock boyfriend drives dad to keel over with a cardiac. Again she takes up with a serious young man with a history of violence: the volatile Martin (Donovan), whose rows with his father and his computer-manufacturer bosses induce ideas of suicide. Again, too, the couple's attempts to forge a trusting relationship, in the face of hostility, rumour and absurd notions of bourgeois respectability, are played out as deadpan farce. This is funnier and more stylish than its predecessor; and for all the bright, brash hues of Michael Spiller's sleek camerawork, it's also darker, slyly combining social comment and satire as it embraces issues like abortion, child abduction, sexual harassment and parental cruelty. GA

Trust Me

(1989, US, 104 min)
d Bobby Houston. *p* George Edwards. *sc* Bobby Houston, Gary M Rigdon. *ph* Thomas Jewett. *ed* Barry Zetlin. *m* Pray for Rain. *cast* Adam Ant, David Packer, Talia Balsam, William DeAcutis, Joyce Van Patten.

● Adam Ant's cash-strapped art dealer will stop at nothing to increase the value of talent-free Packer's latest canvases, even if it means killing him, in this patchy satire on the skewed values of the art market. Not many laughs though, given such an easy target, mainly because of an uncertain cast and half-finished script. Genuine works by Andy Warhol and Keith Haring contextualise the pastiche offerings Packer knocks out. TJ

Truth About Cats & Dogs, The

(1996, US, 97 min)
d Michael Lehmann. *p* Cari-Esta Albert. *sc* Audrey Wells. *ph* Robert Brinkmann. *ed* Stephen Semel. *pd* Sharon Seymour. *m* Howard Shore. *cast* Uma Thurman, Janeane Garofalo, Ben Chaplin, Jamie Foxx, James McCaffrey, Richard Coca, Stanley DeSantis.

● Your fish is depressed, your tortoise won't look you in the eye, and the dog's careering about on roller-skates. Who you gonna call? Abby Barnes, that's who. Abby (Garofalo) is a radio pet-therapist, dispensing sound practical advice to distressed animals and owners alike. Abby is warm, funny and intelligent, but she's made for radio; men never give her a second glance. When a caller, Brian (Chaplin), asks her for a date, Abby panics, and sends her beautiful, dizzy neighbour Noelle (Thurman) in her stead. Heavy petting ensues. A pleasingly old-fashioned romantic comedy, this plays a mildly feminist variation on *Cyrano de Bergerac*, with Abby dishing out amorous advice and promptly regretting it, as Brian falls head over heels with the wrong woman – or rather, with her brains and Noelle's body. Granted, this misunderstanding is pretty silly, but it's a tribute to the cast that we don't lose patience with them. Garofalo, especially, is the cat's meow; in part, it's such an appealing performance because Abby is clearly her own worst enemy. It's a relief to come across a Hollywood comedy which doesn't talk down to the audience. Bravo to screenwriter Audrey Wells for her sophisticated script, and to director Lehmann, who gives the material a light, airy feel. TCh

Truth Game, The

(2000, GB, 80 min)
d Simon Rumley. *p* Piers Jackson, Simon Rumley. *sc* Simon Rumley. *ph* Alistair Cameron. *ed* Colin Sherman. *pd* Alice Herrick. *cast* Paul Blackthorne, Tania Emery, Thomas Fisher, Selina Giles, Stuart Laing, Wendy Wason, Jennifer White.

● The truth will out: hosting dinner parties can be tricky. So too accepting your friends' dinner invitations. As a rule, don't get people together, only monkey business will result. Eddy (Laing) and Lilly (Giles) are a married London couple circling thirty. He's a chummy amateur writer, still dealing on the side, she's plummy and brings home the bacon. That they're happily attached doesn't preclude straying eyes. His friend Dan (Blackthorne) is an abrasive, abusive man of appetites about to put on a piss poor show of cleaning himself up – unsurprisingly, his girlfriend Charlotte (Emery) acts like she can't stand him and she's close to breaking-up point. Then there's Alex (White), and her beau Alan (Fisher), one daffy and gregarious, the other autistic and gauche. They're doing fine with each other, but like everyone else, they've brought a secret to the table. Explosive dinner affrays may not be a cinematic novelty, but Rumley's second feature certainly has the courage of its convictions. It's a raw, frank, eminently naturalistic thumbnail snapshot of how people live with themselves and their intimates, here and now. NB

Truth or Dare (aka In Bed with Madonna)

(1991, US, 119 min, b/w & col)
d Alek Keshishian. *p* Jay Roewe, Tim Clawson. *ph* Robert Leacock. *ed* Barry Alexander Brown. *ad* Christopher Ciccone.

● 'This movie has been worth five years of psychoanalysis,' Madonna has said. Indeed, Keshishian's record of the 'Blonde Ambition' tour is memorable not so much for the live footage (electrifying, but brief), nor for the few risqué moments contrived to provide hype, but for its study of the loneliness of stardom and the ties of family. Madonna's shrink would be interested to meet her father: their love-hate relationship, combined with a Catholic upbringing, might explain the mild SM fetish that surfaces in 'Hanky Panky' and 'Justify My Love'. There's also the classic guilt complex over her mother's death. Madonna comes across as warm, generous, impulsive, casting herself as mother to her dancers. She also comes across as spoilt, bitchy, witty, incapable of sitting still. Her shrink may agree that this is the most intriguing rockumentary since *Don't Look Back*, but he won't advise her to cancel her appointments yet. DW

Try and Get Me

see Sound of Fury, The

Tsuru-Henry (Mugen Ryukyu – Tsuru-Henry)

(1998, Jap/Tai, 85 min)
d Go Takamine. *p* Shinko Nakamura, Zhang Huakun, Ni Zhonghua. *sc* Go Takamine, Isao Nakazato. *ph* Go Takamine. *ed* Kunihiko Ukai, Masahiro Dozaka. *m* Koji Ueno. *cast* Misako Oshiro, Katsuma Miyagi, Miezo Toma, Chen Xiangqi, Susumu Taira.

● Tsuru (folk-blues singer Oshiro) is a roving broadcaster and collector of singing-and-dancing DNA samples, kept in her lunchbox. One day she finds an abandoned script (its penniless author has fled to Taiwan in search of a woman – Chen, from *A Confucian Confusion* and *The River*) and so she moves into the writer's house and sets about staging it as a play. But her son Henry (high-school karate champ Miyagi) over-identifies with his role as a US official, goes crazy and is taken as a prophet... Takamine is still the poet laureate of everything bizarre and musical in Okinawa and this ramshackle mix of separatist politics and conceptual sexuality answers every question about the islands – including the ones nobody's thought of yet. TR

Tua presenza nuda, La

see Night Hair Child

Tube Tales

(1999, GB, 88 min)
d Amy Jenkins ('Mr Cool'), Stephen Hopkins ('Horny'), Menhaj Huda ('Grasshopper'), Bob Hoskins ('My Father, the Liar'), Ewan McGregor ('Bone'), Armando Iannucci ('Mouth'), Jude Law ('A Bird in the Hand'), Gaby Dellal ('Rosebud'), Charles McDougal ('Steal Away'). *p* Richard Jobson, Tony Thompson; Jill Robertson ('Bone'). *sc* Amy Jenkins ('Mr Cool'), Stephen Hopkins ('Horny'), Harsha Patel ('Grasshopper'), Paul Fraser ('My Father, the Liar'), Mark Greig ('Bone'), Armando Iannucci ('Mouth'), Ed Allen ('A Bird in the Hand'), Gaby Dellal, Atlanta Goulandris ('Rosebud'), Nick Perry ('Steal Away'). *ph* Sue Gibson, David Johnson, Brian Tufano. *ed* Niven Howie, Liz Green. *pd* Eva Mavrakis. *m* Mark Hinton Stewart ('Grasshopper'), Simon Boswell ('Bone'), Keith Atack ('Rosebud', 'Steal Away'). *cast* Jason Flemyng, Dexter Fletcher, Kelly Macdonald ('Mr Cool'); Tom Bell, Denise Van Outen ('Horny'); Stephen Da Costa ('Grasshopper'); Ray Winstone ('My Father, the Liar'); Daniela Nardini ('Mouth'); Rachel Weisz ('Rosebud'); Carmen Ejogo, Hans Matheson ('Steal Away').

● Inspired by the American *Subway Stories* and made up of anecdotal tales provided by *Time Out* readers, this compendium is inevitably a varied and variable affair. Some, like McGregor's and Huda's, are overly whimsical or hip; Iannucci's is very funny, Law's sweet, Hoskins' solid, and McDougal's perhaps the most ambitious. Most are pacy, energetic and fairly shrewd in their use of space; few are very coherent, memorable or demonstrate any particular understanding of the short story form. But as a whole it's surprisingly watchable; if it leaves you just a little dissatisfied, that's because there really isn't a single terrific standout, which this kind of film always needs. GA

Tucker: The Man and His Dream

(1988, US, 111 min)
d Francis Coppola. *p* Fred Roos, Fredric S Fuchs. *sc* Arnold Schulman, David Seidler. *ph* Vittorio Storaro. *ed* Priscilla Nedd. *pd* Dean Tavoularis. *m* Joe Jackson. *cast* Jeff Bridges, Joan Allen, Martin Landau, Frederic Forrest, Mako, Elias Koteas, Christian Slater, Lloyd Bridges, Dean Stockwell.

● It's tempting to view Coppola's version of the destruction of a self-promoting American original by the big corporations as a personal metaphor: Preston Tucker's visionary 1948 automobile went the way of Zoetrope Studios. Whatever, *Tucker* is a visually dazzling piece of cinema, though about as psychologically profound a portrait of post-war American optimism as a *Saturday Evening Post* cover. Emphatically, this is not the reverent Paul Muni-Warner Brothers treatment, though it does fling period biopic devices at the screen in exhilarating handfuls. Coppola's dreamer is determinedly loveable, surrounded by moiling dogs and family. Tucker (Bridges) also imbues his crew with fierce loyalty, most movingly embodied by cringing Abe Karatz (Landau), who confesses that he got too close and caught his dreams. Even Howard Hughes (Stockwell), recognising a kindred spirit, offers valuable advice under the wings of his chimerical Spruce Goose. The Motown monopoly works through corrupt Senator Ferguson (Lloyd Bridges), and drags Tucker to court, but not before 50 beautiful cars of the future roll off the production line, causing even the partial judge to smile. The cinematic sleight-of-hand parallels the bombast of its hero, but you never get a glimpse of either visionary. BC

Tueur à Gages

see Killer, The

Tuff Turf

(1984, US, 111 min)
d Fritz Kiersch. *p* Donald P Borchers. *sc* Jette Rinck. *ph* Willy Kurant. *ed* Marc Grossman. *ad* Craig Stearns. *m* Jonathan Elias. *cast* James Spader, Kim Richards, Paul Mones, Matt Clark, Claudette Nevins, Olivia Barash, Robert Downey Jr.

● Scenes from the class war in LA. Preppy rebel Morgan (Spader) goes head to perfectly sculpted head with high school toughs, even hitting on the gang leader's best girl. Morgan's father gets in the way of a bullet as the feud escalates to a messy climax. Traces of *Romeo and Juliet* – or at least *West Side Story* – surface elsewhere in Kiersch's films, notably *Under the Boardwalk*. The intensity of the melodrama here is undermined by a camp-ish turn from Robert Downey Jr as Morgan's leathered friend and by risible musical outbursts from Spader and Kim Richards. DO

Tugboat Annie

(1933, US, 87 min, b/w)
d Mervyn LeRoy. *p* Harry Rapf. *sc* Zelda Sears, Eve Greene, Norman Reilly Raine. *ph* Gregg Toland. *ed* Blanche Sewell. *ad* Merrill Pye. *cast* Marie Dressler, Wallace Beery, Robert Young, Maureen O'Sullivan, Willard Robertson, Frankie Darro.

● Amiable and amusing comedy-drama, uniting for the second time (after *Min and Bill*) MGM's older and uglier alternatives to the likes of Garbo and Gilbert: the admirably cynical, world-worn Dressler and the rumbustious but surprisingly subtle Beery. Most delightful are their scenes of brawling and quarrelling as the husband-and-wife skippers of a tugboat, although Dressler also manages to inject a more sentimental touch into her scenes with upwardly mobile son Young. For sheer uncomplicated professionalism of performance, the old-timers can't be beat. GA

Tulsa

(1949, US, 91 min)
d Stuart Heisler. *p* Walter Wanger. *sc* Frank Nugent, Curtis Kenyon. *ph* Winton Hoch. *ed* Terrell Morse. *ad* Nathan Juran. *m* Frank Skinner. *cast* Susan Hayward, Robert Preston, Pedro Armendariz, Chill Wills, Ed Begley, Lola Albright.

● 'Smart, ambitious and hard as a driller's fist.' Add a confident sexuality and ferocity of spirit, and Cherokee Lansing is well in the mainstream of Susan Hayward heroines. One-quarter Indian, Cherokee begins the film seeking revenge on the oil tycoon responsible for her father's death. But along the way she's seduced by the establishment, and becomes Cherry, heedless socialite. Only after ex-boyfriend Armendariz is declared insane for refusing to have more oil wells drilled on his land does our heroine find moral redemption, during a fiery climax. As scripted, this is an unusually fretful gloss on the American Dream. But it takes a worried man to sing a worried song, and Heisler clearly didn't have a worry in the world. BBa

Tumbleweeds

(1999, US, 102 min)
d Gavin O'Connor. *p* Gregory O'Connor. *sc* Gavin O'Connor, Angela Shelton. *ph* Daniel Stoloff. *ed* John Gilroy. *pd* Bruce Eric Holtshousen. *m* David Mansfield. *cast* Janet McTeer, Jay O Sanders, Kimberly J Brown, Gavin O'Connor, Laurel Holloman, Lois Smith, Michael J Pollard, Ashley Buccille.

● Performances don't come much more vivid than McTeer's Oscar-nominated portrayal of contradictory single mom Mary Jo Walker. Fiercely independent, she'd sooner quit a job than bite her tongue, yet emotionally she's congenitally dependent on whichever man she's with at the time. When we catch up with her, she's throwing her worldly possessions on to the highway, picking up the first guy that comes along. Her 12-year-old, Ava (Brown), has seen it all before, yet her advice always falls on deaf ears. This engaging US indie covers similar ground to *Alice Doesn't Live Here Anymore* and the Susan Sarandon vehicle *Anywhere But Here*, but scores strongly with its simple, unaffected style and earthy humour. Similarly, Mary Jo's relationship with trucker Jack (played by director O'Connor) isn't caricatured: we understand what they see in each other, even if the fault lines are staring them in the face. (O'Connor wrote the script with his then wife Angela Shelton about her relationship with her mother.) The film-makers almost blow it with a tear-crunching scene featuring Sanders as Mr Right, but regain their perspective with an inspired, improvised heart to heart on female plumbing. TCh

Tumult (Gir-Gir)

(1996, Ethiopia/US, 117 min, b/w & col)
d/p/sc Yemane I Demisse. *ph* Costas Kitsos, Jeffret Crum. *ed* Yemane I Demissie. *pd* Yemane I Demissie. *cast* Jima Assefa, Seble Tekle, Eskinder Berhanu, Tabi Gebre-Hiwot, Samson K Guma.

● Seven years in the making, this is a landmark in Ethiopian film-making. It's set during the period of political upheaval pre-dating the dismissal of Haile Selassie in 1974, and personalises the conflicting pulls on the younger members of Ethiopia's middle (and upper) class elite in the story of Yoseph, who joins anti-government rebels following his return from studies in America. Yemane I Demisse (director, producer, writer, editor and production designer) adopts a desultory tone that echoes the feeling of malaise and defeat that met the rebels when the country failed to ignite in opposition. Following the young man on the run, the film observes people and events afresh, albeit now from a hunted perspective. An impressive, sophisticated work, with a controlled handling of mood, actors, and location, but the resonances produced by the use of religious music, ethnic song and poetry may be lost on many non-Ethiopians. WH

Tunde's Film

(1973, GB, 43 min)
d Maggie Pinhorn, Tunde Ikoli. *p* Maggie Pinhorn. *sc* Tunde Ikoli. *ph* Paddy Seale. *ed* Nick Lewin, Robert Frew. *cast* Harry Curran, Lesley Easteale, Colin Hennessy, Tunde Ikoli.

● Written and co-directed by 18-year-old Tunde Ikoli, this was made, he said, 'to show people what we have to put up with'; and its immediacy in dealing with the repressive influences on teenagers living in the East End of London often compensates for its lack of technical gloss. Particularly effective are a pointless search by goon-like policemen, and a café conversation between Tunde's friends, both of which do more to 'explain' delinquency than all of your glib sociological theorising. Like all neo-realism, *Tunde's Film* has the authority of performers re-enacting lived experience rather than acting. RM

Tune in Tomorrow (aka Aunt Julia and the Scriptwriter)

(1990, US, 104 min)
d Jon Amiel. *p* John Fiedler, Mark Tarlov. *sc* William Boyd. *ph* Robert Stevens. *ed* Peter Boyle. *pd* Jim Clay, James L Schoppe. *m* Wynton Marsalis. *cast* Barbara Hershey, Keanu Reeves, Peter Falk, Bill McCutcheon, Patricia Clarkson, Richard Portnow, Jerome Dempsey, Richard B Shull, Henry Gibson, Buck Henry, Hope Lange, John Larroquette, Elizabeth McGovern.

● Transposed in William Boyd's adaptation from Peru to New Orleans in 1951, Mario Vargas Llosa's novel has lost much of its flavour, but enough of its Chinese-box trickery remains. Aunt Julia (Hershey) is the woman with a past who casts a spell over her puppyish nephew Martin (Reeves). The Scriptwriter is the mercurial and possibly dangerous Pedro Carmichael (Falk), dramaturge of the nail-biting radio schlock-opera 'Kings of the Garden District'. With the mad, moustache-curling genius at the helm, the ratings soar – but why the sniping obsession with Albanians, more virulent with each episode? The film ends up rather uneven in its attempt to balance the demands of the love interest (lukewarm) and the spiralling lunacy of the soap. But it has a lot going for it in its playfulness and performances (including a number of guest cameos in the serial). Amiel may not get to ring the reality-fantasy changes as ingeniously as he did in *The Singing Detective*, but a good time was clearly had by all. JRo

Tunes of Glory

(1960, GB, 107 min)
d Ronald Neame. *p* Colin Lesslie. *sc* James Kennaway. *ph* Arthur Ibbetson. *ed* Anne V Coates. *ad* Wilfrid Shingleton. *m* Malcolm Arnold. *cast* Alec Guinness, John Mills, Susannah York, Kay Walsh, Dennis Price, John Fraser, Duncan Macrae, Gordon Jackson, Allan Cuthbertson, Peter McEnery.

● The British cinema is littered with movies (from *Bridge on the River Kwai* to *Tiara Tahiti*) purporting to explore the military mind and caste ethics, but withdrawing into compromise before getting anywhere much. Here (an adaptation by James Kennaway of his own novel), as the English martinet taking over a Highland regiment in its bleak Scottish quarters, Mills comes across with rather more conviction than Guinness as his raffishly pawky predecessor, 'Jock' Sinclair. The clash of native temperaments and military customs between the two, leading both to mental crack-ups, has the stuff of real drama to it, but is gradually frittered away into silly sentimental melodramatics. TM

Tunisian Victory

(1944, GB, 105 min, b/w)
d Hugh Stewart, Roy Boulting, Frank Capra. *m* William Alwyn, Dimitri Tiomkin.

● The sequel to Boulting's *Desert Victory*, in which the British 8th Army's advance is seen as part of an Allied masterplan to drive the Germans out of Africa. Two huge convoys – one British, the other American – meet at a predetermined point in mid-Atlantic; a lengthy flashback takes us back to the previous summer, when the masterplan was conceived, and the remainder of the film follows the course of the North African campaign chronologically. Apart from two sequences – the British attack on Wadi Zig Zaou and the American assault on Hill 609, staged in England and Arizona respectively – the movie is all combat footage. (This was a re-working by Boulting and Capra of Stewart's earlier *Africa Freed*, which had been suppressed for allegedly down-playing the US contibution to the campaign.) MA

Tunnel, The (aka Transatlantic Tunnel)

(1935, GB, 94 min, b/w)
d Maurice Elvey. *p* Michael Balcon. *sc* L DuGarde Peach, Clemence Dane, Kurt Siodmak. *ph* Günther Krampf. *ed* Charles Frend. *ad* Ernö Metzner. *m* Louis Levy. *cast* Richard Dix, Leslie Banks, Madge Evans, C Aubrey Smith, George Arliss, Helen Vinson, Jimmy Hanley, Walter Huston, Basil Sydney.

● League of Nations pacifism bred some strange fruits, but none stranger than this extravagant hymn to peaceful coexistence. In a vaguely futuristic era beyond 1940, the building of a Transatlantic tunnel is suggested as the solution to the world's problems. As the suspiciously Disraeli-like Prime Minister declares, the tunnel will be 'an artery through which will course the life-blood of our two nations, flowing into the hearts of Anglo-American relations'. In a slow-moving but complex melodrama, Dix and Banks, with their radium drills, televisors, and tough, no-nonsense technology, battle their way through tunnel sickness and high finance treachery, subterranean volcanos and feminine intrigue, to reach at last the light at the end of their 2,000 mile tunnel. RMy

Tupamaros

(1972, Swe/Uru, 50 min)
d/p/sc Jan Lindqvist. *m* Numa Moraes, Daniel Viglietti.

● Essentially, the film behind Costa-Gavras' *State of Siege*. Edited by Jan Lindqvist from clandestine footage shot by a whole series of different people, all unaware of the final purpose of the film, it combines polemic and information into a persuasive piece of committed radical film-making. Interviews with Geoffrey Jackson, Dan Mitrione, and others in the Peoples' Prison; interviews with the parents of a Tupamaro who find their house bombed out nightly; interviews with people in the street, alternating with shots of the landed oligarchy enjoying their wealth; information about the domination of foreign companies; information about the history and desperation of the struggle. And that is what comes across most forcefully – the desperation behind the seemingly impudent tactic of what the film calls 'the faceless power' in the Uruguayan situation.

Turbulence

(1997, US, 100 min)
d Robert Butler. *p* Martin Ransohoff, David Valdes. *sc* Jonathan Brett. *ph* Lloyd Ahern II. *ed* John Duffy. *pd* Mayling Cheng. *m* Shirley Walker. *cast* Ray Liotta, Lauren Holly, Brendan Gleeson, Ben Cross, Rachel Ticotin, Jeffrey DeMunn, John Finn, Hector Elizondo.

● The NYPD choose a deserted 747 flight on Christmas Eve to transport two criminals – a bank robber and a serial killer – across country. Lonely stewardess – excuse me, flight attendant – Teri (Holly) takes a shine to the psycho, Ryan (Liotta), who may have been framed and has a way with women. Even when both pilots are dead, the passengers have disappeared and there's a hole in the side of the plane, Ryan can coax Teri out of the cockpit with his soft-spoken schizo charm. Guess Teri picked the wrong week to give up glue sniffing. The ads promise 'over-the-top action', but this is surely a misprint; over-the-top acting is the main attraction here. It's hard to tell with Holly, who sheds her dignity and her uniform with stoic resignation, but Liotta seems well aware just how appalling this movie is, flashing his chops with an alacrity to rival the Big Bad Wolf, pitching his performance several thousand feet above ground level, and refusing to come down. TCh

Turkey Shoot

(1981, Aust, 93 min)
d Brian Trenchard-Smith. *p* Antony I Ginnane, William Fayman. *sc* Jon George, Neill Hicks. *ph* John McLean. *ed* Alan Lake. *pd* Bernard Hides. *m* Brian May. *cast* Steve Railsback, Olivia Hussey, Michael Craig, Carmen Duncan, Noel Ferrier, Lynda Stoner, Roger Ward.

● Turkey shite, more like, a tuppeny ha'penny rehash of *The Most Dangerous Game*. It's 1995, world peace at last, although it takes global totalitarianism to enforce. Dissidents are sent to what looks like *Camp on Blood Island*, only cheaper. As well as being beaten by bullies with whips, they have to wear canary jumpsuits. New arrivals Railsback and Hussey are among those chosen for the sport of CO Thatcher (Craig) and his decadent chums. Five unarmed kids, one jungle, half-a-dozen armed pursuers with transport. So who wins? The film had some 'shock horror' press over its violence. But ghouls won't be satisfied with scenes like one where a nasty gets his hands lopped and advances on the audience with bloody stumps that are the same cuff-over-the-knuckles trick most of us learned before junior school. If it was that funny even a quarter of the time, it wouldn't be so bad. Despite a heap of 'action', the pic's about as lively as a snail full of downers. GD

Turkish Bath – Hamam, The (Il Bagno Turco – Hamam)

(1996, Sp/It/Tur, 94 min)
d Ferzan Ozpetek. *p* Marco Risi, Maurizio Tedesco, Cengiz Ergun, Aldo Sambrell. *sc* Ferzan Ozpetek, Stefano Tummolini. *ph* Pasquale Mari. *ed* Mauro Bonanni. *pd* Virginia Vianello, Mustafa Ziya Ulkenciler. *m* Pivio Also De Scalzi. *cast* Alessandro Gassman, Francesca d'Aloja, Carlo Cecchi, Halil Ergun, Serif Sezer, Mehmet Gunsur.

● Interior designer Francesco (Gassman) leaves Rome and his fading marriage and travels to Istanbul to assess the inheritance left to him by his aunt: an old-fashioned Turkish bath ('hamam') on a quiet backstreet. Lodging with the establishment's kindly retainers, he falls under the spell of the alien city, and strikes up a relationship with the son of the family which promises a freedom he may not have enjoyed at home. This first feature conveys the relaxed rhythm of life in Istanbul with assurance, while the warmth of Francesco's welcome, the story's sexual undercurrent and the film's ethnic influenced score complete a persuasive (if somewhat dramatically unfocused) package. TJ

Turkish Delight (Turks Fruit)

(1973, Neth, 106 min)
d Paul Verhoeven. *p* Mia van't Hof. *sc* Gerard Soeteman. *ph* Jan De Bont. *ed* Jan Bosdriess. *ad* Ralf van der Elst. *m* Rogier van Otterloo. *cast* Monique van de Ven, Rutger Hauer, Tonny Huurdeman, Wim van den Brink, Dolf de Vries.

● An expensive excuse for a love/sex/death porno exercise. Sculptor falls in love with a spoiled rich young thing who is too young and full of sexy life to live, so a brain tumour happens along. Young sexy girls grow up to lose their bloom, and the only way the media mythology can deal with its own limitations is to kill them off while they're still young and beautiful, and use them as an excuse to make a pseudo-philosophical statement about love, life and decay. MV

Turk 182!

(1985, US, 98 min)
d Bob Clark. *p* Ted Field, René Dupont. *sc* James Gregory Kingston, Denis Hamill, John Hamill. *ph* Reginald Morris. *ed* Stan Cole. *pd* Harry Pottle. *m* Paul Zaza. *cast* Timothy Hutton, Robert Urich, Kim Cattrall, Robert Culp, Darren McGavin, Steven Keats, Peter Boyle, James Tolkan, Dick O'Neill, Maury Chaykin.

● Adamantly sincere but utterly redundant populism from Bob *Porky's* Clark, a boy scout's stab at *Bonfire of the Vanities* starring Timothy Hutton's noble adam's apple (gulp!), which he thrusts this way and that for all the world like an ostrich with a social conscience. Hutton's a kind of contemporary James Stewart, a graffiti guerrilla taking on City Hall. And for what? To get some support for his brother, a fireman injured in the line of duty. You can't help wondering why he didn't just find a good lawyer. TCh

Turnabout

(1940, US, 83 min, b/w)
d/p Hal Roach. *sc* Mickell Novak, Berne Giler, John McClain. *ph* Norbert Brodine. *ed* Bert Jordan. *ad* Nicolai Remisoff. *m* Arthur Morton. *cast* John Hubbard, Carole Landis, Adolphe Menjou, William Gargan, Mary Astor, Verree Teasdale, Donald Meek, Franklin Pangborn.

● Adapted from Thorne Smith's fantasy about sexual role reversal, this probably seemed daring once, but hasn't worn well. An Indian sculpture with magical powers, tired of endless quarrels between a married couple (Hubbard, Landis) as to who has the best of the marriage contract, grants their wish to change roles. So while she (Hubbard, dubbed with Landis' voice and indulging excruciatingly stereotyped camp mannerisms) goes to work as an advertising executive, he (Landis, dubbed with Hubbard's voice and striding out a bit) tries to cope with the housewife's lot. Causing endless havoc and confusion, both are relieved when their wish to return to normal – prompted by Hubbard's fearful discovery that he/she is pregnant – is granted. The marital status quo is never questioned for a moment, of course; and the revelation that the statue made a mistake in rectifying matters – the husband is now pregnant – is chickenheartedly thrown away as a curtain line. The best bits come from the supportingcast, especially Pangborn and Meek, archetypal Preston Sturges characters without the Sturges dialogue to bring them fully to life. TM

Turner & Hooch

(1989, US, 99 min)
d Roger Spottiswoode. *p* Raymond Wagner, Michele Ader. *sc* Dennis Shryack, Michael Blodgett, Daniel Petrie Jr, Jim Cash, Jack Epps Jr. *ph* Adam Greenberg. *ed* Garth Craven. *pd* John F DeCuir Jr. *m* Charles Gross. *cast* Tom Hanks, Mare Winningham, Craig T Nelson, Reginald VelJohnson, Scott Paulin, JC Quinn, John McIntire.

● Why does Tom Hanks so often work with unworthy material? Why has Roger Spottiswoode never fulfilled the promise of *Under Fire?* Small-town cop Turner (Hanks) reluctantly adopts an ugly, scene-stealing, monster dog when its ancient owner (McIntire) is murdered. Keen (for no clear reason) to prevent the beast from being put down, and convinced it will prove a key witness in his investigation of the mystery (if such it can be called), Turner lets Hooch demolish his home, imperil his blossoming romance with a local vet, and turn Rin Tin Tin. A couple of vaguely amusing monologues apart, this lame, tame variation on the buddy-buddy comic cop thriller is flaccid, predictable, and as sickeningly anthropomorphic as one might fear. From the moment when Hooch first appears to the strains of Strauss' 'Also sprach Zarathustra', the gags can be smelt a mile off, and the thriller elements are as hackneyed as an episode of *Murder She Wrote*. GA

Turning Gate, The (Saeng-hwal ui Balgyeon)

(2002, SKor, 115 min)
d Hong Sang-Soo. *p* Ahn Byung-Joo, Choi In-Gee, Hanna Lee. *sc* Hong Sang-Soo. *ph* Choi Young-Taek. *ed* Ham Sung-Won. *m* Oh Won-Chul. *cast* Kim Sang-Kyung, Chu Sang-Mi, Yea Ji-Won, Kim Hak-Sun.

● Hong's latest wry dissection of the gap between head and heart is divided into seven chapters, but the plot falls neatly into two halves. In the first, out-of-work actor Kyung-Soo (Kim Sang-Kyung) visits a country town famous for its lakes and has a fling with a dance instructor (Yea); she's crazy for him, but her affection turns him off and he bolts. In the second, he takes a train and chats to Sun-Young (Chu), who recognises him from his stage work; he gets off at Kyungju to follow her home and next day knocks on her door. They have sex in a hotel and he begs her to abandon husband and family to run away with him. She declines – and reminds him that anyway they met in similar circumstances twenty years earlier… As in *The Power of Kangwon Province*, the two halves are riddled with parallels, echoes and contrasts; the plotting is as intricate and detailed as anything you'd find in 19th century fiction (a form explicitly evoked by the descriptive chapter-titles), but the overall aesthetic strategy is as modernist as an ace scratch-mix. Often ruefully funny, too. TR

Turning Point, The

(1977, US, 119 min)
d Herbert Ross. *p* Herbert Ross, Arthur Laurents. *sc* Arthur Laurents. *ph* Robert Surtees. *ed* William H Reynolds. *pd* Albert Brenner. *m* John Lanchbery. *cast* Anne Bancroft, Shirley MacLaine, Mikhail Baryshnikov, Leslie Browne, Tom Skerritt, Martha Scott, Antoinette Sibley, Alexandra Danilova.

● A film about classical ballet which is also about friendship, usually the cinematic prerogative of men. From a deceptively simple script – renewed acquaintance between an ageing ballerina (Bancroft) and a former colleague (MacLaine) who is now a housewife with a daughter just starting out as a dancer – emerge jealousies and resentments about lost chances, maternity-vs-career, comfort-vs-austere dedication; conflicts all purged in Bancroft and MacLaine's magnificent fishwife scene. There's some beautiful dancing and a wealth of detail about the world of classical ballet. Interesting and entertaining. JS

Turtle Beach

(1992, Aust, 88 min)
d Stephen Wallace. *p* Matt Carroll. *sc* Ann Turner. *ph* Russell Boyd. *ed* Lee Smith. *pd* Brian Thompson. *m* Chris Neal. *cast* Greta Scacchi, Joan Chen, Jack Thompson, Art Malik, Norman Kaye, Victoria Langley, Martin Jacobs.

● Australian journalist Judith Wilkes (Scacchi) leaves her estranged husband and children and takes off for Malaysia, where Vietnamese boat people are being slaughtered or moved into makeshift holding camps. Once there, her main contact is Vietnamese ex-prostitute Minou (Chen), now married to the Australian High Commissioner, who seeks to be reunited with the three children she left behind in Saigon. In the process of researching her story, Judith abandons professional objectivity and becomes emotionally involved, both with Minou and with black marketeer Kanan (Malik). Ann Turner's stilted script is burdened by a metaphorical link between the life-cycle of giant sea turtles and that of boat people who land on the same spot. Even worse is the clumsy editing and flat direction, Wallace indulging in innumerable close-ups in an attempt to emphasise emotional tension. CM

Turtle Diary

(1985, GB, 96 min)
d John Irvin. *p* Richard Johnson. *sc* Harold Pinter. *ph* Peter Hannan. *ed* Peter Tanner. *pd* Leo Austin. *m* Geoffrey Burgon. *cast* Glenda Jackson, Ben Kingsley, Richard Johnson, Michael Gambon, Rosemary Leach, Eleanor Bron, Harriet Walter, Jeroen Krabbé, Nigel Hawthorne.

● Jackson plays an unmarried lady who writes children's books under the pseudonym of Delia Swallow, and Kingsley a sales clerk living in limbo between a Bloomsbury bookshop and Fulham bedsitland: two lonely people drawn out of their shells by an elaborate heist to liberate the turtles from London Zoo. Absent, however, is the American-born Russell Hoban's quizzical perspective on his uptight Brits in his novel. What's left is not quite Delia Swallow for grown-ups; but the bland world this film inhabits is almost as quaint, complacent and parochial. SJo

Turtle on Its Back (La Tortue sur le Dos)

(1978, Fr, 109 min)
d Luc Béraud. *p* Luc Béraud, Hubert Niogret. *sc* Luc Béraud, Claude Miller. *ph* Bruno Nuytten. *ed* Joële van Effenterre. *m* Guillaume Lekeu, Mozart, Beethoven, Verdi. *cast* Jean-François Stévenin, Bernadette Lafont, Claude Miller, Virginie Thévenet, Véronique Silver.

● A splendid, unsettling first feature from writer Béraud, about a bad case of writer's block. Béraud's achievement lies in finding a visual and visceral language to describe the process of writing as work (more perspiration than inspiration, and more neurosis than either). After sketching the tense domestic relations between financially supportive girlfriend (Lafont) and impotent writer (Stévenin), the film follows the writer off the rails, sliding into a delirious nightmarish journey through a night-town whose torments and triumphs, though vividly real, may also represent the creative process itself. JD

Tusalava

(1928, GB, 9 min, b/w)
d/pd/animation Len Lye. *m* Jack Ellit.

● A posse of spermatozoa heads briskly wombwards; a string of tadpole spawn drifts past a row of Polo Mints. Lye's not-quite-abstract animation invites this sort of literal-minded response. The title is supposed to be Samoan for 'life cycle', and what we get is an encounter involving a Fernand Leger robot and a Polo

Mint monster. Having finally coalesced, the pair enjoy a kind of interaction, possibly sexual, then feed off and into one another, before fragmenting and flying into a void. *Tusalava!* Seminal stuff for Samoans; for the rest the mysticism, mock biology and primitive animation are quite intriguing. BBa

Tutor in Fear, The (Vychovatel ke Strachu)

(1989, Czech, 16 min)
d/sc Pavel Marek. *cast* Dalibor Fenel.

●Marek appears to practice a sub-Svankmajerian brand of stop-motion surrealism, of some curiosity value but essentially lacking both the master's formal charm and his thematic accessibility. Here a wheelbarrow and tools are led out of Hell (a room of Sissyphian randomness) by the Tutor in Fear – an empty pair of boots – to dig holes around town, before the boots take their leave on a pair of skis. 'Somewhere that senile old man is making an omelette from plaster eggs which seem to hide inside a finger pointing at the Moon.' Ain't that the truth? NB

Tuvalu

(1999, Ger, 100 min, col & b/w)
d/p Veit Helmer. *sc* Michaela Berk, Veit Helmer. *ph* Emil Christov. *ed* Araksi Mouhibjan. *pd* Alexander Manasse. *m* Jürgen Knieper. *cast* Denis Lavant, Chulpan Hamatova, Philippe Clay, Catalma Murgea, EJ Callahan, Terrence Gillespie.

●Playing like a mix of *The Bed Sitting Room* and *Delicatessen*, this pseudo-silent farce (the dialogue is provided by grunts and a variety of pidgin languages; the camerman shoots out of kilter in monocrome given standard tints) is set in a crumbling public baths/swimming pool. It's presided over by the blind father (Clay) of energetic Anton (Lavant), who tries to keep the place from the clutches of his cynical businessman brother Gregor (Gillespie) and the public authorities. It's a tale of desire, dystopia and bad plumbing, a critique of the decay and corruption of ex-Communist Greek Orthodox Europe which owes much to Helmer's evident cinephilia and the teeming satirical comedy of Emir Kusturica, whose scriptwriter Gordan Michic will provide the screenplay for Helmer's next movie. WH

Tva Killar och en Tjej (Happy We/Two Lovers and Their Lass/Two Guys and a Gal)

(1982, Swe, 111 min)
d Lasse Hallström. *sc* Brasse Brännström, Lasse Hallström, Magnus Härenstam. *ph* Roland Lundin, Torbjörn Andersson. *ed* Lasse Hallströn, Jan Persson. *ad* Lasse Westfelt. *m* Anders Berglund. *cast* Brasse Brannstrom, Ivan Oljelund, Magnus Harenstam, Pia Green, Lars Amble.

●Three university friends meet '20 years on'. They're Nordic thesps who all love performing, and are only too keen to relive moments from their old stage successes. Between times, they swap notes on their marriages, divorces and general swings in fortune. Hallström keeps matters light, avoiding a Bergman-like probe into tortured souls. GM

TV Dante: Cantos I–VIII, A

(1989, GB, 88 min, b/w & col)
d Peter Greenaway, Tom Phillips.
cast John Gielgud, Bob Peck, Joanne Whalley-Kilmer, David Rudkin, David Attenborough.

●It's easy to see what attracted Greenaway to Dante. *Inferno*, the first of the three books of *The Divine Comedy* – still the world's most complex account of the male menopause – teems with symbols, allusions, lists and numbers. Preempting the Renaissance, it is an *omnium gatherum* of history, science, animal behaviourism, cosmology and medicine. Collaborating with artist Phillips, Greenaway exploits state-of-the-art video techniques to lay image after image on top of each other, thus creating a picture that corresponds in depth of meaning, colour and excitement to that of the written text. Monologue, mud-wrestling and Muybridge animation are all part of the ordered mêlée. Peck is Dante, Gielgud is Virgil, and Whalley-Kilmer is Beatrice. Each of the eight cantos completed lasts 11 minutes, which is roughly equal to reading time, and is by turns horrifying, beautiful, creepy and fascinating. This is TV designed to be viewed over and over again: 'a pop person's think-video'. MS

Twelfth Night

(1996, GB, 133 min)
d Trevor Nunn. *p* Stephen Evans, David Parfitt. *sc* Trevor Nunn. *ph* Clive Tickner. *ed* Peter Boyle. *pd* Sophie Becher. *m* Shaun Davey. *cast* Imogen Stubbs, Helena Bonham Carter, Nigel Hawthorne, Ben Kingsley, Richard E Grant, Mel Smith, Imelda Staunton, Toby Stephens, Stephen MacKintosh.

●Set in a Hardy-esque English countryside, circa 1890, this starts boldly with a shipwreck and scene-setting voice-over from Kingsley's Feste, whose journeyman troubadour and hedgerow philosopher bestrides the piece like a rustic colossus. Shakespeare's greatest comedy is bitter-sweet, involving parted siblings, a fair amount of sexual confusion, which, thankfully, director/ adaptor Nunn doesn't turn into a tediously modish essay on cross-dressing and sexuality, and the come-uppance of Hawthorne's churlish Malvolio, which deliberately waters down the heady wine of the joyous ending. Filming the play brings an obvious problem: the point of much of both the comedy and the transcendence relies on the audience wearing the fact that Viola, disguised as a bloke, is the spitting image of her brother Sebastian. An impressive Stubbs does everything in her and the make-up department's power to look like Stephen MacKintosh's young blade, but the attempt still falls short. It's not a terminal problem, however: the direction is assured, and the cast is masterly. SGr

12 Angry Men

(1957, US, 95 min, b/w)
d Sidney Lumet. *p* Henry Fonda, Reginald Rose. *sc* Reginald Rose. *ph* Boris Kaufman. *ed* Carl Lerner. *ad* Robert Markel. *m* Kenyon Hopkins. *cast* Henry Fonda, Lee J Cobb, Ed Begley, EG Marshall, Jack Klugman, Jack Warden, Martin Balsam, John Fiedler, George Voskovec, Robert Webber, Edward Binns, Joseph Sweeney.

●Lumet's origins as a director of teledrama may well be obvious here in his first film, but there is no denying the suitability of his style – sweaty close-ups, gritty monochrome 'realism', one-set claustrophobia – to his subject. Scripted by Reginald Rose from his own teleplay, the story is pretty contrived – during a murder trial, one man's doubts about the accused's guilt gradually overcome the rather less-than-democratic prejudices of the other eleven members of the jury – but the treatment is tense, lucid, and admirably economical. Fonda, though typecast as the bastion of liberalism, gives a nicely underplayed performance, while Cobb, Marshall and Begley in particular are highly effective in support. But what really transforms the piece from a rather talky demonstration that a man is innocent until proven guilty, is the consistently taut, sweltering atmosphere, created largely by Boris Kaufman's excellent camerawork. The result, however devoid of action, is a strangely realistic thriller. GA

Twelve Chairs, The

(1970, US, 93 min)
d Mel Brooks. *p* Michael Hertzberg. *sc* Mel Brooks. *ph* Dorde Nikolic. *ed* Alan Heim. *ad* Mile Nikolic. *m* John Morris. *cast* Ron Moody, Frank Langella, Dom DeLuise, Bridget Brice, Robert Bernal, David Lander, Mel Brooks.

●Gambolling about the Balkans is the theme of Mel Brooks' second feature, with comic Moody and personable Langella chasing the one chair out of a set which is stuffed with pre-Russian Revolutionary booty. They run into Dom DeLuise, playing a Zero Mostel-in-*The Producers* role, and Brooks himself as a loony lackey. It's all very fairytale, delightful to watch, and certainly not as self-indulgent as the major Brooks works it slips in between (*The Producers* and *Blazing Saddles*). What's more pleasant about it is the direction, both of the performers and of the action within scenes: the excellent timing can now be seen as preparation for the sort of classical control that made a lot of *Young Frankenstein* so good. AN

12 Monkeys

(1995, US, 129 min)
d Terry Gilliam. *p* Chuck Roven. *sc* David Webb Peoples, Janet Peoples. *ph* Roger Pratt. *ed* Mick Audsley. *pd* Jeffrey Beecroft. *m* Paul Buckmaster. *cast* Bruce Willis, Madeleine Stowe, Brad Pitt, Christopher Plummer, Joseph Melito, Jon Seda.

●In 1996, a virus kills five billion people. 'This already happened,' James Cole (Willis) explains to Dr Railly (Stowe) in 1990. He knows because he's been there. Six years and a matter of minutes after he vanishes from a padded cell, Cole is back in his psychiatrist's life. He must trace the contagion, but he needs Railly's help to track down former patient Goines (Pitt), whose environmental action group, the Army of the 12 Monkeys, may be behind the disaster. With its shifts in tone and style signposted by Pitt's buggy loony-toon and Willis's movingly bewildered introvert, Terry Gilliam's apocalyptic fantasy is even weirder than it sounds. Less a *Terminator*-type action pic than a spectacularly disorienting *inaction* movie, with Cole as a helpless Cassandra hooked on an image from his own past, hoping against hope that he may in fact be crazy…the film's a terrible mess, but a terribly beautiful, tender mess. The screenplay by Janet and David Peoples (*Blade Runner*, *Unforgiven*) takes off from Chris Marker's 1962 short, *La Jetée*, but soon spirals into more pressing millennial obsessions (insanity, chaos and ecological catastrophe), before a vertiginous Hitchcockian make-over in the last reel. Gilliam gives the material a lunatic poetry of his own, but remains impervious to the requirements of narrative pacing. TCh

Twelve O'Clock High

(1949, US, 132 min, b/w)
d Henry King. *p* Darryl F Zanuck. *sc* Sy Bartlett, Beirne Lay Jr. *ph* Leon Shamroy. *ed* Barbara McLean. *ad* Lyle Wheeler, Maurice Ransford. *m* Alfred Newman. *cast* Gregory Peck, Hugh Marlowe, Gary Merrill, Millard Mitchell, Dean Jagger, Paul Stewart.

●Along with *The Gunfighter* (also directed by the erratic but undervalued King), one of Peck's best performances as the martinet required to take over an exhausted World War II American bomber group in England because High Command feels that the present CO (Merrill) is too emotionally involved with his men: appalled by the casualty rates, Merrill is reluctant to turn the screw, and their deteriorating performance is casting doubts in high places about the value of daylight precision bombing, still in its experimental stages. A superb first half dissects the sense of demoralisation, with the group, already bowed under its reputation as a hard-luck outfit, initially wilting even further as Peck applies kill or cure remedies (like segregating the worst misfits and malingerers as a crew known as 'The Leper Colony'). Latterly, with Peck beginning to crack under the emotional strain and go the same way as Merrill, the film sails close to becoming a (less romantic) remake of *The Dawn Patrol*. But King's control, the electric tension, and the performances all hold firm. TM

12 Storeys (Shi-er Lou)

(1997, Singapore, 107 min)
d Eric Khoo. *p* Brian Hong. *sc* Eric Khoo, James Toh. *ph* Ho Yoke Weng. *ed* Ng Jasmine Kin Kia. *pd* Alec Tok. *m* Kevin Matthews. *cast* Jack Neo, Chuan Yi-Fong, Koh Boon-Pin, Lucilla Teoh, Lum May-Yee, Ritz Lim.

●The benign spirit of Kieslowski hovers over Khoo's second feature, which picks up where *Mee Pok Man* left off with more funny/sad accounts of screwed-up lives in a typical Singaporean government-housing block. Khoo focuses on the inhabitants of three apartments: an overweight single woman who can't get her late mother's cruel nagging out of her head, a working-class slob put through the mill by his brought-from-China wife, and a very uptight guy who crashes into the discovery that his younger sister has a sex life. As a social satire of Lee Kuan-Yew's nanny state, this is witty and sophisticated stuff. As an anthology of lives blighted by self-delusion and peer-group pressure, it's so truthful it hurts. TR

Twelve Tasks of Asterix, The (Les 12 Travaux d'Astérix)

(1975, Fr, 82 min)
d René Goscinny, Albert Uderzo. *p* René Goscinny, Albert Uderzo, Georges Dargaud. *sc*

René Giscinny, Albert Uderzo. *ed* René Chaussy, Minouche Gauzins, Isabel Garcia de Herreros, Michèle Nény. *pd* Pierre Watrin, Pierre Leroy, Gérard Calvi. *m* Mickey Nicolas. *cast* voices (English version): George Baker, Sean Barrett, John Ringham, Barbara Mitchell.
● In this product of the Idéfix studio, established by Goscinny, creator of the stocky Gallic hero Astérix, French humour strikes a common note with the British in the struggle of the plucky, apolitical bourgeois against bureaucratic authority. Although the film achieves nothing startling in its use of animation techniques, the narrative moves along at a fair pace as Astérix and Obélix tackle the twelve Herculean labours imposed by Julius Caesar, relying on the virtues of audacity, tenacity, fortitude, sheer ignorance, and the magic potion scored off Getafix the Druid. The most appealing task is a sortie into the Madhouse of Bureaucracy to obtain a permit for their next move. Our heroes find that the only way to combat the insane system is to create further confusion. JS

Twelve Views of Kensal House

(1984, GB, 55 min)
d/p/sc Peter Wyeth. *ph* Patrick Duval. *ed* William Diver. *with* Maxwell Fry, Stephen Bayley, Lady Newall, Margaret Wilson, Eva Wilson.
● Wyeth's documentary investigates Maxwell Fry's ideas when he designed one of Britain's first modern flat complexes in London's Ladbroke Grove. Fry's views were basically well-founded, if a little blinkered and paternalistic, determined to create a better environment for working-class tenants. But what in the late '30s was something of an idyllic community project, has become an archetypal North Ken wasteland, semi-derelict, under-funded, and devoid of any sense of purpose or friendship. It's not so much the fault of Fry and the Gas Board, who constructed the block as a publicity stunt, as of the increasing poverty – both economic and social – of Britain at large. Nor are the tenants entirely blameless. Several of those interviewed sadly and characteristically lay the blame for the death of their community on the influx of immigrants (commonly referred to as 'bad' or 'rough' types). A fascinating look at the aims and effects of social architecture which is warmly human and sharply analytical, and which offers insights, by implication, on the changes in postwar British society. GA

Twentieth Century

(1934, US, 91 min, b/w)
d/p Howard Hawks. *sc* Ben Hecht, Charles MacArthur. *ph* Joseph August. *ed* Gene Havlick. *cast* John Barrymore, Carole Lombard, Walter Connolly, Roscoe Karns, Etienne Girardot, Ralph Forbes, Edgar Kennedy.
● Hecht and MacArthur never wrote a better film script (or play) than this madcap tale of a theatrical producer chasing after his absconding star. Barrymore was an actor (and a drinker) after their own hearts, particularly since his grandiloquent gestures and delivery were then edging towards self-parody – exactly what the part of Oscar Jaffe, Broadway producer extraordinary, demands. And Lombard's mercurial beauty, Lily Garland, is a perfect match. Thanks to Hawks, the film not only takes place on an express train, it moves like one too. GB

Twenty Days Without War (Dvadtsat Dnei bez Voini)

(1976, USSR, 100 min, b/w)
d Alexei Gherman. *sc* Konstantin Simonov. *ph* Valeri Fedosov. *ed* E Makhankovoi. *pd* Yevgeny Gukov. *m* V Lavrov. *cast* Yuri Nikulin, Liudmila Gurchenko, R Sadykov, A Petrenko, A Stepanova.
● Banned for a decade, Gherman's anti-war film avoids all butchery to make its case through a subtly layered interplay between fact, fiction, and the evidence of the landscape and the human face. Lopatin (Nikulin), a writer and war correspondent, is on leave from the front during World War II. Travelling home by train, he listens impassively to a soldier's marital problems, and watches a young woman in tears; most of the incidents appear at a tangent to the theme, yet evoke the feel of an emotional destitution. Lopatin's responses are at their least dislocated in his reaction to the filming of one of his books, which processes his reality into inspirational propaganda. His brief affair with the woman who cried on the train is the sole positive in this portrait of an unremittingly anguished era. IC

28 Days

(2000, US, 104 min)
d Betty Thomas. *p* Jenno Topping. *sc* Susannah Grant. *ph* Declan Quinn. *ed* Peter Teschner. *pd* Marcia Hinds-Johnson. *m* Richard Gibbs. *cast* Sandra Bullock, Viggo Mortensen, Dominic West, Diane Ladd, Elizabeth Perkins, Steve Buscemi, Alan Tudyk, Michael O'Malley, Marianne Jean-Baptiste.
● Gwen Cummings (Bullock) has a problem with booze. We know this because we see her dancing on a table and making a tit of herself at her sister's wedding. Soon she's drying out in a ward of rehabilitating coke fiends, smack heads and morphine addicts under the beady gaze of counsellor Cornell (Buscemi). And does Gwen like Pacific Haven? Not one jot. But does she learn the error of her ways, earn her sister's forgiveness, come to terms with her rotten childhood, dump her unctuous English boyfriend Jasper (West), lay off the hard stuff and emerge a clean and sober, righteous Gwen? You betcha. Trust Hollywood to come up with a feelgood movie about AA. This is a botch, but you can see it wants to be warm, witty and wise. Bullock dispenses with the lip gloss and the blush, and enjoys some choice moments. Director Thomas goes for a jitter-cam feel that's supposed to read as intense, gritty and raw, but comes across as TV, while screenwriter Grant aims for feisty self-determination but hits cute self-absorption. TCh

25 Watts

(2000, Uru, 94 min, b/w)
d Juan Pablo Rebella, Pablo Stoll. *p* Fernando Epstein. *sc* Juan Pablo Rebella, Pablo Stoll. *ph* Barbara Alvarez. *ed* Fernando Epstein. *pd* Gonzalo Delgado. *cast* Daniel Hendler, Jorge Temponi, Alfonso Tort, Valentín Rivero, Valeria Mendieta, Roberto Suárez.
● This slow-burning slacker comedy from Montevideo clearly owes a debt to Rick Linklater, Kevin Smith and, especially, early Jarmusch. It's shot in b/w, and its three feckless young anti-heroes do nothing much over the weekend quite stylishly, pondering the implications of getting dogshit on their shoes, for example, or riffing on what it means if your girlfriend gives you a hamster (definitely nothing good). If the characters sound like dim bulbs, well, there's plenty to relate to – and co-directors Rebella and Stoll have lots of cool tricks up their sleeves. Just get a load of that vinyl rpm PoV shot, for example. Fun. TCh

25 Years

(1977, GB, 77 min)
d/p/sc Peter Morley. *ph* Tony Coggans, Eric van Haren Noman, Mike Delaney, Harvey Harrison. *ed* Trevor Pyke, Jeff Harvey.
● Anyone staying awake through this compilation celebrating the Queen's Silver Jubilee deserves a medal. What it is, is 'a highly personal selection picked from an infinite variety of home and world events, all jostling for inclusion', designed to show that 'through good times and bad, and there have been many of both, through tumultuous changes for better and for worse, the monarchy in the person of Queen Elizabeth II has provided continuity and stability'. It starts off seductively enough with the Royal Yacht steaming serenely into Boston while the Yanks go ape trying to get ready in time. But then we're into the Pathé News footage, a barrage of Danvers-Walker, making you shut your eyes and stuff up your ears. The Queen looks and sounds fed up throughout, as well she might; horses, investitures, state visits, all are presented as being dull as hell. AN

24 Hour Party People

(2001, GB, 117 min)
d Michael Winterbottom. *p* Andrew Eaton. *sc* Frank Cottrell Boyce. *ph* Robby Müller. *ed* Trevor Waite. *pd* Mark Tildesley. *cast* Steve Coogan, Rob Brydon, Ron Cook, Paddy Considine, Sean Harris, Shirley Henderson, Andy Serkis, Keith Allen, Chris Coghill, Dave Gorman, Danny Cunningham, Enzo Cilenti.
● 'I'm a minor character in my own story,' complains Tony Wilson, music impresario, club owner, and living legend within the Granada TV region. The film-makers pack in so much, from the Sex Pistols in 1976 to the birth of the rave scene at the Hacienda club in the late 1980s, it's difficult to know where to start – but Wilson is the common link. He was in the right place at the right time, and, crucially, he had the good sense to know it. Snugly personified here by Coogan, Wilson comes off as a pragmatic dreamer, an idealistic opportunist with an eye for the genius of anarchy and accident. All of which makes him a lively, unreliable guide to the tangled roots of Madchester. The merry casting, too, throws up a dozen memorable vignettes (best of all, Sean Harris, intense and haunting as Joy Division's Ian Curtis). Encouraging improvisation and shooting on DV, Winterbottom has come up with a raucous and unruly mob of a movie, which pulls this way and that with drunken abandon, stepping on toes left and right, stumbling more than once, probably pissing all over the floor with the facts, but always having a high old time. TCh

24 Hours in London

(1999, GB, 90 min)
d Alexander Finbow. *p* Fergal McGrath. *sc* Alexander Finbow. *ph* Chris Plevin. *ed* Ian Farr. *pd* Matthew Davies. *m* Ed Butt. *cast* Gary Olsen, Anjela Lauren Smith, Sara Stockbridge, John Benfield, Amita Dhiri, Tony London, David Sonnenthal.
● A London gangsters movie in which Olsen does his hardman act as peroxided crime boss Christian Writer/director Finbow's attempt to fashion a thriller while simultaneously guying it has landed him with a stylistic mess. The plot has a spine of sorts. Caught in a gunplay between rival gangs, innocent Martha (Smith) is persuaded by cop Duggan (Benfield) to risk her life helping track Mr Big. But Finbow adds complication after complication until you end up not knowing who's who or what's what, and caring even less. On the plus side, he shows talent in comic set pieces and mounts an inventively OTT three-way shoot-out. WH

TwentyFourSeven

(1997, GB, 96 min, b/w)
d Shane Meadows. *p* Imogen West. *sc* Shane Meadows, Paul Fraser. *ph* Ashley Rowe. *ed* William Diver. *pd* John-Paul Kelly. *m* Neill MacColl, Boo Hewerdine. *cast* Bob Hoskins, Danny Nussbaum, Bruce Jones, Frank Harper, Annette Badland.
● Those who have seen Shane Meadows' camcorder gem *Smalltime* will already know the young writer/director is one of Britain's most promising talents. This, his first full length feature, lives up to expectations splendidly. Though it's never quite as funny as the earlier movie, and the bigger (£1.5m) budget has resulted in more conventional characterisation and plotting, the extra polish comes with no significant drop in energy, flair or invention. Darcy (Hoskins) decides to inject a sense of community and purpose into the disaffected youth of a Nottingham suburb by reopening a club. While determination and a canny ability to win over most people he meets results in camaraderie and a modicum of sporting success, resentment, cynicism and even violence are so deeply ingrained in certain locals that the club is never entirely without enemies. What lifts the film beyond the constraints of this potentially corny story is Meadows' engagingly blend of authentic naturalism, robust rapscallion humour, jaunty editing and off-the-cuff lyricism. GA

20 Million Miles to Earth

(1957, US, 82 min, b/w)
d Nathan Juran. *p* Charles H Schneer. *sc* Bob Williams, Christopher Knopf. *ph* Irving Lippman, Carlos Ventigmilia. *ed* Edwin Bryant. *ad* Cary Odell. *m* Mischa Bakaleinikoff. *cast* William Hopper, Joan Taylor, Frank Puglia, Thomas Browne Henry, John Zaremba, Tito Vuolo.
● There is nothing that master animator Ray Harryhausen likes more than going on a wrecking spree. Over the years, his monsters, painstakingly galvanised frame by frame, have laid Washington to waste, devastated New York, and wrapped their clammy tentacles round the Golden Gate Bridge. Here, a blubbery-looking beastie from Venus ends up careering through Rome. The showdown in the Colosseum is a treat. Don't worry about the dotty script or cardboard performances – just sit back and watch this gelatinous blob in action. GM

Twenty-One

(1991, GB, 101 min)
d Don Boyd. *p* Morgan Mason, John Hardy. *sc* Don Boyd, Zoe Heller. *ph* Keith Goddard. *ed* David Spiers. *ad* Roger Murray Leach. *m* Phil Sawyer. *cast* Patsy Kensit, Jack Shepherd, Patrick Ryecart, Maynard Eziashi, Rufus Sewell, Sophie Thompson, Susan Wooldridge.
● There's plenty of frank sex talk when director/co-writer Boyd takes his Steadicam through doors normally marked private. No sooner have the credits rolled than we're with Katie (Kensit) in the bathroom of her New York apartment, where she scrubs her feet in the bidet and delivers her first direct-to-camera monologue about sex and friendship. Cue a series of flashbacks to her life in London: Dad (Shepherd) endures a failed marriage, her lovers (Sewell and Ryecart) are respectively on drugs and married, and her confidante (Thompson) is a compulsive eater. The discursive approach is strangely alienating, and too often the relationships smack of contrivance. Kensit brings the right buoyancy to some of her monologues, but there's not enough introspection for the more demanding emotional exchanges. CM

20000 Leagues Under the Sea

(1954, US, 126 min)
d Richard Fleischer. *p* Walt Disney. *sc* Earl Felton. *ph* Franz Planer. *ed* Elmo Williams. *ad* John Meehan. *m* Paul Smith. *cast* Kirk Douglas, James Mason, Paul Lukas, Peter Lorre, Robert J Wilke, Carleton Young.
● Still one of Disney's most ambitious live action adaptations, only marginally vulgarising Jules Verne's original and notable for some staggering designs, including the beautiful 'Nautilus' submarine itself, with its lush Victorian interior. It was the first Disney film to use very big stars, with Mason contributing a thoroughly sympathetic performance as the anguished Captain Nemo, and Lorre as one of his foils. Time hasn't been quite so kind to Kirk Douglas' role as a lusty harpooner, who looks as though he was inserted to reassure American audiences in the face of what might seem to be a sternly anti-colonial plot. Otherwise this is one of the great movie adventures, fully deserving its canonisation in Disney World, where an elaborate underwater ride attempts – with mixed success – to duplicate some of the film's major thrills. DP

20,000 Years in Sing Sing

(1932, US, 78 min, b/w)
d Michael Curtiz. *p* Robert Lord. *sc* Wilson Mizner, Brown Holmes. *ph* Barney McGill. *ed* George Amy. *ad* Anton F Grot. *m* Bernhard Kaun. *cast* Spencer Tracy, Bette Davis, Arthur Byron, Lyle Talbot, Warren Hymer, Louis Calhern, Grant Mitchell, Sheila Terry, Edward J McNamara.
● Cagney was Warners' first choice for Tommy Connors, the 'tough bird' who eventually goes to the electric chair with a touch of cool resignation. Tracy, however, is suitably gritty in this taut but somewhat implausible moral drama which puts its protagonist through riots, solitary confinement and an escape before he realises that the warden (Byron) is a 'swell guy' deserving his trust. Connors' girl Bette Davis rather overdoes the acid tongue, but the quasi-documentary scenes of prison life are compelling. Based on a book by Sing Sing's liberal warden Lewis E Lawes who believed in rewarding good behaviour and facilitated location shooting inside the walls of the New York prison. TJ

23:58 (23h58)

(1995, Fr, 85 min)
d Pierre-William Glenn. *sc* Pierre-William Glenn, Edith Vergne, Frédéric Leroy. *ph* Jean-Claude Vicquery. *ed* Anita Perez. *pd* Jacques Voizet. *m* Laurent Cugny. *cast* Jean-François Stévenin, Jean-Pierre Malo, Gérald Garnier, Yan Epstein, Kader Boukanef, Sophie Tellier.
● While cinematographer Glenn (best known for his work with Truffaut and Tavernier) has come up with a diverting update of Kubrick's racetrack-heist thriller *The Killing*, it's easy to accuse him of indulgence. For one thing, there's rather too much stock footage of the Le Mans 24-hour motorcycle race, setting for the daring robbery planned by former track stars Bernard (Stévenin), Thierry (Garnier) and their team of assorted little criminals and low-lifes. For another, making Morin (Malo), the top cop on the case, not only a bike connoisseur but a movie-buff, tends to tip the whole thing into anorak territory. Finally, a framing story, in which a couple of kids (one the offspring of a dead biker champ) read a letter from Bernard while playing on the beach, never manages to convince that it's anything more than poetic whimsy. That said, it's an amiably brief spin, fair on atmosphere (though the promise of the opening Melville-like shots of an empty grey northern coastline is never fulfilled), and strong on occasional quirky detail. Minor, for sure, but sufficiently different to pass the time. GA

Twice in a Lifetime

(1985, US, 117 min)
d/p Bud Yorkin. *sc* Colin Welland. *ph* Nick McLean. *ed* Robert C Jones. *pd* William J Creber. *m* Pat Metheny. *cast* Gene Hackman, Ann-Margret, Ellen Burstyn, Amy Madigan, Ally Sheedy, Brian Dennehy, Stephen Lang, Darrell Larson.
● Yorkin sets up a family drama with Hackman as paterfamilias, Burstyn devoted wife, Dennehy drinking chum, Madigan married daughter, Sheedy unmarried daughter. Having given us the satiric *Divorce American Style* two decades ago, he now serves up 'Divorce Serious Style', with Hackman falling for barmaid Ann-Margret. But while there is an admirable depiction of 'real' people at work or settling down for the big match with a six-pack, the material is still no more than the great middle class drama of adultery, worked out with its very familiar rows and guilts. The acting, however, is a fascinating primer in just who can handle the medium. Burstyn and Madigan come out as if born to the art. CPea

Twilight

(1998, US, 95 min)
d Robert Benton. *p* Arlene Donovan, Scott Rudin. *sc* Robert Benton, Richard Russo. *ph* Piotr Sobocinski. *ed* Carol Littleton. *pd* David Gropman. *m* Elmer Bernstein. *cast* Paul Newman, Susan Sarandon, Gene Hackman, Stockard Channing, Reese Witherspoon, Giancarlo Esposito, James Garner, Liev Schreiber, M Emmet Walsh.
● Though Robert Benton's film may not be as richly rewarding as underrated *Nobody's Fool*, it does share the earlier film's its leading actor (Newman) and writer (Richard Russo), and its gentle, semi-comic humanism which investigates the themes of ageing and failure while paying tribute to the enduring virtues of honour and friendship. It tells the labyrinthine but fundamentally familiar *noir* story of a private dick – ex-cop, ex-husband and father, and ex-drunk Harry Ross (Newman) – getting entangled in a web of blackmail, corruption and murder after he reluctantly agrees to deliver an envelope for his former movie-star pal Jack (Hackman). But friendship, it seems, has its limits: not only is Harry, who lodges with and works as a handyman for the cancer-stricken Jack and his wife Catherine (Sarandon), ready to indulge his long-harboured desires for the latter, but when he delivers Jack's package to the mysterious Gloria, he finds instead a dying man. If there's nothing particularly original about Benton's film, there's still much to enjoy – notably, a crop of solid, charismatic performances and cameraman Piotr Sobocinski's restoration LA to its near-mythic *noir* glory. Far from breeding contempt, familiarity here produces its own peculiar pleasures. Indeed, what makes the film satisfying is its quiet, effortless assurance, as easy-going as in a late Hawks movie. Modest, intelligent and very engaging. GA

Twilight City

(1989, GB, 52 min)
d Reece Auguiste. *p* Avril Johnson. *sc* Edward George, John Akomfrah. *ph* Jonathan Collinson. *ed* Brand Thumis. *m* Trevor Mathison. *cast* Homi Bhaba, Andy Coupland, Paul Gilroy, Gail Lewis, Savriti Hensman, Femi Otitoju, George Shire, Rosina Visram, David Yallop.
● In his novel *The Moviegoer*, Walker Percy writes about how seeing your everyday surroundings up on a cinema screen somehow authenticates them, conferring a reality they never had before. This is partly what the Black Audio Film Collective's work achieves, for London is the Twilight City now. As in *Handsworth Songs* and *Testament*, the BAFC adopts an evocative, poetic free form, comprised of powerful documentary and archival footage, narrative devices, and symbolic imagery. Liberating documentary from its didactic conventions, they synthesise the emotional and the political; the effect is urgent and memorable. 'Sacrifice a piece of the past for the whole of the future': the slogan reverberates through the film like a bell, a nightmarish Orwellian alarm and an elegiac knell. Other voices speak of other Londons: remembered, imagined, dreaded… cities of the mind. Immigrant experience, Section 28, architecture, Big Bang, the Docklands development, down-and-outs – there is too much here for the 52-minute running time, but Trevor Mathison's cacophonous score pulls it together in a cinematic stream of consciousness. TCh

Twilight of the Ice Nymphs, The

(1997, Can, 91 min)
d Guy Maddin. *p* Ritchard Findlay. *sc* George Toles. *ph* Michael Marshall. *ed* Reginald Harkena. *pd* Rejean Labrie. *m* John McCulloch. *cast* Pascale Bussières, Shelley Duvall, Frank Gorshin, Alice Krige, RH Thomson.
● An acquired taste they may have been, but from the mock early sound-era Nordic saga *Tales from the Gimli Hospital* to the deconstructed, de-Nazified mountain film *Careful*, the camp pastiche melodramas of Canadian experimentalist Maddin had a compelling (if confounding) hallucinatory logic of their own: surreally funny, but halo'd by a haze of 'lost age' romantic nostalgia. Forsaking at last the creaky conventions of '20s cinema, Maddin takes his inspiration here from the equally kitsch but more ethereal magical reaches of such '30s movies as the Reinhardt/ Dieterle *A Midsummer Night's Dream*. Sadly, it collapses dizzily amid a baroque shower of bejewelled costumes, Kenneth Anger style colour overload, mock fairytale purple prose, and pixillated anti-naturalistic performances: mournful ugly sister Amelia (Duvall); mesmerist Dr Solti (Thomson), the object of her affection; widowed Zephyr (Krige); a returned convict, and a dog called Aesop among them. Finally pretty tedious. WH

Twilight's Last Gleaming

(1977, US/WGer, 146 min)
d Robert Aldrich. *p* Merv Adelson. *sc* Ronald M Cohen, Edward Huebsch. *ph* Robert B Hauser. *ed* Michael Luciano, Maury Winetrobe, William Martin. *pd* Rolf Zehetbauer. *m* Jerry Goldsmith. *cast* Burt Lancaster, Richard Widmark, Charles Durning, Melvyn Douglas, Paul Winfield, Burt Young, Joseph Cotten, Roscoe Lee Browne, Gerald S O'Loughlin, Richard Jaeckel.
● Nuclear missiles raise their warheads, but this time the paranoia is inward, and it's American vs American as Lancaster's renegade Air Force General captures a Montana missile base in order to 'blackmail' the President into revealing the shameful secrets of former administrations. The plea for 'open' government makes this in many ways the first film of the Carter administration. On reflection, the script is often contrived and the acting less than dynamic. But praise to Aldrich for his no-nonsense direction, which fashions the material into a fairly riveting computer hardware thriller. His handling of the countdown – 'It stopped at 8. Next time they go!' – is sufficiently convincing for one to think that the film and everything else might end prematurely. Aldrich turns in a neat, professional job, and even his use of split-screen is unusually uncluttered. CPe

Twilight Zone – The Movie

(1983, US, 101 min)
d John Landis, Steven Spielberg, Joe Dante, George Miller. *p* Steven Spielberg, John Landis. *sc* John Landis, George Clayton Johnson, Richard Matheson, Josh Rogan. *ph* Stevan Larner, Allen Daviau, John Hora. *ed* Malcolm Campbell, Michael Kahn, Tina Hirsch, Howard Smith. *pd* James D Bissell. *m* Jerry Goldsmith. *cast* Dan Aykroyd, Albert Brooks, Vic Morrow, Scatman Crothers, Bill Quinn, Kathleen Quinlan, Jeremy Licht, Kevin McCarthy, John Lithgow.

●These revamped episodes from the old supernatural TV series begin splendidly with Aykroyd and Brooks driving down a dark road at night, singing along to Creedence Clearwater and trying to guess TV theme songs. Four episodes follow, and it's ironic that producer Spielberg's geriatric remake of *Peter Pan* set in an Old People's home is easily the weakest of the lot, exhibiting all the churning sentimentality of a great film-maker going OTT. The others have a comic strip zeal which makes them intensely watchable, but ultimately it's left to *Mad Max* wizard Miller to steal the show with an extraordinary remake of Richard Matheson's story about an airline passenger who spies a demon noshing the starboard engine. DP

Twin Dragons (Shuangiong Hui)

(1991/1998, HK/US, 89 min)
d Tsui Hark, Ringo Lam. *p* Teddy Robin. *sc* Barry Wong, Tsui Hark, Joe Cheung, Wong Yik. *ph* Wong Wing-Hang. *ed* Mark Chi-Sin. *ad* Bill Lui, Ray Lam. *m* Lowell Lo. *cast* Jackie Chan, Maggie Cheung, Teddy Robin, Anthony Chan, Philip Chan, Sylvia Chang, Alfred Cheung, Jacob Cheung.
●This dreadful Jackie Chan caper (made in the early '90s and redubbed in '98) kicks off in 1965 with identical twins John and Boomer Ma separated when a gangster grabs the latter from his mother's arms. The infant is later dumped and grows up streetwise and well-equipped for fighting the thugs with whom he's soon to become acquainted. His brother is a successful composer and conductor. Years later, the twins (Chan) are reunited when an episode in Boomer's troubled life spills into John's ordered world. The script (as translated) is facile, the dubbing atrocious and the direction all over the place; the cast is mostly inadequate and the editing haphazard. What you don't expect from a Chan movie, though, is such poorly choreographed and shot fight sequences as these here. DA

Twin Falls Idaho

(1998, US, 110 min)
d Michael Polish. *p* Marshall Persinger, Rena Ronson, Steven J Wolfe. *sc* Mark Polish, Michael Polish. *ph* M David Mullen. *ed* Leo Trombetta. *pd* Warren Alan Young. *m* Stuart Matthewman. *cast* Mark Polish, Michael Polish, Michele Hicks, Jon Gries, Patrick Bauchau, Garrett Morris, William Katt, Lesley Ann Warren, Holly Woodlawn.
●In an era when Jerry Springer and his ilk are grooming every boondock hick with a sister for a wife and a rinky-dink tale to tell, let's applaud two film-makers bestowing dignity on misfits everywhere. Blake (Mark Polish) and Francis (Michael Polish) are conjoined twins. Two heads, two arms, three legs. And two hearts, one of which, Blake's, is gradually lost to kindly prostitute Penny (Hicks). Tentatively, she returns his love, but, well, three's a crowd. While director Michael Polish has picked an artful, brooding path between TV movie melodrama, Cronenberg-style show-and-tell, and Harmony Korine's ironic freak shows, for the first 30 minutes he appears to be on a collision course with B-grade David Lynch. Thankfully, the opening's uneasy gothic whimsy is shown to be just that – a purposely discomfiting curtainraiser for the brothers' own distinct vision and remarkable manipulation of mood. Minimally lit by David Mullen, the film's literal darkness lifts almost imperceptibly before the searing light of its conclusion. Conversations are barely audible, and a tight-lipped screenplay discloses only the most tantalising of personal details. And, yes, ypu do get a three-way love scene – but it's a testament to this sure footed, singular debut that you'll be hard pushed to find a more moving clinch at the cinema this year. MHi

Twinkle, Twinkle, Killer Kane

see Ninth Configuration, The

Twin Pawns (aka The Curse of Greed)

(1920, US, 74 min, b/w)
d/sc Léonce Perret. *ph* Alfred Ortlieb. *cast* Mae Murray, Warner Oland.
●Perret first worked with Feuillade as an actor, and obviously picked up a flair for poetic hokum which is displayed to great effect in this fast-paced melodrama (made during a four-year spell in America). The 'twin pawns' are identical sisters whose fortunes are manipulated by a greedy bookmaker suitably called Bent. The story (from Wilkie Collins' *The Woman in White*) may be nothing special, but the treatment certainly is, for Perret shows astonishing mastery of all the elements of cinema. The lighting, sets, compositions (impeccable use of doors, windows, and mirrors), editing, use of close-ups, even the design of the linking titles – all are pertinently stylish, full of the kind of visual texture usually associated with Sternberg, Sirk or Welles. GB

Twin Peaks

(1989, US, 112 min)
d David Lynch. *p* David J Latt. *sc* Mark Frost, David Lynch. *ph* Ron Garcia. *ed* Duwayne Dunham. *pd* Patricia Norris. *m* Angelo Badalamenti. *cast* Kyle MacLachlan, Michael Ontkean, Peggy Lipton, Jack Nance, Russ Tamblyn, Joan Chen, Piper Laurie, Troy Evans.
●Although financed by television, this – the first episode of a 30-episode serial, with a specially taken ending tacked on – was shot on film, allowing Lynch free rein to work in the partly surreal, partly expressionist style that has suffused his work to date. Set in the eponymous small lumber town in the Pacific Northwest, it begins with the discovery of a girl's corpse on a lakeside beach. Her parents are devastated, and when another girl is found wandering into town, dazed and speechless after having suffered unthinkably horrific torture, the local sheriff (Ontkean) calls in the FBI to help investigate the case. Already the spiritual unease and corruption of the community has been signalled, but when agent Dale Cooper (MacLachlan) drives into town, entranced by the Douglas firs, conversing endlessly with a cassette recorder, and grinning like a madman, the inimitable Lynch vision begins to grip like a strangler. Nightmare merges with comedy, and normality flies out the window. The result, like a soap reimagined by a Bosch or Magritte, is more genuinely cinematic than many a big screen thriller. See it, and shudder. GA

Twin Peaks: Fire Walk with Me

(1992, US, 134 min)
d David Lynch. *p* Gregg Fienberg. *sc* David Lynch, Robert Engels. *ph* Ron Garcia. *ed* Mark Sweeney. *pd* Patricia Norris. *m* Angelo Badalamenti. *cast* Kyle MacLachlan, Sheryl Lee, Harry Dean Stanton, Kiefer Sutherland, Moira Kelly, David Bowie, Chris Isaak, Ray Wise, James Marshall, Pamela Gidley, Grace Zabriskie, Jürgen Prochnow, David Lynch.
●'Goddamn, these people are peculiar!' opines Harry Dean Stanton's trailer-park manager in Lynch's big screen prequel to his cult TV series. He's right: not only are his fellow-characters weird, but the film's makers must be pretty odd too. For one thing, they evidently never felt that the tortuous narrative need make sense to audiences; for another, they appear to have made no attempt to conceal the cynicism that presumably motivated their desire to cash in on their TV success. It begins a year before Laura Palmer's death, with FBI agent Desmond (Isaak) investigating the murder of one Teresa Banks (Gidley); meanwhile, Dale Cooper (MacLachlan) has his usual premonitory dreams. The whole thing looks like off-cuts from the series that were eliminated because they were either too nasty or too inept. Moreover, the cast consists largely of the series' weakest performers (Lee, particularly, as Laura Palmer, proves she can't carry a movie). Self-parody would seem too generous an assessment of Lynch's aims and achievement. GA

Twins

(1988, US, 107 min)
d/p Ivan Reitman. *sc* William Davies, William Osborne, Timothy Harris, Herschel Weingrod. *ph* Andrzej Bartowiak. *ed* Sheldon Kahn, Donn Cambern. *pd* James D Bissell. *m* Georges Delerue. *cast* Arnold Schwarzenegger, Danny DeVito, Kelly Preston, Chloe Webb, Bonnie Bartlett, Marshall Bell, Trey Wilson.
●Tailor-made for Schwarzenegger and DeVito, this slick comedy about a pair of genetically-engineered twins is too tight for comfort, and works best when the odd couple parody their familiar personae and play off one another. The result of a scientific experiment, in which their mother was impregnated with a 'sperm milkshake' derived from six male geniuses, the twins were separated at birth. Arnie is now a naive, super-intelligent virgin, DeVito a small-time hustler. So when Arnie finally tracks down his long-lost brother, it's hardly fraternal love at first sight. The subplots about DeVito's problems with loan sharks, exposing his residual avarice, help to flesh out what is essentially a one-joke scenario; but more emotionally revealing are DeVito's selfish, venal desire for Chloe Webb, and Arnie's innocent affection for her long-limbed sister (Preston). DeVito displays his remarkable ability to shift from fast-talking cynicism to affecting sentiment, while Arnie reveals a reasonable talent for light comedy. NF

Twins of Evil

(1971, GB, 87 min)
d John Hough. *p* Harry Fine, Michael Style. *sc* Tudor Gates. *ph* Dick Bush. *ed* Spencer Reeve. *ad* Roy Stannard. *m* Harry Robinson. *cast* Madeleine and Mary Collinson, Peter Cushing, Kathleen Byron, Dennis Price, Harvey Hall, Isobel Black, Damien Thomas, David Warbeck, Katya Keith.
●Hammer climaxed scriptwriter Tudor Gates's Sheridan Le Fanu trilogy (*The Vampire Lovers* and *Lust for a Vampire*) with this little number: Puritan witch-hunting and rum goings-on at Castle Karnstein in Pinewood Austria. The centrefold Collinson twins are a sabre-toothed fiend (Madeleine) and a damsel in distress (Mary), effectively marking out the tension between virginal repression and unchecked licentiousness lying at the core of the genre. Some moments of Gothic atmosphere though, don't quite dispel the feeling that much of the plot is devoted to developing situations where its leading ladies might be disrobed for the camera. TJ

Twin Town

(1997, GB, 99 min)
d Kevin Allen. *p* Peter McAleese. *sc* Kevin Allen, Paul Durden. *ph* John Mathieson. *ed* Norrie Ottey. *pd* Pat Campbell. *m* Mark Thomas. *cast* Llyr Evans, Rhys Ifans, Dorien Thomas, Dougray Scott, Biddug Williams.
●Port Talbot, and school dropout twins Julian and Jeremy are revelling in daily joyriding, solvent abuse and petty vandalism. Meanwhile, over in the chintzier reaches of twin town Swansea, coppers Terry and Greyo, mates of bent building contractor Cartwright, argue about the appropriate scale of their drug deals. Their fates intertwine when the kids' father Fatty, engaged on a job for Cartwright, is hospitalised but refused compensation, triggering tit-for-tat threats, humiliations, slaughtered dogs and finally arson and multiple murder. This urban black comedy is a plain misfire. Strangely, for all its pulse-taking pretensions, it most resembles some old-fashioned criminal caper movie, albeit psyched-up and overdone for the '90s: the moral perspective has merely been flipped from the majority's to that of the confused offender, keeping the facile narrative and quaint social caricature intact. Llyr Evans (Julian) and Rhys Ifans (Jeremy), on the other hand, display a louche rude-boy energy that betokens fine things for the future. WH

Twister

(1990, US, 93 min)
d Michael Almereyda. *p* Wieland Schulz-Keil, William J Quigley. *sc* Michael Almereyda. *ph* Renato Berta. *ed* Roberto Silvi. *ad* David Waso. *m* Hans Zimmer. *cast* Harry Dean Stanton, Suzy Amis, Crispin Glover, Dylan McDermott, William Burroughs.
●An engagingly slapdash tale of an everyday American family: soda pop billionaire Dad (Stanton), *fin de siècle* fop son (Glover), teenage single-parent daughter (Amis), and her moppet progeny who drags around her pet plastic lizard in a jar. When Amis' lovelorn suitor and Dad's evangelist fiancée come a-calling, all hell doesn't *quite* break out, but there's some entertainingly freaky dialogue – and even freakier acting – to liven things up along the way. With verbal, visual and narrative non-sequiturs at every turn – the freak weather conditions of the title, a mysterious helicopter, and a wildly incongruous William Burroughs cameo – *Twister* is clearly lost without a map from the first frame. Languorous pace

and uneasy self-consciousness notwithstanding, it's in a similar bracket to the work of Hal Hartley and Atom Egoyan; it has a spaced-out charm of its own. And Glover's ludicrous wardrobe and whip-dancing skills make this a must for completists of Crazy Crispin. JRo

Twister

(1996, US, 113 min)
d Jan De Bont. *p* Kathleen Kennedy, Ian Bryce, Michael Crichton. *sc* Michael Crichton, Anne-Marie Martin. *ph* Jack N Green. *ed* Michael Kahn. *pd* Joseph Nemec III. *m* Mark Mancina. *cast* Helen Hunt, Bill Paxton, Jami Gertz, Cary Elwes, Lois Smith, Philip Seymour Hoffman, Alan Ruck, Sean Whalen.

●Effects apart, this is dire: predictable, clichéd, sloppily written, pitifully performed and surprisingly short of real shocks and suspense. The story can be described in two ways: as a rip-off of *Only Angels Have Wings*, in which Paxton's implausibly intuitive tornado expert is torn between two women, his ex (Hunt) and his fiancée (Gertz), and two lives, a safe weatherman job, or a risky return to the group of crazily devoted storm-chasers trying to get a gizmo up inside a twister's 'suck-zone'; or as a repetitive spectacle where all that happens is that the objects hurled around in the air simply get bigger. Forget the many redundant references to *The Wizard of Oz*, this hasn't a fraction of that movie's logic, imagination or ambitions. Seriously depressing. GA

Two Daughters

see Teen Kanya

2 Days in the Valley

(1996, US, 107 min)
d John Herzfeld. *p* Jeff Wald, Herb Nanas. *sc* John Herzfeld. *ph* Oliver Wood. *ed* Jim Miller, Wayne Wahrman. *pd* Catherine Hardwicke. *m* Anthony Marinelli. *cast* James Spader, Danny Aiello, Teri Hatcher, Paul Mazursky, Jeff Daniels, Eric Stoltz, Glenne Headly, Greg Cruttwell, Marsha Mason, Robert Carradine, Louise Fletcher.

●Hatcher hires Spader to kill her ratbag of a husband. That's the stone tossed into the pool: the ripples take in Mazursky's suicidal film director, Daniels' and Stoltz's variously troubled cops, Cruttwell's travails with a kidney stone, and more. The result is not so much complexity as a mildly entertaining collection of rather superficial short stories; or perhaps it's best described as an elementary elaboration of a greater number of subsidiary characters than usual, inside a piece of pulp fiction. Smoothly constructed, for such a busy piece of work, and Hatcher's ascent to stardom continues. BBa

Two Deaths

(1994, GB, 103 min)
d Nicolas Roeg. *p* Carolyn Montagu, Luc Roeg. *sc* Allan Scott. *ph* Witold Stok. *ed* Tony Lawson. *pd* Don Taylor. *m* Hans Zimmer. *cast* Michael Gambon, Sonia Braga, Patrick Malahide, Ion Caramitru, Sevilla Delofski, Nickolas Grace.

●Secrets and lies in Bucharest. Dr Daniel Pavenic (Gambon) hosts the annual evening get-together of four old friends. Outside, civil war rages. Inside, everything's perfect: delicious food and self-effacing service by the beautiful housekeeper Ana (Braga). Pressed by his companions, Pavenic tells Ana's story – a tale that turns into a sordid confession. Gradually the war outside seeps through the walls of these well-appointed male bourgeois lives, and long-established convictions and relationships crumble to dust. Although Roeg and screenwriter Allan Scott have transposed Stephen Dobyns' novel *The Two Deaths of Señora Puccini* from Chile to Romania, the budget seems not to have stretched much further east than a soundstage at Pinewood – giving this dinner party conversation piece a dourly theatrical air. This impression is exacerbated by ungainly chunks of speechifying and pontificating, some uneven performances, choppy editing and hand-held camerawork. Visually, this must be the least distinguished of Roeg's films. There's enough sting in the tale to keep you watching, but *Two Deaths* marks no career resurrection – indeed it only rarely comes to life at all. TCh

2 Duo

(1996, Jap, 90 min)
d Nobuhiro Suwa. *p* Takenori Sento, Koji Kobayashi. *sc* Nobuhiro Suwa. *ph* Masaki Tamura. *ad* Toshihiro Isomi. *m* Nick Wood. *cast* Eri Yu, Hidetoshi Nishijima, Makiko Watanabe.

●A low-budget first feature with an exemplary grasp of what it's doing (and why it was worth doing in the first place), this account of a young couple falling apart together has real bite. The guy is an aspiring actor, the girl works in a smart boutique; her sense that things are going really really wrong starts when he turns a trivial apology into a proposal of marriage. Suwa began with a full script but told his actors to forget it and invent their own actions, reactions and dialogue. He shoots the results in long takes from fixed angles, and compounds the quasi-documentary feel by adding sequences in which the characters respond to questions about themselves from an off-screen interviewer. The resulting feeling of truthfulness makes it all remarkably moving. TR

Two English Girls

see Deux Anglaises et le Continent, Les

Two-Faced Woman

(1941, US, 94 min, b/w)
d George Cukor. *p* Gottfried Reinhardt. *sc* SN Behrman, Salka Viertel, George Oppenheimer. *ph* Joseph Ruttenberg. *ed* George Boemler. *ad* Cedric Gibbons, Daniel Cathcart. *m* Bronislau Kaper. *cast* Greta Garbo, Melvyn Douglas, Constance Bennett, Roland Young, Ruth Gordon, Robert Sterling.

●Garbo's last film, graced by some charming scenes and directed with Cukor's usual flair, but hardly sending her off in a blaze of glory. A sophisticated comedy, it has Garbo vamping it up as her imaginary twin sister in order to re-seduce the wandering attention of her husband (Douglas). The Garbo persona is really too dreamy for this sort of flightiness, and although she amiably parodies her own image, she tends to be upstaged by Constance Bennett as the other woman. The script, in any case, is something of a disaster area, not least because the film was denounced by the Legion of Decency, hurriedly withdrawn, and partially redubbed into a blandness that sometimes becomes meaningless. TM

Two Faces of Dr Jekyll, The (aka House of Fright)

(1960, GB, 88 min)
d Terence Fisher. *p* Michael Carreras. *sc* Wolf Mankowitz. *ph* Jack Asher. *ed* James Needs, Eric Boyd-Perkins. *ad* Bernard Robinson. *m* Monty Norman, David Heneker. *cast* Paul Massie, Dawn Addams, Christopher Lee, David Kossoff, Francis De Wolff.

●Robert Louis Stevenson in the mincer again, courtesy of Sir James Carreras' K-Tel strategy and the appropriately named Wolf Mankowitz at the typewriter. Jekyll is a whiskery and sinister scientist, and Hyde a debonair charmer wenching through those familiar London stews where Hammer's wardrobe department always kept their wenches' dumplings on the boil. This is Explicit City sex-wise, with a snake-dancing floor show. Oliver Reed appears in a bijou part. The mantis-like Christopher Lee displays his usual grip as Hyde's friend, despite inner discontent at keeping decomposing company. Mediocre, but all right for late-night viewing. BC

Two for Tea (Tomándote)

(1999, Sp, 99 min)
d Isabel Gardela. *p* Carlos Benpar. *sc* Isabel Gardela. *ph* Núria Roldós. *ed* Domi Parra, Victor Vidal. *pd* Salvador Ferrer. *m* Alex Solana. *cast* Núria Prims, Zack Qureshi, Olalla Moreno, Teresa Gimpera, Txell Sust, Mònica Van Campen, Xavier Graset.

●Regardless of it billing, this grim Catalan 'romantic comedy' is neither funny nor romantic. It charts the blossoming of a problematic relationship between a successful novelist who has just returned to Barcelona amid accusations that she's exploited and betrayed friends as research material for her books, and an Indian florist's assistant. Not only do religious, cultural and gender differences get in the way of an otherwise satisfying affair, but the novelist's parents are as upset by the fling as those in *Guess Who's Coming to Dinner* – which is occasionally echoed in this naive, annoyingly didactic, even sometimes unwittingly racist dross. One of those self-consciously 'modern' Spanish films in which the heroine and her friends are all ludicrously into sexual liberation, drugs, art, and other fashionable hedonisms, it's actually as old fashioned and unappealing as a threadbare afghan. GA

Two for the Road

(1966, GB, 111 min)
d/p Stanley Donen. *sc* Frederic Raphael. *ph* Christopher Challis. *ed* Richard Marden, Madeleine Gug. *ad* Willy Holt. *m* Henry Mancini. *cast* Audrey Hepburn, Albert Finney, Eleanor Bron, William Daniels, Claude Dauphin, Nadia Gray, Jacqueline Bisset.

●Old-fashioned romantic comedy tricked out with some new-fangled ideas. Donen does some tricksy time-jumping between past and present as a couple (Hepburn and Finney) look back over their twelve years of marriage, while Frederic Raphael's script provides some crisply disillusioned dialogue for their quarrels. The trouble is that smart direction and smart dialogue slide off the glossily idealised couple like water off a duck's back. Arid, crowd-pleasing stuff, in which the soul-searchings take place very conveniently on annual holidays in France and in a variety of luxuriously furnished interiors. TM

Two Friends

(1986, Aust, 76 min)
d Jane Campion. *p* Jan Chapman. *sc* Helen Garner. *ph* Julian Penney. ed Bill Russo. *pd* Janet Patterson, Martin Armiger. *cast* Emma Coles, Kris Bidenko, Kris McQuade, Stephen Leeder, Peter Hehir, Tony Barry.

●The first feature-length film from Jane Campion; made for TV, like *An Angel at My Table*, and still a little unpolished, it is nevertheless a remarkable picture. It's the story of two inseparable schoolmates, Kelly and Louise (Bidenko and Coles), and how over the course of ten months they become, in fact, separated. Campion's films are acutely personal and absolutely distinctive. They combine an oblique, detached point of view with startling human insight. She has the knack of invading private space by standing back; a sort of estranged intimacy. Here, she tells this very simple story (written by Helen Garner) in reverse. It begins in July, cuts back to February, to January, December, and finally October. The effect is puzzling at first, but stimulating, and it ends appropriately on a note of unforeseen poignancy. TCh

Two Girls and a Guy

(1997, US, 84 min)
d James Toback. *p* Edward R Pressman, Chris Hanley. *sc* James Toback. *ph* Barry Markowitz. *ed* Alan Oxman. *pd* Kevin Thompson. *cast* Heather Graham, Natasha Gregson Wagner, Robert Downey Jr, Angel David, Frederique Van Der Wal.

●Basically a three-hander set in a spacious NY loft, Toback's conversation piece charts the recriminations, apologies, explanations and accusations that occur when two rather different women suddenly discover not only that they've unwittingly been sharing the same lover, an actor, for the last 10 months, but that they also share contempt for his pathetic deceits and self-delusions. That's it, really, but the excellent performances, the authenticity of the dialogue, the subtle, fluid direction – it nearly all takes place in 'real time' – and the fact that it's all so unquestionably adult make it a thoroughly engrossing, intelligent and enjoyable experience. Oh, and its one sex scene is, for an American movie, quite raunchy. GA

Two Guys and a Gal

see Tva Killar och en Tjej

Two Hands

(1999, Aust, 102 min)
d Gregor Jordan. *p* Marian Macgowan. *sc* Gregor Jordan. *ph* Malcolm McCulloch. *ed* Lee Smith. *pd* Steven Jones-Evans. *m* Cezary Skubiszewski. *cast* Heath Ledger, Bryan Brown, Rose Byrne, David Field, Tom Long, Tony Forrow, Mariel McClorey, Evan Sheaves, Steve Vidler, Susie Porter.

●Would-be goofy crime thriller pastiche which sets up young-blood Ledger (the wild-haired hunk in *10 Things I Hate About You*) with Brown's semi-competent Mob outfit, whose $10,000 he instantly loses. A couple of deadbeat dads help on a bank job to make up his loss; and Porter is the love interest. More perplexingly, Ledger's battle-scarred brother looks like he's dug himself up from hell to watch the show. The deadpan tone intermittently hits home, but for the most part the OTT construction – hyperactive plotting, bovine philosophical musings in voice-over, wailing guitars over the soundtrack – just seems crude. NB

200 Motels

(1971, GB, 98 min)
d Frank Zappa, Tony Palmer. *p* Jerry Good, Herb Cohen. *sc* Frank Zappa. *ph* Barrie Dodd, Mike Fitch, John Howard. *ed* Rich Harrison. *pd* Calvin Schenkel. *m* Frank Zappa. *with* Frank Zappa, Mothers of Invention, Ringo Starr, Theodore Bikel, Keith Moon.
●A real dinosaur, this purports to give a warts 'n' all snapshot of life in Zappa's touring rock circus. Along the way Frank indulges in time-locked psychedelic frippery, and there's a certain amount of dodgy cavorting with the groupies. Mocked-up at Pinewood, shot on video. TJ

Two if by Sea (aka Stolen Hearts)

(1996, US, 96 min)
d Bill Bennett. *p* James G Robinson. *sc* Denis Leary, Mike Armstrong. *ph* Andrew Lesnie. *ed* Bruce Green. *pd* David Chapman. *m* Nick Glennie-Smith, Paddy Moloney. *cast* Denis Leary, Sandra Bullock, Stephen Dillane, Yaphet Kotto, Mike Starr, Jonathan Tucker, Wayne Robson, Michael Badalucco.
●Co-written by spitball comedian Leary, whose previous, far superior vehicle *Hostile Hostages*, met with similar lack of attention by its distributors both in Britain and the US, this is a romantic comedy from the wrong side of the tracks. Leary's a small-time, small-thinking Boston thief and decorator, who takes along girlfriend Bullock when he steals a 'Henry Matis' painting so they can enjoy a weekend away from it all in Rhode Island, where he's to make the sale. Kotto reprises his *Midnight Run* role as the FBI man on their (very exposed) tail, and Dillane is the wealthy sophisticate who romances Bullock right in front of her blue-collar beau. It begins smartly, and occasionally serves up the kind of venomous, vulgar put-down at which Leary excels, but the invention fades and Bullock is really just along for the ride. TCh

Two Jakes, The

(1990, US, 138 min)
d Jack Nicholson. *p* Robert Evans, Harold Schneider. *sc* Robert Towne. *ph* Vilmos Zsigmond. *ed* Anne Goursaud. *pd* Jeremy Railton, Richard Sawyer. *m* Van Dyke Parks. *cast* Jack Nicholson, Harvey Keitel, Meg Tilly, Madeleine Stowe, Eli Wallach, Ruben Blades, Frederic Forrest, David Keith, Richard Farnsworth, Tracey Walter, Perry Lopez, Joe Mantell, Tom Waits.
●Neither the glittering sequel to *Chinatown* nor the expected mess that its distribution troubles and production history would suggest, this is often pretty good and never less than intriguing. The problem is the plot, which is dense indeed – a Robert Towne hallmark – and a recent viewing of the Polanski might come in handy. Jake Gittes (Nicholson) is still the loyal gumshoe, and eleven years on, remains in thrall to his tragic past. 'You might think you know what's going on, but you don't,' the bent real estate developer Jake Berman (Keitel) tells him, after which the gumshoe lights a cigarette and is blown sky high, confirming the statement. *Chinatown* was conspiratorial about water, the sequel concerns oil. Both women in the case (Tilly and Stowe) move in mysterious ways. LA earth tremors interrupt the action at random, bringing a surreal air to social interchange. It's beautifully acted with a fine '40s feel to it, and lingers in the mind long after you've left the cinema. BC

Two-Lane Blacktop

(1971, US, 101 min)
d Monte Hellman. *p* Michael Laughlin. *sc* Rudy Wurlitzer, Will Corry. *ph* Jack Deerson. *ed* Monte Hellman. *m* Billy James. *cast* James Taylor, Warren Oates, Laurie Bird, Dennis Wilson, David Drake, Rudolph Wurlitzer.
●Hellman, as his later inactivity testifies, seems to have turned himself into box-office anathema by toying once too often with his beloved *actes gratuites*, so open-ended that they would delight even the most demanding existentialist. Here two young hot-rodders (Taylor, Wilson), making their way across America by picking up racing bets on the side, challenge (or are challenged by) the boastful middle-aged owner of a gleaming new Pontiac (Oates). As their mesmeric duel unfolds within a landscape that narrows down to a claustrophobic tunnel of highways, filling stations and roadside cafés, it soon becomes apparent that Hellman is less interested in allegory (class and generation conflicts as in *Easy Rider*) or in the race itself (which simply fizzles out), than in the mysterious process whereby a challenge is subtly metamorphosed into an obsession. Self-enclosed, self-absorbed, and self-destructive (as the last shot of the film catching in the projector and burning suggests), it's absolutely riveting. TM

Two Lovers and Their Lass

see Tva Killar och en Tjej

Two-Minute Warning

(1976, US, 115 min)
d Larry Peerce. *p* Edward S Feldman. *sc* Edward Hume. *ph* Gerald Hirschfeld. *ed* Eve Newman, Walter Hannemann. *ad* Herman A Blumenthal. *m* Charles Fox. *cast* Charlton Heston, John Cassavetes, Martin Balsam, Beau Bridges, Marilyn Hassett, David Janssen, Jack Klugman, Gena Rowlands, Walter Pidgeon, Brock Peters.
●More unsettling in its implications than in execution, this places a faceless gunman in a tower overlooking a Los Angeles football stadium filled to capacity. The persistent high-angle shots, use of long lenses (equivalent to the rifle's telescopic sight), and subjective camerawork inevitably distance the 'human' vignettes being enacted on the terraces below. Coldly and unemotionally, the film portrays the crowd individually as losers, collectively as innocent bystanders in a struggle between two sinister psychopathic forces, the assassin and the cops. The paranoid, edgy movie (best represented by Cassavetes' SWAT sergeant) finally erupts when the crowd turns almost effortlessly and devours itself in a climax of panic. Efficient enough as formula suspense, but it fails to confront the implications of its subject, preferring instead evasiveness and fast cynicism to pull it through. CPe

Two Moon Junction

(1989, US, 105 min)
d Zalman King. *p* Donald P Borchers. *sc* Zalman King. *ph* Mark Plummer. *ed* Marc Grossman. *pd* Michelle Minch. *m* Jonathan Elias. *cast* Sherilyn Fenn, Richard Tyson, Louise Fletcher, Burl Ives, Kristy McNichol, Martin Hewitt, Juanita Moore, Millie Perkins, Don Galloway, Herve Villechaise, Screamin' Jay Hawkins.
●Fenn plays pampered April Delongpre, irritatingly dubbed Princess, Baby, Sugar and Darlin' (but then she *is* a Southern belle) and engaged to be married to the finest beau in the state. Perry (Tyson) is the fairground worker who teases, pursues, menaces and finally beds her. April is without doubt a corker; the same cannot be said for the wholly unappetising Perry, all rippling ringlets and pug features. What tiny tension the plot affords rests in April's choice between privilege and passion, and typically it's fudged: she gets to keep her swanky marriage *and* her bit of rough. Sex sequences are disappointingly non-specific: blurred nipples and vaguely flickering tongues, set to That Disco Beat and invariably followed by post-coital blubbing. Louise Fletcher is sinister as April's deeply creepy gran, and Kristy McNichol puts in a likeable performance as chirpy drifter Patti Jean, despite the ill-advised flirtation with lesbianism. 'Times like this ah know why men like women so much' she chirrups at April's uncorseted bosom. Sick-making. SFe

Two Much (Loco de amor)

(1996, Sp/US, 118 min)
d Fernando Trueba. *p* Christina Huete. *sc* Fernando Trueba, David Trueba, Menno Meyjes. *ph* José Luis Alcaine. *ed* Nena Bernard. *pd* Juan Botella. *m* Michel Camilo. *cast* Antonio Banderas, Melanie Griffith, Daryl Hannah, Danny Aiello, Joan Cusack, Eli Wallach, Austin Pendleton.
●Banderas is Art Dodge, a Miami art dealer, and Griffith is Betty Kerner, a fabulously wealthy divorcee. She thinks he'll make a virile third husband; he thinks she's the answer to his financial problems – and we think she's far too old for him. No surprise, then, when he falls for her younger sister Liz (Hannah). He dons wire-rimmed specs, wears his hair down, and – hey presto! – meet Art's twin Bart. Cue bed-hopping, wardrobe changes and contrivance. A big hit in Spain, and a considerable flop in the US, the film was adapted from a Donald Westlake novel and goes through the motions of classic screwball farce. Everything, however, feels stilted and second-hand. TCh

Two Mules for Sister Sara

(1969, US, 116 min)
d Don Siegel. *p* Martin Rackin, Carroll Case. *sc* Albert Maltz, Budd Boetticher. *ph* Gabriel Figueroa, Gabriel Torres. *ed* Robert F Shugrue, Juan José Marino. *ad* José Rodriguez Granada. *m* Ennio Morricone. *cast* Shirley MacLaine, Clint Eastwood, Manolo Fabregas, Alberto Morin, Armando Silvestre.
●A witty and slightly whimsical Western, which teams MacLaine – as a whore playing at being a nun – with the ever-chivalrous Eastwood as the man who steps in and prevents a three-way desert rape by drunken bandits. They go on to become involved with the Mexican revolutionary movement, with Eastwood's respect for her chastity becoming increasingly strained and her true profession coming in handy for infiltrating an enemy fort. Siegel devotees will find much to enjoy in the languid but not unexciting story by Budd Boetticher (who was originally to direct himself). VG

Two of a Kind

(1983, US, 87 min)
d John Herzfeld. *p* Roger M Rothstein, Joe Wizan. *sc* John Herzfeld. *ph* Fred J Koenekamp. *ed* Jack Hofstra. *pd* Albert Brenner. *m* Patrick Williams. *cast* John Travolta, Olivia Newton-John, Charles Durning, Oliver Reed, Beatrice Straight, Scatman Crothers, Richard Bright, Vincent Bufano.
●God, returning to heaven after a holiday, decides to wipe out the errant human race. The archangels, earning a stay of execution provided two randomly selected specimens prove to be Good, rest their case upon Zack (Travolta) and Debbie (Newton-John): he immediately holds up a bank, and she walks off with the loot. What follows is a rather complicated orchestration, with musical interludes, of this simple story in which Good and Evil battle it out with Zack and Debbie in between, as oblivious to all these earth-stopping machinations as the teenagers flocking to see Hollywood's best-brushed teeth will be to superior antecedents like *A Matter of Life and Death*. There are worse ways to spend an afternoon. FD

Two of Them, The (Ök Ketten/aka Two Women)

(1977, Hun, 95 min)
d Márta Mészáros. *sc* Ildikó Korody, József Balazs, Géza Bereményi. *ph* János Kende. *ed* Andrásné Karmentö. *ad* Tamás Banovich. *m* György Kovacs. *cast* Marina Vlady, Lili Monori, Jan Nowicki, Miklós Tolnay.
●After 20-odd years of documentary work, Mészáros trusts what and who she puts in front of her camera and rarely relies on heavily plotted scripting. Here she establishes two drifting marriages and the relationship that evolves between the two women surviving within them. Such is the worthiness of intent – as much humanist as feminist – that it feels churlish to note that in truth it's not very exciting to watch. DO

Two of Us, The

see Vieil Homme et l'Enfant, Le

Two or Three Things I Know About Her

see Deux ou Trois Choses que Je Sais d'Elle

Two Rode Together

(1961, US, 109 min)
d John Ford. *p* Stan Shpetner. *sc* Frank S Nugent. *ph* Charles Lawton Jr. *ed* Jack Murray. *ad* Robert Peterson. *m* George Duning. *cast* James Stewart, Richard Widmark, Shirley Jones, Linda Cristal, Andy Devine, John McIntire, Mae Marsh, Anna Lee.
●Dismissed by Ford as a casual favour to Columbia's boss Harry Cohn, this neglected Western repays careful attention. Stewart is the cynical marshal hired to repatriate pioneer children captured by the Comanche, and Widmark the cavalry officer who accompanies him. Gone is the clean frontier as would-be garden of *The Searchers* and earlier; instead, Ford offers us a nightmare vision, the frontier overrun by hysteria and (Eastern/Yankee) hypocrisy, with even the Indians seen as primitive entrepreneurs. PH

Two Stage Sisters (Wutai Jiemei)

(1964, China, 114 min)
d Xie Jin. *sc* Lin Gu, Xu Jin, Xie Jin. *ph* Zhen Zhenxiang, Zhou Taming. *ed* Zhang Liqun. *ad* Ge Schicheng. *m* Huang Zhun. *cast* Xie Fang, Cao Yindi, Feng Ji, Gao Yuansheng, Shen Fengjuan.
●A real delight, attractive on many levels. The story concerns two women who start out working for a travelling musical theatre company. As they become more famous, their friendship weakens and they take radically different paths; one becomes increasingly politically committed, the other is attracted to the trappings of urban success. Made before the Cultural Revolution by a man, the film manages to embrace feminist issues, political ideologies, thriller and musical motifs, and a surprisingly Hollywood-style sense of 'weepie' melodrama. The performances are terrific, but what really distinguishes this amazing hybrid (in Western terms, that is) is the director's fluid and elegant style. Colour, composition, pace, and above all, camera movement, create an exhilarating spectacle that is never thematically shallow. Imagine Sirk's colours and emotional sense, Scorsese or Minnelli's craning camera shots, allied to a politically perceptive treatment, and you're half way to imagining this film. GA

2001: 100 (100) 10 A Space Odyssey

(1968, GB, 141 min)
d/p Stanley Kubrick. *sc* Stanley Kubrick, Arthur C Clarke. *ph* Geoffrey Unsworth. *ed* Ray Lovejoy. *pd* Tony Masters, Harry Lange, Ernest Archer. *m* Richard Strauss, Johann Strauss Jr, Aram Khachaturian. *cast* Keir Dullea, Gary Lockwood, William Sylvester, Daniel Richter, Leonard Rossiter, Margaret Tyzack, Robert Beatty.
●A characteristically pessimistic account of human aspiration from Kubrick, this tripartite sci-fi look at civilisation's progress from prehistoric times (the apes learning to kill) to a visionary future (astronauts on a mission to Jupiter encountering superior life and rebirth in some sort of embryonic divine form) is beautiful, infuriatingly slow, and pretty half-baked. Quite how the general theme fits in with the central drama of the astronauts' battle with the arrogant computer HAL, who tries to take over their mission, is unclear; while the final farrago of light-show psychedelia is simply so much pap. Nevertheless, for all the essential coldness of Kubrick's vision, it demands attention as superior sci-fi, simply because it's more concerned with ideas than with Boy's Own-style pyrotechnics. GA

2010

(1984, US, 116 min)
d/p/sc/ph Peter Hyams. *ed* James Mitchell, Mia Goldman. *pd* Albert Brenner. *m* David Shire. *cast* Roy Scheider, John Lithgow, Helen Mirren, Bob Balaban, Keir Dullea, Madolyn Smith, Dana Elcar, Taliesin Jaffe.
●Hyams' sequel to Kubrick's big daddy of sci-fi movies may not have the novelty of *2001: A Space Odyssey*, but it is still a better film than anyone could have dared to expect. Scheider plays the American space agency boss trying to find out what happened to the ill-fated 'Discovery' spacecraft and its surviving crew-member. He joins a Russian space mission to Jupiter captained by the formidable Mirren, but things get pretty sticky when news comes through that back on Earth the super-powers are on the point of war. Hyams has not come up with a climax to match Kubrick's rush through the star-gate; but this is still space fiction of a superior kind, making the *Star Trek* movies look puny by comparison. DP

Two Thousand Women

(1944, GB, 97 min, b/w)
d Frank Launder. *p* Edward Black. *sc* Frank Launder. *ph* Jack Cox. *ed* RE Dearing. *ad* John Bryan. *m* Louis Levy. *cast* Phyllis Calvert, Patricia Roc, Jean Kent, Flora Robson, Reginald Purdell, Renee Houston, Thora Hird, Dulcie Gray, Carl Jaffe.
●Typically lively wartime offering from Launder and Gilliat, made under the Gainsborough banner and set in a women's prison in Nazi-occupied France. The prisoners attempts to conceal three daring RAF chaps from the authorities. On the one hand, it stands as a progenitor of Launder and Gilliat's later, equally zestful St Trinian's movies, coming complete with lashings of knockabout humour and a chaotic fight which would have done the Fifth Form proud. On the other, however, in its own *Tenko*-like way, it's also surprisingly touching. GM

2 x 50 Years of French Cinema

(1995, GB/Fr, 52 min)
d Anne-Marie Miéville, Jean-Luc Godard. *with* Michel Piccoli.
●You might have guessed that Miéville/Godard's contribution to the BFI's 'Century of Cinema' would be a demolition job on the series' premises. Godard invites Michel Piccoli (in his capacity as chairman of the official Centenary Committee) to a hotel lake and asks him what there is to celebrate. Isn't the cinema dead? Isn't French cinema forgotten? Disturbed by his host's harangue, Piccoli spends the rest of the movie asking hotel staff what they know of French cinema and discovering Godard was right. His hilariously hangdog field research is overlaid with stills and lines of dialogue from everyone's best-loved French movies, and the whole is rounded off with Godard and Miéville's elegy for the great tradition which has died. More of a wake than a funeral, and wickedly funny. TR

Two-Way Stretch

(1960, GB, 87 min, b/w)
d Robert Day. *p* M Smedley Aston. *sc* John Warren, Len Heath. *ph* Geoffrey Faithfull. *ed* Bert Rule. *ad* John Box. *m* Ken Jones. *cast* Peter Sellers, Wilfrid Hyde-White, Maurice Denham, Irene Handl, David Lodge, Lionel Jeffries, Liz Fraser, Bernard Cribbins, Thorley Walters, Beryl Reid.
●Convicts Sellers, Cribbins and Lodge treat prison like a holiday camp and hatch a plan with bogus clergyman Hyde-White to escape from the joint, deprive a maharaja of his jewels, then break back in again to ensure a watertight alibi. Unfortunately, new warden Jeffries is determined to initiate a tougher regime, which puts the gang's plans in jeopardy. With a tight narrative and a raft of top British character actors, this ebullient comedy could hardly go wrong – and it didn't. Reliably amusing stuff.

Two Weeks in Another Town

(1962, US, 107 min)
d Vincente Minnelli. *p* John Houseman. *sc* Charles Schnee. *ph* Milton Krasner. *ed* Adrienne Fazan, Robert J Kern Jr. *ad* George W Davis, Urie McCleary. *m* David Raksin. *cast* Kirk Douglas, Edward G Robinson, Daliah Lavi, George Hamilton, Claire Trevor, Rosanna Schiaffino, Cyd Charisse, James Gregory, George Macready.
●Having dealt superbly with Hollywood ten years earlier in *The Bad and the Beautiful*, Minnelli returned to the topic of movie-making, this time changing the location to Rome's Cinecittà, and using Douglas not as a ruthless producer but as a washed-up actor reduced largely to dubbing international movies. While the plot nominally deals cynically and sensationally with corruption and intrigue within the movie world's jet set as it follows Douglas' attempts to persuade producer Robinson to help him make a comeback, it really concerns itself more with failure, compromise, and disillusionment. Superb performances throughout, although it's Minnelli's remarkable direction that really lifts the movie up among the classics. Described by some as gaudy or overheated, it is in fact imbued with a thoroughly appropriate expressionism. (From a novel by Irwin Shaw.) GA

Two Weeks with Love

(1950, US, 92 min)
d Roy Rowland. *p* Jack Cummings. *sc* John Larkin, Dorothy Kingsley. *ph* Alfred Gilks. *ed* Irvine Warburton. *ad* Cedric Gibbons, Preston Ames. *songs* Arthur Fields, Walter Donovan, others. *cast* Jane Powell, Ricardo Montalban, Louis Calhern, Ann Harding, Debbie Reynolds, Phyllis Kirk, Carleton Carpenter, Clinton Sundberg.
●Nostalgic, turn-of-the-century musical set in the Catskills, and dealing with the romantic adventures of sisters Powell and Reynolds while on holiday with their parents. Busby Berkeley supervised the dance routines, but it's the lively Reynolds who steals the show, singing 'Aba Daba Honeymoon' with her gangling boyfriend Carpenter. There's a weird Freudian dream sequence, too, with Reynolds' underdeveloped sister (Powell) longing to be fitted with a corset, as well as swept off her feet by the handsome Montalban. NF

Two Women

see Two of Them, The

Two Women (Iki Kadin)

(1992, Tur, 124 min)
d/p/sc/ph Yavuz Özkan. *ed* Mevlüt Koçak. *m* Muzikotek. *cast* Zuhal Olcay, Serap Aksoy, Haluk Bilginer.
●When a high-class prostitute taunts a cop client about his sexual drive, he rapes her and has her thrown on the street. She decides to prosecute. The woman, who has a blind daughter, later becomes best friends with the culprit's wife. A bit of a haul. GA

Two Years Before the Mast

(1946, US, 98 min, b/w)
d John Farrow. *p* Seton I Miller. *sc* Seton I Miller, George Bruce. *ph* Ernest Laszlo. *ed* Eda Warren. *ad* Hans Dreier, Franz Bachelin. *m* Victor Young. *cast* Alan Ladd, Brian Donlevy, William Bendix, Esther Fernandez, Howard da Silva, Barry Fitzgerald, Albert Dekker, Darryl Hickman.
●Well-to-do, Harvard-educated Richard Henry Dana went to sea for his health, and his experiences as a common sailor determined him to 'redress the grievances and sufferings of that class of beings with whom my lot had so long been cast'. This he attempted to do in *Two Years Before the Mast*, published way back in 1840. Farrow, an authentic sea-dog himself, directs this adaptation (with Donlevy as Dana) as a labour of love. Despite its *Mutiny on the Bounty* overtones, and the latent sensationalism of flogging scenes, the film is most impressive for its sobriety, and the way Farrow gets an ensemble-type feel from a cast as disparate as he has here. There are no star turns or glamorous set pieces, no sea battles and very little 'action' as such, but it's an engrossing mix of formula/genre/humanism. CW

Typewriter, the Rifle & the Movie Camera, The

(1996, GB, 55 min)
d Adam Simon. *p* Colin MacCabe, Paula Jalfon, Tim Robbins. *sc* Adam Simon. *ph* Caroline Champetier. *ed* Bill Diver. *cast* Sam Fuller, Tim Robbins, Quentin Tarantino, Jim Jarmusch, Martin Scorsese.
●This documentary covers all the main facets of Sam Fuller's life and career: his years as a copyboy and crime reporter for the Hearst press; his experiences during World War II; his first time behind a camera, at a concentration camp liberated by the US army; and the two decades as a bona fide Hollywood *auteur*. The format is fun: Tim Robbins interviewing the inimitably brash old codger in Paris; Robbins and Tarantino gleefully checking out the memorabilia in Sam's LA garage; Jim Jarmusch commenting on how Fuller films were preoccupied with the 'American Lie' and how the man himself is not exactly rational; Scorsese on his camera style, the films' emotional authenticity and the ferocious primal force of Fuller's characters; Sam babbling on about Balzac and the art of storytelling, and finally revealing the identity of 'Griff', a moniker that turns up in just about every movie he ever made. Mouth-watering clips. GA

U

The Unsinkable Molly Brown

Uccellacci e Uccellini (Hawks and Sparrows)

(1966, It, 88 min, b/w)
d Pier Paolo Pasolini. *p* Alfredo Bini. *sc* Pier Paolo Pasolini. *ph* Tonino Delli Colli, Mario Bernardo. *ed* Nino Baragli. *ad* Luigi Scaccianoce. *m* Ennio Morricone. *cast* Totò, Ninetto Davoli, Femi Benussi, Rossana Di Rocco, Lena Lin Solaro.

● Given Italy's shameful record of allowing the wholesale slaughter of just about everything with wings, it's ironic that the only movie (outside of Disney) with a talking crow as one of its leads should have been made by Pasolini. Unsurprisingly, it's a mess. Its human leads, comedian Totò and Ninetto Davoli, take double roles: as a father and son discussing politics and philosophy as they wander a bleakly absurd landscape, and – in a parable told them by a wise Marxist crow they meet – as two hapless disciples of St Francis, sent forth to convert the hawks and their feathered prey to the Christian ideal of universal love. Intended as a darkly comic allegory on class conflict and the injustice of the world, the film looks and sounds good (the music, including sung opening credits, is by Morricone), but suffers throughout from obscure whimsicality. The crow's performance is the best thing in it. GA

Uccello dalle Piume di Cristallo, L' (The Bird with the Crystal Plumage/The Gallery Murders)

(1969, It/Ger, 98 min)
d Dario Argento. *p* Salvatore Argento. *sc* Dario Argento. *ph* Vittorio Storaro. *ed* Franco Fraticelli. *ad* Dario Micheli. *m* Ennio Morricone. *cast* Tony Musante, Suzy Kendall, Eva Renzi, Umberto Raho, Enrico Maria Salerno, Mario Adorf.

● Now king of the spaghetti slasher, Argento made his directorial debut with this tightly constructed thriller in which an American writer is witness to an attempted knife attack, and then finds himself obsessed with tracking down a serial killer whose next victims could be himself and his lover.. There are some extravagant false leads, but tension is well sustained with the aid of Vittorio Storaro's stylish 'Scope photography and a Morricone score. Particularly effective are the opening attack, viewed through a maze of locked windows, and a scene with the victim caught on a stairway suddenly plunged into darkness. Certain elements seem to have been an influence on *Dressed to Kill* and *The Shining*, but Argento himself zoomed into more and more abstract shock effects, neglecting the Hitchcockian principles observed here. DT

Udienza L'

see Audience, The

U-571

(2000, US, 116 min)
d Jonathan Mostow. *p* Dino De Laurentiis, Martha De Laurentiis. *sc* Jonathan Mostow, Sam Montgomery, David Ayer. *ph* Oliver Wood. *ed* Wayne Wahrman. *pd* Wm Ladd Skinner, Götz Weidner. *m* Richard Marvin. *cast* Matthew McConaughey, Bill Paxton, Harvey Keitel, Jon Bon Jovi, David Keith, Thomas Kretschmann, Jake Weber, Jack Noseworthy, Thomas Guiry.

● In 1942, to frustrate the Nazis decimating the Atlantic convoys, the US Navy plans to capture a stricken U-boat – carrying the Enigma coding device – with a fake German rescue sub. The operation goes disastrously wrong. However, Lt Tyler (McConaughey, sonambulent), a popular but frustrated officer, proves his worth by navigating the U-boat plus its vital device into safe waters. Aided by persuasive effects and authoritative production design from Götz (*Das Boot*) Weidner, writer/director Mostow pays his dues to the genre, but without much charge and even less depth. After an overextended landlocked prologue, the film pits Tyler and his sub against the German navy in a series of efficient if predictable cat and mouse encounters. A natural climax eludes the filmmakers and instead an endnote asks us, with some gall, to view this Americanised composite as a tribute to largely British actions during WWII. MHi

Ugetsu Monogatari 

(1953, Jap, 96 min, b/w)
d Kenji Mizoguchi. *p* Masaichi Nagata. *sc* Matsutaro Kawaguchi, Yoshikata Yoda. *ph* Kazuo Miyagawa. *ed* Matsuzo Miyata. *ad* Kisaku Ito. *m* Fumio Hayasaka. *cast* Masayuki Mori, Machiko Kyo, Sakae Ozawa, Mitsuko Mito, Kinuyo Tanaka.

● Mizoguchi's best-known work, based on two stories by the 18th century writer Akinari Ueda (often described as the Japanese Maupassant), was one of a handful of Japanese films to sweep up numerous awards at European festivals in the early '50s. Its reputation as one of Mizoguchi's finest works and a landmark of the Japanese 'art' cinema has remained undented ever since. Mizoguchi's unique establishment of atmosphere by means of long shot, long takes, sublimely graceful and unobtrusive camera movement, is everywhere evident in his treatment of the legend of a potter who leaves his family to market his wares during the ravages of a civil war, and is taken in and seduced by a ghost princess. A ravishingly composed, evocatively beautiful film. RM

Ugliest Woman in the World, The (La Mujer más fea del mundo)

(1999, Sp, 108 min)
d Miguel Bardem. *sc* Nacho Faerna. *ph* Alain Bainee. *ed* Iván Aledo. *m* Juan Bardem. *cast* Elia Galera, Otero Roberto Álvarez, Javivi, Héctor Alterio, Alberto San Juan, Enrique Villén, Guillermo Toledo, David Pinilla, Pablo Pinedo, Saturnino García.

● Similar in style to the fantastic satires of Alex de la Iglesia (*Acción Mutante, The Day of the Beast*), this vaguely futuristic, feminist schlock begins in Madrid, 2010, with the savage knife murder of an old woman by a mysterious nun – or perhaps that was just her party costume. Lt Arribas' investigation leads him to a scientist specialising in 'morphogenetics', Lola Otero, the 'most beautiful woman in the world,' and the haunting tale of a little girl dubbed 'the Malaysian foetus' by her classmates. Bardem's dissection of social hyprocrisy is only skin deep, but this cartoony fairytale is fun all the same. TCh

Ugly, The

(1996, NZ, 91 min)
d Scott Reynolds. *p* Jonathan Dowling. *sc* Scott Reynolds. *ph* Simon Raby. *ed* Wayne Cook. *pd* Grant Major. *m* Victoria Kelly. *cast* Paolo Rotondo, Rebecca Hobbs, Roy Ward, Jennifer Ward-Lealand, Darien Takle.

● Invited by multiple murderer Rotondo to say whether he's sane enough to stand trial, publicity-seeking shrink Rebecca Hobbs is determined to control the assessment interviews. Instead, she's drawn into the killer's world, where past and present are fluid, logic's skewed, and figures called The Visitors haunt his disturbed mind. Writer/director Reynolds knows his horror movies, but this is no fanboy knock-off – having absorbed his influences, he's able to take bold formal risks. Although there's a nagging doubt that this is just a low concept horror pic, tricked out with clever stylistic flourishes and a complex narrative structure, it's an auspicious debut that refuses to resolve the psychological ambiguities or tie up the worrying loose ends. NF

Ugly, Dirt and Mean

see Brutti, sporchi e cattivi

Ugly, Dirty and Bad

see Brutti, sporchi e cattivi

UHF

(1989, US, 97 min)
d Jay Levey. *p* Gene Kirkwood, John Hyde. *sc* Jay Levey, 'Weird Al' Yankovic. *ph* David Lewis. *ed* Dennis O'Connor. *pd* Ward Preston. *m* John Du Prez. *cast* 'Weird Al' Yankovic, Victoria Jackson, Kevin McCarthy, Michael Richards, David Bowe, Emo Philips.

● Installed as the chief exec of a local TV station that his uncle's just won in a poker game, the self-proclaimed strange one's wacky ideas on programme development – like turning janitor Richards into the operation's biggest onscreen asset – soon prove surprisingly powerful in the ratings battle. Moments of off-centre humour, but an hour and a half of parodist Weird Al is a severe test. TJ

Ulee's Gold

(1997, US, 113 min)
d/p/sc Victor Nunez. *ph* Virgil Mirano. *ed* Victor Nunez. *pd* Pat Garner. *m* Charles Engstrom. *cast* Peter Fonda, Patricia Richardson, Jessica Biel, J Kenneth Campbell, Tom Wood, Christine Dunford.

● Vietnam vet Ulysses (Ulee) Jackson (Fonda) lives in the swampy backwoods of the Florida panhandle, patiently farming Tupelo honey. On the one hand, since his wife Penelope died, Ulee has been content to withdraw into gruff self-dependence. On the other, blood will out, and the combination of Ulee's remoteness and the younger generation's hotheaded reaction have rent the Jackson family. While Ulee tends his two granddaughters, his son Jimmy (Wood) sits out a sentence for a robbery. Jimmy's wife Helen (Dunford), who has disappeared, surfaces in Orlando with a heroin habit and in the custody of her husband's two ex-partners in crime. She lets slip that Jimmy had secretly hidden bank money on Ulee's land, and the hoods are calling it in. Part vehicle for Fonda's seasoned presence, part depiction of the honey harvest, this low-key drama is played slow and sage. NB

Ultima Donna, L'

see Last Woman, The

Ultimas Imágenes del naufragio

See Last Images of the Shipwreck

Ultimate Solution of Grace Quigley, The

see Grace Quigley

Ultrà (Ultras: Some Lose, Some Die...Some Win)

(1990, It, 86 min)
d Ricky Tognazzi. *p* Claudio Bonivento. *sc* Graziano Diana, Simona Izzo, Giuseppe Manfredi. *ph* Alessio Gelsini. *ed* Carla Simoncelli. *m* Antonella Venditti. *cast* Claudio Amendola, Ricky Memphis, Gianmarco Tognazzi.

● This second feature by Ugo Tognazzi's son offers a thoroughly joyless hour and a half in the company of football hooligans, much of it spent on the train from Rome to Turin. The moral core of the piece is the struggle of one guy to get married, go straight, and get a job – ambitions tragically thwarted when he decides to take the rap for a murder accidentally committed by his best friend. The emphasis on mindless adolescent violence and vulgarity is convincing enough, but the drama, alternately muffled and overstated, has neither grip nor punch. The climactic football match, by the way, occurs off-screen. TR

Ulysses

(1967, GB, 132 min, b/w)
d/p Joseph Strick. *sc* Joseph Strick, Fred Haines. *ph* Wolfgang Suschitzky. *ed* Reginald Mills. *ad* Graham Probst. *m* Stanley Myers. *cast* Milo O'Shea, Barbara Jefford, Maurice Roëves, TP McKenna, Anna Manahan, Maureen Potter, Martin Dempsey.

● A completely foolish venture, which only looks promising when put beside the even worse adaptation of *Portrait of the Artist* Strick went on to make a decade later. Naturally the naughty bits of James Joyce's great and revolutionary novel caused quite a rumpus in their screen transposition, but while certain sections work well as naturalistic comedy, Strick's embarrassingly literal interpretation of the more fantastical passages sink the film completely. Barbara Jefford's rapturous reading of Molly Bloom's final monologue deserves commendation, however. DT

Ulysses' Gaze (To Vlemma Tou Odyssea/ aka The Gaze of Ulysses)

(1995, Greece/It/Fr, 180 min)
d Theo Angelopoulos. *p* Eric Heumann, Giorgio Silvagni, Dragan Ivanonic-Hevi, Ivan Milovanovic. *sc* Theo Angelopoulos, Tonino

Guerra, Giorgio Silvagni, Petros Markaris. *ph* Yorgos Arvanitis. *ed* Giannis Tsitsopoulos. *pd* Yorgos Patsas, Mile Nicolic. *m* Eleni Karaindrou. *cast* Harvey Keitel, Erland Josephson, Maia Morgenstern.
● When film-maker A… (Keitel) returns, after 35 years in the US, to his hometown in Greece for a retrospective of his work, he takes the opportunity to pursue an obsession: to track down the missing three reels of the first film footage ever shot (by the Manakia brothers) in the Balkans. His odyssey, from Ptolemais through Albania, Macedonia, Bulgaria and Romania, to Belgrade and Sarajevo, allows for a meditation on changing borders, national identity, and the relationship of film to historical and political reality. Angelopoulos' stately epic is hugely ambitious, and despite some art movie clichés – A's encounters with various women, each played by the same actress – and some clumsiness in the English dialogue, by and large it succeeds. Constructed from long elegant takes, and moving fluidly between naturalism and tableaux-like theatricality, it's a mesmerising work of arresting beauty and impressive emotional power. GA

Ulzana's Raid

(1972, US, 103 min)
d Robert Aldrich. *p* Carter De Haven Jr. *sc* Alan Sharp. *ph* Joseph Biroc. *ed* Michael Luciano. *ad* James D Vance. *m* Frank de Vol. *cast* Burt Lancaster, Bruce Davison, Jorge Luke, Richard Jaeckel, Joaquin Martinez, Lloyd Bochner, Karl Swenson.
● Even though Aldrich himself proclaimed a certain amount of dissatisfaction with the way this Western turned out, it's still one of his very finest films. A bleak and complex account of a platoon's hunt for a small group of Apaches who have escaped from their wretched reservation and committed acts of rape, murder, and mutilation, it never strays into the pitfall of portraying the Indians either as noble savages or as evil barbarians. Rather, Alan Sharp's marvellous script elucidates the issues and psychological causes of racial warfare, with Lancaster's weary army scout as the mouthpiece for unusually honest perceptions about both the Indians and the whites who have simply failed to comprehend them. It's brutally but never gratuitously violent, laden with images of death and destruction (beautifully caught by Joseph Biroc's camerawork), and far more than just an extraordinarily intelligent horse opera: the parallels with America's involvement in Vietnam should be easy to see. GA

Umberto D.

(1952, It, 89 min, b/w)
d Vittorio De Sica. *sc* Cesare Zavattini, Vittorio De Sica. *ph* GR Aldo. *ed* Eraldo Da Roma. *ad* Virgilio Marchi. *m* Alessandro Cicognini. *cast* Carlo Battisti, Maria Pia Casilio, Lina Gennari, Memmo Carotenuto, Alberto Albani Barbieri.
● Judging by his demeanour, the D stands for Deep Depression. But the old man at the centre of De Sica's famous film from the heyday of Italian neo-realism hasn't got much to be happy about, stripped bare as he is of all money and all friends except a little fox terrier. There's no denying the director's compassion, nor the dignity and strength of Carlo Battisti's performance, but there's nothing so wilting as doom and gloom couched in sweetly sentimental terms. GB

Umbrellas of Cherbourg, The

see Parapluies de Cherbourg, Les

Umbrella Woman, The (aka The Good Wife)

(1986, Aust, 97 min)
d Ken Cameron. *p* Jan Sharp. *sc* Peter Kenna. *ph* James Bartle. *ed* John Scott. *pd* Sally Campbell. *m* Cameron Allan. *cast* Rachel Ward, Bryan Brown, Steven Vidler, Sam Neill, Jennifer Claire, Bruce Barry.
● Hot thighs under the cold tap, blood-kin and wife-sharing in the shack – no, not Erskine Caldwell, but New South Wales in the late '30s. Marge (Ward) tries hard to be a pillar of the community, to live down her infamous mother's horizontal career, and marries the dependable Sonny (Brown). Her life seems humdrum, however, and when Sonny's weak younger brother Sugar (Vidler) proposes sex, she lets her husband decide with the comment that one man is much like another. Sugar proves even less exciting than Sonny, and boasts of his conquest in town, which sets tongues wagging. Becoming obsessed with the new bartender at the hotel (Neill), an unscrupulous womaniser, Marge lays embarrassing siege to him... This could easily have been one of those old devil-in-the-flesh absurdities, but the plot is full of surprises, with Marge's hunger for a grand passion resulting in humiliation all round and a sadly chastening ending. Within its small compass, a moving experience. BC

Unbearable Lightness of Being, The

(1987, US, 172 min)
d Philip Kaufman. *p* Saul Zaentz. *sc* Jean-Claude Carrière, Philip Kaufman. *ph* Sven Nykvist. *ed* BJ Sears, Vivien Hillgrove Gilliam, Stephen A Rotter. *pd* Pierre Guffroy. *m* Mark Adler. *cast* Daniel Day Lewis, Juliette Binoche, Lena Olin, Derek de Lint, Erland Josephson, Pavel Landovsky, Donald Moffat, Daniel Olbrychski, Laszlo Szabo.
● Prague, 1968: womanising doctor Tomas (Day Lewis) and his lover Sabina (Olin) are giddy with the social and sexual liberation of Czech communism. But when Tomas meets shy, sensitive Teresa (Binoche), he is forced to re-think his self-protective irresponsibility towards others, just as Prague suffers traumatic changes when the Russian tanks arrive. Kaufman's intelligent, faithful version of Milan Kundera's novel wisely jettisons the woolly philosophising, focusing on characters, relationships, and the many facets of loyalty and betrayal. It's a rich, ambitious film, repetitive and voyeuristic in its eroticism, but exhilarating in its blend of documentary and fictional recreation to depict the Soviet invasion. The narrative, now linear (unlike the book), is leisurely, the camerawork evocative; the progress from cynical irony to something more heartfelt rarely falters. Binoche and Olin avoid being reduced to symbols of Tomas' polarised soul, and Day Lewis seems increasingly one of the most versatile actors of his generation. GA

Unbelievable Truth, The

(1989, US, 90 min)
d Hal Hartley. *p* Bruce Weiss, Hal Hartley. *sc* Hal Hartley. *ph* Michael Spiller. *ed* Hal Hartley. *pd* Carla Gerona. *cast* Adrienne Shelly, Robert Burke, Christopher Cooke, Julia McNeal, Mark Bailey, Gary Sauer, Katherine Mayfield.
● Undecided whether to go to college, burdened by anxieties about nuclear apocalypse, forever at loggerheads with her Mom and Dad, teenager Audry (Shelly) finds life in her small Long Island home-town impossibly tedious. But when tall, dark, handsome Josh (Burke) arrives on the scene cloaked in mystery, her mundane world is transformed, not only by the erotic attraction she feels for the silent stranger, but by the rumours concerning his past: is he a priest, a mechanic, or – as most townsfolk would have it – a mass murderer? Like *Mystery Train* and *Metropolitan*, Hartley's independent first feature partly concerns problems of knowledge and truth: how do hearsay and personal bias relate to reality? He adopts an engagingly low-key form of farce to make his point, and to paint an affectionate, accurate satire on the shortcomings of small-town life. The director's delicately turned script is well served by colourful but credible performances, and by Michael Spiller's stark but stylish camerawork. GA

Unberührbare, Die

see No Place to Go

Unbreakable

(2000, US, 107 min)
d M Night Shyamalan. *p* M Night Shyamalan, Barry Mendel, Sam Mercer. *sc* M Night Shyamalan. *ph* Eduardo Serra. *ed* Dylan Tichenor. *pd* Larry Fulton. *m* James Newton Howard. *cast* Bruce Willis, Samuel L Jackson, Robin Wright Penn, Spencer Treat Clark, Charlayne Woodard, Eamonn Walker, Leslie Stefanson.
● Following *The Sixth Sense* was always going to be a nightmare for writer/director Shyamalan, even with Willis and Jackson on board. Yet this study of comic-book heroism and human destiny challenges rather than meets the audience's expectations. The miraculous sole survivor of a train crash, Philadelphia security guard David Dunn (Willis) is told by Elijah Price (Jackson) – a dealer in comic-book art with a fertile imagination and brittle bones – that he is 'unbreakable'. Like indestructible comic-book heroes, David has been put on Earth to vanquish evil. The movie then swerves into deeper, murkier territory, as the bewildered David ponders the cosmic consequences of this knowledge. Is this crazy, Biblical soothsayer right? If so, does he have a responsibility to develop and use his super-powers? Whereas *The Sixth Sense* left audiences surprised but surprisingly comfortable, this more mature and ambitious movie preserves its ambiguities and keeps everyone guessing. As David's wife Audrey, Wright Penn is mostly sidelined, although a brief exchange about their shaky marriage provides the film's most compelling emotional moment. If anything, the near somnambulant Willis is a little too restrained, as if to counter-balance Jackson's flamboyant, mesmerising portrayal of the mysterious stranger Elijah. NF

Uncanny, The

(1977, Can/GB, 85 min)
d Denis Héroux. *p* Claude Héroux, René Dupont. *sc* Michel Parry. *ph* Harry Waxman, James Bawden. *ed* Peter Weatherley, Keith Palmer, Michel Guay. *pd* Wolf Kroeger, Harry Pottle. *m* Wilfred Josephs. *cast* Peter Cushing, Ray Milland, Susan Penhaligon, Joan Greenwood, Simon Williams, Roland Culver, Alexandra Stewart, Chloe Franks, Donald Pleasence, Samantha Eggar, John Vernon.
● Truly terrible trio of tales, all based on the (false) premise that, since a shot of an ordinary domestic cat is already fairly scary, then shots of several hundred cats must be very frightening indeed. Yet the animals come out of it better than the poor actors, forced to do their best with such dusty Amicus anthology-type plots as the bedridden aunt with the cats and the changed will; the child with the cat and the occult power (using the girl from *The House That Dripped Blood*, but here dubbed by what sounds like a middle-aged Canadian); and the self-parodying horror film star and starlet (Pleasence and Eggar, making you wish you were watching *Dr Crippen* instead) who own a cat. The stories are linked by cat-crazy Cushing and purring Milland – as sad a pair of back tax-payers as you could wish to see. AN

Uncertainty Principle, The (O Princípio da Incerteza)

(2002, Port, 133 min)
d Manoel de Oliveira. *p* Paulo Branco. *sc* Manoel de Oliveira. *ph* Renato Berta. *ed* Manoel de Oliveira, Catherine Krassovsky. *ad* Maria José Branco. *cast* Leonor Baldaque, Leonor Silveira, Isabel Ruth, Ricardo Trepa, Ivo Canelas, Luís Miguel Cintra, José Manuel Mendes, Carmen Santos, Cecília Guimarães.
● A typically eccentric, playful post-post-modern account of dynastic and domestic intrigue involving a seemingly pure heroine, her wealthy husband, his childhood friend the maid's son (who has always loved the girl), and his friend, a seductive and seemingly Machiavellian brothel madame. If that sounds complex, it's as nothing compared to the ludicrously ornate opening exegesis (complete with speculation on bizarre nicknames) offered by two men on the fringes of what little action there is – mostly the film comprises static, stylised tableaux of often impenetrable talk. Then there are the endless, minimally varied shots of the Douro valley, from trains or from high above Oporto. For admirers in the right mood, the parodic absurdity and syntactical experimentation is deliciously funny; otherwise, the discussions over split characters, tragic heroines and so forth may leave you cold. (From the novel *Jóia de Família* by Augustina Bessa-Luís.) GA

Unchain

(2000, Jap, 97 min)
d Toshiaki Toyoda. *p* Miyoshi Kikuchi, Tomoo Tsuchii. *sc/ph* Toshiaki Toyoda. *ed* Mototaka Kusakabe. *m* Soul Flower Union. *with* Toshiro 'Unchain' Kaji, 'Garuda' Tetsu, Seiichiro Nishibayashi, Osamu Nagaishi, Sachiko Fujii.
● Toyoda's excellent documentary plays like a rock'n'soul lament for the limits of a testosterone-driven life. Toshiro Kaji nicknamed himself 'Unchain' after the Ray Charles song 'Unchain My Heart'. He became a pro boxer in

1988 and had just seven bouts (lost six, drew one) before nerve paralysis in his eyes forced him to stop. He went on to drive trucks, work as a radio DJ and help disabled kids, but a bizarre raid on an Osaka job centre landed him a spell in a mental hospital. He's fiercely devoted to Sachiko, but while he was in hospital after a road accident she married his Korean-Japanese friend Nagaishi. Toyoda is obviously close to Kaji and his circle of equally unsuccessful friends; the film is a group portrait without condescension, sentimentality or prurience. These people may, objectively, be losers, but this glimpse of lives on the bottom rung is remarkably heartening. TR

Unchanged Heart in Life and Death (Shengsi Tong Xin)

(1936, China, 95 min, b/w)
d Ying Yunwei. *sc* Yang Hansheng. *ph* Wu Yinxian. *ed* Huang Shengpu, Qian Xiaochang. *ad* Ma Shouhong. *m* Jiang Dingxian. *cast* Yuan Muzhi, Chen Bo'er, Liu Shangwen, Chen Yiting, Liu Liying, Hao Enxing.

● Probably the most sheerly entertaining of all the films made in 1930s Shanghai by 'underground' leftists, this riff on *The Prisoner of Zenda* is funny and engaging from first to last. The irresistible Yuan Muzhi (director of *Street Angel* the following year) plays both Li Tao, a revolutionary on the run, and Liu Yuanjie, an American-Chinese teacher visiting China with his fiancée. Liu is mistaken for Li and thrown into jail; Li teams up with the fiancée (Chen Bo'er, Yuan's real life wife) to get him out of prison and into the spirit of revolution. Ying Yunwei (who started out playing female roles in Chinese opera) uses chiaroscuro lighting, highly mobile camerawork and zippy pacing to give it maximum impact, but it's Yuan who really keeps you watching. TR

Uncle Buck

(1989, US, 100 min)
d John Hughes. *p* John Hughes, Tom Jacobson. *sc* John Hughes. *ph* Ralf D Bode. *ed* Lou Lombardo, Tony Lombardo, Peck Prior. *ad* John W Corso. *m* Ira Newborn, Matt Dike, Michael Ross. *cast* John Candy, Jean Louisa Kelly, Gaby Hoffman, Macauley Culkin, Amy Madigan, Elaine Bromka, Garrett M Brown, Laurie Metcalf, Jay Underwood.

● Tia (Kelly) is an unlovely specimen, her face fixed in a scowl of post-pubescent parent-hating, generated by mom's inattentiveness. When granny has a heart attack, mom and dad rush to her bedside, leaving the kids in the care of the family's black sheep, Uncle Buck (Candy). While the younger brats soon take to the slobby, loveable newcomer, Buck and Tia swiftly settle down to a war of attrition (he demobilises her dating power by fending off suitors with axes and power-drills, she throws a spanner in his affair with Amy Madigan). It's clear from the outset that by the time the parents return all will be reconciled; what is unclear is quite why this formulaic film fails to click, providing only interludes of satisfying Candy comicry amid the peculiarly meandering plot expositions. Set piece scenes arrive without warning and depart without conclusion, notably a painfully unfunny interview with a pimpled school principal in which crass 'don't-mention-the-melonoma' jokes fly thick and fast. Candy still raises laughs simply by playing himself, but the film is a heavy weight for even his imposing form to carry. MK

Uncle from Brooklyn, The (Lo Zio di Brooklyn)

(1995, It, 98 min, b/w)
d Daniele Ciprì, Franco Maresco. *p* Galliano Juso. *sc* Daniele Ciprì, Franco Maresco. *ph* Luca Bigazzi. *ed* Jacopo Quadri. *pd* Enzo Venezia. *m* Joseph Vitale. *cast* Pippo Augusta, Francesco Arnao, Antonio Bruno, Rosario Carollo, Luigi Cina, Bruno Di Benedetto, Giuseppe Di Stefano, Angelo Prollo.

● This deliriously weird first feature from Daniele Ciprì and Franco Maresco starts with the removal of a glass eye and the casual fucking (for money) of a donkey. It continues along a likewise coarse path as it charts the relationship between a boorish Palermo family and the local *mafiosi*. It's got great visual gags, and endless farting, belching, gluttony, mother-fixation and masturbation. All the roles (including the mothers) are played by unattractive men. There are unexpected musical and Brechtian interludes, and allusions to various films including *Bicycle Thieves*. It's a little protracted, and the touch of the Fellinis at the end is regrettable, but otherwise it's a gloriously bawdy black comedy which gives a whole new meaning to the term '*cosa nostra*'. GA

Uncle Silas (aka The Inheritance)

(1947, GB, 103 min, b/w)
d Charles Frank. *p* Josef Somlo, Laurence Irving. *sc* Ben Travers. *ph* Robert Krasker. *ed* Ralph Kemplen. *pd* Laurence Irving. *m* Alan Rawsthorne. *cast* Jean Simmons, Katina Paxinou, Derrick de Marney, Derek Bond, Esmond Knight, Guy Rolfe.

● It was a rum idea, hiring the author of all those trouser-dropping Whitehall farces to adapt Sheridan Le Fanu's 1864 gothic thriller. The opening shot of a girl's hand brushing aside a cobweb and plucking some berries symbolically encapsulates what's to come, and several other moments in this wildly inconsistent movie suggest that Travers, or someone, was still rooted in the silent era. Its most relishable aspects are the lavishly designed, atmospherically shot interiors, Travers' ear for the comic possibilities of stilted conversation, the naturalness of Jean Simmons as the much-menaced teenage heiress and, for some tastes, Paximou's fruity performance as a batty governess, swigging her claret straight from the bottle. Lacking a strong director, though, the material never coheres, while Rawsthorne's score and de Marney's lacklustre villain are major liabilities. BBa

Uncle Tom (Addio, zio Tom)

(1971, It, 130 min)
d/p/sc Gualtiero Jacopetti, Franco Prosperi. *ph* Claudio Cirillo, Antonio Climati, Benito Frattari. *ed* Gualtiero Jacopetti, Franco Prosperi. *m* Riz Ortolani.

● A documentary on American slavery by the makers of *Mondo Cane*. Using reconstructions of how black slaves were transported, sold, bred like cows, chained, raped, abused, the film purports to be a testament to the barbarism of our ancestors. In fact, with its wheeling camera movements over slave markets, its concentration on eccentric slave owners (massaging the breasts of their 'prize bitches'), its jaunty music, its obsession with black sensuality, it turns out as nasty sensationalism. Ironically, it was made in Haiti before Papa Doc died, but never for a moment conveys the idea that slavery, in a 20th century form, still exists. CAub

Uncommon Senses

(1987, US, 117 min)
d/with Jon Jost.

● Jost's documentary about how America constructs and consumes its own mythology begins as an oblique attack on its subject, but in an odd way ends up as American as the Constitution it criticises. Divided into ten parts, each looking at different aspects of the USA – its centre, its coasts, its roads, people, money, military power and so on – the film amounts to a lengthy and eloquent broadside on the 'entrepreneurial' ethic in America, and ends with a controversial straight-to-camera speech from the director that might be described as a contemporary and cinematic version of Thoreau's *On Civil Disobedience*. Funny, sinister and engrossingly watchable, a riveting vision of a country and the forces that shape it, it's a surprising and accessible success for a director notorious for his low-budget minimalism. JG

Uncommon Valor

(1983, US, 105 min)
d Ted Kotcheff. *p* John Milius, Buzz Feitshans. *sc* Joe Gayton. *ph* Stephen H Burum. *ed* Mark Melnick. *pd* James Schoppe. *m* James Horner. *cast* Gene Hackman, Robert Stack, Fred Ward, Reb Brown, Randall 'Tex' Cobb, Patrick Swayze, Harold Sylvester, Tim Thomerson.

● Kotcheff's film may look like a none too subtle piece of wish fulfilment, but is in fact grounded in one of the many painful emotional outcomes of the Vietnam war. Hackman is haunted by his son's fate – MIA (missing in action) – and so assembles a team of the usual veterans: the jock, the pilot, the war-junkie, the Tai Chi freak, and the one who can't sleep at nights. They then undergo the classic 'mission movie' format: first they train in a model camp, then they do it for real, where nothing goes as planned and acts of uncommon valour are called for. After *North Dallas Forty* and *First Blood*, Kotcheff seems to be moving into the action picture arena, and he acquits himself admirably with the more strenuous details of firefighting. CPea

Unconcealed Poetry (Puisi Yang Tak Terkuburkan/A Poet)

(1999, Indonesia, 86 min, b/w & col)
d/p Garin Nugroho. *sc* Nana Mulyana, Garin Nugroho. *ph* Winaldha E Melalatoa. *ed* Rahmat YP, Arturo GP. *cast* Ibrahim Kadir, El Manik, Pietrajaya Burnama, Amak Baljun, Atiek Cancer.

● Timely in terms of current Indonesian politics but in other respects long overdue, Nugroho's extraordinary film looks back to 1965, when the assassination of seven army officers was unconvincingly pinned on communists – giving the dictator Suharto all the excuse he needed for decades of authoritarian rule and arbitrary arrests. There were mass arrests and executions in Aceh, then as now considered Indonesia's most fractious province. One lucky survivor was the poet Ibrahim Kadir. Nugroho invites Kadir (now 56) to perform some of the *didong* narrative poems he has written in the intervening years, amid a recreation of events in the Takengon Prison. The film focuses on cells 7 (for men) and 8 (for women); the inmates keep their spirits up with songs, stories of local courtships and tales of government stupidity. More elegiac than angry, the film is presented – very poetically – as a slow transition from monochrome to delicate colour. TR

Unconquered

(1947, US, 147 min)
d/p Cecil B DeMille. *sc* Charles Bennett, Fredric M Frank, Jesse L Lasky Jr. *ph* Ray Rennahan. *ed* Anne Bauchens. *ad* Hans Dreier, Walter Tyler. *m* Victor Young. *cast* Gary Cooper, Paulette Goddard, Howard da Silva, Boris Karloff, Cecil Kellaway, Ward Bond, Katherine DeMille, C Aubrey Smith, Henry Wilcoxon.

● Paulette Goddard runs a typically lusty DeMille gamut from torture by Indians to saucy bath scene as an English wench deported to America for theft in the 1760s (she's innocent, of course), and finding a champion in Gary Cooper's Virginia militiaman. Nicely shot in colour, but overlong and curiously listless despite all the bustling adventures (and hilariously ludicrous dialogue). It isn't exactly improved by the lumbering right wing allegory which has Howard da Silva being un-American in subverting the Indians while Coop upholds the anti-Red American way of life. TM

Un©ut

(1997, Can, 92 min)
d/p/sc John Greyson. *ph* Kim Derko. *ed* Dennis Day. *pd* Bill Layton. *m* Andrew Zealley. *cast* Michael Achtman, Matthew Ferguson, Damon D'Oliveira, Maria Reidstra.

● 'Learn your alphabet,' this genre bending exercise in cut-and-paste film polemic exhorts us. 'C' is for copyright, censorship and circumcision, which are central, and to some extent connected, themes at play here. There are three principals – Peter (Achtman), Peter (Ferguson) and Peter (Damon) – whose various projects and passions provide an index to the film's own: Peter is writing a thesis on 'The psychosexual meanings of circumcision and the foreskin'; Peter has a crush on Pierre Trudeau, manifested in pastel cartoons of doubtful taste and authenticity; and Peter is compiling a scrapbook home video barrage of whatever material comes to hand, set to a rewrite of the Jackson 5's 'ABC'. How else to describe it? The film perhaps does for the docu-drama what Mark Rappaport's ciné-essays (*From the Journals of Jean Seberg*, etc) do for the film course lecture: it's a witty, imaginative and frequently subversive reappraisal of cinematic form, technique and focus, although it lacks Rappaport's discipline and depth. NB

...und der Himmel steht still

see Innocent, The

Undead, The

(1956, US, 75 min, b/w)
d/p Roger Corman. *sc* Charles B Griffith, Mark Hanna. *ph* William Sickner. *ed* Frank Sullivan. *m* Ronald Stein. *cast* Pamela Duncan, Richard Garland, Allison Hayes, Val Dufour, Mel Welles, Billy Barty, Bruno VeSota, Richard Devon.

● An early low-budget Corman effort which begins in the realms of modern science – troubled callgirl (Duncan) consults psychiatrist (Garland) – before shamelessly leaping back centuries to a tale of witches, virgins and knights, which thinly covers the movie's selling point, sexual temptation. The results are pretty nutty, especially the energetic cod Shakespearean dialogue provided by Charles Griffith and Mark Hanna. Good moments include the heroine in a coffin with a corpse, and a reasonable pay-off. CPe

Undeclared War, The

see Guerre sans nom, La

Undefeated, The

(1969, US, 118 min)
d Andrew V McLaglen. *p* Robert L Jacks. *sc* James Lee Barrett. *ph* William H Clothier. *ed* Robert Simpson. *ad* Carl Anderson. *m* Hugo Montenegro. *cast* John Wayne, Rock Hudson, Tony Aguilar, Roman Gabriel, Bruce Cabot, Lee Meriwether, Ben Johnson, Harry Carey Jr, Paul Fix, Jan-Michael Vincent, Royal Dano, Richard Mulligan, John Agar.

● A characteristically folksy Western, sprawling around in the post-Civil War rivalries between Union (Wayne) and Confederacy (Hudson, remarkably good). Wayne, discovering that the Union army intends to cheat him on a horse-trading deal, decides instead to drive his herd down to Mexico to sell to the Emperor Maximilian; Hudson, meanwhile, is leading a wagon train of disgruntled Southerners to settle in Mexico at the Emperor's invitation. Their odysseys converge, and when their arrival in Mexico coincides with the Juarez revolt, they decide that the good old USA is better than these pesky foreigners after all. It's all stirringly traditional stuff, with a lively supporting cast, and made very easy on the eye by William Clothier's camerawork. TM

UndeRage

(1982, GB, 57 min)
d Kim Longinotto, Lizzie Lemon. *ph* Kim Longinotto. *ed* Kim Longinotto, Lizzie Lemon.

● This documentary on no-hope teenagers in Coventry naturally had sections of the press crying scandal. But simply applauding the film's 'honest realism' in its depiction of a daily round of glue-sniffing, aggressive racism, and sexism isn't adequate defence. The problem is that the self-effacing method blocks any attempt by the film-makers to analyse/account for the disturbing discourses which speak through their subjects. Instead, the latter are simply given screen space to perform – see them weep, throw up, abuse blacks, and threaten violence. Realism or voyeuristic exploitation? Predictably, the only hint of contradiction comes from the teenagers themselves, some of whom display an ironic self-awareness at odds with the project's low-key miserabilism. Towards the end, a freeze-frame unites black and white at a Specials concert: a revealingly artificial gesture, which in this context seems desperately and pathetically romantic. SJ

Under a Spell (Un Embrujo)

(1998, Mex, 130 min)
d Carlos Carrera. *p* Bertha Navarro, Guillermo del Toro. *sc* Carlos Carrera, Martín Salinas. *ph* Rodrigo Prieto. *ed* Sigfrido Barjau. *m* José María Vitier. *cast* Damián Delgado, Blanca Guerra, Mario Zaragoza, Daniel Acuña, Luisa Huertas, Guillermo Gil, Vanessa Bauche, Elpidia Carrillo.

● Young Eliseo grows up in a provincial port in Progreso, Mexico, in the late 1920s under the mighty influence of his formidable father, a stevedore and a union rep, and under the more sensual sway of his school teacher, Felipa (Guerra). Produced by Guillermo del Toro, this takes promising material (think Tom Sawyer with sex), and turns up something rather ho-hum. There's plenty of incident and some depth to the treatment of themes of gender and revolutionary politics, superstition, and so on, but Carrera's lack of visual flair leaves it feeling more like a TV mini series than a movie. TCh

Under Capricorn

(1949, GB, 117 min)
d Alfred Hitchcock. *p* Sidney Bernstein, Alfred Hitchcock. *sc* James Bridie, Hume Cronyn. *ph* Jack Cardiff. *ed* Bert Bates. *pd* Tom Morahan. *m* Richard Addinsell. *cast* Ingrid Bergman, Joseph Cotten, Michael Wilding, Margaret Leighton, Cecil Parker, Jack Watling.

● A strangely unexciting but emotionally intriguing Hitchcock costume drama with echoes of *Rebecca* and *Suspicion*. Set in the 1830s, it details the aristocratic Bergman's disastrous marriage to rakish stable-hand Cotten, who is deported to Australia convicted of murder. When the Governor's nephew (Wilding) visits them, he finds her an alcoholic wreck, and suspects she is being poisoned. Slow, a mite predictable, and rather verbose, the film nevertheless has an elegance (thanks to long, sweeping takes) and a poignant romanticism that looks forward to Hitchcock's more pessimistic account of human relationships in *Vertigo*. GA

Undercover Blues

(1993, US, 90 min)
d Herbert Ross. *p* Mike Lobell. *sc* Ian Abrams. *ph* Donald Thorin. *ed* Priscilla Nedd-Friendly. *pd* Ken Adam. *m* David Newman. *cast* Kathleen Turner, Dennis Quaid, Fiona Shaw, Stanley Tucci, Larry Miller, Obba Babatunde, Tom Arnold.

● Jeff and Jane Blue (Quaid and Turner) are vacationing in New Orleans with their baby. But the plans of these amorous FBI agents are spoiled when arch-enemy Novacek (Shaw) turns out to be the mastermind of an arms-smuggling ring. One can understand how this project might have appealed to the leads: the sassy by-play and brassy derring do is reminiscent of *Romancing the Stone*, while Quaid is back in *Big Easy* territory. Herbert Ross, however, appears to think he's directing a spin-off from *Police Academy*. Disappointingly infantile. TCh

Undercover Man, The

(1949, US, 89 min, b/w)
d Joseph H Lewis. *p* Robert Rossen. *sc* Sydney Boehm, Malvin Wald. *ph* Burnett Guffey. *ed* Al Clark. *ad* Walter Holscher. *m* George Duning. *cast* Glenn Ford, Nina Foch, James Whitmore, Barry Kelley, Howard St John, David Wolfe, Leo Penn, Anthony Caruso.

● A superior crime thriller in the semi-documentary style beloved by Hollywood in the late '40s. With the Big Fellow clearly inspired by Capone (he's prosecuted for tax evasion when normal policing methods fail to nail him), and Glenn Ford's Federal Treasury agent wading through piles of paperwork (as well as resorting to the customary action-packed physical pursuit), it achieves an authenticity rare in the genre. Perhaps even more impressive is the acknowledgment that mob crime affects not only cops and criminals, but innocents too: witnesses are silenced, bystanders injured. And Lewis – one of the B movie greats – directs in admirably forthright, muscular fashion, making superb use of Burnett Guffey's gritty monochrome camerawork. GA

Undercurrent

(1946, US, 116 min, b/w)
d Vincente Minnelli. *p* Pandro S Berman. *sc* Edward Chodorov. *ph* Karl Freund. *ed* Ferris Webster. *ad* Cedric Gibbons, Randall Duell. *m* Herbert Stothart. *cast* Katharine Hepburn, Robert Taylor, Robert Mitchum, Edmund Gwenn, Marjorie Main, Jayne Meadows.

● Although best known for his marvellous MGM musicals, Minnelli also directed several superbly stylish melodramas (*The Bad and the Beautiful*, *Some Came Running*). This early example is a sombre, faintly *noir*-ish romantic thriller, with Hepburn marrying the handsome, wealthy, but cruel Taylor, and finding help when she needs it from his mysterious brother (Mitchum). Echoes of *Rebecca*, *Gaslight*, etc, but in its quiet understatement it becomes less of a full-blown weepie, more a haunting and subtle study of malevolence and gullibility. Surprisingly, it finally impresses by the very absence of those memorably hysterical, stylistically baroque touches that make Minnelli's musicals and later dramas so wonderful. GA

Under Fire

(1983, US, 127 min)
d Roger Spottiswoode. *p* Jonathan Taplin. *sc* Ron Shelton, Clay Frohman. *ph* John Alcott. *ed* Mark Conte. *ad* Agustin Ytuarte, Toby Carr Rafelson. *m* Jerry Goldsmith. *cast* Nick Nolte, Gene Hackman, Joanna Cassidy, Jean-Louis Trintignant, Ed Harris, Richard Masur, Hamilton Camp, Alma Martinez, Holly Palance, René Enriquez, Martin Lasalle.

● Riding to another Central American firefight come three journalists: reporter Hackman, tired of Third World wars; Nolte, Hackman's colleague and obsessive lensman; Cassidy, a radio reporter shifting her affections from Hackman to Nolte. Spottiswoode constructs a true portrait of these people, with no part of their lives, personal, moral, or political, which is not deeply informed by journalism; everything they do is subsumed in the great quest for the major scoop. Cassidy gives us a generous, no-nonsense Hawksian woman; Nolte is superb, American cinema's nearest thing to a tiger and a true heir to Robert Mitchum. As an immediate picture of what it feels like to be under fire, the black fear of being shot for nothing in a rubble-strewn street, the movie is way ahead of earlier examples like *Missing*; indeed, it takes an honourable place alongside classic war-torn romance pictures like *Casablanca* and *To Have and Have Not*; and there are ways in which it exceeds them. A thrilling film, with a head, a heart, and muscle. CPea

Underground

(1928, GB, 81 min, b/w)
d Anthony Asquith. *p* H Bruce Woolfe. *sc* Anthony Asquith. *ph* Stanley Rodwell, Karl Fischer. *ad* Ian Campbell-Gray. *cast* Elissa Landi, Brian Aherne, Cyril McLaglen, Norah Baring.

● Asquith's first solo feature is set in the strangely surreal world of the Northern Line in the 1920s, with shopgirls and porters, dressmakers and power station workers tangling and untangling their love lives between Leicester Square and Stockwell. Asquith virtually dispenses with titles, and relies on some splendid acting – particularly from lynx-eyed Landi and weaselly cloth-capped womaniser McLaglen – and on Karl Fischer's sensitively expressionistic lighting to carry his trite but well-constructed story from light romance to brooding melodrama, with an emotional triangle leading to murder and a chase through the Battersea Power Station. RMy

Underground

(1976, US, 88 min)
d/p Emile de Antonio. *sc* Emile De Antonio, Haskell Wexler. *ph* Haskell Wexler. *ed* Mary Lampson. *cast* Billy Ayers, Kathy Boudin, Bernadine Dohrn, Jeff Jones, Cathy Wilkerson.

● With a somewhat greater reputation as a 'cause' than as a film (FBI subpoenas on de Antonio, Haskell Wexler and Mary Lampson to surrender all footage brought an outcry from left-liberal Hollywood, before being withdrawn), this clandestinely-shot interview with five leading members of the Weather Underground marks both de Antonio's weakness and his strength as a radical film-maker. Soft-pedalling the analysis of the Weather-people's position on revolutionary armed struggle in the States (the questioning suggests reverence for 'the outlaw' rather than rigorous enquiry), and accordingly obtaining a number of rather woolly theoretical self-justifications, he none the less firmly situates the group in a recent US political history constructed largely from his own previous films and those of his followers, constantly relating his almost anonymous (obliquely shot) fugitive subjects to the events and conditions that radicalised them and sent them underground. PT

Underground

(1995, Fr/Ger/Hun, 192 min)
d Emir Kusturica. *p* Pierre Spengler. *sc* Dusan Kovacevic, Emir Kusturica. *ph* Vilko Filac. *ed* Branka Caperac. *pd* Miljen Kljakovic. *m* Goran Bregovich. *cast* Miki Manojlovic, Lazar Ristovski, Mirjana Jokovic, Slavko Stimac.

● There's no denying Kusturica's technical virtuosity as he mounts one hectic, large-scale set-piece after another, but in the end it's hard to fathom the exact purpose of this epic allegory. Starting in 1941 with the German bombing of Belgrade, and moving through the post-war Tito years to the present, it follows the antics of two irrepressible con-men who become, in different ways, national heroes. One, having hidden his friend, along with many others, in a cellar to save them from the Gestapo, neglects to tell them of the war's end, profiting from their arms-making industry, until they finally break free to discover that some things never change (even though countries may disappear). Played as broad, noisy black farce, the film is about the deception of politics and heroism, dog-eat-dog morals and the propensity for violence, but one can't help thinking that behind the sometimes sensational apocalyptic imagery, there's less here than meets the eye. GA

Underground

(1998, GB, 98 min)
d Paul Spurrier. *p* Christopher Leeson. *sc/ph/ed* Paul Spurrier. *pd* Natalie Ashby. *cast* Billy Smith, Zoe Smale, Chrissie Cotterill, Nick Sutton, Alison Lintott, Terry Randall, Ben McCosker, Alex Barker.
● The title has it down: this low budget British indie boasts plenty of style and an authentic street feel – it's probably the first credible picture of the '90s 'E' scene. Yet, following a night in the life of a London juvenile, Rat, who gets out of his depth with an ill-advised pharmaceutical sideline, it can't make up its mind if it wants to be a gritty thriller or a *Nil by Mouth*-style slice of life. There's not enough plot for the former, and some wobbly performances don't help – though young Smith is both resourceful and sympathetic – but it builds up a fair amount of tension and gets the thudding, spacey vibe of the clubs exactly right (the trance soundtrack recalls the heady days when Tangerine Dream and Wang Chung scored Hollywood's hottest thrillers). Visually striking, with an edgy, ambient style, it's an impressive directorial debut for Spurrier. TCh

Underground Orchestra, The (Het Ondergronds Orkest)

(1998, Neth, 105 min)
d Heddy Honigmann. *p* Pieter van Huystree. *sc* Heddy Honigmann. *ph* Eric Guichard. *ed* Mario Steenbergen.
● As this feature-length documentary reveals, the musicians who perform on the Paris Métro are 'underground' in more ways than one. They're often illegal immigrants, eking out an existence in a twilight world. There are some remarkable characters here – the Argentinian pianist and political activist who escaped torture to come to France, the Venezuelan harp player struggling for the rent, the Sarajevan violinist, and the Romanian citar player at odds with his son. Writer/director Honigmann tells their stories with humour and delicacy. They're all exiles, they all share a sense of loss, and (unlike most of their counterparts on the London Underground) they all play their instruments beautifully. GM

Underground U.S.A.

(1980, US, 85 min)
d/p/sc Eric Mitchell. *ph* Tom DiCillo. *ed* JP Roland-Levy. *pd* Jedd Garet. *m* James White and the Blacks, Walter Stedding, Lounge Lizards, Seth Tillet. *cast* Patti Astor, Eric Mitchell, Rene Ricard, Tom Wright, Jackie Curtis, Cookie Mueller, Taylor Mead, Duncan Smith.
● The *Sunset Blvd.* of underground cinema, and a suitably ambivalent retrospect on the star-game casualties of New York's upper depths, with Patti Astor statuesquely hysterical as a 20-year-old Norma Desmond, made up to recall Edie Sedgwick and surrounded by Warhol's lost children. We've been here before, but without the hindsight: a camera cruise along a hustler's meat-rack, kitchen-talk over cold canned spaghetti, Taylor Mead grimacing in a spastic dance, the silent stud a sullenly passive observer. Mitchell's ear for campy native wit and eye for figures in a loft-scape happily keep at bay the otherwise contagious NY ennui. PT

Under Milk Wood

(1971, GB, 88 min)
d Andrew Sinclair. *p* Hugh French, Jules Buck. *sc* Andrew Sinclair. *ph* Bob Huke. *ed* Willy Kemplen. *ad* Geoffrey Tozer. *m* Brian Gascoigne. *cast* Richard Burton, Elizabeth Taylor, Peter O'Toole, Glynis Johns, Vivien Merchant, Sian Phillips, Victor Spinetti, Angharad Rees.
● An appallingly pedestrian adaptation of Dylan Thomas' radio play, reverently rendered as a cultural exercise, simply waiting for the script to drop a particularly fulsome poetic image and then illustrating it with stultifying literalness. Burton wanders zomboidally through the night as the Narrator (sonorous but peculiarly toneless), while O'Toole hams it up no end as Captain Cat (energetic but peculiarly un-Welsh). TM

Underneath, The

(1995, US, 99 min)
d Steven Soderbergh. *p* John Hardy. *sc* Sam Lowry, Daniel Fuchs. *ph* Elliott Davis. *ed* Stan Salfas. *pd* Howard Cummings. *m* Cliff Martinez. *cast* Peter Gallagher, Alison Elliott, William Fichtner, Paul Dooley, Joe Don Baker, Shelley Duvall, Elisabeth Shue, Adam Trese.
● Michael Chambers (Gallagher), a reformed gambler, follows his losing streak back home to Austin, Texas. Moving in with mom and her new husband Ed (Dooley), Michael finds work driving an armoured car, but he runs straight into trouble when he looks up his ex-wife Rachel (Elliott), now the jealously guarded property of local hood Tommy Dundee (Fichtner). Rachel needs an escape route, and Michael wants her back, but the odds are stacked against a happy ending. Michael is 'not very present tense', we're told, and nor is Soderbergh, who uses colour-coded overlapping time-frames to tease us into the story and filter our responses. A remake of Siodmak's *Criss Cross*, the film is like a sci-fi *noir*, emotionally inhibited, sparse and strange in oppressive blues, reds and greens. It could use more humour, and some of the supporting roles are sketchy, but it's a slow-burner and never less than intelligent and engrossing. Gallagher is particularly good as the cocksure anti-hero who can barely see past his own nose, and take note of Fichtner's scary turn in the old Dan Duryea role. A rather remote film on the surface, but eventually it gets right under your skin. TCh

Underneath the Arches

(1937, GB, 72 min, b/w)
d Redd Davis. *p* Julius Hagen. *sc* H Fowler Mear. *ph* Sydney Blythe. *cast* Bud Flanagan, Chesney Allen, Lyn Harding, Stella Moya, Enid Stamp-Taylor, Aubrey Mather.
● Routine, seedy vehicle for Flanagan and Allen as stowaways in a silly spy plot, with less songs and more daftness than needed. Some gems: a suicide pact with a policeman in a London fog, a drunk Scotsman, a rigged boxing match. But overall, 'orrible. This was the film that set the pattern for the series of Crazy Gang comedies that followed. DMacp

Under Satan's Sun

see Sous le Soleil de Satan

Under Siege

(1992, US, 102 min)
d Andrew Davis. *p* Arnon Milchan, Steven Reuther, Steven Seagal. *sc* Larry Ferguson, JF Lawton. *ph* Frank Tidy. *ed* Robert A Ferretti. *pd* Bill Kenney. *m* Gary Chang. *cast* Steven Seagal, Tommy Lee Jones, Gary Busey, Erika Eleniak, Patrick O'Neal, Damian Chapa, Troy Evans, David McKnight.
● Action-man Seagal plays Casey, whose position as cook aboard the USS Missouri hides a past as a Navy SEAL and top-level combat operative in Vietnam and Panama. Right from the beginning, it's clear that he hates Commander Krill (Busey, wonderfully demented), who spits in his bouillabaisse before holing him up in the meat locker. But worse is to come. Krill and the even loonier William Strannix (Jones) hijack the ship, planning to steal its nuclear arsenal. So Casey has to bust out of the freezer, organise a rescue team, and kick ass to save the world from nuclear war. Davis handles the pacy action sequences confidently, with dark, claustrophobic interiors enhancing the suspense; so it's all the more disappointing when corny dialogue and barely-sketched characters let things down. CM

Under Siege 2

(1995, US, 99 min)
d Geoff Murphy. *p* Steven Seagal, Arnon Milchan, Steve Perry. *sc* Richard Hatem, Matt Reeves. *ph* Robbie Greenberg. *ed* Michael Tronick. *pd* Albert Brenner. *m* Basil Poledouris. *cast* Steven Seagal, Katherine Heigl, Eric Bogosian, Everett McGill, Morris Chestnut, Brenda Bakke, Nick Mancuso, Andy Romano.
● A superior train-board Seagal adventure featuring bug-eyed bastard Bogosian, backed up by mean-as-a-Doberman henchman McGill. Whenever the star threatens to get sincere or sentimental, Kiwi director Murphy cuts to bone-crunching violence or cliff-hanging suspense. Shortly after his estranged brother's death in an air crash, Casey Ryback (Seagal) and his orphaned 17-year-old niece Sarah (Heigl) board the Grand Continental train from Denver to LA. Uncomfortable in his new surrogate father role, Ryback is relieved when the train is hijacked by megalomaniac scientist Travis Dane (Bogosian) and his terrorist gang. Using state-of-the-art technology, Dane seizes control of a military satellite he designed before being sacked, then demonstrates its awesome power by wiping out China (yes, all of it). Next up is the Pentagon and the entire Eastern seaboard – unless Uncle Sam stumps up $1bn. The one duff element is young black porter Bobby (Chestnut), a reluctant back-up man whose underwritten role is a cynical sop to the non-white segment of Seagal's fan base. That aside, this is Seagal's best movie since *Out for Justice*. NF

Understanding Jane

(1998, GB, 99 min)
d Caleb Lindsay. *p* Daniel M San. *sc* Jim Mummery. *ph* Christian Koerner. *ed* Caleb Lindsay. *pd* Shlomo Abecassis. *cast* Kevin McKidd, John Simm, Amelia Curtis, Louisa Milwood Haigh.
● Two very laddish lads meet up with a couple of girls through a Lonely Hearts ad, get ripped off and decide to wreak revenge. This meeting-cute premise paves the way for a troubled, tentative relationship between two of the quartet – Jane being unpredictable, abrasive and morose (well, she's a girl, ain't she). Despite its downbeat, modish pretensions (it sometimes comes across as a British response to Kevin Smith), this is in the end a conventionally romantic affair which never quite distances itself enough from its relentlessly male point of view. But the sometimes implausible plotting, the very evident limitations of the budget, and the excessive use of pop cultural allusions are offset by sturdy performances, a number of decent gags, and the enthusiasm and commitment of all involved. GA

Under Suspicion

(1991, GB, 100 min)
d Simon Moore. *p* Brian Eastman. *sc* Simon Moore. *ph* Vernon Layton. *ed* Tariq Anwar. *pd* Tim Hutchinson. *m* Christopher Gunning. *cast* Liam Neeson, Kenneth Cranham, Laura San Giacomo, Maggie O'Neill, Alan Talbot, Malcolm Storry, Stephen Moore, Alphonsia Emmanuel.
● Tony Aaron (Neeson) is a private investigator with a seedy line in divorce work and dogged charm fraying with desperation. Then the bottom drops out of his low-rent world: his wife and a wealthy client are slaughtered in a bloody double murder, and naturally Aaron is the prime suspect. Cannily set in downtown Brighton on the very brink of the '60s, *Under Suspicion* is the sort of polished British crime melodrama that might have been made in the '50s with Richard Todd and some circumspection. Modern audiences may have doubts about the enterprise: the denouement hinges on a series of shameless contrivances and a last gasp race against the gallows. More damagingly, perhaps, Aaron's relationship with an American *femme fatale* (San Giacomo) smacks less of *amour fou* than an affair of convenience. Nevertheless, it's an engrossing mystery, snappily written and smartly directed by Moore in a promising debut. TCh

Under Suspicion

(1999, Fr/US, 111 min)
d Stephen Hopkins. *p* Lori McCreary, Anne Marie Gillen, Stephen Hopkins. *sc* Tom Provost, W Peter Iliff. *ph* Peter Levy. *ed* John

Smith. *pd* Cecilia Montiel. *m* BT. *cast* Morgan Freeman, Gene Hackman, Thomas Jane, Monica Bellucci, Nydia Caro, Miguel Angel Suárez, Pablo Cunquiero, Isabel Algaze.

●This sweaty two-hander about a police interrogation is a remake of *Garde à Vue*, Claude Miller's claustrophobic 1981 suspenser, relocated from provincial France to a small Caribbean island in carnival week. World-weary cop Freeman invites bigwig lawyer Hackman down to the station for some routine inquiries which turn out to be anything but. Three young girls have been raped and murdered in the past month, and the suspect's stumbling account of his movements serves only to heighten his inquisitor's conviction of the man's guilt. Circumstantial evidence, however, will have to be backed up by some notion of motive. From here, the psychology starts getting rather murky. You can understand the stars' attraction to the material, since it obviously offers a good chew on middle-aged regrets, sexual guilt and frustration, a rich old stew. All director Hopkins had to do was put these two guys in a room together, turn them loose and watch the fur fly, right? Well, you would think so, but what the maestro of *Lost in Space* actually does is to open out the action at every opportunity, revel in gimmicky flashbacks and sensationalise the lurid background detail, leaving the gritty central performances to go for very little. TJ

Under the Cherry Moon

(1986, US, 100 min, b/w)
d Prince. *p* Robert Cavallo, Joseph Ruffalo, Steven Fargnoli. *sc* Becky Johnston. *ph* Michael Ballhaus. *ed* Eva Gardos. *pd* Richard Sylbert. *m* Prince and the Revolution. *cast* Prince, Jerome Benton, Kristin Scott-Thomas, Steven Berkoff, Emmanuelle Sallet, Alexandra Stewart, Francesca Annis, Victor Spinetti.

●Prince portrays a pianist/gigolo, on the make on the French Riviera until true love puts an end to his philandering and, ultimately, to his life. A moral tale indeed. Wiry and perched on high heels, he makes an unlikely gigolo, which any amount of coy pouting and flashing eye contact cannot disguise. He is, of course, lampooning himself wildly (isn't he?). His buddy (Benton, currently one of his backing singers) is a far more believable character, in what is rather a wasted supporting cast. Shot in black-and-white in an attempt to evoke the sophisticated burr of '40s films, its intent is hamstrung by over-familiar gags, though the script comes more to life when Prince and Benton lapse into black street talk during their pursuit of moneyed women. GBr

Under the City's Skin

see Under the Skin of the City

Under the Clock

see Clock, The

Under the Doctor

(1976, GB, 86 min)
d Gerry Poulson. *p/sc* Ron Bareham. *ph* Ray Parslow. *ed* Mike Kaufman. *ad* Norman Vertigan. *m* Jean Bouchéty. *cast* Barry Evans, Liz Fraser, Hilary Pritchard, Penny Spencer, Jonathan Cecil, Elizabeth Counsell.

●Amused by 'confessional sex comedies' like Tudor Gates' *Intimate Games*? Then here's your chance to guffaw at another remarkably similar bit of British rubbish. Harley Street psychiatrist listens to the stupefying fantasies of three women patients, and is at last – not surprisingly – driven bonkers by his work. Liz Fraser, a veteran of this sort of nonsense, is allowed to keep her bra on; the other women strip with the usual offhand indifference. No male genitalia, but a superabundance of wilting puns. JPy

Under the Gun

(1950, US, 83 min, b/w)
d Ted Tetzlaff. *p* Ralph Dietrich. *sc* George Zuckerman. *ph* Henry Freulich. *ed* Virgil W Vogel. *ad* Bernard Herzbrun, Edward L Ilou. *m* Joseph Gershenson. *cast* Richard Conte, Audrey Totter, Sam Jaffe, John McIntire, Royal Dano, Shepperd Strudwick.

●No forgotten masterpiece, but a neat little crime thriller, ingeniously plotted by George Zuckerman (who also provided source material for *Border Incident* and *99 River Street*) around the teasing legal anomaly that a prison trusty who kills an escaping convict can earn himself a pardon. Worth watching for the admirable Conte, the Florida locations, and fitful direction by Tetzlaff, a fine cameraman (*My Man Godfrey*, *Notorious*) who never quite hit his director's stride again after the excellent *The Window* in 1949. TM

Under the Moonlight (Zir-e Nour-e Mah)

(2001, Iran, 96 min)
d Reza Mir-Karimi. *p* Manouchehr Mohammadi. *sc* Reza Mir-Karimi. *ph* Hamid Khozouee-Abyaneh. *ed* Nazanin Mofakham. *pd* Reza Torabi. *m* Mohammad Reza Aligholi. *cast* Hossein Paras, Hamad Rajabali, Mehran Rajabi, Ali Bokaian, Mahmoud Nazaralian.

●A young man, Seyyed, goes through a crisis of faith as he approaches 'taking the turban' – becoming a cleric – in accordance with his father's wishes. Sceptical of the dogma taught him in the seminary, Seyyed nevertheless buys the necessary vestments – but a street kid makes off with them, forcing the trainee mullah to venture into a shocking Tehran subculture to retrieve them. With its explicit references to prostitution, drug pushing and the plight of the homeless, writer/director Mir-Karimi's neo-realism ties in with *The Circle* and *Under the Skin of the City*, evidence of an emboldened reformist imperative in new Iranian cinema. Unlike those two, however, this is also a religious film, a kind of Islamic Pilgrim's Progress. TCh

Under the Olive Trees

see Through the Olive Trees

Under the Red Robe

(1937, GB, 82 min, b/w)
d Victor Sjöström. *p* Robert T Kane. *sc* Arthur Wimperis, Lajos Biro, JL Hodson, Philip Lindsay. *ph* Georges Périnal, James Wong Howe. *ed* James B Clark. *ad* Frank Wells. *m* Arthur Benjamin. *cast* Conrad Veidt, Raymond Massey, Romney Brent, Annabella, Sophie Stewart, Wyndham Goldie, Lawrence Grant.

●As one might expect from a director famous for his ability to concretise interior struggles on celluloid, this adaptation of Stanley Weyman's costume romance of 17th century France (dealing with Cardinal Richelieu's hounding of the Huguenots) is a swashbuckler more concerned with character than action. Set in a deliciously stylised Sternbergian world – a contrast to the realistic tone of most of Sjöström's films – it follows Conrad Veidt's attempts to square his role as a mercenary with his conscience and his eventual salvation in love. Massey is equally sombre as Richelieu, and the photography by Georges Périnal and James Wong Howe is stunning. PH

Under the Sand (Sous le sable)

(2000, Fr, 95 min)
d François Ozon. *p* Olivier Delbosc, Marc Missonnier. *sc* François Ozon; Emmanuèle Bernheim, Marina de Van, Marcia Romano. *ph* (Winter) Jeanne Lapoirie, (Summer) Antoine Héberlé. *ed* Laurence Bawedin. *ad* [set decorator] Sandrine Canaux. *m* Philippe Rombi. *cast* Charlotte Rampling, Bruno Cremer, Jacques Nolot, Alexandra Stewart, Pierre Vernier, Andrée Tainsy, Maya Gaugler, Damien Abbou.

●The subject matter of prolific young French auteur François Ozon's fourth feature – a happily married, childless woman's traumatised denial of her husband's sudden death by drowning – may, superficially, suggest a move on the director's part to calmer, more classical, waters after the sly, shocking tactics of his more transgressive early melodramas. Indeed, in focusing so sharply on Charlotte Rampling's tautly controlled, subtly nuanced performance as the elegant, Paris-based university lecturer who painstakingly, if psychotically, maintains a pretence of continuity, Ozon's film can be appreciated as a quality star vehicle, and as a tribute to the graceful mystique, sexual potency and fractured sensibility that the now 56-year-old actress brings to the screen. The movie's emphasis, however, gradually becomes more philosophical, abstract and quietly macabre. Hence a persuasive, intimate study of grief is transformed into a more general critique of romantic self-delusion in conventional marriage, made all the more unsettling by Rampling's film persona which, ultimately, remains impenetrable. WH

Under the Skin

(1997, GB, 83 min)
d Carine Adler. *p* Kate Ogborn. *sc* Carine Adler. *ph* Barry Ackroyd. *ed* Ewa J Lind. *pd* John Paul Kelly. *m* Ilona Sekacz. *cast* Samantha Morton, Claire Rushbrook, Rita Tushingham, Christine Tremarco, Stuart Townsend, Matthew Delamere, Mark Womack.

●Iris (Morton) has always been jealous of sister Rose (Rushbrook), but when their mother (Tushingham) dies, she's thrown into numb, furious confusion. Rejecting her old life (Rose and boyfriend Gary), Iris turns instead to the discomfort of strangers. At first glance, writer/director Adler's film seems extremely thin. Morton has charisma in spades and wears oddball clothes well. Such blasted poise proves irresistible to Adler, whose frenetic camera feasts on Morton as if she were a piece of meat. We never believe Iris is part of a community; she's more a wandering Lolita, slumming it among ignorant, treacherous low life. And though the sexual commentary is clearly intended to be cold, it's also tiresome. Are the sex scenes exploitative? Who can say. In the last third, however, Adler's strategy becomes clear: she's been playing a waiting game. Rose acquires an integrity that goes beyond mere respectable virtue, and when Iris's grief thaws, her helpless, animal-like pain is overwhelming. More surprisingly, our sense of the will-o'-the-wisp mother gathers force, the 'story' of her complex mothering told through the daughters' pinches, pokes and eventual tender fumblings towards each other. In its own twisty way, then, the film avoids both sentimentality and art-school cool, and with the help of superlative performances from Morton and Rushbrook, digs deep into the psyche. CO'Su

Under the Skin of the City (Zir-e Poost-e Shahr/aka Under the City's Skin)

(2001, Iran, 92 min)
d Rakhshan Bani Etemad. *p* Rakhshan Bani Etemad, Jahangir Kosari. *sc* Rakhshan Bani Etemad, Farid Mostafavi. *ph* Hossein Jafarian. *ed* Mostafa Kherghepoush. *pd* Omid Mohit. *cast* Golab Adineh, Mohammad Reza Foroutan, Baran Kosari, Ebrahim Shaybani, Mohsen Ghazi Moradi, Homeira Riazi, Ali Osivand.

●Even after all the great films that have emerged from Iran in recent years (or maybe especially after them), this is striking for its outspoken anger and its unflinching focus on a country torn between Islamic tradition and modernity, crippling poverty and corruption. Writer/director Rakhshan Bani Etemad serves up one close-knit family as a microcosm for the tensions in Iranian society: elderly traditionalist parents (Touba works in a textile factory, her husband is unfit for work) keep a concerned eye on their chief breadwinner Abbas – a charismatic go-getter who dreams of moving to Japan to make some real money – and their younger children. One sister is married but regularly runs away from her violent husband, another brother is involved in student political demonstrations, and the youngest daughter starts playing truant from school with her best friend and neighbour. Neo-realist in style, this compassionate, devastating film leads inexorably to the most tragic and damning conclusions. TCh

Under the Volcano

(1984, US, 111 min)
d John Huston. *p* Moritz Borman, Wieland Schulz-Keil. *sc* Guy Gallo. *ph* Gabriel Figueroa. *ed* Roberto Silvi. *pd* Gunther Gerzso. *m* Alex North. *cast* Albert Finney, Jacqueline Bisset, Anthony Andrews, Ignazio Lopez Tarzo, Katy Jurado, James Villiers.

●Everyone will be doing Huston's film a favour if they try hard not to compare it with the now classic Malcolm Lowry novel. In fact it captures the doomed spirit of the original, while – rightly – in no way apeing its dense, poetic style. Huston opts for straightforward narrative, telling the story of Geoffrey Firmin, an alcoholic English ex-diplomat who embraces his own destruction in Mexico shortly before the outbreak of World War

II. As the limp-wristed observers of this manic process, Andrews and Bisset are at best merely decorative, at worst an embarrassment, and the film's success rests largely on an (often literally) staggering performance from Finney as the dipso diplo. Slurring sentences, sweating like a pig, wobbling on his pins, he conveys a character who is still, somehow, holding on to his sense of love and dignity. Not for the purists, maybe, but the last half-hour, as Firmin plunges ever deeper into his self-created hell, leaves one shell-shocked. RR

Underworld

(1927, US, 7,643 ft, b/w)
d Josef von Sternberg. *p* Hector Turnbull. *sc* Robert N Lee, Charles Furthman. *ph* Bert Glennon. *ad* Hans Dreier. *cast* George Bancroft, Evelyn Brent, Clive Brook, Larry Semon, Fred Kohler, Helen Lynch, Jerry Manda.

● Ex-reporter Ben Hecht drafted the script for *Underworld*, and clearly saw the project as a reflection of his experiences on the crime beat. Sternberg had no interest in Chicago realities, but it took him a while to muster the confidence to abandon Hecht's outline. Hence the clumsiness of the opening scenes, which introduce the central triangle (bank-robber Bancroft, his girl Brent, and alcoholic lawyer Brook) and establish the deadly rivalry between Bancroft and gangster Buck Mulligan (Kohler), whose front is a flower-shop that specialises in wreaths. Sternberg comes into his own with the scene of the gangsters' ball, where emotional and physical violence erupt amid a storm of confetti and streamers. Thereafter, the film radiates total confidence in its own means and methods, and the themes are wholly Sternberg's: a woman breaks free of the codes that imprison her, a macho thug discovers the depths of his own feelings, and sexual love proves stronger than hand-guns, prison bars, and the entire police force. Hecht wanted his name taken off the film, but that didn't stop him from accepting an Oscar for it the following year. TR

Underworld U.S.A.

(1960, US, 99 min, b/w)
d/p/sc Samuel Fuller. *ph* Hal Mohr. *ed* Jerome Thoms. *ad* Robert Peterson. *m* Harry Sukman. *cast* Cliff Robertson, Beatrice Kay, Larry Gates, Richard Rust, Dolores Dorn, Robert Emhardt, Paul Dubov.

● In typical fashion, Fuller transforms the 'organised crime on the move' plot into that of a war film, with the FBI and the Syndicate each housed in their own skyscrapers overlooking the battlefield of America on which their troops are locked in conflict. The film's opening sees the Syndicate and the FBI at war, but it is the behind-the-scenes skirmishings and double-dealings of Tolly Devlin (Robertson), fighting his own no-holds-barred war of revenge (the Syndicate killed his father), which finally win the day for the FBI. For Fuller, the State is maintained not by its own machinery, but by the personal efforts of its citizens. PH

Un Deux Trois Soleil (1, 2, 3, Sun)

(1993, Fr, 105 min)
d Bertrand Blier. *p* Patrice Ledoux. *sc* Bertrand Blier. *ph* Gérard de Battista. *ed* Claudine Merlin. *m* Cheb Khaled. *pd* Jean-Jacques Caziot. *cast* Anouk Grinberg, Marcello Mastroianni, Olivier Martinez, Myriam Boyer.

● An absurdist comedy about a poor family living in an ugly housing project in the South of France. Anouk Grinberg (from *Merci la Vie*) plays 15 or so years beneath her actual age as the six-year-old daughter of alcoholic Mastroianni and the unstable Boyer. Sufficiently provocative to put it beyond the pale as far as the BBFC goes, but Blier's ruminations are becoming tediously circular (and even sentimental). TCh

Undying Monster, The

(1942, US, 60 min, b/w)
d John Brahm. *p* Bryan Foy. *sc* Lillie Hayward, Michel Jacoby. *ph* Lucien Ballard. *ed* Harry Reynolds. *ad* Richard Day, Lewis H Creber. *m* Emil Newman, David Raksin. *cast* James Ellison, Heather Angel, John Howard, Bramwell Fletcher.

● A curse hangs over the ancestral home of the Hammonds. These English toffs are all destined to die at the claws of the hairiest monster the make-up department can cobble together. Fox made a foray into Universal territory with this admirably eerie werewolf pic. Lucien Ballard, one of Sternberg's protégés, provided the gloomy chiaroscuro photography. The story's a howler, but direction and performances have plenty of bite. GM

Uneasy Riders (Nationale 7)

(1999, Fr, 95 min)
d Jean-Pierre Sinapi. *p* Jacques Fansten. *sc* Jean-Pierre Sinapi, Anne-Marie Catois. *ph* Jean-Paul Meurisse. *ed* Catherine Schwartz. *ad* Ermina Sinapi, Jean-Noël Borecek. *cast* Nadia Kaci, Olivier Gourmet, Lionel Abelanski, Chantal Neuwirth, Julien Boisselier, Saïd Taghmaoui, Gérald Thomassin, Jean-Claude Frissung.

● A DV experiment which grows on you big time. Opening with a neat introduction to its disabled and handicapped characters, riding in a minibus on the Southern French Route Nationale 7A ('The Pleasure Trail'), this challenging faux documentary is a piercing examination of society's attitude to the less favoured among us, an inadvertent (but who knows?) essay on form and, finally, an affecting love story. Set in a Roman Catholic centre, the film uses mainly disabled, non-professionals and follows the routine of residents and carers with refreshing handheld immediacy, shorn of the usual tricks, and with little or no music. Of the performers, that of Dardenne brothers' regular Olivier Gourmet stands out. As gruff, candid ex-union militant René, his efforts to make kind nurse Julie (Kaci, excellent) find him a prostitute set the home into often hilarious turmoil. Writer/director Sinapi's transparent humanism dignifies carers and patients alike, and by never losing sight of our common needs to be understood, recognised and loved, he turns the film into a quiet celebration of the fruits of that recognition. WH

Une Chante, l'Autre Pas, L'

see One Sings, the Other Doesn't

Unfaithful, The

(1947, US, 109 min, b/w)
d Vincent Sherman. *p* Jerry Wald. *sc* David Goodis, James Gunn. *ph* Ernest Haller. *ed* Alan Crosland. *ad* Leo K Kuter. *m* Max Steiner. *cast* Ann Sheridan, Lew Ayres, Zachary Scott, Eve Arden, Steve Geray, Jerome Cowan, John Hoyt.

● A fine melodrama loosely updating Somerset Maugham's *The Letter* to take in the problem of lonely wartime wives. The magnificent Sheridan gives one of her best performances as the woman who falls from grace, and is then forced to kill her importunate lover (alleging that he is an intruder) to prevent the husband she loves from finding out. A little florid as her trial builds to an impassioned plea for understanding (though Scott as the husband, and Ayres as the sympathetic defence counsel, both give good support); but the rest, co-scripted by David Goodis and including a blackmailer among its tortuous thriller-style ramifications, is beautifully handled. TM

Unfaithfully Yours

(1948, US, 105 min, b/w)
d/p/sc Preston Sturges. *ph* Victor Milner. *ed* Robert Fritch. *ad* Lyle R Wheeler, Joseph C Wright. *m* Alfred Newman. *cast* Rex Harrison, Linda Darnell, Kurt Kreuger, Barbara Lawrence, Rudy Vallee, Robert Greig, Lionel Stander, Edgar Kennedy.

● The Sturges film with the odd flavour. As nutty as usual in its treatment of character and language, it adds a strong dash of poison to its tale of a famous conductor (Sir Thomas Beecham wickedly parodied) who comes to suspect his wife's fidelity. His imagination, fed by Rossini, Wagner and Tchaikovsky, conceives scenes of delirious revenge, reconciliation, and renunciation, only to find reality letting it down with a humiliating bang on each occasion. A bitter black comedy, some of it (like Harrison's struggles with a recalcitrant recording machine in preparing the perfect murder) is incredibly funny, but the rest is shot through with a painful tang of despair. Not much liked at the time, but a small masterpiece just the same in its skilful blending of moods, genuinely moving and quite beautifully played by Harrison and Darnell. TM

Unfaithfully Yours

(1983, US, 96 min)
d Howard Zieff. *p* Marvin Worth, Joe Wizan. *sc* Valerie Curtin, Barry Levinson, Robert Klane. *ph* David M Walsh. *ed* Sheldon Kahn. *pd* Albert Brenner. *m* Bill Conti. *cast* Dudley Moore, Nastassja Kinski, Armand Assante, Albert Brooks, Cassie Yates, Richard Libertini, Richard B Shull.

● Amiable but half-baked remake of what was anyway one of Preston Sturges' least satisfactory comedies. Moore plays the old Rex Harrison role of the egocentric conductor convinced his beloved (Kinski at her most coquettish) has been cheating on him with the devilishly good-looking lead violinist. The mood here is far less menacing or unsettling than in the original. Instead of the sleek and murderous elegance of Harrison, we have to put up with cuddly Dudley's gooey, Arthur-like grimaces. He's trying so hard to ingratiate himself that it's impossible to believe he could ever really entertain the idea of killing Kinski. GM

Unfaithful Wife

see Femme Infidèle, La

Unfinished Piece for Mechanical Piano (Neokonchennaya Pyesa dlya Mekhanicheskogo Pianin)

(1976, USSR, 100 min)
d Nikita Mikhalkov. *sc* Nikita Mikhalkov, Alexander Adabashian. *ph* Pavel Lebeshev, Eduard Artemiev. *cast* Alexander Kalyagin, Elena Solovei, Eugenia Glushenko, Antonina Shuranova, Yuri Bogatyrev, Nikita Mikhalkov.

● Mikhalkov's version of Chekhov's first play, *Platonov*, has a lyrical naturalism that Chekhov would have loved. Beautifully paced, the film knows when to draw back from its lethargic liberals, impotent idealists, and hedonists in hock. Stolidly unlikely to inflame even provincial female hearts, Alexander Kalyagin's once promising schoolmaster rings uncomfortably true as he rouses a sleeping household with the tragic self-realisation of the non-achiever down the ages. 'I'm thirty-five!' he shrieks, yesterday's radical now a blubbering clown. The household clucks, consoles, squabbles, goes back to sleep as dawn breaks. Chilly for some. MHoy

Unfish, The (Der Unfisch)

(1997, Aus, 98 min)
d Robert Dornhelm. *cast* Maria Schrader.

● Dornhelm returns to home turf for this offbeat, so-called fairytale about the fortunes of a picturesque Austrian village, following the arrival of a giant model whale and its owner Sophie (Schrader) – who finds she has the powers of a benign sorceress. She invites the males of the village one by one to have sex with her and their wishes fulfilled (they include a priest, a 'capitalist' who rapes her and – pushing it over the edge – a dog), with chaotic and communally destructive results. The narration annoyingly parades the story's absurdity. The elements of French frivolity, Germanic folkloredom and leaden Central European comedy make for a discombobulating concoction. WH

Unforgettable

(1996, US, 117 min)
d John Dahl. *p* Dino De Laurentiis, Martha De Laurentiis. *sc* Bill Geddie. *ph* Jeff Jur. *ed* Eric L Beason, Scott Chestnut. *pd* Rob Pearson. *m* Christopher Young. *cast* Ray Liotta, Linda Fiorentino, Peter Coyotte, Christopher McDonald, Kim Cattrall, Kim Coates.

● *The Last Seduction* looked like a career maker for director Dahl and star Fiorentino, but four long years on, this dire effort suggests it could have been a flash in the pan. Liotta is Dr David Krane, a forensic scientist in the coroner's department. An ex-alcoholic, he's still suspected of his wife's murder, a night he can't remember but will never forget. Then he meets neuro-biologist Martha Briggs (Fiorentino), who claims to have identified a serum which enables her to transfer the memory of lab rats, and the movie takes a terminal credibility dive. Inspired by the rats, and undeterred by potentially lethal side effects, Krane volunteers as a human guinea pig, sampling memory cells taken from his wife's autopsy and sundry victims of a serial killer. Bill Geddie's script is a lame whodunit with a lunatic gimmick and a bad dose of the flashbacks. Fiorentino does her best, but her hands are tied. TCh

Unforgettable Summer, An (Un Eté inoubliable)

(1994, Fr/Romania, 82 min)
d Lucian Pintilié. *p* Marin Karmitz, Constantin Popescu. *sc* Lucien Pintilié. *ph* Calin Ghibu. *ed* Victorita Nae. *m* Anton Suteu. *cast* Kristin Scott-Thomas, Claudiu Bleont, Olga Tudorache, Marcel Iurès.

●1925, in Dobroujda, an area of Romania on the Bulgarian border, populated by a variety of nationalities: to an isolated army garrison come captain Bleont and his wife Scott-Thomas. To avenge the massacre of frontier guards by Macedonian bandits, Bleont takes Bulgarian villagers hostage; but when he's ordered to shoot them, encouraged by his wife's humane sympathy for their captives, he refuses. Firmly rooted in history, this is far more than just another costume drama; the insane savagery of the conflict depicted inevitably recalls more recent Balkan hostilities and 'ethnic cleansing'. It's a tough, unsentimental film, fuelled by a hatred of nationalistic delirium and tribal aggression, its anguish wonderfully incarnated by Scott-Thomas's characteristically fine (albeit dubbed) performance. GA

Unforgiven

(1992, US, 131 min)
d/p Clint Eastwood. *sc* David Webb Peoples. *ph* Jack N Green. *ed* Joel Cox. *pd* Henry Bumstead. *m* Lennie Niehaus. *cast* Clint Eastwood, Gene Hackman, Morgan Freeman, Richard Harris, Jaimz Woolvett, Saul Rubinek, Frances Fisher, Anna Thomson, David Mucci, Anthony James.

●A magnificent movie that transcends its familiar tale of a reformed gunman forced by circumstance to resume his violent ways. When a cowhand cuts up a prostitute and a bounty is placed on his head, killer-turned-farmer Will Munny (Eastwood) joins his old partner (Freeman) and a bluff youngster (Woolvett) in the hunt. But in Big Whiskey, they must face the rough justice of Sheriff Daggett (Hackman)... While Eastwood's muscular direction shows he's fully aware of genre traditions, he and writer David Webb Peoples have created something fresh, profound, complex. It's not only a question of the excellent characterisations, but of situations given a new spin: the prostitutes and the spirit of Munny's dead wife introduce a feminist angle; there are insights into the thin line dividing law from justice; and the accent on ageing, fear and death establishes a dark tone perfectly complemented by Jack Green's sombre images. All of which links with the way this very violent film shows the cost of violence, painting a persuasive portrait of people increasingly given to emotions they have no control over. Refuting conventional cowboy heroics, Eastwood presents an alternative myth whereby a man, goaded by Furies to yield to a past that still haunts him, despatches himself to a living Hell. In this dark, timeless terrain, the film achieves a magnificent intensity. GA

Unforgiven, The

(1959, US, 125 min)
d John Huston. *p* James Hill. *sc* Ben Maddow. *ph* Franz Planer. *ed* Russell Lloyd. *ad* Stephen Grimes. *m* Dimitri Tiomkin. *cast* Burt Lancaster, Audrey Hepburn, Audie Murphy, Charles Bickford, Lillian Gish, John Saxon.

●Though neglected, and not entirely convincing in its treatment of racial identity, prejudice and tension, Huston's Western is one of his more intriguing films. Hepburn is an Indian girl adopted by Gish after her family was killed by whites. Raised as a white, she becomes the centre of a maelstrom of hatred, bigotry and violence when her true history is discovered: the Indians want her back, while local whites turn against her and her adoptive family. Notable chiefly for Franz Planer's fine photography and for a brace of sturdy performances (with Gish admirably evoking the pioneer spirit), the film is sadly flawed by its stereotyped depiction of the Indians, strangely at odds with its anti-racist impulses. It is, however, mercifully lacking in the sort of dry, clumsy solemnity that mars many of Huston's more self-consciously 'serious' movies, and remains unusually affecting. GA

Unheimliche Geschichten

see Living Dead, The

Unholy, The

(1987, US, 102 min)
d Camilo Vilo. *p* Matthew Hayden. *sc* Philip Yordan, Fernando Fonseca. *ph* Henry Vargas. *ed* Marck Melnick. *pd* Fernando Fonseca, Jim Darfus, Cathy Carlisle. *m* Roger Bellon. *cast* Ben Cross, Ned Beatty, William Russ, Jill Carroll, Hal Holbrook, Trevor Howard, Peter Frechette, Claudia Robinson.

●A tediously solemn horror pic which abandons an intriguing conflict between repressed sexuality and disruptive desire in favour of the usual battle between Christian good and Satanic evil. Having survived a fall from a 17th floor window, young New Orleans priest Cross is made the pastor of a church whose last two incumbents have been murdered. Unsettled by a series of strange omens, he heeds the advice of cop Beatty and tracks down a frightened girl (Carroll), who used to help out at the church but now dances at a nightclub run by a sleazoid reptile (Russ) who uses chic Devil worship as an erotic floorshow. This sort of daft dabbling Cross can cope with; more disturbing are the warnings of blind Father Howard, who says that he must face a terrifying demon called 'The Unholy'. Sadly, for all the emphasis on diabolism and kinky sex, the toothy, red-eyed rubber monster simply preys on the devout and innocent. Unlikely to generate any fervour, religious or otherwise. NF

Unholy Garden, The

(1931, US, 74 min, b/w)
d George Fitzmaurice. *sc* Ben Hecht, Charles MacArthur. *ph* Gregg Toland, George Barnes. *ed* Grant Whytock. *ad* Richard Day. *m* Alfred Newman. *cast* Ronald Colman, Fay Wray, Estelle Taylor, Tully Marshall, Mischa Auer, Warren Hymer.

●Ever urbane Colman is the gentleman thief in this picturesque Sam Goldwyn trifle. Hiding out in a desert hotel that's a refuge for a coterie of international criminals, he joins the plot to rob blind innkeeper Marshall and ward Wray of their hard-earned nest egg, but romance is on the menu. Colman apparently didn't think much of the piece, though screenwriters Ben Hecht and Charles MacArthur found it hard to turn in a completely duff assignment. TJ

Unholy Three, The

(1925, US, 86 min, b/w)
d Tod Browning. *p* Irving Thalberg. *sc* Waldemar Young. *ph* David Kesson. *ed* Daniel J Grey. *ad* Cedric Gibbons, Joseph Wright. *cast* Lon Chaney, Mae Busch, Victor McLaglen, Harry Earles, Matt Moore, Matthew Betz.

●Although they had worked together twice before, this is the first in the remarkable series of Browning/Chaney collaborations which served as a source for all t hat is best in the horror movie. Based like *Freaks* on a story by Tod Robbins, it is curiously muted compared to the macabre fancies dreamed up later in the series. But there is many a pleasing frisson to be had from the weird family circle formed by three carnival refugees – ventriloquist in drag as granny (Chaney), malevolent midget as baby (Earles), strong man in moronic attendance (McLaglen) – to further their criminal activities with the reluctant aid of Mae Busch's heroine, using a thriving pet shop as their HQ. Slightly tongue-in-cheek (baby sporting a huge cigar as he checks his and bootees; a murderous ape thrown in for the finale), it also displays considerable subtlety in depicting the perverse passions that tear the trio apart. TM

Unholy Three, The

(1930, US, 72 min, b/w)
d Jack Conway. *sc* JC Nugent, Elliot Nugent. *ph* Percy Hilburn. *ed* Frank Sullivan. *ad* Cedric Gibbons. *cast* Lon Chaney, Lila Lee, Elliott Nugent, Harry Earles, Ivan Linow, John Miljan.

●Chaney's final film (and his only talkie) is far from wonderful but it's certainly weird, with its tale of crimes committed by a gang comprising a ventriloquist disguised as a bird-shop proprietress, a strong man, and a midget who dresses and babbles like a baby when the occasion warrants. As if these weren't enough, there's also a romantic hero (played by chipper Elliott Nugent, pal of James Thurber and later a movie director) and a very bad-tempered gorilla. With that cast list, coherence is the last thing you should expect, and you certainly never get it. Much more slackly directed than Browning's original (which it often cribs from), it's still fun of a creaky historical kind. GB

Unhook the Stars (Décroches les étoiles)

(1996, Fr, 105 min)
d Nick Cassavetes. *p* René Cleitman. *sc* Nick Cassavetes, Helen Caldwell. *ph* Phedon Papamichael Sr. *ed* Petra von Oelffen. *pd* Phedon Papamichael Sr. *m* Steven Hufsteter. *cast* Gena Rowlands, Marisa Tomei, Gérard Depardieu, Jake Lloyd, David Sherrill, David Thornton, Moira Kelly.

●Though her husband died leaving her financially secure, life isn't exactly great for Mildred (Rowlands). Her teenage daughter Ann Mary Margaret (Kelly) is an argumentative ungrateful sort who only visits when she wants something; her beloved son Ethan (Thornton) is supportive and solicitous, but he's keen to take her with his family to San Francisco and install her in a granny flat, and Mildred's not sure she wants to move. Mildred's a little bored and lonely – not that she'd complain – so when a new neighbour, foul-mouthed, frequently drunk Monica (Tomei), asks her to babysit for six-year-old JJ (Lloyd), Mildred's happy to oblige. Little does she know the encounter will change her life. Nick Cassavetes' debut as writer/director is a sensitive, honest, touching study of the seemingly limited options faced by a woman whose age belies her energy, enthusiasm and ability to enjoy herself whenever the opportunity presents itself. If it lacks the raw intensity and brilliant insights of his father John's work, Cassavetes Jr still provides enough subtly observed moments to suggest he's a talent to watch. The film features a clutch of terrific performances, headed by the director's mother – sweet, strong, vulnerable and iron-willed, Rowlands is entirely credible and affecting throughout. The film's only misjudgment is the inclusion of Depardieu in a minor but important role: while there's nothing wrong with his performance, we're just too aware of who he really is to be properly convinced that he's a French-Canadian trucker. GA

Unidentified Flying Oddball, The (aka The Spaceman and King Arthur)

(1979, US, 93 min)
d Russ Mayberry. *p* Ron Miller. *sc* Don Tait. *ph* Paul Beeson. *ed* Peter Boita. *ad* Albert Witherick. *m* Ron Goodwin. *cast* Dennis Dugan, Jim Dale, Ron Moody, Kenneth More, John Le Mesurier, Rodney Bewes, Sheila White, Robert Beatty.

●An intelligent film with a cohesive plot and an amusing script, this is one of the better Disney attempts to hop on the sci-fi bandwagon. Based on Mark Twain's *A Connecticut Yankee in King Arthur's Court,* it has a strong cast of British character actors who keep things ticking over nicely, and sweeten the rather depressingly obvious opening at NASA, where a freak accident sends Dugan and his lookalike robot back in time. Arthur (More) and Gawain (Le Mesurier) are rather touchingly portrayed as friends who have grown old together and, no longer really capable of holding the reins, are being jostled for power by evil Sir Mordred (Dale), abetted by the wicked Merlin (Moody). The final 'big battle' is fought with imaginative special effects, no blood is shed, good triumphs, love is requited, and peace once more reigns in good King Arthur's green and pleasant land. FF

Uninvited, The

(1944, US, 98 min, b/w)
d Lewis Allen. *p* Charles Brackett. *sc* Dodie Smith, Frank Partos. *ph* Charles Lang Jr. *ed* Doane Harrison. *ad* Hans Dreier, Ernst Fegté. *m* Victor Young. *cast* Ray Milland, Gail Russell, Ruth Hussey, Donald Crisp, Cornelia Otis Skinner, Barbara Everest, Alan Napier.

●Set in a distinctly Hollywoodian but nevertheless persuasive Cornwall, this is an impressive supernatural thriller, not unlike *Rebecca* in its use of an eerily atmospheric house and a sense of morbid brooding about the troubled past. Milland and Hussey are the siblings who buy the old house, only to find it haunted and exerting a sinister influence over the previous owner's granddaughter (Russell). Allen's direction tightens the screws of tension to genuinely frightening effect, aided by an intense performance from Russell as the girl who believes herself haunted by the malevolent ghost of her mother, and by beautiful camerawork in the *noir* style from Charles Lang. The real strength of the film, though, is its atypical stance part way between psychology and the supernatural, achieving a disturbingly serious effect. GA

Union City

(1979, US, 87 min)
d Mark Reichert. *p* Graham Belin. *sc* Mark Reichert. *ph* Ed Lachman. *ed* Eric Albertson. *ad* George Stavrinos. *m* Chris Stein. *cast* Dennis Lipscomb, Deborah Harry, Irina Maleeva, Everett McGill, Sam McMurray, Taylor Mead.

● A film of relentless tediousness. Based loosely on a Cornell Woolrich story, it's about a placid accountant, with a bored, frustrated wife, who gets so worked up by someone stealing his milk delivery every day that he eventually turns to murder. Admittedly Edward Lachman's gaudy camerawork is very accomplished, and the attention to period detail (New Jersey, '53) is admirable, if superfluous; but the monotonous acting, total lack of suspense, and endless punk chic makes it less a tribute than an insult to classic *film noir*. GA

Union Maids

(1976, US, 50 min, b/w & col)
d Julia Reichert, James Klein, Miles Mogeluscu. *ph* Sherry Novick, Tony Heriza. *ed* Julia Reichert, James Klein. *with* Kate Hyndman, Stella Nowicki, Sylvia Woods.

● A clear-eyed documentary look at the rise of the Union movements in Chicago during the '30s, combining archive material and contemporary interviews with three women union organisers. The women, two white, one black, talk separately with clarity and conviction about working conditions during the Depression and the need to organise into unions. In the ensuing battle between big businesses and an increasingly militant labour force, the police were frequently called upon to intervene brutally: 'To us it was class warfare' says one of the women. The film uses its hindsight well, resisting over-simplification. Problems of racial prejudice, problems of women organisers working alongside men, the decline of the unions into conservatism, current difficulties between the middle class women's movement and its working class counterpart – all are discussed or touched upon. CPe

Union Station

(1950, US, 80 min, b/w)
d Rudolph Maté. *p* Jules Schermer. *sc* Sydney Boehm. *ph* Daniel L Fapp. *ed* Ellsworth Hoagland. *ad* Hans Dreier, Earl Hedrick. *m* David Buttolph, Heinz Roemheld. *cast* William Holden, Nancy Olson, Barry Fitzgerald, Lyle Bettger, Jan Sterling, Allene Roberts.

● Despite implausibilities in its police procedural aspects, a sharp, brilliantly staged thriller about the kidnapping of a blind girl (Roberts), and the massive surveillance operation set up at Chicago's Union Station, the contact point established with the girl's father. Luck aiding, the kidnapper's plan starts to unravel almost immediately, with one associate trampled to death by cattle after being pursued into the stockyards; another spilling all he knows when cops threaten to throw him under a train; and a third (Sterling) left dying in the gutter when the hideout has to be abandoned. Undeterred, the dementedly vindictive kidnapper (Bettger) stashes the blind girl alone in a tunnel under the station strewn with naked high tension wires, then proceeds to try to collect the ransom... Agreeably ruthless on both sides of the law, the whole thing is considerably boosted by being shot on location (though not actual locations). Good performances down the line too, from Holden as the caring cop, Fitzgerald as the cynical one, and Olsen (secretary to the girl's father) as the bystander whose sharp eyes help crack the case. TM

Universal Soldier

(1992, US, 103 min)
d Roland Emmerich. *p* Craig Baumgarten, Allen Shapiro, Joel B Michaels. *sc* Richard Rothstein, Christopher Leitch, Dean Devlin. *ph* Walter Lindenlaub. *ed* Michael J Duthie. *pd* Holger Gross. *m* Christopher Franke. *cast* Jean-Claude Van Damme, Dolph Lundgren, Ally Walker, Ed O'Ross, Jerry Orbach, Leon Rippy.

● Martial arts hero Van Damme finally joins the major league Action Men with this futuristic picture, originally developed as a Sylvester Stallone vehicle. He and Lundgren are UniSols – Vietnam vets brought back from the dead and transformed into state-of-the-art cyborg soldiers. Their memories have been wiped, but during an SAS-style action, Van Damme flashes back to a My Lai-type incident in 'Nam... Mostly this is an amalgam of ideas, images and whole scenes lifted from other movies. Emmerich, director of the low-budget stiff *Moon 44*, moves things along at a cracking pace, staging the fights and senseless destruction with savage efficiency. No prizes for originality, then, but full marks for giving Van Damme ample opportunity to display his limited talents to maximum advantage. NF

Universal Soldier: The Return

(1999, US, 83 min)
d Mic Rodgers. *p* Craig Baumgarten, Allen Shapiro, Jean-Claude Van Damme. *sc* William Malone, John Fasano. *ph* Michael A Benson. *ed* Peck Prior. *pd* David Chapman. *m* Don Davis. *cast* Jean-Claude Van Damme, Michael Jai White, Heidi Schanz, Xander Berkeley, Justin Lazard, Kiana Tom, Daniel von Bargen, Bill Goldberg.

● This begins with an impressive set-piece: Luc Deveraux (Van Damme) and partner Maggie (Tom) are pursued by baddies on jet skis; predictably, however, the sequence turns out to be a test, by super computer SETH for his UniSols – soldiers brought back from the dead to be made into even more ruthless killing machines. Later, taking a break from babysitting Deveraux's daughter, SETH turns evil and sets out to kill Deveraux. Director Rodgers' debut comically tries to inject romance and pathos into what should, like part one, simply be a routine action movie. Filling out and greying at the temples, Van Damme is far from convincing, even in the tedious fight sequences.TH

Univers de Jacques Demy, L'

(1995, Fr, 91 min, b/w & col)
d/sc Agnès Varda. *ph* Stefan Kraus, Peter Pilafian, Georges Strouvé. *ed* Marie-Jo Audiard. *with* Agnès Varda, Anouk Aimée, Michel Legrand, Claude Berri, Françoise Fabian, Jacques Perrin, Catherine Deneuve, Michel Piccoli, Bernard Evein, Harrison Ford, Bertrand Tavernier, Jeanne Moreau.

● Continuing her memorial to her late husband, Varda turns from the life (*Jacquot de Nantes*) to the work, with a mixture of extracts, documentary footage and interviews. Essential viewing, obviously, for anyone at all in sympathy with Demy's 'universe'. Surprises include a glimpse of Jim Morrison visiting the set of *Peau d'Ane*, and Harrison Ford relating how he was picked by Demy to play the lead in *Model Shop* but was fired by Columbia for lacking star potential. Varda consults not only ex-colleagues but fans as well, all of whom are impressively fluent, in the French manner: 'For me, that film was a shining star, each point representing a Demy theme…' BBa

Unknown, The

(1927, US, 65 min, b/w)
d Tod Browning. *sc* Waldemar Young. *ph* Merritt Gerstad. *ed* Harry Reynolds, Errol Taggart. *ad* Cedric Gibbons, Richard Day. *cast* Lon Chaney, Joan Crawford, Norman Kerry, Nick de Ruiz, John George.

● As with Browning's *Freaks*, one wonders how MGM ever got conned into making this resplendent study in morbid psychology. As much a casebook as a horror movie, it tells the truly marvellous tale of Alonzo the Armless Wonder (Chaney, of course), who uses his feet to perform a circus knife-throwing act. Only masquerading as armless (wanted by the police for a strangling, he's concealing the telltale evidence of a hand with two thumbs), he falls for pretty Estrellita (Crawford), the bareback rider. But she has a trauma about being touched by men, so he besottenly decides to have his arms amputated, only to find a handsome strong man emerging as a successful rival for her heart...cue for a fiendishly vengeful Grand Guignol finale staged during the strong man's act. One of the great silent movies, astonishing in its intensity, this is by far the best of the remarkable series of Browning/Chaney collaborations. TM

Unknown Pleasures (Ren Xiaoyao)

(2002, Jap/HK/SKor, 113 min)
d Jia Zhangke. *p* Shozo Ichiyama, Li Kit-Ming. *sc* Jia Zhangke. *ph* Yu Lik-Wai. *ed* Chow Keung. *ad* Liang Jiangdong. *m* Xiao Chong, Ren Xianqi. *cast* Zhao Tao, Zhao Weiwei, Wu Qiong, Zhou Qingfeng, Wang Hongwei, Bai Ru.

● After the historical panorama of *Platform*, Jia's third feature (shot on DV) returns to the scale and style of *Xiao Wu*. Indeed, Xiao Wu himself (the inimitable Wang Hongwei) makes a couple of reappearances here, latterly back on the streets as a loan shark. But the central characters are Xiao Ji and Binbin, jobless 19-year-olds in Datong, fairly typical of China's current 'no future' generation. Xiao Ji (Wu) makes a shy play for the dancer Qiao Qiao (Zhao Tao, from *Platform*), undaunted by the fact that she's a gangster's mistress; Binbin (Zhao Weiwei) sings karaoke with a girl who's about to leave to study in Beijing. Eventually they get around to thinking about robbing a bank. Jia integrates both fact (the awarding of the Olympics to Beijing, ads for the Shanxi provincial lottery) and references to news events (the detonation of a block of flats by a laid-off worker) to build up a credible sense of the fast-changing present, but he's interested in a lot more than social reportage. As in the other films, his perspective is essentially spiritual: this lays bare the *tao* of contemporary China, like a doctor taking a pulse. TR

Unlawful Entry

(1992, US, 111 min)
d Jonathan Kaplan. *p* Charles Gordon. *sc* Lewis Colick. *ph* Jamie Anderson. *ed* Curtiss Clayton. *pd* Lawrence G Paull. *m* James Horner. *cast* Kurt Russell, Ray Liotta, Madeleine Stowe, Roger E Mosley, Ken Lerner, Deborah Offner, Carmen Argenziano , Andy Romano, Dick Miller.

● When a knife-wielding intruder invades the spacious LA home of Michael and Karen Carr (Russell and Stowe), along comes friendly neighbourhood policeman Pete Davis (Liotta), whose concern leads the trio towards an unlikely friendship. But that's before the cop turns out to be a psycho who gets Michael caught up in a spiralling nightmare and starts making moves on Karen. Kaplan is in his element in the first half, neatly stressing social differences; but the contrivances which alienate the couple become more glaring as we approach the OTT climax demanded of the genre. It's all designed to keep you on the edge of your seat (none too excusably in an over-extended prelude preying on fundamental fears of rape). Solid performances lend weight to the flakier elements, with Liotta turning crazed excess into something wild. CM

Unloved

(2001, Jap, 117 min)
d Kunitoshi Manda. *p* Takenori Sento. *sc* Kunitoshi Manda, Tamani Manda. *ph* Akiko Ashizawa. *ed* Suichi Kakesu. *m* Kenji Kawai. *cast* Mitsuko Kageyama, Shunsuke Matsuoka, Youko Moriguchi, Toru Nakamura.

● A quiet, thirty-ish secretary attracts the eye of her wealthy boss and bemuses him, during their affair, with her apparent lack of ambition or materialist desire. Maybe the guitar-playing hippy who is her neighbour would make a more promising match? An odd film, this: though it initially seems to offer a facile black and white account of sexual and social issues, it's actually rendered rather more interesting by a visual and narrative style so formal it sometimes veers on the abstract. Cool, ironic and impressively attuned to nuance. GA

Unmarried Woman, An

(1977, US, 124 min)
d Paul Mazursky. *p* Paul Mazursky, Tony Ray. *sc* Paul Mazursky. *ph* Arthur J Ornitz. *ed* Stuart H Pappé. *pd* Pato Guzman. *m* Bill Conti.

cast Jill Clayburgh, Alan Bates, Michael Murphy, Cliff Gorman, Pat Quinn, Kelly Bishop, Lisa Lucas.

●Very much the product of its New York setting, in the well-established tradition of *Annie Hall* or a novel like *Fear of Flying*. The heroine is a woman suddenly deserted by her husband. Though enviably rich, smart and healthy, she suffers. She moves towards a kind of feminism, motivated by her touchiness concerning the men who step blithely into her life offering help, homes, approval, sex, or just a friendly drink. They're all the young middle-aged. They jog, take pills, vacations, analysis, and laugh at themselves. They're absurd and at the same time perfectly believable. JS

Unnatural Causes: The Agent Orange Story

(1986, US, 100 min)
d Lamont Johnson. *cast* John Ritter, Alfre Woodard, Patti LaBelle, John Sayles, Sean McCann, John Vargas, Gwen E Davis.

●John Sayles scripted (and appears in) this true-life telemovie about Vietnam vet Ritter (atoning for the *Problem Child*) trying to prove that his chronic ill health can be directly traced to the ill effects of the US military's use of the defoliant Agent Orange. Woodard's tremendous as the counsellor who takes on her superiors to battle it out for him. Impassioned and involving, it's far, far superior to the usual run of small-screen fare from the US networks, a credit to all concerned – including experienced director Johnson, who made his name on series like *The Twilight Zone* some two decades earlier. TJ

Un Nos Ola Leuad

see One Full Moon

Unsaid, The

(2001, Can/US, 108 min)
d Tom McLoughlin. *p* Tom Berry, Matthew Hastings, Kelly Feldstott Reynolds. *sc* Miguel Tejada-Flores, Scott Williams. *ph* Lloyd Ahern II. *ed* Charles Bornstein. *pd* Gregory Bolton. *m* Don Davis. *cast* Andy Garcia, Vincent Kartheiser, Linda Cardellini, Sam Bottoms, August Schellenberg, Chelsea Field, Brendan Fletcher, Teri Polo.

●Something of a vanity project for its star, who also exec produced, Garcia plays Dr Michael Hunter, a psychiatrist so obsessed with his career that he fails to notice the family tragedy hatching in his midst. We're barely 10 minutes into this psychological thriller when his son commits suicide. Some months later, the shrink takes on a new patient, a delinquent adolescent who just happens to be the spitting image of his dead child. Director McLoughlin (*Friday the 13th Part VI*) is uncertain whether he's making a teen movie, an exploitation pic or a family drama. In the original story, the son actually possessed the body of the other child, but Garcia reportedly insisted on straining all the supernatural elements from the plot. What's left is a plodding, self-righteous drama about redemption and family values. GM

Unseen, The

(1945, US, 82 min, b/w)
d Lewis Allen. *p* John Houseman. *sc* Hagar Wilde, Raymond Chandler, Ken England. *ph* John Seitz. *ed* Doane Harrison. *ad* Hans Dreier, Earl Hedrick. *m* Ernst Toch. *cast* Joel McCrea, Gail Russell, Herbert Marshall, Phyllis Brooks, Isobel Elsom, Norman Lloyd, Richard Lyon, Nona Griffith.

●Taken from Ethel Lina White's Midnight House – she also wrote the excellent The Wheel Spins, which became The Lady Vanishes – and co-scripted by Raymond Chandler, this follow-up to The Uninvited is labyrinthine, New England atmospheric, and delivers what the New York Herald Tribune called `bona fide creeps'. Maybe some of it was down to the creaking of unidexter Herbert Marshall, the doctor from over the road. `The last one was pretty, too' says a retainer to new governess Gail Russell, with heavy foreboding. One of her charges (the more mutinously sinister one) was played by the very junior Richard Lyon, son of Ben and Bebe, paying his dues for the subsequent radio hit, Life with the Lyons. Bad-tempered Chandler had one contretemps with producer John Houseman. 'Look, John, I'm the fucking writer.' BC

Uns et les Autres, Les (Bolero/The Ins and the Outs)

(1981, Fr, 173 min)
d/p/sc Claude Lelouch. *ph* Jean Boffety. *ed* Hugues Darmois, Sophie Bhaud. *m* Francis Lai, Michel Legrand. *cast* Robert Hossein, Nicole Garcia, Geraldine Chaplin, James Caan, Daniel Olbrychski, Evelyne Bouix.

●To cinema's cognoscenti, Lelouch's name is mud, yet this three-hour folly makes the mud seem not so much unjustified as inappropriate. True, Lelouch rarely finds images to match the ambitions of his story (there are four multinational musical families, journeying through the 20th century); and for all the inspiration in authentic histories, the lives of his dancers, bandleaders, Auschwitz survivors, conductors, pop stars, waifs and strays, are still gilded clichés. But there is a point when the director's fatuity becomes sublime. The growling spectator is swept along by plot absurdities, camera pirouettes, and the unfashionable drift towards happiness; by the time the finale is reached, with Ravel's 'Bolero' played, danced and sung in front of the Eiffel Tower (in Dolby stereo), one's scruples lie in smithereens. At one point the narrator berates history for lacking imagination; history, as revealed here, certainly lacks taste, and its imagination could be toned up, but there's no shortage of silly entertainment. SJo

Unsinkable Molly Brown, The

(1964, US, 127 min)
d Charles Walters. *p* Lawrence Weingarten. *sc* Helen Deutsch. *ph* Daniel L Fapp. *ed* Fredric Steinkamp. *ad* George W Davis, Preston Ames. *songs* Meredith Willson. *cast* Debbie Reynolds, Harve Presnell, Ed Begley, Jack Kruschen, Hermione Baddeley, Martita Hunt, Audrey Christie, Harvey Lembeck.

●A minor but likeable musical, partly based on fact, with Debbie Reynolds as the innocent backwoods orphan who, thanks to a combination of push, shove and money from her placid husband's lucky silver strike, makes good her burning ambition to gate-crash turn-of-the-century Denver society, finally conquering the snobs and achieving her finest hour during the 'Titanic' disaster. As ebulliently energetic as ever, Reynolds makes the brash social climbing both funny and touching, but the film itself gets trapped in two minds between satire and sentimentality. The score, by Meredith Willson of *The Music Man*, though pleasant, is rather thinly spread; but the sets are a delight in the best traditions of the MGM musical, and Walters does a wonderfully graceful job of direction. TM

Unstable Elements – Atomic Stories 1939–85

(1985, GB, 90 min)
d Paul Morrison, Andy Metcalf. *p* Gillian Slovo. *sc* Stephen Lowe. *ph* Ian McMillen, David Read, Pascoe McFarlane, Robert Smith, Luke Cardiff, Tim Broad. *ed* Trevor Williamson. *ad* Piers Lea. *m* Piers Partridge. *cast* Donald Sumpter, Caroline Hutchison, Susanna Kleeman, Sam Kolpe, David Henry.

●Two-thirds documentary, one-third dramatic moral exemplar, this traces a new history of the bomb and its domestic spin-offs: the World War II race between the Allies and the Axis to get there first, the complicity of politicians and scientists, the international bullying antics of America (riding to world domination on the back of the bomb), and the fallacy of the 'Atoms for Peace' campaign, portrayed here as a whitewash over a deliberate policy of using nuclear power stations to produce plutonium for the bomb. Using documentary footage, interviews with Manhattan Project scientists and their UK counterparts, excellent montages from Peter Kennard, and interviews with the relatives of dead nuke industry workers, it's a powerful indictment. But the final part – a mystifyingly oblique drama about the human, emotional effect of the nuke industry, based around Sizewell B – presents such an abrupt change as to almost scupper what went before. JG

Unstrung Heroes

(1995, US, 93 min)
d Diane Keaton. *p* Susan Arnold, Donna Roth, Bill Badalato. *sc* Richard LaGravenese. *ph* Phedon Papamichael. *ed* Lisa Churgin. *pd* Garreth Stover. *m* Thomas Newman. *cast* Andie MacDowell, John Turturro, Nathan Watt, Michael Richards, Maury Chaykin, Kendra Krull, Joey Andrews.

●Twelve-year-old Steven Lidz (Watt) lives a pleasant if unexceptional sort of life in early '60s suburban LA. Dad (Turturro) is a boffin, whose family input consists largely of unusual labour-saving inventions; mom (MacDowell) takes care of home and isn't averse to the occasional ciggie. Cancer duly strikes, dad can't cope with both a dying wife and the demands of his kids, and Steven runs away to live with his uncles Danny and Arthur in the city. Under their diligent tutelage, he's soon changed his name to Franz, trawls the city sewers for collectable objects, and has caught religion. Cue worried parents. Keaton's first feature is a highly enjoyable, predictably wacky family drama. The zestful direction captures the kid's-eye-view wonderfully, and the performances are exemplary. If the film succeeds, though, it's primarily thanks to the strength of Richard LaGravenese's script (from a novel by Franz Lidz); some of the most endearing moments recall the Gothic abandon of his earlier *The Fisher King*. A film to be enjoyed for its numerous surface charms – above all, the gloriously paranoiac Danny's broadside against Steven's odious rival for class president. NB

Unsuitable Job for a Woman, An

(1981, GB, 94 min)
d Christopher Petit. *p* Michael Relph, Peter McKay. *sc* Elizabeth McKay, Brian Scobie, Christopher Petit. *ph* Martin Schäfer. *ed* Mick Audsley. *pd* Anton Furst. *m* Chas Jankel, Philip Bagenal, Peter Von-Hooke. *cast* Billie Whitelaw, Pippa Guard, Paul Freeman, Dominic Guard, Elizabeth Spriggs, David Horovitch.

●Toss a girl down a disused well, and watch her struggle to get out: a scene which deserves a corner in cinema history. Based on the novel by PD James, this is a stinging *film noir* played out in the long, russet shadows of an English summer: the story of a young woman (Guard) who, after the quiet suicide of her partner, takes control of the private detective agency he has bequeathed to her, and is asked (by Whitelaw) to investigate another suicide – the son of a prominent businessman – found hanged in a rented cottage. The plot is spare, bitter, and buried in the past. All the more credit to director and co-writer Petit (in his second film) for not resorting to the easy recourse of flashback; it's a restraint that contributes to the film's special, uneasy quality of the here-and-now. JS

Unsuspected, The

(1947, US, 103 min, b/w)
d Michael Curtiz. *p* Charles Hoffman. *sc* Ranald MacDougall, Bess Meredyth. *ph* Woody Bredell. *ed* Frederick Richards. *ad* Anton F Grot. *m* Franz Waxman. *cast* Claude Rains, Joan Caulfield, Audrey Totter, Constance Bennett, Hurd Hatfield, Michael North, Fred Clark, Jack Lambert.

●A gilt-edged performance from Rains, revelling in sinister ambiguities as a radio personality/criminologist who, while regaling his fans with titillating tales of true crime and learned speculations as to the tortuous ways of the criminal mind, secretly commits a murder of his own. Based on a marvellous novel by Charlotte Armstrong, the film is considerably weakened by the fact that her intricate plot is partly discarded. But this hardly matters, since Curtiz wraps the rest up in a pyrotechnic display of expressionistic effects, including one shot in which a girl dying of poison is coolly watched through the bubbles in a champagne glass, and another in which a reluctant killer broods in his sleazy hotel room while Rains (who is blackmailing him into killing again) can be heard droning away on the radio and part of a neon sign seen flashing on and off outside urges 'kill...kill...kill'. The use Curtiz makes of the weirdly opulent mansion in which most of the action takes place is almost as psychologically acute as in Losey's *The Prowler*. TM

Untama Giru

(1989, Jap, 120 min)
d Go Takamine. *p* Junichi Ito, Natsuki Hariu. *sc* Go Takamine. *ph* Masaki Tamura. *ed* Hiroshi Yoshida. *pd* Keiko Hoshino. *m* Koji Ueno. *cast* Kaoru Kobayashi, Jun Togawa, John Sayles, Chikako Aoyama, Susumu Taira, Edie.

●Another paean to Okinawa's 'sacred indolence', this reunites the stars of *Paradise View* in a mythic/poetic social satire which plays like a fullscale orchestration of the themes and plotlines of the earlier film. The original Untama Giru was an Okinawan Robin Hood; the film's Giru (Kobayashi) is an exploited worker in 1969 who flees into the Untama forest after learning that his boss's adopted daughter is actually a crazed sow in human guise. While he teaches himself to levitate, the rest of the island debates what should become of Okinawa when the US (represented by John Sayles as a commissioner who gets off on blood transfusions from monkeys and pigs) hands it back to Japan. With the most unlikely barbershop quintet in film history serving as a chorus, this is doubtless the most spaced-out agit-prop ever filmed. TR

Untamed

(1955, US, 111 min)
d Henry King. *p* Bert E Friedlob, William A Bacher. *sc* Talbot Jennings, Frank Fenton, Michael Blankfort. *ph* Leo Tover. *ed* Barbara McLean. *ad* Lyle Wheeler, Addison Hehr. *m* Franz Waxman. *cast* Tyrone Power, Susan Hayward, Richard Egan, Agnes Moorehead, Rita Moreno, John Justin.

●Expensive, long and dreary attempt at a South African Western with the Zulus as makeshift Indians. Power is the rugged trekking Boer, Susan Hayward the love interest, a fiery Irishwoman who emigrated in the wake of the potato famine. Shot in 'Scope, with matte shots and back projection masking the fact that none of the principals ventured to Africa. GM

Untamed Heart

(1993, US, 102 min)
d Tony Bill. *p* Tony Bill, Helen Buck Bartlett. *sc* Tom Sierchio. *ph* Jost Vacano. *ed* Mia Goldman. *pd* Steven Jordan. *m* Cliff Eidelman. *cast* Marisa Tomei, Christian Slater, Rosie Perez, Kyle Secor, Willie Garson.

●Tony Bill's Minneapolis melodrama begins with washed-out, anaemic shots of an orphanage and a fey bedtime story passed from a nun to a young invalid about a boy with a baboon heart. It's a shock how suddenly the film is back on course after such a sickly sentimental prologue, kick started by a happening actress firing on all cylinders. Tomei's after-hours waitress, Caroline, is vulnerable, funny and wholly unaffected. Her banter with friend Rosie Perez is like verbal pinball. Slater's busboy Adam is an angelic wild child, so shyly distant his work mates assume he'd retarded. When he saves Caroline from two rapists, she becomes curious…and falls in love. Slater's greasy-haired 'Beast' is not for the hard-boiled, but see the film for Tomei's sensitive, doe-eyed 'Beauty', and for Bill's sure feel for an authentic downtown milieu. TCh

Until Death

see Hasta Morir

Until the End of the World (Bis ans Ende der Welt)

(1991, Ger/Fr/Aust, 158 min)
d Wim Wenders. *p* Jonathan Taplin, Anatole Dauman. *sc* Peter Carey, Wim Wenders. *ph* Robby Müller. *ed* Peter Przygodda. *pd* Thierry Flamand, Sally Campbell. *m* Graeme Revell. *cast* Solveig Dommartin, William Hurt, Sam Neill, Jeanne Moreau, Max von Sydow, Chick Ortega, Eddy Mitchell, Adella Lutz, Ernie Dingo, Rüdiger Vogler, Chishu Ryu, Allen Garfield, Lois Chiles, David Gulpilil.

●Wenders' stab at making the ultimate road movie is a severe disappointment. Co-scripted by Wenders and novelist Peter Carey, it's set somewhat portentously during the last weeks of 1999. The Indian nuclear satellite is out of control, but Claire (Dommartin) is too busy with her own chaotic existence to get caught up in apocalyptic panic. Carrying a stash of dirty money to Paris for two hoods, she meets an American (Hurt) also involved in a mysterious mission. As her odyssey continues via Berlin, Lisbon, Moscow, Beijing, Tokyo and San Francisco to the Australian outback, others join the chase: notably her novelist ex (Neill), a missing persons investigator (Vogler), and Hurt himself, whose plans to help his blind mother (Moreau) see again, with a camera his dad (von Sydow) has devised, set the limits for the film's geographically static last hour or so. If all this sounds needlessly complicated, it is. The first half is simply an over-plotted caper, devoid of suspense, comedy or anything else. The second gets heavily philosophical, and muses none too illuminatingly on dreams, images, obsessions, love, the mystery of life, etc. Despite a few felicitous moments, the film is turgid, pretentious, and dramatically lifeless. GA

Untouchables, The

(1987, US, 120 min)
d Brian De Palma. *p* Art Linson. *sc* David Mamet. *ph* Stephen H Burum. *ed* Jerry Greenberg, Bill Pankow. *ad* Patrizia von Brandenstein. *m* Ennio Morricone. *cast* Kevin Costner, Sean Connery, Charles Martin Smith, Andy Garcia, Robert De Niro, Richard Bradford, Jack Kehoe, Brad Sullivan, Billy Drago.

●Time-honoured mayhem in the Windy City, and if there are few set-ups you haven't seen in previous Prohibition movies, it's perhaps because De Palma and scriptwriter David Mamet have settled for the bankability of enduring myth. And boy, it works like the 12-bar blues. The director's pyrotechnical urge is held in check and trusts the tale; the script doesn't dally overmuch on deep psychology; the acting is a treat. Connery's world-weary and pragmatic cop, Malone, steals the show because he's the only point of human identification between the monstrously evil Al Capone (De Niro) and the unloveably upright Eliot Ness (Costner), and when he dies the film has a rocky time recovering. Costner looks like the kid who got a briefcase for Xmas and was pleased, but painfully learns under Malone's tutelage how to fight dirty. De Niro establishes his corner courtesy of a bloody finger in close-up, and unleashes uncontrollable rage to electrifying effect, most notably at the blood-boltered baseball-bat board meeting. The Odessa Steps set piece at the railway station could maybe do with one more angle to shuffle, and the battle at the border bridge diminishes the claustrophobic grip of the corrupt city, but the narrative thunders to its conclusion like a locomotive. BC

Unzipped

(1994, US, 73 mn, b/w & col)
d Douglas Keeve. *p* Michael Alden. *ph* Ellen Kuras. *ed* Paula Heredia. *with* Isaac Mizrahi, Kate Moss, Linda Evangelista, Cindy Crawford, Naomi Campbell, Christy Turlington, Ertha Kitt, Sandra Bernhardt.

●'It's about women not wanting to look like cows, I guess…' So says fashion designer *extraordinaire* Isaac Mizrahi in this witty, insightful 'fly on the changing-room wall' documentary by his then lover, photographer Douglas Keeve. The film begins with Mizrahi reading the reviews for his latest show, and charts the progress of his next (New York, 1994) – ''50s cheesecake meets eskimo fake fur' – bursting into colour for the fabulously decadent climax. Not only does the film establish the credentials of the art of fashion, it's also a whole lot funnier than Altman's *Prêt-à-Porter*. TCh

Uomo avvisato mezzo ammazzato...parola di Spirito Santo

see Blazing Guns

Uomo delle stelle, L' (The Starmaker)

(1994, It, 113 min)
d Giuseppe Tornatore. *p* Vittorio Cecchi Gori, Rita Cecchi Gori. *sc* Giuseppe Tornatore, Fabio Rinaudo. *ph* Dante Spinotti. *ed* Massimo Quglia. *pd* Franco Bronzi. *m* Ennio Morricone. *cast* Sergio Castellitto, Tiziana Lodato, Leopoldo Trieste, Nicola Di Pinto, Franco Scaldati, Tony Sperandeo, Jane Alexander.

●Back in his native Sicily, where he scored his greatest triumph with *Cinema Paradiso*, director Tornatore confronts the magic of celluloid with distinctly less happy results in this story of a man with a movie camera. It's 1953, television hasn't yet reached Italy's poverty-stricken South, and Joe Morelli has little difficulty in persuading the locals to part with their hard-earned lire for the price of a screen test. Here's their big chance at movie stardom, since the footage is sent back to the studios in Rome and the right face might just be plucked from obscurity for a glittering new career. That's how the theory goes, but even the hustling, bustling Joe can't fail to notice the burden of dreams he carries around with him, particularly when the teenage orphan Beata pins all her hopes on his battered van and its travels across the Sicilian landscape. As the unprepossessing Joe, Castellitto tries hard to veil the ugly truth behind his character's money-making scheme, but the effort is so obvious it's hard to care about him either way, especially when his treatment of newcomer Tiziana Lodato's striking Beata veers on the neolithic side of macho. Much more palatable is the notion that the villagers' open-hearted confessions to Morelli's camera prove more touching and true than anything in the Italian movies of the time. Disappointing. TJ

Up at the Villa

(1999, US/GB, 116 min)
d Philip Haas. *p* Geoff Stier. *sc* Belinda Haas. *ph* Maurizio Calvesi. *ed* Belinda Haas. *pd* Paul Brown. *m* Pino Donaggio. *cast* Kristin Scott Thomas, Sean Penn, Anne Bancroft, James Fox, Jeremy Davies, Derek Jacobi, Massimo Ghini, Dudley Sutton, Lorenza Indovina.

●Florence, 1938. Cosseted by the blithe company of Anglo-American expats like Princess San Ferdinando (Bancroft), widowed Mary Panton (Scott Thomas) is barely aware of the rise of fascism, so concerned is she with keeping her head above water in a sea of luxury. A proposal from Sir Edgar (Fox), due to become Governor of Bengal, promises stability, status and security, but a riskier temptation presents itself almost simultaneously when playboy Rowley Flint (Penn) advises her to choose passion instead. To their adaptations of Paul Auster's *The Music of Chance* and AS Byatt's *Angels and Insects*, Philip and Belinda Haas brought visual and literary elegance and a welcome, almost perverse quirkiness both in terms of tone and content. Those elements are again present in this intelligent version of Somerset Maugham's novella – except, crucially the perverse quirkiness. Yes, it's engaging and psychologically astute, despite some occasional clunky lines, while the lush Tuscan milieu is counterpointed by a subtle, sustained whiff of complacency and corruption. But somehow it never quite sheds that peculiar blend of predictability and polite discretion that tethers so much period drama. Still, Scott Thomas is as fine as you'd expect, Penn once again steals the laurels and, if you like a decent, undemanding romance, it's quite watchable. GA

Up Close & Personal

(1996, US, 124 min)
d Jon Avnet. *p* Jon Avnet, David Nicksay, Jordan Kerner. *sc* Joan Didion, John Gregory Dunne. *ph* Walter Lindenlaub. *ed* Debra Neil-Fisher. *pd* Jeremy Conway. *m* Thomas Newman. *cast* Robert Redford, Michelle Pfeiffer, Stockard Channing, Joe Mantegna, Kate Nelligan, Glenn Plummer, James Rebhorn, DeDee Pfeiffer.

●A soppy May-December romance masquerading as a deadly earnest issues movie (script by Joan Didion and John Gregory Dunne, 'suggested' by the book *Golden Girl* by Alanna Nash). Pfeiffer is Tally Atwater, a perky klutz who dreams of being a TV news anchor. She's picked up by respected old pro Warren Justice (Redford). If Nicole Kidman had had a Warren, she'd have had no reason *To Die For*. Warren thinks Tally 'eats the lens'. She's 'hungry', so he gives her a 'live feed'. With a little mood music from Celine Dion, they do the do, but Tally's career takes off, while the obstinately sanctimonious Warren is deemed too political for TV (think *Broadcast News* without the wit, *A Star Is Born* without the alcohol). Somehow the film-makers spin this dramatic vacuum out for another hour or so, putting Ms Pfeiffer in a new hairdo every few minutes to relieve the tedium, until finally they come up with the TV-reporter-in-a-prison-riot routine. Blow-dried, bleached blonde-on-bland entertainment. TCh

Up in Arms

(1944, US, 106 min)
d Elliott Nugent. *p* Samuel Goldwyn. *sc* Don Hartman, Robert Pirosh, Allen Boretz. *ph* Ray Rennahan. *ed* Daniel Mandell, James Newcom. *ad* Perry Ferguson, Stewart Chaney. *songs* Harold Arlen, Ted Koehler, Sylvia Fine. *cast* Danny Kaye, Dinah Shore, Dana Andrews, Constance Dowling, Louis Calhern, Elisha Cook Jr, Walter Catlett.

●Kaye's very scrappy first starring vehicle, in which he plays a hypochondriac drafted in World War II and packed off to the Pacific sector along with the Goldwyn Girls (handy for filling in when inspiration flags). The tiresome patter song with which he had already wowed Broadway ('Malady in 4-F'), and which set the pattern for his frenzied double-talk speciality, is much in evidence. So, as Parker Tyler noted, is the shameless fixation on the camera which made him rather unprepossessing for all his obvious talents. Still, there are moments of genuine splendour in his bizarre satire on screen musicals ('Manic-Depressive Presents'). TM

Up in Smoke

(1978, US, 86 min)
d Lou Adler. *p* Lou Adler, Lou Lombardo. *sc* Tommy Chong, Cheech Marin. *ph* Gene Polito. *ed* Lou Lombardo, Scott Conrad. *ad* Leon Ericksen. *m* Danny Kortchmar, Waddy Wachtel. *cast* Cheech Marin, Tommy Chong, Strother Martin, Edie Adams, Stacy Keach, Tom Skerritt.

●Cheech and Chong's first movie is the epitome of the serious doper's heaven and hell. Heaven: they drive around in a van made entirely from 100% 'Fibreweed'. Hell: they don't know it. Heaven: they find a whole plateful of coke in the aftermath of a party. Hell: they also find a lady with a nose like the Blackwall tunnel and sniffing power equal to any Jet-vac. Covering the gamut of a laid-back, laid-out LA dope bum's world – dumb cops, 'Nam, being busted, the eternal search for a 'lid' – the movie eventually gets too out of it, and tails off into easy visual gags rather than maintaining the spaced-out repartee that made Cheech and Chong so memorable. As the most fun comes not from watching the movie but from recalling great lines later, it would seem that the audio success of C & C has not translated too well into visuals. FF

Up 'n' Under

(1997, GB, 90 min)
d John Godber. *p* Mark Thomas. *sc* John Godber. *ph* Alan Trow. *ed* Chris Lawrence. *pd* Hayden Pearce. *m* Mark Thomas. *cast* Gary Olsen, Richard Ridings, Samantha Janus, Ralph Brown, Neil Morrissey, Tony Slattery, Griff Rhys-Jones, Brian Glover.

●Based on characters from a play by director John Godber, this patronising feel-good comedy is set in the world of Yorkshire pub seven-a-side rugby. Ex-pro Olsen bets flash git entrepreneur Slattery his house that the Wheatsheaf team of lifelong losers will beat the seemingly invincible Cobblers Arms squad of brick shithouses. Olsen is ordinary and vulnerable enough to be convincing. Samatha Janus, too, as the gym owner who helps whip the team into shape, is sufficiently feisty and natural in the 'strong woman' role to mask the script's contrivance. However, the 'money shot' of her in the nude – 'You've had a look, now piss off!' – is typical of the film's casual sexual-political hypocrisy. Too concerned with courting sympathy, thin on laughs – and the rugby's a joke. WH

Up on the Roof

(1997, GB, 101 min)
d Simon Moore. *p* Jane Prowse, Pippa Cross, Brian Eastman. *sc* Jane Prowse, Simon Moore. *ph* Nic Morris. *ed* Peter Hollywood. *pd* Tim Hutchinson. *m* Alan Parker. *cast* Billy Carter, Adrian Lester, Clare Cathcart, Amy Robbins, Daniel Ryan.

●Adapted by Simon Moore and Jane Prowse from their successful stage musical, this concerns five friends from the university of Hull, class of '79. Golden couple Bryony and Scott (Robbins and Lester), tubby geek Angela (Cathcart), cheery hanger-on Tim (Carter) and scaly Keith (Ryan) all belong to an a cappella group. On the last day of term, they vow to meet again in 1989. First problem: as a group, they fail to convince. As for the singing, Prowse and Moore are obviously going for heartfelt sweetness, but only Lester has a really fine voice, while the arrangements are literally soul-destroying. Would the sight of the singing, grinning five, high on a building, overwhelm a whole campus of laidback dudes? A far more likely response would be a unanimous 'Jump!' CO'Su

Upper Hand, The

see Rififi à Paname

Uproar in Heaven (Danao Tiangong)

(1961–64, China, 110 min)
d Wan Lai-Ming.

●Wan Lai-Ming and his brothers were China's pioneers in animation, but their work was suppressed after the Cultural Revolution of 1966. This ambitious animated feature is adapted from the first seven chapters of the 16th century novel *Journey to the West* (best known here in Arthur Waley's translation as *Monkey*), and it celebrates the mischievous Monkey King's challenge to the celestial autocracy. Wan makes no real effort to produce 'charming' or sympathetic characters, and so his main appeal is to those familiar with the book – which means everyone in China. His figure animation is like simplified Disney without the sentimentality, but his backgrounds derive rather beautifully from traditional Chinese painting. TR

Upstairs and Downstairs

(1959, GB, 101 min)
d Ralph Thomas. *p* Betty E Box. *sc* Frank Harvey. *ph* Ernest Steward. *ed* Alfred Roome. *ad* Maurice Carter. *m* Philip Green. *cast* Michael Craig, Anne Heywood, Mylène Demongeot, James Robertson Justice, Claudia Cardinale, Sidney James, Joan Hickson, Joan Sims, Daniel Massey.

●Oh, the problems of nice upper-class couples in British comedies of the '50s. Newly-weds Craig and Heywood simply can't find the right domestic and they've got to do lots of entertaining for her wealthy father's business clients. After trying and failing with the likes of Claudia Cardinale (her first English-speaking role) and Joan Hickson, they hit pay-dirt with Sid James. Very genteel. Began life as a novel by Ronald Scott Thorne. TJ

Up the Down Staircase

(1967, US, 123 min)
d Robert Mulligan. *p* Alan J Pakula. *sc* Tad Mosel. *ph* Joseph Coffey. *ed* Folmer Blangsted. *ad* George Jenkins. *m* Fred Karlin. *cast* Sandy Dennis, Patrick Bedford, Eileen Heckart, Ruth White, Jean Stapleton, Sorrell Booke, Roy Poole, Ellen O'Mara.

●Documentary-style drama dealing with the problems that face an idealistic young schoolteacher when she is assigned to a rough school in a slum area. Some of the characters are very accurately drawn (by Sandy Dennis as the teacher, Ellen O'Mara as a lovesick schoolgirl); others are stereotypes. Some of the situations work (the plot is little more than a catalogue of events), others don't. It comes to precious few conclusions, but does at least provide a talking-point of sorts in its portrayal of a frighteningly unenlightened American educational system. DMcG

Up the Junction

(1967, GB, 119 min)
d Peter Collinson. *p* Anthony Havelock-Allan, John Brabourne. *sc* Roger Smith. *ph* Arthur Lavis. *ed* John Trumper. *ad* Ken Jones. *m* Mike Hugg, Manfred Mann. *cast* Suzy Kendall, Dennis Waterman, Adrienne Posta, Maureen Lipman, Michael Gothard, Liz Fraser, Hylda Baker, Alfie Bass, Susan George.

●Hard to see what all the fuss was about (at least from this movie cash-in on Kenneth Loach's teleplay version of Nell Dunn's novel). The idea that the decision of middle class Polly (Kendall) to forsake Chelsea and move to Battersea should provide enough substance for either a book or a film now seems ludicrous. Nevertheless here it all is. In the shadow of the power station, she helps working class Rube (Posta) cope with abortion and death: part of the short-lived and generally muffed attempt by the film industry to make a foray of sorts into the realities of working class life in Britain. VG

Up the Sandbox

(1972, US, 98 min)
d Irvin Kershner. *p* Irwin Winkler, Robert Chartoff. *sc* Paul Zindel. *ph* Gordon Willis. *ed* Robert Lawrence. *pd* Harry Horner. *m* Billy Goldenberg. *cast* Barbra Streisand, David Selby, Jane Hoffman, Jacobo Morales, John C Becher, Paul Benedict, Paul Dooley.

●Good old Hollywood doing its bit to keep the giggles going about Women's Lib. The wife of a radical prof at Columbia, Streisand feels somewhat dissatisfied with life. Egged on by the more forthright comments of housewife/mother friends, and hormonally motivated by the fact that she is pregnant for the third time, she enacts the problems of her marriage through a series of fantasies: a confrontation with a South American revolutionary who turns out to be a woman, a hair-tearing session with her possessive Jewish mother, a cathartic attack on her devoted husband, and one about abortion where she drifts through a children's playground in a white gown on the operating-table. In spite of a number of funny lines, it all ends up as though happy-ever-after had only just been invented. Well, we always knew that women – especially stars – were really content just to be wives and mothers. MV

Uptown Saturday Night

(1974, US, 104 min)
d Sidney Poitier. *p* Melville Tucker. *sc* Richard Wesley. *ph* Fred J Koenekamp. *ed* Pembroke J Herring. *pd* Alfred Sweeney. *m* Tom Scott. *cast* Sidney Poitier, Bill Cosby, Harry Belafonte, Flip Wilson, Richard Pryor, Rosalind Cash, Roscoe Lee Browne, Paula Kelly, Calvin Lockhart.

●An efficient enough comedy in which Poitier directs himself as straight man to Cosby's slightly demented taxi driver. The film takes off from the first night of their vacation, when a winning lottery ticket is stolen and their attempts to retrieve it involve them in a movie fantasy world of gangsters. Radiating professionalism rather more than inspiration, it boils down to the sum of its star turns, and with the exception of a fairly nauseous opening sequence sketching in Poitier's 'happy marriage', emerges not unlikeably. Calvin Lockhart etches a neat thumb-nail sketch of a ghetto gangster; Belafonte takes off Brando's Godfather; Roscoe Lee Browne adds a touch of acid to his portrayal of a black congressman. But it's Richard Pryor's fleeting yet totally three-dimensional Sharp Eye Washington, a perspiring and achingly nervous phony private eye, who really walks away with the honours. VG

Upworld

see Gnome Named Gnorm, A

Up Your Alley

(1988, US, 88 min)
d Bob Logan. *p* Murray Langston. *sc* Murray Langston, Bob Logan. *ph* Mark Melville. *ed* Tom Silter. *m* Paul Ventimiglia. *cast* Linda Blair, Murray Langston, Bob Zany, Kevin Benton, Ruth Buzzi, Glen Vincent, Jack Hanrahan, Melissa Shear.

●Here we have Linda Blair in her 'comedy debut' as a yuppy junior reporter dressing up as a bag lady in order to write a tear-jerking piece about 'street people'. In no time at all she's falling in lurve with the cutest derelict in town (Langston), giving her smarmy editor the thumbs-down for the hot-tub option, and helping to solve a murder. And all without the aid of make-up! Unusually, she manages to make it through the entire movie without getting imprisoned, raped, abused, possessed or murdered. The whole thing is fittingly low budget: it looks like it was filmed in about four days. MK

Uranus

(1990, Fr, 99 min)
d Claude Berri. *sc* Claude Berri, Arlette Langmann. *ph* Renato Berta. *ed* Hervé de Luze. *ad* Bernard Vezat. *m* Jean-Claude Petit. *cast* Philippe Noiret, Gérard Depardieu, Jean-Pierre Marielle, Michel Blanc, Michel Galabru, Gérard Desarthe, Fabrice Luchini, Daniel Prévost, Florence Darel.

●The troubled mood of guilt, recrimination and persecution that plagued France at the end of WWII has rarely been even hinted at by that country's cinema, and one would like to be able to commend Berri's adaptation of Marcel Aymé's novel for bravery, if nothing else. But while this account of vicious, hypocritical intrigue in a small, recently liberated town certainly admits to the existence of both collaborators and communist fanatics, the histrionic performances, excessively eventful narrative, and two-dimensional characterisations make for ludicrous melodrama. The sense of quiet drama that made *Jean de Florette* so popular is conspicuously absent, and *everyone* overacts. It may aspire to tragedy, but the overblown script and emphatically drab period dressing reduce it to little more than an indulgent wallow in petty corruption. GA

Urban Cowboy

(1980, US, 135 min)
d James Bridges. *p* Robert Evans, Irving Azoff. *sc* James Bridges, Aaron Latham. *ph* Reynaldo Villalobos. *ed* David Rawlins. *pd* Stephen Grimes. *cast* John Travolta, Debra Winger, Scott Glenn, Madolyn Smith, Barry Corbin, Brooke Alderson, Cooper Huckabee.

● In Hollywood parlance, *Urban Cowboy* is just like *Saturday Night Fever* but completely different. It began life as a factual article in *Esquire* about the weekend cowboys of Houston, who live a split existence between their factories and the fantasy world of the honky-tonk bars. Bridges builds this material into a well acted, eye-catching romance about the aspirations and romances of a new kid in town (Travolta). But the stream of incidents and pick-ups around the mechanical rodeo bull in the ballroom cannot disguise the fact that the film badly lacks a central narrative hook. It is too obviously a starring vehicle, and – unlike *Saturday Night Fever*, which did present some insights into a subculture – its major events are crudely imposed on the setting. In fact, the film's virtues derive not from Travolta at all, but from Bridges' obvious enjoyment of the country milieu, and the fine performances he wins from Travolta's co-stars. Debra Winger, as his wife, lends her part far more spirit and sympathy than the writing deserves; but the trump card is Scott Glenn as the villain, looking uncannily like a new Eastwood. DP

Urban Ghost Story

(1998, GB, 88 min)
d Genevieve Jolliffe. *p* Chris Jones. *sc* Chris Jones, Genevieve Jolliffe. *ph* Jon Walker. *ed* Eddie Hamilton. *pd* Simon Pickup. *m* Rupert Gregson Williams. *cast* Heather Ann Foster, Stephanie Buttle, Jason Connery, Nicola Stapleton, James Cosmo, Alan Owen, Andreas Wisniewski.

● A drug-fuelled teenage joyride is the unlikely catalyst for this modern horror with a social conscience. Foster survives the car crash which kills her boyfriend, but going back home to a Glasgow tower block fails to provide the expected rest and recuperation. Moving furniture and strange noises suggest the presence of poltergeist activity, but could it just be the disturbed aftershocks on a young mind? Buttle is the hard-pressed mother and Connery the cynical tabloid journalist on the case, as medical and eventually spiritual help is called on for answers. It may not quite have enough story to go round, but the film makes its point about the demoralisation of the urban disenfranchised while delivering a fair quotient of chills. Excellent use of suggestive sound and an impressive action finale, all done on a tiny budget. TJ

Urban Legend

(1998, US/Fr, 100 min)
d Jamie Blanks. *p* Neal H Moritz, Gina Matthews, Michael McDonnell. *sc* Silvio Horta. *ph* James Chressanthis. *ed* Jay Cassidy. *pd* Charles Breen. *m* Christopher Young. *cast* Jared Leto, Alicia Witt, Rebecca Gayheart, Joshua Jackson, Natasha Gregson Wagner, Robert Englund, Brad Dourif.

● The most frightening aspect of the post-*Scream* horror revival is how quickly the knowing smile of Craven's original turned into the lazy smirk of its imitators. Worse, the sloppy spin-offs have leap-frogged backwards over *Scream*'s post-modern ingenuity to ape crude '70s teen slasher pics. But since the teen leads are no longer by-the-yard disposables but the bankable stars of such glossy TV series as *Beverly Hills 90210* and *Dawson's Creek*, these watered-down '90s versions lack the gratuitous nudity and gleeful gore that was their '70s equivalents' raison d'être. First time director Jamie Blanks lacks the intellectual firepower to make the most of a script that junks its promising premise – a hooded psycho's murders mirror popular urban myths – halfway through. The usual blandly attractive teenagers run around campus at night, walk into dark rooms without switching on the lights, and are surprised when they suffer the painful demise they deserve. NF

Urban Legends Final Cut

(2000, US/Fr, 98 min)
d John Ottman. *p* Neal H Moritz, Gina Matthews, Richard Luke Rothschild. *sc* Paul Harris Boardman, Scott Derrickson. *ph* Brian Pearson. *ed* John Ottman, Ron Kobrin. *pd* Mark Zuelzke. *m* John Ottman. *cast* Jennifer Morrison, Matthew Davis, Hart Bochner, Joseph Lawrence, Anson Mount, Anthony Anderson, Eva Mendes, Michael Bacall, Jessica Cauffiel, Loretta Devine.

● This horror sequel opens with an out of control passenger plane, then plummets to intellectual ground zero. Substituting *Scream*-style movie references for any semblance of story, characterisation or suspense, it links with the half-baked original via sparky security guard Reese (Devine), now performing similar duties at Alpine University. Inspired by Reese's account of the urban legend-related killings at Pendleton High, film student Amy makes her thesis project a psychological thriller based on those murders. But competition for the prestigious Hitchcock Award is so fierce that members of Amy's crew are soon bumped off in ways echoing classic horror movies. Ottman, an editor/composer turned director, serves up plenty of gruesome nastiness, but he'd be unwise to give up either day job. Of the actors, the only one to escape 'irritating, disposable teen' status is Morrison, whose increasingly paranoid Amy has more psychological depth than the sloppy script deserves. NF

Urga

(1990, Fr/USSR, 118 min)
d Nikita Mikhalkov. *p* Michel Seydoux. *sc* Rustam Ibragimbekov. *ph* Vilen Kaliuta. *ed* Joëlle Hache. *pd* Alexei Levchenko. *m* Eduard Artemiev. *cast* Badema, Bayaertu, Vladimir Gostukhin, Babushka, Larissa Kuznetsova, Jon Bochinski.

● Best known for his Chekhov adaptations, Mikhalkov here came up with a film full of narrative surprises. Set for the most part in the vast, empty steppes of Chinese Mongolia, it's partly a docudrama detailing the day-to-day existence of a herdsman's family, partly a fable about the material and spiritual threats facing a robust but largely forgotten culture (the *urga* is a herdsman's lasso, but also a symbol of traditions in harmony with nature). Into this strange, remote world comes a Russian ex-soldier, working on a road-building project. Nothing here is quite as it seems, and as Mikhalkov guides us on a voyage into a fascinating but unfamiliar landscape, he deploys dreamy images, rapturous music, and bizarre incongruities to undermine our assumptions about 'primitive' Mongolian life. Admittedly, towards the end the narrative gets a little out of control, but much of it is very funny, and the engagingly naturalistic performances, the ravishing camerawork, and the mostly subtle use of natural symbols sustain interest throughout. GA

Urinal

(1988, Can, 100 min)
d/p/sc John Greyson. *ph* Adam Surica. *ed* David McIntosh. *m* Glenn Schellenberg. *cast* Pauline Carey, Paul Bettis, George Spelvin.

● This overly ambitious film, part documentary and part fantasy, is centered around a research project on the policing of cottaging (or 'washroom sex', as Canadians term it) in Ontario. The most interesting parts of the film (revealing the lengths that the Canadian police go to, including the use of *agents provocateurs* and video surveillance, in order to make easy arrests and bump up prosecution figures) are the interviews with men who have been charged with 'gross indecency', with gay activists, with a lawyer working on behalf of prosecuted gay men, and with Svend Robinson, Canada's first 'out' gay MP. Unfortunately, you also have to wade through a nonsensical framework involving the ghosts of famous lesbian, gay and bisexual figures (including Eisenstein, Frida Kahlo, Mishima and Langston Hughes), who are summoned to the garden of two dead Toronto sculptors to talk about the history of lavatories and debate the question of police entrapment. Aiming for imagination, it just becomes weird… and boring. MG.

Ursula and Glenys

(1985, GB, 54 min)
d John Davies. *sc* John Davies, Brid Brennan, Gaylie Runciman. Ric Morgan. *ph* Robert Smith. *ed* John Davies. *m* Nick Garvey. *cast* Brid Brennan, Gaylie Runciman, Ric Morgan, Joe Davies, Kieran Davies.

● This is a spiky film with a certain trenchant humour contributed by the Glenys character (Runciman), a Soho hooker. This is played off against the slightly soured strength of Ursula (Brennan). They are respectively the 'bad' and 'good' half-sisters who provide the focus for this rather disengaged exploration of fragmented families, incest, and moral disenchantment. Perhaps appropriately for a stagnant Britain (that image of parked car, doors open against a flat landscape, 'Islands in the Stream' on the radio), the only form of communication is confession. Hallmark of the '80s? The film has surprising charm, and the locations are well used. VG

Used Cars

(1980, US, 111 min)
d Robert Zemeckis. *p* Bob Gale. *sc* Robert Zemeckis, Bob Gale. *ph* Donald M Morgan. *ed* Michael Kahn. *pd* Peter Jamison. *m* Patrick Williams. *cast* Kurt Russell, Jack Warden, Gerrit Graham, Frank McRae, Deborah Harmon, Joseph P Flaherty, Michael McKean, David L Lander, Wendie Jo Sperber.

● With their unerring eye for potential, the distributors didn't release this hilarious black comedy to cinemas in Britain. Zemeckis subsequently went on to make *Romancing the Stone*, *Back to the Future*, *Who Framed Roger Rabbit* and loadsa money. Infinitely more caustic than these blockbusters, *Used Cars* runs on a contemporary screwball motor with a slapstick chassis. Centred on the outrageous rivalry of two car dealerships (both owned by Jack Warden, as twins), it's an amoral celebration of the all-American wheeler-dealer – like *Tin Men* on speed. Even Jimmy Carter lends his support! TCh

Used People

(1992, US, 116 min)
d Beeban Kidron. *p* Peggy Rajski. *sc* Todd Graff. *ph* David Watkin. *ed* John Tintori. *pd* Stuart Wurtzel. *m* Rachel Portman. *cast* Shirley MacLaine, Marcello Mastroianni, Bob Dishy, Kathy Bates, Jessica Tandy, Marcia Gay Harden, Sylvia Sidney.

● Kidron's beguiling American debut sprinkles moments of everyday oddity and genuine pain into the usual Hollywood syrup of think-positive platitudes. Queens in 1969 bustles with Jewish familial ructions when middle-aged mum Pearl Berman (MacLaine) gets picked up at her husband's funeral by spiv-suited Italian Joe Meledandri (Mastroianni), a long-time secret admirer. Initially awkward, eventually rejuvenating, this romantic late late show puts Pearl's toiling years of marriage into proper perspective and throws the rest of the household's problems into sharper relief... MacLaine bristles to touching effect as a woman at last grasping some time for herself; Mastroianni's Casanova codger is a hangdog charmer of a Hollywood debut. Elsewhere, myriad minor characters and switchback shifts from tears to whimsy jostle for attention in Todd Graff's densely populated script. More lunatic than *Moonstruck*, sweeter than *Sweetie*, the film's breezy domesticity is the acceptable face of sentimental guff. TJ

U.S. Marshals

(1998, US, 131 min)
d Stuart Baird. *p* Arnold Kopelson, Anne Kopelson. *sc* John Pogue. *ph* Andrzej Bartkowiak. *ed* Terry Rawlings. *pd* Maher Ahmad. *m* Jerry Goldsmith. *cast* Tommy Lee Jones, Wesley Snipes, Robert Downey Jr, Joe Pantoliano, Irène Jacob, Kate Nelligan, Patrick Malahide, Tom Wood.

● A sequel to *The Fugitive* starring Jones' hardass marshal is not a bad idea; but this lazy follow-up is simply a carbon of the original, with a few token changes. This time, it's Snipes, not Harrison Ford, on the run. The wrongfully imprisoned Snipes escapes after a crash involving a plane not a train; and the jaw-dropping stunt is a Tarzan swing from a high rise not a swan dive from a dam. When Jones utters the words, 'We have a fugitive,' we know we're in *Die Hard 2* territory. The cosmetic changes, though, alter the balance of the story significantly. We must divide our sympathies between Snipes, set up as a fall guy by his former government employers, and Jones' no nonsense lawman, who always gets his man; but Snipes plays second fiddle to Jones' pursuing hero. Director Baird stages the buttock clenching plane crash with skill, and despite letting the chase drag on too long keeps things moving brisk, if sometimes fitful pace. NF

Usual Suspects, The (100)

(1995, US, 108 min)
d Bryan Singer. *p* Bryan Singer, Michael McDonnell. *sc* Christopher McQuarrie. *ph* Tom Sigel. *ed* John Ottman. *pd* Howard Cummings. *m* John Ottman. *cast* Gabriel Byrne, Kevin Spacey, Stephen Baldwin, Chazz Palminteri, Pete Postlethwaite, Giancarlo Esposito.

● This labyrinthine, very well played thriller – a huge improvement on the Bryan Singer's intriguing but awkward debut, *Public Access* – never lets up. It begins with the explosion of a docked ship, before one of the two survivors goes on to detail, to the cops and the audience, the events of the previous six weeks that led him to the vessel. It's a yarn involving five criminals unwittingly brought together in a police cell due to one thing they have in common: the master criminal Keyser Soze, who may or may not exist…Working from Christopher McQuarrie's marvellously tortuous, colourful script, Singer creates a classy, thought-provoking mystery that is pleasingly old-fashioned (the settings, characters and sassy mood recall Hammett and Chandler) and absolutely modern in the sly, slightly self-conscious play it makes with myth and methods of storytelling. GA

Utamaro o Meguru Go-nin no Onna

see Five Women Around Utamaro

Utu

(1983, NZ, 104 min)
d Geoff Murphy. *p* Geoff Murphy, Don Blakeney. *sc* Geoff Murphy, Keith Aberdein. *ph* Graeme Cowley. *ed* Michael Horton, Ian John. *pd* Ron Highfield. *m* John Charles. *cast* Anzac Wallace, Bruno Lawrence, Tim Elliott, Kelly Johnson, Wi Kuki Kaa, Tania Bristowe.

● This does for the 19th century Land Wars in New Zealand what *Ulzana's Raid* did for the contemporary Apache campaign in the USA, making it clear that the white man's destiny to conquer new and fertile corners of the earth was totally irreconcilable with the interests and culture of the previous inhabitants. The story of a series of revenge raids by Maori rebel Te Wheke is violent in every sense: in the action of many scenes; in the abrupt changes of tone, from the horror of the opening massacre, through spaghetti Western-style confrontations, to the almost mystical ending; and in the violence it does to the idea of liberal democratic understanding as a universal panacea. There are rough passages and uncertain performances, but both Lawrence as a sort of serio-comic Eastwood figure, and Wallace as the brooding, mercurial Te Wheke, are excellent. A film both fascinating and disconcerting, all but bringing off the gamble of combining a serious look at history with a thrills'n'spills action movie. NR

U Turn

(1997, US/Fr, 125 min)
d Oliver Stone. *p* Don Halsted, Clayton Townsend. *sc* John Ridley. *ph* Robert Richardson. *ed* Hank Corwin, Thomas J Nordberg. *pd* Victor Kempster. *m* Ennio Morricone. *cast* Sean Penn, Jennifer Lopez, Nick Nolte, Powers Boothe, Claire Danes, Joaquin Phoenix, Billy Bob Thornton, Jon Voight.

● When his Mustang breaks down in Superior, Arizona, gambler Bobby Cooper (Penn) has no idea how low his luck has sunk. He picks up the lusty Grace (Lopez), or she picks up him – either way, her husband Jake (Nolte) isn't happy. In fact, he has his own proposition for the stranger. He wants his wife dead and reckons Bobby's the man for the job. He might be, too, if Grace can't make a better offer. John Ridley's script (from his book *Stray Dogs*) affects the tortuous contrivances of a malign and witty fate, in the manner of James M Cain, Jim Thompson, or more recently *Red Rock West*. But it's this affectation which kills the film. Stone directs with the same inebriated three-second attention span he adopted for *Natural Born Killers*, experimenting with different film gauges, stocks and speeds every other shot. To be fair, going by Ennio Morricone's spaghetti-and-meatballs score, Stone is fishing for laughs much of the time. Penn turns in a crisp, unfussy comic performance, Lopez vamps like a scorpion in heat, Nolte sustains a pretty good John Huston impression, and Thornton is mighty peculiar as the mechanic from hell. TCh

U2 Rattle and Hum

(1988, US, 99 min)
d Phil Joanou. *p* Michael Hamlyn. *ph* Jordan Cronenweth, Robert Brinkman. *ed* Phil Joanou. *m* U2. *with* Bono, The Edge, Adam Clayton, Larry Mullen, BB King.

● Joanou perpetuates the image of U2 as Eastwood-style Men with No Name: dressed like extras from a spaghetti Western, in interview they fumble over answers with brows furrowed as if words can't express their depth of feeling. The implication is that U2's music speaks for them. A shame, then, they don't get down to it earlier. U2's place as rock regents is emphasised by a visit to Graceland, with drummer Larry Mullen contemplating Elvis's grave, and by a wonderful moment in which singer Bono shows BB King how to play a U2 song. A gospel version of 'I Still Haven't Found What I'm Looking For' provides a rare glimpse of the band's feeling for their craft, but for the most part the documentary footage is unsatisfactory, saying nothing new about the men behind the myth. The live footage, shot at one of the later American 'Joshua Tree' concerts, is another matter. Seamlessly edited, the camera entirely unobtrusive, and the sound impeccably produced by Jimmy Iovine, this gives you a front row seat at a textbook stadium show. Bono's visionary poetic preaching, which takes in a little Irish/American history and a brave tirade against the IRA's Enniskillen massacre before launching into the utterly inspired 'Sunday Bloody Sunday', is something you can stomach or not, but it won't leave you unmoved. EP

V

Vertigo

Vacances au Pays

see Trip to My Country, A

Vacances de M. Hulot, Les (Monsieur Hulot's Holiday/ Mr Hulot's Holiday)

(1952, Fr, 91 min, b/w)
d Jacques Tati. *p* Fred Orain. *sc* Jacques Tati, Henri Marquet. *ph* Jacques Mercanton, Jean Mousselle. *ed* Jacques Grassi. *ad* Henri Schmitt. *m* Alain Romans. *cast* Jacques Tati, Nathalie Pascaud, Michèle Rolla, Louis Perrault, André Dubois, Valentine Camax.

● Tati's most consistently enjoyable comedy, a gentle portrait of the clumsy, well-meaning Hulot on vacation in a provincial seaside resort. The quiet, delicately observed slapstick here works with far more hits than misses, although in comparison with, say, Keaton, Tati's cold detachment from his characters seems to result in a decided lack of insight into human behaviour. But at least in contrast to later works like *Playtime* and *Traffic*, there's enough dramatic structure to make it more than simply a series of one-off gags. GA

Vacas (Cows)

(1992, Sp, 96 min)
d Julio Medem. *sc* Julio Medem, Michel Gaztambide. *ph* Carles Gusi. *ed* Maria Elena Sainz. *pd* Rafael Palermo. *m* Alberto Iglesias. *cast* Emma Suárez, Carmelo Gómez, Ana Torrent, Karra Elejalde.

● The second Carlist war, 1875. Panicking under fire, Basque woodcutter Irigibel drops to the earth and smears himself with blood gushing hot from the neck of his mortally wounded neighbour, Mendiluze. The battle over, he crawls out from a cart-load of the dead, naked but unremarked, except by a curious, solitary cow. Medem's trenchant, daring directorial debut cuts through the decades like an axe. 1905: the neighbours' sons feud and Irigibel embarks on a clandestine affair with his counterpart's sister. 1915: her bastard son Peru grows up alongside his half-sister, while the boy's parents elope to America and take him with them. 1936: Peru returns to photograph the Spanish Civil War. Medem is unexpectedly impatient with that old standby of Spanish cinema, the epic historical melodrama. His movie is swift and urgent – it's closer to Jane Campion than Carlos Saura – and he has a sharp eye for *la vida loca*. Captured at moments of crisis and decision, his characters are forced to confront the precariousness of their rural existence and the great black hole of their own mortality. Imperviously, implacably bovine – it's somehow typical of this startlingly original picture that cows should carry the bulk of the symbolism. TCh

Vacation from Marriage

see Perfect Strangers

Vache et le Prisonnier, La (The Cow and I)

(1959, Fr/It, 123 min, b/w)
d Henri Verneuil. *p* Roland Girard. *sc* Henri Verneuil, Henri Jeanson, Jean Manse. *ph* Roger Hubert. *ed* James Cuenet. *m* Paul Durand. *cast* Fernandel, Ellen Schwiers, Pierre Louis, René Havard, Albert Rémy, Bernard Musson.

● On the same principle that so long as you're holding a clipboard, you can saunter around any workplace in the world, escaped PoW Fernandel crosses Germany virtually unchallenged, leading a cow with one hand and carrying a milk pail in the other. This is a sturdy, even affecting tale, with whimsy mostly held at bay.The cow is not made to do cute things and remains an admirably cow-like, anonymous sort of cow. Fernandel is as restrained as he ever gets, the German characters are uncommonly affable and pacific, and the mood is one of wistfulness, notably in the underplayed ending when our hero jumps the wrong freight train and goes rattling straight back to where he started from. BBa

Vagabonde (Sans Toit ni Loi)

(1985, Fr, 106 min)
d Agnès Varda. *p* Oury Milshtein. *sc* Agnès Varda. *ph* Patrick Blossier. *ed* Agnès Varda, Patricia Mazuy. *m* Joanna Bruzdowicz. *cast* Sandrine Bonnaire, Macha Méril, Yolande Moreau, Stéphane Freiss, Marthe Jarnias, Joël Fosse.

● Varda's lyrical requiem to Mona, a teenage tramp discovered dead from exposure, shows (in flashback) her last few months and her effect on people she met briefly and variously: a smart middle class professor (Méril) mesmerised and repelled by the fierce young woman, peasant drudges in whom she inspires romantic dreams of freedom, a dour ageing *soixante-huitard*, now the most conventional of them all. Varda boldly explains nothing about Mona, who simply holds up an unflattering mirror to others' follies, prejudices, and fears. Spare, poetic images of the midwinter Midi are offset by the warmth and vigour of the well-chosen, largely non-professional cast, with a formidable central performance from Sandrine Bonnaire. SJo

Vagabonding Images

(1999, Ger, 48 min, col & b/w)
d/p/ph/ed Nicolas Humbert, Simone Fürbringer.

● A dire experimental film in which, purportedly, a seemingly random collage of lyrical and treated images (kites, cows, kids, pregnant women) gradually coalesces into a twin narrative outlining the history of cinema and the story of a couple. GA

Vaghe Stelle dell'Orsa (Of a Thousand Delights/Sandra)

(1965, It, 100 min, b/w)
d Luchino Visconti. *p* Franco Cristaldi. *sc* Suso Cecchi D'Amico, Luchino Visconti, Enrico Medioli. *ph* Armando Nannuzzi. *ed* Mario Serandrei. *ad* Mario Garbuglia. *m* César Franck. *cast* Claudia Cardinale, Jean Sorel, Michael Craig, Marie Bell, Renzo Ricci.

● Visconti's retelling of the Electra story starts with Sandra/Electra (Cardinale) returning to her ancestral home in Italy – and reviving an intimate involvement with her brother (Sorel) which troubles her naive American husband (Craig) – on the eve of an official ceremony commemorating the death of her Jewish father in a Nazi concentration camp. As ever with Visconti, he is ambivalently drawn to the decadent society he is ostensibly criticising; and Armando Nannuzzi's camera lovingly caresses the creaking old mansion, set in a landscape of crumbling ruins, where the incestuous siblings determine to wreak revenge on the mother (Bell) and stepfather (Ricci) who supposedly denounced their father. Something like a Verdi opera without the music, the result may not quite achieve tragedy, but it *looks* marvellous. The title, culled from a poem by Leopardi, has been better rendered as 'Twinkling Stars of the Bear'. TM

Valdez Horses, The

see Valdez il Mezzosangue

Valdez il Mezzosangue (Chino/The Valdez Horses/ Valdez the Halfbreed)

(1973, It/Sp/Fr, 97 min)
d John Sturges. *p* Duilio Coletti. *sc* Dino Maiuri, Massimo De Rita, Clair Huffaker. *ph* Armando Nannuzzi. *ed* Vanio Amici, Peter Zinner. *ad* Mario Garbuglia. *m* Guido De Angelis, Maurizio De Angelis. *cast* Charles Bronson, Jill Ireland, Vincent Van Patten, Marcel Bozzuffi, Melissa Chimenti, Fausto Tozzi, Ettore Manni.

● Bronson suffers from galloping symbolism as Valdez, a wild horse-taming Mexican halfbreed representing different things to different people. Overall, he is the mustang, caught in a wild West which is being tamed and fenced in by white settlers. To Jamie, a young white boy, he is manhood, tough and tender. To the white English lady (Ireland), he is mustang again. And to her brother, he is contaminating dirty devilry. The wild and the tame correlate with the old and the new, against the backdrop of a magnificent herd of wild horses, led by a superb stud. Despite a few dodgy moments when one really fears for Valdez' co-optability by Ireland's well-kept fragility, the film maintains its contradictory stance right through to a bitter-sweet ending. Valdez leaves, sans wife, sans house, but on his own terms, and after ensuring that if he can't tame the wild horses no one else will. MV

Valdez Is Coming

(1970, US, 90 min)
d Edwin Sherin. *p* Ira Steiner. *sc* Roland Kibbee, David Rayfiel. *ph* Gabor Pogany. *ed* James T Heckert. *ad* José Maria Tapiador. *m* Charles Gross. *cast* Burt Lancaster, Susan Clark, Jon Cypher, Barton Heyman, Richard Jordan, Frank Silvera, Hector Elizondo, Phil Brown.

● A fairly impressive Western adapted from Elmore Leonard's novel, with Lancaster as the Mexican Valdez, working part-time as a shotgun guard for a powerful rancher (Cypher) in the South West, who is forced to kill a negro in self-defence while on the rancher's business. Mindful of his status as a local constable, he demands compensation for the dead man's widow; and when this is refused, aware that Cypher was up to no good in the first place, he declares a private war. It's a little cramped, but Sherin's background as a Broadway director (this was his first movie) serves him well in his lucid delineation of the characters, while Lancaster brings a subtle ambiguity to his central role as the outsider-idealist fighting against unfeeling prejudice and materialism. GA

Valdez the Halfbreed

see Valdez il Mezzosangue

Vale Abraão

see Abraham Valley

Valentine

(2000, US/Aust, 96 min)
d Jamie Blanks. *p* Dylan Sellers. *sc* Donna Powers, Wayne Powers, Gretchen J Berg, Aaron Harberts. *ph* Rick Bota. *ed* Steve Mirkovich. *pd* Stephen Geaghan. *m* Ron Davis. *cast* David Boreanaz, Denise Richards, Marley Shelton, Katherine Heigl, Jessica Capshaw, Jessica Cauffiel, Johnny Whitworth.

● Back in 1988, five adolescent girlfriends were mean to class geek Jeremy Melton at the middle-school Valentine's Day dance. Twelve years later, the girls are in their mid-20s and have forgotten all about little Jeremy's abject humiliation. Until Shelly is brutally murdered, and the others start getting nasty valentines from someone who signs himself 'JM'. The culprit may be obvious, but 12 years is a long time – with a new name, Jeremy could be almost anyone. Cue spooky music, grotesquely inventive murder scenes and, of course, the running and screaming. Director Blanks made his debut with the derivative *Urban Legend* and apparently plans to continue strip-mining slasher-movie clichés until audiences wise up. MMc

Valentino

(1977, GB, 127 min)
d Ken Russell. *p* Robert Chartoff, Irwin Winkler. *sc* Ken Russell, Mardik Martin. *ph* Peter Suschitzky. *ed* Stuart Baird. *ad* Philip Harrison. *m* Ferde Grofé, Stanley Black. *cast* Rudolf Nureyev, Leslie Caron, Michelle Phillips, Carol Kane, Felicity Kendal, Seymour Cassel, Peter Vaughan, Huntz Hall, Alfred Marks, Anton Diffring.

● Structured as a series of flashbacks from Valentino's funeral to his early years in America, the first hour or so of this biopic is Russell's sanest and most controlled work in several years, despite its hollow cynicism. About halfway through, though, the movie degenerates into a series of typical Russell hyperboles. There is also a shift in tone from comedy to pathos, resulting in a dismal drop in entertainment value. Nureyev (in his debut) dances agreeably often, but his acting is hopelessly under-directed. TR

Valerie and Her Week of Wonders (Valerie a Tyden Divu)

(1970, Czech, 77 min)
d Jaromil Jires. *sc* Jaromil Jires, Ester Krumbachová. *ph* Jan Curik. *ed* Josef Valusiak. *ad* Jan Oliva. *m* Jan Klusák. *cast* Jaroslava Schallerová, Helena Anyzková, Petr Kopriva, Jiri Prymek, Jan Kluzák.

● Shot in the lyrical *Elvira Madigan* mode, this celebrates the 'first stirrings of adolescence' of a beautiful young girl in a vaguely-defined Transylvanian townscape sometime in the last century. A student of folklore and mythology could perhaps detect a logical thread in the continuous sequence of vampires, devils, black magic, ritual and dance that the film presents, but for most people it will be a simpler and undemanding pleasure to sit back and be agreeably surprised as the images unfold. There is no clearly-defined story; the film's logic is that of the subconscious, its images those of the Gothic fairytale and the psychiatrist's couch, and its overall effect is stunning. JC

Valiant Ones, The (Zhonglie Tu)

(1974, HK, 106 min)
d/p/sc King Hu. *ph* Chen Qingqu. *ed/pd* King Hu. *cast* Roy Chiao, Pai Ying, Hsu Feng, Zhao Lei, Tu Guangqi, Liu Jiang.

●No surprise that a movie which reunites the director/writer and three stars of *A Touch of Zen* should offer hitherto untasted pleasures. *The Valiant Ones* delivers as an exemplary piece of Ming Dynasty Chinese historiography, and at the same time as a daringly innovative action adventure, quite different in tone and visual style from the pyrotechnics of *A Touch of Zen*. An enfeebled emperor appoints a loyal official to tackle the problem of Sino-Japanese pirate bands who are pillaging the south coast of China; the official assembles a team of peasants and intellectuals, and plans a war of strategies, not confrontations. Plot developments, however, occur between scenes rather than in them. The film dreams a series of martial set pieces, with increasingly abstract action once again derived from the Peking Opera tradition. The glittering images include a chess game that suddenly becomes a battle plan, a silent woman with heightened sight and hearing, and a rumbustious zen archer. TR

Vallée, La (The Valley Obscured by Clouds)

(1972, Fr, 114 min)
d/p/sc Barbet Schroeder. *ph* Nestor Almendros. *ed* Denise de Casablanca. *m* Pink Floyd. *cast* Jean-Pierre Kalfon, Bulle Ogier, Michael Gothard, Valérie Lagrange, Jérôme Beauvarlet, Monique Giraudy.

●Journey to the Centre of a Cliché. Assorted Anglo-French hippies set off in search of a 'lost' valley in uncharted New Guinea, accompanied by the spaciest Pink Floyd music, and expose assorted bourgeois neuroses en route. Nestor Almendros' landscape photography is succulent. TR

Valley, The (Volgy)

(1969, Hun, 76 min, b/w)
d Tamás Rényi. *sc* Gyula Hernadi. *ph* Otto Forgacs. *ed* Sandor Boroknay. *ad* Béla Zeichan. *m* András Mihaly. *cast* Gábor Koncz, István Avar, Tibor Molnár, György Bardi, János Koltai.

●An arresting, ambitious anti-war drama, shot in widescreen and stunning black-and-white, about a group of army deserters (from an unspecified conflict) who seek refuge in a remote village populated entirely by women and girls (their menfolk are presumably in war service). The women are persuaded to let them stay, an act that carries a severe penalty... The film is as interested in sexual politics and the survival of traditional (and repressive) social forms as it is in its overall pacifist thrust, and sets up a series of remarkable tableaux (the envious, hardened faces of the black-clad elders) and formal, almost ritualist, set pieces (a sexually frenzied dance between one of the deserters and the virgin white-dressed girls, for instance). There is a pained, poetic quality to the film and its imagery that produces a strong pull on the imagination, but the (deliberate) omission of specific references (what is the film-maker saying, if anything, about the Hungary of 1969?) leads to a slightly disconcerting obscurity. WH

Valley of Abraham

see Abraham Valley

Valley Obscured by Clouds, The

see Vallée, La

Valley of Gwangi, The

(1968, US, 95 min)
d James O'Connolly. *p* Charles H Schneer. *sc* William E Bast. *ph* Erwin Hillier. *ed* Henry Richardson. *ad* Gil Parrondo. *m* Jerome Moross. *cast* James Franciscus, Gila Golan, Richard Carlson, Laurence Naismith, Freda Jackson, Gustavo Rojo.

●A Charles Schneer/Ray Harryhausen fantasy for Dynamation special effects fans only: a reworking of the *King Kong* structure that has turn-of-the-century Wild West show boss Franciscus venturing into Mexico's Forbidden Valley in search of prehistoric specimens. A formula writing credit for William Bast, one of the very few screenwriters to have been characterised on screen: by Michael Brandon in the telemovie *James Dean*, which tracked the friendship between the actor and Bast from UCLA to Dean's death. PT

Valley of Song (aka Men Are Children Twice)

(1953, GB, 74 min, b/w)
d Gilbert Gunn. *p* Vaughan N Dean. *sc* Phil Park, Cliff Gordon. *ph* Lionel Banes. *ed* Richard Best. *ad* Robert Jones. *m* Robert Gill. *cast* Mervyn Johns, Clifford Evans, Maureen Swanson, John Fraser, Rachel Thomas, Rachel Roberts, Kenneth Williams, Alun Owen.

●Who will sing the contralto role in *The Messiah*? Two families, the Davies and the Lloyds, fall to feuding in this small-town Welsh comedy based on Cliff Gordon's successful radio play *Choir Practice*. Sub-Ealing whimsy memorable for Rachel Roberts' debut as gossip Bessie the Milk. GM

Valley of the Dolls

(1967, US, 123 min)
d Mark Robson. *p* David Weisbart. *sc* Helen Deutsch, Dorothy Kingsley. *ph* William H Daniels. *ed* Dorothy Spencer. *ad* Jack Martin Smith. *songs* André Previn, Dory Previn. *cast* Barbara Parkins, Patty Duke, Paul Burke, Sharon Tate, Susan Hayward, Tony Scotti, Martin Milner, Charles Drake, Alex Davion, Lee Grant.

●Jacqueline Susann's 'exposé' of Hollywood gets the cliché-ridden treatment it deserves from Robson. Parkins, Tate, Duke and Hayward are the actresses whose career vicissitudes take us on the round tour of drink, drugs, sex, disillusion, infidelity, and clawing up to the top or sliding down to the bottom. That said, the film is regarded in some quarters as a marvellous piece of camp. The songs, curiously, are by André and Dory Previn. CPe

Valmont

(1989, Fr/GB, 137 min)
d Milos Forman. *p* Paul Rassam, Michael Hausman. *sc* Jean-Claude Carriere. *ph* Miroslav Ondricek. *ed* Alan Heim, Nena Danevic. *pd* Pierre Guffroy. *m* Christopher Palmer. *cast* Colin Firth, Annette Bening, Meg Tilly, Fairuza Balk, Sian Phillips, Jeffrey Jones, Henry Thomas, Fabia Drake, TP McKenna, Ian McNeice.

●Comparisons may be odious, but here they are unavoidable. *Valmont* and Stephen Frears' *Dangerous Liaisons* were both based on the same 18th century French novel, and shot at the same time; but the latter's phenomenal success quite eclipsed Forman's more lavish effort, and its British release was held back. The basic story is the same: the Marquise de Merteuil and the Vicomte de Valmont spin an intricate web of deception, using sex as a weapon and destroying lives for fun. But the claustrophobic interiors of *Dangerous Liaisons* are here replaced with horseback rides and landscaped gardens, beautifully shot by Miroslav Ondricek; and where the acid cynicism of Glenn Close and John Malkovich provided a clash of titans, *Valmont* gives us, in the youthful enthusiasm of Bening (too naive) and Firth (too nice), little more than a childish spat. It's a warm, energetic, humorous film, with some excellent ensemble playing; but the cruelty and psychological complexity are lost, and the ensuing tragedy has little resonance. DW

Valseuses, Les (Going Places/Making It)

(1974, Fr, 118 min)
d Bertrand Blier. *p* Paul Claudon. *sc* Bertrand Blier, Philippe Dumarçay. *ph* Bruno Nuytten. *ed* Kénout Peltier. *ad* Jean-Jacques Caziot. *m* Stéphane Grappelli. *cast* Gérard Depardieu, Patrick Dewaere, Miou-Miou, Jeanne Moreau, Jacques Chailleux, Michel Peurelon, Brigitte Fossey, Isabelle Huppert.

●A huge hit in France, about two youths waving a finger at society. Their pursuits include car theft, robbery, three-way sex, and general impulsive offensiveness, while their development is limited to the degree of selectivity they start showing towards their compulsive fucking. Forsaking a girl who can't have an orgasm, they cultivate an older woman just out of prison, on the assumption that she must be dying for it (which she is, literally). With a couple of deaths sending them on the run, their rambling delinquency takes on rather more romantic fugitive connotations. The physical robustness and frankness prevails (the film deliberately evokes the sounds and smells of sex), but as the characters develop into something approaching human beings, much of the bite is lost. It ends relatively tame: an unfocused comedy whose sense of the outlandish extends little further than screwing on the back seat of a Rolls. A lot of good points, though. CPe

Value for Money

(1955, GB, 93 min)
d Ken Annakin. *p* Sergei Nolbandov. *sc* RF Delderfield, William Fairchild. *ph* Geoffrey Unsworth. *ed* Geoffrey Foot. *ad* Alex Vetchinsky. *m* Malcolm Arnold. *cast* John Gregson, Diana Dors, Susan Stephen, Derek Farr, Ernest Thesiger, Joan Hickson, Donald Pleasence, Leslie Phillips.

●Despite inheriting his old man's millions, rag magnate Gregson still counts every penny, so much so that fiancée Stephen turns down his marriage proposal, unable to face a life of drudgery as his replacement housekeeper. Rejection leaves the moneybags skinflint to drag his sorrows down to London, where Cup Final night throws him together with gold-digging chorus gal Ruthine West (Dors) who knows a good thing when she sees it. Cliché piles on cliché in this moderate '50s comedy spun out from a novel by Derrick Boothroyd. TJ

Vamos a Matar, Compañeros!

see Compañeros

Vamp

(1986, US, 94 min)
d Richard Wenk. *p* Donald P Borchers. *sc* Richard Wenk. *ph* Elliot Davis. *ed* Marc Grossman. *pd* Alan Roderick-Jones. *m* Jonathan Elias. *cast* Chris Makepeace, Sandy Baron, Robert Rusler, Dedee Pfeiffer, Gedde Watanabe, Grace Jones, Billy Drago.

●Want a stripper for your frat party? Of course you do, so make your way to the After Dark Club, where Katrina and her girls offer a novel blood transfusion service on the side. Blink and you'll miss Grace Jones, as menacing as they come. (Fans of her legendary sweet nature should head straight for the out-takes option on the DVD.) Using an approach to a meagre budget that Lewton or Ulmer would have approved, Wenk lays on atmospheric lighting to disguise the cheap sets. Worth watching for the sake of a scene containing a genuine innovation in vampire-staking. DO

Vampira (aka Old Dracula)

(1974, GB, 88 min)
d Clive Donner. *p* Jack H Wiener. *sc* Jeremy Lloyd. *ph* Anthony B Richmond. *ed* Bill Butler. *ad* Philip Harrison. *m* David Whitaker. *cast* David Niven, Teresa Graves, Peter Bayliss, Jennie Linden, Nicky Henson, Linda Hayden, Bernard Bresslaw.

●Clive Donner had been living in limbo since the famous disaster of *Alfred the Great*, but making a movie like *Vampira* is no way to set any man's career to rights. It's a horror spoof with no sense of style and no sense of humour, for which Jeremy Lloyd's infantile script is as much to blame as Donner's slap-happy direction. Count Dracula's beloved Vampira is mistakenly brought back to life black rather than white, and Dracula (Niven) runs amok in a still-swinging London trying to find an antidote – a plotline which provides sufficient excuse for jokes and wheezes that one thought had gone out with *The Munsters*. One consolation is that the movie wasn't called 'Fangs Ain't Wot They Used To Be'. GB

Vampire at Midnight

(1987, US, 93 min)
d Gregory McClatchy. *p* Jason Williams, Tom Friedman. *sc* Dulany Ross Clements. *ph* Daniel Yarussi. *ed* Kaye Davis. *ad* Beau

Peterson. *m* Robert Etoll. *cast* Jason Williams, Gustav Vintas, Lesley Milne, Jeanie Moore, Esther Alise, Ted Hamaguchi, Robert Random.

●Count Drac (Vintas) is unalive and well and living in Beverly Hills. He is a hypnotherapist. As might be expected, there's a lot of necking of one form or another. The barely existent plot is padded out with a sequence of dirty dancing and several pairs of naked breasts. Also, the dumb detective (Williams) gets handcuffed to his bed and raped by a lustful colleague. It's OK, she's a woman. Scares don't come into it, and the general corn-flakiness of the whole enterprise just goes to show that old Terror Teeth was one of the very first cereal killers. MS

Vampire Bat, The

(1933, US, 71 min, b/w)
d Frank R Strayer. *p* Phil Goldstone. *sc* Edward T Lowe. *ph* Ira Morgan. *ed* Otis Garrett. *ad* Daniel Hall. *cast* Lionel Atwill, Melvyn Douglas, Fay Wray, Dwight Frye, Maude Eburne, George E Stone.

●As creaky as an old church door, but with some of the same antique charm, this is a B horror picture shot on the village sets of Universal's *Frankenstein* (1931), and using the interiors from *The Old Dark House* (1932). Bat-loving village idiot Frye is suspected of a series of vampyric murders, but when obsessive doctor Atwill's soon-to-be-married assistant (Wray) stumbles on the truth, she's menaced by the real culprit. New wine in old bottles, but hardly vintage. NF

Vampire Beast Craves Blood, The

see Blood Beast Terror, The

Vampire Circus, The

(1971, GB, 87 min)
d Robert Young. *p* Wilbur Stark. *sc* Jud Kinberg. *ph* Moray Grant. *ed* Peter Musgrave. *ad* Scott MacGregor. *m* David Whitaker. *cast* Adrienne Corri, Laurence Payne, Thorley Walters, John Moulder Brown, Lynne Frederick, Elizabeth Seal.

●The circus of the title is an evocative 19th century troupe which weaves magic spells around a naive woodland village in Serbia. For a while, Young (here making his first feature) manages to use this basic premise to establish a delicate fairy-tale atmosphere, with a genuine sense of strangeness as the circus people gradually take over the imaginative life of the community (isolated from the rest of the world by plague), changing back and forth into animals nightly before their eyes; and he is greatly aided by some unusually restrained performances (from the girls in particular). But sadly the whole fragile effect eventually gives way to formula, and as clichés mount, the fashionably explicit sexuality of the vampires jars badly against the rest of the film. Lines like 'One lust feeds another' can't disguise the awkwardness of the transition from vampirism to sex. DP

Vampire de Dusseldorf, Le

(1964, Fr/It/Sp, 90 min, b/w)
d Robert Hossein. *p* Georges de Beauregard. *sc* Robert Hossein, Claude Desailly, Georges-André Tabet. *ph* Alain Levent. *ed* Marie-Sophie Dubus. *ad* François de Lamothe, Pierre Guffroy. *m* André Hossein. *cast* Robert Hossein, Marie-France Pisier, Roger Dutoit, Paloma Valdès, Tanya Lopert, Danik Patisson.

●The years have been surprisingly kind to this sanitised sketch of compulsive killer Peter Kürten, guillotined in 1930 for nine murders, whose case inspired Fritz Lang's *M* and Ulli Lommel's *Tenderness of the Wolves*. Combining a mincing, stiff-armed walk with a fastidious, courtly manner, Hossein turns Kürten into a cross between a timid Truffaut hero and some bright-eyed, remorseless rodent. The background of political upheaval (the film opens with a mini-documentary on the Weimar Republic) is pseudo-significant: anomalies like Kürten are hardly a product of social conditions. Still, the sullen strikers and cruising Brownshirts all add to the atmosphere of disturbance and hysteria. The quirky tone is sustained by the score – written by the director's father – which like the whole film manages to be simultaneously jaunty and funereal. BBa

Vampire in Brooklyn

(1995, US, 102 min)
d Wes Craven. *p* Eddie Murphy, Mark Lipsky. *sc* Charles Murphy, Michael Lucker, Christopher Parker. *ph* Mark Irwin. *ed* Patrick Lussier. *ad* Gary Diamond, Cynthia Charette. *m* J Peter Robinson. *cast* Eddie Murphy, Angela Bassett, Allen Payne, Kadeem Hardison, John Witherspoon, Zakes Mokae, Joanna Cassidy.

●Introducing classy production values and comedy to the blackvampire cycle that surfaced in the '70s, Murphy plays a modern debonair Nosferatu (as well as adding some unnecessary icing to the cake by impersonating an alcoholic preacher and an Italian hood). Caribbean-born Maximillian sails to New York in search of his unwitting blood sister, troubled cop Rita (Bassett). With the help of reluctant ghoul Julius (Hardison), he tries to seduce her with promises of eternal life and untold riches. Things get complicated when Maximillian falls for his blood relative, and she in turn rejects her shy, sensitive police partner (Payne) in favour of the suave vamp. Murphy's choice of director was shrewd: making good use of his biggest budget to date, Craven brings his knowledge of the genre to bear, allowing time for humour while ensuring that the requisite shocks arrive on cue. Bassett brings a little extra to her role as a woman torn between the calling of her blood and fear for her eternal soul. There's some scary fun to be had here. NF

Vampire Lovers, The

(1970, GB, 91 min)
d Roy Ward Baker. *p* Harry Fine, Michael Style. *sc* Tudor Gates. *ph* Moray Grant. *ed* James Needs. *ad* Scott MacGregor. *m* Harry Robinson. *cast* Ingrid Pitt, Pippa Steele, Madeleine Smith, Peter Cushing, George Cole, Dawn Addams, Douglas Wilmer, Jon Finch, Kate O'Mara, Ferdy Mayne.

●The film which made Ingrid Pitt a major horror movie cult figure (she plays a voracious lesbian vampire). Based on Sheridan Le Fanu's *Carmilla*, it is well mounted and enjoyable, with solid performances: the pre-credits sequence, in particular, has a dreamy beauty. But some of the action is a bit flat; and overall it marks the point at which vampirism in British movies became so overtly erotic that the films virtually ceased to be about anything except sex. Later examples of the strain were to become terribly monotonous. DP

Vampires (aka John Carpenter's Vampires)

(1997, US, 108 min)
d John Carpenter. *p* Sandy King. *sc* Don Jakoby. *ph* Gary B Kibbe. *ed* Edward A Warschilka. *pd* Thomas A Walsh. *m* John Carpenter. *cast* James Woods, Daniel Baldwin, Sheryl Lee, Thomas Ian Griffith, Maximilian Schell, Tim Guinee, Gregory Sierra.

●This throwback vampire Western wastes the talent of James Woods, and revels in mean-spirited gore, gratuitous female nudity and repellent violence against women. Derived from John Steakley's novel *Vampire$*, it pitches Vatican-backed vampire slayer Jack Crow (Woods), his portly sidekick Tony Montoya (Baldwin) and naive young priest Adam Guiteau (Guinee) against Valek (Griffith). The 600-year-old bloodsucker is seeking the legendary Berziers Cross, a religious relic that will allow his nocturnal cohorts to stalk the Earth in broad daylight. Eschewing what Crow characterises as the 'Eurotrash fag' approach to vampire mythology, Carpenter opts for a tough, macho beat-'em-up style. The bloodthirsty creatures get staked, decapitated and torched, the last accomplished by dragging them into the New Mexico sunlight to spontaneously and spectacularly combust. Only one scene, in which Valek and his followers emerge from beneath the desert sand at dawn, hints at the stylish genre film-making with which Carpenter established his reputation. NF

Vampires, Les

(1915, Fr, 440 min approx, b/w)
d/sc Louis Feuillade. *ph* Manichoux. *ad* Garnier. *cast* Musidora, Edouard Mathe, Marcel Levesque, Jean Aymé, Louis Leubas.

●1915: Slaughter at Gallipoli; first use of gas on the Western Front; *Lusitania* sunk. And as diversion, this serial saga (in 10 episodes) of a band of robbers whose principals include Satanas, who keeps a howitzer behind the fireplace and a bomb under his top hat, and Irma Vep, the notorious anagram, to whom Olivier Assayas rendered homage 80 years later. There's a hero (a resolute reporter), but all the interest goes to Irma and Co – their heists, their feuds with a rival gang and with the agents of law and order, all conducted by means of slaughter, gassing and sinking, on a scale and insouciance appropriate to the time. There's a comic strip aspect ('Episode 1: The Severed Head'), a roundelay of disguises, kidnappings, secret codes and acrobatic getaways. And simultaneously there's the poetry of the grey deserted Paris streets, our consciousness that the trenches are only a bus ride away; and the idea of a separate world of mischief and anarchy, situated just beyond the everyday. It's possible to overstate the extent to which all this is a bunch of fun: if shown, as it often is, in one great unnatural marathon, it can be sheer torture. Best viewed on tape. BBa

Vampires in Venice (Nosferatu a Venezia)

(1988, It, 90 min)
d/p/sc Augusto Caminito. *ph* Antonio Nardi. *ed* Claudio Cutry. *ad* Joseph Teichner, Luca Antonucci. *m* Luigi Ceccarelli. *cast* Klaus Kinski, Christopher Plummer, Barbara De Rossi, Yorgo Voyagis, Donald Pleasence, Anne Knecht, Elvire Audray.

●Nosferatu vanished, we're told, from plague-stricken Venice during the Carnival of 1786. Called back to the city by a present-day Transylvanian princess, he compels an old lady to impale herself on a railing, ravishes a young woman in a church and causes a vampire hunter (Plummer) to jump despairingly into a canal. Klaus Kinski's Nosferatu longs wearily for death, but the end will come only when a virgin surrenders to him willingly. The princess obliges. Unpersuasive. JPy

Vampire's Kiss

(1988, US, 103 min)
d Robert Bierman. *p* Barbra Zitwer, Barry Shils. *sc* Joseph Minion. *ph* Stefan Czapsky. *ed* Angus Newton. *pd* Christopher Nowak. *m* Colin Towns. *cast* Nicolas Cage, Maria Conchita Alonso, Jennifer Beals, Elizabeth Ashley, Kasi Lemmons, Bob Lujan, Jessica Lundy.

●Cage gives a manically mannered performance as Peter Loew, a literary agent whose obsession with a missing contract pushes him over the edge. Increasingly alienated, he alternates between harassing his timid secretary (Alonso), clubbing all night, and visiting his shrink (Ashley). One night, in a moment of orgasmic pleasure, the mysterious Rachel (Beals) bites his neck. Obsessed with the idea that he is a vampire's victim, he starts pulling down shades, hunches over in a grotesque parody of Max Schreck's Nosferatu, and – sporting plastic fangs – stalks the dark streets and pulsing discos in search of necks to bite. Cage's excessive acting style has been called neo-expressionist, a term that might also be applied to the moody, burnished colours of Stefan Czapsky's photography, which transforms New York into the Gothic city of Loew's distorted imagination. A viciously funny study of yuppy alienation, scripted by Joseph Minion (who wrote *After Hours*), Bierman's striking first feature leaves one trembling between corrosive laughter, edgy terror, and a residual sadness at Loew's pitiful plight. NF

Vampire Thrills

see Frisson des Vampires, Le

Vampyr

(1932, Ger/Fr, 83 min, b/w)
d Carl Theodor Dreyer. *p* Carol Theodor Dreyer, Nicolas de Gunzburg. *sc* Carl Theodor Dreyer, Christen Jul. *ph* Rudolph Maté. *ed* Tonka Taldy. *ad* Hermann Warm, Hans Bittman, Cesare Silvagni. *m* Wolfgang Zeller. *cast* Julian West [Nicolas de Gunzburg], Henriette Gérard, Jan Hieronimko, Maurice Schutz, Sybille Schmitz, Rena Mandel.

●Based on Sheridan Le Fanu's novel *In a Glass Darkly* and shot in France using real locations, *Vampyr* is one of the first psychological horror films. Helped by a dream-like logic, the film takes its main character on a voyage through light and darkness to a point where he can imagine his own burial (disturbingly shot from a subjective point of view). With the help of Rudolph Maté's luminous photography, Dreyer creates a film of great beauty. Often the close-ups are particularly haunting, but the main achievement is the correctness of each shot, and their relationship to each other; notably, in the climactic juxtapositions of the trapped doctor being buried alive in the mill, and of the young couple in a boat, inching their way to safety through the fog. CPe

Van, The

(1996, Ire/GB, 100 min)
d Stephen Frears. *p* Lynda Myles. *sc* Roddy Doyle. *ph* Oliver Stapleton. *ed* Mick Audsley. *pd* Mark Geraghty. *m* Eric Clapton, Richard Hartley. *cast* Colm Meaney, Donal O'Kelly, Ger Ryan, Caroline Rothwell, Neili Conroy, Ruaidhri Conroy, Jack Lynch.

●In the winter of '89, Bimbo (O'Kelly), a baker from Dublin's Barrytown, is made redundant, but the last thing he wants is to loaf all day in a pub like his jobless mates. The mobile chip-and-burger business beckons. By the spring he and Larry (Meaney) have gone into partnership, buying a filthy run-down van in the hope of cashing in on the euphoria igniting Ireland during the 1990 World Cup. It's tough work, but both men's families chip in. Indeed, Larry's so keen to keep his own brood in work that Bimbo sometimes feels the need to remind him who's boss. The final film adaptation of Roddy Doyle's Barrytown trilogy is a jauntily enjoyable comedy about unemployment. Occasionally the direction is too determinedly feel-good, but as the film proceeds and the men's partnership becomes increasingly strained, the jokes are underpinned by something more substantial: it gradually becomes clear that Larry's larky ways are partly symptomatic of irresponsibility, partly a defence against despondency; and that friendship depends on some sort of equality. Fun, on the whole. GA

Vanessa

(1976, WGer, 91 min)
d Hubert Frank. *sc* Joos de Ridder. *ph* Franz X Lederle. *ed* Eva Zeyn, Mimi Werkmann. *ad* Klaus Haase. *m* Gerhard Heinz. *cast* Olivia Pascal, Anton Diffring, Günter Clemens, Uschi Zech, Eva Eden.

●The virginal Vanessa – 'sexual plaything of lewd lechers', as the expensive bilingual publicity handout cheerfully announces – is in fact a putty-faced actress (an animated centrefold) whisked to Hong Kong for the usual wearisome round of softcore shenanigans. The fun includes a bout of love-making in a barn beneath a cascade of grain, and in conclusion, the devilish Diffring flaying our heroine with an understandably half-hearted lack of conviction. JPy

Van Gogh

(1991, Fr, 159 min)
d Maurice Pialat. *p* Daoneil Toscan Du Plantier. *sc* Maurice Pialat. *ph* Gilles Henry, Emmanuel Machuel. *ed* Yann Dedet, Nathalie Hubert. *m* Léo Delibes. *cast* Jacques Dutronc, Alexandra London, Bernard Le Coq, Gérard Sety, Corinne Bourdon, Elsa Zylberstein, Leslie Azoulai, Jacques Vidal.

●This stunningly photographed and skilfully acted film uses an accretion of naturalistic detail to present an emotionally restrained but utterly compelling account of the last three months of Van Gogh's life. Living in Auvers-sur-Oise with his sensitive and knowledgeable patron Gachet (Sety), Van Gogh (Dutronc) works quietly and steadily, meanwhile flirting with Gachet's precocious daughter Marguerite (London). However, his ill health, a brief return to the debauchery of brothels and drink, and his irrational resentment of his brother Theo's failure to sell his work, provoke erratic swings from brooding introspection to frustrated anger. Since Pialat has no desire to canonise the artist, there is no attempt to trace the origins and development of his 'creative genius'; nor, avoiding the hazards of biopic cliché, does he seek to illuminate these dark corners of his subject's troubled soul. In the leading role, Dutronc has exactly the right quality of physical frailty and stooped sadness to complement Pialat's beautiful, poignant images. NF

Vanilla Sky

(2001, US, 136 min)
d Cameron Crowe. *p* Tom Cruise, Paula Wagner, Cameron Crowe. *sc* Cameron Crowe. *ph* John Toll. *ed* Joe Hutshing, Mark Livolsi. *pd* Catherine Hardwicke. *m* Nancy Wilson. *cast* Tom Cruise, Penélope Cruz, Kurt Russell, Jason Lee, Noah Taylor, Cameron Diaz, Timothy Spall, Tilda Swinton, Michael Shannon, Delaina Mitchell, Shalom Harlow.

●This is a very straight remake of Alejandro Amenábar's Spanish-language *Abre los Ochos* (*Open Your Eyes*). Admittedly, that film stands a second viewing – a provocative post-modern fairytale which kept pulling the rug out from under – but Hollywood inflation does the story no favours. Easy to imagine what attracted Cruise to the role of David, the mega-rich, handsome playboy disfigured by spurned harpy Julie (Diaz, miscast), just as he finds true love in the form of Sofia (Cruz, reprising her soulful muse bit from the original). David finds it hard to readjust, and not just because he's lost his toothy smile. He goes to bed with Sofia and wakes up with Julie – reality ain't what it used to be. Whether this is an example of rampant egoism or a dissection of same, the face mask sure fits. But writer/director Crowe is a bland film-maker who shows no affinity for schlock and never threatens to make us care. There are no surprises here, and worse, no suspense. Spinning out the earnest and unenlightening psychiatric sessions, Crowe misses the delirium of Amenábar's climax. If *Open Your Eyes* could be filed under 'fantasy horror', *Vanilla Sky* comes closer to 'pretentious psychodrama'. TCh

Vanishing, The

(1993, US, 110 min)
d George Sluizer. *p* Larry Brezner, Paul Schiff. *sc* Todd Graff. *ph* Peter Suschitzky. *ed* Bruce Green. *pd* Jeannine C Oppewall. *m* Jerry Goldsmith. *cast* Jeff Bridges, Kiefer Sutherland, Nancy Travis, Sandra Bullock, Lisa Eichhorn, Park Overall.

●In directing this misjudged, compromised Hollywood remake of his Dutch-French thriller, Sluizer has held down his waywardly inspired child while studio and scriptwriter Todd Graff have lobotomised it with a sharp, cruel scalpel. Worse, by replacing cerebral dread with knee-jerk reaction, this depressing travesty taints forever our memory of the devastating original. Shifting emphasis from Sutherland's impotent obsession with his missing girlfriend to abductor Bridges' coldly calculating psychopathology, the film-makers pander to the lowest common denominator – beefing up Bridges' misconceived role as the villain and transforming Sutherland into an active, albeit perversely motivated hero. NF

Vanishing, The (Spoorloos)

(1988, Neth/Fr, 106 min)
d George Sluizer. *p* Anne Lordon, George Sluizer. *sc* Tim Krabbé. *ph* Toni Kuhn. *ed* George Sluizer, Lin Friedman. *ad* Santiago Isidro Pin, Cor Spijk. *cast* Bernard-Pierre Donnadieu, Gene Bervoets, Johanna Ter Stegge, Gwen Eckhaus, Bernadette Le Saché.

●An unforgettably chilling psychodrama which twists the slenderest of plots into a hellish exploration of human potential. On a driving holiday in France, a young Dutch couple, Saskia and Rex (Ter Steege and Bervoets), stop at a service station to refuel; as Rex waits, Saskia walks to a nearby toilet, and vanishes without trace. Three years later, an embittered Rex finds himself drawn into a nightmarish relationship with Saskia's awesomely mundane abductor, Raymond Lemorne (Donnadieu), who via taunting postcards promises to reveal the fate of his lost love. Consumed by his desire for knowledge, Rex resolves to confront his nemesis and end the Nietzschean conflict of wills in which he is embroiled...Adapted from Tim Krabbé's novel *The Golden Egg*, this is a beautifully understated study of obsession that investigates the edges of rationality and the destructive capacity of idealistic devotion. at the heart of its icy spell is Donnadieu's utterly plausible evocation of everyday madness, a resolutely banal picture of evil. Sluizer's direction is seamless throughout, effortlessly juggling domesticity and damnation as it ploughs inexorably towards an appaling *dénouement*. MK

Vanishing Corporal, The

see Caporal Epinglé, Le

Vanishing Point

(1971, GB, 107 min)
d Richard Sarafian. *p* Norman Spencer. *sc* Guillermo Cain. *ph* John A Alonzo. *ed* Stefan Arnsten. *pd* Glen Daniels, Jerry Wunderlich. *m* Jimmy Brown. *cast* Barry Newman, Cleavon Little, Dean Jagger, Victoria Medlin, Paul Koslo, Bob Donner, Karl Swenson, Severn Darden.

●Having just driven 1,500 miles non-stop from California to Colorado, Sarafian's sullenly uncommunicative anti-hero pauses long enough to grab a supply of bennies, accept a bet that he won't make it back in 15 hours, and zooms off again. It's a marvellous idea: a strange, obsessive odyssey by a man driven like the lemmings by an inexplicable need to keep on going. Then the script starts explaining in embarrassing memory flashes, the echoes of *Easy Rider* multiply, bits of mysticism and a blind black DJ called Super-Soul are injected, and the woodenness of both direction and Newman's performance becomes increasingly apparent. Marvellously shot on location by John A Alonzo, though. TM

Vanya on 42nd Street

(1994, US, 120 min)
d Louis Malle. *p* Fred Berner. *sc* David Mamet. *ph* Declan Quinn. *ed* Nancy Baker. *pd* Eugene Lee. *m* Joshua Redman. *cast* Wallace Shawn, Julianne Moore, André Gregory, George Gaynes, Brooke Smith, Larry Pine, Phoebe Brand, Lynn Cohen, Jerry Mayer, Madhur Jaffrey.

●A select audience gathers for André Gregory's workshop production of *Uncle Vanya* in Broadway's crumbling New Amsterdam theatre. The staging is sparse – a table, a few chairs – and Malle's direction is as discreetly self-effacing as Gregory's, shifting from *cinéma vérité* in the establishing sequence to a more intimate style as the drama casts its spell (intervals are respected with the minimum of fuss). Thus we can concentrate on David Mamet's fluent, sensitive adaptation and some (unexpectedly) enthralling performances: Shawn as the wretched, resentful Vanya; Gaynes – a long way from the 'Police Academy' – as the Professor; and Julianne Moore as his lovely, long-suffering wife Yelena. Moore is simply outstanding, composed and modulated, shouldering her companions' pain with a compassion and forbearance that's also a kind of defeat. Chekhov's astonishingly modern *fin de siècle* concerns are expressed with a rare and vivid clarity: ennui, environment, old age, the difficulty of change, and the disappointments of love. There's more power here than in all the multi-million dollar fireworks of Hollywood. TCh

Varieté (Variety/Vaudeville)

(1925, Ger, 9,331 ft, b/w)
d EA Dupont. *p* Erich Pommer. *sc* EA Dupont, Leo Birinski. *ph* Karl Freund. *ad* Oscar Friedrich Werndorff. *m* Ernö Rapée. *cast* Emil Jannings, Lya de Putti, Warwick Ward, Mady Delschaft, Georg John, Kurt Gerron.

●Dupont's most celebrated film (it was one of the most famous films in the world in 1925) unfolds in a long series of flashbacks from a prison straight out of a Van Gogh painting: prisoner No 28 (Jannings, with his back to the camera more often than not) is granted remission, and in return tells the story of his crime to the governor. The story itself is a banal triangle melodrama: a trapeze duo in the Berlin music-hall becomes a trio, and the lady switches gentlemen, driving the cuckold to murder his rival. The treatment, though, is something else again. Impressionistic lighting, lingering expressionist imagery, and giddily mobile camerawork are all pushed to unprecedented extremes, like Murnau on speed. Hard to take it too seriously, but the bravura style and Lya de Putti's coquettish performance remain as impressive as ever. TR

Varietes

(1985, Greece, 100 min)
d Nikos Panayotopoulos. *p* Marianna Spanoudaki. *sc* Nikos Panayotopoulos. *ph* Aris Stavrou. *ed* Kostas Iordanidis. *ad* Dionysus Fotopoulos. *m* Frederic Chopin. *cast* Minis Chrysomallis, Vangelis Germanos, Lefteris Yoyiatzis, Nikitas Tsakiroglou, Olia Lazaridou, Despina Geroulanou.

●Evening on a reservoir road and a film director exchanges his viewfinder for the gun of a passing motorcycle cop . He then proceeds to shoot himself – or so it seems – in a kaleidoscope of collapsing geography and personality. Starting from the point of a fatally tarnished relationship, the director's life melds with the prerogatives of film as he seeks adventure over thought. This is a manifesto for cinema and life. Employing his regular motifs – the road, travel, walls, isolation and brief, urgent unions – to illuminate the images as much as whatever narrative or psychology they advance, Panayotopoulos' film is complex but rewarding. Its closing image of the director colouring snow like he wants to fill the empty frame is a poignant illustration of the imperatives of creativity. GE

Variety

(1983, US, 100 min)
d Bette Gordon. *p* Renee Shafansky. *sc* Kathy Acker. *ph* Tom DiCillo, John Foster. *ed* Ila von Hasperg. *m* John Lurie. *cast* Sandy McLeod, Luis Guzman, Will Patton, Nan Goldin, Richard Davidson.

●Written by blood-and-guts flavour of the month Kathy Acker, and directed by New York feminist film-maker Gordon, this boldly goes into feminine response to pornography – and the results are by no means predictable. Christine (McLeod) takes a job as a ticket vendor at a porn cinema; she finds herself slowly drawn towards both the ambience depicted on the screen and to one of the older clients, Louis (Davidson), a suave shark with apparent Mafia connections. She follows him around, eavesdropping on his world of very masculine power and money, while simultaneously indulging her curiosity in the equally voyeuristic roles played out in sex shops and movie houses. The elision of the two worlds is a good device, and well handled, for is not every sexual adventure also a form of detection? The film is not prescriptive in its designs, nor is it remotely prurient. A brave foray across a minefield. CPea

Variety Lights

see Luci del Varietà

Varsity Blues

(1998, US, 105 min)
d Brian Robbins. *p* Tova Laiter, Mike Tollin, Brian Robbins. *sc* W Peter Iliff. *ph* Charles Cohen. *ed* Ned Bastille. *pd* Jaymes Hinkle. *m* Mark Isham. *cast* James Van Der Beek, Jon Voight, Paul Walker, Ron Lester, Scott Caan, Amy Smart, Thomas F Duffy.

●This hackneyed teen sports movie marks hardly any advance on *All The Right Moves*. A nonconformist high school quarterback Mox (Van Der Beek) hopes for a scholarship to escape the confines of his Texas locality. In the meantime he leads a pitch mutiny against the team's tyrannical coach Kilmer (Voight). The characters are personable, as stereotypes go, and the film displays some scepticism about small town America's sporting meritocracy – it turns out everyone down to the head cheerleader is looking for an escape, in their different ways – although the matter found richer expression in two minutes' worth of Richard Linklater's *Dazed and Confused*. NB

Va Savoir (Who Knows?)

(2001, Fr/It/Ger 154 min)
d Jacques Rivette. *p* Martine Marignac. *sc* Pascal Bonitzer, Christine Laurent, Jacques Rivette. *ph* William Lubtchansky. *ed* Nicole Lubtchansky. *pd* Manu de Chauvigny. *cast* Jeanne Balibar, Sergio Castellitto, Marianne Basler, Jacques Bonnaffé, Hélène de Fougerolles, Bruno Todeschini.

●Rivette revisits familiar ground with this leisurely tale of romantic intrigue and possibly dark deeds among members of a theatrical troupe and their various acquaintances, but while it certainly lacks the edge of *Paris Nous Appartient*, it nevertheless exerts immense charm. Balibar is the Parisian diva returning after three years in Italy in a production of Pirandello's *Come tu mi vuoi*; Castellitto is her lover, leading man and manager, jealous that she's in touch with her (now married) ex, seeking out an apocryphal play by Goldoni, and drawn to the daughter of a woman who may have the text. As ever, it's about different kinds and levels of performance and falsehood, and shifts from 'realist' elements to something more fancifully theatrical (a delightful duel – by drinking). Funny, sentimental but ironic, and wondrously assured. GA

Vassa

(1983, USSR, 136 min)
d Gleb Panfilov. *sc* Gleb Panfilov. *ph* Leonid Kalashnikov. *ad* Nikolai Dvigubsky. *m* Vadim Bibergan. *cast* Inna Churikova, Vadim Medvedev, Nikolai Skorobogatov, Valentina Yakunina, Olga Mashnaya, Yana Poplavskaya.

●For the wondrously sour-mouthed Vassa Zheleznova (Churikova), troubles come not in threes but in great swinging clusters. Her husband is accused of child-molesting, her brother is a lush who has got the maid pregnant, one of her daughters is 'wrong in the head', while the other is scampering through puberty towards nymphean alcoholism. Add murder, suicide and hefty dollops of greed, and you have Maxim Gorky's version of *Dynasty* on the Volga, with the ripples extending out to embrace imminent revolution. Set in 1913, this presents a portrait of a society fit for rupture, viewed with sad disgust. Panfilov wisely never forces the pace, letting the richness of the piece come through in a host of finely tailored performances. An unexpected delight. JP

Vatel

(2000, Fr, 117 min)
d Roland Joffé. *p* Alain Goldman, Roland Joffé. *sc* Jeanne Labrune, (English adaptation) Tom Stoppard. *ph* Robert Fraisse. *ed* Noëlle Boisson. *pd* Jean Rabasse. *m* Ennio Morricone. *cast* Gérard Depardieu, Uma Thurman, Tim Roth, Julian Glover, Timothy Spall, Julian Sands, Richard Griffiths, Murray Lachlan Young, Hywel Bennett, Arielle Dombasle.

●Despite a sturdy, occasionally subtle performance from Depardieu, cast (predictably) as the life-loving master of entertainments, burdened by his debt-ridden aristo employer (Glover) with the responsibility of providing food, music, theatre, etc, for the visiting Louis XIV (Sands), this tepid costumer is as much a hollow, purposelessly extravagant spectacle as the court shenanigans it depicts. The plot, such as it is, centres on the triangular romantic/sexual intrigues between principled lady-in-waiting Thurman, salt-of-the-earth Depardieu, and the king's malicious righthand wig Roth. For a movie about food, sensuality and passion, it's strikingly undernourished. GA

Vaudeville

see Varieté

Vault of Horror

(1973, GB, 86 min)
d Roy Ward Baker. *p* Max J Rosenberg, Milton Subotsky. *sc* Milton Subotsky. *ph* Denys Coop. *ed* Oswald Hafenrichter. *ad* Tony Curtis. *m* Douglas Gamley. *cast* Daniel Massey, Anna Massey, Terry-Thomas, Glynis Johns, Curt Jürgens, Dawn Addams, Michael Craig, Edward Judd, Tom Baker, Denholm Elliott.

●Amicus' sixth portmanteau film. Following up *Tales from the Crypt* with another selection from the William Gaines horror comics, it simply slaps down its Grand Guignol climaxes after hopefully buttressing them with dreary slabs of plot and chatter. The result is paralysingly pedestrian, despite the fact that each of the stories harbours an ingeniously ghoulish conceit (like the suburban wife driven to murder, and an impeccably tidy disposal of the corpse, by her house-proud husband's constant nagging about her housekeeping). As tedious as anything is the framing device whereby the five heroes (Massey, Terry-Thomas, Jürgens, Craig and Baker) confide their recurring nightmares in turn after delivery by lift to a no-exit room in the basement of a skyscraper. TM

Veillées d'Armes (The Troubles We've Seen)

(1994, Fr, (First Journey) 74 min, (Second Journey) 135 min)
d Marcel Ophuls. *p* Bertrand Tavernier, Frédéric Bourboulon. *sc* Marcel Ophuls. *ph* Pierre Boffety, Pierre Milon. *ed* Sophie Brunet. *with* Marcel Ophuls, John Burns, John Simpson, Martha Gellhorn, Philippe Noiret.

●The title is significant: Ophuls' Sarajevo documentary is concerned less with the Serbo-Croatian war than with our perception of the conflict, the way journalists filter their experience of the frontline, and how our inaction in the West translates as moral complicity – as Philippe Noiret points out at the beginning of the film, people used to say that if they'd known about the Nazi atrocities, things would have been different; today, we know what's going on in the former Yugoslavia, and it makes no difference. This is a personal, rogue (and often roguish) vision. Ophuls shows us clips from his father's film *De Mayerling à Sarajevo*, about the start of WWI, which was shooting just as WWII broke out. He counterpoints news footage with sequences from *Annie Hall* and *Henry V*, and he reveals elements in the manufacture of 'the truth' no other film-maker would consider – more than anything, this is a film about self-censorship, a condition which is often unconscious and, perhaps, inevitable. Startling, candid, intelligent – and essential viewing. TCh

Velvet Goldmine

(1998, GB, 123 min)
d Todd Haynes. *p* Christine Vachon. *sc* Todd Haynes. *ph* Maryse Alberti. *ed* James Lyons. *pd* Christopher Hobbs. *m* Carter Burwell. *cast* Jonathan Rhys Meyers, Ewan McGregor, Toni Collette, Christian Bale, Eddie Izzard.

●This witty, evocative re-creation of the heady days of glam rock is loosely structured on the lines of a *Citizen Kane*-style flashback narrative, with a journalist (Bale) sent back from New York to Britain to investigate, ten years on, the disappearance of Bowie-like star Brian Slade (Meyers) after an on-stage assassination is revealed to have been a publicity stunt. Partly a *film à clef* which retranslates real-life events and personalities into a dazzling fiction, partly an unsentimental celebration of an era of (potential) pan-sexual liberation (complete with unexpected but fitting tribute to Oscar Wilde), and partly a typically Haynesian study of transgression, identity and the gulf between private and public image, it's superbly shot, edited and performed, and exhilaratingly inventive throughout. GA

Velvet Vampire, The (aka Cemetery Girls/ The Waking Hour)

(1971, US, 80 min)
d Stephanie Rothman. *p* Charles S Swartz. *sc* Maurice Jules, Charles S Swartz, Stephanie Rothman. *ph* Daniel Lacambre. *ed* Stephen Judson, Barry Simon. *ad* Teddi Peterson. *m* Clancy B Grass III, Roger Dollarhide. *cast* Sherry Miles, Michael Blodgett, Celeste Yarnall, Paul Prokop, Gene Shane, Jerry Daniels.

●It's hard to dislike a movie that strives so hard to offend the vampire fan base. No dripping Gothic piles here. The in-your-face and on-your-neck vamp strides through sun-bleached Los Angeles without a care and is defiantly female, as a first reel would-be rapist discovers. Under whichever title, it's a lightweight treatise on voyeurism and domination given a classier look, courtesy Lacambre, than the run of New World releases, though characteristically low-rent in all other departments. DO

Vendetta

(1950, US, 84 min, b/w)
d Mel Ferrer. *p* Howard Hughes. *sc* WR Burnett. *ph* Franz Planer, Alfred Gilks. *ed* Stuart Gilmore. *ad* Robert Usher. *m* Roy Webb. *cast* Faith Domergue, George Dolenz, Hillary Brooke, Nigel Bruce, Joseph Calleia, Hugo Haas, Donald Buka.

●A typical Howard Hughes folly, begun in 1946, in which his aim of making Faith Domergue as mean, moody and magnificent as Jane Russell ran him through an intriguing palette of directors (Max Ophüls, Preston Sturges, Stuart Heisler, Hughes himself) before Ferrer made whatever grade he was after. It also led to a betrayal of Prosper Mérimée's source novella *Colomba*, a coolly ironic account of a Corsican blood feud which here becomes imbued with heavy-breathing romanticism. Overblown and somewhat turgid, the film is quite striking visually, with Franz Planer's moody camerawork making the most of the rocks, gaunt trees and desolate moorlands that stand in for the Corsican exteriors. TM

Vengeance (Joko, Invoca Dio...e Muori)

(1968, It/WGer, 100 min)
d Anthony Dawson. *sc* Anthony M Dawson, Renato Savino. *ph* Riccardo Pallottini. *ed* Otello Colangeli. *m* Carlo Savina. *cast* Richard Harrison, Claudio Camaso, Werner Pochat, Paolo Gozlino.
● This spaghetti Western stars Richard Harrison, a more than competent cowboy actor who refused the lead in *A Fistful of Dollars*, and, in fact, suggested that Sergio Leone check out the young guy who played Rowdy Yates in *Rawhide*. We have, however, Anthony Dawson's film to judge what might have been. Harrison is Joko, a half-breed with a lethal grudge against the bandits who betrayed his sidekick (brother? – lover?). The English title says it all. Crude sensibilities are the price of brute force. There's a sterling score by Carlo Savina, a juicy climax in a sulphur mine, and a remarkable opening shot – a God's-eye view of a man scrabbling in the dirt with a noose round each limb and four banditos on horseback straining to be off. You don't see that in many John Ford flicks. TCh

Vengeance, the Demon

see Pumpkinhead

Vengo

(2000, Fr/Sp, 97 min)
d/p Tony Gatlif. *sc* Tony Gatlif, David Trueba. *ph* Thierry Pouget. *ed* Pauline Dairou. *pd* Brigitte Brassart, Denis Mercier. *cast* Antonio Canales, Orestes Villasan Rodriguez, Antonio Perez Dechent, Bobote, Juan Luis Corrientes, Fernando Guerrero Rebollo.
● The cinema's leading chronicler of gypsy life bounces back from the disastrous *Children of the Stork* with an infectiously exuberant film set amid Andalusia's flamenco culture. A clumsy mix of suspense (a lackadaisical plot about the vendettas of two clans) and semi-documentary dance musical, it gets by on authentic observations of Spain's macho, belligerent, proud and vibrant Rom culture and on magnificent music, which embraces Asian and North African fare. GA

Venial Sin (Peccato Veniale)

(1973, It, 97 min)
d Salvatore Samperi. *p* Silvio Clementelli. *sc* Ottavio Jemma, Allesando. *ph* Tonino Delli Colli. *ed* Sergio Montanari. *ad* Ezio Altieri. *m* Fred Bongusto. *cast* Laura Antonelli, Alessandro Momo, Orazio Orlando, Lilla Brignone, Tino Carraro.
● The sin is venial but the film is barely excusable: yet another saga of a boy's sentimental education, softcore in format and with a nasty puritanism beneath a wafer-thin fashionable permissiveness (we are supposed to laugh when father thanks the Lord that his boy is not gay after all). Basically, on a family vacation by the seaside, kid brother (Momo) works out his adolescent pangs through a crush, eventually consummated, on his big sister-in-law (Antonelli). The generally lame and/or slushy performances are not even relieved by the bursts of humour, which are on a par with tenth rate graffiti; the camerawork is ploddingly intimate, with – of course – the climactic misty lens; and the score is spectacularly awful pasta muzak. IB

Venice: Theme and Variations

(1957, US, 28 min)
d/p/sc/ph James Ivory. *ed* Stelios Roccos. *narrator* Alexander Scourby.
● Ivory's first, slightly intoxicated film (part of his MA thesis for the University of Southern California) is a documentary on the history of Venice as revealed through the work of some of the artists who have painted its architecture and citizens (from Gentile Bellini to Saul Steinberg). In *The Europeans*, Ivory cast himself as an austere silent collector eyeing an objet d'art; in *A Room with a View*, Cecil Vyse mounts a chair to take a closer look at a portrait; in *Hullabaloo Over Georgie and Bonnie's Pictures*, Saeed Jaffrey flicks back a sheet of tissue to reveal an erotic Indian miniature for the delectation of Peggy Ashcroft; *Slaves of New York* finds keen young artists frantically painting in New York lofts; and in *Savages*, one of the Mudpeople goes so far as to lick an oil painting to discover, perhaps, if it is real. Thesis writers start here. JPy

Venom

(1971, GB, 91 min)
d Peter Sykes. *p* Michael Pearson, Kenneth F Rowles. *sc* Donald Ford, Derek Ford. *ph* Peter Jessop. *ed* Stephen Collins. *ad* Hayden Pearce. *m* John Simco Harrison. *cast* Simon Brent, Neda Arneric, Derek Newark, Sheila Allen, Gerard Heinz, Gertan Klauber.
● Shelved for nearly five years after completion (reputedly for tax reasons), this was Sykes' feature debut: not – contrary to appearances in an opening sequence involving nude bathing and a mysterious nymph – sexploitation but a spirited horror/adventure movie. The script, about mysterious goings-on in a Bavarian forest (with the hero tangling with a supposed spider goddess, murderous villagers, and evilly-experimenting Nazis) is full of holes; but the action remains tautly visual, and the direction is imaginative enough to gloss over the worst narrative clichés. DP

Venom

(1981, GB, 92 min)
d Piers Haggard. *p* Martin Bregman. *sc* Robert Carrington. *ph* Gilbert Taylor. *ed* Michael Bradsell. *ad* Tony Curtis. *m* Michael Kamen. *cast* Sterling Hayden, Klaus Kinski, Sarah Miles, Oliver Reed, Cornelia Sharpe, Nicol Williamson, Susan George.
● Woefully archaic in its British B-pic reliance on very cheap thrills and very worn dramatic clichés, and without any self-parodic saving grace, *Venom* spells box-office poison. A kidnapped kid, a killer snake loose in the house, sibilant Teuton Kinski and sneering Bulldog Reed hamming villainy against each other, and Nicol Williamson the sorely tried bobby out in the sealed-off London street. Get the picture? There is more (by way of disgressive star turns, that is), but never enough to raise a glimmer of interest or tension in the static rituals of siege cinema. PT

Vent d'Est (Wind from the East)

(1970, It/Fr/WGer, 95 min)
d/p Jean-Luc Godard. *sc* Jean-Luc Godard, Daniel Cohn-Bendit, Sergio Bazzini. *ph* Mario Vulpani. *cast* Gian Maria Volonté, Anne Wiazemsky, Glauber Rocha, Jean-Luc Godard, George Götz.
● Godard's target is representational cinema (Nixon-Paramount/Brezhnev-Mosfilm), and this film is one step in his struggle to create images and sounds that lie outside all ruling hegemonies. It's formulated as a barrage of angry sounds and a trickle of dramatically minimal images, returning constantly to a set of very basic questions: how can you represent oppression without being oppressive? Can you articulate revolutionary ideas without forging a new language to express them? Is any representation of a reactionary society bound to be politically wrong? TR

Vent de la Nuit, Le

(1999, Fr, 95 min)
d Philippe Garrel. *p* Alain Sarde. *sc* Philippe Garrel, Marc Cholodenko, Xavier Beauvois, Arlette Langmann. *ph* Caroline Champetier. *ed* Françoise Collin. *pd* Mathieu Menut, Giacomo Macchi, Gino Diomaiuto, Laurent Baude. *m* John Cale. *cast* Catherine Deneuve, Daniel Duval, Xavier Beauvois, Jacques Lassalle, Daniel Pommereulle, Marc Fauré, Marie Vialle, Laurence Girard, Anita Blond, Juliette Poissonnier.
● Unconscionable pretentious tosh about three upper middleclass French intellectuals, all either talking about or actually working on suicide bids. Deneuve has the least screen time as Beauvois' older, married lover, and has a couple of very intense scenes, but much of the rest consists of non-conversations between the unappealing young man and '60s radical Duval, mostly as they traverse the autoroutes of Europe. Before long, most of the audience will also have considered ending it all. TCh

Vent nous emportera, Le

see Wind Will Carry Us, The

Venus Beauty (Vénus Beauté (Institut))

(1998, Fr, 107 min)
d Tonie Marshall. *p* Gilles Sandoz. *sc* Tonie Marshall. *ph* Gérard de Battista. *ed* Jacques Comets. *ad* Michel Vandestien. *m* Khalil Chahine. *cast* Nathalie Baye, Bulle Ogier, Samuel LeBihan, Jacques Bonnaffé, Mathilde Seigner, Audrey Tautou, Robert Hossein, Edith Scob, Marie Rivière, Clair Denis.
● The beauty parlour of the title offers sanctuary, a window on the world and, perhaps, a somewhat misleading display. Here come women, and men, from various walks, seeking respite and repose, sometimes solace, and a therapeutic lift. Behind the counter, too, the women and girls who work the parlour alternately share and conceal their interior lives – the latter especially in the case of veteran beautician Angèle (Baye), who seems to have resigned from romantic pursuits, negotiating her nocturnal liaisons with business-like dispassion. Plainly, she's ill-disposed for the declaration of helpless love proferred by a perfect stranger, Antoine (LeBihan). A study of relationships in wintertime in the classical French mode, this covers familiar ground to underwhelming effect. NB

Venus in Furs (Venus im Pelz)

(1968, WGer, 87 min)
d Massimo Dallamano. *p* Luggi Waldleitner. *sc* Inge Hilger. *ph* Sergio D'Offizi. *ed* Hans Zeiler. *pd* Alida Cappellini. *m* Gianfranco Riverberi. *cast* Laura Antonelli, Renate Kasche, Ewing Loren, Peter Heeg, Mady Rahl, Werner Pochath.
● Not to be confused with the Jess Franco version released the following year, this is an updated, softcore adaptation of Leopold Sacher-Masoch's novel about voyeurism, the fetishistic thrill of fur, and the desire to be sexually dominated. Through fantasy, role-playing and sexual experiment, bland hunk Severin (Kasche) and his blonde lover Wanda (Antonelli) explore the power dynamics of their relationship: 'Each day Wanda seems more beautiful to me,' reflects Severin, 'but what is a woman's beauty compared with her cruelty?' Much of the coupling and lashing is coyly filmed from behind strategically placed foreground objects, but those with a tolerance for repeated zoom shots, atrocious dubbing and irritating '60s muzak may find this titillating. More problematic is an extended scene, filmed subjectively through the manacled Severin's mask, which depicts the rape of a maid by an animalistic man. Surely it is the maid and not Severin who is being humiliated here, a misogynist slide that is compounded by the suggestion that she eventually begins to enjoy it. Sleazy this may be, subversive it ain't. NF

Venus Peter

(1989, GB, 94 min)
d Ian Sellar. *p* Christopher Young. *sc* Ian Sellar, Christopher Rush. *ph* Gabriel Beristain. *ed* David Spiers. *pd* Andy Harris. *m* Jonathan Dove. *cast* Ray McAnally, David Hayman, Sinead Cusack, Gordon R Strachan, Sam Hayman, Caroline Paterson, Alex McAvoy, Emma Dingwall, Robin McCaffrey.
● Growing up in the Orkneys in the late '40s, young Peter leads a strange and magical life. Christened with sea water, he sometimes fancies he is a boat; his wise-old-fisherman grandfather (McAnally) rails against human greed and burbles on about whales and eternity; his ancient aunt extols the virtues of poetry; and his teacher (Cusack) is heavily into the appreciation of beauty. Not surprisingly, Peter spends much of his time in dreams, usually about his father, who is either dead or (sensibly) a fugitive from this inbred island community, where harsh prejudice, acts of cruelty towards beached whales, and vacuous, whimsical mysticism are the norm. Sellar's first feature looks nice enough, in a picture-postcard sort of way, but its script is so much nonsense: the film dishes up a series of loosely connected, impressionist vignettes that appear to have no narrative rhyme or reason. Someone, somewhere along the line, should have put the brake on the indulgently fanciful poeticism and insisted on rather more plot logic. GA

Vera Cruz

(1954, US, 94 min)
d Robert Aldrich. *p* James Hill. *sc* Roland Kibbee, James R Webb. *ph* Ernest Laszlo. *ed* Alan Crosland Jr. *ad* Alfred Ynarra. *m* Hugo Friedhofer. *cast* Burt Lancaster, Gary Cooper,

Denise Darcel, Cesar Romero, Sarita Montiel, George Macready, Ernest Borgnine, Jack Elam, Jack Lambert, Charles Bronson.
●A brash, lively, and totally appealing Western about a couple of American adventurers – Cooper, a decent but cynical Southern gentleman, and Lancaster, a supremely conniving crook – getting involved with Maximilian's imperial court and the Juarez revolutionaries in 1860s Mexico. Basically, the film is played as a game of bluff and betrayal, with the pair continually voicing their distrust of each other as they transport a countess and her crock of gold to Vera Cruz, allowing Aldrich to alternate with ease between earthy comedy and taut suspense. Beautifully shot by Ernest Laszlo, it conjures up a Mexico that in some ways looks forward to Peckinpah's *The Wild Bunch*, a country at once romantic and treacherous, wild and lovely, an outpost of freedom for exiles yet oppressed by a corrupt government. And the performances, as you might expect, are highly professional. GA

Verboten!

(1958, US, 94 min, b/w)
d/p/sc Samuel Fuller. *ph* Joseph Biroc. *ed* Philip Cahn. *ad* John Mansbridge. *m* Harry Sukman, Richard Wagner, Ludwig van Beethoven. *cast* James Best, Susan Cummings, Tom Pittman, Paul Dubov, Steven Geray.
●The great Fuller at his punchy, unsubtle best, beginning with a long tracking shot of an American GI clambering through the grim rubble of war-torn Berlin (the rifle shotd of snipers intercut with the opening chords of Beethoven's 5th), and ending with an image of raging flames. In between, the film, set mostly in the immediate postwar period, charts the troubled relationship of the American, working for the occupying Allied Forces, with a German woman who saved his life and whi is surrounded by compatriots – including her younger brother – determined to revive the power of the Nazi movement. It's a tale of betrayal, violence, confusion and stark ironies, and takes in bravura action sequences, scenes of argumentative discourse, and documentary footage of the Nazi atrocities shown at the Nuremberg War Criminals Tribunal. Fuller's methods may not be sophisticated, but they are complex; as such, his own inimitably brash brand of didactism makes for riveting and powerful cinema. GA

Verbrechen am Seelenleben eines Menschens

see Kaspar Hauser

Verdict (The Verdict)

(1974, Fr/It, 97 min)
d André Cayatte. *p* Carlo Ponti. *sc* André Cayatte, Paul Adreota, Pierre Dumayet. *ph* Jean Badal. *ed* Paul Cayatte. *ad* Robert Clavel. *m* Louiguy. *cast* Sophia Loren, Jean Gabin, Henri Garcin, Julien Bertheau, Muriel Catala.
●Cayatte is the Frenchman's Stanley Kramer, with an unswerving penchant for expounding knotty points of law and morals in a narrative framework, giving audiences a lot of fun and education all at once. Here, Sophia Loren's worthless son is up for trial under clauses 296, 297, 302, 304 and 332 of the French penal code. Despite this daunting array of transgressions, the judge (Gabin) urges his jurors to acquit the wretch, for Loren has his diabetic wife locked up, and his conscience goes to pot as a result. Acting and direction are uniformly sober, and you don't learn a thing. GB

Verdict, The

(1946, US, 86 min, b/w)
d Don Siegel. *p* William Jacobs. *sc* Peter Milne. *ph* Ernest Haller. *ed* Thomas Reilly. *ad* Ted Smith. *m* Frederick Hollander. *cast* Sydney Greenstreet, Peter Lorre, Joan Lorring, George Coulouris, Rosalind Ivan, Paul Cavanagh, Morton Lowry.
●Siegel's first film, an ingenious locked room mystery set in London in 1890, adapted from a novel by Israel Zangwill (often described as the father of the genre). Greenstreet plays a genial Scotland Yard inspector who, dismissed after thirty years of distinguished service when an oversight results in the hanging of an innocent man, deviously stages a second case; this not only sees justice done (the victim is himself a killer), but puts Greenstreet's baffled successor (Coulouris, the ambitious underling who shopped him in the first place) on the road to perpetrating a similar miscarriage of justice in solving it. Fascinatingly, though, Siegel deliberately plays on ambivalences throughout, leaving motivations not quite explained and opening up dark, speculative avenues of paranoia and perversity, not least through Greenstreet's teasing, subtly suggestive intimacy with Lorre as an amiably decadent, inimitably sinister artist friend. The result, impeccably performed and beautifully shot by Ernest Haller, emerges as splendid cross between Gothic melodrama and *film noir*. TM

Verdict, The

(1982, US, 128 min)
d Sidney Lumet. *p* Richard D Zanuck, David Brown. *sc* David Mamet. *ph* Andrzej Bartkowiak. *ed* Peter C Frank. *pd* Edward Pisoni. *m* Johnny Mandel. *cast* Paul Newman, Charlotte Rampling, Jack Warden, James Mason, Milo O'Shea, Lindsay Crouse, Edward Binns, Julie Bovasso, Roxanne Hart, Wesley Addy.
●Newman as a washed-up lawyer, given one last chance to prove himself with a rather squalid medical malpractice suit. David Mamet has delivered a fast-paced, eloquent, and suspenseful screenplay which, like all the best genre movies, plunges its hero so far into the abyss that it seems impossible for him to climb out. And for once Lumet makes story rather than performance his first priority, with the paradoxical result – so familiar in American movies – that the acting sometimes reaches a near-invisible perfection. Admittedly this is a legal *Rocky*, convincing rather than realistic, witty rather than analytical, but it amounts to a far more effective indictment of the US legal system than *...and justice for all*, and is the first courtroom drama in years to recapture the brilliance of the form. DP

Verdugo, El (The Executioner/ Not On Your Life)

(1963, Sp/It, 110 min, b/w)
d Luis Berlanga. *sc* Luis Garcia Berlanga, Rafael Azcona, Ennio Flaiano. *ph* Tonino Delli Colli. *ed* Alfonso Santacana. *ad* José Antonio de la Guerra. *m* Miguel Asins Arbo. *cast* Nino Manfredi, Emma Penella, José Isbert, José Luis López Vázquez, Angel Alvarez.
●Regularly voted by its country's critics as the best Spanish film of all time, Berlanga's brilliantly dark comedy on the peculiar horror of the garotte has not lost its power over the years. Manfredi plays an undertaker's hapless assistant who marries the executioner's daughter, then discovers that they can keep their precious apartment only if he agrees to become his father-in-law's successor. Full of sharp and disturbing insights into the corrupt world engendered by the Francoist mentality, the film's build-up to its terrifying conclusion – when Manfredi, as the new executioner, is dragged literally kicking and screaming to perform his duty – is inexorable. DT

Verhängnis

see Fate

Vérité, La (The Truth)

(1960, Fr/It, 130 min, b/w)
d Henri-Georges Clouzot. *p* Raoul J Lévy. *sc* Henri-Georges Clouzot, Jérome Géronimi, Simone Drieu, Michèle Perrein, Christiane Rochefort. *ph* Armand Thirard. *ed* Albert Jurgenson. *ad* Jean André. *m* Igor Stravinsky. *cast* Brigitte Bardot, Charles Vanel, Marie-Josée Nat, Paul Meurisse, Louis Seigner, Sami Frey.
●A dissection of life and amorality among the young and disaffected in the late '50s, with Bardot giving her finest ever performance as the girl whose headlong rush from her stiff bourgeois home into a series of frustrating affairs with Parisian intellectuals leads to her trial for murder. Clouzot, the man who made the wonderful but terribly cynical *Le Corbeau*, *The Wages of Fear* and *Les Diaboliques*, is as cold and savage as ever in his observation of French manners, although the courtroom scenes that frame the flashbacks to Bardot's past tend to decrease the tension inherent in the subject. Far from his finest work, but still compelling viewing: compared to Clouzot, even Fassbinder seemed a romantic. GA

Verlorene, Der (The Lost One)

(1951, WGer, 98 min, b/w)
d Peter Lorre. *p* Arnold Pressburger. *sc* Peter Lorre, Benno Vigny, Axel Eggebrecht. *ph* Vaclac Vich. *ed* Carl-Otto Bartning, K Weber. *ad* Franz Schroedter. *m* Willy Schmidt-Gentner. *cast* Peter Lorre, Karl John, Helmut Rudolph, Renate Mannhardt, Johanna Hofer, Lotte Rausch.
●*Der Verlorene* would have been remarkable in virtually any context; as a product of the depressed German film industry of the post-war years, it's absolutely phenomenal. It was Lorre's only film as writer/director, and it clearly represents a personal comment on the side of Germany that forced him into exile in 1933, just as his own performance in the lead is a rethinking of the psychopath roles that he played in *M* and many Hollywood movies. The plot, developed entirely in flashbacks, shows how research doctor Rothe (Lorre) is forced into political complicity with the Nazis by their shrewd, cold-blooded exploitation of his emotional and psychological weaknesses; everything about it (including the spasms of expressionism in the imagery) is haunted by a sense of the German past, until the powerhouse melodrama of the ending rockets the film into the even bleaker present. TR

Verlorene Ehre der Katharina Blum, Die

see Lost Honour of Katharina Blum, The

Vernon, Florida

(1980, US, 60 min)
d/p Errol Morris. *ph* Ned Burgess. *ed* Brad Fuller. *cast* Claude Register, Albert Bitterling, Henry Shipes, Snake Reynolds, Roscoe Collins.
●Anyone who saw *Gates of Heaven* will need no inducement to try Errol Morris' second idiosyncratic foray into documentary. While less sharply focused than the pet cemetery film, this is equally delightful in its loving – but detached – portrait of the more eccentric inhabitants of small-town America, in this case the backwater community of the title. The subjects discussed include turkey hunting, sand-growth (a couple have a jarful from Los Alamos, New Mexico, which they insist is growing apace), and people with multiple brains. Morris, thankfully, never patronises his subjects' loony views. Touching and funny, the film is a real-life predecessor to David Byrne's fictional *True Stories*. GA

Verónico Cruz (La Deuda Interna)

(1987, Arg/GB, 96 min)
d Miguel Pereira. *p* Julio Lencina, Sasha Manocki. *sc* Eduardo Leiva Muller, Miguel Pereira. *ph* Gerry Feeny. *ed* Gerry Feeny. *ad* Kiki Aguiar. *m* Jaime Torres. *cast* Juan José Camero, Gonzalo Morales, René Olaguivel, Guillermo Delgado.
●Despite its very evident sincerity, Pereira's feature debut offers a sometimes muddled, wanly liberal response to the human waste incurred during the Falklands War. In a tiny, remote village high in the Argentinian mountains, the uneducated population is barely aware of events in the outside world; only a teacher from the city – whose growing friendship with shepherd boy Veronico forms the core of the film's narrative – seems conscious of the implications of 1976's military coup. True, life in the village changes; but any real political criticism would seem to lie in the character of Veronico's father, whose absentee status may serve to tug the heartstrings in regard to our perception of his son's predicament, but does little to clarify either the mechanisms of Argentine fascism or the war itself. Finally, both strengths and weaknesses are rooted in the film's decidedly poetic humanism; only the most bigoted Brits could find such a well-meaning anti-war movie offensive. GA

Veronika Voss (Die Sehnsucht der Veronika Voss)

(1982, WGer, 104 min, b/w)
d Rainer Werner Fassbinder. *p* Thomas Schühly. *sc* Peter Märthesheimer, Pea Fröhlich, Rainer Werner Fassbinder. *ph* Xaver Schwarzenberger. *ed* Juliane Lorenz. *pd* Rolf Zehetbauer. *m* Peer Raben. *cast* Rosel Zech, Hilmar Thate, Annemarie Düringer, Doris Schade, Cornelia Froboess, Erik Schumann.

● Intended as just another chapter in the continuing indictment of the post-war German economic recovery, but Fassbinder's death means that this will have to take its place as a loose third panel of the *Maria Braun/Lola* triptych. Unlike those heroines, however, Veronika (Zech) doesn't even pretend to any kind of upward social mobility. When 'discovered' by a crusading journalist (Thate), she is already on the skids, a washed-up Third Reich film star. His infatuation and subsequent investigation reveals her dependency on a snow white clinic, and her sadomasochistic relationship with the female doctor who feeds her morphine habit; and that's just the beginning of the downward slide. If Sirk's colourful melodramas were once Fassbinder's models, this is closer to Wilder's monochrome *Sunset Boulevard*, not just in theme, but in the reductive cynicism that views all human motivation as grounded on folly and greed; a world in which love is just a power struggle, dirty 'habits' are murderous, and happiness is simply the art of being well deceived. CPea

Versailles

see Si Versailles m'était conté...

Versailles rive gauche (A Night in Versailles)

(1991, Fr, 47 min)
d Bruno Podalydès. *sc* Bruno Podalydes, Denis Podalydes. *ph* Pierre Stoeber. *ed* Marie-France Cuenot. *ad* Anne Carlier. *m* Dominique Paulin. *cast* Isabelle Candelier, Denis Podalydès, Philippe Linchan, Michel Vuiuermoz.

● A beautifully elaborated, extended gag about a bumbling intellectual and Tintin fan (Podalydès) who invites his dream date (Candelier) for an intimate evening in, but gets hopelessly entangled in his own fastidious embarrassment. Nothing could be simpler than this deliciously excruciating comedy of errors (it's as if a bunch of Rohmer characters had accidentally stumbled into a Feydeau farce), but Podalydès (who also co-scripted and plays the lead) carries it off with perfect timing. JRo

Verso sera

see By Nightfall

Versprechen, Das

see Promise, The

Vertical Limit

(2000, US/Ger, 124 min)
d Martin Campbell. *p* Lloyd Phillips, Robert King, Martin Campbell. *sc* Robert King, Terry Hayes. *ph* David Tattersall. *ed* Thom Noble. *pd* Jon Bunker. *m* James Newton Howard. *cast* Chris O'Donnell, Bill Paxton, Robin Tunney, Scott Glenn, Izabella Scorupco, Temuera Morrison, Stuart Wilson, Nicholas Lea.

● Campbell knows how to make the best of vertiginous jeopardy, but second-rank stars and a contrived, over-plotted screenplay prove an insurmountable object to this amalgam of *Cliffhanger* and *The Wages of Fear*. There's an effective pre-credits attention grabber as we join siblings O'Donnell and Tunney on a family climbing expedition which slips into fatal tragedy, leaving the pair with a potent legacy of guilt. Years later, chance brings them together on the slopes of K2, where he's taking wildlife photographs and she's now a top climber assisting entrepreneur Paxton's publicity-seeking assault on the summit. Inevitably, her expedition lands in trouble, and O'Donnell must lead the effort to dig them out of the ice. At times, this is undeniably nail-chewing stuff, but when it'snot unleashing avalanches or dangling disposable supporting players over snowy precipices, the movie's found decidedly wanting. TJ

Vertical Ray of the Sun

see At the Height of Summer

Vertiges

(1985, Fr/GB, 107 min)
d Christine Laurent. *p* Paulo Branco. *sc* Christine Laurent. *ph* Acacio de Almeida. *ed* Francine Sandberg. *cast* Magali Noël, Krystyna Janda, Paulo Autran, Hélène Lapiower, Henri Serre, Thierry Bosc.

● A moonstruck enterprise, from the maverick independent international producer Paulo Branco, in which, on the first night of a fraught production of *The Marriage of Figaro*, Serre, playing the count, shoots dead Bosc, playing Figaro, with the latter's own pearl-handled pistol. This is no more than the lippy servant deserves since throughout rehearsals he's tormented the conductor with hints of some old injustice. The conductor, meanwhile, has grown increasingly obsessed with the memory of his former mistress, La Gravida, and her perfect voice. One of the singers (Janda) loses her voice. 'You have to be a *real* diva to lose your voice,' the conductor's current mistress says, comfortingly. News arrives of La Gravida's retirement. The conductor swoons and expires. The Countess swears vengeance, and the Count, in the event, acts the gentleman. Vertigo, indeed. JPy

Vertigo 100 (100) 10

(1958, US, 128 min)
d/p Alfred Hitchcock. *sc* Alec Coppel, Samuel Taylor. *ph* Robert Burks. *ed* George Tomasini. *ad* Hal Pereira, Henry Bumstead. *m* Bernard Herrmann. *cast* James Stewart, Kim Novak, Barbara Bel Geddes, Tom Helmore, Henry Jones, Ellen Corby, Lee Patrick.

● Brilliant but despicably cynical view of human obsession and the tendency of those in love to try to manipulate each other. Stewart is excellent as the neurotic detective employed by an old pal to trail his wandering wife, only to fall for her himself and then crack up when she commits suicide. Then one day he sees a woman in the street who reminds him of the woman who haunts him... Hitchcock gives the game away about halfway through the movie, and focuses on Stewart's strained psychological stability; the result inevitably involves a lessening of suspense, but allows for an altogether deeper investigation of guilt, exploitation, and obsession. The bleakness is perhaps a little hard to swallow, but there's no denying that this is the director at the very peak of his powers, while Novak is a revelation. Slow but totally compelling. GA

Verweigerung, Die

see Refusal, The

Very Annie-Mary

(2000, Fr/GB, 104 min)
d Sara Sugarman. *p* Graham Broadbent, Damian Jones. *sc* Sara Sugarman. *ph* Barry Ackroyd. *ed* Robin Sales. *pd* Alice Normington. *m* Stephen Warbeck. *cast* Rachel Griffiths, Jonathan Pryce, Ioan Gruffudd, Matthew Rhys, Kenneth Griffith, Ruth Madoc, Grafton Radcliffe.

● Welsh writer/director Sugarman's second feature is an uneven, sometimes awkward but ultimately winning parable about female emancipation and small town claustrophobia. It's set in the Valleys, in the former mining community of Ogw, and Sugarman revels in its looped cadence. Here Annie-Mary (Griffiths) cooks and cleans for her da, Jack Pugh (Pryce), the town baker. Pugh is loved for his wonderful tenor voice, but he's a tyrannical father who treats his daughter more like a maid than his own flesh and blood. Very broad, this opening, with Annie-Mary apparently still a teenager at heart, her development forestalled by the death of her mam just as she was on the point of taking up a singing scholarship in Milan. Sugarman finds more emotional focus when Pugh suffers a stroke but selfishly refuses to die. So the cruel indignities add up. It's only when she joins some local lassies for a talent contest that Annie-Mary gets a chance to prove herself. Griffiths throws herself into this ugly duckling role with characteristic aplomb: hair in buns, dressed in hand-me-downs, but with those beseeching eyes – it's as if this time she gets to play Hilary *and* Jackie. TCh

Very Bad Things

(1998, US, 100 min)
d Peter Berg. *p* Michael Schiffer, Diane Nabatoff, Cindy Cowan. *sc* Peter Berg. *ph* David Hennings. *ed* Dan Lebental. *pd* Dina Lipton. *m* Stewart Copeland. *cast* Cameron Diaz, Christian Slater, Jon Favreau, Jeanne Tripplehorn, Daniel Stern, Jeremy Piven.

● The writing/directing debut of actor Peter Berg (from *The Last Seduction*) is a black comedy about a stag trip to Las Vegas that ends in the accidental death of a prostitute, and the murder of the hotel security man who notices her body. Jon Favreau is understandably anxious that his imminent marriage to control freak Cameron Diaz is ruined, but ruthless, self-serving Christian Slater insists all will be well if they just dispose of the 'problems'. He's only half right: the law seems to pose no threat, but guilt, mutual distrust and fear of discovery inevitably – and predictably – take their toll on the five friends and their wives. However, despite a frantic pace, snazzy visuals and the eager embrace of supposedly outrageous bad taste, this isn't very funny. Berg seems so keen to shock us with his laddish amorality (or is that what he's satirising? – if so, it doesn't come off) that the tone soon turns sour and tiresomely hysterical. The film lacks both the goofy, charmingly juvenile innocence of the Farrelly brothers' work, and the rigour that makes, say, Clouzot's misanthropic fables about the wages of sin compelling from beginning to end. GA

Very Curious Girl, A

see Fiancée du Pirate, La

Very Important Person

(1961, GB, 98 min, b/w)
d Ken Annakin. *p* Julian Wintle, Leslie Parkyn. *sc* Jack Davies. *ph* Ernest Steward. *ed* Ralph Sheldon. *ad* Harry Pottle. *m* Reg Owen. *cast* James Roberton Justice, Leslie Phillips, Stanley Baxter, Eric Sykes, Richard Wattis, John Le Mesurier.

● Dated British comedy poking fun at *Wooden Horse* and *Colditz*-style PoW movies. Bellowing beard James Robertson Justice, always good value, plays a distinguished radar scientist who takes very badly to life in a Nazi camp. When his fellow prisoners realise he's vital to Britain's war efforts, they reluctantly agree to help him escape. All sorts of radio and TV comedians pop up in the supporting cast, but if some of the jokes fall a little flat, it's hardly a surprise – Norman Wisdom's regular screenwriter, Jack Davies, helped provide the script. GM

Very Moral Night, A (Egy Erkölcsös Ejszaka)

(1977, Hun, 99 min)
d Károly Makk. *sc* István Örkény, Péter Bacsó. *ph* János Tóth. *ed* György Sivó. *ad* Tamás P Balassa. *m* Frédéric Chopin, Leo Fall, Ferenc Erkel, György Forrai, István Major, Béla Radics, Johann Strauss, Jacques Offenbach, Léo Delibes. *cast* Margit Makay, Irén Psota, Carla Romanelli, Györgyi Tarján, György Cserhalmi.

● Makk's film suffers by comparison with his later, more serious *Another Way*; a certain turn-of-the-century light-weightedness is not quite the same thing as buoyancy. A small town's brothel takes a medical student as a lodger, much to the all round delight of the girls, student, and madame. When his mother arrives to visit unexpectedly, the girls rally round with a charade to keep up appearances. The mask slips occasionally, but the old lady is beyond corruption, and to the pure all things are pure. Indeed, the film's main delight rests on Margit Makay's performance as the mother, a strong portrait of kindness and innocence preserved into old age. CPea

Very Private Affair, A

see Vie Privée

Vessel of Wrath (aka The Beachcomber)

(1938, GB, 93 min, b/w)
d/p Erich Pommer. *sc* Bartlett Cormack, B Van Thal. *ph* Jules Kruger. *ed* Robert Hamer. *ad* Tom Morahan. *m* Richard Addinsell. *cast* Charles Laughton, Elsa Lanchester, Tyrone Guthrie, Robert Newton, Dolly Mollinger, Eliot Makeham.

●Laughton's venture into independent production, of which this was the first fruit, afforded him a welcome opportunity to escape typecasting as a monster. Set in the Dutch East Indies, the Somerset Maugham story – gradual defrosting of a frigid spinster by a drunken reprobate ('I suppose I'm jealous of the reckless way he squanders the precious treasure of life') – may be clichéd, but Laughton's performance adds an extra dimension. Burdened and embarrassed by his homosexual inclinations, he obviously entered with gusto into this portrayal of a man with problems in every area of his life apart from sex. Playing opposite his real life wife, he carefully combines conventions of masculinity with the self-doubt and inadequacy of his own persona to create an almost Falstaffian screen character. RMy

Veuve de Saint-Pierre, La (The Widow of Saint-Pierre)

(2000, Fr/Can, 112 min)
d Patrice Leconte. *p* Frédéric Brillion, Gilles Legrand. *sc* Claude Faraldo. *ph* Eduardo Serra. *ed* Joëlle Hache. *ad* Ivan Maussion. *m* Pascale Estève. *cast* Juliette Binoche, Daniel Auteuil, Emir Kusturica, Michel Duchaussoy, Philippe Magnan, Christian Charmetant, Philippe Du Janerand, Reynald Bouchard, Ghyslain Tremblay.
●Saint-Pierre is a small island off Newfoundland. The year is 1850. Fog and scandal enwrap the island in the wake of a brutal random murder committed by two drunken locals, who are quickly arrested and tried. Neel Auguste (Serbian director Kusturica) is sentenced to the guillotine but, while the device is shipped from Paris, he's turned over to the supervision of Le Capitaine (Auteuil) for hard labour. The latter and his wife (Binoche) are very much in love, and her growing interest and faith in their prisoner's scope for redemption leads Le Capitaine into increasingly serious confrontation with the island's bigoted governing elite. Thus prejudices are tested, loyalties torn and love rent asunder – all of which ought not to come across as so commonplace, but the film is resolutely unsurprising. NB

Viaggio in Italia (Journey to Italy/The Lonely Woman/ Strangers/Voyage to Italy)

(1953, It, 100 min, b/w)
d Roberto Rossellini. *p* Roberto Rossellini, Adolfo Fossataro, Alfredo Guarini. *sc* Roberto Rossellini, Vitaliano Brancati. *ph* Enzo Serafin. *ed* Jolanda Benvenuti. *ad* Piero Filippone. *m* Renzo Rossellini. *cast* Ingrid Bergman, George Sanders, Maria Mauban, Paul Muller, Leslie Daniels, Natalia Ray, Anna Proclemer.
●Some films have to be seen to be believed: the secret of this most beautiful and magical of films is 'nothing happens'. From the slight tale of a bored English couple holidaying in Italy, Rossellini builds a magnificently passionate story of cruelty and cynicism swirling into a renewal of love: life is so short, we must make the most of it... Rarely has screen chemistry worked so indefinably well; Sanders' suave, caddish businessman superbly complements Bergman's Garbo-like presence and the sensuous locations in which they feel so ill at ease. And though critics may have always praised it as 'one of the most beautiful films ever made', its genuinely romantic tenderness (it ends in 'I love you') mark it as never so unfashionable, never so moving. DMacp

Viaje, El

see Voyage, The

Via Satellite

(1998, NZ, 90 min)
d Anthony McCarten. *p* Philippa Campbell. *sc* Anthony McCarten, Greg McGee. *ph* Simon Riera. *ed* John Gilbert. *pd* Clive Memmott. *m* David Bergeaud. *cast* Danielle Cormack, Rima Te Wiata, Tim Balme, Brian Sergent, Jodie Dorday, Karl Urban.
●Swimmer Carol (Cormack) could well provide New Zealand with an Olympic gold medal, so, desperate to catch a satellite 'moment', a TV camera crew descends on her hapless family. Carol's twin Chrissy (Cormack again) is loath to join the circus, but in the ensuing chaos it's she who has most to learn. Set in the anti-cool, drab 1970s suburbs, this first feature, based on the director's own play, is a crude, raucous shadow of Mike Leigh's *Secrets & Lies*. Thanks to Cormack, though, who boasts beautiful, root-vegetable features reminiscent of Sandrine Bonnaire, you find yourself drawn in. Chrissy's sour rage, in particular, proves haunting. CO'Su

Vicar of Vejlby, The (Præsten i Vejlby)

(1931, Den, 101 min, b/w)
d George Schnéevoigt. *sc* Fleming Lynge. *ph/ed* Valdemar Christensen. *m* Bent Froda. *cast* Henrik Malberg, Karin Nellemose, Kai Holm, Gerhard Jessen, Eyvind Johan-Svendsen, Holger-Madsen, Mathilde Nielsen, Gudrun Nissen, Aage Winther-Jørgensen.
●The first Danish talkie is a stern tragedy, from a novel by Steen Steensen Bilcher, about the fall of a pious but intemperate preacher at the hands of his daughter's spurned suitor. The tale unfolds with classical implacability, but the characterisation is thin and the drama ponderous. The iron grip of gravity rules: what is down must stay down. Claus Orsted directed a remake in 1972. NB

Vice and Virtue

see Vice et la Vertu, Le

Vice et la Vertu, Le (Vice and Virtue)

(1963, Fr, 105 min, b/w)
d Roger Vadim. *p* Alain Poiré. *sc* Roger Vadim, Roger Vailland, Claude Choublier. *ph* Marcel Grignon. *ed* Victoria Mercanton. *ad* Jean André. *m* Michel Magne. *cast* Catherine Deneuve, Annie Girardot, Robert Hossein, OE Hasse, Philippe Lemaire, Luciana Paluzzi, Paul Gégauff.
●De Sade was all over the publicity for this film, but is excluded from its credits. Nevertheless, it's *Justine* and *Juliette* updated to 1944–45. Justine (Deneuve), churchgoing, loyal to her fiancé in the Resistance, is forcibly consigned to an SS brothel in the Tyrol. Meanwhile her sister Juliette (Girardot) is infatuated with a Gestapo brute who lets her sit in on his torture sessions. Only the cast makes this worth a look. The sex contrives to be both tame and vulgar, and Vadim's fancy lighting effects – dimming out the set in mid-scene and putting a spot on the characters – just looks silly. What with this and Pasolini's odious *Salò*, it's clear that Sade and WWII are subjects best treated separately. BBa

Vices in the Family (Vizio di Famiglia)

(1975, It, 94 min)
d Mariano Laurenti. *p* Gianfranco Couyoumdjian. *sc* Cesare Frugoni, Marino Onorati, Gianfranco Couyoumdjian. *ph* Federico Zanni. *ed* Alberto Moriani. *ad* Gianfranco Fantacci. *m* Gianni Ferrio. *cast* Edwige Fenech, Renzo Montagnani, Juliette Mayniel, Susan Scott, Gigi Ballista, Roberto Cenci.
●An incomprehensible black comedy (any charm it may have had has gone in the dubbing and cutting of the version released in Britain), this concerns the cack-handed efforts of a group of scheming ladies to relieve a dying Count of his fortune. It borrows shamelessly from Polanski's *What?*, and throws in a few nods towards Pasolini, but basically attempts no more than a bit of absent-minded titillation. Laurenti directs as though he were being paid by the minute, and the result is a crashing bore. VG

Vice Squad

(1981, US, 98 min)
d Gary A Sherman. *p* Brian Frankish. *sc* Sandy Howard, Robert Vincent O'Neil, Kenneth Peters. *ph* John Alcott. *ed* Roy Watts. *pd* Lee Fischer. *m* Michael Montgomery. *cast* Season Hubley, Gary Swanson, Wings Hauser, Pepe Serna, Beverly Todd.
●Sadistic pimp (Hauser) beats LA prostitute to death; her friend (Hubley) collaborates with police to trap him; he escapes and seeks murderous revenge. Apart from a marginally more lurid approach to sex and violence, this could be any old episode from any old TV cop series, right down to the appalling sub-disco score. There's also a pretty insulting opening which reveals that (gasp) prostitutes have feelings too. DP

Vice Versa

(1947, GB, 111 min, b/w)
d Peter Ustinov. *p* Peter Ustinov, George H Brown. *sc* Peter Ustinov. *ph* Jack Hildyard. *ed* John D Guthridge. *ad* Carmen Dillon. *m* Antony Hopkins. *cast* Roger Livesey, Kay Walsh, Petula Clark, David Hutcheson, Anthony Newley, James Robertson Justice.
●Ustinov was in his mid-20s when he wrote and directed this sparkling comedy about a Victorian businessman (Livesey) who ends up trapped in his young son's body after meddling with a magical Indian gem. (The son, a very cheeky Anthony Newley, takes over his father's body.) A sort of cross between the *Arabian Nights* and a Whitehall farce, it's every bit as funny as Penny Marshall's *Big*, made from a similar premise 40 years later. GM

Vice Versa

(1988, US, 98 min)
d Brian Gilbert. *p/sc* Dick Clement, Ian La Frenais. *ph* King Baggot. *ed* David Garfield. *pd* James Schoppe. *m* David Shire. *cast* Judge Reinhold, Fred Savage, Corinne Bohrer, Swoosie Kurtz, Jane Kaczmarek, David Proval, William Prince.
●Divorced workaholic department store executive (Reinhold) and his 11-year-old son (Savage) both wish they could lead each other's lives: a magical skull, mysteriously come into Dad's possession during a trip to Thailand, makes the wish come true. After a tedious prologue, Dick Clement and Ian La Frenais' role-reversal script settles for bland farce, with son (in Dad's body) forced to negotiate the executive boardroom, while Dad (in son's body) takes on school bullies. Moments of rather tasteless complexity arise with Dad's girlfriend (Bohrer), but mostly the hoary gags give rise to less tantalising ideas. Reinhold does his darnedest, but both script and direction are instilled with a numbing predictability. GA

Vicious Circle

see Huis Clos

Victim

(1961, GB, 100 min, b/w)
d Basil Dearden. *p* Michael Relph. *sc* Janet Green, John McCormick. *ph* Otto Heller. *ed* John D Guthridge. *ad* Alex Vetchinsky. *m* Philip Green. *cast* Dirk Bogarde, Sylvia Syms, John Barrie, Peter McEnery, Anthony Nicholls, Dennis Price, Norman Bird, Charles Lloyd Pack, Nigel Stock, Derren Nesbitt, Hilton Edwards.
●A fascinating slice of social history. Bogarde plays a homosexual barrister being blackmailed by a young man who commits suicide when arrested. Bogarde can either shut up or 'come out', and opts for the latter, putting a strain on his marriage and his reputation. Bogarde, the Rank matinee idol, risked almost everything by playing the role, and he gives an open and sincere performance, with Sylvia Syms also good as his appalled but supportive wife. By today's standards the film is of course compromised, and in 1961 it could be nothing else (Dearden apparently insisted that homosexuals should be called 'inverts'). It flirts with the subject, as did the same team's exposé of racism in the earlier *Sapphire*; but although treated as a thriller, it does seek to normalise (rather than glamourise) homosexuality by finding it in every side street, every Rolls Royce, and every club in town. ATu

Victoire en Chantant, La

see Black and White in Colour

Victor – pendant qu'il est trop tard

(1999, Fr, 90 min)
d Sandrine Veysset. *p* Humbert Balsam. *sc* Denis Belloc, Sandrine Veysset. *ph* Hélène Louvart. *ed* Mathilde Grosjean. *pd* Thomas Peckre. *cast* Jérémy Chaix, Lydia Andrei, Mathieu Lané, Skan Guenin, Chantal Malebert, Paulette Benson, Nicole Richard.
●Less Bressonian, stylistically and spiritually, than Veysset's *Will It Snow for Christmas?*, this concerns an unlikely encounter between a runaway kid and a hard-nosed young whore who reluctantly provides shelter. A potentially clichéd tale of innocence and experience made palatable and poignant by the bold, Vigo-style mix of realism and fairytale. (From Denis Belloc's novel *Les Ailes de Julien*.) GA

Victors, The

(1963, GB, 175 min, b/w)
d/p/sc Carl Foreman. *ph* Christopher Challis. *ed* Alan Osbiston. *ad* Geoffrey Drake. *m* Sol Kaplan. *cast* George Hamilton, George Peppard, Eli Wallach, Vincent Edwards, Rosanna Schiaffino, James Mitchum, Maurice Ronet, Jeanne Moreau, Romy Schneider, Michael Callan, Peter Fonda, Melina Mercouri, Mervyn Johns, Albert Lieven, Senta Berger, Elke Sommer, Albert Finney.

● A World War II picture with a weightiness all its own that follows an American infantry unit from Sicily, up through Europe, to the fall of Berlin and after. Foreman adds nothing to William Wellman's portrait of an ordinary GI unit in *Battleground* (1949). Instead of the emotional complexity of the earlier film, Foreman offers a rather cheap and shallow sense of irony, sometimes effective, more often ponderous. Interludes between campaigns are beefed up by the presence of various sexy European actresses; Hamilton, Peppard, Wallach and Fonda play some of the soldiers who get theirs at various stages of the long slog towards the death of the last one at the hands of a drunken Russian soldier (Finney) in a knife fight in Occupied Berlin. CPe

Victor/Victoria

(1982, GB, 134 min)
d Blake Edwards. *p* Blake Edwards, Tony Adams. *sc* Blake Edwards. *ph* Dick Bush. *ed* Ralph E Winters, Alan Killick. *pd* Rodger Maus. *m* Henry Mancini. *cast* Julie Andrews, James Garner, Robert Preston, Lesley Ann Warren, Alex Karras, John Rhys-Davies, Graham Stark, Peter Arne.

● There is so much to like and admire in Edwards' intricate comedy about sexual identity which is neither vulgar nor preachy, combining a Clouseau-esque bedroom farce – and the prospect of characters coming out of the closet in all possible ways – with a convincing love story and just enough show-stopping musical numbers. It gives Andrews her best role ever as the beanpole English soprano peddling 'Cherry Ripe' to unimpressed cabaret managers in a wonderfully fake 'Paris 1934'. Befriended by Toddy (Preston), a very together 'gay' (much of the excellent dialogue's zip comes from the conscious use of anachronisms), Victoria is easily persuaded to pass herself off as a Bowie-elegant young man, and develops a scintillating drag act which delights Paris, confuses devout hetero King Marchan (Garner), and broadens the implications of the film, forcing the audience to ponder its own response to our sweet, safe and usually unsexy Julie suddenly coming on so attractive as a fella in a dress. Well, as the song says, climb every mountain. Don't miss this one. It sends sparks. JS

Victory

(1940, US, 77 min, b/w)
d John Cromwell. *p* Anthony Veiller. *sc* John J Balderston. *ph* Leo Tover. *ed* William Shea. *ad* Hans Dreier. *m* Frederick Hollander. *cast* Fredric March, Betty Field, Cedric Hardwicke, Jerome Cowan, Sig Ruman, Rafaela Ottiano.

● A curious adaptation of Joseph Conrad's novel, with March as the tender-hearted misanthrope whose ivory tower on an island in the Dutch East Indies is simultaneously invaded by a downtrodden girl (Field) he rescues from a lecherous hotel-keeper, and by an unscrupulous gentleman adventurer (Hardwicke) – attended by his male 'secretary' and a brutish thug – who is after the mythical treasure supposedly hidden there. No prizes for guessing that subtleties go by the board, with Hollywood romance winning the day as a tropical storm orchestrates the passions. But the characterisations are vivid, the relationships (Hardwicke's sadistic sexual domination of Cowan, for example) surprisingly explicit, and the camerawork (Leo Tover) lushly atmospheric. TM

Victory

(1995, GB/Fr/Ger, 99 min)
d Mark Peploe. *p* Simon Bosanquet. *sc* Mark Peploe. *ph* Bruno De Keyzer. *ed* Tony Lawson, Michael Bradsell. *pd* Luciana Arrighi. *m* Richard Hartley. *cast* Willem Dafoe, Sam Neill, Irène Jacob, Rufus Sewell, Jean Yanne, Ho Yi, Bill Paterson, Simon Callow.

● Watching Peploe's Conrad adaptation spurs on a bit of a guessing game: what's so terrible about it that it was consigned to three years on the shelf? It's the saga of Axel Heyst, a reclusive American living in the ruins of his failed mining operation in the Dutch East Indies. Dafoe looks characteristically careworn as the man with a past – did he sell out his best friend to amass his fortune? – who rescues Alma (Jacob) from a life of virtual prostitution. It seems like a new start for both of them, but soon the couple must face up to the arrival of malevolent con-men Neill and Sewell, drawn to Heyst's island refuge by the rumours of treasure. The film has a lot going for it: South Sea locations, a persuasive period feel, a lush orchestral score that is among the decade's best, and neatly turned performances. Disappointingly, though, the central drama is the film's weakest point. Dafoe and Jacob seem drawn together by the vagaries of international casting rather than by any dynamic between their characters, and motivations get cloudier the more we learn about the pair of them. Since grandiose Conradian themes of honour, choice and redemption hang so heavy over the proceedings, events on screen can't help but seem overwhelmed by the ideas behind them. TJ

Victory (aka Escape to Victory)

(1981, US, 117 min)
d John Huston. *p* Freddie Fields. *sc* Evan Jones, Yabo Yablonsky. *ph* Gerry Fisher. *ed* Robert Silvi. *pd* J Dennis Washington. *m* Bill Conti. *cast* Sylvester Stallone, Michael Caine, Max von Sydow, Amidou, Daniel Massey, Pele, Bobby Moore, Osvaldo Ardiles.

● Unsatisfactory both for fans of star-studded prison escape dramas and for football fans hoping to see cunningly devised tactics from Pele and his squad of internationals (half the Ipswich team in addition to Moore and Ardiles). If one buys the barely plausible notion of a squad of PoW soccer stars escaping from a Paris stadium, one is still constantly reminded by the rip-off music score just how inferior this is to *The Great Escape*. Stallone comes off best among the familiar gallery of Nazi and prisoner stereotypes. RM

Victory at Entebbe

(1976, US, 119 min)
d Marvin J Chomsky. *p* Robert Guenette. *sc* Ernest Kinoy. *ph* James Kilgore. *ed* David Saxon, Jim McElroy, Mike Gavaldon. *pd* Edward Stephenson. *m* Charles Fox. *cast* Helmut Berger, Linda Blair, Kirk Douglas, Richard Dreyfuss, Julius Harris, Helen Hayes, Anthony Hopkins, Burt Lancaster, Christian Marquand, Elizabeth Taylor, Jessica Walter, Harris Yulin.

● Six months after the event came the first of the action replays of the Entebbe hijack. Flatly directed and poorly shot on video (the TV version ran 150 minutes), it offers a sorry approximation to a sub-standard disaster movie rather than any semblance of truth. That Mrs Bloch has become the uncommonly wise Mrs Wise (Helen Hayes, angelically wistful) is fair example of the confection on offer. Rather than examine the hijacking in context, the film instead revives the spectre of Nazi Jewish oppression. Amin (atrociously portrayed by Harris) is 'the builder of a memorial to Hitler', the hijackers relentless Teutonic fanatics, which causes the Jewish hijacked to indulge in much emoting and dredging of their collective consciousness. Of all the stars paraded to no effect, the wooden Helmut Berger gives the most flexible performance. CPe

Vida Criminal de Archibaldo de la Cruz, La

see Criminal Life of Archibaldo de la Cruz, The

Vida en Sombras

see Life in Shadows

Vida es silbar, La

see Life Is to Whistle

Vidas Secas

see Barren Lives

Videodrome

(1982, Can, 89 min)
d David Cronenberg. *p* Claude Héroux. *sc* David Cronenberg. *ph* Mark Irwin. *ed* Ron Sanders. *ad* Carol Spier. *m* Howard Shore. *cast* James Woods, Sonja Smits, Deborah Harry, Peter Dvorsky, Les Carlson, Jack Creley, Lynne Gorman.

● Cronenberg has always crossed the line between taste and distaste with his combinations of vile glop-horror and social criticism, and this is no exception. A cable TV programmer (Woods) becomes increasingly intrigued by the hardcore S/M movies he is beaming down from satellite, and so does his girlfriend (Harry), a dead-eyed sensation-seeker with cigarette brands on her breast to prove it. The plotline becomes too contorted to go into here, and far, far too weird; sufficient to note that Cronenberg's most interesting trick is to eradicate the difference between hardware and software by giving his hero a pulsing vagina-like slot in his stomach through which he can be programmed by ..it gets much worse. There are distinct signs of strain in the plot convolutions, not least in the spectator's loss of faith over indiscriminate and cheating use of hallucination; what certainly survives is Cronenberg's wholesale disgust with the world in general. CPea

Vie à l'Envers, La (Life Upside-Down)

(1964, Fr, 92 min, b/w)
d Alain Jessua. *sc* Alain Jessua. *ph* Jacques Robin. *ed* Nicole Marko. *ad* Olivier Girard. *m* Jacques Loussier. *cast* Charles Denner, Anna Gaylor, Guy Saint-Jean, Nicole Gueden, Jean Yanne, Yvonne Clech.

● This first feature from Jessua, who made the wonderful *Jeu de Massacre*, coolly and wittily watches its central character, a serious but unexceptional estate agent, withdraw from things into a world of his own. First he lets go his job, and then his wife of only two weeks. The strength of the film, which begins with a calculated mundaneness, is its lack of either explanation or interpretation of the man's behaviour. Whether he is retreating into a life of inner contemplation, as some have claimed, or whether he is cracking up, is left deliberately unclear. As a piece of observation and as a description of human behaviour, particularly domestic, it's rather fine and consistently droll. CPe

Vie de Bohème, La (Bohemian Life)

(1991, Fin, 100 min, b/w)
d/p/sc Aki Kaurismäki. *ph* Timo Salminen. *ed* Veikko Aaltonen. *pd* John Ebden. *cast* Matti Pellonpää, Evelyne Didi, André Wilms, Kari Väänänen, Jean-Pierre Léaud, Samuel Fuller, Louis Malle.

● British audiences have thus far shown stoic indifference to the work of Finnish fashion victim Kaurismäki, and this straight-faced adaptation of Henri Murger's melodramatic novel (1851) is unlikely to quicken their pulses. A polyglot cast (most of them long-haired Finns) enact the depressed lives of failed artists and their consumptive muse Mimi in fractured French, spurred on by names from the director's address-book and a dog named Baudelaire. The one-note joke palls fast, and Kaurismäki's endless quest for emotional truth at the heart of miserabilist clichés winds up in its usual cul-de-sac. TR

Vie devant Soi, La

see Madame Rosa

Vie de Jésus, La (The Life of Jesus)

(1996, Fr, 96 min)
d Bruno Dumont. *p* Jean Bréhat, Rachid Bouchareb. *sc* Bruno Demont. *ph* Philippe Van Leeuw. *ed* Guy Lecorne, Yves Deschamps. *ad* Frédéric Suchet. *m* Richard Cuvillier. *cast* David Douche, Marjorie Cottreel, Geneviève Cottreel, Kader Chaatouf, Sébastien Delbaere.

● Making use of locals instead of professional actors lends authenticity to this impressive look at a group of otherwise innocuous teenage lads in a boring northern French town (Bailleul in Flanders), driven to violence by a mixture of boredom, jealousy, macho pride and ingrained racism. Essentially it's a work of low key 'realism' in the Bressonian tradition (albeit less obviously 'spiritual'), though it includes odd touches, such as the local marching band's unexpectedly dissonant music, and a couple of brief sequences (involving body doubles) so sexually frank they look like out-takes from *Ai No Corrida*. Perhaps strangest of all is that the protagonist's girlfriend seems for most of the film to be the only young female in town, but that's a very minor criticism when compared to writer/director Dumont's tough, confident handling of mood, milieu, pace, performance and theme. GA

Vie en rose, La (Changmi Bit Insaeng)

(1994, SKor, 95 min)
d Kim Hong-Joon. *p* Le Tae-Won. *sc* Yook Sang-Hyo. *ph* Park Seoung-Bai. *ed* Park Soon-duk. *cast* Choi Myung-Gil, Choi Jae-Sung, Cha Kwang-Su, Lee Ji-Hyung, Hwang Mi-Sun.

●Remarkably original and recklessly emotive, this debut feature by a former assistant to Im Kwon-Taek takes elements from gangster thrillers, melodramas, martial arts movies and *film noir* to colour an hallucinatory descent into Seoul's 'lower depths'. The setting is a rough part of town in the months just before the 1988 Olympics, a time when the military dictatorship slackened its grip in the hope of presenting a more liberal face to the visiting world. A young woman runs a basement flop-house, renting out comic books and screening soft-porn videos on the side; her life gets turned upside down by a taciturn macho man with enough trouble on his back to fill several flashbacks. TR

Vie est à nous, La (The People of France)

(1936, Fr, 66 min, b/w)
d Jean Renoir. *sc* André Zwobada. [*d/sc collaborators* Jacques Becker, Jean-Paul Le Chanois, Henri Cartier-Bresson, Pierre Unik, Jacques Brunius, André Vaillant-Couturier.] *ph* Alain Douarinar, Claude Renoir, Jean Isnard, Jean Bourgoin. *ed* Marguerite Renoir. *cast* Jean Dasté, Jacques Brunius, Simone Guisin, Teddy Michaux, Pierre Unik, Max Dalban, Madeleine Sologne, Charles Blavette, Jean Renoir, Roger Blin, Gaston Modot, Jacques Becker.

●Described in its original credits simply as 'a film made collectively by a group of technicians, artists and workers' with no names appearing, *La Vie est à nous* was the most overt work of the French Popular Front, made by Renoir with the assistance of Jacques Becker and Henri Cartier-Bresson, among others, and produced by the Communist Party. Basically a collection of documentary footage and vignettes satirising bourgeois society, offering up plenty of Communist-inspired optimism; but what marks it out from most propagandist tracts is the familiar Renoir theme of community ideals transcending social classes, expressed so eloquently in his previous feature, *Le Crime de Monsieur Lange*. A film of its time, conceived in the shadow of Hitler, it still communicates its message with an irrepressible joy and swagger. DT

Vie est belle, La

(1987, Bel/Fr/Zaire, 72 min)
d Benoit Lamy, Ngangura Mweze. *p* Benôit Lamy. *sc* Ngangura Mweze, Maryse Léon, Benôit Lamy. *ph* Michel Baudour. *ed* Martine Giordano. *ad* Mutoke Wa Mputu, Barly Baruti. *m* Papa Wemba, Zaiko Langa Langa, Tshala Muana, Klody. *cast* Papa Wemna, Bibi Krubwa, Landu Nzunzimbu Matshia, Kanku Kasongo, Lokinda Menji Feza.

●Papa Wemba, one of Zaire's most exuberant and enterprising musicians, plays Kouru, a traditional musician whose popularity dwindles when local villagerslatch on to the more exciting possibilities of electric instruments. Kouru decides to travel to the city to pursue his dream of becoming a superstar. In his eventful, funny journey to success, he lands a job as a houseboy and falls in love. Only problem is, he and his boss fall for the same woman…Set against the bustling backdrop of the town of Kinshasa, the film paints a more honest and vivid picture of African life than any blockbuster with sunset safari scenes ever could. And Wemba is given plenty of scope to perform, leading to a joyous all's well that ends well musical finale, 'La Vie est belle'. IA

Vie est un long fleuve tranquille, La

see Life Is a Long Quiet River

Vie est un Roman, La (Life Is a Bed of Roses)

(1983, Fr, 111 min)
d Alain Resnais. *p* Philippe Dussart. *sc* Jean Gruault. *ph* Bruno Nuytten. *ed* Albert Jurgenson, Jean-Pierre Besnard. *ad* Jacques Saulnier, Enki Bilal. *m* M Philippe-Gérard. *cast* Vittorio Gassman, Ruggero Raimondi, Geraldine Chaplin, Fanny Ardant, Pierre Arditi, Sabine Azéma, Robert Manuel, André Dussollier.

●Resnais speculates on the utopian dream that life is infinitely perfectable, that human chaos, despair and horror can be spirited or educated out of existence. There are two stories, to correspond to each of these possibilities. In the first, set in 1914, Count Forbek (Raimondi), aristocrat, aesthete and visionary, erects a Temple of Happiness in which a select few will be drugged into a state of original innocence. In the second, set in the present, a gaggle of theorists (Gassman, Chaplin) have taken over Forbek's castle to conduct a seminar on the 'education of the imaginative'. Both enterprises come to grief, though in the process Resnais does realise his own utopia, a realm of vast imaginative possibility. A third story, a simple but charming fairytale on similar themes, is offered as 'objective' proof. RC

Vie et rien d'autre, La

see Life and Nothing But

Viehjud Levi

see Jew-Boy Levi

Vieil Homme et l'Enfant, Le (The Two of Us)

(1966, Fr, 90 min, b/w)
d Claude Berri. *p* Paul Cadéac. *sc* Claude Berri. *ph* Jean Penzer. *ed* Sophie Coussein, Denis Charvein. *ad* Georges Lévy, Maurice Petri. *m* Georges Delerue. *cast* Michel Simon, Alain Cohen, Luce Fabiole, Roger Carel, Paul Préboist, Charles Denner.

●Berri's fictionalised memoir – the Jewish child, Claude, billeted on a curmudgeonly old anti-Semite, was the director himself in the final months of the World War II Occupation – wears its heart stitched on to its sleeve like a Star of David. But, though compromised by the facility with which its glib antitheses (old age/childhood, country/city, Gentile/Jew) are reconciled by the (un)likely friendship of the ill-matched pair, the film's good humour and discretion, plus Simon's virtuoso performance, make it never less than watchable. GAd

Vieille Canaille (The Old Crook)

(1992, Fr, 99 min)
d/p Gérard Jourd'hui. *sc* Gérard Jourd'hui, Dominique Roulet. *ph* Georges Barsky. *ed* Nicole Saunier. *ad* Dominique André. *m* Bruno Coulais. *cast* Michel Serrault, Anna Galiena, Pierre Richard, Jean-Pierre Bouvier, Catherine Frot.

●More French recycling of American pulp fiction. Fredric Brown's 1954 novel *His Name Was Death* is mainstream *noir*, the tale of a forger's efforts to retrieve some incriminating bills, every step plunging him deeper into nightmare. This adaptation is reasonably faithful to the letter of the novel, but radically modifies it as regards tone and intention. The geographical setting is now Lyon, the spiritual setting in the vicinity of Ealing, with much whimsical detail and a central role for Serrault that allows him Guinness-like scope for disguises and eccentric comportment. Admirers of the star will find this a highly congenial vehicle, but *noir* addicts may feel somewhat let down. BBa

Vieille Dame indigne, La (The Shameless Old Lady)

(1965, 94 min, b/w)
d René Allio. *p* Claude Nedjar. *sc* René Allio. *ph* Denys Clerval. *ed* Sophie Coussein. *ad* Hubert Monloup. *m* Jean Ferrat. *cast* Sylvie, Malka Ribovska, Etienne Bierry, Victor Lanoux, Jean Bouise, François Maistre.

●81-year-old Sylvie is magnificent in this adaptation of Brecht's fable about an old woman who suddenly starts a new life of delightful irresponsibility after the death of her husband, wonderfully wry and funny as she breaks out of a lifetime of devoted household drudgery to enjoy a round of whipped cream sundaes, movies and fast cars. Equally (or more) importantly, Allio never loses sight of Brecht. For the first time in her life, in her new friendship with the local whore (Ribovska) and an anarchist shoemaker (Bouise), the old lady begins to respond to people on their own terms instead of out of duty. Meanwhile her family, outraged at her irresponsibility, are seen to be irresponsibly frittering away their lives, toiling at jobs which serve only to build prisons for their souls. Witty, wise and gently funny, it is also, in its quiet way, a genuinely subversive film. TM

Vieille qui Marchait dans la Mer, La

see The Old Lady Who Walked in the Sea

Viens chez moi, j'habite chez une copine

(1981, Fr, 85 min)
d Patrice Leconte. *p* Christian Fechner. *sc* Patrice Leconte, Michel Blanc. *ph* Bernard Zitzermann. *ed* Jacqueline Thiedot. *ad* Yvan Maussion. *m* Renaud. *cast* Michel Blanc, Bernard Giraudeau, Thérèse Liotard, Anémone, Marie-Anne Chazel, Jean Champion.

●Guy (Blanc) is temperamentally incapable of going about anything in an honest, straightforward way. Thrown out of his job and his flat, he is taken in by Giraudeau and Liotard, a friendly couple. But he's no liberating spirit like Renoir's Boudu, and the damage starts mounting up. Still, everything sorts itself out in a playful shrug of an ending, and with the balance of Guy's persona, as between the despicable and the sympathetic, tilting decisively towards the latter. The quiet efficiency of the exposition (from a play by Luis Rego and Didier Kaminka) and Guy's self-absorbed loopiness (cf *Monsieur Hire, The Hairdresser's Husband*) identify the movie as embryonic Leconte. BBa

Vie Privée (A Very Private Affair)

(1962, Fr/It, 103 min)
d Louis Malle. *p* Christine Gouze-Rénal. *sc* Louis Malle, Jean-Paul Rappeneau, Jean Ferry. *ph* Henri Decae. *ed* Kenout Peltier. *ad* Bernard Evein. *m* Fiorenzo Carpi. *cast* Brigitte Bardot, Marcello Mastroianni, Eleonore Hirt, Ursula Kubler, Dirk Sanders.

●Difficult to say exactly what Malle thought he was up to with his tale of Jill, a poor little rich girl who takes up a film career and becomes a poor little superstar. Though incorporating elements from Bardot's own life, the film has the feel of a misty, quite unreal romance. Certainly it's hard to believe in the hapless Jill who's presented as merely a victim with no resources of her own whatever. One of Bardot's least affecting performances and one of Malle's least interesting movies – certainly in its American dubbed and cut (to 94 min) version. BBa

Vie Rêvée, La

see Dream Life

Vie Rêvée des Anges, La (The Dream Life of Angels)

(1998, Fr, 113 min)
d Erick Zonca. *p* François Marquis. *sc* Erick Zonca, Roger Bohbot. *ph* Agnès Godard. *ed* Yannick Kergont. *ad* Jimmy Vansteenkiste. *cast* Elodie Bouchez, Natacha Régnier, Grégoire Colin, Jo Prestia, Patrick Mercado.

●This first feature starts out looking as if it's simply going to be a well-observed female buddy movie about two 20-year-olds: drifter Isa (Bouchez) and seamstress Marie (Régnier) meet when the former turns up virtually penniless in Lille. As the film progresses, however, with Marie falling, against both her own and her friend's better instincts, for a callous but wealthy young womaniser (Colin), it enters darker, more troubling territory. It's a beautifully insightful movie which views its characters (the type of 'marginal' folk rarely shown in the cinema) sympathetically but unsentimentally, and after the scene setting of the first half-hour, it grips like a vice as it proceeds to a shocking and profoundly moving conclusion. GA

Vie Sexuelle des Belges 1950–1978, La

see Sexual Life of the Belgians 1950–1978, The

Vie sur Terre, La

see Life on Earth

Vietnam Journey

(1974, US, 64 min)
d Christine Burrill, Bill Yahrhaus, Jane Fonda, Tom Hayden, Haskell Wexler. *p* Jane Fonda, Tom Hayden. *ph* Haskell Wexler. *ed* Christine Burrill, Bill Yahraus. *with* Jane Fonda, Tom Hayden.

● A deceptively quiet and relaxed film, almost a home movie of Jane Fonda's travels within North Vietnam with her husband Tom Hayden (including a visit to Hanoi film studios, where she interviews actress Tra Giang). Certainly no political tract, it is, in fact, the tour as covered by Fonda in *Rolling Stone*. While the film perhaps doesn't solve the central problem of coping with Fonda's status as a personality, its openness, warmth, and occasional gaucheness lend it notably radical dimensions by comparison with the relentlessly single-note coverage of the war and its bizarre aftermath on TV and in the press. VG

View to a Kill, A

(1985, GB, 131 min)
d John Glen. *p* Albert R Broccoli, Michael Wilson. *sc* Richard Maibaum, Michael Wilson. *ph* Alan Hume. *ed* Peter Davies. *pd* Peter Lamont. *m* John Barry. *cast* Roger Moore, Christopher Walken, Tanya Roberts, Grace Jones, Patrick Macnee, Patrick Bauchau, David Yip, Fiona Fullerton.

● Bond struck camp long ago, so it would seem pointless to complain about the dilution of Fleming's cruel stud into a smirking dinner-jacket with a crude line in double entendres. But the problem here is that the elements which act as consolation in late Bondage are missing. Chiefest of these is a strong villain: Walken, far from being able to flood Silicon Valley by imploding the San Andreas faultline, looks more like an effete gigolo, just waiting to scratch Roger's eyes out. Grace Jones is badly wasted. The digital countdown to Armageddon trick has been worn smooth with overuse. The operatic sets of yore have shrunk, and something has gone very wrong when the climax belongs to something as serene and harmless as an airship. Even the tottering finale, high up on the Golden Gate Bridge supports, left this vertigo sufferer in a deep state of lacquered composure. Once 007 was licensed to kill; now he not only eats quiche, he cooks it himself. CPea

Vigil

(1984, NZ, 90 min)
d Vincent Ward. *p* John Maynard. *sc* Vincent Ward, Graeme Tetley. *ph* Alun Bollinger. *ed* Simon Reece. *pd* Kai Hawkins. *m* Jack Body. *cast* Bill Kerr, Fiona Kay, Gordon Shields, Penelope Stewart, Frank Whitten.

● Though often in danger of sinking into a heavy mythical mud of its own making, Ward's would-be visionary account of life on a remote New Zealand sheep farm does achieve occasional moments of striking visual beauty. Following the death of farmer Justin Peers, his wife Liz (Stewart) and daughter Lisa (Kay) labour on with the help of senile grandfather (Kerr) and Ethan (Whitten), an itinerant hunter who hires on as help. Ward creates a powerful sense of the struggle between the farmers, their machines, and the elemental forces of nature, while the sexual tension between Liz and Ethan, and Lisa's strange dreams, suggest deeper mysteries. Ultimately, though, the images and rather portentous soundtrack tend to hint at more than they actually deliver. NF

Vigilante Force

(1975, US, 89 min)
d George Armitage. *p* Gene Corman. *sc* George Armitage. *ph* William Cronjager. *ed* Morton Tubor. *ad* Jack Fisk. *m* Gerald Fried. *cast* Kris Kristofferson, Jan-Michael Vincent, Victoria Principal, Bernadette Peters, Brad Dexter, Judson Pratt.

● Californian small town becomes lawless boom town after the re-working of dormant oil deposits. To restore order, the helpless legal guardians draft Vietnam hero Kristofferson, the town's erstwhile rebel. What emerges is an awkward combination of cheapo war and cowboy comics: gold replaced by black gold; a near-parody of saloon rowdiness; a brooding anti-hero; urban guerilla warfare that explodes into open hostilities. Kristofferson (long-haired) shuffles through quite convincingly, especially as his inability to adapt to a peacetime situation becomes more apparent. His Abel-like brother Jan-Michael Vincent (short-haired) does more driving than acting, and Victoria Principal is almost totally self-effacing as his girlfriend, but Bernadette Peters plays an ill-treated, down-at-heel, after-hours singer with real style. The dialogue veers towards the self-consciously smart-ass (enraged drinker attacks jukebox playing '70s rock: 'There must be a Buddy Holly record here somewhere!'), and the direction has irritatingly jagged, grisly violence alternating with manly introspection. IB

Vigo Passion for Life (Vigo Histoire d'une passion)

(1997, GB/Jap/Fr/Sp/Ger, 103 min)
d Julien Temple. *p* Amanda Temple, Jeremy Bolt. *sc* Peter Ettedgui, Anne Devlin, Julien Temple. *ph* John Mathieson. *ed* Marie-Thérèse Boiché. *pd* Caroline Greville-Morris. *m* Bingen Mendizabal. *cast* Romane Bohringer, James Frain, Jim Carter, Diana Quick, William Scott-Masson, Lee Ross, Nicholas Hewetson, Brian Shelley, Kenneth Cranham.

● Jean Vigo (1905–34) suffered from TB and paranoia. His anarchist father was murdered when Vigo was 12, and the event haunted him. Yet in a career that encompassed only three short scraps and one heavily compromised feature (*L'Atalante*), Vigo ensured his place in history as a poet of cinema. Best known for *The Great Rock'n'Roll Swindle*, Julien Temple doubtless identified with Vigo the proto-punk and master metteur-en-scène, yet the character here, filtered through a gauzy screenplay, is an impetuous, immature prankster whose love for cinema seems to be a symptom of congenital irresponsibility. Constructed as a romance of sorts, the film begins with Vigo (Frain) meeting his future wife Lydu (Bohringer) in an alpine sanatorium, whisking her off to marriage and motherhood in Nice, and then abandoning her to his career. While Frain strikes a boyish, charismatic note, and Bohranger brings her trademark pursed soulfulness to Lydu, they're surrounded by as excruciating a contingent of channel-hopping Frenchmen as you'll find this side of TV's *'Allo, 'Allo*. TCh

Viking Queen, The

(1966, GB, 91 min)
d Don Chaffey. *p* John Temple-Smith. *sc* Clarke Reynolds. *ph* Stephen Dade. *ed* Peter Boita. *ad* George Provis. *m* Gary Hughes. *cast* Don Murray, Carita, Adrienne Corri, Donald Houston, Andrew Keir, Niall MacGinnis, Wilfred Lawson, Nicola Pagett, Percy Herbert.

● Imported Finnish sexpot Carita plays the peace loving Queen of the Iceni, a Boadicea figure, forced into the war with the Romans that no one except the audience wants. Basically this is a British Western – never a good idea – with the Iceni subbing for the Cherokees, Druids instead of medicine men, and the Romans as the encroaching palefaces. It was shot in Ireland with the Irish army, co-opted as extras, required to kick the bejasus out of the Ancient Brits. They and Donald Houston as a ga-ga Druid are the only ones having much fun. Boadicea's grave is supposed to be under Platform 10 at King's Cross station: commuters may have felt something turning under their feet when this farrago was released. BBa

Vikings, The

(1958, US, 114 min)
d Richard Fleischer. *p* Jerry Bresler. *sc* Calder Willingham, Dale Wasserman. *ph* Jack Cardiff. *ed* Elmo Williams. *ad* Harper Goff. *m* Mario Nascimbene. *cast* Kirk Douglas, Tony Curtis, Ernest Borgnine, Janet Leigh, Alexander Knox, Frank Thring, James Donald, Maxine Audley. *narrator* Orson Welles.

● Viking half-brothers Douglas and Curtis fight it out for the throne of Northumbria. Plenty of pillaging, axe-throwing, hearty quaffing of ale, storming of castles, heroic jumping into wolf pits, and manly talk about the glories of entering Valhalla with sword in hand. Handsomely shot by Jack Cardiff, and directed with muscle and verve by Fleischer, this thoroughly entertaining historical epic stands up to umpteen viewings. NF

Viking Women and Their Voyage to the Waters of the Great Sea Serpent, The

(1957, US, 66 min, b/w)
d/p Roger Corman. *sc* Lawrence Louis Goldman. *ph* Monroe P Askins. *ed* Ronald Sinclair. *ad* Robert Kinoshita. *m* Albert Glasser. *cast* Abby Dalton, Susan Cabot, Brad Jackson, Richard Devon.

● As sundry Nordic lasses set off to rescue their menfolk from the Monster of the Vortex, little do they suspect the brief glimpses of laughable effects work that lie in store for them. TJ

Village Has No Walls, The (Bangarwadi)

(1995, India, 130 min)
d Amol Palekar. *p* Ravi Gupta. *sc* Madgulkar Vyankatesh. *ph* Debu Deodhar. *ed* Waman Bhonsle. *pd* Guruji Brothers. *m* Vanraj Bhatia. *cast* Chandrakant Madray, Adhishree Athray, Chandrakant Kulkarni.

● Into the 1940s Maharashtra village comes a fledgling teacher on a mission from the Raja to provide the local children with an education. It takes time for him to win the elders' confidence; to persuade the shepherd villagers to spare their children for lessons; to allay fears that he's after their women; to overcome the jealous threats of one inhospitable local; to come to terms with traditional disciplines and superstitions – until eventually he finds himself an indispensible part of the community. This leisurely, well-populated film has ethnological and historical interest, but as drama it rather saps one's patience. (Adapted by Vynakatesh Madgulkar from his own famous 1953 Marathi novel.) NB

Village in the Mist (Angemaeul)

(1983, SKor, 90 min)
d Lim Kwon-Taek. *p* Park Chong-chan. *sc* Song Kil-han. *ph* Jong Il-song. *ed* Kim Chang-soon. *pd* Kim U-Chun. *m* Kim Jong-kil. *cast* Ahn Song-Ki, Chong Yun-Hee, Lee Yea-Min, Kim Ji-Yung, Choi Dong-Jun, Jin Bong-Jin.

● A startling Korean variation on *Straw Dogs*. A young woman schoolteacher is posted to a remote village for a year, and senses something odd about it as soon as she gets off the bus; by the time she's been raped (with total impunity) by the mysterious village tramp, she's on the way to uncovering its strange and guilty secret. Hard to judge the film's contribution to Korean sexual politics, but it's certainly expert film-making by a world-class director. TR

Village of Dreams (E No Naka no Boku no Mura)

(1996, Jap, 112 min)
d Yoichi Higashi. *p* Tetsujiro Yamagami. *sc* Yoichi Higashi. *ph* Yoshio Shimizu. *ed* Yoichi Higashi. *pd* Akira Naito. *cast* Keigo Matsuyama, Shogo Matsuyama, Mieko Harada, Kyozo Nagatsuka.

● Co-scripted by Takehiro Nakajima, the director of *Okoge*, this magic-realist evocation of a rural childhood is chiefly interesting for its undercurrent of homosexual panic: twin boys are warned that the thunder god will steal their penises if they go naked and imagine being smothered by their gruff landlord's animated fundoshi loincloth. Elsewhere, the film rehearses the standard Freudian reading of the approach to puberty: ground already well-covered by Hou Xiaoxian in *A Summer at Grandpa's*. Amusing and skilfully executed, but nothing new. TR

Village of the Damned

(1960, GB, 78 min, b/w)
d Wolf Rilla. *sc* Stirling Silliphant, Wolf Rilla, George Barclay. *ph* Geoffrey Faithfull. *ed* Gordon Hales. *ad* Ivan King. *m* Ron Goodwin. *cast* George Sanders, Barbara Shelley, Martin Stephens, Michael Gwynne, Laurence Naismith, Richard Vernon, John Phillips.

● A modest but intelligent and extremely effective adaptation of John Wyndham's novel *The Midwich Cuckoos*, about a small English village which mysteriously and inexplicably succumbs to a 24-hour trance-like sleep, after which the womenfolk all discover that they are pregnant. The alien children, strangely alike in appearance, prove to be endowed with telepathic and kinetic powers...You don't get much explanation, and the overall plot may not withstand detailed analysis. But the atmosphere and pace are superbly handled, and the performances of the sinister, inhumanly intelligent 'children' never falter. The allegorical possibilities (generation gap?) are there, but they don't get in the way. DP

Villain

(1971, GB, 98 min)
d Michael Tuchner. *p* Alan Ladd Jr, Jay Kanter. *sc* Dick Clement, Ian La Frenais. *ph* Christopher Challis. *ed* Ralph Sheldon. *ad* Maurice Carter. *m* Jonathan Hodge. *cast* Richard Burton, Ian McShane, Nigel Davenport, Donald Sinden, Fiona Lewis, TP McKenna, Joss Ackland, Cathleen Nesbitt.

●An underworld saga scripted by Dick Clement and Ian La Frenais, who look as though they were disgorging a semi-masticated lesson culled from Nic Roeg, Donald Cammell and *Performance*. A ludicrous exposé of the lower depths of London crime, it tarts up the hoariest old gangster clichés with a bit of homosexuality and a lot of thuggery, and manages to be both brutish and maudlin. Burton gives a performance of ripe grotesquerie as the gay gang boss who is the spirit of devotion to his mother and a leering Marquis de Sade to his victims. TM

Villain, The (aka Cactus Jack)

(1979, US, 89 min)
d Hal Needham. *p* Mort Engelberg. *sc* Robert G Kane. *ph* Bobby Byrne. *ed* Walter Hannemann. *ad* Carl Anderson. *m* Bill Justis. *cast* Kirk Douglas, Ann-Margret, Arnold Schwarzenegger, Paul Lynde, Foster Brooks, Ruth Buzzi, Jack Elam, Strother Martin.

●Having flopped in the States as *The Villain*, this abysmally unfunny comedy Western would need a lot more changed than just its title to even begin to fulfil its implicit promise as a live-action Roadrunner cartoon. Douglas mugs his way through a tedious routine of graceless, mistimed slapstick as his incompetent outlaw repeatedly fails to waylay the miscast Schwarzenegger and Ann-Margret, while director Needham – apparently lost without Burt Reynolds – resorts to hackneyed camera trickery, and only stops the rot with a truly offensive resolution. PT

Villa Rides!

(1968, US, 124 min)
d Buzz Kulik. *p* Ted Richmond. *sc* Robert Towne, Sam Peckinpah. *ph* Jack Hildyard. *ed* David Bretherton. *pd* Ted Howarth. *m* Maurice Jarre. *cast* Yul Brynner, Robert Mitchum, Grazia Buccella, Charles Bronson, Robert Viharo, Frank Wolff, Herbert Lom, Alexander Knox, Fernando Rey, John Ireland, Jill Ireland.

●The Mexican revolution according to Hollywood. Scripted by Robert Towne and Sam Peckinpah, it makes some gestures towards indicating the political and personal complexities behind the career of Pancho Villa (played by Brynner with hair for once). Unfortunately, these are rather nullified by the need to centre the whole thing on an American identification figure – Mitchum as a freebooting pilot – who can serve as a focus for the statutory clichés about simple peasant loyalties and not killing people when you don't hate them. Bronson steals the picture as Villa's brutal lieutenant, who likes to shoot prisoners personally, then have his trigger-finger gently massaged by a pretty wench. Filmed in Panavision in Spain. TM

Ville des Pirates

see City of Pirates

Ville est tranquille, La

(2000, Fr, 133 min)
d Robert Guédiguian. *p* Gilles Sandoz, Michel Saint-Jean, Robert Guédiguian. *sc* Jean-Louis Milesi, Robert Guédiguian. *ph* Bernard Cavalié. *ed* Bernard Sasia. *ad* Michel Vandestien. *cast* Ariane Ascaride, Jean-Pierre Darroussin, Gérard Meylan, Jacques Boudet, Christine Brücher, Jacques Pieiller, Pascale Roberts.

●Marseilles, 2000: the city may appear peaceful, even prosperous, but for all the sun, sea and civic rhetoric, life can be tough. Take Michèle, who gets tired enough toiling at the fish market without having to return home to rows with a husband who refuses to deal with their daughter's drug addiction. Or Paul, brushing aside a residue of guilt over having abandoned his striking docker mates to buy a car and set up as a cabbie, he's lonely, too. Then there's the local politician whose cynicism disgusts his social worker wife; and Aderramane, inspired by a stretch inside to help the brothers react more fruitfully to racism and injustice; or the jobless guy blaming blacks and Arabs for his plight; or Gérard, still so hooked on Michèle after all these years, he'd do anything to help her. Guédiguian has forged a reputation as one of the finest, most distinctive French film-makers around. A humanist in the Renoir mould, here he offers something larger and darker than the whimsy of *A l'attaque!*: his *Short Cuts*-style social tapestry weaves a host of vivid, credible characters into a multi-layered narrative as dramatically engrossing as it's emotionally powerful. GA

Villeggiatura

see Black Holiday, La

Vincent & Theo (Vincent et Theo)

(1990, Fr/GB, 140 min)
d Robert Altman. *p* Ludi Boeken, Emma Hayter, David Conroy. *sc* Julian Mitchell. *ph* Jean Lepine. *ed* Françoise Coipeau, Geraldine Peroni. *pd* Stephen Altman. *m* Gabriel Yated. *cast* Tim Roth, Paul Rhys, Johanna Ter Steege, Wladimir Yordanoff, Jip Wijngaarden, Jean-Pierre Cassel, Hans Kesting.

●Scripted by Julian Mitchell, this covers much the same period (from Van Gogh's decision to paint full-time to the death of his art-dealer brother) as Minnelli's *Lust for Life*. Indeed, the films are not so very different. True, the focus on the brothers' close but troubled relationship not only mirrors the uneast symbiosis between art and finance, but offers through their parallel experiences a quasi-mystical dimension entirely in keeping with Vincent's art. But the film goes further than Minnelli's in its palpable – sordid, even – physicality and readiness to depict vincent's less endearing qualities. Tim Roth, superb as Vincent, veers convincingly between morose introspection and fervered intensity, while Paul Rhys' twitchy Theo lends depth to a traditionally shadowy figure. Best of all is Altman's simple, uncluttered direction, which makes sensitive use of a strong cast, Jean Lepine's evocative location photography, and Gabriel Yared's compulsive music. Nowhere does Altman sermonise about the artist's greatness; his achievement is allowed to speak for itself. If only more film-makers had such confidence and integrity. GA

Vincent: The Life and Death of Vincent Van Gogh

(1987, Aust, 99 min)
d Paul Cox. *p* Tony Llewellyn-Jones. *sc/ph/ed* Paul Cox. *pd* Richard Stringer, Neil Angwin. *m* Jean-François Rogeon, Philip Faiers, Norman Kaye. *cast* John Hurt (narrator), Gabi Trsek, Marika Rivera.

●Cox's version of the life and work of Van Gogh will surprise those unfamiliar with the painter's correspondence with his brother Theo, where what emerges is a far cry from the fevered illiterate loony of popular mythology. Read by Hurt, the letters, besides being intensely moving, reveal an artist both mystical and intellectual, and a practical man taking steps to defend himself from the well-known enemy of madness within. The words are wonderful, and of course the paintings too. Each time the screen commemorates that perfectly poised tug between the precision of the draughtsmanship and the expressionist writhings of the brushwork, you can guess at the strength of mind necessary to produce such art. Cox's film presents a more complex man than the Kirk Douglas of Minnelli's gorgeous *Lust for Life*. There isn't much on the turbulent relationship with Gauguin at Arles, and the self-mutilation, like the suicide, favours reeling subjective camera. At times the filmed landscape is flooded with the subject's psychology – fields of flowers whoosh past into an exaltation of abstract colour, the windmills of Van Gogh's native land revolve like the windmills of the mind. Like most of Cox's work, unclassifiable and considered. BC

Violated Angels (Okasareta Byakui)

(1967, Jap, 56 min, b/w & col)
d/p/sc Koji Wakamatsu. *ph* Hideo Ito. *ed* Fumio Miyata. *m* Koji Takamura. *cast* Juro Kara, Reiko Koyonagi, Miki Hayashi, Shoko Kidowaki, Makiko Saegusa, Kyoko Yayoi.

●Based on the factual case of a young man who broke into a nurses' home in Chicago, mutilating and killing several of the inmates, Wakamatsu's film mercifully has nothing to do with casebook killings. What emerges from the film's rigorous beauty, sense of ceremony, and unsparingly attentive gaze, is a precise, sad delineation of a particular aspect of masculine sexual consciousness. The finale, in which the arrest of the murderer merges with police suppression of student protest, underlines its political relevance. VG

Violation of Justine, The (Justine)

(1974, Fr/It/Can, 110 min)
d/p Claude Pierson. *sc* Huguette Boisvert. *ph* Jean-Jacques Tarbès. *ed* Françoise Ceppi, Ronald Sinclair. *m* Françoise Cotte, Roger Cotte. *cast* Alice Arno, France Verdier, Yves Arcanel, Georges Beauvillier, Dominique Santarelli.

●Exceedingly dull porno version of de Sade's *Justine*, which half-heartedly strives for respectability. To prove that they're performing a classic, no one says one word when ten will do, and the film kicks off with a mini-documentary on de Sade's life and times, concluding with the cheeky suggestion that the whole is designed as a stiff warning against 'unbridled perversity'. But there's nothing unbridled about the perversity on display: as the pure-in-heart heroine, the strapping Alice Arno receives the most routine chastisements before being charmingly struck down by a lightning flash obviously borrowed from one of Corman's Poe adaptations. GB

Violator, The

see Act of Vengeance

Viol du Vampire, Le

(1967, Fr, 90 min, b/w)
d Jean Rollin. *p* Sam Selsky. *sc* Jean Rollin. *ph* Guy Leblond. *ed* Jean-Denis Bonon. *ad* Alain-Yves Beaujoue. *m* Francois Tusques, Yvon Geraud. *cast* Bernard Letrou, Solange Pradel, Ursule Pauly.

●Two wan French babes think they're vampires and sit around their gloomy mansion fretting about the night 60 years ago when peasants burst in and blinded one and raped the other. A group of youngsters turn up and free the girls from their obsession. It's incomprehensible, unscary, but prettily shot in b/w, and everyone looks like Juliet Greco. SFe

Violence at Noon (Hakuchu no Torima)

(1966, Jap, 99 min, b/w)
d Nagisa Oshima. *p* Masayuki Nakajima. *sc* Tsutomu Tamura. *ph* Akira Takeda. *ed* Keiichi Uradka. *ad* Jusho Toda. *m* Hikaru Hayashi. *cast* Saeda Kawaguchi, Akiko Koyama, Kei Sato, Matsuhiro Toura, Fumio Watanabe.

●As in several other films, Oshima takes the story of a real-life criminal (here, a rapist and murderer) and uses it as the key to a sweeping analysis of the ills of post-war Japanese society. Very little time is wasted on the nuts-and-bolts of the police manhunt; the focus is on two women who know the criminal, and – through them – on the history of the village in Shinshu where the wretched man was born and raised. Oshima reveals his real subject gradually, piecing it together like a mosaic. It is an account of the decay of post-war idealism, the collapse of brave ventures like a collectively run farm, the inexorable restoration of old inequalities and injustices. The visual approach, too, is like a mosaic: there are incessant changes of camera angle, as if to stress that no one point of view is 'true'. TR

Violent Cop, The (Sono Otoko Kyobo ni Tsuki)

(1989, Jap, 103 min)
d Takeshi Kitano. *p* Hisao Nabeshima, Takio Yoshida, Shozo Ichiyama. *sc* Hisashi Nozawa. *ph* Yashuchi Sakakibara. *ed* Nobutake Kamiya. *m* Daisaku Kume. *cast* Takeshi Kitano, Haku Ryu.

●From its updated Erik Satie score to its shockingly sadistic gay villain, this 'rogue cop' thriller has very obvious debts to western precedents: it tells a not-very-surprising story about a lone detective who takes on both a *yakuza* gang and his own corrupt superiors, and generates considerable mayhem in the process. But this formulary material makes for electrifying entertainment in the hands of Takeshi Kitano (remember him as Sergeant Hara in *Merry Christmas, Mr Lawrence?*), who stars and directs. The whole movie is imbued with his personality, a mix of stubborn pig-headedness, blatant prejudices, committed violence, and hard, self-deprecatory humour. It's also superbly paced. TR

Violent Professionals, The (Milano Trema: La Polizia Vuole Giustizia)

(1973, It, 100 min)
d Sergio Martino. *p* Carlo Ponti. *sc* Ernesto Gastaldi. *ph* Giancarlo Ferrando. *ed* Eugenio Alabiso. *ad* Giantito Burchiellaro. *m* Guido De Angelis, Maurizio De Angelis. *cast* Luc Merenda, Silvano Tranquilli, Richard Conte, Martine Brochard, Carlo Alighiero.

●A direct crib from Siegel's *Dirty Harry* (in fact almost every scene can be matched from one or other of Siegel's films), given a pernicious Red Scare overlay, and with clean-cut Prince Valiant-cum-Captain Marvel (referred to as such in the script) Luc Merenda as Caneparo, 'The Man', whose methods get him suspended from the police force. He vows to go it alone after the death of a colleague, and infiltrates an underworld composed entirely of drugged-out hippies and anarchists trying to force the birth of a new order by robbing banks. A text-book example of smear-type propaganda of the simplest sort, plus a quota of the formula shocks, dispensed at the press of a button, that seem to be Martino's forte. Luc Merenda's expression of non-comprehending idiocy has to be seen to be believed. VG

Violent Saturday

(1955, US, 91 min)
d Richard Fleischer. *p* Buddy Adler. *sc* Sydney Boehm. *ph* Charles G Clarke. *ed* Louis Loeffler. *ad* Lyle Wheeler, George W Davis. *m* Hugo Friedhofer. *cast* Victor Mature, Richard Egan, Stephen McNally, Lee Marvin, Sylvia Sidney, Ernest Borgnine, Tommy Noonan, J Carrol Naish.

●A competent bank job movie that takes place in the widescreen DeLuxe Color burning light of the Midwest noonday sun, without a shadow in sight. Any movie which features Mature, Borgnine and Marvin has to be some kind of primer in slobdom; but in fact Borgnine plays a religious fundamentalist farmer, and hero Mature soon becomes marginal when up against Marvin's minimal performance as a loose-lipped killer with a permanent head cold. Growling that women and children 'make me nervous', he can make his continual inhalation of benzedrine look like deep degeneracy. When a boy knocks the nasal spray out of his hand, he treads all over the kid's fingers. Sadly, Fleischer takes attention away from the action and into a moral battleground back at the farm, but Borgnine finally gets his pitchfork into Marvin's back. The devil you know...CPea

Violent Streets

see Thief

Violent Tradition

(1996, US/Can, 96 min)
d John Woo. *sc* Glenn Davis, William Laurin. *ph* Bill Wong. *ed* David Wu. *pd* Douglas Higgins. *m* Amin Bhatia. *cast* Sandrine Holt, Ivan Sergei, Nicholas Lea, Michael Wong, Jennifer Dale.

●The title and the packaging are misleading. This isn't the ultra-violent action bonanza they would have us believe, but a kinder, gentler John Woo flick, a made-as a-cable pilot introducing an eccentric crime-fighting trio: two refugees from the Hong Kong triads, Li Ann (Holt), and Mac (Sergei), who is in love with her, and an ex-cop (Lea) who is her fiancé. Li Ann's admirers don't stop there: there's also Michael (Wong), heir to a powerful crime family. Inspired by Woo's 1991 HK comedy *Once a Thief*, this conceit harks back further to classy crime capers like *Topaz* or *Gambit*. Very minor, but quite watchable. TCh

Violette et François

(1977, Fr, 98 min)
d Jacques Rouffio. *p* Jacques-Eric Strauss. *sc* Jean-Loup Dabadie. *ph* Andréas Winding. *ed* Geneviève Winding. *ad* Jean André. *m* Philippe Sarde. *cast* Isabelle Adjani, Jacques Dutronc, Serge Reggiani, Lea Massari, Sophie Daumier, Françoise Arnoul.

●Cashing in on the powerful combination of crime, passion and conjugal bliss, Rouffio has his young couple (Adjani and Dutronc) resort to shoplifting, a practice which keeps them in bohemian comfort and stunning clothes. Typically European, it's superiority they're after, not just shekels. Accordingly they display an inbred aristocratic anarchism, have madcap adventures, and do cutesy things. All this is silly enough and not unfunny, but François' growing angst and his (sadly) unfulfilled suicidal urges destroy the last vestiges of irresponsible charm. JS

Violette Nozière

(1977, Fr/Can, 122 min)
d Claude Chabrol. *p* Eugène Lepicier, Denis Héroux. *sc* Odile Barski, Hervé Bromberger, Frédéric Grendel. *ph* Jean Rabier. *ed* Yves Langlois. *pd* Jacques Brizzio. *m* Pierre Jansen. *cast* Isabelle Huppert, Jean Carmet, Stéphane Audran, Mario David, Bernadette Lafont, Lisa Langlois, Jean-François Garreaud.

●The Chabrol film for people who don't really like Chabrol films. Based, like the infinitely superior but much maligned *Les Noces Rouges*, on a real-life murder case – the 18-year-old Violette poisoned her parents in 1933 – it begins brilliantly with a characteristic demolition job on the dreary, furtive squalors of petit bourgeois life that drive Violette to murder. But the political and social implications thus raised are never really confronted. Instead, leaving all sorts of questions unanswered and avenues unexplored, Chabrol ('I fell in love with *Violette Nozière* he roundly declared) settles down latterly to canonise her for no very apparent reason as a patient and saintly Grizelda. The period evocation is gorgeous, but ultimately it's an empty slice of sleight-of-hand. TM

Violino Rosso, Il

see Red Violin, The

Violon de Rothschild, Le

see Rothschild's Violin

Violons du Bal, Les

(1974, Fr, 108 min, b/w & col)
d/p/sc Michel Drach. *ph* William Lubtchansky, Yann Le Masson. *ed* Geneviève Winding. *ad* Eric Simon. *m* Jean-Manuel de Scarano, Jacques Bulostin. *cast* Michel Drach, Jean-Louis Trintignant, David Drach, Christian Rist, Nathalie Roussel, Marie-Josée Nat, Guido Alberti.

●More personal memories of France under the German Occupation in World War II: the director Michel Drach (charmingly played by his son David) was, however, no Lucien Lacombe, ready to accommodate the conqueror, but a wide-eyed Jewish boy who, despite a spell in hiding with the family of a canny, treacherous peasant, was blessed with a handsome, wealthy mother and survived the war with his trusting nature still intact. *Les Violons du Bal* comprises episodes in Michel's escape to Switzerland, intercut with semi-humorous scenes of the still-trusting Drach (played as an adult by Trintignant) attempting to finance the film ('When are you shooting the sex scenes?' a fat, pin-headed producer enquires). Drach's earnest confusion about the sort of film he is making does not ultimately diminish these deeply-felt, nostalgic, and often affecting memories. JPy

V.I.P.s, The

(1963, GB, 119 min)
d Anthony Asquith. *p* Anatole De Grunwald. *sc* Terence Rattigan. *ph* Jack Hildyard. *ed* Frank Clarke. *ad* William Kellner. *m* Miklós Rozsa. *cast* Elizabeth Taylor, Richard Burton, Louis Jourdan, Elsa Martinelli, Margaret Rutherford, Maggie Smith, Rod Taylor, Orson Welles, Linda Christian, Dennis Price.

●Asquith, once a card-carrying member of the Communist Party and a determinedly radical film-maker, subsided in the '50s and '60s into lavish productions which were in some cases entertaining and glossy, but politically middle-of-the-road conservative. This one concerns the various problems and predicaments of a group of wealthy people stranded at London Airport by fog. The level of the Terence Rattigan script is typified by the episode in which 'devoted secretary' Maggie Smith persuades millionaire Richard Burton to write a cheque for a vast sum of money in order to save her boss (Rod Taylor) from ruin. The performances are all reasonably enjoyable, but it's the sort of film the British cinema could well do without. DP

Virgen de los Sicarios, La

see Our Lady of the Assassins

Virgin (36 Fillette)

(1988, Fr, 88 min)
d Catherine Breillat. *p* Emmanuel Schlumberger, Valerie Seydoux. *sc* Catherine Breillat. *ph* Laurent Dailland. *ed* Yann Dedet. *ad* Olivier Paultre. *cast* Delphine Zentout, Etienne Chicot, Olivier Parnière, Jean-Pierre Léaud, Jean-François Stévenin.

●Yet another film that catches the thrills and fears of a young girl's sexual awakening. Unromantic and shot in long, unflinching takes, Breillat's film sees 14-year-old Lili (Zentout), on a family camping holiday, accept a lift in a flash car from balding smoothie Maurice (Chicot). They meet later at a nightclub, and a mating ritual based on his lust and her paralysed desire begins. Things get complex. In the course of alternately teasing Maurice to distraction and insulting him cruelly – in his hotel room, on the beach, in his ex-girlfriend's bed – Lili reveals a fragility that arouses affection and protectiveness in her playboy seducer. He falls in love, and when he does, Lili senses that her use for him is over. In Lili, Breillat has created a new kind of sex symbol: a voluptuous ingénue who is sharp-tongued, quick-witted, and independent of spirit to the bitter end. But will that appeal to men? Probably not. EP

Virgin (Virgina)

(1991, Yugo/Fr, 118 min)
d Srdjan Karanovic. *p* Rajko Grlic, Mladen Koceic, Djordje Milojevic, Laudie Ossard, Cedomir Kolar. *sc* Srdjan Karanovic. *ph* Slobodan Trninic. *m* Soran Simjanovic. *cast* Marta Keler, Miodrag Kreivokapic.

●Until recently, in certain areas of Yugoslavia, families without male children were regarded as cursed; accordingly, they would select a daughter to live as a son. In exploring the fate of one such family, this fascinating drama has hapless young 'Stephen' struggling with the deception, though defying both her father and repressive religious orthodoxy to find illicit joy in femininity. Karanovic's framing sets characters against the harsh, stark landscape to convey a sense of lives completely integrated with nature, while domestic scenes capture back-breaking hardship. Forceful and tender by turns, this boasts sequences of haunting intensity. CM

Virgin and the Gypsy, The

(1970, GB, 95 min)
d Christopher Miles. *p* Kenneth Harper. *sc* Alan Plater. *ph* Bob Huke. *ed* Paul Davies. *pd* Terence Knight. *m* Patrick Gowers. *cast* Joanna Shimkus, Franco Nero, Honor Blackman, Mark Burns, Maurice Denham, Fay Compton, Kay Walsh.

●If casting were everything, this sensitive adaptation of DH Lawrence's novella would rate very high indeed: Joanna Shimkus is painfully convincing as the clergyman's virginal daughter trembling on the brink of womanhood when she falls for the smouldering sexual magnetism of gypsy Franco Nero. Despite Alan Plater's faithful screenplay, however, Miles' direction tends too much towards the pictorial, lacking the visual brio that brought Ken Russell's *Women in Love* so much closer to the dark, physical essence of Lawrence's writing. Miles later directed the turgid Lawrence biopic, *Priest of Love*. NF

Virgin and the Soldier, The

see Petit Matin, Le

Virgin for Saint Tropez, A (Une Vierge pour St Tropez)

(1975, Fr/It, 85 min)
d Gregory Freed. *p* Marius Lesoeur. *sc* Gregory Freed. *ph* Raymond Heil. *m* Daniel

Janin, Robert Hermel. *cast* Marianne Remont, Jean-Pierre Delamour, Georges Alexandre, Favre Bertin, Gilda Arrancio.
●Had the ingredients of this mishmash been more expertly blended, one might have credited the writer/director with the intention of sending us out of the theatre ruminating on the wisdom of unmarried girls defending their virginity. In the event – having endured this wholly implausible tale of a devout Spanish girl and a mercenary Frenchman who finally deflowers her for the entertainment of some ageing swingers – one is left merely yawning. Set in the '60s Côte d'Azur; zero for titillation, in case you wondered. JPy

Virgin Machine (Die Jungfrauenmaschine)

(1988, WGer, 85 min)
d/p/sc Monika Treut. *ph* Elfi Mikesch. *ed* Renate Merck. *m* Mona Mur. *cast* Ina Blum, Marcello Uriona, Dominique Gaspar, Peter Kern.
●Journalist Dorothee (doe-eyed Blum) pedals around Hamburg in print dresses and heavy eye make-up. She's writing a book about romantic love, fuel for which are two doomed relationships. She visits the zoo and a hormone specialist, but it isn't until she hears an American feminist speak about reclaiming porn that she decides to head for California in pursuit of her runaway mother and her undiscovered libido. The San Francisco conjured up by director Treut is charged with sexuality, from the purring sex-line ads on TV to the SM shenanigans of Dorothee's plump neighbour. Soon Dorothee is belting around SF on her bike, in flat cap and britches, but still with the eye-make-up, and though her quest for love continues she has at least made some very special friends, and has gained an entry into the fabulous dyke scene. SFe

Virgins and Vampires

see Requiem pour un Vampire

Virgins of the Seven Seas

see Enter the 7 Virgins

Virgin Spring, The (Jungfrukällan)

(1959, Swe, 88 min, b/w)
d Ingmar Bergman. *p* Carl Anders Dymling. *sc* Ulla Isaksson. *ph* Sven Nykvist. *ed* Oscar Rosander. *ad* PA Lundgren. *m* Erik Nordgren. *cast* Max von Sydow, Birgitta Valberg, Gunnel Lindblom, Birgitta Pettersson, Axel Düberg, Tor Isedal, Allan Edwall.
●Bergman won his first Oscar for this cruel but unsensational medieval allegory, a tale of superstition, religious faith, rape and revenge set in a 14th century Sweden where the populace is vacillating between Christianity and paganism. On her way to church, the 15-year-old virgin daughter (Pettersson) of peasant parents (von Sydow and Valberg) is raped by two goatherds. Later, in a bizarre twist of fate, the culprits ask for food and shelter at the house of the dead girl's parents. Discovering the truth when the goatherds offer to sell them their dead daughter's blood-stained clothes, the parents exact a brutal revenge. The formal simplicity and overt symbolism (light and dark, fire and water) undercut the potentially sensationalist elements of the material, Sven Nykvist's luminous black-and-white photography conspiring with the austerity of Bergman's imagery to create an extraordinary metaphysical charge. NF

Virgin Stripped Bare by Her Bachelors (Oh! Soojung)

(2000, SKor, 126 min, b/w)
d Hong Sang-Soo. *p* Ahn Byung-Joo, Choi In-Ki, Lee Yujin. *sc* Hong Sang-Soo. *ph* Choi Young-Taek. *ed* Ham Sung-Won. *m* Ok Gil-Sung. *cast* Lee Eun-Joo, Jung Bo-Suk, Moon Sung-Kuen.
●Hong's third feature is built on the same narrative intricacies and ambiguities as before, but it extends the uncertainty principle into the areas of memory and subjective consciousness. Soojung (Lee), a bright young woman who has been saving her virginity for the right man, is quite close to her married boss Youngsoo (Moon) but finds herself more attracted to his gallery-owning friend Jaehoon (Jung), eventually promising to go to bed with him. The film is in five chapters; the first, third and fifth detail events on the day Soojung is supposed to surrender her virginity to Jaehoon in a Seoul hotel room. The longer second and fourth chapters offer different and mutually contradictory takes on the earlier stages in their relationship, reflecting the different perceptions, memories and fantasies of the three central characters. Often very funny and always spot-on in its observation of middle-class mores and secrets. TR

Virgin Suicides, The

(1999, US, 97 min)
d Sofia Coppola. *p* Francis Ford Coppola, Julie Costanzo, Chris Hanley, Dan Halsted. *sc* Sofia Coppola. *ph* Edward Lachman. *ed* James Lyons, Melissa Kent. *pd* Jasna Stefanovic. *m* Air. *cast* James Woods, Kathleen Turner, Kirsten Dunst, Josh Hartnett, AJ Cook, Hanna Hall, Leslie Hayman, Chelse Swain, Anthony DiSimone, Lee Kagan, Scott Glenn, Danny DeVito.
●This extremely assured directorial debut from Sofia Coppola finds an unexpected perspective on what should by rights be difficult subject matter – teenage suicide. Adapting Jeffrey Eugenides' best-seller, Francis Coppola's daughter tells the story of the Lisbon sisters – five delicious blondes who set teenage hormones raging in Grosse Point, Michigan, some 20-odd years ago. On her second suicide attempt, Cecilia impales herself on the railings outside the house. In the ensuing months, the remaining (older) sisters cast a troubling shadow over the neighbourhood, especially for the boys at school. Kept on a tight leash by their religious parents (Turner and Woods, both cast against type and underplaying effectively), the girls come to represent the intangible mysteries and sorrows of all women. As a rule of thumb, one should approach any movie constructed around a metaphor with caution. Nevertheless,Coppola casts quite a spell. She has a deft sense of composition and a great ear for music (particularly an original ambient score by Air). The tone of wistful regret and longing doesn't preclude a good deal of gentle humour. It's a restrained, subtly suggestive piece which disintegrates if you try to get a fix on it. TCh

Viridiana

(1961, Sp/Mex, 91 min, b/w)
d Luis Buñuel. *p* Ricardo Muñoz Suay. *sc* Luis Buñuel, Julio Alejandro. *ph* José F Aguayo. *ed* Pedro del Rey. *ad* Francisco Canet. *cast* Silvia Piñal, Francisco Rabal, Fernando Rey, Margarita Lozano, Victoria Zinny, Teresa Rabal.
●After years in Mexican exile, Buñuel returned to his native Spain to make this dark account of corruption, which was immediately banned. A young nun, full of charity, kindness, and idealistic illusions about humanity, visits her uncle and tries to help some local peasants and beggars. But her altruism is greeted with ridicule and cruelty. Pinal gives a superb performance in the title role, and Buñuel's clear-eyed wit is relentless in its depiction of human selfishness, ingratitude, and cynicism. The final beggars' orgy – a black parody of the Last Supper, performed to the ethereal strains of Handel's *Messiah* – is one of the director's most memorably disturbing, funny, and brutal scenes. A masterpiece. GA

Virtual Sexuality

(1999, GB, 92 min)
d Nick Hurran. *p* Christopher Figg. *sc* Nick Fisher. *ph* Brian Tufano. *ed* John Richards. *pd* Chris Edwards. *m* Rupert Gregson-Williams. *cast* Laura Fraser, Rupert Penry-Jones, Kieran O'Brien, Luke De Lacey, Marcelle Duprey, Natasha Bell.
●At 17, Justine (Fraser) reckons she's ready to lose her virginity, but where can she find Mr Right? The obvious answer is school stud Alex (O'Brien), but it all goes awry when her geeky friend Chas (De Lacey) fails to lure him to a rendezvous at a computer show. Left to her own devices, Justine has a go at designing her own virtual dream date, but just when she's come up with 'Jake', an explosion rips through the venue. Out of the rubble crawls a blonde hunk draped in Justine's ragged clothes, and 'Jake' (Penry-Jones) is ready to face the world, having morphed with his creator, a girl in a guy's body. How on earth will (s)he go about explaining that to decent, sensible Chas? Quite a pleasant surprise to find a British movie offering a high concept plot and character comedy more familiar from yesteryear's John Hughes pictures. The news is not entirely positive, since director Hurran is fooling nobody with electro hardware straight out of the Children's Film Foundation. More persuasive is the device that allows the heroine to learn all about boys by becoming one of them. This one's an awkward customer, but so puppy-dog keen it's very hard to dislike.TJ

Virus

(1998, US, 99 min)
d John Bruno. *p* Gale Anne Hurd. *sc* Chuck Pfarrer, Dennis Feldman. *ph* David Eggby. *ed* Scott Smith. *pd* Mayling Cheng. *m* Joe McNeely. *cast* Jamie Lee Curtis, William Baldwin, Donald Sutherland, Joanna Pacula, Marshall Bell, Julio Oscar Mechoso, Sherman Augustus, Cliff Curtis.
●Based on the *Dark Horse* comics series, this plays like a jerky computer game infected with the *Alien* clone virus. A crackling ball of electrical energy is transmitted via the Mir space station to a hi-tech Russian research ship. By the time the crew of a storm-lashed salvage tug climbs aboard, the ship is a latter-day *Marie Celeste*. Their drunken captain (Sutherland) plans to salvage the empty vessel, but then a terrified Russian scientist (Pacula) emerges from hiding, raving about a force that has occupied the ship and killed the crew. Tiny mechanoid creatures skitter about, an android-manufacturing workshop operated by larger mechanoids is discovered below decks, and the force uses the on-board computer system to state its intentions: the humans are a virus that must be eliminated. Having worked with James Cameron on *The Abyss* and *Terminator 2*, director and sfx wizard John Bruno has the technical credentials. But while he can fling together a competent action or special effects sequence, his handling of the plot and actors is strictly routine. NF

Virus (Fukkatsu no Hi)

(1980, Jap/Can, 155 min)
d Kinji Fukasaku. *p* Haruki Kadakawa. *sc* Kinji Fukasaku, Koji Takada, Gregory Knapp. *ph* Daisaku Kimura. *m* Teo Macero. *cast* Sonny Chiba, Chuck Connors, Glenn Ford, Olivia Hussey, George Kennedy, Cec Linder, Bo Svenson, Henry Silva, Robert Vaughn, Stephanie Faulkner, Masao Kusakari, Edward James Olmos.
●A rip-roaring apocalypse thriller about a germ warfare virus that escapes and devastates the world. Bearing strong echoes of Stephen King's book *The Stand* and Romero's *The Crazies*, plus more than a hint of *On the Beach*, the film has as many locations and characters as a fat paperback, but is saved from the anonymity that sometimes afflicts such ventures by its wonderfully fatalistic tone: in this English-speaking co-production, Kinji Fukasaku allows his Japanese masochism full rein ('How can the entire Japanese population have died in three months?' someone pleads) and dispatches an all-star American cast with happy abandon. Admittedly his film contains some slightly repellent notions about the submission of sexuality to reason, which are as hard to swallow as Chuck Connors playing a British Naval Captain, but you can forgive a lot to a film-maker audacious enough to destroy the world twice over in one movie. DP

Visible Secret (Youling Ren Jian)

(2001, HK, 98 min)
d Ann Hui. *p/sc* Abe Kwong. *ph* Arthur Wong. *ed* Kong Chi-Leung. *m* Tommy Wai. *cast* Shu Qi, Eason Chan, Sam Lee, James Wong, Wai Ying-Hung, Anthony Wong.
●Hairdresser Peter (Chan) meets the mysterious June (Shu, unrecognisable in a dark wig and heavy make-up) as she's busy ditching her ex in a crowded disco. They start dating and soon shack up together, but weird shit starts happening around them: possessed neighbours, friends with inexplicable compulsions to paint rooms red, dad gibbering in the bathroom when he's supposed to be secure in a nursing home – that sort of thing. Turns out that June can see ghosts through one eye, but the amulet that keeps this unwelcome talent under control is losing its potency. Time to get a new one – which leads the couple into ever deeper waters, including those of Peter's own memory. Maybe Hui was forced into this by the commercial failure of *Ordinary*

Heroes, or maybe she wanted to revisit the ghost-story sites of her early hit *The Spooky Bunch*. Either way, this is a likeable entertainment. TR

Vision Quest (aka Crazy for You)

(1985, US, 105 min)
d Harold Becker. *p* Jon Peters, Peter Guber. *sc* Darryl Ponicsan. *ph* Owen Roizman. *ed* Maury Winetrobe. *pd* Bill Malley. *m* Tangerine Dream. *cast* Matthew Modine, Linda Fiorentino, Michael Schoeffling, Ronny Cox, Harold Sylvester, Roberts Blossom, Madonna, Forest Whitaker.

●Like his French namesake, Becker seems most at ease with masculine institutions: the cops of *The Onion Field*, the cadets of *Taps* and, here, a team of high-school wrestlers. The imposing Fiorentino helps adjust the gender balance, Modine gives his customary un-showy performance and Ponicsan tries to find a few fresh-seeming angles in his coming-of-age scenario. Still, it does cover awfully familiar ground. BBa

Visions of Eight

(1973, US, 110 min)
d Juri Ozerov, Mai Zetterling, Arthur Penn, Michael Pfleghar, Kon Ichikawa, Claude Lelouch, Milos Forman, John Schlesinger. *p* Stan Margulies. *sc* Deliara Ozerova, David Hughes, Arthur Penn, Michael Pfleghar, Shuntaro Tanikawa, Claude Lelouch, John Schlesinger. *ph* Igor Slabnevich, Prem Huna, Rune Ericson, Mike Matthews, Walter Lassally, Stewart Harris, Ernst Wild, Ernst Stritzinger, Masuo Yamaguchi, Mike Davies, Alan Hume, Daniel Bocly, Alain Basnier, Elie Chouraqui, Jörgen Persson, Shaun O'Dell, Arthur G Wooster, Drummond Challis. *ed* Robert K Lambert. *m* Henry Mancini.

●The 1972 Munich Olympics as seen by eight directors; eight sequences devoted entirely to sport, with only passing reference to the intrusion of politics. About half of them work. Perhaps Lelouch on the losers is the most surprising, given his indifferent films; his study of private humiliation in a public place succeeds almost to the point of intrusion. Penn's sequence on the pole vault, shot almost entirely in slow motion and silence by Walter Lassally, is the most beautiful to look at. Penn lets the event speak for itself, unlike Ichikawa, who tries to show the 100 metres as representative of modern human existence, takes 34 cameras, shoots 20,000 feet of film, and still fails. Schlesinger's treatment of the marathon emerges as the most individual piece, but with its straining after hallucinatory and atmospheric effects, ends up overdone. Mai Zetterling's study of weightlifters deserves mention, while the other three are forgettable. The final impression that remains is of a public relations campaign – what makes the Games transcend the physical into the spiritual, as the press handout said – for an event that is becoming increasingly complex and out-of-hand; a pity that no one explored those implications. CPe

Visions of Light

(1992, US/Jap, 92 min, b/w & col)
d Arnold Glassman, Todd McCarthy, Stuart Samuels. *p* Stuart Samuels. *sc* Todd McCarthy. *ph* Nancy Schreiber. *ed* Arnold Glassman. *with* Nestor Almendros, Bill Butler, Michael Chapman, Allen Daviau, Caleb Deschanel, James Wong Howe, Sven Nykvist, Haskell Wexler, Gordon Willis, Vilmos Zsigmond.

●Subtitled 'The Art of Cinematography', this American Film Institute documentary turns the camera back on the people (mostly men) behind the lens: the directors of photography. As this intelligently structured interview-based film implicitly recognises, the history of cinematography is also an alternative history of cinema itself. Hence, we start with the silent era and the innovations of Billy Bitzer, DW Griffith's cameraman, and move on to the glamorous monochrome photography of the '30s, Gregg Toland's contribution to *Citizen Kane* and the 'primal imagery' of *film noir*. The documentary really comes into its own, however, when the interviewees – Allen Daviau (*E.T.*), Gordon Willis (*The Godfather*), Nestor Almendros (*Days of Heaven*), Michael Chapman (*Raging Bull*) and many others – reminisce about their own experience: the switch from the 'more abstract' b/w to colour, the anamorphic space, and, most intriguingly, the way in which new technology subtly redefines the texture of the movies. TCh

Visiteurs, Les

(1993, Fr, 107 min)
d Jean-Marie Poiré. *p* Alain Terzian. *sc* Jean-Marie Poiré, Christian Clavier. *ph* Jean-Yves Le Mener. *ed* Catherine Kelber. *pd* Hugues Tissandier. *m* Eric Lévi. *cast* Christian Clavier, Jean Reno, Valérie Lemercier, Marie-Anne Chazel, Christian Bujeau.

●This quixotic time-travel movie comes on like a lunatic blend of *Time Bandits*, Tati and Benny Hill. Tall 12th century knight Godefroy de Montmirail (Reno) and his short-arse servant Jacquouille (Clavier) return to France from foreign wars. Under a witch's curse, Godefroy mistakes his intended father-in-law for a bear and shoots him with an arrow. A potion from wizard Eusebius intended to take him back in time instead hurtles him and his servant into contemporary France, where he finds their castle is now an upmarket chateau-restaurant run by Godefroy's distant relative, the effete Béatrice (Lemercier). Shot in the verdant hills of Languedoc, this puerile caper is likely to appeal more to fans of Will Hay and Mr Bean than those of Monty Python. Exquisite period detail and sophisticated effects. WH

Visiteurs du Soir, Les (The Devil's Envoys)

(1942, Fr, 110 min, b/w)
d Marcel Carné. *p* Andre Paulvé. *sc* Jacques Prévert, Pierre Laroche. *ph* Roger Hubert. *ed* Henri Rust. *ad* Alexandre Trauner, Georges Wakhevitch. *m* Maurice Thiriet, Joseph Kosma. *cast* Arletty, Alain Cuny, Jules Berry, Marie Déa, Marcel Herrand, Fernand Ledoux, Gabriel Gabrio, Roger Blin.

●Forced to retreat into the past during the German Occupation, the poetic realism of Carné and Prévert degenerated into fey surrealism in this lazy medieval ballad about the Devil's malicious meddling in affairs of the heart. The opening sequences, with two mysterious strangers riding out of the desert and beginning to work their magic in the magnificent white castle created by Trauner, have a true fairytale touch. But as the hearts get tangled, with the devil's emissary falling despairingly in love with the beautiful princess, the dialogue gets increasingly lachrymose, and the slow pace begins to take its toll. Wonderful performances, though, and graced with an undeniable visual splendour. TM

Visiteurs en Amérique, Les

see Just Visiting

Visiting Hours

(1981, Can, 105 min)
d Jean-Claude Lord. *p* Claude Héroux. *sc* Brian Taggart. *ph* René Verzier. *ed* Jean-Claude Lord. *ad* Michel Proulx. *m* Jonathan Goldsmith. *cast* Michael Ironside, Lee Grant, Linda Purl, William Shatner, Lenore Zann, Harvey Atkin.

●A fatuous attempt to amalgamate the maniac-with-the-knife format of *Halloween* with the street realism of *Taxi Driver*. As any horror fan knows, *Halloween* worked so well precisely because it was not set in any gritty urban context but in a dream-like adolescent world. In contrast, this film concerns a fascist sicko (Ironside) who terrorises a liberal woman TV reporter (Grant) just seen making an outspoken contribution to a discussion on battered wives, continuing after she has been hospitalised: a thuddingly literal theme that not only shatters any spooky atmosphere the film might have, but makes its lingeringly voyeuristic style all the more reprehensible. Not content with flashbacks to the villain's childhood, the sexist script also takes time out to congratulate the heroine on being worth killing: 'He's after you because you're a strong woman' says Grant's boss Shatner, conveniently ignoring about eight other victims. The fact that the film is not tacky in appearance, and is energetically acted, only makes it more depressing. If you want horror in a hospital, try *Halloween II*. DP

Visitor, The (Cugini Carnali)

(1974, It, 99 min)
d Sergio Martino. *p* Carlo Ponti. *sc* Sergio Martino, Sauro Scavolini, Fernando Popoli. *ph* Giancarlo Ferrando. *ed* Eugenio Alabiso. *ad* Francesco Calabrese. *m* Claudio Mattone. *cast* Riccardo Cucciolla, Alfredo Pea, Claudio Nicastro, Susan Player, Hugh Griffith, Fiorella Masselli.

●One of those Italian sex'n'satire movies, this deliberates for most of its ponderous 99 minutes over the problems leading up to that magical first fuck. The boy's skinny, keeps his head in his Latin text and his mind elsewhere; the girl's more beautiful than one can reasonably expect of a cousin; and there's a muscle-bound friend to kick sand around and complicate the plot. Meanwhile the clergy, fat mothers, and constipated fathers are lampooned in a heavy-handed sort of way, while maids stand around and scratch their legs. An hour and a half leading up to something that probably only lasted thirty seconds (there's a discreet fadeout), and you have an idea of what a huge waste of time it all is. Worth noting in passing that it was exactly this type of film that Polanski took apart so effectively in *What?*. The fact that Carlo Ponti produced both is also fairly revealing. CPe

Visitor Q

(2000, Jap, 84 min)
d Takashi Miike. *p* Susumu Nakajima, Reiko Arakawa, Seiichiro Kobayashi. *sc* Itaru Era. *ph* Hideo Yamamoto. *ed* Yasuji Shimamura. *ad* Yutaka Ogi. *m* Koji Endo. *cast* Kenichi Endo, Shungiku Uchida, Kazushi Watanabe, Shoko Nakahara, Fujiko, Jun Muto, Iko Suzuki.

●Made for peanuts and shot on DV, this phenomenally provocative film may well turn out to be Miike's masterpiece. A mysterious stranger (Watanabe, himself a talented indie director) moves into an ultra-dysfunctional middle-class home – and destroys it by leading each member of the Yamazaki family to his or her most secret, solipsistic desire. Only one of them (the bullied son, given to beating up his mother) ultimately has the courage to break free. The junkie mother (Uchida, a famous author) learns to get high on hyper-lactation and rediscovers her maternal role, welcoming her erring husband and daughter back to suckle at her breasts: a regression to infantilism more scary than any of the preceding incest, violence, murder and necrophilia. Funnier and less cerebral than Pasolini's *Theorem*, its obvious model, this is perhaps the most devastating attack on the nuclear family ever made. TR

Vita è Bella, La

see Life Is Beautiful

Vitelloni, I

(1953, It, 109 min, b/w)
d Federico Fellini. *p* Lorenzo Pegoraro. *sc* Federico Fellini, Ennio Flaiano, Tullio Pinelli. *ph* Otello Martelli. *ed* Rolando Benedetti. *ad* Mario Chiari. *m* Nino Rota. *cast* Franco Interlenghi, Alberto Sordi, Franco Fabrizi, Leopoldo Trieste, Riccardo Fellini, Leonora Ruffo, Achille Majeroni.

●The best of Fellini went into this bleakly funny study of five young men adrift in the wasteland of their provincial home town. Middle class layabouts living by cadging off their families, aimlessly spending their days in pursuit of amusement and girls while nursing vague ambitions never likely to be more than pipe-dreams, they are trapped as much by their own moral bankruptcy as by the futureless society in which they have never quite grown up. Beautifully shot and performed, and governed by an inextricable mixture of affectionate sympathy and acid satire, it clearly (and beneficially) trails the neo-realist roots which Fellini later shook off. TM

Vivacious Lady

(1938, US, 90 min, b/w)
d/p George Stevens. *sc* PJ Wolfson, Ernest Pagano. *ph* Robert de Grasse. *ed* Henry Berman. *ad* Van Nest Polglase, Carroll Clark. *m* Roy Webb. *cast* James Stewart, Ginger Rogers, James Ellison, Charles Coburn, Beulah Bondi, Frances Mercer, Grady Sutton, Franklin Pangborn, Jack Carson.

●Mostly a light-hearted fable in which nightclub dancer Rogers meets, falls for, and marries Professor James Stewart. Much humour is derived from the couple's inability to consummate their wedding owing to family and social pressures, but there are also traces of a critique of the institution of marriage itself: it is always the women who have to adapt and make sacrifices for the sake of monogamy. Rogers is the accomplished centrepiece of the film, slightly atypical as the soft-focus romantic heroine, but with welcome eruptions of her tough and shrewd persona throughout. JCl

Viva Erotica! (Seqing Nan Nü)

(1996, HK, 97 min)
d Derek Yee, Lo Chi-Leung. *p* Raymond Chow Man-Wai. *sc* Lo Chi Leung, Derek Yee. *ph* Ma Choh-Shing. *ed* Kwong Chi-leung. *ad* Ringo Fung. *m* Clarence Hui. *cast* Leslie Cheung, Karen Mok, Shu Qi, Tsui Kam-Kong, Law Kar-Ying, Lau Ching-Wan.
●One of the first mainstream movies tailored for 'Category III' (adults only) release in Hong Kong, this opens with a wildly orgasmic sex scene between Leslie Cheung and Karen Mok and ends with the cheering sight of an entire film crew working in the nude. In between the two it's a not-very-sharp satire of the Hong Kong film industry, centred on an art movie director with two flops to his name (Cheung) who wrestles with his conscience as he shoots a porno movie for the money. The mix of parodies, sentimentality, melodrama and earnest pretensions never really gels, but the overall anti-moralist thrust is decent enough. TR

Viva Knievel!

(1977, US, 106 min)
d Gordon Douglas. *p* Stan Hough. *sc* Antonio Santillan, Norman Katkov. *ph* Fred Jackman. *ed* Harold F Kress. *pd* Ward Preston. *m* Charles Bernstein. *cast* Evel Knievel, Gene Kelly, Lauren Hutton, Leslie Nielsen, Red Buttons, Cameron Mitchell, Albert Salmi, Marjoe Gortner.
●A mountain of self-love, revealing stunt biker Knievel as a saintly combination of Batman and Billy Graham. Anyone who saw the Ray Charles vehicle *Ballad in Blue* knows the format: sole object is to show the star (playing Himself) in the best light, preferably with some orphans or cripples around to be nice to. Knievel comes out of it badly, since he also has thespian cripple Hutton to cope with, plus Gene Kelly – 'an embittered ex-champ whose wife died in childbirth on the day of his big accident ten years before' – who, with his croaking voice and shambling appearance, is in line for a 'Most Pitiful Come-down' Oscar. Gordon Douglas, handling the action sequences adequately and gritting his teeth at the rest of the drug-busting plot nonsense, deserves sympathy as well. AN

Viva la Muerte

(1970, Fr/Tun, 90 min)
d Fernando Arrabal. *sc* Fernando Arrabal, Claudine Lagrive. *ph* Jean-Marc Ripert. *ed* Lawrence Leininger. *pd* Hechmi Marzouk. *cast* Mahdi Chaouch, Nuria Espert, Anouk Ferjac, Ivan Henriques, Jazia Klibi.
●Arrabal's first feature as director generalises out from a series of autobiographical memories, in time-honoured surrealist fashion; personal Oedipal anguish is meshed with strands of social and political criticism, until the two become indistinguishable. Various 'psychedelic' colour effects serve to blur the drama's focus even more. Bourgeois 'outrage' is generated quite mechanically, by showing shit, carcasses, maggots, and so on; when hints of authentic feeling peep through, they turn out to be outrageous only in their sentimentality – as in the fantasy images of Lorca's funeral, thronged with naked street-boys. TR

Viva Las Vegas (aka Love in Las Vegas)

(1963, US, 86 min)
d George Sidney. *p* Jack Cummings, George Sidney. *sc* Sally Benson. *ph* Joseph Biroc. *ed* John McSweeney. *ad* George W Davis, Richard Carfagno. *songs* Doc Pomus, Sid Tepper, Ray Charles, others. *cast* Elvis Presley, Ann-Margret, Cesare Danova, William Demarest, Nicky Blair, Jack Carter.
●Thin even by Presley standards, this has him as a racing driver yearning to win the Las Vegas Grand Prix, and filling in as a singing waiter while Ann-Margret revs her chassis at him. Directed with lethargic brashness, it matches the gaudy vulgarity of Las Vegas pretty well. There's a generous quota of songs, pretty unimaginatively staged apart from an impromptu rendering of 'The Yellow Rose of Texas'. TM

Viva la Vie

(1984, Fr, 110 min)
d Claude Lelouch. *sc* Claude Lelouch, Jérôme Tonnerre. *ph* Bernard Lutic. *ed* Hugues Darmois. *ad* Jacques Bufnoir. *m* Didier Barbelivien. *cast* Michel Piccoli, Charlotte Rampling, Jean-Louis Trintignant, Evelyne Bouix, Charles Aznavour, Anouk Aimée.
●This sci-fi is a decidedly un-Lelouchian Lelouch. At a time of international tension, a businessman and an actress vanish at precisely the same time and in similar circumstances. A few days later they reappear, apparently traumatised and with a message of peace and tolerance from some all powerful Beyond. Reality, hoax, or feature length dream sequence? All of the above. Bags of swank, of course (Lelouch hasn't changed that much), plus an impression of slightly more substance than usual. But be advised Trintignant keeps performing a chant of such insidious, brainwashing monotony that it's impossible to flush out of your system. BBa

Viva Maria!

(1965, Fr/It, 120 min)
d Louis Malle. *p* Oscar Dancigers, Louis Malle. *sc* Louis Malle, Jean-Claude Carrière. *ph* Henri Decaë. *ed* Kénout Peltier, Suzanne Baron. *ad* Bernard Evein. *m* Georges Delerue. *cast* Jeanne Moreau, Brigitte Bardot, George Hamilton, Gregor Von Rezzori, Paulette Dubost, Claudio Brook, Carlos López Moctezuma.
●Bardot and Moreau in irresistibly carefree mood as a pair of chorines who invent the striptease and become twin inspirations for a Latin American revolution, 1907 vintage. Like *Zazie dans le Métro*, this is Malle in his freewheeling guise, casually tossing out gags like so many fireworks, and shortly afterwards he embarked for India as a spiritual refresher course in countering the hollowness of commercial filmmaking. *Viva Maria* is certainly empty, but fun. A fair percentage of its gags may fall by the wayside (especially if you happen on the English dubbed version), but nothing can dim the pyrotechnics of Henri Decaë's camerawork, which has all the colour and charm of a carnival. And the songs Georges Delerue provides for the two stars in their act are delightful. TM

Viva Max!

(1969, US, 92 min)
d Jerry Paris. *p* Mark Carliner. *sc* Elliot Baker. *ph* Henri Persin. *ed* Bud Molin, David Berlatsky. *pd* James Hulsey. *m* Hugo Montenegro. *cast* Peter Ustinov, Pamela Tiffin, Jonathan Winters, John Astin, Keenan Wynn, Harry Morgan, Alice Ghostley, Kenneth Mars.
●A sort of Ealing comedy transplant, with Ustinov in his element as a bumbling Mexican generalissimo who leads an army of 87 men into Texas to recapture the Alamo, huffed because his lady friend scoffed that his troops wouldn't follow him even into a whorehouse. He gets there just before closing time – the Alamo now being a museum – and raises the Mexican flag before realising he has forgotten to issue any ammunition. But that's all right, since the American National Guardsmen haven't any either. In the ensuing stand-off, gentle satirical swipes are taken at bureaucracy, nationalism, militarism and anti-Commie hysteria. It is amusing enough, if whimsical and distinctly patchy, but is given a lift by some fine supporting performances (Keenan Wynn and Harry Morgan, especially) and by location shooting in the streets of San Antonio. The scenes in the Alamo, however, were staged at Cinecittà in Rome: the Daughters of the Republic of America were not amused by the threat of desecration to their national souvenir shop. TM

Viva Portugal

(1975, WGer/Fr, 99 min)
d/p/sc/ph/ed Christiane Gerhards, Malte Rauch, Samuel Schirmbeck, Serge July, Peer Oliphant.
●Made by a group of French and West German journalists (the English version was assembled by Cinema Action), this traces the first year of the Portuguese revolution. Besides documenting the political changes, from the overthrow of Caetano's dictatorship to the failure of a right wing coup in March 1975 (largely because soldiers questioned their officers' orders), the film deals with the effect of the revolution on the people. Factory and village committees, independent trade unions, are shown being set up; the plight of the farmworkers and the power of the anti-Communist Church are dealt with. It culminates with the occupation of an empty manor house, which is converted into a people's hospital. CPe

Viva Villa!

(1934, US, 115 min, b/w)
d Jack Conway. *p* David O Selznick. *sc* Ben Hecht. *ph* James Wong Howe, Charles G Clarke. *ed* Robert J Kern. *ad* Harry Oliver. *m* Herbert Stothart. *cast* Wallace Beery, Leo Carrillo, Fay Wray, Donald Cook, Stuart Erwin, George E Stone, Katherine DeMille.
●An uncredited Howard Hawks directed some of the material in this rumbustious traversal of the Mexican revolutionary leader's rise and fall, with Beery leading from the front as future president Pancho, part moral crusader, part crazy bandito. The big MGM production typically plays fast and loose with the facts so it's as much an action spectacular as a genuine historical chronicle, but there's much good humour and a terrifically hammy death scene where one unfortunate villain is coated in honey and left under the sun for the ants. TJ

Viva Zapata!

(1952, US, 113 min, b/w)
d Elia Kazan. *p* Darryl F Zanuck. *sc* John Steinbeck. *ph* Joseph MacDonald. *ed* Barbara McLean. *ad* Lyle Wheeler, Leland Fuller. *m* Alex North. *cast* Marlon Brando, Jean Peters, Anthony Quinn, Joseph Wiseman, Margo, Frank Silvera, Mildred Dunnock, Henry Silva.
●Covered in an unconvincing mess of Mexican make-up, Brando adds a touch of fire to this otherwise frequently dull tale of the outlaw who became a revolutionary hero in the struggle against the tyrannical President Diaz. An actorly film, of course – what else would one expect from Kazan? – but the direction and John Steinbeck's script seem stranded in a no man's land between straightforward adventure and a pessimistic allegory about the corrupting nature of power. GA

Vive l'Amour (Aiqing Wansui)

(1994, Tai, 118 min)
d Tsai Ming-liang. *p* Hsu Li-kong. *sc* Tsai Ming-Liang, Yang Pi-Ying, Tsai Yi-Chun. *ph* Liao Pen-Jung, Lin Ming-Kuo. *ed* Sung Shin-Cheng. *ad* Lee Pao-Lin. *cast* Yang Kuei-mei, Chen Chao-jung, Lee Kang-sheng.
●A lot of city life flows through Tsai's masterly follow-up to *Rebels of the Neon God*, but our attention is focused on just three people. Mei, a woman pushing middle age, lives alone, sells real estate and longs to be loved. Hsiao Kang has left home and sells burial lockers in a new designer cemetery; possibly gay, he longs to love someone. And the cocky Ah Jung sometimes sells clothes at the night market; he neither loves anyone, nor feels any need to be loved. Watching Tsai manoeuvre these people into proximity with each other so that their lives may be changed is a large part of the film's pleasure, but it doesn't eclipse the sheer joy of discovering gradually where the film's own heart lies. Funny and heartbreakingly sad. TR

Vivement Dimanche! (Confidentially Yours/ Finally, Sunday!)

(1983, Fr, 111 min, b/w)
d François Truffaut. *p* Armand Barbault. *sc* François Truffaut, Suzanne Schiffman, Jean Aurel. *ph* Nestor Almendros. *ed* Martine Barraque-Curie. *pd* Hilton Mac Connico. *m* Georges Delerue. *cast* Fanny Ardant, Jean-Louis Trintignant, Philippe Laudenbach, Caroline Sihol, Philippe Morier-Genoud, Jean-Pierre Kalfon, Jean-Louis Richard.
●Based on an American novel (Charles Williams' *The Long Saturday Night*, but set in small-town South of France, the plot introduces Trintignant as the owner of an estate agency and Ardant as his long-suffering secretary. Trintignant is first implicated in one murder. Then his wife is killed. While he is on the run, it falls to Ardant to solve the crimes, with the neat role reversal allowing Truffaut both to cover familiar genre ground in unfamiliar manner, and to reflect on the fragility of the male ego. Thoughtfully composed, elegantly performed, and shot atmospherically in

black-and-white, it could so easily have become a brittle exercise in form. But the sentimentality is constantly undercut, and almost every scene is infused with deft, sometimes dark humour, even as the corpses pile high on the sidewalks of those not particularly mean French streets. RR

Vivre pour Vivre (Live for Life)

(1967, Fr/It, 130 min)
d Claude Lelouch. *p* Alexandre Mnouchkine, Georges Dancigers. *sc* Claude Lelouch, Pierre Uytterhoeven. *ph* Claude Lelouch. *ed* Claude Barrois, Claude Lelouch. *m* Francis Lai. *cast* Yves Montand, Candice Bergen, Annie Girardot, Irène Tunc, Anouk Ferjac.

● Whatever else, Lelouch must have acquired a super tan making this successor to *Un Homme et une Femme*, so generously does he allow the sun to dazzle his camera lens. An unsalvageably meretricious melodrama (Montand's TV reporter torn between patient wife Girardot and fashion model Bergen) played out against the glamorous backdrops of downtown Manhattan and up-country Vietnam, it is rendered even more preposterous by the pretentious dialogue, inept performances, cross-eyed cross-cutting, and a score by Francis Lai more suited to a hotel lounge than a film. GAd

Vivre sa Vie (It's My Life/My Life to Live)

(1962, Fr, 85 min, b/w)
d Jean-Luc Godard. *p* Pierre Braunberger. *sc* Jean-Luc Godard. *ph* Raoul Coutard. *ed* Agnès Guillemot. *m* Michel Legrand. *songs* Jean Ferrat. *cast* Anna Karina, Sady Rebbot, André S Labarthe, Guylaine Schlumberger, Brice Parain, Peter Kassowitz.

● Twelve Brechtian tableaux chronicle the life and death of a whore, starting out as a documentary on prostitution, ending as a Monogram B movie. In retrospect, Godard expressed doubts about the cheap gangster pyrotechnics as being merely a nod to cinephilia. But like the highly stylised prostitution scenes, they are in fact a distantiating device forcing a more direct confrontation with the film's true subject: the enigmatic beauty and troubling presence of Karina, and the mystery of Godard's own passionate involvement with her. This film, as Godard has noted, was the first stage in the inevitable dissolution of their marriage, as described in *Pierrot le Fou*; and every scene in the film obliquely pinpoints that crisis as originating in the awareness that, as director to star actress, he found himself rapturously but humiliatingly playing client to her prostitute. TM

V I Warshawski

(1991, US, 89 min)
d Jeff Kanew. *p* Jeffrey R Lurie. *sc* David Aaron Cohen, Edward Taylor, Nick Thiel. *ph* Jan Kiesser. *ed* C Timothy O'Meara, Debra Neil. *pd* Barbara Ling. *m* Randy Edelman. *cast* Kathleen Turner, Jay O Sanders, Charles Durning, Angela Goethals, Nancy Paul, Frederick Coffin, Charles McCaughan, Stephen Meadows, Wayne Knight.

● Even stripped of her liberal politics and souped up to Emma Peel levels of retaliation, thriller-writer Sara Paretsky's private eye V I Warshawski (Turner) should have been a plausible alternative to the screen's male peepers. Kanew's vehicle, however, proves a wheel-clamped affair. Hired by foul-mouthed but vulnerable 13-year-old Kat (Goethals) to find out who killed her dad, V I digs into the case, which turns out to be a disappointing piece of all-purpose fluff about an inheritance. Since she's out there on her own, V I has a pit-stop team comprising on-off lover Murray (Sanders) and a caring cop who knew her way back when (Durning); and some of the interchanges between them recall, in a debased form, the old Howard Hawks routines for bantering buddies. The hook is Warshawski's feminism, delivered, and the relationship with the kid, vastly borrowed from Cassavetes' wonderful *Gloria*. Not good. BC

Vixen

(1968, US, 71 min)
d/p Russ Meyer. *sc* Robert Rudelson. *ph* Russ Meyer. *ed* Russ Meyer, Richard Brummer. *ad* Wilfred Kues. *m* Igo Kantor. *cast* Erica Gavin, Harrison Page, Garth Pillsbury, Michael Donovan O'Donnell, Vincene Wallace.

● Voracious Erica Gavin indulges a little choreographed foreplay with a wet fish; a black draft-dodging biker discovers during a mid-air hijack that even Cuba-bound IRA commies hate niggers. Just two cherishably iconic moments from *Vixen*, the film that showed Meyer to have the most dynamic editing style in American cinema, and took him from nudie king to national monument via the most outrageous exploitation of bosom buddydom ever. PT

Vizi Privati, Pubbliche Virtú

see Private Vices & Public Virtues

Vizontele

(2000, Tur, 105 min)
d Yilmaz Erdogan, Ömer Faruk Sorak. *p* Necati Akpinar. *sc* Yilmaz Erdogan. *ph* Omer Faruk Sorak. *ed* Mustafa Presheva. *ad* Yasar Kartoglu. *m* Bosphorus University Show Art Group. *cast* Yilmaz Erdogan, Demet Akbag, Altan Erekli, Cem Yilmaz.

● Or 'tele-vision', being the strange beast brought to an isolated southeastern Turkish township in 1974, by a less than helpful government delivery unit who don't stop even to set it working. Bemused and baffled, the characters confer an air of mystery on the box, which it preserves in its stony inoperability. The believers comprise the mayor, a fondly mocked paternal figure, and 'crazy' Emin, a Mr Fixit eccentric who lives on the edge of town. The doubters are led by the perturbed cinema owner and the preening local bullshitter. But there's plenty more life beyond the simple bounds of the plot. A blockbuster hit in Turkey, this is a gentle, rambling comedy with a minor point to make. Odd to see a film so positive about TV, the eternal enemy. NB

Vladimir et Rosa (Vladimir and Rosa)

(1970, Fr/WGer/US, 103 min)
d/p/sc/ed Groupe Dziga-Vertor [Jean-Luc Godard, Jean-Pierre Gorin, others]. *cast* Anne Wiazemsky, Jean-Pierre Gorin, Juliette Berto, Ernest Menzer, Jean-Luc Godard, Yves Alfonso.

● *Wind from the East* and the other Dziga-Vertov Group films put themselves forward as positive steps. *Vladimir and Rosa* does the same, but it's dominated by an angry sense of defeat. It centres on a grotesque parody/reconstruction of the Chicago Conspiracy Trial, but the actors playing the defendants are also seen in a few domestic scenes (dominated by discussions of feminism), while Godard and Gorin themselves continually interrupt the proceedings to mull over the film's implications and reassess their strategies. The black humour and the new emphasis on the material processes of film-making give the film a distinctive place in the Group's researches, even if its discussion is a rather defeatist rehash of arguments rehearsed more cogently elsewhere. TR

Voce della luna, La

see Voice of the Moon, The

Voce del Silenzio, La

see House of Cards

Voice of Kurdistan, The

(1980, GB/Aust, 109 min, b/w)
d Georges Drion, Jacqueline Bottagisio. *p* Georges Drion. *m/songs* Dilman group Zakho, Samir, Sivan Perwer, Suleimaniyeh group, Zadîna Sekir, O Bedelî.

● National liberation movements rarely have any tradition in cinema, for obvious reasons: celluloid is not a major priority in guerrilla warfare. When films do emerge from or about such struggles, the makers often understandably try to make up for lost time by cramming a whole complex history and current context into one giant macro-statement. But are such ambitious, all-embracing projects tactically the best vehicles for eliciting solidarity in the West? Certainly the first part of this film about the struggle of the Middle East's 18 million Kurds is somewhat intimidating, with its barrage of names, groups, uprisings, and incomprehensible archive footage (rarely labelled). But once the broad outlines have been established, the later material (from 1961 to 1978) is fascinating, particularly on the role of the Shah, and the realignment and move to the left of the Kurdish movement since the defeat by the Ba'ath regime in 1975. As 'one of the largest nations to have been denied a state', Kurdistan, divided among four Middle East dictatorships, certainly deserved to have its revolution popularised. CG

Voice of the Moon, The (La Voce della luna)

(1989, It, 115 min)
d Federico Fellini. *sc* Tullio Pinelli, Federico Fellini, Ermanno Cavazzoni. *ph* Tonino Delli Colli. *ed* Nino Baragli. *pd* Dante Ferretti. *m* Nicola Piovani. *cast* Roberto Benigni, Paolo Villaggio, Nadia Ottaviani, Marisa Tomasi.

● A noisome, sprawling slab of pretentious nonsense, charting the odyssey of a dreamy simpleton-cum-poet (Benigni) through an Emilian landscape populated by the usual Fellini collection of grotesque eccentrics, and clearly intended to evoke the various ills of the modern world. Profoundly reactionary, almost without narrative structure, and embarrassingly self-indulgent, it is virtually unwatchable. GA

Voice Over

(1981, GB, 105 min)
d/p/sc Chris Monger. *ph* Roland Denning. *ed* Chris Monger, Laurie McFadden. *ad* Triple M Productions. *m* Edward Klak. *cast* Ian McNeice, Bish Nethercote, John Cassady, Sarah Martin, David Pearce.

● When shown at the Edinburgh Festival, this caused a minor furore over its supposed misogyny; and indeed its story of radio personality Fats Bannerman (McNeice), writer and presenter of a bland romantic costume serial, far outdoes John Fowles' *The Collector* as an instance of ultimate male possessiveness of the female object. When Fats is accused in an interview of escapism, the programme begins to darken; and when he comes across and takes in a catatonic rape victim (Nethercote), it gets farther and farther out (Gothic vampires, improvised sax doodlings), as does his mental state, finally erupting in (predictably phallic) violence. Accompanying Fats' decline is some increasingly obvious visual and aural symbolism: attempts to strangle himself with his own tape recordings, regression to a childhood stammer. Sick and disturbing. RM

Voices

(1973, GB, 91 min)
d Kevin Billington. *p* Robert Enders. *sc* George Kirgo, Robert Enders. *ph* Geoffrey Unsworth. *ed* Peter Thornton. *ad* Len Townsend. *m* Richard Rodney Bennett. *cast* David Hemmings, Gayle Hunnicutt, Lynn Farleigh, Russell Lewis, Eva Griffiths, Adam Bridge.

● Hemmings and Hunnicutt arrive at their auntie's dilapidated mansion; she (brooding over the death of their son) hears ghostly voices, he (brooding over his failure as a writer) doesn't. That's about all there is to it. There's a surprise twist ending, but its impact is somewhat reduced by the one-and-a-half hours of circuitous chit-chat that's gone before. Based on a play by Richard Lortz, it's staggeringly boring (and blatantly illogical into the bargain).

Voices from the Front

(1990, US, 90 min)
d/p/ed Sandra Elgear, Robyn Hutt, David Meieran.

● A combative documentary from the New York AIDS activist group Testing the Limits, its point being that people with AIDS are on a war footing. It takes an unapologetically polemical line, diametrically opposed to the 'neutral' reportage found in the mainstream media, and begins by looking at the media's subtly prejudicial rhetoric of 'victims' and ghettoisation, before focusing on the work of the American 'empowerment movements' and direct-action groups like ACT-UP and People With AIDS Coalition. What's at stake in this battle, the film argues, is a genuinely insurrectionary groundswell that not only proposes a radical challenge to institutionalised exclusions – of women, racial minorities and gay men – but also calls for a direct confrontation of the power structures of the US Government and the drugs multinationals. The film's technique – collaging interviews, demo footage and TV excerpts – makes for a punchy broadsheet approach, punctuated with info-crammed flashes of text, and (unfortunately) a rousing anthem in the 'We are the World' school. Potent stuff, although at times it wears its pamphleteering a little heavily. JRo

Voie Lactée, La (The Milky Way)

(1968, Fr/It, 102 min)
d Luis Buñuel. *p* Serge Silberman. *sc* Luis Buñuel, Jean-Claude Carrière. *ph* Christian Matras. *ed* Louisette Hautecoeur. *ad* Pierre Guffroy. *m* Luis Buñuel. *cast* Laurent Terzieff, Paul Frankeur, Delphine Seyrig, Edith Scob, Bernard Verley, Georges Marchal, Jean-Claude Carrière, Pierre Clémenti, Marcel Pérès, Michel Piccoli, Alain Cuny, Claudio Brook.

●One of the least accessible (and successful) of Buñuel's later films, it is mainly of interest for its pre-*Discreet Charm of the Bourgeoisie* narrative structure: as it follows a couple of tramps on their pilgrimage from Paris to a shrine in Spain, they encounter various characters and slip through time-warps, space-warps, and numerous narrative digressions en route. It is of course beautifully put together, and there are frequently very amusing interludes. But much of the humour is either too obvious in its general anti-clerical stance, or conversely, too obscure in its examination of the niceties of different Catholic doctrines. One for the Buñuel collectors, or for those knowledgeable about religious dogma. GA

Volcano

(1976, Can, 99 min)
d Donald Brittain. *p* Donald Brittain, RA Duncan. *sc* Donald Brittain. *ph* Douglas Kiefer. *ed* John Kramer. *ad* Denis Boucher. *m* Alain Clavier. *with* narrator: Donald Brittain.

●Malcolm Lowry, author of the highly charged, semi-autobiographical *Under the Volcano*, seems to have had more problems than hot dinners, and this film portrait produced by the National Film Board of Canada puts them all on to the screen with enough clarity to wipe the grin off anyone's face. Here are alcoholic bouts, homosexual traumas, practical catastrophes (a late draft of his painfully written novel went up in smoke), everything culminating in the numbing loss of creativity in 1947, and death through whisky and pills in a Sussex village ten years later. It's a survey which digs deeper and longer than most such jobs, and presents its findings in a complex manner, with strong bursts of visual symbolism (derived from location footage of Lowry landscapes) constantly peppering the conventional interview material (with Lowry's widow, college chums, and knights of the bottle). Topping off the heady brew, passages from Lowry's writings are read by Richard Burton. GB

Volcano

(1997, US, 104 min)
d Mick Jackson. *p* Neal Moritz, Andrew Z Davis. *sc* Jerome Armstrong, Billy Ray. *ph* Theo van de Sande. *ed* Michael Tronick, Don Brochu. *pd* Jackson De Govia. *m* Alan Silvestri. *cast* Tommy Lee Jones, Anne Heche, Gaby Hoffmann, Don Cheadle, Jacqueline Kim, Keith David, John Corbett.

●Only emergency chief Jones and spunky seismologist Heche stand between Los Angeles and meltdown. The most striking aspect of this fun, old-fashioned disaster movie is the novelty of seeing the most familiar of backdrops used as a creative resource in its own right. Throwing in-jokes and tourist landmarks on to the fire with a pyromaniac's passion, Mick Jackson turns the city into a kind of postmodern theme park. Such is the lightness of touch, it's possible even to interpret the pat sermonising which mars the later sequences as a subtle joke – what would this kind of film be without moral closure? Jones and Heche work hard to dig up an emotional rapport from next to nothing, while the slow but inexorable progress of the lava makes for more suspense than the usual slam bang firework display. TCh

Volcano High (Hwa San Go)

(2001, SKor, 117 min)
d Kim Tae-Gyun. *p* Tcha Sung-Jai, Kim Jae-Won. *cast* Jang Hyuk, Shin Min-Ah, Huh Jun-Ho, Kim Soo-Roh, Chae Shi-Ah, Byun Hee-Bong.

●The perfect *Harry Potter* antidote, this comic-derived action fantasy imagines a 108-year-old high school for the magically and martially adept, fills it with colourful stereotypes and lets rip with the digital effects. Dyed-blonde Kim Kyung-Soo (Jang) has been expelled from eight previous schools for failing to keep his awesome powers under control; he arrives at Volcano High – his last-chance saloon – and finds himself facing the power-hungry Dark Oxen gang, top supernatural fighter Song, a tough-but-righteous women's kendo team, and a principal nicknamed Cold-Blooded Venom who is the current guardian of the secret manuscript that can end the chaos. Hong Kong film-makers used to do this kind of stuff with their eyes closed; Kim's advantage is that he does it with both eyes open, one of them focused on a script with enough structural integrity and dramatic impact to shame both Tsui Hark's *Zu* movies put together. A shortened 'international version' is reportedly on the way. TR

Volere, Volare

(1991, It, 96 min)
d Maurizio Nichetti, Guido Manuli. *p* Ernesto di Sarro, Mario Cecchi Gori, Vittorio Cecchi Gori. *sc* Maurizio Nichetti, Guido Manuli. *ph* Roberto Brega. *ed* Rita Rossi. *ad* Maria Angelini. *cast* Angela Finocchiaro, Maurizio Nichetti, Mariella Valentini, Patrizio Roversi, Remo Remotti.

●Maurizio (Nichetti) is a shy sound effects man who wanders around the city in search of the perfect honk, creak or squeak for whatever cartoon he is dubbing. Martina (Finocchiaro) likes to describe herself as a social worker, but is in fact a callgirl catering to a kinky clientèle. Of course these two lonely romantics meet, and Maurizio begins to feel strange stirrings. Little does he realise, he is turning into a cartoon! Like Nichetti's *Icicle Thief* (Manuli is responsible for the animation), this harks back to a golden cinematic era from a bold, post-modernist perspective. Nichetti evokes comparison with the great slapstick comedians; indeed, he is referred to occasionally as 'Little Moustache', surely a nod to Chaplin's 'little fellow'. But Chaplin the on-screen moralist would probably have had a heart attack if he'd seen the outrageous climax contrived here: a sex scene to titillate the most jaded palate, with the fully-animated Maurizio hilariously credible. The film takes a good half-hour to find its feet, and Nichetti himself is sometimes a rather graceless clown, but there are brilliantly inventive gags even in the slack passages. TCh

Voleurs, Les

(1996, Fr, 116 min)
d André Téchiné. *p* Alain Sarde. *sc* André Téchiné, Gilles Taurand. *ph* Jeanne Lapoirie. *ed* Martine Giordano. *ad* Ze Branco. *m* Philippe Sarde. *cast* Daniel Auteuil, Catherine Deneuve, Laurence Côte, Benoît Magimel, Fabienne Babe, Ivan Desny.

●Kicking off with a scene in which a young boy, woken by his mother's scream, discovers that for some reason his father has been killed, Téchiné's ambitious attempt to deconstruct (and put a less generic, more humanist slant on) the crime thriller continues by telling the story through a variety of 'voices', including Auteuil as the dead man's detective brother, Deneuve as a philosophy professor, and Côte as the tortured young woman involved, at one time or another, with all three. Ambitious, yes; successful, no. Though script and direction have their moments, as a whole the film is simply too diffuse to add up to very much, either intellectually or emotionally; notwithstanding the strong performances, it all seems rather academic and, well, pointless. GA

Voleuse de Saint-Lubin, La

see Thief of Saint Lubin, The

Volpone

(1940, Fr, 94 min, b/w)
d Maurice Tourneur. *sc* Jules Romains. *ph* Armand Thirard. *ed* Marcel Cohen. *ad* Jean Perrier, Jacques Gut, André Barsacq. *m* Marcel Delannoy. *cast* Louis Jouvet, Harry Baur, Charles Dullin, Fernand Ledoux, Jacqueline Delubac, Alexandre Rignault.

●'Good morning to the day! And next, my gold...' Ben Jonson's avaricious con-man is altered, however, in this adaptation from a Venetian Magnifico to a 'Levantine' outsider – though as rendered by Baur (who specialised in Jewish roles: Shylock, Rothschild), Volpone seems rather a Semitic caricature, putty nose and all. The film was completed just before the Occupation: dreadful timing in the circumstances. Romains further offends by reforming the conniving servant Mosca (Jouvet), who here outwits Volpone, humiliates him and gives away his gold to the poor! The film's cinematic virtues are not negligible, but the fact that Baur died in 1943 after being tortured by the Gestapo only adds to its troubling undertones. BBa

Volunteers

(1985, US, 107 min)
d Nicholas Meyer. *p* Richard Shepherd, Walter F Parkes. *sc* Ken Levine, David Isaacs. *ph* Ric Waite. *ed* Ronald Roose, Steven Polivka. *pd* James Schoppe, Delia Castaneda Millan. *m* James Horner. *cast* Tom Hanks, John Candy, Rita Wilson, Tim Thomerson, Gedde Watanabe, George Plimpton, Allan Arbus.

●Compulsive gambler Lawrence Bourne III (Hanks) joins the Peace Corps to evade a pack of creditors. In Thailand (oh yeah? And this is Patagonia) he encounters a manic blancmange (Candy), defeats the local black marketeer, an army of gooks and CIA, and gets his girl (Wilson). From titles to credits, this is a cynical exploitation of every film in the book – *The Bridge on the River Kwai*, *Apocalypse Now*, *Indiana Jones and the Temple of Doom*, even *Casablanca* – but is by no means as good as this might suggest. A blasé Hanks redeems this string of sexist, racist, comic clichés with winning charm. It's funny. MS

Von Richthofen and Brown (aka The Red Baron)

(1971, US, 97 min)
d Roger Corman. *p* Gene Corman. *sc* John William Corrington, Joyce H Corrington. *ph* Michael Reed. *ed* George Van Noy. *ad* Jimmy Teru Murakami. *m* Hugo Friedhofer. *cast* John Phillip Law, Don Stroud, Barry Primus, Karen Huston, Corin Redgrave, Hurd Hatfield, Peter Masterson, Stephen McHattie.

●Corman's Poe-derived motifs are transposed exuberantly to the skies as WWI biplanes fight it out with romantic heroism. Law's Baron von Richthofen, an airborne Teutonic knight, carries the seed of inevitable disaster within him: his mistake being that he removes the goggles from the first pilot he shoots down (the eye fixation again) and looks into the dead man's eyes; his perversion, that he needs to remember each kill. The Baron is firmly identified with the past, and his plebeian Canadian counterpart Brown (Stroud), representative of the new generation, ends up not with grudging respect for a gentlemanly enemy, but with the growing realisation that both of them are instruments of a destructive force. Good fights evil as in the regulation war movie, only here good and evil are neither separable nor where you'd expect to find them. Corman may have risen through the ranks, but his production economies are still blatant. Period reconstruction is abandoned, and each plane, one would swear, crashes to the same whizzbang soundtrack. Originally the German segments were shot in natural Yankee, now they are dubbed into German-accented English: 'Effry moment I am in ze air viz zees schpandaus in my hands – zat iss forever!' Schterling schtuff.

Von Ryan's Express

(1965, US, 117 min)
d Mark Robson. *p* Saul David. *sc* Wendell Mayes, Joseph Landon. *ph* William H Daniels. *ed* Dorothy Spencer. *ad* Jack Martin Smith, Hilyard Brown. *m* Jerry Goldsmith. *cast* Frank Sinatra, Trevor Howard, Raffaella Carra, Sergio Fantoni, Brad Dexter, John Leyton, Wolfgang Preiss, James Brolin, Adolfo Celi.

●Set in a World War II PoW camp in Italy, this starts with what looks like becoming solemn *Bridge on the River Kwai* stiff-upper-lippery, but soon turns into a ripping adventure. Directed with amused panache by Robson, and helped no end by a fine cast, it's action all the way as Sinatra contrives a mass escape which culminates in the theft of a train and a wild dash through German-occupied Italy to Switzerland and liberty. There's the masquerade in German uniforms to obtain the papers which will permit them to proceed; a sinister encounter with a Gestapo agent who turns out to be more interested in black marketeering; an attack on the main railway control tower at Milan; a superb final battle with the train perched precariously on a slender viaduct high in the Alps while the prisoners struggle to free a blocked tunnel, ward off attacking aircraft, and halt their pursuers. As much fun as an old-time serial. TM

Voodoo Man

(1944, US, 62 min, b/w)
d William Beaudine. *p* Sam Katzman. *sc* Robert Charles. *ph* Marcel Le Picard. *ed* Carl Pierson. *ad* Dave Milton. *m* Edward Kay. *cast* Bela Lugosi, John Carradine, George Zucco, Michael Ames, Henry Hall, Wanda McKay.
● White voodoo in American suburbia, '40s style! A pleasantly tacky Monogram B movie, with paper-thin action and Bela Lugosi hamming wildly from start to finish as the mad doctor who tries to bring his wife back to life by kidnapping young women for use in psycho-surgery. Two retarded henchmen and a tongue-in-cheek finale save the day. CA

Voodoo Woman

(1956, US, 77 min, b/w)
d Edward L Cahn. *p* Alex Gordon. *sc* Russell Bender, VI Voss. *ph* Frederick E West. *ed* Ronald Sinclair. *ad* Bartlett A Carré. *m* Darrell Călker. *cast* Tom Conway, Marla English, Michael Connors, Lance Fuller.
● No budget nonsense in which mad scientist Conway turns jungle adventuress Marla English into a psychopathic monster. See if you can work out what's going on – and why. TJ

Vortex

(1982, US, 87 min)
d Scott B, Beth B. *p* Jonathan Auerbach. *sc* Scott B, Beth B. *ph* Steven Fierberg. *ed* Scott B, Beth B. *m* Adele Bertel, Richard Edson, Lydia Lunch, Scott B, Beth B. *cast* James Russo, Lydia Lunch, Bill Rice, Ann Magnuson, Brent Collins, Bill Corsair, Tom Webber, Scott B.
● The very accomplished (and self-consciously wry) first 16mm feature by the NY new wave underground film-makers Scott and Beth B finds private eye Angel Powers (poet, singer and playwright Lydia Lunch) – hard boozing, foul mouthed, clad in black leather, and her mind not always on the job – set to solve the mystery of a Congressman's assassination, against a background of serpentine paranoia and 'Star Wars' gadgetry. Bill Rice plays a Howard Hughes-like recluse (in the cadaverous manner of Klaus Kinski) who commissioned the hit to ensure that a defence contract went to a rival. Made on a tiny budget, with striking chiaroscuro visual effects, the movie pulses with a punk sensibility. It meanders and is sometimes chaotically makeshift, but it's all of a part: tough and buzzing with New York zip. JPy

Vortex, The

(1928, GB, 6,281 ft, b/w)
d Adrian Brunel. *p* Michael Balcon. *sc* Eliot Stannard, (titles) Roland Pertwee. *ph* Jimmy Wilson. *ad* Clifford Pember. *cast* Ivor Novello, Frances Doble, Willete Kershaw, Simeon Stewart.
● A tale of fraught emotional intrigues set among the wealthy and sophisticated: a prig, pianist and wimp Nicky has a hard time with journalist Bunty, who's still attracted to old flame and cad Tom, who is Nicky's age – concealing mother's paramour. First staged in 1924, Noël Coward's *succès de scandale* about incest, promiscuity, and morphine addiction was not surprisingly toned down for the screen; and now the hoohah about adultery on the tennis court, pill popping in the studio, and other such beastly japes, seems stale and dated. Novello as Nicky is irritatingly wet, while the succession of hounders, rotters, and chic shams looks like the creation of a posturing moraliser with a puritannically reactionary message. A dreadfully stagey curio. GA

Vou Para Casa

see I'm Going Home

Vous Intéressez-vous à la Chose?

see First Time with Feeling

Voyage

(1993, It/GB/Malta, 58 min)
d John MacKenzie. *p* Tarak Ben Ammar, Peby Guisez, John Davis, Merrill Karpf. *sc* Mark Mongomery. *ph* Clive Tickner. *ed* Graham Walker. *pd* Enrico Fiorentini. *m* Carl Davis. *cast* Rutger Hauer, Eric Roberts, Karen Allen, Connie Nielsen.
● A somewhat pale shadow of *Dead Calm*. Before going on a Mediterranean sailing trip to help their ailing marriage, Morgan (Hauer) and Kit Norvell (Allen) meet Gil Freeland (Roberts) at their Class of '72 college reunion. Gil, now a dentist, and wife Ronnie (Nielsen) invite themselves on board and proceed in the nasty, psychotic behaviour we just knew lay behind those sweet smiles. In the end, Hauer works out the murderous plot, and, clutching Roberts' dental bag, exclaims, 'These teeth were meant for us!' Heavy signposting, insistent Carl Davis score; not bad performances. FM

Voyage, The (El Viaje)

(1991, Arg/Fr, 150 min)
d/p/sc Fernando E Solanas. *ph* Felix Monti. *ed* Alberto Borello, Jacqueline Meppiel, Jacques Gaillard. *m* Egberto Gismonti, Astor Piazzolla, Fernando Solanas. *cast* Walter Quiroz, Soledad Alfaro, Ricardo Bartis, Cristina Becerra, Marc Berman.
● Solanas's cinematic trip – ramble, rather – from tip to toe of South America comes as a disappointment after the melancholic pleasures of *Sur*. This is a voyage round my fatherland: part magic-realist travelogue, part politico-satirical parable. It follows the journey taken by 17-year-old Martin – by bicycle! – from his snow-frozen school in Tierra del Fuego in search of his 'real' father, a cartoonist turned anthropologist believed to be in the Amazon. On his way north – visiting his grandmother in a drowned valley outside Buenos Aires, then on through the Andes to Nicaragua, the gold mines of Peru and Mexico – he meets various 'characters' from his father's work, a mysterious girl, a blind Jamaican, a drummer. Where *Sur* was suffused with fragile optimism, reflecting the hope that came with the return of democracy, *The Voyage* presents a more diffuse, enervated vision, expressive of an anomie of political failure and neglect. As a sad state-of-the-nations address to the younger generation it has pertinence, but its length and aimlessness often prove tedious. WH

Voyage au début du monde

see Journey to the Beginning of the World

Voyage Home: Star Trek IV, The

(1986, US, 119 min)
d Leonard Nimoy. *p* Harve Bennett. *sc* Steve Meerson, Peter Krikes, Harve Bennett, Nicholas Meyer. *ph* Don Peterman. *ed* Peter E Berger. *pd* Jack T Collis. *m* Leonard Rosenman. *cast* William Shatner, Leonard Nimoy, DeForest Kelley, James Doohan, George Takei, Walter Koenig, Nichelle Nichols, Jane Wyatt, Catherine Hicks, John Schuck, Brock Peters.
● Kirk & Co return to present-day San Francisco to save the whales in the most enjoyable film of the series so far, also returning to the simplistic morality-play format that gave the original TV series its strength. The crew embark on a chase through contemporary California: Spock gets to put the Vulcan pinch on a punk, Kirk gets lost on a downtown bus, and Chekov hits the street to find a nuclear 'wessel' (in order to get enough juice for the ship, whales and water to make the jump through time). Nimoy's irreverent tone makes it more digestible than it sounds: a myth whose heart lies 20 years in the past, and whose eyes look 2,000 years into the future. SGo

Voyage of the Damned

(1976, GB, 155 min)
d Stuart Rosenberg. *p* Robert Fryer. *sc* Steve Shagan, David Butler. *ph* Billy Williams. *ed* Tom Priestley. *pd* Wilfrid Shingleton. *m* Lalo Schifrin. *cast* Faye Dunaway, Max von Sydow, Oskar Werner, Malcolm McDowell, James Mason, Orson Welles, Katharine Ross, Ben Gazzara, Lee Grant, Sam Wanamaker, Lynne Frederick, Julie Harris, Helmut Griem, Luther Adler, Wendy Hiller, Maria Schell, Fernando Rey, José Ferrer, Denholm Elliott.
● In May 1939, to define the Jewish 'problem' to the world, Goebbels had 937 German Jews shipped to the apparent safety of Cuba. Refused entry into Havana, the luxury liner was forced back towards Hamburg and the camps. Rosenberg here confuses seriousness with tedious solemnity, and with the star glut has produced a compacted TV series. Too many dramas vie for attention on board. The political doings in Havana are confusing; and the prelude to each Cuban scene – maracas, rumbas, cut-price Carmen Mirandas – irritates. Very idiosyncratic performances from the big shots: Welles' wryly charitable Cuban magnate; Captain von Sydow, humane and anguished; steward McDowell hitting new heights in public school deference; Dunaway in jackboots and monocle. The best moments, such as they are, come in the big passenger scenes; though awkwardly filmed, they generate hysteria, a sense of despair. JS

Voyager

(1991, Ger/Fr, 117 min)
d Volker Schlöndorff. *p* Eberhard Junkersdorf. *sc* Rudy Wurlitzer. *ph* Pierre Lhomme, Yorgos Arvanitis. *ed* Dagmar Hirtz. *pd* Nicos Perakis. *m* Stanley Myers. *cast* Sam Shepard, Julie Delpy, Barbara Sukowa, Dieter Kirchlechner, Traci Lind, Deborah Lee-Furness, August Zirner.
● The fifty-year-old man revitalised by a love affair with a twenty-year-old girl is one of life's clichés, but Schlöndorff's film, adapted from Max Frisch's novel *Homo Faber* (and filmed in English), also examines the price. Faber, laconically played by Shepard, is the rational man who has no time for emotion, and his relationships are cursory. Dodging an intimate dinner-for-two in his New York apartment, he makes his excuses, impulsively hops on a liner bound for France – and falls in love with fellow-passenger Delpy, of the Pre-Raphaelite looks. By the time they dock, they can't bear to say goodbye, and he hires a car to take her to Greece, where a tragic irony from the past awaits him. Unfortunately, audiences will see this coming a mile off, and may also resent the symbolic signposts. At least Schlöndorff isn't afraid of ideas, even if they derive from literary sources. BC

Voyages (Tracks)

(1999, Fr/Pol, 115 min)
d Emmanuel Finkiel. *p* Yael Fogiel. *sc* Emmanuel Finkiel. *ph* Jean-Claude Larrieu, Hans Meier. *ed* Emmanuelle Castro. *pd* Dorota Ignaczak, Katia Wyszkop. *cast* Shulamit Adar, Liliane Rovère, Esther Gorintin, Natan Cogan, Moscu Alcalay, Maurice Chevit, Michael Shillo.
● A very impressive feature about the present-day legacy of the Holocaust, this delicate, deceptively simple film consists of three separate episodes. A group of mainly elderly Jews from France, Germany and elsewhere visit Poland, where their coach breaks down en route to Auschwitz; a middle-aged Parisian is contacted by a Lithuanian man claiming to be her father, unseen since the war and long believed dead; an elderly Moscow woman takes up Israeli citizenship in Tel Aviv, and finds her newly adopted country bewildering. The stories are loosely, but powerfully linked, not merely through the characters but through theme: it's a movie about memory, lost time, the diaspora, identity, exile, searching, trying to find a way to make sense of the past. It's all done with sensitivity, intelligence and not a little humour. GA

Voyage-Surprise

(1947, Fr, 85 min, b/w)
d Pierre Prévert. *sc* Jacques Prévert, Pierre Prévert, Claude Accursi. *ph* Jean Bourgoin. *ed* Jacqueline Desagneaux. *ad* Alexandre Trauner. *m* Joseph Kosma. *cast* Maurice Baquet, Martine Carol, Etienne Decroux, Pierre Piéral, Annette Poivre, Marcel Pérès, Max Revol, Sinoël.
● Dazzlingly masterminded by Jacques and Pierre Prévert, first generation Surrealists both, this is not only the movie that Buñuel wanted *Discreet Charm of the Bourgeoisie* to be, but also one of the most laceratingly funny provocations ever launched in France. A guileless old tour proprietor trumps his new-fangled rival by offering a genuine mystery trip; the takers are a crowd of eccentrics and dropouts from all backgrounds and classes, who find themselves experiencing all their wildest dreams and fears as they follow their truly arbitrary itinerary. Jacques Prévert's effortlessly brilliant dialogue points up the fact

that the comedy is founded on benign-but-tough assumptions about eroticism, social attitudes, and revolution. It's an ecstatic experience. TR

Voyage to Cythera (Taxidi sta Kithira)

(1984, Greece/WGer/It/GB, 136 min)
d Theo Angelopoulos. *p* Nikos Angelopoulos. *sc* Theo Angelopoulos, Theo Valentinos, Tonino Guerra. *ph* Yorgos Arvanitis. *ed* Georgios Triantafyllou. *m* Eleni Karaindrou. *cast* Julio Brogi, Manos Katrakis, Mary Chronopoulou, Dionyssis Papayannopoulos, Dora Volanaki.

● A film-maker, Alexandros (Brogi), auditions a succession of old men who speak the line, 'It's me, it's me.' Tiring of the task, he goes to a café and sees his perfect actor, a lavender-seller. Alexandros follows the man to Piraeus where, it transpires, the film-maker is to meet his father, a resistance fighter (Katrakis) returning to Greece after 32 years in the USSR. The father descends from a huge anonymous vessel to an empty quay. 'It's me,' he says. Not knowing what to do, Alexandros reaches to take the old man's violin case. 'Aren't you going to kiss me?' his father asks. Angelopoulos once again plays a variation on the theme of what it means to be a modern Greek artist living in the shadow of the civil war. The first half of the film, which is told naturalistically, with the father visiting his native village and resolving not to sell his barren ancestral land (now required for a winter sports centre), is suffused with that peculiar melancholy which Angelopoulos has made entirely his own. One begins to lose the thread in the second half, however, when the old man and his wife are cast adrift on a symbolic voyage to Cythera, birthplace of Aphrodite, the goddess of love and regeneration. JPy

Voyage to Italy

see Viaggio in Italia

Vraie Nature de Bernadette, La

see True Nature of Bernadette, The

Vredens Dag

see Day of Wrath

Vroom

(1988, GB, 89 min).
d Beeban Kidron. *p* Paul Lister. *sc* Jim Cartwright. *ph* Gale Tattersall. *ed* Stephen Singleton. *ad* Caroline Hanania. *m* Adam Kidron. *cast* Clive Owen, Diana Quick, David Thewlis.

● Down those cobbled streets a man must go in Beeban Kidron's feature debut, about two Lancashire lads – Owen the smooth guy all the girls want to kiss, Thewlis a spiky-haired loon – who decide to kick it all in and joyride off to nowhere. The brightly promising first half has Owen conducting a passionate affair with sultry divorcée Quick, and the direction has zip and sensuality to spare, with especially atmospheric photography. However, Jim Cartwright's script is thin on the ground and detours into road movie clichédom, losing the film its early exuberance and eventually flying off into unconvincing whimsy. But then that's probably the message – that pure fantasy is the only way out of the mortgage repayments. DT

W

Willy Wonka and the Chocolate Factory

Wackiest Ship in the Army, The

(1960, US, 100 min)
d Richard Murphy. *p* Fred Kohlmar. *sc* Richard Murphy. *ph* Charles Lawton Jr. *ed* Charles Nelson. *ad* Carl Anderson. *m* George Duning. *cast* Jack Lemmon, Ricky Nelson, John Lund, Chips Rafferty, Tom Tully, Joby Baker, Patricia Driscoll.

●Lemmon flaps amiably enough as the lieutenant in charge of scrap-bound gunship 'The Echo', surprisingly charged with providing an escort through Japanese-controlled waters in the South Pacific in 1943, yet the vessel's real role is to provide an erratic decoy that'll suitably bamboozle enemy strategists. Passable blend of laughter and heroics, thankfully never quite as 'zany' as the title suggests. TJ

Wages of Fear

see Sorcerer

Wages of Fear, The (Le Salaire de la Peur)

(1953, Fr/It, 144 min, b/w)
d Henri-Georges Clouzot. *p* Raymond Borderie, Henri-Georges Clouzot. *sc* Henri-Georges Clouzot. *ph* Armand Thirard. *ed* Madeleine Gug, Henri Rust. *ad* René Renoux. *m* Georges Auric. *cast* Yves Montand, Charles Vanel, Peter Van Eyck, Folco Lulli, Véra Clouzot, Dario Moreno, William Tubbs.

●Buried at the time of William Friedkin's shabby remake (*Sorcerer*) but now blessedly with us again, this confirms the view of Clouzot as one of the sourest of modern film-makers. A slow first hour establishes a world of sweating, poor expatriates hanging out in the feverish bars in French colonial Latin America, which inevitably brings to mind such far-flung adventurer films as *Only Angels Have Wings*. But Hawks' classic depends upon the fraternal bonds forged among his existential heroes by flying in the face of death. When Clouzot's foursome decide to drive a load of nitroglycerine through the jungle in order to raise some cash, the motive is greed and the results are as black a vision of human infidelity as any since *Othello*. The cliff-edge tension wracks the nerves, of course, but never obscures the fact that men in contest with each other will crack up and die; one truck blows away without reason; the other only arrives by running over its co-driver, in an oil-pool that looks like the pit of hell. A reeking bandana movie, with all the expected thrills, but a vision of men as scurrying insects with no redeeming features. CPea

Wagner

(1983, GB/Hun/Aust, 300 min)
d Tony Palmer. *p* Alan Wright. *sc* Charles Wood. *ph* Vittorio Storaro. *ed* Graham Bunn. *ad* Kenneth E Carey. *cast* Richard Burton, Vanessa Redgrave, Gemma Craven, László Gálffi, John Gielgud, Ralph Richardson, Laurence Olivier, Ronald Pickup, Joan Plowright, Arthur Lowe, Franco Nero.

●Palmer's 5-hour biopic of Wagner (nine hours in the TV version) is a long haul for anyone: sumptuous, overblown, lumbering, and riddled with narrative non sequiturs. The strangest aspect is that the music often seems peripheral rather than central, relegated to being film music as though we might as well be watching a biopic about Ennio Morricone. The visuals are splendid and you can play spot the cast, but somehow it's all a bit sub-Ken Russell, without the redeeming vulgarity and with a lot less cinematic energy. SM

Wagon Master

(1950, US, 86 min, b/w)
d John Ford. *p* John Ford, Merian C Cooper. *sc* Frank S Nugent, Patrick Ford. *ph* Bert Glennon. *ed* Jack Murray. *ad* James Basevi. *m* Richard Hageman. *cast* Ben Johnson, Joanne Dru, Harry Carey Jr, Ward Bond, Alan Mowbray, Jane Darwell, Charles Kemper, Russell Simpson, James Arness.

●Another Fordian epic positing the American community as the sum of its bands of outsiders, with a Mormon wagon train bound for the westward Promised Land in alliance with a pair of rootless horse-traders, a trio of theatricals, and a tribe of nomadic Navajos, tested by the landscape and the threat of their perverse familial mirror image, the villainous Uncle Shiloh Clegg and his boys. A moral fable, but with a refreshing lack of rhetoric to its poetry. Athlete/actor Jim Thorpe, here playing the Navajo leader, was himself portrayed by Burt Lancaster the following year in the biopic *Jim Thorpe – All-American*. PT

Wagons East!

(1994, US, 107 min)
d Peter Markle. *p* Gary M Goodman, Barry Rosen, Robert Newmyer, Jeffrey Silver. *sc* Matthew Carlson, Jerry Abrahamson. *ph* Frank Tidy. *ed* Scott Conrad. *pd* Vince Cresciman. *m* Michael Small. *cast* John Candy, Joe Bays, Abe Benrubi, Jill Boyd, Ellen Greene, Robert Picardo, Ed Lauter, Rodney A Grant.

●John Candy takes his place at the head of a wagon train leading a handful of disenchanted pioneers back to the home comforts of the East. Alarmed that the quitters may set a trend, a railway baron hires assorted gunslingers and even the US Cavalry to stop them, while by the same token, formerly hostile Indians are only too happy to provide safe passage. The humour is sufficiently scattershot to hit the mark once or twice, but basically a no-brains comedy. TCh

Wag the Dog

(1997, US, 95 min)
d Barry Levinson. *p* Jane Rosenthal, Robert De Niro, Barry Levinson. *sc* Hilary Henkin, David Mamet. *ph* Robert Richardson. *ed* Stu Linder. *pd* Wynn Thomas. *m* Mark Knopfler. *cast* Dustin Hoffman, Robert De Niro, Anne Heche, Denis Leary, Willie Nelson, Andrea Martin, Kirsten Dunst, William H Macy, Woody Harrelson.

●A sex scandal is about to break around the President, threatening to derail his re-election bandwagon less than two weeks before polling day. Veteran Conrad Brean (De Niro) quickly formulates a rescue policy: to deflect public attention, the US will go to war. Not in real life, but where it matters, on America's TV screens. He co-opts veteran Hollywood producer Stanley Motss (Hoffman) and they thrash out the details: the rumours and denials of military mobilisation, the video footage of terrified refugees, the rousing patriotic anthem. And the venue? How about Albania. Adapted from Larry Beinhart's novel *American Hero* by Hilary Henkin and David Mamet, this is intended as an airy semi-political comedy. Lazily assembled by director Levinson, it slides into a series of soft, extended skits on engineering a media war, not helped by several badly handled leaps in the story. In short, a telling symptom of the malaise of mainstream American cinema – once capable of producing such taut political thrillers as *The Candidate* and *The Parallax View*. NB

Wahlverwandtschaften, Die

see Elective Affinities

Waikiki Brothers, The

(2001, SKor, 105 min)
d Im Soon-Rye. *p* Lee Eun. *sc* Im Soon-Rye, Choi Soonshik. *ph* Choi Jeeyul. *ed* Kim Sangbum. *pd* Oh Sangman. *cast* Lee Uhl, Park Won-Sang, Hwang Jungmin, Oh Jeehae, Ryu Sungbum.

●This has a great first line: 'Thanks for coming to see Waikiki Brothers. Unfortunately, due to unforeseen circumstances this will be our last song.' Seems that since the introduction of karaoke machines, the market for lounge covers of 'La Bamba' has dried up all over Korea. As the band disintegrates around him, the taciturn, half-defeated Sung-Woo retreats to his home town, scene of youthful flirtations, hopes and dreams. An old flame proffers renewed hope, possibly, if only he could stir himself to make a move. Poignant, understated and bittersweet, but the drama is never as moving as you think it's going to be. TCh

Waiting

(1990, Aus, 94 min)
d Jackie McKimmie. *p* Ross Matthews. *sc* Jackie McKimmie. *ph* Steve Mason. *ed* Michael Honey. *pd* Murray Picknett. *m* Martin Arminger. *cast* Noni Hazlehurst, Deborah Lee-Furness, Frank Whitten, Helen Jones, Denis Moore, Fiona Press, Ray Barrett.

●When Clare (Hazlehurst) agrees to become a surrogate mother for her friend Sandy (Jones), the pregnancy proves less worrying than the behaviour of old friends. With the big day approaching, the friends converge on Clare's rambling farmhouse outside Sydney to help, hinder, bicker and worry. Sandy is accompanied by her right-on husband (Whitten) and adopted children; feminist film-maker Terry (Press) brings her daughter and throws herself into making a documentary; and glamorous fashion editor Diane (Lee-Furness) comes with wealthy boyfriend (Moore) in tow. Writer-director McKimmie creates an almost casual rhythm, concentrating on character and incidental details in the build-up to a series of confrontations and revelations. Some longueurs strain patience, and compounding our detachment is the way certain characters observe and analyse others' behaviour. Still, sympathetic performances and a fair amount of humour deflate pomposity. CM

Waiting for Godot

(2000, Ire/GB, 120 min)
d Michael Lindsay-Hogg. *p* Michael Colgan, Alan Moloney. *sc* Samuel Beckett. *ph* Seamus Deasy. *ed* Lori Ball, Dody Dorn. *pd* Charles Garrad. *cast* Barry McGovern, Johnny Murphy, Alan Stanford, Stephen Brennan, Sam McGovern.

●The set is suitably spare: a misty grey sky squats on a foreshortened horizon – scree mounds of small, equally grey splinters of rock. A path runs between the two nearest hillocks, with the inevitable blackened tree skeleton to the side. Bare and barren it might be, but the camera movement and facial close-ups provide freshness – a fluidity and emotional connection – which take us beyond the claustrophobia that defines Beckett's bleak vision of the human condition. With Barry McGovern as Vladimir and Johnny Murphy as Estragon, this production will have you pondering the big questions all over again. EPe

Waiting for the Light

(1989, US, 94 min)
d Christopher Monger. *p* Caldecot Chubb, Ron Bozman. *sc* Christopher Monger. *ph* Gabriel Beristain. *ed* Eva Gardos. *pd* Phil Peters. *m* Michael Storey. *cast* Teri Garr, Shirley MacLaine, Colin Baumgartner, Hillary Wolf, Clancy Brown, Vincent Schiavelli, John Bedford Lloyd, Jeff McCracken.

●Monger's engaging comedy is set against the unlikely backdrop of the Cuban missile crisis. The political turmoil provides the springboard for an exploration of superstition and religion, which are treated with equal doses of scepticism and wonderment. When Kay (Garr) inherits a diner in the Pacific Northwest, she and her two young children uproot from Chicago in order to transform the ramshackle eatery. An attempt by their amateur magician Aunt Zena (MacLaine) to scare reclusive neighbour Mullins (Schiavelli) backfires – he mistakes her ghostly apparition for an angel – and the community starts buzzing with the news that Mullins' orchard is a hot-spot for divine visitations. This somewhat incredible plot is embellished with curious details and carried along by the sheer professionalism of Garr and MacLaine, who make entirely convincing relatives. If the characters are fairly two-dimensional, Monger compensates with odd observation and dry humour. CM

Waiting for the Messiah (Esperando al Mesias)

(2000, Arg/Sp/It, 97 min)
d Daniel Burman. *p* Amedeo Pagani, Daniel Burman, Luis Angel Bellaba. *sc* Daniel Burman, Emiliano Torres. *ph* Ramiro Civita. *ed* Veronica Chen. *pd* Paula Taratuto. *m* César Lerner, Marcelo Moguilevsky. *cast* Daniel Hendler, Stefania Sandrelli, Chiara Caselli, Enrique Piñeyro, Hector Alterio, Imanol Arias, Melina Petriella.

●Following a Tokyo financial crash, Buenos Aires bank clerk Santamaria (Piñeyro) loses his job, sees his marriage fall apart and winds up on the street. Scraping a living by returning stolen wallets, he meets Ariel (Hendler), a confused Jewish boy who wants to change the future mapped out future in his father's restaurant business and with the 'girl next door'. Through these carefully constructed, unconventional characters, ideas of Jewishness, sexual difference, loneliness and social exclusion are explored with humour and sensitivity. JFu

Waiting to Exhale

(1995, US, 123 min)
d Forest Whitaker. *p* Ezra Swerdlow, Deborah Schindler. *sc* Terry McMillian, Ron Bass. *ph* Toyomichi Kurita. *ed* Richard Chew. *pd* David Gropman. *m* Kenneth 'Babyface' Edmonds. *cast* Whitney Houston, Angela Bassett, Loretta Devine, Lela Rochon, Gregory Hines, Dennis Haysbert, Mykelti Williamson, Michael Beach.

● As Hollywood genres go, the black women's film is a non-entity, so any effort should be welcomed. It's New Year's Eve in Phoenix, Arizona, and Savannah (Houston) arrives in town on the look out for a good man. Fat chance: simultaneously, Bernardine (Bassett) is dumped by her husband for his white secretary; Gloria (Devine) discovers the reason she can't persuade her ex-husband back into the sack is that he's gay; and Robin (Rochon) is finding her rotund lover's sexual technique spectacularly uninvolving. The odd honky temptress apart, race isn't an issue here. Trysts with married men, widowers, widowers-to-be and crackheads are interspersed with the four friends getting together for some quality bitching therapy about the men in their lives. This is about girls-together solidarity, as the audience I was in loudly demonstrated. For every crowd-pleasing set-piece, there's the shambolic structure, uncomfortable shifts of tone, overglossed visuals, and the music: rightly not trusting his scenes to stand alone, Whitaker wallpapers his film with unconscionably bland slush-pop. Shallow, semi-coherent, overlong, but a likely hit. NB

Wait Till the Sun Shines, Nellie

(1952, US, 108 min)
d Henry King. *p* George Jessel. *sc* Allan Scott. *ph* Leon Shamroy. *ed* Barbara McLean. *ad* Lyle Wheeler, Maurice Ransford. *m* Alfred Newman. *cast* David Wayne, Jean Peters, Hugh Marlowe, Albert Dekker, Alan Hale Jr, Warren Stevens, Helene Stanley.

● Diverting slice of turn-of-the-century nostalgia has Wayne as the small-town barber left to raise two children when spouse Peters skips off for the delights of city living. Trial and tribulation follow, including a fire and the influence of bad company on the younger son. Adapted by Allan Scott from the novel by Ferdinand Reyher, and very capably put together. TJ

Wait Until Dark

(1967, US, 108 min)
d Terence Young. *p* Mel Ferrer. *sc* Robert Carrington, Jane-Howard Carrington. *ph* Charles Lang Jr. *ed* Gene Milford. *ad* George Jenkins. *m* Henry Mancini. *cast* Audrey Hepburn, Alan Arkin, Richard Crenna, Efrem Zimbalist Jr, Jack Weston, Samantha Jones.

● An effective shocker which has the blind Hepburn alone in the house when psychotic villain Arkin and his hoodlum pals (Crenna and Weston) arrive to retrieve a doll containing heroin which her husband (Zimbalist) unwittingly brought through customs for them. The nail- biting climax, during which Hepburn turns the tables by smashing the light-bulbs and leaving the place in darkness, is a classic. Though based on a stage play (by Frederick Knott), the skilful use of interiors for once transcends the visual limitations. NF

Wake in Fright (aka Outback)

(1970, Aust, 109 min)
d Ted Kotcheff. *p* George Willoughby. *sc* Evan Jones. *ph* Brian West. *ed* Anthony Buckley. *ad* Dennis Gentle. *m* John Scott. *cast* Donald Pleasence, Gary Bond, Chips Rafferty, Sylvia Kay, Jack Thompson, Peter Whittle, Al Thomas, John Meillon.

● A sadly confused film, shot with something like a social realist's eye for accurate documentation – clothes, faces, sex habits, furniture, buildings, language. Into this very precise context, however, is dropped the melodramatic tale of a schoolteacher from the city (Bond) who goes to pieces in a remote desert township (a favourite piece of Australian mythology) under the impact of the hard-drinking, gambling, nihilistic pressures of life there, and is finally raped by Pleasence's renegade doctor. The end result is crudely exploitative.

Wake Up, Love (Despabilate Amor)

(1996, Arg, 90 min)
d Eliseo Subiela. *p* Damián Kirzner, Jorge Rocca. *sc* Eliseo Subiela. *ph* Daniel Rodriguez Maseda. *ed* Marcela Saenz. *pd* Ricardo Farfan. *m* Martin Bianchedi. *cast* Darío Grandinetti, Juan Leyrado, Soledad Silveyra, Marilyn Solaya, Gustavo Garzón.

● This romantic drama follows the efforts of one Ricardo (Leyrado) – nicknamed 'Elvis' for his all too evident belief in rock'n'roll as a way of keeping young at heart – to reassemble the old college crowd of 30 years back. During preparations for the reunion, his wife Ana (Silveyra) rekindles her torch for Ernesto 'The King of Insomnia' (Grandinetti), a senior journalist of Hamlet-like melancholy, who in turn breaks his carnal fast with attractive cellist Silvia. Its nostalgic bent is expressed in a character's complaint that compared to the '60s, these days 'people's hearts are dry – it's ages since it rained dreams!' Using amusing kitschy flashbacks to old trysts, and Paul Anka-dominated parties (this is Argentina, don't forget), it's full of genuine feeling, nice comic touches (Ana pulling on her old jeans with the aid of coat hanger hook), all poetically swooned in sad but defiant music (Bach's Cello Suites 1–6) and poetry (Mario Beneddetti's). WH

Waking Hour, The

see Velvet Vampire, The

Waking Life

(2001, US, 101 min)
d Richard Linklater. *p* Anne Walker-McBay, Tommy Pallotta, Palmer West, Jonah S Smith. *sc* Richard Linklater. *ph* Richard Linklater, Tommy Pallotta. *ed* Sandra Adair. ad Bob Sabiston. *m* Glover Gill. *cast* Trevor Jack Brooks, Lorelei Linklater, Wiley Wiggins, Glover Gill, Lara Hicks, Ames Asbell, Leigh Mahoney, Sara Nelson, Jeanine Attaway, Erik Grostic, Bill Wise, Ethan Hawke, Julie Delpy, Steven Soderbergh, Richard Linklater.

● Acclaimed in the US, Linklater's movie has Wiley Wiggins, the lanky longhair in *Dazed & Confused*, bumping pinball-style from one encounter to the next, with each acquaintance offloading his or her own pet theory of life, the universe and everything. Among them are the likes of Ethan Hawke and Julie Delpy, Austin, Texas's finest characters and crazies, and Linklater himself. It would be easy to dismiss as 'Slackers – Part Deux', but for the inspired conceit of shooting the film twice: once as a conventional DV feature, which then became the template for computer animator Bob Sabiston. Sabiston's woozy, pulsing dream imagery is something else. Wiley gradually realises that (a) he's in the middle of the weirdest dream of his life, and (b) he can't wake up. This is one movie where nodding off would seem an appropriate response. The endless philosophising is a bit sophomoric and more jokes would help, but this is one of a kind that grows more absorbing the longer it runs. TCh

Waking Ned (aka Waking Ned Devine)

(1998, GB/Fr/US, 91 min)
d Kirk Jones. *p* Glynis Murray, Richard Holmes. *sc* Kirk Jones. *ph* Henry Braham. *ed* Alan Strachan. *pd* John Ebden. *m* Shaun Davey. *cast* Ian Bannen, David Kelly, Fionnula Flanagan, James Nesbitt, Susan Lynch, Maura O'Malley, Robert Hickey.

● Rural Ireland, and the village of Tullymore is about to receive a rude awakening. According to the newspaper, someone in the community has just won the Irish national lottery, and it shouldn't be long before the truth will out. Bannen and Kelly are the two old codgers sniffing out the likely recipient, but the discovery that the lucky winner dropped dead on the spot before he could claim the dosh brings with it a new challenge – how to step into his shoes and collect the loot. Charming performances and easygoing humour are the strengths of Jones's enjoyable Oirish romp, even if the romantic sub-plot's as flat as a peat bog. TJ

Waking the Dead

(2000, US, 105 min)
d Keith Gordon. *p* Keith Gordon, Stuart Kleinman, Linda Reisman. *sc* Robert Dillon. *ph* Tom Richmond. *ed* Jeff Wishengrad. *pd* Zoé Sakellaropoulo. *m* Tomandandy (Tom Hajdu, Andy Milburn). *cast* Billy Crudup, Jennifer Connelly, Molly Parker, Janet McTeer, Paul Hipp, Sandra Oh, Hal Holbrook, Bill Haughland, Nelson Landrieu.

● This strange, beguiling work from Keith Gordon, one of America's more ambitious and idiosyncratic film-makers (*The Chocolate War*, *Mother Night*), was written by Robert Dillon (*The River*) from a novel by Scott Spencer. In précis it sounds like the worst kind of potboiler – and this straight to small screen UK release is being marketed as a romance, pure and simple. 1972: Fielding is a young man brought up to entertain serious Presidential ambitions, but he falls headlong for an unsuitably radical and outspoken chick, Sarah, who dies suddenly in suspicious circumstances. Ten years later, on the verge of getting into Congress, Fielding keeps seeing his lost lover. Is this a ghost, or didn't she die after all? Or maybe he's losing his mind? The timeshift structure and an arresting jump cut style preserves these ambiguities to the end. You can see it as straight melodrama or nightmarish black comedy; either way Gordon teases out questions about the extent our destinies are shaped by others, the clash between personal obligations and social ambitions (even responsibilities), and the limits and possibilities of romantic love. The way the consummately groomed Billy Crudup unravels before our eyes – then puts himself back together again – is absolutely extraordinary. TCh

Walkabout

(1970, Aust, 100 min)
d Nicolas Roeg. *p* Si Litvinoff. *sc* Edward Bond. *ph* Nicolas Roeg. *ed* Antony Gibbs, Alan Pattillo. *pd* Brian Eatwell. *m* John Barry. *cast* Jenny Agutter, Lucien John, David Gumpilil, John Meillon.

● Roeg's second film (made after the massively delayed *Performance*) is at first sight uncharacteristic: the story of two posh English kids abandoned in the Australian outback and left to fend for themselves when their father commits suicide. In fact, the shimmering light and colour, the conflict of cultures, and the emergence of semimystic sexual forces in the desert landscape make this as Roeg-ian a film as *The Man Who Fell to Earth* or *Bad Timing*. Only the rather cute casting of Jenny Agutter as an English Rose and some implausibly romantic moments detract. CA

Walk East on Beacon!

(1952, US, 98 min, b/w)
d Alfred Werker. *p* Louis De Rochemont. *sc* Leo Rosten. *ph* Joseph Brun. *ed* Angelo Ross. *ad* Herbert Andrews. *m* Jack Shaindlin. *cast* George Murphy, Finlay Currie, Virginia Gilmore, Karel Stepanek, George Roy Hill, Louisa Horton.

● Documentary-style Cold War spy picture, shot on location in Boston and produced by Louis de Rochemont, best known for the *March of Time* newsreel. A celebration of the FBI, it makes frightening and/or funny viewing today. Says one apologetic Commie, finding you have a Party card is like 'finding yourself married to a woman you hate'. Made of sterner stuff is Red George Roy Hill: resisting arrest with the original 'You can't pin anything on me!', he went on to direct subversive classics like *Butch Cassidy and the Sundance Kid* and *The Sting*. More surprisingly, journalist Nora Sayre learned that the CIA was leasing some ten prints a year from Columbia, including a number dubbed into foreign languages, as late as 1977. TCh

Walker

(1987, US, 94 min)
d Alex Cox. *p* Lorenzo O'Brien, Angel Flores Marini. *sc* Rudy Wurlitzer. *ph* David Bridges. *ed* Carlos Puente, Alex Cox. *pd* Bruno Rubeo, J Rae Fox. *m* Joe Strummer. *cast* Ed Harris, Richard Masur, René Auberjonois, Keith Szarabajka, Sy Richardson, Xander Berkeley, John Diehl, Peter Boyle, Marlee Matlin.

● Funded by grasping capitalist Cornelius Vanderbilt (Boyle), 19th century American adventurer Walker (Harris) and his band of mercenaries invade Nicaragua and join forces with the liberals against the country's corrupt ruler. Despite his disastrous military campaigns and political naïveté Walker eventually falls into the president's chair (a historical figure, he was self-proclaimed president of Nicaragua from 1855-57). He even makes the cover of *Newsweek*, because to drive home the obvious contemporary parallels, Cox litters the screen with historical anomalies: Zippo lighters, a

Mercedes limo, journos with tape recorders. He presents this fascinating episode, which would have had far more potential as a straight political allegory, as a shambolic, Pythonesque satire. Only Ed Harris seems to have grasped this point: his controlled and credible performance is curiously at odds with a chaotic plot that shoots off in all directions without once finding its target. NF

Walkers on the Tiger's Tail

see Tora no O o Fumu Otokotachi

Walking and Talking

(1996, GB/US, 85 min)
d Nicole Holofcener. *p* Ted Hope, James Schamus. *sc* Nicole Holofcener. *ph* Michael Stuhler. *ed* Alisa Lepselter. *pd* Anne Stuhler. *m* Billy Bragg. *cast* Catherine Keener, Anne Heche, Todd Field, Liev Schreiber, Kevin Corrigan, Randall Batinkoff, Joseph Siravo.

●Amelia (Keener) and Laura (Heche) have been best friends since childhood, but when Laura agrees to marry live-in lover Frank (Field), Amelia begins to feel abandoned. True, she decides to try giving up therapy once and for all, but her support system – an adored but ailing cat, an ex (Schreiber) now addicted to phone sex with a woman in California – isn't all it might be, while an ill-starred date with a weirdo video-store assistant (Corrigan) doesn't do much for her confidence either. Still, at least she has some idea of what she wants, whereas Laura, once engaged, starts finding fault with everything Frank does and says, and fantasising (irony of ironies – she's a trainee shrink) about her clients. Writer/director Nicole Holofcener's deliciously witty first feature is a perceptive comedy-drama which, despite its New York setting and its fascination with neuroses, anxieties, desire and relationships, is far fresher and more rewarding than the 'female Woody Allen' tag invoked by some critics. The sassy, snappy dialogue is less a matter of one- liners than a wryly amusing exploration of personality; story and gags alike are at the service of characterisation, so that we're never allowed to forget the very real pain, confusion, guilt and affection that underpins the movie. Great cast, immense fun. GA

Walking a Tightrope

see Equilibristes, Les

Walking Dead, The

(1936, US, 66 min, b/w)
d Michael Curtiz. *p* Louis F Edelman. *sc* Ewart Adamson, Peter Milne, Robert Hardy Andrews, Lillie Harward. *ph* Hal Mohr. *ed* Thomas Pratt. *ad* Hugh Reticker. *cast* Boris Karloff, Edmund Gwenn, Ricardo Cortez, Marguerite Churchill, Barton MacLane.

●No great shakes in terms of plot – Karloff's wronged innocent, executed for murder, returns from the dead to wreak vengeance on his persecutors – but Curtiz' fondness for the heavy shadows of Gothic expressionism, and Karloff's characteristically committed performance, lend this moody chiller a welcome touch of class. *Mystery of the Wax Museum* it ain't, but for all the creaky clichés of the story, it still generates the odd frisson. GA

Walking Stick, The

(1970, GB, 101 min)
d Eric Till. *p* Alan Ladd Jr. *sc* George Bluestone. *ph* Arthur Ibbetson. *ed* John Jympson. *pd* John Howell. *m* Stanley Myers. *cast* David Hemmings, Samantha Eggar, Emlyn Williams, Phyllis Calvert, Ferdy Mayne, Francesca Annis, Dudley Sutton.

●A romantico-psychological thriller, with fine, persuasively detailed performances from Eggar as a crippled girl with a sexual chip on her shoulder, and Hemmings as the enigmatic artist who melts it, gradually persuading her to abandon the walking-stick on which she has leaned since a childhood bout with polio, but also leading her to a dark brink of crime and betrayal. Rather too stolidly directed by Till, with meticulous fidelity to Winston Graham's novel, it is reminiscent enough of *Marnie* (also from a novel by Graham) – here, rather than the colour red, the heroine's problem is a claustrophobic aftermath of her time in an iron lung – to make one wonder whether Hitchcock could have screwed excitement out of the situation as well as sympathetic character studies. TM

Walking Tall

(1973, US, 125 min)
d Phil Karlson. *p/sc* Mort Briskin. *ph* Jack Marta. *ed* Harry Gerstad. *pd* Stan Jolley. *m* Walter Scharf. *cast* Joe Don Baker, Elizabeth Hartman, Gene Evans, Noah Beery, Rosemary Murphy, Brenda Benet, John Brascia, Bruce Glover, Arch Johnson.

●Based on the real life experiences of Sheriff Buford Pusser's lone fight against gambling, moonshining, and prostitution in an effort to make Tennessee's McNairy County the sort of place decent folks could live. He cudgels his opposition into submission with the huge stick he carries wherever he goes, and suffers a few hundred stitches, a couple of shootings, and a dead wife in return. But he comes through walking tall, leaving a trail of cardboard villains splattered in his wake. As much as anything, the film is about Nixon's silent majority. They emerge at the end once the enemy are scattered or dead, to tear down and burn the local gambling saloon-cum-cathouse. Even more depressing is that American readers of *Photoplay* voted the film their 'Favorite Motion Picture of the Year'. It's an interesting example of how a stock Western plot can assume some fairly explicit political ramifications once it is transposed to a modern setting (not that that is any recommendation). CPe

Walk in the Clouds, A

(1995, US, 102 min)
d Alfonso Arau. *p* Gil Netter, David Zucker, Jerry Zucker. *sc* Robert Mark Kamen, Mark Miller, Harvey Weitzman. *ph* Emmanuel Lubezki. *ed* Don Zimmerman. *pd* David Gropman. *m* Maurice Jarre. *cast* Keanu Reeves, Aitana Sanchez-Gijon, Anthony Quinn, Giancarlo Giannini, Angelica Aragon, Evangelina Elizondo, Freddy Rodriguez.

●Watching Arau's follow-up to *Like Water for Chocolate* is like finding yourself in Shangri-La, a lost valley where time has stood still for decades, and movies still end with 'The End'. Reeves is Paul Sutton, a GI recently returned from WWII. He has a wife who doesn't love him, nightmares from the front (dream sequences by Alejandro Jodorowsky), a two-bit job as a travelling chocolate salesman, and no prospects. A chance encounter with Victoria Aragon (Sanchez-Gijon) changes all that. She's on her way home to face the music: pregnant, alone, and terrified of her father (Giannini), who oversees the family vineyard in Southern California. Paul agrees to play her husband and then disappear into the night, but he's waylaid by what he finds there, and the kindly efforts of the elderly Don Pedro (Quinn). This is shameless stuff: happy, barefoot peasants sing that traditional Latin *cancion*, 'Crush the grapes, crush the grapes,' the moonlight is so strong you could get burned, and the metaphors are writ large as tabloid headlines; it's all about putting down roots. See it, if you must, for Keanu's pure puppy-love, and for a peerless drunken duet with Quinn. TCh

Walk in the Spring Rain, A

(1969, US, 98 min)
d Guy Green. *p/sc* Stirling Silliphant. *ph* Charles Lang Jr. *ed* Ferris Webster. *ad* Malcolm C Bert. *m* Elmer Bernstein. *cast* Anthony Quinn, Ingrid Bergman, Fritz Weaver, Katherine Crawford, Tom Fielding.

●A dish of tripe that has to be seen to be believed. Quinn does his nature boy act yet again as a Tennessee backwoodsman who always knows where to find the first darling buds of spring and can lay fires in the hearth so that the smoke isn't twisted. Whatever that means, it makes him irresistible enough to ensnare poor Ingrid Bergman ('You're full of love, ain't you?'), a college professor's wife down in the menopausal dumps and seemingly bent on becoming a dropout grandmother. Since both have family ties and problems, the course of their true love doesn't run smooth, but Quinn is philosophical to the last: 'You know what I found out? The clouds just keep on moving'. Stirling Silliphant scripted, if you can call it that. TM

Walk in the Sun, A

(1945, US, 117 min, b/w)
d/p Lewis Milestone. *sc* Robert Rossen. *ph* Russell Harlan. *ed* Duncan Mansfield. *ad* Max Bertisch. *m* Fredric Efrem Rich. *cast* Dana Andrews, John Ireland, Richard Conte, Sterling Holloway, Norman Lloyd, Lloyd Bridges, George Tyne, Herbert Rudley, Huntz Hall.

●One of the best movies to have come out of World War II literately scripted by Robert Rossen from Harry Brown's fine novel, and making marvellous use of the repetitive rhythms of GI banter (with the cheery Conte's Nobody dies!, for instance, gradually assuming the quality of an ironic incantation). Discreet, dispassionate, and subtly poetic, it traces the experiences, through one brief action, of an infantry platoon which 'came across the sea to sunny Italy and took a little walk in the sun'. Characterisation is sharp and simple, the focus kept strictly to the immediate realities of fear and boredom, so that there is none of the special pleading of Milestone's earlier *All Quiet on the Western Front.* Here messages are left to take care of themselves, although the introspective Ireland's habit of composing letters to his sister in his head is used more than once to subversive effect. 'We just blew a bridge and took a farmhouse' he begins after the action in which a lot of his platoon died, 'It was easy…so terribly easy': a rare acknowledgement at that time of every soldier's innocently selfish joy that he didn't die. TM

Walk Like a Man

(1987, US, 86 min)
d Melvin Frank. *p* Leonard Kroll. *sc* Robert Klane. *ph* Victor J Kemper. *ed* Bill Butler, Steve Butler. *pd* Bill Malley. *m* Lee Holdridge. *cast* Howie Mandel, Christopher Lloyd, Cloris Leachman, Colleen Camp, Amy Steel, George DiCenzo.

●Scraggy slapstick comedy which attempts to give the Kaspar Hauser myth a new twist. Bobo Shand, son of a wealthy family, is lost in the woods as a kid and raised by wolves. Twenty-eight years pass before he's found by an animal behaviourist and reintroduced into human society. Needless to say, his grasping, wheedling family is considerably less civilised than his old feral friends. Neither Leachman's class nor Lloyd's clowning can put meat on this very dry bone. GM

Walk on the Moon, A

(1998, US, 107 min)
d Tony Goldwyn. *p* Dustin Hoffman, Tony Goldwyn, Jay Cohen, Neil Koenigsberg, Lee Gottsegen, Murray Schisgal. *sc* Pamela Gray. *ph* Anthony Richmond. *ed* Dana Congdon. *pd* Dan Leigh. *m* Mason Daring. *cast* Diane Lane, Viggo Mortensen, Liev Schreiber, Anna Paquin, Tovah Feldshuh, Bobby Boriello, Stewart Bick, Jess Platt.

●It's 1969. As moon-walking Apollo astronauts take giant steps for mankind, hippies invade Woodstock and students protest against the Vietnam War, Jewish housewife Pearl Kantrowitz (Lane) enjoys her own summer of love at a traditional Catskills holiday resort. While her TV repairman husband Marty (Schreiber) slaves away back in town, and her teenage daughter Alison (Paquin) flirts with adulthood, Pearl wears tie-dye, goes skinny dipping and gets it on with Walker Jerome (Mortensen), a handsome hippie who finances his freewheeling lifestyle by selling blouses. As the frustrated wife, Lane is both sensual and sympathetic, although the scrupulously fair screenplay is clear about the costs of her liberation. Schreiber conveys a stolid dignity as the hardworking husband whose limited worldview is shattered by his wife's infidelity. A modest, lovingly crafted melodrama, but regrettably, this first feature from actor-turned-director Goldwyn (who played Patrick Swayze's duplicitous colleague in *Ghost*) never integrates its parochial setting and intimate emotional conflicts with the broader social canvas, which in the event feels more like a historical backdrop than a dramatic context. NF

Walk on the Wild Side

(1962, US, 114 min, b/w)
d Edward Dmytryk. *p* Charles K Feldman. *sc* John Fante, Edmund Morris. *ph* Joseph MacDonald. *ed* Harry Gerstad. *ad* Richard Sylbert. *m* Elmer Bernstein. *cast* Laurence Harvey, Capucine, Jane Fonda, Barbara Stanwyck, Anne Baxter, Richard Rust, Karl Swenson.

●A prowling black cat taking a 'walk on the wild side' creates the brilliant promise of Saul Bass' famous credit sequence. The rest just doesn't match it, despite the tale of passion: Laurence Harvey seeking his former love (Capucine), now a high-class 'harlot' for 'Madame' Barbara Stanwyck, who is also in love with her; meanwhile a full-blooded Anne Baxter and a raunchy Jane Fonda succumb to Harvey's moralising Texan. If Dmytryk had only concentrated more on the women instead of the dull central male, this might have been a superb dark work, not just a fairly steamy melodrama. Still, it certainly has its moments. HM

Walk Through H, A

(1978, GB, 41 min)
d/sc Peter Greenaway. *ph* John Rosenberg. *ed/pd* Peter Greenaway. *m* Michael Nyman. *cast* Jean Williams. *narrator* Colin Cantlie.

● Greenaway's unique short feature is one of the best British movies of the decade. It defeats efforts at description. You could call it a cross between a vintage Borges 'fiction' and a Disney True Life Adventure, but that wouldn't get close to its humour or the compulsiveness of Michael Nyman's romantic score. It's nominally a narrative about an ornithologist following a trail blazed by the legendary Tulse Luper, but it's a narrative without characters... See it at all costs. TR

Walk with Love and Death, A

(1969, US, 90 min)
d John Huston. *p* Carter De Haven. *sc* Dale Wasserman, John Huston, Hans Koningsberger [Hans Koning]. *ph* Ted Scaife. *ed* Russell Lloyd. *pd* Stephen Grimes. *m* Georges Delerue. *cast* Anjelica Huston, Assaf Dayan, Anthony Corlan, John Hallam, Eileen Murphy, Anthony Nicholls, Robert Lang, Michael Gough, John Huston.

● A Huston curiosity, deliberately contemporary in preoccupation despite its medieval setting: two young lovers rove through strife-torn France making love not war, seeking involvement only with each other. In emphasising youthful passion and integrity, questioning accepted values, and setting the film in a period of social and civil unrest, it becomes a self-evident reflection of the moods of the late '60s; but a mere reflection, and unsatisfyingly inconclusive, because Huston is far too sceptical and knowing to believe in his subject. As the lovers become more committed, the film grows less certain; the essential simplicity of their relationship eludes Huston, who is far more interested in the deviant characters who take up the rest of the film. Further dislocation is caused by the inexperienced leading couple; most of the film's coherence comes from the source novel by Hans Koningsberger, lustrous photography, and a brief appearance from Huston as a wily old fox. CPe

Wall, The (Le Mur)

(1983, Fr, 116 min)
d Yilmaz Güney. *p* Marin Karmitz. *sc* Yilmaz Güney. *ph* Izzet Akay. *ed* Sabine Mamou. *m* Ozan Garip Sahin, Setrak Bakirel, Ali Dede Altuntas, Robert Kempler. *cast* Tuncel Kurtiz, Ahmet Ziyrek, Emel Mesci, Isabelle Tissandier, Ali Berktay.

● There has never been a prison movie like this, but then it's doubtful that any major film-maker ever spent as long behind bars as Güney. It's not a bleeding chunk of autobiography, but an imaginative reconstruction of the events that led up to the revolt in the children's dormitory in Ankara Prison in March 1976. *Yol* saw all of Turkey as a kind of prison; *The Wall* reverses the metaphor, seeing the prison as a microcosm of the country, crippled both spiritually and physically under its fascistic government. Güney has no need of melodrama or extremes of violence or horror. He simply demonstrates the mechanisms of tyranny: the way that mindless and arbitrary routines stunt jailers and prisoners alike, creating a desperate conspiracy of ignorance and defeat. A deeply provocative vision of what happens when idealism runs out, it's not easy to watch or think about, but Güney sees it and shows it as unflinchingly as Buñuel would have done in his prime. TR

Wall of Silence, A

see Totschweigen

Walls of Glass

(1985, US, 86 min)
d Scott Goldstein. *p* Scott Goldstein, Mark Slater. *sc* Edmond Collins, Scott Goldstein. *ph* Ivan Strasburg. *ed* Scott Vickrey. *pd* Ruth Ammon. *m* Scott Goldstein. *cast* Philip Bosco, Geraldine Page, Linda Thorson, Olympia Dukakis, Brian Bloom, Steven Weber, Louis Zorich.

● Taxi driver Flanagan (Bosco) dreams of the stage, but with middle age setting in, feels time is running out. Imprisoned by his work, he sees no escape. Down on his luck, all Flanagan has left is the comfort of the printed word (Shakespeare), and the love of an ageing mother (Page). Granted flashbacks to whisky-swigging immigrant fathers quoting sonnets are tough to swallow, but if you can get past the mechanics, you're in for some warm moments. Top marks to Goldstein, in his first feature, for tasting the flavour of New York's outer boroughs. His contemporary taxi trip, despite the affected aftertaste, grasps the traditional essence: all the world's a stage, even the back seat of Flanagan's cab. SGo

Wall Street

(1987, US, 126 min)
d Oliver Stone. *p* Edward R Pressman. *sc* Stanley Weiser, Oliver Stone. *ph* Robert Richardson. *ed* Claire Simpson. *pd* Stephen Hendrickson. *m* Stewart Copeland. *cast* Michael Douglas, Charlie Sheen, Daryl Hannah, Martin Sheen, Terence Stamp, Hal Holbrook, Sean Young, Sylvia Miles, Richard Dysart, Annie McEnroe, Millie Perkins.

● Remove the restless camera pyrotechnics and incomprehensible jargon, and you have a corny old melo: broker Charlie Sheen (green) perpetrates illegal practices to please surrogate poppa/company-trader Douglas (tough), a mega-villain mastermind who spits out absurdities like 'Lunch is for wimps' and longs to destroy his rival Stamp (lost). Soon Charlie's climbing the ladder in search of a fast buck and a flash fuck: Hannah (vacuous). Inevitably, he descends into a mire of insider-dealing, Faustian intrigue, and personal betrayal, culminating in his responsibility for Douglas' near-liquidation of the company where Sheen Sr (natch) is an Incorruptible Working Class Hero union rep. Charlie's cured, of course, by the most clichéd comeuppance of 'em all – family illness – which he should have foreseen, given the homespun homilies about abysses and doom repeatedly offered by full-time office soothsayer Holbrook (solemn). Dramatically inept, the film also muddles its naïve moralising: though condemnatory of avarice and dishonesty, Stone seems seduced by the financiers' luxurious lives and frantic energy, and even expects us to sympathise with the ghastly Charlie's final regret and redemption. GA

Walter (aka Loving Walter)

(1982, GB, 65 min)
d Stephen Frears. *p* Nigel Evans. *sc* David Cook. *ph* Chris Menges. *ed* Mick Audsley. *ad* Michael Minas. *m* George Fenton. *cast* Ian McKellen, Barbara Jefford, Arthur Whybrow, Tony Melody, Jim Broadbent, Nabil Shaban.

● This short feature film, set in straitened postwar England about the fate of a mentally handicapped young man institutionalised after the death of his parents, was adapted from a novel by David Cook and memorably inaugurated Channel 4's 'Film on Four' series in November 1982. It's a copybook exercise in bleak unvarnished realism, punctuated by moments of operatic violence and emotion, but what makes it special is its unsentimental tone of melancholy inevitability, and, above all, McKellen's perfectly pitched performance. (The film was amalgamated with its somewhat histrionic sequel, *Walter & June*, and retitled *Loving Walter* for its US release.) JPy

Wanda

(1970, US, 100 min)
d Barbara Loden. *p* Harry Shuster. *sc* Barbara Loden. *ph/ed* Nicholas Proferes. *cast* Barbara Loden, Michael Higgins, Charles Dosinan, Frank Jourdano.

● A remarkable one-off from Elia Kazan's wife. Shot in 16mm and blown up to 35, it's a subtly picaresque movie about the wanderings of a semi-destitute American woman. Directing herself, Barbara Loden manages to make the character at once completely convincing in her soggy and directionless amorality, yet gradually sympathetic and even heroic. After a desultory involvement with a bank robber, to whom she becomes attached despite his unpredictable temper, Wanda botches everything – having agreed to drive a getaway car for him – by getting lost in a traffic jam; and our last glimpse of her is back on the road, being picked up in a bar. The film is all the more impressive for its refusal to get embroiled in half-baked political attitudinising; it's good enough to make one regret that the director/star produced nothing else before her untimely death from cancer. DP

Wanda Nevada

(1979, US, 105 min)
d Peter Fonda. *p* Neal Dobrofsky, Dennis Hackin. *sc* Dennis Hackin. *ph* Michael Butler. *ed* Scott Conrad. *ad* Lynda Paradise. *m* Ken Lauber. *cast* Peter Fonda, Brooke Shields, Fiona Lewis, Luke Askew, Ted Markland, Severn Darden, Paul Fix, Henry Fonda.

● The easy rider exchanges motorbike for horse, but the tempo rarely rises above a trot in this clod-hopping Western. Fonda is a gambler. When he wins cowgirl Brooke Shields in a poker game, he's obliged to take her along in his search for gold. Perhaps bent on some oedipal revenge trip, the director/star casts his more illustrious father in a thankless bit-part as a bearded old loon of a prospector – it was the only time these two Fondas worked together.

Wanderer, The (Le Grand Meaulnes)

(1967, Fr, 110 min)
d Jean-Gabriel Albicocco. *p* Gilbert de Goldschmidt. *sc* Isabelle Riviere, Jean-Gabriel Albicocco. *ph* Quinto Albicocco. *ed* Georges Klotz. *ad* Daniel Louradour. *m* Jean-Pierre Bourtayre. *cast* Brigitte Fossey, Jean Blaise, Alain Libolt, Alain Noury, Juliette Villard, Christian de Tilière.

● A film made with vaseline and railway tracks, which takes some adjusting to; but you soon forget to read the subtitles, because you can understand all you need without them. It's based on the book *Le Grand Meaulnes* by Alain-Fournier, and explores a strange adolescence in provincial France at the end of the last century. In the film, Roger Corman meets Proust, *Elvira Madigan* rides again, and Renoir takes acid. JC

Wanderers, The

(1979, US/Neth, 117 min)
d Philip Kaufman. *p* Martin Ransohoff. *sc* Rose Kaufman, Philip Kaufman. *ph* Michael Chapman. *ed* Ronald Roose, Stuart H Pappé. *ad* Jay Moore. *cast* Ken Wahl, John Friedrich, Karen Allen, Toni Kalem, Alan Rosenberg, Jim Youngs, Tony Ganios, Linda Manz, Val Avery.

● The Bronx, 1963. Gangland. Rumbles, racism, and rock'n'roll; but the times they are a-changin'. Kennedy's dead and the Marines are calling. This adaptation of Richard Price's episodic novel plays like the urban flip-side of *American Graffiti*: a macho mini-community grows up and apart in the cultural gulf between Dion and Dylan. The comic indulgence is streaked with hindsight analysis and irony, but thankfully avoids moral schematics as the wonderfully-cast characters confront a world beyond their tenement horizons and, well...wander. The film survives cuts to deliver some great, gross, comic book capers. And rock history gets its most intelligent illustration since *Mean Streets*. PT

Wanted Dead or Alive

(1987, US, 106 min)
d Gary Sherman. *p* Robert C Peters. *sc* Michael Patrick Goodman, Brian Taggert, Gary Sherman. *ph* Alex Nepomniaschy. *ed* Ross Albert. *pd* Paul Eads. *m* Joseph Renzetti. *cast* Rutger Hauer, Gene Simmons, Robert Guillaume, Mel Harris, William Russ, Susan McDonald, Jerry Hardin.

● A fast, high-powered political thriller, with Hauer as ex-CIA agent turned bounty hunter, renowned for hauling in hardened criminals – dead or alive. He has his work cut out when a group of Middle Eastern terrorists start a bombing campaign in leafy LA. Led by Malak Al Rahim (played by Simmons like an evil comic book character), the group has already killed scores in a cinema bombing, and now plan to blow up a chemical plant containing lethal cyanide. Hauer is unwittingly being used as bait by CIA schemers, and following the loss of his girlfriend and best pal in a mistaken identity mishap, he's provoked into seeking personal revenge...The film is enjoyably tense, explicitly violent, yet at times quite humorous; and Hauer, having collared the psycho market, here makes a similarly irresistible claim in the hard-man-with-heart stakes. DA

Wanton, The

see Manèges

Wanton Countess, The

see Senso

War (aka Troma's War)

(1988, US, 99 min)
d Michael Herz, Samuel Weil [Lloyd Kaufman]. *p* Michael Herz, Lloyd Kaufman. *sc* Mitchell Dana, Lloyd Kaufman. *ph* James London. *pd* Alexis Grey. *cast* Carolyn Beauchamp, Sean Bowen, Michael Ryder, Patrick Weathers, Jessica Dublin, Steven Crossley.

●After their airliner crashes on a deserted island, a group of survivors stumble upon a terrorist training camp, from which the Commies plan to infiltrate and take over the United States. Can the gutsy blonde heroine, the hunky hero, the psycho Vietvet, and other assorted *Airplane!* types frustrate their fiendish plans and save democracy? The budget, slightly higher than usual by Troma standards, is mostly eaten up by endless gunfire, feeble explosions and monotonously repeated stunts, while the one-dimensional villans speak in funny accents, and the good guys (and gals) do what they gotta do. Come back, Chuck norris, all is forgiven. NF

War, The

(1994, US, 125 min)
d Jon Avnet. *p* Jon Avnet, Jordan Kerner. *sc* Kathy McWorter. *ph* Geoffrey Simpson. *ed* Debra Neil-Fisher. *pd* Kristi Zea. *m* Thomas Newman. *cast* Kevin Costner, Elijah Wood, Mare Winningham, Lexi Randall, LeToya Chisholm, Christopher Fenell, Donald Sellers.

●Oozing sincerity and restraint, this coming-of-age tale submerges under the weight of its own worthiness. If you go with the flow, the languorous atmosphere and fine acting may draw you in, but a lack of dramatic focus frequently leads to a blurring of the edges. For young Stu Simmons (Wood) and his sister Lidia (Randall), growing up in small-town Mississippi in the early '70s is tough. Their father, Vietnam vet Costner, is unemployed and withdrawn due to post-traumatic stress, their mother struggles to make ends meet, and their clashes with the bullying Lipnicki boys repeatedly threaten to escalate into violence. The siblings' sole refuge is a tree-house they're building out of scrap metal; but unbeknown to Stu, his sister and her two black friends have been taking time out from their dance routines to steal these materials from the Lipnickis' scrapyard. With their feral, shaven-headed enemies now hellbent on revenge, Stu and Lidia must either fight for what's theirs or embrace the pacifism espoused by their repentant father. Once the film spills over into blatant anti-war allegory, everything starts to unravel. Already over-written to within an inch of its life, it lurches from one climax to the next, tugging at the heart-strings until they snap. NF

War and Peace

(1956, US/It, 208 min)
d King Vidor. *p* Dino De Laurentiis. *sc* Bridget Boland, King Vidor, Mario Camerini, Ennio De Concini, Ivo Perilli, Robert Westerby. *ph* Jack Cardiff. *ed* Leo Cattozzo, Stuart Gilmore. *ad* Mario Chiari. *m* Nino Rota. *cast* Audrey Hepburn, Henry Fonda, Mel Ferrer, Vittorio Gassman, John Mills, Herbert Lom, Anita Ekberg, Barry Jones, Oscar Homolka, Jeremy Brett, Helmut Dantine.

●Hepburn apart, a miscast and largely misconceived – but not unenjoyable – epic. The fact that six writers collaborated on the screenplay tells its own story of a lavish, respectful, essentially hollow reduction-by-committee of Tolstoy's novel. The first couple of hours, rambling episodically on, seems less a panoramic view of the social scene than a gaggle of characterisations with nowhere much to go. But after Borodino, Vidor and the film seem to be pulling together for the first time in the flurry of magnificently staged battle scenes (the retreat from Moscow, the crossing of the Beresina). As Vidor has commented, 'My favourite subject is the search for truth. This is also the essential theme of Tolstoy's book. It is Pierre who forces himself to discover what is at the heart of man. All that we see, he sees. I wanted to show his point of view'. Although this point of view is never really anchored in the film, it does lend a belated sense of purpose. TM

War and Peace (Voina i Mir)

(1967, USSR, 357 min)
d Sergei Bondarchuk. *sc* Sergei Bondarchuk, Vasily Solovyov. *ph* Anatoly Petritsky, Dmitri Korzhikin, A Zenyan. *ed* Tatiana Likhacheva. *ad* Mikhail Bogdanov, Gennady Myasnikov. *m* Vyacheslav Ovchinnikov. *cast* Ludmila Savelyeva, Sergei Bondarchuk, Vyacheslav Tikhonov, Anastasia Vertinskaya, Vasily Lanovoi.

●Compared to this 70mm monster (five years in the making, and running 507 minutes in its original Russian version), most other epics have the visual dimensions of an Edgar Wallace potboiler. Battles, duels, ballroom scenes, and even trips in a troika are staged with unsparing picturesqueness; at the battle of Borodino, a staggering twenty thousand extras mill around the cannons, smoke, and horses. But spectacle apart, Bondarchuk's version of Tolstoy falls into the category of respectable mediocrity, and matters aren't helped by the loud American voices with which everyone speaks in this much-edited and dubbed version. As a movie excursion into Russian literature, *Love and Death* still wins hands down. GB

War at Home, The

(1996, US, 123 min)
d Emilio Estevez. *p* Emilio Estevez, Brad Krevoy, Steve Stabler, James Duff. *sc* James Duff. *ph* Peter Levy. *ed* Craig Bassett. *pd* Eve Cauley. *m* Basil Poledouris. *cast* Kathy Bates, Martin Sheen, Kimberly Williams, Emilio Estevez, Carla Gugino, Geoffrey Blake, Penny Allen.

●As a director Estevez is probably best remembered for *Men at Work*, a film most impressive for the stunted development and general hopelessness of the two leads. In years gone by a good parent might have reacted by packing the boys off to war to make men of them; in this gentler age Martin Sheen instead settled for forwarding his elder lad a copy of James Duff's Broadway play *Homefront*, concerning a traumatised young Viet vet doing battle back home in Texas with his uncomprehending family. The good news is that Estevez is showing distinct signs of maturity. Although he plays Jeremy, the protagonist barely in his twenties, Estevez the director keeps enough distance to allow that Jeremy suffers indulgent self-pity among his several problems, and gives as unreasonably as he gets. Indeed, there's some power in the film's depiction of this upstanding, traditional family unit (solidly acted by Sheen, Bates and Williams) as being the problem rather than the solution: Jeremy's past and not his future. It's never anything more than middlebrow, obvious and quite laboured – and, for good and ill, very earnest NB

War Bride, The

(2001, GB/Can, 103 min)
d Lyndon Chubbuck. *p* Alistair Maclean-Clark, Doug Bergquist. *sc* Angela Workman. *ph* Ron Orieux. *ed* Alan Strachan. *pd* Ken Rempel. *m* John Sereda. *cast* Anna Friel, Aden Young, Brenda Fricker, Loren Dean, Molly Parker, Julie Cox.

●This Canadian-British production sees Friel and fellow seamstress Cox whisked away from the London Blitz by dashing Canadian soldiers. Cox gets the rich guy, Friel the short straw in a nowheresville Cold Comfort Farm presided over by unsmiling mother-in-law Fricker. Friel does well playing the embodiment of the optimistic spirit beset by petty prejudice, envy and xenophobia, but shows the limitations of her acting when dealing with her traumatised husband (the excellent Young) on his return from war. Decently directed and nicely shot, the film nevertheless rarely rises above the conventional. WH

WarGames

(1983, US, 113 min)
d John Badham. *p* Harold Schneider. *sc* Lawrence Lasker, Walter F Parkes. *ph* William A Fraker. *ed* Tom Rolf. *pd* Angelo Graham. *m* Arthur B Rubinstein. *cast* Matthew Broderick, Dabney Coleman, John Wood, Ally Sheedy, Barry Corbin, Juanin Clay, Dennis Lipscomb.

●'Or How We Learned to Stop Worrying, Because Nuclear Brinksmanship Is as Simple as Tick-Tack-Toe.' Badham's movie was one of the first to pick up on home computer power – with schoolboy whiz Broderick hacking into his school files, and later chancing across a new 'game': Global Thermonuclear War. The first half has a sardonic edge to it, but the more seriously the movie takes itself the sillier it gets. TCh

War Gods of the Deep

see City Under the Sea

War Is Over, The

see Guerre est finie, La

Warlock

(1959, US, 122 min)
d/p Edward Dmytryk. *sc* Robert Alan Aurthur. *ph* Joseph MacDonald. *ed* Jack W Holmes. *ad* Lyle Wheeler, Herman A Blumenthal. *m* Leigh Harline. *cast* Richard Widmark, Henry Fonda, Anthony Quinn, Dorothy Malone, Dolores Michaels, Wallace Ford, Tom Drake, Richard Arlen.

●An incredibly overwrought Freudian Western, with Fonda as the notorious killer hired by the cowardly citizens of Warlock to defend them from a vicious gang. Fonda brings with him his lifelong partner (and possible lover), the blond, neurotic, club-footed Anthony Quinn. After a few rousing shoot-outs, one of the opposition (Widmark) joins them, and he is appointed sheriff. Enter Dorothy Malone, whose fiancé has been murdered by Quinn, and she falls in love with Widmark, whom she hopes will avenge her. It all ends with a Viking-style funeral, and with Fonda starting to think beyond his guns. Dmytryk (after the blacklist days, at least) was usually one of Hollywood's dullest directors, but not here. The movie is overlong yet dynamic, juxtaposing moments of repose, when the script shuffles relationships like a stacked deck, and bursts of action which have something of the operatic stylisation of Sergio Leone. ATu

Warlock

(1988, US, 102 min)
d/p Steve Miner. *sc* David N Twohy. *ph* David Eggby. *ed* David Finfer. *pd* Roy Forge Smith. *m* Jerry Goldsmith. *cast* Richard E Grant, Julian Sands, Lori Singer, Kevin O'Brien, Mary Woronov, Richard Kuss, Juli Burkhart.

●This updated witch-finder movie eschews hardcore horror in favour of supernatural action adventure, with enjoyable results. Its master-stroke is the inspired casting of blond-haired wimp Sands as the suavely malevolent warlock, and raven-haired Grant as the witch-hunter. None too keen on being hanged and then burned over a basket of live cats, Sands uses his magic powers to escape across time, from 17th century Massachusetts to modern day Los Angeles, where waitress Singer is a little put out when she finds a cool-looking guy with a weird accent in her apartment, then really pissed off when Grant turns up in pursuit. But when Sands casts a spell which causes her to age 20 years every day, she teams up with Grant. Marred only by some silly dialogue and naff flying effects, the ensuing cross-country chase is confidently handled; and with the help of Sands' subtly evil performance, Miner tones down the violence while hinting at some really nasty stuff. NF

War Lord, The

(1965, US, 122 min)
d Franklin Schaffner. *p* Walter Seltzer. *sc* John Collier, Millard Kaufman. *ph* Russell Metty. *ed* Folmar Blangsted. *ad* Alexander Golitzen, Henry Bumstead. *m* Jerome Moross. *cast* Charlton Heston, Richard Boone, Rosemary Forsyth, Maurice Evans, Guy Stockwell, Niall MacGinnis, Henry Wilcoxon, James Farentino, Michael Conrad.

●An interesting attempt to break away from stereotype epic. Heston plays the war lord in 11th century Normandy who finds that the land he controls is steeped in primitive tradition. The rituals of pagan mythology are well observed – cabalistic idols, sacrifices – as is Heston's disintegration in the face of a mental force that he can't understand. Well put together by Schaffner (it's one of his best films, along with *Planet of the Apes* and *Patton*), and strongly photographed by Russell Metty. CPe

Warlords of Atlantis

(1978, GB, 96 min)
d Kevin Connor. *p* John Dark. *sc* Brian Hayles. *ph* Alan Hume. *ed* Bill Blunden. *pd* Elliot Scott. *m* Mike Vickers. *cast* Doug McClure, Peter Gilmore, Shane Rimmer, Lea Brodie, Michael Gothard, Hal Galili, John Ratzenberger, Robert Brown, Cyd Charisse, Daniel Massey.

●Although the title promises something new, this is a rehash of exactly the same old fantasy formula used by Connor and producer John Dark in *The Land That Time Forgot*, *At the Earth's Core* and *The People That Time Forgot*: the discovery of a lost community, the imprisonment of one of the party, a rescue attempt, and final escape from the lost world as it's about to be destroyed. The structure has so little to commend it that it's amazing they pursue it with such dogged persistence. As always, Connor's approach is commendably stolid, but this production lacks almost all the more pleasing elements of the earlier movies, and is sickeningly vulgar in its portrayal of Atlantis, right down to the leering emphasis on Cyd Charisse's legs. DP

Warm December, A

(1972, GB/US, 101 min)
d Sidney Poitier. *p* Melville Tucker. *sc* Lawrence Roman. *ph* Paul Beeson. *ed* Pembroke J Herring, Peter Pitt. *ad* Elliot Scott. *m* Coleridge-Taylor Perkinson. *cast* Sidney Poitier, Esther Anderson, Yvette Curtis, George Baker, Johnny Sekka, Earl Cameron, Hilary Crane.
●Black radical chic with a tragic twist. Poitier, a widowed doctor, runs a ghetto clinic in Washington DC, races motor-bikes on the side, and has enough money to live in style. While in London on holiday with his 10-year-old daughter, he meets and falls in love with Catherine (Anderson), daughter of an ambassador from a new African state. Punctuated by unnecessary mystery music and mysterious-looking foreigners in raincoats, the secret emerges that Catherine is dying of sickle cell disease. The love is short-lived. She is beautiful, bright, and brave. We all leave in tears. MV

Warning Shadows

see Schatten

Warning Shot

(1966, US, 100 min)
d/p Buzz Kulik. *sc* Mann Rubin. *ph* Joseph Biroc. *ed* Archie Marshek. *ad* Hal Pereira, Roland Anderson. *m* Jerry Goldsmith. *cast* David Janssen, Ed Begley, Keenan Wynn, Sam Wanamaker, Lillian Gish, Stefanie Powers, Eleanor Parker, George Grizzard, George Sanders, Steve Allen, Carroll O'Connor, Joan Collins, Walter Pidgeon, John Garfield Jr.
●Staking out an apartment block on the watch for a psycho killer, Detective Sergeant Valens of the LA police (Janssen) is forced to shoot a man who keeps on coming with a gun when challenged. The dead man turns out to be a highly respected doctor, and there is no trace of the gun. Suspended with the threat of a manslaughter charge hanging over him, Valens goes rogue to clear his name. Neatly scripted from Whit Masterson's novel *711 – Officer Needs Help*, the film is very enjoyable in the time-honoured private eye manner, even though the parade of vivid 'guest cameos' uncovered during Janssen's dogged trek through the spiralling mystery smacks less of *noir* tradition than of TV practice (Kulik had only recently graduated to movies). TM

Warnung vor einer heiligen Nutte

see Beware of a Holy Whore

War of the Buttons, The

see Guerre des Boutons, La

War of the Buttons

(1993, GB/Fr, 94 min)
d John Roberts. *p* David Puttnam. *sc* Colin Welland. *ph* Bruno de Keyser. *ed* David Freeman. *pd* Jim Clay. *m* Rachel Portman. *cast* Gregg Fitzgerald, John Coffey, Paul Batt, Gerard Kearney, Eveanna Ryan, Frank Grimes, Declan Mulholland.
●Slim pickings from David Puttnam, reunited with *Chariots of Fire* screenwriter Colin Welland: this mildly diverting entertainment is a remake of Yves Robert's *La Guerre des Boutons* (1962). Transposed to County Cork, the film charts the feud between the pupils of neighbouring village schools, the Carricks and the Ballys. While the dispute's origins remain hazy, it soon escalates via public humiliation and private recrimination to 'all-out war', sticks and stones – and buttons – at the ready. Relatively unsentimental. TCh

War of the Colossal Beast

(1958, US, 68 min, b/w & col)
d/p Bert I Gordon. *sc* George Worthing Yates. *ph* Jack Marta. *ed* Ronald Sinclair. *ad* Walter Keller. *m* Albert Glasser. *cast* Sally Fraser, Roger Pace, Dean Parkin, Russ Bender, Charles Stewart.
●Sci-fi schlock merchant Gordon followed *The Amazing Colossal Man* with this reprise of the same 'tall actor knocks over miniature sets' formula. Eschewing the Cold War paranoia of the previous offering, this one has Roger Pace as a 60ft giant with the mind of a wild beast, and a handy loincloth, who goes on the rampage when the powers that be whisk him from the wilds of Mexico to LA captivity. Watch out for the climactic burst of colour. TJ

War of the Monsters (Gojira Tai Gaigan)

(1972, Jap, 89 min)
d Jun Fukuda. *p* Tomoyuki Tanaka. *sc* Shinichi Sekizawa. *ph* Kiyoshi Hasegawa. *ed* Yoshio Tamura. *ad* Yoshibumi Honda. *m* Akira Ifukube. *cast* Hiroshi Ishikawa, Yuriko Hishimi, Tomoko Umeda, Minoru Takashima.
●Although Godzilla doesn't really cut it in the special effects department, he does have a certain lumbering charm. So does the script: Godzilla fights off monsters from outer space to save Tokyo from colonisation by a group of intelligent cockroaches with imperialist tendencies (the only species to have survived pollution on their planet). The monster battle is overlong, though the one with a rotary saw in his chest (a Texan?) is a novelty, and like the others, all too obviously a man in a moth-eaten suit. They bump into each other to see how often they can fall down, and Godzilla takes some time to find his pace. As he's floored again and again but comes back fighting, his performance more and more resembles Stallone in *Rocky*, even to the mumbling. If you're in the right silly mood, kind of fun. SM

War of the Roses, The

(1989, US, 116 min)
d Danny DeVito. *p* Arnon Milchan, James L Brooks. *sc* Michael Leeson. *ph* Stephen H Burum. *ed* Lynzee Klingman. *pd* Ida Random. *m* David Newman. *cast* Michael Douglas, Kathleen Turner, Danny DeVito, Marianne Sägebrecht, GD Spradlin, Peter Donat.
●Adapted from Warren Adler's novel, this portrait of a disintegrating marriage is a riotous mix of of wicked and wince-inducing humour. After seventeen years of marital bliss, Barbara Rose (Turner) asks her lawyer husband (Douglas) for a divorce. The reason? 'Because when I watch you sleeping, when I see you eating, when I look at you now, I just want to smash you face in'. From then on, their showcase home – complete with two kids, dog and cat – becomes a battlefield. She smashes his collection of porcelain figures, he saws the heels off all her shoes; he disrupts her gourmet evening by pissing on the fish dish, she trashes his Morgan sports car. This dark comic tone, though, is lightened into a cautionary fairytale by the pro-marriage moralising of a framing device in which divorce lawyer De Vito relates the events to a prospective client. There is also a sneaking suspicion that what the couple are tearing to shreds is not so much the emotional fabric of their relationship as the soft furnishings of their home. Still, De Vito's quirky camera angles and Kathleen Turner's steely-eyed spite inject a sadistic comic-strip madness into a film that for once has the nerve to see its nastiness through. NF

War of the Satellites

(1958, US, 66 min, b/w)
d/p Roger Corman. *sc* Lawrence Louis Goldman. *ph* Floyd Crosby. *ed* Irene Morra. *ad* Daniel Haller. *m* Walter Greene. *cast* Susan Cabot, Dick Miller, Richard Devon, Robert Shayne, Jerry Barclay, Eric Sinclair.
●In which Dick Miller hushes the United Nations, saves the world, and wins Ms Cabot in mid-space. In which alien-controlled scientist Devon walks off in two directions at once. In which Corman himself is glimpsed auteuristically knob-twiddling at Mission Control. Compared to which even *The Outer Limits* looks opulent. Which is no surprise for a flick started the day after Sputnik was launched, and on-screen only eight weeks later. Cheap, but very cheerful. PT

War of the Worlds

(1953, US, 85 min)
d Byron Haskin. *p* George Pal. *sc* Barré Lyndon. *ph* George Barnes. *ed* Everett Douglas. *ad* Hal Pereira, Albert Nozaki. *m* Leith Stevens. *cast* Gene Barry, Ann Robinson, Les Tremayne, Henry Brandon, Robert Cornthwaite, Jack Kruschen.
●Updated from London 1890 to contemporary California, George Pal's version of the HG Wells novel still works pretty well, thanks to its attractive special effects. You can on occasion see the wires manipulating the Martian ships, but their graceful sting-ray design (replacing Wells' tripod conception) is sleekly sinister; the wholesale destruction of (miniature) cities is surprisingly convincing; and the one-eyed humanoid/octopoid alien with the sucker fingers is an engaging creation. Too bad about the wooden cast, the tackily conventional romance, and a draggy religious message; but at least, given the time it was made, it isn't imbued with Cold War hysteria. TM

War Party

(1989, US, 97 min)
d Franc Roddam. *p* John Daly, Derek Gibson. *sc* Spencer Eastman. *ph* Brian Tufano. *ed* Sean Barton. *pd* Michael Bingham. *m* Chaz Jankel. *cast* Billy Wirth, Kevin Dillon, Tim Sampson, Jimmie Ray Weeks, M Emmet Walsh, Kevyn Major Howard, Jerry Hardin, Tantoo Cardinal, Bill McKinney.
●Sonny (Wirth) leads a mundane life on a Montana reservation, and only reluctantly agrees to participate in a local re-enactment of the battle which killed his Indian ancestors. The gala occasion brings out Cavalry uniforms and racial prejudice; there are real-life killings on both sides, prompting Sonny, his best friend (Dillon) and a couple of pals to take to the hills. What starts out promisingly enough as a firmly deglamorised depiction of reservation life declines into a routine chase thriller. Roddam shifts fluently between depictions of the original conflict and modern-day tensions, but there's a stagy atmosphere to the historic sequences which weakens their dramatic impact. The film's political will is more forcefully evident in exchanges between the tribal council leader and his wife as they discuss the circumstances leading to Sonny's defiant gesture. Their opportunity to air long-standing grievances is all too brief; but at least the film commendably refuses to offer an easy, upbeat resolution. CM

Warren Oates: Across the Border

(1992, US, 54 min)
d/p Tom Thurman. *sc* Tom Marksbury. *ph* Walter Brock. *ed* Tom Thurman. *m* Frank Schaap. *with* Peter Fonda, Ned Beatty, Stacy Keach, Harry Dean Stanton, Thomas McGuane, David Thomson, Monte Hellman, Sam Peckinpah.
●'Nobody loses all the time,' mused Warren Oates in his greatest role, Benny, in *Bring Me the Head of Alfredo Garcia*. But if anyone was born to play losers it was Oates. As Ned Beatty recalls, 'You could smell whisky and bad breath on him; he was toothy and small, with eyes that have seen too much solitary confinement – but for some of us, he was the only human being in motion pictures.' Although he never made it as a star, you only have to look at the friends and collaborators Thurman has assembled here to know the ragged glory of the man: novelist Thomas McGuane; directors Hellman and Peckinpah; Harry Dean Stanton and Peter Fonda. He was a 'constitutional anarchist', says Harry Dean, and the movies bear him out. TCh

War Requiem

(1988, GB, 93 min, b/w & col)
d Derek Jarman. *p* Don Boyd. *ph* Richard Greatrex. *ed* Rick Elgood. *pd* Lucy Morahan. *m* Benjamin Britten. *cast* Nathaniel Parker, Tilda Swinton, Laurence Olivier, Patricia Hayes, Rohan McCullough, Nigel Terry, Owen Teale.
●Jarman's finest work to date takes as its soundtrack/score Benjamin Britten's masterly religious/poetic choral work. A work of unrelieved mourning – an unfashionable sentiment – it mingles Wilfred Owen's World War One poems (written in the trenches) with the text of the Latin mass. The score is complex, long, non-narrative, and uninterrupted, which demands much of Jarman; and he delivers. His script subtly intertwines the poems' slight strains of a story – guns, dying,

death, hell, loss, and reconciliation – with imagined scenes around the poet at war, along with cruelly honest, uncensored found footage of wars distant and current. He also wrings remarkable silent performances from Swinton, who embodies the awful roles traditionally allotted the female principle in war; from Parker as the poet; and Teale as an unknown soldier transmuted by war. TC

War Room, The

(1993, US, 96 min)
d DA Pennebaker, Chris Hegedus. *p* RJ Cutler, Wendy Ettinger, Frazer Pennebaker. *ph* Nick Doob, DA Pennebaker, Kevin Rafferty. *ed* Chris Hegedus, Erez Laufer, DA Pennebaker. *with* James Carville, George Stephanopolis.

●'The most expensive single act of masturbation in history' – James Carville on Ross Perot's 1992 campaign for the US presidency. If this documentary record of the Clinton team's own campaign doesn't quite warrant such abusive language, it nevertheless comes across as an indulgent piece of self-preening. The film follows campaign manager Carville (see him in *The People vs. Larry Flynt*) and George Stephanopolis, director of communications, from a pre-Primary February breakfast with Clinton to the night of the November election results. The two 'stars', Carville, a 'ragin' Cajun' with fiercely intelligent Simian features and a forthright approach to the press corps, and Stephanopolis, telegenic Harvard boy, twinkle-eyed and soft-spoken, make a great double-act, though Carville is the stand-out. But the focus is way too far over on the side of personalities. There's scant political revelation: it's less behind-the-scenes than the scenes from a different perspective. NB

Warrior, The

(2001, GB/Fr/Ger/Ind, 86 min)
d Asif Kapadia. *p* Bertrand Faivre. *sc* Asif Kapadia, Tim Miller. *ph* Roman Osin. *ed* Ewa J Lind. *pd* Adrian Smith. *m* Dario Marianelli. *cast* Irfan Khan, Puru Chhibber, Sheikh Annuddin, Manadakini Goswani, Sunita Sharma, Noor Mani.

●NW India, ages ago. Sent by his warlord boss to punish a village defaulting on tithes, warrior Lafcadia (Khan) finds himself unable to slay a young girl after noticing his son's pendant around her neck. But the tyrant won't tolerate deserters: when Lafcadia, laying aside his sword, tries to leave for his native village in the Himalayas, his former second-in-command, Biswas, captures and kills his son. Devastated, he continues his journey into the wilderness, meeting various loners as he goes, while Biswas follows in bloody pursuit. If some of the above sounds familiar, that's because the plot of Kapadia's fine feature debut echoes *The Outlaw Josey Wales* and several Mann and Boetticher Westerns; stylistically, however, Kurosawa and Leone are reference points. In other words, this is basically a Western transposed to India, but the brazenly mythic tone aligns it less closely with Hollywood models than with more reflexive storytelling traditions. With its stark narrative simplicity, its timeless setting and cipher characters, the epic mode may not produce psychological complexity, but it does score in terms of scale, sweep and sheer panache. GA

Warriors, The

see Dark Avenger, The

Warriors, The

(1979, US, 94 min)
d Walter Hill. *p* Lawrence Gordon. *sc* David Shaber, Walter Hill. *ph* Andrew Laszlo. *ed* David Holden, Freeman Davies Jr, Billy Weber, Susan E Morse. *ad* Don Swanagan, Bob Wightman. *m* Barry DeVorzon. *cast* Michael Beck, James Remar, Thomas Waites, Dorsey Wright, Brian Tyler, David Harris, Deborah Van Valkenburgh.

●From its powerhouse opening, in which all the gangs of New York gather in tribal splendour in Riverside Drive Park, to the last ditch stand in dilapidated Coney Island, Hill has elevated his story of a novice gang on the run into a heroic epic of Arthurian dimensions, with sex as sorcery and the flick-knife as sword. Anyone expecting gritty realism will be disappointed, because Hill is offering something better: shooting entirely on NY locations at night, he has transformed the city into a phantasmagoric labyrinth of weird tribes in fantastic dress and make-up who move over (and under) the streets as untouched as troglodytes by the civilisation sleeping around them. The novice gang from Coney accidentally encounters some middle class swingers on the subway, and the two groups stare at each other like aliens from different galaxies (while the gang's new female recruit has to be gently restrained from instinctively putting a hand up to straighten her hair). Mixing ironic humour, good music, and beautifully photographed suspense, it's one of the best of 1979. DP

Warriors of Virtue

(1996, US/HK, 103 min)
d Ronny Yu. *p* Dennis Law, Ronald Law, Christopher Law, Jeremy Law, Patricia Ruben. *sc* Michael Vickerman, Hugh Kelley. *ph* Peter Pau. *ed* David Wu. *pd* Eugenio Zanetti. *m* Colorado Symphony Orchestra. *cast* Angus MacFadyen, Mario Yedidia, Marley Shelton, Jack Tate, Doug Jones, Don W Lewis, J Todd Adams.

●Stuntmen in kangaroo suits knock the stuffing out of one another. Yedidia's the kid with a gammy leg who disappears down a whirlpool when he's bullied by schoolmates, only to wake in the magical kingdom of Tao – a land whose harmony is threatened by the rampant ham of MacFadyen's warlord Komodo. Only the reunion of the five Warriors of Virtue, super-marsupials using the power of the elements to defeat their enemies without killing them, can save the day. Hong Kong director Yu's flashy combat sequences and the fairytale production design by Eugenio Zanetti unfortunately count for little when the exposition holding it all together is both cluttered and hamfisted. TJ

Warsaw Ghetto Uprising, The

(1993, Pol, 70 min, b/w & col)
d Jolanta Dylewska. *with* Marek Edelman.

●This moving documentary, subtitled 'Chronicle According to Marek Edelman', begins with 15 minutes of archive footage, presumably taken by the Nazis, of the Warsaw Ghetto between 1940 and 1943, to the accompanying music of Jan Kanty Pawluskiewicz. This is the background to the testimony of Edelman, a young leader of the Jewish Battle Organisation during the 53 days of the Warsaw Ghetto Uprising. Edelman recalls in perfect detail the suffering and courage of the Jews. WH

Warshots

(1996, Ger, 93 min)
d/p Heiner Stadler. *sc* Harald Göckeritz, Heiner Stadler. *ph* Hu Yusef. *ed* Micki Joanni. *pd* Hamze Nasrallah. *m* Roman Bunka. *cast* Herbert Knaup, Peter Franke, Özay Fecht, Hassan Farhat, David Kehoe, Jamal Hamdan.

●February 1995: Having witnessed the shooting of an Irish rebel by British soldiers in Belfast, German conflict-photographer Jan Loy (Knaup) ventures into a Somalia-like civil war constituted by warlords, journalists and UN troops. With his experience in Ireland still hanging over him – despite a press award for his shots of the incident, fellow reporter (Franke) blames him for the Irishman's death – Loy meets a local sniper and is struck by the similarities between their trades, furthering his doubts about the ethics of his profession. It could be promising, but, with director and co-writer Stadler's elliptical, disjointed style and low word count, the effect is ponderous and unrevealing. NB

War Wagon, The

(1967, US, 101 min)
d Burt Kennedy. *p* Marvin Schwartz. *sc* Clair Huffaker. *ph* William H Clothier. *ed* Harry Gerstad. *ad* Alfred Sweeney. *m* Dimitri Tiomkin. *cast* John Wayne, Kirk Douglas, Howard Keel, Robert Walker, Keenan Wynn, Bruce Cabot, Valora Noland, Gene Evans, Bruce Dern.

●Kennedy is very nearly at his tongue-in-cheek best in this Western which affably carries on the mood and manner of Hawks' *El Dorado*. Wayne and Douglas play the old friends from way back, one hired to kill the other but joining forces – along with a pleasingly motley band of helpers – to turn the tables on the villainous Cabot with a handsome profit on the side. 'Mine hit the ground first' Douglas boasts as they simultaneously out-draw two opponents. 'Mine was taller' says Wayne laconically. No masterpiece, but very engaging. TM

War Zone

(1986, WGer, 99 min)
d Nathaniel Gutman. *p* Elisabeth Wolters-Alfs. *sc* Hanan Peled. *ph* Amnon Salomon, Thomas Mauch. *ed* Peter Przygodda. *pd* Jürgen Henze. *m* Jacques Zwart, Hans Jansen. *cast* Christopher Walken, Marita Marschall, Hywel Bennett, Arnon Zadock, Amos Lavie, Etti Ankri.

●The approach employed here is so unimaginative, the format so tired, that electro-cardiac shock couldn't save this melodrama (filmed in English) from its own dubiously oversimplified politics. Don Stevens (Walken), jaded war correspondent, finds himself in the Lebanon, a disengaged hack who wanders somnolently through the gunfire, until an exclusive (which turns out to be a set-up) plunges him into the middle of the battle. Another chapter of recent history reduced to an amalgam of censored memory, romance, and imagination. SGo

War Zone, The

(1998, GB, 99 min)
d Tim Roth. *p* Sarah Radclyffe, Dixie Linder. *sc* Alexander Stuart. *ph* Seamus McGarvey. *ed* Trevor Waite. *pd* Michael Carlin. *m* Simon Boswell. *cast* Ray Winstone, Lara Belmont, Freddie Cunliffe, Tilda Swinton, Kate Ashfield, Aisling O'Sullivan.

●Scripted by Alexander Stuart from his own novel, Roth's ambitious and very decent directorial debut tells of a teenage boy's suspicions that his slightly elder sister (Belmont) is caught up in a sexual relationship with their father (Winstone); but is he just bored, confused and angry that the family left London for a remote Devon farmhouse? It's a tough, uncompromising movie, beautifully acted by all concerned (though one does wonder how the very different Winstone and Swinton, as the Earth Mother mum, ever got together in the first place), and imaginatively shot by Seamus McGarvey in broodingly dark 'Scope. A few scenes are perhaps needlessly and voyeuristically explicit, and it's not as emotionally affecting as it would like to be, but it's a confident, intelligent work for all that. GA

Waschen und Legen

see Shampoo and Set

Washington Square

(1997, US, 116 min)
d Agnieszka Holland. *p* Roger Birnbaum, Julie Bergman. *sc* Carol Doyle. *ph* Jerzy Zielinski. *ed* David Siegel. *pd* Allan Starski. *m* Jan AP Kaczmarek. *cast* Jennifer Jason Leigh, Albert Finney, Ben Chaplin, Maggie Smith, Judith Ivey, Betsy Brantley.

●When Wyler made *The Heiress*, he was, of course, filming a Broadway adaptation of Henry James's novel. This version goes back to the original book, jettisoning the stage-related business, and retrieving details and scenes lost in the translation from page to stage. Other 'corrections' include a greater teasing of the audience concerning the affections of the heroine's suitor: is anything stirring there besides opportunism? And Wyler's ending – a melodramatically decisive balancing of the moral books – here becomes a faithful transcription of the low key but equally deadly last interview described by James. But one does miss the severe monochrome of 1949, amid all this colour, all this brightness. BBa

Wasp Woman, The

(1959, US, 73 min, b/w)
d/p Roger Corman. *sc* Leo Gordon. *ph* Harry C Newman. *ed* Carlo Lodato. *ad* Daniel Haller. *m* Fred Katz. *cast* Susan Cabot, Fred Eisley, Barboura Morris, Michael Marks, William Roerick, Frank Gerstle.

●A film that highlights Corman's ability to ring interesting changes on proven formulas. The she-creature and the havoc she wreaks are both predictable enough, but it's a novel touch that she's a beautician, and that her metamorphosis is caused by experiments with new cosmetics ingredients. Susan Cabot (always Corman's favourite female sadist-figure) anchors the sexual mayhem in a very credible characterisation. TR

Watcher, The

(2000, US, 97 min)
d Joe Charbanic. *p* Christopher Eberts, Elliot Lewitt, Jeff Rice, Nile Niami. *sc* David Elliot, Clay Ayers. *ph* Michael Chapman. *ed* Richard

Nord. *pd* Brian Eatwell, Maria Caso. *m* Marco Beltrami. *cast* James Spader, Marisa Tomei, Ernie Hudson, Chris Ellis, Keanu Reeves, Robert Cicchini, Yvonne Niami, Jennifer McShane, Gina Alexander.
●Spader and Tomei, as the haunted ex-cop and his lonely shrink, add a human dimension to a derivative scenario. Based on the premise that serial killers, whose obsession is with their victims, also like to play cat-and-mouse games with the cops, this has voyeuristic strangler Reeves (comatose) following the burnt-out Spader to Chicago. Reeves believes that they have a vitalising 'yin and yang'-type relationship, so he starts sending Spader photos of his intended victims, 24 hours in advance. Spader takes the bait, cleans up his act and discovers new meaning in his life. Tomei, meanwhile, unwittingly offers psychoanalytical solace to both cop and killer. Veteran cinematographer Michael Chapman adds an unearned class to the cityscapes and over-designed interiors, but the director's penchant for MTV-style flashbacks and shaky-cam killer's-eye shots merely induces headaches. And the more Marco Beltrami's overpitched score tries to crank up the suspense level, the more vapid, pointless and unexciting it gets. NF

Watcher in the Woods, The

(1982, US, 100 min)
d John Hough. *p* Ron Miller. *sc* Brian Clemens, Harry Spalding, Rosemary Anne Sisson. *ph* Alan Hume. *ed* Geoffrey Foot. *pd* Elliot Scott. *m* Stanley Myers. *cast* Bette Davis, Carroll Baker, David McCallum, Lynn-Holly Johnson, Kyle Richards, Ian Bannen, Richard Pasco, Frances Cuka, Eleanor Summerfield, Georgina Hale.
●The horror movie, Disney-style. After an American couple and their two daughters move into an English country house, one of the girls (Johnson) imagines she is being watched by a creature that lurks in the woods. Her experiences seem to be linked to the disappearance, thirty years before, of another young girl, creepy old crone Davis' daughter. When it became obvious that the film's mix of cutesy sentiment and vague scariness wasn't working, the company ordered whole sequences to be rewritten, re-shot or re-edited, then imposed a stupid ending that explains precisely nothing. NF

Watchers

(1988, Can, 91 min)
d John Hess. *p* Damian Lee, David Mitchell. *sc* Bill Freed, Damian Lee. *ph* Richard Leiterman. *ed* Bill Freda, Carolle Alain, Rick Fields. *pd* Richard Wilcox. *m* Joel Goldsmith. *cast* Michael Ironside, Lala, Corey Haim, Dale Wilson, Blu Mankuma.
●A secret government laboratory, which has been genetically engineering animals for combat, unaccountably explodes, allowing two creatures to escape: a super-intelligent golden retriever that only wants to be loved, and a super-nasty hairy beastie. The dog befriends a kid called Travis, who's basically a good sort; but because the beastie has been trained to kill, Travis is soon surrounded by dead people with missing eyeballs. The obligatory mad scientists run around attempting to catch their creations, and don't care who they walk over in the process, so pretty soon it's 'young boy and wonder dog against the world' time. Produced under the guiding influence of Roger Corman, this low budget adaptation of Dean R Koontz's novel is a Boy's Own adventure all the way, a cross between *Lassie Come Home* and *Predator*, with a terrifically evil performance from Ironside. The script is enjoyably laughable, and the special effects are reassuringly tacky. Good cheap nonsense. MK

Watching the Detective (Aru Tantei no Yu-utsu)

(1998, Jap, 71 min)
d Junichi Yagi. *p* Junichi Yagi, Yuko Kameda. *sc* Junichi Yagi. *ph* Hiroaki Niizuma. *ed* Junichi Yagi. *ad* Masashi Nagata. *m* Susumu Obata. *cast* Eiji Oki, Haruko Mabuchi, Miki Ozawa.
●A lazy young gumshoe (Oki) is hired to stake out the apartment of an elderly woman. He sets up his video-cam in a room across the road and watches – until he starts to go a little stir-crazy. Then a stranger appears in the apartment opposite, an attractive young woman who sometimes seems to be aware of his furtive gaze… Yagi's debut feature (he was Kitano's assistant on *Boiling Point*) is the smartest Japanese indie of the year, less a 'who watches the watchmen?' parable than a cunning riff on Berkeley's dictum *esse est percipi* – to be is to be perceived. The mildly sadistic denouement risks cancelling out some of the more intriguing interpretations, but it remains one of the least boring films ever made about boredom. TR

Watch It

(1993, US, 102 min)
d Tom Flynn. *p* Thomas J Mangan IV. *sc* Tom Flynn. *ph* Stephen M Katz. *ed* Dorian Harris. *ad* Jeff Steven Ginn. *m* Stanley Clarke. *cast* Peter Gallagher, Suzy Amis, John C McGinley, Jon Tenney, Cynthia Stevenson, Lily Taylor, Tom Sizemore, Jordana Capra.
●John (Gallagher) moves in with Rick, Danny and Michael – all aimless twenty-somethings – and finds himself caught up in a life of parties, pranks and perfidy. But if their laid-back ways at first seem innocent, they mask a reluctance to grow up, and a fear of responsibility that sours their view of the world and hurts those who come close to them. So when John falls for one of Michael's cast-offs (Amis), it provokes a spate of jealousy and one-upmanship among the four – and a reassessment of their various relationships. NB

Watchmaker of Saint-Paul, The

see Horloger de St Paul, L'

Watch Out, We're Mad (Altrimenti ci Arrabbiamo)

(1974, It/Sp, 102 min)
d Marcello Fondato. *p* Mario Cecchi Gori. *sc* Francesco Scardamaglia, Marcello Fondato. *ph* Arturo Zavattini. *ed* Sergio Montanari. *ad* Francesco Vanorio. *m* Guido De Angelis, Maurizio De Angelis. *cast* Bud Spencer [Carlo Pedersoli], Terence Hill [Mario Girotti], Donald Pleasence, John Sharp, Deogratias Huerta.
●The double act from the 'Trinity' Westerns lend themselves rather absent-mindedly to this fairly resistible comedy geared to the great Italian fetish for gadgetry on wheels. The plot revolves around a highly-prized dune buggy, and is decorated with herds of trail-bikes, which at one point are involved in a joust-style contest. It is as bright and relentless as can be, with some of the side characters admittedly carrying a certain bite; but Fondato is a great one for never using a nuance if he can belabour the audience with a signpost. VG

Watch Your Stern

(1960, GB, 88 min, b/w)
d Gerald Thomas. *p* Peter Rogers. *sc* Alan Hackney, Vivian A Cox. *ph* Ted Scaife. *ed* John Shirley. *ad* Carmen Dillon. *m* Bruce Montgomery. *cast* Kenneth Connor, Leslie Phillips, Eric Barker, Joan Sims, Noel Purcell, Hattie Jacques, Sidney James, Eric Sykes, Spike Milligan, Victor Maddern.
●The 'Carry On' crew edge out of port under a flag of convenience as able seaman Connor dons a variety of disguises to stop the Admiralty top brass discovering he's accidentally destroyed a set of hush-hush torpedo plans. Milligan and Sykes steal the picture as a couple of chatty electricians, otherwise the awful puns and dodgy double entendres are all shipshape and Bristol-fashion. TJ

Water

(1985, GB, 97 min)
d Dick Clement. *p* Ian La Frenais. *sc* Dick Clement, Ian La Frenais, Bill Persky. *ph* Douglas Slocombe. *ed* John Victor Smith. *pd* Norman Garwood. *m* Mike Moran. *cast* Michael Caine, Valerie Perrine, Brenda Vaccaro, Leonard Rossiter, Billy Connolly, Dennis Duggan, Fulton Mackay, Dick Shawn, Fred Gwynne.
●This movie has the conviction of a farce negligently translated from an obscure foreign dialect. The action takes place on the fictional island of Cascara, which becomes the subject of international dispute when a long-neglected oil well is reopened and strikes…Perrier. American oilmen, Brit paratroopers, film crews, assorted mercenaries and revolutionaries move in as the plot trickles towards a conclusion in which a gang comprising executive producer George Harrison's old mates (Starr, Clapton, et al) gives an exquisitely embarrassing rock performance. Fine actors such as Vaccaro, Connolly and Rossiter, recognising a lame horse when they see one, camp it up for all they're worth, and it is left to Caine, giving yet another understated and perfectly timed performance as Cascara's beleaguered governor, to push *Water* limping across the finishing line. Eau-ful. RR

Water and Power

(1993, US, 58 min)
d Pat O'Neill.
●Though the title of Pat O'Neill's ciné-poem evokes Los Angeles and southern California – ostensibly its subject – it might more fittingly be called 'Movements of the Sun' or 'Ghosts in the Machine'. For while this visually striking, technologically remarkable movie acknowledges water as the life force that enables LA to prosper in what would otherwise be a virtual desert, most of O'Neill's time-lapse camerawork, multi-layered superimpositions and dynamic optical effects are concerned with changes in light, whether they be shadows shifting over baking sands or concrete canyons, or the Bacon-esque contortions of wraithlike figures in surreal cloud-walled rooms. Whatever, rather like *Koyaanisqatsi* with even less narrative but far more imaginative sense, this immaculately edited, kaleidoscopic collage of densely textured images and sounds paints a persuasive picture of LA and its environs as a feverishly dreamlike state of mind. GA

Water and Salt (Água e Sal)

(2001, Port/It, 117 min)
d Teresa Villaverde. *p* Paolo Branco. *sc* Teresa Villaverde. *ph* Emmanuel Machuel. *ed* Andrée Davanture. *pd* Ana Louro. *cast* Galatea Ranzi, Joaquim de Almeida, Alexandre Pinto, Clara Jost, Joel Miranda, Maria De Medeiros.
●Set in a small Portuguese coastal town, this intimate drama focuses on the breakdown of a relationship between introspective artist Ana (Ranzi) and her husband (de Almeida). She's terrified that he might abduct their four-year-old daughter. There's also an element of mystery: Ana becomes slowly drawn into the lives and problems of various misfits who live in the sleepy town. Seen almost entirely from Ana's perspective, the storytelling style is impressionistic. It's her emotions and thoughts that writer/director Villaverde concentrates on to the exclusion of almost everything else, throwing up some baffling non sequiturs. For instance, Ana's friend (De Medeiros) flits in and out of the film with no explanation why's she's there. The film might be somewhat puzzling, but it's also beautifully acted and quietly moving in its own lyrical, understated way. GM

Water Babies, The

(1978, GB/Pol, 92 min)
d Lionel Jeffries. *p* Peter Shaw. *sc* Michael Robson. *ph* Ted Scaife. *ed* Peter Weatherley. *ad* Herbert Westbrook. *m* Phil Coulter. *cast* James Mason, Billie Whitelaw, Bernard Cribbins, Joan Greenwood, David Tomlinson, Paul Luty, Tommy Pender, Samantha Gates.
●Charles Kingsley ended his amazing Victorian tale of chimney-sweep Tom's underwater odyssey with the earnest wish that his child readers learn their lessons and wash themselves in cold water 'like a true Englishman'. Times have obviously changed, and any modern adaptation has to soft-pedal the pious author's whimsical allegories of spiritual and social improvement. Jeffries' film achieves this by plunging into tepid animation when Tom (Pender) plunges into water. But with the allegories submerged, the string of animated adventures involving the smiling band of pure, fearless babies and the gallery of talking (and singing) fish seem just idle amusement, lacking all the driving force of the live-action framework. There's no cute buffoonery in those scenes, which are replete with solid Yorkshire atmosphere, narrative tension, and excellent acting (even from David Tomlinson). It's really two films in one. (Animation directed by Miroslaw Kijowicz.) GB

Waterboy, The

(1998, US, 90 min)
d Frank Coraci. *p* Robert Simonds, Jack Giarraputo. *sc* Tim Herlihy, Adam Sandler. *ph* Steven Bernstein. *ed* Tom Lewis. *pd* Perry Andelin Blake. *m* Alan Pasqua. *cast* Adam Sandler, Kathy Bates, Fairuza Balk, Jerry Reed, Henry Winkler, Blake Clark, Larry Gillard Jr.

●Sandler deals in the Chapline-like whimsy of the triumphant little man – in this case a vengeful nerd. Agreed, he hasn't the simpering narcissism of Chaplin at his most sentimental, though you have to wonder what Sandler thinks he's doing with his one-note, instantly unconvincing, blink-and-stutter performance. He's Bobby Boucher, a 31-year-old virginal retard who takes his job (a football team's 'water distribution engineer') too seriously, despite the ceaseless abuse of the jocks, and who bows to his Mama (Bates, hopeless), despite her instruction that 'little girls are the devil'. Sacked by one team, he takes up with Winkler's hopeless Coach Klein and discovers the ability to channel years of victimisation into prowess on the field, winning games and girls. The direction is as blunt and vacant as the plotting, the jokes are obvious and the performances (with a couple of exceptions) charmless. NB

Waterboys

(2001, Jap, 91 min)
d Shinobu Yaguchi. *p* Akifumi Takuma, Daisuke Sekiguchi. *sc* Shinobu Yaguchi. *ph* Yuichi Nagata. *ed* Ryuji Miyajima. *ad* Takeshi Shimizu. *m* Gakuji Matsuda. *cast* Satoshi Tsumabuki, Naoto Takenaka, Kaori Manabe, Akira Emoto, Hiroshi Tamaki, Akifumi Miura, Kondo Kuen.
●Nice idea: the hopeless swimmers of Tadano High put themselves through hell to become Japan's first male synchronised swimming team in order to fulfil the dream of their coach, even though she's away having a baby. Sadly, the film itself is not so great. Yaguchi's previous, smaller movies didn't strain for humour, but this big ensemble comedy tries much too hard. Yaguchi constantly goes for live-action cartoon-style visual gags and botches the tone or timing of most of them. Worse, he was obviously unable to control Takenaka, who plays an aquarium owner with such 'brio' that the film becomes unwatchable whenever he's on. And the handling of a gay subplot, although very PC, is so perfunctory that it simply isn't funny. Still, the boys are cute and the show they finally manage to put on is quite something. TR

Waterdance, The

(1991, US, 107 min)
d Neal Jimenez, Michael Steinberg. *p* Gale Anne Hurd, Marie Cantin, Michael Steinberg. *sc* Neal Jimenez. *ph* Mark Plummer. *ed* Jeff Freeman. *pd* Bob Ziembicki. *m* Michael Convertino. *cast* Eric Stoltz, Wesley Snipes, William Forsythe, Helen Hunt, Elizabeth Peña, William Allen Young.
●In 1985, Neal Jimenez, a successful young screenwriter, was left paralysed for life after breaking his neck. The same fate befalls novelist Joel Garcia (Stoltz) in Jimenez's first film as director, a moving drama set in a rehabilitation ward for paraplegics. At first Garcia maintains a degree of equanimity – he can still write, after all – but his latent frustration becomes more apparent in contact with his married girlfriend (Hunt) and the other patients in his ward, Raymond (Snipes) and Bloss (Forsythe). In essence another 'triumph-over-adversity' picture, its ensemble nature is both its strongest asset and its weakness. Neither lonely, black Raymond nor redneck biker Bloss has Joel's mental escape route: his talent. If this helps to ground things in a less sanguine vision than is usual, the movie cannot quite bring itself to resist the balm of male bonding, so that at worst it comes perilously close to something like a buddy movie on wheels. Even then, script, direction and performances are all right on the nose. It's frank and funny with it. TCh

Water Drops on Burning Rocks (Gouttes d'eau sur pierres brûlantes)

(1999, Fr/Jap, 85 min)
d François Ozon. *p* Olivier Delbosc, Marc Missonier. *sc* François Ozon. *ph* Jeanne Lapoirie. *ed* Laurence Bawedin. *ad* Arnaud de Moleron. *cast* Bernard Giraudeau, Malik Zidi, Ludivine Sagnier, Anna Thomson.
●Cynics would argue that this is so much more achieved than Ozon's first two features because there was a real script: it's based on an early, unproduced play by Fassbinder. The plot is quintessential Fassbinder: middle-aged businessman picks up a young straight, seduces him, installs him as his lover/housekeeper and begins to tire of him. Then the boy's jilted fiancée shows up, soon followed by the transsexual who sacrificed everything for love of the businessman. Emotional recriminations ensue. With French actors playing German characters, quoting Rilke in German and, in one show-stopping scene, grooving to German pop of the '70s, it manages to be 90 per cent pure Fassbinder *and* 90 per cent pure Ozon. A perfect co-feature for *Chinese Roulette*. TR

Waterland

(1992, GB, 95 min)
d Stephen Gyllenhaal. *p* Patrick Cassavetti, Katy McGuinness. *sc* Peter Prince. *ph* Robert Elswit. *ed* Lesley Walker. *pd* Hugo Luczyc-Wyhiwski. *m* Carter Burwell. *cast* Jeremy Irons, Sinead Cusack, Ethan Hawke, Grant Warnock, Lena Headey, David Morrissey, John Heard, Callum Dixon, Pete Postlethwaite.
●Graham Swift's Fenland novel paid homage to a part of Britain that's been ignored by film, unless you count *Dakota Road*. Gyllenhaal rises to the challenge of Swift's prose, capturing a flat land bogged down in its past, and creating an extravagant historical picture that avoids the traps of the Hovis-ad picturesque. The crazy-paving narrative and musings on the nature of history have inevitably been reduced in Peter Prince's script, but the essentials are there: memory, madness, incest, eels and real ale. History teacher Tom Crick (Irons), about to be axed by headmaster Heard, interrupts his classes to deliver a rambling memoir about his youth in the Fens, delving back to WWI and beyond to explain the multiple reasons behind the crack-up of his wife Mary (Cusack). There are obvious concessions to the US market; and as in his previous film, *Paris Trout*, Gyllenhaal bites off more narrative than he can chew, so that, for example, Cusack's character gets lost somewhere en route. Still, it's a brave endeavour, held together by Robert Elswit's poetic photography, and by Irons' authoritative impression of the crumbling desperation behind the chalk-dusted facade of a pensive history man. JRo

Waterloo

(1970, It/USSR, 132 min)
d Sergei Bondarchuk. *p* Dino De Laurentiis. *sc* HAL Craig, Sergei Bondarchuk, Vittorio Bonicelli. *ph* Armando Nannuzzi. *ed* Richard C Meyer. *pd* Mario Garbuglia. *m* Nino Rota. *cast* Rod Steiger, Christopher Plummer, Orson Welles, Jack Hawkins, Virginia McKenna, Dan O'Herlihy, Rupert Davies, Philippe Forquet, Michael Wilding.
●Visually impressive, but a rather silly attempt to explain Napoleon, tracing his career from exile in Elba, through resurgence to power, to his defeat by Wellington at Waterloo. The main problem seems to lie in Bondarchuk's reliance on eye-catching gimmickry, and in his indecision as to whether to make a spectacular epic about nations at war, or an intimate portrayal of Bonaparte as a person. The early scenes, with less action, suffer most from this fault, although the whole thing is also blighted by Steiger's eccentrically mannered performance. GA

Waterloo Road

(1944, GB, 76 min, b/w)
d Sidney Gilliat. *p* Edward Black. *sc* Sidney Gilliat. *ph* Arthur Crabtree. *ed* Alfred Roome. *ad* Alex Vetchinsky. *m* Bob Busby. *cast* John Mills, Stewart Granger, Alastair Sim, Joy Shelton, Alison Leggatt, Beatrice Varley, George Carney, Jean Kent, Wylie Watson.
●Set in the mean streets around Waterloo Station in 1941, Gilliat's second feature is, like *Millions Like Us*, a populist drama commendably unpatronising in its view of the way the war left 'folks battling with themselves' at home. The simple narrative thread concerns Shelton as a young newly-wed left alone when her husband (Mills) is whisked away by the army. Unhappy, parked with in-laws, longing for the baby it didn't seem the right time to contemplate, she is fair game for a smooth spiv (Granger) proud of having bought himself medical exemption from the forces (which, ironically, it turns out he could have earned for free). But the meat of the film lies in the sleazy odyssey through the local pleasure domes (dance hall, pub, amusement arcade, hairdressing parlour, tattooist's shop) as the frantic Mills gets wind of the affair and goes AWOL to look for his wife. The hunt ends in happy reconciliation after a cleansing fist-fight between Mills and Granger (none too subtly waged to the sound of noises off from the blitz). No masterpiece, certainly, but it's often funny, sometimes touching, and always wonderfully evocative of the period. TM

Watermelon Man

(1970, US, 100 min)
d Melvin Van Peebles. *p* John B Bennett. *sc* Herman Raucher. *ph* W Wallace Kelley. *ed* Carl Kress. *ad* Malcolm C Bert, Sydney Z Litwack. *m* Melvin Van Peebles. *cast* Godfrey Cambridge, Estelle Parsons, Howard Caine, D'Urville Martin, Mantan Moreland, Kay Kimberly.
●Cambridge plays (admirably) a high-powered all-American insurance salesman, bursting with health, dirty jokes, and bigotry, who wakes up one morning to find that his skin has turned black. His frenzied attempts to explain the metamorphosis as an excess of tan and/or soya sauce won't wash any more than his skin will, so he finds himself forced to adjust. Often very funny in its topsy-turvy comments on racism, the script unfortunately has to battle against a director determined to use every gaudy trick in the book. The real pity, though, is that it fails to follow through on the logic of its premise whereby the hero is so heartily extrovert that everybody (wife and kids included) dislikes him. When he turns black, he also turns sympathetic, so nobody's reflex responses are really tested. TM

Watermelon Woman, The

(1997, US, 80 min)
d Cheryl Dunye. *p* Barry Swimar, Alexandra Juhasz. *sc* Cheryl Dunye. *ph* Michelle Crenshaw. *ed* Annie Taylor. *pd* Robert Holtzman. *m* Paul Shapiro. *cast* Cheryl Dunye, Guinevere Turner, Valerie Walker, Lisa Marie Bronson, Irene Dunye, Camille Paglia.
●A witty exploration of black American culture, past and present. Shooting in breezy, boppy fashion, Dunye soon has two narratives on the go: her quest for the 'truth' behind 'the Watermelon Woman', a beautiful, undocumented '30s film actress forever cast as a 'black mammy', and her own life working in a video store, bickering with her pal Tamara (Walker) and finding a girlfriend. Both these criss-crossing Philadelphia stories work in their own right. Dunye is fiercely charismatic, and while Tamara may seem like the stereotypically hardline, 'narrow' best friend, she also gets some great lines. It's the search for the Watermelon Woman, though, that really engrosses, throwing up a host of *Looking for Langston*-style images, as well as marvellous clips of Dunye's camera-shy mother suddenly denying all knowledge of the subject at hand. (Camille Paglia is a hoot, delivering patronising pearls of wisdom with irritable gusto.) CO'Su

Watership Down

(1978, GB, 92 min)
d/p/sc Martin Rosen. *m* Angela Morley. *cast* voices: John Hurt, Richard Briers, Ralph Richardson, Roy Kinnear, Denholm Elliott, Zero Mostel, Harry Andrews, Michael Hordern.
●All one can say about this animated feature is thank God for myxomatosis. The book is another matter: once you've got past fey footnotes explaining that rabbits can count up to five, Richard Adams presents a good solid story, ingeniously and effectively told from the rabbit's minuscule perspective. Had the original director John Hubley been allowed to persevere, maybe some of the virtues would have remained; but as rejigged by producer Martin Rosen, there is nothing. The 'camera' takes a conventionally objective viewpoint, perpetually rolling over rolling countryside, which effectively robs the plot of all its terror and tension. And the bunnies are a crudely drawn, charmless bunch, with the final nail provided by the soundtrack's famous voices, who help turn the film into a radio play. GB

Water, Wind, Dust (Ab, Bad, Khak)

(1989, Iran, 72 min)
d/sc Amir Naderi. *ph* Reza Pakzad. *ed* Amir Naderi. *cast* Majid Niromand.
●Naderi made this for Iranian TV right after *The Runner*, and it plays like an expressionist twin to the earlier film. A boy searches for his missing parents in a huge, parched desert while the last inhabitants of the region flee as refugees and the sandstorms rise. There's no plot to speak of, but the boy faces a crisis of conscience when he finds himself responsible for an abandoned baby. There's hardly any dialogue either, just harsh, elemental imagery and a grim vision of life

at the point of extinction. The slightly misjudged ending (which involves a burst of Beethoven on the soundtrack) confirms that allegorical interpretations are there for the asking. TR

Waterworld

(1995, US, 134 min)
d Kevin Reynolds. *p* Charles Gordon, John A Davis, Kevin Costner. *sc* Peter Rader, David N Twohy, Joss Whedon. *ph* Dean Semler. *ed* Peter Boyle. *pd* Dennis Gassner. *m* James Newton Howard. *cast* Kevin Costner, Jeanne Tripplehorn, Dennis Hopper, Tina Majorino, Zakes Mokae.

● Water, water everywhere, and recycled urine to drink. The ice-caps have melted, and humans have split into three groups: eco-communities living together on deep-anchored, heavily guarded atolls; piratical 'Smokers' monopolising the scant reserves of oil; and lone mariners sailing in search of trade. Led by the Deacon (Hopper), the Smokers burn out an atoll looking for Enola (Majorino), a girl with a map to the mythical 'Dryland' tattooed on her back – but she escapes with the aid of her guardian Helen (Tripplehorn) and a mutant mariner with webbed feet and gills (Costner). After all the expense and negative speculation, the first thing to say about *Waterworld* is that it works – up to a point. The film inhabits its own brave new world and it's a real eyeful: witness the rusted techno-junk design of the atoll, the Smokers' kamikaze jet-ski attacks, and the Mariner's surprisingly nifty trimaran. Costner's acrobatic, taciturn hero is a charismatic figure, and his terse, uncomfortable relationship with the two female stowaways is the movie's dramatic strong point, but things drift when the Mariner softens, and the last half-hour is an inert retread of the familiar kidnap-rescue formula of contemporary action movies. A *Mad Max* rip-off at heart, but a blockbuster none the less. TCh

Wattstax

(1973, US, 102 min)
d Mel Stuart. *p* Larry Shaw, Mel Stuart. *sc* Mel Stuart. *ph* Roderick Young, Robert Marks, Jose Mignone, Larry Clark, John A Alonzo. *ed* Robert K Lambert. *with* Richard Pryor, Isaac Hayes, The Staple Singers, Luther Ingram, Johnnie Taylor, Rufus Thomas, Carla Thomas, The Emotions.

● A record of an all-day concert put on by Stax as part of the Watts Summer Festival to celebrate the riots. There isn't enough music, but Stax have at least had the wit to hire Richard Pryor to deliver one of his characteristic monologues (the rest of the time is filled out by chats with the denizens of Watts). Much good music all the same, from Carla Thomas and others, with an anti-climactic appearance from Isaac Hayes. See it for Rufus Thomas doing 'Funky Chicken', and for the genuinely stirring 'I am Somebody', the National Black Litany led, incredibly, by Jesse Jackson with the 100,000 auditorium joining in – a strong experience. VG

Wave (Nami)

(2001, Jap, 111 min)
d Hiroshi Okuhara. *p* Masafumi Fukui, Tatsuji Omori, Kensaku Watanabe. *sc* Hiroshi Okuhara. *ph* Masahiro Miki. *ed* Hiroshi Okuhara. *m* Sangatsu. *cast* Kensaku Watanabe, Sakutaro Inui, Asako Kobayashi, Chiharu Konno, Tatsuji Omori.

● Much less elusive than Okuhara's debut *Timeless Melody*, but still not exactly plot-heavy, this chronicles the shifting relationships between four young people (two boys, two girls) one summer by the sea. Both girls and one of the boys are just visiting; the main focus is on the kid who lives in the sleepy seaside town, working as night-clerk in the hotel, hung up on both girls and deeply jealous of his friend's success with them. There's an interesting tension between the film's formal precision and the desultory nature of much of the action; it lifts the film above the ruck of 'freewheeling' youth pics and allows Okuhara to get to grips with adolescent fears, rivalries and solipsisms. TR

Wavelength

(1967, Can, 45 min)
d Michael Snow. *cast* Hollis Frampton.

● Snow is the uncontested master of the structural movement. *Wavelength*, his first major work, is a relentless 45-minute voyage across a loft that perpetually transforms, questions and illuminates everything in its path. Proposing and requiring a radically different form of perception of what a film experience entails, it repels passive attention as much as it rewards participation. As Snow describes it: 'The space starts at the camera's (spectator's) eye, is in the air, then is on the screen, then is within the screen (the mind)'. JR

Wax, or The Discovery of Television Among the Bees

(1991, US, 85 min)
d/p/sc David Blair. *ph* Mark Kaplan. *cast* David Blair, William Burroughs.

● A curious pot-pourri of found footage, fantasy narrative and electronic visual trickery, this is proof that stylistic innovation and a taste for the bizarre don't always add up to galvanising effect. The narrative concerns a post-WWI English beekeeper, James 'Hive' Maker (William Burroughs in his most fleeting film cameo to date), with a miraculous swarm of Mesopotamian bees, and his descendant Jacob, who works in a military computer graphics unit in New Mexico. Starting off with a stack of antique documentary footage, Blair builds up an intrigue narrative that aspires to the po-faced absurdity of Peter Greenaway's early pseudo-documentaries. But it loses momentum when Blair himself takes centre stage as the protection-suited Jacob.

Waxwork

(1988, US, 97 min)
d Anthony Hickox. *p* Staffan Ahrenberg. *sc* Anthony Hickox. *ph* Gerry Lively. *ed* Christopher Cibelli. *pd* Gianni Quaranta. *m* Roger Bellon. *cast* Zack Galligan, Deborah Foreman, Michelle Johnson, Dana Ashbrook, David Warner, Patrick MacNee.

● The portmanteau horror movie makes a hesitant comeback with this jokey teen splatter pic. Invited to a midnight show by the owner (Warner) of a mysterious waxwork exhibit, six teenagers are spooked by lifelike tableaux depicting the 18 most evil men who ever lived. Drawn into the victimless displays, they catapult back through time, and find themselves on the business end of the Wolfman's claws, Dracula's fangs, or the Marquis de Sade's riding whip. The clunking inconsistencies which litter the episodic plot mar enjoyment of the striking set designs and outrageous (censored) gore. The final showdown degenerates into a cross between a Western saloon brawl and a custard pie fight. In short, this cannot hold a candle to its AIP and Amicus predecessors, and mostly just gets on one's wick. NF

Waxworks (Das Wachsfigurenkabinett)

(1924, Ger, 7,028 ft, b/w)
d Paul Leni. *sc* Henrik Galeen. *ph* Helmar Lerski. *ad* Paul Leni, Fritz Maurischat, Alfred Junge. *cast* Conrad Veidt, Emil Jannings, Werner Krauss, Wilhelm Dieterle, John Gottowt, Olga Belajeff.

● Leni, a former designer for Reinhardt, seems to have conceived *Waxworks* as an inventory of expressionistic effects, using a different style, motif, and mood for each of its three episodes. The first is erotic and very funny, with Jannings as a wicked Caliph whose rotundity is echoed by the Bagdad sets, all bulbous walls and secret orifices. The second is a sadistic fantasia, with Veidt as Ivan the Terrible, eventually driven mad by his own tortures. The last is a phantasmagoria of Jack the Ripper (Krauss), pursuing young lovers through a nightmare London of cobblestones and fog. The result is consistently enthralling, years ahead of its time. The poet seen dreaming up the stories, incidentally, was to become the Hollywood director William Dieterle. TR

Way Ahead, The

(1944, GB, 115 min, b/w)
d Carol Reed. *p* Norman Walker, John Sutro. *sc* Eric Ambler, Peter Ustinov. *ph* Guy Green. *ed* Fergus McDonell. *ad* David Rawnsley. *m* William Alwyn. *cast* David Niven, Stanley Holloway, Raymond Huntley, William Hartnell, James Donald, John Laurie, Leslie Dwyer, Hugh Burden, Jimmy Hanley, Renee Asherson.

● Scripted by Eric Ambler and Peter Ustinov, this is more complex than Dick Lester's scornful '60s parody of it in *How I Won the War* suggests. Reed achieves his transformation of a bunch of lazy, quarrelsome civilians into a proficient fighting force with a minimum of machismo and glory. Unlike today's sinister professional force, this is a people's army. Niven's officer is a car mechanic up from the ranks, and Hartnell's thin-lipped sergeant scourges out class differences with a rigorous application of army discipline. Despite a framework which stresses regimental traditions and military valour, the film's celebration of the ordinary man as soldier leaves a residue of radicalism. RMy

Way Down East

(1920, US, 123 min, b/w)
d/p DW Griffith. *sc* Anthony Paul Kelly, DW Griffith. *ph* Billy Bitzer, Hendrik Sartov. *ed* James Smith, Rose Smith. *ad* Charles O Seessel, Clifford Pember. *cast* Lillian Gish, Richard Barthelmess, Lowell Sherman, Burr McIntosh, Edgar Nelson.

● Griffith's Victorian perspective on illegitimacy (plus his view of maternity as 'woman's Gethsemane', etc) threatens for a while to make *Way Down East* the tract on monogamy that it announces itself as. It has two lifelines out of that morass: one is Lillian Gish, whose virtuoso performance makes the heroine's growth from gullible innocence to bitter experience credible; the other is Griffith's old standby, the reliable mechanism of suspense melodrama, here escalating busily and inventively right up to the famous ice-floe climax. The result is a good deal more interesting than camp, but Russ Meyer fans won't have any problem perceiving this as a rural prototype for *Beyond the Valley of the Dolls*, with its classical simplicity, its comic relief yokels, its villainous squire, and its matchless moral. TR

Way I Killed My Father, The (Comment j'ai tué mon père/ Cómo maté a mi padre)

(2001, Fr/Sp, 98 min)
d Anne Fontaine. *p* Philippe Carcassonne. *sc* Jacques Fieschi, Anne Fontaine. *ph* Jean-Marc Fabre. *ed* Guy Lecorne. *ad* Sylvain Chauvelot. *m* Jocelyn Pook. *cast* Michel Bouquet, Charles Berling, Natacha Régnier, Amira Casar, Stéphane Guillon, Hubert Koundé, Karole Rocher, Marie Micla.

● Jean-Luc (Berling) seems to have it all: he's a wealthy doctor with a beautiful wife (Régnier), and well respected by the affluent Versailles society whom he works to keep young. He even employs his younger brother as his chauffeur. Then, out of the blue, his father returns from Africa, opening up all manner of secrets and wounds festering in the subconscious. The French have a reputation for dissecting the bourgeoisie with exquisite taste and discretion, and this has the accoutrements (and the fine performances) of something by Claude Sautet, say. Unfortunately, the longer it goes on, the emptier it feels, and its emptiness's all the more glaring for director and co-writer Fontaine's desperate recourse to melodrama in the final reel. TCh

Wayne's World

(1992, US, 95 min)
d Penelope Spheeris. *p* Lorne Michaels. *sc* Mike Myers, Bonnie Turner, Terry Turner. *ph* Theo van de Sande. *ed* Malcolm Campbell. *pd* Gregg Fonseca. *m* J Peter Robinson. *cast* Mike Myers, Dana Carvey, Rob Lowe, Tia Carrere, Brian Doyle-Murray, Lara Flynn Boyle, Michael DeLuise, Meat Loaf, Ed O'Neill.

● Bill & Ted never quite got beyond cult status, while this low-budget imitator became the US box-office phenomenon of the year. Why? Wayne & Garth don't have the charisma and telepathic rapport that made B & T such a terrific comic duo, and the only significant addition to the B & T lexicon is a new range of sexist epithets and the all-conquering 'NOT!'. And, bizarrely, Wayne (Myers) still lives in his parents' house, though he's clearly well into his thirties. They are the acceptable mascots of Metal; boys you could take home to your parents. Much of the credit for the film's success lies with Spheeris, whose confident if rough-edged direction keeps it on track and cooking. The jokes come thick and fast, mostly deconstructing TV: 'Wayne's World' is a public access TV show hosted by Wayne and his dweebish best friend Garth (Carvey). They play games with film, too: Wayne and Garth's to-camera monologues always hit the spot, and there's a signposted 'gratuitous sex scene'. Lowe is suitably slimy as the TV mogul who offers them fame and wealth without obligation (not!), and the whole thing chunters along nicely to the climax(es). DW

Wayne's World 2

(1993, US, 95 min)
d Stephen Surjik. *p* Lorne Michaels. *sc* Mike Myers, Bonnie Turner, Terry Turner. *ph* Francis Kenny. *ed* Malcolm Campbell. *pd* Gregg Fonseca. *m* Carter Burwell. *cast* Mike Myers, Dana Carvey, Tia Carrere, Christopher Walken, Ralph Brown, Kim Basinger, James Hong.
● A year has passed, Wayne and Garth (Myers and Carvey) are a little older, a little wiser, and 'starting to grow hair in really weird places'. While Cassandra (Carrere) pursues her rock career under the auspices of shady producer Bobby Cahn (Walken) and Garth falls into the welcoming arms of Honey Hornée (Basinger), Wayne is visited in his dreams by Jim Morrison and promises to put on a huge concert: Waynestock! Despite typically hip disclaimers, *WW2* is in many respects a standard sequel, careful to rerun not only the (very sketchy) form of the original, but often the content as well. Odd, then, that this should be much funnier than the first film. A headbanger with brains, Wayne is a teen hero for ex-teens, and while the film isn't exactly 'mature', it must be baffling to anyone who doesn't remember the '70s with at least a modicum of embarrassed amusement. TCh

Way of a Gaucho

(1952, US, 91 min)
d Jacques Tourneur. *p/sc* Philip Dunne. *ph* Harry Jackson. *ed* Robert Fritch. *ad* Lyle Wheeler, Mark-Lee Kirk. *m* Sol Kaplan. *cast* Rory Calhoun, Gene Tierney, Hugh Marlowe, Richard Boone, Everett Sloane, Enrique Chaico, Lidia Campos.
● Calhoun certainly makes an authentic cowboy. An ex-lumberjack, ranch hand and forester, he was given an unlikely break in movies after a chance meeting with Alan Ladd. He stars as the gaucho, a renegade from the Argentine pampas who bitterly resents the way that 'civilisation' is transforming his backyard. Despite the South American settings, this unfolds like a very conventional Western, and doesn't bear comparison with Tourneur's masterly *Out of the Past*, or his cult horror films *Cat People* and *I Walked with a Zombie*. GM

Way of the Dragon, The (Meng Long Guo Jiang/aka Return of the Dragon)

(1972, HK, 99 min)
d Bruce Lee. *p* Raymond Chow. *sc* Bruce Lee. *ph* Ho Lan Shan. *ed* Chang Yao Ching. *ad* Chien Hsin. *m* Joseph Koo. *cast* Bruce Lee, Nora Miao, Chuck Norris, Wei Ping Ao, Robert Wall, Wang Ing Sik.
● The only film written, produced, and directed by Bruce Lee was to have been the first of a series in which he cast himself as Tan Lung, out-of-town strong-arm, here hired by the Chinese owner of a restaurant in Rome to sort out their problems with the local syndicate. The film has the roughness you might expect in a first directorial effort, and also a perhaps unexpected leaning towards comedy. Lee makes great play on his character as the country boy without weapons confronting the denizens of the technologically-powerful West and winning hands down. Fight fest addicts will relish confrontations with Chuck Norris, Robert Wall and Wang Ing Sik, professionals all. VG

Way of the Gun, The

(2000, US, 119 min)
d Christopher McQuarrie. *p* Kenneth Kokin. *sc* Christopher McQuarrie. *ph* Dick Pope. *ed* Stephen Semel. *pd* Maia Javan. *m* Joe Kraemer. *cast* Ryan Phillippe, Benicio Del Toro, Juliette Lewis, Taye Diggs, Nicky Katt, Geoffrey Lewis, Dylan Kussman, Scott Wilson, James Caan.
● With an Oscar under his belt for the screenplay of *The Usual Suspects*, McQuarrie makes his directorial bow with this arresting attempt at a contemporary thriller filtered through the spirit of Peckinpah. Hoods Del Toro and Phillippe like to think they're the last word in ruthless cool, but they may have to reconsider when they kidnap pregnant Lewis and discover her unlikely connection to a scary crime figure, who soon has veteran fixer Caan on the case. With its elliptical gunfights, deliberate echoes of *The Wild Bunch* and probing moral sense, the film shows that, post-Tarantino, there's life left in the genre yet, even if the much signposted childbirth finale goes seriously off the rails, and Phillippe's badass credentials never really persuade. TJ

Way Out West

(1937, US, 65 min, b/w)
d James W Horne. *p* Stan Laurel. *sc* Charles Rogers, Felix Adler, James Parrott. *ph* Art Lloyd, Walter Lundin. *ed* Bert Jordan. *ad* Arthur I Royce. *m* Marvin Hatley. *cast* Stan Laurel, Oliver Hardy, Sharon Lynn, James Finlayson, Rosina Lawrence, Stanley Fields.
● Arguably the most assured of Stan and Ollie's features, with the sparkling duo sent to Brushwood Gulch to deliver the deed for a gold mine to the daughter (Lawrence) of a deceased prospector. Looking for a quick buck, saloon-keeper Finlayson directs them to his own brassy girlfriend (Lynn). Some classic moments, such as the pair's soft-shoe shuffle outside the saloon, and their vocal duet at the bar on 'The Blue Ridge Mountains of Virginia', as well as a razor-sharp satire of B Western conventions. ATu

Way Through the Bleak Woods, The (Cesta pustym lesem)

(1997, Czech Republic, 86 min, b/w)
d Ivan Vojnár. *p* Galina Sustová, Ivana Jaroschy, Petr Morávek. *sc* Ivan Arsenjev. *ph* Jaromir Kacer. *ed* Alois Fisárek. *pd* Vladimir Labsc. *m* Irena Havel, Vojtech Havel. *cast* Václav Koubek, Pavel Landovsky, Jana Dolanská, Eliska Sirová, Jirí Soukup.
● One of the most beautiful b/w films of the last 30 years, this is a romantic tone poem, set in a remote Eastern European community on the eve of WWI. Vojnár is less interested in plot than situation: only gradually does he suggest the social fissures that may tear the village apart through a subtle, elliptical succession of images and echoes. (Typical scene: bearded man walks through the woods in the snow, stops and sits.) Frustrating until you adjust to the pace, the film is deeply evocative, with some of the eerie resonance of faded still-life photography, a sense of time and place you can practically taste on your breath. TCh

Way to the Stars, The (aka Johnny in the Clouds)

(1945, GB, 109 min, b/w)
d Anthony Asquith. *p* Anatole De Grunwald. *sc* Terence Rattigan. *ph* Derrick Williams. *ed* Fergus McDonell. *ad* Paul Sheriff. *m* Nicholas Brodszky. *cast* Michael Redgrave, John Mills, Rosamund John, Douglass Montgomery, Renee Asherson, Stanley Holloway, Trevor Howard, Basil Radford, Bonar Colleano, David Tomlinson, Jean Simmons.
● Good performances distinguish this evocation of a World War II bomber base in Britain, studiously anti-heroic in its concentration on human relationships rather than stirring combat (as one might expect with a script by Terence Rattigan). But it has dated badly in its genteelly romantic view of the hazards and heartbreaks, and in its cosy cementing of Anglo-American relationships. The best things in it are moments of pure atmosphere, like the opening shot in which the camera prowls through the deserted post-war airfield, picking up forlorn tokens of the past – a torn photograph, a scribbled signature – whose history is recounted in flashback. TM

Way Upstream

(1986, GB, 102 min)
d Terry Johnson. *p* Andrée Molyneaux. *sc* Terry Johnson. *ph* Peter Hall. *ed* Howard Billington. *pd* Geoff Powell. *m* Alan Brown. *cast* Barrie Rutter, Marion Bailey, Nick Dunning, Joanne Pearce, Stuart Wilson, Lizzie McInnerny, Veronica Clifford.
● More point in filming this Alan Ayckbourn comedy than most, perhaps, since the floating motor launch on stage frequently got stuck. In Johnson's hands, everything but the launch gets stuck in an interminable tale of bickering couples on a Thames holiday cruise. The playwright is revered by actors for his plotting, but things go badly adrift in this TV movie, with horror film dream sequences and a bloodthirsty fight. Way offbeam. BC

Wayward Bus, The

(1957, US, 89 min, b/w)
d Victor Vicas. *p* Charles Brackett. *sc* Ivan Moffatt. *ph* Charles G Clarke. *ed* Louis Loeffler. *ad* Lyle R Wheeler, Walter M Simonds. *m* Leigh Harline. *cast* Joan Collins, Jayne Mansfield, Dan Dailey, Rick Jason, Dolores Michaels, Betty Lou Keim, Will Wright.
● A cleaned up adaptation of a Steinbeck novel, this centres on Sweetheart, a boneshaker of a bus rattling over the 'washboard roads' of Southern California. On board are, among others, salesman Dailey, loud-mouthed but lonesome; Mansfield, a soiled stripper with an unsullied heart; mixed-up rich kid Michaels. During a journey beset by flood, landslide and a collapsing bridge, the characters' assorted predicaments get more or less ironed out. To compensate for excessive contrivance, the film is rough-edged and rather awkwardly composed for a 1957 Fox production – presumably the result of the project being assigned to an obscure French documentary maker. BBa

Way West, The

(1967, US, 122 min)
d Andrew V McLaglen. *p* Harold Hecht. *sc* Ben Maddow, Mitch Lindemann. *ph* William H Clothier. *ed* Otho Lovering. *ad* Ted Haworth. *m* Bronislau Kaper. *cast* Kirk Douglas, Robert Mitchum, Richard Widmark, Lola Albright, Michael Witney, Sally Field, Stubby Kaye, Jack Elam, Harry Carey Jr, William Lundigan.
● A mishandled version of AB Guthrie Jr's award-winning novel about a wagon train of pioneers charting the Oregon trail in 1843. The cast – Douglas as a frantically visionary senator, Mitchum as the veteran trail scout, Widmark as the leader of the settlers – is fine, and William Clothier's location photography impressive. But the script meanders badly, even taking time off for a bit of teenage romance involving nymphet Sally Field in her film debut, while McLaglen's direction is simply lacklustre. GA

Way We Were, The

(1973, US, 118 min)
d Sydney Pollack. *p* Ray Stark, Sydney Pollack. *sc* Arthur Laurents. *ph* Harry Stradling Jr. *ed* Margaret Booth. *pd* Stephen Grimes. *m* Marvin Hamlisch. *cast* Barbra Streisand, Robert Redford, Bradford Dillman, Lois Chiles, James Woods, Patrick O'Neal, Viveca Lindfors, Allyn Ann McLerie, Murray Hamilton, Herb Edelman.
● A *Love Story* with Redford and Streisand making an undeniably attractive pair. Though doomed from the start (by class, ethnic background, commitment), they get in their share of mileage, from college days of '37 to the break-up of their marriage in '50s Hollywood, where he's a compromised writer. Like their relationship, the film works best when they are alone. But with the script glossing whole areas of confrontation (from the communist '30s to the McCarthy witch-hunts), it often passes into the haze of a nostalgic fashion parade. Although Streisand's liberated Jewish lady is implausible, and emphasises the period setting as just so much dressing, Redford's Fitzgerald-type character, whose easy success carries the seeds of his possible destruction, is an intriguing trailer for his later *Great Gatsby*. It's a performance that brings more weight to the film than it deserves, often hinting at depths that are finally skated over.

W.C. Fields and Me

(1976, US, 112 min)
d Arthur Hiller. *p* Jay Weston. *sc* Bob Merrill. *ph* David M Walsh. *ed* John C Howard. *pd* Robert Boyle. *m* Henry Mancini. *cast* Rod Steiger, Valerie Perrine, John Marley, Jack Cassidy, Bernadette Peters, Dana Elcar, Paul Stewart, Billy Barty.
● Based on the ghost-written memoirs of the comedian's 'last mistress' Carlotta Monti (played here by Perrine), this witless biopic leaps through pseudo-history with cretinous inaccuracy. Sloppily slung together, hell-bent on wringing hearts with the drama of the last, lonely, drink-sodden years, it can't get even the simplest facts straight, and doesn't do much of a job on the tear-jerking either. Nose heavily reinforced and voice caressing insults in the approved manner, Steiger makes a brave stab at the part, but the reality and genius of Fields never get a look in. TM

We Are Not Alone

(1939, US, 112 min, b/w)
d Edmund Goulding. *p* Henry Blanke. *sc* Milton Krims, James Hilton. *ph* Tony Gaudio. *ed* Warren Low. *ad* Carl Jules Weyl. *m* Max Steiner. *cast* Paul Muni, Jane Bryan, Flora Robson, Raymond Severn, Una O'Connor, Henry Daniell, Cecil Kellaway, Montagu Love.
● A modest James Hilton tale (mild mannered husband, domineering wife, sweet other woman) is subtly invested with more potent themes and a darker than expected edge in the excellent hands of Edmund Goulding. Muni, the De Niro of his day, gives a superb, meticulous performance as an unexceptional Englishman under exceptional duress: in love with the governess (Bryan), he finds himself accused of murdering his wife (Robson). It was his favourite film role, and you can see why. The film is set in a sufficiently credible backlot England, immediately prior to the First World War. Its sympathetic portrait of an Austrian abroad (the Bryan character) was thought to have put paid to its box-office chances just before WWII, though in any case Jack Warner considered it too long 'for this kind of suffering picture'. He was mistaken; a thoughtful and engrossing melodrama, it's no masterpiece but it was underrated. TCh

Weak and The Wicked, The

(1953, GB, 88 min, b/w)
d J Lee Thompson. *p* Victor Skutezky. *sc* J Lee Thompson, Anne Burnaby. *ph* Gilbert Taylor. *ed* Richard Best. *ad* Robert Jones. *m* Leighton Lucas. *cast* Glynis Johns, John Gregson, Diana Dors, Sidney James, AE Matthews, Athlene Seyler, Sybil Thorndike, Rachel Roberts.
●Gambling debts land Glynis Johns in stir, where she's befriended by streetwise Diana Dors in this homegrown tilt at women-in-prison melodrama (from Joan Henry's novel *Who Lie in Gaol*). The focus is as much on the events that put the girls behind bars as on the inmates' daily grind, and if it doesn't exactly look hard-hitting these days, the performances (Dors especially) are game enough to avoid crassness. TJ

Weak at Denise

(2000, GB, 87 min)
d/p Julian Nott. *sc* Graham Williams, Julian Nott. *ph* Marco Windham. *ed* Simon Beeley, Melanie Adams. *pd* Kate Woodman. *m* Julian Nott. *cast* Bill Thomas, Chrissie Cotterill, Craig Fairbrass, Tilly Blackwood, Claudine Spiteri, Edna Doré, Indira Joshi.
● This concerns a model aeroplane enthusiast's none too hilarious entanglement in a chain of inheritance-related murder plots, which look like falling apart when his new wife Denise (Cotterill), touched by his kindly ways and romantic warblings, has doubts about poisoning his sweets as arranged with her scheming boyfriend. Could it be she's falling in love? So much for the plot. For all its would-be surrealist shock tactics, the directorial debut of Julian Nott, composer of the music for the Wallace and Gromit shorts, provides mere nostalgia-soaked dregs. Proving the rule that what works for a Plasticine nerd doesn't transfer too well to humans, anti-hero Colin (Thomas) cuts a desperately lame figure. SS

Weapons of Mass Distraction

(1997, US, 92 min)
d Stephen Surjik. *sc* Larry Gelbart. *cast* Gabriel Byrne, Ben Kingsley, Mimi Rogers, Illeana Douglas, Chris Mulkey, Kathy Baker, Paul Mazursky.
●Stephen Surjik directed the superior *Wayne's World* sequel, but the key credit here belongs to screenwriter Larry Gelbart – best known for *Tootsie* and the TV *MASH*. A fictional companion piece to his award winning 1993 cable movie *Barbarians at the Gate* (a satire about the corporate buy out of RJR Nabisco), it features Kingsley and Byrne as feuding multimedia tycoons whose one-upmanship escalates to the point of mutual destruction. This is cruder than *Barbarians* and lacks the same true-story sting, but it's even more savage in its portrait of capitalism run rampant. (Look out for Paul Mazursky in a cameo as a penis transplant specialist.) TCh

Weavers: Wasn't That a Time, The

(1981, US, 73 min)
d James B Brown. *p* James B Brown, George C Stoney, Harold Leventhal. *sc* Lee Hays. *ph* Daniel Ducovny, Jim Brown, Tom Hurwitz. *ed* Paul Barnes. *with* Pete Seeger, Lee Hays, Ronnie Gilbert, Fred Hellerman, Studs Terkel, Don McLean, Arlo Guthrie.
●An enormous influence upon the US folk boom of the late '50s and early '60s, the Weavers also brought a breath of fresh air to the charts when the quartet's version of Leadbelly's 'Goodnight Irene' became a No. 1 hit single. Formed in the late '40s when mainstream popular music was big band slickness and moon-in-June love songs, the group began by singing in such uncommercial venues as trade halls. When the group's resident wit, double-amputee Lee Hays, decided that it was time for a last reunion before he died, he invited documentarist Jim Brown to film the picnic performance. The result is a fascinating and very moving mix of concert film and historical reminiscence (Hays: 'If it weren't for the honour, I'd just as soon not been blacklisted'). RM

Weber, Die

(1927, Ger, 8,727 ft, b/w)
d Friedrich Zelnik. *cast* Paul Wegener, Dagny Servaes, Wilhelm Dieterle, Theodor Loos, Hans von Twardowski.
●Proletarian kitsch from a director who subsequently proved himself more at home in the field of Viennese operetta. The film was quite ambitious for its time (the sets and costumes are lavish period reconstructions), but its main claim to cultural legitimacy was its derivation from a Gerhart Hauptmann play; this attracted a starrier cast than was usual, including Paul *Golem* Wegener and director-to-be Dieterle. The result was the most picturesque presentation of poverty and squalor until Hollywood discovered the visual possibilities of the Depression. Its main interest now is that it serves as a reminder of the fact that German cinema of the late '20s turned to 'left wing' subjects as much for reasons of fashion as from political commitment. TR

Web of Passion

see A Double Tour

We Can't Go Home Again

(1973, US, 90 min)
d Nicholas Ray. *sc* Nicholas Ray, Susan Ray. *cast* Nicholas Ray, students of Harpur College - New York State University.
●Subtitled 'A Film By Us', this began life as a practical exercise in film-making in which Ray and his students sought to redefine/reinvent cinema (much as Godard, years earlier, had predicted he might) through on-going experimentation. A disjointed narrative (assembled from an often bewildering plethora of simultaneously projected images, shot on 35, 16, 8mm and video) attempts to explore the sexual, social and political unrest in America in the late '60s. Certainly it's something of a mess, but there's no denying either Ray's unsentimental sympathy for the plight of the young, or the raw emotional power of scenes in which students act out their own real-life psychodramas. (The film ran approximately 90 minutes when it was first shown in Cannes in 1973. It was later re-edited by various hands about half a dozen times, and new material was shot, but evidently the film never reached a definitive form beofre Ray died.) GA

Wedding, A

(1978, US, 125 min)
d/p Robert Altman. *sc* John Considine, Patricia Resnick, Allan Nicholls, Robert Altman. *ph* Charles Rosher Jr. *ed* Tony Lombardo. *cast* Carol Burnett, Paul Dooley, Amy Stryker, Mia Farrow, Geraldine Chaplin, Vittorio Gassman, Lillian Gish, Nina Van Pallandt, Viveca Lindfors, John Cromwell, Pat McCormick, Desi Arnaz Jr, Lauren Hutton, Howard Duff, Dina Merrill, Peggy Ann Garner.
● Altman's attempt to repeat the magic formula of *Nashville*, by concentrating on the interweaving relationships between a large number of guests at a wealthy society wedding, is flawed by an often sadly unimaginative script, which lampoons obvious targets as it clears the skeletons out of the two families' closets. The staging of the action is as exhilarating as ever, and there are glorious moments in the twisted, kaleidoscopic narrative; finally, however, the effect seems curiously contrived and complacent. Entertaining, though, thanks to the top-notch ensemble acting. GA

Wedding, The (Wesele)

(1972, Pol, 110 min)
d Andrzej Wajda. *sc* Andrzej Kijowski. *ph* Witold Sobocinski. *ad* Tadeusz Wybult. *m* Stanislaw Radwan. *cast* Ewa Zietek, Daniel Olbrychski, Andrzej Lapicki, Wojciech Pszoniak, Maja Komorowska.
●In Poland, Stanislaw Wyspianski's verse play *The Wedding* carries huge historical resonance. First performed in 1901, it deals with the provincial wedding of a peasant girl to an urban poet, at which the guests encounter dramatic figures from Poland's tortured past – a wise court jester, the Black Knight, a ghostly peasant who led a revolt against the gentry in 1848, and so on. Particular significance is attached to a golden horn – a symbol of national mission – that goes missing in the increasingly frenzied proceedings. Wajda goes for all of this with full romantic abandon. The camera swings wildly like a drunken wedding guest, the actors cast caution (and verse speaking) to the winds, and there is a great deal of blood and smoke. Whether you find this bewildering or exhilarating depends on your sympathies for such an extreme approach to a nation's artistic sensibility. DT

Wedding, The (La Noce)

(2000, Fr/Ger/Rus, 114 min)
d Pavel Lounguine. *p* Catherine Dussart. *sc* Pavel Lounguine, Alexandre Galine. *ph* Alexandre Burov. *ed* Sophie Brunet. *ad* Ilya Amursky. *m* Vladimir Chekassine, Lipki town folk band, Borodinski village veterans band. *cast* Marat Basharov, Maria Mironova, Andrei Panine, Alexandre Semtchev, Vladimir Simonov, Maria Goloubkina.
●A young, sexy woman returns to her impoverished mining village and proposes to her childhood sweetheart. He accepts, but his folks reckon her a slut (she left their son for a Moscow modelling career), and her big-cheese former sugar daddy will do anything – with the inevitable help of a self-seeking local police chief – to get her back, even, of course, at the raucous reception. Oh, those boisterous Russian comedies which evoke society's foibles through a micro-cosmic social gathering! Lounguine proffers every cliché in the book, sentimental ending included; sloppily overactive hand-held camera notwithstanding, this could have been made years ago. GA

Wedding Banquet, The (Xiyan)

(1993, Tai/US, 108 min)
d Ang Lee. *p* Ted Hope, James Schamus, Ang Lee. *sc* Ang Lee, Neil Feng, James Schamus. *ph* Jong Lin. *ed* Tim Squyres. *pd* Steve Rosenzweig. *m* Mader. *cast* Winston Chao, May Chin, Mitchell Lichtenstein, Sihung Lung, Ah-Leh Gua.
●Wai-Tung's life seems near perfect: a Taiwanese in New York, he's a natural at real estate, and shares an apartment with his long-time lover Simon (Lichtenstein). There's just one problem: he hasn't come out to his folks who still write from Taiwan of their desire for grandchildren. To forestall an arranged marriage, Wai-Tung persuades his tenant Wei-Wei (May Chin), a Shanghai woman in need of a Green Card, to join in a marriage of mutual convenience. His parents then announce they're coming for the wedding. Never patronising his characters, Ang Lee combines comedy, both subtle and raucous, with acute social asides. There's genuine pain and confusion amid the jokes, so that the bitter-sweet, tentatively positive coda packs real punch. Winston Chow's Wai-Tung is initially rather stilted, but the rest of the cast performs excellently, and the script is admirably matter-of-fact in its treatment of the threatened gay relationship. GA

Wedding Bells

see Royal Wedding

Wedding in Blood

see Noces Rouges, Les

Wedding in Galilee (Noce en Galilée)

(1987, Bel/Fr, 116 min)
d Michel Khleifi. *p* Jacqueline Louis, Bernard Lorais. *sc* Michel Khleifi. *ph* Walther van der Ende. *ed* Marie Castro Vasquez. *m* Jean-Marie Sénia. *cast* Ali M El-Akili, Bushra Karaman, Makram Khouri, Anna Achdian, Sonia Amar.

●An excellent first feature from the Palestinian Khleifi, in which the mayor of an Israeli-controlled Palestinian village insists that his son be married in traditional Arabic style. But the village is divided when the Israeli governor, fearing a political demonstration, agrees to suspend martial law for the occasion only on condition that he himself be allowed to attend. Performed mainly by local people, shot in Galilee and the occupied West Bank, the film is intelligent, surprisingly sensuous, and a moving plea for liberty and understanding. GA

Wedding March, The

(1927, US, 10, 170 ft, b/w)
d Erich von Stroheim. *p* Pat Powers. *sc* Harry Carr, Erich von Stroheim. *ph* Hal Mohr, Ben Reynolds. *ad* Erich von Stroheim, Richard Day. *cast* Erich von Stroheim, Fay Wray, George Fawcett, Maude George, Cesare Gravina, Dale Fuller, Matthew Betz, ZaSu Pitts.

●Like *Foolish Wives*, *Greed* and *Queen Kelly*, *The Wedding March* (originally made in two parts, of which only the first is extant) survives as a mutilated masterpiece, even this first part having been cut from 14 reels to ll. Charting the ill-starred romance between a Viennese prince (Stroheim in an unusually sympathetic role) and a lowly commoner (Wray), the film would perhaps appear to be its cynical creator's most romantic work, were it not for the marvellously detailed portrait of the corruption of society in general, rich and poor. Nevertheless, it is the love scenes, played beneath shimmering apple blossoms in lyrical soft focus, that stick in the memory, ironically turning what is now the film's ending – the frustration of that love – into one of the director's most bitterly pessimistic scenes. GA

Wedding Moon (Noces de lune)

(1998, Tun, 90 min)
d Taïeb Louhichi. *sc* Taïeb Louhichi, Rafic Sabban. *ph* Dominique Le Rigoleur. *ed* Arbi Ben Ali. *pd* Claude Bennys. *m* Luis Bacalov. *cast* Mess Hattou, Rym Riahi, Mohamed Hedi Moumen, Mohamed Ali Nehdi, Mohamed Ali Ben Jemaa, Mohamed Choura, Samia Rehaiem, Hichem Rostom.

●Energetic but somewhat tiresome tale of a close-knit bunch of bikers, repeatedly partying around the outskirts of Tunis to a heavy metal soundtrack. Facing opposition from parents, bosses and the like, it turns out that the kids are all right! – when they help to matchmake a (patronisingly portrayed) couple of misfits with disabilities. Then an argument leads to disaster, and the story finally kicks in. Repetitive, none too effectively acted, and saddled with an uneven, meandering narrative that combines clichés and melodrama, the film never once lives up to the promise of its opening credits. GA

Wedding Night, The

(1935, US, 83 min, b/w)
d King Vidor. *p* Samuel Goldwyn. *sc* Edith Fitzgerald. *ph* Gregg Toland. *ed* Stuart Heisler. *ad* Richard Day. *m* Alfred Newman. *cast* Gary Cooper, Anna Sten, Ralph Bellamy, Walter Brennan, Helen Vinson, Sig Ruman.

●Basically a weepie about the star-crossed love between an unhappily married man and an immigrant girl being forced into an arranged marriage. Discreetly lavish (it was the last, following *Nana* and *We Live Again*, of Sam Goldwyn's three attempts to promote Sten as a major star) and beautifully shot by Gregg Toland, it is handled with sensitivity by Vidor. But Cooper is rather miscast as a writer escaping the New York socialite round to get back to the soil; the ethnic customs of the Polish tobacco-growing community are too sketchy as well as too picturesque (especially in the wedding sequence); and in determinedly avoiding the statutory happy ending, the film achieves melodrama rather than the tragedy it is aiming for. TM

Wedding Planner, The

(2000, Ger/GB/US, 103 min)
d Adam Shankman. *p* Peter Abrams, Robert L. Levy, Jennifer Gibgot, Gigi Pritzker, Deborah Del Prete. *sc* Pamela Falk, Michael Ellis. *ph* Julio Macat. *ed* Lisa Zeno Churgin. *pd* Bob Ziembicki. *m* Mervyn Warren. *cast* Jennifer Lopez, Matthew McConaughey, Bridgette Wilson-Sampras, Justin Chambers, Judy Greer, Alex Rocco, Joanna Gleason, Charles Kimbrough.

●In these days of personal shoppers, trainers and life coaches, it's no surprise to learn there are people who make a living planning other people's weddings. The immaculately groomed Lopez is ideally cast as Mary Fiore, the queen of wedding planners. To young, admiring girls she appears to be having a ball, but, a self-declared magnet for unsuitable men, she's less than clued-up about her own love life. Mary's loving dad Salvatore tries fixing her up with goodhearted Italian boy Massimo, but as he's presented as some kind of halfwit it's small wonder she's not too keen. Infinitely more suitable is dishy doctor Steve (McConaughey), who is charm itself and pretty stuck on her too – but as the fiancé of Mary's latest client Fran (Wilson-Sampras), he's hardly ideal either. Aspiring to ape classic screwball comedies of the '30s and '40s, this has the dance numbers and glossy photography of a good old-fashioned romance. But while Lopez and McConaughey are an appealing couple, the clunking script denies them any chance of doing a Hepburn and Tracy. KW

Wedding Rehearsal

(1932, GB, 84 min, b/w)
d/p Alexander Korda. *sc* Arthur Wimperis, Helen Gardom. *ph* Leslie Rowson. *ed* Hal Young. *pd* OF Werndorff, Vincent Korda. *m* Kurt Schroeder. *cast* Merle Oberon, Roland Young, George Grossmith, John Loder, Maurice Evans, Lady Tree, Wendy Barrie.

●Escapism par excellence, with high society weddings, country house romances on warm summer nights, and the working class strange 'men in green baize aprons with long hairs on their arms'. Korda has an acute mid-European appreciation of English foibles, and is able to poke fun at, yet still celebrate, traditional concern with dogs, cats and debutantes. A witty, if structurally inconsequential script, superb performances from Grossmith and delicately twittering old Lady Tree, Korda's enthusiasm, and the presence (it's little more) of breathtakingly beautiful Oberon, sweep one into a hypnotic if sickly world of Gerties and Berties, where problems revolve around whether Rose-Marie should marry Bimbo and Mary-Rose should marry Tootles. RMy

Wedding Singer, The

(1998, US, 97 min)
d Frank Coraci. *p* Robert Simonds, Jack Giarraputo. *sc* Tim Herlihy. *ph* Tim Suhrstedt. *ed* Tom Lewis. *pd* Perry Andelin Blake. *m* Teddy Castellucci. *cast* Adam Sandler, Drew Barrymore, Christine Taylor, Allen Covert, Angela Featherstone, Alexis Arquette, Jon Lovitz, Steve Buscemi.

●Sandler, a cult comedian here submerging himself in the mainstream, plays Robbie Hart, a wannabe rock star stuck on the wedding band circuit. He's happy enough, until his own bride leaves him standing at the altar – which prompts the film's funniest scene, a bitter breakdown in professional decorum at his next gig, when he turns into the wedding singer from hell. Luckily for Robbie, the delicious Julia (Drew Barrymore) is waitressing in the wings. Her fiancé Glenn is bad news, so it can only be a matter of time before Robbie and Julia figure out they're made for each other. The movie is set in 1985 and won't let you forget it for a second. Culture Club, Huey Lewis, Nena, Billy Idol, Hall & Oates, The Cars, Kajagoogoo, Wham!, it's frightening how innocent all this stuff sounds now. Sandler himself sings in a personably reedy register, and sports an authentic, dopily romantic David Essex wig which somehow doesn't preclude our sympathy. As for Barrymore, playing a good girl at last, she deserves nothing less – you can't help pulling for the kids. Anyway, it's hard to be cynical about a film which finds time to let Alexis Arquette do Boy George and Buscemi tear up Spandau Ballet's 'True'. TCh

Wedding Tackle, The

(1999, GB, 93 min)
d Rami Dvir. *p/sc* Nigel Horne. *ph* Shelley Hirst. *ed* Matthew Tabern, Mike Latham. *pd* Sarah Beaman. *m* Charles Hodgkinson, Kirk Zavieh. *cast* Adrian Dunbar, James Purefoy, Tony Slattery, Neil Stuke, Leslie Grantham, Victoria Smurfit, Susan Vidler, Amanda Redman, Martin Armstong, Sara Stockbridge.

●Writer/producer Horne declares ominously in the press notes: 'I first thought of the idea of a film based around an all-day pub crawl when I was living in Newcastle-upon-Tyne.' At Hal's stag festivities, a group of thirty-something men spends 24 hours cuckolding one another. The film lingers interminably on every lame gag, narrative inconsistency and ill-constructed scene. MHi

Wednesday 19.7.1961 (Sreda)

(1997, Rus/Ger/GB/Fin, 93 min)
d Viktor Kossakovsky. *p* Viola Stephan. *sc/ed* Viktor Kossakovsky. *m* Alexander Popov.

●A new-born baby: the greatest manifestation of hope, our belief in a future, the recognition of our mortality. That Kossakovsky should thus begin his documentary of contemporary Russian life is no coincidence. For many Russians, wealth is measured not in kopecks but in the value of a child born against all odds. Setting out to trace the other 100 people born, like him, in St Petersburg on 19 July 1961, Kossakovsky found 70 still living in the city; without introduction or voice-over, he presents them apparently at random, until the craft of his richly woven tapestry becomes evident. The unflinching camera is at times disarming. Nor is he averse to ambushing subjects, some of whom are less than impressed by his nerve. Others are pleased to find their lives deemed worthy of recording. One couple features repeatedly. She, heavily pregnant, is an alcoholic, he a drug addict. Their thoughts on life pepper the film until, eventually, we watch the birth of their daughter. Then film's intent becomes clear: the couple's decision to become parents is symbolic of whatever drives Russians to face each new day. 'Why isn't she crying? Is something wrong?' asks the mother. Kossakovsky makes us wait for the answer. Minutes drag until we return to the hospital – he's telling us we must have faith. FM

We Don't Want to Talk About It (De eso no se habla)

(1993, Arg/It, 105 min)
d María Luisa Bemberg. *p* Oscar Kramer, Roberto Cicutto. *sc* María Luisa Bemberg, Jorge Goldenberg. *ph* Felix Monti. *ed* Juan Carlos Macias. *pd* Jorge Sarudiansky. *m* Nicola Piovani. *cast* Marcello Mastroianni, Luisina Brando, Alejandra Podestá, Betiana Blum, Roberto Carnaghi, Alberto Segado, Jorge Luz.

●The title of Bemberg's subtle, touching film refers to the determination expressed by the proud widow Leonor (Brando) regarding the condition of her daughter Charlotte (Podestá). Quite simply, Leonor will not accept the fact that the girl is a dwarf. Instead, she showers her beloved progeny with kindness and encourages her interest in the arts – an interest which forms the basis of a friendship between the teenager and Don Ludovico D'Andrea (Mastroianni), an elderly bachelor of mysterious origins who falls profoundly in love with the girl. Set in a small Argentinian town in the '40s, Bemberg's poignant fable succeeds largely through understatement and the principals' superb performances. Mercifully, while there are a few faintly surreal touches, the magic here derives from the cool, unsentimental, down-to-earth appraisal of the trio's tangled emotions. It's a tender movie, but never needlessly romanticised, and not without its quiet cruelties. GA

Wee Geordie

see Geordie

Weekend (Week-end)

(1967, Fr/It, 103 min)
d Jean-Luc Godard. *sc* Jean-Luc Godard. *ph* Raoul Coutard *ed* Agnès Guillemot. *m* Antoine Duhamel, Wolfgang Amadeus Mozart. *cast* Mireille Darc, Jean Yanne, Jean-Pierre Kalfon, Yves Beneyton, Jean-Pierre Léaud, Juliet Berto, Anne Wiazemsky.

●Godard's vision of bourgeois cataclysm, after which he began the retreat from commercial cinema to contemplate his ideological navel. A savage Swiftian satire, it traces a new Gulliver's travels through the collapsing consumer society as a married couple set out for a weekend jaunt, passing through a nightmare landscape of highways strewn with burning cars and bloody corpses (a stunning ten-minute take) before emerging into a brave new world peopled by Maoist revolutionaries living like redskins in the woods off murder, pillage and rape. What takes the film one stage further into inimitable Godard territory is the note of despairing romanticism he first mined in *Pierrot le Fou*. Here too, his hero and heroine emerge as oddly tragic figures, modern Robinson Crusoes wandering helplessly in limbo because, even if they could find a desert island free of abandoned cars, they are incapable of surviving without consumer goods. TM

Weekend at Bernie's

(1989, US, 99 min)
d Ted Kotcheff. *p* Victor Drai. *sc* Robert Klane. *ph* François Protat. *ed* Joan E Chapman. *pd* Peter Jamison. *m* Andy Summers. *cast* Andrew McCarthy, Jonathan Silverman, Catherine Mary Stewart, Terry Kiser, Don Calfa, Catherine Parks, Louis Giambalvo, Ted Kotcheff.
● A one-joke movie which moves puerile party humour from the Animal House to the yuppie world of work. Pals Larry (McCarthy) and Dick (Silverman) – one a smooth-talking sloppy-Joe, the other a tongue-tied whizz-kid-in-waiting – share desks and frustration on the trading floor at Trans Allied Insurance. When Dick finds a million-dollar discrepancy in payouts, they force their way into an audience with jet-setter boss Bernie (Kiser), who invites them, with Bela Lugosi smile, for a weekend at his Hamptons beach-house. Death is in the offing, but it's Bernie who gets stiffed (by his Mafia associates), not the boys. Question is, how long can they party, party, party with the bathing-suited bimbos and cool cat coke-sniffers before anybody notices that Bernie's a corpse? Kotcheff aims straight for the juvenile and spends most of his effort, successfully, on getting the timing right for the endless gags with Bernie's cadaver propped up on the sofa, falling downstairs, etc. But it's strictly kids'stuff and quickly palls. WH

Weekend Plot (Miyu Shi Qi Xiaoshi)

(2001, China, 91 min)
d Zhang Ming. *p* Zhang Ming, Zou Jingzi. *sc* Zhang Ming. *ph* Xu Wei. *ed* Zhang Ming. *ad* Ma Chengyun. *m* Wen Zi. *cast* Zhang Yalin, Guo Xiaodong, Huang Zhizhong, Li Na, Wang Kuen, Chen Hongchi.
● Zhang's follow-up to *Rainclouds over Wushan* is again set on the Yangtze River, an area that will be flooded when the Three Gorges Dam is completed. Six twenty-somethings convene for a summer weekend on the river; four are old schoolfriends (one guy still works locally as a cop, the others now live in Beijing) and the group includes two couples. The cop, whose marriage is in trouble, feels out of place and takes off early, promising to return with the boat later to pick them up. While he's away, the group falls apart: an unsigned billet doux provokes paranoia and jealousy, one couple breaks up and one woman goes missing. Zhang planned this as a thriller and had to rethink/rewrite it extensively when his script didn't pass censorship; the surviving mystery elements are actually the weakest links in a rather striking group-portrait of China's emerging middle-class, riven by insecurities and backbiting. The cool, distanced visuals, the unhurried pacing and the missing girl motif inevitably recall *L'Avventura* – by no means to the film's detriment. TR

Week in the Life of a Man, A (Tydzien z zycia mezczyzny)

(1999, Pol, 90 min)
d Jerzy Stuhr. *p* Juliusz Machulski. *sc* Jerzy Stuhr. *ph* Edward Klosinski. *ed* Elzbieta Kurkowska. *pd* Monika Sajko-Gradowska. *m* Wojciech Kilar. *cast* Jerzy Stuhr, Gosia Dobrowolska, Danuta Szaflarska, Alex Mozdzynski, Krzysztof Stroinski.
● A solid, well-mounted and nicely performed drama by actor turned writer/director Stuhr (best known from his work with Kieslowski) which presents something of a state of the nation address on Poland's 'new reality' as the century draws to a close. Adam (Stuhr) is a state prosecutor (handling depressing cases of corruption, racism, etc), who's doing the rounds of press for a book of his cases, finishing off an adulterous affair while his infertile wife thinks he's attending choir practice. His wife is keen to adopt, but the representative is a member of the ex-Communist democratic left; his best friend is a psychiatric case with whom he feels unable to sympathise; and his wife finds giving love to a child over-challenging. *Memories of Underdevelopment*, Polish-style. WH

Week's Holiday, A

see Semaine de Vacances, Une

We from Kronstadt (My iz Kronshtadta)

(1936, USSR, 89 min, b/w)
d Efim Dzigan. *p* I Weissfeldt. *sc* Vsevolod Vishnevski. *ph* N Naumov-Straj. *ad* V Egorov. *m* N Krukov. *cast* V Zaichikov, G Bushuev, N Ivakin, O Zhakov, R Esipova.
● 1919: a detachment of Bolshevik sailors defending an outpost of Petrograd is wiped out but for one man, who escapes back to the Red lines, returns with reinforcements and wins the day. Graham Greene's unqualified rave (see his collected film criticism) was presumably more a matter of ideology than aesthetics. Hard otherwise to imagine him being impressed by the B-Western characterisation, the humourlessness, the blanket denial of complexity – though the energetically arranged battle scenes may have appealed to the child in him. His description, 'an unusual mixture of poetry and heroics,' suggests Ford but, really, this is totalitarian film-making at its most dispiriting. BBa

Weight of Water, The

(2000, US/Fr, 119 min)
d Kathryn Bigelow. *p* Janet Yang, Sigurjon Sighvatsson, A Kitman Ho. *sc* Alice Alen, Christopher Kyle. *ph* Adrian Biddle. *ed* Howard E Smith. *pd* Karl Juliusson. *m* David Hirschfelder. *cast* Sean Penn, Catherine McCormack, Elizabeth Hurley, Josh Lucas, Sarah Polley, Vinessa Shaw, Ulrich Thomsen, Anders Berthelsen, Katrin Cartlidge, Ciaran Hands.
● A curious movie from Bigelow, this marks a departure from 'male' genre pics in favour of a double helping of melodrama, based on Anita Shreve's novel. In the present tense, McCormack, poet husband Penn, brother Lucas and sexpot Hurley go sailing off Smuttynose Island. A century earlier, Polley had been found there, the sole survivor of a senseless axe murderer who had slaughtered her sisters. It's often quite brilliantly directed – Bigelow even gets a performance out of Hurley – and the sexual politics are intriguing, but you can't get away from the problem that the plot is all in the past. TCh

Weird Science

(1985, US, 94 min)
d John Hughes. *p* Joel Silver. *sc* John Hughes. *ph* Matthew F Leonetti. *ed* Mark Warner, Chris Lebenzon, Scott Wallace. *pd* John W Corso. *m* Ira Newborn. *cast* Anthony Michael Hall, Kelly LeBrock, Ilan Mitchell-Smith, Bill Paxton, Suzanne Snyder, Judie Aronson, Robert Downey.
● John Hughes' half-cocked exercise in teen-flick wish-fulfilment centres on a couple of friendless nerds (Hall and Mitchell-Smith) who decide to build the perfect woman on a computer. Implausibly, they succeed. In a puff of smoke, LeBrock appears, soon revealing herself to be part sex object, part mother, part fairy godmother; in other words, Hollywood's idea of every boy's dream woman. That this folly is not completely loathsome is due largely to the efforts of Hall, to some extent reprising his *Breakfast Club* role, and LeBrock, who couldn't be any camper or more knowing had she made the entire film with one eyebrow arched. Otherwise, though, this is ordinary stuff that's aged about as well as Mitchell-Smith's clunky computer. WFJ

Weisse Hölle vom Piz Palu, Die

see White Hell of Piz Palu, The

Welcome Back Mr McDonald (Radio No Jikan)

(1997, Jap, 103 min)
d Koki Mitani. *p* Chaiki Matsushita, Hisao Masuda, Takashi Ishihara, Kanjiro Sakuro. *sc* Koki Mitani. *ph* Kenji Takama, Junichi Tozawa. *ed* Hirohide Abe. *pd* Tomia Ogawa. *m* Takayuki Hattori. *cast* Jun Inoue, Shunji Fujimura, Akira Fuse, Toshiaki Karasawa, Kyoka Suzuki, Masahiko Nishimura, Toshiyuki Hosokawa.
● Winner (and only entrant) in Radio Beng Teng's drama competition, a shy housewife is about to have her emotive drama about married romance turned into chaotic farce when the temperamental star decides she does not want the lead to be a pachinko-parlour flunky but a high-powered New York lawyer. Changes are duly made, but then the other cast members start complaining too, and soon the hassled station manager and studio director find themselves forced to fake burst dams and rocket flight in the studio. Having worked on stage and in radio, first time writer/director Mitani displays pure brilliance at keeping the mayhem on the right side of plausibility and never letting the performers run away with themselves. The textbook comic construction offers a master class in setting a gag up then topping it, since Mitani always has another winning notion in reserve. In pure entertainment terms, this is easily the equal of *Tampopo* and *Shall We Dance?*, yet it somehow failed to find the same international distribution. TJ

Welcome Home

(1989, US, 92 min)
d Franklin J Schaffer. *p* Martin Ransohoff. *sc* Maggie Kleinman. *ph* Fred J Koenekamp. *ed* Bob Swink. *pd* Dan Yarhi, Dennis Davenport. *m* Henry Mancini. *cast* Kris Kristofferson, JoBeth Williams, Sam Waterston, Trey Wilson, Ken Pogue, Brian Keith, Thomas Wilson Brown.
● Seventeen years after being declared missing in action in Cambodia, pilot Jake Robbins (Kristofferson) turns up in his American home town, where he is reunited with his wife Sarah (now happily remarried) and teenage son. Jake, it appears, has a new wife and kids in Cambodia, where he would have stayed had he not been wounded, hospitalised, and duly identified by the military. His reappearence causes Sarah (Williams) to reassess her marriage to Woody (Waterston), and shatters son Tyler's glorified image of his heroic father. Yes, it's big family crisis time, with little to commend it other than Waterston, who anchors the film in some form of credible behaviour while all around is mushy, tear-jerking melodrama. As the last drop of emotional manipulation is squeezed from the turmoil (accompanied throughout by Willie Nelson's nasal whining), the movie attempts to transform itself into a thriller about government secrecy and gung-ho rescue operations, but by then who cares? MK

Welcome Home, Roxy Carmichael

(1991, US, 98 min)
d Jim Abrahams. *p* Penney Finkelman Cox. *sc* Karen Leigh Hopkins. *ph* Paul Elliott. *ed* Bruce Green. *pd* Dena Roth. *m* Thomas Newman. *cast* Winona Ryder, Jeff Daniels, Laila Robins, Thomas Wilson Brown, Joan McMurtrey, Graham Beckel, Frances Fisher, Robby Kiger, Dinah Manoff, Stephen Tobolowsky, Ava Fabian.
● Local bad girl Roxy (Fabian) left her small-town Ohio home in search of fame and fortune. Fifteen years later, as the burghers of Clyde prepare to pay awestruck homage to her homecoming, adopted teen misfit Dinky (Ryder) is also obsessed with the living legend, for her own neurotic reasons. From a script by Karen Leigh Hopkins, Abrahams has concocted an initially intriguing mishmash: part high school angst opera, part suburban schlocker (Daniels, always dependable as the dentist-next-door type, is surpassingly dull here), part 'search for origins' family romance. There are a few piquant ironies at work, but the selling point is Ryder, again doing her coming-of-age turn for the camera, with a performance that wavers between gangling fragility and a tough-girl Matt Dillonism. Otherwise, the movie falls flat, because of its leaden pacing, and because deep down it believes in the moral imperative of having perfect hair and teeth. JRo

Welcome to Blood City

(1977, Can/GB, 96 min)
d Peter Sasdy. *p* Marilyn Stonehouse. *sc* Stephen Schneck, Michael Winder. *ph* Reginald Morris. *ed* Keith Palmer. *pd* Jack McAdam. *m* Roy Budd. *cast* Jack Palance, Keir Dullea, Samantha Eggar, Barry Morse, Hollis McLaren, Chris Wiggins.
● An utterly spineless sci-fi Western. The plot premise has possibilities: Dullea is hauled out of some unspecified urban crisis and into an equally unspecified laboratory, where a 'Western drama' is computer-programmed into his brain to test his ruthlessness quotient. The main dramatic problem is the feebleness of the Western (which occupies

most of the running time); even Jack Palance as an urbane, unbeatable sheriff can't lend it more credibility than a playground version of *Gunfight at the OK Corral*. But what finally sinks the film is Sasdy and his writer Stephen Schneck's refusal to commit themselves to any social or political meaning; the way they trot out some newsreel atrocity footage to fuel a supposedly common paranoia about the Horrors of the Modern World is both facile and deeply offensive. TR

Welcome to Britain

(1976, GB, 70 min)
d Ben Lewin. *ph* Roger Deakins, Brian Huberman. *ed* Ben Lewin.

●Lewin's documentary concerns the appalling treatment meted out to immigrants and Commonwealth visitors on arrival in Britain rather than the question of whether immigration controls should exist. He chose the colourful and unorthodox entrepreneur Reuben 'Mr Fixit' Davis to illustrate his point about the system: that a man who (according to the Home Office) was able to earn thousands from helping his clients enter the country, was actually preferable to the insular bureaucracy of the official advisory service, let alone the immigration officers themselves. Well-made documentary that it is, it insists on taking sides, but without ever entering the realms of dogma: the scenes at Harmondsworth Detention Centre, peopled by the 'suspect' friends and relatives of those whom 'we don't need' any more, say it all. HM

Welcome to Hard Times (aka Killer on a Horse)

(1966, US, 105 min)
d Burt Kennedy. *p* Max E Youngstein, David Karr. *sc* Burt Kennedy. *ph* Harry Stradling Jr. *ed* Aaron Stell. *ad* George W Davis, Carl Anderson. *m* Harry Sukman. *cast* Henry Fonda, Janice Rule, Keenan Wynn, Janis Paige, John Anderson, Warren Oates, Fay Spain, Edgar Buchanan, Aldo Ray, Denver Pyle, Lon Chaney, Royal Dano, Elisha Cook.

●Adapted from EL Doctorow's novel, Kennedy's film casts a cold eye on the career of a one-horse frontier town, from its initial destruction by an itinerant hellraiser (Ray), through its redevelopment (initiated by a travelling whorehouse) and final near-extinction by the returning villain. Intriguing for its use of Fonda, whose personal cowardice is responsible for the town's internal death wish, and whose peace-making liberal intentions bring about the nihilistic ending: three-quarters of the population lying dead among the smoking ruins. There's also an immaculate cast of standard Western supporting actors. CPea

Welcome to L.A.

(1976, US, 106 min)
d Alan Rudolph. *p* Robert Altman. *sc* Alan Rudolph. *ph* David Myers. *ed* William A Sawyer, Tom Walls. *pd* Dennis J Parrish. *m* Richard Baskin. *cast* Keith Carradine, Sally Kellerman, Geraldine Chaplin, Harvey Keitel, Lauren Hutton, Viveca Lindfors, Sissy Spacek, Denver Pyle, John Considine, Richard Baskin

●In retrospect, more an intriguing taste of things to come than a throwback to the free-form, large-scale interactions of *Nashville* (on which Rudolph served time as Altman's assistant). Here, in his debut, the precise *La Ronde*-style choreography of its nine principal characters – assorted inhabitants of LA, all connected somehow or another with self-centred rock-writer Carradine's sexual one-night stands – tends to prefigure *Choose Me* in its elegance, dry wit, and flawless visual sense. Sadly, however, it lacks both the inspirational spontaneity of his producer and mentor Altman's best work, and the warmth of his own later films, since many of the characters are so bloody unsympathetic. That said, it's finely performed and well worth seeing. GA

Welcome to Sarajevo

(1997, GB, 102 min)
d Michael Winterbottom. *p* Graham Broadbent, Damian Jones. *sc* Frank Cottrell-Boyce. *ph* Dafydd Hobson. *ed* Trevor Waite. *pd* Mark Geraghty. *m* Adrian Johnston. *cast* Stephen Dillane, Woody Harrelson, Kerry Fox, James Nesbitt, Goran Visnjic, Emira Nusevic, Marisa Tomei, Emily Lloyd.

●The first Western feature to pick over the bones of the Bosnian conflict, this applies the trusty 'foreign correspondent finds his conscience' ploy to some effect. Dillane is Michael Henderson – based on ITN reporter Michael Nicholson – a hardened pro who none the less becomes obsessed with the plight of a Sarajevo orphanage during the 1992 siege, and promises refuge to one young girl. A crisp, rigorously unsentimental director, Winterbottom was a good choice for this project. Mixing film, video and a good deal of news footage, he captures a powerful sense of the jogging, jagged rhythms of life and death under siege, takes an unapologetically polemical line against Europe's hands-off policy, and consequently earns the emotional dividends. TCh

Welcome to the Dollhouse

(1995, US, 88 min)
d Todd Solondz. *p* Ted Skillman, Todd Solondz. *sc* Todd Solondz. *ph* Randy Drummond. *ed* Alan Oxman. *pd* Susan Block. *m* Jil Wisoff. *cast* Heather Matarazzo, Victoria Davis, Christina Brucato, Christina Vidal, Siri Howard, Brendan Sexton Jr, Telly Pontidis.

●Whether at school or at home in the New Jersey suburbs, 11-year-old Dawn Wiener has a miserable time of it. Ostracised and vilified by classmates as a 'lesbo', the 'Wienerdog' comes a cropper sticking up for herself against rough tough Brandon (Sexton): he responds by promising to rape her when school's out. Meanwhile, Mom makes it all too obvious she prefers her youngest, Missy, while Dawn's snooty brother Mark is reluctant to let her anywhere near his guitarist friend Steve, whose looks, musical skills and unthinking displays of kindness ensure she develops a crush on him. But would the high school hunk ever go out with a seventh-grader, or even join the exclusive 'Special Persons' club Dawn has founded with her only friend, poor little Ralphy next door? Admirably unsentimental exploration of the bewildering, cruel nightmare that is early adolescence: astutely perceptive, darkly comic and often profoundly and provocatively unsettling. If the film veers a little too closely to melodramatic parody towards the end, for the most part script and direction are spot-on, with writer/director Solondz carefully balancing insight and irony, humour and real tenderness. Sterling acting, particularly from Heather Matarazzo, whose remarkable blend of vulnerability and determination, dignity and vivacity effortlessly enrols our sympathies. Talents to watch. GA

Welcome II the Terrordome

(1994, GB, 94 min)
d Ngozi Onwurah. *p* Simon Onwurah. *sc* Ngozi Onwurah. *ph* Alwin H Kuchler. *ed* Liz Webber. *pd* Lindi Pankiv, Miraphora Mina. *m* John Murphy, David A Hughes, Black Radical Mk II. *cast* Suzette Llewellyn, Saffron Burrows, Brian Bovell, Felix Joseph, Valentine Nonyela, Ben Wynter.

●This feature debut is an angry uncompromising take on race relations, guaranteed to put liberals on edge. Set ten or 15 years on in a claustrophobic black ghetto, it's the story of Spike (Nonyela) and his girlfriend Jodie (Burrows). Tensions are already running high – Jodie's pregnant and white – when a black kid is killed in a police raid and his mother goes on a vengeful killing spree. Onwurah's dystopia isn't a comfortable place to be and the film isn't easy to watch. The makers have done wonders with a minuscule budget, creating a stylised but still credible environment hemmed in by metal cages, pierced by strobing searchlights and a bombardment of urgent rap. This is a world which doesn't breathe so much as pant. The acting, however, is variable, and the movie is sometimes both naive and repetitive. Imperfect, then, but also provocative: it never lies down on you. TCh

Welcome to Woop Woop

(1997, Aust/GB, 96 min)
d Stephan Elliott. *p* Finola Dwyer. *sc* Michael Thomas. *ph* Mike Molloy. *ed* Martin Walsh. *pd* Owen Paterson. *m* Guy Gross. *cast* Johnathon Schaech, Rod Taylor, Noah Taylor, Paul Mercurio, Susie Porter, Dee Smart, Barry Humphries, Richard Moir, Rachel Griffiths.

●In this skewed follow-up to *The Adventures of Priscilla, Queen of the Desert*, Stephan Elliott once more braves the Outback to find a cultural enclave which has long since isolated itself from modern Australia. Waylaid by a local maiden, New York con artist Scheach finds himself trapped in the desert community of Woop Woop, where macho patriarch Taylor holds unbending sway, women are women, kangaroos are dinner, and there's no escape. Elliott is out to uncover the heart of darkness in the Aussie national identity, but the ferocity of his attack soon pays diminishing returns. With Taylor hamming away to the nines and *The Sound of Music* replayed as the town's only entertainment, strident kitsch is the order of the day, and it becomes very wearing indeed. TJ

Welfare

(1975, US, 167 min, b/w)
d/p/sc Frederick Wiseman. *ph* William Brayne. *ed* Frederick Wiseman, Oliver Kool.

●Wiseman's unsparing *vérité* camera takes us to a New York Welfare Center, where America's victims (all races, ages, and emotional conditions) parade their misery to receive enough money to survive. The film has a sharp eye for the exhausted, melancholy, and angry faces of social workers and clients, both groups ensnared in a vicious, heartless system – where who is responsible becomes the prime question, fatalism the reigning philosophy, and the general atmosphere one of claustrophobic bedlam. Wiseman avoids facile stereotypes: his case-workers are not callous heavies, nor are the clients members of a heroic, politically conscious mass. Some of the Center's staff attempt to ease the bureaucracy's dehumanising red tape, but given the hopelessness of the institution, their gestures are almost quixotic. The film never editorialises, sentimentalises, or attempts to be dramatic, but its cumulative effect is to make one enraged enough to cry out for the dismantling of the whole welfare (or is it the capitalist?) system. LQ

We Live Again

(1934, US, 84 min, b/w)
d Rouben Mamoulian. *p* Samuel Goldwyn. *sc* Preston Sturges, Maxwell Anderson, Leonard Praskins. *ph* Gregg Toland. *ed* Otho Lovering. *ad* Richard Day, Sergei Soudeikin. *m* Alfred Newman. *cast* Anna Sten, Fredric March, Jane Baxter, C Aubrey Smith, Ethel Griffies, Gwendolyn Logan, Sam Jaffe, Dale Fuller, Leonid Kinsky.

●Conceived as a vehicle for Goldwyn's protégée Anna Sten, this adaptation of Tolstoy's novel *Resurrection* was turned into something more by Mamoulian's superb direction. He opens with an airy Dovzhenko pastiche to introduce the light-hearted farmyard flirtation between Prince Dmitri (March) and serving maid Katusha (Sten). Then, clearly drawing on his own background, he stages a stunning evocation of the Russian Orthodox Easter Mass, carrying the richly sensuous mood over into the seduction scene that immediately follows. The inescapable parallel between worship by the soul and by the senses intimates that Dimitri is motivated as much by love as by lust; and this lends conviction to his 'resurrection' when, seven years later, he realises his culpability in the girl's physical (though not spiritual) degradation, and follows her into Siberia. The second half of the film rather loses its momentum in a flurry of explanatory plot and scratchily staged scenes, but is sustained by the performances. Gregg Toland's camerawork is superlative throughout. TM

Well, The

(1951, US, 85 min, b/w)
d Leo Popkin, Russell Rouse. *p* Clarence Greene, Leo Popkin. *sc* Russell Rouse, Clarence Greene. *ph* Ernest Laszlo. *ed* Chester W Schaeffer. *pd* Rudolph Sternad. *m* Dimitri Tiomkin. *cast* Richard Rober, Henry Morgan, Barry Kelley, Christine Larson, Maidie Norman, Ernest Anderson.

●Rouse's first film as director (co-written with Clarence Greene, with whom he had scripted *DOA* the previous year). The first half is a vividly etched portrait of small-town unease as a black child is reported missing, the suspicions deepening a racial divide that threatens to escalate into racial violence on both sides as circumstances suggest that a white transient (Morgan) had something to do with her disappearance. The discovery that the little girl, scarcely more than a baby, has in fact fallen down an abandoned well, opens a safety valve; and the rest of the film is devoted to the rescue operation. It still grips, but in a more overtly crowd-pleasing way, what with even the most bigoted coming round to the side of the angels, and the hazards of the rescue milked for all they are worth. An impressive piece, all the same, brilliantly shot by Ernest Laszlo. TM

Well, The

(1997, Aust, 102 min)
d Samantha Lang. *cast* Pamela Rabe, Miranda Otto, Paul Chubb.

●Out on a remote farm, Rabe takes on as home-help young Miranda Otto, an emotionally unstable waif who soon responds gratefully to Rabe's various kindnesses; but their blossoming relationship hits trouble when a car accident forces them to dump a body down the farm's well. Lang's portentous, hysterical psycho-drama about desire, guilt and repressed emotions wears its metaphors and symbols all too conspicuously on its sleeve. Undecided as to whether it's a horror pic or an art movie, and unconcerned with plot logic (why don't the women just tell the cops about their accident?), it resorts increasingly to contrived shop-worn melodrama. As a bonus, it includes one of the most risible dream sequences in years. GA

Well-Founded Fear

(1999, US, 119 min)
d/p Shari Robertson, Michael Camerini. *ph* Michael Camerini. *ed* Christopher Osborn, Suzanne Pancrazi, Karen Schmeer. *m* Mark Suozzo.

●The title refers to the wording of the UN Convention on Refugees, detailing the degree of threatened persecution which establishes a person as a political refugee. There are 16 million claimed refugees in the world; one in 200 applicants for refugee status are actually admitted into the US. This documentary follows a number of such stories through the chambers of the US Immigration and Naturalization Service, recording their interviews and the thoughts and feelings of their interrogators. The nuances of story and character upon which the applicants' hopes turn are brought out in cogent detail. A shame, then, that the initially effective two by two case study structure is drastically overused. NB

Wendy Cracked a Walnut

(1990, Aust, 90 min)
d Michael Pattinson. *p* John Edwards. *sc* Suzanne Hawley. *ph* Jeffrey Malouf. *ed* Michael Honey. *pd* Leigh Tierney. *m* Bruce Smeaton. *cast* Rosanna Arquette, Bruce Spence, Hugo Weaving, Kerry Walker.

●The Australian cinema has built up a reputation for quirky, low-budget gems, but this comedy-romance succeeds only on the first two counts. Arquette tries hard, but is hopelessly miscast as a dowdy housewife (even with spectacles, you can't believe it) who is whisked off her feet by the man of her dreams (Spence). There's a bit of a twist at the end, and some good intentions, but you'd be better off staying home and reading Mills & Boon. DW

Went the Day Well?

(1942, GB, 92 min, b/w)
d Alberto Cavalcanti. *p* Michael Balcon. *sc* John Dighton, Diana Morgan, Angus MacPhail. *ph* Wilkie Cooper. *ed* Sidney Cole. *ad* Tom Morahan. *m* William Walton. *cast* Leslie Banks, Elizabeth Allan, Frank Lawton, Basil Sydney, Valerie Taylor, Mervyn Johns, Marie Lohr, Edward Rigby, David Farrar, Thora Hird, Harry Fowler, John Slater.

●An extremely effective wartime thriller which transcends its propagandist impulse (about the need to look out for fifth columnists or Germans in disguise), thanks to a tremendous story base by Graham Greene and to Cavalcanti's firm direction. As a small, remote village is taken over and cut off by a platoon of undercover German paratroopers, tensions and suspicions mount, and confusion reigns as to how to deal with the problem. What really distinguishes the film is not so much the impressive exploration of the way the invasion threatens the accepted hierarchy within the village, but Cavalcanti's cool, brutal depiction of suddenly erupting violence and death; not only are British 'heroes' often despatched with shocking realism, but quiet, cosy housewives find themselves killing the enemy with almost hysterical relish. And any film that includes Thora Hird as a flighty seductress has to be worth watching. GA

We of the Never Never

(1982, Aust, 134 min)
d Igor Auzins. *p* Greg Tepper. *sc* Peter Schreck. *ph* Gary Hansen. *ed* Clifford Hayes. *pd* Josephine Ford. *m* Peter Best. *cast* Angela Punch McGregor, Arthur Dignam, Tony Barry, Tommy Lewis, Lewis Fitz-Gerald, Martin Vaughan.

●Down under, *We of the Never Never* is a well-loved turn-of-the-century classic by a Mrs Aeneas Gunn, who as a genteel Melbourne bride was expected to add a woman's touch to her husband's isolated cattle station. Phlegmatic British audiences, not much in touch with the pioneer spirit, will find in this adaptation an unashamedly old-fashioned celebration of corseted pluck as Jeannie Gunn rolls up her lacey sleeves and wins the grudging respect of the hitherto misogynistic stockmen. It's a pleasurably predictable formula, kept afloat by plangent orchestration, glorious cinematography, and a continuous supply of death-beds and simple outback funerals. The film's real difficulty lies in Jeannie's treatment of the Aborigines. She's nice to them but patronising (makes the gardener wear trousers). Is Auzins inviting us to make up our own minds about her naive colonialism, or just dodging what could have been the film's central issue? JS

Werckmeister Harmonies (Werckmeister harmóniák)

(2000, Hun/Fr/Ger/It/Switz, 145 min, b/w)
d Béla Tarr. *p* Joachim von Vietinghoff. *sc* Béla Tarr, László Krasznahorkai, (additional dialogue) Péter Dobrai, Gyuri Dósa Kiss, György Fehér. *ph* Miklós Gurban, Erwin Lanzensberger, Gábor Medvigy, Emil Novák, Rob Tregenza, Patrick de Ranter. *ed* Agnes Hranitzky. *m* Mihály Vig. *cast* Lars Rudolph, Peter Fitz, Hanna Schygulla, János Derzsi, Djoko Rosic, Tamás Wickmann, Ferenc Kállai.

●Adapted from László Krasznahorkai's novel *The Melancholy Resistance*, Tarr's visually and formally stunning fable explores the havoc wreaked on a small town when a giant stuffed whale is put on display by a visiting circus. Weird, wonderful, witty and unsettling. Good to see Schygulla back, too. GA

We're Alive

(1974, US, 48 min, b/w & col)
d Women's Film Workshop, UCLA, Video Workshop, California Institution for Women.

●Made jointly by the Women's Film Workshop and some of the inmates of the California Institution for Women, this is a moving analysis of why the women are in prison, what's happening to them, what's to become of them. It begins and ends with film taken outside the walls, while the rest is videotape transferred to film of the prisoners talking about race, sex and religion, class, economics and drugs. Occasionally statistics are inserted, but generally the women show such a degree of articulacy and radical thought that what they have to say is explanation enough. A remarkably undated combination of political anger and collective tenderness. HM

We're All Stars

see Todos Somos Estrellas

We're No Angels

(1954, US, 106 min)
d Michael Curtiz. *p* Pat Duggan. *sc* Ranald MacDougall. *ph* Loyal Griggs. *ed* Arthur P Schmidt. *ad* Hal Pereira, Roland Anderson. *m* Frederick Hollander. *cast* Humphrey Bogart, Peter Ustinov, Aldo Ray, Joan Bennett, Basil Rathbone, Leo G Carroll.

●The ill-assorted trio of Bogart, Ray and Ustinov play escapees from Devil's Island who take refuge with a French shopkeeper's family, and demonstrate that beneath their rascally exteriors lie hearts of 40 carats. The lowest point comes when they all line up to croak Christmas carols. Based on a French play (*La Cuisine des Anges* by Albert Husson), it's static and laden with leaden talk, with nothing to interest the eye as recompense. Curtiz was going to the dogs at the time, but it's doubtful whether anyone could have worked wonders with such material. Bogart looks particularly ill-at-ease and silly. GB

We're No Angels

(1989, US, 102 min)
d Neil Jordan. *p* Art Linson. *sc* David Mamet. *ph* Philippe Rousselot. *ed* Mick Audsley, Joke Van Wijk. *pd* Wolf Kroeger. *m* George Fenton. *cast* Robert De Niro, Sean Penn, Demi Moore, Hoyt Axton, Bruno Kirby, Ray McAnally, James Russo, Wallace Shawn.

●Those who wrote off Neil Jordan as a director of comedy after *High Spirits* will have to think again. His first American film, scripted by David Mamet, is a nicely paced comedy of errors in which two escaped convicts, Ned (De Niro) and Jim (Penn) are mistaken for priests. The prison opening – a souped-up pastiche of old Warner Bros big-house movies, with the late Ray McAnally as the slavering, sadistic warden – is such a nightmare setting that you have to laugh. On the run, baying hounds on their trail, Ned and Jim take refuge in a monastery. Their only chance of getting across the border into Canada lies with the annual procession of monks bearing their miracle-working shrine across the bridge. Ned falls for sluttish Molly (Moore), mother of a deaf-and-dumb child, Jim for religion. De Niro's gift for pantomime, glimpsed in his plumber for *Brazil*, is a non-stop bombardment of mugging on the silent screen scale. There isn't much left for Penn, which is okay by me. Very entertaining. BC

Werewolf of London

(1935, US, 75 min, b/w)
d Stuart Walker. *sc* John Colton, Harvey Gates, Rupert Harris. *ph* Charles Stumar. *ed* Russell Schoengarth. *ad* Albert S D'Agostino. *m* Karl Hajos. *cast* Henry Hull, Warner Oland, Lester Matthews, Valerie Hobson, Spring Byington, JM Kerrigan, Zeffie Tilbury, Ethel Griffies.

●Guy Endore created the definitive werewolf myth in his superb novel *The Werewolf of Paris*, published in 1933. Since Endore was snapped up under contract by MGM, Universal – determined to get in first with werewolves – had to go with a feeble myth about a rare Tibetan flower which is the only known control for lycanthropy. In Walker's patchy but mostly ineffective film, this flower becomes a bone of contention between an Oriental werewolf (Oland) and a distinguished London botanist (Hull). Oland is impeccably sinister and contributes most of the best moments, while Hull, dull as the botanist, becomes even duller in transformation after he is bitten. His make-up, designed by Jack Pierce to leave his face as nakedly expressive as Karloff's in *Frankenstein*, merely makes him look like a toothily hairy cretin in a rotten temper. TM

Werewolf of Washington, The

(1973, US, 90 min)
d Milton Moses Ginsberg. *p* Nina Schulman. *sc* Milton Moses Ginsberg. *ph* Robert Baldwin. *ed* Milton Moses Ginsberg. *ad* Nancy Miller-Corwin. *m* Arnold Freed. *cast* Dean Stockwell, Biff McGuire, Clifton James, Beeson Carroll, Jane House, Michael Dunn.

●A hit-or-miss comedy which blends political satire and lycanthropic laughs, but lacks bite. Stockwell plays a White House aide who is bitten by a werewolf while in Hungary, then returns to Washington to wreak havoc in the corridors of power. The President (McGuire) and his pragmatic psychiatrist effect a cover-up (cf. Watergate), fearing the press will use Stockwell's senatorial snacks to discredit the presidency. A poorly integrated subplot involving a mad-dwarf scientist (Dunn) is good for a few laughs, but like the half-hearted pastiche of Universal's *The Wolf Man*, it goes nowhere. NF

Wes Craven's New Nightmare

(1994, US, 112 min)
d Wes Craven. *p* Marianne Maddalena. *sc* Wes Craven. *ph* Mark Irwin. *ed* Patrick Lussier. *pd* Cynthia Charette. *m* J Peter Robinson. *cast* Robert Englund, Heather Lagenkamp, Miko Hughes, John Saxon, Robert Shaye, Wes Craven.

●In this post-modern take on the enervated *Elm Street* series, the director of the original uses a complex film-within-a-film structure to reassess and revitalise the moribund Freddy Krueger mythology. Craven's conceptual coup is to cast himself; the man behind the Freddy mask (Englund), the heroine of the original (Lagenkamp), and even the supremo of New World Pictures (Bob Shaye) as both themselves and their fictional counterparts. Thus, he explicitly confronts the previous sequels' cynical softening of Freddy's once horrifying persona. During preparations for yet another sequel, Freddy is born again, spilling over from the pages of Craven's script-in-progress to threaten those involved with its making. Skilfully blending fairy-tale clarity with the skewed logic of nightmares, Craven also blurs the boundary between reality and fiction. There is creepy subversive stuff going on here, not to mention sly sideswipes at the censors. The climactic punch-up fails to match the power of the first film's true ending, but in deconstructing his own bastardised creation, Craven redeems both the series and his own tarnished reputation. NF

West Beirut (West Beyrouth)

(1998, Fr/Leb/Bel/Nor, 110 min)
d Ziad Doueiri. *p* Rachid Bouchareb, Jean Bréhat. *sc* Ziad Doueiri. *ph* Richard Jacques Gale. *ed* Dominique Marcombe. *ad* Hamzé Nasrallah. *m* Stuart Copeland. *cast* Rami Doueiri, Mohammad Chamas, Rola Al Amin, Carmen Loubbos, Joseph Bou Nassar, Liliane Nemry, Leila Karam.

● Much has been made of Ziad Doueiri's service as assistant or second unit cameraman on all Tarantino's films, but his assured, semi-autobiographical debut as writer and director is strong enough to be judged on its own terms. Set in 1975, it recreates the initial stages of Lebanon's civil war through the experiences of three teenagers: Muslim friends Tarek (the director's younger brother Rami) and Omar (Chamas), and the former's Christian neighbour May (Al Amin). Not that religion or politics concern them very much; while Tarek is happy to torment teachers at his French high school and spout a few fashionable slogans now and then, he's more preoccupied with pop, sex, smoking and his beloved cine camera, and barely understands why mum wants to leave the city against dad's wishes. Indeed, the division of Beirut into Christian-controlled East and Muslim West is simply an excuse to skip school… until he needs to get his Super-8 film printed up over the frontline. With a light touch wisely applied both to the chaos of a city in turmoil and to the rites-of-passage narrative arc, Doueiri's film succeeds by offering up sturdy performances, attention to detail, humour, drama and a refusal to sermonise or take sides. It marks Doueiri as a talent to watch. GA

Western

(1997, Fr, 134 min)
d Manuel Poirier. *p* Maurice Bernart, Michael Saint-Jean. *sc* Manuel Poirier, Jean-François Goyet. *ph* Nara Keokosal. *ed* Yann Dedet. *ad* Roland Mabille. *m* Bernardo Sandoval. *cast* Sergi Lopez, Sacha Bourdo, Elisabeth Vitali, Marie Matheron, Basile Siekoua.

● This amiable road movie follows two misfits – Catalan shoe salesman Paco and vertically challenged Russian-Italian Nino who meet under inauspicious circumstances – as they travel with no particular purpose through Brittany, the former giving himself and his new love a little space to consider their future, the latter in search of his own inamorata. Nothing extraordinary happens, the highlights of their journey being a drunken dinner with a barmaid and her cousin, and a survey conducted about the ideal man, but it's often funny and touching, mainly because the focus is on the credible, charming but never sentimentalised characters. Modest, but immensely engaging. GA

Western Approaches (aka The Raider)

(1944, GB, 83 min)
d Pat Jackson. *p* Ian Dalrymple. *sc* Pat Jackson, Gerry Bryant. *ph* Jack Cardiff. *ed* Jocelyn Jackson, Willy Freeman. *ad* Edward Carrick, Peggy Gick. *m* Clifton Parker.

● This highly respected documentary tells the story of a group of British merchant seamen adrift in the Atlantic after their ship has been torpedoed by a German U-Boat. In essence it's a fictionalised account (using men on active naval service rather than actors) of a typical World War Two disaster, whereby merchant ships returning to Britain with vital supplies of food and goods from America ran the gamut of the Nazi subs in their attempt to beat the blockade. As a tribute to heroism, it's easier to take than many from the same period, and the outstanding colour camerawork by Jack Cardiff is all the more remarkable when you consider that it was shot under dangerous conditions similar to those portrayed in the film. MA

Westerner, The

(1940, US, 100 min, b/w)
d William Wyler. *p* Samuel Goldwyn. *sc* Jo Swerling, Niven Busch. *ph* Gregg Toland. *ed* Daniel Mandell. *ad* James Basevi. *m* Dimitri Tiomkin. *cast* Gary Cooper, Walter Brennan, Doris Davenport, Fred Stone, Forrest Tucker, Chill Wills, Dana Andrews.

● A minor divertissement from Wyler in between the heavyweight stuff of *Wuthering Heights* and *The Letter*, this works primarily as an affectionate reminiscence by the director of the dozens of B-Westerns he cut his teeth on in the 1920s. It's the cattlemen vs homesteaders plot, present in all its particulars, but refracted through the star personae of Cooper and Brennan. The former takes the opportunity to run through his entire repertoire – shrewd bumpkin, simpering lover, tight-lipped man of action – without much regard to consistency of characterisation. Brennan as Judge Roy Bean (a surrogate cattle baron for the purposes of the plot) is an excessively loveable villain, but he won an Oscar, so he must have known what he was doing. Toland's landscapes are superb. BBa

Western Union

(1941, US, 93 min)
d Fritz Lang. *p* Harry Joe Brown. *sc* Robert Carson. *ph* Edward Cronjager, Allen M Davey. *ed* Robert Bischoff. *ad* Richard Day, Wiard B Ihnen. *m* David Buttolph. *cast* Robert Young, Randolph Scott, Dean Jagger, Virginia Gilmore, John Carradine, Slim Summerville, Chill Wills, Barton MacLane.

● Perhaps the most memorable moment in this fine and feisty Western comes with the superb 180-degree pan which starts at a cut telegraph line, moves slowly over to a coil of wire with an arrow through it, and then suddenly discovers a band of hostile Indians, fearsome and beautiful in startlingly brilliant warpaint and feathered headdresses. Lang was the first director really to exploit the possibilities of colour in the Western, and his marvellous sense of composition lifts an otherwise conventional story – the laying of the first trans-continental telegraph wire in 1861, with the inevitable conflict between brothers backing opposing interests – clear out of the rut. TM

Westfront 1918 (aka Vier von der Infanterie)

(1930, Ger, 97 min, b/w)
d GW Pabst. *sc* Ladislao Vajda, Peter Martin Lampel. *ph* Fritz Arno Wagner. *ed* Hans Oser. *ad* Ernö Metzner. *cast* Gustav Diessl, Fritz Kampers, Claus Clausen, Hans Joachim Moebis, Gustav Püttjer, Jackie Monnier.

● Pabst's first talkie offered a grim, humanitarian perspective on trench warfare, not unlike that in the almost contemporary *All Quiet on the Western Front.* Hardly any film since has given such an unremittingly horrific picture of warfare-in-action, from the agonising lulls to the surprise attacks, from harsh resilience to the release of madness or a death wish. The point is ultimately a simple pacifism, with all the political limitations that implies. But Pabst's brilliant tracking shots along the trenches, through ruins, and across no man's land, remain more haunting than anything in 'expressionist' cinema. TR

Westler: East of the Wall

(1985, WGer, 94 min)
d Wieland Speck. *cast* Sigurd Rachman, Rainer Strecker, Andy Lucas, Sala Kogo.

● A refreshing, direct, and effective gay love story that displays the irrelevance of big budgets where honesty, imagination, and something to say takes their place. West Berliner Felix meets out-of-work waiter Thomas in Alexanderplatz while taking his Amerikanischer Freund for a day trip to East Berlin; they fall in love, but political, border, and visiting restrictions conspire to pull them apart. This low-budget first feature, composed partly of illegal video footage shot in the East, is full of fascinating semi-documentary-style detail and unforced insights into the lives of its protagonists, and provides a quietly uplifting, totally unpretentious attack on the absurdity and inhumanity of repression, whatever its form. WH

West Side Story 100 (100)

(1961, US, 151 min)
d Robert Wise, Jerome Robbins. *p* Robert Wise. *sc* Ernest Lehman. *ph* Daniel L Fapp. *ed* Thomas Stanford, Marshall M Borden. *pd* Boris Leven. *songs* Leonard Bernstein, Stephen Sondheim. *cast* Natalie Wood, Richard Beymer, George Chakiris, Rita Moreno, Russ Tamblyn, Tucker Smith, Simon Oakland.

● Jerome Robbins, who choreographed and directed the Broadway production (book by Arthur Laurents), was originally hired to direct this lavish film version. He got about three weeks into rehearsal before his painstaking perfectionism looked like doubling the budget, and in a state of panic, United Artists brought in Robert Wise to direct the non-musical sequences. More intrigue followed, and finally Robbins was sacked altogether. But before leaving the set, he had completed four song sequences which remain the unchallenged highlights of the film: the whole of the opening sequence ('The Jet Song'), 'America', 'Cool', and 'I Feel Pretty'. If only he had been allowed to do it all… DP

Westworld

(1973, US, 89 min)
d Michael Crichton. *p* Paul N Lazarus III. *sc* Michael Crichton. *ph* Gene Polito. *ed* David Bretherton. *ad* Herman A Blumenthal. *m* Fred Karlin. *cast* Yul Brynner, Richard Benjamin, James Brolin, Norman Bartold, Alan Oppenheimer, Victoria Shaw.

● Despite faults (chiefly a dispersal of its energies), a wonderfully enjoyable fantasy about a futuristic holiday resort offering robot worlds of exotic sex, romance or violence amid the licence of ancient Rome, the gallantries of a medieval chateau, or the gunslinging frontier town. Best and most fully realised of these worlds is the Western, with Brynner (brilliant) as the robot gunman required to die, bloodily, every time a greenhorn tourist challenges him to the draw. Until, that is, the robots begin to malfunction – or rebel: only the computers that designed them know exactly how they work – and the Brynner machine sets out, now part mad killer and part Frankenstein monster, in quest of revenge. Great stuff. TM

We the Living (Noi vivi)

(1942, It, 174 min, b/w)
d Goffredo Alessandrini. *p* Franco Magli. *sc* Corrado Alvaro, Orio Vergani. *ph* Giuseppe Caracciolo. *ed* Eraldo Da Roma. *m* Renzo Rossellini. *cast* Fosco Giachetti, Alida Valli, Rossano Brazzi, Giovanni Grasso, Emilio Cigoli, Annibale Betrone.

● Based (unauthorised) on Ayn Rand's first, partly autobiographical novel, this was banned by the Fascist authorities, who disapproved of its anti-totalitarian stance. It was originally prepared for release in two parts, running 270 minutes in all; the present version was re-edited in 1986 under the supervision of Rand's attorneys. The setting is post-revolutionary Russia, where 18-year-old Kira (Valli) and her family oppose the new order. Her ambitions for further education and a career as an engineer are disrupted – and the seeds for disaster sown – when two very different men fall in love with her: a former aristocrat on the run from the secret police (Brazzi), and a Party official committed to Communist ideals (Giachetti). Giuseppe Caracciolo's exquisite cinematography sets up a brooding, melodramatic atmosphere, and as Valli's and Brazzi's eyes sparkle into the lens, it's hard not to feel soppily sympathetic toward their cause. This is intended, of course. The romantic triangle defines the political debate (as it did in *Senso*, but with far more passion). Still, there is a luminous quality to the lead performances which lifts some of the weightier passages. CM

Wetherby

(1985, GB, 102 min)
d David Hare. *p* Simon Relph. *sc* David Hare. *ph* Stuart Harris. *ed* Chris Wimble. *pd* Hayden Griffin. *m* Nick Bicat. *cast* Vanessa Redgrave, Ian Holm, Judi Dench, Stuart Wilson, Joely Richardson, Robert Hines, Tim McInnerny, Suzanna Hamilton.

● A man shoots himself in the head in a film that's dead from the neck down. Harsh? Possibly, but Hare's first film as director, set in Yorkshire, does seem to be playing mind games. McInnerny is the uninvited guest who twice turns up at the Wetherby home of schoolteacher Jean Travers (Redgrave) – first at a dinner party and then, the following day, to commit suicide in front of her. Flashbacks, to the night before and a dark episode in the teacher's past, with Richardson fittingly playing the young Travers, seek to cast light. Redgrave's performance is superb and she's ably supported by Holm, Dench, and Hamilton in particular. Perhaps lacking the truly cinematic qualities of Hare's later *Paris by Night*, but avoiding the stagebound theatricality of *The Designated Mourner*, *Wetherby* is – if you can track it down – worth the detour. NRo

We Think the World of You

(1988, GB, 91 min)
d Colin Gregg. *p* Tommaso Jandelli. *sc* Hugh Stoddart. *ph* Mike Garfath. *ed* Peter Delfgou. *pd* Jamie Leonard. *m* Julian Jacobson. *cast* Alan Bates, Gary Oldman, Frances Barber, Liz Smith, Max Wall.

●JR Ackerley's wonderfully moving novel wouldn't work without the central relationship between an ageing lonely gay and his Alsatian. Colin Gregg hasn't solved that one – how can you on screen? – and concentrates elsewhere, losing the point in a plethora of Brit caricatures, Liz Smith prominent among them. Bates does his over-familiar mannered queen in melancholy circs, effectively shafting any chance of sympathy, and only Oldman as his unreliable lover gives any sense of layered life, earning a pang as the trap snaps shut upon his prospects. BC

We Three

see Noi tre

We Were One Man (Nous Etions un Seul Homme)

(1978, Fr, 90 min)
d/p/sc Philippe Vallois. *ph* François About. *ed* Philippe Vallois. *m* Jean-Jacques Ruhlmann. *cast* Serge Avédikian, Piotr Stanislas, Catherine Albin.

●A low-budget but highly acclaimed study of love doubly forbidden by sexual and (because of its World War II setting) national taboos. Valois makes good use of his lonely Landes landscapes and the interestingly contrasted characters: an erratic, mercurial Frenchman; his blond German lover, reserved, slower, almost stolid; and the female figure in the triangle, treated – despite the film's title – with surprising generosity. It's not without its longueurs, nor certain of the clichés (love across the barricades; love among the trees) that often attend this particular mode of the Historical-Pastoral. But there's still a freshness and lyricism in the showing of shared activities (fishing, fighting, felling trees), and a delicacy in indicating how these small epiphanies, moments of elation familiar from many films of 'straight' mateships, can shade imperceptibly into a more overtly erotic passion. SJo

We Were Soldiers

(2002, US/Ger, 138 min)
d Randall Wallace. *p* Bruce Davey, Stephen McEveety, Randall Wallace. *sc* Randall Wallace. *ph* Dean Semler. *ed* William Hoy. *pd* Tom Sanders. *m* Nick Glennie-Smith. *cast* Mel Gibson, Madeleine Stowe, Greg Kinnear, Sam Elliott, Chris Klein, Keri Russell, Barry Pepper, Don Duong, Ryan Hurst, Marc Blucas, Josh Daugherty.

●The Valley of Death, La Drang, Vietnam, 1965. Lt-Col Hal Moore (Gibson) and 400 of his fellow Seventh Cavalrymen encounter 2,000 dug-in Viet Cong, who they engage in a severe four-day rearguard action, until the remnants are pulled out. The major part of this serious-minded war movie, adapted by the scriptwriter of *Braveheart* and *Pearl Harbor* from Col Moore's book, depicts this savage battle in graphic, protracted and often confusing scenes. A forward party is separated; we watch them being picked off relentlessly. 'I'm glad I could die for my country – tell my wife I love her,' says a dying GI, sounding too much like a movie soldier. There's no 'gook' talk here, and few die from 'friendly fire'. Gibson's fatherly commander, whose dictum is 'we're coming back together – dead or alive,' steadfastly strives for iconic status as the image of military professionalism. The movie is as predictable as Gibson's performance; not gung ho, but tokenistic in its effort to present both sides impartially, and celebratory despite the director's determination to show the fighting men as fathers, sons and lovers. WH

Whales of August, The

(1987, US, 91 min)
d Lindsay Anderson. *p* Carolyn Pfeiffer, Michael Kaplan. *sc* David Berry. *ph* Mike Fash. *ed* Nick Gaster. *pd* Jocelyn Herbert. *m* Alan Price. *cast* Bette Davis, Lillian Gish, Vincent Price, Ann Sothern, Harry Carey Jr, Margaret Ladd, Tisha Sterling, Mary Steenburgen.

●Anderson's version of David Berry's play opens with a sepia-tinted Steenburgen joyfully watching the spouters of the title, before fast-forwarding into the future. Sixty years later, Libby (Davis) and Sarah (Gish) are still on the island where they spent the summers with their husbands who, like the leviathans themselves, have long since gone. Libby, who is blind, treats her sister with disdain, but allows her to brush her long ivory hair. When Sarah invites the exiled Russian charmer Mr Maranov (Price) to dinner, Libby expresses her disapproval by refusing to permit Joshua (Carey) to install a picture window. Sarah's patience begins to run out…Nothing much happens in this curious chamber piece – the pair of crumblies chinwag with their blowsy friend Tisha (Sothern); Mr Maranov catches a fish; Sarah pegs out the washing – but the dragonish Ms Davis is in fine form, and Ms Gish is as captivating as ever. A gentle interlacing of memory, comedy and pathos, this is a golden opportunity to enjoy, if not whale music, then the probable swansong of two giants of cinema. MS

What? (Che?)

(1972, It/Fr/WGer, 113 min)
d Roman Polanski. *p* Carlo Ponti. *sc* Gérard Brach, Roman Polanski. *ph* Marcello Gatti, Giuseppe Ruzzolini. *ed* Alastair McIntyre. *pd* Aurelio Crugnola. *m* Schubert, Mozart, Beethoven. *cast* Sydne Rome, Marcello Mastroianni, Hugh Griffith, Romolo Valli, Guido Alberti, Roman Polanski.

●Polanski takes American innocence (Sydne Rome) abroad to Italy, and places her in the middle of a droll and inconsequential sex (or perversion) comedy. What lifts the film out of its one-joke level is Polanski's civilised handling of his material. Avoiding obvious laughs, he opts for a mixture of satire and comedy of embarrassment (as our heroine finds herself more and more preyed and pryed upon), with everyone playing games where only you don't know the rules. All suitably throwaway, it's held together by our own curiosity and Polanski's obvious delight in observing such strange goings-on in rich summer villas. CPe

What About Bob?

(1991, US, 99 min)
d Frank Oz. *p* Laura Ziskin. *sc* Tom Schulman. *ph* Michael Ballhaus. *ed* Anne V Coates. *pd* Leigh Dilley. *m* Miles Goodman. *cast* Bill Murray, Richard Dreyfuss, Julie Hagerty, Charlie Korsmo, Kathryn Erbe, Tom Aldredge, Susan Willis, Roger Bowen, Fran Brill.

●With Dreyfuss and Murray on top form, not even the familiar plotline – uptight rich person meets free-wheeling poor person and learns about life – can prevent this lunatic comedy from being funny. Ideally cast and perfectly matched as an anal-retentive shrink and his multi-phobic patient, the stars generate laughs a-plenty. As the author of a bestselling self-help manual, Dr Leo Marvin (Dreyfuss) should have no trouble coping with a deeply dependent patient who follows him to his lakeside holiday home. But Bob (Murray) fails to heed Leo's professional advice and wreaks havoc in Leo's messed-up family, liberating them from their neuroses. Leo's reaction is neither grateful nor rational… Occasionally, something dark and disturbing threatens to rise to the surface, but this being a formulaic comedy, the ripples caused by Bob's anarchic antics soon give way to the flat calm of normality. NF

What About Me?

(1993, US, 87 min)
d/p/sc Rachel Amodeo. *cast* Rachel Amodeo, Richard Edson, Judy Carne, Richard Hell, Rockets Redglare.

●In Los Angeles, they say, everyone has a script. In New York, though, everybody goes ahead and actually makes their movie – usually in b/w and preferably with a rock guitar soundtrack, in this case by Johnny Thunders. Written, produced, directed and starring Rachel Amodeo, this is a late example of that old new wave scene which crested in the early '80s. Amodeo (formerly a drummer with Vacuum Bag and Das Furlines, apparently) is Lisa, lonely, unemployed and sharing her aunt's low-rent apartment. She buys a coffee cup from a bag lady (Carne) and spends her last dollar on a palm reading. Returning home, the landlord (Rockets Redglare) says her aunt is dead. Then he rapes her. Then he evicts her. Lisa becomes a bag lady. She is struck by a motorbike. She witnesses a mob hit. The victim dies in her arms. The film ends with her death on a bench beneath the Statute of Liberty. TCh

What About Me?

(1996, US, 34 min)
d Benjamin Allanoff. *cast* Benjamin Allanoff, Nicole Holofcener.

●Men! Do you feel lonely, abandoned, jealous and resentful when the woman you love achieves something in her working life that you're also proud of? If so, you'll identify with this often hilarious documentary about the way director, writer, cameraman and co-producer Ben Allanoff felt when his romantic and professional partner Nicole Holofcener got to make her feature debut, *Walking and Talking*. Men! Aren't we impossible? (Or is it the women?) GA

What a Carve Up

(1961, GB, 88 min, b/w)
d Pat Jackson. *p* Robert S Baker. *sc* Ray Cooney, Tony Hilton. *ph* Monty Berman. *ed* Gordon Pilkington. *ad* Ivan King. *m* Muir Mathieson. *cast* Sidney James, Kenneth Connor, Shirley Eaton, Dennis Price, Donald Pleasence, Esma Cannon, Michael Gough, Adam Faith.

●Frank King and Leonard Hines' story *The Ghoul* has twice served as a straight shocker (once with Boris Karloff in 1933), but here it's treated as a spoof (co-written by Ray Cooney) with pals James and Connor knee-deep in horror-flick clichés (thunderstorms, mad relatives, Donald Pleasence) as they get caught in a a series of slayings at ye olde dark house, Blackshaw Towers on the Yorkshire moors. Fluff and nonsense, of course, but competently acted and directed. With appeal for fans of *Carry On Screaming* (and Jonathan Coe's 1994 novel *What a Carve Up!*). TJ

What a Man!

see Never Give a Sucker an Even Break

What Are You Doing After the Orgy? (Rötmånad)

(1970, Swe, 104 min)
d Jan Halldoff. *p* Bengt Forslund. *sc* Jan Halldoff, Bengt Forslund, Lars Forssell. *ph* Lars Johnsson. *ed* Siv Lundgren. *ad* PA Lundgren. *m* Lars Färnlöf. *cast* Carl Gustav Lindstedt, Ulla Sjöblom, Ernst Günther, Ulf Palme, Christina Lindberg, Eddie Axberg.

●Despite the come-on of the English title, not a sex pic but a long, lugubrious, and finally quite engaging black comedy in which a woman believed dead these two years (Sjöblom) suddenly descends on her bored but relatively peaceful holidaying family. Now a hooker by trade, she organises herself a procession of paying customers, and for her daughter a financially beneficial line in 'amateur photographers', while downtrodden dad mends the roof and gets the drinks. Her plots founder on young love, but there's a suitably murky ending. Slow and sometimes predictable, the film often commits virtual acts of aggression on its characters and actors in an attempt to exact humour or pathos; nevertheless Halldorf does manage to take it towards a bleakly amusing analysis of family relationships.

What Changed Charley Farthing?

(1974, GB, 101 min)
d Sidney Hayers. *p* Tristam Cones, Sidney Hayers. *sc* David Pursall, Jack Seddon. *ph* Graham Edgar. *ed* Bernard Gribble. *pd* Enrique Alarcon. *m* Angel Arteaga. *cast* Doug McClure, Lionel Jeffries, Hayley Mills, Warren Mitchell, Dilys Hamlett, Alberto De Mendoza.

●This very inevitable adventure comedy, involving the attempts of a group of expatriates to escape from a revolutionary island, shows off with an excess of loveable rascals: McClure as the fun-loving sailor who falls for Hayley's incomprehensible accent; Jeffries as her stepfather, the wily, scheming last outpost of the Empire; and Mitchell as a blaspheming Scot. The only notable points are that the numerous brawls serve as very obvious time-fillers, and that all three men prove fairly game at showing off their buttocks – indeed, McClure can scarcely be induced to keep his trousers on. Wild horses shouldn't drag you to this film, but if they do, you might find Jeffries' desperate mugging sufficient to stave off utter despondency. CPe

What Did You Do in the War, Daddy?

(1966, US, 119 min)
d/p Blake Edwards. *sc* William Peter Blatty. *ph* Philip H Lathrop. *ed* Ralph E Winters. *pd* Fernando Carrere. *m* Henry Mancini. *cast* James Coburn, Dick Shawn, Sergio Fantoni, Giovanna Ralli, Aldo Ray, Harry Morgan, Carroll O'Connor, Leon Askin, Kurt Kreuger.
● An engaging comedy, scripted by William Peter Blatty, with Shawn as a keen young company commander eager to prove his valour in the Italian campaign of 1943. Disconcerted to discover that the Italian unit he is supposed to attack asks nothing better than to surrender, but insists that the village first be allowed to hold its annual wine festival, he is persuaded to agree by his more worldly-wise lieutenant (Coburn); and both armies duly get so drunk that, to save face, they decide to stage a mock battle. This, alas, is observed and taken seriously by both German and American troops, who prepare to intervene, and complications pile up until the whole thing gets wildly out of hand. Some of it is very funny, like the mock battle, with attempts at choreographed strategy ruined by tired combatants sneaking away for refreshment. Some of it (especially the volubly excitable Italian bits) are tiresome. But it is held together by terrific performances, Philip Lathrop's exquisite, pastel-shaded photography, and Blake Edwards' instinct for composition and design, let loose in some pleasantly fantastical images. TM

What Dreams May Come

(1998, US/NZ, 113 min)
d Vincent Ward. *p* Stephen Simon, Barnet Bain. *sc* Ron Bass. *ph* Eduardo Serra. *ed* David Brenner, Maysie Hoy. *pd* Eugenio Zanetti. *m* Michael Kamen. *cast* Robin Williams, Annabella Sciorra, Cuba Gooding Jr, Max von Sydow, Jessica Brooks Grant, Josh Paddock.
● The blissful existence of Dr Chris Nielsen (Williams) and his wife Annie (Sciorra) shatters when their children are killed in a car smash. Later, Chris too dies in an accident. But, as it says on the poster, 'The end is only the beginning': we follow Chris to a celestial afterlife, where his burning will to be reunited with his family is complicated by his guilt about the kids and the discovery that Annie has committed suicide. How to find her again, when her soul has been consigned to the underworld? Ambitious is too small a word for Ward's film: it encompasses a visionary journey into the beyond and considers the power of emotions to contend with death itself. Since Annie is a painter working in traditional landscapes, the film allows Chris to construct his own heaven out of the art history they shared, from Caspar David Friedrich to Salvador Dali. Even in today's effects sated market, this conjures a real sense of wonder, imagining hell as a Sargasso Sea of twisted metal and doomed human faces. On the downside, the script spews Californian psycho-babble as friendly guides (Gooding and Sydow) explain the ground rules of paradise. As we make an Orphean trek towards a conventional finale, Ward dazzles the eye and boggles the mind, but leaves the heart relatively untouched. TJ

Whatever (Extension du domaine de la lutte)

(1999, Fr, 121 min)
d Philippe Harel. *p* Adeline Lecallier. *sc* Philippe Harel, Michel Houellebecq. *ph* Gilles Henry. *ed* Bénédicte Teiger. *ad* Louise Marzaroli. *cast* Philippe Harel, José Garcia, Catherine Mouchet, Cécile Reigher, Marie Charlotte LeClaire, Philippe Agael, Alain Guillo, Yvan Garouel, Christophe Rossignon.
● A computer systems engineer (director and co-writer Harel) has been accelerating on the downward slope ever since his girl finished with him, leaving him listless, cynical, socially timid, touched by self-pity, and so passive and prey to confusion that the very idea of buying a new bed becomes impossibly problematic. He's lucid enough to know he's suffering some sort of breakdown, but still finds it increasingly difficult just to survive. His masturbatory fantasies become ever more misogynistic and violent, while the camaraderie offered by a likewise lonely but considerably less taciturn colleague, Tisserand (Garcia), offers little respite. Meanwhile, Our Hero's private philosophy, juggling notions of injustice and inequality in the economic and sexual arenas, gets more garbled. Adapted from Michel Houellebecq's best-selling first novel, this is certainly fascinating as a foray into the darker byways of the male psyche. For sure, the protagonist's miserabilism sometimes verges on black comedy, and, until Tisserand turns up, the secondary characters tend towards caricature. But the relationship between the two workmates is beautifully handled and the creation and control of atmosphere deftly managed. The closing moments are both unexpected and affecting. GA

What Ever Happened to Aunt Alice?

(1969, US, 101 min)
d Lee H Katzin. *p* Robert Aldrich. *sc* Theodore Apstein. *ph* Joseph Biroc. *ed* Frank J Urioste. *ad* William Glasgow. *m* Gerald Fried. *cast* Geraldine Page, Ruth Gordon, Rosemary Forsyth, Robert Fuller, Mildred Dunnock.
● Reasonably enjoyable suspenser in the post-Aldrich manner. Geraldine Page – almost two decades before her Oscar for *The Trip to Bountiful* – is the impoverished Arizona widow who's gotten through a succession of housekeepers by nobbling them for their savings. But she meets her match in Ruth Gordon, the post's latest incumbent, a lady of natural curiosity and great strength of character. The oldsters clearly relish their roles, even if you can see the plot coming from miles off. TJ

What Ever Happened to Baby Jane?

(1962, US, 133 min, b/w)
d/p Robert Aldrich. *sc* Lukas Heller. *ph* Ernest Haller. *ed* Michael Luciano. *ad* William Glasgow. *m* Frank De Vol. *cast* Bette Davis, Joan Crawford, Victor Buono, Anna Lee, Maidie Norman, Marjorie Bennett.
● Faded child star of the '20s (Davis) terrorises faded matinee star of the '30s (Crawford) in a decaying Hollywood mansion, after a mysterious accident has confined the latter to a wheelchair. Aldrich didn't have the courage to break with mystery-thriller conventions, and so the whole thing turns out to hinge on the true responsibility for the accident, but the film's real centre of interest is its *Sunset Boulevard*-type acerbity about Hollywood. Clips from authentic old Crawford movies are used to represent her past, to teasingly 'biographical' effect, and much hinges on Bette Davis' real-life reputation for bitchery. The Grand Guignol elements themselves are relatively forced and unconvincing. TR

Whatever Happened to Harold Smith?

(1999, GB, 96 min)
d Peter Hewitt. *p* Ruth Jackson. *sc* Ben Steiner. *ph* David Tattersall. *ed* Martin Walsh. *pd* Gemma Jackson. *m* Rupert Gregson-Williams. *cast* Tom Courtenay, Michael Legge, Laura Fraser, Stephen Fry, Charlotte Roberts, Amanda Root, Lulu, David Thewlis, Matthew Rhys, Rosemary Leach.
● It's 1977, and when dopey young legal clerk Vince Smith (Legge) isn't clock watching, he's making eyes at fellow desk jockey Joanna (Fraser), comely daughter of the local university's super-don (Fry). Back home, dad (Courtenay) is an ineffectual couch potato, resigned to the philandering of his wife (Lulu) and the contempt of his eldest son (Rhys). Whereupon Vince spies a strangely familiar punk girl out and about, and Pa Smith modestly reveals to the family his long hidden psychic powers. Given his delightful film of *The Borrowers*, it's no pleasure to report that director Hewitt has come a cropper with this desperately uneven comedy. To be fair, Ben Steiner's lumpen attempt at a feelgood screenplay must shoulder some blame. After a neat, if predictable, opening pastiche of *Saturday Night Fever*, the film abandons everything but the most facile notion of its punk/disco period setting. MHi

What Happened to Kerouac?

(1986, US, 97 min)
d Richard Lerner, Lewis MacAdams. *p/ph* Richard Lerner. *ed* Nathaniel Dorsky, Robert Estrin. *cast* Gregory Corso, Jan Kerouac, William Buckley, Allen Ginsberg, Edie Parker Kerouac, William Burroughs, Gary Snyder, Neal Cassady, Ann Charters, Steve Allen.
● A lovingly assembled mosaic of testimonials to the late lamented Daddy-O of the Beats. What did happen? Gregory Corso's guess is as good as any: 'The American media is a fucker'. The reclusive small-town boy simply shrivelled under the glare of publicity, and vowed that he'd drink himself to death since suicide was off-limits to Catholics. The dispiriting process is illustrated by footage of Kerouac reading his work on TV's Steve Allen Show in 1959, but reduced to impersonations of bleary bigotry a few years later on Buckley's 'Firing Line'. The Snyder and Burroughs interviews reveal sealed systems leaking no emotion, but Ginsberg gushes like a man in need of a washer. Biographer Ann Charters is reliable, but Corso, sounding like Mel Blanc reading from Slim Gaillard's *Dictionary of Vouteroonie*, is easily the best turn. Those who cling to the image of the handsome young writer toting 40 pounds of on-the-hoof manuscript in a doctor's bag will be pierced by the last twilight photos of the knock-nutty Marciano face. BC

What Have I Done to Deserve This? (¿Qué he hecho YO para merecer esto?)

(1984, Sp, 101 min)
d Pedro Almodóvar. *p* Tadeo Villalba. *sc* Pedro Almodóvar. *ph* Angel Luis Fernandez. *ed* José Salcedo. *m* Bernardo Bonezzi. *cast* Carmen Maura, Luis Hostalot, Angel De Andres-López, Gonzalo Suarez, Verónica Forque.
● Gloria is a typical Spanish housewife – or is she? Her small apartment would seem enough to keep her occupied, housing as it does her indifferent taxi-driver husband, two sons who have discovered the fringe benefits of drug-dealing, and a self-reliant mother-in-law with a pet lizard. But Gloria craves a better life, or at least, for starters, sex with a potent man. In Almodóvar's early feature, the mad inversions and absurdities familiar from *Law of Desire* and *Women on the Verge of a Nervous Breakdown* are delivered without the fuss of incorporating the imperatives of, respectively, melodrama and farce. The result is undiluted scabrous humour, with short, sharp scenes and a crazy string of plots involving the forging of Hitler's diaries, murder by hambone, and keeping a neighbour company during her bonking hour. Almodóvar directs throughout with splendid zip; all in all, the film's piquant look at high-rise life is far more cutting *and* funnier than his later box-office hits. DT

What I Have Written

(1996, Aust, 102 min)
d John Hughes. *p* Peter Sainsbury, John Hughes. *sc* John A Scott. *ph* Dion Beebe. *ed* Uri Mizrahi. *m* John Phillips, David Bridie. *cast* Angie Milliken, Jacek Koman.
● When a poet suffers a near fatal stroke, his wife receives the manuscript of an erotic novella he'd written (unbeknown to her) from a lecturer friend; suspecting it contains autobiographical elements about an intense, liberating affair, she begins to investigate and finds her ideas about her marriage, masculinity, sex and truthfulness overturned. This low-budget feature, while a tad predictable, is an intriguing, intelligent study in erotic obsession; if the narrative, with its flashbacks constructed largely from stills, is occasionally clumsy and overarty, this is still a sporadically rewarding foray into territory previously charted by the likes of Resnais, Roeg and Kieslowski. GA

What Is Democracy? (¿Qué es la Democracia?)

(1971, Col, 42 min, b/w)
d Carlos Alvarez.
● A critique of party political democracy in Colombia. Using cartoon, old newsreel, and a barrage of photo-material, it exposes the way in which clerical, military and business interests colluded with the American government against the peasantry and workers. Alvarez demonstrates the futility of voting for a series of figurehead personalities, none of whom, liberal or conservative, are prepared to instigate the enormous changes necessary in the

Colombian social system. While the Colombian people continue to believe in the party machine, while they continue to vote, while they continue not supporting the revolutionary vanguard, they will remain oppressed. Alvarez' points were brought home by subsequent events in Colombia. He himself was imprisoned without trial in 1972, on charges of 'conspiracy' against the state.

What Lies Beneath

(2000, US, 130 min)
d Robert Zemeckis. *p* Steve Starkey, Robert Zemeckis, Jack Rapke. *sc* Clark Gregg. *ph* Don Burgess. *ed* Arthur Schmidt. *pd* Rick Carter, Jim Teegarden. *m* Alan Silvestri. *cast* Harrison Ford, Michelle Pfeiffer, Diana Scarwid, Victoria Bidewell, Joe Morton, James Remar, Miranda Otto, Amber Valletta, Katharine Towne, Wendy Crewson.

●Norman Spencer (Ford, slothful) and his wife Claire (Pfeiffer) are so happily in love in their lakeside mansion that you know something dreadful's going to occur. It's just a case of when. But Zemeckis keeps the ambiguities coming. While Norman is content to pursue his career as a research scientist, Claire still suffers the psychological after effects of a car accident and prefers to stay at home with her thoughts. Then the strangeness begins: she starts hearing noises. Echoing *Rear Window*, she even begins to suspect her new neighbour has killed his wife. Worse, turning off the bath, she briefly catches the horrifying reflection of a young woman. Either she's off her rocker or the woman's trying to tell her something. But what, and why? Who is she anyway? Claire stumbles into her own investigation and proceeds to put her foot right in it. At which point – after a slow build that at times makes every hair stand on end – Zemeckis rolls out every thriller cliché there is. A pity, because until then it's a smart, realistically staged, adult-oriented and extraordinarily effective domestic chiller. DA

What Lola Wants

see Damn Yankees

What Maisie Knew

(1975, US, 55 min)
d/p/sc/ph/ed Babette Mangolte. *cast* Epp Kotkas, Kate Manhein, Saskia Noordhoek-Hegt, Linda Patton, Yvonne Rainer, Philip Glass.

●It takes a certain audacity to adapt one's first film from a novel that has been described as 'one of the most remarkable technical achievements in fiction'. But Henry James' vision of venery seen through innocent eyes proves the perfect vehicle for Mangolte's own fascination with the peculiar ambivalence of the filmic, its ability to render perceptions that can be at the same time subjective and impersonal. Here her evocative sensual imagery traces out fragments of memories, glimpses of gestures from a remote, mysterious adult world of erotic desires, all observed with a detached curiosity which approaches the Jamesian ideal of allowing each scene 'to emerge and prevail – vivid, special and wrought hard to the hardness of the unforgettable'. SJo

What Makes David Run? (Qu'est-ce qui fait courir David?)

(1982, Fr, 99 min)
d Elie Chouraqui. *p* Xavier Gélin. *sc* Elie Chouraqui. *ph* Robert Alazraki. *ed* Georges Klotz. *m* Michel Legrand. *cast* Francis Huster, Nicole Garcia, Charles Aznavour, Magali Noël, Michel Jonasz, Nathalie Nell, Anouk Aimée, André Dussollier.

●David (Huster) – a frantic scriptwriter from an upwardly mobile Jewish family – struggles at both his relationship with his adoring but independent girlfriend, and with his latest movie project, a semi-comic, semi-autobiographical account of family life, the main scenes of which are shown as he dreams them up. The film's strengths and faults are similar to those in Fellini, to whose *8½* and *Amarcord* there are clear resemblances. Family rituals are remembered with grotesque emphasis on their larger-than-life absurdity; history pokes its nervous nose in now and again; nostalgia is allowed free rein. Problems arise from the fact that the central character is such a self-obsessed, approval-seeking little shit that we never really care about his situation, even when the too-neatly muted moments of pain occur. Still, never taking itself too seriously, it is lively and amusing enough. GA

What Next?

(1974, GB, 56 min)
d Peter Smith. *p* Carole K Smith. *sc* Derek Hill. *ph* Ray Orton. *ed* Brian Tomkins. *ad* Evan Hercules. *m* Carl Davis. *cast* Peter Robinson, Perry Benson, Lynne White, James Cossins, Laurence Carter, Jerold Wells, Derek Deadman.

●Presumably it was the plot of this Children's Film Foundation adventure that led one American critic to call it the teenies' *Chinatown*: blustering right-wing property developer of eminent respectability (Cossins) is uncovered by three kids as the man behind the Great Plane Robbery. Rather, we're back in the world of the *Dandy* and *Beano*, where a hit on the head means a sudden acquisition of prophetic powers, where kids become super-sleuths moving through a world of half-disguised names (Pentonmarsh Prison, Whittlewoods Pools) and get their picture on the front page of the local paper. What's more, the kids actually look as though they were thought up by a DC Thompson artist. The film develops a refreshingly conspiratorial attitude to grown-ups, and a healthy irreverence towards figures of authority. Just the right amount of laughs and a scary sequence in the Ghost Train for kids. Excellent use of London locations, natural performances, and enough wit for attendant adults.

What Planet Are You From?

(2000, US, 104 min)
d Mike Nichols. *p* Neil A Machlis, Mike Nichols, Garry Shandling. *sc* Garry Shandling, Michael Leeson, Ed Solomon, Peter Tolan. *ph* Michael Ballhaus. *ed* Richard Marks. *pd* Bo Welch. *m* Carter Burwell. *cast* Garry Shandling, Annette Bening, John Goodman, Greg Kinnear, Ben Kingsley, Judy Greer, Linda Fiorentino.

●Men are from Mars, women are down to earth, according to this embarrassing vehicle for Shandling (TV's 'Larry Sanders'). He's an extra-terrestrial on a mission to propagate the race as quickly as possible. Beeping radio-activated phallus at the ready – and eager to compliment earth women on their smell and their footwear – Harold gets a job in a bank and sets his sights on Bening, who inexplicably falls for his line. Meanwhile in an even less funny subplot FAA official Goodman becomes convinced he's on the trail of an unknown life form. It's an incredibly evolved metaphor for gender alienation, but sadly it's so sour and so crass it might just scupper the movie career of one of TV's sharpest comedians. The DVD comes with a 'making of' doc and the option of watching it in German, which may help. TCh

What Price Hollywood?

(1932, US, 88 min, b/w)
d George Cukor. *p* David O Selznick. *sc* Gene Fowler, Rowland Brown. *ph* Charles Rosher. *ed* Jack Kitchin. *ad* Carroll Clark. *m* Max Steiner. *cast* Constance Bennett, Lowell Sherman, Neil Hamilton, Gregory Ratoff, Brooks Benedict, Louise Beavers.

●Terrific performances, a sharp story by Adela Rogers St John, and characteristically elegant, subtle direction from Cukor make this largely affectionate but sometimes biting satire on Hollywood and its star system a perennial delight. Its story – waitress-turned-actress Bennett's star rises while that of her mentor/director, the cynically self-loathing alcoholic Sherman, fades – served as a run-through for the more famous *A Star Is Born* (also produced by Selznick), and the steady shift from light, bubbly comedy to the genuine darkness of the scenes leading to Sherman's suicide is effortlessly made. Funny, moving, and unusually honest. GA

What's Cooking?

(2000, US/GB, 110 min)
d Gurinder Chadha. *p* Jeffrey Taylor. *sc* Gurinder Chadha. *ph* Lin Jong. *ed* Janice Hampton. *pd* Stuart Blatt. *m* Craig Pruess. *cast* Mercedes Ruehl, Victor Rivers, Douglas Spain, Maria Carmen; Joan Chen, François Chau, Will Yun Lee, Kristy Wu; Lainie Kazan, Maury Chaykin, Kyra Sedgwick, Julianna Margulies; Alfre Woodard, Dennis Haysbert, Eric K George, Brittany Jean Henry.

●Four LA families prepare for Thanksgiving. Well-off African-American Audrey Williams (Woodard) wants an elegant dinner with fare like shiitake and oyster mushroom stuffing, but her meddling mother-in-law's macaroni also fights for table space, while her son's antagonism further strains her crumbling marriage. Recently separated Elizabeth Avila (Ruehl) prepares an Hispanic feast, though she hasn't anticipated the presence of her new lover and her estranged husband. Vietnamese Trinh Nguyen (Chen), livening up a bird with East Asian spice, is disappointed that her kids prefer McDonald's, but saddened mostly by the absence of her eldest. The Seeligs try to accept their daughter's lesbianism, but they still wish she'd married a nice Jewish boy, while praying she'll pass her girlfriend off as a 'roommate'. This is a studied representation of races and cultures, generational differences and changing notions of family, co-written and directed by Gurinder Chadha (*Bhaji on the Beach*) with humour and insight. The performances are uniformly well judged; Ruehl and Chen exude their customary class, while Sedgwick and Margulies provide a non-stereotypical portrayal of a lesbian relationship. A pity, then, that the film can't suppress an occasional tendency to dispaly its political correctness in neon. KW

What's Eating Gilbert Grape

(1993, US, 118 min)
d Lasse Hallström. *p* Meir Teper, David Matalon, Bertil Ohlsson. *sc* Peter Hedges. *ph* Sven Nykvist. *ed* Andrew Mondshein. *pd* Bernt Capra. *m* Alan Parker, Björn Isfält. *cast* Johnny Depp, Juliette Lewis, Mary Steenburgen, Leonardo DiCaprio, John C Reilly, Darlene Cates.

●Hallström's finally struck a chord with the Americans, though it's much the same cocktail of whimsy and worry, the eccentric and the banal, that he's been mixing all along. The frustrated Gilbert (Depp) lives at home in Endora, Iowa, with his two younger sisters, his mentally disabled brother Arnie (DiCaprio), and his sofa-crushing 600lb mother (Cates). Deep in a Midwestern rut, Gilbert holds down a job at the local store, maintains a bored affair with housewife Betty Carver (Steenburgen), and tries to keep Arnie out of trouble, but his patience is running out – it's only when he meets teen traveller Becky (Lewis) that he can really take stock. Cute adolescent poetry with a sentimental kick. TCh

What's Love Got to Do With It

see Tina: What's Love Got to Do With It

What's New Pussycat

(1965, US/Fr, 108 min)
d Clive Donner. *p* Charles K Feldman. *sc* Woody Allen. *ph* Jean Badal. *ed* Fergus McDonell. *ad* Jacques Saulnier. *m* Burt Bacharach. *cast* Peter Sellers, Peter O'Toole, Romy Schneider, Capucine, Paula Prentiss, Woody Allen, Ursula Andress, Edra Gale, Michel Subor, Annette Poivre.

●At the time, Richard Williams' credit titles were thought to be better than the film they introduced. In retrospect, it is clear that while Woody Allen, who wrote the script and appears as the hero's friend, saw it as a satire on womanising – the O'Toole character is based on Warren Beatty – Clive Donner saw it as a morality tale in the form of a farce. The mixed results are entertaining, if flawed. O'Toole is the promiscuous hero, with Schneider, Andress, Prentiss and Capucine as some of his women, and Sellers the decidedly camp psychoanalyst he goes to for help. PH

What's the Matter with Helen?

(1971, US, 101 min)
d Curtis Harrington. *p* Edward S Feldman, James C Pratt, George Edwards. *sc* Henry Farrell. *ph* Lucien Ballard. *ed* William H Reynolds. *ad* Eugène Lourié. *m* David Raksin. *cast* Debbie Reynolds, Shelley Winters, Dennis Weaver, Agnes Moorehead, Michael MacLiammoir, Timothy Carey, Harry Dean Stanton.

●With a script by Henry Farrell (author of the source novel on which *What Ever Happened to Baby Jane?* was based), Baby Jane in effect slays again…except that this time she's directed by Curtis Harrington, erstwhile buddy of Kenneth Anger (he acts in *Inauguration of the Pleasure Dome*), who knows what's camp and what's not, and the difference between melodrama and expressionism. He films this as Sternberg might have, with a great emphasis on masks and facades, underpinned with gorgeous fairytale motifs. Plus he stages the best tango since *The Conformist*. TR

What's Up, Doc?

(1972, US, 94 min)
d/p Peter Bogdanovich. *sc* Buck Henry, David Newman, Robert Benton. *ph* Laszlo Kovacs. *ed* Verna Fields. *ad* Polly Platt. *m* Artie Butler. *cast* Barbra Streisand, Ryan O'Neal, Kenneth Mars, Austin Pendleton, Sorrell Booke, Stefan Gierasch, Mabel Albertson, Michael Murphy, Madeline Kahn, John Hillerman, Randy Quaid, M Emmet Walsh.

●A homage to Hollywood screwball comedy that by and large gets its pace and cartoon/slapstick timings right, this began life with a call from Bogdanovich (hot from the Hawksian *Last Picture Show*) to screenwriting team Robert Benton and David Newman (even hotter from *Bonnie and Clyde*): 'I've got a deal with Streisand and O'Neal, and no script. I want to do a remake of *Bringing Up Baby*, and we can do it just like that'. A remake it's not, but the spirit of Hawks (and of Preston Sturges and Frank Tashlin) survived two rapid drafts from Benton & Newman and a polish from Buck Henry, to infuse the misalliance of absent-minded musicologist O'Neal and all-purpose kook Streisand with about the right amount of madcap frenzy. PT

What's Up Tiger Lily?

(1966, US/Jap, 79 min)
d Senkichi Taniguchi, Woody Allen. *p* Woody Allen. *sc* Kazuo Yamada, Woody Allen. *ph* Kazuo Yamada. *ed* Richard Krown. *m* Jack Lewis, The Lovin' Spoonful. *cast* Tatsuya Mihashi, Miyi Hana, Eiko Wakabayashi, Tadao Nakamaru, Woody Allen, The Lovin' Spoonful, China Lee.

●Sweet revenge for anyone who has sat through a foreign film suffering from a torrent of bad dubbing. For his first *auteur*-credit (!), Woody Allen got hold of a 1964 Japanese exploitation thriller and exploited it for his own ends, dubbing it delightfully with gags and Hollywood clichés. Invention flags, and the then hip interjections from The Lovin' Spoonful now seem quaint, but there are enough one-liners to leave you with happy memories. A jolly oddity. AN

What the Peeper Saw

see Night Hair Child

What Time Is It There? (Ni Neibian Ji Dian/Et là-bas quelle heure est-il?)

(2001, Tai/Fr, 116 min)
d Tsai Ming-Liang. *p* Bruno Pesery, Chinlin Hsieh. *sc* Tsai Ming-Liang, Yang Pi-Ying. *ph* Benoît Delhomme. *ed* Chen Sheng-Chang. *pd* Yip Kam-Tim. *cast* Lee Kang-Sheng, Chen Shiang-Chyi, Lu Yi-Ching, Miao Tien, Jean-Pierre Léaud.

●Is Tsai ploughing the same furrow once too often? Soon after the death of his father (Miao), Hsiao Kang (Lee) sells a wrist-watch to a girl (Chen) who's about to fly to France. The film then crosscuts between her miserable time in Paris and his increasingly manic behaviour in Taipei (stealing public clocks, resetting timepieces to French time, coping with his batty mother) – until the twin storylines move towards a mysterious synthesis, helped along by Léaud, who enters Kang's life on tape (as Antoine Doinel in *Les Quatre Cents Coups*) and hers in person (as a randy old man in a cemetery). It all looks and feels a little too much like a rerun of *The River*, but the emphases on time, coping with bereavement and possible reincarnations give it a reasonably fresh spin. And the underlying black humour is still present and correct: how can you destroy time when some idiot invents a new unbreakable watch? TR

What Women Want

(2000, US, 127 min)
d Nancy Meyers. *p* Matt Williams, Susan Cartsonis, Gina Matthews, Bruce Davey, Nancy Meyers. *sc* Josh Goldsmith, Cathy Yuspa. *ph* Dean Cundey. *ed* Stephen A Rotter, Thomas J Nordberg. *pd* Jon Hutman. *m* Alan Silvestri. *cast* Mel Gibson, Helen Hunt, Marisa Tomei, Mark Feuerstein, Lauren Holly, Ashley Johnson, Judy Greer, Alan Alda, Delta Burke, Valerie Perrine, Bette Midler.

●Gibson's chauvinist adman suffers electrocution by hairdryer and wakes up hearing voices subjecting him to torrents of abuse. It isn't schizophrenia. Hexed by the dryer, Nick Marshall can now read women's minds. Turns out they really do hate him. If the premise for Meyer's superficially good-looking romantic comedy stinks, it doesn't help that she's toeing the John Gray 'Mars and Venus' line of reductionist claptrap. There's precious little in these minds for anyone to read: waitress Lola (Tomei) is afraid of getting hurt again; new boss and putative ball-breaker Darcy (Hunt) is quite nice at heart. It's easy to take candy from these babies, and so Nick does, putting his new-found skill to work and poaching Darcy's ideas. So far, so insipid. Hunt's career woman is paper-thin, while Gibson trespasses awkwardly on Clooney territory, as he explores mysterious girly products, waxing his legs and trying on tights. After his transformation, irritation levels mount as 'feminisation' sets in. Alongside an automatic identification with gay men, Nick develops a taste for spilling his emotional guts and jumping headlong into the romantic mushpot. SS

Wheels & Deals

(1991, Ger, 96 min, b/w)
d Michael Hammon. *p* Pierre de C Hinch. *sc/ph* Michael Hammon. *ed* Simone Bräuer. *ad* Mark Wilby. *m* William Ramsay. *cast* Sello Ke Maake-Ncube, Kimberley Stark, Dominic Tyawa, Archie Mogorosi.

●Do we really need a 'politically correct' footnote to *Mapantsula*, directed by another young, white South African keen to establish Sowetan street-cred? Laid off during a strike at the metal foundry, the stolidly principled BT comes under pressure from the members of his late brother's gang to get into the car-theft business. No big problem, until he presents a stolen car to the woman he has a crush on – getting her and her right-on activist friends into trouble, and bringing BT himself under the thumb of a ruthless Mr Big. The real trouble is that this is written as a pessimistic lefty tract, rather amateurishly acted, and shot without flair. The old label fits: worthy but dull. TR

Wheels on Meals (Kuai-can Che)

(1984, HK, 102 min)
d Samo Hung. *p* Leonard KC Ho. *sc* Edward Tang, Johnny Lee. *cast* Jackie Chan, Yuen Biao, Samo Hung, Richard Ng.

●Jackie Chan is more than the sum of his stunts: it's his knack for comedy, as much as his martial arts virtuosity that makes him Asia's top star. This delirious comedy, set in Barcelona, is one of his better efforts. He and Yuen Biao are fast-food operators who somehow become entangled in a plot involving a prostitute, a lunatic and a missing heiress. The sheer haphazardness of the happenings recalls Hollywood's golden slapstick comedies. GM

When a Man Loves a Woman

(1994, US, 125 min)
d Luis Mandoki. *p* Jon Avnet, Jordan Kerner. *sc* Ronald Bass, Al Franken. *ph* Lajos Koltai. *ed* Garth Craven. *pd* Stuart Wurtzel. *m* Zbigniew Preisner. *cast* Andy Garcia, Meg Ryan, Ellen Burstyn, Tina Majorino, Mae Whitman, Lauren Tom, Gail Strickland.

●Ryan excels as Alice Green, teacher and mother of two young children, whose apparently idyllic marriage cracks open to reveal a dependence on drink. The emphasis here, though, is neither on Alice's drinking and (self-)deception, nor on the gruelling drying-out period, but on the guilt, confusion and disruption provoked by her return to the dysfunctional family unit that caused her breakdown and which must now adjust to accommodate a wife/mother who is not only sober but irrevocably changed. Having spent much of her marriage rummaging in the laundry cupboard for vodka, Alice now starts to delve into her past for the missing pieces of an unfulfilled life. Ryan, with her trademark sobbing to the fore, gives a showier performance than Garcia, who nevertheless impresses as the husband unable to cope with Alice's growing self-confidence. Mandoki transforms what might have been a familiar story of personal redemption into a coruscating dissection of a marriage built on shifting sand. NF

When a Stranger Calls

(1979, US, 97 min)
d Fred Walton. *p* Doug Chapin, Steve Feke. *sc* Steve Feke, Fred Walton. *ph* Don Peterman. *ed* Sam Vitale. *pd* Elayne Ceder. *m* Dana Kaproff. *cast* Charles Durning, Carol Kane, Colleen Dewhurst, Tony Beckley, Rachel Roberts, Ron O'Neal.

●An anonymous phonecaller urges the babysitter to check the children… Two competently handled sequences of protracted suspense, featuring the killer at large in a darkened house, bracket a less effectively realised murder hunt through the city streets. However, this stab at the soft underbelly of American middle class paranoia looks increasingly contrived once the film loses direction in the daylight outside, and a realism intrudes that the film-makers just don't know how to handle. Not as atmospherically eerie as *Halloween* nor as mechanically effective as *Black Christmas*, but there's one great moment when the husband in bed turns into a stranger. Kane is the babysitter (later wife and mother), Beckley the killer, and Durning the cop. CPe

When Brendan Met Trudy

(2000, Ire/GB, 95 min)
d Kieron J. Walsh. *p* Lynda Myles. *sc* Roddy Doyle. *ph* Ashley Rowe. *ed* Scott Thomas. *pd* Fiona Daly. *m* Richard Hartley. *cast* Peter McDonald, Flora Montgomery, Marie Mullen, Pauline McLynn, Don Wycherley, Maynard Eziashi, Eileen Walsh, Barry Cassin.

●Cinephile fantasies come up against the altogether more unpredictable yearnings of real life in Roddy Doyle's first original screenplay. When solitary celluloid dreamer and Dublin teacher Brendan (McDonald) falls for the street-level life force of Trudy (Montgomery), he finds himself rapidly embroiled in an escalating series of comic misadventures, engineered with nods to numerous movies. Briefly suspecting her of city-wide serial castrations, he uncovers a spirit of personal rebellion, propelling him off the sofa. The set-up is clearly stock, but there's an easy-going vitality to the playing and pacing, while the relative predictability of the centre allows the eye to drift towards the edges, where some of the more interesting business is unfolding. There's a strain of gentle satire on nouveau Ireland. Indeed, some *Airplane!*-style spoofing around is laugh out loud stuff – stay with the end credits for amusing updates on the characters' afterlives. But the picture works most intriguingly as an unintentional elegy to the passing of repertory cinema, and with it any real notion of a shared filmic history. GE

When Dinosaurs Ruled the Earth

(1969, GB, 100 min)
d Val Guest. *p* Aida Young. *sc* Val Guest. *ph* Dick Bush. *ed* Peter Curran. *ad* John Blezard. *m* Mario Nascimbene. *cast* Victoria Vetri, Robin Hawdon, Patrick Allen, Drewe Henley, Sean Caffrey, Magda Konopka, Imogen Hassall, Patrick Holt.

●Rousing tribal squabbles among scantily clothed men and women clambering amid the rocks, jungle foliage, and lumbering monsters of Shepperton Studios. The script is couched entirely in prehistoric syllables – a testament to Guest's valiant attempt at creating science-fact rather than fiction. Alas, the budget was too small for the facts to convince, but the film still includes a few of the strangest shots in British cinema. GB

When Eight Bells Toll

(1971, GB, 94 min)
d Etienne Périer. *p* Elliott Kastner. *sc* Alistair MacLean. *ph* Arthur Ibbetson. *ed* John Shirley. *ad* Jack Maxsted. *m* Wally Stott. *cast* Anthony Hopkins, Robert Morley, Nathalie Delon, Jack Hawkins, Corin Redgrave, Ferdy Mayne.

●Adapted by Alistair MacLean from his own novel, this has young Hopkins as a secret service agent investigating the disappearance of gold bullion from vessels in the Irish Sea, with shipping magnate Hawkins apparently up to no good. It's a decent production job if you can work up any interest in this sort of espionage thriller. Great Panavision location photography by Arthur Ibbetson. TJ

When Father Was Away on Business (Otac na Sluzbenom Putu)

(1985, Yugo, 136 min)
d Emir Kusturica. *p* Mirza Pasic. *sc* Abdulah Sidran. *ph* Vilko Filac. *ed* Andrija Zafranovic. *ad* Predrag Lukovac. *m* Zoran Simjanovic. *cast* Moreno de Bartoli, Miki Manojlovic, Mirjana Karanovic, Mustafa Nadarevic.
●In the wake of the Tito/Kremlin split in the early '50s, little Malik's dad is despatched 'on business' to a labour camp for his Stalinist leanings (and philandering habits). His son stolidly observes the hardship this brings upon the family, takes to sleepwalking, and experiences first love. A few smiles, a few tears, all most unexceptionable: the very stuff, in short, of a festival laureate. Meticulously crafted and full of delightful touches, but there is little to lift this Cannes prize-winner above the ordinary. SJo

When Harry Met Sally...

(1989, US, 95 min)
d Rob Reiner. *p* Rob Reiner, Andrew Scheinman. *sc* Nora Ephron. *ph* Barry Sonnenfeld. *ed* Robert Leighton. *pd* Jane Musky. *m* Marc Shaiman. *cast* Billy Crystal, Meg Ryan, Carrie Fisher, Bruno Kirby, Steven Ford, Lisa Jane Persky, Michella Nicastro.
●1977: cynical womaniser Harry (Crystal) and clean-living would-be journo Sally (Ryan) are thrown together on an 18-hour trip to New York. They don't exactly hit it off, but ten years later, having suffered the traumas of break-up and divorce, they meet again and find they can offer mutual support. Will their friendship move from platonic to romantic? It seems likely, but there's a problem: Harry is reluctant to commit himself, while Sally won't countenance one-night stands. Reiner's Woody Allen-ish comedy is, for all its up-front discussion of matters sexual, disarmingly old-fashioned. A mite too pat, it never really probes or challenges Harry and Sally's attitiudes; but Nora Ephron's extended, slightly sentimental, and none-too-original meeting cute scenario includes enough funny one-liners to hold the attention of all but the most jaded viewer. As ever, Reiner clearly likes his characters, and elicits sturdy performances from a proficient cast (Kirby and Fisher are especially fine as friends and confidants to the pair). GA

When I Fall In Love

see Everybody's All-American

When in London

(2000, GB, 99 min)
d Nina Carbone. *p* Nina Carbone, Hugh Whitworth. *sc* Nina Carbone, Hugh Whitworth, James Innes Smith. *ph* Hugh Whitworth. *cast* James Innes Smith, Rupam Maxwell, Tania Levey.
●The film's full titling – 'the rise and fall of the world's worst escort agency' – says it all. An enthusiastic mock-doc about hopeless public school types out to run a companion operation (initially) without the sex, it's a UK DV take on the Dogme manifesto, and filmed intervention-style in streets and clubs around the capital. Some likeable performances and camerawork, along with the film's snappy pace, work most of the time, but it's uneven and overlong, and lacks rigour in pursuit of its theme. GE

When Joseph Returns (Ha Megjön József)

(1975, Hun, 88 min)
d/sc Zsolt Kézdi Kovács. *ph* János Kende. *ed* Zoltán Farkas. *pd* Tibor Nell. *cast* György Pogány, Lili Monori, Eva Ruttkai, Gábor Koncz.
●In the East European tradition of low-key, observational cinema, blending naturalistic acting styles into workaday urban backgrounds. Middle-aged woman shares small city apartment with new daughter-in-law while merchant seaman son is at sea. They soon find themselves on an emotional collision course: the older woman's furtive liaisons, and the girl's more open if bewildered drift into promiscuity, nurture mutual accusations of hypocrisy. The film's harmonious resolution rather belies what has gone before (the intense antagonism and misunderstanding that grows between generations); but writer/director Kézdi Kovács displays a special feeling for everyday lives forever skirting boredom, and draws well-pitched performances from Monori (the daughter-in-law) and Ruttkai (the mother). CPe

When Ladies Meet

(1941, US, 108, b/w)
d Robert Z Leonard. *p* Robert Z Leonard, Orville O Dull. *sc* SK Lauren, Anita Loos. *ph* Robert Planck. *ed* Robert J Kern. *ad* Cedric Gibbons, Randall Duell. *m* Bronislau Kaper. *cast* Joan Crawford, Robert Taylor, Greer Garson, Herbert Marshall, Spring Byington.
●Adapted from Rachel Crothers' play, previously filmed in 1933 with Ann Harding and Myrna Loy. When the ladies in question are the supremely vulgar Joan Crawford and the svelte-but-deadly Greer Garson, quite a lot happens. Both in love with Herbert Marshall, the ladies have a lot of girl-talk before fighting it out. The screenplay, by Anita Loos (*Gentlemen Prefer Blondes)*, ensures maximum bitch-factor. Crawford, playing a sophisticated (and ridiculously well-dressed) novelist, loses Marshall but gets Robert Taylor as a kind of consolation prize. No fool, our Joan; she trades romance for looks, in which department Taylor could beat any contender in Tinseltown. Hovering over the whole proceedings is the motherly form of Spring Byington. ATu

When Love Comes

(1998, NZ, 94 min)
d Garth Maxwell. *p* Michele Fantl, Jonathan Dowling. *sc* Garth Maxwell, Rex Pilgrim, Peter Wells. *ph* Darryl Ward. *ed* Cushla Dillon. *pd* Grace Mok. *cast* Rena Owen, Dean O'Gorman, Simon Prast, Nancy Brunning, Sophia Hawthorne, Simon Westaway, Judith Gibson.
●'A sexy movie with music' is promised This modern love yarn does indeed have music, and the odd spot of sex, which doesn't automatically make it 'sexy' – it's cute but pretty enervated. The film's only heartfelt interest is in the doubt and diminished fortitude of its forty-something characters. The three younger cast members provide adrenalin relief mainly. Two of them – riot grrrl bandmates Fig (Brunning) and Sally (Hawthorne) – are used as tousle-haired muppets, full of carefree insouciance; their songwriter pal Mark (O'Gorman), a sex 'n' booze binger, is a placid cliché of a turbulent rebel poet. Moving on, Mark's would-be older lover, Stephen (Prast), is a warm if undistinguished man of means, patiently abiding his love object's agitation. It's his old disco diva pal Katie (Owen) who stirs the story, when she returns home from LA at an impasse in her career. Director and co-writer Maxwell's compassion for his characters is agreeable, but he's soft on their problems and vague, too. It's handsomely rendered; from Auckland to the beach house where everyone ends up, the scenery's there, but the scenario ain't. NB

When Mother Comes Home for Christmas (Otan Erhtli Mama Gia ta Christougenna)

(1995, Greece, 109 min)
d/p/sc Nilita Vachani. *ph* Vangelis Kalambakas. *ed* Nilita Vachani. *m* Ross Daly.
●One in six Sri Lankan women work abroad, often as home-helps and nannies, sending money back to their families. This documentary, by a US-trained Indian film-maker based in Athens, focuses on Josephine, a nanny who hasn't seen her own kids in 8 years. They're having trouble with school and their love lives. Josephine gets on well with her charge and is more of a mother to the infant girl than the vain and horrendously selfish middle-class woman for whom she works. Chastening but over-extended. GA

When Night Is Falling

(1995, Can, 94 min)
d Patricia Rozema. *p* Barbara Tranter. *sc* Patricia Rozema. *ph* Douglas Koch. *ed* Susan Shipton. *pd* John Dondertman. *m* Lesley Barber. *cast* Pascale Bussières, Rachael Crawford, Henry Czerny, David Fox, Don McKellar, Tracy Wright, Clare Coulter.
●Grief takes Protestant academic Camille to the laundrette, where circus performer Petra supplies tissues, sympathy and a sly switcheroo on the holdalls containing their respective smalls. The meeting-cute hurdle negotiated, the story proceeds to run a relatively fresh spin on ye old eternal threesome. The man in Camille's life is Martin, fellow lecturer at the College of New Faith, but how can the call of duty compete with this new woman winkling out the new woman in her. After all, tweed jackets and keynote speeches can't compete with tight black leather, arrows of desire fired through your window, and an epochal hang-gliding trip. No, it's not much of a contest, but Rozema provides ample pleasures to compensate for the lack of surprise, not the least of which is a warm sensuality that never feels exploitative, plus the good heart to make Czerny's boyfriend a decent stick and even to have the stern college principal question his own homophobia. While the surrounding Sirkus of Sorts frippery is endearing without being pushy, and Lesley Barber's terrific score provides emotional thrust, the key to the film's mercurial charm is the performances of the two leads: Bussières ranging engagingly from prim to perky, and Crawford a bewitching presence as the impish seductress. Cynics may demur, but the result is quite delicious. TJ

When Saturday Comes

(1995, GB, 98 min)
d Maria Giese. *p* James Daly, Christopher Lambert. *sc* Maria Giese. *ph* Gerry Fisher. *ed* George Akers. *pd* Hugo Luczyc-Wyhowski. *m* Anne Dudley. *cast* Sean Bean, Emily Lloyd, Pete Postlethwaite, Craig Kelly.
●Roy of the Rovers meets *Emmerdale* in this tale of soccer-mad Jimmy Muir (Bean) and his fight to make it as a professional footballer for local team Sheffield United. From the kick off, the omens aren't good. Jimmy has always shone in amateur teams, but suffers from a temperament problem. Yet when sprightly Irish lass Annie Doherty (Lloyd) starts at the brewery where he works, his luck begins to improve. First there's the snogging, then there's the fact that her uncle (Postlethwaite) runs a highly regarded local football team. It's difficult to convey how thoroughly dreadful this film is. It's like watching the football episode of Michael Palin's *Ripping Yarns*, but without the jokes. En route to its tedious, inevitable conclusion, every cliché about life oop north gets a good airing. The script is leaden and the direction has that unmistakable 'made for TV' look about it. Bean, Lloyd and Postlethwaite struggle dutifully with the material. NKe

When Strangers Marry (aka Betrayed)

(1944, US, 67 min, b/w)
d William Castle. *p* Frank King, Maurice King. *sc* Philip Yordan, Dennis Cooper. *ph* Ira Morgan. *ed* Martin G Cohn. *ad* F Paul Sylos. *m* Dimitri Tiomkin. *cast* Robert Mitchum, Kim Hunter, Dean Jagger, Neil Hamilton, Lou Lubin, Milton Kibbee.
●The Monogram B-picture that gave Mitchum his first starring role. Hunter's the innocent one, turning to former boyfriend Mitchum, when husband Jagger disappears after a couple of months of marriage. A trip to the cops reveals that the latter may not be quite the man she thought and thus the plot thickens. Future horror showman Castle keeps it simple, leaving the cast and the cracking dialogue to make the running. Mitchum shows promise. TJ

When the Cat's Away... (Chacun cherche son chat)

(1996, Fr, 90 min)
d Cédric Klapisch. *p* Farid Lahoussa, Aïssa Djabri. *sc* Cédric Klapisch. *ph* Benoît Delhomme. *ed* Francine Sandberg. *ad* François Emmanuelli. *cast* Garance Clavel, Renée Lecalm, Zinedine Soualem, Olivier Py.
●When make-up artist Chloé (Clavel) takes a week's holiday, the only person who'll look after her beloved cat Gris-Gris is Mme Renée (Lecalm), an eccentric old biddy who promptly loses the animal during the girl's absence. In addition to Chloé and her gay flat-mate Michel (Py), the search party which Mme Renée helps to mobilise includes numerous elderly matrons and Djamel (Soualem), a kindly if somewhat naive Arab who develops a crush on Chloé. She, however, finds herself taking an unexpected shine to a local young drummer. The third feature from writer/director Klapisch is a beautifully observed comedy vaguely in the Rohmer tradition: light, spontaneous, seemingly inconsequential, but packed with deft, delicate insights into loneliness, love, the comforts of community and the changing nature of Paris. Crucial to the film's emotional pull is an unsentimental generosity extended to each character. The naturalistic performances help no end in this respect, while the affection

stretches even to Gris-Gris, filmed, inspirationally, to the strains of Al Green's 'So Tired of Being Alone'. Witty, touching, refreshingly nonchalant, and very French. GA

When the Legends Die

(1972, US, 105 min)
d/p Stuart Millar. *sc* Robert Dozier. *ph* Richard H Kline. *ed* Luis San Andres. *ad* Angelo Graham. *m* Glenn Paxton. *cast* Richard Widmark, Frederic Forrest, Luana Anders, Vito Scotti, Herbert Nelson, John War Eagle.

● A fine contemporary Western, about a young Indian (Forrest) whose strange affinity for horses attracts the attention of an ageing rodeo rider (Widmark), who buys his freedom from the reservation by becoming his guardian, teaches him the trade, and builds him into a minor star. Simultaneously exploited by Widmark, who drinks away their winnings and tries to double them by rigging bets, Forrest determines to break away, convinced he can make the grade honestly. He finally manages his escape (although Widmark 'owns' him until he is 21), only to find himself still imprisoned, this time by the American dream of success. Elegiacally framed as an allegory (noble savage vs ignoble civilisation), the film is saved from pretension by the fact that its real flesh is the superbly detailed world of grubby towns and back street bars, of endless days and nights on the road or in faceless hotels, which forms a laconic background to the rough, tumbling, touchingly funny relationship in which Widmark simultaneously tears Forrest to pieces and becomes his only friend. Widmark's performance is absolutely magnificent. TM

When the Mountains Tremble

(1983, US, 83 min)
d Pamela Yates, Thomas Sigel. *p* Peter Kinoy. *ph* Thomas Sigel. *ed* Peter Kinoy. *ad* Randy Barcelo. *m* Rubén Blades. *with* Shawn Elliot, Eddie Jones, Linda Segura, Shelly Desai, Ron Ryan.

● A documentary with a dramatic framework, made by a team which provides CBS News coverage of Guatemala, this tells the story of 30 years of US-initiated and backed military dictatorships in that country, through the family saga of Rigoberta Menchú, the Indian peasant woman narrator, whose father and brother were both burned alive by security forces. Made with the cooperation of both government and guerrillas, it is perhaps strongest in presenting attitudes: from the brutal, no-nonsense frankness of the military, through the even more repulsive blinkered stupidity of Americans, to the desperation of the poor and the optimism of the guerillas. With *El Salvador: Another Vietnam* and John Pilger's Nicaragua documentary, this helps to complete the picture of a region to which America, not Russia, is exporting revolution. JCo

When the North Wind Blows

(1974, US, 113 min)
d Stewart Raffill. *p* Joseph Raffill, Stewart Raffill. *sc* Stewart Raffill. *ph* Gerard Alcan. *ed* K Hansel Brown, Ken Koch. *m* Jimmie Haskell. *cast* Henry Brandon, Herbert Nelson, Dan Haggerty, Henry Olek, Sander Johnson.

● There is a distant place in north Alaska, far from where the caribou roam. Here a man is judged by his strength, not by how many books he has read. A man like Avacum (Brandon), who accidentally shoots the son of his best friend, Boris the storekeeper. Fleeing to the wilds, Avacum makes a new friend – the tigress who has been terrorising the village. They protect each other, she has a pair of cubs, he adopts them when mother is gunned down by anti-conservationists. Avacum survives a year of hardship, finally turning his back on so-called civilisation. The question remains: who got the tigress pregnant? In other words, an overbearingly solemn slice of life-in-the-raw, whose often beautiful photography is let down by the Woody Allen-ish character of the peasantry involved. Some interest is kept going by the spectacle of large tigers on the attack and at play. It's a long winter, though. AN

When the Sky Falls

(1999, Ire/US, 107 min)
d John MacKenzie. *p* Nigel Warren-Green, Michael Wearing. *sc* Michael Sheridan, Ronan Gallagher, Colum McCann. *ph* Seamus Deasy. *ed* Graham Walker. *pd* Mark Geraghty. *m* Pól Brennan. *cast* Joan Allen, Patrick Bergin, Liam Cunningham, Kevin McNally, Jimmy Smallhorne, Gerard Flynn, Jason Barry, Pete Postlethwaite, Des McAleer, Owen Roe.

● How do you sell the real-life story of journalist Victoria Guerin (here renamed Sinead Hamilton), killed for speaking out against Dublin's drug barons? As with *Erin Brockovich*, a feisty mother juggles a dangerous crusade with the demands of family life, but where Erin's enemies were anonymous businessmen, Sinead's are rough and ruined hustlers. Erin's victims were in the dark about the poison entering their blood, but Sinead's have a choice. John (*The Long Good Friday*) MacKenzie would seem well placed to appreciate such muddy details. For much of the time he does well, treating Sinead (Allen) not as a heroine, but as an ordinary complex individual. She enjoys a charged relationship with one of her sources, Mickey (Smallhorne). Does he provide some sort of sexuality – raciness – lacking in her life, or is that just what she wants him to think? As in *Nixon* and *The Ice Storm*, Allen's disheartened eyes keep her secrets locked tight. The Dublin police with whom she joins forces, meanwhile, are incompetent and occasionally vicious, with the most shocking scene saved for the murder of a drug addict forced to act as a mole. It's all the stranger then, that elsewhere the film plays like a dreary TV movie. CO'Su

When the Whales Came

(1989, GB, 100 min)
d Clive Rees. *p* Simon Channing-Williams. *sc* Michael Morpurgo. *ph* Bob Paynter. *ed* Andrew Boulton. *pd* Bruce Grimes. *m* Christopher Gunning. *cast* Helen Mirren, Paul Scofield, David Suchet, Barbara Jefford, David Threlfall, Barbara Ewing, Jeremy Kemp, Max Rennie, Helen Pearce.

● A rather simple-minded tale of magic, friendship and conflict, scripted by Michael Morpurgo from his own children's novel set on one of the Scilly Isles at the start of WWI, with soaring strings, sweeping landscapes, and a no-sex, no violence, uplifting storyline about redemption through being kind to animals and befriending lonely oldsters. Mirren perfects her beautiful, battered but unbowed act; Scofield is magisterial as the Birdman, a kindly hermit; while the two children central to the action are played with delightful spontaneity by Max Rennie and lithping Helen Pearce. The endangered animal is an authentically mournful beached narwhal. A climactic, cinematically beautiful sequence has torch-wielding villagers wading into a twilt sea to ward off more of the beasts, but mostly Rees just points his camera at the wonders of nature. Don't even try to swallow the preposterously happy, mythic ending. SFe

When the Wind Blows

(1986, GB, 84 min)
d Jimmy T Murakami. *p* John Coates. *sc* Raymond Briggs. *ed* John Cary. *ad* Richard Fawdry. *m* Roger Waters. *cast* voices: Peggy Ashcroft, John Mills, Robin Houston.

● There have been enough post-holocaust nuclear winter films nearly to constitute a genre, but there has never been anything quite like veteran animator Murakami's version of Raymond Briggs' cartoon book. Jim and Hilda Bloggs are living out an unexceptional retirement, when the unthinkable happens. Happily prattling about their World War II adventures in the blitz, they duly follow the government brochure advice and build a shelter with doors and cushions, then go about their business as their hair falls out and the dust rains down. The animation is at its best – and the film most effective – during sequences of their reminiscences, when the daily round of their past lives is seen as a delight in the ordinary and in a history which is not just forgotten but literally obliterated. But their slow degradation is almost unbearably moving. The only note of hope is that it might just get through to some people who have a say in such matters. Jim and Hilda are worth preserving. CPea

When Time Ran Out

(1980, US, 121 min)
d James Goldstone. *p* Irwin Allen. *sc* Carl Foreman, Stirling Silliphant. *ph* Fred J Koenekamp. *ed* Edward Biery, Freeman Davies. *pd* Philip M Jefferies. *m* Lalo Schifrin. *cast* Paul Newman, Jacqueline Bisset, William Holden, Red Buttons, Valentina Cortese, Burgess Meredith, Ernest Borgnine, James Franciscus, Veronica Hamel, Barbara Carrera, Edward Albert.

● Well, there's this island in the Pacific where maverick oil-driller Newman hits the black stuff, much to the delight of Franciscus, screwy scion of the island's ruling family. A wooden effigy of Holden jets in with Bisset, summoned by Franciscus to locate one of his luxury hotels there. Bisset was mean to Newman, so he glowers at her. Franciscus' daddy was mean to him, so he glowers at daddy's portrait. Holden suspects Franciscus of telling whoppers about the future intentions of the island's volcano, so he glowers. (The subsidiary characters glower a lot too). Amid all the tension, the volcano blows its stack. 'Is anything wrong?' someone asks. 'No, nothing's wrong' says someone else. Something is very wrong. There's a tidal wave and an earthquake, flaming balls of fire and a menacing lava flow, and Newman decides to get the hell out with the major stars. A real movie disaster, scripted by Carl Foreman and Stirling Silliphant. DSi

When We Were Kings

(1996, US, 87 min, col & b/w)
d Leon Gast. *p* David Sonenberg, Leon J Gast, Taylor Hackford. *ph* Maryse Alberti, Paul Goldsmith, Kevin Keating, Albert Maysles, Roderick Young. *ed* Leon J Gast, Taylor Hackford, Jeffrey Levy-Hinte, Keith Robinson. *with* Muhammad Ali, George Foreman, Don King, James Brown, BB King, Norman Mailer, George Plimpton, Spike Lee, Thomas Hauser, Miriam Makeba.

● Leon Gast's time-capsule of a film transports us to Zaire in 1974 (when most of the material was shot), and the heavyweight encounter between Muhammad Ali and George Foreman – the famous 'rumble in the jungle'. Gast was on hand to record the three-day music festival which preceded the bout, but stayed when the fight was delayed after Foreman was cut in a training session. Press conferences, gym sessions, and all the cultural paradox which accompanied two African-American superstars stranded with the world's media in Kinshasa for six weeks. Apparently Taylor Hackford, who has a producer credit, came up with the idea of using commentaries from Norman Mailer, George Plimpton and Spike Lee to structure the material, and though Lee (who wasn't there) has little to say, Plimpton and Mailer (who were) make enthralling guides. Mailer, especially, acknowledges the ironies congruent on this gladiatorial showpiece for black pride being staged by the Mobutu dictatorship and the Don King machine, and produces a penetrating emotional analysis of the boxing which is nothing short of inspired. TCh

When We Were Young (Kak Molody My Byli)

(1985, USSR, 92 min)
d Mikhail Belikov. *p* A Vishnyevsky, N Fedyuk. *sc* Mikhail Belikov. *ph* Vasily Trushkovsky. *ed* N Akaemovoi. *ad* Alexei Levchenko. *m* Y Vinnik, Frédéric Chopin, George Gerschwin. *cast* Taras Denisenko, Elena Shkurpelo, N Sharolapova, A Pashutin, A Sviridovsky.

● Set in the '50s, this follows the teenage hero, a trainee sanitary engineer, as he undergoes rites of passage of various kinds before marrying his mortally ill childhood sweetheart. The tone moves between mawkish comedy and melodrama, with the shadows of still fresh war memories falling exceedingly lengthily and darkly. Not brilliant, but very desperate, and offering a window on Russia during the high years of the Cold War. It also implies criticism of the high price of space technology. VG

When Willie Comes Marching Home

(1950, US, 82 min, b/w)
d John Ford. *p* Fred Kohlmar. *sc* Mary Loos, Richard Sale. *ph* Leo Tover. *ed* James B Clark. *ad* Lyle Wheeler, Chester Gore. *m* Alfred Newman. *cast* Dan Dailey, Corinne Calvet, Colleen Townsend, William Demarest, James Lydon, Lloyd Corrigan, Evelyn Varden.

● One of Ford's most underrated films, this isn't as beady-eyed as Sturges' *Hail the Conquering Hero* in its take on patriotic fervour, but is still immensely engaging. Dailey plays small-town boy Bill Kluggs, son of a flag-waving American Legion stalwart (Demarest), who earns a civic send-off as the first to enlist after Pearl Harbor. After training, unfortunately, he is posted back home as an instructor. Repeated requests for combat duty are turned down; and cordiality turns to contempt among the townsfolk as other local boys meanwhile win glory. His chance finally comes as last-minute replacement on a bomber heading for London, leading to an inadvertent adventure in Occupied France, and an escape, engineered by the Resistance, with vital information concerning the new German rocket. He's back home within four days; and with the matter classified, everybody thinks he's lying or crazy until news comes of a pending decoration. Ford, steering a more naturalistic path than Sturges through the quirkish characters and semi-slapstick action, makes the central irony ring loud and clear: while doing his despised duty as an aerial gunnery instructor, Bill Kluggs demonstrates considerable heroism; while earning his decoration at the hands of a grateful President, he is either asleep or dead drunk the entire time. TM

When Worlds Collide

(1951, US, 83 min)
d Rudolph Maté. *p* George Pal. *sc* Sydney Boehm. *ph* John F Seitz, W Howard Greene. *ed* Arthur P Schmidt. *ad* Hal Pereira, Albert Nozaki. *m* Leith Stevens. *cast* Richard Derr, Barbara Rush, Peter Hanson, Larry Keating, John Hoyt, Judith Ames.

● Exciting science fantasy movie about the end of the world, no less. A dying star is on a crash course with the earth. Flyer Dave Randall (Derr) and astronomer Doc Hendron (Keating) put their heads together and organise the construction of a space ark to transport forty lucky workers to the nearest hospitable planet and save the human race. Based on a novel by Philip Wylie and Edwin Balmer once envisaged as a Cecil B DeMille project back in 1934, George Pal's production is better remembered for its apocalyptic special effects than for the perfunctory dialogue, but the gripping story keeps you watching. TCh

Where Angels Fear to Tread

(1991, GB, 112 min)
d Charles Sturridge. *p* Jeffrey Taylor, Kent Walwin, Derek Granger, Olivia Stewart. *sc* Derek Granger, Tim Sullivan Charles Sturridge. *ph* Michael Coulter. *ed* Peter Couldon. *pd* Simon Holland. *m* Rachel Portman. *cast* Helena Bonham Carter, Judy Davis, Rupert Graves, Giovanni Guidelli, Barbara Jefford, Helen Mirren, Thomas Wheatley.

● The fostering of Forster in a rash of movies since the mid-'80s continues with this adaptation of the novel in which Lilia Herriton (Mirren), a widow of a certain age, shocks her strait-laced in-laws by wedding the son of an Italian toothpuller (played by Guidelli with dewy eyes and pouts). When this frightful news reaches Sawston, Mrs Herriton (Jefford) dispatches her son Philip (Graves) to Monteriano to rescue her. He fails. After Lilia dies in childbirth, he returns with his sister Harriet (Davis) to retrieve the *bambino*, only to fail again – but not before he's fallen for Lilia's former companion Caroline Abbott (Bonham Carter). Stiff upper lips prove no protection against the ancient charms of tourist Tuscany. The performances and scenery cannot be faulted. Mirren, defiantly vulnerable as ever, dominates the movie while she's in it. Thereafter, Davis steals the show as a hilariously hysterical spinster. Graves, too, proves he's not just a pretty face. But though things connect much better than they did in Sturridge's *A Handful of Dust*, the screenplay degenerates into a static succession of talking heads. Sturridge's work still seems to be TV masquerading as cinema. MS

Where Danger Lives

(1950, US, 84 min, b/w)
d John Farrow. *p* Irving Cummings Jr. *sc* Charles Bennett. *ph* Nick Musuraca. *ed* Eda Warren. *ad* Albert S D'Agostino, Ralph Berger. *m* Roy Webb. *cast* Robert Mitchum, Faith Domergue, Claude Rains, Maureen O'Sullivan, Charles Kemper, Ralph Dumke, Billy House, Jack Kelly.

● Odd casting for Mitchum as a solid citizen, first cousin to Dr Kildare, who finds himself on the run after succumbing to the siren songs of a psychotic patient (Domergue, who asphyxiates her husband Rains, letting Mitchum think he killed him in a fight). Nick Musuraca's superb camerawork stresses the *noir* that is synonymous with the Mitchum persona; Charles Bennett's script seems to be hankering after all those innocent thrillers he wrote for Hitchcock in the '30s. The result is an impasse of cross-purposes which lends the film a sort of bleak abstraction, curious and rather compelling. TM

Where Eagles Dare

(1968, GB, 155 min)
d Brian G Hutton. *p* Elliott Kastner. *sc* Alistair MacLean. *ph* Arthur Ibbetson. *ed* John Jympson. *ad* Peter Mullins. *m* Ron Goodwin. *cast* Richard Burton, Clint Eastwood, Mary Ure, Patrick Wymark, Michael Hordern, Donald Houston, Peter Barkworth, Robert Beatty, William Squire, Derren Nesbitt, Anton Diffring.

● A conscientiously large World War II adventure, drawn from the novel by Alastair MacLean, about a 7-man team parachuted into the Bavarian Alps to rescue a high-ranking Allied officer held prisoner by the Germans in an impregnable mountain Schloss. It may be devoid of significance of any sort, but it is nevertheless passably entertaining, and certainly better viewing than most MacLean adaptations. Its ability to sustain interest depends on fine cinematography (Arthur Ibbetson), and a handful of genuinely exciting action sequences, notably two extended scenes involving death-defying feats on a cable car slung between two snow-covered peaks. The climax simply involves blowing up everything in sight. VG

Where Is My Friend's House? (Khaneh-Je Doost Kojast)

(1987, Iran, 85 min)
d Abbas Kiarostami. *p* Ali Reza Zarrin. *sc* Abbas Kiarostami. *ph* Farhad Saba. *ed* Naamet Allah Alizadah. *m* Amine Allah Hessine. *cast* Babek Ahmed Poor, Ahmed Ahmed Poor, Kheda Barech Defai, Iran Outari, Aït Ansari.

● Familiar in Britain only to those who've caught his work at festivals or noted his name as writer of *The White Balloon*, Iran's Abbas Kiarostami has been acclaimed a key film-maker of the '90s. Judging by this (and by *And Life Goes On*…), he's a major talent – his work an enthralling blend of low-key realism and a more thought-provoking, sometimes playful formalism. Here young Ahmed tries to return a schoolmate's notebook he's unwittingly taken home. (Its loss might get its owner expelled.) Obstacles abound, chiefly in the shape of unhelpful, domineering adults, but also because, while Ahmed knows his pal lives in the next village, he's no idea of the address. While the film is often funny, it's also very moving. The repetitive structure of the boy's quest, and the poetic evocation of the landscape he moves through, highlight his vulnerability, frustration and, finally, his sterling determination. GA

Where No Vultures Fly (aka Ivory Hunter)

(1951, GB, 107 min)
d Harry Watt. *p* Michael Balcon. *sc* WP Lipscomb, Ralph Smart, Leslie Norman. *ph* Geoffrey Unsworth. *ed* Gordon Stone. *m* Alan Rawsthorne. *cast* Anthony Steel, Dinah Sheridan, Harold Warrender, Meredith Edwards.

● Ealing moved from their modest studios to the wide open spaces of Kenya for this time-locked colonial adventure. Steel is square-jawed as the warden of Mt Kilimanjaro Game Reserve, seeing off ivory hunter Warrender and the local tribesmen he's stirred into helping him. Former documentarist Watt slightly makes up for the shortcomings in the plotting with some evocative wildlife footage (by Paul Beeson). TJ

Where's Jack?

(1968, GB, 119 min)
d James Clavell. *p* Stanley Baker. *sc* Rafe Newhouse, David Newhouse. *ph* John Wilcox. *ed* Peter Thornton. *pd* Cedric Dawe. *m* Elmer Bernstein. *cast* Tommy Steele, Stanley Baker, Fiona Lewis, Alan Badel, Dudley Foster, Sue Lloyd.

● Years before the *Shogun* millions rolled in, Clavell was the writer and director of some distinguished movies, like this one. Eighteenth century England is recreated with care as government agent Baker (who also produced) shakes down notorious highwayman Jack Sheppard, but the film never gets over the fact that some bright spark cast Tommy Steele in the lead. TJ

Where's Poppa?

(1970, US, 82 min)
d Carl Reiner. *p* Jerry Tokofsky, Marvin Worth. *sc* Robert Klane. *ph* Jack Priestley. *ed* Bud Molin, Chic Ciccolini. *ad* Warren Clymer. *m* Jack Elliott. *cast* George Segal, Ruth Gordon, Trish Van Devere, Ron Leibman, Rae Allen, Vincent Gardenia, Barnard Hughes, Rob Reiner.

● Scripted by Robert Klane from his own novel, this is the ultimate in Jewish Momma jokes, with a despairing Segal dressing up in a King Kong suit in hopes of scaring his obstructively senile parent to death, while she, indestructibly played by Ruth Gordon at her battiest, serenely continues turning his sex life into an everlasting coitus interruptus while herself bearing a charmed life. Meanwhile the plot is assaulted by a riot of topsy-turvy New York neuroses: a brother-in-law who insists on walking home through Central Park because he has a cosy arrangement with the muggers waiting there to attack him every night; a General who gets so carried away while being cross-examined about military codes of conduct that he launches into a Molly Bloom monologue about the orgiastic delights of killing goons; a cop who refuses to press charges after being raped while disguised as a policewoman, instead sending a bouquet of roses to his assailant. An irresistible black comedy, it's probably Reiner's best film, not least because it shows such affection for all its crazies. TM

Where the Boys Are

(1984, US, 94 min)
d Hy Averback. *p* Allan Carr. *sc* Stu Krieger, Jeff Burkhart. *ph* James A Contner. *ed* Melvin Shapiro, Bobbie Shapiro. *pd* Michael Baugh. *m* Sylvester LeVay. *cast* Lisa Hartman, Lorna Luft, Wendy Schaal, Lynn-Holly Johnson, Russell Todd, Howard McGillin.

● Social scientists might care to run this in comparison with the 1960 original (the one with the Connie Francis title song) to measure how much more mature teenagers are about bodily functions 24 years on: not very, but they've learned lots of new synonyms for 'urinate'. Four college girls descend on a Florida resort to get laid (1960: looking for romance). The first version played with moral dilemmas but reached only Bible-class conclusions. By '84 independent and liberated women can pay to see themselves represented as slutty, avaricious and brutal. ('Get undressed! When I buy a piece of meat I sure as hell want to see what's under the wrapper.') The next remake is presumably due around 2008. Can't wait? DO

Where the Buffalo Roam

(1980, US, 99 min)
d/p Art Linson. *sc* John Kaye. *ph* Tak Fujimoto. *ed* Chris Greenbury. *pd* Richard Sawyer. *m* Neil Young. *cast* Peter Boyle, Bill Murray, Bruno Kirby, René Auberjonois, RG Armstrong, Danny Goldman, Rafael Campos, Leonard Frey.

● The Drury Lane stage version of Hunter S Thompson's imaginary biog stank, but Linson's movie lists closer to the vicarious thrill of the loathsome baby's fictitious experiences. Bill Murray passes well as Thompson, although Peter Boyle's occasional appearances as his 600lb Samoan attorney can't help but upstage him. It's all here: the copious drink, the superhuman drug intake, and the wind-ups shot at whatever symbol of authority Thompson considers as fair game; but, as with his writing, the attacks always fall short of delivering the final payload. Laughs aplenty for people who use drugs as a pose, but most will be left wondering if half a pint of Bass doesn't qualify as a revolutionary action. JG

Where the Green Ants Dream (Wo die grünen Ameisen träumen)

(1984, WGer, 100 min)
d Werner Herzog. *p* Lucki Stipetic. *sc* Werner Herzog. *ph* Jörg Schmidt-Reitwein. *ed* Beate Mainka-Jellinghaus. *ad* Ulrich Bergfelder. *m*

Fauré, Wagner. *cast* Bruce Spence, Wandjuk Marika, Roy Marika, Ray Barrett, Norman Kaye, Colleen Clifford.
●A bunch of inscrutable Aboriginals occupy a patch of Australian desert, sitting down in the path of oil prospectors. Why these surly Abos? Why these belligerent Diggers? It's all because the land is a sacred burial site for mythical green ants – except that no such creatures figure in Aboriginal mythology, they're just bugs in Herzog's brain. That doesn't matter. We follow the protesting Aboriginals through a court case (the most laughable scene in this badly acted, sloppily directed movie), and back to their sit-down strike, still uncertain whether this is meant to be an adventure in anthropology, an exercise in environmental agit-prop, or just an excuse for Herzog to spend someone else's fortune laying classical music over shots of empty desert. MA

Where the Heart Is

(1990, US, 107 min)
d/p John Boorman. *sc* John Boorman, Telsche Boorman. *ph* Peter Suschitzky. *ed* Ian Crafford. *pd* Carol Spier. *m* Peter Martin. *cast* Dabney Coleman, Uma Thurman, Joanna Cassidy, Crispin Glover, Suzy Amis, Christopher Plummer, David Hewlett, Maury Chaykin.
●Boorman's ambitious and clearly allegorical black comedy explores (and exorcises?) a variety of problems facing modern youth: family tension, unemployment, ecology. To his wife's dismay, and in the hope that hardship fosters maturity, self-made demolition-tycoon Stewart McBain (Coleman) dumps their three spoiled, dreamy progeny – body-painter Chloe (Amis), computer fanatic Jimmy (Hewlett), and flaky no-hoper Daphne (Thurman) – in a derelict Brooklyn house. Inevitably, with a little help from their motley assortment of friends, the kids begin to make good, even as Dad's rugged individualism comes a cropper. While never less than a lively tribute to communal life, the script (by Boorman and his daughter Telsche) is sadly short of real focus and bite, and it's left to the director's keen visual sense, and fluent choreography of the ensemble scenes, to hold the interest. Moments of surrealism abound, but the actors are indulged, and the allusions to rain forests, conservation etc, are squeezed awkwardly into a farcical narrative, so that real issues are softened and sentimentalised. GA

Where the Heart Is

(2000, US, 120 min)
d Matt Williams. *p* Matt Williams, Susan Cartsonis, David McFadzean, Patricia Whitcher. *sc* Lowell Ganz, Babaloo Mandel. *ph* Richard Greatrex. *ed* Ian Crafford. *pd* Paul Peters. *m* Mason Daring. *cast* Natalie Portman, Ashley Judd, Stockard Channing, Joan Cusack, James Frain, Dylan Bruno, Keith David, Sally Field, Richard Jones.
●In which poor pregnant Tennessee teenager Novalee Nation (Portman) lands up alone in a car park in Sequoyah, Oklahoma, puts herself up in the local Wal-Mart and gives birth to a son she calls Americus. And in which the single mother and child find shelter with a kindly, kooky old couple, and befriend nurse Lexie Coop (Judd) and her ever growing brood. And … and … and. Adapted from Billie Letts' sudsy bestseller, this is a dementedly episodic, over-plotted story of secular faith, community and fortitude. Technically, it's terrible. Besides the dud storytelling, there's bad dialogue and wooden acting. It would be patronising too, but for the commitment of its leads – most impressively Portman, who brings a precocious moral conviction to the film's pappy wholesomeness. NB

Where the Money Is

(1999, Ger/US/GB, 88 min)
d Marek Kanievska. *p* Ridley Scott, Charles Weinstock, Chris Zarpas, Christopher Dorr. *sc* E Max Frye, Topper Lilien, Carroll Cartwright. *ph* Thomas Burstyn. *ed* Garth Craven, Samuel Craven, Dan Lebental. *pd* André Chamberland. *m* Mark Isham. *cast* Paul Newman, Linda Fiorentino, Dermot Mulroney, Susan Barnes, Anne Pitoniak, Bruce MacVittie, Irma St Paul.
●Paul Newman has nothing left to prove, so we can be thankful that he's still generous enough to turn it on for this modest caper movie. We first see him being wheeled into hospital, but nurse Fiorentino soon suspects there's more life behind the drooping mouth and empty eyes than the medical report suggests. When she eventually gets him to drop his guard, he shares the secret that he's a veteran thief who's tricked his way out of jail by feigning a stroke. He's waiting to collect on a stash, but not before putting naughty ideas in Fiorentino's head. While there's just about enough plot to be getting on with, most of the pleasure in the film is simply watching Newman get on with it, sparking dialogue off Fiorentino, playing gruff and grizzled with the driest sense of humour. He's so comfortable on screen you never catch him acting, and it's a bespoke role. Thankfully, Fiorentino has enough presence to go a few rounds with him. TJ

Where the Red Fern Grows

(1974, US, 97 min)
d Norman Tokar. *p* Lyman D Dayton. *sc* Douglas C Stewart, Eleanor Lamb. *ph* Dean Cundey. *ed* Bob Bring. *ad* Michael D Devine. *m* Lex De Azevdo. *cast* James Whitmore, Beverly Garland, Jack Ging, Lonny Chapman, Stewart Peterson.
●Depression? What Depression? It may be 1930s Oklahoma, but a 12-year-old boy (Peterson) can still hoard $50 to buy himself a pair of raccoon hounds and start adventuring towards manhood. A syrupy kids' yarn from former Disney animal-movie specialist Tokar, backed by appropriate soundtrack odes from the Osmonds and Andy Williams. PT

Where There's a Will

see Good Morning, Boys!

Where the River Bends

see Bend of the River

Where the Rose Wilted (Gülün Bittigi Yer)

(1999, Tur, 95 min)
d Ismail Günes. *cast* Cüneyt Arkın, Tolga Tibet, Yagmur Kasifoglu.
●A depressed exposé of Turkish torture practices, this has righteous conviction to spare; also a few cinematic ideas, but none terribly dramatic. It opens and closes with the same tracking shot past fragments of standard small town street life, and the casual family and official curses and abuse that, it suggests, breeds the monstrous institutional violence that has destroyed its young protagonist. He sits in a train carriage, unshaven and scarred by the memories of official interrogation now triggered by every passing sight or sound. Opposite him sits a solicitous elderly public prosecutor who wants to connect; ditto his faithfully waiting wife at home. Most of the tale's in the editing, which is awkward – though at least once you pick up on its strategy, nothing much changes. NB

Where Were You When the Lights Went Out?

(1968, US, 94 min)
d Hy Averback. *p* Everett Freeman, Martin Melcher. *sc* Everett Freeman, Karl Tunberg. *ph* Ellsworth J Fredricks. *ed* Rita Roland. *ad* George W Davis, Urie McCleary. *m* David Grusin. *cast* Doris Day, Robert Morse, Patrick O'Neal, Terry-Thomas, Lola Albright, Steve Allen, Jim Backus, Ben Blue, Robert Emhardt.
●A sprightly comedy, set during the great American East Coast power failure of 1965, which mercifully doesn't get all sniggery about the aftermath of the unexpected blackout (an unprecedented rise in the birthdate nine months later). Instead, it has Doris Day, gently satirising her own image, playing an actress tired of being known as 'The Constant Virgin', especially after catching her husband (O'Neal) almost in the act with a voluptuous journalist (Albright) sent to interview her. She runs off to sulk, a young business executive (Morse) runs off with his company's funds, the lights go out, and a perfectly logical series of circumstances finds the pair in bed together, happily unaware of each other's existence, when O'Neal arrives on the scene. A brilliantly funny sequence ensues as the enraged O'Neal threatens to run riot with a gun, but all the dazed 'guilty couple' want (since both are heavily sedated) is to be allowed to go back to bed. Not all of the film is as good, but the performances are superb (Morse, O'Neal and Albright, especially), and Averback's comic timing is spot on. TM

Which Way to the Front? (aka Ja, Ja, Mein General! But Which Way to the Front?)

(1970, US, 96 min)
d/p Jerry Lewis. *sc* Gerald Gardner, Dee Caruso. *ph* W Wallace Kelley. *ed* Russell Wiles. *ad* John Beckman. *m* Louis Brown. *cast* Jerry Lewis, Jan Murray, Willie Davis, John Wood, Kaye Ballard, Steve Franken, Dack Rambo, Robert Middleton.
●Perhaps not classic Lewis (his directorial invention flagging a bit, even if his gibbering performance genius remains intact), but audaciously anachronistic enough in its retread of the Nazi impersonation schtick to bring tears to the eyes. A World War II draft reject, Lewis' millionaire sets up his own private army to help out the Allies in Italy, producing an outrageous inversion of *The Dirty Dozen*. PT

Whiffs (aka C.A.S.H.)

(1975, US, 92 min)
d Ted Post. *p* George Barrie. *sc* Malcolm Marmorstein. *ph* David M Walsh. *ed* Robert Lawrence. *ad* Fernando Carrere. *m* John Cameron. *cast* Elliott Gould, Eddie Albert, Harry Guardino, Godfrey Cambridge, Jennifer O'Neill.
●Gould is discharged from the US Army on grounds of medical disability after years of being a guinea pig for the Medical Corps. Embittered, he takes revenge by putting the gases he knows and loves so well to use in a series of robberies. 'C.A.S.H.' (Chemical Air-Spray Holdup) is a perfect example of a film constructed around an idea that must have seemed funny to someone once.

While Parents Sleep

(1935, GB, 72 min, b/w)
d Adrian Brunel. *p* Paul Soskin. *sc* Edwin Greenwood, John Paddy Carstairs, Jack Marks. *ph* Ernest Palmer. *ed* Michael Hankinson. *ad* LP Williams. *m* Percival Mackey. *cast* Jean Gillie, Enid Stamp-Taylor, Mackenzie Ward, Romilly Lunge, Athole Stewart, Davy Burnaby.
●Brunel was the great might-have-been of British cinema. Tactless, radical, idiosyncratic, he was allowed frustratingly few outlets for his talents. His most prolific period was the mid '30s, when his sheer efficiency ensured him regular work making ultra-cheap 'quota quickies'. Thematic consistency is hardly likely where the sole consideration is cost, but Brunel's effectiveness as a stylist is remarkable. Here, with a stage play script, a couple of tatty sets, and a bunch of unknown actors, he produces a witty, sharply paced, economical essay on class and manners in inter-war Britain. It's ironic that while Brunel was energetically devoting his talents to programme fillers, the moguls of film production were bent on importing American and continental directors for their disastrously expensive 'prestige' productions. RMy

While the City Sleeps

(1956, US, 100 min, b/w)
d Fritz Lang. *p* Bert Friedlob. *sc* Casey Robinson. *ph* Ernest Laszlo. *ed* Gene Fowler Jr. *ad* Carroll Clark. *m* Herschel Burke Gilbert. *cast* Dana Andrews, Ida Lupino, Rhonda Fleming, George Sanders, Howard Duff, Thomas Mitchell, Vincent Price, Sally Forrest, John Barrymore Jr, James Craig, Robert Warwick.
●A group of newsmen hunt for a sex murderer. Their motive is greed; the prize is control of a newspaper. 'Noble' Dana Andrews initially refuses to participate, but finally offers his fiancée (Forrest) as bait for the killer (Barrymore) who, naturally, is the film's most sympathetic character. Lang makes inspired use of glass-walled offices, where all is seen and nothing revealed, and traces explicit parallels between Andrews and the murderer. Lang's most underrated movie. SJ

While You Were Sleeping

(1995, US, 103 min)
d Jim Turteltaub. *p* Joe Roth, Roger Birnbaum. *sc* Daniel G Sullivan, Fredric Lebow. *ph* Phedon Papamichael. *ed* Bruce Green. *pd* Garreth Stover. *m* Randy Edelman. *cast* Sandra Bullock, Bill Pullman, Peter Gallagher, Peter Boyle, Jack Warden, Glynis Johns, Micole Mercurio, Jason Bernard.
●Disney's fairytale romance is as cute and cuddly a bedtime story as anyone could wish for. Bullock stars as Lucy Moderatz, who sells tick-

ets for the Chicago el-train. Lonesome Lucy has the hots for Peter (Gallagher): tall, dark, handsome – and he doesn't even know she's alive. Then, one day before Christmas, Peter collapses in a coma and Lucy pulls him from the tracks. After a mix-up at the hospital, she's introduced as Peter's fiancée and embraced to the bosom of his eccentric family (father Boyle, mother Johns, godfather Warden). Only brother Jack (Pullman) harbours any doubts – doubts Lucy is too ashamed to confirm. If *Sleepless in Seattle* was designer romance, *While You Were Sleeping* is comfortable fit: loose-knit sweaters, lumberjack shirts, blue jeans and Timberland boots. It's the difference between uptown Manhattan and blue-collar Chicago. There are no hip riffs on 'movie love' here, it's all the real McCoy. If there's a problem with the film, it's that this emphasis on authenticity is essentially just another style option, one that sits oddly with such an outrageously unlikely scenario. It's a mark of Bullock's radiant star quality that we're rooting for Lucy from the start. The movie coasts home on her charm. TCh

Whip Hand, The

(1951, US, 82 min, b/w)
d William Cameron Menzies. *p* Lewis J Rachmil. *sc* George Bricker, Frank L Moss. *ph* Nick Musuraca. *ed* Robert Golden. *pd* William Cameron Menzies. *m* Paul Sawtell. *cast* Elliott Reid, Carla Balenda, Raymond Burr, Edgar Barrier, Lurene Tuttle.

●Cut from Kremlin top brass scrutinising a wall-map of America to a holidaying reporter stumbling across an unfriendly US small town where all the fish have died and Raymond Burr eavesdrops on all outgoing phone calls. *The Whip Hand* progresses into such clinically clear-cut Cold War paranoia that it can hardly get through its multiple process shots quickly enough to warn that the resident Red scientists and fellow-travellers are all (gasp!) ex-Nazis; and inevitably about to destroy civilisation as we know it, unless...The delicious, delirious whirlwind of a plot affords sufficient uniquely '50s black'n'white fun to make recognition of the auteurist hand of William Cameron Menzies a decided bonus. Here Hollywood's most versatile art director/production designer (and inadequately-credited mastermind behind *Gone With the Wind*) manages (as director) a Hitchcockian playfulness with back-projection and wooden actors, even with the budget tying one hand behind his back. The tacky essence of B+. PT

Whipped

(2000, US, 82 min)
d/p/sc Peter M Cohen. *ph* Peter B Kowalski. *ed* Tom McArdle. *pd* Katherine M Szilagyi. *m* Michael Montes. *cast* Amanda Peet, Brian Van Holt, Jonathan Abrahams, Zorie Barber, Judah Domke, Callie Thorne.

●This dire sex comedy stakes out territory somewhere between *Swingers* and *American Pie*. Guys sit around trading descriptions of how last night's date, quote, 'cleaned my tailpipe' and how they wanked themselves off. Brad (Holt) is a smarmy Wall Street operator whose favourite scam is to approach a woman and pretend they have a mutual friend. Zeke (Barber) is an aspiring screenwriter with an outsize ego; Jonathan (Abrahams) the weirdo who's scared of meaningless sex. Then there's Eric (Domke), their married ex-pal, who hangs around for vicarious kicks and drinks grapefruit juice to improve the taste of his sperm. 'There is a bit of me in all these characters, all my friends are like this,' the writer/director declares. The guys get their comeuppance – sort of – when they all fall in love with Mia (Peet), a character every bit as unconscionable as they are. TCh

Whirlpool

(1950, US, 97 min, b/w)
d/p Otto Preminger. *sc* Ben Hecht ['Lester Barstow' on GB release prints], Andrew Solt. *ph* Arthur Miller. *ed* Louis Loeffler. *ad* Lyle Wheeler, Leland Fuller. *m* David Raksin. *cast* Gene Tierney, Richard Conte, José Ferrer, Charles Bickford, Barbara O'Neil, Eduard Franz, Fortunio Bonanova, Constance Collier.

●The same themes and the same cool style as in *Laura* and *Angel Face* are at work in this portrait of the wealthy and sophisticated cracking apart at the seams, under pressure from psychological hang-ups, repressed passion, and innocent gullibility. When rich kleptomaniac Tierney turns for help not to her psychoanalyst husband (Conte) but to a hard-hearted hypnotherapist (Ferrer), she finds herself bereft of memory and implicated in a murder. Preminger translates the rather daft story (scripted by a pseudonymous Ben Hecht, loosely adapting Guy Endore's novel *Methinks the Lady*) into a typically unhysterical and lucid examination of people under stress: as the crime is investigated, currents of distrust, fear, and falsehood disturb the smooth waters of an apparently happy marriage. Content to observe rather than moralise, he creates a world of sympathetically flawed characters, the magnificent exception being the swindling quack, a manipulating charmer whose underplaying by Ferrer suggests credible evil. With its *noir* themes played out in cold, bright interiors, it's a fine example of the way Preminger, on occasion, managed to deflect routine melodrama into something more personal and profound. GA

Whirlpool of Fate, The

see Fille de l'Eau, La

Whisky Galore! (aka Tight Little Island)

(1949, GB, 82 min, b/w)
d Alexander Mackendrick. *p* Michael Balcon. *sc* Compton Mackenzie, Angus MacPhail. *ph* Gerald Gibbs. *ed* Joseph Sterling. *ad* Jim Morahan. *m* Ernest Irving. *cast* Basil Radford, Joan Greenwood, Jean Cadell, Gordon Jackson, James Robertson Justice, Wylie Watson, John Gregson, Duncan Macrae, Catherine Lacey.

●Classic Ealing comedy about the no-holds-barred battle waged by a Hebridean island community, parched by wartime shortages, determined to put a shipwrecked cargo of whisky to proper use before officialdom can lay claim to it. Reminiscent of *Passport to Pimlico* in its amiable puncturing of bureaucracy, but a good deal sharper as a parable of colonialism, with the Scots contriving a humiliating double-edged comeuppance for their English laird and master (Radford). Delightful characterisations, lovely locations on the island of Barra. TM

Whisperers, The

(1966, GB, 106 min, b/w)
d Bryan Forbes. *p* Michael Laughlin, Ronald Shedlo. *sc* Bryan Forbes. *ph* Gerry Turpin. *ed* Anthony Harvey. *ad* Ray Simm. *m* John Barry. *cast* Edith Evans, Eric Portman, Avis Bunnage, Nanette Newman, Gerald Sim, Ronald Fraser, Leonard Rossiter, Kenneth Griffith.

●Forbes' ambitious but finally unsuccessful adaptation of Robert Nicolson's novel about an old working class woman, abandoned in her impoverished flat, who retreats into paranoid delusions of faded grandeur. Dame Edith Evans gives a spirited performance in the central role, but Forbes' direction is typically over-emphatic and obvious, underlining the social conscience of the film ad nauseam, and even putting its message into the mouth of a social worker (who asks a psychiatrist if the old lady wasn't happier with her illusions than with society's attempts to cure them). Forbes' daughter Sarah appears as the old lady when she was a child. DP

Whispering Corridors (Yeogo Goedam)

(1998, SKor, 110 min)
d Park Ki-Hyung. *p* Lee Chun-Yun. *sc* In Jung-Ok, Park Ki-Hyung. *ph* Suh Jung-Min. *ed* Ham Sung-Won. *ad* Kang Chang-Kil. *m* Moon Seung-Hyun, Park Jung-Ho. *cast* Lee Mi-Yeon, Park Yong-Su, Kim Kyu-Li, Choi Sae-Yun, Park Jin-Hee.

●The highest grossing Korean film of its year, a gory supernatural thriller set in a high school for girls. Teachers who have maltreated pupils meet grisly deaths one by one; eventually pupil-turned-teacher Eun-Young (Lee Mi-Yeon, from *Motel Cactus*) consults the old yearbooks and realises that the vengeful ghost of a suicide is regularly re-manifesting herself. *Carrie*-like menstruation metaphors count for less than the underlying critique of the Korean education system, which is what made the film such a hot item on domestic release. As Park's debut feature (after the excellent short *Great Pretenders*), it's a little disappointing that so much of it is so generic. But it has enough flair to suggest interesting work ahead. TR

Whistle Blower, The

(1986, GB, 104 min)
d Simon Langton. *p* Geoffrey Reeve. *sc* Julian Bond. *ph* Fred Tammes. *ed* Robert Morgan. *pd* Morley Smith. *m* John Scott. *cast* Michael Caine, James Fox, Nigel Havers, John Gielgud, Felicity Dean, Barry Foster, Gordon Jackson.

●We've been here before. Bob Jones (Havers) is a translator in the Russian section at GCHQ. Following the trial of an employee, convicted of spying for the Eastern bloc, all personnel are requested to report any inconsistencies in the behaviour of their colleagues, and Bob becomes convinced that British intelligence is no better than the KGB. Meanwhile the CIA, worried about the apparent lack of security in England, begins to act with extreme prejudice. When Bob is bumped off, his father enters the fray to see that justice is done. In this role, Caine glides imperiously along, allowing none of the surrounding dross to tarnish his image. The rest of the cast do not come out of it so well. There are a couple of surprises, and the cynicism prevents the film from becoming overtly old-fashioned, but in general it is dreadful. The locations – Gloucester Cathedral, tourist Cheltenham, the Remembrance Day service at the Cenotaph – are stagy, the pace is slack, and the script pretentious. MS

Whistle Down the Wind

(1961, GB, 99 min, b/w)
d Bryan Forbes. *p* Richard Attenborough. *sc* Keith Waterhouse, Willis Hall. *ph* Arthur Ibbetson. *ed* Max Benedict. *ad* Ray Simm. *m* Malcolm Arnold. *cast* Hayley Mills, Alan Bates, Bernard Lee, Norman Bird, Elsie Wagstaffe, Alan Barnes.

●Forbes' first film, a reef-ridden whimsy about three Lancashire farm kids who find a fugitive murderer (Bates) hiding in the barn and think he is Jesus. Done with a kind of grubby lyricism borrowed from *Jeux Interdits*, the early scenes are quite effective as the children matter-of-factly wonder how to react (should they curtsey, steal the family bottle of port?). But as the parable (and the parallels) extend towards a scene in which the killer is apprehended and adopts the posture of crucifixion as he is searched, it all becomes more than faintly embarrassing. TM

White Angel

(1993, GB, 96 min)
d Chris Jones. *p* Genevieve Jolliffe. *sc* Chris Jones, Genevieve Jolliffe. *ph* Jon Walker. *ed* John Holland. *ad* Kay Minter. *m* Harry Gregson-Williams. *cast* Harriet Robinson, Peter Firth, Don Henderson, Anne Catherine Arton, Harry Miller, Joe Collins.

●A 'thriller' which purports to examine the psychology of the banal 'blend-into-the-crowd' type that supposedly characterises the British serial killer. Leslie (Firth), a dentist transvestite and slayer of women-in-white, is, however, a signposted oddball: note his string singlets and see-through polyester shirts. He answers an ad placed by American crime writer Ellen (Robinson) and takes a room in her north London house. Ellen's no angel herself. Leslie seems to have twigged that she has, in fact, murdered her missing husband and presumes a bond of complicity between them – but the net is closing. This plays like a kitchen-sink horror movie, much of the action confined to the semi, all cramped camera angles and ill-lit close-ups, and more sofa fabric than a furniture ad. Hard to take seriously. WH

White Balloon, The (Badkonak-E Sefid)

(1995, Iran, 84 min)
d Jafar Panahi. *p* Kurosh Mozkouri. *sc* Abbas Kiarostami. *ph* Fardaz Jowdat. *ed/pd* Jafar Panahi. *cast* Aïda Mohammadkhani, Mohsen Kafili, Fereshteh Sadr Orfani, Anna Bourkowska, Mohammad Shahani.

●This extraordinary debut feature, about a 7-year-old's first journey alone into the streets of Tehran, is a movie of audacious subtlety and simplicity, and a deserving Cannes prize-winner. It takes place in 'real time', the 84 minutes leading to New Year (March 21), as little Razieh (Aïda Mohammadkhani) goes off to purchase, with her mother's last 500 *toman*, the 'chubby' gold-fish that has taken her fancy. Along the way, she encounters snake-charmers, irate shopkeepers, a country-born soldier, a young

Afghan boy with a white balloon – a whole world hitherto 'forbidden'. Scripted in collaboration with leading Iranian director Abbas Kiarostami, this is a film of small incident, minute, telling observations, and enormous heart and intelligence. Tethering the movie to the child's point of view (both literal and metaphorical), Panahi absorbs us so entirely into his heroine's delicate, enquiring world, that the loss of her money and her separation from her brother create an atmosphere of suspense as gripping as that of any Hitchcock thriller. Moreover, suggestive intimations of the troubled adult world – the mother's anxiety in the bazaar, the lonely 'outsiders' – combine to produce a feeling of almost metaphysical tension. WH

White Buffalo, The

(1977, US, 97 min)
d J Lee Thompson. *p* Pancho Kohner. *sc* Richard Sale. *ph* Paul Lohmann. *ed* Michael F Anderson. *pd* Tambi Larsen. *m* John Barry. *cast* Charles Bronson, Jack Warden, Will Sampson, Kim Novak, Clint Walker, Stuart Whitman, Slim Pickens, John Carradine, Ed Lauter.

●Bronson plays Wild Bill Hickok, whose nemesis is the giant white buffalo of the title which haunts his nightmares. But the major struggle in the film is over whether it is a 'big' or 'small' picture. Biggest are: the buffalo, another Dino (*King Kong*) De Laurentiis presentation; the cast of mainly fading stars featured in cameo roles; and the self-consciously epic character names like Hickok, Crazy Horse and Custer. All of which suggests a thunderously empty yarn mounted around yet another mechanical gimmick. Yet Richard Sale's adaptation of his own novel hints at something more intimate. His Hickok is haunted, ageing, and diseased, trapped and uncertain in his own myth. Because of this, the movie occasionally takes an interesting turn, but less often than it should, because J Lee Thompson's direction clings to the increasing number of action set pieces with all the relief of a drowning man clutching a life raft. CPe

White Bus, The

(1967, GB, 41 min, b/w & col)
d/p Lindsay Anderson. *sc* Shelagh Delaney. *ph* Miroslav Ondricek. *ed* Kevin Brownlow. *ad* David Marshall. *m* Misha Donat. *cast* Patricia Healey, Arthur Lowe, John Sharp, Julie Perry, Anthony Hopkins, Fanny Carby, Stephen Moore.

●Originally designed to be part of a feature called *Red, White and Zero*, a planned reunion of three 'Free Cinema' directors. When Karel Reisz' *Morgan, A Suitable Case for Treatment* turned into a feature, Lindsay Anderson and Tony Richardson were joined by Peter Brook, but their three contributions were never released together, and only Anderson's has stood the test of time. Shelagh Delaney's script takes an impassive young girl (Healey) out of her suicidal London office back to her Northern home town, which she views as part of a bizarre bus tour. The film looks forward to Anderson's blurring of the fantastic and the naturalistic in *If*..., and benefits from the poetic eye of the same Czech cameraman, Miroslav Ondricek. Fitting no conventional genre, the offbeat humour often hits the mark as a non-specific satire on British moribundity. DT

White Dawn, The

(1974, US, 110 min)
d Philip Kaufman. *p* Martin Ransohoff. *sc* James Houston, Tom Rickman. *ph* Michael Chapman. *ed* Douglas Stewart. *m* Henry Mancini. *cast* Warren Oates, Timothy Bottoms, Lou Gossett, Simonie Kopapik, Joanasie Salomonie, Pilitak.

●A surprisingly hypnotic B feature based on a true story that took place in the Canadian Arctic around 1900. Three sailors (Oates, Bottoms and Gossett), marooned on the ice cap, are taken in by a tribe of nomadic Eskimos. At a lyrically measured pace, the film unfolds how the three cultural aliens, ironically mistaken as 'dog children' by their protectors, variously adapt to and influence their new way of life. Bottoms, with misty-eyed reverence, drinks it up like a fish (the occasional moments of cloying sentiment are carefully structured around his character), while Gossett enjoys himself from the sidelines. A splendidly cantankerous Oates grudgingly accepts the help, and as his sole contribution to cultural exchange, initiates the Eskimos into alcohol. Most successful, however, is the presentation of the natural rhythms of the Eskimo life cycle, from religious rituals to hunting practices and recreation pursuits. The Baffin Island location, resonantly photographed, is in constant evidence, underlining its key position in the overall pattern. Even Henry 'Moon River' Mancini has come up trumps with a delicately pitched score. A treat. IB

White Dog

(1981, US, 90 min)
d Samuel Fuller. *p* Jon Davison. *sc* Samuel Fuller, Curtis Hanson. *ph* Bruce Surtees. *ed* Bernard Gribble. *pd* Brian Eatwell. *m* Ennio Morricone. *cast* Kristy McNichol, Paul Winfield, Burl Ives, Jameson Parker, Lynne Moody, Marshall Thompson, Christa Lang, Samuel Fuller, Paul Bartel, Dick Miller.

●From the opening shot of a white flashlight piercing a black screen, Fuller's film is a model of intelligent simplicity. McNichol runs over a beautiful white Alsatian, takes it home to care for it, and discovers that the beast has been conditioned as a 'white dog' which attacks any black that it encounters. Rather than destroy it, she takes it to a black animal trainer (Winfield) to try to de-condition it…Just one of the many remarkable things about Fuller's impeccable treatment of racism is that it investigates that vile trait without showing a racist character; the dog is a perfect symbol for the confused and vicious conditioning that runs riot throughout the human world. Fuller has never heeded the false optimism of liberal creeds, and is well aware that there are no easy solutions to the problem; as the film's ending possibly suggests, you might just eradicate racism, but you'll never be rid of hatred. With Bruce Surtees' uncluttered camerawork, a superb score from Ennio Morricone, and fine acting throughout, this is one film of Fuller's which is most complex in its emotional sway: compassionate towards both animal and humans in the error of their ways, but fuelled by a seething anger. There is certainly no finer film on its subject. GA/CPea

White Fang (Zanna Bianca)

(1974, It/Sp/Fr, 101 min)
d Lucio Fulci. *p* Henry Alan Towers. *sc* Roberto Gianviti, Piero Regnoli, Harry Alan Towers, Guy Elmes, Thom Keyes, Guillaume Roux. *ph* Pablo Ripoli. *ed* Ornella Micheli. *ad* Emilio Ruitz. *m* Carlo Rustichelli. *cast* Franco Nero, Virna Lisi, Fernando Rey, Missaele, John Steiner.

●An unambitious, comic strip adaptation of Jack London's superb novel that nevertheless manages to capture something of the essence of London's world – the purity of the struggle with (not against) nature in the icy wastes, the corruption of the money-grabbing mining towns. One gets only glimpses of the original's intrepid reporter in Nero's performance, although Fernando Rey carries some resonance as the drink-sodden priest. The Indian child is suitably unwinsome, and the hound most mercifully un-Lassie-like. The overall feeling of the romance of the wilds survives the picture-book interpretation, making the film one any kid with an ounce of imagination should enjoy. VG

White Fang

(1990, US, 109 min)
d Randal Kleiser. *p* Marykay Powell. *sc* Jeanne Rosenberg, Nick Thiel, David Fallon. *ph* Tony Pierce-Roberts. *ed* Lisa Day. *pd* Michael Bolton. *m* Basil Poledouris. *cast* Klaus Maria Brandauer, Ethan Hawke, Seymour Cassel, Susan Hogan, James Remar, Bill Moseley.

●This Disney version of Jack London's tale is run-of-the-mill stuff, offering spectacular icy locations set to a soapy orchestral score. Young Jack Conroy (Hawke) arrives in Alaska during the turn-of-the-century gold rush, determined to find his recently deceased father's claim. He enlists the aid of prospectors Alex (Brandauer) and Skunker (Cassel), and along the way develops a bond with White Fang, half-wolf and half-dog. The film charts their relationship, with White Fang at one point languishing in the hands of money-grubbing villain Beauty Smith (Remar) before Jack can stage a dramatic rescue. Despite moments of bravura and shameless tugs at the heart-strings, the film simply meanders towards a resolution. What's Brandauer doing here? CM

White Feather

(1955, US, 102 min)
d Robert Webb. *p* Robert L Jacks. *sc* Delmer Daves, Leo Townsend. *ph* Lucien Ballard. *ed* George A Gittens. *ad* Jack Martin Smith. *m* Hugo Friedhofer. *cast* Robert Wagner, John Lund, Debra Paget, Jeffrey Hunter, Noah Beery Jr, Hugh O'Brian, Eduard Franz.

●Can it be possible? Co-scripted by Delmer Daves five years after his *Broken Arrow*, another white man (Wagner) strives for peace with Jeffrey Hunter and the Indians, and falls in love with a squaw (Paget again). If you can withstand the feelings of *déjà vu* from the descendants of *Broken Arrow*, this is, in all fairness, a cut above its relatives. It looks convincing (it's based on fact – the defeat of the last of the Cheyenne warriors in 1877), the Indians are portrayed as human beings and not pantomime characters, and an exciting climax is well handled. DMcG

White Heat

(1949, US, 114 min, b/w)
d Raoul Walsh. *p* Louis Edelman. *sc* Ivan Goff, Ben Roberts. *ph* Sid Hickox. *ed* Owen Marks. *ad* Edward Carrere. *m* Max Steiner. *cast* James Cagney, Virginia Mayo, Edmond O'Brien, Margaret Wycherly, Steve Cochran, John Archer, Paul Guilfoyle, Fred Clark.

● *White Heat = Scarface + Psycho*. Cagney sits in his mother's lap as they plan their heists together with plans provided by classical mythology. In the prison canteen, they tell him she's dead, and he lurches, whimpers, and punches everybody in his way. Finally cornered by the cops on top of an oil refinery, he yells 'Made it Ma, to the top of the world, Ma!' and empties his gun into the gas tank to join her in gangster heaven. Despite chronology (deranged by the censor's influence on the studios), this is really the fitting climax of the '30s gangster movie. PH

White Hell of Piz Palu, The (Die Weisse Hölle vom Piz Palu)

(1929, Ger, 133 min for 1998 restoration, 83 min for 1930 GB/US sound version, b/w)
d Arnold Fanck, GW Pabst. *p* HR Sokal. *sc* Ladislaus Vajda, Arnold Fanck. *ph* Sepp Allgeier, Richard Angst, Hans Schneeberger. *ed* Arnold Fanck. *ad* Ernö Metzner. *m* Ashley Irwin (1998), Heinz Roemheld (1930). *cast* Gustav Diessl, Leni Riefenstahl, Ernst Petersen, Mizzi Götzel, Ernst Udet, Otto Spring.

●The title of this late silent mountain picture refers to a sequence in which a party of rescuers brandishing flares enter a crevasse to retrieve the bodies of some students caught in an avalanche. The imagery is indeed hellish, the scene itself the only one to suggest that Fanck and Pabst might genuinely have collaborated. For the rest, a lengthy passage in which a grim, grief-stricken Diessl shares a mountain hut with a sexy couple (Riefenstahl and Petersen) is echt-Pabst, while Fanck's trademarks – distant figures traversing fantastic ice-scapes, the theme of endurance in the face of hostile Nature – are overwhelmingly present. The plot is rudimentary, with WWI ace Ernst Udet, as himself, flying in to round things up. Altogether a curious example of bifurcated auteur syndrome. BBa

White Hunter, Black Heart

(1990, US, 112 min)
d/p Clint Eastwood. *sc* James Bridges, Peter Viertel, Burt Kennedy. *ph* Jack N Green. *ed* Joel Cox. *pd* John Graysmark. *m* Lennie Niehaus. *cast* Clint Eastwood, Jeff Fahey, George Dzundza, Alun Armstrong, Mel Martin, Marisa Berenson, Charlotte Cornwell, Timothy Spall, Boy Mathias Chuma.

●In this adaptation by Peter Viertel from his thinly fictionalised account of John Huston's arrogant antics immediately prior to filming *The African Queen*, Eastwood – directing himself as Huston/'Wilson' – proffers a supremely intelligent study of a man of monstrous selfishness and often irresistible charm, whose overwhelming passion for hunting drives him inexorably toward what even he acknowledges as an irredeemable sin: killing an elephant. Friendship, the film, and ordinary ethics are sacrificed on the altar of his ego. Wisely, however, Eastwood doesn't preach or condemn, but simply reveals the man's magnetism while admitting to the terrible consequences of his ambition. After a comparatively stodgy opening in London, the film shifts to Africa, and at once settles into a tone of semi-comic high adventure which never allows the serious themes – wanton ecological destruction, colonial racism, and the necessity of remaining true to oneself – to lapse into portentousness. Ably aided by a fine cast and Jack Green's no-nonsense photography, Eastwood constructs a marvellously pacy, suspenseful movie which is deceptively easy on both eye and ear. GA

White Lies (Mentiras piadosas)

(1988, Mex, 100 min)
d Arturo Ripstein. *sc* Paz Alicio Garciadiego. *ph* Angel Goded. *ed* Carlos Puente. *m* Luis Alvarez. *cast* Alonso Echanove, Delia Casanova, Ernesto Yanez, Luisa Hertas, Fernando Palavicini.

● Virtually from the opening shots, when the stall-holder Israel's magical music-box plays 'Love is a Many Splendoured Thing', we know that this is a film more about love than lies. And, since love means dreams, Israel's fantasies take off in the direction of his Phenomenal Museum, north of the Mexican border, which is intended to house a mechanical light-and-music show that Israel has built with his gay friend Matilde. The stars of the show are a collection of fine porcelain dolls, which are forsaken as Israel finds himself falling for Clara, the municipal inspector who threatens to close his market stall. To her he shows a side of life he dare not show his wife: his love of astrology, necromancy and clairvoyance. In so doing, he puts the knowledge of her fate into Clara's hands…Alongside the sadness and inadequacies of the ordinary lives it describes, this is a rich and witty film that prises open the little secrets of the human condition. AH

White Lightning

(1973, US, 101 min)
d Joseph Sargent. *p* Arthur Gardner, Jules V Levy. *sc* William Norton. *ph* Edward Rosson. *ed* George Jay Nicholson. *m* Charles Bernstein. *cast* Burt Reynolds, Jennifer Billingsley, Ned Beatty, Bo Hopkins, Matt Clark, Louise Latham, Diane Ladd, RG Armstrong.

● An example of what can go wrong with a movie. Ned Beatty as the corrupt Southern sheriff who drowns two long-hairs in a backwater; the down-home photography; the minor characters who bootleg whisky – they all make it look as if the film has something to say. But with Burt Reynolds, playing it light though all out for revenge as the brother of one of the dead boys, everything becomes one long car chase, and in the end it's just a matter of the fat bald bully getting his comeuppance at the hands of the not-so-fat toupeed hero. Reynolds returned to the character in *Gator* three years later. CPe

White Line Fever

(1975, US, 92 min)
d Jonathan Kaplan. *p* John Kemeny. *sc* Ken Friedman, Jonathan Kaplan. *ph* Fred J Koenekamp. *ed* O Nicholas Brown. *ad* Sydney Z Litwack. *m* David Nichtern. *cast* Jan-Michael Vincent, Kay Lenz, Slim Pickens, LQ Jones, Leigh French, Don Porter, Sam Laws, RG Armstrong, Dick Miller.

● 'You're a very charismatic man, Mr Hummer' says the smooth, evil corporation magnate (thereby pointing out something that hadn't hitherto been in evidence) to the young truck-driver who has taken a single-handed stand in refusing to carry stolen goods in his rig. Indeed, Jan-Michael Vincent looks decidedly puny trying to fill a part that would have given Eastwood trouble. This 'youth' movie, in which the lithe Vincent takes on the ageing, paunchy and corrupt – and wins, despite some heavy muscle from the organisation – gives evidence of little more than the recurring need to re-adapt various fantasies from Westerns. But as Vincent takes his stand and cleans up town, he joins a long line of American heroes whose capacity for punishment borders on masochism. There's also some particularly gratuitous agonising over the question of abortion, which is promptly resolved by having the mother-to-be beaten up and losing the child. CPe

White Man's Burden

(1995, US/Fr, 89 min)
d Desmond Nakano. *p* Lawrence Bender. *sc* Desmond Nakano. *ph* Willy Kurant. *ed* Nancy Richardson. *pd* Naomi Shohan. *m* Howard Shore. *cast* John Travolta, Harry Belafonte, Kelly Lynch, Margaret Avery, Tom Bower, Andrew Lawrence, Bumper Robinson.

● An off-the-peg crime thriller with a reversible lining, screenwriter Nakano's first film as an indie hyphenate relies for effect on a crude racial twist meant to 'jar viewers out of their polarised complacency'. Sadly, his portrait of a contemporary American society in which the polarities of race and power are merely turned around – rich black boss, put-upon white worker – is so obvious and reductive as to be pointless. Given this, it's hard to imagine how his facile 'What if?' scenario could have lured elder statesman Belafonte out of retirement and attracted the attention of Travolta. Sacked from his job over a simple misunderstanding, Louis Pinnock (loyal working stiff) seeks justice from Thomas (suave, complacent factory owner), but never gets past the security gates of his suburban mansion; later, when he and his family are evicted from their home, Pinnock abducts Thomas at gun-point, and goes on the run. Since it's clear where the film's headed, the fitful plot is forced to tread a fine line between fatalistic inevitability and tedious predictability. NF

White Men Can't Jump

(1992, US, 114 min)
d Ron Shelton. *p* David V Lester, Don Miller. *sc* Ron Shelton. *ph* Russell Boyd. *ed* Paul Seydor. *pd* Dennis Washington. *m* Bennie Wallace. *cast* Wesley Snipes, Woody Harrelson, Rosie Perez, Tyra Ferrell, Cylk Cozart, Kadeem Hardison, Ernest Harden Jr.

● America's homeboy comedy of the year is about basketball only in the sense that writer-director Shelton's *Bull Durham* was about baseball. It's a truly terrific piece of entertainment propelled by the magic and dynamism of its stars. Sidney Deane (Snipes) meets Billy Hoyle (Harrelson) on a public court where the game is played as a mix of macho combat, stand-up comedy and con-artistry. The jokes and banter are wonderful. But this is also a most unlikely buddy movie, where the black/white pair team up as hustlers floating around the rougher areas of Los Angeles, turn on each other, and finally bury the hatchet to get Billy out of hock to some surprisingly obliging hoods. Sadly, in doing so, the duo alienate Billy's long-suffering Hispanic girlfriend (Perez), who dreams of the straight life and spends her time memorising trivia in hopes of a TV game show break. Snipes and Harrelson bounce off the screen like Michael Jordan, while Shelton and cinematographer Russell Boyd perfectly capture the agile thrills of the game itself. A double-whammy slam-dunker of a movie. SGr

White Mischief

(1987, GB, 107 min)
d Michael Radford. *p* Simon Perry. *sc* Michael Radford, Jonathan Gems. *ph* Roger Deakins. *ed* Tom Priestley. *pd* Roger Hall. *m* George Fenton. *cast* Charles Dance, Greta Scacchi, Joss Ackland, Sarah Miles, John Hurt, Geraldine Chaplin, Ray McAnally, Trevor Howard, Susan Fleetwood, Alan Dobie, Jacqueline Pearce.

● Just in case you miss the point that one's betters are scum, Radford's version of the James Fox book opens on the decadent rich drinking champers in a London underground shelter during an air-raid. They took the party to Kenya, where one adultery too many led to the shooting of Josslyn Hay, twenty-second Earl of Erroll. Since we are never in much doubt that murder is inevitable, know the murderer's identity, and have no sympathy for any of the Happy Valley set, all that's on offer are hopefully scandalous tableaux of rude goings-on. Diana (Scacchi) hooks rich old Sir Jock (Ackland), but falls for the rogering Earl (Dance). Sir Jock bumps him off, gets acquitted, but tops himself anyway. So much for the story. On the sociological side, there's wife-swapping, Trevor Howard peering through a peephole at Scacchi in the bath, lots of drugs and drink, transvestite parties, Sarah Miles smearing her vaginal secretions on the lips of her dead lover in the morgue, and roomy shorts. Irising out on a cocktail party in a cemetery, we say farewell or toodle-pip to the most stunningly boring crew this side of the Ralph Reader show. BC

White Nights (Le Notti Bianche)

(1957, It/Fr, 105 min, b/w)
d Luchino Visconti. *p* Franco Cristaldi. *sc* Suso Cecchi D'Amico, Luchino Visconti. *ph* Giuseppe Rotunno. *ed* Mario Serandrei. *ad* Mario Chiari, Mario Garbuglia. *m* Nino Rota. *cast* Maria Schell, Marcello Mastroianni, Jean Marais, Clara Calamai.

● Visconti's version of the Dostoievsky story – about the chance encounter of a couple as she is waiting in vain for her lover, and the obsessive, panic-stricken relationship which then develops between them – later filmed by Bresson as *Four Nights of a Dreamer*. Visconti traps his characters (three excellent performances) within a claustrophobic canal-side set, and the film is a series of brief walks, chases, attempted escapes, always frustrated. Shot as neo-realist high tragedy, the film offers its characters only one strange moment of escape from their night-time obsessions – a raucous, sexual, subversive scene in a dance-hall. Then the snow comes down, and with it a chilly desperation about the extent of human self-delusion. CA

White Nights

(1985, US, 135 min)
d Taylor Hackford. *p* Taylor Hackford, William S Gilmore. *sc* James Goldman, Eric Hughes. *ph* David Watkin, Alan Jone. *ed* Fredric Steinkamp, William Steinkamp. *pd* Philip Harrison. *m* Michel Colombier. *cast* Mikhail Baryshnikov, Gregory Hines, Jerzy Skolimowski, Helen Mirren, Geraldine Page, Isabella Rossellini, John Glover.

● After the romance of *An Officer and a Gentleman* and the frequent excitement of *Against All Odds*, one would never have guessed that Taylor Hackford would prove just plain boring. Indeed, the premise of *White Nights* is good: the plane on which a Russian ballet dancer (Baryshnikov) is travelling makes a forced landing in Russia, the land from which he defected to the US ten years previously. But the grinding ins and outs of just what the KGB will use him for are constantly held up for long sequences in which he dances in partnership with Gregory Hines, a black American tap dancer who went to Moscow in protest over Vietnam; nor are these sequences filmed with the formal rigour that dance requires. The virulence of the film's anti-Russian stance makes *Rambo* looks distinctly spineless; and the happy ending is risible. Sole point of interest: Skolimowski as a KGB officer with a smile like liquid nitrogen. CPea

White of the Eye

(1986, GB, 111 min)
d Donald Cammell. *p* Cassian Elwes, Brad Wyman. *sc* China Cammell, Donald Cammell. *ph* Larry McConkey, Alan Jones. *ed* Terry Rawlings. *pd* Philip Thomas. *m* Nick Mason, Rick Fenn. *cast* David Keith, Cathy Moriarty, Alan Rosenberg, Art Evans, Michael Greene, Danko Gurovich, David Chow, China Cammell.

● Cammell transforms a stalk'n'slash thriller into a complex, cubist kaleidoscope of themes and images. Paul and Joan White (Keith and Moriarty) lead a happy enough life in a quiet Arizona mining town, until Paul suddenly finds himself chief suspect in a police investigation of a series of violently misogynistic murders. Matters are complicated by the reappearance of Joan's gun-crazy ex-husband (Rosenberg). A determinedly offbeat murder mystery, delving into dotty Indian mysticism and throwing up symbols, red herrings, and Steadicam flourishes for the asking, this nevertheless remains oddly effective. Imbued with a brooding, oppressive atmosphere and coloured by vivid performances, though often murkily motivated, it is genuinely nightmarish in its portrait of relationships where love is blinding and the past casts an intolerably heavy spell. GA

Whiteout

(2000, Jap, 129 min)
d Setsuro Wakamatsu. *p* Shohei Kotaki, Nobuyuki Toya, Takashi Ishihara, Hirotsugu Usui. *sc* Yuichi Shimpo, Yasuo Hasegawa. *ph* Hideo Yamamoto. *m* Ken Ishii, Norihito Sumitomo. *cast* Yuji Oda, Nanako Matsushima, Koichi Sato.

● A mega-hit in Japan, this fairly spectacular adaptation of a pulp novel by co-scripter Shimpo is a Japanese *Die Hard* set in a mountain blizzard. The power plant next to Japan's largest dam is seized by terrorists from the Red Moon group, ostensibly to demand freedom for imprisoned colleagues, but actually because the leader Utsugi (Sato) wants to bury the group (and his own former idealism) and flee with crates of cash. The only man who can save the dam is plucky engineer Togashi (Oda), not yet over the self-sacrificing death of his best friend, but seemingly immune to frostbite and hypothermia. The action-suspense set-pieces follow the Hollywood template, but the film is more intriguing when it's most Japanese: no US blockbuster would go for such a boyish, grief-stricken hero, or waste time on the dead man's mistakenly resentful fiancée (Matsushima). TR

White Palace

(1990, US, 103 min)
d Luis Mandoki. *p* Mark Rosenberg, Amy Robinson, Griffin Dunne. *sc* Ted Tally, Alvin Sargent. *ph* Lajos Koltai. *ed* Carol Littleton. *pd* Jeannine C Oppewall. *m* George Fenton. *cast* Susan Sarandon, James Spader, Jason Alexander, Kathy Bates, Eileen Brennan, Spiros Focas, Gina Gershon, Steven Hill.

●In the years following his wife's death, Max (Spader) leads a carefully controlled life: a sense of purpose is found through work, and passion confined to a love of classical music. Then he meets no-nonsense Nora (Sarandon), for whom culture consists of Marilyn Monroe, and whose apartment boasts the Just-Ransacked look. He's 27, Jewish, and an affluent copy-writer; she's 44, Catholic, and a fast-food waitress. Will their affair survive differences in background, the age gap, and Thanksgiving dinner with Max's over-solicitous friends? Glenn Savan's novel offered a stronger exploration of Reaganism and consumerism, but overall he's served well by this intelligent, involving adaptation. There's an unmistakable charge between the two leads, and an acute sense of their mutual confusion. Acting honours go to Sarandon, who brings off a complex depiction of vulgarity, defiance and vulnerability. CM

White Rock

(1976, GB, 76 min)
d Tony Maylam. *p* Michael Samuelson. *sc* Tony Maylam. *ph* Arthur G Wooster. *ed* Gordon Swire. *m* Rick Wakeman. *narrator* James Coburn.

●The official film of the 1976 Winter Olympics held at Innsbruck isn't even satisfactory as a documentary record of the major events. The trouble is that writer (Maylam) and narrator (Coburn) reduce virtually all the events – ski-jumping, ice hockey, the biathlon, bobsled, slalom, downhill racing – to the rock-bottom level of beefy American locker-room speed, thrills and spills, neglecting to pay any attention to the individual athletes, or (as in Herzog's *The Great Ecstasy of Woodcarver Steiner*) the inherent spiritual attraction of the sports on view. Coburn's running commentary seems more interested in recording his own participation in death-defying stunts (taking front position on a two-man bobsleigh, for instance) than in interviewing any of the athletes; while Rick Wakeman's 'bubble and squeak' synthesiser soundtrack and much flashy editing do little to gloss over the poverty of this tedious film. RM

White Room

(1990, Can/GB, 90 min)
d Patricia Rozema. *p* Alexandra Raffé. *sc* Patricia Rozema. *ph* Paul Sarossy. *ed* Patricia Rozema. *pd* Valanne Ridgeway. *m* Mark Korven. *cast* Kate Nelligan, Maurice Godin, Margot Kidder, Sheila McCarthy, Barbara Gordon.

●A distinct change of tack for writer-director Rozema after the quirky *I've Heard the Mermaids Singing*, this strange, arty film follows a weedy voyeur (Godin) who witnesses a pop star's murder and meets a reclusive mystery woman who has the dead singer's voice. Although Sheila McCarthy provides a little light relief as the voyeur's wacky sidekick, and Kate Nelligan makes a strong impression as the recluse, the film virtually falls into abstraction. Imagine a Brian De Palma script directed by Jane Campion – or, better yet, watch it for yourself. TCh

White Sands

(1992, US, 101 min)
d Roger Donaldson. *p* William Sackheim, Scott Rudin. *sc* Daniel Pyne. *ph* Peter Menzies Jr. *ed* Nicholas Beauman, Sue Blainey. *pd* John Graysmark. *m* Patrick O'Hearn. *cast* Willem Dafoe, Mary Elizabeth Mastrantonio, Mickey Rourke, Sam Jackson, M Emmet Walsh, Mimi Rogers, James Rebhorn, Maura Tierney.

●Deputy sheriff Ray Dolezal (Dafoe, in an assured performance) is an upstanding citizen, complete with wife (Rogers), son and white stetson. But life in his backwater New Mexico town is thrown into turmoil after the discovery of an apparent suicide victim, together with a case containing $500,000. Assuming the corpse's identity to investigate the mystery, Ray encounters villains who relieve him of the loot and the clothes off his back; but worse is to come in a meeting with FBI agent Meeker (Jackson), who reveals that the money belonged to the Bureau. It's all down to the do-good deputy to get it back, which means making friends with both shady-lady Lane Bodine (Mastrantonio) and Gorman Lennox (Rourke), who has the money earmarked for a weapons deal. In the absence of real substance, Donaldson's stylish direction borders on the self-conscious, though cinematographer Peter Menzies Jr captures images of startling richness and clarity. CM

White Sheik, The (Lo Sceicco Bianco)

(1951, It, 88 min, b/w)
d Federico Fellini. *p* Luigi Rovere. *sc* Federico Fellini, Tullio Pinelli, Ennio Flaiano. *ph* Arturo Gallea. *ed* Rolando Benedetti. *ad* Raffaello Tolfo. *m* Nino Rota. *cast* Alberto Sordi, Brunella Bovo, Leopoldo Trieste, Giulietta Masina, Lilia Landi.

●Fellini's first solo feature, a delightful satirical comedy about a young honeymoon couple (Bovo and Trieste) who arrive in Rome with the wife yearning after her romantic ideal, *The White Sheik*, star of one of the *fumetti* (the photographic comic strips so popular in Italy). While she dashes off for a glimpse of her hero (Sordi), incarnated by a bedraggled hack actor who vainly tries to preen himself to meet her expectations, the disconsolate husband spends a lonely night wandering the streets until he meets a friendly prostitute. Agreeably abrasive in its attitude to illusions and the self-delusions that fuel them, vitriolically funny in evoking the world of the fumetti, Fellini lapses only briefly into his later mystico-sentimentality in the character of the prostitute (played, of course, by Masina). (From a story by Fellini, Tullio Pinelli and Michelangelo Antonioni.) TM

White Squall

(1996, US, 129 min)
d Ridley Scott. *p* Mimi Polk, Rocky Lang. *sc* Todd Robinson. *ph* Hugh Johnson. *ed* Gerry Hambling. *pd* Peter J Hampton. *m* Jeff Rona. *cast* Jeff Bridges, Caroline Goodall, Scott Wolf, John Savage, Jeremy Sisto, Ryan Phillippe, David Lascher, Balthazar Getty.

●Based on a real-life memoir, this nautical rites-of-passage story set in 1960 sees a crew of teenage boys on a school ship maturing rapidly under the hard-but-fair tutelage of 'Skipper' Sheldon (Bridges). They gain valuable lessons in character, responsibility and individual integrity as the 'Albatross' sails from the Caribbean into a ferocious hurricane that will fatefully test the mettle of all on board. Although the early sequences win no prizes for originality, Scott bathes his handsome young charges in plenty of tropical sun and draws a convincing partnership between brooding old hand Sheldon and his ship's doctor spouse (an impressively natural Goodall), which gives the material an emotional core later to prove deceptively potent. It is, however, the 'white squall' sequence that stands way above anything else in the movie, detailing with you-are-there intensity the vessel's helpless plight as she's buffeted by a series of enormous waves and the Skipper battles to keep her upright. This particular landlubber felt like jelly for the rest of the day, notwithstanding the hokey courtroom showdown that closes the picture. TJ

White Tower, The

(1950, US, 98 min)
d Ted Tetzlaff. *p* Sid Rogell. *sc* Paul Jarrico. *ph* Ray Rennahan. *ed* Samuel E Beetley. *ad* Albert S D'Agostino, Ralph Berger. *m* Roy Webb. *cast* Glenn Ford, Claude Rains, Alida Valli, Oscar Homolka, Cedric Hardwicke, Lloyd Bridges.

●Against a daunting Swiss mountain, pit an ill-assorted bunch of climbers: gruff guide (Homolka), diffident Yank (Ford), ex-Hitler Youth member (Bridges), alcoholic writer (Rains), English no-hoper (Hardwicke), and a woman trying to live up to her father's reputation (Valli). Then watch the mountain polarise their characters; the uncommitted find true grit, the weak go to the wall, and blond Teutons who rely on the 'Will to Power' tend to flake off and die. Even the heroine forsakes the summit for true love on the south col, and Glenn Ford becomes as obsessed as he was in *Gilda*, except that here it's a rock pile rather than Rita Hayworth. Can you take a Freudian *Eiger Sanction*? Come to that, has there ever been a great mountain movie? CPea

White Wall, The (Den Vita Vüggen)

(1974, Swe, 79 min)
d Stig Björkman. *p* Bengt Forslund. *sc* Stig Björkman. *ph* Petter Davidsson, Bertil Rosengren. *ed* Stig Björkman, Margit Nordqvist. *ad* Anders Barréus. *m* Sven-Olof Walldoff. *cast* Harriet Andersson, Lena Nyman, Sven Wollter, Tomas Pontén, Rolf Larsson.

●Given that its central performance by Harriet Andersson is technically perfect, this study of female frustration displays hardly any other redeeming features. Settling for a one-track, frankly boring delineation of the tribulations of a newly-separated woman of 35, it progresses (infinitely slowly) by means of a line of clichéd encounters with representative boorish males and sympathetic girlfriend towards a cop-out fadeout that is the ultimate in arty pretentiousness. Throughout, the film treats Andersson's character as a 'specimen' under glass, even going so far as to parallel her situation with that of her son's goldfish. A sign of Björkman's inability to think his subject through is that he has to despatch the young son from the narrative halfway through; while his oblique references to Bergman merely highlight the emptiness of his own concept. PT

White Zombie

(1932, US, 73 min, b/w)
d Victor Halperin. *p* Edward Halperin. *sc* Garnett Weston. *ph* Arthur Martinelli. *ed* Harold MacLernon. *ad* Ralph Berger, Conrad Tritschler. *cast* Bela Lugosi, Madge Bellamy, Robert Frazer, Brandon Hurst, John Harron, Joseph Cawthorn.

●A dream-like encounter between Gothic romance and 'primitive' mythology, with an American innocent (Bellamy) plucked from her wedding feast and consigned to walk with the Haitian living dead by voodoo master Lugosi. Halperin shoots this poetic melodrama as trance; insinuating ideas and images of possession, defloration, and necrophilia into a perfectly stylised design, with the atmospherics conjuring echoes of countless resonant fairytales. The unique result constitutes a virtual bridge between classic Universal horror and the later Val Lewton productions. PT

Who?

(1974, GB, 93 min)
d Jack Gold. *p* Barry Levinson. *sc* John Gould. *ph* Petrus Schloemp. *ed* Norman Wanstall. *ad* Peter Scharff. *m* John Cameron. *cast* Elliott Gould, Trevor Howard, Joseph Bova, Ed Grover, James Noble, John Lehne.

●Looking rather better on TV than on the big screen, where its rough edges show up more, this is a very passable adaptation of a fine sci-fi/espionage novel by Algis Budrys. The basic premise is vividly laid out as an American scientist (Bova), injured in a car crash on the Russian border, is returned to the West after advanced medical treatment which has him looking like a Martian invader with a prosthetic metal head. Thereafter the script develops cold feet, and obscures its detective theme – is this the same man, and can he be safely returned to his secret research? – by making tiresome concessions to action adventure (routine car chase and so forth). MA

Who Am I This Time?

(1982, US, 60 min)
d Jonathan Demme. *p/sc* Neal Miller. *ed* Marc Leif. *m* John Cale. *cast* Susan Sarandon, Christopher Walken, Robert Ridgeley, Dorothy Paterson.

●Made for television, Demme's adaptation of a Kurt Vonnegut story is totally delightful. Sarandon is the new girl in town who joins an amateur dramatics group and falls for local star

Walken. The only trouble is that, offstage, he is terminally shy. Finally, of course, she gets her man, but not before Demme has fleshed out the slim plot with vivid, likeable characters (both leads are superb), and a great deal of charm and wit. One of his very best. GA

Who Are You Polly Maggoo? (Qui êtes-vous Polly Maggoo?)

(1966, Fr, 102 min, b/w)
d William Klein. *p* Robert Delpire. *sc* William Klein. *ph* Jean Boffety. *ed* Anne-Marie Cotret. *ad* Bernard Evein. *m* Michel Legrand. *cast* Dorothy McGowan, Jean Rochefort, Sami Frey, Philippe Noiret, Grayson Hall, Delphine Seyrig, Joanna Shimkus.

● First feature for Klein, the American expatriate king of visual razzmatazz and strident satire, drawing on his own early background in fashion photography. Polly Maggoo (McGowan) is a suddenly famous model whose true personality is probed by a multitude of people, including a TV interviewer (Noiret) and a lovelorn Ruritanian prince (Frey) who dispatches two secret agents to grab her for his own. Klein's satiric targets may be nothing more than clay pigeons (we all know about media madness), but it's churlish to complain when he shoots at them in such an agreeably nutty way. GB

Who Dares Wins (aka The Final Option)

(1982, GB, 125 min)
d Ian Sharp. *p* Euan Lloyd. *sc* Reginald Rose. *ph* Philip Meheux. *ed* John Grover. *pd* Syd Cain. *m* Roy Budd, Jerry Donahue, Marc Donahue. *cast* Lewis Collins, Judy Davis, Richard Widmark, Edward Woodward, Robert Webber, Tony Doyle, John Duttine, Kenneth Griffith, Rosalind Lloyd, Ingrid Pitt, Norman Rodway, Patrick Allen.

● Inspired by the Iranian Embassy siege, a kiddie-comic yarn about hardcore terrorists who subvert the 'Peace Lobby' and mount an armed attack on the American ambassador's London residence, holding the assembled VIP company to ransom. The terrorists are, of course, a hamfisted bunch led by a sexy American bourgeoise (Davis), and they haven't reckoned with the superhuman skills and no-nonsense brutality of the SAS. Beneath the gung-ho action, the ideology of the movie stinks. Peace lobbyists are portrayed as spineless liberals, women are epitomised as the power-crazed rich bitch or the faithful wife-and-mother, and the SAS (following their 'heroic' image in the popular press) is depicted as an élite of supermen. A film to make the uncommitted want to join the next antinuclear demonstration from sheer outrage. MA

Whoever Says the Truth Will Die

(1984, Neth, 52 min)
d Philo Bregstein. *p* Frank Diamand. *ph* Michele Pensato, Ali Movahed, Richard Laurent. *ed* Mario Steenbergen. *with* Laura Betti, Bernardo Bertolucci, Alberto Moravia, Antonietta Macciochi.

● Even for someone disillusioned by the fall-off in originality of Pasolini's later films, this neat little documentary exerts considerable interest. Hardly surprising, given that the director led a pretty colourful life, making his name first as a poet and novelist, hanging out with the denizens of Rome's poorest suburbs, and repeatedly coming into conflict with the authorities (tried and acquitted 33 times) for his homosexuality and political views. Bregstein's film attempts to understand the man himself and his place in Italian art and politics, while also questioning the verdict that had Pasolini killed by a single 17-year-old boy in 'self-defence after sexual threats'. From various pieces of evidence, it does indeed seem that no one person could have carried out such a brutal mutilation, nor would have wanted to. Whatever one feels about the answer posited here, however, it's a fascinating and provocative look at a complex and disturbing man. GA

Who Framed Roger Rabbit

(1988, US, 104 min)
d Robert Zemeckis. *p* Robert Watts, Frank Marshall. *sc* Jeffrey Price, Peter S Seaman. *ph* Dean Cundey. *ed* Arthur Schmidt. *ad* Elliot Scott, Roger Cain. *m* Alan Silvestri. *cast* Bob Hoskins, Christopher Lloyd, Joanna Cassidy, Stubby Kaye, Alan Tilvern.

● Ever since his brother's death, seedy gumshoe Eddie Valiant (Hoskins) has hated Toons – the animated inhabitants of the '40s LA suburb of Toontown, most of whom make a living appearing in Hollywood cartoons. But when studio head Marvin Acme asks him to check up on the extramarital activities of Jessica Rabbit, the humanoid, torch-singing, Toon spouse of our eponymous stunt-Toon hero, Eddie finds himself up to his fedora in murder, blackmail, and conspiracy. Zemeckis and animation director Richard Williams' comedy-thriller blends live action, Warners-style animation, and a typically tortuous film *noir* plot to delirious effect. Virtually faultless on the technological front, it also excels in terms of a breathless, wisecracking script, deft characterisation (both human and Toon), and rousing action. At its best, the humour is as cruel, violent, and surreal as vintage Chuck Jones. Supremely entertaining – especially for adults. BC

Who Is Harry Kellerman and Why Is He Saying Those Terrible Things About Me?

(1971, US, 108 min)
d Ulu Grosbard. *p* Ulu Grosbard, Herb Gardner. *sc* Herb Gardner. *ph* Victor J Kemper. *ed* Barry Malkin. *pd* Harry Horner. *songs* Shel Silverstein. *cast* Dustin Hoffman, Barbara Harris, Jack Warden, David Burns, Dom DeLuise, Betty Walker, Gabriel Dell, Regina Baff.

● Hoffman (oddly cast but excellent) as a fabulously successful rock musician driven to a headshrinker by problems of ageing, loneliness, and the mysterious caller who is alienating his harem of women by casting libellous aspersions on his character. Waywardly whimsical in its satire of material success and the analyst's couch, the film suffered a critical clobbering. But it is also strangely moving, peopled by marvellously vivid characters dredged out of the hero's past and lending undertones of real pain and longing to the otherwise formulary comedy as he becomes a minor league Citizen Kane, beleaguered by sad ghosts in his lonely Xanadu (a New York penthouse lined with golden discs and *Time* magazine covers). Barbara Harris is outstanding as the would-be singer who belatedly shows him what-might-have-been. TM

Who Is Killing the Great Chefs of Europe? (aka Too Many Chefs)

(1978, US/WGer, 112 min)
d Ted Kotcheff. *p* William Aldrich. *sc* Peter Stone. *ph* John Alcott. *ed* Thom Noble. *pd* Rolf Zehetbauer. *m* Henry Mancini. *cast* George Segal, Jacqueline Bisset, Robert Morley, Jean-Pierre Cassel, Philippe Noiret, Jean Rochefort, Madge Ryan.

● With exotic food providing the ground-bass imagery, it is only fitting that the film's one funny line should be delivered by walk-on Mr Chow, restaurateur to the rich and famous. The rest is a heavy plough through all the familiar routes along which comedy-thrillers frequently get lost: travelogue backdrops of Venice, Paris and London, gourmet Robert Morley doing battle with super-Wildean courage against unspeakable lines, a plot involving the methodical extinction of European chefs in various nasty ways (Noiret in a duck-press), and a level of joking which never exceeds puns on *Bombe Surprise*. Saddest of all is Segal's vulgarity, unleavened by his usually strong sense of irony. The only funny thing about all this is why Robert Aldrich was at one time interested in directing it. CPea

Who Killed Vincent Chin?

(1988, US, 87 min)
d Christine Choy, Renee Tajima. *ph* Christine Choy, Nick Doob, Kyle Kibbe, Al Santana. *ed* Holly Fisher.

● In June 1982, Vincent Chin, a Chinese American draftsman, was beaten to death by two thugs wielding baseball bats outside a McDonald's in Detroit. Despite protests from the local Asian community, the murderers received three years' probation for manslaughter and a fine of $3,750: neither spent more than one night in jail. This documentary charts the growth of an emotive civil rights protest, the murderers' subsequent re-trial, and the personal confusion of all involved. Through extensive interviews with killer Ronald Ebens, a honey-tongued redneck, and Lily Chin, Vincent's mother, an icon of inarticulate grief, the film builds to an outraged climax as the case continues to evade the much-vaunted American way of justice. Detailed, terse, and politically compelling. RS

Who Knows?

see Va Savoir

Whole Nine Yards, The

(2000, US, 99 min)
d Jonathan Lynn. *p* David Willis, Allan Kaufman. *sc* Mitchell Kapner. *ph* David Franco. *ed* Tom Lewis. *pd* David L Snyder. *m* Randy Edelman. *cast* Bruce Willis, Matthew Perry, Rosanna Arquette, Michael Clarke Duncan, Natasha Henstridge, Amanda Peet, Kevin Pollak, Harland Williams.

● Hitman Jimmy 'the Tulip' Tudesk (Willis clad in a white vest) flees to Canada with a contract on his head and moves next door to debt-ridden dentist Nicholas 'Oz' Oseransky (Perry). Oz is persuaded to grass on Jimmy for an all-important finder's fee. Meanwhile, Oz's ex-wife (Arquette) seeks the services of any available assassin to do away with Oz for his hefty life insurance. Hilarious double-cross capers ensue, but this popcorn comedy misses the dark humour and cynicism of a genre gem like *Grosse Point Blank* by a country mile. AL

Whole Town's Talking, The (aka Passport to Fame)

(1935, US, 95 min, b/w)
d John Ford. *p* Lester Cowan. *sc* Jo Swerling, Robert Riskin. *ph* Joseph August. *ed* Viola Lawrence. *cast* Edward G Robinson, Jean Arthur, Wallace Ford, Arthur Hohl, Edward Brophy, Arthur Byron, Donald Meek.

● A brisk, snappy comedy with Robinson in a double role: as the timid, dependable clerk Jones, and the notorious gangster, Killer Mannion. An accountant with a cat he calls Abelard and a canary named Heloise, Jones dreams of exotic places and his spunky colleague Miss Clark (Arthur). It is only after he has been mistaken for his doppelgänger (who then 'borrows' the special ID card issued to the clerk by the police to avoid similar errors in the future) that Jones finds the courage of his convictions. Adapted from a WR Burnett story by Frank Capra's regular collaborators Robert Riskin and Jo Swerling, this low budget comedy sneaked past the Hays Office ban on gangster movies, but proved so popular that the genre was immediately revived. Ford may parody the conventions of the crime film, but his picture is as subversive as any *Little Caesar*: when the worm turns, it might as well be on his boss or on the police as on the hoods who have kidnapped his precious Miss Clark. TCh

Whole Wide World, The

(1996, US, 116 min)
d Dan Ireland. *p* Carl-Jan Colpaert, Kevin Reidy, Dan Ireland, Vincent D'Onofrio. *sc* Michael Scott Myers. *ph* Claudio Rocha. *ed* Luis Colina. *pd* John Frick. *m* Hans Zimmer. *cast* Vincent D'Onofrio, Renée Zellweger, Ann Wedgworth, Harve Presnell.

● Small town Texas in the mid-'30s. Robert Howard lives with his parents – clinging mother, remote father – spending his time banging out a series of fantasy yarns for the pulps, many featuring a warrior super-hero named Conan. A schoolteacher, Novalyne Price, tries with fluctuating degrees of resolve, to turn this intriguing but unpromising case into conventional boyfriend material. Conan buffs will already know how it all comes out. Somewhat repetitive, though declining any temptations to melodrama or overt psychoanalysis, it's an insightful two-hander, beautifully played by D'Onofrio and Zellweger. Based on a memoir by Ms Price. BBa

Who'll Stop the Rain? (aka Dog Soldiers)

(1978, US, 126 min)
d Karel Reisz. *p* Herb Jaffe, Gabriel Katzka. *sc* Judith Rascoe, Robert Stone. *ph* Richard H Kline. *ed* Chris Ridsdale, Mark Conte. *pd*

Dale Hennesy. *m* Laurence Rosenthal. *cast* Nick Nolte, Tuesday Weld, Michael Moriarty, Anthony Zerbe, Richard Masur, Ray Sharkey, Gail Strickland, Charles Haid, David Opatoshu.
● A traumatised Vietnam war correspondent can draw 'no more cheap morals' from the bloody absurdity around him. 'In a world where elephants are pursued by flying men, everyone's gonna want to get high' he reasons, as he blindly steps into the heroin business and joins the 'Dog Soldiers' of Robert Stone's novel and Reisz's excellent adaptation. Involving old buddy Nolte and his own wife Weld in his doomed dope deal, he precipitates a compelling chase through the corrupt moral wasteland of counter-culture/CIA-culture America. On the way, Washington power-play is mirrored in the casual sadism of the pursuers, and the conventional 'MacGuffin' role of the 2kg bag takes on a metaphorical charge. Reisz nimbly avoids the Big Theme style, finds the pace of his material early, and sustains it brilliantly, emerging with a contemporary classic of hard-edged adventure and three superb character studies. PT

Wholly Moses!

(1980, US, 109 min)
d Gary Weis. *p* Freddie Fields. *sc* Guy Thomas. *ph* Frank Stanley. *ed* Sidney Levin. *pd* Dale Hennesy. *m* Patrick Williams. *cast* Dudley Moore, Laraine Newman, James Coco, Paul Sand, Jack Gilford, Dom DeLuise, John Houseman, Madeline Kahn, David L Lander, Richard Pryor, John Ritter.
● An opportunistic attempt to cash in on the diminutive Moore's post-*10* stardom by shamelessly ripping off the premise of *The Life of Brian*. Here we have, instead of the Gospels, a Funny Thing Happened on the Way to the Promised Land, with Moore cast as the character denied his rightful place in Biblical history by some upstart called Moses. The director of *Saturday Night Live* opts for a comic style which falls uneasily between the New American anarchic comic farce and that pioneered by the 'Python' team. A string of promising cameos – DeLuise, Kahn, Pryor – none of which come off, and an underwritten script leave one very unsatisfied. Cecil B DeMille was cubits more comical than anything on show here. RM

Who Needs a Heart

(1991, GB, 80 min, b/w & col)
d John Akomfrah. *p* Lina Gopaul. *sc* John Akomfrah, Eddie George. *ph* Nancy Schiesari. *ed* Brand Thumim. *m* Trevor Mathison. *cast* Caroline Burghard, Treva Ettiene, Ruth Gemmell.
● Another very lively experimental film from the Black Audio Film Collective in the wake of *Handsworth Songs*, this is akin to a sophisticated home-movie history, a record of life on the fringes in London between 1965 and 1975. Inspired by the black political figurehead and/or criminal Michael X, the film nevertheless holds him at a distance, tracing his career through contemporary TV and radio bulletins which counterpoint and parallel the lives of a group of (racially mixed) friends and lovers involved in the Black Power movement. Dialogue is strictly a subsidiary element in Trevor Mathison's allusive, inventive sound design; narrative emerges in snatches, as Akomfrah flashes back from 1972 to the early '60s, and then forwards, recalling the properties of the times in music, fashion and art. It's an outside-in approach to cinema, and to politics, but there's more humour than pretension here. An intriguing, rewarding film. TCh

Whooping Cough (Szamárköhögés)

(1987, Hun, 87 min)
d Péter Gárdos. *sc* András Osvat, Péter Gárdos. *ph* Tibor Máthé. *ed* Mária Rigó. *pd* Jozsef Romvári. *m* James Novák. *cast* Marcell Tóth, Eszter Kárász, Deszö Garas, Judit Hernádi, Mari Törőcsik, Anna Fehér.
● The Hungarian cinema tackles the October 1956 uprising again, this time seen through the eyes of two mischievous children in a family of confused and desperate adults. For the most part, the film is attractive and well staged, but the grinning brats are allowed to hog the camera too much, and the climactic intrusion of reality on their playground is badly fudged. DT

Whoops Apocalypse

(1986, GB, 91 min)
d Tom Bussmann. *p* Brian Eastman. *sc* Andrew Marshall, David Renwick. *ph* Ron Robson. *ed* Peter Boyle. *pd* Tony Noble. *m* Patrick Gowers. *cast* Loretta Swit, Peter Cook, Michael Richards, Rik Mayall, Ian Richardson, Alexei Sayle, Herbert Lom, Joanne Pearce.
● Charting the course of international misunderstanding, writers Andrew Marshall and David Renwick – of the original TV series – return with this feature length comedy lampooning events of the 'near future'. The film centres on a South American invasion by the 'Maguadorans' of British 'Santa Maya', and a British PM determined to give the public what it demands – a nuclear strike in retaliation. Despite the potential, the film sticks meekly to a conventional framework, with gags that never manage to sink their teeth into the tenuous absurdity of international affairs as *Dr Strangelove* did. The mechanical antics, though at times amusing, amount to a timid distraction – kind of like riding the underground in the rush hour. SGo

Whore

(1991, US, 92 min)
d Ken Russell. *p* Ronaldo Vasconcellos, Dan Ireland. *sc* Ken Russell, Deborah Dalton. *ph* Amir Mokri. *ed* Brian Tagg. *pd* Richard Lewis. *m* Michael Gibbs. *cast* Theresa Russell, Benjamin Mouton, Antonio Fargas, Sanjay, Elizabeth Morehead, Michael Crabtree, John Diehl, Jack Nance, Frank Smith.
● Released in a version cut by 7 minutes, one part downbeat docudrama and two parts Russell rant, this adaptation of David Hines' play *Bondage* lacks the visual imagination and cutting edge of the director's earlier *Crimes of Passion*. He seems constrained by the seedy naturalism as low-rent hooker Liz (Theresa Russell) walks the streets, keeping one eye out for the vicious pimp she fled earlier. Delivering most of her lines direct to camera, the foul-mouthed Liz lectures the audience on the routine abuse and humiliations she suffers in her line of work. Bullied, beaten and branded by her sadistic pimp (Mouton), Liz has a sneaking affection for some of her older clients, but knows that most of them 'don't want sex, they want revenge'. Flashbacks to a broken marriage and a son taken into care bespeak an equally unhappy past, but there are occasional, fleeting moments of human tenderness. What is most depressing, given the hectoring tone of Liz's monologues, is the way the film comes alive when her hateful pimp usurps the voice-over to brag about his entrepreneurial skills. NF

Whores, The (Le Buttane)

(1994, It, 85 min, b/w)
d Aurelio Grimaldi. *p* Maurizio Tedesco. *sc* Aurelio Grimaldi. *ph* Maurizio Calvesi. *ed* Mauro Bonanni. *m* Aurelio Grimaldi. *cast* Ida di Benedetto, Guia Jelo, Lucia Sardo, Sandra Sindoni.
● An engagingly ramshackle, mostly light-hearted look at the lives of a group of prostitutes (one of them male), shot in b/w with a simplicity at times faintly reminiscent of Pasolini. Without moralising, Grimaldi proffers (largely inconsequential) vignettes revelling in the details of everyday life: the bitching, the camaraderie, the dealings with pimps and clients, the lack of business on Christmas Day. The overall matter-of-fact tone creates, for the most part, a surprising aura of sweet innocence, though odd moments involving violence and racism (a number of the women's johns are Turks and Moroccans) acknowledge the potential dangers of prostitution. Minor, then, but funny, perceptive and, now and then, touching. GA

Who's Afraid of Virginia Woolf?

(1966, US, 132 min, b/w)
d Mike Nichols. *p/sc* Ernest Lehman. *ph* Haskell Wexler. *ed* Sam O'Steen. *pd* Richard Sylbert. *m* Alex North. *cast* Elizabeth Taylor, Richard Burton, George Segal, Sandy Dennis.
● Edward Albee's vitriolic stage portrayal of domestic blisslessness translated grainily and effectively to the screen. Taylor gives what is probably her finest performance as the blowsy harridan Martha, while Burton is not quite so hammy as usual as her angst-ridden college professor husband. The verbal fireworks that occur when they invite a young couple to dinner are surprisingly convincing. In an interview much later, Sandy Dennis said that, amazingly, Taylor and Burton were in fact very happy together at the time. It doesn't show on screen. The film's one problem, however, is that it's played so relentlessly for realism, when in fact the subject is at least half fantasy. A very loud film. GA

Whose Life Is It Anyway?

(1981, US, 118 min)
d John Badham. *p* Lawrence P Bachmann. *sc* Brian Clark, Reginald Rose. *ph* Mario Tosi. *ed* Frank Morriss. *pd* Gene Callahan. *m* Arthur Rubinstein. *cast* Richard Dreyfuss, John Cassavetes, Christine Lahti, Bob Balaban, Kenneth McMillan, Kaki Hunter, Janet Eilber.
● To be fair, this is a livelier film than you'd expect, considering that its subject is a paralysed patient's struggle for the right to die. Badham has done his best to see that this adaptation of Brian Clark's play is filled with humour and emotion, and he's helped by a verbally energetic performance from Dreyfuss. But popular cinema is ultimately not about talk, and for all its verbal pyrotechnics, the film has the unmistakable narrative thinness of the filmed play. One of the results is that our sympathy for the eternally wisecracking Dreyfuss is stretched to the limit. 'So far as I am concerned' says Dreyfuss at one point, 'I am dead already'. Yet, despite some moving scenes, this is precisely what the film never conveys. DP

Who's Harry Crumb?

(1989, US, 90 min)
d Paul Flaherty. *p* Arnon Milchan. *sc* Robert Conte, Peter Martin Wortmann. *ph* Stephen M Katz. *ed* Danford B Greene. *pd* Trevor Williams. *m* Michel Colombier. *cast* John Candy, Jeffrey Jones, Annie Potts, Tim Thowerson, Barry Corbin, Shawnee Smith.
● Candy makes the transition from sidekick to stardom as Harry Crumb, bumbling private eye. The plot is a lightweight concotion for a heavyweight hero, concerning the kidnapped daughter of multi-millionaire PJ Downing (Corbin). The incompetent sleuth has been given the assignment because the corrupt head of the investigation agency (Jones) is involved in the kidnapping and has every confidence that Crumb will fail. But, as always in such cases, stupidity triumphs over cynicism. Things plod to their inevitable conclusion, helped along by the script's assortment of stereotypical underdogs and manipulators, and with Candy hamming up the oppourtunity to get into lots of tight spots while wearing funny disguises. At their silliest, such moments actually provide light relief from an otherwise unremarkable comedy caper. CM

Who's That Girl

(1987, US, 94 min)
d James Foley. *p* Rosilyn Heller, Bernard Williams. *sc* Andrew Smith, Ken Finkleman. *ph* Jan De Bont. *ed* Pembroke J Herring. *pd* Ida Random. *m* Stephen Bray. *cast* Madonna, Griffin Dunne, Haviland Morris, John McMartin, Bibi Besch, John Mills, Robert Swan, Drew Pillsbury.
● Would-be madcap comedy wallowing in the wake of *Bringing Up Baby*. Inoffensive Dunne, who wouldn't even park next to a fire hydrant, is sent to collect Madonna from jail and put her on a bus out of town, and to collect a species of cougar from the docks. The girl and the cat are kindred spirits, of course, and demonstrate their emancipation from dreary old straight life at every opportunity, to the mortification of their keeper. She's out to clear her name, the bad guys are out to stop her, but in the nick of time Dunne resurrects his skill with a rapier. Sir John Mills appears, briefly and embarrassingly, as a life-affirming zoo owner, and the billing and cooing in his menagerie finally activates our hero's libido. Tiring stuff. BC

Who's That Knocking at My Door? (aka I Call First)

(1968, US, 90 min, b/w)
d Martin Scorsese. *p* Joseph Weill, Haig Manoogian, Betzi Manoogian. *sc* Martin Scorsese. *ph* Michael Wadleigh. *ed* Thelma Schoonmaker. *ad* Victor Magnotta. *cast* Harvey Keitel, Zina Bethune, Lennard Kuras, Ann Collette, Michael Scala, Catherine Scorsese.

●Scorsese's first feature. Set in New York's Little Italy, and what amounts to a dress rehearsal for *Mean Streets*, this displays all the excesses of a first effort. Although technically under the spell of European cinema (Godard et al), the film is just as much a tribute to Hollywood (Ford, Hawks) and more experimental Americans, particularly Anger and Cassavetes. But behind this melange there's no doubting the talent. In the aggressive self-confidence, the use of rock music, and the perceptive observation, Scorsese reveals an anthropological feel for street life and the attitudes of male adolescence, particularly how introversion and weakness are reserved for moments with the opposite sex, kept carefully apart from the mainstream of life. CPe

Who's the Man?

(1993, US, 85 min)
d Ted Demme. *p* Maynell Thomas, Charles Stettler. *sc* Seth Greenland. *ph* Adam Kimmel. *ed* Jeffrey Wolf. *pd* Ruth Ammon. *m* Michael Wolff, Nic tenBroek. *cast* Richard Bright, Dr Dré, Ed Lover, Denis Leary, Badja Djola, Cheryl 'Salt' James, Jim Moody, Ice T, Andre B Blake.

●A celebration of the hold that hip-hop's extended family of megastar rappers and DJs has on America, Demme's second film has rounded up a roster of stars. It's ostensibly about the threat posed to the community when evil property developer Demetrius (Bright) unveils his plans for Harlem. The only building in the way of his scheme is a barber shop, owned by pillar of the community, Nick. With the plot established, the film turns into a platform for rap stars Dr Dré and Ed Lover. Styled as a sort of black Abbott and Costello for the '90s, the pair exercise their appalling hairdressing skills in Nick's shop, until they become too much of a liability. Their natural timing goes a long way towards making the movie an effortless 85 minutes, but the 'raucous comedy' billing is justified only occasionally once they join the NYPD. Some diverting cameos. PP

Who Shot Patakango? (aka Who Shot Pat?)

(1990, US, 102 min)
d Robert Brooks. *p* Halle Brooks. *sc* Robert Brooks, Halle Brooks. *ph* Robert Brooks. *cast* David Knight, Sandra Bullock, Kevin Otto, Aaron Ingram, Brad Randall.

●This slice of teen nostalgia (featuring an early appearance by Sandra Bullock) captures the life and times of a Brooklyn high school in 1957, during the moment of transition when a wave of migrant blacks arrived from the South and populated what had till then been a predominantly white down-home territory. Matters are enlivened somewhat by a plethora of vintage hits. TJ

Why? (Detenuto in Attesa di Giudizio)

(1971, It, 102 min)
d Nanni Loy. *p* Gianni Hecht Lucari. *sc* Sergio Amidei, Amilio Sanna. *ph* Sergio D'Offizi. *ed* Franco Fraticelli. *ad* Gianni Polidori. *m* Carlo Rustichelli. *cast* Alberto Sordi, Elga Andersen, Lino Banfi, Giuseppe Anatrelli, Tano Cimarosa.

●A film that attracted a certain amount of attention as an indictment of the hopelessly corrupt and inhuman Italian penal system. Sordi plays an expatriate engineer returning to Italy on holiday with his Swedish wife and kids. He is promptly arrested for no apparent reason, shipped from jail to jail, jumps through absurd legal hoops, and worries himself into an asylum for the criminally insane before even getting near a trial. The film suffers from looking like an American light comedy, and Sordi's performance diverts events away from an excursion into Kafka territory. It occasionally manages to rise above itself: a homosexual near-rape; a sharp portrayal of a prison governor; the boredom and discomfort of long train journeys; the indignity of being watched while trying to shit. But for the most part it plays safe. CPe

Why Bother to Knock

see Don't Bother to Knock

Why Did Bohdi-Dharma Leave for the Orient? (Dharmaga tongjoguro kan kkadalgun?)

(1989, SKor, 135 min)
d/p/sc/ph/ed Bae Yong-Kyun. *m* Chin Kyn-Yong. *cast* Yi Pan-Yong, Sin Won-Sop, Huang Hae-Jin, Ko Su-Myong.

●Made completely outside the Korean film industry, this was a four-year labour of love for Bae, a 38-year-old teacher of painting. The title (an unanswerable zen riddle) gives a fair indication of his purpose and methods, which have nothing to do with drama but everything to do with Frommian notions of self-realisation and spiritual fulfillment. A zen master on the verge of physical death has two disciples, a young monk and an orphaned boy novice; the film shows their ascetic lives in a mountain retreat, and traces a cycle of death and rebirth that seems to guide the two disciples towards enlightenment. Of course, hardly anything happens in action terms. But the photography (worthy of Ansel Adams) and the imagery cast a potent spell, and the film comes as close as any other movie of the '80s to expressing the inexpressible. TR

Why Me?

(1989, US, 87 min)
d Gene Quintano. *p* Marjorie Israel. *sc* Donald E Westlake, Leonard Maas Jr. *ph* Peter Deming. *ed* Alan Balsam. *pd* Woody Crocker. *m* Phil Marshall. *cast* Christopher Lambert, Kim Greist, Christopher Lloyd, JT Walsh, Gregory Millar, Wendel Meldrum, Michael J Pollard, John Plana.

●A lacklustre action comedy that woefully fails to exploit the talents of its stars. When bungling safe-cracker Gus Cardinal (Lambert, miscast) and his eccentric accomplice Bruno (Lloyd) accidentally steal a cursed Turkish ruby known as the Byzantine Fire, much contrived capery ensues. The hapless pair are pursued by Turks, the CIA, the LAPD, and a bunch of deranged Armenians obsessed with preventing the rise of the Ottoman Empire. Based (very loosely) on a novel by Donald Westlake, this bears all the hallmarks of a straight-to-video production: functional script, limp direction, workaday performances and perfunctory stunt sequences, all played out amid the drab, tedious surroundings of Los Angeles. Lloyd attempts half-heartedly to enliven the proceedings with his characteristic blend of deadpan daftness, but it's a losing battle. Kim Greist is entirely wasted as the obligatory love interest. Less a case of why me than what for? MK

Why Not Me?

see Pourquoi pas moi?

Why Shoot the Teacher

(1976, Can, 99 min)
d Silvio Narizzano. *p* Lawrence Hertzog. *sc* James DeFelice. *ph* Marc Champion. *ed* Max Benedict. *ad* Karen Bromley. *m* Ricky Hyslop. *cast* Bud Cort, Samantha Eggar, Chris Wiggins, Gary Reineke, John Friesen, Michael J Reynolds, Kenneth Griffith.

●Earnest amiability is both the keynote and the principal weakness of this movie, in which Cort stars as an adolescent Montreal teacher who takes up a post in the wilds of Depression Saskatchewan, where he learns about Life, Love, and Manhood the hard way. Impeccably good intentions are betrayed by occasional lapses of probability, and the project suffers from predictable faults: no reason is offered for the hardship of the people's lives other than the harsh climate; the 'realism' of it all breeds lush landscape photography. But as a hesitant testimony to a historical period (the growth of a Dominion into a nation), it manages its clichés with considerable grace. CA

Why Worry?

(1923, US, 6 reels, b/w)
d Fred Newmeyer, Sam Taylor. *sc* Sam Taylor. *ph* Walter Lundin. *cast* Harold Lloyd, Jobyna Ralston, John Aasen, Leon White, Wallace Howe.

●Not so much one of Harold Lloyd's thrill comedies, more a gag-packed celebration of/satire on the American go-getter determination that was an essential part of his persona. Here he's a wealthy hypochondriac advised to take the sun, and landing up in a strife-torn banana republic where, with the help of a giant he befriends in jail after pulling his sore tooth, he quells a revolution… simply to ensure peace and quiet for himself. There's no denying the technical expertise behind the endless gags, but the remorseless optimism, coupled with the general blandness of Lloyd's character (there's no development here), makes the film somewhat wearying. GA

Why Would I Lie?

(1980, US, 105 min)
d Larry Peerce. *p* Pancho Kohner. *sc* Peter Stone. *ph* Gerald Hirschfeld. *ed* John C Howard. *ad* James Schoppe. *m* Charles Fox. *cast* Treat Williams, Lisa Eichhorn, Gabriel Swann, Susan Heldfond, Anne Byrne, Valerie Curtin, Jocelyn Brando.

●Comedy-romance with Williams as an habitual liar who's set to pick up a family inheritance if he can demonstrate he's doing something worthwhile with his life. Enter seven-year-old orphan Swann and love interest Eichhorn to try to prove his case. Heldfond makes for a feminist caricature villainess, and to tell the truth the overall point remains somewhat opaque. TJ

Wichita

(1955, US, 81 min)
d Jacques Tourneur. *p* Walter Mirisch. *sc* Daniel B Ullman. *ph* Harold Lipstein. *ed* William Austin. *ad* David Milton. *m* Hans J Salter. *cast* Joel McCrea, Vera Miles, Wallace Ford, Edgar Buchanan, Lloyd Bridges, Peter Graves, Robert Wilke, Jack Elam, Mae Clarke.

●'Everything Goes in Wichita' boast the signposts. The railroad has put the town on the map, but those businessmen set to become rich off the influx of hungry, thirsty, rowdy cattlemen are also concerned that their property should be protected against the cowboys' worst excesses. They persuade the reluctant Wyatt Earp (McCrea) to accept the marshal's badge, but have second thoughts when his civic law and order policies contradict their commercial instincts. This smooth, unassuming Western fits in neatly between the idealism of Ford's *My Darling Clementine* (1946) and the cynicism of Dmytryk's *Warlock* (1959). It ends optimistically enough, with Earp and his new bride leaving for a date with destiny in Dodge City, but not before the loss of at least two innocents, and many more gunmen, TCh

Wicked City, The (Yaoshou Dushi)

(1992, HK, 90 min)
d Mai Tai Kit. *p* Raymond Lee. *sc* Tsui Hark, Roy Szeto. *ph* Andrew Lau, Joe Chan. *ed* Mak Chi-Sin. *m* Richard Yuen. *cast* Jackie Cheung, Leon Lai, Michelle Li, Yuen Wo Ping.

●Special-effects hi-jinks from Tsui Hark's Film Workshop framed as a cross between Blade Runner and Japanese manga. Pop stars Jackie Cheung and Leon Lai, special-unit cops of the future, are assigned to hunt down and rub out shape-shifting monsters masquerading as humans. They are let down by dodgy visual effects (the climax, involving a 747 and IM Pei's Bank of China Tower, is particularly weak) and by the sheer monotony of the pacing. TR

Wicked Lady, The

(1945, GB, 104 min, b/w)
d Leslie Arliss. *p* RJ Minney. *sc* Leslie Arliss. *ph* Jack Cox. *ed* Terence Fisher. *ad* John Bryan. *m* Hans May. *cast* Margaret Lockwood, James Mason, Patricia Roc, Griffith Jones, Michael Rennie, Enid Stamp-Taylor, Felix Aylmer, Martita Hunt, Jean Kent.

●Post-war uplift becomes almost exclusively a matter of Ms Lockwood's cleavage in this period melodrama from Gainsborough that caused a censorious and highly profitable controversy in a teacup for its quaint bawdiness. Lockwood is the amoral aristo thrill-seeker who takes to highway robbery alongside Mason; former critic and screenwriter Arliss the unfortunate director having to contend with the recalcitrant mechanics of Lime Grove studio ruralism. PT

Wicked Lady, The

(1983, GB, 99 min)
d Michael Winner. *p* Menahem Golan, Yoram Globus. *sc* Leslie Arliss, Michael Winner. *ph* Jack Cardiff. *ed* Michael Winner. *ad* John

Blezard. *m* Tony Banks. *cast* Faye Dunaway, Alan Bates, John Gielgud, Denholm Elliott, Prunella Scales, Oliver Tobias, Glynis Barber, Joan Hickson.
● 'Bawdy', 'full-blooded', 'boisterous romp' – jaded adjectives hover over this particular filmic carcass, and popular British cinema gets another Carry On Up the Restoration. Charles II is squeezing Nell's oranges ho ho, and the very wonderful Dunaway becomes a roaring girl by night, cantering out from secret back passages and getting their money or their lives from rentacrowd in full-bottomed wigs. No village green without a rollicking maypole, no keyhole without a rutting doxy behind it; Tyburn's in there somewhere, and so is that whip-fight which almost constituted a case for censorship. CPea

Wicked Reporter, The (Gokudo Kisha)

(1993, Jap, 100 min)
d Rokuro Mochizuki. *cast* Eiji Okuda, Haku Ryu, Maiko Kawakami, Keiko Suzuki, Makoto Kakeda.
● More than his indie debut *Skinless Night*, this was the film that launched Mochizuki on his distinctive trajectory through the crime and yakuza genres. Matsuzaki is a racing tipster for a sports paper, a lowlife who spends half his time drunk, hangs out with yakuza and other riff-raff and complicates his sex life by succumbing to advances from his girlfriend's sister. As played by Okuda, he's also a figure of considerable hangdog charm. Less a plot-based movie than a guide to the several forms of high stakes gambling in Japan, this centres on his attempt to help a friend swindled in a bent mahjong game. Korean-Japanese actor Haku Ryu appears (memorably) as an inscrutable yakuza in a black leather jacket. The film's success led to two sequels. TR

Wicked Stepmother

(1988, US, 92 min)
d Larry Cohen. *p* Robert Littman. *sc* Larry Cohen. *ph* Bryan England. *ed* David Kern. *ad* Gene Abel. *m* Robert Folk. *cast* Bette Davis, Lionel Stander, Colleen Camp, David Rasche, Barbara Carrera, Richard Moll, Seymour Cassel, Evelyn Keyes, Tom Bosley.
● A vegetarian Los Angeles couple return from vacation to find that her father, a widower (Stander), has married a chain-smoking carnivorous weirdo (Davis) and undergone a worrying personality change. The crack-voiced stepmother has a familiar, a cigarette-smoking cat, and a seductive daughter (Carrera), who from time to time appears to take over her body. A ramshackle supernatural spoof, beset with production difficulties, in which Bette Davis made her last, best forgotten screen appearance. JPy

Wicked, Wicked

(1973, US, 95 min)
d/p/sc Richard L Bare. *ph* Frederick Gately. *ed* John F Schreyer. *ad* Walter McKeegan. *m* Philip Springer. *cast* David Bailey, Tiffany Bolling, Randolph Roberts, Scott Brady, Edd Byrnes, Diane McBain.
● A silly, wretchedly derivative psycho movie in which a hotel handyman (Roberts), sexually humiliated as a child by his foster mother, goes around in a fright mask dismembering blondes. Bailey is the house dick doing most of the investigating, and Bolling is his ex-wife, conveniently hired by the hotel as resident singer and sporting a blonde wig while performing so that she's up for grabs as the climactic victim. As a gimmick, the film offers 'Duo-vision', which is simply a split screen offering the killer on one side, his victim (or his traumatic memories) on the other. TM

Wicker Man, The (100)

(1973, GB, 102 min)
d Robin Hardy. *p* Peter Snell. *sc* Anthony Shaffer. *ph* Harry Waxman. *ed* Eric Boyd-Perkins. *ad* Seamus Flannery. *m* Paul Giovanni. *cast* Edward Woodward, Britt Ekland, Diane Cilento, Ingrid Pitt, Christopher Lee, Lesley Mackie, Walter Carr, Lindsay Kemp.
● A bona fide British eccentric near-classic: devoutly virginal protestant cop Edward Woodward is lured to a Scottish island to investigate a schoolgirl disappearance, and finds himself embroiled in a pottage of erotic paganism. Expertly scripted by Anthony Shaffer, and cast to get Christopher Lee into drag and Britt Ekland to play Lindsay Kemp's daughter, the movie is let down only by ham-fisted direction. A cult favourite in the US. TR

Wide Sargasso Sea

(1992, Aust, 98 min)
d John Duigan. *p* Jan Sharp. *sc* Jan Sharp, Carole Angier, John Duigan. *ph* Geoff Burton, Gabriel Beristain. *ed* Anne Goursaud, Jimmy Sandoval. *m* Stewart Copeland. *cast* Karina Lombard, Nathaniel Parker, Rachel Ward, Michael York, Martine Beswicke, Claudia Robinson.
● Jean Rhys's last novel unlocked the secret behind the door: who was the mysterious madwoman in Rochester's attic in *Jane Eyre*? Rhys imagined her as a Creole Jamaican plantation-owner's daughter and voodoo-child who becomes a victim of clashing cultural loyalties, degenerate family inheritance and disappointed love. Duigan's version retains much of the period detail, but wisely avoids getting swamped by diffuse political allegory, and settles instead as a full blown bodice-ripper. Presumably Karina Lombard was cast as the daughter to embody sensuality and suggest mixed-blood inheritance, but her limitations as an actress forbid audience identification. Likewise, Parker's Rochester, shipped from Albion for the fateful arranged marriage, is merely a dashing cad. There's little sense of any of the proceedings, but the movie has a fascinating charged quality: Geoff Burton films the Jamaican locations in an intoxicating profusion of colour, and the colonialist soirées and the plantation-house fire are superbly mounted. A strange, dark, muddled dream of a movie, occasionally risible but rarely boring. WH

Widow of Saint-Pierre, The

see Veuve de Saint-Pierre, La

Widows' Peak

(1993, GB, 101 min)
d John Irvin. *p* Jo Manuel. *sc* Hugh Leonard. *ph* Ashley Rowe. *ed* Peter Tanner. *pd* Leo Austin. *m* Carl Davis. *cast* Mia Farrow, Joan Plowright, Natasha Richardson, Adrian Dunbar, Jim Broadbent, Gerard McSorley, Tina Kellegher.
● A peculiar concept, this hill where only single women and widows are permitted to live, but such a place forms the setting for director Irvin's first foray into comedy. Set in 1920s Ireland, it tells of a community of widows, spearheaded by Plowright, which is disrupted by the arrival of spirited war widow Edwina (Richardson, with American accent). Farrow plays the downtrodden Miss O'Hare who immediately takes a violent dislike to Edwina. Both seem to have a difficult past they want hidden, the unravelling of which forms a strong whodunit narrative and, ultimately, a clever plot twist. The robust characterisation of the trio is the film's main strength. JBa

Wifemistress (Mogliamante)

(1977, It, 106 min)
d Marco Vicario. *p* Franco Cristaldi. *sc* Rodolfo Sonego, Marco Vicario. *ph* Ennio Guarnieri. *ed* Nino Baragli. *ad* Mario Garbulia. *m* Armando Trovaioli. *cast* Laura Antonelli, Marcello Mastroianni, Leonard Mann, William Berger, Olga Karlatos.
● A sickly Antonelli emerges from a moribund marriage to become a New Woman in the course of this classic comedy of concealment, deception, and revelation, played out in Northern Italy in the early 1900s. Vicario, through velvety, sensual camerawork, captures an era of intense intellectual and physical restlessness, when Italy dusted off the *Belle Epoque* and feverishly embraced anarchism, atheism, science, social reform, egalitarianism, and when political and sexual excitement might have seemed interchangeable. The film's shimmering eroticism is delicious. Bertolucci might have made this, if he wasn't such a prig. JS

Wilby Conspiracy, The

(1974, GB, 105 min)
d Ralph Nelson. *p* Martin Baum. *sc* Rod Amateau, Harold Nebenzal. *ph* John Coquillon. *ed* Ernest Walter. *pd* Harry Pottle. *m* Stanley Myers. *cast* Sidney Poitier, Michael Caine, Nicol Williamson, Prunella Gee, Persis Khambatta, Saeed Jaffrey, Rutger Hauer, Patrick Allen.
● Handcuffed together, white Caine and black Poitier pursue smuggled diamonds across the veld, and are themselves chased by the Jo'burg fuzz. Mix in some interracial screwing and violence, and Ralph Nelson's got himself a South African *Soldier Blue*, a sort of tin *Gold*. Assets there are: Caine is served with some nice deadpan lines by Rod Amateau, and John Coquillon's photography is characteristically cool. But this is an unpleasant and invidious film, like *Soldier Blue* creaming the surface off profound racial issues to ease the killing along. Its basic attitude is as leering as Nicol Williamson's security cop. AN

Wild About Harry

(2000, GB, 100 min)
d Declan Lowney. *p* Laurie Borg, Robert Cooper. *sc* Colin Bateman. *ph* Ron Fortunato. *ed* Tim Waddell. *pd* Shane Bunting, Claire Kenny. *m* Murray Gold. *cast* Amanda Donohoe, Brendan Gleeson, Adrian Dunbar, James Nesbitt, George Wendt, Henry Deazley, Bronagh Gallagher.
● Womanising, boozy, cheeky presenter (Gleeson) of TV North's 'What's Cooking?' programme is kicked senseless by louts on a night-time cigarette hunt, causing him to lose his memories and old ways, much to the relief and eventual pleasure of his son and seriously pissed-off wife (Donohoe). But is this rejuvenation just an act? This lightweight, but enjoyable comedy is directed by the creator of TV's *Father Ted* and is full of satisfying detail (notably in the programme itself) and neatly timed broad comedy, but its bid for romantic appeal turns it sentimental. The leads are on the money. WH

Wild Angels, The

(1966, US, 93 min)
d/p Roger Corman. *sc* Charles B Griffith. *ph* Richard Moore. *ed* Monte Hellman. *pd* Rick Beck-Meyer. *m* Mike Curb. *cast* Peter Fonda, Nancy Sinatra, Bruce Dern, Lou Procopio, Coby Denton, Marc Cavell, Michael J Pollard, Diane Ladd, Joan Shawlee, Gayle Hunnicutt.
● First shot: a kid on a trike pedals furiously away from his mother, to be stopped abruptly by a chopper's front wheel. Final shot: Peter Fonda shovels dirt over fellow-Angel Bruce Dern's grave, as police sirens wail closer. Moral: none. Roger Corman's notorious classic remains perhaps the most explicitly nihilistic movie ever made; revealed in retrospect to be less a rebellious youth picture than the extremist culmination of his horror movie cycle. Organised around Dern's death and protracted funeral rites, the film focuses a dispassionate scrutiny on the limits of inarticulate anarchy, with the Hell's Angels characterised with suitably satanic literalness as they 'fall' in the no-choice gulf between the cross and the swastika. Paradise Lost, indeed, as *non serviam* leads inexorably, and very sourly, to 'nothing to say'...'nowhere to go'. Discomfiting, but timely. PT

Wild at Heart

(1990, US, 124 min)
d David Lynch. *p* Monty Montgomery, Steve Golin, Sigurjon Sighvatsson. *sc* David Lynch. *ph* Frederick Elmes. *ed* Duwayne Dunham. *pd* Patricia Norris. *m* Angelo Badalamenti. *cast* Nicolas Cage, Laura Dern, Diane Ladd, Willem Dafoe, Isabella Rossellini, Harry Dean Stanton, Crispin Glover, Grace Zabriskie, JE Freeman, W Morgan Shepherd.
● As petty criminal Sailor (Cage) and his lover Lula (Dern) go on the run through a murderous Deep South, fleeing but meeting sleazy oddballs hired by Lula's mom (Ladd) to end their relationship, Lynch evokes a surreal, sinister world a mite too reminiscent of his earlier work: bloody murder, violent sexual passion, kooky kitsch, freaky characters immersed in private fantasies, digressive metaphors, symbols and cultish references, and bizarre humour to lighten the nightmare. This *déjà vu* weakens the film; sometimes the weirdness seems so forced that Lynch appears merely to be giving fans what they expect. But it's churlish to focus on flaws when so much is exhilaratingly unsettling. Even more than a virtuoso shoot-out, two scenes – Stanton tortured by a gang of grotesques, a truly nasty car crash – exemplify Lynch's ability to disturb through carefully contrived atmosphere; while

the performances lend a consistency of tone lacking in the narrative (but ever-present in Fred Elmes' fine camerawork). The film, finally, is funny, scary and brilliantly cinematic. GA

Wild Bill

(1995, US, 97 min, b/w & col)
d Walter Hill. *p* Richard D Zanuck, Lili Zanuck. *sc* Walter Hill. *ph* Lloyd Ahern. *ed* Freeman Davies. *pd* Joseph C Nemec III. *m* Van Dyke Parks. *cast* Jeff Bridges, James Remar, David Arquette, Ellen Barkin, John Hurt.

● Hill's portrait of Wild Bill Hickok – trapper, gambler, sometime marshal, showman and drifter – is a touch disappointing. It's not the lead performance that's at fault: Bridges is as natural and easy as ever and gives Hickok a complexity and depth barely hinted at by Hill's script which, despite switching deftly between time frames, never really gets beyond the conceit that the legendary hard-livin' shootist cherished surprisingly tender, opium-induced memories of an old flame. In other words, we're more or less in *Judge Roy Bean* territory, with echoes of Leone, Ford and others thrown in for good measure. As various glory hunters turn up in 1870s Deadrock hoping to dispatch the West's fastest draw, and while Hickok himself loses his sight, his desire for Calamity Jane (Barkin) and, perhaps, his lust for life, Hill and cameraman Lloyd Ahern litter the plot proper with attractively bleached b/w flashbacks to 'explain' his reputation and state of mind. The uneven tone shifts between mythic elegy, heroic action and broad, ironic comedy, while the narrative's rapid pace reduces certain characters to mere cameos and, worse, undermines the film's aspirations to epic drama. Both as a modern Western and as a Hill movie, this is efficient but middling – which still, finally, means that it's worth catching. GA

Wild Bill: A Hollywood Maverick

(1995, US, 95 min, b/w & col)
d/sc Todd Robinson. *ph* Theodor M Angell. *ed* Leslie Jones. *m* David Bell. *with* William Wellman, Clint Eastwood, Robert Redford, Sidney Poitier, Gregory Peck, Charles Buddy Rogers, Nancy Reagan, Robert Mitchum, Martin Scorsese. *narrator* Alec Baldwin.

● William Augustus Wellman ('My father gave me that name so I'd learn how to fight') came back from the Great War with a new nickname, a steel plate in his head, and enough experience to fuel 76 tough and tender movies, 'films you have to reach for', as Tab Hunter puts it. A handful are classics – the original *A Star Is Born, The Public Enemy, Nothing Sacred* – but somehow the oeuvre has escaped the critical attention it deserves. At the very least, this thorough, impressive documentary will have you desperate to catch up with half a dozen lesser known titles, but it also serves as a probing biography of a fascinating life. Unusually astute anecdotes and insights come from an all-star line-up: Eastwood, Redford, Peck, Poitier, Mitchum, Scorsese, even Nancy Reagan, marred only slightly by the Alec Baldwin's purple narration ('directing a motion picture might be akin to helming a ship called Genesis'). TCh

Wild Bunch, The 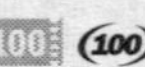 (100)

(1969, US, 145 min)
d Sam Peckinpah. *p* Phil Feldman. *sc* Walon Green, Sam Peckinpah. *ph* Lucien Ballard. *ed* Lou Lombardo. *ad* Edward Carrere. *m* Jerry Fielding. *cast* William Holden, Ernest Borgnine, Robert Ryan, Edmond O'Brien, Warren Oates, Jaime Sanchez, Ben Johnson, Emilio Fernandez, Strother Martin, LQ Jones, Albert Dekker, Bo Hopkins.

● From the opening sequence, in which a circle of laughing children poke at a scorpion writhing in a sea of ants, to the infamous blood-spurting finale, Peckinpah completely rewrites John Ford's Western mythology – by looking at the passing of the Old West from the point of view of the marginalised outlaws rather than the law-abiding settlers. Though he spares us none of the callousness and brutality of Holden and his gang, Peckinpah nevertheless presents their macho code of loyalty as a positive value in a world increasingly dominated by corrupt railroad magnates and their mercenary killers (Holden's old buddy Ryan). The flight into Mexico, where they virtually embrace their death at the hands of double-crossing general Fernandez and his rabble army, is a nihilistic acknowledgment of the men's anachronistic status. In purely cinematic terms, the film is a savagely beautiful spectacle, Lucien Ballard's superb cinematography complementing Peckinpah's darkly elegiac vision. NF

Wildcats

(1986, US, 107 min)
d Michael Ritchie. *p* Anthea Sylbert. *sc* Ezra Sacks. *ph* Donald E Thorin. *ed* Richard A Harris. *pd* Boris Leven. *m* Hawk Wolinski, James Newton. *cast* Goldie Hawn, Swoosie Kurtz, Robyn Lively, Brandy Gold, James Keach, Jan Hooks, Bruce McGill, Nipsey Russell, Wesley Snipes, Woody Harrelson, M Emmet Walsh, Ann Doran, Gloria Stuart.

● Football-crazy Goldie Hawn gets her wish to coach a high school team, but there's a catch. It's the roughest, toughest school in the city: Dobermans patrol the halls. Greeted with universal derision by a team of no-hopers, Goldie's got her work cut out for her; but sticking to her credo that 'you can be anything you want to be', she's soon kicking ass. Goldie's inspirational shot at playing Sly Stallone *and* Burgess Meredith is undone by the trite, inner-city Hollywood context she always favours. Instead of 'believe in yourself', the message becomes simply 'make believe'. TCh

Wildcats of St Trinian's, The

(1980, GB, 91 min)
d Frank Launder. *p* EM Smedley Aston. *sc* Frank Launder. *ph* Ernest Steward. *ed* Antony Gibbs. *ad* John Beard. *m* James Kenelm Clarke. *cast* Sheila Hancock, Michael Hordern, Joe Melia, Thorley Walters, Rodney Bewes, Deborah Norton, Maureen Lipman, Julia McKenzie.

● Launder and Gilliat's series about the dreadful girls' boarding school, inspired by Ronald Searle's cartoons, revived after a 14-year absence from the screen. Too late. The '60s versions were already failing in their attempt to find contemporary material on which to hang the myth (for that's what it had become – weekend wet dreams for suburbia). This one should never have been made: the old stock actors (Grenfell, Sim, et al) have died; the storyline is feebly offensive (the girls kidnap the daughter of a rich Arab to press their demand for Trade Union recognition of their strike); and the repressed anarchic energy of the '50s originals (Amazons for Chaos) has just dribbled away into more page three cheesecake. CA

Wild Child, The

see Enfant Sauvage, L'

Wilde

(1997, GB/US/Jap/Ger, 117 min)
d Brian Gilbert. *p* Marc Samuelson, Peter Samuelson. *sc* Julian Mitchell. *ph* Martin Fuhrer. *ed* Michael Bradsell. *pd* Maria Djurkovic. *m* Debbie Wiseman. *cast* Stephen Fry, Jude Law, Vanessa Redgrave, Jennifer Ehle, Gemma Jones, Judy Parfitt, Michael Sheen, Zoë Wanamaker, Tom Wilkinson, Peter Barkworth.

● If anybody was born to play Oscar Wilde, it must have been Stephen Fry: not only does he look like the Green Carnation Man, but he himself is often portrayed as being too clever, too complex for his own good. Gilbert's film, with an intelligent screenplay by Julian Mitchell based on Richard Ellmann's biography, looks curiously old-fashioned. More lavish than Merchant Ivory, it's a '60s-style Technicolor affair with a grown-up '90s feel. Unlike its predecessors, it's able to be frank about the sexual encounters: with devoted friend Robbie Ross; with rent boys to whom Wilde was indulgently generous; and, fatefully, with the love of his life, the beautiful, wilful, spoilt brat Lord Alfred ('Bosie') Douglas, who didn't fancy Wilde, but saw him as the alternative father to his brutal, bullying pater, the Marquess of Queensberry. As Wilde, descending from would-be-doting husband and father to follower of his own 'nature', and finally ruined and disgraced martyr on the tree of English hypocrisy, Fry is utterly convincing. He speaks the witty lines as if he invented them and manages to square Wilde's weakness and arrogance with his immense generosity of spirit, while his prison cell reunion with dying wife Constance (Ehle) would make a traffic warden cry. The cast oozes real class: Redgrave is superb as Wilde's tigerish Irish mother; Wilkinson suitably revolting as Queensberry; Sheen perfect as Ross; and Law explosively arresting as the capricious, finally destructive Douglas. SGr

Wild Flowers (Les Fleurs Sauvages)

(1982, Can, 153 min, b/w & col)
d Jean-Pierre Lefebvre. *p* Marguerite Duparc. *sc* Jean-Pierre Lefebvre. *ph* Guy Dufaux. *ed* Marguerite Duparc. *m* Raoul Duguay. *cast* Marthe Nadeau, Michèle Magny, Pierre Curzi, Claudia Aubin, Eric Beauséjour.

● Anyone who has spent Christmas in the company of an ageing relative, and by Boxing Day felt a strangling fit coming on, will be on familiar territory here, with an elderly woman (Nadeau), tight-lipped and fussy, coming to stay for a week in the country with her daughter and grandchildren. Perhaps at two hours-plus of fairly slow-moving action you feel the tedium of the old lady's visit almost as much as her daughter (Magny) – a potter trying to reject a stereotyped role of wife and mother – but the film also raises many interesting questions about the importance of families and the nature of relationships within them. Its main purpose, though, working through this clash between generations, is a plea for tolerance, most effectively expressed in the portions of the film which lapse into black-and-white to indicate what the characters really feel about each other. CS

Wild Flowers

(1989, GB, 69 min)
d Robert Smith. *p* Chris Harvey. *sc* Sharman Macdonald. *ph* Witold Stok. *ed* John Davies. *pd* Caroline Hanania. *m* Kenny Craddock, Colin Gibson. *cast* Beatie Edney, Sheila Keith, Colette O'Neil, Stevan Rimkus, Amanda Walker, Kay Gallie.

● Robert Smith's film is set in a tight Scottish coastal community. Annie (O'Neil), a woman who loves women, is daggers drawn with her mother Marguerite (Keith, a superb performance of implacable bottled-up fury). Annie is a child of her mother's middle age, and Marguerite has laid out the corpses of all four of her brothers. At the centre of this intense, unexpected film, scripted by Sharman Macdonald and handsomely photographed by Witold Stok, is Annie's son Angus (Rimkus), who has returned home from Edinburgh with his friend Sadie (Edney). The trouble is that Angus lacks mettle. He adores nothing so much as the sweet sound of his own singing voice. And Annie finds herself compelled to save Sadie, a fellow free spirit, from this fastidious young man. JPy

Wild for Kicks

see Beat Girl

Wild Game (Wildwechsel)

(1972, WGer, 102 min)
d Rainer Werner Fassbinder. *p* Gerhard Freund. *sc* Rainer Werner Fassbinder. *ph* Dietrich Lohmann. *ed* Thea Eymesz. *ad* Kurt Raab. *cast* Eva Mattes, Harry Baer, Jörg von Liebenfels, Ruth Drexel, Rudolf Waldemar, Hanna Schygulla, Kurt Raab.

● Fassbinder made this (for TV) right after *The Bitter Tears of Petra von Kant*, in the year that Godard made *Tout va Bien*. Like Godard's film, Fassbinder's is about a male-female relationship in a 'political' context, but here the boy is 19 and the girl only 14, so that their mutual love outrages more than one lower middle class taboo. Despite a final flourish of misogyny (the girl betrays the boy after he's laid his life on the line for her), Fassbinder's stance is very sympathetically unsentimental; and his mixture of caricature (her parents), materialism (the depiction of a factory production line), carefully stylised realism (the central relationship), and a bold physical frankness, is more than usually adroit. The movie created a censorship furore in Germany, not least because the author of the original play (Franz Kroetz) denounced Fassbinder's 'obscene' depiction of his characters. TR

Wild Games (Combat des fauves/Der Mann im Lift)

(1995, Bel/Ger/Fr, 92 min)
d Benoît Lamy. *p* Alfred Hürmer, Jacques Perrin, Jacqueline Pierreux, Dagmar Jacobson. *sc* Gabrielle Borile, Benoît Lamy. *ph* Charles

van Damme. *ed* Denise Vindevogel. *pd* Pierre-François Limbosch. *m* Bruno Coulais. *cast* Richard Bohringer, Ute Lemper, Papa Wemba, Jacqueline Nicolas, Roland Depauw.

● Featuring Wemba (from Lamy's earlier *La Vie est belle*) as the lament-singing janitor, this slightly clunking, though well-shot, lift drama sees advertising ace Bohringer caught between floors in an old elevator. He is at turns taunted, neglected or seduced by haughty, recently widowed Lemper in semi-vamp get-up, a possible crazy suicide living in a neighbouring flat. Unconvincing, psychologically or dramatically, this adaptation of a novel by Henri-Frédéric Blanc is neither droll nor satiric enough to get us through the rather obvious mechanics of the sexual role-reversal game play. WH

Wild Geese, The

(1977, GB, 134 min)
d Andrew V McLaglen. *p* Euan Lloyd. *sc* Reginald Rose. *ph* Jack Hildyard. *ed* John Glen. *pd* Syd Cain. *m* Roy Budd. *cast* Richard Burton, Roger Moore, Richard Harris, Hardy Krüger, Stewart Granger, Jack Watson, Winston Ntshona, John Kani, Frank Finlay, Kenneth Griffith, Barry Foster, Jeff Corey.

● Dried-out 'hellraisers' Burton and Harris totter together for this mercenary outing which transfers the fundamental plotline of *The Professionals* to Africa: sinister businessman Granger hires Burton as head of a private army to rescue imprisoned black liberal leader. Harris' gooey relationship with his son sets him up for the chop from the start; racist Krüger, to whom niggers are the white man's burden, ends up carrying black leader cross country and undergoes a last-minute change of heart; 'camp' doctor Kenneth Griffith gets ripped apart by lithe black men, much to his delight. The natives are more primitive than they were in *Zulu*. It's also the kind of film that would be deeply misogynist…if there were any women in it. CPe

Wild Geese II

(1985, GB, 125 min)
d Peter Hunt. *p* Euan Lloyd. *sc* Reginald Rose. *ph* Michael Reed. *ed* Keith Palmer. *pd* Syd Cain. *m* Roy Budd. *cast* Scott Glenn, Barbara Carrera, Edward Fox, Laurence Olivier, Robert Webber, Robert Freitag, Kenneth Haigh, Stratford Johns, Ingrid Pitt.

● A pseudo-'good idea' for a movie: springing Hitler's ancient deputy Hess from Spandau prison. To what end, though? Eschewing any scenario about buried Nazi gold, the writer (Reginald Rose, a long way from *12 Angry Men*) opts for the batty notion that a TV executive would hire a flock of mercenaries to lift Hess so he can appear as guest on a chat show. In the run-up to the big event a familiar assortment of Arab terrorists, KGB colonels and whatnot bustle around the scene exchanging gunfire, waylaying one another and generally reproducing the adolescent ambience of *Wild Geese* the first. BBa

Wild in the Country

(1961, US, 114 min)
d Philip Dunne. *p* Jerry Wald. *sc* Clifford Odets. *ph* William C Mellor. *ed* Dorothy Spencer. *ad* Jack Martin Smith. *m* Kenyon Hopkins. *cast* Elvis Presley, Hope Lange, Tuesday Weld, Millie Perkins, John Ireland, Gary Lockwood.

● 'I'm carrying a cupful of anger and trying not to spill it' says Elvis, backwoods literary genius, to Hope Lange's psychiatrist in this extraordinary film. Actually, he's carrying scriptwriter Clifford Odets' cupful, much diluted since the '30s when he was hailed as the white hope of leftist drama. Odets' characteristic cascades of metaphors sit strangely on almost everyone in the cast. Only Tuesday Weld's small town gal dreaming of the big time convinces as a character, not a mouthpiece. There are just a few songs, and the whole's as wild as a glass of milk, but its curio quotient is enormous. GB

Wild in the Streets

(1968, US, 96 min)
d Barry Shear. *p* James H Nicholson, Samuel Z Arkoff. *sc* Robert Thom. *ph* Richard Moore. *ed* Fred R Feitshans, Eve Newman. *ad* Paul Sylos. *m* Les Baxter. *cast* Shelley Winters, Christopher Jones, Diane Varsi, Ed Begley, Hal Holbrook, Millie Perkins, Richard Pryor, Bert Freed, Michael Margotta.

● A wild, uneven frolic about a teenage takeover, directed with great verve by Shear from a witty script by Robert Thom. It's a nightmare fantasy about a millionaire pop star (Jones) who enters politics, gets the voting age lowered to 15, and is swept to the White House. Soon everyone over 35 is being herded off to 'Paradise Camps' to be force-fed LSD. But there's a small problem left for the new dictator: a small child crossly observes how old he is at 24… Despite its rough edges and airy trimmings, the film has a chilling nub of possibility to it, neatly underlined in a scene where the hero's mother (Winters) is dragged out of hiding by youthful guards deaf to her plea that she is a teenager. As she is dragged away, her despairing cry floats back: 'But I'm aryan…I mean, I'm young, I'm young'. TM

Wild Man Blues

(1997, US, 105 min)
d Barbara Kopple. *p* Jean Doumanian. *ph* Tom Hurwitz. *ed* Lawrence Silk. *with* Woody Allen, Soon-Yi Previn, Letty Aronson, Jean Doumanian, Nettie Konigsberg, Eddy Davis.

● After *Deconstructing Harry* comes this record of clarinetist Woody Allen's 1996 European tour with his New Orleans jazz band (18 concerts, seven countries). The film was commissioned by Allen's producer Jean Doumanian, and the director apparently secured editorial freedom and 'access all areas'. This is a standard rockumentary: concert footage plus backstage eavesdropping, played out against the highs and lows of a sell-out tour. True to type, Allen gets seasick gliding round Venice in a gondola, and insists on twin suites everywhere he and companion Soon-Yi Previn stay – he needs his own personal shower. It's hardly a revelation, but Allen emerges as genuinely neurotic. He's also funny (especially on the discrepancy between the adulation of the crowds and his films' meagre takings) and not particularly likeable (there's no interplay with the band off-stage, for example). The horrors of *Stardust Memories* are very real to him. The only person who seems to break through this self-protective bubble is the singularly no nonsense, thoroughly unfazed and self-assured Soon-Yi. TCh

Wild One, The

(1953, US, 79 min, b/w)
d Laslo Benedek. *p* Stanley Kramer. *sc* John Paxton. *ph* Hal Mohr. *ed* Al Clark. *pd* Rudolph Sternad. *m* Leith Stevens. *cast* Marlon Brando, Mary Murphy, Robert Keith, Lee Marvin, Jay C Flippen, Peggy Maley, Ray Teal.

● Effectively banned in Britain until 1968, Brando's biker seems disarmingly tame by comparison with the wild angels he spawned. Yet the film isn't half bad as it sets up characters and situation with neat economy, tracing the seeds of explosion when the Black Rebels ride into town, are detained by a minor accident, and hang around trading insults with a rival gang. A distinct bonus is the echt '50s insolence with which Brando handles bits like his famous response to the girl in the drugstore who asks what he's rebelling against: a pause, a quirk of the eyebrow, a drawled 'Whaddya got?'. But all too soon one is reminded that Stanley Kramer produced. Dissolving into a flurry of melodrama, it emits no more than a faint liberal yap about the misunderstood youth saved by an understanding girl. TM

Wild Orchid

(1989, US, 111 min)
d Zalman King. *p* Mark Damon, Tony Anthony. *sc* Zalman King, Patricia Louisianna Knop. *ph* Gale Tattersall. *ed* Marc Grossman, Glenn A Morgan. *pd* Carlos Conti. *m* Geoff MacCormack, Simon Goldenberg. *cast* Mickey Rourke, Jacqueline Bisset, Carré Otis, Assumpta Serna, Bruce Greenwood.

● You are now entering soft-porn country. Your guides – Zalman King, co-scriptwriter Patricia Louisianna Knop, masterful stud Rourke – brought you *Nine ½ Weeks*, so you know what you're getting. Three acts: set-up, foreplay, bonk. Kansas boondocks ingénue Emily Reed (Otis, ex-model, no actress), a lawyer, gets a corporation job in sensuous, throbbing Rio de Janeiro, handling the papers for a complex hotel buy-out. The savage, passionate fucking she witnesses in an abandoned warehouse begins to distract her from work, as does interested party James Wheeler (Rourke), with his 16 inches of applied suntan, gitano bandana and Harley Davidson. He wines and dines Emily, asking challenging questions like 'Have you ever felt that primal, insatiable hunger?' How long can she resist? Even within its own terms the film is a disaster: all the acting is pathetic, the pacing poor, and the pay-off copulation scene merely mechanical. WH

Wild Party, The

(1929, US, 77 min, b/w)
d Dorothy Arzner. *sc* E Lloyd Sheldon. *ph* Victor Milner. *ed* Otho Lovering. *cast* Clara Bow, Fredric March, Shirley O'Hara, Marceline Day, Joyce Compton, Jack Oakie, Phillips Holmes.

● A mischievous silent film featuring Clara Bow as Stella, a flighty girl with hair of fluff and heart (finally) of gold. In a transatlantic tale of the Angela Brazil genre, Stella's good-time girl stereotype is challenged a) by another student for whom studying is a serious thing, and b) by a heroic professor whose savage heart beats beneath a pocket of tweed and a respect for learning. Despite the dashing moral ending, it's a very enjoyable film, and Arzner handles the exposition of and challenge to the stereotype very astutely, especially in a scene of sexually violent response by some men in a bar to a deliberately provocative bevy of girls. MV

Wild Party, The

(1974, US, 100 min)
d James Ivory. *p* Ismail Merchant. *sc* Walter Marks. *ph* Walter Lassally. *ed* Kent McKinney. *ad* David Nichols. *m* Laurence Rosenthal. *cast* James Coco, Raquel Welch, Perry King, Tiffany Bolling, Royal Dano, David Dukes, Dena Dietrich, Jennifer Lee.

● Based on the bizarre narrative poem by Joseph Moncure March which celebrates the decadence of the Roaring Twenties in cheerful Kiplingesque doggerel, this tells of a chubby silent comedian who throws a Hollywood shindig that ends in murder. No doubt to emphasise the titillating (but misleading) echoes of the Fatty Arbuckle scandal, the film was originally released in Britain in a version cut and 'rearranged' by American International. Coming on like a sexploiter but failing to deliver, this naturally died the death. Ivory's original cut is a delightful tour de force, choreographed entirely around the serpentine party which represents the fading comedian's last desperate bid for success and happiness, but which ends by swallowing its own wild tail. An acid-tinted elegy for the Dream factory, it features some fine musical numbers and wonderfully baroque settings, but also takes a look at the skull beneath the skin just as the extravagance, the glamour, and the licence were beginning to wear thin under pressure from the coming of sound and of Hays Code censorship. TM

Wild Reeds, The

see Roseaux Sauvages, Les

Wild River

(1960, US, 109 min)
d/p Elia Kazan. *sc* Paul Osborn. *ph* Ellsworth J Fredricks. *ed* William H Reynolds. *ad* Lyle Wheeler, Herman A Blumenthal. *m* Kenyon Hopkins. *cast* Montgomery Clift, Lee Remick, Jo Van Fleet, Jay C Flippen, Albert Salmi, Barbara Loden, James Westerfield, Bruce Dern.

● Maybe it's the location shooting, maybe it's the performances, but Kazan's lyrical, liberal account of a Tennessee Valley Authority agent (Clift) struggling to persuade an obstinate old woman (Fleet) to abandon her home before it is flooded by a new project, is one of his least theatrical and most affecting films. Partly that's because the battle lines – between city and country, old and new, expediency and commitment – are effectively blurred, making the conflict more dramatically complex than one might expect; but Kazan's evident nostalgia for the '30s (New Deal) setting also lends the film greater depth and scope than is usually to be found in his work. GA

Wild Rovers

(1971, US, 132 min)
d Blake Edwards. *p* Blake Edwards, Ken Wales. *sc* Blake Edwards. *ph* Philip H Lathrop. *ed* John F Burnett. *ad* George W Davis, Addison Hehr. *m* Jerry Goldsmith. *cast* William Holden, Ryan O'Neal, Karl Malden, Lynn Carlin, Tom Skerritt, Joe Don Baker, James Olson, Leora Dana, Moses Gunn, Rachel Roberts, Charles Gray.

●Arguably one of Blake Edwards' best films, this is a faintly derivative but highly enjoyable Western in the nostalgic, anti-heroic mould. Holden and O'Neal are the innocents tired of their unremarkable lives who team up for a bank robbery, and head off on a picaresque odyssey to Mexico with dreams of amounting to something as cattle barons. If most of the film is gently comic and lyrical, the harshness of the West is never played down, so that the duo's cruel destiny is foreshadowed throughout. Marvellous performances and elegiac photography (by Philip Lathrop) are well complemented by Edwards' unusually light touch. GA

Wild Side (aka Donald Cammell's Wild Side/Wild Side – The Director's Cut)

(1995/2000, US, 115 min)
d Donald Cammell [as Franklin Brauner, 1995 version]. *p* (1995) Elie Cohn, John Langley; (2000) Hamish McAlpine, Nick Jones, Frank Mazzola. *sc* China Kong, Donald Cammell. *ph* Sead Mutarevic. *ed* Frank Mazzola. *pd* Claire Bowin. *m* (1995) John Hassell; (2000) Ryuichi Sakamoto. *cast* Christopher Walken, Joan Chen, Steven Bauer, Anne Heche, Allen Garfield, Adam Novack, Zion, Richard Palmer.

●Twenty minutes longer than the 1995 version released on video in the US, this arrives restored to the late Donald Cammell's original intentions. Hopes for a late rally from the maverick behind *Performance* may not be fully realised, but this awkward crossbreed of erotic thriller, black farce and lyrical love story certainly has the gumption to risk absurdity for the sake of cavalier spirit. Money problems compel California bank exec Alex (Heche) to moonlight as an expensive call girl. As such, she encounters Walken's fugitive money launderer, who's sexually taken with her and eager to exploit her access to the banking system. His oafish driver (Bauer) has his eye on Heche too, but as soon as she meets Walken's spouse Chen a spark ignites. Can the purity of their desire extricate them from the surrounding cycle of money, power and sexual domination? Walken connoisseurs will doubtless enjoy his declamatory style, but he turns this shark with skewed morals into a show-off routine, making the rest of the movie rather hard to take seriously. TJ

Wild Side, The (aka Suburbia)

(1983, US, 96 min)
d Penelope Spheeris. *p* Bert Dragin. *sc* Penelope Spheeris. *ph* Tim Suhrstedt. *ed* Ross Albert. *ad* Randy Moore. *m* Alex Gibson. *cast* Chris Pederson, Bill Coyne, Jennifer Clay, Timothy O'Brien, Grant Miner, Andrew Pece, Don Allen.

●Far from the mad pretensions of Coppola's Camus-for-kids, far from the puerile pranks of *Porky's*, this combines intelligent social comment with the conventions of the teens-in-revolt exploiter to gripping effect. The group of nihilist punks who scandalise one of LA's seedier neighbourhoods are never glamorised, but shown warts and all. Eventually, however, they gain our sympathy, partly because Spheeris reveals why they have become so anti-social, partly because the irate locals who persecute them as scapegoats for every crime imaginable are even less attractive. A justifiably angry film, fast and full of violent action, though there's plenty of humour too; and the lack of originality is amply compensated for by its manifest sincerity. GA

Wild Strawberries (100) (Smultronstället)

(1957, Swe, 94 min, b/w)
d Ingmar Bergman. *p* Allan Ekelund. *sc* Ingmar Bergman. *ph* Gunnar Fischer. *ed* Oscar Rosander. *ad* Gittan Gustafson. *m* Erik Nordgren. *cast* Victor Sjöström, Bibi Andersson, Ingrid Thulin, Gunnar Björnstrand, Naima Wifstrand, Björn Bjelvenstam, Max von Sydow.

●One of Bergman's warmest, and therefore finest films, this concerns an elderly academic – grouchy, introverted, dried up emotionally – who makes a journey to collect a university award, and *en route* relives his past by means of dreams, imagination, and encounters with others. It's an occasionally over-symbolic work (most notably in the opening nightmare sequence), but it's filled with richly observed characters and a real feeling for the joys of nature and youth. And Sjöström – himself a celebrated director, best known for his silent work (which included the Hollywood masterpiece *The Wind*) – gives an astonishingly moving performance as the aged professor. As Bergman himself wrote of his performance in the closing moments: 'His face shone with secretive light, as if reflected from another reality…It was like a miracle'. GA

Wild Style

(1982, US, 82 min)
d/p/sc Charlie Ahearn. *ph* Clive Davidson. *ed* Steve Brown. *m* Frederick Brathwaite. *cast* 'Lee' George Quinones, Sandra 'Pink' Fabara, Frederick Brathwaite, Patti Astor, Zephyr, Busy Bee.

●As teenage lovers, Raymond and Rose are as gauche and uninteresting as other people's holiday snaps, but Ahearn fleshes out the bare bones of their story with characters and action that exercise an alien charm: saluting the rappin', breakin', and graffiti people of New York's run-down South Bronx, his film features many key figures from the city's street culture. Quinones, infamous wall and subway train-sprayer, plays the mild-mannered Raymond, who at night becomes the enigmatic Zoro, always painting one step ahead of the law; 'Pink' Fabara, whose 'writings' hang in New York art galleries, plays his 'Lady Bug' Rose, leader of the media-conscious Graffiti Union. Yet despite the sharp pace and Chris Stein's slick soundtrack, the movie doesn't quite succeed in presenting the essentially repetitious rappin' and breakin' without itself becoming repetitive. FD

Wild Target

see Cible émouvante

Wild Things

(1998, US, 108 min)
d John McNaughton. *p* Rodney Liber, Steven A Jones. *sc* Stephen Peters. *ph* Jeffrey L Kimball. *ed* Elena Maganini. *pd* Edward T McAvoy. *m* George S Clinton. *cast* Kevin Bacon, Matt Dillon, Neve Campbell, Theresa Russell, Denise Richards, Carrie Snodgress, Bill Murray, Robert Wagner.

●Lombardo (Dillon) is 'Educator of the Year' at Florida's Blue Bay high school, a popular teacher with a taste for the good life. When Kelly (Richards), one of his students, accuses him of rape, the police don't give much credence to a rich bitch on heat. But when punky low class Suzie (Campbell) echoes her claims, Lombardo only has two-bit lawyer Ken Bowden (Murray) standing between him and jail. For about an hour, this shapes up promisingly: it's so blatant, you know it's got to be a tease. The director zooms in on wet T-shirts in slo-mo and maps out the social and sexual hierarchies with glee: think John Waters crossed with John Hughes. When the film-makers pull the rug out from under us, it's a doozy of a twist. Too bad there's still an hour to go, because then all bets are off. McNaughton double and triple-crosses the audience with such reckless abandon, it's impossible to care any more. This is one of those puzzle movies that's quite intriguing while it's feigning superficiality – and truly funny when Bill Murray is around – but really dumb once it thinks it's being smart. TCh

Wildwechsel

see Wild Game

Wild West

(1992, GB, 85 min)
d David Attwood. *p* Eric Fellner. *sc* Harwant Bains. *ph* Nic Knowland. *ed* Martin Walsh. *pd* Caroline Hanania. *m* Dominic Miller. *cast* Naveen Andrews, Sarita Choudhury, Ravi Kapoor, Ronny Jhutti, Ameet Chana.

●Spurred cowboys are stalking down Southall Broadway, and stetsons bob up and down suburban streets in this engaging film about Country & Western-obsessed British Asian kids who form themselves into a band, the 'Honky Tonk Cowboys'. Likely to be referred to as an Asian version of *The Commitments*, this cuts much deeper than Alan Parker's Irish ensemble piece. Harwant Bains' script makes pertinent points about culture and identity, but without pushing them in your face. Naveen Andrews (wasted in *London Kills Me*) gets a chance to show what he can do, and Sarita Choudhury (from *Mississippi Masala*) gives a nice performance as the female lead. Attwood's direction is a touch undisciplined, but there are some nice allusions to classic Westerns. AJ

Wild Wild West

(1999, US, 106 min)
d Barry Sonnenfeld. *p* Jon Peters, Barry Sonnenfeld. *sc* SS Wilson, Brent Maddock, Jeffrey Price, Peter S Seaman. *ph* Michael Ballhaus. *ed* Jim Miller. *pd* Bo Welch. *m* Elmer Bernstein. *cast* Will Smith, Kevin Kline, Kenneth Branagh, Salma Hayek, M Emmet Walsh, Ted Levine, Frederique Van Der Wal, Musetta Vander.

●Nominally a modern update on a long-forgotten '60s TV show, this monument to the vacuous excesses of chequebook cinema highlights the desperation of those who throw money at the screen hoping it will buy them a blockbuster. Back in the Old West, sassy marshal James West (Smith) and gadget master Artemus Gordon (Kline) are the two federal agents assigned to track down just who has been kidnapping the country's top scientists. Rita (Hayek) is the gal along for the ride since her dad is one of the disappeared. Dr Arliss Loveless (Branagh, beyond excruciating) is the megalomaniac techno wizard behind it all, a vengeful Confederate who now plans the overthrow of the US government. What happens? Lots of explosions as Branagh's giant mechanical tarantula runs amok, lots of gizmos as Kline rigs up a secret weapon on rails, and absolutely – repeat absolutely – no laughs from a pitiful script. A profound fog of boredom swiftly descends, quite unrecognisable as the work of the Barry Sonnenfeld who put such zip into *Men in Black*. TJ

Wild Women of Wongo

(1958, US, 70 min)
d James L Wolcott. *p* George R Black. *sc* Cedric Rutherford. *ph* Harry Walsh. *ed* David Cazalet. *cast* Jean Hawkshaw, Johnny Walsh, Mary Ann Webb, Ed Fury, Adrienne Bourbeau.

●Only the most dedicated follower of camp, the most ardent devotee of '50s hair lacquer and leopard-skin kitsch, will be kept genuinely amused throughout this High School Beach Party movie, thinly disguised as true tribal romance between the determined teenage virgins of Wongo (it's not their ethnic roots that are showing) and the dumb Caucasian hunks from the neighbouring Goona tribe – selected in preference to the neanderthal Wongo males. It's like a John Waters film without any disgusting bits, and as a conscious comedy one might argue that it lacks the innocent solemnity of the truly great bad movie. Needless to say, its prevailing ideology will prove deeply offensive to women, ugly people, and stuffed alligators everywhere.

William Christie et Les Arts Florissants ou la Passion du Baroque

(1994, Fr, 70 min)
d Andrea Kirsch. *with* William Christie.

●Whether you're already a devotee of the astringent melodious sound of the French baroque, or you enjoyed the music of *Tous les Matins du Monde* and want to hear more, this portrait of conductor William Christie and his gifted group of players Les Arts Florissants should please and inform in almost equal measure. An American who has reawakened in the French a delight in their own musical heritage, notably through his performances of Charpentier and Rameau, Christie is seen here in rehearsal, in concert and at home, and is revealed as an aesthete, disciplinarian and enthusiast. TJ

William Shakespeare's Romeo & Juliet

(1996, US, 120 min)
d Baz Luhrmann. *p* Gabriella Martinelli, Baz Luhrmann. *sc* Craig Pearce, Baz Luhrmann. *ph* Donald McAlpine. *ed* Jill Bilcock. *pd* Catherine Martin. *m* Nellee Hooper. *cast* Leonardo DiCaprio, Claire Danes, Harold Perrineau, Pete Postlethwaite, Miriam Margolyes, Brian Dennehy, John Leguizanmo, Paul Sorvino.

●Leone-style face-off between gun-toting gangs at a gas station: outright street-warfare is evidently imminent, which presents something of a problem for young Montague when, at an absurdly extravagant costume ball thrown at the Capulets' mansion, he falls head over heels for Juliet. So starts *WS's Romeo & Juliet.* Baz Luhrmann's gleefully cinematic version of the play is so relentlessly inventive and innovative, it takes 20 minutes to get a grasp on how appropriate is his approach to the material. Bravely (but sensibly) sticking with the original dialogue, Luhrmann makes the central element of his audacious adaptation visual: as the camera races wildly around, or rests on luminous close-ups and ornate tableaux, the striking sets, costumes, characters, the colours and compositions serve perfectly to evoke the forces of wealth and poverty, love and hate, power and pride, prejudice and superstition that infest the chaotically sprawling post-punk, post-industrial, multi-ethnic world of millennial Verona (Mexico City and Vera Cruz, heavily made over). Fine as the rest of the cast is, it's DiCaprio and Danes – vulnerable, innocent, impassioned and beautiful, both of them – who steal the honours. GA

Willie & Phil

(1980, US, 116 min)
d Paul Mazursky. *p* Paul Mazursky, Tony Ray. *sc* Paul Mazursky. *ph* Sven Nykvist. *ed* Donn Cambern. *pd* Pato Guzman. *m* Claude Bolling. *cast* Michael Ontkean, Margot Kidder, Ray Sharkey, Jan Miner, Tom Brennan, Julie Bovasso, Natalie Wood.

●For sheer consistency in chronicling a decade's evolution of chic American manners, mores, and ménages, Mazursky has few rivals. But as Bob & Carol & Ted & Alice have been supplemented in his trend-spotter's log-book by the likes of Alex & Blume & Harry & Tonto (and the strangely anonymous *Unmarried Woman*), his satirical edge has become blunted to a dull indulgence. Accordingly, *Willie & Phil* – optimistically and improbably rhymed with Truffaut's *Jules and Jim* – are let off much too lightly as they pussyfoot around Margot Kidder (as the quicksilver Jeannette) while the '70s trickle away in the background. Undecided whether he's shooting an upmarket buddy-love saga or simply shuffling a modish three-card deck, Mazursky piles on the nostalgic Age-of-Aquarius ephemera and shies away from the sexual grit, while Ontkean and the likeable Sharkey wrestle in awe with roles once earmarked for Pacino and Woody Allen. Wry, but on the rocks. PT

Will It Snow for Christmas? (Y'aura t'il de la neige à Noël?)

(1996, Fr, 91 min)
d Sandrine Veysset. *p* Danny Lebigot. *sc* Sandrine Veysset. *ph* Hélène Louvart. *ed* Nelly Quettier. *ad* Jacques Dubus. *m* Henri Ancillotti. *cast* Dominique Reymond, Daniel Duval, Jessica Martinez, Alexandre Roger, Xavier Colonna.

●A remarkable debut from writer/director Veysset, this depiction of farm life in the south of France mercilessly explodes the sentimentality and picturesqueness of, say, Claude Berri's films. Autobiographically inspired, it focuses on the hard frugal life of a mother (Reymond) and her seven children. Cinematographer Hélène Louvart keeps the camera close to the family's field of vision, making the viewer a kind of house guest, witness to the intimate rituals of family life – it takes time to become familiar with the children's names and their relationships with their older, emotionally distant stepbrothers, and to realise that their tyrannical father is keeping another 'legitimate' family some miles away. No music guides our attitude, merely 'natural' sound and the evidence of our eyes. The period and time are deliberately vague. Veysset concentrates instead on incident and detail, and nurtures an array of naturalistic performances. Her cinematic maturity and clarity of vision allow her to express passionate feelings with impressive restraint, while her feminism is one of acute understanding, avoiding both censure of the Reymond character, for continuing to love a man who makes her suffer to the point of suicide, and demonisation of the father. A movie of majestic non-judgmental authenticity. WH

Will My Mother Go Back to Berlin?

(1992, Ger/US, 53 min)
d Micha Peled.

●Micha Peled's mother left her native German for Palestine in 1937, never to return. As her 80th birthday approaches, Peled cooks up a plan with his producer. He will visit her armed with a personal invitation from the mayor of Berlin and an air ticket. The woman turns out to be a stern, rigorous thinker, and still an activist (she's seen Shoah twice, she says: 'Like a whip on my back…pointless of course'). It's clear to us, if not to Peled, that this plan is a mistake. In seeking some personal/political reconciliation, he only throws into relief the chasm between the generations. Worse, he brings a film crew along with him. At the end of this absorbing, ambivalent documentary, mother and son can only talk about the weather. TCh

Will o' the Wisp

see Feu Follet, Le

Willow

(1988, US, 126 min)
d Ron Howard. *p* Nigel Wooll. *sc* Bob Dolman. *ph* Adrian Biddle. *ed* Daniel Hanley, Michael Hill, Richard Hiscott. *pd* Allan Cameron. *m* James Horner. *cast* Val Kilmer, Joanne Whalley, Warwick Davis, Jean Marsh, Patricia Hayes, Billy Barty, Pat Roach.

●It is a dark and stormy night. In the bowels of evil Queen Bavmorda's fortress, a child is born with a birthmark. According to the prophecy, this innocent child signifies the end of Bavmorda's rule, and must die. However, a floating tussock carries her to safety in the land of the Nelwyns, a race of friendly munchkins. The chase is on…George Lucas may just be producing *Star Wars* in furs, but it's still a great Christmas movie. The bulk of it concerns the attempts of Willow Ufgood (Davis) to take the child Elora Danan to the good witch Raziel (Hayes). On the quest he falls in with Madmartigan (Kilmer), a plausible rogue who develops the screaming thigh sweats for Sorsha (Whalley), daughter of bad Bavmorda (Marsh). Along the way they encounter Death Dogs, Brownies, Faeries, Trolls, and a two-headed, fire-breathing monster. The pace is breakneck, the plot so thin that it threatens to fragment into so many pieces, the SFX out of this world. MS

Will Penny

(1967, US, 108 min)
d Tom Gries. *p* Fred Engel, Walter Seltzer. *sc* Tom Gries. *ph* Lucien Ballard. *ed* Warren Low. *ad* Hal Pereira, Roland Anderson. *m* David Raksin. *cast* Charlton Heston, Joan Hackett, Donald Pleasence, Lee Majors, Anthony Zerbe, Jon Francis, Bruce Dern, Ben Johnson, Slim Pickens, Clifton James.

●This mean, moody and magnificent Western still remains Tom Gries' sole claim to fame: before it he directed mid-'50s piffle about the Korean War and lumberjacks; afterwards he went on till the mid-'70s directing piffle about absolutely anything, mostly for TV. It's a downbeat tale of hardships and loneliness out on the cattle trail, with Heston as the ageing, illiterate cowpuncher brought face to face with his own hopeless, dead end existence in an encounter with a good but unattainable woman (Hackett), while simultaneously tangling with a psycho preacher (Pleasence) and his three murderous sons. It's blessed with crystal-clear photography by Lucien Ballard, understated performances (Pleasence naturally excepted), and a neatly idiomatic script by Gries himself. GB

Will Success Spoil Rock Hunter? (aka Oh! For a Man)

(1957, US, 94 min)
d/p/sc Frank Tashlin. *ph* Joseph MacDonald. *ed* Hugh S Fowler. *ad* Lyle Wheeler, Leland Fuller. *m* Cyril J Mockridge. *cast* Jayne Meadows, Tony Randall, Betsy Drake, Joan Blondell, John Williams, Henry Jones, Mickey Hargitay.

●A frantic, scattershot satire on '50s morals, advertising, sex and television. The not inconsiderable charms of Jayne Mansfield are much to the fore, but it's Randall's performance as timid advertising executive Rockwell Hunter that holds the whole thing together. While trying to persuade Mansfield to employ her oh-so-kissable lips in a commercial for Stay-Put lipstick, Randall finds himself inadvertently promoted as the world's hottest lover – much to the chagrin of his fiancée (Drake). Not in the same league as the wonderful *Girl Can't Help It*, but possessed of the same comic strip vitality and frenzied humour. NF

Willy Wonka and the Chocolate Factory

(1971, US, 100 min)
d Mel Stuart. *p* David L Wolper, Stan Margulies. *sc* Roald Dahl. *ph* Arthur Ibbetson. *ed* David Saxon. *ad* Harper Goff. *songs* Leslie Bricusse, Anthony Newley. *cast* Gene Wilder, Jack Albertson, Peter Ostrum, Michael Bollner, Roy Kinnear, Aubrey Woods.

●Despite indifferent Leslie Bricusse/Anthony Newley songs, an adaptation of Roald Dahl's charmingly eccentric novella (a Grimm-style moral tale) which has the true magic touch of fantasy. Slow to start, but once the youthful hero and four greedy companions arrive for their prize tour of the mysterious chocolate factory – hitherto operating behind locked gates, as hostile as Kane's Xanadu – the film really takes off. Whole landscapes of candy-striped trees, rivers of chocolate negotiable by gondola, sinister caverns manned by orange-faced dwarfs into which the greedier children disappear to suffer torments of their own devising. Great fun, with Wilder for once giving an impeccably controlled performance as the factory's bizarre owner. TM

Wilson

(1944, US, 154 min)
d Henry King. *p* Darryl F Zanuck. *sc* Lamar Trotti. *ph* Leon Shamroy. *ed* Barbara McLean. *ad* Wiard Ihnen, James Basevi. *m* Alfred Newman. *cast* Alexander Knox, Charles Coburn, Geraldine Fitzgerald, Cedric Hardwicke, Thomas Mitchell, Vincent Price, Mary Anderson, Eddie Foy Jr, Francis X Bushman.

●This three-hour biopic was well reviewed in its day and nominated for a raft of Oscars, but the box-office tills did not ring. Knox, more a character actor then a leading man, made an excellent Woodrow Wilson, the President who founded the League of Nations in 1920, only for Congress to vote against US participation in it. Producer Darryl Zanuck, fresh from his experiences of WWII, was keen to make a movie which addressed the problems of the age. The result's handsome, worthy and solemn. GM

Wilt

(1989, GB, 93 min)
d Michael Tuchner. *p* Brian Eastman. *sc* Andrew Marshall, David Renwick. *ph* Norman Langley. *ed* Chris Blunden. *pd* Leo Austin. *m* Anne Dudley. *cast* Griff Rhys Jones, Mel Smith, Alison Steadman, Diana Quick, Jeremy Clyde, Roger Allam, David Ryall.

●Griff Rhys Jones may not be everybody's idea of the hero of Tom Sharpe's delightfully black-humoured novel, but despite pedestrian direction, he does pull off the difficult task of sustaining interest and creulity throughout the accelerating absurdity (intentional and otherwise) of this bleak tale of misunderstandings. Wilt is a Liberal Studies lecturer at a Cambridge 'tec whose day-release students – leather-clad butcher's apprentices and the like – spend their time disputing the negligibility of his penis and fucking- rate. Wilt has no drive, but his socially aspirant, ball-breaking wife Eva (Steadman) has. Of the many incompetents around, Detective Inspectot Flint (Smith, wasted) takes the wooden spoon. After various country house shenanigans involving predatory moves made towards Eva by over-attentice 'friend' Sally (Quick), which end in a prolonged scene with Wilt humiliatingly strapped to a life-size female doll, he and Flint finally clash. Wilt has disposed of the doll in concrete, his wife has disappeared, and Flint can add two and two and get the wrong answer. It all adds up to little more than a poorly paced, sporadically amusing farce which never finds a visual equivalent for Sharpe's wickedly acute social observations. WH

Wimbledon Stage, The (Le Stade de Wimbledon)

(2001, Fr, 80 min)
d Mathieu Amalric. *p* Paulo Branco. *sc* Mathieu Amalric. *ph* Christophe Beacarne. *ed* François Gédigier. *cast* Jeanne Balibar, Esther Gorintin, Anna Prucnal, Ariella Reggio, Peter Hudson.

●Leading French actor Amalric's second feature as director, which he adapted by him from a novel by Daniele del Giudice, sends his wife Balibar on an improvised search for the life of a writer, as recounted by friends and colleagues. The destination is Trieste, which is protrayed as provisional, ambiguous, meditative and 'other', like a mobile version of much contemporary photography, emphasising the quiet and transitional spaces. An unashamedly European picture of ideas and mood, it's a beautiful, open and enigmatic fable, and it's puzzling title finds an anchorage of sorts in the final London scenes, which significantly echoes *Blow-Up* in its use of absence as the often strongest form of presence. GE

Winchell

(1998, US, 108 min)
d Paul Mazursky. *p* Stan Wlodkowski. *sc* Scott Abbott. *ph* Robert Greenberg. *ed* Stuart Pappé. *pd* Marcia Hinds-Johnson. *m* Bill Conti. *cast* Stanley Tucci, Glenne Headley, Christopher Plummer, Kevin Tighe, Paul Giamatti, Paul Mazursky.

● Walter Winchell, star gossip columnist/broadcaster from the '30s to the '50s here gets the telefeature treatment. Bit of a hero, bit of a heel, he seems an altogether more banal figure than the monstrous extrapolation played by Burt Lancaster in *Sweet Smell of Success* – which may have been less 'true' but which felt much more convincing. Superficiality is the rule, from Plummer's Santa Claus of an FDR to Tighe's lightweight Hearst. Tip for budding broadcasters: a bit before going on air Winchell would allegedly guzzle pints of water, so that the famous urgency with which he tore through his script was absolutely genuine. BBa

Winchester Conspiracy, The

(1990, Aust, 90 min)
d Ken Cameron. *cast* Gerald Kennedy, Terry Gill.

● Fact-based Australian police thriller detailing the controversial Operation Seville, in which the Federal and NSW forces collaborated with organised crime to cultivate and sell marijuana: the prize was a number of convictions, the price an influx of soft drugs on the streets of Melbourne and Sydney. Compelling material, efficiently handled. Raises tough questions about the motivation behind such doubtful methods of investigation. TJ

Winchester '73

(1950, US, 92 min, b/w)
d Anthony Mann. *p* Aaron Rosenberg. *sc* Robert L Richards, Borden Chase. *ph* William H Daniels. *ed* Edward Curtiss. *ad* Bernard Herzbrun, Nathan Juran. *m* Frank Skinner. *cast* James Stewart, Shelley Winters, Dan Duryea, Stephen McNally, Charles Drake, Millard Mitchell, John McIntire, Jay C Flippen, Will Geer, Rock Hudson, Tony Curtis.

● Mann's first film with James Stewart, with whom he was to make a series of classic Westerns, this offers the clearest example of Mann's use of the revenge plot. Hero (Stewart) and villain (McNally) are brothers who have been taught to shoot by their father. After McNally murders the father, Stewart sets out to seek revenge and so prove himself worthy of his father's name, symbolised by the perfect Winchester Stewart wins in a shooting contest and McNally steals from him. So begins the long chase to one of the most neurotic shootouts in the history of the Western. PH

Wind

(1992, US, 126 min)
d Carroll Ballard. *p* Mata Yamamoto, Tom Luddy. *sc* Rudy Wurlitzer, Kimball Livingston, Roger Vaughan, Mac Gudgeon. *ph* John Toll. *ed* Michael Chandler. *pd* Laurence Eastwood. *m* Basil Poledouris. *cast* Matthew Modine, Jennifer Grey, Cliff Robertson, Jack Thompson, Stellan Skarsgard, Rebecca Miller, Ned Vaughn, James Rebhorn.

● On the surface, Ballard's effervescent celebration of the joys of competitive yachting seems little more than a formulaic gung-ho sports movie. With its risibly romantic plot (boy deserts girl to pursue ambitions, screws up big-time, realises he cannot win trophies without winning back girl's love), its surging musical score and multiple orgasm-style climaxes, this could easily be the sort of film Ron Howard knocks out in an afternoon. But dive beneath the shimmering surface, and some mysterious treasures can be found. While cinematographer John Toll's daredevil camerawork assaults the eyes, swooping impressively in and out of the crashing waves, it is the relentless undercurrent of Alan Splet's creaking, crunching sound effects accompanying the images that holds the key to the film's power, perfectly enhancing the exhilaration of Ballard's tale. Solid performances by Modine and Grey lend a much-needed air of credibility to the proceedings, but Robertson delightfully scuppers their understated efforts by playing cantankerous old Captain Morgan Weld (Modine's Nemesis) as a camp pastiche of Robert Shaw's Quint in *Jaws*. MK

Wind, The

(1928, US, 6,824 ft, b/w)
d Victor Sjöström. *sc* Frances Marion. *ph* John Arnold. *ed* Conrad A Nervig. *ad* Cedric Gibbons, Edward Withers. *cast* Lillian Gish, Lars Hanson, Montagu Love, Dorothy Cumming, Edward Earle, William Orlamond.

● One of cinema's great masterpieces. The lovely Lillian Gish gives her finest performance ever as the young Virginian innocent who travels West to stay with relatives on the Texan prairie, only to be pushed into a harsh, unwanted marriage, and to find herself immersed in a maelstrom of rape, murder and madness. Swedish emigré Sjöström directs with immaculate attention to psychological detail, while making perfectly credible the film's transition from low-key, naturalistic comedy of manners to full-blown hysterical melodrama. Filmed under extremely difficult conditions on location in the Mojave desert, its climactic sandstorm sequence has to be seen to be believed, although the entire film – erotic, beautiful, astonishing – demonstrates such imagination and assurance that it remains, sixty years after it was made, completely modern. GA

Wind, The

see Finyé

Wind, The (aka Edge of Terror)

(1986, US, 92 min)
d/p Nico Mastorakis. *sc* Nico Mastorakis, Fred C Perry. *ph* Andrew Bellis. *ed* Nico Mastorakis, Bruce Cannon. *m* Stanley Myers, Hans Zimmer. *cast* Meg Foster, Wings Hauser, David McCallum, Steve Railsback, Robert Morley.

● Mystery writer Meg Foster, seeking peace and inspiration in the ancient, strangely deserted Greek town of Monemvassia, witnesses scythe-wielding psycho Wings Hauser polishing off Robert Morley. What's more, Wings has witnessed the witnessing. Movies usually present Meg with this sort of trouble. Eventually she recalls Morley mentioning hunting weapons locked in a closet. Finding a sub-machine-gun there (just what is it that Greeks hunt?), she empties the clip into a potted plant. With only the moon, a candle and many powerful arc lamps to show the way, she lures the demented Wings on to a promontory just in time for the wind to lift a not quite Wings-like dummy over the cliff. End of short but interminable feature. DO

Wind Across the Everglades

(1958, US, 93 min)
d Nicholas Ray. *p* Stuart Schulberg. *sc* Budd Schulberg. *ph* Joseph Brun. *ed* Georges Klotz, Joseph Zigman. *ad* Richard Sylbert. *cast* Burl Ives, Christopher Plummer, Gypsy Rose Lee, George Voskovec, Emmett Kelly, Mackinlay Kantor, Tony Galento, Peter Falk.

● One of Ray's most beautifully bizarre projects (though he never fitted easily into the restrictions of genre), merging Western conventions with ecological and philosophical concerns as, in turn-of-the-century Florida, teacher-turned-game warden Plummer takes on a gang of unruly, primitive poachers led by the awesomely charismatic Burl Ives, who are killing off the local rare birds for their fashionable, valuable plumage. With an often poetic script by Budd Schulberg and Joseph Brun's glistening location photography (in ravishing Technicolor), it effortlessly combines artifice with realism, and besides offering a strong argument in favour of conservation, also develops into an oblique meditation on the relativity of good and evil. Ives may spit in the face of God to win his hard-earned money through killing and commerce, but Ray makes no bones about his being closer to nature than Plummer. GA

Wind and the Lion, The

(1975, US, 119 min)
d John Milius. *p* Herb Jaffe. *sc* John Milius. *ph* Billy Williams. *ed* Robert L Wolfe. *pd* Gil Parrondo. *m* Jerry Goldsmith. *cast* Sean Connery, Candice Bergen, Brian Keith, John Huston, Geoffrey Lewis, Steve Kanaly, Roy Jenson, Vladek Sheybal.

● Based very loosely on a historical incident which took place in 1904, involving president Teddy Roosevelt in vote-catching reprisals for the kidnapping of an American citizen (here transformed into Candice Bergen and her two children) by a group of Arab 'bandits' in Morocco, Milius' film revives the desert epic with wit, style and a compelling brilliance in his handling of the Panavision format. Milius once more reveals that his overriding concern is with the formation of myth rather than realism, as he balances the fates of his two legendary figures – Brian Keith's Roosevelt and Sean Connery's kidnapper Raisuli – to dynamic effect. The result compares interestingly with the Paul Schrader-scripted *The Yakuza*, also much bound up with 'proving' an identity between two apparently alien codes. Towards the end, Milius does allow his film to become a distinctly naïve fanfare on behalf of American interventionist policies, but then it is a film that thrives on a species of *naïveté*. VG

Windbag the Sailor

(1936, GB, 85 min, b/w)
d William Beaudine. *p* Michael Balcon. *sc* George Edgar, Stafford Dickens, Will Hay. *ph* Jack Cox. *ed* RE Dearing, Terence Fisher. *ad* Alex Vetchinsky. *cast* Will Hay, Moore Marriott, Norma Varden, Graham Moffatt, Dennis Wyndham.

● British comedy from a bygone age, produced by Michael Balcon at Gainsborough studios. Pub bore Hay, veteran of many a fabricated maritime tall story, gets his comeuppance when the local Sea Scouts trick him into captaining a dodgy old tub whose mutinous crew land them on an island populated by cannibals. Rudimentary. TJ

Wind Cannot Read, The

(1958, GB, 114 min)
d Ralph Thomas. *p* Betty E Box. *sc* Richard Mason. *ph* Ernest Steward. *ed* Frederick Wilson. *ad* Maurice Carter. *m* Angelo Francesco Lavagnino. *cast* Dirk Bogarde, Yoko Tani, John Fraser, Ronald Lewis, Anthony Bushell, Michael Medwin.

● Grisly romantic twaddle set during WWII, with Bogarde's chipper air force chappie arriving in Delhi for a language course, falling for and then marrying a Japanese dish (Tani), getting sent to Burma, enduring torture in a PoW camp, and escaping when he hears that his wife has a brain tumour. Love scenes are played against the Taj Mahal, and dear Dirk looks as if he wishes he hadn't read the script, which is all wind. ATu

Wind Echoing in My Being (Nae-an e Unn Param)

(1997, SKor, 40 min)
d Jeon Soo Il. *cast* Cho Jae Hyun.

● A film about time: a writer, unable to finish his book, loses himself in memories, dreams, fantasies. Though elegantly shot in an oneiric, measured, not to say ploddingly slow style vaguely reminiscent of Tarkovsky, Angelopoulos and Antonioni, this very 'Zen' study in alienation looks more like a student exercise than the work of a 38-year-old professor of cinema. Beneath the emphatically arty veneer there lies little but empty clichés. (The director later expanded the film into a 113 minute feature.) GA

Wind from the East

see Vent d'Est

Windhorse

(1998, US, 97 min)
d Paul Wagner, Thupten Tsering. *p* Paul Wagner, Julia Elliot. *sc* Julia Elliot, Thupten Tsering, Paul Wagner. *ph* Steve Schecter. *ed* Paul Wagner, Tony Black. *m* Tommy Hayes, John Dana, Sam Chapin, Dadon. *cast* Dadon, Jampa Kelsang, Richard Chang, Lu Yü, Taije Silverman, Pema Choekyi, Nima Bhuti.

● A very different take on Tibet from Scorsese's *Kundun*, this contemporary drama focuses on young people living under Chinese rule today. A girl pursues a pop career; her brother takes a shine to a young Western tourist. Initially apathetic, they are confronted with the limits of their freedom when their sister (a nun) is arrested and beaten. Shot clandestinely in Tibet and Nepal as a drama of conscience, the film is rudimentary, but offers a fascinating and authentic glimpse of an oppressed society. TCh

Wind in the Willows, The

(1996, GB, 87 min)
d Terry Jones. *p* John Goldstone, Jake Eberts. *sc* Terry Jones. *ph* David Tattersall. *ed* Julian Doyle. *pd* James Acheson. *m* John Du Prez. *songs* John Du Prez, André Jacquemin, Terry Jones, Dave Howman. *cast* Terry Jones, Steve Coogan, Eric Idle, Antony Sher, Nicol Williamson, John Cleese, Stephen Fry, Bernard Hill, Michael Palin, Nigel Planer, Julia Sawalha, Victoria Wood.

● Terry Jones' version of Kenneth Grahame's classic echoes Alan Bennett's successful stage play, but on the whole it's a dire miscalculation. Things start unpromisingly when Mole (Coogan, serviceably velveteen) quits his burrow, not to avoid spring cleaning, but to get away from the developer's bulldozer. Apart from turning up the impact on Toad's multiple car crashes and adding a big explosive ending, Jones introduces a nightmarish Dog Food Factory which, with its cogs and sprockets and steel-edged mincers, drags the gentle animals into its maw. It's showtime too, with a parade of stars bunged in to do tiny turns. The suitably threatening weasel dance in the woods is one of the film's few inventive moments. BC

Windjammer, The

(1930, GB, 58 min, b/w)
d John Orton. *p* H Bruce Woolfe. *sc* John Orton, AP Herbert. *ph* Alan Villiers, RJ Walker, Jack Parker. *ed* John Orton. *with* Michael Hogan, Tony Bruce, Hal Gordon, Charles Levey, Gordon Craig.

● This account of the five month voyage of the 'Grace Harwar' from Wallaroo in Australia to London in 1929 is an extraordinary combination of documentary and low-life drama. Working class hero Bert is as bloody-minded as Arthur Seaton in *Saturday Night and Sunday Morning*, and leads a chorus of eccentrically seedy sailors in grousing about the patched and battered old sailing ship. AP Herbert's phlegmatically salty dialogue, and the stunning photography of angry seas and men swinging through the rigging like gibbons (which the young cameraman paid for with his life), give the film an almost hallucinatory resonance. An authentic glimpse into a lost world. RMy

Windom's Way

(1957, GB, 108 min)
d Ronald Neame. *p* John Bryan. *sc* Jill Craigie. *ph* Christopher Challis. *ed* Reginald Mills. *pd* Michael Stringer. *m* James Bernard. *cast* Peter Finch, Mary Ure, Natasha Parry, Michael Hordern, Robert Flemyng, Marne Maitland.

● Colonial drama in which a caring medic, Alec Windom (Finch), is sent to Malaya where he intervenes in local affairs and encourages the villagers to resist the Communist takeover of the newly independent territory. Decent performances and a genuine sense of concern throughout; scripted by Jill Craigie (Mrs Michael Foot) from a novel by James Ramsay Ullman. TJ

Window, The

(1949, US, 73 mn, b/w)
d Ted Tetzlaff. *p* Frederick Ullman. *sc* Mel Dinelli. *ph* William Steiner. *ed* Frederick Knudtson. *ad* Albert S D'Agostino, William E Keller, Sam Corso. *m* Roy Webb. *cast* Bobby Driscoll, Barbara Hale, Arthur Kennedy, Paul Stewart, Ruth Roman.

● A superior RKO B thriller variant on the boy who cried wolf fable, adapted from a short story by Cornell Woolrich. Driscoll is the kid who, from the fire escape one hot night, witnesses the couple in the apartment above killing a drunken seaman, only to have no one believe his story since they're all so used to his lying ways. Thrills begin when the culprits (Stewart and Roman) realise he knows the truth, and decide to ensure his silence. Pleasingly performed and shot, the film benefits from its evocative creation of the grimy New York tenements as a claustrophobic haven of crime and paranoia. Taut and gripping. GA

Window to the Sky, A

see Other Side of the Mountain, The

Windprints

(1989, GB, 100 min)
d David Wicht. *p* Michael L Games, Raymond Day. *sc* David Wicht. *ph* Brian Tufano. *ed* Robin Sales. *pd* Michael Phillips. *m* John Keane. *cast* John Hurt, Sean Bean, Lesley Fong, Marius Weyers.

● Wicht, a white South African, here tells a factually-based story of the hunting down of Nhadiep (Fong), a mute Namibian outlaw and killer legendary for his elusiveness. It's set in pre-independence Namibia in 1982, SWAPO is engaged in bloody war against South Africa, and there's increasing local unrest between Afrikaaner farmers and native Nama workers. Liberal Johannesburg cameraman Anton van Heerden (Bean) is despatched to work on Nhadiep's story with an out-of-touch English journo (Hurt) given to hanging out with 'colonial relics'. Why has Nhadiep killed only members of his own people? Is he in the pay of racist Afrikaaner Henning (Weyers), who is cynically buying up abandoned farmsteads? Wicht's use of van Heerden to examine contradictions within the white liberal consciousness (including his own?) – the cameraman's objectivity as reporter of events, his status as an Afrikaaner, the significance of his personal involvement in tracking the killer – is, despite its conventionality, brave and honest if not entirely successful. Despite the usual adumbration of roles for blacks, Wicht has the guts to admit the complexity of varying points of view without resorting to simplistic messages. WH

Wind Will Carry Us, The (Le Vent nous emportera/ Bad mara khahad bourd)

(1999, Fr/Iran, 118 min)
d Abbas Kiarostami. *p* Marin Karmitz, Abbas Kiarostami. *sc* Abbas Kiarostami. *ph* Mahmoud Kalari. *ed* Abbas Kiarostami. *m* Peyman Yazdanian. *cast* Behzad Dourani, Farzad Sohrabi, Shahpour Ghobadi, Masood Mansouri, Masoameh Salimi.

● Another subtle, deceptively simple and richly rewarding work of genius from Kiarostami, this Venice prizewinner opens on a long shot of a car negotiating a dusty mountain road, with driver and passengers arguing about where they are. Those who have seen the Koker Trilogy, especially *And Life Goes On...*, may ask whether Kiarostami is simply repeating himself, but fans will know there's always more to his work than first meets the eye. Sure enough, once the car reaches the Kurdistan village of Siaf Dareh, the ambiguities and mysteries proliferate and interweave. Are the men in the village treasure-hunters, as they tell a boy, the telecom engineers as the villagers assume to be, or something more sinister? Why is their apparent leader curious about the boy's dying grandma? And why, when Tehran calls on his mobile and he needs to move to higher ground, does he always drive to the cemetery, where an invisible man sings from a hole in the ground? This engrossing and beautiful film succeeds on many levels. As witty, almost absurdist comedy, it offers lovely visual and verbal gags. And as an ethnographic/philosophical study of the relationships between ancient and modern, rural and urban, devotion and directionlessness, it's intriguing and illuminating. GA

Wing and the Thigh, The

see Aile ou la Cuisse, L'

Winged Serpent, The (aka Q – The Winged Serpent)

(1982, US, 93 min)
d/p/sc Larry Cohen. *ph* Fred Murphy. *ed* Armond Lebowitz. *m* Robert O Ragland. *cast* Michael Moriarty, Candy Clark, David Carradine, Richard Roundtree, James Dixon, Malachy McCourt, John Capodice.

● A plumed serpent ('Whaddya mean? That fuckin' bird?') is nesting in the top of the Chrysler Building, from where it swoops and gobbles up hapless New Yorkers. Cop Carradine and robber Moriarty form an uneasy alliance to flush out the beast. This is the kind of movie that used to be indispensable to the market: an imaginative, popular, low-budget picture that makes the most and more of its limited resources, and in which people get on with the job instead of standing around talking about it. Cohen knows there isn't the time or money to question the logic of anything, so he keeps his assembly so fast and deft that we're prepared to swallow whatever he tells us; and his script has much droll fun with a plot that keeps losing things ('Maybe his head just got loose and fell off'). He also gets great performances from Carradine as the cop who treats it all as part of a day's work, and (especially) Moriarty as the jittery criminal whose 15 minutes of fame ('I'm just asking for a Nixon-like pardon') leave him wondering if on some days it's better just to stay home in bed. We have no hesitation in awarding Oscars all round. CPe

Wings

(1927, US, 12, 240 ft, b/w)
d William A Wellman. *p* Lucien Hubbard. *sc* Hope Loring, Louis D Lighton. *ph* Harry Perry. *ed* E Lloyd Sheldon. *cast* Clara Bow, Charles 'Buddy' Rogers, Richard Arlen, Jobyna Ralston, Gary Cooper, Arlette Marchal, El Brendel.

● Long touted as a classic by cinema historians, and justifying almost every adjectival extravagance. A spectacular tribute to the American flyers of World War I, born of Wellman's and John Monk Saunders' own experiences with the Lafayette Flying Corps, it's distinguished by matchless aerial photography, logistically-detailed battle scenes and dogfights, a unique blend of 'European' directorial touches with Hollywood pace, and solid performances holding the straightforward love/duty/camaraderie plotline together. Clara Bow leaves 'It' behind to work as a volunteer ambulance driver, while the boy-next-door she loves (Buddy Rogers) performs airborne heroics with his friend and rival-in-love Arlen, and Gary Cooper makes a brief but telling early appearance. PT

Wings of Desire (Der Himmel über Berlin) (100)

(1987, WGer/Fr, 128 min, b/w & col)
d Wim Wenders. *p* Anatole Dauman. *sc* Wim Wenders. *ph* Henri Alekan. *ed* Peter Przygodda. *ad* Heidi Lüdi. *m* Jürgen Knieper. *cast* Bruno Ganz, Solveig Dommartin, Otto Sander, Curt Bois, Peter Falk.

● Part romance, part comedy, part meditation on matters political and philosophical, Wenders' remarkable movie posits a world haunted by invisible angels listening in to our thoughts. Such plot as there is concerns two kindly spirits (Ganz and Sander), posted to contemporary Berlin, who encounter a myriad of mortals, including an ageing writer blighted by memories of a devastated Germany; actor Peter Falk, on location shooting a film about the Nazi era; and a lonely trapeze artist, with whom Ganz falls in love, thus prompting his desire to become mortal at last. A film about the Fall and the Wall, it's full of astonishingly hypnotic images (courtesy veteran Henri Alékan), and manages effortlessly to turn Wenders' and Peter Handke's poetic, literary script into pure cinematic expression. Masterpiece? Maybe not, but few films are so rich, so intriguing, or so ambitious. GA

Wings of Eagles, The

(1957, US, 110 min)
d John Ford. *p* Charles Schnee. *sc* Frank Fenton, William Wister Haines. *ph* Paul C Vogel. *ed* Gene Ruggiero. *ad* William A Horning, Malcolm Brown. *m* Jeff Alexander. *cast* John Wayne, Maureen O'Hara, Dan Dailey, Ward Bond, Ken Curtis, Edmund Lowe, Kenneth Tobey, Sig Ruman.

● Almost wholly incestuous, but about as impenetrable as a marshmallow for all that. Ford's biopic tribute to naval air ace Frank 'Spig' Wead is simultaneously a tip of the hat to the screenwriter of his earlier films *Air Mail* and *They Were Expendable* (Wead turned to cinema after an accident paralysed him), and it also includes Ward Bond's muted parody of Ford himself. There's a strange imbalance between knockabout comedy and reverential drama, but enough cherishable moments – like a post-operative Wayne going through actorly agonies to wiggle his toes again. PT

Wings of Fame

(1990, Neth, 109 min)
d Otakar Votocĕk. *p* Laurens Geels, Dick Maas. *sc* Herman Koch, Otakar Votocĕk. *ph* Alex Thomson. *ed* Hans van Dongen. *m* Paul M van Brugge. *cast* Peter O'Toole, Colin Firth, Marie Trintignant, Ellen Umlauf, Andrea Ferreol, Maria Becker, Gottfried John, Robert Stephens.

● Outside a festival première of his latest movie, celebrated '60s actor Cesar Valentin (O'Toole) is shot by agitated fan Brian Smith (Firth), who is in turn killed by a falling spotlight. Transported across a Styx-like river to a purgatorial hotel, they join a variety of celebrities whose continuing occupancy (and quality of accommodation) depends on how well their mortal fame is holding up. Einstein plays violin while Lassie sniffs around, and Hemingway rubs shoulders with such lesser immortals as Horace T Merrick (Stephens), famous for refusing the Nobel Prize for literature. So while O'Toole probes his assassin's obscure motives, Firth sustains his fit of pique and concentrates on pursuing the beautiful, amnesiac Bianca (Trintignant). Although the pacing is a shade too measured, the striking hotel setting and deft plot twists hold the attention throughout, especially in the weirdly funny finale, a game show lottery in which contestants are given the chance to return to the real world. Classily shot by veteran British cinematographer Alex Thomson, filmed in English by Czech director Votocek, this gentle allegory is slyly funny and quietly satisfying. NF

Wings of Honneamise, The (Oneamisu No Tsubasa)

(1987, Jap, 121 min)
d Hiroyuki Yamaga. *p* Hirohiko Sueyoshi, Hiroaki Inoue. *sc* Hiroyuki Yamaga. *ed* Harutoshi Ogata. *m* Ryuichi Sakamoto. *cast* voices: Robert Matthews, Melody Lee, Lee Stone, Alfred Thev.

● An animated *manga* feature set in an alternative reality where the north and south hemispheres of the world are locked in eternal combat and the hero is a member of the Royal Space Force. The sci-fi elements, however, are played down, and the journey into space is presented as a moral fable, the stars being 'a place where all mankind can find a new freedom'. Whether or not you swallow this, let alone the subplot of specifically Christian redemption, depends on whether tears spring to your eyes when you listen to 'Imagine'. First-rate score by Ryuichi Sakamoto, lighting effects that would shame Ridley Scott, lushly detailed background and a great eye for composition. A weak story, however, is required to go a long way. DW

Wings of the Apache

see Firebirds

Wings of the Dove, The

(1997, US/GB, 102 min)
d Iain Softley. *p* Stephen Evans, David Parfitt. *sc* Hossein Amini. *ph* Eduardo Serra. *ed* Tariq Anwar. *pd* John Beard. *m* Edward Shearmur. *cast* Helena Bonham Carter, Linus Roache, Alison Elliott, Elizabeth McGovern, Michael Gambon, Alex Jennings, Charlotte Rampling.

● Kate Croy (Bonham Carter) loves Merton (Roache), a comparatively impoverished, 'progressive' journalist, but the aunt on whom she depends (Rampling) prefers a wealthier suitor and forbids them to meet. Reluctant to lose either her lover or her allowance, Kate takes advantage of her blossoming friendship with visiting American heiress Milly (Elliott), travelling with her to Venice and, unknown to her aunt, inviting her 'friend' Merton to join them. But things get still more complicated when it looks like Milly is starting to fall for Merton herself. For the early London scenes, Hossein Amini's adaptation of Henry James' novel (updated to 1910) seems merely an imaginatively designed Edwardian costumer about frustrated love. In Venice, however, it soon becomes noticeably more interesting, with Kate's motives and methods turning increasingly murky as she appears to drive Merton into Milly's arms. The familiar Jamesian conflict of American innocence and Old World intrigue emerges, darker and crueller than a conventional romantic triangle, and a palpable sense of anguish, guilt and confusion takes hold. The performances are sensitive and sturdy, most impressively so in a beautifully judged sex scene (between Merton and Kate) that is authentically despairing. GA

Wings of the Morning

(1937, GB, 89 min)
d Harold Schuster. *p* Robert T Kane. *sc* Tom Geraghty. *ph* Ray Rennahan, Jack Cardiff. *ed* James B Clark. *ad* Ralph Brinton. *m* Arthur Benjamin. *cast* Henry Fonda, Annabella, Stewart Rome, John McCormack, Leslie Banks, Irene Vanbrugh, Harry Tate, Edward Underdown, Helen Haye.

● So few British colour films survive from the '30s that one is inclined to be indulgent toward this misconceived cross between a screwball comedy and a gypsy melodrama. Fonda overacts even more than the stage Oirish and wooden gypsies, but really the characters and plot are of secondary importance. This was Britain's first Technicolor movie, and the green/blue/grey of the Killarney landscapes, and the bright rainbow colours of Epsom on Derby Day, must have had an overwhelming effect on contemporary audiences. What impresses most now, though, are the scenes shot within the baronial interior of Denham studios. They have that shimmering, iridescent quality only possible with (now fast-decaying) nitrate film. RMy

Winner, The

(1996, US/Aust, 89 min)
d Alex Cox. *p* Kenneth Schwenker. *sc* Wendy Riss. *ph* Denis Maloney. *ed* Carlos Puente. *pd* Cecilia Montiel. *m* Daniel Licht. *cast* Rebecca DeMornay, Vincent D'Onofrio, Richard Edson, Saverio Guerra, Delroy Lindo, Michael Madsen, Billy Bob Thornton, Frank Whaley.

● At one point, casino boss Delroy Lindo says, 'Nobody likes anybody who goes too far.' Well, maybe Cox is desperate to be liked, for his story of Phillip (D'Onofrio), the holy fool who keeps hitting the jackpot in Las Vegas, stays way too close to home. The visuals are nice enough – *Wizard of Oz* colours beslimed by brutish '80s tack – but the characters are painfully predictable (all shysters or whores), and as if to make up for the duff gags and fortune cookie lines, a host of 'cult' faces (Whaley, Madsen) chew up the scenery. CO'Su

Winslow Boy, The

(1998, US, 104 min)
d David Mamet. *p* Sarah Green. *sc* David Mamet. *ph* Benoît Delhomme. *ed* Barbara Tulliver. *pd* Gemma Jackson. *m* Alaric Jans. *cast* Nigel Hawthorne, Jeremy Northam, Rebecca Pidgeon, Gemma Jones, Matthew Pidgeon, Lana Bilzerian, Sarah Flind, Aden Gillett.

● Previously filmed by Anthony Asquith in 1948, Terence Rattigan's play – about the trials and tribulations of an upper middle class Edwardian family determined to clear the name of a young son expelled from Naval Academy for stealing a postal order – isn't the kind of material you'd expect David Mamet to adapt and direct. That said, it's an elegant, engrossing film and surprisingly faithful. It could, of course, be seen as just another costume drama, but Mamet's decision not to open it out – it almost all takes place within the confines of the Winslow household – is wise. Kept offscreen, the unquestioning adherence to the status quo of the naval and political establishments is as frustratingly vague and intractable as it is for the family, just as the media fuss about their predicament is seen literally to hem it in. Mamet never tips the balance. Young Ronnie's innocence remains open to question, his father's fight is as much a matter of stubborn pride as a petition for justice, and the economic and human cost of his quest is all too evident. As ever with such films, much rests on the performances, and Northam (as barrister Sir Robert Morton), Jones (Grace Winslow), and Rebecca and Matthew Pidgeon (as the suffragette daughter and feckless elder son) do the play proud. Again, however, Nigel Hawthorne steals the laurels, his understatement investing the driven patriarch with complexity and emotional depth. GA

Winstanley

(1975, GB, 96 min, b/w)
d/p/sc Kevin Brownlow, Andrew Mollo. *ph* Ernest Vincze. *ed* Sarah Ellis. *ad* Andrew Mollo. *cast* Miles Halliwell, Jerome Willis, Terry Higgins, Phil Oliver, David Bramley, Alison Halliwell.

● In this adaptation of David Caute's novel *Comrade Jacob*, the story of England's first commune – the settlement formed by the Diggers, under the leadership of Gerrard Winstanley, on St George's Hill in Surrey in 1649 – is decorated with unromantic details of Cromwell's era, and edited with the emphasis one expects from Brownlow. But that's about all there is to it: overriding solemnity crushes the sympathy that is clearly demanded for the story's characters, almost inviting a shrug. The old problem of portraying misery without being miserable yourself hasn't been solved. AN

Winter Guest, The

(1997, US/GB, 104 min)
d Alan Rickman. *p* Ken Lipper, Edward R Pressman. *sc* Sharman Macdonald, Alan Rickman. *ph* Seamus McGarvey. *ed* Scott Thomas. *pd* Robin Cameron Don. *m* Michael Kamen. *cast* Phyllida Law, Emma Thompson, Sheila Reid, Sandra Voe, Arlene Cockburn, Gary Hollywood, Douglas Murphy, Sean Biggerstaff.

● This confident directorial debut is unashamed of its theatrical origins. Alan Rickman, who helped create (and directed) Sharman Macdonald's play in Leeds and London, wrote the script with the playwright, and retains Phyllida Law as the meddling Elspeth who tries to rekindle a relationship with her grieving daughter Frances (Emma Thompson, Law's real daughter). Set against the snow, wind and ice-blasted landscape of a Fife fishing village, it follows and contrasts the diffident, often quarrelsome relationships of four pairs of characters – two teenage boys playing hooky; two ageing 'funeral' junkies; Frances' son and an independent young woman; and the mother and daughter. The distraction of the Pinter-esque pauses and use of language notwithstanding, it's well acted (with child actors Murphy and Biggerstaff especially winning), sensitively directed and expressively shot (by Seamus McGarvey), but finally a shade too dramatically sealed up. WH

Winter Kills

(1979, US, 96 min)
d William Richert. *p* Fred Caruso. *sc* William Richert. *ph* Vilmos Zsigmond. *ed* David Bretherton. *pd* Robert Boyle. *m* Maurice Jarre. *cast* Jeff Bridges, John Huston, Anthony Perkins, Sterling Hayden, Eli Wallach, Dorothy Malone, Ralph Meeker, Belinda Bauer, Richard Boone, Elizabeth Taylor, Brad Dexter.

● An excellent conspiracy thriller of unusual blackness and wit, from a novel by Richard Condon, author of *The Manchurian Candidate* and *Prizzi's Honour*. A dazzling cast is assembled for its helter-skelter narrative about the brother (Bridges) of a murdered US President, searching for the real assassin and stumbling across the bloodstained pieces of a jigsaw that refuses to be completed. For once the tag of 'any similarity' hardly stands up, since the family patriarch – richly played by Huston, even in red underwear – owns most of America, and the name begins with K. Richert's direction negotiates the plot's many pleasurably sharp bends with such skill that one emerges a little dazed, more than a little amused, and nagged by a worrying sense that it could just all be true. DT

Winter Light

see Nattvardsgästerna

Winter of Our Dreams

(1981, Aust, 90 min)
d John Duigan. *p* Richard Mason. *sc* John Duigan. *ph* Tom Cowan. *ed* Henry Dangar. *pd* Lee Whitmore. *m* Sharyn Calcraft. *cast* Judy Davis, Bryan Brown, Cathy Downes, Baz Luhrmann, Peter Mochrie, Mervyn Drake.

● Contemporary urban life in the lucky country found wanting. Alas, this offering from the New Australian Cinema wears its heart and its didacticism on a rather tired old sleeve. The storyline bulges with stereotypes. The suicide of a folksy idealist turned hooker brings about the meeting of two people from two different realms of her past: her agitprop, Richard Neville-clone former lover, Rob (Brown), now owner of an arty Sydney bookshop; and fellow pro and junkie, Lou (Davis). Armed with her loser's uniform of peroxide crew-cut, kitsch togs, and aggressive vulnerability, Lou sets out to win

Rob from his cosy refuge of bland materialism. Against a tritely sentimental screenplay and an eerily inert performance from Brown, Davis fights an uphill battle to provide convincing emotional light and shade. BPa

Winter People

(1988, US, 111 min)
d Ted Kotcheff. *p* Robert H Solo. *sc* Carol Sobieski. *ph* François Protat. *ed* Thom Noble. *pd* Ron Foreman. *m* John Scott. *cast* Kurt Russell, Kelly McGillis, Lloyd Bridges, Mitchell Ryan, Amelia Burnette, Eileen Ryan, Lanny Flaherty, Jeffrey Meek.

●Men proving their manhood, women feisty and maternal by turns: Appalacian sexual politics during the depression are certainly basic in these backwoods where Collie (McGillis) rears an illegitimate child after being spurned by her clean-cut kinfolk. Into her life wanders gentle, clock-making widower Wayland (Russell) and his daughter. Does Collie choose Wayland or her brutish ex-lover (Meek), who hails from an uncouth rival family? Will the two clans ever agree on matters of personal hygiene? No prizes for guessing the outcome. Adapted from John Ehle's novel, this is highly predictable romantic melodrama, of the kind you find in fat paperbacks. We're meant to draw some significant parallels between the title, the harsh landscape, and emotional isolation, but the contrived connections lack substance. Even a murder mystery is introduced, too late to kick life into events, such is the certainty that wholesomeness will triumph over the eye-for-an-eye crudity of the villans. CM

Winter Sleepers (Winterschläfer)

(1997, Ger/Fr, 124 min)
d Tom Tykwer. *p* Stefan Arndt. *sc* Tom Tykwer, Anne-Françoise Pyszora. *ph* Frank Griebe. *ed* Katja Dringenberg. *ad* Alexander Manasse. *m* Reinhold Heil, Johnny Klimek, Tom Tykwer. *cast* Ulrich Matthes, Josef Bierbichler, Marie-Lou Sellem, Floriane Daniel, Heino Ferch, Laura Tonke, Sebastian Schipper.

●Germany, the dead of winter: fate's frosty hand entwines itself around the lives of four lonely young souls who come together in a chalet at the foot of the mountains. Trudging home after a long night in the Sleepers bar, Rene (Matthes) passes the chalet and impulsively drives away the car parked outside; further down the road he collides with a truck in which a farmer, Theo (Bierbichler), is unwittingly transporting his young daughter. Dazed, Rene walks away; Theo is shaken to find his daughter in a coma by the roadside. His confusion is compounded by the police's subsequent assertion that there was no other car involved. Further coincidences deepen the mystery. Though this is just the set-up, the hermetic melodrama sits a little uncomfortably throughout. Neat coincidences aside, it's never clear how a plot turning on various degrees of amnesia should illustrate the film's thematic interest in the hesitancies and elusiveness of emotional intimacy. It's all rather glacially opaque. You can see how the film means well, and holds promise, but ultimately it doesn't come together. (From Anne-Françoise Pyszora's novel *Expense of the Spirit.*) NB

Winter's Tale, A

see Conte d'hiver

Winter's Tale, The

(1966, GB, 151 min)
d Frank Dunlop. *p* Peter Snell. *ph* Oswald Morris. *ed* Gordon Pilkington. *pd* Carl Toms. *m* Jim Dale, Anthony Bowles. *cast* Laurence Harvey, Jane Asher, Diana Churchill, Moira Redmond, Jim Dale, Esmond Knight, Richard Gale.

●A ludicrously stagebound record by Frank Dunlop of his own 'Pop Theatre' production of Shakespeare's play for the Edinburgh Festival in 1966. Shot on the original stage set, with lumbering cameras and inadequate lighting, it's a fair old shambles in which the colour varies from shot to shot and the use of close-ups is almost invariably disruptive. With no attempt made to scale the acting from stage to screen, the performances – obviously no great shakes to start with – are something posterity is unlikely to be grateful to find preserved for its benefit. TM

Winter Tan, A

(1987, Can, 91 min)
d Jackie Burroughs, Louise Clark, John Frizzell, John Walker, Aerlyn Weissman. *cast* Jackie Burroughs, Erando González, Javier Torres Zarragoza, Anita Olanick, Diane d'Aquila.

●Strange movie, impossible to classify. It's based on letters by American feminist Maryse Holder, sent to girlfriends back home while she was abandoning herself to lust in Mexico, published (after her death at the hands of a Mexican stud) under the title *Give Sorrow Words.* The movie is framed as a sexual monologue: we see much more of the author (played by co-director Burroughs in a performance of awesome spiritual nakedness) than we do of the Mexican cocks she craves. The result is a bit like a female rewrite of Genet, a meditation in strictly physical terms on sex, desire, and frustration. Whatever else you think about it, it's certainly the only film of its kind. TR

Wired

(1989, US, 109 min)
d Larry Peerce. *p* Edward S Feldman, Charles R Meeker. *sc* Earl Mac Rauch. *ph* Tony Imi. *ed* Eric A Sears. *pd* Brian Eatwell. *m* Basil Poledouris. *cast* Michael Chiklis, Patti D'Arbanville, JT Walsh, Lucinda Jenney, Gary Groomes, Ray Sharkey, Alex Rocco, Jerre Burnes.

●It isn't easy to leave aside the Hollywood conspiracy against this John Belushi biopic, since threats of litigation have left such raw gaps in the action. One's sympathy for the underdog – producer Ed Feldman – is counterbalanced by one's boredom about Belushi and all his works, plus the high stultifying factor in Bob Woodward's biography. Perhaps the worst thing about *Wired* is that it is totally unfunny. Michael Chiklis works hard to bring the fat comic to life, but none of the routines work, and the samurai baseball-player sketch is embarrassing. This Dan Aykroyd (Groomes), perhaps haunted by the actual Aykroyd's curse, scarcely registers; Woodward (Walsh) is suitably beady as the investigator, but his function in the screenplay is clearly that of connective tissue. God knows why they decided to resurrect the dead Belushi from his slab in the morgue and take him on a tour of his life under the ageis of a guardian angel (Sharkey). Probably desperation. BC

Wisconsin Death Trip

(1999, GB/US, 76 min, col & b/w)
d/sc James Marsh. *ph* Eigil Bryld, (additional) Frank DeMarco. *ed* Jinx Godfrey. *cast* Jo Vukelich, Marilyn White, John Baltes, Nathan Butchart, Zeke Dasho, Krista Grambow, Raeleen McMillion, Marcus Monroe.

●If you tarried a few days in Black River Falls, Wisconsin, a hundred years ago, it would have seemed a forward-looking community, bustling with the enterprise of Scandinavian and German immigrants. Get stuck there over a long cold winter, though, and you might begin to sense the creeping madness of the place, the disease, hunger and suffering. That is, if you survived that long. James Marsh's documentary, made for the BBC's 'Arena' series, is stylish and mordantly witty. It's derived from a book, edited by Michael Lesy, which trawled through an archive of local newspaper stories and photographic portraits (many of the recently deceased). Even by the standards of British tabloids, and dispassionately voiced by Ian Holm, these dispatches from the *Badger State Banner* consist of truly toe-curling tales of murder, mania and mortal illness – with the exploits of notorious window-smasher Mary Sweeney a running sore. The material is cleverly arranged. The stark, staring portraiture of the time is augmented with crisp dramatic vignettes, shot in sepia and b/w to resemble the earliest days of cinema. What emerges is primal American Gothic: a blighted pathos which is also irrepressibly, grotesquely funny. TCh

Wisdom

(1986, US, 109 min)
d Emilio Estevez. *p* Bernard Williams. *sc* Emilio Estevez. *ph* Adam Greenberg. *ed* Michael Kahn. *pd* Dennis Gassner. *m* Danny Elfman. *cast* Emilio Estevez, Demi Moore, Tom Skerritt, Veronica Cartwright, William Allen Young, Richard Minchenberg.

●A bathtub wallow in teenage narcissism. John Wisdom (Estevez), convicted of drunk driving at eighteen, finds it tough getting a decent job. Five years later, he's still living with Mom and Pop, and spending a great deal of time in front of the mirror (but it's OK folks, he's got a girl). Fired from Cityburger for lying, he opts for a career in felony. A TV programme on the social effects of bank foreclosure shows him what to do. Armed with home-made bombs, our suburban guerilla holds up banks, not for megabucks but to destroy all traces of mortgage agreements. With his chick (Moore) as chauffeuse, he travels the road pursued by the FBI. The cute couple become public heroes. It all ends in tears. As Wisdom (the name represents the single feeble attempt at irony), Estevez demonstrates an undeniable charisma, but in the roles of writer and director he is less successful. What initiative there is in this retread gets swamped by silliness, slackness and sentiment. MS

Wisdom of Crocodiles, The

(1998, GB, 99 min)
d Po Chih Leong. *p* David Lascelles, Carolyn Choa. *sc* Paul Hoffman. *ph* Oliver Curtis. *ed* Robin Sales. *pd* Andy Harris. *m* John Lunn, Orlando Gough. *cast* Jude Law, Elina Löwensohn, Timothy Spall, Kerry Fox, Jack Davenport, Colin Salmon.

●Po-Chih Leong's film begins strikingly with a car wreck suspended in the treetops. The female driver had the misfortune to be involved with one Steven Grlscz (Law). It's not until Grlscz's next girlfriend meets with an equally grisly fate that Inspector Healey (Spall) takes an interest – although the suspect could scarcely be more cooperative. He even saves the inspector from a gang of muggers on the Underground. Meanwhile, Steven has taken up with an engineer, Anne Levels (Löwensohn), who can't figure out her charming, mysterious lover for the life of her. A strange, enigmatic, stylish and stimulating picture, this toys with tropes from the horror movie, the thriller and romantic melodrama with singular results. The closest comparison is with Harry Kümel's elegant philosophical fantasy films *Daughters of Darkness* and *Malpertuis*; the original screenplay has similar mytho-poetic pretensions, with its ruminations on the nature of good and evil, love, death and the whole damn thing. Po Chih Leong brings a stately sense of foreboding to the proceedings, hints at a contorted, expressionist shadow behind Law's brooding beauty and charisma, and uses the dissolve almost as a fleeting totem of impermanence. TCh

Wise Blood

(1979, US/WGer, 108 min)
d John Huston. *p* Michael Fitzgerald, Kathy Fitzgerald. *sc* Benedict Fitzgerald, Michael Fitzgerald. *ph* Gerry Fisher. *ed* Roberto Silvi. *m* Alex North. *cast* Brad Dourif, Ned Beatty, Harry Dean Stanton, Daniel Shor, Amy Wright, Mary Nell Santacroce, John Huston.

●A comedy? A tragedy? Philosophical farce, rather…in which a young fanatic (Dourif) returns from the army to his home town in the Bible-belt South, and stages a doomed private rebellion against the evangelism and repression of his upbringing. The enemy is neither tangible, nor simply a feature of his lived memory, but permeates the whole town: Jesus is celebrated in neon, on the street, in the language of everyday chatter. The young heretic's 'Church of Truth Without Jesus Christ' finally founders under the weight of human deception, driving its twisted creator into a real-life imitation of the martyrdom of Christ. Tragically, desperately funny: this adaptation of Flannery O'Connor's novel is John Huston's best film for many years. CA

Wise Guys

(1986, US, 91 min)
d Brian De Palma. *p* Aaron Russo. *sc* George Gallo. *ph* Fred Schuler. *ed* Jerry Greenberg. *pd* Edward Pisoni. *m* Ira Newborn. *cast* Danny DeVito, Joe Piscopo, Harvey Keitel, Ray Sharkey, Dan Hedaya, Julie Bovasso, Patti LuPone.

●Made in between *Scarface* and *The Untouchables*, De Palma's third gangster movie of the '80s is something completely different: a light-hearted and extremely wacky caper in which DeVito and Piscopo play small-time errand-runners for a local mobster. Failing in their efforts to essay a little double-crossing, each finds himself faced with a contract to kill the other. Instead they go on the run, and end up on a spending spree using the mob's credit card. Some great laughs, but it isn't hard to see why the film was never released theatrically in Britain: at times it just gets bogged down with over-the-top performances. The ending is great, though. DA

Wishing Tree, The (Drevo Zhelanya)

(1976, USSR, 107 min)
d Tenghiz Abuladze. *sc* Revaz Inanishvili, Tengiz Abuladze. *ph* Lomer Akhvlediani. *ed* Revaz Kveselava, Nino Natroshvili. *ad* Revaz Mirzashvili. *m* Bidzina Kvernadze, Yakov Bobohidze. *cast* Lika Kavzharadze, Soso Dzhachvliani, Zaza Kolelishvili, Kote Daushvili.
●Abuladze's film is a magically sustained fantasia about life in a Georgian village on the eve of the revolution, poetry rather than narrative thrust carrying it from one incident to another. The characters are eccentric, and their dreams and longings are gently indulged, from the simpleton who searches for the tree that will fulfil his wishes, to the dishevelled lady fortune-teller who promises herself the return of a long-lost lover. The central focus is a tragic love story (sweethearts denied marriage by the village elders), and this, more than any overtly political points, serves to intimate the social changes to come. Best seen in the original Georgian version (rather than the Russian-dubbed one), with its delicate aural lyricism matching the pictorial splendours. TR

Wishmaster

(1997, US, 90 min)
d Robert Kurtzman. *p* Pierre David, Clark Peterson, Noel Zanitsch. *sc* Peter Atkins. *ph* Jacques Haitkin. *ed* David Handman. *pd* Deborah Raymond, Dorian Vernacchio. *m* Harry Manfredini. *cast* Tammy Lauren, Andrew Divoff, Kane Hodder, Tony Todd, Robert Englund, Chris Lemmon.
●A psycho genie turns every wish put to him into an atrocity, until at long last Lauren tricks his nasty ass back into the lamp for good (unless, of course, he's required for a sequel). Englund goes all Peter Cushing, donning dressing gown and cravat to explain the plot, a simple-minded affair, structured around an explosion of body parts and giblets roughly every eight minutes. Wes Craven executive produced, a man without shame. BBa

Wish You Were Here

(1987, GB, 92 min)
d David Leland. *p* Sarah Radclyffe. *sc* David Leland. *ph* Ian Wilson. *ed* George Akers. *pd* Caroline Amies. *m* Stanley Myers. *cast* Emily Lloyd, Clare Clifford, Barbara Durkin, Geoffrey Hutchings, Charlotte Barker, Tom Bell, Pat Heywood, Neville Smith.
●With mother dead and father emotionally ditto, 16-year-old Linda (Lloyd) hungers for love with a foul-mouthed exhibitionism that horrifies the strait-laced elders of her '50s South Coast home town. More scandalously, after an initiation into the disappointments of sex with a silly young bus clippie, she takes to sleeping with the local fleapit's limp projectionist (Bell), one of her dad's masonic mates. For his writer/director debut, Leland filches a few incidents from the early life of Cynthia Payne to create a teenage rebel whose frustrations lead her to kick against the pricks of repressively status-conscious, middle class Britain, double standards and all. The trouble is that Lloyd's loud, brattish performance makes Linda less a socially purgative Free Spirit than a pain in the neck. More a well-meaning romp than a credible analysis of the state of the nation, now or then. GA

Wissen vom Heilen, Das

see Knowledge of Healing, The

Wit

(2001, GB/US, 99 min)
d Mike Nichols. *p* Simon Bosanquet. *sc* Emma Thompson, Mike Nichols. *ph* Seamus McGarvey. *ed* John Bloom. *pd* Stuart Wurtzel. m Henryk Mikolaj Gorecki, Charles Ives, Arvo Pärt, Dimitri Shostakovich. *cast* Emma Thompson, Christopher Lloyd, Eileen Atkins, Audra McDonald, Jonathan M Woodward, Harold Pinter, Rebecca Laurie.
●An HBO adaptation of Margaret Edson's Pulitzer-winning play in which a respected professor of 17th century poetry (Thompson) diagnosed with ovarian cancer. She decides to treat the disease as a new challenge. For once, this is a terminal illness drama which refuses to resort to mushy melodrama. The downside is that it's also unremittingly grim, full of windy sermonising about John Donne's poetry, and Thompson's asides to camera rapidly begin to grate. GM

Witch, The

see Superstition

Witchcraft Through the Ages (Häxan)

(1921, Swe, 6,840 ft, b/w)
d/sc Benjamin Christensen. *ph* Johan Ankerstjerne. *ad* Richard Louw. *cast* Maren Pedersen, Clara Pontoppidan, Tora Teje, Benjamin Christensen, Oscar Stribolt.
●A weird and rather wonderful brew of fiction, documentary and animation based on 15th and 16th century witchcraft trials, Christensen's film has a remarkable visual flair that takes in Bosch, Breughel and Goya (no wonder it was a particular favourite of the Surrealists). The director himself plays Satan, seducing a woman while she is in bed with her husband; another episode follows an accused witch through the tortures of the Inquisition. The film is now most commonly seen in a sound version, running 76 minutes, made in 1967 with a commentary by William Burroughs; a later restoration with tinted sequences is far preferable. DT

Witches, The

(1989, US, 91 min)
d Nicolas Roeg. *p* Mark Shivas. *sc* Allan Scott. *ph* Harvey Harrison. *ed* Tony Lawson. *pd* Voytek, Andrew Sanders. *m* Stanley Myers. *cast* Anjelica Huston, Mai Zetterling, Jasen Fisher, Charlie Potter, Bill Paterson, Brenda Blethyn, Rowan Atkinson.
●A gutsy version of Roald Dahl's story, reasonably faithful despite the changed ending. Luke (Fisher) and his Norwegian grandmother (Zetterling), both clued up on witch-lore, end up sharing a seaside hotel with a coven. Led by the Grand High Witch (Huston), the witches plan to turn all of England's children into mice. Distinctive casting has paid off, (Huston splendidly glam, camp and evil; Zetterling the voice of maternal moderation; Rowan Atkinson an obsessive hotel manager), and the adaptation recreates the sense of foreboding that gives way to gruesome reality. Customary Roeg concerns are evident, but issues of identity are given darkly humourous expression, while directorial extravagance is held in check by an outrageous plot about supernatural transformation, and there are some wonderful special effects from Jim Henson's crew. Strange and scary enough to fascinate parents and offspring alike. CM

Witches of Eastwick, The

(1987, US, 118 min)
d George Miller. *p* Neil Canton, Peter Guber, Jon Peters. *sc* Michael Cristofer. *ph* Vilmos Zsigmond. *ed* Richard Francis-Bruce, Hubert C De La Bouillerie. *pd* Polly Platt. *m* John Williams. *cast* Jack Nicholson, Cher, Susan Sarandon, Michelle Pfeiffer, Veronica Cartwright, Richard Jenkins, Keith Jochim, Carel Struycken.
●Very loosely based around the John Updike novel. Three women, bored by life in a small, sleepy New England town, find that they can make bizarre things happen. Cher, Pfeiffer and Sarandon are fine as the trio who conjure up their perfect man (Nicholson in the most manic part of his career to date). The four set up home together, but after a succession of mishaps, the girls realise that the decadent idyll has to come to an end. For three-quarters of the film, Miller triumphantly welds a strong comic element on to a taut, truly menacing atmosphere, but the last 20 minutes dive straight to the bottom of the proverbial barrel with a final crass orgy of special effects. Such a shame. DPe

Witchfinder General

(1968, GB, 87 min)
d Michael Reeves. *p* Arnold Louis Miller. *sc* Michael Reeves, Tom Baker. *ph* John Coquillon. *ed* Howard Lanning. *ad* Jim Morahan. *m* Paul Ferris. *cast* Vincent Price, Ian Ogilvy, Hilary Dwyer, Rupert Davies, Robert Russell, Patrick Wymark, Wilfrid Brambell.
●Filmed on location in the countryside of Norfolk and Suffolk on a modest budget, this portrait of backwoods violence – set in 1645, it deals with the infamous witchhunter Matthew Hopkins, and the barbarities he practised during the turmoils of the Civil War – remains one of the most personal and mature statements in the history of British cinema. In the hands of the late Michael Reeves (this was his last film, made at the age of 23), a fairly ordinary but interestingly researched novel by Ronald Bassett, with a lot of phony Freudian motivation, is transformed into a highly ornate, evocative, and poetic study of violence, where the political disorganisation and confusion of the war is mirrored by the chaos and superstition in men's minds. The performances are generally excellent, and no film before or since has used the British countryside in quite the same way. DP

Witch Hunt

(1996, US, 94 min)
d Paul Schrader. *p* Gale Ann Hurd, Michael R Joyce. *sc* Joseph Dougherty. *ph* Jean Yves Escoffier. *ed* Kristina Boden. *pd* Curtis A Schnell. *m* Angelo Badalamenti. *cast* Dennis Hopper, Penelope Ann Miller, Eric Bogosian, Sheryl Lee Ralph, Julian Sands.
●You can see why Schrader thought he might make something of this made-for-cable satire, in which the Hollywood of the early 1950s becomes the target for a corrupt egomaniacal Senator whose bid for the presidency is built on a campaign to expose practicing magicians. The film's gimmick is that the magic is real: it conjures up dream hookers, turns a plain stenographer into a star, brings back Shakespeare to write additional dialogue and forces the bad guy to disgorge his evil 'inner twin'. Sadly it all runs aground on the pitifully feeble dialogue and the parallel attempt to spoof the gumshoe genre, while Hopper (as private eye HP Lovecraft!) and Sands (as his evil-eyed foe, with the world's dodgiest Oirish accent) look as if they don't care. TR

Witch's Curse, The

see Maciste all'Inferno

With a Friend Like Harry...

see Harry, He's Here to Help

With a Song in My Heart

(1952, US, 117 min)
d Walter Lang. *p/sc* Lamar Trotti. *ph* Leon Shamroy. *ed* J Watson Webb Jr. *ad* Lyle Wheeler, Joseph C Wright. *songs* Alfred Newman, Eliot Daniel, Ken Darby. *cast* Susan Hayward, Rory Calhoun, David Wayne, Thelma Ritter, Una Merkel, Robert Wagner.
●The story of star radio singer and entertainer Jane Froman is the sort of stuff Hollywood would have gladly made up had not reality beaten them to it. Hayward was Froman's choice for the lead (although the singer dubbed her own songs) in this rags-to-riches story, capped by a near-fatal aircrash during WWII, a tough fight-back from illness, and a big finale that has Froman out entertaining the troops again. Hideously schmaltzy and Hayward's not exactly anyone's idea of musical sparkle. But what songs! 'Blue Moon', 'Give My Regards to Broadway', 'Embraceable You', 'Get Happy'. Alfred Newman won an Oscar for musical direction. TJ

With Babies and Banners

(1976, US, 45 min, b/w & col)
d Lorraine Gray. *p* Lorraine Gray, Lyn Goldfarb. *ph* Ting Barrow. *ed* Mary Lampson, Melanie Maholick. *with* Genora Dollinger, Babe Gelles, Lillian Hatcher, Mary Handa, Helen Hauer.
●A group of American grannies pore over old scrapbooks, pointing freckled fingers at tattered cuttings: not the obvious starting point for the stirring political documentary which this unashamedly is. They're not the Daughters of the Revolution, more like the instigators; women who joined the successful 1937 sit-down strike at the vast General Motors plant in Flint, Michigan, called to force GM into union recognition. Like *Salt of the Earth* and *Harlan County USA*, the film makes admirably clear that the women fought on two fronts: against management/

politicians, and against male workers who took them to be 'on the make'. During the strike, the men occupied the plant, while the women (who left rather than provide the press with an opportunity to comment on sexual shenanigans within) formed an effective auxiliary and foil to police lines embarrassed about clubbing women or shooting them in the back. JS

With Honors

(1994, US, 193 min)
d Alek Keshishian. *p* Paula Weinstein, Amy Robinson. *sc* William Mastrosimone, Israel Horovitz. *ph* Sven Nykvist. *ed* Michael R Miller. *pd* Barbara Long. *m* Patrick Leonard. *cast* Joe Pesci, Brendan Fraser, Moira Kelly, Josh Hamilton, Gore Vidal, Deborah Fortson.
●Monty, a Harvard politics student (Fraser), is struggling to finish his thesis when the only copy falls into the hands of Simon, a wily bum (Pesci). Attempting to retrieve it, Monty realises he has much to learn and Simon that he has much to teach. As an entertaining demonstration, Simon delivers an impromptu lecture on the role of the common man in the US Constitution, hence the presence of Gore Vidal as a supercilious tutor who hopes that the repetition of his cynical ideals will allow Monty to graduate 'With Honors'. A slight film, reiterating the simpler aspects of its theme (making your way in the world), but one with brains and heart. Attractive performances, handsome photography by Sven Nykvist, and charming music by Patrick Leonard, go some way to offset the clichés and sentimentality. AO

Withnail & I (100)

(1986, GB, 107 min)
d Bruce Robinson. *p* Paul Heller. *sc* Bruce Robinson. *ph* Peter Hannan. *ed* Alan Strachan. *pd* Michael Pickwoad. *m* David Dundas, Rick Wentworth. *cast* Richard E Grant, Paul McGann, Richard Griffiths, Ralph Brown, Michael Elphick, Daragh O'Malley.
●That rare thing: an intelligent, beautifully acted, and gloriously funny British comedy. At the butt-end of the '60s, two 'resting' young thesps – Withnail (Grant, a revelation), a cadaverous upper middle class burning-out case with an acid wit and soleless shoes, and the seemingly innocent unnamed 'I' (McGann) – live on a diet of booze, pills, and fags in their cancerous Camden flat, until a cold comfort Lakeland cottage is offered for their use. For all its '60s arcana, this is no mere semi-autobiographical nostalgia trip, but an affecting and open-eyed rites-of-passage movie. Robinson's debut as writer/director (he scripted *The Killing Fields*) exhibits the value of the old virtues: characterisation, detail, and engagement. His characters are oddball, degenerate even, but rounded – none more so than the elephantine figure of Griffiths as Withnail's gay uncle Monty. Beautifully scripted, indecent, honest, and truthful, it's a true original. WH

With or Without You

(1999, GB, 90 min)
d Michael Winterbottom. *p* Andrew Eaton, Gina Carter. *sc* John Forte. *ph* Benoît Delhomme. *ed* Trevor Waite. *pd* Mark Tildesley. *m* Adrian Johnson. *cast* Christopher Eccleston, Dervla Kirwan, Yvan Attal, Julie Graham, Alun Armstrong, Lloyd Hutchinson, Michael Liebmann, Doon MacKichan, Gordon Kennedy, Fionnula Flanagan.
●This humdrum drama about a thirty-something couple trying to have a baby lacks the ambition and intensity that Winterbottom usually brings to his work. There's something perverse about hiring a cinematographer with the visual flair of Delhomme and then making him shoot the film as if it's a small scale TV drama. Eccleston is Vince, the dour, suspicious husband, an ex-RUC man now working for his father-in-law. Kirwan is his wife, Rosie. They're trying to have a baby, but Rosie can't conceive and Vince grows increasingly jealous of her friendship with her French pen pal (Attal), who – again true to national stereotype – is as sleek, witty and romantic as her husband is boorish. Winterbottom's one real achievement is to make a movie set in Belfast in which, for once, the Troubles don't intrude. GM

Without a Clue

(1988, GB, 107 min)
d Thom Eberhardt. *p* Marc Stirdivant. *sc* Gary Murphy, Larry Strawther. *ph* Alan Hume. *ed* Peter Tanner. *pd* Brian Ackland-Snow, Martyn Hebert. *m* Henry Mancini. *cast* Michael Caine, Ben Kingsley, Jeffrey Jones, Lysette Anthony, Paul Freeman, Nigel Davenport, Pat Keen, Peter Cook.
●You'd think it would make your toes curl: a period buddy movie set in Victorian England, top names in top hats, carriages clattering on cobbles, puffer trains puffing through the Lake District. *Without a Clue* has all this, but the buddies are Sherlock Holmes and Dr Watson, and the usual set-up has been reversed: Watson (Kingsley) is the clever one, Holmes (Caine) is really Reginald Kincaid, an out-of-work actor hired to maintain Watson's credibility. When the boozy Kincaid begins to revel in his role, Watson becomes jealous and gives him the boot, but soon discovers that he can't do without him. Thanks to inspired casting, the result is superior schlock. The plot concerns the theft of the Treasury's £5 note plates; Moriarty (Freeman) is of course the culprit, and Inspector Lestrade of the Yard (Jones) is of course a dimwit. Although a bit long, it's full of incidental pleasures, and the climax in an empty gaslit theatre is slapstick at its silliest and best. MS

Without a Trace

see Que no quede huella

Without a Trace

(1983, US, 120 min)
d/p Stanley R Jaffe. *sc* Beth Gutcheon. *ph* John Bailey. *ed* Cynthia Scheider. *pd* Paul Sylbert. *m* Jack Nitzsche. *cast* Kate Nelligan, Judd Hirsch, David Dukes, Stockard Channing, Jacqueline Brookes, Keith McDermott, Kathleen Widdoes.
●If Jaffe's previous production credits aren't sufficient warning that this is one for Sensitive Drama suckers, the opening shot's a giveaway. The camera may be prowling Kate Nelligan's bedroom as if setting up a creepshow, but it's focused on a line of framed group photos on the mantelpiece. Nelligan's going to cry a lot, but she's not going to be conventionally imperilled. For this is another saga of the Ordinary Kramers, and it's the nuclear family itself that's once more in jeopardy. Hubby's already walked out, but ten minutes into the movie it's the pre-teen kid who goes missing. Kidnapped? Killed? Mum goes through the tear-jerk agonies as her son's disappearance becomes a case, an issue, and as time drags on, (almost) a statistic. The sickies, the psychics, and the media swoop briefly and indistinguishably, though Judd Hirsch is on hand as the concerned cop with a family of his own. One interlude of gay-baiting apart, everything else from here on in is designed to be drowned in sobs. PT

Without Limits

(1998, US, 118 min)
d Robert Towne. *p* Tom Cruise, Paul Wagner, *sc* Robert Towne, Kenny Moore. *ph* Conrad L Hall. *ed* Claire Simpson, Robert K Lambert, Charles Ireland. *pd* William Creber. *m* Randy Miller. *cast* Billy Crudup, Donald Sutherland, Monica Potter, Jeremy Sisto, Matthew Lillard, Billy Burke, Dean Norris, Gabriel Olds, Judith Ivey, William Mapother, William Friedkin.
●The 5,000m runner, Steve Prefontaine, represented the US at the 1972 Munich Olympics, but despite expectations failed to pick up even a Bronze medal. Then again, when he died at the age of 24, he held seven US records between 2,000 and 10,000m. The rest, as they say, is footnotes. Judging by Robert Towne's fine, rather old-fashioned film, the athlete's association with his coach Bill Bowerman afforded him this belated honour – not least because Bowerman took the running shoe he tinkered up for his favourite student and turned it into Nike's designer footwear. Produced by Tom Cruise, the film tells of a young man who simply loved to run from the front, and a coach (Sutherland) who tried to instill some sophistication in him. It's a long time since Towne matched the calibre of his screenplays for *Chinatown* and *The Last Detail*, but he's still a solid bet for three-dimensional characters; as a director, his third effort has a fluidity and coherence lacking in *Personal Best* and *Tequila Sunrise*. The understated cinematography by Conrad Hall and sterling work from Crudup and Sutherland lend a patina of class, yet it's in the end a po-faced film; you can't help thinking Ron (*Tin Cup*) Shelton wouldn't have abandoned these characters to their pedestals without a joke or two. TCh

Without Memory (Kioku-ga Ushinawareta-toki)

(1996, Jap, 84 min)
d Hirokazu Koreeda. *with* Hiroshi Sekine and his family.
●Begun before *Maborosi*, this documentary records nearly two years in the life of a family faced with an exceptional difficulty. Severe Thiamin deficiency can cause Wernicke's Encephalopathy, a brain disorder which results in total loss of short term memory. Hiroshi Sekine was hospitalised in 1992 for a stomach operation; for five weeks he was fed on a glucose drip which starved his bódy of vitamins. He emerged with WE and (along with his wife and two sons) has been trying to cope with it ever since. It took the family three years to get a disability pension out of the authorities, and even longer for the government to admit that health service cuts have cost at least 41 lives and damaged many others. In part, Koreeda's film is a protest against medical malpractice and bureaucratic inertia. But it also offers a vision stranger than anything William Gibson might dream up of what it means to start each day with no memory more recent than 1992. TR

Without *You* I'm Nothing

(1990, US, 94 min)
d John Boskovich. *p* Jonathan D Krane. *sc* John Boskovich, Sandra Bernhard. *ph* Joseph Yacoe. *ed* Pamela Malouf-Cundy. *pd* Kevin Rupnik. *m* Patrice Rushen. *cast* Sandra Bernhard, John Doe, Steve Antin, Lu Leonard, Ken Foree, Cynthia Bailey.
●More of a pop video than a movie, this is the film version of outrageous comedienne Sandra Bernhard's off-Broadway show. Her pastiche of the Hollywood dream is a hilarious hit parade of tormented lesbian lullabies, awesomely bad '70s go-go girl costumes, and 'in your face' sexual politics. Bernhard, the original wide-mouthed frog, shimmies her way through a star-spangled show: an anorexic, Madonna-style strippergram one minute and a bad-assed impression of a 'sexpert' in the mould of Dr Ruth the next. She turns the old soul classic 'Me and Mrs Jones' into a sexually ambiguous anthem, and she kidnaps Prince's 'Little Red Corvette', transforming it into a bump-and-grind strip show. She also sends up her own life, from growing up in Michigan to revealing a hidden yearning to be a Gentile on Christmas Day. This is sure to catapult Bernhard (best known previously as the crazed groupie in *King of Comedy*) into the mainstream as a performer; whether the mainstream is ready for her is another matter. ACh

Witman Boys, The (Witman Fiúk)

(1997, Hun, 93 min)
d János Szász. *p* Ferenc Kardos. *sc* János Szász, Geza Csath. *ph* Tibor Mathé. *ed* Anna Kornis. *pd* József Romvari. *cast* Alpár Fogarasi, Szaboles Gergely, Maia Morgenstein, Dominika Ostalowska, Péter Andorai.
●A stylish, slightly pretentious but finally effective little movie, set in 1913, about two brothers who react to their disciplinarian father's death by retreating into a shared secret world of rituals involving sex, cruelty and death. When they also become involved with a prostitute, their distaste for their mother begins to verge on pure hatred. Though the measured pace and overall glumness make the movie sometimes feel a little strained, Producer/director Szász elicits superb performances from his young leads, while the vibrant, near expressionist photography lends the proceedings the feel of a feverish dream. It's a dark tale of pain, confusion and misplaced desire, helped considerably by sensitive borrowings from the likes of Schubert and Richard Strauss on the soundtrack. GA

Witness, The (A Tanu)

(1968, Hun, 108 min)
d Pèter Bacsó. *p* Lajos Gulyas. *sc* Péter Bacso. *ph* János Zsombolyai. *ed* Sándor Boronkay. *ad* László Blaho. *m* György Yukan. *cast* Ferenc Kállai, Lajos Oze, Zoltán Fábri, Béla Both, Lili Monori.
●Bureaucratically blocked in its homeland for a decade, Bacsó's anti-Stalinist comedy confronts the historical trauma of the post-war purges and

show trials with the iconoclastic wit of true absurdism – tracking the farcical travails of a good, simple communist dyke-keeper as he's unwittingly targeted to become a key prosecution witness in the rigged case against a former comrade. The treacherous currents of party-line politics prove beyond the poor man's comprehension – he knows only those of the Danube – as he is buffeted, under sinisterly ludicrous secret police supervision, through a bewildering switchback of imprisonment and (invariably inappropriate) rehabilitation. As agit-prop clichés become running gags, the horrific ironies emerge from a series of classic comic set pieces: the well-meaning creation of a Socialist Ghost Train in the people's amusement park; the ceremonial passing off of a lemon as the first 'Hungarian orange'; the eventual unscripted débâcle of the trial. Exorcism through echoing laughter: brilliant. PT

Witness

(1985, US, 112 min)
d Peter Weir. *p* Edward S Feldman. *sc* Earl W Wallace, William Kelley. *ph* John Seale. *ed* Thom Noble. *pd* Stan Jolley. *m* Maurice Jarre. *cast* Harrison Ford, Kelly McGillis, Josef Sommer, Lukas Haas, Jan Rubes, Alexander Godunov, Danny Glover.

● Weir's first film set in America explores a theme familiar from his earlier work: the discovery of an all but forgotten culture in modern society: in this case the Amish, a puritanical sect whose life in Pennsylvania has remained unchanged since the 18th century. Threat explodes into this community when an Amish boy witnesses a murder; cop Ford investigates the case and, finding his own life endangered, is forced to hot-foot it back to the Amish ranch with the bad guys in pursuit. The film also allows Ford to fall in love with the boy's mother (McGillis), and comments on the distance between the messy world Ford leaves behind and the cloistered one in which he takes refuge. Powerful, assured, full of beautiful imagery and thankfully devoid of easy moralising, it also offers a performance of surprising skill and sensitivity from Ford. RR

Witness for the Prosecution

(1957, US, 114 min, b/w)
d Billy Wilder. *p* Arthur Hornblow Jr. *sc* Billy Wilder, Harry Kurnitz, Larry Marcus. *ph* Russell Harlan. *ed* Daniel Mandell. *ad* Alexandre Trauner. *m* Matty Malneck. *cast* Marlene Dietrich, Tyrone Power, Charles Laughton, Elsa Lanchester, John Williams, Henry Daniell, Norma Varden, Una O'Connor.

● The undisputed star of this courtroom drama is Alexander Trauner's magnificent recreation of the Old Bailey, which is just as well, since the presence of Charles Laughton as the defence counsel, and the film's origins as an Agatha Christie novel and play, combine to give the movie a heavy – almost stolid – theatrical flavour. Tyrone Power is surprisingly good as the man accused of murdering his mistress, but the swift twists and turns of Ms Christie's plot soon drain Dietrich and Laughton's roles of any dramatic credibility. PH

Wits to Wits

see Conman and the Kung Fu Kid

Wittgenstein

(1993, GB, 75 min)
d Derek Jarman. *p* Tariq Ali. *sc* Derek Jarman, Terry Eagleton, Ken Butler. *ph* James Welland. *ed* Budge Tremlett. *ad* Annie Lapaz. *m* Jan Latham-Koenig. *cast* Karl Johnson, Michael Gough, Tilda Swinton, John Quentin, Kevin Collins, Clancy Chassay, Jill Balcon, Sally Dexter, Nabil Shaban.

● Jarman's biopic brings to life the *seriously* eccentric philosopher Ludwig Wittgenstein: Viennese millionaire's son, schoolteacher, WWI infantry officer, hospital porter, gardener, naturalised Briton and homosexual. Initiated as a small-budget educational TV programme, then produced for the BFI by one-time Trot Tariq Ali from a script by Marxist professor Terry Eagleton, it hardly sounds enticing. But thanks to genuinely engaging performances by Johnson and Chassay (as Ludwig, man and boy), as well as a witty script and economical direction, this turns treatise into treat. It's shot on the simplest of sets against black backgrounds, with all the money spent on costumes, actors and lights, and framed like dark Enlightenment paintings. If it ranges wide rather than deep – the philosophy is either dropped into conversation or presented like a blackboard primer – Jarman still manages to capture the spirit and complexity of his fascinating subject. Of the entertaining cameos, Quentin's epicene John Maynard Keynes (in a delightful series of pastel shirts) and Gough's miffed Bertrand Russell are the most telling. WH

Wittstock, Wittstock

(1997, Ger/Aus, 119 min, b/w)
d Volker Koepp. *p* Herbert Kruschke. *sc* Volker Koepp. *ph* Christian Lehmann. *ed* Angelika Arnold.

● A feature culled from one of those '7-Up' style documentaries in which the film-makers revisit a handful of characters every so often for updates. Here, the subjects are three women in a textile plant, in Wittstock, East Germany, and the period ranges from 1964 to 1996. The women are personable enough, but the film covers too much time to go into a lot of detail, and there's an inordinate amount of footage devoted to the comely Elsbeth smirking into the camera (her aspirations are tragically funny: a trip to Bulgaria and a Trabant – no, it's not funny, really). Boredom is averted by dismantling the Berlin Wall, with sorry results. TCh

Wives (Hustruer)

(1975, Nor, 84 min)
d Anja Breien. *p* Hans Lindgren. *sc* Anja Breiein. *ph* Halvor Naess. *ed* Jan Horne. *m* Finn Ludt. *cast* Anne-Marie Ottersen, Froydis Armand, Katja Medboe, Noste Schwab, Helge Jordal.

● 'We want fun – we can screw at home!' This manifesto voiced by one of the three wives, part way through a spree begun in the wake of a school reunion, gives a small clue as to the direction taken by Breien's film. It is of course a reply to Cassavetes' *Husbands*, and a cheerful, relaxed, and good-humoured one, with some of the conspiratorial overtones of a school adventure story, and with some deliciously peppery gags. The script, with its astute contributions to script as well as performance from Breien's lead actresses, is quite a landmark in feminist cinema. VG

Wives: Ten Years After (Hustruer ti ar etter)

(1985, Nor, 88 min)
d Anja Breien. *p* Bente Erichsen. *sc* Anja Breien, Knut Faldbakken. *ph* Erling Thurmann-Anderson. *ed* Lasse Hagström. *ad* Madla Hruzova. *cast* Froydis Armand, Katja Medboe, Anne-Marie Ottersen, Brasse Brännström, Henrik Scheele.

● A decade after their reckless spree together, the three friends from *Wives* meet up again at a pre-Christmas fancy dress party. However, when they try to relive the past, the changes wrought in them by age and the failure of their relationships with men generate unsettling tensions. Even when they hole up together in a deserted Malmö hotel, where they were waited on hand and foot by the manager, they find little comfort in one another's company. A painfully honest film which benefits greatly from the reuniting of the original cast, all of whom again collaborated with Breien on the scenario. NF

Wives III (Hustruer III)

(1996, Nor, 80 min)
d Anja Breien. *sc* Anja Breien, Armand Froydis, Katja Medboe, Anne-Marie Ottersen. *ph* Halvor Naess. *ed* Trygve Hagen. *pd* Anne Siri Bryhai. *m* Edvard Grieg, Franz Schubert. *cast* Froydis Armand, Katja Medboe, Anne-Marie Ottersen, Noste Schwab, Hedda Sandvig, Mathias Armand.

● Ten years after *Wives: Ten Years After*, and the three friends reconvene aboard a tram touring the late-night streets of Oslo: a surprise birthday-party for Kaja (Medboe), who's reached the 50 mark. She, Heidrun (Armand) and Mie (Ottersen) spend the next two days together, recounting, recollecting, reflecting, revaluating, bemoaning and celebrating life as 'wrinkled and weathered, wonderful women', with the city's Independence Day celebrations in the background, and a stolen bust of Norway's national poet somewhere in between. Breien again collaborated with her three leads on the writing, to similarly naturalistic effect. If formally slight, this well-seasoned and eccentric blend of wry comedy and candour provides a rare perspective on a constituency sorely under-represented in cinema. NB

Wiz, The

(1978, US, 134 min)
d Sidney Lumet. *p* Rob Cohen. *sc* Joel Schumacher. *ph* Oswald Morris. *ed* Dede Allen. *pd* Tony Walton. *m* Quincy Jones. *songs* Charlie Smalls. *cast* Diana Ross, Michael Jackson, Nipsey Russell, Ted Ross, Mabel King, Theresa Merritt, Lena Horne, Richard Pryor.

● Dorothy and her entourage of malfunctioning under-achievers move on from rural Kansas to face the contemporary perils of cocaine-sniffing, disco-chic New York in this all black, or rather Motown, version of Frank Baum's *The Wonderful Wizard of Oz*, adapted from the Broadway hit musical (with Charlie Smalls' original score augmented by Quincy Jones). Lumet adopts a bravely vacillating tone, alternating between tear-jerking schmaltz and smart-ass humour; both work, though you may well giggle when Lena Horne (as Glinda the Good) is spotted, hanging in the sky in sequined shower-cap, urging you to 'Believe in Yourself'. On the plus side are vast, brilliant sets by Tony Walton, a couple of well-staged show-stoppers ('Everybody Rejoice' in the Wicked Witch's sweat-shop, and 'Emerald City Ballet'), Michael Jackson (the Scarecrow), Richard Pryor (The Wiz), and Diana Ross who, as Dorothy, is just gorgeous. JS

Wizard of Darkness (Eko Eko Azaraku)

(1995, Jap, 81 min)
d Shimako Sato. *p* Yoshi Chiba. *sc* Junki Takegami, Shimako Sato. *ph* Shoei Sudo. *ed* Shimako Sato. *m* Ali Project. *cast* Kimika Yoshino, Miho Kanno, Shu-ma, Naozumi Takahoshi.

● The most striking element of Shimako (*Tale of a Vampire*) Sato's subtly erotic horror film about a Japanese high school at the centre of a satanic pentagram of evil is once again the juxtaposition of charged stillness with eruptions of blood-bolted violence. New student Missa impresses some but scares others with her apparently magical powers. Later, kept behind with 12 other pupils, she's trapped and hunted by an unseen assailant. Fluid direction; accomplished sfx. NF

Wizard of Oz, The (100)

(1939, US, 101 min, b/w & col)
d Victor Fleming. *p* Mervyn LeRoy. *sc* Noel Langley, Florence Ryerson, Edgar Allan Woolf. *ph* Harold Rosson. *ed* Blanche Sewell. *ad* Cedric Gibbons. *songs* EY Harburg, Harold Arlen. *cast* Judy Garland, Ray Bolger, Bert Lahr, Jack Haley, Frank Morgan, Billie Burke, Margaret Hamilton.

● The niece of Kansas homesteaders dreams of a magical land, over the rainbow. She and her dog Toto meet the Munchkins – the little people – who tell her to follow the yellow brick road, which will bring her to the Wizard. She joins up with a scarecrow who hasn't a brain, a tin man who hasn't a heart, and a lion who's cowardly. A good witch protects them from a wicked witch. But the Wizard is not what he seems...It's hard to imagine now the impact this classic fantasy must have had on a world sliding into war. Garland became a legend at 16. Bolger, Haley and Lahr were immortalised as her three blighted pals. It's still a potent dreamworld. The dubbing and some of the visual effects may creak a bit, but the songs, make-up, costumes and sets are magical. Infinitely preferable to Boorman's nightmare gloss for the '70s, *Zardoz*. SG

Wizard of Speed and Time, The

(1988, US, 98 min)
d Mike Jittlov. *p* Richard Kaye, Mike Jittlov, Deven Chierighino. *sc* Mike Jittlov. *ph* Russell Carpenter. *ed* Mike Jittlov. *m* John Massari. *cast* Mike Jittlov, Richard Kaye, Paige Moore, David Conrad, Steve Brodie, John Massari, Gary Schwartz.

● This bizarre and wacky conglomeration of sfx and fantasy slapstick is based around a fable-like tale mirroring Jittlov's own experiences: eccentric effects wiz (Jittlov) spends months touting his work around the big studios before he is finally offered a particle of air time on a high-rating TV show. The most amusing moments occur in the first quarter, as Jittlov attempts to secure the US equivalent of the Equity card. For the rest, the film labours through repeated scenes of the crew shooting in adverse conditions, lengthy car chases involving camera dollies, hired punks, and unscrupulous moguls hell-bent on disrupting the production. The effects themselves (brilliantly created through stop-motion and literally making a film studio come to life) unfortunately appear in their entirety only during the last 10 minutes. DA

Wizard of Waukesha, The

(1980, US, 59 min)
d Catherine Orentreich, Susan Brockman. *p* Catherine Orentreich. *ph* Mark Obenhaus, Don Lenzer, Ed Gray. *ed* Susan Brockman. *with* Les Paul.

● A straightforward documentary, enlivened by the charisma of its puckish subject, the guitarist Les Paul. It follows the life story of the one-time Broadway entertainer ('We died'), inventor of the electric guitar, and granddaddy of rock recording. Likeable Les will retain even the uncommitted viewer's attention, although the deadbeat rockers wheeled on to give an expert's opinion may have the opposite effect. Full of lovely pop media kitsch, and a genuine rags-to-riches story. JG

Wizards

(1977, US, 81 min)
d/p/sc Ralph Bakshi. *ed* Donald W Ernst. *m* Andrew Belling. *cast* voices: Bob Holt, Jesse Wells, Richard Romanus, David Proval.

●Bakshi, maker of *Fritz the Cat* and *Heavy Traffic*, is still waving a tattered flag for Underground Culture in this sentimental animated satire on the future ways of the world. Two brother wizards battle for supremacy. One's good, with a vast ginger beard and a George Burns voice, and is supported by a host of elf and fairy helpers (fairies are the true ancestors of man, we're told). The other's evil, all bones and no flesh; he fuels the hatred of his subjects with Nazi propaganda films found along with a movie projector in the rubble of the 20th century. Provided one can stomach the combination of elves and Nazis (and it's a big proviso), then there's moderate fun here and there. But the film shows all the signs of an economic freeze: it has quite lavish backgrounds, but bare, unimaginative character movement, and frequent use of still drawings to fill in portions of the narrative. GB

Wobblies, The

(1979, US, 89 min, b/w & col)
d/p Stewart Bird, Deborah Shaffer. *ph* Sandi Sissel, Judy Irola, Peter Gessner, Bonnie Friedman. *ed* Deborah Shaffer, Stewart Bird. *m* Richard Bell, Anna Chairetakis, Sam Eskin. *narrator* Roger Baldwin.

● 'Trust in the Lord and sleep in the streets': just one of the iconoclastic maxims coined by the Industrial Workers of the World ('The Wobblies') in song and agitation, and given new voice in this documentary. In the currently depressing US political situation, any recovery of that continent's militant, socialist tradition is welcome; especially the first two decades of this century, when the Wobblies tried to organise the whole booming, unskilled working class into one industrial union. Guided by the memories of several old World War I activists on film, this is a fascinating and often moving compilation of newsreel, photographs, and those amazing songs. But given its classic US documentary strategy, based primarily on 'personal testament', there are weaknesses. In particular, the film is unable to transcend the naive syndicalist politics of the IWW itself. As a film it has no critical distance on its chosen subject, so the movement is presented in celluloid aspic, with no past and, more importantly, no legacy. And the shooting style, characterised by the endemic docu-makers' disease of zoomitis, only serves to park the film more firmly in the labour movement museum. Despite this, one still emerges stunned and angry, admiring and amused. The World War I failed, the film half-fails, but both are still more than worthy of our attention. CG

Wolf

(1994, US, 125 min)
d Mike Nichols. *p* Douglas Wick. *sc* Elaine May, Jim Harrison, Wesley Strick. *ph* Giuseppe Rotunno. *ed* Sam O'Steen. *pd* Bo Welch. *m* Ennio Morricone. *cast* Jack Nicholson, Michelle Pfeiffer, James Spader, Kate Nelligan, Richard Jenkins, Christopher Plummer, Eileen Atkins, Om Puri, Prunella Scales, Madhur Jaffrey.

●Quite frankly, it's hard to fathom why exactly anyone would have wanted to make this slick, glossy, but utterly redundant werewolf movie. Okay, maybe Nicholson sympathised with his Will Randall, a middle-aged New York book editor anxious about his job and his marriage, who finds his powers and senses not only restored but greatly sharpened when he's bitten by a wolf he ran into with his car. And maybe Spader, as Randall's smarmy, back-stabbing colleague Swinton, reckoned here was a juicy, villainous part to sink his teeth into. But for Pfeiffer – as Randall's love interest Laura – there's little of substance, while Nichols makes it clear that directing a horror movie was the last thing on his mind. Even make-up wiz Rick Baker is stymied by the air of restraint. Overall, this is needlessly polished nonsense: not awful; just toothless, gutless and bloodless. GA

Wolf Brigade, The

see Jin-Roh

Wolfen

(1981, US, 115 min)
d Michael Wadleigh. *p* Rupert Hitzig. *sc* David Eyre, Michael Wadleigh. *ph* Gerry Fisher. *ed* Chris Lebenzon, Dennis Dolan, Martin J Bram, Marshall M Borden. *pd* Paul Sylbert. *m* James Horner. *cast* Albert Finney, Diane Venora, Edward James Olmos, Gregory Hines, Tom Noonan, Dick O'Neill.

●School-leavers whose ambitions lean towards criminal pathology will pick up useful tips on wielding the scalpel and the white sheet in this foray into the bleakly explicit world of the contemporary shocker: a werewolf movie for an ecology-conscious age. The last-reel process whereby the lurking terror breaks cover and is transformed into a 'sympathetic' but unconquerable force is smoothly convincing: we are a long way here from simply feeling a bit sorry for King Kong. The setting is two New Yorks: that of the multinational, politically-amoral corporations, and that of the slum wastelands, both with the same landlords. The camera's vision is a fresh one, and though the wolf's eye view sequences threaten at first to become a nuisance, they are soon justified as a dramatic device, and ultimately as essential to the plot. JC

Wolf Man, The

(1941, US, 70 min, b/w)
d/p George Waggner. *sc* Curt Siodmak. *ph* Joseph Valentine. *ed* Ted J Kent. *ad* Jack Otterson. *m* Hans Salter, Frank Skinner. *cast* Lon Chaney Jr, Evelyn Ankers, Claude Rains, Maria Ouspenskaya, Ralph Bellamy, Patric Knowles, Warren William, Bela Lugosi, Fay Helm.

● 'It's only in your mind' says Claude Rains to his screen son Lon Chaney Jr, as he straps the suspected werewolf to a chair in Universal's second try at the Wolf Man saga. But he's three corpses too late, and we've already seen the transformation as Chaney stomps through a never-never land of foggy glades outside English villages set in Alpine scenery. Suspension of disbelief aside, this is interesting for its relatively modern equation between Chaney's wolfish desires and his unhappy fate, for its concern over the victims, and for the fact that – despite all odds – there's undeniable magic within the staid format. DMacp

Wolfshead: The Legend of Robin Hood

(1969, GB, 56 min)
d Johnny Hough. *p* Bill Anderson. *sc* David Butler. *ph* David Holmes. *ed* Bob Dearberg. *m* Jack Sprague, Bernie Sharp. *cast* David Warbeck, Kathleen Byron, Dan Meaden, Ciaran Madden, Kenneth Gilbert, Joe Cook.

●How Robert of Locksley became an outlaw ('wolfshead') and took the name Robin Hood. A rather grave and pedantic account, short on zip and long on hammering the points. It's actually a TV pilot that never made it to your living room. Come back Richard Greene, nearly all is forgiven.

Wolves Cry Under the Moon (Guo Dao Feng Bi)

(1997, Tai, 121 min)
d Ho Ping. *p* Lee Yao-ting. *sc* Kuo Cheng. *ph* Han Yun-chung. *ed* Chen Po-wen. *pd* Chang Hung. *m* Jerry Huang. *cast* Chang Shih, Annie Shizuka Inoh, To Tzong-hua, Gu Bao-ming.

●Touching, funny and quirkily inventive, this interweaves the stories of four groups of characters during one long night when Taiwan's main north-south highway is closed to traffic. Taking to the side roads are a wacky punkette who conducts a mobile phone conversation with the stranger whose car she's just stolen; a chauffeur so stressed by doubts about his wife's fidelity that he begins to crack up; a hitman who hijacks a bus to take him to his next assignment and builds an unexpected relationship with the driver; and a trio of puppeteers who never seem to get anywhere. Clearly a reflection on contemporary Taiwanese life (generational and family problems; confusion about crime, jobs and relationships; everyone going round in circles), the film is at times reminiscent of Altman but still works admirably in terms of its individual characters. GA

Wolves of Willoughby Chase, The

(1988, GB, 93 min)
d Stuart Orme. *p* Mark Forstater. *sc* William M Akers. *ph* Paul Beeson. *ed* Martin Walsh. *pd* Christopher Hobbs. *m* Colin Towns. *cast* Stephanie Beacham, Mel Smith, Geraldine James, Richard O'Brien, Emily Hudson, Aleks Darowska, Jane Horrocks, Eleanor David, Jonathon Coy, Lynton Dearden.

●Any fidelity to Joan Aiken's classic for kids is captured in the opening sequences, with their snowbound landscapes, helpless orphan traveller, and treacherous forests. Thereafter, bogged down in Victorian gloom, some of the book's more glorious passages are neglected, while there seems no dramatic point in beefing up the relationship between evil governess Slighcarp and her henchman Grimshaw, only to pit the two young heroines Bonnie and Sylvia against each other. They squabble over Sylvia's lack of courage, while Bonnie rebounds of life's knocks with distictly unappealing, gormless innocence. Eventually the pair are carted off from a life of splendour to a grim orphanage, while the greedy oppressors work in the wings. Budgetary restraints presumably worked against a more imaginative, broad-ranging use of locations, but this doesn't explain the casting of Stephanie Beacham as Slighcarp (playing on her soap opera associations) and of Emily Hudson as the dreadful Bonnie. Better are Geraldine James, Mel Smith, and Aleks Darowska (as Sylvia), who have just the right degree of moderation. A big disappointment. CM

Woman for Joe, The

(1956, GB, 91 min)
d George More O'Ferrall. *p* Leslie Parkyn. *sc* Neil Paterson. *ph* Georges Périnal. *ed* Alfred Roome. *ad* Maurice Carter. *m* Malcolm Arnold. *cast* George Baker, Diane Cilento, David Kossoff, Jimmy Kairoubh, Sydney Tafler, Miriam Karlin.

●Very minor homegrown drama in dubious taste has fairground hawker Baker finding a new top attraction in midget Kairoubh – 'The World's Smallest Man' – and then having to sort out some female company to keep him happy, hiring Cilento to sing in the lion's den. TJ

Woman in a Dressing Gown

(1957, GB, 93 min, b/w)
d J Lee Thompson. *p* Frank Godwin, J Lee Thompson. *sc* Ted Willis. *ph* Gilbert Taylor. *ed* Richard Best. *ad* Robert Jones. *m* Louis Levy. *cast* Yvonne Mitchell, Anthony Quayle, Sylvia Syms, Andrew Ray, Carole Lesley, Olga Lindo.

●Proof that the kitchen sink wasn't invented in the 1960s. Ted Willis' domestic drama was originally produced on television, then filmed (from his own script) to some contemporary acclaim. Yvonne Mitchell gives it the works in the juicy role of a drudge who fights to rekindle the affection of her husband (Quayle) when he asks for a divorce. There's a great bit when a rainstorm ruins her new hairdo, but it's heavy weather throughout; a depressing reminder of prevailing British sexual attitudes. TCh

Woman in a Twilight Garden

see Femme entre Chien et Loup, Une

Woman in Flames, A (Die flambierte Frau)

(1983, WGer, 105 min)
d Robert van Ackeren. *sc* Robert van Ackeren, Catharina Zwerenz. *ph* Jürgen Jürges. *ed* Tanja Schmidbauer. *pd* Herbert Weinand, Heidrun Brandt. *m* Peer Raben. *cast* Gudrun Landgrebe, Mathieu Carrière, Hanns Zischler, Gabriele Lafari, Matthias Fuchs.

●In the middle of a stuffy dinner party, Eva (Landgrebe) walks out of her marriage and into the world of high-class prostitution. She finds customers, a lover (Chris, a male prostitute), and that the thin veneer of chic separating her life from the ordinary world can be pierced by the new emotional strains. Van Ackeren casts a cold eye upon the German middle classes, for whom post-war prosperity has brought expectations of comfort, culture and sterile sex. The subject is not prostitution. Quite what it is, is hard to fathom, for the sexual politics and psychology are complex, and the shifts in tone – from carnal comedy to tragedy – dramatic. But for Eva it is about emotional and economic freedom, bought with sexual favours and too precious to surrender, even to the benign imperialism of Chris' love. Landgrebe spikes Eva's stubborn docility with an icy poise, in a performance which is mesmerising and the key that unlocks the strange pleasures of this film. FD

Woman in Love

see Enamorada

Woman in Red, The

(1984, US, 86 min)
d Gene Wilder. *p* Victor Drai. *sc* Gene Wilder. *ph* Fred Schuler. *ed* Christopher Greenbury. *pd* David L Snyder. *m* John Morris. *cast* Gene Wilder, Charles Grodin, Joseph Bologna, Judith Ivey, Michael Huddleston, Kelly Le Brock, Gilda Radner, Kyle T Heffner, Michael Zorek.

●Menopausal male Wilder gets the frustrated hots for comely Ms Le Brock in this broad, unfunny Hollywood remake of the broad, only vaguely funny French original *Pardon Mon Affaire* (which at least had long-faced Jean Rochefort in its favour). Here writer/director/star Wilder's hankering after extra-marital excitement is indulged without question, while the female characters come off abominably: spouse Ivey is a kindly frump, spinster co-worker Radner's suspicion that she may have a secret admirer a comic delusion, much-ogled Le Brock unaccountably eager to bed her crinkly leading man. Stevie Wonder's songs would be instantly forgettable were it not for the inexplicable fact that the queasy 'I Just Called to Say I Loved You' spent weeks at the top of the UK charts. TJ

Woman in the Moon (Frau im Mond)

(1929, Ger, 14,292 ft, b/w)
d/p Fritz Lang. *sc* Thea von Harbou, Fritz Lang. *ph* Curt Courant, Oskar Fischinger, Otto Kanturek. *pd* Otto Hunte, Emil Hasler, Karl Vollbrecht. *m* Willy Schmidt-Gentner. *cast* Gerda Maurus, Willy Fritsch, Fritz Rasp, Gustav von Wangenheim, Klaus Pohl.

●Lang's last silent movie was planned as another giant sci-fi film in the vein of *Metropolis*. It didn't work out like that, partly because the design and trick-work are cramped and unimaginative, partly because Thea von Harbou's script centres on the exceedingly banal character conflicts on board the first rocket to the moon. As a result, it looks considerably more dated than other Lang silents: it's badly acted melodrama, and the sci-fi trimmings remain entirely secondary. One scene is distinguished by Lang's magnificent sense of spatial drama: the actual launching of the rocket. Otherwise, it's chiefly notable for being one of the rare Lang movies with a deliriously happy ending. TR

Woman in the Window, The

(1944, US, 99 min, b/w)
d Fritz Lang. *p/sc* Nunnally Johnson. *ph* Milton Krasner. *ed* Marjorie Johnson. *ad* Duncan Cramer. *m* Arthur Lange. *cast* Edward G Robinson, Joan Bennett, Dan Duryea, Raymond Massey, Edmund Breon.

●A classic *noir* thriller with Robinson in top form as the likeable professor of criminal psychology who finds his most vivid fantasies and fears fulfilled when his wife and kids take a vacation and leave him alone to cope with the evils of the big city. Meeting up (innocently, it seems) with the woman of his dreams – the subject of a painting in a gallery window he passes regularly – he becomes involved first in the violent killing of a man, then in blackmail. Meanwhile his DA pal (Massey) keeps him in touch with the police's search for the killer. With Bennett and Duryea superb as the eponymous heroine and the blackmailer, and atmospheric camerawork by Milton Krasner, it's not merely a dazzling piece of suspense, but also a characteristically stark demonstration of Lang's belief in the inevitability of fate: Robinson, basically a good man, makes one small slip in a moment of relaxation, and he's doomed. GA

Woman Is a Woman, A

see Femme est une Femme, Une

Woman Next Door, The (La Femme d'à côté)

(1981, Fr, 106 min)
d François Truffaut. *sc* François Truffaut, Suzanne Schiffman, Jean Aurel. *ph* William Lubtchansky. *ed* Martine Barraque-Curie, Marie-Aimée Debril. *ad* Jean-Pierre Kohut-Svelko. *m* Georges Delerue. *cast* Gérard Depardieu, Fanny Ardant, Henri Garcin, Michèle Baumgartner, Véronique Silver.

●For all the period charm of his historical pieces – from *Jules and Jim* to *The Last Métro* – Truffaut increasingly looks more comfortable with contemporary domestic dramas drawn from the bourgeois milieu so successfully explored by Chabrol in the early '70s. In this context, *The Woman Next Door* recounts its tale of *amour fou* in a provincial town – Depardieu (plus wife and kid) moves in next door to a newly-married woman (Ardant) with whom he had an obsessional affair eight years earlier – with absolute narrative confidence. But as Truffaut steers his audience towards the tragic dénouement, the effect is a curiously passive experience, as if, like passengers on a bus tour, we are offered a scenic excursion without ever being driven to the precipice from which his protagonists will fall. A long way from Hitchcock (and Chabrol), but a consistently watchable subthriller none the less. MA

Woman Obsessed

(1959, US, 102 min)
d Henry Hathaway. *p/sc* Sydney Boehm. *ph* William C Mellor. *ed* Robert Simpson. *ad* Lyle Wheeler, Jack Martin Smith. *m* Hugo Friedhofer. *cast* Susan Hayward, Stephen Boyd, Barbara Nichols, Dennis Holmes, Theodore Bikel, Ken Scott.

●Susan Hayward is a widow attempting to run a farm on the rugged plains of Canada. Boyd is the handsome hobo she falls in love with and eventually marries. Conditions are pretty bad – cyclones, blizzards, forest fires – and their relationship is on the stormy side too. It's up to Hayward to rid her new husband of his wife-beating, child-abusing tendencies, and to remould him as a decent cowboy. Hathaway made some fine Westerns, but this 'Scope epic wasn't one of them. GM

Woman of Paris, A

(1923, US, 8,395 ft, b/w)
d/p/sc Charles Chaplin. *ph* Roland Totheroh, Jack Wilson. *ed* Monta Bell. *ad* Arthur Stibolt. *m* Charles Chaplin. *cast* Edna Purviance, Adolphe Menjou, Carl Miller, Lydia Knott, Charles French, Henry Bergman, Charles Chaplin.

●Emerging after being placed on the shelf by Chaplin for almost fifty years, with a reputation as the film that made all directors fall on their knees, *A Woman of Paris* had a lot to live up to. It's easy enough to appreciate the deftness with which Chaplin propels the narrative in this 'first serious drama written and directed by myself' (to quote the opening preamble); in particular, his use of objects (a pipe on the floor, a collar falling from a chest-of-drawers) to relay facts about events and relationships. Easy enough also to enjoy the insouciant charm of Menjou's lecher, who languishes in pyjamas, and tootles on a tiny saxophone while his mistress (Purviance) grows more and more bored at the frenzy of Parisian high society. Yet despite its wealth of detail and sharp observations about morality, the film remains curiously insubstantial with its refined dabbling in the elements of satire, sentiment and melodrama exploited with such panache in Chaplin's starring comedies. The final verdict has to be: fascinating, but... GB

Woman of Straw

(1964, GB, 117 min)
d Basil Dearden. *p* Michael Relph. *sc* Robert Muller, Stanley Mann, Michael Relph. *ph* Otto Heller. *ed* John D Guthridge. *pd* Ken Adam. *m* Beethoven, Berlioz, Mozart, Rimsky-Korsakov. *cast* Gina Lollobrigida, Sean Connery, Ralph Richardson, Johnny Sekka, Laurence Hardy, Alexander Knox.

●Richardson is the wheelchair-bound scourge of his family, hated by his nephew Connery, and nursed by Lollobrigida. Connery hatches a scheme to inherit the old man's money by marrying him off to La Lollo, but of course it goes rather awry, with Richardson getting bumped off earlier than expected. Despite good performances from the three stars, and a plot whose convolutions keep you awake, Dearden treats it rather timidly, afraid to go for the dramatic jugular. ATu

Woman of the Dunes (Suna no Onna)

(1964, Jap, 127 min, b/w)
d Hiroshi Teshigahara. *p* Kiichi Ichikawa, Tadashi Ohono. *sc* Kobo Abé. *ph* Hiroshi Segawa. *ed* F Sushi. *m* Toru Takemitsu. *cast* Eiji Okada, Kyoko Kishida.

●An entomologist finds himself trapped by mysteriously tribal villagers, and forced to cohabit with a desirable but inarticulate woman in an escape-proof sandpit. Leaving aside all the teasing questions of allegorical meaning, Teshigahara's film is a tour de force of visual style, and a knockout as an unusually cruel thriller. It builds on its blatantly contrived premise (taken from Kobo Abé's novel) with absolute fidelity and conviction, which leaves the manifest pretensions looking both credible and interesting, and centres its effects on the erotic attraction between the man and woman, filmed with a palpable physicality that remains extraordinary. TR

Woman of the Port

see Mujer del puerto, La

Woman of the Year

(1942, US, 112 min, b/w)
d George Stevens. *p* Joseph L Mankiewicz. *sc* Ring Lardner Jr, Michael Kanin. *ph* Joseph Ruttenberg. *ed* Frank Sullivan. *ad* Cedric Gibbons, Randall Duell. *m* Franz Waxman. *cast* Spencer Tracy, Katharine Hepburn, Fay Bainter, Reginald Owen, William Bendix, Roscoe Karns, Dan Tobin.

●Tracy and Hepburn were a great team, and this, their first outing together, set the seal on the pattern to follow into the next decade. He's a sports journalist, she's an influential political columnist, and after they marry he wants her to be a woman as well. The comic byplay between opposites – everyday guy Spence and haughty Kate – is a consistent pleasure, even if its sexual politics are ambiguous: Spence scores many more points than Kate, and the whole film is geared toward the climax when she cooks him breakfast like a good little housewife. Produced by Joseph L Mankiewicz, the film has that MGM glitter and literary sparkle. ATu

Woman on Her Own, A (Kobieta samotna)

(1981, Pol, 110 min)
d Agnieszka Holland. *sc* Maciej Karpinski, Agnieszka Holland. *ph* Jacek Petrycki. *ed* Roman Kolski. *m* Jan Kanty Pawluszkiewicz. *cast* Maria Chwalibog, Boguslaw Linda, Pawel Witczak.

●One of the 'missing ten' films which ran into censorship trouble in Poland, not so much a cry from the heart as a hectoring scream of miserabilism. Agnieszka Holland traces the life, and love affair with an epileptic, club-footed no-hoper, of a prematurely-aged postwoman struggling to bring up her son. She lives in a rented cesspit of a one-bed flat by the railway tracks (the recurrent metaphorical image is of trains passing her by), sans TV set but replete with banging pans, totally unsympathetic landlord, and a chip the size of the Polish national debt. She faints from overwork in scene three, is made homeless in scene 17, then things start getting *really* bad. The three lead actors show considerable ability, but collapse, like the audience, under the farcical catalogue of woe they are required to endure. WH

Woman on Pier 13, The

see I Married a Communist

Woman on the Beach, The

(1946, US, 71 min, b/w)
d Jean Renoir. *p* Jack J Gross. *sc* Frank Davis, Jean Renoir, Michael Hogan. *ph* Leo Tover, Harry J Wild. *ed* Roland Gross, Lyle Boyer. *ad* Albert S D'Agostino, Walter Keller. *m* Hanns Eisler. *cast* Joan Bennett, Robert Ryan, Charles Bickford, Nan Leslie, Walter Sande, Irene Ryan.

● The last film from Renoir's wartime exile in America, considered too obscure, too erotic, and cut by nearly a third of its running time by RKO after a preview. What might have been is anybody's guess (not least because it freely rewrites the emphases of its source novel, Mitchell Wilson's *None So Blind*), but what's left is great Renoir: a tormented triangle involving a blind painter (Bickford), his passionate wife (Bennett), and a shell-shocked sailor (Ryan), all three of them outcasts in different ways. A *film noir* in mood, with terrific performances, wonderful use made of the dead-end settings (the lonely clifftop house, the beach strewn with dead hulks), and darkly elemental overtones to the emotional battle (Ryan's recurring nightmare of drowning; Bickford's cleansing by fire of his past). Fragments, maybe, but remarkable all the same. TM

Woman on Top

(2000, US, 92 min)
d Fina Torres. *p* Alan Poul. *sc* Vera Blasi. *ph* Thierry Arbogast. *ed* Leslie Jones. *pd* Philippe Chiffre. *m* Luis Bacalov. *cast* Penélope Cruz, Murilo Benício, Harold Perrineau Jr, Mark Feuerstein, John De Lancie, Anne Ramsay, Ana Gasteyer.

● It's something of a disappointment that this frothy romantic comedy is riddled with soap opera clichés about Latin America. From the Technicolor holiday brochure scene-setting to the salsa-lite soundtrack and the sparkly bits of coy magical realism, it's about as authentically Latin as Doritos. The freakishly beautiful Cruz stars as Isabella, a sultry Brazilian babe whose traffic-stopping looks come with a curse: she's plagued by chronic motion sickness. To overcome this affliction, she must always be in the driver's seat, a situation that eventually tries her husband's macho ego to breaking point. After discovering him with another woman, Isabella sets off for a new life in San Francisco with friend Monica, a lurid transvestite. Within weeks, she's the star of her own live TV cooking show. Desperate to win her back, the errant husband follows her to the States, and effectively begins stalking her with a small samba band in tow. It's a sweet-natured film with some charming and gently funny moments, but ultimately pretty insipid. WI

Woman or Two, A (Une Femme ou Deux)

(1985, Fr, 97 min)
d Daniel Vigne. *p* Michel Choquet. *sc* Daniel Vigne, Elisabeth Rappeneau. *ph* Carlo Varini. *ed* Marie-Josèphe Yoyotte. *ad* Jean-Pierre Kohut-Svelko. *m* Kevin Mulligan, Evert Verhees, Jean Thielemans. *cast* Gérard Depardieu, Sigourney Weaver, Ruth Westheimer, Michel Aumont, Zabou, Jean-Pierre Bisson, Yann Babilée.

● Depardieu is an archaeologist who stumbles across the bones of the first French woman, a two million-year-old number called (in his sculptured model of her) Laura. Alas, he is taken for a ride by a scheming American advertising executive (Weaver), who wants to use his eternal woman in a campaign to sell perfume, and deceives him into thinking she is the director of a foundation which will give money for his digs. Then the real director (Westheimer) turns up…and the perfume woman gets kidnapped…and it all gets very silly. Depardieu coasts through it with his customary felicitousness and charm; Weaver's vaunted ambitions to do comedy are less well realised. There is more to it than crossing your eyes and sticking your tongue out. CPea

Woman Rebels, A

(1936, US, 88 min, b/w)
d Mark Sandrich. *p* Pandro S Berman. *sc* Anthony Veiller, Ernest Vajda. *ph* Robert de Grasse. *ad* Van Nest Polglase, Darrell Silvera. *m* Roy Webb. *cast* Katharine Hepburn, Herbert Marshall, Van Heflin, Elizabeth Allan, Donald Crisp, David Manners, Doris Dudley.

● Interesting proto-feminist movie, adapted from Netta Syrett's novel *Portrait of a Rebel*. Hepburn is the Victorian miss saddled with a stern father (Crisp), despite which she manages to get herself pregnant in a headily romantic affair with Van Heflin. A visit to a married sister in Italy enables her to pass the child off as her niece; after which, determined to stand on her own feet, she rejects an offer of marriage from an understanding diplomat (Marshall) and goes to work. Twenty years later, through journalism, she has become a leading campaigner for women's rights. The gradual growth of her militancy, fuelled by her own experience, is effectively detailed; but Hollywood crassness has to get its word in by way of one of those fatuous coincidences (the threat of incest rears its head when her daughter falls for a young man who happens to be her half-brother), and the inevitable happy ending (Marshall, still patient, faithful, and infinitely understanding, gets Hepburn in the end). With all faults, it's nevertheless held together by Hepburn's superb performance. TM

Woman's Face, A

(1941, US, 105 min, b/w)
d George Cukor. *p* Victor Saville. *sc* Donald Ogden Stewart, Elliot Paul. *ph* Robert Planck. *ed* Frank Sullivan. *ad* Cedric Gibbons, Wade B Rubottom. *m* Bronislau Kaper. *cast* Joan Crawford, Melvyn Douglas, Conrad Veidt, Osa Massen, Reginald Owen, Albert Basserman, Marjorie Main.

● An absurdly melodramatic story, about a nursemaid with a hideously scarred face, who beats a gradual retreat from her embittered life of blackmail and murder-plotting into a world of love and righteousness when she undergoes plastic surgery. Despite some rather silly dialogue (Veidt: 'Do you like music? Symphonies? Concertos?' – Crawford: 'Some symphonies, most concertos'), scripted by the usually reliable Donald Ogden Stewart from a French play (*Il était une Fois* by Francis de Croisset), Cukor's civilised handling of the actors and his often expressionist visuals lend credence to the tale, with atmosphere thick and juicy enough to cut with a knife. Crawford herself was acclaimed for her courage in spending half the film with her distinctive beauty disfigured, but in fact it is Veidt who steals the show, satanic and sinister, as a decadent connoisseur of evil. For Cukor fans, it's also of interest as a peculiarly explicit example of his abiding obsession with the relationship between inner reality and external appearances. GA

Woman's Secret, A

(1949, US, 85 min, b/w)
d Nicholas Ray. *p/sc* Herman J Mankiewicz. *ph* George Diskant. *ed* Sherman Todd. *ad* Albert S D'Agostino, Carroll Clark. *m* Frederick Hollander. *cast* Maureen O'Hara, Melvyn Douglas, Gloria Grahame, Bill Williams, Victor Jory, Mary Philips, Jay C Flippen.

● Something of an RKO chore for Ray, to be sure. But a nicely structured script by Herman J Mankiewicz (from a novel by Vicki Baum) – repeating the investigative flashback structure of *Citizen Kane* as it examines the events leading up to the death of ex-singer O'Hara's devious and ungrateful protégée (beautifully incarnated by Grahame) – is well served by the civilised direction, which not only turns the Vicki Baum melodrama into a *noir*-ish mystery, but also stresses, as so often in Ray, the importance of interior space and the way it reflects/influences action. Entertaining, and less routine than it sounds. GA

Woman's Tale, A

(1991, Aust, 94 min)
d Paul Cox. *p* Paul Cox, Sanantha Naidu. *sc* Paul Cox, Barry Dickins. *ph* Nino Martinetti. *ed* Russell Hurley. *ad* Neil Angwin. *m* Paul Grabowski. *cast* Sheila Florance, Chris Haywood, Gosia Dobrowolska, Norman Kaye, Ernest Gray, Myrtle Woods.

● Australia's art house maestro deals here with the life of an eccentric 80-year-old woman suffering from terminal cancer. Martha (spunkily played by the delightful Florance) is not one to be daunted by the failure of the flesh. Her spirit is alive and well, and she gives to her friend, district nurse Anna (Dobrowolska), as good as she gets: love and support. Martha's son (Haywood) doesn't understand her fierce independence (or much else, to her chagrin) and tries to place her in a home – over her dead body! She's happier with her budgie Jesus, her books and painting, her confused and bedridden ex-RAF officer neighbour, and the prostitutes in the local park. It's an affirmative film, and a restrained one for Cox, who uses Florance to explicate his askance view on life: one that has little sympathy for landlords, closed minds, or people who refuse to take responsibility for (and joy in) their own lives. WH

Woman's World

(1954, US, 94 min)
d Jean Negulesco. *p* Charles Brackett. *sc* Claude Binyon, Mary Loos, Richard Sale. *ph* Joseph MacDonald. *ed* Louis Loeffler. *ad* Lyle Wheeler, Mark-Lee Kirk. *m* Cyril J Mockridge. *cast* Clifton Webb, June Allyson, Van Heflin, Arlene Dahl, Lauren Bacall, Fred MacMurray, Cornel Wilde.

● A well-cast rehash by 20th Century-Fox of MGM's *Executive Suite* (made the same year) that reads like a Neil Simon comedy, with Webb playing an automobile tycoon trying to choose a deputy. He summons the three top candidates and their wives to New York: Cornel Wilde and Allyson are homespun and want to remain in Kansas; MacMurray and Bacall are ambitious and divorcing; Heflin is a wimp, but his wife Arlene Dahl sets out to seduce Webb on her husband's behalf. The result is a victory for feminism and sexism, and it's fun getting there. The tendency to have characters on the edges of the frame, and the frequent travelogue shots of Manhattan, are there to advertise CinemaScope. ATu

Woman to Woman

(1975, US, 48 min)
d Donna Deitch. *m* Barbara Jackson, Sandy Ajita, Cindy Fitzpatrick, Virgina Rubino.

● This documentary, in which women speak to each other about themselves, leaves one with a residual and positive sense of shared problems and collective strength. By involving women from as many social levels as possible, Deitch manages to avoid the aura of elitism and in-group morale-boosting that tends to haunt much of West Coast independent film-making. Opening with a montage of clips illustrating the history of women at work, *Woman to Woman* becomes even more assured once Deitch begins to talk to specific groups of women face-to-face. Perhaps her greatest asset, an infinitely valuable one, is the ability to convey, unfiltered, an immediate impression of the individual women and their particular experience. One comes out feeling stimulated by their company, rather than thinking they have been marshalled into the film as specimens illustrating a predetermined argument. VG

Woman Under the Influence, A

(1974, US, 155 min)
d John Cassavetes. *p* Sam Shaw. *sc* John Cassavetes. *ph* Mitch Breit. *ed* Elizabeth Bergeron, David Armstrong, Sheila Viseltear. *ad* Phedon Papamichael. *m* Bo Harwood. *cast* Peter Falk, Gena Rowlands, Katherine Cassavetes, Lady Rowlands, Fred Draper, OG Dunn.

● One of Cassavetes' best films, with a suitably ambiguous title for a plot that manages to be political in its social implications without succumbing to any crass statements. Rowlands and Falk play a lower middle class couple with three kids, whose combined temperaments produce a potentially explosive emotional energy. He can let off steam in his work; she tries to do it at home, but ends up by turning her household into a cross between an encounter group and an adventure playground, to the fury of neighbours and mother-in-law. The brilliance of the film lies in its sympathetic and humorous exposure of social structure. Rowlands unfortunately overdoes the manic psychosis at times, and lapses into a melodramatic style which is unconvincing and unsympathetic; but Falk is persuasively insane as the husband; and the result is an astonishing, compulsive film, directed with a crackling energy. DP

Woman Who Dreamed, The (I Gynaki pou evlepe ta oneira)

(1988, Greece, 105 min)
d/p Nikos Panayotopoulos. *sc* Nikos Panayotopoulos, Christos Yakalopoulos. *ph* Aris Stavrou. *ad* Dionysus Fotopoulos. *cast* Myrto Paraschi, Yannis Bezos, Theodoris Moridis.

● Dreams fuse with reality in this idiosyncratic relationship drama, the twist being that they are clearly allied to feminine and masculine ways of perceiving reality. Anna recounts her dreams to her work-obsessed husband. During a murder trial, at which the husband is the defence lawyer, a dream prophesies the predisposition of a journalist. As the couple drift apart – he feeling caged by her visions, she by his poor reception of them – so the value and significance of the dreams change. Anna is associated with movement and transition: with roads, water (some immaculate images of flooded floors), thresholds and windows. He is interior, courtroom-defined and rational. But his world is also disturbed by a terrorist organisation which publicly broadcasts Brahms from concealed speakers. In the process, the film becomes as much about exploring cinematic manipulation of emotion and meaning, as it is about the ceaseless negotiation of contemporary relationships and love's fluid role within them. GE

Wombling Free

(1977, GB, 96 min)
d Lionel Jeffries. *p* Ian Shand. *sc* Lionel Jeffries. *ph* Alan Hume. *ed* Peter Tanner. *ad* Jack Shampan. *m* Mike Batt. *cast* David Tomlinson, Frances de la Tour, Bonnie Langford, Bernard Spear, Yasuko Nagazumi, John Junkin, Reg Lye.

● A bit late for TV's Womble-mania gravy train, this feature spin-off does itself no favours by leading its 4ft, fat, and furry heroes into close encounters with a (purportedly) human family to press home the simple ecological message, or by relegating Mike Batt's inventive lyrics and music to backing for a few variable set pieces. There's a certain perverse joy in watching the shaggy creatures in a pastiche of the Hollywood musical, but there's little more than sheer perversity involved in the casting of Bernard Spear as a Japanese car salesman whose genuinely Oriental wife never speaks a word of English. Frances de la Tour is great, and is given great lines, but they belong to a different movie; the rest of her family belong to Disneyland. Lionel Jeffries' previous kids' films promised much, but this unfortunately doesn't begin to deliver. Shame, 'cos Wombles definitely rule Muppets, OK? PT

Women, The

(1939, US, 132 min, b/w & col)
d George Cukor. *p* Hunt Stromberg. *sc* Anita Loos, Jane Murfin. *ph* Oliver T Marsh, Joseph Ruttenberg. *ed* Robert J Kern. *ad* Cedric Gibbons, Wade B Rubottom. *m* Edward Ward, David Snell. *cast* Joan Crawford, Norma Shearer, Rosalind Russell, Mary Boland, Paulette Goddard, Joan Fontaine, Lucile Watson, Phyllis Povah, Ruth Hussey, Virginia Weidler, Margaret Dumont, Marjorie Main.

● A real treat, and an unusual one in that it not only has an all-female cast, but it was scripted by Anita Loos and Jane Murfin from a play by Clare Boothe. Men are present, however, not just in the form of Cukor (rightly acclaimed as one of Hollywood's most sympathetic directors of women), but also in that the group of middle class socialites who make up the cast spend virtually the entire film discussing the men they love, hate, desire, or have just left. The bitchiness comes to the boil when go-getter shopgirl Crawford makes a play for, and wins, one of the group's men, resulting in divided loyalties, devious scheming, and delightfully sharp dialogue all round. Hardly a subversive proto-feminist manifesto, given that Shearer goes back to her faithless hubby with gooey eyes; but enough points are made *en route* about male pride and foibles, and enough laughs are had by all, to leave the abiding impression of a joyous, unsentimental celebration of womanhood. And the performances are wonderful. GA

Women from the Medina (El Batalett)

(2001, Fr/Mor, 60 min)
d Dalila Ennadre. *p* Samir Abdallah. *ph* Dalila Ennadre. *ed* Barbara Pueyo. *with* Saadi Daji, Zainebi Naji, Najate Arafa, Zhor Hourmatallah.

● The heroines of the title are a group of housewives living in Casablanca who openly tell their stories to camera, whether in the *hammam* (the baths), at home or on the streets during the International Women's March of 2000. This intimate account of their lives exposes grinding poverty, endless work, including prostitution, and myriad other hardships associated with being a woman, particularly an Arab woman. But it's far from humourless: as one struggles to get through the washing that piled up during Ramadan, she speaks of her red-raw hands, 'When I get up, they get up,' before addressing them directly : 'Help me make money – then I'll buy you a washing machine!' Such lighter moments contrast sharply with the more disturbing topical tales about racist attacks on Arabs in Spain, difficulties facing immigrants looking for work in France and the continuing lack of equal rights for women under Islam. JFu

Women in Love

(1969, GB, 130 min)
d Ken Russell. *p/sc* Larry Kramer. *ph* Billy Williams. *ed* Michael Bradsell. *ad* Ken Jones. *m* Georges Delerue. *cast* Glenda Jackson, Oliver Reed, Alan Bates, Jennie Linden, Eleanor Bron, Michael Gough, Alan Webb.

● Despite a growing portentousness towards the end, and moments of silliness (memorably, the fireside nude wrestling scene between Bates and Reed) scattered throughout, a surprisingly restrained, even respectful adaptation of DH Lawrence's novel. Much of the credit lies with the cast, camerawork (by Billy Williams), the art direction and Georges Delerue's score, though it must be said that Russell, if seemingly unconcerned with the novel's political thrust, is in fruitful sympathy with Lawrence's sexual politics. Far from good, but better than one might fear or expect. GA

Women in Revolt

(1971, US, 98 min)
d Paul Morrissey. *p* Andy Warhol. *sc/ph/ed* Paul Morrissey. *cast* Jackie Curtis, Candy Darling, Holly Woodlawn, Jonathan Kramer, Johnny Minute, Michael Sklar.

● Three transvestites play at being women playing at being Women. Candy tries for a job as an actress, but has a hard time avoiding the casting couch. Holly plays a spaced-out model who ends up on the Bowery. Jackie ends up looking after the kids. Some find the film anti-women in its parody of the notion of a women's movement…but after all, who better equipped to depict those male fantasies about women than transvestites? VG

Women in Tropical Places

(1990, GB, 90 min)
d Penny Woodcock. *cast* Alison Doody, Scarlett O'Hara, Huffty Reah, Alan Igbon.

● 'I just have affairs with strangers who make things up' confesses elegant Argentinian Celia (Doody). Arriving in Newcastle to meet businessman George, she is dumped by one of his henchmen in a hotel suite, shared by bizarre cabaret artistes Scarlet (O'Hara) and her bald daughter Charmaine (Reah), plus assorted wacky visitors. George is nowhere in sight, but to the horror of Celia, an active member of the International Revolutionary League, a local hate campaign has been launched against his proposal to redevelop the town using non-union labour. This first feature is full of half-realised ideas, but quickly loses all sense of pace and direction. The combination of cabaret turns, social commentary and frustrated libidos, while potentially intriguing, is ultimately too incohesive. Where is George? Why is he buying an ice-cream in one of Celia's fantasies? Why so many flashbacks of Celia's half-hearted ministrations to cheerfully posed peasants? Is she bored, patronising, or just well-dressed? You give up wondering. CM

Women on the Roof, The (Kvinnorna på taket)

(1989, Swe, 90 min)
d Carl-Gustaf Nykvist. *p* Katinka Farago. *sc* Carl-Gustaf Nykvist, Lasse Summanen. *ph* Ulf Brantas, Jorgen Persson. *ed* Lasse Summanen. *ad* Birgitta Brenson. *m* Haken Möller. *cast* Amanda Ooms, Helena Bergström, Stellan Skarsgård, Percy Brandt.

● 'The light…See how it comes in. Licht, light, lumière. But Nordic light is the most beautiful in Europe'. If this sounds like Woody Allen satirising Bergman, it isn't, but you're close. In fact this is a first feature by the son of great Swedish cameraman (and Bergman/Allen collaborator) Sven Nykvist. We are in Stockholm, 1914. Anna (Bergström) is a sophisticated, tempestuous photographer with a mysterious history; innocent, timid Linnea (Ooms) gradually falls under her spell, and into her bed, before Anna's past interrupts their idyll. This falls into most of the pitfalls associated with the continental art movie, flirting as it does with pornography and proving strictly a tease on the intellectual front. The pensive piano score and pretty photography are par for the course, but the film, like the vapid Linnea, only threatens to come to life when events take a macabre turn towards the end; even then, the effect is chilly and rather too pat to convince. TCh

Women on the Verge of a Nervous Breakdown (Mujeres al Borde de un Ataque de Nervios)

(1988, Sp, 89 min)
d Pedro Almodóvar. *p* Agustin Almodóvar. *sc* Pedro Almodóvar. *ph* José Luis Alcaine. *ed* José Salcedo. *m* Bernardo Bonezzi. *cast* Carmen Maura, Antonio Banderas, Julieta Serrano, María Barranco, Rossy de Palma.

● To attempt a synopsis of this extravagantly stylish farce would be daft and forgettable: suffice it to say that a lot happens in the absence of anything actually happening. What lingers in the memory is a sustained desperation, and scenes of Wilder-like sophistication dotted with improbable props, actions, inflated campery, and most of Almodóvar's usual repertory-style company. Somehow a deranged and oddly distanced plot is contrived from elements including infidelity, tranquiliser-spiked gazpacho, interior decor, bad fashion, beds on fire, caged animals, demented telephone answering machines, Shi-ite terrorists, motorbikes, sentimentalism, property rental, and madness. Don't expect the delirious, hilarious eroticism of Almodóvar's previous *Law of Desire*, although the two films share a taste for the thriller elements of high comedy. This is an altogether stranger film – looser, more dream-like, as if directed in the state to which the title refers. TC

Women Talking Dirty

(1999, US/GB, 97 min)
d Coky Giedroyc. *p* David Furnish, Polly Steele. *sc* Isla Dewar. *ph* Brian Tufano. *ed* Patrick Moore, Budge Tremlett. *pd* Lynne Whiteread. *m* Elton John. *cast* Helena Bonham Carter, Gina McKee, Eileen Atkins, Kenneth Cranham, James Nesbitt, James Purefoy, Ken Drury, Richard Wilson.

● 'A wank a day keeps the doctor away,' laugh Cora (Bonham Carter) and Ellen (McKee). And that – apart from the occasional obscenity – is it, as far as women talking dirty goes. The title's such a glaring misnomer, it might have been calculated to lure as many men as women. Few fellas, however, would rush to see a female buddy chickflick set in Edinburgh. Twenty-year-old Ellen and 19-year-old Cora are good people who make bad choices: Ellen marries sleazy Daniel (Purefoy), a gambler who claims to be doing a PhD in women's post-coital chat; Cora falls pregnant by accident and drops out of university. Despite their differences – sullen Ellen is a successful illustrator, Cora a buoyant kid in psychedelic duds – the two become best pals. Then Daniel seduces Cora without her realising who he is, but what does that matter now she's pregnant again. Even with girlish fringe and kooky bunches, McKee and Bonham Carter look too old to play the first flush of youth, while the genuine affection they express for each other is marred by wavering Scottish accents. Still, it's mostly innocuous enough fare, and funny at times. CF

Wonder Boys

(2000, US/Ger/GB/Jap, 111 min)
d Curtis Hanson. *p* Scott Rudin, Curtis Hanson. *sc* Steve Kloves. *ph* Dante Spinotti. *ed* Dede Allen. *pd* Jeannine Oppewall. *m* Christopher Young. *cast* Michael Douglas, Tobey Maguire, Frances McDormand, Robert Downey Jr, Katie Holmes, Rip Torn, Richard Knox, Jane Adams, Michael Cavadias, Philip Bosco.
●Seven years after his first novel was hailed a 'modern classic', Grady Tripp can't finish the follow-up. It just keeps growing. Then there's his writing student James Leer (Maguire), who's enviably gifted, even if he's suicidal, a congenital liar and a thief. On the eve of the university's WordFest festival, Grady's wife leaves, his lover the Dean (McDormand) announces she's pregnant and, worst of all, his editor (Downey) comes calling. Douglas gives one of the most appealing performances of his career as the well meaning but hopelessly befuddled Tripp. On the surface, Hanson's film of Michael Chabon's novel has little in common with the labyrinthine iniquities of *LA Confidential*. But you don't have to peek far into this insular campus setting to unearth discontents and a comparable pattern of people in different social trajectories, inadvertently plotting a collision course – though here it happens to be more comic than tragic. *Wonder Boys* digresses so entertainingly, you forget how quickly Grady got into the mess he's in, and can't imagine where we might be headed. That confusion is unusual in an American movie, only enhancing the pleasure of Steve Kloves' sophisticated dialogue, and the quality of the craftsmanship. The film also elicited a fine new Dylan song, 'Things Have Changed', for its rock-strewn soundtrack. TCh

Wonderful Country, The

(1959, US, 98 min)
d Robert Parrish. *p* Chester Erskine. *sc* Robert Ardrey. *ph* Floyd Crosby, Alex Phillips. *ed* Michael Luciano. *pd* Harry Horner. *m* Alex North. *cast* Robert Mitchum, Julie London, Gary Merrill, Pedro Armendariz, Albert Dekker, Jack Oakie, Charles McGraw, 'Satchel' Paige.
●There's something to be said for letting a project get out of hand when the result is as sympathetic as this. Bursting with characters, sub-plots, themes, symbols, the movie centres on Mitchum, a gringo pistolero operating South of the Border. Crossing the river (a recurring image) on a gun running mission, he painfully rediscovers the blessings and burdens of home and belonging. A German immigrant, an unhappy army wife and a troop of black cavalry reflect different aspects of his situation. Photographically and musically it's a continuous treat, though having the hero ride a horse called Lágrimas – Tears – was carrying portentousness too far. From a novel by the artist Tom Lea, who has a cameo as a barber. BBa

Wonderful Lie, The

see Wunderbare Lüge der Nina Petrowna, Die

Wonderful Life

(1964, GB, 113 min)
d Sidney J Furie. *p* Kenneth Harper. *sc* Peter Myers, Ronnie Cass. *ph* Ken Higgins. *ed* Jack Slade. *pd* Stanley Dorfman. *songs* Peter Myers, Ronnie Cass. *cast* Cliff Richard, Walter Slezak, Susan Hampshire, Melvyn Hayes, Richard O'Sullivan, Una Stubbs, The Shadows.
●Frustrated by shooting a movie with a stuffy veteran director (Slezak) who's not hip to the scene, Cliff and the Shadows conspire to make their own musical version. Lively but contrived star vehicle, chiefly notable for the 'We Love Movies' sequence in which Cliff gets to dress up as Valentino, Jolson and Groucho Marx. NF

Wonderful Visit, The

see Merveilleuse Visite, La

Wonderland

(1999, GB, 109 min)
d Michael Winterbottom. *p* Michele Camarda, Andrew Eaton. *sc* Laurence Coriat. *ph* Sean Bobbitt. *ed* Trevor Waite. *pd* Mark Tildesley. *m* Michael Nyman. *cast* Shirley Henderson, Gina McKee, Molly Parker, Ian Hart, John Simm, Stuart Townsend, Kika Markham, Jack Shepherd, Enzo Cilenti, Sarah-Jane Potts.
●A long weekend in the lives of an extended family of strangers in South London. Dad and mum (Shepherd and Markham) have long since settled for habitual resentment, their general disappointment accentuated by runaway son Darren. They also have three grown daughters: Nadia (McKee) has resorted to the lonely hearts columns; Debbie (Henderson) is the eldest, with an 11-year-old boy and a good-for-nothing ex (Hart); the youngest, Molly (Parker), is pregnant, and blissfully happy with her partner, Eddie (Simm). Only Eddie's getting cold feet. Winterbottom's best film by some measure offers an intimate, suburban panorama of London life now. In the past, this director has slapped style over substance with more vigour than sensitivity; here he's opted for handheld 16mm cameras and a skeleton crew to shoot on the streets of Soho and SW1. The result rings true in a way precious few London films have managed, so that the experience of going to the movie in a local cinema practically blurs with what you've seen on screen. Not that the technique obscures the humanity in Laurence Coriat's fine screenplay, which keeps tabs on half-a-dozen emotionally deprived lives, and endows mundane occurrences with an unforced resonance. Shored up with a memorable Michael Nyman score, this achingly tender film makes most new British cinema look downright frivolous. TCh

Wonder Man

(1945, US, 98 min)
d H Bruce Humberstone. *p* Samuel Goldwyn. *sc* Don Hartman, Melville Shavelson, Philip Rapp. *ph* Victor Milner, William Snyder. *ed* Daniel Mandell. *ad* Ernst Fegte, McClure Capps. *songs* Sylvia Fine, Leo Robin, David Rose. *cast* Danny Kaye, Virginia Mayo, Vera-Ellen, Donald Woods, SZ Sakall, Allen Jenkins, Ed Brophy, Otto Kruger.
●Kaye is notably adept in a dual role: as a song-and-dance man murdered after witnessing a mob killing, and as the entertainer's timid 'intellectual' twin. Since the shy half of the family is unwilling to get involved in the case, the dead brother's restless spirit comes back to share his body while exacting his revenge, causing romantic complications for the two respective girlfriends who now find themselves in love with the same man. John P Fulton's effects work won a deserved Oscar.

Woo

(1998, US, 85 min)
d Daisy VS Mayer. *p* Beth Hubbard, Michael Hubbard. *sc* David C Johnson. *ph* Jean Lépine. *ed* Nicholas Eliopoulos, Janice Hampton. *pd* Ina Mayhew. *m* Michel Colombier. *cast* Jada Pinkett Smith, Tommy Davidson, Dave Chappelle, Paula Jai Parker, LL Cool J, Darrel Heath, Girlina.
●Woo is a flaky but strong-minded girl who gets to choose between a string of willing males. But the film, a would-be latter-day *She's Gotta Have It*, suffers an early failure of nerve. The first shot of the anonymous heroine takes in her legs, her short skirt, her tight top – and finally her glossy face. We're meant to see Woo (Pinkett Smith) as a maverick, but the film has already marked her out as a 'classy lady'; the sort of female who always takes on the black macho male and remains utterly unreal. Equally unengaging are hero Tim (Davidson), the wimpish buppie who loves her, and his male buddies, who provide the requisite quota of chauvinism – an endless flow of sexism and homophobia apparently challenged by the film, but actually endorsed. The script does occasionally surge into life, and there's also something interesting about Woo's close friendship with drag queen Celestrial (Girlina), because Pinkett looks rather draggy herself here. CO'Su

Wood, The

(1999, US, 107 min)
d Rick Famuyiwa. *p* Albert Berger, Ron Yerxa, David Gale. *sc* Rick Famuyiwa. *ph* Steven Bernstein. *ed* John Carter. *pd* Roger Fortune, Maxine Shepard. *m* Robert Hurst. *cast* Taye Diggs, Omar Epps, Richard T Jones, Sean Nelson, Trent Cameron, Duane Finley, Malinda Williams, De'Aundre Bonds, Sanaa Lathan, LisaRaye, Tamala Jones.
●In this thoughtful but flat coming-of-age comedy-drama, Roland (Diggs) has gone AWOL with a bout of wedding day jitters. His oldest friends Mike (Epps) and Slim (Jones) are despatched to find him and deliver him up the aisle. In the ensuing tour of ex-girlfriends and old neighbourhood haunts, the best men get their man, prompting the three to reminisce about their middle class '80s adolescence in suburban Inglewood. The film's opening and the playground dare – a spot of bum pinching – which brings the three together don't bode well for the sexual politics, so it comes as something of a surprise to see the boys' scruples quietly putting paid to a wager as to who will lose his virginity first. MHi

Wooden Crosses

see Croix de Bois, Les

Wooden Horse, The

(1950, GB, 101 min, b/w)
d Jack Lee. *p* Ian Dalrymple. *sc* Eric Williams. *ph* CM Pennington-Richards. *ed* John Seabourne, Peter Seabourne. *ad* William Kellner. *m* Clifton Parker. *cast* Leo Genn, David Tomlinson, David Greene, Anthony Steel, Bryan Forbes, Peter Finch.
●Solid retelling of one of WWII's most audacious and enduring escape stories as Genn, Tomlinson and Steel tunnel under a vaulting horse to escape Nazi captivity in Stalag Luft III and head for neutral Sweden courtesy of fake passports. Detailed handling gives a good idea of the men's ingenuity and courage in this dignified, reasonably tense Britflick. TJ

Wooden Man's Bride, The (Yan Shen)

(1993, Tai, 114 min)
d Huang Jianxin. *p* Wang Ying-Hsiang. *sc* Yang Zhengguang, Jia Pingau. *ph* Zhang Xiaoguang. *ed* Lei Qin. *pd* Teng Jie. *m* Zhang Dalong. *cast* Chang Shih, Wang Lan.
●From the director of *The Black Cannon Incident*, this is a piece of raunchy myth-making in the vein of *Red Sorghum* and *The Swordsman in Double-Flag Town*. A peasant bride is hijacked by bandits on the way to her wedding. Her intended husband meanwhile meets an untimely accident and bites the dust. Undaunted the groom's family presses ahead with the wedding ceremony, marrying the rescued girl to a wooden effigy of the dead man. The melodramatics and sexual exotica are routine for the genre, but the film looks good and plays well. Its most intriguing element is the gay subplot involving the bandit chief, a cross-dressing aesthete who gets a crush on the strapping hero. TR

Woodlanders, The

(1997, GB, 98 min)
d Phil Agland. *p* Barney Reisz, Phil Agland. *sc* David Rudkin. *ph* Ashley Rowe. *ed* David Dickie. *pd* Andy Harris. *m* George Fenton. *cast* Rufus Sewell, Jodhi May, Polly Walker, Tony Haygarth, Cal MacAninch, Emily Woof, Walter Sparrow, Sheila Burrell.
●Best known for spending a year in a remote Chinese village for his documentary series *Beyond the Clouds*, Agland comes down to earth with this, his first fiction film (scripted by David Rudkin). On the edge of the New Forest, the daughter of a sawmill owner (Woof), whose father has hopes for her betterment, loves a woodsman (Sewell), but is edged into marriage to a doctor (MacAninch). Result, tragedy. Underplaying the extreme melodramatics of Thomas Hardy's novel (a self-defeating exercise, perhaps) while hammering home the class theme, the movie feels tired and draggy even at ninety-odd minutes – and the blame rests squarely with Agland, whose direction is flat and uninspired. The scenes simply don't breathe, though the women in particular perform heroic acts of hopeless resuscitation. TCh

Woodstock

(1970, US, 184 min)
d Michael Wadleigh. *p* Bob Maurice. *ph* Michael Wadleigh, David Myers, Richard Pearce, Don Lenzer, Al Wertheimer. *ed* Michael Wadleigh, Thelma Schoonmaker, Martin Scorsese. *with* Joan Baez, Joe Cocker, Country Joe and the Fish, Crosby Stills & Nash, Arlo Guthrie, Richie Havens, Jimi Hendrix, The Who.
●As the roaches moulder in the gutters of Haight Ashbury, and the Love generation consider their bank statements, we're left with this

legendary piece of trend-setting opportunism to reflect on. The screen shatters into fragments of middle class kids in rags, of super-lays offering their love to millions, of nipples al fresco. Of course there's Hendrix coming orgasmically alive, Richie Havens shot from below and carved from granite, Joe Cocker timelessly manic, Crosby Stills & Nash in some peace-sodden heaven. A time capsule, yes, and a hallowed memory, perhaps. But gimme shelter. SG

Woodstock: The Director's Cut

(1994, US, 224 min)
d Michael Wadleigh. *p* Bob Maurice. *ph* Michael Wadleigh, David Myers, Richard Pearce, Don Lenzer, Al Wertheimer. *ed* Thelma Schoonmaker, Martin Scorsese, Stan Warnow, Yeu-Bun Yee. *cast* Jimi Hendrix, The Who, Janis Joplin, Crosby Stills & Nash, Sly & the Family Stone, Country Joe & the Fish, Canned Heat, Jefferson Airplane.

● The 'director's cut' has digitally improved sound and imagery and about 40 minutes of extra footage, including previously unseen performances by Jefferson Airplane, Janis Joplin and Canned Heat. Pride of place goes to Jimi Hendrix, looking saintly for what was to be a last screen appearance. Remember a time when sex didn't carry the death penalty and records didn't come from commercials on the telly? SGr

Woo Woo Kid, The (aka In the Mood)

(1987, US, 98 min)
d Phil Alden Robinson. *p* Gary Adelson, Karen Mack. *sc* Phil Alden Robinson. *ph* John Lindley. *ed* Patrick Kennedy. *pd* Dennis Gassner. *m* Ralph Burns. *cast* Patrick Dempsey, Talia Balsam, Beverly D'Angelo, Michael Constantine, Betty Jinnette, Kathleen Freeman, Peter Hobbs.

● The beguiling true-life case of Sonny Wisecarver – who, aged 14, married two married women in their twenties in the dog days of World War II, and shared tabloid covers with Hitler and D-Day – was a moment's monument, and a perfect vehicle for the likes of Jonathan Demme. In Robinson's hands, it is sometimes crude, sometimes wonderfully small-print human, bailed out by the gravitational pull of documentary truth, and generally worth a look. The soundtrack alone is sharp enough to sell the movie to blind swing band fans. For Sonny (Dempsey) it was always true love, though the ladies suffer the strictures of the law for corrupting a minor. Sonny is played adenoidally open-mouthed and innocently goodhearted, and both wives (Balsam, D'Angelo) are experienced but achingly vulnerable. The movie, validly, doesn't take a stance, but plays a cheeky catch-as-catch-can between tethered fact and sometimes surreal guesswork. Nice little film. BC

Word, The

see Ordet

Word Is Out

(1977, US, 135 min)
d/p/sc/ph/ed Mariposa Film Group (Peter Adair, Veronica Selver, Nancy Adair, Andrew Brown, Robert Epstein, Lucy Massie Phenix. *m* Trish Nugent.

● A documentary by the San Francisco-based Mariposa Film Group, comprising interviews with 26 gay American men and women of varied classes and ethnic origins. It is neither militant (although it does contain some footage of civil rights demos) nor analytic (although the careful selection of interviewees bespeaks one level of analysis), and is an important film for those very reasons. It doesn't intimidate or alienate any potential viewer, but uses techniques of simple reasoning, and elements of mild surprise, to catch attention and hold it. If two hours of talking heads sounds like a long time, then it's a measure of the film-makers' success that the result is as gripping and persuasive as the most accomplished fiction. TR

Working Class Go to Heaven, The

see Classe Operaia Va in Paradiso, La

Working Girl

(1988, US, 113 min)
d Mike Nichols. *p* Douglas Wick. *sc* Kevin Wade. *ph* Michael Ballhaus. *ed* Sam O'Steen. *pd* Patrizia von Brandenstein. *m* Carly Simon. *cast* Harrison Ford, Sigourney Weaver, Melanie Griffith, Alec Baldwin, Joan Cusack, Philip Bosco, Kevin Spacey, Olympia Dukakis, David Duchovny.

● A New York romantic comedy which exhibits a touch, timing and inventiveness that puts the much acclaimed *Moonstruck* in its place, and the interaction between the female leads is so funny that you don't care if the leading man never turns up – the film's only problem. Tess McGill (Griffith) aches to graduate from the secretarial pool to executive level in the brokerage industry, but her male colleagues promise breaks and pass her round. The deal is no fairer under a female boss, Katharine Parker (Weaver), who never makes the coffee and steals Tess' best idea. When the boss breaks her leg skiing, Tess takes over her office, and meets investment broker Jack Trainer (Ford), with whom she works well until her boss returns breathing fire. Kevin Wade's screenplay is so sharply witty in all directions on class differences that the man in the middle appears neutral and all-purpose. All the women steal his scenes, including the wonderfully funny Joan Cusack as a back-combed secretary. A treat. BC

Working Girls

(1986, US, 91 min)
d Lizzie Borden. *p* Lizzie Borden, Andi Gladstone. *sc* Lizzie Borden, Sandra Kay. *ph* Judy Irola. *ed* Lizzie Borden. *pd* Kurt Ossenfort. *m* David Van Tieghem. *cast* Louise Smith, Deborah Banks, Liz Caldwell, Marusia Zach, Amanda Goodwin, Boomer Tibbs, Ellen McElduff.

● Lizzie Borden takes an axe to the Hollywood image of the prostitute. Focusing on Molly (Smith), a college girl who's trying to make some cash, prostitution is viewed as an economic alternative, another business in the world's financial capital. The overriding unsung leitmotif is that of a procession (of clients, rituals, preparations); the cold reality of Borden's vision is reminiscent of Frederick Wiseman's examinations of American institutions. But where Wiseman's seemingly neutral recording of a nightmare works, Borden's calculated dramatic reconstruction falters as one set of stereotypes is substituted for another. Wooden lines stand in lieu of dialogue, caricatures in place of characters. SGo

Work in Progress (En Construcción)

(2001, Sp/Fr, 126 min)
d José Luis Guerín. *p* Antoni Camín. *sc* José Luis Guerín. *ph* Alex Gaultier. *ed* Mercedes Alvarez, Núria Esquerra. *cast* Juana Rodríguez, Iván Guzmán, Juan López López, Santiago Segade, Antonio Atar, Abdel Aziz el Mountassir.

● Fascinating semi-documentary traces the building of a new apartment block in a rundown corner of Barcelona. Guerín shot more than 100 hours of footage over 18 months – some partially staged for the camera – then whittled it down, to concentrate on a squatting couple (Rodríguez, Guzmán), a tramp (Atar), the workers and their foreman (López). Several sequences, including the discovery of a Roman cemetery, are still far too long. But, without any narration, the writer/director achieves startling moments of urban poetry and unexpected anthropological insight, as the future takes shape among the rubble of the past. NY

Work Is a Four Letter Word

(1967, GB, 93 min)
d Peter Hall. *p* Thomas Clyde. *sc* Jeremy Brooks. *ph* Gilbert Taylor. *ed* Jack Harris. *ad* Philip Harrison. *m* Guy Woolfenden. *cast* David Warner, Cilla Black, Elizabeth Spriggs, Zia Mohyeddin, Joe Gladwin, Julie May, Alan Howard.

● A disastrous reworking of Henry Livings' play *Eh?*, recognisable only in that the hero still grows aphrodisiac mushrooms in the boiler-room of the automated factory where he works and is currently honeymooning with his new bride. Livings' wonderful mental slapstick (with not so much his characters' bottoms as their minds exposed in long woolly underwear as their spiritual trousers fall down) has been reduced to a pitifully trite satire on automation. A few amusing bits survive the gaudily trendy direction. TM

Work on the Grass (Kusa no Ue no Shigoto)

(1993, Jap, 42 min)
d Tetsuo Shinohara. *p* Tetsuo Shinohara, Akemi Sugawara, Shogo Ueno. *sc* Tetsuo Shinohara. *ph* Shogo Ueno. *ed* Yoko Nishioka. *m* Hiroyuki Murakami. *cast* Naoki Goto, Hikari Ota.

● Two young men cut grass in what appears to be a huge countryside park. The younger, more butch one is a pro; he does this every day. The other, slightly nerdy and clumsy with the equipment, is a temp; he wants to be a writer. The day starts badly, but they reach a truce during lunch-break. And then, in the afternoon, they drift towards – what? Emotional intimacy? Sex? A glimmer of mutual understanding? Shinohara's prizewinning short shows the collision of two personalities, two approaches to life, and yields some moving and curiously melancholy perceptions of the world as young men see it. A minor classic of Japanese indie cinema. TR

World According to Garp, The

(1982, US, 136 min)
d George Roy Hill. *p* George Roy Hill, Robert L Crawford. *sc* Steve Tesich. *ph* Miroslav Ondricek. *ed* Stephen A Rotter, Ronald Roose. *pd* Henry Bumstead. *m* David Shire. *cast* Robin Williams, Mary Beth Hurt, Glenn Close, John Lithgow, Hume Cronyn, Jessica Tandy, Swoosie Kurtz.

● John Irving's bestselling book – one of those huge, baggy, scattergun novels that Americans imagine contain all human life – is noticeably shortened and not improved by Steve Tesich's script, which loses Irving's perceptions of Garp's life existing within a much larger flow of experience. All we are left with are some of those telling symbolic nuggets from another cradle-to-the-grave saga of a New England writer and his proto-feminist Mom. Williams is cuddly enough as the man whose talents for nurturing a family are constantly undermined by a malign fate, and there is a performance of some dignity from Lithgow as a six-and-a-half-foot ex-pro footballer transsexual. But it's the kind of movie which is brave – or stupid – enough to ask the meaning of life without having enough arse in its breeches to warrant a reply. CPea

World and His Wife, The

see State of the Union

World Apart, A

(1987, GB, 113 min)
d Chris Menges. *p* Sarah Radclyffe. *sc* Shawn Slovo. *ph* Peter Biziou. *ed* Nick Gaster. *pd* Brian Morris. *m* Hans Zimmer. *cast* Jodhi May, Jeroen Krabbé, Barbara Hershey, Nadine Chalmers, Maria Pilar, Kate Fitzpatrick, Tim Roth.

● What lifts cinematographer Menges' directorial debut above the worthiness of most anti-apartheid movies is the child's viewpoint. Like Maisie in *What Maisie Knew*, 13-year-old Molly (May) is walled off from much of the high passion of the adult world, but a casualty of the fall-out. With her communist father (Krabbé) on the run, and her liberal journalist mother Diane (Hershey) totally preoccupied with the struggle against apartheid, Molly is resentful about her loveless and lonely upbringing. When Diane – whose involvement with the banned ANC brings down the brutality of the South African police on their comfortable white Johannesburg suburb – is imprisoned under the 90 Day Detention Act, Molly's schoolfriends ostracise her; meanwhile, subjected to intense psychological pressure driving at her maternal guilts, released and immediately imprisoned again, Diane attempts suicide. Few cause-movies point out how uncomfortable martyrs are to live with, and few stars are prepared to play them that way, but Hershey does. Intelligent, unsensational, and painful, it's a film to applaud. BC

World Apartment Horror

(1991, Jap, 97 min)
d Katsuhiro Otomo. *p* Hiro Osaki, Kazama Yasuhisa. *sc* Katsuhiro Otomo, Nobumoto Keiko. *ph* Shinoda Noboru. *cast* Hiroki Tanaka, Yuji Nakamura, Weng Huarong, Kimiko Nakagawa.

● The global success of *Akira* earned Otomo the freedom to make this live-action feature, which launched a cycle of films about the situation of

Asian immigrants in Japan, most of them earnestly sociological. Otomo's film, though, is a yakuza horror comedy. The Black Dragon gang has its eye on a tumbledown apartment building rented to poor students and workers from Taiwan, China, Pakistan, the Philippines and Bangladesh. The first heavy sent to force the tenants out goes crazy. The second is Itta (Tanaka, now better known as a director under the name Sabu), who rushes in ego-first and finds himself facing not only uncowed Asians but also some very strong voodoo. TR

World for Ransom

(1954, US, 82 min, b/w)
d Robert Aldrich. *p* Robert Aldrich, Bernard Tabakin. *sc* Lindsay Hardy. *ph* Joseph Biroc. *ed* Michael Luciano. *ad* William Glasgow. *m* Frank De Vol. *cast* Dan Duryea, Gene Lockhart, Patric Knowles, Reginald Denny, Nigel Bruce, Marian Carr, Arthur Shields, Douglas Dumbrille.

● A Monogram cheapie derived from the NBC TV series *China Smith*, this is a seminal Aldrich movie with Duryea, as private eye Mike Callahan, the first in a long line of compromised idealists who recur throughout the director's work. The plot concerns a kidnapped nuclear scientist – we're in Cold War country here – and the story's set in a Poverty Row Singapore. 'It was a parody on the usual exotic espionage adventure films' Aldrich remarked in an interview. He thought it 'interesting', indeed 'pretty good', but was sore about the excision of a scene which portrayed the girl Duryea loves as a lesbian (after Dietrich in *Morocco*). The whole point, he explained, was that Duryea could forgive her past life with men, but couldn't handle her love for women. Nor could the censors, it seems. Boy's Own material on the surface, maybe, but on the level of characterisation a compelling exploration of partnerships, brotherly bonds, and the fallibility of trust. MA

World Is Full of Married Men, The

(1979, GB, 106 min)
d Robert Young. *p* Malcolm J Fancey, Oscar Lerman. *sc* Jackie Collins. *ph* Ray Parslow. *ed* David Campling. *ad* Tony Curtis. *m* Frank Musker, Dominic Bugatti. *cast* Anthony Franciosa, Carroll Baker, Sherrie Cronn, Paul Nicholas, Gareth Hunt, Georgina Hale, Anthony Steel.

●Dreadful moral tale-cum-sex comedy, with Franciosa as an adulterous director of TV commercials, living a hypocritical double life with wife (Baker) and model (Cronn), until wife throws him out in favour of a rock star (Nicholas). Scripted by Jackie Collins from her own novel, it's a repeat of the formula of *The Stud*, with the same mixture of softcore jollies and 'comedy' scenes of humiliation/embarrassment. RM

World Is Not Enough, The

(1999, GB/US, 128 min)
d Michael Apted. *p* Michael G Wilson, Barbara Broccoli. *sc* Neal Purvis, Robert Wade, Bruce Feirstein. *ph* Adrian Biddle. *ed* Jim Clark. *pd* Peter Lamont. *m* David Arnold. *cast* Pierce Brosnan, Sophie Marceau, Robert Carlyle, Denise Richards, Robbie Coltrane, Desmond Llewelyn, Maria Grazia Cucinotta, Samantha Bond, Michael Kitchen, Judi Dench, John Cleese, Patrick Malahide.

● At least you know what to expect with a Bond movie: it will begin with a spectacular chase after which Bond pulls off a miraculous escape; it will involve a dangerous megalomaniac with plans to rule the world; there'll be plenty of exotic locations, guns, gadgets and girls; and the finale will feature another successful shoot-out in the baddies' headquarters, followed by a closing shot of Bond having a snog. You know this because you've seen it all 18 times before. That said, some Bonds are more watchable than others, and this, the 19th addition to the franchise, is certainly one of the better ones. An oil magnate friend of Commander Bond (Brosnan) is murdered, and his heir, the beautiful Elektra King (Marceau), is threatened with the same treatment unless she changes the route of her father's proposed pipeline. The terrorist in question is one Renard (Carlyle), a dying, dark-eyed psycho who feels no pain. Worse, he's got a missile in his silo. Bond hotfoots it to several exotic climes, nearly dies a few times, enlists the help of an old adversary, ex-KGB man Valentin (Coltrane), and even endures a few minutes of auto-eroticism, all in the course of active duty. Midway through it becomes apparent that someone's overcooked the story with too many incidentals and locations (not to mention too many puns). Nevertheless, director Michael Apted ensures it all passes by efficiently enough. And his extraordinarily well staged opening salvo is one of the most impressive Bond sequences yet. DA

World of Gilbert & George, The

(1981, GB, 69 min)
d Gilbert & George. *with* Gilbert & George.

● Art world dabblings with the fringe culture of the New Right bear all the slightly risible hallmarks of a hermetically-sealed conceptual con(troversy), though there are apparently some who claim the status of key political text for this Arts Council-funded effort. A first film by the 'living sculpture' pose-artists, the Morecambe and Wise of sober-suited, straight-faced pretension, it's a cumulatively noxious set of discreet statements, visual and musical quotes, and appropriated testimonies representing a claimed triumph of the artistic will over national decay and the inarticulate dead end. A manifesto for a troublesome, truthless Beauty, it's a thoughtfully cinematic provocation that inventively formalises the clichés of agit-prop and turns them around, but probably further marginalises itself in the process. Odd, though, that 'Jerusalem' makes as much sense ending this as it did *Chariots of Fire*. PT

World of Glory (Härlig är Jorden)

(1991, Swe, 15 min)
d Roy Andersson. *p* Göran Lindström, Freddy Olsson. *sc* Roy Andersson. *ph* István Borbás. *m* Allan Pettersson. *cast* Klas-Gösta Olsson, Lennart Björklund, Christer Christensen, Bernard Eiger, Rolf Engstrom, Gun Fors, Udo Kühnapas, Hans Söderblom, Anne Tubin.

● Where *Songs from the Second Floor* envisages the apocalypse through the workings of a city, this shorter antecedent focuses on one 'ordinary' individual, who addresses viewers directly as he introduces the people and places that figure in his life. It's a compassionate yet savage indictment of human cruelty, complacency, conformism and alienation. It's often very funny, even as it's haunted by its creator's sheer horror at acts perpetrated against humans by other humans during the Holocaust. GA

World of Suzie Wong, The

(1960, GB, 129 min)
d Richard Quine. *p* Hugh Perceval. *sc* John Patrick. *ph* Geoffrey Unsworth. *ed* Bert Bates. *ad* John Box. *m* George Duning. *cast* William Holden, Nancy Kwan, Sylvia Syms, Michael Wilding, Laurence Naismith, Jackie Chan.

● Holden plays the aspiring young artist in Hong Kong who falls for a Chinese prostitute (Kwan), and despite major difficulties – like his loathing of her way of life, a poor script, and the restrictions that taste demanded of films in those days – their relationship flourishes for a while. But denied the chance of being honest about its subject, it soon degenerates into euphemistic soap opera, with vague gestures towards bohemianism and lukewarm titillation. Wisely, Quine seems to have devoted most of his attention to the Hong Kong locations. CPe

World's Greatest Lover, The

(1977, US, 89 min)
d/p/sc Gene Wilder. *ph* Gerald Hirschfeld. *ed* Anthony A Pellegrino. *pd* Terence Marsh. *m* John Morris. *cast* Gene Wilder, Carol Kane, Dom DeLuise, Fritz Feld, Carl Ballantine, Matt Collins.

● Heading for Tinsel Town to compete for stardom as the World's Greatest Lover in an ailing studio's last ditch attempt at finding its own Valentino, Wilder's newly-wed small town baker is undaunted by the vast competition or by an embarrassing nervous disorder, and ignorant of the hunger harboured by his new wife (Kane) for the Divine Rudy. Wilder's second feature as writer/director hovers uneasily between homage and pastiche, and on occasion his specialised hysteria stretches too thin for comfort, particularly with several supporting characters being cut from the selfsame cloth. He also succumbs to the same kind of icky True Romance sentimentality that all but poleaxed Woody Allen's early features, thereby wasting much of Carol Kane's potential. For all that, there are enough laughs – DeLuise and Feld sparkle beautifully – to justify the price of a ticket. GD

World Without Pity, A

see Monde sans pitié, Un

Worm Eaters, The

(1977, US, 94 min)
d Herb Robins. *p* Ted V Mikels. *sc* Herb Robins. *ph* Willis Hawkins. *ed* Soly Bina. *pd* Jack DeWolf. *m* Theodore Stern. *cast* Herb Robins, Lindsay Armstrong Black, Robert Garrison, Joseph Sackett, Mike Garrison, Muriel Cooper.

● Fish-bait entrepreneur Herman breeds a worm that chews up fishermen, who return to dry land in ill-fitting worm suits demanding, reasonably, that Herman supply worm girls for them. Meanwhile, the crooked mayor of Subplot City and his Klan buddies plan to steal Worm Guy's land. Herman's revenge is, it goes without saying, of a worm-related nature. The producer is Ted V Mikels, the Ed Wood of this end of the market, and, perhaps due to a volunteer shortage, Herman is played by the director. Aspiring Max Bialystocks might consider adapting this for their next Broadway musical. DO

Wot! No Art

(1978, GB, 55 min)
d/p/sc Christopher Mason. *ph* Clive Tickner. *ed* Polly Bindloss. *cast* narrator: Tom Kempinski.

● An entertaining if undeniably muddled retrospective on the social context of the arts in the period 1945-51, the years of the first post-war Labour government and the birth of the Arts Council: days of hope (and austerity) when public patronage for 'public art' was intended to promote a cultural renaissance to complement that in education, health and housing. The film is sound in tracing the dissipation of the dream (making good use of representative newsreels, with their uniquely patronising commentaries), but falters in drawing parallels with today's situation, and is insufficiently rigorous or coherent in its polemical assertion of the status of art as a social priority. Provocative, none the less. PT

Would You Kill a Child?

see ¿Quién Puede Matar a un Niño?

Wounds, The (Rane)

(1998, Serbia/Fr, 103 min)
d Srdjan Dragojevic. *p* Dragan Bjelogrlic. *sc* Srdjan Dragojevic. *ph* Dusan Joksimovic. *ed* Petar Markovic. *pd* Aleksandar Denic. *m* Aleksandar Sasa Habic. *cast* Dusan Pekic, Milan Maric, Dragan Bjelogrlic, Branka Katic, Predrag Miki Manojilovic, Vesna Trivalic.

● Kicking off in 1996 Belgrade, where the director's previous feature, *Pretty Villlage, Pretty Flame*, left off, this presents, if anything, a sourer version of recent Serbian history than its predecessor. Tracking back to the beginnings of the Bosnian conflict, it follows the descent of two barely adolescent boys, degraded by fighting, hunger and homelessness into a life of crime, drugtaking and lost idealism. To emphasise the tragi-farcical, writer/director Dragojevic adopts a rumbustious quasi-Kusturica style of frenetic action, broad acting and ironic musical bombast. Dedicated to the post-Tito generation. WH

Woyzeck

(1978, WGer, 81 min)
d/p/sc Werner Herzog. *ph* Jörg Schmidt-Reitwein. *ed* Beate Mainka-Jellinghaus. *ad* Henning von Gierke. *m* Fiedelquartett Telc, Antonio Vivaldi, Benedetto Marcello. *cast* Klaus Kinski, Eva Mattes, Wolfgang Reichmann, Willy Semmelrogge, Josef Bierbichler.

● An anarchist's morality play; the tale of an army private tormented in private by visions of apocalypse, in public by the unbearable weight of social and sexual oppression; he flips. Herzog's harsh vision of human suffering beyond despair, adapted from the Georg Büchner play, casts Woyzeck as a proletarian King Lear (Kinski, extraordinary once again), but there are echoes, too, of Beckett and Brecht. A sharp parable on social oppression and dormant rebellion, made with a dispassionate, deliberate formality that some may find hard to take. CA

Woyzeck

(1994, Hun, 93 min, b/w)
d János Szász. *p* Peter Barbalics. *sc* Janos Szasz. *ph* Tibor Mathé. *ed* Anna Kornis. *ad* Peter Mandoki. *cast* Lajos Kovács, Diana Vâcaru, Alexandr Porohovschikov, Péter Haumann.

●Visually extraordinary version of Büchner's oft-adapted play, with a sturdy performance from Kovács as the hapless, humiliated Woyzeck, here a railway signalman, who finally cracks when he discovers his wife's infidelity. The combination of high-contrast b/w and some telling, unusual angles makes for a strikingly poetic version that verges on the abstract, but it is slow, a little too studied and far less poignant than Herzog's more romantic account. GA

Wraith, The

(1986, US, 92 min)
d Mike Marvin. *p* John Kemeny. *sc* Mike Marvin. *ph* Reed Smoot. *ed* Scott Conrad, Gary Rocklen. *ad* Dean Tschetter. *m* Michael Hoenig, J Peter Robinson. *cast* Charlie Sheen, Nick Cassavetes, Sherilyn Fenn, Randy Quaid, Griffin O'Neal, Matthew Barry.

●Gang of comic-strip killer car-thieves is led by lip-curling psycho Packard (Cassavetes). New kid in town Sheen is sometimes himself, sometimes a leathered-up RoboDredd available for chicken run assignments in his blacked-out turbo roadster. Sherilyn Fenn is Packard's girl 'or nobody's', but was previously the squeeze of a Packard victim and is starting to come on strong to Sheen, apparently or spasmodically the deceased boyfriend reincarnated. The town (comprising one house, a burger joint and no citizen who isn't a teenager or a cop) is overseen by Sheriff Randy Quaid, who displays all the reverence the script deserves. Best joke is having one of the thugs know a word like 'wraith'. DO

Wrestlers, The (Uttara)

(1999, Ind, 99 min)
d/sc Buddhadeb Dasgupta. *ph* Asim Bose. *ed* Rabi Ranjan Maitra. *ad* Ashok Bose. *m* Biswadeb Dasgupta. *cast* Jaya Seal, Tapas Pal, Shankar Chakraborty, RI Asad, Tapas Adhikari, Saurav Das.

●Lofty claims are made for Indian poet and film-maker Dasgupta, who has been compared to everybody from Ray to Fellini. Adapted from a story by Samaresh Bose, this rambling, quietly surrealist tale of two friends who love to wrestle is slow-burning but beguiling. The humour is very deadpan. We see passing parades of midgets and circus folk. The trees and fields are exquisitely photographed, and the film is lit throughout in a magical, crepuscular light. At first, this seems like sheer whimsy, but gradually the mood darkens as Dasgupta begins to hint at all sorts of tensions – religious and sexual – lurking beneath the surface of a deceptively placid rural world. GM

Wrestling Ernest Hemingway

(1994, US, 123 min)
d Randa Haines. *p* Joe Wizan, Todd Black. *sc* Steven Conrad. *ph* Lajos Koltai. *ed* Paul Hirsch. *pd* Waldermar Kalinowski. *m* Michael Convertino. *cast* Robert Duvall, Richard Harris, Shirley MacLaine, Sandra Bullock, Nicole Mercurio, Piper Laurie.

●Frank (Harris) is an Irish sea-salt marooned in a quiet Florida backwater. Lonely and forgotten, he strikes up a friendship with a retiring old man in the park, Walt (Duvall), a hairdresser from Chicago. Frank is loud and full of blarney; Walt is dapper, shy and in love with the sunny young waitress (Bullock) at the local diner. They become inseparable. The relationship between two grumpy old codgers is not what you'd immediately expect from director Haines (*Children of a Lesser God*), or from a 21-year-old screenwriter (Steve Conrad), but then this is a film of discreet pleasures and minor miracles. There aren't really any surprises, but it's a delight to see a movie which idles away without anything more pressing on its mind than people. As good a way as any of watching the world go by. TCh

Writing in the Sand, The

(1991, GB, 45 min, b/w)
d Amber Films.

●A cinepoem from the Amber Collective evoking a day at the seaside, through a collage of recorded snippets of conversation and Sirkka Lüsa-Konttinen's superb photographs of holidaymakers at play. Atmospheric and frequently funny, it is imbued with an unsentimental nostalgia for simpler summertimes, but the coda about environmental pollution seems rather tagged on, and therefore less forceful than it might have been. GA

Writing on the Wall, The (Nous Etions Tous des Noms d'Arbres)

(1982, Fr/Bel, 114 min)
d Armand Gatti. *p* Jean-Jacques Hocquard, François Leclerc, Colm Cavanagh, Jacques Gouverneur, Gérard Martin, Marc Minon. *sc* Armand Gatti. *ph* Armand Marco, Ned Burgess, Jean-Pierre Dardenne, Stéphane Gatti. *ed* Olivier van Malderghem, Véronique Lange, Danièle Delvaux. *ad* Pierre-Henri Madnin, Raphaël Gattegno, Clarisse Gatti, Catherine Renson, Rouben Ter-Minassian. *m* Philippe Hemon-Tamie, Demons. *cast* John Deehan, Brendan 'Archie' Deeney, Paddy Doherty, Nigel Haggan, John Keegan, Neil McCaul.

●A youth workshop in Derry is mounting various projects, including a dramatised enquiry into the death of a soldier. But when a squaddy is shot on the doorstep, then real life intrudes in the shape of the police and security forces. Gatti's brave and honourable film forcefully engages with a subject with which we on the 'mainland' are often too ignorant – the images of violence are plainly visible day after day, but the means to interpret them is absent. By a diligent inclusion of the background cultural elements to the drama, Gatti builds a penetrating account of the Irish 'question' that does justice to the complexities of its condition. The film's confusions might be said to mirror those of its subject, but it demonstrates better than any other film to date the passion that lies behind a whole community's grievances. CPea

Written Face, The (Das Geschriebene Gesicht)

(1995, Switz/Jap, 93 min)
d Daniel Schmid. *p* Marcel Hoehn, Kenzo Horizuka. *sc* Daniel Schmid. *ph* Renato Berta. *ed* Daniela Roderer. *with* Tamasaburo Bando, Han Takehara, Karuko Sugimura, Kazuo Ohno, Yajuro Bando, Kai Shishido.

●This portrait of kabuki artist Tamasaburo Bando explores the art of the *Onnagata*, the male performer who specialises in female parts. Alongside lengthy stage excerpts, where music, movement and dazzling costume changes trace the refined expression of loss and longing, the man himself attests that he's 'never seen the world with the eyes of a woman', while several actresses who've inspired him attest to the longevity of their own careers – Tsutakiyomatsu Asaji, for instance, still singing at 101. Schmid's approach is reverent, if slightly functional, but he comes a cropper when attempting a kabuki-style celluloid drama of his own, and the use of *Madame Butterfly* is surely a misjudgment. Occasionally captivating none the less. TJ

Written on the Wind

(1956, US, 99 min)
d Douglas Sirk. *p* Albert Zugsmith. *sc* George Zuckerman. *ph* Russell Metty. *ed* Russell Schoengarth. *ad* Alexander Golitzen, Robert Clatworthy. *m* Frank Skinner. *cast* Lauren Bacall, Robert Stack, Dorothy Malone, Rock Hudson, Robert Keith, Grant Williams.

●How many movies evoke the period in which they were made and yet still look both fresh and modern as well? This seems like one of the quintessential films of the '50s: a high-powered Texas oil-family drama, detailing the mis-matches between the spoiled and variously bent children of the family and the relatively 'normal' outsiders. Sirk plays it as a conspicuously fierce critique of a particular sector of American society, the disintegrating middle class, but one in which all the sympathy goes to the 'lost' children rather than to the straights. The acting is dynamite, the melodrama is compulsive, the photography, lighting, and design share a bold disregard for realism. It's not an old movie; it's a film for the future. TR

W.R. – Mysteries of the Organism (W.R. – Misterije Organizma)

(1971, Yugo/WGer, 86 min)
d/sc Dusan Makavejev. *ph* Pega Popovic, Aleksandar Petkovic. *ed* Ivanka Vukasovic. *ad* Dragoljub Ivkov. *m* Bojana Marijan. *cast* Milena Dravic, Jagoda Kaloper, Zoran Radmilovic, Tuli Kupferberg, Jackie Curtis, Betty Dodson, Jim Buckley, Nancy Godfrey.

●Although it seemed like some kind of breakthrough at the time, Makavejev's film isn't improving with age. Its comedy rests flimsily on cross-cutting between two distinct sets of material: the American footage starts with the life and ideas of Wilhelm Reich, and goes on to explore some of the more bizarre fringes of 'permissive' America; the Yugoslav footage comprises a risible hymn to Stalin from the archives, plus a satirical account of an affair between a liberated Yugoslav woman and a repressed Russian skating star. The Reichian notion that everybody needs better orgasms has a certain credibility; but neither Tuli Kupferberg prowling New York as a 'hippie guerilla', nor the juxtaposition of Stalin with Jim Buckley's erect cock, says anything interesting about sex, power politics, or the relation between them. TR

Wrong Arm of the Law, The

(1962, GB, 94 min, b/w)
d Cliff Owen. *p* Aubrey Baring. *sc* Ray Galton, Alan Simpson, John Antrobus. *ph* Ernest Steward. *ed* Tristam Cones. *ad* Harry White. *m* Richard Rodney Bennett. *cast* Peter Sellers, Lionel Jeffries, Bernard Cribbins, Davy Kaye, Nanette Newman, Bill Kerr, John Le Mesurier.

●On the face of it, a TV-style comedy inspired by Ealing Studios, most notably *The Lavender Hill Mob*. But somehow Owen, the cast, and a large team of writers turn it into a very superior piece of work, with both an eye and an ear for dialogue and the absurd situation. Sellers, a smooth Bond Street couturier, is also the rough-diamond leader of a bunch of inept criminals. He keeps them happy with luncheon vouchers, home movies, and paid holidays in Spain. But their welfare state criminality is undermined by the arrival of a gang of Australians, forcing Scotland Yard to get its act together. Not only is it genuinely funny, it's also a sly portrait of Britain slowly emerging from the 'Never Had It So Good' days into the Wilson era. ATu

Wrong Is Right (aka The Man With the Deadly Lens)

(1982, US, 118 min)
d/p/sc Richard Brooks. *ph* Fred J Koenekamp. *ed* George Grenville. *pd* Edward C Carfagno. *m* Artie Kane. *cast* Sean Connery, George Grizzard, Robert Conrad, Katharine Ross, GD Spradlin, John Saxon, Henry Silva, Leslie Nielsen, Robert Webber, Rosalind Cash, Hardy Krüger, Dean Stockwell.

●Perhaps the oddest major Hollywood feature of 1982. Veering wildly between a quite well-written satire on the contemporary American political scene and a very ham-fisted nuclear blackmail thriller, its sheer eccentricity is quite engaging. Connery is excellent as a superstar TV reporter, but he deserves a better plot; and the adulation his character receives from Arab leaders seems as ridiculous as his network's apparently effortless ability to transmit live anywhere, any time. Writer/director Brooks is on stronger ground when tilting at the extraordinary contradictions in America's political morality, but his one major coup is to demonstrate just how good a TV performer Connery could indeed be. DP

Wrong Man, The

(1956, US, 105 min, b/w)
d/p Alfred Hitchcock. *sc* Maxwell Anderson, Angus MacPhail. *ph* Robert Burks. *ed* George Tomasini. *ad* Paul Sylbert. *m* Bernard Herrmann. *cast* Henry Fonda, Vera Miles, Anthony Quayle, Harold J Stone, Nehemiah Persoff, Charles Cooper, Richard Robbins.

●Hitchcock's long-standing fear of the police is what originally attracted him to a newspaper account of a family man wrongly identified as an armed robber. *The Wrong Man* pays scrupulous attention to such things as the details of police procedure and the eventual apprehension of the real culprit – before the conviction of the wrongly accused man (Fonda), but after the stress has driven his wife (Miles) to mental breakdown. The result is Hitchcock's most sombre film, unrelieved by his usual macabre humour; the black-and-white photography and the persecuted Fonda's sharply chiselled features lend an impressive documentary feel. It's not generally rated among the master's best works, largely because of the intractability of the source material (or Hitchcock's unwillingness to dramatise the events). But there's still plenty here for Hitchcockophiles: a Jesuitical strain (the man happened to be a devout Catholic), a complicity of guilt (as the wife irrationally comes to blame herself); and it's pure *noir*. RM

Wrong Man, The

(1992, US, 110 min)
d Jim McBride. *p* Chris Chesser, Alan Beattie. *sc* Michael Thoma. *ph* Affonso Beato. *ed* Lisa Churgin. *pd* Jeannine Oppewall. *m* Los Lobos. *cast* Kevin Anderson, Rosanna Arquette, John Lithgow, Robert Harper, Jorge Cervera Jr, Ernesto LaGuardia.

● An exotic modern-day *film noir* from the director of *The Big Easy* with a promising cast and a soundtrack by Los Lobos. Drifting through Mexico, Anderson finds himself wanted for murder. He hitches a fast ride to town with two fellow Americans, bickering couple Lithgow and Arquette, but his troubles are only just beginning. Scrappy, obnoxious, shrill and tiresome, though Rosanna Arquette fans may disagree. TCh

Wrong Movement (Falsche Bewegung)

(1975, WGer, 103 min)
d Wim Wenders. *p* Peter Genée. *sc* Peter Handke. *ph* Robby Müller, Martin Schäfer. *ed* Peter Przygodda, Barbara von Weitershausen. *ad* Heidi Lüdi. *m* Jürgen Knieper. *cast* Rüdiger Vogler, Hanna Schygulla, Ivan Desny, Marianne Hoppe, Hans Christian Blech, Nastassja Kinski, Peter Kern.

● Made between *Alice in the Cities* and *Kings of the Road*, this is an odd and rather uncharacteristic work for Wenders. Basically, the problem arises from Peter Handke's script ('inspired' by Goethe's *Wilhelm Meister*), which tends towards a symbolism and explicitness Wenders usually steers clear of. The film follows the attempts of the central character (Vogler) to get a grip on an embryonic vocation as a writer, at the same time coming to some kind of working arrangement with the spectres of Germany's past. But Wenders' strengths are also tantalisingly in evidence: the highly-charged road sequences, the meditative use of landscape, and the tensions beneath apparently desultory encounters. VG

Wrony

see Crows

Wunderbare Lüge der Nina Petrowna, Die (The Wonderful Lie)

(1929, Ger, 105 min approx, b/w)
d Hanns Schwarz. *p* Erich Pommer. *sc* Hans Szekely. *ph* Carl Hoffmann. *ad* Robert Herlth, Walter Röhrig. *m* Willy Schmidt-Gentner. *cast* Brigitte Helm, Franz Lederer, Warwick Ward, Harry Hardt, Lya Jan.

● Helm and Lederer eye one another across a St Petersburg nightclub; cut to a waiter igniting the brandy around a phallically rearing ice cream bombe. But Lederer is a mere lieutenant while Helm is already his colonel's mistress, and although the colonel sees off this upstart rival with practised ease, he reckons without true love: tragedy ensues. Few surprises in the narrative of this late silent, which refers throughout to existing models, notably *Camille*. But Schwarz had an eye for sensuous detail, and sends his camera prowling stylishly around some imposing sets: the split level nightclub, Helm's chic apartment, the smoky officers' mess with empty champagne bottles stacked in the corner. BBa

W USA

(1970, US, 117 min)
d Stuart Rosenberg. *p* Paul Newman, John Foreman. *sc* Robert Stone. *ph* Richard Moore. *ed* Robert Wyman. *ad* Philip M Jefferies. *m* Lalo Schifrin. *cast* Paul Newman, Joanne Woodward, Anthony Perkins, Laurence Harvey, Pat Hingle, Cloris Leachman, Don Gordon, Moses Gunn, Bruce Cabot.

● Adapted from Robert Stone's novel *A Hall of Mirrors*, this is a sophisticated political satire set in New Orleans, with Newman as a DJ on a right wing station (it's being used to propagandise a neo-Fascist movement) whose tough cynicism finally shatters his relationship with a timid girl he picks up (Woodward). The film is intelligent and well directed, but what makes it exceptional is Anthony Perkins' extraordinary performance as the neurotic liberal Rainey, which builds – after a few rather shaky scenes – into an agonisingly real force in the narrative. Someone had the astonishingly appropriate idea of taking Norman Bates out of *Psycho* and turning him into a torn and anguished liberal/revolutionary: it's less a character study than a kind of visible expression of the raw liberal conscience, a twitching, convulsive mass of uncertainty and pain. Newman's visual, verbal and structural dialogue with Perkins throughout the film is so impressive that it makes this one of the more important political statements to have come out of Hollywood in the early '70s. DP

Wuthering Heights

(1939, US, 103 min, b/w)
d William Wyler. *p* Samuel Goldwyn. *sc* Ben Hecht, Charles MacArthur. *ph* Gregg Toland. *ed* Daniel Mandell. *ad* James Basevi. *m* Alfred Newman. *cast* Merle Oberon, Laurence Olivier, David Niven, Flora Robson, Donald Crisp, Geraldine Fitzgerald, Hugh Williams, Leo G Carroll, Cecil Kellaway.

● From the (prolific) output of a largely unfashionable director, Wyler's *Wuthering Heights* has a distinctive look that elevates it above the blandness Goldwyn productions are so often charged with. Handsomely designed by James Basevi and shot by Gregg Toland, the much-filmed tale of Cathy's passion for Heathcliff succeeds as fulsome melodrama; and while it has little to do with Emily Bronte's sense of environment and pre-Victorian society, it's nevertheless strong on performances – especially Olivier, seen here at the peak of his romantic lead period. MA

Wuthering Heights

see Abismos de pasión

Wuthering Heights

(1992, GB, 106 min)
d Peter Kosminsky. *p* Mary Selway. *sc* Anne Devlin. *ph* Mike Southon. *ed* Tony Lawson. *pd* Brian Morris. *m* Ryuichi Sakamoto. *cast* Juliette Binoche, Ralph Fiennes, Janet McTeer, Sophie Ward, Simon Shepherd, Jeremy Northam, Simon Ward, John Woodvine.

● Restoring the dangerous passion and morbid obsession crucial to Emily Bronte's novel, Kosminsky's debut feature eschews melodrama in favour of Gothic romance, with Anne Devlin's skilful screenplay delving deep into the swirling currents of Cathy's forbidden love for the gypsy foundling Heathcliff, whom she later abandons for sensitive, refined Mr Linton. Where the film falls down is in confining itself too much to gloomy rooms, thus failing to point up the contrast between imprisoning social conventions and the pagan pleasures of the moors. Similarly, while Fiennes' flowing black locks and piercing blue eyes make Heathcliff, striding the moors swathed in animal skins, a powerful, darkly attractive figure, Binoche's Cathy lacks the wild sensuality that should underpin her wilfulness. There are problems, too, with the French actress' wavering accent. Nevertheless, this is superior to the 1939 Hollywood version in one other respect: instead of ending with the romantic tragedy of Cathy's death, it continues into the next generation, when the spurned Heathcliff returns to claim Wuthering Heights and to take a cruel revenge. A brave stab, but it doesn't always pierce the heart. NF

W.W. and the Dixie Dancekings

(1975, US, 94 min)
d John G Avildsen. *p* Stanley S Canter. *sc* Thomas Rickman. *ph* James Crabe. *ed* Richard Halsey, Robbe Roberts. *ad* Lawrence G Paull. *m* David Grusin. *cast* Burt Reynolds, Art Carney, Conny Van Dyke, Jerry Reed, Ned Beatty, Richard D Hurst, Don Williams, Furry Lewis.

● Reynolds at his best as a hillbilly conman (he robs gas stations with a water-pistol in hopefully swashbuckling imitation of his idol Errol Flynn) who finds himself steering a minor-league bunch of musicians to stardom in a Nashville considerably sleazier than Altman's. Quirky Deep South locations, fine '50s atmosphere (back street bars full of young hopefuls imitating Elvis), a wonderful interlude in which Furry Lewis sings 'Dirty Car Blues'. With all faults (chiefly Art Carney as a tiresome lawman-cum-hellfire preacher), a refreshingly irrepressible movie. TM

Wyatt Earp

(1994, US, 190 min)
d Lawrence Kasdan. *p* Jim Wilson, Kevin Costner, Lawrence Kasdan. *sc* Lawrence Kasdan, Dan Gordon. *ph* Owen Roizman. *ed* Carol Littleton. *pd* Ida Random. *m* James Newton Howard. *cast* Kevin Costner, Gene Hackman, Dennis Quaid, Michael Madsen, Bill Pullman, Jeff Fahey, Isabella Rossellini, Tom Sizemore, JoBeth Williams, James Gammon.

● Costner's Earp is a 'deliberate' man, and Kasdan's big-budget over-long epic is deliberate to a fault. Depicting Wyatt's youth, his first, tragic marriage, and especially the stern injunctions of paterfamilias Hackman, this prologue is ponderous and predictable. Where Kasdan/Costner insist on going back and crossing every 't', Eastwood might have conveyed the same information in the blinking of an eye. Costner creates a complex individual, but he's in virtually every scene, and one yearns for a less monotonous presence. There's a tremendous lift when Quaid's emaciated, debauched, wise-cracking Doc Hol-liday appears. Despite its longueurs, however, this is not a negligible movie. When Earp pins a badge on his pathology the picture begins to add up (the famous feud with the Clantons is tense and brutal); and when the Earp family falls apart, it's clear the mess is largely of Wyatt's making. Breathtakingly photographed by Owen Roizman, this serious picture slowly reveals the festering wounds at the at the heart of a key Western myth. TCh

xyz

Yankee Doodle Dandy

Xala

(1974, Sen, 123 min)
d Ousmane Sembene. *p* Paulin Soumanou Vieyra. *sc* Ousmane Sembene. *ph* Georges Caristan, Orlando R Lopez, Seydina D Saye, Farba Seck. *ed* Florence Eymon. *m* Samba Diabara Samb. *cast* Thierno Leye, Seune Samb, Miriam Niang, Younouss Seye, Dieynaba Niang.

● An invigorating film which tells, in leisurely fashion, of a middle-aged Dakar businessman whose social standing begins to slip when he takes a third wife and finds that he's lost his touch in bed ('xala' means impotence). There's no sniggering humour, though; instead, Sembene aims satirical thrusts at the Senegalese bourgeoisie, who impotently ape the worst aspects of their former colonial masters, particularly their corruption and extravagance (our hero, for instance, uses imported mineral water to wash his car). The jokes and details are delightful, yet there's real anger behind them, and it bursts spectacularly into view in the concluding frames. GB

Xanadu

(1980, US, 96 min)
d Robert Greenwald. *p* Lawrence Gordon, Joel Silver. *sc* Richard Christian Danus, Marc Reid Rubel. *ph* Victor J Kemper. *ed* Dennis Virkler. *pd* John W Corso. *m* Barry DeVorzon. *cast* Olivia Newton-John, Gene Kelly, Michael Beck, James Sloyan, Dimitra Arliss, Katie Hanley, Sandahl Bergman.

● An experience so vacuous it's almost frightening. Built around a threadbare Hollywood fairytale which has Newton-John (on roller-skates) playing a muse despatched by Zeus to help mortals realise their fantasies, it turns out in fact to be an unashamed show-case for Livvy's multifarious 'talents'. Alas, as the film grinds from one epic production routine to another, it becomes painfully clear that she can't deliver a line (the script, full of gnomic punchlines, is admittedly abysmal), hold a note (the Jeff Lynne/John Farrar songs are lowest common denominator), or step a pas de deux (despite the helping hand of Gene Kelly, who can still cut it on the dance floor). Not even Michael Beck, fresh out of *The Warriors*, can salvage the disaster. IB

Xenolith

(1994, US, 96 min)
d YN Wong-Ho. *ph* Chan Kam-yuen. *ed* Ying Nam-ko. *cast* Tsui Wing-Chi, Tsui Wing-Sing, Pak Yiu-Charn, Chan Fung-Ping.

● Shot entirely in Hong Kong and nearly eight years in post-production, this no-budget indie feature looks like any number of HK social-realist TV films but dares to do without a storyline or any hint of hyped-up drama. A working-class man struggles to bring up his two school-age sons; his wife has divorced him and emigrated, but remains a significant absence in the minds of the boys. That's more or less it as far as the content goes. Wong-Ho centres her interest on the minutiae of the kids' lives in the cramped apartment, implicitly challenging the orthodox Confucian view that father-son relations are the core of Chinese society. Unmomentous, but modestly impressive. TR

X Files, The

(1998, US, 122 min)
d Rob Bowman. *p* Chris Carter, Daniel Sackheim. *sc* Chris Carter. *ph* Ward Russell. *ed* Stephen Mark. *pd* Christopher Nowak. *m* Mark Snow. *cast* David Duchovny, Gillian Anderson, John Neville, William B Davis, Martin Landau, Mitch Pileggi, Blythe Danner, Armin Mueller-Stahl.

● It would probably take a team of top FBI investigators years to figure out what's going on in writer/producer Chris Carter's big screen expansion of his TV series. The truth may be out there, but it's certainly not in here as agents Mulder and Scully (Duchovny and Anderson) spend two hours running around failing to reveal the conspiracy to cover up the existence of aliens among us. To the neophyte, it will make little sense: there's an Oklahoma-style bombing, gooey extra-terrestrials lurking underground in Texas, enigmatically powerful men plotting in rooms, Landau off his trolley and an awful lot of bees. Money has been spent on massive set-pieces and expensive hardware to remind us we're not watching the box, though those who have never seen the series may be at a loss to fathom the appeal of the Duchovny-Anderson duo. TJ

Xiao Wu

(1997, China/HK, 113 min)
d Jia Zhangke. *p* Li Kitming, Jia Zhangke. *sc* Jia Zhangke. *ph* Nelson Yu Lik-Wai. *ed* Lin Xiaoling. *ad* Liang Jingdong. *cast* Wang Hongwei, Hao Hongjian, Zu Baitao, Ma Jinrei, Liu Junying, Liang Yonghao, An Qunyan.

● Xiao Wu is a likeable but scummy petty criminal, lifting wallets from visitors to the provincial dirt town he calls home. Times are getting hard. His oldest friend, now a respected citizen, doesn't want to know him any more; the leggy girl from the karaoke hostess bar is stringing him along; and the cops are mounting an anti-crime campaign. This wonderful debut feature (like most decent Chinese films of the 1990s, it was made outside what remains of the studio system) takes an almost Bressonian path to the core of one man's psyche, stripping away layer after layer of his loser's armour until he's left as 'naked' as a person can be. Acted with absolute conviction by a cast of non-professionals and resourcefully shot by HK indie film-maker Yu Lik-Wai, this is an engrossing and moving achievement. TR

X-Men

(2000, US, 104 min)
d Bryan Singer. *p* Lauren Shuler Donner, Ralph Winter. *sc* David Hayter. *ph* Newton Thomas Sigel. *ed* Steven Rosenblum, Kevin Stitt, John Wright. *pd* John Myhre. *m* Michael Kamen. *cast* Hugh Jackman, Patrick Stewart, Ian McKellen, Famke Janssen, James Marsden, Halle Berry, Anna Paquin, Tyler Mane, Ray Park, Rebecca Romijn-Stamos, Bruce Davison.

● Stewart's Dr Xavier – from the Marvel comic strip – runs his boarding school as a refuge for mutants with special powers, and as an undercover operation against Magneto (McKellen), whose mutant forces are plotting warfare on humans in response to proposed legislation against the growing percentage of 'freaks' in the population. Aiming to stop such damaging conflict are Xavier's X-Men. His latest recruit Wolverine (Jackman) produces metal spikes from his knuckles; Rogue (Paquin) can cause death with a touch; Storm (Berry) has the weather at her command; while Cyclops (Marsden) delivers withering looks from ray-gun eyes. The conflict between Xavier and Magneto couches a dilemma familiar from ethnic and gay politics: assimilation or direct action. It's good to find an action movie which has at least one idea in its head, but apart from the brushed metal production design and pin-sharp camerawork, this offers only moderate excitement. TJ

X – the Man with X-Ray Eyes (aka The Man with the X-Ray Eyes)

(1963, US, 80 min)
d/p Roger Corman. *sc* Robert Dillon, Ray Russell. *ph* Floyd Crosby. *ed* Anthony Carras. *pd* Daniel Haller. *m* Les Baxter. *cast* Ray Milland, Diana Van Der Vlis, Harold J Stone, John Hoyt, Don Rickles, John Dierkes, Lorie Summers, Vicki Lee.

● Corman's intelligent sci-fi movie has a powerful performance from Milland as Dr Xavier, whose experiments with X-Ray eye-drops allow him to cheat at cards, diagnose patients' internal complaints, and see through women's clothing (fortunately for them, they're all standing with their naughty bits shielded by inexplicably opaque plants and pieces of furniture). As the treatment continues, however, Milland becomes terrified as he starts to see beyond the material world into the heart of the universe. The rudimentary special effects and cheapo production notwithstanding, this is an undoubted cult classic. ATu

X the Unknown

(1956, GB, 81 min, b/w)
d Leslie Norman. *p* Anthony Hinds. *sc* Jimmy Sangster. *ph* Gerald Gibbs. *ed* James Needs. *ad* Edward Marshall. *m* James Bernard. *cast* Dean Jagger, Edward Chapman, Leo McKern, William Lucas, Peter Hammond, Anthony Newley, Kenneth Cope.

● 1956 – the year of the Suez crisis, a sharp increase in the crime rate, and uneasy preparation for WWIII – spawned a series of gloomy thrillers (both in Britain and in America) in which the weight of the military is mobilised against various alien organisms from the bowels of the earth or outer space. This Hammer entry is photographed in shadowy monochrome by Gerald Gibbs, with a sense of muted hysteria and despair underlying the stalwart attempts to defeat a radioactive thing which erupts in the Scottish highlands. Trash to people who don't like sci-fi or horror movies, but in a lot of ways it communicates the atmosphere of Britain in the late '50s more effectively than the most earnest social document. As one example, note the film's obsession with radioactivity (the monster feeds on it), which even becomes the background to an assignation between a doctor and a nurse in a nearby hospital. (The film was started by Joseph Losey, who left the production after a few days, due to illness – officially at least.) DP

Xtro

(1982, GB, 86 min)
d Harry Bromley Davenport. *p* Mark Forstater. *sc* Iain Cassie, Robert Smith. *ph* John Metcalfe. *ed* Nick Gaster. *ad* Andrew Mollo. *m* Harry Bromley Davenport. *cast* Bernice Stegers, Philip Sayer, Danny Brainin, Simon Nash, Maryam D'Abo.

● A British horror picture incompetent enough to be prime drive-in fodder, if only we had such a thing, this throws together in random fashion a mish-mash of all the half-remembered elements from recent hungry alien films. Telekinesis, melting telephones, randy au pair girls getting sliced in the shower, pumas in the living-room, and – nastiest scene of the month – a woman giving birth to a fully-grown man, who then bites off his own placenta. The Xtro creature is a warty lizard which snatches family men off to its space craft for three years at a stretch; but its greatest service to mankind seems to be a taste for eating the drivers of Volvo estate cars, which is very heartening. CPea

X, Y and Zee

see Zee & Co.

Yaaba

(1989, Burkina Faso/Fr/Switz, 90 min)
d Idrissa Ouedraogo. *p* Pierre Alain Meier, Freddy Denaes, Idrissa Ouedraogo. *sc* Idrissa Ouedraogo. *ph* Matthias Kalin. *ed* Loredana Cristelli. *m* Francis Bebey. *cast* Fatima Sanga, Noufou Ouedraogo, Barry Roukietou, Adama Ouedraogo, Amade Toure.

● In the Mooré language of Burkina Faso, 'yaaba' means grandmother, in the sense of respect towards an elder touched with wisdom and grace. And 'yaaba' is the name given by a young village boy to an old woman ostracised by the community and forced to live alone outside their walls. Ouedraogo's beautifully controlled film gently illustrates how the villagers' prejudice towards the old woman reveals to the boy an adult world of folly and generosity that he's about to join himself. Amid the palpable heat and dust, characters are confidently drawnin the great cinema tradition of the rural poor, wit more than an occasional nod to Satyajit Ray's *Pather Panchali*. Oudraogo's direction of actors is superb, and as in Cissé's *Yeelen*, an input of European money and talent gives the film a polished surface. Unlike *Yeelen*, though, this seeks not to create a magical universe, but to tell a direct, affecting story of superstition and love that marks Ouedraogo as a talent to watch. DT

Yaacov Ben Dov: Father of the Hebrew Film

(1989, Isr, 31 min)
d Yaacov Gross.

● Ukrainian Yaacov Ben Dov began as a still photographer before becoming Palestine's first documentary-maker. His footage of the emerging state of Israel is full of optimism – children plant groves of trees, schools rise, harvests are reaped. Palestine, Kafka wrote in his diary after seeing Ben Dov's work, needs earth, not lawyers. There's no shortage of Brits in pith helmets – General Allenby in 1917; Churchill and Balfour; High Commissioner Sir Herbert Samuel watching a camel race. BC

Ya – Cuba

see I Am Cuba

Yakuza, The

(1974, US, 112 min)
d Sydney Pollack. *p* Sydney Pollack, Michael Hamilburg. *sc* Paul Schrader, Robert

Towne. *ph* Kozo Okazaki, Duke Callaghan. *ed* Thomas Stanford, Don Guidice. *pd* Stephen Grimes. *m* David Grusin. *cast* Robert Mitchum, Ken Takakura, Brian Keith, Keiko Kishi, Eiji Okada, James Shigeta, Herb Edelman, Richard Jordan.

●Writer Paul Schrader's homage to the Japanese gangster movie, with the standard plot opened out to accommodate Mitchum and American support, who share the screen with Ken Takakura (the No 1 star of such pictures) and some attractive Japanese locations. Behind an excessively wordy script, obligatory twists and double-crosses, and the celibate stance of the two leads, there emerges the familiar and increasingly explicit nostalgic celebration of the chivalric male relationships of countless American Westerns. The exposition is often laughably inscrutable, and obligations to both Japanese and American audiences frequently land in the mid-Pacific, but the film succeeds in casting its own slow spell. Takakura's terse, spring-coiled performance nicely complements Mitchum's somnolent bulk, and despite falterings in build-up, the formalised violence is rivetingly choreographed. The final show-down is one not to be missed. CPe

Yana's Friends (Hachaverim shel Yana)

(1999, Isr, 90 min)
d Arik Kaplun. *p* Marek Rozenbaum, Moshe Levinson, Uri Sabag, Einat Bikel. *sc* Arik Kaplun, Simeon Vinokur. *ph* Valentin Belanogov. *ed* Tali Halter, Einat Glazer-Zarchin. *pd* Ariel Roshko. *m* Avi Binyamin. *cast* Evlyn Kaplun, Nir Levi, Shmil Ben-Ari, Dalia Friedland, Vladimir Friedman, Israel Damidov, Lena Sachnova.

●Lively, enjoyable comedy drama set in Tel Aviv during the Gulf War, charting the fortunes of various inhabitants of a flatshare – notably a womanising video artist and a pregnant Russian immigrant abandoned by her husband – and the people they encounter in the street. The plotting and the gags are predictable, perhaps, but the essentially goodnatured tone is engaging, there are some subtle, imaginative visual and aural touches, the music is catchy, and the central theme of regeneration through new responsibilities and relationships, even in times of war, is lightly handled. Fun. GA

Yang ± Yin: Gender in Chinese Cinema (Nansheng Nüxiang)

(1996, HK, 77 min)
d Stanley Kwan. *p* Thomas Chow. *sc* Stanley Kwan, Edward Lam. *ph* Christopher Doyle. *ed* Maurice Lee. *m* Yo Yo Yu. *cast* Leslie Cheung, John Woo, Edward Yang, Chen Kaige, Tsui Hark, Hou Hsiao-Hsien, Tsai Ming-Liang, Ang Lee, Stanley Kwan.

●Made for the BFI's 'Century of Cinema' series, this remarkable film combines ultra-candid autobiography (Kwan not only comes out as gay but also discusses his sexuality with his mother) with a highly original investigation of the ways that Chinese cinema has constructed images of masculinity and dealt with sexual ambivalence. Many directors chip in comments on the roles of fathers in Chinese families, male bonding and the sexual lure of elder-brother figures. Stand-out sequences include a celebration of drag king Yam Kin-Fai, a survey of Brigitte Lin's many androgynous roles, and an interview with veteran martial arts director Chang Cheh about the Freudian symbolism in his all male extravaganzas – which Kwan illustrates with a hair-raising clip of a half-naked man being impaled by the arse on a huge metal spike. TR

Yang Kwei Fei

see Empress Yang Kwei Fei, The

Yangtse Incident (aka Battle Hell/Escape of The Amethyst)

(1957, GB, 113 min, b/w)
d Michael Anderson. *p* Herbert Wilcox. *sc* Eric Ambler. *ph* Gordon Dines. *ed* Basil Warren. *ad* Ralph Brinton. *m* Leighton Lucas. *cast* Richard Todd, William Hartnell, Akim Tamiroff, Donald Houston, Keye Luke, Robert Urquhart, Barry Foster, Sam Kydd.

●This well-worn '50s actioner of the stiff-upper-lip school has Richard Todd as the Lt Commander of HMS *Amethyst*, a crippled British cruiser caught on the Yangtse in 1949 and narrowly escaping capture by the Chinese communist forces. Screenwriter Eric Ambler marshals the facts into the usual account of true-Brit resolve, and the production looks the part. TJ

Yankee Doodle Dandy

(1942, US, 126 min, b/w)
d Michael Curtiz. *p* Hal B Wallis, William Cagney. *sc* Robert Buckner, Edmund Joseph. *ph* James Wong Howe. *ed* George Amy. *ad* Carl Jules Weyl. *songs* George M Cohan. *cast* James Cagney, Joan Leslie, Walter Huston, Irene Manning, Rosemary De Camp, Richard Whorf, Jeanne Cagney, SZ Sakall, Walter Catlett, Frances Langford, George Barbier.

●Who but theatre historians now bother with George M Cohan, author of songs like 'Mary's a Grand Old Name' and shows like *45 Minutes from Broadway*? No one. But everyone remembers Cagney's impersonation, pitched as it is at fever level, even higher up the thermometer than Curtiz' direction or Ray Heindorf's musical arrangements. This was just the film to bombard American theatres with after Pearl Harbor: full of rousing sentiments and songs ('You're a Grand Old Flag', 'Over There' – Cohan's chief contribution to WWI), all designed to steel the morale of every patriot. Now it seems raucous, vulgar, over long; but if you like slick jobs, this is certainly one of the slickest. GB

Yankee in King Arthur's Court, A

see Connecticut Yankee in King Arthur's Court, A

Yank in London, A

see I Live in Grosvenor Square

Yank in the RAF, A

(1941, US, 98 min, b/w)
d Henry King. *p* Darryl F Zanuck. *sc* Darrell Ware, Karl Tunberg. *ph* Leon Shamroy. *ed* Barbara McLean. *ad* Richard Day, James Basevi. *m* Alfred Newman. *cast* Tyrone Power, Betty Grable, John Sutton, Reginald Gardiner, Donald Stuart, Morton Lowry.

●Producer Darryl Zanuck provided the outline for this tiresome WWII yarn about lending a hand 'over there'. Power plays an experienced civil pilot who, because the pay is good, agrees to ferry a bomber to England. In London, he bumps into old flame Grable, a showgirl doing volunteer ambulance work on the side; and determined to stick around to win her back (she tired of his other women), he cynically joins the RAF. Cockily convinced that the war effort needs his knowhow, he meanwhile leads Grable an unhappy dance by his unreliability and busy skirt-chasing. Redeeming himself through a heroic deed or two, he originally died in action; preview audiences refused to buy this; so now he ends apparently reunited with Grable, but still, in his own wry but apt term, 'a worm'. As perfunctory in its action sequences as in its personal relationships – with a couple of song-and-dance routines for Grable thrown in to crowd-please – it is unpersuasive, to say the least. TM

Yanks

(1979, GB, 141 min)
d John Schlesinger. *p* Joseph Janni, Lester Persky. *sc* Colin Welland, Walter Bernstein. *ph* Dick Bush. *ed* Jim Clark. *pd* Brian Morris. *m* Richard Rodney Bennett. *cast* Vanessa Redgrave, Richard Gere, William Devane, Lisa Eichhorn, Chick Vennera, Rachel Roberts, Tony Melody, Wendy Morgan.

●From the arrival of a platoon of GIs in Northern England to their departure for D-Day, this chronicles three wartime romances, supposedly illuminating the fears and tensions that riddled the Anglo-American alliance. Good cast, scrupulous period reconstruction, and sentimentality; but it doesn't do much to redeem Schlesinger from the 'less-than-meets-the-eye' category.

Yara

(1998, Tur/Ger, 98 min)
d/p/sc Yilmaz Arslan. *ph* Jürgen Jürges. *ed* André Bendocchi Alves. *pd* Ahmet Sisman. *m* Rabih Abou-Khalil. *cast* Yelda Reynaud, Halil Ergün, Nur Sürer, Necmettin Cobanoglu.

●Like Arslan's first feature *Passages*, this fable about loss of cultural identity is harsh, uncompromising and sometimes hard to take. Hülya (Reynaud), a Turkish girl raised in Germany by her divorced father, is taken back to Turkey for what she thinks is a vacation – to find herself dumped on her uncle and effectively imprisoned. The first half details her attempted escape, heading for the German border by any means available and trampling on every Turkish/Islamic tradition she encounters en route. The second, following her inevitable breakdown, shows her sojourn in an appalling mental hospital. Himself an émigré in Germany, Arslan knows whereof he speaks: all the hysteria, neuroses and self-hatred of 'emigrant rage' are here, softened only by the seductive vision of rural Turkey and by serene, surreal dream sequences which get inside Hülya's dysfunctional ego. TR

Yards, The

(2000, US, 108 min)
d James Gray. *p* Nich Wechsler, Paul Webster, Kerry Orent. *sc* James Gray, Matt Reeves. *ph* Harris Savides. *ed* Jeffrey Ford. *pd* Kevin Thompson. *m* Howard Shore.*cast* Mark Wahlberg, Joaquin Phoenix, Charlize Theron, James Caan, Ellen Burstyn, Faye Dunaway, Victor Argo, Tomas Milian.

●A sensitive, intelligent and ambitious variation on the traditional going-straight story. Wahlberg is just out of prison and determined to stay out of trouble. Inevitably he runs straight into it when, under the influence of his uncle (Caan) and old pal (Phoenix), he gets involved in railyard sabotage and unforeseen murder. In terms of conventional suspense, the film is too muted and sombre to deliver the goods convincingly, but as a character study and an exploration of different notions of family, friendship, duty and loyalty, the careful attention to detail pays off. A great cast helps, as does the sometimes surprising use of music (notably Holst's 'Saturn'). GA

Y'aura t'il de la neige à Noël?

see Will It Snow for Christmas?

Year My Voice Broke, The

(1987, Aust, 105 min)
d John Duigan. *p* Terry Hayes, Doug Mitchell, George Miller. *sc* John Duigan. *ph* Geoff Burton. *ed* Neil Thumpson. *pd* Roger Ford. *cast* Noah Taylor, Loene Carmen, Ben Mendelsohn, Graeme Blundell, Lynette Curran, Malcolm Robertson, Bruce Spence.

●A film to restore one's faith in films about the transition from adolescence to adulthood. It's 1962 in the Australian backwater town where callow teenager Danny (Taylor) has grown up with the slightly older Freya (Carmen), an orphan child with a murky past who feels like an outsider. *The Man Who Shot Liberty Valance* is showing at the Astor, The Shadows strum 'Apache' on the radio, and car-stealing delinquent Trevor (Mendelsohn) fancies himself as the local rebel without a cause. Using telepathy, 'force fields', and hypnosis, Danny tries to win Freya's love, but the bad boy hunk aims lower and scores… So sure is writer/ director Duigan's feel for the characters, the period, and the prevailing moral climate, that the faintly supernatural elements are effortlessly integrated: as the mystery surrounding the local 'haunted house' unfolds, there is an uncanny sense of a scandalous episode in the community's history repeating itself. A lovingly crafted and deeply affecting film, this might be likened, in terms of both quality and perception, to Rob Reiner's excellent *Stand By Me*. NF

Year of Juliette, The

see Année Juliette, L'

Year of Living Dangerously, The

(1982, Aust, 115 min)
d Peter Weir. *p* Jim McElroy. *sc* Alan Sharp, David Williamson, Peter Weir, CJ Koch. *ph* Russell Boyd. *ed* William Anderson. *ad* Herbert Pinter. *m* Maurice Jarre. *cast* Mel Gibson, Sigourney Weaver, Linda Hunt, Bembol Roco, Domingo Landicho, Hermino de Guzman, Michael Murphy, Bill Kerr, Noel Ferrier.

●Bedeviled by much-publicised script wrangles (between Weir and source novelist Christopher Koch) and production difficulties (death threats to the crew on location in the Philippines), this bears too many signs of compromise betokening an at least partly US financed project. Gibson is adequate as the Aussie news journalist on assignment in the turbulent Indonesia of late 1965, teamed up romantically with the assistant to the British military attaché (Weaver), and professionally with a dwarf Chinese-Australian camera-man (actress Hunt, extraordinary as the movie's Tolstoy-quoting social conscience). Weir's steamy atmospherics often have the camera standing in for the unwelcome, uncomprehending Westerner in South East Asia to impressive effect; but the delineation of the political forces at work in the last days of Sukarno's regime is often less than clear. The result is a curiously languid affair, rather than the breathless Costa-Gavras-style thriller which was the least one might have expected from this kind of material. RM

Year of My Japanese Cousin, The

(1995, US, 70 min)
d Maria Gargiulo. *p* Maria Gargiulo, Sheila Kelly. *sc* Maria Gargiulo. *ph* Lulu Gargiulo. *ed* Maria Gargiulo. *pd* Geoff Spencer. *cast* Selene Vigil, Janis Tanaka, Jasper Streak.
●Un film de Gargiulo (she wrote, directed and edited), this slight tale concerns Stevie (Vigil), a rock guitar wannabe in trendy downtown Seattle, who's well and truly (and rather predictably) upstaged by cousin Yukari (Tanaka). It's hip, flashily edited and features lots and lots of grunge complaint rock, so much, in fact, that it resembles an audio-visual demo tape. Fans of Silly Rabbit, Deflowers and The Smugglers won't want to miss it, but Elvis movies have more substance. TCh

Year of the Beaver

(1985, GB, 771 min)
d Steve Sprung, Sylvia Stevens, Dave Fox. *with* narrators: Anne Lamont, Steve Sprung.
●Transport and General Workers Union boss Jack Jones dubbed 1977 'Year of the Beaver', a time to encourage productivity and smoother union-management relations. It was also the year of the strike at the Grunwick photo processing plant. This documentary investigation into the 'staged media event' surrounding that strike, compiled from a mass of material (TV and independent interviews, news, radio and newspaper reports), builds up to a powerful indictment of the vacillation, compromise, and eventual betrayal by the official labour movement leadership, faced with the defence of the largely immigrant and female staff of George Ward's 'little photographic works' in West London. All the familiar spectacle of recent years is there: massed police ranks, hysterical reporting, Thatcher's dulcet tones urging the destruction of union power… Essential viewing for anyone interested in the mechanics of the evolving media show of industrial relations in our 'civilised state'. WH

Year of the Dragon

(1985, US, 134 min)
d Michael Cimino. *p* Dina De Laurentiis. *sc* Oliver Stone, Michael Cimino. *ph* Alex Thomson. *ed* Françoise Bonnot. *pd* Wolf Kroeger. *m* David Mansfield. *cast* Mickey Rourke, John Lone, Ariane, Leonard Termo, Ray Barry, Caroline Kava, Eddie Jones, Joey Chin, Victor Wong.
●Cimino's heroes have always been insufferably self-righteous, and Captain Stanley White (Rourke) is no exception. Standing alone, in the teeth of public opinion and police distrust, he conducts a clean-up campaign on New York's Chinatown which amounts to declared warfare (appropriate, since he is NYPD's most decorated veteran). His feud is conducted with such savage relentlessness and disregard for procedural nicety that he finds himself fighting his own police force, his wife, and his girlfriend as much as the local tong. Once again Cimino's ability to handle furious action set pieces is well to the fore: a shootout in a Chinese restaurant and a battle with two pistol-packing Chinese punkettes put him in the Peckinpah class. The connecting material, however, is by turns muddled, crass and dull, amounting mostly to Stanley's interminable self-justification. His anger directed at any yellow skin, and his inability to distinguish between Asiatic races, mark him down as a racist. Whether this applies, by extension, to Cimino and the film as a whole, is a moot point. CPea

Year of the Gun

(1991, US, 111 min)
d John Frankenheimer. *p* Edward R Pressman. *sc* David Ambrose. *ph* Blasco Giurato. *ed* Lee Percy. *pd* Aurelio Crugnola. *m* Bill Conti. *cast* Andrew McCarthy, Sharon Stone, Valeria Golino, John Pankow, George Murcell, Mattia Sbragia, Roberto Posse.
●Frankenheimer's affinity for political subjects involving assassination, conspiracy and terrorism was proved by *The Manchurian Candidate*, *Seven Days in May* and *Black Sunday*, so what went so horribly wrong with this movie about Italy's Red Brigades? Rather than a viable script, it seems to be chunks from Michael Mewshaw's source novel, several of them leading nowhere, while the complicated political background is left to a university professor to pass off as conversation. The casting is dreadful, particularly smug McCarthy as the investigating American journalist, and Stone as a veteran war photographer, coiffured like one of Charlie's Angels. The Red Brigades are strictly pantomime: you expect them to carry round black fizzing bombs. Is our hero compiling a report on the revolutionaries or is he writing a novel about them? Much seems to depend upon this, though the outcome is far from clear. In short, Frankenheimer kneecaps himself. BC

Year of the Horse

(1997, US, 107 min, b/w & col)
d Jim Jarmusch. *p* LA Johnson. *ph* LA Johnson, Jim Jarmusch. *ed* Jay Rabinowitz. *songs* Neil Young. *with* Neil Young and Crazy Horse.
●Since indie maestro Jarmusch made imaginative use of Young's soundtrack for *Dead Man*, it's fitting that he should have shot this documentary of the veteran band in concert on their 1996 tour, interspersed with interviews (some stoned, some illuminating) and footage from tours in the '70s and '80s. In contrast with the Young/Shakey-directed *Rust Never Sleeps*, Jarmusch uses film and video, colour and b/w to emphasise the music's rawness and immediacy, and by shooting mostly in medium and long shot, he catches the feel of actually being at a gig. Incidentally, the director also provides the film's funniest moment as he enlightens Young about God's mysterious ways. GA

Year of the Quiet Sun, A (Rok Spokojnego Slonca)

(1984, Pol/US/WGer, 108 min)
d/sc Krzysztof Zanussi. *ph* Slawomir Idziak. *ed* Marek Denys. *ad* Janusz Sosnowski. *m* Wojciech Kilar. *cast* Maja Komorowska, Scott Wilson, Hanna Skarzanka, Ewa Dalkowska, Vadim Glowna.
●1946, and amid the wreckage of a devastated town in West Poland, love grows between a Polish war widow and a shy American soldier too shattered by his experience of suffering to return home. As the troubled couple, barely able to communicate in words, try tentatively to find happiness together in a bleak landscape of doubt, suspicion, and hardship, Zanussi effortlessly avoids all the usual pitfalls, directing with exemplary restraint and an assured sense of period and place. With excellent performances from Wilson and the truly wonderful Komorowska, the film transcends its status as a sombre, sensitive love story, and becomes a moving meditation on the dignity and indomitability of the human spirit when beset by pain, cruelty, despair and death. Deeply human, with acute observation, wry humour, and a startling finale, it is as powerful and uplifting as Zanussi's earlier *The Contract*. GA

Year One

see An 01, L'

Years Without Days

see Castle on the Hudson

Yeelen (Brightness/The Light)

(1987, Mali, 105 min)
d/p/sc Souleymane Cissé. *ph* Jean-Noël Ferragut. *ed* Dounamba Coulibaly, Andrée Davanture, Marie-Cathérine Miqueau, Jenny Frenck, Seipati N'Xumalo. *ad* Kossa Mody Keita. *m* Michel Portal, Salif Keita. *cast* Issiaka Kané, Aoua Sangaré, Niamanto Sanogo, Balla Moussa Keita.
●This luminous and beautiful film is set, at an indeterminate period, among the Bambara peoples of Cissé's Mali homeland, in Central North-West Africa. At its core is a spiritual battle waged to the death between a father and son (Kané); the son coming to full maturity and potency, physically through his joining with one of a local chief's wives, and spiritually through his self-driven initiation into the ancient knowledge of the Bambara, encoded in the Komo. This is no ethnographic tract, despite being uniquely informed and filled with the fetishes, rituals and codes of this threatened culture. It is a film of complete integrity: the landscape stunning, the performances (non-professional) remarkable; full of light and fire, quiet passion and profundity, pure and simple. WH

Yellow Balloon, The

(1952, GB, 80 min, b/w)
d J Lee Thompson. *p* Viktor Skutezky. *sc* Anne Burnaby, J Lee Thompson. *ph* Gilbert Taylor. *ed* Richard Best. *ad* Robert Jones. *m* Philip Green. *cast* Andrew Ray, Kathleen Ryan, Kenneth More, William Sylvester, Bernard Lee, Veronica Hurst, Sidney James.
●Britain's second 'X' certificate picture. Young master Ray loses papa More's sixpence and snatches a yellow balloon from another boy, who appears to fall to his death in the ensuing chase. Bad egg Sylvester, however, is the only other witness to the dreadful event, and blackmails the kid into taking part in a planned robbery. Tense direction from a promising newcomer and a strong central performance contribute to a '50s Britflick (from a story by Anne Burnaby) with a touch more bite than usual. (The balloon's colour must be taken on trust.) TJ

Yellowbeard

(1983, US, 101 min)
d Mel Damski. *p* Carter De Haven. *sc* Graham Chapman, Peter Cook, Bernard McKenna. *ph* Gerry Fisher. *ed* William H Reynolds. *pd* Joseph R Jennings. *m* John Morris. *cast* Graham Chapman, Peter Boyle, Richard 'Cheech' Marin, Tommy Chong, Marty Feldman, Peter Cook, Martin Hewitt, Michael Hordern, Eric Idle, Madeline Kahn, James Mason, John Cleese, Spike Milligan, Nigel Planer, Susannah York, Beryl Reid, David Bowie.
●Rollicking is the word the publicity people grab for when trying to sell a tedious piece of period-comic trash like this pirate spoof. Here it signifies the embarrassing sight of three generations of British comedy – Fringe to Python to Comic Strip – gritting their teeth through a series of gags in the meekest of bad taste, about sheep-shagging, cowflop, and big tits (Madeline Kahn in the Barbara Windsor parts), accompanied by token Americans to make it more acceptable to people in Idaho wondering why the accents are so weird. The script, for which Chapman and Cook must bear some responsibility, is a three-minute Python skit bloated out to feature length, involving buried treasure, revenge, and machinations close to the throne. Depressing stuff. KJ

Yellow Bride, The (Sari Gyalin)

(1999, Azerbaijan, 87 min)
d/sc Yaver Rzayev. *ph* Rovshan Dzhavanshir-ogly. *ed* Yaver Rzayev. *pd* Rafig Nasirov. *m* Siyavush Kerimi. *cast* Haci Ismayilov, Cahargas Novruzov, Dzhamilya Kyamal, Siyavush Kerimi, Gyseymaga Yachyaev, Elshan Gasymov.
●Billed as the first independent Azerbaijan production, this film begins with a table of statistics illustrating Azerbaijan's fate at the hands of the Armenians and others, not least in the Karabach War of 1988, when it lost 30,000 nationals and suffered economic devastation. Perhaps the body counts were required for home consumption, because writer/director Rzayev's war drama is basically a humanistic entreaty about the dark, destructive, yet often farcical nature of war. It pairs an incompetent Azerbaijani hero in the Chaplin or Benigni mould with a sympathetic Armenian soldier who have deserted from their respective armies. The desertions prompt opposing armies to join forces in tracking them down, proving that, to the military, pacifism is less acceptable than nationalism. This is Renoir territory, of course, but the film plays it as satire, much in the up and down manner of recent Balkan war dramas. The soundtrack, repetitiously featuring the Azer's deep gasps, is very annoying. WH

Yellow Canary, The

(1943, GB, 98 min, b/w)
d/p Herbert Wilcox. *sc* Miles Malleson, DeWitt Bodeen. *ph* Max Greene. *ed* Vera Campbell. *ad* William C Andrews. *m* Clifton Parker. *cast* Anna Neagle, Richard Greene, Albert Lieven, Margaret Rutherford, Nova Pilbeam, Valentine Dyall, Cyril Fletcher.

● Anna Neagle in bed with Adolf Hitler? Hardly likely, yet that's the set-up in this wartime spy drama, a sprightly collaboration between the husband-and-wife team of Neagle and Wilcox, which also boasts a curious meeting of minds in the screenplay department: Hollywood pro DeWitt Bodeen, and mild-mannered English actor and playwright Miles Malleson.

Yellow Dog

(1973, GB, 101 min)
d/p Terence Donovan. *sc* Shinobu Hashimoto. *ph* David Watkin. *ed* Fergus McDonell. *pd* Roger Burridge. *m* Ron Grainer. *cast* Jiro Tamiya, Robert Hardy, Carolyn Seymour, Joseph O'Conor, Hilary Tindall.

● The script credits list Kurosawa's writer Shinobu Hashimoto, Professor Alan Turney, and John Bird – which just about sums it up. This is a highly eccentric spy fable about a 'yellow dog' (Japanese private eye) who comes to London on a mission, only to find himself working in rather strained tandem with MI5. Kimura is given to making rice balls, moving into his superior's garden shed, and running round (literally) in small circles. The film is directed with much amiable if incoherent humour by Donovan, image maker of the '60s, who apparently gave in to his passion for things Japanese and even financed it himself; but somewhere along the line the original thread of Hashimoto's story seems to have got lost. Which doesn't help anyone follow the plot, but does make for a strange experience. CPe

Yellow Earth (Huang Tudi)

(1984, China, 89 min)
d Chen Kaige. *p* Guo Keqi. *sc* Zhang Ziliang. *ph* Zhang Yimou. *ed* Pei Xiaonan. *ad* He Qun. *m* Zhao Jiping. *cast* Xue Bai, Wang Xueqi, Tan Tuo, Liu Qiang.

● The first 'modern' film to emerge from China, and one of the most thrilling debut features of the '80s. Its storyline couldn't be simpler. A Communist soldier visits a backward village in 1939, and is billeted with a taciturn widower and his teenage daughter and son. The soldier's mission is to collect folk songs, and it's through the exchange of songs that he gradually wins the trust and affection of his hosts. But the girl is to be sold into marriage with a much older man, and all the soldier's talk of breaking with feudal tradition fills her with unrealistic hopes of escaping her fate. The soldier returns to his base, leaving her to take her future in her own hands...There are political undercurrents here that got the film into trouble in China: the encounter between the CP and China's peasants is shown not as an instant meeting of minds, but as the uneasy, frustrating, and ultimately unresolved process that it actually was. But what really stirred things up in old Beijing was the film's insistence on going its own way. Chen Kaige and his cinematographer Zhang Yimou have invented a new language of colours, shadows, glances, spaces, and unspoken thoughts and implications; and they've made their new language sing. TR

Yellow Sky

(1948, US, 98 min, b/w)
d William A Wellman. *p/sc* Lamar Trotti. *ph* Joseph MacDonald. *ed* Harmon Jones. *ad* Lyle Wheeler, Albert Hogsett. *m* Alfred Newman. *cast* Gregory Peck, Anne Baxter, Richard Widmark, Robert Arthur, John Russell, Henry Morgan, James Barton, Charles Kemper.

● A fine Western, harshly shot by Joe MacDonald in Death Valley locations, inevitably conjuring comparisons with *Greed* and *The Treasure of the Sierra Madre* as six bankrobbers on the run all but die in the desert salt flats before stumbling on a ghost town where a lone prospector (Barton) guards twin secrets: his rich gold strike and his fiercely tomboyish granddaughter (Baxter). Like a pack of wolves, the strangers are soon snarling lustfully after gold and/or the girl, with their leader (Peck) gradually detaching himself as his presence causes the girl to discover her femininity, and hers revives in him something of the man he was before Quantrill's Raiders descended on his home. Intriguingly, Lamar Trotti's screenplay develops WR Burnett's source story with *The Tempest* in mind, the subtler analogies serving to provide resonances. The situation again harks back to fraternal conflict (the year is 1867, in the aftermath of the Civil War); *Yellow Sky* also has its malign spirits, a band of renegade Apaches under the uneasy control of the prospector; and the conflict similarly resolves strangely, at its violent climax, into a sense of conciliation. Beautifully cast and characterised, this is one of Wellman's best films. TM

Yellow Smile, The (Sari Tebessum)

(1992, Tur, 120 min)
d Secklin Yasar. *cast* Sahika Tekland, Mahir Gunsiray, Leventn Ozdilek.

● Passions flair among the Turkish glitterati when art gallery owner Eda (Tekland), frustrated by her poet husband's alcohol-induced impotence, wanders from the straight and narrow and gets involved with artist friend Erdal (Gunsiray). The film adds little to the myriad other variations on the eternal triangle, but leading lady Tekland goes through the motions with a modicum of physical commitment. Be prepared for the odd splash of unintentional hilarity in this would-be sophisticated milieu (earnest discussions of Leonard Cohen's poetry and music rub shoulders with some of the most embarrassing disco scenes since *Basic Instinct*). TJ

Yellow Submarine

(1968, GB, 87 min)
d George Dunning. *p* Al Brodax. *sc* Lee Minoff, Al Brodax, Jack Mendelsohn, Erich Segal. *ed* Brian J Bishop. *pd* Heinz Edelman, John Cramer, Gordon Harrison. *m* John Lennon, Paul McCartney. *cast* voices: John Clive, Geoffrey Hughes, Paul Angelus, Dick Emery, Lance Percival.

● Inspired by Beatlemania, this was the first feature-length animated movie made in Britain for 14 years, and it seemed determined to give a break to all those valiant animators who had been sweating to produce under-budgeted shorts throughout the '60s. Which is doubtless why there's such a wide disparity of graphic styles from sequence to sequence. Some of them, though, still look terrific: director George Dunning's own contribution is the 'Lucy in the Sky with Diamonds' fantasia, with swirling, colour-washed couples counterpointing the song in a totally unexpected way. Speculation: maybe the banality of the over-long 'Love Conquers All' finale has less to do with John Lennon than with Erich (*Love Story*) Segal, who had a hand in the script. TR

Yentl

(1983, GB, 133 min)
d Barbra Streisand. *p* Barbra Streisand, Rusty Lemorande. *sc* Jack Rosenthal, Barbra Streisand. *ph* David Watkin. *ed* Terry Rawlings. *pd* Roy Walker. *m* Michel Legrand. *lyrics* Alan Bergman, Marilyn Bergman. *cast* Barbra Streisand, Mandy Patinkin, Amy Irving, Nehemiah Persoff, Steven Hill, Allan Corduner.

● Despite Streisand's apparently hypnotic hold over a large portion of the earth's population, it's still almost impossible to equate the critical plaudits already bestowed on *Yentl* with the movie itself. This lumbering, overwrought, and wildly self-indulgent adaptation of Isaac Bashevis Singer's frail short story is clearly cranked up with the full quotient of sincerity and conviction. But it is this very earnestness of tone that topples a pretty dubious premise – Streisand dresses up as a boy in order to learn the Talmud – into galloping bathos. The end result looks like nothing so much as the raw material for every Woody Allen Jewish joke ever coined. JP

Yepeto

(1999, Arg, 107 min)
d/sc Eduardo Calcagno. *ed* Juan Carlos Macias. *m* Mariano Nuñez West. *cast* Ulises Dumont, Nicolás Cabré, Malena Figo, Alejandra Flechner, Villanueva Cosse, Pepe Nuvoa, Margara Alonso.

● 'It's my duty as a teacher to bore people,' declares the eponymous professor – drinking, cussing, all polonecks and solitary anger – as he seeks to do the exact opposite, testing extra-curricular friendship, jealousy and the generation gap with a pair of students. Dumont's is a spirited and unconventional part, not especially endearing, but clearly committed to the project we call living. He writes a novel, it affects those around him. Visually unremarkable but imbued with a reasonable melancholy, this captures well the loneliness beneath the surface of city life and is successful in creating a palpable sense of the ambiguous possibilities of the urban night. Long on longing, short on innovation, it's a familiar tale but does the job, questioning fiction and life, and even hinting occasionally at a fetish of reading. GE

Yes, Giorgio

(1982, US, 110 min)
d Franklin J Schaffner. *p* Peter Fetterman. *sc* Norman Steinberg. *ph* Fred J Koenekamp. *ed* Michael F Anderson. *pd* William J Creber. *m* Michael J Lewis. *cast* Luciano Pavarotti, Kathryn Harrold, Eddie Albert, Paolo Borboni, James Hong.

● An MGM extravaganza in which Pavarotti, not a natural film actor, plays an Italian opera star who falls for doctor Harrold after she helps him regain his voice which one day fails him completely in rehearsal. Best quietly to close the curtain on this one.

Yessongs

(1973, GB, 75 min)
d Peter Neal. *p* David Speechley. *sc* Peter Neal. *ph* Ian McMillan, Brian Grainger, Anthony Stern, Richard Stanley. *ed* Philip Howe. *with* Jon Anderson, Steve Howe, Chris Squire, Alan White, Rick Wakeman.

● Yes-freaks might use this footage of the group's 1972 Rainbow concert to plumb the topographic oceans of their consciousness; otherwise it's tedium in extremis. Jon Anderson's lyrics, given the extended arrangements in concert (long and indulgent solos, disjunctive and arbitrary time changes), are exposed as even slighter than on record. His vocals are reminiscent of a lone refugee from the Hollies (okay, if only he had some singles of that standard to trot out). Rick Wakeman and Steve Howe, with their respective instrumental prowess, should know better. Wakeman provides the film's only moment of humour, wrenching an atrocious 'Hallelujah Chorus' from his vast synthesiser bank. Howe slips into ragtime (for which he doesn't have the necessary sense of syncopation or off-rhythm) or flashy fingerboard runs at every opportunity. Apart from some Roger Dean graphics and opticals, the visuals are exceedingly murky, flattened by the stage lighting. Sound separation behind the vocals or lead guitar is equally muddy. RM

Yesterday Girl (Abschied von Gestern)

(1966, WGer, 90 min, b/w)
d/sc Alexander Kluge. *ph* Edgar Reitz, Thomas Mauch. *ed* Beate Mainka-Jellinghaus. *cast* Alexandra Kluge, Günther Mack, Eva Maria Meinecke, Hans Korte, Edith Kuntze-Pellogio.

● Kluge's first feature traces the misadventures of Anita G. (played by his sister Alexandra), a young refugee from East Germany, as she wanders through the Economic Miracle but fails to find a place in it. Always penniless and often involved in petty crime, she meets a string of people who try to 'improve' and/or seduce her, but never gets to the root of her problems. Kluge makes it clear that she's a product of Germany's past, and his basic point is the simple one that Germany is trying to sweep its history under the carpet. But his Godardian wit and informality give the argument countless resonances, and keep the movie surprisingly fresh. TR

Yesterday's Hero

(1979, GB, 95 min)
d Neil Leifer. *p* Oscar S Lerman, Ken Regan. *sc* Jackie Collins. *ph* Brian West. *ed* Antony Gibbs. *pd* Keith Wilson. *songs* Domenic Bugatti, Frank Musker. *cast* Ian McShane, Suzanne Somers, Adam Faith, Paul Nicholas, Sam Kydd, Glynis Barber.

● Not content with getting Leicester City relegated during his brief foray into management, 'football adviser' Frank McLintock compounds the sin by having Ian McShane's decadent Roy of the Rovers make his cup final comeback with two winning goals against the insultingly dubbed 'Leicester Forest'. Jackie Collins' script is a paste job of scandal-sheet sports page headlines (boozing striker, hard-line manager, rock star chairman), while US sports photographer Leifer works backwards from footage of the Southampton/ Nottingham Forest League Cup Final to give a hilarious sense of skewed felicity to the comic strip giant-killing progress of The Saints and their repentant super-sub sinner. John Motson commentates. Irresistibly bad. PT

Yeux sans Visage, Les (Eyes Without a Face/The Horror Chamber of Dr Faustus)

(1959, Fr, 90 min, b/w)
d Georges Franju. *p* Jules Borkon. *sc* Jean Redon, Pierre Boileau, Thomas Narcejac, Claude Sautet. *ph* Eugen Schüfftan. *ed* Gilbert Natot. *ad* Auguste Capelier. *m* Maurice Jarre. *cast* Pierre Brasseur, Alida Valli, Edith Scob, Juliette Mayniel, François Guérin, Béatrice Altariba.

● An incredible amalgam of horror and fairytale in which scalpels thud into quivering flesh and the tremulous heroine (Scob) remains a prisoner of solitude in a waxen mask of eerie, frozen beauty. Having crashed the car which destroyed her face, her doctor father (Brasseur) feverishly experiments with skin grafts, each failure requiring his devoted assistant (Valli) to prowl the Latin Quarter in search of another suitable 'donor'. Finally, despair breeds madness and rebellion, erupting in an extraordinary sequence where the victim looses the dogs from the doctor's vivisection chambers to turn on their common torturer. Illuminated throughout by Franju's unique sense of poetry – nowhere more evident than in the final shot of Scob wandering free through the night, her mask discarded but her face seen only by the dogs at her feet and the dove on her shoulder – it's a marvellous movie in the fullest sense. TM

Yiddle with His Fiddle (Judel gra na Skrzypkach/ Yidl mitu fidl)

(1936, Pol, 92 min, b/w)
d Joseph Green, Jan Nowina Przybylski. *p* Joseph Green, Jacob Kalich. *sc* Konrad Tom. *ph* J Jonilowicz. *m* Abe Ellsted. *cast* Molly Picon.

● This lively musical comedy was a big hit in its day. It stars the vaudevillian Picon, an infectious mugger of strange bird-like mien who was then probably the biggest stage and film star in the Yiddish firmament. The tale – the prototype for Streisand's *Yentl* – has Picon as the optimistic street violinist who, disguised as a boy, leaves her shtetl with her bassist father in search of fame and fortune. It turns into an entertaining, if cheaper, version of a Hollywood staple, but especially in the early rural scenes, before the big-city success and the ocean-liner trip to America, Green injects a deeply lyrical atmosphere, with dream interludes and rhapsodic Renoir-esque shots of swaying trees and the countryside. Even more poignant, given how close this was to the coming Holocaust, is the incorporation of location work and the use of non-professionals: the shots of the old Polish shtetl courtyards and the villagers' faces which were shortly to vanish forever. WH

Yield to the Night

(1956, GB, 99 min, b/w)
d J Lee Thompson. *p* Kenneth Harper. *sc* John Cresswell, Joan Henry. *ph* Gilbert Taylor. *ed* Richard Best. *ad* Robert Jones. *m* Ray Martin. *cast* Diana Dors, Yvonne Mitchell, Michael Craig, Geoffrey Keen, Olga Lindo, Mary Mackenzie, Joan Miller, Marie Ney.

● Loosely based, like *Dance with a Stranger*, on the Ruth Ellis case, this oddly austere thriller has Dors as the unrepentant murderess waiting in prison, thinking back over the events that made her kill, and agonising over whether she'll be given the death sentence or not. Decidedly anti-capital punishment, the film never actually excites, but thanks to the downbeat mood and the surprisingly effective performances, it does grip the attention. It never, however, attempts to explore in any depth the relationship between the legal practice of hanging and society's attitudes to crime. GA

Yojimbo

(1961, Jap, 110 min, b/w)
d Akira Kurosawa. *sc* Ryuzo Kikushima, Akira Kurosawa. *ph* Kazuo Miyagawa. *ad* Yoshiro Muraki. *m* Masuru Sato. *cast* Toshiro Mifune, Eijiro Tono, Kamatari Fujiwara, Takashi Shimura, Seizaburo Kawazu, Isuzu Yamada, Tatsuya Nakadai.

● Far from being just another vehicle for Mifune, this belongs in that select group of *films noirs* which are also comedies. It's not as uproarious as its sequel *Sanjuro*, but the story of a mercenary samurai selling his services to two rival factions in a small town, and then sitting back to watch the enemies destroy each other, certainly marks a departure from the predominantly sentimental moralising of earlier Kurosawa movies. Ultrapragmatic, unheroic Sanjuro is the centre-piece: his laziness matches the sleepiness of the town, his quirky mannerisms echo the town's gallery of grotesques, and his spasms of violence reflect the society's fundamental cruelty. If the plot sounds familiar, it's probably because Leone stole it for *A Fistful of Dollars*. TR

Yol

(1982, Switz, 114 min)
d Serif Gören. *p* Edi Hubschmid, KL Puldi. *sc* Yilmaz Güney. *ph* Erdogan Engin. *ed* Yilmaz Güney, Elisabeth Waelchli, Laura Montoya, Hélène Arnal, Serge Guillemin. *m* Sebastian Argol, Kendal. *cast* Tarik Akan, Halil Ergün, Necmettin Cobanoglu, Serif Sezer.

● In Yilmaz Güney's extraordinary Turkish odyssey (filmed by Gören from his script and detailed instructions while he was in jail), five prisoners are allowed a week's parole to journey home. In many ways it's a story about the tragedy of distances: the geographical and historical ones that still separate Turkey, and the distances imposed upon people by a military state and by a heritage that still expects husbands to punish by death wives taken in adultery. A kind of distance, too, makes this a film of the highest order. Its homesickness, for freedom above all, is very particular. Güney can't go home, and completed the film in exile. This perspective gives great clarity to his picture of the state of the nation, a state in suspense where something has to change, which gathers complexity and shifts effortlessly into universal allegory. The film's poetry, its combination of sound and image especially, has an unconscious innocence no longer available to most European and American narratives, and it is inspired by an enormous compassion for the suffering people endure at each other's hands in a world where the strong pick upon the weak, the weak upon the weaker. CPe

Yo, la peor de todas

see I, the Worst of All

Yo soy así

(2000, Neth, 80 mins)
d Sonia Herman Dolz. *p* Pieter van Huystee. *sc* Sonia Herman Dolz. *ph* Hans Fels. *ed* Andrez De Jong. *m* Paul M van Brugge.

● This documentary charts the last days of La Bodega Bohemia, a famous Barcelona nightclub about to close. For more than 100 years, the city's bohemians used to gather here – where, as the sign outside proclaimed, 'Every day a new artist was born.' The performers are an extraordinary bunch: singing plumbers, variety artists and raddled transvestites. Offstage, they're grey, anonymous figures, but as soon as they take the microphone, they're transformed. The singers may not be as silken voiced as the Cubans in Wenders' *Buena Vista Social Club*, but writer/ director Dolz captures their double lives with such tenderness and humour that we scarcely notice the missed notes. The film's undertow of melancholy acknowledges that the old owner has died, and the regulars know that La Bodega will soon be history. There will never be another nightclub quite like it. GM

You and Me

(1938, US, 90 min, b/w)
d/p Fritz Lang. *sc* Virginia Van Upp. *ph* Charles Lang Jr. *ed* Paul Weatherwax. *ad* Hans Dreier, Ernst Fegte. *m* Kurt Weill. *cast* Sylvia Sidney, George Raft, Robert Cummings, Barton MacLane, Roscoe Karns, Harry Carey, Warren Hymer.

● In most interviews, Lang dismisses *You and Me* – within Hollywood categories, his only attempt at straight comedy – as a failure; but even if it were much more of a failure than it actually is, it would remain an utterly fascinating film. Raft and Sidney play a pair of ex-cons employed by a benign liberal (Carey) in his large department store. Sidney knows about Raft's past, but he is ignorant of hers; they marry secretly, breaking the terms of their parole, and the marriage is threatened when he accidentally discovers the truth. Lang's intention was a Brechtian *Lehrstück* (lesson-play); Kurt Weill worked on some of the songs, including the brilliant opening number; and for ideas about the criminal underworld, Lang borrowed as much from *The Threepenny Opera* as from his own *M*. It perhaps lacks stylistic unity, but still has many fine scenes. (From a story by Norman Krasna.) RM

You Are My Only Love

(1993, Rus, 92 min)
d Dimitri Astrakhan. *p* Arkadij Tulchin. *sc* Oleg Danilov, Dmitri Astrakhan. *ph* Jurij Voroncov. *ed* Dmitri Astrakhan, V Rubanov. *pd* M Petrova. *m* Aleksandr Pantykin. *cast* Aleksander Zbruev, Marina Neelova, Svetlana Riabova.

● A girl tells her uncle Evgeny that 'I'll love you all my life', as she leaves Leningrad for New York, only to return years later, now an important sales executive, to work on a Russo-American project, involving the engineering company where hard-pressed Evgeny is now employed. Astrakhan's sour comedy uses this relationship as a springboard for analysing the post-communist malaise, with everyone jumping to the Yankee dollar. The flashback sequences to the Beatles-dominated '70s will please retro fans who like three-quarter length plastic macs, but they may be less impressed by the movie's enervated old-fashioned neo-realist feel. Here's an instance of a director finding a subject before he's found a style. WH

You Can Count on Me

(2000, US, 111 min)
d Kenneth Lonergan. *p* John N Hart, Jeffrey Sharp, Barbara De Fina, Larry Meistrich. *sc* Kenneth Lonergan. *ph* Stephen Kazmierski. *ed* Anne McCabe. *pd* Michael Shaw. *m* Lesley Barber. *cast* Laura Linney, Mark Ruffalo, Matthew Broderick, Jon Tenney, Rory Culkin, J Smith Cameron, Josh Lucas, Kenneth Lonergan.

● This won best screenplay prize at Sundance, and justly so. The tone is a little uncertain at first, as writer/director Lonergan introduces his four characters: Linney's single mom, a Christian who still works in a bank in the town she grew up in; her young son (Culkin); her new boss, the smug and officious Broderick; and her tearaway brother, Ruffalo, who has never settled at anything with anyone. It's not long, though, before we discover that these people have much more in common than they imagine. Lonergan has the rare gift of allowing comic tribulation to deepen his characters, not degrade them (he also has a cameo as the local priest). Linney especially responds with a warm and sympathetic performance. TCh

You Can't Cheat an Honest Man

(1939, US, 76 min, b/w)
d George Marshall. *p* Lester Cowan. *sc* George Marion Jr, Richard Mack, Everett Freeman. *ph* Milton Krasner. *ed* Otto Ludwig. *ad* Jack Otterson. *m* Charles Previn. *cast* WC Fields, Edgar Bergen, Constance Moore, James Bush, Mary Forbes, Edward Brophy, Eddie 'Rochester' Anderson.

● 'It is overloaded with two-reel comedy and no story, no pathos, no believable characters': the perceptive critic is Fields himself, who helplessly watched Universal mishandle his heartwarming story of a roguish circus owner. Most of the comedy is put into the sticky hands of Edgar Bergen, known now as the father of Candice, known then as a ventriloquist and the manipulator of dummy Charlie McCarthy, whose radio feud with Fields had all America doubled up. But their antics now seem far more historical than hysterical, and Fields' character emerges sadly belittled and coarsened. Still, good moments survive here and there. GB

You Can't Sleep Here

see I Was a Male War Bride

You Can't Take It With You

(1938, US, 127 min, b/w)
d/p Frank Capra. *sc* Robert Riskin. *ph* Joseph Walker. *ed* Gene Havlick. *ad* Stephen Goosson.

m Dimitri Tiomkin. *cast* Jean Arthur, James Stewart, Lionel Barrymore, Edward Arnold, Mischa Auer, Ann Miller, Spring Byington, Eddie 'Rochester' Anderson.
● How true that is. And how revealing. Capra is at his most sentimental here, with James Stewart, the son of a munitions tycoon, falling for dizzy Jean Arthur, who comes from a poor but happy family of eccentrics. There are fireworks when the two fathers meet, but mostly the picture is a damp squib, trite, preachy, and desperately sincere. If the poor were a vocal minority, this would be denounced as the equivalent of Uncle Tomism. The cast is appealing, particularly Stewart and Arthur, but it's not enough. Polly Wolly Doodle indeed. BC

You Light Up My Life

(1977, US, 91 min)
d/p/sc Joseph Brooks. *ph* Eric Saarinen. *ed* Lynzee Klingman. *ad* Tom Rasmussen. *m* Joseph Brooks. *cast* Didi Conn, Joseph Silver, Michael Zaslow, Stephen Nathan, Melanie Mayron.
● With the American singles charts in their worst state since the days of Frankie Laine and Johnnie Ray, it was only a matter of time before some joker set about transposing the world of 'hip easy listening' to the screen. Joseph Brooks did just that with a vengeance. Not content with producing, writing, and directing, he also penned the title tune which drove US radio to new heights of palsied schmaltz. But what is unbearable on record can be hypnotically funny on screen. With breathtaking assurance, *Light Up My Life* follows a young soft-rock Angeleno hopeful (in moments of great emotion, she looks like an asphyxiated Pinocchio) in encounters with a beautiful movie producer who also happens to produce beautiful records, but who finally gives her a beautiful nervous breakdown on TV. Connoisseurs of LA sentiment will love it. DP

You'll Find Out

(1940, US, 97 min, b/w)
d/p David Butler. *sc* James V Kern. *ph* Frank Redman. *ed* Irene Morra. *ad* Van Nest Polglase, Carroll Clark. *m* Roy Webb. *songs* Johnny Mercer, Jimmy McHugh. *cast* Kay Kyser, Peter Lorre, Boris Karloff, Bela Lugosi, Helen Parrish, Ginny Simms, Ish Kabibble.
● Considering the cast, this is disappointing fare. Fake swami Lugosi, family medic Karloff and mad scientist Lorre are actually a trio of crooks out to bump off heiress Parrish and claim her dosh, but the most horrifying thing about the movie is that someone in the front office thought it was just the place to dump five numbers by crazy bandleader Kay Kyser and his College of Musical Knowledge. TJ

You'll Like My Mother

(1972, US, 93 min)
d Lamont Johnson. *p* Mort Briskin. *sc* Jo Heims. *ph* Jack Marta. *ed* Edward Abroms. *ad* William DeCinces. *m* Gil Mellé. *cast* Patty Duke, Richard Thomas, Rosemary Murphy, Sian Barbara Allen, Dennis Rucker.
● The tale of a pregnant girl (Duke), widow of a soldier killed in action, who undertakes a long journey to visit the mother-in-law (Murphy) she has never met. She finds herself snowbound in a sinister house on the edge of town inhabited by a subnormal girl (Allen), a shadowy figure (much is made of facial distortion through stained glass), and the mother-in-law, whose strident manner and skill as a nurse speak volumes. Johnson's direction tends to lay on the spooks a bit heavily, while the over-familiar situation (with echoes of *Rosemary's Baby*) is a further strait-jacket. That said, though, several risky scenes are brought off with some aplomb.

You'll Never Get Rich

(1941, US, 88 min, b/w)
d Sidney Lanfield. *p* Samuel Bischoff. *sc* Michael Fessier, Ernest Pagano. *ph* Philip Tannura. *ed* Otto Meyer. *ad* Lionel Banks. *songs* Cole Porter. *cast* Fred Astaire, Rita Hayworth, John Hubbard, Robert Benchley, Osa Massen, Frieda Inescort, Guinn Williams, Donald MacBride, Cliff Nazarro.
● Fred and Rita were a dream partnership, even better than Fred and Ginger, but with a stumbling script and so-so Cole Porter score, this musical never really gets off the ground. Astaire and Hayworth, he a star Broadway dancer, she in the chorus, are involved in one of those irritating on-off romances, courtesy of misunderstandings generated by their producer Benchley's penchant for pursuing chorines and then putting the blame on Astaire to pacify his wife. Astaire is drafted, and the misunderstandings then come wrapped up in acres of leaden boot camp comedy (much of it involving Nazarro, a dire double-talk comedian). Astaire has a joyous two-part solo while languishing in the guardhouse, and shares a fine, romantic Robert Alton routine with Hayworth to Porter's 'So Near and Yet So Far'. Otherwise, the pickings are thin. TM

You, Me, Jerusalem

(1995, US, 54 min)
d George Khleifi, Micha Peled.
● Directed by a Palestinian and an Israeli, this modest documentary sounds a note of muted optimism. Focusing on the Palestinian/Jewish paramedic volunteers who crew the Jerusalem emergency service, and their families on either side of the divide, the film-makers find a nostalgia among the elders for peaceful coexistence – but also, of course, the ancient current of recrimination. TCh

Young Americans, The

(1993, GB, 103 min)
d Danny Cannon. *p* Paul Trijbits, Alison Owen. *sc* Danny Cannon, David Hilton. *ph* Vernon Layton. *ed* Alex MacKie. *pd* Laurence Dorman. *m* David Arnold. *cast* Harvey Keitel, Iain Glen, John Wood, Craig Kelly, Viggo Mortensen, Terence Rigby.
● Visually assured but unevenly paced, Cannon's ambitious first feature recalls such gritty British pictures as *Get Carter* and *The Long Good Friday*. Promising newcomer Kelly exudes vulnerability and confusion as Chris, a young club barman who is sucked into a maelstrom of greed and violence, after two criminals are gunned down by a posse of young wannabe gangsters, and a subsequent trial uncovers an international drugs operation. Keitel is the American cop, drafted in to 'advise' the drug squad, who cynically exploits Chris to settle an old score with dealer Mortensen. A sleek, violent, designer crime movie for style-conscious twenty-somethings. NF

Young and Dangerous (Guhuozai zhi Ren zai Jianghu)

(1995, HK, 99 min)
d Andrew Lau. *p* Wong Jing. *sc* Manfred Wong. *ph* Andrew Lau. *cast* Ekin Cheng, Jordan Chan, Gigi Lai, Francis Ng, Simon Yam, Ng Chi-Hung, Michael Tse, Jerry Lamb, Jason Chu.
● Based on a popular graphic novel (itself a thinly fictionalised commentary on real-life power struggles in the Hong Kong-Macau triad underworld), this low-budget firecracker is the kind of movie that gives immorality a good name. Shot (mostly hand-held) by its director and scripted by its producer Manfred Wong, it's founded on a clash between 'good' triads and 'bad' triads. The five adorable heroes are foot soldiers in the Hung Hing gang, laddish as they come but dedicated to ideals of loyalty, righteousness and 'brotherhood'. The bad guy is Hung Hing branch leader Kwan (Francis Ng), who usurps leadership of the gang but then overdoes the power thing. A huge – and largely deserved – hit in Hong Kong, it rocketed all its young leads to stardom. TR

Young and Dangerous 2 (Guhuozai 2 zhi Menglong Guo Jiang)

(1996, HK, 98 min)
d Andrew Lau. *p/sc* Manfred Wong. *ph* Andrew Lau. *ed* Marco. *cast* Ekin Cheng, Jordan Chan, Chingmy Yau, Gigi Lai, Anthony Wong, Simon Yam, Jerry Lamb, Michael Tse, Jason Chu.
● Already in production before the first film went ballistic, this is a direct sequel which fills in gaps in the story-so-far (a long flashback reveals how the Jordan Chan character Chicken got ahead during a period of exile in Taiwan) and goes on to chronicle a large-scale clash between the Hung Hing gang and Taiwan's San Luen gang over control of a new Macau casino. The main hero Ho Nam (singer Ekin Cheng) rises to the rank of branch leader in this episode, but much of the focus is on the high-baroque supporting roles, notably the femme fatale villain (Chingmy Yau). The incidental exposé of the links between triads and politicians in Taiwan is daringly forthright. TR

Young and Dangerous 3 (Guhuozai 3 zhi Zhishou Zhetian)

(1996, HK, 98 min)
d Andrew Lau. *cast* Ekin Cheng, Jordan Chan, Gigi Lai, Karen Mok, Roy Cheung, Ng Chi-Hung, Simon Yam, Jerry Lamb.
● Best to date in this on-going series, even if the emphasis on 'family' and the constant references back to the other episodes evoke soap opera. Hung Hing's dominance of Causeway Bay comes under threat from the rival Tung Sing gang, whose officers Crow and Tiger have forged secret links with drug lords in Amsterdam. Murders, double-crosses and entrapments ensue, some of them on location in Holland, although Ho Nam and Chicken incidentally get to spend more time than usual with girlfriends. Structure and pacing are very strong, and Roy Cheung's psychopathic Crow is the series' scariest villain yet. TR

Young and Innocent

(1937, GB, 82 min, b/w)
d Alfred Hitchcock. *p* Edward Black. *sc* Charles Bennett, Edwin Greenwood, Anthony Armstrong, Gerald Savary, Alma Reville. *ph* Bernard Knowles. *ed* Charles Frend. *ad* Alfred Junge. *m* Jack Beaver. *cast* Nova Pilbeam, Derrick de Marney, Percy Marmont, Edward Rigby, George Curzon, Mary Clare, John Longden, Basil Radford.
● Not top-notch Hitchcock, but engrossing enough. At the centre is another of his odd couples: an innocent man accused of murder and on the run (de Marney), and the young daughter of a policeman (18-year-old Pilbeam) who finds herself helping him along the way. Both leads are very mannered: de Marney has a most odd whine of a voice, and Pilbeam is too gawky, too jolly-hockey-sticks (though she's fine in other films). So their parts, and their relationship, aren't as believable as they might be, with the result that most of the film is a bit loose. But there are at least two splendid sequences, with menace and suspense hovering, in typical Hitchcock fashion, over innocent amusements: first a children's party, and finally a hotel thé-dansant, where everything finally jells. (From the novel by Josephine Tey.) GB

Young and the Damned, The

see Olvidados, Los

Young at Heart

(1954, US, 117 min)
d Gordon Douglas. *p* Henry Blanke. *sc* Julius J Epstein, Lenore J Coffee. *ph* Ted McCord. *ed* William Ziegler. *ad* John Beckman. *songs* George Gershwin, Ira Gershwin, Harold Arlen, Johnny Mercer, others. *cast* Doris Day, Frank Sinatra, Robert Keith, Dorothy Malone, Ethel Barrymore.
● Fascinating attempt to bring together a number of disparate elements – whimsical comedy, songs, death – plus big city slum rat Sinatra and wholesome Day in the same frame. Sinatra's character has to pay a terrible price for daring to encroach on Andy Hardy-world, a reminder perhaps that the Fannie Hurst story ('Sister Act'), from which this derives, dates back to 1924, and that consequently there's a collision of eras going on here, as well as one of genres. As usual with Gordon Douglas movies, it's very mixed: Sinatra's rendition of the title song and 'One for My Baby' are certainly classics, even if the film itself scarcely qualifies as a musical. BBa

Young Bess

(1953, US, 112 min)
d George Sidney. *p* Sidney A Franklin. *sc* Arthur Wimperis, Jan Lustig. *ph* Charles Rosher. *ed* Ralph E Winters. *ad* Cedric Gibbons, Urie McCleary. *m* Miklós Rozsa. *cast* Jean Simmons, Stewart Granger, Charles Laughton, Deborah Kerr, Kay Walsh, Kathleen Byron, Guy Rolfe, Cecil Kellaway, Leo G Carroll.
● MGM's contribution to the coronation of Elizabeth II was this piece of Tudor tosh about the early years of Elizabeth I. Simmons suppresses giggles, Granger makes Thomas Seymour

a pompous ass, Laughton catches up on his Henry VIII, and Kerr plays well below Parr. All it lacks is a commentary by Richard Dimbleby. ATu

Youngblood

(1986, US, 110 min)
d Peter Markle. *p* Peter Bart, Patrick Wells. *sc* Peter Markle. *ph* Mark Irwin. *ed* Stephen Rivkin, Jack Hofstra. *ad* Alicia Keywan. *m* William Orbit, Torchsong. *cast* Rob Lowe, Cynthia Gibb, Patrick Swayze, Ed Lauter, Jim Youngs, Eric Nesterenko, George Finn.

●The kind of film you'd sooner forget, an ice-hockey romance aimed squarely at a sub-teenage audience. Teen heart-throb Lowe plays Dean Youngblood, the young hick from the sticks who wants to try his luck as an ice-hockey pro, and who joins up with a Canadian Junior League team, Hamilton Mustangs. There he is confronted both by the realities of his chosen sport, in the shape of a bully (Finn) who wants to grind his face into the ice, and by the traumas of puppy love as he falls for the nubile daughter (Gibb) of the team's macho coach (Lauter). Everything is predictable, except perhaps for the searching close-ups of the star's behind. In other respects, Lowe's performance is quite decent, and he cannot be blamed for the puerile humour of a director who considers putting false teeth into someone's beer to be a good joke. TRi

Young Cassidy

(1964, GB, 110 min)
d Jack Cardiff. *p* Robert D Graff, Robert Emmett Ginna. *sc* John Whiting. *ph* Ted Scaife. *ed* Anne V Coates. *ad* Michael Stringer. *m* Seán O'Riada. *cast* Rod Taylor, Flora Robson, Maggie Smith, Julie Christie, Edith Evans, Michael Redgrave, Jack MacGowran, Sian Phillips, TP McKenna.

●Started by John Ford, who retired because of illness, this is an intelligent, powerfully cast, if slightly too pretty-pretty looking biography of Sean O'Casey. Taylor is excellent in the title role, digging ditches to support his mother (Robson) and sickly sister (Phillips), screwing his way through Julie Christie's chorus girl and Maggie Smith's demure librarian, dropping in on Michael Redgrave's WB Yeats and Edith Evans' literary sponsor, and still finding time to pen a line or two and support revolutionary causes. Ending with the first night of *The Plough and the Stars*, which Ford filmed in 1936, this undervalued picture deserves a look. ATu

Young Couples (Yuanyang lou)

(1987, China, 125 min)
d Zheng Dongtian. *sc* Wang Peigong. *ph* G Wenkai, Qu Jianwei. *ed* Zhang Lanfang. *pd* Liu Ying. *m* Zhang Ruishen. *cast* Ji Ling, Tian Shaojun, Song Xiaoying, Xiao Xiong.

●Zheng's flim comprises six episodes, each featuring a young married couple and aiming to sketch a particular economic, moral or psychological problem; the cumbersome link is that they all live in the same high-rise in the Beijing suburbs. This was actually made to launch the careers of twelve new graduates from the Beijing Film Academy's acting classes, and it never manages to look anything but contrived. The script is weak, the performances are flat, and it all feels like TV drama. TR

Young Dillinger

(1965, US, 102 min, b/w)
d Terry Morse. *p* Al Zimbalist. *sc* Arthur Hoerl, Don Zimbalist. *ph* Stanley Cortez. *ed* Terry Morse. *ad* Don Ament. *m* Shorty Rogers. *cast* Nick Adams, Mary Ann Mobley, Robert Conrad, John Ashley, Victor Buono, John Hoyt, Reed Hadley.

●Hoping to marry Mobley, yet desperately short of money, Adams' Dillinger attempts to rob her father's grain store. He's sent to prison where his association with Conrad's Pretty Boy Floyd and Ashley's Baby Face Nelson later sparks a crime spree that's to make him the Most Wanted Man in America. Unexceptional crime biopic, lacking the kind of compelling '30s detail seen two years later in *Bonnie and Clyde*. The brassy score is by jazzer Shorty Rogers. TJ

Young Doctors in Love

(1982, US, 96 min)
d Garry Marshall. *p* Jerry Bruckheimer. *sc* Michael Elias, Rich Eustis. *ph* Don Peterman. *ed* Dov Hoenig. *pd* Polly Platt. *m* Maurice Jarre. *cast* Michael McKean, Sean Young, Harry Dean Stanton, Patrick Macnee, Hector Elizondo, Dabney Coleman, Pamela Reed, Taylor Negron, Saul Rubinek.

●A top US TV comedy director used to a mere half-hour slot isn't going to hang around for punchlines when he goes feature-length. No surprise, then, that Marshall directs this parody of TV hospital dramas at a maniacal pace. Meet the brilliant, callous young doctor with the secret fear, and the secret love for lovely Dr Brody, who has mysterious pain spasms; meet the overworked and oversexed intern turned speed freak, etc. And should the general idea and intermittently sharp dialogue fail to please, there are endless childish visual jokes and pieces of slapstick (fortunately the blithe egomania of the medics is matched only by the indestructibility of the patients) which come and go faster than the nurse on roller-skates. The effect is crass, crowded, and pretty funny, as though the characters from half-a-dozen episodes of *General Hospital* had strayed onto a big screen and decided to misbehave. JS

Young Einstein

(1988, Aust, 91 min)
d Yahoo Serious. *p* Yahoo Serious, Warwick Ross, David Roach. *sc* Yahoo Serious, David Roach. *ph* Jeff Darling. *ed* Yahoo Serious. *ad* Steve Marr, Laurie Faen, Colin Gibson, Ron Highfield. *m* William Motzing, Martin Armiger, Tommy Tycho. *cast* Yahoo Serious, Odile le Clezio, John Howard, Peewee Wilson, Su Cruickshank.

●Hyped with much the same spirit of vigorous nationalism as Paul Hogan and Castlemaine XXXX, this proves decidedly less successful. As writer/director/co-producer, Yahoo Serious (born Greg Pead) casts himself as turn-of-the-century entrepreneur Albert Einstein, who creates the theory of atomic energy in order to put bubbles into beer. Setting off from his parents' Tasmanian apple farm, he heads for Sydney to patent his idea. A human dynamo, he falls in love with scientist Marie Curie (studying at Sydney University), dreams up the Theory of Relativity, invents the surfboard, and devises rock'n'roll. The episodic structure and slapstick humour keep the pace superficially bubbling along, but given a flimsy intellectual base, form and content are at odds with one another. Ultimately, a delirious sense of unwavering optimism lacks the perspective of decent comedy. CM

Young Emmanuelle, A

see Néa

Younger and Younger

(1993, Ger, 93 min)
d Percy Adlon. *p* Eleonore Adlon, Percy Adlon. *sc* Percy Adlon, Felix Adlon. *ph* Bernd Heinl. *ed* Suzanne Fenn. *ad* Steven Legler. *m* Hans Zimmer. *cast* Donald Sutherland, Lolita Davidovich, Brendan Fraser, Julie Delpy, Sally Kellerman.

●The title refers to the Glendale depository business run by anglophile fantasist Sutherland – or rather prematurely-aged wife Davidovich, until her premature death during one of her husband's many bouts of sexual infidelity. Wandering in and out of the warehouse concourses are a variety of odd-ball characters – ex-star ZigZag Lillian (Kellerman) and daughter Melody (Delpy) among them – who are regularly entertained by Younger Snr's 'encouragements' and his turns on the upstairs Wurlitzer. Adlon's film sees him paddling headlong down the wish-fulfilling pseudo-feminist day-glo painted creek he has made his home since moving from Germany to America with *Bagdad Café*. It ends in a kitsch dance duet sequence, sprinkled with broken glass stardust, that would make fans of Fellini stare at their toes with embarrassment. WH

Young Frankenstein

(1974, US, 108 min, b/w)
d Mel Brooks. *p* Michael Gruskoff. *sc* Gene Wilder, Mel Brooks. *ph* Gerald Hirschfeld. *ed* John C Howard. *ad* Dale Hennesy. *m* John Morris. *cast* Gene Wilder, Peter Boyle, Marty Feldman, Madeline Kahn, Cloris Leachman, Teri Garr, Kenneth Mars, Gene Hackman, Richard Haydn.

●By and large, a rather pitiful parody of the Universal 'Frankenstein' movies, taking typically Brooksian liberties with characters and plot, resorting to juvenile mugging, and relying to a great extent on fairly authentic sets and photography for its better moments. A few gags work (notably when Brooks extends the spirit of the original, or comments on it, as in the Monster's scenes with the little girl and with the blind hermit). But for a really delightful parody, James Whale's own *Bride of Frankenstein* is far better value. GA

Young Giants

(1983, US, 97 min)
d Terrell Tannen. *p* Tom Moyer, Megan Moyer. *sc* Tom Moyer, Terrell Tannen, Mike Lammers. *ph* Raoul Lomas. *ed* Denine Rowan, Marion W Cronin, Daniel Gross. *ad* Dan Webster. *m* Rick Patterson. *cast* John Huston, Pelé, Peter Fox, Lisa Wills, F William Parker, Severn Darden.

●Pelé (pronounced alternately 'pale ale' and 'play') comes to the aid of his childhood mentor, a dying priest (Huston) whose orphanage is under threat from corporate baddies, who want to kick the kids' football team out onto the streets. 'Who are those men?' – 'I don't know' (cut to close-up on features hardening), 'but I'm sure gonna find out'. Yes, it's the Lone Ranger meets Tinkerbell. In the end, under Pale Ale's coaching, the kids win a fund-raising/feud match against the local rich kids' school. Well, they could hardly lose with God and Play on their side. PBu

Young Girls of Rochefort, The

see Demoiselles de Rochefort, Les

Young Guns

(1988, US, 107 min)
d Christopher Cain. *p* Joe Roth, Christopher Cain. *sc* John Fusco. *ph* Dean Semler. *ed* Jack Hofstra. *pd* Jane Musky. *m* Anthony Marinelli, Brian Banks. *cast* Emilio Estevez, Kiefer Sutherland, Lou Diamond Phillips, Charlie Sheen, Dermot Mulroney, Casey Siemaszko, Terence Stamp, Jack Palance, Patrick Wayne, Sharon Thomas, Brian Keith, Alice Carter.

●Cain doesn't so much tip his hat to the Western as thumb his nose affectionately. The plot is a pastiche of the Doc Holliday and Billy the Kid legends, with a smattering of *The Magnificent Seven*, all wrapped up in the silliness of *Bonanza*. Stamp plays John Tunstall, an educated English gent with a dubious fondness for the youthful tearaways he hires as 'regulators' to guard his ranch, where new recruit Estevez is introduced to a life of cattle lassoing by day and poetry reading by night. If Stamp's namby-pamby ways endear him to his young charges, they don't go down too well with the wild and woolly townsfolk (led by Palance), who eventually shoot him down. What follows, as Estevez (Billy) and Sutherland (Doc Scurlock) lead the gang (including Sheen and Phillips) in a vengeful chase that culminates in a classic shootout, is a mixed homage to the craggy Arizona landscape and the pert boyishness of the bratpack cast. Little more than a flawed romp, but energetic and enjoyable, with sterling performances from Sutherland and Estevez. EP

Young Guns II

(1990, US, 104 min)
d Geoff Murphy. *p* Paul Schiff, Irby Smith. *sc* John Fusco. *ph* Dean Semler. *ed* Bruce Green. *pd* Gene Rudolph. *m* Alan Silvestri. *cast* Emilio Estevez, Kiefer Sutherland, Lou Diamond Phillips, Christian Slater, William Petersen, Alan Ruck, RD Call, James Coburn, Balthazar Getty, Viggo Mortensen, Scott Wilson, Jack Kehoe.

●Those 'regulators' left standing at the end of *Young Guns* reassemble for another romp around a landscape shot in homage to John Ford. Phillips and Sutherland are back, while Charlie Sheen has been more than adequately replaced by Getty. Billy the Kid (Estevez, frantically scene-stealing) still leads the gang, and as the film opens with him stumbling out of the desert at (seemingly) the age of 120 to tell his story, he'll no doubt ride the teen-Western for some time. The plot is all pot-shots and posses, with a bit of Indian hocus-pocus thrown in for comic relief. In other words, more of the same. The Kid is dismayed to discover that, to save his own hide, his buddy Pat Garrett (Petersen, wasted) is hot on his trail. A tentative subtext plays with the psychology behind being the fastest gun, and with a little imagination you could make something of the group dynamics –

but this is not the point. The point is that the soundtrack includes Jon Bon Jovi, and that the stars play to the audience with a nod and a wink that says, 'Well, no one takes Westerns seriously any more, do they?' EP

Young Ladies of Wilko, The (Panny z Wilka)

(1979, Pol/Fr, 116 min)
d Andrzej Wajda. *sc* Zbigniew Kaminski. *ph* Edward Klosinski. *ed* Halina Prugar. *ad* Allan Starski. *m* Karol Szymanowski. *cast* Daniel Olbrychski, Anna Seniuk, Christine Pascal, Maja Komorowska, Stanislawa Celinska, Krystyna Zachwatowicz.

● 'You've sort of wilted since then…' one of five sisters tells the brooding Viktor (Olbrychski), revisiting the family with whom he spent an idyllic summer as an adolescent. 'Then' was the eve of the Great War, 'now' is late 1920s Poland, and for Viktor it's the autumn of his life. Essentially a piece about lost romance, missed chances, and the doomed attempts of the youngest sister (Pascal) to revive Viktor's passion with the breath of summer, and thereby ensure that she doesn't become an 'old maid' like her sisters. This is minor key Wajda (made before *Man of Iron* and *Danton*), wistful, elegiac, seductive. MA

Young Lions, The

(1958, US, 167 min, b/w)
d Edward Dmytryk. *p* Al Lichtman. *sc* Edward Anhalt. *ph* Joseph MacDonald. *ed* Dorothy Spencer. *ad* Lyle Wheeler, Addison Hehr. *m* Hugo Friedhofer. *cast* Marlon Brando, Montgomery Clift, Dean Martin, Hope Lange, Barbara Rush, Maximilian Schell, Mai Britt, Lee Van Cleef.

● This version of Irwin Shaw's lengthy WWII novel, adapted by Edward Anhalt, is three movies for the price of one. We follow idealistic German Brando, American soldier Clift and crooner Martin from the time of enlistment until their paths eventually cross outside a concentration camp towards the end of the war. Clift, who accused Brando of turning the character of Diestl into a 'fucking Nazi pacifist', blocked his fellow Method actor from dying with his arms outstretched as if on the Cross; and director Dmytryk dissuaded Brando from delivering an improvised speech about the plight of American blacks. Clift gave his deliberately unattractive Jewish GI, Noah Ackerman, a shuddering intensity. Perhaps wisely, Clift and Brando, shared no scenes together. Motivation, Dean Martin observed, is a lot of crap. 'Hell, I just played myself. A likeable coward.' BC

Young Man With a Horn (aka Young Man of Music)

(1950, US, 112 min, b/w)
d Michael Curtiz. *p* Jerry Wald. *sc* Carl Foreman, Edmund H North. *ph* Ted McCord. *ed* Alan Crosland Jr. *ad* Edward Carrere. *cast* Kirk Douglas, Lauren Bacall, Doris Day, Hoagy Carmichael, Juano Hernandez, Jerome Cowan, Mary Beth Hughes, Dan Seymour.

● Originally released in Britain as *Young Man of Music*, lest anyone got the wrong idea about Kirk Douglas' instrumentation, this Warner Bros biopic plays typically fast and loose with the life of its inspiration, legendary jazzer Bix Beiderbecke. Douglas' devotion to his (Harry James dubbed) trumpet drags him on to a stock melodramatic switchback, embracing booze and Bacall before submitting to a redemptive realliance with sweet-singing Doris Day. Hoagy Carmichael tells the tale from his time-honoured ringside seat, the piano stool; while the soundtrack bops along nicely with jazz-tinged standards. (From a novel by Dorothy Baker.) PT

Young Mr Lincoln

(1939, US, 101 min, b/w)
d John Ford. *p* Kenneth MacGowan. *sc* Lamar Trotti. *ph* Bert Glennon. *ed* Walter Thompson. *ad* Richard Day, Mark-Lee Kirk. *m* Alfred Newman. *cast* Henry Fonda, Alice Brady, Marjorie Weaver, Arleen Whelan, Richard Cromwell, Ward Bond, Donald Meek, Eddie Quillan, Milburn Stone, Francis Ford, Pauline Moore.

● This first product of the Ford-Fonda partnership – reputedly a favourite not only of Ford but of Eisenstein too – today commands classic status. Composed of serio-comic scenes from small town life, heavy with a future perfect sense of Myth-in-the-making, it's riven by tensions between insignificance and monumentality (Fonda: 'For me it was like playing Jesus Christ') that explode in the histrionic splendour and 'excess' of the celebrated final sequence: Abe Lincoln setting out to scale unseen heights against the portentous gloom of a gathering storm. SJo

Young Mr Pitt, The

(1942, GB, 118 min, b/w)
d Carol Reed. *p* Edward Black. *sc* Sidney Gilliat, Frank Launder. *ph* Freddie Young. *ed* RE Dearing. *ad* Alex Vetchinsky. *m* Charles Williams. *cast* Robert Donat, Robert Morley, Phyllis Calvert, John Mills, Max Adrian, Felix Aylmer, Raymond Lovell, Stephen Haggard, Herbert Lom.

● This sturdy biopic, written by Frank Launder and Sidney Gilliat, demonstrates Prime Minister Pitt's steadfast conduct during the Napoleonic era and did its bit as a WWII morale-booster. The roll call includes Donat as the handsome Pitt, Morley as his rival, the hissable Fox, Mills as William Wilberforce, Adrian as the playwright Sheridan, Haggard as Nelson, Aylmer as Lord North…and the 25-year-old Lom as Napoleon, a role he'd later reprise to even greater effect in the Vidor's *War and Peace*. TJ

Young One, The (La Joven)

(1960, Mex/US, 95 min, b/w)
d Luis Buñuel. *p* George P Werker. *sc* Luis Buñuel, Hugo Butler. *ph* Gabriel Figueroa. *ed* Carlos Savage. *ad* Jesús Bracho. *m* Jesus Zarzosa. *cast* Zachary Scott, Bernie Hamilton, Kay Meersman, Crahan Denton, Claudio Brook.

● Not one of Buñuel's more celebrated films, *The Young One* may be relatively crude in its production values and acting, but it is nevertheless thematically complex. A black jazz musician (Hamilton), escaping a wrongful rape charge, lands up on an island inhabited only by a gamekeeper (Scott) and his teenage ward (Meersman), an unspoilt nymphet. The gamekeeper's racial prejudice bursts forth, though it is he who eventually deflowers the consenting innocent. Buñuel has made of his potentially exploitative material an amoral parable, outlining the ways 'civilisation' can prove as harmful or as beneficial as untamed nature. DT

Young Poisoner's Handbook, The

(1994, GB/Ger, 105 min)
d Benjamin Ross. *p* Sam Taylor. *sc* Jeff Rawle, Benjamin Ross. *ph* Herbert Taczanowski. *ed* Anne Sopel. *pd* Maria Djorkovic. *m* Robert Lane, Frankie Strobel. *cast* Hugh O'Conor, Antony Sher, Ruth Sheen, Roger Lloyd Pack, Charlotte Coleman, Paul Stacey, Samantha Edmonds.

● Teenage toxicologist Graham Young (O'Conor) is a budding genius with a predilection for ketchup and difficulties at home and school. Girls are turned off by his fascination with decapitation, and his family resent the chemical residue which clings to the kitchen utensils after his experiments. Undaunted, Graham resolves to solve his social problems once and for all, and make a name for himself in the process. He will be Neasden's most famous poisoner. Recounted by the arch-criminal himself, Graham's exploits have an unsettling rationality about them. O'Conor plays him unblinking and wide-eyed. Like a downwardly mobile *Kind Hearts and Coronets*, the film is at its sharpest satirising the suburban domestic kitsch of the '60s and '70s, the trendy psychological theories prison psychiatrist Dr Zeigler (Sher) uses to 'cure' Graham, and the doleful social camaraderie at the photographics laboratory where he's placed for rehabilitation. Director Ross has the confidence to pitch his malicious wit very close to the bone, so that at times you don't know whether to laugh or cry (or both). TCh

Young Sherlock Holmes (Young Sherlock Holmes and the Pyramid of Fear)

(1985, US, 109 min)
d Barry Levinson. *p* Mark Johnson. *sc* Chris Columbus. *ph* Stephen Goldblatt. *ed* Stu Linder. *pd* Norman Reynolds. *m* Bruce Broughton. *cast* Nicholas Rowe, Alan Cox, Sophie Ward, Anthony Higgins, Susan Fleetwood, Freddie Jones, Nigel Stock.

● Levinson (with a script by Chris Columbus of *Gremlins* and *The Goonies*) uses an apocryphal version of the early life of Holmes as the peg for an adventure which romps with the schoolboy Holmes and Watson through a London predictably shrouded in fog. Less predictably, it is populated by shrieking Egyptian fanatics who use a hallucinatory drug to kill their victims. This plot device is the cue for a series of virtuoso special effects sequences: hat-stands come malevolently to life, a roast pheasant bites back, and the youthful, portly Watson undergos torture by patisserie. It's all a long way from Conan Doyle. But while lacking the clarity and breathtaking speed which Spielberg brings to this type of material, it's agreeable enough entertainment. RR

Young Soul Rebels

(1991, GB, 105 min)
d Isaac Julien. *p* Nadine Marsh-Edwards. *sc* Derrick McClintock, Isaac Julien, Paul Hallam. *ph* Nina Kellgren. *ed* John Wilson. *pd* Derek Brown. *m* Simon Boswell. *cast* Valentine Nonyela, Mo Sesay, Dorian Healy, Frances Barber, Sophie Okonedo, Jason Durr, Gary McDonald, Debra Gillet, Eamon Walker.

● 1977: Queen's Silver Jubilee year. Two London soul-boys want their pirate radio station to reach a wider public; but Chris (Nonyela) is distracted both by the big-time lure of the mainstream 'Metro' station and by Tracy (Okonedo), while Caz (Sesay) reacts to what he sees as his old friend's betrayal by taking up with gay socialist-worker punk Billibud (Durr). Worse, the cops suspect Chris of murdering one of Caz's gay friends in the park. Julien's brave, ambitious first feature makes all the right noises in terms of its sensitive treatment of thorny problems like racism and homophobia, and is largely successful in recreating various alternative cultural realities to the jingoistic claptrap which stands as the 'official' history of Britain during the summer of '77. Sadly, despite a strong soul soundtrack and fine camerawork, the film suffers from weak performances and an undernourished script that never frames its ideas within a gripping narrative. GA

Young Stranger, The

(1957, US, 84 min, b/w)
d John Frankenheimer. *p* Stuart Miller. *sc* Robert Dozier. *ph* Robert Planck. *ed* Robert Swink, Edward Biery Jr. *ad* Albert S D'Agostino, John B Mansbridge. *m* Leonard Rosenman. *cast* James MacArthur, James Daly, Kim Hunter, James Gregory, Jeff Silver, Marian Seldes, Whit Bissell.

● Frankenheimer had already directed MacArthur in the original play (Deal a Blow) for television, and his movie debut still smacks somewhat of small-screen ambitions in its emphasis on low-key 'realism' and dramatic intimacy. Nevertheless, it's one of the better generation gap dramas of the '50s, since at least its tale of a movie executive's neglected and embittered son, who gets into trouble with the law after he assaults a cinema manager, is for the most past psychologically acute and sensitively acted. There's the usual explanatory pleading about lack of parental love, and the film lacks the force, dramatic unity and stylistic flair of Rebel Without a Cause. Still, Frankenheimer manages to avoid the pitfalls of most Hollywood portrayals of flaming youth, with MacArthur providing a performance of impressive depth and understatement. GA

Young Törless (Der junge Törless)

(1966, WGer/Fr, 87 min, b/w)
d Volker Schlöndorff. *p* Franz Seitz. *sc* Volker Schlöndorff. *ph* Franz Rath. *ed* Claus von Boro. *ad* Maleen Pacha. *m* Hans Werner Henze. *cast* Mathieu Carrière, Bernd Tischer, Marian Seidowsky, Alfred Dietz, Barbara Steele.

● An adaptation of Robert Musil's novel (written in 1906) about schoolboy sadism in turn-of-the-century Germany, notable for its stylish period evocation. As young Törless arrives at school, a new senior pupil shepherded by a fond mamma, he looks a likely candidate for persecution. As it turns out, another boy (Seidowsky) – a Jew, as it happens – becomes the victim after being caught stealing; and Törless watches with clinical interest as the hapless boy is driven to despair by fiendish tortures and humiliations. Only an accidental encounter during the holidays makes Törless realise that this is, after all, happening to a human being; he duly brings it to the attention of the school authorities as a matter of moral obligation, but remains chiefly concerned with justifying his position as an intellectual observer. Beautifully acted, this bitter little anecdote is all the better in that Schlöndorff, sticking to the disturbing rites and mercurial friendships of the boarding-school world, resists the temptation to dress up its prophetic intimations of Nazism. TM

Young Warriors

(1983, US, 103 min)
d Lawrence D Foldes. *p* Victoria Paige Meyerink. *sc* Lawrence D Foldes, Russell W Colgin. *ph* Mac Ahlberg. *ed* Ted Nicolaou. *pd* Karl Pogany. *m* Rob Walsh. *cast* Ernest Borgnine, Richard Roundtree, Lynda Day George, James Van Patten, Anne Lockhart, Tom Reilly, Mike Norris, Dick Shawn.

●Taking its inspiration from *Death Wish*, *National Lampoon's Animal House*, and Enid Blyton's Famous Five, this opens in the wacky world of college fraternity funsters, and descends by way of the rape and murder of hero Kevin's sister into a social, psychological, and cinematic sewer of destruction and revenge, taking in the usual dialogue clichés and softcore teen-exploitation hooks on the way. Young Kev (Van Patten), an intense young man whose decline into violent paranoia is symbolised by the animated movies he makes ('Kevin, that was so meaningful – where do you get your ideas?'), brushes aside his cop father Borgnine's advice and, accompanied by a guerilla-garbed white pet poodle (no kidding), leads four college chums into a bloodbath of vigilante vengeance. In the final scene the camera focuses on an ad on the wall: 'Schlitz' it says, 'makes everything great'. A high-tack classic. SPr

Young Werther

see Jeune Werther, Le

Young Winston

(1972, GB, 157 min)
d Richard Attenborough. *p/sc* Carl Foreman. *ph* Gerry Turpin. *ed* Kevin Connor. *pd* Geoffrey Drake, Don Ashton. *m* Alfred Ralston. *cast* Simon Ward, Robert Shaw, Anne Bancroft, Jack Hawkins, John Mills, Ian Holm, Anthony Hopkins, Patrick Magee, Edward Woodward.

●A frightfully Boering biopic chronicling the adventures of 2nd Lt Winston Churchill, and ending with his election to the House of Commons. It comes across rather like an episode of the *Antiques Road Show* on location at Blenheim. Well, here we have a very fine example of John Mills that has been handed down over the generations, in perfect nick, about £10 at auction. Simon Ward, as the British bulldog pup, fetches rather less than Jeffrey Hunter as Jesus. ATu

You Only Live Once

(1937, US, 86 min, b/w)
d Fritz Lang. *p* Walter Wanger. *sc* Gene Towne, Graham Baker. *ph* Leon Shamroy. *ed* Daniel Mandell. *ad* Alexander Toluboff. *m* Alfred Newman. *cast* Sylvia Sidney, Henry Fonda, Barton MacLane, Jean Dixon, William Gargan, Warren Hymer, Margaret Hamilton, Jerome Cowan, Ward Bond.

●Looking back to the boldly-stated fatalism of his German films, and – in the on-the-run figures of Sidney and Fonda – forward to the likes of *Bonnie and Clyde* and *Pierrot le Fou*, Lang's superb *film noir* constantly breaks the boundaries of the 'social consciousness' movie category within which it was originally pigeonholed. Determinism is here at the crux of a social, psychological, and generic network, as three-time-loser Fonda finds his guilt or innocence merely the stuff of ready-set alternative newspaper headlines; and Lang constantly queries the narrative thrust with visuals that pose their own ambiguous riddles. Even the title is challenged by the movie's final shot: less a sentimental cop-out than the rigorous working through of a schema that incorporates three essential levels of perception: Fonda's own, society's, and the audience's. PT

You Only Live Twice

(1967, GB, 116 min)
d Lewis Gilbert. *p* Harry Saltzman, Albert R Broccoli. *sc* Roald Dahl. *ph* Freddie Young. *ed* Peter Hunt. *pd* Ken Adam. *m* John Barry. *cast* Sean Connery, Akiko Wakabayashi, Tetsuro Tamba, Mie Hama, Teru Shimada, Karin Dor, Donald Pleasence, Tsai Chin, Alexander Knox, Robert Hutton.

●Agent 007 travels to Japan, where he fakes his own death, gets married (?!), and thwarts a plan by cat-loving SPECTRE mastermind Blofeld (Pleasence) to use hijacked US and Soviet space capsules to blackmail the world super-powers. Roald Dahl's implausible script is padded out with the usual exotic locations, stunts, and trickery. Connery left the series after this one, but was lured back for *Diamonds Are Forever* four years later. NF

Your Beating Heart

see Coeur qui bat, Un

You're a Big Boy Now

(1966, US, 97 min)
d Francis Ford Coppola. *p* Phil Feldman. *sc* Francis Ford Coppola. *ph* Andrew Laszlo. *ed* Aram Avakian. *ad* Vassele Fotopoulos. *m* Bob Prince. *cast* Peter Kastner, Elizabeth Hartman, Geraldine Page, Julie Harris, Rip Torn, Karen Black, Tony Bill, Michael Dunn, Dolph Sweet.

●Coppola's second feature, a free-wheeling comedy about a young man (Kastner) and his frenzied efforts to rid himself of sexual and other inhibitions inculcated by smugly protective/possessive parents (Torn and Page). Though boarded out with a neurotically strait-laced landlady (Harris) whose brief is to keep him pure, he nevertheless contrives to be pursued by a nice girl who loves him (Black), while he perversely lusts after an all-too available actress (Hartman), only to be let down by his rebellious member. Very much of its time (i.e influenced by Godard, Dick Lester and the whole dropout thing), it now looks archly dated rather than spontaneous. But Coppola's style had healthy roots in the screwball comedies of the Thirties, and the glorious performances litter the film with moments to treasure (like Julie Harris' anguished cry when locked into a library vault with the innocent Torn: 'Trapped in the pornography collection of a fiend!'). TM

You're Dead...

(1999, US/Ger, 97 min)
d Andy Hurst. *p* Marco Weber. *sc* Andy Hurst. *ph* Wedigo von Schultzendorff. *ed* Andrew Starke. *pd* Frank Bollinger. *m* Robert Folk. *cast* John Hurt, Rhys Ifans, Claire Skinner, Barbara Flynn, John Benfield, David Schneider, Roger Ashton-Griffiths.

●Actually, one feels all too alive when gaping incredulously at witless, fatuous, ludicrously unnecessary lumber like this. Someone or something, however, clearly spoke to Hurt, Ifans and Skinner persuasively enough that they've gamely debased themselves in this ridiculous pastiche bank job thriller. Most remarkable is the preposterously baroque flashback-and-forward-and-inside-out narrative structure in which, to cut a lot of crap short, two bowler-hatted wasters (Ifans, Schneider) spring an ageing con (Hurt) to abet their raid. After it all goes wrong a corrupt cop (Benfield) vies with a mysterious private agency chief (Flynn) to piece things together. Director Hurst starts out with dead bodies, flaming banknotes and the sort of grandiose orchestral swell usually found at the finale of the more shameless Hollywood thriller, leaving nowhere to go but over the top. NB

You're in the Army Now

see O.H.M.S.

You're Lying (Ni Ljuger)

(1969, Swe, 107 min, b/w)
d Vilgot Sjöman. *p* Göran Lindgren. *sc* Vilgot Sjöman. *ph* Olle Ohlsson. *ed* Carl-Olov Skeppstedt. *m* Ulf Björlin, Cornelis Vreeswuk. *cast* Stig Engström, Börje Ahlstedt, Sif Ruud, Anita Ekström.

●This indictment of the comparatively liberal Swedish penal system argues that a prison system is still a prison system. Caught between pleading a cause and producing a drama, the film never entirely reconciles the two elements. Filmed as social realism in an almost *cinéma-vérité* style, it tells of a talented but highly-strung young artist whose instability is partly of his own making – through his compulsive exploitation of others, and of himself through drink – partly because of an overworked and uncaring prison system. The film is at its best in dealing with prison days, particularly when contrasting behaviour in isolation and in groups. Towards the end of two hours, things look increasingly unsteady as Sjöman concentrates on the destruction of the artist's individual creative impulse, but Stig Engström's strong, starry performance always remains a focal point. CPe

Your Friends & Neighbors

(1998, US, 100 min)
d Neil LaBute. *p* Steve Golin, Jason Patric. *sc* Neil LaBute. *ph* Nancy Schreiber. *ed* Joel Plotch. *pd* Charles Breen. *cast* Amy Brenneman, Aaron Eckhart, Catherine Keener, Nastassja Kinski, Jason Patric, Ben Stiller.

●If you didn't go for the caustic analysis of male insecurity and cruelty in Neil LaBute's previous film, *In the Company of Men*, you'll probably hate this one. It's a similarly cold, detached study of human foibles as exemplified by the sordid sexual shenanigans of three friends and their partners, but despite the strong performances, with Keener excelling as always, the slightly theatrical framing and narrative repetitions and the gloating emphasis on deviousness, weakness and self-obsession not only suggest that the writer/director may just have only one idea in his head, but that he may be genuinely misanthropic. GA

Your Past is Showing!

see Naked Truth, The

Yours and Mine (Wo de Shenjingbing)

(1997, Tai, 114 min)
d Wang Shaudi. *p* Huang Liming, Wang Mingtai. *sc* Wang Shaudi. *ph* Cai Chengtai. *ed* Meng Peixiong. *ad* Yang Zhengyi. *m* Wu Bai & China Blue. *cast* Bai Bingbing, Lin Chengsheng, Hsieh Li-Jin, Hsu Jie-Hui, Gu Bao-Ming, Jeffrey Xu.

●Maybe a little too protractedly raucous for its own good, Wang's scabrous black comedy satirises four contemporary obsessions: cars, homes, bodies and love. It's divided into four chapters with those titles, but its intersecting storylines cut across them just as the main characters cut across lines of class and wealth. The working class scenes succeed best in teasing out the pathos underlying the satire, and Lin Chengsheng (a fine director in his own right) is indelible as the grumpy proprietor of a scuzzy noodle restaurant with a hang-up about the size of his penis. TR

Yours, Mine and Ours

(1968, US, 110 min)
d Melville Shavelson. *p* Robert F Blumofe. *sc* Melville Shavelson, Mort Lachman. *ph* Charles F Wheeler. *ed* Stuart Gilmore. *ad* Arthur Lonergan. *m* Fred Karlin. *cast* Lucille Ball, Henry Fonda, Van Johnson, Jennifer Leak, Tom Bosley, Tim Matheson.

●A horrendously cute premise: Navy widower with ten children meets and marries Navy widow with eight. There's worse to come, since all eighteen kids resent the new arrangement, and a nineteenth is shortly on the way. It's saved by the sheer professionalism of Lucille Ball and Henry Fonda, who share several very funny scenes, the best of which is a meeting in a crowded pub where he struggles with recalcitrant drinks and she with a descending undergarment as they try to make mutual confession as to the enormity of the contribution each is going to make to their marriage. TM

Your Three Minutes Are Up

(1973, US, 92 min)
d Douglas N Schwartz. *p* Jerry Gershwin, Mark C Levy. *sc* James Dixon. *ph* Stephen M Katz. *ed* Aaron Stell. *ad* Joseph Crowingham. *m* Perry Botkin Jr. *cast* Beau Bridges, Ron Liebman, Janet Margolin, Kathleen Freeman, David Ketchum, Stu Nisbet, Read Morgan.

●A modest buddy picture about straight Bridges and scam-artist pal Liebman, who doesn't mind bending the rules to get ahead, which adds up to a witty, well-observed tale of skewed American values. TJ

You Talkin' to Me?

(1987, US, 90 min)
d Charles Winkler. *p* Michael Polaire. *sc* Charles Winkler. *ph* Paul Ryan. *ed* David

Handman. *ad* Alexandra Kicenik. *m* Joel McNeely. *cast* Jim Youngs, James Noble, Faith Ford, Mykel T Williamson.
● Obsessed by Robert De Niro's Travis Bickle character from *Taxi Driver*, unemployed actor Youngs arrives in Hollywood to be seduced by a white supremacist TV producer before coming to his senses and doing what Travis might have done in the same circumstances. A 'comedy' which insults its proclaimed inspiration. TJ

Youth of the Beast (Yaju no Seishun)

(1963, Jap, 92 min)
d Seijun Suzuki. *p* Keinosuke Kubo. *sc* Ichiro Ikeda, Tada-aki Yamazaki. *ph* Kazue Nagatsuka. *ed* Ko Suzuki. *ad* Karyo Yokoo. *m* Hajime Okumara. *cast* Joe Shishido, Akiji Kobayashi, Kinzo Shin, Hideaki Esumi, Misako Watanabe.
● This was the Nikkatsu programmer in which contract director Suzuki first asserted his voice – and assertive is the word. Soon after the apparent love-suicide of a cop and his mistress, the tough Mizuno (Shishido, whey-faced as ever) muscles his way to prominence in yakuza circles. He gets himself hired by two rival gang bosses who hate each other as much as they hate the cops. But who is Mizuno really and what is his secret agenda? And what does it have to do with the Takeshita School of Knitting? Suzuki films this nonsense with a keen sense of its absurdity, but also raises the genre's visual rhetoric to a new high. Who else would park a gay yakuza in a pink limo under matching cherry blossoms? Or whip up an unexplained sandstorm outside the room where a sadist is indulging his vile passions? Hot stuff. TR

You've Got Mail

(1998, US, 119 min)
d Nora Ephron. *p* Lauren Shuler Donner, Norah Ephron. *sc* Norah Ephron, Delia Ephron. *ph* John Lindley. *ed* Richard Marks. *pd* Dan Davis. *m* George Fenton. *cast* Tom Hanks, Meg Ryan, Parker Posey, Jean Stapleton, Dave Chappelle, Steve Zahn, Dabney Coleman, Greg Kinnear.
● Few acquainted with the work of Nora Ephron and Ernst Lubitsch would expect her remake of his *The Shop Around the Corner* (1940) to be anything but inferior to one of the most delicate, poignant romantic comedies ever made. But in updating to the e-mail era the still potentially fertile story of anonymous pen pals who never knowingly meet but whose letters grow intimate in inverse proportion to their professional animosity, Ephron has produced a travesty, opting for every manipulative trick available. First, from her earlier *Sleepless in Seattle*, she reunites Ryan, sickeningly ditzy but earnest from her first appearance as the chintzy indie kids' bookseller, and Hanks, flabby and implausibly flexible as the superstore tycoon who threatens to put her out of business but finally does the right thing. Second, there's the ludicrously twee brownstone Manhattan setting. Third, the clumsily loaded characterisation not only treats almost every other figure as dispensable, but doesn't even bother to make Meg and Tom properly sympathetic. GA

You Were Meant for Me

(1948, US, 92 min, b/w)
d Lloyd Bacon. *p* Fred Kohlmar. *sc* Elick Moll, Valentine Davies. *ph* Victor Milner. *ed* William H Reynolds. *ad* Lyle Wheeler, Richard Irvine. *songs* Nacio Herb Brown, Irving Caesar, others. *cast* Jeanne Crain, Dan Dailey, Oscar Levant, Barbara Lawrence, Selena Royle, Percy Kilbride.
● A virtual remake of 1942's *Orchestra Wives*, this Fox musical has small-town high school student Crain swept off her feet by bandleader Dailey and only to discover at length the difficulties of Depression life on the road and the ups-and-downs of the record industry. A half-decent script means you're not twiddling your thumbs between the production numbers (a raft of jazz standards), but Levant steals it entirely as the band's cynical manager and even puts in a storming, if abbreviated performance at the keyboard for Gershwin's Piano Concerto in F. TJ

You Were Never Lovelier

(1942, US, 97 min, b/w)
d William A Seiter. *p* Louis F Edelman. *sc* Michael Fessier, Ernest Pagano, Delmer Daves. *ph* Ted Tetzlaff. *ed* William Lyon. *ad* Lionel Banks, Rudolph Sternad. *m* Jerome Kern. *songs* Jerome Kern, Johnny Mercer. *cast* Fred Astaire, Rita Hayworth, Adolphe Menjou, Leslie Brooks, Adele Mara, Xavier Cugat, Larry Parks, Gus Schilling.
● Columbia's second teaming of Astaire and Hayworth is a vast improvement on *You'll Never Get Rich*, even though the script is merely adequate, and it keeps threatening to let Xavier Cugat and his Latin rhythms run riot (it doesn't). Astaire plays a Broadway hoofer stranded in Buenos Aires after a bad day at the races. His efforts to secure an engagement at the plushy Hotel Acuna (his insolently playful audition piece is a delight) founder on the temperamental preoccupation of the millionaire proprietor (Menjou), but he subsequently finds himself involved in the latter's devious plot to stoke fires in his supposedly cold-fish daughter (Hayworth). Naturally, both Astaire and Hayworth get caught up in more than mere masquerade; and with love blooming to dreamily romantic Jerome Kern standards (the title song, 'I'm Old-Fashioned', 'Dearly Beloved'), the musical sequences are marvellous, especially an ecstatic dance that whisks all over a moonlit garden. TM

Yoyo

(1965, Fr, 97 min, b/w)
d Pierre Etaix. *p* Paul Claudon. *sc* Pierre Etaix, Jean-Claude Carriere. *ph* Jean Boffety. *ed* Henri Lanoe. *ad* Raymond Tournon, Raymond Gabutti. *m* Jean Paillaud. *cast* Pierre Etaix, Luce Klein, Philippe Dionnet, Claudine Auger.
● The second and possibly the best of Etaix's features, which starts out by dogging Buster Keaton's footsteps as he plays a bored millionaire waited on hand and foot in his château. This first half-hour, set during the last days of the silents, is shot without dialogue (though not without sound effects) and at slightly accelerated speed. Come 1929, the film shifts into a Chaplin mood when, ruined by the Wall Street crash, the millionaire joins a circus to rediscover his first love (who became an equestrienne after bearing him a son). Etaix has just enough astringency to keep sentimentality at bay, and his mastery of the sight gag amply justifies Jerry Lewis' enthusiasm for the film, which is singularly beautifully shot by Jean Boffety. TM

Y tu mamá también

see And Your Mother Too

Yukinojo Henge

see Actor's Revenge, An

Yumeji

(1991, Jap, 128 min)
d Seijun Suzuki. *p* Genjiro Arato. *sc* Yozo Tanaka. *ph* Junichi Fujisawa. *ed* Akira Suzuki. *ad* Noriyoshi Ikeya. *m* Kaname Kawachi, Shigeru Umebayashi. *cast* Kenji Sawada, Tomoko Mariya, Yoshio Harada.
● The final segment of Suzuki's Taisho trilogy suffers somewhat seen in isolation, without the earlier films *Zigeunerweisen* and *Heat-Haze Theatre*. Nevertheless, it's a spirited showing for a veteran director: a sensual, absurdist ghost story spun around the character and work of real-life painter and poet Yumeji Takehisa (1884-1934), seen as a chronic philanderer and dreamer. Kenji Sawada, the effete pop star featured as a glamorous masochist in Paul Schrader's *Mishima*, does his utmost to give the hero some substance, but Suzuki's saturated colours, delirious imagery, and narrative ellipses swamp all attempts at characterisation. The film goes nowhere, slowly, but the mood along the way is seductive enough. TR

Z

(1968, Fr/Alg, 125 min)
d Costa-Gavras. *p* Jacques Perrin. *sc* Costa-Gavras, Jorge Semprun. *ph* Raoul Coutard. *ed* Françoise Bonnot. *ad* Jacques d'Ovidio. *m* Mikis Theodorakis. *cast* Yves Montand, Jean-Louis Trintignant, Jacques Perrin, François Périer, Irene Papas, Georges Géret, Charles Denner.
● Costa-Gavras' crowd-pleasing left wing thriller was based on the 1965 Lambrakis affair, in which investigation of the accidental death of a medical professor uncovered a network of police and government corruption. As Greece was under the Generals at the time, the film was shot in Algeria, with a script by Spaniard Jorge Semprun and music by Theodorakis. The recreation of the murder and the subsequent investigation uses the techniques of an American thriller to gripping effect, though conspiracies are so commonplace nowadays that it's hard to imagine the impact it made at the time. DT

Zabriskie Point

(1970, US, 110 min)
d Michelangelo Antonioni. *p* Carlo Ponti. *sc* Michelangelo Antonioni, Fred Gardner, Sam Shepard, Tonino Guerra, Clare Peploe. *ph* Alfio Contini. *ed* Michelangelo Antoniou. *pd* Dean Tavoulis. *m* Pink Floyd. *cast* Mark Frechette, Daria Halprin, Rod Taylor, Paul Fix, GD Spradlin, Kathleen Cleaver.
● Antonioni's sorrowing, stranger's-eye view of modern America is sadly flawed by the way his 'story' (a rambling, jumbled and mumbling mess scripted by a variety of writers including Sam Shepard, Tonio Guerra and Claire Peploe) is bogged down in the mood of student revolt dogging the nation in the late '60s. Frechette, suspected of shooting a cop during a campus riot, steals a plane, meets Halprin, and makes love with her in Death Valley before returning to give himself up; she meanwhile goes off to meet prospective employer and capitalist pig Taylor. It's clear that the director's interest in America was less political than visual: the painted slogans and billboards seem important less for their content than for their appearance, just as the repeated metaphor of the desert is picturesque rather than telling. That said, the final explosion of a house and its contents in slow-motion is a dazzling, almost celebratory symbol of youthful dreams of ending consumerism. GA

Zandalee

(1990, US, 104 min)
d Sam Pillsbury. *p* William Blaylock, Eyal Rimmon. *sc* Mari Kornhauser. *ph* Walt Lloyd. *ed* Michael Horton. *pd* Michael Corenblith. *m* Pray For Rain. *cast* Nicolas Cage, Judge Reinhold, Erika Anderson, Joe Pantoliano, Viveca Lindfors, Aaron Neville, Steve Buscemi.
● Every few years, a film redefines the boundaries of screen sexuality: *Last Tango in Paris* or *Ai no Corrida*, for example. On the other hand, there is trite soft-porn rubbish like *Nine ½ Weeks* or *Full Moon Junction*. This flaccid effort from Kiwi director Pillsbury wants to be 'Last Tango in New Orleans', but feels like nine-and-a-half weeks in Full Moon Junction. 'I wanna shake you naked and eat you alive, Zandalee' pants passionate artist Nicolas Cage. Amazingly, his best friend's wife (Anderson) falls for this line, immediately consenting to torrid sex. Zandalee's journey through the empire of the senses (from wanton knee-trembler to forced anal sex in a confessional) plumbs the usual depths of female masochism. Meanwhile, husband Judge Reinhold ponders the loss of his poetic muse, then cracks up completely. The plot is daft, the dialogue worse. Asked about working with naked female models, Cage admits: 'When that big red snatch is comin' at yer like a freight train, it's pretty hard to paint, I'll tell yer'. NF

Zandy's Bride (aka For Better, For Worse)

(1974, US, 116 min)
d Jan Troell. *p* Harvey Matofsky. *sc* Marc Norman. *ph* Jordan Cronenweth. *ed* Gordon Scott. *pd* Albert Brenner. *m* Michael Franks. *cast* Gene Hackman, Liv Ullmann, Eileen Heckart, Harry Dean Stanton, Susan Tyrrell, Joe Santos, Sam Bottoms, Frank Cady.
● Swedish director Troell, having won an international reputation with his sweeping historical saga *The Emigrants* and *The New Land*, headed off to America himself, where his career soon ground to a halt after this picturesque but rather vacant tale from the Old West. Hackman's the gruff rancher who's initially antagonistic when he sends off for a mail-order bride and gets Ullmann back, but her fighting spirit is soon to win him over. The performances strike sparks occasionally, but Jordan (*Alien*) Cronenweth's rural cinematography steals all the attention. TJ

Zapatista

(1998, Nor, 55 min)
d Benjamin Eichert, Richard Rowley, Staale Sandberg. *m* Neil Young, Ozomatli. *narrators* Geronimo Pratt, Mumia Abdul Jamal, Edward James Olmos, Daryl Hannah.

●There's a fascinating and important story here – the struggle of the exploited, betrayed and oppressed Chiapas Indians against a corrupt Mexican government quick to use military force to protect its relationship with international capitalist conglomerates. And there's no denying either the clarity of the telling or the impressive interviews obtained by the film-makers. Sadly, however, they botch it, partly by making such an openly facile propaganda piece, but mainly by the infuriatingly tricksy visuals, which are ironically at odds with the traditional culture being celebrated. A wasted opportunity. GA

Zardoz

(1973, GB, 105 min)
d/p/sc John Boorman. *ph* Geoffrey Unsworth. *ed* John Merritt. *pd* Anthony Pratt. *m* David Munrow. *cast* Sean Connery, Charlotte Rampling, Sara Kestelman, Sally Anne Newton, John Alderton, Niall Buggy.
●A bizarre futurist fantasy which seems to have substituted itself when Boorman's plans to film Tolkien's *Lord of the Rings* fell through. Zardoz (joke ref: Wizard of Oz) is a vast, Blakean bust of a bearded Zeus which roams the air spewing arms and ammunition to its Exterminators on earth so that they may enforce the law: 'The gun is good, the penis is evil'. Liberated by the memory of a rape committed in the course of his liberties, one of these Exterminators (Connery) enters the godhead, kills the magician manipulating it, and finds he has penetrated the Vortex, a world of sterilised stasis established to preserve the sum of man's knowledge. At which point, poised to take off from its make love not war springboard, perhaps to explore the dichotomy between physical and spiritual forces, the script gradually falls apart into a mess of philosophical pottage under the whimsically pretentious Tolkien influence. But visually the film remains a sparkling display of fireworks, brilliantly shot and directed. TM

Zaza

(1939, US, 83 min, b/w)
d George Cukor. *p* Albert Lewin. *sc* Zoë Akins. *ph* Charles Lang Jr. *ed* Edward Dmytryk. *ad* Hans Dreier, Earl Hedrick. *m* Frederick Hollander. *cast* Claudette Colbert, Herbert Marshall, Bert Lahr, Constance Collier, Helen Westley, Genevieve Tobin, Walter Catlett, Monty Woolley.
●Minor but typically elegant and enjoyable Cukor, taken from a French stage success (by Pierre Barton and Charles Simon), in which Colbert's vivacious can-can dancer falls (somewhat implausibly) for Marshall, only to find that he's married. Hardly a blazingly original story, but Cukor makes the most of the turn-of-the-century theatrical milieu, rhyming Zaza's on-stage performances (with Colbert herself singing) with the various deceptions that define Marshall's treatment both of her and of his own family. It's a fine example of Colbert at her very engaging best. GA

Zazie

(1989, Jap, 95 min)
d Go Riju. *p* Akira Morishige, Hideaki Tsushima, Tatsuo Hatanaka. *sc* Go Riju. *ph* Joji Ide. *m* Odd-Bowz. *cast* Yoshito Nakamura, Masumi Miyazaki, Rikaco, Tetta Sugimoto, Yuki Matsushita.
●Zazie – a name given him by his many Tokyo waterfront buddies, ex-girlfriends, and ex-members of his successful punk-rock band 'Junk' – is trying to simplify his life. He resists flattery ('You're a legend, man'), and also invitations to join the re-formed band or get back together with his girl. He takes to wandering the waterfront and mooching about his large, dilapidated house, filming and talking philosophy to his new acquisition, a state of the art video camera. A waitress at his favourite café gently mocks his attempts at honesty ('It's a form of selfishness'); Buddha is invoked in hyperbolic comparison ('He had no responsibilities'); Zazie starts finding it easier to communicate with people by sending them videos. Riju's film wears its heart delightfully on its sleeve: exploratory, noisy, energetic, stylistically experimental and very moving though it may be, it avoids self-consciousness by a special brand of wry humour and its mood of knowing introspection. What surprises is Riju's control and vitality; his camera finds interest everywhere it shoots, and beauty too, not least in the bright industrial Tokyo landscapes. WH

Zazie dans le Métro

(1960, Fr, 88 min)
d Louis Malle. *p* Irénée Leriche. *sc* Louis Malle, Jean-Paul Rappeneau. *ph* Henri Raichi. *ed* Kénout Peltier. *ad* Bernard Evein. *m* Fiorenzo Capri. *cast* Catherine Demongeot, Philippe Noiret, Vittorio Caprioli, Yvonne Clech, Hubert Deschamps, Antoine Roblot, Annie Fratellini, Jacques Dufilho.
●Malle's third feature plunges us straight back into the world of New Wave jiggery-pokery, with jump-cuts, lavish in-jokes, and a whirlwind narrative (taken from Raymond Queneau's delightful novel) centred around a precocious brat (Demongeot) lewd enough to give a few tips to the Jodie Foster of *Taxi Driver*. It has survived the years much better than other indulgent frolics, mainly because Malle really does seem motivated by gleeful malice and anarchy – he's not just toying with a fashionable mood. This spirit captured even underground guru Jonas Mekas, who commented on the original US release, 'The fact that the film is a failure means nothing. Didn't God create a failure too?' GB

Zed & Two Noughts, A

(1985, GB/Neth, 115 min)
d Peter Greenaway. *p* Peter Sainsbury, Kees Kasander. *sc* Peter Greenaway. *ph* Sacha Vierny. *ed* John Wilson. *pd* Ben van Os, Jan Roelfs. *m* Michael Nyman. *cast* Andrea Ferreol, Brian Deacon, Eric Deacon, Frances Barber, Joss Ackland, Jim Davidson.
●A car accident caused by a swan outside Rotterdam Zoo leaves ex-Siamese twin brothers (Brian and Eric Deacon, the two noughts) widowers, so they take up with the driver, Alba Bewick (Ferreol), who had one leg amputated and is considering the other. Grief also propels them into investigations at the Zoo into death and decay. Then there is Van Meegeren, surgeon brother to the Vermeer forger, with designs on Alba's legs...As usual with Greenaway, the ideas are large, endless and perverse; and they are teased out with the exquisite formal perfection of a court minuet. Moreover he frames, colours, and shoots with a top dollar perfection (the camerawork is by Sacha Vierny). A film with all the cool, intellectual thrill of the Kasparov-Karpov game. CPea

Zee & Co (X, Y and Zee)

(1971, GB, 109 min)
d Brian G Hutton. *p* Jay Kanter, Alan Ladd Jr. *sc* Edna O'Brien. *ph* Billy Williams. *ed* Jim Clark. *ad* Peter Mullins. *m* Stanley Myers. *cast* Elizabeth Taylor, Michael Caine, Susannah York, Margaret Leighton, John Standing, Mary Larkin.
●One of those follies that everyone involved (especially writer Edna O'Brien) must look back on with cringing embarrassment. Arch-bitch Zee (Taylor, wearing an incredibly unflattering Beatrice Dawson wardrobe) fights tooth and manicured nail to retrieve her philandering husband (Caine) from his sensitive mistress (York), only to end up in the sack with the woman herself. The real highpoint is the sight of Margaret Leighton in a see-thru blouse with a pet faggot in tow. TR

Zelig

(1983, US, 79 min, b/w & col)
d Woody Allen. *p* Robert Greenhut. *sc* Woody Allen. *ph* Gordon Willis. *ed* Susan E Morse. *pd* Mel Bourne. *m* Dick Hyman. *cast* Woody Allen, Mia Farrow, Garrett Brown, Stephanie Farrow, Mary Louise Wilson, Sol Lomita, John Rothman.
●One of Allen's miniaturist exercises in style, *Zelig* is a one-joke movie about a man so self-effacing that he takes on the physical appearance of the person he is with. In addition to the chameleon-like ability for personal metamorphosis, Zelig manifests an equally unique capacity for materialising at important social gatherings and significant historical events – at a garden party given by novelist Scott Fitzgerald, on the balcony of the Vatican during a Papal address, behind a ranting Adolf Hitler at a Nazi rally. Employing skilfully doctored black-and-white photographs and newsreel footage, Allen has created a painstaking and mildly amusing fictional documentary about a non-person who never lived. NF

Zéro de Conduite (Zero for Conduct)

(1933, Fr, 44 min, b/w)
d/sc Jean Vigo. *ph* Boris Kaufman. *ed* Jean Vigo. *m* Maurice Jaubert. *cast* Louis Lefèvre, Gilbert Pluchon, Gérard de Bédarieux, Constantin Goldstein-Kehler, Jean Dasté, Robert Le Flon.
●Vigo's anarchic, disorienting vision of life in a French boarding school, banned until 1945 when Vigo had been dead for eleven years. Outwardly it appears to be an accurate picture; and yet nothing is real. The teachers, their idiosyncrasies appropriately magnified, are seen through the eyes of their pupils. The boys' revolt against mindless discipline culminates in a surreal battle in the playground on speech day. Thirty years later, Lindsay Anderson re-used the same symbols in his own attack on the Establishment, *If*.... DMcG

Zero Effect

(1997, US, 116 min)
d Jake Kasdan. *p* Lisa Henson, Janet Yang, Jake Kasdan. *sc* Jake Kasdan. *ph* Bill Pope. *ed* Tara Timpone. *pd* Gary Frutkoff. *m* The Greyboy Allstars. *cast* Bill Pullman, Ben Stiller, Ryan O'Neal, Kim Dickens, Angela Featherstone, Hugh Ross, Sara DeVincentis.
●Daryl Zero (Pullman) may be the world's greatest, most expensive private detective, but in his personal life he's such a neurotic, unsophisticated mess that he employs a frontman, Steve Arlo (Stiller), to meet clients and generally serve as gofer. Inevitably, his demands strain Arlo's relationship with his lover Jess; not that Zero cares since he himself has no time for attachments – until, that is, an investigation into the blackmailing of Gregory Stark (O'Neal) leads him to suspect attractive, strangely sympathetic paramedic Gloria Sullivan (Dickens). The press notes for this, the first feature by Lawrence Kasdan's son Jake, claim it provides a fresh twist on the private eye genre; well, not if you see Zero, with his logic, erudition, eccentricity and emotional reticence, as a latter-day Holmes and Arlo as his Watson, in which case the sentimental education at the story's core echoes that in Billy Wilder's considerably more affecting *The Private Life of Sherlock Holmes*. That said, Kasdan's is a very promising debut, its own dearth of feeling offset by able writing, engaging playing and a sure sense of pace. GA

Zero Hour

see Stunde Null

Zero Patience

(1993, Can, 100 min)
d John Greyson. *p* Louise Garfield, Anna Stratton. *sc* John Greyson. *ph* Miroslaw Baszak. *ed* Miume Jan. *pd* Sandra Kybartas. *m* Glenn Schellenberg. *cast* John Robinson, Normand Fauteux, Dianne Heatherington, Richardo Keens-Douglas, Bernard Behrens.
●A witty riposte to *And the Band Played On*, this is Canadian AIDS activist Greyson's personal take on 'official' AIDS history. Picking up where Randy Shilts left off, he introduces us to 'Patient Zero', the Air Canada flight attendant alleged to have brought AIDS to America. But scapegoating couldn't be further from the picture. Slyly inverting popular wisdom, the movie offers a sassy commentary on the epidemic of blame. The plot follows the fortunes of notorious Victorian explorer and sexologist Sir Richard Burton as he works to assemble a multi-media museum display on the origin of AIDS. His plans are thwarted when he runs into Zero, back from the dead and determined to clear his name. The film offers a timely reminder that AIDS movies needn't be all Kodak moments and earnest posturing. Matching a flagrant disregard for sentimental pieties with a passion for undermining generic conventions, Greyson has produced a film which engages your mind as much as your heart, and leaves you laughing. PBur

Ziegfeld Follies

(1945, US, 110 min)
d Vincente Minnelli. *p* Arthur Freed. *sc* George White, William K Wells, Al Lewis, Robert Alton, Kay Thompson, Roger Edens, Irving Brecher, others. *ph* George Folsey, Charles Rosher. *ed* Albert Akst. *ad* Cedric

Gibbons, Merrill Pye, Jack Martin Smith. *songs* George Gershwin, Ira Gershwin, Harry Warren, Arthur Freed, Roger Edens, Kay Thompson, Hugh Maltin, Ralph Blane. *cast* William Powell, Fred Astaire, Judy Garland, Lucille Ball, Lena Horne, Gene Kelly, Lucille Bremer, Esther Williams, Red Skelton, Fanny Brice, Edward Arnold, Victor Moore, Keenan Wynn, Feodor Chaliapin, Hume Cronyn, Kathryn Grayson.

●Only partly directed by Minnelli, who took over from George Sidney (responsible for the opening girlie number with Lucille Ball) and suffered various meddlings. From his plushy celestial penthouse, Ziegfeld (Powell) dreams up a posthumous revue which proves predictably lavish and surprisingly garish. No plot, just thirteen items which drag in most of MGM's stars, include some horrendously unfunny sketches (Red Skelton's drunk act is the worst; Fanny Brice's famous 'Baby Snooks' sketch must be an acquired taste), and intermittently display the Minnelli touch (notably an operatic scene brilliantly conceived in black and white except for the diva's crimson dress). As so often, the honours are taken by Astaire's three numbers (including his only duet with Kelly, 'The Babbitt and the Bromide'), best of which is the gorgeous 'Limehouse Blues', danced with Lucille Bremer and partly shot on a foggy street set held over from *The Picture of Dorian Gray*. TM

Ziegfeld Girl

(1941, US, 131 min, b/w)
d Robert Z Leonard. *p* Pandro S Berman. *sc* Marguerite Roberts, Sonya Levien. *ph* Ray June. *ed* Blanche Sewell. *ad* Cedric Gibbons. *songs* Roger Edens, Gus Kahn, Nacio Herb Brown, Ralph Freed, others. *cast* James Stewart, Lana Turner, Judy Garland, Hedy Lamarr, Tony Martin, Jackie Cooper, Dan Dailey, Philip Dorn, Ian Hunter, Charles Winninger, Eve Arden, Edward Everett Horton, Al Shean.

●Classic MGM musical with Busby Berkeley pulling all stops out to retell the story of legendary showman Ziegfeld by way of the mixed fortunes of three of his girls, with Turner as the one who hits the skids, Lamarr as the one who settles for marriage, and Garland as the one who makes the grade. An oddly intriguing mix of production numbers and melodrama, with Dailey outstanding as a sadistic prizefighter who gives Turner a hard time, and Garland at the height of her powers. Favourite numbers include: 'You Stepped Out of a Dream' and 'I'm Always Chasing Rainbows'. MA

Zigeunerweisen

(1980, Jap, 145 min)
d Seijun Suzuki. *p* Genjiro Arato. *sc* Yozo Tanaka. *ph* Kazue Nagatsuka. *ed* Nobutake Kaniya. *ad* Takeo Kimura, Yoshito Tada. *m* Kaname Kawase, Pablo de Sarasate. *cast* Yoshio Harada, Naoko Otani, Toshiya Fujita, Michiyo Okusu, Akaji Maro.

●The first and arguably best achieved part of Suzuki's 'Taisho Trilogy' (*Kagero-za* and *Yumeji* followed) is a shaggy-ghost-dog story in which assorted ambiguities of identity and memory turn on a 78rpm record of Pablo de Sarasate playing *Zigeunerweisen*. Nakasago (Harada) is a wild and crazy hedonist obsessed by the geisha Koine (Otani); he marries her dead ringer (Otani again) but abandons her for Koine as she is about to give birth to their child – later installing the geisha as a surrogate mother when his wife dies of flu. These events repercuss on his one-time colleague Aochi (Fujita), a stolid professor of German, who remembers hearing the Sarasate record but is sure he never borrowed it… Playful, sensuous and performed and shot with élan, this looks very much like a riddle without a solution. TR

Ziggy Stardust and the Spiders from Mars

(1982, GB/US, 90 min)
d DA Pennebaker. *ph* Jim Desmond, DA Pennebaker, Mike Davis, Nick Doob, Randy Franken. *ed* Lorry Whitehead. *with* David Bowie, Mick Ronson, Trevor Bolder, Mick Woodmansy, Ringo Starr.

●The whole flashy, rockist affair is based on a wobbly premise of sentimentality. It's a record of the Ziggy character's farewell dates at the Hammersmith Odeon in 1973, and while the likes of 'Oh You Pretty Things' and 'All the Young Dudes' still raise a smile, the presiding image is of those flesh-crawling glam-rock costumes and stage antics. Go for the music, or not at all. JG

Zina

(1985, GB, 94 min)
d/p Ken McMullen. *sc* Terry James, Ken McMullen. *ed* Robert Hargreaves. *pd* Paul Cheetham. *m* Barrie Guard, David Cunningham. *cast* Domiziana Giordano, Ian McKellen, Philip Madoc, Paul Geoffrey, Tusse Silberg, Maureen O'Brien.

●This revisits the twin 20th century traumas of Revolution and Reich, as witnessed by the self-styled 'good-for-nothing daughter of the most important man of our time', namely Leon Trotsky. 1932 finds him in Turkey rallying forces against Stalin and Hitler, while she, both victim and visionary, lies on a couch in Berlin, where McKellen's neo-Freudian shrink sees her morbid insanity as mirroring a Germany in thrall to Thanatos. Is there more than a coincidental (anagrammatic?) link between Zina's and the Nazis' different madnesses? McMullen isn't entirely convincing, but his elegantly prowling camera, careful compositions, and astute use of locations ranging from Berlin and Blackpool to Lanzarote, create a powerful, onerous mood with much more assurance than the otherwise similar '1919'; and the wild and woolly Giordano, emotions scudding across her face like clouds, is simply magnificent as the volatile Zina. SJo

Zio di Brooklyn, Lo

see Uncle from Brooklyn, The

Zipper and Tits (Fastener to Chibusa)

(2001, Jap, 70 min)
d/p/sc/ph/ed Koji Shirakawa. *m* Kiyohito Komatsu. *cast* Kentaro Takayama, Manami Ogawa, Yoshifumi Tsubota, Sachiko Eijiri.

●No less demanding than Shirakawa's earlier first-person films, this two-part DV feature gets inside the heads of two prostitutes, one male, one female, and reveals gaping holes where their self-esteem should be. 'Zipper' centres on a rent-boy who works the Tokyo streets and back alleys, despised by his johns and taken completely for granted by the boyfriend he lives with. The 30-year-old woman in 'Tits' works in the apartment she shares with her boyfriend/banker; the episode centres on the day she gets her first female client, a brittle woman who turns out to have ulterior motives for being there. Shirakawa's brooding, expressionist visuals and the sexual frankness build a wounding sense of what it means to lose even your sense of loss. TR

Zombie Flesh-Eaters (Zombi 2)

(1979, It, 91 min)
d Lucio Fulci. *p* Ugo Tucci, Fabrizio De Angelis. *sc* Elisa Livia Briganti. *ph* Sergio Salvati. *ed* Vincenzo Tomassi. *pd* Walter Patriarca. *m* Fabio Frizzi, Giorgio Tucci. *cast* Tisa Farrow, Ian McCulloch, Richard Johnson, Al Cliver, Auretta Gay, Olga Karlatos.

●A slight but very gory pulp zombie tale in true spaghetti style: on a lurid voodoo isle (complete with white doctor), fading stars and clones slug it out with the living dead. A massacre. One twist: the cannibal-zombies eventually take over New York ('They're breaking through the door… aaargh!'), where they no longer look out of place. But the lack of suspense amid the Technicolor carnage disappoints. Subtle it ain't, but the title alone should keep art lovers away. DMacp

Zombies

see Dawn of the Dead

Zone Troopers

(1985, US, 86 min)
d Danny Bilson. *p* Paul DeMeo. *sc* Danny Bilson, Paul DeMeo. *ph* Mac Ahlberg. *ed* Ted Nicolaou. *pd* Philip Dean Foreman. *m* Richard Band. *cast* Tim Thomerson, Timothy Van Patten, Art La Fleur, Biff Manard, William Paulson, Alviero Martin.

●The playful, plagiaristic Poverty Row spirit of early Roger Corman is not dead. Starting off as a conventional war film (Italy 1944), with a bunch of American GIs stranded behind enemy lines, it soon escalates/degenerates into an absurd semi-sci-fi thriller when an enormous rocket is discovered smouldering in the forest: it's a Martian spaceship, and a benign, burbling alien survivor is on the loose. Not as good as producer Charles Band's own *Trancers*, and it would be unfair to recommend too highly any film featuring a distinctly un-Hitlerish Führer (Martin) and a daring escape ludicrously accompanied by the sounds of big band swing. But as inventive nonsense scarcely tainted by plot logic, it's more rewarding viewing than any Hugh Hudson film. GA

Zoo in Budapest

(1933, US, 85 min, b/w)
d Rowland V Lee. *p* Jesse Lasky. *sc* Dan Totheroh, Louise Long, Rowland V Lee. *ph* Lee Garmes. *ed* Harold Schuster. *ad* William Darling. *m* Louis de Francisco. *cast* Gene Raymond, Loretta Young, OP Heggie, Paul Fix, Wally Albright.

●A strange, ecstatically beautiful little fantasy, set almost entirely within a quaint Douanier Rousseau zoo, all trailing palm fronds and swirling mists, where three innocents – a pair of lovers and a runaway child – seek refuge one night from the cruelties of the world outside. At first a hostile jungle, the zoo mysteriously mutates by night into a Garden of Eden, a transformation subtly painted in light by Lee Garmes' incredible camerawork, which draws delicate analogies in captivity between humans and animals, and culminates with the fantastic sequence of the revolt of the caged beasts, which points the way to freedom. Only marginally let down by the final scene – a brief coda showing the couple happily settled into their own little cottage 'just like anybody else' – the whole film reverberates like one of Blake's 'Songs of Innocence'. TM

Zoolander

(2001, US/Ger/Aust, 89 min)
d Ben Stiller. *p* Scott Rudin, Ben Stiller, Stuart Cornfield. *sc* Drake Sather, Ben Stiller. *ph* Barry Peterson. *ed* Greg Hayden. *pd* Robin Standefer. *m* David Arnold. *cast* Ben Stiller, Owen Wilson, Will Ferrell, Christine Taylor, Milla Jovovich, Jerry Stiller, Jon Voight, David Duchovny, Judah Friedlander, Nathan Lee Graham.

●A fashion spoof draped over the bones of a puerile conspiracy adventure, this vanity comedy fails at every level barring its incidental details. Stiller directs, co-writes and stars, casting or flash-cameoing a host of real models and designers, personalities and family members. In the process he stretches himself as thin as the film's original idea, sparked by his 1996 onstage appearance as a dumb male supermodel for the VH1 Fashion Awards ceremony. We have to suffer much preening and prancing catwalk capers, the most absurd and least funny of which is the grudge match/private wager Zoolander (Stiller) conducts with the über-model who has taken his crown. Zoolander agrees to model for evil designer Mugatu's Derelicte collection, only to find himself being indoctrinated to assassinate the Malaysian premier for introducing new child-labour legislation. Funny, yes? The self-absorbed world of fashion proves notoriously hard to parody or satirise, and Stiller's insights are neither original nor artful. WH

Zoo la Nuit, Un

see Night Zoo

Zorba the Greek

(1965, Greece/US, 146 min, b/w)
d/p/sc Michael Cacoyannis. *ph* Walter Lassally. *ed* John Dwyre. *ad* Vassilis Photopoulos. *m* Mikis Theodorakis. *cast* Anthony Quinn, Alan Bates, Irene Papas, Lila Kedrova, George Foundas.

●The dreadful movie (from the novel by Nikos Kazantzakis) that launched a million package tours: timid writer Bates falls spellbound to the outsize folkloric 'charm' of Quinn's philosophically boisterous Cretan Character, a role he's revamped with minor cultural compensations in almost every one of his films since. PT

Zorro the Gay Blade

(1981, US, 93 min)
d Peter Medak. *p* George Hamilton, CO Erickson. *sc* Hal Dresner. *ph* John A Alonzo. *ed* Hillary Jane Kranze. *pd* Herman A Blumenthal.

m Ian Fraser. *cast* George Hamilton, Lauren Hutton, Brenda Vaccaro, Rob Leibman, Donovan Scott, James Booth, Clive Revill.
●This 'affectionate parody' of the swashbuckling Zorro myth is so determinedly amiable that one feels distinctly caddish for regretting that the laughs are not even more frequent. It fails only in that Leibman's villain shouts too much, and that the set pieces, the skeleton of most film comedy, are under-considered. The simple idea, for example, of every male guest at a masked ball turning up disguised as Zorro, making the villain's task of identifying the real one trickier than he expected, is almost hysterically thrown away: the scene is just good enough to make it doubly frustrating. This said, Hamilton's hamming is a delight rather than an annoyance, the sets and stuntwork well achieved. JC

Zouzou

(1934, Fr, 90 min, b/w)
d Marc Allégret. *sc* Carlo Rim. *ph* Michel Kelber. *ad* Lazare Meerson, Alexandre Trauner. *m* Vincent Scotto, Georges Van Parys. *cast* Josephine Baker, Jean Gabin, Pierre Larquey, Yvette Lebon, Madeleine Guitry, Palau.
●Basically a vehicle for Josephine Baker, who bubbles effervescently through some Busby Berkeley-ish production numbers, and also gets to sing her classic 'Pour moi, y'a qu'un homme à Paris', with a tearful eye on her adored but roving-eyed foster brother. It is Gabin who really catches the eye in this part, with his persona already almost fully developed. Impassive as ever, he is first glimpsed as a soldier in an oriental dive, reigning benignly over the pretty girls but still a stranger in a strange land. Then the fatal encounter with his dream during a *bal musette* waltz which he hoarsely croons in her ear; and finally the misunderstanding, the accusations of murder. Happy ending apart, you can already see the romantically doomed gangster of *Pépé le Moko*, stubbornly proletariat, eternally yearning for the purity denied by the world in which he is mired. TM

Zulu

(1963, GB, 135 min)
d Cy Endfield. *p* Stanley Baker, Cy Endfield. *sc* John Prebble, Cy Endfield. *ph* Stephen Dade. *ed* John Jympson. *ad* Ernest Archer. *m* John Barry. *cast* Stanley Baker, Jack Hawkins, Michael Caine, Ulla Jacobsson, James Booth, Nigel Green, Ivor Emmanuel, Paul Daneman, Glynn Edwards.
●A film which comes with two heavy strikes against it: it was made during the '60s boom for epic adventures in exotic climes (which now look like a breed of cinematic dinosaur), and it recounts one of those heroic tales of the thin red line holding out against hordes of fuzzy-wuzzies that endlessly fuelled *Boy's Own*. In fact, *Zulu* is a fairly tough-minded and interesting account of a company of Welsh soldiers doing their bit for somebody else's Queen and Country in an alien land (the script was co-written by the chronicler of the Highland Troubles, John Prebble), and is a more honest account of imperialism than the belated follow-up, *Zulu Dawn*, supposedly telling the Zulus' side of things. In his first starring role, Cockney wide boy Caine actually assumes an upper crust, but is finally one-upped by Baker's officer of Engineers. MA

Zulu Dawn

(1979, US/Neth, 117 min)
d Douglas Hickox. *p* Nate Kohn. *sc* Cy Endfield, Anthony Storey. *ph* Ousama Rawi. *ed* Malcolm Cooke. *pd* John Rosewarne. *m* Elmer Bernstein. *cast* Burt Lancaster, Peter O'Toole, Simon Ward, John Mills, Nigel Davenport, Michael Jayston, Ronald Lacey, Denholm Elliott, Freddie Jones, Christopher Cazenove.
●A motion picture epic of (and about) timeless stupidity. Belonging to the 'overwhelming odds' school of cinematic dross, this recounts the massacre at Isandhlwana in 1879, the worst defeat ever suffered by British forces at the hands of natives, with the big-name colonials battling against well-oiled and statuesque blacks. Embarrassed by the fundamental attraction of this ripping yarn, the film abandons *Zulu*-style Celtic punk and sells itself instead on spectacle, in a wrap-around package of documentation and social insight (meaning shots of rows of native boobs vs elaborate Brit table manners). You can't fail to be staggered by the discrepancy between the film's wet-nosed anxiety to please, to affect, and its wide-screen parade of nervy little cosmetic clichés. RP

Zu: Warriors from the Magic Mountain (Shu Shan: Xin Shushan Jianxia)

(1983, HK, 97 min)
d Tsui Hark. *cast* Brigitte Lin, Samo Hung, Yuen Biao, Meng Hai, Adam Cheng, Judy Ong, Feng Ke'an, Tsui Hark.
●Reverend Long-brows (Hung) holds a ravening blood monster at bay for 49 days while four fallible humans comb the universe for the two celestial swords which can save the world. Tsui brought in technicians from *Star Wars*, *Star Trek* and *Tron* to help him make 'the ultimate Chinese mythological spectacular', inspired by a newspaper serial of the late 1920s by Li Shoumin. Thanks to Hollywood know-how (and William Chang's designs), it does look pretty good, and the starry cast just about holds its own amid all the special visual effects. But where was the script? So much effort has gone into the set-pieces that pacing, coherence and even dramatic impact all go hang. TR

Zweite Erwachen der Christa Klages, Das

see Second Awakening of Christa Klages, The

Film Categories

As a quick reference guide for readers hiring or buying videos and DVDs, there follows lists of films under 15 different category headings. The categorising of any film is a risky business – many films fall into several possible categories – so we have used headings similar to those of most video/DVD libraries, as well as some commonly recognised genres. The Appendices that follow do not include every film in the Guide, as many are simply beyond categorisation, but all the titles in them will be found in the main text. Also, Appendices 16 to 21 (*pages* 1403–1416) list films from the producer countries, other than the USA and Britain, most represented in the Guide.

The category headings we have adopted are:

Action/Adventure	Appendix 1	*page* 1377
Children's Films	Appendix 2	*page* 1379
Comedy	Appendix 3	*page* 1380
Documentaries	Appendix 4	*page* 1386
Epics	Appendix 5	*page* 1388
Fantasy	Appendix 6	*page* 1388
Film Noir	Appendix 7	*page* 1389
Gangsters	Appendix 8	*page* 1390
Horror	Appendix 9	*page* 1390
Musicals	Appendix 10	*page* 1392
Period/Swashbucklers	Appendix 11	*page* 1393
Science Fiction	Appendix 12	*page* 1395
Thrillers	Appendix 13	*page* 1396
War	Appendix 14	*page* 1400
Westerns	Appendix 15	*page* 1401

Appendix 1

Action/Adventure

Accidental Legend
Accidental Spy
Adventures of Captain Marvel, The
African Queen, The
Africa – Texas Style
Air Force One
Airport
Airport 1975
Airport '77
Airport '80
Alaska
Alien Thunder
Amazing Captain Nemo, The
Ambassador, The
American Ninja
Another Stakeout
Appât, L'
Appointment in Honduras
Arena
Around the World in 80 Days
Asoka
Assassination
Assault on a Queen
Assault on Precinct 13
Atlantic Adventure
Avalanche
Avengers, The
A.W.O.L.

Backdraft
Back from Eternity
Badge 373
Bamboo Gods and Iron Men
Bandido!
Bandit, The
Band of the Hand
Bard Wire
Barquero
Battlefield Earth
Battle Royale
Beach of the War Gods
Bear, The
Bear Island
Beau Geste
Beneath the 12-Mile Reef
Bengazi
Best of the Best
Best of the Best 2
Better Tomorrow, A
Better Tomorrow II, A

Beyond the Poseidon Adventure
Big Bad Mama
Big Boss, The
Big Brawl, The
Big Trouble in Little China
Big Zapper
Billy Jack
Bird People in China, The
Black Belt Jones
Black Eagle
Blind Fury
Blood of the Dragon
Blood on the Sun
Bloodsport
Bloody Fists, The
Blue Fin
Bodo
Body
Bootleggers
Born Losers, The
Botany Bay
Boxcar Bertha
Breakout
Brigand of Kandahar, The
Broken Arrow
Bronx Warriors, The
Brotherhood of the Wolf
Bucktown
Bullet Ballet
Bulletproof
Bullfighter and the Lady, The
Burning Paradise

Cannonball
Caper of the Golden Bulls, The
Cape Town Affair, The
Captains Courageous
Caravans
Caravan to Vaccarès
Cast a Giant Shadow
Catchfire
Ça va Barder
Ceiling Zero
Challenge
Charlie's Angels
Chase, The
Cherry 2000
Chill Factor
China Seas
Chinese Connection, The
City Beneath the Sea
City on Fire
Clan of the Cave Bear, The
Cleopatra Jones
Cleopatra Jones and the Casino of Gold
Cliffhanger
Cobra
Cockfighter
Codename: The Soldier
Code of Silence
Coffy
Collateral Damage
Commando
Comrade X
Con Air
Condorman
Congo
Congo Crossing
Conman and the Kung Fu Kid, The
Convoy
Countdown
Countryman
Crash
Crimson Tide
Crocodile Dundee
Crocodile Dundee II
Crocodile Dundee in Los Angeles
Crouching Tiger, Hidden Dragon
Cuba
CutThroat Island

Dandy, the All-American Girl
Danger: Diabolik
Dante's Peak
Dark Journey
Daylight
Days of Thunder
Death in the Sun
Death Kick
Death Race 2000
Death Wish
Death Wish II
Death Wish 3
Death Wish 4
Deep, The
Deep Impact
Deep Rising
Defiance
Deliverance
Delta Force, The
Demolition Man
Desperate Search
Devil at 4 O'Clock, The
Devil's Island (Clemens)
Diamond Mercenaries
Diamonds
Diamonds are Forever
Dirigible
Dirty Ho
Dirty Mary, Crazy Larry
Dixie Dynamite
Dr No
Dogs of War, The
Donovan's Reef
Double Impact
Double Team
Dove, The
Downhill Racer
Dragon Dies Hard, The
Driven
Drive-In
Drop Zone
Drum, The
Dynasty

Eagle Has Landed, The
Earthquake
East of Sumatra
Eat My Dust!
Edge, The
Eiger Sanction, The
8 Million Ways to Die
8-Wheel Beast, The
Elephant Boy
Emerald Forest, The
Emperor of the North Pole, The
Enter the Ninja
Enter the 7 Virgins
Escape from New York
Escape from Zahrain
Escape to Burma
Evel Knievel
Evil That Men Do, The
Exterminator 2
Extreme Prejudice
Eye for an Eye, An
Eye of the Needle

Face/Off
Far Off Place, A
Fast Charlie, the Moonbeam Rider
Fast Company
Fate of Lee Khan, The
Fathom
Ferry to Hong Kong
Fighting Back
Fighting Mad
Figures in a Landscape
Finders Keepers
Fine Mess, A
Fire
Firebirds
Firefox
First Blood
First Great Train Robbery
First Strike
F.I.S.T.
Fist of Fury
Fist of Fury Part II
Fist of the North Star
Five Came Back
Fled
Flight from Ashiya
Flight of the Doves
Flight of the Phoenix, The
Force: Five
Force of One, A
Fort Apache, the Bronx
For Your Eyes Only
Four Feathers, The (Korda)
Four Feathers, The (Sharp)
Four Men and a Prayer
Fourth Protocol, The
Freebie and the Bean
Freedom Road
From Russia With Love
Fugitive, The

Game for Vultures
G.I. Jane
Giù la Testa
Gladiator
Glimmer Man, The
Glory Stompers, The
Gods Must Be Crazy, The
Gods Must Be Crazy II, The
Gojoe
Gold
Golden Child, The
GoldenEye
Golden Lady, The
Golden Needles
Golden Rendezvous
Goldfinger
Gone in 60 Seconds
Gone in Sixty Seconds
Good Guys Wear Black
Good to Go
Goodbye Pork Pie
Gordon's War
Grand Jeu, Le
Grand Prix
Grand Theft Auto
Gray Lady Down
Great Texas Dynamite Chase, The
Great Waldo Pepper, The
Green Fire
Greystoke – The Legend of Tarzan of the Apes
Grizzly
Gunga Din
Gulag
Gunmen
Guns and the Fury, The
Guns for San Sebastian
Guns of Darkness
Gymkata
Gypsy Moths, The

Hap-Ki-Do
Hard Times
Harley Davidson and the Marlboro Man
Hatari!
Heartbreak Ridge
Helicopter Spies, The
Hellhounds of Alaska, The
Hell's Angels on Wheels
Hell Up In Harlem
Heroes, The
High Risk
High Road to China
Hit!
Homme de Rio, L'
House on Garibaldi Street, The
How to Destroy the Reputation of the Greatest Secret Agent
Hudson Hawk
Hunter, The
Hurricane
Hurricane, The

Iceman Cometh, The
Ice Palace
Ice Station Zebra
I Escaped from Devil's Island
Impasse
Indiana Jones and the Last Crusade
Indiana Jones and the Temple of Doom
Inferno
In Like Flint
Inside Out
Into the Night
Invasion U.S.A.
Iron Eagle
Iron Eagle II
Island, The

Jackal, The
Jaguar Lives
Jaws
Jaws 2
Jaws 3-D
Jaws – The Revenge
Jet Pilot
Jet Storm
Jewel of the Nile, The
Joan of Arc of Mongolia
John Carpenter's Escape from L.A.
Jungle 2 Jungle

Karate Kid, The
Karate Kid: Part II, The
Karate Kid: Part III, The
Karate Killers, The
Kawashima Yoshiko
Kickboxer
Killer, The (Chu Yuan)
Killer Elite, The
Killer Fish
Killers of Kilimanjaro
Killpoint
Kim
King of Kung Fu
Kings of the Sun
King Solomon's Mines (Stevenson)
King Solomon's Mines (Thompson)
King Solomon's Treasure
Kiss of the Dragon
Knock Off
Krakatoa – East of Java
K2
Kung Fu Fighting
Kung-Fu Gangbusters
Kung Fu Girl, The
Kung Fu – Girl Fighter
Kung Fu Street Fighter
Kung Fu – The Headcrusher

Lassiter
Last Castle
Last Dinosaur, The
Last Dragon, The
Last Hard Men, The
Last Hurrah for Chivalry
Last Voyage, The
Legend of Bruce Lee
Legend of the Lost
Legend of Zu, The
Le Mans
Licence to Kill
Live and Let Die
Living Daylights, The
Lock Up
Long Ride, The
Long Voyage Home, The
Lost World, The (Allen)
Lost World, The (Hoyt)
Love and Bullets
Low Down Dirty Shame, A
Lustful Amazon, The
Lone Wolf McQuade
Longest Yard, The
Long Kiss Goodnight, The

Macao
Mackenna's Gold
Mackintosh Man, The
Macon County Line
Madame Sin
Mad Bomber, The
Mad Dog Morgan
Magnum Force
Mama's Dirty Girls
Man from Hong Kong, The
Man from Snowy River, The
Man With the Golden Gun, The
Marked for Death
Maximum Risk
Medicine Man

Mercenaries, The
Mighty Joe Young (Schoedsack)
Mighty Joe Young (Underwood)
Missing in Action
Mission Impossible
Mission: Impossible II
Mr Forbush and the Penguins
Mr Majestyk
Mr Nice Guy
Moby Dick
Mogambo
Molly Maguires, The
Montagna del Dio Cannibale, La
Moonraker
Moonrunners
Moonshine War, The
Morning Departure
Morocco
Mort en ce Jardin, La

Naked Jungle, The
Navy Seals
Ned Kelly
Neptune Factor, The
Never Cry Wolf
Never Say Never Again
New One-Armed Swordsman, The
Nickel Queen
Ninja III – The Domination
No Highway
No Retreat, No Surrender
North Sea Hijack
North to Alaska
North West Frontier

Octopussy
Odessa File, The
Oklahoma Crude
Old Man and the Sea
Once a Jolly Swagman
One, The
One Armed Boxer
On Her Majesty's Secret Service
Only Angels Have Wings
Open Season
Operation Thunderbolt
Orca
Osterman Weekend, The
Outcast of the Islands
Out for Justice
Overlanders, The
Over the Top

Papillon
Passage, The
Peacemaker, The
Penitentiary
People That Time Forgot, The
Perfect Weapon, The
Police Story (Chan)
Poseidon Adventure, The
Postman, The
Predator
Predator 2
Prisoner of Rio
Prisoner of Shark Island, The
Professionals, The
Project A
Punisher, The

Queimada!
Quest, The
Quigley Down Under

Race for the Yankee Zephyr
Raiders of the Lost Ark
Raid on Entebbe
Raise the Titanic!
Rambo: First Blood, Part II
Rambo III
Rampage
Rapid Fire
Raw Deal
Red Corner
Red Dawn
Red Dust
Red Line 7000
Remo Williams: The Adventure Begins
Return of the Dragon
RevelationRiddle of the Sands, The
Right Stuff, The
Road House
Robbery Under Arms
Robinson Crusoe
Rock, The
Rocky
Rocky II
Rocky III
Rocky IV
Rocky V
Rollerball
Romancing the Stone
Romeo Must Die
Rookie, The
Rosebud
Rules of Engagement
Rumble in the Bronx
Runaway Train
Run for the Sun
Running Man, The (Glaser)
Rush Hour
Rush Hour 2

Saadia
Sahara (McLaglen)
Sammy Going South
Sand Pebbles, The
Santiago
Satan Bug, The
Satan Never Sleeps
Savage Innocents, The
Scorpion King, The (Russell)
Scorpion King, The (Lai)
Scott of the Antarctic
Secret Invasion, The
Seven (Sidaris)
Seven-Ups, The
Shadow Conspiracy
Shaft (Parks)
Shaft (Singleton)
Shaft in Africa
Shaft's Big Score!
Shaker Run
Shanghai Lil
Shanghai Noon
Shaolin Soccer
Sharks' Cave, The
Sharks' Treasure
She
She Demons
Sheena
She Gods of Shark Reef
Shogun Assassin
Shooter, The
Shout at the Devil
Siege
Silent Rage
Skullduggery
Sky Pirates
Sky Riders
Sniper
Soldier, The
Sorcerer
S.O.S. Titanic
Southern Comfort
SpaceCamp
Spider-Man
Spoor
Spy Game
S.T.A.B.
Starflight: The Plane That Couldn't Land
Station Six – Sahara
Stick, The
Stormriders, The
Stone Cold
Stoner
Strange Days
Steet Fighter
Streets of Fire
Streets of Gold
Stunts
Sudden Death
Surf Nazis Must Die
Sword of Doom
Tank Girl
Tarzan and the Mermaids
Tarzan, The Ape Man
Ten Fingers of Steel
Terminal Velocity
Terra-Cotta Warrior, A
That Lucky Touch
That Man Bolt
Thunder and Lightning
Thunderball
Thunderbolt and Lightfoot
Tigers Don't Cry
Tiger Shark
Till There Was You
Time After Time
Time and Tide
Tintorera
Tomorrow Never Dies
Too Hot to Handle
Top Gun
Top of the World
Toward the Unknown
Towering Inferno, The
Toy Soldiers
Treasure of the Four Crowns
Treasure of the Sierra Madre, The
True Lies
Tunnel, The
Turbulence
Turkey Shoot
Twin Dragons
Twister (Du Bont)
Two Lane Blacktop
Two Years Before the Mast

Uncommon Valor
Under Fire
Under Siege
Under Siege II
Universal Soldier
Universal Soldier: The Return
U.S. Marshals
Vendetta
Vertical Limit
Victory at Entebbe
View to a Kill, A
Vigilante Force
Villa Rides!
Viva Knievel!
Viva Maria!
Vixen
Volcano
Wages of Fear, The
Walkabout
War
Warriors, The
War Zone
Way of the Dragon, The
What Changed Charley Farthing
When the North Whiteout
Wind Blows
When Time Ran Out…
Where No Vultures Fly
White Dawn, The
White Fang (Fulci)
White Fang (Kleiser)
White Hell of Piz Palu, The
White Squall
White Tower, The
Who Dares Wins
Wilby Conspiracy, The
Wild Angels, The
Wild Geese, The
Wild Geese II
Wind
Wind Across the Everglades
Wind and the Lion, The
Windjammer, The
World Is Not Enough, The

Young Warriors
You Only Live Twice

Zulu
Zulu Dawn

Appendix 2

Children's Films

Adventures of Frontier Fremont, The
Adventures of Huck Finn, The
Adventures of Mark Twain, The
Adventures of Milo and Otis,The
Adventures of Pinocchio, The
Adventures of Rocky & Bullwinkle, The
Adventures of Tom Sawyer, The
Aladdin
All Creatures Great and Small
All Dogs Go to Heaven
All I Want for Christmas
Amazing Mr. Blunden, The
American Tail, An
American Tail: Fievel Goes West, An
Anastasia
Andre
Anne of Green Gables
Antz
Aristocats, The
Asterix & Obelix Take on Caesar
Asterix and the Big Fight
Asterix Conquers America
Asterix in Britain
Atlantis – The Lost Empire

Babar: The Movie
Babe
Babe – Pig in the City
Baby – Secret of the Lost Legend
Ball, The
Bambi
Barney's Great Adventure
Beauty and the Beast (Trousdale/Wise)
Belstone Fox, The
Benji
Best of Walt Disney's True Life Adventures, The
Biggles
Big Mouth, The
Big Wheels and Sailor
Black Beauty
Black Cauldron, The
Black Stallion, The
Black Stallion Returns, The
BMX Bandits
Borrowers, The
Boy Named Charlie Brown, A
Boy Who Could Fly, The
Brave Litte Toaster, The
Bug's Life, A
Bugsy Malone
Buster's World

Captain Stirrick
Care Bears Adventure in Wonderland, The
Care Bears Movie, The
Casper
Cat From Outer Space, The
Cats & Dogs
Charlotte's Web
Cheetah
Children of Heaven
Children's Midsummer Night's Dream, The
Chitty Chitty Bang Bang
Christmas Carol – The Movie
Cinderella
Clarence, the Cross-Eyed Lion
Colour of Paradise, The
Courage Mountain

Daemon
Danny the Champion of the World
Darby O'Gill and the Little People
Dark Enemy
Digby – The Biggest Dog in the World
Digimon Digital Monsters – The Movie
Dimples
Disney's The Kid
Dr Dolittle
Doctor Dolittle 2
Dr Seuss's How the Grinch Stole Christmas
Dougal and the Blue Cat
Doug's 1st Movie
Dumbo
Dunston Checks In

Emil & the Detectives
Escape from the Dark
Escape to Witch Mountain
Ewok Adventure, The

FairyTale – A True Story
Far from Home: The Adventures of Yellow Dog
Father, The
Feast at Midnight
Felix the Cat: The Movie
FernGully: The Last Rainforest
Flintstones, The
Flipper
Fly Away Home
Fox and the Hound, The
Freddie as F.R.O.7.
Free Willy
Free Willy II
Free Willy 3: The Rescue
Frog Dreaming

George of the Jungle
Gift, The
Girl with Brains in Her Feet, The
Glitterball, The
GoBots: Battle of the Rocklords
Golden Seal, The
Goonies, The
Grandma and Her Ghosts
Great Mouse Detective, The
Gulliver's Travels

Hambone and Hillie
Hard Road
Harriet the Spy
Harry and the Hendersons
Harry Potter and the Philosopher's Stone
Heidi's Song
Help! I'm a Fish
Herbie Goes Bananas
Herbie Goes to Monte Carlo
Herbie Rides Again
Hercules
Huckleberry Finn
Hugo the Hippo

Ice Age
Ichabod and Mr Toad
Ikíngut
Incredible Journey, The
Indian in the Cupboard, The
International Velvet
It Shouldn't Happen to a Vet

James and the Giant Peach
Jetsons: The Movie
Jingle All the Way
Journey of Natty Gann, The
Jungle Book, The (Reitherman)
Jungle Book, The (Sommers)
Just Ask for Diamond

King and I, The (Rich)
King of the Wind

Lady and the Tramp
Land Before Time, The
Last Flight of Noah's Ark, The
Last Unicorn, The
Lion King, The
Little Mermaid, The
Little Nemo Adventures in Slumberland
Little Princess, A
Little Rascals, The
London Connection, The

Madeline
Magic Sword: Quest for Camelot, The
Mighty Morphin Power Ranger: The Movie
Mighty Mouse in the Great Space Chase
Miracle on 34th Street
Mister Skeeter
Monsters, Inc.
Mouse and His Child, The
Mulan
Muppet Christmas Carol, The
Muppet Movie, The
Muppets Take Manhattan, The
Muppet Treasure Island
My Little Pony

Namu, The Killer Whale
Napoleon and Samantha
NeverEnding Story, The
NeverEnding Story II: The Next Chapter, The
NeverEnding Story III: Escape from Fantasia, The
Night Crossing
Nightmare Before Christmas, The
North Avenue Irregulars, The

Oliver & Company
Once Upon a Forest
One Hundred and One Dalmatians (Reitherman/ Luske/Geronimi)
101 Dalmatians (Herek)
102 Dalmatians
One of Our Dinosaurs Is Missing

Pagemaster, The
Paulie
Peter Pan
Pete's Dragon
Phantom Tollbooth, The
Pied Piper, The
Pinocchio
Pinocchio and the Emperor of the Night
Pippi Longstocking
Point, The
Pokémon – The First Movie: Mewtwo Strikes Back
Pokémon 2: The Power of One
Pokémon 3: Spell of the Unown
Prince of Egypt, The
Princess Bride, The

Railway Children, The
Rescuers, The
Rescuers Down Under, The
Return from Witch Mountain
Richie Rich
Ride a Wild Pony
Road to El Dorado, The
Roald Dahl's Matilda
Robin Hood (Reitherman)
Rock-a-Doodle
Rugrats in Paris: The Movie
Rugrats Movie, The

Scalawag
School for Vandals
Sea Gypsies, The
Secret Garden, The (Wilcox)
Secret Garden, The (Holland)
Secret of NIMH, The
Secret of the Sword, The
Short Circuit
Short Circuit 2
Shrek
Singing Ringing Tree, The
Sleeping Beauty
Small Soldiers
Snow White and the Seven Dwarfs
Song of the South
Spy Kids
Starchaser: The Legend of Orin
Star Kid
Stuart Little
Suburban Commando
Summer Magic

Tadpole and the Whale
Tarka the Otter
Tarzan
Teenage Mutant Ninja Turtles
Teenage Mutant Ninja Turtles II: The Secret of the Ooze
Teenage Mutant Ninja Thomas and the Magic Railroad
Turtles III
Terry on the Fence
3 Ninja Kids
Thumbelina
Tiger Walks, A
Tommy Tricker and the Stamp Traveller
Tom's Midnight Garden
Tom Thumb
Toy Story
Toy Story 2
Twelve Tasks of Asterix, The

Warriors of Virtue
Water Babies, The
Watership Down
What Next?
When the Whales Came
Whistle Down the Wind
Willy Wonka and the Chocolate Factory
Wind in the Willows,
Wolves of Willoughby Chase, The
Wombling Free

Young Sherlock Holmes

Appendix 3

Comedy

Abel
Abbott and Costello Meet Frankenstein
Accidental Hero
Ace Ventura, Pet Detective
Ace Ventura – When Nature Calls
Adam's Rib
Addams Family, The
Addams Family Values
Addicted to Love
Adhemar ou Le Jouet de la Fatalité
Admirable Crichton, The
Adolf Hitler – My Part in His Downfall
Adrenaline Drive
Advance to the Rear
Adventure in Baltimore
Adventures of a Private Eye
Adventure of Sherlock Holmes' Smarter Brother
Adventures of Barry McKenzie, The
Adventures of Ford Fairlane, The
Adventures of Gerard, The
Affairs of Annabel, The
Affair to Remember, An
After Hours
A-Haunting We Will Go
Aile ou la Cuisse, L'
Air America
Air Bud
Airheads
Airplane!
Airplane II the Sequel
A l'attaque!
Alfredo Alfredo
Alice (Allen)
All Night Long
All of Me
All or Nothing
All Through the Night
Almost an Angel
Almost You
Alvin Purple
Amazon Women on the Moon
Ambulance, The
American Tickler or The Winner of 10 Academy Awards
American Dreamer
American Graffiti
Americanization of Emily, The
American Pie
American Pie 2
American Success Company, The
American Way, The
American Werewolf in London, An
Analyze This
And Now for Something Completely Different
Angels in the Outfield
Animal Crackers
Animalympics
Annie Hall
Anniversary, The
Another Man, Another Woman
Another You
A Nous la Liberté
Any Which Way You Can
Apartment, The
Apple Dumpling
Appointment with Venus
Apprentis, Les
April Fools, The
Are You Being Served?
Armed and Dangerous
Army of Darkness: The Medieval Dead
Arnold
Arsenic and Old Lace
Arthur
Arthur 2: On the Rocks
Artists and Models
Art of Love
Ashanti
Ask Any Girl
Asking for Trouble
Associate, The
Assassination Bureau, The
Attack on a Gas Station!
Attack of the Killer Tomatoes
At the Circus
Auberge Rouge, L'
Austin Powers: International Man of Mystery
Austin Powers: The Spy Who Shagged Me
Author! Author!
Avanti!
Awful Truth, The
Ay! Carmela

Baby Boom
Baby's Day Out
Bachelor, The
Bachelor Mother
Back-Room Boy
Back to School
Back to the Future
Back to the Future Part II
Back to the Future Part III
Bad News Bears, The
Bagdad Café

Baisers Volés
Ball of Fire
Bamboozled
Bananas
Bank Dick, The
Bank Holiday
Bank Shot
BAPS
Barefoot in the Park
Bargee, The
Barking Dogs Never Bite
Barnacle Bill
Battle of the Sexes, The
Battling Butler
Beaches
Bean
Beavis and Butt-head Do America
Bedazzled (Donen)
Bedazzled (Ramis)
Bedknobs and Broomsticks
Bedrooms and Hallways
Bed Sitting Room, The
Beetlejuice
Beethoven
Beethoven's 2nd
Being There
Bellboy, The
Belle Fille comme moi, Une
Belles of St Trinian's, The
Bellissima
Bernie
Best Age, The
Best Defence
Best Friends
Best in Show
Best Men
Best of Times, The
Betsy's Wedding
Better Late Than Never
Betty Boop Follies, The
Beverly Hillbillies, The
Bewegte Mann, Der
Beyond Therapy
Beyond the Valley of the Dolls
Big
Big Animal, The
Big Banana Feet
Big Bus, The
Big Business
Big Fella
Big Girls Don't Cry… They Get Even
Big Job, The
Big Lebowski, The
Big Meat Eater
Big Momma's House
Big Night
Big Picture, The
Big Steal, The (Tass)
Big Store, The
Big Top Pee-Wee
Bill & Ted's Bogus Journey
Bill & Ted's Excellent Adventure
Biloxi Blues
Bingo Long Travelling All Stars & Motor Kings, The
Birdcage, The
Bird on a Wire
Birds and the Bees, The
Bishop's Wife, The
Blackbeard's Ghost
Black Bird, The
Black Cat White Cat
Black Joy
Black Sheep
Black Sheep of Whitehall, The
Blame It on Rio
Blame It on the Bellboy
Blank Check
Blast from the Past
Blazing Saddles
Blind Date (Edwards)
Bliss of Mrs Blossom, The
Blithe Spirit
Blockheads
Blondie
Blood and Concrete
Blow Dry

Bluebeard's Eighth Wife
Blue Mountains
Blue Murder at St Trinian's
Blume in Love
Bob & Carol & Ted & Alice
Bobo, The
Bob Roberts
Bollywood Calling
Bonnie Scotland
Book of Love
Book That Wrote Itself, The
Boomerang (Hudlin)
Born Yesterday (Cukor)
Born Yesterday (Madoki)
Boudu Sauvé des Eaux
Bowfinger
Boy Meets Girl
Boys in Blue, The
Boys Will Be Boys
Brady Bunch Movie, The
Braindead
Bread and Chocolate
Breakfast at Tiffany's
Breakfast of Champions
Breaking In
Brewster's Millions (Dwan)
Brewster's Millions (Hill)
Bridget Jones's Diary
Brighton Beach Memoirs
Bringing Up Baby
Broadway Bill
Broadway Bound
Broadway Danny Rose
Bronzés, Les
Brother from Another Planet, The
Brothers in Law
Brutti, porchi e cattivi
BS I Love You
Buddy Buddy
Buddy's Song
Buffalo '66
Buffy the Vampire Slayer
Bulldog Jack
Bull Durham
Bullets Over Broadway
Bullseye!
Bullshot
Bulworth
Bunny O'Hare
Buona Sera, Mrs Campbell
'burbs, The
Bus Stop
Bustin' Loose
Butcher's Wife, The
Buttoners

Cabaret Balkan
Cable Guy, The
Cadillac Man
Canadian Bacon
Candy
Candy Mountain
Cannery Row
Cannibal Women in the Avocado Jungle of Death
Cannonball Run, The
Cannonball Run II
Can She Bake a Cherry Pie?
Can't Buy Me Love
Can You Keep It Up for a Week?
Caporal Epinglé, Le
Caprice
Captain Jack
Captain Ron
Captain's Paradise, The
Captain's Table, The
Carbon Copy
Card, The
Carry On Admiral
Carry On Columbus
Carry On Sergeant
Car Trouble
Car Wash
Casanova's Big Night
Casino Royale
Castle, The
Casual Sex?
Cat and the Canary, The (Leni)

Cat and the Canary, The (Metzger)
Cat Ballou
Catch Me a Spy
Cat's-Paw, The
Ça va Barder…
Cecil B. Demented
Celebrity
Chain, The
Champagne Charlie
Chance of a Lifetime
Chapter Two
Charles and Lucie
Chateau, The
Cheap Detective, The
Cheaper by the Dozen
Checking Out
Cheech & Chong's Next Movie
Cheer, Boys, Cheer
Chicken and Duck Talk
Chicken Run
Chikin Bizniz
Chiltern Hundreds, The
Chorus of Disapproval, A
Christmas in July
Christmas Story, A
'Chubby' Down Under and Other Sticky Regions
Chuck & Buck
Chump at Oxford, A
Cinderfella
Circus, The
Citizens Band
City Lights
City Slickers
City Slickers II: The Legend of Curly's Gold
Class
Class of Nuke 'Em High
Claudine
Clerks
Clinic, The
Clockwise
Closely Observed Trains
Closer You Get, The
Club de Femmes
Cluny Brown
Coca Cola Kid, The
Cocoanuts, The
Cocoon
Cocoon: The Return
Cold Comfort Farm
Cold Dog Soup
Cold Feet
Cold Turkey
College
Come Blow Your Horn
Comedy of Terrors, The
Come on George
Come Play with Me
Comfort and Joy
Comic Magazine
Coming to America
Coming Up Roses
Confessions from a Holiday Camp
Confessions of a Bigamist
Confessions of a Driving Instructor
Confessions of a Pop Performer
Confessions of a Window Cleaner
Confucian Confusion, A
Consul, The
Consuming Passions
Conte d'Automne
Convoyeurs Attendent, Les
Cookie
Cool Runnings
Cop & ½
Couch Trip, The
Country Dance
Coupe de Ville
Courage, Fuyons
Court Jester, The
Coyote Ugly
Cracksman, The
Crazy Family
Crazy Mama
Crazy People
Creator

Cremator, The
Crime Busters
Crossing Delancey
Crooks' Tour
Cruel Intentions
Cry-Baby
Curdled
Curly Sue
Curse of the Pink Panther
Curtain Call
Cutting It Short
Cyclone, The

Daddy's Dyin' – Who's Got the Will?
Dad's Army
Daisies
Dance, Girl, Dance
Danger – Love at Work
Dark Habits
Darling Lili
Dave
David Holzman's Diary
Day at the Races, A
Daydream Believer
Day for Night
Day the Fish Came Out, The
D.C. Cab
Dead Men Don't Wear Plaid
Death Becomes Her
Death in Brunswick
Decline and Fall…of a Birdwatcher!
Deconstructing Harry
Deep End
Defending Your Life
Delicate Delinquent, The
Delirious
Dennis the Menace
Dentist in the Chair
Dernier Milliardaire, Le
Desert Mice
Design for Living
Designing Woman
Desire
Desk Set
Desperate Living
Desperately Seeking Susan
Deuce Bigalow: Male Gigolo
Devil and Max Devlin, The
Devil and Miss Jones, The
Devils on the Doorstep
Diary of a Mad Housewife
Didn't You Kill My Brother?
Different Story, A
Dîner de cons, Le
Dinner at Eight
Dirty Rotten Scoundrels
Dish, The
Disorderly Orderly, The
Distinguished Gentleman, The
Disturbed
Divine Intervention
Divorce American Style
Divorcing Jack
Doc Hollywood
Docteur Popaul
Doctor in the House
Dr Jekyll and Ms Hyde
Dr Strangelove: or, How I Learned to Stop Worrying and Love the Bomb
Dog Eat Dog
Dogma
Dogpound Shuffle
Doña Flor and Her Two Husbands
Doña Herlinda and Her Son
Don Juan DeMarco
Do Not Disturb
Don't Just Lie There, Say Something!
Don't Make Waves
Don't Take it To Heart
Don't Tell Her It's Me
Don't Tell Mom the Babysitter's Dead
Do the Right Thing
Double Agent 73
Down Among the Z Men

Down and Out in Beverly Hills
Down by Law
Down Memory Lane
Down Periscope
Down to Earth
Dracula: Dead and Loving It
Dragnet
Dramma della Gelosia
Dream Team, The
Drop Dead Fred
Dry Rot
Duck Soup
Dudes
Dude, Where's My Car?
Duets
Dumb & Dumber
Dunston Checks In
During the Summer
Dutch
Dynamite Chicken

Early Bird, The
East is East
Easy Living
Easy Money
Eating Raoul
Eat the Rich
Ecole des Facteurs, L'
Eddie
Eddie Murphy Raw
Educating Rita
8 Heads in a Duffel Bag
18 Again!
Electric Moon
Eléna et les Hommes
Emmerdeur,L'
Emperor's New Groove, The
Encino Man
End, The
End of the Road
End Play
Entertaining Mr Sloane
Epoque formidable..., Une
Equinox
Ernest Saves Christmas
Everybody Dance
Every Little Crook and Nanny
Everything You Always Wanted to Know About Sex But Were Afraid to Ask
Every Which Way But Loose
Experts, The

Face in the Crowd, A
Falling For You
Family Business (Lumet)
Family Game
Family Jewels, The
Fandango
Fanny & Elvis
Fantome du Moulin Rouge, Le
Farmer's Wife, The
Fast Food, Fast Women
Fast Lady, The
Fast Talking
Fast Times at Ridgemont High
Fatal Beauty
Father Brown
Father Goose
Father of the Bride (Minnelli)
Father of the Bride (Shyer)
Father of the Bride Part II
Fathers' Day
Favourites of the Moon
Favour, the Watch and the Very Big Fish, The
Fear of a Black Hat
Feds
Feet First
Female Trouble
Femme du Boulanger, La
Ferris Bueller's Day Off
Fiancée du Pirate, La
Fiddlers Three
Fierce Creatures
5th Avenue Girl
51st Sate, The
Filofax
Fils de Deux Mères ou Comédie de l'Innocence

Finances of the Grand Duke, The
Finding North
Fine Madness, A
Firemen's Ball, The
First Effort
Fish Called Wanda, A
Flamingo Kid, The
Flap
Fletch
Fletch Lives
Flim-Flam Man, The
Flintstones in Viva Rock Vegas, The
Flubber
Folies Bergère
Folks!
Follow a Star
Folly to be Wise
Footman, The
Forces of Nature
Foreign Affair, A
For Keeps
For Love or Money
For Pete's Sake
Fortunat
Fortune, The
Fortune Cookie, The
Foul Play
Four Weddings and a Funeral
Fracture du myocarde, La
Francis
Freaked
Freaky Friday
French Mistress, A
French Mustard
French Without Tears
Freshman, The
Friday
Front Page
Front Page, The (Milestone)
Front Page, The (Wilder)
Front Page Woman
Full Monty, The
Full Moon in Blue Water
Full of Life
Funeral Rites
Funny About Love
Fun With Dick and Jane

Gabriel Over the White House
Galaxy Quest
Garde du Corps, Le
Gasbags
Gas-s-s-s, or it became necessary to destroy the world in order to save it
'Gator
Gazebo, The
Gazon maudit
Geisha Boy, The
General, The
Genevieve
Gentlemen Prefer Blondes
Gen-X Cops
Gen-Y Cops
German Chainsaw Massacre, The
George and Mildred
Georgy Girl
Gert and Daisy's Weekend
Get Real
Getting Any
Getting It Right
Getting Straight
Ghost and Mrs Muir, The
Ghost Breakers, The
Ghostbusters
Ghostbusters II
Ghost Catchers
Ghost Chase, The
Ghost Goes West, The
Ghost of St Michael's, The
Ginger & Fred
Girl from Maxim's, The
Girl in Every Port, A
Girl in the Picture, The
Girl Shy
Global Affair, A
Go for a Take
Going in Style

Going Steady
Golden Coach, The
Gold Rush, The
Good Burger
Goodbye, Columbus
Goodbye Girl, The
Good Morning, Boys!
Good Morning Vietnam
Goofy Movie, A
Go West (Keaton)
Go West (Buzzell)
Grace Quigley
Graduate, The
Grand Amour, Le
Grandma's Boy
Grazie Zia
Greased Lightning
Great Dictator, The
Great McGinty, The
Great McGonagall, The
Great Man Votes, The
Great White Hype, The
Green Card
Green Ice Greetings
Greenkeeping
Green Man, The
Gregory's Girl
Groundhog Day
Groove Tube, The
Grosse Point Blank
Guerre des boutons, La
Guest House Paradiso
Guide for the Married Man, A
Gumball Rally, The
Gumshoe
Guru in Seven

Hail the Conquering Hero
Hairspray
Hallelujah the Hills
Hamlet Goes Business
Hands Across the Table
Hanky Panky
Happening, The
Happiest Days of Your Life, The
Happiness
Happy Birthday Wanda June
Happy Gilmore
Happy Hooker, The
Happy Texas
Happy Time
Hardbodies
Hard Day's Night, A
Hard to Handle
Hard Way, The
Harlem Nights
Harold and Maude
Harry and Tonto
Harry and Walter Go to New York
Harvey
Harvey Middleman, Fireman
Has Anybody Seen My Gal
Haunted Honeymoon
Having It All
Hawks
Head
Head over Heels
Health
Hear My Song
Heartbreakers
Heartbreak Kid, The
Heart Condition
Heathers
Heaven Can Wait (Lubitsch)
Heaven Can Wait (Beatty/Henry)
Heaven Help Us
Heavenly Pursuits
Heavens Above
Hello Again
Hell of a Day, A
Hellzapoppin'
Help!
Her Alibi
Herod's Law
Hercules Returns
Here We Go Round the Mulberry Bush
Her Majesty, Love

Hero at Large
Héros très discret, Un
High Anxiety
High Hopes
High School High
High Spirits
Hi, Mom!
Hi, Nellie!
His Girl Friday
Histoire inventée, Une
History of the World Part One
Hobson's Choice
Hocus Pocus
Hog Wild
Hold Me, Thrill Me, Kiss Me
Hole in the Head, A
Holiday
Hollywood or Bust
Hollywood Shuffle
Holy Man
Home Alone
Home Alone 2: Lost in New York
Home Alone 3
Homebodies
Home for the Holidays
Homework
Homme de Marrakech, L'
Honey, I Blew Up the Kid
Honey, I Shrunk the Kids
Honeymoon in Vegas
Honey Pot, The
Honky Tonk Freeway
Hooper
Hoots Mon!
Hopscotch
Horse Feathers
Hospital, The
Hôtel de la Plage, L'
Hotel de Love
Hotel Sahara
Hot Enough for June
Hot Rock, The
Hot Shots!
Hot Shots! Part Deux
Hot Stuff
Hot Times
House!
House Calls
House on Trubnaya, The
House Party
Housesitter
How I Won the War
How to Be Very, Very Popular
How to Commit Marriage
How to Get Ahead in Advertising
How to Marry a Millionaire
Huggetts Abroad, The
Husbands and Wives

Iceland
Icicle Thief
Idle on Parade
If I Had a Million
I Hired a Contract Killer
Ikinai
I Love Trouble
I Love You Again
I Love You, Alice B. Toklas!
I Love, You Love
I Love You to Death
I'm All Right, Jack
I'm Gonna Git You Sucka
I Married a Witch
Importance of Being Earnest, The
Impostors, The
Incredible Shrinking Woman, The
Indiscreet
In July
In-Laws, The
Innocents in Paris
International House
In the Spirit
Intimate Games
Invitation, The
I Ought to Be in Pictures
Irma la Douce
Ishtar

Is there Sex After Marriage?
It Came from Hollywood
It Happened One Night
I Think I Do
It's a Gift
It's a Mad, Mad, Mad, Mad World
It's a 2'6" Above the Ground World
It's Great to Be Young
It Should Happen to You
It's Love I'm After
It's Only Money
It Started in Naples
It Started With Eve
It's the Old Army Game
It Takes Two
It Was an Accident
I Wanna Hold Your Hand
I Want to Go Home
I Was a Male War Bride
I Was Born, But
I Was on Mars
I Will…I Will…for Now

Jabberwocky
Jack
Jack Frost
Jake Speed
Jane and the Lost City
Jay and Silent Bob Strike Back
Jerk, The
Jerry Maguire
Jimmy the Kid
Jit
Jitterbugs
Johnny Suede
Jolly Bad Fellow, A
Jolly Boys' Last Stand
Josie and the Pussycats
Jour de Fête
Juha
Julia Has Two Lovers
Jumping for Joy
Jumpin' Jack Flash
Jump Tomorrow
Junior
Just Another Date
Just Like a Woman
Just the Ticket
Just Visiting

Keep Cool
Keeping the Faith
Keep It Up, Jack!
Kentucky Fried Movie, The
Kermesse Héroique, La
Kevin & Perry Go Large
Kicked in the Head
Kick the Moon
Kid, The
Kid Brother, The
Kids in the Hall: Brain Candy
Kids Return
Killer Klowns from Outer Space
Killing Dad
Kindergarten Cop
Kind Hearts and Coronets
Kingdom, The
Kingdom II, The
King in New York, A
King of Hearts
Kingpin
King Ralph
King Ubu
Kissing a Fool
Kiss Me Goodbye
Kiss Me, Stupid
Kleiner Liebt Mich
Klondike Annie
Knack… and how to get it, The
Knave of Hearts
Knickers Ahoy
K-9
Knock on Wood

Labyrinth of Passion
Ladies' Man, The (Lewis)
Ladies Man, The (Hudlin)
Lady Eve, The
Lady Godiva Rides Again
Lady Killer
Ladykillers, The
Landlord, The
Larger Than Life
Lásky Jedné Plavovlásky (A Blonde in Love)
Last Boy Scout, The
Last Holiday
Last Italian Tango, The
Last Married Couple in America, The
Last of the Red Hot Lovers
LA Story
Late for Dinner
Laughter in Paradise
Lavender Hill Mob, The
Law and Disorder
Laxdale Hall
League of Gentlemen, The
Le Cop
Le Cop 2
Left, Right and Centre
Legally Blonde
Leon the Pig Farmer
Leningrad Cowboys Go America
Lenny Bruce Performance Film, The
Lenny Bruce Without Tears
Lenny Live and Unleashed
Let It Ride
Let's Do It Again
Let's Get Laid!
Let's Hope It's A Girl
Let the People Sing
Lewis & Clark & George
Liar Liar
Libero Burro
Libert Heights
Licence to Live
Life
Life Is a Long Quiet River
Life Is Cheap…But Toilet Paper Is Expensive
Life Is Sweet
Life Less Ordinary, A
Life Stinks
Life of Stuff, The
Like Father, Like Son
Likely Lads, The
Lily Tomlin
Limey, The
Limit Up
Lincoln County Incident
Linguini Incident, The
Little City
Little Hut, The
Little Shop of Horrors, The (Corman)
Littlest Rebel, The
Little Tony
Lonely in America
Loners
Long Live the Lady!
Long Shot
Long Way Home
Look Who's Talking
Look Who's Talking Now
Look Who's Talking Too
Loose Cannons
Lord Love a Duck
Loser
Losers
Losin' It
Lost in America
Lost Paradise, The
Love and Death
Love and Other Catastrophes
Love at First Bite
Love Crazy
Loved One, The
Love Happy
Love in the Afternoon (Wilder)
Love on the Run
Loverboy
Lovers!, The
Lovesick
Love Test, The
Loving
Lock Up Your Daughters!
Lonely Hearts
Lukewarm Water Under the Red Bridge
Luna e l'Altra
Lunatic, The

Macunaima
Mad Adventures of 'Rabbi' Jacob, The
Made
Made in America
Madhouse
Mad Miss Manton, The
Magnificent Seven Deadly Sins, The
Magnificent Two, The
Maids
Main Event, The
Major and the Minor, The
Major League
Major League II
Make Mine a Million
Making Mr Right
Malcolm
Malizia
Man Alive
Man, a Woman and a Bank, A
Man Friday
Man from Africa and Girl from India
Manhattan
Man of the House
Manolito Four-Eyes
Manifesto
Man in the White Suit, The
Man Is Not a Bird
Mannequin
Mannequin 2: On the Move
Man of the Moment
Man on the Flying Trapeze, The
Man's Favorite Sport?
Man Trouble
Man Who Came to Dinner, The
Man With Two Brains, The
Married to the Mob
Marrying Kind, The
Marrying Man, The
Mars Attacks!
Martins, The
Masala
Matinee
Matinee Idol, The
Matter of Honour, A
Mazel Tov ou le mariage
Meet the Applegates
Meet the Parents
Memoirs of an Invisible Man
Me, Myself & Irene
Me Myself I
Men at Work
Merci pour le chocolat
Mermaids
Métisse
Metropolitan
Me You Them
Micki + Maude
Mickey Blue Eyes
Midnight
Midsummer Night's Sex Comedy, A
Mighty Aphrodiet
Milk
Million, Le
Millionairess, The
Million Pound Note, The
Milou en mai
Miracle of Morgan's Creek, The
Miracles
Miss Congeniality
Missionary, The
Miss Robin Hood
Mr and Mrs Smith
Mr Billion
Mr Blandings Builds His Dream House
Mister Cory
Mr Deeds Goes to Town
Mr Drake's Duck
Mr Hobbs Takes a Vacation
Mr Jolly Lives Next Door
Mr Mom
Mr Nanny
Mr Peabody and the Mermaid
Mr Saturday Night
Mr Smith Goes to Washington
Mistress
Mrs Pollifax – Spy
Mixed Company
Mixed Nuts
Modern Times
Modesty Blaise
Moment d'Egarement, Un
Mo' Money
Mondo Trasho
Money Pit, The
Monkey Business (McLeod)
Monkey Business (Hawks)
Mon Oncle
Mon Père, ce héros
Monsieur Verdoux
Monty Python and the Holy Grail
Monty Python's Life of Brian
Monty Python's Meaning of Life
Moon is Blue, The
Moon Over Parador
Moonstruck
More American Graffiti
More Bad News
More the Merrier, The
Morgan, a Suitable Case for Treatment
Morons from Outer Space
Moscow on the Hudson
Mother, Jugs & Speed
MouseHunt
Mouse on the Moon, The
Mouse that Roared, The
Movie Crazy
Movie Movie
Moving
Mozart in Love
Multiplicity
Murder By Death
Murder, He Says
Muse, The
Mutiny on the Buses
My Best Friend's Girl
My Best Friend's Wedding
My Blue Heaven
My Cousin Vinny
My Dad Is a Jerk
My Father Is Coming
My Favorite Blonde
My Favorite Brunette
My Favorite Wife
My Favorite Year
My Girl
My Girl II
My Learned Friend
My Little Chickadee
My Man Godfrey (La Cava)
My Man Godfrey (Koster)
My New Gun
Myra Breckinridge
My Silly Mother
My Stepmother Is an Alien
Mystery Men
Mystery of the Leaping Fish, The
My Young Auntie

Nadine
Naked Gun, The
Naked Gun 2½: The Smell of Fear, The
Naked Gun 33⅓
Naked Man, The
Naked Truth, The
Nasty Habits
National Lampoon Goes to the Movies
National Lampoon's Animal House
National Lampoon's Class Reunion
National Lampoon's Loaded Weapon 1
National Lampoon's Vacation
Navigator, The

Necessary Roughness
Neighbors
Never Give a Sucker an Even Break
Never on Sunday
Never Say Die
New Leaf, A
New Morning of Billy the Kid, The
Next Friday
Next Stop, Greenwich Village
Nick Carter in Prague
Nickelodeon
Night After Night
Night at the Opera, A
Night at the Roxbury, A
Night in Casablanca, A
Night Shift
Nine Lives of Fritz the Cat, The
1988: The Remake
1941
Nine to Five
Ninotchka
Nobody's Fool
No Deposit, No Return
Noises Off
Norman…Is That You?
Norman Loves Rose
Northerners, The
No Surrender
Not for Publication
Nothing in Common
Nothing to Lose
Nothing Sacred
Not Now, Comrade
Notre Histoire
Notting Hill
Novocaine
No Way to Treat a Lady
Nude Bomb, The
Nuns on the Run
Nutty Professor, The (Lewis)
Nutty Professor, The (Shadyac)
Nutty Professor II: The Klumps

O.C. & Stiggs
Ocean's 11 (Milestone)
Ocean's Eleven (Soderbergh)
Odd Couple, The
Odd Couple II, The
Odd Job, The
Off and Running
Off Beat
Oh, God!
Oh, Men! Oh, Women!
Oh, Mr Porter
O-Kay for Sound
Old-Fashioned Way, The
Old Flames
Old Lady Who Walked in the Sea, The
On Approval
Once Upon a Honeymoon
Once Upon a Time
One and Only, The
One Flew Over the Cuckoo's Nest
One Hamlet Less
One More Time
One, Two, Three
Only Game in Town, The
Only the Lonely
Only Two Can Play
Only When I Laugh
On purge Bébé
On the Beat
On the Buses
Ooh…You Are Awful
Operation Petticoat
Orders are Orders
Orgazmo
Oscar
Osmosis Jones
Otesánek
Other People's Money
Otley
Our Hospitality
Our Man in Havana
Our Relations
Our Town
Outlaw Blues
Out of Order
Out-of-Towners, The (Hiller)
Out-of-Towners, The (Weisman)
Outrageous!
Outrageous Fortune
Overboard
Over Her Dead Body
Over the Brooklyn Bridge
Owl and the Pussycat, The
Oxford Blues

Pack Up Your Troubles
Paleface, The
Palm Beach Story, The
Palookaville
Papa, les Petits Bateaux…
Paper, The
Paperback Hero
Parade
Pardners
Pardon Mon Affaire
Pardon Mon Affaire, Too
Pardon Us
Parenthood
Parents
Parent Trap, The
Paris qui Dort
Parlor, Bedroom and Bath
Parole Officer, The
Parting Shots
Party, The
Party Party
Pas de Scandale
Passport to Pimlico
Pat and Mike
Paternity
Patsy, The
Paws
Pecker
Peeper
Pee-Wee's Big Adventure
Pelvis
People of the North Sea
People Will Talk
Percy
Percy's Progress
Perfect Couple, A
Perfectly Normal
Permis de Conduire, Le
Personal Services
Pete 'n' Tillie
Peter's Friends
Petomane, Il
Petticoat Pirates
Philadelphia Story, The
Philosopher's Stone, The
Pigs
Pillow Talk
Pink Panther, The
Pink Panther Strikes Again, The
Pirates
Plaff! or Too Afraid of Life
Planes, Trains and Automobiles
Platinum Blonde
Player, The
Play It Again, Sam
Playtime
Please Don't Eat the Daisies
Pleasure Principle, The
Plot Against Harry, The
Plunder
Police Academy
Police Academy 2: Their First Assignment
Police Academy 3: Back in Training
Police Academy 4: Citizens on Patrol
Police Academy 5: Assignment Miami Beach
Police Academy 6: City Under Siege
Police Academy 7: Mission to Moscow
Polyester
Pope Must Die, The
Porky's
Porky's II: The Next Day
Porky's Revenge
Porridge
Postman Blues
Posto, Il
Pot Luck
Pourquoi pas moi?
Practical Magic
Préparez Vos Mouchoirs
President's Analyst, The
Press for Time
Pretty Woman
Primrose Path, The
Prince and the Showgirl, The
Prisoner of Second Avenue, The
Prisoner of Zenda, The (Quine)
Private Benjamin
Private Club
Private Function, A
Private Parts
Privates on Parade
Private's Progress
Producers, The
Promise Her Anything
Protocol
P Tinto's Miracle
Pulp
Punch-Drunk Love
Punchline
Punch Me in the Stomach
Pure Hell of St Trinian's, The
Pure Luck
Purple Rose of Cairo, The
Pushing Hands
Putney Swope
Pyrates

Queenie in Love
Queen of Hearts
Quick
Quick Change
Quiet Man, The

Radio Days
Rain or Shine
Raising Arizona
Raising the Wind
Rake's Progress, The
Rally 'round the Flag, Boys!
Randonneurs, Les
Ratboy
Rat Race
Raven, The (Corman)
Reaching for the Moon
Ready to Rumble
Real Genius
Real Life
Real Blonde, The
Real Howard Spitz, The
Rebel, The
Recess: School's Out
Remember Last Night?
Remember Me?
Remember the Night
Rentadick
Repo Man
Repossessed
Restless Natives
Return of Captain Invincible, The
Return of the Pink Panther, The
Reuben, Reuben
Revenge of the Nerds
Revenge of the Pink Panther
Rhubarb
Richard Pryor… Here & Now
Richard Pryor Live in Concert
Richard Pryor Live on the Sunset Strip
Rien ne va plus
Rien sur Robert
Riff-Raff
Rigolboche
Rise and Rise of Michael Rimmer, The
Rising Damp
Risky Business
Rita, Sue and Bob Too
Ritz, The
Roadie
Road to Morocco
Road to Utopia
Road Trip
Robin Hood – Men in Tights
Rock-a-Bye Baby
Rockets Galore
Rock'n'Roll High School
Roger Corman's Frankenstein Unbound
Romance with a Double Bass
Roman d'un Tricheur, Le
Roman Holiday
Romuald et Juliette
Romy and Michelle's High School Reunion
Rookery Nook
Room Service
Rosalie Goes Shopping
Rosie Dixon, Night Nurse
Rotten to the Core
Roxanne
Roxie Hart
Royal Tenenbaums, The
Rude Awakening
Ruggles of Red Gap
Ruling Class, The
Run for Your Money, A
Rushmore
Ruthless People

Sabrina
Safe Men
Safety Last
Sailor Beware
Sallah
Salt & Pepper
Salvation! Have You Said Your Prayers Today?
Same Time, Next Year
Santa Clause, The
Saphead, The
Saps at Sea
Saturday the 14th
Sauvage, Le
Savage Honeymoon
Saving Grace
Saving Silverman
Say It Isn't So
Scary Movie
Scenes from a Mall
Scenes from the Class Struggle in Beverly Hills
Schizopolis
School Daze
School for Scoundrels
Schtonk!
Screwballs
Screwballs II – Loose Screws
Scrooges
Seclusion Near a Forest
Secret Admirer
Secret Agent Club, The
Secret Life of an American Wife, The
Secret of Santa Vittoria, The
Secret Policeman's Ball, The
Secret Policeman's Other Ball, The
Secret Policeman's Third Ball, The
Seems Like Old Times
See No Evil, Hear No Evil
See Spot Run
Semi-Tough
Senator Was Indiscreet, The
Send Me No Flowers
Seniors, The
Sgt Bilko
Serial Lover
Serial Mom
Seven Chances
Seven Year Itch, The
Sex and the Single Girl
Sex Shop
Sexy Beast
Shadows and Fog
Shaggy D.A., The
Shakespeare in Love
Shallow Hal
Shall We Dance?
Shanghai Surprise
She-Devil

She Done Him Wrong
Sherlock Junior
She's Gotta Have It
She's Having a Baby
She's Out of Control
Shirley Valentine
Short Time
Shot in the Dark, A
Sibling Rivalry
Sidewalk Stories
Silence of the Hams, The
Silent Movie
Silver Bears
Silver Streak
Simon
Singles
Sin of Harold Diddlebock, The
Sir Henry at Rawlinson's End
Sister Act
Sister Act II: Back in the Habit
Sitcom
Sitting Ducks
Six Days Seven Nights
Skin Deep
Skinless Night
Ski Patrol
Skyline
Slacker
Sleeper
Sleepless in Seattle
Sleep With Me
Sliding Doors
Slight Case of Murder, A (Bacon)
Slight Case of Murder, A (Schachter)
Slightly Pregnant Man, The
Slogans
Slums of Beverly Hills
Smallest Show on Earth, The
Small Time Crooks
Smiles of a Summer Night
Smiling Ghost, The
Smoke Signals
Smokey and the Bandit
Smokey and the Bandit II
Snobs
Soapdish
S.O.B.
So Fine
Soft Top, Hard Shoulder
So I Married an Axe Murderer
Solarwarriors
Solid Gold Cadillac, The
Solitaire for 2
Soliti Ignoti, I
Somebody Killed Her Husband
Some Girls
Some Kind of Hero
Some Like It Hot
Something Big
Son in Law
Son of Paleface
Sons of the Desert
Soul Man
Soupirant, Le
Sour Grapes
Southern Yankee, A
Spaceballs
Space Cowboys
Spagnola, La
Spanish Fly
Special Treatment
Speedy
Spies Like Us
Spite Marriage
Spitfire
Splash
Splitting Heirs
Spotswood
Spy Hard
SPYS
Squeeze, The
Squibs
Stan and George's New Life
Stand-In
Stand Up, Don't Grovel!
Stand Up Virgin Soldiers
Stardust Memories
Stars and Bars
State and Main
State of the Union
Static
Stay Hungry
Stay Tuned
Steamboat Bill Jr
Steelyard Blues
Stiff Upper Lips
Still Crazy
Stir Crazy
Stop! or My Mom Will Shoot
Stork
Story of Us, The
Straight Talk
Straight to Hell
Strange Brew
Strictly Ballroom
Stripes
Strong Man, The
Stroszek
Stuart Saves His Family
Student Teachers, The
Stuff, The
Stunt Man, The
Stupids, The
Such Good Friends
Sugarbaby
Sugarland Express, The
Survivors, The
Sullivan's Travels
Summer School
Sweethearts
Sweetie
Sweet November
Swing
Switch
Sylvia Scarlett

Take the Money and Run
Taking Off
Tall Guy
Tampopo
Tango
Tank
Tant qu'on a la Santé
Tao of Steve, The
Tapeheads
Tatie Danielle
Taxi 2
Taxing Woman, A
Teahouse of the August Moon, The
Teen Wolf
Teen Wolf Too
Teeth
Telephone Book, The
'10'
Tenue de Soirée
That Gang of Mine
That Riviera Touch
That's Carry On
That Sinking Feeling
'That's Life'
That Summer!
Theodora Goes Wild
There's a Girl in My Soup
There's Something About Mary
They All Laughed
They Call Me Bruce
They Knew What They Wanted
They Might Be Giants
They're a Weird Mob
Things Change
30 Is a Dangerous Age, Cynthia
This Is My Life
This Is Spinal Tap
Those Wonderful Movie Cranks
Three Ages, The
¡Three Amigos!
Three Fugitives
Three Men and a Baby
3 Men and a Cradle
Three Men and a Little Lady
Three Men in a Boat
3 Ring Circus
Three to Tango
3 Women in Love
Throw Momma from theTrain
Tiger's Tale, A
Till Death Us Do Part
Till Sex Do Us Part
Tin Men
Titfield Thunderbolt, The
To Be or Not To Be (Lubitsch)
To Be or Not To Be (Johnson)
Tokyo Chorus
Tokyo Raiders
Tommy Boy
Tootsie
Topper
Top Secret!
Torrente, the Dumb Arm of the Law
Totò Who Lived Twice
Touch and Go
Touch of Class, A
Tough Guys
Tout ça… pour ça!!!
Town & Country
Toy, The
Toys
Trading Places
Traffic (Tati)
Trafico
Trail of the Pink Panther
Tramp, Tramp, Tramp
Transformers – The Movie, The
Trapped in Paradise
Travelling Executioner, The
Traversée de Paris, La
Treasure of Matecumbe
Trial By Combat
Trois Vies et une Seule Mort
Tropical Fish
Trouble in Paradise
Trouble in Store
Trou Normand, Le
Truck Stop Women
True Confession
True Identity
True Love
True Nature of Bernadette, The
True Nature of Eskimo Nell, The
Tugboat Annie
Tune in Tomorrow
Turnabout
Turner & Hooch
Twelve Chairs, The
Twentieth Century
Twins
Twister
Two-Faced Woman
Two for Tea
Two for the Road
Two if by Sea
Two-Way Stretch

UHF
Uncle Buck
Uncle from Brooklyn, The
Undercover Blues
Underneath the Arches
Under the Doctor
Understanding Jane
Un Deux Trois Soleil
Unfaithfully Yours (Sturges)
Unfaithfully Yours (Zieff)
Up in Smoke
Uptown Saturday Night
Up Your Alley
Used Cars
Used People

Vacances de M. Hulot, Les
Valley of Song
Valseuses, Les
Value for Money
Van, The
Verdugo, El
Versailles rive gauche
Vices in the Family
Vice Versa (Gilbert)
Vice Versa (Ustinov)
Victor/Victoria
Vieille Dame Indigne. La
Violette et François
Visitor, The
Vivacious Lady
Viva Max!
Vizontele
Volcano High
Volere, Volare
Volunteers
Voyage-Surprise

Wackiest Ship in the Army, The
Wagons East!
Wag the Dog
Waiting for Godot
Waiting for the Light
Waking Ned
Walking and Talking
Walk Like a Man
Wanderers, The
War of the Roses, The
Watch Out, We're Mad
Watch Your Stern
Water
Waterboy, The
Watermelon Man
Wayne's World
Wayne's World II
Way Out West
Way Upstream
Wedding, A
Wedding, The (Lounguine)
Wedding Planner, The
Weekend at Bernie's
Welcome Back Mr McDonald
Wendy Cracked a Walnut
We're No Angels
Werewolf of Washington, The
What?
What About Bob?
What a Carve Up!
What Are You Doing After the Orgy?
What Did You Do in the War, Daddy?
Whatever Happened to Harold Smith
What Have I Done to Deserve This?
What Makes David Run?
What Price Hollywood?
What's New Pussycat?
What's Up Doc?
What's Up Tiger Lily?
Wheels on Meals
When Brendan Met Trudy
When Harry Met Sally…
Where's Poppa?
Where the Boys Are
Where the Heart Is
Where Were You When the Lights Went Out?
Which Way to the Front?
Whiffs
While Parents Sleep
While You Were Sleeoing
Whipped
Whisky Galore!
White Men Can't Jump
White Sheik, The
Who Am I This Time?
Who Are You Polly Maggoo?
Who Framed Roger Rabbit?
Who Is Harry Kellerman and Why Is He Saying ThoseTerrible Things About Me?
Who Is Killing the Great Chefs of Europe?
Whole Town's Talking, The
Wholly Moses!
Whoops Apocalypse
Who's Harry Crumb?
Who's the Man
Who's That Girl?
Why Me?
Why Worry?
Wild About Harry
Wildcats
Wildcats of St Trinian's, The
Wild in the Streets
Wild Party, The
Wild West

Wild Women of Wongo
Will Success Spoil Rock Hunter?
Wilt
Windbag the Sailor
Wise Guys
Wish You Were Here
Witches of Eastwick, The
Withnail & I
Without a Clue
Witness, The
Wizard of Speed and Time, The
Wood, The
Woman in Red, The
Woman of the Year
Woman on Top
Woman or Two, A
Woman's World
Women on the Verge of a Nervous Breakdown
Working Girl
Work is a Four Letter Word
World is Full of Married Men, The
World's Greatest Lover, The
Wrong Arm of the Law, The
W.W. and the Dixie Dancekings

Yana's Friends
Yellowbeard
You and Me
You Can't Cheat an Honest Man
Young Doctors in Love
Young Einstein
Young Frankenstein
You're a Big Boy Now
Yours and Mine
Yours, Mine and Ours
Yoyo

Zelig
Zero de Conduite
Zorba the Greek
Zorro the Gay Blade

Appendix 4

Documentaries

A
Abba, The Movie
A.B.C. Africa
Above Us the Earth
Adventures of a Brown Man in Search of Civilization
Africa Addio
African Elephant, The
After the Fall
Ah-Ying
A.K.
Alcohol Years, The
All Visitors Must Be Announced
Alternative Miss World, The
Always for Pleasure
Amazonia: Voices from the Rainforest
America – from Hitler to M-X
American Boy
American Pictures: A Personal Journey Through Black America
Amour Existe, L'
...and the pursuit of happiness
Angel on My Shoulder
Angst
Animals Film, The
Anou Banou or the Daughters of Utopia
Army of Lovers or Revolt of the Perverts
Art Pepper: Notes from a Jazz Survivor
Atlantis
Atomic Café, The
At Sundance
Attica
Attila '74

Ballad of Ramblin' Jack, The
Ballet Black
Bantsuma: The Life and Times of Tsumasaburo
Bando
Bari-Zogon
Basic Training
Battle of Chile, The
Battle of the Somme, The
Battle of the Ten Million, The
Beautiful People
Because of That War
Before Hindsight
Before Stonewall
Before the Nickelodeon: The Early Cinema of Edwin S Porter
Behind Closed Eyes
Behind the Rent Strike
Benjamin Smoke
Berlin – die Sinfonie der Grosstadt
Best Boy
Best Hotel on Skid Row
Best Man
Beyond the Mat
Big Bang, The (Toback)
Big Time
Bird Now
Bit of Scarlet, A
Bitter Cane
Bix: 'Ain't None of Them Play Like Him Yet'.
Black Diamond Rush
Black Fox
Blacks Britannica
Black Wax
Blind Alley
Blood is Not Fresh Water
Blue Note: A History of Modern Jazz
Blue Notes and Exiled Voices
Blue Water, White Death
Boatman
Bombay Our City
Bongo Man
Bonjour, Monsieur Dosineau
Born to Boogie
Bosna!
Bowling for Columbine
Bring On the Night
British Sounds
Broken Arrow 29
Broken Noses
Brother, Can You Spare a Dime?
Buena Vista Social Club, The
Burden of Dreams
Burning Wall, The
Burra Sahib
...But Then, She's Betty Carter
Bye-Bye Babushka

Cane Toads – an Unnatural History
Carl Th. Dreyer: My Work
Carlo Giuliani, Ragazzo
Carmen Miranda: Bananas Is My Business
Carry Greenham Home
Celluloid Closet, The
Chagrin et le Pitié, Le
Chantons sous l'Occupation
Chariots of the Gods
Charlie Mingus: The Triumph of the Underdog
Children of Theatre Street, The
Children Underground
Citizen Langlois
Chronique d'un Eté
Ciao! Manhattan
Cinema Cinema
Circle of Gold
Classified X
Clowns, The
Coal Face
Color of Honor, The
Comic Book Confidential
Common Threads: Stories from the Quilt
Completely Pogued
Confessions of a Suburban Girl
Confessions of Winifred Wagner, The
Conquest of the Air
Contre l'Oubli
Conversations with Willard Van Dyke
Cool & Crazy
Coraje del Pueblo, El
Correction Please, or How We Got Into Pictures
Cortazar
Courtesans of Bombay, The
Cousin Bobby
Crazy English
Cross and Passion
Cruise, The
Crumb

Dance Craze
Dark Circle
Dark Days
Day After Trinity, The
Dealers Among Dealers
Dear America: Letters Home From Vietnam
Decline of the Western Civilization, The
Decline of the Western Civilization Part II, The Metal Years
De l'Autre Côté du Périph'
Délits Flagrants
Demon Lover Diary
Derby
Desert Victory
Deus, Patria e Autoridade
Deutschland, Erwache!
Devil's Accordion, The
¡Devils Don't Dream! Research on Jacobo Arbenz Guzmán
Diaries
Dick
Diplomat, The
Directed by Andrei Tarkovsky
Directed by William Wyler
Divine Madness
Dogtown and Z-Boys
Domestic Violence
Donald Cammell: The Ultimate Performance
Don't Look Back
Double Headed Eagle, The
Down from the Mountain
Driving Me Crazy

Eadweard Muybridge, Zoopraxographer
East Side Story
Eight-Tray Gangster: The Making of a Crip
80 Blocks from Tiffany's
El Salvador: Another Vietnam
El Salvador – Decision to Win
El Salvador – Portrait of a Liberated Zone
El Salvador – The People Will Win
Elvis on Tour
Elvis – That's the Way It Is
Emperor's Naked Army Marches On, The
Enfants de Lumière, Les
Eric Clapton and His Rolling Hotel
Escape Route to Marseilles
Europe After the Rain
Everest
Every Little Thing
Execution Protocol, The
Exodus – Bob Marley Live

Falconer, The
Fall of the Romanov Dynasty, The
Family Business
Far From Vietnam
Farm, The
Farrebique
Fast Trip, Long Drop
Fatal Reaction: Singapore
Fellini A Director's Notebook
Femi Kuti: What's Going On
Fetishes
F for Fake
Fillmore
Film from the Clyde
Fires Were Started
Fly a Flag for Poplar
For All Mankind
Force More Powerful, A
Forest of Bliss
For Love or Money
Fortini/Cani
Fountain, The
4 Little Girls
François Truffaut, Portraits Volés
Frank Capra's American Dream
Frantz Fanon: Black Skin, White Mask
From Mao to Mozart: Issac Stern in China
From Pole to Equator
From Russia to Hollywood: The 100-Year Odyssey of Chekhov and Shdanoff
From Russia with Rock
From the Cloud to the Resistance
From the Journals of Jean Seberg
F.T.A.
Full Tilt Boogie

Gaea Girls
Galahad of Everest
Garlic Is as Good as Ten Mothers
Gates of Heaven
General Amin
Germany in Autumn
Get Back
Gifted City
Gilsodom
Gimme Shelter
Glastonbury: The Movie
Gleaners and I, The
God's Alcatraz
Good Fight, The
Good People of Portugal, The
Good Wife of Tokyo, The
Good Woman of Bangkok, The
G'Ole!
Grass (Cooper/Shoedsack)
Grass (Mann)
Great Day in Harlem, A
Great Ecstasy of Woodcarver Steiner, The
Greatness of the Small Man, The
Grey Gardens
Gringo in Mañanaland, A
Guerre sans nom, La

Hail! Hail! Rock'n'Roll
Half Life
Hamster Factor and Other Tales of Twelve Monkeys, The
Handsworth Songs
Happiness in Twenty Years
Harlan County, U.S.A.
Havanna Mi Amor
Heartland Reggae
Hearts and Minds
Hearts of Darkness: A Filmmaker's Apocalypse

Heaven
Heaven, Man, Earth
Heaven-6-Box
Heavy Petting
Heidi Fleiss – Hollywood Madam
Hero
Hillbrow Kids
Hitler – A Career
Hitmakers: The Teens Who Stole Pop Music
Hollywood on Trial
Home Game
Homme au Chapeau de Soie, L'
Hoop Dreams
Hotel Terminus: The Life and Times of Klaus Barbie
Housing Problems
How Does It Feel

I Am Cuba
I Am a Dancer
I Am Anna Magnani
I Am a Sex Addict
I Am My Own Woman
I.F. Stone's Weekly
Imagine
Imago – Meret Oppenheim
Improper Conduct
In Cane for Life
Indian Story, An
In Georgia
In Ismail's Custody
In My Father's House
In Search of Famine
In the Name of the People
Into the Arms of Strangers: Stories of the Kindertransport
Invocation Maya Deren
Ireland Behind the Wire
Italianamerican
It's All True
Ivan Mosjoukine, or The Carnival Child
I Was, I Am, I Shall Be

Jabula – A Band in Exile
James Baldwin: The Price of the Ticket
James Dean Story, The
James Dean – The First American Teenager
Jane
Jang Sun-Woo Variations, The
Janis
Jazz in Exile
Jazz on a Summer's Day
Jazzwomen
Jimi Hendrix
Joe Albany…A Jazz Life
Joe Louis – For All Time
John Heartfield: Photomonteur
John Huston War Stories
Joli mai, Le
Joseph Cornell: Worlds in a Box
Journey to Beijing
Jung (War) – in the Land of the Mujaheddin
Juvenile Court
Juvenile Liaison
Juvenile Liaison 2

Kamikaze Hearts
Kanehsatake (Oka) – 270 Years of Resistance
Kashima Paradise
Kerouac
Kids Are Alright, The
Kids of Survival: The Art and Life of Tim Rollins & K.O.S.
Knowledge of Healing, The
Koyaanisqatsi
Krzysztof Kieslowski: I'm So So
Kurosawa
Kurt & Courtney

Ladies and Gentlemen, The Rolling Stones
Land of Silence and Darkness
Last Date
Last Days, The
Last Grave at Dimbaza
Last of the Blue Devils, The
Last Waltz, The
Law and Order
Lebanon…Why?
Legend of Teddy Edwards, The
Lessons in Darkness
Let It Be
Let It Come Down: The Life of Paul Bowles
Let's Get Lost
Letter to Jane
Letter Without Words, A
Let the Good Times Roll
Libertad, La
Life and Times of Allen Ginsberg, The
Life and Times of Rosie the Riveter, The
Listen Up: The Lives of Quincy Jones
Litany for Survival: The Life and Work of Audre Lord
Little People
Live a Life
Lodz Ghetto
London Rock and Roll Show, The
Long Night's Journey into Day
Looking for Richard
Lord of the Dance
Louis Prima: The Wildest
Loving the Dead
Luck, Trust & Ketchup: Robert Altman in Carver Country
Lumière

Mad Dogs and Englishmen
Mandela
Man of Africa
Man of Aran
Man of the Year
Manson
Manufacturing Consent: Noam Chomsky and the Media
Man Who Drove with Mandela
Man With A Movie Camera
Martha & Ethel
Me & My Matchmaker
Mechanics of the Brain
Mexico: The Frozen Revolution
Microcosmos
Milestones
Militia Battlefield
Millhouse, a White Comedy
1974, Une Partie de Campagne
Minamata
Miners' Film, The
Miniskirted Dynamo
Mirror Phase
Mississippi Blues
Mobutu: King of Zaire
Model
Monde du Silence, Le
Monster in a Box
Montand
Monterey Pop
Moon and the Sledgehammer, The
Moonwalker
More About the Language of Love
Motel
Mother Dao the Turtlelike
Motion and Emotion: the Films of Wim Wenders
Mouth Wide Open – A Journey in Film with Ted Coubray
Mueda – Memory and Massacre
Muhammad Ali: The Greatest
Musicals Great Musicals: The Arthur Freed Unit at MGM
Music for the Movies: Bernard Herrmann
Music for the Movies: Toru Takemitsu
Mustang…The House that Joe Built
My Crasy Life
My Dearest Enemy
My Generation
My Journey, My Islam
My New Friends
My Private War
Mystère Picasso, Le

Nela
Nicaragua – No Pasarán
Nice Time
Nico Icon
Nightcleaners
Night in Havana: Dizzy Gillespie in Cuba, A
Niños Abandonados, Los
Nobody Someday
No Maps on My Taps
No Nukes
Not a Love Story
Notebook on Cities and Clothes
November Days Voices and Choices

O Amor Natural
Occupied Palestine
Occupy!
Ode to Cologne
O Dreamland
Of Great Events and
Oporto of My Childhood
Ordinary People
Original Kings of Comedy, The
Olympische Spiele 1936
On Any Sunday
On Boys, Girls and the Veil
On Company Business
Ondeko-za on Sado, The
One by One
One Day in September
One Day in the Life of Andrei Arsenevitch
100 Years of Polish Cinema
One Man's War
One PM
One Way or Another
On Our Land
On the Bridge
On the Game
Ornette: Made in America
Osaka Story
Other One, The
Our Wall
Out of the Present
Over Our Dead Bodies

Package Tour, The
Painters Painting
Paolozzi Story, The
Paperback Vigilante
Paragraph 175
Paris Is Burning
Paris Mil Neuf Cent Chronique de 1900 à 1914
Paris Was a Woman
Passion of Remembrance, The
Pasternaks, The
Patriot Game, The
Patu!
Peasants of the Second Fortress, The
Pink Floyd Live at Pompeii
Platz, Der
Plow That Broke the Plains, The
Plutonium Circus, The
Point Is to Change It, The
Point of Order
Pop and Me
Pop Gear
Portrait of a 60% 'Perfect' Man: Billy Wilder
Portrait of Jason
Portrait of Teresa
Poto and Cabengo
Powaqqatsi
Pretty as a Picture: The Art of David Lynch
Primate
Prince – Sign o' the Times
Promised Lands
Promises
Proud to be British
Public Enemy Number One
Pumping Iron
Pumping Iron II: the Women
Punk in London
Punk Rock Movie, The

Queen, The
Queens of the Big Time
Quince Tree Sun, The

Race, the Spirit of Franco
Raga
Rate It X
Refusal, The
Reggae
Reggae Sunsplash II
Reminiscences of a Journey to Lithuania
Repubblica Nostra
Requiem for Dominic
Return Engagement
Right Out of History: the Making of Judy Chicago's Dinner Party
Roar
Robert Altman's Jazz '34: Remembrances of Kansas City Swing
Rockshow
Roger & Me
Roger Corman: Hollywood's Wild Angel
Roots Rock Reggae
Rough Cut and Ready Dubbed
Route One/USA
Rush to Judgement
Rust Never Sleeps

Sacrifice
St Ann's
Sang des Bêtes, Le
São Paulo, SP
Saudade do Futuro
Savage Man…Savage Beast
Schiele in Prison
Scratch
Screamin' Jay Hawkins: I Put a Spell on Me
Seacoal
Sense of Loss, A
Será Posible el Sur
Sex Is…
Sex Life in L.A.
Shampoo and Set
Shark Callers of Kontu, The
Shattered Dreams: Picking Up the Pieces
She Lives to Ride
Shtetl
Shvitz, The
Sick: The Life & Death of Bob Flanagan, Supermasochist
Signed: Lino Brocka
Silent Witness, The
Slanted Vision
Small Wonder
Soft on the Inside
Soldier Girls
Sometimes I Look at My Life
Song for Tibet
Song of Ceylon
Sonic Outlaws
So That You Can Live
Soufrière, La
Soul to Soul
Sound of Brazil
South
South Africa Belongs to Us
Southpaw
Spare Time
Specialist, The
Spin
Split William to Chrysis: Portrait of a Drag Queen

Square, The
Srebrenica: A Cry from the Grave
Stepping Razor – Red X
Stop Making Sense
Streetwise
Strip Jack Naked: Nighthawks II
Silent Witness, The
Sud
Summer in the City
Sunless Days
Superstar: the Karen Carpenter Story
Sword and the Flute, The

Tales from a Hard City
Talking History
Talmage Farlow
Tapdancin'
Target Shoots First, The
Tattooed Tears
T. Dan Smith
Teenage Kicks – The Undertones
Terrorists in Retirement
Theatre Girls
Thelonious Monk: Straight No Chaser
Thin Blue Line, The
'36 to '77
This is Elvis
Tibet: A Buddhist Trilogy
Tibetan New Year, A
Tickle in the Heart, A
Tidikawa and Friends
Tierische Liebe
Tigrero – A Film That Was Never Made
Time and Judgement
Times of Harvey Milk, The
Time Will Tell
Tokyo-Ga
Tokyo Olympiad 1964
To Live in Freedom
Tom Simpson: Something to Aim At
Tongues Untied
Tonite Let's All Make Love in London
Too White for Me
To Speak the Unspeakable: The Message of Elie Wiesel
To the Heart
To the Last Drop
Totschweigen
Town Bloody Hall
Trade Off
Trances
Travelling Light: a Portrait of Lindsay Kemp
Trials of Alger Hiss, The
Tribulation 99: Alien Anomalies Under America
Triumph of the Will
True Glory, The
Truth or Dare
Tunisian Victory
Tupamaros
Twelve Views of Kensal House
25 Years
Twilight City
Typewriter, the Rifle & the Movie Camera, The

Uncle Tom
Uncommon Senses
UndeRage
Underground
Underground Orchestra, The
Union Maids
Univers de Jacques Demy, Le
Unstable Elements – Atomic Stories
Unzipped
Urinal
U2 Rattle and Hum

Veillées d'Armes
Vernon, Florida
Vietnam Journey
Vincent: the Life and Death of Vincent Van Gogh
Visions of Eight
Visions of Light
Viva Portugal
Voice of Kurdistan, The
Voices from the Front
Volcano

Warren Oates: Across the Border
War Room, The
Warsaw Ghetto Uprising, The
Wattstax
Weavers, The: Wasn't That a Time?
Wednesday 19.7.1961
Welcome to Britain
Welfare
Well-Founded Fear
We're Alive
What About Me?
What Happened to Kerouac?
What Is Democracy?
When Mother Comes Home for Christmas
When the Mountains Tremble
When We Were Kings
White Rock
Whoever Says the Truth Will Die
Who Killed Vincent Chin?
Wild Bill: A Hollywood Maverick
Wild Man Blues
William Christie et Les Arts Florissants
Will My Mother Go Back to Berlin?
Wisconsin Death Trip
Witchcraft Through the Ages
With Babies and Banners
Without Memory
Without You I'm Nothing
Wittstock, Wittstock
Wizard of Waukesha, The
Wobblies, The
Woman to Woman
Woodstock
Word Is Out
Wot! No Art
Writing in the Sand, The

Yaacov Ben Dov: Father of the Hebrew Film
Year of the Beaver
Year of the Horse
Yessongs
You, Me, Jerusalem

Zapatista
Ziggy Stardust and the Spiders from Mars

Appendix 5

Epics

Al-Risalah
Alexander Nevsky
Alexander the Great
Andrei Rublev
Apollo 13

Barabbas
Ben-Hur (Niblo)
Ben-Hur (Wyler)
Bible…In the Beginning, The
Birth of a Nation, The

Cabeza de Vaca
Cleopatra (DeMille)
Cleopatra (Mankiewicz)
Conqueror, The
Deluge, The
Demetrius and the Gladiators
Doctor Zhivago
Don Quichotte

El Cid
Emperor's Shadow
Ercole alla conquista di Atlantide

Fabiola
Fall of the Roman Empire, The
55 Days in Peking
Flametop

Gandhi
Gladiator (Scott)
Goliath and the Barbarians
Gone With the Wind
Good Earth, The
Greatest Show on Earth, The
Greatest Story Ever Told, The

Hero (Platts-Mills)
Horsemen, The
Hwa-om-Kyong

Jason and the Argonauts

King David
King of Kings

Land of the Pharaohs
Last Days of Pompeii, The
Last Emperor, The
Lawrence of Arabia
Les Misérables (Boleslawski)
Les Miserables (Milestone)
Lion of the Desert
Little Buddha
Lord Jim
Lord of the Rings: The Fellowship of the Ring, The
Markéta Lazarová
Misérables, Les (Le Chanois)
Misérables, Les (Lelouch)
Moses
Mother India
Mountains of the Moon

Napoléon (Gance)
Napoléon (Guitry)
Nicholas and Alexandra
Noah's Ark

Pathfinder
Perfect Storm, The
Pride and the Passion, The

Quo Vadis?

Regeneration
Robe, The
Romance of Book & Sword, The

Saladin
Samson and Delilah
Shackleton's Antarctic Adventure
Sign of the Cross, The
Sign of the Gladiator
Sign of the Pagan
Sodom and Gomorrah
Solomon and Sheba
Spartacus

Taebaek Mountains, The
Ten Commandments,The
13th Warrior, The
Titanic (Cameron)
Touch of Zen, A

Ulysses' Gaze

Valiant Ones, The
Vikings, The

War and Peace (Vidor)
War and Peace (Bondarchuk)
Waterloo
Waterworld

Appendix 6

Fantasy

Adventures of Baron Munchhausen, The (Gilliam)
Adventures of Baron Munchhausen, The (von Baky)
Adventures of Buckaroo Banzai Across the 8th Dimension, The
Adventures of Goopy and Bagha, The
Alice
Alice in Wonderland (McLeod)
Alice in Wonderland (Bower/Bunin)
Alice's Adventures in Wonderland
Amélie
Angel Who Pawned Her Harp, The
Anger Magick Lantern Cycle, The
Animal Farm
Arabian Adventure
Arabian Nights
Ashik Kerib
Attack of the 50ft Woman
At the Earth's Core
Aurora Encounter, The

Barb Wire
Baron Munchhausen
Batman (Martinson)
Batman (Burton)
Batman Forever
Batman Returns
Batman & Robin
Bearskin
Being Human
Being John Malkovich
Belles de nuit, Les
Blood Brothers, The
Blue Bird, The
Book of Life, The
Brazil
Butterfly Murders, The

Captain Kronos – Vampire Hunter
Captain Nemo and the Underwater City
Case for a Young Hangman, A
Chinese Ghost Story, A
Chinese Ghost Story II, A
Chinese Ghost Story III, A
Cinderella – Italian-style
Cité des enfants perdus, La
City of Angels
City of Pirates
City Under the Sea
Clash of the Titans
Company of Wolves, The
Conan the Barbarian
Conan the Destroyer
Conquest
Conspirators of Pleasure
Craft, The
Creatures the World Forgot
Cremaster 5
Crow, The
Cyberworld 3D

Dark Crystal, The
Dead Forest
Deaf and Mute Heroine, The
Delicatessen
Désert des Tartares, Le
Destiny
Dinosaur
Dinosaurus!
DragonHeart
Dragonslayer
Dreamchild
Dungeons & Dragons
Dybbuk, The

Edward Scissorhands
Electric Dragon 80,000
Eraserhead
Erik the Viking

Fantasia
Faust
Fire and Ice
Fisher King, The
5000 Fingers of Dr T, The
From Hell It Came

Gabriel & Me
Game, The
Gamera: The Guardian of the Universe
Gnome Named Gnorm, A
Godzilla
Golden Voyage of Sinbad, The
Goto, l'île d'amour
Gremlins
Gremlins 2: the New Batch
Gunhed

Hawk the Slayer
Highlander
Highlander II – The Quickening
Highlander III –The Sorcerer
Hole, The
Hook
Hungarian Fairy Tale, A

Inhumaine, L'
Invincible Barbarian, The

Joe Versus the Volcano
Jumanji
Jurassic Park
Jurassic Park III

Knightriders
Krull

Lara Croft: Tom Raider
Last Action Hero
Last Valley, The
Little Vampire, The
Lord of Illusions
Lost World: Jurassic Park, The

Maciste all'Inferno
Maciste Contro i Mostri
Mahabharata, Le
Man Called Hero, A
Mansion of the Ghost Cat, The
Man Who Could Work
Merlin: The Return
Meteor Man, The
Merveilleuse Visite, La
Michael
Miracles, The
Monkeybone
Moon Warriors
Mortal Kombat
Mortal Kombat 2: Annihilation

Navigator: A Medieval Odyssey, The
Nez au Vent, Le
Nibelungen, Die
No Escape
Nothing Lasts Forever
Nuit fantastique, La
Nutcracker – the Motion Picture

Offending Angels
One Million Years B.C.
Orlando

Parking
Peau d'Ane
Phantom, The
Preacher's Wife, The
Prince Valiant
Princess Mononoke

Rainbow
Raining in the Mountain
Red Sonja
Return to Never Land
Return to Oz
Rocketeer, The
Romantic Agony, The

Santa Sangre
Schatten
Secret Life of Walter Mitty, The
Seventh Voyage of Sinbad, The
Shadow, The
Silent Flute, The
Sinbad and the Eye of the Tiger
Slipstream
Snow White: A Tale of Terror
Soultaker
Spawn
Spider-Man
Spider-Man Strikes Back
Spider-Man – the Dragon's Challenge
Super Mario Bros.
Swordsman
Swordsman II
Swordsman in Double-Flag Town, The

Teenage Caveman
Thief of Bagdad, The (Walsh)
Thief of Bagdad, The (Powell/Berger/Whelan/Korda)
Thief of Baghdad, The (Donner)
Three Worlds of Gulliver, The
Tiger of Eschnapur, The/The Indian Tomb
Time Bandits
Topo, El
Touche pas à la femme blanche
Tromeo and Juliet
Troll
Truman Show, The
12 Monkeys
20000 Leagues Under the Sea
Twilight of the Ice Nymphs, The
Twilight Zone – the Movie

Unbreakable
Unidentified Flying Oddball, The
Uproar in Heaven
Unsuspected, The

Valley of Gwangi, The
Viking Women and Their Voyage to the Waters of the Great Sea Serpent
Visiteurs, Les
Visiteurs du Soir, Les

Warlords of Atlantis
War of the Colossal Beast
What Planet Are You From?
When Dinosaurs Ruled the Earth
Willow
Witches, The
Wizard of Oz, The
Wizards

Younger and Younger
Yumeji

Zardoz
Zoo in Budapest
Zu: Warriors from the Magic Mountain

Appendix 7

Film Noir

A Bout de Souffle
Across the Pacific
After Dark, My Sweet
American Friend, The
American Gigolo
Among the Living
Angel Dust
Asphalt Jungle, The
Au Nom de la Loi

Beyond Reasonable Doubt (Laing)
Big Clock, The
Big Sleep, The (Hawks)
Big Steal, The (Siegel)
Black Angel
Blood Simple
Body and Soul
Blue Dahlia, The
Body Heat
Border Incident
Born to Kill
Brasher Doubloon, The
Breathless
Brute Force

Call Northside 777
Captive City, The
Caught
Cause for Alarm!
Chinatown
Christmas Holiday
Città si Difende, La
City That Never Sleeps
Clash by Night
Clay Pigeon, The
Conflict
Criss Cross (Siodmak)
Criss Cross (Soderbergh)
Cry Danger
Cutter's Way

Dangerous Mission
Dark City
Dark Corner, The
Dark Mirror, The
Dark Passage
Deadline at Dawn
Dead Reckoning
Dernier Tournant
Desperate
Desperate Hours, The
Detective Story
Detour
D.O.A (Maté)
Double Indemnity
Doulos, Le

Edge of Doom
Enforcer, The
Everybody Wins

Farewell, My Lovely (Dmytryk)
Farewell, My Lovely (Richards)
Fear in the Night
File on Thelma Jordon, The
Force of Evil

Garment Jungle, The
Gilda
Great Gatsby, The (Nugent)
Grifters, The
Gun Crazy

Hammett
Hangmen Also Die!
Hard Eight
He Died With His Eyes Open
He Walked By Night
High Sierra
His Kind of Woman
Hitch-hiker, The
Hot Spot, The
House of Strangers
Hustle

In a Lonely Place

Johnny O'Clock

Key Largo
Killers, The
Killing, The
Killing Me Softly
Kiss Me Deadly
Kiss of Death

Lady from the Shanghai Cinema, The
Lawless, The
Light Sleeper

Maltese Falcon, (Huston)
Man Hunt
Man I Love, The
Moonrise
Murder by Contract
Mystery Street

Naked City, The
Narrow Margin, The
Night and the City (Dassin)
Night and the City (Winkler)
Nightfall
Night Has a Thousand Eyes
Nightmare
Nightmare Alley
No Man of Her Own

On Dangerous Ground
Out of the Fog
Out of the Past

Palmetto
Panic in the Streets
Pitfall
Public Eye, The

Quai des Brumes, Le
Quai des Orfèvres

Raw Deal (Mann)
Reckless Moment, The
Reservoir Dogs
Road House
Run for Money
Ruthless

Samourai, Le
Scarlet Street
Shockproof
Singapore Sling
Slightly Scarlet
So Dark the Night
So Evil My Love
Somewhere in the Night
Sorry, Wrong Number
Strange Affair of Uncle Harry, The
Strange Love of Martha Ivers, The

Tête d'un Homme, La
They Live by Night
They Won't Believe Me
Thief, The
Thieves' Highway
This Gun For Hire
This World, Then the Fireworks
T-Men
Touch of Evil
Twilight
Twin Peaks

Union Station
Unsuspected, The

Where Danger Lives
While the City Sleeps
Whirlpool
Window, The

Woman in the Window, The
Woman on the Beach, The
Woman's Secret, A
Wrong Man, The (Hitchcock)
Wrong Man, The (McBride)

You Only Live Once

Appendix 8

Gangsters

Agitator
Al Capone
Angels With Dirty Faces
Another Battle
Another Lonely Hitman
Assassin(s)
As Tears Go By

Baby Face Morgan
Back of Beyond
Big Shot, The
Billy Bathgate
Black Hand, The
Bloody Mama
Boiling Point (Kitano)
Bonnie and Clyde
Borsalino
Borsalino & Co
Bound by Honor
Branded to Kill
Brother orchid
Bugsy
Bullets or Ballots

Capone
Carlito's Way
Casino
City Streets
Cyclo

Dang Bireley's and the Young Gangsters
Dead End
Dead Presidents
Dick Tracy
Dillinger (Nosseck)
Dillinger (Milius)
Dobermann
Donnie Brasco

Each Dawn I Die
Essex Boys

Fire Within, The
Flic, Un
Frightened City
Full Contact
Funeral, The

Gang, Le
Gangster No. 1
'G' Men
Godfather, The
Godfather Part II, The
Godfather Part III, The
God's Favorite
GoodFellas
Gotti
Great Jewel Robber, The
Grissom Gang, The

Heat
Hi, Dharma!
Honest
Honor Thy Father
Hoodlum Empire

I Am the Law
I, Mobster
In Nome della Legge
Invisible Stripes

Joe Macbeth
Johnny Dangerously
Johnny Eager
Just Heroes

King of New York

King of the Roaring 20's – The Story of Arnold Rothstein
Kiss Tomorrow Goodbye
Killing of a Chinese Bookie, The

Lady in Red, The
Last Gangster, The
Lepke
Little Caesar
Lock, Stock and Two Smoking Barrels
Long Good Friday, The
Lucky Luciano

Machine Gun Kelly
Manhattan Melodrama
Marked Woman
Men of Respect
Miller's Crossing
Mob, The
Mobsters
Môme Pigalle, La

Noose
No. 3

Once Upon a Time in Triad Society
Once Upon a Time in Triad Society 2
One Generation of Tattoos
Original Gangstas
Outer Way, The

Painted Desert
Party Girl
Pépé le Moko
Pete Kelly's Blues
Placido Rizzotto
Portland Street Blues
Prime Cut
Public Enemy, The

Racket, The
Rise and Fall of Legs Diamond, The

St Valentine's Day Massacre,The
Scarface (Hawks)
Scarface (De Palma)
Shanghai Triad
Sicilian, The
Sicilian Clan, The
State of Grace
Street With No Name, The
Sugartime

Tchao Pantin
This Day and Age
Thunderbolt
Touchez pas au Grisbi
24 Hours in London

Underworld
Untouchables, The

Violent Tradition

White Heat
Wicked Reporter, The

Yakuza, The
Young and Dangerous
Young and Dangerous 2
Young and Dangerous 3

Appendix 9

Horror

Abominable Dr Phibes, The
Abominable Snowman, The
Adrenalin – Fear the Rush
Alchemist, The
Alligator
Alone in the Dark
Amazing Stories
American Nightmare, The
American Werewolf in Paris, An
Amityville Horror, The
Amityville II: The Possession
Amityville 3-D
Anaconda
And Now the Screaming Starts!
Angel Heart
Anguish
Anticristo, L'
Arachnophobia
Asylum
Attack of the 50 Foot Woman
Attack of the Puppet People
Audrey Rose
Awakening, The

Baby, The
Bad Taste
Basket Case
Basket Case 2
Bats
Beast from Haunted Cave
Beast from 20,000 Fathoms
Beast in the Cellar, The
Beast Must Die, The
Before I Hang
Beyond, The
Beyond, Bedlam
Billy the Kid vs Dracula
Birds, The
Black Cat, The
Black Knight, The
Black Sabbath
Black Torment
Blacula
Blade
Blade II
Blair Witch Project, The
Blood Beach
Blood Beast Terror, The
Blood from the Mummy's Tomb
Bloodline
Blood of the Vampire
Blood Reincarnation
Bluebeard
Body Bags
Body Melt
Body Parts
Body Snatcher, The
Boogie Man Will Get You, The
Book of Shadows Blair Witch 2
Brain Damage
Brainscan
Bride, The
Bride of Chucky
Bride of Frankenstein, The
Brides of Dracula, The
Brood, The
Bucket of Blood, A
Bug
Buried Alive
Burning, The
Burnt Offerings

Cameron's Closet
Candyman
Candyman 2: Farewell to the Flesh
Car, The
Carnival of Souls
Carrie (De Palma)
Cars That Ate Paris, The
Cat Girl
Cathy's Curse
Cat People (Tourneur)

Cat People (Schrader)
Cat's Eye
Cellar, The
Chamber of Horrors
Changeling, The
Chat, Le
Cherry Falls
Children of the Corn
Child's Play
Child's Play 2
Chi Sei?
Christine
Chute de la Maison Usher, La
Circus of Fear
Circus of Horrors
Colossus of New York, The
Come Back, The
Communion (Sole)
Corridors of Blood
Count Dracula
Countess Dracula
Count Yorga, Vampire
Craze
Crazies, The
Creature from the Black Lagoon
Creature Walks Among Us, The
Creepers
Creeping Flesh, The
Creepshow
Creepshow 2
Crimes of the Future
Critters
Critters 2: The Main Course
Cronos
Crucible of Terror
Cry of the Banshee
Cujo
Curse of Frankenstein, The
Curse of the Cat People, The
Curse of the Crimson Altar
Curse of the Mummy's Tomb, The
Curse of the Werewolf, The

Damien – Omen II
Dance of the Vampires
Dark Eyes of London
Dark Half, The
Darklands
Darkman
Daughters of Darkness
Daughters of Satan
Dawn of the Dead
Day of the Animals
Day of the Beast
Day of the Dead
Dead and Buried
Dead Can't Lie, The
Deadly Blessing
Deadly Friend
Dead Men Don't Die
Dead of Night (Hamer/Dearden/Crichton/Cavalcanti)
Dead of Night (Clark)
Dead Ringers
Dead Zone, The
Death Line
Death Trap
Death Valley
Death Weekend
DEF by Temptation
Dementia 13
Demons (O'Hara)
Demons (Bava)
Demons 2
Demons of the Mind
Deranged
Destroy All Monsters
Devil Commands, The
Devil-Doll, The
Devil Rides Out, The
Devil's Backbone, The
Devil's Rain, The
Disciple of Death

Disturbing Behavior
Docteur Jekyll et les Femmes
Doctor Blood's Coffin
Doctor Death: Seeker of Souls
Dr Jekyll and Mr Hyde (Robertson)
Dr Jekyll and Mr Hyde (Fleming)
Doctor Jekyll and Sister Hyde
Dr Phibes Rises Again
Dr Terror's House of Horrors
Doctor X
Dogs
Dog Soldiers
Dominique
Donovan's Brain
Don't Answer the Phone!
Doppelganger: The Evil Within
Dracula (Browning)
Dracula (Fisher)
Dracula (Curtis)
Dracula (Badham)
Dracula (Coppola)
Dracula A.D. 1972
Dracula Has Risen from the Grave
Dracula, Prince of Darkness
Dracula's Daughter
Dracula 2000
Driller Killer, The

Ebirah – Terror of the Deep
Ed Gein
Edge of Sanity
Elvira, Mistress of the Dark
Empire of the Ants
End of Days
Entity, The
Evictors, The
Evil Dead, The
Evil Dead II
Exorcist, The
Exorcist – Director's Cut, The
Exorcist II: The Heretic
Exorcist III, The
Eye of the Cat

Face Behind the Mask
Face of Darkness, The
Feverhouse
Fiend Without a Face
Final Conflict, The
Final Destination
Final Terror, The
Flesh & Blood
Flesh and the Fiends, The
Flesh for Frankenstein
Fly, The (Cronenberg)
Fly, The (Neumann)
Fly II, The
Fog, The
Food of the Gods, The
Frankenhooker
Frankenstein
Frankenstein and the Monster from Hell
Frankenstein Created Woman
Frankenstein Meets the Wolf Man
Frankenstein Must Be Destroyed
Frankenstein: The True Story
Freaks
Freddy's Dead: The Final Nightmare
Friday the 13th
Friday the 13th Part Two
Friday the 13th Part VIII: Jason Takes Manhattan
Frightmare
Frighteners, The
Fright Night
Fright Night Part 2
Frisson des Vampires, Les
Frogs
From Beyond
From Beyond the Grave
From Hell
Full Circle
Funhouse, The
Funny Games
Funny Man
Fury, The

Galaxy of Terror
Gate, The
Ghost of Frankenstein, The
Ghost Ship, The
Ghost Story
Ghoul, The (Hunter)
Ghoul, The (Francis)
Ghoulies
Giant Spider Invasion, The
Ginger Snaps
Godsend, The
God Told Me To
Godzilla 1985
Godzilla vs the Smog Monster
Golem, The
Gorgo
Gorgon, The
Graveyard Shift
Grim Prairie Tales
Guardian, The

Halloween
Halloween II
Halloween III
Halloween 4: The Return of Michael Myers
Halloween H20 – 20 Years Later
Halloween: The Curse of Michael Myers
Hand, The
Hands of Orlac, The
Hands of the Ripper
Hannibal
Harlequin
Haunted Place
Haunting, The
Headhunter
Hellbound: Hellraiser II
Hell Night
Hellraiser
Hellraiser III: Hell on Earth
Hellstrom Chronicle, The
Hex
Hills Have Eyes, The
Histoires Extraordinaires
Hitcher, The
Holocaust 2000
Homicidal
Horror Express
Horror Hospital
Horrors of the Black Museum
House
House II
House by the Cemetery
House in Nightmare Park, The
House of Dracula
House of Exorcism, The
House of Fear, The
House of Frankenstein
House of Mortal Sin
House of the Long Shadows, The
House of Usher, The
House of Wax
House of Whipcord
House on Haunted Hill
House on Sorority Row, The
House that Dripped Blood, The
Howling, The
Hunter's Blood
Hush…Hush, Sweet Charlotte

I Bought a Vampire Motorcycle
I Don't Want to Be Born
I Know What You Did Last Summer
I, Monster
Impulse
Incense for the Damned
Incredible Melting Man
Incredibly Strange Creatures Who Stopped Living and Became Mixed-Up Zombies, The
Incubus
Inferno
Innocents, The
In the Mouth of Madness
Invisible Ray, The
Island of Dr Moreau, The (Taylor)
Island of Dr Moreau, The (Frankenheimer)
Island of Lost Souls
Island of Mutations
Isle of the Dead
I Still Know What You Did Last Summer
It Lives Again
It's Alive
I Walked With a Zombie
I Was a Teenage Werewolf

Jacob's Ladder

Keep, The
Kichiku
Killer Nun
Killer Tongue
Kindred, The
Kingdom of the Spiders
King Kong (Cooper/Shoedsack)
King Kong (Guillermin)
Kiss, The
Kiss of the Vampire
Kitami
Konga
Kuroneko
Kwaidan

Ladies in Retirement
Lady Vampire, The
Lair of the White Worm, The
Lake Placid
Last Broadcast, The
Last House on the Left, The
Leatherface: The Texas Chainsaw Massacre III
Legacy, The
Legend of Hell House, The
Legend of the Mountain
Legend of the Werewolf
Leopard Man, The
Leviathan
Lift, The
Link
Living Dead, The
Living Dead at the Manchester Morgue, The
Lost Boys, The
Lost Continent, The
Lost Souls
Lovecraft

Macabre
Mad Doctor of Market Street, The
Mad Genius, The
Madhouse
Mad Love
Mad Magician, The
Mad Room, The
Magic
Magician, The
Mangler, The
Maniac Cop
Maniac Cop 2
Manitou, The
Man-Made Monster
Mansion of the Doomed
Man Who Changed His Mind, The
Mary Reilly
Maximum Overdrive
Mindwarp
Monkey Shines
Monolith Monsters, The
Monster and the Girl, The
Monster Club, The
Monster from Green Hell
Monster of Terror
Monster on the Campus
Monster Squad, The
Most Dangerous Game, The
Mothman Prophecies, The
Mummy, The (Freund)
Mummy, The (Fisher)
Mummy, The (Sommers)
Mummy Returns, The
Mummy's Hand, The
Mummy's Shroud, The
Murders in the Rue Morgue, The (Florey)
Murders in the Rue Morgue, The (Hessler)
Murders in the Zoo
Mutant
Mutations, The
Mystery of the Wax Museum

Near Dark
Necronomicon
Nightbreed
Nightmare on Elm Street, A
Nightmare on Elm Street Part 2: Freddy's Revenge, A
Nightmare on Elm Street 3: Dream Warriors, A
Nightmare on Elm Street 4: The Dream Master, A
Nightmare on Elm Street 5: The Dream Child, A
Nightmares
Night of the Comet
Night of the Creeps
Night of the Demons
Night of the Eagle
Night of the Ghouls
Night of the Lepus
Night of the Living Dead (Romero)
Night of the Living Dead (Savini)
Nightwing
976-Evil
Nocturna
Nosferatu – eine Symphonie des Grauens
Nosferatu the Vampyre
Nothing But the Night

Oblong Box, The
Old Dark House, The
Omen, The
Omen IV: The Awakening
Organ
Out of the Dark

Pack, The
Paperhouse
Parasite Murders, The
Parts: The Clonus Horror
Patrick
Paura nella Città dei Morti Viventi
People Under the Stairs, The
Pet Sematary
Phantom of the Opera, The (Julian)
Phantom of the Opera (Lubin)
Phantom of the Opera, The (Fisher)
Phantom of the Opera (Little)
Piranha
Piranha II: Flying Killers
Pit and the Pendulum, The (Corman)
Pit and the Pendulum, The (Gordon)
Place of One's Own, A
Plague of the Zombies, The
Poltergeist
Poltergeist II: The Other Side
Poltergeist III
Possession
Possession of Joel Delaney, The
Premature Burial
Prince of Darkness
Prison
Prom Night
Prophecy
Prowler, The
Psychic Killer
Psycho (Hitchcock)
Psycho (Van Sant)
Psycho II
Psycho III
Pumpkinhead

Queen of the Damned
¿Quién Puede Matar a un Niño?

Rabid
Rabid Grannies
Race with the Devil
Rage: Carrie 2, The
Rats, The
Raven, The (Friedlander)
Ravenous
Razorback
Razor Blade Smile
Re-Animator
Re-Animator 2
Refrigerator, The
Relic, The
Reptile, The
Repulsion
Retribution
Return of Count Yorga, The
Return of Doctor X, The
Return of Dracula, The
Return of the Fly
Return of the Living Dead
Return of the Living Dead Part II
Return of the Living Dead III
Return of the Swamp Thing, The
Return of the Vampire, The
Revenge of Frankenstein, The
Revenge of the Creature
Revenge of the Dead
Ring 0 – Birthday
Ring
Ring 2
Roadgames
Rosemary's Baby
Ruby (Harrington)

Salem's Lot
Satanic Rites of Dracula, The
Satan's Skin
Satan's Slave
Savage Bees, The
Scarecrows
Scars of Dracula, The
Scary Movie
Scary Movie 2
Schizophrenia
Scream
Scream 2
Scream 3
Scream and Scream Again
Sect, The
Sender, The
Sentinel, The
Seven Women for Satan
Severed Arm, The
Shadow of the Hawk
Shanks
Shining, The
Shocker
Silver Bullet
Sisters
Sixth Sense, The
Skull, The
Sleepless
Sleepwalkers
Sleepy Hollow
Slumber Party Massacre, The
Society
Son of Dracula
Son of Frankenstein
Son of Godzilla
Sorcerers, The
Sorum
Soul Survivors
Spiral Staircase, The (Siodmak)
Spiral Staircase, The (Collinson)
Squirm
Sssssss
Stepfather, The
Stepfather II, The
Stepfather III
Stephen King's Thinner
Stir of Echoes
Strait-Jacket
Strange Door, The
Straw Dogs
Succubus
Sundown
Superstition
Swamp Thing

Tale of a Vampire
Tales from the Crypt Presents Demon Knight
Tales from the Darkside: The Movie
Tales of Terror
Tarantula
Taste the Blood of Dracula
Tenebrae
Tentacles
Terror (Warren)
Terror, The (Corman)
Terror in the Aisles
Testament du Docteur Cordelier, Le
Texas Chain Saw Massacre, The
Texas Chainsaw Massacre 2, The
Theatre of Blood
Ticks
Thing with Two Heads, The
Tingler, The
Tomb of Ligeia, The
Torture Garden
To the Devil a Daughter
Tower of the Seven Hunchbacks, The
Toxic Avenger, The
Toxic Avenger Part II, The
Traitement de Choc
Trauma
Trick or Treat
Twins of Evil
Two Faces of Dr Jekyll, The

Ugly, The
Uncanny, The
Undead, The
Undying Monster, The
Unholy, The
Unholy Three, The (Browning)
Unholy Three, The (Conway)
Uninvited, The
Unknown, The
Unseen, The
Urban Ghost Story
Urban Legend
Urban Legends Final Cut

Valentine
Vamp
Vampira
Vampire at Midnight
Vampire Bat, The
Vampire Circus, The
Vampire Lovers, The
Vampires in Venice
Vampire's Kiss
Vampyr
Vault of Horror
Velvet Vampire, The
Vendetta, The
Venom
Videodrome
Visiting Hours
Voice Over
Voodoo Man

Walking Dead, The
Wasp Woman, The
Watcher in the Woods, The
Waxwork
Waxworks
Werewolf of London
Wes Craven's New Nightmare
White Zombie
Wishmaster
Witchfinder General
Wizard of Darkness
Wolf
Wolfen
Wolf Man, The
Wraith, The

Xtro

Yeux sans visage, Les
You'll Like My Mother

Zombie Flesh Eaters

Appendix 10

Musicals

Absolute Beginners
All This and World War 2
American in Paris, An
Anchors Aweigh
Annie
Annie Get Your Gun
Auntie Mame

Bal, Le
Balalaika
Babes in Arms
Babes on Broadway
Babymother
Band Wagon, The
Band Waggon
Barkleys of Broadway, The
Bawdy Adventures of Tom Jones, The
Beggar's Opera, The
Belle of New York, The
Bells are Ringing
Bert Rigby, You're a Fool
Best Foot Forward
Best Little Whorehouse in Texas, The
Best Things in Life Are Free, The
Billy Rose's Jumbo
Bloodhounds of Broadway
Blood Wedding
Blossom Time
Bluebeard's Castle
Blue Hawaii
Blue Skies
Blues Brothers, The
Blues Broithers 2000
Blues Under the Skin
Body Rock
Bohème, La
Bolero (Ruggles)
Born to Dance
Bowery to Broadway
Boy Friend, The
Breakin'
Breaking Glass
Brigadoon
Broadway Melody of 1936
Buddy Holly Story, The
Bundle of Joy
Butterfly Ball, The
Bye Bye Birdie
By the Light of the Silvery Moon

Can-Can
Can't Help Singing
Can't Stop the Music
Captain January
Carefree
Carmen (DeMille)
Carmen (Saura)
Carmen (Rosi)
Carmen Jones
Carousel
Catch My Soul
Centennial Summer
Chocolate Soldier, The
Chorus Line, A
Comedian Harmonists
Commitments, The
Congress Dances
Connecticut Yankee in King Arthur's Court, A
Cotton Club, The
Cover Girl
Crossover Dreams
Cry-Baby

Daddy Long Legs
Dames
Damn Yankees
Damsel in Distress, A
Dancer in the Dark
Dancers
Dangerous When Wet
Daughter of Rosie O'Grady, The
Days in London
Demoiselles de Rochefort, Les
Dick Deadeye, or Duty Done
Dirty Dancing
Dr Rhythm
Don't Knock the Rock
Double Trouble
Dreigroschenoper, Die
DuBarry Was a Lady

Earth Girls Are Easy
Easter Parade
Ek Baar Phir
Elstree Calling
Elvis
Emperor Waltz, The
Evergreen
Everyone Says I Love You
Expresso Bongo

Fame
Fantasticks, The
Fast Forward
Ferry Cross the Mersey
Fiddler on the Roof
Finian's Rainbow
First a Girl
Five Heartbeats, The
Flame
Flashdance
Flying Down to Rio
Follow That Dream
Follow the Fleet
Footlight Parade
Footloose
Forget me not
For Me and My Gal
42nd Street
French Cancan
French Line, The
Funny Face
Funny Girl
Funny Lady
Funny Thing Happened on the Way to the Forum, A

Gang's All Here, The
Gay Divorcee, the
GI Blues
Gigi (Minnelli)
Giovanna d'Arco al Rogo
Girl Can't Help It, The
Girl Most Likely, The
Girls! Girls! Girls!
Girls Just Want to Have Fun
Give My Regards to Broad Street
Glenn Miller Story, The
Go, Johnny, Go!
Gold Diggers of 1933
Gold Diggers of 1935
Gold Diggers of 1937
Golden Eighties
Good Companions, The
Goodnight Vienna
Grease
Grease 2
Great Waltz, The (Duvivier)
Great Waltz, The (Stone)
Green Pastures, The
Greenwich Village
Guys and Dolls
Gypsy (LeRoy)
Gypsy (Ardolino)

Hair
Half a Sixpence
Hans Christian Andersen
Happiest Millionaire, The
Happiness of the Katakuris, The
Harvey Girls, The
Heaven Tonight
Hello Dolly!
Hello, Frisco, Hello!

Here Come the Waves
High Society
Holiday Inn
Hound-Dog Man
How to Succeed in Business Without Really Trying
Hypnotised and Hysterical (Hairstylist Wanted)

I Love Melvin
Inside Daisy Clover
It Happened in Brooklyn
It's All Happening

Jailhouse Rock
Jeanne et le Garçon Formidable
Jesus Christ Superstar
Joy of Living
Jupiter's Darling

Kazablan
Kid from Spain, The
Kid Galahad
King and I, The
King Creole
King of Jazz, The
King Steps Out, The
Kismet
Kissin' Cousins
Kiss Me Kate
Kiss Me Kate: 3D

Lady in the Dark
Lambada
Les Girls
Let's Make Love
Li'l Abner
Lili
Little Nellie Kelly
Little Night Music, A
Little Prince, The
Little Shop of Horrors (Oz)
Lost in the Stars
Love Bewitched, A
Love Me or Leave Me
Love Me Tonight
Love's Labour's Lost
Lullaby of Broadway

Madame Butterfly
Magic Flute, The
Mambo Kings, The
Mame
Meet Me at the Fair
Meet Me in St Louis
Meet the Feebles
Message of Love: The Isle of Wight Festival
Mikado, The
Mr Music
Mister Quilp
Mo' Better Blues
Mother Wore Tights
Music Machine, The
Music Man, The
My Fair Lady
My Sister Eileen
Nashville
Naughty but Nice
Naughty Marietta
Never Too Young to Rock
New Moon
Newsies
New York, New York
Night and Day
Nijinsky

Off the Dole
Oh Rosalinda!
Oh! What a Lovely War
Oh, You Beautiful Doll
Oklahoma!
Oliver!
On a Clear Day You Can See Forever
One From the Heart
One Heavenly Night
One Hour With You
One Hundred Men and a Girl
One in a Million
One Touch of Venus
On Moonlight Bay
On the Town
Opera do Malandro
Opposite Sex, The
Orchestra Wives
Otello

Pagliacci
Paint Your Wagon
Pajama Game, The
Pakeezah
Pal Joey
Palmy Days
Paradise – Hawaiian Style
Parapluies de Cherbourg, Les
Pin Up Girl
Pirate, The
Pirates of Penzance, The
Play It Cool
Popeye
Princesse Tam Tam

Raise the Roof
Rappin'
Red Detachment of Women
Red Shoes, The
Rhapsody in Blue
Rigoletto
Roberta
Rock, Rock, Rock
Rocky Horror Picture Show, The
Romance on the High Seas
Roman Scandals
Rooftops
Rose, The
Rose of Washington Square
Route enchantée, La
Royal Wedding

Sarafina!
Scrooge
Sensations of 1945
Sgt Pepper's Lonely Hearts Club Band
Sevillanas
Seven Brides for Seven Brothers
1776
Shall We Dance? (Sandrich)
Shock Treatment
Show Boat (Whale)
Show Boat (Sidney)
Silk Stockings
Sing
Singin' in the Rain
Sky's the Limit
Slipper and the Rose, The
Song Is Born, A
Song of Norway
Song of Scheherazade
Sound of Music, The
South Pacific
Stardust
Star Is Born, A (Cukor)
Star Is Born, A (Pierson)
Starstruck
State Fair
Staying Alive
Stepping Out
Stormy Weather
Strike Up the Band
Summer Stock
Sweethearts of the Campus

Take Me Out to the Ball Game
Tales of Beatrix Potter
Tales of Hoffmann, The
Tap
Teenage Hooker Became Killing Machine in Daehakroh
Thank God It's Friday
That'll Be the Day
That's Dancing
That's Entertainment!
That's Entertainment! Part II
That's Entertainment! III
That Thing You Do
There's No Business Like Show Business
Thoroughly Modern Millie
Three For All
Times Square
Tommy
Tommy Steele Story, The
Top Hat
Torch Song
Tosca
Traviata, La
Trois Places pour le 26
Two of a Kind
Two Weeks With Love

Under the Cherry Moon
Unsinkable Molly Brown, The
Up in Arms
Up on the Roof

Vie est Belle, La
Viva Las Vegas

West Side Story
Wild in the Country
Wild Style
Wiz, The

Xanadu

Yankee Doodle Dandy
Yiddle with His Fiddle
You'll Never Get Rich
Young Man With a Horn
You Were Meant for Me
You Were Never Lovelier

Zaza
Ziegfeld Follies
Ziegfeld Girl
Zouzou

Appendix 11

Period/Swashbucklers

Adventures of Don Juan
Adventures of Michael Strogoff, The
Adventures of Robin Hood, The
Affaire du Courrier de Lyon, L'
Affair of the Necklace, The
Affairs of Cellini, The
Age of Innocence, The
Agony and the Ecstasy, The
Allonsanfan
All This and Heaven Too
Amistad
Anastasia
Angela's Ashes
Anna and the King
Anna Karenina (Brown)
Anna Karenina (Duvivier)
Anna Karenina (Rose)
Anne of the Indies
Anne of the Thousand Days
Anthony Adverse
Arena, The
Ars Amandi
Artemisia
Assassin of the Tsar

Bandit of Sherwood Forest, The
Bang Rajan – Legend of the Village Warriors
Barber of Siberia, The
Barretts of Wimpole Street, The
Barry Lyndon
Baron Fantôme, Le
Beaumarchais
Becky Sharp
Billy Budd
Blackbeard the Pirate
Black Jack
Black Pirate, The
Black Swan, The
Blanche
Blanche Fury
Blood Brothers, The
Bossu, Le
Bostonians, The
Boule de Suif
Bounty, The
Bowery, The
Braveheart
Bride of Vengeance
Buccaneer, The

Camille Claudel
Canterbury Tales, The
Capitaine Fracasse, Le
Captain Blood
Captain Boycott
Carlota Joaquina, Princess of Brazil
Catherine the Great
Charge of the Light Brigade, The (Curtiz)
Charge of the Light Brigade, The (Richardson)
Chartreuse de Parme, La
Charulata
Chess Players, The
Christopher Columbus
Christopher Columbus: The Discovery
Clandestine Marriage, The
Colonel Chabert, Le (Le Hénaff)
Colonel Chabert, Le (Angelo)
Colossus of Rhodes, The
Count of Monte-Cristo, The (Greene)
Count of Monte Cristo, The (Reynolds)
Cousin Bette
Crimson Pirate, The
Cromwell
Crucible, The
Cruel Story of the Shogunate's Downfall
Curse of the Wraydons, The
Cyrano de Bergerac

Dangerous Beauty
Dangerous Liaisons
Dark Avenger, The
Decameron, The
Deceivers, The
Destin Fabuleux de Désirée Clary, Le
Destiny (Chahine)
Devils, The
Devil's Eye, The
Dialogue des Carmelites
Dog of Flanders, A
Doll, The
Don Quixote
Draughtman's Contract, The
Drum
Duellists, The

East-West
Effi Briest
8-Diagram Pole Fighter, The
Eijanaika
El Dorado (Saura)
Elective Affinities
Elephant Man, The
Eline Vere
Elizabeth
Elusive Pimpernel, The
Emigrants,The
Emma
Emperor and the Assassin, The
Empress Yang Kwei Fei, The
Enchanted April
Enfant Sauvage, L'

Enfants du Paradis, Les
Enfants du siècle, Les
Ethan Frome
Ever After
Evita
Excalibur
Executioners from Shaolin
Execution in Autumn
Exile, The

Fabiola
Fanny Hill
Far and Away
Farinelli Il Castrato
Feast of July
Femme Française, Une
Fencing Master, The
Fille de D'Artagnan, La
Firelight
Fire Over England
First Knight
Five Women Around Utamaro
Fixer, The
Flame and the Arrow, The
Flowers of Shanghai
Folk Tales of Lu Ban
Forever Amber
Four Musketeers: The Revenge of Milady, The
1492: Conquest of Paradise
Francesco, giullare di Dio
French Lieutenant's Woman, The
Frenchman's Creek
Fury

Galileo (Cavani)
Galileo (Losey)
Gambler, The
Gawain and the Green Knight
Gentleman Jim
Gervaise
Ghost and the Darkness, The
Giant of Marathon, The
Goat Horn, The
Golden Swallow
Gonza the Spearman
Gorgeous Hussy, The
Gosford Park
Governess, The
Goya in Bordeaux
Great Expectations (Lean)
Great Expectations (Hardy)
Great Expectations (Cuarón)
Great Garrick, The
Great Sinner, The
Gypsy and the Gentleman, The

Hamlet (Plumb)
Hamlet (Olivier)
Hamlet (Kozintsev)
Hamlet (Richardson)
Hamlet (Coronado)
Hamlet (Zeffirelli)
Hamlet (Branagh)
Hamlet (Almereyda)
Haunted Summer
Hellfire Club, The
Henry VIII and His Six Wives
Henry V (Olivier)
Henry V (Branagh)
Heritage, The
Herr Arnes Pengar
Hidden Fortress, The
HMS Defiant
House of Rothschild, The
Howards End
Hungry Hill
Hussard sur le toit, Le

Ideal Husband, The (Korda)
Ideal Husband, The (Parker)
Impromptu
Inheritance, The
In Love and War
Intolerance
Iron Mask, The
I, the Worst of All
Ivanhoe
Ivan the Terrible

Jamaica Inn
Jane Eyre (Stevenson)
Jane Eyre (Mann)
Jane Eyre (Zeffirelli)
Jefferson in Paris
Journey to the Western Xia
Juarez
Jude
Julius Caesar
Justine

Kagemusha
Kama Sutra: A Tale of Love
Karakter
Keep the Aspidistra Flying
Kidnapped
King Lear (Brook)
King Lear (Kozintsev)
Knight's Tale, A
Kundun

Lady & the Duke, The
Lady Caroline Lamb
Lady Jane
Lady L
Lancelot du Lac
Last Emperor, The
Last Supper, The
Les Miserables (Milestone)
Les Misérables (Boleslawski)
Les Misérables (August)
Liaisons Dangereuses 1960, Les
Libertin, Le
Life of Emile Zola, The
Life of Oharu, The
Light at the Edge of the World, The
Li Lianying, the Imperial Eunuch
Lion in Winter, The
Long Ships, The
Love in the Mirror
Little Women (Cukor)
Little Women (Armstrong)
Lucie Aubrac
Ludwig

Macbeth (Welles)
Macbeth (Polanski)
Madame Curie
Madness of King George, The
Magnificent Doll
Mandingo
Man for All Seasons, A
Man in Grey, The
Man in the Iron Mask, The (Whale)
Man in the Iron Mask, The (Wallace)
Mansfield Park
Man Who Would Be King, The
Marquise
Masada
Mask, The (Infascelli)
Mask of Zorro, The
Mayerling
Michael Collins
Michael Kohlhaas
Middleton's Changeling
Misérables, Les (Le Chanois)
Misérables, Les (Lelouch)
Mission, The (Joffe)
Mrs Brown
Mrs Dalloway
Mistress Pamela
Moll Flanders
Month by the Lake, A
Moonfleet
Music Teacher, The
Mutiny on the Bounty (Lloyd)
Mutiny on the Bounty (Milestone)
Name of the Rose, The
Nana
Nell Gwyn
Nemuri Kyoshiro: The Book of Killing-Rules
Nest of Gentlefolk, A
1900
Nicholas Nickleby
Night Sun
Noi Tre
Norseman, The
Northwest Passage
Nostradamus
November 1828
Nun and the Devil, The

Oblomov
Old Curiosity Shop, The
Oliver Twist (Lean)
Oliver Twist (Donner)
Once Upon a Time in China
Once Upon a Time in China II
Once Upon a Time… We Were Colored
Onegin
Onibaba
Orphans of the Storm
Oscar and Lucinda

Pandaemonium
Passion Béatrice, La
Passion de Jeanne d'Arc, La
Passione d'Amore
Passion in the Desert
Peg of Old Drury
Peking Opera Blues
Père Goriot, Le
Photographing Fairies
Plaisir, Le
Plunkett & Macleane
Pope Joan
Portrait of a Lady, The
Pride and Prejudice
Prince of Foxes
Prince of Homburg, The
Prince of Jutland
Princess Caraboo
Prise de Pouvoir par Louis XIV, La
Prisoner of Zenda, The (Cromwell)
Prisoner of Zenda, The (Thorpe)
Private Affairs of Bel Ami, The
Private Life of Henry VIII, The
Private Lives of Elizabeth and Essex, The
Procès de Jeanne d'Arc
Profession of Arms, The

Queen Christina
Queen Kelly
Queen of Spades. The
Que la Fête Commence
Quills
Quiz Show

Rachel's Man
Raintree County
Ran
Rashomon
Rasputin and the Empress
Rebecca's Daughters
Rebellion
Rebel Nun, The
Red Beard
Red Peony Gambler: Flower-cards Match
Reign of Terror
Reine Margot, La
Religieuse, La
Rembrandt
Remains of the Day, The
Retour de Martin Guerre, Le
Return of the Three Musketeers, The
Revolution
Richard III (Olivier)
Richard III (Loncraine)
Ridicule
Road to Wellville, The
Robin and Marian
Robin Hood (Dwan)
Robin Hood (Irvin)
Robin Hood: Prince of Thieves
Rob Roy
Roi de Paris, Le
Rollicking Adventures of Eliza Fraser, The
Ronde, La
Room With a View, A
Rosa Luxemburg
Royal Flash
Royal Hunt of the Sun, The
Royal Scandal, A

Sade
Sailor's Return, The
Saint-Ex
Sansho Dayu
Saraband for Dead Lovers
Saratoga Trunk
Sasuke and His Comedians
Savage Islands
Scaramouche
Scarlet Blade, The
Scarlet Empress, The
Scarlet Letter, The
Scarlet Pimpernel, The
Scarlet Tunic, The
Scent of Green Papaya, The
Sea Hawk, The
Secret Agent, The
Secret de Mayerling, Le
Serpent's Kiss, The
Seven Years in Tibet
Shadowlands
Shawshank Redemption, The
Shin Heike Monogatari
Shogun
Silas Marner
Simon Magus
Sinful Davey
Si Versailles m'était conté…
Slavers
Sommersby
Spanish Main, The
Sparrow
Surrogate Mother

Tartuffe
Taste of the Black Earth
Tess
That Hamilton Woman
That Lady
That Night In Varennes
36th Chamber of Shaolin, The
Three Musketeers: The Queen's Diamonds, The (Lester)
Three Musketeers, The (Herek)
Three Sisters
Throne of Blood
'Tis Pity She's a Whore
Tom Jones
Torrents of Spring
Total Eclipse
Tournoi, Le
Tous les matins du monde
Treasure Island
Twefth Night

Under Capricorn
Under the Red Robe
Unfinished Piece for Mechanical Piano
Utu

Valmont
Vatel
Victory (Cromwell)
Victory (Peploe)
Vikings, The
Viking Queen, The

Virgin Spring, The
Volpone

Walk with Love and Death, A
War Lord, The
Warrior, The
Washington Square
We Live Again
Where Angels Fear to Tread
Where's Jack?
Wicked Lady, The (Arliss)
Wicked Lady, The (Winner)
Wifemistress
Wilde
William Shakespeare's Romeo & Juliet
Wings of the Dove, The
Woodlanders, The
Wolfshead: The Legend of Robin Hood
Wuthering Heights (Wyler)
Wuthering Heights (Kosminsky)

Young Bess
Young Mr Lincoln
Young Mr Pitt, The
Young Winston

Appendix 12

Science Fiction

Abyss, The
Abyss: Special Edition,The
Acción Mutante
Accumulator 1
A.I. Artificial Intelligence
Akira
Alien
Alien Nation
Alien Resurrection
Aliens
Alien^3
Alphaville
Amazing Colossal Man, The
Android
Andromeda Strain, The
Armageddon
Arrival, The
Astronaut's Wife, The
August in the Water

Barbarella
Barren Illusion
Batteries Not Included
Battle Beyond the Stars
Battlefield Earth
Battle for the Planet of the Apes
Battlestar Galactica
Belle Verte, La
Beneath the Planet of the Apes
Bermuda Triangle, The
Beware! the Blob
Bicentennial Man
Black Hole, The
Blade Runner
Blade Runner – The Director's Cut
Blob, The
Body
Body Snatchers
Body Stealers, The
Born in Flames
Borrower, The
Boy and His Dog, A
Brainstorm
Buck Rogers in the 25th
Bunker Palace Hotel

Century
Capricorn One
Children of the Damned
Choke Canyon
Close Encounters of the Third Kind
Close Encounters of the Third Kind (Special Edition)
Communion (Mora)
Conquest of Space
Conquest of the Earth
Conquest of the Planet of the Apes
Contact
Crack in the World
Cube

Daleks – Invasion Earth 2150 AD
Damnation Alley
Damned, The (Losey)
Dark Angel
Dark City
Dark Star
D.A.R.Y.L.
Day of the Triffids, The
Day the Earth Caught Fire, The
Day the Earth Stood Still, The
Day the World Ended, The
Day Time Ended, The
Deathsport
DeepStar Six
Demon Seed
Destination Moon
Doc Savage – the Man of Bronze
Dr Cyclops
Dr Who and the Daleks
Dune

Earth vs the Flying Saucers
Earth vs the Spider
Empire Strikes Back, The
Empire Strikes Back: Special Edition, The
Enemy Mine
Escape from the Planet of the Apes
E.T. The Extra-Terrestrial
Event Horizon
Eve of Destruction
Evolution
Explorers

Faculty, The
Fahrenheit 451
Fantastic Planet
Fantastic Voyage
Fifth Element, The
Final Countdown, The
Final Fantasy: The Spirits Within
Final Programme, The
Fire in the Sky
First Men in the Moon
Flaming Ears
Flash Gordon
Flesh Gordon
Flight of the Navigator
Forbidden Planet
Forbidden World
Forbin Project, The
Fortress
Fortress II: Re-entry
Freejack
Friendship's Death
Futureworld

Gawin
Ghost in the Shell
Ghosts of Mars

Halbe Welt
Hardware
Health Warning
Heavy Metal
Hidden, The
Hollow Men
Humanoid, The
Illustrated Man, The
I Married a Monster from Outer Space
Incredible Hulk, The
Incredible Shrinking Man,The
Independence Day
Innerspace
In the Belly of the Dragon
Invaders from Mars (Menzies)
Invaders from Mars (Hooper)
Invasion
Invasion of the Body Snatchers (Siegel)
Invasion of the Body Snatchers (Kaufman)
Invasion of the Saucermen
Invisible Man, The
Invisible Man Returns, The
It Came from Beneath the Sea
It Came from Outer Space
It Conquered the World

Jimmy Neutron Boy Genius
Johnny Mnemonic
Journey to the Centre of the Earth
Judge Dredd
Jules Verne's Rocket to the Moon

Kamikaze
K-PAX

Laserblast
Last Starfighter, The
Lawnmower Man, The
Lifeforce
Liquid Dreams
Liquid Sky
Logan's Run
Looker
Lost in Space

Mac and Me
Mad Max
Mad Max 2
Mad Max Beyond Thunderdome
Magnetic Monster, The
Malevil
Man from Planet X, The
Man Who Fell to Earth, The
Memories
Metalstorm: the Destruction of Jared-Syn
Meteor
Metropolis (Lang)
Metropolis (Lang/Moroder)
Metropolis (Rintaro)
Millennium
Mimic
Mission to Mars
Monolith
Moon 44
Most Dangerous Man Alive
My Favourite Martian

New Barbarians, The
Night Caller
Night of the Big Heat
Nine Lives of Tomas Katz, The
Nineteen Eighty-Four
No Answer from F.P.1
Not of This Earth

Omega Man, The
Outland

Parasite
Phantasm
Phantasm II
Phase IV
Phenomenon
Philadelphia Experiment, The
Pitch Black
Planet of the Apes (Burton)
Planet of the Apes (Schaffner)
Plan 9 from Outer Space
Prayer of the Rollerboys
Projected Man, The
Proteus
Power, The

Quatermass and the Pit
Quatermass Experiment, The
Quatermass II
Queen of Outer Space
Quest for Love
Quiet Earth, The
Quintet

Red Planet
Red Planet Mars
Return of the Jedi
Return of the Jedi: Special Edition
Rift, The
Robinson Crusoe on Mars
RoboCop
RoboCop 2
RoboCop 3
Robot
Rub Love
Runaway

Salute of the Jugger, The
Santa Claus Conquers the Martians
Saturn 3
Scanners
Scanners II: The New Order
Screamers
Shape of Things to Come, The
Silent Running
6th Day, The
Slaughterhouse Five
Solaris
Soylent Green
Spaced Invaders
Spacehunter: Adventures in the Forbidden Zone
Space Truckers
Species
Species II
Sphere
Split Second
Starcrash
Stargate
Starman
Starship Troopers
Star Trek – The Motion Picture
Star Trek II: The Wrath of Khan
Star Trek III: The Search for Spock
Star Trek V: The Final Frontier
Star Trek VI: The Undiscovered Country
Star Trek: Generations
Star Trek: First Contact
Star Trek: Insurrection
Star Wars
Star Wars Episode I: The Phantom Menace
Star Wars Episode II Attack of the Clones
Star Wars, Episode IV, A New Hope
Sticky Fingers of Time, The
Strange Invaders
Superman
Superman II
Superman III
Superman IV: The Quest for Peace
Supernova

Teenagers from Outer Space
Terminal Man, The
Terminator, The
Terminator 2: Judgment Day
Terminus
TerrorVision
Tetsuo
Tetsuo II: Bodyhammer
Them!
They Live
Thing, The
Thing from Another World, The
Things to Come
This Island Earth

THX 1138
Timecop
Time Machine, The
Timescape
Timeslip
Time Travellers, The
Titan A.E.
Titan Find, The
Total Recall
Trancers
Tremors
Tron
2001: A Space Odyssey
2010
20 Million Miles to Earth

Village of the Damned
Virus
Viva la Vie
Voyage Home:
  Star Trek IV, The

War of the Monsters
War of the Satellites
War of the Worlds
Watchers
Weird Science
Welcome to Blood City
Westworld
When Worlds Collide
Who?
Woman in the Moon

X Men
X – the Man with X-Ray Eyes
X the Unknown

Zone Troopers

Appendix 13

Thrillers

Absolute PowerAbduction
Above Suspicion
Above the Law
Absolution
Accused, The
Across 110th Street
Action Jackson
Act of Vengeance
Addiction, The
Addition, L'
Adult Fun
Adventures of PC 49, The
Adventures of Sherlock
  Holmes, The
Adversary, The
Afraid of the Dark
After Office Hours
After the Thin Man
Against All Odds
Against the Wind
Agency
Albino Alligator
Alias Nick Beal
Alligator Eyes
All the President's Men
All the Way
Alone
Along Came a Spider
Alphabet Murders, The
Amateur, The
Amazing Doctor
  Clitterhouse, The
Ambushers, The
American Dream, An
American Psycho
American Roulette
Amore Molesto, L'
Amores perros
Amsterdamned
Anatomy of a Murder
Anderson Tapes, The
And Soon the Darkness
And Then There Were None
  (Clair)
And Then There Were None
  (Collinson)
Angel (Jordan)
Angel City
Angel Dust
Angel Eyes
Angel Face
Another 48 HRS
Another Life
Antitrust
Apartment Zero
Appointment With Death
Arabesque
Argent des Autres, L'
Arlington Road
Arnelo Affair, The
Arsenal Stadium
  Mystery, The
Art of War, The
Ascenseur pour l'Echafaud
Assassin
Assassin Habite au 21, L'
Assassins (Donner)
Assassin(s) (Kassovitz)
Atlantic City

Babysitter, The
Backfire
Background to Danger
Backlash
Bad Blood
Bad Day at Black Rock
Bad Influence
Bad Seed, The
Balance, La
Bande à Part
Bangkok: Dangerous
Basic Instinct
Bayan Ko: My Own Country
Beat the Devil
Beck
Bedlam
Bedroom Window, The
Before and After
Believers, The
Bellman and True
Benefit of the Doubt
Best Laid Plans
Best Revenge
Best Seller
Betrayed
Between Midnight and Dawn
Beverly Hills Cop
Beverly Hills Cop II
Beverly Hills Cop III
Beware, My Lovely
Beyond a Reasonable Doubt
Beyond Forgivin'
Big Bang Theory
Big Brass Ring, The
Big Easy, The
Big Fix, The
Big Heat, The
Big Hit, The
Big Man, The
Big Sleep, The (Winner)
Big Trouble
Billion Dollar Brain
Black Christmas
Black Eye
Black Gunn
Blackmail (Hitchcock)
Blackmail (Potter)
Black Marble, The
Black Moon Rising
Blackout (Adams)
Blackout (Ferrara)
Black Rain (Scott)
Black Rainbow
Black Sunday
Black Widow (Johnson)
Black Widow (Rafelson)
Black Windmill, The
Bless the Child
Blind Alley
Blind Corner
Blind Date (Losey)
Blind Date (Mastorakis)
Blindfold
Blink
Blood and Wine
Blood Relatives
Blood of Revenge
Blood Ties
Bloody Angels
Blow
Blown Away
Blow Out
Blue Collar
Blue Ice
Blue Knight
Blue Lamp, The
Blues Harp
Blue Steel
Blue Sunshine
Blue Thunder
Blue Tiger
B Monkey
B. Must Die
Bob le Flambeur
Body Control
Body Double
Bodyguard, The
Body in the Forest, A
Boiler Room
Boiling Point (Harris)
Bone Collector
Boomerang (Kazan)
Border, The
Borderline
Boucher, Le
Bound
Boys from Brazil, The
Brainwaves
Brannigan
Brass Target
Breakdown
Breaking Point (Clark)
Breaking Point, The (Curtiz)
Breaking Point, The (Comfort)
Bribe, The
Brides of Fu Manchu
Bride Wore Black, The
Brighton Strangler, The
Bringing Out the Dead
Bring Me the Head of
  Alfredo Garcia
Brink's Job, The
Broken Mirrors
Brotherhood, The
Brother
Brothers and Sisters
Brown's Requiem
Buffet Froid
Bulldog Drummond
Bulldog Drummond
  Comes Back
Bulldog Drummond Escapes
Bullet Train, The
Bullitt
Bunny Lake is Missing
Bureau of Missing Persons
Burglars, The
Burke and Hare
Business of Strangers, The
Busting

Cairo Road
Caged
Call Me
Camera Obscura
Cape Fear (Thompson)
Cape Fear (Scorsese)
Captive
Careful, Soft Shoulder
Carey Treatment, The
Cash on Demand
Cassandra Crossing, The
Cast a Dark Shadow
Castle on the Hudson
Cat Chaser
Cat's Meow, The
Cell, The
Chain Reaction, The
Chamber, The
Champagne Murders, The
Chance to Die, A
Charade
Charisma
Charley Varrick
Charlie Chan and the
  Curse of the Dragon
  Queen (Donner)
Charlie Chan at the Opera
Chase a Crooked Shadow
Cheap Shots
Chiens, Les
China Moon
China Syndrome, The
Choirboys, The
Circle of Danger
Circus
Cisco Pike
City Heat
City of Fear
City of God
City of Industry
City on Fire
Civil Action, A
Clairvoyant, The
Clean, Shaven
Clean Slate
Clear and Present Danger
Client, The
Cloak and Dagger
Closed Circuit
Clouded Yellow, The
Club, The (Wong)
Clue
Cobra (Boisset)
Cohen and Tate
Cold Heaven
Cold Sweat
Colors
Colour of Lies, The
Coma
Come Back Charleston Blue
Comme un Aimant
Company Business
Compromising Positions
Compulsion
Confessions of a Nazi Spy
Confidential Agent
Consenting Adults
Conspiracy Theory
Conspirators, The
Contraband
Conversation, The
Coogan's Bluff
Cool Breeze
Cop
Cop au Vin
CopLand
Cops and Robbers
Cop's Honour
Copycat
Cornered
Corruptor, The
Counsellor, The
Counterfeiters
Courier, The
Cousin, Le
Crackers
Crack in the Mirror
Crack-Up (St Clair)
Crack-Up (Reis)
Crazy Joe
Crescendo
Cri du Hibou, Le
Crime and Punishment
  (von Sternberg)
Crime and Punishment
  (Kaurismäki)
Crime in the Streets
Crime Story
Crimetime
Crimewave
Criminal, The (Losey)
Criminal. The (Simpson)
Criminal Code, The
Criminal Law
Crimson Kimono, The
Crimson Rivers
Croupier
Crossfire
Crossroads (Conway)
Cruising
Crying Freeman
Crying Game, The
Cry of the Hunted

Cry Wolf
Cure
Custodian, The

Dancing With Crime
Dandy in Aspic, A
Danger by My Side
Dangerously They Live
Dangerous Summer, A
Danger Route
Darker Than Amber
Darkness Falls
Dark Waters
Dark Wind, The
Day of the Dolphin, The
Day of the Jackal, The
Dead Again
Dead Bang
Deadbeat at dawn
Deadfall
Dead Heat
Deadly
Deadly Affair, The
Deadly Females, The
Deadly Run
Deadly Strangers
Deadly Trap, The
Dead Calm
Dead Man's Curve
Dead of Winter
Dead or Alive
Dead or Alive 2 – Birds
Dead Pigeon on Beethoven Street
Dead Pool, The
Death at Broadcasting House
Death Collector
Death on the Nile
Death Sentence
Death Ship
Deaths in Tokimeki
Deathtrap
Deceived
Deep Blue Sea
Deep Cover
Deep Crimson
Defence of the Realm
Delinquent Schoolgirls
Dementia
Desperate Hours
Desperate Measures
Desvio al Paraiso
Detective
Detective, The
Détour, Le
Deux Hommes dans Manhattan
Deuxième Souffle, Le
Devil's Advocate, The
Devil's Own, The
Diaboliques, Les
Diabolique
Diagnosis: Murder
Dial M for Murder
Dias Contados
Die Hard
Die Hard 2
Die Hard with a Vengeance
Diggstown
Dinner Rush
Diplomatic Courier
Dirty Harry
Dirty Weekend
Disappearance, The
Dishonoured
Disparen a Matar
Disparus de Saint-Agil, Les
Diva
Dr M
Dr Mabuse, the Gambler
D.O.A. (Morton/Jankel)
Dog Day Afternoon
$
Domestic Disturbance
Domino Principle. The
Donato and Daughter
Don is Dead, The
Don't Look Now
Don't Play With Fire
Don't Say a Word
Doomwatch
Dossier 51, Le
Double Headed Eagle, The
Double Jeopardy
Double Man, The
Double X
Down Three Dark Streets
Dream Demon
Dreamscape
Dressed to Kill
Drive, The
Driver, The
Drôle de Drame
Drowning Pool, The
D-Tox
Duel
Due to an Act of God
Duffy
Dumb Die Fast, the Smart Die Slow, The
Du Rififi à Paname
Du Rififi Chez les Hommes

Ecoute Voir…
Eel, The
8MM
Eight O'Clock Walk
Electra Glide in Blue
Element of Crime, The
11 Harrowhouse
Emergency
Emergency Call
Empire State
Enchantment, The
Encounter at Raven's Gate
Endangered Species
Endless Night
End of Violence, The
Enemy of the State
Enfer, L'
Enforcer, The (Windust/Walsh)
Enforcer, The (Fargo)
Enigma
Eraser
Escape (Dean)
Escape from Alcatraz
Espion Lève-toi
Etoile du Nord, L'
Etrange Monsieur Victor, L'
Entrapment
Evil Under the Sun
Executive Action
Executive Decision
eXistenZ
Experiment, The
Experiment in Terror
Exposé
Exposed
Exquisite Tenderness
Extreme Measures
Extremities
Eye for an Eye
Eyes of a Stranger
Eyes of Laura Mars
Eyewitness (Hough)
Eyewitness (Yates)

Face
Face at the Window, The
Face of Fu Manchu, The
Fade to Black
Fail Safe
Fair Game (Sipes)
Falcon and the Co-eds, The
Falcon and the Snowman, The
Fallen
Fallen Angels
Falling Down
Family Plot
Fan, The (Bianchi)
Fan, The (Scott)
Fanatic
Fantasist, The
Fargo
Fatal Attraction
Fatal Bond
Fear (O'Bannon)
Fear (Foley)
Fear in the Night
Fear is the Key
Fellow Traveller
Femme Infidèle, La
15 Minutes
52 Pick-Up
Fille de l'Air, La
Final Analysis
Final Combination
Fingers
Firepower
Firestarter
Firm, The
First Deadly Sin
First Power, The
Five Corners
5 Fingers
Flatliners
Flesh and Fantasy
Flight of the Innocent
Florentine Dagger, The
Flowers in the Attic
Flying Fool, The
Fog Over Frisco
Folle à Tuer
Following
Footsteps in the Fog
Foreign Correspondent
Formula, The
For Them That Trespass
48 HRS
Four Flies on Grey Velvet
Four Just Men, The
Fourteen Hours
Fourth Man, The
Foxy Brown
Framed
Franchise Affair, The
Frantic
Freelance
French Connection, The
French Connection II
Frenzy
Frequency
Frieda
Friends of Eddie Coyle, The
Frisk
From Dusk Till Dawn
Fruit Machine, The
Fugitive, The (Ford)
Fugitive, The (Davis)
Full Confession
Funeral in Berlin
Funny Money
Further Gesture
Fury
F/X
F/X2

Gambit
Gang Related
Garde a Vue
'Gator Bait
Gauntlet, The
Gaunt Stranger, The
General's Daughter, The
Gentle Gunman, The
Getaway, The (Peckinpah)
Getaway, The (Donaldson)
Get Carter
Get Shorty
Ghost Dog: The Way of the Samurai
Ghosts of the Mississippi
Gingerbread Man, The
Giro City
Give Us Tomorrow
Gleaming the Cube
Glissements Progressifs du Plaisir
Glitter Dome, The
Gloria
God's Army
Gold Coast
Golden Salamander
Gonin
Gonin 2
Gorky Park
Grand Central Murder
Great Jewel Robber, The
Green for Danger
Gridlock'd
Grievous Bodily Harm
Grip of the Strangler
Groundstar Conspiracy, The
Guilty as Sin
Guncrazy

Haine, La
Hana-Bi
Handgun (Garnett)
Handgun (Ransick)
Hand That Rocks the Cradle, The
Hanged Man, The
Happy Now?
Hard-Boiled
Hard Contract
Hard Men
Hard Rain
Hard to Kill
Harper
Harry, He's Here to Help You
Harvest, The
Haunting, The
Head Above Water
Hear No Evil
Heart of Midnight
Heat (Mann)
Heatwave
Heaven's Burning
Heaven's Prisoners
Heist
He Knows You're Alone
Hell Drivers
Hell Is a City
Hets
Hider in the House
High and Low
Highly Dangerous
Highways by Night
History is Made at Night
Hit List
Holcroft Covenant, The
Hole, The
Hollow Triumph
Home at Seven
Homicide
Homme de Désir, L'
Honeymoon Killers, The
Honorary Consul, The
Hot War
Hound of the Baskervilles, The (Lanfield)
Hound of the Baskervilles, The (Fisher)
House of Bamboo
House on Carroll Street, The
'Human' Factor, The (Dmytryk)
Human Factor, The (Preminger)
Hunted
Hunt for Red October, The

Ichi the Killer
Illustrious Corpses
Impulse (Locke)
In Cold Blood
In Crowd, The
In Dreams
Innocent Man, An
Innocents With Dirty Hands
Inspecteur Lavardin
Internal Affairs
Internecine Project, The
In the Heat of the Night
In the Line of Fire
Intimate Stranger, The
In Too Deep
Intruder, The
Ipcress File, The
I Saw What You Did
I Start Counting
Italian Job, The
I, the Jury
Ivy
I Wake Up Screaming
I Went Down

Jackie Brown
Jack's Wife
Jade
Jaguar
January Man, The
Jeepers Creepers
Jennifer

Jennifer 8
Jeopardy
Jerusalem File, The
Jinxed!
Jo
John Q
Johnny Allegro
Johnny Angel
Johnny Handsome
Journey Into Fear
Joy Ride
Judex
Judgement in Stone, A
Juggernaut
Juice
Jump into the Void
Juror
Just Before Nightfall
Just Cause

Kaleidoscope
Kalifornia
Kansas
Kansas City
Kennel Murder Case, The
Keys to Tulsa
Kid
Kid Glove Killer
Kidnapping of the
President, The
Killer, The (Woo)
Killer: A Journal of Murder
Killer Inside Me, The
Killer Is Loose, The
Killer Is on the Phone, The
Killers, The (Siodmak)
Killers, The (Siegel)
Killer's Kiss
Killing of Angel Street, The
Killing Zoe
Kill Me Again
Kill-Off, The
King of Alcatraz
Kings and Desperate Men
Kiss Before Dying, A (Oswald)
Kiss Before Dying, A (Dearden)
Kiss of Death (Schroeder)
Kiss the Girls
Klute
Knife in the Head
Knight Moves
Kremlin Letter, The

Labyrinth of Dreams
LA Confidential
Ladder of Swords
Lady from Shanghai, The
Lady Ice
Lady in Cement
Lady in the Car with
Glasses and a Gun, The
Lady in the Lake
Lady in White
Lady of Burlesque
Lady on a Train
Lady Vanishes, The
(Hitchcock)
Lady Vanishes, The (Page)
Lancer Spy
Last Embrace
Last Man Standing
Last of Sheila, The
Last of the Finest, The
Last Rites
Last Seduction, The
Laughing Policeman, The
Lava
Lethal Weapon
Lethal Weapon 2
Lethal Weapon 3
Lethal Weapon 4
Letters to an Unknown Lover
Liar
Liebestraum
Lies
Lifespan
Like a Rolling Stone
Lineup, The
Lipstick
Lisboa
List of Adrian Messenger, The
Little Drummer Girl, The
Little Nikita
Little Odessa
Live Flesh
Lodger, The (Hitchcock)
Lodger, The (Brahm)
Lolly-Madonna XXX
London Belongs to Me
Lone Star
Long Arm, The
Long Goodbye, The
Looking Glass War, The
Loophole
Lost Highway
Lost Moment, The
Lost Son, The
Love and Action in Chicago
Love at Large
Love, Cheat & Steal
Lovely Way to Die, A
L.627
Lumière Noire
Lured

M (Lang)
M (Losey)
Macorelle Affair, The
Madame Claude
Mädchen Rosemarie, Das
Mad City
Mad Dog Time
Madigan
Mad Monkey, The
Madre Muerta, La
Maledetto Imbroglio, Un
Malice
Malicious
Man Between, The
Manchurian Candidate, The
Man from Majorca, The
Manhunter
Manhunt in Milan
Man in the Road, The
Mani Sulla Città
Manny & lo
Man on Fire
Man on the Roof, The
Man to Respect, A
Man Upstairs, The
Man Who Had His Hair Cut
Short, The
Man Who Knew Too Little,
The
Man Who Knew Too Much,
The (Hitchcock, 1934)
Man Who Knew Too Much,
The (Hitchcock, 1956)
Man Who Saw Too Much, The
Man Who Watched Trains
Go By, The
Man With a Cloak, The
Matrix, The
Melancholia
Memento
Mercury Rising
Metro
Mexican, The
Miami Blues
Midas Run
Midnight
Midnight Express
Midnight Man, The
Midnight Run
Mighty Quinn, The
Mike's Murder
Mike Yokohama – A Forest
with No Name
Ministry of Fear
Miracle Mile
Mirage
Mirror Crack'd, The
Misery
Mission, The (Sayyad)
Mississippi Burning
Miss Pinkerton
Mr Moto's Gamble
Mitchell
Moments
Mona Lisa
Money Movers
Monkey's Mask, The
Moon in the Gutter, The
Morning After, The
Mortal Thoughts
Moss Rose
Most Wanted
Mother's Boys
Ms .45
Mulholland Falls
Murder
Murder at 1600
Murder by Decree
Murder Is a Murder…
Is a Murder, A
Murder on the Orient Express
Murphy's Law
Mute Witness
My Name Is Julia Ross
Mystery in Mexico

Nada
Naked Are the Cheaters
Naked City, The
Naked Killer
Naked Runner, The
Nanny, The
Narrow Margin
Near Room, The
Negotiator, The
Net, The
Never Talk to Strangers
New Centurions, The
New Jack City
Newman's Law
Next of Kin
Next of Kin, The
Nick Carter – Master Detective
Nick of Time
Night Caller
Nightcomers, The
Night Falls on Manhattan
Night Has Eyes
Nighthawks (Malmuth)
Night Holds Terror, The
Nightmare (Whelan)
Nightmare (Shane)
Nightmare (Francis)
Night Moves
Night Must Fall (Thorpe)
Night Must Fall (Reisz)
Night Nurse
Night of the Demon
Night of the Following
Day, The
Night of the Hunter, The
Night of the Party, The
Night Train to Munich
Night Watch (Hutton)
Nightwatch (Bornedal, 1994)
Nightwatch (Bornedal, 1998)
Night Zoo
Nikita
99 to 44/100% Dead
92 in the Shade
Ninth Configuration, The
Nobody Knows Anybody
Nobody Runs Forever
Nobody Will Speak of Us
When We're Dead
Noces Rouges, Les
Nocturne
No Man's Land (Werner)
No Mercy
No Orchids for Miss Blandish
Normal Life
North by Northwest
North Dallas Forty
Notorious
November Plan, The
No Way Home
No Way Out (Donaldson)
Nowhere to Hide
Nowhere to Run
Nuit de Carrefour, La
Nuits Rouges
Number One (Blair)
Number Seventeen

Obsession (Dmytryk)
Obsession (De Palma)
Obsession, An
October Man, The
Odd Man Out
Odds Against Tomorrow
Offence, The
Off Limits
O.H.M.S.
Once a Thief
Once Upon a Time in America
Once Upon a Time…
This Morning
On Deadly Ground
One Deadly Summer
One False Move
One Good Cop
One of Those Things
Onion Field, The
Open Your Eyes
Opera
Ordeal by Innocence
Order of Death
Order to Kill
Organization, The
Organized Crime and
Triad Bureau
Orion's Belt
Outfit, The
Out of Order (Schenkel)
Outside Man, The
Outsider, The
Other, The
Out of Sight

Pacific Heights
Package, The
Painted Heart
Panic Room
Paper Mask
Paradine Case, The
Parallax View, The
Paris by Night
Partners
Pasolini, un Delitto Italiano
Patriot Games
Payback
Payroll
Pearl of Death, The
Peeping Tom
Pelican Brief, The
Penny Gold
Perfect Friday
Perfect Murder, A
Perfect World, A
Permission to Kill
Persecution
Persons Unknown
Petrified Forest, The
Phantom Lady
Phantom Light, The
Phenix City Story, The
Physical Evidence
π [Pi]
Piccadilly Third Stop
Pickup on South Street
Pièges
Pierre dans la Bouche, Une
Pistol Opera
PJ
Place Vendôme
Playbirds, The
Playing God
Playmaker, The
Play Misty for Me
Pledge, The
Plein Soleil
Point Blank
Point Break
Poison Ivy
Police Story (Graham)
Police Story (Chan)
Poodle Springs
Post Mortem
Power Play
Prayer for the Dying, A
Presumed Innocent
Pretty Maids All in a Row
Prey of the Chameleon
Private Hell 36
Prize of Arms, A
Prize of Pertil. The
Prizzi's Honor
Proof of Life
Prowler, The (Losey)

Pulp Fiction
Pulse
Puppet on a Chain
Purple Storm
Pursuit to Algiers
Pusher

Q & A
Que la Bête Meure
Que no quede huella
Quiller Memorandum, The

Rage in Harlem, A
Rainmaker, The
Rainy Dog
Raising Cain
Rancid Aluminium
Random Hearts
Ransom (Wrede)
Ransom (Howard)
Rape, The
Rear Window
Rebecca
Red Circle, The
Redheads
Red Heat
Red Nightmare
Red Rings of Fear
Red Rock West
Reefer and the Model
Regarde la Mer
Regarde les hommes tomber
Reincarnation of Peter Proud, The
Reindeer Games
Remember My Name
Renegades
Replacement Killers, The
Report to the Commissioner
Resurrection Man
Resurrection of Zachary Wheeler, The
Retroactive
Revenge (Scott)
Reward, The
Ricco
Rich Kids
Ricochet
Rider on the Rain
Ring
Ring 2
Riot in Cell Block 11
Rising Sun
River's Edge
River Wild, The
Road Flower
Robbery
Roberto Succo
Rock n'Roll Cop
Rogue Cop
Rollercoaster
Rope
Ronin
Rosary Murders, The
Rough Cut
Rough Shoot
Rounders
Route de Corinthe, La
Running Hot
Running Man, The (Reed)
Running Scared
Rupture, La
Russia House, The
Russian Roulette
Russicum

Sabotage
Saboteur
Saint in New York, The
St Ives
Sandman, The
Sapphire
Satan Met a Lady
Scarlet Claw, The
Scènes de Crimes
Scenes of the Crime
Schizo
Scissors
Score
Scorpio
Scorpion, The
Scorta, La
Scoumoune, La
Scream for Help
Seance on a Wet Afternoon
Sea of Love
Second Awakening of Christa Klages, The
Second Chance (Maté)
Secret, The (Enrico)
Secret, The (Hui)
Secret Agent, The
Secret Beyond the Door
Secret People
Seins de glace, Les
Sellout, The
Serpent, The
Serpent and the Rainbow, The
Serpico
Set It Off
Seven (Sidaris)
Seven (Fincher)
Seven Days in May
Seven Days to Noon
Seven Sinners (de Courville)
Seventh Sign, The
Shadow of a Doubt
Shadows in the Night
Shakedown
Shallow Grave
Shamus
Shark
Shark-skin Man and Peach-hip Girl
Sharky's Machine
Shattered (Leroy)
Shattered (Petersen)
Shattered Image
Sheba Baby
Sheriff, Le
Sherlock Holmes and the Spider Woman
Shiner
Shinjuku Triad Society
Ship That Died of Shame, The
Shock to the System, A
Shooters
Shooting Stars
Shoot to Kill
Show of Force, A
Showtime
Siege, The
Silence of the Lambs, The
Silencieux, Le
Silent Partner, The
Simple Plan, A
Single White Female
Sirène du Mississipi, La
Sister My Sister
Skin & Bone
Skip Tracer
Skulls, The
Skyjacked
Slam Dance
Slaughter
Slaughter's Big Rip-Off
Slayground
Sleepers
Sleeping Car Murder, The
Sleeping Dogs
Sleeping Tiger, The
Sleeping with the Enemy
Sleepless Town
Sleep, My Love
Sleuth
Slither
Sliver
Slow Attack
Smilla's Feeling for Snow
Snake Eyes
Sneakers
Sniper, The
So Close to Paradise
Someone to Watch Over Me
Sonatine
Sound of Fury, The
Spanish Prisoner, The
Special Effects
Specialist, The
Specter of the Rose
Speed
Speed 2: Cruise Control
Spellbound
Spider and the Fly, The
Spinnen, Die
Spione
Spy in Black, The
Spy Story
Spy Who Came In From the Cold, The
Spy Who Loved Me, The
Squeaker, The
Squeeze, The (Apted)
Stacy's Knights
Stakeout
Star Chamber, The
State of Siege
State Secret
Stepford Wives, The
Stick
Still of the Night
Stone Killer, The
Stoolie, The
Storyville
Straight Out of Brooklyn
Strange Affair, The
Strange Case of Dr Rx, The
Stranger, The (Welles)
Stranger (Nagasaki)
Stranger on the Third Floor
Strangers
Strangers on a Train
Strangler, The
Strapped
Stray Dog
Street of Shadows
Strictly Sinatra
Striking Distance
Striptease
Study in Terror, A
Sudden Death
Sudden Fear
Sudden Impact
Suddenly
Sugar Hill
Summerfield
Surveillance
Surviving the Game
Suture
Sweet Scent of Death, A
Swordfish

Taffin
TAG, The Assassination Game
Tailor of Panama, The
Take, The
Taking of Pelham One Two Three, The
Talented Mr Ripley, The
Tall Target, The
Tango & Cash
Tank Malling
Target (Penn)
Taste of Fear
Tattoo
Taxi!
Telefon
Tell Me Something
Temptation Harbour
Tenant, The
Ten Days' Wonder
Ten Little Indians
Ten Seconds to Hell
10 to Midnight
Tequila Sunrise
Terror By Night
Terror Train
Testament of Dr Mabuse, The
Tête contre les murs, La
Theft Under the Sun
They Call Me MISTER Tibbs!
They Call That an Accident
They Came to Rob Las Vegas
They Drive By Night (Woods)
They Drive By Night (Walsh)
They're Playing With Fire
They Won't Forget
Thief
Thieves Like Us
Things to Do in Denver When You're Dead
Thin Man, The
Third Man, The
39 Steps (Hitchcock)
39 Steps (Thomas)
Thirty-Nine Steps, The (Sharp)
This Is My Affair
This Is Not a Love Story
Thomas Crown Affair, The (Jewison)
Thomas Crown Affair, The (McTiernan)
1000 Eyes of Dr Mabuse, The
Three Days of the Condor
Three Hours to Kill
301-302
Three the Hard Way
Throwing Down
Thunderheart
Thunder Road
Thursday
Tiger by the Tail
Tightrope
Time to Kill (Leeds)
Time to Kill, A (Schumacher)
Time Without Pity
To Catch a Thief
Todd Killings, The
To Have and Have Not
Tokyo Drifter
Tolerance
To Live and Die in LA
Tomorrow Never Comes
Tony Rome
Toolbox Murders, The
Topaz
Topkapi
Torn Curtain
Tough Guys Don't Dance
Traces of Red
Trackdown
Traffic (Soberbergh)
Training Day
Traitor Spy
Trapped
Traveller
Tree of Hands
Trenchcoat
Trespass
Trial by Jury
Trial Run
Triple Cross, The
Trouble in Mind
Trout, The
True Believer
True Confessions
True Crime
25 Watts
Twilight's Last Gleaming
Two Jakes, The
Two-Minute Warning

Uccello dalle Piume de Cristallo, L'
Uncle Silas
Undercover Man
Undercurrent
Underground (Asquith)
Under Suspicion
Under the Gun
Underworld U.S.A.
Unfaithful, The
Unforgettable
Unlawful Entry
Unsaid, The
Unsuitable Job for a Woman, An
Usual Suspects, The
U Turn

Vanishing, The (Sluizer, 1988)
Vanishing, The (Sluizer, 1993)
Vanishing Point
Venom (Haggard)
Verdict, The (Siegel)
Verdict, The (Lumet)
Vérité, La
Vertigo
Vice Squad
Victim

Villain
Violent Cop
Violent Professionals, The
Violent Saturday
Virus
Vivement Dimanche!
V I Warshawski
Voleurs, Les
Voyage

Wait Until Dark
Walk East on Beacon
Walking Stick, The
Wanted Dead or Alive
Warning Shot
War Party
Watcher, The
Way of the Gun, The
What Ever Happened to Baby Jane?
What's the Matter With Helen?
What Lies Beneath
When a Stranger Calls
When Eight Bells Toll
Whip Hand, The
Whispering Corridors
Whistle Blower, The
White Angel
White Dog
White Lightning
White Line Fever
White Man's Burden
White of the Eye
White Sands
Who'll Stop the Rain?
Wicked, Wicked
Wicker Man, The
Wind, The (Mastorakis)
Winged Serpent, The
Winter Kills
Wisdom of Crocodiles, The
Witness
Witness for the Prosecution
Woman Next Door, The
World for Ransom
Wrong Is Right

X Files, The

Year of the Dragon
Year of the Gun
Yellow Dog
Yield to the Night
Young and Innocent
Younger and Younger

Z
Zero Effect

Appendix 14

War

Above Us the Waves
Action in the North Atlantic
Aimée & Jaguar
Albert, RN
All Quiet on the Western Front (Milestone)
All Quiet on the Western Front (Mann)
Along the Sungari River
American Guerilla in the Philippines
Annapolis Story, An
Apocalypse Now
Apocalypse Now Redux
Attack!
Austerlitz
Away All Boats

Back Door to Hell
Back to Bataan
Ballad of a Soldier
Bataan
BAT 21
Battleground
Battle of Algiers, The
Battle of Britain
Battle of the Bulge
Battle of the River Plate, The
Battle of the Somme, The
Beach Red
Beast, The
Behind Enemy Lines
Between Heaven and Hell
Big Red One, The
Bitter Victory
Black Hawk Down
Blood of Others
Bloody Sunday
Blue Max, The
Boat, The
Boat, Director's Cut, The
Born on the Fourth of July
Boys in Company C, The
Breaker Morant
Bridge at Remagen, The
Bridge on the River Kwai, The
Bridges at Toko-Ri, The
Bridge Too Far, A
Brylcreem Boys, The
Bullet in the Head
Bunker, The

Captain Corelli's Mandolin
Capitaine Conan
Captive Heart, The
Carve Her Name With Pride
Castle Keep
Casualties of War
Catch-22
Chambre des officiers, La
Charge of the Light Brigade, The (Curtiz)
Charge of the Light Brigade, The (Richardson)
Charlotte Gray
Chico
Civilised People
Cockleshell Heroes
Colditz Story, The
Come and See
Confidence
Confirm or Deny
Corvette K-225
Courgae Under Fire
Croix de Bois, Les
Cross of Iron
Cruel Sea, The

Dam Busters, The
Dangerous Moonlight
Dark Blue World
Dawn Patrol,The (Goulding)
Dawn Patrol, The (Hawks)
Days of Glory
Deer Hunter, The
Deserter and the Nomads, The
Desert Fox, The
Desperate Journey
Destination Gobi
Devil's Brigade, The
Dirty Dozen, The
Dunkirk

84 Charlie Mopic
Empire of the Sun
Enemy at the Gates
Enemy Below, The
Enigma
Era Notte a Roma
Escape
Escape to Athena
Espoir, L'
Every Time We Say Goodbye

Farewell to the King
Fifth Rider Is Fear, The
Fighting Seabees, The
Fighting 69th, The
First of the Few, The
First Yank into Tokyo
Five Graves to Cairo
Fixed Bayonets!
Flight of the Intruder
Flying Leathernecks
Flying Tigers
Force 10 from Navarone
Foreman Went to France,The
For Freedom
49th Parallel
For Whom the Bell Tolls
From Hell to Victory
Full Metal Jacket

Gallipoli
Generation, A
Gettysburg
Girl with the Red Hair, The
Glory
Go Tell the Spartans
Grande Illusion, La
Graveyard of Dreams
Great Escape, The
Green Berets, The
Guadalcanal Diary
Guns of Navarone, The

Halls of Montezuma
Hamburger Hill
Hanna's War
Hannibal Brooks
Heaven & Earth
Hell and High Water
Hellcats of the Navy
Hell is for Heroes
Heroes of Telemark, The
Hill in Korea, A
Hitler's Madman
Hunters, The

Ice Cold in Alex
I Live in Grosvenor Square
Ill Met by Moonlight
Immortal Sergeant, The
In Harm's Way
In Love and War (Dunne)
In Which We Serve
Iron Triangle, The
It Happened Here
Ivan's Childhood
I Was Nineteen

J'Accuse (Gance, 1918)
J'Accuse (Gance, 1937)
Journey's End
Journey Together

Kanal
Kapo
Kedma
Kelly's Heroes
Key, The
Kings Go Forth
Kiss Them for Me

Left Hand of God, The
Libertarias
Lighthorsemen, The
Ligne de Démarcation, La
Long Day's Dying, The
Longest Day, The
Lost Patrol, The

Malaya
Memphis Belle
Midnight Clear, A
Midway
Millions Like Us
Miracle in the Rain
Mosquito Squadron
Mrs Miniver
Murphy's War

Naked and the Dead, The
Neige était sale, La
Never So Few
New Lot, The
Night of San Lorenzo, The
Night of the Generals, The
Night Paths
Nine Lives
None But the Brave
North Star, The

Objective, Burma!
Occupation in 26 Pictures, The
Odd Angry Shot, The
Odette
One Minute to Zero
One of Our Aircraft Is Missing
One That Got Away, The
1,000 Plane Raid, The
Operation Amsterdam
Operation Crossbow
Operation Daybreak
Orders to Kill
Overlord

Paisà
Paradie Road
Paris After Dark
Password Is Courage, The
Pearl Harbor
Père Tranquille, Le
Perfect Circle
Perfect Strangers
Pianist, The
Platoon
Play Dirty
Pork Chop Hill
Pretty Village, Pretty Flame
Prisoner of the Mountains

Reach for the Sky
Real Glory, The
Red Badge of Courage, The
Regeneration
Return from the River Kwai
Retreat, Hell!
Road to Glory, The

Sac de Billes, Un
Sahara (Korda)
San Demetrio, London
Sands of Iwo Jima
Saving Private Ryan
Savior
Sbarco di Anzio, Lo
Sea Chase, The
Sea of Sand
Search, The
Sea Wolves, The
Sergeant York
Shop on the High Street, A
Silence de la mer, Le
67 Days
Soldier of Orange
Stalingrad
Steel Bayonet, The
Steel Helmet, The
Storm Over Asia
Story of GI Joe, The
Submarine Patrol
Submarine X-1

Tell England
That Summer of White Roses
They Were Expendable
They Were Not Divided
The Thin Red Line
36 Hours
This Above All
This Land is Mine
Three Came Home
Three Kings
Tiara Tahiti
Tigerland
Too Late the Hero
Tora! Tora! Tora!
Torpedo Run
Traversée de Paris, La
Train, The
Trial on the Road
Twelve O'Clock High

Vache et la Prisonnier, La
Valley, The
Verboten
Victors, The

Victory
Von Richthofen and Brown
Von Ryan's Express

Walk in the Sun, A
War Bride
Way Ahead, The
Way to the Stars, The
We from Kronstadt
Welcome to Sarajevo
Went the Day Well?
Westfront 1918

We Were Soldiers
Where Eagles Dare
Wind Cannot Read, The
Wings
Wings of Eagles, The
Wooden Horse, The

Yank in the RAF, A
Yangtse Incident
Yellow Bride, The
Young Lions, The

Appendix 15

Westerns

Across the Wide Missouri
Adventures of Bullwhip Griffin, The
Alamo, The
All the Pretty Horses
Along Came Jones
Americano, The
American Outlaws
Annie Oakley
Apache
Appache Drums
Appaloosa, The
At Gunpoint
Autre Homme une Autre Chance, Un

Bad Company
Bad Girls
Badlanders, The
Bad Man's River
Ballad of Cable Hogue, The
Ballad of Gregorio Cortez
Ballad of Little Jo, The
Bandolero!
Barbarosa
Barquero
Beautiful Blonde from Bashful Bend, The
Bend of the River
Big Country, The
Big Hand for the Little Lady, A
Big Jake
Big Silence, The
Big Sky, The
Big Trail, The
Billy the Kid
Billy Two Hats
Bite the Bullet
Blazing Guns
Blazing Saddles
Blindman
Blood Money
Blood on the Moon
Blood Red
Blood River
Blue
Border Shootout
Boss Nigger
Bravados, The
Breakheart Pass
Brigham Young – Frontiersman
Broken Arrow
Broken Lance
Buchanan Rides Alone
Buck and the Preacher
Buffalo Bill and the Indians
Bugles in the Afternoon
Bullet for the General, A
Burning Hills, The
Butch and Sundance: The Early Days
Butch Cassidy and the Sundance Kid

Cahill – US Marshal
Calamity Jane
Canadians, The
Carson City
Car Ballou
Catlow
Cattle Annie and Little Britches
Cattle Queen of Montana
Charge at Feather River, The
Charley-One-Eye
Charro!
Chato's Land
Cheyenne Autumn
Cheyenne Social Club, The
China 9, Liberty 37
Chisum
Chuka
Cimarron
Cisco Kid and the Lady, The
Claim, The
Colorado Territory
Colt .45
Comanche Station
Comes a Horseman
Command, The
Companeros
Cowboy
Cowboys, The
Cry Onion
Culpepper Cattle Co., The
Custer of the West

Dakota Incident
Dallas
Dances With Wolves
Dances With Wolves – Special Edition
Day of the Evil Gun
Day of the Outlaw
Deadly Companions
Deadly Trackers, The
Dead Man
Deaf Smith & Johnny Ears
Death of a Gunfighter
Desert Trail, The
Devil's Doorway
Dirty Little Billy
Distant Drums
Distant Trumpet, A
Django
Django Kill
Doc
Dodge City
Dragoon Wells Massacre
Drums Along the Mohawk
Duchess and the Dirtwater Fox, The
Duel at Diablo
Duel at Silver Creek, The
Duel in the Sun
Dust

Eagle's Wing
El Condor
El Dorado (Hawks)
Electric Horseman, The
Escape from Fort Bravo

Far Country, The
Fastest Gun Alive, The
Fistful of Dollars, A
5 Card Stud
Flaming Star
For a Few Dollars More
Fort Apache
40 Graves for 40 Guns
Forty Guns
From Hell to Texas
From Noon Till Three
Furies, The

Geronimo: An American Legend
Glory Guys, The
Goin' South
Good Guys and the Bad Guys, The
Good, the Bad and the Ugly, The
Grayeagle
Great Day in the Morning
Great K & A Train Robbery, The
Great Northfield Minnesota Raid, The
Great Scout & Cathouse Thursday, The
Grey Fox, The
Gunfight, A
Gunfight at the OK Corral, The
Gunfighter, The
Gun Fury

Half-Breed, The
Halliday Brand, The
Hang 'em High
Hannie Caulder
Heartland
Heaven's Gate
Heller in Pink Tights
High Noon
High Plains Drifter
Hired Hand, The
Hondo
Honkers
Horizons West
Horse Soldiers
Hour of the Gun
How the West Was Won
Hud

Indian Fighter, The
Iron Horse, The
I Shot Jesse James

Jeremiah Johnson
Jesse James
Joe Kidd
Johnny Guitar
Junior Bonner

Kentuckian, The
Kid Blue
King and Four Queens, The

Last Challenge, The
Last Command, The
Last Hunt, The
Last of the Mohicans, The
Last Sunset, The
Last Train from Gun Hill
Last Wagon, The
Law and Jake Wade, The
Lawless Street, A
Lawman
Left Handed Gun, The
Legend of Frenchie King, The
Legend of the Lone Ranger, The
Legends of the Fall
Life and Times of Judge Roy Bean, The
Little Big Man
Lone Hand, The
Lonely Are the Brave
Long Riders, The
Love Me Tender
Lucky Texan, The

McCabe and Mrs Miller
Madron
Magnificent Seven, The
Magnificent Seven Ride!, The
Major Dundee
Man Alone, A
Man Called Horse, A
Man Called Noon, The
Man from Colorado, The
Man from Laramie, The
Man in the Wilderness
Man of the West
Man Who Loved Cat Dancing, The
Man Who Shot Liberty Valance, The
Man Without a Star
Maverick
Mercenario, Il
Misfits, The
Missouri Breaks, The
Mohawk
Monte Walsh
Mule Train
Mustang Country
My Darling Clementine
My Heroes Have Always Been Cowboys
My Name is Nobody

Naked Dawn, The
Naked Spur, The
Night Passage
North to Alaska
Northwest Passage

Oklahoma Woman
Once Upon a Time in the West
One-Eyed Jacks
Outlaw, The
Outlaw Josey Wales, The
Ox-Bow Incident, The

Pale Rider
Pat Garrett and Billy the Kid
Plainsman, The
Pocket Money
Pony Soldier
Posse (Douglas)
Posse (Van Peebles)
Professionals, The
Proud Ones, The
Pursued

Quantrill's Raiders
Quattro dell'Ave Maria, I
Quick and the Dead, The

Rachel and the Stranger
Raid, The
Ramrod
Rancho Deluxe
Rancho Notorious
Randy Rides Alone
Rare Breed, The
Ravenous
Rawhide
Reason to Live, a Reason to Die, A
Red River
Red Sun
Restless Breed, The
Return of a Man Called Horse, The
Return of Frank James, The
Return of the Cisco Kid, The
Return of Sabata
Return of the Seven
Revengers, The
Ride in the Whirlwind
Ride Lonesome
Ride in the High Country
Riders of Destiny
Ride with the Devil
Rio Bravo
Rio Conchos
Rio Grande
Rio Lobo
River of No Return
Robin Hood of El Dorado,The
Rooster Cogburn
Rough Night in Jericho
Rounders, The
Run for Cover
Run of the Arrow

Sabata
Saddle the Wind
Sam Whiskey

Santa Fe Trail
Santee
Scalphunters, The
Searchers, The
Secrets
Sergeant Rutledge
Seven Men from Now
7th Cavalry
Shalako
Shane
Sheepman, The
Sheriff of Fractured Jaw, The
She Wore a Yellow Ribbon
Shooting, The
Shootist, The
Sierra
Silent Tongue
Silverado
Silver Lodge
Singer Not the Song, The
Smoke Signal
Smoky
Soldier Blue
South of St Louis
Spikes Gang, The
Stagecoach (Ford)
Stagecoach (Douglas)
Strada per Forte Alamo, La
Stranger on the Run
Sunchaser, The

Take a Hard Ride
Tall Men, The
Tall T, The
Tell Them Willie Boy is Here
Tennessee's Partner
Tension at Table Rock
Terror in a Texas Town
Texas, Addio
Texas Rangers
There Was a Crooked Man
They Call Him Marcado
They Call Me Trinity
They Died With Their
Boots On
They Passed This Way
Three Bullets for a Long Gun
Three Godfathers
3.10 to Yuma
Ticket to Tomahawk, A
Time for Dying, A
Tin Star, The
Tombstone
Tom Horn
Touche pas à la femme blanche
Town Called Bastard, A
Track of the Cat
Train Robbers, The
Tribute to a Bad Man
Triumphs of a Man Called
Horse
True Grit
True Story of Jesse James, The
Two Mules for Sister Sara
Two Rode Together

Ulzana's Raid
Unconquered
Undefeated, The
Unforgiven (Eastwood)
Unforgiven, The (Huston)

Valdez il Mezzosangue
Valdez is Coming
Vampires
Vengeance
Vera Cruz
Villain, The
Viva Villa

Wagon Master
Wanda Nevada
Warlock
War Wagon, The
Way of a Gaucho
Welcome to Hard Times
Westerner, The
Western Union
When the Legends Die
White Buffalo, The
White Feather
Wichita
Wild Bill
Wild Bunch, The
Wild Rovers
Wild Wild West
Will Penny
Winchester '73
Woman Obsessed
Wonderful Country, The
Wyatt Earp

Yellow Sky
Young Guns
Young Guns II

Zandy's Bride

Appendices of Major Film-Producing Countries

Appendix 16

Australian Films

ABBA The Movie (Swe/Aust)
Adventures of Barry McKenzie, The
Adventures of Priscilla Queen of the Desert, The
Age of Consent
Alvin Purple
American Roulette (GB/Aust)
Angel Baby
Angst
Annie's Coming Out

Babe
Babe – Pig in the City (US/Aust)
Backlash
Back of Beyond
Backroads
Bank, The
Bedevil
Better Than Sex
Between Wars
Big Boy Bubby (Aust/It)
Big Steal, The
Black River
Black Robe (Can/Aust)
Bliss
Blood Oath
Blue Fin
BMX Bandits
Body Melt
Bootmen (Aust/US)
Boys, The (Aust/GB)
Boy Who Had Everything, The
Breaker Morant
Brilliant Lies

Cactus
Caddie
Cane Toads – An Unnatural History
Captain Johnno
Careful, He Might Hear You
Cars That Ate Paris, The
Castle, The
Cathy's Child
Cats & Dogs (US/Aust)
Celia
Chain Reaction, The
Chant of Jimmie Blacksmith, The
Charlotte Gray (GB/US/Aust)
Chopper
Clinic, The
Club, The
Coca Cola Kid, The
Country Life
Crocodile Dundee
Crocodile Dundee in Los Angeles (US/Aust)
Crocodile Dundee II
Cry in the Dark, A
Cup, The
Custodian, The

Dance Me to My Song
Dangerous Summer, A
Dark City (US/Aust)
Dawn!
Daydream Believer
Dead Calm
Dead Heart
Dead Letter Office
Deadly
Death in Brunswick
Death of a Soldier
Delinquents, The
Devil's Playground, The
Diplomat, The
Dish, The
Disturbing Behavior (US/Aust)
Dogs in Space
Doing Time for Patsy Cline
Don Quixote
Don's Party
Don't Say a Word (US/Aust)
Down to Earth (US/Ger/Aust)
Emma's War
Encounter at Raven's Gate
End Play
Everlasting Secret Family, The
Exit Wounds (US/Aust)
Eye of the Beholder (Can/GB/US/Aust)

Fast Talking
Fatal Bond
Father
Feeling Sexy
FernGully: The Last Rainforest
15 Amore
Fighting Back (Caulfield)
Fistful of Flies
Flirting
Floating Life
Force More Powerful, A
For Love or Money
Fortress, The (US/Aust)
Frauds
Fringe Dwellers, The
Frog Dreaming

Gallipoli
Getting of Wisdom, The
Ghosts…of the Civil Dead
Goddess of 1967, The
Golden Braid
Goodbye, Norma Jean (US/Aust)
Good Woman of Bangkok, The
Gossip (US/Aust)
Greenkeeping
Grievous Bodily Harm

Half Life
Hammers Over the Anvil
Harlequin
Head On
Hearts in Atlantis
Heatwave
Heaven's Burning
Heaven Tonight
Hercules Returns
High Tide
Hotel de Love
Hotel Sorrento

In a Savage Land
Indecent Obsession, An
In the Winter Dark
Isabelle Eberhardt (Fr/Aust)

Just Us

Kangaroo (Burstall)
Killing of Angel Street, The
Kiss or Kill

Last Crop, The (GB/Aust)
Last Days of Chez Nous, The
Last Wave, The
Les Patterson Saves the World
Lightning Jack
Lonely Hearts
Long Weekend
Love and Other Catastrophes
Love in Limbo
Love Letters from Teralba Road, The
Lucky Break

Mad Dog Morgan
Mad Max
Mad Max Beyond the Thunderdome
Mad Max 2
Malcolm
Mallboy
Malpractice
Man from Hong Kong, The (Aust/HK)
Man from Snowy River, The
Manganinnie
Mango Tree
Man of Flowers
Map of the Human Heart (GB/Aust/Fr/Can)
Matrix, The (US/Aust)
Me Myself I (Fr/Aust)
Miniskirted Dynamo, The
Mr Reliable (a True Story)
Miss Congeniality (US/Aust)
Money Movers
Monkey Grip
Monkey's Mask, The (Aust/Fr/Jap/It)
Mortgage
Mullaway
Muriel's Wedding
My Brilliant Career
My First Wife
My Journey, My Islam
My Life Without Steve

Navigator: A Medieval Odyssey, The
Nickel Queen
Norman Loves Rose

Ocean's Eleven (US/Aust)
Odd Angry Shot, The
Only the Brave

Outback
Over the Hill

Paperback Hero
Paradise Road (US/Aust)
Patrick
Paws (GB/Aust)
Personal History of the Australian Surf, A
Petersen
Phantom, The (US/Aust)
Phar Lap
Piano, The
Picnic at Hanging Rock
Picture Show Man, The
Pitch Black (US/Aust)
Praise
Prejudice
Proof
Puberty Blues
Public Enemy Number One
Punisher, The

Queen of the Damned (US/Aust)
Quiet Room, The

Race for the Yankee Zephyr (NZ/Aust)
Radiance
Razorback
Redheads
Red Planet (US/Aust)
Return of Captain Invincible
Return to Never Land (US/Can/Aust)
Roadgames
Road to Nhill
Robbery Under Arms
Rollicking Adventures of Eliza Fraser, The
Rough Diamonds

Salute of the Jugger, The
Say a Little Prayer
Secrets
Shame
Shanghai Panic (China/Aust)
Shark Caller of Kontu, The
Shine (Aust/GB)
Showtime (US/Aust)
Siam Sunset (Aust/GB)
Silver City
Sirens (Aust/GB)
Sky Pirates
Slate, Wyn & Me
SLC Punk (US/Aust)
Southern Cross
Space Cowboys (US/Aust)
Spagnola, La
Spider and Rose
Spotswood
Stan and George's New Life
Starstruck
Stork
Strange Planet
Strictly Ballroom
Strikebound
Summerfield
Sunday Too Far Away
Survivor, The
Sweetie
Swordfish (US/Aust)

Terra Nova
That Eye, the Sky
Three Kings (US/Aust)
They're a Weird Mob (Aust/GB)
Till There Was You
Tim
To Have & to Hold
Training Day (US/Aust)
Travelling North
True Story of Eskimo Nell, The
Turkey Shoot
Turtle Beach
Two Friends
Two Hands

Umbrella Woman, The
Until the End of the World (Ger/Fr/Aust)

Vincent: The Life and Death of Vincent Van Gogh
Voice of Kurdistan, The (GB/Aust)

Waiting
Wake in Fright
Walkabout
Welcome to Woop Woop (Aust/GB)
Well, The
Wendy Cracked a Walnut
We of the Never Never
What Have I Written
Wide Sargasso Sea
Winchester Conspiracy, The
Winner, The (US/Aust)
Winter of Our Dreams
Woman's Tale, A

Year My Voice Broke, The
Year of Living Dangerously, The
Young Einstein

Zoolander (US/Ger/Aust)

Appendix 17

Canadian Films

Adjuster, The
Agency
Air Bud (US/Luxembourg/Can)
Alien Thunder
American Psycho (US/Can)
Anne Trister (Can/Switz)
Apprenticeship of Duddy Kravitz, The
Ararat
Archangel
Around the Pink House (Can/Fr/Leb)
Art of War (Can/US)
Atanarjuat: The Fast Runner
Atlantic City (Can/Fr)
August 32nd on Earth

Babar: The Movie (Can/Fr)
Bay Boy, The (Can/Fr)
Bear Island (Can/GB)
Beautiful Dreamers
Being at Home with Claude
Best Revenge
Between Friends
Big Meat Eater
Bix
Black Christmas
Black Robe (Can/Aust)
Blood of Others (Can/Fr)
Blood Relatives (Can/Fr)
Breaking Point
Brood, The
Buffalo '66 (Can/US)
Butley (US/GB/Can)
Bye Bye Blues

Calendar (Can/Arm/Ger)
Camilla (Can/GB)
Candy Mountain (Switz/Fr/Can)
Care Bears Adventure in Wonderland!, The
Careful
Cathy's Curse (Fr/Can)
Cat's Meow, The (Can/Ger/GB)
Chance or Coincidence (Fr/Can)
Changeling, The
Child Under a Leaf
Circle of Two
City on Fire (Can/US)
Claim, The (GB/Can/Fr)
Class of 1984
Cold Comfort
Comic Book Confidential
Company of Strangers, The
Confessional, The
Crash (Cronenberg)
Crimes of the Future
Crying Freeman (Fr/Can/US/Jap)
Cry-Woman (Can/SKor/Fr)
Cube
Curtis's Crimes

Dancing in the Dark
Dead of Night
Dead Ringers
Death Ship (Can/GB)
Death Weekend
Decline of the American Empire, The
Diplomatic Immunity
Disappearance, The (GB/Can)
Distant Thunder (Rosenthal – US/Can)
Dogpound Shuffle
Dream Life
D-Tox (Us/Ger/Can)
Dunston Checks In

Earth (Mehta – Ind/Can)
Eclipse
eXistenZ (Can/GB)
Exotica
Eye of the Beholder (Can/GB/US/Aust)

Family Viewing
Fast Company
Felicia's Journey (US/Can)
51st State, The (Can/GB)
Finding Forrester (US/Can)
Fire
Five Senses
Fortune and Men's Eyes (Can/US)
Freeway II: Confessions of a Trickbaby (US/Fr/Can)
Full Circle (GB/Can)

Galileo (Losey – GB/Can)
Gate, The
Ginger Snaps
Glitter (US/Can)
Goin' Down the Road
Grey Fox, The
Grey Owl (US/Can)

Hathi (Can/Ind)Head On
Heartaches
Heartland Reggae
Heart of the World, The
Highland III – The Sorcerer (Can/Fr/GB)
Histoire inventée, Une
Hochelaga
Hog Wild
Homme de ma vie, L' (Fr/Can)
Hot Money
Hounds of Notre Dame, The
House
House with a View of the Sea, The (Ven/Can/Sp)

If Only (Sp/Fr/Can/GB/Luxembourg)
I Love a Man in Uniform
In Celebration (GB/Can)
Incubus
In Praise of Older Women
In the Belly of the Dragon
Intimate Relations (GB/Can)
Iron Eagle II
I've Heard the Mermaids Singing

J.A. Martin, Photographer
Janis
Jesus of Montreal (Can/Fr)
Joy (Fr/Can)
Judgement in Stone, A

Kabloonak (Fr/Can)
Kanehsatake (Oka) – 270 Years of Resistance
Kidnapping of the President, The
Kings and Desperate Men
King Solomon's Treasure
Kissed

Last Night (Can/Fr)
Last Supper, The (Roberts)
Last Temptation of Christ, The (US/Can)
Law of Enclosures, The
Let It Come Down: The Life of Paul Bowles
Léolo
Leopard in the Snow (GB/Can)
Lilies
Love and Death on Long Island (GB/Can)
Love and Human Remains
Luck of Ginger Coffey, The (Can/US)
Luther (US/GB/Can)

Maids, The (GB/Can)
Man, a Woman and a Bank, A
Manufacturing Consent: Noam Chomsky and the Media
Map of the Human Heart (GB/Aust/Fr/Can)
Margaret's Museum (Can/GB)
Marie s'en va-t-en ville
Married Couple, A
Masala
Mask, The
Middle Age Crazy
Mon Oncle Antoine
Montreal Main
Morvern Callar (GB/Can)
Mourir à Tue-Tête
Murder by Decree (Can/GB)
My American Cousin

Naked Lunch (GB/Can)
Neptune Factor, The
Never Talk to Strangers (Can/US)
Night Zoo
90 Days
Nô
No Skin Off My Ass
No Surrender (GB/Can)
Not a Love Story

Outrageous!

Painted Angels (Can/GB)
Paperback Hero
Paper Wedding, A
Parasite Murders, The
Paris France
Perfectly Normal (GB/Can)
Pippi Longstocking (Swe/Ger/Can)
Polygraph, The (Can/Fr/Ger)
Porky's
Porky's II: The Next Day
Porky's Revenge
Pornographer, The (Fr/Can)
Possible Worlds
Post Mortem
Power Play (GB/Can)
Punch Me in the Stomach (NZ/Can)

Quest for Fire (Can/Fr)

Rabid
Rainbow (GB/Can)
Real Howard Spitz, The (GB/Can)
Reason Over Passion
Red Violin, The (Can/It/US/GB)
Réjeanne Padavani
Return to Never Land (US/Can/Aust)
Revolving Doors, The
Room for Romeo Brass, A (GB/Can)

Scanners
Scanners II: The New Order
Screamers (Can/US/Jap)
Screwballs
Screwballs II – Loose Screws
Secret Laughter of Women, The (GB/Can)
Secret Wedding (Arg/Neth/Can)
September Songs: The Music of Kurt Weill
Shadow of the Hawk
Shape of Things to Come, The
Shoemaker
Siege
Silent Partner The
Sitting in Limbo
Skin Flick (Ger/GB/Can/Jap)
Skip Tracer
Song for Tibet
Soul Investigator
Sparklehorse
Speaking Parts
Special Day, A (It/Can)
Spider
Stardom (Can/Fr)
Stepping Razor – Red X
Such a Long Journey (Can/GB)
Sunday in the Country (Trent)
Sunshine (Hun/Ger/Can/Aus/GB)
Super 8½
Suspicious River
Swan Lake – The Zone (USSR/Can/US/Swe)
Swann
Sweet Angel Mine (GB/Can)
Sweet Hereafter , The
Sweet Movie (Fr/Can/WGer)

Tadpole and the Whale
Tales from the Gimli Hospital
Tendresse Ordinaire
Terra-Cotta Warrior, A (HK/Can)
Terror Train
Terry Fox Story, The
Tête de Normande St-Onge, La
That Cold Day in the Park
Thirty Two Short Films About Glenn Gould
Ticket to Heaven
Tommy Tricker and the Stamp Traveller
Tomorrow Never Comes (Can/GB)
To Walk with Lions (Can/GB/Kenya)
Tribute (US/Can)
True Nature of Bernadette, The
Twilight of the Ice Nymphs, The

Uncanny, The (GB/Can)
Un©ut
Unsaid, The (Can/US)
Urinal

Veuve de Saint-Pierre, La (Fr/Can)
Videodrome
Violation of Justine, The (Fr/It/Can)
Violent Tradition (US/Can)
Violette Nozière (Fr/Can)
Virus (Jap/Can)
Visiting Hours
Volcano

War Bride, The (GB/Can)
Watchers
Wavelength
Welcome to Blood City (Can/GB)
When Night Is Falling
White Room (Can/GB)
Why Shoot the Teacher?
Wild Flowers
Winter Tan, A

Zero Patience

Appendix 18

French Films

A.B.C. Africa (Iran/Fr)
About a Boy (Ger/US/Fr/GB)
A Bout de Souffle
Abraham Valley (Fr/Switz)
Accompagnatrice, L'
Aces High (GB/Fr)
Addition, L'
Adhemar ou Le Jouet de la Fatalité
Adieu Bonaparte (Fr/Egypt)
Adieu Philippine (Fr/It)
A Double Tour (Fr/It)
Adventures of Pinocchio, The (GB/Fr/Ger/Czech Rep/US)
Adversary, The (Fr/Switz/Sp)
Affaire du Courrier de Lyon, L'
Affiche Rouge, L'
Afraid of the Dark (GB/Fr)
Age d'Or, L'
Agression, L' (Fr/It)
Aïd el Kébir (Fr/Tun)
Aigle à Deux Têtes, L'
Aile ou la Cuisse, L'
Ai No Corrida (Jap/Fr)
Air de Famille, Un
A.K. (Fr/Jap)
A la Place du Coeur
A l'attaque
Albino Aligator (US/Fr)
Alexandre
Alexandria Encore (Egypt/Fr)
Alfredo Alfredo (It/Fr)
Algiers/Beyrouth: pour mémoire (Fr/Leb)
Alice et Martin (Fr/Sp/US)
Alice in Wonderland (US/Fr/GB)
Ali G Indahouse (Ger/US/Fr/GB)
Ali Zaoua: Prince de la Rue (Mar/Tun/Fr)
All About My Mother (Sp/Fr)
All Men Are Mortal (GB/Neth/Fr)
All or Nothing (GB/Fr)
Alphaville (Fr/It)
Amants, Les
Amants du Pont-Neuf, Les
Amants de Verone, Les
Amarcord (It/Fr)
A ma soeur! (Fr/It/Sp)
Amateur (Fr/GB)
Amazons, The (It/Fr)
Amélie (Fr/Ger)
American Friend, The (WGer/Fr)
American Stories (Fr/Bel)
American Werewolf in Paris, An (US/Luxembourg/Fr/GB)
Ames Fortes, Les (Fr/Bel)
Amour à Mort, L'
Amour d'enfance
Amour Existe, L'
Amour Fou, L'
Amour par terre, L'
Amy Foster (GB/US/Fr)
And Now My Love (Fr/It)
And the Ship Sails On (It/Fr)
Année Juliette, L'
Angel Dust
Angel Sharks
Anges du Péché, Les
Annabelle partagée
Année Dernière à Marienbad, L' (Fr/It)
A Nous la Liberté
A Nous les Petites Anglaises!
An 01, L'
Appartement, L (Fr/Sp/It)
Appât, L'
Appel du Silence, L'
Après l'Amour
Apt Pupil (US/Fr)
Arabian Nights (It/Fr)

Araignée de Satin, L'
Arbre, le Mairie et la Médiathèque ou Les Sept Hasards, L'
Arche du désert, L' (Alg/Fr/Ger/Switz)
Argent, L' (L'Herbier)
Argent, L' (Bresson – Switz/Fr)
Argent de Poche, L'
Argent des Autres, L'
Arizona Dreaming (Fr/Former Yugo)
Armée des Ombres, L' (Fr/It)
Around the Pink House (Can/Fr/Leb)
Ars Amandi (It/Fr)
Artemisia (Fr/Ger/It)
As a Man
Ascenseur pour l'Echafaud
Assassination of Trotsky, The (Fr/It/GB)
Assassin Habite au 21, L'
Assassin(s)
Asterix & Obelix Take on Caesar (Fr/Ger/It)
Asterix and the Big Fight (Fr/WGer)
Asterix in Britain
Astragale, L' (Fr/WGer)
Atalante, L'
Atlantic City, (Can/Fr)
Atlantis (Fr/It)
A Toute Vitesse
Attentat, L' (Fr/It/WGer)
At the Height of Summer (Fr/Vietmnam)
Auberge Rouge, L'
Au Hasard, Balthazar (Fr/Swe)
Au Nom de la Loi
Au Revoir les Enfants (Fr/WGer)
Austerlitz (Fr/It/Liechtenstein)
Australia (Fr/Bel/Switz)
Autre, L' (Egypt/Fr)
Autre Homme une Autre Chance, Un
Aux Yeux du monde
Aveu, L' (Fr/It)
Aviator's Wife, The

Babar: The Movie (Can/Fr)
Baba Yaga (It/Fr)
Bab El-Oued City (Alg/Fr)
Baby of Mâcon, The (GB/Neth/Fr/Ger)
Bad Man's River (Sp/It/Fr)
Baie des Anges, La
Baise-moi
Baisers Volés
Bal, Le (Fr/It/Alg)
Balance, La
Ballon d'Or, Le (Guinea/Fr)
Balzac and the Little Chinese Seamstress (Fr/China)
Bande à Part
Barbarella (Fr/It)
Barber of Siberia, The (Rus/Fr/It/Czech Rep)
Barnabo of the Mountains (Fr/It/Switz)
Baron Fantôme, Le
Bas-Fonds, Les
Bataille du Rail, La
Battle of the Ten Million, The (Fr/Bel/Cuba)
Bayan Ko: My Own Country (Phil/Fr)
Bay Boy, The (Fr/Can)
Beach Café
Bear, The
Beaumarchais
Beau Mariage, Le
Beau Serge, Le
Beau Travail
Beauté du Diable, La (Fr/It)

Bee Keeper, The (Fr/Greece)
Before the Rain (Macedonia/GB/Fr)
Behind the Sun (Braz/Switz/Fr)
Beijing Bicycle (Tai/China/Fr)
Belle (Bel/Fr)
Belle Captive, La
Belle de Jour (Fr/It)
Belle Equipe, La
Belle et la Bête, La
Belle Fille Comme Moi, Une
Belle Noiseuse, La
Belle Noiseuse – Divertimento, La
Belles de nuit, Les (Fr/It)
Belle Verte, La
Benvenuta (Bel/Fr/It)
Berlin Jerusalem
Bernadette
Bernie
Best Way to Walk, The
Bête, La
Bête Humaine, La
Betelnut Beauty (Tai/Fr)
Betty Blue (versions 1 & 2)
Beyond Evil (It/Fr/WGer)
Beyond the Clouds (Fr/It/Ger)
Biches, Les (Fr/It)
Bidone, Il (It/Fr)
Big Bang, The (Fr/Bel)
Big Silence, The (Fr/It)
Bilitis
Bird Now (Bel/Fr)
Bisexual (Fr/It)
Bitter Moon (Fr/GB)
Bitter Victory
Black and White in Colour (Fr/Switz/Ivory C)
Black Cat White Cat (Fr/Ger)
Black Moon
Black Orpheus (Fr/It/Braz)
Blackout, The (Ferrara – US/Fr)
Black Sabbath (It/Fr)
Black Shack Alley
Blaise Pascal (Fr/It)
Blanche
Blood for Dracula (It/Fr)
Blood of Others, The (Can/Fr)
Blood Relatives (Can/Fr)
Blow-Out (Ferreri – Fr/It)
Blues Under the Skin
Blue Villa, The (Bel/Fr/Switz)
Bob le Flambeur
Boesman & Lena (Fr/SAf)
Bof!
Bohème, La (Fr/It)
Bonheur, Le
Bonheur est dans le Pré, Le
Bonjour, Monsieur Dosineau
Bonne Année, La (Fr/It)
Bonne Nouvelle
Bonnes Femmes, Les (Fr/It)
Bonzesse, La
Book of Life, The (US/Fr)
Boomerang (Giovanni – Fr/It)
Borsalino (Fr/It)
Borsalino & Co (Fr/It/WGer)
Bosna!
Bossu, Le (Fr/It/Ger)
Both Sides of the Street
Boucher, Le (Fr/It)
Boudu Sauvé des Eaux
Boulangère de Monceau, La
Boule de Suif
Boy from Mercury, The (GB/Fr/Ire)
Boy Meets Girl
Branches of the Tree (Ind/Fr)
Breaking the Waves (Den/Swe/Fr/Neth/Nor)
Bread and Roses (GB/Ger/Sp/Fr/It)
Bride Wore Black, The (Fr/It)
Bridget (Fr/US)
Bridget Jones's Diary (US/Fr/GB)
Brigands
Bronzés, Les
Brotherhood of the Wolf
Bûche, La

Buffet Froid
Bully (Fr/US)
Bunker Palace Hote
Burglars, The (Fr/It)
Burnt by the Sun (Rus/Fr)
Business Affair, A (GB/Fr/Ger/Sp)
Butterfly Effect (Sp/Fr/GB)
Bye Bye Brasil (Braz/Fr)

Cabaret Balkan(Fr/Greece/Macedonia/Tur/Yugo)
Cachetonneurs, Les
Cage aux Folles, La (Fr/It)
Cage aux Folles II, La (Fr/It)
Cage aux Folles III: The Wedding, La (Fr/It)
Calle Mayor (Sp/Fr)
Call of the Wild, The (GB/WGer/Sp/It/Fr)
Camille Claudel
Camisards, Les
Campana del Infierno, La (Sp/Fr)
Candy (US/It/Fr)
Candy Mountain (Switz/Fr/Can)
Canterbury Tales, The (It/Fr)
Capitaine Conan
Capitaine Fracasse, Le
Caporal Epinglé, Le
Captain Corelli's Mandolin (US/Fr/GB)
Captains of April (Fr/It/Port/Sp)
Captive (GB/Fr)
Captive, La (Fr/Bel)
Captive du Désert, La
Carabiniers, Les (Fr/It)
Caravan to Vaccares (GB/Fr)
Carmen (Rosi – Fr/It)
Carné
Carnet de Bal, Un
Carrière de Suzanne, La
Casanova '70 (It/Fr)
Casque d'Or
Catch Me a Spy (GB/Fr/US)
Catherine and Co. (Fr/It)
Cathy's Curse (Fr/Can)
Cat o'Nine Tails, The (It/WGer/Fr)
Ca va Barder... (Fr/It)
Cavafy (Greece/Fr)
Cecil B. Demented (US/Fr)
Cecilia, La (It/Fr)
Cela s'appelle l'Aurore (Fr/It)
Celestine, Maid at Your Service
Céline and Julie Go Boating
Cement Garden, The (GB/Ger/Fr)
Cérémonie, La
César
César and Rosalie (Fr/It/WGer)
Chambre des officiers, La
Chambre Verte, La
Champagne Murders, The
Chance or Coincidence (Fr/Can)
Chanel Solitaire (Fr/GB)
Chantons sous l'Occupation
Charles and Lucie
Charlotte (Fr/It/WGer)
Chartreuse de Parme, La (Fr/It)
Chat, Le
Chateau, The (US/Fr)
Château de ma mère, Le
Chère Louise (Fr/It)
Cherry Orchard, The (Greece/Cyp/Fr)
Cheval d'Orgueil, Le
Chien Andalou, Un
Chienne, La
Chiens, Les (Fr/Tahiti)
Chinese Box (US/HK/Fr)
Chinese Roulette (WGer/Fr)
Chinoise, La
Chocolat
Choses de la Vie, Les (Fr/It)
Christ Stopped at Eboli (It/Fr)
Chronicle of a Death Foretold (It/Fr)

Chronique d'un Eté
Chute de la Maison Usher, La
Cinderella – Italian Style (It/Fr)
Ciel, les Oiseaux et... Ta Mère!, Le
Ciénaga, La (Arg/USJap/Fr/Switz/Sp/Braz)
Cinema Cinema (Fr/US)
Cinema Paradiso (It/Fr)
Cinema Paradiso: The Special Edition (It/Fr)
Circle of Deceit (WGer/Fr)
Cité des enfants perdus, La
Citizen Langlois
City of Joy (GB/Fr)
City of Pirates (Fr/Port)
City of Women (It/Fr)
Civilised People (Fr/Switz/Leb)
Claim, The (GB/Can/Fr)
Claire Dolan (Fr/US)
Claire's Knee
Classified X (Fr/US)
Class Relations (WGer/Fr)
Class Trip
Clean Slate
Cléo de 5 à 7 (Fr/It)
Clowns, The (It/Fr/WGer)
Clubbed to Death (Fr/Port/Neth)
Club de Femmes
Cobra (Boisset – Fr/It)
Cocaine
Code Unknown
Coeur en hiver, Un
Coeur qui bat, In
Cold Sweat (Fr/It)
Collectionneuse, La
Colobane Express (Fr/Sen)
Colonel Chabert, Le (Le Hénaff)
Colonel Chabert, Le (Angelo)
Colossus of Rhodes, The (It/Sp/Fr)
Colour of Lies, The
Comedians, The (US/Bermuda/Fr)
Comme un Aimant
Condamné à Mort s'est Echappé, Un
Confessional, The (Can/GB/Fr)
Conformist, The (It/Fr/WGer)
Conte d'automne
Conte de printemps
Conte d'été
Conte d'hiver
Contre l'Oubli
Convent, The (Port/Fr)
Conversation Piece (It/Fr)
Convoyeurs Attendent, Les (Bel/Fr/Switz)
Cook, the Thief, His Wife and Her Lover, The (GB/Fr)
Cop au Vin
Cop's Honour
Corbeau, Le
Couch in New York, A (Bel/Fr/Ger)
Coup de Foudre
Coup de Grâce (WGer/Fr)
Coup pour Coup (WGer/Fr)
Courage Fuyons
Cousin, Le
Cousin Cousine
Cousins in Love (Fr/WGer)
Crazy Horse of Paris, The
Créatures, Les (Fr/Swe)
Cri du Coeur, Le
Cri du Hibou, Le (Fr/It)
Crime de Monsieur Lange, Le
Criminal Lovers
Crimson Rivers, The
Crise, La
Croix de Bois, Les
Croupier (GB/Ire/Ger/Fr)
Crying Freeman (Fr/Can/US/Jap)
Cry-Woman (Can/SKor/Fr)
Cyclo
Cyrano de Bergerac

Daens (Bel/Fr/Neth)
Damage (GB/Fr)
Dame aux Camélias, La (Fr/It)
Dames du Bois de Boulogne, Les
Dance of the Wind (GB/Fr/Ger/Neth)
Dandy
Danger: Diabolik (Fr/It)
Danton (Fr/Pol)
Darkest Light, The (GB/Fr)
Daughters of Darkness (Bel/Fr/WGer/It)
Day After Day (Fr/Isr)
Day of the Jackal, The (GB/Fr)
Deadly Run
Deadly Trap, The (Fr/It)
Dear Diary (It/Fr)
Dear Inspector
Death and the Maiden (GB/US/Fr)
Death in a French Garden
Death in the Seine (GB/Fr)
Death of Mario Ricci, The (Switz/Fr/WGer)
Death Watch (Fr/WGer)
Decameron, The (It/Fr/WGer)
Déjeuner sur l'Herbe, Le
De l'Autre Côté du Périph'
Delicatessen
Délits Flagrants
Demoiselles de Rochefort, Les
Dentellière, La (Fr/Switz/WGer)
Dernières Vacances, Les
Dernier Milliardaire, Le
Dernier Tournant, Le
Dérobade, La
Des Enfants Gâtés
Désert des Tartares, Le (Fr/It/WGer)
Des Nouvelles du Bon Dieu
Despair (WGer/Fr)
Destinées Sentimentales, Les
Destin Fabuleux de Désirée Clary, Le
Destiny
Détective
Détour, Le
Deux Anglaises et le Continent, Les
Deux Hommes dans Manhattan
Deuxième Souffle, Le
Deux ou Trois Choses que Je Sais d'Elle
Diable au Corps, La
Diable Probablement, Le
Diaboliques, Les
Diabolo Menthe
Dialogue des Carmélites, Le (Fr/It)
Diary of a Chambermaid, The (Buñuel – Fr/It)
Diary of a Country Priest
Diavolo in Corpo, Il (It/Fr)
Djomeh (Fr/Iran)
Dimenticare Venezia (It/Fr)
Dîner de cons, Le
Disappearance of Finbar, The (Ire/GB/Swe/Fr)
Discreet Charm of the Bourgeoisie, The
Discrète, La
Disparus de Saint-Agil, Les
Diva
Divine Intervention
Divorcing Jack (GB/Fr)
Dobermann
Doc's Kingdom (Port/Fr/GB)
Docteur Jekyll et les Femmes
Docteur Petiot
Docteur Popaul (Fr/It)
Dr M (WGer/It/Fr)
Dolce Vita, La (It/Fr)
Dôlé (Gabon/Fr)
Doll's House, A (Losey – GB/Fr)
Domicile Conjugal (Fr/It)
Don Giovanni (It/Fr/WGer)
Don Juan or If Don Juan Were a Woman (Fr/It)
Don Quichotte

Doom Generation, The (Fr/US)
Dossier 51, Le (Fr/WGer)
Dougal and the Blue Cat
Douce
Doulos, Le (Fr/It)
Down the Ancient Stairs (It/Fr)
Downtime (GB/Fr)
Drama of the Rich (It/Fr)
Drifting Clouds (Fin/Ger/Fr)
Drôle de Drame
Drôle de Félix
Durian Durian (HK/Fr)
Du Rififi à Paname (Fr/It/WGer)
Du Rififi chez les Hommes
Dust (Bel/Fr)

East Side Story (Ger/US/Fr)
East-West (Fr/Rus/Bulg/Sp)
Eau Froide, L'
Eclipse, The (It/Fr)
Ecole de la Chair, L' (Fr/Bel)
Ecole des Facteurs, L'
Ecoute Voir…
Edith and Marcel
Eighth Day, The (Fr/Bel/GB)
8-Wheel Beast, The (It/Fr)
8 Women
El Dorado (L'Herbier)
El Dorado (Saura – Sp/Fr)
Elective Affinities (It/Fr)
Eléna et les Hommes (Fr/It)
Eline Vere (Bel/Fr/Neth)
Elisa
Eloge de l'amour
Emmanuelle
Emmanuelle 2
Emmène-moi
Emmerdeur, L' (Fr/It)
Emperor and the Assassin, The (China/Jap/Fr)
Empire of Passion (Fr/Jap)
En avoir (ou pas)
En Cas de Malheur (Fr/It)
En Compagnie d'Antonin Artaud
End of Violence, The (US/Fr/Ger)
Enfance nue, L'
Enfant Sauvage, L'
Enfants du Lumière, Les
Enfants du Marais, Les
Enfants du Paradis, Les
Enfants du siècle, Les (Fr/GB)
Enfants Terribles, Les
Enfer, L'
Enigma (GB/Fr)
Ennui, L'
Entre Nous
Epoque formidable…, Une
Equilibristes, Les
Era Notte a Roma (It/Fr)
Ercole alla conquista di Atlantide (It/Fr)
Erendira (Fr/Mex/WGer)
Escalier C
Escort, The (Fr/GB)
Espion Lève-toi
Espions, Les
Espoir (Fr/Sp)
Esther Kahn (Fr/GB)
Et Dieu Créa la Femme
Eternel Retour, L'
Eternity and a Day (Greece/Fr/It/Ger)
Etoile du Nord, L'
Etoile Sans Lumière
Etrange Monsieur Victor, L'
Europa, Europa (Fr/Ger)
Eve (Fr/It)
Everybody's Fine (It/Fr)
Every Little Thing

Fabiola (It/Fr)
Falbalas
Fanny (Allégret)
Fantastic Planet (Fr/Czech)
Fantômas
Fantômas contre Fantômas
Fantôme de la Liberté, Le
Fantôme du Moulin Rouge, Le
Fantômes du Chapelier, Les
Far Away (Fr/Sp)
Farewell, Home Sweet Home (Fr/Switz/It)
Farrebique
Fatherland (GB/WGer/Fr)
Fatma (Tun/Fr)
Faust (Czech Rep/Fr)
Fausto
Faute à Voltaire, La
Faute de l'Abbé Mouret, La (Fr/It)
Faute de Soleil
Favourites of the Moon
Favour, the Watch and the Very Big Fish, The (Fr/GB)
Fellini-Satyricon (It/Fr)
Fellini's Roma (It/Fr)
Female Vampires
Femi Kuti: What's Going On (Nigeria/Fr)
Femme Défendue, La
Femme Douce, Une
Femme du Boulanger, La
Femme entre Chien et Loup, Une (Bel/Fr)
Femme est une Femme, Une
Femme française, Une (Fr/GB/Ger)
Femme Infidèle, La (Fr/It)
Femme Mariée, Une
F for Fake (Fr/Iran/WGer)
Fiancée du Pirate, La
Fidélité, La
Fièvre Monte à El Pao, La (Fr/Mex)
Fifth Element, The
Fille de D'Artagnan, La
Fille de l'Air, La
Fille de l'Eau
Fils de Deux Mères ou Comédie de l'Innocence
Fin du Jour, La
Fiorile (It/Fr/Ger)
First Name: Carmen (Fr/Switz)
First Time with Feeling (Fr/WGer)
Five and the Skin (Fr/Phil)
Flame (Zim/Fr/Mamibia)
Flame in My Heart, A (Fr/Switz)
Flesh for Frankenstein (It/Fr)
Flic, Un (Fr/It)
Flower Island (SKor/Fr)
Flower of My Secret, The (Sp/Fr)
Food of Love (GB/Fr)
Folle à Tuer (Fr/It)
For Ever Mozart
Forfaiture
Fortini/Cani (It/Fr/WGer/GB/US)
Fortunat (Fr/It)
4 Adventures of Reinette & Mirabelle
Four Flies on Grey Velvet (It/Fr)
Four Nights of a Dreamer (Fr/It)
Fracture du myocarde, La
Fragments of Life (Cameroon/Bel/Ger/Fr)
Franc, Le (Switz/Fr/Senegal)
François Truffaut, Portraits Volés
Frantz Fanon: Black Skin, White Mask (GB/Fr)
Freedom (Fr/Lithuania/Port)
Freeway II: Confessions of a Trickbaby (US/Fr/Can)
French Cancan
French Mustard
Fresh (US/Fr)
Friends (GB/Fr)
Friends and Husbands (WGer/Fr)
Frisson des Vampires, Le
From Hell to Victory (Fr/It/Sp)
From the Cloud to the Resistance (It/Fr/WGer/GB)
Fruits of Passion, The (Fr/Jap)
Full Moon in Paris
Future Is Woman, The (It/Fr/WGer)
Future of Emily, The (Fr/WGer)

Gabbeh (Iran/Fr)
Gadjo Dilo
Gai Savoir, Le (Fr/WGer)
Gang, Le (Fr/It)
Garde à Vue
Garde du Corps, Le
Gawin
Gazon maudit
General Amin
Genesis (Fr/Ind/Bel/Switz)
Gens de la rizière, Les (Cambodia/Fr)
Germinal (Fr/Bel/It)
Gervaise
Giant of Marathon, The (It/Fr)
Gigi (Audry)
Ginger & Fred (Fr/It/WGer)
Giovanna d'Arco al Rogo (It/Fr)
Girl from Lorraine, A (Fr/Switz)
Girl on a Motorcycle (GB/Fr)
Girl on the Bridge, The
Gito, the Ungrateful (Burundi/Switz/Fr)
Gleaners and I, The
Glissements Progressifs du Plaisir
Gloire de mon père, La
Godard on TV: 1960–2000
Golden Coach, The (Fr/It)
Golden Eighties (Fr/Bel/Switz)
Goodbye Emmanuelle
Good Morning Babylon (It/Fr/US)
Gospel According to St Matthew, The (It/Fr)
Goto, l'île d'amour
Goupi-Mains-Rouges
Goût des autres, Le
Governess, The (GB/Fr)
Grand Amour, Le
Grand Chemin, Le
Grande Illusion, La
Grandes Manoeuvres, Les
Grand Jeu, Le
Green Ray, The
Grosse Fatigue
Guerre des Boutons, La
Guerre est Finie, La (Fr/Swe)
Guerre sans nom, La
Gueule d'Amour
Guns for San Sebastian (Fr/Mex/It)

Hail, Mary (Fr/Switz)
Haine, La
Hairdresser's Husband, The
Happiness in Twenty Years
Hard Men (GB/Fr)
Harem
Harem Suare (Fr/It/Tur)
Harry, He's Here to Help
Haut les Coeurs
He Died with His Eyes Open
Hell of a Day, A
Heroes, The (It/Fr/Sp)
Héros très discret, Un
Hideous Kinky (GB/Fr)
Highlander III – The Sorcerer (Can/Fr/GB)
Himalaya (Fr/Switz/GB/Nepal)
Hiroshima, Mon Amour (Fr/Jap)
Histoires Extraordinaires (Fr/It)
Hitler, a Film from Germany (WGer/GB/Fr)
Ho! (Fr/It)
Hole, The (Tsai – Tai/Fr)
Hole, The (Hamm – GB/Fr)
Homme au Chapeau de Soie, L'
Homme de Désir, L'
Homme de Marrakech, l' (Fr/It/Sp)
Homme de ma vie, L' (Fr/Can)
Homme de Rio, L' (Fr/It)
Homme et une Femme, Un
Homme qui Dort, Un (Fr/Tun)
Honest (GB/Fr)
Horloger de St Paul, L'
Hors la vie (Fr/It/Bel)
Hôtel de la Plage, L'
Hôtel du Nord
Hôtel du Paradis (GB/Fr)
Hotel Splendide (GB/Fr)
Hour of the Pig (GB/Fr)
How Harry Became a Tree (Ire/It/GB/Fr)
How to Destroy of the Reputation of the Greatest Secret Agent (Fr/It)
Huis Clos
Humanité, L'
Human Resources (Fr/GB)
Hunchback of Notre Dame, The (Delannoy – Fr/It)
Hussard sur le toit, Le
Hyenas (Switz/Fr/Sen)
Hypnotised and Hysterical (Hairstylist Wanted)
Hypothesis of the Stolen Painting, The

I Am a Dancer
I Am Frigid…Why?
I Could Read the Sky (Ire/GB/Fr)
Identification of a Woman (It/Fr)
If Only (Sp/Fr/Can/GB/Luxembourg)
Ile au trésor, L' (Fr/US)
Illustrious Corpses (It/Fr)
I Love You, I Don't
I'm Going Home (Port/Fr)
Immoral Tales
Immortal Story, The
Immortelle, L' (Fr/It/Tur)
Improper Conduct
Impudent Girl, An
In All Innocence
Indians Are Still Far Away, The (Switz/Fr)
India Song
Indochine
Infernal Trio, The (Fr/It/WGer)
Inhumaine, L'
Innocent, The (Visconti – It/Fr)
Innocents with Dirty Hands (Fr/It/WGer)
Inspecteur Lavardin
In the French Style (Fr/US)
In the Mood for Love (HK/Fr)
Intimacy (Fr/GB)
Inutile Envoyer Photo
Invitation, The (Switz/Fr)
Invitation to Bed
IP5
Irma Vep
Isabelle Eberhardt (Fr/Aust)
I Stand Alone
It All Starts Today
It's All True (Fr/US)
I Want to Go Home

J'Accuse (Gance – 1918)
J'Accuse (Gance – 1937)
Jacquot de Nantes
Jane Eyre (GB/It/Fr/US)
Jaya Ganga (Ind/Fr/US)
Jean de Florette (Fr/It)
Jeanne Dielman, 23 Quai du Commerce, 1080 Bruxelles (Bel/Fr)
Jeanne et le Garçon Formidable
Jeanne la Pucelle
J'embrasse pas
Je suis né d'une cigogne
Jesus of Montreal (Can/Fr)
Je t'aime, Je t'aime
Jetée, La
Jeu de l'oie, Le
Jeune Wether, Le
Jeux Interdits
Jeux Sonts Faits, Les

Jo
Joan of Arc
Johnny Suede (US/Switz/Fr)
Joli mai, Le
Jonah Who Will Be 25 in the Year 2000
Jour de Fête
Journal de Lady M (Switz/Bel/Sp/Fr)
Journey to the Beginning of the World (Port/Fr)
Jour se Lève, Le
Joy (Fr/Can)
Jules et Jim
Juliet of the Spirits (It/Fr)
Jungle Burger (Fr/Bel)
Just Before Nightfall (Fr/It)

Kabloonak (Fr/Can)
Kadosh (Isr/Fr)
Kafka (US/Fr)
Kamikaze
Kandahar (Iran/Fr)
Kapo (It/Fr)
Katia Ismaïlova (Rus/Fr)
Këita! The Voice of the Griot (Fr/Burkina Faso)
Khrustalyov, My Car! (Fr/Rus)
Killer, The (Omirbaev – Kazakhstan/Fr)
Kippur (Isr/Fr)
Kiss of the Dragon (Fr/US0
Korczak (Pol/Ger/Fr/GB)

La Baule-les-Pins
Lacho Drom
Lacombe Lucien (Fr/It/WGer)
Lac aux Dames
Lady & the Duke, The (Fr/Ger)
Lady Chatterley's Lover (GB/Fr)
Lady in the Car with Glasses and a Gun, The
Lady L (Fr/It)
Lancelot du Lac (Fr/It)
Land Girls, The (GB/Fr)
Landru (Fr/It)
Landscape in the Mist (Greece/Fr/It)
Last Battle, The
Last Melodrama, The
Last Metro, The
Last Night (Can/Fr)
Last September, The (Fr/Ire/GB)
Last Tango in Paris (Fr/It)
Last Woman, The (Fr/It)
Late August, Early September
Late Marriage (Isr/Fr)
Laughter in the Dark (GB/Fr)
Laura (Hamilton)
Lautrec (Fr/Sp)
LA Without a Map (GB/Fr/Fin/Luxembourg)
Leap into the Void (Fr/It)
Le Cop
Le Cop 2
Lectrice, La
Legend of Frenchie King, The (Fr/It/Sp/GB)
Leon
Leon Morin, Priest (Fr/It)
Lessons in Darkness (Fr/Ger)
Let's Hope It's a Girl (It/Fr)
Letter, The (Fr/Port/Sp)
Letters to an Unknown Lover (GB/Fr)
Letter to Jane
Lettres de Mon Moulin, Les
Level Five
Liaisons Dangereuses 1960, Les
Liaison Pornographique, Une (Fr/Bel/Luxembourg/Switz)
Libera Me
Libertin, Le
Lie, The
Life and Extraordinary Adventures of Private Ivan Chonkin, The (GB/Fr/It/Czech Rep/Rus)
Life and Nothing But
Life Is a Long Quiet River
Life on Earth
Life Size (Fr/It/Sp)
Light Years Away (Fr/Switz)
Ligne de Démarcation, La
Lion Has Seven Heads, The (Fr/It)
Lisbon Story (Fr/Port)
Little Buddha (Fr/GB)
Little Darling
Little Girl Who Sold the Sun, The (Sen/Switz/Fr)
Live Flesh (Sp/Fr)
Loin des Barbares
Lola (Demy – Fr/It)
Lola Montès (Fr/WGer)
Lolita (Lyne – Fr/US)
Loulou
Lord of the Dance (Fr/Switz/WGer)
Lost Son, The (GB/Fr)
Love etc.
Love in Germany, A (WGer/Fr)
Love in the Afternoon
Love in the Strangest Ways
Love Is the Devil – Study for a Portrait of Francis Bacon (GB/Fr/Jap)
Love on the Run (Truffaut)
Lover, The (Fr/GB)
Lovers – Dogma 5
Lovers of the Arctic Circle, The (Sp/Fr)
Love's Labour's Lost (GB/Fr/US)
L.627
Lucie Aubrac
Lucky Luciano (It/Fr)
Lucky Luke (Fr/Bel)
Ludwig (Fr/It/WGer)
Lumière
Lumière et Compagnie
Lumière Noire
Lumumba (Fr/Bel/Ger/Haiti)
Lust and Desire
Luzin Defence, The (GB/Fr/It/Hun/US)

Madadam Tribu (Fr/Zaire)
Mad Adventures of 'Rabbi' Jacob, The (Fr/It)
Madame Bovary (Renoir)
Madame Bovary (Chabrol)
Madame Butterfly (Fr/Jap/Ger/GB)
Madame Claude
Madame de… (Fr/It)
Madame Rosa
Mademoiselle (GB/Fr)
Mademoiselle Docteur
Mahabharata, Le
Maid for Pleasure
Maison de Jade, La
Maîtresse
Maladie de Sachs, Le
Maldone
Malevil (Fr/WGer)
Malpertuis (Bel/Fr/WGer)
Manèges
Man by the Shore, The
Man in Love, A
Man Is a Woman
Manon des Sources (Fr/It/Switz)
Man on Fire (Fr/It)
Man Who Cried, The (GB/Fr/US)
Man Who Loved Women, The (Truffaut)
Map of the Human Heart (GB/Aust/Fr/Ger)
Marchands de Sable, Les
Marcorelle Affair, The
Marge, La
Marie-Jo and Her Two Loves
Mario and the Magician (Ger/Fr/Aus)
Marius
Marius et Jennette
Marquis (Bel/Fr)
Marquise (Fr/It/Switz/Sp)
Marquise von O…, Die (WGer/Fr)
Marseillaise, La
Marseilles Contract, The (GB/Fr)
Ma Saison Préférée
Mascara (Bel/Neth/Fr/US)
Masculin Féminin (Fr/Swe)
Masques
Massacre in Rome (Fr/It)
Mata-Hari, Agent H.21 (Fr/It)
Mauvais Sang
Ma Vie en Rose (Fr/Bel/GB/Switz)
Ma vie sexuelle (Paul Dedalus' Journey)
Max Mon Amour (Fr/US)
Maybe Baby (GB/Fr)
Mayerling
Mazel Tov ou le Mariage
Medea (It/Fr/WGer)
Medusa Touch, The (GB/Fr)
Me Ivan, You Abraham
Mektoub (Mor/Fr)
Mélo
Me Myself I (Fr/Aust)
Ménilmontant
Men, Women: User's Manual
Mémoire des apparences
Mépris, Le (Fr/It)
Merci la vie
Merci pour le chocolat (Fr/Switz)
Merlusse
Merveilleuse Visite, La (Fr/It)
Mes Petites Amoureuses
Messiah
Messidor
Métisse
Metroland (GB/Fr)
Microcosmos (Fr/Switz/It)
Middle of the World, The (Switz/Fr)
Middle Passage, The (Fr/Martinique)
Midnight (Salles – Fr/Braz)
Mignon Has Left (It/Fr)
Milk of Human Kindness, The (Fr/Bel)
Millennium Mambo (Tai/Fr)
Million, Le
1974, Une Partie de Campagne
Milou en mai (Fr/It)
Mina Tannenbaum
Miroir a deux faces, Le (Fr/It)
Misadventures of Margaret, The (GB/Fr)
Misérables, Les (le Chanois)
Misérables, Les (Lelouch)
Mississippi Blues (Fr/US)
Mister Freedom
Mister Frost (Fr/GB)
Mistons, Les
Moine, Le (Fr/It/WGer)
Moi, Pierre Rivière, ayant égorgé ma mère, ma soeur et mon frère…
Môme Pigalle, La
Moment d'Egarement, Un
Moment of Innocence (Iran/Fr/Switz)
Monde du Silence, Le
Monde sans Pitié, Un
Money Order, The (Fr/Sen)
Mon Homme
Monkey's Mask, The (Aust/Fr/Jap/It)
Monkey's Tale, A (Fr/GB/Ger/Hun)
Mon Oncle
Mon Oncle d'Amérique
Mon Père, ce héros
Mon Pierre Amour
Monsieur Hire
Monsoon Wedding (US/It/Ger/Fr)
Montalvo et l'enfant
Montand
Moon in the Gutter, The (Fr/It)
Moonraker (GB/Fr)
Mort en ce Jardin, La (Fr/Mex)
Moses and Aaron (WGer/Fr)
Mother and the Whore, The
Mouchette
Moulin Rouge (US/Fr)
Mouth Agape, The
Mr Arkadin (Sp/Fr)
Mr Klein (Fr/It)
Muhammad Ali
Mulholland Dr. (US/Fr)
Murder Is a Murder…Is a Murder, A (Fr/It)
Muriel (Fr/It)
Music for the Movies: Bernard Herrmann (US/Fr)
Music for the Movies: The Hollywood Sound (US/Jap/Fr)
My Best Friend's Girl
My Girlfriend's Boyfriend
My Name Is Nobody (Fr/It/WGer)
My Night With Maud
Mystère Picasso, Le
Mystery of Alexina, The

Nada (Fr/It)
Name of the Rose, The (WGer/Fr/It)
Nana
Nanou (GB/Fr)
Napoléon (Gance)
Napoléon (Guitry)
Nathalie Granger
Néa (Fr/WGer)
Neige était sale, La
Nelly & Monsieur Arnaud
Nénette et Boni
News from Home (Fr/Bel)
New Year's Day (GB/Fr)
Nez au Vent, Le (Bel/Fr)
Night and Day
Night Caller (Fr/It)
Night of the Generals, The (GB/Fr)
Nightshift
Night Sun (It/Fr/Ger)
Nikita (Fr/It)
1900 (Fr/It/WGer)
1999 Madeleine
Nineth Gate, The (Fr/Sp)
Noce blanche
Noces Rouges, Les (Fr/It)
Noir et Blanc
No Man's Land (Tanner – Switz/Fr/WGerGB)
No Man's Land (Tanovic – Fr/It/GB/Bel/Slovenia)
Nord
Nosferatu the Vampire (WGer/Fr)
Notre Histoire
Notte, La (It/Fr)
Notti di Cabiria, Le (It/Fr)
N'oublie pas que tu vas mourir
Nouvelle Eve
Nouvelle Vague
November Moon (WGer/Fr)
Nowhere (US/Fr)
Nuit du Carrefour, La
Nuit fantastique, La
Nuits Rouges (Fr/It)
Numéro Deux
Nun and the Devil, The (It/Fr)

Of Great Events and Ordinary People
Old Lady Who Walked in the Sea, The
Olivia
Olivier Olivier
Ombre du Doute, L'
One Day in the Life of Andrei Arsenevitch
One Deadly Summer
101 Reykjavik (Ice/Den/Nor/Fr/Ger)
One Man's War (Fr/WGer)
One Sings, The Other Doesn't (Fr/Bel/Cur)
On purge Bébé

Open Your Eyes (Sp/Fr/It)
Opera do Manlandro (Fr/Braz)
Oporto of My Childhood (Port/Fr)
Orgueilleux, Les (Fr/Mex)
Original Sin (US/Fr)
Orlando (GB/Rus/Fr/It/Neth)
Orphée
Ossos (Port/Fr/Den)
Ostrich Has Two Eggs, The
Our Lady of the Assassins (Fr/Col)
Out of the Present (Ger/Fr/Bel/Rus)
Out 1: Spectre
Outside Man, The (Fr/It)

Paltoquet, Le
Papa, les Petits Bateaux
Parade (Fr/Swe)
Paradis Perdu
Parallel Worlds (Czech Rep/Fr)
Paranoia (It/Fr)
Parapluies de Cherbourg, Les (Fr/WGer)
Pardon Mon Affaire
Pardon Mon Affaire, Too
Parents Terribles, Les
Parfait Amour!
Parfum d'Yvonne, Le
Paris Mil Neuf Cent Chronique de 1900 à 1914
Paris Nous Appartient
Paris qui Dort
Paris s'éveille
Paris, Texas (WGer/Fr/GB)
Paris vu par…
Paris: XY
Parking
Parsifal (Fr/WGer)
Partie de Campagne, Une
Partie de Plaisir, Une (Fr/It)
Pasolini, un Delitto Italiano (It/Fr)
Passenger, The (It/Fr/Sp)
Passe ton Bac d'Abord
Passion (Fr/Switz)
Passion Béatrice, La
Passion de Jeanne d'Arc, La
Passione d'Amore (It/Fr)
Pasteur
Pas trés Catholique
Patriot Game, The
Pau and His Brother (Sp/Fr)
Paul and Michelle (Fr/GB)
Paulina 1880
Pauline à la Plage
Pauline & Paulette (Bel/Neth/Fr)
Peau d'Ane
Peau Douce, La
Peau Neuve
Pension Mimosas
Pépé le Moko
Perceval le Gallois
Père Goriot, Le
Père Tranquille, Le
Perfect Circle
Péril Jeune, Le
Perles de la Couronne, Les
Permis de Conduire, Le
Pétain
Petite Marchande d'allumettes, La
Petite Voleuse, La
Petit Matin, Le
Petit Price a dit, Le (Fr/Switz)
Petits Frères, Les
Petit Soldat, Le
Petit Théâtre de Jean Renoir, Le (Fr/It/WGer)
Peu de Soleil dans l'Eau Froide, Un
Phantom India
Piaf
Pianist, The
Piano Teacher, The (Aus/Fr)
Pickpocket
Pièges
Pierre dans la Bouche, Une
Pierrot le Fou (Fr/It)
Pigsty (It/Fr)
Pillow Book, The (Neth/Fr/Ger)
Pink Floyd Live at Pompeii (Fr/Bel/WGer)
Pink Telephone, The
Pirates
Place Vendôme (Fr/Bel/GB)
Plaisir, Le
Platform, The (HK/Jap/Fr)
Playing from Plates (Pol/Fr)
Playtime
Pleins Feux sur l'assassin
Plein Soleil (Fr/It)
Po di Sangui (Fr/Port/Guinea Bissau)
Pola X (Fr/Jap/Ger/Switz)
Police
Polygraph, The (Can/Fr/Ger)
Ponette
Pont du Nord, Le
Pornographer, The (Fr/Can)
Porte des Lilas
Portrait of a '60% Perfect' Man: Billy Wilder
Portrait of a Young Girl at the End of the '60s in Brussels
Portraits Chinois (Fr/GB)
Possession (Fr/WGer)
Postino, Il (It/Fr)
Pourquoi pas moi? (Fr/Sp/Switz)
Prague (GB/Fr)
Pravda
Préparez Vos Mouchoirs (Fr/Bel)
Présence réelle, La
Presque Rien (Fr/Bel)
P..... Respectueuse, La
Price Above Rubies, A (US/Fr/GB)
Prince of Jutland (Fr/GB/Den/Neth/GB)
Princes, Les
Princesa (GB/Fr/Ger/It/Sp)
Princesse Tam Tam
Prise de Pouvoir par Louis XIV, La
Private Club
Prix de Beauté
Prize of Peril, The (Fr/Yugo)
Procès de Jeanne d'Arc
Profession of Arms, The (It/Fr/Ger)
Promise, The, The (Dardenne – Bel/Fr/Lux)
Promise, The (von Trotta – Ger/Fr)
Promised Lands
Proprietor, The (Fr/GB/Ger)
Prospero's Books (Neth/Fr/It)
Providence (Fr/Switz)
Pull-Over Rouge, Le
Pure Formality, A (It/Fr)
Puritan, The
Purple Taxi, The (Fr/It/Eire)
Pussy Talk

Quai des Brumes, Le
Quai des Orfèvres
Quarry, The (Bel/Fr/Neth/Sp)
Quartet (Ivory – GB/Fr)
Quatorze Juillet
Quatre Cents Coups, Les
Queimada! (Fr/It)
Que la Bête Meure (Fr/It)
Que la Fête Commence
Querelle (WGer/Fr
Quest for Fire (Can/Fr)
Quiet Days in Clichy (Fr/It/Ger)

Ramparts of Clay (Fr/Alg)
Ran (Fr/Jap)
Randonneurs, Les
Real Cool Time
Reason to Live, a Reason to Die, A (It/Fr/Sp/WGer)
Rebel Nun, The (It/Fr)
Red Circle, The (Fr/It)
Red Desert, The (It/Fr)
Red Sun (Fr/It/Sp)
Regarde le Mer
Regarde les hommes tomber
Règle du Jeu, La
Rein à Faire
Reine Margot, La (Fr/Ger/It)
Religieuse, La
Remorques
Rempart des Béguines, Le (Fr/It)
Rendez-vous d'Anna, Les (Fr/Bel/WGer)
Rendez-vous de juillet
Rendez-vous de Paris, Les
Requiem pour un Vampire (Fr/Ger)
Retour d'Afrique, Le (Switz/Fr)
Retour de Martin Guerre, Le
Return of Sabata (It/Fr/WGer)
Return of the Musketeers, The (GB/Fr/Sp)
Reunion (Fr/WGer/GB)
Revolving Doors, The (Can/Fr)
Riaba Ma Poule
Rider on the Rain (Fr/It)
Ridicule
Rien ne va plus
Rien sur Robert
Rigolboche
Rise and Fall of a Little Film Company from a Novel by James Hadley Chase
Road, The (Fr/Jap/Kazakhstan/Neth)
Roads of Exile, The (Fr/Switz/GB)
Road to Salina (Fr/It)
Roberto Succo (Fr/Switz)
Rocco and His Brothers (It/Fr)
Roi de Paris, Le (Fr/GB)
Roi des Aulnes, Les (Fr/Ger/GB)
Romance
Roman de Renard
Roman d'un Tricheur, Le
Romantic Englishwoman, The (GB/Fr)
Romuald et Juliette
Ronde, La
Room to Rent (GB/Fr)
Roseaux Sauvages, Les
Roselyne and the Lions
Rosetta (Bel/Fr)
Rothschild's Violin (Fr/Switz/Fin/Hun)
Rouge Baiser (Fr/WGer)
Rough Magic (GB/Fr)
'Round Midnight (US/Fr)
Route enchantée, La
Route de Corinthe, La (Fr/It/Greece)
Route One/USA (US/Fr/GB/It)
Rupture, La (Fr/It/Bel)

Sac de Billes, Un
Sacrifice, The (Swe/Fr)
Sade
Salaam Bombay! (Ind/Fr/GB)
Saló, o le Centoventi Giornate de Sodoma (It/Fr)
Salomé (Fr/It)
Salon Kitty (It/Fr/WGer)
Salsa
Salut Cousin! (Fr/Bel/Alg/Luxembourg)
Same Old Song (Fr/Switz/GB)
Samourai, Le (Fr/It)
Sang des Bêtes, Le
Sang d'un Poète, Le
Sans Soleil
Sarraounia (Fr/Burkina Faso)
Saudade do Futuro (Braz/Fr/Bel)
Sauvage, Le (Fr/It)
Sauve Qui Peut-la Vie (Switz/Fr)
Savage Innocents, The (It/Fr/GB)
Savage Nights
Scene of the Crime, The
Scènes de Crimes
Scènes de lit
Scent of Green Papaya, The
Scoumoune, La (Fr/It)
Season Five (Iran/Fr)
Season of Men, The (Fr/Tun
Second Chance (Lelouch)
Second Time, The (It/Fr)
Secret, Le
Secret, The (Fr/It)
Secret Défense (Fr/Switz/It)
Secret de Mayerling, Le
Section Spéciale (Fr/It/WGer)
Seins de glace, Les
Sélect Hotel
Selon Mathieu
Semaine de Vacances, Une
S'en fout la mort
Sentinelle, La
Séparation, La
Serial Lover
Serpent, The (Fr/It/WGer)
Servante et Maîtresse
Seven Nights in Japan (GB/Fr)
17 rue Bleue
Seven Women for Satan
Sex and Lucía (Sp/Fr)
Sex Shop (Fr/It/WGer)
Shanghai Triad (HK/China/Fr)
Shark's Son
Shattered (Fr/It)
Sheriff, Le
Shooting Stars
Siberia (Neth/Fr)
Sicilian Clan, The
Sicily! (Fr/It)
Signe du Lion, Le
Sign of the Gladiator (It/Fr/WGer)
Si Jolie Petite Plage, Une
Silence de la mer, Le
Silence est d'Or, Le
Silences of the Palaces, The (Fr/Tun)
Silencieux, Le (Fr/It)
Silent Cry, The (GB/WGer/Fr)
Simon Magus (GB/Ger/It Fr)
Simpatico (US/Fr)
Simple Plan, A (US/GB/Jap/Ger/Fr)
Sin Compasión (Peru/Mex/Fr)
Sirène du Mississipi, La (Fr/It)
Sitcom
Si tous les gars du monde…
Si Versailles m'était conté…
Skin of Man, Heart of Beast
Sleeping Car Murder, The
Slightly Pregnant Man, The (Fr/It)
Slogans (Albania/Fr)
Smalltime Thief
Smoking/No Smoking
Snobs (Fr/Switz)
Sodom and Gomorrah (Fr/It)
Soigne ta Droite (Fr/Switz)
Soir, un Train, Un (Bel/Fr)
Sombre
Someone Else's America (Fr/GB/Ger)
Sommersby (US/Fr)
Son's Room, The (It/Fr)
So there,
Souffle au Coeur, Le (Fr/It/WGer)
Soupirant, Le
Souriante Madame Beudet, La
Sous le Soleil de Satan
Sous les Toits de Paris
South, The (Sp/Fr)
Specialist, The (Fr/Ger/Bel/Aus/Isr)
Spirit of Mopti, The (Fr/Mali)
Splendor (It/Fr)
Spring into Summer
Spy Games (Ger/US/Jap/Fr)
Squale, La
Stardom (Can/Fr)
State of Siege (Fr/It/WGer)
Stavisky… (Fr/It)
Stealing Beauty (It/GB/Fr)

Stepfather
Story of Adèle H., The
Story of O, The (Fr/WGer)
Strada per Forte Alamo, La (It/Fr)
Straight Story, The (US/Fr)
Strange Place to Meet, A
Stranger (Ind/Fr)
Subway
Success Is the Best Revenge (GB/Fr)
Sud (Fr/Bel)
Summer in La Goulette, A (Fr/Tun)
Sunday in the Country
Sunflower (It/Fr)
Sur (Arg/Fr)
Swann in Love
Sweet Movie (Fr/Can/WGer)
Symphonie Pastorale, La

Tales of Ordinary Madness (Fr/It)
Tango (Leconte)
Tango Lesson, The (GB/Fr/Arg/Jap/Ger)
Tant qu'on a la Santé
Tartuffe
Tatie Danielle
Tavaszi Zápor (Hun/Fr)
Taxandria (Fr/Bel/Ger)
Taxi (Pirès)
Taxi Blues (USSR/Fr)
Taxi 2
Tchao Pantin
10
Tenant, The
Ten Days' Wonder
Tendre Ennemie, La
Tenue de Soirée
Terminus (Fr/WGer)
Terres Froides, Les
Terrorists in Retirement
Tess (Fr/GB)
Testament du Docteur Cordelier, Le
Testament d'Orphée, Le
Tête Contre les Murs, La
Tête d'un Homme, La
That Night in Varennes (Fr/It)
That Obscure Object of Desire (Fr/Sp)
Théâtre de Monsieur et Madame Kabal
Themroc
Thérèse
There's Only One Jimmy Grimble (GB/Fr)
These Are Not My Images (neither there nor here) (US/Fr/Ger/GB)
These Foolish Things
Thief of Saint-Lubin, The
Time for Drunken Horses, A (Fr/Iran)
Time Out
Time Regained (Fr/It/Port)
TGV (Sen/Fr)
They Call That an Accident
They Came to Rob Las Vegas (Sp/Fr/WGer/It)
Thief, The (Rus/Fr)
Thief of Baghdad, The (Donner – GB/Fr)
This Sweet Sickness
Thomas l'Imposteur
Those Who Love Me Will Take the Train
1000 Eyes of Dr Mabuse, The (WGer/Fr/It)
Three Brothers (It/Fr)
Three Colours: Blue
Three Colours: Red (Fr/Switz/Pol)
Three Colours: White (Fr/Pol)
Three Crowns of the Sailor
3 Men and a Cradle
Three Sisters (It/Fr/Ger)
Tiger of Eschnapur, The (WGer/It/Fr)
Tilaï (Burkina Faso/Switz/Fr)
Tin Drum, The (WGer/Fr)
Tiré à Part
Tirez sur le Pianiste
Titanic Town (GB/Ger/Fr)
Tit and the Moon, The (Sp/Fr)
To Kill a Priest (US/Fr)
Tombes du Ciel
Toni
Tontaine et Tonton
Too Late (Fr/Romania)
To Our Loves
Topaze (Pagnol)
Torrents of Spring (It/Fr)
Tosca (Fr/GB/Ger/It)
To Speak the Unspeakable: The Message of Elie Wiesel (Hun/Fr)
Total Eclipse (Fr/GB/Bel)
Toto the Hero (Bel/Fr/Ger)
Touch (US/Fr)
Touche pas à la femme blanche (Fr/It)
Touchez pas au Grisbi (Fr/It)
Tous les matins du monde
Tournoi, Le
Tout ça… pour ça!!!
Toute une Nuit (Fr/Bel)
Tout Va Bien (Fr/It)
Traffic (Fr/It)
Trafico (Port/Fr/Den)
Tragedy of Carmen, The
Train, The (US/Fr/It)
Traitement de Choc (Fr/It)
Trances (Mor/Fr)
Trans-Europ-Express
Traversée de Paris, La (Fr/It)
Trench, The (GB/Fr)
Trial, The (Welles – Fr/It/WGer)
Trip to My Country, A (Cameroon/Fr)
Tristana (Sp/Fr/It)
Trois Places pour le 26
Trois Vies et une Seule Morte
Trop Belle Pour Toi!
Trop de Bonheur
Trou, Le (Fr/It)
Trouble Every Day
Trou Normand, Le
Trout, The
Truce, The (It/Fr/Ger)
Turtle on Its Back
Twelve Tasks of Asterix, The
23:58
2 x 50 Years of French Cinema (GB/Fr)

Ulysses' Gaze (Greece/It/Fr)
Underground (Fr/Ger/Hun)
Under Suspicion (Fr/US)
Under the Sand
Un Deux Trois Soleil
Uneasy Riders (Nationale 7)
Unforgettable Summer, An (Fr/Romania)
Unhook the Stars
Univers de Jacques Demy, L'
Uns et les Autres, Les
Until the End of the World (Ger/Fr/Aust)
Uranus
Urban Legend (US/Fr)
Urban Legends Final Cut (US/Fr)
Urga (Fr/USSR)
U Turn (US/Fr)

Vacances de M. Hulot, Les
Vache et la Prisonnier, La (Fr/It)
Vagabonde
Valdez il Mezzosangue (It/Sp/Fr)
Vallée, La
Valmont (Fr/GB)
Vampyr (Ger/Fr)
Valseuses, Les
Vampire de Dusseldorf, Le (Fr/It/Sp)
Vampires, Les
Van Gogh
Vanishing, The (Neth/Fr)
Va Savoir (Fr/It/Ger)
Vatel
Veillées d'Armes
Vengo (Fr/Sp)
Vent de la Nuit, Le
Vent d'Est (Fr/It/WGer)
Venus Beauty
Verdict (Cayatte – Fr/It)
Vérité, La (Fr/It)
Versailles rive gauche
Vertiges (Fr/GB)
Very Annie-Mary (Fr/GB)
Veuve de Saint-Pierre, La (Fr/Can)
Vice et la Vertu, Le
Victor – pendant qu'il est trop tard
Victory (Peploe – GB/Fr/Ger)
Vie à l'Envers, La
Vie de Jésus, La
Vie est à Nous, La
Vie est Belle, La (Bel/Fr/Zaire)
Vie est un Roman, La
Vieil Homme et l'Enfant, Le
Vieille Canaille
Vieille Dame Indigne, La
Viens chez moi, j'habite chez une copine
Vie Privée (Fr/It)
Vie Rêvée des Anges, La
Vigo Passion for Life (GB/Jap/Fr/Sp/Ger)
Ville est tranquille, La
Vincent & Theo (GB/Fr)
Violation of Justine, The (Fr/It/Can)
Viol de Vampire, Le
Violette et François
Violette Nozière (Fr/Can)
Violons du Bal, Les
Virgin (Breillat)
Virgin (Karanovic – Yugo/Fr)
Virgin for Saint Tropez, A (Fr/It)
Visiteurs, Les
Viva la Muerte (Fr/Tun)
Viva la Vie
Viva Maria! (Fr/It)
Viva Portugal (WGer/Fr)
Vivement Dimanche!
Vivre pour Vivre (Fr/It)
Vivre sa Vie
Vladimir et Rosa (Fr/WGer/US)
Voie Lactée, La (Fr/It)
Voleurs, Les
Volpone
Voyage, The (Arg/Fr)
Voyager (Ger/Fr)
Voyages (Fr/Pol)
Voyage-Surprise
Wages of Fear, The (Fr/It)
Waking Ned (GB/Fr/US)
Wall, The
Wanderer, The
War of the Buttons (GB/Fr)
Warrior, The (GB/Fr/Ger/Ind)
Water Drops on Burning Rocks (Fr/Jap)
Way I Killed My Father, The (Fr/Sp)
Wedding, The (Lounguine – Fr/Ger/Rus)
Wedding in Galilee (Bel/Fr)
Weekend (Fr/It)
Weight of Water (US/Fr)
Werckmeister Harmonies (Hun/Fr/Ger/It/Switz)
West Beirut (Fr/Leb/Bel/Nor)
Western
We Were One Man
What? (Fr/It/WGer)
Whatever
What Makes David Run?
What's New Pussycat? (US/Fr)
What Time Is It There?
When the Cat's Away…
White Fang (It/Fr/Sp)
White Man's Burden (US/Fr)
White Nights (Visconti – Fr/It)
Who Are You Polly Maggoo?
Wild Games (Bel/Ger/Fr)
William Christie at Les Arts Florissants
Will It Snow for Christmas?
Wimbledon Stage, The
Wind Will Carry Us, The (Fr/Iran)
Wings of Desire (WGer/Fr)
Winter Sleepers
Woman Next Door, The
Woman or Two, A
Women from the Medina (Fr/Mor)
Work in Progress (Sp/Fr)
Wounds, The (Serbia/Fr)
Writing on the Wall, The (Fr/Bel)

Yaaba (Burkina Faso/Fr/Switz)
Yeux sans Visage, Les
Young Ladies of Wilko, The (Pol/Fr)
Young Törless (WGer/Fr)
Yoyo

Z (Fr/Alg)
Zazie dans le Métro
Zéro de Conduite
Zouzou

Appendix 19

German Films

About a Boy (Ger/US/Fr/GB)
Adventures of Baron Munchausen, The (Gilliam – GB/WGer)
Adventures of Baron Munchhausen, The (von Baky)
Adventures of Elmo in Grouchland, The (US/Ger)
Adventures of Pinocchio (GB/Fr/Czech Rep/US)
Adventures of Prince Achmed, The
Adventures of Rocky & Bullwinkle, The (US/Ger)
Adventures of Werner Holt, The
After the Fall
After the Truth (Ger/US)
Aguirre, Wrath of God
Aimée & Jaguar
Alice in the Cities
Ali G Indahouse (Ger/US/Fr/GB)
All-Round Reduced Personality – Redupers, The
Along Came a Spider (US/Ger)
Amélie (Fr/Ger)
American Friend, The (WGer/Fr)
American Soldier, The
Amour, l'Argent, l'Amour, L'
Anita: Dances of Vice
Anou Banou or the Daughters of Utopia
Arche du désert, L' (Alg/Fr/Ger/Switz)
Army of Lovers or Revolt of the Perverts
Artemisia (Fr/Ger/It)

Artistes at the Top of the Big Top: Disorientated
Asphalt Night
Asterix & Obelix Take on Caesar (Fr/Ger/It)
Asterix and the Big Fight (Fr/WGer)
Asterix Conquers America
Astragale, L' (Fr/WGer)
Attentat, L' (WGer/Fr/It)
Au Revoir les Enfants (Fr/WGer)
Autumn Sonata

Baby of Mâcon, The (GB/Neth/Fr/Ger)
Bagdad Café
Baker's Bread
Ball, The (Bel/Switz/Ger/Neth)
Bedazzled (Ramis – US/Ger)
Be My Star (Aus/Ger)
Bend It Like Beckham (Ger/GB)
Benefit of the Doubt (US/Ger)
Berlin Affair, The (It/WGer)
Berlin Alexanderplatz
Berlin – Die Sinfonie der Grosstadt
Berlin Is in Germany
Beware of a Holy Whore
Bewegte Mann, Der
Beyond Evil (It/Fr/WGer)
Beyond Silence
Beyond the Clouds (Fr/It/Ger)
Big Momma's House (US/Ger)
Birth of a Nation, The (Wyborny)
Bitter Tears of Petra von Kant, The
Black Cannon Incident, The (China/WGer)
Black Cat White Cat (Fr/Ger)
Blade II (US/Ger)
Blau Licht, Das
Bless the Child (US/Ger)
Blind Spot
Bloodline (US/WGer)
Blow Dry (Ger/GB/US)
Blue Angel, The
Bluebeard's Castle
Blue Exile, The (Tur/Ger)
Blue Note: A History of Modern Jazz
Boat, The
Body, The (US/Ger)
Bolwieser
Bongo Man
Borsalino & Co (Fr/It/WGer)
Bossu, Le (Fr/It/Ger)
Bread and Roses (GB/Ger/Sp/Fr/It)
Buena Vista Social Club, The
Burning Life
Business Affair, A (GB/Fr/Ger/Sp)

Cabinet of Dr Caligari, The
Calendar (Can/Arm/Ger)
Call of the Wild, The (GB/WGer/Fr/It/Sp)
Capitano, Il (Swe/Fin/Ger/Den)
Carla's Song (GB/Ger/Sp)
Cassandra Crossing, The (GB/It/WGer)
Catamount Killing, The
Cat o'Nine Tails, The (It/Fr/WGer)
Cat's Meow, The (Can/Ger/GB)
Céleste
Cell, The (US/Ger)
Cement Garden, The (GB/Ger/Fr)
Center Stage (US/Ger)
César and Rosalie (It/Fr/WGer)
Chagrin et la Pitié, Le (WGer/Switz)
Chariots of the Gods
Charlie's Angels (US/Ger)
Charlotte (Fr/It/WGer)
Charlotte Gray (GB/Aust/Ger)
Chico (Hun/Ger/Croatia/Chile)
Child's Play
Chinese Boxes
Chinese Roulette (WGer/Fr)
Christiane F
Christmas Carol – The Movie (GB/Ger)
Chronicle of Anna Magdalena Bach (It/WGer)
Circle of Deceit
City of Angels (US/Ger)
City of Lost Souls
Class Relations (WGer/Fr)
Climax
Clowns, The (It/Fr/WGer)
Cobra Verde
Cold Fever (Ice/Ger/Switz/US)
Colonel Redl (Hun/WGer/Aus)
Comedian Harmonists (Ger/Aus)
Coming Out
Companeros (It/Sp/WGer)
Conamara (Ger/Ire)
Confessions of a Bigamist (It/WGer)
Confessions of a Sixth Form Girl
Confessions of Winifred Wagner, The
Conformist, The (It/Fr/WGer)
Congress Dances
Consequence, The
Contender, The (Ger/US/GB)
Couch in New York, A (Bel/Fr/Ger)
Count Dracula (Sp/It/WGer)
Coup de Grâce (WGer/Fr)
Coup pour Coup (Fr/WGer)
Cousins in Love (Fr/WGer)
Crazy
Crimetime (GB/US/Ger)
Criminal
Cross of Iron (GB/WGer)
Croupier (GB/Ire/Ger/Fr)
Cry Onion (It/Sp/WGer)

Damned, The (Visconti – It/WGer)
Dance of Love
Dance of the Wind (GB/Ger/Fr/Neth
Dark Blue World (Czech Rep/GB/Ger/Den/It)
Daughters of Darkness (Bel/Fr/WGer/It)
Dead Pigeon on Beethoven Street
Dead Man (US/Ger)
Dealer
Dear Mother, I'm All Right
Death in the Sun
Death Is My Trade
Death of Maria Malibran, The
Death of Mario Ricci, The (Switz/Fr/WGer)
Death Watch (Fr/WGer)
Decameron, The (It/Fr/WGer)
Deep End (WGer/US)
Degree of Murder, A
Dentellière, La (Fr/Switz/WGer)
Désert des Tartares, Le (Fr/It/WGer)
Despair (WGer/Fr)
Destiny
Deutschland, Erwache!
Devil's Accordion, The (Switz/Ger)
Devil's Advocate, The (Green)
Devil's Island (Fridriksson – Ice/Nor/Ger/Den)
Diary of a Lost Girl
Dirnentragödie
Dirt for Dinner
Divine Intervention (Fr/Ger/Mor)
Dr M (Ger/It/Fr)
Dr Mabuse, The Gambler
Don Giovanni (It/Fr/WGer)
Don't Cry for Me Little Mother (WGer/Yug)
Don't Get Me Started (GB/Ger)
Dossier 51, Le (Fr/WGer)
Double Jeopardy (US/Ger)
Down to Earth (US/Ger/It)
Dreigroschenoper, Die
Drifting Clouds (Fin/Ger/Fr)
Drop Dead Gorgeous (US/Ger)
D-Tox (US/Ger/Can)
Due to an Act of God
Du Rififi à Paname (Fr/It/WGer)
Dust (GB/Ger/It/Macedonia/US/Sp/Switz)

East Side Story (Ger/US/Fr)
Effi Briest
8½ Women (Neth/GB/Ger/Luxembourg)
8MM (US/Ger)
Eika Katappa
Elective Affinities
Emil & the Detectives
End of the Affair (US/Ger)
End of Violence, The (US/Fr/Ger)
Enemy at the Gates (Ger/GB/Ire/US)
Enigma (Neth/US/GB/Ger)
Enter the 7 Virgins (HK/WGer)
Entrapment (US/Ger)
Erendira (Fr/Mex/WGer)
Erotic Quartet (US/WGer/It)
Erotique (US/Ger/HK)
Escape Route to Marseilles
Eternity and a Day (Greece/Fr/It/Ger)
Europa, Europa (Fr/Ger)
Even Dwarfs Started Small
Exquisite Tenderness (US/Ger)

Faithless (Swe/Nor/Fr/It/Ger)
Faraway, So Close
Farewell
Farewell, Stranger
Farewell to False Paradise (WGer/Tur)
Fast and the Furious, The (Ger/US)
Fata Morgana
Fate
Fatherland (GB/WGer/Fr)
Fat World
Faust
Faustrecht der Freiheit
Fear (It/WGer)
Fear Eats the Soul
Fedora
Female Perversions (US/Ger)
Femme française, Une (Fr/GB/Ger)
F for Fake (Fr/Iran/WGer)
15 Minutes (US/Ger)
Fight Club (US/Ger)
Finances of the Grand Duke, The
Fiorile (It/Fr/Ger)
First Time With Feeling (Fr/WGer)
Fistful of Dollars, A (It/WGer/Sp)
Fitzcarraldo
Flickering Roads
Flight to Berlin
Forbidden (GB/WGer)
Fortini/Cani (It/Fr/WGer/GB/US)
40 Metre Square Germany
Fragments of Life (Cameroon/Bel/Ger/Fr)
Friends and Husbands (WGer/Fr)
From Pole to Equator (It/WGer)
From the Cloud to the Resistance (It/Fr/WGer/GB)
From the Life of the Marionettes
Frost
Further Gesture, A (GB/Ger/Jap/Ire)
Future Is Woman, The (It/Fr/WGer)
Future of Emily, The (Fr/WGer)
Gai Savoir, Le (Fr/WGer)
Gangster No. 1 (GB/Ger)
Garden of the Finzi-Continis, The (It/WGer)
Gathering of Old Men, A (US/GB/WGer)
General's Daughter, The (US/Ger)
Genuine
Georgette Meunier
German Chainsaw Massacre, The
German Sisters, The
Germany in Autumn
Germany, Pale Mother
Germany, Year Zero (It/WGer)
Ghost Chase
Gigantic
Ginger & Fred (It/Fr/WGer)
Girlfriend, The (Arg/WGer)
Girl in a Boot
Gods of the Plague
Golem, The
Goodbye Lover (US/Ger)
Gorilla Bathes at Noon
Grass Is Always Greener, The
Gregory's Two Girls (GB/Ger)
Guy (GB/Ger)

Handmaid's Tale, The (US/Ger)
Hanussen (Hun/WGer)
Hard Rain (US/GB/Jap/Ger/Den)
Havanna Mi Amor (Ger/Cuba)
Heartbreakers, The
Heart of Glass
Heaven (Ger/US)
Heimat
Held for Questioning
Help! I'm a Fish (Den/Ger/Ire)
Hellhounds of Alaska, The
Highway Society (Ger/Fin)
Hillbrow Kids (Ger/SAf)
Hindered (GB/WGer)
Hitler – a Career
Hitler, a Film from Germany (WGer/Fr/GB)
Hollow Men (US/Ger)
Hollow Reed (GB/Ger)
Home Game
House of Spirits, The (Ger/Den/Port)
How Sweet Is Her Valley

I Am My Own Woman
I Am Sam (US/Ger)
i.d.
I Love You, I'll Kill You
Imposters (US/WGer)
In a Year with 13 Moons
Infernal Trio, The (Fr/It/WGer)
In Georgia
Inheritors, The (Aus/Ger)
In July
Innocent, The (Schlesinger – GB/Ger)
Innocents with Dirty Hands (Fr/It/WGer)
Inside Out (GB/WGer)
Invincible (Ger/Ire/GB/US)
Isn't She Great (US/Ger/GB/Jap)
I Still Know What You Did Last Summer
I Was, I Am, I Shall Be
I Was Nineteen
I Was on Mars

Jeder für sich und Gott gegen alle (The Engima of Kaspar Hauser)
Jeepers Creepers (Ger/US)
Jew-Boy Levi
Joan of Arc of Mongolia
John Heartfield: Photomonteur
Josephine
Journey to the Sun (Tur/Neth/Ger)
Joyless Street
Just a Gigolo

Kama Sutra: A Tale of Love (Ind/GB/Jap/Ger)
Kämeradschaft (Ger/Fr)
Karl May
Kaspar Hauser
Katzelmacher
Keiner Liebt Mich
King, Queen, Knave (US/WGer)
Knickers Ahoy (WGer/It)
Knife in the Head
Knight Moves (US/Ger)
Komitas
Korczak (Pol/Ger/Fr/GB)
K-PAX (US/Ger)
Kühle Wampe

Labyrinth (Jires – Ger/Czech)
Lacombe Lucien (Fr/WGer/It)
Lady & the Duke, The (Fr/Ger)
Land and Freedom (GB/Sp/Ger)
Land of Silence and Darkness
Lara Croft: Tomb Raider
Last Exit to Brooklyn
Last Hole, The
Last Orders (GB/Ger)
Last Yellow, The (GB/Ger)
Late Night Shopping (GB/Ger)
Latin Boys Go to Hell (US/Ger/Sp/Jap)
Left-Handed Woman, The
Legends of Rita, The
Lessons in Darkness (Fr/Ger)
Letters from the East (GB/Ger/Fin/Swe)
Liam (GB/Ger/It)
Liebelei
Life Is All You Get
Life on a String (China/GB/Ger)
Lightning Over Water (WGer/Swe)
Lili Marleen
Lina Braake
Little Angel
Little Godard, A
Little Night Music, A (Aus/WGer)
Little Vampire, The (Ger/Neth/GB/US)
Living Dead, The
Lola (Fassbinder)
Lola Montès (Fr/WGer)
Lola + Bilidikid
Lord of the Dance (Fr/Switz/WGer)
Lost Honour of Katharina Blum, The
Love in Germany, A (Fr/WGer)
Love Is Colder than Death
Lovely Rita (Aus/Ger)
Lucky Break (GB/Ger/US)
Ludwig (Fr/It/WGer)
Ludwig – Requiem for a Virgin King
Ludwig's Cook
Lumumba (Fr/Bel/Ger/Haiti)

M (Lang)
Madame Butterfly (Fr/Jap/Ger/GB)
Madame X
Mädchen in Uniform
Mädchen Rosemarie, Das
Madeline (US/Ger)
Magician of Lublin, The (WGer/Isr)
Main Actor, The
Making Up
Maldoror (GB/Ger)
Malevil (Fr/WGer)
Malou
Malpertuis (Bel/Fr/WGer)
Manhunt in Milan (It/WGer)
Man Like Eva, A
Man to Respect, A (It/WGer)
Man Who Knew Too Little, The (US/Ger)
Mario and the Magician (Ger/Fr/Aus)
Marlene
Marquise von O…, Die (WGer/Fr)
Marriage of Maria Braun, The
Martha
Mau Mau
Medea (It/Fr/WGer)
Memory of Justice, The (GB/US/WGer)
Men
Merchant of Four Seasons, The
Me Without You (GB/Ger)
Michael
Michael Kohlhaas
Midsummer Night's Dream, A (Hoffman – US/Ger)
Million Dollar Hotel, The (Ger/US)
Mirror, The (WGer/GB)
Mission, The (Sayyad – US/WGer)
Mission: Impossible II (US/Ger)
Moine, Le (Fr/It/WGer)
Moloch (Rus/Ger)
Monkey's Tale, A (Fr/GB/Ger/Hun)
Monsoon Wedding (US/It/Ger/Fr)
Moon 44
Moses and Aaron (Fr/WGer)
Mostly Martha (Aus/Ger/It/Switz)
Motel (US/WGer)
Mother and Son (Rus/Ger)
Mother Küster's Trip to Heaven
Mute Witness (GB/Ger/Rus)
My Brother Tom (GB/Ger)
My Dearest Enemy (Ger/GB)
My Father Is Coming (Ger/US)
My Mother's Courage (Ger/GB/Aus)
My Name Is Nobody (It/Fr/WGer)
My Private War
My 20th Century (Hun/WGer/Cuba)

Name of the Rose, The (WGer/It/Fr)
Nasty Girl, The
Néa (Fr/WGer)
Negotiator, The (US/Ger)
Nela
NeverEnding Story, The
NeverEnding Story II: The Next Chapter, The
NeverEnding Story III: Escape from Fantasia, The
Nibelungen, Die
Nicht Versöhnt
Nico Icon
Nightfall
Night Hair Child (GB/It/WGer/Sp)
Night Paths
Night Sun (It/Fr/Ger)
Nine Lives of Tomas Katz, The (Ger/GB)
1900 (It/Fr/WGer)
No Answer from F.P.1
No Man's Land (Switz/Fr/WGer/GB)
No Mercy, No Future
No Place to Go
Nora (GB/Ire/Ger/It)
Nora Helmer
Nosferatu – eine Symphonie des Grauens
Nosferatu the Vampyre (WGer/Fr)
Nostradamus (GB/Ger)
Notebook on Cities and Clothes
November Days Voices and Choices (GB/Ger)
November Moon (WGer/Fr)

Oberwald Mystery, The (It/WGer)
Occasional Work of a Female Slave
Odessa File, The (GB/WGer)
Ode to Cologne
101 Reykjavík (Ice/Den/Nor/Fr/Ger)
One Man's War (Fr/WGer)
1 + 1 = 3
One, Two, Three (US/WGer)
Orchestra Rehearsal (It/WGer)
Ordinary Decent Criminal (Ire/Ger/US/GB)
Othon (WGer/It)
Out of Order
Out of the Present (Ger/Fr/Bel/Rus)
Outside In (GB/WGer)

Palermo or Wolfsburg (WGer/It)
Palmetto (US/Ger)
Paolozzi Story, The (GB/WGer)
Paragraph 175 (GB/Ger/US)
Parapluies de Cherbourg, Les (Fr/WGer)
Paris, Texas (WGer/Fr/GB)
Parsifal (WGer/Fr)
Party – Nature Morte, The
Passages
Passion of Darkly Noon, The (GB/Ger/Bel)
Patriot, The (Kluge)
Patriot, The (Emmerich – US/Ger)
Pedestrian, The (WGer/Switz)
Peppermint Freedom
Petit Théâtre de Jean Renoir, Le (Fr/It/WGer)
Pied Piper (Barta – Czech/WGer)
Pink Floyd Live at Pompeii (Fr/Bel/WGer)
Pippi Longstocking (Swe/Ger/Can)
Platz, Der
Point Is to Change It, The
Pola X (Fr/Jap/Ger/Switz)
Policewoman, The
Polygraph, The (Can/Fr/Ger)
Possession (Fr/WGer)
Poto and Cabengo (WGer/US)
Power of Men Is the Patience of Women, The
Prince of Jutland (Fr/GB/Den/Neth/Ger)
Princesa (GB/Fr/Ger/It/Sp)
Princess + the Warrior, The
Prince Valiant (Ger/GB/Ire/US)
Private Popsicle (Isr/WGer)
Profession of Arms, The (It/Fr/Ger)
Promise, The (von Trotta – Ger/Fr))
Punk in London

Quante Volte… Quella Notte (It/WGer)
Querelle (WGer/Fr)
Quick
Quiet Days in Clichy (Fr/It/Ger)
Quills (US/Ger)

Radio On (GB/WGer)
Rainmaker, The (Ger/US)
Raskolnikow
Reason to Live, a Reason to Die, A (It/Fr/Sp/WGer)
Rebecca's Daughters (GB/Ger)
Red Rings of Fear (It/Sp/WGer)
Reggae Sunsplash II
Reine Margot, La (Fr/Ger/It)
Requiem pour un Vampire (Fr/Ger)
Reunion (Fr/WGer/GB)
Roi des Aulnes, Le (Fr/Ger/GB)
Rosalie Goes Shopping
Rosa Luxemburg
Rouge Baiser (Fr/WGer)
Rugrats in Paris: The Movie (US/Ger)
Rules of Engagement (US/Ger)
Run Lola Run
Salmonberries
Salon Kitty (It/WGer/Fr)
Samsara (Ger/Ind)
Sandman, The
Sankofa (US/Ger/Ghana/Burkina Faso)
Satan's Brew
Sátántangó (Hung/Ger/Switz)
Scarlet Letter, The (WGer/Sp)
Scenes of the Crime (Ger/US)
Schatten
Schizophrenia
Schramm
Schtonk!
Score, The (US/Ger)
Scorpion King, The (US/Ger)
Second Awakening of Christa Klages, The
Secret Face, The
Secrets of a Soul
Section Spéciale (Fr/It/WGer)
Será Posible el Sur
Serbian Girl, The
Sgt Pepper's Lonely Hearts Club Band (US/WGer)
Serpent, The (Fr/It/WGer)
Serpent's Egg, The (WGer//US)
Servicer, The (WGer/US)
Seven Minutes (US/WGer)
71 Fragments of a Chronology of Chance (Aus/Ger)
Sex Life in a Convent
Sex Life in L.A.
Sex Shop (Fr/It/WGer)
Shaft (Singleton – US/Ger)
Shallow Hal (US/Ger)
Shampoo and Set
Shirin's Wedding
Signed: Lino Brocka (US/GB/WGer)
Sign of the Gladiator (It/Fr/WGer)
Signs of Life
Silent Cry, The (GB/WGer/Fr)
Simon Magu (GB/Ger/It/Fr)
Simple Plan, A (US/GB/Jap/Ger/Fr)
Simply Irresistible (US/Ger)
Singing Ringing Tree, The
Sisters or the Balance of Happiness
Skin Flick (Ger/GB/Can/Jap)
Sleepy Hollow (US/Ger)
Slow Attack
Smilla's Feeling for Snow (Ger/Den/Swe)
Snow Day (US/Ger)
Someone Else's America (Fr/GB/Ger)
Something to Believe In (GB/Ger)
Somewhere in Berlin…
Song for Beko, A (Ger/Arm)
Souffle au Coeur, Le (Fr/It/WGer)
Soufrière, La
Sound of Brazil (Ger/Braz/Fin)
South Africa Belongs to Us (WGer/SAf)
Specialist, The (Fr/Ger/Bel/Aus/Isr)
Spicy Rice (WGer/Switz)
Spinnen, Die
Spione
Spring Symphony
Spy Games (Ger/US/Jap/Fr)
Stalingrad
Stammheim
Stamping Ground
Starke Ferdinand, Der
Star! Star! (US/Ger)
State of Siege (It/Fr/WGer)
Station Six – Sahara (GB/WGer)
Story of O, The (Fr/Ger)
Stranger Than Paradise (US/WGer)
Strasse, Die
Stroszek
Stunde Null

Subjective Factor, The
Succubus
Sudden Fortune of the Good People of Kombach, The
Sugarbaby
Summer in the City
Sumo Bruno
Sumurun
Sun Alley
Sunshine (Hun/Ger/Can/Aus/GB)
Super 8½
Suzhou (China/Ger)
Sweet Movie (Fr/Can/WGer)
Swing, The
Swiss Conspiracy, The (US/WGer)
Sylvester Countdown

Tales from the Vienna Woods (Aus/WGer)
Tango Lesson, The (GB/Ger/Arg/Jap/Ger)
Taxandria (Fr/Bel/Ger)
Taxi zum Klo
Tenderness of the Wolves
Ten Minutes Older – The Trumpet (GB/Ger)
Terminus (Fr/WGer)
Terror 2000
Testament of Dr Mabuse, The
There's No Sex Like Snow Sex
These Are Not My Images (neither there nor here) (US/Fr/Ger/BGB)
hey Came to Rob Las Vegas(Sp/Fr/WGer/It)
Third Generation, The
1000 Eyes of Dr Mabuse, The (WGer/It/Fr)
3 Women in Love
Three Sisters (It/Fr/Ger)
Tickle in the Heart, A
Tigerland (US/Ger)
Tiger of Eschnapur (It/Fr/WGer)
Titanic (Selpin – 1943)
Titanic Town (GB/Ger/Fr)
Tödliche Maria, Die
Tokyo-Ga (WGer/US)
Tosca (Fr/GB/Ger/It)
To the Devil a Daughter (GB/WGer)
Toto the Hero (Bel/Fr/Ger)
Tour Abroad
Trial, The (Welles – Fr/It/WGer)
Truce, The (It/Fr/Ger)
Tuvalu
Twilight's Last Gleaming (US/WGer)

Uccello dalle Piume di Cristallo,L' (It/Ger)
Underground (Fr/Ger/Hun)
Until the End of the World (Ger/Fr/Aust)

Vagabond Images
Vampyr (Ger/Fr)
Vanessa
Varieté
Va Savoir (Fr/It/Ger)
Vengeance (It/WGer)
Vent d'Est (It/WGer/Fr)
Venus in Furs
Verlorene, Der
Veronika Voss
Vertical Limit (US/Ger)
Victory (Peploe – GB/Fr/Ger)
Vigo Passion for Life (GB/Jap/Fr/Sp/Ger)
Virgin Machine
Viva Portugal (WGer/Fr)
Vladimir et Rosa (Fr/WGer/US)
Voyager (Ger/Fr)
Voyage to Cythera (Greece/WGer/It/Fr)

Warrior, The (GB/Fr/Ger/Ind)
Warshots
War Zone
Weber, Die
Wedding, The (Lounguine – Fr/Ger/Russia)
Wedding Planner, The (Ger/GB/US)
Wednesday 19.7.1961 (Rus/Ger/GB/Fin)
Werckmeister Harmonies (Hun/Fr/Ger/It/Switz)
Westler: East of the Wall
We Were Soldiers (US/Ger)
What? (It/Fr/WGer)
Wheels & Deals
Where the Green Ants Dream
Where the Money Is (Ger/US/GB)
White Hell of Piz Palu, The
Who Is Killing the Great Chefs of Europe? (WGer/US)
Wilde (GB/US/Jap/Ger)
Wild Game
Wild Games (Bel/Ger/Fr)
Will My Mother Go Back to Berlin? (Ger/US)
Wings of Desire (WGer/Fr)
Winter Sleepers (Ger/Fr)
Wise Blood (US/WGer)
Wittstock, Wittstock (Ger/Aus)
Woman in Flames, A
Wonder Boys (US/Ger/GB/Jap)
Woyzeck
W.R. – Mysteries of the Organism (Yugo/WGer)
Wrong Movement
Wunderbare Lüge der Nina Petrowna, Die

Yara (Tur/Ger)
Year of the Quiet Sun, A (Pol/US/WGer)
Yesterday Girl
Younger and Younger
Young Poisoner's Handbook, The (GB/Ger)
Young Törless (WGer/Fr)
You're Dead (US/Ger)

Zoolander (US/Ger/Aust)

Appendix 20

Italian Films

Accattone
Adieu Philippine (Fr/It)
A Double Tour (Fr/It)
Adventures of Gerard, The (GB/It/Switz)
Africa Addio
After the Fo\x (It/US)
Age of Cosimo de Medici, The
Agony and the Ecstasy, The (US/It)
Agression, L' (Fr/It)
Alexander the Great (Angelopoulos – Greece/It)
Alfredo Alfredo (It/Fr)
Allegro Non Troppo
Allonsanfan
Alphaville (Fr/It)
Amarcord (It/Fr)
A ma soeur! (Fr/It/Sp)
Amazons, The (It/Fr)
Amiche, Le
Amore, L'
Amore Molesto, L'
And Now My Love (Fr/It)
And the Ship Sails On (It/Fr)
Année Dernière à Marienbad, L' (Fr/It)
Anticristo, L'
Appartement, L (Fr/Sp/It)
Aprile
Arabian Nights (It/Fr)
Armée des Ombres, L' (Fr/It)
Ars Amandi (It/Fr)
Artemisia (Fr/Ger/It)
Assassination of Trotsky, The (Fr/It/GB)
Asterix & Obelix Take on Caesar (Gr/Ger/It)
Atlantis (Fr/It)
Attentat, L' (Fr/It/WGer)
Audience, The
Augustine of Hippo
Austerlitz (Fr/It/Liechtenstein/Yug)
Avventura, L'
Ay! Carmela (Sp/It)

Baba Yaga (It/Fr)
Bad Boy Bubby (Aust/It)
Bad Man's River (Sp/It/Fr)
Bal, Le (Fr/It/Alg)
Barabbas
Barbarella (Fr/It)
Barber of Siberia, The (Rus/Fr/It/Czech Rep)
Barnabo of the Mountains (Fr/It/Switz)
Battle of Algiers, The (Alg/It)
Beauté du Diable, La (Fr/It)
Before and After Sex
Before the Revolution
Behind Convent Walls
Belle de Jour (Fr/It)
Belles de nuit, Les (Fr/It)
Bellissima
Belly of an Architect, The (GB/It)
Benvenuta (Bel/Fr/It)
Berlin Affair, The (It/WGer)
Besieged
Beyond, The
Beyond Evil (It/Fr/WGer)
Beyond the Clouds (Fr/It/Ger)
Beyond the Door
Bible…In the Beginning, The (It/US)
Biches, Les (Fr/It)
Bicycle Thieves
Bidone, Il (It/Fr)
Big Silence, The (Fr/It)
Bisexual (Fr/It)
Bits and Pieces
Bitter Rice
Blackboards (Iran/It)
Black Emanuelle
Black Holes
Black Holiday
Black Orpheus (Fr/It/Braz)
Black Sabbath (It/Fr)
Blaise Pascal (Fr/It)
Blazing Guns (It/Sp)
Blindman (US/It)
Blood for Dracula (It/Fr)
Blood Is Not Fresh Water (Ethiopia/It)
Blood Money (HK/It/Sp/US)
Blood River (It/Sp)
Blood Ties
Blow Out (Ferreri – Fr/It)
Blow to the Heart
Blue Belle (GB/It)
B Monkey (It/GB/US)
Boatman
Boccaccio '70
Bonne Année, La (Fr/It)
Boomerang (Giovanni – Fr/It)
Borsalino (Fr/It)
Borsalino & Co (Fr/It/WGer)
Bossu, Le (Fr/It/Ger)
Boucher, Le (Fr/It)
Bread and Chocolate
Bread and Roses (GB/Ger/Sp/Fr/It)
Bread and Tulips
Bride Wore Black, The (Fr/It)
Brief Vacation, A (It/Sp)
Bronx Warriors
Brother Sun, Sister Moon (It/GB)
Brutti, sporchi e cattivi
Bullet for the General, A
Burglars, The (Fr/It)
By Nightfall

Cage aux Folles, La (Fr/It)
Cage aux Folles II, La (Fr/It)
Cage aux Folles III: The Wedding (Fr/It)
Call of the Wild, The (WGer/GB/Fr/It/Sp)
Caligula (US/It)
Cammina Cammina
Candido Erotico
Candy (US/It/Fr)
Cannibal
Cannibal Holocaust (It/Col)
Cannibals, The
Canterbury Tales, The (It/Fr)
Captains of April (Fr/It/Port/Sp)
Carabiniers, Les (Fr/It)
Carlo Giuliani, Ragazzo
Carmen (Rosi – Fr/It)
Casanova '70 (It/Fr)
Cassandra Crossing, The (GB/It/WGer)
Catherine and Co (Fr/It)
Cat o' Nine Tails, The (It/WGer/Fr)
Ca va barder… (Fr/It)
Cecilia, La (It/Fr)
Cela s'Appelle l'Aurore (Fr/It)
César and Rosalie (Fr/It/WGer)
Charlotte (Fr/It/WGer)
Chartreuse de Parme, La (Fr/It)
Chère Louise (Fr/It)
China Is Near
China 9, Liberty 37 (It/Sp)
Chi Sei?
Choses de la Vie, Les (Fr/It)
Christ Stopped at Eboli (It/Fr)
Chronicle of a Death Foretold (It/Fr)
Chronicle of Anna Magdalena Bach (It/WGer)
Cinderella – Italian Style (It/Fr)
Cinema Paradiso (It/Fr)
Cinema Paradiso: The Special Edition (It/Fr)
Circumstance, The
Città si Difende, La
City of Women (It/Fr)
Classe Operaia Va in Paradiso, La
Cléo de 5 à 7 (Fr/It)
Closed Circuit
Clowns, The (It/Fr/WGer)
Cobra (Boisset – Fr/It)
Cold Sweat (Fr/It)
Colossus of Rhodes, The (It/Sp/Fr)
Comfort of Strangers, The (It/GB)
Commare Secca, La
Companeros (It/Sp/WGer)
Confessions of a Bigamist (WGer/It)
Conformist, The (It/Fr/WGer)
Conquest (It/Sp/Mex)
Conversation Piece (It/Fr)
Coraje del Pueblo, El (Bol/It)
Counsellor, The (It/Sp)
Count Dracula (Sp/It/WGer)
Crazy Joe (US/It)
Creepers
Cri du Hibou, Le (Fr/It)
Crime Busters
Cronaca di un amore
Cry Onion (It/Sp/WGer)
Cuba Libre – Velocipedi ai Tropici (It/Cuba)
Cyclone, The

Dame aux Camélias, La (Fr/It)
Damned, The (Visconti – It/WGer)
Danger: Diabolik (It/Fr)

Dark Blue World (Czech Rep/GB/Ger/Den/It)
Dark Eyes
Daughters of Darkness (Bel/Fr/WGer/It)
Day of the Beast, The (Sp/It)
Deadly Trap, The (Fr/It)
Deaf Smith & Johnny Ears
Dear Diary (It/Fr)
Death in Venice
Death of a Cameraman
Decameron, The (It/Fr/WGer)
Demons
Demons 2
Désert des Tartares, Le (Fr/It/WGer)
Deserter and the Nomads, The (Czech/It)
Dialogue des Carmélites, Le (Fr/It)
Diary of a Chambermaid, The (Buñuel – Fr/It)
Diavolo in Corpo, Il (It/Fr)
Dimenticare Venezia (It/Fr)
Django (It/Sp)
Django Kill (It/Sp)
Docteur Popaul (Fr/It)
Dr M (Ger/It/Fr)
Dolce Vita, La (It/Fr)
Domicile Conjugal (Fr/It)
Domenica
Don Giovanni (It/Fr/WGer)
Don Juan or If Don Juan Were a Woman (Fr/It)
Don't Look Now (GB/It)
Doulos, Le (Fr/It)
Down the Ancient Stairs (It/Fr)
Drama of the Rich (It/Fr)
Dramma della Gelosia (It/Sp)
Du Rififi à Paname (Fr/It/WGer)
During the Summer
Dust (GB/Ger/Macedonia/US/Sp/Switz)

Eclipse, The (It/Fr)
8½
8-Wheel Beast, The (It/Fr)
Elective Affinities (It/Fr)
Eléna et les Hommes (Fr/It)
Emanuelle and the Last Cannibals
Emmerdeur, L' (Fr/It)
En Cas de Malheur (Fr/It)
Enzo, Domani a Palermo!
Era Notte a Roma (It/Fr)
Ercole alla conquista di Atlantide (It/Fr)
Erotic Quartet (US/WGer/It)
Eternity and a Day (Greece/Fr/It/Ger)
Eve (Fr/It)
Everybody's Fine (It/Fr)

Fabiola (It/Fr)
Fair Game
Faithless (Swe/Nor/Fin/It/Ger)
Farinelli Il Castrato (It/Bel)
Farewell, Home Sweet Home (Fr/Switz/It)
Faute de l'Abbé Mouret, La (Fr/It)
Fear (It/WGer)
Fellini A Director's Notebook
Fellini-Satyricon (It/Fr)
Fellini's Casanova
Fellini's Roma (It/Fr)
Femme Infidèle, La (Fr/It)
Ferroviere, Il
Fiorile (It/Fr/Ger)
Firemen's Ball, The (Czech/It)
First Light of Dawn
Fistful of Dollars, A (It/WGer/Sp)
Fists in the Pocket
Fit To Be Untied
Flesh for Frankenstein (It/Fr)
Flic, Un (Fr/It)
Flight of the Innocent
Folle à Tuer (Fr/It)
Footman, The
For a Few Dollars More (It/Sp/WGer)
Forever Mary
Fortini/Cani (It/Fr/WGer/GB/US)
Fortunat (Fr/It)
Four Flies on Grey Velvet (It/Fr)
Four Nights of a Dreamer (Fr/It)
Francesco, giullare di Dio
From Hell to Victory (Fr/It/Sp)
From Pole to Equator (It/WGer)
From the Cloud to the Resistance (It/Fr/WGer/GB)
Fury (It/GB)
Future Is Woman, The (It/Fr/WGer)

Galileo (Cavani – It/Bulg)
Gang, Le (Fr/It)
Garage Olimpio (Arg/It)
Garden of the Finzi-Continis, The (It/WGer)
Germany, Year Zero (It/WGer)
Germinal (Fr/Bel/It)
Giant of Marathon, The (It/Fr)
Ginger & Fred (Fr/It/WGer)
Giorno della prima di 'Close Up', Il
Giovanna d'Arco al Rogo (It/Fr)
Girl from Trieste, The
Giù la Testa
Golden Coach, The (Fr/It)
Goliath and the Barbarians (It/US)
Good Morning Babylon (It/Fr/US)
Good, the Bad and the Ugly, The
Gospel According to St Matthew, The (It/Fr)
Goya in Bordeau (Sp/It)
Grazie Zia
Guns for San Sebastian (Fr/Mex/It)

Haren Suare (Fr/It/Tur)
Heroes, The (Sp/It/Fr)
Histoires Extraordinaires (Fr/It)
History Lessons
Hitler: the Last Ten Days (GB/It)
Ho! (Fr/It)
Hold Back the Night (GB/It)
Holocaust 2000 (It/GB)
Homme de Marrakech, L' (Fr/It/Sp)
Homme de Rio, L' (Fr/It)
Honey Pot, The (US/It)
Hors la vie (Fr/It/Bel)
Hotel (GB/It)
House of Cards (US/It)
House by the Cemetery, The
House of Exorcism, The
House of Smiles
How Harry Became a Tree (Ire/It/GB/Fr)
How to Destroy the Reputation of the World's Greatest Secret Agent (Fr/It)
Humanoid, The
Hunchback of Notre Dame, The (Delannoy – Fr/It)

Icicle Thief
Identification of a Woman (It/Fr)
Illustrious Corpses (It/Fr)
Immortelle, L' (Fr/It/Tur)
Imperfect Love
Infernal Trio (Fr/It/WGer)
Inferno
Inheritance, The
Inhibitions
Inner Circle, The
Innocent, The (Visconti – Fr/It)
Innocents with Dirty Hands (Fr/It/WGer)
In Nomme della Legge
Intervista
In the Name of the Father
Invincible Barbarian, The
Island of Mutations
Italy: Year One

Jane Eyre (GB/It/Fr/US)
Jazzwomen (It/US)
Jean de Florette (Fr/It)
Jung (War) – in the Land of the Mujaheddin
Just Before Nightfall (Fr/It)

Kapo (It/Fr)
Killer Fish
Killer Nun

LaCapaGira
Lacombe Lucien (Fr/It/WGer)
Lady L (Fr/It)
Lancelot du Lac (Fr/It)
Landru (Fr/It)
Landscape in the Mist (Greece/Fr/It)
Last Emperor, The (China/It)
Last Feelings
Last Italian Tango, The
Last Moments
Last Snows of Spring, The
Last Tango in Paris (Fr/It)
Last Woman, The (Fr/It)
Leap Into the Void, (It/Fr)
Legend of Frenchie King, The (Fr/It/Sp/GB)
Legend of 1900, The
Legend of the Holy Drinker, The
Leon Morin, Priest (Fr/It)
Leopard, The
Let's Hope It's a Girl (It/Fr)
Leviathan (US/It)
Liam (GB/Ger/It)
Libera
Libero Burro
Lies to Live by (Babylon)
Life and Extraordinary Adventures of Private Ivan Chonkin, The (GB/Fr/It/Czech Rep/Rus)
Life Is Beautiful
Life Size (Sp/Fr/It)
Light of My Eyes
Lion Has Seven Heads, The (Fr/It)
Living Blood
Living Dead at the Manchester Morgue, The (Sp/It)
Living It Up
Lizards, The
Lola (Demy – Fr/It)
Long Live the Lady!
Lost Lover, The (It/GB)
Love in a Women's Prison
Love in the Mirror
Luci del Varietà
Lucky Luciano (It/Fr)
Ludwig (Fr/It/WGer)
Luna, La
Luna e l'Altra
Luzhin Defence, The (GB/Fr/It/Hun/US)

Macaroni
Machine That Kills Bad People, The
Maciste all'Inferno
Maciste Contro i Mostri
Mad Adventures of 'Rabbi' Jacob, The (Fr/It)
Madame de...(Fr/It)
Maledetto Imbroglio, Un
Malenà (It/US)
Malizia
Mamma Roma
Manhunt in Milan (It/WGer)
Man Named John, A
Manon des Sources (Fr/It/Switz)
Man on Fire (Fr/It)
Man to Respect, A (It/WGer)
Marquise (Fr/It/Switz/Sp)
Maschera del Demonio, La
Mask, The
Massacre in Rome (Fr/It)
Master and Margarita, The (Yugo/It)
Master of Love
Mata-Hari, Agent H21 (Fr/It)
Maternale
Mattei Affair, The
Medea (Fr/It/WGer)
Mediterraneo
Mépris, Le (Fr/It)
Mercenario, Il (It/Sp)
Merveilleuse Visite, La (Fr/It)
Microcosmos (Fr/Switz/It)
Mignon Has Left (It/Fr)
Milou en mai (Fr/It)
Miracle in Milan
Miroir a deux faces, Le (Fr/It)
Moine, Le (Fr/It/WGer)
Moment of Truth, The (It/Sp)
Monkey's Mask, The (Aust/Fr/Jap/It)
Monsoon Wedding (US/It/Ger/Fr)
Montagna del Dio Cannibale, La
Moon in the Gutter, The (Fr/It)
Moses (It/GB)
Mostly Martha (Aus/Ger/It/Switz)
Mr Klein (Fr/It)
Murder Is a Murder...Is a Murder, A (Fr/It)
Muriel (Fr/It)
My First 40 Years
My Name Is Nobody (It/Fr/WGer)

Nada (Fr/It)
Name of the Rose, The (Fr/It/WGer)
Nana
Naples Connection, The
Necropolis
Nest of Vipers
New Barbarians, The
Night Caller (Fr/It)
Night Hair Child (GB/It/WGer/Sp)
Night of San Lorenzo
Night Porter, The
Night Sun (It/Fr/Ger)
Nikita (Fr/It)
1900 (It/Fr/WGer)
Noces Rouges (Fr/It)
Noi Tre
No Man's Land (Tanovic – Fr/It/GB/Bel/Slovenia)
Nora (GB/Ire/Ger/It)
Notte, La (Fr/It)
Notti di Cabiria, Le (It/Fr)
Nuits Rouges (Fr/It)
Nun and the Devil, The (It/Fr)

Oberwald Mystery, The (It/WGer)
Oedipus Rex
Off to the Revolution by 2CV
Once Upon a Time in the West
One Hamlet Less
Open Doors
Open Your Eyes (Sp/Fr/It)
Opera
Operation Crossbow (GB/It)
Orchestra Rehearsal (It/WGer)
Order of Death
Order to Kill (Sp/It/Dom)
Orlando (GB/Rus/Fr/It/Neth)
Ossessione
Otello
Othon (WGer/It)
Outside Man, The (Fr/It)

Padre Padrone
Paisà
Palermo or Wolfsburg (WGer/It)
Paranoia (It/Fr)
Partie de Plaisir, Une (Fr/It)
Partner
Pasolini, un Delito Italiano (It/Fr)
Passenger, The (Fr/It/Sp)
Passione d'Amore (Fr/It)

Paura nella Città dei Morti Viventi
Petit Théâtre de Jean Renoir, Le (Fr/It/WGer)
Petomane, Il
Pierrot le Fou (Fr/It)
Pigsty (It/Fr)
Placido Rizzotto
Plein Soleil (Fr/It)
Postino, Il (It/Fr)
Posto, Il
Prince of Homburg, The
Princesa (GB/Fr/Ger/It/Sp)
Private Vices and Public Virtues (It/Yugo)
Profession of Arms, The (It/Fr/Ger)
Prospero's Books (Neth/Fr/It)
Prostitution Racket, The
Protagonists, The
Puerto Escondido
Pure Formality, A (It/Fr)
Purple Taxi, The (Fr/It/Ire)

Quattro dell'Ave Maria, I
Quante Volte… Quella Notte (It/WGer)
Queimada!
Que la Bête Meure (Fr/It)
Quiet Days in Clichy (Fr/It/Ger)

Reason to Live, a Reason to Die, A (It/Fr/Sp/WGer)
Rebel Nun, The (It/Fr)
Recuperanti, I
Red Circle (Fr/It)
Red Desert, The (It/Fr)
Red Rings of Fear (It/Sp/WGer)
Red Sun (Fr/It/Sp)
Red Violin, The (Can/It/US/GB)
Reine Margot, La (Fr/Ger/It)
Rempart de Béguines, Le (Fr/It)
Repubblica Nostra
Return of Sabata (Fr/It/WGer)
Rider on the Rain (Fr/It)
Rigoletto
Road to Salina (Fr/It)
Rocco and His Brothers (It/Fr)
Roma, Città Aperta
Romeo and Juliet (GB/It)
Rosa e Cornelia
Route de Corinthe, La (Fr/It/Greece)
Route One/USA (US/Fr/GB/It)
Rupture, La (Fr/It/Bel)
Russicum

Sabata
Saló, o le Centoventi Giornate di Sodoma (It/Fr)
Salomé (Fr/It)
Salon Kitty (It/Fr/WGer)
Salvatore Giuliano
Samourai, Le (Fr/It)
Santa Sangre
Sauvage, Le (Fr/It)
Savage Innocents, The (It/Fr/GB)
Savage Man, Savage Beast
Sbarco di Anzio, Lo (Anzio)
Scalawag (US/It)
School
Scorta, La
Scoumoune, La (Fr/It)
Second Time, The (It/Fr)
Secret, The (Fr/It)
Secret Ballot (Iran/It)
Secret Défense (Fr/Switz/It)
Sect, The
Section Spéciale (Fr/It/WGer)
Sellout, The (Fr/It)
Senso
Serpent, The (Fr/It/WGer)
Seven Beauties
Seventeen Years (China/It)
Sexorcist, The
Sex Shop (Fr/It/WGer)
Shark's Cave, The (It/Sp)
Shattered (Fr/It)
Sheltering Sky, The (GB/It)
Sicilian Cross

Sign of the Gladiator (It/Fr/WGer)
Signora di Tutti, La
Signora Senza Camelie, La
Silence of the Hams (It/US)
Silencieux, Le (Fr/It)
Simon Magus (GB/Ger/It)
Sirène du Mississipi, La (Fr/It)
Sleepless
Slightly Pregnant Man, The (Fr/It)
Sodom and Gomorrah (Fr/It)
Son's Room, The (It/Fr)
Souffle au Coeur, Le (Fr/It/WGer)
Sparrow
Special Day (It/Can)
Splendor (It/Fr)
State of Seige (Fr/It/WGer)
Stavisky… (Fr/It)
Stealing Beauty (It/GB/Fr)
Stolen Children, The
Strada, La
Strada per Forte Alamo, La
Stromboli, Terra di Dio
Sunflower (It/Fr)
Superargo (It/Sp)
Suspiria
Swept Away…by an Unusual Destiny in the Blue Sea of August

Take a Hard Ride (US/It)
Tales of Ordinary Madness (Fr/It)
Tano da Morire
Tea with Mussolini (It/GB)
Teeth
Tempter, The (It/GB)
Tenebrae
Tentacles
Terminal Station (It/US)
Texas, Addio (It/Sp)
That Night in Varennes (Fr/It)
Theorem
They Call Me Trinity
They Came to Rob Las Vegas (Sp/Fr/WGer/It)
This Is the Garden
1000 Eyes of Dr Mabuse, The (WGer/Fr/It)
Three Brothers (It/Fr)
Three Sisters (It/Fr/Ger)
Tiger of Eschnapur, The (WGer/Fr/It)
Time Regained (Fr/It/Port)
'Tis Pity She's a Whore
Today It's Me…Tomorrow You!
Together (Swe/Den/It)
Torrents of Spring
Tosca (Fr/GB/Ger/It)
Totò Who Livved Twice
Touche pas à la femme blanche (Fr/It)
Touchez pas au Grisbi (Fr/It)
Tout Va Bien (Fr/It)
Traffic (Fr/It)
Train, The (US/Fr/It)
Traitement de Choc (Fr/It)
Trauma
Travelling Light: a Portrait of Lindsay Kemp
Traversée de Paris, La (Fr/It)
Tree of Wooden Clogs, The
Trial, The (Welles – Fr/It/WGer)
Tristana (Sp/Fr/It)
Trou, Le (Fr/It)
Truce, The (It/Fr/Ger)
Turkish Bath – Hamam, The (Sp/It/Tur)

Uccellacci e Uccellini
Uccello dalle Piume di Cristallo, L' (It/WGer)
Ulysses' Gaze (Greece/It/Fr)
Ultrà
Umberto D.
Uncle from Brooklyn, The
Uncle Tom
Uomo delle stelle, L'

Vache et la Prisonnier, La (Fr/It)
Vaghe Stelle dell'Orsa
Valdez il Mezzosangue (It/Sp/Fr)
Vampire de Dusseldorf, Le (Fr/It/Sp)
Vampires in Venice
Va Savoir (Fr/It/Ger)
Vengeance (It/WGer)
Venial Sin
Vent d'Est (Fr/It/WGer)
Verdict (Fr/It)
Verdugo, El (Sp/It)
Vérité, La (Fr/It)
Viaggio in Italia
Vices in the Family
Vie Privée (Fr/It)
Violation of Justine (Fr/It/Can)
Violent Professionals, The
Virgin for St Tropez, A (Fr/It)
Visitor, The
Vitelloni, I
Viva Maria! (Fr/It)
Vivre pour Vivre (Fr/It)
Voice of the Moon, The
Voie Lactée, La (Fr/It)

Volere, Volare
Voyage
Voyage to Cythera (Greece/WGer/It/GB)

Wages of Fear, The (Fr/It)
Waiting for the Messiah (Arg/Sp/It)
War and Peace (Vidor – US/It)
Watch Out, We're Mad (It/Sp)
Water and Salt (Port/It)
Waterloo (It/USSR)
We Don't Want to Talk About It (Arg/It)
Weekend (Fr/It)
Werckmeister Harmonies (Hun/Fr/Ger/It/Switz)
We the Living
What? (It/Fr/WGer)
White Fang (It/Sp/Fr)
White Nights (Visconti – Fr/It)
White Sheik, The
Whores, The
Why?
Wifemistress

Zombie Flesh-Eaters

Appendix 21

Japanese Films

A
Abnormal Family: Brother's Wife
About Love, Tokyo
Actor's Revenge, An
Adrenaline Drive
Adventures of Milo and Otis, The
After Life
Afternoon Breezes
Agitator
Ai No Corrida (Fr/Jap)
A.K. (Fr/Jap)
Akira
Alone on the Pacific
Angel Dust
Annyong Kimchi
Another Battle
Another Lonely Hitman
April Story
Asako in Ruby Shoes (SKor/Jap)
Attack on a Bakery
Audition
August in the Water
Autumn Afternoon, An
Autumn Moon (HK/Jap)

Bad Company
Bad Sleep Well, The
Ballad of Narayama, The
Bantsuma: The Life and Times of Tsumasaburo Bando
Bari-Zogon
Barren Illusion
Battle Royale
Beautiful Mystery – Legend of Big Horn
Bent (GB/US/Jap)
Bird People in China, The
Black Lizard, The
Black Rain (Imamura)
Blind Alley
Blood of the Dragon
Blood of Revenge
Blood: The Last Vampire
Blues Harp
Blue Spring
Body Drop Asphalt
Boiling Point (Kitano)
Boxer, The (Terayama)
Boy
Boy Called Third Base, A
Boy's Choir
Branded to Kill
Brother and Sister
Bullet Ballet
Bullet Train, The
Burmese Harp, The

Ceremony, The
Chance to Die, A (Tai/Jap)
Charisma
Chikamatsu Monogatari
Ciénaga, La (Arg/US/Jap/Fr/Switz/Sp/Braz)
Circus Boys
City of Lost Souls
Comic Magazine
Crazy Family
Crossways
Cruel Story of the Shogunate's Downfall
Crying Freeman (Fr/Can/US/Jap)
Cure

Dead or Alive
Dead or Alive 2 – Birds
Dear Summer Sister
Death by Hanging
Death on a Full Moon Day (Sri Lanka/Jap)
Deaths in Tokimeki
Delbaran (Iran/Jap/Neth)
Dersu Uzala (USSR/Jap)
Destroy All Monsters
Diary of a Shinjuku Thief
Digimon Digital Monsters – The Movie (Jap/US)
Discipline for the Left-Handed
Distance
Dodes'ka-den
Dora-Heita
Double Suicide
Drive, The
Drowning Man, A

Early Spring
Early Summer
Ebirah – Terror of the Deep
Eel, The
Eijanaika
Electric Dragon 80,000
Elephant Song
Emmanuelle in Tokyo
Emperor and the Assassin, The (China/Jap/Fr)
Emperor's Naked Army Marches On, The
Empire of Passion (Fr/Jap)
Empress Yang Kwei Fei, The (Jap/HK)
Empty Table, The
Enchantment, The
Eureka

Face
Family Game
Fancy Dance
Fighting Elegy
Fire Festival
Fire Within
Fist of the North Star
Five Women Around Utamaro
Flavour of Green Tea Over Rice
Flight from Ashiya (US/Jap)
Flirt (US/GB/Jap)
[Focus]
Four Days of Snow and Blood
Fruits of Passion, The (Fr/Jap)
Fufu the Worldweary
Funeral Parade of Roses
Further Gesture, A (GB/Ger/Jap/Ire)

Gamera: The Guardian of the Universe
Gate of Flesh
Getting Any?
Ghost in the Shell (Jap/GB)
Ghosts of Kasane Swamp, The
Ghost Story of Yotsuya
Gion Festival Music
Gips
Girl, She Is 100%, A
Godzilla 1985
Godzilla vs the Bionic Monster
Godzilla vs the Smog Monster
Gojoe
Gonin
Gonin 2
Gonza the Spearman
Good Men, Good Women (Jap/Tai)
Gunhed

Hair Opera, The
Hana-Bi
Happiness of the Katakuris, The
Hard Rain (US/GB/Jap/Ger/Den)
Hazy Life
Heart, Beating in the Dark
Heaven-6-Box
Hell
Hen in the Wind, A
Hidden Fortress, The
High and Low
Hiroshima, Mon Amour (Fr/Jap)
History of a Man's Face, The
History of Post-War Japan as Told by a Bar Hostess
Hole in the Sky
Hometown
How Old Is the River?
Humanity and Paper Balloons
Hush!
Hysteric

I Am an S+M Writer
Ichi the Killer (Jap/SKor/HK)
Idiot, The
Ikinai
Ikiru
I Like You, I Like You Very Much
Irezumi – Spirit of Tattoo
Iron Maze (US/Jap)
Island, The (Shindo)
Island Tale, The (HK/Jap)
Isn't She Great (US/Ger/GB/Jap)
I, the Executioner
I Was Born, But…

Jam (Tai/Jap)
Jam Session: The Official Bootleg of Kikujiro
Jin-Roh
Ju Dou (China/Jap)

Kagero-za
Kama Sutra: A Tale of Love (Ind/GB/Jap/Ger)
Kamizake Taxi
Kaza-hana
Kichiku
Kids Return
Kikuchi
Kikujiro
Kitami
Kitchen, The
KT
Kuroneko
Kwaidan

Labyrinth of Dreams
Lady Vampire, The
Lara Croft: Tomb Raider (US/Ger/GB/Jap)
Late Spring
Latin Boys Go to Hell (US/Ger/Sp/Jap)
Leaving
Ley Lines
Licence to Live
Life of Chikuzan, The
Life of Oharu, The
Lightning Swords of Death
Like a Rolling Stone
Like Grains of Sand
Little Cheung (HK/Jap)
Little Nemo Adventures in Slumberland (US/Jap)
Looking for an Angel
Lost Sex
Lost World of Sinbad, The
Love Is the Devil – Study for a Portrait of Francis Bacon (GB/Fr/Jap)
Love/Juice
Love Letter
Lower Depths, The
Loyal 47 Ronin of the Genroku Era, The
Luna Papa

Maborosi
Madadayo
Madame Butterfly
Mansion of the Ghost Cat, The
Man Vanishes, A
Man Who Left His Will on Film, The
March Comes in Like a Lion
MARKS
Memories
Metropolis (Rintaro)
Mike Yokohama – a Forest with No Name
Minamata
Minbo Woman – Or the Gentle Art of Japanese Extortion
Mishima: A Life in Four Chapters (US/Jap)
Mr Baseball (US/Jap)
Miyamoto Musashi
Monday
Monkey's Mask, The (Aust/Fr/Jap/It)
Moon Has Risen, The
Most Terrible Time of My Life (Jap/Tai/China)
M/other
Moving
Muddy River
Music for the Movies: The Hollywood Sound (US/Fr/Jap)
My Love Has Been Burning
Mystery of Rampo, The
My Sons

Nemuri Kyoshiro: The Book of Killing-Rules
New God, The
New Morning of Billy the Kid, The
None But the Brave (US/Jap)
Nostalgia for Countryland (Vietnam/Jap)
Not Forgotten
Nowhere Man
Obsession, The
Ohayo
Okaeri
Okoge
Ondeko-za on Sado, The
One and a Two…, A
One Fine Spring Day (SKor/Jap/HK)
One Generation of Tattoos
On Equal Terms (Tajikistan/Switz/Jap)
Onibaba
Organ
Osaka Elegy
Ososhiki
Outer Way, The

Page of Madness, A
Painful Pair, A
Painted Desert
Pandemonium
Paradise View
Pastoral Hide-and-Seek
Patlabor – The Movie
Patlabor 2
Pigs and Battleships
Pokémon – the First Movie (Jap/US)
Pokémon 3: Spell of the Unown
Postman Blues
Peasants of the Second Fortress, The
Perfect Blue
Pistol Opera
Platform, The (HK/Jap/Fr)
Pola X (Fr/Jap/Ger/Switz)
Princess Mononoke
Profound Desire of the Gods: Tales from a Southern Island
Promise

Rainy Dog
Ran (Fr/Jap)
Rashomon
Rebellion
Record of a Tenement Gentleman
Red Beard
Red Peony Gambler: Flower-cards Match
Remembrance (Nakajima)
Rhapsody in August
Ring 0 – Birthday
Ring
Ring 2
Road, The (Fr/Jap/Kazakhstan/Neth)
Roujin Z

Sadistic City
Saga of Anatahan, The
Sanjuro
Sansho Dayu
Sasuke and His Comedians
Scene at the Sea, A
Screamers (Can/US/Jap)
Seance
Seven Samurai
7/25
Shall We Dance?
Shark-skin Man and Peach-hip Girl
Shikoku
Shin Heike Monogatari
Shinjuku Triad Society
Shogun Assassin (Jap/US)
Sight Behind the Bandaged Eye
Simple Plan, A (US/GB/Jap/Ger/Fr)
Sisters of Gion
Skin Flick (Ger/GB/Can/Jap)
Skinless Night
Sleeping Man
Sleepless Town
Some Kinda Love
Sonatine
Son of Godzilla
Space Firebird
Spirited Away
Spriggan
Spy Game (Ger/US/Jap/Fr)
Stakeout
Sting of Death, The
Story of the Late Chrysanthemums, The
Stranger
Stray Dog
Street of Shame
Stroller in the Attic, The
Suicide Club
Sukiyaki
Summer Soldiers
Summer Vacation 1999
Sumo Do, Sumo Don't
Sunless Days (HK/Jap)
Suzaku
Swallowtail Butterfly
Sweet Degeneration (Tai/Jap)
Swimming Prohibited
Swimming with Tears
Sword of Doom, The

Taboo
Tango Lesson, The (GB/Fr/Arg/Jap/Ger)
Taxing Woman, A
Tel-Club
Tender Place, A
Tetsuo
Tetsuo II: Bodyhammer
That Night's Wife
This Window Is Yours
Three Resurrected Drunkards
Throne of Blood
Throw Away Your Books, Let's Go into the Streets
Timeless Melody
Tokyo Chorus
Tokyo Daughter
Tokyo Decadence
Tokyo Fist
Tokyo Kyodai
Tokyo Olympiad 1964
Tokyo Story
Tom's Midnight Garden (US/GB/Jap)
Tora no O o Fumu Otokotachi
Tora! Tora! Tora! (US/Jap)
To Sleep, So As to Dream
Town of Love and Hope, A
Triple Cross, The
Tsuru-Henry (Jap/Tai)
2 Duo

Ugetsu Monogatari
Unchain
Unknown Pleasures (Jap/HK/SKor)
Unloved
Untama Giru

Vigo Passion for Life (GB/Jap/Fr/Sp/Ger)
Village of Dreams
Violated Angels
Violent Cop, The
Virus (Jap/Can)
Visions of Light (US/Jap)
Visitor Q

Wave
War of the Monsters
Watching the Detective
Water Drops on Burning Rocks (Fr/Jap)
Welcome Back Mr McDonald
What's Up Tiger Lily? (US/Jap)
Whiteout
Wicked Reporter, The
Wings of Honneamise, The
Wilde (GB/US/Jap/Ger)
Without Memory
Wizard of Darkness
Woman of the Dunes
Wonder Boys (US/Ger/GB/Jap)
Work of the Grass
World Apartment Horror
Written Face, The (Switz/Jap)

Yojimbo
Youth of the Beast
Yumeji

Zazie
Zigeunerweisen
Zipper and Tits

Actors' Index

Adjani, Isabelle *Camille Claudel; Deadly Run (Mortelle Randonnée); Diabolique* (Chechik); *Driver, The; Ishtar; Nosferatu the Vampyre (Nosferatu: Phantom der Nacht); One Deadly Summer (L'Eté Meurtrier); Possession; Quartet* (Ivory); *Reine Margot, La; Story of Adèle H., The (L'Histoire d'Adèle H.); Subway; Tenant, The (Le Locataire); Violette et François.*

Ameche, Don *Cocoon; Cocoon: The Return; Confirm or Deny; Corrina, Corrina; Folks!; Four Sons; Greenwich Village; Harry and the Hendersons (aka Bigfoot and the Hendersons); Heaven Can Wait* (Lubitsch); *Hollywood Cavalcade; Homeward Bound: The Incredible Journey; In Old Chicago; Lillian Russell; Midnight; One in a Million; Oscar; Sleep, My Love; That Night in Rio; Things Change; Trading Places.*

Andrews, Dana *Airport 1975; Ball of Fire; Battle of the Bulge; Best Years of Our Lives, The; Beyond a Reasonable Doubt; Boomerang* (Kazan); *Crack in the World; Daisy Kenyon; Devil's Brigade, The; Edge of Doom (aka Stronger Than Fear); Fallen Angel; Good Guys Wear Black; In Harm's Way; Iron Curtain, The (aka Behind the Iron Curtain); I Want You; Last Tycoon, The; Laura; Loved One, The; My Foolish Heart; Night of the Demon (aka Curse of the Demon); North Star (aka Armored Attack); Ox-Bow Incident, The (aka Strange Incident); Satan Bug, The; Smoke Signal; State Fair; Swamp Water; Take a Hard Ride; Three Hours to Kill; Tobacco Road; Up in Arms; Walk in the Sun, A; Westerner, The; While the City Sleeps.*

Andrews, Julie *Americanization of Emily, The; Darling Lili; Duet for One; Hawaii; Little Miss Marker; Man Who Loved Women, The; Mary Poppins; Princess Diaries, The; Relative Values; S.O.B.; Sound of Music, The; Star!; Tamarind Seed, The; '10'; 'That's Life'; Thoroughly Modern Millie; Torn Curtain; Victor/ Victoria.*

Arthur, Jean *Devil and Miss Jones, The; Easy Living* (Leisen); *Foreign Affair, A; History Is Made at Night; Lady Takes a Chance, A; Mr Deeds Goes to Town; Mr Smith Goes to Washington; More the Merrier, The; Only Angels Have Wings; Plainsman, The; Shane; Talk of the Town, The; Whole Town's Talking, The (aka Passport to Fame); You Can't Take It With You.*

Astaire, Fred *Band Wagon, The; Barkleys of Broadway, The; Belle of New York, The; Blue Skies; Carefree; Daddy Long Legs; Damsel in Distress, A; Easter Parade; Finian's Rainbow; Flying Down to Rio; Follow the Fleet; Funny Face; Gay Divorcee, The; Ghost Story; Holiday Inn; Midas Run (aka A Run on Gold); On the Beach; Purple Taxi, The (Le Taxi Mauve); Roberta; Royal Wedding (aka Wedding Bells); Shall We Dance?* (Sandrich); *Silk Stockings; Sky's the Limit, The; Story of Vernon and Irene Castle, The; Swing Time; That's Entertainment!; That's Entertainment Part II; Top Hat; Towering Inferno, The; You'll Never Get Rich; You Were Never Lovelier; Ziegfeld Follies.*

Attenborough, Richard *And Then There Were None (aka Ten Little Indians); Angry Silence, The; Bliss of Mrs Blossom, The; Boys in Brown; Brannigan; Brighton Rock; Brothers in Law; Chess Players, The (Shatranj ke Khilari); Conduct Unbecoming; Dancing With Crime; Dunkirk; Eight O'Clock Walk; Elizabeth; Flight of the Phoenix, The; Great Escape, The; Guinea Pig, The (aka The Outsider); Hamlet* (Branagh); *Human Factor, The* (Preminger); *I'm All Right, Jack; In Which We Serve; Jet Storm; Journey Together; Jurassic Park; League of Gentlemen, The; London Belongs to Me (aka Dulcimer Street); Loot; Jurassic Park; Magic Box, The; Magic Christian, The; Man Upstairs, The; Matter of Life and Death, A (aka Stairway to Heaven); Miracle on 34th Street; Morning Departure (aka Operation Disaster); Only Two Can Play; Only When I Larf; Private's Progress; Rosebud; Sand Pebbles, The; Scamp, The; Seance on a Wet Afternoon; Sea of Sand; Shadowlands; Ship That Died of Shame, The; 10 Rillington Place.*

Audran, Stéphane *And Then There Were None (aka Ten Little Indians); Babette's Feast (Babettes Gaestebud); Bay Boy, The; Biches, Les (The Does); Big Red One, The; Black Bird, The; Blood of Others, The (Le Sang des Autres); Blood Relatives (Liens de Sang); B Must Die (Hay que Matar a B); Bonnes Femmes, Les (The Girls); Boucher, Le (The Butcher); Cage aux Folles III: The Wedding, La; Champagne Murders, The (Le Scandale); Clean Slate (Coup de Torchon); Cop au Vin (Poulet au Vinaigre); Cousins, Les (The Cousins); Deadly Run (Mortelle Randonée); Dead Pigeon on Beethovenstrasse; Devil's Advocate, The (Des Teufels Advokat); Discreet Charm of the Bourgeoisie, The (Le Charme Discret de la Bourgeoisie); Eagle's Wing; Femme Infidèle, La (Unfaithful Wife); Just Before Nightfall (Juste avant la Nuit); Lady in the Car with Glasses and a Gun, The (La Dame dans l'auto avec des lunettes et un fusil); Landru; Ligne de Démarcation, La; Madeline; Maximum Risk; Murder Is a Murder…Is a Murder, A (Un Meurtre est un Meurtre); Noces Rouges, Les (Blood Wedding/Red Wedding/ Wedding in Blood); Paris vu par… (Six in Paris); Quiet Days in Clichy (Jours Tranquilles à Clichy)* (Chabrol); *Rupture, La; Signe du Lion, Le (The Sign of Leo); Silver Bears; Sons* (Rockwell); *Violette Nozière.*

Aykroyd, Dan *Blues Brothers, The; Blues Brothers 2000; Canadian Bacon; Casper; Chaplin; Couch Trip, The; Crossroads; Dragnet; Driving Miss Daisy; Exit to Eden; Feeling Minnesota; Ghostbusters; Ghostbusters II; Grosse Pointe Blank; House of Mirth, The; Indiana Jones and the Temple of Doom; Into the Night; It Came from Hollywood; Loose Cannons; Loser; My Girl; My Girl 2; My Stepmother Is an Alien; Neighbors; 1941; North; Nothing Lasts Forever; Pearl Harbor; Rainbow; Sgt Bilko; She's Having a Baby; Sneakers; Spies Like Us; Stardom; This Is My Life; Tommy Boy; Trading Places; Twilight Zone: The Movie.*

Bacall, Lauren *All I Want for Christmas; Appointment with Death; Big Sleep, The* (Hawks); *Cobweb, The; Confidential Agent; Dark Passage; Designing Woman; Fan, The; Harper (aka The Moving Target); Health; How to Marry a Millionaire; Key Largo; Mirror Has Two Faces, The; Misery; Mr North; Murder on the Orient Express; North West Frontier (aka Flame Over India); Sex and the Single Girl; Shootist, The; To Have and Have Not; Tree of Hands; Woman's World; Written on the Wind; Young Man with a Horn (aka Young Man of Music).*

Baker, Stanley *Accident; Alexander the Great* (Rossen); *Blind Date (aka Chance Meeting); Captain Horatio Hornblower R.N.; Criminal, The (aka The Concrete Jungle); Cruel Sea, The; Eve; Good Die Young, The; Guns of Navarone, The; Hill in Korea, A (aka Hell in Korea); Hell Drivers; Hell Is a City; In the French Style; Jet Storm; Perfect Friday; Prize of Arms, A; Richard III; Robbery; Sodom and Gomorrah (Sodoma e Gomorra); Where's Jack?; Zulu.*

Bardot, Brigitte *Don Juan or If Don Juan Were a Woman (Don Juan 1973 ou si Don Juan était une Femme); En Cas de Malheur (La Ragazza del Peccato/Love Is My Profession); Et Dieu Créa la Femme (And God Created Woman/And Woman…Was Created); Grandes Manoeuvres, Les (Summer Manoeuvres); Histoires Extraordinaires (Spirits of the Dead/Tales of Mystery); Legend of Frenchie King, The (Les Pétroleuses); Masculin Féminin (Masculine Feminine); Mépris, Le (Contempt); Shalako; Si Versailles m'était conté… (Versailles/ Royal Affairs at Versailles); Trou Normand, Le (Crazy for Love); Vérité, La (The Truth); Vie Privée (A Very Private Affair); Viva Maria!.*

Bates, Alan *Britannia Hospital; Butley; Caretaker, The (aka The Guest); Cherry Orchard, The (O Visinokipos/La Cerisaie); Dr M (aka Club Extinction); Duet for One; Entertainer, The; Far From the Madding Crowd; Fixer, The; Georgy Girl; Go-Between, The; Gosford Park; Grotesque, The (aka Gentlemen Don't Eat Poets); Hamlet* (Zeffirelli); *Hamlet* (Branagh); *Hands Up! (Rece do Góry); In Celebration; Kind of Loving, A; King of Hearts (Le Roi de Coeur); Mister Frost; Mothman Prophecies, The; Nijinsky; Nothing But the Best; Prayer for the Dying, A; Quartet* (Ivory); *Return of the Soldier, The; Rose, The; Royal Flash; Running Man, The* (Reed); *Secret Friends; Shout, The; Silent Tongue; Three Sisters* (Olivier); *Unmarried Woman, An; We Think the World of You; Whistle Down the Wind; Wicked Lady, The* (Winner); *Women in Love; Zorba the Greek.*

Beatty, Warren *All Fall Down; Bonnie and Clyde; Bugsy; Bulworth; Dick Tracy; $ (aka The Heist); Fortune, The; Heaven Can Wait* (Beatty/ Henry); *Ishtar; Kaleidoscope; Lilith; Love Affair (aka An Affair to Remember); McCabe and Mrs Miller; Mickey One; Only Game in Town, The; Parallax View, The; Promise Her Anything; Reds; Roman Spring of Mrs Stone, The; Shampoo; Splendor in the Grass; Town & Country.*

Belmondo, Jean-Paul *A Bout de Souffle (Breathless); A Double Tour (Leda/Web of Passion); Borsalino; Burglars, The (Le Casse); Casino Royale; Docteur Popaul (High Heels/ Scoundrel in White); Doulos, Le (The Finger Man); Enfants de Lumière, Les (The Children of Lumière); Femme est une Femme, Une (A Woman Is a Woman); Ho! (aka Criminal Face); Homme de Rio, L' (That Man from Rio); How to Destroy the Reputation of the Greatest Secret Agent (Le Magnifique); Leon Morin, Priest (Léon Morin, Prêtre); Misérables, Les (aka Les Misérables du vingtième siècle); Night Caller (Peur sur la Ville); Pierrot le Fou; Scoumoune, La (Hit Man/ Scoundrel); Sirène du Mississipi, La (Mississippi Mermaid); Stavisky…*

Bennett, Joan *Bulldog Drummond; Confirm or Deny; Father of the Bride* (Minnelli); *Hollow Triumph (aka The Scar); Little Women; Macomber Affair, The; Man Hunt; Man I Married, The (aka I Married a Nazi); Man in the Iron Mask, The; Man Who Broke the Bank at Monte Carlo, The; Reckless Moment, The; Scarlet Street; Secret Beyond the Door; Suspiria; There's Always Tomorrow; We're No Angels* (Curtiz); *Woman in the Window, The; Woman on the Beach, The.*

Berenger, Tom *At Play in the Fields of the Lord; Betrayed; Beyond the Door (Oltre la Porta); Big Chill, The; Butch and Sundance: The Early Days; Chasers; Dogs of War, The; D-Tox (D-Tox Im Auge der Angst); Eddie and the Cruisers; Field, The; Gettysburg; Gingerbread Man, The; In Praise of Older Women; Last of the Dogmen; Last Rites; Looking for Mr Goodbar; Love at Large; Major League; Major League II; Platoon; Sentinel, The; Shattered; Shoot to Kill (aka Deadly Pursuit); Sliver; Sniper; Someone to Watch Over Me; Substitute, The; Training Day.*

Bergman, Ingrid *Anastasia; Arch of Triumph; Autumn Sonata (Herbstsonate); Bell's of St Mary's, The; Casablanca; Dr Jekyll and Mr Hyde* (Fleming); *Eléna et les Hommes (Paris Does Strange Things); Fear (La Paura); For Whom the Bell Tolls; Gaslight (aka The Murder in Thornton Square); Giovanna d'Arco al Rogo (Jeanne au Bûcher/Joan at the Stake); Indiscreet; Inn of the Sixth Happiness, The; Intermezzo (aka Escape to Happiness); Murder on the Orient Express; Notorious; Rage in Heaven; Saratoga Trunk; Spellbound; Stromboli, Terra di Dio (Stromboli); Under Capricorn; Viaggio in Italia (Journey to Italy/The Lonely Woman/ Strangers/Voyage to Italy); Walk in the Spring Rain, A.*

Binoche, Juliette *Alice et Martin; Amants du Pont-Neuf, Les; Chocolat* (Hallström); *Code Unknown (Code Inconnu); Couch in New York, A (Un Divan à New York); Damage; Enfants du siècle, Les; English Patient, The; Hail, Mary (Je Vous Salue, Marie); Hussard sur le toit, Le (The Horseman on the Roof); Mauvais Sang (The Night Is Young); Three Colours: Blue (Trois Couleurs: Bleu); Three Colours: Red (Trois Couleurs: Rouge); Three Colours: White (Trois Couleurs: Blanc); Unbearable Lightness of Being, The; Veuve de Saint-Pierre, La (The Widow of Saint-Pierre); Wuthering Heights* (Kosminsky).

Bogarde, Dirk *Accident; Blue Lamp, The; Boys in Brown; Bridge Too Far, A; Cast a Dark Shadow; Damned, The (La Caduta degli Dei/Götterdämmerung); Darling; Death in Venice (Morte a Venezia); Despair; Doctor in the House; Esther Waters; Fixer, The; Gentle Gunman, The; High Bright Sun, The (aka McGuire Go Home!); HMS Defiant (aka Damn the Defiant); Hot Enough for June; Hunted (aka The Stranger in Between); I Could Go On Singing; Ill Met by Moonlight (aka Night Ambush); Justine* (Cukor); *King & Country; Libel; Modesty Blaise; Night Porter, The (Il Portiere di Notte); Oh! What a Lovely War; Once a Jolly Swagman (aka Maniacs on Wheels); Our Mother's House; Password Is Courage, The; Permission to Kill; Providence; Quartet* (Smart/ French/Crabtree/Annakin); *Serpent, The (Le Serpent); Servant, The; Simba; Singer Not the Song, The; Sleeping Tiger, The; So Long at the Fair; Song Without End; Spanish Gardener, The; These Foolish Things (Daddy Nostalgie); Victim; Wind Cannot Read, The.*

Bogart, Humphrey *Across the Pacific; Action in the North Atlantic; African Queen, The; All Through the Night; Amazing Doctor Clitterhouse, The; Angels with Dirty Faces; Barefoot Contessa, The; Beat the Devil; Big Shot, The; Big Sleep, The* (Hawks); *Brother Orchid; Bullets or Ballots; Caine Mutiny, The; Casablanca; China Clipper;*

Conflict; Dark Passage; Dark Victory; Dead End; Deadline – USA (aka Deadline); Dead Reckoning; Desperate Hours, The; Enforcer, The (aka Murder, Inc.); Harder They Fall, The; High Sierra; In a Lonely Place; In This Our Life; Invisible Stripes; Key Largo; Kid Galahad (Curtiz); *Knock on Any Door; Left Hand of God, The; Love Lottery, The; Maltese Falcon, The; Marked Woman; Passage to Marseille; Petrified Forest, The; Return of Doctor X, The; Roaring Twenties, The; Sabrina (aka Sabrina Fair); Sahara* (Korda); *Stand-In; Thank Your Lucky Stars; They Drive By Night (aka The Road to Frisco)* (Walsh); *To Have and Have Not; Treasure of the Sierra Madre, The; We're No Angels* (Curtiz).

Bonham Carter, Helena *Fight Club; Getting It Right; Hamlet* (Zeffirelli); *Howards End; Keep the Aspidistra Flying; Lady Jane; Margaret's Museum; Mary Shelley's Frankenstein; Mask, The (La Maschera); Maurice; Mighty Aphrodite; Novocaine; Planet of the Apes* (Burton); *Portraits Chinois; Room With a View, A; Theory of Flight, The; Twelfth Night; Where Angels Fear to Tread; Wings of the Dove, The; Women Talking Dirty.*

Boyer, Charles *Algiers; All This and Heaven Too; April Fools, The; Arch of Triumph; Around the World in 80 Days; Back Street; Barefoot in the Park; Buccaneer, The; Casino Royale; Cluny Brown; Cobweb, The; Confidential Agent; Fanny* (Logan); *First Legion, The; Flesh and Fantasy; Garden of Allah, The; Gaslight (aka The Murder in Thornton Square); History Is Made at Night; Hold Back the Dawn; Lost Horizon* (Jarrott); *Love Is a Ball (aka All This and Money Too); Madame de… (The Earrings of Madame de…); Mayerling; Stavisky…; Tovarich.*

Branagh, Kenneth *Book That Wrote Itself, The; Celebrity; Dead Again; Gingerbread Man, The; Hamlet* (Parker); *Henry V* (Branagh); *High Season; In the Bleak Midwinter (aka A Midwinter's Tale); Looking for Richard; Love's Labour's Lost; Mary Shelley's Frankenstein; Month in the Country, A; Much Ado About Nothing; Othello* (Branagh); *Peter's Friends; Proposition, The; Swing Kids; Theory of Flight, The; Wild Wild West.*

Brando, Marlon *Apocalypse Now; Apocalypse Now Redux; Appaloosa, The (aka Southwest to Sonora); Brave, The; Candy; Chase, The; Christopher Columbus: The Discovery; Countess from Hong Kong, A; Don Juan DeMarco; Dry White Season, A; Formula, The; Freshman, The; Fugitive Kind, The; Godfather, The; Guys and Dolls; Island of Dr Moreau, The* (Frankenheimer); *Julius Caesar; Last Tango in Paris; Men, The; Missouri Breaks, The; Mutiny on the Bounty* (Milestone); *Nightcomers, The; Night of the Following Day, The; One-Eyed Jacks; On the Waterfront; Queimada! (Burn!); Reflections in a Golden Eye; Sayonara; Score, The; Streetcar Named Desire, A; Superman; Teahouse of the August Moon, The; Viva Zapata!; Wild One, The; Young Lions, The.*

Bridges, Beau *Daddy's Dyin' – Who's Got the Will?; Fabulous Baker Boys, The; Greased Lightning; Heart Like a Wheel; Honky Tonk Freeway; Hotel New Hampshire, The; Iron Triangle, The; Jerry Maguire; Landlord, The; K-PAX; Lovin' Molly; Night Crossing; Norma Rae; Other Side of the Mountain, The (aka A Window to the Sky); Positively True Adventures of the Alleged Texas Cheerleader-Murdering Mom, The; Runner Stumbles, The; Scenes of the Crime; Silver Dream Racer; Swashbuckler (The Scarlet Buccaneer); Two-Minute Warning; Your Three Minutes Are Up.*

Bridges, Jeff *Against All Odds; American Heart; American Success Company, The (aka Success); Arlington Road; Bad Company; Big Lebowski, The; Blown Away; Cold Feet; Company She Keeps, The; Contender, The; Cutter's Way (aka Cutter and Bone); 8 Million Ways to Die; Fabulous Baker Boys, The; Fat City; Fearless; Fisher King, The; Hearts of the West (aka Hollywood Cowboy); Heaven's Gate; Jagged Edge; King Kong* (Guillermin); *Kiss Me Goodbye; Last American Hero, The; Last Picture Show, The; Last Unicorn, The; Lolly-Madonna XXX (aka The Lolly-Madonna War); Mirror Has Two Faces, The; Morning After, The; Muse, The; Nadine; Rancho Deluxe; See You in the Morning; Simpatico; Somebody Killed Her Husband; Starman; Stay Hungry; Texasville; Thunderbolt and Lightfoot; Tron; Tucker: The Man and His Dream; Vanishing, The; White Squall; Wild Bill; Winter Kills.*

Bronson, Charles *Apache; Assassination; Borderline; Breakheart Pass; Breakout; Caboblanco; Chato's Land; Cold Sweat (De la Part des Copains); Death Wish; Death Wish II; Death Wish 3; Death Wish 4: The Crackdown; Diplomatic Courier; Dirty Dozen, The; Donato and Daughter; Evil That Men Do, The; From Noon Till Three; Great Escape, The; Guns for San Sebastian (La Bataille de San Sebastian); Hard Times (aka The Streetfighter); House of Wax; Indian Runner, The; Kid Galahad* (Karlson); *Love and Bullets; Machine Gun Kelly; Magnificent Seven, The; Marrying Kind, The; Master of the World; Mechanic, The (aka Killer of Killers); Miss Sadie Thompson; Mr Majestyk; Mob, The (aka Remember That Face); Murphy's Law; Never So Few; Once Upon a Time in the West (C'era una Volta il West); Pat and Mike; Raid on Entebbe; Red Sun (Soleil Rouge); Rider on the Rain (Passager de la Pluie); Run of the Arrow; St Ives; Sandpiper, The; Stone Killer, The; Telefon; 10 to Midnight; This Property Is Condemned; Valdez il Mezzosangue (Chino/The Valdez Horses/Valdez the Halfbreed); Vera Cruz; Villa Rides!; White Buffalo, The.*

Brooks, Louise *Beggars of Life; Diary of a Lost Girl (Das Tagebuch einer Verlorenen); Girl in Every Port, A; It's the Old Army Game; Pandora's Box (Die Büchse der Pandora); Prix de Beauté (Miss Europe).*

Brynner, Yul *Anastasia; Brothers Karamazov, The* (Brooks); *Buccaneer, The; Cast a Giant Shadow; Catlow; Double Man, The; Escape from Zahrain; File of the Golden Goose; Flight from Ashiya; Futureworld; King and I, The; Kings of the Sun; Light at the Edge of the World, The; Magic Christian, The; Magnificent Seven, The; Return of the Seven (aka Return of the Magnificent Seven); Romance of a Horsethief; Serpent, The (Le Serpent); Solomon and Sheba; Ten Commandments, The; Testament d'Orphée, Le (Testament of Orpheus); Villa Rides!; Westworld.*

Bullock, Sandra *Demolition Man; Forces of Nature; Hope Floats; In Love and War* (Attenborough); *Miss Congeniality; Net, The; Practical Magic; Speed; Speed 2: Cruise Control; Time to Kill, A; 28 Days; Two if by Sea (aka Stolen Hearts); Vanishing, The; While You Were Sleeping; Who Shot Patakango? (aka Who Shot Pat?); Wrestling Ernest Hemingway.*

Burton, Richard *Absolution (aka Murder by Confession); Alexander the Great* (Rossen); *Anne of the Thousand Days; Assassination of Trotsky, The; Bitter Victory (Amère Victoire); Boom; Bramble Bush, The; Candy; Circle of Two; Cleopatra* (Mankiewicz); *Comedians, The; Equus; Exorcist II: The Heretic; Green Grow the Rushes (aka Brandy Ashore); Ice Palace; Klansman, The; Longest Day, The; Look Back in Anger; Massacre in Rome (Rappresaglia); Medusa Touch, The; My Cousin Rachel; Night of the Iguana, The; Nineteen Eighty-Four; Rains of Ranchipur, The; Robe, The; Sandpiper, The; Seawife; Spy Who Came in from the Cold, The; Staircase; Under Milk Wood; Villain; V.I.P.s, The; Wagner; What's New Pussycat?; Where Eagles Dare; Who's Afraid of Virginia Woolf?; Wild Geese, The.*

Buscemi, Steve *Airheads; Animal Factory; Armageddon; Barton Fink; Big Daddy; Big Lebowski, The; Billy Bathgate; Call Me; Con Air; Desperado; Domestic Disturbance; Fargo; Final Fantasy: The Spirits Within; Ghost World; Heart at Midnight; Hudsucker Proxy, The; In the Soup; John Carpenter's Escape from L.A.; Kansas City; King of New York; Living in Oblivion; Miller's Crossing; Monsters, Inc.; Mystery Train; New York Stories; Parting Glances; Pulp Fiction; Real Blonde, The; Reservoir Dogs; Rising Sun; Slaves of New York; Somebody to Love; Tales from the Darkside: The Movie; Things to Do in Denver When You're Dead; Trees Lounge; 28 Days; Wedding Singer, The; Zandalee.*

Caan, James *Alien Nation; Autre Homme une Autre Chance, Un (Another Man, Another Woman/Another Man, Another Chance); Bottle Rocket; Boy Called Hate, A; Bridge Too Far, A; Chapter Two; Cinderella Liberty; Comes a Horseman; Countdown; Dick Tracy; El Dorado; Eraser; Flesh and Bone; For the Boys; Freebie and the Bean; Funny Lady; Gambler, The; Gardens of Stone; Glory Guys, The; Godfather, The; Harry and Walter Go to New York; Hide in Plain Sight; Honeymoon in Vegas; Irma la Douce; Godfather Part 2, The; Killer Elite, The; Kiss Me Goodbye; Mickey Blue Eyes; Misery; Poodle Springs; Rain People, The; Red Line 7000; Rollerball; Silent Movie; Slither; Submarine X-1; Thief (aka Violent Streets); Uns et les Autres, Les (Bolero/The Ins and the Outs); Way of the Gun, The; Yards, The.*

Cage, Nicolas *Birdy; Bringing Out the Dead; Captain Corelli's Mandolin; City of*

Angels; Con Air; Cotton Club, The; 8MM; Face/Off; Family Man, The; Firebirds (aka Wings of the Apache); Gone in Sixty Seconds; Guarding Tess; Honeymoon in Vegas; It Could Happen to You; Kiss of Death (Schroeder); *Leaving Las Vegas; Moonstruck; Peggy Sue Got Married; Racing with the Moon; Raising Arizona; Red Rock West; Rock, The; Rumble Fish; Shadow of the Vampire; Snake Eyes; Trapped in Paradise; Wild at Heart; Zandalee.*

Cagney, James *Angels With Dirty Faces; Blood on the Sun; Boy Meets Girl* (Bacon); *Ceiling Zero; Come Fill the Cup; Each Dawn I Die; Fighting 69th, The; Footlight Parade; G-Men; Hard to Handle; Kiss Tomorrow Goodbye; Lady Killer; Lion Is in the Streets, A; Love Me or Leave Me; Mayor of Hell, The; Midsummer Night's Dream, A* (Reinhardt/Dieterle); *Mister Roberts; One, Two, Three; Other Men's Women; Picture Snatcher; Public Enemy, The; Ragtime; Roaring Twenties, The; Run for Cover; Taxi!; Torrid Zone; Tribute to a Bad Man; White Heat; Yankee Doodle Dandy.*

Caine, Michael *Alfie; Ashanti; Battle of Britain; Beyond the Poseidon Adventure; Billion Dollar Brain; Black Windmill, The; Blame It On Rio; Blood and Wine; Blue Ice; Bridge Too Far, A; Bullseye!; California Suite; Cider House Rules, The; Curtain Call; Day the Earth Caught Fire, The; Deadfall; Deathtrap; Dirty Rotten Scoundrels; Dressed to Kill; Eagle Has Landed, The; Educating Rita; Fourth Protocol, The; Funeral in Berlin; Gambit; Get Carter; Half Moon Street; Hand, The; Hannah and Her Sisters; Harry and Walter Go to New York; Hill in Korea, A (aka Hell in Korea); Holcroft Covenant, The; Honorary Consul, The (aka Beyond the Limit); Hurry Sundown; Ipcress File, The; Island, The* (Ritchie); *Italian Job, The; Jaws – The Revenge; Key, The* (Reed); *Kidnapped; Last Orders; Last Valley, The; Little Voice; Magus, The; Man Who Would Be King, The; Marseille Contract, The; Miss Congeniality; Mona Lisa; Muppet Christmas Carol, The; Noises Off; On Deadly Ground; Peeper; Play Dirty; Pulp; Quills; Romantic Englishwoman, The; Shiner; Shock to the System, A; Silver Bears; Sleuth; Surrender; Swarm, The; Sweet Liberty; Tonite Let's All Make Love in London; Too Late the Hero; Victory (aka Escape to Victory); Water; Whistle Blower, The; Wilby Conspiracy, The; Without a Clue; Wrong Arm of the Law, The; Zee & Co (aka X, Y and Zee); Zulu.*

Callow, Simon *Ace Ventura – When Nature Calls; Amadeus; Bedrooms and Hallways (Des Chambres et Des Couloirs); Christmas Carol – The Movie; Four Weddings and a Funeral; Good Father, The; Howards End; Jefferson in Paris; Manifesto; Maurice; Mr and Mrs Bridge; No Man's Land* (Tanovic); *Notting Hill; Old Flames; Postcards from the Edge; Room With a View, A; Scarlet Tunic, The; Shakespeare in Love; Soft Top Hard Shoulder; Street Fighter; Victory* (Peploe).

Carradine, Keith *Almost Perfect Affair, An; Andre; Backfire; Ballad of the Sad Café, The; Choose Me; Cold Feet; Daddy's Dyin' – Who's Got the Will?; Duellists, The; Emperor of the North Pole, The (aka Emperor of the North); Gunfight, A; Hex; Long Riders, The; Maria's Lovers; McCabe and Mrs Miller; Mrs Parker and the Vicious Circle; Moderns, The; Nashville; Old Boyfriends; Pretty Baby; Southern Comfort; Thieves Like Us; Thousand Acres, A; Tie That Binds, The; Trouble in Mind; Welcome to L.A.*

Cassavetes, John *Brass Target; Capone; Crime in the Streets; Dirty Dozen, The; Edge of the City (aka A Man Is Ten Feet Tall); Fury, The; Husbands; Incubus; Killers, The* (Siegel); *Love Streams; Mikey and Nicky; Minnie and Moskowitz; Night Holds Terror, The; Opening Night; Rosemary's Baby; Saddle the Wind; Shadows; Tempest; Two-Minute Warning; Whose Life Is It Anyway?.*

Chaney, Lon (Sr) *He Who Gets Slapped; Hunchback of Notre Dame, The* (Worsley); *Phantom of the Opera, The* (Julian); *Unholy Three, The* (Browning); *Unholy Three, The* (Conway); *Unknown, The.*

Chaplin, Charles *Circus, The; City Lights; Countess from Hong Kong, A; Gold Rush, The; Great Dictator, The; Kid, The; King in New York, A; Limelight; Modern Times; Monsieur Verdoux; Show People; Woman of Paris, A.*

Cheung, Leslie *Ashes of Time (Dong Xie Xi Du); Better Tomorrow, A (Yingxiong Bense); Better Tomorrow II, A (Yingxiong Bense II); Buenos Aires Zero Degree; Chinese Ghost Story, A (Qian Nü Youhun); Chinese Ghost Story II, A; Days of Being Wild (Ahfei Zhenjuang); Farewell My Concubine (Ba Wang Bie Ji); Happy Together (Chunguang Zhaxie); He's a Woman, She's a Man (Jinzhi Yuye); Once a Thief (Zonheng Sihai); Phantom Lover, The (Xin Yeban Gesheng); Rouge (Inji Kau); Temptress Moon (Fengyue).*

Cheung, Maggie *Actress (Ruan Ling Yu); Ashes of Time (Dong Xie Xi Du); As Tears Go By; Chinese Box; Comrades, Almost a Love Story (Tian Mimi); Crouching Tiger, Hidden Dragon (Wo Hu Zang Long); Days of Being Wild (Ahfei Zhenjuang); Full Moon in New York (Ren zai Niu-Yue); Heroic Trio, The (Dongfang San Xia); Iceman Cometh, The (Jidong Qixia); In the Mood for Love (Huayang Nianhua); Irma Vep; Moon Warriors; Police Story (Jingcha Gushi); Sausalito (Yi Jian Zhongqing); Song of the Exile (Ke Tu Chiu Hen); Twin Dragons (Shuanglong Hui).*

Chow Yun-Fat *Anna and the King; Better Tomorrow, A (Yingxiong Bense); Better Tomorrow II, A (Yingxiong Bense II); City on Fire; Corruptor, The; Full Contact (Xia Dao Gao Fei); Hard-Boiled (Lat Sau San Tam); Killer, The (Diexue Shuang Xiong); Love in a Fallen City (Qingchengzhi Lian); Love Unto Waste (Deiha Tsing); Once a Thief (Zonheng Sihai); Replacement Killers, The; Story of Woo Viet, The (Hu Yue de Gushi).*

Christie, Julie *Afterglow; Billy Liar; Darling; Demon Seed; Doctor Zhivago; Don't Look Now; DragonHeart; Fahrenheit 451; Far From the Madding Crowd; Fast Lady, The; Fools of Fortune; Go-Between, The; Gold Diggers, The; Hamlet* (Branagh); *Heat and Dust; Heaven Can Wait* (Beatty/Henry); *McCabe and Mrs Miller; Memoirs of a Survivor; Miracle Maker, The; Miss Mary; No Such Thing; Petulia; Power; Return of the Soldier, The; Shampoo; Tonite Let's All Make Love in London; Young Cassidy.*

Clift, Montgomery *Big Lift, The; Freud; From Here to Eternity; Heiress, The; I Confess; Judgment at Nuremberg; Lonelyhearts; Misfits, The; Place in the Sun, A; Raintree County; Red River; Suddenly Last Summer; Terminal Station (Stazione Termini/ aka Indiscretion of an American Wife); Wild River; Young Lions, The.*

Close, Glenn *Air Force One; Big Chill, The; Cookie's Fortune; Dangerous Liaisons; Fatal Attraction; House of Spirits, The; Jagged Edge; Hamlet* (Zeffirelli); *Mary Reilly; Mars Attacks!; Maxie; Meeting Venus; Natural, The; 101 Dalmatians* (Herek); *102 Dalmatians; Paper, The; Paradise Road; Reversal of Fortune; Stone Boy, The; Things You Can Tell Just by Looking at Her; World According to Garp, The.*

Colbert, Claudette *Arise, My Love; Bluebeard's Eighth Wife; Boom Town; Cleopatra* (DeMille); *Drums Along the Mohawk; Imitation of Life* (Stahl); *It Happened One Night; Midnight; Palm Beach Story, The; Phantom President, The; Remember the Day; Sign of the Cross, The; Since You Went Away; Si Versailles m'était conté… (Versailles/Royal Affairs at Versailles); Sleep, My Love; Three Came Home; Tovarich; Zaza.*

Colman, Ronald *Around the World in 80 Days; Bulldog Drummond; Double Life, A; Lost Horizon* (Capra); *Man Who Broke the Bank at Monte Carlo, The; Prisoner of Zenda, The* (Cromwell); *Raffles; Random Harvest; Talk of the Town, The; Unholy Garden, The.*

Connery, Sean *Anderson Tapes, The; Another Time, Another Place* (Allen); *Avengers, The; Bridge Too Far, A; Cuba; Diamonds Are Forever; Darby O'Gill and the Little People; Dr No; Entrapment; Family Business; Fine Madness, A; Finding Forrester; First Great Train Robbery, The (aka The Great Train Robbery); First Knight; Five Days One Summer; Frightened City, The; From Russia With Love; Goldfinger; Good Man in Africa, A; Hell Drivers; Highlander; Highlander II – The Quickening; Hill, The; Hunt for Red October, The; Indiana Jones and the Last Crusade; Just Cause; Man Who Would Be King, The; Marnie; Medicine Man; Meteor; Molly Maguires, The; Murder on the Orient Express; Name of the Rose, The (Der Name der Rose); Never Say Never Again; Offence, The; Outland; Playing by Heart; Presidio, The; Ransom; Rising Sun; Robin and Marian; Robin Hood: Prince of Thieves; Rock, The; Russia House, The; Shalako; Sword of the Valiant – The Legend of Gawain and the Green Knight, The; Thunderball; Time Bandits; Untouchables, The; Wind and the Lion, The; Woman of Straw; Wrong Is Right (aka The Man With the Deadly Lens); You Only Live Twice; Zardoz.*

Cooper, Gary *Alice in Wonderland* (McLeod); *Along Came Jones; Ball of Fire; Beau Geste; Blowing Wild; Bluebeard's Eighth Wife; City Streets; Cloak and Dagger; Court-Martial of*

Billy Mitchell, The (aka One Man Mutiny); Dallas; Design for Living; Desire; Distant Drums; Farewell to Arms, A (Borzage); *For Whom the Bell Tolls; Fountainhead, The; Friendly Persuasion; High Noon; If I Had a Million; Love in the Afternoon* (Wilder); *Man of the West; Meet John Doe; Mr Deeds Goes to Town; Morocco; Peter Ibbetson; Plainsman, The; Real Glory, The; Saratoga Trunk; Unconquered; Vera Cruz; Wedding Night, The; Westerner, The; Wings.*

Costner, Kevin *Amazing Stories; American Flyers; Bodyguard, The; Bull Durham; Dances with Wolves; Dances with Wolves – Special Edition; Fandango; Field of Dreams; For Love of the Game; Frances; JFK; Message in a Bottle; Night Shift; No Way Out* (Donaldson); *Perfect World, A; Postman, The* (Costner); *Revenge* (Scott); *Robin Hood: Prince of Thieves; Silverado; Stacy's Knights; Table for Five; Testament* (Littman); *Thirteen Days; Tin Cup; Truth or Dare (aka In Bed with Madonna); Untouchables, The; War, The; Waterworld; Wyatt Earp.*

Cotten, Joseph *Abominable Dr Phibes, The; Airport '77; Beyond the Forest; Caravans; Citizen Kane; Delicate Balance, A; Duel in the Sun; F for Fake (Vérités et Mensonges); Gaslight (aka The Murder in Thornton Square); Guyana: Crime of the Century (Guyana: El Crimen del Siglo); Halliday Brand, The; Hearse, The; Heaven's Gate; Hush…Hush, Sweet Charlotte; I'll Be Seeing You; Island of Mutations (L'Isola degli Uomini Pesce); Journey into Fear; Killer Is Loose, The; Last Sunset, The; Love Letters* (Dieterle); *Lydia; Magnificent Ambersons, The; Man With a Cloak, The; Niagara; Oscar, The; Petulia; Portrait of Jennie; Shadow of a Doubt; Since You Went Away; Soylent Green; Survivor, The; Third Man, The; Tora! Tora! Tora!; Touch of Evil; Twilight's Last Gleaming; Under Capricorn.*

Crawford, Joan *Above Suspicion; Autumn Leaves; Gorgeous Hussy, The; Grand Hotel; Humoresque; I Saw What You Did; Johnny Guitar; Karate Killers, The; Love on the Run; Mildred Pierce; Possessed; Rain; Shining Hour, The; Strait-Jacket; Strange Cargo; Sudden Fear; Torch Song; Tramp, Tramp, Tramp; Unknown, The; What Ever Happened to Baby Jane?; When Ladies Meet; Woman's Face, A; Women, The.*

Crosby, Bing *Bells of St Mary's, The; Birth of the Blues; Blue Skies; Connecticut Yankee in King Arthur's Court, A (aka A Yankee in King Arthur's Court); Dixie; Dr Rhythm; Emperor Waltz, The; Going My Way; Here Comes the Groom; Here Come the Waves; High Society; High Time; Holiday Inn; King of Jazz, The; Let's Make Love; Mr Music; My Favorite Brunette; Reaching the Moon; Road to Morocco; Road to Utopia; Robin and the 7 Hoods; Son of Paleface; Stagecoach* (Douglas); *That's Entertainment!*

Cruise, Tom *All the Right Moves; Born on the Fourth of July; Cocktail; Color of Money, The; Days of Thunder; Eyes Wide Shut; Far and Away; Few Good Men, A; Firm, The; Interview with the Vampire; Jerry Maguire; Legend; Losin' It; Magnolia; Mission Impossible; Mission: Impossible II; Outsiders, The* (Coppola); *Rain Man; Risky Business; Taps; Top Gun; Vanilla Sky.*

Curtis, Jamie Lee *Amazing Grace and Chuck (aka Silent Voice); Blue Steel; Dominick and Eugene (aka Nicky and Gino); Escape from New York; Fierce Creatures; Fish Called Wanda, A; Fog, The; Forever Young* (Miner); *Grandview, U.S.A.; Halloween; Halloween II; Halloween H20 – 20 Years Later; Love Letters* (Jones); *Man in Love, A (Un Homme Amoureux); Mother's Boys; My Girl; My Girl 2; Perfect; Prom Night; Queens Logic; Roadgames; Tailor of Panama, The; Terror Train; Trading Places; True Lies.*

Curtis, Tony *Bad News Bears Go to Japan, The; Boston Strangler, The; Brainwaves; Celluloid Closet, The; Count of Monte-Cristo, The; Criss Corss* (Siodmak); *Defiant Ones, The; Don't Make Waves; Francis; Insignificance; Kings Go Forth; Last Tycoon, The; Lepke; List of Adrian Messenger, The; Little Miss Marker; Manitou, The; Mirror Crack'd. The; Mister Cory; Naked in New York; Operation Petticoat; Sex and the Single Girl; Sierra; Some Like It Hot; Spartacus; Sweet Smell of Success; Vikings, The; Winchester '73.*

Cushing, Peter *Abominable Snowman, The; Alexander the Great* (Rossen); *…And Now the Screaming Starts (aka Fengriffen); Arabian Adventure; Asylum; At the Earth's Core; Beast Must Die, The; Biggles; Black Night, The; Blood Beast Terror, The (aka The Vampire Beast Craves Blood); Brides of Dracula, The; Cash on Demand; Chump at Oxford, A; Creeping Flesh, The; Curse of Frankenstein, The; Daleks – Invasion Earth 2150 A.D.; Dr Phibes Rises Again; Dr Terror's House of Horrors; Dr Who and the Daleks; Dracula (aka Horror of Dracula); Dracula A.D. 1972; Fear in the Night; Flesh and the Fiends, The (aka Mania/Psycho Killers/The Fiendish Ghouls); Frankenstein and the Monster from Hell; Frankenstein Created Woman; Frankenstein Must Be Destroyed; From Beyond the Grave; Ghoul, The* (Francis); *Gorgon, The; Horror Express (Pánico en el Transiberiano); Hound of the Baskervilles, The* (Fisher); *House of the Long Shadows, The; House That Dripped Blood, The; I, Monster; Incense for the Damned; Legend of the 7 Golden Vampires, The; Legend of the Werewolf; Madhouse* (Clark); *Mummy, The* (Fisher); *Night of the Big Heat; No Secrets (aka Touch of the Sun); Nothing But the Night; Revenge of Frankenstein, The; Satanic Rites of Dracula, The (aka Count Dracula and His Vampire Bride); Scream and Scream Again; She; Skull, The; Star Wars; Sword of the Valiant – The Legend of Gawain and the Green Knight, The; Time Without Pity; Top Secret!; Torture Garden; Trial by Combat (aka A Choice of Weapons/Dirty Knight's Work); Twins of Evil; Uncanny, The; Vampire Lovers, The.*

Darrieux, Danielle *Alexander the Great* (Rossen); *Club de Femmes; Demoiselles de Rochefort, Les (The Young Girls of Rochefort); 8 Women (8 Femmes); 5 Fingers; Greengage Summer, The (aka Loss of Innocence); Landru; Madame de… (The Earrings of Madame de…); Mayerling; Napoléon* (Guitry); *Plaisir, Le (House of Pleasure); Ronde, La; Scene of the Crime, The (Le Lieu du Crime).*

Davis, Bette *All About Eve; All This and Heaven Too; Anniversary, The; Beyond the Forest; Bordertown; Bunny O'Hare; Bureau of Missing Persons; Burnt Offerings; Cabin in the Cotton, The; Connecting Rooms; Dangerous; Dark Victory; Death on the Nile; Deception; Fog Over Frisco; Front Page Woman; Great Lie, The; Hush…Hush, Sweet Charlotte; In This Our Life; It's Love I'm After; Jezebel; Juarez; Kid Galahad* (Curtiz); *Letter, The; Little Foxes, The; Madame Sin; Man Who Came to Dinner, The; Marked Woman; Mr Skeffington; Nanny, The; Now, Voyager; Old Acquaintance; Petrified Forest, The; Phone Call from a Stranger; Private Lives of Elizabeth and Essex, The; Return from Witch Mountain; Satan Met a Lady; Sisters, The; Star, The; Stolen Life, A; Storm Center; Thank Your Lucky Stars; 20,000 Years in Sing Sing; Watcher in the Woods, The; Whales of August, The; What Ever Happened to Baby Jane?; Wicked Stepmother.*

Davis, Geena *Accidental Hero; Accidental Tourist, The; Angie; Beetlejuice; Cut Throat Island; Earth Girls Are Easy; Fletch; Fly, The* (Cronenberg); *Quick Change; League of Their Own, A; Long Kiss Goodnight, The; Speechless; Stuart Little; Thelma & Louise.*

Day-Lewis, Daniel *Age of Innocence, The; Bounty, The; Boxer, The; Crucible, The; In the Name of the Father; Last of the Mohicans, The; My Beautiful Laundrette; My Left Foot; Nanou; Room With a View, A; Stars and Bars; Unbearable Lightness of Being, The.*

Dean, James *East of Eden; Giant; Has Anybody Seen My Gal?; Rebel Without a Cause.*

de Havilland, Olivia *Adventurers, The; Adventures of Robin Hood, The; Airport '77; Anthony Adverse; Captain Blood; Charge of the Light Brigade, The* (Curtiz); *Dark Mirror, The; Devotion; Dodge City; Gone With the Wind; Great Garrick, The; Heiress, The; Hold Back the Dawn; Hush…Hush Sweet Charlotte; In This Our Life; It's Love I'm After; Libel; Light in the Piazza; Midsummer Night's Dream, A* (Reinhardt/ Dieterle); *My Cousin Rachel; Not As a Stranger; Pope Joan; Private Lives of Elizabeth and Essex, The; Santa Fe Trail; Snake Pit, The; Swarm, The; Thank Your Lucky Stars; That Lady; They Died With Their Boots On.*

Deneuve, Catherine *Agression, L' (Aggression); April Fools, The; Argent des Autres, L' (Other People's Money); Belle de Jour; Contre l'Oubli (Against Oblivion); Book That Wrote Itself, The; Convent, The (O Convento); Courage Fuyons (Courage – Let's Run); Créatures, Les; Dancer in the Dark; Demoiselles de Rochefort, Les (The Young Girls of Rochefort); Drama of the Rich (Fatti di Gente Perbene); East-West (Est-Ouest); Ecoute Voir… (See Here My Love); 8 Women (8 Femmes); Flic, Un (Dirty Money); Hunger, The; Hustle; I'm Going Home*

(Vou Para Casa/Je Rentre à la Maison); Indochine; Last Metro, The (Le Dernier Métro); Let's Hope It's a Girl (Speriamo che sia Femmina); March or Die; Ma Saison Préférée; Parapluies de Cherbourg, Les (The Umbrellas of Cherbourg); Peau d'Ane (The Magic Donkey); Place Vendôme; Pola X; Repulsion; Sauvage, Le; Scene of the Crime, The (Le Lieu du Crime); Second Chance (Si c'était à refaire); Sirène du Missisipi, La (Mississippi Mermaid); Slightly Pregnant Man, The (L'Evénement le plus Important depuis que l'Homme a Marché sur la Lune); Strange Place to Meet, A (Drôle d'Endroit pour une Rencontre); Time Regained (Le Temps retrouvé); Touche pas à la femme blanche (Don't Touch the White Woman); Tristana; Univers de Jacques Demy, L'; Vice et la Vertu, Le (Vice and Virtue); Vent de la Nuit, Le; Voleurs, Les.

De Niro, Robert *Adventures of Rocky & Bullwinkle, The; Analyze This; Angel Heart; Awakenings; Backdraft; Bloody Mama; Brazil; Bronx Tale, A; Cape Fear* (Scorsese); *Casino; CopLand; Deer Hunter, The; Falling in Love; Fan, The* (Scott); *15 Minutes; Flawless; Godfather Part II, The; GoodFellas; Great Expectations* (Cuáron); *Greetings; Guilty by Suspicion; Heat* (Mann); *Hi, Mom!; Jackie Brown; Jacknife; King of Comedy, The; Last Tycoon, The; Mad Dog and Glory; Marvin's Room; Mary Shelley's Frankenstein; Mean Streets; Meet the Parents; Men of Honor; Midnight Run; Mission, The; Mistress; New York, New York; Night and the City* (Winkler); *1900 (Novecento); Once Upon a Time in America; Raging Bull; Ronin; Score, The; Showtime; Sleepers; Stanley & Iris; Taxi Driver; This Boy's Life; True Confessions; Untouchables, The; Wag the Dog; We're No Angels* (Jordan).

Depardieu, Gérard *An 01, L'; Buffet Froid; Camille Claudel; Chiens, Les (The Dogs); Cible émouvante (Moving Target); Colonel Chabert, Le* (Angelo); *Cyrano de Bergerac; Danton; 1492: Conquest of Paradise; Germinal; Green Card; Hamlet* (Branagh); *Hussard sur le toit, Le (The Horseman on the Roof); I Love You, I Don't (Je t'aime, moi non plus); I Want to Go Home (Je veux rentrer à la maison); Jean de Florette; Last Metro, The (Le Dernier Métro); Last Woman, The (L'Ultima Donna); Left-Handed Woman, The (Die linkshändige Frau); Loulou; Maîtresse; Man in the Iron Mask, The* (Wallace); *Merci la vie (Thank You, Life); Mon Oncle d'Amérique (My American Uncle/My Uncle from America); Mon Père, ce héros; Moon in the Gutter, The (La Lune dans le Caniveau); My Father, the Hero* (Milner); *Nathalie Granger; 1900 (Novecento); 102 Dalmatians; Peu de Soleil dans l'Eau Froide, Un (Sunlight on Cold Water); Police; Préparez Vos Mouchoirs (Get Out Your Handkerchiefs); Pure Formality, A (Un Pura Formalità); Retour de Martin Guerre, Le (The Return of Martin Guerre); Secret Agent, The (aka Joseph Conrad's The Secret Agent); Sous le Soleil de Satan (Under Satan's Sun); Stavisky…; Strange Place to Meet, A (Drôle d'Endroit pour une rencontre); Tartuffe, Le; Tenue de Soirée (Evening Dress); This Sweet Sickness (Dites-lui que Je l'aime); Tous les matins du monde; Trop belle pour toi! (Too Beautiful for You); Unhook the Stars (Décroches les étoiles); Uranus; Valseuses, Les (Going Places/Making It); Vatel; Woman Next Door, The (La Femme d'à côté); Woman or Two, A (Une Femme ou Deux).*

Depp, Johnny *Arizona Dreaming; Astronaut's Wife, The; Before Night Falls; Benny and Joon; Blow; Brave, The; Chocolat* (Hallström); *Cry-Baby; Dead Man; Don Juan DeMarco; Donnie Brasco; Edward Scissorhands; Ed Wood; Fear and Loathing in Las Vegas; From Hell; Man Who Cried, The; Nick of Time; Nightmare on Elm Street, A; Ninth Gate, The; Platoon; Sleepy Hollow; What's Eating Gilbert Grape.*

DeVito, Danny *Batman Returns; Erin Brokovich; Get Shorty; Heist; Hoffa; Jack the Bear; Jewel of the Nile, The; Johnny Dangerously; Junior; LA Confidential; Living Out Loud; Man on the Moon; Mars Attacks!; My Little Pony; Other People's Money; Renaissance Man; Roald Dahl's Matilda; Romancing the Stone; Ruthless People; Scalawag; Terms of Endearment; Throw Momma from the Train; Tin Men; Twins; Virgin Sicides, The; War of the Roses, The; Wise Guys.*

Dietrich, Marlene *Angel* (Lubitsch); *Around the World in 80 Days; Black Fox; Blonde Venus; Blue Angel, The (Der blaue Engel); Desire; Destry Rides Again; Devil Is a Woman, The; Dishonored; Flame of New Orleans, The; Foreign Affair, A; Garden of Allah, The; Judgment at Nuremberg; Just a Gigolo (Schöner Gigolo – Armer Gigolo); Knight Without Armour; Manpower; Morocco; No Highway (aka No Highway in the Sky); Rancho Notorious; Scarlet Empress, The; Seven Sinners; Shanghai Express; Song of Songs; Stage Fright; Touch of Evil; Witness for the Prosecution.*

Donat, Robert *Captain Boycott; Citadel, The* (Vidor); *Ghost Goes West, The; Goodbye, Mr Chips* (Wood); *Inn of the Sixth Happiness, The; Knight Without Armour; Lease of Life; Magic Box, The; New Lot, The; Perfect Strangers (aka Vacation from Marriage); Private Life of Henry VIII, The; 39 Steps, The* (Hitchcock); *Young Mr Pitt, The.*

Douglas, Kirk *Ace in the Hole (aka The Big Carnival); Arrangement, The; Bad and the Beautiful, The; Bi Sky, The; Brotherhood, The; Cast a Giant Shadow; Catch Me a Spy (Les Doigts Croisés/aka To Catch a Spy); Champion; Cinderella Liberty; Detective Story; Final Countdown, The; Fury, The; Gunfight, A; Gunfight at the O.K. Corral; Heroes of Telemark, The; Holocaust 2000 (aka The Children); Indian Fighter, The; In Harm's Way; Jacqueline Susann's Once Is Not Enough; Last Sunset, The; Last Train from Gun Hill; Letter to Three Wives, A; Light at the Edge of the World, The; List of Adrian Messenger, The; Lonely Are the Brave; Lovely Way to Die, A (aka A Lovely Way to Go); Lust for Life; Man from Snowy River, The; Man to Respect, A (Un Uomo da Rispettare); Man Without a Star; Oscar; Out of the Past (aka Build My Gallows High); Paths of Glory; Posse; Saturn 3; Scalawag; Seven Days in May; Spartacus; Strange Love of Martha Ivers, The; Strangers When We Meet; There Was a Crooked Man…; Tough Guys; 20000 Leagues Under the Sea; Two Weeks in Another Town; Victory at Entebbe; Vikings, The; Villain, The (aka Cactus Jack); War Wagon, The; Way West, The; Young Man With a Horn (aka Young Man of Music).*

Douglas, Melvyn *Advance to the Rear; Americanization of Emily, The; Angel* (Lubitsch); *Annie Oakley; As You Desire Me; Being There; Billy Budd; Candidate, The; Captains Courageous; Changeling, The; Ghost Story; Gorgeous Hussy, The; Great Sinner, The; Hud; I Never Sang for My Father; Mr Blandings Builds His Dream House; My Forbidden Past; Ninotchka; Old Dark House, The; Seduction of Joe Tynan, The; Shining Hour, The; Tell Me a Riddle; Tenant, The (Le Locataire); Theodora Goes Wild; Twilight's Last Gleaming; Two-Faced Woman; Vampire Bat, The; Woman's Face, A; Woman's Secret, A.*

Douglas, Michael *American President, The; Basic Instinct; Big Sky, The; Black Rain* (Scott); *China Syndrome, The; Chorus Line, A; Coma; Disclosure; Don't Say a Word; Falling Down; Fatal Attraction; Jewel of the Nile, The; Napoleon and Samantha; One Night at McCool's; Perfect Murder, A; Romancing the Stone; Shining Through; Star Chamber, The; Traffic* (Soberbergh); *Wall Street; War of the Roses; Wonder Boys.*

Dreyfuss, Richard *Addicted to Love; Always* (Spielberg); *American Graffiti; American President, The; Another Stakeout Apprenticeship of Duddy Kravitz, The; Big Fix, The; Close Encounters of the Third Kind; Close Encounters of the Third Kind – Special Edition; Competition, The; Dillinger* (Milius); *Down and Out in Beverly Hills; Game, The; Goodbye Girl, The; Inserts; Jaws; Let It Ride; Lost in Yonkers; Mad Dog Time (aka Trigger Happy); Mr Holland's Opus; Moon Over Parador; Night Falls on Manhattan; Nuts; Once Around; Postcards from the Edge; Rosencrantz and Guildenstern Are Dead; Silent Fall; Stakeout; Stand by Me; Tin Men; Victory at Entebbe; What About Bob?; Whose Life Is It Anyway?*

Dunaway, Faye *Albino Alligator; Arizona Dreaming; Arrangement, The; Barfly; Bonnie and Clyde; Burning Secret; Chamber, The; Champ, The; Chinatown; Deadly Trap, The (La Maison sous les Arbres); Doc; Don Juan DeMarco; Dunston Checks In; Eyes of Laura Mars; First Deadly Sin, The; Four Musketeers: The Revenge of Milady, The; Handmaid's Tale, The; Happening, The; Hurry Sundown; Joan of Arc (Jeanne d'Arc); Little Big Man; Mommie Dearest; Network; Oklahoma Crude; Ordeal by Innocence; Puzzle of a Downfall Child; Scorchers; Supergirl; Thomas Crown Affair, The* (Jewison); *The Thomas Crown Affair* (McTiernan); *Three Days of the Condor; Three Musketeers: The Queen's Diamonds, The; Towering Inferno, The; Voyage of the Damned; Wicked Lady, The* (Winner); *Yards, The.*

Duryea, Dan *Along Came Jones; Ball of Fire; Battle Hymn; Black Angel; Criss Cross; Flight of the Phoenix, The; Lady on a Train; Little Foxes, The; Ministry of*

Fear; Night Passage; None But the Lonely Heart; Sahara; Scarlet Street; Silver Lode; Winchester '73; Woman in the Window, The; World for Ransom.

Duvall, Robert *Apocalypse Now; Apostle, The; Badge 373; Betsy, The; Breakout; Bullitt; Chase, The; Civil Action, A; Colors; Conversation, The; Countdown; Days of Thunder; Deep Impact; Detective, The; Eagle Has Landed, The; Falling Down; Geronimo: An American Legend; Gingerbread Man, The; Godfather, The; Godfather Part II, The; Gone in Sixty Seconds; Greatest, The; Great Northfield Minnesota Raid, The; Great Santini, The; Handmaid's Tale, The; Invasion of the Body Snatchers* (Kaufman); *Joe Kidd; John Q; Killer Elite, The; Lady Ice; Lawman; Lightship, The; M*A*S*H; Natural, The; Network; Newsies (aka The News Boys); Outfit, The; Paper, The; Phenomenon; Rain People, The; Rambling Rose; Revolutionary, The; Scarlet Letter, The; Seven-Per-Cent Solution, The; Show of Force, A; 6th Day, The; Sling Blade; Something to Talk About; Stone Boy, The; Tender Mercies; Terry Fox Story, The; THX 1138; To Kill a Mockingbird; True Confessions; True Grit; Wrestling Ernest Hemingway.*

Eastwood, Clint *Absolute Power; Any Which Way You Can; Away All Boats; Beguiled, The; Bridges of Madison County, The; Bronco Billy; City Heat; Coogan's Bluff; Dead Pool, The; Dirty Harry; Eiger Sanction, The; Enforcer, The* (Fargo); *Escape from Alcatraz; Every Which Way But Loose; Firefox; Fistful of Dollars, A (Per un Pugno di Dollari); For a Few Dollars More (Per Qualche Dollari in Più); Gauntlet, The; Good, the Bad and the Ugly, The (Il Buono, il Brutto, il Cattivo); Hang 'em High; Heartbreak Ridge; High Plains Drifter; Honkytonk Man; In the Line of Fire; Joe Kidd; Kelly's Heroes; Magnum Force; Outlaw Josey Wales, The; Paint Your Wagon; Pale Rider; Perfect World, A; Play Misty for Me; Revenge of the Creature; Rookie, The; Space Cowboys; Sudden Impact; Tarantula; Thunderbolt and Lightfoot; Tightrope; Two Mules for Sister Sara; True Crime; Unforgiven; Where Eagles Dare; White Hunter, Black Heart; Wild Bill: A Hollywood Maverick.*

Falk, Peter *All the Marbles (aka The California Dolls); Big Trouble; Brink's Job, The; Castle Keep; Cheap Detective, The; Cookie; Faraway, So Close (In weiter Ferne, so nah!); Husbands; In-Laws, The; In the Spirit; It's a Mad, Mad, Mad, Mad World; Lakeboat; Luv; Made; Mikey and Nicky; Murder by Death; Princess Bride, The; Sbarco di Anzio, Lo (Anzio/The Battle for Anzio); Tune in Tomorrow (aka Aunt Julia and the Scriptwriter); Wind Across the Everglades; Wings of Desire (Der Himmel über Berlin); Woman Under the Influence, A.*

Farrow, Mia *Alice* (Allen); *Another Woman; Avalanche; Broadway Danny Rose; Crimes and Misdemeanors; Dandy in Aspic, A; Death on the Nile; Docteur Popaul (High Heels/ Scoundrel in White); Full Circle (aka The Haunting of Julia); Great Gatsby, The* (Clayton); *Hannah and Her Sisters; Hurricane; Husbands and Wives; John and Mary; Miami Rhapsody; Midsummer Night's Sex Comedy, A; New York Stories; Purple Rose of Cairo, The; Radio Days; Rosemary's Baby; Secret Ceremony; September; Shadows and Fog; Supergirl; Wedding, A; Widows' Peak; Zelig.*

Fields, WC *Alice in Wonderland* (McLeod); *Bank Dick, The; David Copperfield; Her Majesty, Love; If I Had a Million; International House; It's a Gift; It's the Old Army Game; Man on the Flying Trapeze, The; My Little Chickadee; Never Give a Sucker an Even Break (aka What a Man!); Old-Fashioned Way, The; Sally of the Sawdust; Sensations of 1945 (aka Sensations); You Can't Cheat an Honest Man.*

Fiennes, Ralph *Avengers, The; Baby of Mâcon, The; End of the Affair, The; English Patient, The; Onegin; Oscar and Lucinda; Quiz Show; Schindler's List; Spider; Strange Days; Sunshine (A napfény íze/Ein Hauch von Sonnenschein)* (Szabó); *Wuthering Heights* (Kosminsky).

Finch, Peter *Abdication, The; Battle of the River Plate, The (aka Pursuit of the Graf Spee); Bequest to the Nation (aka The Nelson Affair); Dark Avenger, The (aka The Warriors); England Made Me; Far From the Madding Crowd; Father Brown; First Men in the Moon; Flight of the Phoenix, The; Girl with Green Eyes; Heart of the Matter, The; Judith; Legend of Lylah Clare, The; Lost Horizon* (Jarrott); *Network; Nun's Story, The; Operation Amsterdam; Passage Home; Pumpkin Eater, The; Raid on Entebbe; Simon and Laura; Sins of Rachel Cade, The; Something to Hide; Story of Gilbert and Sullivan, The (aka The Great Gilbert and Sullivan); Sunday, Bloody Sunday; 10:30 P.M. Summer; Town Like Alice, A (aka The Rape of Malaya); Trials of Oscar Wilde, The (aka The Man With the Green Carnation); Train of Events; Windom's Way; Wooden Horse, The.*

Finney, Albert *Annie; Breakfast of Champions; Browning Version, The; Charlie Bubbles; Dresser, The; Duellists, The; Entertainer, The; Erin Brokovich; Gumshoe; Looker; Loophole; Man of No Importance, A; Miller's Crossing; Murder on the Orient Express; Night Must Fall* (Reisz); *Orphans; Playboys, The; Rich in Love; Run of the Country, The; Saturday Night and Sunday Morning; Scrooge; Shoot the Moon; Simpatico; Tom Jones; Two For the Road; Under the Volcano; Victors, The; Washington Square; Wolfen.*

Fishburne, Laurence *Apocalypse Now; Apocalypse Now Redux; Boyz N the Hood; Class Action; Count a Lonely Cadence (aka Stockade); Deep Cover; Event Horizon; Fled; Higher Learning; Just Cause; King of New York; Matrix, The; Nightmare on Elm Street 3: Dream Warriors, A; Once in the Life; Othello* (Parker); *Red Heat; Rumble Fish; School Daze; Searching for Bobby Fischer (aka Innocent Moves); Tina: What's Love Got to Do With It (aka What's Love Got to Do With It).*

Flynn, Errol *Adventures of Don Juan (aka The New Adventures of Don Juan); Adventures of Robin Hood, The; Another Dawn; Dark Avenger, The (aka The Warriors); Captain Blood; Charge of the Light Brigade, The* (Curtiz); *Cry Wolf; Dawn Patrol, The; Desperate Journey; Dive Bomber; Dodge City; Edge of Darkness; Gentleman Jim; Green Light; Kim; Objective, Burma!; Private Lives of Elizabeth and Essex, The; Santa Fe Trail; Sea Hawk, The; Sisters, The; Sun Also Rises, The; Thank Your Lucky Stars; They Died With Their Boots On.*

Fonda, Henry *Advise and Consent; Alpha Caper, The (aka Inside Job); Ash Wednesday; Battle of the Bulge; Best Man, The; Big Hand for the Little Lady, A (aka Big Deal at Dodge City); Big Street, The; Blockade; Boston Strangler, The; Chad Hanna; Cheyenne Social Club, The; City on Fire; Daisy Kenyon; Drums Along the Mohawk; Fail Safe; Fedora; Fort Apache; Fugitive, The* (Ford); *Grapes of Wrath, The; How the West Was Won; Immortal Sergeant, The; In Harm's Way; Jesse James; Jezebel; Lady Eve, The; Last of the Cowboys, The (aka The Great Smokey Roadblock); Lillian Russell; Longest Day, The; Long Night, The; Madigan; Mad Miss Manton, The; Meteor; Midway (aka Battle of Midway); Mister Roberts; My Darling Clementine; My Name Is Nobody (Mio Nome è Nessuno); Once Upon a Time in the West (C'era una Volta il West); On Golden Pond; Ox-Bow Incident, The (aka Strange Incident); Return of Frank James, The; Rollercoaster; Rounders, The; Serpent, The (Le Serpent); Sex and the Single Girl; Sometimes a Great Notion (aka Never Give an Inch); Stranger on the Run; Swarm, The; Tentacles (Tentacoli); There Was a Crooked Man…; Tin Star, The; Too Late the Hero; 12 Angry Men; Wanda Nevada; War and Peace* (Vidor); *Warlock* (Dmytryk); *Welcome to Hard Times (aka Killer on a Horse); Wings of the Morning; Wrong Man, The; Young Mr Lincoln; You Only Live Once; Yours, Mine and Ours.*

Fonda, Jane *Agnes of God; Any Wednesday (aka Bachelor Girl Apartment); Barbarella; Barefoot in the Park; Blue Bird, The; California Suite; Cat Ballou; Chapman Report, The; Chase, The; China Syndrome, The; Comes a Horseman; Coming Home; Dollmaker, The; Doll's House, A* (Losey); *Electric Horseman, The; F.T.A.; Fun With Dick and Jane; Histoires Extraordinaires (Spirits of the Dead/Tales of Mystery); Hurry Sundown; Julia; Klute; Morning After, The; Nine to Five; Old Gringo; On Golden Pond; Period of Adjustment; Rollover; Stanley & Iris; Steelyard Blues; They Shoot Horses, Don't They?; Tout Va Bien; Walk on the Wild Side.*

Fontaine, Joan *Beyond a Reasonable Doubt; Bigamist, The; Born to Be Bad; Casanova's Big Night; Damsel in Distress, A; Emperor Waltz, The; Frenchman's Creek; From This Day Forward; Gunga Din; Island in the Sun; Ivanhoe; Ivy; Jane Eyre* (Stevenson); *Letter from an Unknown Woman; Rebecca; Suspicion; This Above All; Women, The.*

Ford, Glenn *Advance to the Rear; Americano, The; Appointment in Honduras; Big Heat, The; Blackboard Jungle, The; Border Shootout; Cimarron; Cowboy; Day of the Evil Gun; Experiment in Terror (aka The Grip of Fear); Fastest*

Gun Alive, The; Gazebo, The; Gilda; Human Desire; Last Challenge, The (aka The Pistolero of Red River); Love Is a Ball (aka All This and Money Too); Man from Colorado, The; Midway (aka Battle of Midway); Rounders, The; Santee; Secret of Convict Lake, The; Sheepman, The; Stolen Life, A; Superman; Teahouse of the August Moon, The; 3.10 to Yuma; Torpedo Run; Undercover Man; Virus (Fukkatsu no Hi); White Tower, The.

Ford, Harrison *Apocalypse Now; Apocalypse Now Redux; Air Force One; American Graffiti; Blade Runner; Blade Runner – The Director's Cut; Clear and Present Danger; Devil's Own, The; Empire Strikes Back, The; Empire Strikes Back: Special Edition, The; Force 10 from Navarone; Frantic; Fugitive, The* (Davis); *Hanover Street; Heroes; Indiana Jones and the Last Crusade; Indiana Jones and the Temple of Doom; More American Graffiti; Mosquito Coast, The; Patriot Games; Presumed Innocent; Raiders of the Lost Ark; Random Hearts; Regarding Henry; Return of the Jedi; Return of the Jedi: Special Edition; Sabrina Fair; Six Days Seven Nights; Star Wars; Star Wars, Episode IV, A New Hope; Univers de Jacques Demy, L'; What Lies Beneath; Witness; Working Girl.*

Foster, Jodie *Accused, The; Anna and the King; Blood of Others, The (Le Sang des Autres); Bugsy Malone; Candleshoe; Carny; Catchfire; Contact; Five Corners; Foxes; Freaky Friday; Hotel New Hampshire, The; Kansas City Bomber; Little Man Tate; Maverick; Napoleon and Samantha; Nell; Panic Room; Shadows and Fog; Siesta; Silence of the Lambs, The; Sommersby; Stealing Home; Taxi Driver; Tom Sawyer.*

Freeman, Morgan *Along Came a Spider; Amistad; Bonfire of the Vanities, The; Brubaker; Clean and Sober; Deep Impact; Driving Miss Daisy; Glory; Hard Rain; Harry & Son; Johnny Handsome; Marie; Kiss the Girls; Moll Flanders; Nurse Betty; Outbreak; Power of One, The; Robin Hood: Prince of Thieves; Seven (aka Se7en); Shawshank Redemption, The; That Was Then... This Is Now; Under Suspicion; Unforgiven.*

Gabin, Jean *Bas-Fonds, Les (The Lower Depths); Belle Equipe, La; Bête Humaine, La (The Human Beast/Judas Was a Woman); Chat, Le (The Cat); Du Rififi à Paname (Rififi in Paris/The Upper Hand); En Cas de Malheur (La Ragazza del Peccato/Love Is My Profession); French Cancan; Grande Illusion, La; Gueule d'Amour; Jour se lève, Le (Daybreak); Misérables, Les* (Le Chanois); *Napoléon* (Guitry); *Pépé le Moko; Plaisir, Le (House of Pleasure); Quai des Brumes, Le (Port of Shadows); Remorques (Stormy Waters); Sicilian Clan, The (Le Clan des Siciliens); Touchez pas au Grisbi (Grisbi/Honour Among Thieves); Traversée de Paris, La (Pig Across Paris/Four Bags Full); Verdict (The Verdict); Zouzou.*

Gable, Clark *Across the Wide Missouri; After Office Hours; Boom Town; China Seas; Command Decision; Comrade X; Gone With the Wind; Idiot's Delight; It Happened One Night; It Started in Naples; Love on the Run; Manhattan Melodrama; Misfits, The; Mogambo; Mutiny on the Bounty* (Lloyd); *Night Nurse; No Man of Her Own; Red Dust; San Francisco; Strange Cargo; Tall Men, The; Too Hot to Handle.*

Garbo, Greta *Anna Christie; Anna Karenina* (Brown); *As You Desire Me; Camille* (Cukor); *Flesh and the Devil; Grand Hotel; Joyless Street, The (Die freudlose Gasse); Kiss, The* (Feyder); *Mata Hari* (Fitzmaurice); *Ninotchka; Painted Veil, The; Queen Christina; Two-Faced Woman.*

Gardner, Ava *Around the World in 80 Days; Barefoot Contessa, The; Bhowani Junction; Bible...In the Beginning, The (La Bibbia); Blue Bird, The; Bribe, The; Cassandra Crossing, The; City on Fire; Earthquake; 55 Days at Peking; Great Sinner, The; Hitler's Madman; Kid Glove Killer; Kidnapping of the President, The; Killers, The* (Siodmak); *Life and Times of Judge Roy Bean, The; Little Hut, The; Mogambo; My Forbidden Past; Night of the Iguana, The; One Touch of Venus; On the Beach; Pandora and the Flying Dutchman; Permission to Kill; Priest of Love; Sentinel, The; Seven Days in May; Show Boat* (Sidney); *Snows of Kilimanjaro, The; Sun Also Rises, The; Thank Your Lucky Stars.*

Garfield, John *Air Force; Body and Soul* (Rossen); *Breaking Point, The* (Curtiz); *Dangerously They Live; Force of Evil; Gentleman's Agreement; Humoresque; Juarez; Nobody Lives Forever; Out of the Fog; Postman Always Rings Twice, The* (Garnett); *Pride of the Marines (aka Forever in Love); Saturday's Children; Sea Wolf, The.*

Garland, Judy *Babes in Arms; Babes on Broadway; Child Is Waiting, A; Clock, The (aka Under the Clock); Easter Parade; For Me and My Gal; Harvey Girls, The; I Could Go On Singing; In the Good Old Summertime; Judgment at Nuremberg; Little Nellie Kelly; Meet Me in St Louis; Pirate, The; Pigskin Parade; Star Is Born, A* (Cukor); *Strike Up the Band; Summer Stock (aka If You Feel Like Singing); Wizard of Oz, The; Ziegfeld Follies; Ziegfeld Girl.*

Gazzara, Ben *Anatomy of a Murder; Big Lebowski, The; Bloodline (aka Sidney Sheldon's Bloodline); Bridge at Remagen, The; Buffalo '66; Capone; First Knight; Girl from Trieste, The (La Ragazza di Trieste); Happiness; Husbands; Killing of a Chinese Bookie, The; Neptune Factor, The; Opening Night; Road House* (Herrington); *Saint Jack; Spanish Prisoner, The; Strange One, The (aka End as a Man); Summer of Sam; Tales of Ordinary Madness (Storie di Ordinaria Follia); They All Laughed; Thomas Crown Affair, The* (McTiernan); *Voyage of the Damned.*

Gere, Richard *American Gigolo; And the Band Played On; Autumn in New York; Baby Blue Marine; Bloodbrothers; Breathless; Cotton Club, The; Days of Heaven; Dr T & the Women; Final Analysis; Honorary Consul, The (aka Beyond the Limit); Internal Affairs; Intersection; Jackal, The; King David; Looking for Mr Goodbar; Miles from Home; Mr Jones; Mothman Prophecies, The; No Mercy; Officer and a Gentleman, An; Power; Pretty Woman; Red Corner; Report to the Commissioner (aka Operation Undercover); Rhapsody in August (Hachigatsu no Kyoshikyoku); Runaway Bride; Sommersby; Yanks.*

Gibson, Mel *Air America; Bird on a Wire; Bounty, The; Braveheart; Conspiracy Theory; FairyTale – A True Story; Fathers' Day; Forever Young* (Miner); *Gallipoli; Hamlet* (Zeffirelli); *Lethal Weapon; Lethal Weapon 2; Lethal Weapon 3; Lethal Weapon 4; Mad Max; Mad Max 2; Mad Max Beyond Thunderdome; Man Without a Face, The; Maverick; Million Dollar Hotel, The; Mrs Soffel; Patriot, The; Payback; Ransom; River, The* (Rydell); *Tequila Sunrise; Tim; We Were Soldiers; What Women Want; Year of Living Dangerously, The.*

Gielgud, John *Aces High; Appointment With Death; Around the World in 80 Days; Arthur; Arthur 2: On the Rocks; Caligula; Charge of the Light Brigade, The* (Richardson); *Chariots of Fire; Chimes at Midnight (Campanadas a Medianoche); Conductor, The (Dyrygent); Elephant Man, The; 11 Harrowhouse; Elizabeth; Formula, The; Frankenstein: The True Story; Gandhi; Getting It Right; Gold; Good Companions, The; Hamlet* (Branagh); *Haunted; Human Factor, The* (Preminger); *Joseph Andrews; Julius Caesar; Lion of the Desert; Looking for Richard; Lost Horizon* (Jarrott); *Loved One, The; Murder by Decree; Murder on the Orient Express; Oh! What a Lovely War; Plenty; Portrait of a Lady, The; Portrait of the Artist as a Young Man, A; Power of One, The; Priest of Love; Prospero's Books; Providence; Richard III* (Olivier); *Saint Joan; Scandalous; Secret Agent, The; Shine; Shining Through; Shoes of the Fisherman, The; Shooting Party, The; Sphinx; Tichborne Claimant, The; TV Dante: Cantos I–VIII, A; Wagner; Whistle Blower, The; Wicked Lady, The* (Winner).

Gish, Lillian *Birth of a Nation, The* (Griffith); *Broken Blossoms* (Griffith); *Cobweb, The; Comedians, The; Duel in the Sun; Hambone and Hillie (aka The Adventures of Hambone and Hillie); Intolerance; Night of the Hunter, The; Orders to Kill; Orphans of the Storm; Portrait of Jennie; Scarlet Letter, The* (Sjöström); *Sweet Liberty; Unforgiven, The; Warning Shot; Way Down East; Wedding, A; Whales of August, The; Wind, The.*

Goldberg, Whoopi *Adventures of Rocky & Bullwinkle, The; Associate, The; Boys on the Side; Burglar; Celluloid Closet, The; Clara's Heart; Color Purple, The; Corrina, Corrina; Eddie; Fatal Beauty; Ghost; Ghosts of Mississippi (aka Ghosts from the Past); Jumpin' Jack Flash; Lion King, The; Little Rascals, The; Made in America; Monkeybone; Moonlight and Valentino; Naked in New York; Pagemaster, The; Player, The; Rat Race; Sarafina!; Sister Act; Sister Act 2: Back in the Habit; Soapdish; Star Trek: Generations.*

Goldblum, Jeff *Adventures of Buckaroo Banzai Across the 8th Dimension, The; Between the Lines; Beyond Therapy; Big Chill, The; California Split; Cats & Dogs; Deep Cover; Earth Girls Are Easy; Favour, the Watch and the Very Big*

Fish, The (Rue Saint-Sulpice); Fly, The (Cronenberg); *Great White Hype, The; Holy Man; Independence Day; Into the Night; Invasion of the Body Snatchers* (Kaufman); *Jurassic Park; Lost World: Jurassic Park, The; Lush Life; Mad Dog Time (aka Trigger Happy); Mad Monkey, The (El Mono Loco); Mister Frost; Nine Months; Powder; Remember My Name; Right Stuff, The; St Ives; Sentinel, The; Silverado; Tall Guy, The; Thank God It's Friday.*

Grable, Betty *Beautiful Blonde from Bashful Bend, The; Follow the Fleet; Gay Divorcee, The; How to Be Very, Very Popular; How to Marry a Millionaire; I Wake Up Screaming (aka Hot Spot); Mother Wore Tights; Pigskin Parade; Pin Up Girl; Yank in the RAF, A.*

Grahame, Gloria *Bad and the Beautiful, The; Big Heat, The; Cobweb, The; Crossfire; Good Die Young, The; Greatest Show on Earth, The; Head Over Heels; Human Desire; In a Lonely Place; It Happened in Brooklyn; It's a Wonderful Life; Macao; Mama's Dirty Girls; Man on a Tightrope; Mansion of the Doomed (aka The Terror of Dr Chaney); Melvin and Howard; Not as a Stranger; Odds Against Tomorrow; Oklahoma!; Sudden Fear; Todd Killings, The; Woman's Secret, A.*

Grant, Cary *Affair to Remember, An; Alice in Wonderland* (McLeod); *Arsenic and Old Lace; Awful Truth, The; Bishop's Wife, The; Blonde Venus; Bringing Up Baby; Charade; Crisis; Father Goose; Grass Is Greener, The; Gunga Din; His Girl Friday; Holiday; Houseboat; I'm No Angel; Indiscreet; In Name Only; I Was a Male War Bride (aka You Can't Sleep Here); Kiss Them for Me; Merrily We Go to Hell; Mr Blandings Builds His Dream House; Monkey Business* (Hawks); *My Favorite Wife; Night and Day; None But the Lonely Heart; North by Northwest; Notorious; Once Upon a Honeymoon; Once Upon a Time; Only Angels Have Wings; Operation Petticoat; Penny Serenade; People Will Talk; Philadelphia Story, The; Pride and the Passion, The; She Done Him Wrong; Suspicion; Sylvia Scarlett; Talk of the Town, The; To Catch a Thief; Topper.*

Grant, Hugh *About a Boy; Awfully Big Adventure, An; Big Man, The; Bitter Moon (Lunes de Fiel); Bridget Jones's Diary; Dawning, The; Englishman Who Went Up a Hill But Came Down a Mountain, The; Extreme Measures; Four Weddings and a Funeral; Impromptu; Lair of the White Worm, The; Maurice; Mickey Blue Eyes; Nine Months; Notting Hill; Privileged; Remains of the Day, The; Restoration; Sense and Sensibility; Small Time Crooks; Sirens; White Mischief.*

Greenstreet, Sydney *Across the Pacific; Background to Danger; Casablanca; Conflict; Conspirators, The; Devotion; In This Our Life; Malaya (aka East of the Rising Sun); Maltese Falcon, The; Mask of Dimitrios, The; Passage to Marseille; Ruthless; They Died With Their Boots On; Verdict, The* (Siegel).

Griffith, Melanie *Another Day in Paradise; Body Double; Bonfire of the Vanities, The; Born Yesterday; Cecil B. Demented; Celebrity; Cherry 2000; Close to Eden; Crazy in Alabama; Drowning Pool, The; In the Spirit; Lolita* (Lyne); *Milk Money; Mulholland Falls; Night Moves; Nobody's Fool; Now and Then; One on One; Pacific Heights; Paradise; Roar; Shining Through; Smile; Something Wild; Stormy Monday; Two Much (Loco de amor); Working Girl.*

Guinness, Alec *Barnacle Bill (aka All at Sea); Bridge on the River Kwai, The; Brother Sun, Sister Moon (Fratello Sole, Sorella Luna); Captain's Paradise, The; Card, The (aka The Promoter); Comedians, The; Cromwell; Doctor Zhivago; Empire Strikes Back, The; Fall of the Roman Empire, The; Father Brown; Great Expectations* (Lean); *Handful of Dust, A; Hitler: the Last Ten Days; HMS Defiant (aka Damn the Defiant); Horse's Mouth, The; Kafka; Kind Hearts and Coronets; Ladykillers, The; Last Holiday; Lavender Hill Mob, The; Lawrence of Arabia; Little Dorrit; Little Lord Fauntleroy; Lovesick; Man in the White Suit, The; Mudlark, The; Murder by Death; Mute Witness; Oliver Twist* (Lean); *Our Man in Havana; Passage to India, A; Prisoner, The; Quiller Memorandum, The; Raise the Titanic!; Return of the Jedi; Return of the Jedi: Special Edition; Run for Your Money, A; Scrooge; Star Wars; Star Wars, Episode IV, A New Hope; Tunes of Glory.*

Hackman, Gene *Absolute Power; All Night Long; Another Woman; Bat 21; Behind Enemy Lines; Birdcage, The; Bite the Bullet; Bonnie and Clyde; Bridge Too Far, A; Chamber, The; Cisco Pike; Class Action; Company Business; Conversation, The; Crimson Tide; Domino Principle, The (aka The Domino Killings); Downhill Racer; Enemy of the State; Eureka; Extreme Measures; Firm, The; French Connection, The; French Connection II; Full Moon in Blue Water; Geronimo: An American Legend; Get Shorty; Gypsy Moths, The; Hawaii; Heartbreakers; Heist; Hoosiers (aka Best Shot); I Never Sang for My Father; Lilith; Loose Cannons; Lucky Lady; March or Die; Marooned; Mexican, The; Mississippi Burning; Narrow Margin; Night Moves; No Way Out; Package, The; Poseidon Adventure, The; Postcards from the Edge; Power; Prime Cut; Quick and the Dead, The; Reds; Royal Tenebaums, The; Scarecrow; Split, The; Superman; Superman II; Superman IV: The Quest for Peace; Target; Twice in a Lifetime; Twilight; Uncommon Valor; Under Fire; Under Suspicion; Unforgiven; Wyatt Earp; Young Frankenstein; Zandy's Bride.*

Hanks, Tom *Apollo 13; Bachelor Party; Big; Bonfire of the Vanities, The; 'burbs, The; Cast Away; Celluloid Closet, The; Dragnet; Every Time We Say Goodbye; Forrest Gump; Green Mile, The; He Knows You're Alone; Joe Versus the Volcano; League of Their Own, A; Money Pit, The; Nothing in Common; Philadelphia; Punchline; Radio Flyer; Saving Private Ryan; Sleepless in Seattle; Splash; That Thing You Do!; Turner & Hooch; Volunteers; You've Got Mail.*

Harlow, Jean *China Seas; Dinner at Eight; Hell's Angels; Platinum Blonde; Public Enemy, The; Red Dust.*

Harris, Richard *Barber of Siberia, The (Sibirskii tsiriulniki); Bible…In the Beginning, The (La Bibbia); Bloomfield (aka The Hero); Camelot; Caprice; Cassandra Crossing, The; Cromwell; Count of Monte Cristo, The; Deadly Trackers, The; Field, The; Game for Vultures; Gladiator* (Scott); *Golden Rendezvous; Gulliver's Travels; Guns of Navarone, The; Harry Potter and the Philosopher's Stone (aka Harry Potter and the Sorcerer's Stone); Hawaii; Heroes of Telemark, The; Juggernaut; King of the Wind; Long and the Short and the Tall, The; Major Dundee; Man Called Horse, A; Man in the Wilderness; Molly Maguires, The; Mutiny on the Bounty* (Milestone); *99 and 44/100% Dead (aka Call Harry Crown); Orca (aka Orca…Killer Whale); Patriot Games; Red Desert, The (Deserto Rosso); Return of a Man Called Horse, The; Robin and Marian; Silent Tongue; Smilla's Feeling for Snow (Fräulein Smillas Gespür für Schnee/aka Smilla's Sense of Snow); Tarzan, The Ape Man; Terrible Beauty, A (aka Night Fighters); This Is the Sea; This Sporting Life; To Walk with Lions; Triumphs of a Man Called Horse (El Triunfo de un Hombre Llamado Caballo); Trojan Eddie; Unforgiven; Wild Geese, The; Wrestling Ernest Hemingway.*

Harrison, Rex *Agony and the Ecstasy, The; Anna and the King of Siam; Ashanti; Blithe Spirit; Citadel, The* (Vidor); *Cleopatra* (Mankiewicz); *Ghost and Mrs Muir, The; Honey Pot, The; I Live in Grosvenor Square (aka A Yank in London); Major Barbara; Men Are Not Gods; My Fair Lady; Night Train to Munich; Prince and the Pauper, The (aka Crossed Swords); Rake's Progress, The (aka Notorious Gentleman); St Martin's Lane (aka Sidewalks of London); Staircase; Unfaithfully Yours* (Sturges).

Hawkins, Jack *Adventures of Gerard, The; Angels One Five; Autumn Crocus; Ben-Hur* (Wyler); *Bridge on the River Kwai, The; Cruel Sea, The; Death at Broadcasting House; Elusive Pimpernel, The; Fallen Idol, The; Home at Seven (aka Murder on Monday); Jane Eyre* (Mann); *Judith; I Lived With You; Kidnapped; Land of the Pharoahs; Lawrence of Arabia; League of Gentlemen, The; Long Arm, The (aka The Third Key); Lord Jim; Mandy (aka Crash of Silence); Masquerade* (Dearden); *Nicholas and Alexandra; No Highway (aka No Highway in the Sky); Peg of Old Drury; Prisoner, The; Rampage; Shalako; Small Back Room, The; State Secret (aka The Great Manhunt); Theatre of Blood; Waterloo; When Eight Bells Toll; Young Winston; Zulu.*

Hayworth, Rita *Angels Over Broadway; Blood and Sand* (Mamoulian); *Cover Girl; Dante's Inferno; Down to Earth; Gilda; Lady from Shanghai, The; Miss Sadie Thompson; Only Angels Have Wings; Pal Joey; Road to Salina (Sur la Route de Salina); You'll Never Get Rich; You Were Never Lovelier.*

Hepburn, Audrey *Always* (Spielberg); *Bloodline (aka Sidney Sheldon's Bloodline); Breakfast at Tiffany's; Charade; Funny Face; Lavender Hill Mob, The; Laughter in Paradise; Love in the Afternoon* (Wilder); *My Fair Lady; Nun's Story, The; Robin and Marian;*

Roman Holiday; Sabrina (aka Sabrina Fair); Secret People; They All Laughed; Two For the Road; Unforgiven, The; Wait Until Dark; War and Peace (Vidor).

Hepburn, Katharine *Adam's Rib; African Queen, The; Alice Adams; Bill of Divorcement, A; Bringing Up Baby; Christopher Strong; Delicate Balance, A; Desk Set (aka His Other Woman); Grace Quigley; Guess Who's Coming to Dinner; Holiday; Keeper of the Flame; Lion in Winter, The; Little Women* (Cukor); *Long Day's Journey into Night; Love Affair (aka An Affair to Remember); Love Among the Ruins; Mary of Scotland; On Golden Pond; Pat and Mike; Philadelphia Story, The; Rooster Cogburn; Spitfire; Stage Door* (La Cava); *State of the Union (aka The World and His Wife); Suddenly Last Summer; Summertime (aka Summer Madness); Sylvia Scarlett; Undercurrent; Woman of the Year; Woman Rebels, A.*

Heston, Charlton *Agony and the Ecstasy, The; Airport 1975; Alaska; Almost an Angel; Antony and Cleopatra; Any Given Sunday; Awakening, The; Beneath the Planet of the Apes; Ben-Hur* (Wyler); *Big Country, The; Buccaneer, The; Call of the Wild, The; Dark City; Earthquake; El Cid; 55 Days at Peking; Four Musketeers: The Revenge of Milady, The; Gray Lady Down; Greatest Show on Earth, The; Greatest Story Ever Told, The; Gringo in Mañanaland, A; Hamlet* (Branagh); *In the Mouth of Madness; Khartoum; Last Hard Men, The; Major Dundee; Midway (aka Battle of Midway); Naked Jungle, The; Number One (aka Pro); Omega Man, The; Planet of the Apes* (Schaffner); *Planet of the Apes* (Burton); *Prince and the Pauper, The (aka Crossed Swords); Ruby Gentry; Skyjacked; Soylent Green; Ten Commandments, The; Town & Country; Three Musketeers: The Queen's Diamonds, The; Tombstone; Touch of Evil; Treasure Island; Two-Minute Warning; War Lord, The; Will Penny.*

Hoffman, Dustin *Accidental Hero; Agatha; Alfredo Alfredo; All the President's Men; American Buffalo; Billy Bathgate; Death of a Salesman; Dick Tracy; Family Business; Graduate, The; Hook; Ishtar; Joan of Arc (Jeanne d'Arc); John and Mary; Kramer vs Kramer; Lenny; Little Big Man; Mad City; Marathon Man; Midnight Cowboy; Outbreak; Papillon; Rain Man; Sleepers; Sphere; Straight Time; Straw Dogs; Tootsie; Wag the Dog; Walk on the Moon, A; Who Is Harry Kellerman and Why Is He Saying Those Terrible Things About Me?*

Holden, William *Ashanti; Blue Knight, The; Born Yesterday; Breezy; Bridge on the River Kwai, The; Bridges at Toko-Ri, The; Casino Royale; Damien – Omen II; Dark Past, The; Devil's Brigade, The; Escape from Fort Bravo; Executive Suite; Fedora; Golden Boy; Horse Soldiers, The; Invisible Stripes; Key, The; Lion, The; Love Is a Many-Splendored Thing; Man from Colorado, The; Moon Is Blue, The; Network; Open Season (Los Cazadores); Our Town; Picnic; Proud and Profane, The; Rachel and the Stranger; Revengers, The; Sabrina (aka Sabrina Fair); Satan Never Sleeps (aka The Devil Never Sleeps); 7th Dawn, The; S.O.B.; Stalag 17; Sunset Blvd.; Toward the Unknown (aka Brink of Hell); Towering Inferno, The; Union Station; When Time Ran Out; Wild Bunch, The; Wild Rovers; World of Suzie Wong, The.*

Hope, Bob *Beau James; Casanova's Big Night; Cat and the Canary, The* (Nugent); *Ghost Breakers, The; Global Affair, A; How to Commit Marriage; Muppet Movie, The; My Favorite Blonde; My Favorite Brunette; Never Say Die; Paleface, The; Road to Morocco; Road to Utopia; Son of Paleface.*

Hopkins, Anthony *All Creatures Great and Small; Amistad; Audrey Rose; August; Bounty, The; Bridge Too Far, A; Change of Seasons, A; Chaplin; Chorus of Disapproval, A; Dawning, The; Desperate Hours; Doll's House, A* (Garland); *Dracula (aka Bram Stoker's Dracula); Edge, The; 84 Charing Cross Road; Elephant Man, The; Freejack; Good Father, The; Hamlet* (Richardson); *Howards End; Innocent, The* (Schlesinger); *Instinct; International Velvet; Juggernaut; Legends of the Fall; Lion in Winter, The; Looking Glass War, The; Magic; Mask of Zorro, The; Meet Joe Black; Nixon; Remains of the Day, The; Road to Wellville, The; Shadowlands; Silence of the Lambs, The; Spotswood; Surviving Picasso; Trial, The* (Jones); *Victory at Entebbe; When Eight Bells Toll; White Bus, The; Young Winston.*

Hopper, Dennis *American Friend, The (Der Amerikanische Freund); American Way, The (aka Riders of the Storm); Apocalypse Now; Apocalypse Now Redux; Basquiat; Blackout, The; Black Widow* (Rafelson); *Blood Red; Blue Velvet; Boiling Point* (Harris); *Carried Away (aka Acts of Love); Catchfire; Chasers; Chattahoochee; Cool Hand Luke; Easy Rider; EDtv; From Hell to Texas (aka Manhunt); Giant; Glory Stompers, The; Hang 'em High; Hoosiers (aka Best Shot); Indian Runner, The; Jesus' Son; Kid Blue; Last Movie, The; Mad Dog Morgan (aka Mad Dog); O.C. & Stiggs; Paris Trout; Osterman Weekend, The; Out of the Blue; Rebel Without a Cause; Red Rock West; River's Edge; Rumble Fish; Space Truckers; Speed; Super Mario Bros.; Texas Chainsaw Massacre 2, The; Tracks; Trip, The; True Grit; True Romance; Waterworld; Witch Hunt.*

Hoskins, Bob *Blue Ice; Brazil; Captain Jack; Cotton Club, The; Cousin Bette; Favour, the Watch and the Very Big Fish, The (Rue Saint-Sulpice); Felicia's Journey; God's Favorite; Heart Condition; Honorary Consul, The (aka Beyond the Limit); Hook; Inner Circle, The (Il Proiezionista); Inserts; Lassiter; Last Orders; Lonely Passion of Judith Hearne, The; Long Good Friday, The; Mermaids; Mona Lisa; National Health, The; Nixon; Parting Shots; Pink Floyd: The Wall; Prayer for the Dying, A; Raggedy Rawney, The; Rainbow; Room for Romeo Brass, A; Secret Agent, The (aka Joseph Conrad's The Secret Agent); Shattered; Spice World; Super Mario Bros.; Sweet Liberty; Tube Tales; TwentyFourSeven; Who Framed Roger Rabbit?*

Howard, Leslie *First of the Few (aka Spitfire); 49th Parallel; Gentle Sex, The; Gone With the Wind; Intermezzo (aka Escape to Happiness); It's Love I'm After; Petrified Forest, The; Outward Bound; Pimpernel Smith; Pygmalion; Scarlet Pimpernel, The; Secrets* (Borzage); *Stand-In.*

Howard, Trevor *Aces High; Around the World in 80 Days; Battle of Britain; Bawdy Adventures of Tom Jones, The; Brief Encounter; Catch Me a Spy (Les Doigts Croisés/aka To Catch a Spy); Charge of the Light Brigade, The* (Richardson); *Clouded Yellow, The; Cockleshell Heroes; Conduct Unbecoming; Count of Monte-Cristo, The; Craze; Dawning, The; Death in the Sun (Der Flüsternde Tod); Doll's House, A* (Losey); *Dust; 11 Harrowhouse; Father Goose; Foreign Body; Gandhi; Golden Salamander; Green for Danger; Heart of the Matter, The; Hennessy; Hurricane; I See a Dark Stranger (aka The Adventuress); Key, The; Kidnapped; Lady Godiva Rides Again; Light Years Away; Lion, The; Ludwig; Manuela (aka Stowaway Girl); Mary, Queen of Scots; Meteor; Missionary, The; Mutiny on the Bounty* (Milestone); *Odette; Offence, The; Operation Crossbow; Outcast of the Islands; Passionate Friends, The (aka One Woman's Story); Persecution; Pope Joan; Rollicking Adventures of Eliza Fraser, The (aka A Faithful Narrative of the Capture, Sufferings and Miraculous Escape of Eliza Fraser); Run for the Sun; Ryan's Daughter; Sea Wolves, The; Sir Henry at Rawlinson's End; Slavers; Sons and Lovers; Stevie; Superman; Sword of the Valiant – The Legend of Gawain and the Green Knight, The; Third Man, The; Unholy, The; Von Ryan's Express; Way to the Stars, The (aka Johnny in the Clouds); White Mischief; Who?*

Hudson, Rock *All That Heaven Allows; Ambassador, The; Avalanche; Battle Hymn; Bend of the River (aka Where the River Bends); Blindfold; Darling Lili; Farewell to Arms, A* (Vidor); *Gathering of Eagles, A; Giant; Gun Fury; Has Anybody Seen My Gal?; Horizons West; Ice Station Zebra; Last Sunset, The; Magnificent Obsession; Man's Favourite Sport; Mirror Crack'd, The; Pillow Talk; Pretty Maids All in a Row; Seconds; Send Me No Flowers; Something of Value; Tarnished Angels, The; Undefeated, The; Winchester '73; Written on the Wind.*

Hunter, Holly *Always* (Spielberg); *Blood Simple; Broadcast News; Burning, The; Copycat; Crash; Firm, The; Gathering of Old Men, A; Home for the Holidays; Jesus' Son; Life Less Ordinary, A; Living Out Loud; Miss Firecracker; O Brother, Where Art Thou?; Once Around; Piano, The; Positively True Adventures of the Alleged Texas Cheerleader-Murdering Mom, The; Raising Arizona; Swing Shift; Things You Can Tell Just by Looking at Her; Timecode.*

Huppert, Isabelle *Amateur; Après l'Amour; Bedroom Window, The; Cactus; Cérémonie, La (A Judgement in Stone); César and Rosalie (César et Rosalie); Clean Slate (Coup de Torchon); Contre l'Oubli (Against Oblivion); Coup de Foudre (At First Sight/Entre Nous); Dame aux Camélias, La; Dentellière, La (The Lacemaker); Destinées Sentimentales, Les; Ecole de la Chair, L' (The School of*

Flesh); 8 Women (8 Femmes); Elective Affinities (Le Affinità Elettive); Fils de Deux Mères ou Comédie de l'Innocence; Heaven's Gate; Indians Are Still Far Away, The (Les Indiens Sont Encore Loin); Loulou; Madame Bovary; Merci pour le chocolat; My Best Friend's Girl (La Femme de Mon Pote); Pas de Scandale (Keep It Quiet/No Scandal); Passion; Piano Teacher, The (La Pianiste); Rien ne va plus; Rosebud; Sauve Qui Peut – la Vie (Every Man for Himself/Slow Motion); Séparation, La; Trout, The (La Truite); Valseuses, Les (Going Places/Making It); Violette Nozière.

Hurt, John *Alien; All the Little Animals; Aria; Before Winter Comes; Champions; Contact; Dead Man; Disappearance, The; East of Elephant Rock; Elephant Man, The; Even Cowgirls Get the Blues; Field, The; From the Hip; Ghoul, The* (Francis); *Harry Potter and the Philosopher's Stone (aka Harry Potter and the Sorcerer's Stone); Heaven's Gate; History of the World Part I; Hit, The; Jake Speed; King Ralph; Krapp's Last Tape; Little Malcolm and His Struggle Against the Eunuchs; Lord of the Rings, The; Love and Death on Long Island; Man for All Seasons, A; Midnight Express; Mr Forbush and the Penguins (aka Cry of the Penguins); Monkey's Tale, A (Le Château des singes); Monolith; Night Crossing; Night Train; Nineteen Eighty-Four; Osterman Weekend, The; Partners; Pied Piper, The* (Demy); *Rob Roy; Rocinante; Roger Corman's Frankenstein Unbound; Sailor from Gibraltar, The; Scandal; Shout, The; Sinful Davey; Spaceballs; Success is the Best Revenge; 10 Rillington Place; White Mischief; Wild Bill; Windprints; You're Dead…*

Hurt, William *Accidental Tourist, The; A.I. Artificial Intelligence; Alice; Altered States; Big Brass Ring, The; Big Chill, The; Body Heat; Broadcast News; Children of a Lesser God; Dark City; Doctor, The; Eyewitness (aka The Janitor); Gorky Park; I Love You to Death; Jane Eyre; Kiss of the Spider Woman; Lost in Space; Loved; Michael; Miracle Maker, The; Mr Wonderful; One True Thing; Proposition, The; Second Best; Smoke; Sunshine (A napfény ize/Ein Hauch von Sonnenschein); Time of Destiny, A; Trial by Jury; Until the End of the World (Bis ans Ende der Welt).*

Huston, Anjelica *Addams Family, The; Addams Family Values; Agnes Browne; And the Band Played On; Buffalo '66; Crimes and Misdemeanors; Crossing Guard, The; Dead, The; Enemies, a Love Story; Ever After; Gardens of Stone; Golden Bowl, The; Grifters, The; Hamlet* (Richardson); *Handful of Dust, A; Manhattan Murder Mystery; Mr North; Perez Family, The; Postman Always Rings Twice, The* (Rafelson); *Prizzi's Honor; Royal Tenenbaums, The; Swashbuckler (The Scarlet Buccaneer); Walk with Love and Death, A; Witches, The.*

Huston, John *Battle for the Planet of the Apes; Bible…In the Beginning, The (La Bibbia); Candy; Cardinal, The; Chinatown; Head On (aka Fatal Attraction); Jaguar Lives; Kremlin Letter, The; Life and Times of Judge Roy Bean, The; Lovesick; Man in the Wilderness; Myra Breckinridge; Tentacles (Tentacoli); Treasure of the Sierra Madre, The; Walk with Love and Death, A; Wind and the Lion, The; Winter Kills; Wise Blood; Young Giants.*

Huston, Walter *All That Money Can Buy (aka The Devil and Daniel Webster/Daniel and the Devil); American Madness; And Then There Were None (aka Ten Little Niggers); Criminal Code, The; Dragonwyck; Duel in the Sun; Edge of Darkness; Furies, The; Gabriel Over the White House; Great Sinner, The; In This Our Life; Mission to Moscow; North Star; Outlaw, The; Rain; Shanghai Gesture, The; Swamp Water; Treasure of the Sierra Madre, The; Tunnel, The (aka Transatlantic Tunnel); Yankee Doodle Dandy.*

Irons, Jeremy *Australia; Betrayal; Chinese Box; Chorus of Disapproval, A; Damage; Danny the Champion of the World; Dead Ringers; Die Hard with a Vengeance; Dungeons & Dragons; French Lieutenant's Woman, The; House of Spirits, The; Kafka; Lolita* (Lyne); *Man in the Iron Mask, The* (Wallace); *Mission, The* (Joffé); *M. Butterfly; Moonlighting; Nijinsky; Reversal of Fortune; Stealing Beauty (Io ballo da sola/Beauté Volée); Swann in Love (Un Amour de Swann); Waterland.*

Jackson, Glenda *Bequest to the Nation (aka The Nelson Affair); Beyond Therapy; Boy Friend, The; Business As Usual; Class of Miss MacMichael, The; Giro City; Health; Hedda; Hopscotch; House Calls; Incredible Sarah, The; King of the Wind; Lost and Found; Maids, The; Mary, Queen of Scots; Music Lovers, The; Nasty Habits; Persecution and Assassination of Jean-Paul Marat as Performed by the Inmates of the Asylum of Charenton Under the Direction of the Marquis de Sade, The; Rainbow, The; Return of the Soldier, The; Romantic Englishwoman, The; Salome's Last Dance; Stevie; Sunday, Bloody Sunday; Tempter, The (Il Sorriso del Grande Tentatore); Touch of Class, A; Triple Echo, The; Turtle Diary; Women in Love.*

Jackson, Samuel L *Betsy's Wedding; Coming to America; Deep Blue Sea; DEF by Temptation; Die Hard with a Vengeance; Do the Right Thing; Eddie Murphy Raw; Eve's Bayou; Exorcist III, The; 51st State, The; Fresh; GoodFellas; Great White Hype, The; Hard Eight; Jackie Brown; Johnny Suede; Juice; Jungle Fever; Jurassic Park; Kiss of Death* (Schroeder); *Long Kiss Goodnight, The; Menace II Society; Mo' Better Blues; National Lampoon's Loaded Weapon 1; Negotiator, The; New Age, The; One Eight Seven; Out of Sight ; Patriot Games; Pulp Fiction; Ragtime; Red Violin, The (Il Violino Rosso); Rules of Engagement; School Daze; Sea of Love; Shaft* (Singleton); *Shock to the System, A; Sphere; Star Wars Episode I The Phantom Menace; Star Wars Episode II Attack of the Clones; Time to Kill, A; Trees Lounge; True Romance; Unbreakable; White Sands.*

Johnson, Ben *Angels in the Outfield (aka Angels); Bite the Bullet; Breakheart Pass; Champions; Cherry 2000; Chisum; Dillinger* (Milius); *Evening Star; Getaway, The* (Peckinpah); *Grayeagle; Greatest, The; Hang 'em High; Hunter, The; Hustle; Junior Bonner; Kid Blue; Last Picture Show, The; Major Dundee; Mighty Joe Young; My Heroes Have Always Been Cowboys; One-Eyed Jacks; Rare Breed, The; Radio Flyer; Red Dawn; Rio Grande; Savage Bees, The; Shane; She Wore a Yellow Ribbon; Something Big; Sugarland Express, The; Swarm, The; Terror Train; Three Godfathers; Train Robbers, The; Undefeated, The; Wagon Master; Wild Bunch, The; Will Penny.*

Jones, Tommy Lee *Back Roads; Batman Forever; Betsy, The; Big Town, The; Black Moon Rising; Blown Away; Blue Sky; Client, The; Coal Miner's Daughter; Cobb; Double Jeopardy; Executioner's Song, The; Eyes of Laura Mars; Firebirds (aka Wings of the Apache); Fugitive, The* (Davis); *Heaven & Earth; House of Cards (La Voce del Silenzio); Jackson County Jail; JFK; Love Story* (Hiller); *Men in Black; Natural Born Killers; Package, The; River Rat, The; Rules of Engagement; Savage Islands; Space Cowboys; Stormy Monday; Under Siege; U.S. Marshals; Volcano* (Jackson).

Karloff, Boris *Bedlam; Before I Hang; Black Cat, The (aka House of Doom); Black Room, The; Black Sabbath (I Tre Volti della Paura); Body Snatcher, The; Boogie Man Will Get You, The; Bride of Frankenstein, The; Charlie Chan at the Opera; Comedy of Terrors, The; Corridors of Blood; Criminal Code, The; Curse of the Crimson Altar (aka The Crimson Cult); Devil Commands, The; Devil's Island* (Clemens); *Five Star Final; Frankenstein; Ghoul, The* (Hunter); *Grip of the Strangler (aka The Haunted Strangler); House of Frankenstein; House of Rothschild, The; Invisible Ray, The; Isle of the Dead; Lost Patrol, The; Lured (aka Personal Column); Mad Genius, The; Mad Monster Party; Man Who Changed His Mind, The (aka The Man Who Lived Again); Mask of Fu Manchu, The; Monster of Terror (aka Die, Monster, Die); Mummy, The* (Freund); *Old Dark House, The; Raven, The* (Friedlander/Landers); *Raven, The* (Corman); *Scarface* (Hawks); *Secret Life of Walter Mitty; Son of Frankenstein; Sorcerers, The; Strange Door, The; Targets; Terror, The; Unconquered; Walking Dead, The; You'll Find Out.*

Keaton, Buster *Adventures of Huckleberry Finn, The; Around the World in 80 Days; Battling Butler; Beach Blanket Bingo; Cameraman, The; College; Film; Funny Thing Happened on the Way to the Forum, A; General, The; Go West* (Keaton); *In the Good Old Summertime; It's a Mad, Mad, Mad, Mad World; Limelight; Navigator, The; Our Hospitality; Parlor, Bedroom and Bath (aka Romeo in Pyjamas); Saphead, The; Seven Chances; Sherlock Junior; Spite Marriage; Steamboat Bill, Jr; Sunset Blvd.; Three Ages.*

Keaton, Michael *Batman; Batman Returns; Beetlejuice; Clean and Sober; Despoerate Measures; Dream Team, The; Gung Ho; Jack Frost; Jackie Brown; Johnny Dangerously; Mr Mom (aka Mr Mum); Much Ado About Nothing; Multiplicity; My Life; Night Shift; One Good Cop; Out of Sight; Pacific Heights; Paper, The; Speechless; Squeeze, The* (Young); *Touch and Go.*

Keitel, Harvey *Bad Lieutenant; Bad Timing; Blue Collar; Blue in the Face; Border, The; Buffalo Bill and the Indians, or Sitting Bull's History Lesson; Bugsy; City of Industry; Clockers; CopLand; Death Watch (La Mort en Direct); Duellists, The; Eagle's Wing; Exposed; FairyTale – A True Story; Falling in Love; Finding Graceland; Fingers; From Dusk Till Dawn; Full Tilt Boogie; Head Above Water; Holy Smoke; Imaginary Crimes; January Man, The; Last Temptation of Christ, The; Mean Streets; Men's Club, The; Monkey Trouble; Mortal Thoughts; Mother, Jugs & Speed; Naples Connection, The (Un Complicato Intrigo di Donne, Vicoli e Delitti); Off Beat; Order of Death (aka Corrupt); Piano, The; Pierre dans la Bouche, Une (aka Le Fugitif); Point of No Return (aka The Assassin); Pulp Fiction; Reservoir Dogs; Rising Sun; Saturn 3; Sister Act; Smoke; Snake Eyes; Somebody to Love; Taxi Driver; That Night in Varennes (La Nuit de Varennes); Thelma & Louise; Three Seasons; Two Jakes, The; Ulysses' Gaze; U–571; Welcome to L.A.; Who's That Knocking at My Door? (aka I Call First); Wise Guys; Young Americans.*

Kelly, Gene *American in Paris, An; Anchors Aweigh; Black Hand, The; Brigadoon; Christmas Holiday; Cover Girl; Demoiselles de Rochefort, Les (The Young Girls of Rochefort); DuBarry Was a Lady; For Me and My Gal; Inherit the Wind; It's Always Fair Weather; Les Girls; Let's Make Love; On the Town; Pirate, The; Singin' in the Rain; Summer Stock (aka If You Feel Like Singing); Take Me Out to the Ball Game (aka Everybody's Cheering); That's Dancing!; That's Entertainment!; That's Entertainment Part II; Viva Knievel!; Xanadu; Ziegfeld Follies.*

Kelly, Grace *Bridges at Toko-Ri, The; Dial M for Murder; Green Fire; High Noon; High Society; Mogambo; Rear Window; To Catch a Thief.*

Kilmer, Val *At First Sight; Batman Forever; Doors, The; Heat* (Mann); *Island of Dr Moreau, The* (Frankenheimer); *Kill Me Again; Pollock; Real Genius; Real McCoy, The; Red Planet; Saint, The; Thunderheart; Tombstone; Top Gun; Top Secret!; True Romance; Willow.*

Kinski, Klaus *Aguirre, Wrath of God (Aguirre, der Zorn Gottes); Android; Big Silence, The (Il Grande Silenzio); Buddy Buddy; Bullet for the General, A (¿Quién Sabe?); Circus of Fear (aka Psycho-Circus); Cobra Verde; Count Dracula (El Conde Dracula); Fitzcarraldo; For a Few Dollars More (Per Qualche Dollari in più); Fruits of Passion, The (Les Fruits de la Passion); Lifespan; Little Drummer Girl, The; Madame Claude; Nosferatu the Vampyre (Nosferatu: Phantom der Nacht); Operation Thunderbolt; Soldier, The (aka Codename: The Soldier); Time to Love and a Time to Die, A; Titan Find, The (aka Creature); Vampires in Venice (Nosferatu a Venezia); Venom* (Sykes); *Woyzeck.*

Kinski, Nastassja *Cat People* (Schrader); *Claim, The; Exposed; Harem; Hotel New Hampshire, The; Farway, So Close (In weiter Ferne, so nah!); Fathers' Day; Lost Son, The; Maria's Lovers; Moon in the Gutter, The (La Lune dans le Caniveau); Night Sun (Il Sole anche di notte); One From the Heart; One Night Stand; Paris, Texas; Revolution; Savior; Spring Symphony (Frühlingssinfonie); Terminal Velocity; Tess; Torrents of Spring (Acque di primavera); To the Devil a Daughter; Town & Country; Unfaithfully Yours* (Zieff); *Wrong Movement (Falsche Bewegung); Your Friends & Neighbors.*

Kline, Kevin *Big Chill, The; Chaplin; Consenting Adults; Cry Freedom; Dave; Fierce Creatures; Fish Called Wanda, A; French Kiss; Grand Canyon; I Love You to Death; Ice Storm, The; In & Out; January Man; Looking for Richard; Midsummer Night's Dream, A* (Hoffman); *Pirates of Penzance, The; Princess Caraboo; Silverado; Soapdish; Sophie's Choice; Wild Wild West.*

Ladd, Alan *And Now Tomorrow; Badlanders, The; Black Cat, The* (Rogell); *Black Knight, The; Blue Dahlia, The; Botany Bay; Glass Key, The; Calcutta; Great Gatsby, The* (Nugent); *My Favourite Brunette; Santiago (aka The Gun Runner); Shane; This Gun for Hire; Two Years Before the Mast.*

Lake, Veronica *Blue Dahlia, The; Glass Key, The; Hold Back the Dawn; I Married a Witch; Ramrod; Sullivan's Travels; This Gun for Hire.*

Lamarr, Hedy *Algiers; Boom Town; Comrade X; Conspirators, The; Crossroads; Experiment Perilous; Extase (Ecstasy/aka Symphony of Love); I Take This Woman; Lady Without Passport, A; Samson and Delilah; Ziegfeld Girl.*

Lancaster, Burt *Airport; Apache; Atlantic City (aka Atlantic City U.S.A.); Bird Man of Alcatraz; Brute Force; Buffalo Bill and the Indians, or Sitting Bull's History Lesson; Cassandra Crossing, The; Castle Keep; Cattle Annie and Little Britches; Child Is Waiting, A; Come Back, Little Sheba; Conversation Piece (Gruppo di Famiglia in un Interno); Crimson Pirate, The; Criss Cross; Elmer Gantry; Executive Action; Field of Dreams; Flame and the Arrow, The; From Here to Eternity; Go Tell the Spartans; Gunfight at the O.K. Corral; Gypsy Moths, The; Island of Dr Moreau, The; Judgment at Nuremberg; Kentuckian, The; Killers, The* (Siodmak); *Lawman; Leopard, The (Il Gattopardo); List of Adrian Messenger, The; Local Hero; Midnight Man, The; Moses; 1900 (Novecento); Osterman Weekend, The; Professionals, The; Scalphunters, The; Scorpio; Seven Days in May; Sorry, Wrong Number; Sweet Smell of Success; Swimmer, The; Tough Guys; Train, The; Twilight's Last Gleaming; Ulzana's Raid; Unforgiven, The; Valdez Is Coming; Vera Cruz; Victory at Entebbe; Zulu Dawn.*

Lange, Jessica *All That Jazz; Cape Fear* (Scorsese); *Blue Sky; Country; Cousin Bette; Crimes of the Heart; Everybody's All-American (aka When I Fall in Love); Far North; Frances; King Kong* (Guillermin); *Men Don't Leave; Music Box; Night and the City* (Winkler); *Postman Always Rings Twice, The* (Rafelson); *Rob Roy; Sweet Dreams; Thousand Acres, A; Titus; Tootsie.*

Laughton, Charles *Advise and Consent; Arch of Triumph; Barretts of Wimpole Street, The; Big Clock, The; Bribe, The; Hobson's Choice; Hunchback of Notre Dame, The* (Dieterle); *If I Had a Million; Island of Lost Souls; It Started with Eve; Jamaica Inn; Les Misérables; Mutiny on the Bounty* (Lloyd); *O. Henry's Full House (aka Full House); Old Dark House, The; Paradine Case, The; Piccadilly; Private Life of Henry VIII, The; Rembrandt; Ruggles of Red Gap; St Martin's Lane (aka Sidewalks of London); Sign of the Cross, The; Spartacus; Strange Door, The; Suspect, The; They Knew What They Wanted; This Land Is Mine; Vessel of Wrath (aka The Beachcomber); Witness for the Prosecution; Young Bess.*

Laurel, Stan, and Hardy, Oliver *A-Haunting We Will Go; Blockheads; Bonnie Scotland; Chump at Oxford, A; Jitterbugs; Our Relations; Pack Up Your Troubles; Pardon Us; Saps at Sea; Sons of the Desert (aka Fraternally Yours); Way Out West.*

Léaud, Jean-Pierre *Baisers Volés (Stolen Kisses); Bunker Palace Hotel; Chinoise, La (La Chinoise, ou plutôt à la Chinoise); Day for Night (La Nuit Américaine); Départ, Le; Détective; Deux Anglaises et le Continent, Les (Anne and Muriel/Two English Girls); Domicile Conjugal (Bed and Board); Gai Savoir, Le; I Hired a Contract Killer; Ile au trésor, L' (Treasure Island); Irma Vep; Last Tango in Paris; Lion Has Seven Heads, The (Der Leone Have Sept Cabecas); Love on the Run (L'Amour en Fuite); Marcorelle Affair (L'Affaire Marcorelle); Masculin Féminin (Masculine Feminine); Mon Homme; Mother and the Whore, The (La Maman et la Putain); Out 1: Spectre; Paris s'éveille (Paris Awakens); Pierrot le Fou; Pigsty (Porcile); Ponographer, The (Le Pornographe); Quatre Cents Coups, Les (The 400 Blows); Rise and Fall of a Little Film Company from a Novel by James Hadley Chase (Grandeur et Décadence d'un Petit Commerce de Cinéma d'après un roman de JH Chase); Testament d'Orphée, Le (Testament of Orpheus); Vie de Bohème, La (Bohemian Life); Virgin (36 Fillette); Weekend (Week-end); What Time Is It There? (Ni Neibian Ji Dian/Et là-bas quelle heure est-il?).*

Lee, Bruce *Big Boss, The (Tangshan Daxiong/aka Fists of Fury); Enter the Dragon; Fist of Fury; Marlowe; Way of the Dragon, The.*

Lee, Christopher *Airport '77; Arabian Adventure; Battle of the River Plate, The (aka Pursuit of the Graf Spee); Bear Island; Beat Girl (aka Wild for Kicks); Bitter Victory (Amère Victoire); Brides of Fu Manchu, The; Caravans; Circus of Fear (aka Psycho-Circus); Corridors of Blood; Count Dracula (El Conde Dracula); Creeping Flesh, The; Curse of Frankenstein, The; Curse of the Crimson Altar (aka The Crimson Cult); Death in the Sun (Der Flüsternde Tod); Death Line (aka Raw Meat); Devil Rides Out, The; Diagnosis: Murder; Diamond Mercenaries, The; Dr Terror's House of Horrors; Dracula (aka Horror of Dracula); Dracula A.D. 1972; Dracula Has Risen from the Grave; Dracula, Prince of Darkness; Eye for an Eye, An; Face of Fu Manchu, The; Feast at Midnight, A; Four Musketeers: The Revenge of Milady, The; Funny Man;*

Gorgon, The; Gremlins 2: The New Batch; Hannie Caulder; Horror Express (Pánico en el Transiberiano); Hound of the Baskervilles (Fisher); *House of the Long Shadows, The; House That Dripped Blood, The; Ill Met by Moonlight (aka Night Ambush); I, Monster; Innocents in Paris; Jaguar Lives; Lord of the Rings: The Fellowship of the Ring, The; Magic Christian, The; Man With the Golden Gun, The; Moulin Rouge; Mummy, The* (Fisher); *Night of the Big Heat; 1941; Nothing But the Night; Oblong Box, The; Passage, The; Police Academy &: Mission to Moscow; Private Life of Sherlock Holmes, The; Return from Witch Mountain; Return of Captain Invincible, The; Return of the Musketeers, The; Revenge of the Dead; Satanic Rites of Dracula, The (aka Count Dracula and His Vampire Bride); Scars of Dracula, The; Scott of the Antarctic; Scream and Scream Again; She; Silent Flute, The (aka Circle of Iron); Skull, The; Sleepy Hollow; Star Wars Episode II Attack of the Clones; Stupids, The; Taste of Fear (aka Scream of Fear); Taste the Blood of Dracula; That Lady; Three Musketeers: The Queen's Diamonds, The; To the Devil a Daughter; Treasure Island; Two Faces of Dr Jekyll, The (aka House of Fright); Wicker Man, The.*

Leigh, Vivien *Anna Karenina* (Duvivier); *Caesar and Cleopatra; Dark Journey; Fire Over England; Gone With the Wind; Roman Spring of Mrs Stone, The; St Martin's Lane (aka Sidewalks of London); Ship of Fools; Streetcar Named Desire, A; That Hamilton Woman (aka Lady Hamilton).*

Lemmon, Jack *Airport '77; Alex & the Gypsy; Apartment, The; April Fools, The; Avanti!; Buddy Buddy; China Syndrome, The; Cowboy; Dad; Days of Wine and Roses; Fortune Cookie, The (aka Meet Whiplash Willie); Front Page, The* (Wilder); *Grass Harp, The; Glengarry Glen Ross; Grumpy Old Men; Hamlet* (Branagh); *Irma la Douce; It Should Happen to You; JFK; Legend of Bagger Vance, The; Luv; Macaroni (Maccheroni); Missing; Mister Roberts; My Sister Eileen; Odd Couple, The; Odd Couple II, The (aka Neil Simon's The Odd Couple II); Out-of-Towners, The* (Hiller); *Prisoner of Second Avenue, The; Save the Tiger; Short Cuts; Some Like It Hot; 'That's Life'; Tribute; Wackiest Ship in the Army, The.*

Lewis, Jerry *Arizona Dreaming; Artists and Models; Bellboy, The; Big Mouth, The; Cinderfella; Cookie; Delicate Delinquent, The; Disorderly Orderly, The; Family Jewels, The; Funny Bones; Geisha Boy, The; Hollywood or Bust; It's Only Money; King of Comedy, The; Ladies' Man, The; Nutty Professor, The* (Lewis); *Pardners; Patsy, The; Rock-a-Bye Baby; 3 Ring Circus; Which Way to the Front? (aka Ja, Ja, Mein General! But Which Way to the Front?).*

Lloyd, Harold *Cat's-Paw, The; Feet First; Girl Shy; Grandma's Boy; Kid Brother, The; Movie Crazy; Safety Last; Sin of Harold Diddlebock, The (aka Mad Wednesday); Speedy; Why Worry?.*

Lollobrigida, Gina *Bad Man's River (El Hombre del Rio Malo); Beat the Devil; Belles de nuit, Les (Beauties of the Night/Night Beauties); Buona Sera, Mrs Campbell; Città si Difende, La (Four Ways Out); Go Naked in the World; Hunchback of Notre Dame, The (Notre Dame de Paris); King, Queen, Knave (Herzbube); Never So Few; Solomon and Sheba; Woman of Straw.*

Lombard, Carole *Bolero* (Ruggles); *Hands Across the Table; In Name Only; Mr and Mrs Smith; My Man Godfrey; No Man of Her Own; Nothing Sacred; Rumba; Supernatural; They Knew What They Wanted; To Be or Not To Be* (Lubitsch); *True Confession; Twentieth Century.*

Loren, Sophia *Arabesque; Black Orchid, The; Boccaccio '70; Brass Target; Cassandra Crossing; Cinderella – Italian Style (C'era una Volta); Countess from Hong Kong, A; Desire Under the Elms; El Cid; Fall of the Roman Empire, The; Firepower; Heller in Pink Tights; Houseboat; It Started in Naples; Judith; Key, The; Lady L; Legend of the Lost; Millionairess, The; Operation Crossbow; Pride and the Passion, The; Ready to Wear (aka Prêt-à-Porter); Special Day, A (Una Giornata Particolare); Sunflower (I Girasoli); Verdict (The Verdict).*

Lorre, Peter *All Through the Night; Arsenic and Old Lace; Background to Danger; Beast With Five Fingers, The; Beat the Devil; Big Circus, The; Black Angel; Boogie Man Will Get You, The; Casablanca; Comedy of Terrors, The; Confidential Agent; Congo Crossing; Conspirators, The; Crack-Up* (St Clair); *Crime and Punishment* (von Sternberg); *Face Behind the Mask, The; In This Our Life; Lancer Spy; M* (Lang); *Mad Love (aka The Hands of Orlac); Maltese Falcon, The; Man Who Knew Too Much, The* (1934); *Mask of Dimitrios, The; Mr Moto's Gamble; My Favourite Brunette; No Answer from F.P.1 (F.P.1 antwortet nicht); Passage to Marseille; Patsy, The; Raven, The* (Corman); *Secret Agent, The; Silk Stockings; Strange Cargo; Stranger on the Third Floor, The; Tales of Terror; 20000 Leagues Under the Sea; Verdict, The* (Siegel); *Verlorene, Der (The Lost One); You'll Find Out.*

Loy, Myrna *After the Thin Man; Airport 1975; April Fools, The; Best Years of Our Lives, The; Broadway Bill (aka Strictly Confidential); Cheaper by the Dozen; End, The; From the Terrace; Girl in Every Port, A; I Love You Again; Lonelyhearts; Love Crazy; Love Me Tonight; Manhattan Melodrama; Mask of Fu Manchu, The; Mr Blandings Builds His Dream House; Noah's Ark; Rains Came, The; Senator Was Indiscreet, The; Stamboul Quest; Thin Man, The; Too Hot to Handle.*

Lugosi, Bela *Abbott and Costello Meet Frankenstein (aka Abbott and Costello Meet the Ghosts); Black Cat, The (aka House of Doom); Black Cat, The* (Rogell); *Body Snatcher, The; Dark Eyes of London (aka The Human Monster); Dracula* (Browning); *Frankenstein Meets the Wolf Man; Ghost of Frankenstein, The; Glen or Glenda? (aka I Led Two Lives/I Changed My Sex); International House; Invisible Ray, The; Island of Lost Souls; Mark of the Vampire; Murders in the Rue Morgue* (Florey); *Ninotchka; Plan 9 from Outer Space; Raven, The* (Friedlander/Landers); *Return of the Vampire, The; Son of Frankenstein; Voodoo Man; White Zombie; Wolf Man, The; You'll Find Out.*

McCrea, Joel *Banjo on My Knee; Barbary Coast; Colorado Territory; Come and Get It; Dead End; Foreign Correspondent; Great Moment, The; Lone Hand, The; Lost Squadron, The; More the Merrier, The; Most Dangerous Game, The (aka The Hounds of Zaroff); Mustang Country; Palm Beach Story, The; Primrose Path, The; Ramrod; Ride the High Country (aka Guns in the Afternoon); Rough Shoot (aka Shoot First); South of St Louis; Sullivan's Travels; These Three; They Passed This Way (aka Four Faces West); Unseen, The; Wichita.*

MacLaine, Shirley *Apartment, The; Around the World in 80 Days; Artists and Models; Ask Any Girl; Being There; Bliss of Mrs Blossom, The; Can-Can; Cannonball Run II; Celluloid Closet, The; Change of Seasons, A; Career; Evening Star, The; Gambit; Guarding Tess; Irma la Douce; Loving Couples; Madame Sousatzka; Mrs Winterbourne; Ocean's 11* (Milestone); *Possession of Joel Delaney, The; Robe, The; Sheepman, The; Some Came Running; Steel Magnolias; Sweet Charity; Terms of Endearment; Trouble with Harry, The; Turning Point, The; Two Mules for Sister Sara; Used People; Waiting for the Light; Wrestling Ernest Hemingway.*

MacMurray, Fred *Above Suspicion; Alice Adams; Apartment, The; At Gunpoint (aka Gunpoint); Caine Mutiny, The; Dive Bomber; Double Indemnity; Hands Across the Table; Happiest Millionaire, The; Miracle of the Bells, The; Murder, He Says; Rains of Ranchipur, The; Remember the Night; Smoky; Swarm, The; Texas Rangers, The; There's Always Tomorrow; True Confession; Woman's World.*

McQueen, Steve *Baby the Rain Must Fall; Blob, The* (Yeaworth); *Bullitt; Cincinnati Kid, The; Enemy of the People, An* (Schaefer); *Getaway, The* (Peckinpah); *Great Escape, The; Hell Is for Heroes; Hunter, The; Junior Bonner; Le Mans; Love With the Proper Stranger; Magnificent Seven, The; Never So Few; On Any Sunday; Papillon; Reivers, The; Sand Pebbles, The; Somebody Up There Likes Me; Thomas Crown Affair, The* (Jewison); *Tom Horn; Towering Inferno, The.*

Magnani, Anna *Amore, L'; Bellissima; Fellini's Roma (Roma); Fugitive Kind, The; Golden Coach, The (La Carrozza d'Oro/Le Carrosse d'Or); Mamma Roma; Roma, Città Aperta (Open City/Rome, Open City); Secret of Santa Vittoria, The.*

March, Fredric *Adventures of Mark Twain, The* (Rapper); *Affairs of Cellini, The; Alexander the Great, The* (Rossen); *Anna Karenina* (Brown); *Anthony Adverse; Barretts of Wimpole Street, The; Best Years of Our Lives, The; Bridges at Toko-Ri, The; Christopher Columbus; Dark Angel, The; Design for Living; Desperate Hours, The; Dr Jekyll and Mr Hyde* (Mamoulian); *Executive Suite; Hombre; I Married a Witch; Inherit the Wind; Laughter; Les Misérables; Mary of Scotland; Merrily We Go to Hell; Nothing Sacred; Road to Glory, The; Seven Days in May; Sign of the Cross, The; Star Is Born, A* (Wellman);

Victory (Cromwell); *We Live Again; Wild Party, The* (Arzner).

Martin, Steve *All of Me; And the Band Played On; Bowfinger; Dead Men Don't Wear Plaid; Dirty Rotten Scoundrels; Fantasia/2000 (aka Fantasia 2000); Father of the Bride* (Shyer); *Father of the Bride Part II; Grand Canyon; Housesitter; Jerk, The; Joe Gould's Secret; Kids Are Alright, The; L.A. Story; Leap of Faith; Little Shop of Horrors* (Oz); *Man with Two Brains, The; Movers and Shakers; Muppet Movie, The; My Blue Heaven; Novocaine; Out-of-Towners, The* (Weisman); *Parenthood; Pennies from Heaven; Planes, Trains & Automobiles; Roxanne; Sgt Bilko; Sgt. Pepper's Lonely Hearts Club Band; Simple Twist of Fate, A; Spanish Prisoner, The; ¡Three Amigos!*

Marvin, Lee *Attack; Avalanche Express; Bad Day at Black Rock; Big Heat, The; Big Red One, The; Caine Mutiny, The; Cat Ballou; Delta Force, The; Dirty Dozen, The; Donovan's Reef; Duel at Silver Creek, The; Emperor of the North Pole, The (aka Emperor of the North); Gorky Park; Great Scout & Cathouse Thursday, Gun Fury; The; Hell in the Pacific; I Died a Thousand Times; Killers, The* (Siegel); *Klansman, The; Man Who Shot Liberty Valance, The; Monte Walsh; Not As a Stranger; Paint Your Wagon; Pete Kelly's Blues; Pocket Money; Point Blank; Prime Cut; Professionals, The; Raid, The; Raintree County; Seven Men from Now; Ship of Fools; Shout at the Devil; Spikes Gang, The; Violent Saturday; Wild One, The.*

Marx Brothers, *Animal Crackers; At the Circus; Big Store, The; Cocoanuts, The; Day at the Races, A; Duck Soup; Go West* (Buzzell); *Horse Feathers; Love Happy; Monkey Business* (McLeod); *Mr Music; Night at the Opera, A; Night in Casablanca, A; Room Service.*

Mason, James *Age of Consent; Autobiography of a Princess; Bad Man's River (El Hombre del Rio Malo); Bells Go Down, The; Bigger Than Life; Bloodline (aka Sidney Sheldon's Bloodline); Blue Max, The; Botany Bay; Boys from Brazil, The; Caught; Child's Play* (Lumet); *Cold Sweat (De la Part des Copains); Cross of Iron; Dangerous Summer, A; Deadly Affair, The; Desert Fox, The (aka Rommel – Desert Fox); Duffy; 11 Harrowhouse; Escape from Zahrain; Evil Under the Sun; Fall of the Roman Empire, The; Fire Over England; 5 Fingers; Frankenstein: The True Story; Georgy Girl; Great Expectations* (Hardy); *Hatter's Castle; Heaven Can Wait* (Beatty/Henry); *Inside Out; Island in the Sun; Journey to the Centre of the Earth; Julius Caesar; Last of Sheila, The; Lolita* (Kubrick); *Lord Jim; Mackintosh Man, The; Man Between, The; Mandingo; Marseille Contract, The; Murder by Decree; Night Has Eyes, The (aka Terror House); North by Northwest; North Sea Hijack; Odd Man Out; Pandora and the Flying Dutchman; Passage, The; Place of One's Own, A; Prisoner of Zenda, The* (Thorpe); *Pumpkin Eater, The; Reckless Moment, The; Salem's Lot; Sea Gull, The; Seventh Veil, The; Shooting Party, The; Spring and Port Wine; Star Is Born, A* (Cukor); *They Were Sisters; Thunder Rock; Tiara Tahiti; 20000 Leagues Under the Sea; Verdict, The* (Lumet); *Voyage of the Damned; Water Babies, The; Wicked Lady, The* (Arliss); *Yellowbeard.*

Mastroianni, Marcello *Allonsanfan; Bee Keeper, The (O Melissokomos); Beyond the Door (Oltre la Porta); Blow-Out (La Grande Bouffe); By Nightfall (Verso sera); Casanova '70; City of Women (La Città delle Donne); Dark Eyes (Oci Ciornie); Dolce Vita, La (The Sweet Life); Down the Ancient Stairs (Per le Antiche Scale); Dramma della Gelosia (Jealousy, Italian Style/The Pizza Triangle); 8½ (Otto e Mezzo); Everybody's Fine (Stanno tutti bene); Gabriela; Ginger & Fred (Ginger e Fred); Intervista; Journey to the Beginning of the World (Viagem ao pricipio do mundo/Voyage au début du monde); Leo the Last; Macaroni (Maccheroni); Massacre in Rome (Rappresaglia); Notte, La; Ready to Wear (aka Prêt-à-Porter); Slightly Pregnant Man, The (L'Événement le plus Important depuis que l'Homme a Marché sur la Lune); Soliti Ignoti, I (Big Deal on Madonna Street/Persons Unknown); Special Day, A (Una Giornata Particolare); Splendor; Sunflower (I Girasoli); That Night in Varennes (La Nuit de Varennes); Trois Vies et une Seule Mort (Three Lives and Only One Death); Un Deux Trois Soleil (1, 2, 3, Sun); Used People; Vie Privée (A Very Private Affair); We Don't Want to Talk About It (De eso no se Habla); What? (Che?); White Nights (Le Notti Bianche); Wifemistress (Mogliamante).*

Matthau, Walter *Bad News Bears, The; Bigger Than Life; Buddy Buddy; California Suite; Candy; Casey's Shadow; Charade; Charley Varrick; Couch Trip, The; Dennis the Menace (aka Dennis); Earthquake; Ensign Pulver; Face in the Crowd, A; Fail Safe; First Monday in October; Fortune Cookie, The (aka Meet Whiplash Willie); Front Page, The* (Wilder); *Grass Harp, The; Grumpy Old Men; Guide for the Married Man, A; Hanging Up; Hello, Dolly!; Hopscotch; House Calls; Indian Fighter, The; I Ought to Be in Pictures; JFK; Kentuckian, The; King Creole; Kotch; Laughing Policeman, The (aka An Investigation of Murder); Little Miss Marker; Lonely Are the Brave; Mirage; Movers and Shakers; New Leaf, A; Odd Couple, The; Odd Couple II, The (aka Neil Simon's The Odd Couple II); Pete'n'Tillie; Pirates; Plaza Suite; Secret Life of an American Wife, The; Strangers When We Meet; Sunshine Boys, The; Survivors, The; Taking of Pelham One Two Three, The.*

Mature, Victor *After the Fox (Caccia alla Volpe); Androcles and the Lion; Big Circus, The; Cry of the City; Dangerous Mission; Demetrius and the Gladiators; Easy Living* (Tourneur); *Every Little Crook and Nanny; Head; I Wake Up Screaming (aka Hot Spot); Kiss of Death* (Hathaway); *Las Vegas Story, The; Moss Rose; My Darling Clementine; Samson and Delilah; Shanghai Gesture, The; Violent Saturday.*

Mifune, Toshiro *Bad Sleep Well, The (Warui Yatsu Hodo Yoko Nemuru); Challenge, The; Grand Prix; Hell in the Pacific; Hidden Fortress, The (Kakushi Toride no San-Akunin); High and Low (Tengoku to Jigoku); Idiot, The (Hakuchi); I Live in Fear (Ikimono no Kiroku); The Life of Oharu (Saikaku Ichidai Onna); Lost World of Sinbad, The (Daitozoku); Lower Depths, The (Donzoko); Midway (aka Battle of Midway); Miyamoto Musashi (Musashi Miyamoto); 1941; Paper Tiger; Picture Bride; Rashomon; Rebellion (Joi-Uchi); Red Beard (Akahige); Red Sun (Soleil Rouge); Sanjuro (Tsubaki Sanjuro); Seven Samurai (Shichinin no Samurai); Shogun; Stray Dog (Nora Inu); Sword of Doom, The (Daibosatu Toge); Throne of Blood (Kumonosu-jo); Yojimbo.*

Milland, Ray *Aces High; Alias Nick Beal (aka The Contact Man); Arise, My Love; Battlestar Galactica; Beau Geste; Big Clock, The; Bolero* (Ruggles); *Bugles in the Afternooon; Bulldog Drummond Escapes; Circle of Deceit; Dial M for Murder; Easy Living* (Leisen); *Escape to Witch Mountain; French Without Tears; Frogs; Game for Vultures; Gold; House in Nightmare Park, The; Kitty; Lady in the Dark; Last Tycoon, The; Lost Weekend, The; Love Story* (Hiller); *Major and the Minor, The; Man Alone, A; Ministry of Fear; Night into Morning; Oliver's Story; Panic in Year Zero; Piccadilly; Premature Burial, The; Rhubarb; River's Edge, The; Slavers; So Evil My Love; Starflight: The Plane That Couldn't Land (aka Starflight One); Swiss Conspiracy, The; Thief, The; Thing With Two Heads, The; Uncanny, The; Uninvited, The; X – the Man with X-Ray Eyes (aka The Man with the X-Ray Eyes).*

Mills, John *Above Us the Waves; Africa – Texas Style; Bean; Big Blockade, The; Big Sleep, The* (Winner); *Black Sheep of Whitehall, The; Chuka; Colditz Story, The; Cottage to Let (aka Bombsight Stolen); Deadly Advice; Devil's Advocate, The (Des Teufels Advokat); Dulcima; Dunkirk; Flame in the Streets; Forever England (aka Bound for Glory/Brown on Resolution); Gandhi; Gentle Gunman, The; Ghost Camera, The; Goodbye, Mr Chips* (Wood); *Great Expectations* (Lean); *Grotesque, The (aka Gentlemen Don't Eat Poets); Hamlet* (Branagh); *History of Mr Polly, The; Hobson's Choice; Human Factor, The* (Dmytryk); *Ice Cold in Alex; In Which We Serve; It's Great to Be Young; I Was Monty's Double; King Rat; Lady Caroline Lamb; Long Memory, The; Morning Departure (aka Operation Disaster); October Man, The; O.H.M.S. (aka You're in the Army Now); Oh! What a Lovely War; Oklahoma Crude; Operation Crossbow; Rocking Horse Winner, The; Ryan's Daughter; Sahara* (McLaglen); *Scott of the Antarctic; Singer Not the Song, The; Thirty-Nine Steps, The* (Sharp); *Tiara Tahiti; Tiger Bay; This Happy Breed; Trial by Combat (aka A Choice of Weapons/Dirty Knight's Work); Tunes of Glory; War and Peace* (Vidor); *Waterloo Road; Way to the Stars, The (aka Johnny in the Clouds); Who's That Girl; Young Winston; Young Mr Pitt, The; Zulu Dawn.*

Mitchum, Robert *Agency (aka Mind Games); Ambassador, The; Amsterdam Kill, The; Angel Face; Bandido!; Big Sleep, The* (Winner); *Big Steal, The* (Siegel); *Blood on the Moon; Cape Fear* (Thompson); *Cape Fear* (Scorsese); *Crossfire; Dead Man; El Dorado; Enemy*

Below, The; Farewell, My Lovely (Richards); *5 Card Stud; Friends of Eddie Coyle, The; Good Guys and the Bad Guys, The; Grass Is Greener, The; Heaven Knows, Mr Allison; His Kind of Woman; Home from the Hill; Hunters, The; Last Tycoon, The; List of Adrian Messenger, The; Locket, The; Longest Day, The; Lusty Men, The; Macao; Maria's Lovers; Midway (aka Battle of Midway); Mr North; My Forbidden Past; Night of the Hunter, The; Not As a Stranger; One Minute to Zero; Out of the Past (aka Build My Gallows High); Pursued; Rachel and the Stranger; Racket, The; Rampage; River of No Return; Ryan's Daughter; Sbarco di Anzio, Lo (Anzio/The Battle for Anzio); Scrooged; Second Chance* (Maté); *Secret Ceremony; Story of GI Joe, The; Sundowners, The; Terrible Beauty, A (aka Night Fighters); That Championship Season; Thunder Road; Track of the Cat; Undercurrent; Villa Rides!; Way West, The; When Strangers Marry (aka Betrayed); Where Danger Lives; Wild Bill: A Hollywood Maverick; Wonderful Country, The; Yakuza, The.*

Monroe, Marilyn *All About Eve; Asphalt Jungle, The; Bus Stop; Clash By Night; Don't Bother to Knock* (Baker); *Gentlemen Prefer Blondes; How to Marry a Millionaire; Ladies of the Chorus; Let's Make Love; Love Happy; Misfits, The; Monkey Business* (Hawks); *Niagara; O. Henry's Full House (aka Full House); Prince and the Showgirl, The; River of No Return; Seven Year Itch, The; Some Like It Hot; There's No Business Like Show Business; Ticket to Tomahawk, A.*

Montand, Yves *Aveu, L' (The Confession); César and Rosalie (César et Rosalie); Etoile sans Lumière (Star Without Light); Grand Prix; Guerre est finie, La (The War Is Over); IP5; Jean de Florette; Let's Make Love; Manon des Sources; Mister Freedom; Napoléon* (Guitry); *On a Clear Day You Can See Forever; Portes de la Nuit, Les (Gates of the Night); Red Circle, The (Le Cercle Rouge); Sanctuary; Sauvage, Le; Sleeping Car Murder, The (Compartiment Tueurs); Soir, un Train, Un; State of Siege (Etat de Siège); Tout Va Bien; Trois Places pour le 26 (Three Seats for the 26th); Vivre pour Vivre (Live for Life); Wages of Fear, The (Le Salaire de la Peur); Z.*

Moreau, Jeanne *Alex in Wonderland; Amants, Les (The Lovers); Ascenseur pour l'Echafaud (Frantic/Lift to the Scaffold); Baie des Anges, La (Bay of Angels); Bride Wore Black, The (La Mariée était en Noir); Chère Louise (Louise); Chimes at Midnight (Campanadas a Medianoche); Dialogue des Carmélites, Le; Diary of a Chambermaid, The (Le Journal d'une Femme de Chambre); Eve; Ever After; Femme est une Femme, Une (A Woman Is a Woman); Feu Follet, Le (A Time to Live and a Time to Die/The Fire Within/Fox Fire/Will o'the Wisp); Immortal Story, The (Histoire Immortelle); Jules and Jim (Jules et Jim); Last Tycoon, The; Liaisons Dangereuses 1960, Les; Mademoiselle; Map of the Human Heart; Mata-Hari, Agent H.21; Mr Klein; Monte Walsh; Nathalie Granger; Nikita; Notte, La; Old Lady Who Walked in the Sea, The (La Vieille qui Marchait dans la Mer); Paltoquet, Le; Petit Théâtre de Jean Renoir, Le (The Little Theatre of Jean Renoir); Proprietor, The (Le Propriétaire); Querelle; Sailor from Gibraltar, The; Touchez pas au Grisbi (Grisbi/Honour Among Thieves); Train, The; Trial, The (Le Procès); Trout, The (La Truite); Univers de Jacques Demy, L'; Until the End of the World (Bis ans Ende der Welt); Valseuses, Les (Going Places/Making It); Victors, The; Viva Maria!.*

Mui, Anita *Au revoir, mon amour (He Rijun Zai Lai); Eighteen Springs (Ban Sheng Yuan); Heroic Trio, The (Dongfang San Xia); July Rhapsody (Nanren Sishi); Kawashima Yoshiko (Chuandao Fangzi/aka The Last Princess of Manchuria); Moon Warriors; Rouge (Inji Kau); Rumble in the Bronx (Hongfan Qu).*

Muni, Paul *Black Fury; Bordertown; Good Earth, The; Hi, Nellie!; I Am a Fugitive from a Chain Gang; Juarez; Life of Emile Zola, The; Scarface* (Hawks); *Song to Remember, A; We Are Not Alone.*

Murphy, Eddie *Another 48 HRS; Best Defence; Beverly Hills Cop; Beverly Hills Cop II; Beverly Hills Cop III; Boomerang* (Hudlin); *Bowfinger; Coming to America; Distinguished Gentleman, The; Doctor Dolittle; Dr Dolittle 2; 48 HRS; Golden Child, The; Harlem Nights; Holy Man; Life; Metro; Nutty Professor, The* (Shadyac); *Nutty Professor II: The Klumps; Showtime; Trading Places; Vampire in Brooklyn.*

Murray, Bill *Caddyshack; Charlie's Angels; Cradle Will Rock; Ed Wood; Ghostbusters; Ghostbusters II; Groundhog Day; Hamlet* (Almereyda); *Kingpin; Larger Than Life; Little Shop of Horrors* (Oz); *Mad Dog and Glory; Meatballs; Next Stop, Greenwich Village; Nothing Lasts Forever; Osmosis Jones; Quick Change; Royal Tenenbaums, The; Rushmore; Scrooged; She's Having a Baby; Space Jam; Stripes; Tootsie; What About Bob?; Where the Buffalo Roam; Wild Things.*

Newman, Paul *Absence of Malice; Blaze; Buffalo Bill and the Indians, or Sitting Bull's History Lesson; Butch Cassidy and the Sundance Kid; Cat on a Hot Tin Roof; Color of Money, The; Cool Hand Luke; Drowning Pool, The; Exodus; Fat Man and Little Boy (aka Shadow Makers); Fort Apache, the Bronx; From the Terrace; Harper (aka The Moving Target); Harry & Son; Hombre; Hud; Hudsucker Proxy, The; Hustler, The; Lady L; Left-Handed Gun, The; Life and Times of Judge Roy Bean, The; Long, Hot Summer, The; Mackintosh Man, The; Message in a Bottle; Mr and Mrs Bridge; New Kind of Love, A; Nobody's Fool; Pocket Money; Quintet; Rally 'round the Flag, Boys!; Slap Shot; Somebody Up There Likes Me; Sometimes a Great Notion (aka Never Give an Inch); Sting, The; Sweet Bird of Youth; Torn Curtain; Towering Inferno, The; Twilight; Verdict, The* (Lumet); *When Time Ran Out; Where the Money Is; W USA.*

Nicholson, Jack *About Schmidt; As Good As It Gets; Back Door to Hell; Batman; Blood and Wine; Border, The; Broadcast News; Carnal Knowledge; Chinatown; Crossing Guard, The; Easy Rider; Evening Star, The; Few Good Men, A; Five Easy Pieces; Fortune, The; Goin' South; Head; Heartburn; Hell's Angels on Wheels; Hoffa; Ironweed; King of Marvin Gardens, The; Last Detail, The; Last Tycoon, The; Little Shop of Horrors, The* (Corman); *Man Trouble; Mars Attacks!; Missouri Breaks, The; On a Clear Day You Can See Forever; One Flew Over the Cuckoo's Nest; Passenger, The (Professione: Reporter); Pledge, The; Postman Always Rings Twice, The* (Rafelson); *Prizzi's Honor; Psych-Out; Raven, The* (Corman); *Rebel Rousers; Reds; Ride in the Whirlwind; Safe Place, A; Shining, The; Shooting, The; Terms of Endearment; Terror, The; Tommy; Two Jakes, The; Witches of Eastwick, The; Wolf.*

Niven, David *Appointment with Venus (aka Island Rescue); Around the World in 80 Days; Ask Any Girl; Bachelor Mother; Before Winter Comes; Beloved Enemy; Better Late Than Never; Birds and the Bees, The; Bishop's Wife, The; Bluebeard's Eighth Wife; Bonjour Tristesse; Candleshoe; Carringto VC (aka Court Martial); Casino Royale; Charge of the Light Brigade, The* (Curtiz); *Curse of the Pink Panther; Dawn Patrol, The; Death on the Nile; Elusive Pimpernel, The; Escape to Athena; 55 Days at Peking; First of the Few (aka Spitfire); Four Men and a Prayer; Guns of Darkness; Guns of Navarone, The; Happy Ever After (aka Tonight's the Night); King, Queen, Knave (Herzbube); Lady L; Little Hut, The; Love Lottery, The; Magnificent Doll; Matter of Life and Death, A (aka Stairway to Heaven); Moon Is Blue, The; Murder by Death; My Man Godfrey* (Koster); *No Deposit, No Return; Oh, Men! Oh, Women!; Paper Tiger; Pink Panther, The; Please Don't Eat the Daisies; Prisoner of Zenda, The* (Cromwell); *Real Glory, The; Rough Cut; Sea Wolves, The; Thank You, Jeeves!; Toast of New Orleans, The; Trail of the Pink Panther; Vampira (aka Old Dracula); Way Ahead, The; Wuthering Heights* (Wyler).

Noiret, Philippe *Alexandre (Alexandre le Bienheureux); Assassination Bureau, The; Attentat, L' (Plot); Blow-Out (La Grande Bouffe); Bossu, Le (On Guard!); Cinema Paradiso (Nuovo Cinema Paradiso); Cinema Paradiso: The Special Edition; Clean Slate (Coup de Torchon); Contre l'Oubli (Against Oblivion); Dear Inspector (Tendre Poulet); Désert des Tartares, Le; Etoile du Nord, L' (The Northern Star); Fille de D'Artagnan, La (D'Artagnan's Daughter); Grosse Fatigue; Horloger de St Paul, L' (The Clockmaker/The Watchmaker of Saint-Paul); J'embrasse pas (I Don't Kiss); Justine* (Cukor); *Lady L; Le Cop (Les Ripoux); Le Cop 2 (Ripoux contre ripoux); Let's Hope It's a Girl (Speriamo che sia Femmina); Life and Nothing But (La Vie et Rien d'autre); Masques; Mister Freedom; Murphy's War; Night of the Generals, The; Postino, Il (The Postman); Purple Taxi, The (Le Taxi Mauve); Que la Fête Commence (Let Joy Reign Supreme); Return of the Musketeers, The; 'Round Midnight (Autour de Minuit); Secret, The (Le Secret); Semaine de Vacances, Une (A Week's Holiday); Serpent, The (Le Serpent); Tango; Three Brothers (Tre Fratelli); Time for Loving; Topaz; Touche pas à la femme blanche (Don't Touch the White Woman); Uranus; Who Are*

You Polly Maggoo? (Qui êtes-vous Polly Maggoo?); Who Is Killing the Great Chefs of Europe? (aka Too Many Chefs); Zazie dans le Métro.

Nolte, Nick *Affliction; Afterglow; Another 48 HRS; Blue Chips; Breakfast of Champions; Cannery Row; Cape Fear* (Scorsese); *Deep, The; Down and Out in Beverly Hills; Everybody Wins; Extreme Prejudice; Farewell to the King; 48 HRS; Golden Bowl, The; Grace Quigley; Heart Beat; I Love Trouble; Jefferson in Paris; Lorenzo's Oil; Mother Night; Mulholland Falls; New York Stories; Nightwatch* (Bornedal – 1998); *North Dallas Forty; Prince of Tides, The; Q & A; Simpatico; Teachers; Thin Red Line, The; Three Fugitives; Under Fire; Who'll Stop the Rain? (aka Dog Soldiers).*

Oates, Warren *Badlands; Barquero; Blue Thunder; Border, The; Bring Me the Head of Alfredo Garcia; Brink's Job, The; China 9, Liberty 37; Cockfighter; Dillinger* (Milius); *Dixie Dynamite; Drum; Hired Hand, The; In the Heat of the Night; Kid Blue; Major Dundee; 1941; 92 in the Shade; Race with the Devil; Return of the Seven (aka Return of the Magnificent Seven); Ride the High Country (aka Guns in the Afternoon); Rise and Fall of Legs Diamond, The; Shooting, The; Sleeping Dogs; Split, The; Stripes; There Was a Crooked Man…; Tom Sawyer; Two-Lane Blacktop; U Turn; Welcome to Hard Times (aka Killer on a Horse); White Dawn, The; Wild Bunch, The.*

O'Hara, Maureen *Battle of the Villa Fiorita, The; Big Jake; Black Swan, The; Dance, Girl, Dance; How Green Was My Valley; Hunchback of Notre Dame, The* (Dieterle); *Immortal Sergeant, The; Jamaica Inn; Kangaroo* (Milestone); *Little Romance, A; Long Gray Line, The; Mr Hobbs Takes a Vacation; Only the Lonely; Our Man in Havana; Quiet Man, The; Rare Breed, The; Rio Grande; Sentimental Journey; Sitting Pretty; Spanish Main, The; This Land Is Mine; Wings of Eagles, The; Woman's Secret, A.*

Olivier, Laurence *As You Like It* (Czinner); *Battle of Britain; Beggar's Opera, The; Betsy, The; Bounty, The; Boys from Brazil, The; Bridge Too Far, A; Bunny Lake Is Missing; Carrie* (Wyler); *Clash of the Titans; Demi-Paradise, The (aka Adventure for Two); Divorce of Lady X, The; Dracula* (Badham); *Entertainer, The; Fire Over England; 49th Parallel; Hamlet* (Olivier); *Henry V* (Olivier); *Jazz Singer, The; Khartoum; Lady Caroline Lamb; Love Among the Ruins; Magic Box, The; Marathon Man; Nicholas and Alexandra; Oh! What a Lovely War; Othello* (Burge); *Pride and Prejudice; Prince and the Showgirl, The; Rebecca; Richard III* (Olivier); *Seven-Per-Cent Solution, The; Shoes of the Fisherman, The; Sleuth; Spartacus; Term of Trial; That Hamilton Woman (aka Lady Hamilton); Three Sisters* (Olivier); *Wagner; War Requiem; Wild Geese II; Wuthering Heights* (Wyler).

O'Toole, Peter *Bible…In the Beginning, The (La Bibbia); Caligula; Country Dance (aka Brotherly Love); Creator; FairyTale – A True Story; Goodbye, Mr Chips* (Ross); *High Spirits; Isabelle Eberhardt; King Ralph; Last Emperor, The; Lawrence of Arabia; Lion in Winter, The; Lord Jim; Man Friday; Masada (aka The Antagonists); Molokai: The Story of Father Damien; Murphy's War; My Favorite Year; Night of the Generals, The; Power Play; Rebecca's Daughters; Rosebud; Ruling Class, The; Savage Innocents, The; Stunt Man, The; Supergirl; Under Milk Wood; What's New Pussycat?; Wings of Fame; Zulu Dawn.*

Pacino, Al *…and justice for all; Any Given Sunday; Author! Author!; Bobby Deerfield; Carlito's Way; City Hall; Cruising; Devil's Advocate, The; Dick Tracy; Dog Day Afternoon; Donnie Brasco; Frankie & Johnny; Glengarry Glen Ross; Godfather, The; Godfather Part II, The; Godfather Part III, The; Heat* (Mann); *Insider, The; Looking for Richard; Panic in Needle Park, The; Revolution; Scarecrow; Scarface* (De Palma); *Scent of a Woman; Sea of Love; Serpico.*

Palance, Jack *Alone in the Dark; Attack!; Austerlitz (aka The Battle of Austerlitz); Bagdad Café (aka Out of Rosenheim); Barabbas (Barabba); Batman; Big Knife, The; Chato's Land; Che!; City Slickers; City Slickers II: The Legend of Curly's Gold; Companeros (Vamos a Matar, Companeros!); Craze; Dracula* (Curtis); *Hawk the Slayer; Horsemen, The; I Died a Thousand Times; Mépris, Le (Contempt); Mercenario, Il (The Mercenary/A Professional Gun); Monte Walsh; Oklahoma Crude; Panic in the Streets; Professionals, The; Second Chance* (Maté); *Shane; Shape of Things to Come, The; Sign of the Pagan; Sudden Fear; Tango & Cash; Ten Seconds to Hell; They Came to Rob Las Vegas (Las Vegas 500 Millones); Torture Garden; Welcome to Blood City; Young Guns.*

Paltrow, Gwyneth *Bounce; Duets; Emma; Flesh and Bone; Great Expectations* (Cuarón); *Hard Eight; Hook; Jefferson in Paris; Malice; Moonlight and Valentino; Mrs Parker and the Vicious Circle; Perfect Murder, A; Royal Tenenbaums, The; Seven (aka Se7en)* (Fincher); *Shakespeare in Love; Shallow Hal; Shout; Sliding Doors; Talented Mr Ripley, The.*

Peck, Gregory *Amazing Grace and Chuck (aka Silent Voice); Arabesque; Beloved Infidel; Big Country, The; Billy Two Hats; Boys from Brazil, The; Bravados, The; Cape Fear* (Thompson); *Cape Fear* (Scorsese); *Captain Horatio Hornblower; Days of Glory; Designing Woman; Duel in the Sun; Gentleman's Agreement; Great Sinner, The; Gunfighter, The; Guns of Navarone, The; How the West Was Won; MacArthur – The Rebel General; Mackenna's Gold; Macomber Affair, The; Marooned; Million Pound Note, The (aka Man With a Million); Mirage; Moby Dick; Old Gringo; Omen, The; On the Beach; Other People's Money; Paradine Case, The; Pork Chop Hill; Roman Holiday; Sea Wolves, The; Snows of Kilimanjaro, The; Spellbound; To Kill a Mockingbird; Twelve O'Clock High; Yellow Sky; Wild Bill: A Hollwood Maverick.*

Penn, Sean *At Close Range; Bad Boys; Before Night Falls; Carlito's Way; Casualties of War; Colors; Crackers; Dead Man Walking; Falcon and the Snowman, The; Fast Times at Ridgemont High (aka Fast Times); Game, The; Hurly Burly; I Am Sam; Judgment in Berlin; Loved; Racing with the Moon; Shanghai Surprise; She's So Lovely; State of Grace; Sweet and Lowdown; Taps; Up at the Villa; U Turn; Weight of Water, The; We're No Angels.*

Perkins, Anthony *Actress, The; Black Hole, The; Catch-22; Champagne Murders, The (Le Scandale); Crimes of Passion; Desire Under the Elms; Edge of Sanity; Fear Strikes Out; Friendly Persuasion; In the Deep Woods; Life and Times of Judge Roy Bean, The; Lovin' Molly; Mahogany; Murder on the Orient Express; North Sea Hijack; On the Beach; Phaedra; Pretty Poison; Psycho* (Hitchcock); *Psycho II; Psycho III; Remember My Name; Ten Days' Wonder (La Décade Prodigieuse); Tin Star, The; Trial, The (Le Procès); Winter Kills; W USA.*

Pfeiffer, Michelle *Age of Innocence; Batman Returns; Dangerous Liaisons; Dangerous Minds; Deep End of the Ocean, The; Fabulous Baker Boys, The; Frankie & Johnny; Grease 2; I Am Sam; Into the Night; Ladyhawke; Love Field; Married to the Mob; Midsummer Night's Dream, A* (Hoffman); *One Fine Day; Russia House, The; Scarface* (De Palma); *Story of Us, The; Sweet Liberty; Tequila Sunrise; Thousand Acres, A; Up Close & Personal; What Lies Beneath; Witches of Eastwick, The; Wolf.*

Philipe, Gérard *Beauté du Diable, La (Beauty and the Devil); Belles de nuit, Les (Beauties of the Night/Night Beauties); Chartreuse de Parme, La; Diable au corps, Le (Devil in the Flesh); Fièvre Monte à El Pao, La (Republic of Sin); Grandes Manoeiuvres, Les (Summer Manoeuvres); Knave of Hearts (aka Lovers, Happy Lovers!/Monsieur Ripois); Liaisons Dangereuses 1960, Les; Orgueilleux, Les (The Proud Ones); Ronde, La; Si Jolie Petite Plage, Une (Such a Pretty Little Beach); Si Versailles m'était conté… (Versailles/Royal Affairs at Versailles).*

Piccoli, Michel *Adieu Bonaparte (Al-wedaa ya Bonaparte); Atlantic City (aka Atlantic City U.S.A.); Attentat, L' (Plot); Audience, The (L'Udienza); Belle de Jour; Belle Noiseuse, La; Belle Noiseuse – Divertimento, La; Beyond the Door (Oltre la Porta); Blow-Out (La Grande Bouffe); Choses de la Vie, Les (The Things of Life); Contre l'Oubli (Against Oblivion); Créatures, Les; Danger: Diabolik (Diabolik); Dangerous Moves (La Diagonale du Fou); Death in a French Garden (Péril en la Demeure); Demoiselles de Rochefort, Les (The Young Girls of Rochefort); Des Enfants Gâtés (Spoiled Children); Diary of a Chambermaid, The (Le Journal d'une Femme de Chambre); Doulos, Le (The Finger Man); Equilibristes, Les (Walking a Tightrope); Espion Lève-toi; Fantôme de la Liberté, Le (The Phantom of Liberty); French Cancan; Guerre est finie, La (The War Is Over); I'm Going Home (Vou Para Casa/Je Rentre à la Maison); Infernal Trio, The (Le Trio Infernal); Lady L; Last Woman, The (L'Ultima Donna); Leap into the Void (Salto nel Vuoto); Libero Burro; Life Size (Tamaño Natural); Masquerade* (Dearden); *Mauvais Sang (The Night Is Young); Mépris, Le*

(Contempt); Milou en mai (Milou in May); Mort en ce Jardin, La (Evil Eden); Noces Rouges, Les (Blood Wedding/ Red Wedding/Wedding in Blood); Paltoquet, Le; Passion; Passion in the Desert; Prize of Peril, The (Le Prix du Danger); Sleeping Car Murder, The (Compartiment Tueurs); Rien sur Robert; Success Is the Best Revenge; Ten Days' Wonder (La Décade Prodigieuse); Themroc; Topaz; Touche pas à la femme blanche (Don't Touch the White Woman); 2 x 50 Years of French Cinema; Univers de Jacques Demy, L'; Viva la Vie; Voie Lactée, La (The Milky Way).

Pitt, Brad *Cool World; Devil's Own, The; Fight Club; Happy Together* (Damski); *Interview With the Vampire; Johnny Suede; Kalifornia; Legends of the Fall; Meet Joe Black; Mexican, The; No Man's Land* (Werner); *Ocean's Eleven* (Soderbergh); *River Runs Through It, A; Seven (aka Se7en)* (Fincher); *Seven Years in Tibet; Sleepers; Snatch; Spy Game; Thelma & Louise; True Romance; 12 Monkeys.*

Poitier, Sidney *Bedford Incident, The; Blackboard Jungle, The; Buck and the Preacher; Defiant Ones, The; Duel at Diablo; Edge of the City (aka a Man is Ten Feet Tall); Greatest Story Ever Told, The; Guess Who's Coming to Dinner; In the Heat of the Night; Jackal, The; Let's Do It Again; Little Nikita (aka Sleepers); Long Ships; No Way Out* (Mankiewicz); *Organization, The; Patch of Blue, A; Piece of the Action, A; Shoot to Kill (aka Deadly Pursuit); Sneakers; Something of Value; They Call Me MISTER Tibbs!; To Sir, With Love; Uptown Saturday Night; Warm December, A; Wilby Conspiracy, The; Wild Bill: A Hollywood Maverick.*

Powell, Dick *Bad and the Beautiful, The; Christmas in July; Cornered; Cry Danger; Dames; Farewell, My Lovely (aka Murder My Sweet); Footlight Parade; 42nd Street; Gold Diggers of 1933; Gold Diggers of 1935; Gold Diggers of 1937; It Happened Tomorrow; Johnny O'Clock; Midsummer Night's Dream, A* (Reinhardt/Dieterle); *Naughty but Nice; Page Miss Glory; Pitfall; Susan Slept Here; Tall Target, The.*

Powell, William *After the Thin Man; Crossroads; How to Marry a Millionaire; I Love You Again; Kennel Murder Case, The; Last Command, The* (von Sternberg); *Life with Father; Love Crazy; Manhattan Melodrama; Mr Peabody and the Mermaid; Mister Roberts; My Man Godfrey* (La Cava); *Senator Was Indiscreet, The; Thin Man, The; Ziegfeld Follies.*

Power, Tyrone *American Guerilla in the Philippines; Black Swan, The; Blood and Sand* (Mamoulian); *Brigham Young – Frontiersman; Diplomatic Courier; In Old Chicago; Jesse James; Long Gray Line, The; Mark of Zorro, The; Nightmare Alley; Pony Soldier; Prince of Foxes; Rains Came, The; Rawhide (aka Desperate Siege); Razor's Edge, The; Rose of Washington Square; Suez; Sun Also Rises, The; Thin Ice (aka Lovely to Look at); This Above All; Untamed; Witness for the Prosecution; Yank in the RAF, A.*

Price, Vincent *Abominable Dr Phibes, The; Big Circus, The; Bloodbath at the House of Death; Bribe, The; Brigham Young – Frontiersman; Casanova's Big Night; Catchfire; City Under the Sea (aka War Gods of the Deep); Comedy of Terrors, The; Cry of the Banshee; Dangerous Mission; Dr Phibes Rises Again; Dragonwyck; Edward Scissorhands; Eve of St Mark, The; Fly, The* (Neumann); *Haunted Palace, The; His Kind of Woman; House of the Long Shadows, The; House of Usher, The (aka The Fall of the House of Usher); House of Wax; Invisible Man Returns, The; Las Vegas Story, The; Laura* (Preminger); *Leave Her to Heaven; Long Night, The; Madhouse* (Clark); *Mad Magician, The; Masque of the Red Death, The; Master of the World; Monster Club, The; Moss Rose; Oblong Box, The; Percy's Progress; Pit and the Pendulum, The; Private Lives of Elizabeth and Essex, The; Raven, The* (Corman); *Return of the Fly; Royal Scandal, A; Scream and Scream Again; Song of Bernadette, The; Tales of Terror; Ten Commandments, The; Theatre of Blood; Tingler, The; Tomb of Ligeia, The; Whales of August, The; While the City Sleeps; Wilson; Witchfinder General.*

Quinn, Anthony *Across 110th Street; Al-Risalah (The Message/Mohammed, Messenger of God); Back to Bataan; Barabbas (Barabba); Black Orchid, The; Black Swan, The; Blood and Sand* (Mamoulian); *Blowing Wild; Caravans; City Beneath the Sea; Deaf Smith & Johnny Ears (Los Amigos); Don Is Dead, The; Dream of Kings, A; East of Sumatra; Flap (aka The Last Warrior); From Russia to Hollywood: The 100-Year Odyssey of Chekhov and Shdanoff; Ghost Breakers, The; Gotti; Greek Tycoon, The; Guadalcanal Diary; Guns for San Sebastian (La Bataille de San Sebastian); Guns of Navarone, The; Happening, The; Heller in Pink Tights; High Risk; High Wind in Jamaica, A; Hunchback of Notre Dame, The (Notre Dame de Paris); Inheritance, The (L'Eredità Ferramonti); Jungle Fever; King of Alcatraz; Last Action Hero, The; Last Train from Gun Hill; Last Train from Madrid, The; Lawrence of Arabia; Lion of the Desert; Lust for Life; Magus, The; Marseille Contract, The; Mobsters (aka Mobsters – The Evil Empire); Only the Lonely; Ox-Bow Incident, The (aka Strange Incident); Passage, The; Plainsman, The; Revenge* (Scott); *River's Edge, The; Road to Morocco; Savage Innocents, The; Secret of Santa Vittoria, The; Shoes of the Fisherman, The; Somebody to Love; Strada, La (The Road); They Died With Their Boots On; Tigers Don't Cry; Viva Zapata!; Walk in the Clouds, A; Walk in the Spring Rain, A; Warlock* (Dmytryk); *Zorba the Greek.*

Rains, Claude *Adventures of Robin Hood, The; Anthony Adverse; Caesar and Cleopatra; Casablanca; Clairvoyant, The; Deception; Greatest Story Ever Told, The; Here Comes Mr Jordan; Invisible Man, The; Juarez; Kings Row; Lawrence of Arabia; Lost World, The; Man Who Watched Trains Go By, The (aka Paris Express); Mr Skeffington; Mr Smith Goes to Washington; Notorious; Now, Voyager; Passage to Marseille; Passionate Friends, The (aka One Woman's Story); Phantom of the Opera* (Lubin); *Saturday's Children; Sea Hawk, The; They Won't Forget; Unsuspected, The; Where Danger Lives; White Tower, The; Wolf Man, The.*

Rampling, Charlotte *Angel Heart; Asylum (Baker); Caravan to Vaccarès; Cherry Orchard, The; D.O.A.* (Morton); *Damned, The (La Caduta degli Dei/ Götterdämmerung); Farewell, My Lovely* (Richards); *Georgy Girl; Hammers Over the Anvil; He Died with His Eyes Open (On ne Meurt que Deux Fois); Henry VIII and His Six Wives; Knack…and how to get it, The; Mascara; Max Mon Amour (Max My Love); Night Porter, The (Il Portiere di Notte); Orca (aka Orca…Killer Whale); Paris by Night; Purple Taxi, The (Le Taxi Mauve); Rotten to the Core; Ski Bum, The; Stardust Memories; 'Tis Pity She's a Whore (Addio, Fratello Crudele); Verdict, The* (Lumet); *Viva la Vie; Under the Sand (Sous le Sable); Wings of the Dove, The; Zardoz.*

Reagan, Ronald *Angels Wash Their Faces, The; Boy Meets Girl* (Bacon); *Cattle Queen of Montana; Gringo in Mañanaland, A; Hellcats of the Navy; Killers, The* (Siegel); *Kings Row; Naughty but Nice; Santa Fe Trail; Tennessee's Partner.*

Redford, Robert *All the President's Men; Barefoot in the Park; Bridge Too Far, A; Brubaker; Butch Cassidy and the Sundance Kid; Candidate, The; Chase, The; Downhill Racer; Electric Horseman, The; Great Gatsby, The* (Clayton); *Great Waldo Pepper, The; Havana; Horse Whisperer, The; Hot Rock, The (aka How to Steal a Diamond in Four Uneasy Lessons); Indecent Proposal; Inside Daisy Clover; Jeremiah Johnson; Last Castle, The; Legal Eagles; Natural, The; Out of Africa; Sneakers; Spy Game; Sting, The; Tell Them Willie Boy Is Here; This Property Is Condemned; Three Days of the Condor; Up Close & Personal; Way We Were, The; Wild Bill: A Hollywood Maverick.*

Redgrave, Michael *Battle of Britain; Big Blockade, The; Browning Version, The; Captive Heart, The; Connecting Rooms; Dam Busters, The; Dead of Night; Fame Is the Spur; Go-Between, The; Goodbye, Mr Chips* (Ross); *Heroes of Telemark, The; Hill, The; Importance of Being Earnest, The; Innocents, The; Lady Vanishes, The* (Hitchcock); *Law and Disorder; Loneliness of the Long Distance Runner, The; Magic Box, The; Mr Arkadin (aka Confidential Report); Nicholas and Alexandra; Night My Number Came Up, The; Oh Rosalinda!!; Oh! What a Lovely War; Quiet American, The; Secret Agent, The; Secret Beyond the Door; Stars Look Down, The; Thunder Rock; Time Without Pity; Way to the Stars, The (aka Johnny in the Clouds); Young Cassidy.*

Redgrave, Vanessa *Agatha; Ballad of the Sad Café, The; Bear Island; Blow-Up; Bostonians, The; Camelot; Charge of the Light Brigade, The* (Richardson); *Comrades; Consuming Passions; Cradle Will Rock; Deep Impact; Déjà Vu; Devils, The; Girl, Interrupted; House of Spirits, The; Howards End; Isadora; Julia; Little Odessa; Looking for Richard; Man for all Seasons, A; Mary, Queen of Scots; Mission Impossible; Mrs Dalloway; Month by the Lake, A; Morgan, a Suitable Case for Treatment; Mother's Boys; Murder on the Orient Express; Oh! What a Lovely War; Out of Season; Pledge, The; Prick Up Your Ears;*

Sailor from Gibraltar, The; Sea Gull, The; Seven-Per-Cent Solution, The; Smilla's Feeling for Snow (Fräulein Smillas Gespür für Schnee/aka Smilla's Sense of Snow); Sparrow (Storia di una Capinera); Steaming; Wagner; Wetherby; Wilde; Yanks.

Reggiani, Serge *Amants de Vérone, Les (The Lovers of Verona); Armée des Ombres, L' (The Army in the Shadows); Bee Keeper, The (O Melissokomos); Casque d'Or (Golden Marie); Doulos, Le (The Finger Man); Etoile sans Lumière (Star Without Light); I Hired a Contract Killer; Leopard, The (Il Gattopardo); Napoléon* (Guitry); *Mauvais Sang (The Night Is Yours); Misérables, Les* (Le Chanois); *Portes de la Nuit, Les (Gates of the Night); Ronde, La; Secret People; Touche pas à la femme blanche (Don't Touch the White Woman); Violette et François.*

Reynolds, Burt *Angel Baby; At Long Last Love; Bean; Best Friends; Best Little Whorehouse in Texas, The; Boogie Nights; Breaking In; Cannonball Run, The; Cannonball Run II; City Heat; Deliverance; Driven; End, The; Cop and ½ (aka Cop and a Half); Everything You Always Wanted to Know About Sex, But Were Afraid to Ask; Gator; Hooper; Hotel; Hustle; Impasse; Longest Yard, The (aka The Mean Machine); Lucky Lady; Mad Dog Time (aka Trigger Happy); Man Who Loved Cat Dancing, The; Man Who Loved Women, The; Modern Love; Nickelodeon; Paternity; Physical Evidence; Rough Cut; Sam Whiskey; Semi-Tough; Shamus; Shark; Sharky's Machine; Silent Movie; Skullduggery; Smokey and the Bandit; Smokey and the Bandit II (aka Smokey and the Bandit Ride Again); Starting Over; Stick; Striptease; Switching Channels; White Lightning; W.W. and the Dixie Dancekings.*

Richardson, Ralph *Alice's Adventures in Wonderland; Anna Karenina* (Duvivier); *Battle of Britain; Bed Sitting Room, The; Bulldog Jack (aka Alias Bulldog Jack); Citadel, The* (Vidor); *Divorce of Lady X, The; Doctor Zhivago; Doll's House, A* (Garland); *Dragonslayer; Exodus; Fallen Idol, The; Four Feathers, The* (Korda); *Frankenstein: The True Story; Ghoul, The* (Hunter); *Give My Regards to Broad Street; Greystoke – The Legend of Tarzan Lord of the Apes; Heiress, The; Home at Seven (aka Murder on Monday); Khartoum; Lady Caroline Lamb; Long Day's Journey Into Night; Looking Glass War, The; Man Who Could Work Miracles, The; Midas Run (aka A Run on Gold); Oh! What a Lovely War; O Lucky Man!; Our Man in Havana; Outcast of the Islands; Richard III* (Olivier); *Rollerball; Sound Barrier, The (aka Breaking the Sound Barrier); South Riding; Things to Come; Time Bandits; Wagner; Woman of Straw.*

Robards, Jason *Adventures of Huck Finn; All the President's Men; Any Wednesday (aka Bachelor Girl Apartment); Ballad of Cable Hogue, The; Big Hand for the Little Lady, A (aka Big Deal at Dodge City); Black Rainbow; Boy and His Dog, A; Bright Lights, Big City; Capoblanco; Comes a Horseman; Divorce American Style; Good Mother, The; Hour of the Gun; Hurricane; Isadora; Johnny Got His Gun; Julia; Legend of the Lone Ranger, The; Little Big League; Long Day's Journey Into Night; Magnolia; Melvin and Howard; Murders in the Rue Morgue* (Hessler); *Once Upon a Time in the West (C'era una Volta il West); Paper, The; Parenthood; Pat Garrett and Billy the Kid; Philadelphia; Quick Change; Raise the Titanic; Reunion (L'Ami Retrouvé); St Valentine's Day Massacre, The; Something Wicked This Way Comes; Square Dance; Storyville; Thousand Acres, A; Tora! Tora! Tora!; Trial, The* (Jones).

Robbins, Tim *Antitrust; Arlington Road; Austin Powers: The Spy Who Shagged Me; Bob Roberts; Bull Durham; Cadillac Man; Erik the Viking; Five Corners; The; High Fidelity; Howard the Duck (aka Howard…a new breed of hero); Hudsucker Proxy, The; I.Q.; Jacob's Ladder; Jungle Fever; Miss Firecracker; Mission to Mars; Nothing to Lose; Player, The; Ready to Wear (aka Prêt-à-Porter); Shawshank Redemption, The; Short Cuts; Sure Thing, The; Tapeheads.*

Roberts, Julia *America's Sweethearts; Blood Red; Conspiracy Theory; Dying Young; Erin Brockovich; Everyone Says I Love You; Flatliners; Hook; I Love Trouble; Mary Reilly; Mexican, The; Michael Collins; My Best Friend's Wedding; Mystic Pizza; Notting Hill; Ocean's Eleven* (Soderbergh); *Pelican Brief, The; Player, The; Ready to Wear (aka Prêt-à-Porter); Pretty Woman; Runaway Bride; Satisfaction; Sleeping with the Enemy; Something to Talk About; Steel Magnolias; Stepmom.*

Robinson, Edward G *Amazing Doctor Clitterhouse, The; Barbary Coast; Blackmail* (Potter); *Brother Orchid; Bullets or Ballots; Cheyenne Autumn; Cincinnati Kid, The; Confessions of a Nazi Spy; Dr Erlich's Magic Bullet; Double Indemnity; Five Star Final; Flesh and Fantasy; Hatchet Man, The (aka The Honourable Mr Wong); Hole in the Head, A; House of Strangers; I Am the Law; Journey Together; Key Largo; Kid Galahad* (Curtiz); *Last Gangster, The; Little Caesar; Mackenna's Gold; Manpower; Neither By Day Nor By Night; Night Has a Thousand Eyes; Nightmare* (Shane); *Our Vines Have Tender Grapes; Red House, The; Robin and the 7 Hoods; Sammy Going South (aka A Boy Ten Feet Tall); Scarlet Street; Sea Wolf, The; Slight Case of Murder, A; Song of Norway; Soylent Green; Stranger, The; Ten Commandments, The; Tiger Shark; Two Weeks in Another Town; Whole Town's Talking, The (aka Passport to Fame); Woman in the Window, The.*

Rogers, Ginger *Bachelor Mother; Barkleys of Broadway, The; Black Widow* (Johnson); *Carefree; Fifth Avenue Girl; Flying Down to Rio; Follow the Fleet; 42nd Street; Gay Divorcee, The; Gold Diggers of 1933; I'll Be Seeing You; Lady in the Dark; Magnificent Doll; Major and the Minor, The; Monkey Business* (Hawks); *Oh, Men! Oh, Women!; Once Upon a Honeymoon; Primrose Path, The; Roberta; Roxie Hart; Shall We Dance?* (Sandrich); *Stage Door* (La Cava); *Story of Vernon and Irene Castle, The; Swing Time; Tender Comrade; Top Hat; Vivacious Lady.*

Russell, Jane *Born Losers, The; Darker Than Amber; French Line, The; Gentlemen Prefer Blondes; His Kind of Woman; Hot Blood; Las Vegas Story, The; Macao; Outlaw, The; Paleface, The; Revolt of Mamie Stover, The; Son of Paleface; Tall Men, The.*

Ryan, Meg *Addicted to Love; Amityville 3-D (aka Amityville: The Demon); Armed and Dangerous; City of Angels; Courage Under Fire; D.O.A.* (Morton); *Doors, The; Flesh and Bone; French Kiss; Hanging Up; Hurlyburly; Innerspace; I.Q.; Joe Versus the Volcano; Kate & Leopold; Prelude to a Kiss; Presidio, The; Promised Land; Proof of Life; Restoration; Rich and Famous; Sleepless in Seattle; Top Gun; When a Man Loves a Woman; When Harry Met Sally…; You've Got Mail.*

Ryan, Robert *About Mrs Leslie; Back from Eternity; Bad Day at Black Rock; Battle of the Bulge; Berlin Express; Beware, My Lovely; Billy Budd; Born to Be Bad; Boy With Green Hair, The; Canadians, The; Captain Nemo and the Underwater City; Caught; City Beneath the Sea; Clash By Night; Crossfire; Custer of the West; Day of the Outlaw; Dirty Dozen, The; Escape to Burma; Executive Action; Flying Leathernecks; God's Little Acre; Horizons West; Hour of the Gun; House of Bamboo; Ice Palace* (Sherman); *I Married a Communist (aka The Woman on Pier 13); Inferno* (Baker); *King of Kings; Lawman; Lolly-Madonna XXX (aka The Lolly-Madonna War); Lonelyhearts; Longest Day, The; Love Machine, The; Men in War; Naked Spur, The; Odds Against Tomorrow; On Dangerous Ground; Outfit, The; Professionals, The; Proud Ones, The; Racket, The; Sbarco di Anzio, Lo (Anzio/The Battle for Anzio); Set-Up, The; Sky's the Limit, The; Tall Men, The; Tender Comrade; Wild Bunch, The; Woman on the Beach, The.*

Sarandon, Susan *Anywhere but Here; Atlantic City (aka Atlantic City U.S.A.); Client, The; Bob Roberts; Bull Durham; Celluloid Closet, The; Compromising Positions; Cradle Will Rock; Crash; Dead Man Walking; Dry White Season, A; Front Page, The* (Wilder); *Great Waldo Pepper, The; Hunger, The; January Man, The; Joe Gould's Secret; King of the Gypsies; Last of the Cowboys, The (aka The Great Smokey Roadblock); Light Sleeper; Little Women* (Armstrong); *Lorenzo's Oil; Loving Couples; Lovin' Molly; Other Side of Midnight, The; Pretty Baby; Rocky Horror Picture Show, The; Safe Passage; Sweet Hearts Dance; Stepmom; Tempest; Thelma & Louise; Twilight; White Palace; Who Am I This Time?; Witches of Eastwick, The.*

Scheider, Roy *All That Jazz; Blue Thunder; Cohen and Tate; 52 Pick-up; Fourth War, The; French Connection, The; Jaws; Jaws 2; Klute; Last Embrace; Listen to Me; Loving; Marathon Man; Men's Club, The; Myth of Fingerprints, The; Naked Lunch; Outside Man, The (Un Homme est Mort); Puzzle of a Downfall Child; Romeo Is Bleeding; Russia House, The; Seven-Ups, The; Sorcerer (aka Wages of Fear); Still of the Night; 2010.*

Schneider, Romy *Assassination of Trotsky, The; Bloodline (aka Sidney Sheldon's*

Bloodline); Bloomfield (aka The Hero); Boccaccio '70; Cardinal, The; César and Rosalie (César et Rosalie); Choses de le Vie, Les (The Things of Life); Death Watch (La Mort en Direct); Garde à Vue (The Inquisitor); Infernal Trio, The (Le Trio Infernal); Innocents with Dirty Hands (Les Innocents aux Mains Sales); Ludwig; Otley; Plein Soleil (Delitto in pieno sole/Blazing Sun/ Purple Noon); 10:30 P.M. Summer; Trial, The (Le Procès); Victors, The; What's New Pussycat?

Schwarzenegger, Arnold *Batman & Robin; Collateral Damage; Commando; Conan the Barbarian; Conan the Destroyer; End of Days; Eraser; Jingle All the Way; Junior; Kindergarten Cop; Last Action Hero, The; Predator; Pumping Iron; Raw Deal; Red Heat; Red Sonja; Running Man, The* (Glaser); *6th Day, The; Stay Hungry; Terminator, The; Terminator 2: Judgment Day; Total Recall; True Lies; Twins; Villain, The (aka Cactus Jack).*

Schygulla, Hanna *Berlin Alexanderplatz; Beware of a Holy Whore (Warnung vor einer heiligen Nutte); Bitter Tears of Petra von Kant, The (Die Bitteren Tränen der Petra von Kant); Blue Exile, The (Mavi Sürgün); Circle of Deceit (Die Fälschung); Dead Again; Delta Force, The; Effi Briest; Friends and Husbands (Heller Wahn); Future Is Woman, The (Il Futuro è Donna); Gods of the Plague (Götter der Pest); Hunting Scenes from Lower Lower Bavaria (Jagdszenen aus Niederbayern); Katzelmacher; Lili Marleen; Love in Germany, A (Eine Liebe in Deutschland); Love Is Colder than Death (Liebe ist kälter als der Tod); Marriage of Maria Braun, The (Die Ehe der Maria Braun); Merchant of Four Seasons, The (Händler der vier Jahreszeiten, Der); Passion; That Night in Varennes (La Nuit de Varennes); Third Generation, The (Die Dritte Generation); Werckmeister Harmonies (Werckmeister harmóniák); Wild Game (Wildwechsel); Wrong Movement (Falsche Bewegung).*

Scofield, Paul *Bartleby; Carve Her Name with Pride; Crucible, The; Delicate Balance, A; Hamlet* (Zeffirelli); *Henry V* (Branagh); *King Lear* (Brook); *Man for All Seasons, A; Nineteen Nineteen; Quiz Show; Scorpio; That Lady; Train, The; When the Whales Came.*

Scott, George C *Anatomy of a Murder; Angus; Bank Shot; Beauty and the Beast* (Cook); *Bible…In the Beginning, The (La Bibbia); Changeling, The; Christmas Carol, A; Day of the Dolphin, The; Dr Strangelove: or, How I Learned to Stop Worrying and Love the Bomb; Exorcist III, The; Firestarter; Flim-Flam Man, The (aka One Born Every Minute); Formula, The; Gloria* (Lumet); *Hardcore (aka The Hardcore Life); Hindenburg, The; Hospital, The; Hustler, The; Islands in the Stream; Jane Eyre* (Mann); *Last Run, The; List of Adrian Messenger, The; Malice; Movie Movie; New Centurions, The (aka Precinct 45: Los Angeles Police); Oklahoma Crude; Oliver Twist* (Donner); *Patton (aka Patton: Lust for Glory); Petulia; Prince and the Pauper, The (aka Crossed Swords); Taps; They Might Be Giants.*

Sellers, Peter *After the Fox (Caccia alla Volpe); Alice's Adventures in Wonderland; Battle of the Sexes, The; Being There; Blockhouse, The; Bobo, The; Casino Royale; Dr Strangelove: or, How I Learned to Stop Worrying and Love the Bomb; Down Among the Z Men; Fiendish Plot of Dr Fu Manchu, The; Great McGonagall, The; Heavens Above!; I Love You, Alice B Toklas; I'm All Right, Jack; Ladykillers, The; Lolita* (Kubrick); *Magic Christian, The; Millionairess, The; Mouse That Roared, The; Murder By Death; Naked Truth, The (aka Your Past Is Showing); Never Let Go; Only Two Can Play; Optimists of Nine Elms, The; Orders are Orders; Party, The; Pink Panther, The; Pink Panther Strikes Again, The; Prisoner of Zenda, The* (Quine); *Return of the Pink Panther, The; Revenge of the Pink Panther; Shot in the Dark, A; Smallest Show on Earth, The; Soft Beds, Hard Battles; There's a Girl in My Soup; Tom Thumb; Trail of the Pink Panther; Two-Way Stretch; What's New Pussycat?; Wrong Arm of the Law, The.*

Serrault, Michel *Argent des Autres, L' (Other People's Money); Artemisia; Assassin(s); Beaumarchais (Beaumarchais l'insolent); Bonheaur est dans le pré, Le; Buffet Froid; Cage aux Folles, La (Birds of a Feather); Cage aux Folles II, La; Cage aux Folles III: The Wedding, La; Deadly Run (Mortelle Randonnée); Diaboliques, Les (Diabolique/The Fiends); Docteur Petiot; Garde à Vue (The Inquisitor); Enfants du Marais, Les (Children of the Marshland); Fantômes du Chapelier, Les (The Hatter's Ghosts); He Died With His Eyes Open (On ne Meurt que 2 Fois); King of Hearts (Le Roi de Coeur); Libertin, Le; Malevil; Murder Is a Murder…Is a Murder, A (Un Meurtre est un Meurtre); Nelly & Monsieur Arnaud (Nelly and Mister Arnaud); Old Lady Who Walked in the Sea, The (La Vieille qui Marchait dans la Mer); Préparez vos Mouchoirs (Get Out Your Handkerchiefs); Rien ne va plus; Vieille Canaille (The Old Crook).*

Seyrig, Delphine *Accident; Année Dernière à Marienbad, L' (Last Year in Marienbad); Baisers Volés (Stolen Kisses); Black Windmill, The; Daughters of Darkness (Les Lèvres Rouges); Day of the Jackal, The; Discreet Charm of the Bourgeoisie, The (Le Charme Discret de la Bourgeoisie); Doll's House, A* (Losey); *Golden Eighties; India Song; Jeanne Dielman, 23 Quai du Commerce, 1080 Bruxelles; Joan of Arc of Mongolia (Johanna d'Arc of Mongolia); Mister Freedom; Muriel (Muriel, ou le Temps d'un Retour); Peau d'Ane (The Magic Donkey); Voie Lactée, La (The Milky Way); Who Are You Polly Maggoo? (Qui êtes-vous Polly Maggoo?).*

Shaw, Robert *Avalanche Express; Battle of Britain; Battle of the Bulge; Birthday Party, The; Black Sunday; Caretaker, The (aka The Guest); Custer of the West; Deep, The; Diamonds; Figures in a Landscape; Force 10 from Navarone; From Russia With Love; Hill in Korea, A (aka Hell in Korea); Hireling, The; Jaws; Lavender Hill Mob, The; Luck of Ginger Coffey, The; Man for All Seasons, A; Robin and Marian; Royal Hunt of the Sun, The; Sting, The; Swashbuckler (aka The Scarlet Buccaneer); Taking of Pelham One Two Three, The; Town Called Bastard, A; Young Winston.*

Sheen, Martin *American President, The; Apocalypse Now; Apocalypse Now Redux; Badlands; Believers, The; Beverly Hills Brats; Beyond the Stars (aka Personal Choice); Cassandra Crossing, The; Catch-22; Count a Lonely Cadence (aka Stockade); Da; Dead Zone, The; Eagle's Wing; Enigma; Entertaining Angels: The Dorothy Day Story; Final Countdown, The; Firestarter; Gandhi; Gettysburg; Hear No Evil; In the King of Prussia; Judgment in Berlin; Killing Box, The (aka Ghost Brigade); Loophole; Man, Woman and Child; No Drums, No Bugles; Siesta; Subject Was Roses, The; That Championship Season; Wall Street; War at Home, The.*

Signoret, Simone *Against the Wind; Armée des Ombres, L' (The Army in the Shadows); Aveu, L' (The Confession); Casque d'Or (Golden Marie); Chat, Le (The Cat); Deadly Affair, The; Diaboliques, Les (Diabolique/The Fiends); Etoile du Nord, L' (The Northern Star); Madame Rosa (La Vie devant Soi); Manèges (The Wanton); Mort en ce Jardin, La (Evil Eden); Ronde, La; Room at the Top.*

Sim, Alastair *Belles of St Trinian's, The; Blue Muder at St Trinian's; Captain Boycott; Cottage to Let (aka Bombsight Stolen); Escape from the Dark (aka The Littlest Horse Thieves); Folly to Be Wise; Geordie (aka Wee Geordie); Green for Danger; Green Man, The; Happiest Days of Your Life, The; Hue and Cry; Innocents in Paris; Inspector Calls, An; Laughter in Paradise; Left, Right and Centre; Let the People Sing; London Belongs to Me (aka Dulcimer Street); Millionairess, The; Royal Flash; Ruling Class, The; School for Scoundrels; Scrooge; Squeaker, The; Stage Fright; Waterloo Road.*

Simon, Michel *Atalante, L'; Beauté du Diable, La (Beauty and the Devil); Blanche; Boudu Sauvé des Eaux (Boudu Saved from Drowning); Chienne, La; Disparus de Saint-Agil, Les; Drôle de Drame (Bizarre, Bizarre); Fabiola (Fighting Gladiator); Fin du Jour, La (The End of the Day); Lac aux Dames; On Purge Bébé; Passion de Jeanne d'Arc, La (The Passion of Joan of Arc); Quai des Brumes, Le (Port of Shadows); Saadia; Train, The; Vieil Homme et l'Enfant, Le (The Two of Us).*

Sinatra, Frank *Anchors Aweigh; Around the World in 80 Days; Assault on a Queen; Can-Can; Cannonball Run II; Cast a Giant Shadow; Come Blow Your Horn; Detective, The; Devil at 4 O'Clock, The; First Deadly Sin, The; From Here to Eternity; Guys and Dolls; High Society; Hole in the Head, A; It Happened in Brooklyn; Kings Go Forth; Lady in Cement; List of Adrian Messenger, The; Manchurian Candidate, The; Man With the Golden Arm, The; Miracle of the Bells, The; Naked Runner, The; Never So Few; None But the Brave; Not As a Stranger; Ocean's 11* (Milestone); *On the Town; Pal Joey; Pride and the Passion, The; Robin and the 7 Hoods; Some Came Running; Suddenly; Take Me Out to the Ball*

Game (aka Everybody's Cheering); That's Entertainment!; Tony Rome; Von Ryan's Express; Young at Heart.

Smith, Maggie *Better Late Than Never; California Suite; Clash of the Titans; Curtain Call; Death on the Nile; Evil Under the Sun; First Wives Club, The; Gosford Park; Harry Potter and the Philosopher's Stone (aka Harry Potter and the Sorcerer's Stone); Honey Pot, The; Hook; Last September, The; Lonely Passion of Judith Hearne, The; Missionary, The; Murder by Death; Oh! What a Lovely War; Othello* (Burge); *Prime of Miss Jean Brodie, The; Private Function, A; Pumpkin Eater, The; Quartet* (Ivory); *Richard III* (Loncraine); *Room with a View, A; Secret Garden, The* (Holland); *Sister Act; Sister Act II: Back in the Habit; Tea with Mussolini (Te con il Duce); V.I.Ps, The; Washington Square; Young Cassidy.*

Snipes, Wesley *Art of War, The; Blade; Blade II; Boiling Point; Demolition Man; Drop Zone; Fan, The* (Scott); *Jungle Fever; King of New York; Major League; Mo' Better Blues; Money Train; Murder at 1600; New Jack City; One Night Stand; Passenger 57; Rising Sun; Streets of Gold; Sugar Hill; To Wong Foo, Thanks For Everything! Julie Newmar; U.S. Marshals; Waterdance, The; White Men Can't Jump; Wildcats.*

Spacey, Kevin *American Beauty; Consenting Adults; Dad; Glengarry Glen Ross; Heartburn; Henry & June; Hurlyburly; K-PAX; LA Confidential; Looking for Richard; Midnight in the Garden of Good and Evil; Negotiator, The; Ordinary Decent Criminal; Outbreak; Pay It Forward; Ref, The (aka Hostile Hostages); Seven (aka Se7en)* (Fincher); *See No Evil, Hear No Evil; Shipping News, The; Show of Force, A; Swimming with Sharks; Time to Kill, A; Usual Suspects, The; Working Girl.*

Stallone, Sylvester *Assassins; Bananas; Capone; Cliffhanger; Cobra* (Cosmatos); *CopLand; Daylight; Death Race 2000; Demolition Man; Driven; D-Tox (D-Tox Im Auge der Angst); Farewell, My Lovely* (Richards); *First Blood; F.I.S.T.; Judge Dredd; Lock Up; Lords of Flatbush, The; Nighthawks* (Malmuth); *Oscar; Over the Top; Paradise Alley; Prisoner of Second Avenue, The; Rambo: First Blood, Part II; Rambo III; Rocky; Rocky II; Rocky III; Rocky IV; Rocky V; Specialist, The; Stop! or My Mom Will Shoot; Tango & Cash; Victory (aka Escape to Victory).*

Stamp, Terence *Adventures of Priscilla Queen of the Desert, The; Alien Nation; Billy Budd; Blue* (Narizzano); *Bowfinger; Collector, The; Company of Wolves, The; Directed by William Wyler; Far from the Madding Crowd; Histoires Extraordinaires (Spirits of the Dead/Tales of Mystery); Hit, The; Legal Eagles; Limey, The; Link; Modesty Blaise; Poor Cow; Real McCoy, The; Red Planet; Revelation; Sicilian, The; Star Wars Episode I The Phantom Menace; Superman; Superman II; Term of Trial; Theorem (Teorema); Thief of Baghdad, The* (Donner); *Tiré à Part; Wall Street; Young Guns.*

Stanton, Harry Dean *Alien; Black Marble, The; Blue Tiger; Care Bears Movie, The; Christine; Cisco Pike; Cockfighter; Cool Hand Luke; Day of the Evil Gun; Death Watch (La Mort en Direct); Dillinger* (Milius); *Down Periscope; Escape from New York; Farewell, My Lovely* (Richards); *Fear and Loathing in Las Vegas; Fool for Love; Fourth War, The; Kelly's Heroes; Last Temptation of Christ, The; Man Trouble; Man Who Cried, The; Mighty, The; Missouri Breaks, The; Mr North; Never Talk to Strangers; 92 in the Shade; Paris, Texas; Pat Garrett and Billy the Kid; Pledge, The; Pretty in Pink; Private Benjamin; Rafferty and the Gold Dust Twins; Rancho Deluxe; Rebel Rousers; Red Dawn; Renaldo & Clara; Repo Man; Ride in the Whirlwind; Rose, The; She's So Lovely; Slam Dance; Stars and Bars; Straight Story, The; Straight Time; Titanic; Twin Peaks: Fire Walk with Me; Twister; What's the Matter With Helen?; Wild at Heart; Wise Blood; Young Doctors in Love; Zandy's Bride.*

Stanwyck, Barbara *All I Desire; Annie Oakley; Baby Face; Ball of Fire; Banjo on My Knee; B.F.'s Daughter; Bitter Tea of General Yen, The; Blowing Wild; Cattle Queen of Montana; Clash By Night; Crime of Passion; Cry Wolf; Double Indemnity; Escape to Burma; Executive Suite; File on Thelma Jordan, The; Flesh and Fantasy; Forbidden; Forty Guns; Furies, The; Golden Boy; Jeopardy; Lady Eve, The; Lady of Burlesque (aka Striptease Lady); Mad Miss Manton, The; Man With a Cloak, The; Meet John Doe; Miracle Woman, The; Night Nurse; No Man of Her Own; Remember the Night; Sorry, Wrong Number; Stella Dallas; Strange Love of Martha Ivers, The; There's Always Tomorrow; This Is My Affair (aka His Affair); Walk on the Wild Side.*

Steiger, Rod *Al Capone; Amityville Horror, The; Back from Eternity; Ballad of the Sad Café, The; Big Knife, The; Cattle Annie and Little Britches; Chosen, The; Court-Martial of Billy Mitchell, The (aka One Man Mutiny); Crazy in Alabama; Doctor Zhivago; End of Days; F.I.S.T.; Giù la Testa (Duck, You Sucker/A Fistful of Dynamite/Once Upon a Time – the Revolution); Happy Birthday, Wanda June; Harder They Fall, The; Hennessy; Heroes, The (Gli Eroi); Hurricane, The; Illustrated Man, The; Incognito; Innocents With Dirty Hands (Les Innocents aux Mains Sales); In the Heat of the Night; January Man, The; Kindred, The; Lion of the Desert; Lolly-Madonna XXX (aka The Lolly-Madonna War); Love and Bullets; Loved One, The; Lucky Luciano; Mani sulla Città, Le (Hands Over the City); Man Named John, A (E Venne un Uomo); Mars Attacks!; Men of Respect; Naked Face, The; No Way to Treat a Lady; Oklahoma!; On the Waterfront; Pawnbroker, The; Run of the Arrow; Specialist, The; That Summer of White Roses; Three Into Two Won't Go; Waterloo; W.C. Fields and Me.*

Stewart, James *After the Thin Man; Airport '77; Anatomy of a Murder; Bandolero!; Bend of the River (aka Where the River Bends); Big Sleep, The* (Winner); *Born to Dance; Broken Arrow; Call Northside 777; Cheyenne Autumn; Cheyenne Social Club, The; Destry Rides Again; Far Country, The; Flight of the Phoenix, The; Glenn Miller Story, The; Gorgeous Hussy, The; Greatest Show on Earth, The; Harvey; How the West Was Won; It's a Wonderful Life; Last Gangster, The; Magic of Lassie, The; Magic Town; Malaya (aka East of the Rising Sun); Man from Laramie, The; Man Who Knew Too Much, The* (1956); *Man Who Shot Liberty Valance, The; Mr Hobbs Takes a Vacation; Mr Smith Goes to Washington; Mortal Storm, The; Naked Spur, The; Night Passage; No Highway (aka No Highway in the Sky); Philadelphia Story, The; Rare Breed, The; Rear Window; Rope; Seventh Heaven* (King); *Shootist, The; Shop Around the Corner, The; Spirit of St. Louis, The; That's Entertainment!; Two Rode Together; Vertigo; Vivacious Lady; Winchester '73; You Can't Take It With You; Ziegfeld Girl.*

Streep, Meryl *Before and After; Birdges of Madison County, The; Cry in the Dark, A; Dancing at Lughnasa; Death Becomes Her; Deer Hunter, The; Defending Your Life; Falling in Love; French Lieutenant's Woman, The; Heartburn; Ironweed; House of Spirits, The; Julia; Kramer vs Kramer; Manhattan; Marvin's Room; Music of the Heart; One True Thing; Out of Africa; Plenty; Postcards from the Edge; River Wild, The; Seduction of Joe Tynan, The; She-Devil; Silkwood; Sophie's Choice; Still of the Night.*

Sutherland, Donald *Alex in Wonderland; Alien Thunder (aka Dan Candy's Law); Art of War, The; Backdraft; Bear Island; Bedford Incident, The; Benefit of the Doubt; Blood Relatives (Liens de Sang); Buffy the Vampire Slayer; Crackers; Day of the Locust, The; Disclosure; Dirty Dozen, The; Disappearance, The; Dr Terror's House of Horrors; Don't Look Now; Dry White Season, A; Eagle Has Landed, The; Eye of the Needle; Fallen; Fanatic (aka Die! Die! My Darling!); Fellini's Casanova (Il Casanova di Federico Fellini); Final Fantasy: The Spirits Within; First Great Train Robbery, The (aka The Great Train Robbery); F.T.A.; Heaven Help Us (aka Catholic Boys); Instinct; Interlude* (Billington); *Invasion of the Body Snatchers* (Kaufman); *JFK; Johnny Got His Gun; Kelly's Heroes; Kentucky Fried Movie, The; Klute; Lady Ice; Little Murders; Lock Up; Lost Angels (aka The Road Home); Man, a Woman and a Bank, A; M*A*S*H; Murder by Decree; National Lampoon's Animal House; 1900 (Novecento); Oedipus the King; Ordeal by Innocence; Ordinary People; Outbreak; Puppet Masters, The (aka Robert Heinlein's The Puppet Masters); Revolution; Rosary Murders, The; Shadow Conspiracy; Six Degrees of Separation; Space Cowboys; Split, The; S*P*Y*S; Steelyard Blues; Time to Kill, A; Virus; Without Limits; Younger and Younger.*

Swanson, Gloria *Airport 1975; Queen Kelly; Sadie Thompson; Sunset Blvd.*

Taylor, Elizabeth *Ash Wednesday; Blue Bird, The; Boom; BUtterfield 8; Cat on a Hot Tin Roof; Cleopatra* (Mankiewicz); *Comedians, The; Father of the Bride; Flintstones, The; Giant; Ivanhoe; Jane Eyre* (Stevenson); *Lassie Come Home; Last Time I Saw Paris; Life with Father; Little Night Music, A; Mirror Crack'd, The; National Velvet; Night Watch; Only*

Game in Town, The; Place in the Sun, A; Raintree County; Reflections in a Golden Eye; Sandpiper, The; Secret Ceremony; Suddenly Last Summer; Sweet Bird of Youth; That's Entertainment!; Under Milk Wood; Victory at Entebbe; V.I.P.s, The; Who's Afraid of Virginia Woolf?; Winter Kills; Zee & Co (aka X, Y and Zee).

Taylor, Robert *Adventures of Quentin Durward, The (aka Quentin Durward); Bataan; Beat Street; Billy the Kid; Bribe, The; Broadway Melody of 1936; Camille* (Cukor); *Devil's Doorway; Escape* (LeRoy); *Gorgeous Hussy, The; Ivanhoe; Johnny Eager; Killers of Kilimanjaro; Last Hunt, The; Law and Jake Wade, The; Party Girl; Quo Vadis?; Rogue Cop; Saddle the Wind; This Is My Affair (aka His Affair); Three Comrades; Undercurrent; When Ladies Meet.*

Temple, Shirley *Adventure in Baltimore (aka Bachelor Bait); Captain January; Dimples; Fort Apache; I'll Be Seeing You; Littlest Rebel, The; Since You Went Away.*

Tierney, Gene *Advise and Consent; Black Widow* (Johnson); *Dragonwyck; Ghost and Mrs Muir, The; Heaven Can Wait* (Lubitsch); *Iron Curtain, The (aka Behind the Iron Curtain); Laura; Leave Her to Heaven; Left Hand of God, The; Night and the City* (Dassin); *Pleasure Seekers, The; Razor's Edge, The; Return of Frank James, The; Secret of Convict Lake, The; Shanghai Gesture, The; Tobacco Road; Way of a Gaucho; Whirlpool.*

Tracy, Spencer *Actress, The; Adam's Rib; Bad Day at Black Rock; Boom Town; Broken Lance; Captains Courageous; Dante's Inferno; Desk Set (aka His Other Woman); Devil at 4 O'Clock, The; Dr Jekyll and Mr Hyde* (Fleming); *Edison the Man; Father of the Bride; Fury* (Lang); *Guess Who's Coming to Dinner; Inherit the Wind; I Take This Woman; It's a Mad, Mad, Mad, Mad World; Judgment at Nuremberg; Keeper of the Flame; Last Hurrah, The; Malaya (aka East of the Rising Sun); Man's Castle; Northwest Passage; Old Man and the Sea, The; Pat and Mike; Power and the Glory, The; San Francisco; Seventh Cross, The; State of the Union (aka The World and His Wife); 20,000 Years in Sing Sing; Woman of the Year.*

Travolta, John *Battlefield Earth; Blow Out; Broken Arrow; Carrie* (De Palma); *Civil Action, A; Devil's Rain, The; Domestic Disturbance; Experts, The; Face/Off; General's Daughter, The; Get Shorty; Grease; Look Who's Talking; Look Who's Talking Now; Look Who's Talking Too; Mad City; Michael; Moment by Moment; Perfect; Phenomenon; Primary Colors; Pulp Fiction; Saturday Night Fever; She's So Lovely; Shout; Staying Alive; Swordfish; Thin Red Line, The; Two of a Kind; Urban Cowboy; White Man's Burden.*

Trevor, Claire *Amazing Doctor Clitterhouse, The; Born to Kill (aka Lady of Deceit); Cape Town Affair, The; Crack-Up* (Reis); *Crossroads* (Conway); *Dante's Inferno; Dead End; Farewell, My Lovely (aka Murder My Sweet); Hard, Fast and Beautiful; Hoodlum Empire; Johnny Angel; Key Largo; Kiss Me Goodbye; Man Without a Star; Raw Deal* (Mann); *Stagecoach* (Ford); *Two Weeks in Another Town.*

Trintignant, Jean-Louis *Agression, L' (Aggression); Argent des Autres, L' (Other People's Money); Attentat, L' (Plot); Biches, Les (The Does); Big Silence, The (Il Grande Silenzio); Blow to the Heart (Colpire al Cuore); Bunker Palace Hotel; Conformist, The (Il Conformista); Désert des Tartares, Le; Et Dieu Créa la Femme (And God Created Woman/And Woman… Was Created); Glissements Progressifs du Plaisir; Héros très discret, Un (A Self-Made Hero); Homme et une Femme, Un (A Man and a Woman); Liaisons Dangereuses 1960, Les; Malevil; Mata Hari, Agent H.21; Merci la vie (Thank You, Life); My Night with Maud (Ma Nuit chez Maud); Outside Man, The (Un Homme est Mort); Passione d'Amore; Pleins Feux sur l'assassin; Regarde les hommes tomber (See How They Fall); Secret, The (Le Secret); Shattered (Les Passagers); Si tous les gars du monde… (Race for Life/If All the Guys in the World…); Sleeping Car Murder, The (Compartiment Tueurs); That Night in Varennes (La Nuit de Varennes); Those Who Love Me Will Take the Train (Ceux qui m'aiment prendront le train); Three Colours: Red (Trois Couleurs: Rouge); Trans-Europ-Express; Under Fire; Violons du Bal, Les; Viva la Vie; Vivement Dimanche! (Confidentially Yours/ Finally, Sunday!); Z.*

Turner, Kathleen *Accidental Tourist, The; Body Heat; Crimes of Passion; House of Cards (La Voce del Silenzio); Jewel of the Nile; Love and Action in Chicago; Man With Two Brains, The; Moonlight and Valentino; Naked in New York; Peggy Sue Got Married; Prizzi's Honor; Romancing the Stone; Serial Mom; Simple Wish, A; Switching Channels; Undercover Blues; Virgin Suicides, The; V I Warshawski; War of the Roses, The.*

Valentino, Rudolph *Blood and Sand* (Niblo); *Camille* (Smallwood); *Cobra, The; Eagle, The; Isle of Love, The.*

Veidt, Conrad *Above Suspicion; All Through the Night; Cabinet of Dr Caligari, The (Das Kabinett des Dr Caligari); Casablanca; Congress Dances (Der Kongress tanzt); Contraband (aka Blackout); Dark Journey; Escape* (LeRoy); *Hands of Orlac, The (Orlacs Hände); King of the Damned; Spy in Black, The; Thief of Bagdad, The* (Powell/Berger/Whelan/ Korda); *Under the Red Robe; Waxworks (Das Wachsfigurenkabinett); Woman's Face, A.*

von Stroheim, Erich *As You Desire Me; Blind Husbands; Disparus de Saint-Agil, Les; Five Graves to Cairo; Foolish Wives; Grande Illusion, La; Lost Squadron, The; Napoléon* (Guitry); *North Star, The (aka Armored Attack); Pièges (Personal Column/ Snares); Sunset Blvd.; Wedding March, The.*

von Sydow, Max *Ansiktet (The Face/The Magician); Best Intentions, The (Den Goda Viljan); Brass Target; Conan the Barbarian; Death Watch (La Mort en Direct); Désert des Tartares, Le; Dreamscape; Duet for One; Dune; Emigrants, The (Utvandrarna); Exorcist, The; Exorcist – The Director's Cut, The; Exorcist II: The Heretic; Father; Flash Gordon; Greatest Story Ever Told, The; Hannah and Her Sisters; Hawaii; Hour of the Wolf (Vargtimmen); Hurricane; Illustrious Corpses (Cadaveri Eccellenti); Judge Dredd; Kiss Before Dying, A* (Dearden); *Kremlin Letter, The; March or Die; Nattvardsgästerna (The Communicants/Winter Light); Needful Things; Never Say Never Again; Ox, The (Oxen); Passion, A (En Passion); Pelle the Conqueror (Pelle Erobreren); Quiller Memorandum, The; Reward, The; Seventh Seal, The (Det Sjunde Inseglet); Shame, The (Skammen); Silent Touch, The; Sleepless (Nonhosonno/aka Non ho sonno); Snow Falling on Cedars; Steppenwolf; Strange Brew; Three Days of the Condor; Through a Glass Darkly (Sasom i en Spegel); Touch, The; Until the End of the World (Bis ans Ende der Welt); Victory (aka Escape to Victory); Virgin Spring, The (Jungfrukällan); Voyage of the Damned; Wild Strawberries (Smultronstället).*

Washington, Denzel *Bone Collector, The; Carbon Copy; Courage Under Fire; Crimson Tide; Cry Freedom; Devil in a Blue Dress; Fallen; For Queen and Country; Glory; Heart Condition; He Got Game; Hurricane, The; John Q; Malcolm X; Mighty Quinn, The; Mississippi Masala; Much Ado About Nothing; Mo' Better Blues; Pelican Brief, The; Philadelphia; Power; Preacher's Wife, The; Remember the Titans; Ricochet; Siege, The; Soldier's Story, A; Training Day.*

Wayne, John *Alamo, The; Baby Face; Back to Bataan; Big Jake; Big Trail, The; Brannigan; Cahill – US Marshal; Cast a Giant Shadow; Chisum; Conqueror, The; Cowboys, The; Desert Trail, The; Donovan's Reef; El Dorado; Fighting Seabees, The; Flying Leathernecks; Flying Tigers; Fort Apache; Greatest Story Ever Told, The; Green Berets, The; Hatari!; Hondo; Horse Soldiers, The; How the West Was Won; I Married a Woman; In Harm's Way; Jet Pilot; Lady from Louisiana; Lady Takes a Chance; Legend of the Lost; Longest Day, The; Long Voyage Home, The; Lucky Texan, The; Man Who Shot Liberty Valance, The; McQ; Quiet Man, The; North to Alaska; Randy Rides Alone; Red River; Riders of Destiny; Rio Bravo; Rio Grande; Rio Lobo; Rooster Cogburn; Sands of Iwo Jima; Sea Chase, The; Searchers, The; Seven Sinners; She Wore a Yellow Ribbon; Shootist, The; Stagecoach* (Ford); *They Were Expendable; Three Godfathers; Train Robbers, The; True Grit; Undefeated, The; War Wagon, The; Wings of Eagles, The.*

Weaver, Sigourney *Alien; Aliens; Alien³; Alien Resurrection; Annie Hall; Copycat; Dave; Death and the Maiden; Eyewitness (aka The Janitor)* (Yates); *1492: Conquest of Paradise; Galaxy Quest; Ghostbusters; Ghostbusters II; Gorillas in the Mist; Half Moon Street; Heartbreakers; Ice Storm, The; Jeffrey; Map of the World, A; Snow White: A Tale of Terror; Woman or Two, A (Une Femme ou Deux); Working Girl; Year of Living Dangerously, The.*

Welles, Orson *Austerlitz (aka The Battle of Austerlitz); Butterfly* (Cimber); *Casino Royale; Catch-22; Chimes at Midnight (Campanadas a*

Medianoche); Citizen Kane; Compulsion; Ferry to Hong Kong; F for Fake (Vérités et Mensonges); Hot Money; Immortal Story, The (Histoire Immortelle); Jane Eyre (Stevenson); *Journey into Fear; Kremlin Letter, The; Lady from Shanghai, The; Long Hot Summer, The; Macbeth* (Welles); *Malpertuis; Man for All Seasons, A; Mr Arkadin (aka Confidential Report); Moby Dick; Muppet Movie, The; Napoléon* (Guitry); *Oedipus the King; Othello* (Welles); *Prince of Foxes; Safe Place, A; Sailor from Gibraltar, The; Si Versailles m'était conté… (Versailles/Royal Affairs at Versailles); Someone to Love; Stranger, The; Ten Days' Wonder (La Décade Prodigieuse); Third Man, The; Touch of Evil; Trial, The (Le Procès); V.I.P.s, The; Voyage of the Damned; Waterloo.*

West, Mae *I'm No Angel; Klondike Annie; My Little Chickadee; Myra Breckinridge; Night After Night; She Done Him Wrong.*

Whitaker, Forest *Battlefield Earth; Bird; Bloodsport; Blown Away; Body Count; Body Snatchers; Consenting Adults; Crying Game, The; Ghost Dog: The Way of the Samurai; Good Morning Vietnam; Jason's Lyric; Johnny Handsome; Lush Life; Panic Room; Phenomenon; Platoon; Rage in Harlem, A; Smoke; Species; Stakeout.*

Widmark, Richard *Against All Odds; Alamo, The; Bear Island; Bedford Incident, The; Broken Lance; Cheyenne Autumn; Cobweb, The; Coma; Death of a Gunfighter; Destination Gobi; Domino Principle, The (aka The Domino Killings); Don't Bother to Knock* (Baker); *Flight from Ashiya; Gathering of Old Men, A; Halls of Montezuma; Hanky Panky; Hell and High Water; How the West Was Won; Judgment at Nuremberg; Kiss of Death* (Hathaway); *Last Wagon, The; Law and Jake Wade, The; Long Ships, The; National Lampoon Goes to the Movies (aka National Lampoon's Movie Madness); Madigan; Moonshine War, The; Murder on the Orient Express; Night and the City* (Dassin); *No Way Out* (Mankiewicz); *Panic in the Streets; Pickup on South Street; Road House* (Negulesco); *Rollercoaster; Run for the Sun; Sellout, The; Street with No Name, The; Swarm, The; To the Devil a Daughter; Twilight's Last Gleaming; Two Rode Together; Warlock* (Dmytryk); *Way West, The; When the Legends Die; Who Dares Wins; Yellow Sky.*

Williams, Robin *Aladdin; Adventures of Baron Munchausen, The* (Gilliam); *Awakenings; Being Human; Best of Times, The; Bicentennial Man; Birdcage, The; Cadillac Man; Dead Again; Dead Poets Society; Deconstructing Harry; Fathers' Day; Fisher King, The; Flubber; Good Morning Vietnam; Good Will Hunting; Hamlet* (Branagh); *Hook; Jack; Jakob the Liar; Jumanji; Mrs Doubtfire; Moscow on the Hudson; Nine Months; Patch Adams; Popeye; Secret Agent, The (Joseph Conrad's The Secret Agent); Seize the Day; Survivors, The; Toys; What Dreams May Come; World According to Garp, The.*

Winger, Debra *Betrayed; Black Widow* (Rafelson); *Cannery Row; Dangerous Woman, A; Everybody Wins; Forget Paris; Leap of Faith; Legal Eagles; Made in Heaven; Mike's Murder; Officer and a Gentleman, An; Shadowlands; Sheltering Sky, The; Slumber Party '57; Terms of Endearment; Thank God It's Friday; Urban Cowboy.*

Winters, Shelley *Alfie; Big Knife, The; Bloody Mama; Blume in Love; Buona Sera, Mrs Campbell; Chapman Report, The; City on Fire; Cleopatra Jones; Cry of the City; Delta Force, The; Diamonds; Diary of Anne Frank, The; Double Life, A; Elvis (aka Elvis – The Movie); Executive Suite; Fanny Hill; Flap (aka The Last Warrior); Greatest Story Ever Told, The; Great Gatsby, The* (Nugent); *Harper (aka The Moving Target); Heavy; I Am a Camera; I Died a Thousand Times; King of the Gypsies; Lolita* (Kubrick); *Mad Room, The; Magician of Lublin, The; Next Stop, Greenwich Village; Night of the Hunter, The; Odds Against Tomorrow; Over the Brooklyn Bridge; Patch of Blue, A; Pete's Dragon; Phone Call from a Stranger; Place in the Sun, A; Portrait of a Lady, The; Poseidon Adventure, The; Scalphunters, The; Sex Symbol, The; Silence of the Hams, The (Il silenzio dei prosciutti); S.O.B.; Something to Hide; Stepping Out; Tenant, The (Le Locataire); Tentacles (Tentacoli); That Lucky Touch; What's the Matter with Helen?; Wild in the Streets; Winchester '73.*

Woods, James *Against All Odds; Alex & the Gypsy; Another Day in Paradise; Any Given Sunday; Best Seller; Black Marble, The; Boost, The; Casino; Cat's Eye; Chaplin; Choirboys, The; Citizen Cohn; Contact; Cop; Diggstown (aka Midnight Sting); Dirty Pictures; Eyewitness (aka The Janitor); Fast-Walking; Final Fantasy: The Spirits Within; Gambler, The; General's Daughter, The; Getaway, The* (Donaldson); *Ghosts of the Mississippi (aka Ghosts of the Past); Hickey & Boggs; John Q; Kicked in the Head; Killer: A Journal of Murder; Night Moves; Nixon; Once Upon a Time in America; Onion Field, The; Raid on Entebbe; Recess: School's Out; Riding in Cars with Boys; Salvador; Scary Movie 2; Specialist, The; Straight Talk; True Believer (aka Fighting Justice); True Crime; Vampires (aka John Carpenter's Vampires); Videodrome; Virgin Suicides, The.*

Directors' Index

Aaron, Paul *Different Story, A; Force of One, A; Maxie.*

Abashidze, Dodo *Ashik Kerib (Ashug Qaribi/aka Kerib the Minstrel); Legend of the Suram Fortress, The (Legenda Suramskoi Kreposti).*

Abbott, George *Damn Yankees (aka What Lola Wants); Pajama Game, The.*

Abdelsalam, Shadi *Night of Counting the Years, The (El Mumia).*

Abdrashitov, Vadim *Parade of the Planets (Parad Planyet); Plumbum, or a Dangerous Game (Plyumbum, ili opasnaya igra).*

Abel, Robert *Elvis on Tour; Let the Good Times Roll.*

Abey, Dennis *Never Too Young to Rock.*

Abrahams, Jim *Airplane!; Big Business; Hot Shots!; Hot Shots! Part Deux; Ruthless People; Top Secret!; Welcome Home, Roxy Carmichael.*

Abuladze, Tenghiz *Repentance (Monanieba); Wishing Tree, The (Drevo Zhelanya).*

Acevski, Jon *Freddie as F.R.O.7.*

Achbar, Mark *Manufacturing Consent: Noam Chomsky and the Media.*

Achternbusch, Herbert *Last Hole, The (Das letzte Loch).*

Ackerman, Robert Allan *Safe Passage.*

Adams, Catlin *Sticky Fingers.*

Adams, Doug *Blackout (aka The Attic).*

Adams, Marcus *Long Time Dead.*

Adamson, Andrew *Shrek.*

Adelson, Alan *Lodz Ghetto.*

Adidge, Pierre *Elvis on Tour; Mad Dogs and Englishmen.*

Adler, Carine *Under the Skin.*

Adler, Lou *Up In Smoke.*

Adlon, Percy *Bagdad Café (aka Out of Rosenheim); Céleste; Rosalie Goes Shopping; Salmonberries; Sugarbaby (Zuckerbaby); Swing, The (Die Schaukel); Younger and Younger.*

Aduaka, Newton I *Rage.*

Aghion, Gabriel, *Libertin, Le.*

Agland, Phil *Woodlanders, The.*

Agnes Kirchner, Alice *Shampoo and Set (Waschen und Legen).*

Agosti, Silvano *Fit to Be Untied (Matti da Slegare).*

Agostini, Philipe *Dialogue des Carmélites, Le.*

Agresti, Alejandro *Buenos Aires Vice Versa; Cross, The (La Cruz); Secret Wedding (Boda Secreta).*

Aguiluz, Tikoy *Boatman (Ang Bangkero).*

Aguirre, Monti *Amazonia: Voices from the Rainforest (Amazonia: Vozes da Floresto).*

Ahearn, Charlie *Wild Style.*

Ahwesh, Peggy *Deadman, The.*

Aïnouz, Karim *Madame Satã.*

Aitken, Doug *Big Wheels and Sailor.*

Akerman, Chantal (Anne) *American Stories (Histories d'Amérique: Food, Family and Philosophy); Captive, La (The Captive); Contre l'Oubli (Against Oblivion); Couch in New York, A (Un Divan à New York); Golden Eighties; Jeanne Dielman, 23 Quai du Commerce, 1080 Bruxelles; Je tu il elle (I…You… He…She); News from Home; Night and Day (Nuit et Jour); Portrait of a Young Girl at the End of the '60s in Brussels; Rendez-vous d'Anna, Les (The Meetings of Anna); Sud; Toute une Nuit (All Night Long).*

Akhénaton *Comme un Aimant (The Magnet).*

Akin, Fatih *In July (Im Juli).*

Akkad, Moustapha *Al-Risalah (The Message/Mohammad, Messenger of God); Lion of the Desert.*

Akomfrah, John *Handsworth Songs; Speak Like a Child; Testament; Who Needs a Heart.*

Alaux, Myriam *Animals Film, The.*

Albacete, Alfonso *I Will Survive (Sobreviviré).*

Albaladejo, Miguel *Manolito Four-Eyes (Manolita Gatofotas); Ten Days Without Love (El Cielo Abierto).*

Albertini, Adalberto *Black Emanuelle (Emanuelle Nera).*

Albicocco, Jean-Gabriel *Petit Matin, Le (The Virgin and the Soldier); Wanderer, The (Le Grand Meaulnes).*

Albou, Karin *Aïd el Kébir.*

Alda, Alan *Betsy's Wedding; Four Seasons, The; New Life, A; Sweet Liberty.*

Alderman, Thomas S *Severed Arm, The.*

Aldiss, Will *Stealing Home.*

Aldrich, Robert *All the Marbles (aka The California Dolls); Apache; Attack!; Autumn Leaves; Big Knife, The; Choirboys, The; Dirty Dozen, The; Emperor of the North Pole, The (aka Emperor of the North); Flight of the Phoenix, The; Garment Jungle, The; Hush…Hush, Sweet Charlotte; Hustle; Killing of Sister George, The; Kiss Me Deadly; Last Sunset, The; Legend of Lylah Clare, The; Longest Yard, The (aka The Mean Machine); Sodom and Gomorrah (Sodoma e Gomorra); Ten Seconds to Hell; Too Late the Hero; Twilight's Last Gleaming; Ulzana's Raid; Vera Cruz; What Ever Happened to Baby Jane?; World for Ransom.*

Alemann, Claudia von *Blind Spot (Die Reise nach Lyon); Point Is to Change It, The (Es Kommt drauf an, sie zu Verändern).*

Alessandrini, Goffredo *We the Living (Noi Vivi).*

Alexander, Mike *Mairi Mhor.*

Alexandrov, Grigori *Oktyabr (October/Ten Days That Shook the World).*

Alfredson, Daniel *Tic Tac.*

Algar, James *Best of Walt Disney's True Life Adventures, The; Fantasia/2000 (aka Fantasia 2000).*

Al Ghosaini, Samir *Days in London (Ayam fi London).*

Algrant, Dan *Naked in New York.*

Alk, Howard *Janis.*

Allan, Irvine *Daddy's Girl.*

Allanhof, Benjamin *What About Me?*

Allcroft, Britt *Thomas and the Magic Railroad.*

Allégret, Marc *Blanche Fury; Fanny; Lac aux Dames; Lumière; Zouzou.*

Allégret, Yves *Manèges (The Wanton); Orgueilleux, Les (The Proud Ones); Si Jolie Petite Plage, Une (Such a Pretty Little Beach).*

Allen, Corey *Avalanche; Thunder and Lightning.*

Allen, Davida *Feeling Sexy.*

Allen, Irwin *Beyond the Poseidon Adventure; Lost World, The; Swarm, The.*

Allen, Kevin *Big Tease, The; Twin Town.*

Allen, Lewis *Another Time, Another Place; So Evil My Love; Suddenly; Uninvited, The; Unseen, The.*

Allen, Woody *Alice; Annie Hall; Another Woman; Bananas; Broadway Danny Rose; Bullets Over Broadway; Celebrity; Crimes and Misdemeanors; Deconstructing Harry; Everyone Says I Love You; Everything You Always Wanted to Know About Sex, But Were Afraid to Ask; Hannah and Her Sisters; Hollywood Ending; Husbands and Wives; Interiors; Love and Death; Manhattan; Manhattan Murder Mystery; Midsummer Night's Sex Comedy, A; Mighty Aphrodite; New York Stories; Purple Rose of Cairo, The; Radio Days; September; Shadows and Fog; Sleeper; Small Time Crooks; Stardust Memories; Sweet and Lowdown; Take the Money and Run; What's Up Tiger Lily?; Zelig.*

Allers, Roger *Lion King, The.*

Allio, René *Camisards, Les; Contre l'Oubli (Against Oblivion); Moi, Pierre Rivière, ayant égorgé ma mère, ma soeur et mon frère…; Vieille Dame indigne, La (The Shameless Old Lady).*

Allouache, Merzak *Algiers/Beyrouth: pour mémoire (Algiers/Beirut: A Souvenir); Bab El-Oued City; Salut Cousin! (Hey Cousin!); Lumière et Compagnie.*

Almendros, Nestor *Improper Conduct (Mauvaise Conduite).*

Almereyda, Michael *Another Girl, Another Planet; At Sundance; Hamlet; Nadja; Twister.*

Almodóvar, Pedro *All About My Mother (Todo Sobre Mi Madre); Dark Habits (Entre Tinieblas); Flower of My Secret, The (La Flor di me Secreto/La Fleur de mon secret); High Heels (Tacones Lejanos); Kika; Labyrinth of Passion (Laberinto de Pasiones); Law of Desire, The (La Ley del Deseo); Live Flesh (Carne Trémula/En chair et en os); Matador; Pepi, Luci, Bom… (Pepi, Luci, Bom y otras chicas del montón); Tie Me Up! Tie Me Down! (¡Atame!); What Have I Done to Deserve This? (¿Qué He Hecho Yo para Merecer Esto?); Women on the Verge of a Nervous Breakdown (Mujeres al Borde de un Ataque de Nervios).*

Alonso, Lisandro *Libertad, La (Freedom).*

Alonzo, John A *FM.*

Altioklar, Mustafa *Elevator (Asansör).*

Altman, Robert *Aria; Beyond Therapy; Brewster McCloud; Buffalo Bill and the Indias, or Sitting Bull's History Lesson; California Split; Cookie's Fortune; Come Back to the 5 & Dime Jimmy Dean, Jimmy Dean; Countdown; Dr T & the Women; Fool for Love; Gingerbread Man, The; Gosford Park; Health; Images; James Dean Story, The; Long Goodbye, The; M*A*S*H; McCabe and Mrs Miller; Nashville; O.C. & Stiggs; Perfect Couple, A; Player, The; Popeye; Quintet; Ready to Wear (aka Prêt-à-Porter); Robert Altman's Jazz '34: Remembrances of Kansas City Swing; Kansas City; Secret Honor; Short Cuts; Streamers; That Cold Day in the Park; Thieves Like Us; 3 Women; Vincent & Theo (Vincent et Theo); Wedding, A.*

Alvarez, Carlos *What Is Democracy? (¿Qué es la Democracia?).*

Alves, Joe *Jaws 3-D.*

Amalou, JK *Hard Men.*

Amalric, Mathieu *Wimbledon Stage, The (Le Stade de Wimbledon).*

Amar, Denis *Addition, L' (The Patsy); Contre l'Oubli (Against Oblivion).*

Amaral, Suzana *Hour of the Star (A Hora da Estrela).*

Amateau, Rod *Drive-In; Seniors, The (aka The Senior).*

Amber Films/Amber Production Team *Dream On; Eden Valley; In Fading Light; Letters to Katja; Like Father; Seacoal; T. Dan Smith; Writing in the Sand, The.*

Ambrose, Anna *Phoelix.*

Ameli, Rassul Sadr *Girl in the Sneakers, The (Dokhtari Ba Kafsh-Hay-e Katani).*

Amelio, Gianni *Blow to the Heart (Colpire al Cuore); Open Doors (Porte Aperte); Stolen Children, The (Il Ladro di Bambini).*

Amenábar, Alejandro *Open Your Eyes (Abre los ojos/Ouvre les Yeux/Apri gli occhi); Others, The (Los Otros); Thesis (Tesis).*

Amenta, Pino *Heaven Tonight.*

Amero, John *Blonde Ambition.*

Amero, Len *Blonde Ambition.*

Amiel, Jon *Copycat; Entrapment; Queen of Hearts; Man Who Knew Too Little, The; Sommersby; Tune in Tomorrow (aka Aunt Julia and the Scriptwriter).*

Amodeo, Rachel *What About Me?*

Amrohi, Kamal *Pakeezah.*

Amurri, Franco *Flashback; Monkey Trouble.*

Amyes, Julian *Hill in Korea, A (aka Hell in Korea).*

Anciano, Dominic *Final Cut.*

Anders, Allison *Four Rooms; Gas Food Lodging; Grace of My Heart; Love, Honour and Obey; My Crazy Life (Mi Vida Loca)'; Things Behind the Sun.*

Andersen, Knut *I Was Fifteen (Den Sommeren jeg fylte 15).*

Andersen, Thom *Eadweard Muybridge, Zoopraxographer.*

Anderson, Brad *Next Stop Wonderland.*

Anderson, John *Mouth Wide Open – A Journey in Film with Ted Coubray.*

Anderson, John Murray *King of Jazz, The.*

Anderson, J. Todd *Naked Man, The.*

Anderson, Laurie *Home of the Brave.*

Anderson, Lindsay *Britannia Hospital; If…; In Celebration; O Dreamland; O Lucky Man!; This Sporting Life; Whales of August, The; White Bus, The.*

Anderson, Michael *Around the World In 80 Days; Chase a Crooked Shadow; Conduct Unbecoming; Dam Busters, The; Doc Savage – The Man of Bronze; Dominique; Flight from Ashiya; Logan's Run; Millennium; Operation Crossbow; Orca (aka Orca… Killer Whale); Pope Joan; Quiller Memorandum, The; Shoes of the Fisherman, The; Yangtse Incident (aka Battle Hell/Escape of The Amethyst).*

Anderson, Paul *Event Horizon; Mortal Kombat; Shopping.*

Anderson, Paul Thomas *Boogie Nights; Hard Eight; Magnolia; Punch-Drunk Love.*

Anderson, Steve *South Central.*

Anderson, Wes *Bottle Rocket; Royal Tenenbaums, The; Rushmore.*

Andersson, Kjell *Greatness of the Small Man, The.*

Andersson, Roy *Giliap; Songs from the Second Floor (Sånger från Andra Våningen); Something Happened; World of Glory (Härlig är Jorden).*

Andonov, Metodi *Goat Horn, The (Koziyat Rog).*

Andrade, Joaquim Pedro do *Macunaima.*

Andrea, Dree *All Visitors Must Be Announced.*

Andreacchio, Mario *Captain Johnno.*

Andrien, Jean-Jacques *Australia.*

Ang Lee *Crouching Tiger, Hidden Dragon (Wo Hu Zang Long); Eat Drink Man Woman (Yinshi Nan Nü); Ice Storm, The; Pushing Hands (Tui Shou); Ride with the Devil; Sense and Sensibility; Wedding Banquet, The (Xiyan).*

Angel, Hélène *Skin of Man, Heart of Beast (Peau d'homme coeur de bête).*

Angelo, Yves *Colonel Chabert, Le.*

Angelopoulos, Theo *Alexander the Great (O Megalexandros); Bee Keeper, The (O Melissokomos); Eternity and a Day (Mia Eoniotita Ke Mia Mera); Landscape in the Mist (Topio stin Omichli); Lumière et Compagnie; Travelling Players, The (O Thiassos); Ulysses' Gaze (To Vlemma Tou Odyssea/aka The Gaze of Ulysses); Voyage to Cythera (Taxidi sta Kithira).*

Anger, Kenneth *The Anger Magick Lantern Cycle.*

Annakin, Ken *Battle of the Bulge; Call of the Wild, The; Fast Lady, The; Holiday Camp; Hotel Sahara; Huggets Abroad, The; Longest Day, The; Loser Takes All; Paper Tiger; Quartet; Trio; Three Men in a Boat; Value for Money; Very Important Person.*

Annaud, Jean-Jacques *Bear, The (L'Ours); Black and White in Color (La Victoire en Chantant); Enemy at the Gates (Duell – Enemy at the Gates); Lover, The (L'Amant); Name of the Rose, The (Der Name der Rose); Seven Years in Tibet; Quest for Fire.*

Annett, Paul *Beast Must Die, The.*

Ansah, Kwaw *Heritage…Africa.*

Anspach, Sólveig *Haut les Coeurs (Chin Up!/aka Battle Cries).*

Anspaugh, David *Fresh Horses; Hoosiers (aka Best Shot); Moonlight and Valentino; Rudy.*

Anstey, Edgar *Housing Problems.*

Antamoro, Giulio *see* Gant

Anthony, Joseph *Career.*

Antonelli, John *Kerouac.*

Antonijevic, Peter *Savior.*

Antonioni, Michelangelo *Amiche, Le (The Girlfriends); Avventura, L' (The Adventure); Beyond the Clouds (Par-delà les Nuages/Al di là nuvole/ Jenseits der Wolken); Blow-Up; Cronaca di un Amore (Chronicle of a Love Affair); Eclipse, The (L'Eclisse); Identification of a Woman (Identificazione di una Donna); Oberwald Mystery, The (Il Mistero di Oberwald); Notte, La; Passenger, The (Professione: Reporter); Red Desert, The (Deserto Rosso); Signora senza camelie, La (Camille without Camellias/The Lady without Camellias); Zabriskie Point.*

Aoyama, Shinji *Eureka; Mike Yokohama – A Forest with No Name (Hama Mike – Namae no nai Mori); Obsession, An (Tsumetai Chi).*

Appleby, Daniel B *Bound and Gagged: A Love Story.*

Apted, Michael *Agatha; Blink; Bring On the Night; Class Action; Coal Miner's Daughter; Enigma; Extreme Measures; Gorillas in the Mist; Gorky Park; Nell; P'Tang, Yang, Kipperbang; Squeeze, The; Stardust; Thunderheart; Triple Echo, The; World Is Not Enough, The.*

Araki, Gregg *Doom Generation, The; Living End, The; Nowhere; Totally F***ed Up.*

Aranda, Vicente *Jealousy (Celos); Libertarias; Lovers (Amantes); Lumière et Compagnie.*

Arau, Alfonso *Like Water for Chocolate (Como Agua para Chocolate); Walk in the Clouds, A.*

Aravindan, G *Bogey Man, The (Kummatty); Masquerade (Marattom); Sometime, Somewhere (Oridathu).*

Arcand, Denys *Decline of the American Empire, The (Le Déclin de l'Empire Américain); Jesus of Montreal (Jésus de Montréal); Love and Human Remains; Réjeanne Padovani; Stardom.*

Arcelin, Jacques *Bitter Cane.*

Archainbaud, George *Lost Squadron, The.*

Archibugi, Francesca *By Nightfall (Verso Sera); Mignon Has Left (Mignon è partita).*

Ardolino, Emile *Chances Are; Dirty Dancing; Gypsy; Nutcracker, The (aka George Balanchine's The Nutcracker); Sister Act; Three Men and a Little Lady.*

Argento, Dario *Cat o' Nine Tails, The (Il Gatto a Nove Code); Creepers (Phenomena); Four Flies on Grey Velvet (Quattro Mosche di Velluto Grigio); Inferno; Opera (Terror at the Opera); Sleepless (Nonhosonno/aka Non ho sonno); Suspiria; Tenebrae (Sotto gli Occhi dell'Assassino); Trauma; Uccello dalle Piume di Cristallo, L' (The Bird with the Crystal Plumage/The Gallery Murders).*

Ariç, Nizamettin *Song for Beko, A (Ein Lied für Beko/Klamek ji bo Beko).*

Arioli, Don *Charles Dickens' David Copperfield.*

Aristakisyan, Artur *Hands (Ladoni/aka Palms).*

Aristarain, Adolfo *Place in the World, A.*

Arkin, Alan *Little Murders.*

Arkush, Allan *Deathsport; Hollywood Boulevard; Rock'n'Roll High School.*

Arliss, Leslie *Love Story; Man in Grey, The; Wicked Lady, The; Night Has Eyes, The (aka Terror House).*

Armanet, François *Dandy (La Bande du Drugstore).*

Armendáriz, Montxo *Secrets of the Heart (Secretos del corazón); Stories of the Kronen (Historias del Kronen).*

Armitage, George *Grosse Pointe Blank; Miami Blues; Vigilante Force.*

Armiñán, Jaime de *Nest, The (El Nido).*

Armstrong, Gillian *Charlotte Gray; High Tide; Last Days of Chez Nous, The; Little Women; Mrs Soffel; My Brilliant Career; Oscar and Lucinda; Starstruck.*

Arnfred, Morten, *Me and Charly (Mig og Charly); Kingdom, The (Riget); Kingdom II, The (Riget II).*

Arnold, Jack *Black Eye; Boss Nigger (aka The Black Bounty Killer); Creature from the Black Lagoon; Global Affair, A; Incredible Shrinking Man, The; It Came from Outer Space; Marilyn – The Untold Story; Monster on the Campus; Mouse That Roared, The; Revenge of the Creature; Sex Play (aka The Bunny Caper); Swiss Conspiracy, The; Tarantula.*

Arnold, Newt *Bloodsport.*

Aronofsky, Darren *Pi; Requiem for a Dream.*

Aronson, Jerry *Life and Times of Allen Ginsberg, The.*

Arrabal, Fernando *Viva la Muerte.*

Arslan, Thomas *Dealer; Fine Day, A (Der Schöne Tag).*

Arslan, Yilmaz *Passages (Langer Gang); Yara.*

Artenstein, Isaac *Break of Dawn.*

Arteta, Miguel *Chuck & Buck.*

Arthur, Karen *Legacy; Mafu Cage, The.*

Arthy, Natasha *Miracle (Mirakel).*

Arvelo, Alberto *House with a View of the Sea, A (Una Casa con Vista al Mar).*

Arzner, Dorothy *Christopher Strong; Craig's Wife; Dance, Girl, Dance; Merrily We Go to Hell; Nana (aka Lady of the Boulevards); Wild Party, The.*

Ash *Big Bang Theory, The (aka Bang).*

Ashburne, Derek *Naked Are the Cheaters.*

Ashby, Hal *Being There; Bound for Glory; Coming Home; 8 Million Ways to Die; Harold and Maude; Landlord, The; Last Detail, The; Let's Spend the Night Together (aka Time Is On Our Side); Shampoo.*

Asher, Robert *Early Bird, The; Follow a Star; Intelligence Men, The; Movers and Shakers; On the Beat; Press for Time.*

Asher, William *Beach Blanket Bingo.*

Ashida, Toyoo *Fist of the North Star.*

Ashley, Christopher *Jeffrey.*

Askarian, Don *Komitas; On the Old Roman Road.*

Askoldov, Alexander *Commissar, The (Komissar).*

Asquith, Anthony *Browning Version, The; Carrington VC (aka Court Martial); Cottage to Let (aka Bombsight Stolen); Demi-Paradise (aka Adventure for Two); French Without Tears; Guns of Darkness;*

Importance of Being Earnest, The; Libel; Millionairess, The; Orders to Kill; Pygmalion; Tell England; Underground; V.I.P.s, The; Way to the Stars, The (aka Johnny in the Clouds).

Assayas, Olivier *Destinées Sentimentales, Les; Eau Froide, L' (Cold Water); Irma Vep; Late August, Early September (Fin août, début septembre); Paris s'éveille (Paris Awakens).*

Asseo, André *Enfants de Lumière, Les (The Children of Lumière).*

Astrakhan, Dimitri *You Are My Only Love.*

Atalla, Jorge Wolney *In Cane for Life (A Vida em Cana).*

Ataman, Kutlug *Lola + Bilidikid.*

Athens, JD *Cannibal Women in the Avocado Jungle of Death (aka Piranha Women in the Avocado Jungle of Death).*

Athié, Francisco *Lolo.*

Atkins, David *Novocaine.*

Atkinson, Jim *Can You Keep It Up for a Week?*

Attenborough, Richard *Bridge Too Far, A; Chaplin; Chorus Line, A; Cry Freedom; Gandhi; Grey Owl; In Love and War; Magic; Oh! What a Lovely War; Shadowlands; Young Winston.*

Attias, Daniel *Silver Bullet.*

Attwood, David *Shot Through the Heart; Wild West.*

Au, Tony *Au revoir, mon amour (He Rijun Zai Lai).*

Audiard, Jacques *Héros très discret, Un (A Self-Made Hero); Regarde les hommes tomber (See How They Fall).*

Audry, Jacqueline *Gigi; Huis Clos (No Exit/Vicious Circle); Olivia.*

Auer, John H *City That Never Sleeps.*

Auguiste, Reece *Twilight City.*

August, Bille *Best Intentions, The (Den Goda Viljan); Buster's World (Busters Vedren); House of Spirits, The; Les Misérables; Pelle the Conqueror (Pelle Erobreren); Smilla's Feeling for Snow (Fräulein Smillas Gespür für Schnee/aka Smilla's Sense of Snow).*

Austen, Chris *South Africa Belongs to Us.*

Auster, Paul *Blue in the Face.*

Austin, Michael *Killing Dad; Princess Caraboo.*

Autant-Lara, Claude *Affaire du Courrier de Lyon, L'; Auberge Rouge, L' (The Red Inn); Diable au corps, Le (Devil in the Flesh); Douce; En Cas de Malheur (La Ragazza del Peccato/Love Is My Profession); Traversée de Paris, La (Pig Across Paris/Four Bags Full).*

Auzins, Igor *We of the Never Never.*

Avakian, Aram *Cops and Robbers; 11 Harrowhouse; End of the Road.*

Avalos, Stefan *Last Broadcast, The.*

Avary, Roger *Killing Zoe.*

Avati, Pupi *Festival; Noi tre (The Three of Us/We Three).*

Avdeliodis, Demos *Four Seasons of the Law, The (I Earni Synaxis ton Agrofylakon).*

Avedis, Howard (Hikmet) *Stepmother, The; They're Playing With Fire.*

Averback, Hy *Chamber of Horrors; I Love You, Alice B. Toklas!; Where the Boys Are; Where Were You When the Lights Went Out?*

Avila, Carlos *Price of Glory.*

Avildsen, John G *Cry Uncle (aka Super Dick); 8 Seconds; For Keeps (aka Maybe Baby); Formula, The; Karate Kid, The; Karate Kid: Part II, The; Karate Kid Part III, The; Neighbors; Power of One, The; Rocky; Rocky V; Save the Tiger; Slow Dancing in the Big City; Stoolie, The; W.W. and the Dixie Dancekings.*

Avnet, Jon *Fried Green Tomatoes at the Whistle Stop Café; Red Corner; Up Close & Personal; War, The.*

Axel, Gabriel *Babette's Feast (Babettes Gaestebud); Lumière et Compagnie; Prince of Jutland.*

Axelrod, George *Lord Love a Duck; Secret Life of an American Wife, The.*

Ayouch, Nabil *Ali Zaoua: Prince de la Rue (Ali Zaoua: Prince of the Street); Mektoub.*

Azéma, Sabine *Bonjour, Monsieur Doisneau.*

Azpurúa, Carlos *Disparen a Matar (Shoot to Kill).*

B, Beth *Salvation! Have You Said Your Prayers Today? (aka Salvation!); Vortex.*

B, Scott *Vortex.*

Babenco, Hector *At Play in the Fields of the Lord; Ironweed; Kiss of the Spider Woman; Pixote (Pixote a lei do mais fraco).*

Babbit, Jamie *But I'm a Cheerleader.*

Bach, Jean *Great Day in Harlem, A.*

Bacon, Lloyd *Action in the North Atlantic; Boy Meets Girl; Brother Orchid; Footlight Parade; 42nd Street; French Line, The; Gold Diggers of 1937; In Caliente; Invisible Stripes; Marked Woman; Miss Pinkerton; Picture Snatcher; Slight Case of Murder, A; You Were Meant for Me.*

Bacsó, Péter *Witness, The (A Tanu).*

Badham, John *American Flyers; Another Stakeout; Bingo Long Travelling All-Stars & Motor Kings, The; Bird on a Wire; Blue Thunder; Dracula; Drop Zone; Hard Way, The; Incognito; Nick of Time; Point of No Return (aka The Assassin); Saturday Night Fever; Short Circuit; Stakeout; Sunshine Part II (aka My Sweet Lady); WarGames; Whose Life Is It Anyway?*

Baer, Max *Ode to Billy Joe.*

Bae Yong-Kyun *Why Did Bohdi-Dharma Leave for the Orient? (Dharmaga tongjoguro kan kkadalgun?).*

Bafaloukos, Theodoros *Rockers.*

Bagdadi, Maroun *Fille de l'Air, La; Hors la vie (Out of Life).*

Bahr, Fax *Hearts of Darkness: A Filmmaker's Apocalypse.*

Baichwal, Jennifer *Let It Come Down: The Life of Paul Bowles.*

Baigelman, Steven *Feeling Minnesota.*

Bail, Chuck *Choke Canyon (aka On Dangerous Ground); Cleopatra Jones and the Casino of Gold; Gumball Rally, The.*

Bailey, John *China Moon.*

Baily, John *Amir.*

Baird, Stuart *Executive Decision; U.S. Marshals.*

Bakari, Imruh *Blue Notes and Exiled Voices.*

Baker, David *Libido.*

Baker, Fred *Lenny Bruce Without Tears.*

Baker, Graham *Alien Nation; Final Conflict, The; Impulse.*

Baker, Robert S *Hellfire Club, The; Siege of Sidney Street, The.*

Baker, Roy Ward *...And Now the Screaming Starts! (aka Fengriffen); Anniversary, The; Asylum; Dr Jekyll and Sister Hyde; Don't Bother to Knock; Flame in the Streets; Higly Dangerous; Inferno; Legend of the 7 Golden Vampires, The; Monster Club, The; Morning Departure (aka Operation Disaster); Night to Remember, A; October Man, The; One That Got Away, The; Passage Home; Quatermass and the Pit; Scars of Dracula, The; Singer Not the Song, The; Vampire Lovers, The; Vault of Horror.*

Bakshi, Ralph *Cool World; Fire and Ice; Fritz the Cat; Heavy Traffic; Lord of the Rings, The; Wizards.*

Balaban, Bob *Last Good Time, The; Parents; Subway Stories Tales from the Underground.*

Balabanov, Alexei (Aleksei) *Brother (Brat); Happy Days (Stchastlivye Dni); Of Freaks and Men (Pro Ourodov i Lioudiei).*

Balasko, Josiane *Gazon maudit (French Twist).*

Balayan, Roman *Dream Flights (Polioty Vo Sne Naiavou).*

Balch, Antony *Horror Hospital.*

Baldi, Ferdinando *Blindman; Comin' at Ya!; Texas, Addio (aka The Avenger); Treasure of the Four Crowns.*

Baldwin, Craig *Tribulation 99: Alien Anomalies Under America; Sonic Outlaws; Spectres of the Spectrum.*

Ballard, Carroll *Black Stallion, The; Fly Away Home; Never Cry Wolf; Nutcracker – the Motion Picture; Wind.*

Balletbò-Coll, Marta *Costa Brava (Family Album).*

Balling, Erik *One of Those Things (Haendeligt Uheld).*

Ballmann, Herbert *Girl in a Boot (Einmal Ku'damm und Zurück).*

Balshofer, Fred J *Isle of Love, The.*

Bancroft, Tony *Mulan.*

Banderas, Antonio *Crazy in Alabama.*

Band, Charles *Alchemist, The; Metalstorm: The Destruction of Jared-Syn; Parasite; Trancers (aka Future Cop).*

Bangura, Roberto *Girl with Brains in Her Feet.*

Banham, Derek *Last Day of Summer.*

Banks, Monty *Shipyard Sally.*

Banno, Yoshimitsu *Godzilla vs the Smog Monster (Gojira tai Hedora).*

Baran, Jack *Destiny Turns on the Radio.*

Baratier, Jacques *Araignée de Satin, L' (Satin Spider); First Time with Feeling (Vous Intéressez-vous à la Chose?).*

Barba, Norbert *Blue Tiger.*

Barbash, Uri *Beyond the Walls (Me'Achorei Hasoragim); One of Us (Echad Mi'Shelanu).*

Barbera, Joseph *Jetsons: The Movie.*

Bardem, Juan Antonio *Calle Mayor (The Love Maker/ Main Street).*

Bardem, Miguel *Ugliest Woman in the World, The (La Mujer más fea del mundo).*

Bare, Richard L *Wicked, Wicked.*

Barkas, Geoffrey *Tell England.*

Barker, Clive *Hellraiser; Lord of Illusions; Nightbreed.*

Barker, Mike *Best Laid Plans; James Gang, The.*

Barnet, Boris *House on Trubnaya, The (Dom na Trubnoi).*

Barnett, Steve *Mindwarp.*

Barney, Matthew *Cremaster 5.*

Barr, Jean-Marc *Lovers – Dogme 5.*

Barreto, Bruno *Carried Away (aka Acts of Love); Doña Flor and Her Two Husbands (Doña Flor e Seus Dois Maridos); Four Days in September (O Que é Isso, Companheiro?); Gabriela; Show of Force, A.*

Barrett, Lezli-An *Business As Usual.*

Barris, Chuck *Gong Show Movie, The.*

Barron, Arthur *Jeremy.*

Barron, Steve *Adventures of Pinocchio, The; Electric Dreams; Mike Bassett England Manager; Teenage Mutant Ninja Turtles.*

Barron, Zelda *Secret Places; Shag.*

Barroso, Mariano *Extasis.*

Barry, Ian *Chain Reaction, The.*

Barta, Jirí *Pied Piper, The (Krysar).*

Bartas, Sharunas *Freedom.*

Bartel, Paul *Cannonball (aka Carquake); Death Race 2000; Eating Raoul; Lust in the Dust; Not for Publication; Private Parts; Scenes from the Class Struggle in Beverly Hills; Secret Cinema, The.*

Bartkowiak, Andrzej *Exit Wounds; Romeo Must Die.*

Bartlett, Hall *Jonathan Livingston Seagull.*

Barton, Charles T *Abbott and Costello Meet Frankenstein (aka Abbott and Costello Meet the Ghosts).*

Barua, Jahnu *It's a Long Way to the Sea (Hkhagoroloi Bohu Door).*

Basaran, Tunç *Abuzer Baklava (Abuzer Kadayif).*

Baser, Tevfik *Farewell, Stranger (Lebewohl Fremde); Farwell to False Paradise (Abschied vom Falschen Paradies/Yalanci Cennete Elveda); 40 Metre Square Germany (40 Metrekare Almanya).*

Bashore, Juliet *Kamikaze Hearts.*

Baskin, Richard *Sing.*

Bass, Jules *Mad Monster Party; Last Unicorn, The.*

Bass, Saul *Phase IV.*

Batchelor, Joy *Animal Farm.*

Batsry, Irit *These Are Not My Images (neither there nor here).*

Battersby, Roy *Mr Love.*

Battiato, Giacomo *Blood Ties (Il Cugino Americano).*

Bauer, Evgenij *Dying Swan, The (Umirajuseij lebed).*

Bauer, Tristán *Borges, Books and the Night (Borges, los libros y las noches); Cortazar.*

Bava, Lamberto *Demons (Demoni); Demons 2 (Demoni 2).*

Bava, Mario *Black Sabbath (I Tre Volti della Paura); Danger: Diabolik (Diabolik); Maschera del Demonio, La (Black Sunday/Mask of the Demon/Revenge of the Vampire); Quante Volte… Quella Notte (Four Times That Night); Strada per Forte Alamo, La (Arizona Bill/The Road to Fort Alamo).*

Baxley, Craig R *Action Jackson; Dark Angel; Stone Cold.*

Baxter, John *Common Touch, The; Crooks' Tour; Let the People Sing; Love on the Dole; Song of the Road.*

Bay, Michael *Armageddon; Bad Boys; Pearl Harbor; Rock, The.*

Bayly, Stephen *Coming Up Roses; Just Ask for Diamond.*

Beaird, David *It Takes Two; Scorchers.*

Bean, Henry *Believer, The.*

Bean, Robert B *Made for Each Other.*

Beatt, Cynthia *Party – Nature Morte, The.*

Beatty, Warren *Bulworth; Dick Tracy; Heaven Can Wait; Reds.*

Beaudin, Jean *Being at Home with Claude (Seul, avec Claude); J.A. Martin Photographer (J.A. Martin Photographe).*

Beaudine, William *Billy the Kid vs. Dracula; Boys Will Be Boys; Old-Fashioned Way, The; Voodoo Man; Windbag the Sailor.*

Beaufoy, Simon *Darkest Light, The.*

Beaumont, Gabrielle *Godsend, The.*

Beauvois, Xavier *N'oublie pas que tu vas mourir (Don't Forget You're Going to Die); Nord (North); Selon Mathieu.*

Beaver, Chris *Dark Circle.*

Bechis, Marco *Garage Olimpo.*

Beck, Steve *Thirteen Ghosts (aka Thir13teen Ghosts).*

Becker, Harold *Black Marble, The; Boost, The; City Hall; Domestic Disturbance; Malice; Mercury Rising; Onion Field, The; Ragman's Daughter, The; Sea of Love; Taps; Vision Quest (aka Crazy for You).*

Becker, Jacques *Casque d'Or (Golden Marie); Falbalas; Goupi Mains Rouges (It Happened at the Inn); Rendez-vous de juillet; Touchez pas au Grisbi (Grisbi/Honour Among Thieves); Trou, Le (The Hole/The Night Watch).*

Becker, Jean *Contre l'Oubli (Against Oblivion); Elisa; Enfants du Marais, Les (Children of the Marshland); One Deadly Summer (L'Eté Meurtrier).*

Becker, Lutz *Double Headed Eagle, The.*

Becker, Wolfgang *Child's Play (Kinderspiel); Life Is All You Get (Das Leben ist eine Baustelle).*

Bedford, Terry *Slayground.*

Beeman, Greg *License to Drive.*

Beesley, Mark *Savage Honeymoon.*

Bégéja, Liria *Loin des Barbares (Far from the Barbarians).*

Behi, Rihda *Hyenas' Sun (Soleil des Hyènes).*

Beineix, Jean-Jacques *Betty Blue (37°2 le Matin)* [versions 1 & 2]; *Diva; IP5; Moon in the Gutter, The (La Lune dans le Caniveau); Roselyne and the Lions (Roselyne et les lions).*

Bekolo, Jean-Pierre *Aristotle's Plot (Le Complot de Aristote).*

Bélanger, Louis *Post Mortem.*

Belén, Ana *How to Be a Woman and Not Die in the Attempt (Como ser mujer y no morir en el intento).*

Belikov, Mikhail *When We Were Young (Kak Molody My Byli).*

Bell, Martin *American Heart; Streetwise.*

Bellamy, Earl *Fire; Speedtrap.*

Beller, Hava Kohav *Burning Wall, The.*

Bellew, Bonner *Scratch.*

Bellisario, Donald P *Last Rites.*

Bellocchio, Marco *China Is Near (La Cina è vicina); Diavolo in Corpo, Il (Le Diable au corps/Devil in the Flesh); Fists in the Pocket (I Pugni in Tasca); Fit To Be Untied (Matti da Slegare); In the Name of the Father (Nel Nome del Padre); Leap into the Void (Salto nel Vuoto); Prince of Homburg, The (Il Principe di Homburg).*

Belmont, Véra *Marquise; Rouge Baiser.*

Belson, Jerry *Surrender.*

Belvaux, Rémy *Man Bites Dog (C'est arrivé près de chez vous).*

Belzberg, Edet *Children Underground.*

Bemberg, María Luisa *Camila; I, the Worst of All (Yo, la Peor de Todas); Miss Mary; We Don't Want to Talk About It (De eso no se habla).*

Benabib, Roberto *Little City.*

Ben-Dor Niv, Orna *Because of That War (Biglal Hamilkhama Hahi).*

Bene, Carmelo *One Hamlet Less (Un Amleto di Meno).*

Benedek, Laslo *Namu, The Killer Whale; Wild One, The.*

Benedict, Richard *Impasse.*

Benedikt, Julian *Blue Note: A History of Modern Jazz.*

Benegal, Shyam *Ankur (The Seeling); Ascending Scale (Arohan); Boon, The (Kondura); Role, The (Bhumika); Trikal: Past, Present and Future (Trikal).*

Benigni, Roberto *Life Is Beautiful (La Vita è Bella).*

Benjamin, Richard *City Heat; Little Nikita (aka Sleepers); Made in America; Mermaids; Milk Money; Mrs Winterbourne; Money Pit, The; My Favorite Year; My Stepmother Is an Alien; Racing with the Moon.*

Benner, Richard *Outrageous!*

Bennett, Bill *Backlash; In a Savage Land; Kiss or Kill; Malpractice; Mortgage; Spider and Rose; Two If by Sea (aka Stolen Hearts).*

Bennett, Compton *Seventh Veil, The; So Little Time.*

Bennett, Edward *Ascendancy; Life Story of Baal, The.*

Bennett, Leroy *Cure Show, The.*

Benoit, Patricia *Subway Stories Tales from the Underground.*

Bensalah, Djamel *Ciel, les Oiseaux et… Ta Mère, Le (Boys on the Beach).*

Benson, Robby *Crack in the Mirror; Modern Love.*

Benson, Leon *Sunshine Part II (aka My Sweet Lady).*

Bentley, Thomas *Old Curiosity Shop, The.*

Benton, Robert *Bad Company; Billy Bathgate; Kramer vs Kramer; Late Show, The; Nadine; Nobody's Fool; Places in the Heart; Still of the Night; Twilight.*

Benveniste, Michael *Flesh Gordon.*

Benz, Obie *Heavy Petting.*

Béraud, Luc *Turtle on Its Back (La Tortue sur la Dos).*

Bercovici, Luca *Ghoulies.*

Beresford, Bruce *Adventures of Barry McKenzie, The; Aria; Black Robe; Breaker Morant; Club, The; Crimes of the Heart; Don's Party; Double Jeopardy; Driving Miss Daisy; Fringe Dwellers, The; Getting of Wisdom, The; Good Man in Africa, A; Her Alibi; King David; Last Dance; Mister Johnson; Money Movers; Paradise Road; Puberty Blues; Rich in Love; Side by Side; Silent Fall; Tender Mercies.*

Berg, Peter *Very Bad Things.*

Bergenstråhle, Johan *Foreigners (Jag Heter Stelius).*

Berger, Ludwig *Thief of Bagdad, The.*

Bergeron, Eric *Road to El Dorado, The.*

Bergman, Andrew *Freshman, The; Honeymoon in Vegas; Isn't She Great; It Could Happen to You; So Fine; Striptease.*

Bergman, Daniel *Söndags Barn (Sunday's Children).*

Bergman, Ingmar *Ansiktet (The Face/The Magician); Autumn Sonata (Herbstsonate); Cries and Whispers (Viskingar och Rop); Devil's Eye, The (Djävulens Öga); Face to Face (Ansikte mot Ansikte); Fanny and Alexander (Fanny och Alexander); From the Life of the Marionettes (Aus dem Leben der Marionetten); Gycklarnas Afton (The Naked Night/Sawdust and Tinsel); Hour of the Wolf (Vargtimmen); Kvinnodröm (Dreams/Journey Into Autumn); Magic Flute, The (Trollflöjten); Nattvardsgästerna (The Communicants/Winter Light); Passion, A (En Passion); Persona; Rite, The (Riten); Scenes from a Marriage (Scener ur ett äktenskap); Serpent's Egg, The (Das Schlangenei); Seventh Seal, The (Det Sjunde Inseglet); Shame, The (Skammen); Silence, The (Tystnaden); Smiles of a Summer Night (Sommarnattens Leende); Sommaren med Monika (Monika/Summer with Monika); Sommarlek (Illicit Interlude/Summer Interlude); Through a Glass Darkly (Sasom i en Spegel); Touch, The; Wild Strawberries (Smultronstället); Virgin Spring, The (Jungfrukällan).*

Bergon, Serge *Joy.*

Bergqvist, Stig *Rugrats in Paris: The Movie.*

Berkeley, Busby *Babes in Arms; Babes on Broadway; For Me and My Gal; Gang's All Here, The (aka The Girls He Left Behind); Gold Diggers of 1935; Strike Up the Band; Take Me Out to the Ball Game (aka Everybody's Cheering).*

Berkoff, Steven *Decadence.*

Berlanga, Luis Garcia *Life Size; Verdugo, El (The Executioner/Not On Your Life).*

Berlanti, Greg *Broken Hearts Club, The.*

Berliner, Alain *Ma Vie en Rose.*

Berlinger, Joe *Book of Shadows Blair Witch 2.*

Berman, Brigitte *Bix: 'Ain't None of Them Play Like Him Yet'.*

Berman, Jonathan *Shvitz, The.*

Berman, Monty *Hellfire Club, The.*

Berman, Ted *Black Cauldron, The; Fox and the Hound, The.*

Bernal, Ishmael *Manila After Dark (aka City After Dark).*

Bernard, Chris *Letter to Brezhnev, A.*

Bernard, Raymond *Croix de Bois, Les (Wooden Crosses).*

Bernardin, Alain *Crazy Horse of Paris, The (Crazy Horse de Paris).*

Bernds, Edward *Quantrill's Raiders; Queen of Outer Space; Return of the Fly.*

Bernhardt, Curtis *Conflict; Devotion; Miss Sadie Thompson; Possessed; Stolen Life, A.*

Bernstein, Walter *Little Miss Marker.*

Berri, Claude *Germinal; Jean de Florette; Lucie Aubrac; Manon des Sources; Mazel Tov ou le mariage (Marry Me! Marry Me!); Moment d'Egarement, Un (In a Wild Moment/One Wild Moment/ A Summer Affair); Sex Shop; Tchao Pantin; Uranus; Vieil Homme et l'Enfant, Le (The Two of Us).*

Berruti, Giulio *Killer Nun (Suor omicidio).*

Berry, John *Bad News Bears Go to Japan, The; Boesman & Lena; Ça va Barder… (Give 'em Hell/Silenzio…Si Spara!); Claudine; From This Day Forward.*

Bertoglio, Edo *Downtown 81 (aka Glenn O'Brien's New York Beat Movie).*

Bertolucci, Bernardo *Before the Revolution (Prima della Rivoluzione); Besieged (L'Assedio); Commare Secca, La (The Grim Reaper); Conformist, The (Il Conformista); Last Emperor, The; Last Tango in Paris; Little Buddha; Luna, La; 1900 (Novecento); Partner; Sheltering Sky, The; Spider's Stratagem, The (Strategia del Ragno); Stealing Beauty (Io ballo da sola/Beauté Volée); Tragedy of a Ridiculous Man, The (La Tragedia di un Uomo Ridicolo).*

Bertuccelli, Jean-Louis *Paulina 1880; Ramparts of Clay (Remparts d'Argile).*

Berwick Street Film Collective *Ireland: Behind the Wire; Nightcleaners.*

Besson, Luc *Atlantis; Big Blue, The; Fifth Element, The (Le Cinquième Elément); Joan of Arc (Jeanne d'Arc); Last Battle, The (Le Dernier Combat); Leon (aka The Professional); Nikita; Subway.*

Beyer, Frank *Held for Questioning (Der Aufenthalt).*

Bharadwaj, Radha *Closet Land.*

Bhattacharya, Uday *Circle of Gold.*

Bianchi, Edward *Fan, The; Off and Running.*

Biberman, Herbert J *Master Race, The; Salt of the Earth.*

Bicat, Tony *Skinflicker.*

Bielinsky, Fabián, *Nine Queens (Nueve Reinas).*

Bierman, Robert *Keep the Aspidistra Flying (aka A Merry War); Vampire's Kiss.*

Bigas Luna, (JJ) *Anguish (Angustia); Golden Balls (Huevos de Oro); Jamón Jamón; Lumière et Compagnie; Tit and the Moon, The (La Teta y la luna/La teta i la lluna/La Lune et le téton).*

Bigelow, Kathryn *Blue Steel; Loveless, The; Near Dark; Point Break; Strange Days; Weight of Water, The.*

Bijl, Jacob *Beck (aka The Locked Room).*

Bilal, Enki *Bunker Palace Hotel.*

Bill, Tony *Crazy People; Five Corners; Home of Our Own, A; My Bodyguard; Six Weeks; Untamed Heart.*

Billard, Pierre *Enfants de Lumière, Les (The Children of Lumière).*

Billington, Kevin *Interlude; Light at the Edge of the World, The; Reflections; Rise and Rise of Michael Rimmer, The; Voices.*

Bilson, Bruce *North Avenue Irregulars, The (aka Hill's Angels).*

Bilson, Danny *Zone Troopers.*

Binder, Mike *Crossing the Bridge.*

Binzer, Roland *Ladies and Gentlemen, the Rolling Stones.*

Birch, Patricia *Grease 2.*

Bird, Antonia *Face; Mad Love; Priest; Ravenous.*

Bird, Brad *Iron Giant, The.*

Bird, Stewart *Wobblies, The.*

Birkin, Andrew *Burning Secret; Cement Garden, The.*

Birkin, Jane *Contre l'Oubli (Against Oblivion).*

Bishop, Larry *Mad Dog Time (aka Trigger Happy).*

Bishop, Terry *Cover Girl Killer.*

Bistiskas, Alexis *Dawn, The (To Harama).*

Björkman, Stig *White Wall, The (Den Vita Väggen).*

Blaché, Herbert *Saphead, The.*

Black, Cathal *Korea; Pigs.*

Black, Michael *Pictures.*

Black, Noel *Man, a Woman and a Bank, A; Pretty Poison.*

Blackwood, Christian *Motel; Roger Corman: Hollywood's Wild Angel; Signed; Lino Brocka; Tapdancin'.*

Blackwood, Maureen *Passion of Remembrance, The.*

Blair, David *Wax, or The Discovery of Television Among the Bees.*

Blair, Les *Bad Behaviour; Jump the Gun; Number One.*

Blakemore, Michael *Country Life; Personal History of the Australian Surf, A; Privates on Parade.*

Blanc, Christophe *Faute de Soleil (For Want of Sun).*

Blanc, Michel *Escort, The (Mauvaise Passe); Grosse Fatigue.*

Blanco, Jorge *Argie.*

Blank, Les *Always for Pleasure; Burden of Dreams; Garlic Is as Good as Ten Mothers.*

Blanks, Jamie *Urban Legend; Valentine.*

Blasetti, Alessandro *Fabiola (aka Fighting Gladiator).*

Blatty, William Peter *Exorcist III, The; Ninth Configuration, The (aka Twinkle, Twinkle Killer Kane).*

Blaustein, Barry W *Beyond the Mat.*

Blier, Bertrand *Buffet Froid; Merci la vie (Thank You Life); Mon Homme; My Best Friend's Girl (La Femme de Mon Pote); Notre Histoire (Our Story/Separate Rooms); Préparez Vos Mouchoirs (Get Out Your Handkerchiefs); Stepfather (Beau-père); Tenue de Soirée (Evening Dress); Trop belle pour toi! (Too Beautiful for You); Un Deux Trois Soleil (1, 2, 3, Sun); Valseuses, Les (Going Places/Making It).*

Bliss, Barry *Fords on Water.*

Blistène, Marcel *Etoile sans Lumière (Star Without Light).*

Blom, Per *Ice Palace, The (Isslottet).*

Bloom, Jeffrey *Bloody Beach; Flowers in the Attic; Dog pound Shuffle (aka Spot).*

Bloomfield, George *Child Under a Leaf (aka Love Child).*

Blum, Chris *Big Time.*

Bluth, Don *All Dogs Go to Heaven; American Tail, An; Anastasia; Land Before Time, The; Pebble and the Penguin, The; Rock-a-Doodle; Secret of NIMH, The; Thumbelina; Titan A.E.*

Blystone, John G *Block-heads; Our Hospitality.*

Blyth, Jeff *Cheetah.*

Bobrova, Lidia *In That Land (V toi Stranje).*

Bochner, Hart *High School High.*

Bodrov, Sergei *Freedom Is Paradise (SER); I Wanted to See Angels (Ja Chtela Uwidetj Angelow); Prisoner of the Mountains (Kavkazski Plennik).*

Bodrov Jr, Sergei *Sisters (Sestry).*

Boetticher, Budd *Buchanan Rides Alone; Bullfighter and the Lady, The; City Beneath the Sea; Comanche Station; East of Sumatra; Horizons West; Killer Is Loose, The; Ride Lonesome; Rise and Fall of Legs Diamond, The; Seven Men from Now; Tall T, The; Time for Dying, A.*

Bogart, Paul *Broadway Bound; Class of '44; Marlowe; Torch Song Trilogy.*

Bogayevicz, Yurek *Anna; Three of Hearts.*

Bogdanovich, Peter *At Long Last Love; Cat's Meow, The; Daisy Miller; Last Picture Show, The; Mask; Nickelodeon; Noises Off; Paper Moon; Saint Jack; Targets; Texasville; They All Laughed; Thing Called Love, The; What's Up Doc?*

Boger, Chris *Cruel Passion.*

Bogle, James *In the Winter Dark.*

Boisrond, Michel *Catherine and Co (Catherine et Cie),*

Boisset, Yves *Attentat, L' (Plot); Cobra (La Saut de l'Ange); Espion Lève-toi; Folle à Tuer (The Evil Trap); Prize of Peril The (Le Prix du Danger); Purple Taxi, The (Le Taxi Mauve); Sheriff, Le (Le Juge Fayard dit le Sheriff).*

Bokova, Jana *Hôtel du Paradis; Love Is Like a Violin; Militia Battlefield.*

Bolado, Jorgé *Second Century (Segundo Siglo).*

Boldt, Rainer *Due to an Act of God (Im Zeichen des Kreuzes).*

Boleslawski, Richard *Garden of Allah, The; Les Misérables; Painted Veil, The; Rasputin and the Empress; Theodora Goes Wild.*

Böll, Heinrich *Germany in Autumn (Deutschland im Herbst).*

Bollaín, Iciar *Hi, Are You Alone? (Hola, estás sola?).*

Bolognini, Mauro *Dame aux Camélias, La; Down the Ancient Stairs (Per le Antiche Scala); Drama of the Rich (Fatti di Gente Perbene); Inheritance, The (L'Eredità Ferramonti).*

Bolotin, Craig *That Night.*

Bolt, Ben *Arm, The (aka The Big Town).*

Bolt, Robert *Lady Caroline Lamb.*

Bond, Jack *It Couldn't Happen Here.*

Bond III, James *DEF by Temptation.*

Bondarchuk, Sergei *War and Peace (Voina i Mir); Waterloo.*

Bondy, Luc *Josephine (Die Ortliebschen Frauen).*

Bonello, Bertrand *Pornographer, The (Le Pornographe).*

Bonerz, Peter *Police Academy 6: City Under Siege.*

Bonitzer, Pascal *Rien sur Robert.*

Bonzel, André *Man Bites Dog (C'est arrivé près de chez vous).*

Boon Joon-Ho *Barking Dogs Never Bite (Puhran Dah Suh ui Geh/aka A Higher Animal).*

Boorman, John *Beyond Rangoon; Catch Us If You Can (aka Having a Wild Weekend); Deliverance; Emerald Forest, The; Excalibur; Exorcist II: The Heretic; General, The; Hell in the Pacific; Hope and Glory; Leo the Last; Lumière et Compagnie; Point Blank; Tailor of Panama, The; Where the Heart Is; Zardoz.*

Booth, Harry *Go for a Take; Mutiny on the Buses; On the Buses.*

Borau, José Luis *B. Must Die (Hay que Matar a B); Poachers (Furtivos).*

Borden, Lizzie *Born in Flames; Erotique; Working Girls.*

Bordowitz, Gregg *Fast Trip, Long Drop.*

Boris, Robert *Oxford Blues.*

Bork, Miroslav *Consul, The (Konsul).*

Bornedal, Ole *Nightwatch (Nattevagten,* 1994); *Nightwatch* (1998).

Boros, Phillip *Grey Fox, The; Mean Season, The.*

Borowczyk, Walerian *Ars Amandi (L'Art d'Aimer/The Art of Love); Behind Convent Walls (L'Interno di un Convento); Blanche; Bête, La (The Beast); Docteur Jekyll et les Femmes (The Blood of Doctor Jekyll/ Doctor Jekyll and Miss Osbourne); Goto, l'île d'amour (Goto, Island of Love); Immoral Tales (Contes Immoraux); Marge, La (The Streetwalker); Story of Sin, The (Dzieje Grzechu); Théâtre de Monsieur et Madame Kabal.*

Borsos, Phillip *Far from Home: The Adventures of Yellow Dog.*

Borthwick, Dave *Secret Adventures of Tom Thumb, The.*

Borzage, Frank *Desire, Farewell to Arms, A; Green Light; History Is Made at Night; Little Man, What Now?; Lucky Star; Magnificent Doll; Man's Castle; Moonrise; Mortal Storm, The; Secrets; 7th Heaven; Shining Hour, The; Spanish Main, The; Strange Cargo; Street Angel; Three Comrades; Till We Meet Again.*

Bose, Tapan K *Indian Story, An.*

Boskovich, John *Without You I'm Nothing.*

Botelho, João *Hard Times (Tempos Dificeis, Este Tempo); Other One, The (Conversa Acabada); Portuguese Goodbye, A (Un Adeus Português); Trafico; Três Palmeiras (Three Palm Trees).*

Bottagisio, Jacqueline *Voice of Kurdistan, The.*

Böttcher, Jürgen *In Georgia (In Georgien).*

Boucault, Mosco *Terrorists in Retirement (Des Terroristes à la retraite).*

Boughédir, Férid *Summer in La Goulette, A (Un été à La Goulette).*

Bouhnik, Laurent *1999 Madeleine; Sélect Hotel.*

Boulting, John *Brighton Rock; Heavens Above!; I'm All Right, Jack; Journey Together; Lucky Jim; Magic Box, The; Private's Progress; Rotten to the Core; Seven Days to Noon.*

Boulting, Roy *Brothers in Law; Desert Victory; Fame Is the Spur; French Mistress, A; Guinea Pig, The (aka The Outsider); Pastor Hall; Run for the Sun; Soft Beds, Hard Battles; There's a Girl in My Soup; Thunder Rock; Tunisian Victory.*

Bourguignon, Serge *Reward, The.*

Bowen, Jenny *Street Music.*

Bower, Dallas *Alice In Wonderland.*

Bowers, George *Body and Soul; Hearse, The; My Tutor.*

Bowman, Antony J *Paperback Hero.*

Bowman, Rob *X Files, The.*

Bowser, Kenneth *Frank Capra's American Dream.*

Box, Muriel *Beachcomber, The; Happy Family, The (aka Mr Lord Says No); This Other Eden; Simon and Laura.*

Boyd, Don *East of Elephant Rock; Intimate Reflections; Lucia; Twenty-One.*

Boyd, Joe *Jimi Hendrix.*

Boyd, William *Trench, The (Tranchée, La).*

Boyer, Jean *Trou Normand, Le (Crazy for Love).*

Boyle, Danny *Beach, The; Shallow Grave; Life Less Ordinary, A; Trainspotting.*

Boytler, Arcady *Mujer del puerto, La (Woman of the Port).*

Bozzetto, Bruno *Allegro Non Troppo.*

Brabant, Charles *P..... Respectueuse, La (The Respectful Prostitute/The Respectable Prostitute).*

Brabec, FA *King Ubu (Král Ubu).*

Brabec, Jaroslav *Melancholic Chicken, The (Kure Melancholik).*

Brabin, Charles *Mask of Fu Manchu, The.*

Bradbeer, Harry *As the Beast Sleeps.*

Bradbury, David *Nicaragua – No Pasarán; Public Enemy Number One.*

Bradbury, Robert N *Lucky Texan, The; Riders of Destiny.*

Braddock, Reb *Curdled.*

Brady, Eugene *Nephew, The.*

Brahm, John *Bengazi; Brasher Doubloon, The (aka The High Window); Broken Blossoms; Hangover Square; Locket, The; Lodger, The; Mad Magician; Undying Monster, The.*

Brakhage, Stan *Dog Star Man.*

Brambilla, Marco *Excess Baggage; Demolition Man.*

Branagh, Kenneth *Dead Again; Hamlet; Henry V; In the Bleak Midwinter (aka A Midwinter's Tale); Love's Labour's Lost; Mary Shelley's Frankenstein; Much Ado About Nothing; Peter's Friends.*

Brand, Joshua *Pyromaniac's Love Story, A.*

Brandauer, Klaus Maria *Mario and the Magician (Mario und der Zauberer); Seven Minutes (Georg Elser).*

Brandner, Uwe *I Love You, I'll Kill You (Ich liebe Dich, Ich töte Dich).*

Brando, Marlon *One-Eyed Jacks.*

Brandstrom, Charlotte *Business Affair, A.*

Brant, Beto *Friendly Fire (Ação entre Amigos).*

Brass, Tinto *Caligula; Salon Kitty.*

Brault, Michel *Ordres, Les (Orders); Paper Wedding, A (Les Noces de papier).*

Brauner, Franklin *see* Cammell, Donald

Brealey, Gil *Annie's Coming Out.*

Breashears, David *Everest.*

Breathnach, Paddy *Ailsa; Blow Dry; I Went Down.*

Bregstein, Philo *Whoever Says the Truth Will Die.*

Breien, Anja *Wives (Hustruer); Wives: Ten Years After (Hustruer ti ar etter); Wives III (Hustruer III).*

Breillat, Catherine *A ma soeur! (A mia Sorella!); Parfait Amour! (Perfect Love!); Romance; Virgin (36 Fillette).*

Breiman, Valerie *Love & Sex.*

Brenon, Herbert *Someone at the Door.*

Brenta, Mario *Barnabo of the Mountains (Barnabo delle Montagne).*

Bressan Jr, Arthur J *Buddies.*

Bresson, Robert *Anges du Péché, Les; Argent, L' (Money); Au Hasard, Balthazar (Balthazar); Condamné à mort s'est échappé, Un (A Man Escaped); Dames du Bois de Boulogne, Les; Diable Probablement, Le (The Devil, Probably); Diary of a Country Priest (Journal d'un Curé de Campagne); Femme Douce, Une (A Gentle Creature); Four Nights of a Dreamer (Quatre Nuits d'un Rêveur); Lancelot du Lac (Lancelot of the Lake); Mouchette; Pickpocket; Procès de Jeanne d'Arc (Trial of Joan of Arc).*

Brest, Martin *Beverly Hills Cop; Going in Style; Meet Joe Black; Midnight Run; Scent of a Woman.*

Brewster, Joe *Keeper, The.*

Bricken, Jules *Danny Jones.*

Brickman, Marshall *Lovesick; Simon.*

Brickman, Paul *Men Don't Leave; Risky Business.*

Bridges, Alan *Hireling, The; Invasion; Out of Season; Return of the Soldier, The; Shooting Party, The.*

Bridges, James *Bright Lights; Big City; China Syndrome, The; Mike's Murder; Paper Chase, The; Perfect; Urban Cowboy.*

Bright, Matthew *Freeway; Freeway II Confessions of a Trickbaby (aka Confessions of a Trickbaby).*

Brignone, Guido *Sign of the Gladiator (Nel segno di Roma).*

Brinckerhoff, Burt *Dogs.*

Bringmann, Peter F *Heartbreakers, The (Die Heartbreakers).*

Brisseau, Jean-Claude *Noce Blanche.*

Brittain, Donald *Volcano.*

Britten, Lawrence (Gerry O'Hara) *Feelings.*

Brittenden, Tony *Lincoln County Incident.*

Brizzi, Gaëtan Fantasia/2000 (aka Fantasia 2000).

Brizzi, Paul *Fantasia/2000 (aka Fantasia 2000).*

Brocani, Franco *Necropolis.*

Brocka, Lino *Bayan Ko: My Own Country (Bayan Ko-Kapit Sa Patalim); Jaguar; Manila: In the Claws of Darkness (Maynila, sa mga Kuko ng Liwanag).*

Brockman, Susan *Wizard of Waukesha, The.*

Brody, Hugh *Nineteen Nineteen.*

Bromly, Alan *Angel Who Pawned Her Harp, The.*

Brook, Clive *On Approval.*

Brook, Peter *Beggars' Opera, The; King Lear; Lord of the Flies; Mahabharata, Le (The Mahabharata); Persecution and Assassination of Jean-Paul Marat as Performed by the Inmates of the Asylum of Charenton Under the Direction of the Marquis de Sade, The; Tragedy of Carmen, The (La Tragédie de Carmen).*

Brookfield, William *Milk.*

Brookner, Howard *Bloodhounds of Broadway.*

Brooks, Adam *Almost You; Invisible Circus, The.*

Brooks, Albert *Defending Your Life; Lost in America; Modern Romance; Mother; Muse.*

Brooks, James L *As Good As It Gets; Broadcast News; Terms of Endearment.*

Brooks, Joseph *You Light Up My Life.*

Brooks, Mel *Blazing Saddles; Dracula: Dead and Loving It; High Anxiety; History of the World Part I; Life Stinks; Producers, The; Robin Hood – Men in Tights; Silent Movie; Spaceballs; Twelve Chairs, The; Young Frankenstein.*

Brooks, Richard *$ (aka The Heist); Bite the Bullet; Blackboard Jungle; Brothers Karamazov, The; Cat on a Hot Tin Roof; Crisis; Deadline – USA (aka Deadline); Elmer Gantry; Fever Pitch; In Cold Blood; Last Hunt, The; Last Time I Saw Paris, The; Looking for Mr Goodbar; Lord Jim; Professionals, The; Something of Value; Sweet Bird of Youth; Wrong Is Right (aka The Man With the Deadly Lens).*

Brooks, Robert *Who Shot Patakango? (aka Who Shot Pat?).*

Brooks, Sue *Road to Nhill, The.*

Broomfield, Nick *Behind the Rent Strike; Diamond Skulls; Driving Me Crazy; Fetishes; Heidi Fleiss – Hollywood Madam; Juvenile Liaison; Juvenile Liaison 2; Kurt & Courtney; Monster in a Box; Lily Tomlin; Proud to Be British; Soldier Girls; Tattooed Tears; Too White for Me.*

Brophy, Philip *Body Melt.*

Brougher, Hilary *Sticky Fingers of Time, The.*

Brown, Barry Alexander *Lonely in America.*

Brown, Bruce *On Any Sunday.*

Brown, Clarence *Anna Christie; Anna Karenina; Eagle, The; Edison the Man; Flesh and the Devil; Gorgeous Hussy, The; Idiot's Delight; Intruder in the Dust; National Velvet; Rains Came, The.*

Brown, Clifford *Celestine, Maid at Your Service (Célestine, Bonne à Tout Faire).*

Brown, James B *Weavers: Wasn't That a Time, The.*

Browne, Chris *Third World Cop.*

Browning, Tod *Devil-Doll, The; Dracula; Freaks; Mark of the Vampire; Unholy Three, The; Unknown, The.*

Brownlow, Kevin *It Happened Here; Winstanley.*

Bruce, Nichola *I Could Read the Sky.*

Bruck Jr, Jerry *I.F. Stone's Weekly.*

Bruckberger, RL *Dialogue des Carmélites, Le.*

Bruckman, Clyde *Feet First; General, The; Man on the Flying Trapeze, The; Movie Crazy.*

Brummer, Alois *How Sweet Is Her Valley (Unterm Dirndl wird gejodelt); There's No Sex Like Snow Sex (Beim jodeln juckt die Lederhose).*

Brunel, Adrian *Elstree Calling; Vortex, The; While Parents Sleep.*

Bruno, Ellen *Sacrifice.*

Bruno, John *Virus.*

Brusati, Franco *Bread and Chocolate (Pane e Cioccolata); Dimenticare Venezia (Forget Venice/To Forget Venice).*

Brustellin, Alf *German in Autumn (Deutschland im Herbst).*

Bryant, Charles *Salome.*

Bryant, Gerard *Tommy Steele Story, The (aka Rock Around the World).*

Bryden, Bill *Aria; Ill Fares the Land.*

Brynych, Zbynek *Fifth Rider Is Fear, The (...a páty jezdec je Strach/aka The Fifth Horseman Is Fear).*

Bu Wancang *see* Richard Poh.

Buba, Tony *No Pets.*

Buch, Franziska *Emil & the Detectives (Emil & die Detective).*

Buchanan, Larry *Goodbye, Norma Jean.*

Buck, Chris *Tarzan.*

Buck, Roger *Fly a Flag for Poplar.*

Buckley, David *Saturday Night at the Baths.*

Buckner, Noel *Good Fight, The.*

Bucksey, Colin *Dealers.*

Bucquoy, Jan *Sexual Life of the Belgians 1950–1978, The (La Vie Sexuelle des Belges 1950–1978).*

Budd, Robin *Return to Never Land.*

Buechler, John Carl *Troll.*

Bugajski, Ryszard *Interrogation (Przesluchanie).*

Bui, Tony *Three Seasons.*

Büld, Wolfgang *Punk in London.*

Bunce, Alan *Babar: The Movie.*

Bunin, Lou *Alice in Wonderland.*

Buntzman, Mark *Exterminator 2.*

Buñuel, Joyce Sherman *Salsa.*

Buñuel, Luis *Age d'Or, L'; Abismos de pasión (Cumbres borrascosas/ Wuthering Heights); Belle de Jour; Bruto, El (The Brute); Cela s'appelle l'Aurore; Criminal Life of Archibaldo de la Cruz (Ensayo de un Crimen/La Vida Criminal de Archibaldo de la Cruz); Chien Andalou, Un (An Andalusian Dog); Diary of a Chambermaid, The (Le Journal d'une Femme de Chambre); Discreet Charm of the Bourgeoisie, The (Le Charme Discret de la Bourgeoisie); El; Exterminating Angel, The (El Angel Exterminador); Fièvre Monte à El Pao, La (Republic of Sin); Mort en ce Jardin, La (Evil Eden); Nazarin; Olvidados, Los (The Young and the Damned); The Phantom of Liberty (Fantôme de la Liberté, Le); Robinson Crusoe (aka Adventures of Robinson Crusoe); Simon of the Desert (Simón del Desierto); That Obscure Object of Desire (Cet Obscur Objet du Désir); Tristana; Viridiana; Voie Lactée, La (The Milky Way); Young One, The (La Joven).*

Burch, Noël *Correction, Please or how we got into pictures.*

Burge, Stuart *Othello.*

Burke, Erik *Loser.*

Burke, Martyn *Power Play.*

Burman, Daniel *Waiting for the Messiah (Esperando al Mesias).*

Burnett, Charles *Glass Shield, The; Killer of Sheep; My Brother's Wedding; To Sleep with Anger.*

Burnley, Fred *Neither the Sea Nor the Land.*

Burns, Allan *Just Between Friends.*

Burns, Edward *Brothers McMullen, The; She's the One; Sidewalks of New York.*

Burr, Jeff *Leatherface: The Texas Chainsaw Massacre III; Stepfather II, The.*

Burrill, Christine *Vietnam Journey.*

Burroughs, Jackie *Winter Tan, A.*

Burrowes, Michael *Incense for the Damned.*

Burrows, James *Partners.*

Burstall, Tim *Alvin Purple; End Play; Kangaroo; Libido; Petersen; Rollicking Adventures of Eliza Fraser, The (aka A Faithful Narrative of the Capture, Sufferings and Miraculous Escape of Eliza Fraser); Stork.*

Burton, Norman *Lady by Choice.*

Burton, Tim *Batman; Batman Returns; Beetlejuice; Edward Scissorhands; Ed Wood; Mars Attacks!; Pee-Wee's Big Adventure; Planet of the Apes; Sleepy Hollow.*

Buscemi, Steve *Animal Factory; Trees Lounge.*

Bussemaker, Jan Bernard *Jabula – A Band in Exile.*

Bussmann, Tom *Whoops Apocalypse.*

Bute, Mary Ellen *Finnegans Wake (aka Passages from James Joyce's Finnegans Wake).*

Butler, David *By the Light of the Silvery Moon; Calamity Jane; Captain January; Command, The; Daughter of Rosie O'Grady, The; Kentucky; Littlest Rebel, The; Lullaby of Broadway; Pigskin Parade; Road to Morocco; Thank Your Lucky Stars; You'll Find Out.*

Butler, George *Pumping Iron; Pumping Iron II: The Women; Shackleton's Antarctic Adventure.*

Butler, Robert *Blue Knight, The; Turbulence.*

Butoy, Hendel *Fantasia/2000 (aka Fantasia 2000); Rescuers Down Under, The.*

Butterworth, Jez *Mojo.*

Buttgereit, Jörg *Schramm.*

Buzzell, Edward *At the Circus; Best Foot Forward; Go West.*

Bye, Ed *Kevin & Perry Go Large.*

Byrne, David *True Stories.*

Byrum, John *Heart Beat; Inserts.*

Caan, James *Hide In Plain Sight.*

Cabanne, Christy *Mummy's Hand, The.*

Cabréra, Dominique *Milk of Human Kindness, The (Le Lait de la tendresse humaine).*

Cabrera, Sergio *Matter of Honour, A (Técnicas de Duelo); Strategy of the Snail, The (La Estratagia del Caracol).*

Caccia, Antonia *On Our Land.*

Cacoyannis, Michael *Attila '74; Cherry Orchard, The (O Visinokipos/La Cerisaie); Day the Fish Came Out, The; Zorba the Greek.*

Cadena, Jordi *Senyora, La.*

Caesar, David *Greenkeeping.*

Caetano, Israel Adrián *Bolivia.*

Caffé, Eliane *Kenoma.*

Caffrey, David *Divorcing Jack.*

Cahn, Edward L *Invasion of the Saucermen; She Creature, The; Voodoo Woman.*

Cain, Christopher *Stone Boy, The; That Was Then...This Is Now; Young Guns.*

Caiozzi, Silvio *Moon in the Mirror, The (La Luna en el Espejo).*

Calcagno, Eduardo *Yepeto.*

Calder, Alexander *Dreams That Money Can Buy.*

Calenda, Antonia *Fury (Il Giorno del Furore).*

Callis, James *Beginner's Luck.*

Callow, Simon *Ballad of the Sad Café, The.*

Calopresti, Mimmo *Second Time, The (La Seconda Volta).*

Calparsoro, Daniel *Jump into the Void (Salto al Vacio).*

Cameron, James *Abyss, The; Abyss: Special Edition, The; Aliens; Piranha II: Flying Killers; Terminator, The; Terminator 2: Judgment Day; Titanic; True Lies.*

Cameron, Ken *Fast Talking; Monkey Grip; Umbrella Woman, The (aka The Good Wife); Winchester Conspiracy.*

Cameron, Ray *Bloodbath at the House of Death.*

Caminito, Augusto *Vampires in Venice (Nosferatu a Venezia).*

Camino, Jaime *Long Holidays of 1936, The (Las Largas Vacaciones del 36).*

Cammell, Donald *Demon Seed; Performance; White of the Eye.*

Cammell, Donald (as Franklin Brauner) *Wild Side (aka Donald Cammell's Wild Side/Wild Side – The Director's Cut).*

Camp, Joe *Benji.*

Campanella, Juan José *Boy Who Cried Bitch, The.*

Campbell, Dirk *I Bought a Vampire Motorcycle.*

Campbell, Martin *Criminal Law; Lovecraft (aka Cast a Deadly Spell); GoldenEye; Mask of Zorro, The; No Escape; Three for All; Vertical Limit.*

Campbell, Nicholas *Stepping Razor – Red X.*

Campion, Anna *Loaded.*

Campion, Jane *Angel at My Table, An; Holy Smoke; Piano, The; Portrait of a Lady, The; Sweetie; Two Friends.*

Campogalliani, Carlo *Goliath and the Barbarians (Il Terrore dei Barbari).*

Camurati, Carla *Carlota Joaquina, Princess of Brazil.*

Camus, Marcel *Black Orpheus (Orfeu Negro).*

Camus, Mario *Holy Innocents, The (Los Santos Inocentes); House of Bernarda Alba, The (La Casa de Bernarda Alba).*

Cannon, Danny *I Still Know What You Did Last Summer; Judge Dredd; Strangers; Young Americans, The.*

Cantet, Laurent *Human Resources (Ressources Humaines); Time Out (L'Emploi du temps).*

Capaldi, Peter *Strictly Sinatra.*

Capetanos, Leon *Servicer, The (Cream – Schwabing-Report).*

Capra, Frank *American Madness; Arsenic and Old Lace; Bitter Tea of General Yen, The; Broadway Bill (aka Strictly Confidential); Dirigible; Forbidden; Here Comes the Groom; Hole in the Head, A; It Happened One Night; It's a Wonderful Life; Lady for a Day; Lost Horizon; Matinee Idol, The; Meet John Doe; Miracle Woman, The; Mr Deeds Goes to Town; Mr Smith Goes to Washington; Platinum Blonde; Rain or Shine; State of the Union (aka the World and his Wife); Strong Man, The; Tramp, Tramp, Tramp; Tunisian Victory; You Can't Take It With You.*

Carax, Léos *Amants du Pont-Neuf, Les; Boy Meets Girl; Mauvais Sang (The Night Is Young); Pola X.*

Carbone, Nina *When in London.*

Cardiff, Jack *Girl on a Motorcycle (La Motocyclette/Naked Under Leather); Lion, The; Long Ships, The; Mercenaries, The (aka Dark of the Sun); Mutations, The; Penny Gold; Sons and Lovers; Young Cassidy.*

Cardona, René (Sr) *Survive! (Supervivientes de los Andes).*

Cardona, René (Jr) *Guyana: Crime of the Century (Guyana: El Crimen del Siglo); Tintorera.*

Cardone, JS *Forsaken, The; Thunder Alley.*

Cardos, John 'Bud' *Day Time Ended, The; Kingdom of the Spiders; Mutant.*

Carle, Gilles *True Nature of Bernadette, The (La Vraie Nature de Bernadette); Tête de Normande St-Onge, La.*

Carlei, Carlo *Flight of the Innocent (La Corsa dell'innocente).*

Carlino, Lewis John *Class; Great Santini, The; Sailor Who Fell from Grace with the Sea, The.*

Carné, Marcel *Drôle de Drame (Bizarre, Bizarre); Enfants du Paradis, Les (Children of Paradise); Hôtel du Nord; Jour se lève, Le (Daybreak); Merveilleuse Visite, La (The Wonderful Visit); Portes de la Nuit, Les (Gates of the Night); Quai des Brumes, Le (Port of Shadows); Visiteurs du Soir, Les (The Devil's Envoys).*

Carnimeo, Giuliano (Anthony Ascott) *Blazing Guns (Uomo avvisato, mezzo ammazzato…parola di Spirito Santo).*

Caro, Marc *Cité des enfants perdus, La (The City of Lost Children); Delicatessen.*

Caron, Glenn Gordon *Clean and Sober; Love Affair (aka An Affair to Remember); Picture Perfect.*

Caron, Pierre *Route enchantée, La.*

Carow, Heiner *Coming Out.*

Carpenter, John *Assault on Precinct 13; Big Trouble in Little China; Body Bags; Christine; Dark Star; Elvis (aka Elvis – The Movie); Escape from New York; Fog, The; Ghosts of Mars; Halloween; In the Mouth of Madness; John Carpenter's Escape from L.A.; Memoirs of an Invisible Man; Prince of Darkness; Soul Survivors; Starman; They Live; Thing, The; Vampires (aka John Carpenter's Vampires).*

Carpenter, Stephen *Kindred, The.*

Carr, Steve *Dr Dolittle 2; Next Friday.*

Carradine, David *Americana.*

Carré, Jean-Michel *Contre l'Oubli (Against Oblivion).*

Carrera, Carlos *No Return Address (Sin Remitente); Under a Spell (Un Embrujo).*

Carreras, Michael *Blood from the Mummy's Tomb; Curse of the Mummy's Tomb, The; Lost Continent, The; Steel Bayonets, The.*

Carri, Albertina *I Won't Go Back Home (No quiero volver a casa).*

Carroll, Willard *Playing by Heart; Tom's Midnight Garden.*

Carson, David *Star Trek: Generations.*

Carstairs, John Paddy *Chiltern Hundreds, The (aka The Amazing Mr Beecham); Dancing With Crime; Jumping for Joy; Man of the Moment; Trouble in Store.*

Carter, Thomas *Metro; Save the Last Dance; Swing Kids.*

Cartwright, Justin *Rosie Dixon, Night Nurse.*

Carver, Steve *Arena, The; Big Bad Mama; Bulletproof; Capone; Drum; Eye for an Eye, An; Fast Charlie the Moonbeam Rider; Lone Wolf McQuade; Steel.*

Casaril, Guy *L'Astragale (Ankle Bone); Piaf (aka Piaf – The Early Years/The Sparrow of Pigalle); Rempart des Béguines, Le (The Beguines).*

Cass, Henry *Blood of the Vampire; Glass Mountain, The; Last Holiday.*

Cassavetes, John *Big Trouble; Child Is Waiting, A; Faces; Gloria; Husbands; Killing of a Chinese Bookie, The; Love Streams; Minnie and Moskowitz; Opening Night, Shadows; Too Late Blues; Woman Under the Influence, A.*

Cassavetes, Nick *John Q; Unhook the Stars (Décroches les étoiles); She's So Lovely.*

Cassenti, Frank *Affiche Rouge, L'.*

Castellari, Enzo G *Bronx Warriors, The (1990 I Guerrieri del Bronx); Cry Onion (Cipolla Colt); New Barbarians, The (I Nuovi Barbari).*

Castellitto, Sergio *Libero Burro.*

Castle, Nick *Boy Who Could Fly, The; Dennis the Menace (aka Dennis); Last Starfighter, The; TAG, The Assassination Game; Tap.*

Castle, William *Americano, The; Homicidal; I Saw What You Did; Macabre; Shanks; Strait-Jacket; Tingler, The; When Strangers Marry (aka Betrayed).*

Castro, Rick *Hustler White.*

Cates, Gilbert *Affair, The; Backfire; I Never Sang for My Father; Last Married Couple in America, The; Summer Wishes, Winter Dreams.*

Caton-Jones, Michael *Doc Hollywood; Jackal, The; Memphis Belle; Rob Roy; Scandal; This Boy's Life.*

Cattaneo, Peter *Full Monty, The; Lucky Break.*

Caulfield, Michael *Fighting Back.*

Caumon, Yves *Amour d'enfance (Boyhood Loves).*

Cavalcanti, Alberto *Champagne Charlie; Coal Face; Dead of Night; For Them That Trespass; Nicholas Nickleby; Pett and Pott; Went the Day Well?*

Cavalier, Alain *Libera Me; Thérèse.*

Cavani, Liliana *Berlin Affair, The (Interno Berlinele); Beyond Evil (Al di là del Bene e del Male); Beyond the Door (Oltre la Porta); Cannibals, The (I Cannibali); Galileo; Night Porter, The (Il Portiere di Notte).*

Cavara, Paolo *Deaf Smith & Johnny Ears (Los Amigos).*

Cayatte, André *Amants de Verone, Les (The Lovers of Verona); Miroir a deux faces, Le (Lo Specchi a due facce/The Mirror Has Two Faces); Verdict (The Verdict).*

Cellan Jones, James *Bequest to the Nation (aka The Nelson Affair).*

Cellan Jones, Simon *Some Voices.*

'Cero a la Izquierda' Film Collective *El Salvador – Decision to Win (El Salvador – La Decisión de Vencer).*

Cervi, Tonino *Nest of Vipers (Ritratto di Borghesia in Nero); Today It's Me… Tomorrow You! (Oggi a me… domani a te!).*

Ceylan, Nuri Bilge *Clouds of May (Mayis Sikintisi).*

Cha Chuen-Yee *Once Upon a Time in Triad Society (Wangjiao Cha-fit-ren); Once Upon a Time in Triad Society 2 (Qua ba! Cha-fit-ren Bingtuan); Theft Under the Sun (Haoqing Gai Tian).*

Chabrol, Claude *A Double Tour (Leda/Web of Passion); Beau Serge, Le; Biches, Les*

(The Does); Blood of Others (Le Sang des Autres); Blood Relatives (Liens de Sang); Bonnes Femmes, Les (The Girls); Boucher, Le (The Butcher); Cérémonie, La (A Judgement in Stone); Champagne Murders, The (Le Scandale); Cheval d'Orgueil, Le (The Proud Ones); Colour of Lies, The (Au Coeur du mensonge); Cop au Vin (Poulet au Vinaigre); Cousins, Les (The Cousins); Cri du Hibou, Le (The Cry of the Owl); Dr M (aka Club Extinction); Docteur Popaul (High Heels/Scoundrel in White); Enfer, L' (Torment); Fantômes du Chapelier, Les (The Hatter's Ghost); Femme Infidèle, La (Unfaithful Wife); Innocents with Dirty Hands (Les Innocents aux Mains Sales); Inspecteur Lavardin; Just Before Nightfall (Juste avant la Nuit); Landru; Ligne de Démarcation, La; Madame Bovary; Masques; Merci pour le chocolat; Nada; Noces Rouges, Les (Blood Wedding/Red Wedding/ Wedding in Blood); Paris vu par… (Six in Paris); Partie de Plaisir, Une (Love Match); Que la Bête Meure (Killer!); Quiet Days in Clichy (Jours Tranquilles à Clichy); Rien ne va plus; Route de Corinthe, La (The Road to Corinth); Rupture, La; Ten Days' Wonder (La Décade Prodigieuse); Violette Nozière.

Chadha, Gurinder *Bend It Like Beckham; Bhaji on the Beach; What's Cooking?*

Chaffey, Don *Charley-One-Eye; Creatures the World Forgot; Jason and the Argonauts; Jolly Bad Fellow, A; Magic of Lassie, The; Man Upstairs, The; One Million Years B.C.; Persecution; Pete's Dragon; Ride a Wild Pony; Viking Queen, The.*

Chahine, Youssef *Adieu Bonaparte (Al-wedaa ya Bonaparte); Alexandria Encore (Eskendereya kaman we kaman); Autre, L' (The Other); Destiny (Al Massir); Egyptian Story, An (Hadduta Misriya); Lumière et Compagnie; Saladin (An-Nasr Salah ad-Din).*

Chamchoum, FN Georges *Lebanon…Why? (Liban…Pourquoi?).*

Champion, Gower *Bank Shot.*

Champion, Gregg *Short Time.*

Champion, John *Mustang Country.*

Chan, Benny *Gen-X Cops (Tejing Xin Renlei); Gen-Y Cops (Tejin Xin Renlei 2).*

Chan, Evans *Journey to Beijing (Bei Zheng); Map of Sex and Love, The (Qingse Ditu).*

Chan, Fruit *Durian Durian (Liulian Piaopiao); Little Cheung (Xilu Xiang); Longest Summer, The (Qunian Yanhua Tebie Duo); Made in Hong Kong (Xianggang Zhizao).*

Chan Ho-sun, Peter *He's a Woman, She's a Man; Love Letter, The.*

Chan, Jackie *Armour of God, The (Long Xiong Hu Di); Police Story (Jingcha Gushi); Project A (A Jihua).*

Chan, Joe *'92 The Legendary La Rose Noire (Heimeigui dui Heimeigui).*

Chan, Peter *Comrades, Almost a Love Story (Tian Nimi).*

Chan, Philip *Front Page (Xin Ban Jin Ba Liang).*

Chanan, Michael *El Salvador – Portrait of a Liberated Zone.*

Chang Cheh *Blood Brothers, The (Ci Ma/aka Chinese Vengeance); Chinese Connection, The (Quan Ji/aka Duel of Fists); Golden Swallow (Jin Yanzi); New One-Armed Swordsman, The (Xin Dubi Dao).*

Chang Hwa-Kun *Cabby, The (Yun Zhuanshou de Lian).*

Chang, Sylvia *Siao Yu (Shaonü Xiao Yu).*

Chang Tso-Chi *Ah Chung (Zhong-zai); Darkness and Light (Heian zhi Guang).*

Chang Yi *Jade Love (Yu Qing sao); This Love of Mine (Wo de Ai).*

Chang Youn-Hyun *Contact, The (Jeopsok); Tell Me Something.*

Chaplin, Charles *Circus, The; City Lights; Countess from Hong Kong, A; Gold Rush, The; Great Dictator, The; Kid, The; King in New York, A; Limelight; Modern Times; Monsieur Verdoux; Woman of Paris, A.*

Chapman, Brenda *Prince of Egypt, The.*

Chapman, Matthew *Hussy; Heart of Midnight; Strangers Kiss.*

Chapman, Michael *All the Right Moves; Clan of the Cave Bear, The.*

Chappell, Peter *El Salvador – Portrait of a Liberated Zone.*

Chappelle, Joe *Halloween: The Curse of Michael Myers.*

Charbanic, Joe *Watcher, The.*

Charell, Erik *Congress Dances (Der Kongress tanzt).*

Charlot, André *Elstree Calling.*

Chart, Paul *American Perfekt.*

Chatiliez, Etienne *Bonheur est dans le pré, Le; Life Is a Long Quiet River (La Vie est un long fleuve tranquille); Tatie Danielle.*

Chatri-Chalerm Yukol *Song of Chao-Phrya, The (Nong Mia).*

Chaudhri, Amin Q *Tiger Warsaw.*

Chavarri, Jaime *To an Unknown God (A un Dios Desconocido).*

Chechik, Jeremiah *Avengers, The; Benny and Joon; Diabolique.*

Che-Kirk Wong *see* Wong, Kirk.

Chelsom, Peter *Funny Bones; Hear My Song; Mighty, The; Serendipity; Town & Country.*

Chen, Joan *Autumn in New York.*

Chen Kaige *Big Parade (Da Yuebing); Emperor and the Assassin, The (Jing Ke Ci Qin Wang); Farewell My Concubine (Ba Wang Bie Ji); Killing Me Softly; King of the Children (Haizi Wang); Life on a String (Bian Zou Bian Chang); Temptress Moon (Fengyue); Ten Minutes Older – The Trumpet; Yellow Earth (Huang Tudi).*

Chen, Singing *Bundled (Wo Jiao A-Ming-la).*

Chen, Teddy *Accidental Spy, The (Tewu Mi Ching); Purple Storm (Ziyu Fengbao).*

Chen Yiwen *Cabby, The (Yun Zhuanshou de Lian); Chance to Die, A (Xiang Si Chen Xianzai); Jam (Guojiang).*

Chen Yu-Hsun *Tropical Fish (Redai Yu).*

Chenal, Pierre *Dernier Tournant, Le.*

Cheng Andre YS *Shanghai Panic (Women hai Pa).*

Cheng Sheng-Fu *Silent Thrush, The (Shisheng Huamei).*

Chenouga, Chad *17 rue Bleue.*

Cher *If These Walls Could Talk.*

Chéreau, Patrice *Contre l'Oubli (Against Oblivion); Intimacy (Intimité); Reine Margot, La; Those Who Love Me Will Take the Train (Ceux qui m'aiment prendront le train).*

Cherry, John *Ernest Saves Christmas.*

Cheung Tung Cho *My Dad Is a Jerk (Dui-bu-qi, Dou Xie Ni).*

Cheung Yeun Ting *Eight Taels of Gold (Ba Liang Jin).*

Chiesa, Alcides *Amigomio.*

Chiesa, Guido *Lies to Live by (Babylon) (Babylon: la paura e la migliore amica dell'uomo).*

Chilvers, Colin *Moonwalker.*

Ching Siu-Tung *Chinese Ghost Story, A (Qiannü Youhun); Chinese Ghost Story II, A (Qiannü Youhun zhi Renjian Dao); Chinese Ghost Story III, A (Qiannü Youhun III Dao Dao Dao); Swordsman (Xiao'ao Jianghu); Swordsman II (Xiao'ao Jianghu zhi Dongfang Bu Bai); Terra-Cotta Warrior, A (Qin Yong).*

Chiodo, Stephen *Killer Klowns from Outer Space.*

Chionglo, Mel *Midnight Dancers (Sibak).*

Cholodenko, Lisa *High Art.*

Chomsky, Marvin J *Evel Knievel; Tank; Victory at Entebbe.*

Chong, Thomas *Cheech & Chong's Next Movie (aka High Encounters of the Ultimate Kind).*

Chopra, Joyce *Lemon Sisters, The; Smooth Talk.*

Chouikh, Mohamed *Arche du désert, L'; Citadel, The (El Kalaa).*

Chouraqui, Elie *Man on Fire; Mon Premier Amour; What Makes David Run? (Qu'est-ce qui fait courir David?).*

Chow, Stephen *Shaolin Soccer (Shaolin Zuqiu/aka Kung-fu Soccer).*

Choy, Christine *Best Hotel on Skid Row; Who Killed Vincent Chin?*

Christensen, Benjamin *Witchcraft through the Ages (Häxan).*

Christensen, Bent *Harry and the Butler (Harry og Kammertjeneren).*

Christian, Roger *Battlefield Earth; Nostradamus; Sender, The.*

Christian-Jaque *Chartreuse de Parme, La; Disparus de Saint-Agil, Les; Legend of Frenchie King, The (Les Pétroleuses); Perles de la Couronne, Les (The Pearls of the Crown); Rigolboche; Si tous les gars du monde… (Race For Life/If All the Guys in the World…).*

Christopher, Frank *In the Name of the People.*

Christopher, Mark *54.*

Chrysanthou, Panicos *Our Wall (Duvarimiz).*

Chu Yuan *Intimate Confessions of a Chinese Courtesan (Ai Nu); Killer, The (Da Sha Shou).*

Chubbuck, Lyndon *War Bride, The.*

Chukhrai, Grigori *Ballad of a Soldier (Ballada o Soldate).*

Chukhrai, Pavel *Thief, The (Vor).*

Churchill, Joan *Juvenile Liaison; Juvenile Liaison 2; Lily Tomlin; Soldier Girls; Tattooed Tears.*

Chytilová, Vera *Daisies (Sedmikrásky); Pearls of the Deep (Perlicky na dne).*

Cicero, Nando *Last Italian Tango, The (Ultimo Tango a Zagarol).*

Cimber, Matt *Butterfly.*

Cimino, Michael *Deer Hunter, The; Desperate Hours; Heaven's Gate; Sicilian, The; Sunchaser, The; Thunderbolt and Lightfoot; Year of the Dragon.*

Cinema Action *Film from the Clyde; Miners' Film, The; So That You Can Live.*

Cipri, Daniele *Enzo, Domani a Palermo!; Totò Who Lived Twice (Totò che visse due volte); Uncle from Brooklyn, The (Lo Zio di Brooklyn).*

Cissé, Souleymane *Brightness (Yeelen); Finyé (The Wind).*

Clair, René *A Nous la Liberté (Freedom for Us); And Then There Were None (aka Ten Little Niggers); Beauté du Diable, La (Beauty and the Devil); Belles de nuit, Les (Beauties of the Night/Night Beauties); Dernier Milliardaire, Le; Fantôme du Moulin Rouge, Le; Flame of New Orleans, The; Ghost Goes West, The; Grandes Manoeuvres, Les (Summer Manoeuvres); I Married a Witch; It Happened Tomorrow; Million, Le; Paris qui Dort (The Crazy Ray); Porte des Lilas (Gate of Lilacs); Quatorze Juillet, Le (July 14th); Silence est d'Or, Le (Man About Town); Sous les Toits de Paris.*

Clark, Bob *Black Christmas; Breaking Point; Christmas Story, A; Dead of Night (aka Deathdream); From the Hip; Loose Cannons; Murder by Decree; Porky's; Porky's II: The Next Day; Tribute; Turk 182!*

Clark, Bruce *Galaxy of Terror; Ski Bum, The.*

Clark, Curtis *Shut Down.*

Clark, Duane *Shaking the Tree.*

Clark, James B *Dog of Flanders, A; Flipper.*

Clark, Jim *Madhouse; Rentadick.*

Clark, Larry *Another Day in Paradise; Bully; Kids.*

Clark, Louise *Winter Tan, A.*

Clark, Matt *Da.*

Clarke, Alan *Billy the Kid and the Green Baize Vampire; Rita, Sue and Bob Too; Scum.*

Clarke, Frank *Blonde Fist.*

Clarke, James Kenelm *Exposé; Funny Money; Let's Get Laid!*

Clarke, Shirley *Connection, The; Cool World, The; Ornette: Made in America; Portrait of Jason.*

Clavell, James *Last Valley, The; To Sir, With Love; Where's Jack?*

Claxton, William F *Night of the Lepus.*

Claydon, Phil *Alone.*

Clayton, Jack *Great Gatsby, The; Innocents, The; Lonely Passion of Judith Hearne, The; Our Mother's House; Pumpkin Eater, The; Room at the Top; Something Wicked This Way Comes.*

Clayton, Susan *Disappearance of Finbar, The; Last Crop, The; Song of the Shirt, The.*

Clegg, Tom *G'Olé!; McVicar; Sweeney 2.*

Clemens, Brian *Captain Kronos Vampire Hunter.*

Clemens, William *Devil's Island; Falcon and the Co-eds, The.*

Clement, Dick *Bullshot; Catch Me a Spy (Les Doigts Croisés/aka To Catch a Spy); Otley; Porridge; Water.*

Clément, René *Bataille du Rail, La (Battle of the Rails); Gervaise; Jeux Interdits (Forbidden Games/The Secret Game); Knave of Hearts (aka Lovers, Happy Lovers!/ Monsieur Ripois); Père Tranquille, Le (Mr Orchid); Plein Soleil (Delitto in pieno sole/Blazing Sun/Purple Noon); Rider on the Rain (Passager de la Pluie).*

Clements, Ron *Aladdin; Great Mouse Detective, The (aka Basil the Great Mouse Detective); Hercules; Little Mermaid, The.*

Clifford, Graeme *Frances; Gleaming the Cube; Past Tense; Ruby Cairo.*

Clifton, Peter *London Rock and Roll Show, The; Song Remains the Same, The.*

Climati, Antonio *Savage Man…Savage Beast (Ultima Grida della Savana).*

Cline, Edward F *Bank Dick, The; Ghost Catchers; My Little Chickadee; Never Give a Sucker an Even Break (aka What a Man!).*

Cloos, Hans Peter *Germany in Autumn (Deutschland im Herbst).*

Clouse, Robert *Amsterdam Kill, The; Big Brawl, The; Black Belt Jones; Darker Than Amber; Enter the Dragon; Force: Five; Golden Needles; Gymkata; London Connection, The (aka The Omega Connection); Pack, The; Rats, The (aka Deadly Eyes).*

Clouzot, Henri-Georges *Assassin Habite au 21, L' (The Murderer Lives at Number 21); Corbeau, Le (The Raven); Diaboliques, Les (Diabolique/The Fiends); Espions, Les; Quai des Orfèvres; Mystère Picasso, Le; Vérité, La (The Truth); Wages of Fear, The (Le Salaire de la Peur).*

Clowes, St John L *No Orchids for Miss Blandish.*

Clucher, EB (Enzo Barboni) *Crime Busters (Due Superpiedi quasi Piatti); They Call Me Trinity (Lo Chiamavano Trinità).*

Clunes, Martin *Staggered.*

Clurman, Harold *Deadline at Dawn.*

Clément, René *Deadly Trap, The (La Maison sous les Arbres); Jeux Interdits (Forbidden Games/The Secret Game); Rider on the Rain (Passager de la Pluie).*

Coates, Lewis (Luigi Cozzi) *Starcrash.*

Cobham, David *Tarka the Otter.*

Coccoritti, Gérard *Paris France.*

Cochran, Stacy *Boys; My New Gun.*

Cocteau, Jean *Aigle à Deux Têtes, L' (The Eagle Has Two Heads/Eagle With Two Heads); Belle et la Bête, La (Beauty and the Beast); Orphée (Orpheus); Parents Terribles, Les (The Storm Within); Sang d'un Poète, Le (The Blood of a Poet); Testament d'Orphée, Le (Testament of Orpheus).*

Coe, Peter *Lock Up Your Daughters!*

Coe, Wayne *Grim Prairie Tales.*

Coen, Joel *Barton Fink; Big Lebowski, The; Blood Simple; Fargo; Hudsucker Proxy; Man Who Wasn't There, The; Miller's Crossing; O Brother, Where Art Thou?; Raising Arizona.*

Cohen, David *Pleasure Principle, The.*

Cohen, Eli *Summer of Aviya, The (Hakayitz shel Aviya).*

Cohen, Howard R *Saturday the 14th.*

Cohen, Jem *Benjamin Smoke; Instrument: Ten Years with the Band Fugazi.*

Cohen, Larry *Ambulance, The; Black Caesar (aka The Godfather of Harlem); Bone (aka Dial Rat for Terror/ Beverly Hills Nightmare); God Told Me To (aka Demon); Hell Up in Harlem; It Lives Again; It's Alive; Original Gangstas; Private Files of J Edgar Hoover, The; Special Effects; Stuff, The; Wicked Stepmother; Winged Serpent, The (aka Q – The Winged Serpent).*

Cohen, Martin B *Rebel Rousers.*

Cohen, Nick *Beginner's Luck.*

Cohen, Norman *Adolf Hitler – My Part in His Downfall; Confessions from a Holiday Camp; Confessions of a Driving Instructor; Confessions of a Pop Performer; Dad's Army; Stand Up Virgin Soldiers; Till Death Us Do Part.*

Cohen, Peter M *Whipped.*

Cohen, Rob *Daylight; DragonHeart; Dragon: The Bruce Lee Story; Fast and the Furious, The; Scandalous; Skulls, The.*

Cohen, Tom *Family Business.*

Cohn, Michael *Snow White: A Tale of Terror.*

Coixet, Isabel *Things I Never Told You.*

Cokliss, Harley *Black Moon Rising; Dream Demon; Glitterball, The; That Summer!*

Cole, Henry *Mad Dogs and Englishmen.*

Cole, Nigel *Saving Grace.*

Cole, Sidney *Train of Events.*

Coleman, Graham *Tibet: A Buddhist Trilogy.*

Colizzi, Giuseppe *Blood River (Dio Perdona…Io No!); Quattro dell'Ave Maria, I (Ace High/Revenge in El Paso).*

Colla, Richard A *Battlestar Galactica.*

Collard, Cyril *Savage Nights (Les Nuits Fauves).*

Collectives:
Amber Films/Amber Production Team *Dream On; Eden Valley; In Fading Light; Letters to Katja;*

Seacoal; T. Dan Smith; Writing in the Sand, The.
Anon., China *Red Detachment of Women (Hung Sik Leung Dje Ching).*
Berwick Street Film Collective *Ireland: Behind the Wire; Nightcleaners.*
'Cero a la Izquierda' Film Collective *El Salvador – Decision to Win (El Salvador – La Decisión de Vencer).*
Cinema Action *Film from the Clyde; Miners' Film, The; So That You Can Live.*
Dziga Vertov Group *Pravda.*
Mariposa Film Group *Word Is Out.*
Women's Film Workshop *We're Alive.*

Collie-Cousins, Philippa *Happy Now?*

Collier, James FR *Cry from the Mountain; Hiding Place, The.*

Collins, Arthur Greville *Thank You, Jeeves!*

Collins, Boon *Spirit of the Eagle.*

Collins, Lewis D *see* Lewis Cullen.

Collins, Tom *Teenage Kicks – The Undertones.*

Collinson, Peter *And Then There Were None (aka Ten Little Indians); House on Garibaldi Street, The; Italian Job, The; Long Day's Dying, The; Man Called Noon, The; Open Season (Los Cazadores); Sellout, The; Spiral Staircase, The; Tigers Don't Cry; Tomorrow Never Comes; Up the Junction.*

Colomo, Fernando *Butterfly Effect, The (El Efecto Mariposa); Skyline (La Linea del Cielo).*

Colpaert, Carl *Delusion.*

Columbus, Chris *Adventures in Babysitting (aka A Night on the Town); Bicentennial Man; Harry Potter and the Philosopher's Stone (aka Harry Potter and the Sorcerer's Stone); Home Alone; Home Alone 2: Lost in New York; Mrs Doubtfire; Nine Months; Only the Lonely; Stepmom.*

Comencini, Francesca *Annabelle partagée; Carlo Giuliani, Ragazzo.*

Comencini, Luigi *Bohème, La.*

Comerford, Joe *High Boot Benny; Reefer and the Model; Traveller.*

Comfort, Lance *Bang! You're Dead (aka Game of Danger); Blind Corner; Breaking Point, The (aka The Great Armored Car Swindle); Eight O'Clock Walk; Hatter's Castle; Make Mine a Million; Man in the Road, The; Pit of Darkness; Temptation Harbour.*

Comolli, Jean-Louis *Cecilia, La.*

Compton, Richard *Macon County Line.*

Concini, Ennio De *Hitler: the Last Ten Days.*

Condon, Bill *Candyman 2: Farewell to the Flesh; Gods and Monsters.*

Connell, Merle *Test Tube Babies (aka The Pill).*

Connell, Myles *Opportunists, The.*

Connelly, Marc *Green Pastures, The.*

Connolly, Ray *James Dean – the First American Teenager.*

Connolly, Robert *Bank, The.*

Connolly, Tom *Five Seconds to Spare.*

Connor, Kevin *At the Earth's Core; Arabian Adventure; From Beyond the Grave; Land That Time Forgot, The; People That Time Forgot, The; Trial by Combat (aka A Choice of Weapons/Dirty Knight's Work); Warlords of Atlantis.*

Conrad, Patrick *Mascara.*

Conway, Jack *Arsene Lupin; Boom Town; Crossroads; Love Crazy; Too Hot to Handle; Unholy Three, The; Viva Villa!*

Coninx, Stijn *Daens.*

Cook, Barry *Mulan.*

Cook, Fielder *Beauty and the Beast; Big Hand For the Little Lady, A (aka Big Deal at Dodge City); Patterns (aka Patterns of Power); Seize the Day.*

Cooke, Alan *Nadia.*

Coolidge, Martha *Angie; Lost in Yonkers (aka Neil Simon's Lost in Yonkers); Not a Pretty Picture; Rambling Rose; Real Genius; Three Wishes.*

Cooney, Ray *Not Now, Comrade.*

Cooper, Merian C *Grass; King Kong.*

Cooper, Stuart *Disappearance, The; Little Malcolm and His Struggle Against the Eunuchs; Overlord.*

Coppola, Francis Ford *Apocalypse Now; Apocalypse Now Redux; Conversation, The; Cotton Club, The; Dementia 13 (aka The Haunted and the Hunted); Dracula (aka Bram Stoker's Dracula); Gardens of Stone; Finian's Rainbow; Godfather, The; Godfather Part II, The; Godfather Part III, The; Jack; New York Stories; One From the Heart; Outsiders, The; Peggy Sue Got Married; Rainmaker, The (aka John Grisham's The Rainmaker); Rain People, The; Rumble Fish; Tucker: The Man and His Dream; You're a Big Boy Now.*

Coppola, Sofia *Virgin Suicides, The.*

Coraci, Frank *Waterboy, The; Wedding Singer, The.*

Corarito, Gregory *Delinquent School Girls (aka Sizzlers).*

Corbiau, Gérard *Farinelli Il Castrato; Music Teacher, The (Le Maître de musique).*

Corbucci, Sergio *Big Silence, The (Il Grande Silenzio); Companeros (Vamos a Matar, Companeros!); Django; Mercenario, Il (The Mercenary/A Professional Gun); 8-Wheel Beast, The (Il Bestione).*

Corcuera, Javier *Back of the World, The (La Esplada del Mundo).*

Cordero, Sebastian *Rodents (Ratas, Ratones, Rateros).*

Cordero, Viviana *Sensations.*

Corman, Roger *Bloody Mama; Bucket of Blood, A; Day the World Ended, The; Gas-s-s-s, or it became necessary to destroy the world in order to save it; Haunted Palace, The; House of Usher, The (aka The Fall of the House of Usher); I, Mobster (aka The Mobster); Intruder, The (aka The Stranger/I Hate Your Guts); It Conquered the World; Last Woman on Earth, The; Little Shop of Horrors, The; Machine Gun Kelly; Masque of the Red Death, The; Not of This Earth; Oklahoma Woman, The; Pit and the Pendulum, The; Premature Burial, The; Raven, The; Rock All Night; Roger Corman's Frankenstein Unbound; St Valentine's Day Massacre, The; Secret Invasion, The; She Gods of Shark Reef; Sorority Girl; Tales of Terror; Teenage Caveman; Terror, The; Tomb of Ligeia, The; Trip, The; Undead, The; Viking Women and Their Voyage to the Waters of the Great Sea Serpent, The; Von Richthofen and Brown (aka The Red Baron); War of the Satellites; Wasp Woman, The; Wild Angels, The; X – the Man with X-Ray Eyes (aka The Man with The X-Ray Eyes).*

Corneau, Alain *Contre l'Oubli (Against Oblivion); Cousin, Le; Enfants de Lumière, Les (The Children of Lumière); Lumière et Compagnie; Tous les matins du monde.*

Cornelius, Henry *Genevieve; I Am a Camera; Passport to Pimlico.*

Cornell, John *Almost an Angel; Crocodile Dundee II.*

Cornfield, Hubert *Night of the Following Day, The.*

Coronado, Celestino *Hamlet; Midsummer Night's Dream, A.*

Corr, Eugene *Desert Bloom.*

Correll, Charles *In the Deep Woods.*

Correll, Richard *Ski Patrol.*

Corrente, Michael *American Buffalo.*

Corsicato, Pappi *Black Holes, The (I Buchi Neri); Libera.*

Corsini, Catherine *Nouvelle Eve, La.*

Corson, Ian *Malicious.*

Cortazar, Octavio *Teacher, The (El Brigadista).*

Corti, Alex *Refusal, The (Die Verweigerung).*

Coscarelli, Don *Beastmaster, The; Phantasm; Phantasm II.*

Cosmatos, George Pan *Cassandra Crossing, The; Cobra; Escape to Athena; Leviathan; Massacre in Rome (Rappresaglia); Rambo: First Blood, Part II; Shadow Conspiracy; Tombstone.*

Costa, Pedro *Ossos (Bones).*

Costa-Gavras *Aveu, L' (The Confession); Betrayed; Contre l'Oubli (Against Oblivion); Lumière et Compagnie; Mad City; Missing; Music Box; Section Spéciale (Special Section); Sleeping Car Murder, The (Compartiment Tueurs); State of Siege (Etat de Siège); Z.*

Costard, Hellmuth *Little Godard, A (Der kleine Godard).*

Costner, Kevin *Dances with Wolves; Dances with Wolves – Special Edition; Postman, The.*

Coto, Manny *Star Kid.*

Cottafavi, Vittorio *Ercole alla conquista di Atlantide (Hercules and the Captive Women/Hercules Conquers Atlantis).*

Couffer, Jack *Darwin Adventure, The; Ring of Bright Water.*

Cousteau, Jacques-Yves *Monde du Silence, Le (The Silent World).*

Coutaz, Gérad Frot *Contre l'Oubli (Against Oblivion).*

Couturie, Bill *Dear America: Letters Home from Vietnam.*

Covert, Michael *Dirt.*

Coward, Noël *In Which We Serve.*

Cox, Alex *Repo Man; Highway Patrolman (El Patrullero); Sid and Nancy; Straight to Hell; Walker; Winner, The.*

Cox, Paul *Cactus; Golden Braid; Lonely Hearts; Man of Flowers; Molokai: The Story of Father Damien; My First Wife; Vincent: The Life and Death of Vincent Van Gogh; Woman's Tale, A.*

Cozarinsky, Edgardo *Citizen Langlois; One Man's War (La Guerre d'un Seul Homme); Rothschild's Violin (Le Violon de Rothschild/ Rothschildin Viulu).*

Crabtree, Arthur *Fiend Without a Face; Horrors of the Black Museum; Madonna of the Seven Moons; Quartet; They Were Sisters.*

Crain, William (Bill) *Blacula; Midnight Fear.*

Crane, Barry *Conquest of the Earth.*

Crane, Kenneth *Monster from Green Hell.*

Crane, Peter *Assassin; Moments.*

Craven, Wes *Deadly Blessing; Deadly Friend; Hills Have Eyes, The; Last House on the Left, The (aka Krug and Company/Sex Crime of the Century); Music of the Heart; Nightmare on Elm Street, A; People Under the Stairs, The; Scream; Scream 2; Scream 3; Serpent and the Rainbow, The; Shocker; Swamp Thing; Vampire in Brooklyn; Wes Craven's New Nightmare.*

Creme, Lol *Lunatic, The.*

Crichton, Charles *Against the Wind; Another Shore; Battle of the Sexes, The; Dance Hall; Dead of Night; Divided Heart, The; Fish Called Wanda, A; Hue and Cry; Hunted (aka The Stranger in Between); Lavender Hill Mob, The; Law and Disorder; Love Lottery, The; Painted Boats; Titfield Thunderbolt, The; Train of Events.*

Crichton, Michael *Coma; First Great Train Robbery, The (aka The Great Train Robbery); Looker; Physical Evidence; Runaway; Westworld.*

Crisci, Giovanni *Before and After Sex (Prima e Dopo l'Amore…Un Grido d'Allarme).*

Crisp, Donald *Navigator, The.*

Cristofer, Michael *Body Shots; Original Sin (Péché originel).*

Croghan, Emma-Kate *Love and Other Catastrophes; Strange Planet.*

Crombie, Donald *Caddie; Cathy's Child; Killing of Angel Street, The; Robbery Under Arms; Rough Diamonds.*

Crome, John *Naked Cell, The.*

Cromwell, John *Algiers; Anna and the King of Siam; Banjo on My Knee; Caged; Company She Keeps, The; Dead Reckoning; Enchanted Cottage, The; Goddess, The; In Name Only; Prisoner of Zenda, The; Racket, The; Since You Went Away; Spitfire; Victory.*

Cronenberg, David *Brood, The; Crash; Crimes of the Future; Dead Ringers; Dead Zone, The; eXistenZ; Fast Company; Fly, The; M. Butterfly; Naked Lunch; Parasite Murders, The (aka Shivers/They Came from Within); Rabid; Scanners; Spider; Videodrome.*

Crowe, Cameron *Almost Famous; Jerry Maguire; Say Anything; Singles; Vanilla Sky.*

Crowe, Christopher *Off Limits (aka Saigon).*

Crumlish, Brian *Tickets for the Zoo.*

Cruze, James *If I Had a Million.*

Crystal, Billy *Forget Paris; Mr Saturday Night.*

Csaky, Mick *How Does It Feel.*

Cuarón, Alfonso *And Your Mother Too (Y tu mamá también); Great Expectations; Little Princess, A.*

Cuerda, José Luis *Butterfly's Tongue (La Lengua de las Mariposas/aka The Tongue of the Butterfly).*

Cukor, George *Actress, The; Adam's Rib; Bhowani Junction; Bill of Divorcement, A; Blue Bird, The; Born Yesterday; Camille; Chapman Report, The; David Copperfield; Dinner at Eight; Double Life, A; Gaslight (aka The Murder In Thornton Square); Heller in Pink Tights; Holiday; It Should Happen to You; Justine; Keeper of the Flame; Les Girls; Let's Make Love; Little Women; Love Among the Ruins;. Marrying Kind, The; My Fair Lady; One Hour With You; Pat and Mike; Philadelphia Story, The; Rich and Famous; Star Is Born, A; Sylvia Scarlett; Two-Faced Woman; What Price Hollywood?; Woman's Face, A; Women, The; Zaza.*

Culp, Robert *Hickey & Boggs.*

Cummings, Irving *Hollywood Cavalcade; Lillian Russell; That Night in Rio.*

Cundieff, Rusty *Fear of a Black Hat.*

Cunha, Richard E *She Demons.*

Cunningham, Sean S *Deep Star Six; Friday the 13th; Together (aka Sensual Paradise).*

Curling, Jonathan *Song of the Shirt, The.*

Curran, John *Praise.*

Curran, Peter *No Secrets! (aka Touch of the Sun); Penelope 'Pulls It Off'.*

Curran, William *Love, Cheat & Steal.*

Currier, Lavinia *Passion in the Desert.*

Curteis, Ian *Projected Man, The.*

Curtis, Dan *Burnt Offerings; Dracula.*

Curtis-Hall, Vondie *Glitter; Gridlock'd.*

Curtiz, Michael *Adventures of Huckleberry Finn, The; Adventures of Robin Hood, The; Angels With Dirty Faces; Best Things in Life Are Free, The; Black Fury; Breaking Point, The; Cabin in the Cotton, The; Captain Blood; Casablanca; Charge of the Light Brigade, The; Dive Bomber; Kid Galahad; King Creole; Life with Father; Mad Genius; Mildred Pierce; Mission to Moscow; Mystery of the Wax Museum; Night and Day; Noah's Ark; Passage to Marseille; Private Lives of Elizabeth and Essex, The; Romance on the High Seas (aka It's Magic); Santa Fe Trail; Sea Hawk, The; Sea Wolf, The; 20,000 Years in Sing Sing; Unsuspected, The; Walking Dead, The; We're No Angels; Yankee Doodle Dandy; Young Man With a Horn (aka Young Man of Music).*

Cutts, Graham *Rat, The.*

Czinner, Paul *As You Like It; Catherine the Great.*

Daalder, Renee *Massacre at Central High (aka Blackboard Massacre).*

Da Costa, Morton *Auntie Mame; Music Man, The.*

Dahl, John (R) *Joy Ride (aka Roadkill); Kill Me Again; Last Seduction, The; Red Rock West; Rounders; Unforgettable.*

Dai Sijie *Balzac and the Little Chinese Seamstress (Balzac et la petite tailleuse chinoise).*

Daldry, Stephen *Billy Elliot.*

Dalen, Zale R *Hounds of Notre Dame, The; Skip Tracer.*

Dallamano, Massimo *Blue Belle; Venus in Furs (Venus im Pelz).*

Dalrymple, Ian *Esther Waters.*

Dalva, Robert *Black Stallion Returns, The.*

D'Amato, Joe (Aristide Massaccesi) *Emanuelle and the Last Cannibals (Emanuelle e gli Ultimi Cannibali).*

Damiani, Damiano *Amityville II: The Possession; Bullet for the General, A (¿Quién Sabe?); Tempter, The (Il Sorriso del Grande Tenatore).*

Damiano, Gerard *Devil in Miss Jones, The; Memories Within Miss Aggie.*

Damiano, Gerard (as Jerry Gerard) *Deep Throat.*

Damski, Mel *Happy Together; Yellowbeard.*

Dang Nhât Minh *Nostalgia for Countryland (Thuong Nho Dong Que); Return, The (Tro' Vé).*

Daniel, Rod *Beethoven's 2nd; K-9; Like Father, Like Son; Teen Wolf.*

Daniels, Frank *Classified X (aka Melvin Van Peebles' Classified X).*

Daniels, Godfrey *Insatiable.*

Danielsson, Tage *Out of an Old Man's Head (I Huvet på en Gammal Gubbe).*

Danino, Nina *Temenos.*

D'Anna, Claude *Salomé.*

Danot, Serge *Dougal and the Blue Cat (Pollux et le Chat Bleu).*

Danquart, Didi *Jew-Boy Levi (Viehjud Levi).*

Danquart, Pepe *Home Game (Heimspiel).*

Dansereau, Mireille *Dream Life (La Vie Rêvée).*

Dante, Dominique *Contre l'Oubli (Against Oblivion).*

Dante, Joe *Amazon Women on the Moon; 'burbs, The; Explorers; Gremlins; Gremlins 2: The New Batch; Hollywood Boulevard; Howling, The; Innerspace; Matinee; Piranha; Small Soldiers; Twilight Zone – The Movie.*

Danton, Raymond *Psychic Killer.*

D'Antoni, Philip *Seven-Ups, The.*

Darabont, Frank *Green Mile, The; Shawshank Redemption, The.*

Dardenne, Jean Pierre, *Promise, The (La Promesse); Rosetta; Son, The (Le Fils).*

Dardenne, Luc, *Promise, The (La Promesse); Rosetta; Son, The (Le Fils).*

Darling, Joan *First Love.*

Darnborough, Anthony *Astonished Heart, The; So Long at the Fair.*

Darnell, Eric *Antz.*

D'Arrast, Harry D'Abbadie *Laughter; Raffles.*

Dasgupta, Buddhadeb *Wrestlers, The (Uttara).*

Dash, Julie *Daughters of the Dust; Illusions; Subway Stories Tales from the Underground.*

Dassin, Jules *Brute Force; Circle of Two; Dream of Passion, A; Du Rififi chez les Hommes (Rififi); Naked City, The; Never on Sunday (Pote tin Kyriaki); Night and the City; Phaedra; 10.30 P.M. Summer; Thieves' Highway; Topkapi.*

Davenport, Harry Bromley *Xtro.*

Daves, Delmer *Badlanders, The; Battle of the Villa Fiorita, The; Broken Arrow; Cowboy; Dark Passage; Demetrius and the Gladiators; Kings Go Forth; Last Wagon, The; Pride of the Marines (aka Forever in Love); Red House, The; 3.10 to Yuma.*

David, Charles *Lady on a Train.*

David, Larry *Sour Grapes.*

Davide, Giovanni *This Is the Garden (Questo è il giardino).*

Davidson, Boaz *Going Steady (Yotz'im Kavna); Last American Virgin, The; Lemon Popsicle (Eskimo Limon); Private Popsicle (Sapiches); Salsa.*

Davidson, John-Paul *Galahad of Everest; Grotesque, The (aka Gentlemen Don't Eat Poets).*

Davidson, Martin *Almost Summer; Eddie and the Cruisers; Hero at Large; Lords of Flatbush, The.*

Davies, Colin *Cyberworld 3D.*

Davies, Howard *Secret Rapture, The.*

Davies, John *Acceptable Levels; City Farm; Maeve; Ursula and Glenys.*

Davies, Robert *Saturday Night at the Palace.*

Davies, Terence *Distant Voices, Still Lives; House of Mirth, The; Long Day Closes, The; Neon Bible, The; Terence Davies Trilogy, The.*

Davis, Andrew *Above the Law (aka Nico); Code of Silence; Collateral Damage; Final Terror (aka Campsite Massacre); Fugitive, The; Package, The; Perfect Murder, A; Steal Big, Steal Little; Under Siege.*

Davis, Desmond *Clash of the Titans; Country Girls, The; Girl with Green Eyes; I Was Happy Here; Ordeal by Innocence.*

Davis, John A *Jimmy Neutron Boy Genius.*

Davis, Mick *Match, The.*

Davis, Ossie *Gordon's War.*

Davis, Peter *Best Hotel on Skid Row; Hearts and Minds; Paperback Vigilante.*

Davis, Philip *Hold Back the Night; i.d.*

Davis, Redd *Underneath the Arches.*

Davis, Tamra *Best Men; CB4; Crossroads; Guncrazy.*

Dawson, Anthony M (Antonio Margheriti) *Blood Money (aka The Stranger and the Gunfighter); Killer Fish (Agguato sul Fondo); Take a Hard Ride; Vengeance (Joko, Invoca Dio…e Muori).*

Day, Ernest *Green Ice.*

Day, Robert *Corridors of Blood; Green Man, The; Grip of the Strangler (aka The Haunted Strangler); Rebel, The; She; Sunshine Part II (aka My Sweet Lady); Two-Way Stretch.*

Deák, Krisztina *Jadviga's Pillow (Jadviga Párája).*

de Almeida, Guilherme *Magic Hour, The (A Hora Mágica).*

Dean, Basil *Autumn Crocus; Escape!*

de Antonio, Emile *In the King of Prussia; Millhouse, a White Comedy; Painters Painting; Point of Order; Rush to Judgement; Underground.*

Dear, William *Amazing Stories; Angels in the Outfield (aka Angels); Harry and the Hendersons (aka Bigfoot and the Hendersons); Teen Agent.*

Dearden, Basil *Assassination Bureau, The; Bells Go Down, The; Black Sheep of Whitehall, The; Blue Lamp, The; Cage of Gold; Captive Heart, The; Dead of Night; Frieda; Gentle Gunman, The; Green Man, The; Khartoum; League of Gentlemen, The; Masquerade; My Learned Friend; Only When I Larf; Pool of London; Rainbow Jacket, The; Sapphire; Saraband for Dead Lovers; Ship That Died of Shame, The (aka PT Raiders); Smallest Show on Earth, The; Train of Events; Victim; Woman of Straw.*

Dearden, James *Kiss Before Dying, A; Pascali's Island; Rogue Trader.*

Deasy, Frank *Courier, The.*

DeBello, John *Attack of the Killer Tomatoes.*

De Bont, Jan *Haunting, The; Speed; Speed 2: Cruise Control; Twister.*

De Bosio, Gianfranco *Moses.*

Debrauwer, Lieven *Pauline & Paulette.*

de Broca, Philippe *Bossu, Le (On Guard!); Chère Louise (Louise); Dear Inspector (Tendre Poulet); Homme de Rio, L' (That Man from Rio); How to Destroy the Reputation of the Greatest Secret Agent (Le Magnifique); King of Hearts (Le Roi de Coeur).*

de Chalonge, Christian *Argent des Autres, L', (Other People's Money); Docteur Petiot; Malevil.*

de Clerq, Dimitri *Blue Villa, The (Un bruit qui rend fou).*

de Courville, Albert *Seven Sinners (aka Doomed Cargo).*

De Felitta, Frank *Scissors.*

Degregori, Luis Felipe *Todos Somos Estrellas (We're All Stars).*

de Gregorio, Eduardo *Aspern; Sérail.*

de Heer, Rolf *Bad Boy Bubby; Dance Me to My Song; Encounter at Raven's Gate; Quiet Room, The.*

Dehlavi, Jamil *Blood of Hussain, The; Born of Fire (aka The Master Musician); Immaculate Conception.*

Deitch, Donna *Angel on My Shoulder; Desert Hearts; Prison Stories: Women on the Inside; Woman to Woman.*

DeJarnatt, Steve *Cherry 2000; Miracle Mile.*

De Jong, Ate *All Men Are Mortal; Drop Dead Fred.*

de Jong, Mijke *Love Hurts (Hartverscheurend/Heart-Rending).*

Dekker, Fred *Monster Squad, The; Night of the Creeps; RoboCop 3.*

de Kuyper, Eric *Casta Diva.*

de la Iglesia, Alex *Acción Mutante; Day of the Beast, The (El día de la bestia); Perdita Durango.*

Delannoy, Jean *Bernadette; Eternel Retour, L' (Eternal Love/Love Eternal); Hunchback of Notre Dame, The (Notre Dame de Paris); Jeux sont Faits, Les; Secret de Mayerling, Le; Symphonie Pastorale, La.*

de la Parra, Pim *My Nights with Susan, Sandra, Olga and Julie (Mijn Nachten med Susan Olga Albert Julie Piet & Sandra).*

de la Patellière, Denys *Du Rififi à Paname (Rififi in Paris/ The Upper Hand).*

de la Texera, Diego *El Salvador – The People Will Win (El Salvador – El Pueblo Vencerá).*

Del Balzo, Raimondo *Last Snows of Spring, The (L'Ultima Neve di Primavera).*

de Leon, Mike *Kisapmata.*

Deleuze, Emilie *Peau Neuve (A New Skin).*

Dell, Jeffrey *Don't Take It To Heart.*

Dellal, Gaby *Tube Tales.*

Delon, Nathalie *They Call That an Accident (Ils Appellent ça un Accident).*

Delouche, Dominique *Homme de Désir, L'.*

Delpeut, Peter *Felice… Felice…*

Del Ruth, Roy *Born to Dance; Broadway Melody of 1936; Bureau of Missing Persons; Chocolate Soldier, The; DuBarry Was a Lady; Folies Bergère; Lady Killer; Maltese Falcon, The (aka Dangerous Female); My Lucky Star; On Moonlight Bay; Taxi!*

del Toro, Guillermo *Blade II; Devil's Backbone, The (El Espinazo del Diablo); Cronos; Mimic.*

DeLuise, Dom *Hot Stuff.*

Delvaux, André *Belle; Benvenuta; Femme entre Chien et Loup, Une (Woman In a Twilight Garden); Man Who Had His Hair Cut Short, The (De Man die Zijn Haar Kort Liet Knippen); Rendez-vous à Bray (Rendezvous at Bray); Soir, un Train, Un.*

De Martino, Alberto *Anticristo, L' (The Antichrist/The Tempter); Counsellor, The (Il Consigliori); Holocaust 2000 (aka The Chosen); Killer Is on the Phone, The (Assassino…è al Telefono).*

Dembo, Richard *Dangerous Moves (La Diagonale du Fou).*

De Medeiros, Maria *Captains of April (Capitães de Abril/Capitanes d'avril/aka April Captains).*

Demetrakas, Johanna *Right Out of History: The Making of Judy Chicago's Dinner Party.*

Demeyer, Paul *Rugrats in Paris: The Movie.*

Demicheli, Tullio *Ricco (Une Tipo con una Faccia Strana Ti Cerca per Ucciderti).*

DeMille, Cecil B *Carmen; Cleopatra; Greatest Show on Earth, The; Plainsman, The; Samson and Delilah; Sign of the Cross, The; Ten Commandments, The; This Day and Age; Unconquered.*

Demirkubuz, Zeki *Third Page, The (Ügüznuk Safya).*

Demisse, Yemane I *Tumult (Gir-Gir).*

Demme, Jonathan *Beloved; Caged Heat; Citizens Band; Cousin Bobby; Crazy Mama; Fighting Mad; Last Embrace; Married to the Mob; Melvin and Howard; Philadelphia; Silence of the Lambs, The; Something Wild; Stop Making Sense; Subway Stories Tales from the Underground; Swimming to Cambodia; Swing Shift; Who Am I This Time?*

Demme, Ted *Beautiful Girls; Ref, The (aka Hostile Hostages); Blow; Life; Who's the Man?; Subway Stories Tales from the Underground.*

De Molinis, Claudio *Candido Erotico.*

DeMott, Joel *Demon Lover Diary.*

Demy, Jacques *Baie des Anges, La (Bay of Angels); Demoiselles de Rochefort, Les (The Young Girls of Rochefort); Lola; Model Shop; Parapluies de Cherbourg, Les (The Umbrellas of Cherbourg); Parking; Peau d'Ane (The Magic Donkey); Pied Piper, The; Slightly Pregnant Man, The (L'Evénement le plus Important depuis que l'Homme a Marché sur la Lune); Trois Places pour le 26 (Three Seats for the 26th).*

Denham, Reginald *Death at Broadcasting House.*

De Niro, Robert *Bronx Tale, A.*

Denis, Claire *Beau Travail; Chocolat; Contre l'Oubli (Against Oblivion); S'en fout la mort (No Fear, No Die); Nénette et Boni; Trouble Every Day.*

Dennis, Jonathan *Mouth Wide Open – A Journey in Film with Ted Coubray.*

Densham, Pen *Kiss, The; Moll Flanders.*

Deodato, Ruggero *Cannibal (Ultimo Mondo Cannibale); Cannibal Holocaust; Last Feelings (L'Ultimo Sapore dell'Aria).*

De Palma, Brian *Blow Out; Body Double; Bonfire of the Vanities, The; Carlito's Way; Carrie; Casualties of War; Dressed to Kill; Fury, The; Greetings; Hi, Mom!; Mission Impossible; Mission to Mars; Obsession; Phantom of the Paradise; Raising Cain; Scarface; Sisters (aka Blood Sisters); Snake Eyes; Untouchables, The; Wise Guys.*

Depardieu, Gérard *Tartuffe, Le.*

Depardon, Raymond *Captive du Désert, La (Captive of the Desert); Contre l'Oubli (Against Oblivion); Délits Flagrants (Caught in the Act); Lumière et Compagnie; 1974, Une Partie de Campagne.*

de Poligny, Serge *Baron Fantôme, Le (The Phantom Baron).*

Depp, Johnny *Brave, The.*

Deprez, Dany *Ball, The (Der Ball/De Bal).*

Deray, Jacques *Borsalino; Borsalino & Co (Blood on the Streets); Contre l'Oubli (Against Oblivion); Gang, Le; He Died with His Eyes Open (On ne Meurt que 2 Fois); Homme de Marrakech, L' (Our Man in Marrakesh/ That Man George); Outside Man, The (Un Homme est Mort); Peu de Soleil dans l'Eau Froide, Un (Sunlight on Cold Water).*

Dercout, Denis *Cachetonneurs, Les (The Music Freelancers/ aka The Freelancers).*

Derek, John *Bolero (aka Bo's Bolero); Tarzan, the Ape Man.*

Deruddere, Dominique *Crazy Love; Suite 16.*

De Santis, Giuseppe *Bitter Rice (Riso Amaro).*

Deschanel, Caleb *Crusoe.*

De Sica, Vittorio *After the Fox (Caccia alla Volpe); Bicycle Thieves (Ladri di Biciclette); Boccaccio '70; Brief Vacation, A (Una Breve Vacanza); Garden of the Finzi-Continis, The (Il Giardino dei Finzi-Contini); Miracle in Milan (Miracolo a Milano); Sunflower (I Girasoli); Terminal Station (Stazione Termini/ Indiscretion of an American Wife); Umberto D.*

De Simone, Thomas *Hell Night; Prison Girls.*

De Sisti, Vittorio *Private Lesson, The (Lezioni Private).*

de Souza, Steven E *Street Fighter.*

Despentes, Virginie *Baise-moi.*

Despins, Elaine *Cyberworld 3D.*

Despins, Joseph *Duffer; Moon Over the Alley, The.*

Desplechin, Arnaud *Esther Kahn; Ma vie sexuelle (Paul Dedalus' Journey) (Comment je me suis disputé… ('ma vie sexuelle')); Sentinelle, La (The Sentinel).*

DeStefano, Lorenzo *Talmage Farlow.*

Deswarte, Benie *Kashima Paradise.*

De Toth, André *Carson City; Dark Waters; Day of the Outlaw; House of Wax; Indian Fighter, The; None Shall Escape; Pitfall; Play Dirty; Ramrod.*

Deutch, Howard *Getting Even With Dad; Odd Couple II, The (aka Neil Simon's The Odd Couple II); Pretty in Pink; Some Kind of Wonderful.*

Deval, Jacques *Club de Femmes.*

Devenish, Ross *Boesman and Lena; Marigolds in August.*

Devers, Claire *Noir et Blanc; Thief of Saint Lubin, The (La Voleuse de Saint-Lubin).*

Deville, Michel *Contre l'Oubli (Against Oblivion); Death in a French Garden (Péril en la Demeure); Dossier 51, Le; Lectrice, La; Maladie de Sachs, La; Paltoquet, Le.*

DeVito, Danny *Hoffa; Roald Dahl's Matilda; Throw Momma from the Train; War of the Roses, The.*

DeVito, Ralph *Death Collector.*

Dexter, John *I Want What I Want.*

Dey, Tom *Shanghai Noon; Showtime.*

Dhouailly, Alain *Inutile Envoyer Photo.*

Diaz-Abaya, Marilou *In the Navel of the Sea (Sa Pusod Ng Dagat).*

Díaz Yanes, Agustín *Nobody Will Speak of Us When We're Dead (Nadie Hablará de Nostras cuando Hayamos Muerto).*

DiCillo, Tom *Box of Moon Light; Johnny Suede; Living in Oblivion; Real Blonde, The.*

Dick, Kirby *Sick: The Life & Death of Bob Flanagan, Supermasochist.*

Dick, Nigel *Final Combination; P.I. Private Investigations.*

Dickerson, Ernest R *Juice; Surviving the Game; Tales from the Crypt Presents Demon Knight.*

Dickinson, Thorold *Arsenal Stadium Mystery, The; Gaslight; Men of Two Worlds; Next of Kin, The; Queen of Spades, The; Secret People.*

Diegues, Carlos *Bye Bye Brasil; Orfeu; Tieta of Agreste (Tieta do Agreste).*

Dieterle, William *All That Money Can Buy (aka The Devil and Daniel Webster/ Daniel and the Devil); Another Dawn; Dark City; Dr Erlich's Magic Bullet; Blockade; Fog Over Frisco; Her Majesty, Love; Hunchback of Notre Dame, The; I'll Be Seeing You; Juarez; Last Flight, The; Life of Emile Zola, The; Love Letters; Midsummer Night's Dream, A; Portrait of Jennie; Satan Met a Lady; Searching Wind, The.*

Dietl, Helmut *Schtonk!*

Dieutre, Vincent *Bonne Nouvelle.*

Dignam, Erin *Loved.*

Di Leo, Fernando *Manhunt in Milan (La 'Mala' Ordina).*

Di Mello, Victor *Giselle.*

Dindal, Mark *Emperor's New Groove, The.*

Ding, Loni *Color of Honor, The.*

Dingwall, John *Custodian, The.*

Dinner, Michael *Heaven Help Us (aka Catholic Boys); Off Beat.*

DiNovis, Kevin *Surrender Dorothy.*

Diop-Mambéty, Djibril *Franc, Le; Hyenas (Hyènes/ Ramatou); Little Girl Who Sold the Sun, The (La Petite Vendeuse de Soleil).*

Dippé, Mark AZ *Spawn.*

DiSalle, Mark *Kickboxer; Perfect Weapon.*

Di Silvestro, Rino *Love in a Women's Prison (Diario Segreto da un Carcere Femminile).*

Disney, Walt *Snow White and the Seven Dwarfs.*

Dissanayake, Somaratne *Saroja.*

Dizdar, Jasmin *Beautiful People.*

Dmytryk, Edward *Back to Bataan; Broken Lance; Caine Mutiny, The; Cornered; Crossfire; Devil Commands, The; Farewell, My Lovely (aka Murder My Sweet); 'Human' Factor, The; Left Hand of God, The; Mirage; Obsession (aka The Hidden Room); Raintree Country; Sbarco di Anzio, Lo (Anzio/The Battle for Anzio); Shalako; Sniper, The; Sweetheart of the Campus (aka Broadway Ahead); Tender Comrade; Walk on the Wild Side; Warlock; Young Lions, The.*

Dobson, Kevin *Mango Tree, The.*

Docter, Pete *Monsters, Inc.*

Dohany, Gael *Occupy!*

Doillon, Jacques *Contre l'Oubli (Against Oblivion); Jeune Werther, Le (Young Werther); Petits Frères, Les; Ponette; Sac de Billes, Un.*

Dolmatovskaya, Galina *Ivan Mosjoukine, or The Carnival Child (Ivan Mosjoukin ili Ditya Karnavala).*

Dolz, Sonia Herman *Yo soy así.*

Dominici, Paolo (Domenico Paolella) *Nun and the Devil, The (Le Monache di Sant'Arcangelo).*

Dominik, Andrew *Chopper.*

Donald, Simon *Life of Stuff, The.*

Donaldson, Roger *Bounty, The; Cadillac Man; Cocktail; Dante's Peak; Marie; Getaway, The; No Way Out; Sleeping Dogs; Smash Palace; Species; Thirteen Days; White Sands.*

Donehue, Vincent J *Lonelyhearts.*

Donen, Stanley *Arabesque; Bedazzled; Blame It On Rio; Charade; Damn Yankees (aka What Lola Wants); Funny Face; Grass Is Greener, The; Indiscreet; It's Always Fair Weather; Kiss Them for Me; Little Prince, The; Lucky Lady; Movie Movie; On the Town; Pajama Game, The; Royal Wedding (aka Wedding Bells); Saturn 3; Seven Brides for Seven Brothers; Singin' in the Rain; Staircase; Two for the Road.*

Donnelly, Dennis *Toolbox Murders, The.*

Donner, Clive *Caretaker, The (aka The Guest); Charlie Chan and the Curse of the Dragon Queen; Christmas Carol, A; Here We Go Round the Mulberry Bush; Luv; Maverick; Nothing But the Best; Nude Bomb, The; Oliver Twist; Stealing Heaven; Thief of Baghdad, The; Vampire (aka Old Dracula); What's New Pussycat?*

Donner, Jörn *Black on White (Mustaa Valkoisella).*

Donner, Richard *Assassins; Conspiracy Theory; Goonies, The; Inside Moves; Ladyhawke; Lethal Weapon; Lethal Weapon 2; Lethal Weapon 3; Lethal Weapon 4; Omen, The; Radio Flyer; Salt & Pepper; Scrooged; Superman; Toy, The.*

Donoghue, Mary Agnes *Paradise.*

Donohue, Jack *Assault on a Queen.*

Donovan, Martin *Apartment Zero.*

Donovan, Paul *Siege.*

Donovan, Terence *Yellow Dog.*

Donskoi, Mark *Childhood of Maxim Gorki, The (Detstvo Gorkovo); Orlovs, The (Suprugi Orlovy).*

Doob, Nick *Down from the Mountain.*

Dore, Mary *Good Fight, The.*

Doring, Jef *Tidikawa and Friends.*

Doring, Su *Tidikawa and Friends.*

Dornhelm, Robert *Children of Theatre Street, The; Cold Feet; Echo Park; Further Gesture, A (aka The Break); Requiem for Dominic; Unfish, The (Der Unfisch).*

Dorr, John *Luck, Trust & Ketchup: Robert Altman in Carver Country.*

Dörrie, Doris *Keiner Liebt Mich (Nobody Loves Me); Men (Männer).*

Dos Santos, Nelson Pereira *Barren Lives.*

Douchet, Jean *Paris vu par… (Six in Paris).*

Doueiri, Ziad *West Beirut (West Beyrouth).*

Douglas, Bill *Comrades; My Childhood/My Ain Folk/My Way Home.*

Douglas, Gordon *Barquero; Between Midnight and Dawn; Charge at Feather River, The; Chuka; Come Fill the Cup; Detective, The; First Yank into Tokyo (aka First Man into Tokyo/ Mask of Fury); Follow That Dream; In Like Flint; Kiss Tomorrow Goodbye; Lady in Cement; Rio Conchos; Robin and the 7 Hoods; Santiago (The Gun Runner); Saps at Sea; Skullduggery; Sins of Rachel Cade, The; Slaughter's Big Rip-Off; Stagecoach; Them!; They Call Me MISTER Tibbs!; Tony Rome; Viva Knievel!; Young at Heart.*

Douglas, John *Milestones.*

Douglas, Kirk *Posse; Scalawag.*

Douglas, Peter *Tiger's Tale, A.*

Doukas, Bill *Feedback.*

Doukouré, Cheik *Ballon d'Or, Le (The Golden Ball).*

Dovzhenko, Alexander *Earth (Zemlya).*

Downey, Robert *Putney Swope.*

Doyle, Jim *Going Off Big Time.*

Drach, Michel *Pull-Over Rouge, Le; Violons du Bal, Les.*

Dragin, Sinisa *Every Day God Kisses Us on the Mouth (In fiecare zi Dumnezeu ne saruta pe gura).*

Dragojevic, Srdjan *Pretty Village, Pretty Flame (Lepa sela lepo gore); Wounds, The (Rane).*

Dragoti, Stan *Dirty Little Billy; Love at First Bite; Mr Mom (aka Mr Mum); Necessary Roughness; She's Out of Control.*

Drake, Jim *Police Academy 4: Citizens on Patrol.*

Drazan, Anthony *Hurlyburly; Imaginary Crimes.*

Dreifuss, Arthur *Baby Face Morgan.*

Dresen, Andreas *Policewoman, The (Die Polizistin).*

Dreyer, Carl Theodor *Day of Wrath (Vredens Dag); Gertrud; Michael (Mikaël); Ordet (The Word); Passion de Jeanne d'Arc, La (The Passion of Joan of Arc); President, The (Praesidenten); Vampyr.*

Drion, Georges *Voice of Kurdistan, The.*

Drury, David *Defence of the Realm; Forever Young.*

Duan Jinchuan *Square, The (Guangchang).*

DuBoc, Claude *One By One.*

Dubov, Adam *Dead Beat.*

Ducastel, Olivier *Jeanne et le Garçon Formidable.*

Duchamp, Marcel *Dreams That Money Can Buy; Drôle de Félix.*

Du Chau, Frederick *Magic Sword: Quest for Camelot, The.*

Duchemin, Rémy *Fausto.*

Duckworth, Jacqui *Home-Made Melodrama.*

Dudow, Slatan *Kuhle Wampe.*

Duffell, Peter *England Made Me; Experience Preferred But Not Essential; House That Dripped Blood, The; Inside Out; King of the Wind; Letters to an Unknown Lover (Les Louves).*

Duffy, Martin *Boy from Mercury, The.*

Dufort, Glenn *Shooters.*

Dugan, Dennis *Big Daddy; Happy Gilmore; Problem Child; Saving Silverman (aka Evil Woman).*

Dugdale, George *Living Doll.*

Dugowson, Martine *Mina Tannenbaum; Portraits Chinois.*

Duguay, Christian *Art of War, The; Scanners II: The New Order; Screamers.*

Duigan, John *Flirting; Lawn Dogs; Leading Man, The; Parole Officer, The; Romero; Sirens; Wide Sargasso Sea; Winter of Our Dreams; Year My Voice Broke, The.*

Duke, Bill *Deep Cover; Killing Floor, The; Rage in Harlem, A; Sister Act 2: Back in the Habit.*

Duke, Daryl *Payday; Silent Partner, The.*

Dulac, Germaine *Seashell and the Clergyman, The (La Coquille et le Clergyman; Souriante Madame Beudet, La (The Smiling Madame Beudet).*

Dumaresq, William *Duffer.*

Dumont, Bruno *Humanité, L'; Vie de Jésus, La (The Life of Jesus).*

Duncan, Patrick *84 Charlie Mopic.*

Dunkerton, Martin *Brothers.*

Dunlop, Frank *Winter's Tale, The.*

Dunne, Griffin *Addicted to Love; Practical Magic.*

Dunne, Philip *Blindfold; Blue Denim (aka Blue Jeans); In Love and War; Wild in the Country.*

Dunning, George *Yellow Submarine.*

Dunye, Cheryl *Stranger Inside; Watermelon Woman, The.*

Dupeyron, François *Chambre des officiers, La (The Officers' Ward); Coeur qui bat, Un (Your Beating Heart); Strange Place to Meet, A (Drôle d'Endroit pour une rencontre).*

Dupont, EA *Piccadilly; Varieté (Variety/Vaudeville).*

Dupontel, Albert *Bernie.*

Durán, Rodolfo *Close to the Border (Cerca de la Frontera).*

Durand, Rudy *Tilt.*

Durant, Alberto *Courage (Coraje).*

Duras, Marguerite *India Song; Nathalie Granger.*

Durham, Duwayne *Homeward Bound: The Incredible Journey.*

Duty, Claude *Hypnotised and Hysterical (Hairstylist Wanted) (Filles Perdues, Cheveux Gras).*

Duval, Daniel *Dérobade, La (The Life).*

Duvall, Robert *Angelo My Love; Apostle, The.*

Duvivier, Julien *Anna Karenina; Belle Equipe, La; Carnet de Bal, Un; Fin du Jour, La (The End of the Day); Flesh and Fantasy; Great Waltz, The; Lydia; Pépé le Moko; Tête d'un Homme, La (A Man's Neck).*

Dvir, Rami *Wedding Tackle, The.*

Dwan, Allan *Angel in Exile; Brewster's Millions; Cattle Queen of Montana; Driftwood; Escape to Burma; Iron Mask, The; Most Dangerous Man Alive; Robin Hood; Restless Breed; River's Edge, The; Sands of Iwo Jima; Silver Lode; Slightly Scarlet; Suez; Tennessee's Partner.*

Dwoskin, Stephen *Ballet Black; Dyn Amo; Further and Particular; Hindered (Behindert); Outside In; Silent Cry, The.*

Dylan, Bob *Renaldo & Clara.*

Dylewska, Jolanta *Warsaw Ghetto Uprising, The.*

Dzhordzhadze, Nana *My English Grandfather (Robinsonada anu Chemi Ingliseli Papa).*

Dzigan, Efim *We from Kronstadt (My iz Kronshtadta).*

Dziga Vertov Group (Groupe Dziga Vertov) *Pravda; Vladimir et Rosa (Vladimir and Rosa).*

E J-Yong *Asako in Ruby Shoes (Sun Ae Bo).*

Eagles, Bill *Beautiful Creatures.*

East, John M *Hellcat Mud Wrestlers.*

Eastwood, Clint *Absolute Power; Bird; Bridges of Madison County, The; Breezy; Bronco Billy; Eiger Sanction, The; Firefox; Gauntlet, The: Heartbreak Ridge; High Plains Drifter; Honkytonk Man; Midnight in the Garden of Good and Evil; Outlaw Josey Wales, The; Pale Rider; Perfect World, A; Play Misty for Me; Rookie, The; Space Cowboys; Sudden Impact; True Crime; Unforgiven; White Hunter, Black Heart.*

Eberhardt, Thom *Captain Ron; Gross Anatomy (aka A Cut Above); Night of the Comet; Without a Clue.*

Ecaré, Désiré *Faces of Women (Visages de Femmes).*

Echevarria, Nicolas *Cabeza de Vaca.*

Edel, Ulrich [Uli] *Body of Evidence; Christiane F. (Christiane F. wir Kinder vom Bahnhof Zoo); Last Exit to Brooklyn (Letzte Ausfahrt Brooklyn); Little Vampire, The (Die kleine Vampir).*

Eder, Harriet *My Private War (Mein Krieg).*

Edmondson, Adrian *Guest House Paradiso; More Bad News.*

Edwards, Blake *Blind Date; Breakfast at Tiffany's; Carey Treatment, The; Curse of the Pink Panther; Darling Lili; Days of Wine and Roses; Experiment in Terror (aka The Grip of Fear); Fine Mess, A; High Time; Man Who Loved Women, The; Micki + Maude; Mister Cory; Operation Petticoat; Party, The; Pink Panther, The; Pink Panther Strikes Again, The; Return of the Pink Panther, The; Revenge of the Pink Panther; S.O.B.; Shot in the Dark, A; Skin Deep; Sunset; Switch; Tamarind Seed, The; Trail of the Pink Panther; '10'; 'That's Life'; Victor/ Victoria; What Did You Do in the War, Daddy?; Wild Rovers.*

Edwards, Harry *Tramp, Tramp, Tramp.*

Edwards, Henry *Squibs.*

Edzard, Christine *As You Like It; Biddy; Fool, The; Children's Midsummer Night's Dream, The; Little Dorrit; Stories from a Flying Trunk.*

Eggleston, Colin *Long Weekend; Sky Pirates.*

Egleson, Jan *Shock to the System, A.*

Egoyan, Atom *Adjuster, The; Ararat; Calendar; Exotica; Family Viewing; Felicia's Journey; Krapp's Last Tape; Speaking Parts; Sweet Hereafter, The.*

Eichert, Benjamin *Zapatista.*

Eisenman, Rafael *Lake Consequence.*

Eisenstein, Sergei *Alexander Nevsky; Battleship Potemkin (Bronenosets Potyomkin); General Line, The (Staroye i Novoye; aka Old and New); Ivan the Terrible (Ivan Grozny); Oktyabr (October/Ten Days That Shook the World); Strike (Stachka).*

Elçi, Umit *Cockroach, The (Böcek).*

Eldridge, John *Conflict of Wings (aka Fuss Over Feathers); Laxdale Hall (aka Scotch on the Rocks).*

Elek, Judit *To Speak the Unspeakable: The Message of Elie Wiesel (Mondani a mondhatatlant: Elie Wiesel uzenete).*

Elfick, David *Love in Limbo.*

Elfont, Harry *Josie and ther Pussycats.*

Elgear, Sandra *Voices from the Front.*

El Hagar, Khalid, *Room to Rent.*

Elias, Michael *Lush Life.*

Ellin, Doug *Kissing a Fool.*

Elliott, Aiyana *Ballad of Ramblin' Jack, The.*

Elliott, Scott *Map of the World, A.*

Elliott, Stephan *Adventures of Priscilla Queen of the Desert, The; Eye of the Beholder; Frauds; Welcome to Woop Woop.*

Ellis, Arthur *Don't Get Me Started (aka Psychotherapy).*

Else, Jon *Day After Trinity, The.*

Elton, Arthur *Housing Problems.*

Elton, Ben *Maybe Baby.*

Eltringham, Bille *Darkest Light, The; This Is Not a Love Song.*

Elvey, Maurice *Beware of Pity; Clairvoyant, The; Dry Rot; For Freedom; I Lived With You; Princess Charming; Tunnel, The (aka Transatlantic Tunnel).*

Emerson, John *Mystery of the Leaping Fish, The.*

Emery, Ted *Craic, The.*

Emlyn, Endaf *Leaving Lenin (Gadael Lenin); Making of Maps, The (Y Mapiwr); One Full Moon (Un Nos Ola Leuad).*

Emmerich, Roland *Ghost Chase; Godzilla; Independence Day; Moon 44; Patriot, The; Stargate; Universal Soldier.*

Enders, Robert *Stevie.*

Endfield, Cyril (Cy) *Hell Drivers; Jet Storm; Mysterious Island; Sound of Fury, The (aka Try and Get Me); Zulu.*

Engel, Andi *Melancholia.*

English, John *Adventures of Captain Marvel, The (aka The Return of Captain Marvel); Mule Train.*

Englund, Robert *976-Evil.*

Engström, Ingemo *Escape Route to Marseilles (Fluchtweg nach Marseilles).*

Ennadre, Dalila *Women from the Medina (El Batalett).*

Enrico, Robert *Ho! (aka Criminal Face); Secret, The (Le Secret).*

Enright, Ray *Angels Wash Their Faces; China Clipper; Dames; Man Alive; Naughty but Nice; South of St Louis.*

Enyedi, Ildikó *My 20th Century (Az én XX századom).*

Ephron, Nora *Michael; Mixed Nuts; Sleepless in Seattle; This Is My Life; You've Got Mail.*

Epstein, Jean *Chute de la Maison Usher, La (The Fall of the House of Usher).*

Epstein, Marcelo *Body Rock.*

Epstein, Robert (Rob) *Celluloid Closet, The; Common Threads: Stories from the Quilt; Paragraph 175; Times of Harvey Milk, The.*

Equino, Antonio *Chuquiago.*

Erdem, Reha *Run for Money (Kaç Para Kaç).*

Erdogan, Yilmaz *Vizontele.*

Erdöss, Pál *Princess, The (Adj Király Katonát!).*

Erice, Victor *Quince Tree Sun, The (El Sol del Membrillo); South, The (El Sur); Spirit of the Beehive, The (El Espíritu de la Colmena); Ten Minutes Older – The Trumpet.*

Erkenov, Khusein *100 Days Before the Command (Sto Dnei Do Prikaza…).*

Erlingsson, Gisli Snaer *Ikingut.*

Erman, John *Making It; Stella.*

Erne, Eduarde *Totschweigen (A Wall of Silence).*

Ernst, Max *Dreams That Money Can Buy.*

Erskine, Chester *Androcles and the Lion.*

Eshetu, Theo *Blood Is Not Fresh Water; Travelling Light: a Portrait of Lindsay Kemp.*

Esteban, Juan *Sensations.*

Estevez, Emilio *Men at Work; War at Home, The; Wisdom.*

Estrada, Luis *Herod's Law (La Ley de Herodes).*

Esway, Alexander *Conquest of the Air.*

Etaix, Pierre *Grand Amour, Le; Soupirant, Le (The Suitor); Tant qu'on a la Santé (As Long as You're Healthy); Yoyo.*

Etemad, Rakhshan Bani *Under the Skin of the City (Zir-e Poost-e Shahr/aka Under the City's Skin).*

Eustache, Jean *Mes Petites Amoureuses; Mother and the Whore, The (La Maman et la Putain).*

Evans, Betsan Morris *Dad Savage.*

Evans, Bruce A *Kuffs.*

Evans, David *Fever Pitch.*

Evans, David Mickey *Sandlot, The (aka The Sandlot Kids).*

Evans, Marc *Gift, The; House of America; Resurrection Man.*

Everett, DS *see* Shebib, Donald.

Export, Valie *Invisible Adversaries (Unsichtbare Gegner).*

Eyre, Chris *Smoke Signals.*

Eyre, Richard *Imitation Game, The; Iris; Laughterhouse (aka Singleton's Pluck); Loose Connections; Ploughman's Lunch, The.*

Eyres, John *Monolith.*

Faenza, Roberto *Order of Death (L'Assassino del Poliziotti/aka Corrupt); Lost Lover, The (L'Amante Perduto).*

Faiman, Peter *Crocodile Dundee; Dutch (aka Driving Me Crazy).*

Fairfax, Ferdinand *Savage Islands; True Blue.*

Falk, Feliks *And There Was Jazz (Byl Jazz); Top Dog (Wodzirej).*

Falkenstein, Jun *Tigger Movie, The.*

Fall, Jim *Trick.*

Famuyiwa, Rick *Wood, The.*

Fanaka, Jamaa *Penitentiary.*

Fanck, Arnold *White Hell of Piz Palu, The (Die Weisse Hölle vom Piz Palu).*

Fansten, Jacques *Fracture du myocarde, La (Cross My Heart).*

Faraldo, Claude *Bof!; Themroc.*

Färberböck, Max *Aimée and Jaguar.*

Fargo, James *Caravans; Enforcer, The; Every Which Way But Loose; Game for Vultures.*

Farhang, Dariush *Spell, The (Telesm).*

Faringer, Asa *Daughter of the Puma, The.*

Farino, Julian *Last Yellow, The.*

Farmanara, Bahman *Smell of Camphor, Fragrance of Jasmine (Booye Kafoor, Atre Yas).*

Farrelly, Bobby *Kingpin; Me, Myself & Irene; Osmosis Jones; Shallow Hal; There's Something About Mary.*

Farrelly, Peter *Dumb & Dumber; Kingpin; Me, Myself & Irene; Osmosis Jones; Shallow Hal; There's Something About Mary.*

Farrina, Corrado *Baba Yaga – The Devil Witch (Baba Yaga).*

Farrow, John *Alias Nick Beal (aka The Contact Man); Back from Eternity; Big Clock, The; Botany Bay; Calcutta; Five Came Back; Full Confession; His Kind of Woman; Hitler Gang, The; Hondo; Night Has a Thousand Eyes; Sea Chase, The; Two Yeas Before the Mast; Where Danger Lives.*

Fassbinder, Rainer Werner *American Soldier, The (Der Amerikanische Soldat); Berlin Alexanderplatz; Beware of a Holy Whore (Warnung vor heiligen Nutte); Bitter Tears of Petra von Kant, The (Die Bitteren Tränen der Petra von Kant); Bolwieser (The Stationmaster's Wife); Chinese Roulette (Chinesisches Roulette); Despair; Effi Briest; Faustrecht der Freiheit (Fox/Fox and His Friends); Fear Eats the Soul (Angst essen Seele auf); Germany in Autumn (Deutschland im Herbst); Gods of the Plague (Götter der Pest); In a Year with 13 Moons (In einem Jahr mit 13 Monden); Katzelmacher; Lili Marleen; Lola; Love Is Colder than Death (Leibe is kälter als der Tod); Marriage of Maria Braun, The (Die Ehe der Maria Braun); Martha; Merchant of Four Seasons, The (Der Händler der vier Jahreszeiten); Mother Küster's Trip to Heaven (Mutter Küsters Fahrt zum Himmel); Nora Helmer; Querelle; Satan's Brew (Satansbraten); Third Generation, The (Die Dritte Generation); Veronika Voss (Die Sehnsucht der Veronika Voss); Wild Game (Wildwechsel).*

Fasulino, Cristina *South of a Passion, The (El Sur de una Pasion/aka From South to South).*

Faty Sow, Thierno *Camp Thiaroye (Camp de Thiaroye).*

Favio, Leonardo *Gatica.*

Favreau, Jon *Made.*

Fawcett, John *Ginger Snaps.*

Fehèr, György *Passion (Szenvedély).*

Fei Mu *Spring in a Small Town (Xiao Cheng zhi Chun).*

Feig, Rebecca *Bye-Bye Babushka.*

Feigenbaum, William *Hugo the Hippo.*

Feist, Felix *Donovan's Brain.*

Fejos, Paul (Pál Fejös) *Tavaszi Zápor (Marie – a Hungarian Legend/Marie, légende hongroise/Spring Shower).*

Fekete, Ibolya *Bolshe Vita (Bolse Vita); Chico.*

Feldman, John *Alligator Eyes; Dead Funny.*

Fellini, Federico *Amarcord; And the Ship Sails on (E la Nave Va); Bidone, Il (The Swindlers); Boccaccio '70; City of Women (La Città delle Donne); Clowns, The (I Clowns); Dolce Vita, La (The Sweet Life); 8½ (Otto e Mezzo); Fellini A Director's Notebook (Block-Notes di un Regista); Fellini-Satyricon; Fellini's Casanova (Il Casanova di Federico Fellini); Fellini's Roma (Roma); Ginger & Fred (Ginger e Fred); Histoires Extraordinaires (Spirits of the Dead/Tales of Mystery); Intervista; Juliet of the Spirits (Giulietta degli Spiriti); Luci del Varietà (Lights of Variety/Variety Lights); Notti di Cabiria, Le (Cabiria/Nights of Cabiria); Orchestra Rehearsal (Prova d'Orchestra); Strada, La (The Road); Vitelloni, I; Voice of the Moon, The (La Voce della Luna); White Sheik, The (Lo Sceicco Bianco).*

Fenady, Georg *Arnold.*

Fenton, Leslie *Lulu Belle.*

Féret, René *Mystery of Alexina, The (Mystère Alexina).*

Ferguson, Graeme *Love Goddesses, The.*

Ferland, Guy *Babysitter, The; Telling Lies in America.*

Fernandel *Adhemar ou Le Jouet de la Fatalité (Adhemar or Destiny's Plaything).*

Fernández, Emilio *Enamorada (Women in Love); Río Escondido (Hidden River); Salón México.*

Ferrara, Abel *Addiction, The; Bad Lieutenant; Blackout, The; Body Snatchers; Cat Chaser; China Girl; Driller Killer, The; Funeral, The; King of New York; Ms.45 (aka Angel of Vengeance); Snake Eyes (aka Dangerous Game); Subway Stories Tales from the Underground.*

Ferrari, Alain *Bosna!*

Ferrer, José *Cockleshell Heroes; I Accuse!*

Ferrer, Mel *Vendetta.*

Ferreri, Marco *Audience, The (L'Udienza); Blow-Out (La Grande Bouffe); Future Is Woman, The (Il Futuro è Donna); House of Smiles (La Casa del Sorriso); Last Woman, The (L'Ultima Donna); Tales of Ordinary Madness (Storie di Ordinaria Follia); Touche pas à la femme blanche (Don't Touch the White Woman).*

Fesser, Javier *P Tinto's Miracle (El Milagro de P Tinto).*

Fest, Joachim C *Hitler – a Career (Hitler eine Karriere).*

Festa Campanile, Pasquale *Girl from Trieste, The (La Ragazza di Trieste); Petomane, Il (The Windbreaker).*

Feuillade, Louis *Fantômas; Vampires, Les.*

Feyder, Jacques *Grand Jeu, Le (Card of Fate); Kermesse Héroique, La (Carnival in Flanders); Kiss, The; Knight Without Armour; Pension Mimosas.*

Field, Connie *Life and Times of Rosie the Riveter, The.*

Field, Todd *In the Bedroom.*

Fiennes, Martha *Onegin.*

Figgis, Mike *Browning Version, The; Hotel; Internal Affairs; Leaving Las Vegas; Liebestraum; Loss of Sexual Innocence, The; Miss Julie; Mr Jones; One Night Stand; Stormy Monday; Timecode.*

Finbow, Alexander *24 Hours in London.*

Finbow, Colin *Captain Stirrick; Custard Boys, The; Daemon; Dark Enemy; Hard Road; Mister Skeeter; School for Vandals, Swarm in May, A.*

Finch, Nigel *Stonewall.*

Fincher, David *Alien³; Fight Club; Game, The; Panic Room; Seven (aka Se7en).*

Findlay, Seaton *Janis.*

Finkiel, Emmanuel *Voyages (Tracks).*

Finkleman, Ken *Airplane II The Sequel.*

Finney, Albert *Charlie Bubbles.*

Fiore, Robert *Pumping Iron.*

Firestone, Cinda *Attica.*

Firstenberg, Sam *American Ninja (aka American Warrior); Ninja III – The Domination.*

Firth, Michael *Sylvia.*

Fischer, Hans Conrad *Nela.*

Fishburne, Laurence *Once in the Life.*

Fisher, Danny Paul *Inbetweeners.*

Fisher, Terence *Astonished Heart, The; Brides of Dracula, The; Curse of Frankenstein, The; Curse of the Werewolf, The; Devil Rides Out, The; Dracula (aka Horror of Dracula); Dracula, Prince of Darkness; Frankenstein and the Monster from Hell; Frankenstein Created Woman; Frankenstein Must Be Destroyed; Gorgon, The; Hound of the Baskervilles, The; Mummy, The; Night of the Big Heat (aka Island of the Burning Heat); Phantom of the Opera, The; Revenge of Frankenstein, The; So Long at the Fair; Spaceways; Stranglers of Bombay, The; Two Faces of Dr Jekyll, The.*

Fishman, Bill *Tapeheads.*

Fisk, Jack *Daddy's Dyin' – Who's Got the Will?; Raggedy Man.*

Fitzgerald, Thom *Hanging Garden, The.*

Fitzmaurice, George *As You Desire Me; Mata Hari; One Heavenly Night; Unholy Garden, The.*

Fiveson, Robert S *Parts: The Clonus Horror (aka Clonus).*

Fjeldmark, Stefan *Help! I'm a Fish (Hjælp! Jeg er en fisk/Hilfe! Ich bin ein Fisch).*

Flaherty, Paul *18 Again!; Who's Harry Crumb?*

Flaherty, Robert *Elephant Boy; Louisiana Story; Man of Aran.*

Fleder, Gary *Don't Say a Word; Kiss the Girls; Things to Do in Denver When You're Dead.*

Fleischer, Dave *Betty Boop Follies, The.*

Fleischer, Richard *Amityville 3-D (aka Amityville: The Demon); Arena; Armoured Car Robbery; Ashanti; Bandido!; Barabbas (Barabba); Between Heaven and Hell; Boston Strangler, The; Che!; Child of Divorce; Clay Pigeon, The; Compulsion; Conan the Destroyer; Don Is Dead, The; Fantastic Voyage; Incredible Sarah, The; Jazz Singer, The; Last Run, The; Mandingo; Mr Majestyk; Narrow Margin, The; New Centurions, The (aka Precinct 45: Los Angeles Police); Prince and the Pauper, The (aka Crossed Swords); Red Sonja; Soylent Green; Spikes Gang, The; 10 Rillington Place; Tora! Tora! Tora!; Trapped; 20,000 Leagues Under the Sea; Vikings, The; Violent Saturday.*

Fleischmann, Peter *Hunting Scenes from Lower Bavaria (Jagdszenen aus Niederbayern).*

Fleming, Andrew *Craft, The; Threesome.*

Fleming, Victor *Captains Courageous; Dr Jekyll and Mr Hyde; Gone With the Wind; Red Dust; Wizard of Oz, The.*

Flemyng, Gordon *Daleks – Invasion Earth 2150 A.D.; Dr Who and the Daleks; Split, The.*

Fletcher, Mandie *Deadly Advice.*

Flicker, Florian *Halbe Welt (Half World).*

Flicker, Theordore J *President's Analyst, The.*

Flitcroft, Kim *Tales from a Hard City.*

Florey, Robert *Beast With Five Fingers, The; Cocoanuts, The; Dangerously They Live; Face Behind the Mask, The; Florentine Dagger, The; King of Alcatraz; Murders in the Rue Morgue; Tarzan and the Mermaids.*

Flynn, John *Best Seller; Brainscan; Defiance; Jerusalem File, The; Lock Up; Marilyn – The Untold Story; Outfit, The; Out for Justice.*

Flynn, Tom *Watch It.*

Foldes, Lawrence D *Young Warriors.*

Foley, James *After Dark, My Sweet; At Close Range; Chamber, The; Corruptor, The; Fear; Glengarry Glen Ross; Who's That Girl.*

Fonda, Jane *Vietnam Journey.*

Fonda, Peter *Hired Hand, The; Wanda Nevada.*

Fondato, Marcello *Watch Out, We're Mad (Altrimenti ci Arrabbiamo).*

Fong, Allen *Ah Ying (Banbianren); Dancing Bull (Wuniu); Father and Son (Fuzi Qing); Just Like Weather (Meiguo Xin).*

Fong, Eddie *Kawashima Yoshiko (Chuandao Fangzi/aka The Last Princess of Manchuria).*

Fons, Jorge *Jory (Un Niño Llamado Muerte); Midaq Alley (El Callejon de los Milagros).*

Fontaine, Anne *Way I Killed My Father, The (Comment j'ai tué mon père/Cómo maté a mi padre).*

Fonteyne, Frédéric *Liaison Pornographique, Une (An Intimate Affair).*

Fonvielle, Lloyd *Dead Can't Lie, The.*

Forbes, Bryan *Better Late Than Never; Deadfall; International Velvet; King Rat; L-Shaped Room, The; Naked Face, The; Raging Moon, The (aka Long Ago, Tomorrow); Seance on a Wet Afternoon; Slipper and the Rose, The; Whisperers, The; Whistle Down the Wind.*

Forcier, André *Histoire inventée, Une (An Imaginary Tale).*

Ford, Clarence (Fok Yiu-Leung) *Before Dawn (Di Ba Zhan); Iceman Cometh, The (Jidong Qixia); Naked Killer (Chiklo gouyeung).*

Ford, Derek *Keep It Up, Jack!*

Ford, John *Cheyenne Autumn; Donovan's Reef; Drums Along the Mohawk; Fort Apache; Four Men and a Prayer; Fugitive, The; Grapes of Wrath, The; Horse Soldiers, The; How Green Was My Valley; How the West Was Won; Hurricane, The; Informer, The; Iron Horse, The; Judge Priest; Last Hurrah, The; Long Gray Line, The; Long Voyage Home, The; Lost Patrol, The; Man Who Shot Liberty Valance, The; Mary of Scotland; Mister Roberts; Mogambo; My Darling Clementine; Prisoner of Shark Island, The; Quiet Man, The; Rio Grande; Searchers, The; Sergeant Rutledge; Seven Women; She Wore a Yellow Ribbon; Stagecoach; Submarine Patrol; Sun Shines Bright, The; They Were Expendable; Three Godfathers; Tobacco Road; Two Rode Together; Wagon Master; When Willie Comes Marching Home; Whole Town's Talking, The (aka Passport to Fame); Wings of Eagles, The; Young Mr Lincoln.*

Ford, Maxim *Live a Life.*

Ford, Philip *Angel in Exile.*

Forde, Eugene *Michael Shayne Private Detective; Shadows in the Night.*

Forde, Walter *Bulldog Jack (aka Alias Bulldog Drummond); Cheer Boys Cheer; Chu-Chin-Chow; Forever England (aka Born for Glory/ Brown on Resolution); Four Just Men, The; Gaunt Stranger The (aka The Phantom Strikes); King of the Damned.*

Forder, Timothy *Mystery of Edwin Drood, The.*

Foreman, Carl *Victors, The.*

Forma, Dominique *Scenes of the Crime.*

Forman, Milos *Amadeus; Fireman's Ball, The (Horí, má Panenko); Hair; Lásky Jedné Plavovlásky (A Blonde in Love/Loves of a Blonde); Man on the Moon; One Flew Over the Cuckoo's Nest; People vs. Larry Flynt, The; Peter and Pavla (Cerny Petr); Ragtime; Taking Off; Valmont; Visions of Eight.*

Forst, Willi *Bel Ami.*

Forster, Marc *Monster's Ball.*

Forsyth, Bill *Being Human; Breaking In; Comfort and Joy; Gregory's Girl; Gregory's Two Girls; Housekeeping; Local Hero; That Sinking Feeling.*

Fortenberry, John *Night at the Roxbury, A.*

Fosse, Bob *All That Jazz; Cabaret; Lenny; Star 80; Sweet Charity.*

Foster, Giles *Consuming Passions; Silas Marner; Tree of Hands.*

Foster, Harve *Song of the South.*

Foster, Jodie *Home for the Holidays; Little Man Tate.*

Foster, Lewis R *Dakota Incident; Top of the World.*

Foster, Norman *Journey Into Fear; Rachel and the Stranger.*

Fotopoulos, James *Back Against the Wall.*

Fournier, Claude *Alien Thunder (aka Dan Candy's Law).*

Fowler Jr, Gene *I Married a Monster from Outer Space; I Was a Teenage Werewolf.*

Fowler, Robert *Below the Belt.*

Fox, Dave *Year of the Beaver.*

Fox, Eytan *Song of the Siren (Shirat Ha'Sirena).*

Fraim, Trace *Dirt.*

Fraker, William A *Legend of the Lone Ranger, The; Monte Walsh.*

Frakes, Jonathan *Star Trek: First Contact; Star Trek: Insurrection.*

France, Chuck *Jazz in Exile.*

Francis, Freddie *Craze; Creeping Flesh, The; Doctor and the Devils, The; Dr Terror's House of Horrors; Dracula Has Risen from the Grave; Ghoul, The; Legend of the Werewolf; Nightmare; Skull, The; Torture Garden.*

Francis, Karl *Above Us the Earth; Boy Soldier; Giro City; Rebecca's Daughters; Streetlife.*

Franck, Martin *Contre l'Oubli (Against Oblivion).*

Franco, Jesús (as Clifford Brown) *Lustful Amazon, The (Maciste contre la Reine des Amazones).*

Franco, Jesús (Jess) *Count Dracula (El Conde Dracula); Female Vampires; Succubus (Necronomicon – Geträumte Sünden).*

Francovich, Allan *On Company Business.*

Franju, Georges *Faute de l'Abbé Mouret, La (The Sin of Father Mouret); Judex; Last Melodrama, The (Le Dernier Mélodrame); Nuits Rouges (Shadowman); Pleins Feux sur l'assassin; Sang des Bêtes, Le; Thomas l'Imposteur (Thomas the Imposter); Tête contre les Murs, La (The Keepers); Yeux sans Visage, Les (Eyes Without a Face/The Horror Chamber of Dr Faustus).*

Frank, Charles *Uncle Silas (aka The Inheritance).*

Frank, Christopher *Love in the Strangest Way (Elles n'oublient pas).*

Frank, Hubert *Vanessa.*

Frank, Melvin *Buona Sera, Mrs Campbell; Court Jester, The; Duchess and the Dirtwater Fox, The; Knock on Wood; Li'l Abner; Lost and Found; Prisoner of Second Avenue, The; Touch of Class, A; Walk Like a Man.*

Frank, Robert *Candy Mountain; CS Blues; Me and My Brother; Pull My Daisy.*

Frank, TC *Billy Jack; Born Loser, The.*

Frankel, Cyril *Don't Bother to Knock (aka Why Bother to Knock); It's Great to Be Young; Man of Africa; No Time for Tears; Permission to Kill.*

Frankel, David *Miami Rhapsody.*

Frankenheimer, John *All Fall Down; Bird Man of Alcatraz; Black Sunday; Challenge, The; Dead Bang; 52 Pick-up; Fixer, The; Fourth War, The; French Connection II; Grand Prix; Gypsy Moths, The; Holcroft Covenant, The, Horsemen, The; Island of Dr Moreau, The; Manchurian Candidate, The; 99 and 44/100% Dead (aka Call Harry Crown); Prophecy; Reindeer Games (aka Deception); Ronin; Seconds; Seven Days in May; Train, The; Year of the Gun; Young Stranger, The.*

Franklin, Carl *Devil in a Blue Dress; One False Move; One True Thing.*

Franklin, Howard *Larger Than Life; Public Eye, The; Quick Change.*

Franklin, Richard *Brilliant Lies; F/X2 (aka F/X2 – The Deadly Art of Illusion); Hotel Sorrento; Link; Patrick; Psycho II; Roadgames; True Story of Eskimo Nell, The (aka Dick Down Under).*

Franklin, Sidney *Barretts of Wimpole Street, The; Dark Angel, The; Good Earth, The.*

Fraser, Harry *Randy Rides Alone.*

Fratzscher, Peter *Asphalt Night (Asphaltnacht).*

Frawley, James *Big Bus, The; Kid Blue, Muppet Move, The.*

Frazer Jones, Peter *George and Mildred.*

Frears, Stephen *Accidental Hero; Bloody Kids; Dangerous Liaisons; Grifters, The; Gumshoe; High Fidelity; Hi-Lo Country, The; Hit, The; Liam; Mary Reilly; Mr Jolly Lives Next Door; My Beautiful Laundrette; Prick Up Your Ears; St Ann's'; Sammy and Rosie Get Laid; Snapper, The; Van, The; Walter (aka Loving Walter).*

Freda, Riccardo *see* Hampton, Robert

Freed, Gregory *Virgin for Saint Tropez, A (Une Vierge pour St Tropez).*

Freedman, Jerrold *Borderline; Kansas City Bomber.*

Freeland, Jason *Brown's Requiem.*

Freeland, Thornton *Brass Monkey, The (aka Lucky Mascot); Flying Down to Rio.*

Freeman, Joan *Satisfaction; Streetwalkin'.*

Freeman, Morgan *Bopha!*

Freeman, Morgan J *Hurricane Streets.*

Fregonese, Hugo *Apache Drums; Blowing Wild; Raid, The.*

French, Harold *Blind Goddess, The; Encore; Major Barbara; Man Who Watched Trains Go By, The (aka Paris Express); Quartet; Trio.*

Frend, Charles *Barnacle Bill (aka All At Sea); Big Blockade, The; Cruel Sea, The; Foreman Went to France, The; Johnny Frenchman; Lease of Life; Long Arm, The (aka The Third Key); San Demetrio, London; Run for Your Money, A; Scott of the Antarctic.*

Freund, Karl *Mad Love (aka The Hands of Orlac); Mummy, The.*

Freundlich, Bart *Myth of Fingerprints, The.*

Fricke, Ron *Baraka.*

Fridman, Eugen *Treasure Island (Ostrov Sokrovishch).*

Fridriksson, Fridrik Thór *Children of Nature (Börn Náttúrunnar); Devil's Island (Djöflaeyjan); Cold Fever; Movie Days (Biodagar).*

Friedberg, Rick *Spy Hard.*

Friedenberg, Richard *Adventures of Frontier Fremont, The (aka Spirit of the Wild); Bermuda Triangle, The.*

Friedgen, Bud *That's Entertainment! III.*

Friedkin, William *Birthday Party, The; Blue Chips; Brink's Job, The; Cruising; Exorcist, The; Exorcist – Director's Cut, The; French Connection, The; Guardian, The; Jade; Rules of Engagement; Sorcerer (aka Wages of Fear); To Live and Die in L.A.*

Friedman, Ed *Mighty Mouse in the Great Space Chase; Secret of the Sword, The.*

Friedman, Jeffrey *Celluloid Closet, The; Common Threads: Stories from the Quilt.*

Friedmann, Anthony *Bartleby.*

Frizzell, John *Winter Tan, A.*

Frost, Lee *Dixie Dynamite; Thing with Two Heads, The.*

Frost, Mark *Storyville.*

Fruet, William *Death Weekend (aka The House by the Lake).*

Fucci, Thomas A *Don't Call Me Frankie.*

Fuest, Robert *Abominable Dr Phibes, The; And Soon the Darkness; Devil's Rain, The; Dr Phibes Rises Again; Final Programme, The (aka The Last Days of Man on Earth).*

Fujiwara, Ken *Organ.*

Fukasaku, Kinji *Battle Royale; Black Lizard, The (Kuro Tokage); Triple Cross, The (Itsuka giragirasuruhi/ aka Double Cross); Virus (Fukkatsu no Hi).*

Fukuda, Jun *Ebirah – Terror of the Deep (Nankai no Daiketto); Godzilla vs the Bionic Monster (Gojira tai Mekagojira); Son of Godzilla (Gojira no Musuko); War of the Monsters (Gojira Tai Gaigan).*

Fulci, Lucio *Beyond, The (…E Tu Vivrai nelTerrore! L'Aldila); Conquest (La Conquista de la Tierra Perdida); House by the Cemetery, The (QuellaVilla accanto al Cimitero); Paura nella Città dei Morti Viventi (City of the Living Dead/The Gates of Hell); White Fang (ZannaBianca); Zombie Flesh-Eaters (Zombi 2).*

Fuller, Samuel *Big Red One, The; Crimson Kimono, The; Dead Pigeon on Beethoven Street (Kressin und die tote Taube in der Beethovenstrasse); Fixed Bayonets!; Forty Guns; Hell and High Water; House of Bamboo; I Shot Jesse James; Merrill's Marauders; Naked Kiss, The; Park Row; Pickup on South Street; Run of the Arrow; Shark; Shock Corridor; Steel Helmet, The; Underworld U.S.A; Verboten!; White Dog.*

Fuller, Tex *Prey of the Chameleon.*

Fulton, Keith *Hamster Factor and Other Tales of Twelve Monkeys, The.*

Fung, Stephen *Heroes in Love (Lian'ai Qi Yi).*

Fuqua, Antoine *Replacement Killers, The; Training Day.*

Fürbriner, Simone *Vagabonding Images.*

Furie, Sidney J *Appaloosa, The (aka Southwest to Sonora); Boys in Company C, The; Doctor Blood's Coffin; Entity, The; Gable and Lombard; Hit!; Ipcress File, The; Iron Eagle; Iron Eagle II; Lady Sings the Blues; Lawyer, The; Naked Runner, The; Superman IV: The Quest for Peace; Wonderful Life.*

Furumaya, Tomoyuki *Bad Company (Mabudachi); This Window Is Yours (Kono Mado wa Kimi no Mono).*

Gabel, Martin *Lost Moment, The.*

Gabizon, Savi *Lovesick on Nana Street (Hole ahava be'shikun gimel); Shuroo.*

Gábor, Pál *Angi Vera; Horizon (Horizont); Long Ride, The.*

Gabrea, Radu *Man Like Eva, A (Ein Mann wie Eva).*

Gabriel, Enrique *Fading Memories (Las Huellas Borradas).*

Gabriel, Mike *Pocahontas; Rescuers Down Under, The.*

Gad, Urban *Abyss, The (Afgrunden).*

Gage, George *Skateboard.*

Gagliardo, Giovanna *Maternale.*

Gainsbourg, Serge *I Love You, I Don't (Je t'aime, moi non plus).*

Gallardo, Cesar *Bamboo Gods and Iron Men.*

Gallo, George *Trapped in Paradise.*

Gallo, Vincent *Buffalo '66.*

Galperin, Mariano *Rich Kids (Chicos Ricos).*

Gance, Abel *Austerlitz (aka The Battle of Austerlitz); J'Accuse* (1918); *J'Accuse* (1937); *Paradis Perdu; Capitaine Fracasse, Le; Napoléon.*

Gans, Christophe *Brotherhood of the Wolf (Le Pacte des loups);Crying Freeman; Necronomicon (aka H.P. Lovecraft's Necronomicon).*

Gant [Giulio Antamoro] *Pinocchio.*

Gantillon, Bruno *Servante et Maîtresse.*

Garbus, Liz *Farm, The (aka The Farm: Angola, USA).*

Garci, José Luis *To Begin Again (Volver a Empezar).*

Garcia, Nicole *Adversary, The (L'Adversaire); Place Vendôme.*

Garcia, Rodrigo *Things You Can Tell Just by Looking at Her.*

García Agraz, Carlos *My Dear Tom Mix (Mi Querido Tom Mix).*

García Guevara, Mercedes *Río Escondido (Hidden River).*

Gardela, Isabel *Two for Tea (Tomándote).*

Gardner, Danielle *Soul in the Hole.*

Gardner, Robert *Clarence and Angel; Forest of Bliss.*

Gárdos, Péter *Whooping Cough (Szamárköhögés).*

Garen, Leo *Hex.*

Garfein, Jack *Strange One, The (aka End As a Man).*

Gargiulo, Maria *Year of My Japanese Cousin, The.*

Gariazzo, Mario *Last Moments (Venditore di Palloncini); Sexorcist, The (L'Ossessa).*

Garland, Patrick *Doll's House, A.*

Garmes, Lee *Angels Over Broadway.*

Garnett, Tay *Bataan; Black Knight, The; Cause for Alarm!; China Seas; Connecticut Yankee in King Arthur's Court, A (aka A Yankee in King Arthur's Court); Joy of Living; One Minute to Zero; Postman Always Rings Twice, The; Seven Sinners; Stand-In; Terrible Beauty, A (aka Night Fighters).*

Garnett, Tony *Handgun (aka Deep in the Heart); Prostitute.*

Garrel, Philippe *Vent de la Nuit, Le.*

Garrett, Oliver HP *Careful, Soft Shoulder.*

Garris, Mick *Critters 2: The Main Course; Sleepwalkers.*

Gasnier, Louis *Reefer Madness.*

Gast, Leon *When We Were Kings.*

Gates, Tudor *Intimate Games.*

Gatlif, Tony *Gadjo Dilo (The Crazy Stranger); Je suis né d'une cigogne (Children of the Stork); Lacho Drom; Princes, Les (The Princes); Vengo.*

Gatti, Armand *Writing on the Wall, The (Nous Etions Tous des Noms d'Arbres).*

Gaubert, Jean-Marie *see* Poiré, Jean-Marie.

Gaudino, Lucio *First Light of Dawn (Prime Luci dell'alba).*

Gaulke, Uli *Havanna Mi Amor.*

Gaup, Nils *Pathfinder (Veiviseren).*

Gautier, Philippe *Hathi.*

Gavaldón, Roberto *Otra, La (The Other Sister).*

Gayor, Richard *Alternative Miss World, The.*

Gazdag, Gyula *Hungarian Fairy Tale, A (Hol Volt, Hol nem Volt); Package Tour, The (Társasutazás).*

Gedeon, Sasa *Closed for Family Mourning (Zavreno pro rodinny smutek); Indian Summer (Indiánské Léto); Return of the Idiot (Návrat Idiota).*

Geller, Bruce *Harry In Your Pocket; Savage Bees, The.*

Geller, Daniel *Kids of Survival: The Art and Life of Tim Rollins & K.O.S.*

Genée, Heidi *1 + 1 = 3.*

Genestal, Fabrice *Squale, La.*

Genina, Augusto *Forget Me Not (aka Forever Yours); Prix de Beauté (Miss Europe).*

George, George W *James Dean Story, The.*

George, Peter *Surf Nazis Must Die.*

George, Terry *Some Mother's Son.*

Gerard, Francis *Private Life, A.*

Gerard, Jerry *see* Damiano, Gerard

Gerbase, Carlos *Tolerance (Tolerância).*

Gerber, Paul *Private Pleasures (I Lust och Nöd).*

Gerber, Paul (as Gerhard Poulsen) *Keyhole, The (Noeglehullet).*

Gerber, Tony *Side Streets.*

Gerhards, Christiane *Viva Portugal.*

Gerima, Haile *Sankofa.*

Gering, Marion *Rumba.*

Germi, Pietro *Alfredo Alfredo; Città si Difende, La (Four Ways Out); Ferroviere, Il (Man of Iron/The Railroad Man); In Nome della Legge (In the Name of the Law); Maledetto Imbroglio, Un (A Sordid Affair/The Facts of Murder).*

Geronimi, Clyde *Lady and the Tramp; One Hundred and One Dalmatians; Peter Pan; Sleeping Beauty.*

Ghatak, Ritwik *Cloud-capped Star (Meghe Dhaka Tara).*

Gherman, Alexei *Khrustalyov, My Car! (Khrustalyov, mahinu!/Khroustaliov, ma voiture!); My Friend Ivan Lapshin (Moi Drug Ivan Lapshin); Trial on the Road (Proverka na Dorogakh); Twenty Days Without War (Dvadtsat Dnei bez Voini).*

Ghobadi, Bahman *Time for Drunken Horses, A (Zamani Barayé Masti Asbha/Un Temps pour l'ivresse des chevaux).*

Ghorbal, Khaled *Fatma.*

Ghose, Goutam *Doll, The (Gudia).*

Giacobetti, Francis *Emmanuelle 2.*

Gianikian, Yervant *From Pole to Equator (Dal Polo all'Equatore).*

Giannaris, Constantine (Konstantinos) *Caught Looking; From the North of the City (Apo tin Akri tis Polis); North of Vortex.*

Giarrusso, Vincent *Mallboy.*

Gibbins, Duncan *Eve of Destruction; Fire with Fire.*

Gibson, Alan *Crash; Crescendo; Dracula A.D. 1972; Satanic Rites of Dracula, The (aka Count Dracula and His Vampire Bride).*

Gibson, Angus *Mandela.*

Gibson, Brian *Breaking Glass; Juror, The; Poltergeist 2: The Other Side; Still Crazy; Tina: What's Love Got to Do With It (aka What's Love Got to Do With It).*

Gibson, Mel *Braveheart; Man Without a Face, The.*

Giedroyc, Coky *Stella Does Tricks; Woman Talking Dirty.*

Giese, Maria *When Saturday Comes.*

Gifford, Nick *Burra Sahib; Pasternaks, The.*

Gil, Mateo *Noboby Knows Anybody (Nadie conoce a nadie).*

Gilbert & George *World of Gilbert & George, The.*

Gilbert, Brian *Frog Prince, The; Not Without My Daughter; Tom & Viv; Vice Versa; Wilde.*

Gilbert, Lewis *Admirable Crichton, The; Adventurers, The; Albert, RN (aka Break to Freedom); Alfie; Carve Her Name with Pride; Cast a Dark Shadow; Educating Rita; Cosh Boy (aka The Slasher); Emergency Call; Ferry to Hong Kong; Friends; Good Die Young, The; Greengage Summer, The (aka Loss of Innocence); Haunted; HMS Defiant (aka Damn the Defiant); Moonraker; Not Quite Jerusalem (aka Not Quite Paradise); Operation Daybreak; Paul and Michelle (Paul et Michelle); Reach for the Sky; Seven Nights in Japan; 7th Dawn, The; Shirley Valentine; Spy Who Loved Me, The; Stepping Out; You Only Live Twice.*

Giler, David *Black Bird, The.*

Gillard, Stuart *Teenage Mutant Ninja Turtles III.*

Gillen, Jeff *Deranged.*

Gillespie, Jim *I Know What You Did Last Summer.*

Gilliam, Terry *Adventures of Baron Munchausen, The; Brazil; D-Tox (D-Tox Im Auge der Angst); Fear and*

Loathing in Las Vegas; Fisher King, The; Jabberwocky; Monty Python and the Holy Grail; Time Bandits; 12 Monkeys.

Gilliat, Sidney *Endless Night; Green for Danger; Left, Right and Centre; London Belongs To Me (aka Dulcimer Street); Millions Like Us; Only Two Can Play; Rake's Progress, The (Notorious Gentleman); State Secret (aka The Great Manhunt); Story of Gilbert and Sullivan, The (aka The Great Gilbert and Sullivan); Waterloo Road.*

Gilling, John *Brigand of Kandahar, The; Flesh and the Fiends, The (aka Mania/Psycho Killers/The Fiendish Ghouls); Idle on Parade; Mummy's Shroud, The; Night Caller, The (aka Blood Beast from Outer Space); Plague of the Zombies, The; Reptile, The; Scarlet Blade, The (aka The Crimson Blade); Tiger by the Tail (aka Crossup).*

Gilmore, Stuart *Half-Breed, The.*

Gilroy, Frank D *From Noon Till Three; Once in Paris…*

Gimbel, Peter *Blue Water, White Death.*

Ginsberg, Milton Moses *Werewolf of Washington, The.*

Giordana, Marco Tullio *Pasolini, un Delitto Italiano (Pasolini, an Italian Crime).*

Giovanazzo, Buddy *No Way Home.*

Giovanni, José *Boomerang (Comme un Boomerang); Scoumoune, La (Hit Man/Scoundrel).*

Giraldi, Bob *Dinner Rush; Hiding Out; National Lampoon Goes to the Movies (aka National Lampoon's Movie Madness).*

Girard, Bernard *Mad Room, The.*

Girard, François *Red Violin, The (Il Violino Rosso); Thirty Two Short Films About Glenn Gould.*

Girault, Jean *Jo; Permis de Conduire, Le (The Driving Licence).*

Girdler, William *Day of the Animals; Grizzly; Manitou, The; Sheba Baby.*

Giritlioglu, Tomris *80th Step (80. Adim).*

Girod, Francis *Contre l'Oubli (Against Oblivion); Infernal Trio, The (Le Trio Infernal); Lumière et Compagnie.*

Gist, Robert *American Dream, An (aka See You in Hell, Darling).*

Gitai, Amos *Berlin Jerusalem; Day after Day (Yom Yom); Kadosh; Kippur; Kedma.*

Gladwell, David *Memoirs of a Survivor, Requiem for a Village.*

Giusti, Stéphane *Pourquoi pas moi? (Why Not Me?).*

Glaser, Paul Michael *Air Up There, The; Band of the Hand; Cutting Edge, The; Running Man, The.*

Glassman, Arnold *Visions of Light.*

Glatter, Lesli Linka *Now and Then; Proposition, The.*

Glatzer, Richard *Fluffer, The; Grief.*

Glazer, Jonathan *Sexy Beast.*

Glebas, Francis *Fantasia/2000 (aka Fantasia 2000).*

Glen, Gordon *Just Us.*

Glen, John *Christopher Columbus: The Discovery; For Your Eyes Only; Licence to Kill; Living Daylights, The; Octopussy; View to a Kill, A.*

Glenn, Pierre-William *Terminus; 23:58 (23h58).*

Glenville, Peter *Comedians, The; Prisoner, The; Summer and Smoke; Term of Trial.*

Gleyzer, Raymundo *Mexico; The Frozen Revolution.*

Glickenhaus, James *Shakedown (aka Blue Jean Cop); Soldier, The (aka Codename: The Soldier).*

Glimcher, Arne *Just Cause; Mambo Kings, The.*

Glinski, Robert *Hi, Tereska (Czesc, Tereska).*

Godard, Jean-Luc *A Bout de Souffle (Breathless); Alphaville (Alphaville, Une Etrange Aventure de Lemmy Caution); Aria; Bande à part (The Outsiders/Band of Outsiders); British Sounds; Carabiniers, Les (The Riflemen/The Soldiers); Chinoise, La (La Chinoise, ou plutôt à la Chinoise); Contre l'Oubli (Against Oblivion); Détective; Deux ou Trois Choses que Je Sais d'Elle (Two or Three Things I Know About Her); Eloge de l'amour (In Praise of Love); Far from Vietnam (Loin du Viêtnam); Femme Mariée, Une (A Married Woman); Femme est une Femme, Une (A Woman Is a Woman); First Name: Carmen (Prénom Carmen); For Ever Mozart; Gai Savoir, Le; Hail, Mary (Je Vous Salue, Marie); King Lear; Letter to Jane; Masculin Féminin (Masculine Feminine); Mépris, Le (Contempt); Nouvelle Vague; Numéro Deux (Number Two); One Plus One (aka Sympathy for the Devil); Paris vu par… (Six in Paris); Passion; Petit Soldat, Le (The Little Soldier); Pierrot le Fou; Pravda; Rise and Fall of a Little Film Company from a novel by James Hadley Chase (Grandeur et Décadence d'un Petit Commerce de Cinéma d'après un roman de J H Chase); Sauve Qui Peut – la Vie (Every Man for Himself/Slow Motion); Soigne ta Droite; Tout Va Bien; 2 x 50 Years of French Cinema; Vent d'Est (Wind from the East); Vivre sa Vie (It's My Life/My Life to Live); Vladimir et Rosa (Vladimir and Rosa); Weekend (Week-end).*

Godber, John *Up 'n' Under.*

Goddard, Gary *Masters of the Universe.*

Goddard, Jim *Parker; Shanghai Surprise.*

Godfrey, Peter *Cry Wolf; Great Jewel Robber, The (aka After Nightfall); Highways by Night.*

Godmilow, Jill *Roy Cohn/ Jack Smith.*

Godwin, Frank *Terry on the Fence.*

Golan, Menahem *Delta Force, The; Diamonds; Enter the Ninja; Hanna's War; Kazablan; Lepke; Magician of Lublin, The; Operation Thunderbolt (Mitzva Yonatan/aka Entebbe: Operation Thunderbolt); Over the Brooklyn Bridge; Over the Top.*

Gold, Jack *Aces High; Bofors Gun, The: Chain, The; Little Lord Fauntleroy; Man Friday; Medusa Touch, The; National Health, The; Sailor's Return, The; Who?*

Gold, Mick *Europe After the Rain; Schiele in Prison.*

Goldbacher, Sandra *Governess, The; Me Without You.*

Goldberg, Danny (Dan) *Feds; No Nukes.*

Goldberg, Eric *Fantasia/2000 (aka Fantasia 2000); Pocahontas.*

Goldberg, Gary David *Dad.*

Goldblatt, Mark *Punisher, The.*

Goldenberg, Michael *Bed of Roses.*

Goldfine, Danya *Kids of Survival: The Art and Life of Tim Rollins & K.O.S.*

Goldie, Caroline *Fly a Flag for Poplar.*

Golding, Paul *Pulse.*

Goldman, Gary *Anastasia; Thumbelina; Titan A.E.*

Goldman, Henrique *Princesa.*

Goldschmidt, John *She'll Be Wearing Pink Pyjamas.*

Goldstein, Jacques *Femi Kuti: What's Going On.*

Goldstein, Scott *Walls of Glass.*

Goldstone, James *Red Sky at Morning; Rollercoaster; Swashbuckler (The Scarlet Buccaneer). When Time Ran Out.*

Goldwyn, Tony *Someone Like You… (aka Animal Attraction); Walk on the Moon, A.*

Gollings, Franklin *Connecting Rooms.*

Gomer, Steve *Barney's Great Adventure.*

Gomes, Flora *Blue Eyes of Yonta, The (Udju Azul di Yonta); Poi di Sangui.*

Gómez, Manuel Octavio *Days of Water, The (Los Días del Agua).*

Gomez, Nick *Laws of Gravity; New Jersey Drive.*

Gómez Pereira, Manuel *Mouth to Mouth (Boca a Boca).*

Gómez Yera, Sara *One Way or Another (De Cierta Manera).*

Gomis, Alain *As a Man (L'Afrance).*

Gonzáles Iñárritu, Alejandro *Amores perros (Love's a Bitch).*

Goo-Bi, CG *Heroes in Love (Lian'ai Qi Yi).*

Goode, Frederic *Pop Gear.*

Goodell, Gregory *Human Experiments.*

Goodhew, Philip *Another Life; Intimate Relations.*

Goodman, Jenniphr *Tao of Steve, The.*

Gopalakrishnan, Adoor *Rat-Trap (Elippathayam).*

Gordon, Bert I *Amazing Colossal Man, The; Attack of the Puppet People (aka Six Inches Tall); Earth vs the Spider (aka The Spider); Empire of the Ants; Food of the Gods, The; Mad Bomber, The; War of the Colossal Beast.*

Gordon, Bette *Variety.*

Gordon, Keith *Chocolate War, The; Midnight Clear, A; Mother Night; Waking the Dead.*

Gordon, Michael *Pillow Talk; Secret of Convict Lake, The.*

Gordon, Robert *It Came from Beneath the Sea.*

Gordon, Steve *Arthur.*

Gordon, Stuart *Fortress; From Beyond; Pit and the Pendulum, The; Re-Animator; Space Truckers.*

Gordy, Berry *Mahogany.*

Gören, Serif *Yol.*

Goretta, Claude *Death of Mario Ricci, The (La Mort de Mario Ricci); Dentellière, La (The Lacemaker); Girl from Lorraine, A (La Provinciale). Invitation, The (L'Invitation); Nice Time; Roads of Exile, The (Les Chemins de l'Exil).*

Gorin, Jean-Pierre *Letter to Jane; My Crasy Life; Poto and Cabengo; Tout Va Bien; Vladimir et Rosa (Vladimir and Rosa).*

Goritsas, Sotiris *Balkanisator (Valkanisater).*

Gomley, Charles *Heavenly Pursuits.*

Gornich, Michael *Creepshow 2.*

Gorris, Marleen *Antonia's Line (Antonia); Broken Mirrors (Gebroken Spiegels); Luzhin Defence, The; Mrs Dalloway; Question of Silence, A (De Stilte Rond Christine M).*

Goscinny, René *Lucky Luke; Twelve Tasks of Asterix, The (Les 12 Travaux d'Astérix).*

Gosha, Hideo *Four Days of Snow and Blood (226).*

Goslar, Jürgen *Death in the Sun (Der Flüsternde Tod); Slavers.*

Gosnell, Raja *Big Momma's House; Home Alone 3; Never Been Kissed.*

Gothár, Péter *Passport (Paszport); Time Stands Still (Megáll az Idó).*

Gottlieb, Carl *Amazon Women on the Moon.*

Gottlieb, Michael *Mannequin; Mr Nanny.*

Gough, Steve *Elenya.*

Gould, Heywood *One Good Cop; Trial by Jury.*

Goulding, Alfred *Chump at Oxford, A; Dick Barton – Special Agent.*

Goulding, Edmund *Dark Victory; Dawn Patrol, The; Everybody Does It; Grand Hotel; Great Lie, The; Nightmare Alley; Razor's Edge, The; Reaching for the Moon; We Are Not Alone.*

Goupil, Romain *Contre l'Oubli (Against Oblivion).*

Gover, Victor M *Curse of the Wraydons, The (aka Stranglers Morgue).*

Graef, Roger *Secret Policeman's Ball, The.*

Graeff, Tom *Teenagers from Outer Space (aka The Gargon Terror).*

Graef Marino, Gustavo *Johnny 100 Pesos (Johnny Cien Pesos).*

Graffin, Benoît *Beach Café (Le Café de la plage).*

Graham, Bob *End of August, The.*

Graham, William *Police Story; Return to the Blue Lagoon; Submarine X-1.*

Grandrieux, Philippe *Sombre.*

Granier-Deferre, Pierre *Etoile du Nord, L' (The Northern Star); Chat, Le (The Cat).*

Grant, Lee *Staying Together; Tell Me a Riddle.*

Grant, Michael *Head On (aka Fatal Attraction).*

Grasshoff, Alex *Last Dinosaur, The.*

Grau, Jorge *Living Dead at the Manchester Morgue, The (Fin de Semana para los Muertos).*

Gray, F Gary *Friday; Negotiator, The; Set It Off.*

Gray, James *Little Odessa; Yards, The.*

Gray, John *Glimmer Man, The.*

Gray, Lorraine *With Babies and Banners.*

Grayson, Godfrey *Adventures of PC 49, The.*

Green, Alfred E *Baby Face; Dangerous; Jolson Story, The; Sierra; They Passed This Way (aka Four Faces West).*

Green, David *Buster; Car Trouble; Firebirds (aka Wings of the Apache).*

Green, David Gordon *George Washington.*

Green, Guy *Angry Silence, The; Devil's Advocate, The (Des Teufels Advokat); Jacqueline Susann's Once Is Not Enough; Light in the Piazza; Luther; Magus, The; Patch of Blue, A; Sea of Sand; Walk in the Spring Rain, A.*

Green, Jack *Traveller.*

Green, Joseph *Yiddle with His Fiddle (Judel gra na Skrzypkach/Yidle mitn Fidl).*

Green, Rob *Bunker, The.*

Green, Walon *Hellstrom Chronicle, The.*

Greenaway, Peter *Baby of Mâcon, The; Belly of an Architect, The; Cook, the Thief, His Wife & Her Lover, The; Death in the Seine; Draughtsman's Contract, The; Drowning by Numbers; 8½ Women; Falls, The; Lumière et Compagnie; Pillow Book, The; Prospero's Books; TV Dante: Cantos I–VIII, A; Walk Through H, A; Zed & Two Noughts, A.*

Greene, David *Count of Monte-Cristo, The; Gray Lady Down; I Start Counting; Madame Sin; People Next Door, The; Strange Affair, The.*

Greenfield, Luke *Animal.*

Greengrass, Paul *Bloody Sunday; Resurrected; Theory of Flight, The.*

Greenough, George *Crystal Voyager.*

Greenwald, Maggie *Ballad of Little Jo, The; Kill-Off, The.*

Greenwald, Robert *Breaking Up; Hear No Evil; Sweet Hearts Dance; Xanadu.*

Greenwalt, David *Rude Awakening; Secret Admirer.*

Gregg, Colin *Begging the Ring; Lamb; Remembrance; We Think the World of You.*

Greggio, Ezio *Silence of the Hams, The (Il silenzio dei prosciutti).*

Gregor, Manfred (Erwin C Dietrich) *Swedish Massage Parlour (Blutjunge Masseusen).*

Greif, Leslie *Keys to Tulsa.*

Grémillon, Jean *Etrange Monsieur Victor, L'; Gueule d'Amour; Maldone; Remorques (Stormy Weather).*

Gréville, Edmond T *Beat Girl (aka Wild for Kicks); Brief Ecstasy; Noose; Princesse Tam Tam.*

Grewal, Shani S *Double X; Guru in Seven.*

Greyson, John *Law of Enclosures, The; Lilies (Les Feluettes, ou La Répétition d'un drama romantique); Un©ut; Urinal; Zero Patience.*

Gries, Tom *Breakheart Pass; Breakout; Greatest. The; Helter Skelter; Lady Ice; Number One (aka Pro); Will Penny.*

Grieve, Andrew *Letters from the East; On the Black Hill.*

Griffin, Ada Gay *Litany for Survival: The Life and Work of Audre Lorde, A.*

Griffith, Charles B *Eat My Dust!*

Griffith, DW *Birth of a Nation, The; Broken Blossoms; Intolerance; Orphans of the Storm; Sally of the Sawdust; Struggle, The; Way Down East.*

Griffith, Edward H *Sky's the Limit, The.*

Griffiths, Mark *Hardbodies; Running Hot (aka Highway to Hell).*

Grigor, Murray *Big Banana Feet.*

Grigsby, Michael *Living on the Edge.*

Grimaldi, Antonello *Bits and Pieces (Il cielo è sempre più blu).*

Grimaldi, Aurelio *Whores, The (Le Buttane).*

Grimault, Paul *King and Mister Bird, The (Le Roi et l'Oiseau).*

Grimond, Philippe *Asterix and the Big Fight (Le Coup de Menhir).*

Grinde, Nick *Before I Hang.*

Grisebach, Anja *Be My Sat (Mein Stern).*

Grlic, Rajko *That Summer of White Roses.*

Grodecki, Wiktor *Mandragora.*

Gröning, Philip *Amour, l'Argent, l'Amour, L'.*

Grønlykke, Jacob *Heart of Light (Lysets Hjerte).*

Grosbard, Ulu *Deep End of the Ocean, The; Falling in Love; Straight Time; Subject Was Roses, The; True Confessions; Who Is Harry Kellerman and Why Is He Saying Those Terrible Things About Me?*

Grosvenor, Charles *Once Upon a Forest.*

Gross, Terence *Hotel Splendide.*

Gross, Yaacov *Yaacov Ben Dov: Father of the Hebrew Film.*

Grosso, Nick *Peaches.*

Grounds, Tony *Martins, The.*

Grousset, Didier *Kamikaze.*

Grune Karl *Pagliacci (aka A Clown Must Laugh); Strasse, Die (The Street).*

Guadagnino, Luca *Protagonists, The.*

Gudmundsson, Agúst *Land and Sons (Land og Symir).*

Guedes, Ann *Bearskin; Rocinante.*

Guedes, Eduardo *Bearskin; Rocinante.*

Guédiguian, Robert *A la Place du Coeur; A l'attaque!; Marie-Jo and Her Two Loves (Marie-Jo et ses deux amours); Marius et Jeannette; Ville est tranquille, La.*

Guercio, James William *Electra Glide in Blue.*

Guerín, José Luis *Train of Shadows (Tren de Sombras); Work in Progress (En Construcción).*

Guerra, Ruy *Erendira; Mueda – Memory and Massacre (Mueda – Memoria e Massacre); Opera do Malandro; Sweet Hunters.*

Guerrier, Dominique *Nez au Vent, Le (Scent of Deceit).*

Guest, Christopher *Attack of the 50ft Woman; Best in Show; Big Picture, The.*

Guest, Val *Abominable Snowman, The; Au Pair Girls; Beauty Jungle, The; Boys in Blue, The; Carry On Admiral (aka The Ship Was Loaded); Casino Royale; Confessions of a Window Cleaner; Dance Little Lady; Day the Earth Caught Fire, The; Dentist in the Chair; Diamond Mercenaries, The; Expresso Bongo; Hell Is a City; It's a Wonderful World; Mr Drake's Duck; Quatermass Experiment, The; Quatermass II; When Dinosaurs Ruled the Earth.*

Guggenheim, Davis *Gossip.*

Guilfoyle, Paul *Tess of the Storm Country.*

Guillermin, John *Blue Max, The; Bridge at Remagen, The; Death on the Nile; El Condor; I Was Monty's Double; King Kong; P.J. (aka New Face in Hell); Miss Robin Hood; Never Let Go; Shaft in Africa; Sheena (aka Sheena – Queen of the Jungle); Skyjacked; Towering Inferno, The.*

Guiraudie, Alain *Du Soleil pour les Gueux (Sunshine for Scoundrels); Real Cool Time (Ce vieux rêve qui bouge).*

Guit, Graham *Shooting Stars (Le Ciel est à nous).*

Guitry, Sacha *Destin Fabuleux de Désirée Clary; Napoléon; Pasteur; Perles de la couronne, Les (The Pearls of the Crown); Roman d'un Tricheur, Le (The Story of a Cheat); Si Versailles m'était conté… (Versailles/Royal Affairs at Versailles).*

Güney, Ismail *Where the Rose Wilted (Gülün Bittigi Yer).*

Güney, Yilmaz *Wall, The (Le Mur).*

Gunn, Bill *Ganja and Hess.*

Gunn, Gilbert *Valley of Song (aka Men Are Children Twice).*

Gunnarsson, Sturla *Diplomatic Immunity; Such a Long Journey.*

Guralnick, Robert *Mustang… The House that Joe Built.*

Guterman, Lawrence *Cats & Dogs.*

Gutiérrez, Chus *Gypsy Soul (Alma Gitana).*

Gutiérrez Alea, Tomás *Death of a Bureaucrat (Muerte de un Burocrata); Guantanamera; Last Supper, The (La Ultima Cena); Memories of Underdevelopment (Memorias del Subdesarrollo); Strawberry and Chocolate (Fresa y Chocolate).*

Gutiérrez Aragón, Manuel *Maravillas.*

Gutman, Nathaniel *War Zone.*

Guttfreund, André *Femme Fatale.*

Guzman, Patricio *Battle of Chile, The (La Batalla de Chile).*

Gyarmathy, Livia *Escape (Szökés).*

Gyles, Anna Benson *Swann.*

Gyllenhaal, Stephen *Dangerous Woman, A; Paris Trout; Waterland.*

Haas, Philip *Angels and Insects; Music of Chance, The; Up at the Villa.*

Hackford, Taylor *Against All Odds; Bound by Honor (aka Blood In Blood Out); Devil's Advocate, The; Dolores Claiborne; Everybody's All-American (aka When I Fall in Love); Hail! Hail! Rock'n'Roll; Officer and a Gentleman, An; Proof of Life; White Nights.*

Hadjithomas, Joana *Around the Pink House (Al bayt al zahr/Autour de la maison rose).*

Haggard, Piers *Fiendish Plot of Dr Fu Manchu, The; Satan's Skin (aka Blood on Satan's Claw); Summer Story, A; Venom.*

Hagman, Larry *Beware! The Blob (aka Son of Blob).*

Hagmann, Stuart *Believe in Me.*

Hahn, Don *Fantasia/2000 (aka Fantasia 2000).*

Hahn, Gerhard *Asterix Conquers America (Asterix in Amerika).*

Hahn, Steven *Starchaster: The Legend of Orin.*

Hai, Zafar *Perfect Murder, The.*

Haigney, Michael*Pokémon – The First Movie: Mewtwo Strikes Back.*

Haines, Fred *Steppenwolf.*

Haines, Randa *Children of a Lesser God; Dance With Me; Doctor, The; Wrestling Ernest Hemingway.*

Haines, Richard W *Class of Nuke 'Em High.*

Halas, John *Animal Farm.*

Hale, William *S.O.S. Titanic.*

Haley Jr, Jack *Love Machine, The; That's Dancing!; That's Entertainment!*

Halicki, HB *Gone in 60 Seconds.*

Halimi, André *Chantons sous l'Occupation.*

Hall, Alexander *Down to Earth; Here Comes Mr Jordan; I Am the Law.*

Hall, Peter *Akenfield; Homecoming, The; Never Talk to Strangers; Perfect Friday; She's Been Away; Three Into Two Won't Go; Work Is a Four Letter Word.*

Hallam, Paul *Nighthawks.*

Halldoff, Jan *What Are You Doing After the Orgy? (Rötmånad).*

Hallek, Dee Dee *Gringo in Mañanaland, A.*

Haller, Daniel *Buck Rogers in the 25th Century; Monster of Terror (aka Die, Monster, Die!); Pieces of Dreams; Sunshine Part II (aka My Sweet Lady).*

Hallström, Lasse *ABBA The Movie; Chocolat; Cider House Rules, The; Jag Är Med Barn (Father-to-Be/I'm Expecting); Lumière et Compagnie; My Life as a Dog (Mit Liv som Hund); Once Around; Shipping News, The; Something to Talk About; Tva Killar och en Tjej (Happy We/Two Lovers and Their Lass/Two Guys and a Gal); What's Eating Gilbert Grape.*

Hallum, Alister *News from Nowhere.*

Halperin, Victor *Supernatural; White Zombie.*

Halvorson, Gary *Adventures of Elmo in Grouchland, The.*

Hamburg, John *Safe Men.*

Hamer, Robert *Dead of Night; Father Brown; It Always Rains on Sunday; Kind Hearts and Coronets; Long Memory, The; Pink String and Sealing Wax; School for Scoundrels; Spider and the Fly, The.*

Hamermesh, Mira *Loving the Dead.*

Hamilton, David *Bilitis; Cousins in Love (Tendres Cousines). Laura (Laura, les Ombres de l'Eté).*

Hamilton, Guy *Battle of Britain; Colditz Story, The; Diamonds Are Forever; Evil Under the Sun; Force 10 from Navarone; Funeral in Berlin; Goldfinger; Inspector Calls, An; Live and Let Die; Manuela (aka Stowaway Girl); Man With the Golden Gun, The; Mirror Crack'd, The; Remo Williams: The Adventure Begins (aka Remo – Unarmed and Dangerous).*

Hamilton, Strathford *Proposition, The (Y Fargen); Set Up, The.*

Hamm, Nick *Hole, The; Martha – Meet Frank, Daniel and Laurence.*

Hammer, Robert *Don't Answer the Phone!*

Hammerich, Rumle *Premonition, The (Svart Lucia).*

Hammon, Michael *Hillbrow Kids; Wheels & Deals.*

Hammond, Peter *Spring and Port Wine.*

Hampton, Christopher *Carrington; Secret Agent, The (aka Joseph Conrad's The Secret Agent).*

Hampton, Robert (Riccardo Freda) *Maciste all'Inferno (Maciste in Hell/The Witch's Curse).*

Hanak, Dusan *I Love, You Love (Ja Milujem, Ty Milujes).*

Hancock, John *Baby Blue Marine.*

Hand, David *Bambi.*

Handke, Peter *Left-Handed Woman, The (Die linkshändige Frau).*

Haneke, Michael *Code Unknown (Code Inconnu); Benny's Video; Castle, The; Funny Games; Lumière et Compagnie; Piano Teacher, The (La Pianiste); 7th Continent, The (Siebente Kontinent); 71 Fragments of a Chronology of Chance (71 Fragmente einer Chronologie des Zufalls).*

Hanig, Josh *Men's Lives.*

Hanks, Tom *That Thing You Do!*

Hanna, William *Jetsons: The Movie.*

Hannam, Ken *Dawn!; Robbery Under Arms; Summerfield; Sunday Too Far Away.*

Hänsel, Marion *Dust; Quarry, The (La Faille); Maestro, Il (The Maestro/Double Game/Conductor).*

Hanson, Curtis *Bad Influence; Bedroom Window, The; Hand That Rocks the Cradle, The; LA Confidential; Losin' It; River Wild, The; Sweet Kill (aka The Arousers); Wonder Boys.*

Hanson, John *Northern Lights.*

Hara, Kazuo *Emperor's Naked Army Marches On, The (Yuki Yukite Shingun).*

Harada, Masato *Gunhed; Kamikaze Taxi; Leaving (Bounce – Ko Gals); Painted Desert.*

Harbutt, Sandy *Stone.*

Hardwick, Gary *Brothers, The.*

Hardy, Joseph *Great Expectations.*

Hardy, Justin *Feast at Midnight, A.*

Hardy, Robin *Fantasist, The; Wicker Man, The.*

Hare, David *Designated Mourner, The; Paris by Night; Strapless; Wetherby.*

Harel, Philippe *Femme Défendue, La (The Forbidden Woman); Randonneurs, Les (The Back-Packers); Whatever (Extension du domaine de la lutte).*

Harkin, Margo *Hush-a-Bye Baby.*

Harlin, Renny *Adventures of Ford Fairlane, The; Cliffhanger; CutThroat Island; Deep Blue Sea; Die Hard 2; Driven; Long Kiss Goodnight, The; Nightmare on Elm Street, 4: The Dream Master, A; Prison.*

Harling, Robert *Evening Star, The.*

Harmon, Robert *Gotti; Hitcher, The; Nowhere to Run.*

Harries, Andy *Lenny Live and Unleashed.*

Harrington, Curtis *Mata Hari; Ruby; What's the Matter with Helen?*

Harris, Damian *Deceived; Rachel Papers, The.*

Harris, Ed *Pollock.*

Harris, Frank *Killpoint.*

Harris, James B *Bedford Incident, The; Boiling Point; Cop; Fast-Walking; Some Call It Loving.*

Harris, Leslie *Just Another Girl on the I.R.T.*

Harris, Mark Jonathan *Into the Arms of Strangers: Stories of the Kindertransport.*

Harris, Richard *Bloomfield (aka The Hero).*

Harris Jr, Wendell B *Chameleon Street.*

Harrison, Greg *Groove.*

Harrison, John *Beautiful Dreamers; Tales from the Darkside: The Movie.*

Harrison, Matthew *Kicked in the Head; Rhythm Thief.*

Harrison, Tony *Prometheus.*

Harron, Mary *American Psycho; I Shot Andy Warhol.*

Hart, Harvey *Bus Riley's Back in Town; Fortune and Men's Eyes.*

Hartford-Davis, Robert *Black Gunn; Black Torment, The; Nobody Ordered Love; Take, The.*

Hartl, Karl *No Answer from F.P.1 (F.P.1 antwortet nicht).*

Hartley, Hal *Amateur; Book of Life, The; Flirt; Henry Fool; No Such Thing; Simple Men; Surviving Desire; Trust; Unbelievable Truth, The.*

Hartman, Rivka *Miniskirted Dynamo, The.*

Hatta, Kayo *Picture Bride.*

Harvey, Anthony *Abdication, The; Dutchman; Eagle's Wing; Grace Quigley; Lion in Winter, The; Players; They Might Be Giants.*

Harvey, Herk *Carnival of Souls.*

Harvey, Joan *America – From Hitler to M-X.*

Has, Wojciech *Doll, The (Lalka); Saragossa Manuscript, The (Rekopis Znaleziony w Saragossie).*

Hashiguchi, Ryosuke *Hush!; Like Grains of Sand (Nagisa no Sindbad).*

Hashimoto, Kohji *Gojira 1984 (Godzilla 1985/Return of Godzilla).*

Haskin, Byron *Conquest of Space; Naked Jungle, The; Power, The; Robinson Crusoe on Mars; Rookery Nook; War of the Worlds.*

Hastrup, Jannik *H.C. Andersen's The Long Shadow (H.C. Andersen og Den Skæve Skygge/aka Hans Christian Andersen and The Long Shadow).*

Hata, Masanori *Adventures of Milo and Otis, The (Koneko Monogatari); Little Nemo Adventures in Slumberland.*

Hathaway, Henry *Brigham Young – Frontiersman; Call Northside 777; Dark Corner, The; Desert Fox, The (aka Rommel – Desert Fox); Diplomatic Courier; 5 Card Stud; Fourteen Hours; From Hell to Texas; Hangup; Home in Indiana; House on 92nd Street, The; How the West Was Won; Kiss of Death; Legend of the Lost; Niagara; O. Henry's Full House (aka Full House); North to Alaska; Peter Ibbetson; Rawhide (aka Desperate Siege); Real Glory, The; True Grit; Woman Obsessed.*

Hatton, Maurice *American Roulette; Long Shot; Nelly's Version; Praise Marx and Pass the Ammunition.*

Hatzis, Efthimios *Shores of Twilight.*

Hauff, Reinhard *Knife in the Head (Messer im Kopf); Main Actor, The (Der Hauptdarsteller); Slow Attack (Endstation Freiheit); Stammheim.*

Hausner, Jessica *Lovely Rita.*

Haussmann, Leander *Sun Alley (Sonnenallee).*

Hawks, Howard *Air Force; Ball of Fire; Barbary Coast; Big Sky, The; Big Sleep, The; Bringing Up Baby; Ceiling Zero; Come and Get It; Criminal Code, The; Dawn Patrol, The; El Dorado; Gentlemen Prefer Blondes; Girl in Every Port, A; Hatari!; His Girl Friday; I Was a Male War Bride (aka You Can't Sleep Here); Land of the Pharaohs; Man's Favorite Sport?; Monkey Business; O. Henry's Full House (aka Full House); Only Angels Have Wings; Red Line 7000; Red River; Rio Bravo; Rio Lobo; Road to Glory, The; Scarface; Sergeant York; Song Is Born, A; Tiger Shark; To Have and Have Not; Twentieth Century.*

Hay, John *Steal, The; There's Only One Jimmy Grimble.*

Hay, Will *Black Sheep of Whitehall, The; My Learned Friend.*

Hayakawa, Wataru *7/25 (Nana/Ni-Go).*

Hayashi, Kaizo *Circus Boys (Nijusseiki Shonen Dokuhon); Most Terrible Time in My Life, The (Waga Jinsei Saiaku no Toki); To Sleep, So As to Dream.*

Hayden, Tom *Vietnam Journey.*

Haydn, Richard *Mr Music.*

Hayers, Sidney *Circus of Horrors; Conquest of the Earth; Deadly Strangers; Diagnosis: Murder; Night of the Eagle (aka Burn, Witch, Burn!); Payroll; Revenge (aka Inn of the Frightened People); What Changed Charley Farthing?*

Hayes, Derek *Miracle Maker, The.*

Hayes, John *Mama's Dirty Girls.*

Hayman, David *Hawk, The; Near Room, The; Silent Scream.*

Haynes, Stanley *Carnival.*

Haynes, Todd *Poison; Safe; Superstar: The Karen Carpenter Story; Velvet Goldmine.*

Hazan, Jack *Bigger Splash, A; Rude Boy.*

He Jianjun *Postman (Youchai).*

He Ping *Red Firecracker, Green Firecracker (Paoda Shuang Deng); Sun Valley (Riguang Xiagu); Swordsman in Double-Flag Town, The (Shuang Qi Zhen Dao Ke).*

He Yi *Red Beads (Xuan Lian).*

Head, John *Jimi Hendrix.*

Heap, Jonathan *Benefit of the Doubt.*

Hebendanz, Johannes *Flickering Roads (Asphaltflimmern).*

Hecht, Ben *Angels Over Broadway; Specter of the Rose.*

Hecht, Dina *Broken Arrow 29.*

Heckerling, Amy *Clueless; Fast Times at Ridgemont High (aka Fast Times); Johnny Dangerously; Look Who's Talking; Look Who's Talking Too; Losers.*

Hedden, Roy *Friday the 13th Part VIII: Jason Takes Manhattan.*

Heerman, Victor *Animal Crackers.*

Heffron, Richard T *Fillmore; Futureworld; I, the Jury; Newman's Law; Outlaw Blues; Trackdown.*

Hegedus, Chris *Down from the Mountain; Startup.com; Town Bloody Hall; War Room, The.*

Hegner, Michael *Help! I'm a Fish (Hjælp! Jeg er en fisk/Hilfe! Ich bin ein Fisch).*

Heifits, Josif *Lady With the Little Dog, The (Dama s Sobachkoi).*

Heinrich, Margarete *Totschweigen (A Wall of Silence).*

Heisler, Stuart *Along Came Jones; Among the Living; Blue Skies; Burning Hills, The; Dallas; Glass Key, The; I Died a Thousand Times; Monster and the Girl, The; Smash-Up, The Story of a Woman; Star, The; Tulsa.*

Helgeland, Brian *Knight's Tale, A; Payback.*

Hellman, Monte *Back Door to Hell; Beast from Haunted Cave; China 9, Liberty 37; Cockfighter; Ride in the Whirlwind; Shooting, The; Two-Lane Blacktop.*

Hellman, Oliver [Sonia Assonitis] *Tentacles (Tentacoli); Chi Sei? (Beyond the Door/ Devil Within Her).*

Helmer, Veit *Tuvalu.*

Helpern Jr, David *Hollywood on Trial.*

Helpmann, Robert *Don Quixote.*

Hemmings, David *Just a Gigolo (Schöner Gigolo – Armer Gigolo); Race for the Yankee Zephyr; Running Scared; Survivor, The.*

Henabery, Joseph *Cobra, The.*

Henderson, Anne *Song for Tibet.*

Henderson, John *Bring Me the Head of Mavis Davis; Loch Ness.*

Hendrickson, Robert *Manson.*

Henenlotter, Frank *Basket Case; Basket Case 2; Brain Damage; Frankenhooker.*

Henkel, Peter *Three Bullets for a Long Gun.*

Henning-Jensen, Astrid *Paw (Boy of Two Worlds/The Lure of the Jungle/Pao of the Jungle).*

Henreid, Paul *Ballad in Blue (aka Blues for Lovers).*

Henriques, Julian *Babymother.*

Henry, Buck *Heaven Can Wait.*

Henson, Brian *Muppet Christmas Carol, The; Muppet Treasure Island.*

Henson, Jim *Dark Crystal, The; Great Muppet Caper, The; Labyrinth.*

Henzell, Perry *Harder They Come, The.*

Herbert, Henry *Crossmaheart.*

Herbert, James *Speedy Boys.*

Herbst, Helmut *John Heartfield: Photomonteur.*

Herek, Stephen *Bill and Ted's Excellent Adventure; Critters; Don't Tell Mom the Babysitter's Dead; Holy Man; Mighty Ducks, The (aka Champions); Mr Holland's Opus; 101 Dalmatians; Rock Star; Three Musketeers, The.*

Herman, Mark *Blame It on the Bellboy; Brassed Off; Little Voice; Purely Belter.*

Hermosillo, Jaime Humberto *Doña Herlinda and Her Son (Doña Herlinda y su Hijo); Homework (La Tarea).*

Hernádi, Tibor *Felix the Cat: The Movie.*

Hernández, Antonio *Lisboa (Lisbon).*

Héroux, Denis *Uncanny, The.*

Herralde, Gonzalo *Race, the Spirit of Franco (Raza, el Espiritu de Franco).*

Herrendoerfer, Christian *Hitler – a Career (Hitler eine Karriere).*

Herrero, Gerardo *Desvio al Paraiso (Shortcut to Paradise); Malena Is a Name from a Tango (Malena es un Nombre de Tango).*

Herrington, Rowdy *Gladiator; Road House; Striking Distance.*

Hershman, Joel *Greenfingers; Hold Me, Thrill Me, Kiss Me.*

Herskovitz, Marshall *Dangerous Beauty; Jack the Bear.*

Herz, Juraj *Cremator, The (Spalovac Mrtvol); Morgiana.*

Herz, Michael *Toxic Avenger, The; Toxic Avenger Part II, The; War (aka Troma's War).*

Herzfeld, John *Don King: Only in America; 15 Minutes; 2 Days in the Valley; Two of a Kind.*

Herzog, Werner *Aguirre, Wrath of God (Aguirre, der Zorn Gottes); Cobra Verde; Even Dwarfs Started Small (Auch Zwerge haben klein angefangen); Fata Morgana; Fitzcarraldo; Great Ecstasy of Woodcarver Steiner, The (Die Grosse Ekstase des Bildschnitzers Steiner); Heart of Glass (Herz aus Glas); Invincible; Jeder für sich und Gott gegen alle (The Enigma of Kaspar Hauser/ Every Man for Himself and God Against All/The Mystery of Kaspar Hauser); Land of Silence and Darkness (Land des Schweigens und der Dunkelheit); Lessons in Darkness (Lektionen in Finsternis); My Dearest Enemy (Mein Liebster Fiend); Nosferatu the Vampyre (Nosferatu: Phantom der Nacht); Signs of Life (Lebenszeichen); Soufrière, La; Stroszek; Ten Minutes Older – The Trumpet; Where the Green Ants Dream (Wo die grünen Ameisen träumen); Woyzeck.*

Hess, John *Watchers.*

Hessler, Gordon *Cry of the Banshee; Golden Voyage of Sinbad; Murders in the Rue Morgue; Oblong Box, The; Scream and Scream Again.*

Heston, Charlton *Antony and Cleopatra.*

Heston, Fraser C *Alaska; Needful Things; Treasure Island.*

Hetata, Atef *Closed Doors (El Abwab el Moghalaka).*

Hewitt, Peter *Bill and Ted's Bogus Journey; Borrowers, The; Whatever Happened to Harold Smith?*

Hexter, Russ *Dadetown.*

Heynemann, Laurent *Old Lady Who Walked in the Sea, The (La Vieille qui Marchait dans la Mer).*

Heynowski, Walter *I Was, I Am, I Shall Be (Ich war, ich bin, ich werde sein).*

Hick, Jochen *Sex Life in L.A.*

Hickenlooper, George *Big Brass Ring, The; Hearts of Darkness: A Filmmaker's Apocalypse; Killing Box, The (aka Ghost Brigade); Persons Unknown.*

Hickey, Kieran *Attracta; Exposure.*

Hickner, Steve *Prince of Egypt, The.*

Hickox, Anthony *Hellraiser III: Hell on Earth; Prince Valiant (Prinz Eisenherz); Sundown; Waxwork.*

Hickox, Douglas *Brannigan; Entertaining Mr Sloane; Sky Riders; Theatre of Blood; Zulu Dawn.*

Hicks, Scott *Hearts in Atlantis; Shine; Snow Falling on Cedars.*

Higashi, Yoichi *Boy Called Third Base, A (Third); Village of Dreams (E no Naka no Boku no Mura).*

Higgins, Colin *Best Little Whorehouse in Texas, The; Foul Play; Nine to Five.*

Higson, Patrick *Big Banana Feet.*

Hill, Brian *Nobody Someday.*

Hill, Claudio Guerin *Campana del Infierno, La (The Bell of Hell/The Bell from Hell).*

Hill, George Roy *Butch Cassidy and the Sundance Kid; Great Waldo Pepper, The; Hawaii; Little Drummer Girl, The; Little Romance, A; Period of Adjustment; Slap Shot; Slaughterhouse-Five; Sting The; Thoroughly Modern Millie; World According to Garp, The.*

Hill, Jack *Coffy; Foxy Brown; Switchblade Sisters (aka Playgirl Gang/The Jezebels).*

Hill, James *Belstone Fox, The; Captain Nemo and the Underwater City; Kitchen, The; Lunch Hour; Study in Terror, A.*

Hill, Tim *Mouth Wide Open – A Journey in Film with Ted Coubray.*

Hill, Walter *Another 48 HRS; Brewster's Millions; Crossroads; Driver, The; Extreme Prejudice; Geronimo: An American Legend; 48 HRS; Hard Times (aka The Streetfighter); Johnny Handsome; Last Man Standing; Long Riders, The; Red Heat; Southern Comfort; Streets of Fire; Trespass; Warriors, The; Wild Bill.*

Hill, Walter (as Thomas Lee) *Supernova.*

Hillcoat, John *Ghosts…of the Civil Dead; To Have & to Hold.*

Hiller, Arthur *Americanization of Emily, The; Author! Author!; Babe, The; Filofax; Hospital, The; In-Laws, The; Love Story; Making Love; Man in the Glass Booth, The; Nightwing; Out-of-Towners, The; Outrageous Fortune; Plaza Suite; Promise Her Anything; See No Evil, Hear No Evil; Silver Streak; Teachers; W.C. Fields and Me.*

Hills, Paul *Boston Kickout.*

Hillyer, Lambert *Dracula's Daughter; Invisible Ray, The.*

Hiroki, Ryuichi *I Am an S+M Writer (Futai no Kisetsu); Sadistic City (Ma-o Gai).*

Hirschbiegel, Oliver *Experiment, The (Das Experiment).*

Hirst, Damien *Breath.*

Hitchcock, Alfred *Aventure Malgache; Birds, The; Blackmail; Bon Voyage; Champagne; Dial M for Murder; Downhill; Easy Virtue; Elstree Calling; Family Plot; Farmer's Wife, The; Foreign Correspondent; Frenzy; I Confess; Jamaica Inn; Lady Vanishes, The; Lifeboat; Lodger, The; Man Who Knew Too Much, The* (1934); *Man Who Knew Too Much, The* (1956); *Manxman, The; Marnie; Mr and Mrs Smith; Murder; North by Northwest; Notorious; Number Seventeen; Paradine Case, The; Psycho; Rear Window; Rebecca; Rich and Strange; Ring, The; Rope; Sabotage, Saboteur; Secret Agent, The; Shadow of a Doubt; Spellbound; Stage Fright; Strangers on a Train; Suspicion; 39 Steps, The; To Catch a Thief; Topaz; Torn Curtain; Trouble with Harry, The; Under Capricorn; Vertigo; Wrong Man, The; Young and Innocent.*

Ho Menghua *Death Kick (Huang Feihong/aka The Master of Kung Fu).*

Ho Ping *Wolves Cry Under the Moon (Guo Dao Feng Bi).*

Hobbs, John B *La Passione.*

Hobby, Amy *At Sundance.*

Hoblit, Gregory *Fallen; Frequency; Primal Fear.*

Hodges, Mike *Black Rainbow; Croupier; Flash Gordon; Get Carter; Morons from Outer Space; Prayer for the Dying, A; Pulp; Terminal Man, The.*

Hoessli, Andreas *¡Devils Don't Dream! Research on Jacobo Arbenz Guzmán (¡Devils don't dream! Nachforschungen über Jacobo Arbenz Guzmán).*

Hofbauer, Ernst *Confessions of a Sixth Form Girl (Schulmädchen Report – Was Eltern nicht für moglich halten); Enter the 7 Virgins (Yang Ji/aka Virgins of the Seven Seas).*

Hoffman, Antony *Red Planet.*

Hoffman, Deborah *Long Night's Journey into Day.*

Hoffman, Jerzy *Deluge, The (Potop).*

Hoffman, Michael *Midsummer Night's Dream, A; One Fine Day; Privileged; Promised Land; Restless Natives; Restoration; Soapdish; Some Girls (aka Sisters).*

Hoffs, Tamar Simon *Allnighter, The.*

Hofmann, Nico *Sandman, The (Der Sandmann).*

Hogan, David *Barb Wire; Most Wanted.*

Hogan, James *Bulldog Drummond Escapes; Last Train from Madrid, The.*

Hogan, PJ *Muriel's Wedding; My Best Friend's Wedding.*

Holbeck, Cæcilia *Agnus Dei (Nonnebørn).*

Holcomb, Rod *Donato and Daughter.*

Holden, Lansing C *She.*

Holdt, Jacob *American Pictures: A Personal Journey Through Black America (Amerikanske Billeder).*

Holland, Agnieszka *Europa, Europa; Olivier Olivier; Secret Garden, The; To Kill a Priest; Total Eclipse; Washington Square; Woman on Her Own, A (Kobieta Samotna).*

Holland, John *Night in Havana: Dizzy Gillespie in Cuba, A.*

Holland, Tom *Child's Play; Fatal Beauty; Fright Night; Stephen King's Thinner.*

Hollander, Eli *Out.*

Holleb, Allan *Candy Stripe Nurses.*

Holloway, Graham *Chasing the Deer.*

Holmes, Ben *Saint in New York, The.*

Holofcener, Nicole *Walking and Talking.*

Holst, Marius *Cross My Heart and Hope to Die (Ti Kniver I Hjertet).*

Holt, Seth *Blood from the Mummy's Tomb; Danger Route; Nanny, The; Station Six – Sahara; Taste of Fear (aka Scream of Fear).*

Holzman, Allan *Forbidden World (aka Mutant).*

Honda, Inoshiro *Destroy All Monsters (Kaiju Soshingeki); Mysterians, The (Chikyu Boeigun).*

Hondo, Med *Lumière Noire; Sarraounia.*

Honey, John *Manganinnie.*

Hong, Elliott *They Call Me Bruce.*

Hong Sang-Soo *Day a Pig Fell into the Well, The; Power of Kangwon Province, The (Kangwon-do ui Him); Turning Gate, The (Saenghwal ui Balgyeon); Virgin Stripped Bare by Her Bachelors (Oh! Soojung).*

Honigmann, Heddy *Au Revoir (Tot Ziens); O Amor Natural; Underground Orchestra, The (Het Ondergronds Orkest).*

Honkasalo, Pirjo *Flame Top (Tulipää).*

Hook, Harry *Kitchen Toto, The; Last of His Tribe, The; Lord of the Flies.*

Hooker, Ted *Crucible of Terror.*

Hooks, Kevin *Fled; Passenger 57.*

Hooper, Tobe *Body Bags; Death Trap (aka Eaten Alive); Funhouse, The; Invaders from Mars; Lifeforce; Mangler, The; Poltergeist; Salem's Lot; Texas Chain Saw Massacre, The; Texas Chainsaw Massacre 2, The.*

Hopkins, Anthony *August.*

Hopkins, Ben *Nine Lives of Tomas Katz, The; Simon Magus.*

Hopkins, Joel *Jump Tomorrow.*

Hopkins, Stephen *Blown Away; Ghost and the Darkness, The; Lost in Space; Nightmare on Elm Street 5: The Dream Child, A; Predator 2; Tube Tales; Under Suspicion.*

Hopper, Dennis *Chasers; Colors; Easy Rider; Hot Spot, The; Last Movie, The; Out of the Blue.*

Hopper, Dennis (as Alan Smithee) *Catchfire.*

Hopper, Jerry *Madron; Smoke Signal.*

Hornaday, Jeffrey *Shout.*

Horne, James W *Bonnie Scotland; College; Way Out West.*

Horner Harry *Beware, My Lovely; Red Planet Mars.*

Horton, Peter *Amazon Women on the Moon; Cure, The.*

Horvat, Aleks *Sweethearts.*

Hosada, Mamoru *Digimon Digital Monsters – The Movie.*

Hoskins, Bob *Raggedy Rawney, The; Rainbow; Tube Tales.*

Hossein, Robert *Vampire de Dusseldorf, Le.*

Hou Jing *Kung Fu – Girl Fighter (Can Nü Kongshoudao/aka Karate King – On the Waterfront).*

Hou Xiaoxian (Hou Hsiao-Hsien) *Boys from Fengkuei, The (Fenggui Lai-de Ren/aka All the Youthful Days); City of Sadness, A (Beiqing Chengshi); Daughter of the Nile (Niluohe Nüer); Dust in the Wind (Lian Lian Feng Chen); Flowers of Shanghai (Hai Shang Hua); Goodbye South, Goodbye (Nanguo Zai Jian, Nanguo); Good Men, Good Women (Haonan Haonü); Green, Green Grass of Home, The (Zai na Hepan Qing Cao Qing); Millennium Mambo (Qianxi Manbo); Puppetmaster, The (Ximeng Rensheng); Sandwich Man, The (Erzi de Da Wan'ou); Summer at Grandpa's, A (Dongdong de Jiaqi); Time to Live and the Time to Die, The (Tongnian Wangshi).*

Hough, John *Biggles; Brass Target; Dirty Mary, Crazy Larry; Escape to Witch Mountain; Eyewitness (aka Sudden Terror); Incubus; Legend of Hell House, The; Return from Witch Mountain; Something to Believe In; Triumphs of a Man Called Horse (El Triunfo de un Hombre Llamado Caballo); Twins of Evil; Watcher in the Woods, The.*

Hough, Johnny *Wolfshead: The Legend of Robin Hood.*

Houston, Bobby *Trust Me.*

Hovde, Ellen *Grey Gardens.*

Howard, Cy *Every Little Crook and Nanny.*

Howard, Leslie *First of the Few (aka Spitfire); Gentle Sex, The; Pimpernel Smith; Pygmalion.*

Howard, Ron *Apollo 13; Backdraft; Beautiful Mind, A; Cocoon; Dr Seuss' How the Grinch Stole Christmas (aka The Grinch); EDtv; Far and Away; Grand Theft Auto; Gung Ho; Night Shift; Paper, The; Parenthood; Ransom; Splash; Willow.*

Howard, William K *Fire Over England; Power and the Glory, The; Squeaker, The.*

Howe, JA *Kid Brother, The.*

Howitt, Peter *Antitrust; Sliding Doors.*

Hoyt, Harry *Lost World, The.*

Hrebejk, Jan *Cosy Dens (Pelisky); Divided We Fall (Musíme si Pomáhat).*

Hsiao Ya-chuan *Mirror Image (Ming dai ahui zhu).*

Hsu Hsiao-Ming *Heartbreak Island (Qunian Dongtian).*

Hu Binliu *Live in Peace.*

Hu Fow-Pyng *Jacky.*

Hu Jinquan *see* Hu, King

Hu, King [Hu Jinquan] *Fate of Lee Khan, The (Ying-chun-ge zhi Fengbo); Legend of the Mountain (Shan Zhong Chuanqi); Raining in the Mountain (Kong Shan Ling Yu); Swordsman; Touch of Zen, A (Xia Nü); Valiant Ones, The (Zhonglie Tu).*

Huang Feng *Hap-Ki-Do (Heqidao); Stoner (Tiejin Gang Da Po Zi Yang Guan).*

Huang, George *Swimming with Sharks.*

Huang Jianxin *Back to Back, Face to Face; Black Cannon Incident, The (Heipao Shijan); Signal Left, Turn Right (Da Zuo Deng, Xiang You Zhuan); Stand Up, Don't Grovel! (Zhanzhiluo, Bie Paxia!); Surveillance (Maifu); Wooden Man's Bride, The (Yan Shen).*

Huang Jianzhong *Girl of Good Family, A (Liangjia funü).*

Huang Min-Chen (Huang Mingzheng) *Birdland (Chengshi Feixing); Too Young (Ye Maque).*

Huang Mingchuan *Bodo (Baodao Dameng); Flat Tyre (Po Luntai); Man from Island West, The (Xibu Lai de Ren).*

Hubert, Jean-Loup *Contre l'Oubli (Against Oblivion); Grand Chemin, Le.*

Huda, Menhaj *Tube Tales.*

Hudlin, Reginald *Boomerang; Great White Hype, The; House Party; Ladies Man, The.*

Hudson, Hugh *Chariots of Fire; Greystoke – The Legend of Tarzan Lord of the Apes; Lost Angels (aka The Road*

Home); Lumière et Compagnie; My Life So Far; Revolution.

Huestis, Marc *Sex Is…*

Hughes, Albert *Dead Presidents; From Hell; Menace II Society.*

Hughes, Allen *Dead Presidents; From Hell; Menace II Society.*

Hughes, Bronwen *Forces of Nature; Harriet the Spy.*

Hughes, Carol *Missing Link.*

Hughes, David *Missing Link.*

Hughes, Enda *Act Without Words –II.*

Hughes, Howard *Hell's Angels; Outlaw, The.*

Hughes, John *Breakfast Club, The; Curly Sue; Ferris Bueller's Day Off; Planes, Trains and Automobiles; She's Having a Baby; Sixteen Candles; Uncle Buck; Weird Science; What Have I Written.*

Hughes, Ken *Alfie Darling; Brain Machine, The; Casino Royale; Chitty Chitty Bang Bang; Cromwell; Internecine Project, The; Joe Macbeth; Timeslip (aka The Atomic Man); Trials of Oscar Wilde, The (aka The Man With the Green Carnation).*

Hughes, Robert C *Hunter's Blood.*

Hughes, Terry *Butcher's Wife, The.*

Hui, Ann *Ah Kam (A-Jin/aka The Stuntwoman); Boat People (Touben Nuhai); Eighteen Springs (Ban Sheng Yuan); July Rhapsody (Nanren Sishi); Love in a Fallen City (Qingcheng zhi Lian); Ordinary Heroes (Qianyan Wanyu); Romance of Book & Sword, The (Shujian Enchou Lu); Secret, The (Fengjie); Song of the Exile (Ketu Qiu Hen); Spooky Bunch, The (Zhuang Dao Zheng); Story of Woo Viet, The (Hu Yue de Gushi); Summer Snow (Nüren Sishi); Visible Secret (Youling Ren Jian).*

Huillet, Danièle *Class Relations (Klassenverhältnisse); Fortini/Cani; From the Cloud to the Resistance (Nube alla Resistenza); History Lessons (Geschichtsunterricht); Moses and Aaron (Moses und Aron); Othon (Les Yeux ne peuvent pas en tout temps se fermer); Sicily! (Sicilia!).*

Hulbert, Jack *Elstree Calling; Falling For You.*

Hull, Norman *Ladder of Swords.*

Hultberg, Ulf *Daughter of the Puma, The.*

Humberstone, H Bruce *Charlie Chan at the Opera; Desert Song, The; Hello, Frisco, Hello; Iceland (aka Katina); If I Had a Million; I Wake Up Screaming (aka Hot Spot); Pin Up Girl; Sun Valley Serenade; Wonder Man.*

Humbert, Nicolas *Vagabonding Images.*

Hume, Kenneth *I've Gotta Horse.*

Humfress, Paul *Sebastiane.*

Hung, Samo *Mr Nice Guy (Yige Hao Ren); Moon Warriors (Zhan Shen Chuanshuo); Wheels on Meals (Kuai-can Che).*

Hunsinger, Tom *Boyfriends.*

Hunt, Bonnie *Return to Me.*

Hunt, Claire *Good Wife of Tokyo, The.*

Hunt, Maurice *Pagemaster, The.*

Hunt, Paul *40 Graves for 40 Guns (aka The Great Gundown).*

Hunt, Peter *Assassination; Gold; Gulliver's Travels; On Her Majesty's Secret Service; 1776; Shout at the Devil; Wild Geese II.*

Hunt, Pixote *Fantasia/2000 (aka Fantasia 2000).*

Hunter, Neil *Boyfriends; Lawless Heart, The.*

Hunter, T Hayes *Ghoul, The.*

Hunter, Tim *River's Edge; Saint of Fort Washington, The.*

Huntington, Lawrence *Franchise Affair, The.*

Hur Jin-Ho *Christmas in August (Pal-Wol ui Christmas); One Fine Spring Day (Bomnal eun Ganda).*

Huraux, Marc *Bird Now.*

Hurran, Nick *Girls' Night; Remember Me?; Virtual Sexuality.*

Hurst, Andy *You're Dead…*

Hurst, Brian Desmond *Black Tent; Dangerous Moonlight; Hungry Hill; Scrooge; Simba.*

Hurtz, William *Little Nemo Adventures in Slumberland.*

Hüseyin, Metin *It Was an Accident.*

Hussein, Waris *Henry VIII and His Six Wives; Possession of Joel Delaney, The; Sixth Happiness, The.*

Huston, Anjelica *Agnes Browne.*

Huston, Danny *Mr North.*

Huston, John *Across the Pacific; African Queen, The; Annie; Asphalt Jungle, The; Beat the Devil; Bible…In the Beginning, The (La Bibbia), Casino Royale; Dead, The; Fat City; Freud; Heaven Knows, Mr Allison; In This Our Life; Key Largo; Kremlin Letter, The; Life and Times of Judge Roy Bean, The; List of Adrian Messenger, The; Mackintosh Man, The; Maltese Falcon, The; Man Who Would Be King, The; Misfits, The; Moby Dick; Moulin Rouge; Night of the Iguana, The; Prizzi's Honor; Red Badge of Courage, The; Reflections in a Golden Eye; Sinful Davey; Treasure of the Sierra Madre, The; Under the Volcano; Unforgiven, The; Victory (aka Escape to Victory); Walk with Love and Death, A; Wise Blood.*

Huth, James *Serial Lover.*

Hutt, David *Nearly Wide Awake.*

Hutt, Robyn *Voices from the Front.*

Hutton, Brian G *First Deadly Sin, The; High Road to China; Kelly's Heroes; Night Watch; Where Eagles Dare; Zee & Co (aka X, Y and Zee).*

Huyck, Willard *Best Defence; Howard the Duck(aka Howard…a new breed of hero).*

Hyams, Peter *Busting; Capricorn One; End of Days; Hanover Street; Narrow Margin; Outland; Peeper; Presidio, The; Relic, The; Running Scared; Star Chamber, The; Stay Tuned; Sudden Death; Timecop; 2010.*

Hylkema, Hans *Last Date (De Laatste Sessie).*

Hytner, Nicholas *Center Stage; Crucible, The; Madness of King George, The; Object of My Affection, The.*

Iannuci, Armando *Tube Tales.*

Ibáñez Serrador, Narciso *¿Quién Puede Matar a un Niño? (Death Is Child's Play/Island of the Damned/Would You Kill a Child?).*

Ice Cube, *Players Club, The.*

Ichaso, Leon *Crossover Dreams; Piñero; Sugar Dreams.*

Ichikawa, Jun *Tokyo Kyodai.*

Ichikawa, Kon *Actor's Revenge, An (Yukinojo Henge); Alone on the Pacific (Taiheiyo Hitoribotchi); Dora-Heita; Burmese Harp, The (Biruma no Tategoto); Tokyo Olympiad 1964; Visions of Eight.*

Ichio, Naoko *Drowning Man, A (Oboreru Hito).*

Idemoto, Michael *Sunsets.*

Igliori, Paolo *American Magus.*

Ihnat, Steve *Honkers, The.*

Ikoli, Tunde *Tunde's Film.*

Ilhan, Biket *Boatman (Kayikci); Man in the Street, The (Sokaktaki Adam).*

Illienko, Yuri *Swan Lake – The Zone (Lebedinoie ozero – Zona).*

Illsley, Mark *Happy Texas.*

Imai, Tadashi *Brother and Sister (Ani Imoto/aka Mon and Ino).*

Imamura, Shohei *Ballad of Narayama, The (Narayama Bushi-ko); Black Rain (Kuroi Ame); Eel, the (Unagi); Eijanaika; History of Post-War Japan as Told by a Bar Hostess (Nippon Sengo Shi: Madamu Omboro no Seikatsu); Lukewarm Water Under the Red Bridge (Akai Hashi Noshitano Nurui Mizu); Man Vanishes, A (Ningen Johatsu); Pigs and Battleships (Buta to Gunkan/aka The Flesh Is Hot); Profound Desire of the Gods: Tales from a Southern Island, The (Kamigami no Fukaki Yokubô/aka Legend from Southern Island/ Kuragejima – Legends from a Southern Island).*

Im Kwon-Taek *Chihwaseon (Strokes of Fire); Chunhyang (Chunhyang Dyeon); Come, Come, Come Upward (Aje Aje Bara-Aje); Festival (Chukje); Gilsodum; Mandala; Sopyonje (Seo-Pyon-Jae); Surrogate Mother (Sibaji); Taebaek Mountains, The (Taebaek Sanmaek); Ticket.*

Im Soon-Rye *Waikiki Brothers, The.*

Inagaki, Hiroshi *Miyamoto Musashi (Musashi Miyamoto).*

Incalcaterra, Daniele *Repubblica Nostra (Our Republic).*

Infascelli, Fiorella *Mask, The (La Maschera).*

Ingram, Rex *Magician, The.*

Ingster, Boris *Stranger on the Third Floor, The.*

Iosseliani, Otar *Brigands; Farewell, Home Sweet Home (Adieu, Plancher des Vaches!); Favourites of the Moon (Les Favoris de la Lune); Pastorale.*

Ip, Riley *Metade Fumaça (Ban zhi Yan).*

Ireland, Dan *Whole Wide World.*

Irmas, Matthew *Edie & Pen.*

Irvin, John *Champions; City of Industry; Dogs of War, The; Ghost Story; Hamburger Hill. Month by the Lake; Next of Kin; Raw Deal; Robin Hood; Shiner; Turtle Diary; Widows' Peak.*

Irving, Judy *Dark Circle.*

Isacsson, Kris *Down to You.*

Isaka, Satoshi *[Focus].*

Isasi, Antonio *They Came to Rob Las Vegas.*

Iscove, Robert *She's All That.*

Ishii, Katsuhito *Shark-skin Man and Peach-hip Girl (Samehada Otoko to Momojiro Onna).*

Ishii, Sogo *Angel Dust; August in the Water (Mizu no Naka no Hachigatsu); Crazy Family (Gyakufunsha Kazoku); Electric Dragon 80,000; Gojoe (Gojo Reisen Ki); Labyrinth of Dreams (Yume no Ginga).*

Ishii, Takashi *Gonin; Gonin 2.*

Isitt, Debie *Nasty Neighbours.*

Israel, Neal *Bachelor Party.*

Issermann, Aline *Ombre du Doute, L' (A Shadow of Doubt).*

Itami, Juzo *Minbo Woman – Or the Gentle Art of Japanese Extortion (Minbo No Onna); Ososhiki (Death Japanese Style/Funeral Rites); Tampopo; Taxing Woman, A (Marusa no Onna).*

Ivanga, Imunga *Dôlé (L'Argent).*

Ivens, Joris *Far from Vietnam (Loin du Viêt-nam).*

Ivory, James *Adventures of a Brown Man in Search of Civilization; Autobiography of a Princess; Bombay Talkie; Bostonians, The; Europeans, The; 5:48, The; Golden Bowl, The; Guru, The; Heat and Dust; Householder, The; Howards End; Hullabaloo over Georgie and Bonnie's Pictures; Jane Austen in Manhattan; Jefferson in Paris; Lumière et Compagnie; Maurice; Mr and Mrs Bridge; Quartet; Remains of the Day, The; Room With a View, A; Roseland; Savages; Shakespeare-Wallah; Slaves of New York; Soldier's Daughter Never Cries, A; Surviving Picasso; Sword and the Flute, The; Venice: Theme and Variation; Wild Party, The.*

Iwai, Shunji *April Story (Shigatsu Monogatari); Love Letter; Swallowtail Butterfly.*

Iwamoto, Kenchi *Kikuchi.*

Jackson, Mick *Bodyguard, The; Chattahoochee; L.A. Story; Volcano.*

Jackson, Pat *Encore; Western Approaches (aka The Raider); What a Carve Up.*

Jackson, Peter *Bad Taste; Braindead; Forgotten Silver; Frighteners, The; Heavenly Creatures; Lord of the Rings: The Fellowship of the Ring, The; Meet the Feebles.*

Jackson, Wilfred *Cinderella; Lady and the Tramp; Peter Pan; Song of the South.*

Jacobs, Alan *Nina Takes a Lover.*

Jacobs, Nicholas *Refrigerator, The.*

Jacobs, Steve *Spagnola, La.*

Jacobson, David *Criminal.*

Jacopetti, Gualtiero *Africa Addio (Africa Blood and Guts); Uncle Tom (Addio, Zio Tom).*

Jacquot, Benoît *Ecole de la Chair, L' (The School of Flesh); Pas de Scandale (Keep It Quiet/No Scandal); Sade; Tosca.*

Jaeckin, Just *Emmanuelle; Lady Chatterley's Lover; Madame Claude; Story of O, The (Histoire d'O/Geschichte der O).*

Jafelice, Raymond *Care Bears Adventures in Wonderland!, The.*

Jaffe, Stanley R *Without a Trace.*

Jaglom, Henry *Always; Can She Bake a Cherry Pie?; Déjà Vu; Last Summer in the Hamptons; National Lampoon Goes to the Movies (aka National Lampoon's Movie Madness); New Year's Day; Safe Place, A; Sitting Ducks; Someone to Love; Tracks.*

Jakubisko, Juro *Deserter and the Nomads, The (Zbehovia a Poutnici).*

Jalili, Abolfazl *Daan (Don); Delbaran; Det Means Girl (Det, Yani Dokhtar); Dance of Dust (Raghs-e-Khak); Tales of Kish (Ghessé Hayé Kish).*

Jamal, Ahmed A *Majdhar.*

James, Steve *Hoop Dreams.*

Jameson, Jerry *Airport '77; Raise the Titanic!; Starflight: The Plane That Couldn't Land (aka Starflight One).*

Jancsó, Miklós *Confrontation, The (Fényes Szelek); Elektreia (Szerelmem, Elektra); My Way Home (Igy Jöttem); Private Vices & Public Virtues (Vizi Privati, Pubbliche Virtú); Red Psalm (Még Kér a Nép); Red and the White, The (Csillagosok, Katonák); Round-Up, The (Szegénylegények); Silence and Cry (Csend és Káiltás).*

Jang Sun-Woo *Hwa-om-kyong (Hwa-eom-gyung); Lies (Kojitmai); Lovers in Woomuk-Baemi (Woomuk-Baemi ui Sarang); Petal, A (Kkotyip); Road to the Racetrack (Kyongmachang Kanungil); Timeless Bottomless Bad Movie (Napun Younghwa); To You, From Me (Neo-ege Narul Bonenda).*

Jankel, Annabel *D.O.A.; Super Mario Bros.*

Jann, Michael Patrick *Drop Dead Gorgeous.*

Janthimathron, Surachi *Tongpan.*

Jaoui, Agnès *Goût des autres, Le.*

Jargil, Jesper *Exhibited, The (De Udstillede).*

Jarman, Derek *Blue; Angelic Conversation, The; Aria; Caravaggio; Edward II; Garden, The; In the Shadow of the Sun; Jubilee; Last of England, The; Sebastiane; Tempest, The; War Requiem; Wittgenstein.*

Jarmusch, Jim *Dead Man; Down by Law; Ghost Dog: The Way of the Samurai; Mystery Train; Night on Earth; Permanent Vacation; Stranger Than Paradise; Ten Minutes Older – The Trumpet; Year of the Horse.*

Jarrold, Julian *Some Kind of Life.*

Jarrott, Charles *Amateur, The; Anne of the Thousand Days; Condorman; Dove, The; Escape from the Dark (aka The Littlest Horse Thieves); Last Flight of Noah's Ark, The; Lost Horizon; Mary, Queen of Scots; Other Side of Midnight, The.*

Järvilaturi, Ilkka *Darkness in Tallinn (Tallinn pimeduses/Tallinnan pimeys).*

Jasny, Voytech *All My Good Countrymen (Vsichni Dobri Rodaci/aka All Good Citizens).*

Jason, Leigh *Mad Miss Manton, The.*

Jayaraj *Calmness (Shantham); Journey to Wisdom (Desaadanam).*

Jean, Vadim *Beyond Bedlam; Clockwork Mice; Leon the Pig Farmer; One More Kiss; Real Howard Spitz, The.*

Jean, Vikram *I Am a Sex Addict.*

Jeffrey, Tom *Odd Angry Shot, The.*

Jeffries, Lionel *Amazing Mr Blunden, The; Baxter!; Railway Children, The; Water Babies, The; Wombling Free.*

Jenkins, Amy *Tube Tales.*

Jenkins, Michael *Rebel.*

Jenkins, Tamara *Slums of Beverly Hills.*

Jennings, Humphrey *Fires Were Started (aka I Was a Fireman); Spare Time.*

Jensen, Knut Erik *Cool & Crazy (Heftig & begeistret/Häftig och begeistrad).*

Jensen, Torben Skjødt *Carl Th. Dreyer: My Work (Carl Th. Dreyer: Min metier).*

Jeon Soo Il *Wind Echoing in My Being (Nae-an e Unn Param).*

Jerstad, Jon *Tibetan New Year, A.*

Jessop, Clytie *Emma's War.*

Jessua, Alain *Chiens, Les (The Dogs). Traitement de Choc (The Doctor int he Nude/Shock Treatment); Vie á l'Envers, La (Life Upside-Down).*

Jetté, Michel *Hochelaga.*

Jeunet, Jean-Pierre *Alien Resurrection; Amélie (Le Fabuleux Destin d'Amélie Poulain/Die fabelhaft Welt der Amélie); Cité des enfants perdus, La (The City of Lost Children); Delicatessen.*

Jewison, Norman *...and justice for all; Agnes of God; Art of Love, The; Best Friends; Cincinnati Kid, The; F.I.S.T.; Fiddler on the Roof; Hurricane, The; In Country; In the Heat of the Night; Jesus Christ Superstar; Moonstruck; Only You; Other People's Money; Rollerball; Send Me No Flowers; Soldier's Story, A; Thomas Crown Affair, The; Thrill of It All, The.*

Jha, Prakash *Death Sentence (Mrityudand); Inevitable, The (Parinati).*

Jia Zhangke *Platform, The (Zhantai); Unknown Pleasures (Ren Xiaoyao); Xiao Wu.*

Jiang Hong *Kung Fu – The Headcrusher (Ying Han/aka Tough Guy).*

Jiang Wen *Devils on the Doorstep (Guizi Lai-le); In the Heat of the Sun (Yang-guang Canlan de Rizi).*

Jiang Yixiong *King of Kung Fu (Shi Xiong Chu Ma/aka He Walks Like a Tiger).*

Jian Long *Ten Fingers of Steel (Tangren Biao Ke).*

Jimenez, Neal *Waterdance, The.*

Jiménez Leal, Orlando *Improper Conduct (Mauvaise Conduite).*

Jingle Ma *Hot War (Huan Yin Te Gong).*

Jin Shan *Along the Sungari River (Songhua-jiang Shang).*

Jires, Jaromil *Labyrinth; Pearls of the Deep (Perlicky na dna); Valerie and Her Week of Wonders (Valerie a Tyden Divu).*

Jitnukul, Thanit 'Pued' *Bang Rajan – Legend of the Village Warriors (Bang Rajan); Crime Kings (Sua… Jone Pan Sua).*

Jittlov, Mike *Wizard of Speed and Time, The.*

Joanou, Phil *Heaven's Prisoners; Final Analysis; State of Grace; Three O'Clock High; U2 Rattle and Hum.*

Jobson, Dickie *Countryman.*

Jodrell, Steve *Shame.*

Jodorowsky, Alejandro *Santa Sangre; Topo, El (The Mole).*

Joffé, Alex *Fortunat.*

Joffé, Arthur *Harem.*

Joffe, Mark *Cosi; Grievous Bodily Harm; Spotswood.*

Joffé, Roland *City of Joy; Fat Man and Little Boy (aka Shadow Makers); Goodbye Lover; Killing Fields, The; Mission, The; Scarlet Letter, The; Vatel.*

Jóhannesdóttir, Kristín *As in Heaven (Svo a Jördu sem á Himni).*

Johar, Karan *Kabhi Khushi Kabhie Gham…; Kuch Kuch Hota Hai.*

Johnson, Alan *To Be or Not to Be; Solarbabies (aka Solarwarriors).*

Johnson, Hugh *Chill Factor.*

Johnson, Jed *Andy Warhol's Bad.*

Johnson, Kenneth *Incredible Hulk, The; Short Circuit 2.*

Johnson, Lamont *Cattle Annie and Little Britches; Groundstar Conspiracy, The; Gunfight, A; Last American Hero, The; Lipstick; McKenzie Break, The; One on One; Somebody Killed Her Husband; Spacehunter: Adventures in the Forbidden Zone; Unnatural Causes: The Agent Orange Story; You'll Like My Mother.*

Johnson, Mark Stephen *Simon Birch.*

Johnson, Niall *Big Swap, The.*

Johnson, Nunnally *Black Widow; How to Be Very, Very Popular; Oh, Men! Oh, Women!; Three Faces of Eve, The.*

Johnson, Patrick Read *Angus; Baby's Day Out; Spaced Invaders.*

Johnson, Sandy *Coast to Coast.*

Johnson, Terry *Way Upstream.*

Johnson, Tim *Antz.*

Johnson-Cochran, Dwayne *Love and Action in Chicago.*

Johnston, Joe *Honey, I Shrunk the Kids; Jumanji; Jurassic Park III; October Sky; Pagemaster, The; Rocketeer, The.*

Johnstone, Jyll *Martha & Ethel.*

Jolivet, Pierre *In All Innocence (En plein coeur).*

Jolliffe, Genvieve *Urban Ghost Story.*

Jones, Amy *Love Letters; Slumber Party Massacre, The.*

Jones, Chris *White Angel.*

Jones, Chuck *How the Grinch Stole Christmas! (aka Dr Seuss's How the Grinch Stole Christmas!); Phantom Tollbooth, The.*

Jones, David *Betrayal; 84 Charing Cross Road; Jacknife; Trial, The.*

Jones, F Richard *Bulldog Drummond.*

Jones, Harmon *Pride of St Louis, The.*

Jones, Kirk *Waking Ned (aka Waking Ned Devine).*

Jones, LQ *Boy and His Dog, A.*

Jones, Michael *My Little Pony.*

Jones, Terry *Erik the Viking; Monty Python and the Holy Grail; Monty Python's Life of Brian; Monty Python's The Meaning of Life; Personal Services; Wind in the Willows, The.*

Jongbloed, Marijke *Fatal Reaction: Singapore.*

Jonze, Spike *Being John Malvokich.*

Jordá, Joaquín *Body in the Forest, A (Cuerpo en el Bosque).*

Jordan, Glenn *Only When I Laugh (aka It Hurts Only When I Laugh).*

Jordan, Gregor *Two Hands.*

Jordan, Neil *Angel; Butcher Boy, The; Company of Wolves, The; Crying Game, The; End of the Affair, The; High Spirits; In Dreams; Interview With the Vampire; Michael Collins; Miracle, The; Mona Lisa; Not I; We're No Angels.*

Joreige, Khalil *Around the Pink House (Al bayt al zahr/ Autour de la maison rose).*

Josephson, Erland *One and One (En och En).*

Jost, Jon *Angel City; Last Chants for a Slow Dance; Slow Moves; Sure Fire; Uncommon Senses.*

Jouffa, François *Bonzesse, La.*

Jourdain, Pierre *I Am a Dancer (Un Danseur: Rudolph Nureyev).*

Jourd'hui, Gérard *Vieille Canaille (The Old Crook).*

Joy, Alex *Sorted.*

Joyce, Maurice *Doug's 1st Movie.*

Joyce, Paul *Motion and Emotion: The Films of Wim Wenders.*

Judge, Mike *Beavis and Butt-head Do America.*

Jugnot, Gérard *Epoque formidable…, Une.*

Julian, Rupert *Merry-Go-Round; Phantom of the Opera, The.*

Julien, Isaac *Frantz Fanon: Black Skin, White Mask; Looking for Langston; Passion of Remembrance, The; Young Soul Rebels.*

Julsrdu, Karin *Bloody Angels (1732 Høtten).*

July, Serge *Viva Portugal.*

Jung Jae-Eun *Take Care of My Cat (Goyang Yirul Butakhae).*

Jung Ji-Woo *Happy End.*

Junger, Gil *10 Things I Hate About You.*

Jurácek, Pavel *Case for a Young Hangman, A (Pripad pro Zacinajiciho Kata); Joseph Kilián (Postava k Podpiráni).*

Juran, Nathan *Attack of the 50 Foot Woman; First Men in the Moon; Hellcats of the Navy; Jack the Giant Killer; Seventh Voyage of Sinbad, The; 20 Million Miles to Earth.*

Justiniano, Gonzalo *Amnesia; Caluga o Menta.*

Jutra, Claude *Mon Oncle Antoine (My Uncle Antoine).*

Kabore, Gastone *Lumière et Compagnie.*

Kachivas, Lou *Mighty Mouse in the Great Space Chase; Secret of the Sword, The.*

Kachyna, Karel *Ear, The (Ucho); I'm Jumping Over Puddles Again (Uz zase Skácu pres Kaluze).*

Kaczender, George *Agency (aka Mind Games); Chanel Solitaire; In Praise of Older Women.*

Kadár, Ján *Adrift (Hrst Piná Vody); Angel Levine, The; Freedom Road; Lies My Father Told Me; Shop on the High Street (Obchod na Korze).*

Kagan, Jeremy Paul *Big Fix, The; By the Sword; Chosen, The; Heroes; Journey of Natty Gann, The; Sting II, The.*

Kahn, Cédric *Ennui, L'; Roberto Succo; Trop de Bonheur (Too Much Happiness).*

Kahn, Jonathan *Girl .*

Kaiserman, Connie *My Little Girl.*

Kalatozov, Mikhail *I Am Cuba (Ya – Cuba/Soy Cuba).*

Kal Ng *Soul Investigator, The.*

Kalik, Mikhail *Goodbye, Boys (Do Svidanija, Maltsjiki).*

Kalin, Tom *Swoon.*

Kalvert, Scott *Basketball Diaries, The.*

Kam Kwok-Leung *4 Faces of Eve (4 [Si] Mian Xiawa).*

Kaminski, Janusz *Lost Souls.*

Kampmann, Steven *Stealing Home.*

Kane, David *Born Romantic; This Year's Love.*

Kane, Joseph *Hoodlum Empire.*

Kaneko, Shusuke *Gamera: The Guardian of the Universe (Gamera Daikaiju Kuchu Kessen); Summer Vacation 1999 (Sen-Kyuhayaku-Kyuju-Kyu-Nen no Natsu Yasumi).*

Kaneko, Shu *Necromicon (aka H.P. Lovecraft's Necronomicon).*

Kanevsky, Vitaly *Don't Move, Die and Rise Again! (Zamri, Umri, Voskresni!).*

Kanew, Jeff *Revenge of the Nerds; Tough Guys; V.I. Warshawski.*

Kanievska, Marek *Another Country; Where the Money Is.*

Kang Je-Gyu *Shiri (Swiri).*

Kanin, Garson *Bachelor Mother; Great Man Votes,*

The; My Favorite Wife; They Knew What They Wanted; True Glory, The.

Kanner, Alexis *Kings and Desperate Men.*

Kanter, Hal *I Married a Woman.*

Kapadia, Asif *Warrior, The.*

Kapakas, Costas *Peppermint.*

Kaplan, Deborah *Josie and the Pussycats.*

Kaplan, Jo Ann *Invocation Maya Deren.*

Kaplan, Jonathan *Accused, The; Bad Girls; Brokedown Palace; Heart Like a Wheel; Mr Billion; Over the Edge; Love Field; Project X; Student Teachers, The; Unlawful Entry; White Line Fever.*

Kaplan, Mike *Luck, Trust & Ketchup: Robert Altman in Carver Country.*

Kaplan, Nelly *Charles and Lucie (Charles et Lucie); Fiancée du Pirate, La (Dirty Mary/A Very Curious Girl); Néa (A Young Emmanuelle); Papa, les Petits Bateaux…*

Kaplanoglu, Semih *Away from Home (Herkes Kendi Evinde).*

Kaplun, Arik *Yana's Friends (Hachaverim shel Yana).*

Kapur, Shekhar *Bandit Queen; Elizabeth.*

Karanovic, Srdjan *Virgin (Virgina).*

Karbelnikoff, Michael *F.T.W.; Mobsters (aka Mobsters – The Evil Empire).*

Karel, Russ *Almonds and Raisins.*

Kargl, Gerald *Schizophrenia (aka Angst).*

Karlin, Marc *'33 to '77.*

Karlson, Phil *Ben; Down Memory Lane; Framed; Kid Galahad; Ladies of the Chorus; Phenix City Story, The; Rampage; Walking Tall.*

Karmel, Pip *Me Myself I.*

Karmitz, Marin *Coup pour Coup (Blow for Blow).*

Karson, Eric *Black Eagle.*

Karya, Teguh *Mementos (Doea Tanda Mata); November 1828.*

Karypides, Georges *Dead Liqueur.*

Kasdan, Jake *Zero Effect.*

Kasdan, Lawrence *Accidental Tourist, The; Big Chill, The; Body Heat; French Kiss; Grand Canyon; I Love You to Death; Silverado; Wyatt Earp.*

Kassovitz, Mathieu *Assassin(s); Crimson Rivers, The (Les Rivières Pourpres); Haine, La (Hate); Métisse (Cafe au Lait/Blended).*

Kassovitz, Peter *Jakob the Liar.*

Kastle, Leonard *Honeymoon Killers, The.*

Kaszubowski, Jerzy *Road Home, The.*

Katakouzinos, Yorgos *Angelos.*

Kato, Akira *Emanuelle in Tokyo (Tokyo Emmanuelle Fujin).*

Kato, Tai *Blood of Revenge (Meiji Kyokyakuden Sandaime Shumei); Cruel Story of the Shogunate's Downfall (Bakumatsu Zankoku Monogatari); History of a Man's Face, The (Otoko no Kao wa Rirekisho); I, the Executioner (Minagoroshi no Reika); Red Peony Gambler: Flower-cards Match (Hibotan Bakuto: Hanafuda Shobu); Sasuke and His Comedians (Sanada Fu-unroku).*

Katselas, Milton *Butterflies Are Free; Report to the Commissioner (aka Operation Undercover).*

Katzin, Lee H *Le Mans; What Ever Happened to Aunt Alice?*

Kavur, Omer *Secret Face, The (Gizli Yuz).*

Kaufman, George S *Senator Was Indiscreet, The.*

Kaufman, Lloyd (see also Weil, Samuel) *Class of Nuke 'em High; Toxic Avenger Part II, The; Tromeo & Juliet.*

Kaufman, Philip *Great Northfield Minnesota Raid, The; Henry & June; Invasion of the Body Snatchers; Quills; Right Stuff, The; Rising Sun; Unbearable Lightness Being, The; Wanderers, The; White Dawn, The.*

Kaurismäki, Aki *Ariel; Crime and Punishment (Rikos ja Rangaistus); Drifting Clouds (Kauas Pilvet Karkaavat/Au loin s'en vont les nuages); Hamlet Goes Business (Hamlet Liikemaailmassa); I Hired a Contract Killer; Juha; Leningrad Cowboys Go America; Man Without a Past, The (Mies Vailla Menneisyyttä); Match Factory Girl, The (Tulitikkutehtaan Tytto); Take Care of Your Scarf, Tatjana (Pida Huivista Kinni, Tatjana); Ten Minutes Older – The Trumpet; Total Balalaika Show; Vie de Bohème, La (Bohemian Life).*

Kaurismäki, Mika *Highway Society; LA Without a Map; Sound of Brazil (Moro no Brasil); Tigrero – A Film That Was Never Made.*

Kavur, Ömer *Night Journey (Gece Yolculugu).*

Kawadri, Anwar *Nutcracker.*

Kawasaki, Hirotsugu *Spriggan.*

Kawase, Naomi *Suzaku (Moe no Shuzaku).*

Kay, Stephen *Last Time I Committed Suicide, The.*

Kaye, Tony *American History X.*

Kaylor, Robert *Carny; Derby (aka Roller Derby).*

Kazama, Shiori *How Old Is the River? (Fuyu no Kappa).*

Kazan, Elia *America, America (aka The Anatolian Smile); Arrangement, The; Baby Doll; Boomerang; East of Eden; Face in the Crowd, A; Gentleman's Agreement; Last Tycoon, The; Man on a Tightrope; On the Waterfront; Panic in the Streets; Splendor in the Grass; Streetcar Named Desire, A; Viva Zapata!; Wild River.*

Kazan, Nicholas *Dream Lover.*

Kazanski, Gennadi *Snow Queen, The (Snezhnaya Koroleva).*

Kazui, Fran Rubel *Tokyo Pop.*

Keating, David *Last of the High Kings, The.*

Keaton, Buster *Battling Butler; General, The; Go West; Navigator, The; Our Hospitality; Seven Chances; Sherlock Junior; Steamboat Bill, Jr.*

Keaton, Diane *Hanging Up; Heaven; Unstrung Heroes.*

Kechiche, Abdellatif *Faute à Voltaire, La (Blame It on Voltaire).*

Kedzierzawska, Dorota *Crows (Wrony); Devils, Devils (Diably, Diably).*

Keeler, Toby *Pretty as a Picture: The Art of David Lynch.*

Keen, Bob *Proteus.*

Keeve, Douglas *Unzipped.*

Keeve, Frederick *From Russia to Hollywood: the 100-Year Odyssey of Chekhov and Shdanoff.*

Keighley, William *Adventures of Robin Hood, The; Bullets or Ballots; Each Dawn I Die; Fighting 69th, The; 'G' Men; Green Pastures, The; Man Who Came to Dinner, The; Street with No Name, The; Torrid Zone.*

Keiller, Patrick *London; Robinson in Space.*

Kelemen, Fred *Fate (Verhängnis); Frost; Nightfall (Abendland).*

Keleti, Márton *Loves of Liszt, The (Szerelmi Almok – Liszt).*

Kellett, Bob *Are You Being Served?; Don't Just Lie There, Say Something!; Spanish Fly.*

Kelljan, Bob *Act of Vengeance (aka Rape Squad/The Violator); Count Yorga, Vampire; Return of Count Yorga, The.*

Kellman, Barnet *Straight Talk.*

Kellogg, David *Inspector Gadget.*

Kellogg, Ray *Green Berets, The.*

Kelly, Gene *Cheyenne Social Club, The; Guide for the Married Man, A; Hello, Dolly!; It's Always Fair Weather; On The Town; Singin' in the Rain; That's Entertainment Part II.*

Kelly, James *Beast in the Cellar, The (aka Are you Dying, Young Man?); Night Hair Child (La Tua Presenza Nuda/aka What the Peeper Saw).*

Kelly, Nancy *Thousand Pieces of Gold, A.*

Kelly, Richard *Donnie Darko.*

Kelly, Rory *Sleep With Me.*

Kelly, Sarah *Full Tilt Boogie.*

Kemp, Julian *House!*

Kennedy, Burt *Canadians, The; Good Guys and the Bad Guys, The; Hannie Caulder; Killer Inside Me, The; Return of the Seven (aka Return of the Magnificent Seven); Rounders, The; Suburban Commando; Support Your Local Gunfighter; Support Your Local Sheriff; Train Robbers. The; War Wagon, The; Welcome to Hard Times (aka Killer on a Horse).*

Kennedy, Chris *Doing Time for Patsy Cline.*

Kenovic, Ademir *Perfect Circle (Savresni Krug).*

Kentis, Chris *Grind.*

Kenton, Erle C *Ghost of Frankenstein, The; House of Dracula; House of Frankenstein; Island of Lost Souls.*

Kernochan, Sarah *Marjoe.*

Kerrigan, Justin *Human Traffic.*

Kerrigan, Lodge *Claire Dolan; Clean, Shaven.*

Kershner, Irvin *Empire Strikes Back, The; Empire Strikes Back: Special Edition, The; Eyes of Laura Mars; Fine Madness, A; Flim-Flam Man, The (aka One Born Every Minute); Loving; Luck of Ginger Coffey, The; Never Say Never Again; Raid on Entebbe; Return of a Man Called Horse, The; RoboCop 2; SPYS; Up the Sandbox.*

Kervyn, Emmanuel *Rabid Grannies.*

Keshishian, Alek *Truth or Dare (aka In Bed with Madonna); With Honors.*

Kessler, Bruce *Angels From Hell.*

Keusch, Erwin *Baker's Bread (Das Brot des Bäckers).*

Keys, Gary *Memories of Duke.*

Kézdi-Kovács, Zsolt *Forbidden Relations (Visszaesök); When Joseph Returns (Ha Megjön József).*

Khaindrava, Georgi *Graveyard of Dreams (Ochnebebis Sasaplao).*

Khan, Mehboob *Mother India (Bharat Mata).*

Khleifi, George *You, Me, Jerusalem.*

Khleifi, Michel *Tale of the Three Jewels (Conte des trois diamants); Wedding in Galilee (Noce en Galilée).*

Khoo, Eric *Mee Pok Man; 12 Storeys.*

Khosa, Rajan *Dance of the Wind (Wara Mandel).*

Khudojnazarov, Bakhtiar *Brothers (Bratan); Luna Papa; On Equal Terms (Kosh Ba Kosh).*

Kiarostami, Abbas *A.B.C Africa; And Life Goes On… (Zendegi Va Digar Hich…); Close-Up (Namayeh Nazdik); Lumière et Compagnie; Taste of Cherry, A (Ta'm e Guilass); 10; Traveller, The (Mossafer); Through the Olive Trees (Zir-e darakhtan-e zeyton/aka Under the Olive Trees); Where Is My Friend's House? (Zhaneh-Je Doost Kojast); Wind Will Carry Us, The (Le Vent nous emportera/Bad mara khahad bourd).*

Kibbee, Roland *Midnight Man, The.*

Kidron, Beeban *Amy Foster (aka Swept from the Sea –The Story of Amy Foster); Carry Greenham Home; To Wong Foo, Thanks for Everything! Julie Newmar; Used People; Vroom.*

Kiersch, Fritz *Children of the Corn; Tuff Turf.*

Kieslowski, Krzysztof *Blind Chance (Przypadek); Camera Buff (Amator); Dekalog 1: 'I am the Lord thy God, Thou shalt have no other God but me'; Dekalog 2: 'Thou shalt not take the name of the Lord thy God in vain'; Dekalog 3: 'Honour the Sabbath Day'; Dekalog 4: 'Honour thy father and thy mother'; Dekalog 5: 'Thou shalt not kill'; Dekalog 6: 'Thou shalt not commit adultery'; Dekalog 7: 'Thou shalt not steal'; Dekalog 8: 'Thou shalt not bear false witness'; Dekalog 9: 'Thou shalt not covet thy neighbour's wife'; Dekalog 10: 'Thou shalt not covet thy neighbour's goods'; Double Vie de Véronique, La (The Double Life of Véronique); No End (Bez Konca); Scar, The (Blizna); Short Film About Killing, A (Krótki Film o Zabijaniu); Short Film About Love, A (Krótki Film o Milosci); Three Colours: Blue (Trois Couleurs: Bleu); Three Colours: Red (Trois Couleurs: Rouge); Three Colours: White (Trois Couleurs: Blanc).*

Kikoine, Gerard *Buried Alive; Edge of Sanity.*

Kilner, Clare *Janice Beard 45 WPM.*

Kim Hong-Joon *Jungle Story.*

Kim In-Shik *Roadmovie.*

Kim Jee-Woon *Foul King, The (Ban-Chik Wang).*

Kim Ki-Duk *Bad Guy (Nappun Mamja); Isle, The (Seom).*

Kim Ki-Young *Housemaid, The (Hanyo); Insect Woman, The (Chung Nyo); Iodo; Killer Butterfly (Salin Nabireul Cchotneun Yeoja).*

Kim Sang-Jin *Attack the Gas Station! (Chuyuso Supgyuk Sa Keun); Kick the Moon (Shilla ui Dalbam).*

Kim Si-On *Fly Low (Ha Woo Deung).*

Kim Tae-Yong *Memento Mori (Yeogo Goedam 2); Volcano High (Hwa San Go).*

Kim Ui-Seok *Marriage Story (Kyolhon Iyagi); That Woman, That Man (Ke Yeoja, Ke Namja); Vie en rose, La (Changmi Bit Insaeng).*

Kimiai, Masud *Snake Fang (Dandane Mar).*

Kimmins, Anthony *Captain's Paradise, The; Come on George; Mine Own Executioner.*

King, Allan *Married Couple, A.*

King, George *Crimes at the Dark House; Face at the Window, The.*

King, Henry *Bravados, The; Beloved Infidel; Black Swan, The; Carousel; Chad Hanna; Gunfighter, The; In Old Chicago; Jesse James; Love Is a Many-Splendored Thing; Margie; O. Henry's Full House (aka Full House); Prince of Foxes; Remember the Day; Seventh Heaven; Snows of Kilimanjaro, The; Song of Bernadette, The; Sun Also Rises, The; Twelve O'Clock High; Untamed; Wait Till the Sun Shines, Nellie; Wilson; Yank in the RAF, A.*

King, Louis *Bulldog Drummond Comes Back; Dangerous Mission; Smoky; Thunderhead, Son of Flicka.*

King, Rick *Prayer of the Rollerboys.*

King, Stephen *Maximum Overdrive.*

King, Zalman *Two Moon Junction; Wild Orchid.*

Kinney, Jack *Ichabod and Mr Toad (aka The Adventures of Ichabod and Mr Toad).*

Kinugasa, Teinosuke *Crossways (Jujiro); Page of Madness, A (Kurutta Ippeiji).*

Kiral, Erden *Blue Exile, The (Mavi Sürgün); Mirror, The (Der Spiegel/ Anya).*

Kirsanoff, Dimitri *Ménilmontant.*

Kirsch, Andrea William *Christie et Les Arts Florissants ou la Passion du Baroque.*

Kishon, Ephraim *Sallah.*

Kitakubo, Hiroyuki *Blood: The Last Vampire; Roujin Z (Rojin Z).*

Kitano, Takeshi *Boiling Point (3–4x Jugatsu/San tai Yon x Jugatsu); Getting Any? (Minna Yatteruka); Brother; Hana-Bi; Kids Return; Kikujiro (Kikujiro no Natsu); Scene at the Sea, A (Ano Natsu, Ichiban Shizukana Umi); Sonatine; Violent Cop, The (Sono Otoko Kyobo ni Tsuki).*

Kizer, RJ *Godzilla 1985 (Gojira).*

Kjaerulff-Schmidt, Palle *Once There Was a War (Der var engang en Krig).*

Kjellin, Alf *Midas Run (aka A Run on Gold).*

Klane, Robert *Thank God It's Friday.*

Klapisch, Cédric *Air de Famille, Un; Lumière et Compagnie; Péril Jeune, Le (Good Old Daze); When the Cat's Away… (Chacun cherche son chat).*

Klein, Bonnie Sherr *Not a Love Story.*

Klein, Carola *Mirror Phase.*

Klein, James *Union Maids.*

Klein, Rolando *Chac.*

Klein, William *Far from Vietnam (Loin du Viêt-nam); Messiah (Le Messie); Mister Freedom; Who Are Your Polly Maggoo? (Qui êtes-vous Polly Maggoo?); Muhammad Ali: The Greatest.*

Kleiser, Randal *Big Top Pee-Wee; Blue Lagoon, The; Flight of the Navigator; Getting It Right; Grandview U.S.A.; Grease; Honey, I Blew Up the Kid; It's My Party; Summer Lovers; White Fang.*

Klier, Michael *Grass Is Always Greener, The (Uberall ist es besser, wo wir nicht sind).*

Klimov, Elem *Agony (Agonia); Come and See (Idi i Smotri); Farewell (Proshchanie).*

Klinger, Tony *Butterfly Ball, The.*

Kloetzel, Andre *Savage Capitalism.*

Klos, Elmar *Shop on the High Street (Obchod na Korze).*

Kloves, Steve *Fabulous Baker Boys, The; Flesh and Bone.*

Kluge, Alexander *Artistes at the Top of the Big Top: Disorientated (Die Artisten in der Zirkuskuppel: ratlos); Germany in Autumn (Deutschland im Herbst); Occasional Work of a Female Slave (Gelegenheitsarbeit einer Sklavin); Patriot, The (Die Patriotin); Starke Ferdinand, Der (Strong-Man Ferdinand); Yesterday Girl (Abschied von Gestern).*

Knight, Castleton *For Freedom.*

Knights, Robert *Dawning, The.*

Knobler, Albert *Happiness in Twenty Years (Le Bonheur dans 20 Ans).*

Knowles, Bernard *Jassy; Magic Bow, The; Perfect Woman, The; Place of One's Own, A.*

Knudsen, Mette *Take It Like a Man, Ma'am (Ta' det som en Mand, Frue!).*

Ko, Clifton *Chicken and Duck Talk (Ji Tong ya Jiang).*

Ko I-cheng *Blue Moon (Lan Yue).*

Kobayashi, Masaki *Empty Table, The (Shokutaku no Nai ie); Kaseki; Kwaidan; Rebellion (Joi-Uchi).*

Koch, Chris *Snow Day.*

Koch, Howard W *Badge 373.*

Koenigsberg, Paula de *Rate It X.*

Koepp, David *Stir of Echoes.*

Koepp, Volker *Wittstock, Wittstock.*

Koerfer, Thomas *Alzire, or the New Continent (Alzire, oder der neue Kontinent); Death of the Flea Circus Director, The (Der Tod des Flohzirkusdirektors).*

Koff, David *Black Britannica; Occupied Palestine.*

Kohn, Richard *Lord of the Dance.*

Kokkinos, Ana *Head On; Only the Brave.*

Kokkinos, Antonis *End of an Era (Telos Epochis).*

Kollek, Amos *Bridget; Fast Food, Fast Women; Goodbye New York; Queenie in Love.*

Koller, Xavier *Journey of Hope (Reise der Hoffnung).*

Kolski, Jan Jakub *Johnny Aquarius (Jancio Wodnik); Playing from Plates (Grajacy Z Talerza).*

Komack, James *Porky's Revenge.*

Kon, Satoshi *Perfect Blue.*

Konchalovsky, Andrei *Duet for One; Inner Circle, The (Il Proiezionista); Lumière et Compagnie; Maria's Lovers; Riaba Ma Poule (Ryaba My Chicken); Runaway Train; Shy People; Tango & Cash.*

Konchalovsky, Andrei (as Andrei Mikhalkov-Konchalovsky) *Asya's Happiness (Istoriya Asi Klyachinoi, Kotoraya Lyubila, da nie vshla zamuzh); Nest of Gentlefolk, A (Dvorianskoe Gnezdo).*

Koning, Olivier *São Paolo, SP.*

Kopple, Barbara *Harlan County, U.S.A.; My Generation; Wild Man Blues.*

Korda, Alexander *Girl from Maxim's, The; Ideal Husband, An; Marius; Perfect Strangers (aka Vacation from Marriage); Private Life of Henry VIII, The; Rembrandt; That Hamilton Woman (aka Lady Hamilton); Wedding Rehearsal.*

Korda, Zoltan *Conquest of the Air; Drum, The (aka Drums); Elephant Boy; Forget me not (aka Forever Yours); Four Feathers, The; Macomber Affair, The; Sahara; Thief of Bagdad, The.*

Koreeda (Kore-eda), Hirokazu *After Life; Distance; Maborosi (Maboroshi no Hikari/The Beckoning Light); Without Memory (Kioku-ga Ushinawareta-toki).*

Kormákur, Baltasar *101 Reykjavík.*

Korner, Anthony *Helen, Queen of the Nautch Girls.*

Korine, Harmony *Gummo; Julien Donkey-Boy.*

Korty, John *Alex & The Gypsy; Autobiography of Miss Jane Pittman, The; Ewok Adventure, The (aka Caravan of Courage); Oliver's Story.*

Kosashvili, Dover *Late Marriage (Hatouna Mehuheret/Mariage Tardif).*

Kosminsky, Peter *Wuthering Heights.*

Kossakovsky, Viktor *Wednesday 19.7.1961 (Sreda).*

Koster, Henry *Bishop's Wife, The; Good Morning, Miss Dove; Harvey; It Started with Eve; Man Called Peter, A; Marilyn; Mr Hobbs Takes a Vacation; My Cousin Rachel; My Man Godfrey; No Highway (aka No Highway in the Sky); O. Henry's Full House (aka Full House); One Hundred Men and a Girl; Robe, The.*

Kot, Eric *First Love – The Litter on the Breeze (Chu Chanlian Hou de Liang Ren Shijie); 4 Faces of Eve (4 [Si] Mian Xiawa).*

Kotani, Tom *Last Dinosaur, The.*

Kotcheff, Ted *Apprenticeship of Duddy Kravitz, The; Billy Two Hats; First Blood; Folks!; Fun with Dick and Jane; Life at the Top; North Dallas Forty; Outback; Shooter, The; Switching Channels; Tiara Tahiti; Uncommon Valor; Wake in Fright (aka Outback); Weekend at Bernie's; Who Is Killing the Great Chefs of Europe? (aka Too Many Chefs); Winter People.*

Kotler, Beth *Groove on a Stanley Knife.*

Kötting, Andrew *Gallivant; This Filthy Earth.*

Kotulla, Theodor *Death Is My Trade (Aus einem deutschen Leben).*

Kouf, Jim *Gang Related; Miracles.*

Kounen, Jan *Dobermann.*

Kouyaté, Dani *Këita! The Voice of the Griot (Këita! L'Héritage du Griot).*

Kovacs, Steven *'68.*

Kovalyov, Igor *Rugrats Movie, The.*

Kowlaski, Bernard L *Krakatoa – East of Java; Sssssss (aka Ssssnake).*

Kozintsev, Grigori *Devil's Wheel, The (Chyortovo Koleso); Don Quixote; Hamlet; King Lear (Korol Lir); New Babylon, The (Novyi Vavilon).*

Krabbé, Jeroen *Left Luggage.*

Kragh-Jacobsen, Søren *Mifune (Mifune sidste sang).*

Kramer, Frank (Gianfranco Parolini) *Sabata (Ehi, Amico … C'è Sabata, hai chiuso!); Return of Sabata (E'Tornato Sabata…Hai Chiuso un'Altra Volta).*

Kramer, Jerry *Moonwalker.*

Kramer, Robert *Contre l'Oubli (Against Oblivion); Doc's Kingdom; Ice; Milestones; Route One/USA.*

Kramer, Stanley *Defiant Ones, The; Domino Principle, The (aka The Domino Killings); Guess Who's Coming To Dinner; Inherit the Wind; It's a Mad, Mad, Mad, Mad, World; Judgment at Nuremberg; Not As a Stranger; Oklahoma Crude; On the Beach; Pride and the Passion, The; Runner Stumbles, The; Secret of Santa Vittoria, The; Ship of Fools.*

Krawczyk, Gérard *Taxi 2.*

Krawinkel, Lenard Fritz *Sumo Bruno.*

Krawitz, Jan *Little People.*

Krejcik, Jirí *Divine Emma, The (Bozká Ema).*

Kressl, Vladimir *Gifted City (Mesto Darovane).*

Krish, John *Decline and Fall…of a Birdwatcher!; Man Who Had Power Over Women, The.*

Krishen, Pradip *Electric Moon.*

Krishna, Srinivas *Masala.*

Krishnamma, Suri *Man of No Importance, A; New Year's Day.*

Krishnan, Tine *Groove on a Stanley Knife.*

Kristiansen, Henning *Me and Charly (Mig og Charly).*

Krohn, Bill *It's All True.*

Kroyer, Bill *FernGully: The Last Rainforest.*

Krueger, Lisa *Manny & Lo.*

Kubrick, Stanley *Barry Lyndon; Clockwork Orange, A; Dr Strangelove: or, How I Learned to Stop Worrying and Love the Bomb; Eyes Wide Shut; Full Metal Jacket; Killer's Kiss; Killing, The; Lolita; Paths of Glory; Shining, The; Spartacus; 2001: A Space Odyssey.*

Kuehn, Andrew J *Terror in the Aisles.*

Kuei Chih-Hung *Enter the 7 Virgins (aka Virgins of the Seven Seas).*

Kufus, Thomas *My Private War (Mein Krieg).*

Kühn, Siegfried *Elective Affinities (Die Wahlverwandtschaften).*

Kukunoor, Nagesh *Bollywood Calling.*

Kuleshov, Lev *By the Law (Dura Lex); Extraordinary Adventures of Mister West in the Land of the Bolsheviks, The (Neobychainiye Priklucheniya Mistera Vesta v Stranye Bolshevikov).*

Kulik, Buzz *Hunter, The; Shamus: To Find a Man; Villa Rides!; Warning Shot.*

Kumakiri, Kazuyoshi *Hole in the Sky (Sora no Ana); Kichiku (Kichiku Dai Enkai).*

Kumar, Harbance Mickey *Man from Africa and Girl from India.*

Kumashiro, Tatsumi *Like a Rolling Stone (Bo no Kanashimi).*

Kumble, Roger *Cruel Intentions.*

Kümel, Harry *Daughters of Darkness (Les Lèvres Rouges); Eline Vere; Lost Paradise, The (Het Verloren Paradijs); Malpertuis; Monsieur Hawarden.*

Kunert, Joachim *Adventures of Werner Holt, The (Die Abenteuer des Werner Holt).*

Kunuk, Zacharias *Atanarjuat: The Fast Runner.*

Kureishi, Hanif *London Kills Me.*

Kurosawa, Akira *Akira Kurosawa's Dreams; Bad Sleep Well, The; Dersu Uzala; Dodes'kaden; Hidden Fortress, The (Kakushi Toride no San-Akunin); High and Low (Tengoku to Jigoku); Idiot, The (Hakuchi); Ikiru (Living/To Live); I Live In Fear (Ikimono no Kiroku); Kagemusha; Lower Depths, The (Donzoko); Madadayo (Not Yet); Noro Inu (Stray Dog); Ran; Rashomon; Red Beard (Akahige); Rhapsody in August (Hachigatsu no Kyoshikyoku); Sanjuro (Tsubaki Sanjuro); Seven Samurai (Shichinin no Samurai); Throne of Blood (Kumonosu-jo); Toro no O o Fumu Otokotachi (The Men Who Tread on the Tiger's*

Tail/Walkers on the Tiger's Tail); Yojimbo.

Kurosawa, Kiyoshi *Barren Illusion (Oinaru Genei); Charisma; Cure; Licence to Live (Ningen Gokaku); Seance (Korei).*

Kurtzman, Robert *Wishmaster.*

Kurys, Diane *Après l'Amour; Coup de Foudre (At First Sight/Entre Nous); Diabolo Menthe (Peppermint Soda); Enfants du siècle, Les; La Baule-les-pins (C'est la Vie); Man in Love, A (Un Homme Amoureux).*

Kusama, Karyn *Girlfight.*

Kusturica, Emir *Arizona Dream (aka American Dreamers); Black Cat White Cat; Time of the Gypsies (Dom za Vesanje); Underground; When Father Was Away on Business (Otac na Sluzbenom Putu).*

Kutz, Kazimierz *Beads of One Rosary, The (Paciorki Jednego Rózanca); Converted, The (Zawrócony); Taste of the Black Earth, The (Sól Ziemi Czarnej).*

Kuzui, Fran Rubel *Buffy the Vampire Slayer.*

Kwak Kyung-Taek *Friend (Chingu); Oksutan (3pm Paradise/Bath House).*

Kwan Pun-Leung *Buenos Aires Zero Degree.*

Kwan, Stanley *Actress (Ruan Ling Yu); Full Moon in New York (Ren zai Niu-Yue); Hold You Tight (Yue Kuai Le, Yue Duoluo); Island Tales, The (You Shi Tiaowu); Lan Yu; Love Unto Waste (Dixia Qing); Red Rose, White Rose (Hong Meigui Bai Meigui); Rouge (Yanzhi Kou); Still Love You After All (Nian Ni Hao Xi); Yang ± Yin: Gender in Chinese Cinema (Nansheng Nüxiang).*

Kwapis, Ken *Dunston Checks In; He Said, She Said.*

Kwietniowski, Richard *Love and Death on Long Island.*

Kyrou, Ado *Moine, Le (The Monk).*

Labate, Wilma *Domenica.*

Labib, Jean *Montand.*

LaBruce, Bruce *Hustler White; No Skin Off My Ass, Skin Flick; Super 8½.*

LaBute, Neil *In the Company of Men; Nurse Betty; Your Friends & Neighbors.*

La Cava, Gregory *Affairs of Cellini, The; 5th Avenue Girl; Gabriel Over the White House; My Man Godfrey; Primrose Path, The; Stage Door.*

Lachman, Harry *Dante's Inferno; Man Who Lived Twice; Our Relations.*

Lafia, John *Child's Play 2; Man's Best Friend.*

LaGravenese, Richard *Living Out Loud.*

Laguionie, Jean-François *Monkey's Tale, A (Le Château des singes/A majmok kastélya).*

Lahiff, Craig *Heaven's Burning.*

Lai, David *Scorpion King, The (Jie zi zhan shi/aka Operation Scorpio).*

Lai, Stan *Peach-Blossom Land, The (Anlian Taohuayuan); Red Lotus Society, The (Feixia A-Da).*

Laine, Edvin *Täällä Pohjantähden alla (Here Beneath the North Star/Akseli and Elina).*

Laing, John *Beyond Reasonable Doubt; Other Halves.*

LaLoggia, Frank *Lady in White.*

Laloux, René *Fantastic Planet (La Planète Sauvage).*

Lalou, Serge *Entre Nous.*

Lam, Ringo *City on Fire (Longhu Fengyun); Burning Paradise (Huoshao Honglian Si); Full Contact (Xia Dao Gao Fei); Maximum Risk; Twin Dragons (Shuanglong Hui).*

Lam, Steffan *Paperback Vigilante.*

Lamb, Jan *4 Faces of Eve (4 [Si] Mian Xiawa).*

Lambert, Mary *Grand Isle; In Crowd, The; Pet Sematary; Siesta.*

Lamont, Charles *Bowery to Broadway.*

Lamore, Marsh *Mighty Mouse in the Great Space Chase; Secret of the Sword, The.*

Lamprecht, Gerhard *Somewhere in Berlin... (Iregendwo in Berlin...).*

Lamy, Benoît *Vie est belle, La; Wild Games (Combat des Fauves/Der Mann im Lift).*

Lancaster, Burt *Kentuckian, The; Midnight man, The.*

Landers, Lew *Boogie Man Will Get You, The; Return of the Vampire, The.*

Landers, Lew (as Louis Friendlander) *Raven, The.*

Landis, John *Amazon Women on the Moon; American Werewolf in London, An; Beverly Hills Cop III; Blues Brothers, The; Blues Brothers 2000; Coming to America; Innocent Blood; Into the Night; Kentucky Fried Movie, The; National Lampoon's Animal House; Oscar; Spies Like Us; Stupids, The; ¡Three Amigos!; Trading Places; Twilight Zone – The Movie.*

Landres, Paul *Go, Johnny, Go!; Return of Dracula, The (aka the Fantastic Disappearing Man).*

Landy, Ruth *Dark Circle.*

Lane, Andrew *Jake Speed.*

Lane, Charles *Sidewalk Stories; True Identity.*

Lane, Rocky *All's Fair.*

Lanfield, Sidney *Hound of the Baskervilles, The; King of Burlesquep; My Favorite Blonde; One in a Million; Thin Ice (aka Lovely to Look at); You'll Never Get Rich.*

Lang, Fritz *American Guerilla in the Philippines (aka I Shall Return); Beyond a Reasonable Doubt; Big Heat, The; Blue Gardenia, The; Clash By Night; Cloak and Dagger; Destiny (Der müde Tod); Dr Mabuse, the Gambler (Dr Mabuse, der Spieler); Fury; Hangmen Also Die!; House by the River; Human Desire; M; Man Hunt; Metropolis* (1926); *Metropolis* (1926/1984); *Ministry of Fear; Moonfleet; Nibelungen, Die; Rancho Notorious; Return of Frank James, The; Scarlet Street; Secret Beyond the Door...; Spinnen, Die (The Spiders); Spione (Spies/The Spy); 1000 Eyes of Dr Mabuse, The (Die Tausend Augen des Dr Mabuse); Testament of Dr Mabuse, The (Das Testament des Dr Mabuse); Tiger of Eschnapur, The (Der Tiger von Eschnapur) [Part I]/ The Indian Tomb (Das Indische Grabmal) [Part II]; Western Union; While the City Sleeps; Woman in the Moon (Frau im Mond); Woman in the Window, The; You and Me; You Only Live Once.*

Lang, Krzysztof *Paper Marriage.*

Lang, Michel *A Nous les Petites Anglaises!; Hôtel de la Plage, L'.*

Lang, Richard *Change of Seasons, A.*

Lang, Samantha *Monkey's Mask, The (aka Poetry, Sex); Well, The.*

Lang, Walter *Can-Can; Cheaper by the Dozen; Desk Set (aka His Other Woman); Greenwich Village; King and I, The; Mighty Barnum, The; Mother Wore Tights; Sentimental Journey; Sitting Pretty; State Fair (aka It Happened One Summer); There's No Business Like Show Business; With a Song in My Heart.*

Langer, Carole *Joe Albany...A Jazz Life.*

Langley, Noel *Our Girl Friday (aka The Adventures of Sadie).*

Langton, Simon *Whistle Blower, The.*

Lankesh, Kavitha *Deveeri.*

Lanza, Anthony M *Glory Stompers, The.*

Lanzac, Frédéric *Le Sexe qui Parle (Pussy Talk).*

Lanzmann, Claude *Shoah.*

Lapine, James *Impromptu.*

Laplaine, José *Macadam Tribu.*

Laplaine, Zeka *Paris: XY.*

Lara, Gerardo *One Lost Year (Un Año Perdido).*

Larkin, John *Quiet Please, Murder.*

Larrain, Ricardo *Enthusiasm (El Entusiasmo); Frontera, La.*

Larraz, Joseph/José *Golden Lady, The; Symptoms (aka The Blood Virgin).*

Lasseter, John *Bug's Life, A; Toy Story; Toy Story 2.*

Lathan, Stan *Beat Street.*

Lattuada, Alberto *Luci del Varietà (Lights of Variety/Variety Lights).*

Lau, Andrew *Stormriders, The (Feng Yun Xiongba Tianxia); Man Called Hero, A (Zhonghua Yingxiong); Sausalito (Yi Jian Zhongqing); Young and Dangerous (Guhuozai zhi Ren zai Jianghu); Young and Dangerous 2 (Guhuozai 2 zhi Menglong Guo Jiang); Young and Dangerous 3 (Guhuozai 3 zhi Zhishou Zhetian).*

Lauder, Al *Paolozzi Story, The.*

Laughlin, Tom (Frank Laughlin) *Master Gunfighter, The.*

Laughlin, Michael *Strange Invaders.*

Laughton, Charles *Night of the Hunter, The.*

Lau Kar-Leung (aka Liu Jialiang) *Dirty Ho (Lantou He); 8-Diagram Pole Fighter, The (Wulang Bagua Gun/aka The Invincible Pole Fighters); Executioners from Shaolin (Hong Xiguan); My Young Auntie (Zhangbei);*

36th Chamber of Shaolin, The (Shaolin Sanshiliu Fang).

Lau Kun Wai *Mr Vampire (Jiangshi Xiansheng).*

Launder, Frank *Belles of St Trinian's, The; Blue Lagoon, The; Blue Murder at St Trinian's' Bridal Path, The; Captain Boycott; Folly To Be Wise; Geordie (aka Wee Geordie); Happiest Days of Your Life, The; I See a Dark Stranger (aka The Adventuress); Lady Godiva Rides Again; Millions Like Us; Pure Hell of Trinian's, The; Two Thousand Women; Wildcats of St Trinian's, The.*

Laurent, Christine *Vertiges.*

Laurenti, Mariano *Vices in the Family (Vizio de Famiglia).*

Lauritzen, Lau *People of the North Sea (Vester-Vov-Vov).*

Lautner, Georges *Cage aux Folles III: The Wedding, La (La Cage aux Folles: Elles se Marient); Road to Salina (Sur la Route de Salina); Seins de glace, Les (Someone Is Bleeding).*

Lauzier, Gérard *Mon Père, ce héros.*

Lauzon, Jean-Claude *Léolo; Night Zoo (Un Zoo la Nuit).*

Laven, Arnold *Down Three Dark Streets; Glory Guys, The; Rough Night in Jericho; Sam Whiskey.*

Law, Clara *Autumn Moon (Qiuyue); Erotique; Floating Life; Goddess of 1967, The.*

Law, Jude *Tube Tales.*

Lawrence, Quentin *Cash on Demand.*

Lawrence, Martin *Thin Line Between Love and Hate, A.*

Lawrence, Ray *Bliss.*

Layton, Joe *Richard Pryor Live on the Sunset Strip.*

Lazarus, Ashley *Golden Rendezvous; e'Lollipop.*

Lazzaretti, Fabrizio *Jung (War) – in the Land of the Mujaheddin (Jung (Giang) – nella Terra dei Mujaheddin).*

Lea, Frances *Everyone's Happy.*

Leach, Wilford *Pirates of Penzance, The.*

Leacock, Philip *Brave Don't Cry, The; Kidnappers, The (aka The Little Kidnappers); Spanish Gardener, The.*

Leacock, Richard *Jane.*

Leader, Anton M *Children of the Damned.*

Leahy, Gillian *My Life Without Steve.*

Lean, David *Blithe Spirit; Bridge on the River Kwai, The; Brief Encounter; Doctor Zhivago; Great Expectations; Hobson's Choice; In Which We Serve; Lawrence of Arabia; Madeleine; Major Barbara; Oliver Twist; Passage to India, A; Passionate Friends, The (aka One Woman's Story); Ryan's Daughter; Sound Barrier, The (aka Breaking the Sound Barrier); Summertime (aka Summer Madness); This Happy Breed.*

Lear, Norman *Cold Turkey.*

Le Chanois, Jean-Paul *Misérables, Les.*

Leconte, Jean-Louis *Pierre dans la Bouche, Une (aka Le Fugitif).*

Leconte, Patrice *Bronzés, Les; Contre l'Oubli (Against Oblivion); Girl on the Bridge, The (La Fille sur le Pont); Hairdresser's Husband, The (Le Mari de la coiffeuse); Lumière et Compagnie; Monsieur Hire; Parfum d'Yvonne, Le; Ridicule; Tango; Veuve de Saint-Pierre, La (The Widow of Saint Pierre); Viens chez moi, j'habite chez une copine.*

L'Ecuyer, John *Curtis's Charm.*

Leder, Mimi, *Deep Impact; Pay It Forward; Peacemaker, The.*

Leduc, Jacques *Tendresse Ordinaire, La (Ordinary Tenderness).*

Leduc, Paul *Dollar Mambo; Reed: Insurgent Mexico (Reed: México Insurgente).*

Lee, Bruce *Way of the Dragon, The (Meng Long Guo Jiang/aka Return of the Dragon).*

Lee Chang-Dong *Green Fish (Chorok Mulgoki); Peppermint Candy (Bakha Satang).*

Lee Chi-Ngai *Sleepless Town (Fuya Jyo).*

Lee, Evan *Revenge of the Dead.*

Lee, Iara *Modulations.*

Lee, Jack *Captain's Table, The; Once a Jolly Swagman (aka Maniacs on Wheels); Town Like Alice, A (aka The Rape of Malaya); Wooden Horse, The.*

Lee, Joe *Courier, The.*

Lee Kwang-Mo *Spring in My Hometown (Areumdaun Sijeol).*

Lee Lik-Chee *Shaolin Soccer (Shaolin Zuqiu/aka Kung-fu Soccer).*

Lee, Malcolm D *Best Man, The.*

Lee Min-Yong *Hot Roof, A (Gyaegotun Nalui Ohu).*

Lee Myung-Se *First Love (Chut Sarang); Nowhere to Hide (Injong Sajong Polkot Opta).*

Lee, Rowland V *One Rainy Afternoon; Son of Frankenstein; Zoo in Budapest.*

Lee, Spike *Bamboozled; Clockers; Crooklyn; Do the Right Thing; 4 Little Girls; Get on the Bus; Girl 6; He Got Game; Jungle Fever; Lumière et Compagnie; Malcolm X; Mo' Better Blues; Original Kings of Comedy, The; School Daze; She's Gotta Have It; Summer of Sam; Ten Minutes Older – The Trumpet.*

Lee Suh-Goon *Rub Love.*

Lee, Thomas *see* Hill, Walter

Leeds, Herbert I *Cisco Kid and the Lady, The; Return of the Cisco Kid, The; Time to Kill.*

Leenhardt, Roger *Dernières Vacances, Les.*

Leetch, Tom *Return of the Big Cat.*

Lefebvre, Jean-Pierre *Wild Flowers (Les Fleurs Sauvages).*

Léger, Fernand *Dreams That Money Can Buy.*

Legrand, François (Franz Antel) *Confessions of a Bigamist (Warum hab'ich bloss 2 x ja gesagt); Knickers Ahoy (Frau Wirtins tolle Töchterlein).*

Le Grice, Malcolm *Emily – Third Party Speculation.*

Le Guay, Philippe *Année Juliette, L'; Nightshift (Trois Huit).*

Le Hénaff, René *Colonel Chabert, Le.*

Lehmann, Maurice *Affaire du Courrier de Lyon, L'.*

Lehmann, Michael *Airheads; Heathers; Hudson Hawk; Meet the Applegates; My Giant; Truth About Cats & Dogs, The.*

Lehto, Pekka *Flame Top (Tulipää).*

Leifer, Neil *Yesterday's Hero.*

Leigh, Mike *All or Nothing; Bleak Moments; Career Girls; Four Days in July; High Hopes; Life Is Sweet; Naked; Secrets & Lies; Topsy Turvy.*

Leight, Warren *Night We Never Met, The.*

Leiner, Danny *Dude, Where's My Car?*

Leisen, Mitchell *Arise, My Love; Bride of Vengeance; Easy Living; Frenchman's Creek; Girl Most Likely, The; Hands Across the Table; Hold Back the Dawn; Kitty; Lady in the Dark; Midnight; Murder at the Vanities; No Man of Her Own; Remember the Night.*

Leiser, Erwin *Deutschland, Erwache! (Germany, Awake!).*

Leitch, Christopher *Courage Mountain; Teen Wolf Too.*

Leland, David *Big Man, The; Checking Out; Land Girls, The; Wish You Were Here.*

Lelouch, Claude *And Now My Love (Toute une Vie); Autre Homme une Autre Chance, Un (Another Man, Another Woman/Another Man, Another Chance); Bonne Année, La (Happy New Year); Chance or Coincidence (Hasards ou coïncidences); Edith and Marcel (Edith et Marcel); Far from Vietnam (Loin du Viêt-nam); Homme et une Femme, Un (A Man and a Woman); Lumière et Compagnie; Men, Women: User's Manual (Hommes Femmes Mode d'emploi); Misérables, Les (aka Les Misérables du vingtième siècle); Second Chance (Si c'était à refaire); Tout ça… pour ça!!!; Uns et les Autres, Les (Bolero/The Ins and the Outs); Visions of Eight; Viva la Vie; Vivre pour Vivre (Live for Life).*

Le Masson, Yann *Kashima Paradise.*

Lemmon, Jack *Kotch.*

Lemmons, Kasi *Eve's Bayou.*

Lemoine, Michel *Invitation to Bed (Les Confidences Erotiques d'un Lit Trop Accueillant); Seven Women for Satan (Les Weekends Maléfiques du Comte Zaroff).*

Lemon, Lizzie *UndeRage.*

Lemont, John *And Women Shall Weep; Frightened City, The; Konga.*

Leni, Paul *Cat and the Canary, The; Waxworks (Das Wachsfiguren-kabinett).*

Lenzi, Umberto *Paranoia (Orgasmo).*

Leo, Malcolm *It Came from Hollywood; This Is Elvis.*

Leonard, Brett *Lawnmower Man, The.*

Leonard, Robert Z *After Office Hours; B.F.'s Daughter; Bribe, The; I n the Good Old Summertime; New Moon; Pride and Prejudice; When Ladies Meet; Ziegfeld Girl.*

Leone, John *Last of the Cowboys, The (aka The Great Smokey Roadblock).*

Leone, Sergio *Colosuss of Rhodes, The (Il Colosso di Rodi); Fistful of Dollars, A (Per un Pugno di Dollari); For a Few Dollars More (Per Qualche Dollari in Più); Giù la Testa (Duck, You Sucker/A Fistful of Dynamite/Once Upon a Time – the Revolution); Good, the Bad and the Ugly, The (Il Buono, il Brutto, il Cattivo); Once Upon a Time in America; Once Upon a Time in the West (C'era una Volta il West).*

Leonetti, John R *Mortal Kombat 2: Annihilation.*

Lepage, Marquise *Marie s'en va-t-en ville (Marie in the City).*

Lepage, Robert *Confessional, The (Le Confessionnal); Nô; Polygraph, The (Le Polygraphe); Possible Worlds.*

Le Pêcheur, Didier *Des Nouvelles du Bon Dieu (News from the Good Lord).*

Le Péron, Serge *Marcorelle Affair, The (L'Affaire Marcorelle).*

Lerner, Irving *City of Fear; Murder by Contract; Royal Hunt of the Sun, The.*

Lerner, Murray *From Mao to Mozart: Isaac Stern in China; Message to Love: The Isle of Wight Festival.*

Lerner, Richard *What Happened to Kerouac?*

LeRoy, Mervyn *Anthony Adverse; Bad Seed, The; Blossoms in the Dust; Devil at 4 O'Clock, The; Escape; Five Star Final; Gold Diggers of 1933; Gypsy; Hard to Handle; Hi, Nellie!; I Am a Fugitive from a Chain Gang; Johnny Eager; Little Caesar; Madame Curie; Mister Roberts; Page Miss Glory; Quo Vadis?; Random Harvest; They Won't Forget; Toward the Unknown (aka Brink of Hell); Tugboat Annie.*

Leroy, Serge *Shattered (Les Passagers).*

Leslie, Alfred *Pull My Daisy.*

Lessac, Michael *House of Cards (La Voce del Silenzio).*

Lester, Mark L *Armed and Dangerous; Class of 1984; Commando; Firestarter; Stunts; Truck Stop Women.*

Lester, Richard *Bed Sitting Room, The; Butch and Sundance: The Early Days; Cuba; Finders Keepers; Four Musketeers: The Revenge of Milady, The; Funny Thing Happened on the Way to the Forum, A; Get Back; Hard Day's Night, A; Help!; How I Won the War; It's Trad, Dad!; Juggernaut; Knack…and how to get it, The; Mouse on the Moon, The; Petulia; Ritz, The; Return of the Musketeers, The; Robin and Marian; Royal Flash; Superman II; Superman III; Three Musketeers: The Queen's Diamonds, The.*

Leszczylowski, Michal *Directed by Andrei Tarkovsky (Regi – Andrej Tarkovskij).*

Leterrier, François *Garde du Corps, Le (The Bodyguard); Goodbye Emmanuelle.*

Leth, Jørgen *Sunday in Hell, A (En Forårsdag i Helvede).*

Leto, Marco *Black Holiday (La Villeggiatura).*

Lettich, Sheldon *A.W.O.L.; Double Impact; Only the Strong.*

Letts, Don *Punk Rock Movie, The.*

Leung, Patrick *Task Force (Rexue Zuiqiang).*

Levant, Brian *Beethoven; Flintstones; Flintstones in Viva Rock Vegas, The; Jingle All the Way; Problem Child 2.*

Leven, Jeremy *Don Juan DeMarco.*

Levey, Jay *UHF.*

Levey, William A *Slumber Party '57.*

Levin, Henry *Ambushers, The; Bandit of Sherwood Forest, The; Dark Avenger, The (aka Warriors); Journey to the Centre of the Earth; Man from Colorado, The; That Man Bolt.*

Levin, Mark *Slam.*

Levin, Sid *Let the Good Times Roll.*

Levinson, Barry *Avalon; Bandits; Bugsy; Diner; Disclosure; Everlasting Piece, An; Good Morning Vietnam; Jimmy Hollywood; Liberty Heights; Natural, The; Rain Man; Sleepers; Sphere; Tin Men; Toys; Wag the Dog; Young Sherlock Holmes (Young Sherlock Holmes and the Pyramid of Fear).*

Levitow, Abe *Phantom Tollbooth, The.*

Levring, Kristian *King Is Alive, The.*

Levy, Ben W *Lord Camber's Ladies.*

Lévy, Bernard-Henri *Bosna!*

Levy, Dani *I Was on Mars.*

Levy, Don *Herostratus.*

Levy, Gerry *Body Stealers, The (aka Thin Air/Invasion of the Body Stealers).*

Levy, Jacques *Oh! Calcutta!*

Levy, Jefery *S.F.W.*

Levy, Ralph *Do Not Disturb.*

Lewenz, Lisa *Letter Without Words, A.*

Lewin, Albert *Moon and Sixpence, The; Pandora and the Flying Dutchman; Picture of Dorian Gray, The; Private Affairs of Bel Ami, The; Saadia.*

Lewin, Ben *Favour, the Watch and the Very Big Fish, The (Rue Saint-Sulpice); Lucky Break; Welcome to Britain.*

Lewis, Cullen (Lewis D Collins) *Desert Trail, The.*

Lewis, Everett *Skin & Bone.*

Lewis, George B *Humanoid, The (L'Umanoide).*

Lewis, Gough *Sex – The Annabel Chong Story.*

Lewis, Herschell Gordon *Color Me Blood Red.*

Lewis, Jerry *Bellboy, The; Big Mouth, The; Family Jewels, The; Ladies' Man, The; Nutty Professor, The; One More Time; Patsy, The; Which Way to the Front? (aka Ja, Ja, Mein General! But Which Way to the Front?).*

Lewis, Jim *Heartland Reggae.*

Lewis, Jonathan *Before Hindsight.*

Lewis, Joseph H *Big Combo, The; Cry of the Hunted; Desperate Search; Gun Crazy (aka Deadly Is the Female); Halliday Brand, The; Lady Without Passport, A; Lawless Street, A; Mad Doctor of Market Street, The; My Name Is Julia Ross; Retreat, Hell!; 7th Cavalry; So Dark the Night; Terror in a Texas Town; That Gang of Mine; Undercover Man, The.*

Lewis, Mark *Cane Toads – An Unnatural History.*

Lewis, Robert Michael *Alpha Caper, The (aka Inside Job).*

L'Herbier, Marcel *Argent, L'; El Dorado; Forfaiture (Obligation); Inhumaine, L'; Nuit fantastique, La (The Fantastic Night).*

Li Hsing *Execution in Autumn (Qiu Jue).*

Li Shaohong *Blush (Hongfen); Family Portrait (Sishi Buhuo); Bloody Morning (Xuese Qingchen).*

Li Yu *Fish and Elephant (Yu he Daxiang/aka Jin Nian Xiatian).*

Li Zuonan *Fist of Fury Part II (Jingwu Men Xuji).*

Liddy, Kevin *Country.*

Lieberman, Jeff *Blue Sunshine; Squirm.*

Lieberman, Robert *All I Want for Christmas; Fire in the Sky; Table for Five.*

Lifshitz, Sébastien *Presque rien; Terres Froides, Les (Cold Lands).*

Light, Allie *Dialogues With Madwomen.*

Lim Kwon-Taek *Village in the Mist (Angemaeul).*

Lima, Kevin *Goofy Movie, A; 102 Dalmatians; Tarzan.*

Lima Jr, Walter *Oyster and the Wind, The (A ostra e o vento).*

Liman, Doug *Go; Swingers.*

Lin Bing *Legend of Bruce Lee (Xin Siwang Youxi/aka The New Game of Death).*

Lin Cheng-Sheng *Betelnut Beauty (Ai Ni Ai Wo); Drifting Life, A (Chunhua Menglu); Murmur of Youth (Meili zai Chang-ge); Sweet Degeneration (Fang Lang).*

Lin Ch'ing-Chieh *Student Days (Xuesheng zhi Ai).*

Lindblad, Christian *Ripa Hits the Skids (Ripa Ruostuu).*

Lindblom, Gunnel *Summer Paradise (Paradistorg).*

Linder, Maud *Homme au Chapeau de Soie, L' (The Man in the Silk Hat).*

Lindqvist, Jan *Tupamaros.*

Lindsay, Caleb *Chasing Dreams; Understanding Jane.*

Lindsay-Hogg, Michael *Frankie Starlight; Guy; Let It Be; Nasty Habits; Object of Beauty; Waiting for Godot.*

Lindström, Jon *Dreaming of Rita (Drömmen om Rita).*

Ling Zifeng *Ripples Across Stagnant Water (Sishui Wei Lan).*

Link, Caroline *Beyond Silence (Jenseits der Stille).*

Linklater, Richard *Before Sunrise; Dazed and Confused; Newton Boys, The; Slacker; SubUrbia; Waking Life.*

Linson, Art *Where the Buffalo Roam.*

Lion, Mickey *House of Exorcism, The (La Casa dell'Esorcismo).*

Lioret, Philippe *Tombes du Ciel (Lost in Transit).*

Lipmann, Eric *Bisexual (Les Onze Mille Verges).*

Lipscomb, James *Blue Water, White Death.*

Lipsky, Oldrich *Nick Carter in Prague (Adela Jeste Nevecerela/aka Adele Hasn't Had Her Supper Yet).*

Lipstadt, Aaron *Android.*

Lisberger, Steven M *Animalympics, Slipstream; Tron.*

Litner, Heseng Noung *Sacrifice.*

Litten, Peter *Living Doll.*

Litten, Peter Mackenzie *To Die For.*

Littín, Miguel *Alsino and the Condor (Alsino y el Condor); Jackal of Nahueltoro, The (El Chacal de Nahueltoro); Naufragos, Los (Shipwrecked).*

Little, Dwight H *Free Willy 2; Halloween 4: The Return of Michael Myers; Marked for Death; Murder at 1600; Phantom of the Opera; Rapid Fire.*

Littlewood, Joan *Sparrows Can't Sing.*

Littman, Lynne *Testament.*

Litvak, Anatole *All This and Heaven Too; Amazing Doctor Clitterhouse, The; Anastasia; Castle on the Hudson (aka Years Without Days); Confessions of a Nazi Spy; Lady in the Car with Glasses and a Gun, The (La Dame dans l'auto avec des lunettes et un fusil); Long Night, The; Mayerling; Night of the Generals, The; Out of the Fog; Sisters, The; Snake Pit, The; Sorry, Wrong Number; This Above All; Tovarich.*

Liu Bingjian *Cry-Woman (Kuqi Nüren); Men and Women (Nanna nünü).*

Liu Jialiang *see* Lau Kar-Leung.

Lively, Gerry *Darkness Falls.*

Livingston, Jennie *Paris Is Burning.*

Lizzani, Carlo *Crazy Joe; Prostitution Racket, The (Storie di Vita e Malavita).*

Llobet Gracia, Lorenzo *Life in Shadows (Vida en Sombras).*

Llorca, Pablo *Jardines Colgantes (Hanging Gardens).*

Llosa, Luis *Anaconda; Sniper; Specialist, The.*

Lloyd, Frank *Blood on the Sun; Cavalcade; Last Command, The; Mutiny on the Bounty.*

Lloyd, Ian FH *Face of Darkness, The.*

Lo Chi-Leung *Viva Erotica! (Seqing Nan Nü).*

Lo Wei *Back Alley Princes (Malu Xiao Yingxiong); Big Boss, The (Tangshan Daxiong/aka Fists of Fury); Fist of Fury (Jingwu Men/aka The Chinese Connection); Kung Fu Girl, The (Tiewa/aka None But the Brave).*

Loach, Ken (Kenneth) *Black Jack; Bread and Roses; Carla's Song; Fatherland; Family Life; Gamekeeper, The; Hidden Agenda; Kes; Ladybird Ladybird; Land and Freedom; Looks and Smiles; My Name Is Joe; Poor Cow; Raining Stones; Riff-Raff; Sweet Sixteen.*

Loader, Jayne *Atomic Café, The.*

Locke, Sondra *Impulse; Ratboy.*

Loden, Barbara *Wanda.*

Loftis, Norman *Small Time.*

Logan, Joshua *Bus Stop; Camelot; Ensign Pulver; Fanny; Paint Your Wagon; Picnic; Sayonara; South Pacific.*

Lombardi, Francisco J *Don't Tell Anyone (No se lo digas a nadie); Lion's Den, The (La Boca del Lobo); Sin Compasión (Sans Pitié).*

Lombardo, Lou *Russian Roulette.*

Lommel, Ulli *Brainwaves; Tenderness of the Wolves (Zärtlichkeit der Wölfe).*

Loncraine, Richard *Bellman and True; Brimstone and Treacle; Flame; Full Circle (aka The Haunting of Julia); Missionary, The; Richard III.*

Lonergan, Kenneth *You Can Count on Me.*

London, Jerry *Shogun.*

Long, Stanley *Adventures of a Private Eye; On the Game.*

Longinotto, Kim *Cross and Passion; Gaea Girls; Good Wife of Tokyo, The; Theatre Girls; UndeRage.*

Longo, Robert *Johnny Mnemonic.*

Lopez, Temistocles *Chain of Desire.*

López Moctezuma, Juan *House of Madness (La Mansión de la Locura).*

Lophushansky, Konstantin *Letters from a Dead Man (Pisma Myortvovo Chelovyeka).*

Lorentz, Pare *Plow That Broke the Plains, The.*

Lord, Chip *Motorist.*

Lord, Jean-Claude *Tadpole and the Whale; Visiting Hours.*

Lord, Peter *Chicken Run.*

Loreau, Dominique *Divine Body (Divine Carcasse).*

Lorenzo, Santiago *My Silly Mother (Mamá es boba).*

Lorre, Peter *Verlorene, Der (The Lost One).*

Losey, Joseph *Accident; Assassination of Trotsky, The; Big Night, The; Blind Date (aka Chance Meeting); Boom; Boy with Green Hair, The; Criminal, The (aka The Concrete Jungle); Damned, The (aka These Are the Damned); Doll's House, A; Don Giovanni; Eve; Figures in a Landscape; Galileo; Go-Between, The; Gypsy and the Gentleman, The; King & Country; Lawless, The (aka The Dividing Line); M; Modesty Blaise; Mr Klein; Prowler, The; Romantic Englishwoman, The; Secret Ceremony; Servant, The; Sleeping Tiger, The; Steaming; Time Without Pity; Trout, The (La Truite).*

Losey, Joseph (as Joseph Walton) *Intimate Stranger, The (aka Finger of Guilt).*

Lotianou, Emil *Pavlova – A Woman for All Time (aka Anna Pavlova).*

Lou Ye *Suzhou (Suzhou He/aka Suzhou River).*

Louhichi, Taïeb *Wedding Moon (Noces de lune).*

Louise, Fhiona *Cold Light of Day, The.*

Lounguine, Pavel *Taxi Blues; Wedding, The (La Noce).*

Lounsbery, John *Rescuers, The.*

Lourié, Eugène *Beast from 20,000 Fathoms, The; Colossus of New York, The; Gorgo.*

Louvish, Simon *To Live in Freedom.*

Love, Nick *Goodbye Charlie Bright.*

Low, Adam *Kurosawa.*

Low, Steven *Across the Sea of Time: A New York Adventure.*

Lowenstein, Richard *Dogs in Space; Say a Little Prayer; Strikebound.*

Lowenthal, John *Trials of Alger Hiss, The.*

Lowney, Declan *Time Will Tell; Wild About Harry.*

Loy, Nanni *Why? (Detenuto in Attesa di Giudizio).*

Lozinski, Pawel *100 Years of Polish Cinema (100 Lat w Kine).*

Lu Yue *Mr Zhao (Zhao Xiansheng).*

Lu Wei *Journey to the Western Xia, The (Xi Xia Lu Tiatiao).*

Lubin, Arthur *Footsteps in the Fog; Francis; Phantom of the Opera; Rhubarb.*

Lubitsch, Ernst *Angel; Bluebeard's Eighth Wife; Cluny Brown; Design for Living; Heaven Can Wait; If I Had a Million; Monte Carlo; Ninotchka; One Hour With You; Shop Around the Corner, The; Sumurun (One Arabian Night); To Be or Not To Be; Trouble in Paradise.*

Lucas, George *American Graffiti; Star Wars; Star Wars Episode I: The Phantom Menace; Star Wars Episode II Attack of the Clones; Star Wars, Episode IV, a New Hope; THX 1138.*

Lucas, Kevin *Black River.*

Lucchi, Angela Ricci *From Pole to Equator (Dal Polo all'Equatore).*

Luchetti, Daniele *Footman, The (Il Portaborse); School (la Scuola).*

Lucidi, Maurizio *Scicilian Cross (Gli Esecutori).*

Lucien, Oscar *Colour of Love (Piel).*

Ludwig, Edward *Fighting Seabees, The; Last Gangster, The.*

Luhrmann, Baz *Moulin Rouge; Strictly Ballroom; William Shakespeare's Romeo & Juliet.*

Luketic, Robert *Legally Blonde.*

Lumet, Sidney *Anderson Tapes, The; Bye Bye Braverman; Child's Play; Daniel; Close to Eden; Deadly Affair, The; Deathtrap; Dog Day Afternoon; Equus; Fail Safe; Family Business; Fugitive Kind, The; Gloria; Group, The; Guilty as Sin; Hill, The; Long Day's Journey Into Night; Lovin' Molly; Morning After, The; Murder on the Orient Express; Network; Night Falls on Manhattan; Offence, The; Pawnbroker, The; Power; Prince of the City; Q&A; Running on Empty; Sea Gull, The; Serpico; 12 Angry Men; Verdict. The; Wiz, The.*

Lupino, Ida *Bigamist, The; Hard, Fast and Beautiful; Hitch-hiker, The.*

Lupo, Michele *Man to Respect, A (Un Uomo da Rispettare/aka The Master Touch).*

Luraschi, Tony *Outsider, The.*

Lurie, Rod *Contender, The; Last Castle, The.*

Luruli, Ntshavheni Wa *Chikin Bizniz.*

Lusk, Don *GoBots: Battle of the Rocklords.*

Luske, Hamilton *Lady and the Tramp; One Hundred and One Dalmatians; Peter Pan; Pinocchio.*

Lussanet, Paul de *Dear Boys (Lieve Jongens).*

Lussier, Patrick *Dracula 2000 (aka Dracula 2001).*

Lustig, William *Hit List; Maniac Cop; Maniac Cop 2; Relentless.*

Lutsik, Petr *Outskirts (Okraina).*

Lye, Len *Tusalava.*

Lynch, David *Blue Velvet; Dune; Elephant Man, The; Eraserhead; Lost Highway; Lumière et Compagnie; Mulholland Dr.; Straight Story, The; Twin Peaks; Twin Peaks: Fire Walk with Me; Wild at Heart.*

Lynch, Jennifer Chambers *Boxing Helena.*

Lynch, John *Night Train.*

Lynch, Paul *Prom Night.*

Lynd, Laurie *House.*

Lyne, Adrian *Fatal Attraction; Flashdance; Foxes; Indecent Proposal; Jacob's Ladder; Lolita; Nine ½ Weeks.*

Lynn, Jonathan *Clue; Distinguished Gentleman, The; My Cousin Vinny; Nuns on the Run; Sgt Bilko; Trial and Error; Whole Nine Yards, The.*

Lyon, Danny *Niños Abandonados, Los.*

Lyon, Nelson *Telephone Book, The.*

Lyssy, Rolf *Konfrontation – Assassination in Davos (Konfrontation); Swissmakers, The (Die Schweizermacher).*

Ma, Jingle *Tokyo Raiders (Dongjing Gonglüe).*

Maan, Shakila Taranum *Quiet Desperation, A.*

Maanouni, Ahmed El *Trances (El Hal).*

Maas, Dick *Amsterdamned; Lift, The (De Lift).*

Maben, Adrian *Pink Floyd Live at Pompeii (Pink Floyd à Pompéi).*

MacAdams, Lewis *What Happened to Kerouac?*

McAnuff, Des *Adventures of Rocky & Bullwinkle, The; Cousin Bette.*

McBride, Jim *Big Easy, The; Breathless; David Holzman's Diary; Great Balls of Fire!; Hot Times; Wrong Man, The.*

Mac Caig, Arthur *Patriot Game, The.*

McCall, Anthony *Sigmund Freud's Dora.*

McCall, Rod *Lewis & Clark & George.*

McCallum, John *Nickel Queen.*

McCarey, Leo *Affair to Remember, An; Awful Truth, The; Bells of St Mary's, The; Duck Soup; Going My Way; Kid from Spain, The; Once Upon a Honeymoon; Rally 'round the Flag, Boys!; Ruggles of Red Gap; Satan Never Sleeps (aka The Devil Never Sleeps).*

McCarey, Raymond *Pack Up Your Troubles.*

McCarten, Anthony *Via Satellite.*

MacCarthy, Gerard Michael *Micha.*

McCarthy, Michael *Operation Amsterdam.*

McCarthy, Todd *Visions of Light.*

MacCartney, Sydney *Bridge, The.*

McCay, Jim *Girls Town.*

McClatchy, Gregory *Vampire at Midnight.*

McConnell, Mick *Betty's Brood.*

McCord, Jonas *Body, The.*

McCormack, Dan (see also Usher, Selig) *Minotaur.*

McCowan, George *Frogs; Magnificent Seven Ride!, The; Shadow of the Hawk; Shape of Things to Come, The.*

McCullough Sr, Jim *Aurora Encounter, The.*

MacDonald, David *Bad Lord Byron, The; Cairo Road; Christopher Columbus; Petticoat Pirates.*

MacDonald, Hettie *Beautiful Thing.*

Macdonald, Kevin *Donald Cammell: The Ultimate Performance; One Day in September.*

Macdonald, Peter *Mo' Money; NeverEnding Story III: Escape from Fantasia, The; Rambo III.*

McDougall, Charles *Arrivederci Millwall; Heart; Tube Tales.*

McDougall, Don *Spider Man – The Dragon's Challenge.*

MacDougall, Ranald *Go Naked in the World; Subterraneans, The.*

McDowell, Curt *Thundercrack!*

McElwee, Ross *Sherman's March.*

McElwee, Vincent *Herbie Goes Bananas; Herbie Goes to Monte Carlo; Superdad; Treasure of Matecumbe.*

McEveety, Bernard *Napoleon and Samantha.*

McG [Joseph McGinty Nichol] *Charlie's Angels.*

McGehee, Scott *Deep End, The; Suture.*

MacGillivray, Greg *Dolphins.*

McGlynn, Don *Art Pepper: Notes from a Jazz Survivor; Charles Mingus: Triumph of the Underdog; Legend of Teddy Edwards, The; Louis Prima: The Wildest.*

McGoohan, Patrick *Catch My Soul.*

McGrath, Douglas *Emma.*

McGrath, John *Blood Red Roses.*

McGrath, Joseph *Bliss of Mrs Blossom, The; Casino Royale; Digby – the Biggest Dog in the World; Great McGonagall, The; Magic Christian, The; Rising Damp; 30 Is a Dangerous Age, Cynthia.*

McGrath, Liam *Southpaw.*

McGregor, Ewan *Tube Tales.*

McGuane, Thomas *92 in the Shade.*

McGuckian, Mary *Best; This Is the Sea.*

McGuigan, Paul *Acid House, The; Gangster No. 1.*

McGuire, Don *Delicate Delinquent, The.*

Machaty, Gustav *Erotikon; Extase (Ecstasy/aka Symphony of Love); From Saturday to Sunday (Ze Soboty na Nedeli).*

McHenry, Doug *Jason's Lyric.*

Machulski, Juliusz *Sex Mission, The (Seksmisja).*

McIntyre, CJ *Border Shootout.*

Mack, Earle *Children of Theatre Street, The.*

McKay, Craig *Subway Stories Tales from the Underground.*

McKellar, Don *Last Night.*

Mackendrick, Alexander *Don't Make Waves; High Wind in Jamaica, A; Ladykillers, The; 'Maggie', The (aka High and Dry); Mandy (aka Crash of Silence); Man in the White Suit, The; Sweet Smell of Success; Sammy Going South (aka A Boy Ten Feet Tall); Whisky Galore! (aka Tight Little Island).*

McKenzie, Brian *Stan and George's New Life.*

MacKenzie, John *Fourth Protocol, The; Honorary Consul, The (aka Beyond the Limit); Innocent, The; Last of the Finest, The (aka Blue Heat); Long Good Friday, The; Made; Ruby; Voyage; When the Sky Falls.*

Mackenzie, Midge *John Huston War Stories.*

McKimmie, Jackie *Waiting.*

MacKinnon, Gillies *Conquest of the South Pole; Grass Arena, The; Hideous Kinky; Playboys, The; Regeneration; Simple Twist of Fate, A; Small Faces; Trojan Eddie.*

Mackinnon, Stewart *Justine.*

McLaglen, Andrew V *Ballad of Josie, The; Bandolero!; Cahill – US Marshal; Chisum; Devil's Brigade, The; Last Hard Men, The; Mitchell; North Sea Hijack; Rare Breed, The; Return from the River Kwai; Sahara; Sea Wolves, The; Something Big; Undefeated, The; Way West, The; Wild Geese, The.*

McLaughlin, Sheila *Committed; She Must Be Seeing Things.*

Maclean, Alison *Crush; Jesus' Son; Subway Stories Tales from the Underground.*

McLean, Steve *Postcards from America.*

McLennan, Don *Mullaway; Slate, Wyn & Me.*

McLeod, Norman Z *Alice in Wonderland; Casanova's Big Night; Horse Feathers; If I Had a Million; It's a Gift; Monkey Business; Paleface, The; Secret Life of Walter Mitty, The; Topper.*

McLoughlin, Tom *Unsaid, The.*

MacMillan, Keith *Culture Club – A Kiss Across the Ocean; Exodus – Bob Marley Live.*

McMullen, Ken *1871; Ghost Dance; Zina.*

McMurchy, Megan *For Love or Money.*

McMurray, Mary *Assam Garden, The.*

McNally, David *Coyote Ugly.*

McNaught, Bob *Seawife.*

Macnaughton, Ian *And Now for Something Completely Different.*

McNaughton, John *Borrower, The; Henry: Portrait of a Serial Killer; Mad Dog and Glory; Normal Life; Wild Things.*

McPherson, Connor *Saltwater.*

McQuarrie, Christopher *Way of the Gun.*

McTiernan, John *Die Hard; Die Hard with a Vengeance; Hunt for Red October, The; Last Action Hero, The; Medicine Man; Predator; 13th Warrior, The; Thomas Crown Affair, The.*

Madden, David *Separate Lives.*

Madden, John *Captain Corelli's Mandolin; Ethan Frome; Mrs Brown; Shakespeare in Love.*

Maddin, Guy *Archangel; Careful; Heart of the World, The; Tales from the Gimli Hospital; Twilight of the Ice Nymphs.*

Maderna, Giovanni Davide *Imperfect Love (L'Amore Imperfetto).*

Madsen, Ole Christian *Kira's Reason – A Love Story (Ein Kærlighedshistorie).*

Maeso, José G *Order to Kill (El Clan de los Inmorales).*

Magar, Guy *Retribution; Stepfather III.*

Maggenti, Maria *Incredibly True Adveture of Two Girls in Love, The.*

Magnoli, Albert *Purple Rain; Take It Easy.*

Magnuson, John *Lenny Bruce Performance Film, The.*

Magra, Billy *Completely Pogued.*

Maguire, Sharon *Bridget Jones's Diary.*

Mahomo, Nana *Last Grave at Dimbaza.*

Mahoney, Robin *Glastonbury: The Movie.*

Mahurin, Matt *Mugshot.*

Mailer, Norman *Maidstone; Tough Guys Don't Dance.*

Maillet, Dominique *Roi de Paris, Le (The King of Paris).*

Main, Stewart *Desperate Remedies.*

Mainka, Maximiliane *Germany in Autumn (Deutschland im Herbst).*

Mainka-Jellinghaus, Beate *Germany in Autumn (Deutschland im Herbst).*

Maira, Salvatore *Love in the Mirror (Amor nello specchio).*

Mai Tai Kit *Wicked City, The (Yaoshou Dushi).*

Majewski, Lech *Prisoner of Rio.*

Majidi, Majid *Children of Heaven (Bacheha-Ye aseman); Colour of Paradise, The (Ranghe Khoda); Father, The (Pedar).*

Makavejev, Dusan *Coca Cola Kid, The; Gorilla Bathes at Noon; Innocence Unprotected (Nevinost Bez Zastite); Manifesto; Man Is Not a Bird (Covek nije Tica); Montenegro; Sweet Movie; Switchboard Operator, The (Ljubavni Slucaj); W.R. – Mysteries of the Organism (W.R. – Misterije Organizma).*

Makhmalbaf, Mohsen *Cyclist, The; Gabbeh; Kandahar (Safar é Ghandehar); Moment of Innocence (Noon va Goldoon); Peddler, The (Dastforoush); Silence, The; Tales of the Kish (Ghessé Hayé Kish).*

Makhmalbaf, Samira *Apple, The; Blackboards (Takhté Siah).*

Makin, Kelly *Kids in the Hall: Brain Candy; Mickey Blue Eyes.*

Makk, Károly *Another Way (Egymásra nézve); Gambler, The; Love (Szerelem); Very Moral Night, A (Egy Erkölcsös Ejszaka).*

Malatesta, Guido *Maciste Contro i Mostri (Colossus of the Stone Age/Fire Monsters Against the Son of Hercules/Land of the Monsters).*

Malick, Terrence *Badlands; Days of Heaven; Thin Red Line, The.*

Malle, Louis *Alamo Bay; Amants, Les (The Lovers); ...and the pursuit of happiness; Ascenseur pour l'Echafaud (Frantic/Lift to the Scaffold); Atlantic City (aka Atlantic City U.S.A.); Au Revoir les Enfants; Black Moon; Crackers; Damage; Feu Follet, Le (A Time to Live and a Time to Die/The Fire Within/ Fox Fire/Will o'the Wisp); God's Country; Histoires Extraordinaires (Spirits of the Dead/Tales of Mystery); Lacombe Lucien; Milou en mai (Milou in May); Monde du Silence, Le (The Silent World)My Dinner with André; Phantom India (L'Inde Fantôme); Pretty Baby; Souffle au Coeur, Le (Dearest Heart); Vanya on 42nd Street; Vie Privée (A Very Private Affair); Viva Maria!; Zazie dans le Métro.*

Malmuth, Bruce *Hard to Kill; Nighthawks.*

Malone, Mark *Killer.*

Malone, William *House on Haunted Hill; Titan Find, The (aka Creature).*

Malraux, André *Espoir (Days of Hope/Man's Hope).*

Mambéty, Djibril Diop *see* Diop-Mambéty, Djibril

Mamet, David *Heist; Homicide; House of Games; Oleanna; Spanish Prisoner, The; State amd Main; Things Change; Winslow Boy, The.*

Mamin, Yuri *Fountain, The (Fontan).*

Mamoulian, Rouben *Applause; Becky Sharp; Blood and Sand; City Streets; Dry Jekyll and Mr Hyde; Golden Boy; Love Me Tonight; Mark of Zorro, The; Queen Christina; Silk Stockings; Song of Songs; We Live Again.*

Manchevski, Milcho *Before the Rain (Po Dezju); Dust.*

Manda, Kunitoshi *Unloved.*

Mandel, Robert *F/X (aka F/X – Murder by Illusion); School Ties; Substitute, The; Touch and Go.*

Mandoki, Luis *Angel Eyes; Born Yesterday; Gaby – A True Story; Message in a Bottle; When a Man Loves a Woman; White Palace.*

Mangold, James *CopLand; Girl, Interrupted; Heavy; Kate & Leopold.*

Mangolte, Babette *Camera: Je, The; Cold Eye, The; What Maisie Knew.*

Mankiewicz, Francis *Revolving Doors, The (Les Portes tournantes).*

Mankiewicz, Joseph L *All About Eve; Barefoot Contessa, The; Cleopatra; Dragonwyck; 5 Fingers; Ghost and Mrs Muir, The; Guys and Dolls; Honey Pot, The; House of Strangers; Julius Caesar; Letter to Three Wives. A; No Way Out; People Will Talk; Quiet American, The; Sleuth; Somewhere in the Night; Suddenly Last Summer; There Was a Crooked Man...*

Mankiewicz, Tom *Delirious; Dragnet.*

Mann, Anthony *Bend of the River (aka Where the River Bends); Border Incident; Cimarron; Dandy in Aspic, A; Desperate; Devil's Doorway; El Cid; Fall of the Roman Empire, The; Furies, The; Glenn Miller Story, The; God's Little Acre; Heroes of Telemark, The; Man of the West; Men in War; Naked Spur, The; Raw Deal; Reign of Terror (aka The Black Book); T-Men; Tall Target, The; Tin Star, The; Winchester '73.*

Mann, Daniel *About Mrs Leslie; BUtterfield 8; Come Back, Little Sheba; Dream of Kings, A; Judith; Lost in the Stars; Kidnapped; Revengers, The; Teahouse of the August Moon, The.*

Mann, Delbert *All Quiet on the Western Front; Bachelor Party, The; Dark at the Top of the Stairs, The; Desire Under the Elms; Gathering of Eagles, A; Jane Eyre; Marty; Night Crossing; Torn Between Two Lovers.*

Mann, Farhad *Lawnmower Man 2: Beyond Cyberspace.*

Mann, Michael *Ali; Heat; Insider, The; Jericho Mile, The; Keep, The; Last of the Mohicans, The; Manhunter; Thief (aka Violent Streets).*

Mann, Ron *Comic Book Confidential; Grass.*

Mannas, James *Aggro Seizeman.*

Manning, Michelle *Blue City.*

Manop Udomdej *Beyond Forgivin' (Dokmai nai Tangpuen); Dumb Die Fast, Smart Die Slow, The (Galok Bang Tai Cha, Galok Na Tai Gon).*

Manos, Mark *Liquid Dreams.*

Mantegna, Jo *Lakeboat.*

Mantello, Joe *Love! Valour! Compassion!*

Manthoulis, Robert *Blues Under the Skin (Le Blues entre les Dents).*

Manuli, Guido *Volere, Volare.*

Marboeuf, Jean *Pétain.*

Marcel, Terry *Hawk the Slayer; Jane and the Lost City.*

March, Alex *Amazing Captain Nemo, The (aka The Return of Captain Nemo).*

Marcheschi, Cork *Survivors, The Blues Today.*

Marconi, David *Harvest, The.*

Marcus, Adam *Let It Snow (aka Snow Days).*

Marcus, James *Tank Malling.*

Marcus, Mitch *Boy Called Hate, A.*

Marczewski, Wojciech *Escape from the 'Liberty' Cinema (Ucieczka z Kina 'Wolnosc').*

Marek, Pavel *Dead Forest (Mrtvy Les); Tutor in Fear, The (Vychovatel ke Strachu).*

Maresco, Franco *Enzo, Domani a Palermo!; TTotò Who Lived Twice (Totò che visse due volte); Uncle from Brooklyn, The (Lo Zio di Brooklyn).*

Margolin, François *Lie, The (Mensonge).*

Margolin, Stuart *Glitter Dome, The.*

Margolis, Jeff *Richard Pryor Live in Concert.*

Maria, Guy *Maid for Pleasure (Filles Expertes en Jeux Clandestines).*

Mariage, Benoît *Convoyeurs Attendent, Les (The Carriers Are Waiting).*

Marin, Cheech *Born in East L.A.*

Marin, Edwin L *Colt .45 (aka Thundercloud); Johnny Angel; Nocturne.*

Marinos, Lex *Indecent Obsession, An.*

Mariposa Film Group *Word Is Out.*

Mariscal, Alberto *They Call Him Marcado (Los Marcados).*

Marker, Chris *A.K.; Battle of the Ten Million, The (La Bataille des Dix Millions); Jetée, La (The Jetty/The Pier); Joli mai, Le; Level Five; One Day in the Life of Andrei Arsenevitch (Une Journée dans la Vie de Andrei Arsenevitch); Sans Soleil (Sunless).*

Markle, Fletcher *Incredible Journey, The; Man With a Cloak, The; Night Into Morning.*

Markle, Peter *Bat 21; Hot Dog…The Movie; Wagons East!; Youngblood.*

Markov, Ivan *Ghetto.*

Marks, Arthur *Bucktown.*

Marks, George Harrison *Come Play with Me.*

Marquand, Christian *Candy.*

Marquand, Richard *Eye of the Needle; Hearts of Fire; Jagged Edge; Legacy, The; Return of the Jedi; Return of the Jedi: Special Edition.*

Marquès, José Luis *Fuckland.*

Marmorstein, Malcolm *Dead Men Don't Die.*

Marr, Leon *Dancing in the Dark.*

Marre, Jeremy *Roots Rock Reggae.*

Marsh, William *Dead Babies.*

Marshall, Frank *Alive; Arachnophobia; Congo.*

Marshall, Fred *Popdown.*

Marshall, Garry *Beaches; Exit to Eden; Flamingo Kid, The; Frankie & Johnny; Nothing in Common; Other Sister, The; Overboard; Pretty Woman; Princess Diaries, The; Runaway Bride; Young Doctors in Love.*

Marshall, George *Advance to the Rear (aka Company of Cowards); Blue Dahlia, The; Destry Rides Again; Gazebo, The; Ghost Breakers, The; How the West Was Won; Murder, He Says; Pack Up Your Troubles; Sheepman, The; You Can't Cheat an Honest Man.*

Marshall, Neil *Dog Soldiers.*

Marshall, Noel *Roar.*

Marshall, Penny *Awakenings; Big; Jumpin' Jack Flash; League of Their Own, A; Preacher's Wife, The; Renaissance Man; Riding in Cars with Boys.*

Marshall, Simon *Out of Depth.*

Marshall, Stuart *Over Our Dead Bodies.*

Marshall, Tonie *Pas très Catholique (A Dubious Business); Tontaine et Tonton; Venus Beauty (Vénus Beauté Institut).*

Martel, Lucrecia *Ciénaga, La (The Swamp).*

Martin, Darnell *I Like It Like That.*

Martín, Eugenio *Bad Man's River (El Hombre del Río Malo); Horror Express (Pánico en el Transiberiano).*

Martin Lionel C *Def Jam's How to Be a Player.*

Martin, Richard *Limit Up.*

Martineau, Jacques *Jeanne et le Garçon Formidable.*

Martinez, Rico *Desperate.*

Martino, Sergio *Island of Mutations (L'Isola degli Uomini Pesce); Montagna del Dio Cannibale, La (Prisoner of the Cannibal God/Slave of the Cannibal God); Violent Professionals, The (Milano Trema; La Polizia Vuole Giustizia); The Visitor (Cugini Carnali).*

Martinson, Leslie *Batman; Fathom; Mrs Pollifax – Spy.*

Marton, Andrew *Africa – Texas Style; Ben-Hur; Clarence, the Cross-Eyed Lion; Crack in the World; Green Fire; Longest Day, The.*

Martone, Mario *Amore Molesto, L'.*

Marvin, Mike *Wraith, The.*

Marzynski, Marian *Shtetl.*

Mason, Christopher *Wot! No Art.*

Mason, Herbert *Back-Room Boy.*

Massaciesi, Aristide *Arena, The (La Rivolta delle Gladiatrici).*

Masson, Laetitia *En avoir (ou pas); Love Me.*

Massot, Claude *Kabloonak.*

Massot, Joe *Dance Craze; Song Remains the Same, The.*

Masters, Quentin *Dangerous Summer, A; Stud, The.*

Masterson, Peter *Blood Red; Full Moon in Blue Water; Trip to Bountiful, The.*

Mastorakis, Nico *Blind Date; Wind, The (aka Edge of Terror).*

Mastroianni, Armand *Cameron's Closet; He Knows You're Alone.*

Matalon, Eddy *Cathy's Curse (Cauchemars/Une si Gentille Petite Fille).*

Maté, Rudolph *Dark Past, The; D.O.A.; Miracle in the Rain; No Sad Songs for Me; Second Chance; Union Station; When Worlds Collide.*

Mathias, Sean *Bent.*

Maticevic, Mladen *Ghetto.*

Matsuda, Shunsui *Bantsuma: The Life and Times of Tsumasaburo Bando (Bantsuma: Bando Tsumasaburo no Shogai).*

Matsue, Tetsuaki *Annyong Kimchi.*

Matsumoto, Toshio *Funeral Parade of Roses (Bara no Soretsu); Pandemonium (Shura).*

Matthau, Charles *Grass Harp, The.*

Matthews, Paul *Merlin: The Return.*

Mattinson, Burny *Great Mouse Detective, The (aka Basil the Great Mouse Detective).*

Maxwell, Garth *Jack Be Nimble; When Love Comes.*

Maxwell, Paul (Paolo Bianchini) *Superargo (Superargo e i Giganti Senza Volto).*

Maxwell, Peter *Serena; Southern Cross (aka The Highest Honor – A True Story).*

Maxwell, Ronald F *Gettysburg; Little Darlings.*

May, Elaine *Heartbreak Kid, The; Ishtar; Mikey and Nicky; New Leaf, A.*

May, Joe *Invisible Man Returns, The.*

Mayberry, Russ *Unidentified Flying Oddball, The (aka The Spaceman and King Arthur).*

Maybury, John *Love Is the Devil – Study for a Portrait of Francis Bacon (Ai no Akuma).*

Mayer, Daisy *VS Woo.*

Mayersberg, Paul *Captive.*

Mayfield, Les *American Outlaws; Blue Streak; Encino Man (aka California Man); Flubber; Miracle on 34th Street.*

Maylam, Tony *Burning, The; Hero; Riddle of the Sands, The; Split Second; White Rock.*

Mayo, Archie *Bordertown; Confirm or Deny; Four Sons; It's Love I'm After; Mayor of Hell, The; Night After Night; Night in Casablanca, A; Orchestra Wives; Petrified Forest, The.*

Maysles, Albert *Gimme Shelter; Grey Gardens.*

Maysles, David *Gimme Shelter; Grey Gardens.*

Mazursky, Paul *Alex in Wonderland; Blume in Love; Bob & Carol & Ted & Alice; Down and Out in Beverly Hills; Enemies, a Love Story; Harry and Tonto; Moon Over Parador; Moscow on the Hudson; Next Stop, Greenwich Village; Scenes from a Mall; Tempest; Unmarried Woman, An; Willie & Phil; Winchell.*

Mead, Nick *Swing.*

Meadows, Shane *Once Upon a Time in the Midlands; Room for Romeo Brass, A; Smalltime; TwentyFourSeven.*

Meckler, Nancy *Alive and Kicking (aka Indian Summer); Sister My Sister.*

Medak, Peter *Changeling, The; Krays, The; Let Him Have It; Men's Club, The; Odd Job, The; Romeo Is Bleeding; Species II; Zorro the Gay Blade.*

Medem, Julio *Lovers of the Arctic Circle, The (Los Amantes del Circulo Polar/Les Amants du Cercle Polaire); Red Squirrel, The (La Ardilla Roja); Sex and Lucía (Lucía y el sexo); Tierra (Earth); Vacas (Cows).*

Medford, Don *November Plan, The; Organization, The.*

Medvedkin, Alexander *Happiness (Schaste).*

Meerapfel, Jeanine *Amigomio; Girlfriend, The (aka La Amiga); Malou.*

Megahey, Leslie *Hour of the Pig, The.*

Megahy, Francis *Disappearance of Kevin Johnson, The; Freelance; Real Life; Taffin.*

Megginson, RT *Pelvis.*

Mehrjui, Daryush (Dariush) *Bemani (Stay Alive); Cow, The (Gav); Cycle, The (Dayereh Mina); Leila.*

Mehta, Deepa *Camilla; Earth; Fire.*

Meieran, David *Voices from the Front.*

Meirelles, Fernando *City of God (Cidade de Deus); Maids (Domésticas).*

Meisel, Myron *It's All True.*

Mekas, Adolfas *Hallelujah the Hills.*

Mekas, Jonas *Reminiscences of a Journey to Lithuania.*

Melamed, Jordan *Manic.*

Melchior, Ib *Time Travellers, The.*

Melendez, Bill *Boy Named Charlie Brown, A (aka A Boy Called Charlie Brown); Dick Deadeye, or Duty Done.*

Mellor, Kay *Fanny & Elvis.*

Melville, Jean-Pierre *Armée des Ombres, L' (The Army in the Shadows); Bob le Flambeur (Bob the Gambler); Deux Hommes dans Manhattan; Deuxième Souffle, Le (Second Breath); Doulos, Le (The Finger Man); Enfants Terribles, Les (The Strange Ones); Flic, Un (Dirty Money); Léon Morin, Priest (Léon Morin, Prêtre); Red Circle, The (Le Cercle Rouge); Samourai, Le (The Samurai); Silence de la mer, Le.*

Menaul, Christopher *Feast of July.*

Menczel, Judy *Angst.*

Mendelsohn, Eric *Judy Berlin.*

Mendeluk, George *Kidnapping of the President, The.*

Mendes, Sam *American Beauty.*

Mendes, Lothar *Man Who Could Work Miracles, The.*

Menell, Jo *Dick; Mandela.*

Menendez, Ramon *Stand and Deliver.*

Menges, Chris *Lost Son, The; Second Best; World Apart, A.*

Menotti, Gian Carlo *Medium, The.*

Menshov, Vladimir *Moscow Distrusts Tears (Moskva Slezam ne Verit).*

Menzel, Jirí *Capricious Summer (Rozmarné Leto); Closely Observed Trains (Ostre Sledované Vlaky); Cutting It Short (Postrizini); Larks on a String (Skrivanci na niti); Life and Extraordinary Adventures of Private Ivan Chonkin, The (Zycie i Niezwyklle Przygodv Szeregowca Iwana Czonkina); My Sweet Little Village (Vesnicko má Stredisková); Pearls of the Deep (Perlicky na dne); Seclusion Near a Forest (Na samote u lesa); Those Wonderful Movie Cranks (Bájecni Muzi s Klikou).*

Menzies, William Cameron *Address Unknown; Conquest of the Air; Invaders from Mars; Things To Come; Whip Hand, The.*

Mercer, Shaya *Trade Off.*

Merchant, Ismail *Cotton Mary; Courtesans of Bombay, The; In Custody (Hifazaat); Lumière et Compagnie; Mystic Maseur, The; Proprietor, The (Le Propriétaire).*

Merendino, James *SLC Punk!*

Merhige, E Elias *Shadow of the Vampire.*

Merlet, Agnès *Artemisia; Shark's Son (Le Fils du Requin).*

Merrick, Laurence *Manson.*

Mertz, Arthur *Off the Dole.*

Meshkini, Marziyeh *Day I Became a Woman, The (Roozi Keh Zan Shodam).*

Mészáros, Márta *Adoption (Örökbefogadás); Diary for My Children (Napló Gyermekeimnek); Diary for My Loves (Napló Szerelmeimnek); Nine Months (Kilenc Hónap); Two of Them, The (Ok Ketten/aka Two Women).*

Metcalf, Andy *Unstable Elements – Atomic Stories 1939-85.*

Metcalfe, Tim *Killer: A Journal of Murder.*

Metter, Alan *Back to School; Cold Dog Soup; Girls Just Want to Have Fun; Moving; Police Academy 7: Mission to Moscow.*

Metzstein, Saul *Late Night Shopping.*

Metzger, Alan *Roomates.*

Metzger, Radley *Cat and the Canary, The; Don't Cry for Me Little Mother; Erotic Quartet (aka The Lickerish Quartet).*

Meyer, Kevin *Perfect Alibi.*

Meyer, Muffie *Grey Gardens.*

Meyer, Nicholas *Company Business; Deceivers, The; Star Trek II; The Wrath of Khan; Star Trek VI: The Undiscovered Country; Time After Time; Volunteers.*

Meyer, Russ *Beneath the Valley of the Ultra Vixens; Beyond the Valley of the Dolls; Blacksnake (aka Slaves); Faster, Pussycat! Kill! Kill!; Good Morning…and Goodbye (aka The Lust Seekers); Motor Psycho; Seven Minutes, The; Supervixens; Vixen.*

Meyers, Nancy *Parent Trap, The; What Women Want.*

Michel, Thierry *Mobutu, King of Zaire (Mobutu, Roi du Zaïre).*

Michell, Roger *Notting Hill; Persuasion; Titanic Town.*

Michell, Scott *Innocent Sleep, The.*

Michener, Dave *Great Mouse Detective, The (aka Basil the Great Mouse Detective).*

Middleditch, Paul *Terra Nova.*

Middleton, Jonas *Through the Looking Glass.*

Miéville, Anne-Marie *Contre l'Oubli (Against Oblivion); 2 x 50 Years of French Cinema.*

Miike, Takashi *Agitator (Araburu Tamashii-tachi); Audition; Bird People in China, The (Chugoku no Chojin); Blues Harp; City of Lost Souls (Hyoryu Gai); Dead or Alive; Dead or Alive 2 – Birds; Happiness of the Katakuris, The (Katakuri-ke no Kofuku); Ichi the Killer (Koroshiya Ichi); Ley Lines (Nihon Kuro Shakai – Ley Lines); Rainy Dog (Gokudo Kuro Shakai – Rainy Dog); Shinjuku Triad Society (Shinjuku Kuro Shakai: China Mafia Senso); Visitor Q.*

Mikhalkov, Nikita *Barber of Siberia, The (Sibirskii Tsiriulnik); Burnt by the Sun (Utomlennye solntsem/Soleil trompeur); Dark Eyes (Oci Ciornie); Five Evenings (Pyat Vercherov); Oblomov (Neskolko Dnei iz Zhizni I.I. Oblomova); Private Conservation, A (Bez Svidetelei); Slave of Love, A (Raba Lubvi); Unfinished Piece for Mechanical Piano (Neokonchennaya Pyesa dlya Mekhanicheskogo Pianin); Urga.*

Mikhalkov-Konchalovsky, Andrei see Konchalovsky, Andrei.

Mikkelsen, Laila *Little Ida (Liten Ida).*

Miles, Bernard *Chance of a Lifetime, Tawny Pipit.*

Miles, Christopher *Clandestine Marriage, The; Maids, The; Priest of Love; That Lucky Touch; Time for Loving; Virgin and the Gypsy, The.*

Milestone, Hank *From Hell to Victory (De l'Enfer à la Victoire).*

Milestone, Lewis *All Quiet on the Western Front; Arch of Triumph; Edge of Darkness; Front Page, The; Hallelujah, I'm a Bum (aka Lazybones); Halls of Montezuma; Kangaroo; Les Miserables; Mutiny on the Bounty; North Star, The (aka Armored Attack); Ocean's 11; Of Mice and Men; Pork Chop Hill; Rain; Strange Love of Martha Ivers, The; Walk in the Sun, A.*

Milius, John *Big Wednesday; Conan the Barbarian; Dillinger, Farewell to the King; Flight of the Intruder; Red Dawn; Wind and the Lion, The.*

Milkina, Sofia *Kreutzer Sonata, The (Kreitzerova Sonata).*

Milland, Ray *Man Alone, A; Panic in Year Zero.*

Millar, Gavin *Complicity; Danny the Champion of the World; Dreamchild.*

Millar, Stuart *Rooster Cogburn; When the Legends Die.*

Miller, Allan *Small Wonders.*

Miller, Bennett *Cruise, The.*

Miller, Claude *Accompagnatrice, L' (The Accompanist); Best Way to Walk, The (La Meilleure Façon de Marcher); Class Trip (La Classe de neige); Deadly Run (Mortelle Randonnée); Enfants de Lumière, Les (The Children of Lumière); Garde à Vue (The Inquisitor); Impudent Girl, An (L'Effrontée); Lumière et Compagnie; Petite Voleuse, La; This Sweet Sickness (Dites-lui que Je l'aime).*

Miller, David *Billy the Kid; Diane; Executive Action; Flying Tigers; Lonely Are the Brave; Love Happy; Opposite Sex, The; Sudden Fear.*

Miller, George (1) *Andre; Les Patterson Saves the World; Man from Snowy River, The; Over the Hill; NeverEnding Story II: The Next Chapter, The.*

Miller, George (2) *Babe – Pig in the City; Lorenzo's Oil; Mad*

Max; Mad Max 2; Mad Max Beyond Thunderdome; The; Twilight Zone – The Movie; Witches of Eastwick, The.

Miller, Jason *That Championship Season.*

Miller, Kurt *Black Diamond Rush.*

Miller, Michael *Jackson County Jail; National Lampoon's Class Reunion; Silent Rage; Street Girls.*

Miller, Rebecca *Angela.*

Miller, Robert Ellis *Any Wednesday (aka Bachelor Girl Apartment); Baltimore Bullet, The; Buttercup Chain, The; Hawks; Heart Is a Lonely Hunter, The; Reuben, Reuben; Sweet November.*

Miller, Sam *Among Giants.*

Miller, Troy *Jack Frost.*

Mills, Abbott *Jane.*

Mills, Reginald *Tales of Beatrix Potter (aka Peter Rabbit and Tales of Beatrix Potter).*

Milner, Dan *From Hell It Came.*

Milton, Robert *Outward Bound.*

Mimouni, Gilles *Appartement, L'.*

Minahan, Daniel *Series 7: The Contenders.*

Miner, Steve *Forever Young; Friday the 13th Part 2; Halloween H20 – 20 Years Later; House; Lake Placid; My Father, the Hero; Soul Man; Warlock.*

Mingay, David *Rude Boy.*

Minghella, Anthony *English Patient, The; Mr Wonderful; Play; Talented Mr Ripley, The; Truly, Madly, Deeply.*

Mingozzi, Gianfranco *Rebel Nun, The (Flavia la Monaca Musulmana).*

Ming-Yuen S Ma *Slanted Vision.*

Minkoff, Ron *Lion King, The; Stuart Little.*

Minnelli, Vincente *American in Paris, An; Bad and the Beautiful, The; Band Wagon, The; Bells Are Ringing; Brigadoon; Cabin in the Sky; Cobweb, The; Designing Woman; Father of the Bride; Gigi; Home from the Hill; Kismet; Lust for Life; Meet Me in St Louis; On a Clear Day You Can See Forever; Pirate, The; Sandpiper, The; Some Came Running; Tea and Sympathy; The Clock (aka Under the Clock); Two Weeks in Another Town; Undercurrent; Ziegfeld Follies.*

Mire, Pat *Dirty Rice.*

Mir-Karimi, Seyyed Reza *Child and the Soldier, The (Koudak va Sarbaz); Under the Moonlight (Zir-e Nour-e Mah).*

Mirkin, David *Heartbreakers; Romy and Michele's High School Reunion.*

Misselwitz, Helke *Little Angel (Engelchen).*

Misumi, Kenji *Lightning Swords of Death (Kozure Ohkami – Ko Wo Kashi Ude Kashi Tsukamatsuru); Shogun Assassin.*

Mita, Merata *Patu.*

Mitani, Koki *Welcome Back Mr McDonald (Radio No Jikan).*

Mitchell, Eric *Underground U.S.A.*

Mitchell, John Cameron *Hedwig and the Angry Inch.*

Mitchell, Mike *Deuce Bigalow: Male Gigolo.*

Mitchell, Oswald *Asking for Trouble.*

Mitchell, Sollace *Call Me.*

Mitrotti, Roberto *Snatched (aka Little Girl…Big Tease).*

Mitrovic, Zika *67 Days (Uziska Republiksa).*

Mitta, Alexander *Lost in Siberia (Zateryani v Sibiryi).*

Mitterrand, Frédéric *Madame Butterfly.*

Miyazaki, Hayao *Princess Mononoke (Mononoke Hime); Spirited Aawy (Sen to Chihiro no Kamikakakushi).*

Mizoguchi, Kenji *Chikamatsu Monogatari (The Crucified Lovers); Empress Yang Kwei Fei, The (Yokihi); Five Women Around Utamaro (Utamaro o Meguru Go-nin no Onna); Gion Festival Music (Gion Bayashi/aka a Geisha); Hometown (Furusato); Life of Oharu, The (Saikaku Ichidai Onna); Loyal 47 Ronin of the Genroku Era, The (Genroku Chushingura); My Love Has Been Burning (Waga Koi Wa Moenu); Osaka Elegy (Naiwa ereji); Sansho Dayu (Sansho the Bailiff); Shin Heike Monogatari (New Tales of the Taira Clan); Sisters of Gion (Gion no Shimai); Story of the Late Chrysanthemums, The (Zangiku Monogatari); Street of Shame (Akasen Chitai); Ugetsu Monogatari.*

Mizrahi, Moshe *Every Time We Say Goodbye; Madame Rosa (La Vie devant Soi); Rachel's Man.*

Mochizuki, Rokuro *Another Lonely Hitman (Shin Kanashiki Hitman); Fire Within, The (Onibi); Outer Way, The (Gedo); Skinless Night; Wicked Reporter, The (Gokudo Kisha).*

Mocky, Jean-Pierre *Snobs.*

Moell, B *Dick.*

Moffatt, Tracey *Bedevil.*

Mogeluscu, Miles *Union Maids.*

Moguy, Leonide *Paris After Dark (aka The Night Is Ending).*

Moland, Hans Petter *Last Lieutenant, The (Secondløitnanten).*

Molina Reig, Josefina *Evening Performance (Función de Noche).*

Molinaro, Edouard *Beaumarchais (Beaumarchais l'insolent); Cage aux Folles, La (Birds of a Feather); Cage aux Folles II, La; Emmerdeur, L' (A Pain in the A**); Just the Way You Are; Pink Telephone, The (Le Téléphone Rose).*

Moll, Dominik *Harry, He's Here to Help (Harry, un ami qui vous veut du bien/aka With a Friend Like Harry…).*

Moll, Jim *Last Days, The.*

Mollberg, Rauni *Earth Is a Sinful Song (Maa on Syntinen Laulau).*

Mollo, Andrew *It Happened Here; Winstanley.*

Monger, Christopher *Englishman Who Went Up a Hill, But Came Down a Mountain, The; Just Like a Woman; Voice Over; Waiting for the Light.*

Monicelli, Mario *Boccaccio '70; Casanova '70; Let's Hope It's a Girl (Speriamo che sia Femmina); Soliti Ignoti, I (Big Deal on Madonna Street/Persons Unknown).*

Monnikendan, Vincent *Mother Dao the Turtlelike.*

Montaldo, Giuliano *Closed Circuit (Circuito Chiuso).*

Monteiro, João César *Hips of John Wayne, The (Le Bassin de J.W./aka the Pelvis of J.W.); Recollections of the Yellow House (Recordacões da Casa Amarela).*

Montesi, Jorge *Omen IV: The Awakening.*

Montgomery, Jennifer *Art for Teachers of Children.*

Montgomery, Monty *Loveless, The.*

Montgomery, Robert *Lady in the Lake.*

Moodysson, Lukaş *Show Me Love (Fucking Åmål); Together (Tillsammans).*

Moon, Sarah *Contre l'Oubli (Against Oblivion); Lumière et Compagnie.*

Moore, Eoin *Conamara.*

Moore, John *Behind Enemy Lines.*

Moore, Michael (1) *Paradise – Hawaiian Style.*

Moore, Michael (2) *Bowling for Columbine; Canadian Bacon; Roger & Me.*

Moore, Richard *Silent Flute, The (aka Circle of Iron).*

Moore, Robert *Chapter Two; Cheap Detective, The; Murder by Death.*

Moore, Simon *Under Suspicion; Up on the Roof.*

Moore, Tom *'Night Mother.*

Moorhouse, Jocelyn *How to Make an American Quilt; Proof; Thousand Acres, A.*

Mora, Philippe *Brother, Can You Spare a Dime?; Communion; Death of a Soldier; Mad Dog Morgan (aka Mad Dog); Return of Captain Invincible, The; Swastika.*

Morahan, Andy *Highlander III – The Sorcerer.*

Morahan, Christopher *Clockwise; Old Flames; Paper Mask.*

Morais, José Alvaro *Jester, The (O Bobo).*

Morandi, Gabriella *Jazzwomen.*

Moranis, Rick *Strange Brew.*

Moraz, Patricia *Indians Are Still Far Away, The (Les Indiens Sont Encore Loin).*

Mordillat, Gérard *En Compagnie d'Antonin Artaud (My Life and Times with Antonin Artaud).*

Morel, Gaël *A Toute Vitesses (Full Speed).*

More O'Ferrall, George *Angels One Five; Heart of the Matter, The; Woman for Joe, The.*

Moretti, Nanni *Aprile; Dear Diary (Caro Diario); Giorno della prima di 'Close Up', Il (Day of the Premiere of 'Close Up'); Son's Room, The (La Stanza del Figlio).*

Mori, Jun *Honey and Venom.*

Mori, Tatsuya *A.*

Morimoto, Koji *Memories.*

Morin, Edgar *Chronique d'un Eté (Chronicle of a Summer).*

Morita, Yoshimitsu *Deaths in Tokimeki (Tokimeki ni Shisu); Family Game (Kazoku Game).*

Morley, Carol *Alcohol Years, The.*

Morley, Peter *25 Years.*

Morneau, Louis *Bats; Retroactive.*

Moroder, Giorgio *Metropolis.*

Morra, Mario *Savage Man… Savage Beast (Ultime Grida della Savana).*

Morris, David Burton *Jersey Girl; Patti Rocks; Purple Haze.*

Morris, Errol *Dark Wind, The; Fast, Cheap & Out of Control; Gates of Heaven; Thin Blue Line, The; Vernon, Florida.*

Morrison, Bruce *Constance; Shaker Run.*

Morrison, Paul *Solomon and Gaenor (Solomon a Gaenor); Unstable Elements – Atomic Stories 1939-85.*

Morrissey, Paul *Bike Boy; Blood for Dracula (Dracula Vuole Vivere: Cerca Sangue di Vergine!/aka Andy Warhol's Dracula); Cocaine (Mixed Blood); Flesh; Flesh for Frankenstein (Carne per Frankenstein); Heat; Hound of the Baskervilles, The; Trash; Women in Revolt.*

Morse, Hollingsworth *Daughters of Satan.*

Morse, Terry *Young Dillinger.*

Morton, Rocky *D.O.A.; Super Mario Bros.*

Morton, Vincent *Fatal Bond.*

Mosher, Gregory *Prime Gig, The.*

Moshinsky, Elijah *Genghis Cohn.*

Moskalyk, Antonín *Dita Saxová.*

Mostow, Jonathan *Breakdown; U-571.*

Mottola, Gregg *Daytrippers, The.*

Mouriéras, Claude *Montalvo et l'enfant (Montalvo and the Child).*

Mowbray, Malcolm *Don't Tell Her It's Me (aka The Boyfriend School); Private Function, A.*

Moxey, John *Circus of Fear (aka Psycho-Circus).*

Moyle, Allan *Empire Records; Pump Up the Volume; Times Square.*

Mueller, Kathy *Daydream Believer.*

Mugge, Robert *Black Wax; Sun Ra: A Joyful Noise.*

Müjde, Gani *Byzantium (Kahpe Bizans).*

Mukdasanit, Euthana *Butterfly and Flowers (Peesua lae dokmai); Path of the Brave (Vittee Khon Kla); Tongpan.*

Mulcahy, Russell *Blue Ice; Highlander; Highlander II – The Quickening; Razorback; Reality Bites; Ricochet; Shadow, The.*

Mullan, Peter *Orphans.*

Müller, Jette *Star! Star!*

Mulligan, Robert *Baby the Rain Must Fall; Bloodbrothers; Clara's Heart; Fear Strikes Out; Kiss Me Goodbye; Inside Daisy Clover; Love With the Proper Stranger; Man in the Moon, The; Other, The; Pursuit of Happiness, The; Same Time, Next Year; Summer of '42; To Kill a Mockingbird; Up the Down Staircase.*

Mulloy, Phil *In the Forest; Return, The.*

Mulvey, Laura *Crystal Gazing; Penthesilea: Queen of the Amazons; Riddles of the Sphinx.*

Münch, Christopher *Hours and Times, The; Sleepy Time Gal, The.*

Mune, Ian *Came a Hot Friday; End of the Golden Weather, The.*

Munro, David I *Knots.*

Munro, Ian *Prejudice.*

Murakami, Jimmy T *Battle Beyond the Stars; Christmas Carol – The Movie; When the Wind Blows.*

Murakami, Kenji *Tel-Club (Natsu ni Umareru).*

Murakami, Ryu *Tokyo Decadence (Topazu/aka Topaz).*

Muratova, Kira *Asthenic Syndrome, The (Asteniceskij Sindrom).*

Murch, Walter *Return to Oz.*

Murer, Fredi M *Alpine Fire (Höhenfeuer).*

Murlowski, John *Secret Agent Club, The.*

Murnau, FW *City Girl (aka Our Daily Bread); Faust; Finances of the Grand Duke (Die Finanzen des Grossherzogs); Last Laugh, The (Der letzte Mann); Nosferatu – eine Symphonie des Grauens; Sunrise; Tabu.*

Murphy, Colleen *Shoemaker.*

Murphy, Eddie *Harlem Nights.*

Murphy, Geoff *Fortress II: Re-entry; Freejack; Goodbye Pork Pie; Quiet Earth, The; Under Siege 2; Utu; Young Guns II.*

Murphy, Maurice *15 Amore.*

Murphy, Pat *Anne Devlin; Maeve; Nora.*

Murphy, Richard *Wackiest Ship in the Army, The.*

Murphy, Tab *Last of the Dogmen.*

Murray, Bill *Quick Change.*

Murray, Don *Cross and the Switchblade, The.*

Murray, John B *Libido.*

Murray, Paul *Elstree Calling.*

Musker, John *Aladdin; Great Mouse Detective, The (aka Basil the Great Mouse Detective); Hercules; Little Mermaid, The.*

Musser, Charles *Before the Nickelodeon: The Early Cinema of Edwin S Porter.*

Musso, Jeff *Puritan, The (Le Puritain).*

Mutrux, Floyd *Aloha, Bobby and Rose; American Hot Wax.*

Muyl, Philippe *Contre l'Oubli (Against Oblivion).*

Mweze, Ngangura *Vie est belle, La.*

Mycroft, Walter C *Banana Ridge.*

Myers, Suzanne *Alchemy.*

Myerson, Alan *Police Academy 5: Assignment Miami Beach; Private Lessons; Steelyard Blues.*

Mykkanen, Mafjaana *From Russia with Rock (Sirppi ja Kitara).*

Mylod, Mark *Ali G Indahouse.*

Myrick, Daniel *Blair Witch Project, The.*

Na'Aman, Rami *Flying Camel, The (Hagamal Hameofef).*

Naderi, Amir *Runner, The (Dawandeh); Water, Wind, Dust (Ab, Bad, Khak).*

Nag, Shankar *Swamy.*

Nagasaki, Shunichi *Drive, The (Saigo no Drive); Enchantment, The (Yuwakusha); Heart, Beating in the Dark (Yamiutsu Shinzo); Shikoku; Some Kinda Love (Romance); Stranger (Yoru no Stranger – Kyofu!); Tender Place, A (Yawaraka na Hoo).*

Nahon, Chris *Kiss of the Dragon (Le Baiser mortel du dragon).*

Nair, Mira *Kama Sutra: A Tale of Love; Mississippi Masala; Monsoon Wedding; Perez Family, The; Salaam Bombay!*

Nair, MT Vasudevan *Slender Smile, A (Oru Cheru Punchiri).*

Nakajima, Takehiro *Okoge; Remembrance (Kyoshu).*

Nakagawa, Nobuo *Ghosts of Kasane Swamp, The (Kaidan Kasane ga Fuchi); Ghost Story of Yotsuya (Tokaido Yotsuya Kaidan); Hell (Jigoku); Lady Vampire, The (Onna Kyuke Tsuki); Mansion of the Ghost Cat, The (Borei Kaibyo Yashiki).*

Nakamura, Eric *Sunsets.*

Nakamura, Genji *Beautiful Mystery – Legend of Big Horn (Utsukushiki Nazo: Kyokon Densetu).*

Nakano, Desmond *White Man's Burden.*

Nakata, Hideo *Ring; Ring 2.*

Nakata, Toichi *Osaka Story.*

Nalin, Pan *Samsara.*

Nalluri, Bharat *Downtime.*

Nam Gee-Woong *Teenage Hooker Became Killing Machine in Daehakroh (Daehakno-yeseo maechoon-hadaka tomaksalhae danghan yeogosaeng ajik Daehakno-ye Issda).*

Narizzano, Silvio *Blue; Class of Miss MacMichael, The; Fanatic (aka Die! Die! My Darling!); Georgy Girl; Loot; Why Shoot the Teacher.*

Nasrallah, Yousry *On Boys, Girls and the Veil (Sobyan Wa Banat).*

Natali, Vincenzo *Cube.*

Nava, Gregory *El Norte; My Family (Mi Familia/aka East LA); Time of Destiny, A.*

Nazareth, HO *Talking History.*

Neal, Peter *Ain't Misbehavin'; Yessongs.*

Neame, Ronald *Card, The (aka The Promoter); Escape from Zahrain; First Monday in October; Foreign Body; Gambit; Golden Salamander; Hopscotch; Horse's Mouth, The; I Could Go On Singing; Meteor; Million Pound Note, The (aka Man With a Million); Odessa File, The; Poseidon Adventure, The; Prime of Miss Jean Brodie, The; Scrooge; Tunes of Glory; Windom's Way.*

Neat, Timothy *Play Me Something.*

Needham, Hal *Cannonball Run, The; Cannonball Run II; Hooper; Smokey and the*

Bandit; Smokey and the Bandit II (aka Smokey and the Bandit Ride Again); Villain, The (aka Cactus Jack).

Nee-Owoo, Kwate *Ama.*

Negrin, Alberto *Red Rings of Fear (Enigma Rosso).*

Negulesco, Jean *Conspirators, The; Daddy Long Legs; How to Marry a Millionaire; Humoresque; Mask of Dimitrios, The; Mudlark, The; Nobody Lives Forever; O. Henry's Full House (aka Full House); Phone Call from a Stranger; Pleasure Seekers, The; Rains of Ranchipur, The; Road House; Three Came Home; Three Coins in the Fountain; Titanic; Woman's World.*

Neill, Roy William *Black Angel; Black Room, The; Frankenstein Meets the Wolf Man; Hoots Mon!; House of Fear, The; Pearl of Death, The; Pursuit to Algiers; Scarlet Claw, The; Sherlock Holmes and the Spider Woman; Terror by Night.*

Neill, Sam *Cinema of Unease.*

Neilson, Anthony *Debt Collector, The.*

Neilson, James *Adventures of Bullwhip Griffin, The; Dr Syn, Alias the Scarecrow; Night Passage; Summer Magic.*

Nellis, Alice *Eeny Meeny (Ene Bene).*

Nelson, David *Last Plane Out.*

Nelson, Gary *Black Hole, The; Freaky Friday; Jimmy the Kid; Santee.*

Nelson, Gene *Kissin' Cousins.*

Nelson, Jessie *Corrina, Corrina; I Am Sam.*

Nelson, Ralph *Duel at Diablo; Father Goose; Flight of the Doves; Soldier Blue; Wilby Conspiracy, The.*

Nemec, Jan *Late Night Talks with Mother (Nocni Hovory s Matkou); Martyrs of Love (Mucednici Lásky); Party and the Guest, The (O Slavnosti a Hostech); Pearls of the Deep (Perlicky na dne).*

Nesbitt, Frank *Dulcima.*

Nesher, Avi *Doppelganger: The Evil Within.*

Nesheim, Berit *Other Side of Sunday (Søndagsengler).*

Nettelbeck, Sandra *Mostly Martha (Drei Sterne).*

Neufeld Jr, Sigmund *Conquest of the Earth; Incredible Hulk, The.*

Neumann, Kurt *Fly, The; Mohawk.*

Neville, Edgar *Tower of the Seven Hunchbacks, The (La Torre de los Siete Jorobados).*

Neville, Morgan *Hitmakers: The Teens Who Stole Pop Music.*

Newbrook, Peter *Asphyx, The (aka Horror of Death).*

Newby, Chris *Anchoress (aka La Recluse); Madagascar Skin.*

Newell, Mike *Amazing Grace and Chuck (aka Silent Voice); Awakening, The; Awfully Big Adventure, An; Dance With a Stranger; Donnie Brasco; Enchanted April; Four Weddings and a Funeral; Good Father, The; Into the West; Pushing Tin; Soursweet.*

Newman, Joseph M *Big Circus, The; King of the Roaring 20's – The Story of Arnold Rothstein (aka The Big Bankroll); Pony Soldier; This Island Earth.*

Newman, Paul *Effect of Gamma Rays on Man-in-the-Moon Marigolds, The; Glass Menagerie, The; Harry & Son; Rachel, Rachel; Sometimes a Great Notion (aka Never Give an Inch).*

Newmeyer, Fred *Girl Shy; Grandma's Boy; Safety Last; Why Worry?*

Newton, Joel *Jennifer.*

Ng, Jasmine *Eating Air (Zhi Feng).*

Ngabo, Léonce *Gito, the Ungrateful.*

Ng Sze-Yuen *Bloody Fists, The (Dangkou Tan); Bruce Lee: The Man, The Myth (Li Xiaolong Chuanqi/aka Bruce Lee – True Story).*

Nibbelink, Phil *American Tail: Fievel Goes West, An.*

Niblo, Fred *Ben-Hur; Blood and Sand.*

Niccol, Andrew *Gattaca.*

Nichetti, Maurizio *Icicle Thief (Ladri di Saponette); Luna e l'Altra; Volere, Volare.*

Nicholas, Gregor *Broken English.*

Nicholls Jr, George *Adventures of Michael Strogoff, The (aka The Soldier and the Lady/Michael Strogoff); Anne of Green Gables.*

Nichols, Charles A *Charlotte's Web.*

Nichols, Mike *Biloxi Blues; Birdcage, The; Carnal Knowledge; Catch-22; Day of the Dolphin, The; Fortune, The; Graduate, The; Heartburn; Postcards from the Edge; Primary Colors; Regarding Henry; Silkwood; What Planet Are You From?; Who's Afraid of Virginia Woolf?; Wilt; Wolf; Working Girl.*

Nicholson, Jack *Drive, He Said; Goin' South; Two Jakes, The.*

Nicholson, William *Firelight.*

Nicks, Dewey *Slackers.*

Nicolaidis, Nicos *Singapore Sling.*

Nicolaou, Ted *TerrorVision.*

Nierenberg, George T *No Maps on My Taps.*

Niermans, Edouard *Angel Dust (Poussière d'Ange).*

Nigh, William *Strange Case of Dr Rx, The.*

Nihalani, Govind *Body (Denham); Mother or 1084 (Hazaar Chaurasi ki Maa).*

Nilsson, Bob *Signal 7.*

Nilsson, Rob *Northern Lights.*

Nimibutr, Nonzee *Dang Bireley's and the Young Gangsters (2499 Antapan Krong Muang); Jan Dara; Nang Nak.*

Nimoy, Leonard *Funny About Love; Good Mother, The; Holy Matrimony; Star Trek III: The Search for Spock; Three Men and a Baby; Voyage Home: Star Trek IV, The.*

Ning Ying *For Fun (Zhao Le).*

Nissimoff, Riki Shelach *Last Winter, The (Hakhoref Ha'Acharon).*

Noble, Adrian *Midsummer Night's Dream, A.*

Noé, Gaspar *Carné; I Stand Alone (Seul contre tous).*

Nolan, Christopher *Following; Memento.*

Noonan, Chris *Babe.*

Norbu, Khyentse *Cup, The (Phörpa).*

Nordlund, Solveig *Comédia Infantil.*

Norfolk, Mark *Love Is Not Enough.*

Norman, Leslie *Dunkirk; Long and the Short and the Tall, The; Night My Number Came Up, The; X the Unknown.*

Normand, Michael *Dirty Laundry.*

Norrington, Stephen *Blade.*

Norton, Bill L (aka BWL Norton/Bill WL Norton) *Baby – Secret of the Lost Legend; Cisco Pike; More American Graffiti; Three for the Road.*

Norton, Edward *Keeping the Faith.*

Nosseck, Max *Brighton Strangler, The; Dillinger.*

Nosseck, Noel *Dreamer.*

Nossiter, Jonathan *Sunday.*

Nott, Julian *Weak at Denise.*

Noujaim, Jehane *Startup.com.*

Novak, Blaine *Good to Go.*

Novak, Frank *Good Housekeeping.*

Novaro, Maria *Danzón; Jardin del Eden, El (The Garden of Eden); Que no quede huella (Without a Trace/Leaving No Trace/aka Sin dejar huella).*

Noyce, Phillip *Backroads; Blind Fury; Bone Collector, The; Clear and Present Danger; Dead Calm; Heatwave; Newsfront; Patriot Games; Sliver.*

Nuchtern, Simon *New York Nights.*

Nugent, Elliott *Cat and the Canary, The; Great Gatsby, The; My Favorite Brunette; Never Say Die; Up in Arms.*

Nugroho, Garin *…And the Moon Dances (Bulan Tertusuk Ilalang); Leaf on a Pillow (Daun Di Atas Bantai); Letter from an Angel (Surat Untuk Bidadari); Unconcealed Poetry (Puisi Yang Tak Yerkuburkan/A Poet).*

Nuñez, Victor *Gal Young 'Un; Ruby in Paradise; Ulee's Gold.*

Nunn, Trevor *Hedda; Lady Jane; Twelfth Night.*

Nureyev, Rudolf *Don Quixote.*

Nuridsany, Claude *Microcosmos (Microcosmos: Le Peuple de l'herbe).*

Nutley, Colin *House of Angels (Anglagård).*

Nutter, David *Cease Fire; Disturbing Behavior.*

Nuytten, Bruno *Camille Claudel.*

Nyby, Christian *Thing from Another World, The.*

Nykvist, Carl-Gustaf *Women on the Roof, The (Kvinnorna på taket).*

Nykvist, Sven *One and One (En och En); Ox, The (Oxen).*

Nyswaner, Ron *Prince of Pennsylvania, The.*

O'Bannon, Dan *Return of the Living Dead, The.*

O'Bannon, Rockne S *Fear.*

Obitani, Yuri *Fufu the Worldweary (Ensei Fufu); Hair Opera, The (Mohatsu Kageki).*

Obler, Arch *Arnelo Affair, The; Five.*

Oblowitz, Michael *King Blank; This World, Then the Fireworks.*

Obomsawin, Alanis *Kanehsatake (Oka) – 270 Years of Resistance.*

O'Brien, Jim *Dressmaker, The.*

Obrow, Jeffrey *Kindred, The.*

O'Callaghan, Maurice *Broken Harvest.*

Ockrent, Mike *Dancin' Thru the Dark.*

O'Connell, Maura *Siege.*

O'Connolly, James *Mistress Pamela; Valley of Gwangi, The.*

O'Connor, Gavin *Tumbleweeds.*

O'Connor, Pat *Cal; Circle of Friends; Dancing at Lughnasa; Fools of Fortune; Inventing the Abbotts; January Man, The; Month in the Country, A; Stars and Bars; Sweet November.*

O'Connor, William A *Cocaine Fiends, The (aka The Pace That Kills).*

O'Donnell, Damien *East is East.*

Odets, Clifford *None But the Lonely Heart.*

Oedekerk, Steve *Ace Ventura – When Nature Calls; Nothing to Lose.*

Ofteringer, Susanne *Nico Icon.*

Ogata, Akira *Boy's Choir (Dokuritsu Shonen Gasshodan).*

Ogawa, Shinsuke *Peasants of the Second Fortress, The (Sanrizuka: Daini Toride no Hitobito).*

Ogilvie, George *Mad Max Beyond Thunderdome.*

Ogorodinikov, Valery *Burglar (Vzlomshchik).*

Oguri, Kohei *Muddy River (Doro no Kawa); Sleeping Man (Nemuru Otoko); Sting of Death, The (Shi no Toge).*

O'Hara, Gerry *Bitch, The; Brute, The; Fanny Hill; Leopard in the Snow.*

O'Hara, Mario *Demons (Pangarap ng Puso).*

O'Haver, Tommy *Billy's Hollywood Screen Kiss; Get Over It.*

Okamoto, Kihachi *Sword of Doom, The (Daibosatu Toge).*

Okamura, Tensai *Memories.*

Okan, Tunc *Mercedes Mon Amour (Fikrimin Ince Gülü).*

Okazaki, Steven *Lisa Theory, The.*

Oki, Hiroyuki *Heaven-6-Box; I Like You, I Like You Very Much (Anata-ga suki desu, dai suki des'); Swimming Prohibited (Yuei Kinishi).*

Okpako, Branwen, *Dirt for Dinner (Dreckfresser).*

Ökten, Zeki *Enemy, The (Düsman); Herd, The (Sürü).*

Okuhara, Hiroshi *Timeless Melody; Wave (Nami).*

Okura, Hiroyuki *Jin-Roh (Jinro/ aka The Wolf Brigade).*

Okuyama, Kazuyoshi *Mystery of Rampo, The (Ranpo).*

Old, John *see* Bava, Mario.

Oldman, Gary *Nil by Mouth.*

Olea, Pedro *Fencing Master, The (El Maestro de Esgrima).*

O'Leary, Ronan *Driftwood; Fragments of Isabella.*

Oliansky, Joel *Competition, The.*

Oliphant, Peer *Viva Portugal.*

Olival, Nando *Maids (Domésticas).*

Oliveira, Manoel de *Abraham Valley (Vale Abraão); Convent, The (O Convento); I'm Going Home (Vou Para Casa/Je Rentre à la Maison); Journey to the Beginning of the World, The (Viagem ao pricipio do mundo/Voyage au début du monde); Letter, The (La Lettre/A Carta); Oporto of My Childhood (O Porto de Minha Infância/La Porte de mon enfance); Uncertainty Principle (O Princípio da Incerteza).*

Olivera, Héctor *Funny Dirty Little War, A (No Habrá más Penas ni Olvido).*

Olivier, Laurence *Hamlet; Henry V; Prince and the Showgirl, The; Richard III; Three Sisters.*

Ollé, Alex *Fausto 5.0.*

Olmi, Ermanno *Cammina Cammina; Circumstance, The (La Circostanza); During the Summer (Durante l'Estate); Legend of the Holy Drinker, The (La Leggenda del Santo Bevitore); Long Live the Lady! (Lunga Vita alla Signora!); Man Named John, A (E Venne un Uomo); Posto, Il (The Job/The Sound of Trumpets); Profession of Arms, The (Il Mestiere delle Armi); Recuperanti, I (The Scavengers); Tree of Wooden Clogs, The (L'Albero degli Zoccoli).*

Olofson, Christina *Lines from the Heart (I Rollerna Tre).*

Olsson, Stellan *Close to the Wind (Oss Emellan); Sven Klang's Combo (Sven Klangs Kvintett).*

Omirbaev, Darejan *Killer, The (Tueur à Gages); Road, The (Jol).*

O'Mochain, Liam *Book That Wrote Itself, The.*

Ondricek, David *Loners (Samotari).*

O'Neil, Lawrence *Throwing Down.*

O'Neil, Robert Vincent *Angel.*

O'Neill, Jevon *Bob's Weekend.*

O'Neill, Ken *Secret Policeman's Third Ball, The.*

O'Neill, Tom *Water and Power.*

Onwurah, Ngozi *Welcome II the Terrordome.*

Ophüls, Marcel *Chagrin et la Pitié, Le (The Sorrow and the Pity); Hotel Terminus: The Life and Times of Klaus Barbie; Memory of Justice, The; November Days Voices and Choices; Sense of Loss, A; Veillées d'Armes (The Troubles We've Seen).*

Ophüls, Max *Caught; Exile, The; Letter from an Unknown Woman; Liebelei; Lola Montès; Madame de... (The Earrings of Madame de...); Plaisir, Le (House of Pleasure); Reckless Moment, The; Ronde, La; Signora di Tutti, La; Tendre Ennemie, La.*

Orders, Ron *Fly a Flag for Poplar.*

Orentreich, Catherine *Wizard of Waukesha, The.*

Orfini, Mario *Fair Game (Mamba).*

Orme, Stuart *Puppet Masters, The (aka Robert A. Heinlein's The Puppet Masters); Wolves of Willoughby Chase, The.*

Ormeland, Paul *Like It Is.*

Ormrod, Peter *Eat the Peach.*

Ormsby, Alan *Deranged.*

O'Rourke, Dennis *Good Woman of Bangkok, The; Half Life; Shark Callers of Kontu, The.*

Orr, James *Man of the House.*

Ortega, Kenny *Hocus Pocus; Newsies (aka The New Boys).*

Ortiz, Isidro *Fausto 5.0.*

Orton, John *Windjammer, The.*

Oshii, Mamoru *Avalon; Ghost in the Shell (Kokaku Kidotai); Patlabor – The Movie; Patlabor 2 – The Movie.*

Oshima, Nagisa *Ai No Corrida (L'Empire des Sens/The Realm of the Senses/In the Realm of the Senses); Boy (Shonen); Ceremony, The (Gishiki); Dear Summer Sister (Natsu no Imoto); Death by Hanging (Koshikei); Diary of a Shinjuku Thief (Shinjuku Dorobo Nikki); Empire of Passion (L'Empire de la Passion/Ai no Borei); Man Who Left His Will on Film, The (Tokyo Senso Sengo Hiwa/aka He Died After the War); Max Mon Amour (Max My Love); Merry Christmas Mr Lawrence; Taboo (Gohatto); Three Resurrected Drunkards (Kaettekita Yopparai); Town of Love and Hope, A (Ai to Kibo no Machi); Violence at Noon (Hakuchu no Torima).*

O'Sullivan, Shane *Second Generation.*

O'Sullivan, Thaddeus *December Bride; Nothing Personal; Ordinary Decent Criminal.*

Oswald, Gerd *Bunny O'Hare; Crime of Passion; Kiss Before Dying, A; Screaming Mimi.*

Oswald, Richard *Living Dead, The (Unheimliche Geschichten).*

Othenin-Girard, Dominique *Omen IV: The Awakening.*

Otomo, Katsuhiro *Akira; Memories; World Apartment Horror.*

Ott, Thomas *Little People.*

Ottman, John *Urban Legends Final Cut.*

Ottinger, Ulrike *Joan of Arc of Mongolia (Johanna d'Arc of Mongolia); Madame X.*

Ouane, Moussa *Spirit of Mopti, The (L'Esprit de Mopti).*

Ouazzani, Fatima Jebli *In My Father's House (In Hets Huis van Mijn Vader).*

Ouedraogo, Idrissa *Cri du Coeur, Le; Kini & Adams; Lumière et Compagnie; Samba Traore; Tilaï; Yaaba.*

Oury, Gérard *Mad Adventures of 'Rabbi' Jacob, The (Les Aventures de Rabbi Jacob).*

Ové, Horace *Playing Away; Pressure; Reggae.*

Owen, Cliff *Bawdy Adventures of Tom Jones, The; Magnificent Two, The; Ooh...You Are Awful (aka Get Charlie Tully); Prize of*

Arms, A; That Riviera Touch; Wrong Arm of the Law, The.

Owusu, Kwesi *Ama.*

Oz, Frank *Bowfinger; Dark Crystal, The; Dirty Rotten Scoundrels; Housesitter; In & Out; Indian in the Cupboard, The; Little Shop of Horrors; Muppets Take Manhattan, The; Score, The; What About Bob?*

Ozawa, Shigehiro *Blood of the Dragon (Satsujinken 2); Kung Fu Street Fighter (Gekitotsu! Satsujinken).*

Ozerov, Juri *Visions of Eight.*

Özkan, Yavuz *Two Women (Iki Kadin).*

Ozon, François *Criminal Lovers (Les Amants Criminels); 8 Women (8 Femmes); Regarde la Mer (See the Sea); Scènes de li (Bed Scenes); Sitcom; Under the Sand (Sous le Sable); Water Drops on Burning Rocks (Gouttes d'eau sur pierres brûlantes).*

Ozpetek, Ferzan *Harem Suare (Le Dernier Harem); Turkish Bath – Hamam, The (Il Bagno Turco – Hamam).*

Ozu, Yasujiro *Autumn Afternoon, An (Samma no aji); Early Spring (Soshun); Early Summer (Bakushu); Flavour of Green Tea Over Rice, The (Ochazuke no aji); Hen in the Wind (Kaze no naka no mendori); I Was Born, But… (Umarete wa Mita Keredo); Late Spring (Banshun); Ohayo (Good Morning); Record of a Tenement Gentleman (Nagaya Shinshiroku); That Night's Wife (Sono yo no tsuma); Tokyo Chorus (Tokyo no gassho); Tokyo Story (Tokyo Monogatari).*

Pabst, Georg Wilhelm *Diary of a Lost Girl (Das Tagebuch einer Verlorenen); Don Quichotte; Dreigroschenoper, Die (The Threepenny Opera); Joyless Street, The (Die freudlose Gasse); Kameradschaft; Love of Jeanne Ney, The (Die Liebe der Jeanne Ney); Mademoiselle Docteur (aka Salonique, nid d'espions); Pandora's Box (Die Büchse der Pandora); Secrets of a Soul (Geheimnisse einer Seele); Westfront 1918 (aka Vier von der Infanterie).*

Pachard, Henri *The Devil in Miss Jones Part II.*

Pacino, Al *Looking for Richard.*

Padrissa, Carlos *Fausto 5.0.*

Paes, César *Saudade do Futuro (Saudate for the Future).*

Page, Anthony *Absolution (aka Murder by Confession); Forbidden; I Never Promised You a Rose Garden; Inadmissible Evidence; Lady Vanishes, The.*

Pagnol, Marcel *César; Femme du Boulanger, La (The Baker's Wife); Lettres de Mon Moulin, Les (Letters from My Windmill); Merlusse; Topaze.*

Pagliero, Marcel *P…. Respectueuse, La (The Respectful Prostitute/The Respectable Prostitute).*

Pajaczkowska, Claire *Sigmund Freud's Dora.*

Pakdivijt, Chalong *S.T.A.B. (aka Thong).*

Pakula, Alan J *All the President's Men; Comes a Horseman; Consenting Adults; Devil's Own, The; Dream Lover; Klute; Orphans; Parallax View, The; Pelican Brief, The; Presumed Innocent; Rollover; See You in the Morning; Sophie's Choice; Starting Over; Sterile Cuckoo, The (aka Pookie).*

Pal, George *Time Machine, The; 7 Faces of Dr Lao; Tom Thumb.*

Palcy, Euzhan *Black Shack Alley (Rue Cases Nègres/aka Sugar Cane Alley); Dry White Season, A.*

Palekar, Amol *Square Circle, The (Daayraa); Village Has No Walls, The (Bangarwadi).*

Palmer, John *Ciao! Manhattan.*

Palmer, Tony *Testimony; 200 Motels; Wagner.*

Paltenghi, David *Orders Are Orders.*

Paltrow, Bruce *Duets.*

Panagiotopoulos, Nikos *see* Panayotopoulos, Nikos

Panahi, Jafar *Circle, The (Dayereh); White Balloon, The (Badkonak-E Sefid).*

Panama, Norman *Court Jester, The; How to Commit Marriage; I Will…I Will… For Now; Knock on Wood.*

Panayotopoulos, Nikos *Edge of Night (Afti i Nighita Meni); I Dream of My Friends (Onirevome tous Filous Mou); Melodrama?; Varietes; Woman Who Dreamed, The (I Gynaki pou evlepe ta oneira).*

Pande, Vinod *Ek Baar Phir (Once Again).*

Panfilov, Gleb *Beginning, The (Nachalo); Theme, The (Tema); Vassa.*

Pang, Danny *Bangkok: Dangerous (Krung Thep Antharai).*

Pang, Oxide *Bangkok: Dangerous (Krung Thep Antharai).*

Panh, Rithy *Gens de la rizière, Les (Rice People).*

Papas, Michael *Tomorrow's Warrior (Avrianos Polemistis).*

Papatakis, Nico *Equilibristes, Les (Walking a Tightrope).*

Papousek, Jaroslav *Best Age, The (Nejkrasnejsi Vek).*

Paradjanov, Sergo *Ashik Kerib (Ashug Qaribi/aka Kerib the Minstrel); Colour of Pomegranates, The (Nran Gouyne); Colour of Pomegranates: Director's Cut, The (Nran Gouyne); Legend of the Suram Fortress, The (Legenda Suramskoi Kreposti); Shadows of Our Forgotten Ancestors (Teni Zanytykh Predkov).*

Parello, Chuck *Ed Gein.*

Paris, Jerry *How Sweet It Is!; Police Academy 2: Their First Assignment; Police Academy 3: Back in Training; Viva Max!*

Parisot, Dean *Galazy Quest.*

Park Chan-Wook *Joint Security Area/JSA (Gongdong Gyungbi Guyeok JSA).*

Park Chon-Won *Our Twisted Hero (Uridleui Ilgureojin Youngung).*

Park Chul-Kwan *see* Park, Kwan

Park Chul-Soo *Farewell My Darling (Haksaeng Bukunshinwi); Push! Push! (San-bu In-gwa); 301–302.*

Park Jae-Ho *Broken Branches (Naeil ui Hyahae Hurunun Kang).*

Park Jin-Pyo *Too Young to Die (Jukeodo Jo A).*

Park Ki-Hyung *Secret Tears (Bimil).*

Park Ki-Yong *Motel Cactus (Motel Seoninjang).*

Park, Kwan *Hi, Dharma! (Darmaya Nolja).*

Park Kwang-Su *Berlin Report; Single Spark, A (Jeon Tae-Il).*

Park, Nick *Chicken Run; Close Shave, A.*

Parker, Alan *Angela's Ashes; Angel Heart; Birdy; Bugsy Malone; Come See the Paradise; Commitments, The; Evita; Fame; Midnight Express; Mississippi Burning; Pink Floyd: The Wall; Road to Wellville, The; Shoot the Moon.*

Parker, Albert *Black Pirate, The.*

Parker, Cary *Girl in the Picture, The.*

Parker, David *Hercules Returns.*

Parker, Francine *F.T.A.*

Parker, John *Dementia.*

Parker, Oliver *Ideal Husband, An; Othello.*

Parker, Trey *Orgazmo; South Park: Bigger, Longer & Uncut.*

Parkerson, Michelle D *…But Then, She's Betty Carter; Litany for Survival: The Life and Work of Audre Lorde, A.*

Park Ki-Hyung *Whispering Corridors (Yeogo Goedam).*

Parkinson, Tom *Disciple of Death.*

Park Kwang-Su *Black Republic (Keduldo Urichorum); Chilsu and Mansu (Chilsu oa Mansu); To the Starry Island (Gesom e Kako Shipta).*

Parks, Gordon *Leadbelly; Shaft; Shaft's Big Score!*

Parks Jr, Gordon *Super Cops, The; Superfly; Three the Hard Way.*

Parriott, James D *Heart Condition.*

Parrish, Robert *Bobo, The; Casino Royale; Cry Danger; Duffy; In the French Style; Marseille Contract, The; Mississippi Blues; Mob, The (aka Remember That Face); Rough Shoot (aka Shoot First); Saddle the Wind; Town Called Bastard, A; Wonderful Country, The.*

Parrott, James *Pardon Us.*

Parry, Gordon *Innocents in Paris; Sailor Beware (aka Panic in the Parlor); Tom Brown's Schooldays.*

Parry, Richard *South West Nine.*

Parsons, Nick *Dead Heart.*

Pascal, Christine *Petit Prince a dit, Le.*

Pascal, Gabriel *Caesar and Cleopatra; Major Barbara.*

Pascal, Michel *François Truffaut, Portraits Volés (François Truffaut, Stolen Portraits).*

Pascoe, Ray *Tom Simpson: Something to Aim At.*

Paskaljevic, Goran *Cabaret Balkan (Bure Baruta/ Baril de Poudre/aka The Powder Keg); How Harry Became a Tree; Someone Else's America (L'Amérique des autres); Special Treatment (Poseban Tretman).*

Pasolini, Pier Paolo *Accattone; Arabian Nights (Il Fiore delle Mille e una Notte); Canterbury Tales, The (I Racconti di Canterbury); Decameron, The (Il Decamerone); Gospel According to St Matthew, The (Il Vangelo Secondo Matteo); Mamma Roma; Medea; Oedipus Rex (Edipo Re); Pigsty (Porcile); Saló, o le Centoventi Giornate di Sodoma (Saló, or the 120 Days of Sodom); Theorem (Teorema); Uccellacci e Uccellini (Hawks and Sparrows).*

Pasquin, John *Jungle 2 Jungle; Santa Clause, The.*

Passer, Ivan *Creator; Cutter's Way (aka Cutter and Bone); Haunted Summer; Law and Disorder; Silver Bears.*

Pataki, Michael *Mansion of the Doomed (aka The Terror of Dr Chaney).*

Pate, Jonas *Liar.*

Pate, Josh *Liar.*

Pate, Michael *Tim.*

Patel, Krutin *ABCD.*

Patel, Sharad *Amin, the Rise and Fall (aka Rise and Fall of Idi Amin).*

Patrick, Matthew *Hider in the House.*

Patroni Griffi, Giuseppe *'Tis Pity She's a Whore (Addio, Fratello Crudele).*

Patellière, Denys de la *Ostrich Has Two Eggs, The (Les Oeufs de l'Autruche).*

Patterson, Ray *GoBots: Battle of the Rocklords.*

Patterson, Willi *Don't Go Breaking My Heart.*

Pattinson, Michael *Secrets; Wendy Cracked a Walnut.*

Patton-Spruill, Robert *Body Count.*

Patwardhan, Anand *Bombay Our City (Hamara shaher).*

Paul, Stefan *Bongo Man; Reggae Sunsplash II; Será Posible el Sur.*

Pawlikowski, Pawel *Last Resort.*

Payami, Babak *Secret Ballot (Raye Makhfi).*

Payne, Alexander *About Schmidt; Election.*

Payne, Christopher *Jolly Boys' Last Stand, The.*

Pearce, Richard *Country; Heartland; Leap of Faith; No Mercy.*

Pearson, Peter *Paperback Hero.*

Pécas, Max *I Am Frigid… Why? (Je Suis Frigide… Pourquoi?); Private Club (Club Privé pour Couples Avertis).*

Peck, Raoul *Lumumba; Man by the Shore, The (L'Homme sur les Quais).*

Peck, Ron *Empire State; Nighthawks; Strip Jack Naked: Nighthawks II.*

Peckinpah, Sam *Ballad of Cable Hogue, The; Bring Me the Head of Alfredo Garcia; Convoy; Cross of Iron; Deadly Companions, The; Getaway, The; Junior Bonner; Killer Elite, The; Major Dundee; Osterman Weekend, The; Pat Garrett and Billy the Kid; Ride the High Country (aka Guns in the Afternoon); Straw Dogs; Wild Bunch, The.*

Peerce, Larry *Ash Wednesday; Goodbye Columbus; Other Side of the Mountain, The (aka A Window to the Sky); Two-Minute Warning; Why Would I Lie?; Wired.*

Peeters, Barbara *Humanoids from the Deep (aka Monster).*

Peirce, Kimberly *Boys Don't Cry.*

Peled, Micha *Will My Mother Go Back to Berlin?; You, Me, Jerusalem.*

Pélissier, Anthony *Encore; History of Mr Polly, The; Meet Mr Lucifer; Rocking Horse Winner, The.*

Pellington, Mark *Arlington Road; Going All the Way; Mothman Prophecies, The.*

Pellizzari, Monica *Fistful of Flies.*

Peng Xiaolian *Story of Women, A (San ge Nüren).*

Penn, Arthur *Alice's Restuarant; Bonnie and Clyde; Chase, The; Dead of Winter; Four Friends (aka Georgia's Friends); Left Handed Gun, The; Little Big Man; Lumière et Compagnie; Mickey One; Miracle Worker, The; Missouri Breaks, The; Night Moves; Target; Visions of Eight.*

Penn, Leo *Judgment in Berlin.*

Penn, Sean *Crossing Guard, The; Indian Runner, The; Pledge, The.*

Pennebaker, DA *Don't Look Back; Down from the Mountain; Jane; Monterey Pop; One PM; Town Bloody Hall; War Room, The; Ziggy Stardust and the Spiders from Mars.*

Pennell, Eagle *Last Night at the Alamo.*

Peoples, David *Salute of the Jugger, The.*

Pepe, Louis *Hamster Factor and Other Tales of Twelve Monkeys, The.*

Peploe, Clare *High Season; Rough Magic (Miss Shumway jette un sort).*

Peploe, Mark *Afraid of the Dark; Victory.*

Perakis, Nikos *Female Company (Thiliki Etairia).*

Peralta, Stacy *Dogtown and Z-Boys.*

Pereira, Miguel *Veronico Cruz (La Deuda Interna).*

Perennou, Marie *Microcosmos (Microcosmos: Le Peuple de l'herbe).*

Peretz, Jesse *Chateau, The; First Love, Last Rites.*

Pérez, Fernando *Hello, Hemingway; Life Is to Whistle (La Vida es silbar).*

Périer, Etienne *Murder Is a Murder…Is a Murder, A (Un Meurtre est un Meurtre); When Eight Bells Toll.*

Peries, Sumitra *Mother Alone, A (Duwata Mawaka Misa).*

Perincioli, Cristina *Power of Men Is the Patience of Women, The (Die Macht der Männer ist die Geduld der Frauen).*

Perkins, Anthony *Psycho III.*

Perkins, Rachel *Radiance.*

Perret, Léonce *Twin Pawns (aka The Curse of Greed).*

Perry, Dein *Bootmen.*

Perry, Frank *Compromising Positions; Diary of a Mad Housewife; Doc; Hello Again; Last Summer; Mommie Dearest; Monsignor; On the Bridge; Rancho Deluxe; Swimmer, The.*

Perry, Simon *Eclipse.*

Petersen, Wolfgang *Air Force One; Boat, The (Das Boot); Boat: The Director's Cut, The (Das Boot); Consequence, The (Die Konsequenz); Enemy Mine; In the Line of Fire; NeverEnding Story, The (Die unendliche Geschichte); Outbreak; Perfect Storm, The; Shattered.*

Petit, Christopher *Asylum; Cardinal and the Corpse, The; Chinese Boxes; Falconer, The; Flight to Berlin (Fluchtpunkt Berlin); Radio On; Radio On (Remix); Unsuitable Job for a Woman, An.*

Petreglia, Sandro *Fit To Be Untied (Matti da Slegare).*

Petri, Elio *Class Operaia Va in Paradiso, La (Lulu the Tool/ The Working Class Go to Heaven).*

Petrie, Daniel *Bay Boy, The; Betsy, The; Bramble Bush, The; Buster and Billie; Cocoon: The Return; Dollmaker, The; Fort Apache, the Bronx; Lifeguard; My Favourite Martian; Neptune Factor, The; Resurrection; Square Dance; Stolen Hours; Sybil.*

Petrie Jr, Daniel *Toy Soldiers.*

Petrie, Donald *Associate, The; Grumpy Old Men; Miss Congeniality; Mystic Pizza; Richie Rich.*

Petrovic, Aleksandar *Master and Margarita, The (Majstori i Margarita).*

Pevney, Joseph *Away All Boats; Cash McCall; Congo Crossing; Strange Door, The; 3 Ring Circus; Torpedo Run.*

Pfleghar, Michael *Visions of Eight.*

Philibert, Nicolas *Every Little Thing (La Moindre des Choses).*

Phillippe, Pierre *Enfants de Lumière, Les (The Children of Lumière).*

Phillips, Maurice *American Way, The (aka Riders of the Storm); Another You; Enid Is Sleeping (aka Over Her Dead Body).*

Phillips, Todd *Road Trip.*

Phillips, Tom *TV Dante: Cantos I–VIII, A.*

Pialat, Maurice *Amour Existe, L'; Enfance nue, L' (Naked Childhood/Me); Loulou; Mouth Agape, The (La Gueule Ouverte); Passe ton bac d'abord; Police; Sous le Soleil de Satan (Under Satan's Sun); To Our Loves (A Nos Amours); Van Gogh.*

Pieraccioni, Leonardo *Cyclone, The (Il Ciclone).*

Piccioni, Giuseppe *Light of My Eyes (Luce dei miei occhi).*

Piccoli, Michel *Contre l'Oubli (Against Oblivion); So there, (Alors voilà,).*

Picha (Jean-Paul Walravens/ Boris Szulzinger) *Big Bang, The (Le Big Bang); Jungle Burger (La Honte de la Jungle).*

Pichel, Irving *And Now Tomorrow; Before Dawn; Destination Moon; Man I Married, The (aka I Married a Nazi); Miracle of the Bells, The; Mr Peabody and the Mermaid; Most Dangerous Game, The (aka The Hounds of Zaroff); Pied Piper, The; She; They Won't Believe Me.*

Pichul, Vasili *Little Vera (Malenkaya Vera).*

Pierce, Charles B *Bootleggers; Evictors, The; Grayeagle; Norseman, The.*

Pierson, Claude *Violation of Justine, The (Justine).*

Pierson, Frank R *Citizen Cohn; Dirty Pictures; Looking Glass War, The; King of the Gypsies; Star Is Born, A.*

Pieters, Guido *Romantic Agony, The (Vaarwel).*

Pilafian, Peter *Jimi Plays Berkeley.*

Pillsbury, Sam *Free Willy 3: The Rescue; Scarecrow, The; Starlight Hotel: Zandalee.*

Pincus, Ed *Diaries.*

Pinheiro, José *Cop's Honour (Parole de Flic).*

Pinhorn, Maggie *Tunde's Film.*

Pinoteau, Claude *Silencieux, Le (The Man Who Died Twice/ The Silent One).*

Pinter, Harold *Butley.*

Pintilié, Lucian *Lumière et Compagnie; Too Late (Trop Tard); Unforgettable Summer, An (Eté inoubliable, Un).*

Pintoff, Ernest *Critic, The; Dynamite Chicken; Harvey Middleman, Fireman; Jaguar Lives.*

Piquer-Simon, Juan *Rift, The (La Grieta); Supersonic Man.*

Pirès, Gérard *Agression, L' (Agression); Taxi.*

Pirhasan, Baris *Summer of Love (O Da Beni Seviyor).*

Pitts, Rafi *Season Five (Fassloh Padjom/Cinquième saison).*

Piva, Alessandro *LaCapaGira.*

Planchon, Roger *Lautrec.*

Platt, Lucas *Subway Stories Tales from the Underground.*

Platts-Mills, Barney *Bronco Bullfrog; Hero; Private Road.*

Plumb, Hay *Hamlet.*

Po Chih Leong *Ping Pong; Wisdom of Crocodiles, The.*

Podalydès, Bruno *Versailles rive gauche (A Night in Versailles).*

Podeswa, Jeremy *Eclipse; Five Senses.*

Poe, Amos *Subway Riders; Triple Bogey on a Par Five Hole.*

Poelvoorde, Benoît *Man Bites Dog (C'est arrivé près de chez vous).*

Pogostin, S Lee *Hard Contract.*

Poh, Richard (Bu Wancang) *Love and Duty (Lian'ai yu Yiwu).*

Pohland, Hans Jürgen *Stamping Ground (aka Love and Music).*

Poiré, Jean-Marie [aka Jean-Marie Gaubert] *Just Visiting (Les Visiteurs en Amerique); Visiteurs, Les.*

Poirier, Anne-Claire *Mourir à Tue-Tête (A Scream from Silence).*

Poirier, Léon, *Appel du Silence, L'.*

Poirier, Manuel *Western.*

Poitier, Sidney *Buck and the Preacher; Fast Forward; Hanky Panky; Let's Do It Again; Piece of the Action, A; Stir Crazy; Uptown Saturday Night; Warm December, A.*

Polanski, Roman *Bitter Moon (Lunes de fiel); Chinatown; Cul-de-Sac; Dance of the Vampires (aka The Fearless Vampire Killers); Death and the Maiden; Frantic; Knife in the Water (Noz w Wodzie); Macbeth; Ninth Gate, The; Pianist, The; Pirates; Repulsion; Rosemary's Baby; Tenant, The (Le Locataire); Tess; What? (Che?).*

Polat, Ayse *Tour Abroad (Auslandstournee).*

Poliakoff, Stephen *Century; Close My Eyes; Food for Love; Hidden City.*

Polish, Michael *Jackpot; Twin Falls Idaho.*

Politi, Edna *Anou Banou or the Daughters of Utopia (Anou Banou oder die Töchter der Utopie).*

Pollack, Barry *Booty Call; Cool Breeze.*

Pollack, Jeff *Above the Rim.*

Pollack, Sydney *Absence of Malice; Bobby Deerfield; Castle Keep; Electric Horseman, The; Firm, The; Havana; Jeremiah Johnson; Out of Africa; Random Hearts; Sabrina; Scalphunters, The; They Shoot Horses, Don't They?; This Property Is Condemned; Three Days of the Condor; Tootsie; Way We Were, The; Yakuza, The.*

Pollak, Claire *Cross and Passion; Theatre Girls.*

Pollak, Kay *Elvis! Elvis!*

Pollet, Jean-Daniel *Paris vu par… (Six in Paris).*

Pollock, George *Ten Little Indians.*

Polonsky, Abraham *Force of Evil; Romance of a Horse Thief; Tell Them Willie Boy Is Here.*

Polson, John *Siam Sunset.*

Pommer, Erich *Vessel of Wrath (aka The Beachcomber).*

Ponnelle, Jean-Pierre *Rigoletto.*

Pons, Ventura *Actresses (Actrius); Anita Takes a Chance (Anita no perd el tren); Caresses (Caricies).*

Pontecorvo, Gillo *Battle of Algiers, The (La Battaglia di Algeri); Kapo; Queimada! (Burn!).*

Pool, Lea *Anne Trister.*

Poole, Tom *'Chubby' Down Under and Other Sticky Regions.*

Pope, Angela *Captives; Hollow Reed.*

Pope, Tim *Crow: City of Angels, The; Cure in Orange, The.*

Popkin, Leo *Well, The.*

Post, Ted *Baby, The; Beneath the Planet of the Apes; Go Tell the Spartans; Good Guys Wear Black; Hang 'em High; Harrad Experiment, The; Magnum Force; Whiffs (aka C.A.S.H.).*

Postma, Laurens C *Heaven, Man, Earth.*

Potenza, Anthony *No Nukes.*

Potter, Dennis *Secret Friends.*

Potter, HC *Beloved Enemy; Blackmail; Congo Maisie; Hellzapoppin'; Mr Blandings Builds His Dream House; Story of Vernon and Irene Castle, The.*

Potter, Sally *Gold Diggers, The; Man Who Cried, The; Orlando; Tango Lesson, The.*

Potterton, Gerald *Heavy Metal.*

Poulson, Gerry *Under the Doctor.*

Powell, Aubrey *Cure Show, The.*

Powell, Dick *Conqueror, The; Hunters, The; Enemy Below, The.*

Powell, Michael *Age of Consent; Battle of the River Plate, The (aka Pursuit of the Graf Spee); Black Narcissus; Bluebeard's Castle; Canterbury Tale, A; Contraband (aka Blackout); Edge of the World, The; Elusive Pimpernel, The; 49th Parallel; Gone To Earth; Her Last Affaire; His Lordship; Honeymoon (Luna de Miel); I Know Where I'm Going!; Ill Met by Moonlight (aka Night Ambush); Lazybones; Life and Death of Colonel Blimp, The; Love Test, The; Matter of Life and Death, A (aka Stairway to Heaven); Night of the Party, The; Oh Rosalinda!!; One of Our Aircraft Is Missing; Peeping Tom; Phantom Light, The; Queen's Guards, The; Red Shoes, The; Small Back Room, The; Spy in Black, The; Tales of Hoffmann, The; They're a Weird Mob; Thief of Bagdad, The.*

Powell, Tristram *American Friends.*

Power, John *Father; Picture Show Man, The.*

Powers, John *I Am a Sex Addict.*

Pradal, Manuel *Angel Sharks (Marie Baie des Anges).*

Prado, Guilherme De Almeida *Lady from the Shanghai Cinema, The (A Dama do cine Shanghai).*

Prasad, Udayan *Brothers in Trouble; Gabriel & Me; My Son the Fanatic.*

Pray, Doug *Scratch.*

Preminger, Otto *Advise and Consent; Anatomy of a Murder; Angel Face; Bonjour Tristesse; Bunny Lake is Missing; Cardinal, The; Carmen Jones; Centennial Summer; Court-Martial of Billy Mitchell, The (aka One Man Mutiny); Daisy Kenyon; Danger – Love at Work; Exodus; Fallen Angel; Forever Amber; Human Factor, The; Hurry Sundown; In Harm's Way; Laura; Man With the Golden Arm, The; Moon Is Blue, The; River of No Return; Rosebud; Royal Scandal, A; Saint Joan; Such Good Friends; Tell Me That You Love Me, Junie Moon; Whirlpool.*

Pressburger, Emeric *Battle of the River Plate, The (aka Pursuit of the Graf Spee); Black Narcissus; Canterbury Tale, A; Elusive Pimpernel, The; Gone To Earth; I Know Where I'm Going!; Ill Met by Moonlight (aka Night Ambush); Life and Death of Colonel Blimp, The; Matter of Life and Death, A (aka Stairway to Heaven); Oh Rosalinda!!; One of Our Aircraft is Missing; Red Shoes, The; Small Back Room, The; Tales of Hoffmann, The.*

Pressman, Michael *Bad News Bears in Breaking Training, The; Boulevard Nights; Great Texas Dynamite Chase, The (aka Dynamite Women); Some Kind of Hero; Teenage Mutant Ninja Turtles II: The Secret of the Ooze.*

Price, David F *Dr Jekyll and Ms Hyde.*

Price, Paul (Paolo Poeti) *Inhibitions.*

Price, Will *Rock Rock Rock!*

Primus, Barry *Mistress.*

Prince Prince *– Sign o'the Times; Under the Cherry Moon.*

Prince-Bythewood, Gina *Love & Basketball.*

Prince, Harold *Little Night Music, A; Something for Everyone (aka Black Flowers for the Bride).*

Pringle, Ian *Isabelle Eberhardt.*

Proctor, Elaine *Friends; Kin; On the Wire.*

Prosperi, Franco *Africa Addio (Africa Blood and Guts); Uncle Tom (Addio, Zio Tom).*

Proud, Peter *Esther Waters.*

Proyas, Alex *Crow, The; Dark City.*

Pryor, Richard *Richard Pryor Here & Now.*

Prechezer, Carl *Blue Juice.*

Prévert, Pierre *Voyage-Surprise.*

Przybylski, Jan Nowina *Yiddle with His Fiddle (Judel gra na Skrzypkach/ Yidle mitn Fidl).*

Pudovkin, Vsevolod *End of St Petersburg, The (Konyets Sankt-Peterburga); Mechanics of the Brain, The (Mekhanika Golovnova Mozga); Mother (Mat); Storm Over Asia (Potomok Chingis-Khan).*

Puenzo, Luis *Official Version, The (La Historia Oficial); Old Gringo, The.*

Purcell, Evelyn *Nobody's Fool.*

Pürrer, Ursula *Flaming Ears.*

Pyke, Rex *Eric Clapton and His Rolling Hotel.*

Pyriev, Ivan *Brothers Karamazov, The (Bratya Karamazovy).*

Pytka, Joe *Let It Ride; Space Jam.*

Pyun, Albert *Adrenalin – Fear the Rush; Sword and the Sorcerer, The.*

Quandour, Mohy *Spectre of Edgar Allan Poe, The.*

Quay, Brothers *Institute Benjamenta.*

Querejeta, Gracia *Robert Ryland's Last Journey.*

Quested, John *Loophole.*

Questi, Giulio *Django Kill (Se Sei Vivo, Spara).*

Queysanne, Bernard *Homme qui Dort, Un (A Man in a Dream).*

Quine, Richard *Full of Life; Moonshine War, The; My Sister Eileen; Prisoner of Zenda, The; Sex and the Single Girl; Solid Gold Cadillac, The; Stangers When We Meet; World of Suzie Wong, The.*

Quinn, Anthony *Buccaneer, The.*

Quinn, Bob *Bishop's Story, The.*

Quintano, Gene *National Lampoon's Loaded Weapon 1; Why Me?*

Quintero, José *Roman Spring of Mrs Stone, The.*

Raban, Marilyn *Black and Silver.*

Raban, William *Black and Silver.*

Radclyffe, Curtis *Sweet Angel Mine.*

Rademakers, Fons *Assault, The (De Aanslag); Rape, The (Niet voor de Poesen).*

Radford, Katy *Soft on the Inside.*

Radford, Michael *Another Time, Another Place; B Monkey; Nineteen Eighty-Four; Postino, Il (The Postman); White Mischief.*

Radler, Bob *Best of the Best; Best of the Best 2.*

Rae, Michael *Laserblast.*

Raeburn, Michael *Grass Is Singing, The; Jit.*

Raei, Mojtaba *Birth of a Butterfly (Tavalod-e-yek Parvaneh).*

Rafelson, Bob *Black Widow; Blood and Wine; Five Easy Pieces; Head; King of Marvin Gardens, The; Man Trouble; Mountains of the Moon; Poodle Springs; Postman Always Rings Twice, The; Stay Hungry.*

Rafferty, Kevin *Atomic Café, The.*

Rafferty, Pierce *Atomic Café, The.*

Raffill, Stewart *High Risk; Mac and Me; Mannequin Two: On the Move (aka Mannequin on the Move); Philadelphia Experiment, The; Sea Gypsies, The (aka Shipwreck!); When the North Wind Blows.*

Rahn, Bruno *Dirnentragödie (Tragedy of the Street).*

Raimi, Sam *Army of Darkness: The Medieval Dead; Crimewave; Darkman; Evil Dead, The; Evil Dead II; For Love of the Game; Gift, The; Quick and the Dead, The; Simple Plan, A; Spider-Man.*

Rainer, Yvonne *Film About a Woman Who…; Kristina Talking Pictures; Lives of Performers; MURDER and Murder; Privilege.*

Raizman, Yuli *Private Life (Chastnaya Zhizn).*

Raja, Andrew *Offending Angels.*

Rakoff, Alvin *City on Fire; Death Ship; King Solomon's Treasure.*

Ramis, Harold *Analyze This; Bedazzled; Caddyshack; Groundhog Day; Multiplicity; National Lampoon's Vacation; Stuart Saves His Family.*

Ramsay, Lynne *Morvern Callar; Ratcatcher.*

Randel, Tony *Hellbound: Hellraiser II; Ticks.*

Ranga, Dana *East Side Story.*

Rankin Jr, Arthur *Last Unicorn, The.*

Ransen, Mort *Margaret's Museum.*

Ransick, Whitney *Handgun.*

Rapp, Bernard *Tiré à Part.*

Rappaport, Mark *Casual Relations; From the Journals of Jean Seberg; Impostors; Mozart in Love; Rock Hudson's Home Movies; Scenic Route, The.*

Rappeneau, Jean-Paul *Cyrano de Bergerac; Hussard sur le toit, Le (The Horseman on the Roof); Sauvage, Le.*

Rapper, Irving *Adventures of Mark Twain, The (aka Mark Twain); Christine Jorgensen Story, The; Deception; Now, Voyager; Rhapsody in Blue; Shining Victory.*

Rasool, Kay *My Journey, My Islam.*

Rash, Steve *Buddy Holly Story, The; Can't Buy Me Love; Eddie; Queens Logic; Son in Law.*

Ratanaruang, Pen-ek (Tom Pannet) *Fun Bar Karaoke; Monrak Transistor; 6ixtynin9 (Ruang Talok 69).*

Ratliff, George *Plutonium Circus, The.*

Ratner, Brett *Family Man; Money Talks; Rush Hour; Rush Hour 2.*

Ratoff, Gregory *Intermezzo (aka Escape to Happiness); Lancer Spy; Moss Rose; Rose of Washington Square.*

Rauch, Malte *Viva Portugal.*

Ravich, Rand *Astronaut's Wife, The.*

Rawi, Ousama *Judgement in Stone, A.*

Rawlence, Christopher *Man Who Mistook His Wife for a Hat, The.*

Ray, Man *Dreams That Money Can Buy.*

Ray, Nicholas *Bigger Than Life; Bitter Victory (Amère Victoire); Born to Be Bad; 55 Days at Peking; Flying Leathernecks; Hot Blood; In a Lonely Place; Johnny Guitar; King of Kings; Knock on Any Door; Lightning Over Water (aka Nick's Movie); Lusty Men, The; Macao; On Dangerous Ground; Party Girl; Rebel Without a Cause; Run for Cover; Savage Innocents, The; They Live By Night; True Story of Jesse James, The (aka The James Brothers); We Can't Go Home Again; Wind Across the Everglades; Woman's Secret, A.*

Ray, Sandip *Target.*

Ray, Satyajit *Adventures of Goopy and Bagha, The (Goopy Gyne Bagha Byne); Adversary, The (Pratidwandi); Branches of the Tree (Shakha Proshakha); Charulata (The Lonely Wife); Chess Players, The (Shatranj ke Khilari); Company Limited (Seemabaddha); Days and Nights in the Forest (Aranyer din Ratri); Devi (The Goddess); Distant Thunder (Ashani Sanket); Enemy of the People, An (Ganashatru); Home and the World, The (Ghare-Baire); Jalsaghar (The Music Room); Kanchenjungha; Mahanagar (The Big City); Middleman, The (Jana-Aranya); Pather Panchali; Philosopher's Stone, The (Paras Pathar); Stranger, The (Agantuk); Teen Kanya (Two Daughters).*

Rayns, Tony *Jang Sun-Woo Variations, The (Jang Sun-Woo Pyeonjuguk).*

Read, Melanie *Trial Run.*

Rebane, Bill *Giant Spider Invasion, The.*

Rebella, Juan Pablo *25 Watts.*

Recha, Mar *Pau and His Brother (Pau i el seu Germa).*

Red, Eric *Body Parts; Cohen and Tate.*

Redford, Robert *Horse Whisperer, The; Legend of Bagger Vance, The; Milagro Beanfield War, The; Ordinary People; Quiz Show; River Runs Through It, A.*

Reed, Bill *Secret of the Sword, The.*

Reed, Carol *Agony and the Ecstasy, The; Bank Holiday; Fallen Idol, The; Flap (aka The Last Warrior); Key, The; Kid for Two Farthings, A; Man Between, The; New Lot, The; Night Train to Munich; Odd Man Out; Oliver!; Our Man in Havana; Outcast of the Islands; Running Man, The; Stars Look Down, The; Third Man, The; True Glory, The; Way Ahead, The; Young Mr Pitt, The.*

Reed, Peyton *Bring It On.*

Rees, Clive *Blockhouse, The; When the Whales Came.*

Rees, Jerry *Brave Little Toaster, The; Marrying Man, The (aka Too Hot to Handle).*

Reeve, Geoffrey *Caravan to Vaccarès; Puppet on a Chain; Souvenir.*

Reeves, Michael *Sorcerers, The; Witchfinder General.*

Refn, Nickolas (Nikolas) Winding *Bleeder; Pusher.*

Reggio, Godfrey *Koyaanisqatsi; Powaqqatsi.*

Reichardt, Kelly *River of Grass.*

Reichert, Julia *Union Maids.*

Reichert, Mark *Union City.*

Reichle, Franz *Knowledge of Healing, The (Das Wissen vom Heilen).*

Reid, Alastair *Road Builder, The (aka The Night Digger); Something to Hide.*

Reid, Fiona Cunningham *Thin Ice.*

Reid, Frances *In the Best Interests of the Children; Long Night's Journey into Day.*

Reid, John *Carry Me Back.*

Reid, Tim *Once Upon a Time… When We Were Colored.*

Reilly, William *Men of Respect.*

Reiner, Carl *All of Me; Bert Rigby, You're a Fool; Dead Men Don't Wear Plaid; Jerk, The; Man With Two Brains, The; Oh, God!; One and Only, The; Sibling Rivalry; Summer School; That Old Feeling; Where's Poppa?*

Reiner, Rob *American President, The; Few Good Men, A; Ghosts of Mississippi (aka Ghosts from the Past); Misery; North; Princess Bride, The; Stand by Me; Story of Us, The; Sure Thing, The; This Is Spinal Tap; When Harry Met Sally…*

Reiner, Jeffrey *Blood and Concrete.*

Reinert, Al *For All Mankind.*

Reinhardt, Max *Midsummer Night's Dream, A.*

Reiniger, Lotte *Adventures of Prince Achmed, The (Die Geschicte des Prinzen Achmed).*

Reinl, Harald *Chariots of the Gods (Erinnerungen an die Zukunft); Hellhounds of Alaska (Die Blutigen Geier von Alaska).*

Reis, Irving *Big Street, The; Crack-Up.*

Reisch, Walter *Men Are Not Gods; Song of Scheherazade.*

Reisner, Allen *St Louis Blues.*

Reisner, Charles F *Everybody Dance; Steamboat Bill, Jr.*

Reisz, Karel *Everybody Wins; French Lieutenant's Woman, The; Gambler, The; Isadora; Morgan, a Suitable Case for Treatment; Night Must Fall; Saturday Night and Sunday Morning; Sweet Dreams; Who'll Stop the Rain? (aka Dog Soldiers).*

Reitherman, Wolfgang *Aristocats; Jungle Book, The; One Hundred and One Dalmatians; Rescuers, The; Robin Hood; Sword in the Stone, The.*

Reitman, Ivan *Dave; Evolution; Fathers' Day; Ghostbusters; Ghostbusters II; Junior; Kindergarten Cop; Legal Eagles; Meatballs; Six Days Seven Nights; Stripes; Twins.*

Reitz, Edgar *Germany in Autumn (Deutschland im Herbst); Heimat (Homeland); Stunde Null (Zero Hour).*

Rejtman, Martín *Silvia Prieto.*

Relph, Michael *Desert Mice; Rockets Galore (aka Mad Little Island).*

René, Norman *Longtime Companion; Prelude to a Kiss.*

Rennie, Howard *Spoor (aka Guns Across the Veldt).*

Renoir, Jean *Bas-Fonds, Les (The Lower Depths); Boudu Sauvé des Eaux (Boudu Saved from Drowning); Bête Humaine, La (The Human Beast/Judas Was a Woman); Caporal Epinglé, Le (The Elusive Corporal/The Vanishing Corporal); Chienne, La; Crime de Monsieur Lange, Le (The Crime of Monsieur Lange); Diary of a Chambermaid, The; Déjeuner sur l'Herbe, Le (Lunch on the Grass/Picnic on the Grass); Eléna et les Hommes (Paris Does Strange Things); Fille de l'Eau, La (The Whirlpool of Fate); French Cancan; Golden Coach, The (La Carrozza d'Oro/Le Carrosse d'Or); Grande Illusion, La; Madame Bovary; Marseillaise, La; Nana; Nuit du Carrefour, La; On Purge Bébé; Partie de Campagne, Une; Petite Marchande d'allumettes, La (The Little Matchgirl); Petit Théâtre de Jean Renoir, Le (Little Theatre of Jean Renoir, The); River, The; Règle du Jeu, La (The Rules of the Game); Southerner, The; Swamp Water; Testament du Docteur Cordelier, Le (Experiment in Evil); This Land Is Mine; Toni; Tournoi, Le (The Tournament); Vie est à nous, La (The People of France); Woman on the Beach, The.*

Rényi, Tamás *Valley, The (Volgy).*

Resnais, Alain *Amour à Mort, L'; Année Dernière à Marienbad, L' (Last Year in Marienbad); Contre l'Oubli (Against Oblivion); Far from Vietnam (Loin du Viêt-nam); Guerre est finie, La (The War Is Over); Hiroshima, Mon Amour; I Want to Go Home (Je Veux Rentrer à la Maison); Je t'aime, Je t'aime; Mon Oncle d'Amérique (My American Uncle/My Uncle from America); Muriel (Muriel, ou le Temps d'un Retour); Mélo; Providence; Same Old Song (On connaît la chanson); Smoking/No Smoking; Stavisky…; Vie est un Roman, La (Life Is a Bed of Roses).*

Resnikoff, Robert *First Power, The.*

Retes, Gabriel *Bulto, El (Excess Baggage); Sweet Scent of Death, A (Un Dulce Olor a Muerte).*

Rey-Coquais, Cyrille *Georgette Meunier.*

Reyero, Pablo *South Dock (Dársena Sur).*

Reygadas, Carlos *Japón (Japan).*

Reynolds, Burt *End, The; 'Gator; Stick; Sharkey's Machine.*

Reynolds, Kevin *Beast, The (aka The Beast of War); Count of Monte Cristo, The; Fandango; One Eight Seven; Rapa Nui; Robin Hood: Prince of Thieves; Waterworld.*

Reynolds, Scott *Ugly, The.*

Rezende, Sergio *To the Last Drop (Até a Ultima Gota).*

Rhodes, Michael Ray *Entertaining Angels: The Dorothy Day Story.*

Rhone, Trevor D *Smile Orange.*

Rhys Jones, Gareth *Bodywork.*

Rich, David Lowell *Airport '80 The Concorde (aka The Concorde – Airport '79); Eye of the Cat; Lovely Way to Die, A (aka A Lovely Way to Go); Sex Symbol, The; That Man Bolt.*

Rich, Matty *Straight Out of Brooklyn.*

Rich, Richard *Black Cauldron, The; Fox and the Hound, The; King and I, The; Swan Princess, The.*

Richard, Jean-Louis *Mata-Hari, Agent H.21.*

Richards, Dick *Culpepper Cattle Co., The; Death Valley; Farewell, My Lovely; Man, Woman and Child; March or Die; Rafferty and the Gold Dust Twins.*

Richards, Julian *Darklands.*

Richardson, Amanda *Carry Greenham Home.*

Richardson, Peter *Eat the Rich; Pope Must Die, The; Supergrass, The.*

Richardson, Ralph *Home at Seven (aka Murder on Monday).*

Richardson, Tony *Blue Sky; Border, The; Charge of the Light Brigade, The; Dead Cert.; Delicate Balance, A; Entertainer, The; Hamlet; Hotel New Hampshire, The; Joseph Andrews; Laughter in the Dark; Loneliness of the Long Distance Runner, The; Look Back in Anger; Loved One, The; Mademoiselle; Ned Kelly; Sailor from Gibraltar, The; Sanctuary; Taste of Honey, A; Tom Jones.*

Richert, William *American Success Company, The (aka Success); Night in the Life of Jimmy Reardon, A (aka Jimmy Reardon); Winter Kills.*

Richman, Geoff *Fly a Flag for Poplar.*

Richman, Marie *Fly a Flag for Poplar.*

Richmond, Anthony (Teodoro Ricci) *Sharks' Cave, The (Bermude: La Fossa Maledetta).*

Richter, Hans *Dreams That Money Can Buy.*

Richter, Roland Suso *After the Truth (Nichts als die Wahrheit).*

Richter, WD *Adventures of Buckaroo Banzai Across the 8th Dimension, The; Late for Dinner.*

Ricker, Bruce *Last of the Blue Devils, The.*

Rickman, Alan *Winter Guest, The.*

Rickman, Tom *River Rat, The.*

Ridley, Philip *Passion of Darkly Noon, The (Die Passion des Darkly Noon); Reflecting Skin, The.*

Riefenstahl, Leni *Blaue Licht, Das (The Blue Light); Olympische Spiele 1936 (Olympiad); Triumph of the Will (Triumph des Willens).*

Riesner, Charles *Big Store, The.*

Rifkin, Adam *Chase, The; Detroit Rock City; Night at the Golden Eagle.*

Riggs, Marlon T *Tongues Untied.*

Riju, Go *Blind Alley (Mienai); Elephant Song; Zazie.*

Riker, David *City, The (aka La Ciudad).*

Riklis, Eran *Cup Final.*

Rilla, Wolf *Black Rider, The; Blue Peter, The (aka Navy Heroes); Picadilly Third Stop; Scamp, The; Village of the Damned.*

Rinse Dream [Stephen Sayadian] *Café Flesh.*

Rintaro *Metropolis.*

Riondino, David *Cuba Libre – Velocipedi ai Tropici.*

Ripley, Arthur *Thunder Road.*

Ripoll, Maria *If Only (Lluvia en los zapatos).*

Ripploh, Frank *Taxi zum Klo.*

Ripstein, Arturo *Deep Crimson (Profundo carmesí/Carmin profond); Divine (El Evangelio de las maravillas); Such Is Life (Asi es la Vida); White Lies (Mentiras Piadosas).*

Risi, Marco *Forever Mary (Mery per sempre).*

Rissi, Michael *Soultaker.*

Rissient, Pierre *Five and the Skin (Cinq et la Peau).*

Ritchie, Aileen *Closer You Get, The.*

Ritchie, Guy *Lock, Stock and Two Smoking Barrels; Snatch.*

Ritchie, Michael *Almost Perfect Affair, An; Bad News Bears, The; Candidate, The; Couch Trip, The; Diggstown (aka Midnight Sting); Divine Madness; Downhill Racer; Fantasticks, The; Fletch; Fletch Lives; Golden Child, The; Island, The; Positively True Adventures of the Alleged Texas Cheerleader-Murdering Mom, The; Prime Cut; Semi-Tough; Simple Wish, A; Smile, Survivors, The; Wildcats.*

Rittakol, Bhandit *Moonhunter, The (14 Tula, Songkram Prachachon); Once Upon a Time…This Morning (Kala Krangnung Mua Shao Ni).*

Ritt, Martin *Back Roads; Black Orchid, The; Brotherhood, The; Casey's Shadow; Conrack; Cross Creek; Edge of the City (aka A Man Is Ten Feet Tall); Front, The; Hombre; Hud; Long, Hot Summer, The; Molly Maguires, The; Murphy's Romance; Norma Rae; Nuts; Pete 'n' Tillie; Sounder; Spy Who Came In From the Cold, The; Stanley & Iris.*

Rivette, Jacques *Amour par terre, L' (Love on the Ground); Belle Noiseuse, La (aka The Beautiful Troublemaker); Belle Noiseuse – Divertimento, La; Céline and Julie Go Boating (Céline et Julie Vont en Bateau: Phantom Ladies over Paris); Jeanne la Pucelle (Joan of Arc); Lumière et Compagnie; Mad Love (L'Amour Fou); Out 1: Spectre; Paris Nous Appartient (Paris Belongs to Us); Pont du Nord, Le; Religieuse, La (aka Suzanne Simonin, La Religieuse de Denis Diderot); Secret Défense; Va Savoir (Who Knows?).*

Roach, Hal *Turnabout.*

Roach, Jay *Austin Powers: International Man of Mystery; Austin Powers: The Spy Who Shagged Me; Meet the Parents.*

Robbe-Grillet, Alain *Belle Captive, La; Blue Villa, The (Un bruit qui rend fou); Glissements Progressifs du Plaisir; Immortelle, L'; Trans-Europ-Express.*

Robbins, Brian *Good Burger; Ready to Rumble; Varsity Blues.*

Robbins, Jerome *West Side Story.*

Robbins, Matthew *Batteries Not Included; Bingo; Corvette Summer (aka The Hot One); Dragonslayer; Legend of Billie Jean, The.*

Robbins, Tim *Cradle Will Rock; Dead Man Walking; Bob Roberts.*

Roberson, James W *Superstition (aka The Witch).*

Robert, Genevieve *Casual Sex?*

Robert, Yves *Alexandre (Alexandre le Bienheureux); Château de ma mère, Le (My Mother's Castle); Courage Fuyons (Courage – Let's Run); Gloire de mon père, La (My Father's Glory); Guerre des Boutons, La (The War of the Buttons); Pardon Mon Affaire (Un éléphant ça trompe énormément); Pardon Mon Affaire, Too (Nous Irons Tous au Paradis).*

Roberts, Cynthia *Last Supper, The.*

Roberts, John *Paulie; War of the Buttons; This Boy's Story.*

Roberts, Mel *Intimate with a Stranger.*

Roberts, Stephen *If I Had a Million; Man Who Broke the Bank at Monte Carlo, The.*

Roberts, Steve *Sir Henry at Rawlinson End.*

Roberts, Will *Men's Lives.*

Robertson, Cliff *J.W. Coop.*

Robertson, Hugh A *Bim; Melinda.*

Robertson, John S *Dr Jekyll and Mr Hyde.*

Robertson, Michael *Back of Beyond.*

Robertson, Shari *Well-Founded Fear.*

Robertson-Pierce, Pamela *Imago – Meret Oppenheim.*

Robison, Arthur *Schatten (Warning Shadows).*

Robins, Herb *Worm Eaters, The.*

Robinson, Bruce *How to Get Ahead in Advertising; Jennifer 8; Withnail & I.*

Robinson, Dave *Take It or Leave It.*

Robinson, John Mark *Kid.*

Robinson, Phil Alden *Field of Dreams; Sneakers; Woo Woo Kid, The.*

Robinson, Richard *Is There Sex After Marriage?*

Robinson, Todd *Wild Bill: A Hollywood Maverick.*

Robson, Mark *Avalanche Express; Bedlam; Bridges at Toko-Ri, The; Champion; Earthquake, Edge of Doom (aka Stronger Than Fear); From the Terrace; Ghost Ship, The; Happy Birthday, Wanda June; Harder They Fall, The; Inn of the Sixth Happiness, The; Isle of the Dead; I Want You; Little Hut, The; My Foolish Heart; Peyton Place; Seventh Victim, The; Valley of the Dolls; Von Ryan's Express.*

Rocco, Marc *Murder in the First.*

Rocha, Glauber *Antonio das Mortes (O Dragão da Maldade contra o Santo Guerreiro); Barravento (aka The Brute); Black God, White Devil (Deus e o Diabo na Terra do Sol); Lion has Seven Heads, The (Der Leone Have Sept Cabecas).*

Rochant, Eric *Aux Yeux du monde (Autobus); Monde sans pitié, Un (Tough Life/A World Without Pity).*

Rochat, Eric *Fifth Monkey, The.*

Rocksavage, David *Other Voices Other Rooms.*

Rockwell, Alexandre *Four Rooms; In the Soup; Somebody to Love; Sons.*

Roddam, Franc *Aria; Bride, The; K2; Lords of Discipline, The; Quadrophenia; War Party.*

Rode, Alfred *Môme Pigalle, La (Scandal in Montmartre).*

Rodgers, Mic *Universal Soldier: The Return.*

Rodley, Chris *Donald Cammell: The Ultimate Performance; Tropical Fish.*

Rodriguez, Robert *Desperado; El Mariachi; Faculty, The; Four Rooms; From Dusk till Dawn; Spy Kids.*

Roe, Chris *Pop and Me.*

Roe, Willy *Playbirds, The.*

Roeg, Nicolas *Aria; Bad Timing; Castaway; Cold Heaven; Don't Look Now; Eureka; Full Body Massage; Insignificance; Man Who Fell to Earth, The; Performance; Sweet Bird of Youth; Track 29; Two Deaths; Walkabout; Witches, The.*

Roehler (Röhler), Oskar *No Place to Go; Sylvester Countdown (aka In With the New/Silvester Countdown).*

Roemer, Michael *Haunted; Plot Against Harry, The.*

Roffman, Julian *Mask, The (aka The Eyes of Hell).*

Rogell, Albert S *Atlantic Adventure; Black Cat, The.*

Rogers, JB *American Pie 2; Say It Isn't So.*

Rogers, Maclean *Down Among the Z Men; Gert and Daisy's Weekend.*

Rogosin, Lionel *Come Back Africa.*

Rogozhkin, Alexander *Guard, The (Karaul).*

Röhler, Oskar *see* Roehler, Oskar

Rohmer, Eric *Arbre, le Maire et la Médiathèque ou Les Sept Hasards, L' (The Tree, the Mayor and the Leisure Centre or The Seven Fortuities); Aviator's Wife, The (La Femme de l'Aviateur); Beau Mariage,*

Le (A Good Marriage); Boulangère de Monceau, La; Carrière de Suzanne, La (Suzanne's Profession); Claire's Knee (Le Genou de Claire); Collectionneuse, La (The Collector); Conte d'automne (An Autumn Tale); Conte d'été (A Summer's Tale); Conte d'hiver (A Winter's Tale); Conte de printemps (A Tale of Springtime); 4 Adventures of Reinette & Mirabelle (4 Aventures de Reinette & Mirabelle); Full Moon in Paris (Les Nuits de la Pleine Lune); Green Ray, The (Le Rayon Vert); Lady & the Duke, The (L'Anglaise et le duc/Die Lady und der Herzog); Love in the Afternoon (L'Amour, l'Après-midi); Marquise von O..., Die (The Marquise of O); My Girlfriend's Boyfirend (L'Ami de Mon Amie); My Night with Maud (Ma Nuit chez Maud); Paris vu par... (Six in Paris); Pauline à la Plage (Pauline at the Beach); Perceval le Gallois; Rendez-vous de Paris, Les (Rendez-vous in Paris); Signe du Lion, Le (The Sign of Leo).

Rojas, Orlando *Sometimes I Look at My Life (A Veces Miro Mi Vida).*

Roley, Sutton *How to Steal the World.*

Rolfe, David W *Silent Witness, The.*

Rollin, Jean *Frisson des Vampires, Le (Sex and the Vampire/Vampire Thrills); Requiem pour un Vampire (Requiem for a Vampire/Virgins and Vampires); Viol du Vampire, Le.*

Roman, Phil *Tom and Jerry: The Movie.*

Romanek, Mark *Static.*

Romeo, Roberto *Esperanza & Sardinas.*

Romero, George A *Crazies, The; Creepshow; Dark Half, The; Dawn of the Dead (aka Zombies); Day of the Dead; Jack's Wife (aka Hungry Wives/Season of the Witch); Knightriders; Martin; Monkey Shines; Night of the Living Dead.*

Ronay, Esther *Rapunzel Let Down Your Hair.*

Rondi, Brunello *Master of Love (Racconti Proibiti di Nulla Vestiti).*

Roodt, Darrell James *Dangerous Ground; Jobman; Sarafina!; Stick, The.*

Rooks, Conrad *Chappaqua; Siddhartha.*

Roos, Don *Bounce; Opposite of Sex, The.*

Ropelewski, Tom *Look Who's Talking Now; Madhouse.*

Rosati, Faliero *Death of a Cameraman (Morte di un Operatore).*

Rose, Bernard *Anna Karenina (aka Leo Tolstoy's Anna Karenina); Candyman; Chicago Joe and the Showgirl; Immortal Beloved; ivansxtc.; Paperhouse.*

Rose, Les *Hog Wild.*

Rose, Robina *Jigsaw; Nightshift.*

Rose, Dan *Dead Man's Curve.*

Rosen, Martin *Plague Dogs, The; Season of Dreams (aka Stacking); Watership Down.*

Rosenbaum, Marianne SW *Peppermint Freedom (Peppermint Frieden).*

Rosenberg, Craig *Hotel de Love.*

Rosenberg, Robert *Before Stonewall.*

Rosenberg, Seth *Subway Stories Tales from the Underground.*

Rosenberg, Stuart *Amityville Horror, The; April Fools, The; Brubaker; Cool Hand Luke; Drowning Pool, The; Laughing Policeman, The (aka An Investigation of Murder); Love and Bullets; My Heroes Have Always Been Cowboys; Pocket Money; Pope of Greenwich Village, The; Voyage of the Damned; W USA.*

Rosenthal, Rick *American Dreamer; Bad Boys; Distant Thunder; Halloween II.*

Rosi, Francesco *Carmen; Christ Stopped at Eboli (Cristo si è Fermato a Eboli); Chronicle of a Death Foretold (Cronaca di una Morte Annunciata); Cinderella – Italian Style (C'era una Volta); Illustrious Corpses (Cadaveri Eccellenti); Lucky Luciano; Mani sulla Città (Hands Over the City); Mattei Affair, The (Il Caso Mattei); Moment of Truth, The (Il Momento della Verità); Salvatore Giuliano; Three Brothers (Tre Fratelli); Truce, The (La Tregua).*

Rosi, Gianfranco *Boatman.*

Rosman, Mark *House on Sorority Row, The (aka House of Evil).*

Ross, Benjamin *Young Poisoner's Handbook, The.*

Ross, Gary *Pleasantville.*

Ross, Gaylen *Dealers Among Dealers.*

Ross, Herbert *Boys on the Side; California Suite; Dancers; Footloose; Funny Lady; Goodbye Girl, The; Goodbye, Mr Chips; I Ought to Be in Pictures; Last of Sheila, The; My Blue Heaven; Nijinsky; Owl and the Pussycat, The; Pennies from Heaven; Play It Again, Sam; Protocol; Secret of My Success, The; Seven-Per-Cent Solution, The; Steel Magnolias; Sunshine Boys, The; Turning Point, The; Undercover Blues.*

Rossellini, Roberto *Age of Cosimo de Medici, The (L'Età de Cosimo de'Medici); Amore, L'; Augustine of Hippo (Agostino di Ippone); Blaise Pascal; Era Notte a Roma; Fear (La Paura); Francesco, giullare di Dio (Francis, God's Jester); Germany, Year Zero (Germania, Anno Zero); Giovanna d'Arco al Rogo (Jeanne au Bûcher/Joan at the Stake); Italy: Year One (Anno Uno); Machine That Kills Bad People, The (La Macchina Ammazzacattivi); Paisà; Prise de Pouvoir par Louis XIV, La (The Rise to Power of Louis XIV); Roma, Città Aperta (Open City/Rome, Open City); Stromboli, Terra di Dio (Stromboli); Viaggio in Italia (Journey to Italy/The Lonely Woman/Strangers/Voyage to Italy).*

Rossen, Robert *Alexander the Great; All the King's Men; Body and Soul; Hustler, The; Island in the Sun; Johnny O'Clock; Lilith.*

Rosso, Franco *Babylon; Nature of the Beast, The.*

Rosson, Richard *Corvette K-225 (aka The Nelson Touch).*

Rostrup, Kaspar *Place Nearvy, A (Her i Nærheden).*

Roth, Bobby *Heartbreakers.*

Roth, Joe *American Sweethearts; Coupe de Ville; Streets of Gold.*

Roth, Tim *War Zone, The.*

Rotheroe, Dom *My Brother Tom.*

Rothman, Stephanie *Velvet Vampire, The (aka Cemetery Girls/The Waking Hour).*

Rothschild, Amalie R *Conversations with Willard Van Dyke.*

Rouch, Jean *Chronique d'un Eté (Chronicle of a Summer); Paris vu par... (Six in Paris).*

Rouffio, Jacques *Violette et François.*

Rouquier, Georges *Farrebique.*

Rouse, Russell *Caper of the Golden Bulls, The (aka Carnival of Thieves); Fastest Gun Alive, The; Oscar, The; Thief, The; Well, The.*

Rousselot, Philippe *Serpent's Kiss, The.*

Rowland, Roy *Bugles in the Afternoon; 5000 Fingers of Dr T, The; Our Vines Have Tender Grapes; Rogue Cop; Two Weeks with Love.*

Rowley, Richard *Zapatista.*

Royer, Michel *Godard on TV: 1960–2000 (Godard à la Télé: 1960–2000).*

Rozema, Patricia *I've Heard the Mermaids Singing; Mansfield Park; When Night Is Falling; White Room.*

Rozier, Jacques *Adieu Philippine.*

Rózsa, János *Love, Mother (Csók, Anyu); Sunday Daughters (Vasárnapi Szlüok).*

Ruane, John *Dead Letter Office; Death in Brunswick; That Eye, the Sky.*

Rubbo, Michael *Tommy Tricker and the Stamp Traveller.*

Ruben, Joseph *Dreamscape; Good Son, The; Money Train; Return to Paradise; Sleeping with the Enemy; Stepfather, The; True Believer (aka Fighting Justice).*

Ruben, Katt Shea *Poison Ivy.*

Rubin, Bruce Joel *My Life.*

Rubinstein, Amnon *Heritage, The.*

Rudolf, Carsten *Beast Within, The (Menneskedyret).*

Rudolph, Alan *Afterglow; Breakfast of Champions; Choose Me; Endangered Species; Equinox; Love at Large; Made in Heaven; Mrs Parker and the Vicious Circle; Moderns, The; Mortal Thoughts; Remember My Name; Return Engagement; Roadie; Songwriter; Trouble in Mind; Welcome to L.A.*

Ruggles, Wesley *Bolero; I'm No Angel; No Man of Her Own; True Confession.*

Ruiz, Raúl *Ames Fortes, Les (Savage Souls); City of Pirates (La Ville des Pirates); Fils de Deux Mères ou Comédie de l'Innocence; Hypothesis of the Stolen Painting, The (L'Hypothèse du Tableau Volé); Ile au trésor, L' (Treasure Island); Jeu de l'oie, Le (Snakes and Ladders); Mémoire des apparences (Life Is a Dream); Of Great Events and Ordinary People (De Grands Evénements et des Gens Ordinaires); On Top of the Whale (Het Dak van de Walvis); Présence réelle, La;*

Shattered Image; Three Crowns of the Sailor (Les Trois Couronnes du Matelot); Time Regained (Le Temps retrouvé); Trois Vies et une Seule Mort (Three Lives and Only One Death).

Rulli, Stefano *Fit To Be Untied (Matti da Slegare).*

Rumley, Simon *Strong Language; Truth Game, The.*

Rupé, Katja *Germany in Autumn (Deutschland im Herbst).*

Rush, Richard *Color of Night; Freebie and the Bean; Getting Straight; Hell's Angels on Wheels; Psych-Out; Stunt Man, The.*

Russell, Charles (Chuck) *Bless the Child; Blob, The; Eraser; Mask, The; Nightmare on Elm Street 3: Dream Warriors, A; Scorpion King, The.*

Russell, David O *Flirting with Disaster; Spanking the Monkey; Three Kings.*

Russell, Jay *My Dog Skip.*

Russell, Ken *Altered States; Aria; Billion Dollar Brain; Boy Friend, The; Crimes of Passion; Devils, The; Gothic; Lair of the White Worm, The; Lisztomania; Mahler; Music Lovers, The; Rainbow, The; Salome's Last Dance; Savage Messiah; Tommy; Valentino; Whore; Women in Love.*

Russo, Aaron *Rude Awakening.*

Ruttmann, Walter *Berlin – Die Sinfonie der Grosstadt (Berlin – Symphony of a Great City).*

Ruzowitzky, Stefan *Inheritor, The (Die Siebtelbauern).*

Ryan, Frank *Can't Help Singing.*

Ryan, Terence *Brylcreen Boys, The.*

Rydell, Mark *Cinderella Liberty; Cowboys, The; Crime of the Century; For the Boys; Fox, The; Harry and Walter Go to New York; Intersection; On Golden Pond; Reivers, The; River, The; Rose, The.*

Ryden, Hope *Jane.*

Rygård, Elisabeth *Take It Like a Man, Ma'am (Ta'det som en Mand, Frue!).*

Rymer, Judy *Cinema of Unease.*

Rymer, Michael *Angel Baby; In Too Deep; Queen of the Damned.*

Ryoo Seung-Wan *Die Bad (Juk Gona Ho Gun Napun Gona).*

Rzayev, Yaver *Yellow Bride, The (Sari Gyalin).*

Sábato, Mario *To the Heart (Al Corazón).*

Sabbag, Randa Chahal *Civilised People (Civilisées).*

Sabu [Hiroyuki Tanaka] *Monday; Postman Blues (Posutoman burusu).*

Sachs, Ira *Delta, The.*

Sachs, William *Incredible Melting Man, The.*

Sackheim, Daniel *Glass House, The.*

Saeta, Eddie *Doctor Death: Seeker of Souls.*

Safran, Henri *Norman Loves Rose.*

Sagal, Boris *Helicopter Spies, The; Masada (aka The Antagonists); Mosquito Squadron; Omega Man, The; 1,000 Plane Raid, The.*

Sagan, Leontine *Mädchen in Uniform (Girls in Uniform/Maidens in Uniform).*

Sai, Yoichi *MARKS (MARKS no Yama).*

Saint-Clair, Julien *Lust and Desire (Le Désir et la Volupté).*

St Clair, Malcolm *Crack-Up; Jitterbugs.*

St Paul, Stuart *Scarlet Tunic, The.*

Saito, Hisashi *Painful Pair, A (Itai Futari).*

Sakaguchi, Hironobu *Final Fantasy: The Spirits Within.*

Sakamoto, Junji *Another Battle (Shin Jingi Naki Tatakai); Face (Kao); KT.*

Saks, Gene *Barefoot in the Park; Brighton Beach Memoirs; Last of the Red Hot Lovers; Mame; Odd Couple, The.*

Sale, Richard *Ticket to Tomahawk, A.*

Saleh, Kamel *Comme un Aimant (The Magnet).*

Salles, Walter *Behind the Sun (Abril despedaçado); Central Do Brasil; Foreign Land; Midnight (O Primeiro Dia/Le Premier Jour/aka Meia Noite).*

Salomon, Mikael *Far Off Place, A; Hard Rain.*

Salva, Victor *Jeepers Creepers; Powder.*

Salvadori, Pierre *Apprentis, Les; Cible émouvante (Wild Target); Détour, Le; Marchands de Sable, Les.*

Salvatores, Gabriele *Mediterraneo; Puerto Escondido; Teeth (Denti).*

Salwen, Hal *Denise Calls Up.*

Samperi, Salvatore *Grazie Zia (Thank You, Aunt); Malizia; Venial Sin (Peccato Veniale).*

Samuels, Stuart *Visions of Light.*

Sanborn, Keith *Deadman, The.*

Sanchez, Eduardo *Blair Witch Project, The.*

Sanchez, Nestor *Hidden Witnesses (Testigos Ocultos).*

Sandberg, Staale *Zapatista.*

Sander, Helke *All-Round Reduced Personality – Redupers, The (Die allseitig reduzierte Persönlichkeit – Redupers); Subjective Factor, The (Der subjektive Faktor).*

Sanders, Denis *Elvis – That's the Way It Is; Soul to Soul.*

Sanders, Jon *Painted Angels; '36 to '77.*

Sanders-Brahms, Helma *Future of Emily, The (L'Avenir d'Emilie); Germany, Pale Mother (Deutschland bleiche Mutter); Lumière et Compagnie; No Mercy, No Future (Die Berührte); Shirin's Wedding (Shirins Hochzeit).*

Sandgren, Åke *Slingshot, The (Kådisbellan); Truly Human (Et Rigtigt Menneske).*

Sandig, Frauke, *After the Fall (Nach dem Fall).*

Sándor, Pál *Daniel Takes a Train (Szerencsés Dániel); Improperly Dressed (Herkulesfürdöi emlék).*

Sandrich, Jay *Seems Like Old Times.*

Sandrich, Mark *Carefree; Follow the Fleet; Gay Divorcee, The; Here Come the Waves; Holiday Inn; Shall We Dance?; Top Hat; Woman Rebels, A.*

Sane, Kelley *Franchesca Page.*

Sangster, Jimmy *Fear in the Night.*

Sanjines, Jorge *Bird's Singing, The (Para Recibir el Canto de los Parajos); Blood of the Condor (Yawar Mallku); Coraje del Pueblo, El (The Courage of the People/The Night of San Juan); Secret Nation, The (La Nación Clandestina).*

Santakumar, Subrahmanian *Guardians of the Earth (Mankolangal).*

Santell, Alfred *Aloma of the South Seas; Beyond the Blue Horizon.*

Santiago, Hugo *Ecoute Voir... (See Here My Love).*

Santini, Derrick *In Ismail's Custody.*

Santley, Joseph *Cocoanuts, The.*

Santos, Alberto Seixas *Mal (Evil).*

Santostefano, Damon *Three to Tango.*

Saperstein, David *Beyond the Stars (aka Personal Choice).*

Sarafian, Deran *Back in the USSR; Gunmen; Road Flower; Terminal Velocity.*

Sarafian, Richard C *Lolly-Madonna XXX (aka The Lolly-Madonna War); Man in the Wilderness; Man Who Loved Cat Dancing, The; Sunburn; Vanishing Point.*

Sargent, Joseph *Coast to Coast; Forbin Project, The (aka Colossus – The Forbin Project); Jaws – The Revenge; MacArthur – The Rebel General; Nightmares; Sunshine; Sunshine Part II (aka My Sweet Lady); Taking of Pelham One Two Three, The; White Lightning.*

Sarin, Vic *Cold Comfort.*

Sariñana, Fernando *Hasta Morir (Until Death).*

Sarkissian, Hamlet *Camera Obscura.*

Sarne, Mike (Michael) *Myra Breckinridge; Punk and the Princess, The.*

Sarno, Joseph W *Butterfly (Broken Butterfly/Baby Tramp).*

Sasanatieng, Wisit *Tears of the Black Tiger (Fa Talai Jone).*

Sasdy, Peter *Countess Dracula; Doomwatch; Hands of the Ripper; I Don't Want to Be Born (aka The Devil Within Her); Lonely Lady, The; Nothing But the Night; Taste the Blood of Dracula; Welcome to Blood City.*

Saslavsky, Luis *Neige était sale, La (The Stain on the Snow/The Snow Was Black).*

Sass, Barbara *Tempation (Pokuszenie).*

Sathyu, MS *Hot Winds (Garm Hava).*

Satlof, Ron *Spider-Man Strikes Back.*

Sato, Hisayasu *Kitami (Kurutta Butokai/aka Lunaic Theatre).*

Sato, Junya *Bullet Train, The (Shinkansen Daibakuha).*

Sato, Shimako *Tale of a Vampire; Wizard of Darkness (Eko Eko Azaraku).*

Saunders, Charles *Danger by My Side; Tawny Pipit.*

Saunders, John Monk *Conquest of the Air.*

Saunders, Red *Gift, The.*

Saura, Carlos *Ay! Carmela; Blood Wedding (Bodas de Sangre); Carmen; Caza, La (The Hunt); Cría Cuervos (Raise Ravens); El Dorado; Fast, Fast (Deprisa, Deprisa); Flamenco; Goya in Bordeaux (Goya en Burdeos); Love Bewitched, A (El Amor Brujo); Peppermint Frappé; Sevillanas; Tango; Taxi; Tender Hours (Dulces Horas).*

Sautet, Claude *Choses de la Vie, Les (The Things of Life); César and Rosalie (César et Rosalie); Coeur en hiver, Un (A Heart in Winter); Enfants de Lumière, Les (The Children of Lumière); Nelly & Monsieur Arnaud (Nelly and Mr Arnaud).*

Saville, Philip *Fellow Traveller; Fruit Machine, The; Metroland; Oedipus the King; Secrets; Shadey; Those Glory, Glory Days.*

Saville, Victor *Dark Journey; Evensong; Evergreen; First a Girl; Good Companions, The; Hindle Wakes; Kim; Me and Marlborough; South Riding.*

Savini, Tom *Night of the Living Dead.*

Savoca, Nancy *Dogfight; If These Walls Could Talk; True Love.*

Sayadian, Stephen *see* Rinse Dream

Sayles, John *Baby It's You; Brother from Another Planet, The; City of Hope; Eight Men Out; Lianna; Limbo; Lone Star; Matewan; Men with Guns (aka Hombres Armados); Passion Fish; Return of the Secaucus Seven; Secret of Roan Inish, The; Sunshine State.*

Sayyad, Parviz *Mission, The.*

Schachter, Steven *Slight Case of Murder, A.*

Schaefer, George *Enemy of the People, An.*

Schaeffer, Eric *My Life's in Turnaround.*

Schaeffer, Francis *Headhunter.*

Schaffner, Franklin J *Best Man, The; Boys from Brazil, The; Double Man, The; Islands in the Stream; Nicholas and Alexandra; Papillon; Patton (aka Patton: Lust for Glory); Planet of the Apes; Sphinx; War Lord, The; Welcome Home; Yes, Giorgio.*

Schamoni, Peter *Spring Symphony (Frühlingssinfonie).*

Schatzberg, Jerry *Dandy, the All-American Girl (aka Sweet Revenge); Honeysuckle Rose; Lumière et Compagnie; Panic in Needle Park, The; Puzzle of a Downfall Child; Reunion (L'Ami retrouvé); Scarecrow; Seduction of Joe Tynan, The.*

Scheinman, Andrew *Little Big League.*

Schell, Maximilian *Marlene; Pedestrian, The (Der Fussgänger); Tales from the Vienna Woods (Geschichten aus dem Wiener Wald).*

Schellerup, Henning *Black Bunch, The (aka Jungle Sex).*

Schenck, George *Superbeast.*

Schenk, Otto *Dance of Love (Reigen).*

Schenkel, Carl *Exquisite Tenderness; Knight Moves; Mighty Quinn, The; Out of Order (Abwärts).*

Schepisi, Fred *Barbarosa; Chant of Jimmie Blacksmith, The; Cry in the Dark, A; Devil's Playground, The; Fierce Creatures; I. Q.; Last Orders; Mr Baseball; Plenty; Roxanne; Russia House, The; Six Degrees of Separation.*

Scherfig, Lone *Italian for Beginners (Italiensk for Begyndere).*

Schertzinger, Victor *Birth of the Blues; Mikado, The.*

Scheumann, Gerhard *I Was, I Am, I Shall Be (Ich war, ich bin, ich werde sein).*

Schierl, Angela Hans *Flaming Ears.*

Schiller, Greta *Before Stonewall; Man Who Drove with Mandela, The; Paris Was a Woman.*

Schiller, Lawrence *Executioner's Song, The; Marilyn – The Untold Story.*

Schiller, Tom *Nothing Lasts Forever.*

Schipek, Dietmar *Flaming Ears.*

Schipper, Sebastian *Gigantic (Absolute Giganten).*

Schirmbeck, Samuel *Viva Portugal.*

Schlamme, Thomas *Miss Firecracker; So I Married an Axe Murderer.*

Schlatter, George *Norman…Is That You?*

Schlesinger, John *Believers, The; Billy Liar!; Colf Comfort Farm; Darling; Day of the Locust, The; Eye for an Eye; Falcon and the Snowman, The; Far From the Madding Crowd; Honky Tonk Freeway; Innocent, The (…und der Himmel steht still); Kind of Loving, A; Madame Sousatzka; Marathon Man; Midnight Cowboy; Next Best Thing, The; Pacific Heights; Sunday, Bloody Sunday; Sweeney Todd; Visions of Eight; Yanks.*

Schlingensief, Christoph *German Chainsaw Massacre, The (Das deutsche Kettensagenmassaker); Terror 2000.*

Schlossberg, Julian *No Nukes.*

Schlöndorff, Volker *Circle of Deceit (Die Fälschung); Coupe de Grâce (Der Fangschuss); Death of a Salesman; Degree of Murder, A (Mord und Totschlag); Gathering of Old Men, A; Germany in Autumn (Deutschland im Herbst); Handmaid's Tale, The (Die Geschichte der Dienerin); Legends of Rita, The (Die Stille nach dem Schuss); Lost Honour of Katharina Blum, The (Die verlorene Ehre der Katharina Blum); Michael Kohlhaas; Palmetto; Roi des Aulnes, Le (The Erl King); Sudden Fortune of the Good People of Kombach, The (Der plötzliche Reichtum der armen Leute von Kombach); Swann in Love (Un Amour de Swann); Tin Drum, The (Die Blechtrommel); Voyager; Young Törless (Der junge Törless).*

Schmid, Daniel *Written Face, The (Das Geschriebene Gesicht).*

Schmid, Hans-Christian *Crazy.*

Schmidt, Jan *Joseph Kilián (Postava k Podpírání).*

Schmidt, Richard R *1988: The Remake.*

Schmidt, Rob *Crime + Punishment in Suburbia; Saturn.*

Schmitz, Oliver *Mapantsula.*

Schnabel, Julian *Basquiat; Before Night Falls.*

Schnéevoigt, George *Vicar of Vejlby, The (Præsten i Vejlby).*

Schneider, Alan *Film.*

Schoedsack, Ernest B *Dr Cyclops; Grass; King Kong; Last Days of Pompeii, The; Mighty Joe Young; Most Dangerous Game, The (aka The Hounds of Zaroff).*

Schoendoerffer, Frédéric *Scènes de Crimes.*

Schonfeld, Victor *Animals Film, The; Shattered Dreams: Picking Up the Pieces.*

Schorm, Evald *Pearls of the Deep (Perlicky na dne).*

Schrader, Leonard *Naked Tango.*

Schrader, Paul *Affliction; American Gigolo; Blue Collar; Cat People; Comfort of Strangers, The (Cortesie per gli ospiti); Hardcore (aka The Hardcore Life); Light of Day; Light Sleeper; Mishima: A Life in Four Chapters; Patty Hearst; Touch; Witch Hunt.*

Schrader, Uwe *Mau Mau.*

Schroeder, Barbet *Barfly; Before and After; Desperate Measures; General Amin (Général Idi Amin Dada: Autoportrait); Kiss of Death; Maîtresse; Our Lady of the Assassins (Notre Dame des assassins/Le Virgen de los Sicarios); Reversal of Fortune; Single White Female; Vallée, La (The Valley Obscured by Clouds).*

Schroeder, Eberhard *Sex Life in a Convent (Klosterschülerinnen).*

Schroeder, Michael *Out of the Dark.*

Schroeder, Sebastian C *O for Oblomov (O wie Oblomov).*

Schroeter, Werner *Death of Maria Malibran, The (Der Tod der Maria Malibran); Eika Katappa; Palermo or Wolfsburg (Palermo oder Wolfsburg); Reign of Naples, The (Neapolitanische Geschwister).*

Schubert, Peter *Germany in Autumn (Deutschland im Herbst).*

Schulman, Tom *8 Heads in a Duffel Bag.*

Schultz, Carl *Blue Fin; Careful, He Might Hear You; Seventh Sign, The; To Walk with Lions; Travelling North.*

Schultz, John *Drive Me Crazy.*

Schultz, Michael *Car Wash; Carbon Copy; Cooley High; Greased Lightning; Krush Groove (aka Rap Attack); Last Dragon, The; Sgt Pepper's Lonely Hearts Club Band.*

Schumacher, Joel *Batman & Robin; Batman Forever; Client, The; Cousins; D.C. Cab (aka Street Fleet); Dying Young; 8MM; Falling Down; Flatliners; Flawless; Incredible Shrinking Woman, The; Lost Boys, The; St Elmo's Fire; Tigerland; Time to Kill, A.*

Schunzel, Reinhold *Balalaika.*

Schüppel, Uli M *Platz, Der (The Place).*

Schuster, Harold *Dragoon Wells Massacre; My Friend Flicka; Wings of the Morning.*

Schütte, Jan *Farewell (Abschied); Fat World (Fette Welt); Spicy Rice (Drachenfutter).*

Schwabach, Peter *Secret Laughter of Women, The.*

Schwartz, Douglas N *Your Three Minutes Are Up.*

Schwartz, Robert *Survivors, The Blues Today.*

Schwartz, Stefan *Shooting Fish; Soft Top, Hard Shoulder.*

Schwarz, Hanns *Wunderbare Lüge der Nina Petrowna, Die (The Wonderful Life).*

Schweitzer, Mikhail *Kreutzer Sonata, The (Kreitzerova Sonata).*

Schwietert, Stefan *Devil's Accordion, The (El Acordéon del Diablo); Tickle in the Heart, A.*

Schyfter, Guita *Like a Bride (Novia que te Vea).*

Sciamma, Alberto *Killer Tongue (La lengua asesina).*

Sciarra, Maurizio *Off to the Revolution by 2CV (Alla Rivoluzione sulla Due Cavalli).*

Scimeca, Pasquale *Placido Rizzotto.*

Scoffield, Jon *Max Wall – Funny Man.*

Scola, Ettore *Bal, Le; Brutti, sporchi e cattivi (Ugly, Dirty and Bad/Ugly Dirty and Mean/Down and Dirty); Dramma della Gelosia (Jealousy, Italian Style/The Pizza Triangle); Macaroni (Maccheroni); Passione d'Amore; Special Day, A (Una Giornata Particolare); Splendor; That Night in Varennes (La Nuit de Varennes).*

Scorsese, Martin *After Hours; Age of Innocence, The; Alice Doesn't Live Here Anymore; American Boy; Boxcar Bertha; Bringing Out the Dead; Cape Fear; Casino; Color of Money, The; GoodFellas; Italianamerican; King of Comedy, The; Kundun; Last Temptation of Christ, The; Last Waltz, The; Mean Streets; New York, New York; New York Stories; Raging Bull; Taxi Driver; Who's That Knocking at My Door? (aka I Call First).*

Scott, Campbell *Big Night.*

Scott, Cynthia *Company of Strangers, The.*

Scott, Jake *Plunkett & Macleane.*

Scott, James *'36 to '77; Adult Fun; Chance, History, Art...; Colin & Platonida; Every Picture Tells a Story.*

Scott, Oz *Bustin' Loose.*

Scott, Peter Graham *Bitter Harvest; Cracksman, The.*

Scott, Ridley *Alien; Black Hawk Down; Black Rain; Blade Runner; Blade Runner – The Director's Cut; Boy and Bicycle; Duellists, The; 1492: Conquest of Paradise; G.I. Jane; Gladiator; Hannibal; Legend; Someone to Watch Over Me; Thelma & Louise; White Squall.*

Scott, Tony *Beverly Hills Cop II; Crimson Tide; Days of Thunder; Enemy of the State; Fan, The; Hunger, The; Last Boy Scout, The; Revenge; Spy Games; Top Gun; True Romance.*

Scribner, George *Oliver & Company.*

Seacat, Sandra *In the Spirit.*

Seagal, Steven *On Deadly Ground.*

Seale, John *Till There Was You.*

Searle, Francis *Emergency.*

Sears, Fred F *Don't Knock the Rock; Earth vs the Flying Saucers (aka Invasion of the Flying Saucers).*

Seaton, George *Airport; Big Lift, The; Proud and Profane, The; 36 Hours.*

Sebastian, Beverly *'Gator Bait (aka Swamp Bait).*

Sebastian, Ferd *'Gator Bait (aka Swamp Bait).*

Sébastian, Isabel *Both Sides of the Street (La Contre-allée).*

Sedgwick, Edward *Cameraman, The; Parlor, Bedroom and Bath (aka Romeo in Pyjamas); Spite Marriage; A Southern Yankee (aka My Hero).*

Seed, Paul *Affair, The.*

Segal, Peter *Naked Gun 33⅓: The Final Insult; Nutty Professor II: The Klumps; Tommy Boy.*

Segura, Santiago *Torrente, the Dumb Arm of the Law (Torrente, el brazo tonto de la ley).*

Sehr, Peter *Kaspar Hauser (Verbrechen am Seelenleben eines Menschens); Serbian Girl, The (Das serbische Mädchen).*

Seidl, Ulrich *Dog Days (Hundstage); Tierische Liebe (Animal Love).*

Seidelman, Susan *Confessions of a Suburban Girl; Cookie; Desperately Seeking Susan; Making Mr Right; She-Devil; Smithereens.*

Seiler, Lewis *Guadalcanal Diary; Smiling Ghost, The.*

Seiter, William A *Broadway; Dimples; If I Had a Million; Lady Takes a Chance; Life Begins in College (aka The Joy Parade); One Touch of Venus; Roberta; Room Service; Sons of the Desert (aka Fraternally Yours); This Is My Affair (aka His Affair); You Were Never Lovelier.*

Sekely, Steve *Day of the Triffids, The; Hollow Triumph (aka The Scar).*

Sekers, Alan *Arp Statue, The.*

Selick, Henry *James and the Giant Peach; Monkeybone; Nightmare Before Christmas, The (aka Tim Burton's The Nightmare Before Christmas).*

Selignac, Arnaud *Gawin.*

Sellar, Ian *Prague; Venus Peter.*

Selpin, Herbert *Titanic.*

Seltzer, David Lucas; *Punchline; Shining Through.*

Selznick, Arna *Care Bears Movie, The.*

Sembene, Ousmane *Black Girl (La Noire de...); Camp Thiaroye (Camp de Thiaroye); Ceddo; Emitaï; Money Order, The (Le Mandat); Xala.*

Sen, Aparna *36 Chowringhee Lane.*

Sen, Mrinal *Genesis (Génésis); In Search of Famine (Aakaler Sandhane); Outsiders, The (Oka Oorie Katha).*

Sena, Dominic *Gone in Sixty Seconds; Kalifornia; Swordfish.*

Seresin, Michael *Homeboy.*

Serious, Yahoo *Young Einstein.*

Serrano, Antonio *Sex, Shame and Tears (Sexo, pudor y lágrimas).*

Serreau, Coline *Contre l'Oubli (Against Oblivion); Belle Verte, La (The Good Green World); Crise, La; Romuald et Juliette (Romuald & Juliette); 3 Men and a Cradle (3 Hommes et un Couffin).*

Servais, Raoul *Taxandria.*

Setbon, Philippe *Mister Frost.*

Sevilla, Raphael J *Mujer del puerto, La (Woman of the Port).*

Sewell, Vernon *Blood Beast Terror, The (aka The Vampire Beast Craves Blood); Burke and Hare; Curse of the Crimson Altar (aka The Crimson Cult).*

Seymour, Daniel *CS Blues.*

Sgarro, Nicholas *Happy Hooker, The.*

Shabazz, Menelik *Burning an Illusion; Time and Judgement.*

Shadyac, Tom *Ace Ventura, Pet Detective; Liar Liar; Nutty Professor, The; Patch Adams.*

Shafer, Dirk *Man of the Year.*

Shaffer, Deborah *Wobblies, The.*

Shah, Hasan *Rough Cut and Ready Dubbed.*

Shah, Krishna *Cinema Cinema.*

Shaji *Piravi (The Birth).*

Shakey, Bernard (Neil Young) *Rust Never Sleeps.*

Shakhnazarov, Karen *Assassin of the Tsar (Tsareubiitsa); Full Moon (Denj Polnoluniya).*

Shamberg, Michael H *Souvenir.*

Shane, Maxwell *Fear In The Night; Nightmare.*

Shankman, Adam *Wedding Planner, The.*

Shanley, John Patrick *Joe Versus the Volcano.*

Shannon, Frank (Franco Prosperi) *Invincible Barbarian, The (Gunan il Guerriero).*

Shapiro, Alan *Crush, The; Flipper.*

Shapiro, Ken *Groove Tube, The.*

Shapiro, Justine *Promises.*

Shapiro, Susan *Rapunzel Let Down Your Hair.*

Sharma, Aribam Syam *Chosen One, The (Ishanou).*

Sharman, Jim *Rocky Horror Picture Show, The; Shock Treatment.*

Sharp, Don *Bear Island; Brides of Fu Manchu, The; Callan; Face of Fu Manchu, The; Four Feathers, The; Hennessy; It's All Happening; Jules Verne's Rocket to the Moon; Kiss of the Vampire (aka Kiss of Evil); Psychomania; Secrets of the Phantom Caves; Thirty-Nine Steps, The.*

Sharp, Ian *Music Machine, The; Who Dares Wins.*

Sarp, Kerri *Maldoror.*

Sharpsteen, Ben *Dumbo; Fantasia; Pinocchio.*

Shatner, William *Star Trek V: The Final Frontier.*

Shaughnessy, Alfred *Cat Girl; 6.5 Special (aka Calling All Cats).*

Shavelson, Melville *Beau James; Cast a Giant Shadow; Houseboat; It Started in Naples; Mixed Company; New Kind of Love, A; Yours, Mine and Ours.*

Shaw, AlexanderConquest *of the Air.*

Shaw, Dom *Rough Cut and Ready Dubbed.*

Shaye, Robert *Book of Love.*

Shbib, Bashar *Julia Has Two Lovers.*

Shea, Katt *Rage: Carrie 2, The.*

Shear, Barry *Across 110th Street; Deadly Trackers, The; Karate Killers, The; Todd Killings, The; Wild in the Streets.*

Shebib, Donald *Between Friends; Goin' Down the Road; Heartaches.*

Shebib, Donald (as DS Everett) *Running Brave.*

Sheen, Martin *Count a Lonely Cadence (aka Stockade).*

Sheetz, Chuck *Recess: School's Out.*

Shelton, Ron *Blaze; Bull Durham; Cobb; Play It to the Bone; Tin Cup; White Men Can't Jump.*

Shengelaya, Eldar *Blue Mountains (Golubye Gory Ely Nepravdopodobnaya Istoria).*

Shengelaya, Georgy *Journey of a Young Composer (Akhalgazrda Kompozitoris Mogzauroba); Pirosmani.*

Shen Jiang *Return of the Dragon (Qisha Jieaka Infernal Street).*

Shepard, Richard *Linguini Incident, The.*

Shepard, Sam *Far North; Silent Tongue.*

Shepitko, Larissa *Ascent, The (Voskhozhdenie).*

Sher, Jack *Three Worlds of Gulliver, The.*

Sheridan, Jim *Boxer, The; Field, The; In the Name of the Father; My Left Foot.*

Sheridan, Kirsten *Disco Pigs.*

Sheridan, Michael J *That's Entertainment! III.*

Sherin, Edwin *Valdez Is Coming.*

Sherman, Gary A *Dead and Buried; Vice Squad.*

Sherman, Gary *Death Line (aka Raw Meat); Poltergeist III; Wanted Dead or Alive.*

Sherman, George *Big Jake; Lone Hand, The.*

Sherman, Lowell *She Done Him Wrong.*

Sherman, Vincent *Adventures of Don Juan (aka The New Adventures of Don Juan); All Through the Night; Garment Jungle, The; Hasty Heart, The; Ice Palace; Mr Skeffington; Old Acquaintance; Return of Doctor X, The; Saturday's Children; Unfaithful, The.*

Sherwin, Robert *Dirty Laundry.*

Sherwood, Bill *Parting Glances.*

Sherwood, John *Creature Walks Among Us, The; Monolith Monsters, The.*

Shi Dongshan *8,000 Li Under the Clouds and Moon (Baqian Li Lu Yun he Yue).*

Shi Runjiu *All the Way (Zou Dao Di).*

Shih Ti *Dragon Dies Hard, The (aka The Bruce Lee Story).*

Shi Hui *This Whole Life of Mine (Wo zhei Yibeizi/aka The Life of a Peking Policeman).*

Shimizu, Hiroshi *Ikinai.*

Shin, Nelson *Transformers – The Movie, The.*

Shindo, Kaneto *Island, The (Hadaka no Shima); Kuroneko (Yabu no Naka no Kuroneko); Life of Chikuzan, The (Chikuzan Hitori Tabi); Lost Sex (Honno); Onibaba (The Hole).*

Shinto, Kaze *Love/Juice.*

Shinoda, Masahiro *Double Suicide (Shinju Ten no Amijima); Gonza the Spearman (Yari no Gonza); Ondeko-za on Sado, The.*

Shinohara, Tetsuo *Stakeout (Harikomi); Work on the Grass (Kusa no Ue no Shigoto).*

Shinozaki, Makoto *Jam Session: The Official Bootleg of Kikujiro; Not Forgotten (Wasurerarenu Hitobito); Okaeri.*

Shiota, Akihiko *Gips.*

Shirakawa, Koji *Discipline for the Left-Handed (Hidari Chokyo); Sight Behind the Bandaged Eye, The (Ishiki Saizuri); Zipper and Tits (Fastner to Chibusa).*

Shoaibi, Moody *Dog Eat Dog.*

Sholder, Jack *Alone in the Dark; Hidden, The; Nightmare on Elm Street Part 2: Freddy's Revenge, A; Renegades.*

Shonteff, Lindsay *Big Zapper; Spy Story.*

Shore, Simon *Get Real; Henri.*

Shu Kei *Hu-Du-Men (aka Stage Door); Queer Story, A (Jilao Sishi); Sunless Days (Meiyou Taiyang de Rizi).*

Shub, Esther *Fall of the Romanov Dynasty, The (Padenie Dinasti Romanovikh).*

Shuker, Gregory *Jane.*

Shumlin, Herman *Confidential Agent.*

Shyer, Charles *Affair of the Necklace, The; Baby Boom; Father of the Bride; Father of the Bride Part II; I Love Trouble; Irreconcilable Differences.*

Shyamalan, M Night *Sixth Sense, The; Unbreakable.*

Siberling, Brad *City of Angels.*

Sichel, Alex *All Over Me.*

Sidaris, Andy *Seven.*

Sidney, George *Anchors Aweigh; Annie Get Your Gun; Bye Bye Birdie; Half a Sixpence; Harvey Girls, The; Holiday in Mexico; Jupiter's Darling; Kiss Me Kate; Kiss Me Kate: 3-D; Pal Joey; Scaramouche; Show Boat; Viva Las Vegas (aka Love in Las Vegas); Young Bess.*

Siegel, David *Suture.*

Siegel, Don *Annapolis Story, An (aka The Blue and the Gold); Baby Face Nelson; Beguiled, The; Big Steal, The; Black Windmill, The; Charley Varrick; Coogan's Bluff; Crime in the Streets; Dirty Harry; Duel at Silver Creek, The; Escape from Alcatraz; Flaming Star; Hanged Man, The; Hell Is for Heroes; Hound-Dog Man; Invasion of the Body Snatchers; Jinxed!; Killers, The; Lineup, The; Madigan; Private Hell 36; Riot in Cell Block 11; Rough Cut; Shootist, The; Stranger on the Run; Telefon; Two Mules for Sister Sara; Verdict, The.*

Siegel, Don (as Alan Smithee) *Death of a Gunfighter.*

Siegel, Robert J *Line, The.*

Sigel, Thomas *When the Mountains Tremble.*

Signorelli, Jim *Easy Money; Elvira, Mistress of the Dark.*

Siguion-Reyna, Carlos *Three (Tatlo…magkasalo).*

Silber, Glenn *El Salvador: Another Vietnam.*

Silberg, Joel *Breakin' (aka Breakdance); Lambada; Rappin'.*

Silberling, Brad *Casper.*

Sills, Sam *Good Fight, The.*

Silver, Claudia *Kalamazoo.*

Silver, Joan Micklin *Between the Lines; Big Girls Don't Cry…They Get Even (aka Stepkids); Crossing Delancey; Head Over Heels (aka Chilly Scenes of Winter); Hester Street; Loverboy; Prison Stories: Women on the Inside.*

Silver, Marisa *He Said, She Said; Old Enough; Permanent Record.*

Silver, Scott *Johns.*

Silverstein, Elliot *Car, The; Cat Ballou; Happening, The; Man Called Horse, A.*

Simmons, Anthony *Black Joy; Optimists of Nine Elms, The.*

Simoes, Rui *Deus, Patria e Autoridade (God, Fatherland and Authority); Good People of Portugal, The (Bom Povo Português).*

Simon, Adam *American Nightmare, The; Typewriter, the Writer & the Movie Camera, The.*

Simon, Frank *Queen, The.*

Simon, S Sylvan *Grand Central Murder.*

Simoneau, Yves *In the Belly of Dragon (Dans le Ventre du Dragon); Mother's Boys; Perfectly Normal.*

Simpson, Julian *Criminal, The.*

Sinapi, Jean-Pierre *Uneasy Riders (Nationale 7) (Nationale 7).*

Sinatra, Frank *None But the Brave.*

Sinclair, Andrew *Under Milk Wood.*

Sinclair, Harry *Topless Women Talk About Their Lives.*

Sinclair, Iain *Asylum; Falconer, The.*

Sinclair, Ingrid *Flame.*

Singer, Bryan J *Apt Pupil (Un Elève doué); Public Access; Usual Suspects, The; X-Men.*

Singer, Marc *Dark Days.*

Singh, Digvijay *Maya.*

Singh, Tarsem *Cell, The.*

Singh, Vijay *Jaya Ganga (Jaya, Fille du Gange).*

Singleton, John *Baby Boy; Boyz N the Hood; Higher Learning; Poetic Justice; Shaft.*

Singleton, Ralph S *Graveyard Shift.*

Sinise, Gary *Miles from Home; Of Mice and Men.*

Sinkel, Bernhard *Germany in Autumn (Deutschland im Herbst); Lina Braake.*

Sinyor, Gary *Bachelor, The; Leon the Pig Farmer; Solitaire for 2; Stiff Upper Lips.*

Siodmak, Curt *Magnetic Monster, The.*

Siodmak, Robert *Christmas Holiday; Crimson Pirate, The; Criss Cross; Cry of the City; Custer of the West; Dark Mirror, The; File on Thelma Jordan, The; Great Sinner, The; Killers, The; People on Sunday (Menschen am Sonntag); Phantom Lady; Pièges (Personal Column/ Snares); Quick; Son of Dracula; Spiral Staircase, The; Strange Affair of Uncle Harry, The (aka Uncle Harry); Suspect, The.*

Sipes, Andrew *Fair Game.*

Sirk, Douglas *All I Desire; All That Heaven Allows; Battle Hymn; First Legion, The; Has Anybody Seen My Gal; Hitler's Madman; Imitation of Life; Interlude; Lured (aka Personal Column); Magnificent Obsession; Meet Me at the Fair; Shockproof; Sign of the Pagan; Sleep, My Love; Summer Storm; Take Me to Town; Tarnished Angels, The; There's Always Tomorrow; Time to Love and a Time to Die, A; Written on the Wind.*

Sirk, Douglas (as Detlef Sierck) *Pillars of Society (Stützen der Gesellschaft).*

Sissako, Abderrahmane *Life on Earth (La Vie sur Terre).*

Sitch, Rob *Castle, The; Dish, The.*

Sivan, Eyan *Specialist, The (Ein Spezialist/Un spécialiste, portrait d'un criminel moderne).*

Sivan, Santosh *Asoka; Terrorist, The.*

Sjöberg, Alf *Father, The (Fadern); Hets (Frenzy/Torment).*

Sjöman, Vilgot *I Am Curious – Yellow (Jag är Nyfiken En Film i Gult); Till Sex Us Do Part (Troll); You're Lying (Ni Ljuger).*

Sjöström, Victor *He Who Gets Slapped; Outlaw and His Wife, The (Berg-Ejvind och hans Hustru); Scarlet Letter, The; Under the Red Robe; Wind, The.*

Skeet, Brian *Misadventures of Margaret, The (Les Mésaventures de Margaret).*

Skjoldbjaerg, Erik *Insomnia.*

Skolimowski, Jerzy *Adventures of Gerard, The; Barrier (Bariera); Deep End; Départ, Le; Hands Up! (Rece do Góry); King, Queen, Knave (Herzbube); Lightship, The; Moonlighting; Shout, The; Success Is The Best Revenge; Torrents of Spring (Acque di Primavera).*

Skolnick, Barry *Mean Machine.*

Skouen, Arne *Cold Tracks (Kalde Spor); Nine Lives (Ni Liv).*

Skyler, Lisanne *Getting to Know You.*

Slesin, Aviva *Directed by William Wyler.*

Sletaune, Pål *Junk Mail (Budbringeren/ Postbudet der vidste for meget).*

Sloan, Brian *I Think I Do.*

Sluizer, George *Crimetime; Vanishing, The (Spoorloos)* (1988); *Vanishing, The* (1993).

Smallwood, Ray *Camille.*

Smaragdis, Iannis *Cavafy (Cavafis).*

Smart, Ralph *Curtain Up; Quartet.*

Smight, Jack *Airport 1975; Damnation Alley; Frankenstein: The True Story; Harper (aka The Moving Target); Illustrated Man, The; Kaleidoscope; Loving Couples; Midway (aka Battle of Miday); No Way to Treat a Lady; Traveling Executioner, The.*

Smihi, Moumen *Moroccan Chronicles (Chroniques Marocaines).*

Smith, Charles Martin *Air Bud; Trick or Treat.*

Smith, Chris *American Movie: The Making of Northwestern.*

Smith, Clive *Pippi Longstocking (Pippi Långstrump).*

Smith, Howard *Marjoe.*

Smith, Jack *Flaming Creatures.*

Smith, John N *Dangerous Minds; Sitting in Limbo; Sugartime.*

Smith, Kevin *Chasing Amy; Clerks; Dogma; Jay and Silent Bob Strike Back; Mallrats.*

Smith, Kevin W *Romance and Rejection.*

Smith, Mel *Bean; High Heels and Low Lifes; Radioland Murders; Tall Guy, The.*

Smith, Noella *Hummingbird Tree, The.*

Smith, Peter K *No Surrender; Private Enterprise, A; What Next?*

Smith, Robert *City Farm; Love Child, The; Wild Flowers.*

Smithee, Allen *see* Hopper, Dennis; Siegel, Don; Totten, Robert.

Smyczek, Karle *Just A Little Whistle (Jen si Tak Trochu Pisknout).*

Snoad, Harold *Not Now, Comrade.*

Snow, Michael *Wavelength.*

Soavi, Michele *Sect, The (La Setta).*

Söderberg, Johan *Lucky People Center International.*

Soderbergh, Steven *Erin Brokovich; Kafka; King of the Hill; Limey, The; Ocean's Eleven; Out of Sight; Schizopolis; sex, lies and videotape; Traffic; Underneath, The.*

Softley, Iain *Backbeat; Hackers; K-PAX; Wings of the Dove, The.*

Sokolov, Stanislav *Miracle Maker, The.*

Sokurov, Alexander *Moloch; Mother and Son (Mat i Syn/Mutter und Sohn); Russian Ark; Taurus.*

Solanas, Fernando E *Cloud, The (La Nube/aka Clouds); Sur; Voyage, The (El Viaje).*

Solas, Humberto *Cantata of Chile (Cantata de Chile); Lucia.*

Solberg, Helena *Carmen Miranda: Bananas Is My Business.*

Soldini, Silvio *Bread and Tulips (Pane e Tulipani).*

Sole, Alfred *Communion (aka Holy Terror).*

Sollett, Peter *Long Way Home.*

Solomon, Courtney *Dungeons & Dragons.*

Solondz, Todd *Happiness; Storytelling; Welcome to the Dollhouse.*

Solt, Andrew *Imagine (aka Imagine: John Lennon); It Came from Hollywood; This Is Elvis.*

Solum, Ola *Orion's Belt (Orions Belte).*

Somai, Shinji *Kaza-hana; Moving (Ohikkoshi).*

Somer, Yossi *Burning Memory (Resism).*

Sommers, Stephen *Adventures of Huck Finn; Deep Rising; Jungle Book, The (aka Rudyard Kipling's The Jungle Book); Mummy, The; Mummy Returns, The.*

Son Jae-Gon *Man Who Saw Too Much, The (Nomu Mani Pon Sanai).*

Song Cunshou *At Dawn (Po Xiao Shi Fen).*

Song Il-Gon *Flower Island (Kkot Seom).*

Song Neung-Han *No. 3.*

Songsri, Cherd *Puen-Paeng; Scar, The (Prae Kaow).*

Sonnenfeld, Barry *Addams Family, The; Addams Family Values; For Love or Money (aka The Concierge); Get Shorty; Men in Black; Wild Wild West.*

Sono, Shion *Suicide Club (Jisatsu Circle).*

Sontag, Susan *Promised Lands.*

Sotirakis, Dimitri *Beverly Hills Brats.*

Sözen, Kadir *Cold Nights (Soguk Geceler).*

Spacey, Kevin *Albino Alligator.*

Sparr, Robert *Swingin' Summer, A.*

Speck, Wieland *Westler: East of the Wall.*

Speek, Peter *Black Diamond Rush.*

Spence, Richard *Different for Girls.*

Spheeris, Penelope *Beverly Hillbillies, The; Black Sheep; Boys Next Door, The; Decline of Western Civilization, The; Decline of Western Civilization Part II, The: The Metal Years; Dudes; Little Rascals, The; Prison Stories: Women on the Inside; Wayne's World; Wild Side, The (aka Suburbia).*

Spicer, Bryan *Mighty Morphin Power Rangers: The Movie.*

Spielberg, Steven *A.I. Artificial Intelligence; Always; Amazing Stories; Amistad; Close Encounters of the Third Kind; Close Encounters of the Third Kind – Special Edition; Color Purple, The; Duel; E.T. The Extra-Terrestrial; Empire of the Sun; Hook; Indiana Jones and the Last Crusade; Indiana Jones and the Temple of Doom; Jaws; Jurassic Park; 1941; Lost World: Jurassic Park, The;*

Raiders of the Lost Ark; Saving Private Ryan; Schindler's List; Sugarland Express, The; Twilight Zone – The Movie.

Spiers, Bob *Didn't You Kill My Brother?; Spice World.*

Spinosa, Michel *Emmène-moi (Last Chance Hotel).*

Spoerri, Anselm *Imago – Meret Oppenheim.*

Spottiswoode, Roger *Air America; And the Band Played On; Best of Times, The; God's Favorite; Shoot to Kill (aka Deadly Pursuit); 6th Day, The; Stop! or My Mom Will Shoot; Terror Train; Tomorrow Never Dies; Turner & Hooch; Under Fire.*

Sprackling, Simon *Funny Man.*

Springer, Brian *Spin.*

Springsteen, RG *Come Next Spring.*

Sprinkle, Annie *Annie Sprinkle's Herstory of Porn.*

Sprung, Steve *Year of the Beaver.*

Spurrier, Paul *Underground.*

Squitieri, Pasquale *Russicum.*

Srour, Heiny *Hour of Liberation – the Struggle in Oman, The (Saat el Tahrir Dakkat Barra Ya Isti'Mar); Leila and the Wolves.*

Stabile, Salvatore *Gravesend.*

Stack, Jonathan *Farm, The (aka The Farm: Angola, USA).*

Stadler, Heiner *Warshots.*

Stahl, John M *Back Street; Eve of St Mark; Imitation of Life; Immortal Sergeant, The; Leave Her to Heaven; Oh, You Beautiful Doll; Only Yesterday.*

Stallone, Sylvester *Paradise Alley; Rocky II; Rocky III; Rocky IV; Staying Alive.*

Stanley, Richard *Dust Devil; Hardware.*

Starewicz, Wladyslaw *Romand de Renard, Le (The Tale of the Fox).*

Stark, Graham *Magnificent Seven Deadly Sins, The.*

Starr, Ringo *Born to Boogie.*

Starrett, Jack *Cleopatra Jones; Race with the Devil; Slaughter.*

Stavrakas, Dimitris *Canary Yellow Bicycle, The (To Kanarini Podilato).*

Steckler, Ray Dennis *Incredibly Strange Creatures Who Stopped Living and Became Mixed-Up Zombies, The (aka Teenage Psycho Meets Bloody Mary).*

Stefani, Francesco *Singing Ringing Tree, The (Das singende klingende Baumchen).*

Stein, Jeff *Kids Are Alright, The.*

Stein, Paul L *Blossom Time.*

Steinberg, David *Paternity.*

Steinberg, Michael *Bodies, Rest & Motion; Waterdance, The.*

Stelling, Jos *Pointsman, The (De Wisselwachter).*

Stellman, Martin *For Queen and Country.*

Stembridge, Gerard *About Adam; Guiltrip.*

Sterling, William *Alice's Adventures in Wonderland.*

Stern, Anthony *Ain't Misbehavin'.*

Stern, Bert *Jazz on a Summer's Day.*

Stern, Daniel *Rookie of the Year.*

Stern, James D *All the Rage (aka It's the Rage).*

Stern, Steven Hillard *BS I Love You; Devil and Max Devlin, The; Neither By Day Nor By Night.*

Stern, Tom *Freaked.*

Stettner, Patrick *Business of Strangers, The.*

Stevens, Art *Fox and the Hound, The; Rescuers, The.*

Stevens, David *Clinic, The; Kansas.*

Stevens, Elizabeth *In the Best Interests of the Children.*

Stevens, George *Alice Adams; Annie Oakley; Damsel in Distress, A; Diary of Anne Frank, The Giant; Greatest Story Every Told, The; Gunga Din; I Remember Mama; More the Merrier, The; Only Game in Town, The; Penny Serenade; Place in the Sun, A; Shane; Swing Time; Talk of the Town, The; Vivacious Lady; Woman of the Year.*

Stevens, Sylvia *Year of the Beaver.*

Stevenson, Robert *Back Street; Bedknobs and Bromsticks; Blackbeard's Ghost; Darby O'Gill and the Little People; Falling For You; Herbie Rides Again; I Married a Communist (aka The Woman on Pier 13); Island at the Top of the World, The; Jane Eyre; King Solomon's Mines; Las Vegas Story, The; Love Bug, The; Man Who Changed His Mind, The (aka The Man Who Lived Again); Mary Poppins; My Forbidden Past; One of Our Dinosaurs Is Missing; Owd Bob; (aka To the Victor) Shaggy D.A., The; That Darn Cat.*

Stewart, David A *Honest.*

Stewart, Douglas Day *Listen To Me.*

Stewart, Hugh *Tunisian Victory.*

Stewart, Peter (Sam Newfield) *Counterfeiters.*

Stigliano, Roger *Fun Down There.*

Stiller, Ben *Cable Guy; Reality Bites; Zoolander.*

Stiller, Mauritz *Gunnar Hedes Saga; Herr Arnes Pengar (Sir Arne's Treasure); Johan.*

Stillman, Whit *Barcelona; Last Days of Disco, The; Metropolitan.*

Stirner, Brian *Kind of Hush, A.*

Stöcklin, Tania *Georgette Meunier.*

Stockman, Alex *I Know I'll See Your Face Again (Verboden te zuchten).*

Stockwell, John *Crazy/Beautiful.*

Stoeffhaas, Jerry *Cheap Shots.*

Stöhr, Hannes *Berlin Is in Germany.*

Stokes, Mark *Joseph Cornell: Worlds in a Box.*

Stoll, Pablo *25 Watts.*

Stoloff, Ben *Affairs of Annabel, The.*

Stone, Alice *She Lives to Ride.*

Stone, Andrew L *Great Waltz, The; Last Voyage, The; Night Holds Terror, The; Password Is Courage, The; Sensations of 1945 (aka Sensations); Song of Norway; Stormy Weather.*

Stone, Oliver *Any Given Sunday; Born on the Fourth of July; Doors, The; Hand, The; Heaven & Earth; JFK; Natural Born Killers; Nixon; Platoon; Salvador; Talk Radio; U Turn; Wall Street.*

Stopkewich, Lynne *Kissed; Suspicious River.*

Stoppard, Tom *Rosencrantz and Guildenstern Are Dead.*

Storm, Esben *Deadly.*

Stoumen, Louis Clyde *Black Fox.*

Stout, Boris *God's Alcatraz.*

Straub, Jean-Marie *Chronicle of Anna Magdalena Bach (Chronik der Anna Magdalena Bach); Class Relations (Klassenverhältnisse); Fortini/Cani; From the Cloud to the Reistance (Nube alla Resistenza); History Lessons (Geschichtsunterricht); Moses and Aaron (Moses und Aron); Nicht Versöhnt (Not Reconciled); Othon (Les Yeux ne peuvent pas en tout temps se fermer); Sicily! (Sicilia!).*

Strayer, Frank R *Blondie; Vampire Bat, The.*

Streisand, Barbra *Mirror Has Two Faces, The; Prince of Tides, The; Yentl.*

Streitfeld, Susan *Female Perversions.*

Strick, Joseph *Janice; Portrait of the Artist as a Young Man, A; Tropic of Cancer; Ulysses.*

Strick, Wesley *Tie That Binds, The.*

Strickland, John *G:MT Greenwich Mean Time.*

Stuart, Mel *Mean Dog Blues; Wattstax; Willy Wonka and the Chocolate Factory.*

Stuart-Young, Brian *Aggro Seizeman.*

Stuhr, Jerzy *Big Animal, The (Duze zwierze); Love Stories (Historie Milosnie); Week in the Life of a Man, A (Tydzien z zycia mezczyzny).*

Sturges, John *Bad Day at Black Rock; Eagle Has Landed, The; Escape from Fort Bravo; Great Escape, The; Gunfight at the O.K. Corral; Hour of the Gun; Ice Station Zebra; Jeopardy; Joe Kidd; Last Train from Gun Hill; Law and Jake Wade, The; Magnificent Seven, The; Marooned; McQ; Mystery Street; Never So Few; Old Mand and the Sea, The; Satan Bug, The; Valdez il Mezzosangue (Chino/The Valdez Horses/Valdez the Halfbreed).*

Sturges, Preston *Beautiful Blonde from Bashful Bend, The; Christmas in July; Great McGinty, The; Great Moment, The; Hail the Conquering Hero; Lady Eve, The; Miracle of Morgan's Creek, The; Palm Beach Story, The; Sin of Harold Diddlebock, The (aka Mad Wednesday); Sullivan's Travels; Unfaithfully Yours.*

Sturridge, Charles *Aria; FairyTale – A True Story; Handful of Dust, A; Runners; Where Angels Fear to Tread.*

Styles, Eric *Dreaming of Joseph Lees; Relative Values.*

Subiela, Eliseo *Hombre Mirando al Sudeste; Last Images of the Shipwreck (Ultimas Imágenes del Naufragio); Little Miracles (Pequeños Milagros); Wake Up, Love (Despabilate Amor).*

Sugarman, Sara *Mad Cows; Very Annie-Mary.*

Sugg, Stewart *Fast Food.*

Suik, Martin *Garden, The (Záhrada).*

Suleiman, Elia *Divine Intervention (Yadon Ilaheyya).*

Sullivan, David *Hellcat Mud Wrestlers.*

Sullivan, Kevin Rodney *How Stella Got Her Groove Back.*

Sullivan, Tim *Jack & Sarah.*

Summers, Jeremy *Ferry Cross the Mersey; Punch and Judy Man, The.*

Summers, Walter *Dark Eyes of London (aka The Human Monster); Flying Fool, The; Raise the Roof; Traitor Spy (aka The Torso Murder Mystery).*

Sun, John (Sun Jiawen) *Kung-Fu Gangbusters (Nanzi Han/aka Smugglers).*

Sun, Shirley *Iron & Silk.*

Sun Yu *Folk Tales of Lu Ban (Lu Ban de Chuanshuo); Highway, The (Da Lu); Little Toys (Xiao Wanyi).*

Sun Zhou *Heartstrings.*

Suo, Masayuki *Abnormal Family: Brother's Wife (Hentai Zazoku: Aniki no Yome-san); Fancy Dance; Shall We Dance?; Sumo Do, Sumo Don't (Shiko Funjatta).*

Surjik, Stephen *Wayne's World 2; Weapons of Mass Distraction.*

Suso, Henry *Deathsport.*

Sutherland, A Edward *Dixie; International House; It's the Old Army Game; Murders in the Zoo; Palmy Days.*

Sutherland, Hal *Pinocchio and the Emperor of the Night.*

Suwa, Nobuhiro *M/other; 2 Duo.*

Suzuki, Akihiro *Looking for an Angel (Tenshi no Rakuen).*

Suzuki, Junichi *Sukiyaki.*

Suzuki, Seijun *Branded to Kill (Koroshi No Rakuin); Fighting Elegy (Kenka Elegy); Gate of Flesh (Nikutai No Mon); Kagero-za; One Generation of Tattoos (Irezum Ichidai); Pistol Opera; Tokyo Drifter (Tokyo Nagaremono); Youth of the Beast (Yaju no Seishun); Yumeji; Zigeunerweisen.*

Svankmajer, Jan *Alice; Conspirators of Pleasure (Spiklenci slasti); Faust (Lekce Faust); Otesánek.*

Sverák, Jan *Accumulator 1; Dark Blue World (Tmavomodry svet); Kolya (Kolja); Ride, The (Jízda).*

Swackhamer, EW *Spider-Man.*

Swaim, Bob *Balance, La; Half Moon Street; Masquerade.*

Swenson, Charles *Mouse and His Child, The.*

Swift, David *How to Succeed in Business Without Really Trying; Little Nemo Adventures in Slumberland; Love Is a Ball (aka All This and Money Too).*

Swimmer, Saul *Concert for Bangladesh, The.*

Switkes, Glenn *Amazonia: Voices from the Rainforest (Amazonia: Vozes da Floresto).*

Syberberg, Hans-Jürgen *Confessions of Winifred Wagner, The (Winifred Wagner und die Geschichte des Hauses Wahnfried 1914-1975); Hitler, a Film from Germany (Hitler, ein Film aus Deutschland); Karl May; Parsifal; Ludwig – Requiem for a Virgin King (Ludwig – Requiem für einen jungfräuchlichen König); Ludwig's Cook (Theodor Hierneis oder wie man ein ehemaliger Hofkoch wird).*

Sykes, Peter *Demons of the Mind; House in Nightmare Park, The; To the Devil a Daughter; Venom.*

Sylla, Khady *Colobane Express.*

Szabó, István *Colonel Redl (Redl Ezredes); Confidence (Bizalom); Hanussen; Meeting Venus; Mephisto; Sunshine (A napfény ize/Ein Hauch von Sonnenschein); Sweet Emma, Dear Böbe (Edes Emma, Drága Böbe).*

Szász, János *Woyzeck; Witman Boys, The (Witman Fiúk).*

Szkopiak, Piotr *Small Time Obsession.*

Szumowska, Malgorzata *Happy Man (Szczesliwy czlowiek).*

Szwarc, Jeannot *Bug; Enigma; Extreme Close-Up; Jaws 2; Santa Claus; Somewhere in Time; Supergirl.*

Taav, Michael *Painted Heart.*

Tabio, Juan Carlos *Guantanamera; Plaff! or Too Afraid of Life (Plaf – Demasiado Miedo a la Vida).*

Tacchella, Jean-Charles *Cousin Cousine; Escalier C; Homme de ma vie, L' (The Man in My Life).*

Taghvaï, Nasser *Tales of the Kish (Ghessé Hayé Kish).*

Tait, Margaret *Blue Black Permanent.*

Tajima, Renee *Best Hotel on Skid Row; Who Killed Vincent Chin?*

Takabayashi, Yoichi *Irezumi – Spirit of Tattoo (Sekka Tomurai Zashi).*

Takacs, Tibor *Gate, The.*

Takamine, Go *Paradise View; Tsuru-Henry (Mugen Ryukyu – Tsuru-Henry); Untama Giru.*

Takamoto, Iwao *Charlotte's Web.*

Takenaka, Naoto *Nowhere Man (Muno no Hito).*

Takita, Yojiro *Comic Magazine (Komikku zasshi nanka iranai).*

Talalay, Rachel *Freddy's Dead: The Final Nightmare; Tank Girl.*

Talkington, CM *Love and a .45.*

Talmadge, Richard *Casino Royale.*

Tamahori, Lee *Along Came a Spider; Edge, The; Mulholland Falls; Once Were Warriors.*

Tampa, Harry (Harry Hurwitz) *Nocturna; Projectionist, The.*

Tanaka, Hiroyuki *see* Sabu

Tanaka, Kinuyo *Moon Has Risen, The (Tsuki wa Noborinu).*

Tanaka, Noboru *Stroller in the Attic, The (Yaneura no Sanposha).*

Tanaka, Tokuzo *Nemuri Kyoshiro: The Book of Killing-Rules (Nemuri Kyoshiro: Sappo Cho/aka Sleepy Eyes of Death: The Chinese Jade).*

Taniguchi, Senkichi *Lost World of Sinbad, The (Daitozoku); What's Up Tiger Lily?*

Tannen, Terrell *Young Giants.*

Tanner, Alain *Charles Dead or Alive (Charles Mort ou Vif); Flame in My Heart, A (Une Flamme dans Mon Coeur); In the White City (Dans la Ville Blanche); Jonah Who Will Be 25 in the Year 2000 (Jonas qui aura 25 ans en l'an 2000); Journal de Lady M, Le (The Diary of Lady M); Light Years Away; Messidor; Middle of the World, The (Le Milieu du Monde); Nice Time; No Man's Land; Retour d'Afrique, Le (Return from Africa); Salamandre, La (The Salamander).*

Tanovic, Danis *No Man's Land.*

Taradash, Daniel *Storm Center.*

Tarantino, Quentin *Four Rooms; Jackie Brown; Pulp Fiction; Reservoir Dogs.*

Tarkovsky, Andrei *Andrei Rublev (St Andrei Passion); Ivan's Childhood (Ivanovo Detstvo); Katok i Skrypka (Roller and Violin/The Steamroller and the Violin); Mirror (Zerkalo); Nostalgia (Nostalghia); Sacrifice, The (Offret); Solaris; Stalker.*

Tarlov, Mark *Simply Irresistible.*

Tarr, Béla*Damnation (Kárhozat); Sátántangó (Satan's Tango); Werckmeister Harmonies (Werckmeister harmóniák).*

Tashiro, Hirotaka *Swimming with Tears (Afureru Atsui Namida).*

Tashlin, Frank *Alphabet Murders, The (aka The ABC Murders); Artists and Models; Caprice; Cinderfella; Disorderly Orderly, The; Geisha Boy, The; Girl Can't Help It, The; Hollywood or Bust; It's Only Money; Rock-a-Bye Baby; Son of Paleface; Susan Slept Here; Will Success Spoil Rock Hunter? (aka Oh! For a Man).*

Tass, Nadia *Big Steal, The; Malcolm; Mr Reliable (a True Story); Pure Luck.*

Tati, Jacques *Ecoles des Facteurs, L' (School for Postmen); Jour de Fête; Mon Oncle (My Uncle); Parade; Playtime; Traffic (Trafic); Vacances de M. Hulot, Les (Monsieur Hulot's Holiday/Mr Hulot's Holiday).*

Tatum, Peter *Joe Louis – For All Time.*

Taurog, Norman *Adventures of Tom Sawyer, The; Birds and the Bees, The; Blue Hawaii; Bundle of Joy; Double Trouble; G.I. Blues; Girls! Girls! Girls!; If I Had a Million; Little Nellie Kelly; Pardners; Phantom President, The; Toast of New Orleans, The.*

Tavel, Ronald *Kitch.*

Taverna, Kathryn *Lodz Ghetto.*

Tavernier, Bertrand *Appât, L' (The Bait); Capitaine Conan; Clean Slate (Coup de Torchon); Contre l'Oubli (Against Oblivion); Death Watch (La Mort en Direct); De l'Autre Côté du Périph' (From the Other Side of the*

Tracks); Des Enfants Gâtés (Spoiled Children); Fille de D'Artagnan, La (D'Artagnan's Daughter); Guerre sans nom, La (The Undeclared War); Horloger de St Paul, L' (The Clockmaker/The Watchmaker of Saint-Paul); It All Starts Today (Ça commence aujourd'hui); Life and Nothing But (La Vie et rien d'Autre); L.627; Mississippi Blues; Passion Béatrice, La; Que la Fête Commence (Let Joy Reign Supreme); 'Round Midnight (Autour de Minuit); Semaine de Vacances, Une (A Week's Holiday); Sunday in the Country (Un Dimanche la Campagne); These Foolish Things (Daddy Nostalgie).

Taviani, Paolo *Allonsanfan; Elective Affinities (Le Affinità Elettive); Fiorile; Good Morning Babylon (Good Morning Babilonia); Kaos; Night of San Lorenzo, The (La Notte di San Lorenzo); Night Sun (Il Sole anche di notte); Padre Padrone.*

Taviani, Vittorio *Allonsanfan; Elective Affinities (Le Affinità Elettive); Fiorile; Good Morning Babylon (Good Morning Babilonia); Kaos; Night of San Lorenzo, The (La Notte di San Lorenzo); Night Sun (Il Sole anche di notte); Padre Padrone.*

Taylor, Alan *Palookaville.*

Taylor, Don *Damien – Omen II; Escape from the Planet of the Apes; Final Countdown, The; Great Scout & Cathouse Thursday, The; Island of Dr Moreau, The; Tom Sawyer.*

Taylor, Donald *Conquest of the Air, The.*

Taylor, Finn *Dream with the Fishes.*

Taylor, Robert *Heidi's Song; Nine Lives of Fritz the Cat, The.*

Taylor, Sam *Cat's-Paw, The; Girl Shy; Safety Last; Why Worry?*

Taymor, Julie *Titus.*

Teague, Colin *Shooters.*

Teague, Lewis *Alligator; Cat's Eye; Cujo; Fighting Back (aka Death Vengeance); Jewel of the Nile, The; Lady in Red, The; Navy Seals.*

Téchiné, André *Alice et Martin; Far Away (Loin); J'embrasse pas (I Don't Kiss); Ma Saison Préférée (My Favourite Season); Roseaux Sauvages, Les (The Wild Reeds); Scene of the Crime, The (Le Lieu du Crime); Voleurs, Les.*

Tedesco, Jean *Petite Marchande d'allumettes, La (The Little Matchgirl).*

Tellegen, Duco *Behind Closed Eyes (Achter gesloten ogen).*

Temple, Julien *Absolute Beginners; Aria; Earth Girls Are Easy; Filth and the Fury, The; Great Rock'n'Roll Swindle, The; Pandaemonium; Secret Policeman's Other Ball, The; Vigo Passion for Life (Vigo Histoire d'une Passion).*

Templeman, Conny *Nanou.*

Téno, Jean Marie *Clando (Clandestine).*

Tennant, Andy *Anna and the King; Ever After; Fools Rush In; It Takes Two.*

Tenney, Kevin S *Cellar, The; Night of the Demons.*

Teno, Jean-Marie *Trip to the Country, A (Vacances au Pays).*

Teplitzky, Jonathan *Better Than Sex.*

Terayama, Shuji *Boxer, The; Fruits of Passion, The (Les Fruits de la Passion); Pastoral Hide-and-Seek (Denen ni Shisu); Throw Away Your Books, Let's Go into the Streets (Sho o Suteyo, Machi e Deyo).*

Teshigahara, Hiroshi *Summer Soldiers; Woman of the Dunes (Suna no Onna).*

Tessari, Duccio *Heroes, The (Gli Eroi).*

Teton, Charles *Dark Summer.*

Tetzlaff, Ted *Johnny Allegro (aka Hounded); Under The Gun; White Tower, The; Window, The.*

Tewkesbury, Joan *Old Boyfriends.*

Tezuka, Osamu *Space Firebird.*

Thacker, David *Broken Glass.*

Theuring, Gerhard *Escape Route to Marseilles (Fluchtweg nach Marseilles).*

Thew, Anna *Hilda Was a Goodlooker.*

Thiago, Paulo *Für Elise.*

Thiele, Rolf *Mádchen Rosemarie, Das (The Girl Rosemarie).*

Thomas, Betty *Brady Bunch Movie, The; Doctor Dolittle; Private Parts; 28 Days.*

Thomas, Dave *Experts, The; Strange Brew.*

Thomas, Edward *Rancid Aluminium.*

Thomas, Gerald *Big Job, The; Carry On Columbus; Carry On Sergeant; Iron Maiden, The; Raising the Wind; That's Carry On; Watch Your Stern.*

Thomas, Jeremy *All the Little Animals.*

Thomas, May Miles *One Life Stand.*

Thomas, Pascal *Spring into Summer (Pleure Pas la Bouche Pleine).*

Thomas, Ralph *Above Us the Waves; Appointment with Venus (aka Island Rescue); Clouded Yellow, The; Conspiracy of Hearts; Doctor in the House; High Bright Sun, The (aka McGuire Go Home!); TheHot Enough for June; It's a 2' 6" Above the Ground World (aka The Love Ban); Nobody Runs Forever (aka The High Commissioner); Percy; Percy's Progress; Quest for Love; 39 Steps, The; Upstairs and Downstairs; Wind Cannot Read, The.*

Thomas, Ralph L *Terry Fox Story, The; Ticket to Heaven.*

Thome, Rudolf *3 Women in Love (Der Philosoph).*

Thompson, Caroline *Black Beauty.*

Thompson, Danièle *Bûche, La (Season's Beatings).*

Thompson, David *Musicals Great Musicals: The Arthur Freed Unit at MGM.*

Thompson, Ernest *1969.*

Thompson, J Lee *Ambassador, The; Battle for the Planet of the Apes; Before Winter Comes; Caboblanco; Cape Fear; Conquest of the Planet of the Apes; Country Dance (aka Brotherly Love); Death Wish 4: The Crackdown; Evil That Men Do, The; Good Companions, The; Greek Tycoon, The; Guns of Navarone, The; Huckleberry Finn; Ice Cold in Alex; King Solomon's Mines; Kings of the Sun; Mackenna's Gold; Murphy's Law; North West Frontier (aka Flame Over India); No Trees in the Street; Passage, The; Reincarnation of Peter Proud, The; St Ives; 10 to Midnight; Tiger Bay; Weak and the Wicked, The; White Buffalo, The; Woman in a Dressing Gown; Yellow Balloon, The; Yield to the Night.*

Thompson, Marcus *Middleton's Changeling.*

Thomsen, Christian Braad *Ladies on the Rocks (Koks i Kulissen).*

Thomson, Chris *Delinquents, The.*

Thongkongtoon,Yongyoot *Iron Ladies (Satree Lek).*

Thornhill, Michael *Between Wars; Everlasting Secret Family, The.*

Thornley, Jeni *For Love or Money.*

Thornton, Billy Bob *All the Pretty Horses; Sling Blade.*

Thoroddsen, Asdis *Ingaló.*

Thorpe, Richard *Above Suspicion; Adventures of Quentin Durward, The (aka Quentin Durward); Black Hand, The; Huckleberry Finn (aka The Adventures of Huckleberry Finn); Ivanhoe; Jailhouse Rock; Killers of Kilimanjaro; Last Challenge, The (aka The Pistolero of Red River); Malaya (aka East of the Rising Sun); Night Must Fall; Prisoner of Zenda, The.*

Thorsen, Jens Jorgen *Quiet Days in Clichy (Stille Dage i Clichy).*

Thorsen, Karen *James Baldwin: The Price of the Ticket.*

Thraves, Jamie *Low Down, The; Take Out, The.*

Thulin, Ingrid *One and One (En och En).*

Thurman, Tom *Warren Oates: Across the Border.*

Tian Zhuangzhuang *Blue Kite, The (Lan Fengzheng); Horse Thief (Daoma Zei); Li Lianying, the Imperial Eunuch (Da Taijian Li Lianying); On the Hunting Ground (Liechang Zhasa).*

Tickell, Paul *Christie Malry's Own Double-Entry; Crush Proof.*

Tighe, Fergus *Clash of the Ash.*

Till, Eric *It Shouldn't Happen to a Vet; Walking Stick, The.*

Tillman Jr, George *Men of Honor; Soul Food.*

Tillman, Lynne *Committed.*

Ting Shan-Hsi *Blood Reincarnation (Yin-yang Jie).*

Tinling, James *Mr Moto's Gamble.*

Tirl, Jirí *Pistol, The (Pistolen).*

Title, Stacy *Last Supper, The.*

Tlatli, Moufida *Season of Men, The (La Saison des Hommes); Silences of the Palace, The (Saimt el Qusur/Les Silences du Palais).*

To, Johnny *Heroic Trio (Dongfang San Xia).*

Toback, James *Big Bang, The; Black and White; Exposed; Fingers; Two Girls and a Guy.*

Todorovsky, Valerii *Katia Ismaïlova (Podmoskovnye vechera).*

Tognazzi, Ricky *Scorta, La (The Escort); Ultrà (Ultras: Some Lose, Some Die...Some Win).*

Tokar, Norman *Apple Dumpling Gang, The; Candleshoe; Cat From Outer Space, The; Happiest Millionaire, The; No Deposit, No Return; Tiger Walks, A; Where the Red Fern Grows.*

Tolkin, Michael *New Age, The; Rapture, The.*

Tong, Kevin *Eating Air (Zhi Feng).*

Tong, Stanley *First Strike (Jingcha Gushi 4 zhi Jiandan Renwu); Rumble in the Bronx (Hongfan Qu).*

Toporoff, Ralph *American Blue Note (aka Fakebook).*

Topper, Burt *Strangler, The.*

Tornatore, Giuseppe *Cinema Paradiso (Nuovo Cinema Paradiso); Cinema Paradiso: The Special Edition; Everybody's Fine (Stanno tutti bene); Legend of 1900, The (La Leggenda del pianista sull'oceano); Malèna; Pure Formality, A (Una Pura Formalità); Uomo delle stelle, L' (The Starmaker).*

Torossian, Gariné *Sparklehorse.*

Torre, Robert *Tano da Morire (To Die for Tano).*

Torres, Fina *Woman on Top.*

Totten, Robert (as Alan Smithee) *Death of a Gunfighter.*

Toubiana, Serge *François Truffaut, Portraits Volés (François Truffaut, Stolen Portraits).*

Touré Moussa *TGV.*

Tourneur, Jacques *Anne of the Indies; Appointment in Honduras; Berlin Express; Cat People; Circle of Danger; City Under the Sea (aka War Gods of the Deep); Comedy of Terrors, The; Days of Glory; Easy Living; Experiment Perilous; Flame and the Arrow, The; Giant of Marathon, The (La Battaglia di Maratona); Great Day in the Morning; I Walked with a Zombie; Leopard Man, The; Nick Carter – Master Detective; Nightfall; Night of the Demon (aka Curse of the Demon); Out of the Past (aka Build My Gallows High); Way of a Gaucho; Wichita.*

Tourneur, Maurice *Au Nom de la Loi; Volpone.*

Towne, Robert *Personal Best; Tequila Sunrise; Without Limits.*

Townsend, Robert *BAPS; Eddie Murphy Raw; Five Heartbeats, The; Hollywood Shuffle; Meteor Man, The.*

Toye, Patrice *Rosie.*

Toye, Wendy *Teckman Mystery, The.*

Toyoda, Toshiaki *Blue Spring (Aoi Haru); Unchain.*

Traïdia, Karim *Diseurs de Vérité, Les; Polish Bride, The (De Poolse Bruid).*

Tramont, Jean-Claude *All Night Long.*

Tran Anh Hung *At the Height of Summer (A la verticale de l'été/aka The Vertical Ray of the Sun); Cyclo (Xich Lo); Scent of Green Papaya, The (L'Odeur de la Papaye Verte/Mui Du Du Xanh).*

Trapero, Pablo *Crane World (Mundo Grúa).*

Trauberg, Leonid *Devil's Wheel, The (Chyortovo Koleso); New Babylon, The (Novyi Vavilon).*

Trenchard Smith, Brian *BMX Bandits; Frog Dreaming; Man from Hong Kong, The; Turkey Shoot.*

Trent, John *Best Revenge; Middle Age Crazy; Sunday in the Country.*

Tresgot, Annie *Portrait of a '60% Perfect' Man: Billy Wilder (Portrait d'un Homme 'à 60% Parfait': Billy Wilder).*

Treut, Monika *Erotique; My Father Is Coming; Virgin Machine (Die Jungfrauenmaschine).*

Trevelyan, Humphrey *'36 to '77.*

Trevelyan, Philip *Moon and the Sledgehammer, The.*

Treves, Giorgio *Rosa e Cornelia (Rosa and Cornelia).*

Trevor, Simon *African Elephant, The (aka King Elephant).*

Triana, Jorge Alí *Time to Die (Tiempo de Morir).*

Triandafyllidis, Nicholas *Screamin' Jay Hawkins: I Put a Spell on Me.*

Trigiani, Adriana *Queens of the Big Time.*

Trikonis, Gus *Touched By Love.*

Trinh Thi, Coralie *Baise-moi.*

Trintignant, Nadine *Contre l'Oubli (Against Oblivion); Lumière et Compagnie; Maison de Jade, La.*

Troche, Rose *Bedrooms and Hallways; Go Fish.*

Troell, Jan *Capitano, Il; Emigrants, The (Utvandrarna); Hurricane; Zandy's Bride (aka For Better, For Worse).*

Trombley, Stephen *Execution Protocol, The.*

Trousdale, Gary *Atlantis – The Lost Empire; Beauty and the Beast; Hunchback of Notre Dame, The.*

Troyano, Ela *Latin Boys Go to Hell.*

Trueba, David *Good Life, The (La Buena Vida).*

Trueba, Fernando *Belle Epoque; First Effort (Opera Prima); Lumière et Compagnie; Mad Monkey, The (El Mono loco); Two Much (Loco de amor).*

Truffaut, François *Argent de Poche, L' (Small Change); Baisers Volés (Stolen Kisses); Belle fille comme moi, Une (A Gorgeous Bird Like Me/Such a Gorgeous Kid Like Me); Bride Wore Black, The (La Mariée était en Noir); Chambre Verte, La (The Green Room); Day for Night (La Nuit Américaine); Deux Anglaises et la Continent, Les (Anne and Muriel/Two English Girls); Domicile Conjugal (Bed and Board); Enfant Sauvage, L' (The Wild Child); Fahrenheit 451; Jules and Jim (Jules et Jim); Last Metro, The (Le Dernier Métro); Love on the Run (L'Amour en Fuite); Man Who Loved Women, The (L'Homme qui Aimait les Femmes); Mistons, Les (The Mischief Makers); Peau Douce, La (Silken Skin/The Soft Skin); Quatre Cents Coups, Les (The 400 Blows); Sirène du Mississipi, La (Mississippi Mermaid); Story of Adèle H., The (L'Histoire d'Adèle H.); Tirez sur le Pianiste (Shoot the Pianist/Shoot the Piano Player); Vivement Dimanche! (Confidentially Yours/Finally, Sunday!); Woman Next Door, The (La Femme d'à côté).*

Trumbo, Dalton *Johnny Got His Gun.*

Trumbull, Douglas *Brainstorm; Silent Running.*

Tsabadze, Aleko *Stain, The (Laka).*

Tsai Ming-Liang *Hole, The (Dong); My New Friends (Wo Xin Renshi de Pengyou); Rebels of the Neon God (Qing Shaonian Nezha); River, The (Heliu); Vive l'Amour (Aiqing Wansui); What Time Is It There? (Neibian Ji Dian/Et là-bas quelle heure est-il?).*

Tse, Nicholas *Heroes in Love (Lian'ai Qi Yi).*

Tsering, Thupten *Windhorse.*

Tsintsadze, Dito *Lost Killers.*

Tsiplakova, Elena *In Thee I Trust (Na Tebya Upovayu).*

Tsuchimoto, Noriaki *Minamata.*

Tsuchiya, Yutaka *New God, The (Atarashii Kami-sama).*

Tsui Hark *Blade, The (Dao); Butterfly Murders, The (Die Bian); Don't Play With Fire (Diyi Leixing Weixian/aka Dangerous Encounter – First Kind); Double Team; Knock Off; Legend of Zu, The (Shushan Zhuan); Once Upon a Time in China (Huang Feihong); Once Upon a Time in China II (Huang Feihong zhi Er: Nan'r Dang Zi Qiang); Peking Opera Blues (Dao Ma Dan); Shanghai Blues (Shanghai zhi Ye); Swordsman; Time and Tide (Shunliu Niliu); Twin Dragons (Shuanglong Hui); Zu: Warriors from the Magic Mountain (Shu Shan: Xin Shushan Jianxia).*

Tsukamoto, Shinya *Bullet Ballet; Tetsuo; Tetsuo II: Bodyhammer; Tokyo Fist.*

Tsukerman, Slava *Liquid Sky.*

Tsuruta, Norio *Ring 0 – Birthday.*

Tsymbal, Yevgeny *Defence Counsel Sedov.*

Tucci, Stanley *Big Night; Impostors, The; Joe Gould's Secret.*

Tuchner, Michael *Fear Is the Key; Likely Lads, The; Mister Quilp; Trenchcoat; Villain; Wilt.*

Tucker, Anand *Hilary and Jackie; Saint-Ex.*

Tucker, Joe *Lava.*

Tucker, Phil *Robot Monster.*

Tuggle, Richard *Tightrope.*

Tu Guangqi *Kung Fu Fighting (Tang Shou Taiquandao/aka Crush).*

Tully, Montgomery *Battle Beneath the Earth; Boys in Brown.*

Turell, Saul J *Love Goddesses, The.*

Turgul, Yavuz *Bandit, The (Eskiya).*

Turk, Ellen Fisher *Split William to Chrysis: Portrait of a Drag Queen.*

Turkiewicz, Sophia *Silver City.*

Turko, Rose-Marie *Scarred.*

Turner, Ann *Celia; Dallas Doll; Hammers Over the Anvil.*

Turner, Martin *Nearly Wide Awake.*

Turner, Paul *Hedd Wyn.*

Turpie, Jonnie *Out of Order.*

Turteltaub, Jon *Cool Runnings; Disney's The Kid; Instinct; Phenomenon; 3 Ninjas (aka 3 Ninja Kids); While You Were Sleeping.*

Turturro, John *Mac.*

Tuttle, Frank *Dr Rhythm; Roman Scandals; This Gun for Hire.*

Twist, Derek *Green Grow the Rushes (aka Brandy Ashore).*

Twohy, David N *Arrival, The; Pitch Black; Timescape (aka Grand Tour: Disaster in Time).*

Tykwer, Tom *Heaven; Princess + the Warrior, The (Der Krieger und die Kaiserin); Run Lola Run (Lola Rennt); Tödliche Maria, Die (Deadly Maria); Winter Sleepers (Winterschläfer).*

Tyndall, Andrew *Sigmund Freud's Dora.*

Uchitel, Alexei *His Wife's Diary (Dnevnik Yego Zheny).*

Uderzo, Albert *Twelve Tasks of Asterix, The (Les 12 Travaux d'Astérix).*

Ujica, Andrei *Out of the Present.*

Ullmann, Liv *Faithless (Trolösa); Lumière et Compagnie; Sofie.*

Ulloa, Juanma Bajo *Madre Muerta, La.*

Ulmer, Edgar G *Black Cat, The (aka House of Doom); Bluebeard, Detour; Light Ahead, The (Fishke der Krummer); Man from Planet X, The; Moon Over Harlem; Naked Dawn, The; People on Sunday (Menschen am Sonntag); Ruthless.*

Underwood, Ron *City Slickers; Mighty Joe Young (aka Mighty Joe); Speechless; Tremors.*

Urban, Stuart *Preaching to the Perverted; Revelation.*

Ureles, Jeff *Cheap Shots.*

Uribe, Imanol *Bwana; Dias Contados (Running Out of Time).*

Usher, Kinka *Mystery Man.*

Usher, Selig *Hot Money.*

Usmonov, Jamshed *Flight of the Bee, The (Parvozi Zanbur/aka Bee-Fly).*

Ustaoglu, Yesim *Journey to the Sun (Gunese Yolculuk).*

Ustinov, Peter *Billy Budd; Lady L; Memed My Hawk; Vice Versa.*

U-Wei Bin Haji Saari *Arsonist, The (Kaki Bakar).*

Uys, Jamie *Beautiful People; Gods Must Be Crazy, The; Gods Must Be Crazy II, The.*

Vachani, Nilita *When Mother Comes Home for Christmas (Otan Erhtli Mama Gia ta Christougenna).*

Václav, Petr *Marian; Parallel Worlds (Paraleini svety).*

Vadim, Roger *And God Created Woman; Barbarella; Charlotte (La Jeune Fille Assassinée); Don Juan, or If Don Juan Were a Woman (Don Juan, ou si Don Juan était une Femme); Et Dieu Créa la Femme (And God Created Woman/And Woman… Was Created); Histoires Extraordinaires (Spirits of the Dead/Tales of Mystery); Liaisons Dangereuses 1960, Les; Night Games; Pretty Maids All in a Row; Vice et la Vertu, Le (Vice and Virtue).*

Valdez, Luis *Bamba, La.*

Valerii, Tonino *My Name Is Nobody (Il Mio Nome è Nessuno); Reason to Live, a Reason to Die, A (Una Ragione per Vivere e Una per Morire).*

Valli, Eric *Himalaya (Himalaya – L'Enfance d'un chef).*

Vallois, Phillipe *We Were One Man (Nous Etions un Seul Homme).*

van Ackeren, Robert *Woman in Flames, A (Die flambierte Frau).*

Van Bebber, Jim *Deadbeat at Dawn.*

Van Damme, Jean-Claude *Quest, The.*

van Diem, Mike *Karakter (Character).*

van de Oest, Paula *Another Mother (de Nieuwe Moeder).*

van de Velde, Jean *All Stars.*

Van Dormael, Jaco *Eighth Day, The (Le Huitième Jour); Lumière et Compagnie; Toto the Hero (Toto le héros).*

Van Dyke, WS *After the Thin Man; Bitter Sweet; I Love You Again; I Take This Woman; Journey for Margaret; Love on the Run; Manhattan Melodrama; Naughty Marietta; Rage in Heaven; San Francisco; Thin Man, The.*

Van Horn, Buddy *Any Which Way You Can; Dead Pool, The.*

Van Lamsweerde, Pino *Asterix in Britain (Astérix chez les Brétons).*

Van Passel, Frank *Manneken Pis.*

Van Peebles, Mario *New Jack City; Panther; Posse.*

Van Peebles, Melvin *Sweet Sweetback's Baadasssss Song; Watermelon Man.*

Van Sant, Gus *Drugstore Cowboy; Even Cowgirls Get the Blues; Finding Forrester; Good Will Hunting; Mala Noche; My Own Private Idaho; Psycho; To Die For.*

van Warmerdam, Alex *Abel; Little Tony (Kleine Teune); Northerners, The (Der Noorderlingen).*

Vanzina, Carlo *My First 40 Years (I Miei Primi 40 Anni).*

Varda, Agnès *Bonheur, Le (Happiness); Cléo de 5 à 7 (Cleo from 5 to 7); Créatures, Les; Far from Vietnam (Loin du Viêt-nam); Gleaners and I, The (Les Glaneurs et la Glaneuse); Jacquot de Nantes; Lions Love; One Sings, the Other Doesn't (L'Une Chante, l'Autre Pas); Univers de Jacques Demy, L'; Vagabonde (Sans Toit ni Loi).*

Vargi, Omer *Everything's Gonna Be Great (Hersey Çok Güzel Olacak).*

Varnel, Marcel *Band Waggon; Gasbags; Ghost of St Michael's, The; Good Morning, Boys! (aka Where There's a Will); Oh, Mr Porter!; O-Kay for Sound.*

Vasconcellos, António-Pedro *Jaime.*

Vasconcellos, Tete *El Salvador: Another Vietnam.*

Vasquez, Joseph B *Hangin' with the Homeboys.*

Vávra, Roman *In the Rye (Co Chytnes v Zite).*

Veber, Francis *Dîner de cons, Le; Three Fugitives.*

Védres, Nicole *Paris Mil Neuf Cent Chronique de 1900 à 1914 (aka Paris 1900).*

Vega, Pastor *Portrait of Teresa (Retrato de Teresa).*

Vendramini, Danny *Redheads.*

Vera, Gerardo *Second Skin (Segunda Piel).*

Verbinski, Gore *Mexican, The; MouseHunt.*

Verbong, Ben *Girl with the Red Hair, The (Het Meisje met het Rode Haar); Scorpion, The (De Schorpioen).*

Verhavert, Roland *Pallieter.*

Verhoeven, Michael *My Mother's Courage (Mutters Courage); Nasty Girl, The (Das schreckliche Mädchen).*

Verhoeven, Paul *Basic Instinct; Business Is Business (Wat Zien Ik); Flesh and Blood; Fourth Man, The (De Vierde Man); Hollow Men; RoboCop; Showgirls; Soldier of Orange (Soldaat van Orange); Spetters; Starship Troopers; Total Recall; Turkish Delight (Turks Fruit).*

Vermorcken, Chris *I Am Anna Magnani (Io Sono Anna Magnani).*

Vernay, Robert *Père Goriot, Le; Fantômas contre Fantômas.*

Verneuil, Henri *Burglars, The (La Casse); Guns for San Sebastian (La Bataille de San Sebastian); Night Caller (Peur sur la Ville); Serpent, The (Le Serpent); Sicilian Clan, The (Le Clan des Siciliens); Vache et la Prisonnier, La (The Cow and I).*

Vernon, Richard *Street of Shadows, (aka Shadowman).*

Vernoux, Marion *Hell of a Day, A (Reines d'un jour); Love etc; Rien à Faire (Empty Days).*

Verona, Stephen F *Boardwalk; Lords of Flatbush, The.*

Verow, Todd *Frisk.*

Vertov, Dziga *Man With a Movie Camera (Chelovek s Kinoapparatom).*

Ve Sota, Bruno *Female Jungle, The.*

Veysset, Sandrine *Victor – pendant qu'il est trop tard; Will It Snow for Christmas? (Y'aura t'il de la neige à Noël?).*

Vicario, Marco *Wifemistress (Mogliamante).*

Vicas, Victor *Wayward Bus, The.*

Vidor, Charles *Blind Alley; Cover Girl; Farewell to Arms, A; Gilda; Hans Christian Andersen; Ladies in Retirement; Love Me or Leave Me; Mask of Fu Manchu, The; Song Without End; Song to Remember, A.*

Vidor, King *American Romance, An; Beyond the Forest; Big Parade, The; Citadel, The; Comrade X; Crowd, The; Duel in the Sun; Fountainhead, The; Man Without a Star; Northwest Passage; Our Daily Bread (aka The Miracle of Life); Ruby Gentry; Show People; Solomon and Sheba; Stella Dallas; Texas Rangers, The; War and Peace; Wedding Night, The.*

Vigne, Daniel *Retour de Martin Guerre, Le (The Return of Martin Guerre); Woman or Two, A (Une Femme ou Deux).*

Vigo, Jean *Atalante, L'; Zéro de Conduite (Zero for Conduct).*

Villacèque, Anne *Little Darling (Petite chérie).*

Villaronga, Augustí *Mar, El (The Sea).*

Villaverde, Teresa *Mutants, The (Os Mutantes); Water and Salt (Água e Sal).*

Villeneuve, Denis *August 32nd on Earth (Un 32 août sur terre).*

Vila, Augustí *Bench in the Park, A (Un banco en el parque).*

Villegas, Juan *Saturday (Sábado).*

Vilo, Camilo *Unholy, The.*

Vilsmaier, Joseph *Comedian Harmonists (The Harmonists); Marlene; Stalingrad.*

Vilstrup, Li *Take It Like a Man, Ma'am (Ta'det som en Mand, Frue!).*

Vincent, Christian *Discrète, La; Séparation, La.*

Vincent, Chuck *American Tickler or the Winner of 10 Academy Awards (aka Draws); Bad Blood; In Love (aka Strangers in Love).*

Vinterberg, Thomas *Celebration, The (Festen); Greatest Heroes, The (De Storste Helte/aka The Biggest Heroes).*

Vinton, Will *Adventures of Mark Twain, The.*

Viola, Al *Mr Forbush and the Penguins (aka Cry of the Penguins).*

Viola, Joe *Hot Box, The.*

Virgien, Norton *Rugrats Movie, The.*

Virzi, Paolo *Living It Up (La Bella Vita).*

Visconti, Luchino *Bellissima; Boccaccio '70; Conversation Piece (Gruppo di Famiglia in un Interno); Damned, The (La Caduta degli Dei/ Götterdämmerung); Death in Venice (Morte a Venezia); Innocent, The (L'Innocente); Leopard, The (Il Gattopardo); Ludwig; Ossessione; Rocco and His Brothers (Rocco e i Suoi Fratelli); Senso (The Wanton Countess); Vaghe Stelle dell'Orsa (Of a Thousand Delights/Sandra); White Nights (Le Notti Bianche).*

Vitale, Frank *Montreal Main.*

Vitale, Tony *Kiss Me, Guido.*

Vithanage, Prasanna *Death on a Full Moon Day (Purahanda Kaluwara).*

Vlácil, Frantisek *Markéta Lazarová.*

Vojnár, Ivan *Way Through the Bleak Woods, The (Cesta pustym lesem).*

vom Bruck, Roswitha *Climax (Ich – das Abenteuer heute eine Frau zu sein).*

von Baky, Josef *Adventures of Baron Munchhausen, The (Münchhausen).*

von Fritsch, Gunther *Curse of the Cat People, The.*

von Garnier, Katja *Making Up (Abgeschminkt).*

von Grote, Alexandra *November Moon (Novembermond).*

von Praunheim, Rosa (Holger Mischwitzki) *Anita: Dances of Vice (Anita: Tänze des Lasters); Army of Lovers or Revolt of the Perverts (Armee der Liebenden oder Revolte der Perversen); City of Lost Souls (Stadt der Verlorenen Seelen); I Am My Own Woman (Ich bin meine eigene Frau).*

von Scherler Mayer, Daisy *Madeline.*

von Sternberg, Josef *American Tragedy, An; Blonde Venus; Blue Angel, the (Der blaue Engel); Crime and Punishment; Devil Is a Woman, The; Dishonored; Jet Pilot; King Steps Out, The; Last Command, The; Macao; Morocco; Saga of Anatahan, The (Anatahan); Salvation Hunters, The; Scarlet Empress, The; Sergeant Madden; Shanghai Express; Shanghai Gesture, The; Thunderbolt; Underworld.*

von Stroheim, Erich *Blind Husbands; Foolish Wives; Greed; Merry-Go-Round; Merry Widow, The; Queen Kelly; Wedding March, The.*

von Sydow, Max *Katinka (Ved Vejen).*

von Trier, Lars *Breaking the Waves; Dancer in the Dark; Element of Crime, The (Forbrydelsens Element); Europa; Idiots, The (Idioterne); Kingdom, The (Riget); Kingdom II, The (Riget II).*

von Trotta, Margarethe *Friends and Husbands (Heller Wahn); German Sisters, The (Die Bleierne Zeit); Lost Honour of Katharina Blum, The (Die verlorene Ehre der Katharina Blum); Promise, The (Das Versprechen/La Promesse); Rosa Luxemburg; Second Awakening of Christa Klages, The (Das zweite Erwachen der Christa Klages); Sisters or the Balance of Happiness (Schwestern oder die Balance des Glücks); Three Sisters (Paura e amore).*

Vorhaus, Bernard *Ghost Camera, The; Lady from Louisiana; Last Journey, The.*

Votocek, Otokar *Wings of Fame.*

Voulgaris, Pantelis *Eleftherios Venizelos; Stone Years, The (Petrina Chronia).*

Wachowski, Andy *Bound; Matrix, The.*

Wachowski, Larry *Bound; Matrix, The.*

Wachsman, Daniel *Hamsin.*

Wacks, Jonathan *Just Another Date (aka Mystery Date); Powwow Highway.*

Wada, Junko *Body Drop Asphalt.*

Waddington, Andrucha *Me You Them (Es Tu Eles).*

Wade, Alan *Julian Po.*

Wadleigh, Michael *Wolfen; Woodstock; Woodstock: The Director's Cut.*

Waggner, George *Man-Made Monster (aka The Electric Man); Red Nightmare; Wolf Man, The.*

Wagner, Jane *Moment by Moment.*

Wagner, Paul *Windhorse.*

Wagon, Virginie *Secret, Le.*

Wainwright, Rupert *Blank Check (aka Blank Cheque); Stigmata.*

Waite, Ralph *On the Nickel.*

Wajda, Andrzej *Ashes and Diamonds (Popiól i Diament); Conductor, The (Dyrygent); Danton; Everything for Sale (Wszystko na Sprzedaz); Generation, A (Pokolenie); Innocent Sorcerers (Niewinni Czarodzieje); Kanal; Korczak; Landscape After a Battle (Krajobraz po Bitwie); Love in Germany, A (Eine Liebe in Deutschland); Man of Iron (Czlowiek z Zelaza); Man of Marble (Czlowiek z Marmur); Miss Nobody (Panna Nikt); Rough Treatment (Bez Znieczulenia); Siberian Lady Macbeth (Sibirska Ledi Magbet); Wedding, The (Wesele); Young Ladies of Wilko, The (Panny z Wilka).*

Wakamatsu, Koji *Violated Angels (Okasareta Byakui).*

Wakamatsu, Setsuro *Whiteout.*

Walas, Chris *Fly II, The.*

Waldron, Gy *Moonrunners.*

Waletzky, Joshua *Music for the Movies: Bernard Herrmann; Music for the Movies: The Hollywood Sound.*

Walker, Giles *90 Days.*

Walker, Hal *Road to Utopia.*

Walker, John *Winter Tan, A.*

Walker, Nancy *Can't Stop the Music.*

Walker, Pete *Comeback, The; Frightmare; Home Before Midnight; House of Mortal Sin; House of Whipcord; House of the Long Shadows, The; Schizo; Tiffany Jones.*

Walker, Rob *Circus.*

Walker, Stuart *Werewolf of London.*

Wallace, Randall *Man in the Iron Mask, The; We Were Soldiers.*

Wallace, Richard *Adventure in Baltimore (aka Bachelor Bait).*

Wallace, Stephen *Blood Oath; Boy Who Had Everything, The; Love Letters from Teralba Road, The; Stir; Turtle Beach.*

Wallace, Tommy Lee *Aloah Summer; Fright Night Part 2; Halloween III; Season of the Witch.*

Waller, Anthony *American Werewolf in Paris, An; Mute Witness.*

Waller, Tom *Monk Dawson.*

Walls, Tom *For Valour; Plunder; Pot Luck; Rookery Nook.*

Walmesley, Howard *Feverhouse.*

Walsh, Aisling *Joyriders.*

Walsh, Kieron J *When Brendan Met Trudy.*

Walsh, Raoul *Background to Danger; Big Trail, The; Blackbeard the Pirate; Bowery, The; Captain Horatio Hornblower; Colorado Territory; Desperate Journey; Distant Drums; Distant Trumpet, A; Enforcer, The (aka Murder Inc.); Gentleman Jim; Glory Alley; Gun Fury; High Sierra; King and Four Queens, The; Klondike Annie; Lion Is in the Streets, A; Man I Love, The; Manpower; Naked and the Dead, The; Objective Burma!; O.H.M.S. (aka You're in the Army Now); Pursued; Regeneration; Revolt of Mamie Stover, The; Roaring Twenties, The; Sadie Thompson; Sheriff of Fractured Jaw, The; Tall Men, The; They Died With Their Boots On; They Drive By Night (aka The Road to Frisco); Thief of Bagdad, The; White Heat.*

Walters, Charles *Ask Any Girl; Barkleys of Broadway, The; Belle of New York, The; Billy Rose's Jumbo (aka Jumbo); Dangerous When Wet; Easter Parade; High Society; Lili; Please Don't Eat the Daisies; Summer Stock (aka If You Feel Like Singing); Torch Song; Unsinkable Molly Brown, The.*

Walton, Fred *Rosary Murders, The; When a Stranger Calls.*

Wam, Svend *Sebastian.*

Wan Jen *Super Citizen Ko (Chaoji Da Guomin).*

Wan Lai-Ming *Uproar in Heaven (Danao Tiangong).*

Wanamaker, Sam *Catlow; File of the Golden Goose, The; Sinbad and the Eye of the Tiger.*

Wang Chao *Orphan of Anyang, The (Anyang Ying'er).*

Wang Guangli *Go For Broke (Heng Shu Heng); Maiden Work (Chunü Zuo).*

Wang Jin *Girls to Be Married, The (Chujia Nü).*

Wang, Peter *Great Wall Is a Great Wall, The (aka A Great Wall).*

Wang Shaudi *Accidental Legend (Fei Tian); Grandma and Her Ghosts (Mo-fa A-Ma); Yours and Mine (Wo de Shenjingbing).*

Wang Shuo *Father (Baba).*

Wang Tsai-Sheng *Cha-Cha for the Fugitive, A (Gei Taowangzhe de Qiaqia).*

Wang, Wayne *Anywhere but Here; Blue in the Face; Center of the World, The; Chan Is Missing; Chinese Box; Dim Sum – A Little Bit of Heart; Eat a Bowl of Tea; Joy Luck Club, The; Life Is Cheap…But Toilet Paper Is Expensive; Slam Dance; Smoke.*

Wang Xiaoshuai *Beijing Bicycle (Shiqi Sui de Danche); Days, The (Dong-Chun de Rizi); So Close to Paradise (Yuenan Guniang).*

Wang Yu *Beach of the War Gods (Zhan Shen Tan); One Armed Boxer (Dubi Quan Wang).*

Ward, David S *Cannery Row; Down Periscope; King Ralph; Major League; Major League II.*

Ward, Donal Lardner *My Life's in Turnaround.*

Ward, Nick *Dakota Road; Look Me in the Eye.*

Ward, Vincent *Map of the Human Heart; Navigator: A Medieval Odyssey, The; Vigil; What Dreams May Come.*

Warchus, Matthew *Simpatico.*

Ware, Clyde *No Drums, No Bugles.*

Wargnier, Régis *East-West (Est-Ouest); Femme française, Une (Eine Französische Frau); Indochine; Lumière et Compagnie.*

Warhol, Andy *Bike Boy; Blue Movie; Chelsea Girls; Couch; Kitchen; Lonesome Cowboys; My Hustler.*

Warner, Deborah *Last September, The.*

Warner, Paul *Fall Time.*

Warren, Charles Marquis *Charro!; Tension at Table Rock.*

Warren, Mark *Come Back Charleston Blue.*

Warren, Norman J *Satan's Slave; Terror.*

Waszynski, Michael *Dybbuk, The.*

Watanable, Fumiki *Bari-Zogon.*

Waters, John *Cecil B Demented; Cry-Baby; Desperate Living; Female Trouble; Hairspray; Mondo Trasho; Pecker; Pink Flamingos; Polyester; Serial Mom.*

Waters, Mark *House of Yes, The.*

Watkins, Peter *Culloden; Edvard Munch; Privilege; Punishment Park.*

Watt, Harry *Fiddlers Three; Overlanders, The; Where No Vultures Fly (aka Ivory Hunter).*

Watts, Roy *Hambone and Hillie (aka The Adventures of Hambone and Hillie).*

Wayans, Keenen (Keenan) Ivory *I'm Gonna Git You Sucka; Low Down Dirty Shame, A; Scary Movie; Scary Movie 2.*

Wayne, John *Alamo, The; Green Berets, The.*

Webb, Jack *Pete Kelly's Blues.*

Webb, Peter *Give My Regards to Broad Street.*

Webb, Robert D *Beneath the 12-Mile Reef; Cape Town Affair, The; Love Me Tender; Proud Ones, The; White Feather.*

Weber, Billy *Josh and S.A.M.*

Weber, Bruce *Broken Noses; Let's Get Lost.*

Webster, Nicholas *Santa Claus Conquers the Martians.*

Wedge, Chris *Ice Age.*

Weeks, Andrew *Split William to Chrysis: Portrait of a Drag Queen.*

Weeks, Stephen *Gawain and the Green Knight; I, Monster; Sword of the Valiant – The Legend of Gawain and the Green Knight, The.*

Weerasethakul, Apichatpong *Mysterious Object at Noon (Dogfar Nai Mea Marn).*

Wegener, Paul *Golem, The (Der Golem, Wie er in die Welt Kam).*

Weil, Samuel (Lloyd Kaufman) *Class of Nuke 'Em High; Toxic Avenger, The; War (aka Troma's War).*

Weiland, Paul *City Slickers II: The Legend of Curly's Gold; Roseanna's Grave (aka For Roseanna).*

Weill, Claudia *Girlfriends.*

Weinstein, Bob *Playing for Keeps.*

Weinstein, Harvey *Playing for Keeps.*

Weinstein, Larry *September Songs: The Music of Kurt Weill.*

Weinstock, Jane *Sigmund Freud's Dora.*

Weir, Peter *Cars That Ate Paris, The; Dead Poets Society; Fearless; Gallipoli; Green Card; Last Wave, The; Mosquito Coast, The; Picnic at Hanging Rock; Truman Show, The; Witness; Year of Living Dangerously, The.*

Weis, Don *I Love Melvin.*

Weis, Gary *80 Blocks from Tiffany's; Jimi Hendrix; Wholly Moses!*

Weisman, David *Ciao! Manhattan.*

Weisman, Sam *Bye Bye Love; D2: The Mighty Ducks; George of the Jungle; Out-of-Towners, The.*

Weiss, Andrea *Bit of Scarlet, A.*

Weiss, Rob *Amongst Friends.*

Weiss, Robert K *Amazon Women on the Moon.*

Weissbrod, Ellen *Listen Up: The Lives of Quincy Jones.*

Weissman, Aerlyn *Winter Tan, A.*

Weitz, Chris *Down to Earth.*

Weitz, Paul *About a Boy; American Pie; Down to Earth.*

Weller, Peter *Gold Coast (aka Elmore Leonard's Gold Coast).*

Welles, Orson *Chimes at Midnight (Campanadas a Medianoche); Citizen Kane; F for Fake (Vérités et Mensonges); Immortal Story, The (Histoire Immortelle); Lady from Shanghai, The; Macbeth; Magnificent Ambersons, The; Mr Arkadin (aka Confidential Report); Othello; Stranger, The; Touch of Evil; Trial, The (Le Procès).*

Wellington, David *I Love a Man in Uniform.*

Wellman, William A *Across the Wide Missouri; Battleground; Beau Geste; Beggars of Life; Hatchet Man, The (aka The Honourable Mr Wong); Iron Curtain, The (aka Behind the Iron Curtain); Lady of Burlesque (aka Striptease Lady); Magic Town; Next Voice You Hear…, The; Night Nurse; Nothing Sacred; Other Men's Women; Ox-Bow Incident, The; Public Enemy, The; Robin Hood of El Dorado, The; Roxie Hart; Star Is Born, A; Story of GI Joe, The; Track of the Cat; Wings; Yellow Sky.*

Wells, Peter *Desperate Remedies.*

Wells, Simon *American Tail, An: Fievel Goes West; Balto; Prince of Egypt, The.*

Welz, Peter *Burning Life.*

Wenders, Wim *Alice in the Cities (Alice in den Städten); American Friend, The (Der Amerikanische Freund); Buena Vista Social Club, The; End of Violence, The (Am Ende der Gewalt); Faraway, So Close (In weiter Ferne, so nah!); Goalkeeper's Fear of the Penalty, The (Die Angst des Tormanns beim Elfmeter); Hammett; Kings of the Road (Im Lauf der Zeit); Lightning Over Water (aka Nick's Movie); Lisbon Story; Lumière et Compagnie; Million Dollar Hotel, The; Notebook on Cities and Clothes (Aufzeichnungen zu Kleidern und Städten); Ode to Cologne (Viel Passiert – Der BAP Film); Paris, Texas; Scarlet Letter, The (Der scharlachrote Buchstabe); State of Things, The; Summer in the City; Ten Minutes Older – The*

Trumpet; Tokyo-Ga; Until the End of the World (Bis ans Ende der Welt); Wings of Desire (Der Himmel über Berlin); Wrong Movement (Falsche Bewegung).

Wendkos, Paul *Angel Baby; Gidget; Honor Thy Father; Mephisto Waltz, The.*

Wenk, Richard *Just the Ticket; Vamp.*

Werker, Alfred *A-Haunting We Will Go; Adventures of Sherlock Holmes, The; At Gunpoint (aka Gunpoint); He Walked by Night; House of Rothschild, The; Three Hours to Kill; Walk East on Beacon!*

Werner, Peter *No Man's Land.*

Wertmüller, Lina *Lizards, The (I Basilischi); Naples Connection, The (Un Complicato Intrigo di Donne, Vicoli e Delitti); Seven Beauties (Pasqualino Settebellezze); Swept Away…by an Unusual Destiny in the Blue Sea of August (Travolti da un Insolito Destino nell'Azzurro Mare d'Agosto).*

Wesley, William *Scarecrows.*

West, Jake *Razor Blade Smile.*

West, Robert Jan *Little Sister (Zusje).*

West, Roland *Bat Whispers, The.*

West, Simon *Con Air; General's Daughter, The; Lara Croft: Tomb Raider.*

West, Wash *Fluffer, The.*

Westdijk, Robert Jan *Siberia.*

Weston, Eric *Iron Triangle, The.*

Wetzler, Gwen *Mighty Mouse in the Great Space Chase; Secret of the Sword, The.*

Wexler, Haskell *Latino; Medium Cool; Vietnam Journey.*

Wexler, Mark *Me & My Matchmaker.*

Wexler, Tanya *Finding North.*

Whale, James *Bride of Frankenstein, The; By Candlelight; Frankenstein; Great Garrick, The; Invisible Man, The; Journey's End; Man in the Iron Mask, The; Old Dark House, The; One More River (aka Over the River); Remember Last Night?; Show Boat.*

Whatham, Claude *All Creatures Great and Small; Buddy's Song; Swallows and Amazons; Sweet William; That'll Be the Day.*

Wheat, Jim *Lies.*

Wheat, Ken *Lies.*

Wheatley, David *Magic Toyshop, The.*

Wheeler, Anne *Bye Bye Blues.*

Whelan, Tim *Action for Slander; Camels Are Coming, The; Divorce of Lady X, The; Farewell Again (aka Troopship); Nightmare; St Martin's Lane (aka Sidewalks of London); Thief of Bagdad, The.*

Whitaker, Forest *Hope Floats; Strapped; Waiting to Exhale.*

Whitehead, Peter *Daddy; Tonite Let's All Make Love in London.*

Whitelaw, Alexander *Lifespan.*

Whitesell, John *See Spot Run.*

Whitney, Mark *Matter of Heart.*

Whittaker, Stephen *Closing Numbers.*

Whorf, Richard *It Happened in Brooklyn.*

Wiard, William *Tom Horn.*

Wicht, David *Windprints.*

Wichert, Tony *Fly a Flag for Poplar.*

Wickes, David *Silver Dream Racer; Sweeney!*

Wicki, Bernhard *Longest Day, The.*

Wickman, Torgny *Anita; Language of Love (Kärlekens Språk); More About the Language of Love (Mera ur Kärlekens Språk).*

Widen, Gregory *God's Army (aka The Prophecy).*

Widerberg, Bo *Adalen '31; Elvira Madigan; Joe Hill (aka The Ballad of Joe Hill); Love Lessons (Laererinden/Lust och fägring Stor); Man from Majorca, The (Mannen från Mallorca); Man on the Roof, The (Mannen på Taket); Pram (Barnvagnen); Stubby (Fimpen).*

Wie Desheng *About July (Qiyue Tian).*

Wiederhorn, Ken *Eyes of a Stranger; Return of the Living Dead Part II.*

Wieland, Joyce *Reason Over Passion (La Raison avant la Passion).*

Wiene, Robert *Cabinet of Dr Caligari, The (Das Kabinett des Dr Caligari); Genuine; Hands of Orlac, The (Orlacs Hände); Raskolnikow.*

Wierzbicki, Krzysztof *Krzysztof Kieslowski: I'm So So.*

Wilcha, Christopher *Target Shoots First, The.*

Wilcox, Fred M *Forbidden Planet; Lassie Come Home; Secret Garden, The.*

Wilcox, Herbert *Courtneys of Curzon Street, The (aka The Courtney Affair); Derby Day (aka Four Against Fate); Goodnight Vienna (aka Magic Night); I Live in Grosvenor Square (aka A Yank in London); Nell Gwynn; Odette; Peg of Old Drury; Yellow Canary, The.*

Wilde, Cornel *Beach Red; No Blade of Grass; Sharks' Treasure.*

Wilde, Ted *Kid Brother, The; Speedy.*

Wilder, Billy *Ace in the Hole (aka The Big Carnival); Apartment, The; Avanti!; Buddy Buddy; Double Indemnity; Emperor Waltz, The; Fedora; Five Graves to Cairo; Foreign Affair, A; Fortune Cookie, The (aka Meet Whiplash Willie); Front Page, The; Irma la Douce; Kiss Me, Stupid; Lost Weekend, The; Love in the Afternoon; Major and the Minor, The; One, Two, Three; Private Life of Sherlock Holmes, The; Sabrina (aka Sabrina Fair); Seven Year Itch, The; Some Like It Hot; Spirit of St. Louis, The; Stalag 17; Sunset Blvd.; Witness for the Prosecution.*

Wilder, Gene *Adventure of Sherlock Holmes' Smarter Brother, The; Haunted Honeymoon; Woman in Red, The; World's Greatest Lover, The.*

Wiley, Ethan *House II: The Second Story.*

Williams, David *Thirteen.*

Williams, Hype *Belly.*

Williams, Jano *Gaea Girls.*

Williams, Linda *Maxwell Street Blues.*

Williams, Matt *Where the Heart Is.*

Williams, Paul *November Men, The; Revolutionary, The.*

Willing, Nick *Photographing Fairies.*

Wills, James Elder *Big Fella.*

Wilson, Andy *Playing God.*

Wilson, Hugh *Blast from the Past; Burglar; First Wives Club, The; Guarding Tess; Police Academy.*

Wilson, Jim *Head Above Water; Stacy's Knights.*

Wilson, Richard *Al Capone; It's All True.*

Wilson, Sandy *My American Cousin.*

Wincer, Simon *Crocodile Dundee in Los Angeles; D.A.R.Y.L.; Free Willy; Harlequin; Harley Davidson and the Marlboro Man; Lightning Jack; Lighthorsemen, The; Phantom, The; Phar Lap; Quigley Down Under.*

Windsor, Chris *Big Meat Eater.*

Windust, Bretaigne *Enforcer, The (aka Murder, Inc.).*

Winer, Harry *SpaceCamp.*

Winer, Lucy *Rate It X.*

Wing Shya *Heroes in Love (Lian'ai Qi Yi).*

Wingrove, Nigel *Sacred Flesh.*

Winham, Francine *Rapunzel Let Down Your Hair.*

Winkler, Charles *Disturbed; You Talkin' to Me?*

Winkler, David *Finding Graceland.*

Winkler, Henry *Cop & ½ (aka Cop and a Half); Memories of Me.*

Winkler, Irwin *At First Sight; Guilty by Suspicion; Net, The; Night and the City.*

Winner, Michael *Appointment With Death; Big Sleep, The; Bullseye!; Chato's Land; Chorus of Disapproval, A; Death Wish; Death Wish II; Death Wish 3; Dirty Weekend; Firepower; Hanibal Brooks; Lawman; Mechanic, The (aka Killer of Killers); Nightcomers, The; Parting Shots; Play It Cool; Scorpio; Scream for Help; Sentinel, The; Stone Killer, The; Wicked Lady, The.*

Winslow, Susan *All This and World War II.*

Winsor, Terry *Essex Boys; Party Party.*

Winspeare, Edoardo *Living Blood (Sangue vivo).*

Winston, Stan *Gnome Named Gnorm, A (aka Upworld/Adventures of a Gnome Named Gnorm); Pumpkinhead (aka Vengeance, the Demon).*

Winter, Alex *Freaked.*

Winter, Donovan *Deadly Females, The; Give Us Tomorrow.*

Winterbottom, Michael *Butterfly Kiss; Claim, The; I Want You; Jude; 24 Hour Party People; Welcome to Sarajevo; With or Without You; Wonderland.*

Wintonick, Peter *Manufacturing Consent: Noam Chomsky and the Media.*

Wipf, Louis *Boule de Suif.*

Wise, Herbert *Lovers!, The.*

Wise, Kirk *Atlantis – The Lost Empire; Beauty and the Beast; Hunchback of Notre Dame, The.*

Wise, Robert *Andromeda Strain, The; Audrey Rose; Blood on the Moon; Body Snatcher, The; Born to Kill (aka Lady of Deceit); Destination Gobi; Captive City, The; Curse of the Cat People, The; Day the Earth Stood Still, The; Executive Suite; Haunting, The; Hindenburg, The; I Want to Live!; Mystery in Mexico; Odds Against Tomorrow; Rooftops; Sand Pebbles, The; Set-Up, The; Somebody Up There Likes Me; Sound of Music, The; Star Trek – The Motion Picture; Star!; Tribute to a Bad Man; West Side Story.*

Wiseman, Frederick *Basic Training; Canal Zone; Domestic Violence; High School; Hospital; Juvenile Court; Law and Order; Meat; Model; Primate; Sinai Field Mission; Welfare.*

Wishman, Doris *Deadly Weapons; Double Agent 73.*

Witcher, Theodore *love jones.*

Witney, William *Adventures of Captain Marvel, The (aka The Return of Captain Marvel); I Escaped from Devil's Island; Master of the World.*

Wohl, Ira *Best Boy; Best Man.*

Wolcott, James L *Wild Women of Wongo.*

Wolf, Fred *Mouse and His Child, The; Point, The.*

Wolf, Konrad *I Was Nineteen (Ich war Neunzehn).*

Wolk, Andy *Traces of Red.*

Wollen, Peter *Crystal Gazing; Friendship's Death; Penthesilea; Queen of the Amazons; Riddles of the Sphinx.*

Wolman, Dan *Nana.*

Women's Film Workshop *We're Alive.*

Wong Chi-Keung *Dead Knot (Si Jie).*

Wong, James *Final Destination; One, The.*

Wong Kar-Wai *As Tears Go By (Wangjiao Jiamen); Chungking Express (Chongqing Senlin); Days of Being Wild (A-Fei Zhengchuan); Fallen Angels (Duoluo Tianshi); Happy Together (Chunguang Zhaxie); In the Mood for Love (Huayang Nianhua).*

Wong, Kirk (aka Che-Kirk Wong) *Ashes of Time (Dong Xie Xi Du); Big Hit, The; Club, The (Wuting); Crime Story (Zhong'an Zu); Health Warning (Da Leitai); Organized Crime and Triad Bureau (Zhong'an Shilu O-ji); Rock n'Roll Cop (Sheng-Gang Yihao Tongji Fan).*

Wong, Lawrence *Cross-Harbour Tunnel (Guo Hai Suidao).*

Wong-Ho, YN *Xenolith.*

Woo, John (Wu Yusen) *Better Tomorrow, A (Yingxiong Bense); Better Tomorrow II, A (Yingxiong Bense II); Broken Arrow; Bullet in the Head (Diexue Jietou); Face/Off; Hard-Boiled (Lashou Shentan); Hard Target; Just Heroes; Killer, The (Diexue Shuang Xiong); Last Hurrah for Chivalry (Haoxia); Mission: Impossible II; Once a Thief (Zongheng Sihai); Violent Tradition.*

Wood, Duncan *Bargee, The.*

Wood Jr, Edward D *Glen or Glenda? (aka I Led Two Lives/I Changed My Sex); Night of the Ghouls (aka Revenge of the Dead); Plan 9 from Outer Space.*

Wood, Sam *Command Decision; Day at the Races, A; Devil and Miss Jones, The; For Whom the Bell Tolls; Goodbye, Mr Chips; Ivy; Kings Row; Night at the Opera, A; Our Town; Saratoga Trunk; Stamboul Quest.*

Woodcock, Penny *Women in Tropical Places.*

Woodhead, Leslie *Srebrenica: A Cry from the Grave.*

Woods, Arthur *They Drive By Night.*

Woods, Rowan *Boys, The.*

Woods, Skip *Thursday.*

Wool, Abbe *Roadside Prophets.*

Woolley, Richard *Brothers and Sisters; Telling Tales.*

Worsdale, Andrew *Shot Down.*

Worsley, Wallace *Hunchback of Notre Dame, The.*

Worth, David *Kickboxer.*

Worth, Howard *Raga.*

Worth, Jan *Doll's Eye.*

Wortmann, Sönke *Bewegte Mann, Der (The Most Desired Man/Maybe…Maybe Not).*

Woukoache, François L *Fragments of Life (Fragments de Vies).*

Wrede, Caspar *One Day in the Life of Ivan Denisovich; Ransom.*

Wright, Basil *Song of Ceylon, The.*

Wright, Edgar *Fistful of Fingers, A.*

Wright, Geoffrey *Cherry Falls; Romper Stomper.*

Wright, Kay *Mighty Mouse in the Great Space Chase.*

Wright, Thomas Lee *Eight-Tray Gangster: The Making of a Crip.*

Wright, Tom *Torchlight.*

Wrye, Donald *Ice Castles.*

Wu Di *Goldfish (Huangjin Yu).*

Wu Ma *Conman and the Kung Fu Kid (Langbei wei Jian/aka Wits to Wits); Deaf and Mute Heroine, The (Longya Jian).*

Wu Ming (Wang Xiaoshuai) *Frozen (Jidu Hanleng).*

Wu Nianzhen *Borrowed Life, A (Duo-sang); Buddha Bless America (Taiping Tianguo).*

Wu Tianming *King of Masks (Bian Lian); Old Well (Lao Jing).*

Wu Yigong *My Memories of Old Beijing (Chengnan Jiushi).*

Wu Yonggang *Goddess, The (Shennü).*

Wu Ziniu *Last Day of Winter, The (Zuihou Yige Dongri).*

Wurlitzer, Rudy *Candy Mountain.*

Wyborny, Klaus *Birth of a Nation, The (Die Geburt der Nation).*

Wyeth, Peter *Twelve Views of Kensal House.*

Wyler, William *Ben-Hur; Best Years of Our Lives, The; Big Country, The; Carrie; Collector, The; Come and Get It; Dead End; Desperate Hours, The; Detective Story; Friendly Persuasion; Funny Girl; Heiress, The; Jezebel; Letter, The; Liberation of L.B. Jones, The; Little Foxes, The; Mrs Miniver; Roman Holiday; These Three; Westerner, The; Wuthering Heights.*

Wynn, Bob *Resurrection of Zachary Wheeler, The.*

Wynne-Simmons, Robert *Outcasts, The.*

Wynorski, Jim *Return of the Swamp Thing, The.*

Xhonneux, Henri *Marquis.*

Xhuvani, Gjergj *Slogans.*

Xia Gang *Concerto of Life.*

Xie Fei *Black Snow (Ben Ming Nian).*

Xie Jin *Hibiscus Town (Furong Zhen); Red Detachment of Women (Hongse Niangzijun); Two Stage Sisters (Wutai Jiemei).*

Yagi, Junichi *Watching the Detective (Aru Tantei no Yu-utsu).*

Yaguchi, Shinobu *Adrenaline Drive; Waterboys.*

Yahrhaus, Bill *Vietnam Journey.*

Yakin, Boaz *Fresh; Price Above Rubies, A; Remember the Titans.*

Yamada, Yoji *My Sons (Musuko).*

Yamaga, Hiroyuki *Wings of Honneamise, The (Oneamisu No Tsubasa).*

Yamakawa, Naoto *Attack on a Bakery (Panya Shugeki); Girl She Is 100%, A (Hyaku percent no Onna no Ko); New Morning of Billy the Kid, The (Billy the Kid no Atarashii Yoake).*

Yamashita, Nobuhiro *Hazy Life (Donten Seikatsu).*

Yamauchi, Shigeyasu *Digimon Digital Monsters – The Movie.*

Yanagimachi, Mitsuo *About Love, Tokyo (Ai ni tsuite, Tokyo); Fire Festival (Himatsuri).*

Yang, Edward *Brighter Summer Day, A (Guling Jie Shaonian Sha Ren Shijian); Confucian Confusion, A (Duli Shidai); Mahjong (Majiang); One and a Two…, A (Yi Yi); Taipei Story (Qingmei Zhuma); Terroriser, The (Kongbufenzi).*

Yang Fengliang *Dragon Town Story; Ju Dou.*

Yang Jingchen *Shanghai Lil (Hao Ke/aka The Champion).*

Yasar, Secklin *Yellow Smile, The (Sari Tebessum).*

Yates, David *Tichborne Claimant, The.*

Yates, Pamela *When the Mountains Tremble.*

Yates, Peter *Breaking Away; Bullitt; Curtain Call; Deep, The; Dresser, The; Eleni; Eyewitness (aka The Janitor); For Pete's Sake; Friends of Eddie Coyle, The; Hot Rock, The (aka How to Steal a Diamond in Four*

Uneasy Lessons); House on Carroll Street, The; Innocent Man, An; John and Mary; Krull; Mother, Jugs & Speed; Murphy's War; Robbery; Run of the Country, The; Summer Holiday; Suspect.

Yau, Herman *From the Queen to the Chief Executive (Denghou Dong Jianhua Faluo).*

Yazaki, Hitoshi *Afternoon Breezes (Kazetachi no Gogo); March Comes in Like a Lion (Sangatsu no Raion).*

Yeaworth Jr, Irvin S *Blob, The; Dinosaurus!*

Yee Chih-Yen *Lonely Hearts Club (Jimo Fangxin Julebu).*

Yee, Derek (Yee Tung-shin) *C'est la Vie, Ma Cherie (Xin Buliao Qing); Viva Erotica! (Seqing Nan Nü).*

Yektapanah, Hassan *Djomeh (aka Djomeh, L'Histoire du garçon qui tombait amoreux).*

Yilmaz, Atif *After the Fall (Eylül Firtinasi); Berdel.*

Yim Ho *Buddha's Lock (Tian Pusa); Day the Sun Turned Cold, The (Tianguo Niezi); Homecoming (Si Shui Liu Nian); Kitchen, The (Wo ai Chufang).*

Yim Soon-Rye *Three Friends (Sechinku).*

Ying Yunwei *Plunder of Peach and Plum (Tao Li Jie); Unchanged Heart in Life and Death (Shengsi Tong Xin).*

Yip, Raymond *Portland Street Blues (Hongxing Shisan Mei).*

Yip, Wilson Bullets *Over Summer (Baolie Xingjing).*

Yonfan, Manshi *Bugis Street.*

Yoon Jong-Chan *Sorum.*

York, Steve *Force More Powerful, A.*

Yorkin, Bud *Arthur 2: On the Rocks; Come Blow Your Horn; Divorce American Style; Inspector Clouseau; Love s; Twice in a Lifetime.*

Yoshida, Hiroaki *Iron Maze.*

Yoshida, Kiju *Lumière et Compagnie.*

Yoshida, Yoshihige *Promise (Ningen no Yakusoku).*

Young, Neil *see* Shakey, Bernard.

Young, Harold *Scarlet Pimpernel, The.*

Young, Robert *Captain Jack; Fierce Creatures; Romance with a Double Bass; Splitting Heirs; Vampire Circus, The; World Is Full of Married Men, The.*

Young, Robert M *Alambrista!; Ballad of Gregorio Cortez, The (aka Gregorio Cortez); Dominick and Eugene (aka Nicky and Geno); Extremities; One-Trick Pony; Rich Kids; Roosters; Saving Grace; Triumph of the Spirit.*

Young, Roger *Gulag; Lassiter; Squeeze, The.*

Young, Terence *Amazons, The (Le Guerriere dal Seno Nuda); Bloodline (aka Sidney Sheldon's Bloodline); Cold Sweat (De la Part des Copains); Dr No; From Russia With Love; Klansman, The; Red Sun (Soleil Rouge); That Lady; They Were Not Divided; Thunderball; Wait Until Dark.*

Younger, Ben *Boiler Room.*

Yu Lik-Wai *Love Will Tear Us Apart (Tian Shang Renjian).*

Yu, Ronny *Bride of Chucky; 51st State, The; Phantom Lover, The (Xin Yeban Gesheng); Warriors of Virtue.*

Yuan Kwai *Fong Sai-Yuk (Fang Shiyu).*

Yuan Muzhi *Street Angel (Malu Tianshi).*

Yuen, Corey *No Retreat, No Surrender.*

Yust, Larry *Homebodies.*

Yuyama, Kunihiko *Pokémon – The First Movie: Mewtwo Strikes Back; Pokémon 2: The Power of One (Gekijôban Poketto Monsutâ: Maboroshi no Pokémon Ekkusu – Rugia Bakudan); Pokémon 3: Spell of the Unown.*

Yuzna, Brian *Necronomicon (aka H.P. Lovecraft's Necronomicon); Re-Animator 2; Return of the Living Dead II; Society.*

Zafranovic, Lordan *Occupation in 26 Pictures, The (Okupacija u 26 Slika).*

Zaillian, Steven *Civil Action, A; Searching for Bobby Fischer (aka Innocent Moves).*

Zaim, Dervis *Somersault in a Coffin (Tabutta Rövasata).*

Zaks, Jerry *Marvin's Room.*

Zambrano, Benito *Solas.*

Zampi, Mario *Happy Ever After (aka Tonight's the Night); Laughter in Paradise; Naked Truth, The (aka Your Past Is Showing).*

Zanuck, Lili Fini *Rush.*

Zanussi, Krzysztof *Catamount Killing, The (Lohngelder für Pittsville); Constant Factor, The (Constans); Contract, The (Kontrakt); Family Life (Zycie Rodzinne); Illumination (Iluminacja); Life at a Gallop (Cwal); Night Paths (Wege in der Nacht); Silent Touch, The; Year of the Quiet Sun, A (Rok Spokojnego Slonca).*

Zappa, Frank *200 Motels.*

Zarindast, Tony *Guns and the Fury, The.*

Zaritsky, Raul *Maxwell Street Blues.*

Zaslove, Alan *GoBots: Battle of the Rocklords.*

Zauberman, Yolande *Clubbed to Death; Me Ivan, You Abraham (Moi Ivan, Toi Abraham).*

Zeffirelli, Franco *Brother Sun, Sister Moon (Fratello Sole, Sorella Luna); Champ, The; Endless Love; Hamlet; Jane Eyre; Otello; Romeo and Juliet; Sparrow (Storia di una Capinera); Tea with Mussolini (Te con il Duce); Traviata, La.*

Zelenka, Petr *Buttoners (Knoflikári).*

Zelnik, Friedrich *Lilac Domino, The; Weber, Die.*

Zeltser, Yuri *Playmaker, The.*

Zeman, Karel *Baron Munchhausen (Baron Prasil).*

Zemeckis, Robert *Amazing Stories; Back to the Future; Back to the Future Part II; Back to the Future Part III; Cast Away; Contact; Death Becomes Her; Forrest Gump; I Wanna Hold Your Hand; Romancing the Stone; Used Cars; Who Framed Roger Rabbit; What Lies Beneath.*

Zetterling, Mai *Amorosa; Scrubbers; Visions of Eight.*

Zeze, Takahisa *Hysteric.*

Zhang Meijun *Dynasty (Qian Dao Wan Li Zhui).*

Zhang Ming *Rainclouds Over Wushan (Wushan Yunyu/aka In Expectation); Weekend plot (Miyu Shi Qi Xiaoshi).*

Zhang Nuanxin *Sacrificed Youth (Qingchun Ji).*

Zhang Tielin *Man from China.*

Zhang Yang *Quitting (Zuotian); Shower (Xizao).*

Zhang Yuan *Beijing Bastards (Beijing Zazhong); Crazy English (Fengkuang Yingyu); East Palace, West Palace (Dong Gong Xi Gong); Mama; Seventeen Years (Guonian Hui Jia); Sons (Erzi), Square, The (Guangchang).*

Zhang Yimou *Happy Times (Xingfu Shiguang); Ju Dou; Keep Cool (You Hua Hao Hao Shuo); Lumière et Compagnie; Not One Less (Yi Ge Duo Bu Neng Shao); Raise the Red Lantern (Dahong Denglong Gaogao Gua); Red Sorghum; Road Home, The (Wo de Fuqin Muqin); Shanghai Triad (Yao a Yao Yao dao Waipo Qiao); Story of Qiu Ju, The (Qiu Ju da Guansi); To Live (Huozhe).*

Zhang Zeming *Foreign Moon; Sun and Rain (Taiyang Yu/aka Sunshine and Showers); Swan Song (Juexiang).*

Zheng Changhe *King Boxer (Tianxia Diyi Quan/aka Five Fingers of Death).*

Zheng Dongtian *Young Couples (Yuanyang Iou).*

Zheng Junli *Crows and Sparrows (Wuya yu Maque); Spring River Flows East, The (Yijiang Chunshui Xiang Dong Liu).*

Zheutlin, Cathy *In the Best Interests of the Children.*

Zhou Xiaowen *Emperor's Shadow, The (Qin Song); Ermo.*

Zhou Youchao *Sweet Grass (Huang Sha, Qing Cao, Hong Taiyang).*

Zhu Wen *Seafood (Haixian).*

Zhuge Qingyun *Shanghai Lil (Hao Ke/aka The Champion).*

Zidi, Claude *Aile ou la Cuisse, L' (The Wing and the Thigh); Asterix & Obelix Take on Caesar (Astérix & Obélix contre César); French Mustard (La Moutarde Me Monte au Nez); Le Cop (Les Ripoux); Le Cop 2 (Ripoux contre ripoux).*

Zieff, Howard *Dream Team, The; Hearts of the West (aka Hollywood Cowboy); House Calls; Main Event, The; My Girl; My Girl II; Private Benjamin; Slither; Unfaithfully Yours.*

Ziehl, Scott *Broken Vessels.*

Ziehm, Howard *Flesh Gordon.*

Zielinski, Rafal *Fun; Screwballs; Screwballs II – Loose Screws.*

Ziewer, Christian *Dear Mother, I'm All Right (Liebe Mutter, mir geht es gut).*

Zilbermann, Jean-Jacques *Man Is a Woman (L'Homme est une femme comme les autres).*

Zima, Jorge *Night on the Terrace (Noche en la Terraza).*

Zimmerman, Vernon *Fade to Black.*

Zinnemann, Fred *Day of the Jackal, The; Eyes in the Night; Five Days One Summer; From Here to Eternity; High Noon; Julia; Kid Glove Killer; Man for All Seasons, A; Men, The; My Brother Talks to Horses; Nun's Story, The; Oklahoma!; Search, The; Seventh Cross, The; Sundowners, The.*

Zito, Joseph *Abduction; Invasion U.S.A.; Missing in Action; Prowler, The (aka Rosemary's Killer).*

Zlotoff, Lee David *Spitfire Grill, The.*

Zonca, Eric *Smalltime Thief (Le Petit Voleur); Vie Rêvée des Anges, La (The Dream Life of Angels).*

Zondag, Ralph *Dinosaur.*

Zubrycki, Tom *Diplomat, The.*

Zucker, David *Airplane!; Naked Gun, The; Naked Gun 2½: The Smell of Fear, The; Ruthless People; Top Secret!*

Zucker, Jerry *Airplane!; First Knight; Ghost; Rat Race; Ruthless People; Top Secret!*

Zuckerman, Francine *Punch Me in the Stomach.*

Zukor, Lou *Mighty Mouse in the Great Space Chase.*

Zulawski, Andrzej*Fidélité, La (Fidelity); Possession; Third Part of the Night, The (Trzecia Czesc Nocy).*

Zuniga, Frank *Golden Seal, The.*

Zurlini, Valerio *Désert des Tartares, Le.*

Zwart, Harald *One Night at McCool's.*

Zwerin, Charlotte *Gimme Shelter; Music for the Movies: Toru Takemitsu; Thelonious Monk: Straight No Chaser.*

Zwick, Edward *About Last Night…; Courage Under Fire; Glory; Having It All; Leaving Normal; Legends of the Fall; Siege, The.*

Zwicky, Karl *Paws.*

Zwigoff, Terry *Crumb; Ghost World.*

General Subject Index

Aakeson, Kim Fupz, film adapted from work, *Miracle*

Abelard and Heloise, film about, *Stealing Heaven*

Abortion, *Alfie; Blue Denim; The Cider House Rules; Dekalog 2: 'Thou shalt not take the name of the Lord thy God in vain'; Detective Story; Flesh; Hush-a-Bye Baby; If These Walls Could Talk; Love with the Proper Stranger; Making It; A Night in the Life of Jimmy Reardon; Occasional Work of a Female Slave; Patti Rocks; To Find a Man*

Acker, Kathy, film adapted from work, *Variety*

Ackerley, JR, film adapted from work, *We Think the World of You*

Adams, Richard, films adapted fom work, *The Plague Dogs; Watership Down*

Adolescence (*see also* **Children and childhood, Runaways, Teenagers and teen movies**)
Aus, *Be My Star; Benny's Video; Fistful of Flies; Lovely Rita; Only the Brave*
Aust, *Emma's War; Fighting Back; Flirting; The Mango Tree; Mullaway; Two Friends; Walkabout; The Year My Voice Broke*
Bel, *Crazy Love; Rosie*
Can, *Mon Oncle Antoine; My American Cousin*
China, *In the Heat of the Sun; Not One Less*
Czech, *Peter and Pavla; Valerie and Her Week of Wonders*
Fr, *A Toute Vitesse; The Best Way to Walk; Bonjour Tristesse; Les Dernières Vacances; Le Diable au corps; Diabolo Menthe; Les Enfants Terribles; Farewell, Home Sweet Home; 4 Adventures of Reinette and Mirabelle; An Impudent Girl; The Lover; Les Mistons; Mon Père, ce héros; Montalvo et l'enfant; Nord; Passe Ton Bac d'Abord; Pauline à la Plage; La Petite Voleuse; Mes Petites Amoureuses; Le Petit Matin; Les Quatre Cents Coups; Rouge Baiser; Le Souffle au Coeur; To Our Loves; Virgin* (Breillat); *The Wanderer; Zazie dans le Métro*
GB, *Beat Girl; Boston Kickout; Boy and Bicycle; Conquest of the South Pole; Experience Preferred But Not Essential; Friends; Get Real; The Girl with Brains in Her Feet; Goodbye Charlie Bright; Gregory's Girl; House of America; Into the Arms of Strangers: Stories of the Kindertransport; The Long Day Closes; The Miracle; Romeo and Juliet; A Room for Romeo Brass; Secret Places; Small Faces; Stella Does Tricks; A Summer in La Goulette; Terms of Trial; The War Zone; Wish You Were Here; The Young Poisoner's Handbook*
Ger, *Mädchen in Uniform; The Main Actor; Wild Game*
Greece, *End of an Era*
Hun, *The Princess*
Iran, *The Girl in the Sneakers*
Ire, *Hush-a-Bye Baby; Last of the High Kings*
Isr, *Lemon Popsicle*
It, *Fists in the Pocket; Malèna; Mignon Has Left; Noi Tre; Romeo and Juliet; Stealing Beauty; Venial Sin; The Visitor; I Vitelloni*
Jap, *April Story; A Boy Called Third Base; How Old Is the River?; Love Letter; The Moon Has Risen; Remembrance* (Nakajima); *This Window Is Yours; Wave*
Mex, *And Your Mother Too; Hasta Morir*
Neth, *Spetters*
Nor, *Cross My Heart and Hope to Die; The Ice Palace* (Blom); *I Was Fifteen; The Other Side of Sunday; Sebastian*
NZ, *An Angel at My Table; The End of the Golden Weather*
Pol, *Miss Nobody; A Short Film About Love*
Sp, *The Good Life*
Swe, *Hets; Love Lessons; Sebastian; Show Me Love*
Switz, *The Indians Are Still Far Away*
Tai, *Ah Chung; A Brighter Summer Day; Darkness and Light; Daughter of the Nile*
Tun, *A Summer in La Goulette*
Tur, *Summer Love*
US, *Aloha Summer; American Pie; American Pie 2; Baby Boy; Angus; Beautiful Girls; Big Girls Don't Cry…They Get Even; Billy Bathgate; Book of Love; Boyz N the Hood; Brighton Beach Memoirs; Buster and Billie; The Chocolate War; Class of '44; Clueless;*

Confessions of a Suburban Girl; The Craft; The Delta; Diner; Donnie Darko; Empire Records; Fire with Fire; Five Corners; Gas Food Lodging; Grandview U.S.A.; Gummo; Heaven Help Us; Heavy Petting; Hopscotch; Housekeeping; Imaginary Crimes; I Never Promised You a Rose Garden; Kicked in the Head; The Last American Virgin; The Last Picture Show; Last Summer; Little Darlings; Long Way Home; The Man in the Moon; Manny & Lo; Mermaids; My Bodyguard; My Father, the Hero; My Little Girl; A Night in the Life of Jimmy Reardon; Ode to Billie Joe; Old Enough; Permanent Record; The Power of One; Racing with the Moon; Red Sky at Morning; Running on Empty; Square Dance; Staying Together; Summer of '42; Teenage Caveman; 10 Things I Hate About You; This Day and Age; Virgin Stripped Bare by Her Bachelors; Welcome to the Dollhouse; William Shakespeare's Romeo & Juliet; White Squall; Who's That Knocking at My Door?; The Woo Woo Kid
USSR, *Goodbye, Boys; Plumbum, or a Dangerous Game; When We Were Young*
Vietnam, *Nostalgia for Countryland*
Yugo, *Time of the Gypsies*

Adoption (see also **Orphans**), *Adoption; Auntie Mame; Big Daddy; L'Enfance nue; Flirting with Disaster; A Global Affair; It Takes Two; Mixed Company; The Official Version; Perfect Circle; Problem Child; Problem Child 2; Santee; Secrets & Lies; A Simple Twist of Fate; The Tie That Binds; The Unforgiven*

Advertising, *Agency; Boomerang* (Hudlin); *Christmas in July; Crazy People; A Face in the Crowd; How to Get Ahead in Advertising; Keep the Aspidistra Flying; Nothing in Common; A Shock to the System; Switch; Will Success Spoil Rock Hunter?; A Woman or Two*

Afghanistan, in film, *The Beast; The Horsemen; Jung (War) – in the Land of the Mujaheddin; Kandahar; Rambo III*

Africa, in film (see also individual African nations)
colonial life in (see also **Colonialism**), *Another Dawn; The Black Bunch; Chocolat* (Denis); *Clean Slate; Cobra Verde; A Good Man in Africa; The Grass Is Singing; La Guerre sans nom; The Heart of the Matter; Heritage…Africa; The Kitchen Toto; The Loss of Sexual Innocence; Men of Two Worlds; Mister Johnson; No Secrets; Out of Africa; Sammy Going South; The Sheltering Sky; Simba; The Sins of Rachel Cade; White Mischief*
ethnographic films, *Africa Addio; Man of Africa*
modern, *Black Hawk Down; Fragments of Life*
safari films, exploration, etc, *Ace Ventura – When Nature Calls; Africa – Texas Style; Clarence, the Cross-Eyed Lion; The Desert Song; A Far Off Place; George of the Jungle; The Gods Must Be Crazy; The Gods Must Be Crazy II; Hatari!; King Solomon's Mines* (Stevenson); *King Solomon's Mines* (Thompson); *The Kiss; The Lion; Missing Link; Mogambo; Mountains of the Moon; Passion in the Desert; Roar; The Snows of Kilimanjaro; White Hunter, Black Heart*

African Americans, see **Blacks in USA**

Afterlife, the (*see also* **Heaven-can-wait fantasies, Return to life, Undead, the**), *Almost an Angel; Bad Lord Byron; Bill & Ted's Bogus Journey; Carnival of Souls; Checking Out; Dante's Inferno; Defending Your Life; Flatliners; Heart Condition; Heaven; Huis Clos; Maciste all'Inferno; Made in Heaven; Meet Joe Black; Outward Bound; Parking; Soultaker; Static; Truly, Madly, Deeply; What Dreams May Come; Wings of Fame*

Age and ageing, *The Alpha Caper; An Autumn Afternoon; The Bandit; Batteries Not Included; Bloomfield; Blue Juice; Boardwalk; Branches of the Tree; Un Carnet de Bal; Charles and Lucie; Children of Nature; Cocoon; Cocoon: The Return; The Company of Strangers; Don Quichotte; Driving Miss Daisy; For Fun; Ginger and Fred; Going in Style; Grumpy Old Men; Guarding Tess; Homebodies; House of Smiles; I Could Read the Sky; Iris; Ju Dou; Kotch; Krapp's Last Tape; The Last Good Time; Last Orders; Lina Braake; Love Among the Ruins; Ma Saison Préférée; Middle Age Crazy; My Sons; Not Forgotten; Number One* (Gries); *Old Gringo; On Golden Pond; Out of an Old Man's Head; Le Plaisir; Promise; Rooster Cogburn; Roseland; She's Been Away; The Shootist; A Slender Smile; Söndags Barn; The Sorcerers; Space Cowboys; Spider and Rose; Star Trek: Insurrection; The Sunshine Boys; Take It Like a Man, Ma'am; Tatie Danielle; Tell Me a Riddle; 30 Is a Dangerous Age, Cynthia; Three Brothers; Tokyo Story; Too Young to Die; Touchez pas au Grisbi; Tough Guys; Travelling North; The Trip to Bountiful; True Grit; Twilight; Umberto D; Unforgiven; Used People; La Vieille Dame indigne; The Whales of August; What Ever Happened to Aunt Alice?; The Whisperers; Wild Strawberries; A Woman's Tale; Wrestling Ernest Hemingway*

Age disparity in relationships
older men, younger women, *American Beauty; American Friends; Autumn in New York; Blame It on Rio; The Blue Angel; The Blue Eyes of Yonta; Born Yesterday* (Cukor); *Born Yesterday* (Mandoki); *Breezy; Circle of Two; En Cas de Malheur; Entrapment; The Few Seasons; Five Days One Summer; Le Grand Amour; The Greengage Summer; Gregory's Two Girls; I Know Where I'm Going; The Last Good Time; Laughter; Lies; Lolita* (Kubrick); *Lolita* (Lyne); *Man of Flowers; Manuela; Nelly & Monsieur Arnaud; The Nest; Noce blanche; Rita, Sue and Bob Too; La Senyora; Susan Slept Here; Three into Two Won't Go; Up Close & Personal; Virgin* (Breillat); *Voyager*
older women, younger men, *Les Amants; Boom; And Your Mother Too; Chère Louise; Class; Death in a French Garden; L'Ecole de la Chair; Dekalog 6: 'Thou shalt not commit adultery'; Le Diable au corps; Fear Eats the Soul; The Fugitive Kind; The Graduate; Harold and Maude; In the Bedroom; La Maison de Jade; Night Hair Child; The Old Lady Who Walked in the Sea; Real Life; The Roman Spring of Mrs Stone; A Short Film About Love; A Tiger's Tale; Tim; Tune in Tomorrow; White Palace; The Woo Woo Kid* older men, younger men, *Apt Pupil*

Age reversal and age exchange, *Before I Hang; Big, Damn Yankees; 18 Again!; Flight of the Navigator; Freaky Friday; Jack; Like Father, Like Son; The Major and the Minor; Monkey Business* (Hawks); *Peggy Sue Got Married; The Picture of Dorian Gray; Seconds; Vice Versa* (Ustinov); *Vice Versa* (Gilbert)

Aguirre, Lope de, films about, *Aguirre, Wrath of God; El Dorado*

AIDS and HIV, *The Addiction; Alive and Kicking; And the Band Played On; Being at Home with Claude; Benjamin Smoke; Blue; Boys on the Side; Buddies; Casual Sex?; Chain of Desire; Citizen Cohn; Close My Eyes; Closing Numbers; Common Threads: Stories from the Quilt; The Cure; Fast Trip, Long Drop; Grief; It's My Party; Jeanne et le Garçon Formidable; Jeffrey; Kids; The Last Supper* (Roberts); *The Lie; The Living End; Longtime Companion; Love! Valour! Compassion!; My New Friends; N'oublie pas que tu vas mourir; One Night Stand; Over Our Dead Bodies; Philadelphia; Postcards from America; Rock Hudson's Home Movies; Roomates; Roy Cohn/Jack Smith; Savage Nights; Shanghai Picnic; Slanted Vision; Something Happened; Stonewall; Strip Jack Naked: Nighthawks II; To Die For; Voices from the Front; Zero Patience*

Airships, *Dirigible; The Hindenberg*

Alain-Fournier, film adapted from work, *The Wanderer*

The Alamo, films about, *The Alamo; The Last Command; Viva Max!*

Alaska, in film, *Alaska; By The Law; Asako in Ruby Shoes; Cry from the Mountain; The Golden Seal; The Hellhounds of Alaska; Ice Palace; Jet Pilot; K2; Limbo; Mountain; North to Alaska; Road to Utopia; Runaway Train; Salmonberries; Top of the World; When the North Wind Blows; White Fang* (Fulci); *White Fang* (Kleiser)

Albanian cinema, *Slogans*

Albee, Edward, films adapted from work, *A Delicate Balace; Who's Afraid of Virginia Woolf?*

Alcoholism, *The Alcohol Years; Arthur; Arthur 2; On the Rocks, Barfly; The Blackout; Clean and Sober; Come Back, Little Sheba; Come Fill the Cup; Days of Wine and Roses; Dream On; D-Tox; Fate; Le Feu Follet; Gervaise; The Grass Arena; The Honorary Consul; Ironweed; Jacknife; Leaving Las Vegas; The Legend of the Holy Drinker; Liar; The Lost Weekend; The Morning After; My Name Is Joe; On the Nickel; Porte des Lilas; Sir Henry at Rawlinson's End; Skin Deep; The Small Back Room; Smash-Up, The Story of a Woman; Somersault in a Coffin; Special Treatment; The Squeeze; The Struggle; Time Without Pity; 28 Days; Under the Volcano; W.C. Fields and Me; When a Man Loves a Woman*

Alcott, Louisa May, films adapted from work, *Little Women* (Cukor); *Little Women* (Armstrong)

Aldiss, Brian W, film adapted from work, *Roger Corman's Frankenstein Unbound*

Algeria, in film, *Aïd el Kébir; Algiers; L'Attentat; L'Arche du Désert; Bab El-Oued City; The Battle of Algiers; The Citadel* (Chouikh); *Les Diseurs de Vérité; La Guerre sans nom; Ramparts of Clay; The Sheltering Sky*

Algerian cinema, *L'Arche du Désert; Bab El-Oued City; The Battle of Algiers; The Citadel* (Chouikh); *Ramparts of Clay; Salut Cousin!*

Ali, Muhammad, films about, *Ali; The Greatest; Muhammad Ali: The Greatest; When We Were Kings*

Aliens, from outer space, *see* **Extra-terrestrials on Earth**

Allen, Woody
film about, *Wild Man Blues*
film adapted from work, *Play It Again, Sam*

Allende, Isabel,
film adapted from work, *The House of Spirits*

Altman, Robert, in film, *Luck, Trust & Ketchup: Robert Altman in Carver Country*

Amado, Jorge,
films adapted from work, *Doña Flor and Her Two Husbands; Gabriela; Tieta of Agreste*

Amazonia, *see* **Rain forests**

Ambler, Eric,
films adapted from work, *Background to Danger; Journey into Fear; The Mask of Dimitrios; The October Man; Topkapi*

Ambulances, *The Ambulance; Bringing Out the Dead; Broken Vessels; Mother, Jugs & Speed*

America, in film, (see also individual cities and **Blacks in USA, Small town life** and **South, The American**)
invaded, *The Blob; Bulletproof; Independence Day; Invasion USA; The Mouse That Roared; Prayer of the Rollerboys; The Puppet Masters; Red Dawn; Red Nightmare; Viva Max!; War; The Whip Hand*
anti-Americanism, *Mister Freedom*

American Civil War, *Advance to the Rear; The Beguiled; The Birth of a Nation* (Griffith); *Escape from Fort Bravo; Freedom Road; The General* (Keaton/Bruckman); *Gettysburg; Glory; Gone With the Wind; The Horse Soldiers; The Killing Box; The Littlest Rebel; Little Women* (Cukor); *Little Women* (Armstrong); *Love Me Tender; Mysterious Island; Qunatrill's Raiders; The Raid; Raintree County; The Red Badge of Courage; Ride with the Devil; Santa Fe Trail; Sommersby; A Southern Yankee; South of St Louis; The Undefeated*

American War of Independence, *The Patriot; Revolution; 1776*

Amis, Kingsley, films adapted from work, *Lucky Jim; Only Two Can Play*

Amis, Martin, films adapted from work, *Dead Babies; The Rachel Papers*

Amish, sect, *Witness*

Amnesia, see **Memory,** loss of

Anarchism, *La Cecilia; Lady L; Nada; The Siege of Sidney Street*

Andersen, Hans Christian,
films adapted from work, *La Petite Marchande d'allumettes; The Snow Queen; Stories from a Flying Trunk; Thumbelina*
films about, *Hans Christian Andersen; H.C. Andersen's The Long Shadow*

Anderson, Edward, films adapted from work, *They Live by Night; Thieves Like Us*

Anderson, Maxwell, films adapted from work, *Anne of the Thousand Days; The Bad Seed; The Eve of St Mark; Key Largo; Mary of Scotland; The Private Lives of Elizabeth and Essex; Saturday's Children; The Wrong Man*

Anderson, Robert, films adapted from work, *Tea and Sympathy; I Never Sang for My Father*

Angels and divine manifestations (*see also* **Heaven-can-wait fantasies, Religion**), *Almost an Angel; Angels in the Outfield; The Baby of Mâcon; Bernadette; The Bishop's Wife; The Book of Life; City of Angels; Dogma; Down to Earth; Faraway, So Close; God's Prophecy; Gabriel & Me; Hail, Mary; It Could Happen to You; It's a Wonderful Life; Letter for an Angel; A Life Less Ordinary; La Merveilleuse Visite; Michael; Offending Angels; The Preacher's Wife; A Simple Wish; The Song of Bernadette; Waiting for the Light; Wings of Desire*

Animals and birds, in film (*see also* **Fish, etc, Insects, spiders, etc, Whales**)
apes and monkeys, *Any Which Way You Can; Congo; Dunston Checks In; Every Which Way but Loose; The Fifth Monkey; George of the Jungle; Gorrilas in the Mist; Greystoke – The Legend of Tarzan, Lord of the Apes; Hollow Men; Instinct; King Kong* (Cooper/Schoedsack); *King Kong* (Guillermin); *The Link; Max Mon Amour; Mighty Joe Young* (Schoedsack); *Mighty Joe Young* (Underwood); *Monkeybone; Monkey Shines; Monkey Trouble; Primate; Project X; Tarzan, The Ape Man*
badgers, *The Wind in the Willows*
bats, *Ace Ventura – When Nature Calls; Bats; Nightwing*
bears, *Alaska; The Bear; Day of the Animals; Dr Dolittle 2; Grizzly; The Edge; Hotel New Hampshire*
beavers, *Dr Dolittle 2; Grey Owl*
big cats, *Bringing Up Baby; Cheetah; Clarence, the Cross-Eyed Lion; The Ghost and the Darkness; The Lion; Napoleon and Samantha; Passion in the Desert; Return of the Big Cat; Roar; Roselyne and the Lions; A Tiger's Tale; A Tiger Walks; To Walk with Lions; When the North Wind Blows; Who's That Girl*
birds, *Bird Man of Alcatraz; The Birds; The Falconer; Fly Away Home; Jonathan Livingston Seagull; Kes; Mr Forbush and the Penguins; My Favorite Blonde; Paulie; Shelter of the Wings; Tawny Pipit; Uccellacci e Uccellini*
bisons, *The Last Hunt*
boars, *Razorback*
camels, *The Big Animal; The Camels Are Coming*
cats, *Aristocats; The Cat from Outer Space; Le Chat; Eye of the Cat; Far from Home: The Adventures of Yellow Dog; Harry and Tonto; Homeward Bound: The Incredible Journey; Joseph Kilián; Morgiana; Rhubarb; Sleepwalkers; That Darn Cat; The Uncanny; When the Cat's Away…*
– malevolent, *Cats & Dogs; The Mansion of the Ghost Cat; Tales from the Darkside: The Movie*
chickens *Chicken Run; Chikin Bizniz*
cows, *The Cow; Go West; The Honkers; La Vache et la Prisonnier*
cows, vampiric, *The Little Vampire*
crocodiles, *Lake Placid*
dogs, *Air Bud; Amores Perros; Another Stakeout; Barking Dogs Never Bite; Beethoven; Beethoven's 2nd; Benji; Best in Show; Bingo; A Boy and His Dog; Call of the Wild; Cats & Dogs; Les Chiens; Cujo; Digby – The Biggest Dog in the World; Dogpound Shuffle; Dogs; Eyes in the Night; Hambone and Hillie; Homeward Bound: The Incredible Journey; The Journey of Natty Gann; Jumping for Joy; K-9; Lassie Come Home; Look Who's Talking Now; The Magic of Lassie; Man's Best Friend; Man Trouble; My Dog Skip; 101 Dalmatians* (Herek); *102 Dalmatians; Owd Bob; The Pack; Paws; Les Petits Frères; Return of the Big Cat; See Spot Run; The Shaggy D.A.; Three Wishes; Turner & Hooch; Watchers; We Think the World of You; Where the Red Fern Grows; White Dog; White Fang* (Fulci); *White Fang* (Kleiser)
– dead dogs, as comic motif, *Cold Dog Soup*
donkeys, *Au Hasard Balthazar; Donkey; Peau d'Ane*
ducks, *Mr Drake's Duck*
elephants, *The African Elephant; Elephant Boy; Escape to Burma; Fish and Elephant; Hannibal Brooks; Hathi; Larger Than Life*
foxes, *The Belstone Fox*
frogs, *Frogs*
geese, *Laughterhouse*
horses, *Black Beauty; The Black Stallion; The Black Stallion Returns; Broadway Bill; Casey's Shadow; Daydream Believer; Dry Rot; Eagle's Wing; Francis; Home in Indiana; The Horse Whisperer; I'm Jumping Over Puddles Again; I Gotta Horse; International Velvet; King of the Wind; The Misfits; Mustang Country; My Friend Flicka; National Velvet; Phar Lap; Ride a Wild Pony; Romance of a Horse Thief; Smoky; Thunderhead, Son of Flicka*
lizards, *Godzilla*
meerkats, *Fierce Creatures*
mice, *MouseHunt; Stuart Little*
moles, *The Wind in the Willows*
otters, *Ring of Bright Water; Tarka the Otter*
oxen, *The Mirror*
pigs, *Animal Farm; Babe; Babe – Pig in the City; The Hour of the Pig; Jamón, Jamón; A Private Function*
rats, *Ben; Panic in the Streets; The Pied Piper* (Demy); *The Rats; Sitcom; The Wind in the Willows*
seals, *Andre, The Golden Seal*
sheep, *The Sundowners*
snakes, *Anaconda; Fair Game*
toads, *Cane Toads – An Unnatural History*
turtles, *Turtle Diary*
wolves, *Never Cry Wolf*
yaks, *Himalaya*
animals, slaughter of *The Animals Film; The Last Hunt; Meat; Le Sang des Bêtes*
various, *The Adventures of Milo and Otis; All Creatures Great and Small; Beautiful People; The Best of Walt Disney's True Life Adventures; Dances with Wolves; Dances with Wolves – Special Edition; Doctor Dolittle; Dr Dolittle 2; Gates of Heaven; It Shouldn't Happen to a Vet; The Incredible Journey; Jumanji; The Last Flight of Noah's Ark; Mysterious Island; Paradise View; Rampage; Tierische Liebe; The Truth About Cats & Dogs; Zoo in Budapest*

Animal Experiments and vivisection, *The Animals Film; Fear; The Mechanics of the Brain; Monkey Shines; The Plague Dogs; Primate*

Animation, see **Cartoons and animation**

Anorexia, *Dream On; Life Is Sweet; Superstar; The Karen Carpenter Story; 301–302*

Anouilh, Jean, film adapted from work, *Time for Loving*

Antarctica (*see also* **Ice dramas**), in film, *Conquest of the South Pole; Mr Forbush and the Penguins; Scott of the Antarctic; Shackleton's Antarctic Adventure; South*

Aphrodisiacs, *Blood and Concrete; Spanish Fly*

Arabian Nights, films adapted from, *Adventures of Prince Achmed, The; Arabian Adventure; Arabian Nights; The Seventh Voyage of Sinbad; Sinbad and the Eye of the Tiger; The Thief of Bagdad* (Powell et al); *The Thief of Bagdad* (Walsh); *The Thief of Baghdad* (Donner)

Arabs, in Western film (see also individual Arab nations), *The Ambassador; Bengazi; The Black Stallion Returns; The Delta Force; Escape from Zahrein; The Garden of Allah; The Guns and the Fury; Harem; Iron Eagle; Jerusalem File; Jewel of the Nile; King of the Wind; Lawrence of Arabia; March or Die; Masquerade* (Dearden); *Navy Seals; Room to Rent; Saadia; The Sheltering Sky; The Siege*

Arbenz Guzmán, Jacobo, film about, *¡Devils Don't Dream! Research on Jacobo Arbenz Guzmán*

Architects and architecture, *The Belly of an Architect; Folk Tales of Lu Ban; The Fountain-head; Mortgage; Peter Ibbetson; Three to Tango; Twelve Views of Kensal House*

Ardrey, Robert, film adapted from work, *Thunder Rock*

Argentina, in film, *Apartment Zero; Buenos Aires Vice Versa; La Ciénaga; Close to the Border; Crane World; The Cross; Don't Cry for Me, La Libertad; Little Miracles; Little Mother; Evita; Happy Together; Hidden Witnesses; The Honorary Consul; Naked Tango; Night on the Terrace; Nine Queens; Río Escondido* (García Guevara); *Saturday; Serà Posible el Sur; Silvia Prieto; South Dock; The South of a Passion; Tango* (Saura); *To the Heart; Waiting for the Messiah; Wake Up, Love; Way of a Gaucho; Yepeto*

Argentinian cinema, *Amigomio; Bolivia; Borges, Books and the Night; Buenos Aires Vice Versa; Camila; La Ciénaga; Close to the Border; The Cloud; Cortazar; Crane World; The Cross; Fading Memories; Fuckland; A Funny Dirty Little War; Garage Olimpio; Gatica; The Girlfriend; Hidden Witnesses; Hombre Mirando al Sudeste; I, the Worst of All; I Won't Go Back Home; Last Images of the Shipwreck; La Libertad; Little Miracles; Miss Mary; Night on the Terrace; Nine Queens; The Official Version; A Place in the World; Secret Wedding; Silvia Prieto; Rich Kids; Río Escondido* (García Guevara); *The South of a Passion; Saturday; South Dock; Sur; A Sweet Scent of Death; Tango* (Saura); *The Tango Lesson; To the Heart; Veronico Cruz; The Voyage; Waiting for the Messiah; Wake Up,Love; We Don't Talk About It; Yepeto*

Argentinians in England, *Argie*

Armenian cinema, *On the Old Roman Road*

Armenians, *in film, Ararat*

Armstrong, Charlotte, films adapted from work, *La Rupture; The Unsuspected*

Army Life (for other services see **Flying dramas, Sea dramas,** also **Vietnam, World War I, World War II**)
Aust, *Breaker Morant*
China, *The Big Parade*
GB, *The Bofors Gun; The Charge of the Light Brigade* (Richardson); *Conduct Unbecoming; Dunkirk; Folly to Be Wise; The Gentle Sex; Gunga Din; The Hill; A Hill in Korea; The New Lot; Next of Kin; O.H.M.S.; Orders Are Orders; Overlord; Privates on Parade; A Prize of Arms; The Queen's Guards; Resurrected; Stand Up Virgin Soldiers; Streamers; Tunes of Glory; The Way Ahead; Zulu*
Ger, *Cross of Iron*
Ire, *Guiltrip*
Isr, *Burning Memory, Private Popsicle*
Jap, *Taboo*
SAf, *On the Wire; the Stick*
Sen, *Camp Thiaroye*
Tai, *Bodo; Buddha Bless America*
US, *Basic Training; Biloxi Blues; Blue Sky; Canal Zone; Count a Lonely Cadence; Dogfight; A Few Good Men; A Foreign Affair; The Fourth War; From Here to Eternity; F.T.A.; Full Metal Jacket; Gardens of Stone; The General's Daughter; G.I. Blues; G.I. Jane; The Long Gray Line; The Lords of Discipline; The Ninth Configuration; The Package; Private Benjamin; Reflections in a Golden Eye; Renaissance Man; Sergeant York; Sgt Bilko; Soldier Girls; A Soldier's Story; The Strange One; Taps; The Victors; A Walk in the Sun; You'll Never Get Rich*
USSR/Rus, *The Beast; The Life and Extraordinary Adventures of Private Ivan Chonkin; 100 Days Before the Command*

Art and artists
artists in society, *The Affairs of Cellini; Alchemy; Chihwaseon; Close to the Wind; Cousin Bette; A Dog of Flanders; The Draughtsman's Contract; The Fountainhead; Good Morning Babylon; The Hair Opera; Heartbreakers; Hour of the Wolf; Kids of Survival: The Art and Life of Tim Rollins & K.O.S.; Love Is the Devil – Study for a Portrait of Francis Bacon; Loving; News from Nowhere; Right Out of History: The Making of Judy Chicago's Dinner Party; The Sandpiper; Le Sang d'un Poète; La Traversée de Paris; La Vie de Bohème; The World of Gilbert & George; Wot! No Art*
graffiti and graffiti artists, *Basquiat; Downtown 81*
painters and painting, *The Agony and the Ecstasy; Anne Trister; Artemisia; La Belle Noiseuse; La Belle Noiseuse – Divertimento; A Bigger Splash; Bluebeard; The Bridge; Caravaggio; La Chienne; Chihwaseon; The Dying Swan; Edvard Munch; Europe After the Rain; Every Picture Tells a Story; Favourites of the Moon; Feeling Sexy; Five Women Around Utamaro; Goya in Bordeaux; The Horse's Mouth; Imago – Meret Oppenheim; Incognito; Lautrec; Love Is the Devil – Study for a Portrait of Francis Bacon; Lust for Life; Maiden Work; Man from China; Michael; The Moon and Sixpence; Moulin Rouge* (Huston); *Le Mystère Picasso; New York Stories; Painters Painting; Pirosmani; Pollock; Pretty as a Picture: The Art of David Lynch; The Quince Tree Sun; The Rebel; Rembrandt; Schiele in Prison; Sirens; Sunday in the Country; Surviving Picasso; Trust Me; Van Gogh; Vincent: The Life and Death of Vincent Van Gogh; Venice: Theme and Variation; Vincent & Theo; Yumeji*
sculpture, *A Bucket of Blood; Camille Claudel; Carnival; Daddy; Debt Collector, The; Joseph Cornell: Worlds in a Box; Lies; The Paolozzi Story; Savage Messiah; Song of Songs*

Artaud, Antonin, film about, *En Compagnie d'Antonin Artaud*

Arthurian legends, see **Middle Ages, and chivalric sagas**

Artists' creations coming alive, *Delirious; Genuine; Icicle Thief; Mannequin; Mannequin Two: On the Move; One Touch of Venus*

Art world, *Artists and Models; The Cold Eye; Crack-Up* (Reis); *Favourites of the Moon; F for Fake; The Golden Salamander; I've Heard the Mermaids Singing; Melancholia; The Moderns; Object of Beauty; Painters Painting; Pecker; Slaves of New York; Surviving Picasso*
art schools, *The Best Age*

Asians in Britain, *Adventures of a Brown Man in Search of Civilisation; Ali G Indahouse; Bend It Like Beckham; Bhaji on the Beach; East Is East; Foreign Body; Guru in Seven; Majdhar; My Beautiful Laundrette; A Private Enterprise; A Quiet Desperation; Sammy and Rosie Get Laid; Soursweet; Wild West*

Asians in Canada, *Masala*

Asians in USA, *Lonely in America; Mississippi Masala*

Assassinations, political, *Above the Law; American Roulette; The Art of War; Ashes and Diamonds; Assassin; Assassin of the Tsar; The Assassination of Trotsky; Assassins; L'Attentat; Brass Target; Bulworth; The Conformist; The Day of the Jackal; The Emperor and the Assassin; Executive Action; Four Days of Snow and Blood; Hitler's Madman; In the Line of Fire; The Jackal; JFK; John Carpenter's Escape from L.A.; Konfrontation – Assassination in Davos; The Last Supper* (Title); *The Manchurian Candidate; Manhunt; Manifesto; Melancholia; Most Wanted; Nick of Time; Nobody Runs Forever; The November Men; One Day in September; Operation Daybreak; The Parallax View; Pasolini, un Delitto Italiano; Patriot Games; The Pelican Brief; Ruby; Rush to Judgment; Russian Roulette; Seven Minutes; The Shooter; State of Siege; Suddenly; TAG, The Assassination Game; The Tall Target; Tigers Don't Cry; The Times of Harvey Milk; Winter Kills; Z*

Astronauts and contemporary space travel, *Apollo 13; Armageddon; Beyond the Stars; Capricorn One; Contact; Countdown; Destination Moon; The Dish; For All Mankind; Galaxy Quest; Lost in Space; Marooned; Mission to Mars; Moonraker; The Mouse on the Moon; October Sky; Out of the Present; The Right Stuff; SpaceCamp; Space Cowboys; Spaceways; Virus*

Asylums, see **Mental hospitals and asylums**

Athletics (see also **Olympic Games**), *Bring It On; Chariots of Fire; Don't Go Breaking My Heart; Geordie; Jericho Mile; The Loneliness of the Long Distance Runner; Personal Best; Running Brave; True Blue; Superargo; Without Limits*

Attila the Hun, film about, *Sign of the Pagan*

Atwood, Margaret, film adapted from work, *The Handmaid's Tale*

Austen, Jane, films adapted from/based on work, *Clueless; Emma; Jane Austen in Manhattan; Mansfield Park; Persuasion; Pride and Prejudice; Sense and Sensibility*

Australia, in film
past, *Between Wars; Botany Bay; Caddie; Country Life; For Love or Money; Kangaroo* (Burstall); *Mad Dog Morgan; Manganinnie; My Brilliant Career; Newsfront; Ned Kelly; The Overlanders; Quigley Down Under; Robbery Under Arms; Silver City; Sirens; Sunday Too Far Away; The Sundowners; Under Capricorn; We of the Never Never*
contemporary, *The Adventures of Priscilla Queen of the Desert; Backroads; Bad Boy Bubby; Cane Toads – An Unnatural History; Celia; 'Chubby' Down Under and Other Sticky Regions; The Club; Crocodile Dundee; Crocodile Dundee II; Crocodile Dundee in Los Angeles; A Cry in the Dark; Dallas Doll; Dead Heart; Deadly; Death in Brunswick; The Dish; Doing Time for Patsy Cline; Dogs in Space; Don's Party; Fast Talking; Fatal Bond; First Strike; Floating Life; Geordie; The Goddess of 1967; Grievous Bodily Harm; Hammers Over the Anvil; Heaven's Burning; Holy Smoke; Hotel Sorrento; Kiss or Kill; The Last Crop; Love in Limbo; The Love Letters from Teralba Road; The Man from Snowy River; The Odd Angry Shot; Mr Reliable (a true story); Outback; Over the Hill; A Personal History of the Australian Surf; Public Enemy Number One; The Quiet Room; Redheads; Romper Stomper; Rough Diamonds; Say a Little Prayer; Secrets; Shame; Shine; Siam Sunset; La Spagnola; Spotswood; Strictly Ballroom; That Eye, the Sky; They're a Weird Mob; Walkabout; Welcome to Woop Woop; The Well; What Have I Written?; The Winchester Conspiracy; Winter of Our Dreams; The Year My Voice Broke; Young Einstein*

Australian Aboriginals, *Backlash; Backroads; The Chant of Jimmy Blacksmith; Dead Heart; Deadly; The Fringe Dwellers; The Last Wave; Manganinnie; Quigley Down Under; Radiance; Walkabout; Where the Green Ants Dream*

Australian cinema, see Appendix 16

Austria, in film, *Bad Timing; Burning Secret; Dishonored; The Divine Emma; Dog Days; Funny Games; Hanussen; The Hotel New Hampshire; The King Steps Out; Mayerling; Oh Rosalinda!; The Piano Teacher; La Ronde; The 7th Continent; The Sound of Music; Tales from the Vienna Woods; The Third Man; Totschweigen; The Unfish; The Wedding March*

Austrian cinema, *Be My Star; Benny's Video; The Castle* (Haneke); *Colonel Redl; Dog Days; Funny Games; Halbe Welt; Invisible Adversaries; Hands of Orlac; The Inheritors; Invisible Adversaries; Lovely Rita; Mario and the Magician; Mostly Martha; My Mother's Courage; The Piano Teacher; The Refusal; Requiem for Dominic; The 7th Continent; 71 Fragments of a Chronology of Chance; Sunshine* (Szabó); *Tierische Liebe; Totschweigen; The Unfish; Wittstock, Wittstock*

Autism, *The Boy Who Could Fly; Jigsaw; La Madre Muerta; Mercury Rising; A Place Nearby; Rain Man; Silent Fall*

Avant garde cinema, see **Experimental films**

Averroës, film about, *Destiny*

Axelrod, George, films adapted from work, *The Seven Year Itch; Will Success Spoil Rock Hunter?*

Ayckbourn, Alan, films adapted from work, *A Chorus of Disapproval; Smoking/No Smoking; Way Upstream*

Aymé, Marcel, films adapted from work, *The Favour, the Watch and the Very Big Fish; La Traversée de Paris; Uranus*

Azerbaijan cinema, *The Yellow Bride*

Babies, see **Pregnancy, childbirth and babies**

Babysitting (see also **Nannies, governesses, au pairs**), *Adventures in Babysitting; The Babysitter; Don't Tell Mom the Babysitter's Dead; Dressed to Kill; Sitting Pretty; Uncle Buck; Unhook the Stars; When a Stranger Calls; When the Cat's Away…*

Bach, JS and Anna Magdalena, *Chronicles of Anna Magdalena Bach*

Bacon, Francis, film about, *Love Is the Devil – Study for a Portrait of Francis Bacon*

Bader, Douglas, film about, *Reach for the Sky*

Bainbridge, Beryl, films adapted from work, *An Awfully Big Adventure; The Dressmaker; Sweet William*

Baker, Chet, film about, *Let's Get Lost*

Baldacci, Daniel, film adapted from work, *Absolute Power*

Baldwin, James
film adapted from work, *A la Place du Coeur*
film about, *James Baldwin: The Price of the Ticket*

Ballard, JG,
films adapted from work, *Crash* (Cronenberg); *Empire of the Sun*

Ballooning, *The Conquest of the Air; Night Crossing*

Baltimore, in film, *The Accidental Tourist; Avalon; Cry-Baby; Desperate Living; Diner; Female Trouble; Hairspray; Pecker; Serial Mom; The Tall Target; Tin Men*

Balzac, Honoré de, films adapted from work, *La Belle Noiseuse; La Belle Noiseuse – Divertimento; Le Colonel Chabert* (Le Hénaff); *Le Colonel Chabert* (Angelo); *Cousin Bette; Passion in the Desert; Le Père Goriot*

Banks, Iain, film adapted from works, *Complicity*

Banks, Lynne Reid, films adapted from work, *The Indian in the Cupboard; The L-Shaped Room*

Banks, Russell, films adapted from work, *Affliction; The Sweet Hereafter*

Barber, Elsie Oaks, film adapted from work, *Angel Baby*

Barker, Clive,
films adapted from work, *Candyman; Candyman 2: Farewell to the Flesh; Hellraiser; Hellbound: Hellraiser II; Hellraiser III: Hell on Earth; Nightbreed*

Barmen, *Cocktail*

Barnes, Julian, films adapted from work, *Love, etc; Metroland*

Barnum, PT, film about, *The Mighty Barnum*

Barrie, JM, films adapted from/influenced by work, *The Admirable Crichton; Hook; Peter Pan; Return to Never Land*
film featuring his work, *An Awfully Big Adventure*

Barry, Philip, films adapted from work, *High Society; Holiday; The Philadelphia Story*

Barstow, Stan, film adapted from work, *A Kind of Loving*

Barth, John, film adapted from work, *End of the Road*

Bartók, Béla, film of opera, *Bluebeard's Castle*

Baseball, *Amazing Grace and Chuck; Angels in the Outfield; The Babe; A Boy Called Third Base; Brewster's Millions* (Hill); *Bull Durham; Cobb; Eight Men Out; The Fan* (Scott); *Fear Strikes Out; Field of Dreams; For Love of the Game; A League of Their Own; Little Big League; Major League; Major League II; Mr Baseball; The Natural; The Pride of St Louis; Rhubarb; Rookie of the Year; The Sandlot; Stealing Home; Take Me Out to the Ball Game*

Basketball, *Above the Rim; Air Bud; The Air Up There; The Basketball Diaries; Blue Chips; Eddie; He Got Game; Hoop Dreams; Hoosiers; Love & Basketball; One on One; Soul in the Hole; Space Jam; That Championship Season; White Men Can't Jump*

Bateman, Colin, films adapted from works, *Crossmaheart; Divorcing Jack*

Bates, HE, films adapted from work, *Dulcima; A Month by the Lake; The Triple Echo*

Baum, L Frank, films adapted from work, *Return to Oz; The Wiz; The Wizard of Oz; Zardoz*

Baum, Vicki, film adapted from work, *Lac aux Dames*

Beach movies, *Beach Blanket Bingo; Big Wednesday; Gidget; Last Summer; A Swingin' Summer; Where the Boys Are*

The Beatles, films of/about (see also **Lennon**, John, and **McCartney**, Paul), *Backbeat; A Hard Day's Night; Help; I Wanna Hold Your Hand; Let It Be; Secrets; Yellow Submarine*
musical based on songs, *Sergeant Pepper's Lonely Hearts Club Band*

Beat writers, films about, *A Bucket of Blood; Heart Beat; Kerouac; Last Time I Committed Suicide; The Life and Times of Allen Ginsberg; Whatever Happened to Kerouac?*

Beauty contests and beauty queens, *The Beauty Jungle; Drop Dead Gorgeous; The Fireman's Ball; Happy Texas; Hope Floats; Lady Godiva Rides Again; Miss Congeniality; Miss Firecracker; Page Miss Glory; The Positively True Adventures of the Alleged Texas Cheerleader-Murdering Mom; Prix de Beauté; Smile*

Beckett, Samuel, films adapted from work, *Act Without Words – II; Krapp's Last Tape; Not I; Play; Waiting for Godot*

Beethoven, Ludwig van, film about, *Immortal Beloved*

Behm, Marc, films adapted from work, *Black Widow* (Rafelson); *Eye of the Beholder; Mortelle Randonnée*

Beiderbecke, Bix, films about, *Bix: 'Ain't None of Them Play Like Him Yet'; Young Man With a Horn*

Belafonte, Harry, film about, *Sometimes I Look at My Life*

Belbel, Sergi, film adapted from work, *Caresses*

Belgian cinema, *American Stories; Les Ames Fortes; Anchoress; Australia; Ball, The; Beck; Benvenuta; Bird Now; The Blue Villa; Les Convoyeurs Attendent; A Couch in New York; Daens; Daughters of Darkness; Le Départ; Dust; Divine Body; The Eighth Day; Eline Vere; L'Etoile du Nord; Farinelli Il Castrato; Une Femme entre Chien et Loup; Fragments of Life; Germinal; I Am Anna Magnani; I Know I'll See Your Face Again; Jeanne Dielman, 23 Quai du Commerce, 1080 Bruxelles; Je tu il elle; Le Journal de Lady M; Une Liaison Pornographique; Libertarias; The Lost Paradise; Lumumba; Il Maestro; Malpertuis; Man Bites Dog; The Man Who Had His Hair Cut Short; Manneken Pis; The Man Who Drove with Mandela; Ma Vie en Rose; The Milk of Human Kindness; Mobutu, King of Zaire; Molokai: The Story of Father Damien; The Music Teacher; Le Nez au Vent; No Man's Land* (Tanovic); *Pallieter; Pauline & Paulette; Place Vendôme; Presque rien; The Promise* (Dardenne/Dardenne); *The Quarry; Rendez-vous à Bray; Rosetta; Rosie; Salut Cousin!; The Sexual Life of the Belgians 1950–1978; Un Soir, un Train; Sud; Tale of the Three Jewels; Taxandria; Total Eclipse; West Beirut; Wild Games*

Belgium, in film, *Les Convoyeurs Attendent; Daens; A Dog of Flanders; La Kermesse Héroïque; Pauline & Paulette; Portrait of a Young Girl at the End of the '60s in Brussels; Rosetta; The Sexual Life of the Belgians 1950–1978; Toute une Nuit*

Bellow, Saul, film adapted from work, *Seize the Day*

Belushi, John, film about, *Wired*

Bemelmans, Ludwig, film adapted from work, *Madeline*

Benchley, Peter, films adapted from work, *The Deep; Island; Jaws*

Benin cinema, *Divine Body*

Bennett, Alan, film adapted from work, *The Madness of King George*

Bennett, Arnold, film adapted from work, *The Card*

Bereavement (see also **Death**), *All About My Mother; Cry-Woman; 8½ Women; Le Grand Chemin; Harry and Son; In Country; Komitas; Life and Nothing But; Moonlight and Valentino; Mother Küster's Trip to Heaven; My Girl; My Girl 2; The Nephew; Night Into MorningOne True Thing; Orphans; Paradise; Phone Call from a Stranger; Ponette; A Portuguese Goodbye; Three Colours: Blue; Truly, Madly, Deeply*

Berendt, John, film adapted from work, *Midnight in the Garden of Good and Evil*

Berger, John, film adapted from work, *Play Me Something*

Berger, Thomas, films adapted from work, *Little Big Man; Neighbors*

Berkeley, Busby, musicals choreographed by, *Dames; Footlight Parade; For Me and My Gal; 42nd Street; The Gang's All Here; Gold Diggers of 1933; Gold Diggers of 1935; Gold Diggers of 1937; The Kid from Spain; Palmy Days; Roman Scandals; Strike Up the Band; Take Me Out to the Ball Game; Two Weeks With Love; Ziegfeld Girl*

Berkoff, Steven, film adapted from work, *Decadence*

Berlin, in film, *Aimée & Jaguar; After the Fall* (Sandig/Black); *Anita: Dances of Vice; Berlin Alexanderplatz; Berlin – die Sinfonie der Grosstadt; Berlin Express; Berlin Jerusalem; The Big Lift; Cabaret; Chinese Boxes; City of Lost Souls; Company Business; Dealer; Dr M; Dr Mabuse, the Gambler; England Made Me; Enigma; Fatherland; Une Femme française; Flight to Berlin; Flirt; Forbidden; A Foreign Affair; Funeral in Berlin; Germany, Year Zero; Girl in a Boot; Gorilla Bathes at Noon; The Grass Is Always Greener; I Am a Camera; The Innocent* (Schlesinger); *Invincible; Judgment in Berlin; A Letter Without Words; Little Angel; Lola + Bilidikid; The Man Between; No Mercy, No Future; November Days Voices and Choices; One, Two, Three; Possession; The Quiller; Memorandum; Salmonberries; The Serpent's Egg; Shampoo and Set; Sun Alley; Taxi zum Klo; Ten Seconds to Hell; Torn Curtain; Verboten; Westler: East of the Wall; Will My Mother Go Back to Berlin?; Wings of Desire*

Berlin, Irving, musicals by, *Annie Get Your Gun; Blue Skies; Carefree; Easter Parade; Follow the Fleet; Holiday Inn; There's No Business Like Show Business; Top Hat*

Bermuda, in film, *The Deep*

Bermuda Triangle, *The Bermuda Triangle; The Sharks' Cave*

Bernhard, Sandra, in performance, *Without You I'm Nothing*

Bernhardt, Sarah, film about, *The Incredible Sarah*

Bernstein, Carl, and Woodward, Bob, film about, *All The President's Men*

Berry, Chuck, in performance, *Hail! Hail! Rock'n'Roll!; Let the Good Times Roll; The London Rock'n'Roll Show*

Bessa-Luis, Augustina, film adapted from work, *Abraham Valley*

Bezzerides, AI, films adapted from work, *They Drive By Night* (Walsh); *Thieves' Highway*

Berlusconi, Silvio, film about, *Repubblica Nostra*

Biblical stories (see also **God, Jesus Christ**), *The Bible…In the Beginning; The Greatest Story Ever Told; King David; King of Kings; Moses; Noah's Ark; The Prince of Egypt; Rachel's Man; The Robe; Samson and Delilah; Sodom and Gomorrah; Solomon and Sheba; The Ten Commandments; Wholly Moses!*

Bibliomania, *Quiet Please, Murder*

Bierce, Ambrose, film about, *Old Gringo*

Big Business, see **Boardroom jungle**

Biggs, Ronald, film about, *Prisoner of Rio*

Bikers, *L'Agression; Akira; Another 48 HRS; The Born Losers; Deathsport; Death Weekend; Easy Rider; Electra Glide in Blue; Evel Knievel; The Glory Stompers; Harley Davidson and the Marlboro Man; Hells Angels on Wheels; Hex; Hog Wild; I Bought a Vampire Motorcyle; I Wanted to See Angels; Kikujiro; Knightriders; The Loveless; On Any Sunday; Psychomania; Roadside Prophets; Rebel Rousers; Savage Honeymoon; Shame; She Lives to Ride; Stone; Stone Cold; Viva Knievel; Wanda Nevada; Watch Out, We're Mad; Wedding Moon; The Wild Angels; The Wild One*

Binchy, Maeve, film from work, *Circle of Friends*

Biopics
artists/musicians/performers/writers, etc, *Actress; The Adventures of Mark Twain; Amadeus; American Magus; An Angel at My Table; Before Night Falls; The Best Things in Life Are Free; Bird; Blossom Time; Bound for Glory; The Buddy Holly Story; Camille Claudel; Carrington; Céleste; Chaplin; Chihwaseon; Chronicle of Anna Magdalena Bach; Coal Miner's Daughter; Comedian Harmonists; Committed; The Death of Maria Malibran; The Divine Emma; Dixie; The Doors; The Dragon Dies Hard; Dragon: The Bruce Lee Story; Edith and Marcel; Ed Wood; Elvis – The Movie; Edvard Munch; En Compagnie d'Antonin Artaud; Frances; Funny Girl; Funny Lady; Gable and Lombard; The Glenn Miller Story; Goya in Bordeaux; Great Balls of Fire!; The Great Waltz* (Duvivier); *The Great Waltz* (Stone); *Goodbye Norma Jean; H.C. Andersen's The Long Shadow; His Wife's Diary; Immortal Beloved; The Incredible Sarah; Iris; Isabelle Eberhardt; Isadora; Isn't She Great; Joe Gould's Secret; The Jolson Story; Kabloonak; Kafka; Karl May; Lady Sings the Blues; Lautrec; Leadbelly; Lenny; The Life of Chikuzan; The Life of Emile Zola; Lillian Russell; Lola Montès; Love Me or Leave Me; The Loves of Liszt; Lust for Life; Madame Satã; The Magic Bow; Mahler; A Man Like Eva; Man on the Moon; Marilyn – The Untold Story; Marlene; The Mighty Barnum; Mrs Parker and the Vicious Circle; Mommie Dearest; Moulin Rouge* (Huston); *The Music Lovers; My Left Foot; Night and Day; Nijinsky; Oh! You Beautiful Doll; Pavlova – A Woman for All Time; Piaf; Piñero; Pollock; Postcards from America; Pirosmani;*

Prick Up Your Ears; Priest of Love; Puppetmaster; Rhapsody in Blue; Rose of Washington Square; Saint-Ex; St Louis Blues; Savage Messiah; Schiele in Prison; Shine; The Sex Symbol; Song of Norway; A Song to Remember; Spring Symphony; Star; Stevie; Superstar: The Karen Carpenter Story; Sweet Dreams; Testimony; Tina: What's Love Got to Do With It; Tom & Viv; The Tommy Steele Story; Total Eclipse; Valentino; Van Gogh; Vigo Passion for Life; Vincent & Theo; Wagner; W.C. Fields and Me; When the Sky Fall; The Whole Wide World; Winchell; Wired; With a Song in My Heart; Yankee Doodle Dandy; Young Cassidy; Young Man with a Horn
criminal lives, *Al Capone; Baby Face Nelson; Buster; Capone; Crime Kings; Dillinger* (Nosseck); *Dillinger* (Milius); *The Executioner's Song; Gotti; King of the Roaring 20's – The Story of Arnold Rothstein; The Krays; Landru; Lucky Luciano; McVicar; Ned Kelly; Paperback Vigilante; The Rise and Fall of Legs Diamond; Salvatore Giuliano; Sugartime; Young Dillinger*
politicians/military figures, etc, *Agony; Catherine the Great; Che!; Christopher Columbus; Christopher Columbus: The Discovery; Flame Top; Daens; 1492: Conquest of Paradise; God's Favorite; The Greek Tycoon; Henry VIII and His Six Wives; Joe Hill; Lawrence of Arabia; MacArthur; Mary of Scotland; Mary Queen of Scots; Men of Honor; Michael Collins; Napoléon* (Gance); *Nicholas and Alexandra; Nixon; Patton; Pride of the Marines; The Private Files of J Edgar Hoover; The Private Life of Henry VIII; Reach for the Sky; Reds; The Roads of Exile; Rosa Luxemburg; The Scarlet Empress; Taurus; That Hamilton Woman; They Died with Their Boots On; Viva Zapata; The Wings of Eagles; Young Mr Lincoln; Young Winston*
saints/visionaries/priests, *L'Appel du Silence; Augustine of Hippo; Brother Sun, Sister Moon; Entertaining Angels: The Dorothy Day Story; Kundun; A Man Called Peter; Molokai: The Story of Father Damien; Pastor Hall; Francesco, giullare di Dio; Nostradamus*
scientists/doctors, etc, *A Beautiful Mind; The Darwin Adventure; Dr Ehrlich's Magic Bullet; Edison the Man; Freud; Gorillas in the Mist; The Great Moment; Korczak; Madame Curie; Pasteur*
sportsmen/women, etc *Ali; The Babe; Best; Cobb; Dawn!; Don King: Only In America; 8 Seconds; Evel Knievel; Greased Lightning; The Greatest; Hurricane; Nadia; The Pride of St Louis; Somebody Up There Likes Me; Without Limits*
miscellaneous, *The Autobiography of Miss Jane Pittman; Beyond Evil; Blossoms in the Dust; Born on the Fourth of July; Chanel Solitaire; Courage; Le Destin Fabuleux de Désirée Clary; Grey Owl; The House of Rothschild; The Inn of the Sixth Happiness; Luther; A Man Named John; Patty Hearst; Placido Rizzotto; A Single Spark; The Spirit of St. Louis; Sylvia; The Terry Fox Story; To Walk with Lions; Tucker: The Man and His Dream; Where the Buffalo Roam; Wittgenstein*

Birds, see **Animals and birds**

Birney, Hoffman, film adapted from work, *The Glory Guys*

Bisexuality, *Basic Instinct; Bedrooms and Hallways; Bisexual; Executioners from Shaolin; Fellini-Satyricon; Labyrinth of Passion; Making Love; A Man Like Eva; The Man Who Had Power over Women; The Opposite of Sex; Parking; Pas très Catholique; Skin & Bone; Sunday, Bloody Sunday*

Bizet, Georges, films adapted from work, *Carmen* (DeMille); *Carmen* (Rosi); *Carmen* (Saura); *Carmen Jones; Dias Contados; First Name: Carmen; The Tragedy of Carmen*

Blackmail, *Blackmail* (Hitchcock); *Blackmail* (Potter); *Boy; Cage of Gold; Crossroads* (Conway); *The Dumb Die Fast, the Smart Die Slow; Gator; The Gazebo; Hidden Witnesses; Intimate Stranger; The Naked Truth; The Night of the Party; One of Those Things; The Private Lesson; Private Lessons; The Reckless Moment; The Suspect; The Swiss Conspiracy; The Unsuspected; Victim; The Woman in the Window; Wrong Is Right*

Black marketeering, *Dancing with Crime; Tenderness of the Wolves; The Third Man; La Traversée de Paris*

Blacks in Britain (see also **Asians in Britain**), *Ali G Indahouse; Ama; Babylon; Babymother; Blue Notes and Exiled Voices; Burning an Illusion; Flame in the Streets; For Queen and Country; Handsworth Songs; Leo the Last; The Passion of Remembrance; Playing Away; Pressure; Reggae; '36 to '77; Time and Judgement; Tunde's Film; Twilight City; Who Needs a Heart; Young Soul Rebels*

Blacks in USA
blaxploitation, *Bucktown; Cleopatra Jones; Cleopatra Jones and the Casino of Gold; Coffy; Hell Up in Harlem; Original Gangstas; Penitentiary; Shaft* (Parks); *Shaft in Africa; Shaft's Big Score; Sheba Baby; Slaughter; Slaughter's Big Rip-Off; Superfly; That Man Bolt; Three the Hard Way*
parodies of, *I'm Gonna Git You Sucka*
in Hollywood, *BAPS; Classified X; Hollywood Shuffle; Illusions*
in South, *Amistad; The Autobiography of Miss Jane Pittman; Beloved; Cabin in the Sky; Candyman 2: Farewell to the Flesh; The Color Purple; Conrack; Driving Miss Daisy; Drum; Eve's Bayou; Freedom Road, A Gathering of Old Men; Ghosts of Mississippi; Glory; The Green Pastures; Hurry Sundown; In the Heat of the Night; The Intruder; Intruder in the Dust; The Killing Floor; The Klansman; Law and Order; The Liberation of L.B. Jones; Mandingo; Martha & Ethel; Mississippi Blues; Mississippi Burning; A Night in Havana: Dizzy Gillespie in Cuba; Once Upon a Time…When We Were Colored; Paris Trout; The Players Club; La P..... Respectuese; The Prisoner of Shark Island; The Reivers; Santa Fe Trail; A Soldier's Story; Song of the South; Sounder; Uncle Tom*
urban, etc, *Above the Rim; Across 110th Street; Action Jackson; Ali; Bamboozled; Basquiat; Beverly Hills Cop; Beverly Hills Cop II; Beverly Hills Cop III; Blues Under the Skin; Boomerang* (Hudlin); *Booty Call; Boyz N the Hood; Brewster's Millions* (Hill); *Brother* (Kitano); *The Brother from Another Planet; The Brothers; Bulworth; Bustin' Loose; Carmen Jones; Car Wash; Clara's Heart; Claudine; Clockers; Come Back Charleston Blue; Cool Breeze; Cooley High; The Cool World; The Cotton Club; Count a Lonely Cadence; Crooklyn; D.C. Cab; Dead Presidents; Deep Cover; DEF by Temptation; Devil in a Blue Dress; The Distinguished Gentleman; Don King: Only In America; Do the Right Thing; Downtown 81; Edge of the City; Fatal Beauty; The Five Heartbeats; Get on the Bus; Ghost Dog: The Way of the Samurai; Girlfight; Gladiator* (Herrington); *The Glass Shield; God's Alcatraz; Good to Go; Gordon's War; Grand Canyon; Hangin' with the Homeboys; Harlem Nights; He Got Game; Hoop Dreams; House Party; Hurricane; James Baldwin: The Price of the Ticket; Juice; Jungle Fever; Just Another Girl on the I.R.T.; Killer of Sheep; Lady Sings the Blues; The Landlord; Life; Listen Up: The Lives of Quincy Jones; Looking for Langston; Love and Action in Chicago; love jones; A Low Down Dirty Shame; Mahogany; Malcolm X; Melinda; Menace II Society; Men of Honor; The Meteror Man; Mo' Better Blues; Mo' Money; Moon Over Harlem; My Brother's Wedding; New Jack City; No Maps on My Taps; Norman…Is That You?; The Nutty Professor* (Shadyac); *Nutty Professor II: The Klumps; The Organisation; The Original Kings of Comedy; Panther; A Patch of Blue; A Piece of the Action; Poetic Justice; Portrait of Jason; The Preacher's Wife; The Price of the Ticket; Putney Swope; A Rage in Harlem; Ragtime; Rappin'; School Daze; Set It Off; Shadows; Shaft* (Singleton); *She's Gotta Have It; Shoot to Kill; Sidewalk Stories; Slam; Soul Food; South Central; Straight Out of Brooklyn; Streamers; Sugar Hill; Sun Ra: A Joyful Noise; Sweet Sweetback's Baadasssss Song; Tap; They Call Me MISTER Tibbs!; Tongues Untied; To Sleep with Anger; Uptown Saturday Night; Vampire in Brooklyn; A Warm December; Watermelon Man; The Watermelon Woman; Wattstax; White Men Can't Jump; Who Shot Patakango?; Who's the Man?; The Wiz*
in Westerns, *Boss Nigger; Buck and the Preacher; Charley-One-Eye; El Condor; Posse; Sergeant Rutledge; Silverado; Take a Hard Ride*
black women, *Eve's Bayou; How Stella Got Her Groove Back; Jackie Brown; A Litany for Survival: The Life and Work of Audre Lorde; The Players Club; Thirteen; Waiting to Exhale; Woo*

Blakeley, Kaja, film adapted from work, *Monkeybone*

Blatty, William Peter, films adapted from work, *The Exorcist; The Exorcist – Director's Cut; The Ninth Config-uration; The Exorcist III*

Blindness, *Afraid of the Dark; Alligator Eyes; Les Amants du Pont-Neuf; At First Sight; Blind Date* (Mastorakis); *Blind Fury; Blink; Blue; Butterflies Are Free; Cactus; The Colour of Paradise; The Dark Angel; Dark Eyes of London; Darkness and Light; The Day of the Triffids; Eyes in the Night; Faute de Soleil; The Goddess of 1967; Ice Castles; An Indian Story; Jennifer 8; The Killer* (Woo); *Laura* (Hamilton); *The Life of Chikuzan; Life on a String; The Light Ahead; Love Story* (Arliss); *Magnificent Obsession;*

Mansion of the Doomed; The Miracle Worker; A Patch of Blue; Pride of the Marines; Proof; Scent of a Woman; The Proud Ones; See No Evil, Hear No Evil; The Silence (Makhmalbaf); *La Symphonie Pastorale; These Are Not My Images (neither there nor here); The Toxic Avenger; The Toxic Avenger Part II; The Woman on the Beach*

Bloch, Robert, films adapted from work, *Asylum; The House That Dripped Blood; Psycho* (Hitchcock); *Psycho* (Van Sant); *The Skull; Torture Garden*

Blues, in film, *The Blues Brothers; Blues Brothers 2000; Blues Under the Skin; Crossroads* (Hill); *The Last of the Blue Devils; Leadbelly; Maxwell Street Blues; Mississippi Blues; Screamin' Jay Hawkins: I Put a Spell on Me; Survivors: The Blues Today*

Blythe, Ronald, film adapted from work, *Akenfield*

Boardroom jungle, and business world (see also **Industry and industrial life, Office life**), *L'Argent* (L'Herbier); *L'Argent des Autres; The Bank; Blind Date* (Edwards); *Boiler Room; The Bonfire of the Vanities; The Boost; Caprice; Cash McCall; Company Limited; Dealers; Easy Living; Executive Suite; Filofax; The Fool; The Formula; From the Terrace; Glengarry Glen Ross; Gremlins 2: The New Batch; Hamlet Goes Business; How to Get Ahead in Advertising; How to Succeed in Business Without Really Trying; The Hudsucker Proxy; The Insider; Jerry Maguire; Life at the Top; Limit Up; Make Mine a Million; Other People's Money; Patterns; Pi; The Rise and Rise of Michael Rimmer; Roger & Me; Rogue Trader; Rollover; Romuald et Juliette; Room at the Top; Ruthless; Sabrina* (Pollack); *Sabrina* (Wilder); *The Secret of My Success; A Shock to the System; Silver Bears; The Solid Gold Cadillac; The Survivors; Trading Places; Tucker: The Man and His Dream; Wall Street; Weekend at Bernie's; Woman's World; Working Girl*

Bobsledding, *Cool Runnings*

Boccaccio, Giovanni, film adapted from work, *The Decameron*

Bodybuilding, *Pumping Iron; Pumping Iron II; Stay Hungry*

Bodyguards, *The Bodyguard; Jaguar; A Lovely Way to Die; Man Trouble; Mr Nanny; P.J.*

Bodysnatchers, *The Bodysnatchers; Burke and Hare; Corridors of Blood; The Doctor and the Devils; Flesh and the Fiends*

Boer War, *Breaker Morant; For Valour; Spoor; Young Winston*

Boileau–Narcejac, Pierre Boileau and Thomas Narcejac, films adapted from work, *Body Parts, Les Diaboliques* (Clouzot); *Diabolique* (Chechik); *Vertigo*

Bolivia
Bolivia in film, *Amigomio; Butch Cassidy and the Sundance Kid; Che!*
Bolivian cinema, *The Bird's Singing; Chuquiago; El Coraje del Pueblo; The Secret Nation*

Böll, Heinrich, film adapted from work, *Nicht Versöhnt*

Bolt, Robert, film adapted from work, *A Man for All Seasons*

Bomb disposal, *Blown Away; The English Patient; Heimat; Juggernaut; The Small Back Room; The Specialist; Speed; Speed 2: Cruise Control; Ten Seconds to Hell*

Bond, James, *Casino Royale; Diamonds Are Forever; Dr No; For Your Eyes Only; From Russia with Love; GoldenEye; Goldfinger; Licence to Kill; Live and Let Die; The Living Daylights; The Man with the Golden Gun; Moonraker; Never Say Never Again; Octopussy; On Her Majesty's Secret Service; The Spy Who Loved Me; Thunderball; Tomorrow Never Dies; A View to a Kill; The World Is Not Enough; You Only Live Twice*

Bootlegging, *Al Capone; Bootleggers; Broadway; City Streets; Dixie Dynamite; Last Man Standing; Miller's Crossing; Moonrunners; The Moonshine War; Night after Night; The Roaring Twenties; A Slight Case of Murder; Thunder Road; Underworld; The Untouchables*

Bordewijk, Ferdinand, film adapted from work, *Karakter*

Borges, Jorge Luis,
film about, *Borges, Books and the Night*
film adapted from work, *The Spider's Stratagem*

Bosnia, in film (see also **Serbia, Yugoslavia and former Yugoslavia**), *Bosna!; For Ever Mozart; Perfect Circle; Pretty Village, Pretty Flame; Savior; Shot Through the Heart; Srebrenica: A Cry from the Grave; Welcome to Sarajevo*
Bosnians in exile, *Beautiful People*

Boston, in film, *Blown Away; Body Count; The Bostonians; The Boston Strangler; A Civil Action; The Friends of Eddie Coyle; Good Will Hunting; Headhunter; Malcolm X; Mystery Street; Next Stop Wonderland; The Proposition; The Thomas Crown Affair* (Jewison); *The Verdict* (Lumet); *Walk East on Beacon!*

Boulle, Pierre, films adapted from work, *Planet of the Apes* (Schaffner); *Planet of the Apes* (Burton)

Bouncers, *Road House* (Herrington)

Bounty hunters, *Boss Nigger; The Hunter; Midnight Run; The Naked Spur; Take a Hard Ride; The Tin Star; Unforgiven; Wanted Dead or Alive*

Bowen, Elizabeth, film adapted from work, *The Last September*

Bowie, David, in performance, *Ziggy Stardust and the Spiders from Mars*

Bowling, *The Big Lebowski; Kingpin*

Bowls, *Greenkeeping*

Bowles, Paul,
film about, *Let It Come Down: The Life of Paul Bowles*
film adapted from work, *The Sheltering Sky*

Boxing, *Ali; Ama; Body and Soul* (Rossen); *Body and Soul* (Bowers); *The Boxer* (Terayama); *The Boxer* (Sheridan); *Broken Noses; The Champ; Champion; Don King: Only In America; Edith and Marcel; Fat City; Gatica; Gentleman Jim; Gladiator* (Herrington); *Glory Alley; Golden Boy; The Greatest; The Great White Hype; The Harder They Fall; Hard Times* (Hill); *Homeboy; Hurricane; Joe Louis; Kid Galahad* (Curtiz); *Kid Galahad* (Karlson); *Killer's Kiss; Let's Do It Again; The Main Event; Muhammad Ali: The Greatest; Night and the City* (Winkler); *Play It to the Bone; The Power of One; Price of Glory; Raging Bull; The Ring; Rocky; Rocky II; Rocky III; Rocky IV; Rocky V; The Set-Up; Shiner; Snake Eyes; Somebody Up There Likes Me; Southpaw; Streets of Gold; Tokyo Fist; Triumph of the Spirit; When We Were Kings*
bareknuckle, *Any Which Way You Can; A.W.O.L.; The Big Man; Diggstown; Every Which Way But Loose; Far and Away; Fight Club*
kickboxing, *Kickboxer; Say Anything*
women boxers, *Blonde Fist; Girlfight*

Boyd, William, films adapted from work, *A Good Man in Africa; Stars and Bars*

Boyle, T Coraghessan, film adapted from work, *The Road to Wellville*

Bradbury, Ray, films adapted from work, *The Beast from 20,000 Fathoms; Fahrenheit 451; The Illustrated Man; It Came from Outer Space; Something Wicked This Way Comes*

Braine, John, films adapted from work, *Life at the Top; Room at the Top*

Brainwashing and indoctrination, *Captive; The Ipcress File; The Manchurian Candidate; Patty Hearst; Simon; Telefon; They Live*

Bram, Christopher, film adapted from work, *Gods and Monsters*

Brazil, in film (see also **Rain Forests**), *Anaconda; Behind the Sun; City of God; Cobra Verde; The Fifth Monkey; Flying Down to Rio; Four Days in September; In Cane for Life; Madame Satã; Maids; The Mission* (Joffé); *O Amor Natural; São Paulo, SP; Saudade do Futuro; Sound of Brazil; Tieta of Agreste; Tolerance*

Brazilian cinema, *Amazonia: Voices from the Rainforest; Anaconda; Behind the Sun; Bye Bye Brasil; Carlota Joaquina, Princess of Brazil; Carme Miranda: Bananas Is My Business; Central Do Brasil; La Ciénaga; City of God; Doña Flor and Her Two Husbands; Foreign Land; Four Days in September; Friendly Fire; Für Elise; Gabriela; Giselle; Hour of the Star; In Cane for Life; Kenoma; Killer Fish; Kiss of the Spider Woman; The Lady from the Shanghai Cinema; Macunaima; Madame Satã; Maids; The Magic Hour; Mal; Me You Them; Midnight; Opera do Malandro; Orfeu; The Oyster and the Wind; Pixote; Prisoner of Rio; Saudade do Futuro; Savage Capitalism; Sound of Brazil; Tieta of Agreste; Tolerance; To the Last Drop*

Brecht, Bertolt
Brecht and Kurt Weill, musical by, *Die Dreigroschenoper*
film about *Farewell*
films adapted from work, *Galileo* (Losey); *Hangmen also Die; History Lessons; Kuhle Wampe; The Life Story of Baal; Opera do Malandro; La Vieille Dame indigne*

Brice, Fanny, films about, *Funny Girl; Funny Lady; Rose of Washington Square*

Brighouse, Harold, film adapted from work, *Hobson's Choice*

Brink, André, film adapted from work, *A Dry White Season*

Britain invaded, *The Eagle Has Landed; It Happened Here; Went the Day Well?*

British history, in film (see also **Shakespeare, World War I, World War II**), *Barry Lyndon; The Beggar's Opera; The Bounty; Braveheart; The Charge of the Light Brigade* (Richardson); *Cromwell; Culloden; The Dark Avenger; Elizabeth; The Exile; Fame Is the Spur; Fire Over England; The Fool; Forever Amber; The Gypsy and the Gentleman; Henry VIII and His Six Wives; The House of Rothschild; Ivanhoe; Khartoum; Kitty; Lady Jane; The Lion in Winter; The Madness of King George; A Man for All Seasons; Mary Queen of Scots; Nell Gwyn; Orlando; The Private Life of Henry VIII; The Private Lives of Elizabeth and Essex; Rebecca's Daughters; Restoration; Robinson in Space; Scott of the Antarctic; That Hamilton Woman; The Viking Queen; Winstanley; Young Bess; The Young Mr Pitt; Young Winston*

British Museum, in film, *Blackmail* (Hitchcock); *Bulldog Jack; Maurice*

Britten, Benjamin, choral work in film, *War Requiem*

Brontë, Charlotte, films adapted from work, *I Walked with a Zombie; Jane Eyre* (Stevenson); *Jane Eyre* (Mann); *Jane Eyre* (Zeffirelli)

Brontë, Emily, films adapted from work, *Abismos de pasión; Wuthering Heights* (Wyler); *Wuthering Heights* (Kosminsky)

Brontë family, film about, *Devotion*

Brothers, relationships between (see also **Sisters, Sisters and brothers**), *American Flyers; Australia; Basket Case; Basket Case 2; The Blood Brothers; Booty Call; The Boys; The Brotherhood; Brothers and Sisters; The Brothers Karamazov* (Brooks); *The Brothers Karamazov* (Pyriev); *The Brothers McMullen; China Is Near; Circus Boys; Coupe de Ville; Crumb; December Bride; Dekalog 10: 'Thou shalt not covet thy neighbour's goods'; Dominick and Eugene; Duel in the Sun; The Emperor's Shadow; The Fabulous Baker Boys; Farinelli Il Castrato; Four Men and a Prayer; From Dusk Till Dawn; The Game; Hell's Angels; A Hole in the Head; Horizons West; House by the River; How Old Is the River?; The Indian Runner; Inventing the Abbotts; Johnny Dangerously; Joseph Cornell: Worlds in a Box; Josh and S.A.M.; Kickboxer; The Kid Brother; The Krays; Legends of the Fall; Lost in Yonkers; Mac; Macadam Tribu; The Mambo Kings; The Man from Laramie; Miles from Home; Mo' Money; A Night at the Roxbury; Orphans; Pictures; A River Runs Through It; Rocco and His Brothers; Rogue Cop; Rumble Fish; Sabrina* (Pollack); *Sabrina* (Wilder); *Saddle the Wind; Shark's Son; She Gods of Shark Reef; She's the One; Simple Men; A Simple Plan; Small Faces; Staying Together; The Straight Story; Strangers; Sugar Hill; Three Brothers; Trapped in Paradise; True Confessions; Vincent & Theo; Western Union; While You Were Sleeping; Winchester '73; The Witman Boys*

Brothers and sisters, see **Sisters and brothers**

Brown, Christy, film about/adapted from work, *My Left Foot*

Brown, Fredric, films adapted from work, *Crack Up* (Reis); *Screaming Mimi; Vieille Canaille*

Brown, Rosellen, film adapted from work, *Before and After*

Bruce, Lenny
film about, *Lenny*
in performance, *The Lenny Bruce Performance Film; Lenny Bruce Without Tears*

Bryant, Louise, film about, *Reds*

Buchan, John, films adapted from work, *The 39 Steps* (Hitchcock); *The 39 Steps* (Thomas); *The Thirty-Nine Steps* (Sharp)

Büchner, Georg, films adapted from work, *Woyzeck* (Herzog); *Woyzeck* (Szász)

Buck, Pearl S, films adapted from work, *The Good Earth; Satan Never Sleeps*

Buddhism, *The Burmese Harp; Buddha's Lock; Burning Paradise; Come, Come, Come Upward; The Cup; 8-Diagram Pole Fighter; Fancy Dance; Hi, Dharma!; Hwa-om-kyong; The Horse Thief; The Knowledge of Healing; Kundun; Little Buddha; Lord of the Dance; Mandala; The Outer Way; Samsara; Tibet: A Buddhist Trilogy; A Tibetan New Year; A Touch of Zen; The Valiant Ones; Why Did Bodhi-Dharma Leave for the Orient?*

Buddy movies (see also **Friendship**), *Another 48 HRS; Any Which Way You Can; Beautiful Creatures; Bengazi; The Best of Times; Le Bonheur est dans le pré; Boom Town; Breaking In; Buddy Buddy; Butch and Sundance: The Early Days; Butch Cassidy and the Sundance Kid; Carny; Catlow; Colors; Disco Pigs; Enemy Mine; Every Which Way But Loose; Fandango; The First Great Train Robbery; Flawless; The Fortune; 48 HRS; Freebie and the Bean; A Girl in Every Port; Goodbye Pork Pie; The Great Texas Dynamite Chase; Gunmen; Happy Texas; Heartaches; Heart Condition; The In-Laws; K-9; Kuffs; Larger Than Life; The Last Boy Scout; Lethal Weapon; Lethal Weapon 2; Lethal Weapon 3; Lethal Weapon 4; Mad Dog and Glory; Midnight Cowboy; Midnight Run; Money Train; Renegades; The Rounders; Scarecrow; The Sting; The Sting II; The Sunshine Boys; Tango & Cash; Three Fugitives; Thunderbolt and Lightfoot; Tough Guys; Turner & Hooch; La Vie Rêvée des Anges; White Men Can't Jump; Women Talking Dirty; Your Three Minutes Are Up*

Bukowski, Charles, films adapted from work, *Barfly; Crazy Love; Tales of Ordinary Madness*

Bulgakov, Mikhail, film adapted from work, *The Master and Margarita*

Bulgaria,
Bulgaria in film, *Capitaine Conan*
Bulgarian cinema, *Balkanisateur; Boatman; East-West; The Goat Horn*

Bullfighting, *Carmen* (DeMille); *Carmen* (Rosi); *Blood and Sand* (Niblo); *Blood and Sand* (Mamoulian); *The Bobo; Bolero* (Derek); *The Bullfighter and the Lady; The Kid from Spain; Matador; The Moment of Truth; The Sun Also Rises*

Bunin, Ivan, film about, *His Wife's Diary*

Burgess, Anthony, film adapted from work, *A Clockwork Orange*

Burial alive, *The House of Usher; Isle of the Dead; Macabre; The Pit and the Pendulum* (Corman); *The Premature Burial; Tales of Terror*

Burke, James Lee, film adapted from work, *Heaven's Prisoners*

Burke, John, film adapted from work, *The Sorcerers*

Burkina Faso
Burkina Faso cinema, *Këita! The Voice of the Griot; Samba Traore*
Burkina Faso in film, *Këita! The Voice of the Griot; Tilaï; Yaaba*

Burnett, Frances Hodgson, films adapted from work, *Little Lord Fauntleroy; A Little Princess; The Secret Garden* (Holland); *The Secret Garden* (Wilcox)

Burundian cinema, *Gito, the Ungrateful*

Burnett, WR, films adapted from work, *The Asphalt Jungle; The Badlanders; Colorado Territory; Cool Breeze; High Sierra; I Died a Thousand Times; Little Caesar; Nobody Lives Forever; The Whole Town's Talking*

Burroughs, Edgar Rice, films adapted from work, *At the Earth's Core; Greystoke – The Legend of Tarzan, Lord of the Apes; The People That Time Forgot; Tarzan; Tarzan, The Ape Man*

Burroughs, William
film adapted from work, *Naked Lunch*
in film, *Kerouac; The Life and Times of Allen Ginsberg*

Bushranger sagas, *Mad Dog Morgan; Ned Kelly; Robbery Under Arms*

Business, see **Boardroom Jungle**

Buskers and street musicians, *St Martin's Lane; The Underground Orchestra*

Butterworth, Jez, film adapted from work, *Mojo*

Byatt, AS, film adapted from work, *Angels and Insects*

Byron, Lord, films about/featuring, *Bad Lord Byron; Gothic; Haunted Summer; Lady Caroline Lamb; Pandaemonium; Roger Corman's Frankenstein Unbound*

Cain, James M,
films adapted from work, *Butterfly; Le Dernier Tournant; Double Indemnity; Everybody Does It; Interlude* (Sirk); *Interlude* (Billington); *Mildred Pierce; Ossessione; The Postman Always Rings Twice* (Garnett); *The Postman Always Rings Twice* (Rafelson); *Passion; Slightly Scarlet*

Cajuns, and Cajun music, *Always for Pleasure; Dirty Rice; First Love, Last Rites*

Calderón de la Barca, Pedro, film adapted from work, *Mémoire des apparences*

Caldwell, Erskine, films adapted from work, *God's Little Acre; Tobacco Road*

Calligraphy, in film, *The Pillow Book*

Cambodia, in film, *The Killing Fields*

Cambodian cinema, *Les Gens de la rizière*

Cameroonian cinema, *Clando; Fragments of Life; A Trip to My Country*

Camp/trash, *Archangel; Beyond the Valley of the Dolls; Beneath the Valley of the Ultra Vixens; Blacksnake; Candy Strip Nurses; Cannibal Women in the Avocado Jungle of Death; Color Me Blood Red; Cry-Baby; Desperate Living; Elvira, Mistress of the Dark; Female Trouble; Faster, Pussycat! Kill! Kill!; Forbidden World; God Told Me To; Good Morning… and Goodbye; Hairspray; Hold Me, Thrill Me, Kiss Me; The Incredibly Strange Creatures Who Gave Up Living and Became Mixed-Up Zombies; Liquid Sky; Lust in the Dust; Mondo Trasho; Pink Flamingos; Polyester; Slacker; Supervixens; Tales from the Gimli Hospital; Thundercrack!; Tribulation 99: Alien Anomalies Under America; Tarzan and the Mermaids; Truckstop Women; Vixen; Wild Women of Wongo*

Campbell, John W, films adapted from work, *The Thing; The Thing from Another World*

Camping, *Grim Prairie Tales; She'll Be Wearing Pink Pyjamas*

Canada, in film
past, *The Apprenticeship of Duddy Kravitz; Black Robe; Bye Bye Blues; The Canadians; 49th Parallel; Kabloonak; Lilies; Map of the Human Heart; Margaret's Museum; My American Cousin; Northwest Passage; La Veuve de Saint-Pierre; Why Shoot The Teacher*
contemporary, *Anne Trister; Between Friends; Calendar; Canadian Bacon; Candy Mountain; Cool Runnings; Crossing the Bridge; Dancing in the Dark; The Decline of the American Empire; Desperate Search; Far from Home: The Adventures of Yellow Dog; Fly Away Home; Goin' Down the Road; The Hanging Garden; Hochelaga; Homeward Bound: The Incredible Journey; Jesus of Montreal; Kanehsatake (Oka) – 270 Years of Resistance; Love and Human Remains; Masala; Montreal Main; 90 Days; Nô; Les Ordres; The Luck of Ginger Coffey; Paperback Hero; A Paper Wedding; Réjeanne Padovani; The Shipping News; Shoemaker; Swann; The Sweet Hereafter; La Tête de Normande St-Onge; The True Nature of Bernadette; When Night Is Falling; Why Shoot the Teacher; Woman Obsessed*

Canadian cinema, see Appendix 17

Canals, *Amsterdamned; L'Atalante; The Bargee; La Fille de l'Eau; Painted Boats*

Cannaughton, Shane, films adapted from work, *The Playboys, The Run of the Country*

Cannibalism, *Alive; Cannibal; Cannibal Holocaust; Consuming Passions; Delicatessen; Deathline; Doctor X; Eating Raoul; The Emperor's Naked Army Marches On; Ghosts of Mars; Hannibal; The Hills Have Eyes; Leatherface: The Texas Chainsaw Massacre III; The Living Dead at the Manchester Morgue; Macunaima; Montagna del Dio Cannibale; Ravenous; The Silence of the Lambs; Survive; Sweeney Todd; Tales from the Darkside: The Movie; The Texas Chain Saw Massacre; Windbag the Sailor; Zombie Flesh-Eaters*

Canonization, *Heavenly Pursuits*

Capital punishment, *Bandolero!; Beyond a Reasonable Doubt; The Chamber; Dance with a Stranger; Daniel; Dead Man Walking; Death by Hanging; Dekalog 5: 'Thou shalt not kill'; The Executioner's Song; Execution in Autumn; The Execution Protocol; The Front Page* (Milestone); *The Front Page* (Wilder); *His Girl Friday; The Green Mile; I Want to Live!; The Jackal of Nahueltoro; Joe Hill; Last Dance; Let Him Have It; London Belongs to Me; Monster's Ball; Ordeal by Innocence; Paths of Glory; Picture Snatcher; Le Pull-Over Rouge; Return to Paradise; A Short Film About Killing; Switching Channels; Time Without Pity; The Traveling Executioner; True Crime; 20,000 Years in Sing Sing; The Verdict* (Siegel); *El Verdugo; Yield to the Night; You Only Live Once*
victim surviving, *The First Power; Shocker; The Walking Dead*

Capitalism, *see* **Boardroom Jungle**

Capone, Al, films about, *Al Capone; Capone; The St Valentine's Day Massacre; The Untouchables*

Capote, Truman, films adapted from work, *Breakfast at Tiffany's; The Grass Harp; In Cold Blood; Other Voices Other Rooms*

Capra, Frank, film about, *Frank Capra's American Dream*

Carcaterra, Lorenzo, film adapted from work, *Sleepers*

Carey, Peter, film adapted from work, *Oscar and Lucinda*

Car fetishism, etc, *The Big Steal* (Tass); *Crash* (Cronenberg); *Dandy, the All-American Girl; Le Départ; Motorist; Off the the Revolution by 2CV*

Caribbean islands, in film (see also individual islands), *Black Shack Alley; Blacksnake; The Black Swan; Captain Blood; Death Ship; The Ghost Breakers; Island in the Sun; Islands in the Stream; I Walked with a Zombie; The Mighty Quinn; My Father, the Hero; Once Around; Queimada!; La Soufrière; The Spanish Prisoner; The Tamarind Seed*

Carpenter, Karen, film about, *Superstar: The Karen Carpenter Story*

Carrère, Emmanuel, film adapted from work, *Class Trip*

Carroll, Lewis
films adapted from/ based on work, *Alice; Alice in Wonderland* (McLeod); *Alice in Wonderland* (Bower); *Alice's Adventures in Wonderland; The Care Bears Adventure in Wonderland!*
film about, *Dreamchild*

Car salesmen, *Cadillac Man; Fargo; Used Cars*

Car smash movies (see also **Chase movies**), *Crash* (Gibson); *Crash* (Cronenberg); *Gone in 60 Seconds; Gone in Sixty Seconds; Grand Theft Auto; Grandview U.S.A.; Head On; Steelyard Blues*

Cars operating themselves, *The Car; Christine; Herbie Goes Bananas; Herbie Goes to Monte Carlo; Herbie Rides Again; The Love Bug*

Carter, Rubin 'Hurricane', film about, *Hurricane*

Cartoonists, film about, *Crumb*

Cartoons and animation (see also **Puppets**)
adult, *Adventures of Prince Achmed, The; Akira; Alice* (Svankmajer); *Animal Farm; The Big Bang; Blood: The Last Vampire; Cool World; The Critic; Dick Deadeye, or Duty Done; Faust* (Svankmajer); *Fist of the North Star; Final Fantasy: The Spirits Within; Ghost in the Shell; Heavy Metal; Heavy Traffic; Jin-Roh; Jungle Burger; Memories; Metropolis* (Rintaro); *The Nine Lives of Fritz the Cat; Patlabor – The Movie; Patlabor 2 – The Movie; Perfect Blue; Roujin Z; South Park: Bigger, Longer & Uncut; Sparklehorse; Spirited Away; Spriggan; Théâtre de Monsieur et Madame Kabal; Tusalava; When the Wind Blows; Wizards; Yellow Submarine*
– mixed animation/live action, *The Adventures of Pinocchio; The Adventures of Rocky & Bullwinkle; Balto; Casper; Cats & Dogs; James and the Giant Peach; The Mystery of Rampo; Osmosis Jones; Otesánek; The Pagemaster; Small Soldiers; Song of the South; Space Jam; Volere, Volare; Who Framed Roger Rabbit*
children's
– Disney, *Aladdin; Aristocats; Atlantis – The Lost Empire; Bambi; Basil, the Great Mouse Detective; Beauty and the Beast; The Black Cauldron; A Bug's Life; Cinderella; Dinosaur; Doug's 1st Movie; Dumbo; The Emperor's New Groove; Fantasia; Fantasia/2000; The Fox and the Hound; A Goofy Movie; Hercules; The Hunchback of Notre Dame* (Trousdale/Kirk); *Ichabod and Mr Toad; The Jungle Book* (Reitherman); *Lady and the Tramp; The Lion King; The Little Mermaid; Lord of the Rings; Mulan; Oliver & Company; One Hundred and One Dalmatians* (Reitherman/Luske/Geronimi); *Peter Pan; Pete's Dragon; Pinocchio; Pocahontas; The Rescuers; The Rescuers Down Under; Robin Hood* (Reitherman); *Sleeping Beauty; Snow White and the Seven Dwarfs; Song of the South; The Sword in the Stone; Tarzan; The Tigger Movie*
– other, *Adventures of Prince Achmed, The; All Dogs Go to Heaven; An American Tail; An American Tail: Fievel Goes West; Anastasia* (Bluth/Goldman); *Animalympics; Antz; Asterix and the Big Fight; Asterix Conquers America; Asterix in Britain; Babar: The Movie; A Boy Named Charlie Brown; The Brave Little Toaster; The Care Bears Adventure in Wonderland!; The Care Bears Movie; Charles Dickens' David Copperfield; Charlotte's Web; Chicken Run; Christmas Carol – The Movie; A Close Shave; Cyberworld 3D; Digimon Digital Monsters – The Movie; Felix the Cat: The Movie; FernGully: The Last Rainforest; Final Fantasy: The Spirits Within; Fire and Ice; Freddie as F.R.O.7; Gobots: Battle of the Rocklords; Grandma and Her Ghosts; Gulliver's Travels; H.C. Andersen's The Long Shadow; Heidi's Song; Help! I'm a Fish; How the Grinch Stole Christmas!; Hugo the Hippo; Ice Age; The Iron Giant; Jetsons: The Movie; Jimmy Neutron Boy Genius; The King and I*

(Rich); *The King and Mister Bird; The Land Before Time; The Last Unicorn; Little Nemo Adventures in Slumberland; Lucky Luke; Mad Monster Party; The Magic Sword: Quest for Camelot; Mighty Mouse in the Great Space Chase; The Miracle Maker; A Monkey's Tale; Monsters, Inc.; The Mouse and His Child; My Little Pony; The Nightmare Before Christmas; Once Upon a Forest; The Pebble and the Penguin; The Phantom Tollbooth; The Pied Piper; Pinocchio and the Emperor of the Night; Pippi Longstocking; Plague Dogs; The Point; Pokémon – The First Movie: Mewtwo Strikes Back; Pokémon 2: The Power of One; Pokémon 3: Spell of the Unown; The Prince of Egypt; Princess Mononoke; The Road to El Dorado; Rock-a-Doodle; Le Roman de Renard; Rugrats in Paris: The Movie; The Rugrats Movie; The Secret Adventures of Tom Thumb; The Secret of Nimh; The Secret of the Sword; Shrek; Space Firebird; Spirited Away; Starchaser: the Legend of Orin; The Swan Princess; Thumbelina; Titan A.E.; Tom and Jerry: The Movie; Toy Story; Toy Story 2; Transformers – the Movie; The Twelve Tasks of Asterix; Uproar in Heaven; The Water Babies; Watership Down; The Wings of Honneamise*

Cartwright, Jim, film adapted from work, *Little Voice*

Carver, Raymond, films adapted from work, *Short Cuts; Tropical Fish* (Rodley)

Cary, Joyce films adapted from work, *The Horse's Mouth; Mister Johnson*

Casanova, Giacomo, films about, *Casanova's Big Night; Fellini's Casanova; That Night in Varennes*

Cassady, Neal and Carolyn film about, *Heart Beat* film based on Neal letter, *Last Time I Committed Suicide*

Castration, *Farinelli il Castrato; Li Lianying, the Imperial Eunuch; Stealing Heaven*

Castro, Fidel, films about, *The Battle of the Ten Million; Che; Improper Conduct*

Catherine the Great, Czarina of Russia, films about/featuring, *Catherine the Great; Russian Ark; The Scarlet Empress*

Catholicism, see **Religion**

Caute, David, film adapted from work, *Winstanley*

Cervantes, Miguel de, films adapted from work, *Don Quichotte; Don Quixote*

Chabon, Michael, film adapted from work, *Wonder Boys*

Chamberlain, Lindy, film about, *A Cry in the Dark*

Chandler, Raymond, films adapted from work, *The Big Sleep* (Hawks); *The Big Sleep* (Winner); *The Brasher Doubloon; Farewell My Lovely* (Dmytryk); *Farewell My Lovely* (Richards); *Lady in the Lake; The Long Goodbye; Marlowe; Poodle Springs; Time to Kill*

Chanel, Coco, film about, *Chanel Solitaire*

Chang, Eileen, film adapted from work, *Eighteen Springs*

Channel Islands, in film, *The Story of Adèle H.; The Others*

Chaplin, Charles, films about, *The Cat's Meow; Chaplin*

Charrière, Henri, film adapted from work, *Papillon*

Charteris, Leslie, films adapted from work, *Lady on a Train; The Saint; The Saint in New York*

Chase, James Hadley, films adapted from work, *The Catamount Killing; Eve; The Grissom Gang; No Orchids for Miss Blandish; Palmetto; The Rise and Fall of a Little Film Company from a novel by James Hadley Chase; Rough Magic; The Set Up*

Chase Movies (see also **Car-smash movies**), *Badlands; The Big Steal* (Siegel); *Bird on a Wire; Bonnie and Clyde; Bullitt; Butch Cassidy and the Sundance Kid; Cannonball; The Cannonball Run; Cannonball Run II; Charlie Varrick; The Chase* (Rifkin); *Convoy; Criminal Lovers; Cry of the Hunted; Death Race 2,000; Deathsport; The Driver; Eat My Dust; Escape to Witch Mountain; Fast Charlie, the Moonbeam Rider; The Fugitive* (Davis); *'Gator Bait; The Getaway* (Peckinpah); *The Getaway* (Donaldson); *Gloria* (Cassavetes); *Gloria* (Lumet); *Gone in 60 Seconds; Gone in Sixty Seconds; Goodbye Pork Pie; The Gumball Rally; Guncrazy; The Killing of a Chinese Bookie; Kill Me Again; King of the Gypsies; Ladder of Swords; The Legend of Billie Jean; Love and a .45; Macon County Line; Midnight Run; The Missouri Breaks; Moonrise; Moonrunners; Mr Billion; Night Train; No Man's Land* (Tanner); *Nuns on the Run; The President's Analyst; Quick Change; Race with the Devil; Renegades; Running Hot; The Running Man* (Reed); *Saboteur; The Seven-ups; Shaker Run; Shattered; Le Silencieux; Sitting Ducks; Smokey and the Bandit; Smokey and the Bandit II; Son of Paleface; Speedtrap; The Sugarland Express; Supervixens; Surviving the Game; Tank; Taxi; Thelma and Louise; They Call Me Bruce; Three Fugitives; Thunder and Lightning; U.S. Marshals; War Party; We're No Angels* (Jordan); *Who'll Stop the Rain?; Why Me?; Wisdom*

Chatwin, Bruce, films adapted from work, *Cobra Verde; On the Black Hill*

Chaucer, Geoffrey, film adapted from work, *The Canterbury Tales*

Chaudhuri, Nirad C, film about, *Adventures of a Brown Man in Search of Civilization*

Chauvinism, British, *Arrivederci Millwall; Proud to Be British*

Chayefsky, Paddy, films adapted from work, *Altered States; The Bachelor Party; Marty*

Cheever, John, films adapted from work, *The 5:48; The Swimmer*

Chekhov, Anton, films adapted from work, *August; Black Sabbath; The Cherry Orchard; Country Life; Dark Eyes; The Lady with the Little Dog; Romance with a Double Bass; The Sea Gull; Summer Storm; Three Sisters* (Olivier); *Three Sisters* (von Trotta); *Unfinished Piece for Mechanical Piano; Vanya on 42nd Street*

Chess, *Dangerous Moves; The Grass Arena; Knight Moves; The Luzhin Defence; Searching for Bobby Fischer*

Chesterton, GK, film adapted from work, *Father Brown*

Chicago, in film, *Angel Eyes; Bound; Candyman; 'G' Men; City Streets; City That Never Sleeps; Eight Men Out; The Front Page* (Milestone); *The Front Page* (Wilder); *Gladiator* (Herrington); *Go Fish; High Fidelity; Hoop Dreams; In Old Chicago; Just Visiting; Love and Action in Chicago; Mad Dog and Glory; Message in a Bottle; The Negotiator; Next of Kin; Only the Lonely; Robin and the 7 Hoods; Shaking the Tree; Soul Food; Straight Talk; Switching Channels; Underworld; Union Station; The Untouchables; V I Warshawski; While You Were Sleeping*

Child abuse, *Child's Play* (Becker); *Class Trip; The Lost Son; M* (Lang); *M* (Losey); *The Offence; L'Ombre du Doute; Tenderness of the Wolves; The War Zone*

Childers, Erskine, film adapted from work, The *Riddle of the Sands*

Child prodigies, *Little Man Tate; Searching for Bobby Fischer*

Children and childhood, in film (see also **Adolescence, Family life, Fathers, Mothers** and **Pregnancy, childbirth and babies**)
Aust, *Captain Johnno; Celia; Frog Dreaming; The Miniskirted Dynamo; The Quiet Room*
Bel, *Ma Vie en Rose; Toto the Hero*
Braz, *Central Do Brasil; Pixote*
Burkina Faso, *Këita! The Voice of the Griot; Yaaba*
Can, *Léolo; Lies My Father Told Me; Tommy Tricker and the Stamp Traveller*
Cyprus, *Tomorrow's Warrior*
Czech/Czech Rep, *Kolya; The Search*
Den, *Buster's World; Once There Was a War*
Fr, *L'Argent de Poche; Au Revoir les Enfants; Le Château de ma mère; City of Pirates; Class Trip; L'Enfance nue; La Fracture du myocarde; Fresh; La Gloire de mon père; Le Grand Chemin; La Guerre des Boutons; Jacquot de Nantes; Les Jeux Interdits; La Baule-les-pins; Ponette*
GB, *Afraid of the Dark; The Amazing Mr Blunden; Bloody Kids; The Borrowers; Bugsy Malone; Burning Secret; Captain Stirrick; Children of the Damned; The Children's Midsummer Night's Dream; The Custard Boys; Dance Little Lady; Dark Enemy; Eyewitness* (Hough); *The Fallen Idol; Flight of the Doves; The Full Monty; The Gift; The Go-Between; Hard Road; Harry Potter and the Philosopher's Stone; High Wind in Jamaica; Hope and Glory; Hue and Cry; The Hummingbird Tree; Into the Arms of Strangers: Stories of the Kindertransport; James and the Giant Peach; A Kid for Two Farthings; La Passione; Last Day of Summer; Liam; Little Lord Fauntleroy; Lord of the Flies* (Brook); *The Magic Toyshop; Mandy; Mirror Phase; Mister Skeeter; The Mudlark; My Childhood; The Nanny; The Optimists of Nine Elms; Our Mother's House; The Pagemaster; Paperhouse; Queen of Hearts; The Railway Children; Ratcatcher; The Reflecting Skin; The Scamp; Seance on a Wet Afternoon; This Boy's Story; Tiger Bay; Tree of Hands; Venus Peter; When the Whales Came; The Wolves of Willoughby Chase ; The Yellow Balloon*
Ger, *The Blue Bird; Child's Play* (Becker); *Emil & the Detectives; Peppermint Freedom; Poto and Cabengo; Somewhere in Berlin*

Greece, *Dead Liqueur; Landscape in the Mist*
HK, *Back Alley Princes*
Hun, *Whooping Cough*
Ice, *Ikingut*
Ind, *Deveeri; Salaam Bombay*
Iran, *Under the Skin of the City*
Ire, *Angela's Ashes; A Boy from Mercury; War of the Buttons*
Isr, *Promises*
Iran, *A.B.C. Africa; The Apple; Children of Heaven; Daan; The Father; The Runner; The Traveller; Where Is My Friend's House?; The White Balloon*
It, *Bellissima; Cinema Paradiso; Cinema Paradiso: The Special Edition; Last Moments; The Last Snows of Spring; The Stolen Children*
Jap, *Muddy River; Pastoral Hide and Seek; Summer Vacation 1999 ; Village of Dreams*
Latin America (unspecified), *Los Niños Abandonados*
Mor, *Ali Zaoua: Prince de la Rue*
Moz, *Comédia Infantil*
Nor, *Little Ida*
NZ, *An Angel at My Table*
Palestine, *Tale of the Three Jewels*
Pol, *Crows*
Port, *Oporto of My Childhood*
Sri Lanka, *Saroja*
Sp, *Cria Cuervos; El Mar; ¿Quién Puede Matar a un Niño?; Secrets of the Heart; The South; The Spirit of the Beehive*
Swe, *Fanny and Alexander; My Life as a Dog; Stubby; The Slingshot*
Tai, *Jade Love; Student Days; Summer at Grandpa's; The Time to Live and the Time to Die; Together; Too Young*
Thai, *Butterfly and Flowers; The Song of Chao-Phrya*
Turk, *Cold Nights*
US, *A.I. Artificial Intelligence; The Adventures of Huckleberry Finn; The Adventures of Huck Finn; The Adventures of Tom Sawyer; All I Want for Christmas; The Baby; Bride of Chucky; Captain January; Child of Divorce; Child's Play* (Holland); *Child's Play 2; A Christmas Story; The Client; Cop & ½; Corrina, Corrina; The Cure; The Curse of the Cat People; Curly Sue; Dennis the Menace; Desperate Search; Disney's The Kid; A Dog of Flanders; Don't Tell Mom the Babysitter's Dead; Driftwood; Empire of the Sun; Escape to Witch Mountain; Explorers; The 5,000 Fingers of Dr T; Flipper* (Clark); *Flipper* (Shapiro); *Flowers in the Attic; Free Willy; Free Willy 2; Free Willy 3: The Rescue; Fresh; Getting Even With Dad; The Goonies; Harriet the Spy; Hide in Plain Sight; Home Alone; Home Alone 2: Lost in New York; Home Alone 3; Honey, I Blew Up the Kid; Honey, I Shrunk the Kids; The Indian in the Cupboard; Jack; Jack the Bear; Josh and S.A.M.; Journey for Margaret; Juvenile Court; The Kid; Kids of Survival: The Art and Life of Tim Rollins & K.O.S.; Kindergarten Cop; King of the Wind; Lawn Dogs; Little Big League; The Little Rascals; The Lone Hand; Look Who's Talking Now; Look Who's Talking Too; Lord of the Flies* (Hook); *Mac and Me; Manny & Lo; The Mighty Ducks; Monkey Trouble; The Monster Squad; My Dog Skip; My Girl; My Girl 2; No Deposit, No Return; North; O. Henry's Full House ('The Ransom of Red Chief'); Once Upon a Time…When We Were Colored; Paradise; A Perfect World; Problem Child; Problem Child 2; Return from Witch Mountain; Rich Kids; Ride a Wild Pony; Roald Dahl's Matilda; Rookie of the Year; The Sandlot; A Simple Wish; Stand by Me; Star Kid; Stone Boy; Three Men and a Little Lady; 3 Ninjas; Tom Sawyer; Treasure of Matecumbe; Uncle Buck; Unstrung Heroes; The Witches*
USSR and Rus, *Don't Move, Die and Rise Again!; Katok i Skrypka; Micha; The Thief*
non-specific, *The Adventures of Pinocchio*

Chile
Chilean cinema, *Amnesia; Caluga o Menta; Chico; Enthusiasm; La Frontera; The Jackal of Nahueltoro; Johnny 100 Pesos; Los Naufragos; The Moon in the Mirror*
Chile in film, *The Battle of Chile; Cantata of Chile; La Frontera; Missing; Los Naufragos*

China, in film
pre-1900, *Accidental Legend; Beach of the War Gods; The Blood Brothers; Burning Paradise; A Chinese Ghost Story; A Chinese Ghost Story II; A Chinese Ghost Story III; The Conqueror; Dirty Ho; Crouching Tiger, Hidden Dragon; Dynasty; The Emperor and the Assassin; The Emperor's Shadow; Executioners from Shaolin; The Fate of Lee Khan; Flowers of Shanghai; Folk Tales of Lu Ban; Golden Swallow; Intimate Confessions of a Chinese Courtesan; The Journey to the Western Xia; Li Lianying, the Imperial Eunuch; Love and Duty; Mulan; Once Upon a Time in China; Once Upon a Time in China II; Peking Opera Blues; The Phantom Lover; Raining in the Mountain; Swordsman; Swordsman II; A Terra-Cotta Warrior; The 36th Chamber of Shaolin; A Touch of Zen; The Valiant Ones*
1900–49, *Actress; Along the Sungari River; Au revoir, mon amour; The Bitter Tea of General Yen; Buddha's Lock; Crows and Sparrows; Death Kick; Devils on the Doorstep; 8,000 Li Under the Clouds and Moon; Farewell My Concubine; 55 Days at Peking; The Girls to Be Married; The Good Earth; The Highway; The Inn of the Sixth Happiness; Ju Dou; King of Masks; Kawashima Yoshiko; Kung Fu Girl; The Last Emperor; The Left Hand of God; Little Toys; My Memories of Old Beijing; My Young Auntie; Plunder of Peach and Plum; Raise the Red Lantern; Red Rose, White Rose; Rouge; Satan Never Sleeps; Seven Women; Shanghai Triad; Spring in a Small Town; The Spring River Flows East; Street Angel; Sweet Grass; Temptress Moon; Unchanged Heart in Life and Death; This Whole Life of Mine; To Live; Yellow Earth*
post-revolutionary, *All the Way; Back to Back, Face to Face; Balzac and the Little Chinese Seamstress; Beijing Bicycle; The Big Parade* (Chen Kaige); *The Bird People in China; Black Snow; Bloody Morning; Blush; Concerto of Life; Crazy English; The Days; The Day the Sun Turned Cold; Durian, Durian; East Palace, West Palace; Ermo; Family Portrait; Farewell My Concubine; Father; For Fun; Fish and Elephant; From Mao to Mozart; Frozen; The Goddess; Go For Broke; Goldfish; Happy Times; Heartstrings; Hibiscus Town; Hold You Tight; Homecoming; In the Heat of the Sun; Iron & Silk; Journey to Beijing; Keep Cool; King of the Children; Lan Yu; The Last Day of Winter; Live in Peace; Maiden Work; Mama; Man and Woman; The Man from Island West; M. Butterfly; Mr Zhao; Murmur of Youth; My New Friends; Not One Less; Old Well; On the Hunting Ground; The Peach-Blossom Land; The Platform; Portland Street Blues; Postman; Quitting; Rainclouds Over Wushan; Rapid Fire; Red Corner; Red Detachment of Women* (Collective); *Red Detachment of Women* (Xie Jin); *The Red Lotus Society; The River* (Tsai Ming-Liang); *The Road Home; Rock n'Roll Cop; Sacrificed Youth; Seafood; Seventeen Years; Shower; Signal Left, Turn Right; So Close to Paradise; Sons; Spy Game; The Square; Stand Up, Don't Grovel!; The Story of Qiu Ju; A Story of Women; Sun and Rain; Sunless Days; Sun Valley; Surveillance; Suzhou; Swan Song; Sweet Degeneration; To Live; Tropical Fish* (Chen Yu-Hsun); *Xiao Wu; Yang ± Yin: Gender in Chinese Cinema; Yangtse Incident; Young Couples*
futuristic, *The Hole*

Chinese Americans, *The Cat's-Paw; Chan Is Missing; The Corruptor; Dim Sum; Eat a Bowl of Tea; Eight Taels of Gold; Full Moon in New York; The Great Wall Is a Great Wall; The Joy Luck Club; Pushing Hands; Rapid Fire; Rush Hour; They Call Me Bruce; A Thousand Pieces of Gold; The Wedding Banquet; Who Killed Vincent Chin?; Year of the Dragon*

Chinese in Britain, *Man from China; Ping Pong; Soursweet*

Chinese cinema (see also **Hong Kong cinema, Taiwanese cinema**)
pre-revolutionary, *Crows and Sparrows; 8,000 Li Under the Clouds and Moon; The Highway; Love and Duty; Plunder of Peach and Plum; Spring in a Small Town; The Spring River Flows East; Street Angel; Unchanged Heart in Life and Death*
post-1949, *All the Way; Along the Sungari River; Back to Back, Face to Face; Balzac and the Little Chinese Seamstress; Beijing Bastards; Beijing Bicycle; The Big Parade* (Chen Kaige); *Black Snow; Bloody Morning; Blush; Buddha's Lock; Concerto of Life; Crazy English; Crouching Tiger, Hidden Dragon; The Days; Devils on the Doorstep; East Palace, West Palace; The Emperor and the Assassin; The Emperor's Shadow; Ermo; Family Portrait; Farewell My Concubine; Father; Fish and Elephant; For Fun; Frozen; A Girl of Good Family; The Girls to Be Married; The Goddess; Go For Broke; Goldfish; The Great Wall Is a Great Wall; Happy Times; Hibiscus Town; Horse Thief; In the Heat of the Sun; Keep Cool; King of the Children; The Journey to the Western Xia; Ju Dou; The Last Day of Winter; The Legend of Zu; Li Lianying, the Imperial Eunuch; Life on a String; Live in Peace; Maiden Work; Mama; Man and Woman; A Man Called Hero; The Most Terrible Time in My Life; Mr Zhao; My Memories of Old Beijing; Not One Less; On the Hunting Ground; The Orphan of Anyang; Postman; Quitting; Rainclouds Over Wushan; Red Beads; Red Detachment of Women* (Collective); *Red Detachment of Women* (Xie Jin); *Red Firecracker, Green Firecracker; Red Sorghum; Ripples Across Stagnant Water; The Road Home; Sacrificed Youth; Seafood; Seventeen Years; Shanghai Picnic; Shanghai Triad; Shaolin Soccer; Shower; Signal Left, Turn Right; So Close to Paradise; Sons; The Square; Stand Up, Don't Grovel!; The Story of Qiu Ju; A Story of Women; Sun and Rain; Sun Valley;*

Surveillance; Suzhou; Swan Song; Sweet Grass; The Swordsman in Double-Flag Town; Taipei Story; This Whole Life of Mine; Two Stage Sisters; Uproarious Heaven; Weekend Plot; Xiao Wu; Yellow Earth; Young Couples

Chomsky, Noam, film about, *Manufacturing Consent: Noam Chomsky and the Media*

Chopin, Frederic, films about, *Impromptu; A Song to Remember*

Christie, Agatha
film about, *Agatha*
films adapted from work, *The Alphabet Murders; And Then There Were None* (Clair); *And Then There Were None* (Collinson); *Appointment With Death; Death on the Nile; Endless Night; Evil Under the Sun; The Mirror Crack'd; Murder on the Orient Express; Ordeal by Innocence; Ten Little Indians; Witness for the Prosecution*

Christie, Dorothy and Campbell, film from work, *Carrington VC*

Christina, Queen of Sweden, films about, *The Abdication; Queen Christina*

Christmas and Thanksgiving films, *All I Want for Christmas; La Bûche; A Christmas Carol; Christmas Carol – The Movie; A Christmas Story; Dr Seuss' How the Grinch Stole Christmas; Ernest Saves Christmas; Holiday Inn; Home Alone; Home for the Holidays; How the Grinch Stole Christmas!; It's a Wonderful Life; Jack Frost; Jingle All the Way; Johns; Miracle on 34th Street; Mixed Nuts; The Muppet Christmas Carol; The Myth of Fingerprints; The Nightmare Before Christmas; Santa Claus; The Santa Clause; Santa Claus Conquers the Martians; Scrooge; Scrooged; Trapped in Paradise; What's Cooking?*

Churchill, Winston S, films about, *The Eagle Has Landed; Young Winston*

CIA (see also **Cold War, Spy films**), *Air America; The Amateur; Bulletproof; Clear and Present Danger; Company Business; Conspiracy Theory; Hopscotch; Hot War; Knock Off; KT; Memoirs of an Invisible Man; Mission Impossible; Mission: Impossible II; On Company Business; Paperback Vigilante; Patriot Games; Powerplay; Scorpio; The Sellout; Sneakers; The Soldier; Target* (Penn); *Spy Game; Three Days of the Condor; Wanted Dead or Alive*

Cinema, early years (see also **Film-makers and film-making**), *Before the Nickelodeon: The Early Cinema of Edwin S Porter; Correction Please, or How We Got into Pictures; Eadweard Muybridge, Zoopraxographer; Edison the Man; L'Homme au Chapeau de Soie; Kabloonak; The Magic Box; Nickelodeon; The Picture Show Man; Those Wonderful Movie Cranks*

Cinema owners, projectionists, staff, etc, *Anita Takes a Chance; Apartment Zero; Cinema Paradiso; Cinema Paradiso: The Special Edition; Clash By Night; Coming Up Roses; Il Giorno della prima di 'Close Up'; Hercules Returns; The Inner Circle; The Last Action Hero; Murmur of Youth; The Projectionist; Sabotage; Sherlock Junior; The Smallest Show on Earth; Splendor; The Tingler*

Cinematic novelties
Duo-vision, *Wicked, Wicked*
Fisher-Price PXL 2000, *Another Girl, Another Planet; Nadja*
Grandeur, *The Big Trail*
Hallucinogenic Hypnovision, *The Incredibly Strange Creatures Who Stopped Living and Became Mixed-Up Zombies*
IMAX, *Across the Sea of Time: A New York Adventure; Everest*
Sensurround, *Earthquake; Midway; Rollercoaster*
3-D, *Arena; The Charge at Feather River; Comin' at Ya!; Dynasty; Flesh for Frankenstein; Freddy's Dead: The Final Nightmare; The French Line; Friday the 13th Part III; Jaws 3-D; Inferno; It Came from Outer Space; House of Wax; Kiss Me Kate: 3-D; The Legend of Orin; The Mask* (Roffman); *Metalstorm; Miss Sadie Thompson; Parasite; Revenge of the Creature; Robot Monster; Second Chance* (Maté); *Spacehunter: Adventures in the Forbidden Zone; Starchaser; Treasure of the Four Crowns*

Circuses, *Artistes at the Top of the Big Top; At the Circus; The Big Top; Billy Rose's Jumbo; Chad Hanna; The Circus; Circus Boys; Circus of Fear; Circus of Horrors; The Clowns; Dante's Inferno; Les Equilibristes; Freaked; The Greatest Show on Earth; Gycklarnas Afton; Killer Klowns from Outer Space; Ladder of Swords; Lola Montès; Luna e l'Altra; Man on a Tightrope; The Mighty Barnum; Rain or Shine; Roselyne and the Lions; Sally of the Sawdust; Santa Sangre; 7 Faces of Dr Lao; Shadows and Fog; La Strada; Street Angel; 3 Ring Circus; The Unknown; When Night Is Falling; Wings of Desire; You Can't Cheat an Honest Man*

City-dweller moves to country, *Baby Boom; City Girl; City Slickers; City Slickers II: The Legend of Curly's Gold; Cowboy, Days of Heaven; Dirty Rice; First Love, Last Rites; Le Grand Chemin; Hope Floats; Jean de Florette; Kansas; Outback; Pallieter; Paradise; Pardners; A Passion; Pump Up the Volume; Ruggles of Red Gap; Seclusion Near a Forest; The Shining Hour; Shy People; Wake in Fright; Wild River*

Clairvoyance (see also **Telepathy**), *Ama; Black Rainbow; The Butcher's Wife; The Clairvoyant; The Dead Zone; The Falcon and The Coeds; Ghost; The Gift* (Evans); *The Gift* (Raimi); *Hanussen; House!; In Dreams; It Happened Tomorrow; Ivy; Jassy; Manhunter; The Night Has a Thousand Eyes; Seance; Seance on a Wet Afternoon*

Clancy, Tom,
films adapted from work, *Clear and Present Danger; The Hunt for Red October; Patriot Games*

Class
Can, *Goin' Down the Road*
Den, *Harry and the Butler; Pelle the Conqueror*
Fr, *Douce; Une Epoque formidable…; Human Resources; Life Is a Long Quiet River; Loulou; Un Monde sans pitié; Montalvo et l'enfant; Peau Neuve; La Règle du Jeu; Ridicule; Tatie Danielle*
GB, *Blind Date* (Losey); *Blonde Fist; The Captain's Table; The Card; The Chain; The Chiltern Hundreds; Cold Comfort Farm; The Common Touch; Diamond Skulls; Distant Voices, Still Lives; Don't Take It to Heart; Educating Rita; Escape; Family Life* (Loach); *Farewell Again; Film from the Clyde; Folly to Be Wise; For Them That Trespass; The Gamekeeper; Gert and Daisy's Weekend; The Go-Between; Gosford Park; The Grotesque; The Guinea Pig; The Half a Sixpence; Hireling; HMS Defiant; Howards End; If…; I'm All Right, Jack; In Which We Serve; Juvenile Liaison; Juvenile Liaison 2; Lazybones; The Loneliness of the Long Distance Runner; The Man in the White Suit; Mansfield Park; Maurice; Mrs Brown; Nothing but the Best; On Approval; The Portrait of a Lady; The Rake's Progress; Relative Values; The Remains of the Day; Room at the Top; A Room with a View; The Ruling Class; Saturday Night and Sunday Morning; The Servant; The Shooting Party; Spare Time; Telling Lies; This Above All; This Happy Breed; This Sporting Life; Upstairs and Downstairs; Up the Junction; The Way Ahead; Wedding Rehearsal; While Parents Sleep; The Woodlanders*
Ger, *Faustrecht der Freiheit; The Reckless Moment; The Sudden Fortune of the Good People of Kombach; Die Weber*
Ind, *Distant Thunder; Kama Sutra: A Tale of Love*
It, *China Is Near; Swept Away…by an Unusual Destiny in the Blue Sea of August; Uccellacci e Uccellini*
Swe, *Miss Julie;*
US, *Barcelona; A Dog of Flanders; Fresh Horses; Giant; Golden Boy; Goodbye Columbus; The Great Gatsby* (Clayton); *The Great Gatsby* (Nugent); *Inventing the Abbotts; Jersey Girl; The Mad Miss Manton; Masquerade* (Swaim); *Metropolitan; Midnight in the Garden of Good and Evil; The Portrait of a Lady; Quiz Show; Reversal of Fortune; Roger & Me; Sabrina* (Pollack); *Sabrina* (Wilder); *Salt of the Earth; Scenes from the Class Struggle in Beverly Hills; Stanley & Iris; Stella; Stella Dallas; They Live; Tovarich; Two Moon Junction; Welfare; Working Girl; You Can't Take It with You*

Clavell, James, films adapted from work, *King Rat; Shogun*

Cleaners, *The Last Crop; Nightcleaners; Romuald et Juliette; '36 to '77*

Cline, Patsy, film about, *Sweet Dreams*

Clinton, Bill,
film about, *The War Room*
film à clef, *Primary Colors*

Clock repairers, *Golden Braid; The Green Man; L'Horloger de St Paul*

Clowns (see also **Circuses**), *L'Aile ou la Cuisse; The Clowns; Delicatessen; He Who Gets Slapped; Killer Klowns from Outer Space; Quick*

Clubbing, see **Show business**

Cockfighting, *Cockfighter; Roosters; S'en fout la mort*

Cobain, Kurt, film about, *Kurt & Courtney*

Cocteau, Jean, films adapted from work, *L'Aigle à Deux Têtes; Les Enfants Terribles; L'Eternel Retour; Les Dames du Bois de Boulogne; The Oberwald Mystery; Orphée; La Testament d'Orphée; Thomas l'Imposteur*

Cody, William F, films about, *Annie Get Your Gun; Annie Oakley; Buffalo Bill and the Indians; The Plainsman; Touche pas à la femme blanche*

Coetzee, JM, film adapted from work, *Dust*

Cohan, George M, film about, *Yankee Doodle Dandy*

Cold War, in film
espionage, etc, *Avalanche Express; Black Eagle; Catch Me a Spy; Condorman; A Dandy in Aspic; Danger Route; The Deadly Affair; Diplomatic Courier; The Double Man; Enigma; Les Espions; Experts, The; The Falcon and the Snowman; Firestarter; The Fourth Protocol; From Russia with Love; Funeral in Berlin; Gorky Park; The Innocent* (MacKenzie); *Jumpin' Jack Flash; The Kremlin Letter; The Looking Glass War; The Mackintosh Man; The Man Between; The Manchurian Candidate; Mrs Pollifax – Spy; The Osterman Weekend; Our Man in Havana; The Quiller Memorandum; Rough Shoot; Russian Roulette; Russicum; Scorpio; The Serpent; S.P.Y.S.; The Spy Who Came In From the Cold; The Tamarind Seed; Telefon; Three Days of the Condor; Topaz; Top Secret; Torn Curtain; Walk East on Beacon!; The Whistle Blower*
other themes, *America – From Hitler to MX; Amazing Grace and Chuck; Atomic Café; The Bedford Incident; Before Winter Comes; Blast from the Past; Bulletproof; Carry Greenham Home; Defence of the Realm; Dr Strangelove: or, How I Learned to Stop Worrying and Love the Bomb; Fail Safe; The Hunt for Red October; Invasion USA; The Iron Giant; Judgment in Berlin; Kiss Me Deadly; Man on a Tightrope; Matinee; November Days Voices and Choices; The Plutonium Circus; Rally 'round the Flag, Boys!; Red Dawn; Red Nightmare; Rockets Galore; Satan Never Sleeps; Seven Days in May; Streets of Gold; Tribulation 99: Alien Anomalies Under America; WarGames*
post-Cold War, *Company Business; The Fourth War; The Grass Is Always Greener; The Russia House*

Coleman, Ornette, film about, *Ornette: Made in America*

Colette, films adapted from work, *Gigi* (Audry); *Gigi* (Minnelli)

Collard, Cyril, film adapted from work, *Savage Nights*

Colleges and students, in film (see also **Education and school stories** and **Oxbridge and the Ivy League**)
Arg, *Wake Up, Love*
Aust, *Love and Other Catastrophes*
Can, *Terror Train*
Fr, *Les Cousins; Le Diable, Probablement; Rendez-vous de Juillet*
GB, *American Friends; Butley; Chariots of Fire; Clockwork Mice; Educating Rita; Inbetweeners; Intimate Games; Lucky Jim; Night of the Eagle; True Blue; Up on the Roof; Wilt*
HK, *July Rhapsody*
Hun, *Time Stands Still*
Ind, *Piravi*
Jap, *April Story; Madadayo; Wizard of Darkness*
Mali, *Finyé*
Pol, *Barrier*
SKor, *Black Republic*
US, *The Allnighter; Back to School; Bowling for Columbine; College; Creator; Dazed and Confused; Dead Man's Curve; Dogs; Drive Me Crazy; Flubber; The Freshman; Good Will Hunting; Getting Straight; Happy Together; Happy We; He Got Game; Higher Learning; Horse Feathers; How to Be Very, Very Popular; Life Begins in College; Listen to Me; Loverboy; Love Story; National Lampoon's Animal House; Loser; Lucky Star; The Mirror Has Two Faces; Necessary Roughness; The Nutty Professor* (Lewis); *The Nutty Professor* (Shadyac); *Nutty Professor II: The Klumps; Oxford Blues; The Paper Chase; Return to Paradise; Revenge of the Nerds; Road Trip; The Seniors; The Skulls; Son in Law; Sorority Girl; Surviving Desire; Vamp; With Honors; Wonder Boys; You're a Big Boy Now*

Collins, Jackie, films adapted from work, *The Stud; The World Is Full of Married Men*

Collins, Larry, film adapted from work, *City of Joy*

Collins, Wilkie, films adapted from work, *Crimes at the Dark House; Twin Pawns*

Colombia
Colombia in film, *Cannibal Holocaust; Chronicle of a Death Foretold; The Devil's Accordion; Green Ice; Our Lady of the Assassins; Romancing the Stone*
Colombian cinema, *Amazonia: Voices from the Rainforest; Cannibal Holocaust; A Matter of Honour; Our Lady of the Assassins; The Strategy of the Snail; Time to Die; What Is Democracy?*

Colonialism (see also **Africa, Racism**)
in Africa, *L'Appel du Silence; The Ghost and the Darkness; La Guerre sans nom; Black and White in Color; Camp Thiaroye; Ceddo; Chocolat* (Denis); *Emitai; Flame; The Four Feathers* (Korda); *The Four Feathers* (Sharp); *The Heart of the Matter; Killers of Kilimanjaro; The Kitchen Toto; Mister Johnson; Massacre; Mountains of the Moon; Khartoum; Something of Value; Xala; Zulu; Zulu Dawn*
in India, *Burra Sahib; Brigand of Kandahar; Charulata; Conduct Unbecoming; The Drum; East of Elephant Rock; Elephant Boy; Four Men and a Prayer; Gandhi; Gunga Din; Kim; The Man Who Would Be King; North West Frontier; A Passage to India; The Rains of Ranchipur; The River* (Renoir); *Trikal: Past Present and Future*
in Indochina, *Indochine; The Lover*
in Indonesia, *Mother Dao the Turtlelike; November 1828; The Scorpion*
in Latin America, *Cobra Verde; The Mission*
in Middle East, *The Guns and the Fury*
in Pacific, *Hurricane; The Hurricane*
in Philippines, *The Real Glory*

Columbus, Christopher, films about, *Carry On Columbus; Christopher Columbus; Christopher Columbus: The Discovery; 1492: Conquest of Paradise*

Comaneci, Nadia, film about, *Nadia*

Comedians, in performance, *Big Banana Feet; 'Chubby' Down Under and Other Sticky Regions; Eddie Murphy Raw; House; The Lenny Bruce Performance Film; Lenny Bruce Without Tears; Lenny Live and Unleashed; Lilly Tomlin; Max Wall – Funny Man; The Original Kings of Comedy; Punch Me in the Stomach; Richard Pryor…Here and Now; Richard Pryor Live in Concert; Richard Pryor Live at Sunset Strip; Roy Cohn/Jack Smith; Without You I'm Nothing*

Comic strip characters, in film, *The Addams Family; Addams Family Values; The Adventures of Captain Marvel; Baba Yaga; Barbarella; Batman* (Martinson); *Batman* (Burton); *Batman Forever; Batman Returns; Batman & Robin; Beavis and Butt-head Do America; The Betty Boop Follies; Blondie; A Boy Named Charlie Brown; Buck Rogers in the 25th Century; Conan the Destroyer; Crimewave; The Crow; The Crow: City of Angels; Crying Freeman; Dennis the Menace; Dick Tracy; Doc Savage – the Man of Bronze; Flash Gordon; The Flintstones; George of the Jungle; Howard the Duck; Jake Speed; Jane and the Lost City; Judge Dredd; Lightning Swords of Death; Li'l Abner; Little Nemo Adventures in Slumberland; Nowhere Man; The Phantom; Popeye; The Rocketeer; Spider-Man* (Swackhamer); *Spider-Man* (Raimi); *Spider-Man Strikes Back; Spider-Man – the Dragon's Challenge; Supergirl; Superman III; Superman IV: The Quest for Peace; Tales from the Crypt Presents Demon Knight; Tank Girl; Tiffany Jones*

Comics, writers and artists, *Bunker Palace Hotel; Comic Book Confidential; Flaming Ears; Funny Bones; The King of Comedy; I Want to Go Home; Soft Top, Hard Shoulder*

Communists
in Australia, *Celia*
in France, *Rouge Baiser; La Vie est à nous*
in China, *Homecoming* (Ho)
in Cuba, *I Am Cuba*
in Czechoslovakia, *L'Aveu; The Ear; Happiness in Twenty Years; Larks on a String; The Unbearable Lightness of Being*
in Germany, *Mother Küster's Trip to Heaven; No Place to Go; One, Two, Three; Rosa Luxemburg*
in Greece, *Eleni*
in Estonia, *Letters from the East;*
in Hungary, *Silence and Cry; The Witness*
in Malaya, *Windom's Way*
in Poland, *And There Was Jazz, Blind Chance; A Generation; Man of Iron, Man of Marble; To Kill a Priest* in South Korea, *The Taebeck Mountains*
in US, *Fellow Traveller; I Married a Communist; Invasion USA; The Iron Curtain; Pickup on South Street; Reds; Walk East on Beacon!*
in Vietnam, *Boat People; The Deer Hunter; The Iron Triangle*

Community/collective action
in Australia, *Heatwave; The Killing of Angel Street*
in Britain, *Behind the Rent Strike; Film from the Clyde; Fly a Flag for Poplar; Year of the Beaver*
in France, *Des Enfants Gâtés; Tout va Bien; La Vie est à nous*
in Germany, *The Inheritors*
in Mexico, *El Bruto*
in US, *Matewan; The Milagro Beanfield War; Salt of the Earth; Where the Heart Is; Wisdom*
in USSR, *Strike*

Compilation films
comedy, *Ain't Misbehavin; Homme au Chapeau de Soie, L'; That's Carry On*
horror, *It Came from Hollywood; Terror in the Aisles*
musicals, *That's Dancing!; That's Entertainment!; That's Entertainment Part II; That's Entertainment! III*

Computers and computer games, effects of, *Alphaville; The Amateur; Assassins; Avalon; Blind Date* (Mastorakis);

Brainscan; Demon Seed; Desk Set; Electric Dreams; Enemy of the State; eXistenZ; The Forbin Project; Gunhed; Jumpin Jack Flash; Hackers; The 'Human' Factor (Dmytryk); *Johnny Mnemonic; Lawnmower Man 2: Beyond Cyberspace; Lara Croft: Tomb Raider; A Man, A Woman and a Bank; The Matrix; The Net; Nightmares; Paws; Pi; Pokémon – The First Movie: Mewtwo Strikes Back; Sneakers; The Steal; Superman III; The Terminal Man; THX 1138; Tron; 2001; A Space Odyssey; Swordfish; WarGames; Weird Science; Welcome to Blood City; Westworld*

Conan Doyle, Arthur, films adapted from/based on work
Sherlock Holmes stories, *The Adventure of Sherlock Holmes' Smarter Brother; The Hound of the Baskervilles* (Fisher); *The Hound of the Baskervilles* (Lanfield); *The Hound of the Baskervilles* (Morissey); *House of Fear; Murder by Decree; Pearl of Death; The Private Life of Sherlock Holmes; Pursuit to Algiers; The Scarlet Claw; The Seven-Per-Cent Solution; Sherlock Holmes and the Spider Woman; A Study in Terror; Terror by Night; They Might Be Giants; Without a Clue; Young Sherlock Holmes*
other, *The Adventures of Gerard; The Lost World* (Allen); *The Lost World* (Hoyt)

Condon, Richard, films adapted from work, *The Manchurian Candidate; Prizzi's Honor; Winter Kills*

Congo, see **Zaire/Congo**

Con-men/women, *Aile ou la Cuisse, L'; Another You; The Associate; Il Bidone; Birds and Bees; Boiling Point* (Harris); *Bullseye!; Came a Hot Friday; The Caper of the Golden Bulls; Circus Boys; Close-Up; The Con Man and the Kung Fu Kid; The Consul; The Couch Trip; Curly Sue; Deep Crimson; Dirty Rotten Scoundrels; The Distinguished Gentleman; Extasis; The Flim-Flam Man; Freelance; Funny Money; Gambit; Go; The Grifters; Heartbreakers; Heist; Un Héros très discret; The Hot Spot; House of Games; I Love You Again; The Impostors; The King and Four Queens; The Man Who Would Be King; The Miracle Woman; The Music Man; Nine Queens; Nobody Lives Forever; The Old Lady Who Walked in the Sea; Only When I Larf; Ooh…You Are Awful; Page Miss Glory; Paper Moon; Perfectly Normal; Prime Gig; Princess Caraboo; Rien ne va plus; Le Roman d'un Tricheur; Shooting Fish; Shooting Stars; Six Degrees of Separation; The Spanish Prisoner; Stavisky…; The Sting; The Sting II; Support Your Local Gunfighter; Sylvia Scarlett; Le Tartuffe; This World, Then the Fireworks; The Thomas Crown Affair* (Jewison); *The Thomas Crown Affair* (McTiernan); *Trouble in Paradise; Twin Pawns; Victory* (Cromwell); *Victory* (Peploe); *Volpone; Welcome to Woop Woop; Where the Heart Is; W.W. and the Dixie Dancekings*

Connell, Evan S, film adapted from work, *Mr and Mrs Bridge*

Connell, Richard, films adapted from work, *The Most Dangerous Game; Run for the Sun*

Conrad, Joseph, films adapted from work, *Amy Foster; Apocalypse Now; Apocalypse Now Redux; The Duellists; Lord Jim; Outcast of the Islands; Sabotage; The Secret Agent* (Hampton); *Victory* (Cromwell); *Victory* (Peploe)

Conquistadors, *Aguirre, Wrath of God; Cabeza de Vaca; El Dorado; The Royal Hunt of the Sun*

Conroy, Pat, films adapted from work, *Conrack; The Great Santini; The Lords of Discipline; The Prince of Tides*

Construction workers, *City of Hope; Mac; Riff-Raff; Steel*

Cook, David, film adapted from work, *Walter*

Cook, Robin, films adapted from work, *Coma; He Died with His Eyes Open*

Cooks, kitchens, restaurants, bakeries, etc (see also **Food**), *L'Aile ou la Cuisse; Un Air de Famille; Amélie; Autumn in New York; Babette's Feast; Baker's Bread; Big Night; La Boulangère de Monceau; Chicken and Duck Talk; The Cook, the Thief, His Wife and Her Lover; Death in Brunswick; Dinner Rush; Drifting Clouds; Ermo; Family Business* (Cohen); *Frankie & Johnny; Fried Green Tomatoes at the Whistle Stop Café; Gas Food Lodging; Good Burger; The Harvey Girls; Just the Ticket; Kitchen* (Yim Ho); *The Kitchen; The Kitchen Toto; Life Is Sweet; The Linguini Incident; Long Live the Lady; Ludwig's Cook; Mee Pok Man; Mister Cory; Mr Nice Guy; Mystic Pizza; The New Morning of Billy the Kid; Palmy Days; Perfectly Normal; Queen of Hearts; '68; Small Time Crooks; Soul Food; Sukiyaki; Tampopo; Under Siege; Waiting for the Light; Wheels on Meals; Who Is Killing the Great Chefs of Europe?; Yours and Mine*

Coppel, Alec, films adapted from work, *The Bliss of Mrs Blossom; The Gazebo; Jo; Obsession* (Dmytryk)

Coppola, Francis Ford, film about, *Hearts of Darkness: A Filmmaker's Apocalypse*

Corman, Roger
film about, *Roger Corman: Hollywood's Wild Angel*
productions, *Avalanche; Battle Beyond the Stars; Beast from Haunted Cave; Big Bad Mama; Boxcar Bertha; Cannonball; Capone; Cockfighter; Crazy Mama; Death Race 2000; Deathsport; Dementia 13; Eat My Dust; Fast Charlie, the Moonbeam Rider; Fighting Mad; Forbidden World; Galaxy of Terror; Grand Theft Auto; I Escaped from Devil's Island; I Never Promised You a Rose Garden; Jackson County Jail; The Lady in Red; Piranha; Saint Jack; Streetwalkin'; Thunder and Lightning; The Trip; Watchers; The Wild Side*
cameo appearances by, *Apollo 13; Body Bags; Cannonball; The Godfather Part II; The Howling; Philadelphia; Scream 3; Silence of the Lambs; The State of Things; Swing Shift*

Cornell, Joseph
film about, *Joseph Cornell: Worlds in a Box*

Corpses
comic, *Men at Work; Over Her Dead Body; Serial Lover; The Trouble with Harry; Waking Ned; Weekend at Bernie's*
dead dogs, *Cold Dog Soup*
embarrassing, *Avanti!; The Happiness of the Katakuris; Head Above Water; Sibling Rivalry; Very Bad Things*
other, *Curdled; Elephant Song; The Iceman Cometh; Journey to the Sun; Morvern Callar; Our Mother's House*

Costello, Mary, film adapted from work, *Titanic Town*

Cotterell, Geoffrey, film adapted from work, *Tiara Tahiti*

Country and Western music, *Coal Miner's Daughter; Doing Time for Patsy Cline; Honeysuckle Rose; Honkytonk Man; Nashville; Outlaw Blues; Payday; Songwriter; Sweet Dreams; Tender Mercies; The Thing Called Love; Wild West; W.W. and the Dixie Dancekings*

Country-dweller moving to city, *Ask Any Girl; Bitter Harvest; Butterfly; DEF by Temptation; Dust in the Wind; The Freshman; The Harder They Come; Hearts of the West; J'embrasse pas; The Jerk; Land and Sons; The Last of His Tribe; Manila in the Claws of Darkness; Midnight Cowboy; My Sister Eileen; My Sons; Next of Kin; The Out-of-Towners* (Hiller); *The Out-of-Towners* (Weisman); *The Refrigerator; Rocco and His Brothers; Safety Last; So Close to Paradise; To Sleep with Anger; Urban Cowboy; La Vie est belle; Woman's World*

Courtroom dramas (see also **Judges, Lawyers**)
Aust, *Blood Oath; Breaker Morant; A Cry in the Dark*
China, *Red Corner*
Fr, *Butterfly* (Cimber); *The Hour of the Pig; Procès de Jeanne d'Arc; Le Retour de Martin Guerre; Saint Joan; Verdict* (Cayatte)
GB, *The Blind Goddess; The Brigand of Kandahar; Carrington VC; A Fish Called Wanda; The Franchise Affair; Libel; The Trials of Oscar Wilde; Victim; Witness for the Prosecution*
Hun, *The Witness*
It, *Open Doors*
NZ, *Beyond Reasonable Doubt*
US, *The Accused; Adam's Rib; Anatomy of a Murder; The Caine Mutiny; A Civil Action; Class Action; The Court Martial of Billy Mitchell; Defending Your Life; A Dry White Season; Feedback; A Few Good Men; Final Analysis; First Monday in October; From the Hip; Fury* (Lang); *Ghosts of Mississippi; Guilty as Sin; Inherit the Wind; In the King of Prussia; Jagged Edge; Judgment at Nuremberg; Judgment in Berlin; The Juror; Juvenile Court; The Lawyer; Legal Eagles; Midnight in the Garden of Good and Evil; Music Box; My Cousin Vinny; Nuts; The Paradine Case; Presumed Innocent; Primal Fear; Roxie Hart; Rules of Engagement; The Runner Stumbles; Sergeant Rutledge; Snow Falling on Cedars; Suspect; They Drive by Night* (Walsh); *A Time to Kill; Trial and Error; Trial by Jury; True Believer; True Confession; Twelve Angry Men; The Unfaithful, The Verdict* (Lumet)
USSR, *Defence Counsel Sedov*

Coward, Noël, films adapted from work, *Bitter Sweet; Blithe Spirit; The Astonished Heart; Brief Encounter; Cavalcade; Design for Living; Easy Virtue; Relative Values; This Happy Breed; The Vortex*

Crane, Stephen, film adapted from work, *The Red Badge of Courage*

Crawford, Joan, film about, *Mommie Dearest*

Crichton, Michael, films adapted from work, *The Andromeda Strain; The Carey Treatment; Disclosure; Jurassic Park; Jurassic Park III; The Lost Word: Jurassic Park; Sphere; The Terminal Man; The 13th Warrior*

Cricket, *Playing Away*

Croatian cinema (see also **Bosnia, Serbia, Yugoslavia and former Yugoslavia**), *Chico*

Cromwell, Oliver, film about, *Cromwell*

Cronin, AJ, films adapted from work, *The Citadel* (Vidor); *Hatter's Castle; Shining Victory; The Spanish Gardener; The Stars Look Down*

Cross-dressing and transvestitism, in film, *An Actor's Revenge; The Adventures of Priscilla Queen of the Desert; The Alternative Miss World; The Ballad of Little Jo; Big Momma's House; The Birdcage; Boys Don't Cry; Bugis Street; La Cage aux Folles; La Cage aux Folles II; La Cage aux Folles III; The Crying Game; The Devil-Doll; First a Girl; Flaming Creatures; Flawless; Franchesca Page; The Fruit Machine; Glen or Glenda?; He's a Woman, She's a Man; High Heels; Hu-Du-Men; Improperly Dressed; Isabelle Eberhardt; Isle of Love; I Was a Male War Bride; Just Like a Woman; Last Exit to Brooklyn; Lola + Bilidikid; Madame Satã; Mascara; Ma Vie en Rose; Mrs Doubtfire; M. Butterfly; Monsieur Hawarden; Nuns on the Run; Outrageous; Paris Is Burning; Princesa; The Queen; The Raggedy Rawney; Some Like It Hot; Split William to Chrysis: Portrait of a Drag Queen; Red Firecracker, Green Firecracker; The Square Circle; Starlight Hotel; Summer Vacation 1999; Sylvia Scarlett; Tootsie; Torch Song Trilogy; To Wong Foo, Thanks for Everything! Julie Newmar; The Triple Echo; Victor/Victoria; White Angel; White Mischief; Wings of the Morning; The Written Face; Women in Revolt; Yentl*
children brought up as the opposite sex, *Virgin* (Karanovic)

Crouse, Russell, film adapted from work, *Life with Father*

Cruz Smith, Martin, films adapted from work, *Gorky Park; Nightwing*

Cuba, in film, *Before Night Falls; The Buena Vista Social Club; Cuba; Cuba Libre – Velocipedi ai Tropici; The Godfather Part II; Havana; Havanna Mi Amor; I Am Cuba; Improper Conduct; Life Is to Whistle; The Mambo Kings; A Night in Havana: Dizzy Gillespie in Cuba; Original Sin; Our Man in Havana; The Perez Family; The Teacher; Voyage of the Damned*
Cuban missile crisis, *Matinee; Thirteen Days; Topaz*

Cuban cinema, *Cuba Libre – Velocipedi ai Tropici; The Days of Water; Death of a Bureaucrat; Guantanamera; Hello, Hemingway; The Last Supper; Life Is to Whistle; Lucia; Memories of Underdevelopment; One Way or Another; Plaff! or Too Afraid of Life; Portrait of Teresa; Sometimes I Look at My Life; Strawberry and Chocolate; The Teacher*

Cults,
apocalyptic and terrorist, *A; Distance; Guyana: Crime of the Century; Mike Yokohama – A Forest with No Name*
Hubbard, L Ron, film adapted from work, *Battlefield Earth*
standard, *Holy Smoke; The Mystic Masseur; Not Forgotten*

Custer, General GA, in film, *Bugles in the Afternoon; Custer of the West; Little Big Man; Santa Fe Trail; 7th Cavalry; They Died with Their Boots On; Touche pas à la femme blanche*

Cycling, *American Flyers; Breaking Away; BMX Bandits; The Fast Lady; A Sunday in Hell; Tom Simpson: Something to Aim At*

Cyprus
Cypriot cinema, *The Cherry Orchard; Our Wall*
Cyprus in film, *Attila '74; The High Bright Sun; Our Wall; Tomorrow's Warrior*

Czechoslovakia and Czech Republic (see also **Slovakian cinema**)
Czechoslovakia and Czech Republic in film, *A Case for a Young Hangman; Cosy Dens; Dita Saxová; Erotikon; Extase; The Fifth Rider Is Fear; From Saturday to Sunday; The Golem; Happiness in Twenty Years; Hot Enough for June; Indian Summer; In the Rye; Gifted City; Kafka; Labyrinth* (Jires); *Late Night Talks with Mother; Man on a Tightrope; Martyrs of Love; The Melancholic Chicken; Prague; Pravda; The Shooter; A Shop on the High Street; The Trial* (Welles); *The Trial* (Jones); *The Unbearable Lightness of Being; The Way Through the Bleak Woods*
Czechoslovakian and Czech cinema, *Accumulator 1; The Adventures of Pinocchio; All My Good Countrymen; The Barber of Siberia; Baron Munchhausen; The Best Age; Buttoners; Capricious Summer; A Case for a Young Hangman; Closed for Family Mourning; Closely Observed Trains; Conspirators of Pleasure; Cosy Dens; The Cremator; Cutting It Short; Daisies; Dark Blue World; Dead Forest; The Deserter and the Nomads; Dita Saxová; Divided We Fall; The Divine Emma; The Ear; Eeny Meeny; Erotikon; Extase; Faust* (Svankmajer); *The Fifth Rider Is Fear; The Firemen's Ball; From Hell; From Saturday to Sunday; Gifted City; I Love, You Love; I'm Jumping Over Puddles Again; Indian Summer; In the Rye; Joseph Kilián; Just a Little Whistle; King Ubu; Kolya; Labyrinth* (Jires); *Larks on a String; Lásky Jedné Plavovlásky (A Blonde in Love); Late Night Talks with Mother; The Life and Extraordinary Adventures of Private Ivan Chonkin; Loners; Mandragora; Marian; Markéta Lazarová; Martyrs of Love; The Melancholic Chicken; Morgiana; My Sweet Little Village; Nick Carter in Prague; Otesánek; Parallel Worlds; The Party and the Guests; Pearls of the Deep; Peter and Pavla; The Pied Piper* (Krysar); *Return of the Idiot; The Ride; Seclusion Near a Forest; A Shop on the High Street; Those Wonderful Movie Cranks; The Tutor in Fear; Valerie and Her Week of Wonders; The Way Through the Bleak Woods*

Dadaism, *Dreams That Money Can Buy; Europe After the Rain; John Heartfield, Photomonteur*

Dahl, Roald, films adapted from work, *Danny the Champion of the World; James and the Giant Peach; Roald Dahl's Matilda; The Witches*

Dailey, Robert, film adapted from work, *Night Falls on Manhattan*

Daisne, John, film adapted from work, *The Man Who Had His Hair Cut Short*

Dana, Richard Henry, film adapted from work, *Two Years Before the Mast*

Dance and Dancers
ballet, *Alive and Kicking; Billy Elliot; Carnival; The Children of Theatre Street; Dance Little Lady; Dancers; Don Quixote; The Dying Swan; Honeymoon; I Am a Dancer; Lives of Performers; The Mad Genius; Nijinsky; Nutcracker; The Nutcracker; Nutcracker – the Motion Picture; Pavlova – A Woman for All Time; The Red Shoes; Slow Dancing in the Big City; Specter of the Rose; Suspiria; Tales of Beatrix Potter; The Turning Point; White Nights* (Hackford)
Chinese ballet, *Red Detachment of Women* (Collective)
ballroom, *Dance With Me; Strictly Ballroom*
other, *Anita: Dances of Vice; Dollar Mambo; Bal, Le; Blood Wedding; Body Rock; Bolero; Breakin'; Bootmen; Broadway; Can't Stop the Music; Carmen* (Saura); *Center Stage; A Cha-Cha for the Fugitive; A Chorus Line; The Courtesans of Bombay; The Cyclone; Dance, Girl, Dance; Dance Hall; Dancing Bull; Danzón; Dirty Dancing; Down to Earth; Driving Me Crazy; Fame; Fast Forward; Flamenco; Flashdance; Girls Just Want to Have Fun; Good to Go; Groove; Gypsy Soul; Human Traffic; Isadora; Lambada; Lord of the Dance; A Love Bewitched; The Music Machine; No Maps for My Taps; Rooftops; Roseland; Rumba; Salsa; Saturday Night Fever; Sevillanas; Shall We Dance?; Staying Alive; Sweet Charity; Tango* (Saura); *The Tango Lesson; Tap; Tapdancin'; Thank God It's Friday; They Shoot Horses Don't They?; To the Heart; Travelling Light: a Portrait of Lindsay Kemp; Wild Style*

Danish cinema, see **Denmark**

D'Annunzio, Gabriele, film adapted from work, *The Innocent* (Visconti)

Dante Alighieri, film adapted from/inspired by work, *A TV Dante: Cantos I–VIII*

Darwin, Charles, and Darwinism, *Angels and Insects; The Darwin Adventure; Inherit the Wind*

Day, Dorothy, film about, *Entertaining Angels: The Dorothy Day Story*

Deafness, *Alpine Fire; Beyond Silence; Captain Johnno; Children of a Lesser God; Goya in Bordeaux; Hear No Evil; The Heart Is a Lonely Hunter; In the Company of Men; Junk Mail; Land of Silence and Darkness; Mandy; The Miracle Worker; Psych-Out; A Scene at the Sea; See No Evil, Hear No Evil; Suspect*

Dean, James, films about, *The James Dean Story; James Dean – the First American Teenager*

Death (see also **Bereavement, Corpses** and **Few-months-to-live stories**), *Always* (Spielberg); *The Asphyx; Because of That War; Bye Bye Braverman; Carnival of Souls; The Comedy of Terrors; The Cremator; Death in the Seine; Destiny; Flatliners; La Fracture du myocarde; Frozen; Gates of Heaven; Grace Quigley;*

Guantanamera; Ikiru; July Rhapsody; The Loved One; Maborosi; The Mouth Agape; My Girl; My Girl 2; Nela; Night Shift; Ososhiki; Ponette; Pearls of the Deep; Post Mortem; Ratcatcher; Savage Man…Savage Beast; Short Time; Sibling Rivalry; Terms of Endearment; These Foolish Things; The Trouble with Harry; Weekend at Bernie's; What Dreams May Come
faked/technical, *Frozen; Kill Me Again; Mission Impossible; Nikita; No Man of Her Own* (Leisen); *Point of No Return;*

de Beauvoir, Simone, films adapted from work, *All Men Are Mortal; The Blood of Others*

Defoe, Daniel, films adapted from work, *Crusoe; Man Friday; Moll Flanders; Robinson Crusoe; Robinson Crusoe on Mars*

Deformity and disfigurement (see also **Mutation**), *The Abominable Dr Phibes; The Affair; Basket Case; Basket Case 2; La Chambre des officiers; Circle of Horrors; Darkman; Dr Phibes Rises Again; The Elephant Man; The Enchanted Cottage; The Face Behind a Mask; Freaked; Freaks; House of Wax; How to Get Ahead in Advertising; The Hunchback of Notre Dame* (Worsley); *The Hunchback of Notre Dame* (Dieterle); *The Hunchback of Notre Dame* (Delannoy); *Johnny Got His Gun; Johnny Handsome; Mansion of the Doomed; The Man Without a Face; Mask; The Phantom Lover; The Phantom of the Opera* (Julian); *Phantom of the Opera* (Little); *Phantom of the Opera* (Lubin); *The Phantom of the Opera* (Fisher); *The Phantom of the Paradise; The Raven* (Friedlander); *The Severed Arm; A Woman's Face; Les Yeux sans Visage*

Deighton, Len, films adapted from work, *Billion Dollar Brain; Funeral in Berlin; The Ipcress File; Only When I Larf; Spy Story*

Delaney, Shelagh, film adapted from work, *A Taste of Honey*

Delinquents, juvenile, see **Street gangs and juvenile delinquents**

Delivery boys, *Bed of Roses; Loverboy*

Demy, Jacques, films about, *Jacquot de Nantes; L'Univers de Jacques Demy*

Denmark
Danish cinema, *The Abyss; Agnus Dei; American Pictures: A Personal Journey Through Black America; Babette's Feast; The Beast Within; Bleeder; Breaking the Waves; Buster's World; Carl Th. Dreyer: My Work; The Celebration; Dancer in the Dark; Day of Wrath; The Daughter of the Puma; Devil's Island* (Fridriksson); *The Element of Crime; Europa; The Exhibited; Gertrud; The Greatest Heroes; Hard Rain; Harry and the Butler; H.C. Andersen's The Long Shadow; Help! I'm a Fish; The House of Spirits; The Idiots; Ikingut; Italian for Beginners; Junk Mail; Katinka; The Kingdom; The Kingdom II; The King Is Alive; Kira's Reason – A Love Story; Ladies on the Rockspas; Last of the High Kings; The Legend of Teddy Edwards; Love Lessons; Lucky People Center International; Me and Charly; Mifune; Miracle; Nightwatch* (Bornedal, 1994); *Once There Was a War; 101 Reykjavik; One of Those Things; Ordet; Ossos; Paw; Pelle the Conqueror; People of the North Sea; A Place Nearby; The President; Pusher; Show Me Love; Smilla's Feeling for Snow; Söndags Barn; A Sunday in Hell; Take It Like a Man, Ma'am; Together; Trafico; Truly Human; The Vicar of Vejlby*
Denmark in film, *The Abyss; Agnus Dei; Babette's Feast; The Beast Within; Buster's WorldThe Celebration; Day of Wrath; Gertrud; Hamlet* (Plumb); *Hamlet* (Kozintsev), *Hamlet* (Richardson); *Hamlet* (Zeffirelli); *Hamlet* (Branagh); *The Idiots; Italian for Beginners; Katinka; The Kingdom; The Kingdom II; Ladies on the Rocks; Last of the High Kings; Me and Charly; Nightwatch* (Bornedal, 1994); *Once There Was a War; One of Those Things; Ordet; Paw; Pelle the Conqueror; People of the North Sea; The President; Prince of Jutland; Pusher; Smilla's Feeling for Snow; Take It Like a Man, Ma'am; Truly Human*

Dennis, Patrick, film adapted from work, *Auntie Mame*

Depression era, in film
Aust, *Caddie; Careful, He Might Hear You*
Can, *Why Shoot the Teacher*
GB, *The Innocent* (MacKenzie); *Liam; Love on the Dole; My Childhood*
Ger, *Little Man, What Now?*
Jap, *Tokyo Chorus*
US, *American Madness; Baby Face Nelson; Billy Bathgate; Black Fury; Bloody Mama; Bonnie and Clyde; Bound for Glory; Brother, Can You Spare A Dime; Each Dawn I Die; Dillinger* (Nosseck); *Dillinger* (Milius); *Elmer Gantry; Emperor of the North Pole; From This Day Forward; Gabriel Over the White House; The Grapes of Wrath; The Grissom Gang; Hard Times* (Hill); *Hard to Handle; Ironweed; Journey of Natty Gann; Hallelujah, I'm a Bum; Honkytonk Man; King of the Hill; The Legend of Bagger Vance; Manhattan Melodrama; Man's Castle; The Mayor of Hell; Miller's Crossing; The Night of the Hunter; O Brother, Where Art Thou?; Of Mice and Men* (Milestone); *Of Mice and Men* (Sinise); *Only Yesterday; Paper Moon; Pennies from Heaven; Places in the Heart; The Plow That Broke the Plains; The Rise and Fall of Legs Diamond; The Roaring Twenties; Song of the Road; Sounder; Splendor in the Grass; They Shoot Horses, Don't They?; Thieves Like Us; Union Maids; Where the Red Fern Grows; Wild River; Winter People; Young Dillinger; You Were Meant for Me*

Desai, Anita, film adapted from work, *In Custody*

De Salvo, Albert, film about, *The Boston Strangler*

Desert dramas, *American Perfekt; L'Appel du Silence; Ashanti; Bagdad Café; Bengazi; Bitter Victory; The Black Tent; La Captive du Désert; Crook's Tour; Dance of Dust; Desert Victory; Destination Gobi; The Diamond Mercenaries; Dudes; Encounter at Raven's Gate; The English Patient; Escape from Zahrein; A Far Off Place; Five Graves to Cairo; The Flight of the Phoenix; Garden of Allah; Le Grand jeu; The Guns and the Fury; Ice Cold in Alex; Inferno; Kill Me Again; Lawrence of Arabia; Legend of the Lost; Lion of the Desert; The Lost Patrol; Motel; Road to Morocco; Sahara* (McLaglen); *Sahara* (Korda); *Saladin; The Salute of the Jugger; The Sheltering Sky; Station Six – Sahara; Sundown; Three Kings; Tremors; Tunisian Victory; Wake in Fright; Walkabout; Water, Wind, Dust; Welcome to Woop Woop; Where the Green Ants Dream; The Wind and the Lion; Yellow Sky*

Deserters, from war/military, *Chicago Joe and the Showgirl; The Deserter and the Nomads; King & Country; Le Quai des Brumes; The Triple Echo; The Valley*

Desert islands, *The Admirable Crichton; The Blue Lagoon* (Launder); *The Blue Lagoon* (Kleiser); *Cast Away; Castaway; Crusoe; Dinosaurus!; Father Goose; Hell in the Pacific; The Little Hut; Lord of the Flies* (Brook); *Lord of the Flies* (Hook); *The Mad Doctor of Market Street; Our Girl Friday; Return to the Blue Lagoon; Robinson Crusoe; Saga of Anatahan; Seawife; She Demons; She Gods of Shark Reef; Six Days Seven Nights; Sweet Hunters; Swept Away…by an Unusual Destiny in the Blue Sea of August; Treasure Island* (Heston); *Treasure Island* (Fridman); *War*

Desserts, as extra-terrestial invader, *The Stuff*

Devi, Phoolan, film about, *Bandit Queen*

Devil, The, and Antichrist (see also **Magic and magicians** and **Witchcraft, etc**), *Bedazzled* (Done); *Bedazzled* (Ramis); *The Book of Life; Damien – Omen II; The Final Conflict; The Devil Rides Out; Damn Yankees; The Day of the Beast; The Devil and Max Devlin; End of Days; The First Power; The Gate; God's Army; The Guardian; Holocaust 2000; The Keep; Legend; Lost Souls; The Master and Margarita; Mister Frost; Monster of Terror; The Ninth Gate; The Omen; Omen IV: The Awakening; Prince of Darkness; Satan's Skin; The Sect; The Sentinel; The Seventh Victim; Shadow of the Hawk; Les Visiteurs du Soir; The Witches of Eastwick*

De Vries, Peter, film adapted from work, *Reuben, Reuben*

Diamond, Legs, film about, *The Rise and Fall of Legs Diamond*

Dick, Philip K, films adapted from work, *Blade Runner; Blade Runner – The Director's Cut; Screamers; Total Recall*

Dickens, Charles, films adapted from/based on work, *Charles Dickens' David Copperfield; A Christmas Carol; Christmas Carol – The Movie; David Copperfield; Great Expectations* (Lean); *Great Expectations* (Hardy); *Great Expectations* (Cuarón); *Hard Times* (Botelho); *Little Dorrit; Mister Quilp; The Muppet Christmas Carol; The Mystery of Edwin Drood; Nicholas Nickleby; The Old Curiosity Shop; Oliver!; Oliver & Company; Oliver Twist* (Lean); *Oliver Twist* (Donner); *Scrooge* (Neame); *Scrooge* (Hurst); *Scrooged*

Diderot, Denis,
film about, *Le Libertin*
films adapted from work, *Les Dames du Bois de Boulogne; La Religieuse*

Dietrich, Marlene, films about, *Marlene* (Schell); *Marlene* (Vilsmaier)

Dighton, John, film adapted from work, *The Happiest Days of Your Life*

Dillinger, John, films about, *Baby Face Nelson; Dillinger* (Nosseck); *Dillinger* (Milius); *Young Dillinger*

DiMaggio, Joe, film about, *Insignificance*

Dinesen, Isak, films adapted from work, *The Immortal Story; Out of Africa*

Dinosaurs, *Barney's Great Adventure; Creatures the World Forgot; Dinosaurus!; The Flintstones; Jurassic Park; Jurassic Park III; The Land Before Time; The Lost World* (Allen); *The Lost World* (Hoyt); *The Lost Word: Jurassic Park; One Million Years B.C.; Super Mario Bros.; When Dinosaurs Ruled the Earth*

Dirty Harry series, *The Dead Pool; Dirty Harry; The Enforcer* (Fargo); *Magnum Force; Sudden Impact*

Disability, physical, *An Affair to Remember; The Arp Statue; L'Astragale; The Best Years of Our Lives; Beware of Pity; The Big Parade* (Vidor); *Bitter Moon; Born on the Fourth of July; Coming Home; Crazy; Dance Me to My Song; The First Legion; Gaby – A True Story; Gips; Grazie Zia; Hindered; The Hunchback of Notre Dame* (Worsley); *The Hunchback of Notre Dame* (Dieterle); *The Hunchback of Notre Dame* (Delannoy); *The Idiots; Inside Moves; Johnny Got His Gun; Just the Way You Are; Kings Row; The Light Ahead; Listen to Me; Lucky Break; Lucky Star; Mac and Me; The Mad Genius; The Men; Men of Honor; The Mighty; Monkey Shines; Mute Witness; My Left Foot; The Other Side of the Mountain; Outside In; Passages; Passion Fish; The Raging Moon; Regarding Henry; See No Evil, Hear No Evil; Simon Birch; The Spiral Staircase* (Siodmak); *The Spiral Staircase* (Collinson); *Tell Me That You Love Me, Junie Moon; The Terry Fox Story; Uneasy Riders; The Unknown; The Walking Stick; The Waterdance; What Ever Happened to Baby Jane?; Whose Life Is It Anyway?; Wings of Eagles; Woman of Straw*

Disappearances see **Family members mislaid**

Disaster movies, *Airport; Airport 1975; Airport '77; Airport '80; Avalanche; City on Fire; Deep Rising; Dante's Peak; Daylight; Down; Drive-In; Earthquake; Fire; Godzilla; Gray Lady Down; Hard Rain; The Hindenburg; In Old Chicago; Juggernaut; Krakatoa – East of Java; The Last Voyage; S.O.S. Titanic; Titanic* (Cameron); *Survive!; The Towering Inferno; Volcano; Whiteout*

Disch, Thomas M, film from work, *The Brave Little Toaster*

Disease, see **Illness**

Disney Studios, films produced by
animated, *Aladdin; Aristocats; Bambi; Basil, the Great Mouse Detective; Beauty and the Beast; The Black Cauldron; A Bug's Life; Cheetah; Cinderella; Doug's 1st Movie; Dumbo; The Emperor's New Groove; Fantasia; Fantasia/2000; The Fox and the Hound; A Goofy Movie; Hercules; The Hunchback of Notre Dame* (Trousdale/Wise); *The Jungle Book* (Reitherman); *Lady and the Tramp; The Lion King; The Little Mermaid; Lord of the Rings; Oliver & Company; One Hundred and One Dalmatians* (Reitherman/Luske/Geronimi); *Peter Pan; Pete's Dragon; Pinocchio; Pocahontas; Recess: School's Out; The Rescuers; The Rescuers Down Under; Return to Never Land; Robin Hood* (Reitherman); *Sleeping Beauty; Snow White and the Seven Dwarfs; Song of the South; The Sword in the Stone; Tarzan; The Tigger Movie*
other, *The Apple Dumpling Gang; Baby – Secret of the Lost Legend; Bedknobs and Broomsticks; The Best of Walt Disney's True Life Adventures; Blackbeard's Ghost; Blank Check; The Boy Who Could Fly; Candleshoe; The Cat from Outer Space; Condorman; The Devil and Max Devlin; Disney's The Kid; Dr Syn, Alias the Scarecrow; Escape from the Dark; Escape to Witch Mountain; Freaky Friday; Herbie Goes Bananas; Herbie Goes to Monte Carlo; Herbie Rides Again; Homeward Bound: The Incredible Journey; Inspector Gadget; The Journey of Natty Gann; The Jungle Book* (Sommers); *Jungle 2 Jungle; The Last Flight of Noah's Ark; The London Connection; The Love Bug; Man of the House; Mary Poppins; My Favourite Martian; Napoleon and Samantha; Never Cry Wolf; Newsies; Night Crossing; No Deposit, No Return; The North Avenue Irregulars; One of Our Dinosaurs Is Missing; Popeye; Remember the Titans; Return from Witch Mountain; Return of the Big Cat; Ride a Wild Pony; Superdad; The Shaggy D.A.; Something Wicked This Way Comes; That Darn Cat; A Tiger Walks; Treasure of Matecumbe; Trenchcoat; 20000 Leagues Under the Sea; Summer Magic; The Unidentified Flying Oddball; The Watcher in the Woods; White Fang* (Kleiser)

Divorce, see **Marital breakdown and divorce**

Döblin, Alfred, film adapted from work, *Berlin Alexanderplatz*

Doctorow, EL, films adapted from work, *Billy Bathgate; Daniel; Ragtime; Welcome to Hard Times*

Doctors and medicine (see also **Few-months-to-live stories, Hospital dramas, Illness, Mad scientists, Mental illness**), *Arachnophobia; Awakenings; Beautiful Dreamers; Beyond Bedlam; Beyond Rangoon; Boxing Helena; Century; The Citadel* (Vidor); *City of Joy; Coma; Crimes and Misdemeanors; Crisis; Dead Ringers; Dekalog 2: 'Thou shalt not take the name of the Lord thy God in vain'; Dentist in the Chair; Doc Hollywood; The Doctor; Dr Ehrlich's Magic Bullet; Dr Rhythm; Doctor Zhivago; Exquisite Tenderness; Flatliners; Foreign Body; Green Light; Junior; Kippur; The Knowledge of Healing; Korczak; The Madness of King George; La Maladie de Sachs; The Man Who Lived Twice; Mektoub; Men of Two Worlds; The Miniskirted Dynamo; Mr Zhao; Not as a Stranger; Novocaine; The Nun's Story; Paper Mask; Pasteur; Parts: the Clonus Horror; People Will Talk; Playing God; Red Beard; Restoration; The Road to Wellville; Saadia; State Secret; Strapless; The Sunchaser; Test Tube Babies; To the Last Drop; Traitement de Choc; Whiffs; Windom's Way; You, Me, Jerusalem; Young Doctors in Love*
medical negligence, *Malpractice; They Call That an Accident*
medical schools, *Doctor in the House; Gross Anatomy*

Docu-dramas, *Ah Ying; Bari-Zogon; The Cold Light of Day; Come Back Africa; The Courtesans of Bombay; Culloden; A Cry in the Dark; Graveyard of Dreams; The House on Garibaldi Street; The House on 92nd Street; JFK; Judgment in Berlin; Konfrontation – Assassination in Davos; Mortgage; Painted Boats; The Power of Men Is the Patience of Women; Prejudice; Prostitute; Reversal of Fortune; Rogue Trader; Ruby; San Demetrio, Sons; Too Young to Die; London; Scum; Silkwood; Whore*

Dolls, malevolent, *Bride of Chucky; Child's Play* (Holland); *Child's Play 2*

Dominican Republic, in film, *Order to Kill*

Donofrio, Beverly, film adapted from work, *Riding in Cars with Boys*

Doomsday movies (see also **Nuclear weapons**), *Armageddon; Crack in the World; The Day the Earth Caught Fire; Deep Impact; Dr Strangelove: or, How I Learned to Stop Worrying and Love the Bomb; End of Days; The Fifth Element; Five; Independence Day; Last Night; Meteor; Millennium; Night of the Comet; The Omega Man; Purple Storm; When Worlds Collide*

Dorfman, Ariel, film adapted from work, *Death and the Maiden*

Dostoevsky, Fyodor, films adapted from work, *The Brothers Karamazov* (Brooks); *The Brothers Karamazov* (Pyriev); *Crime and Punishment* (von Sternberg); *Crime and Punishment* (Kaurismäki); *Four Nights of a Dreamer; The Gambler* (Reisz); *The Gambler* (Makk); *The Great Sinner; The Idiot; Une Femme Douce; Raskolnikow; Sin Compasión; White Nights* (Visconti)
inspired by work, *Return of the Idiot*

Double lives (see also **Impersonation, Multiple personalities**) *The Amazing Doctor Clitterhouse; Back Street* (Stahl); *Back Street* (Stevenson); *The Bigamist; Body Parts; The Captain's Paradise; Confessions of a Bigamist; Deceived; Dr Jekyll and Mr Hyde* (Robertson); *Dr Jekyll and Mr Hyde* (Mamoulian); *Dr Jekyll and Mr Hyde* (Fleming); *Dr Jekyll and Ms Hyde; Dr Jekyll et Les Femmes; Dr Jekyll and Sister Hyde; Edge of Sanity; Europa, Europa; Femme Fatale; Fingers; Foolish Wives; Grip of the Strangler; I Monster; Lilies; The Man Who Lived Twice; Me Myself I; Micki + Maude; Mother Night; Outrageous Fortune; The Secret Life of an American Wife; Separate Lives; Sliding Doors; Le Testament du Docteur Cordelier; That Night in Rio; The Two Faces of Dr Jekyll*

Doubles/doppelgängers (see also **Impersonation**), *L'Affaire du Courrier de Lyon; The Avengers; The Big Mouth; Bill & Ted's Bogus Journey; Bullseye!; The Dark Half; Doppelganger: The Evil Within; La Double Vie de Véronique; Eve of Destruction; Grosse Fatigue; How to Get Ahead in Advertising; I Was Monty's Double; Kagemusha; Love Letter; Luna e l'Altra; The Man in the Iron Mask* (Whale); *The Man in the Iron Mask* (Wallace); *Mr Klein; Nouvelle Vague; The Nutty Professor* (Lewis); *The Nutty Professor* (Shadyac); *Nutty Professor II: The Klumps; The Prince and the Pauper; The Prisoner of Zenda*

(Cromwell); *The Prisoner of Zenda* (Thorpe); *The Prisoner of Zenda* (Quine); *Shattered Image; Schizopolis; Two Much; The Whole Town's Talking*

Douglas, Lloyd C, films adapted from work, *Green Light; Magnificent Obsession; The Robe*

Doyle, Roddy, films adapted from work, *The Commitments; The Snapper; The Van*

Dreams, power of, *Akira Kurosawa's Dreams; As in Heaven; Les Belles de nuit; Dream Demon; Dream Lover* (Pakula); *Dreamscape; Dreams That Money Can Buy; Freddy's Dead: The Final Nightmare; Jack's Wife; Little Nemo Adventures in Slumberland; Martyrs of Love; A Nightmare on Elm Street; A Nightmare on Elm Street Part 2: Freddy's Revenge; A Nightmare on Elm Street, 3: Dream Warriors; A Nightmare on Elm Street, 4: The Dream Master; A Nightmare on Elm Street, 5: The Dream Child; Nostradamus; La Nuit fantastique; Nutcracker – The Motion Picture; Paperhouse; Peter Ibbetson; Red Beads; Schatten; Shocker; Venus Peter; Wes Craven's New Nightmare; The Woman Who Dreamed*

Dreiser, Theodore, films adapted from work, *An American Tragedy; Carrie* (Wyler); *A Place in the Sun*

Dreyer, Carl Theodor film about, *Carl Th. Dreyer: My Work.*

Dreyfus, Alfred, films about, *I Accuse!; The Life of Emile Zola*

Drivers, learner, *Car Trouble; Confessions of a Driving Instructor; License to Drive; Le Permis de Conduire*

Dropping out, *Alexandre; All Night Long; Bronco Billy; Horizon; Kids; In the Belly of the Dragon; Lost in America; The Rain People; Reefer and the Model; La Tête Contre les Murs; The True Nature of Bernadette; La Vie à l'Envers; A Walk in the Spring Rain*

Drugs
extra-terrestrial responsibility for, *Dark Angel*
fight against, *Best Revenge; Blow; Brokedown Palace; Cairo Road; The Camels Are Coming; The Crackdown; Death Wish 4; Deep Cover; Fatal Beauty; Firebirds; A Force of One; Foxy Brown; French Connection; French Connection II; Gang Related; Gordon's War; Grass* (Mann); *Heaven; High Risk; Impulse* (Baker); *In Too Deep; K-9; The Last of the Finest; Lethal Weapon; Lethal Weapon 2; L.627; Lucky Luciano; The Marseilles Contract; New Jack City; One False Move; Only the Strong; The Organization; Predator 2; Prince of the City; Proof of Life; Puppet on a Chain; Return of the Dragon; Running Scared* (Hyams); *Shakedown; Sicilian Cross; Stoner; The Super Cops; The Supergrass; Tchao Pantin; Tequila Sunrise; Toy Soldiers; Traffic* (Soderbergh); *When the Sky Fall; Who'll Stop the Rain?; The Winchester Conspiracy*
use, *The Acid House; The Addiction; Altered States; Animal Factory; Bad Boys* (Rosenthal); *Bad Boys* (Bay); *Bad Lieutenant; The Basketball Diaries; The Blackout; Blow; Boogie Nights; Betty's Brood; Bird; Blood and Concrete; Blue Sunshine; The Boost; Boyz N the Hood; Brain Damage; Bridget; Bright Lights; Big City; Cheech and Chong's Next Movie; Christiane F.; Ciao Manhattan; Cisco Pike; City of God; City of Lost Souls; Clockers; Clean and Sober; Cocaine; The Cocaine Fiends; The Connection; The Courier; Crack in the Mirror; Dark Habits; Dealer; Drugstore Cowboy; Easy Rider; Essex Boys; The Falcon and the Snowman; Fast Talking; Fast, Fast; The 51st State; Friday; Gravesend; Greenkeeping; Gridlock'd; Groove; Groove on a Stanley Knife; Harley Davidson and the Marlboro Man; Head On; Hidden Witnesses; Human Traffic; Jackie Brown; Jacob's Ladder; Jesus' Son; Joe Albany…A Jazz Life; Kids in the Hall: Brain Candy; Killer Nun; Lady Sings the Blues; Let's Get Lost; The Life of Stuff; Light Sleeper; Liquid Dreams; Liquid Sky; Lock, Stock and Two Smoking Barrels; Mad Dogs and Englishmen; The Man with the Golden Arm; Marked for Death; Un Monde sans pitié; The Mystery of the Leaping Fish; Naked Lunch; Nico Icon; Nil by Mouth; N'oublie pas que tu vas mourir; Once Upon a Time…This Morning; Our Lady of the Assassins; Panic in Needle Park; The People Next Door; Playing God; Postcards from the Edge; Pusher; Quitting; Reefer Return to Paradise; Madness; Rush; Saving Grace; Shooting Stars; Silent Scream; Slam; Superfly; Slow Dancing in the Big City; South West Nine; Strangers; Sugar Hill; Throwing Down; Thursday; Tiger Warsaw; Torchlight; Traffic* (Soderbergh); *Trainspotting; Trash; Twin Town; Underground* (Spurrier); *Up in Smoke; The Vortex; Wait Until Dark; Where the Buffalo Roam; Wild in the Streets; Wired*

Drummond de Andrade, Carlos, film about, *O Amor Natural*

Dubbing, comic, *What's Up, Tiger Lily?*

Dubois, René-Jean, film adapted from work, *Being at Home with Claude*

Duff, James, film adapted from work, *War at Home, The*

Dukovski, Dejan, film adapted from work, *Cabaret Balkan*

Dumas, Alexandre (fils), films adapted from work, *Camille* (Cukor); *Camille* (Smallwood); *La Dame aux Camélias; La Traviata*

Dumas, Alexandre (père), films adapted from work, *The Count of Monte Cristo; The Four Musketeers: The Revenge of Milady; The Iron Mask; The Man in the Iron Mask* (Whale); *The Man in the Iron Mask* (Wallace); *The Return of the Musketeers; The Three Musketeers: The Queen's Diamonds* (Lester); *The Three Musketeers* (Herek)

du Maurier, Daphne, films adapted from work, *The Birds; Don't Look Now; Frenchman's Creek; Hungry Hill; Jamaica Inn; My Cousin Rachel; Rebecca*

Dumbness and mutism, *The Big Silence; Jobman; Three Fugitives; Lightning Jack; Mute Witness; The Piano; The Quiet Room*

Duncan, Isadora, film about, *Isadora*

Dunn, Nell, films adapted from work, *Steaming; Up the Junction*

Dunne, John Gregory, film adapted from work, *True Confession*

du Pré, Jacqueline, film about, *Hilary and Jackie*

Duras, Marguerite, films adapted from work, *The Lover; The Sailor from Gibraltar; 10:30 P.M. Summer*

Durrell, Lawrence, film adapted from work, *Justine*

Dürrenmatt, Friedrich, films adapted from work, *Hyenas; The Pledge*

Dwarfs, people of restricted growth, etc, *Even Dwarfs Started Small; Frankie Starlight; A Gnome Named Gnorm; Horror Hospital; Little People; Simon Birch; Time Bandits; The Tin Drum; We Don't Talk About It; The Woman for Joe*

Dylan, Bob, in performance, *Don't Look Back; Renaldo and Clara*

Dyslexia, *La Cérémonie* (Chabrol); *A Judgement in Stone* (Rawi)

Earthquakes, *Earthquake; San Francisco; The Sisters; Superman; Tremors; When Time Ran Out…*

Easter Island, in film, *Rapa Nui*

Eco, Umberto, film adapted from work, *The Name of the Rose*

Ecology (see also **Nature**)
cases for, *Akira Kurosawa's Dreams; All the Little Animals: Amazonia: Voices from the Rainforest; L'Arbre, le Maire et la Médiathèque, ou Les Sept Hasards; At Play in the Fields of the Lord; La Belle Verte; Danny the Champion of The World; Day of the Dolphin; Dr M; Doomwatch; The Electric Horseman; The Emerald Forest; Farewell; FernGully: The Last Rainforest; Fire Festival; The Golden Seal; Grey Owl; Hathi; Koyaanisqatsi; Meet the Applegates; Minamata; Montagna del Dio Cannibale; Once Upon a Forest; Powaqqatsi; Prometheus; A River Runs Through It; Savage Capitalism; Tadpole and the Whale; Tieta of Agreste; When the North Wind Blows; Where the Heart Is; Wild River; Wind Across the Everglades; The Writing in the Sand*
thrillers, *Charisma; The China Syndrome; A Civil Action; Due to an Act of God; Endangered Species; Erin Brokovich; Species II; On Deadly Ground*
horrors, *Bug; Day of the Animals; Frogs; Godzilla; Godzilla 1985; Godzilla vs the Smog Monster; Highlander II; The Quickening; Humanoids from the Deep; Impulse* (Baker); *The Mutant; Prophecy; Son of Godzilla; Split Second; Ticks; The Toxic Avenger; The Toxic Avenger Part II*

Ecuador
Ecuadorean cinema, *Rodents; Sensations*
Ecuador in film, *Amigomio; Rodents; Sensations*

Edison, Thomas A, film about, *Edison the Man*

Education and school stories (see also **Colleges and students**)
Aust, *The Devil's Playground; Fighting Back; The Getting of Wisdom*
Bel, *The Music Teacher*
Can, *Class of 1984; Hog Wild; The Hounds of Notre Dame; Why Shoot the Teacher*
China, *Crazy English; Not One Less;*
Fr, *L'Araignée de Satin; L'Argent de Poche; Au Revoir les Enfants; Les Diaboliques* (Clouzot);

Diabolo Menthe; Les Disparus de Saint Agil; L'Enfant Sauvage; It All Starts Today; Merlusse; Olivia; Une Semaine de Vacances; Topaze; Zéro de Conduite
GB, *Absolution; Another Country; The Belles of St Trinian's; Blue Murder at St Trinian's; Boys Will Be Boys; The Browning Version* (Asquith); *The Browning Version* (Figgis); *The Class of Miss MacMichael; Clockwise; Decline and Fall…of a Birdwatcher; Fear in the Night* (Sangster); *A Feast at Midnight; A French Mistress; French Without Tears; The Ghost of St Michael's; Goodbye, Mr Chips* (Wood); *Goodbye Mr Chips* (Ross); *Good Morning, Boys!; Gregory's Girl; Gregory's Two Girls; The Guinea Pig; The Happiest Days of Your Life; Heavenly Pursuits; If…; Institute Benjamenta; It's Great to Be Young; Leaving Lenin; The Loneliness of the Long Distance Runner; The Long Day Closes; Madame Sousatzka; The Man Who Cried; Old Flames; The Prime of Miss Jean Brodie; Pure Hell of St Trinian's; The Rainbow; The Scamp; Term of Trial; Tom Brown's Schooldays; To Sir, With Love; Waterland; The Wildcats of St Trinian's*
Ger, *Coming Out; Mädchen in Uniform; Reunion; Young Törless*
Greece, *The Canary Yellow Bicycle*
Hun, *Sweet Emma, Dear Böbe*
Ind, *The Village Has No Walls*
Iran, *Birth of a Butterfly; Blackboards*
Ire, *Attracta*
It, *Creepers; In the Name of the Father* (Bellocchio); *Noi Tre; Red Rings of Fear; School*
Jap, *Blue Spring; Family Game; Like Grains of Sand; Sumo Do, Sumo Don't*
NZ, *An Angel at My Table; Sylvia*
SAf, *Sarafina!*
SKor, *Memento Mori; Our Twisted Hero; Whispering Corridors*
Swe, *Hets*
US, *Almost Summer; Art for Teachers of Children; Blackboard Jungle; Boys; Breaking In; Carried Away; A Child Is Waiting; Child of Divorce; Child's Play* (Lumet); *The Chocolate War; Clarence and Angel; Clueless; Conrack; Cooley High; Courage Mountain; The Craft; Dangerous Minds; Dazed and Confused; Dead Poets Society; Diabolique* (Chechik); *Disturbing Behavior; Election; The Faculty; Finding Forrester; Get Over It; Girl; Girls Town; Grease; The Great Man Votes; Halloween H20 – 20 Years Later; Harriet the Spy; Heathers; Heaven Help Us; Hiding Out; High School; High School High; High Time; In & Out; The Incredibly True Adventure of Two Girls in Love; Jack; Kindergarten Cop; Lambada; A Little Princess; Lord Love a Duck; Lords of Discipline; Madeline; Making It; Margie; Massacre at Central High; The Mighty; Mr Holland's Opus; Music of the Heart; National Lampoon's Class Reunion; Never Been Kissed; One Eight Seven; Parenthood; Pay It Forward; Permanent Record; The Power of One; Remember the Day; Renaissance Man; Romy and Michele's High School Reunion; Save the Last Dance; School Daze; School Ties; She's All That; Sing; Sister Act II: Back in the Habit; Slackers; Small Wonders; Stand and Deliver; Stanley & Iris; The Substitute; Summer School; Sweetheart of the Campus; Taps; Tea and Sympathy; Teachers; Three O'Clock High; Up the Down Staircase; Who Shot Patakango?; Wildcats; Wild Things*

Egypt, in film
ancient (see also **Undead, the**), *Caesar and Cleopatra; Cleopatra* (DeMille); *Cleopatra* (Mankiewicz); *Land of the Pharoahs*
more recent, *Adieu Bonaparte; L'Autre; Cairo Road; The Camels Are Coming; Closed Doors; Death on the Nile; The Mummy; The Mummy Returns; The Mummy's Shroud; The Night of Counting the Years; On Boys, Girls and the Veil; Passion in the Desert; Saladin; Sea of Sand*

Egyptian cinema, *Adieu Bonaparte; Alexandria Encore; L'Autre; Closed Doors; Destiny; An Egyptian Story; The Night of Counting the Years; On Boys, Girls and the Veil; Saladin*

Ehrenburg, Ilya, film adapted from work, *The Love of Jeanne Ney*

Eichmann, Adolf, films about, *The House on Garibaldi Street; The Specialist*

Einstein, Albert, film about, *I.Q.; Insignificance*

Electrical appliances, in film, *The Brave Little Toaster*

Electricity pylons, *Among Giants*

Eliot, George, films adapted from work, *Silas Marner; A Simple Twist of Fate*

Eliot, TS, film about, *Tom & Viv*

Eliott, Grace, film about, *The Lady & the Duke*

Elizabeth I, Queen of England, films about, *Elizabeth; Fire Over England; Mary of Scotland; Mary Queen of Scots; The Private Lives of Elizabeth and Essex; Shakespeare in Love; Young Bess*

Ellis, Brett Easton, film adapted from work, *American Psycho*

Ellison, Harlan, film adapted from work, *A Boy and His Dog*

Ellington, Duke, film about, *Memories of Duke*

Elliott, Jack, film about, *The Ballad of Ramblin' Jack*

Ellroy, James, films adapted from works, *Brown's Requiem; Cop; LA Confidential*

El Salvador,
in film, *Diplomatic Immunity; El Salvador – Decision to Win; El Salvador – Portrait of a Liberated Zone; El Salvador – The People Will Win; In the Name of the People; Romero; Salvador*

Ende, Michael,
films adapted from work, *The NeverEnding Story; The NeverEnding Story II: The Next Chapter; The NeverEnding Story III: Escape from Fantasia*

End of the world, see **Doomsday movies**

Ephron, Nora, film adapted from work, *Heartburn*

Epilepsy,
Fists in the Pocket; The Innocent (MacKenzie); *Liar; La Tête contre les Murs*

Eskimos, in film, *Atanarjuat: The Fast Runner; Kabloonak; Map of the Human Heart; On Deadly Ground; Salmonberries; The Savage Innocents; Smilla's Feeling for Snow; The White Dawn*

Espionage, industrial (see also **Spy films**), *Adult Fun; Schizopolis*

Estonia
Estonia in film, *Letters from the East*
Estonian cinema, *Darkness in Tallinn*

Ethiopian cinema,
Blood is Not Fresh Water; Tumult

Etting, Ruth, film about, *Love Me or Leave Me*

Eunuchs, see **Castration**

Euripides, films adapted from work, *A Dream of Passion; Phaedra*

Euthanasia, *Ballad of Narayama; Promise; Whose Life Is It Anyway?*

Evangelists, see **Religion**

Evans, Max, film adapted from work, *Hi-Lo Country*

Evans, Nicholas,
film adapted from work, *The Horse Whisperer*

Evers, Medgar, film about, *Ghosts of Mississippi*

Executions, see **Capital punishment**

Exile, *Anna; Argie; The Blue Exile; Carla's Song; Close to the Border; Daniel Takes a Train; The Diplomat; La Frontera; La Guerre est finie; Hotel du Paradis; A King in New York; Man from China; Moscow on the Hudson; A Paper Wedding; Permission to Kill; The Roads of Exile; The Secret Face; Streets of Gold; The Unbearable Lightness of Being*
return from, *Australia; Diary for My Children; Les Diseurs de Vérité; Fading Memories; Melodrama?; Metade Fumaça; Los Naufragos; Reminiscences of a Journey to Lithuania; Requiem for Dominic; Song of the Exile; Sur; To Begin Again; Voyage to Cythera*

Experimental films
Can, *Reason over Passion; Wavelength*
Fr, *L'Amour par terre; Céline and Julie Go Boating; Un Chien Andalou; City of Pirates; La Jetée; Le Jeu de l'oie; Mémoire des apparences; Merci la vie; Out 1: Spectre; La Présence réelle; The Seashell and the Clergyman; Three Crowns for the Sailor*
GB, *Black and Silver; Crystal Gazing; Dust Devil; Dyn Amo; Emily – Third Party Speculation; The Falls; Further and Particular; Ghost Dance; The Gold Diggers; Herostratus; Hilda Was a Goodlooker; In the Shadow of the Sun; Intimate Reflections; Invisible Adversaries; Invocation Maya Deren; Jigsaw; The Last of England; Rocinante; Outside In; Riddle of the Sphinx; Telling Tales; Temenos; The Terence Davies Trilogy; A Walk Through H; A Zed and Two Noughts*
Ger, *The Birth of a Nation; Fata Morgana; Vagabonding Images*
It, *Necropolis*
Jap, *Kagero-za; To Sleep, So As to Dream*
Neth, *Casta Diva; On Top of the Whale*
US, *The Anger Magick Lantern Cycle; The Camera: Je; The Cold Eye; Dog Star Man; Film About a Woman Who…; Flaming Creatures; Kristina Talking Pictures;*

North of Vortex; A Safe Place; Underground USA; We Can't Go Home Again

Explorers and exploration, *Carry On Columbus; Christopher Columbus; Christopher Columbus: The Discovery; Conquest of the South Pole; 1492: Conquest of Paradise; From Pole to Equator; Mountains of the Moon; Scott of the Antarctic*

Extra-terrestrials on Earth (see also **UFOs**)
benign, *The Aurora Encounter; Batteries Not Included; La Belle Verte; A Boy from Mercury; The Brother from Another Planet; The Cat from Outer Space; Close Encounters of the Third Kind – Special Edition; Cocoon; Cocoon; The Return; The Day the Earth Stood Still; The Day Time Ended; Earth Girls Are Easy; Escape to Witch Mountain; E.T. The Extraterrestrial; Explorers; Fire in the Sky; Friendship's Death; Gawin; The Glitterball; Hombre Mirando al Sudeste; It Came from Outer Space; K-PAX; Mac and Me; The Man Who Fell to Earth; Michael; My Favourite Martian; My Stepmother Is an Alien; Phenomenon; Return from Witch Mountain; Santa Claus Conquers the Martians; Spaced Invaders; Star Kid; Starman; Suburban Commando; What Planet Are You From?; Zone Troopers*
nasty, *The Adventures of Buckaroo Banzai Across the 8th Dimension; Alien Nation; The Arrival; The Astronaut's Wife; Bad Taste; Beware! The Blob; The Blob; Body Snatchers; The Body Stealers; The Borrower; Conquest of the Earth; Critters; Critters 2: The Main Course; Daleks – Invasion Earth 2150 AD; Dark Angel; Dark City; The Day of the Triffids; Destroy All Monsters; Dr Who and the Daleks; Earth vs the Flying Saucers; Evolution; The Faculty; Final Fantasy: The Spirits Within; The Hidden; I Married a Monster from Outer Space; Independence Day; Invaders from Mars* (Menzies); *Invaders from Mars* (Hooper); *Invasion; Invasion of the Body Snatchers* (Kaufman); *Invasion of the Body Snatchers* (Siegel); *Invasion of the Saucermen; It Conquered the World; Killer Klowns from Outer Space; Lifeforce; Liquid Sky; Mars Attacks!; The Mysterians; The Night Caller; Night of the Big Heat; Not of This Earth; Parasite; Plan 9 from Outer Space; Predator; Predator 2; The Puppet Masters; Quatermass and the Pit; Quatermass II; Repo Man; Species II; Strange Invasion; Strange Invaders; TerrorVision; They Live; The Thing; The Thing from Another World; Timescape; 20 Million Miles to Earth; Village of the Damned; Virus; War of the Satellites; War of the Worlds; X the Unknown; Xtro*
both, *Highlander; Highlander II – The Quickening; Highlander III – The Sorcerer; Teenagers from Outer Space*

Factory farming, *Laughterhouse*

Fairgrounds, *Capricious Summer; Carny; Carousel; The Fantasticks; Homeboy; Merry-Go-Round; Nightmare Alley; O Dreamland; The Ring; Rollercoaster; Something Wicked This Way Comes; Strangers on a Train; Sunrise; Two Moon Junction; The Unholy Three* (Browning); *The Unholy Three* (Conway)

Fairy stories, fairies and goblins, *Cinderella; Cinderfella; The Company of Wolves; Darby O'Gill and the Little People; Ever After; FairyTale – A True Story; A Hungarian Fairy Tale; Labyrinth* (Henson); *The Lord of the Rings: The Fellowship of the Ring; The NeverEnding Story; The NeverEnding Story II: The Next Chapter; The NeverEnding Story III: Escape from Fantasia; Photographing Fairies; The Singing Ringing Tree; Snow White: A Tale of Terror; Tom Thumb; Troll; Willow; Wizards*

Faith-healing, *Leap of Faith; Marjoe; Resurrection*

Falklands War, *Argie; Arrivederci Millwall; For Queen and Country; Fuckland; The Ploughman's Lunch; Resurrected; Veronico Cruz*

Family life (see also **Adolescence, Fathers, Mothers, Children and Childhood**)
Arg, *Last Images of the Shipwreck; Miss Mary*
Aust, *The Boys; The Last Crop; Mullaway*
Bel, *Ma Vie en Rose*
Cambodia, *Les Gens de la rizière*
Can, *Family Viewing; The Hanging Garden; The Revolving Doors; The Shipping News; Wild Flowers* (Lefebvre)
Chile, *The House of Spirits*
China, *Live in Peace; Spring in a Small Town; Temptress Moon*
Cuba, *Plaff! or Too Afraid of Life*
Czech, *Lásky Jedné Plavovlásky (A Blonde in Love)*
Den, *The Celebration*
Fr, *A Double Tour; Un Air de Famille; Le Château de ma mère; Conte de printemps; Cousin Cousine; Les Destinées Sentimentales; Entre Nous; La Gloire de mon père; La Baule-les-pins; Life Is a Long Quiet River; Milou en mai; Nord; Numéro Deux; The Ostrich Has Two Eggs; Les Parents Terribles; Le Père Tranquille; Sitcom; Skin of Man, Heart of Beast; Un Deux Trois Soleil; Les Uns et Les Autres; La Vieille Dame indigne; What Makes David Run?*
GB, *All or Nothing; Betty's Brood; The Cement Garden; Distant Voices, Still Lives; East Is East; Family Life* (Loach); *Fools of Fortune; Four Days in July; The Homecoming; Ill Fares the Land; In Celebration; The Huggetts Abroad; I Lived With You; The James Gang; The Krays; Ladybird Ladybird; Life Is Sweet; Like Father; The Long Day Closes; The Martins; My Left Foot; Nil by Mouth; Orphans; Queen of Hearts; The Rainbow; Revenge* (Hayers); *The Secret Rapture; Secrets & Lies; Spring and Port Wine; This Happy Breed; Wonderland*
Ger, *Germany, Pale Mother; Josephine; Rosalie Goes Shopping*
Hun, *Love, Mother*
Ind, *The Householder; Journey to Wisdom; Kabhi Khushi Kabhie Gham…; Mother India*
Ire, *Guiltrip, The Snapper*
It, *Brutti, sporchi e cattivi; By Nightfall; China Is Near; The Circumstance; Dimenticare Venezia; Everybody's Fine; Il Ferroviere; Fists in the Pocket; Grazie Zia; Mignon Has Left*
Jap, *Crazy Family; Early Summer; Family Game; Licence to Live; The Moon Has Risen; Ohayo; Osaka Elegy; Ososhiki; Tokyo Story*
Mex, *El Bulto*
Neth, *Abel*
NZ, *Once Were Warriors*
Pol, *Dekalog 7: 'Thou shalt not steal'*
SKor, *Broken Branches; Farewell My Darling; Gilsodom*
Sp, *Caresses; What Have I Done to Deserve This?*
Sri Lanka, *A Mother Alone*
Swe, *Fanny and Alexander; The Father; Söndags Barn; Summer Paradise; Through A Glass Darkly; What Are You Doing After the Orgy?*
Tai, *A City of Sadness; A Drifting Life; A One and a Two…*
Tur, *Clouds of May; The Herd*
US, *ABCD; About Schmidt; The Addams Family; Addams Family Values; Affliction; All I Desire; American Beauty; Among the Living; Avalon; Before and After; Betsy's Wedding; Big Girls Don't Cry…They Get Even; Bloody Mama; The Brady Bunch Movie; Brighton Beach Memoirs; Broadway Bound; The Brothers McMullen; Buffalo '66; Burnt Offerings; Bye Bye Love; Caught; Cheaper by the Dozen; Communion; Cousins; Crooklyn; Daddy's Dyin' – Who's Got the Will?; The Daytrippers; Death of a Salesman; Desert Bloom; Diaries; Domestic Disturbance; Everyone Says I Love You; Family Business* (Cohen); *Far North; The Flintstones; Fools Rush In; Five Easy Pieces; Fool for Love; Forget Paris; Getting to Know You; The Glass Menagerie; Good Housekeeping; God's Little Acre; Happiness; Hider in the House; Hollow Reed; Home for the Holidays; Home from the Hill; A Home of Our Own; House of Cards; The House of Yes; How to Make an American Quilt; The Ice Storm; In the Bedroom; I Remember Mama; Julien Donkey-Boy; King of the Hill; Last Summer in the Hamptons; Life with Father; Little Odessa; Little Women* (Cukor); *Little Women* (Armstrong); *Long Day's Journey into Night; The Long Hot Summer; Lost Angels; Lost in Yonkers; Madhouse; The Man in the Moon; Meet the Applegates; Miami Rhapsody; Miss Firecracker; Mr and Mrs Bridge; Monster's Ball; Mother* (Brooks); *Mother's Boys; Multiplicity; My Heroes Have Always Been Cowboys; The Myth of Fingerprints; National Lampoon's Vacation; The Next Best Thing; The Next Voice You Hear…; Nothing in Common; Nutty Professor II: The Klumps; One Fine Day; One True Thing; Ordinary People; Parenthood; Parents; Pecker; Pleasantville; Please Don't Eat the Daisies; The Plot Against Harry; The Prince of Pennsylvania; The People Next Door; Radio Flyer; The Royal Tenenbaums; Running on Empty; Safe Passage; See You in the Morning; Slums of Beverly Hills; Some Girls; Something to Talk About; Sometimes a Great Notion; Soul Food; Staying Together; The Stepfather; The Stepfather II; Stepfather III; Striptease; The Stupids; Target* (Penn); *There's Always Tomorrow; This Boy's Life; Three Wishes; Tiger Warsaw; To Sleep with Anger; Twice in a Lifetime; Twister* (Almereyda); *Uncle Buck; A Wedding; While You Were Sleeping; Written on the Wind; You Can't Take It with You; Yours, Mine and Ours*
USSR, *Vassa*

Family members mislaid
locked away, *Among the Living; The Apple; The Beast in the Cellar; Jane Eyre* (Stevenson); *Jane Eyre* (Mann); *Jane Eyre* (Zeffirelli); *The Man in the Iron Mask*

(Whale); *The Man in the Iron Mask* (Wallace); *The Oblong Box*
long lost, *Blackout; Deadly Run; Deep End of the Ocean, The; Happy Birthday Wanda June; Licence to Live; The Manxman; My Favorite Wife; Olivier Olivier; Paris, Texas; Le Retour de Martin Guerre; Sunflower; Welcome Home; What Are You Doing After the Orgy?*
disappearing, *Frantic; The Vanishing* (Sluizer, 1988); *The Vanishing* (Sluizer, 1993)

Fanon, Frantz, film about, *Frantz Fanon: Black Skin, White Mask*

Fans, obsessive, *The Fan* (Scott); *The Fan* (Bianchi); *The King of Comedy; Misery; Wings of Fame*

Fante, John, film adapted from work, *Full of Life*

Farley, Walter, films adapted from work, *The Black Stallion; The Black Stallion Returns*

Farmer, Frances, films about, *Committed; Frances*

Fascism (see also **Germany, Politics and politicians, State terror**)
in Britain, *Little Malcolm and His Struggle Against the Eunuchs; The Remains of the Day*
in Burma, *Beyond Rangoon*
in Chile, *La Frontera*
in France, *Les Chiens; The Diary of a Chambermaid; Lacombe Lucien*
in Italy, *The Cannibals; Christ Stopped at Eboli; The Conformist; Down the Ancient Stairs; Garden of the Finzi-Continis; Mario and the Magician; Open Doors; A Special Day; Tea with Mussolini*
in Japan, *Four Days of Snow and Blood*
in US, *American History X; Arlington Road*
anti-fascism, *Fortini/Cani*

Fashion & fashion world (see also **Models**), *Designing Woman; Falbalas; Fausto; Having It All; Notebook on Cities and Clothes; Ready to Wear; The Real Blonde; Salut Cousin!; Slaves of New York; Unzipped; Zoolander*

Fassbinder, Rainer Werner, film about, *A Man Like Eva*

Fathers (see also **Family life**)
and daughters, *An Autumn Afternoon; Benefit of the Doubt; Betsy's Wedding; Beyond the Door; Bonjour Tristesse; Broken Blossoms* (Griffith); *Broken Blossoms* (Brahm); *Carné; Class Action; Cold Comfort; Conte de printemps; Cookie; The Crossing Guard; Dance Little Lady; Dekalog 4: 'Honour thy father and thy mother'; Dialogues With Madwomen; Double X; Eat Drink Man Woman; Elisa; Eternity and a Day; Eve's Bayou; Father of the Bride* (Minnelli); *Father of the Bride* (Shyer); *Father of the Bride Part II; The Furies; The Happiest Millionaire; Hobson's Choice; I Am Sam; Imaginary Crimes; In Fading Light; I Want to Go Home; Jack & Sarah; Kisapmata; Late Spring; Leave Her to Heaven; Mon Père, ce héros; Music Box; My Father, the Hero; The Near Room; L'Ombre du Doute; On Golden Pond; Paperhouse; Le Père Goriot; Le Petit Prince a dit; Ramrod; The Return of the Swamp Thing; Rich in Love; The River Rat; She's Out of Control; A Simple Wish; A Soldier's Daughter Never Cries; Superdad; Spring and Port Wine; These Foolish Things; Timescape; To Our Loves; Violette Nozière; Washington Square; A Woman Rebels; Zina*
and sons, *Abel; Affliction; American Heart; And Life Goes On...; Aprile; At Close Range; Back to School; Because of That War; Bellman and True; Bloodbrothers; Blow to the Heart; A Borrowed Life; Blue Film; Boomerang; Branches of the Tree; Brightness; Broadway Bill; A Bronx Tale; Broken Lance; The Brothers Karamazov* (Brooks); *The Brothers Karamazov* (Pyriev); *Buddy's Song; Carry Me Back; Come and Get It; The Corruptor; Coupe de Ville; Da; Dad; Dance With Me; Danny the Champion of the World; Deconstructing Harry; Dekalog 1: 'I am the Lord thy God, Thou shalt have no other God but me'; East of Eden; Everybody's Fine; Eden Valley; Family Life* (Zanussi); *Family Portrait; Father; Father and Son; Fathers' Day; Fear Strikes Out; A Feast at Midnight; Field of Dreams; Flesh and Bone; Folks!; The Full Monty; Getting Even With Dad; La Gloire de mon père; The Great Santini; The Halliday Brand; Hammers Over the Anvil; Harry & Son; He Got Game; Hollow Reed; Hud; Indiana Jones and the Last Crusade; I Never Sang for My Father; Iron Eagle; The Island; I Was Born, But...; Jack Frost; Jingle All the Way; Jungle 2 Jungle; Korea; The Last Gangster; The Main Actor; The Man from Laramie; Man, Woman and Child; Memories of Me; Mighty Aphrodite; The Miracle; Monster's Ball; My Dad is a Jerk; My Sons; The Ostrich Has Two Eggs; Other Voices Other Rooms; Over the Top; Padre Padrone; Paris s'éveille; Paris, Texas; Peeping Tom; Pet Sematary; Piravi; Pop and Me; Problem Child; Problem Child 2; Rainy Dog; Rebel Without a Cause; The Road Home; The Road to Glory; Rocky V; Saturn; Second Best; Seize the Day; Sergeant Madden; Short Time; Söndags Barn; Spirit of the Eagle; Steamboat Bill, Jr; Swan and Song; Tank; Texas, Addio; Tilaï; To Sleep with Anger; So there,; The Tragedy of a Ridiculous Man; Tribute; Uccellacci e Uccellini; Wait Till the Sun Shines, Nellie; The Voyage; Xenolith; The Young Stranger*
both, *Honey, I Blew Up the Kid; Honey, I Shrunk the Kids; Look Who's Talking; Look Who's Talking Now; Look Who's Talking Too; Mr and Mrs Bridge; Parenthood; La Passion Béatrice; See You in the Morning; Where the Heart Is; Yours, Mine and Ours*
and son-in-law, *Glory Alley*
surrogate, *The Man Without a Face; The Search; Three Men and a Baby; Three Men and a Little Lady*
gay parents, *The Object of My Affection*

Fat women, as objects of sexual fascination, *Alfredo, Alfredo; Bagdad Café; 8½; Sugarbaby; Rosalie Goes Shopping; Shallow Hal*

Faulkner, William
films adapted from work, *The Arsonist; Intruder in the Dust; The Long Hot Summer; The Reivers; Sanctuary; The Tarnished Angels*
home town explored – Oxford, Miss, *Mississippi Blues*

Faulks, Sebastian, film adapted from work, *Charlotte Gray*

Faustian bargains, *Alias Nick Beale; All That Money Can Buy; Angel Heart; Bad Influence; La Beauté du Diable; Bedazzled* (Donen); *Bedazzled* (Ramis); *Crossroads* (Hill); *Death Becomes Her; The Devil's Advocate* (Hackford); *Faust* (Murau); *Faust* (Svankmajer); *Limit Up; Lord of Illusion; Phantom of the Opera* (Little); *Quiz Show; Stay Tuned; Tales from the Darkside: The Movie*

FBI, in film, *Arlington Road, Betrayed; Big Momma's House; Confessions of a Nazi Spy; Donnie Brasco; Down Three Dark Streets; D-Tox; 'G' Men; Feds; Hannibal; The House on Carroll Street; The House on 92nd Street; Manhunter; Miss Congeniality; Mississippi Burning; My Blue Heaven; Panther; Point Break; The Private Files of J Edgar Hoover; Raw Deal; See Spot Run; Shoot to Kill; A Show of Force; The Silence of the Lambs; Stone Cold; Thunderheart; To Live and Die in L.A.; Twin Peaks; Twin Peaks: Fire Walk with Me; Undercover Blues; Underworld USA; The Untouchables; Walk East on Beacon!; White Sands; The X Files*

Feiffer, Jules, films adapted from work, *Little Murders; Oh! Calcutta!*

Feminist cinema, and Feminism in film, *Alchemy; The All-Round Reduced Personality – Redupers; Antonia's Line; Blood Red Roses; Born in Flames; Broken Mirrors; Burning an Illusion; Business as Usual; Cannibal Women in the Avocado Jungle of Death; Carry Greenham Home; Doll's Eye; Dream Life; Female Perversions; The First Wives Club; G.I. Jane; Girlfriend; The Girl with Brains in Her Feet; Grace of My Heart; The Handmaid's Tale; How to Be a Woman and Not Die in the Attempt; How to Make an American Quilt; Jackson County Jail; Jeanne Dielman, 23 Quai du Commerce, 1080 Bruxelles; A Litany for Survival: The Life and Work of Audre Lorde; Madame X; Maeve; Making Up; Malou; Marriage Story; MURDER and Murder; My 20th Century; Nelly's Version; 1+1=3; One Sings, the Other Doesn't; Penthesilea, Queen of the Amazons; The Point Is to Change It; Privilege* (Rainer); *Private Benjamin; A Question of Silence; Rapunzel Let Down Your Hair; Rate It X; Riddles of the Sphinx; Right Out of History: The Making of Judy Chicago's Dinner Party; Salt of the Earth; The Second Awakening of Christa Klages; Sigmund Freud's Dora; The Silent Cry; The Song of the Shirt; The Stepford Wives; Take It Like a Man, Ma'am; Town Bloody Hall; The Two of Them; Variety; Waiting; Waiting to Exhale; A Winter Tan; Wives; Wives: Ten Years After; Wives III; A Woman Rebels; Woman to Woman; The World According to Garp*

Fencing, *By the Sword; The Fencing Master*

Fenimore Cooper, James, film adapted from work, *The Last of the Mohicans*

Feral children, *L'Enfant Sauvage; Jeder für sich und Gott gegen alle (The Enigma of Kaspar Hauser); Kaspar Hauser; Nell; Walk Like a Man*

Ferber, Edna, films adapted from work, *Cimarron; Come and Get It; Dinner at Eight; Giant; Ice Palace; Saratoga Trunk; Show Boat* (Whale); *Show Boat* (Sidney)

Feuillade, Louis, films adapted from/inspired by work, *Irma Vep; Fantômas contre Fantômas; Judex*

Few-months-to-live stories (see also **Death, Illness** and **AIDS and HIV**), *American Flyers; And Your Mother Too; Autumn in New York; The Belly of an Architect; Bobby Deerfield; Christmas in August; Cries and Whispers; The Darkest Light; Dark Victory; Desperate Measures; D.O.A.* (Maté); *D.O.A.* (Morton/Jankel); *Dream with the Fishes; Dying Young; The End; The English Patient; Eternity and a Day; Girls' Night; Ikiru; Hana-Bi; The Hasty Heart; Hawks; Joe Versus the Volcano; John Q; Kaseki; Last Feelings; Last Holiday; Lease of Life; Love Story* (Arliss); *Love Story* (Hiller); *Mon Premier Amour; My Life; Never Say Die; No Sad Songs for Me; One More Kiss; One True Thing; Parting Shots; Le Petit Prince a dit; Roseanna's Grave; Short Time; Sick: The Life & Death of Bob Flanagan, Supermasochist; Six Weeks; The Sleepy Time Gal; Stepmom; Stolen Hours; The Sunchaser; Sunshine* (Sargent); *Sunshine Part II; Sweet November* (Miller); *Sweet November* (O'Connor); *The Theory of Flight; Tribute; The Wind Cannot Read; The Wings of the Dove; Wit*

Feydeau, Georges, films adapted from work, *The Girl from Maxim's; On purge Bébé*

Fielding, Henry, films adapted from work, *The Bawdy Adventures of Tom Jones; Joseph Andrews; Tom Jones*

Fields, WC, film about, *W.C. Fields and Me*

Film-makers and film-making (see also **Cinema owners, projectionists, staff** and **Hollywood and the movie business**)
Arg, *The Cross*
Aust, *Waiting*
Bel, *Man Bites Dog*
Bol, *The Bird's Singing*
Braz, *Anaconda; Carmen Miranda: Bananas Is My Business*
Can, *Ararat; The Confessional; Kabloonak; The Heart of the World; No Skin Off My Ass; Speaking Parts*
China *Maiden Work; Yang ± Yin: Gender in Chinese Cinema*
Czech, *Labyrinth* (Jires)
Den, *Carl Th. Dreyer: My Work*
Egypt, *Alexandria Encore; An Egyptian Story*
Fin, *Ripa Hits the Skids*
Fr, *A.K.; Citizen Langlois; Des Enfants Gâtés; Les Enfants de Lumière; Etoilessans Lumière; First Name: Carmen; For Ever Mozart; Le Gai Savoir; Grosse Fatigue; L'Homme au Chapeau de Soie; Irma Vep; It's All True; Lisbon Story; A Man in Love; One Day in the Life of Andrei Arsenevitch; The Pornographer; Portrait of a 60% Perfect Man: Billy Wilder; Rise and Fall of Little Film Company from a novel by James Hadley Chase; Sauve Qui Peut: la Vie; Le Silence est d'Or; Soigne ta Droite; 2 x 50 Years of French Cinema; L'Univer de Jacques Demy; Vie Privée; Vladimir et Rosa; What Makes David Run?*
GB, *Acceptable Levels; A Bit of Scarlet; Donald Cammell: The Ultimate Performance; For Freedom; In Ismail's Custody; Intimate Stranger; Invocation Maya Deren; Loaded; Long Shot; Motion and Emotion: The Films of Wim Wenders; Final Cut; Peeping Tom; Shadow of the Vampire; Vigo Passion for Life; Wonderful Life*
Ger, *Beware of a Holy Whore; Burden of Dreams; Lightning Over Water; A Little Godard; The Main Actor; A Man Like Eva; My Dearest Enemy; Notebook on Cities and Clothes; Tokyo-Ga*
Greece, *Ulysses' Gaze*
HK, *Actress; Ah-Kam; Buenos Aires Zero Degree; Father and Son; First Love – The Litter on the Breeze; Viva Erotica!; Yang ± Yin: Gender in Chinese Cinema*
Ind, *Bollywood Calling; Bombay Talkie; In Search of Famine*
International Lumière et Compagnie
Iran, *And Life Goes On…; Close-Up; Through the Olive Trees*
Isr, *Yaacov Ben Dov: Father of the Hebrew Film*
It, *Beyond the Clouds; Bits and Pieces; Cinema Paradiso; Cinema Paradiso: The Special Edition; 8½; Enzo, Domani a Palermo!; Fellini A Director's Notebook; Festival* (Avati); *Icicle Thief; Intervista; L'Uomo delle stelle; Volere, Volare*
Jap, *Getting Any?; Jam Session: The Official Bootleg Kikujiro The Hair Opera; Kurosawa*
Mex, *Homework*
Neth, *Little Sister; Wings of Fame*
NZ, *Cinema of Unease; Forgotten Silver; Mouth Wide Open – A Journey in Film with Ted Coubray; Topless Women Talk About Their Lives*
Pol, *Camera Buff; Everything for Sale; Krzysztof Kieslowski: I'm So So; 100 Years of Polish Cinema*
Port, *Journey to the Beginning of the World; Lisbon Story*
SKor, *The Jang Sun-Woo Variations; The Man Who Saw Too Much*
Sp, *The Law of Desire; Life in Shadows; The Mad Monkey; Thesis; Tie Me Up! Tie Me Down!*
Swe, *Directed by Andrei Tarkovsky; The Greatness of the Small Men; Lines from the Heart*
Switz, *O for Oblomov*
Tai, *Good Men, Good Women; Jam*
Tur, *Clouds of May; Night Journey*
US, *An Almost Perfect Affair; Alex in Wonderland; American Movie: The Making of Northwestern; The American Nightmare; America's Sweethearts; At Sundance; BAPS; The Big Picture; The Blackout; Blair Witch Project, The; Boogie Nights; Book of Shadows: Blair Witch 2; Bowfinger; The Bullfighter and the Lady; The Cat's Meow; Cecil B. Demented; The Celluloid Closet; Classified X; Conversations with Willard Van Dyke; Crimes and Misdemeanors; Dadetown; David Holzman's Diary; Demon Lover Diary; Directed by William Wyler; The Disappearance of Kevin Johnson; Dragon: The Bruce Lee Story; Ed Wood; 8MM; 84 Charlie Mopic; The End of Violence; Frank Capra's American Dream; The Freshman; From the Journals of Jean Seberg; From Russia to Hollywood: The 100-Year Odyssey of Chekhov and Shdanoff; Full Tilt Boogie; Gods and Monsters; A Gringo in Mañanaland; Guy; The Hamster Factor and Other Tales of Twelve Monkeys; Hearts of Darkness: A Filmmaker's Apocalypse; Hollywood Cavalcade; Hollywood Ending; Illusions; In Ismail's Custody; Inserts; Inside Daisy Clover; It's All True; In the Soup; Irreconcilable Differences; It's All True; It Should Happen to You; John Huston War Stories; The Last Movie; Leaving Las Vegas; Living in Oblivion; The Lost Squadron; Luck, Trust & Ketchup: Robert Altman in Carver Country; Matinee; Maidstone; Modern Romance; Mute Witness; The Muse; My Life's in Turnaround; National Lampoon Goes to the Movies; Nico Icon; Pretty as a Picture: The Art of David Lynch; Privilege* (Rainer); *The Real Blonde; Robert Altman's Jazz' 34: Remembrances of Kansas City Swing; Roger Corman: Hollywood's Wild Angel; S.F.W.; Signed: Lino Brocka; Snake Eyes; Special Effects; Stardust Memories; State and Main; The State of Things; Storytelling; Strangers Kiss; Sullivan's Travels; ¡Three Amigos!; The Typewriter, the Rifle & the Movie Camera; Urban Legends Final Cut; Visions of Light; Warren Oates: Across the Border; We Can't Go Home Again; Wes Craven's New Nightmare; What About Me?; White Hunter, Black Heart; Wild Bill:*
A Hollywood Maverick
USSR and Rus, *East Side Story; Man With a Movie Camera; Micha; Mute Witness*

Finland
Finland in film, *Ariel; Black on White; Il Capitano; Crime and Punishment* (Kaurismäki); *Drifting Clouds; Earth Is a Sinful Song; Flame Top; Hamlet Goes Business; Highway Society; Juha; Letters to Katja; The Man Without a Past; The Match Factory Girl; Night on Earth; Ripa Hits the Skids; Täällä Pohjantähden alla; Take Care of Your Scarf, Tatjana; Total Balalaika Show*
Finnish cinema, *Ariel; Black on White; Il Capitano; Cool & Crazy; Crime and Punishment* (Kaurismäki); *Darkness in Tallinn; Drifting Clouds; Earth Is a Sinful Song; Flame Top; Hamlet Goes Business; Highway Society; Juha; LA Without a Map; Leningrad Cowboys Go America; Letters from the East; Letters to Katja; The Man Without a Past; The Match Factory Girl; Ripa Hits the Skids; Sound of Brazil; Täällä Pohjantähden alla; Take Care of Your Scarf, Tatjana; Total Balalaika Show*

Finney, Charles G, film adapted from work, *7 Faces of Dr Lao*

Finney, Jack, films adapted from work, *Assault on a Queen; Invasion of the Body Snatchers; Maxie*

Firefighters, *Backdraft; The Firemen's Ball; Fires Were Started; Frequency; Night of the Big Heat; Trespass*

Fish, etc (see also **Whales**), *Atlantis; Blue Water, White Death; Deep Blue Sea; Deep Rising; A Fish Called Wanda; Goldfish; Help! I'm a Fish; It Came from Beneath the Sea; Jaws; Jaws 2; Jaws 3-D; Jaws – The Revenge; Le Monde du Silence; Piranha; Piranha II: Flying Killers; The Shark Callers of Kontu; The Sharks' Cave; Tiger Shark; 20000 Leagues Under the Sea; The White Balloon*

Fishburne, Laurence, film adapted from work, *Once in the Life*

Fisher, Carrie, film adapted from work, *Postcards from the Edge*

Fishing, *As in Heaven; Beneath the 12-Mile Reef; Blue Fin; Clash By Night; In Fading Light; Ingaló; Man's Favourite Sport?; Mystic Pizza; The Old Man and the*

Sea; The Perfect Storm; A River Runs Through It; Tiger Shark; Venus Peter

Fitzgerald, F Scott
films adapted from work, *The Great Gatsby* (Clayton); *The Great Gatsby* (Nugent); *Indian Summer; The Last Time I Saw Paris; The Last Tycoon*
in film, *Beloved Infidel*

Fitzhugh, Louise, film adapted from work, *Harriet the Spy*

Flagg, Fannie, film adapted from work, *Fried Green Tomatoes at the Whistle Stop Café*

Flaherty, Robert, in film, *Kabloonak*

Flatulence, *Il Petomane*

Flaubert, Gustave, films adapted from work, *Abraham Valley, Madame Bovary* (Renoir); *Madame Bovary* (Chabrol)

Flying dramas
wartime, service, etc, *Aces High; Air Force; An Annapolis Story; Battle Hymn; The Battle of Britain; The Big Lift; The Blue Max; The Body Stealers; The Bridges at Toko-Ri; Broken Arrow* (Woo); *Catch-22; Command Decision; Conflict of Wings; Conquest of the Air; The Court Martial of Billy Mitchell; The Dambusters; Dangerous Moonlight; Dark Blue World; Dawn Patrol* (Hawks); *Dawn Patrol* (Goulding); *Desperate Journey; Desperate Search; Dive Bomber; Firebirds; Flight of the Intruder; Flying Leathernecks; Flying Tigers; First of the Few; A Gathering of Eagles; The Great Santini; Hell's Angels; Hot Shots!; The Hunters; Iron Eagle; Iron Eagle II; Jet Pilot; Journey Together; The Lost Squadron; Memphis Belle; Moon 44; Mosquito Squadron; The Night My Number Came Up; One of Our Aircraft Is Missing; The 1,000 Plane Raid; Project X; Reach for the Sky; Top Gun; Top of the World; Tora! Tora! Tora!; Toward the Unknown; Twelve O'Clock High; Von Richthofen and Brown; The Way to the Stars; Wings; The Wings of Eagles; A Yank in the RAF*
non-military, *Air America; Air Force One; Airplane; Airplane II: The Sequel; Airport; Airport 1975; Airport '77; Airport '80; Always* (Spielberg); *The American Way; Back from Eternity; Blue Thunder; Brewster McCloud; Calcutta; Ceiling Zero; China Clipper; Con Air; Crack-Up* (St Clair); *Christopher Strong; Drop Zone; La Fille de l'Air; Five Came Back; Fly Away Home; Forces of Nature; The Great Waldo Pepper; The Gypsy Moths; Jet Storm; Millennium; No Highway; Only Angels Have Wings; Passenger 57; Pushing Tin; The Rocketeer; Rosalie Goes Shopping; Run for the Sun; Saint-Ex; Sky Pirates; The Sound Barrier; The Spirit of St. Louis; Starflight: The Plane That Couldn't Land; The Tarnished Angels; Terminal Velocity; Tombes du Ciel; Too Hot to Handle; Turbulence*

Flynt, Larry, film about, *The People vs. Larry Flynt*

Folk music, see **Music and musicians, folk/traditional/world**

Fonda, Jane, films about, *Jane; Letter to Jane; Vietnam Journey*

Fontane, Theodor, film adapted from work, *Effi Briest*

Food (see also **Cooks, kitchens, restaurants, bakeries, etc**), *Babette's Feast; Baker's Bread; Big Night; Blow Out* (Ferreri); *Chicken and Duck Talk; The Cook, the Thief, His Wife and Her Lover; Doña Flor and Her Two Husbands; Eat Drink Man Woman; Garlic Is as Good as Ten Mothers; Jamón, Jamón; Like Water for Chocolate; The Scent of Green Papaya; Soul Food; Tampopo; What's Cooking?; Who Is Killing the Great Chefs of Europe?*

Football
American, *All the Right Moves; Any Given Sunday; The Best of Times; Easy Living; Everybody's All-American; Heaven Can Wait* (Beatty/Henry); *Horse Feathers; Jerry Maguire; The Last Boy Scout; The Longest Yard; Necessary Roughness; North Dallas Forty; Number One* (Gries); *Pigskin Parade; Remember the Titans; Rudy; School Ties; The Waterboy; Wildcats*
Australian rules, *The Club*
post-nuclear rugby, *The Salute of the Jugger*
rugby league, *This Sporting Life*
rugby, seven-a-side, *Up 'n' Under*
rugby union, *Carry Me Back; A Run for Your Money*
soccer, *All Stars; The Arsenal Stadium Mystery; Le Ballon d'Or; Bend It Like Beckham; Best; Bloomfield; The Cup; Fever Pitch; The Goalkeeper's Fear of the Penalty; G'Olé!; Gregory's Girl; Hero* (Maylan); *i.d.; The Match; Mean Machine; Mike Bassett England Manager; Purely Belter; Shaolin Soccer; Stubby; This Boy's Story; There's Only One Jimmy Grimble; Those Glory Glory Days; The Traveller; Victory; When Saturday Comes; Yesterday's Hero; Young Giants*

Football hooligans, *Arrivederci Millwall; Ultrà*

Foote, Horton, films adapted from work, *Baby the Rain Must Fall; The Chase; The Trip to Bountiful*

Forbes, Kathryn, film adapted from work, *I Remember Mama*

Ford, John (dramatist), film adapted from work, *'Tis Pity She's a Whore*

Foreign Legion, French, *A.W.O.L.; Beau Geste; Beau Travail; Le Grand Jeu; Gueule d'Amour; March or Die; Morocco*

Forester, CS, films adapted from work, *African Queen; Captain Horatio Hornblower; Forever England; The Pride and the Passion*

Forgers and counterfeiters, *F for Fake; Incognito; Johnny Allegro; Schtonk!; T-Men; To Live and Die in L.A.; Vieille Canaille*

Forman, Sir Denis, film about, *My Life So Far*

Forster, EM, films adapted from work, *Howards End; Maurice; A Passage to India; A Room with a View; Where Angels Fear to Tread*

Forsyth, Frederick, films adapted from work, *The Day of the Jackal; The Dogs of War; The Fourth Protocol; The Odessa File*

Fowles, John, films adapted from work, *The Collector; The French Lieutenant's Woman; The Magus*

Frame, Janet, film about/adapted from work, *An Angel at My Table*

France, in film
(see also **Paris**)
pre-revolutionary, *The Adventures of Quentin Durward; Beaumarchais; Le Bossu; Brotherhood of the Wolf; Les Camisards; Cyrano de Bergerac; Dangerous Liaisons; Diane; Ever After; The Four Musketeers: The Revenge of Milady; La Fille de D'Artagnan; The Great Garrick; The Hour of the Pig; The Iron Mask; Joan of Arc; Le Libertin; The Man in the Iron Mask* (Whale); *The Man in the Iron Mask* (Wallace); *Marquise; La Prise de Pouvoir par Louis XIV; Que la Fête Commence; La Reine Margot; Le Retour de Martin Guerre; The Return of the Musketeers; Ridicule; Scaramouche; The Three Musketeers: The Queen's Diamonds* (Lester); *La Religieuse; Si Versailles m'était conté…; The Three Musketeers* (Herek); *Total Eclipse; Le Tournoi; Tous les matins du monde; The Trial of Joan of Arc; Under the Red Robe; Valmont; A Walk with Love and Death; Vatel; Les Visiteurs; The War Lord*
revolutionary/Napoleonic, *L'Affaire du Courrier de Lyon; Affair of the Necklace, The; Becky Sharp; Le Colonel Chabert* (Le Hénaff); *Le Colonel Chabert* (Angelo); *Danton; Le Destin Fabuleux de Désirée Clary; Le Dialogue des Carmélites; DuBarry Was a Lady; The Elusive Pimpernel; Jefferson in Paris; The Lady & the Duke; Marquis; La Marseillaise; Napoléon* (Gance); *Napoléon* (Guitry); *Reign of Terror; The Scarlet Pimpernel; That Night in Varennes; Waterloo*
19th century, *Les Belles de nuit; Boule de Suif; Eléna at les Hommes; French Can Can; Germinal; Gervaise; Goya in Bordeaux; Le Hussard sur le toit; I Accuse!; Juarez; Lautrec; Les Lettres de Mon Moulin; Lumière; Madame Bovary* (Renoir); *Madame Bovary* (Chabrol); *Les Miserables* (Milestone); *Les Misérables* (Boleslawski); *Les Misérables* (Le Chanois); *Les Misérables* (Lelouch); *Les Misérables* (August); *Le Père Goriot*
1900–WWII, *Les Ames Fortes; La Chambre des officiers; Le Château de ma mère; Le Corbeau; Le Diable au corps; The Diary of a Chambermaid* (Buñuel); *Escape Route to Marseilles; Farrebique; Une Femme française; La Gloire de mon père; La Grande Illusion; Les Grandes Manoeuvres; His Wife's Diary; Lacombe Lucien; Landru; Leon Morin, Priest; Letters to an Unknown Lover; Life and Nothing But; One Man's War; Paris Mil Neuf Cent Chronique de 1900 à 1914; Pension Mimosas; La Règle du Jeu; La Route enchantée; Sister My Sister; Surviving Picasso; Train of Shadows; La Vie est à nous; Violette Nozière; Les Violons du Bal; Zéro de Conduite*
since 1945, *Un Air de Famille; Amour d'enfance; L'Amour, l'Argent, l'Amour; L'Arbre, le Maire et la Médiathèque, ou Les Sept Hasards; Baise-moi; La Boulangère de Monceau; Le Bonheur est dans le pré; The Chateau; Chocolat* (Hallstöm); *Comme un Aimant; Conte d'été; La Crise; Un Conte d'Automne; The Day of the Jackal; Le Deuxième Souffle; The Discreet Charm of the Bourgeoisie; Des Enfants Gâtés; Drôle de Félix; Du Soleil pour les Gueux; En avoir (ou pas); Les Enfants du Marais; Farewell, Home Sweet Home; Le Gang; Girl on a Motorcycle; The Gleaners and I; Grosse Fatigue; La Guerre sans nom; Harry, He's Here to Help You; L'Humanité; In the French Style; IP5; It All Starts Today; La Baule-les-pins; The Last Metro; Les Liaisons Dangereuses 1960;*

Life Is a Long Quiet River; Loulou; Marie-Jo and Her Two Lovers; Marius et Jeannette; Ma Saison Préférée; Milou en mai; Un Monde sans pitié; The Pornographer; Real Cool Time; Rendez-vous de juillet; Roberto Succo; Romuald et Juliette; Rouge Baiser; Le Secret; The Secret Laughter of Women; 17 rue Bleue; The Son; La Squale; Subway; Sunday in the Country; A Sunday in Hell; Tango (Leconte); *Tatie Danielle; Themroc; Trop de Bonheur; Un Deux Trois Soleil; Uranus; La Vérité; La Vie de Jésus; La Vie Rêvée des Anges; La Ville est tranquille; Western; Will It Snow for Christmas?*

Franco, General Francisco, films about, *La Guerre est finie; Race, the Spirit of Franco*

Frankenstein, etc, stories (see also **Shelley,** Mary), *The Curse of Frankenstein; Edward Scissorhands; Flesh for Frankenstein; Frankenhooker; Frankenstein; Frankenstein and the Monster from Hell; Frankenstein Created Woman; Frankenstein Meets the Wolf Man; Frankenstein Must Be Destroyed; Frankenstein: The True Story; The Ghost of Frankenstein; The Golem; Mary Shelley's Frankenstein; Re-Animator; Re-Animator 2; The Revenge of Frankenstein; Roger Corman's Frankenstein Unbound*

Fraser, Brad, film adapted from work, *Love and Human Remains*

Fraser, George MacDonald, film adapted from work, *Royal Flash*

Freed, Arthur, film about, *Musicals Great Musicals: The Arthur Freed Unit at MGM*

French cinema, see Appendix 18

Freud, Esther, film adapted from work, *Hideous Kinky*

Freud, Sigmund, films about, *Freud; Nineteen-Nineteen; Sigmund Freud's Dora*

Friedman, Carl, film adapted from work, *Left Luggage*

Friel, Brian, film adapted from work, *Dancing at Lughnasa*

Friendship (see also **Buddy movies**)
between men, *All Stars; Le Beau Serge; The Big Lebowski; The Boys from Fengkuei; Capitaine Conan; Capricious Summer; Dance of Dust; Friend; Going All the Way; The Hasty Heart; Heartbreakers; The Heart Is a Lonely Hunter; Husbands; I Recuperanti; Kids Return; Kings of the Road; Lifeguard; The Mighty; Miller's Crossing; My Sweet Little Village; My Way Home; The Odd Couple; The Odd Couple II; Powwow Highway; Proof; Queens Logic; Return to Paradise; Reunion; Shaking the Tree; Sling Blade; Soldier of Orange; Spicy Rice; State of Grace; That Championship Season; The Waterdance; Wrestling Ernest Heningway*
between women, *Le Amiche; Angel on My Shoulder; Beaches; Both Sides of the Street; The Company of Strangers; The Country Girls; Coup de Foudre; Daisies; Enchanted April; Fried Green Tomatoes at the Whistle Stop Café; Friends and Husbands; The Future of Emily; Ghost World; The Girlfriend; Girlfriends; A Girl from Lorraine; Girls' Night; Girls Town; Golden Eighties; The Group; Heartache; How to Make an American Quilt; I, the Worst of All; The Last Winter; Leaving Normal; Love; Mädchen in Uniform; Making Up; Me Without You; Mina Tannenbaum; Mystic Pizza; Now and Then; One Sings, the Other Doesn't; Salmonberries; She'll Be Wearing Pink Pyjamas; She's Been Away; Steaming; Steel Magnolias; Sticky Fingers; A Summer in La Goulette; Sweet Emma, Dear Böbe; Take Care of My Cat; That Night; Thelma and Louise; Three Women; The Turning Point; Two Friends; The Two of Them; Two Stage Sisters; A Woman's Tale*
between men and women, *The Big Chill; 84 Charing Cross Road; Four Friends; Jacknife; Peter's Friends; Singles; Waiting; When Harry Met Sally…*
between cats and dogs, *The Adventures of Milo and Otis*

Friese Greene, William, film about, *The Magic Box*

Frisch, Max, film adapted from work, *Voyager*

Fry, Maxwell, films about, *Twelve Views of Kensal House*

Fuentes, Carlos, film adapted from work, *Old Gringo*

Fugard, Athol, films adapted from work, *Boesman and Lena* (Devenish); *Boesman & Lena* (Berry)

Fuller, Sam, film about, *The Typewriter, the Rifle & the Movie Camera*

Future, visions of, *Adrenalin – Fear the Rush; Akira; Alien; Aliens; Alien³; Alien Resurrection; Alphaville; August in the Water; Back to the Future Part II; Barb Wire; Battle Royale; Born in Flames; Blade Runner; Blade Runner – The Director's Cut; Brazil; Bunker Palace Hotel; Death Watch; Demolition Man; Dr M; Escape from New York; Fahrenheit 451; The Fifth Element; Fist of the North Star; Flaming Ears; Fortress; Fortress II: Re-entry; Freejack; Futureworld; Gamera: The Guardian of the Universe; Gen-X Cops; Gen-Y Cops; The Handmaid's Tale; Hardware; Highlander II – The Quickening; John Carpenter's Escape from L.A.; Johnny Mnemonic; Judge Dredd; The Last Battle; Light Years Away; Mad Max; Mad Max 2; Mad Max Beyond the Thunderdome; Memoirs of a Survivor; Metropolis* (Lang); *Moon 44; Mortal Kombat; Mortal Kombat 2: Annihilation; Nineteen Eighty-Four; Nothing Lasts Forever; Panic in the Year Zero; Pitch Black; The Postman; Prayer of the Rollerboys; Predator 2; Punishment Park; Quintet; Red Planet; RoboCop; RoboCop 2; RoboCop 3; Rollerball; Rub Love; Runaway; The Running Man* (Glaser); *The Salute of the Jugger; Series 7: The Contenders; The Sex Mission; The 6th Day; Slipstream; Soylent Green; Space Firebird; Split Second; Stargate; Star Trek: Generations; Star Trek – The Motion Picture; Star Trek II: The Wrath of Khan; Star Trek III: The Search for Spock; Star Trek: First Contact; Star Trek V: The Final Frontier; Star Trek VI: The Undiscovered Country; Star Trek: Insurrection; Strange Days; Super Mario Bros.; Supernova; Tank Girl; The Terminal Man; The Terminator; Terminator 2: Judgment Day; Things to Come; THX 1138; The Time Machine; Total Recall; Trancers; The Truman Show; Turkey Shoot; 2001: A Space Odyssey; 2010; The Tunnel; Universal Soldier; The Ugliest Woman in the World; The Voyage Home: Star Trek IV; Waterworld; The Wicked City; Wizards; X-Men; Zardoz*

Gable, Clark, film about, *Gable and Lombard*

Gabon cinema, *Dôlé*

Gaines, Ernest J, film adapted from work, *A Gathering of Old Men*

Galbally, Frank, film adapted from work, *Storyville*

Gallico, Paul, films adapted from work, *Beyond the Poseidon Adventure; Lili; The Poseidon Adventure*

Galsworthy, John, films adapted from work, *Escape!* (Dean); *One More River; A Summer Story*

Gambling, *Action for Slander; American Madness; The Apple Dumpling Gang; The Arm; A.W.O.L.; Back to the Future Part II; La Baie des Anges; Barrier; California Split; Casino; The Cincinnati Kid; Croupier; Dreamscape; Force of Evil; The Gambler* (Reisz); *The Gambler* (Makk); *Gilda; The Great Sinner; The Grifters; Guys and Dolls; Hard Eight; Havana; Hollywood or Bust; Honeymoon in Vegas; House!; Jinxed!; Johnny O'Clock; Kaleidoscope; King of the Roaring 20's – The Story of Arnold Rothstein; Let It Ride; Loser; Loser Takes All; The Man Who Broke the Bank at Monte Carlo; Maverick; Mister Cory; The Music of Chance; My Brother Talks to Horses; No Man of Her Own* (Ruggles); *Oscar and Lucinda; Pension Mimosas; Rat Race; Rounders; Sour Grapes; Stacy's Knights; The Stain; Quintet; Volunteers; The Wicked Reporter; The Winner*

Gangs, see **Street gangs and juvenile delinquents**

García Lorca, Federico, films adapted from work, *Blood Wedding; The House of Bernarda Alba*

García Márquez, Gabriel, films adapted from work, *Bloody Morning; Chronicle of a Death Foretold; Eréndira; Time to Die*

Gardens and gardeners, etc, *Being There; The Draughtsman's Contract; The Garden; Green Card; Greenkeeping; Mr Love; The Secret Garden* (Holland); *The Secret Garden* (Wilcox); *The Serpent's Kiss; The Spanish Gardener; Tim*

Garland, Alex, film adapted from work, *The Beach*

Garrick, David, film about, *The Great Garrick*

Gary, Romain, films adapted from work, *Genghis Cohn; Lady L; The Ski Bum; White Dog*

Gaudier-Brzeska, Henri, film about, *Savage Messiah*

Gautier, Théophile, film adapted from work, *Le Capitaine Fracassé*

Gay, John, films adapted from/based on work, *The Beggar's Opera; Die Dreigroschenoper*

Gays (male) and gay cinema (see also **Lesbians and lesbianism**)
Aust, *The Adventures of Priscilla Queen of the Desert; The Everlasting Secret Family; Wake in Fright*
Bel, *Mascara*
Braz, *Kiss of the Spider Woman; Madame Satã*

Can, *Being at Home with Claude; Eclipse; Fortune and Men's Eyes; The Hanging Garden; Love and Human Remains; Montreal Main; Night Zoo; No Skin Off My Ass; Super 8½; Urinal; Zero Patience*
China, *East Palace, West Palace*
Cuba, *Before Night Falls; Strawberry and Chocolate*
Egypt, *Adieu Bonaparte*
Fr, *La Cage aux Folles; La Cage aux Folles II; La Cage aux Folles III: The Wedding; Escalier C; Les Equilibristes; Improper Conduct; J'embrasse pas; The Ostrich Has Two Eggs; The Pillow Book; Presque rien; We Were One Man*
GB, *Beautiful Thing; Bedrooms and Hallways; A Bit of Scarlet; Blood and Concrete; Boyfriends; Caravaggio; Caught Looking; Closing Numbers; Duffer; Edward II; Entertaining Mr Sloane; Four Weddings and a Funeral; The Fruit Machine; The Garden; Get Real; Love Is the Devil – Study for a Portrait of Francis Bacon; The L-Shaped Room; Madagascar Skin; Man Is a Woman; Maurice; Militia Battlefield; The Music Lovers; My Beautiful Laundrette; Nighthawks* (Peck); *North of Vortex; Over Our Dead Bodies; The Pillow Book; Prick Up Your Ears; Priest; Sebastiane; Skin Flick; Stonewall; Strip Jack Naked: Nighthawks II; Sunday, Bloody Sunday; A Taste of Honey; To Die For; The Trials of Oscar Wilde; Victim; Water Drops on Burning Rocks; We Think the World of You; Wilde; Young Soul Rebels*
Ger, *Army of Lovers or Revolt of the Perverts; Bent; Bewegte Mann, Der; City of Lost Souls; Coming Out; The Consequence; Coup de Grâce; The Devil's Advocate; Eika Katappa; Faustrecht der Freiheit; I Am My Own Woman; I Love You, I'll Kill You; Last Exit to Brooklyn; Ludwig; Ludwig – Requiem for a Virgin King; Ludwig's Cook; A Man Like Eva; Michael; Paragraph 175; Querelle; Sex Life in L.A.; Taxi zum Klo; Westler; East of the Wall*
Greece, *Cavafy*
HK, *Before Dawn; Happy Together; Journey to Beijing; The Killer* (Woo); *The Map of Sex and Love; A Queer Story; Yang ± Yin: Gender in Chinese Cinema*
Ind, *The Sixth Happiness*
It, *Forever Mary; Il Mercenario; Whoever Says the Truth Will Die*
Jap, *Beautiful Mystery – Legend of Big Horn; The Black Lizard; Cruel Story of the Shogunate's Downfall; Funeral Parade of Roses; Gonin; Heaven-6-Box; Hush!; I Like You, I Like You Very Much; Like Grains of Sand; Looking for an Angel; Okoge; Swimming Prohibited; Taboo*
Mex, *Doña Herlinda and Her Son*
Neth, *Casta Diva; Dear Boys; The Fourth Man; The Pillow Book*
Nor, *Sebastian*
Peru, *Don't Tell Anyone*
Phil, *Midnight Dancers*
SKor, *Broken Branches; Roadmovie*
Sp, *I Will Survive; The Law of Desire; Order to Kill; Pourquoi pas moi?; Second Skin*
Tai, *A Cha-Cha for the Fugitive; Too Young*
US, *And the Band Played On; The Anger Magick Lantern Cycle; As Good As It Gets; Billy's Hollywood Screen Kiss; The Birdcage; The Broken Hearts Club; Buddies; Cabaret; Can't Stop the Music; The Celluloid Closet; Chuck & Buck; Citizen Cohn; Couch; Cruising; The Deep End; The Delta; A Different Story; Dog Day Afternoon; Finding North; Flaming Creatures; Flirting with Disaster; The Fluffer; Frisk; Fun Down There; Gods and Monsters; Happy Texas; Hollow Reed; Hustler White; In & Out; I Think I Do; Jeffrey; Johnny Eager; Kiss Me, Guido; Latin Boys Go to Hell; Liquid Sky; The Living End; Lonesome Cowboys; Longtime Companion; Looking for Langston; Love! Valour! Compassion!; Making Love; Mala Noche; Man of the Year; Midnight in the Garden of Good and Evil; My Best Friend's Wedding; My Hustler; My Own Private Idaho; Naked Lunch; Norman…Is That You?; The Object of My Affection; One Night Stand; The Opposite of Sex; Paris Is Burning; Parting Glances; Partners; Philadelphia; Pink Narcissus; Poison; Portrait of Jason; The Ritz; Rock Hudson's Home Movies; Rope; Saturday Night at the Baths; Slanted Vision; Split William to Chrysis: Portrait of a Drag Queen; Staircase; Swoon; Tea and Sympathy; Three to Tango; The Times of Harvey Milk; The Todd Killings; Tongues Untied; Torch Song Trilogy; Totally F***ed Up; Trick; Victor/Victoria; Voices from the Front; The Wedding Banquet; Word Is Out*

Genet, Jean, films adapted from/inspired by work, *Les Equilibristes; The Maids; Poison; Querelle*

Genetic modification *Bats*

Gentileschi, Artemisia, film about, *Artemisia*

Genghiz Khan, film about, *The Conqueror*

George III, King of England, in film, *The Madness of King George*

Georgian cinema, *Graveyard of Dreams*

German cinema, see Appendix 19

Germany, in film
pre-1900, *Dr Ehrlich's Magic Bullet; Effi Briest; Jeder für sich und Gott gegen Alle (The Enigma of Kaspar Hauser); Kaspar Hauser; Ludwig; Ludwig – Requiem for a Virgin King; Ludwig's Cook; Die Marquise von O…; Michael Kohlhaas; The Sudden Fortune of the Good People of Kombach; The Swing; Woyzeck* (Herzog); *Woyzeck* (Szász)
early 20th century, *Berlin – die Sinfonie der Grosstadt; Bolwieser; Das Blau Licht; The Blue Angel; Cabaret; The Cabinet of Dr Caligari; Dr Mabuse, the Gambler; Emil & the Detectives; Georgette Meunier; The Inheritors; Kameradschaft; Karl May; Kühle Wampe; John Heartfield: Photomonteur; Joyless Street; M* (Lang); *Nicht Versöhnt; The 1,000 Eyes of Dr Mabuse; Rosa Luxemburg; Tenderness of the Wolves; Three Comrades; Le Vampire de Dusseldorf; Die Weber; Young Törless*
Nazi Germany (see also **Jews and Jewish life, War criminals, World War II**), *Address Unknown; The Adventures of Werner Holt; After the Truth; Bent; Berlin Express; Berlin Jerusalem; Cabaret; Comedian Harmonists; The Confessions of Winifred Wagner; The Cremator; The Damned* (Visconti); *Death Is My Trade; Deutschland, Erwache!; The Double-Headed Eagle; England Made Me; Europa, Europa; Hannibal Brooks; Hanussen; Heimat; Hitler – A Career; Hitler, A Film from Germany; The Hitler Gang; Hotel Terminus: The Life and Times of Klaus Barbie; Into the Arms of Strangers: Stories of the Kindertransport; I Was Nineteen; Jew-Boy Levi; Korczak; The Last Days; The Last Hole; Lili Marleen; A Love in Germany; The Man I Married; The Man in the Glass Booth; The Master Race; Mephisto; Moloch; The Mortal Storm; Mother Night; My Private War; The Nasty Girl; The Night of the Generals; None Shall Escape; One Mans War; The Package Tour; Paragraph 175; Pastor Hall; Pimpernel Smith; The Refusal; Reunion; Le Roi de Aulnes; Salon Kitty; The Sea Chase; Seven Beauties; Seven Minutes; The Seventh Cross; Sophie's Choice; The Specialist; Swastika; Swing Kids; The Testament of Dr Mabuse; A Time to Love and a Time to Die; The Tin Drum; To Be or Not To Be* (Lubitsch); *To Be or Not To Be* (Johnson); *Totschweigen; Triumph of the Spirit; Triumph of the Will; Der Verlorene; Voyage of the Damned; Will My Mother Go Back to Berlin?; The Wooden Horse*
post-war, West Germany, *Berlin Is in Germany; The Divided Heart; Europa; Fear Eats the Soul; A Foreign Affair; The German Sisters; Germany, Pale Mother; Germany, Year Zero; Germany in Autumn; G.I. Blues; Garage Olimpio; Hunting Scenes from Lower Bavaria; Judgment at Nuremberg; Keiner Liebt Mich; Kings of the Road; The Legends of Rita; Life Is All You Get; The Man Between; The Marriage of Maria Braun; The Merchant of Four Seasons; Mother Küster's Trip to Heaven; The Nasty Girl; Occasional Work of a Female Slave; 1+1=3; Palermo or Wolfsburg; The Point Is to Change It; The Promise* (von Trotta); *Schtonk!; Spicy Rice; Summer in the City; Verboten; Veronika Voss; A Woman in Flames; Wrong Movement; Yesterday Girl*
East Germany, *Berlin Is in Germany; The Burning Wall; Coming Out; Farewell; Held for Questioning; I Was, I Am, I Shall Be; Judgment in Berlin; The Legends of Rita; No Place to Go; November Days Voices and Choices; Stunde Null; Sun Alley; Westler; Wittstock, Wittstock; East of the Wall*
East German cinema, *The Adventures of Werner Holt; Coming Out; Elective Affinities* (Kühn); *Held for Questioning; In Georgia; I Was, I Am, I Shall Be; The Singing Ringing Tree*
Germany post-reunification, *After the Fall* (Sandig/Black); *After the Truth; Clando; The Experiment; Fat World; Frost; The German Chainsaw Massacre; Home Game; In July; Lost Killers; Mau Mau; Mercedes Mon Amour; Passages; The Princess + the Warrior; The Secret Face; The Serbian Girl; Shampoo and Set; Sumo Bruno Wittstock, Wittstock; Yara*

Germ warfare, *The Avalanche Express; The Crazies; Endangered Species; The Satan Bug; Virus*

Gershwin, George
musicals by, *An American in Paris; A Damsel in Distress; The King of Jazz*
film about, *Rhapsody in Blue*

Ghana, in film, *Ama; Heritage…Africa; Sankofa; Testament* (Akomfrah)

Ghanaian cinema, *Heritage…Africa; Sankofa*

Ghosts (see also **Haunted houses**), *The Amazing Mr Blunden; Beetlejuice; Beloved; Blackbeard's Ghost; Blithe Spirit; The Blue Villa;*

Candyman; Candyman 2: Farewell to the Flesh; Casper; The Changeling; A Chinese Ghost Story; A Chinese Ghost Story II; A Chinese Ghost Story III; Curtain Call; Dead of Night (Hamer); *Don't Take It to Heart; Demons; Dream Demon; Full Circle; Ghost; The Ghost and Mrs Muir; The Ghost Breakers; Ghostbusters; Ghostbusters II; Ghost Catchers; Ghost Chase; The Ghost Goes West; The Ghost Ship; The Ghosts of Kasane Swamp; Ghost Story; Ghost Story of Yotsuya; Gojoe; Haunted; The Haunting; Heart Condition; High Spirits; Hush, Hush, Sweet Charlotte; The Innocents; Killer Butterfly; Kiss Me Goodbye; Kwaidan; Lady in White; Legend of the Mountain; Long Time Dead; A Love Bewitched; The Mansion of the Ghost Cat; Maxie; Memento Mori; Nang Nak; The Others; A Place of One's Own; Poltergeist; Poltergeist II; Poltergeist III; Retribution; Ruby; Sir Henry at Rawlinson's End; Shikoku; The Sixth Sense; The Spooky Bunch; Stir of Echoes; Superstition; La Tendre Ennemie; The Terror; Thirteen Ghosts; Topper; The Tower of the Seven Hunchbacks; Truly, Madly, Deeply; Ugetsu Monogatari; The Uninvited; Urban Ghost Story; Whispering Corridors; Yumeji*

Gibbons, Stella, film adapted from work, *Cold Comfort Farm*

Gide, André, film adapted from work, *La Symphonie Pastorale*

Gigolos, *American Gigolo; Deuce Bigalow: Male Gigolo; Hold Back the Dawn; Intimate with a Stranger; Just a Gigolo; Loverboy; Masquerade* (Swaim); *Midnight Cowboy; Speaking Parts; Sweet Bird of Youth* (Brooks); *Sweet Bird of Youth* (Roeg)

Gilbert and Sullivan
films adapted from operas, *Dick Deadeye, or Duty Done; The Mikado; The Pirates of Penzance;*
films about, *The Story of Gilbert and Sullivan; Topsy Turvy*

Gillespie, Dizzy, films about, *A Great Day in Harlem; A Night in Havana: Dizzy Gillespie in Cuba*

Gilliam, Terry, film about, *The Hamster Factor and Other Tales of Twelve Monkeys*

Gilroy, Frank D, films adapted from work, *The Only Game in Town; The Subject Was Roses*

Ginsberg, Allen
film about, *The Life and Times of Allen Ginsberg*
in film, *Pull My Daisy*

Giono, Jean, film adapted from work, *Les Ammes Fortes*

Giordano, Mario, film adapted from work, *The Experiment*

Gipson, Fred, film adapted from work, *Hound-Dog Man*

Gladiators, *The Arena; Gladiator* (Scott); *Demetrius and the Gladiators; Fabiola; Spartacus*

Gloag, Julian, film adapted from work, *Our Mother's House*

God (see also **Biblical stories, Jesus Christ**)
absence of, *Waiting for Godot*
portrayed in film, *Body Drop Ashphalt; Almost an Angel; The Next Voice You Hear…; Oh, God!; Star Trek V: The Final Frontier; Switch; Two of a Kind*
message from, *Des Nouvelles du Bon Dieu; Red Planet Mars*

Godden, Rumer, films adapted from work, *The Battle of the Villa Fiorita; Black Narcissus; The Greengage Summer; The River* (Renoir)

Goethe, Johann Wolfgang, films adapted from work, *Elective Affinities* (Taviani/Taviani); *Elective Affinities* (Kühn); *Faust* (Murnau); *Faust* (Svankmajer); *Fausto 5.0; Le Jeune Werther*

Go-Go music, *Good to Go*

Golding, William, films adapted from work, *Lord of the Flies* (Brook); *Lord of the Flies* (Hook)

Goldman, William, films adapted from work, *Magic, Marathon Man; No Way to Treat a Lady; The Princess Bride*

Gold prospecting and gold rushes, *Aguirre, Wrath of God; Back to the Future Part III; By the Law; The Claim; El Dorado; Eureka; The Gold Rush; Mackenna's Gold; North to Alaska; Road to Utopia; The Robin Hood of El Dorado; Support Your Local Sheriff; A Thousand Pieces of Gold; The Treasure of the Sierra Madre; Way Out West; White Fang* (Fulci); *White Fang* (Kleiser)

Golf, *Caddyshack; Happy Gilmore; The Legend of Bagger Vance; Tin Cup; Triple Bogey on a Par Five Hole*

Goncharov, Mikhail, film adapted from work, *Oblomov*

Goodis, David, films adapted from work, *The Burglars; Dark Passage; The Moon in the Gutter; Nightfall; Tirez sur le Pianiste*

The Goons, *Down Among the Z Men*

Gorki, Maxim, films adapted from work, *Les Bas-Fonds; The Childhood of Maxim Gorki; The Lower Depths; Mother* (Pudovkin); *The Orlovs; Vassa*

Gould, Glenn, film about, *Thirty Two Short Films About Glenn Gould*

Graffiti artists, *IP5; Turk 182!; Wild Style*

Graham, Sheilah, film adapted from work, *Beloved Infidel*

Graham, Winston, films adapted from work, *Marnie; The Walking Stick*

Grahame, Kenneth, films adapted from work, *Ichabod and Mr Toad; The Wind in the Willows*

Grandparents and grandchildren, *Blood is Not Fresh Water; By Nightfall; L'Enfance nue; The Gift; Heartstrings; Lost in Yonkers; Rabid Grannies; The Revolving Doors; A Summer at Grandpa's; Tokyo Story; Venus Peter*

Grass, Günter, film adapted from work, *The Tin Drum*

Graves, Robert, film adapted form work, *The Shout*

Gray, Simon, films adapted from work, *Butley; Old Flames*

Gray, Spalding, in performance, *Monster in a Box; Swimming to Cambodia*

Graziano, Rocky, film about, *Somebody Up There Likes Me*

Greece, in film
Ancient Greece, *Alexander the Great* (Rossen); *The Giant of Marathon*
Greek Myths (and adaptations), *The Cannibals; Clash of the Titans; The Colossus of Rhodes; The Dawn; A Dream of Passion, Elektreia; Ercole alla conquista di Atlantide; Hercules; Jason and the Argonauts; Oedipus Rex; Oedipus the King; Orfeu; Orphée; Phaedra; Prometheus; Such Is Life; Le Testament d'Orphée; Vaghe Stelle dell'Orsa*
Modern Greece, *Alexander the Great* (Angelopoulos); *Balkanisateur; The Bee Keeper; Brothers; Boatman; Captain Corelli's Mandolin; Cavafy; The Day the Fish Came Out; Dead Liqueur; Edge of Night; Eleftherios Venizelos; Eleni; End of an Era; Escape to Athena; Eternity and a Day; Female Company; The Four Seasons of the Law; The Guns of Navarone; High Season; I Dream of My Friends; Ill Met by Moonlight; Landscape in the Mist; Melodrama?; Peppermint; Shirley Valentine; Shores of Twilight; Stone Years; Summer Lovers; The Travelling Players; Ulysses' Gaze; Voyage to Cythera; When Mother Comes Home for Christmas; The Wind* (Mastorakis); *The Woman Who Dreamed; Zorba the Greek*

Greek cinema, *Alexander the Great* (Angelopoulos); *Balkanisateur; The Bee Keeper; Boatman; Cabaret Balkan; The Canary Yellow Bicycle; The Cherry Orchard; The Dawn; The Day the Fish Came Out; Dead Liqueur; Edge of Night; Eleftherios Venizelos; End of an Era; Eternity and a Day; Female Company; The Four Seasons of the Law; From the Edge of the City; I Dream of My Friends; Landscape in the Mist; Melodrama?; Never on Sunday; Peppermint; Screamin' Jay Hawkins: I Put a Spell on Me; Shores of Twilight; Singapore Sling; Stone Years; The Travelling Players; Ulysses' Gaze; Varietes; Voyage to Cythera; When Mother Comes Home for Christmas; The Woman Who Dreamed; Zorba the Greek*

Greene, Graham, films adapted from work, *Brighton Rock; The Comedians; Confidential Agent; The End of the Affair; England Made Me; The Fallen Idol; The Fugitive* (Ford); *The Heart of the Matter; The Honorary Consul; Loser Takes All; Ministry of Fear; Our Man in Havana; The Quiet American; The Third Man; This Gun for Hire*

Greenwood, Walter, film adapted from work, *Love on the Dole*

Grieg, Edvard, film about, *Song of Norway*

Grimm brothers, films adapted from work, *Rapunzel Let Down Your Hair; Tom Thumb*

Grisham, John, films adapted from work, *The Chamber; The Client; The Firm; The Gingerbread Man; The Pelican Brief; The Rainmaker; A Time to Kill*

Grubb, Davis, film adapted from work, *The Night of the Hunter*

Guare, John, film adapted from work, *Six Degrees of Separation*

Guatemala
in film, *¡Devils Don't Dream! Research on Jacobo Arbenz*

Guzmán; El Norte; When the Mountains Tremble
Guatemalan cinema, *The Daughter of the Puma*

Guaspari-Tzaras, Roberta, film about, *Small Wonders*

Guerin, Victoria, film about, *When the Sky Falls*

Guevara, Che, film about, *Che*

Guinea cinema, *Le Ballon d'Or*

Guinea-Bissau cinema, *The Blue Eyes of Yonta; Po di Sangui*

Gulf War, films about, and aftermath, *Courage Under Fire; Lessons in Darkness; Song of the Siren; Three Kings*

Gun fetishism
Gun Crazy; Jackie Brown; My New Gun; Taxi Driver; White of the Eye

Gurley-Brown, Helen, film adapted from work, *Sex and the Single Girl*

Guterson, David, film adapted from work, *Snow Falling on Cedars*

Guthrie, Woody, film about, *Bound for Glory*

Guyana
Guyana in film, *Guyana: Crime of the Century*
Guyanan cinema, *Aggro Seizeman*

Gymnastics, *Nadia; Take It Easy*

Gypsies, travellers, etc, *Black Cat White Cat; Devils, Devils; Gadjo Dilo; The Gypsy and the Gentleman; Gypsy Soul; Hot Blood; Into the West; Jassy; King of the Gypsies; Lacho Dom; Marian; Les Princes; The Raggedy Rawney; Snatch; Stephen King's Thinner; Southpaw; Time of the Gypsies; Traveller; Wings of the Morning*

Haggard, H Rider, films adapted from work, *King Solomon's Mines* (Stevenson); *King Solomon's Mines* (Thompson); *King Solomon's Treasure; She* (Pichel); *She* (Day)

Hailey, Arthur, films adapted from work, *Airport; Airport 1975; Airport '77; Airport '80*

Hair, as fetish, *Golden Braid*

Hairdressers
in film, *The Big Tease; Blow Dry; Closed for Family Mourning; Earth Girls Are Easy; An Everlasting Piece; The Hairdresser's Husband; The Man Who Wasn't There; Married to the Mob; Mortal Thoughts; Shampoo; Shampoo and Set; Staircase; Three Colours: White; Venus Beauty; Who's the Man?; Wish You Were Here*
haircolouring, invention of, *Siam Sunset*

Haiti
Haitian cinema, *Lumumba*
in film, *Bitter Cane; The Comedians; The Man by the Shore; The Serpent and the Rainbow; White Zombie*

Hall, Willis, and Waterhouse, Keith, films adapted from work, *Billy Liar*

Halliday, Brett, film adapted from work, *Michael Shayne Private Detective*

Halliwell, David, film adapted from work, *Little Malcolm and His Struggle Against the Eunuchs*

Hamilton, Jane, film adapted from work, *A Map of the World*

Hamilton, Lady, films about, *Bequest to the Nation; That Hamilton Woman*

Hamilton, Patrick, films adapted from work, *Bitter Harvest; Gaslight* (Dickinson); *Gaslight* (Cukor); *Hangover Square; Rope*

Hamilton, Walker, film adapted from work, *All the Little Animals*

Hammerstein, Oscar
and Kern, Jerome, musicals by, *Centennial Summer; Show Boat* (Whale); *Show Boat* (Sidney)
and Rodgers, Richard, musicals by, *Carousel; The King and I* (Lang); *The King and I* (Rich); *Oklahoma; South Pacific; State Fair*

Hammett, Dashiell, films adapted from work, *The Black Bird; The Glass Key; The Maltese Falcon* (Del Ruth) *The Maltese Falcon* (Huston); *Satan Met a Lady; The Thin Man*
film about, *Hammett*

Hamsun, Knut, film adapted from work, *Nearly Wide Awake*

Handy, WC, film about, *St Louis Blues*

Hang gliding, *Sky Riders*

Han Suyin, film adapted from work, *Love Is a Many-Splendored Thing*

Hardy, Thomas, films adapted from work, *The Claim; Far from the Madding Crowd; Jude; The Scarlet Tunic; Tess; The Woodlanders*

Hare, David, film adapted from work, *Plenty*

Harrer, Heinrich, film adapted from work, *Seven Years in Tibet*

Harris, Joel Chandler, film adapted from work, *Song of the South*

Harris, Robert, film adapted from work, *Enigma*

Harris, Thomas, films adapted from work, *Black Sunday* (Frankenheimer); *Manhunter; The Silence of the Lambs*

Harrison, Jim, films adapted from work, *Carried Away; Legends of the Fall*

Harryhausen, Ray, special effects by, *Clash of the Titans; Earth vs the Flying Saucers; First Men in the Moon; The Golden Voyage of Sinbad; It Came from Beneath the Sea; Jason and the Argonauts; One Million Years B.C.; The Seventh Voyage of Sinbad; Sinbad and the Eye of the Tiger; The Three Worlds of Gulliver; The Valley of Gwangi*

Hart, Lorenz, and Rodgers, Richard, musicals by, *Babes in Arms; Billy Rose's Jumbo; Hallelujah, I'm a Bum; Love Me Tonight; Pal Joey*

Hartley, LP, films adapted from work, *The Go-Between; The Hireling*

Hastings, Michael, film adapted from work, *Tom & Viv*

Haunted houses (see also **Ghosts, Unwanted guests**), *The Bat Whispers; Beetlejuice; The Beyond; The Cat and the Canary* (Leni); *The Cat and the Canary* (Nugent); *The Cat and the Canary* (Metzger); *The Ghost Breakers; Ghost Catchers; The Ghost Goes West; Haunted; Haunted Honeymoon; The Haunted Palace; The Haunting; The Haunting Hell Night; High Spirits; House; The House by the Cemetery; House of Fear; House of The Long Shadows; House on Haunted Hill; The Innocents; Lady in White; The Legend of Hell House; Maid for Pleasure; Mark of the Vampire; Night of the Demons; The Others; The Spell; The Uninvited*

Hauptmann, Gerhart, film adapted from work, *Die Weber*

Hawaii, in film, *Aloha Summer; Blue Hawaii; From Here to Eternity; Hawaii; Molokai: The Story of Father Damien; Picture Bride; The Revolt of Mamie Stover, Tora! Tora! Tora!*

Hawthorne, Nathaniel, films adapted from work, *The Scarlet Letter* (Sjöström); *The Scarlet Letter* (Joffé); *The Scarlet Letter* (Wenders)

Hayes, Joseph, films adapted from work, *Desperate Hours* (Cimino); *The Desperate Hours* (Wyler)

Health clubs, *Perfect*

Hearst, Patty, films about, *Abduction; Patty Hearst*

Hearst, William Randolph, films about, *The Cat's Meow; Citizen Kane*

Heartfield, John, film about, *John Heartfield, Photomonteur*

Heaven-can-wait fantasies (see also **Afterlife, Return to life**), *Always* (Spielberg); *Down to Earth; Frequency; Ghost; Heaven Can Wait* (Lubitsch); *Heaven Can Wait* (Beatty/Henry); *Here Comes Mr Jordan; It's a Wonderful Life; Jacob's Ladder; Les Jeux sont Faits; A Matter of Life and Death; Meet Joe Black; Le Nez au vent; Switch; Truly, Madly, Deeply; Two of a Kind*

Hecht, Ben, films adapted from work, *The Florentine Dagger; The Front Page* (Milestone); *The Front Page* (Wilder); *His Girl Friday; Twentieth Century*

Hedden, Roger, film adapted from work, *Bodies, Rest & Motion*

Heggen, Thomas, films adapted from work, *Ensign Pulver; Mister Roberts*

Heidi stories, *Courage Mountain; Heidi's Song*

Heists and capers, *American Buffalo; The Asphalt Jungle; The Badlanders; Best Laid Plans; Best Men; Bottle Rocket; The Caper of the Golden Bulls; The Catamount Killing; La Città si Difende; Darkness in Tallinn; Dobermann; $; Du Rififi à Paname; Du Rififi chez les hommes; Fantômas; Heist; High Heels and Low Lifes; L'Homme de Marrakech; Hot Rock; Johnny 100 Pesos; The Italian Job; The Killing; The League of Gentlemen; Lewis & Clark & George; The Longest Summer; Love, Honour and Obey; Midas Run; The Newton Boys; Ocean's 11* (Milestone); *Ocean's Eleven* (Soderbergh); *The Parole Officer; Payback; Palookaville; A Prize of Arms; Reservoir Dogs; Ronin; Safe Men; The Set Up; The Spider and the Fly; That Night's Wife; Topkapi; The Triple Cross; You're Dead…*

Hellman, Lillian
film about, *Julia*
films adapted from work, *The Little Foxes; The Searching Wind; These Three*

Hemingway, Ernest
films adapted from work, *The Breaking Point* (Curtiz); *A Farewell to Arms* (Borzage); *A Farewell to Arms* (Vidor); *For Whom The Bell Tolls; Islands in the Stream; The Killers* (Siodmak); *The Killers* (Siegel); *The Macomber Affair; The Old Man and the Sea; The Snows of Kilimanjaro; The Sun Also Rises; To Have and Have Not*
film inspired by life, *In Love and War*

Henley, Beth, films adapted from work, *Crimes of the Heart; Miss Firecracker*

Henry, O, films adapted from work, *The Cisco Kid and the Lady; Dr Rhythm; O. Henry's Full House*

Henry II, King of England, film about, *The Lion in Winter*

Henry VIII, King of England, films about, *Henry VIII and His Six Wives; A Man for All Seasons; The Private Life of Henry VIII*

Herbert, Frank, film adapted from work, *Dune*

Herbert, James, film adapted from his work, *Haunted; The Survivor*

Herbert, Victor, film adapted from work, *Naughty Marietta*

Hermaphroditism, *Fellini-Satyricon; The Final Programme; The Mystery of Alexina; Private Vices & Public Virtues*

Hermits, *Night Sun*

Herriot, James, films adapted from work, *All Creatures Great and Small; It Shouldn't Happen to a Vet*

Hesse, Hermann, films adapted from work, *Siddhartha; Steppenwolf*

Hiaasen, Carl, film adapted from work, *Striptease*

Hickam, Homer H, film adapted from work, *October Sky*

Higgins, George V, film adapted from work, *The Friends of Eddie Coyle*

Higgins, Jack, film adapted from work, *The Eagle Has Landed*

Highsmith, Patricia, films adapted from work, *The American Friend; Le Cri du Hibou; Plein Soleil; Strangers on a Train; This Sweet Sickness; The Talented Mr Ripley; Throw Momma from the Train*

Highwaymen, *Sinful Davey; Tom Jones; Plunkett & Macleane; Where's Jack; The Wicked Lady* (Arliss); *The Wicked Lady* (Winner)

Hijacking, *Air Force One; Airport '77; Aux Yeux du monde; Con Air; Die Hard 2; Executive Decision; Jet Storm; Joan of Arc of Mongolia; Judgment in Berlin; Moon 44; Operation Thunderbolt; The Out-of-Towners* (Hiller); *The Out-of-Towners* (Weisman); *Passenger 57; Raid on Entebbe; Runaway Train; Scarecrows; Skyjacked; The Taking of Pelham One Two Three; Under Siege; Victory at Entebbe*

Hilton, James, films adapted from work, *Goodbye, Mr Chips* (Wood); *Goodbye, Mr Chips* (Ross); *Lost Horizon* (Capra); *Lost Horizon* (Jarrott); *Rage in Heaven; Random Harvest; We Are Not Alone*

Himes, Chester, films adapted from work, *Come Back Charleston Blue; A Rage in Harlem*

Hinduism, *The Chosen One; Devi; The Guru; The Home and the World; Hot Winds; Journey to Wisdom; Man from Africa and Girl from India; Siddhartha*

Hinton, SE, films adapted from work, *The Outsiders* (Coppola); *Rumble Fish; That Was Then... This Is Now*

Hispanic Americans, *La Bamba; The Border; Border Incident; Bordertown; Boulevard Nights; Crossover Dreams; Dance With Me; El Norte; Hangin' with the Homeboys; Lambada; The Lawless; Mala Noche; The Milagro Beanfield War; My Crazy Life; My Family; The Robin Hood of El Dorado; Rooftops; Running Scared* (Hyams); *Salsa; Salt of the Earth; Stand and Deliver; Touch of Evil; Toy Soldiers; West Side Story*

History and historians, *Talking History*

Hitchhikers, *Alligator Eyes; The Hitcher; The Hitchhiker; Soft Top, Hard Shoulder*

Hitler, Adolf, films about, *Black Fox; Hitler – A Career; Hitler, a Film from Germany; The Hitler Gang; Hitler; The Last Ten Days; Moloch; Swastika*

Hitler's diaries, *Schtonk!; What Have I Done to Deserve This?*

Hitmen (and women), *Amateur; The American Friend; Another Lonely Hitman; The Assassination Bureau; Assassin(s); Bangkok: Dangerous; Beyon Forgivin'; The Big Hit; Black Rainbow; Blame It on the Bellboy; B. Must Die; Branded to Kill; Bring Me the Head of Mavis Davis; Buddy Buddy; Catchfire; The Client; Cohen and Tate; Cible émouvante; Crimes and Misdemeanors; Crying Freeman; The Deadly Females; Dead or Alive 2 – Birds; Deaths in Tokimeki; The Disappearance; Dragon Town Story; 8 Heads in a Duffel Bag; L'Emmerdeur; The Enforcer* (Windust/Walsh); *The Evil That Men Do; Fallen Angels; Flight of the Innocent; Ghost Dog: The Way of the Samurai; Gonin; Gonin 2; The Green Man; Grosse Pointe Blank; Hard Contract; Hard Men; The Hatchet Man; Heaven; Hit List; Ichi the Killer; I Hired a Contract Killer; The Internecine Project; Jackie Brown; Killer; The Killer* (Woo); *Last Man Standing; Leon; The Last Yellow; The Lineup; Little Odessa; The Long Kiss Goodnight; Love and Action in Chicago; Mad Dog Time; The Marseille Contract; The Mechanic; Mercury Rising; The Mission* (Sayyad); *The Most Terrible Time in My Life; Murder by Contract; Naked Killer; Nikita; 99 and 44/100% Dead; The Outside Man; Pistol Opera; Point Blank; Point of No Return; Prizzi's Honor; Pulp Fiction; Rainy Dog; Red Rock West; The Replacement Killers; Rub Love; Ruby; Le Samourai; Scorpio; La Scoumoune; Shark-skin Man and Peach-hip Girl; The Soldier; Sonatine; Spawn; Sun Valley; The Survivors; Things to Do in Denver When You're Dead; This Gun for Hire; 2 Days in the Valley; U Turn; The Whole Nine Yards; Wise Guys*

Hoban, Russell, films adapted from work, *The Mouse and His Child; Turtle Diary*

Hochhuth, Rolf, film adapted from work, *A Love in Germany*

Hockney, David
film about, *A Bigger Splash*
in film, *Tonite Let's All Make Love in London*

Høeg, Peter, film adapted from work, *Smilla's Feeling for Snow*

Hoffman, Alice, film adapted from work, *Practical Magic*

Holiday, Billie, film about, *Lady Sings the Blues*

Holidays and holiday camps, *Aloha Summer; The Best Way to Walk; Blame It on Rio; Les Bronzés; Casual Sex?; Claire's Knee; Confessions from a Holiday Camp; The Cruise; Cuba Libre – Velocipedi ai Tropici; Darkness and Light; Girls' Night; Holiday Camp; How Stella Got Her Groove Back; I Still Know What You Did Last Summer; La Baule-les-pins; Meatballs; Un Moment d'Egarement; Mon Père, ce héros; My Father, the Hero; National Lampoon's Vacation; Pauline à la Plage; Les Randonneurs; Shirley Valentine; Summer Holiday; Summer Lovers; Tout ça... pour ça!!!; Les Vacances de M. Hulot*

Holly, Buddy, film about, *The Buddy Holly Story*

Hollywood and the movie business, in film (see also **Film-makers and film-making)**
British film industry, *Go for a Take; Nobody Ordered Love; O-Kay for Sound; Orders Are Orders*
French film industry, *Day for Night; Irma Vep; Ivan Mosjoukine, or The Carnival Child; Prix de Beauté*
Chinese film industry, *Actress*
Hollywood: golden age, *The Bad and the Beautiful; Barton Fink; Beloved Infidel; Best Foot Forward; The Big Knife; Boy Meets Girl; Bugsy; The Bullfighter and the Lady; The Cat's Meow; Chaplin; Classified X; The Day of the Locust; Ed Wood; Fellow Traveller; Frances; Frank Capra's American Dream; Gable and Lombard; The Goddess; Gods and Monsters; Goodbye, Norma Jean; Good Morning Babylon; Guilty by Suspicion; Hearts of the West; Hold Back the Dawn; Hollywood Cavalcade; Hollywood on Trial; Hollywood or Bust; Illusions; In a Lonely Place; It's All True; Ivan Mosjoukine, or The Carnival Child; The James Dean Story; James Dean – The First American Teenager; Lady Killer; The Last Command; The Last Tycoon; The Lost Squadron; Love Goddesses; The Love Lottery; Movie Crazy; Music for the Movies: The Hollywood Sound; Musicals Great Musicals: The Arthur Freed Unit at MGM; Music for the Movies: Bernard Herrmann; Never Give a Sucker an Even Break; Nickelodeon; 1941; The Rocketeer; The Sex Symbol; Show People; Singin' in the Rain; Stand-In; The Star; A Star Is Born* (Wellman); *A Star Is Born* (Cukor); *Sunset; Sunset Blvd.; Susan Slept Here; Thank Your Lucky Stars; Two Weeks in Another Town; Valentino; The Way We Were; W.C. Fields and Me; Whatever Happened to Baby Jane?; What Price Hollywood?; White Hunter, Black Heart; Wild Bill: A Hollywood Maverick; The Wild Party* (Ivory); *The World's Greatest Lover; The Young Stranger*
Hollywood: contemporary, *Alex in Wonderland; America's Sweethearts; An Almost Perfect Affair; Bert Rigby, You're a Fool; Beyond the Valley of the Dolls; The*

Big Picture; The Bodyguard; Boogie Nights; Cecil B. Demented; Celebrity; Classified X; Crocodile Dundee in Los Angeles; Death Becomes Her; The Disappearance of Kevin Johnson; Eloge de l'amour; Fedora; F/X; F/X2; Get Shorty; The Hard Way; Hearts of Darkness: A Filmmaker's Apocalypse; Heidi Fleiss – Hollywood Madam; Hollywood Ending; Hollywood Shuffle; Hurlyburly; Inserts; I Ought to Be in Pictures; Irreconcilable Differences; Jay and Silent Bob Strike Back; Jimmy Hollywood; The Ladies' Man; L.A. Story; LA Without a Map; The Legend of Lylah Clare; Lions Love; The Lonely Lady; A Man in Love; Mistress; Moon Over Parador; Movers and Shakers; My Giant; Night Games; The Party; The Player; Postcards from the Edge; S.O.B.; Somebody to Love; Star 80; A Star Is Born (Pierson); *Sweet Liberty; Swimming to Cambodia; Swimming with Sharks; True Identity; Valley of the Dolls; What's the Matter with Helen?; Wired; The Wizard of Speed and Time*
Indian film industry, *Bombay Talkie; Cinema Cinema; Helen, Queen of the Nautch Girls; The Role*
Italian film industry, *Bellissima; La Signora senza camelie*
Japanese film industry, *Bantsuma: The Life and Times of Tsumasaburo Bando*

Holocaust, Nazi, see **Germany** and **Jews and Jewish life**

Homelessness, *Les Amants du Pont Neuf; Dark Days; Une Epoque formidable…; Fat World; Hands; Leaf on a Pillow; The Mutants*

Homosexuality, see **Gays (male) and gay cinema** and **Lesbians and lesbianism**

Honduras, in film, *Appointment in Honduras; Latino*

Hong Kong cinema
martial arts, etc *The Accidental Spy; Ah-Kam; Beach of the War Gods; Beijing Bastards; A Better Tomorrow; A Better Tomorrow II; The Big Boss; The Blade; The Bloody Fists; Burning Paradise; Bruce Lee: The Man, The Myth; Bullet in the Head; The Chinese Connection; The Conman and the Kung Fu Kid; Crime Story; Death Kick; Dirty Ho; Dynasty; 8-Diagram Pole Fighter; The Empress Yang Kwei Fei; Enter the Dragon; Enter the Seven Virgins; Executioners from Shaolin; The Fate of Lee Khan; First Strike; Fist of Fury; Fong Sai-Yuk; Full Contact; Golden Swallow; Hap-Ki-Do; The Heroic Trio; The Iceman Cometh; Ichi the Killer; The Killer* (Chu Yuan); *King Boxer; King of Kung Fu; Knock Off; Kung Fu Fighting; Kung Fu Gangbusters; The Kung Fu Girl; Kung Fu – The Headcrusher; Last Hurrah for Chivalry; Legend of the 7 Golden Vampires; The Legend of Zu; The Man from Hong Kong; Mr Nice Guy; Moon Warriors; My Young Auntie; The New One-Armed Boxer; Once Upon a Time in China; Once Upon a Time in China II; Once Upon a Time in Triad Society; Once Upon a Time in Triad Society 2; Police Story* (Chan); *Portland Street Blues; Rumble in the Bronx; The Scorpion King* (Lai); *Shanghai Lil; Shanghai Noon; The Stormriders; The Story of Woo Viet; The 36th Chamber of Shaolin; Time and Tide; Tokyo Raiders; Twin Dragons; Warriors of Virtue; The Way of the Dragon; Young and Dangerous; Young and Dangerous 2; Young and Dangerous 3; Zu: Warriors from the Magic Mountain*
non-martial arts, *Ah-Kam; Ah Ying; Actress; The Armour of God; As Tears Go By; Au revoir, mon amour; Autumn Moon; Back Alley Princes; Back to Back, Boat People; Bullets Over Summer; Before Dawn; The Blood Brothers; Buenos Aires Zero Degree; The Butterfly Murders; C'est la Vie, Ma Cherie; Chinese Box; Chungking Express; Chicken and Duck Talk; A Chinese Ghost Story; A Chinese Ghost Story II; A Chinese Ghost Story III; Comrades, Almost a Love Story; City on Fire; The Club* (Wong); *Cross-Harbour Tunnel; Dead Knot; Dancing Bull; Days of Being Wild; The Day the Sun Turned Cold; The Deaf and Mute Heroine; Don't Play With Fire; Dragon Town Story; Durian, Durian; Eight Taels of Gold; Eighteen Springs; The Emperor's Shadow; Face to Face; Fallen Angels; Father and Son; First Love – The Litter on the Breeze; Foreign Moon; 4 Faces of Eve; Full Moon in New York; For Fun; From the Queen to the Chief Executive; Front Page; Gen-X Cops; Gen-Y Cops; Heroes of Love; He's a Woman, She's a Man; Hard-Boiled; Hold You Tight; Homecoming* (Ho); *Hot War; Hu-Du-Men; In the Mood for Love; Intimate Confessions of a Chinese Courtesan; The Island Tales; Journey to Beijing; July Rhapsody; Just Heroes; Just Like Weather; Kawashima Yoshiko; The Killer* (Woo); *King of Masks; Kitchen* (Yim Ho); *Lan Yu; Legend of the Mountain; Li Lianying, the Imperial Eunuch; Little Cheung; The Longest Summer; Love in a Fallen City; Love Unto Waste; Love Will Tear Us Apart; Made in Hong Kong; The Map of Sex and Love; Metade Fumaça; Mr Vampire; Mr Zhao; My Dad is a Jerk; '92 The Legendary La Rose Noire; Naked Killer; One Fine Spring Day; Once a Thief; Ordinary Heroes; Organized Crime and Triad Bureau; Peking Opera Blues; The Phantom Lover; The Platform; Purple Storm; A Queer Story; Raining in the Mountain; Red Beads; Red Firecracker, Green Firecracker; Red Rose, White Rose; Ripples Across Stagnant Water; Rock n'Roll Cop; The Romance of Book and Sword; Rouge; Sausalito; Seafood; The Secret; Shanghai Blues; Shanghai Triad; Shaolin Soccer; Signal Left, Turn Right; The Spooky Bunch; Still Love You After All; The Story of Woo Viet; Summer Snow; Sunless Days; Sun Valley; Swordsman; Swordsman II; Task Force; Temptress Moon; A Terra-Cotta Warrior; Theft Under the Sun; To Live; Unknown Pleasures; The Valiant Ones; Visible Secret; Viva Erotica!; Wheels on Meals; The Wicked City; Xenolith; Yang ± Yin: Gender in Chinese Cinema*

Hong Kong, in film, *Autumn Moon; Back Alley Princes; Before Dawn; Blood Reincarnation; Blood Sport; Bullet in the Head; C'est la Vie, Ma Cherie; Chicken and Duck Talk; Chinese Box; Chungking Express; Cross-Harbour Tunnel; Dancing Bull; Days of Being Wild; Dead Knot; Dragon: The Bruce Lee Story; Fallen Angels; Beach of the War Gods; Father and Son; Ferry to Hong Kong; First Strike; From the Queen to the Chief Executive; Front Page; 4 Faces of Eve; Full Contact; Gambit; Gen-X Cops; Gen-Y Cops; Heaven, Man, Earth; Heroes of Love; In the Mood for Love; The Island Tales; Journey to Beijing; The Island Tales; Just Heroes; Just Like Weather; The Killer* (Woo); *Kitchen* (Yim Ho); *Life Is Cheap…But Toilet Paper Is Expensive; Little Cheung; The Longest Summer; Love in a Fallen City; Love Will Tear Us Apart; Made in Hong Kong; The Map of Sex and Love; Metade Fumaça; My Dad is a Jerk; Once a Thief; Ordinary Heroes; Rouge; Rush Hour 2; Song of the Exile; Still Love You After All; Task Force; That Man Bolt; The World of Suzie Wong*

Hood, Robin, films about, *The Adventures of Robin Hood; The Bandit of Sherwood Forest; Robin and Marian; Robin Hood* (Dwan); *Robin Hood* (Reitherman); *Robin Hood* (Irvin); *Robin Hood – Men in Tights; Robin Hood – Prince of Thieves; Wolfshead – The Legend of Robin Hood*

Hoover, J Edgar, films about/featuring, *Nixon; The Private Files of J Edgar Hoover*

Hornby, Nick, films adapted from work, *About a Boy; Fever Pitch; High Fidelity*

Horse racing, *Bite the Bullet; Brighton Rock; Broadway Bill; Casey's Shadow; Champions; A Day at the Races; Dead Cert; Derby Day; Dry Rot; The Grifters; Kentucky; The killing; My Brother Talks to Horses; National Velvet; Phar Lap; The Rainbow Jacket; The Rocking Horse Winner; That Gang of Mine*

Hospital dramas (see also **Doctors and medicine, Illness, Mental hospitals and asylums**), *The Ambulance; Britannia Hospital; The Carey Treatment; La Chambre des officiers; Clean and Sober; The Clinic; Coma; The Cycle; Dr T & the Women; Extreme Measures; Feverhouse; The Frighteners; Green for Danger; Halloween II; Halloween 4: The Return of Michael Myers; Hard-Boiled; Hospital; House Calls; An Indecent Obsession; John Q; The Kingdom; The Kingdom II; Living Doll; Lorenzo's Oil; Lord Camber's Ladies; Malpractice; M.A.S.H.; The Men; The National Health; Nightwatch* (Bornedal, 1994); *Nightwatch* (Bornedal, 1998); *Not as a Stranger; No Time for Tears; The Orlovs; Paper Mask; Red Beard; The Resurrection of Zachary; Wheeler; Rosie Dixon; Night Nurse; Strapless; Such Good Friends; Tales from the Gimli Hospital; They Call That an Accident; Traitement de Choc; Visiting Hours; A Woman's Tale; Young Doctors in Love*

Hostages (see also **Kidnap dramas, Unwanted guests**), *Albino Alligator; All the Way; Appointment in Honduras; Blind Alley* (Vidor); *Crime Story; The Dark Past; Four Days in September; Jeopardy; Mad City; Metro; The Negotiator; The Night Holds Terror; The Ref; The Rock; S.F.W.; Street Fighter; Toy Soldiers*
political, *La Captive du Désert; The Crying Game; Hors la vie; Hot Shots! Part Deux; A Perfect World; An Unforgettable Summer*

Hotels, etc, *About Mrs Leslie; Barton Fink; The Bellboy; Best Hotel on Skid Row; Blame It on the Bellboy; California Suite; Cat Chaser; Cheap Shots; Club* *des Femmes; Cocoanuts; Connecting Rooms; Crows and Sparrows; Death in Venice; Detective; Don't Bother to Knock* (Baker); *Dunston Checks In; Electric Moon; For Love or Money; Giliap; Gold Diggers of 1935; Guest House Paradiso; The Happiness of the Katakuris; Her Last Affaire; Hotel; Hotel de Love; Hôtel du Nord; Hôtel du Paradis; The Hotel New Hampshire; Hotel Sahara; Hotel Splendide; L'Ile au trésor; International House; Lac aux Dames; The Ladies' Man; Une Liaison Pornographique; London Belongs to Me; Minbo Woman –Or the Gentle Art of Japanese Extortion; The Moon over the Alley; Motel; Motel Cactus; Mystery Train; Necronomicon; Nelly's Version; Out of Season; Pension Mimosas; Playing for Keeps; Private Parts; Room Service; Sélect Hotel; The Shining; Ski Patrol; Smile Orange; Snake Fang; Street Music; Wicked, Wicked; The Witches; Women in Tropical Places*

Houellebecq, Michel, film adapted from work, *Whatever*

Household, Geoffrey, films adapted from work, *Man Hunt; Rough Shoot*

Household appliances, becoming malevolent, *Maximum Overdrive; Pulse; The Refrigerator*

Howard, Leigh, film adapted from work, *Blind Date* (Losey)

Howard, Sidney, film adapted from work, *They Knew What They Wanted*

Howarth, David, film adapted from work, *Nine Lives*

Hrabal, Bohumil, films adapted from work, *Closely Observed Trains; Pearls of the Deep*

Hughes, Howard, film about, *Melvin and Howard*

Hughes, Ted, film adapted from work, *The Iron Giant*

Hughes, Thomas, film adapted from work, *Tom Brown's Schooldays*

Hugo, Victor, films adapted from work, *The Hunchback of Notre Dame* (Worsley); *The Hunchback of Notre Dame* (Dieterle); *The Hunchback of Notre Dame* (Delannoy); *The Hunchback of Notre Dame* (Trousdale/ Wise); *Les Miserables* (Milestone); *Les Misérables* (Boleslawski) *Les Misérables* (Le Chanois); *Les Misérables* (Lelouch); *Les Misérables* (August)

Hungarian cinema, *Another Way; Bolshe Vita; Chico; Colonel Redl; Confidence; The Confrontation; Damnation; Daniel Takes a Train; Diary for My Children; Diary for My Loves; Elektreia; Escape; Forbidden Relations; The Gambler* (Makk); *Hanussen; A Hungarian Fairy Tale; Improperly Dressed; Jadviga's Pillow; Love; Love, Mother; The Loves of Liszt; The Luzhin Defence; A Monkey's Tale; My 20th Century; My Way Home; Nine Months; The Package Tour; Passion; Passport; The Princess; The Red and the White; Red Psalm; The Round Up; Sátántangó; Silence and Cry; Sunday Daughters; Sunshine* (Szabó); *Sweet Emma, Dear Böbe; Tavaszi Zápor; Time Stands Still; The Two of Them; Underground* (Kusturica); *The Valley; A Very Moral Night; Werckmeister Harmonies; When Joseph Returns; Whooping Cough; The Witman Boys; The Witness*

Hunter, Evan, films adapted from work (see also **McBain,** Ed), *Blackboard Jungle; Last Summer; Strangers When We Meet*

Hunting, and blood sports, *The Bear; The Belstone Fox; Cockfighter; The Deer Hunter; The Ghost and the Darkness; The Golden Seal; Hard Target; Harry and the Hendersons; The Lost Word: Jurassic Park; The Most Dangerous Game; Murders in the Zoo; On the Hunting Ground; Quigley Down Under; Superbeast; White Hunter, Black Heart*

Hurling, *Clash of the Ash*

Hurst, Fannie, films adapted from work, *Back Street* (Stahl); *Back Street* (Stevenson); *Imitation of Life* (Sirk); *Imitation of Life* (Stahl); *Young at Heart*

Huston, John, film about, *John Huston War Stories*

Huth, Angela, film adapted from work, *The Land Girls*

Hutterites, in film, *Holy Matrimony*

Huxley, Aldous, film adapted from work, *The Devils*

Hwang, David Henry, film adapted from work, *M. Butterfly*

Hypnosis, *The Cabinet of Dr Caligari; Dead Again; The 5,000 Fingers of Dr T; Heart of Glass; Let's Do It Again; The Magician; Mario and the Magician; Schatten; Whirlpool*

Hypochondria, *Checking Out; Send Me No Flowers; Why Worry?*

Ibsen, Henrik, films adapted from work, *An Enemy of the People* (Ray); *An Enemy of the People* (Schaefer); *A Doll's House* (Garland); *A Doll's House* (Losey); *Hedda; Nora Helmer*

Ice dramas, *Atanarjuat: The Fast Runner; Bear Island; Captain Jack; Careful; Cold Tracks; The Ice Palace* (Blom); *Ice Palace* (Sherman); *Ice Station Zebra; Insomnia; Jeremiah Johnson; Orion's Belt; The Savage Innocents; Scott of the Antarctic; Ski Patrol; The Thing; The Thing from Another World; The White Dawn; White Fang* (Fulci); *White Fang* (Kleiser)

Ice hockey, *The Cutting Edge; D2: The Mighty Ducks; Happy Gilmore; Hgome Game; The Hounds of Notre Dame; The Mightly Ducks; Slap Shot; Sudden Death; Touch and Go; Youngblood*

Iceland
Icelandic cinema, *As in Heaven; Children of Nature; Cold Fever; Devil's Island* (Fridriksson); *Ikíngut; Ingaló; Land and Sons; Movie Days; No Such Thing101 Reykjavík*
Iceland in film, *Devil's Island* (Fridriksson); *Ikingut; The Outlaw and His Wife; No Such Thing; 101 Reykjavík*

Ice skating, *Iceland; Ice Castles; Lucky Star; One in a Million; Sun Valley Serenade; Thin Ice* (Lanfield); *Thin Ice* (Reid)

Identities confused at birth, *The Acid House; Big Business; Life Is a Long Quiet River; Toto the Hero*

Identity, change of, see **Impersonation**

Illegitimacy, *Asya's Happiness; Better Late than Never; Blanche Fury; Blossoms in the Dust; December Bride; Gosford Park; Home from the Hill; How to Commit Marriage; Ju Dou; Man, Woman and Child; The Match Factory Girl; My Childhood/My Ain Folk/My Way Home; People Will Talk; The Playboys; Tavaszi Zápor; Track 29; Trust; Way Down East; Winter People*

Illiteracy, *Central Do Brasil; The Money Order; Stanley & Iris; The Teacher*

Illness (see also **Doctors and diseases, Few-months-to-live stories, Hospital dramas, Mental illness**), *Angel on My Shoulder; August in the Water; Awakenings; Barren Illusion; Le Beau Serge; Cause for Alarm!; Champions; Cléo de 5 à 7; Dad; Dekalog 9: 'Thou shalt not covet thy neighbour's wife'; The Doctor; Don't Tell Her It's Me; Dying Young; An Egyptian Story; Emergency; Emergency Call; The End; The English Patient; Ethan Frome; Folks!; Gattaca; Gawin; Good Morning, Miss Dove; Grazie Zia; Haut les Coeurs; Heart; The Hole; Ikiru; Iris; Kaseki; Last Moments; The Last Snows of Spring; Lorenzo's Oil; Marvin's Room; Men, Women: User's Manual; Molokai: The Story of Father Damien; Mon Premier Amour; Never Say Die; O. Henry's Full House ('The Last Leaf'); On the Beach; One True Thing; Regarding Henry; The Secret Garden* (Holland); *The Secret Garden* (Wilcox); *Sentimental Journey; Sick: The Life & Death of Bob Flanagan, Supermasochist; Si tous les gars du monde…; The Sixth Happiness; Sorry, Wrong Number; Le Souffle au Coeur; Spanking the Monkey; Steel Magnolias; Such Good Friends; Sunshine* (Sargent); *Sunshine Part II; Terms of Endearment; The Theory of Flight; These Foolish Things; Tribute; Unnatural Causes: The Agent Orange Story; Unstrung Heroes; The Wind Cannot Read; Without Memory; A Woman's Tale*

Imaginary companions, *Drop Dead Fred; Harvey; Secret Friends; Toto the Hero*

Immigrants and immigration
in Argentina, *Bolivia*
in Australia, *Captain Johnno; Cathy's Child; Death in Brunswick; Head On; Romper Stomper; Silver City; La Spagnola; They're a Weird Mob*
in Belgium, *The Promise* (Dardenne/Dardenne)
in Britain, *Ama; Argie; Blue Notes and Exiled Voices; Brothers in Trouble; Foreign Body; Foreign Moon; For Queen and Country; Last Resort; Majdhar; My Beautiful Laundrette; My Son the Fanatic; Ping Pong; A Private Enterprise; Queen of Hearts; Soursweet; Twilight City; Welcome to Britain*
in Canada, *The Luck of Ginger Coffey; Masala; A Paper Wedding; Sitting in Limbo*
in Denmark, *Pelle the Conqueror*
in France, *As a Man; La Balance; Comme un Aimant; Le Cri du Coeur; De l'Autre Côté du Périph'; La Faute à Voltaire; Police; Romuald et Juliette; Salut Cousin!; S'en fout la mort; La Squale; The Underground Orchestra*
in Germany, *Dealer; Fear Eats the Soul; 40 Metre Square Germany; The Grass Is Always Greener; Katzelmacher; Little Angel; Lola + Bilidikid; Lost Killers; Mau Mau; Mercedes Mon Amour; Palermo or Wolfsburg; The Serbian Girl;*

17 rue Bleue; Shirin's Wedding; Spicy Rice; Yara In Greece, From the Edge of the City
in Hong Kong, *Love Will Tear Us Apart*
in Iran, *The Cyclist; Delbaran*
in Italy, *Besieged*
in Japan, *About Love, Tokyo; Death by Hanging; Swimming with Tears; Three Resurrected Drunkards*
in Netherlands, *Another Mother; Jacky; The Polish Bride*
in New Zealand *Broken English*
in Portugal, *Foreign Land*
in Spain, *Loin*
in South Korea, *World Apartment Horror*
in Sweden, *Foreigners*
in Switzerland, *Bread and Chocolate; Journey of Hope; The Swissmakers*
in Taiwan, *Birdland*
in US, *ABCD; Alambrista!; Alamo Bay; America, America; An American Romance; American Stories; ...and the pursuit of happiness; Avalon; A.W.O.L.; Black Fury; Blood Red; The Border; Border Incident; Borderline; Born in East L.A.; Bread and Roses; Clara's Heart; Class Relations; Coming to America; Crossover Dreams; Daughters of the Dust; A Dream of Kings; Eat a Bowl of Tea; El Norte; The Emigrants; Enemies, a Love Story; The Face Behind the Mask; Far and Away; Four Friends; Full Moon in New York; The Godfather Part II; Green Card; Hold Back the Dawn; I Remember Mama; I Was on Mars; The Hatchet Man; Heaven's Gate; Hester Street; A Lady Without Passport; Lonely in America; Mala Noche; Mississippi Masala; My Family; Our Vines Have Tender Grapes; The Perez Family; Picture Bride; Pushing Hands; Ruggles of Red Gap; '68; Siao Yu; Side Streets; Skyline; Someone Else's America; Stranger Than Paradise; Streets of Gold; Telling Lies in America; A Time of Destiny; True Believer; The Wedding Night; Well-founded Fear*
returning to mother country, *Dangerous Ground; Eight Taels of Gold; The Great Wall Is a Great Wall; Reminiscences of a Journey to Lithuania; Testament* (Akomfrah)

Immortality (see also **Undead, the**), *The Asphyx; Highlander; Highlander II – The Quickening; Highlander III – The Sorcerer; The Hunger; Lifespan; No Such Thing; Orlando; The Return of the Swamp Thing; Revelation; A Terra-Cotta Warrior*

Impersonation, and exchanged identities (see also **Doubles, Identities confused at birth, Mistaken identity**), *Accidental Hero; L'Année Juliette; L'Auberge Rouge; Bird on a Wire; Charade; Le Colonel Chabert* (Le Hénaff); *Le Colonel Chabert* (Angelo); *The Consul; Crush; Dark Habits; Darkman; Dave; Desperately Seeking Susan; The Devil and Miss Jones; The Devil-Doll; The Distinguished Gentleman; Donnie Brasco; Dora-Heita; Double Jeopardy; The Double Man; Face/Off; Filofax; Folies Bergère; From Noon till Three; Gattaca; The Gaunt Stranger; History Is Made at Night; Hollow Triumph; Housesitter; Irma La Douce; It Started with Eve; I Was Monty's Double; Jimmy Hollywood; Kagemusha; Law and Disorder; Masques; Maximum Risk; Midnight; Mrs Doubtfire; Mrs Winterbourne; Monte Carlo; My Blue Heaven; Naked Tango; Never Been Kissed; No Man of Her Own* (Leisen); *Nuns on the Run; One Heavenly Night; La Otra* (Gavaldón); *The Palm Beach Story; Paperback Hero; Paper Mask; The Passenger; The Phantom President; Pope Joan; The Prisoner of Zenda* (Cromwell); *The Prisoner of Zenda* (Thorpe); *The Prisoner of Zenda* (Quine); *Reign of Terror; Le Retour de Martin Guerre; Romance on the High Seas; Rotten to the Core; Single White Female; Sommersby; Suture; The Tenant; Things Change; 3 Women; The Tichborne Claimant; Trading Places; Trial and Error; The Triple Echo; Two Faced Woman; Vertigo; Virtual Sexuality; We're No Angels* (Jordan); *White Sands*

Impotence (see also **Infertility**), *Clando; Eat a Bowl of Tea; In Country; Lost Sex; sex, lies and videotape; Sweet Hunters; '10'* (Edwards); *Trash; Xala*

Incest
brother and sister, *Alpine Fire; Bride of Vengeance; The Cement Garden; Close My Eyes; Country Dance; Demons of the Mind; Fool for Love; Forbidden Relations; Georgette Meunier; The House of Yes; Little Sister; Lone Star; March Comes in Like a Lion; Souvenir; Tiger Warsaw; 'Tis Pity She's a Whore; Vaghe Stelle dell'Orsa*
father and daughter, *Butterfly* (Cimber); *Trois Places pour le 26; Ursula and Glenys; The War Zone*
mother and son, *The Grifters; La Luna; Mon Premier Amour; Sleepwalkers; Le Souffle au Coeur; Spanking the Monkey; The Vortex*
stepmother and son, *Phaedra*
sister and sister, *The Silence* (Bergman); *Sister My Sister*

India, in film
pre-independence, *Asoka; Autobiography of a Princess; The Brigand of Kandahar; Calcutta; Charulata; The Chess Players; The Deceivers; Distant Thunder; The Drum; Elephant Boy; Four Men and a Prayer; Gandhi; Gunga Din; Heat and Dust; The Home and the World; India Song; Kama Sutra: A Tale of Love; Kim; The Man Who Would Be King; North West Frontier; A Passage to India; The Rains Came; The Rains of Ranchipur; The River* (Renoir); *Seven Years in Tibet; Stiff Upper Lips; Trikal: Past Present and Future; The Village Has No Walls*
post-independence, *Autobiography of a Princess; The Adversary; Ascending Scale; Bandit Queen; Boatman; The Bogey Man; Bollywood Calling; Bombay Our City; Bombay Talkie; The Boor; Calmness; The Chosen One; Circle of Gold; City of Joy; Company Limited; Cotton Mary; The Courtesans of Bombay; The Cup; Dance of the Wind; Days and Nights in the Forest; Death Sentence; Deveeri; Devi; The Doll* (Ghose); *Earth* (Mehta); *Electric Moon; Fire; Forest of Bliss; Genesis; Guardians of the Earth; The Guru; Hathi; Heat and Dust; Hot Winds; Hullabaloo over Georgie and Bonnie's Pictures; In Custody; The Inevitable; In Search of Famine; It's a Long Way to the Sea; Journey to Wisdom; Kabhi Khushi Kabhie Gham...; Kanchenjungah; Kuch Kuch Hota Hai; Mahanagar; Maya; The Middleman; Monsoon Wedding; Mother India; Mother of 1084; The Outsiders; Pakeezah; Pather Panchali; Phantom India; Piravi; Rat-Trap; Salaam Bombay!; Shakespeare-Wallah; Shelter of the Wings; The Sixth Happiness; A Slender Smile; The Square Circle; The Stranglers of Bombay; Such a Long Journey; Swami; Teen Kanya; The Terrorist; These Are Not My Images (neither there nor here); The Warrior*

Indian cinema, *The Adventures of Goopy and Bagha; The Adversary; Ascending Scale; Asoka; Bandit Queen; Body; Bollywood Calling; The Bogey Man; Bombay Our City; Bombay Talkie; The Boon; Branches of the Tree; Calmness; Charulata; The Chess Players; The Chosen One; Cloud-capped Star; Company Limited; Days and Nights in the Forest; Death Sentence; Deveeri; Devi; Distant Thunder; The Doll* (Ghose); *Earth* (Mehta); *Ek Baar Phir; An Enemy of the People* (Ray); *Genesis; Guardians of the Earth; Hathi; The Home and the World; Hot Winds; Hullabaloo over Georgie and Bonnie's Pictures; In Custody; An Indian Story; The Inevitable; In Search of Famine; It's a Long Way to the Sea; Jalsaghar; Jaya Ganga; Journey to Wisdom; Kabhi Khushi Kabhie Gham...; Kama Sutra: A Tale of Love; Kanchenjungha; Kuch Kuch Hota Hai; Mahanagar; Masquerade* (Aravindan); *Maya; The Middleman; Mother India; Mother of 1084; The Mystic Masseur; The Outsiders* (Sen); *Pakeezah; Pather Panchali; The Perfect Murder; The Philosopher's Stone; Piravi; Rat-Trap; The Role; Salaam Bombay; Samsara; Shakespeare-Wallah; Shelter of the Wings; The Sixth Happiness; A Slender Smile; Sometime Somewhere; The Square Circle; The Stranger* (Ray); *Target* (Ray); *Teen Kanya; The Terrorist; 36 Chowringhee Lane; Trikal: Past Present and Future; The Village Has No Walls; The Warrior; The Wrestlers*

Indian music, *Raga*

Indians, American and Canadian
forgotten by the world, *Last of the Dogmen*
in contemporary society, *The Dark Wind; Flap; Grey Owl; Kanehsatake (Oka) – 270 Years of Resistance; The Last of His Tribe; The Manitou; Nightwing; Map of the Human Heart; Powwow Highway; Renegades; Running Brave; Smoke Signals; The Sunchaser; Tell Them Willie Boy Is Here; Thunderheart; Tulsa; War Party; When the Legends Die*
in Westerns,
– standard, *Across the Wide Missouri; Apache Drums; The Canadians; Cattle Queen of Montana; The Charge at Feather River; Chuka; Comanche Station; Dakota Incident; Day of the Evil Gun; The Deadly Companions; Distant Drums; A Distant Trumpet; Dragon Wells Massacre; Duel at Diablo; Escape from Fort Bravo; Flaming Star; The Iron Horse; Madron; Major Dundee; A Man in the Wilderness; Mohawk; Mustang Country; Pony Soldier; 7th Cavalry; The Sheriff of Fractured Jaw; She Wore a Yellow Ribbon; Smoke Signal; Spirit of the Eagle; Stagecoach* (Ford); *Stagecoach* (Douglas); *Two Rode Together; The Unforgiven*
– sympathetic, *Apache; Black Robe; Broken Arrow; Cheyenne Autumn; Dances with Wolves; Dances with Wolves – Special Edition; Devil's Doorway; Geronimo: An American Legend; Grayeagle; The Half-Breed; Hondo; The Indian in the Cupboard; The Last of the*

Mohicans; Little Big Man; A Man Called Horse; The Master Gunfighter; Return of a Man Called Horse; Run of the Arrow; Soldier Blue; Triumph of a Man Called Horse; Ulzana's Raid; White Feather

Indians, Latin American, *Amazonia: Voices from the Rainforest; At Play in the Fields of the Lord; The Bird's Singing; Chac; Savage Capitalism; The Secret Nation; Tigrero – A Film That Was Never Made*

Indonesia, and Dutch East Indies, in film, *The Diplomat; Leaf on a Pillow; Letter for an Angel; Mementos; Mother Dao the Turtlelike; November 1828; Vessel of Wrath; Victory* (Cromwell); *Victory* (Peploe); *The Year of Living Dangerously; Unconcealed Poetry*

Indonesian cinema, *Leaf on a Pillow; Letter for an Angel; Mementos; November 1828; Unconcealed Poetry*

Industry and industrial life, *A l'attaque!; An American Romance; Australia; The Betsy; Blue Collar; Caprice; Cela s'appelle l'Aurore; La Classe Operaia Va in Paradiso; Coup pour Coup; Dadetown; The Formula; The Grind; Gung Ho; Highways by Night; I'm All Right, Jack; Iron Maze; Man Is Not a Bird; The Match Factory Girl; Nightshift; Once a Jolly Swagman; The Pajama Game; Passport; Real Cool Time; Roger & Me; Saturday Night and Sunday Morning; The Scar; The Sound Barrier; Spotswood; Stanley & Iris; Tout va bien; Tucker: The Man and His Dream; Woman's World; Work Is a Four Letter Word*

Industrial relations see **Labour relations**

Infertility, *Feelings; Immaculate Conception; Leon the Pig Farmer; The Proposition; Test Tube Babies*

Infidelity
(see also **Love stories**)
Arg, *Rio Escondido* (García Guevara);
Aust, *Libido; My First Wife; Praise*
Bel, *Une Femme Entre Chien en Loup*
Braz, *Tolerance*
China, *Ju Dou; Keep Cool; Flowers of Shanghai; Ripples Across Stagnant Water; Spring in a Small Town*
Den, *The Abyss; The President*
Fin, *Black on White*
Fr, *A Double Tour; The Aviator's Wife; Les Biches; Le Bonheur; La Chienne; Les Choses de las Vie; Un Coeur qui bat; Courage; Le Dernier Tournant; Fuyons; En Cas de Malheur; La Femme Défendue; Une Femme française; La Femme Infidèle; Une Femme Mariée; Just Before Nightfall; Les Liaisons Dangereuses 1960; Le Libertin; Love in the Afternoon* (Rohmer); *Love in the Strangest Way; Madame de…; A Man in Love; Marie-Jo and Her Two Lovers; Max Mon Amour; Mélo; My Girlfriend's Boyfriend; La Peau Douce; Rein à Faire; Remorques; Trop belle pour toi; Valmont; The Woman Next Door*
GB, *Anna Karenina* (Duvivier); *Betrayal; Brief Ecstasy; Brief Encounter; Closing Numbers; Damage; Diamond Skulls; Do Not Disturb; Don't Bother to Knock* (Frankel); *The End of the Affair; Hanover Street; The Heart of the Matter; Interlude* (Billington); *Intimate Stranger; Knave of Hearts; The Misadventures of Margaret; Mr Love; Only Two Can Play; The Ring; The Romantic Englishwoman; Le Secret; Sliding Doors; Sparrows Can't Sing; Three into Two Won't Go; The Wedding Tackle*
Ger, *Coup de Grâce; Men; The Scarlet Letter* (Wenders); *Varieté; Waterloo Road; Woyzeck* (Herzog)
HK, *In the Mood for Love*
Hun, *Woyzeck* (Szász)
Ind, *The Home and the World*
It, *The Innocent* (Visconti); *Ossessione; Senso*
Jap, *Early Spring*
Mex, *Amores Perros*
Pol, *Dekalog 3: 'Honour the Sabbath Day'; Dekalog 9: 'Thou shalt not covet thy neighbour's wife'; Knife in the Water*
Port, *In the White City*
Sp, *Lovers; The Lovers of the Arctic Circle; Sex and Lucía; Ten Days Without Love*
Swe, *Faithless; Love Lessons; Scenes from a Marriage*
Tai, *This Love of Mine*
US, *Afterglow; Alice* (Allen); *All This and Heaven Too; An Almost Perfect Affair; Anna Karenina* (Brown); *Anna Karenina* (Rose); *Almost You; The April Fools; Baby Doll; Big Trouble; Body Heat; The Bramble Bush; Buona Sera, Mrs Campbell; Cat Chase; A Change of Seasons; Clash By Night; Cold Heaven; Consenting Adults; Criss Cross;* (Siodmak); *Criss Cross* (Soderbergh); *Crimes and Misdemeanors; Dangerous Liaisons; Dirigible; Dirty Laundry; Do Not Disturb; Double Indemnity; Enemies, Love Story; Fatal Attraction; Feeling Minnesota; Forbidden; Fresh Horses; The Fugitive Kind; Harvey Middleman, Fireman; Having It All; The Honey Pot; Honeysuckle Rose; Human Desire; The Ice Storm; I Love You to Death; Indecent Proposal; Interlude* (Sirk); *Intermezzo; Just Between Friends; Kiss Me, Stupid; Love at Large; Manpower; The Man Who Wasn't There; The Marrying Man; Micki and Maude; Niagara; One Hour With You; One Night Stand; Other Men's Women; Over Her Dead Body; The Painted Veil; Pitfall; Reflections in a Golden Eye; Random Hearts; Revenge* (Scott); *Same Time Next Year; The Scarlett Letter* (Joffé); *The Scarlet Letter* (Sjöström); *Scenes from a Mall; Schizopolis; sex, lies and videotape; Shattered; She-Devil; Siesta; Six Days Seven Nights; Skin Deep; Strangers When We Meet; 10.30 P.M. Summer; That's Life; There's Always Tomorrow; They Won't Believe Me; Tin Men; Torn Between Two Lovers; The Touch; Town & Country; wice in a Lifetime; Two Faced Woman; Undercurrent; The Unfaithful; Unfaithfully Yours* (Sturges); *Unfaithfully Yours* (Zieff); *Vertigo; Where Were You When the Lights Went Out?; The Woman on the Beach; Zaza; Zee & Co*
USSR, *Dark Eyes*

Informers, police, *Le Cousin; Le Doulos; The Friends of Eddie Coyle; The Hit; The Informer; Prince of the City; The Stoolie*

Inge, William, films adapted from work, *Come Back, Little Sheba; The Dark at the Top of the Stair; Picnic*

Inheritance, *The Bachelor; Better Late than Never; Beyond the Blue Horizon; Le Bossu; Brewster's Millions* (Dwan); *Brewsters's Millions* (Hill); *Cast A Dark Shadow; Chase a Crooked Shadow; The Chateau; Daddy's Dyin' – Who's Got the Will?; Dark Waters; Dial M for Murder; The Field; Gosford Park; House of Angels; Howards End; If I Had a Million; The Invitation; It's Only Money; The House in Nightmare Park; Kind Hearts and Coronets; Knickers Ahoy; Lazybones; Little Lord Fauntleroy; Man with a Cloak; Milou en mai; Mr Billion; Mr Deeds Goes to Town; A New Leaf; Night Nurse; A Perfect Murder; Pleins Feux sur l'assassin; Rhubarb; Splitting Heirs; Toys; Le Trou Normand; Uncle Silas; V I Warshawski; Woman of Straw*

Innocents accused, *L'Affaire du Courrier de Lyon; Along Came Jones; Beyond Reasonable Doubt; The Big Steal* (Siegel); *Blackmail* (Potter); *The Blue Gardenia; Boomerang* (Kazan); *Break of Dawn; Call Northside 777; The Dark Corner; Dark Passage; Deadline at Dawn; Defence Counsel Sedov; Double Jeopardy; Downhill; El Mariachi; Everybody Wins; For Them That Trespass; Frenzy; Full Confession; Framed; The Fugitive* (Davis); *Fury* (Lang); *'Gator Bait; Her Alibi; Her Last Affaire; I Am a Fugitive from a Chain Gang; I Confess; An Innocent Man; In the Name of the Father* (Sheridan); *The Insider; Intruder in the Dust; The Invisible Man Returns; I Wake Up Screaming; Human Experiments; Just Cause; Knife in the Head; The Lodger; Lumière Noire; Macon County Line; Madeleine; Murder; Murphy's Law; Mystery Street; Nightfall; Ordeal by Innocence; Orders to Kill; The Ox-Bow Incident; Penitentiary; Physical Evidence; La P..... Respectueuse; Presumed Innocent; Red Corner; Ride in the Whirlwind; Saboteur; Sergeant Rutledge; Sierra; Silver Lady; Slam Dance; Strangers on a Train; Tango & Cash; Term of Trial; They Drive by Night* (Walsh); *The Thin Blue Line; This Is My Affair; Thunderbolt; Time Without Pity; Tough Guys Don't Dance; True Believer; True Crime; Under Suspicion; The Walking Dead; Warning Shot; Where Danger Lives; Who's That Girl?; Why?; The Winslow Boy; The Woman in the Window; The Wrong Man* (Hitchcock); *Young and Innocent; The Young One; You Only Live Once*
guilty released, *Criminal Law; Midnight in the Garden of Good and Evil*

Insects, spiders, etc, *Antz; Arachnophobia; The Beekeeper; A Bug's Life; The Butterfly Murders; Earth vs the Spider; The Fly* (Neumann); *The Fly* (Cronenberg); *The Fly II; The Hellstrom Chronicle; Highly Dangerous; Meet the Applegates; Microcosmos; Mimic; Naked Lunch; Once Upon a Time; Phase IV; Return of the Fly; The Savage Bees; Starship Troopers; The Swarm; Ticks; Ulee's Gold; Wax, or The Discovery of Television Among the Bees*

Insurance and insurance investigators, *The Adjuster; Double Indemnity; Entrapment; Frauds; Ikinai; The Killers* (Siodmak); *Mystery in Mexico; Nightfall*

Internet, e-mail, dotcom dramas, etc, *The Center of the World; Little Miracles; The Net; You've Got Mail; Startup.com*

Invalids, see **Illness**

Inventors (see also **Mad scientists**), *Back to the Future, Back to the Future Part II; Back to the Future Part III; The Barber of Siberia; Chitty Chitty Bang*

Bang; Choke Canyon; Darkman; Flubber; Honey, I Blew Up the Kid; Honey, I Shrunk the Kids; Kenoma; The Man in the White Suit; Malcolm; Master of the World; Paris Qui Dort; Short Circuit; Static; The Time Machine; The Time Travellers; Young Einstein

Invisibility, *Alice* (Allen); *The Invisible Man; The Invisible Man Returns; Memoirs of an Invisible Man*

Iran, in film, *And Life Goes On...; The Apple; Bemani; Birth of a Butterfly; Blackboards; The Child and the Soldier; Children of Heaven; The Circle; Close-Up; The Colour of Paradise; The Cow; The Cycle; The Cyclist; Daan; Dance of Dust; The Day I Became a Woman; Delbaran; The Father; Gabbeh; The Girl in the Sneakers; Grass* (Cooper/Schoedsack); *The Guns and The Fury; Iron Eagle II; Leila; Moment of Innocence; Not Without My Daughter; The Peddler; The Runner; Season Five; Secret Ballot; The Silence* (Makhmalbaf); *Smell of Camphor, Fragrance of Jasmine; Snake Fang; A Taste of Cherry; Through the Olive Trees; A Time for Drunken Horses; Under the Moonlight; Where Is My Friend's House?; The White Balloon; The Wind Will Carry Us*

Iranian cinema, *A.B.C. Africa; And Life Goes On...; The Apple; Bemani; Birth of a Butterfly; Blackboards; The Child and the Soldier; Children of Heaven; The Circle; Close-Up; The Cow; The Colour of Paradise; The Cycle; The Cyclist; Daan; Dance of Dust; The Day I Became a Woman; Delbaran; Det Means Girl; Djomeh; Gabbeh; The Girl in the Sneakers; The Father; Kandahar; Leila; Moment of Innocence; The Peddler; The Runner; Season Five; Secret Ballot; The Silence* (Makhmalbaf); *Smell of Camphor, Fragrance of Jasmine; Snake Fang; The Spell; Tales of Kish; A Taste of Cherry; 10* (Kiarostami); *Through the Olive Trees; A Time for Drunken Horses; The Traveller; Under the Moonlight; Where Is My Friend's House?; The White Balloon; The Wind Will Carry Us*

Ireland, in film
pre-1922, and Irish Republic, *About Adam; Agnes Browne; Ailsa; Angela's Ashes; Beloved Enemy; The Bishop's Story; A Boy from Mercury; Broken Harvest; The Brylcreem Boys; The Butcher Boy; Captain Boycott; Circle of Friends; Clash of the Ash; The Closer You Get; Coilin and Platonida; Conamara; The Commitments; Country; The Country Girls; The Courier; Crush Proof; Da; Dancing at Lughnasa; Darby O'Gill and the Little People; The Dawning; The Dead; The Disappearance of Finbar; Driftwood; Eat the Peach; Exposure; The Fantasist; Far and Away; The Field; Finnegans Wake; Flight of the Doves; Fools of Fortune; Frankie Starlight; A Further Gesture; The General* (Boorman); *Girl with Green Eyes; Guiltrip; Happy Ever After; Hear My Song; High Spirits; How Harry Became a Tree; Hungry Hill; I Could Read the Sky; The Informer; Into the West; I See a Dark Stranger; I Went Down; Joyriders; Korea; Last of the High Kings; The Last September; The Lonely Passion of Judith Hearne; Man of Aran; A Man of No Importance; Michael Collins; The Miracle; My Left Foot; The Nephew; Nora; The Outcasts; Ordinary Decent Criminal; Pigs; The Playboys; The Quiet Man; Reflections; The Run of the Country; Ryan's Daughter; The Secret of Roan Inish; The Snapper; Southpaw; Taffin; Traveller; Ulysses; The Van; Waking Ned; War of the Buttons; When Brendan Met Trudy; When the Sky Fall; Widows' Peak; Wings of the Morning; Young Cassidy*
Northern Ireland, *Acceptable Levels; As the Beast Sleeps; Attracta; Bloody Sunday; The Boxer* (Sheridan); *Boy Soldier; Cal; Cross and Passion; Crossmaheart; The Crying Game; December Bride; Divorcing Jack; An Everlasting Piece; Every Picture Tells a Story; Four Days in July; Hennessy; Henri; Hidden Agenda; Hush-a-Bye Baby; In the Name of the Father* (Sheridan); *Ireland: Behind the Wire; Nothing Personal; A Prayer for the Dying; Resurrection Man; A Sense of Loss; Some Mother's Son; A Terribel Beauty; This Is the Sea; Titanic Town; The Writing on the Wall*

Irish abroad
in Australia, *The Craic*
in Britain, *Bad Behaviour; Felicia's Journey; In the Name of the Father* (Sheridan); *The Return*
in South Africa, *Untamed*
in US, *Da; Far and Away; The Fighting 69th; Full Confession; The Cardinal; Gentleman Jim; The Long Gray Line; Looking for Mr Goodbar; The Nephew; Only the Lonely; Q & A; State of Grace; True Confessions*

Irish cinema, *About Adam; Act Without Words – II; Agnes Browne; Ailsa; All Dogs Go to Heaven; Attracta; Avalanche Express; The Bishop's Story; The Book That Wrote Itself; The Boxer* (Sheridan); *A Boy from Mercury; Circle of Friends; Clash of the Ash; The Closer You Get; Completely Pogued; Conamara; Country; The Courier; Croupier; Crush Proof; Dancing at Lughnasa; The Disappearance of Finbar; Driftwood; Eat the Peach; Enemy at the Gates; Exposure; The Fantasist; Fragments of Isabella; Frankie Starlight; A Further Gesture; Gangster No. 1; The General* (Boorman); *Guiltrip; Help! I'm a Fish; High Boot Benny; How Harry Became a Tree; Hush-a-Bye Baby; I Could Read the Sky; Into the West; Invincible; I Went Down; Korea; Krapp's Last Tape; Last of the High Kings; The Last September; Mal; The Match; Mrs Brown; The Nephew; Night Train; Nora; Not I; Ordinary Decent Criminal; The Outcasts; Peaches; Pigs; Play; Reefer and the Model; Saltwater; Southpaw; This Is the Sea; Thumbelina; The Van; When Brendan Met Trudy; When the Sky Fall*

Irish republicanism, *Blown Away; The Crying Game; The Dawning; The Devil's Own; Fools of Fortune; A Further Gesture; The Gentle Gunman; Giù la Testa; The Informer; In the Name of the Father* (Sheridan); *Ireland: Behind the Wire; The Jackal; Maeve; Michael Collins; Odd Man Out; The Outsider; The Patriot Game; Patriot Games; A Prayer for the Dying; Ryan's Daughter; A Sense of Loss; Some Mother's Son; A Terrible Beauty; Warshots*

Irving, John,
films adapted from work, The Cider House Rules; *Hotel New Hampshire; The World According to Garp*
film suggested by work, *Simon Birch*

Irving, Washington, film adapted from work, *Sleepy Hollow*

Isherwood, Christopher, film adapted from work, *I Am a Camera; Cabaret*

Ishiguro, Kazuo, film adapted from work, *The Remains of the Day*

Isolated houses (see also **Haunted houses**)
Fr, *La Belle Noiseuse; La Belle Noiseuse – Divertimento; Ecoute Voir; 8 Women; Maid for Pleasure; Une Pierre dans la Bouche*
GB, *The Beast, Bellman and True; Cul-de-Sac; The Curse of the Crimson Altar; Dead of Night* (Hamer); *Dominique; Eclipse; Exposé; The Ghoul* (Francis); *The Ghoul* (Hunter); *The Legacy; My Name Is Julia Ross; Nightmare* (Francis); *Number Seventeen; The Old Dark House; Symptoms; Ten Little Indians; The Tomb of Ligeia; The Uninvited; Voices; What a Carve Up*
Ger, *Chinese Roulette*
Ire, *Dementia 13; Exposure*
It *Paranoia*
US, *The Black Cat; Burnt Offerings; Curtain Call; Dark Waters; Dead of Winter; Dolores Claiborne; Dragonwyck; Edward Scissorhands; Ghoulies; Homicidal; Jennifer; Key Largo; The List of Adrian Messenger; Misery; Miss Pinkerton; Murder by Death; The People Under the Stairs; The Petrified Forest; The Shining; The Smiling Ghost; Suspicion; The Unseen; The Velvet Vamp; The Watcher in the Woods*

Islam and Islamic culture
Aïd el Kébir; Al-Risalah; L'Autre; Immaculate Conception; In My Father's House; Leila; My Journey My Islam; My Son the Fanatic; Not Without My Daughter; Pretty Village, Pretty Flame; Under the Moonlight

Israel, in film
historical, *Masada*
contemporary, *The Ambassador; Berlin Jerusalem; Bloomfield; Burning Memory; Cast a Giant Shadow; Cup Final; Day after Day; Divine Intervention; Every Time We Say Goodbye; Exodus; The Flying Camel; Fortini/Cani; Hamsin; The Heritage; The Jerusalem File; Judith; Kadosh; Kedma; Kippur; The Last Winter; Late Marriage; Lemon Popsicle; The Lost Lover; Lovesick on Nana Street; Neither by Day or by Night; Not Quite Jerusalem; One of Us; On Our Land; Private Popsicle; Promised Lands; Raid on Entebbe; The Sellout; Shattered Dreams; Picking Up the Pieces; Promises; Sallah; Shuroo; Sinai Field Mission; Song of the Siren; The Specialist; The Summer of Aviya; To Live in Freedom; Victory at Entebbe; Will My Mother Go Back to Berlin?; Yaacov Ben Dov: Father of the Hebrew Film; Yana's Friends; You, Me, Jerusalem*

Israeli cinema, *Because of That War; Beyond the Walls; Burning Memory; Cup Final; Day after Day; The Flying Camel; Going Steady; Goodbye New York; Hamsin; The Heritage; Kadosh; Kazablan; Kedma; Kippur; The Last Winter; Late Marriage; Lemon Popsicle; Lovesick on Nana Street; Operation Thunderbolt; Private Popsicle; Rachel's Man; Sallah; Shuroo; Song of the Siren; The Summer of Aviya; Yaacov Ben Dov: Father of the Hebrew Film; Yana's Friends*

Italian Americans, *Big Night; The Black Hand; Bloodbrothers; The*

Counsellor; Crazy Joe; Cry of the City; The Godfather; The Godfather Part II; The Godfather Part III; GoodFellas; Gotti; Heartaches; House of Strangers; Italianamerican; Mean Streets; Moonstruck; My Cousin Vinny; Queens of the Big Time; Summer of Sam; They Knew What They Wanted; Torn Between Two Lovers; True Love; Used People; Who's That Knocking at My Door?

Italian cinema, see Appendix 20

Italians in Britain, *Another Time, Another Place; Comfort and Joy; Queen of Hearts; Soft Top, Hard Shoulder*

Italy, in film
pre-1900, *The Age of Cosimo de Medici; The Agony and the Ecstasy; Barnabo of the Mountains; Bride of Vengeance; The Decameron; Drama of the Rich; Elective Affinities* (Taviani/Taviani); *Fiorile; Francesco, giullare di Dio; Goliath and the BarbariansThe Last Days of Pompeii; The Leopard; The Mask* (Infascelli); *Much Ado About Nothing; Night Sun; Prince of Foxes; The Portrait of a Lady; The Profession of Arms; Rosa e Cornelia; Romeo and Juliet; Senso; William Shakespeare's Romeo & Juliet*
1900–1945, *Amarcord; The Conformist; Down the Ancient Stairs; The English Patient; Fiorile; The Garden of the Finzi-Continis; The Glass Mountain; Life Is Beautiful; The Luzhin Defence; Malèna; Mario and the Magician; A Month by the Lake; Nest of Vipers; The Night of San Lorenzo; 1900; Open Doors; A Room with a View; Roma, Città Aperta; Saló, o le Centoventi Giornate de Sodoma; Stiff Upper Lips; Tea with Mussolini; The Tree of Wooden Clogs; Up at the Villa; Where Angels Fear to Tread; Wifemistress*
post-WWII, *Accattone; Aprile; Bellissima; China Is Near; Cinema Paradiso; Cinema Paradiso: The Special Edition; The Cyclone; Dear Diary; Il Diavolo in Corpo; La Dolce Vita; Dramma della Gelosia; During the Summer; Enzo, Domani a Palermo!; Fiorile; Flight of the Innocent; The Footman; Forever Mary; The Glass Mountain; The Godfather Part III; Hannibal; Heaven; Illustrious Corpses; Imperfect Love; The Italian Job; It Started in Naples; LaCapaGira; Libero Burro; Lies to Live by (Babylon); Living It Up; The Lizards; The Love Lottery; Il Maestro; Le Mani sulla Città; The Mattei Affair; Le Notti di Cabiria; Only You; Placido Rizzotto; Il Postino; Il Posto; Princesa; The Reign of Naples; Rocco and His Brothers; Roseanna's Grave; Salvatore Giuliano; School; Something to Believe In; The Son's Room; Speedy Boys; Splendor; The Second Time; Stealing Beauty; Three Brothers; The Tragedy of a Ridiculous Man; Ultrà; L'Uomo delle stelle; I Vitelloni; The White Sheik; The Whores; Year of the Gun*

Ivory Coast cinema, *Faces of Women*

Jackson, Michael, in performance, *Moonwalker*

Jackson, Shirley, film adapted from work, *The Haunting*

Jack the Ripper, films about, *From Hell; Hands of the Ripper; Murder by Decree; A Study in Terror; Time After Time*

Jacobs, WW, film adapted from work, *Footsteps in the Fog*

Jacques, Norbert, films adapted from work, *Dr Mabuse, the Gambler; The Testament of Dr Mabuse; The 1000 Eyes of Dr Mabuse*

Jamaica, in film, *The Black Swan; Bongo Man; Cool Runnings; Countryman; CutThroat Island; The Harder They Come; The Lunatic; Reggae Sunsplash II; Rockers; Smile Orange; Stepping Razor – Red X; Time Will Tell; Wide Sargasso Sea*

Jamaican cinema, *The Harder They Come; Rockers; Smile Orange; Third World Cop*

James, CLR, film about, *Talking History*

James, Henry, films adapted from work, *Aspern; The Bostonians; La Chambre Verte; Daisy Miller; The Europeans; The Golden Bowl; The Heiress; The Innocents; The Lost Moment; The Nightcomers; The Portrait of a Lady; Washington Square; What Maisie Knew; The Wings of the Dove*

James, PD, film adapted from work, *An Unsuitable Job for a Woman*

Janowitz, Tama, film adapted from work, *Slaves of New York*

Japan, in film
pre-1900, *Chikamatsu Monogatari; Cruel Story of the Shogunate's Downfall; Eijanaika; Felice… Felice…; Five Women Around Utamaro; Gonza the Spearman; The Ghosts of Kasane Swamp; Ghost Story of Yotsuya; Gojoe; The Hidden Fortress; House of Bamboo; Humanity and Paper Balloons; Kagemusha; Kashima Paradise; The Life of Chikuzan; The Life of Oharu; The Loyal 47 Ronin of the Genroku Era; The Mansion of the Ghost Cat; Miyamoto Musashi; Nemuri Kyoshiro: The Book of Killing-Rules; Ran; Rashomon; Rebellion; Red Peony Gambler: Flower-cards Match; Sansho Dayu; Sasuke and His Comedians; Seven Samurai; Shin Heike Monogatari; The Sword of Doom; Throne of Blood; Tora no O o Fumu Otokotachi; Ugetsu Monogatari; Yojimbo*
1900–1945, *Ai No Corrida; Annyong Kimchi; Another Battle; Blood of Revenge; The Emperor's Naked Army Marches On; Empire of Passion; Four Days of Snow and Blood; A Hen in the Wind; Kawashima Yoshiko; Kurosawa; Madame Butterfly; Osaka Elegy; Pearl Harbor; Sisters of Gion; That Night's Wife; Tokyo Chorus*
modern Japan, *A; Abnormal Family: Brother's Wife; About Love, Tokyo; Angel Dust; Attack on a Bakery; Audition; An Autumn Afternoon; Bad Company; Bari-Zogon; Black Rain* (Scott); *Blue Spring; Boiling Point* (Kitano); *The Boxer* (Terayama); *Boy; A Boy Called Third Base; Boy's Choir; Branded to Kill; Bullet Ballet; The Ceremony; Charisma; Comic Magazine; Crazy Family; Cure; Dead or Alive; Dear Summer Sister; Deaths in Tokimeiki; Diary of a Shinjuku Thief; Distance; Dodes'ka-den; Dora-Heita; The Drive; A Drowning Man; Early Summer; The Eel; Elephant Song; Eureka; Face; Fancy Dance; Fire Festival; The Fire Within; The Flavour of Green Tea Over Rice; Flirt; Fufu the Worldweary; Funeral Parade of Roses; Gaea Girls; Gate of Flesh; The Geisha Boy; Gips; A Girl, She is 100%; Gonin; Gonin 2; The Good Wife of Tokyo; The Hair Opera; Hana-Bi; The Happiness of the Katakuris; Hazy Life; Heaven-6-Box; Hell; The History of a Man's Face; Hole in the Sky; How Old Is the River?; Hush!; Hysteric; I Am a S+M Writer; Ichi the Killer; I, the Executioner; Ikiru; Irezumi – Spirit of Tattoo; Kamikaze Taxi; Kaza-hana; Kichiku; Kids Return; Kikuchi; Kikujiro; KT; Kurosawa; Labyrinth of Dreams; The Lady Vampire; Late Spring; Leaving; Level Five; Ley Lines; Like a Rolling Stone; Like Grains of Sand; Looking for an Angel; Love/Juice; Lukewarm Water Under the Red Bridge; Maborosi; Madadayo; The Mansion of the Ghost Cat; A Man Vanishes; The Man Who Left His Will on Film; MARKS; Minamata; Minbo Woman – Or the Gentle Art of Japanese Extortion; Mishima: A Life in Four Chapters; Mr Baseball; Monday; The Moon Has Risen; My Sons; The Mystery of Rampo; The New God; The New Morning of Billy the Kid; Nô; Not Forgotten; An Obsession; Ohayo; Ondeko-za on Sado; One of Those Things; Organ; Osaka Story; Ososhiki; The Outer Way; A Painful Pair; Perfect Blue; Pigs and Battleships; The Pillow Book; Record of a Tenement Gentleman; Rhapsody in August; Rising Sun; Sadistic City; Sans Soleil; 7/25; Shall We Dance?; Shikoku; Skinless Night; Sleeping Man; Stakeout; Stranger; Street of Shame; Sukiyaki; Summer Soldiers; Sumo Do, Sumo Don't; Swimming with Tears; Tampopo; A Taxing Woman; A Tender Place; Teenage Mutant Ninja Turtles III; Three Resurrected Drunkards; Thow Away Your Books, Let's Go into the Streets; Sayonara; Shinjuku Triad Society; Sleepless Town; Sonatine; Some Kinda Love; Suicide Club; Suzaku; Swallowtail Butterfly; Swimming Prohibited; Tokyo Decandence; Tokyo Drifter; Tokyo Fist; Tokyo-Ga; Tokyo Kyodai; Tokyo Pop; Tokyo Story; A Town of Love and Hope; The Triple Cross; 2 Duo; Unloved; Untama Giru; Village of Dreams; Violence at Noon; Visitor Q; Waterboys; Wave; Welcome Back Mr McDonald; The Wicked Reporter; Wizard of Darkness; Work on the Grass; World Apartment Horror; Without Memory; The Written Face; The Yakuza; Yellow Dog; Youth of the Beast; Zazie; Zigeunerweisn; Zipper and Tits*

Japanese Americans, *The Color of Honor; Come see the Paradise; The Crimson Kimono; Iron Maze; Mr Moto's Gamble; Snow Falling on Cedars; Sunsets*

Japanese cinema, *see* Appendix 21

Japanese music, *The Life of Chikuzan*

Japrisot, Sébastien, films adapted from work, *The Sleeping Car Murder*

Jarry, Alfred, film adapted from work, *King Ubu*

Jazz, in film
documentaries/performance, *Always for Pleasure; Art Pepper: Notes from a Jazz Survivor; Best Foot Forward; Bird Now; Bix: 'Ain't None of Them Play Like Him Yet'; Blue Note: A History of Modern Jazz; Blue Notes and Exiled Voices;*

...But Then, She's Betty Carter; Charles Mingus: Triumph of the Underdog; Dizzy Gillespie in Cuba; A Great Day in Harlem; Jabula – A Band in Exile; Jazz in Exile; Jazz on a Summer's Day; Jazzwomen; Joe Albany...A Jazz Life; The King of Jazz; Last Date; The Last of the Blue Devils; The Legend of Teddy Edwards; Let's Get Lost; Listen Up: The Lives of Quincy Jones; Memories of Duke; Mississippi Blues; A Night in Havana; Ornette; Made in America; Sun Ra: A Joyful Noise; Robert Altman's Jazz' 34: Remembrances of Kansas City Swing; Talmage Farlow; Thelonious Monk: Straight No Chaser; Wild Man Blues
drama/features, *American Blue Note; And There Was Jazz; Bird; Blue Ice; Bye Bye Blues; C'est la Vie, Ma Cherie; The Connection; The Cool World; The Cotton Club; The Glenn Miller Story; It's Trad, Dad!; Jitterbugs; Kansas City; Lady Sings the Blues; The Legend of 1900; Love with the Proper Stranger; Lush Life; The Man with the Golden Arm; Mo' Better Blues; New York, New York; Orchestra Wives; Pete Kelly's Blues; The Revolving Doors; 'Round Midnight; St Louis Blues; Some Call It Loving; A Song Is Born; The Subterraneans; Sun Valley Serenade; Sven Klang's Combo; Sweet and Lowdown; Sweetheart of the Campus; Swing; Swing Kids; Too Late Blues; Young Man With a Horn*

Jefferson Thomas, film about, *Jefferson in Paris*

Jekyll-and-Hyde stories, see **Stevenson,** Robert Louis

Jerome, Jerome K, film adapted from Work, *Three Men in a Boat*

Jessup, Richard, films adapted from work, *The Cincinnati Kid; Chuka*

Jesus Christ, in film (see also **Biblical stories, God**), *The Body; God Told Me To; The Gospel According to St Matthew; The Greatest Story Ever Told; Jesus Christ Superstar; Jesus of Montreal; King of Kings; The Last Temptation of Christ; The Miracle Maker; Monty Python's Life of Brian; The Robe*

Jewel prospecting, *Romancing the Stone*

Jews and Jewish life, in film (see also **Israel, Yiddish films**)
in Argentina, *The Girlfriend*
in Australia, *Angst; Norman Loves Rose; Shine*
in Austria, *Colonel Redl; Into the Arms of Strangers: Stories of the Kindertransport*
in Britain, *The Custard Boys; Esther Kahn; The Governess; The House of Rothschild; Into the Arms of Strangers: Stories of the Kindertransport; Leon the Pig Farmer; The Man Who Cried; Solomon and Gaenor*
in Canada, *The Apprenticeship of Duddy Kravitz; Lies My Father Told Me*
in Czechoslovakia *Dita Saxová; Gifted City; The Golem; Into the Arms of Strangers: Stories of the Kindertransport; Labyrinth* (Jires); *A Shop on the High Street*
in Denmark, *Sofie*
in France, *Mazel Tov ou le mariage; Man Is a Woman; The Man Who Cried; Mina Tannenbaum; Un Sac de Billes; Le Vieil Homme et l'Enfant; Volpone; What Makes David Run?*
in Germany (pre-Nazi), *Young Törless*
in Italy, *Fortini/Cani; The Garden of the Finzi-Continis*
in Mexico, *Gaby – A True Story; Like a Bride*
in the Netherlands *Left Luggage*
in New Zealand *Punch Me in the Stomach*
in Poland, Simon Magus; Voyages
in Spain, *The Heritage*
and Nazi Holocaust (see also **Germany, War Criminals**), *Aimée & Jaguar; Angst; Au Revoir les Enfants; Because of That War; Berlin Jerusalem; Broken Glass; Conspiracy of Hearts; Dekalog 8: 'Thou shalt not bear false witness'; The Diary of Anne Frank; Docteur Petiot; Enemies, a Love Story; Europa, Europa; Fragments of Isabella; Genghis Cohn; Hanna's War; The Hiding Place; Into the Arms of Strangers: Stories of the Kindertransport; Jew-Boy Levi; Judith; Kapo; Korczak; The Last Days; A Letter Without Words; Life Is Beautiful; Lodz Ghetto; Loving the Dead; Madame Rosa; The Man in the Glass Booth; Mr Klein; My Mother's Courage; None Shall Escape; The Package Tour; Reunion; Un Sac de Billes; Schindler's List; Shoah; Shtetl; Sophie's Choice; The Summer of Aviya; To Speak the Unspeakable: The Message of Elie Wiesel; Triumph of the Spirit; The Truce; The Warsaw Ghetto Uprising; Voyage of the Damned*
in Romania, *To Speak the Unspeakable: The Message of Elie Wiesel*
in Russia and Poland, *The Commissar; Fiddler on the Roof; The Fixer; The Magician of Lublin; Me Ivan, You Abraham; Rothschild's Violin; Schindler's List; Shtetl; Taxi Blues; The Warsaw Ghetto Uprising; Yentl*
in US, *American Stories; Avalon; The Believer; Betsy's Wedding; Brighton Beach Memoirs; Broadway Bound; Carbon Copy; The Chosen; Close to Eden; Crossfire; Crossing Delancey; Crimes and Misdemeanors; Dealers Among Dealers; Driving Miss Daisy; Fast Trip, Long Drop; From Here to Eternity; Gentleman's Agreement; Goodbye Columbus; Hester Street; Homicide; Keeping the Faith; Libert Heights; Little Odessa; Me & My Matchmaker; Mr Saturday Night; Once Upon a Time in America; Over the Brooklyn Bridge; The Pawnbroker; The Plot Against Harry; A Price Above Rubies; Quiz Show; Radio Days; School Ties; The Shvitz; Tell Me a Riddle; A Tickle in the Heart; Used People; Where's Poppa?; White Palace*

Jhabvala, Ruth Prawer, films adapted from work, *Heat and Dust; The Householder*

Joan of Arc, films about, *Giovanna d'Arco al Rogo; Jeanne la Pucelle; Joan of Arc; La Passion de Jeanne d'Arc; Procès de Jeanne d'Arc; Saint Joan*

Joffo, Joseph, film adapted from work, *Un Sac de Billes*

John XXIII, Pope, film about, *A Man Named John*

Jolson, Al, film about, *The Jolson Story*

Jones, James,
fictionalised portrayal, *A Soldier's Daughter Never Cries*
films adapted from work, *From Here to Eternity; Some Came Running; The Thin Red Line*

Jones, Kaylie, film adapted from work, *A Soldier's Daughter Never Cries*

Jonson, Ben, film adapted from work, *The Honey Pot; Volpone*

Joplin, Janis, film about, *Janis*

Journalism, in film
newsreel, *The Cameraman; Newsfront; Too Hot to Handle*
photojournalism, *Picture Snatcher; Under Fire; Warshots*
print, *Absence of Malice; Ace in the Hole; After Office Hours; All the President's Men; Almost Famous; Atlantic Adventure; L'Autre; Between the Lines; The Black Rider; The Bonfire of the Vanities; Call Northside 777; The Captive City; Celebrity; Circle of Deceit; Citizen Kane; Complicity; Comrade X; Confirm or Deny; Les Convoyeurs Attendent; Cover Girl Killer; Crossmaheart; Darklands; The Day the Earth Caught Fire; Deadline – USA; Defence of the Realm; Disparen a Matar; Divorcing Jack; La Dolce Vita; Each Dawn I Die; Eleni; Five Star Final; The Front Page* (Milestone); *The Front Page* (Wilder); *Front Page Woman; He Said, She Said; High Art; Hi, Nellie!; His Girl Friday; How to Be a Woman and Not Die in the Attempt; I Love Trouble; It Happened Tomorrow; Jung (War) – in the Land of the Mujaheddin; Kandahar; LA Confidential; The Last Plane Out; The Last Train from Madrid; The Lawless; Lonelyhearts; The Mad Miss Manton; The Mean Season; Meet John Doe; Message in a Bottle; Monk Dawson; The Naked Truth; The Near Room; Never Been Kissed; A New Kind of Love; Newsies; No Orchids for Miss Blandish; Not for Publication; Nothing Sacred; Palmetto; The Paper; The Parallax View; Park Row; The People vs. Larry Flynt; Perfect; Platinum Blonde; Please Don't Eat the Daisies; Prejudice; Press for Time; Public Enemy Number One; Public Eye; Roman Holiday; Rough Treatment; Roxie Hart; Runaway Bride; Salvador; Schtonk!; The Sisters; Souvenir; Straight Talk; Sweet Smell of Success; Tank Malling; Three O'Clock High; True Crime; Turtle Beach; Up Your Alley; War Zone; While the City Sleeps; Who'll Stop the Rain?; Winchell; Woman of the Year; Year of the Gun; The Year of Living Dangerously*
TV, *Broadcast News; The China Syndrome; Comic Magazine; Death of a Cameraman; Extreme Close-Up; Eyes of a Stranger; Eyewitness; Giro City; Mad City; Man of Iron; Man of Marble; Switching Channels; Testament* (Akomfrah); *Visiting Hours; Vivre pour Vivre; When the Sky Fall; Windprints*

Joyce, James,
film about, *Nora*
films adapted from work, *The Dead; Finnegans Wake; A Portrait of the Artist as a Young Man; Ulysses*

Judges (see also **Courtroom dramas, Lawyers**), *Brothers in Law; Leap into the Void; Open Doors; The Star Chamber; The Sun Shines Bright*

Jung, Carl Gustav, film about, *Matter of Heart*

Junger, Sebastian, film adapted from work, *The Perfect Storm*

Jungle dramas (see also **Rain forests**), *Anaconda; Apocalypse Now; Apocalypse Now Redux; Appointment in Honduras; Baby – Secret of the Lost Legend; Back from Eternity;*

Beyond the Blue Horizon; Cannibal; Cannibal Women in the Avocado Jungle of Death; The Emerald Forest; Escape to Burma; Farewell to the King; Five Came Back; Gorillas in the Mist; Greystoke – The Legend of Tarzan Lord of the Apes; To Have & to Hold; Jumanji; Jungle 2 Jungle; Mighty Joe Young (Schoedsack); *Mighty Joe Young* (Underwood); *Mogambo; Monster from Green Hell; La Mort en ce Jardin; Predator; Red Dust; Run for the Sun; The 7th Dawn; Sheena; Sorcerer; Tarzan and the Mermaids; Tarzan, the Ape Man; Voodoo Woman*

Kafka, Franz
films adapted from work, *The Castle* (Haneke); *Class Relations; The Trial* (Welles); *The Trial* (Jones)
in film, *Kafka; Labyrinth* (Jires)

Kanga, Firdaus, film based on autobiography, *The Sixth Happiness*

Kanin, Garson,
films adapted from work, *Born Yesterday* (Cukor); *Born Yesterday* (Mandoki)

Kästner, Erich, film adapted from work, *The Parent Trap*

Katzenbach, John, film adapted from work, *Just Cause*

Kazakhstan cinema, *Killer, The* (Omirbaev); *Prisoner of the Mountains; The Road*

Kazan, Elia,
film adapted from work, *The Arrangement*

Kazantzakis, Nikos, films adapted from work, *The Last Temptation of Christ; Zorba the Greek*

Keane, John B, film adapted from work, *The Field*

Keating, HRF, film adapted from work, *The Perfect Murder*

Keel, John, film adapted from work, *The Mothman Prophecies*

Kemp, Lindsay, film adapted from work, *Travelling Light: a Portrait of Lindsay Kemp*

Kempinski, Tom, films adapted from work, *Duet for One; Wot! No Art*

Kendrick, Baynard, film adapted from work, *Eyes in the Night*

Keneally, Thomas, films adapted from work, *The Chant of Jimmy Blacksmith; Schindler's List*

Kenju, Haku, film adapted from work, *A Boy Called Third Base*

Kennaway, James, films adapted from work, *Country Dance; Tunes of Glory*

Kennedy (Onassis), Jacqueline, films about, *The Greek Tycoon; The Grey Gardens*

Kennedy, John F,
films about, *Executive Action; In the Line of Fire; JFK; Love Field; Ruby; Rush to Judgment; Thirteen Days*

Kennedy, Ludovic,
films adapted from work, *Crime of the Century; 10 Rillington Place*

Kenya, in film, *The Air Up There; Cheetah; The Ghost and the Darkness; The Kitchen Toto; Out of Africa; Simba; To Walk with Lions; Where No Vultures Fly; White Mischief*

Kenyan cinema, *To Walk with Lions*

Kern, Jerome
musicals by, *Roberta; Swing Time; You Were Never Lovelier*
and Hammerstein, Oscar, musicals by, *Centennial Summer; Show Boat* (Whale); *Show Boat* (Sidney)

Kerouac, Jack
films about, *Heart Beat; Kerouac; What Happened to Kerouac?*
film adapted from work, *The Subterraneans*
in film, *Pull My Daisy*

Kesey, Ken
films adapted from work, *One Flew Over the Cuckoo's Nest; Sometimes a Great Notion*
in film, *The Life and Times of Allen Ginsberg*

Ketcham, Hank, film adapted from comic strip, *Dennis the Menace*

Kieslowski, Krzysztof, film about, *Krzysztof Kieslowski: I'm So So*

Kickboxing, *Kickboxer; Say Anything*

Kidnap dramas, *Abduction; After Dark, My Sweet; Alexander the Great; Along Came a Spider; Baby's Day Out; Beach Blanket Bingo; The Big Hit; The Big Lebowski; The Bitter Tea of General Yen; The Black Lizard; Black Windmill; Buffalo '66; Captive; Catchfire; The Chase* (Rifkin); *La Cité des enfants perdus; Crime of the Century; Crime Story; Crows; Darkess Falls; Dirt; Don't Just Lie There, Say Something!; The Drive; The Everlasting Secret Family; Excess Baggage; The Extraordinary Adventures of Mister West in the Land of the Bolsheviks; Fargo; Fille à Tuer; Fog over Frisco; Full Moon in Blue Water; The Grissom Gang; Guarding Tess; The Happening; High and Low; The Honorary Consul; The House on Garibaldi Street; Humanity and Paper Balloons; Ill Met by Moonlight; Joan of Arc of Mongolia; Kansas City; The Kidnappers; Kidnapping the President; King of Comedy; A Life Less Ordinary; Lolly-Madonna XXX; Malpertuis; Manny & Lo; Man on Fire; Mansion of the Doomed; The Man Who Knew Too Much* (Hitchcock, 1934); *The Man Who Knew Too Much* (Hitchcock, 1956); *The Mexican; My Name Is Julia Ross; Nada; The Night of the Following Day; No Deposit, No Return; No Orchids for Miss Blandish; O. Henry's Full House ('The Ransom of Red Chief'); Papa, les Petits Bateaux…; Palmetto; Parker; Proof of Life; Raising Arizona; Ransom; Rosebud; Ruthless People; Scenes of the Crime; School for Vandals; Seance on a Wet Afternoon; The Secret Invasion; Shanghai Noon; Skinflicker; Slow Attack; The Snow Queen; The Sound of Fury; The Squeeze; Streets of Fire; Sudden Death; Tattoo; Taxi 2; That Darn Cat; This Alien Earth; Tie Me Up! Tie Me Down!; Tropical Fish* (Chen Yu-Hsun); *Union Station; Venom* (Sykes); *Voodoo Man; The Way of the Gun; White Man's Burden; A Woman or Two; World for Ransom; Who's Harry Crumb?*

King, Carole, film inspired by life of, *Grace of My Heart*

King, Stephen, films adapted from work, *Apt Pupil; Carrie* (De Palma); *Cat's Eye* (Teague); *Creepshow; Children of the Corn; Christine; Cujo; The Dark Half; The Dead Zone; Dolores Claiborne; Firestarter; Graveyard Shift; The Green Mile; Hearts in Atlantis; The Lawnmower Man; The Mangler; Maximum Overdrive; Misery; Pet Sematary; The Running Man* (Glaser); *Salem's Lot; The Shawshank Redemption; Silver Bullet; Sleepwalkers; Tales from the Darkside: The Movie*

King/Queen for a day, *The King of Comedy; Lady for a Day; The Man Who Could Work Miracles; The Prince and the Pauper*

King-Smith, Dick, films adapted from works, *Babe; Babe – Pig in the City*

Kingsley, Charles, film adapted from work, *The Water Babies*

Kingsley, Sidney, films adapted from work, *Dead End; Detective Story*

Kinski, Klaus, film about, *My Dearest Enemy*

Kipling, Rudyard,
films adapted from work, *Captains Courageous; Elephant Boy; Gunga Din; The Jungle Book* (Reitherman); *The Jungle Book* (Sommers); *Kim; The Man Who Would Be King*

Kleist, Heinrich von, films adapted from work, *Die Marquise von O…; Michael Kohlhaas; Penthesilea: Queen of the Amazons; The Prince of Homburg*

Kleptomania, *The Locket; Marnie; Slightly Scarlet; Whirlpool*

Kneale, Nigel,
films adapted from work, *Halloween III; Quatermass and the Pit; The Quatermass Experiment; Quatermass II*

Knievel, Evel, films about, *Evel Knievel; Viva Knievel*

Koontz, Dean R, films adapted from work, *Shattered; Watchers*

Kopit, Arthur,
film adapted from work, *Buffalo Bill and the Indians*

Korczak, Janusz,
film about, *Korczak*

Korda, Alexander, films produced by, *Catherine The Great; Dark Journey; The Drum; Elephant Boy; The Elusive Pimpernel; Fire over England; The Four Feathers* (Korda); *The Ghost Goes West; The Girl from Maxim's; That Hamilton Woman; The Man Who Could Work Miracles; The Thief of Bagdad* (Powell et al); *Things to Come; Wedding Rehearsal*

Korea, in film, *Annyong Kimchi; Asako in Ruby Shoes; Attack on a Gas Station!; Bad Guy; Barking Dogs Never Bite; Battle Hymn; Black Republic; The Bridges at Toko-Ri; Chihwaseon; Chilsu and Mansu; Christmas in August; Chunhyang; Come, Come, Come Upward; The Contact; Cry-Woman; The Day a Pig Fell into the Well; Die Bad; Farewell My Darling; Festival* (Im Kwon-Taek); *First Love* (Lee Myung-Se); *Flower Island; Fly Low; The Foul King; Gilsodom; Green Fish; Happy End; Hi, Dharma!; The Housemaid; The Hunters; Hwa-om-kyong; The Isle; Joint Security Area/JSA; Jungle Story; The Insect Woman; Iodo; Kick the Moon; Killer Butterfly; Kung Fu Fighting; Lies; Lovers in Woomuk-Baemi; The Man Who Saw Too Much; Marriage Story; Men in War; No. 3; Nowhere to Hide; Oksutan; One Fine Spring Day; One Minute to Zero; Peppermint Candy; A Petal; Pork Chop Hill; The Power of Kangwon Province;*

Push! Push!; Retreat, Hell!; Roadmovie; Road to the Racetrack; Shirl; A Single Spark; Sopyonje; Spring in My Hometown; The Steel Helmet; Surrogate Mother; The Taebeck Mountains; Take Care of My Cat; That Woman, That Man; Teenage Hooker Became Killing Machine in Daehakroh; Three Friends; Ticket; Timeless Bottomless Bad Movie; To the Starry Island; To You, From Me; Turning Gate; La Vie en rose; Village in the Mist; Virgin Stripped Bare by Her Bachelors; The Waikiki Brothers; Why Did Bodhi-Dharma Leave for the Orient?; Wind Echoing in My Being

Korean Americans, *True Believer*

Korean cinema (South), *Asako in Ruby Shoes; Attack on a Gas Station!; Bad Guy; Barking Dogs Never Bite; Berlin Report; Black Republic; Broken Branches; Chihwaseon; Chilsu and Mansu; Christmas in August; Chunhyang; Come, Come, Come Upward; The Contact; Cry-Woman; The Day a Pig Fell into the Well; Die Bad; Farewell My Darling; Festival* (Im Kwon-Taek); *First Love* (Lee Myung-Se); *Flower Island; Fly Low; The Foul King; Friend; Gilsodom; Grandma and Her Ghosts; Green Fish; Happy End; Hi, Dharma!; A Hot Roof; The Housemaid; Hwa-om-kyong; The Insect Woman; Iodo; The Isle; The Jang-Sun Woo Variations; Joint Security Area/JSA; Jungle Story; Kick the Moon; Killer Butterfly; KT; Lies; Lovers in Woomuk-Baemi; Mandala; The Man Who Saw Too Much; There; Marriage Story; Memento Mori; Motel Cactus; No. 3; Nowhere to Hide; Our Twisted Hero; Oksutan; One Fine Spring Day; Peppermint Candy; A Petal; The Power of Kangwon Province; Push! Push!; Roadmovie; Road to the Racetrack; Rub Love; Secret Tears; Shirl; A Single Spark; Something Happened; Sopyonje; Spring in My Hometown; Surrogate Mother; The Taebeck Mountains; That Woman, That Man; Teenage Hooker Became Killing Machine in Daehakroh; Three Friends; 301–302; Ticket; Timeless Bottomless Bad Movie; Too Young to Die; To the Starry Island; To You, From Me; The Turning Gate; Unknown Pleasures; La Vie en rose; Village in the Mist; Virgin Stripped Bare by Her Bachelors; Volcano High; The Waikiki Brothers; Whispering Corridors; Why Did Bodhi-Dharma Leave for the Orient?; Wind Echoing in My Being*

Korean War, and prelude to, *An Annapolis Story; Battle Hymn; The Bridges at Toko-Ri; Fixed Bayonets!; A Hill In Korea; I Want You; The Hunters; M*A*S*H; One Minute to Zero; Period of Adjustment; Pork Chop Hill; Retreat, Hell!; Sayonara; Spring in My Hometown; The Steel Helmet; The Taebeck Mountains; To the Starry Island*

Kotzwinkle, William, film adapted from work, *Book of Love*

Krupin, Al, film adapted from work, *Sisters of Gion*

Kundera, Milan, film adapted from work, *The Unbearable Lightness of Being*

Kurdistan, in film, *Journey to the Sun; A Song for Beko; The Voice of Kurdistan*

Kurosawa, Akira, films about, *A.K.; Akira Kurosawa's Dreams; Kurosawa*

Labour relations (see also **Industry and industrial life**)
in Australia, *Spotswood*
in Britain, *British Sounds; Business as Usual; Chance of a Lifetime; Comrades; Film from the Clyde; Flame in the Streets; I'm All Right Jack; The Man in the White Suit; '36 to '77; Year of the Beaver*
in Chile, *The Battle of Chile; Cantata of Chile*
in France, *Coup pour Coup; Le Crime de Monsieur Lange; Tout Va Bien*
in Germany, *Dear Mother, I'm All Right*
in Philippines, *Bayan Ko: My Own Country*
in Poland, *Man of Iron; Man of Marble*
in Russia, *Strike*
in South Africa, *Wheels & Deals*
in Sweden, *Adalen '31*
in US, *Black Fury; Blue Collar; Boxcar Bertha; The Devil in Miss Jones; Edge of the City; F.I.S.T.; The Garment Jungle; The Grapes of Wrath; Gung Ho; Harlan County USA; Hoffa; I Married a Communist; Joe Hill; The Killing Floor; Last Exit to Brooklyn; Matewan; The Molly Maguires; Newsies; The Pajama Game; Roger & Me; Salt of the Earth; So That You Can Live; Stanley & Iris; Union Maids; With Babies and Banners; The Wobblies*

Laclos, Choderlos de, films adapted from work, *Cruel Intentions; Dangerous Liaisons; Les Liaisons Dangereuses 1960; Valmont*

La Fayette, Mme de, films adapted from work, *La Fidélité; The Letter*

Laing, RD, film adapted from work, *Knots*

Lamb, Lady Caroline, film about, *Lady Caroline Lamb*

Langlois, Henri, film about, *Citizen Langlois*

Laos, in film, *Air America*

Lapland, in film, *Earth Is a Sinful Song; Pathfinder*

Lasdun, James, film adapted from work, *Besieged*

Las Vegas, in film, *Bugsy; Casino; Corvette Summer; The Don Is Dead; Elvis – The Movie; Elvis – That's the Way It Is; Girls' Night; Honeymoon in Vegas; Indecent Proposal; The Las Vegas Story; Leaving Las Vegas; Ocean's 11* (Milestone); *Ocean's Eleven* (Soderbergh); *One from the Heart; The Only Game in Town; Rain Man; Rat Race; Rush Hour 2; Showgirls; Very Bad Things; Viva Las Vegas*

Latin America, unspecified, in film (see also individual countries), *B. Must Die; Commando; The Evil That Men Do; La Fievre Monte à el Pao; The Fugitive* (Ford); *Guns of Darkness; Men with Guns; Moon Over Parador; Los Niños Abandonados; Romancing the Stone; Rude Awakening*

Latvia, in film, *Another Mother*

Laundry-press, malevolent, *The Mangler*

Lawn-mowers, as long-distance transport, *The Straight Story*

Lawrence, DH
film about, *Priest of Love*
films adapted from work, *The Fox; Kangaroo* (Burstall); *Lady Chatterley's Lover; The Rainbow; The Rocking Horse Winner; Sons and Lovers; The Virgin and the Gypsy; Women in Love*

Lawrence, Gertrude, film about, *Star*

Lawrence, TE, film about, *Lawrence of Arabia*

Lawyers (see also **Courtroom dramas, Judges**), *Adam's Rib; ...and justice for all; Bird on a Wire; Bordertown; Brothers in Law; Cape Fear* (Thompson); *Cape Fear* (Scorsese); *The Chamber; Class Action; The Client; A Civil Action; Criminal Law; Danger – Love at Work; Defence Counsel Sedov; The Devil's Advocate* (Hackford); *Erin Brokovich; Fair Game; The Firm; The Fortune Cookie; The Franchise Affair; From the Hip; The Gingerbread Man; Guilty as Sin; The Hour of the Pig; I Am Sam; I Am the Law; In All Innocence; The Lawyer; Legally Blonde; Liar Liar; Loved; The Marcorelle Affair; Mortgage; My Cousin Vinny; Murder in the First; Narrow Margin; Night and the City* (Winkler); *Night Falls on Manhattan; The Paper Chase; The Paradine Case; Pas Trés Catholique; The Pelican Brief; Philadelphia; Physical Evidence; Presumed Innocent; Primal Fear; The Proposition; The Rainmaker; Regarding Henry; Reversal of Fortune; Scenes from a Mall; Seems Like Old Times; Shakedown; Shame; The Star Chamber; The Story of Qiu Ju; Suspect; The Sweet Hereafter; They Might Be Giants; Tout ça… pour ça!!!; True Believer; The Verdict* (Lumet); *The War of the Roses; Wild Orchid*

Lebanon, in film, *Around the Pink House; Circle of Deceit; Civilised People; Cup Final; Hors la vie; Lebanon…Why?; Navy Seals; War Zone*

Lebanese cinema, *Algiers/Beyrouth: pour mémoire; Al-Risalah; Around the Pink House; Civilised People; Days in London; Hour of Liberation – The Struggle in Oman; Lebanon…Why?; Leila and the Wolves; West Beirut*

Lebert, Benjamin, film adapted from work, *Crazy*

Le Carré, John, films adapted from work, *The Deadly Affair; The Little Drummer Girl; The Looking Glass War; The Russia House; The Spy Who Came In From the Cold; The Tailor of Panama*

Lee, Bruce, films about, *Bruce Lee, The Man, the Myth; The Dragon Dies Hard; Dragon: The Bruce Lee Story*

Lee, Harper, film adapted from work, *To Kill a Mockingbird*

Lee, James, film adapted from work, *Career*

Le Fanu, Sheridan, films adapted from work, *Twins of Evil; Uncle Silas; The Vampire Lovers, Vampyr*

Legends, see **Myths and legends**

Lennon, John, films about, *Backbeat; The Hours and Times; Imagine*

Lenz, Siegfried, film adapted from work, *The Lightship*

Leonard, Elmore, films adapted from work, *The Ambassador; Cat Chaser; 52 Pick Up; Get Shorty; Gold Coast; Hombre; Jackie Brown; The Moonshine War; Out of Sight; Stick; The Tall T; 3:10 to Yuma; Touch; Valdez Is Coming*

Leoncavallo, Ruggiero, film adapted from work, *Pagliacci*

Leopold and Loeb case, *Compulsion; Rope; Swoon*

Lerner, Alan J, and Loewe, Frederick, musicals by, *Brigadoon; Camelot; The Little Prince; My Fair Lady; Paint Your Wagon*

Lermontov, Mikhail, films adapted from work, *Ashik Kerib; Fury* (Calenda)

Leroux, Gaston, films adapted from work, *The Phantom of the Opera* (Julian); *Phantom of the Opera* (Little); *Phantom of the Opera* (Lubin); *The Phantom of the Opera* (Fisher); *Phantom of the Paradise*

Lesbians and lesbianism
Aus, *Flaming Ears*
Aust, *The Monkey's Mask*
Bel, *Daughters of Darkness; Je tu il elle*
Can, *Fire; I've Heard the Mermaids Singing; No Skin Off My Ass; When Night Is Falling*
China, *Fish and Elephant; Maiden Work; Portland Street Blues; Sun and Rain*
Fr, *L'Araignée de Satin; L'Astragale; Les Biches; Chanel Solitaire; Club des Femmes; Gazon maudit; Huis Clos; November Moon; Olivia; Le Rempart des Béguines*
GB, *A Bit of Scarlet; Butterfly Kiss; In the Best Interests of the Children; The Killing of Sister George; Home-Made Melodrama; The Pleasure Principle; The Rainbow; Thin Ice* (Reid); *Wild Flowers* (Smith)
Ger, *The Berlin Affair; The Bitter Tears of Petra von Kant; Joan of Arc of Mongolia; Mädchen in Uniform; My Father Is Coming; Paragraph 175; The Second Awakening of Christa Klages; Virgin Machine*
HK, *Hu-Du-Men*
Hun, *Another Way*
Ind, *Fire*
It, *Love in A Women's Prison*
Jap, *Afternoon Breezes; The Enchantment; Fufu the Worldweary; Love/Juice*
Phil, *Three*
SKor, *Memento Mori*
Sp, *Costa Brava (Family Album); Pourquoi pas moi?*;
Swe, *The Silence* (Bergman); *The Women on the Roof*
Tai, *The Silent Thrush*
Thai, *Iron Ladies*
US, *Bound; Bound and Gagged: A Love Story; Boys on the Side; But I'm a Cheerleader; Can't Stop the Music; The Color Purple; Daughters of Darkness; Desert Hearts; Desperate Living; A Different Story; Girlfriends; Go Fish; Headhunter; The Incredibly True Adventure of Two Girls in Love; Internal Affairs; Kamikaze Hearts; Lianna; Liquid Sky; A Litany for Survival: The Life and Work of Audre Lorde; MURDER and Murder; She Must Be Seeing Things; Three of Hearts; Two Moon Junction; Without You I'm Nothing; Word Is Out; Zee & Co*

Leskov, Nikolai, films adapted from work, *Coilin and Platonida; Katia Ismaïlova; Siberian Lady Macbeth*

Lessing, Doris, films adapted from work, *The Grass Is Singing; Memoirs of a Survivor*

Letters in bottles, *Message in a Bottle*

Levi, Carlo, film adapted from work, *Christ Stopped at Eboli*

Levi, Primo, film adapted from work, *The Truce*

Levin, Ira, films adapted from work, *The Boys from Brazil; Deathtrap; A Kiss Before Dying* (Oswald); *A Kiss Before Dying* (Dearden); *Rosemary's Baby; Sliver; The Stepford Wives*

Lewis, CS, film about, *Shadowlands*

Lewis, Jerry Lee, film about, *Great Balls of Fire!*

Librarians, *The Music Man; No Man of Her Own* (Ruggles); *Off Beat; Only Two Can Play; Storm Center*

Libya, in film, *Bengazi; Lion of the Desert*

Lifeguards, *Lifeguard*

Lifts/elevators, *Lift; Living Out Loud; Love Crazy; Out of Order* (Schenkel); *Wild Games*

Lighthouses, *Back-Room Boy; Diva; The Light at the Edge of the World; The Oyster and the Wind; The Phantom Light*

Lincoln, Abraham, films about, *The Prisoner of Shark Island; The Tall Target; Young Mr Lincoln*

Lindbergh, Charles, films about, *Crime of the Century; The Spirit of St Louis*

Linder, Max, film about, *L'Homme au Chapeau de Soie*

Lindsay, Howard, film adapted from work, *Life with Father*

Lindsay, Norman, film about, *Sirens*

Linklater, Eric, film adapted from work, *Laxdale Hall*

Liszt, Franz, films about, *Lisztomania; The Loves of Liszt*

Lithuanian cinema, *Freedom*

Liverpool, in film (see also **North of England**), *Blonde Fist; Business as Usual; Dancin' Thru the Dark; Dark Summer; Distant Voices, Still Lives; The Dressmaker; Educating Rita; Ferry Cross the Mersey; The 51st State; Flight of the Doves; The Fruit Machine; Going Off Big Time; Gumshoe; Hear My Song; A Letter to Brezhnev; Liam; The Long Day Closes; No Surrender; Occupy; Priest; Shirley Valentine; Swing; The Terence Davies Trilogy; This Boy's Story*

Llewellyn, Richard, films adapted from work, *How Green Was My Valley; None But the Lonely Heart; Noose*

Locke, Josef, film about, *Hear My Song*

Loesser, Frank, musical by, *Guys and Dolls; Hans Christian Andersen; How to Succeed in Business Without Really Trying*

Loewe, Frederick, see **Lerner,** Alan J

Lofting, Hugh, films adapted from work, *Doctor Dolittle; Dr Dolittle 2*

Lombard, Carole, film about, *Gable and Lombard*

London, Jack, films adapted from work, *By the Law; Call of the Wild; The Sea Wolf; White Fang* (Fulci); *White Fang* (Kleiser)

London, in film
19th century and earlier, *Corridors of Blood; Dark Eyes of London; David Copperfield; The Elephant Man; Esther Kahn; The Fool; From Hell; Gaslight* (Cukor); *Gaslight* (Dickinson); *Grip of The Strangler; Little Dorrit; The Lodger; Mary Reilly; Nicholas Nickleby; Oliver!; Oliver Twist* (Lean); *Oliver Twist* (Donner); *The Secret Agent* (Hampton); *A Study in Terror; The Suspect; Sweeney Todd; Tom Jones; The Two Faces of Dr Jekyll; Waxworks*
1900–1919, *Carnival; Mrs Dalloway; The Siege of Sidney Street*
1920s–1930s, *Keep the Aspidistra Flying; None but the Lonely Heart; No Trees in the Street; Number Seventeen; Piccadilly; Traitor Spy; Underground* (Asquith); *Underneath the Arches; Werewolf of London*
1940s–1950s, *The Adventures of PC 49; The Blue Lamp; The Brighton Strangler; Chicago Joe and the Showgirl; Contraband; Dance with a Stranger; Dancing with Crime; The Day the Earth Caught Fire; 84 Charing Cross Road; Expresso Bongo; Fires Were Started; Great Balls of Fire!; Hangover Square; The Happy Family; A Kid for Two Farthings; Knave of Hearts; Let Him Have It; London Belongs to Me; Love Is the Devil – Study for a Portrait of Francis Bacon; Lured; Mojo; The Naked Truth; Nice Time; Night and the City* (Dassin); *Noose; Queen of Hearts; The Tommy Steele Story; Waterloo Road*
1960s, *Alfie; Bitter Harvest; Blow-Up; Darling…; Do Not Disturb; Duffy; File of the Golden Goose; Georgy Girl; Here We Go Round the Mulberry Bush; I Don't Want to Be Born; Kaleidoscope; The Krays; Laughter in the Dark; Life at the Top; The Man Who Had Power Over Women; Nobody Runs Forever; Nothing but the Best; One More Time; Otley; Performance; Piccadilly Third Stop; Play It Cool; Popdown; The Queen's Guards; Repulsion; Salt & Pepper; Song of the Exile; There's a Girl in My Soup; Tonite Let's All Make Love in London; To Sir, With Love; Up the Junction; The Wrong Arm of the Law*
1970s, *Bronco Bullfrog; Deep End; Dracula A.D. 1972; Drôle de Drame; Fly a Flag for Poplar; Frenzy; Metroland; Monk Dawson; Nightcleaners; The Optimists of Nine Elms; The Revolutionary; Sweeney!; Theatre Girls; Tunde's Film; Villain; What Next?; Who Needs a Heart; Young Soul Rebels*
1980s, *Bearskin; The Chain; Crystal Gazing; Dealers; Defence of the Realm; Empire State; A Fish Called Wanda; Fords on Water; The Grass Arena; High Hopes; I Hired a Contract Killer; Melancholia; Mona Lisa; Nightshift; Number One* (Blair); *Nuns on the Run; Old Flames; The Rachel Papers; Runners; The Tall Guy; Tree of Hands; Twilight City; Ursula and Glenys; Who Dares Wins*
1990, *Bad Behaviour; Beautiful People; Beautiful Thing; Bedrooms and Hallways; Before the Rain; Brothers in Trouble; Butterfly Effect; Chasing Dreams; Close My Eyes; Crimetime; The Criminal; Croupier; Don't Go Breaking My Heart; The Escort; Face; Fast Food; Following; Foreign Moon; Gangster No. 1; Guru in Seven; If Only; The Innocent Sleep; A Kind of Hush; Ladybird Ladybird; The Leading Man; Lock, Stock and Two Smoking Barrels; London; London Kills Me; Look Me in the Eye; The Lost Son; Love, Honour and Obey; Man from China; The Man Who Knew Too Little; Naked; Nil by Mouth; Notting Hill; Out of Depth; The Punk and the Princess; Rage; Razor Blade*

Smile; Riff-Raff; Shooting Fish; Sliding Doors; Spice World; Tale of a Vampire; This Year's Love; Tiré à Part; Truly, Madly, Deeply; 24 Hours in London; White Angel; Wild West; Wonderland
from 2000, *About a Boy; Ali G Indahouse; All or Nothing; Intimacy; It Was an Accident; Killing Me Softly; Lava; The Low Down; A Quiet Desperation; Room to Rent; Second Generation; Shiner; Shooters; Some Voices; South West Nine; Spider; When in London*
future visions of, *Daleks – Invasion Earth 2150 AD; The Nine Lives of Tomas Katz; Split Second*

Lonely hearts ads, *Beyond Therapy; Lured; Pièges; Sea of Love; Understanding Jane*

Long, Earl K, film about, *Blaze*

Long, Huey, film about, *All the King's Men*

Lorca, see **García Lorca**

Los Angeles, in film
19th century,
The Mask of Zorro
1930s–1940s,
Barfly; The Big Sleep (Hawks); *Bordertown; Chinatown; Conterfeiters; Devil in a Blue Dress; Farewell, My Lovely* (Dmytryk); *Farewell, My Lovely* (Richards); *Lovecraft; The Maltese Falcon* (Del Ruth); *The Maltese Falcon* (Huston); *Nobody Lives Forever; The November Plan; Satan Met a Lady; True Confessions; The Two Jakes; Who Framed Roger Rabbit*
1950s–1960s, *The Graduate; LA Confidential; M* (Losey); *Model Shop; Mulholland Falls; Poodle Springs; War of the Colossal Beast*
1970s, *American Gigolo; Boulevard Nights; Busting; The Choirboys; Cisco Pike; Earthquake; FM; Foxes; Heat* (Morrissey); *Hustle; The Outside Man; Welcome to L.A.; You Light Up My Life*
1980s, *Blue Thunder; The Boys Next Door; Choose Me; Colors; The Couch Trip; The Craft; The Decline of Western Civilization; The Decline of Western Civilization Part II; Down and Out in Beverly Hills; Earth Girls Are Easy; Eating Raoul; Echo Park; El Norte; The Glitter Dome; Hard to Kill; Internal Affairs; Into the Night; Lambada; The Last of the Finest; Pulse; Repo Man; Scenes from the Class Struggle in Beverly Hills; Skin Deep; Tales of Ordinary Madness; Tango & Cash; Them!; They Live; To Live and Die in L.A.; Vampire at Midnight; Wicked Stepmother; The Wild Side*
1990s, *Airheads; Another You; Best Hotel on Skid Row; The Big Bang Theory; The Big Lebowski; Blast from the Past; Blue Streak; Boyz N the Hood; The Brady Bunch Movie; Bread and Roses; Broken Vessels; Brother* (Kitano); *City of Angels; Donato and Daughter; 8MM; Eight-Tray Gangster: The Making of a Crip; The End of Violence; Falling Down; Fathers' Day; Femme Fatale; Filofax; The First Power; Grand Canyon; The Glass Shield; The Guardian; Guy; Heart Condition; Heat* (Mann); *Hustler White; Intimate with a Stranger; It's My Party; Jackie Brown; Julia Has Two Lovers; Johns; L.A. Story; LA Without a Map; The Limey; The Living End; Madhouse; The Million Dollar Hotel; My Crasy Life; My Crazy Life; The New Age; Nick of Time; A Night at the Roxbury; Night on Earth; Nurse Betty; One Eight Seven; Playing by Heart; Pretty Woman; Rush Hour; Scenes from a Mall; Set It Off; Sex Life in L.A.; Skin & Bone; Slums of Beverly Hills; South Central; Speed; Swingers; Totally F***ed Up; Twilight; Water and Power; White Men Can't Jump*
20th century, *My Family*
after 2000, *Baby Boy; Camera Obscura; Crazy/Beautiful; Crocodile Dundee in Los Angeles; ivansxtc.; Showtime*
20th century, *My Family*
future visions of,
Blade Runner; Blade Runner – The Director's Cut; John Carpenter's Escape from L.A.; Predator 2; Strange Days; The Terminator; Terminator 2: Judgment Day; Volcano

Lotteries,
Le Franc; It Could Happen to You; Loser; The Love Lottery; The Million; Waking Ned

Louis XIV,
King of France, films about, *Marquise; La Prise de Pouvoir par Louis XIV; Si Versailles m'était conté…; Vatel*

Louys, Pierre, films adapted from work, *The Devil Is a Woman; That Obscure Object of Desire*

Lovecraft, HP, films adapted from work, *Lovecraft; Monster of Terror; Re-Animator; Re-Animator 2*

Love stories (see also **Infidelity**)
Arg, *Camila; We Don't Talk About It*
Aust, *Cactus; Daydream Believer; The Delinquents; Flirting; Stan and George's New Life; Strictly Ballroom; Wendy Cracked a Walnut*
Bel, *Benvenuta*
Braz, *Gabriela*
Can, *Archangel; Child Under a Leaf; Leopard in the Snow; Map of the Human Heart; La Tendresse Ordinaire*
Fin, *I Hired a Contract Killer*
Fr, *Adieu Philippine; L'Aigle à Deux Têtes; Alice et Martin; Les Amants de Verone; Les Amants du Pont-Neuf; Angel Sharks; La Bonne Année; L'Appartement; La Boulangère de Monceau; La Carrière de Suzanne; Casque d'Or; César and Rosalie; Charlotte Gray; Conte d'été; Conte de printemps; Cyrano de Bergerac; La Dame aux Camélias; Dear Inspector; Delicatessen; Les Demoiselles de Rochefort; Diane; Eléna et les Hommes; Les Enfants du siècle; Falbalas; Faute de Soleil; Le Goût des Autres; Les Grandes Manoeuvres; Gueule d'Amour; Un Homme et une Femme; Lola; La Maison de Jade; A Man in Love; Marius et Jeannette; Mayerling; Noce blanche; Notre Histoire; Les Parapluies de Cherbourg; Parfait Amour!; Paul and Michelle; Quatorze Juillet; Roselyne and the Lions; Le Secret de Mayerling; Le Silence de la mer; A Strange Place to Meet; This Sweet Sickness; Stealing Heaven; Toute Une Nuit; Trop belle pour toi!; A Winter's Tale*
GB, *Alive and Kicking; American Friends; Anna Karenina* (Duvivier); *Blanche Fury; The Blue Lagoon* (Launder); *Breaking the Waves; Bridget Jones's Diary; Brief Ecstasy; Brief Encounter; The Buttercup Chain; Cal; Dangerous Moonlight; The English Patient; Friends; The Gypsy and the Gentleman; Hussy; I Could Go on Singing; If Only; Impromptu; Interlude* (Billington); *Iris; Jude; Like It Is; The Love Test; Lunch Hour; Manuela; Martha – Meet Frank, Daniel and Laurence; Neither the Sea nor the Sand; Notting Hill; Pandora and the Flying Dutchman; A Private Life; The Raging Moon; Real Life; Romeo and Juliet; The Scarlet Tunic; Shakespeare in Love; Strapless; Sweet William; The Tall Guy; The Tamarind Seed; This Is the Sea; Those Glory, Glory Days; Truly, Madly, Deeply; The Wind Cannot Read; The Wings of the Dove; Yanks*
Ger, *Liebelei; A Love in Germany; The Promise* (von Trotta)
Greece, *Captain Corelli's Mandolin; Stone Years*
HK, *Eighteen Springs*
Ind, *Monsoon Wedding*
It, *A Brief Vacation; Malèna; Romeo and Juliet; Stealing Beauty; Terminal Station; Viaggio in Italia; We the Living*
Jap, *A Scene at the Sea; The Story of the Late Chrysanthemums; Summer Vacation 1999*
Mex, *Abismos de pasión; White Lies*
Neth, *Felice… Felice…; The Polish Bride*
Pol, *Love Stories; The Third Part of the Night; A Year of the Quiet Sun; The Young Ladies of Wilko*
Sp, *Jealousy; Tie Me Up! Tie Me Down!*
Swe, *Elvira Madigan*
Switz, *The Middle of the World*
Tai, *The Cabbie*
US, *The Accidental Tourist; Always* (Spielberg); *Anna Karenina* (Brown); *Anna Karenina* (Rose); *Baby, It's You; Big Night; The Black Orchid; The Blue Lagoon* (Kleiser); *Blume in Love; Bobby Deerfield; Bridges of Madison County; Bus Stop; By the Light of the Silvery Moon; Camille* (Smallwood); *Camille* (Cukor); *Casablanca; Catchfire; The Cobra Cousins; The Dark Angel; Déjà Vu; Deception; Desert Hearts; Dirigible; Dogfight; Don't Tell Her It's Me; Dying Young; The Eagle; The Emperor Waltz; Endless Love; The English Patient; Everyone Says I Love You; Falling in Love; A Farewell to Arms* (Borzage); *A Farewell to Arms* (Vidor); *First Love* (Darling); *Flesh and the Devil; Forever Young* (Miner); *Frankie & Johnny; The Garden of Allah; Ghost; The Ghost and Mrs Muir; The Grass Is Greener; Green Card; Green Light; Grosse Pointe Blank; Housesitter; I Love You to Death; The Incredibly True Adventure of Two Girls in Love; In Love; In Love and War; Interlude* (Sirk); *Intermezzo; In the Good Old Summertime; I Take This Woman; It Could Happen to You; Jersey Girl; Joe Versus the Volcano; Johnny Suede; Kate & Leopold; Keeping the Faith; Let It Snow; Little Man, What Now?; A Little Romance; Living Out Loud; Long Way Home; Love Affair; Love & Sex; Love at Large; Love in the Afternoon* (Wilder); *Love Is a Many Splendored Thing; love jones; Made in Heaven; Making Mr Right; Manpower; Man's Castle; Man, Woman and Child; The Marrying Man; Message in a Bottle; Miracle in the Rain; The Mirror Has Two Faces; Moment by Moment; Moonstruck; Neither by Day Nor by Night; Next Stop Wonderland; Now Voyager; Oliver's Story; Once in Paris…; One from the Heart; One More River; The Only Game in Town; The Other Side of the Mountain; Pat and Mike; Peter Ibbetson; Platinum Blonde; Portrait of Jennie; Prelude to a Kiss; Pretty Woman; A Pyromaniac's Love Story; Random Harvest; Rebecca; Roxanne; Say Anything; 7th Heaven* (Borzage); *Serendipity; Seventh Heaven* (King); *She's So Lovely; The Shining Hour; Sleepless in Seattle; Somewhere in Time; Splendor in the Grass;*

Starting Over; The Sterile Cuckoo; Summertime; Sunrise; Sunshine (Sargent); *Sunshine Part II; Sure Thing; Surrender; Sweet Hearts Dance; Tabu; They Live by Night; A Time to Love and a Time to Die; Tin Cup; Titanic* (Cameron); *A Touch of Class; Trouble in Mind; True Romance; The Truth About Cats & Dogs; Two Moon Junction; Used People; A Walk in the Spring Rain; A Walk with Love and Death; A Warm December; The Way We Were; We Are Not Alone; We Live Again; The Wedding March; When Harry Met Sally…; While You Were Sleeping; White Palace ; William Shakespeare's Romeo & Juliet; You've Got Mail*
Ven, *The Colour of Love*
Yugo, *The Switchboard Operator*

Lowndes, Mrs Belloc, films adapted from work, *The Lodger; Ivy*

Lowry, Malcolm
film about, *Volcano*
film adapted from work, *Under the Volcano*

Luciano, Lucky, films about, *Lucky Luciano; Marked Woman; Mobsters*

Ludlum, Robert, film adapted from work, *The Osterman Weekend*

Ludwig II of Bavaria, films about, *Ludwig; Ludwig – Requiem for a Virgin King; Ludwig's Cook*

Lumberjacks, *And Now for Something Completely Different; Sometimes a Great Notion*

Luther, Martin, film about, *Luther*

Luxemburg, Rosa, film about, *Rosa Luxemburg*

Lynch, David, film about, *Pretty as a Picture: The Art of David Lynch*

Lynching (see also **Vigilantes**), *Among the Living; Hang 'em High; Intruder in the Dust; The Lawless; The Ox-Bow Incident; The Sound of Fury; Sud*

Lyndon, Barre, film adapted from work, *The Amazing Doctor Clitterhouse*

Lynn, Loretta, film about, *Coal Miner's Daughter*

MacArthur, Charles
film about, *Mrs Parker and the Vicious Circle*
films adapted from work, *Lulu Belle, The Front Page* (Milestone); *The Front Page* (Wilder); *His Girl Friday; Twentieth Century*

MacArthur, General Douglas, film about, *MacArthur*

McBain, Ed, films adapted from work (see also **Hunter,** Evan), *Blood Relatives; High and Low*

McCabe, Patrick, film adapted from work, *The Butcher Boy*

McCarthy, Cormac, film adapted from work, *All the Pretty Horses*

McCarthy, Senator Joseph, and McCarthyism, *Chaplin; Citizen Cohn; Comic Book Confidential; The Crucible; Daniel; Fellow Traveller; Force of Evil; For the Boys; The Front; Guilty by Suspicion; Hollywood on Trial; The House on Carroll Street; I.F. Stone's Weekly; I Married a Communist; Insignificance; People Will Talk; Point of Order; Storm Center; Roy Cohn/Jack SmithThe Trials of Alger Hiss; Walk East on Beacon*

McCartney, Paul, in performance (see also **The Beatles**), *Get Back; Give My Regards to Broad Street; Rockshow*

MacCauley, Stephen, film adapted from work, *The Object of My Affection*

McCourt, Frank, film adapted from work, *Angela's Ashes*

McCoy, Horace, films adapted from work, *Kiss Tomorrow Goodbye; They Shoot Horses, Don't They?*

McCullers, Carson, films adapted from work, *The Ballad of the Sad Café; The Heart Is a Lonely Hunter; The Member of the Wedding; An Impudent Girl; Reflections in a Golden Eye*

McCullough, Colleen, films adapted from work, *An Indecent Obsession; Tim*

McDermott, Alice, film adapted from work, *That Night*

McDonald, Gregory, films adapted from work, *Fletch; Fletch Lives; Running Scared* (Hemmings)

Macdonald, Philip, films adapted from work, *Circle of Danger; The List of Adrian Messenger; The Lost Patrol*

MacDonald, Ross, films adapted from work, *Blue City; The Drowning Pool; Harper; The Moving Target*

Macdonald, Sharman, film adapted from work, *The Winter Guest*

Macedonian cinema, *Before the Rain; Cabaret Balkan; Dust*

McEwan, Ian, films adapted from work, *The Cement Garden; The Comfort of Strangers; First Love, Last Rites; The Innocent* (Schlesinger); *Last Day of Summer*

McGivern, William P, films adapted from work, *The Big Heat; Odds Against Tomorrow; Rogue Cop*

McGrath, John, film adapted from work, *The Bofors Gun*

McGrath, Patrick, film adapted from work, *Spider*

McGuane, Thomas
in film, *Warren Oates: Across the Border*
films adapted from work, *Cold Feet; 92 in the Shade*

McIlvanney, William, film adapted from work, *The Big Man*

McInerney, Jay, film adapted from work, *Bright Lights, Big City*

MacInnes, Colin, film adapted from work, *Absolute Beginners*

Mackenzie, Colin, film about, *Forgotten Silver*

Mackenzie, Compton, films adapted from work, *Carnival; Rockets Galore; Sylvia Scarlett; Whisky Galore!*

Macklin, Robert, film adapted from work, *Storyville*

MacLaverty, Bernard, films adapted from work, *Cal; Lamb*

Maclean, Alistair, films adapted from work, *Bear Island; Breakheart Pass; Caravan to Vaccarès; Fear Is the Key; Force 10 from Navarone; Golden Rendezvous; The Guns of Navarone; Ice Station Zebra; The Satan Bug; When Eight Bells Toll; Where Eagles Dare*

MacLeod, Wendy, film adapted from play, *The House of Yes*

McMillan, Terry, films adapted from work, *How Stella Got Her Groove Back; Waiting to Exhale*

McMurtry, Larry, films adapted from work, *The Evening Star; The Last Picture Show; Lovin' Molly; Terms of Endearment; Texasville*

McNally, Terrence, film adapted from play, *Love! Valour! Compassion!*

McPherson, Conor, film adapted from work, *Saltwater*

Macumba, sect, *Barravento*

MacVeigh, Sue, film adapted from work, *Grand Central Murder*

Madgulkar, Vynakatesh, film adapted from work, *The Village Has No Walls*

Madonna, film about, *Truth or Dare*

Mad scientists (see also **Frankenstein, etc, stories, Inventors**), *The Amazing Captain Nemo; The Amazing Doctor Clitterhouse; The Animal; Body Melt; Body Parts; The Boogie Man Will Get You; Bug; Buried Alive; Chill Factor; The Colossus of New York; Creator; The Creeping Flesh; The Damned; Deep Blue Sea; The Devil Commands; The Devil-Doll; Dr Cyclops; Doctor Death, Seeker of Souls; Doctor X; Exquisiste Tenderness; The Face at the Window; The Fly* (Neumann); *The Fly* (Cronenberg); *The Fly II; From Beyond; Gremlins 2: The New Batch; Halloween III; Hollow Men; Horror Hospital; The House by the Cemetary; In the Belly of the Dragon; The Invisible Ray; The Island of Dr Moreau* (Taylor); *The Island of Dr Moreau* (Frankenheimer); *Island of Lost Souls; Island of Mutations; Konga; Late for Dinner; Lifespan; The Link; The Mad Doctor of Market Street; Mad Love; Man-Made Monster; Man's Best Friend; The Man with Two Brains; Monkey Shines; The Monster and the Girl; Monster of Terror; Mysterious Island; Necronomicon; Night of the Lepus; Piranha; Raising Cain; Re-Animator; Re-Animator 2; Red Planet Mars; The Reptile; Retroactive; The Return of Doctor X; Return of the Fly; The Return of the Swamp Thing; Roger Corman's Frankenstein Unbound; Scream and Scream Again; She Demons; The Spectre of Edgar Allan Poe; Sundown; Superbeast; Tarantula; Terminus; Three the Hard Way; The Tingler; Unforgettable; Voodoo Man; Watchers; X – the Man with X-Ray Eyes*

Maeterlinck, Maurice, films adapted from work, *The Blue Bird; The Spirit of the Beehive*

The Mafia, in film,
in France, *Borsalino; Borsalino & Co; Détective*
in Italy, *The 8-Wheel Beast; In Nome della Legge; Living Blood; Manhunt in Milan; The Naples Connection; Placido Rizzotto; Ricco; Salvatore Giuliano; La Scorta; The Sicilian; The Sicilian Clan; Sicilian Cross*
in US, *Al Capone; Analyze This; Armed and Dangerous; The Black Hand; Blind Fury; Body and Soul* (Rossen); *A Bronx Tale; The Brotherhood; Bugsy; Bullitt; The Captive City; Casino;*

Catchfire; Charlie Varrick; Cookie; The Counsellor; Crazy Joe; Death Collecter; The Don Is Dead; Donnie Brasco; Every Little Nook and Cranny; F.I.S.T.; The Freshman; F/X2; Gloria (Cassavetes); *Gloria* (Lumet); *The Godfather; The Godfather Part II; GoodFellas; Gotti; Hit List; Honor Thy Father; Hoodlum Empire; Innocent Blood; I, Mobster; In Too Deep; The Juror; Kill Me Again; Kiss of Death* (Hathaway); *Kiss of Death* (Schroeder); *Last Rites; Married to the Mob; Maximum Risk; Men of Respect; Mickey Blue Eyes; Mobsters; My Blue Heaven; Oscar; Painted Desert; The Plot Against Harry; The Pope of Greenwich Village; The Public Enemy; Pulp; The Punisher; Ruby; Rumble in the Bronx; The St Valentine's Day Massacre; Seven; Sister Act; Things Change; The Undercover Man; Underworld USA; Weekend at Bernie's; Wise Guys*
in Rus, *Rancid Aluminium*
mobile, *The Godfather Part III; Lucky Luciano*

Magic and magicians, (see also **Witchcraft**), *The Adventures of Goopy and Bagha; The Bogey Man; The Boon; The Face; Frog Dreaming; The Geisha Boy; Harry Potter and the Philosopher's Stone; Ladyhawke; The Last Wave; Lovecraft; The Mad Magician; The Magician of Lublin; Peau d'Ane; The Philosopher's Stone; The Raven; Saadia; Santa Sangre; The Seventh Voyage of Sinbad; The Sword and the Sorcerer; The Thief of Bagdad* (Walsh); *The Thief of Bagdad* (Powell et al) Korda); *The Thief of Baghdad* (Donner); *To an Unknown God; Volcano High; White Lies; Willow; Wizards*

Mahfouz, Naguib,
film adapted from work, *Midaq Alley*

Mahler, Gustav, film about, *Mahler*

Mailer, Norman,
films adapted from work, *The American Dream; The Executioner's Song; Maidstone; The Naked and the Dead; Tough Guys Don't Dance*
live appearance, *Town Bloody Hall; When We Were Kings*

Malamud, Bernard,
film adapted from work, *The Fixer; The Natural*

Malaya and Malaysia, in film, *The Arsonist; Banana Ridge; Rampage; Return to Paradise; The 7th Dawn; A Town Like Alice; Turtle Beach; Windom's Way*

Malaysian cinema, *The Arsonist*

Mali,
Malian cinema, *Brightness; Finyé; The Spirit of Mopti*
Mali in film, *Life on Earth*

Malraux, André, film adapted from work, *L'Espoir*

Mamet, David,
films adapted from work, *About Last Night; American Buffalo; Glengarry Glen Ross; Oleanna*

Mandela, Nelson, films related to, *Mandela; The Man Who Drove with Mandela*

Manga animation,
Akira; Fist of the North Star; Ghost in the Shell; Jin-Roh; Memories; Perfect Blue; Roujin Z; Spriggan

Mann, Klaus, film adapted from work, *Mephisto*

Mann, Thomas, films adapted from work, *Death in Venice; Mario and the Magician*

Manson, Charles, films about, *Helter Skelter; Manson*

Mapplethorpe, Robert, film about, *Dirty Pictures*

Mariel boatlift, film about, *The Perez Family*

Marital breakdown and divorce (see also **Infidelity**)
Aust, *The Love Letters of Teralba Road*
China, *Sons*
Czech, *Extase*
Den, *Gertrud*
Fr, *La Baule-les-pins; Paris: XY; Une Partie de Plaisir; La Séparation*
GB, *Buddy's Song; The Comfort of Strangers; Damage; Easy Virtue; The Divorce of Lady X; The Good Father; I Was Happy Here; Something to Hide; Woman in a Dressing Gown*
Ger, *Martha*
HK, *Just Like Weather*
Hun, *Passport*
Iran, Leila
It, *The Future Is Woman; La Notte*
Jap, *Early Spring; Moving*
Swe, *Scenes from a Marriage; Sommaren med Monika*
US, *All I Want for Christmas; Always* (Jaglom); *Autumn Leaves; Best Friends; Big Girls Don't Cry…They Get Even; The Brute; Celebrity; The Champ; Child of Divorce; Divorce American Style; Don't Call Me Frankie; Edie & Pen; Faces; Haunted; The Heartbreak Kid; Heartburn; How to Commit Marriage; Interiors; I Will…I Will…for Now; The Kiss* (Feyder); *Love Crazy; Love Hurts* (Yorkin); *Loving Couples; The Marrying Kind; A New Life; North; One More River; Paris, Texas; Rich in Love; See You in the Morning; Shoot the Moon; That Old Feeling; Twice in a Lifetime; The War of the Roses*

Marley, Bob,
film about, *Time Will Tell*
in performance, *Exodus – Bob Marley Live*

Marlowe, Christopher, film adapted from work, *Edward II*

Marlowe, Derek, films adapted from work, *A Dandy in Aspic; The Disappearance*

Marquand, JP, films adapted from work, *B.F.'s Daughter; Mr Moto's Gamble*

Marriage (see also **Marital breakdown and divorce, Polygamy**)
arranged, *Early Summer; East Is East; Fatal Reaction: Singapore; The Flavour of Green Tea Over Rice; Gabbeh; A Girl of Good Family; The Girls to Be Married; Hot Blood; Jump Tomorrow; Kadosh; Late Marriage; Late Spring; Me & My Matchmaker; Monsoon Wedding; Picture Bride; Saraband for Lovers; Teen Kanya; The Wedding Night; Yellow Earth*
by advertisement and mail order, *The Closer You Get; In That Land; Naked Tango; Jacky; La Sirène du Mississipi; Swimming with Tears; A Thousand Pieces of Gold*
of convenience, *The Bachelor; Green Card; Hold Back the Dawn; Paper Marriage; A Paper Wedding*
second marriages, *Yours, Mine and Ours*
Alg, *The Citadel* (Chouikh)
Aust, *In the Winter Dark; Muriel's Wedding*
Burkina Faso, *Tilaï*
Can, *Dancing in the Dark; The Law of Enclosures*
China, *Young Couples*
Den, *Katinka; Sofie*
Fin, *Drifting Clouds*
Fr, *A la Place du Coeur; Les Amants; Une Femme Mariée; Madame Bovary* (Renoir); *Madame Bovary* (Chabrol); *Max Mon Amour; Mazel Tov ou le mariage; Le Miroir a deux faces; Le Plaisir*
GB, *Dancin' Thru the Dark; Emma; Four Weddings and a Funeral; The Heart of the Matter; A Kind of Loving; Lost and Found; Mine Own Executioner; Secrets* (Saville); *Shirley Valentine; Staggered; Sunday, Bloody Sunday; Two for the Road; Woman in a Dressing Gown*
Ger, *Bolwieser; The Marriage of Maria Braun; Nora Helmer*
Hun, *Jadviga's Pillow*
Iran, Leila
Ire, The Closer You Get
Nor, *Wives; Wives: Ten Years After; Wives III*
Palestine, *Wedding in Galilee*
Pol, *The Contract; Happy Man; The Wedding* (Wajda)
Swe, *The Best Intentions; Cries and Whispers; Scenes from a Marriage*
SKor, *Too Young to Die*
Tai, *The Wooden Man's Bride*
Tur, *Berdel; The Enemy*
US, *Another Woman; The Awful Truth; The Best Man; Betsy's Wedding; The Boost; The Brothers; Come Back, Little Sheba; A Guide for the Married Man; Honeymoon in Vegas; How to Commit Marriage; How to Make an American Quilt; How to Marry a Millionaire; Husbands and Wives; I Love You to Death; Inventing the Abbotts; The Last Married Couple in America; A Letter to Three Wives; Man, Woman and Child; The Marrying Man; O. Henry's Full House ('The Gift of the Magi'); Penny Serenade; Plaza Suite; Queens Logic; Runaway Bride; Scenes from a Mall; Sleeping with the Enemy; Someone to Love; Sons of the Desert; State of the Union; They Knew What They Wanted; True Love; Turnabout; Vivacious Lady; The War of the Roses; A Wedding; The Wedding Banquet; Who's Afraid of Virginia Woolf?; The Wind* (Sjöström); *The Wood; Woman of the Year; Woman's World*
USSR, *The Kreutzer Sonata*

Martial arts movies
Hong Kong, *The Accidental Spy; Ah-Kam; Beach of the War Gods, A Better Tomorrow; A Better Tomorrow II; The Big Boss; The Bloody Fists; Bruce Lee: The Man, the Myth; Burning Paradise; The Chinese Connection; The Conman and the Kung Fu Kid; Death Kick; Dirty Ho; 8-Diagram Pole Fighter; Executioners from Shaolin; The Fate of Lee Khan; First Strike; Fist of Fury; Fong Sai-Yuk; Full Contact; Golden Swallow; Hap-Ki-Do; Intimate Confessions of a Chinese Courtesan; The Killer* (Chu Yuan); *King Boxer; King of Kung Fu; Kung Fu Fighting; Kung Fu Gangbusters; The Kung Fu Girl; Kung Fu – The Headcrusher; Last Hurrah for Chivalry; Mr Nice Guy; Moon Warriors; My Young Auntie; The New One-Armed Boxer; Once Upon a Time in China; Once Upon a Time in China II; Police Story* (Chan); *Rumble in the Bronx; Stoner; The Stormriders; The Story of Woo Viet; The 36th Chamber of Shaolin; The Way of the Dragon; Young and Dangerous; Young and Dangerous 2; Young and Dangerous 3*
Hong Kong/China with other countries, *Crouching Tiger, Hidden Dragon; The Dragon Dies Hard; Dynasty; Enter the Dragon; Enter the Seven Virgins; Knock Off; The Legend of the Seven Golden Vampires; The Man from*

Hong Kong; Twin Dragons
other countries, *American Ninja; Best of the Best; Best of the Best 2: The Big Brawl; The Big Zapper; Black Belt Jones; Black Eagle; Blind Fury; Bloodsport; The Challenge; Code of Silence; Double Impact; Dragon: The Bruce Lee Story; Enter the Ninja; An Eye for an Eye; Fist of Fury Part II; Fist of the North Star; Force: Five; A Force of One; The Golden Child; Golden Needles; Good Guys Wear Black; Gymkata; Jaguar Lives; The Karate Kid: Part II; The Karate Kid Part III; Kickboxer; Kiss of the Dragon; Kung Fu – Girl Fighter; Kung Fu Street Fighter; The Last Dragon; Legend of Bruce Lee; Lone Wolf McQuade; Ninja III – The Domination; No Retreat, No Surrender; Only the Strong; Out for Justice; The Perfect Weapon; The Quest; Rapid Fire; Remo Williams: The Adventure Begins; Return of the Dragon; Road House* (Herrington); *Rooftops; Rush Hour; The Silent Flute; Ten Fingers of Steel; That Man Bolt; Take a Hard Ride; 3 Ninjas; Universal Soldier*

Martinican cinema, *The Middle Passage*

Mary Queen of Scots, films about, *Mary of Scotland; Mary Queen of Scots*

Masters, John, films adapted from work, *Bhowani Junction; The Deceivers*

Masterson, Whit, films adapted from work, *Touch of Evil; Warning Shot*

Mata Hari, films about, *Mata Hari* (Fitzmaurice); *Mata Hari* (Harrington); *Mata Hari – Agent H.21*

Mathematics and mathematicians, see **Science and scientists**

Matheson, Richard, films adapted from work, *The Incredible Shrinking Man; The Legend of Hell House; The Omega Man; Les Seins de glace; Stir of Echoes; What Dreams May Come*

Matthiessen, Peter, film adapted from work, *At Play in the Fields of the Lord*

Maugham, W Somerset, films adapted from work, *The Beachcomber; Christmas Holiday; Encore; The Letter; The Magician; Miss Sadie Thompson; The Moon and Sixpence; The Painted Veil; Quartet; Rain; The Razor's Edge; Sadie Thompson; Secret Agent; Trio; The Unfaithful; Up at the Villa; Vessel of Wrath*

Maupassant, Guy de, films adapted from work, *Boule de Suif; Golden Braid; Une Partie de Campagne; Le Plaisir; The Private Affairs of Bel Ami*

Maxwell, Gavin, film adapted from work, *Ring of Bright Water*

Mayas, *King of the Sun*

Mazes, *Cube; Three Men in a Boat*

Medicine, see **Doctors and medicine, Few-months-to-live stories, Hospital dramas, Illness, Mental hospitals and asylums, Mental illness**

Melons, unnatural craving for, *Mademoiselle Docteur*

Melville, Herman, films adapted from work, *Bartleby; Billy Budd; Moby Dick; Pola X*

Memory
implantation of, *Total Recall*
loss of, *Anastasia* (Litvak); *Anastasia* (Bluth/Goldman); *Asylum; As You Desire Me; The Brain Machine; The Brighton Strangler; The Clay Pigeon; Crack-Up* (Reis); *Crossroads* (Conway); *Dangerously They Live; Dark City; Dead Again; The Groundstar Conspiracy; Home at Seven; The Lady in the Car with Glasses and a Gun; Libel; The Long Kiss Goodnight; Love Letters* (Dieterle); *The Man Called Noon; The Man in the Road; The Man Without a Past; March Comes in Like a Lion; Memento; Mirage; Mugshot; Mulholland Dr.; The October Man; Overboard; Pit of Darkness; The Red Squirrel; Random Harvest; Secret Wedding; Shattered* (Petersen); *Somewhere in the Night; Spellbound; Sunflower; Without Memory*
manipulation of, *Death and the Maiden; 36 Hours*
reflections on, *After Life; Blue Black Permanent; Ghost Dance; La Jetée; Journey to the Beginning of the World; Muriel; The Loss of Sexual Innocence; The Polygraph; Rendez-vous à Bray; The Revolving Doors; Tender Hours; Wild Strawberries*
Repressed memory syndrome, *Never Talk to Strangers*

Ménages-à-trois & other romantic triangles, *Alligator Eyes; Annabelle partagée; Bodies, Rest & Motion; Un Coeur en hiver; December Bride; Design for Living; Les Deux Anglaises et le Continent; Les Diaboliques* (Clouzot); *Diabolique* (Chechik); *The Fabulous Baker Boys; Gazon Maudit; The Great Lie; Heart; Henry & June; Home-Made Melodrama; Homme de Désir; Jules et Jim; Kiss Me Goodbye; The Last Woman on Earth; Lovers; Little Tony; Lucky Lady; The Lunatic; Maiden Work; Making Love; Mr Zhao; The More the Merrier; The Naked Dawn; The Party – Nature Morte; Prague; Semi-Tough; Splendor; Summerfield; The Talk of the Town; Tenue de Soirée; Threesome; Two Girls and a Guy; Willie & Phil*

Menchú, Rigoberta, film about, *When the Mountains Tremble*

Menopause, *Privilege* (Rainer)

Mental handicap (see also **Autism, Disability, Dyslexia**), *All the Little Animals; Benny and Joon; A Child Is Waiting; Dominick and Eugene; The Eighth Day; I Am Sam; Jigsaw; Mama; The Man Who Mistook His Wife for a Hat; No Way Home; Pauline & Paulette; Touched by Love; Walter*

Mental hospitals and asylums, *Alone in the Dark; Amorosa; Assassin of the Tsar; Awakenings; Beautiful Dreamers; Bedlam; Blood of the Vampire; The Boy Who Cried Bitch; Chattahoochee; Committed; Cosi Crazy People; Down the Ancient Stairs; The Dream Team; Les Espions; An Everlasting Piece; Every Little Thing; The Exorcist III; Fit to Be Untied; Girl, Interrupted; House on Haunted Hill; King of Hearts; Lies; Manic; Nightmare; One Flew Over the Cuckoo's Nest; A Page of Madness; Patch Adams; The Persecution and Assassination of Jean-Paul Marat as Performed by the Inmates of the Asylum of Charenton Under the Direction of the Marquis de Sade; The Princess + the Warrior; Red Beads; Santa Sangre; The Sender; Shining Victory; Shock Corridor; The Snake Pit; La Tête contre les Murs; Walter; Yara*
release from, *She's Been Away*

Mental illness and disability (see also **Psychiatry, Psychopaths and serial killers**), *An Angel at My Table; A Beautiful Mind; Benny and Joon; Best Boy; Best Man; Camille Claudel; Clean, Shaven; Coast to Coast* (Sargent); *Cotton Mary; Dementia; Dialogues With Madwomen; Disturbed; Don't Bother to Knock* (Baker); *Each Dawn I Die; End of the Road; Experiment Perilous; Face to Face; Family Life* (Loach); *The Father; Une Femme Douce; First Light of Dawn; The 5,000 Fingers of Dr T; The Florentine Dagger; From Noon till Three; Gaslight* (Cukor); *Gaslight* (Dickinson); *The Girl from Trieste; The Grass Is Singing; Hangover Square; Un Homme Qui Dort; The Idiots; Images; I Never Promised You a Rose Garden; Interlude; The Killer Inside Me; King of Hearts; Komitas; Lilith; Love Crazy; Madonna of the Seven Moons; The Mafu Cage; The Man Who Had His Hair Cut Short; The Man Upstairs; Martin; Me and My Brother; Mr Jones; The Nanny; Night Watch; No Mercy, No Future; Nuts; A Page of Madness; Patch Adams; A Petal; Possessed; The Pumpkin Eater; Puzzle of a Downfall Child; Rage in Heaven; Regeneration; Repulsion; La Rupture; The Saint of Fort Washington; Screaming Mimi; Shine; Sling Blade; Some Voices; Strait-Jacket; Sybil; La Tête de Normande St-Onge; They Might Be Giants; The Three Faces of Eve; Through a Glass Darkly*

Mercenaries, *Il Mercenario; Prince of Foxes; Sniper; The Wild Geese; Wild Geese II*

Merchant, Ismail, film about, *In Ismail's Custody*

Mérimée, Prosper, film adapted from work, *Vendetta*

Mermaids, *Mr Peabody and the Mermaid; Splash*

Metalious, Grace, film adapted from work, *Peyton Place*

Metamorphosis into animals (see also **Mutation**), *Cat Girl; Cat People* (Tourneur); *Cat People* (Schrader); *The Curse of the Cat People; The She Creature; The Witches*

Mexican cinema, *Abismos de pasión; Amores Perros; And Your Mother Too; Break of Dawn; El Bruto; Chac; The Criminal Life of Archibaldo de la Cruz; Danzón; Deep Crimson; The Devil's Backbone; Divine; Dollar Mambo; Doña Herlinda and Her Son; El; El Topo; Enamorada; Eréndira; The Exterminating Angel; La Fièvre Monte à El Pao; Hasta Morir; Herod's Law; Highway Patrolman; Homework; House of Madness; Japón; El Jardin del Edén; Jory; Like a Bride; Like Water for Chocolate; Lolo; Midaq Alley; La Mujer del puerto; My Dear Tom Mix; Nazarin; No Return Address; Los Olvidados; One Lost Year; La Otra* (Gavaldón); *Perdita Durango; Que no quede huella; Reed: Insurgent Mexico; Río Escondido* (Fernández); *Robinson Crusoe; Salón México; Second Century; Sex, Shame and Tears; Simon of the Desert; Sin Compasión; Such Is Life; Survive!; A Sweet Scent of Death; They Call*

Him Marcado; Tintorera; Under a Spell; White Lies; The Young One

Mexico, in film, *The Alamo; All the Pretty Horses; Amores Perros; The Appaloosa; The Big Silence; The Big Steal* (Siegel); *Blazing Guns; Blue; Bordertown; Bring Me the Head of Alfredo Garcia; A Bullet for the General; The Bullfighter and the Lady; El Bulto; Chac; Danzón; The Daughter of the Puma; Deep Crimson; Desperado; Django; Django Kill; Doña Herlinda and Her Son; 8 Heads in a Duffel Bag; El Mariachi; Enamorada; Freeway II: Confessions of a Trickbaby; Gaby – A True Story; Guns for San Sebastian; Hasta Morir; The Harvest; Herod's Law; Highway Patrolman; Holiday in Mexico; In Caliente; I, the Worst of All; El Jardin del Eden; Juarez; The Kid from Spain; The Last Command; Like Water for Chocolate; Lolo; Lone Star; Il Mercenario; The Mexican; Mexico: The Frozen Revolution; Midaq Alley; La Mujer del puerto; My Dear Tom Mix; Mystery in Mexico; The Naked Dawn; Old Gringo; Los Olvidados; Perdita Durango; Puerto Escondido; Que no quede huella; Reed: Insurgent Mexico; Return of the Seven; Revenge* (Scott); *The Reward; Río Escondido; The River's Edge; Salón México; The Singer Not the Song; A Sweet Scent of Death; Traffic* (Soderbergh); *The Undefeated; Under a Spell; Under the Volcano; Villa Rides!; Viva Max!; Viva Villa!; Viva Zapata!; White Lies; The Wild Bunch; A Winter Tan; The Wonderful Country; The Wrong Man* (McBride); *Zapatista*

Michelangelo (Buonarrotti), film about, *The Agony and the Ecstasy*

Michener, James A, films adapted from work, *The Bridges at Toko-Ri; Caravans; Hawaii; Sayonara; South Pacific*

Middle Ages, and chivalric sagas
historical, *Anchoress; Brother Sun, Sister Moon; El Cid; Francesco, giullare di Dio; The Hour of the Pig; Jeanne la Pucelle; The Lion in Winter; La Passion Béatrice; La Passion de Jeanne d'Arc; Procès de Jeanne d'Arc; Saint Joan; Le Tournoi; The Virgin Spring; A Walk with Love and Death; The War Lord*
legend, *The Adventures of Robin Hood; Army of Darkness – The Medieval Dead; As In Heaven; The Bandit of Sherwood Forest; The Black Knight; Camelot; Captain Kronos – Vampire Hunter; The Court Jester; DragonHeart; Excalibur; First Knight; The Flame and the Arrow; Flesh and Blood; Gawain and the Green Knight; Hero* (Platts-Mills); *A Knight's Tale; The Magic Sword: Quest for Camelot; Markéta Lazarová; Merlin: The Return; The Navigator: A Medieval Odyssey; The Pied Piper* (Demy); *Prince Valiant; The Rebel Nun; Robin and Marian; Robin Hood* (Dwan); *Robin Hood* (Irvin); *Robin Hood – Men in Tights; Robin Hood: Prince of Thieves; The Sword in the Stone; The Sword of the Valiant – The Legend of Gawain and the Green Knight; Wolfshead; The Legend of Robin Hood; The Unidentified Flying Oddball; Les Visiteurs du Soir*
literary, *The Adventures of Quentin Durward; The Canterbury Tales; A Connecticut Yankee at King Arthur's Court; The Decameron; Ivanhoe; The Name of the Rose*
present-day medieval fantasies, *Just Visiting; Knightriders; Les Visiteurs*

Middler, Bette, in performance, *Divine Madness*

Middleton, Thomas, film adapted from work, *Middleton's Changeling*

Midlands, the English (see also **Hood,** Robin), *The Card; Felicia's Journey; The Girl with Brains in Her Feet; Handsworth Songs; I Bought a Vampire Motorcycle; In Celebration; The Last Yellow; The Loneliness of the Long Distance Runner; Once Upon a Time in the Midlands; Out of Order* (Turpie); *A Private Enterprise; Prostitute; The Ragman's Daughter; The Rainbow; A Room for Romeo Brass; Saturday Night and Sunday Morning; St Ann's; Smalltime; Sons and Lovers; TwentyFourSeven; Women in Love*

Midlife crises, *Alice* (Allen); *The Arrangement; The Beekeeper; Bliss; Le Bonheur est dans le pré; Bye Bye Braverman; Les Choses de la Vie; City Slickers; City Slickers II: The Legend of Curly's Gold; The Decline of the American Empire; Dream Flight; Funny About Love; Husbands and Wives; Inadmissible Evidence; Intersection; Save the Tiger; Steppenwolf; Tempest; 10; That's Life; Walls of Gloss; The Woman in Red*

Mighton, John, film adapted from work, *Possible Worlds*

Miller, Arthur, films adapted from work, *Broken Glass; The Crucible; Death of a Salesman; Everybody Wins*

Miller, Glenn,
film about, *The Glenn Miller Story*
in performance, *Orchestra Wives; Sun Valley Serenade*

Miller, Henry,
film about, *Henry & June*
films adapted from work, *Tropic of Cancer; Quiet Days in Clichy* (Chabrol); *Quiet Days in Clichy* (Thorsen)

Milligan, Spike, film adapted from work, *Adolf Hitler – My Part in His Downfall; The Bedsitting Room*

Millionaires, eccentric, *Broadway Bill; The Happiest Millionaire; Has Anybody Seen My Girl?; The Honey Pot; Melvin and Howard; The Palm Beach Story; Pardners; Rhubarb; Twister* (Almereyda)

Miners and mining, *Above Us the Earth; Bert Rigby, You're a Fool; The Big Man; Billy Elliot; Black Fury; A Borrowed Life; Brassed Off; The Brave Don't Cry; Coal Face; The Citadel* (Vidor); *East of Sumatra; Escape from the Dark; Germinal; Gold; Gold, Carson City; Green Fire; Hungry Hill; In Celebration; I Was, I Am, I Shall Be; Harlan County, USA; How Green Was My Valley; Kameradschaft; Margaret's Museum; Matewan; The Miners' Film; The Molly Maguires; The Prince of Pennsylvania; Salt of the Earth; The Stars Look Down*

Mirbeau, Octave, films adapted from work, *The Diary of a Chambermaid* (Buñuel); *The Diary of a Chambermaid* (Renoir)

Mishima, Yukio
films about, *Beautiful Mystery – Legend of Big Horn; Mishima: A Life in Four Chapters*
films adapted from work, *L'Ecole de la Chair; The Sailor Who Fell from Grace with the Sea*

Missing body part, *8 Heads in a Duffel Bag*

Missionaries, *The African Queen; At Play in the Fields of the Lord; The Beachcomber; The Bitter Tea of General Yen; Black Narcissus; Black Robe; City of Joy; Dancing at Lughnasa; The Devil at 4 O'Clock; The Inn of the Sixth Happiness; Klondike Annie; Miss Sadie Thompson; The Nun's Story; The Painted Veil; Rain; Sadie Thompson; Satan Never Sleeps; Seven Women; Shanghai Surprise*

Mistaken identity, *Along Came Jones; Bachelor Mother; Bad Blood; Bean; It Takes Two; The Pope Must Die; Quick; Spaced Invaders*

Mitchard, Jacquelyn, film adapted from work, *The Deep End of the Ocean*

Mitchell, Gary, film adapted from work, *As the Beast Sleeps*

Mitchell, RJ, film about, *The First of the Few*

Mo, Timothy, film adapted from work, *Soursweet*

Models, fashion, *Cover Girl; Exposed; The French Line; Joy; Kvinnodrom; Lipstick; Mahogany; Model; Nico Icon; Ready to Wear; Star 80; Unzipped; Who Are You Polly Maggoo?*

Mods and Rockers, *Quadrophenia*

Molière,
film about, *Marquise*
film adapted from work, *Le Tartuffe*

Molnar, Ferenc, films adapted from work, *Carousel; The Chocolate Soldier*

Mongolia, in film, *Destination Gobi; Joan of Arc of Mongolia; On the Hunting Ground; Storm Over Asia; Theft Under the Sun; Urga*

Monk, Thelonious
as performer, *Jazz on a Summer's Day*
films about, *A Great Day in Harlem; Thelonious Monk: Straight No Chaser*

The Monkees, film about, *Head*

Monroe, Marilyn, films about/inspired by, *Goodbye Norma Jean; Insignificance; Marilyn; Marilyn – The Untold Story; The Sex Symbol*

Monsarrat, Nicholas, films adapted from work, *The Cruel Sea; The Ship That Died of Shame; Something to Hide*

Montand, Yves, film about, *Montand*

Moorcock, Michael, film adapted from work, *The Final Programme*

Moore, Brian, films adapted from work, *Black Robe; Cold Heaven; The Lonely Passion of Judith Hearne; The Luck of Ginger Coffey*

Moore, George, film adapted from work, *Esther Waters*

Moore, Hal, film adapted from work, *We Were Soldiers*

Moravia, Alberto
films adapted from work, *Closed for Family Mourning; Il Conformista; L'Ennui; Le Mépris; The Peddler*
appearance in, *Whoever Says the Truth Will Die*

More, Sir Thomas, film about, *A Man for All Seasons*

Mormons, in film, *Brigham Young – Frontiersman; Orgazmo; Sure Fire; Wagon Master*

Morocco
Morocco in film, *Ali Zaoua: Prince de la Rue; Beach Café;* **Freedom;** *Le Garde du Corps; Hideous Kinky; Isabelle Eberhardt; Mektoub; The Wind and the Lion; Women from the Medina*
Moroccan cinema, *Ali Zaoua: Prince de la Rue; Best Revenge; Divine Intervention; Mektoub; Moroccan Chronicles; Trances; Women from the Medina*

Morris, William, film adapted from work, *News from Nowhere*

Morris, Willie, film adapted from work, *My Dog Skip*

Moscow, in film, *The Fountain; Full Moon; Gorky Park; I Wanted to See Angels; The Master and Margarita; Moscow Distrusts Tears; Mute Witness; Police Academy 7: Mission to Moscow*

Mosley, Walter, film adapted from work, *Devil in a Blue Dress*

Mothers (see also **Pregnancy, childbirth and babies**)
and daughters, *Antonia's Line; Anywhere but Here; Applause; Autumn Sonata; Beloved; Bellissima; Crazy Mama; Deadly Advice; Dolores Claiborne; Drop Dead Gorgeous; Eeny Meeny; The Effect of Gamma Rays on Man-in-the-Moon Marigolds; The Future of Emily; Gas Food Lodging; Germany, Pale Mother; The Good Mother; The Good Wife of Tokyo; Hard, Fast and Beautiful; High Heels; High Tide; The House of Bernarda Alba; Imitation of Life* (Stahl); *Imitation of Life* (Sirk); *The Joy Luck Club; Life Is Sweet; Like Water for Chocolate; Little Voice; Little Women* (Cukor); *Little Women* (Armstrong); *The Long Kiss Goodnight; Maternale; Mermaids; Mildred Pierce; The Miniskirted Dynamo; Mommie Dearest; 'Night Mother; No Sad Songs for Me; Not Without My Daughter; Panic Room; The Positively True Adventures of the Alleged Texas Cheerleader-Murdering Mom; Postcards from the Edge; Sailor Beware; Season of Dreams; Secrets & Lies; The Silences of the Palace; Song of the Exile; Steel Magnolias; Stella; Stella Dallas; The Summer of Aviya; A Tender Place; Terms of Endearment; This Is My Life; Die Tödliche Maria; Tumbleweeds; Violette Nozière; We Don't Talk About It; Wild at Heart; Wild Flowers* (Lefebvre); *Wild Flowers* (Smith); *The Winter Guest; A World Apart*
and daughters-in-law, *Plaff! or Too Afraid of Life; When Joseph Returns*
and sons, *Abel; Alice Doesn't Live Here Any More; All About My Mother; Bad Blood; Bad Boy Bubby; Because of That War; The Boy Who Cried Bitch; The Boy Who Had Everything; Braindead; Le Château de ma mère; The Day the Sun Turned Cold; The Deep End of the Ocean; The Divided Heart; Fils de Deux Mères ou Comédie de l'Innocence; The Goddess; The Grifters; Killing Dad; The Krays; La Luna; Little Man Tate; Mama; The Manchurian Candidate; The Man I Married; Malizia; Men Don't Leave; Mon Premier Amour; Monster's Ball; Mostly Martha; Mother* (Brooks); *Mother and Son; Mother's Boys; New York Stories; One Full Moon; 101 Reykjavík; Only the Lonely; Les Parents Terribles; Pas trés Catholique; Pau and His Brother; Persecution; The Real McCoy; The Revolving Doors; The Rockinghorse Winner; Santa Sangre; Some Mother's Son; Le Souffle au Coeur; Spanking the Monkey; Spider; Stop! or My Mom Will Shoot; Throw Momma from the Train; Torch Song Trilogy; Track 29; Where's Poppa; White Heat; A Woman on Her Own*
both, *Babymother; Bloody Mama; Look Who's Talking; Look Who's Talking Now; Look Who's Talking Too; Mr and Mrs Bridge; Parenthood; Titanic Town; Yours, Mine and Ours*
surrogate, *Firelight; The Handmaid's Tale; Record of a Tenement Gentleman; The Proposition; Surrogate Mother*

Motor sport, *Bobby Deerfield; The Cannonball Run; Cannonball Run II; Crash* (Gibson); *Days of Thunder; Death Race 2,000; Driven; The Fast and the Furious; Fast Company; Genevieve; Grand Prix; Greased Lightning; Heart Like a Wheel; La Passione; The Last American Hero; Le Mans; Once a Jolly Swagman; One by One; Red Line 7000; Sahara* (McLaglen); *Shut Down; Silver Dream Racer; Spetters; 23:58; Viva Las Vegas*

Mountains and mountaineering, *Alive; Das Blau Licht; Careful; Cliffhanger; The Eiger Sanction; The Englishman Who Went Up a Hill, But Came Down a Mountain; Everest; Five Days One Summer; Galahad of Everest; Himalaya; K2; Seven Years in Tibet; Vertical Limit; The White Hell of Piz Palu; The White Tower*

Mozambican cinema, *Comédia Infantil; Massacre; Shout at the Devil*

Mozart, Wolfgang Amadeus
films about, *Amadeus; Mozart in Love; Noi Tre*
films of/featuring operas, *Con Air; Don Giovanni; The Magic Flute; Vertiges*

Multiple personalities (see also **Double lives, Doubles/doppelgängers**), *Chameleon Street; Raising Cain; The Secret Life of Walter Mitty; Multiplicty; The Three Faces of Eve; Zelig*

Murakami, Haruki, films adapted from work, *Attack on a Bakery; A Girl, She is 100%; The New Morning of Billy the Kid*

Murdoch, Iris, films about, *Iris*

Music and musicians, brass bands, *Brassed Off; Les Cachetonneurs; The Music Man*

Music and musicians, classical, *L'Accompagnatrice; Allegro Non Troppo, Amadeus; Ballad in Blue; Les Belles de nuit; Besieged; Beyond Silence; Blossom Time; Boy's Choir; Chronicle of Anna Magdalena Bach; Un Coeur en hiver; The Competition; Concerto of Life; The Conductor; The Confessions of Winifred Wagner; Deception; Duet for One; Fantasia; Fantasia/2000; Fingers; The 5,000 Fingers of Dr T; From Mao to Mozart; The Great Waltz* (Duvivier); *The Great Waltz* (Stone); *Hilary and Jackie; Immortal Beloved; Hangover Square; Humoresque; Impromptu; Katok i Skrypka; Letter from an Unknown Woman; Lisztomania; Madame Sousatzka; The Magic Bow; Mahler; Meeting Venus; Mélo; The Mephisto Waltz; Messiah; Music for the Movies: Bernard Herrmann; Music for the Movies: The Hollywood Sound; Music for the Movies: Toru Takemitsu; The Music Lovers; Music of the Heart; The Music Teacher; The Night Has Eyes; Nocturne; Noi Tre; Oh, You Beautiful Doll; One Hundred Men and a Girl; Orchestra Rehearsal; Parsifai; Pastorale; The Piano; The Piano Teacher; Raising the Wind; The Red Violin; Rothschild's Violin; The Seventh Veil; The Silent Touch; Small Wonders; Something to Believe In; Song of Norway; Song of Scheherazade; A Song to Remember; Spring Symphony; Swan Song; Thirty Two Short Films About Glenn Gould; Tous les Matins du monde; Unfaithfully Yours* (Zieff); *Les Uns et Les Autres; Up on the Roof; William Christie et Les Arts Florissants ou la Passion du Baroque; Wagner*

Music and musicians, folk/traditional/world
Armenia, *Komitas*
Braz, *Orfeu; Saudade do Futuro; Sound of Brazil*
Can, *September Song: The Music of Kurt Weill*
China, *The Emperor's Shadow; Life on a String*
Colombia, *The Devil's Accordion*
Cuba, *The Buena Vista Social Club; The Mambo Kings*
Ecuador, *Sensations*
Fin, *Total Balalaika Show*
Ger, *Fatherland*
Ind *The Courtesans of Bombay, Dance of the Wind; The Doll* (Ghose)
It, *Living Blood*
Jap, *Ondeko-za on Sado*
Morocco, *Trances*
Nig, *Femi Kuti: What's Going On*
Nor, *Cool & Crazy*
Scotland, *Mairi Mhor*
SKor, *Sopyonje*
US, *Baby the Rain Must Fall; Don't Say a Word; The Ballad of Ramblin' Jack; Benjamin Smoke; Bound for Glory; The Last Waltz; A Tickle in the Heart; The Weavers; Wasn't That a Time*
USSR and Rus, *Ashik Kerib, Total Balalaika Show*
various, *Modulations*
Zaire, *La Vie est belle*

Music and musicians: street musicians, *Saint Martin's Lane; The Underground Orchestra*

Musicals, music hall and vaudeville, *see* **Show business**

Musil, Robert, film adapted from work, *Young Törless*

Muslim culture and Mohammedanism, see **Islam and Islamic culture**

Mutations (see also **Deformity and disfigurement, Metamorphosis into animals, Shrinking**), *Alligator; The Amazing Colossal Man; Attack of the 50 Foot Woman* (Juran); *Attack of the 50ft Woman* (Guest); *Attack of the Killer Tomatoes; Basket Case 2; Beneath the Planet of the Apes; Body Parts; The Borrower; Braindead; The Brood; Class of Nuke 'Em High; Crimes of the Future; Damnation Alley; The Day the World Ended; Deathsport; Fiend Without a Face; The Fly* (Neumann);

The Fly (Cronenberg); *The Fly II; Food of the Gods; Forbidden World; From Beyond; The Giant Spider Invasion; Godzilla; I, Monster; The Incredible Hulk; Innerspace; The Invisible Man; The Invisible Man Returns; The Incredible Melting Man; The Invisible Ray; The Island of Dr Moreau* (Taylor); *The Island of Dr Moreau* (Frankenheimer); *The Island of Lost Souls; The Island of Mutations; It Came from Beneath the Sea; The Hills Have Eyes; Humanoids from the Deep; Man-Made Monster; The Mask* (Russell); *Matinee; Mimic; Monkey Shines; Monster from Green Hell; Monster of Terror; Mutant; Mutations; Mysterious Island; Nightbreed; Night of the Lepus; The Omega Man; The People Under the Stairs; The Projected Man; Proteus; The Relic; The Reptile; Return of the Fly; The Return of the Swamp Thing; The Revenge of Frankenstein; The Rift; The She Creature; Son of Godzilla; Species; Swamp Thing; Tarantula; Teenage Mutant Ninja Turtles; Teenage Mutant Ninja Turtles II: The Secret of the Ooze; Teenage Mutant Ninja Turtles III; Terminus; TerrorVision; Them; This Island Earth; The Toxic Avenger; The Toxic Avenger Part II; Quatermass II; Sssssss; Superbeast; War of the Colossal Beast; The Wasp Woman; Watchers; Who?*

Muybridge, Eadweard, film about, *Eadweard Muybridge, Zoopraxographer*

Myrer, Anton, film adapted from work, *In Love and War* (Dunne)

Myths and legends (see also **Fairies and goblins, Greece**), *The Amazons; Ashik Kerib; The Blood Brothers; A Chinese Ghost Story; A Chinese Ghost Story II; A Chinese Ghost Story III; Darby O'Gill and the Little People; The Deaf and Mute Heroine; DragonHeart; Dungeons & Dragons; Erik the Viking; L'Eternal Retour; Excalibur; First Knight; The Fisher King; The Golem; Hero* (Platts-Mills); *Hercules; The Illustrated Man; Immortal Story; Jason and the Argonauts; Këita! The Voice of the Griot; Lancelot du Lac; The Legend of the Suram Fortress; Le Mahabharata; Die Nibelungen; Onibaba; Pandora and the Flying Dutchman; Parking; Perceval le Gallois; Prince Valiant; The Romantic Agony; The Sword and the Sorceror; The Sword in the Stone; The Sword of the Valiant; Swordsman; Swordsman II; The Swordsman in Double-Flag Town; The Legend of Gawain and the Green Knight; Ugetsu Monogatari; Zu: Warriors from the Magic Mountain; Wishmaster*

Nabokov, Vladimir, films adapted from work, *Despair; King; Queen, Knave; Laughter in the Dark; Lolita* (Kubrick); *Lolita* (Lyne); *The Luzhin Defence*

Nagel, Blake, film adapted from work, *Girl*

Nagel, James, film adapted from work, *In Love and War* (Attenborough)

Naipaul, VS, film adapted from work, *The Mystic Masseur*

Nameless evils, *The Blob; Duel; Encounter at Raven's Gate; Event Horizon; The Fog; Forbidden Planet; The Keep; Leviathan; Scarecrows; Secrets of the Phantom Caves; The Seventh Sign; The Skull*

Namibia
Namibia in film, *Kin; Windprints*
Namibian cinema *Flame*

Nannies, governesses, au pairs, ***Anna and the King;*** *Anna and the King of Siam; Bicentennial Man; Corrina, Corrina; Cotton Mary; Gaby – A True Story; The Governess; The Guardian; The Hand That Rocks the Cradle; The Innocents; Jane Eyre* (Stevenson); *Jane Eyre* (Mann); *Jane Eyre* (Zeffirelli); *The King and I* (Lang); *The King and I* (Rich); *A Little Princess; Martha & Ethel; Mary Poppins; Miss Mary; Mr Nanny; Mrs Doubtfire; The Nanny; Perfect Alibi; The Unseen; When Mother Comes Home for Christmas*

Napoleon I, Emperor of France, films about, *Austerlitz; Le Destin Fabuleux de Désirée Clary; Napoléon* (Gance); *Napoléon* (Guitry); *War and Peace* (Vidor); *War and Peace* (Bondarchuk); *Waterloo*

Narayan, RK, film adapted from work, *Swamy*

Narcejac, Thomas, see **Boileau–Narcejac**

Nash, John Forbes, film about, *A Beautiful Mind*

Native Americans, see **Indians, American and Canadian**

Nature, hymns to/struggle against (see also **Ecology**), *The Adventures of Frontier Fremont; Alaska; The Bear; Dances with Wolves; Dances with Wolves – Special Edition; Day of the Animals; Le Déjeuner sur l'Herbe; Dersu Uzala; Earth* (Dovzhenko); *The Edge; Edge of the World; Farewell; Greystoke – The Legend of Tarzan Lord of the Apes; Hard Rain; Hurricane; The Hurricane; Inferno; The Island; It's a Long Way to the Sea; Jeremiah Johnson; La Libertad; Long Weekend; Man of Aran; Man in the Wilderness; Never Cry Wolf; The Outlaw and His Wife; The River Wild; The Southerner; Twister* (Du Bont); *Urga; When the North Wind Blows; When the Whales Came; The Wind in the Willows*

Naughton, Bill, films adapted from work, *Alfie; Alfie Darling; Spring and Port Wine*

Navy stories, see **Sea dramas**

Necrophilia, *Deranged; Frisk; Kissed; Living Doll; Schramm; Tales of Terror*

Neiderman, Andrew, film adapted from work, *The Devil's Advocate* (Hackford)

Nelson, Admiral Lord, film about, *That Hamilton Woman*

Nepalese cinema, *Himalaya*

Nero, Roman Emperor, films about, *Fiddlers Three; Quo Vadis?; The Sign of the Cross*

Neruda, Pablo, film about, *Il Postino*

Netherlands
Netherlands cinema, *Abel; All Stars; All Visitors Must Be Announced; Amsterdamned; Another Mother; Au Revoir; The Baby of Mâcon; Ball, The; Beck; Behind Closed Eyes; Breaking the Waves; Broken Mirrors; Casta Diva; Crush Proof; Daens; Dance of the Wind; Dear Boys; Delbaran; Les Diseurs de Vérité; Eline Vere; Enigma; Fatal Reaction: Singapore; Felice... Felice...; The Fourth Man; The Gambler* (Makk); *The Girl with the Red Hair; House of America; In My Father's House; Jacky; Karakter; Last Date; Left Luggage; Lifespan; The Lift; Little Sister; The Little Vampire; The Lone Hand; Love Hurts* (de Jong); *The Man Who Drove with Mandela; Molokai: The Story of Father Damien; Mother Dao the Turtlelike; My Nights with Susan, Sandra, Olga and Julie; The Northerners; O Amor Natural; On the Old Roman Road; On Top of the Whale; The Outsider; Pauline & Paulette; Piranha II; The Pointsman; The Polish Bride; The Quarry; A Question of Silence; The Scorpion; Soldier of Orange; Spetters; The Rape; The Road; The Romantic Agony; São Paulo, SP; Siberia; Turkish Delight; The Underground Orchestra; Whoever Says the Truth Will Die; Wings of Fame; Yo soy así*
Netherlands in film, *The Eighth Day; The Lone Hand; Operation Amsterdam*

Neurology, *Awakenings; The Man Who Mistook His Wife for a Hat*

New Ageism, etc, *Holy Man; In the Spirit; Point Break; The Rapture*

New Guinea, in film, *To Have & to Hold; The Shark Callers of Kontu; Tidikawa and Friends; La Vallée*

Newman, Andrea, film adapted from work, *Three into Two Won't Go*

New Orleans, in film, *Albino Alligator; Always for Pleasure; The Big Easy; Candyman 2: Farewell to the Flesh: Christmas Holiday; Dixie; Down by Law; Dracula 2000; The End of August; The Flame of New Orleans; Glory Alley; Hard Target; Hard Times* (Hill); *Heaven's Prisoners; Jezebel; Johnny Handsome; King Creole; My Forbidden Past; Naughty Marietta; New Moon; No Mercy; Panic in the Streets; Pretty Baby; Storyville; A Streetcar Named Desire; The Tarnished Angels; This Property Is Condemned; Tightrope; The Toast of New Orleans; Undercover Blues; Walk on the Wild Side; Zandalee*

Newspapers, see **Journalism**

New York, in film
pre-1910, *The Age of Innocence; The Bowery; Bowery to Broadway; The Heiress; Hester Street; The house of Mirth; A Man Called Hero; The Man With a Cloak; Newsies; O. Henry's Full House; Washington Square*
post-1910, *Entertaining Angels: The Dorothy Day Story*
1920s, *Bloodhounds of Broadway; Bullets Over Broadway; The Crowd; Entertaining Angels: The Dorothy Day Story; The Great Gatsby* (Clayton); *The Great Gatsby* (Nugent); *Greenwich Village; Mrs Parker and the Vicious Circle; Saturday's Children; Speedy*
1930s, *Born to Dance; Bullets or Ballots; The Cotton Club; Cradle Will Rock; Deadline at Dawn; Dinner at Eight; Entertaining Angels: The Dorothy Day Story; The Funeral; Harlem Nights; King of Burlesque; Naughty but Nice; Sergeant Madden; Taxi!*
1940s, *Brighton Beach Memoirs; Broadway Bound; The Chosen; Cry of the City; Eat a Bowl of Tea; Enemies,*

a Love Story; Entertaining Angels: The Dorothy Day Story; The Godfather; The Godfather Part II; Going My Way; Grand Central Murder; Joe Gould's Secret; The New York, New York; On the Town; The Public Eye; Radio Days
1950s, *Ask Any Girl; A Bucket of Blood; Career; Deux Hommes dans Manhattan; Edge of the City; The Garment Jungle; A Great Day in Harlem; Guys and Dolls; Last Exit to Brooklyn; The Mambo Kings; Mr Music; The Mob; My Sister Eileen; Next Stop, Greenwich Village; On the Waterfront; A Rage in Harlem; Stuart Little; Sweet Smell of Success; Woman's World*
1960s, *The Apartment; Breakfast at Tiffany's; A Bronx Tale; Bye Bye Braverman; Ciao Manhattan; The Cool World; A Fine Madness; Five Corners; A Lovely Way to Die; Nico Icon; The Out-of-Towners* (Hiller); *The Plot Against Harry; Used People; The Wanderers; West Side Story; Who's That Knocking at My Door?*
1970s, *Annie Hall; Casual Relations; Come Back, Charleston Blue; Crooklyn; 54; The French Connection; Girlfriends; The Godfather Part III; The Goodbye Girl; GoodFellas; I'm Gonna Git You Sucka; Manhattan; Mean Streets; News from Home; The Prisoner of Second Avenue; Slow Dancing in the Big City; State of Grace; Summer of Sam; The Taking of Pelham One Two Three; Taxi Driver; They Might Be Giants; Trash; The Warriors; Welfare; Where's Poppa?*
1980s, *After Hours; American Stories; Basket Case; Beyond Therapy; Blue Steel; The Bonfire of the Vanities; Bright Lights, Big City; Broadway Danny Rose; Can She Bake a Cherry Pie?; China Girl; Clarence and Angel; Cocaine; Cocktail; Cookie; Crack in the Mirror; Crimes and Misdemeanors; Crocodile Dundee; Crocodile Dundee II; Crossing Delancey; Crossover Dreams; Cruising; Desperately Seeking Susan; Do the Right Thing; The Dream Team; Fame; Family Business* (Lumet); *Fort Apache – The Bronx; The Freshman; Friday the 13th Part VIII: Jason Takes Manhattan; Fun Down There; Ghostbusters; Ghostbusters II; Gremlins 2: The New Batch; Hannah and Her Sisters; The January Man; King of New York; Longtime Companion; Married to the Mob; Metropolitan; A New Life; New Year's Day; New York Stories; Permanent Vacation; The Pope of Greenwich Village; Rooftops; Shakedown; Sidewalk Stories; Sing; Skyline; Slaves of New York; Smithereens; Times Square; True Love; Vampire's Kiss; Walls of Glass; Wall Street; Wild Style; The Winged Serpent; Wolfen; Working Girl; Year of the Dragon*
1990s, *Across the Sea of Time: A New York Adventure; Addicted to Love; The Addiction; Alice* (Allen); *All Over Me; Amateur; American Psycho; All Visitors Must Be Announced; Another Girl, Another Planet; Bad Lieutenant; The Basketball Diaries; Basquiat; Black and White; Blue in the Face; The Book of Life; Bringing Out the Dead; The Butcher's Wife; Carlito's Way; Celebrity; Chain of Desire; The City; City Hall; The Corruptor; Cousin Bobby; Cruel Intentions; The Cruise; Daylight; Dead Funny; Dealers Among Dealers; Denise Calls Up; The Devil's Advocate* (Hackford); *The Devil's Own; Donnie Brasco; Downtown 81; Eddie; Everyone Says I Love You; Fetishes; Finding North; The First Wives Club; The Fisher King; Flawless; Flirt; For Love or Money; Franchesca Page; Frankie & Johnny; Full Moon in New York; A Further Gesture; Girl 6; God's Alcatraz; Gravesend; Green Card; Gridlock'd; Handgun* (Ransick); *Hangin' with the Homeboys; The Hard Way; High Art; Home Alone 2: Lost in New York; Hurricane Streets; Husbands and Wives; I Like It Like That; In the Soup; It Could Happen to You; I Was on Mars; Jeffrey; Jersey Girl; Juice; Jungle Fever; Jungle 2 Jungle; Just Another Girl on the I.R.T.; Just the Ticket; Kids; Kids of Survival: The Art and Life of Tim Rollins & K.O.S.; Kiss Me, Guido; Latin Boys Go to Hell; Laws of Gravity; Leon; Living Out Loud; Lonely in America; Loser; Lost in Yonkers; Mac; Manhattan Murder Mystery; Miracle on 34th Street; The Mirror Has Two Faces; The Misadventures of Margaret; Mr Wonderful; Money Train; Nadja; Never Talk to Strangers; New Jack City; Night and the City* (Winkler); *Night on Earth; One Fine Day; Other People's Money; The Out-of-Towners* (Weisman); *The Paper; A Price Above Rubies; The Proprietor; Q & A; Quick Change; Ransom; The Real Blonde; The Refrigerator; Rhythm Thief; Rumble in the Bronx; Saturn; Searching for Bobby Fischer; She's the One; A Shock to the System; The Shvitz; Siao Yu; Side Streets; The Siege; A Simple Wish; Sleepers; Sliver; Small Time; Smoke; Someone Else's America; The Sticky Fingers of Time; Straight Out of Brooklyn; Strapped; Subway Stories; Sunday; Teenage Mutant Ninja Turtles; Teenage Mutant Ninja Turtles II: The Secret of the Ooze; The Thomas Crown Affair* (McTiernan); *Trick; Triple Bogey on a Par Five Hole; Two Girls and a Guy; Vampire in Brooklyn; Walking and Talking; The Wedding Banquet; What About Me?; Where the Heart Is; Who's the Man?; Wolf*
from 2000, *Autumn in New York; Center Stage; Coyote Ugly; Dark Days; Dinner Rush; Don't Say a Word; Gossip; Hamlet* (Almereyda); *Kate & Leopold; K-PAX; Long Way Home; Made; No Such Thing; Queenie in Love; The Royal Tenenbaums; Serendipity; Shaft* (Singleton); *Sidewalks of New York*
future visions of, *Born in Flames; Bronx Warriors, The; Escape from New York; Exterminator 2; Freejack; Godzilla; Mimic; Nothing Lasts Forever; Zombie Flesh-Eaters*

New Zealand, in film, *An Angel at My Table; Beyond Reasonable Doubt; Broken English; Carry Me Back; Cinema of Unease; Constance; Goodbye Pork Pie; Once Were Warriors; Other Halves; Patu; Pictures; The Quiet Earth; Savage Honeymoon; The Scarecrow; Utu; Via Satellite; When Love Comes*

New Zealand cinema, *An Angel at My Table; Bad Taste; Beyond Reasonable Doubt; Braindead; Broken English; Came a Hot Friday; Carry Me Back; Cinema of Unease; Constance; Crush; Desperate Remedies; The End of the Golden Weather; Forgotten Silver; The Frighteners; Goodbye Pork Pie; Heavenly Creatures; The Lincoln County Incident; Loaded; Mouth Wide Open – A Journey in Film with Ted Coubray; Other Halves; Patu; The Piano; Pictures; Punch Me in the Stomach; The Quiet Earth; Race for the Yankee Zephyr; Romper Stomper; Savage Islands; Savage Honeymoon; The Scarecrow; Shaker Run; Sleeping Dogs; Smash Palace; Starlight Hotel; Sylvia; Topless Women Talk About Their Lives; Trial Run; The Ugly; Utu; Via Satellite; Vigil; What Dreams May Come; When Love Comes*

Nexo, Martin Andersen, film adapted from work, *Pelle the Conqueror*

Nicaragua
Nicaraguan cinema, *Alsino and the Condor*
Nicaragua in film, *Carla's Song; The Last Plane Out; Latino; Nicaragua – No Pasarán; Under Fire; Walker*

Nicholas II, Czar of Russia, films about/featuring, *The End of St Petersburg; Nicholas and Alexandra; Russian Ark*

Nichols, Peter, films adapted from work, *The National Health; Privates on Parade*

Nicholson, William, film adapted from work, *Shadowlands*

Nietzsche, Friedrich, film about, *Beyond Evil*

Nigerian cinema, *Femi Kuti: What's Going On*

Nightclubs, see **Show business**

Nilsson, Harry, musical by, *The Point; Popeye*

Nin, Anaïs, film about, *Henry & June*

Nixon, Richard, films about, *All the President's Men; Millhouse; Nixon; Secret Honor; The Trials of Alger Hiss*

Norman, Marsha, film adapted from work, *'Night Mother*

North of England, in film (see also **Liverpool**), *The Alcohol Years; All Creatures Great and Small; Among Giants; Bert Rigby, You're a Fool; Billy Elliot; Billy Liar; Blow Dry; Bob's Weekend; The Boys in Blue; Brassed Off; Captain Jack; Come on George; East Is East; Escape from the Dark; The Darkest Light; Fame Is the Spur; The Full Monty; Gabriel & Me; The Gamekeeper; Get Carter; Girls' Night; Groove on a Stanley Knife; Hell Is a City; In Fading Light; The Innocent* (MacKenzie); *It Shouldn't Happen to a Vet; Juvenile Liaison; Juvenile Liaison 2; A Kind of Loving; Lease of Life; Like Father; The Likely Lads; Little Voice; Love on the Dole; The Lovers; My Son the Fanatic; The Nature of the Beast; The Night Has Eyes; The Old Dark House; Owd Bob; Paper Marriage; Payroll; Purely Belter; Raining Stones; Rita, Sue and Bob Too; Room at the Top; Seacoal; South Riding; Speak Like a Child; Spring and Port Wine; The Stars Look Down; A Taste of Honey; T. Dan Smith; There's Only One Jimmy Grimble; This Sporting Life; Up 'n' Under; Up on the Roof; Vroom; Walter; Wetherby; What a Carve Up; When Saturday Comes; Whistle Down the Wind; The White Bus; Women in Tropical Places; Wuthering Heights* (Wyler); *Wuthering Heights* (Kosminsky); *Yanks*

Norton, Mary, film adapted from work, *The Borrowers*

Norway, in film, *Bloody Angels; Cold Tracks; Cross My Heart and Hope to Die; Edge of Darkness; Edvard*

Munch; The Ice Palace (Blom); *Junk Mail; The Last Lieutenant; Little Ida; Nine Lives; Orion's Belt; The Other Side of Sunday; Sebastian; Song of Norway; Wives; Wives: Ten Years After; Wives III*

Norwegian cinema, *Bloody Angels; Breaking the Waves; Cold Tracks; Cool & Crazy; Cross My Heart and Hope to Die; Devil's Island* (Fridriksson); *Edvard Munch; The Ice Palace* (Blom); *Ikingut; Insomnia; Junk Mail; I Was Fifteen; The Last Lieutenant; Little Ida; Lucky People Center International; Nine Lives; 101 Reykjavik; Orion's Belt; The Other Side of Sunday; Pathfinder; Sebastian; West Beirut; Wives; Wives: Ten Years After; Wives III; Zapatista*

Nostalgia
for 1900s, *My Brilliant Career*
for 1920s, *Bloodhounds of Broadway; The Boy Friend; The Fortune; Lucky Lady; Thoroughly Modern Millie*
for 1930s, *Borsalino; Borsalino & Co*
for 1940s, *Broadway Bound; Class of 44; Constance; Le Gang; P'Tang, Yang, Kipperbang; Racing with the Moon; Summer of '42*
for 1950s, *Book of Love; Cry-Baby; The Delinquents; Diner; Eddie and the Cruisers; Forever Young; Grease; Grease 2; Hoosiers; The Last Picture Show; Lords of Flatbush; The Man in the Moon; Motorist; Next Stop; Greenwich Village; Radio Days; Slumber Party '57; The Sticky Fingers of Time; That'll Be The Day; Tribulation 99: Alien Anomalies Under America; Union City; W.W. and the Dixie Dancekings*
for 1960s, *American Graffiti; Baby, It's You; Coupe de Ville; Dirty Dancing; The Five Heartbeats; The Flamingo Kid; Goin' Steady; Hairspray; Lemon Popsicle; More American Graffiti; Private Popsicle; Shag; The Wanderers; The Year My Voice Broke*
for 1970s, *Detroit Rock City; Shock Treatment; Stardust*
for world of old movies, *The Cheap Detective; Cinema Paradiso; Cinema Paradiso: The Special Edition; Dead Men Don't Wear Plaid; Fade to Black; Gumshoe; Movie Movie; Nickelodeon; Splendor; The World's Greatest Lover; Yoyo*
for old television, *Down Memory Lane; Dragnet; My Favorite Year; Pleasantville; Twilight Zone – The Movie*

Nuclear energy, *Bari-Zogon; The Chain Reaction; The China Syndrome; City of Fear; Class of Nuke 'Em High; Crack in the World; The Damned* (Losey); *Dark Circle; The Fiend Without a Face; In the King of Prussia; Meet the Applegates; Silkwood; X the Unknown*

Nuclear weapons
development of, *Fat Man and Little Boy; First Yank into Tokyo; The Plutonium Circus*
effects of/threat of, *America – From Hitler to MX; Amazing Grace and Chuck; Atomic Café; The Bedford Incident; Black Rain* (Imamura); *Blast from the Past; Blue Sky; Broken Arrow* (Woo); *Broken Arrow 29; Buttoners; Carry Greenham Home; Crimson Tide; The Day After Trinity; The Day the Earth Caught Fire; The Day the Fish Came Out; Defence of the Realm; Desert Bloom; Dr Strangelove: or, How I Learned to Stop Worrying and Love the Bomb; The Eclipse; Fail Safe; Half Life; Hiroshima, Mon Amour; Home of the Brave; The Hunt for Red October; I Live in Fear; The Iron Giant; It Came from Beneath the Sea; Kiss Me Deadly; Lost Sex; Miracle Mile; The Peacemaker; Rally 'round the Flag, Boys!; Rhapsody in August; Rockets Galore; Seven Days to Noon; Stargate; Superman IV; The Quest for Peace; Them!; True Lies; Twilight's Last Gleaming; Unstable Elements – Atomic Stories 1939–85; Viva la Vie; WarGames; When the Wind Blows*
life after nuclear holocaust, *The Bedsitting Room; The Big Bang; A Boy and His Dog; Buck Rogers in the 25th Century; Café Flesh; Damnation Alley; Dark Enemy; The Day the World Ended; Deathsport; The Deserter and the Nomads; The Falls; Fist of the North Star; The Last Battle; The Last Woman on Earth; Letters from a Dead Man; Lord of the Flies* (Brook); *Lord of the Flies* (Hook); *Malevil; Mindwarp; The New Barbarians; On the Beach; Panic in Year Zero; Planet of the Apes* (Schaffner); *Planet of the Apes* (Burton); *The Quiet Earth; The Sacrifice; The Salute of the Jugger; Surf Nazis Must Die; Testament* (Littman)

Nureyev, Rudolf, in performance, *I Am a Dancer*

Oates, Joyce Carol, film adapted from work, *Getting to Know You*

O'Barr, James, films adapted from work, *The Crow; The Crow: City of Angels*

O'Brien, Edna, films adapted from work, *The Country Girls; Girl with Green Eyes*

Occult, see **Devil, The Antichrist, Witchcraft, etc**

O'Casey, Sean, film about, *Young Cassidy*

O'Connor, Flannery, film adapted from work, *Wise Blood*

O'Connor, Joseph, film adapted from work, *Ailsa*

Odets, Clifford, films adapted from work, *Clash By Night; Golden Boy*

Offenbach, Jacques, film of opera, *The Tales of Hoffmann*

Office life (see also **Boardroom jungle, Work**), *The Apartment; The Associate; The Bachelor Party; The Clock; The Crowd; Desk Set; Glengarry Glen Ross; Janice Beard 45 WPM; Nine to Five; The Paper; The Secret of My Success; Stan and George's New Life; Working Girl*

O'Flaherty, Liam, films adapted from work, *The Informer; The Puritan*

O'Hara, John, films adapted from work, *BUtterfield 8; From the Terrace; Pal Joey*

Oil prospecting, *Blowing Wild; Boom Town; Giant; The Louisiana Story; Oklahoma Crude; Station Six – Sahara; Tulsa; The Two Jakes; When Time Ran Out…*

OK Corral, films featuring, *Doc; Gunfight at the OK Corral; Hour of the Gun; My Darling Clementine; Tombstone; Wyatt Earp*

Olympic Games, and related competitions, in film (see also **Athletics, Swimming**), *Animalympics; Best of the Best; Best in Show; Chariots of Fire; The Cutting Edge; Geordie; Olympische Spiele 1936; One Day in September; One in a Million; Running Brave; Southpaw; Tokyo Olympiad 1964; Via Satellite; Visions of Eight; White Rock; Without Limits*

Oman, in film, *The Hour of Liberation – The Struggle in Oman*

O'Neill, Eugene, films adapted from work, *Desire under the Elms; Long Day's Journey into Night; The Long Voyage Home*

Onstott, Kyle, films adapted from work, *Drum; Mandingo*

Opera and operetta
films of, *Bluebeard's Castle; Bitter Sweet; Black River; La Bohème; Carmen; The Desert Song; Don Giovanni; The King Steps Out; Madame Butterfly; The Magic Flute; The Merry Widow; The Mikado; Otello; Pagliacci; Parsifal; The Pirates of Penzance; Rigoletto; Tosca; La Traviata; The Tales of Hoffmann*
films about, *The Adventure of Sherlock Holmes' Smarter Brother; Aria; The Confessions of Winifred Wagner; The Death of Maria Malibran; Diva; The Divine Emma; Cosi; Eika Katappal; Evensong; Farinelli Il Castrato; The Glass Mountain; Goodnight Vienna; Lucia; Lillian Russell; Il Maestro; The Medium; M. Butterfly; Mozart in Love; Opera; The Phantom Lover; The Phantom of the Opera* (Julian); *Phantom of the Opera* (Little); *Phantom of the Opera* (Lubin); *The Phantom of the Opera* (Fisher); *The Spooky Bunch; The Story of Gilbert and Sullivan; The Toast of New Orleans; Vertiges*
Peking Opera, *Farewell My Concubine; For Fun; Heartstrings; Peking Opera Blues*

Opinion polls, *Magic Town*

Orczy, Baroness, films adapted from/based on work, *The Elusive Pimpernel; Pimpernel Smith; The Scarlet Pimpernel*

Orkney Islands, in film, *Blue Black Permanent; Venus Peter*

Orphans (see also **Adoption**), *Annie; The Apple Dumpling Gang; Babes on Broadway; The Boy with Green Hair; Boy's Choir; Bustin' Loose; Children Underground; Curly Sue; The Devil's Backbone; The Divided Heart; Domenica; Follow That Star; The Glass House; A Global Affair; The Good Life; The Hellfire Club; Home in Indiana; Housekeeping; A Hungarian Fairy Tale; Hwa-om-kyong; In Thee I Trust; It's All Happening; James and the Giant Peach; Jumanji; The Kidnappers; King of the Wind; The Last Flight of Noah's Ark; Letter for an Angel; Meet Me at the Fair; Mister Skeeter; Nothing but the Night; The Orphan of Anyang; Orphans; The Orphans; Our Mother's House; Pack Up Your Troubles; Paw; Rooftops; The Secret Garden* (Holland); *The Secret Garden* (Wilcox); *The Stolen Children; Sun Valley Serenade; The Unsinkable Molly Brown; The Wolves of Willoughby Chase; Young Giants*

Orton, Joe
film about, *Prick Up Your Ears*
films adapted from work, *Entertaining Mr Sloane; Loot*

Orwell, George
films adapted from work, *Animal Farm; Keep the Aspidistra Flying; Nineteen Eighty-Four*
mentioned in the title song of, *Les Uns et Les Autres*

Osborne, John, films adapted from work, *The Entertainer; Inadmissible Evidence; Look Back in Anger; Luther*

Outlaws and outlaw gangs, *American Outlaws; The Bandit; Bandit Queen; Bandits; Bandolero!; Blue; Bonnie and Clyde; Butch Cassidy and the Sundance Kid; Cattle Annie and Little Britches; Charro!; Colorado Territory; Crime Kings; Day of the Outlaw; Dillinger* (Nosseck); *Dillinger* (Milius); *Goin' South; The Great Northfield Minnesota Raid; I Shot Jesse James; Jesse James; The Left Handed Gun; The Lone Hand; Man of the West; The Naked Dawn; The Spikes Gang; The Long Riders; The Man Who Loved Cat Dancing; Minnesota Raid; One-Eyed Jacks; Pat Garrett and Billy the Kid; The Return of Frank James; Ride Lonesome; They Passed This Way; 3:10 to Yuma; A Time for Dying; The True Story of Jesse James; The Villain*

Oxbridge and the Ivy League, *Adventures of a Brown Man in Search of Civilization; American Friends; Another Country; A Beautiful Mind; Chariots of Fire; Dreamchild; Heaven's Gate; Howards End; Iris; Love Story; Legally Blonde; Maurice; The Mystic Masseur; The Paper Chase; Privileged; Robert Ryland's Last Journey; Shadowlands; The Skulls; True Blue; Wilt; With Honors*

Ozu, Yasujiro, film about, *Tokyo-Ga*

Pacific islands (see also **Desert Islands**), *The Bounty; The Devil at 4 O'Clock; Donovan's Reef; East of Sumatra; From Hell It Came; Heaven Knows, Mr Allison; Hurricane; The Hurricane; Joe Versus the Volcano; Miss Sadie Thompson; The Moon and Sixpence; Outcast of the Islands; The Profound Desire of the Gods: Tales from a Southern Island; Rain; Sadie Thompson; Son of Godzilla; South Pacific; Tabu; Tiara Tahiti; Till There Was You; Up in Arms; Victory* (Cromwell); *Victory* (Peploe);

Pacifism, *All Quiet on the Western Front* (Milestone); *All Quiet on the Western Front* (Mann); *The Burmese Harp; Les Carabiniers; Carry Greenham Home; Catch-22; The Day the Earth Stood Still; The Deserter and the Nomads; A Force More Powerful; Friendly Persuasion; Gandhi; La Grande Illusion; Half Life; How I Won the War; Idiot's Delight; The Imitation Game; Jeux Interdits; Johnny Got His Gun; King & Country; Kiss Me Deadly; No Drums; No Bugles; Paths of Glory; Rhapsody in August; Sergeant York; The Tunnel; Twenty Days Without War; The Valley; Veronico Cruz; The War; War Requiem; Westfront 1918*

Paedophilia, see **Child Abuse**

Paganini, Niccolo, film about, *The Magic Bow*

Page, Alain, film adapted from work, *Tchao Pantin*

Pagnol, Marcel, films adapted from work, *César; Le Château de ma mère; Fanny* (Allégret); *Fanny* (Logan); *La Femme du Boulanger; La Gloire de mon père; Jean de Florette; Manon des Sources; Topaze*

Painters, see **Art and artists**

Pakistan, in film, *Blood of Hussein; Earth* (Mehta); *Immaculate Conception*

Palestine and Palestinians
in film, *Divine Intervention; Friendship's Death; Occupied Palestine; On Our Land; Operation Thunderbolt; Raid on Entebbe; Rosebud; Tale of the Three Jewels; Wedding in Galilee; You, Me, Jerusalem*
Palestinian cinema, *Tale of the Three Jewels*

Palminteri, Chazz, film adapted from work, *A Bronx Tale*

Panama
Panama in film, *Canal Zone; Dollar Mambo; God's Favorite; Sniper; The Tailor of Panama*
Panamanian cinema, *Sweet Hunters*

Paolozzi, Eduardo, film about, *The Paolozzi Story*

Paretsky, Sara, film adapted from work, *V I Warshawski*

Paris, in film
pre-1914, *Aristocats; Beaumarchais; Le Bossu; Camille; Can-Can; Casque d'Or; Cousin Bette; Danton; Douce; 1871; Eléna et les Hommes; Les Enfants du Paradis; Les Enfants du siècle; Fantômas; French Can Can; Gervaise; Gigi* (Audry); *Gigi* (Minnelli); *The Girl from Maxim's; Madame de…; Marquise; Moulin Rouge* (Huston); *Moulin Rouge* (Luhrmann); *Nana* (Arzner); *Nana* (Renoir); *Nana* (Wolman); *The New Babylon; The Rat; Le Roi de Paris; Orphans of the Storm; The Spider and the Fly; Total Eclipse; Swann in Love; Zaza*
WWI, *Mata-Hari, Agent H.21; Les Vampires*
1920s–1930s, *Anastasia* (Litvak); *Boudu Sauvé des Eaux; La Chienne; Le Fantôme du Moulin Rouge; The Flying Fool; Folies Bergère; Henry & June; His Wife's Diary; Le Jour se lève; Ménilmontant; The Moderns; One Hour with You; Paris Was a Woman; Pièges; Quatorze Juillet; Quiet Days in Clichy* (Chabrol); *Quiet Days in Clichy* (Thorsen); *Rigolboche; Roberta; The Sun Also Rises; Surviving Picasso; A Woman of Paris; Zouzou*
WWII, *L'Accompagnatrice; Chantons sous l'Occupation; Docteur Petiot; One Man's War; Paris After Dark*
1940s–1950s, *Bob le Flambeur; Charade; Les Cousins; En Compagnie d'Antonin Artaud; Fantômas contre Fantômas; The French Line; Funny Face; Innocents in Paris; The Last Time I Saw Paris; Love in the Afternoon* (Wilder); *Madeline; The Man Who Watched Trains Go By; La Môme Pigalle; Les Portes de la Nuit; Rouge Baiser; 'Round Midnight; Le Signe du Lion; Le Testament du Docteur Cordelier; La Traversée de Paris*
1960s, *A Bout de Souffle; L'Amour Existe; Les Bonnes Femmes; Chronique d'une Eté; Cléo de 5 à 7; Deux ou Trois Choses que Je Sais d'Elle; Do Not Disturb; Le Doulos; Le Feu Follet; The Frog Prince; Le Joli mai; A Soldier's Daughter Never Cries; Zazie dans le Métro*
1970s, *The Aviator's Wife; Buffet Froid; Catherine and Co; Céline and Julie Go Boating; Le Diable Probablement; Des Enfants Gâtés; L'Eau Froide; Four Nights of a Dreamer; Un Homme qui Dort; Loulou; Love in the Afternoon* (Rohmer); *La Marge; A New Kind of Love; Night Caller; Once in Paris; The Red Circle; The Tenant; Themroc; Time for Loving*
1980s, *Les Amants du Pont-Neuf; Boy Meets Girl; Conte de printemps; Diva; Exposed; Frantic; Full Moon in Paris; A Girl from Lorraine; Le Cop; Le Cop 2; Un Monde sans pitié; Notebook on Cities and Clothes; Le Pont du Nord; Subway; Tchao Pantin; Trop belle pour toi!*
1990s, *An American Werewolf in Paris; L'Appartement; L'Appât; Les Apprentis; Bernie; La Bûche; Cible émouvante; Clubbed to Death; Code Unknown; Un Coeur qui bat; De l'Autre Côté du Périph'; Dobermann; Une Epoque formidable…; Everyone Says I Love You; IP5; Irma Vep; French Kiss; The Girl on the Bridge; Jaya Ganga; J'embrasse pas; Killing Zoe; La Haine; Loin des Barbares; L.627; Lumière Noire; Ma vie sexuelle (Paul Dedalus' Journey); Métisse; Men, Women: User's Manual; Mina Tannenbaum; The Misadventures of Margaret; Night and Day; Night on Earth; Nikita; Once a Thief; Pas de Scandale; Place Vendôme; Pola X; The Proprietor; Ronin; Salut Cousin!; Secret Défense; Sélect Hotel; S'en fout la mort; Souvenir; The Tango Lesson; Three Colours: Blue; The Underground Orchestra; When the Cat's Away…*
from 2000, *As a Man; Bonne Nouvelle; Le Détour; La Faute à Voltaire; Fils de Deux Mères ou Comédie de l'Innocence; Hell of a Day; Human Resources; Les Marchands de Sable; Salsa*
timeless, *The Favour, the Watch and the Very Big Fish; The Legend of the Holy Drinker; Tombés du Ciel; La Vie de Bohème*

Parker, Charlie, films about, *Bird; Bird Now*

Parker, Dorothy,
film about, *Mrs Parker and the Vicious Circle*

Parole, life on,
Cookie; Double Jeopardy; I Want You; You and Me

Pascal, Blaise, film about, *Blaise Pascal*

Pasolini, Pier Paolo, films about, *Dear Diary; Pasolini, un Delitto Italiano; Whoever Says the Truth Will Die*

Pasternak, Boris
film about, *The Pasternaks*
film adapted from work, *Doctor Zhivago*

Paterson, Neil, film adapted from work, *The Kidnappers*

Patterson, James, films adapted from work, *Along Came a Spider; Kiss the Girls*

Patterson, Col John, film adapted from work, *The Ghost and the Darkness*

Paton, Alan, film adapted from work, *Lost in the Stars*

Patrick, John, films adapted from work, *The Teahouse of the August Moon; The Hasty Heart*

Patton, General George, films about, *Brass Target; Patton*

Paul, Les, film about, *The Wizard of Waukesha*

Pavese, Cesare, film adapted from work, *Le Amiche*

Pavlova, Anna, film about, *Pavlova – A Woman for All Time*

Peace Corps, *Blood of the Condor; The Hotbox; Volunteers*

Pearce, Philippa,
film adapted from work, *Tom's Midnight Garden*

Peking Opera, see **Opera and operetta**

Pérez Galdos, Benito, film adapted from work, *Tristana*

Pérez-Reverte, Arturo, films adapted from work, *The Fencing Master; The Ninth Gate*

Peron, Eva, films about, *Evita; Don't Cry for Me Little Mother*

Perrault, Gilles, film adapted from work, *Le Pull-Over Rouge*

Personality exchanges, see **Identities confused at birth, Impersonation**

Peru
Peru in film, *Courage; Aguirre, Wrath of God; El Dorado; The Golden Coach; The Last Movie; The Royal Hunt of the Sun; Sin Compasión*
Peruvian cinema, *Courage; Don't Tell Anyone; The Lion's Den; Sin Compasión; Todos Somos Estrellas*

Petrification, *The Monolith Monsters*

Philbrick, Rodman, film adapted from work, *The Mighty*

Philippines, in film, *American Guerilla in the Philippines; Demons; Bayan Ko: My Own Country; In the Navel of the Sea; Jaguar; Kisapmata; Manila by Night; Manila: In the Claws of Darkness; The Real Glory; Signed: Lino Brocka; The Story of Woo Viet*

Philippine cinema, *Bamboo Gods and Iron Men; Bayan Ko: My Own Country; Boatman; Demons; In the Navel of the Sea; Jaguar; Kisapmata; Manila by Night; Manila: In the Claws of Darkness; Midnight Dancers; Three*

Photographers and photography, *The All-Round Reduced Personality – Redupers; Baba Yaga; Billy's Hollywood Screen Kiss; Blow Up; Bonjour, Monsieur Doisneau; The Bridges of Madison County; Calendar; Comrades; Dirty Pictures; The Eyes of Laura Mars; The Favour, the Watch and the Very Big Fish; Felice… Felice…; La Fidélité; Flat Tyre; A Great Day in Harlem; High Art; The Indian Fighter; J.A. Martin, Photographer; John Heartfield, Photomonteur; Liebestraum; Mahogany; Model; Model Shop; My Favorite Brunette; Parting Shots; Pecker; Proof; Photographing Fairies; The Public Eye; Skyline; Under Fire; Visions of Light; Who Are You Polly Maggoo?; The Women on the Roof*

Piaf, Edith, films about, *Edith and Marcel; Piaf*

Picasso, Pablo, films about, *Le Mystère Picasso; Surviving Picasso*

Pickpockets, *Harry in Your Pocket; Oliver!; Oliver Twist* (Lean); *Oliver* (Donner); *Pickpocket; Pickup on South Street*

Pilots, see **Flying**

Pimps, *La Balance; Black Gunn; La Chienne; I'm Gonna Git You Sucka; Saint Jack*

Pink Panther films, *Curse of the Pink Panther; The Pink Panther; The Pink Panther Strikes Again; The Return of the Pink Panther; Revenge of the Pink Panther; A Shot in the Dark; Trail of the Pink Panther*

Pinter, Harold, films adapted from work, *Betrayal; The Birthday Party; The Caretaker; The Homecoming*

Pirandello, Luigi, films adapted from work, *As You Desire Me; Kaos*

Pirates, *Anne of the Indies; Blackbeard's Ghost; Blackbeard the Pirate; The Black Pirate; The Black Swan; The Buccaneer; Captain Blood; China Seas; The Crimson Pirate; CutThroat Island; Frenchman's Creek; High Wind in Jamaica; The Island; Madame X; The Pirate; Pirates; Scalawag; The Sea Hawk; The Spanish Main; Swashbuckler; Treasure Island* (Heston); *Treasure Island* (Fridman); *Yellowbeard*

Pirosmani, film about, *Pirosmani*

Plagues (see also **Germ warfare**), *Mauvais Sang; No Blade of Grass; Outbreak; Panic in the Streets; Rabid; The Swarm; 12 Monkeys*

Planet of the Apes films, *Battle for the Planet of the Apes; Beneath the Planet of the Apes; Conquest of the Planet of the Apes; Escape from the Planet of the Apes; Planet of the Apes* (Schaffner); *Planet of the Apes* (Burton)

Plastic surgery, *Ash Wednesday; Dark Passage; Death Becomes Her; Doc Hollywood; First Yank into Tokyo; Johnny Handsome; Le Miroir a deux faces; Seconds; Shattered* (Petersen); *Stepfather III; A Woman's Face; Les Yeux sans Visage*

Poachers, *Barnabo of the Mountains; Danny the Champion of the World; Poachers; Where No Vultures Fly*

Poe, Edgar Allan
as character in film, etc, *The Mystery of Rampo; The Spectre of Edgar Allan Poe*
films adapted from work, *The Black Cat; Buried Alive; La Chute de la Maison Usher; City Under the Sea; The Haunted Palace; Histoires Extraordinaires; House of Madness; The House of Usher; Masque of the Red Death; Murders in the Rue Morgue* (Florey) *Murders in the Rue Morgue* (Hessler); *The Oblong Box; The Pit and the Pendulum* (Corman); *The Pit and the Pendulum* (Gordon); *The Premature Burial; The Raven* (Friedlander); *The Raven* (Corman); *Tale of a Vampire; Tales of Terror; The Tomb of Ligeia*

Poland, in film (see also **Polish cinema**), *And There Was Jazz; Ashes and Diamonds; Barrier; The Big Animal; Blind Chance; Camera Bluff; The Constant Factor; The Consul; The Contract; The Converted; Escape from the 'Liberty' Cinema; A Generation; The Grass Is Always Greener; Hi, Tereska; Interrogation; Johnny Aquarius; Kanal; Kapo; Korczak; Krzysztof Kieslowski: I'm So So; Life at a Gallop; Lodz Ghetto; Love Stories; Loving the Dead; Man of Iron; Man of Marble; Miss Nobody; No End; 100 Years of Polish Cinema; The Pianist; Playing from Plates; The Road Home; Romance of a Horse Thief; Rough Treatment; Schindler's List; Shtetl; Simon Magus; The Taste of the Black Earth; Temptation; Three Colours: White; To Be or Not To Be* (Lubitsch); *To Be or Not To Be* (Johnson); *To Kill a Priest; Top Dog; The Scar; The Warsaw Ghetto Uprising; A Woman on Her Own; A Year of the Quiet Sun*

Poles in Britain, *Moonlighting; Success Is the Best Revenge*

Police
Aust, *Deadly; Mr Reliable (a true story); The Monkey's Mask*
Can, *Being at Home with Claude; Urinal*
China, *East Palace, West Palace; Rock n'Roll Cop*
Fr, *Au Nom de la Loi; La Balance, The Colour of Lies; Le Cousin; Le Cop; Le Cop 2; The Crimson Rivers; L'Humanité; L.627; Mister Frost; Police; Tchao Pantin*
GB, *The Adventures of PC 49; Blind Date* (Losey); *The Blue Lamp; Eyewitness* (Hough); *Hell Is a City; Hidden Agenda; i.d.; The Innocent Sleep; Juvenile Liaison; Juvenile Liaison 2; Inspector Clouseau; Ladder of Swords; The Lost Son; Nobody Runs Forever; The Offence; The Spider and the Fly; Tank Malling; The Wisdom of Crocodiles; The Wrong Arm of the Law*
Ger, *Dirt fro Dinner; he Policewoman*
HK, *Before Dawn; Bullets Over Summer; Chungking Express; Crime Story; Gen-X Cops; Gen-Y Cops; The Killer* (Woo); *Organized Crime and Triad Bureau; Police Story* (Chan); *Rock n'Roll Cop; Task Force; Theft Under the Sun; The Wicked City*
Ind, *An Indian Story*
Iran, *Moment of Innocence*
Ire, *The Playboys; The Run of the Country*
Isr, *One of Us*
It, *Illustrious Corpses; Un Maledetto Imbroglio; A Pure Formality; La Scorta; The Stolen Children*
Jap, *Cure; Hana-Bi; I, the Executioner; MARKS; The Most Terrible Time in My Life; An Obsession; The Outer Way; The Violent Cop*
Neth, *Beck; The Rape*
Nor, *Bloody Angels; nsomnia*
Mex, *Highway Patrolman*
SAf, *Bopha!; A Dry White Season; A Private Life*
Sp, *A Body in the Forest; Torrente, the Dumb Arm of the Law*
Swe, *The Man from Majorca; The Man on the Roof*
US – cops against the system, *Another 48 HRS; Basic Instinct; The Big Heat; Black Rain* (Scott); *Cobra* (Cosmatos); *Coogan's Bluff; Cop; The Custodian; The Dead Pool; Die Hard; Die Hard 2; Die Hard with a Vengeance; Dirty Harry; 8 Million Ways to Die; The Enforcer* (Fargo); *48 HRS; Hard to Kill; The January Man; Kuffs; Lethal Weapon; Lethal Weapon 2; Lethal Weapon 3; Lethal Weapon 4; A Lovely Way to Die; McQ; Maniac Cop; Maniac Cop 2; Mulholland Falls; The Negotiator; Next of Kin; Off Limits; On Dangerous Ground; Out for Justice; Physical Evidence; Prince of the City; The Punisher; Renegades; The Rookie; Rush Hour; Serpico; Shakedown; Stone Cold; Tango & Cash; 10 to Midnight; Tightrope; The Violent Professionals; Warning Shot; Year of the Dragon*
– corruption, *Bad Lieutenant; The Captive City; CopLand; Cops and Robbers; Deep Cover; Everybody Wins; Exit Wounds; Gang Related; The Glass Shield; Harlem Nights; An Innocent Man; Internal Affairs; LA Confidential; The Last of the Finest; Money Train; Order of Death; Q & A; Ransom; Romeo Is Bleeding; Rush; Snake Eyes; Striking Distance; Touch of Evil; Training Day; Unlawful Entry*
– futuristic/horrific/cartoon, *Adrenalin – Fear the Rush; Dark Angel; Demolition Man; Fallen; Ghosts of*

Mars; Inspector Gadget; Judge Dredd; Monolith; Nightbreed; The One; Predator 2; RoboCop; RoboCop 2; RoboCop 3; Seven; Timecop
– a policeman's lot, *Affliction; Along Came a Spider; Between Midnight and Dawn; The Blue Knight; Blue Streak; The Bone Collector; Bullets or Ballots; Busting; Camera Obscura; Chasers; The Choirboys; City That Never Sleeps; Colors; Cop & ½; The Corruptor; The Dark Wind; Dead Bank; The Detective; Detective Story; Devil in a Blue Dress; The Devil's Own; Donato and Daughter; End of Days; Exit to EdenThe First Power; Fort Apache – The Bronx; The Glimmer Man; The Glitter Dome; A Gnome Named Gnorm; The Hard Way; Heart Condition; Heat* (Mann); *Heaven's Prisoners; Homicide; In the Line of Fire; It Could Happen to You; Jennifer 8; The Killer Inside Me; Kindergarten Cop; K-9; Law and Order; Lone Star; A Low Down Dirty Shame; Miami Blues; The Mob; Mystery Street; National Lampoon's Loaded Weapon 1; The New Centurions; Newman's Law; No Mercy; Normal Life; One False Move; One Good Cop; Only the Lonely; The Onion Field; The Pledge; Police Academy; Policy Academy 2: Their First Assignment; Police Academy 3: Back in Training; Policy Academy 4: Citizens on Patrol; Policy Academy 5: Assignment Miami Beach; Police Academy 6: City Under Siege; Police Academy 7: Mission to Moscow; Police Story* (Graham); *Report to the Commissioner; Ricochet; Sea of Love; Sergeant Madden; Seven; Short Time; Stop! or My Mom Will Shoot; The Super Cops; Traces of Red; Turner & Hooch; Violent Tradition; White Sands*
– women, *Adrenalin – Fear the Rush; Angel Eyes; Blue Steel; A Body in the Forest; The Bone Collector; The Borrower; Close to Eden; Copycat; Exit to Eden; Fargo; Fatal Beauty; Impulse* (Locke)
USSR, *Plumbum, or a Dangerous Game; Red Heat*

Polish cinema, *And There Was Jazz; Ashes and Diamonds; Barrier; The Big Animal; Blind Chance; Camera Buff; The Conductor; The Constant Factor; The Consul; The Contract; The Converted; Dekalog 1: 'I am the Lord thy God, thou shalt have no other God but me'; Dekalog 2: 'Thou shalt not take the name of the Lord thy God in vain'; Dekalog 3: 'Honour the Sabbath Day'; Dekalog 4: 'Honour thy father and thy mother'; Dekalog 5:'Thou shalt not kill'; Dekalog 6: 'Thou shalt not commit adultery'; Dekalog 7: 'Thou shalt not steal'; Dekalog 8: 'Thou shalt not bear false witness'; Dekalog 9: 'Thou shalt not covet thy neighbour's wife'; Dekalog 10: 'Thou shalt not covet thy neighbour's goods'; The Deluge; Devils, Devils; The Doll* (Has); *La Double Vie de Véronique; The Dybbuk; Escape from the 'Liberty' Cinema; Everything for Sale; Family Life* (Zanussi); *A Generation; Hands Up; Happy Man; Hi, Tereska; Illumination; Innocent Sorcerers; Interrogation; Johnny Aquarius; Kanal; Korczak; Krzysztof Kieslowski: I'm So So; Landscape After Battle; Life at a Gallop; Love Stories; Man of Iron; Man of Marble; Miss Nobody; No End; 100 Years of Polish Cinema; Playing from Plates; The Road Home; Rough Treatment; The Saragossa Manuscript; The Scar; The Sex Mission; A Short Film About Killing; A Short Film About Love; The Silent Touch; The Story of Sin; Taste of the Black Earth; Temptation; The Third Part of the Night; Three Colours: Red; Three Colours: White; Top Dog; Voyages; The Warsaw Ghetto Uprising; The Wedding* (Wajda); *A Week in the Life of a Man; A Woman on Her Own; A Year of the Quiet Sun; Yiddle with His Fiddle; The Young Ladies of Wilko*

Polar exploration, see **Antarctica, Ice dramas**

Politics and politicians (see also **Fascism, Racism, State terror, Terrorism**)
in Africa, *A Good Man in Africa*
in Argentina, *A Funny, Dirty Little War*
in Australia, *Don's Party; Harlequin*
in Belgium, *Daens*
in Bolivia, *Chuquiago; El Coraje del Pueblo*
in Brazil, *Opera do Malandro*
in Britain, *Acceptable Levels; As the Beast Sleeps; Blind Date* (Losey); *British Sounds; Business as Usual; The Chiltern Hundreds; Damage; Defence of the Realm; Don't Just Lie There, Say Something!; Fame Is the Spur; Film from the Clyde; Hidden Agenda; An Ideal Husband* (Korda); *An Ideal Husband* (Parker); *Left, Right and Centre; The Madness of King George; Midas Run; The Mudlark; The Naked Truth; O Lucky Man!; Paris by Night; Privilege* (Watkins); *The Rise and Rise of Michael Rimmer; Rosebud; Salt & Pepper; Scandal; The Stars Look Down; Tank Malling; T. Dan Smith; Who Needs a Heart; Whoops Apocalypse; Year of the Beaver; Young Winston*
in Canada, *Les Ordres; Réjeanne Padovani; The True Nature of Bernadette*
in Chile, *Cantata of Chile; The Battle of Chile; Missing*
in Colombia, *What Is Democracy?*
in Cuba, *Days of Water; Havana*
in Cyprus, *Attila '74*
in Czechoslovakia, *The Ear; Joseph Kilián; Pravda*
in El Salvador, *El Salvador – Decision to Win; El Salvador – Portrait of a Liberated Zone; El Salvador – The People Will Win; In the Name of the People; Romero*
in France, *L'Arbre, le Maire et la Médiathèque, ou Les Sept Hasards; L'Argent Des Autres; The Day of the Jackal; Le Dernier Milliardaire; 1871; La Guerre sans nom; 1974, Une Partie de Campagne; Les Noces Rouges; Of Great Events and Ordinary People; Section Spéciale; Stavisky...; La Vie est à nous*
in Germany, *Berlin Jerusalem; Europa; The German Chainsaw Massacre; Germany in Autumn; The Hitler Gang; John Heartfield Photomonteur; Kaspar Hauser; Mother Küster's Trip to Heaven; November Days Voices and Choices; The Point Is to Change It; Rosa Luxemburg; Die Weber*
in Ghana, *Testament* (Akomfrah)
in Greece, *Eleftherios Venizelos; The Travelling Players; Z*
in Guatemala, *When the Mountains Tremble*
in Hong Kong, *From the Queen to the Chief Executive; Ordinary Heroes*
in Hungary, *The Witness*
in India, *Distant Thunder; An Enemy of the People* (Ray); *Gandhi; Piravi; Trikal: Past Present and Future*
in Indonesia, *The Year of Living Dangerously*
in Ireland, *Ireland: Behind the Wire; Divorcing Jack; The Patriot Game*
in Israel, *To Live in Freedom*
in Italy, *The Footman; Illustrious Corpses; Italy: Year One; Mani sulla Città; The Mattei Affair; Open Doors; Repubblica Nostra*
in Jamaica, *Countryman*
in Japan, *The Ceremony; Four Days of Snow and Blood; The Man Who Left His Will on Film*
in Latin America (unspecified), *American Roulette; The Evil That Men Do; La Fièvre Monte à el Pao; Kiss of the Spider Woman*
in Mali, *Finyé*
in Mexico, *Herod's Law*
in Nicaragua, *Nicaragua – No Pasarán; Walker*
in Peru, *The Lion's Den*
in Poland, *Blind Chance; Camera Buff; The Constant Factor; The Consul; Escape from the 'Liberty' Cinema; Man of Iron; Man of Marble; No End; Rough Treatment*
in Portugal, *Deus Patria e Autoridade; The Good People of Portugal; Viva Portugal*
in Romania, *Requiem for Dominic*
in Spain, *La Guerre est finie; Race, the Spirit of Franco*
in South Africa, *Cry Freedom; Mapantsula; Sarafina!; A World Apart*
in South Korea, *Black Republic; KT*
in Switzerland, *Jonah, Who Will Be 25 in the Year 2000*
in Thailand, *Tongpan*
in Turkey, *The Wall; Yol*
in Uganda, *General Amin*
in Uruguay, *State of Siege*
in US, *Absolute Power; Advise and Consent; Alias Nick Beale; The American Way; Amistad; Beau James; The Best Man; Betrayed; The Big Brass Ring; Black Sheep; Blaze; Bob Roberts; Boomerang* (Kazan); *Born on the Fourth of July; Bulworth; The Candidate; Careful, Soft Shoulder; City of Hope; The Contender; Cousin Bobby; Daniel; DaveThe Distinguished Gentleman; Enemy of the State; Everybody Wins; Executive Action; A Face in the Crowd; Fat Man and Little Boy; First Monday in October; F.I.S.T.; F.T.A.; Gabriel Over the White House; The Garment Jungle; Get on the Bus; The Glass Key; The Gorgeous Hussy; The Great McGinty; Hard to Kill; Harlan County, USA; Hoffa; I.F. Stone's Weekly; In the Line of Fire; The Intruder; JFK; Joe Hill; The Last Hurrah; The Last of the Finest; Malcolm X; The Manchurian Candidate; Matewan; Medium Cool; Meet John Doe; Mr Smith Goes to Washington; Murder at 1600; Music Box; Nixon; Northern Lights; The November Men; The November Plan; No Way Out* (Donaldson); *On Company Business; The Package; The Phantom President; Power; Powwow Highway; Primary Colors; Protocol; Punishment Park; Reds; Roy Cohn/Jack Smith; Running on Empty; Rush to Judgment; The Seduction of Joe Tynan; The Senator Was Indiscreet; Seven Days in May; Shadow Conspiracy; A Show of Force; A Simple Twist of Fate; Snake Eyes; Spin; State of the Union; Storyville; Striptease; Thirteen Days; The Times of Harvey Milk; Talk of the Town; Twilight's Last Gleaming; Uncommon Senses; Underground* (de Antonio); *Vladimir et Rosa; Wag the Dog; Waking the Dead; The War Room; Welfare; The Werewolf of Washington; Who Killed Vincent Chin?; Wild in the Streets; Winter Kills; The Wobblies; W USA; Young Mr Lincoln*
in Venezuela, *Disparen a Matar*
in West Indies, *Island in the Sun*

Polygamy, *Berdel; Brigham Young – Frontiersman; The Citadel* (Chouikh); *Raise the Red Lantern; Xala*

Ponicsan, Darryl, films adapted from work, *Cinderella Liberty; The Last Detail*

Pool and snooker, *The Baltimore Bullet; Billy the Kid and the Green Baize Vampire; The Color of Money; The Hustler; Number One* (Blair)

Pornography, see **Sex films, Sex industry**

Porter, Cole
film about, *Night and Day*
musicals by, *At Long Last Love; Born to Dance; Can-Can; DuBarry Was a Lady; The Gay Divorcee; High Society; Kiss Me Kate; Kiss Me Kate: 3-D; Les Girls; The Pirate; Silk Stockings; You'll Never Get Rich*

Porter, Dorothy, film adapted from work, *The Monkey's Mask*

Porter, Edwin S, films about, *Before the Nickelodeon: The Early Cinema of Edwin S Porter*

Portugal, in film, *Abraham Valley; Captains of April; The Conspirators; The Covent; Deus, Patria e Autoridade; Doc's Kingdom; The Good People of Portugal; The Mutants; Off to the Revolution by 2CV; Oporto of My Childhood; In the White City; Journey to the Beginning of the World; Lisbon Story; Mal; Ossos; Três Palmeiras; The Uncertainty Principle; Viva Portugal; Water and Salt*

Portuguese cinema, *Abraham Valley; Bearskin; Captains of April; Comédia Infantil; The Convent; Deus, Patria e Autoridade; Doc's Kingdom;* ***Freedom;*** *The Good People of Portugal; Hard Times* (Botelho); *The Hips of John Wayne; The House of Spirits; I'm Going Home; In The White City; Jaime; Jester; Journey to the Beginning of the World; The Letter; Lisbon Story; Mal; The Mutants; Oporto of My Childhood; Ossos; The Other One; Po di Sangui; A Portuguese Goodbye; Recollections of the Yellow House; Time Regained; Trafico; Três Palmeiras; The Uncertainty Principle; Water and Salt*

Possession, demonic and similar, *Being John Malkovich; Brainwaves; Bride of Chucky; Carrie* (De Palma); *Cathy's Curse; Child's Play* (Holland); *Child's Play 2; Chi Sei?; Craze; Daemon; Demons; Demo Seed; Demons 2; The Entity; The Exorcist; The Exorcist – Director's Cut; Exorcist II: The Heretic; The Exorcist III; Fallen; The First Power; Freddy's Dead: The Final Nightmare; The Fury* (De Palma); *The Ghost and the Darkness; The Godsend; The Guardian; I Don't Want to Be Born; The Innocents; The Hearse; Holocaust 2000; House on Sorority Row; It Lives Again; It's Alive; The Kiss; The Manitou; The Mothman Prophecies; A Nightmare on Elm Street; A Nightmare on Elm Street Part 2; Freddy's Revenge; A Nightmare on Elm Street 3: Dream Warriors; A Nightmare on Elm Street 4: The Dream Master; A Nightmare on Elm Street 5: The Dream Child; 926 – Evil; Ninja III – The Domination; The Possession of Joel Delaney; The Red Violin; Repossessed; Retribution; Ruby; Rosemary's Baby; Society; Stigmata; Supernatural; The Sexorcist; To the Devil a Daughter; Troll; Village of the Damned; Wes Craven's New Nightmare; White Zombie; You'll Like My Mother*

Postmen and post offices, *Dead Letter Office; Dekalog 6: 'Thou shalt not commit adultery'; L'Ecole des Facteurs; Jour de Fête; Junk Mail; Il Postino; Postman; The Postman; Postman Blues; See Spot Run; A Short Film About Love*

Potok, Chaim, film adapted from work, *The Chosen*

Potter, Beatrix, film adapted from work, *Tales of Beatrix Potter*

Potter, Dennis, films adapted from work, *Brimstone and Treacle; Pennies from Heaven*

Powell, Richard, film adapted from work, *Follow that Dream*

Power failures, *Where Were You When the Lights Went Out?*

Predestination, *The Bad Seed; Don't Look Now; Flesh and Fantasy; The Florentine Dagger; Willow*

Prefontaine, Steve, film about, *Without Limits*

Pregnancy, childbirth and babies, *Afternoon Breezes; Asya's Happiness; August 32nd on Earth; Baby Boom; The Baby of Mâcon; Bachelor Mother; Berdel; Brother and Sister; Bundle of Joy; Dr T & the Women; Feelings; Une Femme Est une Femme; Fools Rush In; For Keeps; The Future Is Woman; The Handmaid's Tale; If These Walls Could Talk; Imperfect Love; Jack & Sarah; Jag Är Med Barn; Junior; The Kidnappers; Leila; Look Who's Talking; Look Who's Talking Too; Malpractice; Manny & Lo; The Match Factory Girl; Merci pour le chocolat; Mermaids; The Miracle of Morgan's Creek; A Nightmare on Elm Street 5: The Dream Child; Nine Months; The Paper; Paternity; Le Péril Jeune; Push! Push!; Raising Arizona; Reefer and the Model; Rita, Sue and Bob Too; Rosemary's Baby; She's Having a Baby; The Snapper; A Taste of Honey; Test Tube Babies; Waiting; With or Without You; A Woman Rebels; You'll Like My Mother*
babies in the care of men, *Look Who's Talking; Look Who's Talking Too; Rock-a-Bye Baby; Three Godfathers; Three Men and a Baby; 3 Men and a Cradle*

Prehistoric creatures in the present day, *At the Earth's Core; Baby – Secret of the Lost Legend; Dinosaurus!; Encino Man; Jurassic Park; The Land That Time Forgot; The Last Dinosaur; Loch Ness; The Lost World* (Allen); *The Lost World* (Hoyt); *The Lost World: Jurassic Park; The People That Time Forgot; Skullduggery*

Prehistoric dramas, *The Clan of the Cave Bear; Creatures the World Forgot; Dinosaur; The Flintstones in Viva Rock Vegas; The Land Before Time; Maciste Contro i Mostri; Missing Link; One Million Years B.C.; Quest for Fire; Teenage Caveman; Three Ages; When Dinosaurs Ruled the Earth*

Presley, Elvis
Elvis cultists, etc, *Elvis! Elvis!; Gigantic; Mystery Train*
films about, *Elvis; Elvis on Tour; Elvis – That's the Way It Is; This Is Elvis*
impersonators, etc, *Finding Graceland*

Price, Richard, films adapted from work, *Bloodbrothers; Clockers*

Priestley, JB, films adapted from work, *The Good Companions* (Saville); *The Good Companions* (Thompson); *An Inspector Calls; Last Holiday; Let the People Sing; The Old Dark House*

Prince, films about, *Prince – Sign o' the Times; Purple Rain*

Prisons (see also **Reform schools, etc**)
futuristic, etc, *Escape from New York; Ghosts…of the Civil Dead; John Carpenter's Escape from L.A.; No Escape; Star Trek VI: The Undiscovered Country*
in Australia, *Botany Bay; Chopper; Fortress; Just Us; Stir; Under Capricorn*
in Britain, *Albert RN; Captives; The Criminal; Escape!* (Dean); *Greenfingers; The Hill; Lucky Break; Mean Machine; Porridge; Silent Scream; Two-Way Stretch; The Weak and the Wicked*
in Canada, *Lilies; Night Zoo*
in China, *The Last Day of Winter*
in France, *L'Astragale; Une Belle Fille comme moi; Délits Flagrants; La Fille de l'Air; Second Chance; Le Trou*
– Devil's Island, *The Devil-Doll; Devil's Island; I Escaped from Devil's Island; King of the Damned; Papillon; Passage to Marseille; We're No Angels* (Curtiz)
in Germany, *Held for Questioning; I Was, I Am, I Shall Be; Varieté*
in Hungary, *Escape; Sunday Daughters*
in Ireland *Some Mother's Son*
in Israel, *Beyond the Walls*
in Italy, *Love in A Women's Prison; Why?*
in Poland, *Interrogation*
in Sweden, *You're Lying*
in Turkey, *Midnight Express; The Wall; Yol*
in US, *And God Created Woman; Attica; Bird Man of Alcatraz; Blackmail* (Potter); *Breakout; Brubaker; Brute Force; Caged; Caged Heat; Castle on the Hudson; Cool Hand Luke; Count a Lonely Cadence; Crazy Joe; Criminal Code; Dead Man Walking; The Defiant Ones; Delinquent School Girls; Down by Law; Each Dawn I Die; Escape from Alcatraz; The Execution Protocol; The Farm; Fast-Walking; Fortress; The Great Jewel Robber; The Green Mile; Human Experiments; I Am a Fugitive from a Chain Gang; An Innocent Man; Instinct; Invisible Stripes; Jailhouse Rock; Jericho Mile; Killer: A Journal of Murder; King of Alcatraz; The Last Castle; Last Dance; The Line; Life; Lock Up; The Longest Yard; Monster's Ball; Motel; Mrs Soffel; Murder in the First; O Brother, Where Art Thou?; Out of Sight; Pardon Us; Penitentiary; Prison; The Prisoner of Shark Island; Prison Stories: Women on the Inside; Riot in Cell Block 11; The Rock; Running Hot; The Seventh Cross; The Shawshank Redemption; Slam; Stir Crazy; Stranger Inside; Tango & Cash; There Was A Crooked Man…; Turbulence; 20,000 Years in Sing Sing; Under the Gun; We're Alive; We're No Angels* (Jordan)
in USSR, *The Guard; Gulag; Lost in Siberia; One Day in the Life of Ivan Denisovich*

Prisoners, ex-, and release from prison, *Crush Proof; The Debt Collector; Double Jeopardy; The Limey; Swing*

Prisoners of war, *Albert, RN; Blood Oath; The Bridge on the River Kwai; The Brylcreem Boys; Le Caporal Epinglé; The Captive Heart; Chicken Run; The Colditz Story; Empire of the Sun; Escape to Athena; First*

Yank into Tokyo; La Grande Illusion; The Great Escape; Hannibal Brooks; King Rat; The McKenzie Break; Merry Christmas Mr Lawrence; The Password Is Courage; Return from the River Kwai; Le Roi des Aulnes; Stalag 17; Three Came Home; La Vache et la Prisonnier; Victory; Von Ryan's Express; Welcome Home; The Wind Cannot Read; The Wooden Horse

Projectionists, see **Cinema owners, projectionists, staff, etc**

Property speculation and speculators
problems of, *Blackbeard's Ghost; The Boost; City of Hope; Close My Eyes; Heatwave; The Killing of Angel Street; Liebestraum; Le Mani sulla Città; The Two Jakes*
as vampires, *The Satanic Rites of Dracula*

Propaganda
films about, *Before Hindsight; Deutschland, Erwache!; A Gringo in Mañanaland; Illusions; Slogans*
Nazi Germany, *Triumph of the Will; Olympische Spiele 1936*
Spain, Franco regime, *Race, the Spirit of Franco*
WWII, *Aventure Malgache; Bon Voyage; Days of Glory; Desert Victory; For Freedom; 49th Parallel; Johnny Frenchman; The Gentle Sex; Hangmen Also Die; Here Comes the Waves; A Matter of Life and Death; My Mission to Moscow; Thunder Rock; The True Glory; The Tunnel; Tunisian Victory; The Way Ahead; Went the Day Well?; Western Approaches*

Prostitution, courtesans
(see also **Gigolos**)
in Argentina, *Last Images of the Shipwreck*
in Australia, *Winter of Our Dreams*
in Belgium, *Jeanne Dielman, 23 Quai du Commerce, 1080 Bruxelles*
in Britain, *Fast Food; Half Moon Street; Hussy; Keep It Up Jack!; Moll Flanders; Mona Lisa; On the Game; Personal Services; Prostitute; Soft Beds, Hard Battles; Stella Does Tricks; Tank Malling; Ursula and Glenys*
in Canada, *Marie s'en va-t-en ville; Suspicious River*
in China, *Blush; Flowers of Shanghai; The Goddess; Intimate Confessions of a Chinese Courtesan; Street Angel*
in Czech Republic, *Mandragora*
in Finland, *Juha*
in France, *L'Astragale; Belle de Jour; Both Sides of the Street; Boule de Suif; La Chienne; La Derobade; Deux ou Trois Choses que Je Sais d'Elle; Irma La Douce; Maîtresse; La Marge; Mon Homme; Le Plaisir; Sélect Hotel; Vivre Sa Vie; Private Club*
in Germany, *Amour, l'Argent, l'Amour, L'; Diary of a Lost Girl; Dirnentragödie; From the Life of the Marionettes; Das Mädchen Rosemarie; A Woman in Flames*
in Greece Never on Sunday
in Hong Kong, *The World of Suzy Wong*
in Hungary, *Sweet Emma, Dear Böbe; Tavaszi Zápor; A Very Moral Night*
in India, *The Courtesans of Bombay*
in Italy, *La Commare Secca; Dangerous Beauty; Mamma Roma; Le Notti di Cabiria; Princesa; The Prostitution Racket; The White Sheik; The Whores*
in Japan, *Crossways; Gate of Flesh; Gion Festival Music; A Hen in the Wind; Kaza-hana; The Life of Oharu; Street of Shame; Tokyo Decadence; Zipper and Tits*
in Korea, *Bad Guy; Ticket*
in Mexico, *La Mujer del puerto*
in Netherlands, *Abel*
in South Korea, *Black Republic; The Insect Woman*
in Spain, *What Have I Done to Deserve This?*
in Sweden, *Hets; What Are You Doing After the Orgy?*
in Thailand, *The Good Woman of Bangkok*
in Turkey, *Two Women*
in US, *American Gigolo; Bad Girls; The Best Little Whorehouse in Texas; The Cheyenne Social Club; Claire Dolan; Crimes of Passion; Deuce Bigalow: Male Gigolo; 8 Million Ways to Die; Exit to Eden; Frankenhooker; The Gauntlet; The Happy Hooker; Hardcore; Heidi Fleiss – Hollywood Madam; Hustle; Hustler White; Impulse* (Locke); *Indecent Proposal; Johns; Klute; Last Exit to Brooklyn; McCabe and Mrs Miller; Mighty Aphrodite; Milk Money; Mustang…The House That Joe Built; Naked Are the Cheaters; Nuts; Painted Angels; La P..... Respectueuse; Pretty Baby; Pretty Woman; The Revolt of Mamie Stover; Scarred; The Secret Life of an American Wife; Sharky's Machine; Skin & Bone; Street Girls; Streetwalkin'; This World, Then the Fireworks; Vice Squad; A Walk on the Wild Side; Whore; Wild Side; Working Girls*
male, *J'embrasse pas; A Kind of Hush*
other, *The Blue Villa;*

Proulx, E Annie,
film adapted from work, *The Shipping News*

Proust, Marcel
film about, *Céleste*
films adapted from work, *La Captive; Swann in Love; Time Regained*

Psychiatry/psychiatrists
(see also **Mental hospitals and asylums, Mental illness, Psychopaths and serial killers, Therapy and therapists**)
Aust, *Between Wars*
Can, *La Tête de Normande St-Onge; The Unsaid*
GB, *The Astonished Heart; Equus; Family Life* (Loach); *Fellow Traveller; The Man Who Mistook His Wife for a Hat; Mine Own Executioner; Nineteen-Nineteen; The Seventh Veil; The Sleeping Tiger; Zina*
Ger, *Secrets of a Soul*
It, *Il Diavolo in Corpo*
Jap, *The Enchantment*
Sp, *Ten Days Without Love*
Swe, *Face to Face*
US, *Agnes of God; The Amazing Doctor Clitterhouse; Analyze This; Another Woman; Blind Alley* (Vidor); *Carefree; The Cobweb; Color of Night; A Couch in New York; The Couch Trip; Curdled; The Dark Mirror; The Dark Past; Disturbed; Do Juan DeMarco; Don't Say a Word; The Dream Team; Experiment Perilous; Fear Strikes Out; Final Analysis; A Fine Madness; The Florentine Dagger; Freud; Fun; High Anxiety; I Was A Teenage Werewolf; K-PAX; Lady in the Dark; Lilith; Lost Angels; Lovesick; Matter of Heart; Mr Jones; The Naked Face; The Ninth Configuration; Now Voyager; Nuts; Oh, Men! Oh, Women!; Patch Adams; The President's Analyst; The Prince of Tides; Scenes from a Mall; Scissors; Screaming Mimi; See You in the Morning; Semi-Tough; Shadows in the Night; She's Out of Control; Sigmund Freud's Dora; The Silence of the Hams; Silent Fall; Society; Spellbound; Still of the Night; Suddenly Last Summer; Sybil; They Might Be Giants; What About Bob?; What's New Pussycat?; Who Is Harry Kellerman and Why Is He Saying Those Terrible Things About Me?; The Unsaid; Wild in the Country*
Yugo, *Special Treatment*

Psychopaths and serial killers
Aus, *Benny's Video; Funny Games*
Aust, *The Boys; Chopper; The Cars That Ate Paris; Dead Calm*
Bel, *Man Bites Dog*
Can, *The Brood; Sunday in the Country; Love and Human Remains; Terror in the Country; Terror Train; Tomorrow Never Comes; Visiting Hours*
Den, *Nightwatch* (Bornedal, 1994)
Fr, *Le Boucher; Docteur Petiot; L'Etrange Monsieur Victor; Les Fantômes du Chapelier; Pièges; Plein Soleil; Roberto Succo; Shattered* (Leroy); *Les Seins de glace; Sombre; Le Vampire de Dusseldorf*
GB, *Afraid of the Dark; Alone; Butterfly Kiss; Circus of Fear; The Cold Light of Day; Cover Girl Killer; Deadly Stranger; Driftwood; Exposé; Frightmare; From Hell; Hands of the Ripper; The Hawk; The Lodger* (Hitchcock); *My Name Is Julia Ross; Night Must Fall* (Reisz); *Nothing Personal; Peeping Tom; Resurrection Man; The Road Builder; Scènes de Crimes; The Spiral Staircase* (Collinson); *Split Second; 10 Rillington Place; Voyage; White Angel*
Ger, *M* (Lang); *The Sandman*
Ir, *Driftwood*
It, *Opera; Trauma; L'Uccello dalle Piume di Cristallo*
Jap, *Angel Dust; Boiling Point* (Kitano); *I, the Executioner; Ley Lines; Shinjuku Triad Society; Violated Angels*
Neth, *Amsterdamned; The Vanishing* (Sluizer, 1988)
Nor, *Bloody Angels*
NZ, *The Frighteners; The Ugly*
Sp, *Thesis*
US, *American Perfekt; American Psycho; Beware, My Lovely; Black Widow* (Rafelson); *Blue Steel; The Bone Collector; Born to Kill; The Boston Strangler; Bluebeard; The Brain Machine; Bride of Chucky; The Burning; The Cell; Chamber of Horrors; Cherry Falls; Child's Play* (Holland); *Child's Play 2; Cop; Copycat; Death Valley; Death Trap; Desperate Measures; Domestic Disturbance; Donato and Daughter; Dressed to Kill; Dillinger* (Milius); *Dillinger* (Nosseck); *Don't Answer the Phone!; The Driller Killer; Ed Gein; The Enforcer* (Fargo); *The Exorcist III; Experiment in Terror; Falling Down; The Fan* (Scott); *The Fan* (Bianchi); *Fear; Final Combination; The First Power; Freeway II: Confessions of a Trickbaby; Frequency; The Glimmer Man; The Good Son; Gravesend; Halloween; Halloween II; Halloween 4: The Return of Michael Myers; Hannibal; Hear No Evil; Heart of Midnight; Heat* (Mann); *He Knows You're Alone; Henry; Portrait of a Serial Killer; The Hitcher; The Hitch-hiker; Homicidal; I Know What You Did Last Summer; In Dreams; In the Line of Fire; I Still Know What You Did Last Summer; The January Man; Jennifer 8; Kalifornia; Killer: A Journal of Murder; The Killer Is Loose; A Kiss Before Dying* (Oswald); *A Kiss Before Dying* (Dearden); *Kiss the Girls; Knight Moves; Lady in White; The Last House on the Left; Leatherface: The Texas Chainsaw Massacre III; Lock Up; The Lodger* (Brahm); *Lured; M* (Losey); *The Mad Bomber; Malicious; Manhunter; Maniac Cop; Maniac Cop 2; The Mean Season; Miami Blues; Midnight Fear; Misery; Murders in the Zoo; Natural*

Born Killers; Never Talk to Strangers; Nightbreed; Night Must Fall (Thorpe); *Nightwatch* (Bornedal, 1998); *No Way to Treat a Lady; Out of the Dark; Pacific Heights; Painted Heart; Pet Sematary; Prey of the Chameleon; Prom Night; The Prowler* (Zito); *Psychic Killer; Psycho* (Hitchcock); *Psycho* (Van Sant); *Psycho II; Psycho III; Relentless; Ricochet; Road Flower; The Scarecrow; Scream; Scream 2; Scream 3; Seven; Shocker; The Silence of the Lambs; Silent Rage; Sleeping with the Enemy; Sliver; Slumber Party Massacre; The Sniper; The Spiral Staircase* (Siodmak); *The Stepfather; The Stepfather II; Stepfather III; Strait-Jacket; The Strangler; Summer of Sam; Superbeast; Sweet Kill; The Talented Mr Ripley; Targets; Taxi Driver; The Terminal Man; The Texas Chain Saw Massacre; The Texas Chainsaw Massacre 2; The Todd Killings; The Toolbox Murders; Traces of Red; Two Minute Warning; Turbulence; Unlawful Entry; Urban Legend; Urband Legend Final Cut; The Vanishing* (Sluizer, 1993); *Voodoo Woman; The Watcher; When a Stranger Calls; Where Danger Lives; While the City Sleeps; White Heat; Wicked, Wicked; The Wraith*
WGer, *Schizophrenia*

Public toilets, *Prick Up Your Ears; Taxi zum Klo; Urinal*

Puccini, Giacomo, films of opera, *La Bohème; Madame Butterfly; Tosca*

Puerto Rico, in film, *A Show of Force*

Puig, Manuel, film adapted from work, *Kiss of the Spider Woman*

Punks, and Punk films, *Asphalt Night; Boys Next Door; Breaking Glass; Burglar; Butterfly and Flowers; Il Capitano; The Decline of Western Civilization; Dekalog 10: 'Thou shalt not covet thy neighbour's goods'; Desperate; Dogs in Space; Dudes; The Filth and the Fury; The Great Rock'n'Roll Swindle; Jubilee; Jump into the Void; Kids; Labyrinth of Passion; Liquid Sky; Nightshift* (Rose); *Nikita; No Skin Off My Ass; Out of the Blue; Pepi, Luci, Bom…; Punk in London; The Punk Rock Movie; Repo Man; The Return of the Living Dead; Rough Cut and Ready Dubbed; Rude Boys; Sid and Nancy; Smithereens; Times Square; Tuff Turf; Union City; The Wild Side; Zazie*

Puppets, *The Adventures of Elmo in Grouchland; The Adventures of Pinocchio; Alice; Dougal and the Blue Cat; The Great Muppet Caper; The Dark Crystal; The Flintstones; Meet the Feebles; The Muppet Christmas Carol; The Muppet Movie; Muppets from Space; The Muppets Take Manhattan; Muppet Treasure Island; Pinocchio; Puppetmaster; Le Roman de Renard; To Live*

Pushkin, Alexander, film adapted from work, *Onegin*

Puzo, Mario, films adapted from work, *The Godfather; The Godfather Part II; The Godfather Part III; The Sicilian*

Pygmalion themes, *Born Yesterday* (Cukor); *Born Yesterday* (Mandoki); *Kitty; My Fair Lady; Pretty Woman; Pygmalion*

Pygmies, *Man of Africa*

Quakers, *Friendly Persuasion; Nixon*

Queneau, Raymond, film adapted from work, *Zazie dans le Métro*

Quilting, *Common Threads; Stories from the Quilt; How to Make an American Quilt*

Quindlen, Anna, film adapted from work, *One True Thing*

Rabe, David, film adapted from work, *Hurlyburly*

Race, mixed, and inter-racial relationships, etc, *ABCD; Billy Jack; Billy Two Hats; The Bitter Tea of General Yen; Bhowani Junction; Blacksnake; Bordertown; A Bronx Tale; The Chant of Jimmie Blacksmith; Chato's Land; Chocolat* (Denis); *Come See the Paradise; Crazy/BeautifulEnemies, a Love Story; Fear Eats the Soul; Flame in the Streets; Flaming Star; Flirting; Forfaiture; Gito, the Ungrateful; The Great Scout and Cathouse Thursday; Guess Who's Coming to Dinner; Hangup; Heat and Dust; Hiroshima, Mon Amour; The Hummingbird Tree; Hurricane; Indochine; Island in the Sun; Jungle Fever; Kin; The Lover; Made in America; Métisse; Mississippi Masala; M. Butterfly; Monster's Ball; Not Without My Daughter; Other Halves; A Private Life; Princesse Tam Tam; Pushing Hands; The Rains Came; The Rains of Ranchipur; The Sailor's Return; Sayonara; Secrets & Lies; Shakespeare-Wallah; Solomon and Gaenor; Song of the Exile; The Subterraneans; 36 Chowringhee Lane; Touch and Go; Two for Tea; The Wedding Banquet; Welcome II the Terrordome; The Wind Cannot Read; The World of Suzi Wong*

Racial appearance, change of, *Soul Man; True Identity; Watermelon Man*

Racism (see also **Colonialism, Fascism**)
in Australia, *Backroads; Black River; The Chant of Jimmie Blacksmith; Fistful of Flies; The Fringe Dwellers; Manganinnie; Romper Stomper*
in Britain, *Burning an Illusion; Flame in the Streets; The Sailor's Return; Sapphire; UndeRage*
in France, *A la Place du Coeur; La Haine; I Stand Alone*
in Germany, *Dirt for Dinner; Fear Eats the Soul; Terror 2000*
in Ivory Coast, *Black and White in Colour*
in Senegal, *Emitaï*
in South Africa, *Cry Freedom; Dangerous Ground; e'Lollipop; Jump the Gun; Lost in the Stars; Patu*
in Spain *Bwana*
in Trinidad, *Bim*
in US, *Alamo Bay; American History X; American Pictures: A Personal Journey Through Black America; Amistad; Betrayed; Billy Two Hats; Birth of a Nation; Carbon Copy; The Chamber; Count a Lonely Cadence; The Defiant Ones; The Delta; Do the Right Thing; Dutchman; Freedom Road; 4 Little Girls; Ghosts of Mississippi; The Glass Shield; Glory; Guess Who's Coming to Dinner; The Halliday Brand; Heart Condition; Imitation of Life* (Stahl); *Imitation of Life* (Sirk); *In the Heat of the Night; The Intruder; Intruder in the Dust; Iron Maze; James Baldwin; The Price of the Ticket; The Klansman; The Lawless; The Liberation of L.B. Jones; Lords of Discipline; Mississippi Burning; No Way Out* (Mankiewicz); *Odds Against Tomorrow; Once Upon a Time… When We Were Colored; Paris Trout; The Robin Hood of El Dorado; Running Brave; Sayonara; School Ties; Sergeant Rutledge; Show Boat* (Whale); *Show Boat* (Sidney); *Soul Man; Thunderheart; A Time to Kill; To Kill a Mockingbird; The Unforgiven; Watermelon Man; The Well; White Dog; The Young One*
in Zimbabwe, *The Green Grass Is Singing*
reflections on, *Crusoe*

Rada, Pacho, film about, *The Devil's Accordion*

Radiguet, Raymond, films adapted from work, *Le Diable au corps; Il Diavolo in Corpo*

Radio broadcasting, in film, *Airheads; Band Waggon; Break of Dawn; Broadway Bound; Citizens Band; Comfort and Joy; The Contact; Death at Broadcasting House; A Face in the Crowd; The Fisher King; FM; Good Morning Vietnam; Grosse Pointe Blank; The Ladies Man; The Magic Hour; Once Upon a Honeymoon; Out of Order* (Turpie); *Play Misty for Me; Private Parts; Pump Up the Volume; Radio Days; Radioland Murders; Straight Talk; Talk Radio; The Truth About Cats & Dogs; Tune in Tomorrow; The Unsuspected; Voice Over; Welcome Back Mr McDonald; Winchell; W USA; Young Soul Rebels*

Railways
in Britain, *The First Great Train Robbery; The Last Journey; Oh, Mr Porter!; The Railway Children; Seven Sinners* (de Courville); *Terror by Night; Thomas and the Magic Railroad; The Titfield Thunderbolt; Train of Events*
in Canada, *Terror Train*
in China, *Shanghai Express*
in Czechoslovakia/Slovakia, *Closely Observed Trains; I Love, You Love*
in Europe (international), *Avalanche Express; The Cassandra Crossing; The Lady Vanishes* (Hitchcock); *The Lady Vanishes* (Page); *Murder on the Orient Express; Les Rendez-vous d'Anna; Trans-Europ-Express*
in France, *La Bataille du Rail; The Man Who Watched Trains Go By; Subway; Those Who Love Me Will Take the Train; The Train*
in Germany, *Europa; Night Train to Munich*
in India, *North West Frontier*
in Ireland Night Train
in Italy Il Ferroviere
in Japan, *Angel Dust; The Bullet Train*
in US, *Breakheart Pass; Emperor of the North Pole; Finders Keepers; The General* (Keaton/Bruckman); *Grand Central Murder; The Great K & A Train Robbery; The Great Scout and Cathouse Thursday; Human Desire; The Iron Horse; Money Train; The Narrow Margin; Narrow Margin; Runaway Train; Silver Streak; Subway Riders; Subway Stories; The Taking of Pelham One Two Three; The Tall Target; Tracks; Under Siege 2; Union Station*
in USSR, *Joan of Arc of Mongolia*

Rain forests (see also **Jungle dramas**)
Amazonia, *Aguirre, Wrath of God; Amazonia: Voices from the Rainforest; At Play in the Fields of the Lord; Burden of Dreams; El Dorado; The Emerald Forest; Fitzcarraldo; Jungle 2 Jungle; Macunaima; Medicine Man; The Mission*
other, *FernGully: The Last Rainforest; The Shark Callers of Kontu*

Ramos Horta, José, film about, *The Diplomat*

Rand, Ayn, films adapted from work, *The Fountainhead; We the Living*

Ranpo, Edogawa, film adapted from work, *The Black Lizard*

Ransley, Peter, film adapted from work, *The Hawk*

Ransome, Arthur, film adapted from work, *Swallows and Amazons*

Rap films, *Beat Street; Body Rock; D.C. Cab; Fear of a Black Hat; House Party; Juice; Krush Groove; New Jack City; Out of Order* (Turpie); *Rappin; Slam; Trespass; Wild Style*

Rape, *The Accused; Act of Vengeance; Bad Lieutenant; La Bête; Bone; The Business of Strangers; Casualties of War; Domenica; The Everlasting Secret Family; Extremities; Eyes of a Stranger; Fatma; Handgun* (Garnett); *Hannie Caulder; Humanoids from the Deep; Incubus; Intimate Confessions of a Chinese Courtesan; Girls Town; Jackson County Jail; Kika; Lipstick; Madonna of the Seven Moons; Die Marquise von O…; The Moon in the Gutter; Mourir à Tue-Tête; Ms .45; Not a Pretty Picture; La Passion Béatrice; Pepi, Luci, Bom…; A Petal; The Rape; Revenge* (Hayers); *Sanctuary; Shame; Thelma & Louise; Things Behind the Sun; Village in the Mist; The Virgin Spring; Voice Over; Wake in Fright;*

Rasputin, Grigori, films about, *Agony; Nicholas and Alexandra; Rasputin and the Empress*

Rastafarians, *Heartland Reggae; Rockers*

Rattigan, Terence, films adapted from work, *Bequest to the Nation; The Browning Version* (Asquith); *The Browning Version* (Figgis); *French Without Tears; The Prince and the Showgirl; The Winslow Boy*

Ray, Nicholas, film about, *Lightning over Water*

Read, Piers Paul, films adapted from work, *Alive; Monk Dawson*

Rednecks, hostile, *Death Trap; Deliverance; Easy Rider; The Final Terror; Fighting Mad; Hunter's Blood; Leatherface; The Texas Chainsaw Massacre III; Lolly-Madonna XXX; Murder, He Says; Open Season; Southern Comfort; Tank; The Texas Chain Saw Massacre; The Texas Chainsaw Massacre 2; Walking Tall*

Reed, John, films about, *Reds; Reed: Insurgent Mexico*

Reform schools, etc, *Bad Boys; A Boy Called Third Base; Boys in Brown; Buried Alive; Forever Mary; Freedom Is Paradise; Hi, Tereska; The Loneliness of the Long Distance Runner; The Mayor of Hell; Scrubbers; Scum; Shout; Sleepers; Summer School; Tattooed Tears*

Refuse collectors, *Men at Work*

Reggae music, *Babymother; Bongo Man; Exodus – Bob Marley Live; The Harder They Come; Heartland Reggae; The Lunatic; Reggae; Reggae Sunsplash II; Rockers; Roots Rock Reggae; Stepping Razor – Red X; Time Will Tell*

Reich, Wilhelm, film about, *W.R. – Mysteries of the Organism*

Reincarnation, *The Alchemist; Audrey Rose; The Awakening; Chances Are; Dead Again; I Married a Witch; The Mummy* (Freund); *On a Clear Day You Can See Forever; The Reincarnation of Peter Proud; Rouge; The Wraith*

Religion, Christian (for non-Christian religions see individual listings; see also **Angels and divine manifestations, Biblical stories, God, Jesus Christ, Missionaries)**
Catholicism, *Absolution; The Addiction; The Agony and the Ecstasy; Alive; Anchoress; L'Appel du Silence; L'Auberge Rouge; The Audience; Augustine of Hippo; Bad Lieutenant; The Bells of St Mary's; Bernadette; The Bishop's Story; Black Robe; Brother Orchid; Brother Sun, Sister Moon; Camila; Cammina Cammina; The Cardinal; Child's Play* (Lumet); *The Chocolate War; Communion; Daens; Dekalog 8: 'Thou shalt not bear false witness'; The Devils; The Devil's Playground; Diary of a Country Priest; Edge of Doom; Father Brown; La Faute de l'Abbé Mouret; The Favour, the Watch and the Very Big Fish; The First Legion; The First Power; Foul Play; Four Days in July; The Fourth Man; Francesco, giullare di Dio; The Fugitive* (Ford); *Full Confession; Galileo* (Cavani); *Galileo* (Losey); *The Garden of Allah; Giovanna d'Arco al Rogo; The Godfather Part III; God Told Me To; Going My Way; Hail, Mary; The Heart of the Matter; Heaven Help Us; Heavenly Pursuits; The Heritage; House of Mortal Sin; I Confess; In the Name of the Father* (Bellocchio); *It's a 2'6" Above the Ground World; I, the Worst of All; Jeanne la Pucelle; Jesus of Montreal; Joan of Arc; Juliet of the Spirits; Lamb; Keeping the Faith; The Left Hand of God; The Legend of the Holy Drinker; Leon Morin, Priest; Liam; Lilies; A Man for All Seasons; A Man Named John; The Mission; Monk Dawson; Monsignor; Nazarin; Night Sun; La Passion de Jeanne d'Arc; Paulina 1880; Pieces of Dreams; Pope Joan; The Pope Must Die; Priest; The Prisoner; Procès de Jeanne d'Arc; Queens of the Big Time; The Refusal; La Reine Margot; Repossessed; Romero; The Rosary Murders; The Runner Stumbles; Russicum; Saint Joan; Saving Grace; The Seashell and the Clergyman; The Shoes of the Fisherman; The Silent Witness; The Song of Bernadette; Sous le Soleil de Satan; The Tempter; Till We Meet Again; To Kill a Priest; Le Tournoi; True Confessions; The Unholy; Viridiana; La Voie Lactée*
– convents, nuns, etc, *Agnes of God; Agnus Dei; Behind Convent Walls; Black Narcissus; Come, Come, Come Upward; The Convent; Dark Habits; Dead Man Walking; Le Dialogue des Carmélites; Heaven Knows, Mr Allison; Killer Nun; Madeline; Le Moine; Nasty Habits; The Nun and the Devil; Nuns on the Run; The Nun's Story; The Rebel Nun; La Religieuse; Sex Life in a Convent; The Sexorcist; Sister Act; Sister Act II: Back in the Habit; Temptation; Thérèse; We're No Angels* (Jordan)
ecumenical, *The Big Bang; Dogma; Jesus Christ Superstar; The Rapture; The Sign of the Cross; Whistle Down the Wind*
Protestantism, *Battle Hymn; The Bishop's Wife; Les Camisards; Carnival; Cousin Bobby; December Bride; Fanatic; Four Days in July; Friendly Persuasion; The Green Pastures; Heavens Above; Luther; A Man Called Peter; The Missionary; Nattvardsgästerna; The Night of the Iguana; One Full Moon; On the Wire; Ordet; The Other Side of Sunday; Rain; A River Runs Through It; The Sandpiper; La Symphonie Pastorale; Take Me to Town; The Wicker Man*
– evangelical/fundamentalist, *Angel Baby; Angel Dust; The Apostle; Brigham Young – Frontiersman; Carrie* (De Palma); *The Cross and the Switchblade; Cry from the Mountain; A Cry in the Dark; Deadly Blessing; Divine; Elmer Gantry; Entertaining Angels: The Dorothy Day Story; God's Alcatraz; Guyana: Crime of the Century; Leap of Faith; Marjoe; The Miracle Woman; Mullaway; The Night of the Hunter; The Preacher's Wife; Resurrection; Salvation! Have you Said Your Prayers Today?; Ticket to Heaven; Touch; Treasure of the Four Crowns; Wise Blood; Witness*

Religion, fringe (see also **New Ageism, etc**), *Holy Man*

Remarque, Erich Maria, films adapted from work, *All Quiet on the Western Front; Arch of Triumph; Bobby Deerfield; Three Comrades; A Time to Love and a Time to Die*

Removals, *The Chain; Moving*

Rendell, Ruth, films adapted from work, *La Cérémonie* (Chabrol); *A Judgement in Stone* (Rawi); *Live Flesh; Tree of Hands*

Repossession of goods, *Aggro Seizeman; Brown's Requiem; The Castle* (Sitch); *Repo Man*

Restaurants see **Cooks, kitchens and restaurants**

Retirement, *The Alpha Caper; Cocoon; Cocoon: the Return; Private Life; Umberto D*

Return to life, after death (see also **Afterlife, Frankenstein stories, Heaven-can-wait fantasies, Reincarnation, Undead, the**), *Chances Are; Creator; The Dead Can't Lie; A Drowning Man; The First Power; Hello Again; Jack Frost; The Iceman Cometh; The Kiss; Love Me Tender; Man Alive; The Miracle of the Bells; Pet Sematary; Resurrected; Shocker; Universal Soldier; The Walking Dead; Wonder Man*

Revenge dramas
Aust, *Fistful of Flies; Mad Max*
Braz, *Friendly Fire*
Bulg, *The Goat Horn*
China, *Ju dou*
Col, *Chronicle of a Death Foretold; Time to Die*
Fr, *L'Agression; The Bride Wore Black; Cela s'appelle l'Aurore; Cobra* (Boisset); *Les Dames du Bois de Boulogne; La Haine; One Deadly Summer; Que La Bête Meure; Le Samourai; Selon Mathieu; Smalltime Thief; They Call That an Accident*
GB, *The Abominable Dr Phibes; The Curse of the Crimson Altar; Debt Collector, The; Hannie Caulder; The Hit; The Long Memory; Murphy's War; Old Flames; Parting Shots; Revenge* (Hayers)
HK, *A Better Tomorrow; A Better Tomorrow II; Dragon Town Story*
Iran, *Season Five*
It, *Django; Django Kill; Invincible Barbarian, The; Today It's Me…Tomorrow*

You!; Vengeance
Jap, *The Bad Sleep Well; Bullet Ballet*
Mex, *Such Is Life*
Nor, *Pathfinder*
Sp, *La Campana del Infierno; Django Kill; Live Flesh; Such Is Life; They Came to Rob Las Vegas*
Swe, *The Virgin Spring*
US, *Act of Vengeance; Basket Case; Blood Red; The Bravados; The Burning Hills; The Business of Strangers; Cape Fear* (Thompson); *Cape Fear* (Scorsese); *Cause for Alarm!; Cousin Bette; The Crossing Guard; The Crow; The Crow: City of Angels; Cry Danger; Cutter's Way; Dallas; The Deadly Trackers; Desperado; The Devil-Doll; Dixie Dynamite; Double Jeopardy; Duel at Diablo; Eleni; Eye for an Eye; The Face Behind the Mask; Fear; The First Wives Club; Ghost Story; The Hand; The Hand That Rocks the Cradle; The Hanged Man; Hang 'em High; Hangup; Hard to Kill; High Plains Drifter; Hit List; The 'Human' Factor* (Dmytryk); *The Iron Horse; Johnny Angel; Johnny Handsome; Jory; Kickboxer; The Last House on the Left; Madhouse; Man in the Wilderness; The Mask of Zorro; Massacre at Central High; Motor Psycho; Ms .45; Next of Kin; One-Eyed Jacks; The Outfit; The Patriot; Patriot Games; Pumpkinhead; The Punisher; The Raid; Rancho Notorious; Remember My Name; Renegades; The Restless Breed; The Return of Frank James; Revenge* (Scott); *Rogue Cop; The Rookie; Scaramouche; The Searchers; The Secret of Convict Lake; Seven Men from Now; She-Devil; Silver Lode; Slaughter; Surf Nazis Must Die; The Specialist; Tchao Pantin; Three Hours to Kill; A Time of Destiny; Tin Men; The Toxic Avenger Part II; Underworld USA; The Walking Dead; White Lightning; Winchester '73*

Revolutionaries and radicals, 1960s and after (see also **Sixties counter culture, State terror, Terrorism**)
in Algeria, *Frantz Fanon: Black Skin, White Mask*
in Britain, *Little Malcolm and His Struggle Against the Eunuchs; One Plus One; Praise Marx and Pass the Ammunition; The Revolutionary; Skinflicker*
in Canada, *Nô*
in Congo, *Lumumba*
in France, *Bof!; La Chinoise; Frantz Fanon: Black Skin, White Mask; Le Gai Savoir; Milou en mai; Nada; Themroc; Tout Va Bien; Vent d'Est; Vladimir et Rosa; Weekend*
in Germany, *Germany in Autumn; The Legends of Rita; Melancholia; The Servicer; The Subjective Factor; The Third Generation*
in India, *Mother of 1084*
in Italy, *Carlo Giuliani, Ragazzo; Before the Revolution; China Is Near; Partner*
in Japan, *Diary of a Skinjuku Thief; The Empty Table; Funeral Parade of Roses; The Man Who Left His Will on Film; Throw Away Your Books, Let's Go into the Streets*
in Portugal, *Captains of April*
in Switzerland, *Charles Dead or Alive; Jonah, Who Will Be 25 in the Year 2000; Le Retour d'Afrique*
in Thai, *The Moonhunter*
in US, *Ali; Abduction; Born on the Fourth of July; Drive, He Said; The Enforcer* (Fargo); *Far from Vietnam; Flashback; Getting Straight; Manufacturing Consent: Noam Chomsky and the Media; Medium Cool; 1969; One PM; Patty Hearst; Route One/USA; Rude Awakening; Running on Empty; '68; Trade Off; Underground* (de Antonio)
in general, *Contre l'Oubli*

Rhys, Jean, films adapted from work, *Quartet; Wide Sargasso Sea*

Rice, Anne, films adapted from work, *Interview With the Vampire; Queen of the Damned*

Richardson, Samuel, film adapted from work, *Mistress Pamela*

Richler, Mordecai, film adapted from work, *The Apprenticeship of Duddy Kravitz*

Ridley, John, film adapted from work, *U Turn*

Rimbaud, Arthur, film about, *Total Eclipse*

Rimsky-Korsakov, Nikolai, film about, *Song of Scheherazade*

Rivas, Manuel, film adapted from work, *Butterfly's Tongue*

Riverboats, etc *The African Queen; L'Atalante; Boatman* (Rosi); *The Flame of New Orleans; Lakeboat; Show Boat* (Whale); *Show Boat* (Sidney); *The Song of Chao-Phrya; Steamboat Bill*

Road movies
Aust, *The Adventures of Priscilla Queen of the Desert; Heaven's Burning; Spider and Rose Backlash; Backroads; Over the Hill; Roadgames; Slate, Wyn and Me*
Can, *Candy Mountain*
China, *A Story of Women*
Cuba, *Guantanamera*
Fin, *Take Care of Your Scarf, Tatjana*
Fr, *Aux Yeux du monde; IP5; Je suis né d'une cigogne; The Lady in the Car with Glasses and a Gun; Merci la vie; Pierrot le Fou; A Strange Place to Meet; Les Valseuses; Violette et François; Western*
GB, *The Buttercup Chain; Chicago Joe and the Showgirl; Coast to Coast* (Johnson); *Fords on Water; Gallivant; Hard Road; North of Vortex; Radio On; Radio On (Remix); The Sheltering Sky; Soft Top, Hard Shoulder; Restless Natives; Vroom*
Fin, *Ariel; Il Capitano; Leningrad Cowboys Go America*
Ger, *Alice in the Cities; Burning Life; Flickering Roads; Kings of the Road; The Serbian Girl; Summer in the City; Until the End of the World; Wrong Movement*
Greece, *Balkanisateur; Landscape in the Mist*
Ice, *Cold Fever*
Ire, *Joyriders*
It, *La Strada*
Jap, *Kikujiro*
Neth *Another Mother*
NZ, *Goodbye Pork Pie; Starlight Hotel*
Sp, *Hi, Are You Alone?; Lisboa*
US, *Alice Doesn't Live Here Anymore; American Perfekt; Back Roads; Badlands; Below the Belt; Bonnie and Clyde; Boxcar Bertha; Boys on the Side; Bronco Billy; Coast to Coast* (Sargent); *Cohen and Tate; Cold Feet; Crazy Mama; Crossroads* (Hill); *Detour; Dirty Mary, Crazy Larry; Dutch; Easy Rider; Electra Glide in Blue; Fandango; Harry and Tonto; Hollywood or Bust; Jackpot; Jump Tomorrow; It's a Mad, Mad, Mad, Mad World; The Last of the Cowboys; Leaving Normal; The Living End; Lost in America; Mad Love; Motorist; My Own Private Idaho; National Lampoon's Vacation; Old Boyfriends; Out; Paper Moon; Poetic Justice; Powwow Highway; Rafferty and the Gold Dust Twins; Rain Man; The Rain People; Roadside Prophets; Route One/USA; Ruby Cairo; Sitting Ducks; Slither; Stranger Than Paradise; Sugarland Express; To Wong Foo, Thanks for Everything! Julie Newmar; Thelma & Louise; Three for the Road; Tilt; Two-Lane Blacktop; Vanishing Point; Wanda; The Wayward Bus; Wild at Heart*
USSR, *Freedom Is Paradise*

Robbins, Harold, films adapted from work, *The Adventurers; The Betsy; King Creole; The Lonely Lady*

Robbins, Tom, film adapted from work, *Even Cowgirls Get the Blues*

Robin Hood, see **Hood, Robin**

Robots, *A.I. Artificial Intelligence; The Avengers; Bicentennial Man; Bill & Ted's Bogus Journey; Bunker Palace Hotel; Cherry 2000; D.A.R.Y.L.; The Day the Earth Stood Still; Deadly Friend; The Empire Strikes Back; The Empire Strikes Back: Special Edition; Eve of Destruction; Forbidden Planet; Futureworld; Hardware; Josh and S.A.M.; Making Mr Right; Metropolis* (Lang); *The Perfect Woman; The Return of the Jedi; Return of the Jedi: Special Edition; Robinson Crusoe on Mars; RoboCop; RoboCop 2; RoboCop 3; Robot Monster; Short Circuit; Short Circuit 2; Silent Running; Slipstream; Space Truckers; Star Wars; Star Wars Episode II Attack of the Clones; Star Wars, Episode IV, A New Hope; The Stepford Wives; The Terminator; Terminator 2: Judgment Day; Universal Soldier; Weird Science; Westworld*

Rock and pop music (see also music listed by type) documentaries and concert films, *ABBA – The Movie; Big Time; Black Wax; Born to Boogie; Bring on the Night; Completely Pogued; The Concert for Bangladesh; CS Blues; Culture Club – A Kiss Across the Ocean; The Cure in Orange; The Cure Show; Dance Craze; The Decline of Western Civilization; The Decline of Western Civilization Part II; Divine Madness; Don't Look Back; Down from the Mountain; Eric Clapton and His Rolling Hotel; Exodus – Bob Marley Live; Fillmore; From Russia with Rock; Get Back; Gimme Shelter; Hitmakers: The Teens Who Stole Music; Home of the Brave; Imagine; Instrument: Ten Years with the Band Fugazi; Jimi Hendrix; Jimi Plays Berkeley; The Kids Are Alright; Kurt & Courtney; Ladies and Gentlemen, The Rolling Stones; The Last Waltz; Let It Be; Let's Spend the Night Together; Mad Dogs and Englishmen; Message of Love: The Isle of Wight Festival; Monterey Pop; Moonwalker; Nobody Someday; No Nukes; Ode to Cologne; One Plus One; One-Trick Pony; Pink Floyd Live at Pompeii; Pop Gear; Prince – Sign o' the Times; The Punk Rock Movie; Rockshow; Rock Star; Rough Cut and Ready Dubbed; Rust Never Sleeps; Soft on the Inside; Soigne ta Droite; The Song Remains the Same; Stop Making Sense; Teenage Kicks – The Undertones; Truth or Dare; 200 Motels; U2 Rattle and Hum; Wayne's World II; The Wizard of Waukesha; Woodstock; Woodstrock: The Director's Cut; Year of*

the Horse; Yessongs; Ziggy Stardust and the Spiders from Mars
films about rock/pop world, *The Adventures of Ford Fairlane; Backbeat; Beyond the Valley of the Dolls; Breaking Glass; The Bodyguard; Buddy's Song; Candy Mountain; Catch Us If You Can; The Commitments; Dead Beat; The Doors; Fast Forward; The Five Heartbeats; Four Flies on Grey Velvet; G:MT Greenwich Mean Time; Grace of My Heart; Hairspray; Heartbreakers; Hearts of Fire; Heaven Tonight; Home Before Midnight; Hypnotised and Hysterical (Hairstylist Wanted); It's All Happening; I Wanna Hold Your Hand; Josie and the Pussycats; Jungle Story; Labyrinth of Passion; Leningrad Cowboys Go America; More Bad News; Parking; Pelvis; Perfect Blue; Performance; Phantom of the Paradise; Play It Cool; Privilege* (Watkins); *Queen of the Damned; Renaldo and Clara; Roadie; The Rose; Rude Boy; Satisfaction; Singles; 6.5 Special; Smithereens; Spice World; Stardust; Starstruck; Still Crazy; Suicide Club; Superstar: The Karen Carpenter Story; Take It or Leave It; Tapeheads; This Is Spinal Tap; Thunder Alley; Tina: What's Love Got to Do With It; Tokyo Pop; Trick or Treat; 24 Hour Party People; Velvet Goldmine; The Wedding Singer; Welcome to L.A.; Who Is Harry Kellerman and Why Is He Saying Those Terrible Things About Me?; Wild in the Streets; Wild West; The Year of My Japanese Cousin; You Light Up My Life; Zazie*
rock/pop musicals, *All This and World War Two; Babymother; Body Rock; Breakin'; The Butterfly Ball; Can't Stop the Music; Catch My Soul; Ferry Cross the Mersey; Flame; Flashdance; Girls Just Want to Have Fun; A Hard Day's Night; Head; Help!; It Couldn't Happen Here; The Music Machine; Never Too Young to Rock; Pink Floyd; The Wall; Purple Rain; Quadrophenia; Rock'n'Roll High School; The Rocky Horror Picture Show; Rooftops; Saturday Night Fever; Sergeant Pepper's Lonely Hearts Club Band; Staying Alive; A Swingin' Summer; Thank God It's Friday; Three for All; Times Square; Tommy; Under the Cherry Moon*

Rock'n'roll
original '50s, *Bye Bye Birdie; Don't Knock the Rock; The Girl Can't Help It; Go, Johnny Go!; Idle on Parade; Jailhouse Rock; King Creole; Rock Rock Rock!*
nostalgia, *Almost Famous; American Hot Wax; La Bamba; The Buddy Holly Story; Cry-Baby; Eddie and the Cruisers; Elvis; Grease; Grease 2; Great Balls of Fire!; That'll Be the Day; That Thing You Do;*
documentaries/concert films, *Elvis on Tour; Elvis – That's the Way It Is; Glastonbury: The Movie; Hail Hail! Rock'n'Roll; Let the Good Times Roll; The London Rock and Roll Show; This Is Elvis*

Rodeos, *Arena; 8 Seconds; F.T.W.; The Honkers; Junior Bonner; J.W. Coop; The Lusty Men; The Misfits; My Heroes Have Always Been Cowboys; When the Legends Die*

Rodgers, Richard
and Hammerstein, Oscar, musicals by, *Carousel; The King and I* (Lang); *The King and I* (Rich); *Oklahoma; South Pacific*
and Hart, Lorenz, musicals by, *Babes in Arms; Billy Rose's Jumbo; Hallelujah, I'm a Bum; Love Me Tonight; Pal Joey*

Rodin, Auguste, film about, *Camille Claudel*

Roelfzema, Erik Hazelhoff, film adapted from work, *Soldier of Orange*

Rohmer, Sax, films adapted from work, *The Bride of Fu Manchu; The Face of Fu Manchu; The Fiendish Plot of Dr Fu Manchu; The Mask of Fu Manchu*

Roller skating, *Derby; Kansas City Bomber; Rollerball; Solarbabies; Xanadu*

The Rolling Stones, films about/in performance, *CS Blues; Gimme Shelter; Ladies and Gentlemen; The Rolling Stones; Let's Spend the Night Together; One Plus One*

Rollins, Tim, film about, *Kids of Survival: The Art and Life of Tim Rollins & K.O.S.*

Romania
Romania in film, *Children Underground; Every Day God Kisses Us on the Mouth; Gadjo Dilo; My Giant; Requiem for Dominic; Too Late; Two Deaths; An Unforgettable Summer*
Romanian cinema, *Every Day God Kisses Us on the Mouth; Too Late; An Unforgettable Summer*

Rome, Ancient, and Roman Empire, *The Arena; Ars Amandi; Asterix & Obelix Take on Caesar; Asterix and the Big Fight; Asterix Conquers America; Asterix in Britain; Augustine of Hippo; Barabbas; Ben-Hur* (Niblo); *Ben-Hur* (Wyler); *Caesar and Cleopatra; Caligula; Cleopatra* (DeMille); *Cleopatra* (Mankiewicz); *Demetrius and the Gladiators; Fabiola; The Fall of the Roman Empire; Fellini-Satyricon; Fiddlers Three; A Funny Thing Happened on the Way to the Forum; Gladiator* (Scott); *History Lessons; Julius Caesar; Jupiter's Darling; Masada; Quo Vadis?; The Robe; Roman Scandals; Sebastiane; The Sign of the Cross; Sign of the Gladiator; The Sign of the Pagan; Spartacus; Three Ages; Titus; The Twelve Tasks of Asterix; The Viking Queen*

Rome, post-Roman empire, in film
pre-1900, *The Agony and the Ecstasy; Artemisia*
20th cent, *Bellissima; Besieged; Bits and Pieces; Brutti, sporchi e cattivi; Closed for Family Mourning; La Dolce Vita; Era Notte a Roma; Fellini's Roma; Ginger and Fred; Il Giorno della prima di 'Close Up'; La Luna; Mamma Roma; Night on Earth; Roma, Città Aperta; Roman Holiday; The Roman Spring of Mrs Stone; Russicum; School; The Shoes of the Fisherman; Tenebrae; Terminal Station; Three Coins in the Fountain; 20 Million Miles to Earth; Two Weeks in Another Town; The White Sheik; Whoever Says the Truth Will Die*

Rostand, Edmond, films adapted from work, *Cyrano de Bergerac; Roxanne*

Roth, Joseph, film adapted from work, *The Legend of the Holy Drinker*

Roth, Philip, film adapted from work, *Goodbye Columbus*

Rothschild family, film about, *The House of Rothschild*

Rousseau, Jean-Jacques, film about, *The Roads of Exile*

Rowling, JK, film adapted from work, *Harry Potter and the Philosopher's Stone*

Royalty (see also **British history**)
British, *King Ralph; Royal Wedding; The Mudlark; 25 Years*
generic, etc, *The Princess Diaries; Roman Holiday*

Runaways, teenage (see also **Adolescence, Teenagers and teen movies**), *Adrenaline Drive; Blackout; A Boy Called Hate; Butterfly* (Sarno); *The Delinquents; Foxes; Hardcore; Runners; Mandragora; Marie s'en va-t-en ville; Streetwise; Taking Off; Times Square; Vagabonde; Without a Trace*

Runyon, Damon, films adapted from work, *Bloodhounds of Broadway; Guys and Dolls; Lady for a Day; Lady by Choice; Little Miss Marker; A Slight Case of Murder*

Rural life
in Algeria, *The Citadel* (Chouikh); *Ramparts of Clay*
in Australia, *In the Winter Dark; Sunday Too Far Away; We of the Never Never*
in Bolivia, *The Secret Nation*
in Brazil, *In Cane for Life*
in Britain, *Akenfield; All Creatures Great and Small; Cold Comfort Farm; Dakota Road; Danny the Champion of the World; Dulcima; Far From the Madding Crowd; The Farmer's Wife; Gone to Earth; Ill Fares the Land; It Shouldn't Happen to a Vet; The Land Girls; On the Black Hill; Requiem for a Village; Tess; Waterland; The Woodlanders*
in Burkina Faso, *Tilai; Yaaba*
in Canada, *The Sweet Hereafter; Why Shoot the Teacher*
in China, *Bloody Morning; The Girls to Be Married; The Good Earth; Old Well; On the Hunting Ground; Raise the Red Lantern; Red Sorghum; The Road Home; Sacrificed Youth; The Story of Qiu Ju; Yellow Earth*
in Colombia, *A Matter of Honour*
in Czechoslovakia, *All My Good Countrymen; Cutting It Short; I Love, You Love; Seclusion Near a Forest; The Way Through the Bleak Woods*
in Denmark, *Babette's Feast; Pelle the Conqueror*
in Finland, *Earth Is a Sinful Song; Juha; Täällä Pohjantähden alla*
in France, *Le Beau Serge; Le Cheval d'Orgueil; Farrebique; La Femme du Boulanger; La Fiancée du Pirate; Goupi Mains Rouges; Inutile Envoyer Photo; Jean de Florette; Jour de Fête; Madame Bovary* (Renoir); *Madame Bovary* (Chabrol); *Manon des Sources; One Deadly Summer; Spring into Summer; Will It Snow for Christmas?*
in Germany, *The Inheritors; The Sudden Fortune of the Good People of Kombach*
in Iceland, *Land and Sons*
in India, *The Bogey Man; The Boon; Genesis; Pather Panchali; The Village Has No Walls*
in Iran, *The Cow; Dance of Dust*
in Ireland, *Clash of the Ash; Dancing at Lughnasa; The Field; Fools of Fortune; The Playboys*
in Italy, *Christ Stopped at Eboli; The Tree of Wooden Clogs*
in Japan, *Peasants of the Second Fortress; Sleeping Man; Village of Dreams*
in Netherlands, *Antonia's Line; Little Tony; The Northerners; The Polish Bride*
in New Zealand, *Came a Hot Friday; Vigil*
in Spain, *The Holy Innocents; Jamón, Jamón; The Spirit of the Beehive*
in South Korea, *Village in the Mist*

in Sweden, *The Emigrants; The Ox*
in Taiwan, *At Dawn*
in Thailand, *Puen-Paeng*
in Turkey, *Berdel; Yol*
in US, *Americana; Bloody Mama; Come Next Spring; Country; Cross Creek; Dirty Rice; The Dollmaker; Far North; Field of Dreams; Grandma's Boy; In Country; Kansas; Miles from Home; Northern Lights; Oklahoma; Our Daily Bread; Our Vines Have Tender Grapes; A Place in the Heart; Pumpkinhead; The Reflecting Skin; The River* (Rydell); *The Straight Story; Thunder Road; A Walk in the Spring Rain; Wild in the Country; Winter People*
in USSR and Russia, *Asya's Happiness; Earth* (Dovzhenko); *In That Land; The Orlovs; Outskirts; Riaba Ma Poule; Shadows of Our Forgotten Ancestors; Unfinished Piece for Mechanical Piano; The Wishing Tree*
in Venezuela, *A House with a View of the Sea*
in Vietnam, *Nostalgia for Countryland*
in (former) Yugoslavia, *Virgin* (Karanovic)

Russell, Willy, films adapted from work, *Dancin' Thru the Dark; Educating Rita; Shirley Valentine*

Russia and the Soviet Union, in film (see also **Moscow, Russian and Soviet cinema**)
pre-1917, *Alexander Nevsky; Andrei Rublev; Assassin of the Tsar; The Barber of Siberia; The Battleship Potemkin; The Brothers Karamazov* (Brooks); *The Brothers Karamazov* (Pyriev); *Catherine the Great; The Cherry Orchard; Crime and Punishment* (von Sternberg); *Crime and Punishment* (Kaurismäki); *Dark Eyes; The Dying Swan; The Fixer; Fury* (Calenda); *The Gambler* (Makk); *Ivan the Terrible; Mother* (Pudovkin); *A Nest of Gentlefolk; Nicholas and Alexandra; Oblomov; Of Freaks and Men; Onegin; Rasputin and the Empress; Romance with a Double Bass; A Royal Scandal; The Scarlet Empress; Shadows of Our Forgotten Ancestors; A Slave of Love; Strike; Torrents of Spring; Unfinished Piece for Mechanical Piano; Vassa; War and Peace* (Vidor); *War and Peace* (Bondarchuk); *Waxworks; We Live Again; The Wishing Tree; Die Wunderbare Lüge der Nina Petrowna*
Revolution and after, *Anastasia* (Bluth/Goldman); *Archangel; Assassination of the Tsar; Balalaika; Capitaine Conan; The Commissar; Doctor Zhivago; The End of St Petersburg; The Extraordinary Adventures of Mister West in the Land of the Bolsheviks; The Fall of the Romanov Dynasty; The House on Trubnaya; Knight Without Armour; My English Grandfather; Oktyabr; The Red and the White; Reds; Taurus; The Twelve Chairs; We from Kronstadt; We the Living*
Stalinist era, *Animal Farm; Ballad of a Soldier; Burnt by the Sun; Bye-Bye Babushka; Come and See; Comrade X; Days of Glory; Defence Counsel Sedov; The Devil's Wheel; Don't Move, Die and Rise Again!; Earth* (Dovzhenko); *East-West; Enemy at the Gates; The General Line; Goodbye, Boys; Gulag; The Inner Circle; Khrustalyov, My Car!; Letters from the East; The Life and Extraordinary Adventures of Private Ivan Chonkin; Lost in Siberia; Man With a Movie Camera; The Mechanics of the Brain; Mission to Moscow; Ninotchka; The North Star; One Day in the Life of Ivan Denisovich; Repentance; Red Monarch; Rothschild's Violin; Stalingrad; Sunflower; Testimony; The Thief; We from Kronstadt; When We Were Young*
Late Communist era *Asya's Happiness; The Beast; Blue Mountains; Gorky Park; Moscow Distrusts Tears; Mother and Son; The Orlovs; Pastorale; Red Heat; Streets of Gold; The Theme*
Gorbachev era and after, and post-Communist Russia and former USSR, *The Asthenic Syndrome; Brother; Brothers; Burglar; Bye-Bye Babushka; First Strike; The Flight of the Bee; The Fountain; Freedom Is Paradise; From Russia with Rock; Full Moon; GoldenEye; The Guard; Hands; Happy Days; In Georgia; In That Land; In Thee I Trust; I Wanted to See Angels; The Jackal; Katia Ismaïlova; Killer, The* (Omirbaev); *Leaving Lenin; Little Vera; Micha; 100 Days Days Before the Command; Out of the Present; Outskirts; Plumbum, or a Dangerous Game; Police Academy 7: Mission to Moscow; Prisoner of the Mountains; Mute Witness; Riaba Ma Poule; The Russia House; Russian Ark; Sisters* (Bodrov);*The Stain; Taxi Blues; The Wedding* (Lounguine); *Wednesday 19.7.1961; You Are My Only Love*

Russian and Soviet cinema, *Agony; The Asthenic Syndrome; Asya's Happiness; Ballad of a Soldier; The Barber of Siberia; The Beginning; Brother; Burglar; Burnt by the Sun; By the Law; The Children of Maxim Gorki; Come and See; The Commissar; Defence Counsel Sedov; Dersu Uzala; The Devil's Wheel; Don Quixote; Don't Move, Die and Rise Again!; Dream Flights; The Dying Swan; Earth* (Dovzhenko); *East-West; The End of St Petersburg; The Extraordinary Adventures of Mister West in the Land of the Bolsheviks; The Fall of the Romanov Dynasty; Farewell; Five Evenings; Freedom Is Paradise; Full Moon; The General Line; Goodbye, Boys; The Guard; Hands; Happiness; Happy Days; His Wife's Diary; The House on Trubnaya; I Am Cuba; In That Land; Ivan Mosjoukine, or The Carnival Child; Ivan the Terrible; I Wanted to See Angels; Katia Ismaïlova; Khrustalyov, My Car!; Killer, The* (Omirbaev); *King Lear* (Kozintsev); *The Kreutzer Sonata; The Lady with the Little Dog; Letters from a Dead Man; The Life and Extraordinary Adventures of Private Ivan Chonkin; Little Vera; Man With a Movie Camera; Moscow Distrusts Tears; Mother; Mother and Son; Mute Witness; My Friend Ivan Lapshin; A Nest of Gentle Folk; The New Babylon; Of Fruits and Men; Oktyabr; The Orlovs; Out of the Present; Outskirts; Parade of the Planets; Plumbum, or a Dangerous Game; A Private Conversation; Private Life; Riaba Ma Poule; Russian Ark; Sisters* (Bodrov); *The Snow Queen; Solaris; Storm Over Asia; Strike; Swan Lake – The Zone; Taurus; Taxi Blues; The Theme; The Thief; Treasure Island* (Fridman); *Trial on the Road; Twenty Days Without War; Unfinished Piece for Mechanical Piano; Vassa; War and Peace* (Bondarchuk); *The Wedding* (Lounguine); *We from Kronstadt; Wednesday 19.7.1961; When We Were Young*
non-Russian cinema, *Ashik Kerib; Blue Mountains; The Colour of Pomegranates; The Colour of Pomegranates: Director's Cut; The Flight of the Bee; Journey of a Young Composer; The Legend of the Suram Fortress; My English Grandfather; 100 Days Before the Command; Pastorale; Pirosmani; Repentance; Shadows of Our Forgotten Ancestors; The Stain; The Wishing Tree; You Are My Only Love*

Russo, Richard, film adapted from work, *Nobody's Fool*

Ryan, Cornelius, films adapted from work, *A Bridge Too Far, The Longest Day*

Sabatini, Rafael, films adapted from work, *Captain Blood; Scaramouche; The Sea Hawk*

Sabotage, *La Bataille du Rail; Sabotage; Saboteur*

Sacks, Oliver, films adapted from work, *At First Sight; Awakenings; The Man Who Mistook His Wife for a Hat*

Sade, Marquis de
films about, *Marquis; The Persecution and Assassination of Jean-Paul Marat as Performed by the Inmates of the Asylum of Charenton Under the Direction of the Marquis de Sade; Quills; Sade*
films adapted from work, *Justine; Saló, o le Centoventi Giornate di Sodoma; Le Vice et la Vertu*

Sadism and Sado-masochism, *Blue Velvet; Body of Evidence; Boxing Helena; Broken Mirrors; Brothers and Sisters; Conspirators of Pleasure; Fetishes; Frisk; Gate of Flesh; The General's Daughter; Glissements Progressifs du Plaisir; Hellbound: Hellraiser II; Hellraiser; Hellraiser III: Hell on Earth; Hets; Horrors of the Black Museum; House of Whipcord; Justine; Kitami; Lies; Love Is the Devil – Study for a Portrait of Francis Bacon; The Maids; Maitresse; Mandingo; Martha; The Night Porter; Nine ½ Weeks; Noir et Blanc; Playing God; Preaching to the Perverted; Saló, o le Centoventi Giornate di Sodoma; Seven; Seven Women for Satan; Sick: The Life & Death of Bob Flanagan, Supermasochist; The Story of O; Suite 16; Swept Away…by an Unusual Destiny in the Blue Sea of August; Tie Me Up! Tie Me Down!; Tightrope; Venus in Furs; Voice Over*

Sagan, Carl, film adapted from work, *Contact*

Sagan, Françoise, films adapted from work, *Bonjour Tristesse; Un Peu de Soleil dans l'Eau Froide*

Sailing, see **Sea dramas**

Saint-Exupéry, Antoine de,
film about, *Saint-Ex*
film adapted from work, *The Little Prince*

Saints, films about, *Augustine of Hippo; Brother Sun, Sister Moon; Francesco, giullare di Dio; Giovanna d'Arco al Rogo; Jeanne la Pucelle; La Passion de Jeanne d'Arc; Procès de Jeanne d'Arc; Saint Joan; Sebastiane*

Sale, Richard, films adapted from work, *The Oscar; The White Buffalo*

Salinger, JD, film adapted from work, *My Foolish Heart*

Salsa music, *Crossover Dreams; Hangin' with the Homeboys; Salsa*

Salvation Army, *Guys and Dolls; Major Barbara*

Samoan Americans, *My Crasy Life*

Sams, Gideon, film adapted from work, *The Punk and the Princess*

Samurai, *Cruel Story of the Shogunate's Downfall; The Hidden Fortress; Lightning Swords of Death; The Loyal 47 Ronin of the Genroku Era; Miyamoto Musashi; Nemuri Kyoshiro: The Book of Killing-Rules; Pandemonium; Sanjuro; Sasuke and His Comedians; Seven Samurai; Shin Heike Monogatari; Shogun Assassin; Ninja III – The Domination; The Sword of Doom*
modern, *Ghost Dog: The Way of the Samurai; The New Morning of Billy the Kid; Ronin*

Sand, George, films about, *Les Enfants du siècle; Impromptu; A Song to Remember*

San Francisco, in film
pre-1900, *Gentleman Jim*
1900s–1920, *Barbary Coast; I Remember Mama; San Francisco; The Sisters*
1920s–1930s, *Fog Over Frisco; Greed*
1940s–1950s, *Dark Passage; D.O.A.* (Maté); *Kiss Them For Me; The Sniper; Vertigo*
1960s, *Bullitt; Days of Wine and Roses; '68*
1970s, *The Counsellor; Dirty Harry; The Enforcer* (Fargo); *Family Plot; Fillmore; Foul Play; They Call Me MISTER Tibbs!; Time After Time; The Times of Harvey Milk; What's Up, Doc?*
1980s, *And the Band Played On; Another 48 HRS; Chan Is Missing; Crackers; The Dead Pool; Dim Sum; An Eye for an Eye; 48 HRS; Jagged Edge; Pacific Heights; The Voyage Home; Star Trek IV*
1990s, *Dream with the Fishes; Jade; Kuffs; Metro; Nina Takes a Lover; Signal 7; Sister Act II: Back in the Habit; True Crime*

Santa Claus, see **Christmas films**

Sartre, Jean-Paul, films adapted from work, *Huis Clos; Les Jeux Sont Faits; Les Orgueilleux; La P..... Respectueuse*

Sardinia, in film, *Padre Padrone*

Sargasso Sea, *The Bermuda Triangle; The Lost Continent*

SAS, *Who Dares Wins*

Scarecrows, malevolent, *Scarecrows*

Schine, Cathleen, film adapted from work, *The Misadventures of Margaret*

Schnitzler, Arthur, films adapted from work, *Chain of Desire; Dance of Love; Eyes Wide Shut; La Ronde; New York Nights*

Schools, see **Education and school stories** and **Reform schools**

Schubert, Franz, film about, *Blossom Time*

Schumann, Robert, film about, *Spring Symphony*

Sciascia, Leonardo, film adapted from work, *Open Doors*

Science and scientists (see also **Mad scientists**), *A Beautiful Mind; L'Enfant Sauvage; Enigma; The ExperimentFlatliners; Galileo* (Cavani); *Galileo* (Losey); *The Love Test; Madame Curie; Medicine Man; Mimic; Sphere; The Tingler*

Scotland, in film
pre-1900, *Braveheart; Chasing the Deer; Culloden; The Flesh and the Fiends; The Governess; Kidnapped; Mairi Mhor; Mary of Scotland; Mary Queen of Scots; Mrs Brown; Rob Roy; Sinful Davey*
1900–1940s, *Back-Room Boy; Bonnie Scotland; Cottage to Let; Every Picture Tells a Story; The Ghost of St Michael's; I Know Where I'm Going; Ill Fares the Land; The Kidnappers; Lassie Come Home; My Life So Far; The Prime of Miss Jean Brodie; Shning Victory; Venus Peter; Whisky Galore!*
1950s–1970s, *The Brave Don't Cry; The Bridal Path; Circle of Danger; Geordie; Laxdale Hall; The 'Maggie'; Ratcatcher; Ring of Bright Water; Rockets Galore; Tunes of Glory; The Wicker Man; X the Unknown*
1980s–1990s, *The Acid House; Betty's Brood; The Big Man; Blue Black Permanent; Breaking the Waves; Carla's Song; Comfort and Joy; Conquest of the South Pole; Debt Collector, The; Gregory's Girl; Gregory's Two Girls; The Life of Stuff; Local Hero; Loch Ness; Lucia; The Near Room; Orphans; Play Me Something; Restless Natives; Soft Top, Hard Shoulder; Small Faces; So I Married an Axe Murderer; Staggered; That Sinking Feeling; Tickets for the Zoo; Trainspotting; Urban Ghost Story; Wild Flowers* (Smith); *The Winter Guest*
from 2000, *Complicity; Daddy's Girl; Dog Soldiers; The Little Vampire; One Life Stand; Morvern Callar; Strictly Sinatra; Sweet Sixteen*

Scott, Walter, films adapted from work, *The Adventures of Quentin Durward; Ivanhoe*

Scratching records, film about, *Scratch*

Sea dramas (see also **Pirates, Submarines, Undersea worlds**)
wartime, service, etc, *Above Us the Waves; Action in the North Atlantic; An Annapolis Story; Away All Boats; The Bedford Incident; The Battle of the River Plate; The Battleship Potemkin; Blue Peter; The Boat; The Boat: The Director's Cut; The Bounty; The Bridges at Tokyo-Ri; The Caine Mutiny; Captain Horatio Hornblower; Carry on Admiral; Cockleshell Heroes; Corvette K-225; Crimson Tide; The Cruel Sea; The Enemy Below; Ensign Pulver; Follow the Fleet; Forever England; For Freedom; Gray Lady Down; Hell and High Water; Here Come the Waves; HMS Defiant; The Hunt for Red October; In Harm's Way; In Which We Serve; Islands in the Stream; The Key; Lifeboat; Men of Honor; Mister Roberts; Morning Departure; Murphy's War; Mutiny on the Bounty* (Lloyd); *Mutiny on the Bounty* (Milestone); *Navy Seals; Operation Petticoat; An Officer and a Gentleman; Perfect Strangers; Petticoat Pirates; Remembrance* (Gregg); *Submarine Patrol; They Were Expendable; U-571; Under Siege; The Wackiest Ship in the Army; Watch Your Stern; Yangtse Incident*
other, *Alone on the Pacific; Amistad; Assault on a Queen; Atlantic Adventure; Beyond the Poseidon Adventure; Blue Black Permanent; Captain Jack; Captain Ron; Captains Courageous; The Captain's Table; China Seas; Cinderella Liberty; Dead Calm; Deep Blue Sea; Deep Rising; The Dove; Edge of the World; Fanny; Ferry to Hong Kong; The Ghost Ship; A Girl in Every Port; Golden Rendezvous; Jaws; Jaws 2; Jaws – The Revenge; Juggernaut; King of Alcatraz; The Last Voyage; The Long Voyage Home; Lord Jim; The Lost Continent; The Mad Doctor of Market Street; Manuela; Moby Dick; The Navigator; A Night to Remember; No Answer from F.P.1; The Old Man and the Sea; Orca; Outward Bound; Passage Home; The Perfect Storm; Pirates; The Poseidon Adventure; Raise the Titanic!; Race for the Yankee Zephyr; Remorques; San Demetrio, London; Saps at Sea; Savage Islands; The Sea Chase; The Sea Wolf; Ship of Fools; The Ship That Died of Shame; Sentimental Journey; Si tous les gars du monde…; S.O.S. Titanic; Three Crowns for the Sailor; Titanic* (Selpin); *Titanic* (Negulesco); *Titanic* (Cameron); *Treasure Island* (Heston); *Treasure Island* (Fridman); *Triple Bogey on a Par Five Hole; Tugboat Annie; Two Years Before the Mast; The Viking Women and Their Voyage to the Waters of the Great Sea Serpent; Virus; Waterworld; Western Approaches; White Squall; Wind; Windbag the Sailor; The Windjammer*

Seale, Bobby, film about, *Panther*

Searle, Ronald
films adapted from cartoons, *The Belles of St Trinian's; Blue Murder at St Trinian's; The Pure Hell of St Trinian's; The Wildcats of St Trinian's*
film designed by, *Dick Deadeye, or Duty Done*

Segal, Erich, films adapted from work, *Love Story; Oliver's Story*

Selby Jr, Hubert, films adapted from work, *Last Exit to Brooklyn; Requiem for a Dream*

Senegalese cinema, *Black Girl; Camp Thiaroye; Ceddo; Colobane Express; Emitai; Le Franc; Hyenas; The Little Girl Who Sold the Sun; The Money Order; TGV; Xala*

Sensory awareness, *How Does It Feel?*

Serbia (see also **Croatian cinema, Bosnia, Yugoslavia and former Yugoslavia**)
films about, *Behind Enemy Lines; Pretty Village, Pretty Flame; The Wounds*
Serbian cinema, *Ghetto; The Wounds*

Serial killers, see **Psychopaths and serial killers**

Sex changes and transformations (see also **Hermaphroditism**), *The Christine Jorgensen Story; Come Back to the 5 & Dime, Jimmy Dean, Jimmy Dean; Different for Girls; Dr Jekyll and Sister Hyde; Dog Day Afternoon; Hedwig and the Angry Inch; In a Year with 13 Moons; I Want What I Want; The Law of Desire; Myra Breckenridge; Orlando; Shadey; Swordsman II; The World According to Garp*
by divine/supernatural intervention, *Switch; Turnabout*

Sex films, *Anita; Annie Sprinkle's Herstory of Porn; Ars Amandi; Au Pair Girls; La Bête; Bisexual; Black Emanuelle; Blue Belle; Bolero* (Derek); *La Bonzesse; Café Flesh; Candido Erotico; Celestine, Maid at Your Service; Climax; Confessions of a Window Cleaner; Cousins in Love; The Crush; Cry Uncle; The Deadly Females; Deadly Weapons;*

Deep Throat; The Devil in Miss Jones; The Devil in Miss Jones II; Double Agent 73; Emanuelle and the Last Cannibals; Emmanuelle; Emmanuelle 2; Emmanuelle in Tokyo; Erotic Quartet; Erotique; Female Perversions; Female Vampires; First Time with Feeling; The Fruits of Passion; Girl on a Motorcycle; Goodbye Emmanuelle; House of Whipcord; How Sweet Is Her Valley; I Am Frigid…Why?; Inhibitions; Insatiable; Invitation to Bed; Is There Sex After Marriage?; Le Journal de Lady M; Joy; Laura (Hamilton); *Love in a Women's Prison; Lust and Desire; Madame Claude; Maid for Pleasure; Oh! Calcutta!; Memories within Miss Aggie; My Tutor; Nana* (Wolman); *New York Nights; Penelope 'Pulls It Off'; Prison Girls; Private Lessons; Quante Volte… Quella Notte; Quiet Days in Clichy* (Chabrol); *Quiet Days in Clichy* (Thorsen); *Le Rempart de Béguines; Road to Salina; Sadistic City; Sex Play; Showgirls; Snatched; Street Girls; The Stroller in the Attic; Student Teachers; Succubus; Super 8½; Swedish Massage Parlour; There's No Sex Like Snow Sex; Thundercrack!; Through the Looking Glass; Tierische Liebe; Till Sex Us Do Part; Together; Turkish Delight; The True Story of Eskimo Nell; Under the Doctor; Vanessa; The Violation of Justine; A Virgin for Saint Tropez; The Virgin Machine; The Visitor; Viva Erotica!*

Sex industry (see also **Prostitution**), *Boatman; Boogie Nights; Compromising Positions; Dyn Amo; 8MM; Family Viewing; The Fluffer; The Full Monty; Get Carter; The Glitter Dome; Hardcore; Inserts; Kamikaze Hearts; The Keyhole; La Môme Pigalle; The Lost Son; Love Will Tear Us Apart; Not a Love Story; Of Freaks and Men; Orgazmo; Out of the Dark; The Playbirds; The Players Club; Promise Her Anything; Rate It X; Sex Life in L.A.; Skinless Night; Star 80; Variety*

Sex therapists and sexology, *The Chapman Report; Everything You Always Wanted to Know About Sex, But Were Afraid to Ask; The Harrad Experiment; I Am a Sex Addict; I Will…I Will…for Now; Sex and the Single Girl*

The Sex Pistols, films about, *The Filth and the Fury; The Great Rock'n'Roll Swindle; Sid and Nancy*

Sexual repression, *A Double Tour; The Citadel* (Chouikh); *Claire's Knee; Cockfighter; Crimes of Passion; The Criminal Life of Archibaldo de la Cruz; Deep Throat; Different for Girls; El; Empire of Passion; The Ice Palace* (Blom); *Intersection; Man from Africa and Girl from India; Miss Julie; Morgiana; Paulina; The Piano Teacher; La Senyora; Surrender Dorothy; Tierische Liebe; Tristana; That Obscure Object of Desire; You're a Big Boy Now*

Sexuality, explorations of
Aus, *The Piano Teacher; Tierische Liebe; The Unfish*
Aust, *Sirens; The Umbrella Woman*
Bel, *Je tu il elle; The Sexual Life of the Belgians 1950–1978*
Braz, *The Oyster and the Wind*
Can, *Dreamlife; Eclipse; Family Viewing; Head On; In Praise of Older Women; Kissed; Paris France; 90 Days; A Winter Tan*
China *Shanghai Picnic; Yang ± Yin: Gender in Chinese Cinema*
Cuba, *One Way or Another*
Czech, *Conspirators of Pleasure; Erotikon*
Fr, *Les Amants; A ma soeur!; Amateur; Annabelle partagée; Baise-moi; The Best Way to Walk; La Bête; Bitter Moon; Boy Meets Girl* (Carax); *Charlotte; Un Coeur qui bat; La Collectioneuse; Emmène-moi; A Flame in My Heart; Glissements Progressifs du Plaisir; The Hairdresser's Husband; Immoral Tales; Joy; La Lectrice; Une Liaison Pornographique; The Man Who Loved Women* (Truffaut); *The Mother and the Whore; Néa; N'oublie pas que tu vas mourir; La Nouvelle Eve; Le Parfum d'Yvonne; The Pillow Book; The Pornographer; Pussy Talk; Requiem pour un Vampire; Romance; La Ronde; Sade; Scènes de lit; The Story of O; Sweet Movie; Tango* (Leconte); *Les Valseuses; La Vie de Jésus; Virgin* (Breillat)
GB, *Amateur; The Big Swap; Breaking the Waves; Captives; The Collector; The Cook, the Thief, His Wife and Her Lover; Daddy; Different for Girls; 8½ Women; Further and Particular; I Am a Sex Addict; Inserts; Intimacy; Intimate Relations; Justine; Killing Me Softly; Lady Chatterley's Lover; Look Me in the Eye; Middleton's Changeling; Miss Julie; Naked; The Pillow Book; The Playmaker; The Pleasure Principle; The Rainbow; Sacred Flesh; This Year's Love; Twenty-One; Under the Skin; The Virgin and the Gypsy; Women in Love*
Ger, *Anita; Dances of Vice; Blue Angel; Dance of Love; My Father Is Coming; 3 Women in Love; A Woman in Flames*
Greece, *Female Company*
HK, *Hold You Tight*
Hun, *The Witman Boys*
Ind, *Kama Sutra: A Tale of Love*
Ire, *Nora*
Isr, *Late Marriage*
It, *The Black Holes; Casanova 70; Fellini-Satyricon; Fellini's Casanova; The Last Woman; Malizia; The Naples Connection; Senso; La Signora di Tutti; Stealing Beauty; What?*
Jap, *Abnormal Family: Brother's Wife; Ai No Corrida; Diary of a Shinjuku Thief; Empire of Passion; Gips; The Hair Opera; Heart Beating in the Dark; I Am a S+M Writer; Irezumi – Spirit of Tattoo; Like Grains of Sand; Unloved; Woman of the Dunes*
Mex, *And Your Mother Too; Homework*
Neth, *Au Revoir; The Pillow Book*
NZ, *The Piano*
Phil, *Manila by Night*
Pol, *Dekalog 6: 'Thou shalt not commit adultery'; Dekalog 9: 'Thou shalt not covet thy neighbour's wife'; A Short Film About Love*
Singapore, *Mee Pok Man*
SKor, *Come, Come, Come Upward; Iodo; Motel Cactus; Virgin Stripped Bare by Her Bachelors*
Sp, *Jamón, Jamón; Kika; Life Size; The Mad Monkey; Matador; Mouth to Mouth; Peppermint Frappé; The Red Squirrel; Sex and Lucía; Tie Me Up! Tie Me Down!; The Tit and the Moon*
Swe, *The Devil's Eye; I Am Curious – Yellow; Language of Love; Love Lessons; Miss Julie; More About the Language of Love; The Premonition*
Thai, *The Isle; Jan Dara*
US, *About Last Night; Addicted to Love; American Pie; American Pie 2; Art for Teachers of Children; Blue Movie; Boogie Nights; Born to Be Bad; Boys Don't Cry; Buster and Billie; BUtterfield 8; Call Me Candy; Carnal Knowledge; Casual Sex?; The Centre of the World; The Chapman Report; Crash* (Cronenberg); *The Deadman; Dick; Disclosure; The Doom Generation; Exit to Eden; Eyes Wide Shut; The Fluffer;The General's Daughter; Girl 6; Heavy Petting; I Am a Sex Addict; Jade; John and Mary; The Ladies Man; Last Tango in Paris; Lawn Dogs; Lolita* (Kubrick); *Lolita* (Lyne); *Looking for Mr Goodbar; Love Letters; Man of the Year; The Mafu Cage; The Man Who Loved Women* (Edwards); *Never Talk to Strangers; Oleanna; Orgazmo; Patti Rocks; The People vs. Larry Flynt; A Price Above Rubies; Private Parts; Quills; Schizopolis; Sex Is…; sex, lies and videotape; Sex – The Annabel Chong Story; She Must Be Seeing Things; Skin Deep; Sweet Kill; Swingers; 10; Tropic of Cancer; The Unbearable Lightness of Being; What's New Pussycat?; Whipped; Wild Orchid; Your Friends & Neighbors; Zandalee*
Yugo, *W.R. – Mysteries of the Organism*

Shaffer, Peter, films adapted from work, *Equus; The Royal Hunt of the Sun*

Shakespeare, William
films of plays, *As You Like It* (Cznner); *As You Like It* (Edzard); *The Children's Midsummer Night's Dream; Hamlet* (Plumb); *Hamlet* (Kozintsev), *Hamlet* (Richardson); *Hamlet* (Zeffirelli); *Hamlet* (Branagh); *Hamlet* (Almereyda); *Henry V* (Branagh); *Henry V* (Olivier); *Julius Caesar; King Lear* (Brook); *King Lear* (Kozintsev); *Love's Labour's Lost; Macbeth* (Polanski); *Macbeth* (Welles); *A Midsummer Night's Dream* (Reinhardt); *A Midsummer Night's Dream* (Noble); *A Midsummer Night's Dream* (Hoffman); *Much Ado About Nothing; Othello* (Welles); *Othello* (Burge); *Othello* (Parker); *Richard III* (Olivier); *Richard III* (Loncraine); *Romeo and Juliet; Titus; Twelfth Night; William Shakespeare's Romeo & Juliet; The Winter's Tale*
films based on/influenced by plays, *Beneath the 12-Mile Reef; Best Men; Catch My Soul; Chimes at Midnight; China Girl; Enamorada; Escape from New York; Forbidden Planet; Get Over It; Gypsy Soul; Hamlet* (Coronado); *Hamlet Goes Business; Une Histoire inventée; Joe Macbeth; King Lear* (Godard); *King Ubu; Kiss Me Kate; Kiss Me Kate: 3-D; Men of Respect; A Midsummer Night's Dream* (Coronado); *One Hamlet Less; Prospero's Books; Ran; Rosencrantz and Guildenstern Are Dead; Shakespeare in Love; A Siberian Lady Macbeth; Strange Brew; Tempest; The Tempest; 10 Things I Hate About You; Theatre of Blood; A Thousand Acres; Throne of Blood; Tromeo & Juliet; West Side Story*
miscellaneous, *Beginner's Luck; The Convent; Food of Love; In the Bleak Midwinter; The King Is Alive; Looking for Richard; Men Are Not Gods; Prince of Jutland; Renaissance Man; Shakespeare-Wallah*

Sharpe, Tom, film adapted from work, *Wilt*

Shaw, George Bernard, films adapted from work, *Caesar and Cleopatra; Major Barbara; The Millionairess; My Fair Lady; Pygmalion; Saint Joan*

Shaw, Irwin, films adapted from work, *In the French Style; Out of the Fog; Two Weeks in Another Town; The Young Lions*

Shaw, Robert, film adapted from work, *The Man in the Glass Booth*

Shawn, Wallace, film adapted from work, *The Designated Mourner*

Seberg, Jean, film about, *From the Journals of Jean Seberg*

Sheldon, Edward, film adapted from work, *Lulu Belle*

Sheldon, Sidney, films adapted from work, *The Naked Face; The Other Side of Midnight*

Shelley, Mary (see also **Frankenstein stories**), films about, *Gothic; Haunted Summer; Roger Corman's Frankenstein Unbound*

Shepard, Sam, films adapted from work, *Far North; Fool for Love; Simpatico*

Sherlock Holmes stories, see **Conan Doyle**

Sherman, Martin, film adapted from work, *Bent*

Sherman, Richard and Robert, musical by, *The Slipper and the Rose*

Sherriff, RC, films adapted from work, *Aces High; Home at Seven; Journey's End*

Sherwood, Robert, films adapted from work, *Idiot's Delight; The Petrified Forest*

Shetland Isles, in film, *Edge of the World*

Shields, Carol, film adapted from work, *Swann*

Shilts, Randy, film adapted from work, *And the Band Played On*

Shipyards, *Film from the Clyde; Shipyard Sally*

Shishgall, Oscar, film adapted from work, *The Man I Married;*

Shostakovich, Dmitri, film about, *Testimony*

Show business (see also **Hollywood and the movie business**)
agents and critics, *Broadway Danny Rose; Enzo, Domani a Palermo!; The Man Who Came to Dinner; Naughty but Nice; Sensations of 1945*
child stars, *Bellissima*
life backstage, and backstage musicals, *All That Jazz; The Bandwagon; Blue Skies; Broadway Melody of 1936; Carnival; Dames; Dance Girl, Dance; Dimples; Down to Earth; Driving Me Crazy; DuBarry Was a Lady; East Side Story; The Fan; Footlight Parade; For Me and My Gal; 42nd Street; Franchesca Page; Gold Diggers of 1933; Gold Diggers of 1935; Gold Diggers of 1937; Gypsy; I Love Melvin; Inside Daisy Clover; The Leading Man; Lucky Break; Lullaby of Broadway; 1988: The Remake; The Producers; Raise the Roof; The Silent Thrush; Sing; Stepping Out; Summer Stock; There's No Business Like Show Business; Torch Song; Trois Places pour le 26; You'll Never Get Rich; You Were Never Lovelier; Ziegfeld Girl; Zouzou*
music hall and vaudeville, *Applause; Ay! Carmela; Babes in Arms; Champagne Charlie; The Daughter of Rosie O'Grady; Elstree Calling; The Entertainer; Evergreen; Falling for You; Funny Girl; Funny Lady; Ginger and Fred; Grip of the Strangler; Harry and Walter Go to New York; King of Burlesque; Ladies of the Chorus; Lady of Burlesque; Let the People Sing; Luci del Varietà; Mother Wore Tights; My favorite Blonde; Nana* (Arzner); *Nana* (Renoir); *The Old-Fashioned Way; Piaf; The Sunshine Boys; Tap; Underneath the Arches; Viva Maria; Yankee Doodle Dandy; Zaza*
nightclubs, cabaret, discos, etc, *About Mrs Leslie; Blaze; Bloodhounds of Broadway; The Blue Angel; Broadway; Cabaret; The Cabinet of Dr Caligari; The Cotton Club; The Crazy Horse of Paris; Dark Habits; Dick Tracy; Dr M; Don't Bother to Knock* (Baker); *Exotica; Expresso Bongo; The Fabulous Baker Boys; 54; A Foreign Affair; Ghost Catchers; Girls! Girls! Girls!; Greenwich Village; Harlem Nights; High Tide; Human Traffic; Invincible; Kansas City; Killer's Kiss; The Lemon Sisters; Little Voice; Lola; The Mambo Kings; The Man I Love; Marked Woman; Mickey One; Mr Saturday Night; La Môme Pigalle; Night and the City* (Dassin); *Punchline; Road House* (Negulesco); *Rose of Washington Square; Rub Love; Salón México; Salt & Pepper; Seven Sinners* (Garnett); *The Shining Hour; Side by Side; Song of Songs; Stories of the Kronen; 30 Is a Dangerous Age, Cynthia; This Is My Life; Too Late Blues; Top Dog; Vivacious Lady; Die Wunderbare Lüge der Nina Petrowna; Yo soy así*
photonovels, *The White Sheik*
seaside and street entertainers, *King of Masks; The Punch and Judy Man*
singers and songwriters, *Abuzer Baklava; Beaches; Bert Rigby, You're a Fool; The Best Things in Life Are Free; Cléo de 5 à 7; Coyote Ugly; Duets; For the Boys; Follow a Star; The Girl Can't Help It; Glitter; Hear My Song; I Could Go On Singing; It Happened in Brooklyn; It's a Wonderful World; Lady Sings the Blues; The Lemon Sisters; Louis Prima: The Wildest; Love Me or Leave Me; Lulu Belle; Mr Music; My Generation; Pennies from Heaven; Será Posible el Sur; Strictly Sinatra; Superstar: The Karen Carpenter Story; That Thing You Do!; The Tommy Steele Story; The Wedding Singer*
travelling shows, *Bronco Billy; Matinee Idol; Meet Me at the Fair; The Platform*

Show jumping, *International Velvet; Something to Talk About*

Shrinking, of humans (see also **Carroll, Lewis**), *The Devil-Doll; Dr Cyclops; Fantastic Voyage; Gulliver's Travels; Honey, I Shrunk the Kids; The Incredible Shrinking Man; The Incredible Shrinking Woman; The Indian in the Cupboard; Jumanji; The Three Worlds of Gulliver*

Shute, Nevil, films adapted from work, *No Highway; On the Beach; The Pied Piper; A Town Like Alice*

Siberia, in film, *Dersu Uzala; Farewell; Gulag; Lost in Siberia; One Day in the Life of Ivan Denisovich; We Live Again*

Sicily, in film, *First Light of Dawn; The Godfather; The Godfather Part II; The Godfather Part III; Enzo, Domani a Palermo!; In Nome della Legge; Kaos; Malèna; Placido Rizzotto; Salvatore Giuliano; The Sicilian; Sicilian Cross; Sicily!; Sparrow; Totò Who Lived Twice; The Uncle from Brooklyn*

Sidhwa, Bapsi, film adapted from work, *Earth* (Mehta)

Sienkiewicz, Henryk, films adapted from work, *The Deluge; Quo Vadis?*

Silent films
Aus, *Hands of Orlac*
China, *The Highway; Little Toys*
Czech, *Erotikon*
Den, *People of the North Sea*
Fr, *L'Argent* (L'Herbier); *La Chute de la Maison Usher; El Dorado* (L'Herbier); *Fantômas; Le Fantôme du Moulin Rouge; La Fille de l'Eau; L'Inhumaine* (L'Herbier); *J'Accuse* (Gance, 1918); *Maldone; Napoléon* (Gance); *Ménilmontant; La Passion de Jeanne d'Arc; La Petite Marchande d'allumettes; Prix de Beauté; Le Sang d'un Poète; La Souriante Madame Beudet; Le Tournoi; Les Vampires*
GB, *The Battle for the Somme; Champagne; Downhill; Easy Virtue; The Farmer's Wife; The Lodger; The Manxman; Piccadilly; The Rat; The Ring; Underground* (Asquith)
Ger, *Adventures of Prince Achmed, The; Berlin – die Sinfonie der Grosstadt; Diary of a Lost Girl; Faust* (Murnau); *The Finances of the Grand Duke; The Last Laugh; Die Nibelungen; Nosferatu – Eine Symphonie des Grauens; Pandora's Box; People on Sunday; Schatten; Secrets of a Soul; South; Die Spinnen; Spione; Waxworks; Die Weber; The White Hell of Piz Palu; Woman in the Moon; Die Wunderbare Lüge der Nina Petrowna*
It, *Pinocchio*
Jap, *Crossways; I Was Born, But…; A Page of Madness*
Swe, *Gunnar Hedes Saga; Herr Arnes Pengar; Johan; The Outlaw and His Wife; Witchcraft Through the Ages*
US, *Beggars of Life; Ben-Hur* (Niblo); *The Big Parade* (Vidor); *The Birth of a Nation; Blind Husbands; Blood and Sand; Broken Blossoms* (Griffith); *The Cameraman; Camille; The Cobra; The Crowd; Dr Jekyll and Mr Hyde* (Robertson); *The Eagle; Flesh and the Devil; Foolish Wives; The General* (Keaton/Bruckman); *A Girl in Every Port; The Gold Rush; Go West; Grandma's Boy; The Great K & A Train Robbery; He Who Gets Slapped; Intolerance; The Iron Mask; The Isle of Love; The Kid Brother; The Kiss* (Feyder); *The Last Command; Lucky Star; The Magician; The Merry-Go-Round; The Merry Widow; The Mystery of the Leaping Fish; The Phantom of the Opera; Sadie Thompson; Safety Last; Sally of the Sawdust; Salome; The Salvation Hunters; The Saphead; The Scarlet Letter* (Sjöström); *Spite Marriage; Steamboat Bill; Seven Chances; 7th Heaven* (Borzage); *Show People; Sunrise; The Thief of Bagdad* (Walsh); *Three Ages; Twin Pawns; The Unholy Three* (Browning); *The Unknown; Way Down East; The Wedding March; Why Worry?; The Wind* (Sjöström); *A Woman of Paris*
USSR, *Battleship Potemkin; By the Law; The Devil's Wheel; Earth* (Dovzhenko); *The Dying Swan; The End of St Petersburg; The Fall of the Romanov Dynasty; Happiness; The House on Trubnaya; The Man with the Movie Camera; The Mechanics of the Brain; Mother* (Pudovkin); *The New Babylon; Storm Over Asia; Strike*
modern silents, *Careful; Film; The Island* (Shindo); *Sidewalk Stories; Silent Movie; The Thief*

Sillitoe, Alan, films adapted from work, *The Loneliness of the Long Distance Runner; The Ragman's Daughter; Saturday Night and Sunday Morning*

Simenon, Georges, films adapted from work, *Le Chat; En Cas de Malheur; L'Etoile du Nord; Les Fantômes du Chapelier; L'Horloger de St Paul; In All Innocence; The Man Who Watched Trains Go By; Monsieur Hire; La Neige était sale; La Nuit du Carrefour; Temptation Harbour; La Tête d'un Homme*

Simon, Neil, films adapted from work, *Barefoot in the Park; Biloxi Blues; Brighton Beach Memoirs; Broadway Bound; California Suite; Chapter Two; The Cheap Detective; Come Blow Your Horn; The Goodbye Girl; The Heartbreak Kid; I Ought to Be in Pictures; The Last of the Red Hot Lovers; The Marrying Man; The Odd Couple; The Odd Couple II; Only When I Laugh; The Out-of-Towners* (Hiller); *The Out-of-Towners* (Weisman); *Plaza Suite; Seems Like Old Times*

Singapore
Singapore cinema, *Bugis Street; Eating Air; Mee Pok Man; 12 Storeys*
Singapore, in film, *Bugis Street; Fatal Reaction: Rogue Trader; Singapore; Saint Jack; 12 Storeys; World for Ransom*

Singer, Isaac Bashevis, films adapted from work, *American Stories; Enemies, a Love Story; The Musician of Lublin; Yentl*

Singles bars, *Looking for Mr Goodbar*

Sisters, relationships between (see also **Brothers, Sisters and brothers**), *Angela; Careful, He Might Hear You; Crimes of the Heart; Diabolo Menthe; Female Perversions; The German Sisters; Gert and Daisy's Weekend; Happiness; Hilary and Jackie; Hotel Sorrento; The House of Bernarda Alba; Interiors; In This Our Life; Kadosh; The Invisible Circus; The Last Days of Chez Nous; Little Women* (Cukor); *Little Women* (Armstrong); *The Mafu Cage; The Man I Love; Marvin's Room; The Moon Has Risen; My Sister Eileen; My 20th Century; Nénette et Boni; Orphans of the Storm; Practical Magic; Radiance; sex, lies and videotape; The Silence* (Bergman); *Sisters* (De Palma); *Sisters* (Bodrov); *The Sisters; Sisters of Gion; Sisters or the Balance of Happiness; Skin of Man, Heart of Beast; Slightly Scarlet; Some Girls; Sweetie; They Were Sisters; Three Sisters* (Olivier); *Three Sisters* (von Trotta); *Under the Skin; Ursula and Glenys; The Whales of August*

Sisters and brothers, relationships between, *China Is Near; Close My Eyes; Daddy's Dyin' – Who's Got the Will?; Dancing at Lughnasa; Dead Liqueur; El Norte; Jack Be Nimble; Jacknife; Leap into the Void; The Legend of Billy Jean; Love Streams; Ma Saison Préférée; Mullaway; Organ; The Prince of Tides; Sélect Hotel; Speaking Parts; The Strange Affair of Uncle Harry; Tokyo Kyodai; Triple Bogey on a Par Five Hole*

Sixties counter culture (see also **Revolutionaries and radicals**)
Can, *Comic Book Confidential; The True Nature of Bernadette*
Fr, *L'An 01; La Fiancée du Pirate; Girl on a Motorcycle; La Vallée*
GB, *Donald Cammell: The Ultimate Performance; Hideous Kinky; Last Day of Summer; Petulia; Tonite Let's All Make Love in London; The White Bus*
Port, *Doc's Kingdom*
Swe *I Am Curious – Yellow*
US, *Alice's Restaurant; Between the Lines; The Big Chill; The Big Fix; The Blues Brothers; Bob and Carol and Ted and Alice; BS I Love You; Bunny O'Hare; Chappaqua; Cheech and Chong's Next Movie; Chelsea Girls; Ciao Manhattan; David Holtzman's Diary; Doc's Kingdom; Don't Make Waves; The Doors; Dynamite Chicken; Easy Rider; Fritz the Cat; Girl on a Motorcycle; Gas-s-s-s, or It Became Necessary to Destroy the World in Order to Save It; Getting Straight; The Graduate; Greetings; The Guru; Hair; Head; Heavy Traffic; How to Commit Marriage; I Love You, Alice B. Toklas!; Jimi Plays Berkeley; Kitchen* (Warhol/Tavel); *Lonesome Cowboys; Manson; Milestones; Monterey Pop; 1969; Nobody's Fool; The Nine Lives of Fritz the Cat; Out; Psych-Out; Purple Haze; Return Engagement; Return of the Secaucus Seven; Rude Awakening; The Sandpiper; '68; A Soldier's Daughter Never Cries; Sunshine* (Sargent); *Sunshine Part II; Taking Off; The Trip; We Can't Go Home Again; Wild in the Streets; Woodstock; Woodstock: The Director's Cut; You're a Big Boy Now*
Yugo, *W.R. – Mysteries of the Organism*

Sjöwall and Wahlöö, films adapted from work, *Beck; The Laughing Policeman; The Man from Mallorca; The Man on the Roof*

Skateboarding, *Dogtown and Z-Boys; Gleaming the Cube; Skateboard*

Skiing, *Avalanche; Black Diamond Rush; Downhill Racer; The Great Ecstasy of Woodcarver Steiner; Hot Dog…The Movie; The Other Side of the Mountain; The Ski Bum; Ski Patrol*

Slavery
in Africa, *Amistad; Cobra Verde; The Middle Passage; Sankofa; The Silences of the Palace*
in American South, *The Autobiography of Miss Jane Pittman; Beloved; Freedom Road; Jefferson in Paris; Mandingo; Slavers; Song of the South; Uncle Tom*
in ancient world, *The Arena; Spartacus*
in Caribbean, *Blacksnake; Queimada!*
in China, *Buddha's Lock*
white, *Harem*

Slaughterhouses, *Cal; Meat; Le Sang des Bêtes*

Slovakian cinema, *The Garden; I Love, You Love*

Slovenian cinema, *No Man's Land* (Tanovic)

Small town life
in Argentina, *A Place in the World*
in Australia, *Deadly; Shame*
in Belgium, *Les Convoyeurs Attendent*
in Canada, *The Bay Boy; Bye Bye Blues; Paperback Hero*
in China, *Ju Dou*
in Czechoslovakia, *Capricious Summer; The Firemen's Ball*
in France, *The Colour of Lies; Uranus*
in Germany, *The Nasty Girl*
in Italy, *Cinema Paradiso; Cinema Paradiso: The Special Edition; Splendor; I Vitelloni*
in Japan, *The Outer Way*
in Norway, *Bloody Angels*
in Taiwan, *Darkness and Light*
in US, *Affliction; All the Right Moves; Arachnophobia; Baby Blue Marine; Best Laid Plans; The Best of Times; Beyond the Forest; The Blob; Blue Velvet; The 'burbs; Bus Riley's Back in Town; Citizen's Band; Clash By Night; Confessions of a Suburban Girl; Dadetown; A Dangerous Woman; Doc Hollywood; Earth vs the Spider; Edward Scissorhands; The Experts; Full Moon in Blue Water; God's Country; Gremlins; Groundhog Day; Halloween; Halloween 4; The Return of Michael Myers; Halloween: The Curse of Michael Myers; Heavy; Henry Fool; Hope Floats; The Hot Spot; The Ice Storm; It's a Gift; It's a Wonderful Life; It's the Old Army Game; I Want You; Kid; Has Anybody Seen My Gal; Lady in White; The Last Picture Show; The Lawless; Liebestraum; Lone Star; The Love Letter; Meet Me at the Fair; Meet the Applegates; Motel; Murphy's Romance; The Man on the Flying Trapeze; Matinee; Mystic Pizza; The Next Voice You Hear…; Nobody's Fool; October Sky; One True Thing; Other Men's Women; Our Town; Painted Heart; Parents; Paris Trout; Peyton Place; Phenomenon; The Positively True Adventures of the Alleged Texas Cheerleader-Murdering Mom; The Prince of Pennsylvania; Public Access; Queens of the Big Time; Rally 'round the Flag, Boys!; River's Edge; Rosalie Goes Shopping; Safe Passage; Simon Birch; Storm Center; The Sun Shines Bright; Testament* (Littman); *Texasville; These Three; This Boy's Life; Tremors; True Stories; Trust; Twin Peaks; Twin Peaks: Fire Walk With Me; The Unbelievable Truth; Vernon Florida; The War; Welcome Home, Roxy Carmichael; The Well; When Willie Comes Marching Home; The Wild One*

Smiley, Jane, film adapted from work, *A Thousand Acres*

Smith, Dodie, films adapted from work, *Autumn Crocus; One Hundred and One Dalmatians* (Reitherman/ Luske/Geronimi); *101 Dalmatians* (Herek)

Smith, Lady Eleanor, film adapted from work, *The Man in Grey*

Smith, Harry, film about, *American Magus*

Smith, Stevie, film about, *Stevie*

Smith, Wilbur, films adapted from work, *Gold; The Mercenaries; Shout at the Devil*

Smoking,
giving up, *Cold Turkey*
effects of, *The Insider*

Smuggling, *Air America; Best Revenge; The Breaking Point* (Curtiz); *Butterfly and Flowers; Cold Feet; Desire; Dr Syn, Alias the Scarecrow; The French Connection; French Connection II; Green Grow the Rushes; Highway SocietyJamaica Inn; Loin; The Man in the Street; Moonfleet; No Man's Land* (Tanner); *To Have and Have Not; Whisky Galore!; The Wilby Conspiracy*

Snooker, see **Pool and snooker**

Snowmen, as guardian angel, *Jack Frost*

Social workers, *Welfare; The Whispers*

Soldiers returning (see also **Vietnam veterans**), *Baby Blue Marine; The Blue*

Dahlia; The Best Years of Our Lives; The Big Parade (Vidor); *Crossfire; Dark City; Going All the Way; Green Fish; Hail the Conquering Hero; The Hi-Lo Country; The History of a Man's Face; Maria's Lovers; The Marriage of Maria Braun; The Private Affairs of Bel Ami; Some Kind of Hero; Somewhere in the Night; A Walk in the Clouds*

Somalia, in film, *Black Hawk Down*

Solzhenitsyn, Alexander, film adapted from work, *One Day in the Life of Ivan Denisovich*

Sondheim, Stephen, films adapted from his work, *A Funny Thing Happened on the Way to the Forum; Gypsy* (LeRoy); *A Little Night Music; West Side Story*

Sophocles, films adapted from work, *The Cannibals; Elektreia; Oedipus the King; Oedipus Rex*

Sosa, Mercedes, film about, *Serà Posible el Sur*

Soul music, *The Five Heart; Soul to Soul; Wattstax; The Wiz*

South, The American
Old South, *Beloved; Drum; Freedom Road; Gone With the Wind; The Green Pastures; The Klansmen; The Littlest Rebel; Mandingo; Our Hospitality; Prisoner of Shark Island; Raintree County; Song of the South; Tom Sawyer*
post-Civil War, *Angel Baby; The Apostle; Baby Doll; The Ballad of the Sad Café; Bootleggers; Boxcar Bertha; Brubaker; Buster and Billy; The Cabin in the Cotton; Cape Fear* (Thompson); *Cape Fear* (Scorsese); *Cat on a Hot Tin Roof; The Chamber; The Color Purple; Cookie's Fortune; Cool Hand Luke; Crazy in Alabama; Crimes of the Heart; Crossroads* (Hill); *The Delta; Doc Hollywood; Double Jeopardy; Driving Miss Daisy; The Drowning Pool; Elmer Gantry; Eve's Bayou; Fled; Fried Green Tomatoes at the Whistle Stop Café; Gator; George Washington; The Grass Harp; The Heart Is a Lonely Hunter; Heaven's Prisoners; Hound-Dog Man; The Intruder; Intruder in the Dust; Judge Priest; Just Cause; The Liberation of L.B. Jones; The Little Foxes; The Long Hot Summer; Love Field; Midnight in the Garden of Good and Evil; Miss Firecracker; Mississippi Blues; Mississippi Burning; Mississippi Masala; Monster's Ball; My Cousin Vinny; My Dog Skip; The Neon Bible; O Brother, Where Art Thou?; Ode to Billy Joe; One False Move; Other Voices Other Rooms; Paris Trout; Passion Fish; Period of Adjustment; The Players Club; La P..... Respectueuse; The Rainmaker; Rambling Rose; Reflections in a Golden Eye; The Reivers; Rich in Love; Ruby Gentry; Scorchers; sex, lies and videotape; Sling Blade; A Soldier's Story; Son of Dracula; The Southerner; Steel Magnolias; Stone Cold; Storyville; Sud; Summer and Smoke; Swamp Thing; Sweet Bird of Youth* (Brooks); *Sweet Bird of Youth* (Roeg); *They Won't Forget; This Property Is Condemned; Thunder and Lightning; Tobacco Road; To Kill a Mockingbird; Traveller; The Traveling Executioner; Treasure of Matecumbe; Two Moon Junction; White Lightning; Wild at Heart; Wise Blood; W.W. and the Dixie Dancekings*

South Africa
South African cinema, *Beautiful People; Boesman and Lena* (Devenish); *Boesman & Lena* (Berry); *Chikin Bizniz; Dangerous Ground; Dust; e'Lollipop; Get Real; The Gods Must Be Crazy; The Gods Must Be Crazy II; Headhunter; Hillbrow Kids; Jobman; Jump the Gun; The Long Night's Journey into Day; Man Who Drove with Mandela; Mapantsula; Marigolds in August; Sarafina!; Saturday Night at the Palace; Shot Down; The Stick; he Theory of Flight; Three Bullets for a Long Gun; Tigers Don't Cry*
South Africa in film, *Boesman and Lena* (Devenish); *Boesman & Lena* (Berry); *Bopha!; Breaker Morant; Buried Alive; The Capetown Affair; Chikin Bizniz; Come Back Africa; Cry Freedom; Dangerous Ground; A Dry White Season; Dust Devil; Friends; Gold; Headhunter; Hillbrow Kids; Jump the Gun; Last Grave at Dimbaza; Lethal Weapon 2; Long Night's Journey into Day; Mandela; The Man Who Drove with Mandela; On the Wire; The Power of One; A Private Life; The Quarry; Saturday Night at the Palace; South Africa Belongs to Us; Spoor; Too White for Me; Untamed; Wheels & Deals; The Wilby Conspiracy; Windprints; A World Apart; Young Winston; Zulu; Zulu Dawn*
anti-apartheid movement abroad, *Blue Notes and Exiled Voices; Jabula – A Band in Exile; Patu!*

Southern, Terry, films adapted from work, *Candy; The Magic Christian*

Space travel, see **Astronauts and contemporary space travel**

Spain, in film
pre-1936, *The Adventures of Gerard; Belle Epoque; Carmen* (DeMille); *Carmen* (Rosi); *Christopher Columbus: The Discovery; Don Quichotte; Don Quixote; El Cid; The Fencing Master; 1492: Conquest of Paradise; The Heritage; The House of Bernarda Alba; The Saragossa Manuscript; The Suna Also Rises; That Lady; Tristana*
Civil War, *Ay! Carmela; Blockade; Butterfly's Tongue; Confidential Agent; The Devil's Backbone; L'Espoir; For Whom the Bell Tolls; The Good Fight; Land and Freedom; The Last Train from Madrid; Libertarias; The Long Holidays of 1936; El Mar*
Franco era, *The Bobo; Broken Arrow 29; La Caza; La Guerre est finie; The Holy Innocents; The Pleasure Seekers; Poachers; Race, The Spirit of Franco; The Running Man* (Reed); *The South; The Spirit of the Beehive; Viridiana*
post-Franco, *Anita Takes a Chance; Barcelona; Costa Brava (Family Album); A Body in the Forest; Bwana; Cría Cuervos; Esperanza & Sardinas; Fast, Fast; First Effort; The Flower of My Secret; Golden Balls; Hi, Are You Alone?; How to Be a Woman and Not Die in the Attempt; I Will Survive; Jealousy; Jump into the Void; The Law of Desire; La Madre Muerta; Morvern Callar; Mouth to Mouth; My Silly Mother; Pau and His Brother; The Red Squirrel; Second Skin; Secrets of the Heart; Secrets of the Phantom Caves; Sexy Beast; Siesta; Solas; Stories of the Kronen; Taxi; Ten Days Without Love; The Tit and the Moon; Torrente, the Dumb Arm of the Law; Vacas; What Have I Done to Deserve This?; Wheels on Meals; Women on the Verge of a Nervous Breakdown; Work in Progress; Yo soy así*

Spanish cinema, *Acción Mutante; The Adversary; A ma soeur!; All About My Mother; Anguish; Anita Takes a Chance; Ay! Carmela; Back of the World; Bad Man's River; A Bench in the Park; Blazing Guns; Blood Wedding; B. Must Die; A Body in the Forest; A Business Affair; Butterfly Effect; Butterfly's Tongue; Bwana; Calle Mayor; La Campana del Infierno; Captains of April; Caresses; Carmen* (Saura); *China 9, Liberty 37; La Ciénaga; Costa Brava – A Family Album; Cría Cuervos; La Caza; The Day of the Beast; The Devil's Backbone; Django Kill; Dust; El Dorado* (Saura); *East-West; Esperanza & Sardinas; Evening Performance; Extasis; Fading Memories; Fast, Fast; Far Away; Fausto 5.0; The Fencing Master; First Effort; Flamenco; The Flower of My Secret; La Frontera; Golden Balls; Goya in Bordeaux; Hi, Are You Alone?; Hidden Witnesses; High Heels; The Holy Innocents; Horror Express; The House of Bernarda Alba; A House with a View of the Sea; How to Be a Woman and Not Die in the Attempt; If Only; I Went Down; I Will Survive; Jamón, Jamón; Japón; Jardines Colgantes; Jealousy; Le Journal de Lady M; Jump into the Void; Labyrinth of Passion; Land and Freedom; Latin Boys Go to Hell; The Law of Desire; The Letter; Life in the Shadows; Libertarias; Life Size; Lisboa; Live Flesh; The Long Holidays of 1936; A Love Bewitched; Lovers; The Lovers of the Arctic Circle; Malena Is a Name from a Tango; Manolito Four-Eyes; El Mar; Maravillas; Matador; Il Mercenario; Mr Arkadin; Mouth to Mouth; My Silly Mother; The Nest; Night Hair Child; The Ninth Gate; Nobody Knows Anybody; Nobody Will Speak of Us When We're Dead; Open Your Eyes; The Others; Pau and His Brother; Pepi, Luci, Bom…; Peppermint Frappé; Perdita Durango; Poachers; Pourquoi pas moi?; P Tinto's Miracle; Princesa; The Quarry; Que no quede huella; ¿Quién Puede Matar a un Niño?; The Quince Tree Sun; Race, the Spirit of Franco; The Red Squirrel; Second Skin; Secrets of the Heart; La Senyora; Sevillanas; Skyline; Solas; The South; The Spirit of the Beehive; Such Is Life; Supersonic Man; Tango* (Saura); *Taxi; Ten Days Without Love; Tender Hours; Texas, Addio; Thesis; They Came to Rob Las Vegas; Things I Never Told You; Tie Me Up! Tie Me Down!; The Tit and the Moon; To an Unknown God; To Begin Again; Torrente, the Dumb Arm of the Law; The Tower of the Seven Hunchbacks; The Turkish Bath – Hamam; Train of Shadows; Tristana; Two for Tea; Two Much; Vacas; The Ugliest Woman in the World; Le Vampire de Dusseldorf; Vengo; El Verdugo; Vigo Passion for Life; Viridiana; Waiting for the Messiah; The Way I Killed My Father; What Have I Done to Deserve This?; Women on the Verge of a Nervous Breakdown; Work in Progress*

Spark, Muriel, films adapted from work, *Nasty Habits; The Prime of Miss Jean Brodie*

Spencer, Scott, film adapted from work, *Waking the Dead*

Spiders, see **Insects, spiders, etc**

Spillane, Mickey, films adapted from work, *I, the Jury; Kiss Me Deadly*

Spiritualism, *Before Dawn; Black Rainbow; Family Plot; The Medium; Nightmare Alley; Supernatural*

Spontaneous combustion, by-product of sex, *Pyrates*

Spots, malevolent, *How to Get Ahead in Advertising*

Spring, Howard, film adapted from work, *Fame Is the Spur*

Spy films
(see also **Bond, James**)
Fr, *Le Dossier 51; Espion Lève-toi; Les Espions; Mademoiselle Docteur; Mata Hari – Agent H.21; La Route de Corinthe; La Sentinelle; The Serpent*
China, *Peking Opera Blues*
GB, *American Roulette; Back-Room Boy; Catch Me a Spy; Confidential Agent; Contraband; Cottage to Let; Crook's Tour; Danger Route; A Dandy in Aspic; Dark Journey; The Deadly Affair; The Double Man; Enigma; Eye of the Beholder; Eye of the Needle; Fathom; The Flying Fool; The Four Just Men; The Fourth Protocol; Funeral in Berlin; The Golden Lady; Hidden City; Highly Dangerous; Hot Enough for June; The Human Factor* (Preminger); *The Ipcress File; The Intelligence Men; I See a Dark Stranger; The Looking Glass War; The Mackintosh Man; The Man Between; The Man in the Road; The Man Who Knew Too Much* (Hitchcock, 1934); *Masquerade* (Dearden); *Mata Hari* (Harrington); *Modesty Blaise; The Next of Kin; Not Now, Comrade; Otley; Our Man in Havana; The Quiller Memorandum; Rentadick; Rough Shoot; Salt & Pepper; The Secret Agent* (Hitchcock); *The Secret Agent* (Hampton); *The Sellout; Spy Hard; The Spy Who Came In From the Cold; The Tamarind Seed; The 39 Steps* (Hitchcock); *The 39 Steps* (Thomas); *The Thirty-Nine Steps* (Sharp); *Timeslip; Traitor Spy; When Eight Bells Toll; The Whistle Blower; The Yellow Canary; Yellow Dog*
Ger, *Dead Pigeon on Beethoven Street*
HK, *Kawashima Yoshiko*
Ire, *Avalanche Express*
It, *Danger: Diabolik; Russiccum; Superargo*
SKor, *Shirl*
US, *Above Suspicion; Across the Pacific; The Amateru; Arabesque; Austin Powers: International Man of Mystery; Austin Powers: The Spy Who Shagged Me; Background to Danger; Black Eagle; Blindfold; Blue Ice; The Cape Town Affair; Careful, Soft Shoulder; Cloak and Dagger; Company Business; Condorman; Confessions of a Nazi Spy; The Conspirators; Crack-Up* (St Clair); *Dangerously They Live; Darling Lili; Diplomatic Courier; Dishonoured; The English Patient; The Experts; The Falcon and the Snowman; Firestarter; 5 Fingers; Foreign Correspondent; Gorky Park; The Groundstar Conspiracy; Hanky Panky; Harriet the Spy; The House on 92nd Street; How to Steal the World; The Iron Curtain; Ishtar; Journey into Fear; Jumpin' Jack Flash; The Kremlin Letter; Lancer Spy; The Little Drummer Girl; Little Nikita; Man Hunt; The Man Who Knew Too Much* (Hitchcock, 1956); *Mata Hari* (Fitzmaurice); *Mrs Pollifax – Spy; Midas Run; My Favorite Blonde; Nick Carter – Master Detective; A Night in Casablanca; Nightmare* (Whelan); *Notorious; The Nude Bomb; Once Upon a Honeymoon; The Osterman Weekend; Permission to Kill; The Russia House; Russian Roulette; Scorpio; Shining Through; Spy Kids; Stamboul Quest; TAG, the Assassination Game; Target* (Penn); *The Tailor of Panama; Teen Agent; Telefon; The Thief; This Is My Affair; Three Days of the Condor; Topaz; Top Secret; Torn Curtain; Walk East on Beacon!*

Squatters, *Pigs*

Sri Lanka
in film, *Song of Ceylon; A Mother Alone; When Mother Comes Home for Christmas; Saroja*
Sri Lankan cinema, *A Mother Alone; Death on a Full Moon Day; Saroja*

Stacpoole, H de Vere, films adapted from work, *The Blue Lagoon* (Launder); *The Blue Lagoon* (Kleiser); *Return to the Blue Lagoon*

Stamp-collecting, etc, *Charade; Nine Queens; Penny Gold; Tommy Ticker and the Stamp Traveller*

Stark, Richard, films adapted from work (see also **Westlake,** Donald E), *Payback; Point Blank; The Outfit; The Split*

State terror (see also **Politics and politicians**)
in Argentina, *Garage Olimpio*
in Cambodia, *Les Gens de la rizière*
in Canada, *Les Ordres*
in Chile, *La Frontera*
in China, *Man from China; Sunless Days*
in Eastern Europe and USSR, *Brigands; The Burning Wall; Defence Counsel Sedov; The Ear; Escape from the 'Liberty' Cinema; The Inner Circle; Interrogation; Lost in Siberia; No End; The Party and the Guests; Pravda; The Prisoner; Requiem for Dominic; Rough Treatment; Whooping Cough; The Witness*
in Iran *Moment of Innocence*
in Latin America, *El Coraje del Pueblo; Death and the Maiden; Disparen a Matar; The Evil That Men Do; La Fièvre Monte à el Pao; The Girlfriend; Havana; The Kiss of the Spider Woman; The Lion's Den; Men with Guns; Missing; Romero; Secret Wedding; State of Siege; Sur; When the Mountains Tremble*
in South Africa, *Cry Freedom; Mapantsula; A World Apart*
in Taiwan, *Super Citizen Ko*
in Turkey, *After the Fall* (Yilmaz); *The Wall; Yol*
in Western Europe, *Defence of the Realm, Germany in Autumn; Hidden Agenda; Ireland: Behind the Wire; Open Doors; Section Spéciale; Z*
in US, *The Siege*
unidentified, *Closet Land*

Steinbeck, John
as movie host, *O. Henry's Full House*
films adapted from work, *Cannery Row, East of Eden; The Grapes of Wrath; Of Mice and Men* (Milestone); *Of Mice and Men* (Sinise); *The Wayward Bus*

Stendhal, films adapted from work, *La Chartreuse de Parme; The Nun and the Devil*

Stepmothers, fathers, children, etc, *Big Girls Don't Cry…They Get Even; The Black Orchid; Hollow Reed; Kolya; The Last Gangster; Limbo; The Lion; Paris s'éveille; The People Under the Stairs; Phaedra; Sons; The Stepfather; The Stepfather II; Stepfather III; Stepmom; The Stepmother; Yours, Mine and Ours; Wicked Stepmother*

Stevenson, Robert Louis, films adapted from work
– Jekyll-and-Hyde stories, *Dr Jekyll and Mr Hyde* (Robertson); *Dr Jekyll and Mr Hyde* (Mamoulian); *Dr Jekyll and Mr Hyde* (Fleming); *Dr Jekyll and Ms Hyde; Dr Jekyll et Les Femmes; Dr Jekyll and Sister Hyde; Edge of Sanity; Grip of the Strangler; I Monster; Mary Reilly; Le Testament du Docteur Cordelier; The Two Faces of Dr Jekyll*
– other, *L'Ile au trésor; Kidnapped; Muppet Treasure Island; Scalawag; The Strange Door; Treasure Island* (Heston); *Treasure Island* (Fridman)

Stoker, Bram, films adapted from/inspired by work, *The Awakening; Blood from the Mummy's Tomb; Dracula* (Browning); *Dracula* (Fisher); *Dracula* (Curtis); *Dracula* (Badham); *Dracula* (Coppola); *Dracula A.D. 1972; Dracula: Dead and Loving It; Dracula Has Risen from the Grave; Dracula Prince of Darkness; Dracula's Daughter; The Lair of the White Worm; The Scars of Dracula*

Stone, IF, film about, *I.F. Stone's Weekly*

Stone, Robert, films adapted from work, *Who'll Stop the Rain?; W USA*

Stoppard, Tom, film adapted from work, *Rosencrantz and Guildenstern Are Dead*

Storey, David, film adapted from work, *This Sporting Life*

Strachey, Lytton, in film, *Carrington*

Strauss, Johann, father and son, films about, *The Great Waltz* (Duvivier); *The Great Waltz* (Stone)

Street gangs and juvenile delinquents (see also **Teenagers and teen movies**)
in Brazil, *Pixote*
in Britain, *Arrivederci Millwall; Brighton Rock; Bronco Bullfrog; A Clockwork Orange; Cosh Boy; Juvenile Liaison; Juvenile Liaison 2; Shopping; Small Faces*
in Canada, *Hochelaga*
in France, *L'Astragale; L'Eau Froide; L'Enfance nue; La Petite Voleuse; Les Quatre Cents Coups; Shark's Son; Vagabonde*
in Indonesia, *Leaf on a Pillow*
in Ireland, *Crush Proof*
in Italy, *Ultrà*
in Japan, *Fighting Elegy*
in Korea, *Timeless Bottomless Bad Movie*
in Mexico, *Los Olvidados*
in Spain, *Fast, Fast*
in Taiwan, *A Brighter Summer Day*
in US, *The Angels Wash Their Faces; Assault on Precinct 13; Bad Boys; Blackboard Jungle; The Boy Who Cried Bitch; Boyz N the Hood; Bronx Warriors, The; Colors; Crime in the Streets; The Cross and the Switchblade; Deadbeat at Dawn; Dead End; Death Wish III; Defiance; The Delicate Delinquent; Drugstore Cowboy; Eight-Tray Gangster: The Making of a Crip; 80 Blocks from Tiffany's; Gang Related; Good to Go; Hangin' with the Homeboys; Juice; The Little Rascals; Lords of Flatbush; Lost Angels; Menace II Society; My Crasy Life; Only the Strong; Out of the Blue; The Outsiders* (Coppola); *Prayer of the Rollerboys; Regeneration; Rumble Fish; Streets of Fire; Switchblade Sisters; Touch and Go; Tuff Turf; That Gang of Mine; The Wanderers; The Warriors; West Side Story*
in USSR, *Burglar*

Strindberg, August, films adapted from/inspired by work, *The Father; The Hips of John Wayne; Miss Julie*

Stuart, Alexander, film adapted from work, *The War Zone*

Students, see **Colleges and students**

Stuntmen/women, *Ah-Kam; Hooper; The Stunt Man; Stunts*

Styron, William, film adapted from work, *Sophie's Choice*

Submarines (see also **Undersea worlds**), *Above Us the Waves; The Abyss; The Abyss: Special Edition; The Boat; The Boat: The Director's Cut; Captain Nemo and the Underwater City; City Under the Sea; Cockleshell Heroes; Crimson Tide; DeepStar Six; Down Periscope; The Enemy Below; Gray Lady Down; Hell and High Water; The Hunt for Red October; It Came from Beneath the Sea; Morning Departure; Murphy's War; The Neptune Factor; Operation Petticoat; The Rift; Sphere; Submarine X-1; Torpedo Run; 20000 Leagues Under the Sea; U-571*

Suicide, *About July; An American Werewolf in Paris; Bad Timing; Bemani; The Big Chill; The Black Torment; Bob's Weekend; The Brave; Cookie's Fortune; Dead Man's Curve; Des Nouvelles du Bon Dieu; Le Diable Probablement; Discipline for the Left-Handed; Downtime; Dream with the Fishes; Une Femme Douce; Le Feu Follet; The First Wives Club; The Florentine Dagger; Folks!; Forbidden Relations; Fourteen Hours; The Girl from Trieste; The Girls to Be Married; The Heart Is a Lonely Hunter; Heathers; Herostratus; Housekeeping; Ikinai; India Song; The Indians Are Still Far Away; Inside Moves; I Take This Woman; It's a Wonderful Life; Japón; Je t'aime, je t'aime; Le Jeune Werther; Johnny Got His Gun; Julian Po; Mayerling; Meet John Doe; The Million Dollar Hotel; Mishima: A Life in Four Chapters; Mixed Nuts; Moments; Monster's Ball; Mouchette; New Year's Day; The Odd Job; Pension Mimosas; The Pistol; Running Scared; Scent of a Woman; Seafood; The Seventh Victim; La Signora di Tutti; A Single Spark; Stealing Home; Suicide Club; A Taste of Cherry; Teenagers from Outer Space; The Unsaid; Too Young; Varietes; Le Vent de la Nuit; The Virgin Suicides; Wetherby; What Price Hollywood?; Whispering Corridors; Will It Snow for Christmas?*

Surfing and surfers, *Aloha Summer; Between Friends; Big Wednesday; Crystal Voyager; Gidget; A Personal History of the Australian Surf; Point Break; A Scene at the Sea*

Surrealism, *L'Age d'Or; Alpine Fire; Barrier; Chance, History, Art…; Un Chien Andalou; Conspirators of Pleasure; Dreams That Money Can Buy; Eraserhead; Europe After the Rain; The Exterminating Angel; Le Fantôme de la Liberté; Le Fantôme du Moulin Rouge; Fever House; Happy Days;Imago – Meret Oppenheim; Immoral Tales; Juliet of the Spirits; In the Name of the Father* (Bellocchio); *Hour of the Wolf; King, Queen, Knave; Peppermint Frappé; Malpertuis; Songs from the Second Floor; Viva La Muerte; Voyage – Surprise*

Surrogate motherhood, see **Mothers**

Surveillance and security business, *The Conversation; Enemy of the State; Le Dossier 51; Der Starke Ferdinand; They All Laughed; Three Days of the Condor; Watching the Detective*

Survival, in wilderness, etc, *Alive; Back from Eternity; Crusoe; Day of the Animals; Deliverance; Dersu Uzala; The Edge; Five Came Back; Flight of the Phoenix; Inferno; Jeremiah Johnson; Lord of the Flies* (Brook); *Lord of the Flies* (Hook); *Man in the Wilderness; The River Wild; San Demetrio, London; Surviving the Game*

Survivalism, *The Survivors; TerrorVision*

Susann, Jacqueline, film about, *Isn't She Great* films adapted from/inspired by work, *The Love Machine; The Valley of the Dolls; Beyond the Valley of the Dolls*

Swamps, *Band of the Hand; Cape Fear* (Thompson); *Cape Fear* (Scorsese); *Cry of the Hunted; Dark Waters; Death Trap; The Defiant Ones; Distant Drums; Empire of the Ants; 'Gator Bait; Scorchers; Southern Comfort; Squirm; Swamp Thing; Swamp Water; Wind Across the Everglades*

Sweden, in film, *Adalen '31; Cries and Whispers; The Disappearance of Finbar; Dreaming of Rita; Elvis! Elvis!; The Emigrants; Fanny and Alexander; Faithless; The Father; Foreigners; Giliap; The Greatest Heroes; Happy We; Herr Arnes Pengar; House of Angels; Kvinnodrom; Love Lessons; Lucky People Center International; The Man from Majorca; The Man on the Roof; Montenegro; My Life as a Dog; Out of an Old Man's Head; The Pistol; Pram; The Seventh Seal; The Slingshot; Smiles of a Summer Night; Sommaren med Monika; Söndags Barn; What Are You Doing After the Orgy?; Wild Strawberries; The Women on the Roof; You're Lying*

Swedish cinema, *Adalen '31; Amorosa; Anita; The Best Intentions; Breaking the Waves; Close to the Wind; Comédia Infantil; Cool & Crazy; Les Créatures; Cries and Whispers; Dancer in the Dark; Darkness in Tallinn; The Daughter of the Puma; The Devil's Eye; The Disappearance of Finbar; Dreaming of Rita; Elvira Madigan; Elvis! Elvis!; The Emigrants; The Face; Face to Face; Faithless; Fanny and Alexander; The Father; Foreigners; Giliap; Gycklarnas Afton; The Greatness of the Small Men; Gunnar Hedes Saga; Happy We; Herr Arnes Pengar; Hets; Hour of the Wolf; House of Angels; Jag Är Med Barn (Father-to-Be/I'm Expecting); Joe Hill; Johan; Kvinnodröm; Language of Love; Letters from the East; Lines from the Heart; Love Lessons; ucky People Center International; The Magic Flute; The Man from Majorca; The Man on the Roof; Mifune; Montenegro; More About the Language of Love; My Life as a Dog; Nattvardsgästerna; One and One; The Outlaw and His Wife; Out of an Old Man's Head; The Ox; A Passion; Persona; Pippi Longstocking; The Pistol; Pram; The Premonition; Private Pleasures; The Rite; The Sacrifice; Sebastian; Seventh Seal; The Shame; Show Me Love; The Silence* (Bergman); *The Slingshot; Smiles of a Summer Night; Smilla's Feeling for Snow; Something Happened; Sommaren med Monika; Sommarlek; Söndags Barn; Songs from the Second Floor; Stubby; Summer Paradise; Sven Klang's Combo; Swan Lake – The Zone; Through a Glass Darkly; Tic Tac; Together; Tupamaros; The Virgin Spring; What Are You Doing After the Orgy?; The White Wall; Wild Strawberries; Witchcraft Through the Ages; The Women on the Roof; World of Glory; You're Lying*

Swift, Graham, films adapted from work, *Last Orders; Waterland*

Swift, Jonathan, films adapted from work, *Gulliver's Travels; The Three Worlds of Gulliver*

Swimming, *Amsterdamned; Captain Johnno; Dangerous When Wet; Dawn!; Last Feelings; The Swimmer; Via Satellite; Waterboys*

Swiss cinema, *Abraham Valley; The Adversary; Alice; Alpine Fire; Alzire, or the New Continent; Anne Trister; L'Arche du Désert; Ashanti; Balkanisateur; Ball, The; Barnabo of the Mountains; Behind the Sun; The Blue Villa; Butterfly* (Sarno); *Charles, Dead or Alive; La Ciénaga; Civilised People; Cold Fever; Conspirators of Pleasure; Dangerous Moves; The Death of Marco Ricci; The Death of the Flea Circus Director; La Dentellière; The Devil's Accordion; ¡Devils Don't Dream Research on Jacobo Arbenz Guzmán; Le Franc; Gito, the Ungrateful; Himalaya; Hyenas; Imago – Meret Oppenheim; The Indians Are Still Far Away; The Invitation; Jonah Who Will Be 25 in the Year 2000; Journey of Hope; The Knowledge of Healing; Konfrontation – Assassination in Davos; Une Liaison Pornographique; The Little Girl Who Sold the Sun; Ma Vie en Rose; Merci pour le chocolat; Messidor; The Middle of the World; Mostly Martha; No Man's Land* (Tanner); *Nouvelle Vague; O for Oblomov; Pourquoi pas moi?; Le Retour d'Afrique; Roberto Succo; La Salamandre; Same Old Song; Sátántangó; Soigne ta Droite; Swedish Massage Parlour; Three Colours: Red; Werckmeister Harmonies; The Written Face*

Switzerland, in film, *The Death of Mario Ricci; Espion Lève-toi; Jonah Who Will Be 25 in the Year 2000; Journey of Hope; Konfrontation – Assassination in Davos; Merci pour le chocolat; Messidor; The Middle of the World; No Man's Land* (Tanner); *Le Parfum d'Yvonne; La Retour d'Afrique; La Salamandre; Three Colours: Red*

Tagore, Rabindranath, films adapted from work, *Charulata; The Home and the World; Teen Kanya*

Taiwan, in film, *Accidental Legend; Ah Chung; The Boys from Fengkuei; Betelnut Beauty; Birdland; A Brighter Summer Day; Bundled; The Cabbie; A Chance to Die; A City of Sadness; Eat Drink Man Woman; Execution in Autumn; Flat Tyre; A One and a Two…Pushing Hands; Rainy Dog; Student Days; Summer at Grandpa's; Taipei Story; The Time to Love and the Time to Die*

Taiwanese cinema, *About July; Accidental Legend; Ah Chung; At Dawn; Bangkok: Dangerous; Beijing Bicycle; Betelnut Beauty; Birdland; Blue Moon; Bodo; A Borrowed Life; The Boys from Fengkuei; A Brighter Summer Day; Buddha Bless America; Bundled; The Cabbie; A Cha-Cha for the Fugitive; A Chance to Die; A City of Sadness; A Confucian Confusion; Crouching Tiger, Hidden Dragon; Daughter of the Nile; Darkness and Light; A Drifting Life; Dust in the Wind; Dynasty; Eat Drink Man Woman; Execution in Autumn; Fist of Fury Part II; Flat Tyre; Flowers of Shanghai; Goodbye South, Goodbye; Good Men, Good Women; Grandma and Her Ghosts; The Green, Green Grass of Home; Heartbreak Island; The Hole; Jade Love; Jam; Kung Fu – Girl Fighter; Legend of Bruce Lee; Lonely Hearts Club; Mahjong; The Man from Island West; Millennium Mambo; Mirror Image; The Most Terrible Time in My Life; Murmur of Youth; My New Friends; A One and a Two…The Peach-Blossom Land; Puppetmaster; Pushing Hands; Rebels of the Neon God; The Red Lotus Society; Red Rose, White Rose; Return of the Dragon; The River* (Tsai Ming-Liang); *The Sandwich Man; Sia Yu; The Silent Thrush; Song of the Exile; Still Love You After All; Student Days; Summer at Grandpa's; Super Citizen Ko; Sweet Degeneration; Taipei Story; Ten Fingers of Steel; The Terroriser; This Love of Mine; The Time to Love and the Time to Die; Too Young; A Touch of Zen; Tropical Fish* (Chen Yu-Hsun); *Tsuru-Henry; Vive l'Amour; The Wedding Banquet; What Time Is It There?; Wolves Cry Under the Moon; The Wooden Man's Bride; Yours and Mine*

Tajikistan, in film, and Tajik cinema, *Brothers; The Flight of the Bee; On Equal Terms*

Tarkington, Booth, films adapted from work, *Alice Adams; The Magnificent Ambersons; On Moonlight Bay*

Tarkovksy, Andrei, film about, *One Day in the Life of Andrei Arsenevitch*

Tattoos, tattooing and body painting, *The Illustrated Man; Irezumi – Spirit of Tattoo; The Pillow Book; Tattoo*

Tax investigators, *A Taxing Woman; The Undercover Man*

Taxis, *All or Nothing; The Cabbie; Clando; Cyclo; Eight O'Clock Walk; Kamikaze Taxi; Killer, The* (Omirbaev); *Night and Day; Night on Earth; Sausalito; Stranger; Signal 7; Taxi; Taxi!; Taxi Driver*

Tchaikovsky, Peter, film about, *The Music Lovers*

Teachers, see **Colleges and students** and **Education and school stories**

Teenagers and teen movies (see also **Adolescence, Education and school stories, Runaways, Street gangs and juvenile delinquents**)
Aust, *The Big Steal* (Tass); *The Delinquents; Puberty Blues; Say a Little Prayer*
Bel, *Rosetta*
Can, *Porky's; Porky's II; Porky's Revenge; Screwballs; Screwballs II*
Fr, *A ma soeur!; Le Ciel, les Oiseaux, et… Ta Mère!; Les Roseaux Sauvages; Trop de Bonheur; La Vie de Jésus*
GB, *Bronco Bullfrog; The Damned* (Losey); *The Girl in the Picture; Here We Go Round the Mulberry Bush; The Hole; Human Traffic; Kevin & Perry Go Large; Out of Order* (Turpie); *The Rachel Papers; Rita, Sue and Bob Too; Terry on the Fence; That Sinking Feeling; That Summer!; Tickets for the Zoo; TwentyFourSeven; UndeRage*
Jap, *Leaving*
Sp, *Fast, Fast*
US, *All Over Me; All the Right Moves; Amongst Friends; Blue City; Blue Denim; Body Rock; Boulevard Nights; The Boys Next Door; The Breakfast Club; Breakin'; But I'm a Cheerleader; Candy; Can't Buy Me Love; Class; Corvette Summer; Courage Mountain; Crazy/Beautiful; Crossing the Bridge; Cruel Intentions; Cry-Baby; Dirty Dancing; Don't Tell Mom the Babysitter's Dead; Earth vs the Spider; Fast Talking; Fast Times at Ridgement High; Ferris Bueller's Day Off; The Flamingo Kid; Footloose; For Keeps; Foxes; Friday; Girl; Girls Just Want to Have Fun; Girls Town; Gleaming the Cube; Good to Go; Grease; Grease 2; Gremlins; Heathers; House Party; I Know What You Did Last Summer; I Still Know What You Did Last Summer; I Wanna Hold Your Hand; Hurricane Streets; Jake Speed; Johnny Suede; The Karate Kid; The Karate Kid II; The Karate Kid III; Kid; Lambada; The Last House on the Left; License to Drive; Little Nikita; Lord Love a Duck; Loser; Losin' It; Loverboy; Lucas; Making It; Mallrats; Mobsters; Nowhere; O.C. & Stiggs; One on One; The Opposite of Sex; Out of the Blue; The Outsiders* (Coppola); *Over the Edge; Pump Up the Volume; Pretty in Pink; Rancho Deluxe; Real Genius; Rebel Without a Cause; Risky Business; Rock'n'Roll High School; Rooftops; Rumble Fish; Say Anything; She's All That; She's Out of Control; Sing; Sixteen Candles; Society; Some Kind of Wonderful; Some Girls; Son in Law; Teen Agent; Telling Lies in America; Thank God It's Friday; That Night; That Was Then… This Is Now; Thirteen; Thunder Alley; Tilt; Trick or Treat; Trust; Tuff Turf; Two of a Kind; The Unbelievable Truth; Urban Legend; Vision Quest; The Wanderers; WarGames; The Warriors; Wayne's World; Wayne's World II; Weird Science; What's Eating Gilbert Grape; Where the Boys Are; Wild in the Streets; The Wild One; The Wild Side; Wild Style; Wisdom; Youngblood; Young Guns; Young Guns II; Young Warriors*
US teens threatened by aliens and other strange things, *Bill & Ted's Bogus Journey; Bill & Ted's Excellent Adventure; Buffy the Vampire Slayer; Children of the Corn; Class of Nuke 'Em High; Encino Man; The Faculty; The Incredibly Strange Creatures Who Stopped Living and Became Mixed-Up Zombies; I Was a Teenage Werewolf; Night of the Comet; Night of the Demons; Teenagers from Outer Space; Teen Wolf; Teen Wolf II; The Toxic Avenger; The Toxic Avenger Part II; Waxwork*
USSR, *Burglar; Freedom Is Paradise; Little Vera*

Teeth, outsize, *Teeth*

Tekeuchi, Yoshikazu, film adapted from work, *Perfect Blue*

Telekinesis, *Akira; Cameron's Closet; Carrie* (De Palma); *Escape to Witch Mountain; Firestarter; The Fury* (De Palma); *Harlequin; Lord Love a Duck; The Medusa Touch; Patrick; Retribution; Return from Witch Mountain; Time of the Gypsies; Village of the Damned; Xtro*

Telepathy (see also **Clairvoyance**), *Brainstorm; Eyes of Laura Mars; Fear; Firestarter; The First Power; Manhunter; Powder; Scanners; Scanners II: The New Order; Shadey; The Shining; Shocker; Split Second*

Telephones and callers, *The Bells Are Ringing; Call Me; Family Viewing; Denise Calls Up; Hanging Up; I Saw What You Did; Julia Has Two Lovers; Mouth to Mouth; One Fine Day; Out of Order* (Turpie); *Out of the Dark; Pett and Pott; Pillow Talk; Sorry, Wrong Number; The Telephone Book; The Terroriser; Things I Never Told You*

Television, in film (see also **Journalism**)
life in/satires of, *Adieu Philippine; Accidental Hero; The American Way; Bamboozled; Broadcast News; The Cable Guy; Comic Magazine; Crimes and Misdemeanors; Crimetime; Dead Men Don't Die; Delirious; Desk Set; EDtv; Elevator; A Face in the Crowd; Fellow Traveller; [Focus]; Galaxy Quest; The Gazebo; Ginger and Fred; The Gong Show Movie; Grief; Groundhog Day; High Heels; Holy Man; Icicle Thief; It Should Happen to You; The Insider; Kamikaze; Kentucky Fried Movie; The Killing of Sister George; L.A. Story; The Love Machine; Mad City; Magnolia; Maybe Baby; Meet Mr Lucifer; My Favourite Martian; My Favorite Year; My Silly Mother; No Such Thing; O for Oblomov; Perfect Blue; Quiz Show; The Sandman; Series 7: The Contenders; Showtime; Sion and Laura; Soapdish; Someone Like You…; Stay Tuned; Stuart Saves His Family; Switching Channels; Tapeheads; Testament* (Akomfrah); *There's a Girl in My Soup; The Thrill of It All; To Die For; Todos Somos Estrellas; Tootsie; The Truman Show; UHF; Up Close & Personal; Via Satellite; Wayne's World; Wayne's World II; Windprints; Wrong Is Right*
power of, *Accumulator 1; Benny's Video; Death Watch; Farhrenheit 451; Godard on TV: 1960–2000; Hot War; I Love a Man in Uniform; Liquid Dreams; The Man Who Fell to Earth; Network; Nurse Betty; The Prize of Peril; Public Access; The Running Man* (Glaser); *Speaking Parts; TerrorVision; Tout Va Bien; The Truman Show; Vizontele*

Tenants/visitors, overstaying their welcome (see also **Unwanted guests**), *Apartment Zero; Boudu Sauvé des Eaux; Down and Out in Beverly Hills; Henry: Portrait of a Serial Killer; Madhouse; The More the Merrier; New Year's Day; Pacific Heights; Perfectly Normal; Poison Ivy; Single White Female; To Sleep with Anger; Viens chez moi, j'habite chez une copine; What About Bob?*

Tennis, *Dial M for Murder; Hard, Fast and Beautiful; Players; School for Scoundrels; Strangers on a Train*

Terrorism, and related phenomena, in film (see also **Revolutionaries and radicals, State terror**)
in Algeria, *The Battle of Algiers*
in Africa, *Death in the Sun; Long Night's Journey into Day; Something of Value*

in Britain, *The Secret Agent* (Hampton); *Secret People; Seven Days to Noon; Who Dares Wins*
in Cyprus, *The High Bright Sun*
in France, *Nada; Nanou*
in Germany, *The German Sisters; Germany in Autumn; The Legends of Rita; The Third Generation*
in India, *The Terrorist*
international, *Captive; The Cassandra Crossing; Exposed; Golden Rendezvous; The 'Human' Factor* (Dmytryk); *Kings and Desperate Men; North Sea Hijack; Ransom; That Obscure Object of Desire*
in Ireland, *Cal; The General* (Boorman); *The Gentle Gunman; Ireland: Behind the Wire; Odd Man Out; Ordinary Decent Criminal*
in Italy, *Blow to the Heart; Il Diavolo in Corpo; Illustrious Corpses; The Second Time; Three Brothers; The Tragedy of a Ridiculous Man; Year of the Gun*
in Japan, *A; The Bullet Train*
in Middle East, *The Ambassador; Black Sunday; Hors la vie; Navy Seals; Not Quite Jerusalem; Operation Thunderbolt; Raid on Entebbe; Rosebud; Victory at Entebbe; Wanted Dead or Alive*
in Peru, Courage
in US, *Abduction; Air Force One; The BelieverBulletproof; Die Hard; Die Hard 2; Die Hard with a Vengeance; The Enforcer* (Windust/Walsh); *Executive Action; Face/Off; The Mad Bomber; Nighthawks* (Malmuth); *Patty Hearst; The Peacemaker; Running on Empty; The Siege; Toy Soldiers; War*

Tevis, Walter, films adapted from work, *The Color of Money; The Hustler; The Man Who Fell to Earth*

Tey, Josephine, films adapted from work, *The Franchise Affair; Young and Innocent*

Thackeray, William Makepeace, films adapted from work, *Becky Sharp; Barry Lyndon*

Thailand
Thailand, in film, *Anna and the King; Bangkok: Dangerous; Bang Rajan – Legend of the Village Warriors; The Beach; Crime Kings; Brokedown Palace; The Good Woman of Bangkok; Iron Ladies; Jan Dara; Kickboxer; The King and I* (Lang); *The King and I* (Rich); *Sacrifice; Tears of the Black Tiger*
Thai cinema, *Bang Rajan – Legend of the Village Warriors; Beyond Forgivin'; Butterfly and Flowers; Crime Kings; Dang Bireley's and the Young Gangsters; The Dumb Dies Fast, the Smart Die Slow; Fun Bar Karaoke; Iron Ladies; Jan Dara; Monrak Transistor; The Moonhunter; Mysterious Object at Noon; Nang Nak; Once Upon a Time… This Morning; Path of the Brave; Puen-Paeng; The Scar; 6ixtynin9; The Song of Chao-Phrya; S.T.A.B.; Tears of the Black Tiger; Tongpan*

Thanksgiving, see **Christmas and Thanksgiving films**

Thatcher's Britain, in film, *Arrivederci Millwall; Babylon; Bloody Kids; Britannia Hospital; Business as Usual; Close My Eyes; Coming Up Roses; Crystal Gazing; Dealers; Didn't You Kill My Brother?; Eat the Rich; Empire State; Fords on Water; For Queen and Country; Giro City; High Hopes; How to Get Ahead in Advertising; In Fading Light; The Last of England; Live a Life; Living on the Edge; London; Looks and Smiles; The Love Child; My Beautiful Laundrette; The Nature of the Beast; No Surrender; Out of Order* (Turpie); *Paris by Night; The Return; Riff-Raff; Rita, Sue and Bob Too; Sammy and Rosie Get Laid; Seacoal; UndeRage; Ursula and Glenys; Women in Tropical Places*

Theatre, in film
in Africa, *Desert Mice*
in Argentina, *The Cloud*
in Bosnia *For Ever Mozart*
in Brazil, *Bye Bye Brasil*
in Britain, *An Awfully Big Adventure; Beginner's Luck; The Brighton Strangler; The Children's Midsummer Night's Dream; A Chorus of Disapproval; Curtain Up; The Dresser; Esther Kahn; The Good Companions* (Saville); *The Good Companions* (Thompson); *The Great Garrick; In the Bleak Midwinter; Looking for Richard; Love Is Like a Violin; Madhouse; Peg of Old Drury; The Punk and the Princess; Shakespeare in Love; Sylvia Scarlett; Star; The Tall Guy; Theatre of Blood; Withnail and I*
in Canada, *Une Histoire inventée; Jesus of Montreal*
in China, *8,000 Li Under the Clouds and Moon; Farewell My Concubine; The Peach-Blossom Land; Two Stage Sisters*
in Denmark, *Ladies on the Rocks*
in France, *L'Amour par terre; Le Capitaine Fracassé; Les Enfants du Paradis; Every Little Thing; La Fin du Jour; French Can Can; Le Goût des Autres; I'm Going Home; The Incredible Sarah; The Last Melodrama; The Last Metro; Marquise; Paris Nous Appartient; Le Roi de Paris; Va Savoir*
in Germany, *Veronika Voss*
in Greece, *The Travelling Players*
in Hong Kong, *Hu-Du-Men*
in India, *Masquerade* (Aravindan); *Shakespeare-Wallah*
in Ireland, *The Playboys*
in Italy, *Les Amants de Verone; I Am Anna Magnani; Love in the Mirror*
in Korea, *First Love* (Lee Myung-Se)
in Peru, *The Golden Coach*
in Poland, *To Be or Not To Be* (Lubitsch); *To Be or Not To Be* (Johnson)
in Portugal, *I'm Going Home; The Jester*
in South Africa, *The Man Who Drove with Mandela; Shot Down*
in Spain, *Actresses; Evening Performance*
in Sweden, *The Rite*
in US, *Actress; Anna; Bullets Over Broadway; Career; Cradle Will Rock; Dangerous; A Double Life; Heller in Pink Tights; The Impostors; It's Love I'm After; Jane; Jane Austen in Manhattan; King of Burlesque; Ladies of the Chorus; Last Summer in the Hamptons; Long Day's Journey into Night; Looking for Richard; The Man Who Came to Dinner; Naked in New York; Next Stop, Greenwich Village; Nobody's Fool; Noises Off; Only When I Laugh; Opening Night; Summer Stock; Tootsie; Twentieth Century; Vanya on 42nd Street; Who Am I This Time?*

Therapy and therapists (see also **Psychiatrists**), *After Life; Bedrooms and Hallways; Don't Go Breaking My Heart; The Prince of Tides; Shuroo; Stuart Saves His Family; Vampire at Midnight; What About Bob?*

Theroux, Paul, films adapted from work, *Half Moon Street; The Mosquito Coast; Saint Jack*

Thomas, Dylan, films adapted from work, *The Doctor and the Devils; Rebecca's Daughters; Under Milk Wood*

Thompson, EP, in film, *Talking History*

Thompson, Hunter S
films based on work, *Fear and Loathing in Las Vegas*
film about, *Where the Buffalo Roam*

Thompson, Jim, films adapted from work, *After Dark, My Sweet; Clean Slate; The Getaway* (Peckinpah); *The Getaway* (Donaldson); *The Grifters; The Killer Inside Me; The Kill-Off; This World, Then the Fireworks*

3-D, see **Cinematic novelties**

Thurber, James, films adapted from work, *The Battle of the Sexes; The Secret Life of Walter Mitty*

Tibet and Tibetan culture, in film, *Horse Thief; The Knowledge of Healing; Kundun; Lord of the Dance; Seven Years in Tibet; Song for Tibet; Tibet: A Buddhist Trilogy; A Tibetan New Year; Windhorse*

Time travel, *The Amazing Mr Blunden; Back to the Future; Back to the Future Part II; Back to the Future Part III; Being Human; Biggles; Bill & Ted's Bogus Journey; Bill & Ted's Excellent Adventure; A Connecticut Yankee in King Arthur's Court; The Final Countdown; Flight of the Navigator; Freejack; Highlander; Highlander II – The Quickening; Highland III – The Sorcerer; The Illustrated Man; Je t'aime, Je t'aime; Jubilee; Just Visiting; Kate & Leopold; Millennium; Monkey Bone; The Navigator: A Medieval Odyssey; Phantom of the Opera* (Little); *The Philadelphia Experiment; Retroactive; Roger Corman's Frankenstein Unbound; Sankofa; Somewhere in Time; Star Trek: Generations; Star Trek: First Contact; The Sticky Fingers of Time; The Terminator; Terminator 2: Judgment Day; Time Bandits; Timecop; The Time Machine; Time to Time; The Time Travellers; Timeslip; Trancers; The Unidentified Flying Oddball; The Voyage Home: Star Trek IV; Les Visiteurs; Warlock; Waxwork*
trapped in time, *Groundhog Day*

Tokyo, in film, *City of Lost Souls; Love/Juice; Swallowtail Butterfly; Tokyo-Ga; Tokyo Raiders; Tokyo Story*

Tolkien, JRR, films adapted from work, *The Lord of the Rings; The Lord of the Rings: The Fellowship of the Ring*

Toller, Ernst, film adapted from work, *Pastor Hall*

Tolstoy, Leo, films adapted from work, *Anna Karenina* (Brown); *Anna Karenina* (Duvivier); *Anna Karenina* (Rose); *Black Sabbath; ivansxtc.; The Kreutzer Sonata; Night Sun; War and Peace* (Vidor); *War and Peace* (Bondarchuk); *We Live Again*

Toole, John Kennedy, film adapted from work, *Neon Bible*

Tosh, Peter, film about, *Stepping Razor – Red X*

Toulouse-Lautrec, Henri de, films about, *Lautrec; Moulin Rouge* (Huston); *Moulin Rouge* (Luhrmann)

Tourism and tour guides (see also **Holidays and holiday camps**), *The Cruise; The Day the Fish Came Out; High Season; Hyena's Sun; Smile Orange; Three Coins in the Fountain*

Tournier, Michel, film adapted from work, *Le Roi des Aulnes*

Toys and toymakers, *Attack of the Puppet People; F/X2; The Magic Toyshop; Small Soldiers; Toys*

Tramps (see also **Homelessness**), *Beggars of Life; Boudu Sauvé des Eaux; Dogpound Shuffle; Down and Out in Beverly Hills; Emperor of the North Pole; Hands; Ironweed; Joe Gould's Secret; O. Henry's Full House ('The Cop and the Anthem'); Modern Times; Mon Homme; My Man Godrey* (La Cava); *Waiting for Godot*

Transformation, ugliness to beauty and vice versa (see also **Mutation**), *Beauty and the Beast; La Belle et la Bête; The Enchanted Cottage; The Singing Ringing Tree*

Transsexuality, see **Sex change**

Transvestitism, see **Cross-dressing**

Transplantation
of body parts, *Before I Hang; Body; Doctor Blood's Coffin; Face/Off; The Hand; The Hands of Orlac; Heart; Heart Condition; Mad Love; Mansion of the Doomed; The Man Who Changed His Mind; The Monster and the Girl; Organ; Parts; The Clonus Horror; Percy; Percy's Progress; The Resurrection of Zachary Wheeler; Return to Me; Scream and Scream Again; The Thing with Two Heads*
of brainwaves, *Brainwaves; Sphere; Unforgettable*
from animals, *The Strange Case of Dr Rx*

Traven, B, films adapted from work, *Banana Ridge; The Treasure of the Sierra Madre*

Travers, Ben, films adapted from work, *Plunder; Rookery Nook*

Tremain, Rose, film adapted from work, *Restoration*

Trevor, William, films adapted from work, *Attracta; Felicia's Journey*

Triad gangs, *Ah Chung; Ah-Kam; The Corruptor; Double Impact; Hard-Boiled; Heaven, Man, Earth; Lethal Weapon 4; The Longest Summer; Once Upon a Time in Triad Society; Once Upon a Time in Triad Society 2; Shanghai Triad; Shinjuku Triad Society; Sleepless Town; So Close to Paradise; Theft Under the Sun; Young and Dangerous; Young and Dangerous 2; Young and Dangerous 3*

Trinidad
Trinidad in film, *The Hummingbird Tree; The Mystic Masseur*
Trinidadian cinema, *Bim; Man from Africa and Girl from India*

Trotsky, Leon, films about, *The Assassination of Trotsky; Zina*

Truck-driving films, *Any Which Way You Can; Convoy; Duel; The 8-Wheel Beast; Hell Drivers; Janice; Jeepers Creepers; Joy Ride; The Last of the Cowboys; Sorcerer; They Drive by Night* (Woods); *They Drive by Night* (Walsh); *Thieves' Highway; Truck Stop Women; The Wages of Fear; White Line Fever*

True crime stories
Aust, *Ned Kelly*
Braz, *Prisoner of Rio*
Chile, *The Jackal of Nahueltoro; Johnny 100 Pesos*
Fr, *L'Affaire du Courrier de Lyon; Les Enfants du Paradis; La Fille de l'Air; Landru; Moi, Pierre Rivière, ayant égorgé ma mère, ma soeur et mon frère...; Les Noces Rouges; Le Pull-over Rouge; Sister My Sister; Toni; Violette Nozière*
Ger, *Dirt for Dinner; Schramm; Tenderness of the Wolves; Le Vampire de Dusseldorf*
GB, *Another Life; The Black Panther; Buster; Chicago Joe and the Showgirl; The Cold Light of Day; Dance With a Stranger; The Krays; Let Him Have It; McVicar; Out of Depth; Robbery; Rogue Trader; The Siege of Sidney Street; 10 Rillington Place; White Mischief*
It, *Illustrious Corpses; Lucky Luciano; The Mattei Affair; Salvatore Giuliano; Tano da Morire*
Jap, *Hysteric; The Saga of Anatahan; Violence at Noon*
Kenya *White Mischief*
Mex *Deep Crimson*
NZ, *Heavenly Creatures*
Phil, *Kisapmata*
Thai *Dang Bireley's and the Young Gangsters*
US, *Al Capone; Baby Face Nelson; The Ballad of Gregorio Cortez; Bonnie and Clyde; The Boston Strangler; Bugsy; Bully; Capone; Compulsion; Copycat; Crime of the Century; Dillinger* (Nosseck); *Dillinger* (Milius); *Ed Gein; The Enforcer* (Windust/Walsh); *The Executioner's Song; Ghosts of Mississippi; GoodFellas; Gotti; Helter Skelter; The Honeymoon Killers; In Cold Blood; Killer: A Journal of Murder; King of the Roaring 20's – The Story of Arnold Rothstein; Lepke; The Positively True Adventures of the Alleged Texas Cheerleader-Murdering Mom; Ragtime; Reversal of Fortune; The Rise and Fall of Legs Diamond; Rope; The St Valentine's Day Massacre; Scenes of the Crime; Sugartime; Swoon; The Untouchables; Walking Tall; Who Killed Vincent Chin?; The Wrong Man* (Hitchcock)

Truffaut, François, film about, *François Truffaut, Portraits Volés*

Tug-of-love dramas, *Careful, He Might Hear You; Cathy's Child; The Company She Keeps; The Good Mother; The Great Lie; I Could Go On Singing; Kramer vs Kramer; Not Without My Daughter; Three Men and a Little Lady*

Tunisian cinema, *Aïd el Kébir; Fatma; Hyena's Sun; Ali Zaoua: Prince de la Rue; The Silences of the Palace; A Summer in La Goulette; Wedding Moon*

Tunnelling, hostile, *Battle Beneath the Earth; Tremors*

Turgenev, Ivan, films adapted from work, *A Nest of Gentlefolk; Torrents of Spring*

Turkey, in film, *Abuzer Baklava; The Accidental Spy; After the Fall* (Yilmaz); *America, America; Away from Home; The Bandit; The Blue Exile; Boatman; Born of Fire; Clouds of May; Cold Nights; The 80th Step; Everything's Gonna Be Great; Farewell, Stranger; 5 Fingers; Gallipoli; Harem Suare; L'Immortelle; Journey of Hope; Journey to the Sun; The Man in the Street; The Mirror; Our Wall; Run for Money; Somersault in a Coffin; A Song for Beko; Summer Love; The Third Page; Topkapi; The Turkish Bath – Hamam; Vizontele; The Wall; Where the Rose Wilted; Yara; Yol*

Turkish baths, etc. *Oksutan; The Ritz; Saturday Night at the Baths; Shower; The Shvitz; Steaming; The Turkish Bath – Hamam*

Turkish cinema, *Abuzer Baklava; After the Fall* (Yilmaz); *Away from Home; The Bandit; Berdel; The Blue Exile; Boatman; Byzantium; Cabaret Balkan; Clouds of May; The Cockroach; Cold Nights; The 80th Step; Elevator; The Enemy; Everything's Gonna Be Great; Farewell to False Paradise; Harem Suare; The Herd; The Man in the Street; Mercedes Mon Amour; Night Journey; Run for Money; Somersault in a Coffin; Summer Love; The Third Page; The Turkish Bath – Hamam; Two Women; Vizontele; Where the Rose Wilted; Yara; Yellow Smile*

Turner, Ike and Tina, film about, *Tina: What's Love Got to Do With It*

Twain, Mark
films about, *The Adventures of Mark Twain* (Rapper); *The Adventures of Mark Twain* (Vinton)
films adapted from work, *The Adventures of Huckeberry Finn; The Adventures of Huck Finn; The Adventures of Tom Sawyer; A Connecticut Yankee in King Arthur's Court; The Million Pound Note; The Prince and the Pauper; Tom Sawyer; The Unidentified Flying Oddball*

Twins, *Among the Living; Big Business; The Black Room; The Buttercup Chain; Cat Ballou; The Dark Mirror; Dead Ringers; Double Impact; Eclipse; Equinox; Hamlet* (Coronado); *Here Come the Waves; Hotel de Love; The Krays; Malena Is a Name from a Tango; The Man in the Iron Mask* (Whale); *The Man in the Iron Mask* (Wallace); *Maximum Risk; My 20th Century; The Other* (Mulligan); *La Otra* (Gavaldón); *The Parent Trap; Penny Gold; The Palm Beach Story; Poto and Cabengo; Ring 0 – Birthday; Sisters* (De Palma); *Steal Big, Steal Little; A Stolen Life; This World, Then the Fireworks; Twin Dragons; Twin Falls Idaho; Twin Pawns; Twins; Twins of Evil; Twin Town; Village of Dreams*

UFOs (see also **Extra-terrestrials on Earth**), *Chariots of the Gods; Communion; That Eye, the Sky; Some Kinda Love*

Uganda, in film, *A.B.C. Africa; Man of Africa*

Uhry, Alfred, film adapted from work, *Driving Miss Daisy*

Undead, the (see also **After-life, Heaven-can-wait fantasies, Return to life**)
mummies, *The Awakening; Blood from the Mummy's Tomb; The Curse of the Mummy's Tomb; The Mummy* (Freund); *The Mummy* (Fisher); *The Mummy* (Sommers); *The Mummy's Hand; The Mummy's Shroud*
zombies, etc, *Army of Darkness: The Medieval Dead; Braindead; Dawn of the Dead; Day of the Dead; Dead Men Don't Die; Dead of Night* (Clark); *Disturbed; Doctor Death; Seeker of Souls; The Evil Dead; Evil Dead II; Face of Darkness; Fantômas contre Fantômas; Ghoulies; Hellbound: Hellraiser II; Hellraiser; Hellraiser III: Hell on Earth; The Incredibly Strange Creatures Who Stopped Living and Became Mixed-Up Zombies; In the Mouth of Madness; Isle of the Dead; I Walked with a Zombie; J'Accuse* (Gance, 1918); *J'Accuse* (Gance, 1937); *The Killing Box; The Living Dead at the Manchester*

Morgue; Maniac Cop; Maniac Cop 2; Night of the Comet; Night of the Creeps; Night of the Ghouls; Night of the Living Dead (Romero); *Night of the Living Dead* (Savini); *The Others; Pauranella Città dei Morti Viventi; The Parasite Murders; Phantasm; Phantasm II; The Plague of the Zombies; Re-Animator; Re-Animator 2; The Return of Doctor X; The Return of the Living Dead; Return of the Living Dead Part II; Return of the Living Dead III; The Sixth Sense; Trick or Treat; Voodoo Man; White Zombie; Zombie Flesh-Eaters*

Underground cinema, see **Experimental films**

Undersea worlds, and undersea adventures (see also **Submarines**), *The Abyss; The Abyss: Special Edition; The Big Blue; Captain Nemo and the Underwater City; City Beneath the Sea; City Under the Sea; The Deep; DeepStar Six; Leviathan; The Neptune Factor; The Rift; Shark; The Shark's Cave; Sharks' Treasure; Sphere; 20000 Leagues Under the Sea; Warlords of Atlantis*
documentaries, *Atlantis*

Unemployment
in Britain, *The Big Man; Conquest of the South Pole; The Full Monty; The Innocent* (MacKenzie); *Last Chants for a Slow Dance; Live a Life; Living on the Edge; Looks and Smiles; Love on the Dole; The Nature of the Beast; The Ragman's Daughter; That Sinking Feeling*
in Cuba, *One Way or Another*
in France, *De l'Autre Côté du Périph'; Une Epoque formidable…*
in India, *The Adversary*
in Taiwan, *Taipei Story*
in US, *The Boost; Hallelujah, I'm a Bum; The Journey of Natty Gann; Palookaville; Roger & Me; The Survivors; The Toy*

Unions, see **Labour relations**

United Nations, in film, *A Global Affair*

Universities, see **Colleges and students, Oxbridge and the Ivy League**

Unwanted guests (see also **Tenants/visitors**), *About Adam; Blind Alley* (Vidor); *The Cellar; The Dark Past; Desperate Hours* (Cimino); *The Desperate Hours* (Wyler); *Funny Games; Hardware; Hider in the House; Malice; MouseHunt; Puerto Escondido; Rawhide; Unlawful Entry; Viens chez moi, j'habite chez une copine; Visitor Q; Voyage; Wicked Stepmother*

Updike, John, film adapted from work, *The Witches of Eastwick*

Urban nightmares, *Akira; Angel Dust; Best Hotel on Skid Row; Blade Runner; Blade Runner – The Director's Cut; Bronx Warriors, The; A Clockwork Orange; Cold Dog Soup; Delicatessen; Dr M; The Driller Killer; Eraserhead; Escape from New York; Exterminator 2; Fort Apache – The Bronx; Ice; John Carpenter's Escape from L.A.; Johnny Mnemonic; Jubilee; Koyannisqatsi; Little Murders; Nightbreed; The Out-of-Towners* (Hiller); *The Out-of-Towners* (Weisman); *Predator 2; Quick Change; RoboCop; RoboCop 2; RoboCop 3; Speed; The Taking of Pelham One Two Three; Tetsuo; Tetsuo II: Bodyhammer; Timecop; Traffic; Welcome II the Terrordome; The Warriors*

Uris, Leon, films adapted from work, *Exodus, Topaz*

Uruguay
Uruguayan cinema, *Tupamaros; 25 Watts*
in film, *State of Siege; Tupamaros; 25 Watts*

Vacations, see **Holidays and holiday camps**

Valentino, Rudolph, film about, *Valentino*

Valens, Richie, film about, *La Bamba*

Vampires, *The Addiction; The Alchemist; Blade; Blade II; Blood for Dracula; Blood: The Last Vampire; Brides of Dracula; Buffy the Vampire Slayer; Captain Kronos – Vampire Hunter; Count Dracula; Countess Dracula; Count Yorga, Vampire; Cronos; Dance of the Vampires; Daughters of Darkness; Dead of Night* (Clark); *DEF by Temptation; Discipline of Death; Dracula* (Badham); *Dracula* (Browning); *Dracula* (Fisher); *Dracula* (Coppola); *Dracula A.D. 1972; Dracula: Dead and Loving It; Dracula Has Risen from the Grave; Dracula, Prince of Darkness; Dracula's Daughter; Dracula 2000; Elvira, Mistress of the Dark; Female Vampires; The Forsaken; Fright Night; Fright Night Part 2; Le Frisson des Vampires; Ganga and Hess; I Bought a Vampire Motorcycle; Incense for the Damned; Innocent Blood; Interview With the Vampire; It Conquered the World; Kiss of the Vampire; The Lady Vampire; Legend of the 7 Golden Vampires; Lifeforce; The Little Vampire; The Lost Boys; Love at First Bite; Mark of the Vampire; Martin; Mr Vampire; The Monster Club; Nadja; Near Dark; Nightwing; Nocturna; Nosferatu – Eine Symphonie des Grauens; Nosferatu the Vampire; Queen of the Damned; Razor Blade Smile; Requiem pour un Vampire; The Return of Count Yorga; Return of the Vampire; Salem's Lot; The Satanic Rites of Dracula; The Scars of Dracula; Shadow of the Vampire; Son of Dracula; Tale of a Vampire; Taste the Blood of Dracula; Twins of Evil; Vamp; Vampira; Vampire at Midnight; The Vampire Bat; The Vampire Circus; Vampire in Brooklyn; The Vampire Lovers; Vampires; Vampires in Venice; Vampyr; The Velvet Vampire; Le Viol du Vampire*
imagining oneself to be a vampire, *Vampire's Kiss*
vampire Westerns, *Billy the Kid vs Dracula; Sundown*

Van Druten, John, films adapted from work, *I Am a Camera; Old Acquaintance; Rich and Famous*

Vane, Sutton, film adapted from work, *Outward Bound*

Van Gogh, Vincent,
films about, *Lust for Life; Van Gogh; Vincent: The Life and Death of Vincent Van Gogh; Vincent & Theo*
relationship with Toulouse-Lautrec, Lautrec

Vargas Llosa, Mario, film adapted from work, *Tune in Tomorrow*

Venereal diseases (see also **AIDS and HIV**), *The Clinic*

Venezuelan cinema, *The Colour of Love; A House with a View of the Sea; Disparen a Matar*

Venice, in film, *Blame It on the Bellboy; Blume in Love; Bread and Tulips; The Comfort of Strangers; Dangerous Beauty; Death in Venice; Don't Look Now; Les Enfants du siècle; Eve; Everyone Says I Love You; Festival* (Avati); *Hotel; In Love and War; A Little Romance; Nest of Vipers; Play Me Something; Senso; Summertime; Vampires in Venice; Venice: Theme and Variation; Volpone; The Wings of the Dove*

Ventriloquism, *Dead of Night; The Doll* (Ghose); *Killing Dad; Knock on Wood; Magic*

Vercel, Roger, film adapted from work, *Capitaine Conan*

Verdi, Giuseppe, films of/featuring operas, *The Adventure of Sherlock Holmes' Smarter Brother; Otello; Rigoletto; La Traviata*

Verlaine, Paul, film about, *Total Eclipse*

Verne, Jules, films adapted from work, *The Adventures of Michael Strogonoff; The Amazing Captain Nemo; Around the World in 80 Days; Captain Nemo and the Underwater City; Journey to the Centre of the Earth; Jules Verne's Rocket to the Moon; The Light at the Edge of the World; Mysterious Island; 20000 Leagues Under the Sea*

Victoria, Queen of England, in film, *Mrs Brown; The Mudlark*

Vidal, Gore, films adapted from work, *The Best Man; The Left Handed Gun; Myra Breckinridge*

Videomakers, *Skinless Night; Tapeheads*

Videotapes, malevolent, *Ring, Ring 2*

Vienna, in film, *Before Sunrise; Bitter Sweet; Goodnight Vienna; Letter from an Unknown Woman; The Third Man*

Vietnam
Vietnamese cinema, *At the Height of Summer; Cyclo; Nostalgia for Countryland; The Return; Three Seasons*
Vietnam in film, *At the Height of Summer; Boat People; Cyclo; Nostalgia for Countryland; The Return; The Scent of Green Papaya; Three Seasons*

Vietnam War, *Air America; Apocalypse Now; Apocalypse Now Redux; BAT 21; Born on the Fourth of July; The Boys in Company C; Bullet in the Head; Casualties of War; Dear America: Letters Home from Vietnam; The Deer Hunter; Dogfight; 84 Charlie Mopic; Flight of the Intruder; Full Metal Jacket; Good Morning Vietnam; Go Tell the Spartans; The Green Berets; Hamburger Hill; Heaven & Earth; The Iron Triangle; The Odd Angry Shot; Off Limits; Platoon; Tigerland; We Were Soldiers*
aftermath, *Cyclo; Turtle Beach*
anti-war movement, *Far from Vietnam; Letter to Jane; 1969; Rude Awakening; Running on Empty; Vietnam Journey*

Vietnam veterans, *Accidental Hero; Americana; The American Way; Backfire; The Big Lebowski; Billy Jack; Birdy; Blind Fury; Blue Thunder; Born Losers; Born on the Fourth of July; Ceasefire; Coming Home; Cutter's Way; The Deer Hunter; Desperate Hours* (Cimino); *The Diamond Mercenaries; The Domino Principle; Don't Play with Fire; Extreme Prejudice; Eyewitness; Firefox; First Blood; The Fourth War; Gardens of Stone; Good Guys Wear Black; Gordon's War; Hearts and Minds; Heroes; Hi, Mom!; In Country; The Indian*

Runner; Jacknife; Jacob's Ladder; Jason's Lyric; Lethal Weapon; Lethal Weapon 2; Lethal Weapon 3; Lethal Weapon 4; Missing in Action; Open Season; Rambo: First Blood, Part II; Rambo III; Scent of a Woman; Slaughter; Slaughter's Big Rip-Off; Some Kind of Hero; Summer Soldiers; Taxi Driver; Three Seasons; Tracks; Ulee's Gold; Uncommon Valor; Universal Soldier; Unnatural Causes: The Agent Orange Story; Vigilante Force; The War; War; The War at Home; Welcome Home; Who'll Stop the Rain?*

Vietnamese in USA, *Alamo Bay; Gleaming in the Cuba; Three Seasons*

Vigilantes, *Breaking Point; Cop's Honour; The Crackdown; Death Wish; Death Wish II; Death Wish 3; Death Wish 4; Defiance; Exterminator 2; Eye for an Eye; Falling Down; Fighting Back; Fury* (Lang); *Gordon's War; Handgun* (Garnett); *Hero at Large; Jimmy Hollywood; Law and Disorder; Original Gangstas; The Ox-Bow Incident; Surf Nazis Must Die; Taxi; 10 to Midnight; This Day and Age; Trackdown; Vigilante Force; Young Warriors*

Vigo, Jean, film about, *Vigo Passion for Life*

Villard, Henry S, film adapted from work, *In Love and War* (Attenborough)

Vikings, *Erik the Viking; The Long Ships; The Norseman; The 13th Warrior; The Vikings; The Viking Women and Their Voyage to the Waters of the Great Sea Serpent*

Virtual reality (see also **Computers and Computer games, effects of**), *Avalon; eXistenZ; Hot War; The Lawnmower Man; Lawnmower Man 2: Beyond Cyberspace; The Matrix*

Volcanoes, *Aloma of the South Seas; Dante's Peak; Krakatoa – East of Java; The Last Days of Pompeii; La Soufrière; Stromboli, Terra di Dio; Volcano*

Volleyball, film about, *Iron Ladies*

von Arnim, Elizabeth, film adapted from work, *Enchanted April*

von Bülow, Claus, film about, *Reversal of Fortune*

von Hoffman, Nicholas, film adapted from work, *Citizen Cohn*

Vonnegut, Kurt, films adapted from work, *Breakfast of Champions; Happy Birthday, Wanda June; Mother Night; Slaughterhouse Five; Who Am I This Time?*

Voodoo and similar sects, *Barravento; The Believers; Curtis's Charm; The Ghost Breakers; Island of Mutation; I Walked with a Zombie; Midnight in the Garden of Good and Evil; Mississippi Burning; The Serpent and the Rainbow; Voodoo Woman; White Zombie; Zombie Flesh-Eaters*

Voyeurism, *Addicted to Love; Blind Date* (Mastorakis); *Cheap Shots; Dekalog 6: 'Thou shalt not commit adultery'; Extreme Close-Up; Fetishes; Homework; Jardines Colgantes; Monsieur Hire; Peeping Tom; Rear Window; sex, lies and videotape; A Short Film About Love; Sliver; White Room*

Wagner, Richard
film about, *Wagner*
film of opera, *Parsifal*

Wagner, Winifred, film about, *The Confessions of Winifred Wagner*

Wakefield, Dan, film adapted from work, *Going All the Way*

Wales, in film, *August; Boy Soldier; Circle of Danger; Coming Up Roses; Danny Jones; Les Deux Anglaises et le Continent; Darklands; Elenya; The Englishman Who Went Up a Hill, But Came Down a Mountain; Experience Preferred But Not Essential; Happy Now?; Hedd Wyn; House!; House of America; Human Traffic; The James Gang; One Full Moon; Only Two Can Play; On the Black Hill; The Phantom Light; The Proposition; Rebecca's Daughters; Second Best; Solomon and Gaenor; Streetlife; Tiger Bay; Twin Town; Under Milk Wood; Valley of Song; Very Annie-Mary*

Walker, Alice, film adapted from work, *The Color Purple*

Walker, Bruce, film adapted from work, *Cosh Boy*

Walker, David, films adapted from work, *Geordie; Operation Amsterdam*

Wallace, Edgar, films adapted from work, *Before Dawn; Dark Eyes of London; The Gaunt Stranger; The Squeaker*

Wallace, William, in film, *Braveheart*

Waller, Robert James, film from work, *The Bridges of Madison County*

Walser, Robert, film adapted from work, *Institute Benjamenta*

Walsh, Enda, film adapted from work, *Disco Pigs*

Wambaugh, Joseph, films adapted from work, *The Black Marble; The Choirboys; The Glitter Dome; The New Centurions; The Onion Field*

War criminals (see also **Germany, Jews and Jewish life**), *Apt Pupil; Blood Oath; The Boys from Brazil; Capoblanco; Deadfall; Father; Hotel Terminus: The Life and Times of Klaus Barbie; The House on Carroll Street; The House on Garibaldi Street; Judgment at Nuremberg; The Man in the Glass Booth; The Memory of Justice; Music Box; The Night Porter; None Shall Escape; The Odessa File; The Stranger* (Welles)

Warhol, Andy, films about/associated with, *Basquiat; Bike Boy; Blood for Dracula; Blue Movie; Chelsea Girls; Couch; Downtown 81; Flesh; Heat* (Morrissey); *I Shot Andy Warhol; Lonesome Cowboys; My Hustler; Nico Icon; Trash; Women in Revolt*

Warren, Robert Penn, film adapted from work, *All the King's Men*

Watergate, *All the President's Men; Nasty Habits; Nixon; Paperback Vigilante; Return Engagement; The Werewolf of Washington*

Waterhouse, Keith, and Hall, Willis, films adapted from work, *Billy Liar*

Waugh, Alec, film adapted from work, *Island in the Sun*

Waugh, Evelyn, films adapted from work, *Decline and Fall...of a Birdwatcher; A Handful of Dust; The Loved One*

Waxworks, *Chamber of Horrors; Crucible of Terror; House of Wax; Mystery of the Wax Museum; Waxwork*

Webster, John, film incorporating work, *Hotel*

Wedekind, Frank, film adapted from work, *Pandora's Box*

Weegee, film about, *The Public Eye*

Weill, Kurt
film about, *September Songs: The Music of Kurt Weill*
musical by, *Lady in the Dark; Lost in the Stars*
and Brecht, Bertold, musical by, *Die Dreigroschenoper*

Weiss, Peter, film adapted from work, *The Persecution and Assassination of Jean-Paul Marat as Performed by the Inmates of the Asylum of Charenton under the Direction of the Marquis de Sade*

Weldon, Fay, film adapted from work, *She-Devil*

Welles, Orson, film about, *Cradle Will Rock*

Wellman, William, film about, *Wild Bill: A Hollywood Maverick*

Wells, HG
fictional representation, *Time After Time*
films adapted from/based on work, *Dead of Night* (Crichton episode); *Empire of the Ants; First Men in the Moon; Food of the Gods; Half a Sixpence; The History of Mr Polly; The Invisible Man; The Island of Dr Moreau* (Taylor); *The Island of Dr Moreau* (Frankenheimer); *The Island of Mutations; La Merveilleuse Visite; The Man Who Could Work Miracles; The Passionate Friends; The Shape of Things to Come; Things to Come; Time After Time; The Time Machine; War of the Worlds*

Welsh, Irvine, films adapted from works, *The Acid House; Trainspotting*

Wenders, Wim, film about, *Motion and Emotion: The Films of Wim Wenders*

Werewolves, *An American Werewolf in Paris; The Beast Must Die; Brotherhood of the Wolf; The Curse of the Werewolf; Dog Soldiers; Frankenstein Meets the Wolf Man; Ginger Snaps; The Howling; I Was a Teenage; Werewolf; The Return of the Vampire; Silver Bullet; Teen Wolf; Teen Wolf II; The Undying Monster; Werewolf of London; The Werewolf of Washington; Wolf; Wolfen; The Wolf Man*

Wesker, Arnold, film adapted from work, *The Kitchen*

West, Morris, films adapted from work, *The Devil's Advocate; The Shoes of the Fisherman*

West, Nathanael, film adapted from work, *The Day of the Locust; Lonleyhearts*

Westerns (see Appendix 15 for full listing)
eastern Western, *Dust*
end-of-West, *Comes a Horseman; The Grey Fox; The Hi-Lo Country; Lonely Are the Brave; The Man Who Shot Liberty Valance; The Misfits; Monte Walsh; Once Upon a Time in the West; Pat Garrett and Billy the Kid; Ride the High Country; The Spikes Gang; The Wild Bunch*
influence of, *My Dear Tom Mix*
schnitzel, *The Hellhounds of Alaska*

spaghetti, *Bad Man's River; The Big Silence; Blazing Guns; Blindman; Blood Money; Blood River; A Bullet for the General; China 9, Liberty 37; Comin' at Ya!; Companeros; Cry Onion; Deaf Smith and Johnny Ears; Django; Django Kill; El Condor; A Fistful of Dollars; A Fistful of Fingers; For a Few Dollars More; The Good, the Bad and the Ugly; Guns for San Sebastian; Il Mercenario; My Name Is Nobody; Once Upon a Time in the West; I Quattro dell'Ave Maria; A Reason to Live, a Reason to Die; Red Sun; Return of Sabata; Sabata; Shalako; La Strada per Forte Alamo; Straight to Hell; Take a Hard Ride; Texas, Addio; They Call Me Trinity; Three Buillets for a Long Gun; Today It's Me…Tomorrow You!; A Town Called Bastard; The Triumphs of a Man Called Horse; Valdez il Mezzosangue; Vengeance*

Westlake, Donald E, films adapted from work (see also **Stark,** Richard), *Bank Shot; Cops and Robbers; The Hot Rock; Jimmy the Kid; Slayground; A Slight Case of Murder; Two Much; Why Me?*

Whale, James, film about, *Gods and Monsters*

Whales and dolphins, *Ace Ventura, Pet Detective; Atlantis; Day of the Dolphin; Dolphins; Flipper* (Clark); *Flipper* (Shapiro); *Free Willy; Free Willy 2; Free Willy 3: The Rescue; Moby Dick; Namu, The Killer Whale; Orca; Tadpole and the Whale; The Unfish; Venus Peter; The Voyage Home: Star Trek IV; When the Whales Came*

Wharton, Edith, films adapted from work, *The Age of Innocence; Ethan Frome; The House of Mirth*

Wharton, William, films adapted from work, *Birdy; A Midnight Clear*

Wheatley, Dennis, films adapted from work, *The Devil Rides Out; The Lost Continent; To the Devil a Daughter*

Whipple, Dorothy, film adapted from work, *They Were Sisters*

White, EB, films adapted from work, *Charlotte's Web; Stuart Little*

White, TH, film adapted from work, *The Sword in the Stone*

Whitman, Walt, film about, *Beautiful Dreamers*

Wilde, Oscar
films adapted from work, *Black and Silver; Flesh and Fantasy; An Ideal Husband* (Korda); *An Ideal Husband* (Parker); *The Importance of Being Earnest; The Picture of Dorian Gray; Salome* (Bryant); *Salomé* (d'Anna); *Salomé's Last Dance*
his life retold, *A Man of No Importance*
films about, *The Trials of Oscar Wilde; Wilde*

Wilde, Patrick,
film adapted from work, *Get Real*

Wilder, Thornton
films adapted from work, *Mr North; Our Town*
work in film, *First Love* (Lee Myung-Se)

Willeford, Charles,
films adapted from work, *Cockfighter; Miami Blues*

Williams, Cecil, film about, *The Man Who Drove with Mandela*

Williams, Charles, films adapted from work, *Dead Calm; The Hot Spot; Vivement Dimanche*

Williams, Emlyn, films adapted from work, *Night Must Fall* (Thorpe); *Night Must Fall* (Reisz); *Time Without Pity*

Williams, Robbie, film about, *Nobody Someday*

Williams, Tennessee, films adapted from work, *Baby Doll; Boom; Cat on a Hot Tin Roof; The Fugitive Kind; The Glass Menagerie; The Night of the Iguana; Noir et Blanc; Period of Adjustment; The Roman Spring of Mrs Stone; A Streetcar Named Desire; Suddenly Last Summer; Summer and Smoke; Sweet Bird of Youth* (Brooks); *Sweet Bird of Youth* (Roeg); *This Property Is Condemned*

Williamson, David, films adapted from work, *Brilliant Lies; The Club; Don't Party; Travelling North*

Williamson, Henry, film adapted from work, *Tarka the Otter*

Willingham, Calder, films adapted from work, *Rambling Rose; The Strange One*

Willis, Ted, film adapted from work, *No Trees in the Street*

Wing, Avra, film adapted from work, *Angie*

Winton, Tim,
film adapted from work, *In the Winter Dark*

Wiseman, Cardinal, film adapted from work, *Fabiola*

Witchcraft, etc (see also **Devil, The, and Antichrist, Magic and magicians**), *Baba Yaga – The Devil Witch; Bedknobs and Broomsticks; The Cellar; The Craft; The Crucible; The Curse of the Crimson Altar; Cry of the Banshee; Daughter of Satan; Day of Wrath; The Devil Rides Out; The Devils; The Devil's Rain; The Face of Darkness; Ghoulies; The Guardian; Halloween III; Halloween: The Curse of Michael Myers; The Haunted Palace; Hello Again; Hex; Hocus Pocus; I Married a Witch; Jack's Wife; The Kiss; The Lair of the White Worm; Macciste all'Inferno; Maid for Pleasure; The Manitou; La Maschera del Demonio; The Mask* (Roffman); *The Mask of the Red Death; The Mephisto Waltz; Night of the Demon; Night of the Eagle; Practical Magic; Pumpkinhead; Race with the Devil; Rosemary's Baby; Satan's Skin; Satan's Slave; Supergirl; Superstition; Terror; To the Devil a Daughter; To Sleep with Anger; The Undead; The Unholy; Warlock; Wicked Stepmother; Witchcraft Through the Ages; The Witches; The Witches of Eastwick; Witchfinder General; Wizard of Darkness*

Witness-to-crime stories, *Absolute Power; The Bedroom Window; Blow Out* (De Palma); *Body Double; Call Me; Cheap Shots; The Client; Cohen and Tate; Dangerous Mission; The Eyes of Laura Mars; Eyewitness* (Hough); *Eyewitness* (Yates); *Flight of the Innocent; The Fruit Machine; Highways by Night; Lady on a Train; Love and Bullets; The Mad Miss Manton; Monolith; Mute Witness; Nadine; Off and Running; Rapid Fire; Rear Window; See No Evil, Hear No Evil; The Sleeping Car Murder; Some Like It Hot; Stop! or My Mom Will Shoot; True Identity; Turner and Hooch; L'Uccello dalle Piume di Cristallo; White Room; The Window; Witness*

Wittgenstein, Ludwig, film about, *Wittgenstein*

Wodehouse, PG, film adapted from work, *Thank You, Jeeves!*

Wolfe, Tom, films adapted from work, *The Bonfire of the Vanities; The Last American Hero; The Right Stuff*

Wolfe, Winifred, film adapted from work, *Ask Any Girl*

Wolff, Tobias, film adapted from work, *This Boy's Life*

Women
and ageing, *Bye-Bye Babushka; The Company of Strangers; The First Wives Club; Good Morning, Miss Dove; MURDER and Murder; Unhook the Stars; La Vieille Dame indigne*
and independence, *All's Fair; Anna Karenina* (Brown); *Anna Karenina* (Duvivier); *Anna Karenina* (Rose); *The Associate; The Ballad of Little Jo; Bandit Queen; Bend It Like Beckham; Bhaji on the Beach; Blue Steel; Les Bonnes Femmes; Bye Bye Blues; Camilla; Camille Claudel; Century; Christopher Strong; City of Women; Club des Femmes; Confessions of a Suburban Girl; Courage Under Fire; Cross and Passion; Dance, Girl, Dance; The Day I Became a Woman; Desperately Seeking Susan; Diary of a Mad Housewife; Dr T & the Women; Doll's Eye; The End of August; Erin Brokovich; Fatma; Female Company; The First Wives Club; Fire; Flowers in the Attic; The Flower of My Secret; Fried Green Tomatoes at the Whistle Stop Café; Full Moon in Paris; Gion Festival Music; Good Morning, Miss Dove; Hi, Are You Alone?; Hindle Wakes; Honey and Venom; How to Make an American Quilt; If These Walls Could Talk; I Like It Like That; In My Father's House; Joyriders; Kika; Kiss the Girls; Klute; The Lady & the Duke; Lara Croft: Tomb Raider; A League of Their Own; Leaving Normal; The Left-Handed Woman; Lucie Aubrac; Majdhar; The Major and the Minor; Malou; Mama's Dirty Girls; Monkey Grip; Morvern Callar; MURDER and Murder; My Brilliant Career; My Crazy Life; My Life Without Steve; Mystic Pizza; Nanou; The Net; Nine Months; Nora; Norma Rae; 1+1=3; The Opposite Sex; Osaka Elegy; Paris Was a Woman; Patti Rocks; Place Vendôme; The Prime of Miss Jean Brodie; Privilege* (Rainer); *Rachel, Rachel; The Rainbow; Redheads; Right Out of History: The Making of Judy Chicago's Dinner Party; Passion Fish; Pas Trés Catholique; Salt of the Earth; The Scent of Green Papaya; The Secret of Convict Lake; Set It Off; Shame; She Lives to Ride; Shirley Valentine; Sigmund Freud's Dora; The Silence of the Lambs; Sliding Doors; Strapless; Take Care of My Cat; 10* (Kiarostami); *There's Always Tomorrow; Three Colours: Blue; The Trout; True Lies; Tumbleweeds; Unhook the Stars; Union Maids; An Unmarried Woman; An Unsuitable Job for a Woman; Up the Sandbox; V I Warshawski; Waiting to Exhale; Wanda; The Watermelon Woman; What Have I Written?; The White Wall; Widows' Peak; Wifemistress; The Wild Party* (Arzner); *A Winter Tan; Wives; Wives: Ten*

Years After; Wives III; A Woman Rebels; Woman to Woman; The Women; Women in Love
as victim, *Bridget Jones's Diary; The Burning; Calle Mayor; The Circle; Deceived; La Dentellière; Farewell to False Paradise; Folle à Tuer; 40 Square Metre Germany; Immoral Tales; The Incredible Shrinking Woman; In My Father's House; Intimate Confessions of a Chinese Courtesan; Jackson County Jail; Kadosh; Lucia; Die Marquise von O…; The Match Factory Girl; Occasional Work of a Female Slave; Painted Angels; The Power of Men Is the Patience of Women; La Religieuse; La Signora senza camelie; Sleeping with the Enemy; Stranger; Streetlife; Summer Wishes; Theatre Girls; Thesis; A Thousand Pieces of Gold; We're Alive; Woman in a Dressing Gown; A Woman Under the Influence*
femmes fatales/avengers/ destroyers, *Act of Vengeance; Adrenalin – Fear the Rush; Afternoon Breezes; Another Life; Attack of the Fifty Foot Woman* (Juran); *Attack of the 50ft Woman* (Guest); *Baise-moi; Barb Wire; Becky Sharp; Beyond the Forest; Black Widow* (Rafelson); *The Business of Strangers; Caged Heat; La Cérémonie* (Chabrol); *Crush; Daughters of Darkness; DEF by Temptation; Dirty Weekend; Disclosure; Dolores Caliborne; 8 Women; Elevator; The Enchantment; Eve of Destruction; Everybody Wins; Eye for an Eye; Face; Fatal Attraction; Femme Fatale; Forty Guns; Georgette Meunier; The Gorgon; Handgun* (Garnett); *Hands of the Ripper; Hannie Caulder; The Hawk; The Heroic Trio; A Hot Roof; Innocents with Dirty Hands; Ivy; A Judgement in Stone* (Rawi); *Kawashima Yoshiko; Kill Me Again; The Kiss; Labyrinth of Dreams; LA Confidential; The Lady from the Shanghai Cinema; Lara Croft: Tomb Raider; Lewis & Clark & George; Madame Sin; The Mad Monkey; Marked Woman; Mike's Murder; Ms .45; My Cousin Rachel; The Naked Cell; The Oklahoma Woman; Panic Room; Papa, Les Petits Bateaux; Penthesilea: Queen of the Amazons; Perdita Durango; Prejudice; Queen of Outer Space; Rambling Rose; Red Peony Gambler: Flower Cards Match; Romeo Is Bleeding; Sea of Love; Shatterd Image; She* (Day); *She* (Pichel); *She-Devil; Sherlock Holmes and the Spider Woman; Species; Stranger Inside; La Tendre Ennemie; Thelma & Louise; Truckstop Women; Walking and Talking; The Wasp Woman; Welcome II the Terrordome; Wild Things*
struggling through, *Agnes Browne; About Mrs Leslie; Aïd el Kébir; All About My Mother; Applause; Baby the Rain Must Fall; Bemani; Bridget Jones's Diary; Bye-Bye Babushka; Career Girls; Cloud-capped Star; Cotton Mary; Dancer in the Dark; Dream On; Eve's Bayou; Flame; Flower Island; Full Moon in New York; Haut les Coeurs; Hope Floats; Hypnotised and Hysterical (Hairstylist Wanted); El Jardin del Eden; Lady L; Kira's Reason – A Love Story; The Last Crop; Love and Duty; Mamma Roma; Men Don't Leave; Moonlight and Valentino; Mother India; 1999 Madeleine; Nobody Will Speak of Us When We're Dead; No Sad Songs for Me; Le Notti di Cabiria; Paradise Road; Prison Stories: Women on the Inside; Push! Push!; The Road to Nhill; The Shining Hour; Some Kind of Love; Some Mother's Son; Steel Magnolias; Stella; Stella Dallas; Street of Shame; Summer Magic; Summer Snow; Surrogate Mother; The Thief of Saint Lubin; Ticket; Venus Beauty; The Weak and the Wicked; What Have I Done to Deserve This?; Where the Heart Is; The Whores; Will It Snow for Christmas?; Wittstock, Wittstock; Women from the Medina; Woman Obsessed; Women on the Verge of a Nervous Breakdown*
women artists, *Anne Trister; Artemisia; Camille Claudel; Imago – Meret Oppenheim; Isabelle Eberhardt; Right Out of History: The Making of Judy Chicago's Dinner Party; The Sandpiper*
in Australia, *Caddie; For Love or Money; High Tide; Radiance*
in Brazil, *Hour of the Star*
in China, *The Girls to Be Married; Ripples Across Stagnant Water; The Story of Qiu Ju; A Story of Women; Two Stage Sisters*
in Cuba, *Portrait of Teresa*
in Hungary, *When Joseph Returns*
in India, *Charulata; The Chosen One; Mahanagar; The Role; 36 Chowringhee Lane*
in Israel, *Kadosh*
in Japan, *Five Women Around Utamaro; The Good Wife of Tokyo; My Love Has Been Burning; Onibaba; Sisters of Gion*
in Korea, *Push! Push!*
in Lebanon, *Leila and the Wolves*
in Mexico, *Danzón; El Jardin del Eden*
in Poland, *A Woman on Her Own*
in South Africa, *South Africa Belongs to Us*
in Spain *Malena Is a Name from a Tango*
in Taiwan, *Lonely Hearts Club*
in war, *Firebirds; The Gentle Sex; The Girl with the Red Hair; The Life and Times of Rosie the Riveter; Swing Shift; Tender Comrade; The Unfaithful*

Woodward, Bob
film adapted from work, *Wired*
and Carl Bernstein, film about, *All the President's Men*

Woolf, Virginia,
films adapted from work, *Mrs Dalloway; Orlando*

Woolrich, Cornell, films adapted from work,*Black Angel; The Bride Wore Black; Deadline at Dawn; Fear in the Night* (Sloane); *The Leopard Man; Martha; Mrs Winterbourne; The Night Has a Thousand Eyes; Nightmare* (Shane); *No Man of Her Own* (Leisen); *Original Sin; Phantom Lady; Union City; The Window*

Work, pressures of (see also **Boardroom jungle, Industry and industrial life, Office life**), *Among Giants; The Associate; Blue Collar; Car Wash; Company Limited; The Crowd; Desk Set; Family Business* (Cohen); *Gung Ho; Men Don't Leave; Nightshift; Nine to Five; No Pets; Raining Stones; Riff-Raff; Seacoal; '36 to '77; Work Is a Four Letter Word*

World War I, *Aces High; The African Queen; All Quiet on the Western Front* (Milestone); *All Quiet on the Western Front* (Mann); *Archangel; The Battle of the Somme; The Big Parade* (Vidor); *The Blue Max; Capitaine Conan; La Chambre des officiers; Les Croix de Bois; Dark Journey; Darling Lili; The Dawn Patrol* (Hawks); *The Dawn Patrol* (Goulding); *The Deserter and the Nomads; Dishonoured; A Farewell to Arms* (Borzage); *A Farewell to Arms* (Vidor); *The Fighting 69th; Forever England; Gallipoli; La Grande Illusion; Hedd Wyn; Hell's Angels; In Love and War; J'Accuse* (Gance, 1918); *J'Accuse* (Gance, 1937); *Journey's End; King & Country; King of Hearts; Lawrence of Arabia; Legends of the Fall; Life and Nothing But; The Lighthorsemen; The Lost Patrol; Mademoiselle Docteur; Mata Hari* (Fitzmaurice); *Mata Hari* (Harrington); *Mata Hari, Agent H.21; Oh! What a Lovely War!; Paths of Glory; Regeneration; The Road to Glory; Sergeant York; 7th Heaven* (Borzage); *Seventh Heaven* (King); *The Spy in Black; Stamboul Quest; Tell England; Thomas l'Imposteur; The Trench; Von Richthofen and Brown; Westfront 1918; Wings*

World War II (see also **Sea Dramas**)
in Australia, *Death of a Soldier; Emma's War; Rebel*
in Black Africa, *Camp Thiaroye; Emitaï*
in Britain, *The Affair; Chicago Joe and the Showgirl; The Custard Boys; Dad's Army; Dark Blue World; The Demi-Paradise; The Dressmaker; The Eagle Has Landed; Enigma; Elenya; Eye of the Needle; Fires Were Started; Foreign Correspondent; The Gentle Sex; Hope and Glory; I Live in Grosvenor Square; The Imitation Game; The Land Girls; Millions Like Us; Mrs Miniver; The New Lot; The Next of Kin; Once a Jolly Swagman; Overlord; Perfect Strangers; They Were Not Divided; This Above All; The War Bride; Waterloo Road; The Way Ahead; Went the Day Well?; Yanks*
in Canada, *Bye Bye Blues; 49th Parallel*
in China, *Flying Tigers*
in Czechoslovakia, *Divided We Fall; The Fifth Rider Is Fear; Four Sons; The Search; A Shop on the High Street*
in France, *The Bunker*
in Germany, *The Desert Fox; Escape* (LeRoy); *Europa, Europa; Forbidden; Heimat; I Was Nineteen; The Night of the Generals; The Sea Chase; Shining Through; A Time to Love and a Time to Die; The Tin Drum*
– aftermath, *Une Femme française; Germany, Year Zero; Judgment at Nuremberg; Somewhere in Berlin; Stunde Null*
in Greece *Captain Corelli's Mandolin*
in Hungary *Jadviga's Pillow*
in Ireland, *The Brylcreem Boys; I See a Dark Stranger; A Terrible Beauty*
in Netherlands, *Soldier of Orange*
in Norway, *Edge of Darkness; The Last Lieutenant; Nine Lives; Submarine X-1*
in Palestine, *Every Time We Say Goodbye*
in Philippines, *American Guerilla in the Philippines*
in Poland, *The Pianist*
in Portugal, *The Conspirators*
in Sweden, *Love Lessons*
in Taiwan, *A City of Sadness*
in Turkey, *5 Fingers; Journey into Fear*
in US, *An American Romance; Careful, Soft Shoulder; The Color of Honor; Come See the Paradise; Fat Man and Little Boy; For the Boys; Hail the Conquering Hero; In Love and War* (Dunne); *Journey for Margaret; Kiss Them for Me; A League of Their Own; The Life and Times of Rosie the Riveter; Since You Went Away; Swing Shift; Tender Comrade; A Time of Destiny; When Willie Comes Marching Home*
in USSR, *Ballad of a Soldier; Come and See; Cross of Iron; Days of Glory; The Demi-Paradise; Enemy at the Gates; Ivan's Childhood; My Private War; The North*

Star; The Patriot; Stalingrad; Trial on the Road; Twenty Days Without War
– aftermath, *Before Winter Comes; Letters from the East*
Pacific War, *Air Force; Away All Boats; Back to Bataan; Bataan; Beach Red; Between Heaven and Hell; The Burmese Harp; Destination Gobi; The Emperor's Naked Army Marches On; Ensign Pulver; Farewell to the King; Father Goose; The Fighting Seabees; Flying Leathernecks; Guadalcanal Diary; Halls of Montezuma; Hellcats of the Navy; Hell in the Pacific; An Indecent Obsession; In Harm's Way; Malaya; Merrill's Marauders; Midway; Mister Roberts; None But the Brave; Not Forgotten; Objective, Burma!; Operation Petticoat; Pearl Harbor; Pride of the Marines; Sands of Iwo Jima; They Were Expendable; The Thin Red Line; Too Late the Hero; Tora! Tora! Tora!; Torpedo Run; The Wackiest Ship in the Army; The Wind Cannot Read*
– aftermath, *Blood Oath*
PoW stories, *Blood Oath; The Bridge on the River Kwai; The Brylcreem Boys; Le Caporal Epinglé; The Captive Heart; The Colditz Story; Empire of the Sun; Escape to Athena; First Yank into Tokyo; The Great Escape; Hannibal Brooks; King Rat; The Mackenzie Break; Merry Christmas Mr Lawrence; The One That Got Away; Paradise Road; The Password Is Courage; Return from the River Kwai; Seven Years in Tibet; Slaughterhouse Five; A Town Like Alice; Two Thousand Women; La Vache et la Prisonnier; Victory; Von Ryan's Express; The Wind Cannot Read*
War in the Desert, *Desert Mice; Desert Victory; Five Graves to Cairo; Ice Cold in Alex; The Immortal Sergeant; Play Dirty; Sahara* (Korda); *Sea of Sand; Three Came Home; Tunisian Victory*
War in Western Europe and Atlantic, *Action in the North Atlantic; Attack; Battleground; The Battle of the Bulge; The Battle of the River Plate; The Big Red One; The Boat; The Boat: The Director's Cut; The Bridge at Remagen; A Bridge Too Far; Catch-22; Cockleshell Heroes; Command Decision; The Cruel Sea; The Dambusters; Dangerous Moonlight; Desperate Journey; The Devil's Brigade; Dunkirk; Hell Is for Heroes; Heroes; In Which We Serve; I Was Monty's Double; John Huston War Stories; Journey Together; Kelly's Heroes; The Key; The Long Day's Dying; The Longest Day; The Long Voyage Home; Memphis Belle; A Midnight Clear; Mosquito Squadron; The Naked and the Dead; Reach for the Sky; San Demetrio, London; Saving Private Ryan; Lo Sbarco di Anzio; The Steel Bayonet; The Story of GI Joe; 36 Hours; The True Glory; Twelve O'Clock High; Verboten; The Victors; A Walk in the Sun; The Way to the Stars; Western Approaches; What Did You Do in the War, Daddy?; Where Eagles Dare; Which Way to the Front?; A Yank in the RAF*

World War II: Resistance and life in occupied countries (see also **Germany, Jews and Jewish life**)
in Belgium, *Against the Wind; Une Femme Entre Chien et Loup*
in Burma, *Never So Few*
in China, *Along the Sungari River; Au revoir, mon amour; 8,000 Li Under the Clouds and Moon; The Highway; The Inn of the Sixth Happiness; The Spring River Flows East*
in Czechoslovakia, *Closely Observed Trains; The Deserter and the Nomads; Hangmen Also Die; Hitler's Madman; Operation Daybreak*
in Denmark, *Once There Was A War*
in Europe (unidentified), *This Land Is Mine*
in France, *L'Affiche Rouge; L'Armée des Ombres; Au Revoir les Enfants; La Bataille du Rail; The Blood of Others; Carve Her Name With Pride; Le Chagrin et la Pitié; Chantons sous l'Occupation; Charlotte Gray; Un Condamné à Mort s'est Echappé; Le Corbeau; Coup de Foudre; Docteur Petiot; Escape Route to Marseille; Fortunat; Hotel Terminus: La Ligne de Démarcation; The Life and Times of Klaus Barbie; Les Jeux Interdits; Julia; Lacombe Lucien; The Last Metro; Leon Morin, Priest; Letters to an Unknown Lover; Lucie Aubrac; November Moon; Odette; One Man's War; Orders to Kill; Paris After Dark; Le Père Tranquille; sPétain; Le Petit Matin; Le Roi des Aulnes; Un Sac de Billes; Section Spéciale; Le Silence de la mer; Souvenir; Terrorists in Retirement; Till We Meet Again; The Train; La Traversée de Paris; Uranus; La Vache et la Prisonnier; Le Vice et la Vertu; Le Vieil Homme et l'Enfant; Les Violons du Bal; We Were One Man*
in Fr West Indies, *The Breaking Point* (Curtiz); *To Have and Have Not*
in Greece, *The Guns of Navarone; Ill Met by Moonlight; Mediterraneo; Signs of Life*
in Hong Kong, *Love in a Fallen City*
in Hungary, *Confidence; Hanna's War; My Mother's Courage; My Way Home*
in Italy, *Era Notte a Roma; From the Cloud to the Resistance; Massacre in Rome; The Night of San Lorenzo; Paisà; Roma, Città Aperta*
in Morocco, *Casablanca*
in the Netherlands, *The Girl With the Red Hair; One of Our Aircraft Is Missing; Operation Amsterdam; Operation Crossbow*
in Norway, *Cold Tracks; Force 10 from Navarone; The Heroes of Telemark*
in Philippines *American Guerilla in the Philippines*
in Poland, *Ashes and Diamonds; A Generation; Kanal; Korczak; Lodz Ghetto; Night Paths; None Shall Escape; Jakob the LiarSchindler's List; The Third Part of the Night; To Be or Not To Be* (Lubitsch); *To Be or Not To Be* (Johnson)
in unidentified country *La Neige était sale*
in Yugoslavia, *Innocence Unprotected; The Long Ride; Occupation in 26 Pictures; 67 Days; That Summer of White Roses*

Worms, malevolent, *Squirm; Tremors; The Worm Eaters*

Wouk, Herman, film adapted from work, *The Caine Mutiny*

Wrestling, *Beyond the Mat; The Foul King; Night and the City; The One and Only; Paradise Alley; Ready to Rumble; Vision Quest; The Wrestlers*
arm wrestling, *Over the Top*
female, *...All the Marbles; Below the Belt; Fetishes; Gaea Girls; Hellcat Mud Wrestlers*
sumo, *Sumo Bruno; Sumo Do, Sumo Don't*

Writers and writing
in Argentina, *Cortazar; Last Images of the Shipwreck*
in Australia, *Hotel Sorrento; Kangaroo; Paperback Hero*
in Belgium, *Benvenuta*
in Brazil, *O Amor Natural*
in Britain, *Boom; A Business Affair; Charlie Bubbles; Croupier; Debt Collector, The; The End of the Affair; Eve; Gothic; Haunted Summer; Hedd Wyn; Horrors of the Black Museum; Iris; Keep the Aspidistra Flying; Love and Death on Long Island; Pandaemonium; Play Me Something; Prick Up Your Ears; Priest of Love; Prospero's Books; The Pumpkin Eater; Regeneration; The Romantic Englishwoman; Shadowlands; Shakespeare in Love; Sleuth; Stevie; Tiré à Part; The Trials of Oscar Wilde; Volcano*
in Canada, *Swann*
in Cuba, *Before Night Falls*
in Finland, *Flame Top*
in France, *Beaumarchais; Céleste; Les Créatures; La Discrète; En Compagnie d'Antonin Artaud; Les Enfants du siècle; Les Equilibristes; His Wife's Diary; Impromptu; Jaya Ganga; Jo; The Last Time I Saw Paris; Paris Was a Woman; Pola X; The Proprietor; Tiré à Part; Total Eclipse; Turtle on Its Back; La Vie de Bohème*
in Germany, *Berlin Jerusalem; Satan's Brew; 3 Women in Love; Wrong Movement*
in Greece, *Cavafy; Zorba the Greek*
in India, *Bombay Talkie; In Custody*
in Ireland, *The Book That Wrote Itself; Girl with Green Eyes; My Left Foot; Nora; A Portrait of the Artist as a Young Man; Young Cassidy*
in Italy, *Les Enfants du siècle; The Footman; Il Postino; Tenebrae; L'Uccello dalle Piume di Cristallo*
in Japan, *Body Drop Ashphalt; Mishima: A Life in Four Chapters; The Mystery of Rampo*
in Malta, *Trenchcoat*
in Mexico, *Gaby – A True Story*
in New Zealand, *An Angel at My Table; Crush*
in Portugal, *The Other One*
in South Korea, *Wind Echoing in My Being*
in Spain, *The Flower of My Secret; Sex and Lucía; Tender Hours*
in Sweden, *Amorosa*
in Switzerland, *La Salamandre*
in Trinidad, *The Mystic Masseur*
in US, *The Accidental Tourist; The Adventure of Mark Twain* (Rapper); *The Adventures of Mark Twain* (Vinton); *Another Woman; As Good As It Gets; Author, Author; Barton Fink; Beautiful Dreamers; Beloved Infidel; The Best Man; Best Seller; Breakfast of Champions; A Bucket of Blood; Closet Land; Communion; The Dark Half; Deconstructing Harry; Delirious; Equinox; Finding Forrester; A Fine Madness; The Front; Girl Shy; Hammett; Heartbeat; Henry & June; Henry Fool; Her Alibi; House; House by the River; In a Lonely Place; In the Mouth of Madness; I Remember Mama; Isn't She Great; James Baldwin: The Price of the Ticket; Joe Gould's Secret; Kerouac; Kissing a Fool; Julia; Love Streams; Manhattan; Misery; Monster in a Box; Naked Lunch; Never Give a Sucker an Even Break; The Proprietor; The Real Howard Spitz; Reuben, Reuben; Riding in Cars with Boys; She-Devil; She's Having a Baby; Skin Deep; The Snows of Kilimanjaro; A Soldier's Daughter Never Cries; Some Came Running; Storytelling; Sudden Fear; Surrender; Sweet Liberty; Tales of Ordinary Madness; Theodora Goes Wild; Throw Momma from the Train;*

Tune in Tomorrow; Vampire's Kiss; The Waterdance; The Way We Were; Whatever Happened to Kerouac; When Ladies Meet; The Whole Wide World; Wild in the Country; The Wind (Mastorakis); *A Winter Tan; Wonder Boys; The World According to Garp*
in USSR, *Blue Mountains; The Colour of Pomegranates; The Colour of Pomegranates: Director's Cut; The Theme*

Wyndham, John, films adapted from work, *Children of the Damned; The Day of the Triffids; Quest for Love; Village of the Damned*

X-Ray and abnormal vision, *Blind Date* (Mastorakis); *Eyes of Laura Mars; X – the Man with X-Ray Eyes*

Yakuza, and Japanese organised crime, in film *Adrenaline Drive; Agitator; Another Battle; Another Lonely Hitman; The Bird People in China; Black Rain* (Scott); *Blood of Revenge; Blues Harp; Boiling Point* (Kitano); *Brother* (Kitano); *Dead or Alive 2 – Birds; Gonin; Gonin 2; The History of a Man's Face; Ichi the Killer; Kamizake Taxi; Kikujiro; Like a Rolling Stone; Minbo Woman – Or the Gentle Art of Japanese Extortion; One Generation of Tattoos; Organ; The Outer Way; The Punisher; Rainy Dog; Red Peony Gambler: Flower Cards Match; Shinjuku Triad Society; Sonatine; Taxi 2; Tokyo Drifter; Violent Cop; The Wicked Reporter; World Apartment Horror; The Yakuza; Youth of the Beast*

Yehoshua, AB, film adapted from work, *The Lost Lover*

Yemen, in film, *The Rules*

The Yeti
The Abominable Snowman

Yiddish films, *Almonds and Raisins; The Dybbuk; The Light Ahead; Yiddle with His Fiddle*

Young, Neil, in performance, *Rust Never Sleeps*

Yourcenar, Marguerite, film adapted from work, *Coup de Grâce*

Yugoslavia and former Yugoslavia, in film (see also **Croatian cinema, Bosnia, Serbia**), *Black Cat White Cat; Cabaret Balkan; Chico; Innocence Unprotected; No Man's Land* (Tanovic); *Occupation in 26 Pictures; Pretty Village, Pretty Flame; 67 Days; Special Treatment; That Summer of White Roses; Underground* (Kusturica); *Virgin* (Karanovic); *When Father Was Away on Business; W.R. – Mysteries of the Organism*

Yugoslavian and former Yugoslavian cinema
Arizona Dream; Austerlitz; Cabaret Balkan; Innocence Unprotected; The Long Ships; Man Is Not a Bird; The Master and Margarita; Occupation in 26 Pictures; Pretty Village, Pretty Flame; Siberian Lady Macbeth; 67 Days; Special Treatment; Time of the Gypsies; Ulysses' Gaze; Veillées d'Armes; Virgin (Karanovic); *When Father Was Away on Business; W.R. – Mysteries of the Organism*

Zaire/Congo
Zairean cinema, *Macadam Tribu; La Vie est belle*
Zaire/Congo in film, *Lumumba; The Mercenaries; Mobutu, King of Zaire; When We Were Kings*

Zangwill, Israel, film adapted from work, *The Verdict* (Siegel)

Zapata, Emiliano, film about, *Viva Zapata!*

Zenobia, Queen of Syria, in film, *Sign of the Gladiator*

Zetterling, Mai, film about, *Lines from the Heart*

Ziegfeld, Florenz, films about, *Ziegfeld Follies; Ziegfeld Girl*

Zimbabwe
in film, *Death in the Sun; Flame; Game for Vultures*
Zimbabwean cinema, *Aristotles Plot; Flame; Jit; Kini & Adams*

Zola, Emile
film about, *The Life of Emile Zola*
films adapted from work, *L'Argent* (L'Herbier); *La Bête Humaine; La Faute de l'Abbé Mouret; Germinal; Gervaise; Human Desire; Manifesto; Nana* (Arzner); *Nana* (Renoir); *Nana* (Wolman)

Zoos, *Cat People* (Schrader); *Cat People* (Tourneur); *Fierce Creatures; Le Garde du Corps; Murders in the Zoo; Roselyne and the Lions; A Zed & Two Noughts; Zoo in Budapest*

Zweig, Stefan, films adapted from work, *Beware of Pity; Burning Secret; Letter from an Unknown Woman*

Academy & Festival Awards

Academy of Motion Picture Arts and Sciences (Oscars)

1927/28
Picture: *Wings*
Director: Frank Borzage (*7th Heaven*)
Actor: Emil Jannings (*The Last Command, The Way of All Flesh*)
Actress: Janet Gaynor (*7th Heaven, Street Angel, Sunrise*)

1928/29
Picture: *Broadway Melody*
Director: Frank Lloyd (*The Divine Lady, Weary River, Drag*)
Actor: Warner Baxter (*In Old Arizona*)
Actress: Mary Pickford (*Coquette*)

1929/30
Picture: *All Quiet on the Western Front*
Director: Lewis Milestone (*All Quiet on the Western Front*)
Actor: George Arliss (*Disraeli*)
Actress: Norma Shearer (*The Divorcee*)

1930/31
Picture: *Cimarron*
Director: Norman Taurog (*Skippy*)
Actor: Lionel Barrymore (*A Free Soul*)
Actress: Marie Dressler (*Min and Bill*)

1931/32
Picture: *Grand Hotel*
Director: Frank Borzage (*Bad Girl*)
Actor: Wallace Beery (*The Champ*)
Actress: Helen Hayes (*The Sin of Madelon Claudet*)

1932/33
Picture: *Cavalcade*
Director: Frank Lloyd (*Cavalcade*)
Actor: Charles Laughton (*The Private Life of Henry VIII*)
Actress: Katharine Hepburn (*Morning Glory*)

1934
Picture: *It Happened One Night*
Director: Frank Capra (*It Happened One Night*)
Actor: Clark Gable (*It Happened One Night*)
Actress: Claudette Colbert (*It Happened One Night*)

1935
Picture: *Mutiny on the Bounty*
Director: John Ford (*The Informer*)
Actor: Victor McLaglen (*The Informer*)
Actress: Bette Davis (*Dangerous*)

1936
Picture: *The Great Ziegfeld*
Director: Frank Capra (*Mr Deeds Goes to Town*)
Actor: Paul Muni (*The Story of Louis Pasteur*)
Actress: Luise Rainer (*The Great Ziegfeld*)

1937
Picture: *The Life of Emile Zola*
Director: Leo McCarey (*The Awful Truth*)
Actor: Spencer Tracy (*Captains Courageous*)
Actress: Luise Rainer (*The Good Earth*)

1938
Picture: *You Can't Take It With You*
Director: Frank Capra (*You Can't Take It With You*)
Actor: Spencer Tracy (*Boys Town*)
Actress: Bette Davis (*Jezebel*)

1939
Picture: *Gone With the Wind*
Director: Victor Fleming (*Gone With the Wind*)
Actor: Robert Donat (*Goodbye, Mr Chips*)
Actress: Vivien Leigh (*Gone With The Wind*)

1940
Picture: *Rebecca*
Director: John Ford (*The Grapes of Wrath*)
Actor: James Stewart (*The Philadelphia Story*)
Actress: Ginger Rogers (*Kitty Foyle*)

1941
Picture: *How Green Was My Valley*
Director: John Ford (*How Green Was My Valley*)
Actor: Gary Cooper (*Sergeant York*)
Actress: Joan Fontaine (*Suspicion*)

1942
Picture: *Mrs Miniver*
Director: William Wyler (*Mrs Miniver*)
Actor: James Cagney (*Yankee Doodle Dandy*)
Actress: Greer Garson (*Mrs Miniver*)

1943
Picture: *Casablanca*
Director: Michael Curtiz (*Casablanca*)
Actor: Paul Lukas (*Watch on the Rhine*)
Actress: Jennifer Jones (*The Song of Bernadette*)

1944
Picture: *Going My Way*
Director: Leo McCarey (*Going My Way*)
Actor: Bing Crosby (*Going My Way*)
Actress: Ingrid Bergman (*Gaslight*)

1945
Picture: *The Lost Weekend*
Director: Billy Wilder (*The Lost Weekend*)
Actor: Ray Milland (*The Lost Weekend*)
Actress: Joan Crawford (*Mildred Pierce*)

1946
Picture: *The Best Years of Our Lives*
Director: William Wyler (*The Best Years of Our Lives*)
Actor: Fredric March (*The Best Years of Our Lives*)
Actress: Olivia de Havilland (*To Each His Own*)

1947
Picture: *Gentleman's Agreement*
Director: Elia Kazan (*Gentleman's Agreement*)
Actor: Ronald Colman (*A Double Life*)
Actress: Loretta Young (*The Farmer's Daughter*)

1948
Picture: *Hamlet*
Director: John Huston (*The Treasure of the Sierra Madre*)
Actor: Laurence Olivier (*Hamlet*)
Actress: Jane Wyman (*Johnny Belinda*)

1949
Picture: *All the King's Men*
Director: Joseph L Mankiewicz (*A Letter to Three Wives*)
Actor: Broderick Crawford (*All the King's Men*)
Actress: Olivia de Havilland (*The Heiress*)

1950
Picture: *All About Eve*
Director: Joseph L Mankiewicz (*All About Eve*)
Actor: José Ferrer (*Cyrano de Bergerac*)
Actress: Judy Holliday (*Born Yesterday*)

1951
Picture: *An American in Paris*
Director: George Stevens (*A Place in the Sun*)
Actor: Humphrey Bogart (*The African Queen*)
Actress: Vivien Leigh (*A Streetcar Named Desire*)

1952
Picture: *The Greatest Show on Earth*
Director: John Ford (*The Quiet Man*)
Actor: Gary Cooper (*High Noon*)
Actress: Shirley Booth (*Come Back Little Sheba*)

1953
Picture: *From Here to Eternity*
Director: Fred Zinnemann (*From Here to Eternity*)
Actor: William Holden (*Stalag 17*)
Actress: Audrey Hepburn (*Roman Holiday*)

1954
Picture: *On the Waterfront*
Director: Elia Kazan (*On the Waterfront*)
Actor: Marlon Brando (*On the Waterfront*)
Actress: Grace Kelly (*The Country Girl*)

1955
Picture: *Marty*
Director: Delbert Mann (*Marty*)
Actor: Ernest Borgnine (*Marty*)
Actress: Anna Magnani (*The Rose Tattoo*)

1956
Picture: *Around the World in Eighty Days*
Director: George Stevens (*Giant*)
Actor: Yul Brynner (*The King and I*)
Actress: Ingrid Bergman (*Anastasia*)

1957
Picture: *The Bridge on the River Kwai*
Director: David Lean (*The Bridge on the River Kwai*)
Actor: Alec Guinness (*The Bridge on the River Kwai*)
Actress: Joanne Woodward (*The Three Faces of Eve*)

1958
Picture: *Gigi*
Director: Vincente Minnelli (*Gigi*)
Actor: David Niven (*Separate Tables*)
Actress: Susan Hayward (*I Want To Live*)

1959
Picture: *Ben-Hur*
Director: William Wyler (*Ben-Hur*)
Actor: Charlton Heston (*Ben-Hur*)
Actress: Simone Signoret (*Room at the Top*)

1960
Picture: *The Apartment*
Director: Billy Wilder (*The Apartment*)
Actor: Burt Lancaster (*Elmer Gantry*)
Actress: Elizabeth Taylor (*BUtterfield 8*)

1961
Picture: *West Side Story*
Director: Jerome Robbins, Robert Wise (*West Side Story*)
Actor: Maximilian Schell (*Judgment at Nuremberg*)
Actress: Sophia Loren (*Two Women*)

1962
Picture: *Lawrence of Arabia*
Director: David Lean (*Lawrence of Arabia*)
Actor: Gregory Peck (*To Kill a Mockingbird*)
Actress: Anne Bancroft (*The Miracle Worker*)

1963
Picture: *Tom Jones*
Director: Tony Richardson (*Tom Jones*)
Actor: Sidney Poitier (*Lilies of the Field*)
Actress: Patricia Neal (*Hud*)

1964
Picture: *My Fair Lady*
Director: George Cukor (*My Fair Lady*)
Actor: Rex Harrison (*My Fair Lady*)
Actress: Julie Andrews (*Mary Poppins*)

1965
Picture: *The Sound of Music*
Director: Robert Wise (*The Sound of Music*)
Actor: Lee Marvin (*Cat Ballou*)
Actress: Julie Christie (*Darling*)

1966
Picture: *A Man for All Seasons*
Director: Fred Zinnemann (*A Man for All Seasons*)
Actor: Paul Scofield (*A Man for All Seasons*)
Actress: Elizabeth Taylor (*Who's Afraid of Virginia Woolf?*)

1967
Picture: *In the Heat of the Night*
Director: Mike Nichols (*The Graduate*)
Actor: Rod Steiger (*In the Heat of the Night*)
Actress: Katharine Hepburn (*Guess Who's Coming to Dinner*)

1968
Picture: *Oliver!*
Director: Carol Reed (*Oliver!*)
Actor: Cliff Robertson (*Charly*)
Actress: Katharine Hepburn (*The Lion in Winter*)

1969
Picture: *Midnight Cowboy*
Director: John Schlesinger (*Midnight Cowboy*)
Actor: John Wayne (*True Grit*)
Actress: Maggie Smith (*The Prime of Miss Jean Brodie*)

1970
Picture: *Patton*
Director: Franklin J Schaffner (*Patton*)
Actor: George C Scott (*Patton*)
Actress: Glenda Jackson (*Women in Love*)

1971
Picture: *The French Connection*
Director: William Friedkin (*The French Connection*)
Actor: Gene Hackman (*The French Connection*)
Actress: Jane Fonda (*Klute*)

1972
Picture: *The Godfather*
Director: Bob Fosse (*Cabaret*)
Actor: Marlon Brando (*The Godfather*)
Actress: Liza Minnelli (*Cabaret*)

1973
Picture: *The Sting*
Director: George Roy Hill (*The Sting*)
Actor: Jack Lemmon (*Save the Tiger*)
Actress: Glenda Jackson (*A Touch of Class*)

1974
Picture: *The Godfather Part II*
Director: Francis Ford Coppola (*The Godfather Part II*)
Actor: Art Carney (*Harry and Tonto*)
Actress: Ellen Burstyn (*Alice Doesn't Live Here Anymore*)

1975
Picture: *One Flew Over the Cuckoo's Nest*
Director: Milos Forman (*One Flew Over the Cuckoo's Nest*)
Actor: Jack Nicholson (*One Flew Over the Cuckoo's Nest*)
Actress: Louise Fletcher (*One Flew Over the Cuckoo's Nest*)

1976
Picture: *Rocky*
Director: John G Avildsen (*Rocky*)
Actor: Peter Finch (*Network*)
Actress: Faye Dunaway (*Network*)

1977
Picture: *Annie Hall*
Director: Woody Allen (*Annie Hall*)
Actor: Richard Dreyfuss (*The Goodbye Girl*)
Actress: Diane Keaton (*Annie Hall*)

1978
Picture: *The Deer Hunter*
Director: Michael Cimino (*The Deer Hunter*)
Actor: Jon Voight (*Coming Home*)
Actress: Jane Fonda (*Coming Home*)

1979
Picture: *Kramer vs Kramer*
Director: Robert Benton (*Kramer vs Kramer*)
Actor: Dustin Hoffman (*Kramer vs Kramer*)
Actress: Sally Field (*Norma Rae*)

1980
Picture: *Ordinary People*
Director: Robert Redford (*Ordinary People*)
Actor: Robert De Niro (*Raging Bull*)
Actress: Sissy Spacek (*Coal Miner's Daughter*)

1981
Picture: *Chariots of Fire*
Director: Warren Beatty (*Reds*)
Actor: Henry Fonda (*On Golden Pond*)
Actress: Katharine Hepburn (*On Golden Pond*)

1982
Picture: *Gandhi*
Director: Richard Attenborough (*Gandhi*)
Actor: Ben Kingsley (*Gandhi*)
Actress: Meryl Streep (*Sophie's Choice*)

1983
Picture: *Terms of Endearment*
Director: James L Brooks (*Terms of Endearment*)
Actor: Robert Duvall (*Tender Mercies*)
Actress: Shirley MacLaine (*Terms of Endearment*)

1984
Picture: *Amadeus*
Director: Milos Forman (*Amadeus*)
Actor: F Murray Abraham (*Amadeus*)
Actress: Sally Field (*Places in the Heart*)

1985
Picture: *Out of Africa*
Director: Sydney Pollack (*Out of Africa*)
Actor: William Hurt (*Kiss of the Spider Woman*)
Actress: Geraldine Page (*The Trip to Bountiful*)

1986
Picture: *Platoon*
Director: Oliver Stone (*Platoon*)
Actor: Paul Newman (*The Color of Money*)
Actress: Marlee Matlin (*Children of a Lesser God*)

1987
Picture: *The Last Emperor*
Director: Bernardo Bertolucci (*The Last Emperor*)
Actor: Michael Douglas (*Wall Street*)
Actress: Cher (*Moonstruck*)

1988
Picture: *Rain Man*
Director: Barry Levinson (*Rain Man*)
Actor: Dustin Hoffman (*Rain Man*)
Actress: Jodie Foster (*The Accused*)

1989
Picture: *Driving Miss Daisy*
Director: Oliver Stone (*Born on the Fourth of July*)
Actor: Daniel Day Lewis (*My Left Foot*)
Actress: Jessica Tandy (*Driving Miss Daisy*)

1990
Picture: *Dances with Wolves*
Director: Kevin Costner (*Dances with Wolves*)
Actor: Jeremy Irons (*Reversal of Fortune*)
Actress: Kathy Bates (*Misery*)

1991
Picture: *The Silence of the Lambs*
Director: Jonathan Demme (*The Silence of the Lambs*)
Actor: Anthony Hopkins (*The Silence of the Lambs*)
Actress: Jodie Foster (*The Silence of the Lambs*)

1992
Picture: *Unforgiven*
Director: Clint Eastwood (*Unforgiven*)
Actor: Al Pacino (*Scent of a Woman*)
Actress: Emma Thompson (*Howards End*)

1993
Picture: *Schindler's List*
Director: Steven Spielberg (*Schindler's List*)
Actor: Tom Hanks (*Philadelphia*)
Actress: Holly Hunter (*The Piano*)

1994
Picture: *Forrest Gump*
Director: Robert Zemeckis (*Forrest Gump*)
Actor: Tom Hanks (*Forrest Gump*)
Actress: Jessica Lange (*Blue Sky*)

1995
Picture: *Braveheart*
Director: Mel Gibson (*Braveheart*)
Actor: Nicolas Cage (*Leaving Las Vegas*)
Actress: Susan Sarandon (*Dead Man Walking*)

1996
Picture: *The English Patient*
Director: Anthony Minghella (*The English Patient*)
Actor: Geoffrey Rush (*Shine*)
Actress: Frances McDormand (*Fargo*)

1997
Picture: *Titanic*
Director: James Cameron (*Titanic*)
Actor: Jack Nicholson (*As Good As It Gets*)
Actress: Helen Hunt (*As Good As It Gets*)

1998
Picture: *Shakespeare in Love*
Director: Steven Spielberg (*Saving Private Ryan*)
Actor: Roberto Benigni (*Life Is Beautiful*)
Actress: Gwyneth Paltrow (*Shakespeare in Love*)

1999
Picture: *American Beauty*
Director: Sam Mendes (*American Beauty*)
Actor: Kevin Spacey (*American Beauty*)
Actress: Hilary Swank (*Boys Don't Cry*)

2000
Picture: *Gladiator*
Director: Steven Soderbergh (*Traffic*)
Actor: Russell Crowe (*Gladiator*)
Actress: Julia Roberts (*Erin Brokovich*)

2001
Best Picture: *A Beautiful Mind*
Best Director: Ron Howard (*A Beautiful Mind*)
Best Actor: Denzel Washington (*Training Day*)
Best Actress: Halle Berry (*Monster's Ball*)
Best Supporting Actor: Jim Broadbent (*Iris*)
Best Supporting Actress: Jennifer Connelly (*A Beautiful Mind*)
Best Foreign Film: *No Man's Land* (Danis Tanovic)
Best Animated Feature: *Shrek*
Best Documentary Feature: *Murder on a Sunny Morning* (Jean-Xavier de Lestrade, Denis Poncet)
Best Original Screenplay: *Gosford Park* (Julian Fellowes)
Best Adapted Screenplay: *A Beautiful Mind* (Akiva Goldsman)
Best Cinematography: Andrew Lesnie (*The Lord of the Rings: The Fellowship of the Ring*)
Best Editing: Pietro Scalia (*Black Hawk Down*)
Best Art Direction: Catherine Martin, Brigitte Broch (*Moulin Rouge*)
Best Visual Effects: Jim Rygiel, Randall William Cook, Richard Taylor, Mark Stetson (*The Lord of the Rings: The Fellowship of the Ring*)
Best Original Score: Howard Shore (*The Lord of the Rings: The Fellowship of the Ring*)
Best Original Song: Randy Newman, 'If I Didn't Have You' (*Monsters, Inc.*)
Best Costume Design: Catherine Martin, Angus Strathie (*Moulin Rouge*)

British Academy of Film and Television Arts (BAFTA Awards)

1948
Film: *The Best Years of Our Lives*

1949
Film: *Hamlet*

1950
Film: *Bicycle Thieves*

1951
Film: *All About Eve*

1952
Film: *La Ronde*

1953
Film: *The Sound Barrier*
Actor: Ralph Richardson (*The Sound Barrier*)
Actress: Vivien Leigh (*A Streetcar Named Desire*)

1954
Film: *Jeux Interdits*
Actor: John Gielgud (*Julius Caesar*)
Actress: Audrey Hepburn (*Roman Holiday*)

1955
Film: *The Wages of Fear*
Actor: Kenneth More (*Doctor in the House*)
Actress: Yvonne Mitchell (*The Divided Heart*)

1956
Film: *Richard III*
Actor: Laurence Olivier (*Richard III*)
Actress: Katie Johnson (*The Ladykillers*)
Actress: Betsy Blair (*Marty*)

1957
Film: *Gervaise*
Actor: Peter Finch (*A Town Like Alice*)
Actress: Virginia McKenna (*A Town Like Alice*)

1958
Film: *The Bridge on the River Kwai*
Actor: Alec Guinness (*The Bridge on the River Kwai*)
Actress: Heather Sears (*The Story of Esther Costello*)

1959
Film: *Room at the Top*
Actor: Trevor Howard (*The Key*)
Actress: Irene Worth (*Orders to Kill*)

1960
Film: *Ben-Hur*
Actor: Peter Sellers (*I'm All Right, Jack*)
Actress: Audrey Hepburn (*The Nun's Story*)

1961
Film: *The Apartment*
Actor: Peter Finch (*The Trials of Oscar Wilde*)
Actress: Rachel Roberts (*Saturday Night and Sunday Morning*)

1962
Film: *Ballad of a Soldier*
Actor: Peter Finch (*No Love for Johnnie*)
Actress: Dora Bryan (*A Taste of Honey*)

1963
Film: *Lawrence of Arabia*
Actor: Peter O'Toole (*Lawrence of Arabia*)
Actress: Leslie Caron (*The L-Shaped Room*)

1964
Film: *Tom Jones*
Actor: Dirk Bogarde (*The Servant*)
Actress: Rachel Roberts (*This Sporting Life*)

1965
Film: *Dr Strangelove: or, How I Learned to Stop Worrying and Love the Bomb*
Actor: Richard Attenborough (*Seance on a Wet Afternoon*, *Guns at Batasi*)
Actress: Audrey Hepburn (*Charade*)

1966
Film: *My Fair Lady*
Actor: Dirk Bogarde (*Darling*)
Actress: Julie Christie (*Darling*)

1967
Film: *Who's Afraid of Virginia Woolf?*
Actor: Richard Burton (*Who's Afraid of Virginia Woolf?*, *The Spy Who Came In From the Cold*)
Actress: Elizabeth Taylor (*Who's Afraid of Virginia Woolf?*)

1968
Film: *A Man for All Seasons*
Actor: Paul Scofield (*A Man for All Seasons*)
Actress: Edith Evans (*The Whisperers*)

1969
Film: *The Graduate*
Actor: Spencer Tracy (*Guess Who's Coming To Dinner*)
Actress: Katharine Hepburn (*Guess Who's Coming To Dinner*, *The Lion in Winter*)

1970
Film: *Midnight Cowboy*
Actor: Dustin Hoffman (*Midnight Cowboy*)
Actress: Maggie Smith (*The Prime of Miss Jean Brodie*)

1971
Film: *Butch Cassidy and the Sundance Kid*
Actor: Robert Redford (*Butch Cassidy and the Sundance Kid*)
Actress: Katharine Ross (*Butch Cassidy and the Sundance Kid*, *Tell Them Willie Boy Is Here*, *Downhill Racer*)

1972
Film: *Sunday, Bloody Sunday*
Actor: Peter Finch (*Sunday, Bloody Sunday*)
Actress: Glenda Jackson (*Sunday, Bloody Sunday*)

1973
Film: *Cabaret*
Actor: Gene Hackman (*The French Connection*, *The Poseidon Adventure*)
Actress: Liza Minnelli (*Cabaret*)

1974
Film: *Day for Night*
Actor: Walter Matthau (*Pete 'n' Tillie*)
Actress: Stéphane Audran (*The Discreet Charm of the Bourgeoisie*)

1975
Film: *Lacombe Lucien*
Actor: Jack Nicholson (*Chinatown*, *The Last Detail*)
Actress: Joanne Woodward (*Summer Wishes, Winter Dreams*)

1976
Film: *Alice Doesn't Live Here Anymore*
Actor: Al Pacino (*The Godfather Part II*, *Dog Day Afternoon*)
Actress: Ellen Burstyn (*Alice Doesn't Live Here Anymore*)

1977
Film: *One Flew Over the Cuckoo's Nest*
Actor: Jack Nicholson (*One Flew Over the Cuckoo's Nest*)
Actress: Louise Fletcher (*One Flew Over The Cuckoo's Nest*)

1978
Film: *Annie Hall*
Actor: Peter Finch (*Network*)
Actress: Diane Keaton (*Annie Hall*)

1979
Film: *Julia*
Actor: Richard Dreyfuss (*The Goodbye Girl*)
Actress: Jane Fonda (*Julia*)

1980
Film: *Manhattan*
Actor: Jack Lemmon (*The China Syndrome*)
Actress: Jane Fonda (*The China Syndrome*)

1981
Film: *The Elephant Man*
Actor: John Hurt (*The Elephant Man*)
Actress: Judy Davis (*My Brilliant Career*)

1982
Film: *Chariots of Fire*
Actor: Burt Lancaster (*Atlantic City*)
Actress: Meryl Streep (*The French Lieutenant's Woman*)

1983
Film: *Gandhi*
Actor: Ben Kingsley (*Gandhi*)
Actress: Katharine Hepburn (*On Golden Pond*)

1984
Film: *Educating Rita*
Actor: Michael Caine (*Educating Rita*)
Actor: Dustin Hoffman (*Tootsie*)
Actress: Julie Walters (*Educating Rita*)

1985
Film: *The Killing Fields*
Actor: Haing S Ngor (*The Killing Fields*)
Actress: Maggie Smith (*A Private Function*)

1986
Film: *The Purple Rose of Cairo*
Actor: William Hurt (*Kiss of the Spider Woman*)
Actress: Peggy Ashcroft (*A Passage to India*)

1987
Film: *A Room with a View*
Actor: Bob Hoskins (*Mona Lisa*)
Actress: Maggie Smith (*A Room with a View*)

1988
Film: *Jean de Florette*
Actor: Sean Connery (*The Name of the Rose*)
Actress: Anne Bancroft (*84 Charing Cross Road*)

1989
Film: *The Last Emperor*
Actor: John Cleese (*A Fish Called Wanda*)
Actress: Maggie Smith (*The Lonely Passion of Judith Hearne*)

1990
Film: *Dead Poets Society*
Actor: Daniel Day Lewis (*My Left Foot*)
Actress: Pauline Collins (*Shirley Valentine*)

1991
Film: *GoodFellas*
Actor: Philippe Noiret (*Cinema Paradiso*)
Actress: Jessica Tandy (*Driving Miss Daisy*)

1992
Film: *The Commitments*
Actor: Anthony Hopkins (*The Silence of the Lambs*)
Actress: Jodie Foster (*The Silence of the Lambs*)

1993
Film: *Howards End*
Actor: Robert Downey Jr (*Chaplin*)
Actress: Emma Thompson (*Howards End*)

1994
Film: *Schindler's List*
Actor: Anthony Hopkins (*The Remains of the Day*)
Actress: Holly Hunter (*The Piano*)

1995
Film: *Four Weddings and a Funeral*
Actor: Hugh Grant (*Four Weddings and a Funeral*)
Actress: Susan Sarandon (*The Client*)

1996
Film: *Sense and Sensibility*
Actor: Nigel Hawthorne (*The Madness of King George*)
Actress: Emma Thompson (*Sense and Sensibility*)

1997
Film: *The English Patient*
Actor: Geoffrey Rush (*Shine*)
Actress: Brenda Blethyn (*Secrets & Lies*)

1998
Film: *The Full Monty*
Actor: Robert Carlyle (*The Full Monty*)
Actress: Judi Dench (*Mrs Brown*)

1999
Film: *Shakespeare in Love*
Director: Peter Weir (*The Truman Show*)
Actor: Roberto Benigni (*Life Is Beautiful*)
Actress: Cate Blanchett (*Elizabeth*)

2000
Film: *American Beauty*
Director: Pedro Almodóvar (*All About My Mother*)
Actor: Kevin Spacey (*American Beauty*)
Best Actress: Annette Bening (*American Beauty*)

2001
Film: *Gladiator*
Director: Ang Lee (*Crouching Tiger, Hidden Dragon*)
Actor: Jamie Bell (*Billy Elliot*)
Actress: Julia Roberts (*Erin Brokovich*)

2002
Best Film: *The Lord of the Rings: The Fellowship of the Ring*
Best Director: Peter Jackson (*The Lord of the Rings: The Fellowship of the Ring*)
Best Actor: Russell Crowe (*A Beautiful Mind*)
Best Actress: Judi Dench (*Iris*)
Best Supporting Actor: Jim Broadbent (*Moulin Rouge*)
Best Supporting Actress: Jennifer Connelly (*A Beautiful Mind*)
Best Original Screenplay: Guillaume Laurant, Jean-Pierre Jeunet (*Amélie*)
Best Adapted Screenplay: Ted Elliott, Terry Rossio, Joe Stillman, Roger SH Schulman (*Shrek*)
Best Foreign Film: *Amores perros*
Best Cinematography: Roger Deakins (*The Man Who Wasn't There*)
Best Editing: Mary Sweeney (*Mulholland Dr.*)
Best Production Design: Aline Bonetto (*Amélie*)
Best Costume Design: Jenny Beavan (*Gosford Park*)
Best Music: Craig Armstrong (*Moulin Rouge*)
Best Special Effects: *The Lord of the Rings: The Fellowship of the Ring*

Cannes Film Festival

1946
Director: René Clément (*La Bataille du Rail*)
Director: Mikhail Romm (*Chelovyek No. 217*)
Actor: Ray Milland (*The Lost Weekend*)
Actress: Michèle Morgan (*La Symphonie Pastorale*)

1949
Director: René Clément (*Au-delà des Grilles*)
Actor: Edward G Robinson (*House of Strangers*)
Actress: Isa Miranda (*Au-delà des Grilles*)

1951
Director: Luis Buñuel (*Los Olvidados*)
Actor: Michael Redgrave (*The Browning Version*)
Actress: Bette Davis (*All About Eve*)

1952
Director: Christian-Jaque (*Fanfan la Tulipe*)
Actor: Marlon Brando (*Viva Zapata!*)
Actress: Lee Grant (*Detective Story*)

1953
Actor: Charles Vanel (*The Wages of Fear*)
Actress: Shirley Booth (*Come Back Little Sheba*)

1955
Palme d'Or: *Marty*
Director: Sergei Vasiliev (*Heroes of Shipka*)
Director: Jules Dassin (*Du Rififi Chez les Hommes*)

1956
Palme d'Or: *Le Monde du Silence*
Director: Sergei Yutkevich (*Othello*)

1957
Palme d'Or: *Friendly Persuasion*
Director: Robert Bresson (*Un Condamné à mort s'est échappé*)
Actor: John Kitzmiller (*Dolina Miru*)
Actress: Giulietta Masina (*Le Notti di Cabiria*)

1958
Palme d'Or: *The Cranes Are Flying*
Director: Ingmar Bergman (*So Close to Life*)
Actor: Paul Newman (*The Long Hot Summer*)
Actress: Ingrid Thulin, Eva Dahlbeck, Barbro Hiort af Ornäs (*So Close to Life*)

1959
Palme d'Or: *Black Orpheus*
Director: François Truffaut (*Les Quatre Cents Coups*)
Actor: Bradford Dillman, Dean Stockwell, Orson Welles (*Compulsion*)
Actress: Simone Signoret (*Room at the Top*)

1960
Palme d'Or: *La Dolce Vita*
Actress: Melina Mercouri (*Never on Sunday*)
Actress: Jeanne Moreau (*Moderato Cantabile*)

1961
Palme d'Or: *Une Aussi Longue Absence*
Palme d'Or: *Viridiana*
Director: Yulia Solntseva (*Povest Plamennykh Let*)
Actor: Anthony Perkins (*Aimez-Vous Brahms?*)
Actress: Sophia Loren (*Two Women*)

1962
Palme d'Or: *O Pagador de Promessas*

1963
Palme d'Or: *The Leopard*
Actor: Richard Harris (*This Sporting Life*)
Actress: Marina Vlady (*Queen Bee*)

1964
Actor: Saro Urzi (*Seduced and Abandoned*)
Actor: Antál Pager (*Pacsirta*)
Actress: Anne Bancroft (*The Pumpkin Eater*)
Actress: Barbara Barrie (*One Potato, Two Potato*)

1965
Director: Liviu Ciulei (*The Lost Forest*)
Best Actor: Terence Stamp (*The Collector*)
Best Actress: Samantha Eggar (*The Collector*)

1966
Director: Sergei Yutkevich (*Portrait of Lenin*)
Actor: Per Oscarsson (*The Hunger*)
Actress: Vanessa Redgrave (*Morgan, a Suitable Case for Treatment*)

1969
Director : Glauber Rocha (*Antonio das Mortes*)
Director: Vojtech Jasny (*All Good Citizens*)
Actor: Jean-Louis Trintignant (*Z*)
Actress: Vanessa Redgrave (*Isadora*)

1970
Director: John Boorman (*Leo the Last*)
Actor: Marcello Mastroianni (*Jealousy – Italian Style*)
Actress: Ottavia Piccolo (*Metello*)

1971
Actor: Riccardo Cucciolla (*Sacco & Vanzetti*)
Actress: Kitty Winn (*Panic in Needle Park*)

1972
Director: Miklós Jancsó (*Red Psalm*)
Actor: Jean Yanne (*We Will Not Grow Old Together*)
Actress: Susannah York (*Images*)

1973
Actor: Giancarlo Giannini (*Love and Anarchy*)
Actress: Joanne Woodward (*The Effect of Gamma Rays on Man-in-the-Moon Marigolds*)

1974
Actor: Jack Nicholson (*The Last Detail*)
Actress: Marie-Josée Nat (*Les Violons du Bal*)

1975
Palme d'Or: *Ahdat Sanawouach El-Djamr*
Director: Costa-Gavras (*Section Spéciale*)
Director: Michel Brault (*Les Ordres*)
Actor: Vittorio Gassman (*Profumo di Donna*)
Actress: Valerie Perrine (*Lenny*)

1976
Palme d'Or: *Taxi Driver*
Director: Ettore Scola (*Brutti, sporchi e cattivi*)
Actor: José Luis Gómez (*Pascual Duarte*)
Actress: Dominique Sanda (*The Inheritance*)
Actress: Mari Töröcsik (*Deryne, Hol Van?*)

1977
Palme d'Or: *Padre Padrone*
Actor: Fernando Rey (*Elisa, Vida Mia*)
Actress: Shelley Duvall (*3 Women*)
Actress: Monique Mercure (*J.A. Martin, Photographer*)

1978
Palme d'Or: *The Tree of Wooden Clogs*
Director: Nagisa Oshima (*Empire of Passion*)
Actor: Jon Voight (*Coming Home*)
Actress: Jill Clayburgh (*An Unmarried Woman*)
Actress: Isabelle Huppert (*Violette Nozière*)

1979
Palme d'Or: *Apocalypse Now*
Palme d'Or: *The Tin Drum*
Director: Terrence Malick (*Days of Heaven*)
Actor: Jack Lemmon (*The China Syndrome*)
Actress: Sally Field (*Norma Rae*)

1980
Palme d'Or: *Kagemusha*
Palme d'Or: *All That Jazz*
Actor: Michel Piccoli (*Leap into the Void*)
Actress: Anouk Aimée (*Leap into the Void*)

1981
Palme d'Or: *Man of Iron*
Actor: Ugo Tognazzi (*The Tragedy of a Ridiculous Man*)
Actress: Isabelle Adjani (*Possession, Quartet*)

1982
Palme d'Or: *Yol*
Palme d'Or: *Missing*
Director: Werner Herzog (*Fitzcarraldo*)
Actor: Jack Lemmon (*Missing*)
Actress: Jadwiga Jankowska-Cieslak (*Egymára Nézve*)

1983
Palme d'Or: *The Ballad of Narayama*
Actor: Gian Maria Volonté (*The Death of Mario Ricci*)
Actress: Hanna Schygulla (*Storia di Piera*)

1984
Palme d'Or: *Paris, Texas*
Director: Bertrand Tavernier (*Sunday in the Country*)
Actor: Francisco Rabal, Alfredo Landa (*Los Santos Inocentes*)
Actress: Helen Mirren (*Cal*)

1985
Palme d'Or: *When Father Was Away on Business*
Director: André Téchiné (*Rendez-vous*)
Actor: William Hurt (*Kiss of the Spider Woman*)
Actress: Norma Aleandro (*The Official Version*)

1986
Palme d'Or: *The Mission*
Director: Martin Scorsese (*After Hours*)
Actor: Bob Hoskins (*Mona Lisa*)
Actress: Barbara Sukowa (*Rosa Luxemburg*)
Actress: Fernanda Torres (*Eu Sei Que Vou Te Amar*)

1987
Palme d'Or: *Under Satan's Sun*
Director: Wim Wenders (*Wings of Desire*)
Actor: Marcello Mastroianni (*Dark Eyes*)
Actress: Barbara Hershey (*Shy People*)

1988
Palme d'Or: *Pelle the Conqueror*
Director: Fernando Solanas (*Sur*)
Actor: Forest Whitaker (*Bird*)
Actress: Barbara Hershey, Jodhi May, Linda Mvusi (*A World Apart*)

1989
Palme d'Or: *sex, lies and videotape*
Director: Emir Kusturica (*Time of the Gypsies*)
Actor: James Spader (*sex, lies and videotape*)
Actress: Meryl Streep (*A Cry in the Dark*)

1990
Palme d'Or: *Wild at Heart*
Director: Pavel Lounguine (*Taxi Blues*)
Actor: Gérard Depardieu (*Cyrano de Bergerac*)
Actress: Krystyna Janda (*The Interrogation*)

1991
Palme d'Or: *Barton Fink*
Director: Joel Coen (*Barton Fink*)
Actor: John Turturro (*Barton Fink*)
Actress: Irène Jacob (*The Double Life of Véronique*)

1992
Palme d'Or: *Intentions*
Director: Robert Altman (*The Player*)
Actor: Tim Robbins (*The Player*)
Actress: Pernilla Ostergran (*Den Goda Viljan*)

1993
Palme d'Or: *Farewell My Concubine*
Palme d'Or: *The Piano*
Director: Mike Leigh (*Naked*)
Actor: David Thewlis (*Naked*)
Actress: Holly Hunter (*The Piano*)

1994
Palme d'Or: *Pulp Fiction*
Director: Nanni Moretti (*Dear Diary*)
Actor: Ge You (*To Live*)
Actress: Virna Lisi (*La Reine Margot*)

1995
Palme d'Or: *Underground*
Director: Mathieu Kassovitz (*La Haine*)
Actor: Jonathan Pryce (*Carrington*)
Actress: Helen Mirren (*The Madness of King George*)

1996
Palme d'Or: *Secrets & Lies*
Director: Joel Coen (*Fargo*)
Actor: Daniel Auteuil, Pascal Duquenne (*The Eighth Day*)
Actress: Brenda Blethyn (*Secrets & Lies*)

1997
Palme d'Or: *A Taste of Cherry* (*Ta'me-gilas*) (Abbas Kiarostami)
Palme d'Or: *Unagi* (Shohei Imamura)
Director: Wong Kar-Wai (*Happy Together*)
Actor: Sean Penn (*She's So Lovely*)
Actress: Kathy Burke (*Nil by Mouth*)

1998
Palme d'Or: *Eternity and a Day* (*Mia Eoniotita Ke Mia Mera*) (Theo Angelopoulos)
Director: John Boorman (*The General*)
Actor: Peter Mullan (*My Name Is Joe*)
Actress: Elodie Bouchez, Natacha Régnier (*La Vie Rêvée des Anges*)

1999
Palme d'Or: *Rosetta* (Luc Dardenne, Jean-Pierre Dardenne)
Director: Pedro Almodóvar (*All About My Mother*)
Actor: Emmanuel Schotté (*L'Humanité*)
Actress: Séverine Caneele (*L'Humanité*)
Actress: Emile Dequenne (*Rosetta*)

2000
Palme d'Or: *Dancer in the Dark* (Lars von Trier)
Director: Edward Yang (*A One and a Two…*)
Actor: Tony Leung (*In the Mood for Love*)
Actress: Björk (*Dancer in the Dark*)

2001
Palme d'Or: *The Son's Room* (Nanni Moretti)
Director: David Lynch (*Mulholland Drive*)
Director: Joel Coen (*The Man Who Wasn't There*)
Actor: Benoît Magimel (*The Piano Teacher*)
Actress: Isabelle Huppert (*The Piano Teacher*)

2002
Palme d'Or: *The Pianist* (Roman Polanski)
Best Director: Paul Thomas Anderson (*Punch-Drunk Love*)
Best Director: Im Kwon-Taek (*Chihwaseon*)
Best Actor: Olivier Gourmet (*The Son*)
Best Actress: Kati Outinen (*The Man Without a Past*)
Grand Prize (runner-up to Palme d'Or): Aki Kaurismäki (*The Man Without a Past*)
Best Script: *Sweet Sixteen* (Paul Laverty)
Jury Prize (special recognition): *Divine Intervention* (Elia Suleiman)
Caméra d'Or (best first-time director): *Bord de Mer* (Julie Lopes-Curval)
Special 55th Anniversary Prize: *Bowling for Columbine* (Michael Moore)

Berlin Film Festival

1956
Golden Bear: *Invitation to the Dance*
Actor: Burt Lancaster (*Trapeze*)
Actress: Elsa Martinelli (*Donatella*)

1957
Golden Bear: *12 Angry Men*
Director: Mario Monicelli (*Padri e Figli…*)
Actor: Pedro Infante (*Tizoc*)
Actress: Yvonne Mitchell (*Woman in a Dressing Gown*)

1958
Golden Bear: *Wild Strawberries*
Director: Tadashi Imai (*Jun-Ai Monogatari*)
Actor: Sidney Poitier (*The Defiant Ones*)
Actress: Anna Magnani (*Wild Is the Wind*)

1959
Golden Bear: *Les Cousins*
Director: Akira Kurosawa (*The Hidden Fortress*)
Actor: Jean Gabin (*Archimède le Clochard*)
Actress: Shirley MacLaine (*Ask Any Girl*)

1960
Golden Bear: *El Lazarillo de Tormes*
Director: Jean-Luc Godard (*A Bout de Souffle*)
Actor: Fredric March (*Inherit the Wind*)
Actress: Juliette Mayniel (*Kirmes*)

1961
Golden Bear: *La Notte*
Director: Bernhard Wicki (*Das Wunder des Malachias*)
Actor: Peter Finch (*No Love for Johnnie*)
Actress: Anna Karina (*Une Femme est une Femme*)

1962
Golden Bear: *A Kind of Loving*
Director: Francesco Rosi (*Salvatore Giuliano*)
Actor: James Stewart (*Mr Hobbs Takes a Vacation*)
Actress: Viveca Lindfors, Rita Gam (*No Exit*)

1963
Golden Bear: *Bushido – Samurai Saga*
Golden Bear: *The Devil*
Director: Nikos Koundouros (*Mikres Aphrodites*)
Actor: Sidney Poitier (*Lilies of the Field*)
Actress: Bibi Andersson (*The Swedish Mistress*)

1964
Golden Bear: *Waterless Summer*
Director: Satyajit Ray (*Mahanagar*)
Actress: Sachiko Hidari (*The Insect Woman, She and He*)

1965
Golden Bear: *Alphaville*
Director: Satyajit Ray (*Charulata*)
Actor: Lee Marvin (*Cat Ballou*)
Actress: Madhur Jaffrey (*Shakespeare Wallah*)

1966
Golden Bear: *Cul-de-Sac*
Director: Carlos Saura (*La Caza*)
Actor: Jean-Pierre Léaud (*Masculin Féminin*)
Actress: Lola Albright (*Lord Love a Duck*)

1967
Golden Bear: *Le Départ*
Director: Zivojin Pavlovic (*Budenje Pacova*)
Actor: Michel Simon (*Le Vieil Homme et l'Enfant*)
Actress: Edith Evans (*The Whisperers*)

1968
Golden Bear: *Who Saw Him Die?*
Director: Carlos Saura (*Peppermint Frappé*)
Actor: Jean-Louis Trintignant (*L'Homme qui Ment*)
Actress: Stéphane Audran (*Les Biches*)

1969
Golden Bear: *Rani Radovi*

1971
Golden Bear: *The Garden of the Finzi-Continis*
Actor: Jean Gabin (*Le Chat*)
Actress: Simone Signoret (*Le Chat*)
Actress: Shirley MacLaine (*Desperate Characters*)

1972
Golden Bear: *The Canterbury Tales*
Director: Jean-Pierre Blanc (*La Vieille Fille*)
Actor: Alberto Sordi (*Why?*)
Actress: Elizabeth Taylor (*Hammersmith Is Out*)

1973
Golden Bear: *Distant Thunder*

1974
Golden Bear: *The Apprenticeship of Duddy Kravitz*

1975
Golden Bear: *Örökbefogadas*
Director: Sergei Solovyov (*Sto Dnei Posle Detstva*)
Actor: Vlastimil Brodsky (*Jakob der Lügner*)
Actress: Kinuyo Tanaka (*Sandakan Hachibanshokan Bohkyo*)

1976
Director: Mario Monicelli (*Caro Michele*)
Actor: Gerd Olschewski (*Verlorenes Leben*)

1977
Golden Bear: *Voskhozhdenie*
Director: Manuel Gutiérrez Aragón (*Camada Negra*)
Actor: Fernando Fernán Gómez (*El Anácoreta*)
Actress: Lily Tomlin (*The Late Show*)

1978
Golden Bear: *Las Truchas*
Golden Bear: *Las Palabras de Max*
Director: Georgi Dyulgerov (*Avantazh*)
Actor: Craig Russell (*Outrageous*)
Actress: Gena Rowlands (*Opening Night*)

1979
Golden Bear: *David*
Director: Astrid Henning-Jensen (*Vinterboern*)
Actor: Michele Placido (*Ernesto*)
Actress: Hanna Schygulla (*The Marriage of Maria Braun*)

1980
Golden Bear: *Palermo oder Wolfsburg*
Golden Bear: *Heartland*

1981
Golden Bear: *Fast, Fast*
Director: Markus Imhoof (*Das Boot Ist Voll*)
Actor: Anatoli Solonitsyn (*Twenty-Six Days in the Life of Dostoevsky*)
Actor: Jack Lemmon (*Tribute*)
Actress: Barbara Grabowska (*Fever*)

1982
Golden Bear: *Veronika Voss*
Director: Mario Monicelli (*Il Marchese del Grillo*)
Actor: Michel Piccoli (*Une Etrange Affaire*)
Actor: Stellan Skarsgård (*A Simple-Minded Murderer*)
Actress: Katrin Sass (*Bürgschaft für ein Jahr*)

1983
Golden Bear: *Ascendancy*
Golden Bear: *La Colmena*
Director: Eric Rohmer (*Pauline à la Plage*)
Actor: Bruce Dern (*That Championship Season*)
Actress: Evgenia Glushenko (*Love by Request*)

1984
Golden Bear: *Love Streams*
Actor: Albert Finney (*The Dresser*)
Actress: Inna Churikova (*Wartime Romance*)
Actress: Monica Vitti (*Flirt*)

1985
Golden Bear: *Wetherby*
Golden Bear: *Die Frau und der Fremde*
Director: Robert Benton (*Places in the Heart*)
Actor: Fernando Fernán Gómez (*Stico*)
Actress: Jo Kennedy (*Wrong World*)

1986
Golden Bear: *Stammheim*
Director: Giorgi Shengelaja (*Journey of a Young Composer*)
Actor: Tuncel Kurtiz (*The Smile of the Lamb*)
Actress: Charlotte Valandrey (*Rouge Baiser*)
Actress: Marcélia Cartaxo (*Hour of the Star*)

1987
Golden Bear: *The Theme*
Director: Oliver Stone (*Platoon*)
Actor: Gian Maria Volonté (*The Moro Affair*)
Actress: Ana Beatriz Nogueira (*Vera*)

1988
Golden Bear: *Red Sorghum*
Director: Norman Jewison (*Moonstruck*)
Actor: Jörg Posse, Manfred Möck (*Bear Ye One Another's Burdens*)
Actress: Holly Hunter (*Broadcast News*)

1989
Golden Bear: *Rain Man*
Director: Dusan Hanák (*I Love, You Love*)
Actor: Gene Hackman (*Mississippi Burning*)
Actress: Isabelle Adjani (*Camille Claudel*)

1990
Golden Bear: *Music Box*
Director: Michael Verhoeven (*The Nasty Girl*)
Actor: Iain Glen (*Silent Scream*)
Joint Performance: Jessica Tandy, Morgan Freeman (*Driving Miss Daisy*)

1991
Golden Bear: *House of Smiles*
Silver Bear: Jonathan Demme (*The Silence of the Lambs*)
Silver Bear: Ricky Tognazzi (*Ultrà*)
Silver Bear: Maynard Eziashi (*Mister Johnson*)
Actress: Victoria Abril (*Amantes*)

1992
Golden Bear: *Grand Canyon*
Director: Jan Troell (*Il Capitano*)
Actor: Armin Mueller-Stahl (*Utz*)
Actress: Maggie Cheung (*Actress*)

1993
Golden Bear: *Hsi Yen*
Golden Bear: *Xian Hunnü*
Director: Andrew Birkin (*The Cement Garden*)
Actor: Denzel Washington (*Malcolm X*)
Actress: Michelle Pfeiffer (*Love Field*)

1994
Golden Bear: *In the Name of the Father*
Director: Krzysztof Kieslowski (*Three Colours: White*)
Actor: Tom Hanks (*Philadelphia*)
Actress: Chrissy Rock (*Ladybird Ladybird*)

1995
Golden Bear: *The Bait*
Director: Richard Linklater (*Before Sunrise*)
Actor: Paul Newman (*Nobody's Fool*)
Actress: Josephine Siao (*Nuiyan, Seisap*)

1996
Golden Bear: *Sense and Sensibility*
Director: Richard Loncraine (*Richard III*)
Director: Ho Yim (*The Day the Sun Turned Cold*)
Actor: Sean Penn (*Dead Man Walking*)
Actress: Anouk Grinberg (*Mon Homme*)

1997
Golden Bear: *The People vs Larry Flynt*
Special Jury Prize: *He Liu* (Tsai Ming-Liang)
Best Director: Eric Heumann (*Port Djema*)
Best Actor: Leonardo DiCaprio (*William Shakespeare's Romeo & Juliet*)
Best Actress: Juliette Binoche (*The English Patient*)

1998
Golden Bear: *Central Do Brasil* (Walter Salles)
Special Jury Prize: *Wag the Dog* (Barry Levinson)
Director: Neil Jordan (*The Butcher Boy*)
Actor: Samuel L Jackson (*Jackie Brown*)
Actress: Fernanda Montenegro (*Central Do Brasil*)

1999
Golden Bear: *The Thin Red Line* (Terrence Malik)
Special Jury Prize: *Mifunes Sidste Sang – Dogme 3* (Søren Kragh-Jacobsen)
Director: Stephen Frears (*The Hi-Lo Country*)
Actor: Michael Gwisdek (*Nachtgestalten*)
Actress: Juliane Köhler, Maria Schrader (*Aimée & Jaguar*)

2000
Golden Bear: *Magnolia* (Paul Thomas Anderson)
Special Jury Prize: *The Road Home* (Zhang Yimou)
Director: Milos Forman (*Man on the Moon*)
Actor: Denzel Washington (*The Hurricane*)
Actress: Bibiana Beglau, Nadja Uhl (*The Legends of Rita*)

2001
Golden Bear: *Intimacy* (Patrice Chéreau)
Silver Bear Jury Prize: *Italian for Beginners* (Lone Scherfig)
Director: Lin Cheng-Sheng (*Betelnut Beauty*)
Runner-up Best Director: Wang Xiaoshuai (*Beijing Bicycle*)
Actor: Benicio Del Toro (*Traffic*)
Actress: Kerry Fox (*Intimacy*)

2002
Golden Bear: *Spirited Away* (Hayao Miyazaki)
Golden Bear: *Bloody Sunday* (Paul Greengrass)
Silver Bear Jury Prize: *Halbe Treppe* (Andreas Dresen)
Best Director: Otar Iosseliani (*Lundi Matin*)
Best Actor: Jacques Gamblin (*Laissez-Passer*)
Best Actress: Halle Berry (*Monster's Ball*)
Silver Bear Best Ensemble of Actresses: *8 Women* (François Ozon)
Silver Bear Best Music: Antoine Duhamel (*Laissez-Passer*)
Golden Bear Best Short: *Bror Min* (Jens Jonsson)

Venice Film Festival

1934
Foreign Film: *Man of Aran*
Italian Film: *Teresa Confalonieri*
Actor: Wallace Beery (*Viva Villa!*)
Actress: Katharine Hepburn (*Little Women*)

1935
Foreign Film: *Anna Karenina*
Italian Film: *Casta Diva*
Director: King Vidor (*The Wedding Night*)
Actor: Pierre Blanchar (*Crime and Punishment*)
Actress: Paula Wessely (*Episode*)

1936
Foreign Film: *The Emperor of California*
Italian Film: *Squadrone Bianco*
Director: Jacques Feyder (*La Kermesse Heroique*)
Actor: Paul Muni (*The Story of Louis Pasteur*)
Actress: Annabella (*Veille d'Armes*)

1937
Foreign Film: *Un Carnet de Bal*
Italian Film: *Scipione l'Africano*
Director: Robert Flaherty, Koltan Korda (*Elephant Boy*)
Italian Director: Mario Camerini (*Il Signor Max*)
Actor: Emil Jannings (*Der Herrscher*)
Actress: Bette Davis (*Kid Galahad, Marked Woman*)

1938
Foreign Film: *Olympische Spiele 1936*
Italian Film: *Luciano serra Pilota*
Actor: Leslie Howard (*Pygmalion*)
Actress: Norma Shearer (*Marie Antoinette*)

1940
Foreign Film: *Der Postmeister*
Italian Film: *L'Assedio dell'Alcazar*

1941
Foreign Film: *Ohm Krüger*
Italian Film: *La Corona di Ferro*
Actor: Ermete Zacconi (*Don Buonaparte*)
Actress: Luise Ullrich (*Annelie*)

1947
Grand Prix: *Sirena*
Director: Henri-Georges Clouzot (*Quai des Orfèvres*)
Actor: Pierre Fresnay (*Monsieur Vincent*)
Actress: Anna Magnani (*Angelina*)

1948
Grand Prix: *Hamlet*
Director: GW Pabst (*Der Prozess*)
Actor: Ernst Deutsch (*Der Prozess*)
Actress: Jean Simmons (*Hamlet*)

1949
Director: Augusto Genina (*Cielo sulla Palude*)
Actor: Joseph Cotten (*The Portrait of Jennie*)
Actress: Olivia de Havilland (*The Snake Pit*)

1950
Actor: Sam Jaffe (*The Asphalt Jungle*)
Actress: Eleanor Parker (*Caged*)

1951
Golden Lion: *Rashomon*
Actor: Jean Gabin (*La Nuit est mon Royaume*)
Actress: Vivien Leigh (*A Streetcar Named Desire*)

1952
Golden Lion: *Jeux Interdits*
Actor: Fredric March (*Death of a Salesman*)

1953
Actor: Henri Vilbert (*Le Bon Dieu sans Confession*)
Actress: Lilli Palmer (*The Fourposter*)

1954
Golden Lion: *Romeo and Juliet*
Actor: Jean Gabin (*L'Air de Paris, Touchez pas au Grisbi*)

1956
Actor: Bourvil (*La Traversée de Paris*)
Actress: Maria Schell (*Gervaise*)

1957
Golden Lion: *Aparajito*
Actor: Anthony Franciosa (*A Hatful of Rain*)
Actress: Dzidra Ritenbergs (*Malva*)

1958
Golden Lion: *The Rickshaw Man*
Actor: Alec Guinness (*The Horse's Mouth*)
Actress: Sophia Loren (*The Black Orchid*)

1959
Golden Lion: *Il Generale della Rovere*
Golden Lion: *The Great War*
Actor: James Stewart (*Anatomy of a Murder*)
Actress: Madeleine Robinson (*A Double Tour*)

1960
Golden Lion: *Le Passage du Rhin*
Actor: John Mills (*Tunes of Glory*)
Actress: Shirley MacLaine (*The Apartment*)

1962
Golden Lion: *Family Diary*
Actor: Burt Lancaster (*Birdman of Alcatraz*)
Actress: Emmanuelle Riva (*Thérèse Desqueyroux*)

1963
Golden Lion: *Hands over the City*
Actor: Albert Finney (*Tom Jones*)
Actress: Delphine Seyrig (*Muriel*)

1964
Golden Lion: *The Red Desert*
Actor: Tom Courtenay (*King & Country*)
Actress: Harriet Andersson (*To Love*)

1965
Golden Lion: *Vaghe Stelle dell'Orsa*
Actor: Toshiro Mifune (*Red Beard*)
Actress: ? (*Trois Chambres à Manhattan*)

1967
Golden Lion: *Belle de Jour*
Actor: Ljubisa Samardzic (*Morning*)
Actress: Shirley Knight (*Dutchman*)

1968
Golden Lion: *Artistes at the Top of the Big Top: Disorientated*
Actor: John Marley (*Faces*)
Actress: Laura Betti (*Theorem*)

1980
Golden Lion: *Atlantic City*
Golden Lion: *Gloria*

1981
Golden Lion: *The German Sisters*

1982
Golden Lion: *The State of Things*

1983
Golden Lion: *Prénom Carmen*
Actor: The cast of *Streamers*
Actress: Darling Legitimus (*Black Shack Alley*)

1984
Golden Lion: *A Year of the Quiet Sun*
Actress: Pascale Ogier (*Full Moon in Paris*)
Actor: Naseeruddin Shah (*The Crossing*)

1985
Golden Lion: *Vagabonde*
Actor: Gérard Depardieu (*Police*)

1986
Golden Lion: *The Green Ray*
Actor: Carlo Delle Piane (*Regalo di Natale*)
Actress: Valeria Golino (*Storia d'Amore*)

1987
Golden Lion: *Au Revoir les Enfants*
Actor: Hugh Grant, James Wilby (*Maurice*)
Actor: Kang Soo-Yeon (*The Surrogate Woman*)

1988
Golden Lion: *The Legend of the Holy Drinker*
Director: Theo Angelopoulos
Actor: Don Ameche, Joe Mantegna (*Things Change*)
Actress: Isabelle Huppert (*Une Affaire de Femmes*)
Actress: Shirley MacLaine (*Madame Sousatzka*)

1989
Golden Lion: *City of Sadness*
Actor: Marcello Mastroianni, Massimo Troisi (*What Time Is It?*)
Actress: Peggy Ashcroft and Geraldine James (*She's Been Away*)

1990
Golden Lion: *Rosencrantz and Guildenstern Are Dead*
Direction: Martin Scorsese (*GoodFellas*)
Actor: Oleg Borisov (*The Final Testimony*)
Actress: Gloria Munchmeyer (*The Moon in the Mirror*)

1991
Golden Lion: *Urga*
Actor: River Phoenix (*My Own Private Idaho*)
Actress: Tilda Swinton (*Edward II*)

1992
Golden Lion: *The Story of Qiu Ju*
Actor: Jack Lemmon (*Glengarry Glen Ross*)
Actress: Gong Li (*The Story of Qiu Ju*)

1994
Golden Lion: *Before the Rain*
Golden Lion: *Aiqing Wansui*
Actor: Xia Yu (*Yangguang Canlan de Rizi*)
Actress: Maria de Medeiros (*Três Irmãos*)

1995
Golden Lion: *Cyclo*
Actor: George Götz (*Der Totmacher*)
Actress: Sandrine Bonnaire, Isabelle Huppert (*La Cérémonie*)

1996
Golden Lion: *Michael Collins*
Actor: Liam Neeson (*Michael Collins*)
Actress: Victoire Thivisol (*Ponette*)

1997
Golden Lion: *Hana-Bi*
Actor: Wesley Snipes (*One Night Stand*)
Actress: Robin Tunney (*Niagara*)

1998
Golden Lion: *The Way We Laughed*
Director: Emir Kusturica (*Black Cat, White Cat*)
Actor: Sean Penn (*Hurlyburly*)
Actress: Catherine Deneuve (*Place Vendôme*)

1999
Golden Lion: *Not One Less*
Director: Zhang Yuan (*Seventeen Years*)
Actor: Jim Broadbent (*Topsy-Turvy*)
Actress: Nathalie Baye (*Une Liaison Pornographique*)

2000
Golden Lion: *The Circle*
Runner-up Grand Prix: *Before Night Falls*
Director: Buddhaded Dasgupta (*Uttara*)
Actor: Javier Bardem (*Before Night Falls*)
Actress: Rose Byrne (*The Goddess of 1967*)

2001
Golden Lion: *Monsoon Wedding*
Jury Grand Prix: *Hundstage*
Best Director: Babak Payami (*Raye Makhfi*)
Best Actor: Luigi Lo Cascio (*Light of My Eyes*)
Best Actress: Sandra Ceccarelli (*Light of My Eyes*)
Best Screenplay: *And Your Mother Too*
(Carlos Cuarón, Alfonso Cuarón)
Marcello Mastroianni Prize (best young actor):
Gael García Bernal, Diego Luna (*And Your Mother Too*)
Best Short Film: *Freunde* (Jan Krüger)